HEATH'S

FRENCH AND ENGLISH DICTIONARY

COMPILED FROM THE

BEST AUTHORITIES IN BOTH LANGUAGES

REVISED AND CONSIDERABLY ENLARGED

BY

JAMES BOÏELLE, B. A. (Univ. Gall.)

OFFICIER D'ACADÉMIE, LATELY EXAMINER IN FRENCH IN THE UNIVER-
SITY OF LONDON ; CORRESPONDING MEMBER OF " LA SOCIÉTÉ
DES GENS DE LETTRES DE FRANCE," ETC., ETC.

AIDED BY

DE V. PAYEN-PAYNE

ASSISTANT-EXAMINER IN FRENCH IN THE UNIVERSITY OF LONDON
PRINCIPAL OF KENSINGTON COACHING COLLEGE
AUTHOR OF "FRENCH IDIOMS AND PROVERBS"

D. C. HEATH & CO., Publishers

BOSTON, NEW YORK, CHICAGO

PREFACE

TO REVISED EDITION.

WHEN I was asked to undertake the preparation of this French Dictionary, I had no idea of the formidable nature of the task that lay before me.
It was obvious, of course, that a very great deal would have to be done to
bring up to date a dictionary of a living language that is ever growing, and
in which new words and new meanings of words are being coined almost
daily. But I found, in the course of the four and a half years during which
I have been engaged upon the work, that it assumed proportions altogether
undreamt of, and that I was virtually producing a new work.

Perhaps I may be permitted to direct attention to some of the features
which distinguish the new edition.

Many thousands of new words and phrases, idioms and idiomatic expressions, proverbs and proverbial expressions, have been included. In a great
many instances chapter and verse have been given. Two hundred columns
of print have been added to the book.

For the words in the French-English part, I have closely followed the
smaller Littré as well as Bescherelle, and have taken special care to give, as
far as the compass of the Dictionary would allow, illustrative examples of the
many and various meanings conveyed by the words under review. These
various meanings have also been classified, as far as possible, under their
respective heads. In the English-French portion I have, as far as the selection of words is concerned, closely followed the lines of Cassell's English
Dictionary. The latest classical, general, scientific, commercial, naval, and
military terms are incorporated. In this part, too, the "notation" of the
words has been carefully marked throughout and the pronunciation revised.

Among other features of the work which may justly, I think, be accounted
improvements, I may mention the following, viz.: the different preposi-
tions governing verbs have been printed in heavier type — thus simplifying
one of the greatest difficulties of the language; the pronunciation of the
words, where necessary, has been carefully indicated; and the list of geographical names of countries and places has been largely added to.

The work has occupied me, as I have said, for more than four years; but
the process of revision has been to me most interesting, and while the labour
expended has been far greater than anything I could have anticipated. I
trust that the result will give satisfaction to an even larger circle of readers
than was obtained by previous editions.

J. B.

ON FRENCH PRONUNCIATION

NOTE. — The rules given below must be considered as general. Some are subject to more or less exceptions, which, for the sake of brevity, have not been mentioned, but they will all be found clearly and fully noticed in their respective places.

ALPHABET.

French Alphabet.	Old French Pronunciation.	Approximate English Pronunciation.	Modern French Pronunciation.	Approximate English Pronunciation.
A a	a	ah	a	ah
B b	bé	bay	be	bu-t
C c	cé	say	ce	su-m
D d	dé	day	de	du-ll
E e	é	a	e	u-p
F f	èff	eff	fe	fu-n
G g	jé	zhay	ge	zhu-t
H h	ash	ash	he	hu-g
I i	i	ee	i	ee-l
J j	ji	zhee	je	zhu-g
K k	k	kah	ke	cu-t
L l	èl	el	le	lu-ck
M m	èmm	em	me	mu-d
N n	ènn	en	ne	nu-t
O o	o	o	o	o-ld
P p	pé	pay	pe	pu-n
Q q	qu	ku	ke	cu-rl
R r	èr	air	re	ru-st
S s	èss	ess	se	su-n
T t	té	tay	te	tu-b
U u	u	u	u	u
V v	vé	vay	ve	vu-lgar
X x	iks	eeks	kse	ksu-t
Y y	i grec	ee grek	y	y-ore
Z z	zed	zed	ze	zu-n

FRENCH VOWEL SOUNDS.

The Simple, or Vowel sounds, in the French language, are as follows : —

French.	English.	French.
a (short) like	a in *bat*, exemplified by	*mal.*
â (long) like	a .. *bar* ..	*âge.*
e sounded like a .. *villâ* ..		{ *me.* / *je.* }
è, ê ..	e .. *e'er, there* ..	*père.*
é ..	ai, e .. *air, eh !* ..	*été.*
i ..	ea .. *peak* ..	*pique.*
î ..	ie .. *field* ..	*gîte.*
o ..	o .. *rob* ..	*mol.*
ô ..	o .. *no* ..	*môle.*
u no equivalent in English (nearest approach is *u* in *brunette*) exemplified by		*suc.*
û no equivalent in English ..		*sûre.*
eû sounded like e in *her* (but longer and deeper)		*jeûne.*
ou ..	oo .. *root* exemplified by	*goutte.*
oû ..	oo .. *noose* ..	*voûte.*
an no equivalent in English ..		*tan.*
in ..	.. ..	*fin.*
on ..	.. ..	*bon.*
un ..	.. ..	*brun.*

Y, when alone, or when preceded or followed by a consonant, is pronounced like an *i*; except in *pays, paysan, paysage*. When placed between two vowels, it performs the office of two *i*'s, and is always preceded by *a, e, o*, or *u*. When preceded by *a* or *e*, it unites its first *i* with this vowel, and sounds è, as in *rayon*, which is pronounced *rè-ion*; when preceded by *o*, its first *i* is sounded in conjunction with *o*, like *wa* in the English word *wag*, as in *joyeux*, which is pronounced *joa-ieû*; and when preceded by *u*, its own two *i*'s preserve their natural sound, as in *appuyer*, which is pronounced *appui-ié*.

A is long in the termination *aille*, except in *médäille, je travâille, détäille, émäille, bäille* (I give). It is also long in *ation*, as, *nation, admiration, oblation;* pronounce therefore, *päille, limäille, canäille, nätion, admirätion, oblätion*, etc.

In the terminations of the imperfect of the subjunctive of verbs of the first conjugation, the *a* is always short; as *que je parlâsse, que je donnâsse.*

NASAL SOUNDS.

The nasal syllables are : *aim, ain, am, an, aon; ean, eim, ein, em, en, eon, eun; im, in; om, on; um, un; ym.*

Am, an, ean, are pronounced like *an*, without exception; as *ambition, vendant, songeant.* *Em* and *en* are also pronounced like *an*, as in *emploi, empire, envie;* but not always. In words derived from foreign languages, they are pronounced liked *ème, ène;* as *Jerusalem, hymen.* In words terminating in *en* or *ein*, and in their derivatives, *en* is pronounced like *in;* as *mien, Chrétien, Chrétienté;* and in the verbs *tenir, venir*, and their derivatives, *en* is sounded like *in;* as *tiens, viens.*

In *femme, em* is pronounced like *am.*

Im, in, aim, ain, ein, are all pronounced like *in.* The *i*, however, keeps its natural sound in words taken from foreign languages, as in *Sélim, Ephraim*, which are pronounced as if the *m* were followed by a silent *e;* in all words in which *in* is followed by a vowel; as *in-animé, in-octavo, in-odore, in-humain;* and in the beginning of words commencing with *imm* and *inn.*

Om, on, are pronounced like *on;* as in *pont, tombe;* *complet, donjon. Automne* is pronounced *ôtonn.*

Aen, aon, ean are sounded as *an* in the following words : *Caen, Laon, taon, faon, paon, Jean.*

Eon is sounded *on* when following *g:* *mangeons, plongeons.*

Um, un, eun, are pronounced like *un;* as in *parfum, importun, à jeun.*

Un is, however, sounded *on* in a few words of foreign origin : *punch, de profundis.*

Um is pronounced like *ome* in words of Latin origin, as *duumvir, triumvir; factum, factotum.*

CONSONANTS.

B has the same sound as in English; as *bal*, ball. It is pronounced in the middle and at the end of words.

C has the sound of *k* before *a, o, u, l, n, r,* except when it has a cedilla under it, in which case it is pronounced like *s*, as *reçu*. It is also pronounced like *s* before *e*, *i*, and *y*. *Ch* has the sound of *sh*, except when it is followed by a consonant, in which case it is pronounced like *k*; as in *chronologie*.

D has the same sound as in English. It is sounded in the middle of words, as in *adverbe*. When it is final, and carried to the following word, it sounds like *t*, as in *grand homme*, which is pronounced *gran-tomme*.

F is pronounced like the same letter in English, as in *fleur*, flower. It is sounded at the end of words; but in *neuf* it is pronounced like *v* when followed by a word beginning with a vowel or *h* mute, as in *neuf enfants*, which words are pronounced *neu-van-fan*.

G has the hard sound of *g* in the English word *go*, before *a*, *o*, *u*, *l*, *m*, *r*, as in *gomme*, *gris*, gum, gray. But it has always the soft sound of *s* as in *pleasure* before *e*, *i*, *y*, as in *génie*, *gîte*.

When combined with *n* in the middle of words, it has a liquid sound, somewhat similar to that of *ni* in the English word onion, as *régner*, *saigner*, *agneau*, *compagnon*, etc. Every word in which this sound occurs is preceded by a star(*) throughout this work. Whenever *gn* is not liquid, it sounds as in the English word ignorant.

H is sounded with a guttural impulse, when aspirated, as in *héros*, hero. When mute it has no use but that of showing the etymology of the word, as in *honneur*, honor. It is always silent after *t*, as in *méthode*, *arithmétique*, which are pronounced *métod*, *a-rit-mé-tik*. The aspirated *h* is marked throughout this work with a dagger (†).

J has always the sound of *s* in *pleasure*, and is subject to no irregularity.

K has always a hard sound, as in the English word king, and is subject to no irregularity.

L has two sounds. The first is precisely the same as *l* in the English word lily. The second is liquid. The liquid *l*, whether double or single, is always preceded by *i*. It is similar to the sound of the last *i* in William.

It is to be remarked, that *i*, followed by *l* or *ll*, and preceded by another vowel, is always silent in pronunciation; it only serves to indicate the liquid sound of the *l*, as in *paille*, *soleil*, *patrouille*, which ought to be pronounced *pâ-i*, *solé-i*, *patrou-i*. But when *i* is not preceded by another vowel, as in *fille*, it retains its natural sound, and serves at the same time to indicate the liquid sound of *l*. And here in *fille*, pronounced *fi-i*, we find both the *i* natural and the *i* which stands for *ll*. Whenever *i* begins a word, as in *illusion*, the *l*'s are never liquid. The liquid *l* is marked throughout this work with a star (*).

P has the sound of the same letter in English, as in *peine*, pain. When combined with *h*, it has the sound of *f*, as in *philosophe*, philosopher.

Q has the hard sound of *k*, as in the English word *quaker*. Whether initial or medial, *q* is always followed by *u*, which is not sounded except in a few words that are noticed in the course of this work.

R has the same sound as in English, but is articulated much more strongly, as in *rivière*, river. It is always sounded at the end of words, when preceded by the vowels *a*, *i*, *o*, *u*. In substantives, adjectives, and verbs ending in *er*, it is silent, unless it is followed by a word beginning with a vowel or *h* mute, as in *dernier ouvrage*, which is pronounced *dernié-rouvraj*.

S has two sounds. The first is hissing, as in the English word *sister*; the second is soft, as in the English word *please*. It has uniformly the hissing sound at the beginning of words, and the soft between two vowels. Both sounds occur in *saison*. It preserves its hissing sound in compound words, as in *parasol*, *vraisemblable*; and when it happens to be sounded at the end of words, as in *Pallas*, *Brutus*, *vis*.

When *s* final is joined to the following word, it is always articulated like *z*, as in *dans un cas important*, which must be pronounced *dān-zun-kâ-zin-por-tān*.

T has two sounds; one hard, as in the English word *tutor*, and the other like the hissing *s*, as in *sister*. Both occur in *situation*, which is pronounced *si-tuā-sion*. It has the hissing sound before *i*, connected with some other following vowel or vowels, as in *patience*, *factieux*, which are pronounced *pasian-s*, *fak-sieŭ*.

When *t*, however, is immediately preceded by *s*, it preserves the hard sound, as in *bastion*, *question*, which are pronounced *bas-tion*, *kès-tion*.

X has generally the sound of *ks*. In all words beginning with *x* or *ex*, followed by a vowel, it has the sound of *gz*, as in *Xavier*, *exil*, which are pronounced *gzavié*, *èg-zil*. When final, it is joined to the following word, and sounds like *z*, as in *beaux yeux*, *dix hommes*, which are pronounced *bô-zieŭ*, *di-zom*. X has the sound of *ss* in *Auxerre*, *Auxonne*, and *Bruxelles*.

FINAL CONSONANTS.

The final consonants that are sounded are *b*, *c*, *f*, *k*, *l*, *m*, *q*, *r*.

The final consonants that are not sounded in words which stand alone, or terminate a sentence, are, *d*, *g*, *h*, *n*, *p*, *r* (in the termination *er* only), *s*, *t*, *x*, *z*.

J and v are never final.

D is pronounced like *t* when joined to the following word, as in *quand il parle*, which must be pronounced *kăn-til parle*.

G is pronounced like *k*, as in *sang impur*, which is pronounced *săn-kin-pur*.

P is pronounced only in *Alep*, *cap*, *Gap*, *cep*, *jalap*; and in *beaucoup*, *trop*, when those two words come before a vowel. In *cep de vigne*, the *p* is silent.

R, preceded by e, is frequently silent in conversation before a vowel, but it must always be sounded in poetry, unless it terminates the verse.

S, before a vowel, sounds like *z*, as in *nous avons eu*, which must be pronounced *nou-zavŏn-zu*. S is sounded in *aloès*, *bibus*, *blocus*, *chorus*, *choléra-morbus*, *dervis*, *florès*, *gratis*, *jadis*, *laps*, *maïs*, *mars*, *orémus*, *ours*, *rébus*, *relaps*, *Reims*, *Rubens*, *sinus*, *en sus*, *vasistas*, etc. It is silent in *Jésus-Christ*, but sounded in *le Christ*.

T is generally pronounced before a vowel, except when it is preceded by a sounded consonant, as in *effort étonnant*, pronounced *é-for-éto-nan*; in *quatre-vingt-un* it is not pronounced, but it is sounded in *vingt et un*. In all plural nouns, and in the conjunction *et*; also before a vowel in *fort*, adjective, it is silent, but it is sounded in *fort*, adverb. Final *t* is also sounded in *brut*, *déficit*, *dot*, *mat*, *exact*, *fat*, *infect*, *intact*, *net*, *rapt*, *subit*, *tact*, *toast*, *transit*, *zénith*, etc. It is not heard in *Jésus-Christ*, though it is sounded in *le Christ*.

LIST OF THE NOUNS OF DOUBLE GENDER EXISTING IN THE FRENCH LANGUAGE.

Aide............ { m., a male assistant.
 { f., a female assistant ; aid, help, succor.

Aigle........... { m., male eagle.
 { f., she-eagle ; standard, eagle.

Ange........... { m., angel ; (artil.) chain-shot, bar-shot; angel-shot; (ich.) angel-fish.[1]
 { f., not used.

Apologétique.. { m., Tertullian's treatise in defense of the early Christians.
 { f., apologetics, a part of theology.

Armadille...... { m., wood-louse.
 { f., armadilla, Spanish fleet to defend Spain's possessions in the New World ; Spanish frigate belonging to this fleet.

Asclépiade .... { m., (ancient poet.) asclepiad.
 { f., (bot.) asclepias, swallow-wort.

Aune........... { m., alder tree.
 { f., obsolete French measure = one ell.

Barbe.......... { m., Barbary horse.
 { f., beard.

Barde .... { m., a bard, Celtic poet.
 { f., a thin slice, a rasher of bacon.

Basque........ { m., Biscayan ; Basque (nation and language).
 { f., flap, skirt, tail, of a coat, or any other garment.

Bourgogne.... { m., Burgundy (wine).
 { f., Burgundy (province).

Brie .... { m., Brie (cheese).
 { f., Brie (province); rolling-pin.

Bulbe.......... { m., (anat.) bulb.
 { f., 2(bot.) bulb.

Câpres[3]....... { m., ⊙pirate ; privateer; piratical ship.
 { f., (bot.) caper.

Carpe.......... { m., wrist.
 { f., (ich.) carp.

Cartouche...... { m., (arch.) cartouch, modillion.
 { f., cartridge for small firearms.

Caustique ..... { m., (med.) caustic.
 { f., (geom., phys.) caustic curve.

Champagne .... { m., Champagne (wine).
 { f., Champagne (province).

Chorée......... { m., choreus, choree, trochee.
 { f., (med.) chorea, St. Vitus' dance.

Cinquième.... { m., the fifth part; pupil in the 5th form in public schools.
 { f., 5th form in public schools.

Cistophore .... { m., (antiq.) Asiatic coin marked with a cist.
 { f., (antiq.) a female cist-bearer in the feast of Ceres and Bacchus.

Claque .... { m., opera hat.
 { f., flap, slap, smack; (thea.) claque, paid clappers.

Cloaque .... { m., sink, receptacle of filth ; filthy, dirty place ; filthy person ; (anat.) cloaca.
 { f., (Roman antiq.) common sewer.

Coche .... { m., barge for the conveyance of travelers, track-boat, coach.
 { f., sow, she-pig; notch, nick, indentation.

Connétable.... { m., High-Constable.
 { f., High-Constable's wife.

Contumace.... { m., a man guilty of contumacy (jur.).
 { f., contumacy.

Cornette ...... { m., cornet, ensign-bearer (cavalry).
 { f., cornet, mob-cap ; (milit.) colors of a company of cavalry ; cornetcy ; (nav.) broad pendant.

Cosaque....... { m., Cossack.
 { f., Cossack dance.

Cosmétique ... { m., cosmetic.
 { f., the art of using cosmetics.

Cotte.......... { m., (ich.) bull-head, miller's-thumb.
 { f., ⊙petticoat. — d'armes; coat of arms. — de mailles; coat of mail. — morte; property left by a deceased monk.

Couple........ { m., a married pair, husband and wife.
 { f., a brace, two.

Cravate....... { m., Croatian horse; ⊙trooper of light cavalry regiments which bore the same name.
 { f., cravat, necktie, neckcloth.

Crêpe......... { m., crape.
 { f., pancake.

Critique...... { m., a critic.
 { f., criticism.

Custode....... { m., warden.
 { f., cloth to cover the pyx in which the Host is kept ; curtain of the high altar ; ⊙curtain.

Décime........ { m., copper coin worth 10 centimes, the tenth part of a franc: a war tax.
 { f., tithe formerly levied on ecclesiastical revenues ; pl., tax paid formerly to the king by the holders of benefices.

Dentale ...... { m., (conch.) dentalium, dental, tooth-shell.
 { f., dental, dental consonant.

Didactique.... { m., didactic language, didactic style.
 { f., the art of teaching.

Dixième....... { m., the tenth part; a tax.
 { f., (mus.) tenth.

Ébène[4]........ { m., not used.
 { f., ebony, ebon; (fig.) black color.

Écho.......... { m., echo.
 { f., Echo (nymph).

Élève......... { m., male pupil, school-boy.
 { f., female pupil, school-girl; breeding of horses, cattle, etc.

Enseigne...... { m., ensign, standard-bearer.
 { f., sign-board.

Éphémère..... { m., (ent.) ephemera, ephemeran, dayfly, May-fly.
 { f., spider-wort, tradescantia virginica.

Espace........ { m., space, distance, interval.
 { f., (print.) space, metallic plate to separate words.

Exemple...... { m., example.
 { f., writing-copy.

Faune........ { m., faun (myth.).
 { f., fauna.

Faux......... { m., forgery, falsehood.
 { f., scythe.

Fin .... { m., sharp, astute man ; gist, main point; (metal.) pure metal.
 { f., end, termination ; aim, object, view, design, intention.

Finale........ { m., (mus.) finale.
 { f., (gram.) final letter or syllable.

Flasque....... { m., cheek (of a gun-carriage).
 { f., powder-flask, powder-horn; (nav.) whelp (of the capstan); board (of bellows).

Follicule...... { m., (anat. bot.) follicle.
 { f., 5small sheet of paper; (pharm.) pod of senna.

Forêt6........ { m., drill (to bore holes).
 { f., forest.

Foudre .... { m. (st. e.) thunder-bolt, lightning ; (paint., sculpt.) thunder-bolt, Jupiter's attribute; (fig.) irresistible eloquence; great general, orator, hero; divine anger, vengeance; fulmination of excommunication, etc.: artillery, mines, war; (poet.) catastrophe, destruction. A tun (cask).
 { f., thunder-bolt, lightning ; (fig.) divine anger, vengeance; fulmination of excommunication, etc.; superior eloquence; artillery, mines, etc.

Fourbe........ { m., knave.
 { f., deceit, craftiness.

---

1 Some grammars and dictionaries give ange de mer, angel-fish, as feminine, but it is an error ; ange is masculine in all its acceptations.—(ACAD.)

2 In the language of botany this word is sometimes used in the masculine—(ACAD.)

3 In the sense of pirate, this word has no accent : câpre.

4 Some grammarians and lexicographers give ébène, in the figurative sense of black color, as masculine, but it is an error: ébène is feminine even when used figuratively.—(ACAD.)

5 Voltaire used this word in the feminine, in the sense of a small sheet of paper ; but it is contrary to etymology, and even to common sense. The French Academy does not give this acceptation.

6 When it means forest, its e has a circumflex accent: forêt.

Garde	*m.*, a guard, a keeper.
	f., guarding, guard; watching; keeping.
Garde-robe....	*m.*, lady's apron.
	f., wardrobe; (bot.) artemisia.
Geste	*m.*, gesture, action, movement. *pl.*, ⊙great deeds of generals, princes, etc.
	f., poem in old French.
Givre	*m.*, hoar frost, rime.
	f., (her.) snake, serpent, wyvern.
Grave	*m.*, (phys.) body, heavy body; (lit.) grave style; (mus.) flat ; wine made at Grave (France).
	f., shore, beach (Newfoundland) ; *pl.*, gravelly and clayey soil in the department of Gironde (France).
Greffe	*m.*, record-office of a court of justice.
	f., graft.
Grêle	*m.*, nut-coal.
	f., hail; (med.) chalazion, grando, hailstone.
Guérilla	*m.*, guerilla-soldier.
	f., guerilla, small army of irregulars.
Guide	*m.*, a guide.
	f., rein.
Havane	*m.*, Havana (cigar).
	f., Havana (town).
Hymne	*m.*, ode, hymn.
	f., hymn (church).
Inde	*m.*, indigo, indigo blue; logwood.
	f., India.
Interligne	*m.*, space between printed or written lines; space between the lines of the stave (mus.).
	f., (print.) lead, metallic plate to separate lines.
Jujube	*m.*, the extract of jujube (fruit).
	f., ¹jujube (fruit).
Laque	*m.*, lacker, lacquer.
	f., lac, lake, gum-lake.
Lepte	*m.*, (ent.) leptus, wheal worm, harvest-bug.
	f., (bot.) a triphyllous plant of the order celastraceæ.
Lévite	*m.*, Levite.
	f., surtout, overcoat.
Liquide	*m.*, a liquid.
	f., (gram.) liquid, liquid consonant.
Litre	*m.*, liter, French measure of capacity, less than a quart.
	f., band of black cloth bearing the coat of arms of a deceased person, and hung in church at his funeral.
Livre	*m.*, book.
	f., pound (weight, money).
Louche	*m.*, ambiguity; equivocalness; underhand dealing.
	f., soup-ladle.
Loutre	*m.*, ⊙a hat, a muff, etc., made of otter-skin or hair.
	f., otter.
Maheutre	*m.*, (French hist.) Protestant soldier.
	f., a sleeve that was formerly worn, and did not reach further than the elbow.
Manche	*m.*, handle of a tool, a knife, etc.
	f., sleeve; the English Channel.
Manœuvre....	*m.*, day-laborer ; bricklayer's journeyman; (fig.) bungler ; crafty person.
	f., (milit., nav.) maneuver ; running rigging, cordages of a ship.
Marengo........	*m.*, Oxford gray (color).
	f., (cook.) marengo (sauce for fowl).
Maroufle.......	*m.*, ragamuffin, lout, rascallion, clodhopper.
	f., (paint.) lining-paste.
Martyre	*m.*, martyrdom.
	f., a female martyr.
Masque	*m.*, a mask.
	f., ⊙ugly woman, ugly girl.
Mémoire	*m.*, memorandum ; memoir ; bill (of large amount).
	f., the memory.
Merci..........	*m.*, thanks.
	f., mercy, grace, benevolence, favor.
Mestre de Camp.......	*m.*, ⊙colonel; general.
	f., ⊙the 1st company of a regiment.
Minime	*m.*, minim, Franciscan monk.
	f., ⊙(mus.) minim.
Mobile	*m.*, mover, spring, motive power; motive; soldier in the *garde mobile.*
	f., the *garde mobile,* a French infantry corps no longer in existence.

Mode	*m.*, mood, mode; method.
	f., fashion.
Môle	*m.*, pier, jetty.
	f., (med.) mole.
Mort	*m.*, a dead man.
	f., death.
Moufle²	*m.*, (chem.) muffle.
	f., (mec.) tackle (assemblage of pulleys); fingerless glove.
Moule	*m.*, mold, matrix to cast lead, iron, etc.
	f., (ich.) mussel.
Mousse	*m.*, cabin-boy, apprentice sailor.
	f., moss; froth, foam.
Mulle	*m.*, (ich.) mullet.
	f., ⊙rennet, prepared membrane of the calf's stomach.
Myope	*m.*, myope, short-sighted man ; (ent.) conops.
	f., myope, short-sighted female.
Mystique......	*m.*, mystic (man).
	f., mystic (female); the study of spirituality.
Néphrétique ..	*m.*, (med.) nephritic ; man affected with nephritis.
	f., nephritic, renal colic.
Nielle	*m.*, niello.
	f., blight, smut ; (bot.) rose campion.
Noël	*m.*, Christmas; Christmas carol.
	f.. *la Noël* (ellipsis for *la* fête de *Noël*), Christmas-day.
Œuvre	*m.*, the philosopher's stone ; (arch.) walls ; the whole of the works of an engraver, painter, or composer of music ; argentiferous lead ; (jur.) summons to one who builds upon another man's ground.
	f., work, deed, action ; work of the hand ; handiwork ; (jewel.) bezel ; (nav.) hull of a ship ; the works of a writer.
Office	*m.*, divine service; duty; office³; employment ; formulary of prayers. *Saint——*; holy-office, inquisition.
	f., servants' hall; pantry.
Ombre⁴........	*m.*, (ich.) umbra, chromis, corvo; umber, grayling, char ; (card game) omber.
	f., shade, shadow; spirit, ghost.
Once	*m.*, mountain-cat, catamount.
	f., ounce (weight); jaguar, ounce.
Orphiques....	*m.*, Orpheus' poems ; Pythagoreans, votaries of Orpheus.
	f., orgies, feast in honor of Bacchus.
Page	*m.*, page, young male servant.
	f., page of a book, etc.
Paillasse	*m.*, clown, merry-andrew.
	f., straw-bed, straw-bed ticking.
Palme	*m.*, palm; hand (measures).
	f., palm; palm-branch ; (bot.) palmtree ; pattern of cashmere shawls ; (sculpt., arch.) palm ; (her.) palm ; (bot.) Cuban reed : (nav.) a kind of East Indian ship with two masts.
Pantomime....	*m.*, pantomimist, pantomime.
	f., dumb-show, pantomime.
Pâques⁵........	*m.*, Easter (Christian religion).
	f., Passover, Easter (Jewish religion).
Parallèle	*m.*, comparison ; (geog.) parallel of latitude.
	f., (geom.) parallel line;(fort.) trench, trenches.
Part...........	*m.*,(jur.)new-born child,infant;birth.
	f., share, portion, part ; concern, interest, part, side.
Peau-rouge....	*m.*, American Indian, Red-skin.
	f., (no hyphen) any one's skin when it is red, or redder than usual.
Pendule	*m.*, pendulum.
	f., time-piece.
Période	*m.*, highest point, acme, height.
	f., period, epoch.
Personne	*m.*, (pron.) nobody, anybody.
	f., (noun) a person.
Physique.......	*m.*, a person's constitution, body.
	f., natural philosophy.
Pique	*m.*, spade (cards).
	f., pike (weapon); tiff, pique, quarrel.
Pivoine	*m.*, (orni.) bull-finch.
	f., (bot.) peony, piony.

---

² French mechanicians give to this noun, in the sense of *tackle,* the masculine gender.

³ This word has never in French the meaning of *room, apartment,* for the transaction of business.

⁴ *Ombre,* card game, is also spelt *hombre.*

⁵ *Pâque,* or *Pâques,* Christian religion, is often used in the plural, and is then feminine. *Pâque,* Jewish religion, is always feminine, and never used in the plural.

---

¹ The French Academy gives to *jujube* (fruit) the feminine gender; but it is contrary to general present usage.

Plane	*m.*, (bot.) plane-tree ; inside surface of scissors blades. *f.*, joiner's plane : spoke-shave, drawing-knife ; (ich.) plaice.
Platine	*m.*, (metal.) platinum. *f.*, lock (of small fire-arms) ; metallic-plate.
Podagre	*m.*, a podagrical man, *i. e.* one having the gout in his feet. *f.*, podagra, gout in the feet.
Pôele	*m.*, pall ; stove. *f.*, frying-pan.
Polacre *or* **Polaque** ...	*m.*, ⊙Polish cavalry. *f.*, (nav.) polacca, polacre.
Politique	*m.*, politician. *f.*, politics ; policy.
Ponte	*m.*, punter (gambling). *f.*, laying of eggs.
Poste	*m.* post, situation. *f.*, post, mail, post-office ; buckshot.
Poulpe	*m.*, (mol.) poulp, octopus. *f.*, pulp, pap.
Pourpre	*m.*, purple (color) ; (her.) purpure ; (chem.) purple ; (med.) purples. *f.*, purple, coloring matter extracted from *buccinum lapillus ;* stuff, fabric dyed in purple ; (fig.) vivid red color ; sovereign dignity, cardinal's dignity.
Prétexte	*m.*, pretense, pretext. *f.*, (Rom. ant.) prætexta.
Primevère	*m.*, ⊙spring season. *f.*, (bot.) primrose, cowslip, oxlip.
Pupille	*m.*, a male ward. *f.*, a female ward ; pupil of the eye.
Pyrrhique ...	*m.*, pyrrhic (poet.) *f.*, pyrrhic, military dance.
Quadrille	*m.*, quadrille (card game) ; quadrille, a dance ; (mus.) quadrille. *f.*, troup of horses in a tournament.
Quadruple ...	*m.*, quadruple, fourfold ; (Spanish coin) doubloon. *f.*, Spanish gold coin worth about £3 8s.
Quatrième ...	*m.*, fourth ; 4th floor ; pupil of the 4th form in public schools. *f.*, 4th form in public schools ; (piquet) quart.
Queux	*m.*, ⊙cook. *f.*, whetting-stone, hone.
Réciproque ...	*m.*, like, like for like, tit for tat. *f.*, (log.) converse.
Réclame	*m.*, (hawking) cry, sign to bring back a hawk to the lure or to the fist. *f.*, (print.) catch-word ; primer ; editorial advertisement in newspapers ; (c. rel.) part of the responses recited in the versicle : (thea.) cue.
Régale	*m.*, organ stop imitating the human voice ; regal (musical instrument). *f.*, the king's right to receive the revenue of a vacant bishopric.
Réglisse	*m.*, *du réglisse* (popular ellipsis for *du jus de réglisse*) extract of liquorice, Spanish juice. *f.*, (bot.) liquorice, licorice ; liquorice root.
Relâche	*m.*, (thea.) non-performance. *f.*, (nav.) putting into port.
Remise	*m.*, coach let on hire, livery-coach. *f.*, coach-house ; (com.) remittance.
Rencontre	*m.*, (her.) rencounter. *f.*, encounter, rencounter, accidental meeting ; accident, chance, collision ; meeting ; accidental fight ; opportunity, occurrence, case ; juncture.
Rhingrave ...	*m.*, count of the Rhine. *f.*, ⊙knee-breeches.
Romaïque	*m.*, Romaic, modern Greek language. *f.*, the Greek national dance.
Rossinante ...	*m.*, Rosinante, Don Quixote's horse. *f.*, Rosinante, a sorry horse, a jade.
Sagittaire	*m.*, (astron.) Saggitarius. *f.* (bot.) arrow-head, adder's-tongue.
Sarde	*m.*, a native of Sardinia. *f.*, (ich.) whale ; scomber ; sardan ; Brazilian sardine or pilchard.
Satyre	*m.*, (myth.) satyr. *f.*, (Grec. ant.) satyric tragedy.

Scolastique	*m.*, scholastic ; school-man. *f.*, scholasticism.
Scolie	*m.*, (geom.) scholium. *f.*, scholium, annotation ; (Grec. antiq.) table-song.
Scytale	*m.*, (zoöl.) a species of very venomous snakes. *f.*, (antiq.) staff used in Sparta as a cypher to write secret dispatches.
Septième	*m.*, seventh, seventh part, seventh day. *f.*, (piquet) septième ; (mus.) seventh.
Serpentaire	*m.*, (astron.) Serpentarius ; (orni.) secretary-bird, snake-eater. *f.*, (bot.) dragon's-wort.
Silène	*m.*, (myth.) Silenus ; Satyr, attendant of Bacchus ; (ent.) a South European butterfly. *f.*, (bot.) catch-fly.
Sixième	*m.*, sixth, sixth part ; sixth day ; pupil of the 6th class in public schools. *f.*, (piquet) seizième ; 6th class in public schools.
Solde	*m.*, balance of an account. *f.*, soldier's pay.
Somme	*m.*, nap, slumbers, doze, sleep. *f.*, a sum of money ; total ; load, burden.
Souris	*m.*, smile. *f.*, mouse.
Statère [1]	*m.*, (antiq.) stater (coin). *f.*, (antiq.) statera, Roman balance.
Statuaire	*m.*, sculptor. *f.*, the art of making statues, statuary.
Stipe	*m.*, (bot.) stipe ; caudex. *f.*, (bot.) stipa, feather-grass ; ⊙ a tax on leases.
Superbe	*m.*, proud, haughty man. *f.*, arrogance, haughtiness, vainglory.
Technique	*m.*, (arts) material execution, technicalities. *f.*, technics.
Teneur	*m.*, keeper, accountant ; *teneur de livres ;* book-keeper. *f.*, text, terms, purport, tenor, contents, of writings.
Terre-neuve ...	*m.*, Newfoundland dog. *f.*, Newfoundland.
Tirelire	*m.*, ⊙ song, carol of the lark. *f.*, money-box.
Tonique	*m.*, (med.) tonic. *f.*, (mus.) tonic, key-note, key.
Topique	*m.*, (rhet., med.) tonic. *f.*, (rhet.) the art of finding topics or arguments.
Tour	*m.*, turn ; tour ; lathe ; trick. *f.*, tower.
Triomphe	*m.*, triumph. *f.*, triumph (card-game).
Trochée	*m.*, (poet.) trochee. *f.*, (agri.) brushwood.
Troisième	*m.*, third ; third floor ; pupil of the 3d class in public schools. *f.*, 3d class in public schools.
Trolle	*m.*, globe-flower, trollius. *f.*, (hunt.) trolling.
Trompette	*m.*, trumpeter. *f.*, trumpet.
Trouble	*m.*, confusion, disorder, disturbance ; dispute, quarrel ; *pl.* troubles, broils, commotions. *f.*, hoop-net (for fishing).
Vague	*m.*, space, emptiness ; vagueness ; looseness ; uncertainty. *f.*, sea-wave, billow.
Vapeur	*m.*, steamer, steam-boat. *f.*, steam ; vapor.
Vase	*m.*, vase. *f.*, mud, slime, mire.
Vigogne	*m.*, hat made of vicugna wool. *f.*, (zoöl.) vicugna.
Voile	*m.*, veil. *f.*, sail.
Vulnéraire	*m.*, (pharm.) vulnerary. *f.*, (bot.) kidney-vetch, woundwort

---

[1] When it means a coin, it is also spelt *stater.*

TABLE OF IRREGULAR AND DEFECTIVE VERBS.

THE Imperfect of the Indicative, the Conditional, the Imperative, and the Imperfect of the Subjunctive, are wanting in this Table. These four tenses are formed as follows : —

The imperfect of the indicative is regularly formed from the present participle by changing *ant* into *ais*, as : *parl-ant, je parl-ais ; finiss-ant, je finiss-ais,* &c.

The conditional has always the same root as the future ; so that the first person of the future being known, it is easy to form the conditional, as : *je parlerai, je parlerai-s ; je finirai, je finirai-s.*

The imperative is always regularly formed from the present of the indicative, by suppressing the pronouns, as : *je parle,* imperative, *parle ;* except in the verbs *avoir, être,* and *savoir.* The third person singular and plural of the imperative are always the same as in the present of the subjunctive, and belong to that tense.

The imperfect of the subjunctive is always regularly formed from the preterit indicative by adding *se,* etc., to the second person singular, as : *tu parlas, que je parlas-se ; tu finis, que je finis-se ; tu reçus, que je reçus-se; tu vendis, que je vendis-se.*

FIRST CONJUGATION.

Infinitive.	Present participle.	Past participle.	Present.	Indicative Preterit.	Future.	Subjunctive Present.	English.
Aller	allant	allé	je vais, allons vas, allez va, vont	j'allai	j'irai	aille, allions ailles, alliez aille, aillent	to go.
Envoyer	envoyant	envoyé	j'envoie, envoyons envoies, envoyez envoie, envoient	j'envoyai	j'enverrai	envoie, envoyions envoies, envoyiez envoie, envoient	to send.

SECOND CONJUGATION.

Infinitive.	Present participle.	Past participle.	Present.	Indicative Preterit.	Future.	Subjunctive Present.	English.
Acquérir	acquérant	acquis	j'acquiers, acquérons acquiers, acquérez acquiert, acquièrent	j'acquis	j'acquerrai	acquière, acquérions acquières, acquériez acquière, acquièrent	to acquire.
Assaillir	assaillant	assailli	j'assaille, assaillons assailles, assaillez assaille, assaillent	j'assaillis	j'assaillirai	assaille, assaillions assailles, assailliez assaille, assaillent	to assault.
Avenir[1]	avenant	avenu	il avient	il avint	il aviendra	qu'il avienne	to happen.
Bouillir[2]	bouillant	bouilli	je bous, bouillons bous, bouillez bout, bouillent	je bouillis	je bouillirai	bouille, bouillions bouilles, bouilliez bouille, bouillent	to boil.
Courir	courant	couru	je cours, courons cours, courez court, courent	je courus	je courrai	coure, courions coures, couriez coure, courent	to run.
Cueillir	cueillant[+]	cueilli	je cueille, cueillons cueilles, cueillez cueille, cueillent	je cueillis	je cueillerai	cueille, cueillions cueilles, cueilliez cueille, cueillent	to gather.

---

1 *Advenir* is more often used.
2 The verb *faire* is generally used to conjugate this verb ; as, *faire bouillir,* &c., except in 3d pers. singular and plural when used "*directly*": As, l'eau bout-elle does the water boil ? Ces pommes de terre bouillent-elles ? Do these potatoes boil ?

SECOND CONJUGATION (continued).

Infinitive.	Present participle.	Past participle.	Present.	Indicative Preterit.	Future.	Subjunctive Present.	English.
Défaillir[1]		défailli	nous défaillons vous défaillez ils défaillent	je défaillis ils défaillirent			to faint.
Dormir	dormant	dormi	je dors, dormons dors, dormez dort, dorment	je dormis	je dormirai	dorme, dormions dormes, dormiez dorme, dorment	to sleep.
Ébouillir		ébouilli					to boil away.
Faillir[2]	faillant	failli	je faux, faillons faux, faillez faut, faillent	je faillis	je faudrai		to fail.
Férir[3]		féru					to strike.
Fleurir	fleurissant florissant	fleuri	je fleuris, fleurissons fleuris, fleurissez fleurit, fleurissent	je fleuris	je fleurirai	fleurisse, fleurissions fleurisses, fleurissiez fleurisse, fleurissent	to flourish, to prosper.
Fuir	fuyant	fui	je fuis, fuyons fuis, fuyez fuit, fuient	je fuis	je fuirai	fuie, fuyions fuies, fuyiez fuie, fuient	to flee.
Gésir[4]	gisant		gisons gisez gît, gisent				to lie.
Haïr	haïssant	haï	je hais, haïssons hais, haïssez hait, haïssent	je haïs	je haïrai	haïsse	to hate.
Mésavenir			il mésavient	il mésavint		qu'il mésavienne	to succeed ill.
Mourir	mourant	mort	je meurs, mourons meurs, mourez meurt, meurent	je mourus	je mourrai	meure, mourions meures, mouriez meure, meurent	to die.
Ouïr[5]		ouï	j'ois, oyons ois, oyez oit, oient	j'ouïs	j'oirai	(old, legal)	to hear.
Ouvrir	ouvrant	ouvert	j'ouvre, ouvrons ouvres, ouvrez ouvre, ouvrent	j'ouvris	j'ouvrirai	ouvre, ouvrions ouvres, ouvriez ouvre, ouvrent	to open.
Quérir[6]							to fetch.
Saillir[7]	saillant	sailli	il saille ils saillent		il saillera ils sailleront	qu'il saille qu'ils saillent	to project.
Sentir	sentant	senti	je sens, sentons sens, sentez sent, sentent	je sentis	je sentirai	sente, sentions sentes, sentiez sente, sentent	to feel, smell.
Servir	servant	servi	je sers, servons sers, servez sert, servent	je servis	je servirai	serve, servions serves, serviez serve, servent	to serve.
Sortir[8]	sortissant	sorti	il sortit il sortissent		il sortira ils sortiront	qu'il sortisse qu'ils sortissent	to obtain.
Surgir[9]			il surgit ils surgissent	il surgit	il surgira		to spring up, to arise.
Tenir	tenant	tenu	je tiens, tenons tiens, tenez tient, tiennent	je tins	je tiendrai	tienne, tenions tiennes, teniez tienne, tiennent	to hold.
Vêtir	vêtant	vêtu	je vêts, vêtons vêts, vêtez vêt, vêtent	je vêtis	je vêtirai	vête, vêtions vêtes, vêtiez vête, vêtent	to clothe.

THIRD CONJUGATION.

Infinitive.	Present participle.	Past participle.	Present.	Indicative Preterit.	Future.	Subjunctive Present.	English.
Apparoir[10]			il appert				to appear.
Asseoir	asseyant	assis	j'assieds, asseyons assieds, asseyez assied, asseient	j'assis	j'assiérai or j'assoirai	asseie, asseyions or asseye asseies, asseyiez asseie, asseient	to set.

---

[1] The imperfect of the indicative, je défaillais, is used.
[2] This verb is seldom used but in the preterit, the compound tenses, and in the infinitive after another verb.
[3] The infinitive is only used in the phrase sans coup férir, without striking a blow.
[4] The imperfect of the indicative, je gisais, &c., is used.
[5] This verb is seldom used but in the infinitive present, and in the compound tenses.
[6] Used only in familiar conversation, and in the infinitive after aller, venir, envoyer.
[7] Used only in the third persons. When it means "to gush," or (of a horse) to serve a mare, it is conjugated like finir.
[8] Used as a law term only.
[9] Seldom used but in the infinitive.
[10] Used as a law term only.

THIRD CONJUGATION (continued).

Infinitive.	Present participle.	Past participle.	Present.	Indicative Preterit.	Future.	Subjunctive Present.	English.
Avoir	ayant	eu	j'ai, avons as, avez a, ont	j'eus	j'aurai	aie, ayons aies, ayez ait, aient	to have.
Choir		chu					to fall.
Comparoir[1]							to appear (before a tribunal).
Déchoir[2]		déchu	je déchois, déchoyons déchois, déchoyez déchoit, déchoient	je déchus	je décherrai	déchoie, déchoyions déchoies, déchoyiez déchoie, déchoient	to fall, lose.
Démouvoir							to make one desist.
Échoir[3]	échéant	échu	il échoit or il échet	il échut	il écherra	échoie	to fall due, to expire.
Falloir[4]		fallu	il faut	il fallut	il faudra	qu'il faille	to be necessary.
Mouvoir	mouvant	mu	je meus, mouvons meus, mouvez meut, meuvent	je mus	je mouvrai	meuve, mouvions meuves, mouviez meuve, meuvent	to move.
Pleuvoir	pleuvant	plu	il pleut	il plut	il pleuvra	qu'il pleuve	to rain.
Pourvoir	pourvoyant	pourvu	je pourvois, pour-voyons pourvois, pourvoyez pourvoit, pourvoient	je pourvus	je pourvoi-rai	pourvoie, pour-voyions pourvoies, pourvoyiez pourvoie, pourvoient	to provide.
Pouvoir	pouvant	pu	[5]je puis, pouvons peux, pouvez peut, peuvent	je pus	je pourrai	puisse, puissions puisses, puissiez puisse, puissent	to be able.
Prévaloir[11]	prévalant	prévalu	je prévaux, prévalons prévaux, prévalez prévaut, prévalent	je préva-lus	je prévau-drai	prévale, prévalions prévales, prévaliez prévale, prévalent	to prevail.
Prévoir	prévoyant	prévu	je prévois, pérvoyons prévois, prévoyez prévoit, prévoient	je prévis	je prévoirai	prévoie, prévoyions prévoies, prévoyiez prévoie, prévoient	to foresee.
Promouvoir[6]		promu					to promote.
Ravoir[7]							to recover, to have again.
Savoir[8]	sachant	su	je sais, savons sais, savez sait, savent	je sus	je saurai	sache, sachions saches, sachiez sache, sachent	to know
Seoir[9]	seyant		il sied ils siéent		il siéra ils siéront	qu'il siée qu'ils siéent	to become, to befit.
Seoir[10]	séant	sis					to sit, situate.
Surseoir	sursoyant	sursis	je sursois, sursoyons sursois, sursoyez sursoit, sursoient	je sursis	je surseoirai	sursoie, sursoyions sursoies, sursoyiez sursoie, sursoient	to put off, to suspend.
Valoir[11]	valant	valu	je vaux, valons vaux, valez vaut, valent	je valus	je vaudrai	vaille, valions vailles, valiez vaille, vaillent	to be worth.
Voir	voyant	vu	je vois, voyons vois, voyez voit, voient	je vis	je verrai	voie, voyions voies, voyiez voie, voient	to see.
Vouloir[12]	voulant	voulu	je veux, voulons veux, voulez veut, veulent	je voulus	je voudrai	veuille, voulions veuilles, vouliez veuille, veuillent	to be willing.

1 Used as a law term only.

2 Imperfect of the indicative: *je déchoyais*, &c.

3 Used generally in the third person only.

4 *Il fallait* is used. No imperative.

5 *Je peux* is also used. No imperative.

6 Only used in the infinitive, in the compound tenses, and in the imperfect of the subjunctive.

7 Used in the infinitive only.

8 Imperative: *sache, sachons, sachez. Je ne sache* is rhetorically used in the first person of the indicative present. Ex.: "*Je ne sache* rien de plus grand et de plus beau" (V. Hugo). The imperfect of the indicative is *je savais*, &c.

9 Used in the third person only. No compound tenses.

10 Used in the two participles only.

11 No imperative.

12 The second person plural of the imperative is *veuillez*, please to.

FOURTH CONJUGATION.

Infinitive.	Present participle.	Past participle.	Present.	Indicative Preterit.	Future.	Subjunctive Present.	English.
Absoudre	absolvant	absous, m. absoute, f.	j'absous, absolvons absous, absolvez absout, absolvent		j'absoudrai	absolve, absolvions absolves, absolviez absolve, absolvent	to absolve.
Abstraire	abstrayant	abstrait	j'abstrais, abstrayons abstrais, abstrayez abstrait, abstraient		j'abstrairai	abstraie, abstrayions abstraies, abstrayiez abstraie, abstraient	to abstract.
Accroire[1] (i. e. faire accroire (à))							to make one believe.
Battre	battant	battu	je bats, battons bats, battez bat, battent	je battis	je battrai	batte, battions battes, battiez batte, battent	to beat.
Boire	buvant	bu	je bois, buvons bois, buvez boit, boivent	je bus	je boirai	boive, buvions boives, buviez boive, boivent	to drink.
Braire			il brait ils braient		il braira ils brairont		to bray.
Bruire[2]	bruyant						to roar, to rustle.
Circoncire	circoncisant	circoncis	je circoncis, circoncisons circoncis, circoncisez circoncit, circoncisent	je circoncis	je circoncirai	circoncise, circoncisions circoncises, circoncisiez circoncise, circoncisent	to circumcise.
Clore[3]		clos	je clos clos clôt		je clorai		to close.
Conclure	concluant	conclu	je conclus, concluons conclus, concluez conclut, concluent	je conclus	je conclurai	conclue, concluions conclues, concluiez conclue, concluent	to conclude.
Confire	confisant	confit	je confis, confisons confis, confisez confit, confisent	je confis	je confirai	confise, confisions confises, confisiez confise, confisent	to pickle, preserve.
Coudre	cousant	cousu	je couds, cousons couds, cousez coud, cousent	je cousis	je coudrai	couse, cousions couses, cousiez couse, cousent	to sew.
Croire	croyant	cru	je crois, croyons crois, croyez croit, croient	je crus	je croirai	croie, croyions croies, croyiez croie, croient	to believe.
Croître	croissant	crû	je croîs, croissons croîs, croissez croît, croissent	je crûs	je croîtrai	croisse, croissions croisses, croissiez croisse, croissent	to grow.
Déconfire		déconfit					to discomfit.
Dire	disant	dit	je dis, disons dis, dites dit, disent	je dis	je dirai	dise, disions dises, disiez dise, disent	to say.
Éclore		éclos	il éclôt ils éclosent		il éclora ils écloront	qu'il éclose qu'ils éclosent	to hatch, to blow (of flowers).
Écrire	écrivant	écrit	j'écris, écrivons écris, écrivez écrit, écrivent	j'écrivis	j'écrirai	écrive, écrivions écrives, écriviez écrive, écrivent	to write.
s'Emboire[4]		embu					to imbibe.
s'Ensuivre	ensuivant	ensuivi	il s'ensuit	il s'ensuivit	il s'ensuivra	qu'il s'ensuive	to follow, to result from.
s'Éprendre		épris					to be smitten.
Être	étant	été	je suis, sommes es, êtes est, sont	je fus	je serai	sois, soyons sois, soyez soit, soient	to be.
Faire	faisant	fait	je fais, faisons fais, faites fait, font	je fis	je ferai	fasse, fassions fasses, fassiez fasse, fassent	to make, to do.

[1] Used only in the infinitive, and always with the verb *faire*.
[2] Imperfect of the indicative *il bruyait, ils bruyaient.*
[3] Used in all the compound tenses.
[4] Used in painting only.

FOURTH CONJUGATION (continued).

Infinitive.	Present participle.	Past participle.	Present.	Indicative Preterit.	Future.	Subjunctive Present.	English.
Forfaire (à)[1]		forfait					to forfeit, to trespass, to be false to.
Frire[2]		frit	fris fris frit		je frirai		to fry.
Joindre	joignant	joint	je joins, joignons joins, joignez joint, joignent	je joignis	je joindrai	joigne, joignions joignes, joigniez joigne, joignent	to join.
Lire	lisant	lu	je lis, lisons lis, lisez lit, lisent	je lus	je lirai	lise, lisions lises, lisiez lise, lisent	to read.
Luire	luisant	lui	je luis, luisons luis, luisez luit, luisent		je luirai	luise, luisions luises, luisiez luise, luisent	to shine.
Malfaire							to do mischief.
Maudire	maudissant	maudit	je maudis, maudissons maudis, maudissez maudit, maudissent	je maudis	je maudirai	maudisse, maudissions maudisses, maudissiez maudisse, maudissent	to curse.
Médire (de)	médisant	médit	je médis, médisons médis, médisez médit, médisent	je médis	je médirai	médise, médisions médises, médisiez médise, médisent	to slander.
Méfaire		méfait					to misdo.
Mettre	mettant	mis	je mets, mettons mets, mettez met, mettent	je mis	je mettrai	mette, mettions mettes, mettiez mette, mettent	to put.
Moudre	moulant	moulu	je mouds, moulons mouds, moulez moud, moulent	je moulus	je moudrai	moule, moulions moules, mouliez moule, moulent	to grind.
Naître	naissant	né	je nais, naissons nais, naissez naît, naissent	je naquis	je naîtrai	naisse, naissions naisses, naissiez naisse, naissent	to be born.
Nuire (à)	nuisant	nui	je nuis, nuisons nuis, nuisez nuit, nuisent	je nuisis	je nuirai	nuise, nuisions nuises, nuisiez nuise, nuisent	to hurt, to injure.
Paître	paissant	pu	je pais, paissons pais, paissez paît, paissent		je paîtrai	paisse, paissions paisses, paissiez paisse, paissent	to graze.
Paraître	paraissant	paru	je parais, paraissons parais, paraissez paraît, paraissent	je parus	je paraîtrai	paraisse, paraissions paraisses, paraissiez paraisse, paraissent	to appear.
Plaire	plaisant	plu	je plais, plaisons plais, plaisez plaît, plaisent	je plus	je plairai	plaise, plaisions plaises, plaisiez plaise, plaisent	to please.
Poindre			il point		il poindra		to dawn, to sting.
Prendre	prenant	pris	je prends, prenons prends, prenez prend, prennent	je pris	je prendrai	prenne, prenions prennes, preniez prenne, prennent	to take.
Réduire	réduisant	réduit	je réduis, réduisons réduis, réduisez réduit, réduisent	je réduisis	je réduirai	réduise, réduisions réduises, réduisiez réduise, réduisent	to reduce.
Repaître	repaissant	repu	je repais, repaissons repais, repaissez repait, repaissent	je repus	je repaîtrai	repaisse, repaissions repaisses, repaissiez repaisse, repaissent	to feed.
Résoudre	résolvant	résolu résous	je résous, résolvons résous, résolvez résout, résolvent	je résolus	je résoudrai	résolve, résolvions résolves, résolviez résolve, résolvent	to resolve.
Rire (de)	riant	ri	je ris, rions ris, riez rit, rient	je ris	je rirai	rie, riions ries, riiez rie, rient	to laugh (at).
Rompre	rompant	rompu	je romps, rompons romps, rompez rompt, rompent	je rompis	je romprai	rompe, rompions rompes, rompiez rompe, rompent	to break.

[1] Used only in the infinitive and compound tenses.

[2] The verb *faire* is used to supply the persons and tenses that are wanting; as, *nous faisons frire*, &c.

FOURTH CONJUGATION.

Infinitive.	Present participle.	Past participle.	Present.	Indicative Preterit.	Future.	Subjunctive Present.	English.
Sourdre			il sourd ils sourdent				to issue; to arise.
Suffire (à)	suffisant	suffi	je suffis, suffisons suffis, suffisez suffit, suffisent	je suffis	je suffirai	suffise, suffisions suffises, suffisiez suffise, suffisent	to suffice.
Suivre	suivant	suivi	je suis, suivons suis, suivez suit, suivent	je suivis	je suivrai	suive, suivions suives, suiviez suive, suivent	to follow.
Traire	trayant	trait	je trais, trayons trais, trayez trait, traient		je trairai	traie, trayions traies, trayiez traie, traient	to milk.
Vaincre	vainquant	vaincu	je vaincs, vainquons vaincs, vainquez vainc, vainquent	je vainquis	je vaincrai	vainque, vainquions vainques, vainquiez vainque, vainquent	to conquer.
Vivre (de)	vivant	vécu	je vis, vivons vis, vivez vit, vivent	je vécus	je vivrai	vive, vivions vives, viviez vive, vivent	to live (on or upon).

LIST OF IRREGULAR AND DEFECTIVE VERBS,

CONJUGATED AFTER THE VERBS IN THE FOREGOING TABLE.

FIRST CONJUGATION.

		Conjugated like
Renvoyer	to send back	...envoyer.
s'En aller	to go away	...... aller.

SECOND CONJUGATION.

Conquérir ....to conquer ⎫
Reconquérir ....to reconquer ⎬ ...acquérir.
Requérir ....to request
s'Enquérir ....to inquire ⎭

Tressaillir ....to start up ⎫ ...assaillir.
Rebouillir ....to boil again ⎭ ...bouillir.

Accourir ....to hasten to ⎫
Concourir ....to concur
Discourir (de) ....to talk about
Encourir ....to incur ⎬ .....courir.
Parcourir ....to run over
Recourir (à)...........to have recourse to
Secourir ....to succor ⎭

Accueillir ....to welcome ⎫
Recueillir ....to gather ⎬ ...cueillir.
se Recueillir.........to collect one's self ⎭

Endormir ....to lull asleep ⎫
s'Endormir ....to fall asleep ⎬ ...dormir.
Rendormir ...to lull to sleep again
se Rendormir ...to fall asleep again ⎭

s'Enfuir ....to run away ⎬ ....fuir.

Couvrir ....to cover ⎫
Découvrir ...to uncover, to discover
Entr'ouvrir ...to open a little
Mésoffrir ....to underbid
Offrir ....to offer ⎬ ...ouvrir.
Recouvrir ....to cover again
Rouvrir ....to open again
Souffrir ....to suffer ⎭

Consentir ....to agree ⎫
Départir ....to distribute
se Départir (de)......to desist, to swerve (from)
Démentir ....to belie
Mentir ....to lie
Partir ....to set out ⎬ ...sentir.
Pressentir ....to foresee
Repartir ....to set off again
se Repentir ....to repent
Ressentir ....to feel
se Ressentir (de) ....to feel
Ressortir ....to go out again
Sortir ....to go out
Desservir ..to clear the table, to do an ill office
se Servir (de)............to make use of ⎬ ...servir.

s'Abstenir ....to abstain ⎫
Appartenir ....to belong to
Circonvenir..............to circumvent
Contenir ....to contain
se Contenir ....to refrain (from)
Contrevenir................to infringe
Convenir ..to suit (with avoir), to agree (with être in comp'd tenses)
Déprévenir ...to divest of (prejudice)
Devenir ....to become
Disconvenir................to deny
Entretenir ....to entertain
s'Entretenir ...to discourse with
Intervenir ....to intervene ⎬ .....tenir.
Maintenir ....to maintain
Obtenir ....to obtain
Parvenir ....to arrive
Prévenir ...to prepossess, to forewarn
Provenir ....to proceed from
Redevenir ...to become again
Retenir ....to retain
se Retenir (de)...........to forbear
Revenir ....to come back
se Ressouvenir (de).........to remember
se Souvenir (de) ...to recollect
Soutenir ....to maintain
Subvenir (à)...........to provide for
Survenir ...to happen, to befall
Venir ....to come ⎭

Dévêtir ....to undress ⎫
se Dévêtir...........to divest one's self
Revêtir (de)...........to clothe, to dress ⎬ .....vêtir.
se Vêtir ....to clothe one's self ⎭

THIRD CONJUGATION.

s'Asseoir ....to sit down ⎫
Rasseoir...........to place down again ⎬ ...asseoir.
se Rasseoir...........to sit down again ⎭

Rechoir ....to fall again ⎬ ...choir.

Émouvoir ...to move, to stir up ⎫
s'Émouvoir ...to be moved, to be concerned ⎬ ...mouvoir.

Dépourvoir...........to leave unprovided ⎬ ..pourvoir.

Équivaloir ...to be equivalent ⎫
Revaloir ...to return like for like ⎬ ..prévaloir.
se Prévaloir (de)..to take advantage (of) ⎭

Messeoir...........to be unbecoming ⎬ ......seoir.

Entrevoir ...to catch a glimpse of ⎫
s'Entrevoir...........to see each other ⎬ ...... voir.
Revoir ....to see again ⎭

FOURTH CONJUGATION.

Conjugated like

Dissoudre............to dissolve, to melt } ..absoudre.

Abattre.....................to pull down
s'Abattre......................to fall down
se Battre.........................to fight
Combattre.............to fight, to combat
Débattre...............to debate
se Débattre...................to struggle
s'Ébattre.........to take one's pleasure
Embattre... to lay the tire of a wheel
Rabattre......to abate, to bring down
se Rabattre..to turn off, to turn back, to fall back upon
Rebattre.....................to beat again } ....battre.

Reboire...................to drink again } ......boire.

Déclore.................to unclose
Enclore..................to enclose
Forclore...............to foreclose } ......clore.

Exclure...............to exclude
Reclure..............to shut up } ..conclure.

Découdre.............to unsew
Recoudre.........to sew again } ....coudre.

Mécroire.............to disbelieve } ....croire.

Accroître.............to increase
Décroître............to decrease
Recroître............to grow again
Surcroître............to grow out } ..croître.*

Redire.................to say again } ......dire.

Circonscrire..........to circumscribe
Décrire................to describe
Inscrire................to inscribe
s'Inscrire............to enter one's name
Prescrire..............to prescribe
se Prescrire..to be lost by limitation (law)
Proscrire.......to proscribe, to outlaw
Récrire...............to write again
Souscrire...............to subscribe
Transcrire...........to transcribe } ....écrire.

Contrefaire.........to imitate, to mimic
Défaire....................to undo
se Défaire...............to get rid
Parfaire................to perfect
Redéfaire..............to undo again
Refaire................to make again
se Refaire.............to recover
Satisfaire...............to satisfy
Surfaire.........to ask too much } ......faire.

Refrire..............to fry again } ......frire.

Adjoindre..............to adjoin
Astreindre.............to subject
s'Astreindre.........to confine one's self
Atteindre....to overtake, to reach
Aveindre...to take out or from, to fetch
Ceindre.......to gird, to encompass
Conjoindre...............to conjoin
Contraindre.........to constrain
Craindre...to fear, to be afraid
Déjoindre.............to disjoin
Dépeindre.............to describe
Déteindre............to discolor
Disjoindre.............to disjoin
Empreindre...........to imprint
Enceindre................to enclose
Enfreindre... to transgress, to infringe
Enjoindre................to enjoin
Épreindre............to squeeze out
Éteindre..............to extinguish
Étreindre....to tie close, to clasp
Feindre...................to feign
Geindre.......to whine, to moan
Oindre...................to anoint
Peindre..................to paint
Plaindre...................to pity
se Plaindre.............to complain
Ratteindre............to overtake again
Rejoindre.............to join again
Repeindre..........to paint again
Restreindre...... to restrain, to confine
Teindre..............to dye, to color } ...joindre.

Élire............to elect, to choose
Prélire.....to read over/previously
Réélire........to elect again
Relire........to read again } ....lire.

Reluire.........to glitter, to shine
Entre-luire......to shine a little } ......luire.

Conjugated like

Contredire............to contradict
Dédire....to disown, to unsay, to belie
se Dédire.....to recant, to retract
Interdire...to interdict, to forbid
Prédire.........to foretell, to predict } ....médire.

Admettre....................to admit
Commettre.............to commit
Compromettre........ to compromise, to expose
se Compromettre... to compromise one's self
Démettre...............to dislocate
se Démettre (de)..............to resign
Émettre....to issue, to set forth, to emit
s'Entremettre... to interpose, to meddle
Omettre..................to omit
Permettre........to permit, to allow
Promettre.............to promise
Remettre........ to replace, to set again
Soumettre........to submit, to subdue
Transmettre.................to transmit } ...mettre.

Émoudre..........to whet, to sharpen
Rémoudre...... to grind over again
Rémoudre......to sharpen again } ...moudre.

Renaître....to revive, to be born again } ....naître.

Apparaître..............to appear
Comparaître............to appear
Connaître....to know, to be acquainted with
Disparaître..........to disappear
Méconnaître... to disown, not to know
se Méconnaître.... to forget one's self
Reconnaître....to recognize, to acknowledge
Reparaître............to appear again } ..paraître.

Complaire.......to humor, to please
se Complaire...............to delight
Déplaire...............to displease
se Déplaire........to be displeased with
Taire.....to conceal, to keep secret
se Taire...............to remain silent } .....plaire.

Apprendre........to learn, to hear of
Comprendre..to understand, to include
Déprendre.....to loosen, to disengage
Désapprendre...............to unlearn
Entreprendre............to undertake
se Méprendre............to mistake
Rapprendre........to learn again
Reprendre....to take again, to chide
se Reprendre....to correct one's self
Surprendre....to surprise, to astonish } ...prendre.

Conduire............to conduct, to lead
Construire....to construct, to build
Cuire............to cook, to bake
Décuire........to thin (syrups, etc.)
Déconstruire......to take to pieces
Déduire................to deduct
Détruire..................to destroy
se Détruire...to kill one's self, to decay
Éconduire......to bow out, to refuse
Enduire......to plaster, to do over
Induire................to induce
Instruire.................to instruct
Introduire................to introduce
Produire....to produce, to bring forth
Reconduire........to conduct again
Reconstruire............to build again
Recuire....to bake again, to do again
Renduire........to plaster anew
Reproduire............to reproduce
Séduire.....to seduce, to bribe
Traduire...............to translate } ....réduire.

se Repaître.. to thirst after, to delight in } ...repaître.

se Rire (de).................to laugh at
Sourire.................to smile } ......rire.

Corrompre................to corrupt
Interrompre.............to interrupt } ...rompre.

Poursuivre......to pursue, to prosecute } .....suivre.

Abstraire...........to abstract
Distraire.........to distract, to divert
Extraire.............to extract
Retraire..........to redeem an estate
Rentraire...........to fine-draw
Soustraire......to substract, to deduct
se Soustraire (à)......to avoid, to escape } ......traire.

Convaincre............to convince } ...vaincre.

Revivre...............to revive
Survivre (à)....to survive, to outlive } ......vivre.

*Only recroître takes a circumflex on its past participle.

EXPLANATION OF THE SIGNS USED IN THIS WORK.

---

* Represents the liquid sounds of *gn*, *l*, or *ll*.

† Signifies that the *h* is aspirated.

— Indicates the repetition of the same word.

(—) Indicates the plural of foreign and compound nouns when it is like the singular.

(—*s*) Indicates the plural of foreign nouns when it is formed by adding *s*.

When the plural of foreign and compound nouns is formed by changing the final letter or letters, the whole plural form is given. Thus, *e.g.*, (*Lazaroni*), plural of *Lazarone*; (—*amiraux*), plural of *vice-admiral*.

(—*s*-—*s*), or (—*s*-—*x*), or (—*x*-—*x*), or (—*x*-—*s*) Indicate the plural of compound nouns when it is formed by adding *s* or *x* to each component.

(—*s*-—) or (—*x*-—) Indicate the plural of compound nouns when it is formed by adding *s* or *x* to the first component only.

(—-—*s*) or (—-—*x*) Indicate the plural of compound nouns when it is formed by adding *s* or *x* to the second component only.

(*n.s.*) Indicates foreign and compound nouns not used in the singular.

(*n.p.*) Indicates foreign and compound nouns not used in the plural.

- Before final letters, points out the masculine termination, which is to be changed in the feminine; as, *acti-f*, *-ve*, actif, active; *act-eur*, *-rice*, acteur, actrice; *honteu-x*, *-se*, honteux, honteuse.

The long sound of the vowels is designated by a horizontal mark over the vowel, thus: ā, ē, ī, ō, ū.

The short sound of the vowels is designated by a curved mark, thus: ă, ĕ, ĭ, ŏ, ŭ. This mark seldom occurs but over the unaccented *e*.

When there is no mark over the other vowels, they may be considered as natural; that is, as neither long nor short.

Words in parentheses serve to complete the sense of those words that precede or follow them; or they refer to the object with which they are connected, or indicate the art, trade, profession, etc., to which they relate. They are given in English and in French.

Those words of which the pronunciation is quite irregular are noticed in full; but those that are only partly irregular are noticed in their irregularities only. Therefore, such words as *chiromancie*, *archétype*, *équateur*, which are irregular in one syllable only, are noticed in that syllable alone; as *ki-*, *-ké-*, *-koua-*.

As none but French spelling can give a correct idea of French pronunciation, it is used throughout this dictionary, with the exception of *ch*, which is rendered by *sh*, so that it may not be mistaken for *k*; of *ou*, which is expressed by *oo*; and of *oi*, which is represented by *oa*.

⊙ Indicates obsolete French words. When found in the middle of lines, it indicates that the French word is obsolete in the meaning before which it is placed.

(ant.) Indicates obsolete English words.

When two or more French nouns of the same gender follow, their gender is indicated after the last noun only.

The pronunciation of English words is indicated, in the English-French Division, in the same manner as that of French words in the French-English Division, and represented in *all* cases by means of the French spelling, with the exception of:

1st, *th* hard, which is expressed by (th);

2nd, *th* soft, "   "   (th);

3rd, *g*, when hard before *e*, *i*, or *y*, by (gh).

ABBREVIATIONS USED IN THIS WORK.

a., active, *actif.*
ab., abbreviation, *abréviation.*
Acad., Academy, *Académie.*
adj., adjective, *adjectif.*
adject., adjectively, *adjectivement.*
adv., adverb, *adverbe.*
agri., agriculture, *agriculture.*
alch., alchemy, *alchimie.*
alg., algebra, *algèbre.*
anat., anatomy, *anatomie.*
antiq., antiquity, *antiquité.*
arch., architecture, *architecture.*
arith., arithmetic, *arithmétique.*
art., article, *article.*
artil, artillery, *artillerie.*
astrol., astrology, *astrologie.*
astron., astronomy, *astronomie.*
auxil., auxiliary, *auxiliaire.*
bookbind., bookbinding, *reliure.*
bot., botany, *botanique.*
b. s., bad sense, *mauvaise part.*
carp., carpentry, *charpenterie.*
chem., chemistry, *chimie.*
coin., coining, *monnayage.*
com., commerce, *commerce.*
conch., conchology, *conchologie.*
conj., conjunction, *conjonction.*
cook., cookery, *cuisine.*
c. rel., catholic religion, *religion catholique.*
dy., dyeing, *teinture.*
ecc., ecclesiastical, *ecclésiastique.*
engr., engraving, *gravure.*
ent., entomology, *entomologie.*
exc., exclamation, *exclamation.*
f., feminine, *féminin.*
fam., familiar, *familier.*
fenc., fencing, *escrime.*
fig., figuratively, *au figuré.*
fin., finance, *finances.*
fort., fortification, *fortification.*
foss., fossils, *fossiles.*
gard., gardening, *jardinage.*
geog., geography, *géographie.*
geol., geology, *géologie.*
geom., geometry, *géométrie.*
gold., goldsmith's work, *orfèvrerie.*
gram., grammar, *grammaire.*
her., heraldry, *blason.*
hist., history, *histoire.*
horl., horology, *horlogerie.*
hort., horticulture, *horticulture.*
hunt., hunting, *chasse.*
hydr., hydraulics, *hydraulique.*
ich., ichthyology, *ichtyologie.*
imp., impersonal, *impersonne.*
indecl., indeclinable, *invariable.*
int., interjection, *interjection.*
iron., ironically, *ironiquement.*
jest., jestingly, *par plaisanterie.*

jur., jurisprudence, *jurisprudence.*
l. ex., low expression, *terme bas.*
lit., literature, *littérature.*
log., logic, *logique.*
l. u., little used, *peu usité.*
m., masculine, *masculin.*
mam., mammalogy, *mammalogie.*
man., manege, *manège.*
manu., manufacture, *manufactures.*
mas., masonry, *maçonnerie.*
math., mathematics, *mathématiques.*
mec., mechanics, *mécanique.*
med., medicine, *médecine.*
metal., metallurgy, *métallurgie.*
milit., military art, *art militaire.*
min., mineralogy, *minéralogie.*
mol., mollusk, *mollusque.*
mus., music, *musique.*
myth., mythology, *mythologie.*
n., noun-substantive, *nom substantif.*
nav., navy, *marine.*
opt., optics, *optique.*
orni., ornithology, *ornithologie.*
paint., painting, *peinture.*
part., participle, *participe.*
pers., person, *personne.*
persp., perspective, *perspective.*
pharm., pharmacy, *pharmacie.*
philos., philosophy, *philosophie.*
phys., natural philosophy (physics), *physique.*
pl., plural, *pluriel.*
poet., poetry, *poésie.*
pol., politics, *politique.*
pop., popular, *populaire.*
prep., preposition, *préposition.*
print., printing, *imprimerie.*
pron., pronoun, *pronom.*
prov., proverbially, *proverbialement.*
r., reflected, *réfléchi.*
rel., religion, *religion.*
rhet., rhetoric, *rhétorique.*
sculpt., sculpture, *sculpture.*
sing., singular, *singulier.*
st. e., elevated style, *style soutenu.*
subst., substantively, *substantivement.*
surg., surgery, *chirurgie.*
tech., technology, *technologie.*
thea., theater, *théâtre.*
theol., theology, *théologie.*
triv., trivial, *trivial.*
v., verb, *verbe.*
v. a., verb active, *verbe actif.*
vet., veterinary art, *art vétérinaire.*
v. imp., verb impersonal, *verbe impersonnel.*
v.n., verb neuter, *verbe neutre.*
v.r., verb reflected, *verbe réfléchi.*
V., vide, *voir.*
zoöl., zoölogy, *zoologie.*

A
GENERAL FRENCH–ENGLISH DICTIONARY

a, *n.m.*, the first letter of the alphabet, a. *Panse d'a;* oval of an a. *Il ne sait ni a ni b;* he does not know *a* from *b. Il n'a pas fait une panse d'a;* he has not done a letter, a stroke. *Un homme marqué à l'a;* the beau-ideal of a man, a man thoroughly reliable. *C'est un homme marqué à l'a;* he is the soul of honor.

a (ab.), *Altesse;* Highness.

aa (ab.), *Altesses;* Highnesses.

a, at the beginning of French words, often comes from the privative α of the Greeks, and denotes privation; as, *atonie,* debility; *acéphale,* acephalous.

à, *prep.,* denotes the end or term of the action of the verb, and indicates the person or thing this action tends to. *Aller à Paris;* to go to Paris. *Parler à quelqu'un;* to speak to some one.

à denotes extraction, separation. *Oter une bague à quelqu'un;* to take a ring from any one. *Se soustraire aux poursuites de la justice;* to abscond.

à denotes property, possession. *Cette montre est à mon frère;* this watch is my brother's. *Il a un style, une manière, à lui;* he has a style, a manner, all his own. *Cette ferme appartient à mon père;* that farm belongs to my father.

à denotes period, time. *Au lever du soleil;* at sunrise. *A l'aube du jour;* at daybreak. *Arriver à temps;* to arrive in time. *A mon retour;* on my return.

à indicates what stops on the surface, or penetrates beyond it. *Il a une bague au doigt;* he has a ring on his finger. *Blessé à l'épaule;* wounded in the shoulder.

à establishes the relative distance between things and persons. *A portée de canon;* within cannon-shot. *Il demeure à vingt lieues d'ici;* he lives twenty leagues off. *De vous à moi;* between you and me, from you to me. *De Paris à Rouen;* from Paris to Rouen.

à points out whatever furnishes an inference or ground for conjecture. *A l'œuvre on connaît l'ouvrier;* the workman is known by his work. *Attendre à l'œuvre;* to await results.

à denotes succession, gradation, order. *Petit à petit;* little by little. *Un à un;* one by one. *Traduire mot à mot;* to translate word for word, i.e., literally.

à is used in speaking of goods sold or bought by weight, measure, or quantity. *Vendre du vin à la bouteille;* to sell wine by the bottle. *Vendre de la viande à la livre;* to sell meat by the pound.

à denotes value, price. *Diner à trois francs par tête;* to dine at three francs a head.

à denotes conformity, manner. *S'habiller à la Française;* to dress after the French fashion. *A l'instar de la capitale;* after the manner of the capital. *A mon avis;* in my opinion. *Aller à pied, à cheval;* to go on foot, to ride on horseback. *Marcher à reculons;* to walk backwards.

à, between two nouns, makes the second serve to denote the species or quality of the first. *Canne à sucre;* sugar-cane. *Vache à lait;* milchcow.

à, between two numeral adjectives, signifies *between,* or about. *Un homme de quarante à cinquante ans;* a man between forty and fifty. *Il y a quatre à cinq lieues;* it is about four or five leagues distant.

Remark. —The French say *quatre à cinq lieues,* because leagues are things which may be divided into fractions; but, in speaking of things which cannot be divided, *ou* must be used. For instance, *Quatre ou cinq personnes;* four or five persons.

à, before an infinitive, commonly denotes what is proper to be done. *Un avis à suivre;* an opinion worth following. *Un homme à récompenser ou à pendre;* a man that deserves to be rewarded or hanged.

à, used in speaking of vehicles, signifies *and. Une voiture à quatre chevaux, grandes guides;* a carriage and four.

à is used in description instead of the English *with. Un homme à barbe blanche;* a man with a white beard. *Une maison à pignon;* a house with a gable, gabled.

a, has.

abaca, *n.m.,* abaca, Manila hemp.

abacus (-kuss), *n.m.,* abacus.

abaisse, *n.f.,* the under-crust of pastry, piece of rolled paste.

abaissé, -e, *part.,* lowered, brought low; dejected; diminished, flattened. *Le pal est —* (her.); the pale is abased.

abaissement (-bèss-man), *n.m.,* lowering, falling, abatement, depression; humiliation, abasement; (surg.) couching. *L'— des eaux;* the abatement of the waters. *Opération de la cataracte par —;* couching.

abaisser, *v.a.,* to let down, to let fall, to lower; to bring low down; to diminish, to reduce; to pull down; (gard.) to lop out; to debase, to cry down; to humble; to roll (paste); (surg.) to couch. *— un pont-levis;* to let down a drawbridge. *— la voix;* to lower the voice. *Dieu abaisse les superbes;* God humbles the proud. *Abaisser une cataracte;* (surg.) to couch a cataract.

s'abaisser, *v.r.,* to fall, to decrease, to subside, to abate, to decline; to humble one's self, to stoop, to sink, to cringe. *S'— à le prier;* to stoop so low as to entreat him.

abaisseur, *n.m.,* (anat.) depressor.

abaisseur, *adj.,* (anat.) depriment. *Muscle —;* depriment muscle.

abait, *n.m.,* bait. *V.* appât.

abaiter, *v.a.,* to bait. *V.* appâter.

abajoue, *n.f.,* (mam.) cheek-pouch; gill, gills.

abalourdir, *v.a.,* (fam.) to make dull and stupid.

abandon, *n.m.,* forsaking, relinquishment, surrender; leaving things at random; abandonment, the being forsaken, forlornness, destitution, ease, unconstraint. *Avoir un — séduisant;* to have seductive manners. *Se livrer avec — à;* to indulge in.

à l'abandon, *adv.,* at random, in confusion, at sixes and sevens. *Laisser ses enfants à l'—;* to neglect one's children. *Un champ qui est à l'—;* a field left to run wild.

abandonnataire, *n.m.f.,* (jur.) relessee.

abandonné, -e, *part.,* abandoned, forsaken,

given over. *Un malade abandonné;* a patient given up.

abandonné, -e, *adj.,* abandoned, lost to decency, shameless, graceless, profligate.

abandonné, *n.m.,* **-e,** *n.f.,* profligate, rake; lewd, wicked, abandoned person.

abandonnement (-do-n-mān), *n.m.,* abandonment, abandoning, forsaking; desertion, the being forsaken; the giving up one's effects; leaving, quitting; dissoluteness, debauchery.

abandonner, *v.a.,* to abandon, to quit, to leave, to desert, to forsake; to give up, to give over; to leave one the disposal of; to deliver up; to let loose, let go. *Il abandonna le pays;* he left the country. — *une cause;* to give up a cause. — *ses prétentions;* to give up one's claims. *Mes forces m'abandonnent;* my strength is failing me. — *une corde;* to let go a rope. — *la partie;* to give up the struggle.

s'abandonner, *v.r.,* to give one's self up, to addict one's self, to give way to; to indulge in; to commit one's self to; to prostitute one's self; to be easy in one's manners, to throw off all restraint. *S'— à la colère, au plaisir, au hasard;* to give way to anger, to indulge in pleasure, to trust to fortune.

⊙**abannation** (-ba-na-), *n.f.,* (jur.) abannition.

⊙**abaptiste** (-ba-tist), *adj.,* (surg.) abaptiston.

abaque, *n.m.,* (arch. antiq.) abacus, plinth, the uppermost part of the capital of a column.

abarticulation, *n.f.,* (anat.) abarticulation, diarthrosis.

abas, *n. m.,* shower (bath), blight (in wheat). *V.* **teigne.**

abasourdir, *v.a.,* (fam.) to stun, to dumfound, to astound; to stupefy.

abâtardir, *v.a.,* to render degenerate; to debase, to corrupt, to spoil, to mar, to adulterate. *La servitude abâtardit le courage;* slavery debases courage. *Un homme abâtardi;* a degenerate man.

s'abâtardir, *v.r.,* to degenerate, to grow worse.

abâtardissement (-mān), *n.m.,* degeneracy.

abat-chauvée, *n.f.,* (*n.p.*) flock-wool.

abat-faim (-fin), *n.m.,* (—) large joint, substantial dish.

abat-foin, *n.m.,* (—) opening above the rack to put the hay through; loft-trap.

abat-jour, *n.m.,* (—) (arch.) sky-light, trunk-light; shade for a lamp; window-blind; (bot.) opening.

abattage, *n.m.,* cutting down, felling, clearance (of a forest); (nav.) heaving down; careening; slaughtering (of animals).

⊙**abattant,** *n.m.,* shutter; flap (of a counter); lid.

abattée, *n.f.,* (nav.) casting; falling off to leeward. *Faire son —;* to cast; to fall off.

abattement (-mān), *n.m.,* faintness, low state, weakness, prostration; dejection, despondency, low spirits; (her.) abatement. *Tomber dans l'—;* to become low-spirited. *Jeter dans l'—;* to deject. *Qui jette dans l'—;* depressive.

abatteur, *n.m.,* feller, knocker-off, slaughterer. *C'est un grand — de bois;* he is a great braggart.

abattis, *n.m.,* houses, walls, trees, thrown down; the killing of game; giblets (of poultry); garbage; stones hewn down in a quarry; raw hides; slaughter, destruction. *Abattis en ragoût;* stewed giblets.

abattoir, *n.m.,* slaughter-house.

abattre, *v.a.,* to throw down, to hurl down; to pull down; to beat, to batter down; to bring down; to fell, to cut down, to hew down, to cut off; to knock down; to blow down; to lay (the dust); to let down; to soak (skins); to couch (the cataract); to waste (strength); to dispirit; to dishearten; to unman; to cast down, to depress; to humble. *Le vent abattra le blé;* the wind will throw the corn down. — *un rideau;* to let a curtain down. — *les cuirs;* to skin dead ani-

mals. — *le pantalon;* to remove the trousers. — *les peaux;* to soak the skins. — *un vaisseau pour le caréner;* to careen a ship. *Un vaisseau dur à —;* a ship hard to swing round. — *un mât* (nav.); to carry away a mast. *La moindre chose l'abat;* the least thing unmans him. *Elle a l'air bien abattu;* she looks very dejected. — *l'orgueil de quelqu'un;* to humble any one's pride.

abattre, *v.n.,* to lay down one's cards (at play); (nav.) to fall off to leeward, to cast. *Le vaisseau s'abat;* the ship is driving to leeward.

s'abattre, *v.r.,* to fall, to tumble down; to stoop; to abate; to be cast down, dejected; to break down (of horses); to burst (of a storm); to despond; to pounce upon. *Le vent s'abat;* the wind is falling. *La chaleur s'abat;* the heat is abating. *Un orage terrible va s'abattre sur nous;* a dreadful storm is about to burst upon us.

abattu, -e, *adj.,* pulled, broken, cast down; depressed, dejected; humbled, crest-fallen. *Je me sens tout —;* I am quite out of spirits. *Un visage —;* a woe-begone countenance.

abattures, *n.f. pl.,* (hunt.) abature; foiling (of a stag).

abat-vent, *n.m.,* penthouse (of a steeple); pentice, wind-screen, louvre window.

abat-voix, *n.m.,* sounding-board (of a pulpit).

abbatial (-cial), **-e,** *adj.,* abbatial, abbatical.

abbaye (abéi), *n.f.,* monastery, abbey. *Administration d'une —;* abbacy.

abbé, *n.m.,* abbé, abbot, priest. *Monsieur l'abbé,* your Reverence.

abbesse, *n.f.,* abbess. *Dignité, fonctions d'abbé, d'abbesse;* abbotship.

abc, *n.m.,* a, b, c, alphabet, primer; a, b, c, book; elements, rudiments, spelling-book. *Apprendre son —;* to learn one's letters. *Etre à l'— de;* to be at the a, b, c, of. *Renvoyer quelqu'un à l'—;* to make a person begin all over again.

abcéder, *v.n.,* to form into an abscess, to apostemate, to gather, to come to a head.

abcès, *n.m.,* abscess, apostem, gathering. *Former, vider, un —;* to form, to take the matter out of, an abscess. — *aux gencives;* gumboil.

abcisse, *n.f. V.* **abscisse.**

abdication, *n.f.,* abdication; (jur.) disinheritance of a son during his father's life-time; renunciation (of property). *Faire —;* to abdicate.

abdiquer, *v.a.,* to abdicate, to resign, to forswear.

abdomen (-mè-n), *n.m.,* abdomen.

abdominal, -e, *adj.,* abdominal.

abducteur, *adj.,* (anat.) abducent.

abducteur, *n.m.,* abductor.

abduction, *n.f.,* (anat. and log.) abduction.

s'abéausir, *v.n.,* (nav.) to become fine (of weather at sea).

abécédaire, *adj.,* of the a, b, c. *Ouvrage —;* child's first-book.

abécédaire, *n.m.,* alphabet, primer, spelling-book.

abecquer, *v.a.,* to feed a bird.

abée, *n.f.,* mill-dam.

***abeille,** *n.f.,* bee. — *bourdon;* bumble-bee. — *domestique;* hive bee. — *mère;* queen bee. — *ouvrière;* working bee. *Ruche d'—s;* bee-hive. *Eleveur d'—;* bee-master. *Essaim d'—s;* swarm of bees.

abeillé, -e, *adj. & part.,* covered, ornamented with bees.

abéquer. *V.* **abecquer.**

aberration, *n.f.,* aberration; (sciences) alienation. — *de réfrangibilité;* Newtonian aberration. *Cercle d'—;* crown of aberration.

abêtir, *v.a.,* to stupefy; to stultify. *V.* **hébéter.**

abêter, *v.n.,* **s'abêtir,** *v.r.,* to grow stupid.

ab hoc et ab hac, *adv.,* at random; confusedly.

abhorrer, v.a., to abhor, detest, loathe.

s'abhorrer, v.r., to abominate, loathe one another.

abime, n.m., unfathomable depth, abyss, hell; a thing most abstruse or obscure; dipping-mold (for candles); (her.) the middle of the shield; fesse-point, heart point.

abimé, -e, part., swallowed up, ingulfed, destroyed, spoiled. — de dettes; over head and ears in debt.

abimer, v.a., to overthrow, to ingulf, to swallow up; to destroy entirely, to cut up, to crush; to spoil, to injure.

abimer, v.n., to be destroyed, to be swallowed up, to sink; to perish, to be crushed.

s'abimer, v.r., to fall into an abyss, to sink; to ruin, to undo one's self; to be spoiled.

ab intestat, adv., abintestate. Succession —; intestate's estate; intestacy.

ab irato, adv., in an angry fit. Parler, agir, —; to speak, to act, under the influence of anger.

abject, -e (jèkt), adj., abject, base, mean, low, vile, despicable.

abjectement, adv., abjectly.

abjection, n.f., abjection, baseness; humiliation; vileness, meanness.

abjuration, n.f., solemn renunciation, abjuration.

abjuratoire, adj., abjuratory. — acte; act of abjuration.

abjurer, v.a., to abjure, to deny, to forswear, to renounce. — une opinion; to abandon an opinion.

ablactation, n.f., (med.) ablactation, weaning.

ablais, n.m., (jurisp.) corn, either standing or cut down, but not carried or carted away.

ablaquéation, n.f., (gard.) ablaqueation.

ablatif, n.m., (gram.) ablative.

ablation, n.f., (surg.) ablation.

ablativo, (triv.) adv., in confusion; higgledy-piggledy.

able, n.m., or **ablette**, n.f., (fish) ablet, bleak.

ablégat, n.m., ablegate.

⊙**ablégation**, n.m., ablegation.

ablepsie, n.f., (med.) ablepsy.

ablier, n.m., (fish.) purse-net; hoop-net.

⊙**abluant, -e**, adj., (med.) abluent, cleansing.

⊙**abluer**, v.a., to revive old writing, to wash with gall-nut.

ablution, n.f., ablution, washing, purification. Faire ses —s; to perform one's ablutions.

abnégation, n.f., abnegation, renunciation, sacrifice. — de soi-même; self-denial. Faire — de; to renounce, set aside.

aboi, n.m., barking, baying.

aboiement or **aboîment** (-boa-mãn), n.m., barking, baying.

abois, n.m. pl., despairing condition, last shift, distress. Aux —; at bay, hard up, at one's wits' end. Mettre aux —; to drive to extremities. La place est aux —; the place, citadel, can hold out no longer, is in desperate straits.

abolir, v.a., to abolish, to repeal, to annul. — un impôt; to take off a tax.

s'abolir, v.r., to fall into disuse, to become obsolete.

abolissable, adj., abolishable.

abolissement (-mãn), n.m., abolishment.

abolition, n.f., abolition; royal pardon; repeal.

abolitionniste, n.m., abolitionist.

abominable, adj., abominable, execrable.

abominablement, adv., abominably.

abomination, n.f., abomination, detestation. Avoir en —; to abominate, to hold in detestation. Etre en —; to be detested.

abondamment (-da-mãn), adv., abundantly.

abondance, n.f., abundance, plenty, copiousness, plentifulness; multitude, affluence; richness, fullness (of language); weak wine-and-water (in schools). Corne d' —; horn of plenty, cornucopia. — de biens; opulence. Vivre, être, dans l' —; to live in plenty. Parler avec —; to speak fluently. Ecrire, parler, d' —; to write, to speak, extempore, offhand. — de biens ne nuit pas; store is no sore.

abondant, -e, adj., abounding, plentiful, copious; fruitful, exuberant, teeming, voluble, diffusive. Une langue —e; a copious language.

abonder, v.n., to abound in or with, to be full of; to overflow. Il abonde dans votre sens; he supports your opinion; he has come round to; he concurs in. — dans son sens; to be wedded to one's own opinion.

abonné, n.m., -e, n.f., subscriber (to periodicals, theatres, &c.).

abonnement (-mãn), n.m., subscription (to periodicals, theatres, &c.); agreement. Les —s sont suspendus pour ce soir (of places of amusement); season-tickets not available this evening.

abonner, v.a., to subscribe for.

s'abonner, v.r., to subscribe; to compound for. On s'abonne à; subscriptions are received at.

⊙**abonnir**, v.a., to better, to mend, to improve.

⊙**abonnir**, v.n., **s'abonnir**, v.r., to mend, to grow better.

⊙**abonnissement** (-nis-mãn), n.m., (fam.), improvement, amelioration.

abord, n.m., landing; arrival; access; admittance, approach; attack, onset. Avoir l' — facile; to be easy of access. De prime —; at first sight.

à bord, adv., aboard, on board.

d'abord, adv., first, at first, at first sight. Tout d'abord, au premier abord, dès l'abord; at first, from the very first. Dès l'abord, j'ai senti que je devais . . . I felt, from the very first, that I ought . . . or was to . . .

abordable, adj., accessible, accostable, of easy access; approachable.

abordage, n.m., (nav.) landing; boarding; fouling. Aller or sauter à l' —; to board a ship, grapple.

aborder, v.n., to arrive at; to land.

aborder, v.a., to come near, to come to, to come up with; to board, to run foul of (a ship); to accost; to broach, handle (a subject). — un vaisseau ennemi; to board an enemy's ship. — par accident; to run foul of. Il m'a abordé dans la rue; he accosted me in the street.

s'aborder, v.r., to run foul of each other; to come up with one another.

abordeur, n.m., boarding vessel.

aborigène, adj., first, original, aboriginal.

aborigènes, n.m., pl., aborigines.

abornement, n.m. V. **délimitation**.

aborner, v.a. V. **délimiter**.

aborti-f, -ve, adj., abortive.

abot, n.m., clog (for horses' fore feet).

abouchement (-boosh-mãn), n.m., interview, conference, parley; (anat.) anastomosis, inosculation.

aboucher, v.a., to bring together, to confer.

s'aboucher, v.r., to have an interview; to confer with; to place one's self in communication with; (anat.) to inosculate.

about, n.m., (carp.) end, butt-end.

abouté, -e, adj., placed end to end.

aboutement (-boot-mãn), n.m., (carp.) but, abutment.

abouter, v.a., to join end to end.

aboutir, v.n., to join; to border upon; to meet; (surg.) to burst; to come to; to tend to; to end in. N'— à rien; to come to nothing; to end in smoke. Ce champ aboutit à un marais; this field borders upon a fen. Faire — un abcès; to bring an abscess to a head. S'aboutir (gard.); to bud, be covered with buds.

aboutissant, -e, *adj.*, bordering upon.

aboutissants (rarely used without the word *tenants*), *n.m.*, *pl.*, boundaries of an estate ; abuttals, particulars ; connections. *Je n'aime pas les tenants et — de cet homme ;* I do not like the set by which that man is surrounded. *Savoir les tenants et — d'une affaire ;* to know all about a thing.

aboutissement (-mān), *n.m.*, eking piece (tailoring) ; (surg.) the drawing to a head.

ab ovo, *adv.*, from the very beginning.

aboyant, -e, *adj.*, barking.

aboyer, *v.n.*, to bark, to bay, to yelp ; to dun. *Il aboie après tout le monde ;* he snarls at everybody. *— après quelque chose ;* to long for a thing, covet a thing. *— à la lune ;* to bark when one cannot bite ; to complain in vain.

aboyeur, *n.m.*, barker ; snarler ; dun ; touter ; link-man (at the door of a theatre) ; (orni.) greenshank. *Ce journaliste n'est qu'un — ;* this journalist is nothing but a snarling critic.

abrac, *n.m.*, abraxas.

abracadabra, *n.m.*, abracadabra (magical word).

abraquer, *v.a.*, (nav.) to haul taut.

abrasion, *n.m.*, (med.) abrasion, excoriation.

abraxas, *n.m.*, abracadabra.

abrégé, -e, *adj.*, short, summary.

abrégé, *n.m.*, abridgment, compendium, epitome, abstract, summary. *En — ;* in a few words, briefly. *Réduire en — ;* to epitomize.

abréger, *v.a.*, to abridge, to shorten, to epitomize ; to abbreviate, to cut down, to cut short. *Pour — ;* to be brief.

s'abréger, *v.r.*, to become short, or shorter.

abreuvage, abreuvement, *n.m.*, watering, soaking, steaming, priming.

abreuver, *v.a.*, to water, to give drink to ; to make drink ; to soak, to drench ; to fill ; (paint.) to prepare, to prime ; to soak (wood).

s'abreuver de, *v.r.*, (of animals) to go to water ; to drink plentifully ; to be steeped in. *S'— de larmes ;* to shed copious tears. *S'— de douleurs ;* to be filled with grief ; to drain to the dregs the cup of sorrow. *Un cœur abreuvé de fiel ;* a heart steeped in gall.

abreuvoir, *n.m.*, watering - place, horsepond ; (mas.) abreuvoir. *— à mouches* (burlesque style) ; a large wound or gash on the head or face.

abréviateur, *n.m.*, abbreviator, abridger.

abréviati-f, -ve, *adj.*, abbreviatory, abridging, abbreviating.

abréviation, *n.f.*, abbreviation, contraction.

abri, *n.m.*, shelter, cover. *Etre sous l'— d'un bois ;* to be sheltered by a wood. *Sans — ;* homeless. *Donner un — à ;* to shelter. *A l'— ;* sheltered, under cover. *Etre à l'— ;* to be under shelter. *Etre à l'— du vent ;* to be sheltered from the wind. *A l'— de la persécution ;* safe from persecution. *Mettre à l'— ;* to shelter, screen.

abricot, *n.m.*, apricot.

abricoté, *n.m.*, candied apricot.

abricotier, *n.m.*, apricot-tree.

abrier, *v.a.*, (nav.) to becalm ; to belee.

abriter, *v.a.*, to shelter, to shield, to screen, to shade, to protect ; (nav.) to becalm, belee.

abrité, -e, *adj.*, (gard.) sheltered.

s'abriter, *v.r.*, to shelter one's self ; to take shelter ; to assist. *Abritez-vous mutuellement ;* mutually assist each other.

abrivent, *n.m.*, (gard.) matting, screen ; shelter ; sentry-box ; hut.

abrogation, *n.f.*, abrogation, repeal ; annulment.

abroger, *v.a.*, to abrogate, to repeal, to annul.

s'abroger, *v.r.*, to fall into disuse, to grow obsolete.

abrome, *n.m.*, (bot.) abroma.

abrouti, -e, *adj.*, nipped, browsed.

abroutissement (-mān), *n.m.*, damage done to trees by cattle browsing.

abrupt, -e, *adj.*, rugged, craggy ; (bot.) abrupt.

abruption, *n.f.*, abruption ; (surg.) rupture, fracture.

ex abrupto, *adv.*, *adj.*, suddenly, bluntly, offhand, on the spur of the moment ; abrupt, impetuous.

abrutir, *v.a.*, to stupefy, to besot, to brutalize.

s'abrutir, *v.r.*, to become stupid, to be besotted, to get brutalized.

abrutissant, -e, *adj.*, brutalizing, stupefying.

abrutissement (-mān), *n.m.*, brutishness, stupor, sottishness.

abrutisseur, *n.m.*, brutalizer ; *adj.*, stupefying, brutalizing.

abscisse, *n.f.*, (geom.) abscissa.

absence, *n.f.*, absence, inadvertence, want of. *— d'esprit ;* absence of mind. *Avoir des —s d'esprit ;* to have fits of absence. *Remarquer l'— de ;* to miss.

absent, -e, *adj.*, absent, out of the way, missing, wanting ; (of the mind) wandering.

absent, *n.m.*, one absent, absentee. *Les —s ont toujours tort ;* the absent are always in the wrong.

s'absenter, *v.r.*, to absent one's self ; to keep out of the way.

absentéisme, *n.m.*, absenteeism.

abside, *n.f.*, (arch. and rel.) apse.

absinthe, *n.f.*, absinthe, wormwood ; bitters.

absolu, *n.m.*, absolute, existing independent of any other cause.

absolu, e, *adj.*, absolute ; arbitrary, despotical, unlimited ; peremptory ; magisterial ; positive, unconditional ; full, strict.

absolument, *adv.*, absolutely, arbitrarily, peremptorily ; positively, indispensably, fully. *Il refusa — ;* he gave a flat denial.

absolution, *n.f.*, absolution ; acquittal ; discharge. *Sans avoir reçu l'— ;* unabsolved.

absolutisme, *n.m.*, absolutism.

absolutiste, *n.m.f.*, partisan of absolute power.

absolutoire, *adj.*, absolutory.

absorbable, *adj.*, absorbable.

absorbant, -e, *adj.*, absorptive, absorbent.

absorbent, *n.m.*, absorbent.

absorbé, -e, *part.*, absorbed, engrossed, rapt in *Il est — dans l'étude ;* he is absorbed in study.

absorbement, *n.m.*, absorption (of mind).

absorber, *v.a.*, to absorb, to swallow up ; to drink in, to consume, to waste ; to engross, to occupy entirely ; to take up.

s'absorber, *v.r.*, to be absorbed, or swallowed up.

absorption, *n.f.*, absorption.

absoudre (absolvant, absous), *v.a.*, to absolve, to acquit, to bring in not guilty, to clear ; to give absolution.

absou-s, -te, *part.*, acquitted, absolved, discharged.

absoute, *n.f.*, (c. rel.) general absolution.

abstème, *adj.*, abstemious.

abstème, *n.m.f.*, abstainer.

abstenant, -e, *n.m.f.*, abstainer, total abstainer, teetotaler.

s'abstenir, *v.r.*, to abstain, to refrain, to forbear, to forego. *S'— de vin ;* to abstain from wine.

abstention, *n.f.*, abstention, abstinency ; withdrawal of a judge from a trial.

abstergent, -e, *adj.*, (med.) cleansing ; abstersive ; abstergent.

abstergent, *n.m.*, (med.) abstergent, detergent.

absterger, *v.a.*, to absterge ; to cleanse.

abstersi-f, -ve, *adj.,* (med.) abstersive, cleansing.

abstersion, *n.f.,* (surg.) abstersion.

abstinence, *n.f.,* abstinence, temperance, sobriety, fasting.

abstinent, -e, *adj.,* abstemious, sober.

abstracti-f, -ve, *adj.,* abstractive.

abstraction, *n.f.,* absence of mind, abstraction. *Avoir des —s;* to have fits of absence. *Par —;* abstractedly. *—faite de;* setting aside; exclusive of.

abstractivement (-mǎn), *adv.,* abstractly, separately.

abstraire (abstrayant, abstrait), *v.a.,* to draw from, to separate, to abstract.

abstrait, -e, *adj.,* abstract; abstruse; inattentive, absent-minded.

abstraitement (-trèt-mǎn), *adv.,* abstractedly, separately.

abstrus, -e, *adj.,* abstruse, intricate, difficult; dark, obscure, recondite.

absurde, *adj.,* absurd, nonsensical, foolish, irrational, preposterous. *Réduire une opinion à l'—;* to show the absurdity of an opinion. *Tomber dans l'—;* to fall into the absurd.

absurdement, *adv.,* absurdly, nonsensically.

absurdité, *n.f.,* absurdity, nonsense, preposterousness, foolishness.

abus, *n.m.,* abuse, misuse, breach (of a thing); grievance; error. *Réformer, corriger, les —;* to redress grievances, nuisances. *Appel comme d'—* (leg.); appeal by writ of error.

abuser, *v.n.,* to abuse, to impose on, to misuse, to use ill, to make a bad use of, to misemploy. *Vous abusez de ma patience;* you take advantage of my patience.

abuser, *v.a.,* to cheat, to deceive, to delude, to gull.

s'abuser, *v.r.,* to mistake, to be mistaken, to deceive one's self.

abuseur, *n.m.,* (l.u.), cheat, deceiver, impostor.

abusi-f, -ve, *adj.,* abusive, improper, against rules, custom.

abusivement (-mǎn), *adv.,* abusively, improperly.

abuter, *v.a.,* to throw for first go, aim. *v.n.,* (shipbuilding) to abut.

abyme, *n.m. V.* **abîme.**

acabit, *n.m.,* quality (of fruits, vegetables); quality, stamp, kidney (of persons). *Cet homme est d'un bon —;* he is a good sort of fellow. *Ce sont des gens du même —;* they are all tarred with the same brush.

acacia, *n.m.,* acacia; gum-tree.

académicien (-si-in), *s.m.,* academician.

académie, *n.f.,* academy, society of learned men; academy (division of the University of France); academy (Plato's); university; ⊙riding-school; pupils, school. *Tenir —;* to keep a gaming-house; (paint.) academy figure.

académique, *adj.,* belonging to an academy, academical.

académiquement (-mik-mǎn), *adv.,* academically.

⊙**académiser,** *v.n.,* to paint from a model.

académiste, *s.m.,* academist, pupil.

***acagnarder,** *v.a.,* (fam.) to accustom to sloth; to make idle.

s'acagnarder, *v.r.,* to grow slothful, to lead an idle life; to become besotted.

acajou, *n.m.,* mahogany. *Noix d'—;* cashew nut. *Pomme d'—;* cashew apple.

acanthe, *n.f.,* acanthus, bear's foot.

acare or **acarus,** *n.m.,* acarus, itch, animalcule, mite.

acariâtre, *adj.,* crabbed, cross-grained, waspish, shrewish.

acariâtreté, *n.f.,* peevishness, crabbedness.

acariens, *n.m. pl.,* (ent.) acaridae.

acatalecte, acatalectique, *n.m.* and *adj.,* acatalectic.

acatalepsie, *n.f.,* (med.) acatalepsy.

acataleptique, *adj.,* acataleptic.

acaule, *adj.,* (bot.) acaulous, acaulose.

accablant, -e, *adj.,* grievous, oppressive, insufferable, overwhelming; annoying, crushing, sweltering.

accablé, -e, *adj.,* dejected, depressed. *Etre —;* to be extremely low-spirited.

accablement, *n.m.,* heaviness, languor, grief, dejection of spirits, oppression, discouragement. *Etre dans l'—;* to be in the greatest dejection.

accabler, *v.a.,* to crush, to bear down, to overwhelm; to throw, to weigh, to press down; to overload; to overpower; to afflict; to deject, to depress, to overwhelm; to load with, to heap on.

accalmie, *n.f.,* (nav.) lull.

accaparement (-mǎn), *n.m.,* monopoly, engrossment, forestalling, buying up.

accaparer, *v.a.,* to engross, to monopolize, to forestall; to swallow up, to buy up.

accapareu-r, *n.m.,* **-se,** *n.f.,* monopolist, engrosser, forestaller, monopolizer.

***accastillage,** *n.m.,* the space occupied by the forecastle and quarter-deck; upper-work.

***accastiller,** *v.a.,* to provide a ship with a fore and a hind-castle.

***accastillé, -e,** *adj.,* (of a ship) having a fore and a hind-castle. *Haut —;* with high upper works.

accéder, *v.n.,* to accede, to comply with, to agree to, consent.

accélérat-eur, -rice, *adj.,* accelerative.

accélération, *n.f.,* acceleration, haste, dispatch.

accéléré, -e, *adj.,* accelerated, quickened. *Au pas —;* in double quick time. *Pas —;* quick march.

accélérer, *v.a.,* to accelerate, to quicken; to despatch, to forward, to hasten.

⊙**accenser** or **acenser,** *v.a.,* to lease, to let, to rent, to annex, to join, to unite.

accent, *n.m.,* stress of the voice, accent, note; pronunciation, emphasis, expression. *— aigu, circonflexe, grave;* acute, circumflex, grave, accent. *— nasillard;* twang. *— très-fortement prononcé;* broad accent. *Sans —;* unaccented. *Prêtez l'oreille à mes —s;* hearken to my strain.

accenteur, *n.m.,* (ornith.) accentor.

accentuation, *n.f.,* accentuation.

accentué, -e, *adj.,* accented, accentuated.

accentuer, *v.a.,* to accent, to accentuate, to lay stress on.

acceptable, *adj.,* acceptable, worth accepting.

acceptant, *n.m.,* (jur.) accepter.

acceptation, *n.f.,* acceptance.

accepter, *v.a.,* to accept, to receive, to admit; to resign one's self to. *Qui vaut la peine d'être accepté;* worth accepting.

accepteur, *n.m.,* (com.) acceptor.

⊙**acceptilation,** *n.f.,* acceptilation.

acception, *n.f.,* respect, regard; (of words) sense, meaning, acceptation. *— de personnes;* respect of persons.

accès, *n.m.,* access, approach, admittance, attack, fit (of fever), paroxysm, madness. *Par —;* by fits and starts.

accessibilité, *n.f.,* accessibility.

accessible, *adj.,* accessible, approachable, easy to come at.

accession, *n.f.,* access, entry; accession; adhesion.

accessit (-sit), *n.m.,* the second best, the first after the prizeman (in academies, schools). *Proxime —;* honorable mention.

accessoire, *adj.,* accessory, additional.

accessoire, *n.m.,* accessory, minor; (paint.)

accessory; (thea.) property. *Fournisseur d'—s* or *chef d'—*; property-man.

accessoirement, *adv.*, accessorily.

accident, *n.m.*, accident, incident, casualty; (paint.) accident; (med.) symptom, complication; (mus.) incidental; irregularity, undulation (in ground). *Par —*; accidentally.

accidenté, -e, *adj.*, rough, uneven, unequal, broken, hilly (of ground); picturesque.

accidentel, -le, *adj.*, accidental, adventitious, incidental; fortuitous, eventual, casual.

accidentellement (-mān), *adv.*, accidentally, casually, by chance.

accipitres, *n.m. pl.*, accipiters.

accipitrin, -e, *adj.*, accipitrine.

accise, *n.f.*, inland duty, excise. *Préposé a l'—*; exciseman.

acclamation, *n.f.*, acclamation, shout, cheering, huzza, applause. *Saluer par des —s;* to cheer.

acclamer, *v.a.*, to acclaim, to applaud, to hail, to welcome.

acclamper, *v.a.*, (nav.) to clamp.

acclimatable, *adj.*, acclimatizable.

acclimatation, acclimatement, *n.f.*, acclimatization.

acclimater, *v.a.*, to acclimatize, to accustom to a climate.

*s'***acclimater**, *v.r.*, to become acclimatized.

accointance, *n.f.*, (fam. and b. s.) acquaintance, commerce, intimacy, connection.

*s'***accointer**, *v.r.*, to become or get intimately acquainted with any one.

accoisement, *n.m.*, appeasement.

accoiser, *v.a.*, to appease, calm, quiet. *S'—*, *v.r.*, to become appeased; to end.

accolade, *n.f.*, embrace, hug; accolade; (cook. — mus.— print.) brace; a crooked line. — *brisée* (print.) half-brace. *Une — de lapereaux;* a brace of rabbits *Donner l'— à;* to embrace, to dub a knight. *Recevoir l'—;* to be made a knight.

accolader, *v.a.*, to bracket.

accolage, *n.m.*, tying up; nailing up.

accolé, -e, *part.*, (her.) joined together.

accolement, *n.m.*, joining, uniting; union.

accoler, *v.a.*, to hug, to embrace; to place side by side; to couple; (hort.) to prop, to tie up.

accolure, *n.f.*, (agri.) a band of straw, osier.

accommodable, *adj.*, that may be arranged; accommodable.

accommodage, *n.m.*, the dressing of meat, cooking; hair-dressing.

accommodant, -e, *adj.*, accommodating, complying, courteous.

accommodé, -e, *part.*, favored, fitted up, adjusted; (cook.) dressed; well off, well to do.

accommodement (-mān), *n.m.*, accommodation, agreement, arrangement, composition; settlement; reconciliation; way, medium. *Un homme d'—;* a man easy to deal with. *En venir à un —;* to come to terms.

accommoder, *v.a.*, to adapt, to accommodate, to fit, to make up; to mend, to improve; to reconcile, to conciliate; to adjust; to be convenient; to dress, to trim; to cook; to treat, to serve out; to thrash; to let have, to sell. *Ceci vous accommodera-t-il?* will this suit you?

*s'***accommoder**, *v.r.*, to agree, to come to terms; to accommodate one's self; to suit; to make free with; to be pleased with, to put up with. *— à tout;* to put up with anything. *— de tout*, to be pleased with everything.

*****accompagnat-eur**, *n.m.*, **-rice**, *n.f.*, (mus.) accompanist.

*****accompagnement** (-mān), *n.m.*, accompanying; attendance, retinue; accompaniment; accessory, appendix. *— de quatuor;* accompaniment for stringed instruments. *— d'harmonie;* ac-

companiment for wind instruments. *— à grand orchestre;* full accompaniment.

*****accompagner**, *v.a.*, to accompany, to escort, to wait on, to attend; to be of the retinue, to follow; to match, to suit with; to add, to back; to be the accompanist. *J'ai eu l'honneur de l'— chez elle;* I had the honor of seeing her home.

*s'***accompagner**, *v.r.*, to be accompanied; to accompany one's self (on an instrument).

accompli, -e, *adj.*, accomplished, performed, fulfilled; complete; faultless, perfect. *Une beauté —;* a perfect beauty.

accomplir, *v.a.*, to accomplish, to effect; to finish, to complete; to fulfill, to make good. *— sa promesse;* to carry out one's promise.

*s'***accomplir**, *v.r.*, to be accomplished, to be performed, to be past.

accomplissement (-mān), *n.m.*, accomplishment, fulfillment; completion, execution, observance.

accon, *n.m.*, small lighter, punt.

accoquiner. *V.* acoquiner.

accorage, *n.m.*, propping.

accord, *s.m.*, agreement, bargain, contract, convention, settlement, stipulation; consent, concurrence; good understanding, unity; (mus.) accord, chord; (paint.) harmony, accord. *Etre d'—; demeurer d'—; tomber d'—;* to agree, to be agreed. *Mettre d'—;* to reconcile. *D'—;* granted, done. *D'un commun —;* by common consent. *Etre d'—;* (mus.) to be in tune. *Tenir d'—;* to keep in tune.

accordable, *adj.*, grantable, that may be granted; (mus.) tunable; (of men) reconcilable.

*****accordailles**, *n.f. pl.*, (pop.) the ceremony of signing the articles of marriage, espousals.

accordant, -e, *adj.*, (mus.) accordant, tunable, harmonious, concordant.

accorde! *int.* (nav.) now! (order given to rowers to pull together).

accordé, *n.m.*, **-e**, *n.f.*, bridegroom, bride (after the marriage articles are signed); one who is betrothed, granted.

accordéon, *n.m.*, accordion.

accorder, *v.a.*, to grant, to allow, to accord, to give, to allot, to bestow, to concede; to admit, to give up; to make friends, to reconcile; (gram.) to make agree; (mus.) to tune, to string. *— mal;* to mistune. *Accordez vos flûtes;* agree upon it between you.

*s'***accorder**, *v.r.*, to agree, to suit, to be suited, to accord, to correspond; to square; to join, to concur. *S'— du prix;* to agree upon the price. *Il ne s'accorde pas avec lui-même;* he is inconsistent with himself.

accordeu-r, *n.m.*, **-se**, *n.f.*, tuner (of instruments). *Clef d'—*; tuning-hammer.

accordoir, *n.m.*, tuning-hammer.

accore, *n.f.*, (nav.) shore, prop, stanchion.

accore, *adj.*, bluff, steep.

accorer, *v.a.*, (nav.) to shore up, to prop, to stay, to wedge.

accorné, -e, *adj.*, (her.) horned.

accort, -e, *adj.*, flexible, complying, courteous, affable.

accortise, *n.f.*, complaisance, affability, courtesy.

accostable, *adj.*, (l.u.) accostable, easy of access. *Il n'est pas —;* he is not approachable.

accoste, *n.m.*, (nav.) order to bring alongside.

accoster, *v.a.*, to accost, to make up to, to come or go up to one, to join, to couple; (nav.) to come alongside.

*s'***accoster de**, *v.r.*, to keep company with, to make acquaintance with, to frequent.

accotar, *n.m. V.* accotoir.

accotement, *n.m.*, (engineering) driftway; (rail.) bank, outer way.

accoter, *v.a.*, to prop up, to support, to bear

up, to lean; (hort.) to dung, to match, to screen.

s'accoter, v.r., to lean on anything, to support one's self.

accotoir, n.m., prop, leaning-stock, stanchion; (nav.) stay, shore.

accouchée, n.f., a woman in child-bed, lying-in woman.

accouchement (-koosh-mān), n.m., child-bed; delivery, confinement, accouchement; obstetrics; midwifery. *Hôpital des —s;* lying-in hospital. *Faire un —;* to deliver a woman.

accoucher, v.n., to lie in, to be brought to bed, to be delivered. *— avant terme;* to miscarry. *Accouchez donc!* (fam.) come, out with it!

accoucher, v.a., to deliver a woman.

accoucheur, n.m., man-midwife, accoucheur.

accoucheuse, n.f., a midwife.

s'accouder, v.r., to lean on one's elbow.

accoudoir, n.m., anything to lean the elbow upon, elbow-rest, sill, rail.

accouer, v.a., to tie the halter of the first horse to the tail of the second, and so on; to wound a stag in the shoulder, to ham-string him.

accoulins, n.m. pl., alluvion; clay for making bricks.

accouple, n.f., leash, brace, couple.

accouplement, s.m., coupling, pairing, joining or yoking together; copulation.

accoupler, v.a., to couple; to tack or join together; to yoke; to match, to pair. *— des bœufs;* to yoke oxen.

s'accoupler, v.r., to couple, to copulate; to pair.

accourcie, n.f., short cut; a passage formed in a ship's hold, to go fore and aft.

accourcir, v.a., to shorten, to make shorter, to abridge.

s'accourcir, v.a., to shorten, to grow shorter, to decrease.

accourcissement (-mān), n.m., shortening, diminution.

accourir, v.n., to run to, to hasten, to flock together, to run at, to rush at.

accoutré, -e, part., accoutred, dressed.

accoutrement, n.m., (jest. or iron.) garb, dress, gear.

accoutrer, v.a., (jest or iron.) to dress out, rig out.

s'accoutrer, v.r., to dress one's self out in, to rig one's self out.

⊙**accoutumance**, n.f., habit, custom.

accoutumé, -e, adj., accustomed, habitual, used to. *A l'—e;* as usual, customarily.

accoutumer, v.a., to accustom, to use, to habituate; to inure.

accoutumer, v.n., to use, to be wont.

s'accoutumer, v.r., to accustom, to use, to inure one's self.

⊙**accouvé, -e**, (fam.) adj., brooding over (the fire).

accréditer, v.a., to accredit; to give reputation, credit, sanction to; to bring into vogue, to procure esteem, to confirm, to spread (rumors).

s'accréditer, v.r., to get a name or reputation, to get into credit; to ingratiate one's self.

accrétion, n.f., (med.) accretion.

accroc (-krô), n.m., impediment, hitch, hindrance; rent, tear. *Faire un — à;* to tear.

⊙**accroche**, n.f., hindrance, obstacle, hitch.

accroche-cœur, n.m., (—) (curl) heartbreaker, kiss-curl. *En —;* curled up, twisted.

accrochement, n.m., locking (of carriages); difficulty, hitch, delay.

accrocher, v.a., to hang up or down, to hook; to catch, to tear; to get, to pick up; to lock, to get locked with; to grapple (a ship); to delay, stop, put off, pawn. *— sa montre;* to pawn one's watch. *Il lui a accroché de l'argent;* he has done him out of some money.

s'accrocher, v.r., to catch in; to hang on; to lay hold of, to cling to.

accroire, v.a., to believe. *Faire — à;* to make believe. *En faire — à quelqu'un;* to impose upon any one. *S'en faire —;* to be self-conceited, to overrate one's self.

accroissement, n.m., increase, growth, enlargement, extension, development.

accroître, v.a., to increase, to enlarge, to amplify, to augment, to raise.

accroître, v.n., to increase, to augment.

s'accroître, v.r., to increase, to grow; to be augmented or advanced, to improve.

accroupi, -e, adj., squat, cowering, crouching.

s'accroupir, v.r., to sit down upon the hams or heels, to squat, to crouch.

accroupissement (-mān), n.m., cowering, squatting, crouching.

accru, n.m., sprig produced by roots, shoot.

accrue, n.f., increase of land caused by the retiring of waters; encroachment by trees on adjoining land.

*accueil (-keu), n.m., reception, welcome, greeting; (com.) protection, honor (of bills). *Faire —;* to receive kindly (of bills), to meet. *Recevoir bon —;* to meet with due honor, protection; to be greeted, welcomed; (com.) to be met, honored (of bills).

*accueillir (-keu-), v.a., to receive, to make welcome, to entertain; to hail; to overtake; to assail; (com.) to honor; to protect. *Etre bien accueilli;* to be received with a hearty welcome. *La tempête nous accueillit;* the storm overtook us.

accul, n.m., place that has no egress; blind alley; small bay, cove; (hunt.) terrier, lodge, hole; breeching (of a cannon).

acculer, v.a., to bring to a stand; to drive into a corner; to drive into a place from which there is no escape; (hunt.) to run home.

acculer, v.n., (of carts) to hang backwards.

accumulat-eur, n.m., **-rice**, n.f., accumulator.

accumulation, n.f., accumulation.

accumuler, v.a., to accumulate, to heap up, to store, to amass. *— crime sur crime;* to heap crime upon crime.

s'accumuler, v.r., to accumulate, to increase.

accusable, adj., accusable, impeachable, chargeable.

accusat-eur, n.m., **-rice**, n.f., accuser, indicter, impeacher.

accusatif, n.m., (gram.) accusative case. *A l'—;* in the accusative.

accusation, n.f., accusation, indictment, impeachment, charge; complaint; prosecution. *Chef d'—;* count of an indictment. *Mise en —;* arraignment. *Intenter une —;* to prefer an indictment. *Mettre en —;* to impeach. *Prononcer la mise en —;* to find a true bill.

accusatoire, adj., accusatory.

accusé, n.m., **-e**, n.f., accused, prisoner, culprit. *— de réception;* (com.) acknowledgment of letter, receipt.

accuser, v.a., to accuse of, to charge with; to indict, to impeach; to reproach, to tax; to blame; to dispute the validity of a deed; to mention, to give notice; (fig.) to show, to indicate, to betray, to attest. *— réception d'une lettre;* to acknowledge the receipt of a letter.

s'accuser, v.r., to accuse one's self.

acéphale, adj., acephalous, without a head.

acéphales, n.m. pl., acephala.

acérain, -e, adj., relating to steel, steely.

acerbe, adj., sour, sharp, acerb; harsh, bitter.

acerbité, n.f., acerbity, harshness; bitterness.

acéré, -e, adj., steely, steeled; sharp, keen, sharp-edged; acerose.

acérer, v.a., to steel.

⊙**acéreu-x, -se**, adj., acerose, needle-shaped.

acescence, n.f., acescency, acidifying.

acescent, -e, adj., acescent.

acétabule, *n.m.*, acetabulum.
acétate, *n.m.*, acetate.
acéteu-x, -se, *adj.*, acetous.
acétique, *adj.*, acetic.
achalandage, *n.m.*, custom, connection; good will and fixtures.
achalandé, -e, *part.*, having custom. *Boutique bien —e;* a well-frequented shop, doing or driving a good trade.
achalander, *v.a.*, to get custom, to procure customers, to procure custom to.
*s'*achalander**, *v.r.*, to get or draw, attract, customers.
acharné, -e, *adj.*, fleshed; rabid; infuriated; implacable; desperate; obstinate; intense. *Un combat —;* a desperate fight. *Une haine —e;* an implacable hatred.
acharnement, *n.m.*, tenacity; rancor, blind fury; stubbornness, ill-nature; obstinacy, desperation. *Avec —;* unmercifully. *C'est de l'—;* this is rank fury.
acharner, *v.a.*, to flesh; to rouse, to madden; to set on; to embitter, to envenom.
*s'*acharner**, *v.r.*, to be intent, bent, set upon; to set one's heart upon; to persist in; to be infuriated, implacable. *Il s'acharne à l'étude;* his heart is set upon study.
⊙**achars**, *n.m.pl.*, Indian pickles.
achat, *n.m.*, purchase, purchasing, buying; bargain. *Faire des —;* to purchase.
ache, *n.f.*, (bot.) smallage.
achée, *n.f.*, worms, gentles, bait.
acheminement (ash-mi-n-mān), *n.m.*, step; preparatory measure, means, way, dispatch.
acheminer (ash-mi-né), *v.a.*, to forward, to send on.
*s'*acheminer**, *v.r.*, to set out or forward, to make one's way towards; to begin one's journey; to proceed towards; to get on.
acheter (ash-té), *v.a.*, to buy, to purchase, to bribe. *— cher ou bon marché;* to buy dear or cheap. *— en bloc;* to buy in a lump. *— chat en poche;* to buy a pig in a poke.
*s'*acheter**, to buy for one's self, to be bought.
acheteur (ash-teur), *n.m.*, buyer, purchaser, last bidder.
achevé, -e, *part.*, finished, perfect, exquisite, absolute; downright, consummate, arrant. *Beauté —e;* a perfect beauty. *Sot —;* downright ass.
achèvement (-shev-mān), *n.m.*, completion, finishing, conclusion.
achever (ash-vé), *v.a.*, to finish, to put the finishing hand to; to close, to end, to conclude, to terminate, to perfect, to crown, to consummate; to dispatch, to kill. *— de boire;* to drink up. *Achevez!* out with it! *Il n'acheva pas;* he said no more.
acheveur, -se, *n.m,f.*, finisher.
achillée, *n.f.*, (bot.) milfoil, yarrow.
achit, *n.m.*, wild vine.
achoppement (-shop-mān), *n.m.*, stumbling, impediment. *Pierre d'—;* stumbling-block.
achopper, *v.n.*, to stumble, to knock one's self against anything; (fig.) to fail.
achromatique (-kro-), *adj.*, achromatic.
achromatisme (-kro-), *n.m.*, (opt.) achromatism.
⊙**achronique** (-kro-), *adj.* V. **acronyque**.
aciculaire, *adj.*, acicular, needle-shaped.
acide, *n.m.*, acid.
acide, *adj.*, acid, sour, tart, sharp.
acidifier, *v.a.*, to acidify.
acidité, *n.f.*, acidity, sourness, sharpness, tartness.
acidule, *adj.*, of the nature of acids, acidulous.
acidulé, -e, *adj.*, acidulated.
aciduler, *v.a.*, to acidulate.
acier, *n.m.*, steel. *— fondu;* cast steel. *— indien, — wootz;* wootz. *— poule, — de cémentation;*

blistered steel. *Articles d'—;* steel wares. *Bijouterie d'—;* polished steel wares. *Fil d'—;* steel wire.
aciérage, *n.m.*, (metal.) the hardening of copper, steeling, plating with steel.
aciération, *n.f.*, the converting of iron into steel.
aciérer, *v.a.*, to convert into steel, to steel.
aciérie, *n.f.*, steel manufactory, steel-works.
acineu-x, -se, *adj.*, acinose, acinous.
aciniforme, *adj.*, aciniform.
acmé, *n.m.*, (med.) acme.
acné, *n.f.*, (med.) acne.
acolyte, *n.m.*, acolothist, acolyte; companion, confederate, associate.
acompte, *n.m.*, installment, partial payment.
acon, *n.m.* V. **accon**.
aconit (-nit), *n.m.*, aconite, wolf's-bane, monk's hood. *— tue-chien;* dog's-bane.
acoquinant, -e, *adj.*, (fam.) alluring, engaging, captivating.
acoquiner, *v.a.*, (fam.) to allure, to bewitch; to captivate.
*s'*acoquiner**, *v.r.*, (fam.) to be bewitched, to be greatly attached to. *Il s'acoquine auprès de cette femme;* he is much in love with that woman.
acotylédone, *adj.*, (of plants) acotyledonous.
acoup, *n.m.*, (—s) jerk, sudden stop, or halt.
acoustique, *n.f.* (n.p.), acoustics.
acoustique, *adj.*, acoustic. *Cordon —;* speaking-pipe. *Cornet —;* ear-trumpet. *Voûte —;* whispering dome, gallery.
acquéreur, *n.m.*, buyer, purchaser.
acquérir (acquérant, acquis), *v.a.*, to acquire, to purchase, to buy, to obtain; to get, to achieve, to attain, to gain, to win.
*s'*acquérir**, *v.r.*, to get, to be gotten, to be acquired, obtained, or purchased, to win for one's self.
acquêt, *n.m.*, (jur.) common property of two married people, acquisition, purchase.
acquiescement (-mān), *n.m.*, acquiescence, compliance, consent, willingness.
acquiescer, *v.n.*, to acquiesce, to agree, to assent, to yield, to comply.
acquis, *part.* of Acquérir.
acquis, -e, *adj.*, acquired; added; secured; (med.) adventitious.
acquis, *n.m.*, acquired knowledge, acquirements, attainments.
acquisition, *n.f.*, acquisition, getting, acquiring, attaining, purchase, conquest. *Contrat d'—;* deed of purchase.
acquit, *n.m.*, discharge, receipt; lead (at billiards). *Par manière d'—;* for form's sake. *Jouer à l'—;* to play who shall pay for the whole. *Pour acquit* (on bills), paid. *Donner —de;* to give a receipt for. *Mettre son — à l'* to put "paid" on to receipt.
acquit-à-caution, *n.m.*, (—s —) (customs) permit.
⊙**acquit-patent**, *n.m.*, (—s —s) royal decree granting the remission of a debt.
acquittement (-mān), *n.m.*, payment, clearing off, liquidation; acquittal.
acquitter, *v.a.*, to pay, to pay off, to clear, to quit; to receipt; to acquit, to discharge.
*s'*acquitter**, *v.r.*, to fulfill, to perform; to pay off one's debts, to pay off, to be quits.
acre, *n.f.*, acre.
âcre, *adj.*, sharp, sour, tart, acrimonious; bitter, biting; acrid.
âcreté, *n.f.*, acridity, sharpness, sourness, tartness, acrimony.
acrimonie, *n.f.*, acrimony, sharpness, keenness.
acrimonieu-x. -se, *adj.*, acrimonious, sharp.
acrobate, *n.m.f.*, rope-dancer.
acronyque, *adj.*, (astr.), acronic, acronical.

acropole, *n.f.*, acropolis.

acrostiche, *n.m.*, acrostic.

acrotère, *n.m.*, (arch.) acroterium, blocking course; (nav.) cape, headland.

acte, *n.m.*, act; deed; indenture, instrument; document; charter; *pl.*, records, public registers, rolls, proceedings. — *faux;* forged deed. *Expédition de* un —; copy of a deed. *Donner — de;* to deliver an official certificate of. *Rédiger un —;* to draw up a document. *Faire acte de présence;* to put in an appearance, to show one's self. *Prendre —;* to make a note of, to put down.

act-eur, *n.m.*, **-rice**, *n.f.*, actor; actress; player.

actif, *n.m.*, (n.p.) assets (pl.); (gram.) active voice. *Actif et passif;* assets and liabilities. *Actif;* receipts of a budget.

acti-f, **-ve**, *adj.*, active; real, actual; quick, nimble, brisk, agile, stirring, busy, energetic. *Dettes actives;* assets.

action, *n.f.*, action, act, agency, operation, virtue, motion; deed, feat, performance; gesture, posture; engagement, battle; suit, plea; share, stock. — *cessible* (com.); transferable share. — *nominative;* personal share. *Promesse d'—s;* scrip. *Détenteur de promesse d'—s;* scrip-holder. *Titre d'une —;* document of a share. *Par —s;* joint-stock. — *d'éclat;* splendid achievement. — *s de banque;* bank stock. *Hausse, baisse, des —s;* rise, fall, of shares. — *de grâces;* thanksgiving. *En —;* in motion. *Entrer en —;* to begin operations. *Intenter une — à quelqu'un;* to bring an action against any one. *Mettre en —;* to carry into action, to carry out. *En —;* (mach.) in gear. *Hors d'—;* out of gear.

actionnaire, *n.m.*, shareholder, stockholder.

actionner, *v.a.*, to bring an action, to sue at law. *S'—;* to bestir oneself.

activement (-mān), *adv.*, actively, vigorously.

activer, *v.a.*, to press, to hasten, to forward, to expedite.

activité, *n.f.*, action, activity; nimbleness, expedition, dispatch, employment. *En —;* in activity, in active service.

actualisation, *n.f.*, actualness, adaptation to the times.

actualiser, *v.a.*, to actualize.

actualité, *n.f.*, actuality, passing event; question of the hour.

actuel, **-le**, *adj.*, actual, real; present.

actuellement (-èl-mān), *adv.*, now, at this very time.

acuité, *n.f.*, (mus.) acuteness, keenness.

acuminé, **-e**, *adj.*, (bot.) acuminated.

acuponcture, *n.f.*, (surg.) acupuncture.

acutangle, *adj.*, acute-angled.

acutangulé, **-e**, *adj.*, (bot.) acute-angled.

adage, *n.m.*, adage, proverb; saying.

adagio, *n.m.*, (—*s*) (mus.) adagio.

adagio, *adv.*, (mus.) adagio, slowly.

adamantin, **-e**, *adj.*, adamantine.

adaptation, *n.f.*, adaptation.

adapter, *v.a.*, to apply, to adapt; to suit; to fit. *s'adapter*, *v.r.*, to apply, fit, suit. *Qui peut —;* which is adaptable.

adapteur, *n.m.f.*, adapter.

addition (ad-di-), *n.f.*, addition; accession; bill, reckoning; (print.) marginal note. — *composée;* compound addition. — *en hache* (print.); interlinear matter. *Faire l'— de;* to add, to sum up.

additionnel, **-le**, *adj.*, addditional.

additionner, *v.a.*, to add, to cast up.

adducteur, *n.m.*, (anat.) adductor.

adducteur, *adj.*, (anat.) adducent.

adduction, *n.f.*, (anat.) adduction.

ademption, *n.f.*, (jur.) revocation of a legacy.

adepte, *n.m.f.*, adept.

adéquat, **-e** (-kouat), *adj.*, (philos.) complete, entire, adequate.

adhérence, *n.f.*, adhesion; adherence, attachment.

adhérent, **-e**, *adj.*, adherent, sticking to.

adhérent, *n.m.*, adherer, follower, partisan.

adhérer, *v.n.*, to adhere, to be adherent, to cling, to hold, to cleave, to stick; to adhere to, to approve.

adhési-f, **-ve**, *adj.*, adhesive.

adhésion, *n.f.*, adhesion, adherence; compliance.

ad hoc, *adv.*, to that effect or purpose.

ad hominem, *adv.*, personal, direct. *Argument —; argumentum ad hominem.*

⊙**ad honores**, *adv.*, honorary.

adiante, *n.m.*, (bot.) adiantum, maiden-hair.

adieu, *adv.*, adieu, farewell, good-bye. *Dire —, faire ses adieux* à; to bid adieu. *Sans —;* without bidding you adieu, without saying good-bye. — *va!* (nav.) about ship!

adieu, *n.m.*, farewell, parting, leave. *Faire ses —x;* to take one's leave.

adipeu-x, **-se**, *adj.*, adipous, adipose, fat.

adipocire, *n.f.*, adipocere.

adiposité, *n.f.*, adipose or fatty condition.

adirer, *v.a.*, (jur.) to mislay, to lose.

adition, *n.f.*, (jur.) acceptance of an inheritance.

adjacent, **-e**, *adj.*, adjacent, bordering upon, contiguous.

adjectif, *n.m.*, (gram.) adjective.

adjecti-f, **-ve**, *adj.*, (gram.) adjectival.

adjectivement (-mān), *adv.*, adjectively.

adjoindre, *v.a.*, to adjoin, to associate, to give as an assistant. *S'—;* to take as a partner.

adjoint, *n.m.*, adjunct, associate, colleague, assistant, deputy. *Maire —;* deputy mayor.

adjonction, *n.f.*, adjunction, union, annexation.

adjudant, *n.m.*, adjutant. *Fonctions d'—;* adjutancy. — *de place;* town adjutant.

adjudicataire, *n.m.f.*, purchaser, contractor, highest bidder.

adjudicataire, *adj.*, purchasing; contracting.

adjudicat-eur, *n.m.*, **-rice**, *n.f.*, awarder.

adjudicati-f, **-ve**, *adj.*, (jur.) adjudging.

adjudication, *n.f.*, adjudication; auction; contract, award. *Par —;* by contract. *Mettre en —;* to contract for.

adjuger, *v.a.*, to adjudge, to adjudicate, to award. *Adjugé!* (at auctions) gone!

s'adjuger, *v.r.*, to appropriate to one's own use.

adjuration, *n.f.*, adjuration, imprecation.

adjurer, *v.a.*, to adjure; to conjure, to call upon, to beseech.

adjuvant, *n.m.*, (med.) adjuvant.

ad libitum (-tom), *adv.*, ad libitum, at will, at pleasure.

admettre, *v.a.*, to admit, to receive; to allow, to approve of, to suppose; to adopt; to give admittance, to take in; to let in, to suffer to come into, to let enter.

adminicule, *n.m.*, (jur.) presumptive proof.

administra-teur, *n.m.*, **-trice**, *n.f.*, administrator, administratrix, manager, trustee, governor, curator; guardian (of the poor).

administrati-f, **-ve**, *adj.*, administrative.

administration, *n.f.*, administration, management, direction, government, conduct. *Mauvaise —;* maladministration.

administrativement, *adv.*, administratively.

administré, *n.m.*, **-e**, *n.f.*, person under one's administration or jurisdiction.

administrer, *v.a.*, to administer, to manage, to officiate, to govern; to minister, to dispense; (jur.) to furnish, find. *Droit d'—;* letters of administration. — *des témoins;* to find, produce, witnesses.

s'administrer, *v.r.*, to administer to one's self; to be managed, to be administered.

admirable, *adj.*, admirable, wonderful.

admirablement, *adv.*, admirably, wonderfully.

admirat-eur, *n.m.*, **-rice**, *n.f.*, admirer, praiser.

admirati-f, -ve, *adj.*, of admiration or exclamation, wondering. *D'un air* —; with a wondering look.

admiration, *n.f.*, admiration, wonder, marvel. *Point d'* —; note of exclamation. *Avoir de l'* — *pour*, *Etre dans l'* —; to admire. *Saisir d'* —; to strike with admiration.

admirer, *v.a.*, to admire, to wonder at.

admissibilité, *n.f.*, admissibility.

admissible, *adj.*, allowable, admissible.

admission, *n.f.*, admission, admittance, reception.

admonestation, *n.f.*, admonishment, admonition.

admonester, *v.a.*, (jur.) to admonish, to warn, to reprimand.

admonit-eur, *n.m.*, **-rice**, *n.f.*, adviser.

admonition, *n.f.*, admonition, advice, exhortation, reprimand.

adné, -e, *adj.*, (bot.) adnate.

adolescence, *n.f.*, adolescence.

adolescent, *n.m.*, **-e**, *n.f.*, lad; lass; stripling.

adolescent, -e, *adj.*, adolescent.

adonien, -ne (-in, -è-n), *adj.*, (poet.) adonic.

adonique. *V.* **adonien.**

adonis (-nis), *n.m.*, Adonis, beau; (bot.) adonis, pheasant's-eye.

adoniser, *v.a.*, to deck out, to make fine.

s'adoniser, *v.r.*, to bedizen one's self.

adonner, *v.n.*, (nav.) to veer aft.

s'adonner, *v.r.*, to give, to apply, to devote, to addict one's self, to give one's mind (to a thing — *à quelque chose*), to follow, to take to a thing. *S'* — *au vin*, to become addicted to drinking.

adoptable, *adj.*, that can be adopted.

adoptant, *n.m.*, adopter.

adopté, *n.m.*, **-e**, *n.f.*, adoptive son, daughter, heir, &c.

adopter, *v.a.*, to adopt; to embrace, to espouse, to sanction, to pass, to carry.

adopti-f, -ve, *adj.*, adoptive, by adoption. *Enfant* —; adoptive child. *Père* —; foster-father.

adoption, *n.f.*, adoption.

adorable, *adj.*, adorable, charming, delightful.

adorablement, *adv.*, adorably, delightfully.

adorat-eur, *n.m.*, **-rice**, *n.f.*, adorer, worshiper, great admirer.

adoration, *n.f.*, adoration, worshiping; worship; admiration, respect, reverence.

adorer, *v.a.*, to adore, to worship; to have a passionate love for.

ados, *n.m.*, (gard.) shelving-bed, border (against a wall).

adossé, -e, *adj.*, back to back; resting or standing against; indorsed (of a bill).

adossement, *n.m.*, position back to back; backing, indorsement.

adosser, *v.a.*, to set or lean with the back against a thing, to put back to back. *S'* — *contre un mur;* to lean up against a wall.

adouber, *v.n.*, (chess) to adjust a piece; (nav.) to mend, to repair.

adoucir, *v.a.*, to soften, to mitigate, to sweeten; to modify, to compose, to calm, to soothe; to smooth, to appease; to ease, to allay, to relieve, to cool, to pacify; to tame. *Rien ne peut* — *son chagrin;* nothing can mitigate his sorrow. — *un esprit irrité;* to appease an exasperated mind.

s'adoucir, *v.r.*, to grow cool, soft, mild; to be assuaged, mitigated; to relent; (of weather) to get milder.

adoucissant, *n.m.*, emollient, mollifier.

adoucissant, -e, *adj.*, softening, soothing, emollient.

adoucissement (-mān), *n.m.*, sweetening, softening, mollifying; assuaging, appeasing; ease, mitigation, palliation, alleviation, relief, consolation.

adoucisseur, *n.m.*, glass-polisher.

adoué, -e, *adj.*, (hunt.) coupled, paired.

ad patres (-ess), to kingdom come. *Aller* —; to be gathered to one's fathers.

adrachne (-rakn), *n.m.*, strawberry-tree. *V.* **arbousier.**

adragant, -e, *adj.*, tragacanth.

adragant, *n.m.*, tragacanth; gum-dragon.

ad rem, *adv.*, pertinently. *Répondre* —; to answer pertinently, to the point.

adresse, *n.f.*, speech, direction, address; skill, dexterity, expertness, cleverness, ingenuity; shrewdness, cunning, direction, destination. *Etre à l'* — *de ;* to be directed to. *Faire tenir à son* —; to forward to its destination. *Tour d'* —; legerdemain. *Avoir l'adresse de ;* to be artful enough to.

adresser, *v.a.*, to direct, to address. — *mal ;* to misdirect.

s'adresser, *v.r.*, to be directed; to address one's self, to apply, to make application, to appeal to. — *ici ;* apply within. *Vous vous adressez mal ;* you mistake your man. — *bien ;* you come to the right person.

adroit, -e, *adj.*, dexterous, ingenious, clever, skillful; handy, neat; cunning, shrewd, artful.

adroitement (-droat-mān), *adv.*, adroitly, skillfully, artfully, cleverly, happily; smartly, handily.

adulaire, *n.f.*, (min.) adularia, moon-stone, sun-stone.

adula-teur, *n.m.*, **-trice**, *n.f.*, adulator, flatterer, fawner, sycophant; parasite.

adula-teur, -trice, *adj.*, adulatory, parasitical.

adulation, *n.f.*, adulation, flattery, sycophancy.

aduler, *v.a.*, to fawn upon, to cringe to, to flatter.

adulte, *adj.*, adult, grown-up.

adulte, *n.m.f.*, adult.

adultération, *n.f.*, (pharm.) adulteration.

adultère, *n.f.*, adulteress.

adultère, *n.m.*, adulterer; adultery.

adultère, *adj.*, adulterous; adulterate. *Femme* —; adulteress.

adultérer, *v.a.*, (pharm.) to adulterate.

adultérin, *n.m.*, **-e**, *n.f.*, adulterine child.

adultérin, -e, *adj.*, adulterine.

aduste, *adj.*, (med.) adust, burnt up.

adustion, *n.f.*, (med.) adustion, burning.

advenant, *part.*, occurring, in case, in the event of. — *le décès ;* in the event of the death.

advenir, *v.n.*, to occur, happen, to chance, befall. *Advienne que pourra ;* happen what may.

adventice, *adj.*, adventitious.

adventi-f, -ve, *adj.*, adventive, casual.

adverbe, *n.m.*, (gram.) adverb.

adverbial, -e, *adj.*, adverbial.

adverbialement (-mān), *adv.*, adverbially.

adverbialité, *n.f.*, adverbial nature of.

adversaire, *n.m.*, adversary, opponent, antagonist, opposer.

adversati-f, -ve, *adj.*, (gram.) adversative.

adverse, *adj.*, adverse, opposite. *Avocat* —; counsel on the opposite side.

adversité, *n.f.*, adversity, affliction.

adynamie, *n.f.*, (med.) adynamy, debility.

adynamique, *adj.*, adynamic.

aérage, *n.m.*, ventilation, airing. *Puits d'* —; air-shaft.

aération, *n.f.*, aëration, airing.

aéré, -e, *adj.*, aired, airy.

aérer, *v.a.*, to air, to renew the air; (chem.) to aërate.

aérien, -ne (-in-e-n), *adj.*, aërial.

aériennement, *adv.*, aerially, in the air.

aérifère, *adj.*, aërial.

aériforme, *adj.*, aëriform.

aériser, *v.a.*, to aërify.

aérodynamique, *n.f.*, aëro-dynamics.

aérographie, *n.f.*, aërography.

aérolithe, *n.m.*, aërolite, aërolith.

aérologie, *n.f.*, aërology.

aéromancie, *n.f.*, aëromancy.

aéromètre, *n.m.*, aërometer.

aérométrie, *n.f.*, aërometry.

aéronaute, *n.m.f.*, aëronaut. *Art, science de l'* —; aëronautics.

aérophobie, *n.f.*, aërophobia.

aérostat, *n.m.*, aërostat; air-balloon.

aérostation, *n.f.*, aërostation.

aérostatique, *adj.*, aërostatic.

aétite, *n.f.*, aëtites, eagle-stone.

affabilité, *n.f.*, affability, affableness, kindness, courtesy.   [ners.

affable, *adj.*, affable, courteous, of easy man

affablement, *adv.*, affably, courteously.

affabulation, *n.f.*, the moral of a fable.

affadir, *v.a.*, to make unsavory or insipid; to flatten; to be nauseous, to cloy, to pall, to satiate.

*s'***affadir,** *v.r.*, to become insipid.

affadissement (-măn), *n.m.*, cloying, insipidity, nauseousness.

affaiblir, *v.a.*, to enfeeble, to weaken, to debilitate; to impair, to attenuate; to debase (coins).

affaiblir, *v.n.*, to grow weak, to weaken, to droop.

*s'***affaiblir,** *v.r.*, to grow weak, to be impaired, to become enfeebled; to abate.

affaiblissant, -e, *adj.*, weakening, enfeebling.

affaiblissement (-măn), *n.m.*, weakening, enfeebling, impairment, diminution of strength; allaying, abatement; debasement (of coins).

affaire, *n.f.*, thing, affair, matter; business, concern, job, duty; dealing; trouble, scrape, quarrel; action, case, lawsuit; fight, skirmish, battle; need, occasion, want; work, transaction. *Belle* —; fine thing, pretty mess, trifling matter. —*s courantes;* current business. —*de rien;* trifling affair. — *d'intérêt;* money matter. *Bien, mal, dans ses* —; in good, bad, circumstances. *Homme d'*—*s;* man of business, agent, steward, middleman. *Relation d'*—*s;* mercantile connection. *Dans les* —*s;* in business. *En* —; engaged in business. *Pour* —; on business. *Aller à ses* —*s;* to go to one's business. *S'attirer une* —; to get into a scrape. *Avoir*—*à;* to have to deal with. *Avoir* —*avec;* to have business with. *Avoir bien des* —*s;* to be much employed. *Avoir des* —*s pardessus la tête;* to be over head and ears in business. *Céder ses* —*s;* to give up business. *Etre à ses* —*s;* to attend to business. *Eviter les* —*s;* to keep clear of scrapes. *Faire des* —*s;* to do business. *Faire l'*— *de quelqu'un;* to answer some one's purpose, turn. *Faire son* — *à quelqu'un;* to settle any one's business, do for him. *Faire de grandes* —*s;* to carry on an extensive business. *Ne faire rien à l'*—; not to affect the matter. *Mettre quelqu'un dans les* —*s;* to set any one up in business, to apprentice any one to a business. *Se retirer des* —*s;* to retire from business. *Sortir d'une* — *avec honneur;* to come off honorably. *Tirer d'*—; to extricate, to help out. *Se tirer d'*—; to get out of trouble, to get on in the world. *Vaquer aux* —*s;* to attend to business. *Vider une* —; to settle an affair. *C'est, ce n'est pas, une* —; it is no, it is an, easy matter. *J'ai votre* —; I have what you want, the very thing for you. *Je ferai son* —; I will do for him. *C'est mon* —; leave that to me. *J'en fais mon* —; I take that upon myself. *Ce ne sont pas là mes*

—*s;* that is none of my business. *Au point où en sont les* —*s;* as matters stand. *Son* — *est bonne;* he is in for it, he will catch it. *Son* — *est faite;* he is done for.

affairé, -e, *adj.*, full of business, busy. *Faire l'*—; to ape the busy man; to fuss about.

affaissement (-măn), *n.m.*, depression, sinking, subsiding, giving way, weakness, weighing down; (med.) collapse.

affaisser, *v.a.*, to cause to sink, to weigh down, to press down, to bear down, to weaken.

*s'***affaisser,** *v.r.*, to sink, sink down, subside, settle, to give way.

affaiter, *v.a.*, (falconry) to reclaim and train, tame (hawks).

affaler, *v.a.*, (nav.) to overhaul (a rope); to embay, drive upon a lee-shore. *Affale!* lower away.

*s'***affaler,** *v.r.*, (nav.) to slide down; to be driven upon a lee-shore.

affamé, -e, *adj.*, famished, hungry, starving, craving. *Etre* — *de;* to be greedy of; eager for.

affamer, *v.a.*, to famish, to starve.

affectation, *n.f.*, affectation, distinction; (jur.) mortgage, charge.

affecté, -e, *adj.*, affected, destined; (alg.) affected, assumed.

affecter, *v.a.*, to affect, to pretend, feign; to appropriate, to destine.

*s'***affecter,** *v.r.*, to be affected; to be moved.

affecti-f, -ve, *adj.*, affective.

affection, *n.f.*, affection, love, attachment, liking, inclination, partiality; (med.) affection. *Témoignage d'*—; token, mark, of affection. *Par* —; out of affection. *Prendre quelqu'un en* —; to become attached, to take a fancy to any one. — *nerveuse;* nervous affection.

affectionné, -e, *adj.*, affectionate, loving.

affectionner, *v.a.*, to love, to have an affection for, to fancy, to be fond of, to like; to take an interest in.

*s'***affectionner,** *v.r.*, to apply one's self to a thing with delight, to attach one's self to, to delight in, to take a fancy for.

affectueusement (-măn), *adv.*, affectionately, fondly, heartily, kindly.

affectueu-x, -se, *adj.*, affectionate, warmhearted.

afférent, -e, *adj.*, (jur.) appertaining to, belonging to, accruing to, indivisible. *Portion* —*e;* share of indivisible property.

affermable, *adj.*, farmable, rentable, demisable.

affermage, *n.m.*, farming, renting, demising.

affermer, *v.a.*, to farm or let out by lease; to take a lease of; to rent.

*s'***affermer,** *v.r.*, to be farmed, rented.

affermir, *v.a.*, to strengthen, to give strength to; to make firm or strong; to fasten; to harden, to make hard or firm; to confirm, to establish, to consolidate, to fix firmly.

*s'***affermir,** *v.r.*, to become strong, firm or fast; to grow hard; to fortify one's self; to become established, to persist in.

affermissement (-măn), *n.m.*, strengthening, settling, consolidation, establishment; stay, support, prop.

affété, -e, *adj.*, affected, full of affectation, prim, finical; canting, mincing. *Mine* —*e;* affected looks. *Manières* —*es;* affected manners.

afféterie, *n.f.*, affectation, affectedness; primness, mannerism; affected, formal ways; cant. *Les* —*s d'une coquette;* the affected ways of a coquette.

affichage, *n.m.*, the posting up of placards, bills, &c., bill-sticking, placarding.

affiche, *n.f.*, placard, bill, hand-bill. *Poser une* —; to post up a placard. *Homme* —; sandwich man.

afficher, v.a., to post up; to publish, to proclaim, to make a show of, to parade, to divulge. *Défense d'—*; stick no bills.

s'afficher, v.r., to set up for; to attract public notice. *Cette femme s'affiche;* that woman seeks notoriety.

afficheur, n.m., bill-sticker.

affidé, n.m., -e, n.f., confederate, trusty, confidential agent.

affidé, -e, adj., trusty, trustworthy.

affilage, n.m., whetting, sharpening, grinding, setting.

affilé, -e, adj., sharp; nimble, glib (of the tongue).

affiler, v.a., to set, to put an edge on, to sharpen.

affiliation, n.f., affiliation, association.

affilier, v.a., to receive, to affiliate, to admit.

s'affilier, v.r., to get affiliated, admitted.

affiloir, n.m., hone, whetstone, steel.

affinage, n.m., affinage, refining, fining (of metals, sugar).

affiner, v.a., to fine, to refine; to try.

s'affiner, v.r., to be refined; to be fined, tried, (nav.) (of weather), to clear up.

affinerie (-rî), n.f., (metal.) finery, painting shop.

affineur, n.m., finer; (metal.) refiner.

affinité, n.f., affinity, alliance; congeniality, conformity, relation. *Avoir de l'— avec;* to be congenial to.

affinoir, n.m., hatchel.

affiquet, n.m., a knitting-sheath. —*s,* pl.; gewgaws, knick-knacks, bauble.

affirmati-f, -ve, adj., affirmative; positive.

affirmation, n.f., affirmation, assertion; (log.) predication; affidavit, oath.

affirmative, n.f., affirmative. *Prendre l'— pour ou contre;* to decide for or against.

affirmativement (-măn), adv., affirmatively, positively.

affirmer, v.a., to affirm, to vouch, to assert, to assure, to declare, to state; to confirm by or on oath; (log.) to predicate.

affixe, n.m., affix.

affleuré, -e, adj., level; (arch.) flush.

affleurement, n.m., leveling; making flush; (mining) cropping out, outcrop.

affleurer, v.a., to make even, to level; (arch.) to make flush; (ship-building) to fay; (mining) to crop out.

affleurer, v.n., to be level, on a level with, to be flush with.

afflicti-f, -ve, adj., (jur.) affecting the person corporal (of punishments).

affliction, n.f., affliction, grief, trouble, distress, anguish, sorrow, tribulation; trial, vexation.

affligé, -e, adj., afflicted, grieved, dejected, disconsolate. —*d'une maladie;* laboring under a disease.

affligeant, -e (-jăn, -t), adj., afflicting, afflictive, distressing, grievous, woeful.

affliger, v.a., to afflict, to grieve, to vex, to trouble, to distress, to cast down; to mortify.

s'affliger, v.r., to grieve, to be concerned; to be afflicted, troubled, distressed, cast down, sorrowful; to fret.

affluence, n.f., a flowing together; affluence, abundance, multitude, concourse, crowd.

affluent, -e, adj., (of rivers) falling into, running into.

affluent, n.m., confluence; tributary stream.

affluer, v.a., to fall, to run, to flow into; to abound; to resort, to flock, to come in great numbers; (med.) to flow, to rush.

afflux, n.m., (med.) afflux, affluxion.

affolé, -e, adj., maddened, distracted, frantic; infatuated with; madly in love with; (nav.) er-

roneous, defective (of the magnetic needle). *Une boussole —e;* a compass that is not true.

affoler, v.a., to make extremely fond, to make one dote upon; to madden, to distract, bewitch. *S'— de;* to become infatuated with.

affouage, n.m., the right of cutting wood.

affouillement, n.m., undermining, washing away.

affouiller, v.a., (arch.) to undermine; to wash away.

affourche, n.f., (nav.) small bower. *Ancre d'—*; small bow-anchor.

affourché, -e, part., astraddle, astride, (nav.) moored across.

affourcher, v.n. and a., s'—, v.r., to seat astride, (nav.) to moor across, to moor by the head or by the head and stern.

affranchi, n.m., -e, n.f., freed man; freed woman.

affranchi, -e, part., freed; post-paid, prepaid.

affranchir, v.a., to set free, to free, to enfranchise, to give liberty; to make free; to absolve; to exempt, to discharge; to deliver; to pay the carriage of; to prepay.

s'affranchir, v.r., to rid one's self of, to free one's self, to get free, to shake off, to break through.

affranchissement (-shis-măn), n.m., enfranchisement, manumission; exemption, discharge; delivery, deliverance; payment of postage (of a letter); pre-payment of carriage (of a parcel). *Timbre d'—*; postage-stamp.

affre, n.f., dread, horror, agony. *Les —s de la mort;* the terrors of death.

affrètement (-măn), n.m., chartering, freighting.

affréter, v.a., (nav.) to charter, to freight.

affréteur, n.m., charterer, freighter.

affreusement (-măn), adv., frightfully, horribly, dreadfully, terribly, shockingly.

affreu-x, -se, adj., frightful, hideous, horrible, atrocious, fearful, ghastly, horrid, shocking.

affriander, v.a., to accustom, use, bring up, to dainties; to allure, to entice, to tempt.

affriolement (-măn), n.m., (fam.) act of alluring, enticing, tempting; allurement; enticement.

affrioler, v.a., (fam.) to allure, to entice, to draw by enticement.

affriter, v.a., to season (a frying pan).

affront, n.m., affront, outrage, insult; disgrace, shame, reproach. *Recevoir un — sanglant;* to receive an outrageous affront. *Boire, avaler, un —;* to pocket an affront.

affronté, -e, adj., (her.) affrontee.

affronter, v.a., to affront, to face, to brave; to cheat, to take in.

affronterie, n.f., braving, daring, affronting.

affronteu-r, n.m., -se, n.f., affronter, deceiver, cheat.

affublement, n.m., grotesque make up (of dress), rig, muffling up.

affubler, v.a., to wrap up, (b.s.) to dress out, up, to muffle up. *S'— d'un manteau;* to muffle one's self up in a cloak, to assume (a name).

s'affubler, v.r., to dress ridiculously. *S'— de quelqu'un;* to be wrapped up in.

affusion, n.f., (phar.) affusion.

affût, n.m., gun-carriage, stand, rest; watch, lying in wait. *Etre à l'—*; to be upon the watch, to lie in wait. *Homme d'—*, knowing fellow.

affûtage, n.m., the mounting of a piece of ordnance; a set of tools, implements; sharpening (of tools); the dressing (of a hat).

affûter, v.a., to mount (a cannon); to stock (with tools); to set or sharpen (tools, pencils).

affutiau (-tio), n.m., trifle, bauble, knick-knack.

afin, *conj.*, to, in order to; that, so that.

afistoler, *v.a.*, to make spruce, to dress up.

à fortiori. *V.* **fortiori.**

africain, *n.m.*, **-e,** *n.f.*, African.

africain, -e, *adj.*, African.

aga, *n.m.*, a Turkish officer, aga.

agaçant, -e, *adj.*, inciting, alluring, enticing; vexing, irritating, provoking, worrying.

agace, *n.f.*, magpie.

agacé, -e, *part.*, irritated, worried, set on edge. *Avoir les dents —es;* to have one's teeth on edge.

agacement (-mān), *n.m.*, setting on edge; irritation. *— des nerfs;* irritation of the nerves.

agacer, *v.a.*, to incite, to provoke, to egg on, to spur on, to irritate, to provoke, to entice, to allure, to set on edge.

agacerie, *n.f.*, allurement, incitement, provocation. *Faire des —s à quelqu'un;* to set one's cap at any one, to ogle.

agame, *adj.*, (bot.) agamous.

agami, *n.m.*, (orni.) agami, gold-breasted trumpeter.

agape, *n.f.*, agape, love-feast.

agapètes, *n.m.* and *f.pl.*, agapetæ.

agaric, *n.m.*, (bot.) agaric. *—champêtre;* field agaric, mushroom. *—femelle;* female agaric. *—de chêne;* touch-wood.

agasse, *n.f.* *V.* **agace.**

agate, *n.f.*, agate.

s'agatiser, *v.r.*, (Th. Gautier) to become mellow (of a picture).

agavé, *n.m.*, (bot.) agave, American aloe.

âge, *n.m.*, age; years; generation, century. *Bas —;* infancy. *Jeune —;* childhood. *Moyen —;* middle ages. *— moyen;* middle age, average. *— mûr;* mature age. *— tendre;* early age. *Vieil —;* old age. *— viril;* manhood. *— d'airain;* brazen age. *— d'argent;* silver age. *— de fer;* iron age. *— d'or;* golden age. *— de raison;* age of discretion. *Doyen d'—;* the oldest, senior. *Fleur de l'—;* prime of life. *Avant l'—;* before one's time. *D'— en —;* from age to age, from generation to generation. *D'un certain —;* elderly. *Entre deux —s;* of middle age. *Etre d'— à;* to be old enough to. *Etre bien pour son —;* to wear well, to bear one's years well. *Etre sur l'—;* to be growing old. *Honoré par l'—;* time-honored. *Paraître son —;* to look one's age. *Tirer sur l'—;* to be elderly.

âgé, -e, *adj.*, aged, in years, elderly. *— de vingt ans;* twenty years old. *Un peu —;* somewhat elderly.

agence, *n.f.*, agency, business. *Bureau d'—;* agency office.

agencement (-jāns-mān), *n.m.*, arrangement, grouping, ordering; (arch.) order, composition; (paint.) disposition.

agencer, *v.a.*, to arrange, to dispose, to fit up, to group.

s'agencer, *v.r.*, to dress up, to adorn one's self.

agenda (-jin-da), *n.m.*, (—s) memorandum-book, agenda, diary.

*agenouiller, *v.a.*, to make kneel down, to bring to one's knees.

*s'agenouiller, *v.r.*, to kneel down, (of a horse) to fall on his knees.

*agenouilloir, *n.m.*, hassock, kneeling-stool.

agent, *n.m.f.*, agent; middleman; broker. *— comptable;* accountant. *— d'affaires;* agent, man of business. *— monétaire;* circulating medium. *— de change;* stock-broker. *— de police;* policeman.

agglomération, *n.f.*, agglomeration.

agglomérer, *v.a.*, to agglomerate.

s'agglomérer, *v.r.*, to agglomerate.

agglutinant, -e, *adj.*, agglutinant, adhesive.

agglutinati-f, -ve, *adj.*, agglutinative.

agglutination, *n.f.*, agglutination.

agglutiner, *v.a.*, to agglutinate, to unite.

s'agglutiner, *v.r.*, to agglutinate, to cohere.

aggravant, -e, *adj.*, (jur.) aggravating.

aggravation, *n.f.*, aggravation; addition. *— de peine;* increase of punishment.

aggrave, *n.m.*, (canon law) threat of excommunication; censure, admonition.

aggraver, *v.a.*, to aggravate, to augment, to make worse.

s'aggraver, *v.r.*, to increase, to be aggravated.

aggrégat, aggrégation, aggréger. *V.* **agrégat, agrégation, agréger.**

agile, *adj.*, agile, quick, nimble, active, light-footed.

agilement (-mān), *adv.*, nimbly, with agility, quickly.

agilité, *n.f.*, agility, nimbleness, activity, quickness, lightness.

agio, *n.m.*, agio, premium.

agiotage, *n.m.*, stock-jobbing; jobbing. *Faire l'—;* to deal in stocks.

agioter, *v.n.*, to be a stock-jobber; to gamble in the funds, to job.

agioteur, *n.m.*, stock-jobber, jobber.

agir, *v.n.*, to act, to do; to operate, to have an influence; to negotiate, to manage a business; to sue, to prosecute; to behave; to work. *Faire —;* to set going, to bring to bear upon. *— de concert avec quelqu'un;* to go hand in hand with any one. *Il agit en ami;* he acts like a friend. *— mal envers;* to use ill. *— d'après;* to act upon, after. *C'est mal —;* that is behaving ill.

s'agir, *v.r.*, to be in question; to be the matter. *Il s'agit;* the question is, the point in question is. *De quoi s'agit-il?* what is the matter? *Il ne s'agit pas de cela;* that is not the question. *Il s'agit de votre vie;* your life is at stake. *Il s'agit bien de cela;* I, they, we, have something else to think of.

agissant, -e, *adj.*, active, stirring, busy; efficacious, effectual.

agitateur, *n.m.*, agitator.

agitation, *n.f.*, agitation; tossing, jolting, shaking; trouble, emotion, disturbance; uneasiness, tumult, restlessness.

agiter, *v.a.*, to agitate, to put in motion, to move, to wave; to shake, to pull, to heave, to jolt; to swing; to disturb, to disquiet, to torment, to debate, to dispute. *— un drapeau;* to wave a flag.

s'agiter, *v.r.*, to be agitated or in movement; to get rough; to be restless, disturbed, uneasy; to stir, writhe, wag, struggle; to be debated. *S'— dans l'eau;* to flounder about in the water.

aglomération, &c. *V.* **agglomération.**

aglutinant, &c. *V.* **agglutinant, &c.**

agnat, *n. m.*, agnate.

agnation, *n.f.*, agnation.

agnatique, *adj.*, agnatic.

*agneau, agnelle, *n.m.f.*, lamb. *Laine d'—;* lamb's wool. *Peau d'—;* lamb-skin.

⊙***agnel,** *n.m.*, an old French golden coin, agnel.

*agneler, *v.n.*, to lamb; to bring forth lambs, to yean.

*agnelet, *n.m.*, lambkin, yeanling.

*agneline, *adj.f.*, of a lamb. *Laine —;* lamb's-wool, teg-wool.

*agnès (-ess), *n.f.*, a young raw girl, simpleton.

agnus, *or* **agnus-Dei,** *n.m.*, (—) (c. rel.) Agnus-Dei, Lamb of God.

agnus-castus, *n.m.*, (—) (bot.) chaste-tree.

agon, *n.m.*, (antiq.) agon, agonism.

agonie, *n.f.*, agony, the pangs of death; grief, trouble, anguish, torture. *Etre à l'—;* to be at the point of death.

agonir, *v.a.*, (pop.) to insult grossly, to pull to pieces, to load with abuse.

agonisant, -e, *n.* and *adj.*, a dying person; dying, in a dying condition.

agoniser, *v.n.*, to be at the point of death.

agonistique, *n.f.*, (antiq.) agonistics.

⊙**agonothète,** *n.m.*, agonothete.

agora, n.f., (—s) (from Gr. 'Αγορὰ) market-place, public place.

agouti, n.m., (mam.) agouti.

agrafe, n.f., hook, clasp, hasp ; (arch.) cramp-iron ; sculptured ornament. — et porte ; hook and eye.

agrafer, v.a., to hook, to clasp, to hasp, to fasten with a clasp.

s'agrafer, v.r., to hook, to clasp, to cling, to lay hold on, to be fastened.

agraire, adj., agrarian.

agrandir, v.a., to make greater ; to enlarge ; to augment ; to lengthen, to widen ; to raise, to promote, to advance ; to amplify, to exaggerate ; to give dignity to, to exalt, to promote. — ses prétentions ; to raise one's pretensions. Le génie agrandit les héros ; genius exalts heroes.

s'agrandir, v.r., to become greater, larger ; to widen, to grow long or longer ; to enlarge one's estate, to become richer, to raise or advance one's self.

agrandissement (-mān), n.m., enlargement, aggrandizement, improvement ; the making greater, larger, bigger ; lengthening, widening, increase ; advancement, preferment, exaltation, dignifying.

agravant, &c. V. **aggravant**, &c.

agréable, adj., agreeable, desirable, pleasant, pleasing, comfortable, acceptable, gladsome, grateful. — au goût ; palatable. Feu — ; comfortable fire. Avoir pour — ; to allow, permit. Faire l' — auprès d'une femme ; to be attentive to a lady.

agréablement, adv., agreeably, pleasantly, comfortably, gratefully, gracefully.

agréage, n.m., brokerage.

agréé, n.m., solicitor, attorney (in the tribunals of commerce).

agréer, v.a., to accept, to receive kindly ; to like, to relish ; to approve, to allow ; ⊙to rig. (V. **gréer**.) — un vaisseau ; to rig, to equip a ship.

agréer, v.n., to be liked, to like, to please, to be agreeable. Cela ne m'agrée pas ; I don't like that, it does not suit me.

⊙**agréeur**, n. m. V. **gréeur**.

agrégat, n.m., aggregate.

agrégati-f, -ve, adj., aggregative.

agrégation, n.f., aggregate ; aggregation ; admission (into a society) ; examination for the degree of fellow ; fellowship ; aggregate body, assemblage. Concours d' — ; examination for a fellowship.

agrégé, n.m., fellow (of the university) ; assistant professor.

agrégé, -e, adj., aggregate ; (bot.) clustered.

agréger, v.a., to aggregate, to unite, to join, to incorporate, to receive, to admit into a society, to associate.

agrément, n.m., liking, approbation, consent ; accomplishment ; agreeableness ; pleasingness ; pleasure, charm ; gracefulness ; ornament, embellishment ; advantage, amusement, comfort ; (mus.) grace. Arts d' — ; accomplishments. De grands —s ; great comfort.

agrémenter, v.a., to ornament, to trim, to adorn.

agrener, v.a., to feed, (game-birds) to bait.

agrèner, v.a., to pump water out of a boat.

agrès, n.m. pl., rigging.

agresseur, n.m., aggressor.

agressi-f, -ve, adj., aggressive.

agression, n.f., aggression.

agressiveté, n.f., aggressiveness.

agreste, adj., agrestic, wild, rustic ; ill-bred, clownish, unmannerly.

agricole, adj., agricultural.

agriculteur, n. m., agriculturist, husbandman, farmer.

agriculture, n.f., agriculture, husbandry, tillage.

s'agriffer, v.r., to cling to with claws, to lay hold of.

agriministe, n.m., trimming maker.

agrion, n.m., dragon-fly.

agripaume, n.f., (bot.) mother-wort.

agripper, v.a., (pop.) to gripe, to snatch up.

s'agripper, v.r., (pop.) to lay hold of, to cling to.

agronome, n. m., agriculturist.

agronomie, n.f., agronomy.

agronomique, adj., agricultural.

agrostemme, n.m., (bot.) agrostemma. — des jardins ; rose-campion, corn-cockle.

agrostide, n.f., (bot.) bent-grass.

agrouper, v.a., to group.

aguerri, -e, (-ghè-) part., inured to war ; disciplined. Soldats mal —s ; raw soldiers.

aguerrir (-ghè-), v.a., to train up in, to inure to the hardships of war, to discipline, to accustom to war ; to accustom, to inure, to use.

s'aguerrir, v.r., to grow warlike or martial ; to accustom one's self to a thing, to be inured.

aguets (-ghè-), n.m. pl., watch, watching. Etre aux —, se tenir aux — ; to lie in wait, to be upon the watch.

agueustie (-gheus-tî), n.f., (med.) loss of taste.

agui, n.m., (nav.) sling, bowline, knot.

ah, int., ah ! hah ! oh ! — ça ; now, then !

ahan, n.m., great bodily exertion, effort. Suer d' — ; to perform hard work, to toil and moil.

ahaner, v.n., to groan, sigh, pant ; to toil and moil.

aheurtement, n.m., stubbornness, obstinacy.

s'aheurter, v.r., to maintain a thing obstinately, to be obstinately bent upon a thing, to stick to it, to persist in. — à une opinion ; to be wedded to an opinion.

ahi, int. V. **aïe**.

ahurir, v.a., to amaze, to astound, to strike all of a heap, to bewilder.

ahurissement, s.m., bewilderment, confusion, perplexity.

aï, n.m., (mam.) three-toed sloth.

aide, n.f., aid, help, relief, assistance, succor, support ; chapel of ease ; (man.) aid, coaxing ; aid ; female assistant. pl., subsidies, excise (taxes). A l'— ! help ! A l'— de ; with the help of. Dieu vous soit en — ! God help you !

aide, n.m., helper, assistant, mate, help, coadjutor. — major (—s —s) ; assistant surgeon, (formerly) adjutant. — chirurgien (—s—s) ; assistant surgeon. — de cuisine (—s de cuisine) ; under cook. — de camp (—s de camp) ; aide-de-camp.

aider, v.a., to aid, to help, to relieve, to assist, to succour. — à descendre, à surmonter, à relever ; to help down, over, up.

aider, v.n., to aid, to help, to assist, to succor, relieve. — à la lettre ; to add to the matter, to complete the sense. — au succès ; to contribute to the success.

s'aider, v.r., to help one another, to use, to make use of ; to bestir one's self ; to help one's self, avail one's self. On s'aide de ce qu'on a ; people make use of what they have. — l'un l'autre ; to help one another.

aides, n.f. pl., (man.) aids.

aïe, int., ay ! oh ! ah ! oh dear !

aïeul, n.m., grandfather, grandsire.

aïeule, n.f., grandmother, grandam.

aïeux, n.m. pl., forefathers, ancestors.

aigle, n.m., eagle ; star (noted person) ; reading-desk, lectern (in churches) ; (astron.) Aquila, Eagle. A vol d' — ; eagle - winged. Aux yeux d' — ; eagle-eyed.

aigle, n.f., she-eagle ; (her.) eagle ; eagle standard.

aiglefin, n.m., haddock.

aiglette, n.f. V. **aiglon**. [eaglet.

aiglon, n.m., eaglet, a young eagle ; (her.)

aigre, *n.m.,* sourness; rawness; sharpness; mustiness.

aigre, *adj.,* sour, tart, sharp, bitter; crabbed; ill-natured; rough, harsh; eager, brittle; shrill; musty. *Voix* —; harsh, shrill voice. *Paroles* —*s;* sharp words.

aigre-dou-x, -ce, *adj.,* bitterish, sourish.

aigrefin, *n.m.,* sharper.

aigrelet, -te, adj., sourish, tartish.

aigrement, *adv.,* acrimoniously, sourly, sharply, bitterly, roughly, harshly.

aigremoine, *n.f.,* (bot.) agrimony, liverwort.

aigremore, *n.m.,* aigremore.

aigret, -te, *adj.,* sourish, tartish.

aigrette, *n.f.,* egret, aigret; aigrette, tuft, or plume (of feathers, diamonds); (bot.) egret; (milit.) tuft; horn (of the owl); crest (of the peacock).

aigretté, -e, *adj.,* with an egret, tufted, crested.

aigreur, *n.f.,* sourness, sharpness, tartness, harshness, bitterness; surliness; ill-nature, grudge, spite; *pl.,* (med.) acidity of stomach, heartburn, water-brash; (engrav.) harsh strokes, hatches made too hard.

aigrir, *v.a.,* to make sour or sharp, to sour, to turn sour; to irritate, to embitter, to make worse; to incense, to provoke; to make ill-humored. *Sa disgrâce lui a aigri l'esprit;* his disgrace has soured his temper.

s'aigrir, *v.r.,* to turn sour, to grow sour or sharp; to grow worse, to be exasperated. *Son mal s'aigrit;* his disease gets worse.

aigrissement, *n.m.,* souring, irritation, bitterness.

aigu, -ë, *adj.,* pointed, that has a sharp point; sharp, keen, acute, piercing. *Son*—; sharp, shrill sound. *Douleur* —ë; acute pain. *Faire un son*—; to utter a shrill cry.

aiguade (-gad), *n.f.,* (nav.) fresh water; watering-place. *Faire* —; to take in fresh water.

aiguail (-ga-), *n.m.,* or **aiguaille,** *n.f.,* (hunt.) dewdrop; morning dew.

aiguayer (-gay-), *v.a.,* to water (a horse); to rinse (clothes). [beryl.

aigue-marine, *n.f.,* (—*s*-—*s*), aqua-marina,

aiguichant, -e, *adj.,* enticing.

aiguière (-ghièr), *n.f.,* ewer.

aiguiérée (-ghié-), *n.f.,* ewer-full.

*aiguillade, *n.f.,* goad.

*aiguillage, *n.m.,* (railways) the shifting of the points, shunting.

*aiguillat, *n.m.,* (ich.) dog-fish.

*aiguille, *n.f.,* needle; hand (of a dial, or watch, &c.); cock (balance); spindle (of a compass); spire (of a steeple); (ich.) hornfish, needle-fish; (railways) point. —*d'emballeur;* packing-needle. —*à tricoter;* knitting-needle. —*à reprises;* darning-needle. —*s à contre-poids;* self-acting points (rail.). *Trou d'une* —; eye of a needle. *Ouvrage à l'* —; needle-work. —*aimantée;* magnetic needle. *Disputer sur la pointe d'une* — ; to quarrel about straws. *Enfiler une* —; to thread a needle.

*aiguillée, *n.f.,* needleful.

*aiguiller, *v.a.,* (surg.) to couch (a cataract); (rail.) to shift the points.

*aiguilletage, *n.m.,* tagging, (nav.) seizing.

*aiguilleter, *v.a.,* (nav.) to trap, to seize, to mouse. —*les canons;* to lash the guns.

aiguilletier, *n.m.,* tagger, tag-maker.

*aiguillette, *n.f.,* aglet, point; shoulder-knot; slice (of flesh, skin); (nav.) knittle, tricing-line, laniard. *Le ferret de l'* —; the tag of a point.

aiguilleur, *n.m.,* (rail.) pointsman, switcher.

*aiguillier, *n.m.,* needle-case, book. *V.* **étui.**

*aiguillier, *n.m.,* needle-maker.

aiguillière, *n.f.,* garfish-net, net for catching hornfish; needle-maker.

*aiguillon, *n.m.,* goad, spur, incentive, incitement, encouragement, stimulus, motive; sting (of insects, serpents); (bot.) prickle, stimulus. *Briser l'* — *de;* to take the sting out of.

*aiguillonner, *v.a.,* to goad, to prick; to incite, to spur on, to stimulate.

*aiguillot, *n.m.,* (nav.) pintle.

aiguisé, -e, *part.,* whetted, sharpened. *Une croix aiguisée;* (her.) a pointed cross.

aiguisement (-mān), *n.m.,* whetting, sharpening.

aiguiser, *v.a.,* to whet, to sharpen, to make sharp; to set an edge on; to point. — *l'appétit;* to sharpen the appetite. — *une épigramme;* to give point to an epigram. — *ses couteaux;* to prepare for battle. — *ses dents;* to prepare to eat heartily.

aiguiseur, *n.m.,* knife-grinder, sharpener (*pers.*)

*ail, *n.m.,* (ails), (aulx) (6), garlic. — *stérile;* eschalot. *Une tête d'* —, *une gousse d'* — ; a clove of garlic.

ailante, *n.m.,* (bot.) ailanthus.

aile, *n.f.,* wing, pinion; van, fan; wing (of an army, building); aisle (of churches); fly (horol.); rung (of ships). *Avoir les* —*s rapides;* to be swift-winged. *A tire d'* —; at a single flight. *En avoir dans l'* —; to be smitten, to be in love. *Il en a dans l'* —; there is a screw loose somewhere. *Frapper à l'* —; to wing. *Couper le bout de l'* —; to pinion. *Être sur l'* —; to be on the wing. *Battre des* —*s;* to clap the wings. *Trémousser des* —*s;* to flutter. *Rogner les* —*s à quelqu'un;* to clip a person's wings. *Voler de ses propres* —*s;* to be able to do without the help of others; to stand on one's own legs. *Vouloir voler sans avoir des* —*s;* to undertake a thing beyond one's strength. *Ne battre plus que d'une* —; to be on one's last legs. *Tirer de l'* —; to make wing. *Tirer pied ou* — *de;* to get something out of (a thing), to make the most of (a thing). — *de moulin;* wind-sail.

ailé, -e, *adj.,* winged.

*aileron, *n.m.,* small wing; pinion; fin (of some fish); float-board (of a water-wheel); (arch.) scroll.

ailette, *n.f.,* side-piece, side-lining of a shoe; small wing (of a building); flange (motor).

*aillade, *n.f.,* garlic sauce.

*ailleurs, *adv.,* elsewhere, somewhere else. *D'* —; from another reason, cause; on another account; besides, moreover, in other respects; after all, in addition to which.

aimable, *adj.,* amiable, lovable, lovely, agreeable, worthy to be loved. *Un caractère* —; an amiable temperament.

aimablement, *adv.,* in an amiable manner, amiably.

aimant, -e, *adj.,* loving, affectionate.

aimant, *n.m.,* loadstone, magnet. *La déclinaison de l'* —; the variation of the compass.

aimanté, -e, *adj.,* magnetic.

aimanter, *v.a.,* to rub or touch with a loadstone, to magnetize.

aimé, -e, *adj.,* loved, beloved.

aimer, *v.a.,* to love, to be fond of, to have a passion for; to be in love with; to like, to fancy, to have a fancy for, to admire, to delight in, to have an inclination for. *Il aime à monter à cheval;* he delights in riding. *Il aime sa personne;* he loves his own dear self. *Aimez qu'on vous conseille, et non pas qu'on vous loue;* love to be advised, not to be praised. — *mieux;* to prefer, to like better. — *passionnément;* to be passionately fond of. — *à l'idolatrie;* to idolize. *Se faire* —; to endear one's self to. *Qui aime bien, châtie bien;* he chasteneth that loveth well. *Qui m'aime aime mon chien;* love me, love my dog.

s'aimer, *v.r.,* to love one's self. *S'* — *les uns les autres;* to love one another.

aimez-moi, *n.f.,* marsh scorpion-grass. *V.* **myosotis.**

ain, *n.m.*, woollen thread; the number of threads contained in a given space.

aine, *n.f.*, groin; herring-stick.

aîné, *n.m.*, -e, *n.f.*, elder, senior.

aîné, -e, *adj.*, eldest, elder, the eldest son or daughter; senior.

aînesse, *n.f.*, primogeniture. *Droit d'—;* birthright.

ainsi, *adv.*, thus, so, in this, that, manner. *Je suis — fait;* that's my temper. *Le monde est —; such is the world. — du reste;* and so forth. *Il en est — des autres passions;* thus it is with the other passions. *— soit-il;* amen, so be it. *— va le monde;* so the world goes. *S'il en est —;* if such is the case.

ainsi, *conj.*, thus, therefore, so that. *— que, tout — que;* as, as well as, even as, in the same way as. *Cela s'est passé — que je vous l'ai dit;* that happened in the way I told you.

air, *n.m.*, air, wind; look, appearance, countenance, deportment; aspect; (mus.) tune; (chem., man., paint., sculp.) air. *— abattu;* downcast look. *— chagrin;* sorrowful look. *— éveillé;* sharp look. *— farouche;* forbidding look. *Faire des châteaux en l'—;* to build castles in the air. *Un coup d'—;* a cold chill. *Prendre l'—;* to take the air. *Donner de l'— à une chambre;* to let the air into, to ventilate, a room. *Chasser l'— renfermé;* to let out the confined air. *En plein —;* in the open air. *Se tenir entre deux —s;* to be in a draught. *Il ne fait point d'—;* there is not the least breath of wind. *Être en l'—;* to be in a flutter. *Paroles en l'—;* empty, idle, words. *Parler en l'—;* to talk wildly. *Il forme des desseins en l'—;* he forms extravagant designs. *Il a tiré son coup en l'—;* he has miscarried. *Prendre l'— du bureau;* to go and see how matters stand. *Faire prendre l'—;* to give an airing to. *Les gens du bel —;* gentle folks, fashionable people. *Un homme de méchant —;* an ill-looking man. *Un homme du grand —;* a man of rank, or quality. *Avoir l'— de;* to look like. *Avoir l'— bien portant;* to look well. *Lancer en l'—;* to toss (of horned cattle). *Avoir l'— bon, l'— mauvais;* to look good-natured, ill-natured. *Prendre un — riant;* to put on a smiling countenance. *Prendre un — de feu;* to warm one's self. *Rempli d'— vicié;* filled with foul air. *Cela a l'— grand;* that looks grand. *Elle n'a pas l'— spirituel;* she does n't look sprightly. *Elle a l'— bien étourdi;* she looks very giddy. *Il n'a pas l'— content;* he does n't seem pleased. *Prendre des —s, se donner des —s;* to give one's self airs. *Prendre des —s de bel esprit;* to set up for a wit. *Un — de famille;* a family likeness. *Air de tête* (paint.); the attitude of the head. *Un — gai, triste;* a lively, dull, tune. *Faire un — sur des paroles;* to set words to music. *Jouer un — rapide;* to play a flourish. *Ce cheval va à tout —;* this horse has all his paces.

airain, *n.m.*, brass. *L'âge d'—;* the brazen age. *Avoir un front d'—;* to have a brazen face, to blush at nothing. *Avoir des entrailles d'—;* to have a heart of stone.

aire, *n.f.*, area, barn-floor, threshing-floor; aerie (of a bird of prey); (of ships) impetus, headway. *L'— d'un bâtiment;* (arch.) the area of a building. *— de plancher;* superficies of a floor. *L'— d'un triangle;* (geom.) the area or inside of a triangle. *Une — de vent;* (nav.) a point of the compass.

airée, *n.f.*, the lot of wheat, &c., lying on a barn-floor; batch of dough.

airelle, *n.f.*, whortleberry, bilberry.

airer, *v.n.*, to make its aerie or nest.

ais (ê), *n.m.*, board, shelf, plank; (print.) wetting-board; butcher's block.

aisance, *n.f.*, ease, freedom, easiness, affluence; the comforts or conveniences of life. *—s, pl.,*

water-closet. *Il fait tout avec —;* he does everything with ease. *Avoir de l'— dans les manières;* to have an easy deportment. *Etre dans l'—;* to be in easy circumstances. *Cabinet d'—s, lieux d'—s;* water-closet. *Fosse d'—s;* cess-pool.

aise, *n.f.*, gladness, joy, content; ease, comfort, conveniency. *A l'—;* easily; comfortable. *Se pâmer d'—;* to be overjoyed. *Tressaillir d'—;* to leap for joy. *Elle ne se sent pas d'—;* she is beside herself for joy. *Etre à son —;* to be well off. *Mettre quelqu'un à son —;* to put at ease, to reassure any one. *Vous en parlez bien à votre —;* it is easy for you to say so. *N'en prendre qu'à son —;* to do only what pleases one, to take it easy. *Se sentir mal à l'—;* to feel uncomfortable. *Aimer ses —s;* to love one's ease. *On n'a pas toutes ses —s en ce monde;* we cannot have all we wish for in this world.

aise, *adj.*, glad, joyful, well pleased. *Je suis bien — de vous voir;* I am very glad to see you.

aisé, -e, *adj.*, easy, convenient, commodious; in easy circumstances. *Cela est — à dire;* it is an easy thing to say. *Un homme — à vivre;* an easy, good-natured man. *Des souliers —s;* comfortable shoes. *Un air —;* an easy deportment. *Un style —;* a free, lucid, easy style. *Il est fort —;* he is in very easy circumstances.

aisément, *adv.*, easily, readily, commodiously, freely, comfortably.

aisselle, *n.f.*, arm-pit; (anat., bot.) axil, axilla.

aitiologie. *V.* **étiologie**.

ajointer, *v.a.*, to join end to end, to fit.

ajonc, *n.m.*, furze, thorn-broom, gorse, whin.

ajournement, *n.m.*, adjournment, postponement; (jur.) summons.

ajourner, *v.a.*, to adjourn, to put off; (jur.) to summon.

ajourner, *v.n.*, *s'ajourner*, *v.r.*, to adjourn, to be adjourned, to put off, to defer, to summons.

ajoutage, *n.m.*, piece joined on.

ajouter, *v.a.*, to add, to join, to put to, to tag, to subjoin, to supply, to interpolate. *Ce passage a été ajouté à ce livre;* this passage is an interpolation. *— foi à quelque chose;* to give credit to a thing.

ajoutoir. *V.* **ajoutage**, **ajutage**.

ajustage, *n.m.*, adjusting, or giving the legal weight to a coin.

ajusté, -e, *part.*, adjusted, fitted, accommodated, dressed. *Un style bien —;* a very elaborate style. *Comme vous voilà —!* what a figure you cut.

ajustement, *n.m.*, adjustment, adjusting, fitting, regulation, settlement; laying out; attire, garb, apparel, dress, garment; accommodation, agreement, reconciliation. *L'— d'un poids;* the adjusting of a weight. *L'— d'une machine;* the regulating a machine. *Elle n'est pas belle, elle a besoin d'—;* she is not handsome, she needs dress or adornment.

ajuster, *v.a.*, to adjust, to regulate, to square, to size, to tally; to aim, to take aim at, to aim at; to fit, to adapt, to set in order, to accommodate; to trim, to bedeck, to dress. *— un lievre;* to take aim at a hare. *— de nouveau;* to recompose. *— ses cheveux;* to put one's hair in order. *— deux personnes;* to reconcile two people, to make them agree. *— un différend;* to reconcile a difference. *Ajustez vos flûtes;* understand one another. *On l'a bien ajusté;* they have given it him well. *— des passages d'un livre;* to make passages of a book agree.

s'ajuster, *v.r.*, to prepare one's self, to get one's self ready; to dress, to deck, one's self out; to agree, to take measures, to concert together.

ajusteur, *n.m.*, weigher at the mint, fitter, sizer.

ajustoir, *n.m.*, a pair of scales (used in the mint); assay scales.

ajutage, ajutoir, *n.m.*, adjutage, a tube or pipe (for water-works).

alacrité, *n.f.*, alacrity.

alambic, *v.m.*, alembic, still. *Faire passer par l'*—; to distill, to draw by distillation. *Passer par l'*—; to undergo a careful examination.

alambiqué, -e, *part.*, far-fetched, too subtle, too refined, fine-spun, wire-drawn. *Cette pensée est trop* —*e ;* that thought is too refined.

alambiquer, *v.a.*, to puzzle, to refine too much upon. *S'* — *l'esprit sur quelque chose ;* to beat, puzzle one's brains about a thing, to pore over it.

alanguir (-ghir), *v.a.*, to enfeeble, to make languid.

*s'*alanguir, *v.r.*, to languish, to flag, to become languid.

alarguer (-ghé), *v.n.*, (nav.) to bear off, to put to sea, to sheer off.

alarmant, -e, *adj.*, alarming, dreadful.

alarme, *n.f.*, alarm, sudden fear, fright. *Sonner l'*—, *donner l'*— ; to sound, to give the alarm. *Cloche d'*— ; alarm-bell. *Fausse* — ; false alarm. *Donner des* —*s ;* to cause uneasiness to. *Porter l'* — *dans ;* to alarm. *L'* — *est au camp ;* they are in a great fright. *Tenir en* — ; to keep in constant fear.

alarmer, *v.a.*, to alarm, to raise an alarm, to startle.

*s'*alarmer, *v.r.*, to take alarm, to be alarmed. *Ne vous alarmez point ;* don't frighten yourself.

alarmiste, *n.m.f.*, alarmist.

alaterne, *n.m.*, species of buck-thorn; alatern.

albâtre, *n.m.*, alabaster, whiteness. *D'*— ; of alabaster, snowy white.

albatros, *n.m.*, (orni.) albatross.

alberge, *n.f.*, a small forward peach.

albergier, *n.m.*, an alberge-tree.

albigeois, *n.m. pl.*, Albigenses.

albinos, *n.m.*, albino.

albion, *n.f.*, Albion (England).

albran. *V.* halbran.

albuginé, -e, *adj.*, (anat.) albugineous.

albugineu-x, -se, *adj.*, (anat.) albugineous, whitish.

albugo, *n.m.*, (med.) albugo.

album (-bom), *n. m.*, album, scrap-book, sketch-book.

albumine, *n.f.*, albumen, white (of an egg).

albumineu-x, -se, *adj.*, albuminous.

alcade, *n.m.*, Spanish alcaid, alcade.

alcaïque, *adj.*, alcaic. *Vers* —*s ;* alcaic verses.

alcalescence, *n.f.*, alkalescence.

alcalescent, -e, *adj.*, alkalescent.

alcali, *n.m.*, alkali.

alcalimètre, *n.m.*, alkalimeter.

alcalin, -e, *adj.*, alkaline.

alcalisation, *n.*, alkalization.

alcaliser, *v.a.*, (chem.) to alkalize.

alcaloïde, *n.m.*, (chem.) alkaloid.

alcantara, *n.m.*, a Spanish military order.

alcarraza, *n.m.*, water-cooler.

alcazar, *n.m.*, alcazar (Moorish palace).

alcée, *n.f.*, hollyhock.

alchimie, *n.f.*, alchemy.

*****alchimille,** *n.f.*, (bot.) lady's mantle.

alchimique, *adj.*, alchymical.

alchimiste, *n.m.*, alchymist.

alcool, *n.m.*, alcohol.

alcoolique, *adj.*, alcoholic.

alcoolisation, *n.f.*, alcoholization.

alcooliser, *v.a.*, to alcohclize.

alcoolisme, *n.m.* (med.) alcoholism.

alcoran, *n.m.*, Koran.

alcôve, *n.f.*, alcove, recess.

alcyon, *n.m.*, halcyon, kingfisher.

alcyonien, -ne, (-in, -è-n), *adj.*, halcyon.

aldébaran, *n.m.*, (astron.) Aldebaran.

alderman, *n.m.*, alderman.

aléatoire, *adj.*, (jur.) eventual, aleatory, contingent.

alène, *n.f.*, awl. *Feuilles en* — ; acuminated leaves ; (pisc.) sharp-nosed skate.

alénier, *n.m.*, awl-maker.

alentir, s'alentir. *V.* ralentir and *se* ralentir.

alénois, *n.m.*, common garden cress.

alentour, *adv.*, about, around, round about. *Les bois d'* — ; the neighboring, surrounding woods.

alentours, *n.m. pl.*, the neighboring grounds ; environs, neighborhood ; persons about, around one ; associates, familiars.

alépine, *n.f.*, bombazine.

alérion, *n.m.*, (her.) eaglet without beak or feet.

alerte, *n.f.*, alarm, warning. *En* — ; on the alert.

alerte, *adj.*, alert, vigilant, watchful ; active, stirring, quick, sprightly, brisk, lively, agile.

alerte, *int.*, take care, be quick ; up !

alésage, *n.m.*, (tech.) boring, drilling.

aléser, *v.a.*, (tech.) to hammer planchets ; to drill, bore. — *un canon ;* to bore a cannon.

alésoir, *n.m.*, borer (instrument).

alevin (-vin), *n.m.*, fry, young fish.

alevinage, *n.m.*, small fry.

aleviner (-né), *v.a.*, to stock with fry.

alevinier (-nié), *n.m.*, breeding-pond.

alexandrien, -ne, *adj.*, Alexandrian.

alexandrin, *n.m.*, (poet.) alexandrine.

alexandrin, -e, *adj.*, alexandrine.

alezan (-zăn), *n.m.*, chestnut horse.

alezan, -e, (-zăn, -za-n), *adj.*, chestnut.

alèze, *n.f.*, sheet (placed under sick persons); draw-sheet ; withe.

alfa, *n.m.*, (bot.) an African plant ; alfa-grass.

alfange. *n.f.*, scimiter, phalanx, battalion (Chinese, Tartar). *V.* cimeterre.

algalie, *n.f.*, (surg.) catheter.

alganon, *n.m.*, a chain for galley-slaves.

algarade, *n.f.*, (fam.) insult, affront; rating; blowing up; attack. *Faire une* — ; to insult, to rate any one ; to blow any one up.

algèbre, *n.f.*, algebra.

algébrique, *adj.*, algebraical.

algébriquement. *adv.*, algebraically.

algébriste, *n.m.*, algebraist.

algide, *adj.*, (med.) cold as ice, algid.

algor, *n.m.*, (med.) algor.

algorithme, *n.m.*, algorithm.

alguazil (-goua-zil), (—*s*) *n.m.*, alguazil.

algue, *n.f.*, alga, sea-weed, sea-wrack grass.

alibi, *n.m.*, (—*s*) (jur.) alibi.

alibiforain, *n.m.*, (fam. l.u.) irrelevant, rambling answer ; evasion, shuffling, prevarication.

alibile, *adj.*, (med.) alible.

aliboron, *n.m.*, jackass, a self-conceited fellow. *Maître* — ; ass.

aliboufier, *n.m.*, a fragrant resin, storax.

alidade, *n.f.*, alidade, the index of any surveying instrument, such as a quadrant, sextant, &c.

aliénable, *adj.*, alienable, transferable.

aliénataire, *n.m.*, alienee.

aliénat-eur, *n.m.*, -rice, *n.f.*, alienator.

aliénation, *n.f.*, a legal conveyance of property to another, alienation, transfer ; alienation (of the mind). — *mentale ;* mental derangement, madness.

aliéné, -e, *n.*, lunatic, maniac. *Hospice pour les* —*s ;* lunatic asylum. *Maison d'* —*s ;* madhouse.

aliéné, -e, *adj.*, (of property) alienated, transferred to another ; (affections) estranged, withdrawn ; (of the mind) deranged, mad.

aliéner, *v.a.*, to alienate, to give away, to part with, to make over, to deliver up the possession or right of. — *les affections, les cœurs, les esprits ;* to alienate, to estrange, to disaffect, to lose the affection. *Il a aliéné les esprits ;* he has disaffected all minds. — *l'esprit à quelqu'un ;* to drive one mad. *S'* —, *v.r.*, to lose, to estrange; to be lost; to be alienated; to become deranged.

*aligné, -e, *part.*, in line; laid out in a line; that stands in a right line; formed in line.

*alignement, *n.m.*, laying out by a line; line; (milit.) dressing; (print.) ranging. *Cette maison sort de l'* — ; that house stands out of the row. *Rentrer dans l'* — ; to fall into line. *Prendre l'* — ; to trace the line of. — *!* (milit.) dress !

*aligner, *v.a.*, to lay out by a line; to square; to put in a straight line; (milit.) to dress; (print.) to range. — *des troupes ;* to form troops in a line. — *ses phrases ;* to square one's sentences. — *un compte* (com.); to balance an account.

*s'***aligner**, *v.r.*, (milit.) to dress; (pop.) to have a set to, to fight.

aliment, *n.m.*, food, aliment, nourishment, meat, nutriment, nutrition; fuel; (jur.) allowance.

aliments, *n.m. pl.*, (jur.) alimony, maintenance.

alimentaire, *adj.*, alimentary; alimental. *Pension* — ; alimony, maintenance. *Régime* — ; diet. *Pompe* — ; feed-pump, donkey engine.

alimentation, *n.f.*, alimentation; feeding.

alimenter, *v.a.*, to feed, to nourish; to maintain; to supply with what is necessary, to furnish; to fuel, to keep up. *Le marché ne fournit pas de quoi* — *la ville ;* the market does not furnish enough to supply the town.

alimenteu-x, -se, *adj.*, (med.) nutritive, alimentary, alimental.

alinéa, *n.m.*, (—*s*), new paragraph, break.

aliquante, *adj.*, (math.) aliquant.

aliquote, *adj.*, (math.) aliquot.

alise, *n.f.*, beam-berry, wild-sorb, chess-apple.

alisier, *n.m.*, service-tree, beam-tree.

alité, -e, *part.*, bedridden, laid up.

aliter, *v.a.*, to confine to one's bed.

*s'***aliter**, *v.r.*, to keep one's bed, to be bedridden, to take to one's bed.

alizari, *n.m.*, madder-root.

alize, *adj.*, (nav.). *Vents* —*s ;* trade-winds.

alizé, *n.f. V.* **alise**.

alizier, *n.m. V.* **alisier**.

alkali, &c. *V.* **alcali**, &c.

alkékenge, *n.m.*, winter-cherry.

alkermès (-ess), *n.m.*, alkermes.

allah (al-la), *n.m.*, Alla, Allah.

allaitement (-lèt-mān), *n.m.*, lactation, nursing, suckling.

allaiter, *v.a.*, to suckle, to give suck, to nurse.

allant, *n.m.*, goer. — *et venants ;* goers and comers.

allant, -e, *adj.*, stirring, bustling, fond of going about.

allantoïde, *n.f.*, (anat.) allantois.

allèchement, *n.m.*, allurement, enticement, bait.

allécher, *v.a.*, to allure, to entice, to attract.

allée, *n.f.*, going; passage, entry, alley; lane; walk. *Une* — *couverte ;* a shady walk. *Faire des* —*s et venues ;* to go in and out, to and fro.

allégation (al-lé-), *n.f.*, citation, quotation, allegation.

allège, *n.f.*, lighter, tender; (arch.) window basement, sill of the window; (rail.) tender. *Frais d'* — ; (com.) lighterage.

allégeance (al-lé-jan-s), *n.f.*, (l.u.) allegiance. *Serment d'* — ; oath of allegiance.

allégeance, *n.f.*, alleviation, relief.

allégement (al-léj-mān), *n.m.*, alleviation, ease, relief.

alléger (al-lé-jé), *v.a.*, to ease, to disburden, to lighten, to unload (a boat); to alleviate, to soften, to relieve, to assuage pain or grief; (nav.) to buoy up.

allégir, *v.a.*, to lighten, to reduce.

allégorie (al-lé-), *n.f.*, allegory. *Par* — ; allegorically.

allégorique (al-lé-), *adj.*, allegoric, allegorical.

allégoriquement (-mān), *adv.*, allegorically.

allégoriser (al-lé-), *v.a.*, to allegorize.

allégoriseur (al-lé-), *n.m.*, allegorizer.

allégoriste (al-lé-), *n.m.*, allegorist.

allègre (al-lègr), *adj.*, brisk, nimble, sprightly, jolly, cheerful.

allègrement, *adv.*, briskly, joyfully, merrily, joyously.

allégresse, *n.f.*, mirth, cheerfulness, gladness, joy, gaiety, sprightliness, alacrity, glee, joyfulness. *Cris d'* — ; shouts of gladness ; huzzas.

allégretto (al-lé-grèt-to), *adv.* and *n.m.*, (—*s*) (mus.) allegretto.

allégro (al-lé-), *adv.* and *n.m.*, (—*s*) (mus.) allegro.

alléguer (al-lé-ghé), *v.a.*, to allege ; to quote, to bring in, to cite, to plead, to produce, to advance, to urge.

alléluia, *n.m.*, hallelujah ; (bot.) wood-sorrel.

allemand, -e (-mān, -mānd), *adj.*, German. *Une querelle d'* — ; a groundless quarrel.

allemand, *n.m.*, -e, *n.f.*, German.

allemande, *n.f.*, allemande, a dance.

aller, *n.m.*, going, course of time, run ; (nav.) outward voyage. — *et retour ;* voyage out and in. *Billet d'* — *et retour ;* return ticket. *Au long* — ; in the long run. *Avoir l'* — *pour le venir ;* to lose one's time and trouble. *Au pis* — ; at the worst. *C'est votre pis* — ; it's your last shift.

aller (allant, allé), *v.n.*, to go, to be going ; to move, to be in motion or movement ; to depart, to repair, to resort ; to reach, to come, to lead, to end ; to do ; to be ; to go forward, to go on ; to succeed ; to amount ; to act ; to proceed ; to go about ; to tend, to aim ; to arrive ; to lay ; to stake ; to play ; to go to the water-closet ; to work ; to chance ; to fit, to become, to be matched ; to sail. — *au marché ;* to go to market. *Allez en paix ;* depart in peace. *Allez au diable ;* go to the devil. — *croissant ;* to go on increasing. *La carte va à dix francs ;* the bill amounts to ten francs. *Faire* — ; to make go, to set going. — *à pied ;* to go on foot. — *à cheval ;* to go on horseback, to ride. — *en voiture ;* to ride in a carriage, to drive. — *au pas ;* at a walking pace. — *au trot ;* to trot. — *au galop ;* to gallop. — *au petit galop ;* to canter. — *son train ;* to keep on, to take one's own course. — *bon train ;* to go on at a good round pace, to get on well. — *à tâtons ;* to grope along. — *au devant de quelqu'un, à la rencontre de quelqu'un ;* to go and meet any one. — *çà et là ;* to ramble, roam about. *Ne faire qu'* — *et venir ;* to do nothing but run backwards and forwards. *Je ne ferai qu'* — *et venir ;* I will not stay ; I shall be back again directly. *Ma montre ne va pas ;* my watch does not go. *Va vite ;* go quickly. *Allant à ;* (nav.) bound for. *Cela vous va ;* that suits you. *Allons donc ;* come now ; nonsense ! *Allez, va ;* be gone ; be off. *Ils vont venir ;* they will come presently. — *se promener ;* to go for a walk. *Allez vous promener ;* go about your business. *La rivière va serpentant ;* the river winds about. — *aux informations, aux renseignements ;* to make inquiries. — *aux voix ;* to put to the vote. — *aux provisions ;* to go marketing. *Ce vase va au feu :* this jug stands the fire. — *de pair;* to be equal. — *de pair à compagnon avec quelqu'un;* to be cheek by jowl with any one. *Ce chemin va à l'église;* this way leads to church. *La montagne va jusqu'aux nues;* the mountain reaches to the clouds. — *de mal en pis;* to go from bad to worse. *Comment va la santé?* how is your health? *Comment cela va-t-il?* how are you? *Sa santé va de mieux en mieux;* his health is better and better. *Comment allez-vous?* how do you do? *Tout va bien;* all is well. *Cet homme ira loin;* that man will distinguish himself. *Le feu ne va pas bien;* the fire does not burn well. *Nos affaires vont mal;* our affairs are in a bad way. *Le commerce ne va plus;* trade is at a standstill. *Cela ne va pas mal;* things are in a fair way. *Votre habit vous va mal;* your coat does n't fit you. *Ces deux couleurs-là vont bien ensemble;* those two colors are well matched. *Il y a de bonne foi;* he acts sincerely. *Y — rondement;* to act frankly, openly. *Tous mes désirs vont là;* all my wishes tend that way. *C'est un adroit qui va à ses fins;* he is a cunning fellow, he pushes his point. — *à la gloire;* to aim at glory. *Est-ce ainsi que vous y allez?* is this your way? *Tudieu! comme vous y allez;* egad! you go on at a fine rate. *De combien allez-vous?* how much do you stake? *Va pour du vin!* (fam.) well, let us have some wine. *Allons, mes amis, courage;* come, my friends, cheer up, take courage. *Allez, n'avez-vous point de honte?* fie, are you not ashamed? *Allez, je veux m'employer pour vous;* take heart, I'll interest myself on your behalf. *Voyez où j'en serais, si elle allait croire cela;* see what a plight I should be in, if she should chance to believe that. — *toujours;* to keep on, (b.s.) to rattle on, blunder on. *Allez toujours;* go it. *Se laisser aller;* to yield, to give way, to abandon one's self to a thing. *Se laisser — à la tentation;* to yield to temptation. *Se laisser — à la douleur;* to give one's self up to grief. *Laisser —;* to release, to let go. *Quand il devrait y — de tout mon bien;* though my whole fortune were at stake. *Songez qu'il y va de votre honneur;* reflect that your honor is at stake. *Il y allait de la vie;* it was a question of life or death. *Quand il y irait de ma vie;* although my life were at stake. *Il en va, il en ira;* it is, it will be. *Il en va de cette affaire-là comme de l'autre;* it is with that affair as with the other. *Où va le navire?* (nav.) where are you bound to? — *son chemin;* to pursue one's course. *Il ira son chemin;* he will make his way. *Faire en — tout le monde;* to drive everybody away. *Faire en — des taches;* to take out stains. *Tous chemins vont à Rome;* more ways than one lead to Heaven. *Cela va tout seul;* there is no difficulty in the thing, *or* it is all plain sailing. *Cela ne va pas;* it 's no go, I am not well. *Cela va sans dire;* that goes without saying; of course. *Cela ira;* that will do; we shall succeed. *Cela n'ira pas loin;* that will not last long. *Cela n'ira pas plus loin;* it shall go no further. *N'y pas — de main morte;* to go at it tooth and nail. *N'y pas — par quatre chemins;* not to beat about the bush. *Qui va là?* who goes there? *s'en* **aller**, *v.r.*, to go away, to set out, to go out, to march off, to depart, to take oneself off; to run, to scamper away; to retire; to run out, to boil over, to dwindle away; to evaporate; to die, to wear out; to sneak off. *Va-t'en; allez-vous-en;* go away; be off with you! *Il faut que tout le monde s'en aille;* everybody must go away. *Allons-nous-en;* let us go. *Ils s'en vont;* they are going away. *Mon habit s'en va;* my coat is wearing out. *Il s'en va;* he is dying. *Je m'en fus;* I went away. *Je m'en vais vous dire;* I 'll tell you what. *Tout s'en est allé en fumée;* all came to nothing.

alleu, *n.m.*, allodium. *Franc-— (—s-—s);* a freehold.

alliacé, -e, *adj.*, (bot.) alliaceous.

alliage, *n.m.*, alloyage, alloy, mixture, union; (arith.) alligation. *Sans —;* pure, without alloy, type-metal.

alliaire, *n.f.*, hedge-garlic.

alliance, *n.f.*, alliance, marriage, match; confederacy; union; blending; wedding-ring; covenant.

allié, *n.m.*, **-e**, *n.f.*, ally; relation (by marriage).

allié, -e, *part.*, allied, related (by marriage); akin, kindred. *Les rois alliés;* the confederate kings.

allier, *v.a.*, to mix; to combine, to unite; to match, to marry; to join, to unite, to ally, to reconcile. — *l'or avec l'argent;* to alloy gold with silver. *s'allier*, *v.r.*, to be incorporated or mixed; to match, to enter into an alliance; to unite; to suit; to combine (of metals).

allier, *n.m.*, partridge-net.

⊙**alliez**, *n.m.*, (bot.) tare. *V.* **ivraie**.

alligator, *n.m.*, the American crocodile, alligator.

allitération (al-li-), *n.f.*, alliteration.

allobroge (al-lo-), *n.m.*, clown, lout, boor.

allocation (al-lo-), *n.f.*, allocation, allowance; (*mil. admin.*) entry, item, supply.

allocution (al-lo-), *n.f.*, allocution, address, speech, harangue.

allodial, -e (al-lo-), *adj.*, allodial. *Terres —es;* freehold lands, freeholds.

allodialité (al-lo-), *n.f.*, free-tenure.

allonge, *n.f.*, a piece of stuff to eke out anything; leaf (of a table); rider (of a bill); (nav.) futtock.

allongé, -e, *part.*, lengthened, elongated, outstretched.

allongement (-mān), *n.m.*, lengthening, stretching out, elongation, delaying.

allonger, *v.a.*, to lengthen, to elongate, to piece, to eke out; to stretch out; to wire-draw; to delay, to protract; (fenc.) to allonge, to fetch, to deal, to strike (a blow). *s'allonger*, *v.r.*, to stretch out, to lengthen, to grow longer, to stretch, to lie at full length.

allouable, *adj.*, allowable, permissible.

allouer, *v.a.*, to allow, to grant, to fix.

alluchon, *n.m.*, cog, catch, tooth (of a wheel).

allumer, *v.a.*, to light, to kindle, to set in a flame or on fire, to inflame, to incite, excite, stir up. — *le feu;* to kindle the fire. — *une chandelle;* to light a candle. — *la guerre;* to kindle war. *s'allumer*, *v.r.*, to be lighted, to light, to kindle, to catch or take fire, to be inflamed, to blaze; to brighten up, to sparkle, to glare; to flare up, to break out. *Ce bois a bien de la peine à s'—;* this wood won't kindle.

allumette, *n.f.*, match; fusee; spill. — *chimique;* lucifer-match. — *en copeau;* spill, pipe-light.

allumeur, *n.m.*, lighter, lamp-lighter; (at auctions) puffer.

allure, *n.f.*, gait, pace, way of walking; conduct, behavior, demeanor, carriage, way of proceeding; turn; (nav.) trim, appearance (of a vessel); *pl.*, intrigues. *Je le connais à son —;* I know him by his gait. *Je connais les —s de cet homme;* I know that man's way of dealing.

allusion (al-lu-), *n.f.*, allusion, hint, innuendo. *Faire—à quelque chose;* to allude to something. *Faire une — peu voilée;* to give a broad hint.

alluvial, -e (al-lu-), *adj.*, alluvious.

alluvien, -ne (-in, -è-n), *adj.* *V.* **alluvial**.

alluvion (al-lu-), *n.f.*, alluvion. *D'—;* alluvial.

almageste, *n.m.*, almagest.

almanach (-nä), *n.m.*, almanac, calendar. — *du commerce ;* commercial directory. — *d'adresse* or *des adresses ;* post office directory.

aloès (-èss), *n.m.*, aloe; aloes.

aloétique, *adj.*, aloetical.

aloi, *n.m.*, alloy, standard; quality (of persons). *Argent de bon* — ; good money. *Homme de bas* — ; man of mean birth. *Sans* — ; without alloy. *Noblesse de bon* —; true blue-blood.

⊙**aloïque**, *adj.*, aloetic.

alonge, &c. *V.* **allonge**, &c.

alopécie, *n.f.*, (med.) alopecy, fox-evil.

alors, *adv.*, then, at that time, in that case, in such a case. *D'* — ; of that time. — *même que ;* even when. — *comme* — ; we shall know what to do, all in good time.

alose, *n.f.*, (ich.) shad, alose.

alosier, *n.f.*, **alosière**, *n.f.*, shad-net.

alouchier, *n.m.*, (bot.) white beam tree.

alouette, *n.f.*, (orni.) lark. — *huppée ;* tufted lark. — *des champs ;* sky-lark. — *lulu ;* wood-lark. *Il attend que les* —*s lui tombent tôutes rôties dans le bec ;* he expects a fortune to drop into his mouth. *Pied d'* — ; (bot.) lark's-heel, larkspur.

alourdir, *v.a.*, to make dull, heavy, stupid. *Je suis tout alourdi ;* my head is quite heavy.

*s'***alourdir**, *v.r.*, to grow dull, heavy.

alourdissement, *n.m.*, heaviness, dullness.

aloyage, *n.m.*, alloyage, mixture, pewterer's alloy.

aloyau, *n.m.*, sirloin or ribs of beef.

aloyer, *v.a.*, to alloy gold and silver.

alpaca, *n.m.*, alpaca, llama.

alpaga, *n.m.*, alpaca (stuff).

alpestre, *adj.*, alpine.

alpha, *n.m.*, beginning, alpha.

alphabet, *n.m.*, alphabet.

alphabétique, *adj.*, alphabetical. *Par ordre* —; alphabetically. *Répertoire* —; alphabetical index. [cally.

alphabétiquement (-män), *adv.*, alphabeti-

alpin, -e, *adj.*, alpine.

alpiniste, *n.m.*, Alpine climber.

alpiou, *n.m. Faire un* — ; to stake double.

alpiste, *n.m.*, (bot.) canary-grass, phalaris.

alsacien, *n.m.*, **alsacienne**, *n.f.*, Alsatian, inhabitant of Alsace. — *Lorrain*, native of Alsace-Lorraine, now Elsass-Lothringen.

alsine, *n.f. V.* **morgeline**.

altaïque, *adj.*, altaic, altaian.

altavelle, *n.f.*, (pisc.) string-ray, fire-flaire.

alte, *n.f. V.* **halte**. [rable.

altérable, *adj.*, corruptible, alterable, adulte-

altérable, *n.s.*, (med.) alterative.

altérant, *n.m.*, (med.) alterative. [terative.

altérant, -e, *adj.*, that causes thirst; (med.) al-

altérati-f, -ve, *adj.*, (med.) alterative.

altération, *n.f.*, deterioration, corruption; adulteration, debasing; weakening, impairing, alteration, misrepresentation; excessive thirst. *L'* — *de sa voix ;* the faltering of his voice. *Tous les excès causent de l'* — *dans la santé ;* all excesses impair health.

altercas, *n.m. V.* **altercation**.

altercation, *n.f.*, altercation, contest, wrangle, dispute.

altéré, -e, *part.*, altered, adulterated; thirsty, dry. — *de gloire ;* greedy of glory. — *de sang ;* bloodthirsty, craving for blood.

alter ego, *n.m.*, (*n.p.*) alter ego. *C'est mon* —; he is my other, second, self.

altérer, *v.a.*, to alter, to change, to impair ; to adulterate, to weaken ; to mis-state, to distort, to pervert; to debase; to cause thirst; to disturb, to trouble ; to discompose. *Le soleil altère les couleurs ;* the sun makes colors fade. — *la viande ;* to taint meat. — *le caractère ;* to spoil the temper. — *l'amitié ;* to weaken friendship. — *la monnaie ;* to debase coin. *Cette sauce*

aux anchois m'a fort altéré ; that anchovy sauce has made me very dry, thirsty.

*s'***altérer**, *v.r.*, to be impaired or altered, to degenerate; to taint, to spoil, to falter, to tremble (of the voice). *Le vin s'altère à l'air ;* wine spoils when exposed to the air. *Sa santé commence à s'* — ; his health is beginning to be impaired.

altérer, *v.n.*, to excite thirst, make thirsty.

alternance, *n.f.*, alternation, succession.

alternat, *n.m.*, alternateness; alternacy, rotation of crops.

alternati-f, -ve, *adj.*, alternate, alternative.

alternative, *n.f.*, alternative, choice, option. *Je vous donne l'* — ; I give you your choice.

alternativement (-män), *adv.*, alternately, by turns.

alterne, *adj.*, alternate, reciprocal.

alterné, -e, *adj.*, (her.) alternate (quarters).

alterner, *v.n.*, to alternate, to succeed each other alternately, to take in turns, to fill by turns, to produce a rotation of crops.

alterquer, *v.n.*, to altercate, to dispute.

altesse, *n.f.*, highness. *Son* — *royale ;* his, her, royal highness.

althæa, *n.m.*, (bot.) marsh-mallow.

alti-er, -ère, *adj.*, haughty, proud, arrogant, lordly, lofty elate, stately. *Mine altière ;* haughty look

altimètre, *n.m.*, altimeter. *V.* **hypsomètre**.

altitude, *n.f.*, altitude.

alto, *n.m.*, (—*s*) (mus.) tenor violin, alto.

altruisme, *n.m.*, altruism, altruist.

altruist, -e, *adj.*, altruistic.

alude, *n.f.*, colored sheep-skin, basil.

aludel, *n.m.*, (chem.) aludel, earthen subliming pot.

alumelle, *n.f.*, long and thin knife or sword-blade ; (nav.) handspike-hole ; sheathing.

alumine, *n.f.*, alumina.

aluminé, -e, *adj.*, alumish.

aluminer, *v.a.*, to mix with alum.

alumineux, -se, *adj.*, aluminous.

aluminière. *V.* **alunière**.

aluminium, *n.m.* (*n.p.*), aluminum, aluminium.

alun, *n.m.*, alum.

alunage, *n.m.*, (dye.) steeping in alum.

alunation, *n.f.*, (chem.) alum-making.

aluner, *v.a.*, to steep in alum-water.

alunière, *n.f.*, alum-pit, alum works.

alvéolaire, *adj.*, alveolar.

alvéole, *n.m.*, alveolus, cell (in a honey-comb), socket (of a tooth).

alvin, -e, *adj.*, (med.) alvine.

alysson, *n.m.*, **alysse**, *n.f.*, madwort, gold-dust.

amabilité, *n.f.*, loveliness ; kindness ; amiableness, amiability.

amadis, *n.m.*, tight sleeve.

amadou, *n.m.*, German tinder ; touch-wood, match-wood ; pyrotechnical sponge.

amadouer, *v.a.*, to coax, to wheedle, to cajole, to flatter, to gain over.

amadoueur, -se, *n.m.f.*, tinder-maker ; (fig.) coaxer, wheedler.

amadouvier, *n.m.*, agaric, touch-wood.

amaigrir, *v.a.*, to make lean, meagre, or thin, to emaciate, to reduce, to lessen ; (arch.) to thin. *C'est cela qui l'amaigrit ;* it is that which makes him grow thin.

amaigrir, *v.n.*, to fall away, to grow lean or thin ; (arch.) to shrink.

*s'***amaigrir**, *v.r.*, to grow thin, to fall away.

amaigrissement (-gris-män), *n.m.*, emaciation ; wasting away, falling away, growing thin, leanness.

amalgamation, *n.f.*, amalgamation.

amalgame, *n.m.*, amalgam ; medley, mixture, amalgamation.

amalgamer, *v.a.*, to amalgamate, to combine, to blend.

s'amalgamer, *v.r.*, to amalgamate; to blend together.

amande, *n.f.*, almond, kernel; nucleus. — *amère, douce;* bitter, sweet, almond. —*s lissées;* sugar-plums. —*s à la praline;* burnt almonds. — *d'amazone;* Brazil-nut. *Huile d'—s douces;* oil of sweet almonds. — *de terre;* rush-nut.

amandé, *n.m.*, amygdalate; milk of almonds.

amandier, *n.m.*, almond-tree.

amant, *n.m.*, -**e**, *n.f.*, lover, wooer, suitor; sweetheart, mistress; votary, spark, gallant, paramour. — *de cœur;* favorite, preferred lover.

amarante, *n.f.*, amaranth, purple flower-gentle, cock's-comb, prince's feather.

amarante, *adj.*, amaranthine, amaranth-colored.

amareilleur, *n.m.*, oyster-bed keeper.

amarinage, *n.m.*, manning (a prize).

amariner, *v.a.*, to man (a prize); to inure to sea.

amarrage, *n.m.*, (nav.) anchorage; mooring, lashing, seizure. *Ligne d'—;* lasher.

amarre, *n.f.*, (nav.) cable, rope, hawser. — *de fond;* ground tackle.

amarrer, *v.a.*, (nav.) to moor, to belay, to make fast, to lash, to tie, to seize.

amaryllis (-ril-lis), *n.f.*, amaryllis, lily-asphodel.

amas, *n.m.*, mass, heap, pile, collection, hoard, store, accumulation, cluster; congeries. *Un — de peuple;* a great mob. — *de sable;* heap of sand.

amasser, *v.a.*, to heap up, to hoard up, to lay up, to treasure up, to gather up, to get together, to accumulate, to rake together; to assemble, to congregate, to put together, to cluster. — *de l'argent;* to hoard up money.

s'amasser, *v.r.*, to gather, to get together, to accumulate, to be collected, to crowd, to assemble.

amassette, *n.f.*, a small palette-knife.

amatelotage (-mat-lo-), *n.m.*, (nav.) messmating.

amateloter (-mat-lo-), *v.a.*, (nav.) to class (the crew).

amateur, *n.m.*, lover, admirer; amateur, virtuoso. — *des beaux-arts;* lover of the fine arts. — *de la nouveauté;* fond of novelty.

amati, *n.m.*, an Amati violin.

amatir, *v.a.*, (gold) to deaden; (coin.) to blanch the planchets.

amaurose, *n.f.*, (med.) amaurosis.

amazone, *n.f.*, amazon, lady on horseback. *Habit d'—;* riding-habit.

ambages, *n.f. pl.*, ambages, idle circumlocution.

ambassade, *n.f.*, embassy, embassade; ambassador's house.

ambassadeur, *n.m.*, ambassador; messenger, envoy.

ambassadrice, *n.f.*, ambassadress.

ambe, *n.m.*, series of two numbers.

ambesas (anb-zâs), *n.m.*, ambs-ace, two aces.

ambi, *n.m.*, (surg.) ambe, ambi.

ambiant, -**e**, *adj.*, ambient, surrounding.

ambidextérité, *n.f.*, double dealing; ambidexterity.

ambidextre, *adj.*, ambidextrous, ambidexter.

ambigu, *n.m.*, collation (with everything served up together); (fig.) medley, olio, compound.

ambigu, -**ë**, *adj.*, ambiguous, equivocal.

ambiguïté, *n.f.*, ambiguity. *Parler sans —;* to speak plainly.

ambigument, *adv.*, ambiguously.

ambitieusement (-mān), *adv.*, ambitiously.

ambitieu-x, -**se**, *adj.*, ambitious, aspiring.

ambition, *n.f.*, ambition.

ambitionner, *v.a.*, to desire earnestly, to be ambitious of, to aspire to, to seek after.

amble, *n.m.*, amble, canter. *Aller l'—;* to amble. *Etre franc d'—;* to amble freely. *Ce cheval a l'— doux;* that horse has an easy amble.

ambler, *v.n.*, to amble, to canter.

amblyope, *n.m.f.*, weak-sighted person; *n.m.*, (pisc.) blind-fish.

ambon, *n.m.*, ambo, rood-loft.

ambre, *n.m.*, amber. — *gris;* ambergris. *Il est fin comme l'—;* he is a shrewd fellow.

ambré, -**e**, *adj.*, amber-colored.

ambrer, *v.a.*, to perfume with amber.

ambrette, *n.f.*, amber-seed, musk-seed.

ambroisie, *n.f.*, ambrosia. *D'—;* ambrosial, fragrant, delicious.

ambrosien, -**ne** (-in, -ène), *adj.*, pertaining to St. Ambrose; Ambrosian.

ambulance, *n.f.*, field-hospital, ambulance. *Chirurgien d'—;* field-surgeon. *En —;* (of vendors) itinerant.

ambulant, -**e**, *adj.*, ambulatory, ambulant; itinerant, strolling. *Marchand —;* itinerant dealer. *Comédiens —s;* strolling players. *Érésipèle —;* flying erysipelas. *Mener une vie —e;* to stroll about, to be upon the tramp.

ambulatoire, *adj.*, ambulatory, movable, itinerant.

âme, *n.f.*, soul; mind; genius; conscience; essence; ghost, spirit; feeling, sentiment; person, people; motto; bore (of a gun); small wood (in faggots); (of bellows) clapper; (sculp.) a rough figure of clay; the model made use of to form a mold; (mus.) sounding-post. *Les facultés de l'—;* the faculties of the mind. *Grandeur d'—;* magnanimity. *Du fond de l'—;* from the depths of the soul. *Dieu veuille avoir son —;* God rest his soul. *Avoir la mort dans l'—;* to be grieved to death. *Il n'y a pas — qui vive ici;* there is not a living creature here. *Je le veux de toute mon —;* I wish it with all my soul. *Les bonnes —;* (iron.) good-natured souls. *Sans —;* spiritless. *La vérité est l'— de l'histoire;* truth is the life of history. *La bonne foi est l'— du commerce;* honesty is the very soul of trade. *Il n'y a point d'— dans sa déclamation;* his delivery is spiritless. *Il est l'— damnée du ministre;* he is the minister's tool. *Rendre l'—;* to give up the ghost. *Il a l'— bourrelée;* his conscience wracks him. *Cet homme n'a point d'—;* that man has no soul. *Il n'y a pas d'— dans ce tableau;* there is no life in this picture.

amélioration, *n.f.*, amelioration, improvement, mending. *Susceptible d'—;* improvable.

améliorer, *v.a.*, to ameliorate, to improve, to meliorate, to better, to cultivate, to mend.

s'améliorer, *v.r.*, to mend, to improve.

amen (amè-n), *n.m.*, amen.

aménagement (-naj-mān), *n.m.*, management of a forest, arrangement, fitting up; disposition (of a house).

aménager, *v.a.*, to regulate the felling, replanting, and preserving of a wood or forest, to dispose, arrange, lay out. — *un arbre;* to cut up a tree.

amendable, *adj.*, improvable, mendable.

amende, *n.f.*, fine, penalty, forfeit, compensation, reparation. *Mettre* or *condamner à l'—;* to fine. *Faire — honorable;* to make amends, to apologize.

amendé, -**e**, *part.*, amended, mended, reclaimed.

amendement (-mān), *n.m.*, amendment, mending, bettering, improvement. — *d'une terre;* improvement, manuring of a piece of ground. *La loi a passé sans —;* the bill passed without amendment.

amender, *v.a.*, to amend, to better, to correct, to improve, to manure.

amender, *v.n.,* to grow better, to improve.

s'amender, *v.r.,* to amend, to grow better, to reform ; to mend.

amener, *v.a.,* to bring ; to bring in, to bring up, to bring over, to bring about, to bring round, to bring on ; to lead ; to fetch, to introduce ; to prevail upon, to induce ; to throw (of dice) ; (nav.) to haul down, lower, strike. *Je l'ai amené où je voulais ;* I brought him to do what I wanted. *Il a amené cette affaire à bien ;* he has ended the matter satisfactorily. *— des maladies ;* to bring on diseases. *— des modes ;* to bring in fashions. *— quelqu'un à faire une chose ;* to induce any one to do a thing. *— son pavillon ;* to lower, to strike one's flag. *Cette remarque est bien amenée ; i.e.* cleverly introduced, well to the point. *N'amenez jamais la conversation sur la politique ;* never introduce politics into conversation.

aménité, *n.f.,* amenity, pleasantness, grace.

amentacées, *n.f.pl.,* (bot.) amentaceous plants.

amenuiser, *v.a.,* to make thin, to make smaller ; to lessen.

am-er (amè-r), **-ère,** *adj.,* bitter, sad, painful, grievous ; harsh, biting, galling, briny. *Principe —,* (chem.) bitter principle. *Rendre — ;* to embitter. *Cela est d'un goût — ;* that has a bitter taste. *Avoir la bouche amère ;* to have a bitter taste in the mouth. *Des plaintes amères ;* bitter complaints. *Une raillerie amère ;* cutting raillery.

amer (amè-r), *n.m.,* bitterness, gall (of some animals and fish. *—s ;* (med.) bitters ; (nav.) seamarks, landmarks.

amèrement (-mān), *adv.,* bitterly, grievously.

américain, *n.m.,* -e, *n.f.,* American.

américain, -e, *adj.,* American.

américaine, *n.f.,* (print.) script.

amertume, *n.f.,* bitterness, acerbity ; grief, sorrow ; gall, venom.

améthyste, *n.f.,* amethyst.

améthyste, *n.m.,* humming-bird.

améthystin, -e, *adj.,* amethystine.

ameublement, *n.m.,* furniture, household goods, set of furniture.

ameublir, *v.a.,* (agri.) to make lighter, to mellow ; (law) to make movable.

ameublissement (-mān), *n.m.,* (agri.) dressing, mellowing ; (law) lien upon land.

ameulonner, *v.a.,* to stack hay, corn, &c.

ameuter, *v.a.,* to train dogs to hunt together ; to stir up, gather, rouse, excite.

s'ameuter, *v.r.,* to gather in a mob, to crowd, to riot ; to mutiny, to rebel.

ami, *n.m.,* -e, *n.f.,* friend. *Bon —, véritable — ;* good, true friend. *— de table ;* table companion. *Bonne —e ;* sweetheart. *C'est un de mes vieux —s ;* he is an old pal, chum of mine. *Traiter quelqu'un en — ;* to use one like a friend. *Etre — de ;* to be the companion of, to be partial to. *Les bons comptes font les bons —s ;* short reckonings make long friends. *M'—e* (for *mon amie*)*!* my dear, my love, darling. *Mon — !* my dear *!* *Chambre d'— ;* spare room. *Ami de cour ;* false friend. *— en voie ;* a friend at court.

ami, -e, *adj.,* friendly ; kind, fond of ; (paint.) friendly, favorite, propitious. *— lecteur,* kind reader.

amiable, *adj.,* amiable, kind, friendly, courteous, amicable.

a l'amiable, *adv.,* amicably, by private contract (of sales). *Terminer un différend à l'— ;* to settle a quarrel amicably. *Vente à l'— ;* sale by private contract.

amiablement, *adv.,* amicably, in a friendly manner.

amiante, *n.m.,* amianthus, mountain-flax, earth-flax.

amical, -e, *adj.,* amicable, friendly, kind.

amicalement (-mān), *adv.,* amicably, kindly, in a friendly manner.

amict (a-mi), *n.m.,* amice.

amidon, *n.m.,* starch ; fecula.

amidonner, *v.a.,* to starch.

amidonnerie (-do-n-rî), *n.f.,* starch manufactory, starch-works.

amidonnier, *n.m.,* starch-maker.

⊙**amigdale,** *n.f.* V. **amygdale.**

amincir, *v.a.,* to make thinner, smaller ; to lessen, to edge off, to attenuate.

s'amincir, *v.r.,* to become thinner, to make one's self thin.

amincissement (-mān), *n.m.,* thinning, thinness.

amiral, *n.m.,* admiral. *Vaisseau — ;* flag-ship; (conch.) admiral. *Grand — ;* high-admiral. *Vice — ;* vice-admiral. *Contre — ;* rear-admiral.

amiralat, *n.m.,* admiralship.

amirale, *n.f.,* admiral's wife.

amirauté, *n.f.,* admiralship ; admiralty.

amitié, *n.f.,* friendship, amity ; affection, goodwill ; favor, kindness ; pleasure ; interest ; *pl.,* kind regards, compliments, attentions. *Se lier d'— avec ;* to become intimate with. *Etre sur un pied d'— avec ;* to be on friendly terms with. *Faites-moi l'— de lui en parler ;* do me the kindness to mention it to him. *Par — ;* out of friendship. *Prendre quelqu'un en — ;* to take a liking to any one. *L'— des couleurs ;* the perfect blending of colors. *Il m'a fait des —s ;* he showed me much attention. *Faites-lui mes —s ;* remember me kindly to him. *Mes —s à tout le monde ;* love to all.

amman, *n.m.,* amman, a judge who has cognizance of civil causes, in Switzerland.

ammi, *n.m.,* (bot.) bishop's-wort.

ammon, *n.m.,* ammonite. *Corne d'—,* *n.f.,* sermon-stone.

ammonia-c, -que, *adj.,* ammoniac. *Sel — ;* sal ammoniac. *Gomme —que ;* gum ammoniac. *Gaz — ;* ammoniacal gas.

ammoniacal, *adj.,* ammoniacal.

ammoniaque, *n.m.f.,* ammonia.

ammonite, *n.f.,* (foss.) serpent-stone.

amnios, *n.m.,* (n.p.) (anat.) amnion, amnios.

amnistie (am-nis-tî), *n.f.,* amnesty, pardon.

amnistié (am-nis-tié), *n.m.,* -e, *n.f.,* person pardoned by amnesty.

amnistier (am-nis-tié), *v.a.,* to pardon by amnesty.

amodiataire, *n.m.,* lessor (of a farm).

amodiateur, *n.m.,* tenant of land, lessee, farmer.

amodiation, *n.f.,* leasing, letting out to farm.

amodier, *v.a.,* to farm out an estate ; to rent an estate.

amoindrir, *v.a.,* to lessen, to decrease, diminish.

amoindrir, *v.n.,* to lessen, to grow less, to decrease.

s'amoindrir, *v.r.,* to lessen, to grow less.

amoindrissement (-mān), *n.m.,* lessening, decrease, abating, diminution.

amollir, *v.a.,* to mollify, to soften, to mellow ; to enervate, to effeminate, to unman.

s'amollir, *v.r.,* to soften, to grow tender, to grow soft ; to grow effeminate or weak.

amollissant, -e, *adj.,* enervating, effeminating, softening.

amollissement (-mān), *n.m.,* softening, flagging, enervation, abatement.

amome, *n.m.,* amomum. *— à grappes ;* cardamom-tree.

amonceler, *v.a.,* to heap up, to lay in a heap, to fill up, to pile up, to drift.

s'amonceler, *v.r.,* to gather ; to be filled up ; to accumulate, to drift. *Les nuages s'amoncellent ;* the clouds are gathering.

amoncellement (-sel-mān), *n.m.,* heaping up, accumulation.

amont, *adv.,* up the river, up stream ; above

the town. *Vent d'—*; (nav.) easterly wind. *Aller en —*; to go up. *En — du pont;* above bridge.

amorce, *n.f.*, bait; priming; (percussion) cap; tinder, train; allurement, attraction, enticement, decoy, charm, electro-plating bath. *Douce —, dangereuse —;* sweet, dangerous attraction. *Trompeuses —s;* deceitful allurements. *Sans brûler une —;* without firing a shot.

amorcer, *v.a.*, to bait; to prime; to cap (small arms); to allure, to entice, to decoy, to draw in. *— un hameçon;* to bait a hook. *— une arme à feu;* to prime a gun.

amorçoir, *n.m.*, wimble, auger. *V.* **ébauchoir.**

amoroso, *adv.*, (mus.) amoroso.

amorphe, *adj.*, amorphous.

amorphie, *n.f.*, amorphy.

amortir, *v.a.*, to deaden, allay, moderate; to weaken; to break (a fall); (fin.) to sink; to redeem (land, stock); to pay off; to cool (passions); (jur.) to amortize; (paint.) to flatten; to buy up. *— un coup, le bruit;* to deaden a blow, the sound. *— une pension;* to redeem a pension. *— des dettes;* to pay off debts. *— la fièvre;* to reduce the fever.

amortir, *v.n.*, (nav.) to be neaped, to be dry.

*s'*amortir, *v.r.*, to be broken, deadened; to slacken; to be paid off; to be bought up; to grow weak.

amortissable, *adj.*, (fin.) redeemable.

amortissement (-măn), *n.m.*, redeeming, buying up; liquidation; sinking; deadening, abatement, redemption; amortization; (arch.) the uppermost part of a building, top, pediment, finishing; (nav.) lying aground. *Caisse d'—;* sinking-fund office. *Fonds d'—;* sinking-fund (capital).

amour, *n.m.*, love, lovingness, passion, flame. *L'Amour;* (myth.) Eros; Cupid. *Beau comme l'Amour;* a very Adonis. *Lacs d'—;* love-knot. *Avec —;* lovingly, carefully. *Se marier par —;* to marry for love. *Mourir d'—;* to be lovesick. *Avoir de l'— pour;* to be in love with. *En —;* (of animals) in heat. *Filer le parfait —;* to play the sentimental lover. *Faire l'—;* to court, to make love to. *Pour l'— de Dieu;* for God's sake. *Je voudrais pour l'— de vous que cela fût;* I wish it were so for your sake. *C'est un vrai remède d'—;* she is a perfect fright. *La terre est en —;* the land is ripe for vegetation. *Cette montre est un véritable —;* that is a love of a watch. *Quel — d'enfant!* what a love of a child! *— propre,* self-love, self-respect, conceit, vanity.

amours, *n.f. pl.*, one's love, flame, amours; delight. *Ses premières —;* his first love. *Les —;* (myth.) the Loves. *De folles —;* foolish love. *Les tableaux sont ses —;* pictures are his delight. *Froides mains, chaudes —;* cold hand, warm heart.

amouraché, -e, *part.*, (fam.) smitten, in love with.

amouracher, *v.a.*, to make fall in love.

*s'*amouracher, *v.a.*, (fam.) to become enamored of, smitten with.

amourette, *n.f.*, intrigue; love, love-affair; amour; (bot.) quaking-grass. *—s de veau;* calf's marrow.

amoureusement (-euz-măn), *adv.*, amorously, lovingly; tenderly, softly.

amoureu-x, -se, *adj.*, in love, enamored, amorous; loving. *Il est — de cette femme;* he is in love with that woman. *Regards —;* looks full of love. *Devenir —;* to fall in love. *Etre — des onze mille vierges;* to be a universal lover, a man-flirt.

amoureu-x, *n.m.*, **-se**, *n.f.*, lover, wooer, sweetheart, spark; (thea.) actor, actress, who performs lovers' parts.

amovibilité, *n.f.*, revocableness, removability, liability to removal.

amovible, *adj.*, removable, revocable, at plea-

sure. *Emploi —;* revocable appointment, office held during pleasure.

amphibie, *n.m.*, amphibian; time-server, double-dealer; (pers.) jack of all trades; man of two different trades.

amphibie, *adj.*, amphibious.

amphibologie, *n.f.*, amphibology.

amphibologique, *adj.*, amphibological, ambiguous.

amphibologiquement (-jik-măn), *adv.*, amphibologically, ambiguously.

amphibraque, *n.m.*, (poet.) amphibrach.

amphictyonide, *adj.* *Ville —;* a town having the right of sending a deputy to the Amphictyonic council.

amphictyonique, *adj.*, Amphictyonic.

amphictyons (-ti-ōn), *n.m. pl.*, Amphictyons.

amphigouri, *n.m.*, ludicrous poem, burlesque, or speech; rigmarole, gibberish.

amphigourique, *adj.*, ludicrous, nonsensical, burlesque.

amphigouriquement (-rik-măn), *adv.*, nonsensically.

amphimacre, *n.m.*, (poet.) amphimacer.

amphisciens (-si-in), *n.m.*, (geog.) amphiscians.

amphithéâtral, -e, *adj.*, amphitheatrical.

amphithéâtre, *n.m.*, amphitheatre; first gallery; dissecting-room, lecture-room. *En —;* in the form of an amphitheatre.

amphitryon, *n.m.*, (myth.) Amphitryon; host, entertainer.

amphore, *n.f.*, amphora, pitcher, jug.

ample, *adj.*, ample, full; large, vast, spacious, roomy, wide, broad; copious, diffuse.

amplement, *adv.*, amply, fully; largely, plentifully, broadly, extensively, diffusively.

ampleur, *n.f.*, amplitude, largeness, wideness. *Il n'a pas assez d'—;* it is too scanty, not full enough.

ampliati-f, -ve, *adj.*, (of the Pope's briefs and bulls) additional, enlarging on.

ampliation, *n.f.*, the duplicate (of a receipt). *Pour —;* a true copy (jurisp.). *Lettres d'—;* letters of ampliation.

⊙**amplier**, *v.a.*, (jur.) to prolong, to put off, to defer.

amplificateur, *n.m.*, (b. s.) amplifier.

amplification, *n.f.*, amplification.

amplifier, *v.a.*, to amplify, to enlarge, to enrich, to enlarge upon; to expatiate upon.

amplitude, *n.f.*, (astron., geol.) amplitude.

ampoule, *n.f.*, blister on the hands or feet; (med., bot.) ampulla. *La sainte —;* the holy phial (for holy oil). *Faire venir des —s;* to blister.

ampoulé, -e, *adj.*, blistered; tumid, high-flown, swelling, bombastic, turgid. *Un style —, des vers —s;* high-flown style, bombastic verses.

ampouler, *v.a.*, (metal.) to blister.

ampouler, *v.n.*, to blister.

ampoulette, *n.f.*, (nav.) clock; glass.

amputation, *n.f.*, amputation. *Faire une —;* to perform an amputation.

amputé, *n.m.*, **-e**, *n.f.*, one who has had a limb amputated.

amputer, *v.a.*, to amputate, to cut off.

amulette, *n.f.*, amulet, charm.

amure, *n.f.*, (nav.) tack of a sail. *Première — de misaine;* fore-tack. *Grande —;* main-tack.

amurer, *v.a.*, (nav.) to haul or bring aboard the tack of a sail. *Amure la grande voile!* aboard th.. main tack!

amusable, *adj.*, capable of being amused, amusable.

amusant, -e, *adj.*, amusing, diverting, entertaining.

amusement (-măn), *n.m.*, amusement, pastime, entertainment, sport, diversion; sham, trick, mere put off; fooling, trifling. *Pas tant d'—;* less trifling.

amuser, *v.a.*, to amuse, to divert, to entertain, to recreate, to solace, to beguile; to put one off with fair words and promises; to trifle with; to stop, to detain; to deceive. *Ne m'amusez pas;* don't detain me. *— le tapis;* to talk the time away, to be long in coming to the point. *— l'ennemi;* to deceive the enemy.

s'amuser, *v.r.*, to amuse one's self, to busy one's self; to disport, to sport, to tarry, to stay, to trifle, to stand trifling. *S'— de quelqu'un;* to trifle with any one. *Ne vous amusez pas en chemin;* don't loiter on the way. *S'— à des bagatelles;* to care for nothing but trifles. *S'— à la moutarde;* to stand at trifles.

amusette, *n.f.*, amusement, trifling, child's play.

amuseur, *n.m.*, entertainer, deceiver.

amusoire, *n.f.*, something amusing, toy, trifle.

amygdale, *n.f.*, (anat.) almond, tonsil.

amygdaloïde, *n.f.*, amygdaloid.

amylacé, -e, *adj.*, amylaceous, resembling starch.

an, *n.m.*, year, twelvemonth. *Le jour de l'—* New Year's day. *L'— bissextile;* leap year. *Bon —, mal —;* one year with another. *Au bout d'un —;* twelve months after that. *L'— de notre Seigneur;* the, in the, year of our Lord. *L'— du monde;* the, in the, year of the world. *Il y a un —;* a year ago. *Nouvel —;* New Year. *L'— passé;* last year. *Tous les —s;* every year, yearly. *Tous les deux —s;* every other year. *Elle a quinze —s;* she is fifteen. *Une fois, deux fois, l'—;* once, twice, a year. *Bon jour, bon —;* a happy New Year to you. *Bout de l'—, service du bout de l'—;* service, commemoration. *Je m'en moque comme de l'— quarante;* I don't care two straws about it.

ana, *n.m.*, (—) termination, denoting a collection of sayings, ana; (phar.) ana, āā *or* ā.

anabaptisme (-ba-tism), *n.m.*, anabaptism.

anabaptiste (-ba-tist), *n.m.*, anabaptist.

anacarde, *n.m.*, anacardium, cashew-nut.

anacardier, *n.m.*, anacardium, cashew-tree.

anachorète (-ko-), *n.m.*, anachoret, anchorite, hermit.

anachronisme (-kro-), *n.m.*, anachronism.

anacoluthe, *n.f.*, (gram.) anacoluthon.

anacréontique, *adj.*, anacreontic.

anagallis. *V.* **mouron.**

anagnoste, *n.m.*, (antiq.) a slave who, among the Romans, read during the meals.

anagogique, *adj.*, (theol.) anagogical, mystical.

anagrammatique, *adj.*, anagrammatical.

anagrammatiser, *v.a.*, to anagrammatize.

anagrammatiste, *n.m.*, anagrammatist.

anagramme, *n.f.*, anagram.

anagyris (-rîs), *n.m.*, bean-trefoil.

analectes, *n.m. pl.*, (phil.) analects.

analemme, *n.m.*, (astron.) analemma.

analeptique, *adj.*, (med.) analeptic.

analeptique, *n.m.*, (med.) analeptic.

analogie, *n.f.*, analogy.

analogique, *adj.*, analogous, analogical.

analogiquement (-jik-mān), *adv.*, analogically.

analogisme, *n.m.*, analogism.

analogue (-log), *adj.*, analogous.

analyse, *n.f.*, analysis; outline; parsing. *Faire l'— de l'eau;* to analyze water. *Faire l'— d'un passage;* (gram.) to parse a passage. *En dernière —;* to conclude, to sum up; the upshot of it is.

analyser, *v.a.*, to analyze. *— une fleur;* to dissect a flower.

analyste, *n.m.*, analyzer, analyst.

analytique, *adj.*, analytical.

analytique, *n.f.*, analytics.

analytiquement (-tik-mān), *adv.*, analytically.

anamorphose, *n.f.*, (persp.) anamorphosis.

ananas (-nâ), *n.m.*, pineapple. *Champ d'—;* pinery. *Fraise —;* pine-strawberry.

anapeste, *n.m.*, (poet.) anapæst.

anapestique, *adj.*, anapæstic.

anaphore, *n.f.*, (rhet.) anaphora.

anaphrodisiaque, *adj.*, (pharm.) antaphrodisiac, anti-aphrodisiac.

anaphrodite, *adj.*, (med.) impotent, anaphrodite.

anarchie, *n.f.*, anarchy.

anarchique, *adj.*, anarchical.

anarchiser, *v.a.*, to throw into anarchy.

anarchiste, *n.m.f.*, anarchist.

anarrhique, *n.m.*, wolf-fish. *— loup;* ravenous wolf-fish.

anasarque, *n.f.*, anasarca, dropsy of the skin.

anastomose, *n.f.*, (anat.) anastomosis.

s'anastomoser, *v.r.*, to anastomose.

anastrophe, *n.f.*, (gram.) anastrophe.

anathématiser, *v.a.*, to anathematize.

anathème, *n. m.*, anathema; reprobation, curse. *Frapper d'—;* to anathematize. *— maranatha;* anathema, maranatha.

anathème, *adj.*, anathematized.

anatife, *n.m.*, barnacle.

anatocisme, *n.m.*, anatocism (compound interest).

anatomie, *n.f.*, anatomy, dissection; subject (body under dissection); methodical analysis (of a book). *— comparée;* comparative anatomy.

anatomique, *adj.*, anatomical.

anatomiquement (-mān), *adv.*, anatomically.

anatomiser, *v.a.*, to anatomize. *—un livre;* to dissect a book.

anatomiste, *n.m.*, anatomist.

ancêtre, *n.m.f.*, ancestor, ancestress.

ancêtres, *n.m.pl.*, ancestors, forefathers. *De ses —;* ancestral.

anche, *n.f.*, reed (of a hautboy or other wind instrument); meal-spout (of a mill). *— d'orgue;* reed-stop of an organ.

anché, -e, *adj.*, (her.) curved.

anchilops (-ki-), *n.m.*, (med.) anchilops.

anchois, *n.m.*, anchovy. *Beurre* or *pâte d'—;* anchovy paste.

anchoité, -e, *adj.*, pickled like anchovies.

ancien, -ne (-si-in, -si-è-n), *adj.*, ancient, old; senior; of old times, of ancient standing; former, late, ex. *Une —ne coutume;* an old custom. *L'— et le Nouveau Testament;* the Old and New Testament.

ancien, *n.m.*, senior; ancient; elder; old codger. *Les ouvrages des —s;* the works of the ancients. *Les —s d'une église;* the elders. *L'—;* Old Nick.

anciennement (-è-n-mān), *adv.*, anciently, formerly; of yore, of old; in former times.

ancienneté (-è-n-té), *n.f.*, ancientness, primitiveness; seniority, age, antiquity. *De toute —;* from the earliest times.

ancile, *n.m.*, (antiq.) sacred buckler.

ancolie, *n.f.*, (bot.) columbine.

anconé, *n.m.*, (anat.) ancon.

ancrage, *n.m.*, anchor-ground; anchorage. *Droits d'—;* anchorage dues.

ancre, *n.f.*, anchor; (arch.) brace, an *s. L'— de flot;* the flood anchor. *L'— de jusant;* the ebb anchor. *L'— de large;* the sea anchor. *Maîtresse —;* the sheet anchor. *— de rechange;* spare anchor. *La seconde —;* the best bower anchor. *L'— d'affourche;* the small bower anchor. *L'— de touée;* the stream anchor. *— de miséricorde, de salut;* sheet anchor. *— surjalée;* foul anchor. *Chasser sur ses —s;* to drag one's anchors. *Empenneler une —;* to back an anchor. *Caponner l'—;* to cat the anchor. *Traverser l'—;* to fish the anchor. *Gou-*

verner sur son — ; to steer the ship to her anchor. *Etre à l'* — ; to ride at anchor. *Fatiguer à l'* — ; to ride hard. *Ne pas fatiguer à l'* — ; to ride easy. *Jeter l'* — ; to cast anchor. *Brider l'* — ; to shoe the anchor. *Lever l'* — ; to weigh anchor. *Mettre l'* — *à poste* ; to stow the anchor. *Jeter sa dernière* — ; (fig.) to make a last effort. *C'est notre* — *de salut ;* it is our last resource.

⊙**ancrer,** *v.n.,* to anchor, to come to an anchor. *V.* **mouiller.**

*s'***ancrer,** *v.r.,* to settle one's self, to get a footing in a place, to take deep root in.

ancrure, *n.f.,* small fold made in cloth while shearing it, crease ; (arch.) iron prop.

andabate, *n.m.,* (antiq.) gladiator who fought blindfolded.

andain, *n.m.,* (agr.) swath ; wind-row.

andanté, *adv.,* (mus.) andante.

andante, *n.m.,* (—*s*) (mus.) an air to be played or sung andante.

⊙**andelle,** *n.f.,* beech-wood.

*****andouille,** *n.f.,* (of pigs) chitterlings ; twist (of tobacco). *Cela s'en est allé en brouet d'* — ; it all ended in smoke.

*****andouiller,** *n.m.,* antler. *Les premiers —s ;* the brow-antlers. *Sur —s ;* sur-antlers.

*****andouillette,** *n.f.,* forced-meat ball, small sausage.

androgyne, *n.m.,* androgynous, hermaphrodite.

androgyne, *adj.,* androgynal, androgynous.

androïde, *n.m.,* android, automaton.

andromède, *n.f.,* (astron.) Andromeda.

andropogon, *n.m.,* (bot.) camel's hay.

âne, *n.m.,* ass, jackass, donkey ; blockhead, ignorant fool, idiot ; vice (instrument). *Fait en dos d'* — ; (arch.) made with a shelving ridge ; hog's-back. *Coq-à-l'* — (—) ; cock-and-bull story. *Promenade à* — ; donkey-ride. *Pont aux —s ;* asses' bridge. *C'est le pont aux —s ;* every fool knows that. *A laver la tête d'un* —, *on perd sa lessive ;* there is no washing a blackamoor white. *Faute d'un point, Martin perdît son* — ; a miss is as good as a mile. *Il ne sera jamais qu'un* — ; he will be an ass as long as he lives. *Conte de peau d'* — ; fairy tale. *On ne saurait faire boire un* — *qui n'a pas soif ;* you may take a horse to water, but you can't make him drink. *Têtu comme un* — ; as stubborn as a mule. *Sérieux comme un* — *qu'on étrille ;* as grave as a judge. *Tête d'* — ; ass's head. *Bonnet d'* — ; fool's cap ; (ich.) bull-head, miller's-thumb, cottus.

anéantir, *v.a.,* to annihilate, to put out of existence, to destroy ; to reduce to nothing, to prostrate, to thunderstrike, to dumfound.

*s'***anéantir,** *v.r.,* to be annihilated or destroyed, to come to nothing ; to cease to be, to humble oneself.

anéantissement (-mān), *n.m.,* annihilation, annihilating ; abjection, humiliation ; prostration, depression ; destruction, destroying, ruin, overthrow.

anecdote, *n.f.,* anecdote.

anecdotier (-tié), *n.m.,* anecdote-teller, monger.

anecdotique, *adj.,* anecdotical. *Recueil* — ; collection of anecdotes.

ânée, *n.f.,* load of an ass.

anémie, *n.f.,* (med.) anæmia.

anémique, *adj.,* suffering from anæmia.

anémographie, *n.f.,* anemography.

anémomètre, *n.m.,* anemometer.

anémone, *n.f.,* anemone, wind-flower.

anémoscope, *n.m.,* anemoscope, weather-cock.

ânerie, *n.f.,* gross ignorance ; stupidity ; gross blunder.

ânesse, *n.f.,* she-ass. *Lait d'* — ; ass's milk.

anesthésie, *n.f.,* (med.) anæsthesia.

anesthésique, *adj.,* anæsthetic.

aneth, *n.m.,* (bot.) dill.

anévrismal, -e, *adj.* aneurismal.

anévrisme, *n.m.,* aneurism.

anfractueu-x, -se, *adj.,* anfractuous, rugged, cragged, craggy.

anfractuosité, *n.f.,* anfractuosity, winding, sinuosity, cavity.

⊙**angar,** *n.m. V.* **hangar.**

ange, *n.m.,* a spirit, angel ; (artil.) chain-shot, cross-bar shot ; angel-shot ; (ich.) angel-fish, skate, squatina. — *déchu ;* fallen angel. — *tutélaire ;* guardian angel. *Rire aux —s ;* to have a laughing fit. *Etre aux —s ;* to be in a transport of joy, in raptures. — *bouffi ;* a chubby child. *Lit d'* — ; tent bed.

angélique, *adj.,* angelical, angelic.

angélique, *n.f.,* angelica.

angéliquement (-lik-mān), *adv.,* angelically.

angelot (anj-lo), *n.m.,* angelot cheese.

angélus (ān-), *n.m.,* (*n.p.*) (c. rel.) Angelus. *Sonner l'* — ; to toll the angelus.

angine, *n.f.,* (med.) angina, quinsy, sore throat. — *couenneuse ;* diphtheria.

angineu-x, -se, *adj.,* (med.) attended with angina.

angiographie, *n.f.,* angiography.

angiologie, *n.f.,* angiology.

angiosperme, *adj.,* (bot.) angiospermous.

angiospermie, *n.f.,* (bot.) angiosperm.

angiotomie, *n.f.,* angiotomy.

anglais, -e, *adj.,* English ; British. *Etre poursuivi par des* — ; to be pestered by creditors.

anglais, *n.m.,* English, Englishman.

anglaise, *n.f.,* English girl, woman ; upholsterer's thread or silk lace. *Elle porte des —s ;* she wears long, drooping curls.

anglaiser, *v.a.,* to nick a horse's tail.

angle, *n.m.,* angle, corner, turning. — *aigu ;* acute angle. — *droit ;* right angle. — *rectiligne ;* rectilinear angle. — *rentrant, saillant ;* re-entrant salient angle. *A —s saillants ;* sharp-cornered. *A* — *droit ;* rectangular. — *facial ;* (anat.) facial angle.

anglet, *n.m.,* (arch.) indenture, channel.

angleu-x, -se, *adj.,* (bot.) imbedded in angular cavities. *Une noix —se ;* a walnut difficult to pick out of its shell.

anglican, -e, *adj.,* Anglican, English. *L'Eglise* —*e ;* the Church of England.

anglican, *n.m.,* -e, *n.f.,* Anglican ; member of the Church of England.

angliciser, *v.a.,* to anglicize.

*s'***angliciser,** *v.r.,* to become anglicized, English.

anglicisme, *n.m.,* anglicism.

anglomane, *n.* and *adj.,* anglomaniac.

anglomanie, *n.f.,* anglomania.

angoisse, *n.f.,* anguish, pang ; great distress, affliction, tribulation. *Les —s de la mort ;* the pangs of death. *Poire d'* — ; choke-pear, gag. *Avaler des poires d'* — ; to go through hardships, to eat humble pie.

⊙**angola.** *V.* **angora.**

angon, *n.m.,* (antiq.) javelin ; (fishing) shell-fish hook.

angora, *n.m.,* Angora-cat.

angora, *adj.,* of Angora.

angousse, *n.f.,* (bot.) hell-weed, dodder.

anguichure (-ghi-shur), *n.f.,* huntsman's horn-belt.

*****anguillade** (-ghi-), *n.f.,* lash ; (with a whip) lashing, cut; eel-skin, &c.

*****anguille** (-ghi-), *n.f.,* eel; fly the garter (boy's game); bilge-ways, launching-ways (square bed of timber placed under a vessel's bilge to support her while launching). — *de mer ;* conger. — *plat-bec ;* grig. *Ecorcher l'* — *par la queue ;* to begin a thing at the wrong end. *Il y a quelque* — *sous roche ;* there is a snake in the grass, there is something in the wind.

angulaire, *adj.*, angular, cornered. *Pierre* —; corner-stone.

angulé, -e, *adj.*, angular, angulated.

anguleu-x, -se, *adj.*, angulous; (bot.) angular.

angusticlave, *n.m.*, (antiq.) angusticlave.

anhydre, *adj.*, (chem.) anhydrous.

anicroche, *n.f.*, obstacle; impediment, slight difficulty; screw loose.

anielles, *n.f. pl.*, ram-stones.

âni-er, *n.m.*, **-ère**, *n.f.*, ass-driver.

anil, *n.m.*, (bot.) anil. *V.* **indigo**.

aniline, *n.f.*, aniline.

anille, *n.f.*, *V.* **annille**.

animadversion, *n.f.*, animadversion, reproof, reprimand, blame.

animal, *n.m.*, animal, beast; brute, ass, booby, sot, dolt. *Un ennuyeux* —; a bore. *Un vilain* —; a nasty fellow.

animal, -e, *adj.*, animal; sensual, carnal (in scriptural language): *Règne* —; the animal kingdom.

animalcule, *n.m.*, animalcule.

animalisation, *n.f.*, animalization.

s'animaliser, *v.r.*, to become animalized.

animalité, *n.f.*, animal life.

animation, *n.f.*, animation, bustle, life, excitement, irritation.

animé, -e, *part.*, animated, incensed; enlivened, spirited, gay, sprightly.

animé, *n.f.*, a resin, anime.

⊙**animelles**, *n.f. pl.*, (cook.) lamb's-fry.

animer, *v.a.*, to animate, to give life; to quicken; to hearten, to stir up, to excite, to urge on, to embolden, to rouse; to provoke, to exasperate. — *la conversation;* to enliven the conversation. — *le teint;* to heighten, to give a glow to, the complexion. — *les yeux, les regards;* to give fire to the eyes, to give animation to the looks. — *d'ardeur;* to fill with ardor. — *au combat;* to excite, to combat.

s'animer, *v.r.*, to become animated, to spring into life; to be encouraged, to take courage, to cheer up; to chafe, to take fire, to grow warm, to be angry. *La dispute s'anime;* the dispute waxes hot.

animosité, *n.f.*, animosity; ill-will, spite, rancor, spleen, animus. *Il a de l'*—, *il est porté d'*—, *contre moi;* he has, he is actuated by, a spite against me.

anis, *n.m.*, anise; aniseed. — *de Verdun;* candied aniseed. — *de la Chine* or *étoilé;* Indian anise. *Graine d'*— ; aniseed.

aniser, *v.a.*, to flavor with aniseed, to mix with aniseed.

anisette, *n.f.*, aniseed cordial.

ankylose, *n.f.*, (med.) anchylosis, stiffness in the joints.

ankyloser, *v.a.*, to produce anchylosis. *S'*—, *v.r.*, to become anchylosed, stiff, cramped.

annal, -e (a-n-nal), *adj.*, (jur.) that lasts but one year.

annales (a-n-nal), *n.f. pl.*, annals, public records.

annaliste (a-n-na-), *n.m.*, annalist.

annate, *n.f.*, annats, first year's income of a living; firstfruits.

anneau, *n.m.*, ring; link (of a chain); bow (of a key); ringlet (of hair); (nav.) mooring-ring. *L'*— *de Saturne;* (astron.) Saturn's ring. *L'*— *pécheur;* the Pope's seal.

année, *n.f.*, year, twelvemonth. — *bissextile;* leap-year. *L'*— *qui vient, l'*— *prochaine;* next year. *D'*— *en* —; from year to year. — *lunaire, solaire;* lunar, solar year. *Une bonne* —; a plentiful year, a happy new year. *Ses belles* —*s;* the prime of life. *Cette terre vaut tant,* — *commune, moyenne,* that land yields so much one year with another. *Une* — *dans l'autre;* one year with another. *Payer à l'*— ; to pay by the year. *Plein d'*—*s;* full of years. *Cette* —; this year.

annelé, -e, *adj.*, ring-streaked, having rings; in ringlets; annulated.

anneler, *v.a.*, to curl the hair (locks or ringlets). — *une cavale;* to ring a mare.

annelet, *n.m.*, ringlet, a small ring; (arch.) annulet.

annélides, *n.m. pl.*, (zool.) annelides.

annelure, *n.f.*, crisping of the hair.

annexe (a-n-nèks), *n.f.*, annex; appendant; schedule; rider; chapel of ease. — *d'une terre;* dependence of an estate.

annexer (a-n-nek-sé), *v.a.*, to annex, to add to. *S'*—, *v.r.*, to be annexed.

annexion (a-n-nek-sion), *n.f.*, annexment, annexation.

annihilation (a-n-ni-), *n.f.*, annihilation.

annihiler (a-n-ni-), *v.a.*, to annihilate, to destroy.

annille, *n.f.*, (her.) anille, fer de moline, millrind; (tech.) cramping-iron.

anniversaire, *adj.*, anniversary.

anniversaire, *n.m.*, anniversary. — *de sa naissance;* birthday.

annomination, *n.f.*, annomination.

loi **annonaire**, *adj.*, (antiq.) a Roman law to prevent the price of provisions from rising.

annonce, *n.f.*, announcement, publication, notification, indication, sign, mark; advertisement; banns of matrimony. *Faiseur d'*—*s;* puffer. *Faire insérer une* —; to advertise. — *de spectacle;* play-bill.

annoncer, *v.a.*, to announce, to tell, to declare, to inform, to proclaim, to bespeak, to advertise; to usher in; to publish, to give out, to preach, to set forth; to foretell, to forebode; to augur, to show, to promise. *Faites vous* —; send in your name. *Cela ne nous annonce rien de bon;* that bodes us no good.

s'annoncer, *v.r.*, to present one's self; to manifest itself; to make itself known. *S'*— *bien;* to be promising. *S'*— *mal;* not to be promising, to begin badly.

annonceur, *n.m.*, the actor who gives out the next play, announcer.

annonciade, *n.f.*, annunciade (name of several military and religious orders).

annonciation, *n.f.*, Annunciation; Lady-day (March 25).

annotateur, *n.m.*, annotator, editor (of a book).

annotation, *n.f.*, annotation, editing; inventory of goods attached or distrained.

annoter (a-n-no-), *v.a.*, to make an inventory of goods attached or distrained ; to annotate; to edit.

annuaire (a-n-nu-èr), *n.m.*, annual, almanac. — *de la marine;* nautical almanac.

annuel, *n.m.*, (c. rel.) a mass celebrated every day for a year, for a deceased person.

annuel, -le (a-n-nu-èl), *adj.*, annual, yearly.

annuellement (a-n-nu-èl-mān), *adv.*, annually, yearly.

annuité (a-n-nu-), *n.f.*, annuity. [ble.

annulable (a-n-nu-), *adj.*, defeasible; reversi-

annulaire (a-n-nu-), *adj.*, annulary. *Le doigt* —; the ring finger.

annulation, *n.f.*, annulling, canceling, repeal, abolition; (jur.) abatement.

annuler, *v.a.*, to annul, to make void, to repeal, to rescind, to cancel, to abolish, to set aside, to quash.

anobli, -e, *part.*, newly raised to the peerage.

anobli, *n.m.*, newly-created nobleman.

anoblir, *v.a.*, to raise to the peerage.

anoblissement (-mān), *n.m.*, ennoblement. *Patente d'*— ; patent of nobility.

anodin, -e, *adj.*, (med.) anodyne, paregoric, soothing, assuaging. *Remèdes* —*s;* anodynes.

anodonte, *adj.*, toothless.

anomal, -e, *adj.*, anomalous.

anomalie, *n.f.,* anomaly.

anomalistique, *adj.,* (astron.) anomalistical. *Année* — ; anomalistical, periodical, year.

anomie, *n.f.,* (conch.) anomia, bowl-shell, beaked-cockle.

ânon, *n.m.,* ass's foal, young ass.

ânonnement (-mān), *n.m.,* stuttering, stammering ; foaling.

ânonner, *v.a.n.,* to falter, to stutter, blunder through a lesson, to stammer, to foal.

anonymat, *n.m.,* the quality of being anonymous ; anonymity.

anonyme, *adj.,* anonymous, nameless; joint-stock.

anonyme, *n.m.f.,* anonymous person. *Garder l'*— ; to remain anonymous. *Sous l'*— ; anonymously.

anorexie, *n.f.,* (med.) anorexy.

anormal, *adj.,* abnormal, irregular.

anse, *n.f.,* handle (of a pot, basket, &c.) ; creek, little bay, cove. *Qui a des* —*s ;* ansated. *Faire danser l'*— *du panier ;* (of a servant), to make a market penny. *L'*— *du panier vaut beaucoup à cette cuisinière ;* that cook makes a good deal by her perquisites. *Faire le pot à deux* —*s ;* to set one's arms a-kimbo. *Faire le panier à deux* —*s ;* to walk with a lady on each arm.

anse. *V.* **hanse.**

anséatique, *adj. V.* **hanséatique.**

ansérine, *n.f.,* (bot.) goose-foot.

anspect, *n.m.,* (nav.) handspike.

antagonisme, *n.m.,* antagonism.

antagoniste, *n.m.,* antagonist, adversary ; opponent ; competitor, rival ; (anat.) antagonist.

antagoniste, *adj.,* antagonist, opponent.

⊙**antan,** *n.m.,* last year. *Les neiges d'*— ; the snows of yester-year.

antanaclase, *n.f.,* antanaclasis.

antarctique, *adj.,* antarctic.

antarès (-ès), *n.m.,* (astron.) Antares.

ante, *n.f.,* (antiq. arch.) anta, pilaster, ante.

antécédemment (-da-mān), *adv.,* antecedently, previously, before.

antécédent, *n.m.,* antecedent ; precedent ; *pl.,* previous conduct. *Avoir de bons* —*s ;* to be known for a person of previous good character.

antécédent, *adj.,* antecedent, preceding, foregoing, previous.

⊙**antécesseur,** *n.m.,* a professor of civil law.

antéchrist (-kri), *n.m.,* antichrist.

antédiluvien, -ne (-in, -è-n), *adj.,* antediluvian.

antéfixe, *n.f.,* (antiq. arch.) antefix.

antenne (-tè-n), *n.f.,* (nav.) lateen sail-yard, yard-arm ; (ent.) *pl.,* horns, feelers.

antépénultième, *adj.,* antepenultimate.

antépénultième, *n.f.,* antepenult.

antérieur, -e, *adj.,* anterior, going before, antecedent, prior, previous ; former ; frontal. *La partie* —*e de la tête ;* the forepart of the head.

antérieurement (-mān), *adv.,* previously, before.

antériorité, *n.f.,* anteriority, priority, precedence.

antes, *n.f. pl.,* (arch.) antæ, pilasters.

anthelminthique, *adj.,* (med.) anthelmintic.

anthère, *n.f.,* (bot.) anther, tip.

anthologie, *n.f.,* anthology.

anthracite, *n.m.,* anthracite; coal-stone, glance-coal, blind-coal.

anthrax (-traks), *n.m.,* (med.) anthrax, carbuncle.

anthropographie, *n.f.,* anthropography.

anthropologie, *n.f.,* anthropology.

anthropologique, *adj.,* anthropological.

anthropomorphe, *adj.,* anthropomorphous.

anthropomorphisme, *n.m.,* anthropomorphism.

anthropomorphite, *n.m.,* anthropomorphite.

anthropophage, *adj.,* anthropophagous.

anthropophage, *n.m.f.,* anthropophagus, cannibal, man-eater.

anthropophagie, *n.f.,* anthropophagy, cannibalism.

anthyllide, *n.f.,* (bot.) kidney-vetch, Jupiter's beard.

anti (prefix from Greek ἀντὶ), anti, against, opposite, contrary ; (prefix from Latin *ante*) before.

antiapoplectique, *adj.,* antapoplectic, antiapoplectic.

antibiblique, *adj.,* unscriptural.

antibilieux, -se, *adj.,* antibilious.

antichambre, *n.f.,* antechamber, anteroom, lobby, hall. *Propos d'*— ; servant's gossip. *Faire* — ; to dance attendance.

antichrèse (-krèz), *n.f.,* (jur.) pledge ; mortgage.

antichrétien, -ne (-ti-in, -ti-è-n), *adj.,* antichristian.

antichristianisme, *n.m.,* antichristianity, antichristianism.

anticipation, *n.f.,* anticipation, forestalling ; encroachment, invasion. *Par* — ; anticipatory, beforehand.

anticipé, -e, *part. adj.,* anticipated. *Joie* —*e;* foretaste of joy. *Connaissance* —*e ;* foreknowledge. *Une vieillesse* —*e ;* a premature old age.

anticiper, *v.a.,* to anticipate, to take up beforehand or before the time, to forestall. — *sur les droits de quelqu'un ;* to encroach upon another's rights. — *sur ses revenus ;* to spend one's income beforehand, or to draw upon.

anticœur, *n.m.,* anticor (inflammation in a horse's throat.

antidartreu-x, -se, *adj.,* (med.) antiherpetic.

antidate, *n.f.,* antedate, antedating.

antidater, *v.a.,* to antedate.

antidotaire, *n.m.,* antidotarium (a book containing a collection of antidotes).

antidote, *n.m.,* antidote, counter-poison.

antienne (-ti-è-n), *n.f.,* anthem. *Annoncer une mauvaise* — ; to bring bad news. *Chanter toujours la même* — ; to harp upon the same string. *Pousser l'*— *à quelqu'un ;* to state one's wishes, one's opinion ; to give a broad hint.

antiépileptique, *adj.,* antiepileptic.

antiépiscopal, -e, *adj.,* antiepiscopal.

antiévangélique, *adj.,* antievangelical.

antifébrile, *n.m.,* antifebrile.

antigorium (-riom), *n.m.,* coarse enamel, glazing.

antigoutteux, -se, *adj.,* (med.) antarthritic.

antilaiteu-x, -se, *adj.* and *n.m.,* antilactic, lactifuge.

antilogie, *n.f.,* antilogy.

antiloïmique, *adj.,* (med.) antiloimic.

antilope, *n.f.,* antelope, gazelle.

antimoine, *n.m.,* antimony.

antimonarchique, *adj.,* antimonarchical.

antimonial, -e, *adj.,* antimonial.

antimonié, *n.m.,* antimonial.

antimonié, -e, *adj.,* antimonial.

antinational, -e, *adj.,* antinational.

antinomie, *n.f.,* antinomy, contradiction.

antipape, *n.m.,* antipope.

antiparalytique, *n.m.,* antiparalytic.

antipathie, *n.f.,* antipathy, repugnance.

antipathique, *adj.,* antipathetical, repugnant.

antipéristaltique, *adj.,* antiperistaltic.

antipéristase, *n.f.,* antiperistasis.

antipestilentiel, le, *adj.,* antipestilential.

antiphilosophique, *adj.,* antiphilosophical.

⊙**antiphlogistique,** *adj.,* antiphlogistic.

antiphone, *n.m.,* antiphon.

antiphonier or **antiphonaire,** *n. m.,* antiphonary.

antiphrase, *n.f.,* antiphrasis, irony.

⊙**antipodal, -e,** *adj.,* antipodal, antipodean.

antipode, *n.m.,* antipode.

antipsorique, *adj.*, antipsoric (against the itch).

antipsorique, *n.m.*, antipsoric.

antiptose, *n.f.*, (gram.) antiptosis.

antiputride, *adj.*, antiseptic.

*****antiquaille**, *n.f.*, old piece of antiquity; old stuff; old rubbish; an old coquette. *Ce n'est qu'une —*; she is but an antiquated coquette.

antiquaire, *n.m.*, antiquary.

antique, *adj.*, antique, ancient, old.

antique, *n.f.*, antique, antiquities, ancient works, of art. *A l'—, adv.*, in the old style. *Dessiner d'après —*; to draw from antique models.

antiquer, *v.a.*, (book-bind.) to adorn the edges of books with little figures, &c.

antiquité, *n.f.*, antiquity, ancientness, old times; piece of antiquity. *Les héros de l'—*; the heroes of former ages. *De toute —, adv.*, from the remotest times.

antiscien (-si-in), *n.m.*, (geog.) antiscian.

antiscorbutique, *adj.* and *n.m.*, antiscorbutic.

antiseptique, *n.m.*, (med.) antiseptic.

antisocial, **-e**, *adj.*, anti-social.

antispase, *n.f.*, (med.) antispasis.

antispasmodique, *n.m.*, antispasmodic.

antispaste, *n.m.*, antispast.

antispastique, *adj.*, antispastic.

antistrophe, *n.f.*, antistrophe.

antisyphilitique, *adj.*, antisyphilitic.

antithèse, *n.f.*, antithesis.

antithétique, *adj.*, antithetic.

antitrinitaire, *n.m.*, antitrinitarian, unitarian.

⊙**antitype**, *n.m.*, antitype, symbol.

antivénérien, **-ne**, (-in, -è-n), *adj.*, antivenereal.

antoiser, *v.a.*, to heap up, to manure, to make a dunghill.

antonomase, *n.f.*, antonomasia.

antre, *n.m.*, cave, den, natural grotto, cavern, lair.

anuer, *v.a.*, to aim, to take aim at.

*s'***anuiter**, *v.r.*, to be benighted, to stay till it is night, or too late (on the road).

anus, *n.m.*, (anat., bot.) anus, fundament.

anvoie, *n.m.*, slow-worm, blind-worm.

anxiété (ank-si-), *n.f.*, anxiety, sorrow, anguish, uneasiness.

anxieu-x, **-se** (ank-si-), *adj.*, anxious, uneasy, restless.

anxieusement, *adv.*, anxiously.

aoriste (-o-rist), *n.m.*, (gram.) aorist.

aorte, *n.f.*, (anat.) aorta.

aortique, *adj.*, aortal.

août (oû), *n.m.*, August. *La mi-août;* the middle of August. *Faire l'—*; to harvest, to get in the corn.

aoûté, **-e**, *adj.*, ripened by the heat of August.

*s'***aoûter** (a-ou-té), *v.r.*, to ripen (in August).

aoûteron (ou-tron), *n.m.*, (l. u.) reaper, harvester.

a.p., (com.) abbreviation of the words *à protester;* to be protested.

apagogie, *n.f.*, apagogy.

apaisement, *n.m.*, appeasement, lull, abatement.

apaiser, *v.a.*, to appease, to soothe, to pacify, to calm, to quiet, to alleviate; to assuage, to allay, to quench, to mitigate, to lull. *— un enfant qui crie;* to quiet a crying child. *— une révolte;* to put down a rebellion. *— les flots;* to calm the waves.

*s'***apaiser**, *v.r.*, to be appeased, stilled, assuaged, &c.; to allay one's passion, to grow quiet, calm; to abate, subside. *Sa colère s'est apaisée;* his anger is appeased. *L'orage s'est apaisé;* the storm has subsided. *Le vent s'est apaisé;* the wind has abated.

apalachine, *n.f.*, (bot.) emetic holly.

apalanche, *n.f.*, (bot.) winter-berry.

apanage, *n.m.*, appanage; lot. *Les infirmités sont l'— de la nature humaine;* infirmities are the lot of human nature.

apanager, *v.a.*, to settle an appanage upon any one, to endow.

apanagiste, *adj.*, having an appanage.

apanagiste, *n.m.*, one who has an appanage.

apanthropie, *n.f.*, apanthropy.

à part. *V.* **part.**

aparté, *n.m.*, words spoken aside; separate group in an assembly. *En —, adv.*, aside.

apathie, *n.f.*, apathy, indolence, listlessness.

apathique, *adj.*, apathetic, listless.

apepsie, *n.f.*, (med.) bad digestion, apepsy.

apercevable, *adj.*, perceivable, perceptible.

apercevance, *n.f.*, perception.

apercevoir, *v.a.*, to perceive, to discover, to discern, to descry, to notice; to remark, to observe.

*s'***apercevoir**, *v.r.*, to perceive, to remark; to see, to be aware of; to find out, to discover; to take notice, to be visible. *Ne pas s'—*; to overlook, not to notice.

aperçu, *n.m.*, sketch, rapid view, glance, survey, sketch, vista; idea, hint; estimate at first sight, rough estimate. *En —, adv.*, summarily. *Par —, adv.*, at a rough guess.

apériti-f, **-ve**, *adj.*, aperient, opening, appetizing. *— n.m.*, appetizer, bitters.

apétale, *adj.*, (bot.) apetalous.

apetissement, &c. *V.* **rapetissement**, &c.

apetisser. *V.* **rapetisser**.

à peu près, *n.m.*, approximation, approach, approaching.

aphélie, *n.m.*, (astron.) aphelion.

aphérèse, *n.f.*, (gram.) apheresis.

aphone, *adj.*, suffering from aphonia, voiceless.

aphonie, *n.f.*, aphony, loss of speech.

aphorisme, *n.m.*, aphorism.

aphoristique, *adj.*, aphoristic.

aphrodisiaque, *adj.*, aphrodisiacal.

aphrodisiasme, *n.m.*, (med.) aphrodisia.

aphrodite, *n.m.*, aphrodita, sea-mouse.

aphte, *n.m.*, vesicle in the mouth; *pl.*, thrush, aphthæ.

aphylle, *adj.*, (bot.) aphyllous, leafless.

api, *n.m.*, small red apple. *Avoir un visage de pomme d'—*; (prov.) to have cheeks like rosy apples.

à pic, *adv.*, perpendicularly; (nav.) apeak. *L'ancre est —*; the anchor is apeak. *Virer —*; to heave short.

apicole, *adj.*, apicultural.

apiculteur, *n.m.*, bee-master.

apiculture, *n.f.*, bee-culture, bee-keeping.

apiquer, *v.a.*, (nav.) to top, to peak (a yard).

apitoyer, *v.a.*, to move one to pity, to soften.

*s'***apitoyer**, *v.r.*, to be moved to pity. *Elle s'est apitoyée sur votre sort;* she pitied, bewailed your fate.

aplani, **-e**, *adj.*, level, flat, smooth, even.

aplanir, *v.a.*, to smooth, to level, to make even, smooth, to unrumple; to plane; to make easy, to remove, to clear up. *— le chemin;* to level the road. *— les difficultés;* to clear up difficulties.

*s'***aplanir**, *v.r.*, to grow easy, smooth, flat, &c.

aplanissement (-mǎn), *n.m.*, smoothing, leveling, making even; smoothness, evenness.

aplatir, *v.a.*, to flatten, to make, strike flat, to flat, to silence, to shut up, to floor, to beat hollow.

*s'***aplatir**, *v.r.*, to become flat, to be flattened, to crouch, to cringe.

aplatissement (-mǎn), *n.m.*, flattening, making flat, flatness; depression; silencing.

aplatisseur, *n.m.*, (tech.) flatter.

aplatissoire, *n.f.*, flatting rollers (tool).

aplet, *n.m.*, herring-net, drift-net.

aplomb, *n.m.*, equilibrium, perpendicularity, plumb; assurance, self-command, self-possession, steadiness, coolness. *Ce mur tient bien son —;* this wall keeps plumb very well.

d'aplomb, *adv.*, perpendicularly, plumb. *Cette ligne tombe d'—;* that line falls plumb. *Être d'—;* to stand plumb, upright. *Être hors d'—;* to be out of the perpendicular.

aplysie, *n.f.*, sea-hare.

apocalypse, *n.f.*, Apocalypse, revelation; obscure thing. *C'est un vrai style d'—;* it is a perfectly obscure style. *Cheval d'—;* (prov. and pop.) sorry jade.

apocalyptique, *adj.*, apocalyptical.

apoco, *n.m.*, fool, ninny, nobody.

apocope, *n.f.*, (gram.) apocope, elision, suppression of a letter (as in *Grand'mère*).

apocrisiaire, *n.m.*, nuncio, apocrisiary.

apocryphe, *adj.*, apocryphal, doubtful.

apocyn, *n.m.*, (bot.) apocynum, apocynom. *— gobe-mouches;* dog-bane.

apode, *adj.*, apodal, having no feet, footless.

apode, *n.m.*, apode.

apodictique, *adj.*, apodictical, evident.

apogée, *n.m.*, apogee, acme, height, zenith.

apogée, *adj.*, at its apogee. *La lune est —;* the moon is at her apogee.

apographe, *n.m.*, apograph, transcript, copy.

apologétique, *adj.*, by way of apology, apologetical, exculpatory.

apologétique, *n.m.*, Tertullian's treatise in defense of the early Christians; *n.f.*, apologetics.

apologie, *n.f.*, apology, vindication, excuse, justification. *Faire son —;* to apologize for.

apologiste, *n.m.*, apologist.

apologue (-log), *n.m.*, apologue.

aponévrose, *n.f.*, (anat.) aponeurosis.

aponévrotique, *adj.*, (anat.) aponeurotic.

apophlegmatique, *adj. n.m.*, (med.) apophlegmatic.

apophtegme, *n.m.*, apophthegm, apothegm.

apophyge, *n.f.*, (arch.) apophyge, scape, the spring of a column.

apophyse, *n.f.*, (anat.) process (of a bone), apophysis.

apoplectique, *adj.*, apoplectical; apoplectic.

apoplectique, *n.m.*, apoplectic.

apoplexie, *n.f.*, apoplexy. *— foudroyante;* instantaneously fatal apoplexy. *— congestive;* serous apoplexy. *Attaque d'—;* apoplectic stroke. *Être attaqué, frappé, d'—;* to be struck down with apoplexy. *Tomber en —;* to fall down in a fit of apoplexy.

apostasie, *n.f.*, apostasy.

apostasier, *v.n.*, to apostatize.

apostat, *adj.*, apostate.

apostat, *n.m.*, apostate.

⊙**apostème**, *n.m.*, apasteme. *V.* **apostume**.

aposter, *v.a.*, (b.s.) to secrete, to place in ambush, to station, to set to watch, to place in readiness (witnesses, assassins).

à posteriori, *adv.*, a posteriori.

⊙*****apostillateur**, *n.m.*, (jur.), annotator, commentator.

*****apostille**, *n.f.*, marginal note, postscript, footnote; recommendatory note (to urge or back a petition).

*****apostiller**, *v.a.*, to write notes; to add a postscript to; to write a recommendation on a petition. *Il a apostillé ma pétition;* he has backed my petition with his recommendation.

apostolat, *n.m.*, apostleship.

apostolique, *adj.*, apostolic; papal; apostolical. *Nonce —;* the pope's nuncio.

apostoliquement (-măn), *adv.*, apostolically.

apostrophe, *n.f.*, apostrophe; address; reproach, insult, attack.

apostropher, *v.a.*, to apostrophize, to address, to fall foul of, to fly at.

⊙**apostume**, *n.m.*, (med.) aposteme, apostema, abscess.

⊙**apostumer**, *v.n.*, (med.) to apostemate.

apothéose, *n.f.*, apotheosis, deification.

apothicaire, *n.m.*, (l.u.), apothecary. *Faire de son corps une boutique d'—;* to be always physicking one's self. *Un mémoire d'—;* an exorbitant bill.

apothicairerie (-kèr-rĭ), *n.f.* (l.u.), pharmacy; apothecary's shop; dispensary.

apothicairesse, *n.f.*, (in nunneries) dispenser.

apôtre, *n.m.*, apostle; hypocrite. *Faire le bon —;* to play the saint; to put on a sanctified look.

apozème, *n.m.*, (med.) apozem, decoction.

apparaître, *v.n.*, to come, to be in sight, to appear suddenly. (jurisp.) *S'il apparaît à la cour;* if the court thinks so. *Faire — de son pouvoir;* to produce proofs of one's power.

apparat, *n.m.*, pomp, state, show; ostentation, affectation, parade; index, vocabulary, syllabus. *Un discours d'—;* a set speech.

apparaux, *n.m. pl.*, (nav.) the sails, the rigging, the tackle, yards, guns, &c., of a ship.

*****appareil**, *n.m.*, formal preparation, pomp, show, display, solemnity, magnificence; train, equipage, attendance; apparatus; (surg.) dressing (of wounds); (arch.) dressing; (nav.) gear. *— de guerre;* warlike preparations. *Mettre le premier —;* to give a wound its first dressing. *Lever l'—;* to take off the dressing. *Une assise de haut —;* a layer of large stones; (phot.) camera; *— instantané,* snapshot camera.

*****appareillage**, *n.m.*, (nav.) act of getting under sail, under way.

*****appareillement**, *n.m.*, yoking, pairing, matching. *L'— des bœufs;* the yoking of oxen.

*****appareiller**, *v.a.*, to match; (arch.) to dress.

*****s'appareiller**, *v.r.*, to join one's self to; to pair.

*****appareiller**, *v.n.*, (nav.) to weigh anchor, to get under way. [(of stones); draughtsman.

*****appareilleur**, *n.m.*, (mas.) dresser, trimmer

*****appareilleuse**, *n.f.*, procuress.

apparemment (-ra-măn), *adv.*, apparently.

apparence, *n.f.*, appearance, outside show, seeming; likelihood, probability; sign, semblance. *En —;* seemingly, apparently, outwardly. *Pour les —s;* for show. *Avoir une belle —;* to look well. *Selon toute —;* in all probability; to all appearances. *Sauver les —s;* to save appearances.

apparent, -e, *adj.*, apparent, plain, obvious, manifest, evident; remarkable, chief, eminent, considerable.

apparenté, -e, *adj.*, related, descended, connected. *Il est bien —;* he is well descended. *Il est mal —;* he is of mean descent.

apparenter, *v.a.*, (l.u.) to ally, to connect by marriage.

s'apparenter, *v.r.*, to ally one's self (by marriage).

appariement, or **appariment**, *n.m.*, pairing, matching; coupling, mating.

apparier, *v.a.*, to pair, to sort, to match; to match horses, gloves.

s'apparier, *v.r.*, to couple, to pair.

appariteur, *n.m.*, apparitor, assistant, bedel (in universities); beadle.

apparition, *n.f.*, apparition, appearance, appearing. *— d'anges;* a vision of angels.

apparoir, *v.n.*, to appear, to be evident. *Comme il appert;* as it appears.

appartement, *n.m.*, apartments, suite of rooms, lodgings, flat. *Pièce d'un —;* room, apartment.

appartenance, *n.f.*, appurtenance.

appartenant, -e, *adj.*, belonging, appertaining.

appartenir, *v.n.*, to belong, to appertain; to relate, to concern; to behove, to be incident, to be related, to be given to.

s'appartenir, v.r., to be master of one's own actions, to be free.

il appartient (-ti-in), v. imp., it becomes; it is meet, fit; it is the duty, business of. *Ainsi qu'il appartiendra;* as they shall see fit. *A tous ceux qu'il appartiendra;* to all whom it may concern.

appas, n.m. pl., charms, attractions; allurements.

appât, n.m., bait; allurement, enticement. *C'est trop vieux poisson pour mordre à l'—;* he is too old a bird to be caught with chaff.

appâter, v.a., to bait, to allure; to feed (an infant or an invalid).

appaumé, adj., (her.) apaumé.

appauvrir, v.a., to impoverish; to make poor, to beggar.

s'appauvrir, v.r., to grow poor, to become impoverished, to be beggared.

appauvrissement (-măn), n.m., impoverishment.

appeau, n.m., bird-call; decoy-bird; (horol.) quarter-bell, half-bell.

appel, n.m., appeal, appealing; calling over; levy (recruiting); call (on shareholders); roll-call, muster; ruffle (of a drum); (jur.) call. *Acte d'—;* writ of appeal. *— nominal;* (parliament) call of the House. *Officier d'—;* mustermaster. *Interjeter—;* to lodge an appeal. *Faire l'—;* to call over the names, the muster-roll. *Manquer à l'—;* to be absent from call-call. *Passer l'—;* to pass muster. *Répondre à l'—;* to answer to one's name. *Battre l'—;* to call to arms. *Faire un —de fonds;* to call in one's funds.

appelant, -e (-lăn, -t), n.m.f., (jur.) appellant; (ornith.) decoy-bird.

appelé, -e, part., called. *Beaucoup d'—s et peu d'élus;* many are called, but few are chosen.

appeler, v.a., to call, to name, to appeal; to chuck (of cocks); to term; to call over; to give a call, to call to; to invoke; to send for; to invite; to summon; to call for, to call on (cause); to challenge. *Comment appelez-vous cela?* what do you call that? *— et rappeler;* to call over and over, again and again. *— en duel;* to call out. *— un médecin;* to call in a physician. *Faire —;* to send for. *— les choses par leur nom;* to call a spade a spade. *Voilà ce que j'appelle pleuvoir;* that is rain with a vengeance.

appeler, v.n., to appeal, to chuck (of cocks); to caterwaul (of cats). *En—;* (jur.) to appeal. *J'en appelle à votre honneur;* I appeal to your honor.

s'appeler, v.r., to be called, to call, to style one's self. *Comment s'appelle cet homme-là?* what is that man's name? *Je m'appelle;* my name is.

appellatif (-pèl-la-), adj., (gram.) appellative.

appellation (-pèl-la-), n.f., appealing, calling, naming, appellation.

appendice (-pin-), n.m., appendix, appendage, addition; process (natural sciences).

appendre, v.a., to hang up.

appentis, n.m., shed, penthouse.

il appert, v.imp. V. **apparoir**.

⊙**appertement**, adv., openly.

appesantir, v.a., to make heavy, to weigh down; to impair, to dull, to make dull.

s'appesantir, v.r., to grow heavy and dull, to be weighed down, to lie heavy; to dwell upon, expatiate on.

appesantissement (-măn), n.m., heaviness, dulness.

appétence (ap-pé-), n.f., appetence, appetency.

appéter, v.a., to desire, to crave for, to covet.

appétibilité, n.f., appetibility, desire.

appétible, adj., appetible, desirable.

appétissant, -e, adj., relishing, appetizing, tempting; delicious, desirable.

appétit, n.m., appetite, relish, desire, longing; inclination, taste; stomach. *De bon —;* heartily. *—de cheval;* ravenous appetite. *Bon—! I* wish you a good appetite. *Avoir de l'—;* to have an appetite. *Être sans —;* to have no appetite. *L'— vient en mangeant;* the more one has, the more one wishes to have. *Il n'est chère que d'—;* hunger is the best sauce. *Rester sur son —;* to check one's appetite, inclination. *—de femme grosse;* depraved appetite, longing. *Pain dérobé réveille—;* stolen joys are sweet.

appétiti-f, -ve, adj., appetitive.

appétition, n.f., appetition, desire for.

applaudir, v.n.a., to applaud, to clap, to clap the hands, to cheer; to praise, to commend, to approve. *— un acteur;* to applaud an actor. *Je vous applaudis de vous être conduit si prudemment;* I commend you for having acted so prudently. *Applaudi de tout le monde;* applauded by everybody.

s'applaudir, v.r., to applaud one's self for, to glory in (a thing); to congratulate one's self (on), to rejoice (in or at). *Il s'applaudit lui-même;* he admires himself.

applaudissement (-măn), n.m., applause, public praise, commendation; plaudits, cheering. *Salve d'—s;* round of applause, of cheering.

applaudisseur, n.m., (b.s.) applauder.

applicable, adj., applicable, apposite, relevant, suitable.

application, n.f., application, employment (of a sum of money); attention, care, diligence, sedulousness; (gold.) charging; appliqué lace. *Avec —;* sedulously. *Sans —délibérée;* unappropriated. *D'—;* practical, feasible. *—d'Angleterre;* Honiton lace. *Bras d'—;* bracket.

applique, n.f., (gold.) charging.

appliqué, -e, adj., intent, sedulous, studious, diligent, attentive.

appliquer, v.a., to apply, to stick; to award (judgment); to employ (money); to put, to set, to affix, to bring close; to adapt, to fit; to apply to, to appropriate; to bestow on, to hit, to strike. *— des ventouses;* to cup. *— mal à propos;* to misapply.

s'appliquer, v.r., to apply a thing to one's self, to take it for one's self; to apply one's self, to fall to, to set to, to take to, to labor at, to make it one's study; to stick to.

appoint, n.m., change, odd money, premium; appoint. *Net—;* appoint. *Par net—;* per appoint. *Faire l'—;* to pay the difference. *D'—;* odd.

appointements (-măn), n.m. pl., salary, stipend.

appointer, v.a., to put, to give a salary to; to punish (in the army); to sew strips of cloth, to stitch (as a mattress, cloth); (juris.) to refer, have a referee. *Commis appointé;* salaried clerk.

appointer, v.a., to point, sharpen to a point.

⊙**appointeur**, n.m., (juris.) referee.

appointement, n.m., temporary wooden bridge; (nav.) gang-way, ladder.

apport, n.m., material brought, quantity brought, documents deposited; personal property; share; contribution.

apporter, v.a., to bring; to bring forward; to cause, to bring to bear upon, to procure, to occasion; to use, to cite, to quote, to allege; to adduce, to produce. *— des difficultés;* to raise difficulties. *— de la précaution;* to use precaution. *— de bonnes raisons;* to adduce good reasons. *— des soins à;* to bestow care upon.

apportionner, v.a., to apportion.

apposer, v.a., to set, to put, to insert, to affix.

apposition, n.f., setting, putting, inserting; affixing; accretion; (gram.) apposition. *Faire l'— des scellés;* to affix the seals.

appréciable, adj., appreciable, perceptible.

appréciat-eur, *n.m.*, **-rice**, *n.f.*, valuer, appraiser, rater.

appréciati-f, -ve, *adj.*, denoting the value of. *Etat, devis* —; estimate.

appréciation, *n.f.*, appreciation, apprizement, rating, valuation, estimation.

apprécier, *v.a.*, to value, to rate, to estimate, to judge; to appreciate, to esteem.

appréhender, *v.a.*, to apprehend, to be apprehensive of, to fear; to arrest, to take up. *— au corps;* to arrest.

appréhensible, *adj.*, apprehensible.

appréhensi-f, -ve, *adj.*, timid.

appréhension, *n.f.*, apprehension; fear, dread. *Avoir des —s;* to be under apprehension.

apprendre, *v.a.*, to learn, to be informed of; to hear of; to teach; to train: to tell, to inform of, to advise, to let know. *— par cœur;* to learn by heart. *— des nouvelles;* to hear news. *Je l'ai appris de bonne part;* I have it from good authority. *Il m'a appris l'algèbre;* he taught me algebra. *Faire — un métier à un enfant;* to put a child to a trade. *Je lui apprendrai qui je suis;* I will let him know who I am. *Les malheurs s'apprennent vite;* ill news flies fast.

apprenti, *n.m.*, **-e**, *n.f.*, apprentice; novice, tyro. *Obliger un —;* to bind an apprentice.

apprenti, -e, *adj.*, apprenticed, articled.

apprentissage, *n.m.*, apprenticeship, trial, experiment. *Etre en —;* to be an apprentice. *Faire son —;* to serve one's apprenticeship. *Mettre en —;* to apprentice, to article. *Brevet d'—;* apprentice's indentures. *Sortir d'—;* to finish one's time.

apprêt, *n.m.*, preparation, preparative; cooking, (manu.) dressing; painting on glass; stiffness, affectation. *Faire de grands —s;* to make great preparations. *Sans —;* unstudied (of style).

apprêtage, *n.m.*, (manu.) dressing; finishing.

apprêté, -e, *part.*, prepared, dressed; studied. *Des manières apprêtées;* affected manners.

apprêter, *v.a.*, to prepare, to get ready; to cook; (manu.) to dress; to afford matter for. *— un chapeau;* to dress a hat. *— à dîner;* to prepare dinner. *— à rire;* to afford matter for laughter.

s'apprêter, *v.r.*, to prepare one's self, to make one's self ready, to dress; to be in course of preparation, to be brewing.

⊙**apprêteur**, *n.m.*, painter upon glass.

apprêteu-r, *n.m.*, **-se**, *n.f.* (manu.) dresser.

appris, -e, *part.*, learned, taught. *Bien —;* well-bred. *Mal —;* ill-bred. *Un mal —;* an ill-bred or an unmannerly fellow.

apprivoisement (-voaz-män), *n.m.*, taming.

apprivoiser, *v.a.*, to tame (animals); to make sociable, tractable, (persons); (hunt.) to reclaim.

s'apprivoiser, *v.r.*, to be tamed, to grow tame (of animals); to become sociable, to lose one's shyness (of persons).

approbat-eur, *n.m.*, **-rice**, *n.f.*, approver, applauder.

approbat-eur, -rice, *adj.*, approving, commending.

approbati-f, -ve, *adj.*, approving. *Geste —;* nod of approbation.

approbation, *n.f.*, approbation, consent; approval. *Incliner la tête en signe d'—;* to nod assent, approval.

approbativement (-män), *adv.*, approvingly, with approbation.

approchant, -e, *adj.*, (fam.) something like; like, bordering upon, approximate; near allied, near akin.

approchant, *prep.*, (l.u. fam.) near, about. *Il a reçu dix mille francs —;* he received about ten thousand francs.

approche, *n.f.*, approach, access; coming, advance; (print.) space, closing up. *Lunette d'—;* spy-glass. *Greffe en —;* graft by approach.

approcher, *v.a.*, to bring, put, or draw near; to bring, put, or draw close; to have access (to any one). *Approchez la table du feu;* draw the table near the fire.

approcher, *v.n.*, to approach, to draw nigh or near, to come near, to be easy of access; to be something like. *Il me fit — de lui;* he made me come near him. *— du but;* to come near the mark. *Ceci n'en approche pas;* this does not come near it.

s'approcher, *v.r.*, to approach, to draw near, to come near, to advance. *Approchez-vous du feu;* draw near the fire.

approfondi, -e, *adj.*, deep, profound; thorough, reasoned out.

approfondir, *v.a.*, to deepen, to make deeper; to examine thoroughly; to search, dive into, to fathom. *— une question;* to sift, to fathom a question.

approfondissement, *n.m.*, deepening, sinking lower; fathoming.

appropriation, *n.f.*, appropriation, assimilation; (jur.) conversion.

approprier, *v.a.*, to appropriate, to accommodate, to adapt, to fit, to suit; to clean, to make neat, to tidy. *— une chambre;* to make a room tidy. *— son langage aux circonstances;* to adapt one's language to circumstances.

s'approprier, *v.r.*, to appropriate a thing to one's self, to convert to one's own use.

approuver, *v.a.*, to approve, to approve of, to sanction, to consent to; to ratify, to authorize; to pass (accounts).

approvisionnement (-zio-n-män), *n.m.*, victualing; supply of provisions, stock. *Vaisseau d'—;* (nav.) victualing ship.

approvisionner, *v.a.*, to supply with necessaries; to victual, to cater for, to stock.

s'approvisionner, *v.r.*, to supply one's self; to lay in, take in supplies.

approvisionneur, *n.m.*, victualer, provider, caterer, purveyor.

approximati-f, -ve, *adj.*, approximative.

approximation, *n.f.*, approximation, rough guess. *Détermination par —;* (math.) approximation. [matively.

approximativement (-män) *adv.*, approxi-
⊙**approximer**, *v.a.*, to approximate.

appui, *n.m.*, prop, stay, support, rest; help, protection; buttress, rail, hand-rail, sill (of windows); rail (of stairs); (man.) appui; (mec.) fulcrum. *A hauteur d'—;* breast-high. *Point d'—;* point of support, prop, fulcrum, base. *A l'— de;* in support of, in confirmation of. *Sans —;* unsupported, friendless. *Il est l'— des malheureux;* he is the support of the unfortunate. *Ce cheval a l'— bon;* that horse is soft-mouthed. *Aller à l'— de;* to support (a proposal).

appui-main, *n.m.*, (—s— —) painter's maulstick, hand-rest.

appui-queue, *n.m.*, rest (at billiards), jigger.

appuyer, *v.a.*, to prop up, to stay, to support, to second; to hold up, to sustain; to set upon; to lean upon; to ground, to found; to back, to stand by; to favor, to countenance; to protect; to enforce, to strengthen. *— une maison contre un coteau;* to build a house against a hill. *— le coude sur la table;* to lean one's elbow upon the table. *Son droit est appuyé sur de bons titres;* his claim is founded on just grounds. *Il m'a promis d'— mon placet;* he has promised to back my petition. *— les chiens;* to urge on the hounds.

appuyer, *v.n.*, to bear upon, to lean; to rest; to lay a stress on; to dwell upon; to insist upon, to urge. *— sur un mot;* to lay a stress on a word. *— sur un passage;* to dwell upon a passage. *— sur la droite, la gauche, on à droite, à gauche;* to bear to the right, the left. *Ce cheval appuie sur le mors;* that horse hangs on the bit.

s'appuyer, *v.r.*, to lean, to lean upon ; to lie, to rest, to recline upon ; to confide in, to rely upon, to depend upon, to trust to ; to lay a stress on, to dwell upon. *Appuyez-vous sur moi ;* lean upon me. — *sur un roseau ;* (fig.) to trust to a broken reed.

âpre, *adj.*, rough, harsh ; tart, sharp ; hard, rugged, uneven ; biting, cutting, bitter ; severe ; crabbed, peevish ; violent, greedy, eager. *Chemin — et raboteux ;* rough, rugged way. — *au gain ;* greedy of gain. — *au jeu ;* eager for play (a born gambler). — *à se venger ;* eager for revenge. — *à la curée ;* eager for prey (of animals) ; greedy of gain (of persons).

aprèle, *n.f.*, (bot.) horse-tail.

âprement, *adv.*, harshly, sharply, roughly, rigorously ; severely ; peevishly, crabbedly ; gruffly ; violently, eagerly, greedily.

après, *prep.*, after, next to ; about ; next. *Sa maison vient — la vôtre ;* his house is next to yours. *Il est toujours — moi ;* he is always after me, always teasing, persecuting, scolding me. *Etre — quelque chose ;* to be in pursuit of something. *On est — ;* it is being done. *Soupirer — quelque chose ;* to long for anything. *Ne pas attendre — quelqu'un ;* not to need, to be able to do without any one. — *lui, il faut tirer l'échelle ;* no one can come after him. — *coup ;* too late. *Crier — quelqu'un ;* to scold anybody. *Tout le monde crie — lui ;* everybody cries out against him. *Ci — ;* hereafter, in the sequel. — *quoi ;* after which. *D'— ;* after, from, according to, following. *Peindre d'— nature ;* to paint from nature. — *tout ;* after all. *Jeter le manche — la cognée ;* to throw the helve after the hatchet (or to give up in despair).

après, *adv.*, afterwards, after ; go on ; what next, what then ? *Vous arrivâtes malade ; — ?* you say you were ill after you arrived ; and what then ?

après que, *conj.*, after, when. — — *vous aurez fait ;* after you have done. — — *je l'eus vu ;* when I had seen him.

après-demain, *adv.*, the day after to-morrow.

⊙**après-dînée**, *n.f.*, (— - —*s*) **après-diné**, *n.m.*, '(— - —*s*) after dinner, afternoon.

après-dîner, *n.m.*, (— - —*s*) after dinner, afternoon.

après-midi, *n.m.f.*, (—) afternoon.

⊙**après-soupée**, *n.f.*, (— - —*s*) **après-soupé**, *n.m.*, (— - —*s*) between supper and bedtime ; evening.

après-souper, *n.m.*, (— - —*s*) between supper and bedtime, evening.

âpreté, *n.f.*, harshness, tartness, sharpness ; roughness, ruggedness ; acrimony, asperity ; violence, fierceness, severity ; eagerness ; greediness. — *à l'argent ;* lust of gold.

à priori. *V.* **priori.**

à propos, *adj., adv. ;* **à-propos**, *n.m. V.* **propos.**

apside, *n.f.*, (apsides, apses) (astron.) apsis.

apte, *adj.*, apt, fit, proper, qualified.

aptère, *n.m.*, apter.

aptère, *adj.*, apteral, apterous.

aptitude, *n.f.*, aptitude, aptness, qualification, disposition ; readiness, inclination, taste.

apurement (-mān), *n.m.*, auditing, closing (of accounts).

apurer, *v.a.*, to audit (accounts).

apyre, *adj.*, apyrous, incombustible, fire-proof.

apyrexie, *n.f.*, (med.) apyrexy.

aquarelle (-koua-), *n.f.*, painting in water-colors, aquarelle, water-color drawing.

aquarelliste, *n.m.*, painter in water colors.

aquarium, *n.m.*, (—*s*) aquarium.

aqua-tinta (—), or **aquatinte** (-koua-), (—*s*) *n.f.*, aquatinta, aquatint.

aquatique (-koua-), *adj.*, aquatic, watery.

aqueduc, *n.m.*, water-pipe, aqueduct, conduit, duct. *Petit — ;* culvert.

aqueu-x, -se, *adj.*, aqueous, watery, waterish.

aquilin, *adj.*, aquiline, curving, hooked, prominent, Roman.

aquilon, *n.m.*, north-wind, northerly wind, cold blast, storm, tempest.

⊙**aquilonaire**, *adj.*, northern, boreal.

aquosité (-kouo-), *n.f.*, aqueousness, wateriness.

ara, *n.m.*, (orni.) macaw.

arabe, *n.m.*, Arabian (person) ; miser, screw, dun, usurer ; Arabic (language).

arabe, *adj.*, Arabic, Arabian.

arabesque, *adj.*, arabesque.

arabesque, *n.f.*, arabesque.

arabique, *adj.*, Arabian, Arabic.

arable, *adj.*, arable, tillable.

arachide, *n.f.*, earth-nut.

arachnide (-rak-), *n.m.*, arachnidan.

arachnoïde (-rak-no-id), *n.f.*, (anat.) arachnoid, arachnoid membrane.

arachnoïde, *adj.*, (anat.) arachnoid ; cobwebbed.

arack or **rack**, *n.m.*, a spirituous liquor ; arrack.

araignée, *n.f.*, spider ; (mining) araignee, arraign ; (nav.) crow-foot. *Toile d'— ;* cobweb, spider-work. — *de mer ;* crab. *Pattes d'— ;* spider's legs, scrawling handwriting. *Oter les — s ;* to sweep the cobwebs away. *J'en ai horreur comme d'une — ;* (fam.) I hate it as I do sin. *Avoir une — dans le plafond ;* to have a bee in one's bonnet.

araméen, -ne, *adj.*, aramean.

aramer, *v.a.*, to stretch cloth upon tenters, to tenter.

aranéeu-x, -se, *adj.*, cobwebbed.

arase, *n.f. Pierres d'— ;* leveling course (mas.).

arasement (-mān), *n.m.*, leveling, making even.

araser, *v.a.*, to level (a wall, a building, &c.) ; to make even.

arases, *n.f. pl.*, leveling course (mas.).

aratoire, *adj.*, aratory, farming. *Instruments —s ;* implements of husbandry.

arbalète, *n.f.*, arbalist, cross-bow, dormouse-trap. — *à jalet ;* a stone-bow. *Attelage en — ;* unicorn team.

⊙**arbalester**, *v.a.*, (arch.) to stay, to bear or shore up with pieces of timber.

arbalétrier, *n.m.*, cross-bowman, archer. — *s ;* principal rafters (carp.) ; (orni.) swift (*Cypselus apus*).

arbitrage, *n.m.*, arbitrage, arbitration, arbitrament, umpirage.

arbitraire, *adj.*, arbitrary, optional, despotic, discretional.

arbitrairement (-mān), *adv.*, arbitrarily, despotically.

arbitral, -e, *adj.*, by arbitration.

arbitralement (-mān), *adv.*, by arbitration.

arbitrateur, *n.m.*, arbitrator, arbiter.

arbitration, *n.f.*, decision, award.

arbitre, *n.m.*, will ; arbiter, arbitrator, umpire, referee ; master, sovereign disposer. *Libre, franc — ;* free will. *Tiers — ;* umpire.

arbitrer, *v.a.*, to arbitrate, to decree, to regulate, to award, to judge, to settle.

arbois, *n.m.*, laburnum.

arboré, -e, *adj.*, (bot.) arboreous ; (of flags) hoisted.

arborer, *v.a.*, to put up, to hoist ; to set up for, to proclaim. — *un pavillon ;* to hoist a flag.

arborescence, *n.f.*, arborescence.

arboriculteur, *n.m.*, arboriculturist.

arboriculture, *n.f.*, arboriculture.

arborisation, *n.f.*, arborization.

arborisé, -e, *adj.,* arborised. *Pierres —es ;* arborized stones.

arbouse, *n.f.,* arbute-berry, wilding.

arbousier, *n.m.,* arbute, strawberry-tree.

arbre, *n.m.,* tree ; beam ; piece of timber ; (tech.) arbor, cylinder, shaft, spindle ; (nav.) mast (in the Mediterranean). *Jeune —* ; sapling. *— fruitier ;* fruit-tree. *— en espalier ;* wall-tree. *— sur pied ;* standing tree. *— en buisson ;* bush. *— de haute futaie ;* forest-tree. *— de plein vent ;* standard. *— nain ;* dwarf-tree. *Grand — ;* shaft. *— de couche ;* horizontal shaft. *— moteur ;* main shaft. *— vertical ;* upright shaft. *— de diane,* or *philosophique* (chem.); arbor dianæ. *— vert ;* evergreen. *— chablis ;* tree blown down. *Arbre généalogique ;* genealogical tree. *— à cire ;* myrica. *— de mestre ;* mainmast. *— de trinquet ;* foremast. *Se tenir au gros de l' — ;* to adhere to what is ancient. *Tel —, tel fruit ;* a tree is known by its fruits. *Faire l' — fourchu ;* to walk on one's two hands, with one's legs in the air. *L' — ne tombe pas du premier coup ;* (prov.) Rome was not built in a day. *Entre l' — et l'écorce il ne faut pas mettre le doigt ;* leave family jars severely alone. *— de transmission ;* connecting shaft.

arbrisseau, *n.m.,* tree ; young tree ; small tree ; underwood ; shrub.

arbuste, *n.m.,* shrub ; bush

arc (ark), *n.m.,* bow, long-bow ; (arch.) arch ; (geom.) arc, arch; (astron.) arc ; (nav.) cambering. *Tirer de l' — ;* to draw the bow. *Corde de l' — ;* bow-string. *A portée d' — ;* within bowshot *Avoir plusieurs cordes à son — ;* to have more than one string to one's bow. *— en plein cintre ;* semi-circular arch. *— de biais ;* sloping arch. *— en décharge ;* arch of discharge *—doubleau* (*—s —x*); massive rib, chief arch of a vault. *— de triomphe ;* triumphal arch. *— diurne ;* (astron.) diurnal arc. *Bander, détendre, l' — ;* to bend, to unbend, the bow. (fig.) *Débander l' — ne guérit pas la plaie ;* to cease to do mischief does not undo the harm done

arc-boutant (ar-boo-tän), *n.m.,* (*—s —s*) arc-boutant, abutment, arched buttress ; prop, shore, supporter ; stretcher ; ringleader, supporter, chief man in any business ; (nav.) sparboom. *—s d'un train de carrosse ;* rods that serve to keep the mainbraces of a coach in place. *— de misaine ;* foresail boom. *Grand —* (nav.); mainsail boom.

arc-bouter, *v.a.,* to prop, to support, to buttress.

arcade, *n.f.,* arcade ; (anat.) arch, vault.

arcane, *n.m.,* (chem.) arcanum, secret, mystery.

arcanson, *n.m.,* colophony, black resin, rosin.

arcasse, *n.f.,* (nav.) buttock of a ship, stern-frame.

arc-doubleau, *n.m.,* groin (of vaults).

arceau, *n.m.,* arch, archway, vault ; (nav.) drift-sail.

arc-en-ciel (ark-an-si-èl), *n.m.,* (*—s —*) rainbow, iris.

archaïque, *adj.,* archaical.

archaïsme (-ka-ism), *n.m.,* archaism. (obsolete word.)

archal, *n.m. Fil d' — ;* iron wire.

archange (-kanj), *n.m.,* archangel.

arche, *n.f.,* arch ; ark. *L' — sainte, l' — du Seigneur ;* the ark of the Lord. *L' — de Noé ;* Noah's ark. *L' — d'alliance ;* the ark of the covenant. *C'est l' — du Seigneur ;* it is forbidden ground. *Pont à plusieurs —s ;* bridge of several arches. *Être hors de l' — ;* to be out of the pale of the church. *Cour des arches ;* Arches-Court.

archée, *n.f.,* principle of life, archeus.

archelet, *n.m.,* drill-bow, hoop (of a net).

archéologie (-ké-), *n.f.,* archæology.

archéologique (-ké-), *adj.,* archæological.

archéologue (ar-ké-o-log), *n.m.,* archæologist.

archer, *n.m.,* archer, bowman ; ⊙policeman, constable.

archet, *n.m.,* bow, fiddle-stick ; upper part of a cradle ; turner's poll or bow ; drill-bow ; bow-hand (mus.).

archétype (-ké-), *n.m.,* archetype.

archétype (-ké-), *adj.,* archetypal.

archevêché, *n.m.,* archbishopric, cathedral town ; the archbishop's residence.

archevêque, *n.m,* archbishop.

archi, prefix from Gr. ἀρχειν, arch.

archichancelier, *n.m.,* archchancellor.

archidiaconat, *n.m.,* archdeaconry.

archidiaconé, *n.m.,* archdeaconry.

archidiacre, *n.m.,* archdeacon.

archiduc, *n.m.,* archduke.

archiduché, *n.m.,* archdukedom, archduchy.

archiduchesse, *n.f.,* archduchess.

archiépiscopal, -e (-ki-), *adj.,* archiepiscopal.

archiépiscopat (-ki-), *n.m.,* archiepiscopacy.

archifo-u, -ïle, *adj.,* stark-mad.

archiluth, *n.m.,* archlute.

archimandritat, *n.m.,* the living of an archimandrite ; abbey.

archimandrite, *n.m.,* archimandrite.

archinoble, *adj.,* (iron.) most noble.

archipel, *n.m.,* archipelago.

archipompe, or **arche-de-pompe,** *n.f.,* (*—s —*) (nav.) well, well-pump.

archipresbytéral, *adj.,* appertaining to an archpresbyter.

archipresbytérat, *n.m.,* archpresbytery.

archiprêtre, *n.m.,* archpriest, archpresbyter.

archiprêtré, *n.m.,* archpresbytery.

architecte, *n.m.,* architect ; master-builder. *—paysagiste,* landscape-gardener.

architectonique, *adj.,* architectonic.

architectonique, *n.f.,* architectonics.

architectonographe, *n.m.,* architectonographer.

architectonographie, *n.f.,* architectonography.

architectural, -e, *adj.,* architectural.

architecture, *n.f.,* architecture.

architrave, *n.f.,* (arch.) architrave.

architriclin, *n.m.,* (antiq.) steward ; (fam. and jest.) head-man, host, entertainer.

archives, *n.f.pl.,* archives, records ; record-office, muniment house.

archiviste, *n.m.,* archivist, keeper of the records, registrar.

archivolte, *n.f.,* (arch.) archivolt.

archontat (-kon-ta), *n.m.,* archonship.

archonte (-kont), *n.m.,* archon.

archure, *n.f.,* mill-stone hoop.

arçon, *n.m.,* saddle-bow ; bow (tool). *Perdre or vider les —s ;* to be thrown from one's horse ; (fig.) to hesitate, lose one's presence of mind. *Être ferme dans les —s ;* to have a firm seat ; to be true to one's principles. *Se remettre dans les —s ;* to recover one's stirrups. *Pistolets d' — ;* horse-pistols.

arçonnage, *n.m.,* bowing ; (agric.) layering.

⊙**arçtier** (-tié), *n.m.,* bow-maker. *—fléchier ;* bow and arrow maker.

arctique, *adj.,* ɔrɔtic, north.

arcturus, *n.m.,* (astron.) Arcturus.

ardélion, *n.m.,* (l. u.) a busybody, meddler.

ardemment (-da-män), *adv.,* ardently, intensely, eagerly, passionately, vehemently, spiritedly, fervently, hotly.

ardent, -e, *adj.,* hot, burning, fiery, glowing ; scorching ; ardent, vehement, violent ; strenuous, spirited, mettlesome ; zealous ; hasty, passionate ; sanguine, fervent, earnest ; greedy ; red (of the hair) ; (nav.) griping. *Charbon — ;* burning-coal. *Chapelle —e ;* mortuary chamber (for lying in state). *Chambre —e* (French history) ardent-chamber, criminal court. *Verre —;* burning-glass.

ardent, *n.m.,* ignis fatuus, will-o'-the-wisp.

⊙**arder** *or* **ardre.** *V.* brûler.

ardeur, *n.f.,* ardor, heat, burning heat; ardency, warmth, fervency; vividness, intensity; eagerness, fire, spirit, spiritedness, mettle, fervor; earnestness, forwardness, strenuousness; passion. *Cheval plein d'—;* high-mettled horse. *Avec —;* spiritedly.

*****ardillon,** *n.m.,* tongue (of a buckle); barb (of a hook).

ardoise, *n.f.,* slate; score, account. *Carrière d'—;* slate-quarry. *Crayon d'—;* slate-pencil. *Couvreur en —;* slater. *Couvrir d'—;* to slate.

ardoisé, -e, *adj.,* slate-colored.

ardoiser, *v.a.,* to slate.

ardoisier, *n.m.,* owner of, workman in (a slate-quarry).

ardoisi-er, -ère, *adj.,* slaty.

ardoisière, *n.f.,* slate-quarry.

⊙**ardre.** *V.* brûler.

ardu, -e, *adj.,* arduous, hard, difficult, steep.

are, *n.m.,* are, 119·6046 square yards.

arec, *n.m.,* (bot.) areca, nut.

aréfaction, *n.f.,* arefaction.

arénacé, -e, *adj.,* arenaceous.

arénation, *n.f.,* arenation.

arène, *n.f.,* sand; arena, lists, ring; cock-pit; battle-ground, theatre, scene.

aréneu-x, -se, *adj.,* sandy, arenous.

aréole, *n.f.,* (anat., med.) areola.

aréomètre, *n.m.,* areometer.

aréométrie, *n.f.,* areometry.

aréopage, *n.m.,* areopagus.

aréopagite, *n.m.,* areopagite.

aréostyle, *n.m.,* (arch.) areostyle.

aréotectonique, *n.f.,* areotechtonics (military architecture).

⊙**aréotique,** *n.m.,* (med.) areotic.

aréquier, *n.m.,* (bot.) cabbage palm.

arête, *n.f.,* fish-bone; skeleton of a fish; (bot.) awn, beard, prickle; (arch.) arris; (nav.) quoin; (geom.) corner, edge; (geog.) ridge; (metal.) angle or edge, ridge; ridge (of a sword blade). *— de poisson;* (arch.) herring-bone work. *A vive —;* (carp.) sharp-edged.

arêtier (-tié), *n.m.,* (arch.) hip.

arêtière, *n.f.,* layer of mortar used in slating.

argala, *n.m.,* (orni.) hurgil.

argali, *n.m.,* (mam.) argali (wild sheep).

arganeau, *n.m.,* (nav.) ring-bolt, anchoring; convict-chain.

argémone, *n.f.,* argemone (thorny Mexican poppy).

argent, *n.m.,* silver; money, coin, cash; (her.) argent; pearl. *—vierge;* virgin silver. *Lingot d'—;* silver bullion. *— en feuilles, battu;* silver-leaf. *— vif* (l. u.), vif-argent (n.p.); quicksilver. *Vaisselle d'—;* plate, silver-plate. *— blanc ;* silver money. *— comptant;* ready money. *— monnayé ;* coined money. *— d'Allemagne ;* German silver. *— doré ;* silver-gilt. *— amati;* deadened silver. *— en caisse ;* cash in hand, money put by. *— dormant;* money lying idle. *— mort;* money paying no interest. *— mignon;* pin-money. *Un — fou ;* no end of money. *Bourreau d'—;* spendthrift. *Pigne d'—;* pena silver. *A pomme d'—;* silver-headed. *A tête d'—;* silver-eyed. *Au croissant d'—;* (her.) argent-horned. *D'—;* silvery; (her.) argent. *En avoir pour son —;* to have one's money's worth. *Avoir le temps et l'—;* to have all one can wish for. *Etre brouillé avec l'—comptant;* never to have any ready money. *Etre cousu d'—, avoir de l'— à gogo ;* to be rolling in riches. *Etre court d'—;* to be short of money. *Jeter son — par la fenêtre;* to throw one's money away. *Homme d'—;* mercenary man. *Lâcher de l'—;* to come down with one's money. *Payer — sec, bas, — sur table ;*

to pay money down, on the nail, ready money. *Manger son —;* to squander one's fortune away. *— comptant porte médecine;* money is a cure for all sores. *Faire rentrer de l'—;* to call in money. *Rapporter de l'—;* to bring in money. *Toucher de l'—;* to receive money. *Trouver de l'—;* to raise money. *Y aller bon jeu, bon —;* to be in earnest, to act frankly. *J'ai toujours l'— à la main;* I am always laying money out. *Payer — comptant;* to pay ready money. *Placer de l'—;* to invest money. *Prendre quelque chose pour — comptant;* to take anything for gospel. *Faire — de tout;* to turn everything into money. *C'est de l'— en barre ;* it is as good as ready money, or as the Bank of England. *— fait tout;* money makes the mare go. *Point d'—, point de Suisse;* no pay, no piper; no money, no Swiss; nothing, without paying.

argentage, *n.m.,* silvering, silver plating.

argenté, *adj.,* plated, silvered over; silvery, snowy.

argenter, *v.a.,* to silver over, to plate, to do over with silver.

argenterie (-jan-trî), *n.f.,* plate, silver-plate.

argenteur, *n.m.,* plater, silverer.

argenteu-x. -se, *adj.,* (pop., l. u.) moneyed.

⊙**argentier,** *n.m.,* steward; treasurer; silversmith.

argentifère, *adj.,* argentiferous.

argentin, -e, *adj.,* silvery, argentine; silver-toned, ringing, clear; (paint.) silvery.

argentine, *adj.,* (geog.) Argentine.

argentine, *n.f.,* argentine, silver-weed, wild tansy; (ich.) argentina.

argenture, *n.f.,* silver-plating.

argilacé, -e, *adj.,* clayey, argillaceous.

argile, *n.f.,* clay, potter's clay, argil. *— à porcelaine ;* China-clay.

argileu-x, -se, *adj.,* clayey, clayish, argillous.

argilière, *n.f.,* clay-pit.

argilifère, *adj.,* argilliferous.

argilolithe, *n.m.,* clay-stone.

argo, *n.m.,* (astr.) Argo.

argonaute, *n.m.,* argonaut; (conch.) argonauta; (moll.) nautilus.

argonautes, *n.m.pl.,* Argonauts.

argot, *n.m.,* cant, professional slang; slang; (gard.) the stub of a branch, above an eye or bud, dead-wood.

argoter, *v.a.,* to cut the stub of a tree above the eye.

argotiser, *v.n.,* to talk slang.

argousin, *n.m.,* convict-warder; bobby, peeler, catch-poll.

argue (arg), *n.f.,* (tech.) draw-bench, draw-room (for wire-drawing).

arguer, *v.a.,* (jur.) to accuse; to wire-draw, argue, infer, conclude.

arguer, *v.n.,* to argue; to conclude, to infer; to urge.

argument, *n.m.,* argument, reasoning; conjecture; evidence, proof, reason; theme, subject. *— dans les règles;* argument in due form.

argumentant, *n.m.,* arguer.

argumentateur, *n.m.,* arguer, disputer.

argumentation, *n.f.,* argumentation, arguing; reasoning.

argumenter, *v.n.,* to argue, to quibble.

argus, *n.m.,* (myth.) Argus; (ent., orn.) argus.

argutie (-ci), *n.f.,* quibble, hair-splitting, cavil.

argutieux, -se, *adj.,* quibbling, caviling.

arianisme, *n.m.,* arianism.

aride, *adj.,* arid, dry, sterile. *Une terre —;* a barren ground.

aridité, *n.f.,* aridity, dryness; barrenness, unfruitfulness.

arien, -ne (-in, -èn), *adj.,* Arian.

arien, *n.m.,* **-ne,** *n.f.,* Arian.

ariette, *n.f.,* arietta.

⊙**arigot**, *n.m.*, a kind of fife. *V.* **larigot**.

***arille**, *n.f.*, (bot.) seed-coat, mace, aril.

aristarque, *n.m.*, Aristarchus; hypercritic.

aristocrate, *adj.*, aristocratic.

aristocrate, *n.m.f.*, aristocrat.

aristocratie, *n.f.*, aristocracy.

aristocratique, *adj.*, aristocratic.

aristocratiquement (-mān), *adv.*, aristocratically.

aristoloche, *n.f.*, aristolochia, birth-wort, hard-wort.

aristotélicien, **-ne** (-in, -è-n), *adj.*, Aristotelian.

aristotélicien, *n.m.*, Aristotelian.

aristotélisme, *n.m.*, Aristotelianism, Aristotelian philosophy.

arithméticien (-in), *n.m.*, arithmetician.

arithmétique, *n.f.*, arithmetic; accounts.

arithmétique, *adj.*, arithmetical.

arithmétiquement (-mān), *adv.*, arithmetically.

arithmomancie, *n.f.*, arithmomancy.

arizarum (-rom), *n.m.*, (bot.) friar's cowl.

arlequin, *n.m.*, harlequin, merry-andrew; (orni.) spotted red-shank. *Habit d'—;* patchwork, medley.

arlequinade. *n.f.*, harlequinade.

arlequine, *n.f.*, harlequin's dance.

***armadille**, *n.f.*, armadillo.

***armadille**, *n.m.*, (ent.) wood-louse.

armand, *n.m.*, drench, spiced-mash (for sick horses).

armateur, *n.m.*, owner of a privateer; shipowner; captain of a privateer.

armature, *n.f.*, (arch., tech.) iron braces, stays, binding, cappings, armature (dynamo).

arme, *n.f.*, arm, weapon, arm (of the service); (bot.) weapon. *—s;* (her.) arms, coat of arms, hatchment; troops, forces; warfare; fencing. *—s blanches;* side-arms (the sabre, sword, bayonet). *— à feu;* fire-arms. *—s fausses, à enquerre;* (her.) irregular arms. *—s parlantes;* (her.) allusive heraldry. *Jaque d'—s;* coat of arms. *A —s parlantes;* (her.) exemplary. *Assaut d'—s;* assault at arms. *— de trait;* missile weapon. *Faisceau d'—s;* pile of arms. *Pas d'—s;* passage of arms. *Une salle d'—s;* a fencing school; armory. *Un maître d'—s;* a fencing-master. *Faire des —s, tirer des —s;* to fence. *Avoir les —s belles;* to fence gracefully. *Né pour les —s;* born a soldier. *Quitter les —s;* to leave the army. *Faire ses premières —s;* to make one's first campaign. *Un fait d'—s;* a warlike feat or exploit. *Héraut d'—s;* herald at arms. *Homme d'—s;* man at arms. *Place d'—s;* a fortress. *Port d'—s;* carrying arms; gun license. *En venir aux —s;* to begin the war. *Porter les —s;* to serve as a soldier. *Aux —s!* to arms! *Prendre les —s;* to take up arms. *Rendre déposer les —s;* to lay down one's arms. *Faire passer par les —s;* to shoot, put to the sword. *Suspension d'—s;* cessation of hostilities. *— au bras!* (milit.) stand at ease! *Haut les —s!* lodge arms! *Portez —s!* shoulder arms! *Présentez —s!* present arms! *—à terre!* ground arms! *—à volonté!* slope arms! *Par la force des —s;* by force of arms. *Prendre les —s contre;* to take up arms against. *Sans —s;* unarmed. *Les —s sont journalières;* (fam.) victory is fickle. *Passer l'— à gauche;* (fam.) to be killed; to kick the bucket.

armé, **-e**, *part.*, armed, equipped; (her.) armed, cocked, at full cock. *— de toutes pièces;* armed from top to toe. *A main —e;* by force of arms.

armée, *n.f.*, army; forces, troops; fleet; host; bevy. *La grande —;* Napoleon's army. *— de mer et de terre;* sea and land forces. *Corps d'—;* main body of troops, army corps. *— permanente;* standing army. *Fournisseur de l'—;* army-contractor. *Entrer dans l'—;* to enter the army.

armeline, *n.f.*, ermine (skin).

armement, *n.m.*, armament; arming, raising of forces; warlike preparations; accoutrements.

arménien, **-ne**, (-in, -èn), *adj.*, Armenian.

arménien, *n.m.*, **-ne**, *n.f.*, Armenian.

arménienne, *n.f.*, Armenian stone.

armer, *v.a.*, to arm, to furnish with arms; (artil.) to load, to mount; to provoke; to rouse; to excite; to cock (a gun, &c.); to fortify; to heel (cocks); (nav.) to equip, to fit out; (nav.) to man (a pump); to strengthen, to bind; (phys.) to arm. *— une poutre de bandes de fer;* to strengthen a beam with iron bands. *— un aimant;* to arm a loadstone. *— les avirons;* (nav.) to ship the oars.

*s'***armer**, *v.r.*, to arm one's self, to take up arms, to provide one's self with arms; to fortify, to protect, to secure one's self against a thing; to summon up. *S'— de la prière;* to fortify one's self with prayer. *S'— de tout son courage;* to summon up all one's courage.

armet, *n.m.*, (ant.) helmet, head-piece.

armillaire (-mil-lér), *adj.*, (astron.) armillary. *Sphère —;* armillary sphere.

armille, *n. f.*, (arch.) annulet; ring, circle.

arminianisme, *n.m.*, Arminianism.

arminien, **-ne** (-in, -èn), *adj.*, Arminian.

armistice, *n.m.*, armistice, truce.

armoire, *n.f.*, closet; cupboard; press. *— à glace;* wardrobe.

armoiries, *n.f. pl.*, (her.) coat of arms, arms, armorial bearings, hatchment. *—fausses, à enquerre;* irregular arms.

armoise, *n.f.*, artemisia. *— commune;* mugwort.

armoisin, *n.m.*, sarcenet.

armon, *n.m.*, futchel (of a coach).

armorial, *n.m.*, book of heraldry.

armoricain, *n.m.*, Armorican (of Brittany).

armorier, *v.a.*, to set, put, paint, a coat of arms, to blazon.

armorique, *n.f.*, Armorica.

armoriste, *n.m.*, armorist, heraldic engraver.

armure, *n.f.*, armor, casing; (phys.) armor; (nav.) fish (of a mast, yard). *— de tête;* headpiece. *— à l'épreuve;* armor-proof. *Revêtir son —;* to buckle on one's armor. *— de la clef;* (mus.) signature.

armurerie, *n.f.*, gunsmithery, arm-manufactory; gun-trade, gun-making.

armurier, *n.m.*, armorer, gunsmith.

arnica, *or* **arnique**, *n.f.*, (bot.) arnica.

arnicine, *n.f.*, (chem.) extract of arnica.

arnotto, *n.m.*, (bot.) arnotto. *V.* **roucou**.

aromate, *n.m.*, aromatic.

aromatique, *adj.*, aromatical, fragrant, spicy.

aromatisation, *n.f.*, aromatization.

aromatiser, *v.a.*, to aromatize.

aromatite, *n.f.*, aromatite.

arome, *n.m.*, flavor, aroma.

aronde, *n.f.*, swallow, swallow-fish. *Queue d'—;* (carp.) dove-tail. *Assembler en queue d'—;* to dove-tail.

⊙**arondelle**, *n.f.*, a kind of fishing-tackle. *— de mer;* any small vessel; a brigantine, pinnace, &c.

⊙***arpailleur**, *n.m.*, gold-searcher. *V.* **orpailleur**.

arpège, *n.m.*, (mus.) arpeggio.

arpéger, *v.n.*, (mus.) to perform arpeggios.

arpent, *n.m.*, acre (French); about an acre and a half (English).

arpentage, *n.m.*, land-measuring; survey.

arpenter, *v.a.*, to survey, to measure lands; to walk at a great pace, to stride along, pace up and down.

arpenteur, *n.m.*, land-surveyor.

arpenteuse, *n.f.*, (ent.) span worm.

arqué, **-e**, *part.*, bent, crooked; arched, curved.

arquebusade, *n.f.*, arquebusade.

arquebuse, *n.f.*, arquebuse.

⊙**arquebuser**, *v.a.*, to shoot with an arquebuse.

arquebuserie (-buz-rî), *n.f.*, the business of a gunsmith. *V.* **armurerie**.

arquebusier, *n.m.*, arquebusier, musketeer; gunsmith.

arquer, *v.a.n.*, to bend, to curve, to arch, to crook.

arrachement (-rash-mān), *n.m.*, tearing up, away, pulling up or out, rooting up or out, clearing away, drawing, extraction ; (arch.) toothing.

*d'***arrache-pied**, *adv.*, without intermission, incessantly.

arracher, *v.a.*, to force from, out of, away from, off ; to pull away ; to drag, to draw, to lug away ; to extort ; to snatch from, to wrest, to wring ; to extract (teeth) ; to wring (tears) ; to tear out, down ; to wrest ; to grub up. *— de mauvaises herbes ;* to grub up weeds. *— un secret à quelqu'un ;* to get a secret out of any one.

*s'***arracher**, *v.r.*, to tear ; to tear away, off ; to get away ; to break away. *S'— les cheveux ;* to tear one's hair. *On se l'arrache ;* he or she is all the rage ; there is a great run upon it.

arracheur, *n.m.*, drawer. *— de dents ;* tooth-drawer. *— de cors ;* corn-cutter. *Mentir comme un — de dents ;* to lie unblushingly, or like an epitaph.

arracheuse, *n.f.*, (hat-making) picker.

arrachis, *n.m.*, plant rooted up ; fraudulent rooting up of young trees.

arrachoir, *n.m.*, rooter, digger.

⊙**arraisonner**, *v.a.*, to argue with any one. *— un vaisseau ;* (nav.) to speak, to hail.

arrangé, -e, *part.*, arranged ; affected.

arrangeant, -e, *adj.*, accommodating, easy to deal with, to get on with.

arrangement, *n.m.*, arrangement, disposing, adjusting, setting in order, laying out ; cooking up ; trimming (lamps) ; accommodating ; order, regularity, composure ; method, proper arrangement or disposition ; economy ; composition, compounding ; *pl.*, terms ; measures. *Entrer en — ;* to compound. *J'ai pris des —s avec eux pour le paiement ;* I have come to terms with them respecting payment.

arranger, *v.a.*, to set in order, to arrange, to do up ; to rank, to range, to dispose, to class ; to accommodate, to make up, to compromise, to conciliate, to compose ; to suit, to agree with ; to settle, to manage, to wind up ; to cook up ; to trim (lamps) ; to ill-treat ; to blow up (any one) ; to fit up (a house) ; to trim up, to dress out. *— un jardin ;* to do up a garden. *— quelque chose ;* to contrive something. *— ses affaires ;* to settle one's affairs. *Il l'a arrangé de la bonne manière ;* he gave it him well, gave him his deserts. *Comme vous voilà arrangé !* what a sight you look ! what a figure you cut ! *Arrangez tout cela ;* set all those things in order. *Cela m'arrange ;* that suits me. *Cela ne m'arrange pas ;* that does not suit me. *Arrangez-vous ;* settle it among yourselves.

*s'***arranger**, *v.r.*, to put, place one's self ; to settle ; to set to rights ; to be placed, arranged ; to arrange, to make arrangements ; to set one's house in order ; to compound ; to be all right ; to contrive ; to make shift, to put up (with). *Cela s'arrangera ;* that will be all right. *Il s'est très bien arrangé ;* he has made his house very comfortable. *Qu'il s'arrange comme il voudra ;* let him do as he likes. *Arrangez-vous ;* do as best you can ; that is your lookout. *Je m'en arrange ;* I make shift with it. *Il s'est arrangé avec ses créanciers ;* he has come to terms with his creditors.

arrentement (-mān), *n.m.*, (l. u.) renting ; letting out. *Tenir par — ;* to rent.

arrenter, *v.a.*, (l.u.) to rent, to let out.

arrérager, *v.n.*, to get in arrears.

arrérages, *n.m. pl.*, arrears. *Mandat d'— de rentes ;* dividend warrant. *Laisser courir ses — ;* to let one's arrears run on.

arrestation, *n.f.*, arrest, custody. *Etre en état d'— ;* to be in custody. *Mettre quelqu'un en — ;* to arrest any one. *Opérer l'— d'une bande de voleurs ;* to capture a gang of thieves.

arrêt, *n.m.*, decree ; decision, award, judgment ; sentence ; attachment (of both persons and goods) ; (horol.) stop-work ; (tech.) rest, stop, stay. *— de mort ;* sentence of death. *— par défaut ;* judgment by default. *Chien d'— ;* setter, pointer. *Robinet d'—*, stop-cock. *Maison d'— ;* jail, lock-up. *Mandat d'— ;* warrant. *—s forcés, simples ;* (milit.) close, open, arrest. *Aux —s ;* (milit.) under arrest ; kept in (schol.). *Mettre aux —s ;* (milit.) to put under arrest. *Lever les —s ;* (milit.) to release from arrest. *Prononcer un — ;* to pronounce judgment, to pass sentence. *Mettre la lance en — ;* to couch the lance. *Temps d'— ;* pause, stoppage, intermission. *En — ;* at rest (of a lance) ; locked (of a pistol).

arrêté, *n.m.*, agreement, resolution ; order, decision (of the police). *— de compte ;* (com.) account agreed upon.

arrêté, -e, *part.*, stopped ; hired, agreed for ; decreed, agreed upon, resolved upon ; arrested ; fastened. *Avoir des idées --es ;* to have fixed ideas. *Dessein — ;* settled design.

arrête-bœuf, *n.m.*, (—) (bot.) cammoc, rest-harrow.

arrête-nef, *n.m.*, (—) (ich.) sucking-fish.

arrête-porte, *n.m.*, (—) gate, door-stop ; door-keeper.

arrêter, *v.a.*, to arrest, to stop, to stay ; to make fast, to fasten ; to delay, to detain, to keep back ; to give over ; to put an end to ; to suppress ; to fix the attention of ; to apprehend, to take into custody ; to seize, to distrain ; to hinder, to impede ; to check, to curb ; to staunch ; to alleviate ; to throw out of gear (machinery) ; to hire, to engage ; ⁺ secure ; to resolve upon, to agree ; to conclude, to decree ; to settle (an account) ; to pin ; to scotch. *— un point en cousant ;* to fasten a stitch. *— ses yeux sur ;* to fix one's eyes upon. *— un courrier ;* to delay a courier. *— un volet ;* to fasten a shutter. *Ses créanciers l'ont fait arrêté ;* his creditors have had him arrested. *Qu'a-t-on arrêté dans cette réunion ?* what has been decided at that meeting ? *— un marché ;* to conclude a bargain. *— un domestique, une chambre ;* to secure, engage a servant, a room. *— une place à la diligence ;* to secure a place in the coach. *Rien ne l'arrête ;* he sticks at nothing.

arrêter, *v.n.*, to stand still, to stop, to make a stay ; to stop to bait (horses) ; to point, to set (of dogs).

*s'***arrêter**, *v.r.*, to stop, to pause, to rest, to dwell upon ; to stand still, to halt ; to tarry, to loiter ; to stop ; to remain ; to lag ; to forbear ; to hesitate ; to give over, to suspend ; to leave off ; to be embarrassed ; to be concluded (of bargains) ; to desist ; to resolve upon ; to draw up (of carriages) ; to be allayed (of pain) ; to be thrown out of gear (of machinery) ; to be fastened, to be pinned down. *Ma montre s'arrête ;* my watch stops. *Il s'arrête, la mémoire lui manque ;* he hesitates, his memory fails him. *Il ne faut pas s'arrêter à ce qu'il dit ;* one must not mind what he says. *Vous vous arrêtez à des riens ;* you stop at trifles.

arrêtiste, *n.m.*, compiler of decrees.

⊙**arrhement**, *n.m.*, the giving of earnest money.

arrher, *v.a.*, to give earnest-money.

arrhes (âr), *n.f. pl.*, earnest, earnest-money. *Donner des — ;* to pay a deposit.

arrière, *n.m.*, back part, rear ; (nav.) stern. *D'— ;* (nav.) aft. *En — !* back ! *En — ;* (nav.)

abaft. *En* — ; in arrears. *En* — *de;* behind. *Surveillant de l'* —; (nav.) after-guard. *Se ranger de l'* —; (nav.). *Tomber de l'* —; (nav.) to fall astern. *Avoir le vent* —, or *filer vent* — ; to sail before the wind.

arrière, *adv.*, behind (of time and place); (nav.) aft, abaft. *Droit* —; right abaft. *Avoir vent* —; to go before the wind.

arrière, *int.*, away ! avaunt !

arriéré, -e, *adj.*, in arrears; behindhand.

arriéré, *n.m.*, arrears. *Liquider l'* —; to pay up arrears. *Il a beaucoup d'* — *dans sa correspondance;* he is very much behindhand in his correspondence.

arrière-ban, *n.m.*, (——*s*) arriere-ban, reserve.

arrière-bec, *n.m.*, (——*s*) (arch.) starling; breakwater; cutwater.

arrière-bouche, *n.f.*, (——*s*) (anat.) swallow (of the throat), pharynx, posterior fauces.

arrière-boutique, *n.f.*, (——*s*) back shop.

⊙**arrière-change,** *n.m.*, (——*s*) compound interest.

arrière-corps, *n.m.*, (—) (arch.) recess; back-building.

arrière-cour, *n.f.*, (——*s*) back yard, back court.

arrière-dos, *n.m.*, (—) (arch.) altar-screen, reredos.

arrière-essaim, *n.m.*, (——*s*) after-swarm.

arrière-faix, *n.m.*, (—) (surg.) after-birth.

arrière-fermier, *n.m.*, (——*s*) under-farmer, under-tenant.

arrière-fief, *n.m.*, (——*s*) arriere-fee or mesne-fief.

arrière-fleur, *n.f.*, (——*s*) second blossom.

arrière-garant, *n.m.*, (——*s*) (jur.) double security; security of the bail.

arrière-garde, *n.f.*, (——*s*) rear-guard; (nav.) rear-division.

arrière-goût, *n.m.*, (——*s*) after-taste.

arrière-main, *n.m.*, (——*s*) back stroke; hindquarters (of a horse).

arrière-neveu, *n.m.*, (——*x*) great-nephew. *Les* —*x ;* descendants, the latest posterity.

arrière-pensée, *n.f.*, (——*s*) mental reservation.

arrière-petite-fille, *n.f.*, (———*s*-—*s*) great-grand-daughter.

arrière-petit-fils, *n.m.*, (———*s*-—) great-grandson.

arrière-plan, *n.m.*, (——*s*) (paint.) back-ground.

arrière-point, *n.m.*, (——*s*) back-stitch.

arrière-pointeuse, *n.f.*,(——*s*) back-stitcher.

arrière-port, *n.m.*, inner harbor.

arriérer, *v.a.*, to defer, to put off; to throw behindhand.

*s'***arriérer,** *v.r.*, to stay behind; to be in arrears (of payment).

arrière-saison, *n.f.*, (——*s*) autumn. *L'* — *de la vie ;* the evening of days, old age.

arrière-train, *n.m.*, (——*s*) after-carriage, hind-quarters.

arrière-vassal, *n.m.*, (——*vassaux*) rear-vassal.

arrière-voussure, *n.f.*, (——*s*) back-arch.

arrimage, *n.m.*, (nav.) stowage; trim of the hold.

arrimer, *v.a.*, (nav.) to stow away; to trim the hold.

arrimeur, *n.m.*, stevedore.

arriser, *v.a.*, (nav.) to touch.

arrivage, *n.m.*, (nav.) arrival.

arrivée, *n.f.*, arrival, entrance, approach, landing, coming, advent; (nav.) falling off, lee-way. *A l'* — *de ;* on the arrival of. *Aussitôt son* —; immediately after his arrival. *Jours d'* —; mail days.

arriver, v.n., to come to land; to bear down; to arrive at, to approach, to be coming; to happen, to chance; (nav.) to bear up, to bear down, to veer; to come to pass; to occur; to befall, to chance, to attain, to reach, to succeed. — *à l'âge de ;* to attain the age of. *Le navire arrive de ce côté ;* the ship is bearing down this way. *La voiture arriva ;* the coach arrived. *La nuit arriva ;* night came on. *Un accident lui est arrivé ;* an accident has happened to him. *Il arrivait à grands pas;* he was approaching with rapid strides. — *à bon port ;* to reach home safely, to land; (of letters) to come to hand. — *à ses fins, à son but ;* to compass one's ends. *Il arrive tous les jours que ;* it happens every day that. *Il lui est arrivé de dire ;* he happened to say. *D'où il est arrivé que ;* whence it came to pass that. *S'il arrive que vous ayez besoin de moi ;* if you should chance to want me. *Quel malheur en peut-il arriver ;* what mischief can it entail ? *Quoi qu'il arrive ;* come what may. *Qu'en arrivera-t-il ?* what will be the consequence, or the upshot ? *Cela ne m'arrivera plus ;* I will never do so again. *Un malheur n'arrive jamais seul ;* misfortunes never come singly. *Arrivez !* (fam.) come on ! come in ! *Arrive qui plante, arrive que pourra ;* (prov.) happen what may, in any case. — *comme marée en Carême ;* to come in the nick of time.

arrobe, *n.f.*, Spanish weight, arroba.

arroche, *n.f.*, (bot.) orach, goose-foot; mountain spinach.

arrogamment (-ga-mān), *adv.*, arrogantly, haughtily, insolently.

arrogance, *n.f.*, arrogance; haughtiness; superciliousness.

arrogant, -e, *adj.*, arrogant, haughty, supercilious.

*s'***arroger,** *v.r.*, to arrogate to one's self, to assume, to claim.

⊙**arroi,** *n.m.*, array, equipage. *Etre en mauvais* —; to be in a sad pickle.

arrondi, -e, *part.*, rounded, made round; full. *Un visage* —; a full face.

arrondir, *v.a.*, to make a thing round, to round off; to aggrandize; to extend, increase; (paint.) to round off; (nav.) to double (a cape). — *une période ;* to round off a period. — *une île ;* (nav.) to sail round an island. — *ses biens;* to increase one's estate.

*s'***arrondir,** *v.r.*, to round, to get round; to increase one's estate.

arrondissement (-mān), *n.m.*, rounding, making round; roundness; district, circuit; ward (of a town).

arrosage, *n.m.*, irrigation, watering.

arrosement (a-rôz-mān), *n.m.*, watering, sprinkling, besprinkling; (cook.) basting; paying all round, stake, pool (at play).

arroser, *v.a.*, to water, to irrigate, to besprinkle, to wet; to bedew; to soak; to bathe (with tears); (cook.) to baste; to distribute money. — *des créanciers ;* to pay one's creditors a trifle. *Arrosez ces gens-là ;* keep in with those people (by giving them trifling presents). — *un repas de vin ;* to wash down a meal with wine.

arrosoir, *n.m.*, watering-pot.

arrowroot, *n.m.*, (n.p.) arrow-root.

arrugie, *n.f.*, (mining) drain.

ars, *n.m. pl.*, (vet.) vein of the fore leg; limb. *Saigner un cheval aux quatre* —; to bleed a horse in all four legs.

arsenal, *n.m.*, arsenal. — *de marine ;* dock-yard.

arséniate, *n.m.*, arseniate.

arséniaté, *adj.*, combined with arseniate.

arsenic, *n.m.*, arsenic.

arsenical, -e, *adj.*, arsenical.

arsénieux, *adj.*, arsenious.

arsénique, *adj.*, (chem.) arsenic.

arsénite, *n.m.*, arsenite.

arsis, *n.f.*, (gram., mus.) arsis.

art, *n.m.*, art; skill; cunning, artifice. *Les termes de l'*—; technical terms. *L'—militaire ;* military art. *Les—s libéraux ;* the liberal arts. *Les beaux—s ;* the fine arts. *—s manufacturiers ;* arts and manufactures. *— angélique ;* (hist.) angelic art. *—s d'agrément ;* accomplishments. *Bachelier ès—s ;* bachelor of arts. *Maître ès—s ;* master of arts. *Ouvrage d'—;* work of art. *Maîtres de l'—;* the connoisseurs, the learned, the masters of their craft. *Homme de l'—;* doctor. *Il a l'—de réussir dans tout ce qu'il entreprend ;* he has the art of succeeding in all his undertakings. *L'—perfectionne la nature ;* art improves nature.

artère, *n.f.*, artery. *Piquer une —;* to open an artery.

artériel, -le, *adj.*, arterial.

artériole, *n.f.*, (anat.) small artery.

artériologie, *n.f.*, arteriology.

artériotomie, *n.f.*, arteriotomy.

artérite, *n.f.*, arteritis.

artésien, -ne (-in, -è-n), *adj.*, *n.*, artesian. *Puits —;* artesian well.

arthralgie, *n.f.*, arthritis.

arthrite, *n.f.*, (med.) arthritis.

arthritique, *adj.*, arthritic.

arthrodie, *n.f.*, (anat.) arthrodia.

arthrose, *n.f.*, arthrosis.

artichaut, *n.m.*, artichoke. *—s ;* spikes on a fence or gate. *—des toits ;* house-leek.

article, *n.m.*, article, head; paragraph; matter, thing, subject; point; item; (gram.) article; (anat.) articulation; (bot.) article, ware, goods. *— de fond ;* leading article. *— de Paris ;* Paris speciality. *C'est un autre —;* that's another matter. *Ce n'est pas un — de foi ;* it is not worthy of credit. *Nous reviendrons sur cet —;* we shall resume this subject. *C'est un — à part ;* that is a separate article. *A l'— de la mort ;* at the point of death. *Faire l'—;* to puff one's goods.

articulaire, *adj.*, (med.) articular.

articulation, *n.f.*, articulation, joint; (bot., anat.) joint, articulation; (jur.) allegation.

articulé, -e, *part.*, articulate; articulated, uttered, jointed, vertebrated. *D'une manière—e ;* articulately, distinctly.

articuler, *v.a.*, to articulate, to pronounce; to enumerate; to set forth.

s'articuler, *v.r.*, to be articulated or jointed, to joint.

articuler, *v.n.*, to articulate.

artifice, *n.m.*, art; contrivance; slyness, cunning, craft, deceit; trick, stratagem; shuffle. *Caisse d'—;* (nav.) powder-chest. *Un feu d'—;* fireworks, pyrotechnics. *Tirer un feu d'—;* to let off fireworks.

artificiel, -le, *adv.*, artificial.

artificiellement (-mãn), *adv.*, artificially.

artificier, *n.m.*, fireworks-maker, pyrotechnist.

artificieusement (-euz-man), *adv.*, cunningly, craftily, artfully, slily.

artificieu-x, -se, *adj.*, artful, cunning, crafty; shuffling, sly.

☉**artillé, -e**, *adj.*, (nav.) mounted with cannon. *Vaisseau —;* armored vessel.

*****artillerie**, *n.f.*, artillery, ordnance. *Une pièce d'—;* a piece of ordnance. *Grosse —;* heavy artillery. *— légère ;* light artillery. *— de campagne ;* field artillery. *— de siège ;* battering or siege artillery. *— à pied ;* foot artillery. *— à cheval ;* horse artillery. *Parc d'—;* park of artillery. *Train d'—;* train of artillery. *Comité d'—;* board of ordnance.

*****artilleur**, *n.m.*, artilleryman, gunner.

artimon, *n.m.*, (nav.) mizzen. *Mât d'—;* mizzen mast. *Hune d'—;* mizzen top.

artisan, *n.m.*, artisan, handicraftsman, operative, artificer, mechanic, craftsman; author, architect, contriver.

artison, *n.m.*, (ent.) wood-fretter, moth.

artisonné, *adj.*, worm-eaten.

artiste, *n.m.f.*, artist, player, performer, actor, actress.

artistement, *adv.*, in an artistic manner; skillfully, artistically.

artistique, *adj.*, artist-like; artistic, of art.

arum (-rom), *n.m.*, (bot.) arum, wake-robin.

aruspice, *n.m.*, aruspex, diviner, soothsayer.

aruspicine, *n.f.*, (antiq.) aruspicy.

aryen, -ne, *adj.*, *n.*, Aryan.

aryténoïde, *adj.*, (anat.) arytænoid.

as (âss), *n.m.*, ace (at cards, dice); as (Roman weight).

asaret, *n.m.*, (bot.) asarum.

asarum (-rom), *n.m.*, asarabacca, asarum.

asbeste, *n.m.*, asbestos.

ascaride, *n.m.*, (ent.) ascaris.

ascendant, *n.m.*, ascendant; ascendency, influence; power, ruling passion, ancestor. *Avoir de l'—sur ;* to have influence over. *—s et descendants ;* ancestors and descendants.

ascendant, -e, *adj.*, ascending, ascendant, upwards.

ascenseur, *n.m.*, hoist, lift.

ascension, *n.f.*, ascent; up-stroke (of machinery); ascension; ascending, rising; Ascension-day, Holy Thursday. *Jour de l'—;* Holy Thursday.

ascensionnel, -le, *adj.*, ascensional.

ascète, *n.m.f.*, ascetic, anchoret; monk.

ascétique, *adj.*, ascetic, rigid, severe.

ascétique, *n.m.*, ascetic.

ascétique, *n.f.*, ascetic doctrine.

ascétisme, *n.m.*, ascetism.

asciens (as-si-in), *n.m. pl.*, (geog.) Ascians.

ascite, *n.f.*, ascites, common dropsy.

ascitique, *adj.*, dropsical, ascitic.

asclépiade, *n.m.*, (poet.), asclepiad.

asclépiade, *adj.*, (poet.) formed of asclepiads.

asclépiade, *n.f.*, or **asclépias**, *n.m.*, (bot.) asclepias, swallow-wort.

asiarcat, *n.m.*, dignity of an asiarch.

asiarque, *n.m.*, (hist.) asiarch.

asiatique, *adj.*, *n.*, Asiatic.

asile, *n.m.*, asylum, refuge, place of refuge, shelter, sanctuary; harbor, retreat, protection. *Salle d'—;* infant school. *Servir d'—;* to shelter. *Sans —;* shelterless, homeless.

asile, *n.m.*, wasp-fly.

asine, *adj. f.*, (l.u.) asinine, of the ass. *Bête —;* ass; blockhead.

aspect, *n.m.*, aspect, view, sight; look, countenance; phase, point of view.

asperge, *n.f.*, asparagus (head of). *Botte d'—s ;* bundle of asparagus.

aspergement, *n.m.*, sprinkling.

asperger, *v.a.*, to sprinkle, to besprinkle.

aspergerie or **aspergière**, *n.f.*, asparagus-bed or ground.

aspergès (-jèss), *n.m.*, aspergillum, holy-water sprinkler. *Je suis arrivé à l'—;* I entered the church as the priest was sprinkling the people with holy-water.

aspérité, *n.f.*, asperity, roughness, ruggedness; harshness; unevenness.

aspersion, *n.f.*, aspersion, sprinkling, besprinkling.

aspersoir, *n.m.*, holy-water brush; rose (of a water-pot).

aspérule, *n.f.*, (bot.) wood-ruff.

asphalte, *n.m.*, asphalt, asphaltum.

asphaltique or **asphaltite**, *adj.*, asphaltic, bituminous. *Le lac—;* the asphaltic lake, the Dead Sea.

asphodèle, *n.m.*, (bot.) asphodel, king's-spear, wild daffodil.

asphyxiant, *adj.*, asphyxiating, suffocating.

asphyxie, *n.f.*, (med.) asphyxy, suffocation, suspended animation.

asphyxié, *n.m.*, **-e**, *n.f.*, a person in a state of asphyxia.

asphyxier, *v.a.*, to cause asphyxia, to suffocate. *Le gaz les asphyxia ;* the gas suffocated them.

*s'***asphyxier**, *v.r.*, to destroy one's self by suffocation.

aspic, *n.m.*, aspic ; asp ; (bot.) aspic ; spikenard ; spike-lavender ; (cook.) cold meat or fish, with jelly. *Langue d' — ;* a viper's tongue.

aspirant, **-e**, *adj.*, suction, sucking (of pumps).

aspirant, *n.m.*, **-e**, *n.f.*, candidate, suitor, aspirant, postulant ; midshipman. *— au doctorat ;* candidate for a doctor's degree. *— de marine ;* midshipman.

aspirateur, *n.m.*, (of air-pumps) exhauster.

aspiration, *n.f.*, inhaling, inspiration ; (gram.) aspiration, breathing ; (of pumps) exhaustion, suction ; aspiration, longing after, fervent desire. *Tuyau d' — ;* exhausting pipe.

aspiré, **-e**, *adj.*, aspirate ; (hydr.) exhausted.

aspirée, *n.f.*, (gram.) aspirate.

aspirer, *v.a.*, to inspire ; to inhale ; to draw in ; to suck in ; (gram.) to aspirate ; (hydr.) to exhaust.

aspirer, *v.n.*, to aspire, to covet, to aim at. *— aux honneurs ;* to aspire after honors.

*s'***aspirer**, *v.r.*, to suck ; to be inhaled.

aspre, *n.m.*, asper, a Turkish coin.

assa, *n.f.* (*n.p.*), concrete gum, asa, assa.

assabler, *v.a.*, to fill with sand.

assabler, *v.n.*, to run aground ; to be stranded.

assa dulcis, *n.f.* (*n.p.*), asa-dulcis, benzoin.

assa foetida, *n.f.*, (phar.) assafœtida.

assagir, *v.a.*, to make wise, to impart wisdom. *S' —*, *v.r.*, to become wise.

*****assaillant**, *n.m.*, aggressor, assailant, besieger.

assaillant, **-e**, *adj.*, aggressive.

*****assaillir**, *v.a.*, to assault, to assail, to attack ; to surprise, to beset, to come upon.

assainir, *v.a.*, to make, to render healthy. *S' —*, *v.r.*, to become healthy.

assainissement (-mān), *n.m.*, sanitation, purification, salubrity, drainage.

assaisonnement (-zo-n-mān), *n.m.*, condiment, seasoning, dressing.

assaisonner, *v.a.*, to season, to dress, to spice ; to give a relish to ; to make palatable ; to set off, to give a zest to.

assaisonneu-r, *n.m.*, **-se**, *n.f.*, seasoner.

assassin, *n.m.*, assassin, murderer, murderess ; ruffian. *A l' — !* murder ! *Crier à l' — ;* to call out murder.

assassin, **-e**, *adj.*, killing, murderous.

assassinant, **-e**, *adj.*, exceedingly tiresome, boring ; killing, murdering.

assassinat, *n.m.*, assassination, willful murder, homicide, murder.

⊙**assassinateur**, *n.m.*, assassin, murderer.

assassiner, *v.a.*, to assassinate, to murder, to make away with ; to bore, to tease, to plague any one to death.

assaut, *n.m.*, assault, storm, onset, onslaught ; attack, shock ; fencing match, assault. *Donner l' — à une place ;* to storm a place. *Emporter une ville d' — ;* to carry a town by storm. *Faire — d'esprit ;* to make a trial of wit. *Faire — de ;* to vie with each other in.

asséchage, **assèchement**, *n.m.*, drying up.

assécher, *v.a.*, to drain (mine) ; to dry up.

assemblage, *n.m.*, assemblage, collection, union ; set, combination ; (print.) gathering ; (nav.) tabling ; (carp.) bond, scarf.

assemblé, **-e**, *part.*, assembled, united, joined.

assemblée, *n.f.*, assembly, meeting, company, party ; convocation ; congregation (of churches) ; meeting, meet (of hunters). *Se réunir en — publique ;* to meet in public assembly. *L' — se tient ;* the meeting is being held. *— de jeu ;* card-party.

assembler, *v.a.*, to collect, to gather ; to get, bring, put or lay, together ; to assemble, to convoke, to call together ; (print.) to gather ; (carp.) to trim, to scarf.

*s'***assembler**, *v.r.*, to assemble, to meet ; to come, to get or gather, together ; to congregate, to muster. *Qui se ressemble s'assemble ;* birds of a feather flock together.

assembleu-r, *n.m.*, **-se**, *n.f.*, gatherer, collector.

asséner, *v.a.*, to strike, to deal (a blow). *Il lui asséna un coup de poing ;* he struck him a violent blow with his fist.

assentiment, *n.m.*, assent.

assentir, *v.n.*, to agree to, to assent ; (hunt.) to scent.

asseoir (-soâr), (asseyant, assis), *v.a.*, to seat ; to set or put in a chair ; to set, to lay, to fix ; to establish, to rest, to ground ; to pitch ; to settle, to assess ; to train (a horse). *— les fondements d'une maison ;* to lay the foundations of a house. *— une rente ;* to settle an annuity. *— un camp ;* to pitch a camp. *Faire — quelqu'un à sa table ;* to admit any one to one's table.

*s'***asseoir**, *v.r.*, to sit, to sit down ; to be seated, to settle, to perch. *Asseyez-vous ;* sit down.

assermenté, **-e**, *part.*, sworn.

assermenter, *v.a.*, to swear in, to administer the oath to.

asserti-f, **-ve**, *adj.*, assertive.

assertion, *n.f.*, assertion, affirmation.

asservir. *v.a.*, to enslave, to reduce to servitude or slavery ; to subject ; to enthrall ; to bring under subjection ; to master, to subdue, to conquer.

asservissant, *adj.*, enslaving, subjecting, coercive.

asservissement (-mān), *n.m.*, subjection, enthrallment, bondage, servitude, slavery.

assesseur, *n.m.*, assessor (judge).

assette, *n.f.*, adze, hatchet.

assez, *adv.*, enough, sufficiently ; pretty, rather. *J'en ai — ;* I have had enough of it. *Vous avez — fait ;* you have done enough. *Cela est — bien ;* that is pretty well. *Cette femme est — jolie ;* this woman is rather pretty. *Cela paraît — vraisemblable ;* that appears likely enough. *— et plus qu'il n'en faut ;* enough and to spare. *C'est —, en voilà — ;* enough, that will do. *— parlé ;* enough talking. *C'est — loin ;* it is rather far. *On ne saurait avoir — de soin de sa santé ;* one cannot take too much care of one's health. *Cela est — de mon goût ;* I like it well enough. *Suis-je — malheureux !* could I be more unfortunate ! *— volontiers, d' — bon cœur ;* readily enough.

assidu, **-e**, *adj.*, assiduous, punctual ; diligent, constant, attentive.

assiduité, *n.f.*, assiduity, application, diligence, attention.

assidûment, *adv.*, assiduously, constantly, sedulously, diligently, punctually.

assiégé, *n.m.*, besieged. *Les — s firent une sortie ;* the besieged made a sally.

assiégeant, **-e**, *adj.*, besieging.

assiégeant, *n.m.*, besieger.

assiéger, *v.a.*, to besiege, to lay siege to ; to surround ; to beset, to dun. *Ses créanciers l'assiègent ;* his creditors dun him.

assiette, *n.f.*, plate ; seat, situation, sitting, posture ; tone, state of the mind ; temper, condition of one's mind ; assessment (of taxes) ; (nav.) trim ; (man.) seat ; (arch.) site. *— s blanches ;* clean plates. *Une — à soupe ;* a soup plate. *— d'argent ;* a silver plate. *L' —*

d'une église ; the site of a church. L'— d'un bâtiment ; the situation of a building. Cela n'est pas dans son — ; that is not steady. Il n'est pas dans son — ; he is out of sorts, not at his ease. Faire l'— de ; to assess. Piquer l'— ; to sponge. Pique— ; sponger. L'— d'une rente ; the assignment of an annuity. — d'un vaisseau ; trim of a ship. Casseur d'—s ; swaggerer. Son — dîne pour lui ; present or not, he pays all the same.

assiettée, n.f., a plateful.

assignable, adj., assignable.

⊙**assignant**, n.m. V. **demandeur.**

assignat, n.m., assignat (French paper money. Legs par — ; specific legacy.

assignation, n.f., summons, subpœna, writ; appointment, rendezvous, assignation; assignment; transfer; (com.) check. Signifier une — à quelqu'un ; to serve a writ upon any one. Faire une — de ; to make an assignment of; (com.) appointment. Manquer à l'— ; to break an appointment.

assigné, -e, part., summoned.

assigné, n.m., -e, n.f., defendant. V. **défendeur.**

assigner, v.a., to summon, to subpœna; to assign ; to appoint, to allow, to allot. Obtenir permission d'— quelqu'un ; to take out a writ against any one.

assimilable, adj., assimilable.

assimilation, n.f., assimilation.

assimiler, v.a., to assimilate, to liken, to compare. S'— à quelqu'un ; to compare one's self to any one.

assis, -e, part., seated. Restez — ; keep your seat. Voter par — et levé ; to give one's vote by rising or by remaining seated.

assise, n.f., (arch.) a course; (geol.) layer, stratum.

assises, n.f. pl., assizes, session. Cour d'— ; Assize Court. Tenir les — ; to hold the assizes. Cet homme tient ses — dans la maison ; this man is the oracle of the house.

assistance, n.f., assistance, help, aid; relief, comfort ; audience, company, by-standers; congregation (in a church). —publique ; poor-law relief.

assistant, n.m., -e, n.f., assistant (of religious orders); onlooker, by-stander, beholder, spectator. Il prit tous les —s à témoin ; he took all present to witness.

assistant, -e, adj., assistant, helper.

assister, v.n., to be at, to be present at, to attend, to stand by, to look on, to witness.

assister, v.a., to assist, to help; to succor ; to aid, to support; to attend. — les pauvres ; to relieve the poor. — ses amis de son crédit ; to use one's interest in favor of. Dieu vous assiste ; God help you !

association, n.f., association, partnership, society; combination. Contrat d'— ; deed of partnership. — illégale ; conspiracy. — de secours mutuels ; friendly benefit society. Faire une — avec quelqu'un ; to enter into partnership with any one.

associé, n.m., -e, n.f., associate; fellow; member ; companion ; partner. — bailleur de fonds, — commanditaire ; sleeping partner.

associer, v.a., to associate, to admit or receive as a partner; to take into partnership; to divide or share something with any one.

*s'associer**, v.r., to enter, to get into partnership with one ; to associate one's self with, to join, to combine, to be joined or connected with; to make any one a party to.

assoiffer, v.n., to become thirsty.

assolement, n.m., (agri.) rotation of crops.

assoler, v.a., (agri.) to vary the crops.

assombrir, v.a., to darken, to make gloomy, to throw a gloom over, to sadden, to cloud. S'—,

v.r., to become, grow dark, gloomy ; to darken (of the brow).

assommant, -e, adj., wearisome, tiresome, boring, killing, oppressive (of heat). Cet homme est — ; this man is a great bore.

assommer, v.a., to beat to death, to knock on the head; to beat unmercifully ; to overpower; to overwhelm, to bear down; to pester, to bore; to grieve, to oppress; to plague to death. — à coups de bâton ; to beat to death with a stick. La chaleur m'assomme ; the heat overpowers me.

*s'assommer**, v.r., to kill one's self, to be overwhelmed, to overburden one's self. Vous vous assommez à force de travail ; you are killing yourself by too much labor.

assommeur, n. m., slaughterer, feller (of oxen).

assommoir, n. m., trap; loaded bludgeon. Coup d'— ; overpowering blow. Quel — ! what a bore !

assompti-f, -ve, adj., assumptive.

assomption, n.f., assumption; (rel.) Assumption (Aug. 15).

assonah, n.m. V. **sonna.**

assonance, n.f., assonance.

assonant, -e, adj., assonant.

assorti, -e, part., stocked, furnished ; matched; sorted; paired; suitable. Il n'y a point de marchand mieux — ; no shop-keeper is better stocked. Un mariage bien — ; a very suitable match.

assortiment, n.m., set ; assortment, stock, collection ; match; sorting; combination. Livres d'— ; books on sale (not published by the vendor).

assortir, v.a., to sort, to match, to pair, to stock, to furnish. Mal — ; to mis-match. — des couleurs ; to match colors. — une boutique ; to stock a shop.

assortir, v.n., to match, to sort, to suit, to pair. *s'assortir**, v.r., to match, to agree, to suit; to be a match, to be suitable.

assortissant, -e, adj., suitable, becoming, matching.

assoté, -e, adj., infatuated, extremely fond, doting on.

assoter, v.a., (fam. and iron.) to befool, to infatuate ; to besot. S'—, v.r., to be foolishly fond of.

assoupir, v.a., to make drowsy, heavy, dull ; to lull, to assuage, to allay, to soften ; to deaden; to suppress, to stifle, to still, to quiet, to hush, to hush up.

*s'assoupir**, v.r., to grow drowsy, dull, heavy, sleepy ; to fall asleep ; to doze; to be assuaged, to be weakened; to be appeased, to be stilled.

assoupissant, -e, adj., drowsy, sleepy, soporiferous, soporific. Discours — ; speech that sends one to sleep.

assoupissement (-mān), n.m., drowsiness, sleepiness, heaviness ; carelessness, sloth, negligence, supineness, hushing up ; (med.) coma.

assouplir, v.a., to make supple, to render flexible, tractable ; (man.) to break in. — un cheval ; to break in a horse. — une étoffe ; to make a stuff soft.

*s'assouplir**, v.r., to become supple, manageable.

assourdir, v.a., to deafen, to make deaf ; to stun ; to muffle (a bell, an oar) ; (paint.) to darken.

*s'assourdir**, v.r., to grow deaf.

assourdissant, adj., deafening.

assourdissement, n.m., deafening noise ; muffling, deadening ; temporary deafness.

assouvir, v.a., to glut, to satiate, to cloy, to surfeit, to gratify. — ses passions ; to gratify one's passions. — sa faim ; to satiate one's hunger.

*s'***assouvir**, *v.r.*, to be satiated, glutted, surfeited, cloyed, gratified.

assouvissement (-mān), *n.m.*, glutting, cloying, satiating.

assujettir, *or* **assujétir**, *v.a.*, to subdue, to enthrall, to bring under, into, subjection ; to subject, to tie down ; to oblige ; to fix, to fasten, to wedge in. — *ses passions ;* to master one's passions. *S'*— *à quelque chose ;* to tie one's self down to a thing.

*s'***assujettir**, *v.r.*, to subject one's self to.

assujettissant, -**e**, *adj.*, binding, constraining, fettering, restrictive.

assujettissement (-mān), *n.m.*, subjection, enthrallment ; constraint.

assumer, *v.n.*, to take upon one's self, to assume.

assurance, *n.f.*, assurance, certainty, certitude ; security, safety ; pledge ; trust, confidence ; protestation, promise ; insurance ; boldness, confidence, hardihood. — *maritime ;* marine insurance. — *contre l'incendie ;* fire insurance. — *sur risques ordinaires ;* common insurance. — *sur la vie ;* life insurance. *Bureau d'*— ; insurance-office. *Courtier d'*— ; insurance broker. *Police d'*— ; policy insurance. *Avec* — ; safely. *Il est en lieu d'*— ; he is in a safe place. *Donnez-moi des* —*s ;* give me a security. *Prenez ma montre pour* — ; take my watch as a security. *Il met son* — *en Dieu ;* he puts his trust in God. *Il parle avec* — ; he speaks boldly. *Prenez de l'*— ; put on a little assurance. *Il n'y a pas d'*— *à prendre en vous ;* there is no reliance to be placed in you.

assure, *n.f.*, woof, texture.

assuré, -**e**, *adj.*, sure, safe, secure ; certain ; bold, confident ; impudent ; trusty ; insured. *Une retraite* —*e ;* a safe retreat. *Sa perte est* —*e ;* his ruin is infallible.

assuré, *n.m.*, -**e**, *n.f.*, person insured.

assurément, *adv.*, assuredly, surely, to be sure ; doubtless, undoubtedly ; certainly, sure enough. *Oui,* — ; yes, doubtless. — *non ;* certainly not.

assurer, *v.a.*, to assure (a person of a thing) ; to assert, to affirm, to promise ; to secure, to make sure of ; to guarantee ; to inspire with confidence ; to fix firmly ; to fasten ; to insure ; to underwrite ; (man.) to accustom to the bit. *Il a assuré son argent ;* he has made sure of his money. — *la bouche d'un cheval ;* to accustom a horse to bear the bit. — *une maison contre l'incendie ;* to insure a house against fire. — *pour l'aller ;* (com.) to insure out. — *pour le retour ;* to insure home.

*s'***assurer**, *v.r.*, to secure, to make sure of ; to ascertain ; to be confident of ; to satisfy one's self ; to be assured, to be sure ; to be persuaded, to be convinced. *S'* — *de quelqu'un ;* to secure any one, to engage him. *S'* — *d'un poste ;* to make sure of a position.

assureur, *n.m.*, underwriter, insurer, assurer.

assyrien, -**ne**, *adj.*, *n.*, Assyrian.

astéisme, *n.m.*, (rhet.) asteism, irony.

⊙**astelle**, *n.f.*, (surg.) splint, bolster. *V.* **attelle**.

aster, *n.m.*, (bot.) star-wort, aster.

astérie, *n.f.*, asteria, star-stone ; star-fish.

astérisme, *n.m.*, (astron.) asterism.

astérisque, *n.m.*, asterisk.

astéroïde, *n.m.*, asteroid.

asthénie, *n.f.*, (med.) debility, asthenia.

asthmatique (as-ma-tik), *adj.*, asthmatical.

asthme (as-m), *n.m.*, asthma.

astic, *n.m.*, glazing-stick, polisher.

asticot, *n.m.*, gentle, maggot, worm.

asticoter, *v.a.*, to plague ; to tease, to vex. *Il est toujours à m'*— ; he is always plaguing me.

astiquer, *v.a.*, to polish, to glaze ; to clean up, to dress up.

astracan, *n.m.*, astrakhan (fur).

astragale, *n.m.*, (arch., bot.) astragal ; (anat.) astragalus, talus, ankle-bone ; (gilding, paint.) fillet ; milk-vetch, wild liquorice.

astral, -**e**, *adj.*, astral, starry.

astre, *n.m.*, star, fixed star, luminary. —*s errants ;* wandering stars. *Cette femme est belle comme un* — ; this woman is quite a paragon of beauty.

astrée, *n.f.*, (astron.) Astrea ; (zool.) astrea.

astreindre (astreignant, astreint), *v.a.*, to force, to compel ; to subject ; to bind down, to oblige.

*s'***astreindre**, *v.r.*, to confine one's self, to tie one's self down, to anything.

astriction, *n.f.*, (med.) astriction.

astringence, *n.f.*, astringency.

astringent, -**e**, *adj.*, astringent.

astringent, *n.m.*, astringent.

astroïte, *n.f.*, astroit.

astrolabe, *n.m.*, (astron.) astrolabe.

astrolâtre, *n.m.*, star-worshiper.

astrolâtrie, *n.f.*, astrolatry.

astrolâtrique, *adj.*, star-worshiping.

astrologie, *n.f.*, astrology.

astrologique, *adj.*, astrological.

astrologue (-log), *n.m.*, astrologer.

astronome, *n.m.*, astronomer.

astronomie, *n.f.*, astronomy.

astronomique, *adj.*, astronomical, astronomic.

astronomiquement (-mān), *adv.*, astronomically.

astuce, *n.f.*, craft, guile, wile, cunning.

astucieusement, *adv.*, craftily, cunningly.

astucieu-x, -**se**, *adj.*, crafty, wily.

asyle. *V.* **asile**.

asymétrie, *n.f.*, asymmetry.

asymptote, *n.f.*, (geom.) asymptote.

asymptotique, *adj.*, asymptotical.

asyndète, *n.m.*, (rhet.) asyndeton.

ataraxie, *n.f.*, ataraxy, quietude.

atavisme, *n.m.*, atavism.

ataxie, *n.f.*, (med.) ataxy.

ataxique, *adj.*, (med.) ataxic, irregular.

atelier, *n.m.*, workshop, manufactory ; study ; studio ; office ; shed ; gang (workmen). *Chef d'*— ; foreman. *Tout l'*— *m'a quitté ;* all my workmen have left me. *Jour d'*— ; best, true light.

atellanes, *n.f. pl.*, (hist.) Atellanae.

atermoiement *or* **atermoiment**, *n.m.*, delay of payment ; composition, delay, evasion, shift.

atermoyer, *v.a.*, to put off ; to delay a payment.

atermoyer, *v.n.*, to try to gain time ; to shuffle.

*s'***atermoyer**, *v.r.*, to compound with one's creditors.

athée, *n.m.*, atheist.

athée, *adj.*, atheistical, atheistic.

athéisme, *n.m.*, atheism.

athénée, *n.m.*, athenæum.

athénien, -**ne**, (-ni-in, -ni-è-n), *adj.*, Athenian.

athénien, *n.m.*, -**ne**, *n.f.*, Athenian.

athérome, *n.m.*, (med.) atheroma.

athlète, *n.m.*, athlete ; wrestler ; champion.

athlétique, *n.f.*, athletics.

athlétique, *adj.*, athletic, athletical.

atlante, *n.m.*, (arch.) atlantes.

atlantide, *n.f.*, Atlantis.

atlantides, *n.f. pl.*, (astron.) Atlantides.

atlantique, *adj.*, Atlantic.

atlantique, *n.f.*, Atlantic.

atlas, *n.m.*, atlas ; (anat.) atlas.

atmosphère, *n.f.*, atmosphere.

atmosphérique, *adj.*, atmospherical, atmospheric.

atome, *n.m.*, atom, corpuscle.

atomique, *adj.*, atomical, atomic.

atomisme, *n.m.*, atomism, doctrine of atoms.

atomiste, *n.m.*, atomist.

atomistique, *adj.*, atomical. *Théorie —;* atomic theory.

atone, *adj.*, atonic, dull, lack-lustre, fixed, staring.

atonie, *n.f.*, (med.) atony, debility.

atonique, *adj.*, (med.) atonic, debilitated.

atours, *n.m. pl.*, woman's attire, ornament, dress. *Dame d'—;* lady of the bedchamber. *Être dans ses plus beaux —;* to be dressed in all one's finery. [Generally used in the plural.]

⊙**atourner**, *v.a.*, to attire, to trick out, to dress out, to bedizen.

atout, *n.m.*, a trump; trump-card. *Jouer —;* to play trumps; (fam.) quietus.

atrabilaire, *adj.*, splenetic; gloomy, morose, peevish, bilious; melancholy.

atrabile, *n.f.*, (med.) black bile, hypochondria.

âtre, *n.m.*, fire-place, hearth, floor (of ovens).

atroce, *adj.*, atrocious, odious, grievous, cruel, flagitious, excruciating.

atrocement (-mǎn), *adv.*, atrociously, cruelly, outrageously.

atrocité, *n.f.*, atrociousness, heinousness, grievousness ; atrocity.

atrophie, *n.f.*, (med.) atrophy.

atrophié, -e, *adj.*, wasted, withered, atrophied, stunted.

atrophier, *v.a.*, to waste, to wither. *S'—*, *v.r.*, to waste away.

attaballe, *n.m.*, attabal (Moorish tabor).

attablé, -e, *part.*, seated at table.

attabler, *v.a.*, to set to table.

*s'***attabler**, *v.r.*, to sit down to, to take one's place at, table.

attachant, -e, *adj.*, engaging, captivating, winning, interesting, attractive, pleasing.

attache, *n.f.*, string, cord, strap, leash, tether (for dogs) ; band (of wood, iron) ; tie, fastening, rivet ; attachment, inclination ; consent ; (anat.) attachment, stabling. *Mettre un chien à l'—;* to tie a dog up. *Prendre des chevaux à l'—;* to take in horses. *Vivre sans —;* to live free. *Être à l'—;* to be always slaving.

attaché, -e, *part.*, fastened, fixed, attached ; tied, bound ; intent on, bent on. *— à son opinion ;* wedded to one's own opinion.

attaché, *n.m.*, attaché (of an embassy).

attachement (-tash-mǎn), *n.m.*, attachment ; affection ; inclination ; eagerness, constant application, zeal, tie, bond ; (arch.) *pl.*, memoranda of work done. *— à l'étude ;* fondness for study.

attacher, *v.a.*, to fasten, to make fast, to attach, to fix, to stick, to tack ; to connect, to join ; to apply, to affix ; to suspend, to hang ; to hook, to link, to chain, to rivet ; to engage, to bind, to endear, to captivate ; to interest, to make attentive, to occupy. *— avec une épingle ;* to pin. *— avec une courroie ;* to strap. *— avec un crochet ;* to hook. *— avec de la colle de pâte ;* to paste. *— avec de la colle forte ;* to glue. *C'est ce qui m'attache à vous ;* this is what binds me to you. *— du prix à quelque chose ;* to set a value upon something. *— le grelot ;* to bell the cat.

*s'***attacher**, *v.r.*, to take hold, to hold to, to fasten on ; to cling ; to cleave, to stick, to keep close, to adhere ; to be attached, to have an affection for, to interest one's self in ; to apply one's self to ; to gain over. *La poix s'attache aux doigts ;* pitch sticks to the fingers. *Ils s'attachèrent l'un à l'autre ;* they became attached to each other. *Je m'attachai à lui plaire, mais en vain ;* I used all my efforts to please him, but in vain. *S'— à remplir son devoir ;* to strive to fulfill one's duty.

attaquable, *adj.*, assailable ; that may be attacked ; of doubtful validity.

attaquant, *n.m.*, assailant, aggressor.

attaque, *n.f.*, attack, onset ; assault ; approach ;

insult, reproach ; aggression ; fit, stroke. *Elle a eu une — de nerfs ;* she has had a nervous attack.

attaqué, -e, *part.*, attacked, stricken, assaulted, set upon ; provoked, urged.

attaquer, *v.a.*, to attack, to assail, to assault, to fall *or* set upon one, to come upon ; to sue ; (man.) to spur ; to impugn, to reproach, to censure ; to contest the validity of a document, to sue ; to begin ; to provoke ; (nav.) to near a cape, a coast. *— quelqu'un de paroles ;* to insult any one. *L'— sur sa naissance ;* to reproach him his birth. *— quelqu'un de conversation ;* to address a person. *— le taureau par les cornes ;* to seize the bull by the horns. *Il attaque bien la note ;* (mus.) he strikes the note well. *Il attaque bien la corde ;* he makes the string tell.

*s'***attaquer**, *v.r.*, to challenge, to defy, to set upon ; to find fault with ; to fall foul of any one ; to fall upon, to encounter any one. *Il s'est attaqué à son maître ;* he has encountered one who is more than his match.

attarder, *v.a.*, to delay. *V.* **retarder**.

*s'***attarder**, *v.r.*, to be belated, to loiter on the way, to linger.

atteindre (atteignant, atteint), *v.a.*, to touch, to strike, to hit, to hurt, to injure ; to reach, to attain ; to affect ; to arrive at, to come to ; to come up to, to overtake, to catch, to join ; to equal. *Il n'a pas atteint le but ;* he has not hit the mark. *La balle l'atteignit au front ;* the ball struck him in the forehead. *— son maître ;* to equal one's master. *— l'âge de ;* to attain the age of. *Ce danger ne saurait m'— ;* this danger cannot reach me. *Nous atteindrons le village avant la nuit ;* we shall reach the village before night. *— l'ennemi ;* to come up with the enemy. *Il a beau courir, je l'atteindrai ;* it is in vain for him to run, I shall overtake him. *Etre atteint de ;* to be seized with.

atteindre, *v.n.*, to reach, to come at, to touch ; to attain, to compass. *Je ne saurais y — ;* I cannot reach it, come up to it. *— au but ;* to hit the mark. *— à la perfection ;* to attain to perfection.

atteint, -e, *part.*, hit, struck ; attacked, seized, affected, reached. *— d'un crime ;* arraigned for a crime.

atteinte, *n.f.*, blow, stroke, touch ; attack, fit, seizure (of disease) ; injury, damage, harm, wrong ; reach ; outrage ; (man.) overreach. *Les —s du froid ;* the ill-effects of cold. *Une légère — de goutte ;* a slight touch of the gout. *Sa santé n'a jamais reçu d'— ;* his health has never received any injury. *Porter — à ;* to injure, to impair, to commit an offense against. *Subir une — ;* to receive a blow, an injury. *Je suis hors de ses —s ;* I am out of his reach. *Porter — à l'honneur ;* to sully the fair name of. *Porter — aux droits de ;* to infringe the rights of.

attelage (-laj), *n.m.*, team, yoke, set, pair ; carriage, horses.

atteler (-lé), *v.a.*, to put horses to ; to yoke. *Dites au cocher qu'il attelle ;* tell the coachman to put the horses to. *C'est une charrette mal attelée ;* they are an ill-assorted couple.

attelle, *n.f.*, hame ; (surg.) splint.

attenant, -e (-nǎn, -t), *adj.*, next, contiguous, adjoining.

⊙**attenant**, *prep.*, next to, close by.

en **attendant**, *adv.*, in the mean time, in the interim, meanwhile, till then, temporarily.

en **attendant que**, *conj.*, till, until. *Jouons en — qu'il vienne ;* let us play till he comes. *En — mieux ;* until something better turns up.

attendre, *v.a.*, to wait for, to stay for, to tarry for ; to look forward to ; to expect ; to look for ; to await, to attend, to be in store for. *— la mort ;* to await death. *Le dîner nous attend ;* the dinner is waiting for us. *Nous l'attendons à dîner ;* we expect him to dinner. *Je l'attends à tout moment ;* I expect him every minute. *C'est* *là où je l'attends;* there I shall have him. *Attendez-moi sous l'orme;* you may wait for me till doomsday. *Voilà le sort qui vous attend;* this is the fate in store for you. *Attendez!* stay! hold! *Je suis las d'—;* I am tired of waiting. *Attendons encore un peu;* let us wait a little longer. *Qu'il attende;* let him wait. *Tout vient à point à qui sait —;* patience brings all things about. *Il attend que son fils revienne;* he is waiting till his son returns. *Attendez jusqu'à demain;* wait till to-morrow. *Une question n'attendait pas l'autre;* question followed question.

*s'***attendre,** *v.r.,* to rely upon, to count upon ; to trust, to trust to ; to expect, to look forward to, to anticipate; to reckon upon. *Se faire —;* to keep people waiting. *Il ne faut pas s'— à cela;* we must not rely upon that. *Je m'y attends;* I expect it. *Je ne m'attendais pas à cela;* I did not expect that. *Attendez-vous-y!* I wish you may get it!

attendri, -e, *part.,* moved, affected, touched.

attendrir, *v.a.,* to make tender, to soften; to touch ; to move, to affect. *Cela attendrit la viande;* that makes meat tender. *Ses larmes m'ont attendri le cœur;* his tears have softened my heart.

*s'***attendrir,** *v.r.,* to grow tender ; **to be moved,** to melt, to pity, to relent, to soften. *S'— sur le sort de quelqu'un;* to pity the fate of any one.

attendrissant, -e, *adj.,* moving, affecting, heart-stirring, soul-moving.

attendrissement (-măn), *n.m.,* compassion, feeling; emotion, sensibility; relenting, tenderness.

attendu, *prep.,* considering, on account of, in consideration of. *—que;* seeing that, as, whereas, in *or* for as much as.

attenir, *v.n.,* to adjoin ; **to be contiguous.**

attentat, *n.m.,* attempt at crime ; crime; attempt; criminal attempt; indecent assault ; outrage, infringement, violation. *— à la pudeur;* outrage on decency. *— contre la vie de;* attempt upon the life of. *— contre les lois;* outrage upon the laws.

attentatoire, *adj.,* (jur.) hostile, outrageous, unlawful, in contempt of.

attente, *n.f.,* expectation, waiting; hope, expectation. *Remplir, tromper, l'—;* to come up to, to deceive, expectation. *Pierre d'—;* (arch.) toothing; (fig.) stepping-stone. *Etre dans l'—de;* to be expecting. *Ligature d'—;* (surg.) temporary ligature. *Salle d'—;* waiting-room. (com.) *Dans l'— de vous lire;* awaiting the favor of a reply.

attenter, *v.n.,* to attempt, to make an attempt. *— à la vie de quelqu'un;* to make an attempt upon any one's life. *— contre la liberté publique;* to make an attempt against public liberty. *— à ses jours;* to try to take one's own life.

attenti-f, -ve, *adj.,* attentive, heedful, mindful, considerate ; studious; diligent, careful. *Etre — à;* to look after, to see to.

attentifs, *n.m. pl.,* followers.

attention, *n.f.,* attention, attentiveness, care ; heed, mindfulness, carefulness, vigilance ; regard, respect, consideration. *Faute d'—;* inadvertently. *Force d'—;* intentness. *Avec —;* attentively. *Manque d'—;* heedlessness. *Faire une chose avec —;* to do a thing with care. *Faire — à;* to mind. *— au commandement!* (milit.) attention! *Faites donc —;* mind what you say, what you do. *N'y faites pas —!* do not mind it! *Regarder avec —;* to look fixedly. *Prêtez-y —;* pay attention to it. *Cela mérite —;* that deserves notice. *S'attirer l'— du public;* to attract the notice of the public. *Plein d'—;* regardful, mindful. *Sans —;* reckless. *Il a eu l'— de m'avertir;* he was good enough to warn me. *Il a pour moi de grandes —s;* he has a great regard for me. *Attention!* Look out!

attentionné, -e, *adj.,* attentive.

attentivement (-măn), *adv.,* attentively, carefully.

atténuant, -e, *adj.,* attenuant; (jur.) palliating, extenuating.

atténuant, *n.m.,* (med.) attenuant.

atténuation, *n.f.,* attenuation, weakness; extenuation, mitigation, palliation.

atténué, -e, *adj.,* attenuated, wasted, emaciated, palliated ; tapering.

atténuer, *v.a.,* to attenuate, to weaken, to make thin ; to extenuate, to mitigate, to palliate, to underrate. *— un crime;* to palliate a crime.

atterrage, *n.m.,* (nav.) landing, landfall, making land.

atterrant, -e, *adj.,* astounding, startling, overwhelming.

atterrer, *v.a.,* to throw or strike down, to bring to the ground; to overthrow ; to destroy, to demolish, to ruin; to subvert ; to deject, to cast down ; to astound, to overwhelm.

atterrer, *v.n.,* (nav.) to make land.

atterrir, *v.n.,* (nav.) to land, to make land.

atterrissage, *n.m.,* landing, making land.

atterrissement (-ĕr-ris-măn), *n.m.,* alluvion, accretion, alluvium.

attestation, *n.f.,* attestation, certificate, voucher, oath, affidavit.

attester, *v.a.,* to attest, to certify, to vouch, to witness, to swear, to testify, to call, to take to witness. *J'en atteste le ciel;* I call heaven to witness. *J'en atteste les dieux;* witness, ye gods.

atticisme, *n.m.,* Atticism.

atticiste, *n.m.,* Atticist.

attiédir, *v.n.,* to make lukewarm, to cool, to abate. *Le temps attiedira leur zèle;* time will cool their ardor.

*s'***attiédir,** *v.n.,* to cool, to grow cool, lukewarm, to become cool.

attiédissement (-măn), *n.m.,* lukewarmness, coolness ; abatement.

attifement, *n.m.,* toggery, rig-out.

attifer, *v.a.,* to dress out ; to bedizen.

*s'***attifer,** *v.r.,* to dress oneself out, to rig oneself out.

attifet, *n.m.,* ornament, trinket.

attique (at-tik), *adj.,* Attic; (arch.) attic. *Goût —;* Attic taste. *Sel —;* Attic salt, Attic wit.

attique, *n.m.,* Attic; (arch.) attic, attic story.

attiquement, *adv.,* (gram.) after the Attic dialect.

*****attirail,** *n.m. sing.,* apparatus, implements, utensils, tire, gear, furniture, tackle ; baggage, train, equipage, paraphernalia ; show, pomp. *L'— d'une imprimerie;* the materials and implements of a printing-office. *L'— d'une cuisine;* kitchen apparatus and utensils.

attirant, -e, *adj.,* attractive, alluring, enticing, engaging.

attirer, *v.a.,* to attract, to draw ; to incite ; to bring over, to win over, to gain over ; to lure, to wheedle, to entice, to bring upon, to inspire. *L'aimant attire le fer;* the loadstone attracts iron. *— par des caresses;* to wheedle by caresses. *— l'ennemi dans une embuscade;* to draw the enemy into an ambuscade. *— les yeux, les regards de tout le monde;* to attract the eyes of all the world. *Un malheur en attire un autre;* one misfortune seldom comes alone.

*s'***attirer,** *v.r.,* to draw down upon one, to draw or bring upon oneself ; to incur, to run into, to get into, to attract; to win, to gain, to get. *— l'attention du public;* to attract the notice of the public. *— des affaires;* to get one's self into scrapes.

attiser, *v.a.,* to make up (the fire), to stir up; to poke; (fig.) to incense, to stir up. *— le feu;* to fan the flame.

attisoir or **attisonnoir**, *n.m.*, (in foundries), poker.

attitrer, *v.a.*, (seldom used but in the *past participle*) to appoint, to recognize; to bribe. *Juges attitrés;* appointed judges. *Marchand attitré;* the shopkeeper one usually deals with. *Témoins attitrés;* bribed witnesses.

attitude, *n.f.*, attitude, (paint.) posture.

attouchement (-toosh-mān), *n.m.*, touch, feeling, contact.

attract-eur, -rice, *adj.*, attractile.

attracti-f, -ve, *adj.*, attractive.

attraction, *n.f.*, attraction.

attraire, *v.a.*, to allure, to entice.

attrait, *n.m.*, allurement, attraction, charm; (rel.) comfort. *La beauté est un puissant —;* beauty is a powerful charm.

attrape, *n.f.*, bite, trick, take-in, sell, hoax.

attrape, *n.m.* — *nigaud;* fool-trap. — *mouche;* catch-fly. *C'est un — tout;* he is a grabber.

attrape-lourdaud, *n.m.*, (—, or — —*s*) clap-trap; catch-penny.

attrape-parterre, *n.m.*, (—, or — —*s*) (l.u.) clap-trap for the pit, clap-trap.

attraper, *v. a.*, to entrap, to ensnare, to trap; to take in, to catch; to overreach; to cheat, to trick; to overtake; to get, to secure; to receive; to compass; to take, to surprise; to hit, to reach; to seize. — *un renard dans un piège;* to entrap a fox. *Prenez garde à vous, il vous attrapera;* look to yourself, he 'll take you in. *Il en a attrapé de plus fins que vous;* he has taken in more cunning people than you are. *Attrape qui peut;* scramble for it. *Attrapé!* caught! *Il a attrapé un bon bénéfice;* he has got a good living. — *un rhume;* to catch a cold. — *un coup;* to get a blow. — *quelqu'un sur le fait;* to catch any one in the act. *La pierre l'a attrapé à la tempe;* the stone hit him on the temple. — *le sens, la pensée, d'un auteur;* to catch the sense, to hit upon the meaning of an author. — *un caractère;* to hit off a character. — *la ressemblance;* to hit off the likeness. *Attrape!* take that!

s'attraper, *v.r.*, to be caught; (man.) to clip.

attrapeu-r, *n.m.*, **-se**, *n.f.*, deceiver, deluder, cheat, trickster.

attrapoire, *n.f.*, trap, pit-fall, snare; wile, trick.

attrayant, -e, *adj.*, attractive, inviting, winning, engaging, charming.

attribuer, *v.a.*, to attach, to annex; to attribute, to ascribe, to impute (a thing to any one); to assign, to confer. — *des privilèges à une charge;* to assign; to attach privileges to an office.

s'attribuer, *v.r.*, to assume, to take upon one's self, to arrogate to one's self; to claim. *Il s'attribue de grands droits;* he claims extensive rights.

attribut, *n.m.*, attribute, prerogative; (log.) predicate, attribute, quality; symbol, emblem.

attributi-f, -ve, *adj.*, attributive; (law) relative.

attribution, *n.f.*, conferring; privilege, prerogative; *pl.*, powers; province, department. *(law)* cognizance, competence. *Lettres d'—;* patents conferring power (to act).

attristant, -e, *adj.*, sad, sorrowful, melancholy, grievous.

attrister, *v.a.*, to grieve, to afflict, to trouble, to cast down, to throw a gloom over. *Cette nouvelle l'attriste;* that piece of news grieves him.

s'attrister, *v.r.*, to grieve, to yield to sorrow; to be sad, to become sorrowful.

attrition, *n.f.*, (theol.) attrition; (phys.) attrition, friction.

attroupement (-troop-mān), *n.m.*, gathering, riotous assemblage, mob, rabble. *Loi contre les —s;* Riot Act.

attrouper, *v.a.*, to assemble, to gather together. *Il attroupa toute la canaille;* he gathered all the rabble together.

s'attrouper, *v.r.*, to flock together, to gather in crowds, to get together tumultuously. *Défense de s'—;* no gatherings allowed.

au, contraction of *à le*, to the. *Céder au torrent;* to give way to the torrent. *Sauce — vin blanc;* wine-sauce.

aubade, *n.f.*, morning serenade; reproof, abuse, lecture. *Il en a eu l'—;* he was reproved for it.

⊙**aubain**, *n.m.*, alien, foreigner.

aubainage, *n.m.*, escheatage.

aubaine, *n.f.*, (jur.) aubaine, escheat, escheatage; windfall, piece of good luck.

aube, *n.f.*, the dawn; alb (priest's garment); (hydr.) float-board; float; paddle-board (of steamers). *D'— du jour;* the break of day. —*s de moulin;* flat-boards of a mill. *Roue à —s;* paddle-wheel. — *mobile;* feathering paddle.

aubépine, *n.f.*, hawthorn, whitethorn, may.

aubère, *adj.*, (man.) flea-bitten gray. *Cheval —;* flea-bitten gray horse.

auberge, *n.f.*, inn, public-house, tavern.

aubergine. *V.* **melongène**.

aubergiste, *n.m.*, innkeeper, publican, landlord, host.

auberon, *n.m.*, catch (of a lock).

auberonnière, *n.f.*, clasp (of a lock).

*****aube-vigne**, *n.f.*, (bot.) virgin's-bower, traveler's joy.

aubier, *n.m.*, (bot.) sap-wood, alburnum.

aubifoin, *n.m.*, (bot.) bluebottle, corn-flower.

aubin, *n.m.*, (man.) canter, hand-gallop.

aubiner, *v.n.*, (man.) to canter; (hort.) to earth; (of vines) to layer.

aubour, *n.m.*, (bot.) laburnum.

aucun, -e, *adj.*, any; (negative) none, no one; not any; no. *Je ne connais — de vos juges;* I know none of your judges. — *ne le dira;* no one will say so. *Je doute qu'— de vous le fasse;* I doubt whether any of you will do it. *Il n'y a — de ses sujets qui ne mourût pour lui;* there is not one of his subjects who would not die for him. *De tous ceux qui se disaient mes amis, — m'a-t-il secouru?* did any of all those who called themselves my friends assist me? *Je vous le cède sans bénéfice —;* I let you have it without any profit whatever. *Il n'a fait —es dispositions;* he has made no arrangements. *Sans —s frais;* without any expense.

aucunement (-mān), *adv.*, in no wise, not at all, not in the least. *Je ne le connais —;* I do not know him at all. —, *Monsieur;* not in the least, Sir.

audace, *n.f.*, audacity, insolence, assurance, daring, boldness. *Avec —;* insolently. *Payer d'—;* to brazen it out.

audacieusement (-eûz-mān), *adv.*, audaciously, daringly, boldly.

audacieu-x, -se, *adj.*, audacious, daring; impudent, insolent; presumptuous, bold; high-spirited, enterprising. *Génie —;* daring genius. *Entreprise —se;* bold enterprise.

⊙**au deçà** (ô-dsa), *prep. V.* **deçà**.

au delà (ô-dlà), *prep.*, on the other side, beyond. *V.* **delà**.

audience, *n.f.*, audience, auditory; court, sitting, hearing; hall (where causes are heard); levee. *Jour d'—;* court day. *Ouvrir l'—;* to open the court. — *publique;* open court. — *à huis clos;* a sitting with closed doors, a case heard *in camerâ. En pleine —;* in open court. *L'— est levée;* the sitting is raised. *On le mit hors de l'—;* he was turned out of the court. *L'— est reprise;* the case is resumed. *Donner —;* (of a minister) to hold a levee, to give audience. *Tenir l'—;* (of a judge) to sit, to preside.

audiencier, *adj.m.* *Huissier* —; crier of a court.

audiencier, *n.m.,* usher, crier of a court.

auditeur, *n.m.,* auditor, auditress, hearer ; auditor (of accounts).

auditi-f, -ve, *adj.,* auditory. *Conduit* — *externe ;* cavity of the ear.

audition, *n.f.,* (jur.) hearing, audit, auditing. *L'— des témoins ;* the hearing of the witnesses.

auditoire, *n.m.,* congregation (in a church) ; audience (theatre, &c.) ; auditory, bar, court.

auge, *n.f.,* trough ; a plasterer's hod ; spout (of a water-mill). — *à goudron ;* (nav.) tar-bucket. — *d'écurie ;* manger.

augée, *n.f.,* hodful, troughful.

augelot (ôj-lo), *n.m.,* little ditch ; small trough, ladle.

auger, *v.a.,* (tech.) to hollow out.

auget, *n.m.,* seed-box, drawer (of a bird-cage) ; spout (of a mill-hopper) ; small trough ; bucket (of a water-wheel) ; trough.

augment, *n.m.,* (gram.) augment ; (med.) increase, jointure, dowry.

augmentateur, *n.m.,* augmenter ; *(adj.)* augmenting.

augmentati-f, -ve, *adj.,* (gram.) augmentative.

augmentation, *n.f.,* augmentation, increase, enlargement, addition ; (com.) rise (in salary).

augmenté, -e, *part.,* augmented, increased. *Un livre revu, corrigé et* — ; a book revised, corrected, and augmented.

augmenter, *v.a.,* to augment, to increase, to enlarge, to add to, to raise the salary of ; (com.) to raise. *Il a augmenté sa maison ;* he has enlarged his house. — *le prix ;* to raise the price. *Je vais* — *mon commis ;* I am about to increase my clerk's salary.

augmenter, *v.n.,* to augment, to increase, to grow, to rise (in price), to multiply. *Le sucre a augmenté de prix ;* sugar has risen in price.

s'augmenter, *v.r.,* to increase, to enlarge, to better, to improve.

augural, -e, *adj.,* augural, augurial.

augure, *n.m.,* augury ; omen, token ; augur, soothsayer. *Un bon, un mauvais* — ; a good, bad omen. *De mauvais* — ; ominous, portentous, ill-boding. *Funeste* — ; ill-boding omen. *Un oiseau de mauvais* — ; a bird of ill-omen.

augurer, *v.a.,* to augur, to conjecture, to surmise. *Qu'en pouvez-vous* —? what can you augur from it ? *Je n'en augure rien de bon ;* I foresee no good result.

auguste, *adj.,* august, sacred, venerable.

augustement, *adv.,* (l. u.) in an august manner.

augustin, -e, *n.m.f.,* Austin friar, or nun. *Saint* — ; (print.) English.

aujourd'hui, *adv.,* to-day, this day ; nowadays, now, at present. *D'— en huit ;* this day week. *D'— en quinze ;* this day fortnight. *Dès* — ; from to-day, henceforth. — *il y a huit, quinze, jours ;* it is a week, a fortnight, ago. *La mode d'—* ; the present fashion. *Les hommes d'—* ; the men of the present day. *Ce n'est pas d'— que nous nous connaissons ;* we are no new acquaintances.

aulique, *adj.,* aulic.

aulique, *n.f.,* thesis.

aulnaie, aulne, aulnée. *V.* **aunaie, aune, aunée.**

auloffée, *n.f.,* (nav.) luff.

aulx (ô), *pl.* of **ail.**

aumailles, *adj.* *Bêtes* — ; horned cattle.

aumône, *n.f.,* alms, alms-giving, charity, gift, dole. *Faire l'—* ; to give alms. *Demander l'—* ; to beg. *Vivre d'—* ; to live upon alms. *Etre réduit à l'—* ; to be reduced to beggary. *Faites moi l'— d'un regard ;* bestow but one look upon me. *Qui vit d'—s, meurt de faim ;* beg and starve.

⊙**aumônée,** *n.f.,* sum given to hospitals.

⊙**aumôner,** *v.a.,* to pay a fine to the poor.

aumônerie, *n.f.,* almonry, chaplaincy.

aumônier, *n.m.,* almoner, chaplain, ordinary.

aumônière, *n.f.,* alms-box, alms-purse ; almoner (nun).

aumôni-er, -ère, *adj.,* charitable, lavish of alms.

aumusse or **aumuce,** *n.f.,* amess, hood (priest's garment).

aunage, *n.m.,* alnage, ell-measure.

aunaie, *n.f.,* an alder-plot, grove of alders.

⊙**aune,** *n.f.,* ell ; (fig.) measure, standard. *Acheter à l'—* ; to buy by the ell. *Mesurer les autres à son* — ; to measure another man's peck by one's own bushel. *Les hommes ne se mesurent pas à l'—* ; one must not judge of a man's merit by his stature. *Il sait ce qu'en vaut l'—* ; he knows it to his cost, by experience. *En avoir tout du long de l'—* ; to get it with a vengeance.

aune, *n.m.,* alder-tree.

aunée or **aulnée,** *n.f.,* (bot.) elecampane.

auner, *v.a.,* to measure ; to judge of, to value.

auneur, *n.m.,* alnager, measurer.

auparavant, *adv.,* before, first ; heretofore, previously ; ere now. *Longtemps* — ; a long time before.

auprès, *prep.,* near, by ; close to ; close by ; near to ; with, in, over ; to, in comparison with. *Sa maison est — de la mienne ;* his house is close to mine. *Etre — d'un seigneur ;* to live with a nobleman. *Excusez-le — de son père ;* excuse him to his father. *Il cherche à me nuire — de vous ;* he endeavors to lower me in your esteem. *Etre bien — de quelqu'un ;* to be in anybody's good books. *Elle peut tout — de lui ;* she can do anything with him. *Votre mal n'est rien — du sien ;* your distress is nothing to his. *Vivre — de ses parents ;* to live with one's parents.

auprès, *adv.,* by, hard by, close to.

aurate, *n.m.,* (chem.) aurate.

auréole, *n.f.,* glory, halo, nimbus, crown of glory ; (paint.) aureola ; (anat.) areola.

auriculaire, *adj.,* auricular. *Témoin* — ; ear-witness. *Le doigt* — ; the little finger.

auriculaire, *n.m.,* the little finger.

auricule, *n.f.,* auricle, external ear ; (bot.) bear's ear, auricula.

auriculé, -e, *adj.,* (bot.) auriculate, eared.

aurifère, *adj.,* auriferous.

aurifier, *v.a.,* to stop (teeth) with gold.

aurillard. *V.* **orillard.**

aurique, *adj.,* shoulder - of - mutton shaped. *Voiles* —*s ;* lateen sails.

aurochs (oroks), *n.m.,* (mam.) urus, wild bull.

aurone, *n.f.,* abrotanum, southern-wood.

aurore, *n.f.,* dawn, morning, morn, day-dawn, day ; East ; gold color ; (myth., astron.) Aurora. *A l'—* ; at daybreak. *Avant l'—* ; before dawn. *L'— commençait à poindre ;* day was beginning to dawn. *L'— aux doigts de rose ;* rosy-fingered morn. *Du couchant à l'—* ; from west to east. — *boréale ;* aurora borealis.

auscultation, *n.f.,* (med.) auscultation.

ausculter, *v.a.,* (med.) to auscultate.

auspice, *n.m.,* auspice, omen, presage. *Heureux* —*s ;* a good omen, auspices.

aussi, *adv.,* too, also, likewise ; besides, therefore, moreover ; accordingly ; so ; as much ; as. *Vous le voulez, et moi* — ; you will have it so, and I too. *Donnez-m'en* — ; give me some too. *Il est — sage que vaillant ;* he is as prudent as courageous. *Il est — sot que son ami ;* he is as much a fool as his friend.

aussi, *conj.,* therefore, but then. *Ces dentelles sont belles,* — *coûtent-elles beaucoup ;* these laces are fine, but then they are dear. — *bien :*

for, and the more so as; as well. *Je ne veux point y aller, — bien est-il trop tard;* I won't go there, the more so as it is too late. *Je n'ai que faire de l'en prier, — bien ne m'écouterait-il pas;* it would be in vain for me to entreat him, inasmuch as he would not listen to me. *Je sais cela — bien que vous;* I know that as well as you. — *peu que;* as little as, as few as.

aussière or **haussière**, *n.f.*, (nav.) hawser, small cable, warp.

aussitôt, *adv.*, immediately, directly, as soon as, forthwith. — *après votre départ;* immediately after your departure. — *dit, — fait;* no sooner said than done. — *que;* as soon as, whenever. — *qu'il viendra;* as soon as he comes.

auster (os-tèr), *n.m.*, auster, south-wind.

austère, *adj.*, austere, severe, stern, grave; harsh, sharp (to the taste).

austèrement (-mãn), *adv.*, austerely, severely, rigidly.

austérité, *n.f.*, austerity; severity, sternness; strictness.

austral, -e, *adj.*, austral.

autan, *n.m.*, (poet.) south wind, storm, blast. *Braver les —s;* to face the storm.

autant, *adv.*, as much, as many; so much, so many; as far, as long. *Ce vase contient — que l'autre;* this vase contains as much as the other. *Il y avait — d'hommes que de femmes;* there were as many men as women. *Travaillez — que vous pourrez;* work as much as you can. *Je l'ai vendu tout —;* I sold it for quite as much. *Une fois —;* as much again. *—que jamais;* as much as ever. — *l'esclavage me répugne, — la liberté m'effraie;* liberty alarms me as much as slavery is repugnant to me. — *de têtes, — d'opinions;* so many men, so many minds. *Cela est fini, ou — vaut;* that is as good as done. — *en emporte le vent;* all that is idle talk. *Boire d'—;* to drink a great deal. *A la charge d'—;* on condition of a return. — *ne pas y aller du tout;* might as well not go at all. — *que;* as, as far as. — *que j'en puis juger;* as far as I can conjecture. — *dire;* you might as well say.

d'autant mieux or **d'autant plus** (*adverb. phrase*), the more so, so much the more so, the rather, especially. *Je l'estime d'autant plus qu'il est pauvre;* I esteem him the more because he is poor. *Je l'en aime d'autant mieux;* I love her all the more for it.

d'autant moins (*adverb. phrase*), the less, so much the less. *Il en est d'autant moins à craindre;* he is all the less to be feared.

d'autant que, *conj.*, seeing that, more especially as.

autel, *n.m.*, altar; (astron.) ara. *Le Sacrement de l'—;* the host; the holy Sacrament, Eucharist. *Les —s;* religion. *Grand, maître, —;* high altar. *Nappe d'—;* altar cloth. *Tableau d'—;* altar-piece. *Il mérite qu'on lui élève des —s;* he deserves the greatest honors. *Il en prendrait sur l'—;* he would rob a church. *Qui sert à l'— doit vivre de l'—;* every man must live by his profession.

auteur, *n. m.*, author, authoress; inventor, maker, cause, source, contriver, framer; writer; perpetrator; achiever; artist, engraver, composer, sculptor; owner; informant, authority. *Dieu est l'— de toutes choses;* God is the author of all things. *L'— d'un projet;* the framer of a project. *L'— d'un procédé;* the inventor of a process. *C'est elle qui est l'— de ce livre;* she is the author of that book. *Se faire —;* to turn author. *Nommez votre —;* name your informant, authority. *Droit d'—;* copyright.

authenticité, *n.f.*, authenticity, genuineness.

authentique, *adj.*, original; authentic, genuine.

authentique, *n.f.*, authentics.

authentiquement (-mãn), *adv.*, authentically.

authentiquer, *v.a.*, (jur.) to sign and seal, to authenticate.

autobiographe, *n.m.*, autobiographer.

autobiographie, *n.f.*, autobiography.

autobus, *n.m.*, motor omnibus.

autochtone (-tok-to-n), *n.m.*, (antiq.) autochthon; (*adj.*) autochthonous.   [ing-pan.

autoclave, *adj.*, self-regulating; *n.m.*, steam-

autocrate, *n.m.*, autocrat.

autocratie (-cî), *n.f.*, autocracy.

autocratique, *adj.*, autocratical.

autodafè, *n.m.*, (—s) auto-da-fé.

autographe, *n.m.*, autograph.

⊙**autographe**, *adj.*, autographic, autographical.

autographie, *n.f.*, autography.

autographier, *v.a.*, to autograph.

autographique, *adj.*, autographic.

automate, *n.m.*, automaton.

automatique, *adj.*, automatic, automatical.

automédon, *n.m.*, charioteer, Jehu, driver, cabby.

automnal, -e (-tom-nal), *adj.*, autumnal.

automne (-to-n), *n.m.f.*, autumn; fall of the leaf; fall (of the year).

automot-eur, -rice, *adj.*, self-acting, self-moving, self-propelling.

automobile, *n.m.*, motor-car.

autonome, *adj.*, autonomous.

autonomie, *n.f.*, autonomy, self-government.

autopsie, *n.f.*, post-mortem examination, autopsy, inquest.

autorisation, *n.f.*, authorization; authority, permission; license (of a preacher); warrant; consent.

autoriser, *v.a.*, to authorise, to empower, to commission, to qualify; to allow by authority, to legalize, to license, to warrant. *s'autoriser*, *v.r.*, to get or gain or assume authority, to think one's self warranted (by), to act on the authority of.

autorité, *n.f.*, authority, legal power, rule, command, sway; credit, power, sanction, interest, weight, consideration. *Avoir de l'— sur;* to have power over. *Etre en —;* to be invested with authority. *Il l'a fait de son — privée;* he did it on his own initiative. *Alléguer, apporter des —s;* to quote or cite authorities. *Faire —;* to be an authority.

autour, *n.m.*, goshawk.

autour, *prep.*, about, round, around. — *de sa personne;* about his person. — *du bras;* round the arm. *Tourner — du pot;* to beat about the bush.

autour, *adv.*, about, round, round about. *Il regardait tout —;* he looked all about. *Ici —;* hereabouts.

autourserie, *n.f.*, goshawk training.

autoursier, *n.m.*, goshawk trainer, falconer.

autre, *adj.*, other, different, else, second, another. *L'— jour;* the other day. *Une — fois;* another time. *Tout —;* quite different. *Aucun —;* no one else. *Vous —s;* you people, fellows. *Nous —;* the like of us. *Encore un —;* another, one more. *Il le regarde comme un — lui même;* he looks upon him as a second self.

autre, *pron.*, another, other, else. *Nul — n'y aurait consenti;* nobody else would have consented to it. *Un — le fera;* another will do it. *Tout — l'aurait fait;* any other would have done it. *Les uns se plaisent à une chose, les —s à une —;* some delight in one thing and some in another. *L'un l'—;* one another, each other. *L'un et l'—;* both. *L'un ou l'—;* either. *Ni l'un ni l'—;* neither. *L'un et l'— vous ont obligé;* both have obliged you. *Les uns et les —s;* all. *Ni l'un ni l'— ne valent rien;* both are good for nothing. *A l'un ou à l'—;* to either. *Ni pour l'un ni pour l'—;* for neither. *On les a payés l'un et l'—;* both have been paid. *A l'envi l'un de l'—;* in emulation of one another. *Entre*

—s ; among other people or among other things. *De côté et d'—* ; up and down. *De part et d'—* ; on both sides, on all sides. *C'est un — homme ;* he is no more the same man. *Il ne fait — chose que jouer ;* he does nothing but play. *C'est — chose ;* it is quite another thing. *C'est une — paire de manches ;* that's a horse of another color. *Nous —s Français, nous mangeons beaucoup de pain ;* we French people eat a great deal of bread. *Causer de choses et d'—s ;* to talk of different things. *Il dit d'une façon et il fait d'une —* ; he says one thing and does another. *L'un vaut l'—* ; they are much of a muchness ; or one is as bad as the other. *Comme dit l'—* ; as somebody says ; as the saying is. *Il n'en fait point d'—s ;* he does nothing else, these are his pranks. *L'un dans l'—, l'un portant l'—* ; one with another ; on an average. *Il en sait bien d'—s ;* he knows a trick worth two of that. *J'en ai vu bien d'—s ;* I have outlived worse things than that. *A d'—s !* pshaw ! I know better, you must not tell that to me, tell it to the marines.

autrefois, *adv.,* formerly, in former times ; of old.

autrement, *adv.,* otherwise ; after another manner, another way ; else ; or else. *Faisons —* ; let us go to work another way. *Entrez, — je fermerai la porte ;* come in, or else I 'll shut the door. *C'est un homme qui n'est pas — riche ;* he is a man who is not over rich.

autrichien, -ne, *adj., n.m.f.,* Austrian.

autruche, *n.f.,* (orni.) ostrich. *Avoir un estomac d'—* ; to have the stomach of an ostrich ; to digest anything.

autrui, *n.m., pron.,* others, other people. *Dépendre d'—* ; to depend on others. *Faire à — ce que nous voudrions qu'on nous fît ;* to do by others as we would be done by. *Le bien d'—* ; another's property. *Mal d'— n'est que songe ;* we make light of the ills of others.

auvent, *n.m.,* shed, penthouse, lean-to.

auvernat, *n.m.,* Orléans wine.

aux (*pl.* of au), *art.,* to the. *V.* à.

auxdits, auxdites, *adj.m.f.pl.,* to the said.

auxiliaire, *adj.,* auxiliary, subsidiary. *Verbe —* ; auxiliary verb.

auxiliaire, *n.m.,* auxiliary ; helper, assistant.

s'avachir, *v.r.,* to flag ; to grow fat and flabby ; to get out of shape, to run down at heel.

aval, *adv.,* down, downwards, down stream. *Le vent vient d'—* ; the wind is blowing up stream. *En — de ;* below. *Vent d'—* ; westerly wind.

aval, *n.m.,* (com.) guarantee, indorsement. *Mettez votre — au dos de ce billet ;* indorse that bill.

avalaison, *n.f.,* flood, torrent ; (nav.) a long-continued west or northwest wind.

avalanche, *n.f.,* avalanche, snow-slip.

avalasse, *n.f. V.* **avalaison.**

avalé, -e, *part.,* flagging, hanging down ; sunk, fallen in ; gone down stream.

avaler, *v.a.,* to swallow, to swallow down ; to let down ; to endure, to pocket (affront) ; to lower (things into a cellar) ; to drink, to toss off ; (gard.) to lop ; to gulp down. *— un affront ;* to pocket an insult. *Il ne fait que tordre et —* ; he gobbles up everything. *— du vin dans une cave ;* to let wine down into a cellar. *— une branche ;* to lop off a branch close to the trunk. *— des couleuvres ;* to pocket many affronts.

avaler, *v.n.,* to go down, drop down (the river with the stream).

s'avaler, *v.r.,* to flag, to hang down, to fall down or in ; to be swallowed.

avalette, *n.f.,* a sort of float (angling).

avaleur, *n.m.,* swallower, glutton. *— de pois gris ;* a great glutton. *— de charrettes ferrées ;* a braggadocio.

avaloire, *n.f.,* a large throat or swallow ; (saddlery) breeching ; (hat making) stamper.

avançage, *n.m.,* cab stand, stand.

avance, *n.f.,* advance, start, distance in advance ; projection, prominence ; advance-money ; first step, offer ; gain, benefit. *Il a quatre lieues d'— sur moi ;* he is four leagues ahead of me. *Faire une — de mille écus ;* to advance a thousand crowns. *Faire les —s d'une entreprise ;* to advance the funds for an enterprise. *Faire des —s ;* to make advances to. *Prendre l'—* ; to get the start. *D'—* ; beforehand. *Payer d'—* ; to pay beforehand. *Prévenir d'—* ; to warn beforehand. *A l'—, en — par —* ; beforehand, before one's time, by anticipation.

avancé, -e, *part.,* advanced ; forward, early ; late (of the hour). *Un homme — en âge ;* an elderly man. *Un jeune homme fort —* ; a very forward youth. *Les arbres sont —s ;* the trees are forward. *Je n'en suis pas plus —* ; I am not a bit the better off for it. *Viande —e ;* meat which is getting bad. *Me voilà bien — !* that's all I get for my pains ; I am in a pretty predicament.

avancée, *n.f.,* (milit.) advance guard.

avancement (-mān), *n.m.,* progress, advancement ; improvement ; preferment, promotion, rise.

avancer, *v.a.,* to advance, to bring, to put forward ; to hold out, to stretch out, to set forward ; to bring nearer ; to hasten ; to forward ; to pay beforehand ; to lay out or down ; to assert, to bring forth, to urge ; to hold forth ; to promote, to put on (a clock) ; to broach, to bring forward (opinion) ; to give (a chair). *Avancez la table ;* push the table forward. *— le pied ;* to put one's foot forward. *Faire —* ; to push, to push on. *Cela a avancé sa mort ;* that hastened his death. *— l'horloge ;* to put the clock on. *— le dîner ;* to hasten dinner. *— un ouvrage ;* to forward a piece of work. *Il lui a avancé de l'argent ;* he has advanced him some money. *— les intérêts de quelqu'un ;* to promote any one's interests. *Pouvez-vous prouver ce que vous avancez ?* can you prove your assertion ? *On l'a avancé ;* he has been promoted.

avancer, *v.n.,* to advance, to get on, to proceed, to march on, to move forward, to keep on, to go too fast ; to come out ; to jut out ; to lean over, to bear out ; to encroach ; to improve, to make some progress ; to thrive ; to rise. *Avancez-donc !* come along ! *L'horloge avance ;* the clock is fast. *Cette maison avance trop sur la rue ;* that house juts out too much into the street. *— en âge ;* to advance in years. *Faire — une voiture ;* to call a cab. *Cela m'— bien !* what good is that to me ?

s'avancer, *v.r.,* to advance, to go on, to move forward ; to stand forth ; to draw near, to come up ; to get on, to improve ; to get preferred, to be successful ; to go far ; to jut out, to project. *Cet ambassadeur s'est trop avancé ;* that ambassador has gone too far. *Le temps s'avance ;* time flies. *S'— à cheval ;* to ride up. *S'— en voiture ;* to drive up. *S'— à la voile ;* to sail up. *S'— en courant ;* to run up.

avanceur, *n.m.,* gold-wire drawer.

avanie, *n.f.,* insult, affront, outrage.

avant, *n.m.,* (nav.) prow, head, bow of a ship. *De l'— à l'arrière ;* from stem to stern. *Gagner l'— de ;* to get ahead of, to get a headway (on a ship).

avant, *prep.,* (of time and order) before. *J'ai vu cela — vous ;* I saw that before you. *— toutes choses ;* above all things. *— tout ;* first of all, before all.

avant, *adv.,* far, deep, forward, far advanced. *D'—* ; before. *En —! forward ! march on ! En — de ;* before, in front of. *Mettre en —* ; to bring forward. *N'allez pas si —* ; don't go so far.

Creuser fort — dans la terre; to dig very deep in the ground. *Plus —;* further, deeper. *Bien — dans la nuit;* very late at night. *Nous étions bien — en mer;* we had got a great way out to sea. *Aller de l'—;* (nav.) to go ahead.

avant que, *conj.,* before. *— qu'il soit un an;* before a year is over.

avantage, *n.m.,* advantage, vantage-ground, pleasure; benefit, profit, interest; behalf, behoof; (nav.) weather-gage; (man.) whip-hand; odds (at play). *Avoir l' — sur;* to have the advantage over. *Avoir l' —;* to win, to prevail. *On lui a fait tous les — possibles;* they gave him every possible advantage. *Quel — vous en revient-il?* what benefit do you reap from it? *On peut dire ceci à son —;* this may be said in his favor. *Nos troupes ont eu l'—;* our troop have had the best of it. *Tirer — de tout;* to turn everything to account. *J'ai perdu, vous avez l'—;* I have lost, you have the better of the game. *S'habiller à son —;* to dress to the best advantage.

avantager, *v.a.,* to advantage; to bestow an advantage on; to favor. *La nature l'avait avantagé de beaucoup de qualités précieuses;* nature had endowed him with many inestimable qualities.

avantageusement (-măn), *adv.,* advantageously, to advantage; usefully; beneficially, favorably; highly. *S'habiller —;* to dress to the best advantage. *Parler — de quelqu'un;* to speak highly of any one.

avantageu-x, -se, *adj.,* advantageous, profitable, beneficial, eligible; conceited, presuming; overbearing; (of dress) becoming. *Conditions — ses;* advantageous terms. *Coiffure — se;* a becoming way of dressing the hair. *Un ton —;* a confident, assuming tone. *C'est un homme —;* he is a conceited fellow, vain, presuming.

avant-bec, *n.,* (— — —s) (arch.) starling of a bridge, pier, ice-breaker, cutwater.

avant-bras, *n.m.,* (—) fore-arm.

avant-corps, *n.m.,* (—) (arch.) fore-part.

avant-cour, *n.f.,* (— — —s) fore-court.

avant-coureur, *n.m.,* (— — —s) (mil.) vancourier, forerunner, precursor; harbinger.

avant-courri-er, *n.m.,* **-ère,** *n.f.,* (— — —s) forerunner, harbinger.

avant-derni-er, -ère, *adj.* and *n.,* (— — —s) the last but one. *L'—e syllabe;* the penultimate.

avant-faire-droit, *n.m.,* (—) preventive injunction.

avant-fossé, *n.m.,* (— — —s) (fortif.) advance-fosse.

avant-garde, *n.f.,* (— — —s) vanguard; (nav.) van.

avant-goût, *n.m.,* (— — —s) foretaste, earnest, anticipation.

avant-hier (-ti-ère), *adv.,* the day before yesterday.

avant-jour, *n.m.,* (*n.p.*) morning-twilight.

avant-main, *n.m.,* (— — —s) (man.) fore-hand of a horse; (tennis) fore-hand stroke; (at cards) lead.

⊙**avant-midi,** *n.m.,* (—) forenoon.

avant-mur, *n.m.,* (— — —s) outward wall, screen-wall.

avant-pêche, *n.f.,* (— — —s) early peach.

avant-pied, *n.m.,* (— — —s) vamp, upper-leather of a boot.

⊙**avant-plancher,** *n.m.,* (— — —s) false-ceiling.

avant-poignet, *n.m.,* (— — —s) fore-wrist.

avant-port, *n.m.,* (— — —s) (nav.) outer harbor, tide-dock.

avant-portail, *n.m.,* (— — —s) fore-portal.

avant-poste, *n.m.,* (— — —s) (milit.) out-post.

avant-propos, *n.m.,* (—) preface, preamble; introduction, exordium.

avant-quart, *n.m.,* (— — —s) (horl.) warning-bell.

avant-scène, *n.f.,* (— — —s) front of the stage; proscenium, stage-box.

avant-toit, *n.m.,* (— - — —s) fore-roof, projecting roof, eaves.

avant-train, *n.m.,* (— - — —s) fore-carriage, limber.

*avant-veille,** *n.f.,* (— — —s) two days before.

avare, *adj.,* avaricious, miserly, covetous; stingy, close-fisted, sparing; penurious, niggardly. *Etre — de ses louanges;* to be sparing of praise. *A père — enfant prodigue;* a miserly father has a spendthrift son.

avare, *n.m.,* miser, niggard; pinch-penny.

avarement, *adv.,* avariciously.

avarice, *n.f.,* avarice, avariciousness, covetousness; niggardliness; stinginess. *Par —;* from avarice.

avaricieu-x, -se, *adj.,* (l.u.) avaricious, covetous; stingy.

avarie, *n.f.,* damage (done in conveying goods); (com.) damage, loss, repairs. *— s communes;* (com.) general average. *Menues — s;* small averages. *— s simples;* ordinary damage. *Sans —;* without mishap. *Causer une —;* to damage. *Régler les — s;* to state the averages.

avarié, -e, *adj.,* damaged.   [damaged.

avarier, *v.a.,* to damage. *S'—, v.r.,* to become

avaste, *int.,* (nav.) avast, stop, stay.

à vau-l'eau, *adv.,* with the stream, downstream. *Toutes son entreprises sont allées —;* all his undertakings have come to nought.

à vau-de-route, *adv.,* in flight.

avé, *n.m.,* (—) ave. *— Maria;* ave Maria.

avec, *prep.,* with, together with; among. *Venez — moi;* come with me. *— dessein;* designedly. *— tout cela;* for all that, nevertheless. *Il a pris mon manteau, et s'en est allé —;* he has taken my cloak, and has gone off with it. *Discerner le bien d' — le mal;* to discern good from evil, *— ça!* (coll.) nonsense!

avecque, *prep.,* obsolete spelling of **avec.**

aveindre (aveignant, aveint), *v.a.,* to take out, to fetch out.

aveine, *n.f.   V.* **avoine.**

avelanède, *n.f.,* acorn-cup, valonia.

aveline, *n.f.* filbert, cob-nut.

avelinier, *n.m.,* filbert-tree.

avénage, *n.m.,* avenage (due, paid in oats).

avenant, *part.   V.* **advenant.**

avenant, -e. *adj.,* good-looking, prepossessing, comely, pleasing, taking. *Physionomie — e;* pleasing features. *Manières — es;* prepossessing, engaging manners. *n.,* declaration of altered policy (insurance).

à l'avenant, *adv.,* appropriate; in keeping with. *Le dessert fut à l'— du repas;* the dessert was in keeping with the repast. *Et tout à l'—;* and all corresponding, matching.

avènement (-măn), *n.m.,* coming, accession, succession, advent. *L'— du roi à la couronne;* the king's accession to the crown. *L'— du Messie;* the coming of the Messiah.

avèneron, *n.m.,* wild oats.

avenir, *n.m.,* the future, futurity, existence, future welfare, hopes, prospects; (jur.) venire facias. *A l'—;* in future. *On ne peut répondre de l'—;* one cannot answer for the future. *J'assure un — à mes enfants;* I secure a competence for my children. *Cet homme n'a aucun —;* that man has no prospects. *D'—,* or *qui a de l'—;* promising, rising.

⊙**avenir,** *v.n.   V.* **advenir.**

à-venir, *n.m.,* (—) (jur.) summons to an attorney to appear for his client.

avent, *n.m.,* Advent.

aventure, *n.f.,* adventure, occurrence; chance, accident, luck; fate, lot. *A l'—;* at a venture, at random. *Une plaisante —;* a droll adventure. *Grosse —;* (com.) bottomry. *Dire la bonne —;* to tell people's fortunes. *Se faire dire sa bonne*

—; to have one's fortune told. *Une diseuse de bonne* —; a fortune-teller. *Tenter l'* —; to make a trial, to try one's luck. *Mal d'* —; whitlow. *D'* —, *par* —; by chance, perchance. *Si par* —; if peradventure, if by chance.

aventuré, -e, *part.,* hazardous, hazarded, bold.

aventurer, *v.a.,* to venture, to put to the venture, to risk.

s'aventurer, *v.r.,* to venture, to take one's chance, to hazard, to risk one's self.

aventureu-x, -se, *adj.,* venturous, venturesome, adventurous.

adventuri-er, *n.m.,* **-ère,** *n.f.,* adventurer, adventuress.

aventurine, *n.f.,* avanturine, venturine.

avenu, -e, *part.,* come to pass, happened. *Acte nul et non* —; act that is null and void.

avenue, *n.f.,* avenue, approach, walk.

avéré, -e, *part.,* averred, established by evidence.

avérer, *v.a.,* to aver, to prove the truth of, to confirm, to establish.

averhan. *See* **tétras.**

à verse, *adv.,* fast (of rain). *Il pleut* —; it is pouring with rain.

averse, *n.f.,* shower of rain; down-pour.

aversion, *n.f.,* aversion, hate, hatred; antipathy, dislike, detestation. *Prendre quelqu'un en* —; to take an aversion to one. *Cet homme est ma bête d'* —; that man is my bugbear, my pet aversion.

averti, -e, *part.,* warned, informed. *Se tenir pour* —; to be on one's guard, to take it as a warning. *Un bon — en vaut deux;* forewarned, forearmed.

avertir, *v.a.,* to warn, to caution; to inform of, to acquaint with, to give notice of, to admonish. *Faire* —; to send notice, word.

avertissement (-măn), *n.m.,* information, advice, (b.s.) warning, caution; notification; advertisement (of books); (b.s.) admonition.

avertisseur, *n.m.,* monitor, adviser; (official) public crier; (thea.) call-boy. — *d'incendie;* fire-alarm.

aveu, *n.m.,* avowal, confession, acknowledgment, admission; approbation, consent, recognition. *Homme sans* —; vagrant, vagabond. *Faire l'* — *de;* to confess.

aveugle, *adj.,* blind, sightless; deluded; ignorant, implicit. — *de naissance* or *né;* born blind. *Obéissance* —; implicit obedience. *Changer son cheval borgne contre un* —; to change from bad to worse. *La fortune est* —; fortune is blind.

aveugle, *n.m.f.,* blind person. *Un* — *y mordrait;* a blind man would see it. *C'est un — qui en conduit un autre;* it is the blind leading the blind. *Crier comme un — qui a perdu son bâton;* to cry out before one is hurt.

aveuglement, *n.m.,* blindness, infatuation.

aveuglément, *adv.,* blindly, rashly, implicitly.

aveugler, *v.a.,* to blind, to make blind; to put out the eyes of; to dazzle; to delude; to obscure, to cloud; (nav.) to fother. *La passion aveugle l'entendement;* passion obscures the understanding. — *une voie d'eau;* (nav.) to fother a leak. *La trop grande lumière aveugle;* too much light dazzles the eyes.

s'aveugler, *v.r.,* to blind one's self, to shut one's eyes to, to be blinded, to deceive one's self.

à l'aveuglette, *adv.,* (fam.) groping in the dark. *Aller* — ; to go groping along, blindly, rashly.

avicule, *n.f.,* (mol.). *V.* **aronde.**

avide, *adj.,* greedy of, eager for, thirsting for; voracious; covetous, rapacious. *Un homme* —; a covetous man. — *de gain;* eager for gain.

avidement (-măn), *adv.,* greedily, eagerly, voraciously, covetously.

avidité, *n.f.,* avidity, greediness, eagerness, covetousness.

avilir, *v.a.,* to debase, to demean, to disgrace,

to vilify; to disparage, to discredit, to depreciate, to lower.

s'avilir, *v.r.,* to disgrace one's self, to debase one's self, to grow contemptible.

avilissant, -e, *adj.,* debasing, degrading, humiliating.

avilissement (-măn), *n.m.,* degradation, debasement, depreciation, contempt, vileness.

aviné, -e, *part.,* drunk, drunken, unsteady (from drink). *Il est* —; *c'est un corps* —; he is a regular tippler.

aviner, *v.a.,* to season with wine.

aviron, *n.m.,* (nav.) oar. — *de couple;* scull. *Aller à l'* —; to row. *Donner un coup d'* —; to lend a helping hand.

avironnerie, *n.f.,* oar-maker's shed.

avironnier, *n.m.,* oar-maker.

avis, *n.m.,* opinion, sentiment, mind, judgment; advice, counsel, deliberation, admonition; notice, notification; warning, caution; account, information, intelligence, news; motion; vote; advertisement (in books). *A mon* —; in my opinion. *Je suis d'* — *que vous lui écriviez;* I am of opinion that you should write to him. *Je ne suis pas d'* — *d'y aller;* I am not for going there. *Dire son* —; to say, speak one's mind. *Je profiterai de l'* — *que vous me donnez;* I shall avail myself of the caution you have given me. — *au lecteur;* a note to the reader; a word to the wise. *J'ai changé d'* —; I have altered my mind. *On a reçu — de Paris;* we are advised from Paris. *Lettre d'* —; letter of advice. *Faute d'* —; for want of advice. *Sous* —; with advice. *Suivant l'* — *de;* as per advice. *Donner à quelqu'un un — de quelque chose;* to advise any one of anything. *Ne m'écris plus jusqu'à nouvel* —; write no more till further notice. *Ouvrir un* —; to broach an opinion. *Etre d'* —; to opine. *Prendre les* —; to take the opinion. *Aller aux* —; to put to the vote. *Donner un — assez clair à quelqu'un;* to give a pretty broad hint to any one. *Il m'est* —; I rather think or methinks. *Deux —s valent mieux qu'un;* two heads are better than one. *Il y a jours d'* —; there is no hurry; there is plenty of time.

avisé, -e, *adj.,* wary, discreet, prudent, cautious, advised, circumspect. *Mal* —; ill-advised. *il est fort* —; he is a very discreet man.

aviser, *v.a.,* to apprise; to perceive; to espy; (com.) to advise.

aviser, *v.n.,* to consider, to see to, to think upon, to look to. *Avisez-y;* look to it. *Vous y aviserez;* you will see to it.

s'aviser, *v.r.,* to think of, to consider, to take it into one's head; to bethink one's self, to be so minded, to dare, to presume. *Il ne s'avise jamais de rien;* he thinks of nothing. *Il s'avisa de;* he took it into his head to. *Il n'y a sottise dont il ne s'avise;* there is no folly he does not commit. *Il s'avisa d'un bon expédient;* he bethought himself of a good expedient. *Ne vous en avisez pas;* you had better not.

aviso, *n.m.,* (nav.) dispatch-boat.

*avitaillement, *n.m.,* (nav., milit.) victualing; stores.

*avitailler, *v.a.,* to victual, to furnish with victuals, to store.

⊙*avitailleur, *n.m.,* army or navy contractor.

avivage, *n.m.,* first laying of tin-foil on glass; hewing.

aviver, *v.a.,* to polish, to burnish, to brighten.

avives, *n.f. pl.,* (vet.) vives.

avivoir, *n.m.,* polisher, burnisher (tool).

avocasser, *v.n.,* to be a pettifogger, to drudge at the bar.

avocasserie, *n.f.,* pettifoggery, caviling, quibble, twaddle.

avocat, *n.m.,* counsel, barrister, advocate, pleader, intercessor. — *de causes perdues,* — *de Pilate,* — *de balle,* — *à tort;* briefless barrister. — *consultant;* chamber-counsel. — *principal;*

leading barrister. — *général;* solicitor general. *Plaider par* —; to be represented by counsel.

avecate, *n.f.,* female advocate; mediatrix, intercessor.

avocette, *n.f.,* (orni.) avoset.

avoine, *n.f.,* oats. —*s,* oats still standing. *D'*—; of oats. *Farine d'*—; oatmeal. *Balle d'*—; oatchaff. *Folles*—*s;* wild oats.

avoinerie, *n.f.,* oat-field.

avoir (ayant, eu), *v.a.,* to have; to get, to possess, to enjoy; to be; to be worth; to be the matter with, to ail; to have on. — *pour agréable;* to like. — *honte;* to be ashamed. — *raison;* to be right. — *raison de;* to get the mastery over. — *tort;* to be wrong. — *peur;* to be afraid. — *faim;* to be hungry. — *soif;* to be thirsty. *Vous n'avez qu'à dire;* you need only say the word. *Qu'est-ce que vous avez?* what ails you? what is the matter with you? *Faire* —; to procure for. *Quel âge avez-vous?* how old are you? *Il a quarante ans;* he is forty. *J'ai à vous parler;* I have something to tell you. *Il avait un habit bleu;* he had on a blue coat. *En* —; to catch it. *Il en a;* he has caught it. *En a-t-il?* what a lot he has! *Y* —; there to be, to be the matter. *Il ne saurait y* — *de différence;* there can be no difference. *Il y en a de noirs;* there are some black ones. *C'est une femme comme il n'y en a point;* she has not her like, her match. *Il y a plus;* nay, more. *Il y en a encore;* there is still some left. *Il y a de quoi;* there is enough, or good reason to. *Il n'y a pas de quoi;* don't name or mention it; there is no offense. *Je suis venu ici il y a deux mois;* I came here two months ago. *Il n'y a tel que d'en;* money makes the man. *Il y a un an qu'il est mort;* he has been dead a year. *Il y a deux mois que je suis ici;* I have been here two months. *Il y a une heure que nous écrivons;* we have been writing for the last hour. *Combien y a-t-il de Paris à Londres?* how far is it from Paris to London? *En* — *à;* to owe a grudge to. — *dans la main;* to hold in the hollow of one's hand. — *la parole;* to be entitled to speak, to be in possession of the House. *Vous avez la main, le dé, la boule;* it is your turn to play (at cards, at dice, at billiards).

avoir, *n.m.,* possessions, substance, property, what one is worth; (com.) credit, creditor, creditor-side. *Voilà tout mon* —; this is all I have.

avoir du poids, *n.m.,* (*n.p.*) avoirdupois.

avoisinant, -e, *adj.,* neighboring, adjoining, close by.

avoisiné, *part.,* with neighbors. *Etre bien or mal* —; to have good or bad neighbors.

⊙**avoisinement** (-mān), *n.m.,* nearness, proximity.

avoisiner, *v.a.,* to border upon, to be situated near, to be contiguous to.

avorté, -e, *adj.,* abortive, miscarried; (bot.) abortive; frustrated, baffled; imperfect.

avortement, *n.m.,* abortion, miscarriage, failure.

avorter, *v.n.,* to miscarry; to slip; to prove abortive; to fail. *Faire* —; to cause or procure abortion. *Ce dessein avorta;* that plan failed. *Faire* — *les desseins de quelqu'un;* to baffle any one's designs.

avorton, *n.m.,* abortion; abortive child. (fig.) *Un* — *de mouche;* a wretched, paltry, miserable fly.

avouable, *adj.,* avowable.

avoué, *n.m.,* attorney; solicitor. *Une étude d'*—; a solicitor's office.

avouer, *v.a.,* to confess, to avow; to own, to acknowledge, to declare openly, to grant, to allow; to approve. *Il a avoué le fait;* he has confessed the deed. *Il avoue l'avoir fait;* he confesses to it. *S'* — *vaincu;* to own one's self vanquished. *J'étais, je l'avoue, un peu confus;* I

was rather confused, I must allow. — *un enfant;* to acknowledge a child. *J'avouerai tout ce qu'il fera;* I will approve of all he does.

avoyer, *n.m.,* avoyer (Swiss magistrate).

****avril,** *n.m.,* April. *Donner un poisson d'* — *à quelqu'un;* to make any one an April-fool. *Recevoir un poisson d'*—; to be made an April-fool. *Poisson d'*—; mackerel.

avrillé, -e, *adj.,* sown in April.

avron, *n.m.,* (bot.) wild oats.

avuer, *v.a.,* (hunt.) to mark down, to mark in.

avulsion, *n.f.,* avulsion.

axe, *n.m.,* axis; axle, axle-tree; (artil.) trunnion. — *tournant;* axle-tree. — *de vis;* screw-arbor.

axifuge, *adj.,* centrifugal. *V.* **centrifuge.**

axillaire (ak-sil-lèr), *adj.,* (anat., bot.) axillar, axillary. *Fleurs* —*s;* axillary flowers.

axiome, *n.m.,* axiom.

axiomètre, *n.m.,* (nav.) tell-tale (of the tiller).

axonge, *n.f.,* (phar.) hog's lard.

ayan, *n.m.,* (—*s*) ayan (Turkish official).

ayant cause, *n.m.,* (—*s* —) (jur.) assign.

ayant droit, *n.m.,* (—*s* —) (jur.) party entitled.

aynet, *n.m.,* skewer (for herrings).

azalée, *n.f.,* (bot.) azalea.

azédarac, *n.m.,* azedarach, bead-tree.

azerole, *n.f.,* (bot.) azarole.

azerolier, *n.m.,* azarole-tree.

⊙**azime,** *adj.* *V.* **azyme.**

azimut (-mut), *n.m.,* (astron.) azimuth.

azimutal, -e, *adj.,* azimuthal.

azotate, *n.m.,* (chem.) nitrate.

azote, *n.m.,* (chem.) azote, nitrogen.

azote, *adj.,* azotic, nitric.

azoté, *adj.,* azotized, nitrogenized.

azotique, *adj.,* azotic, nitric.

azur, *n.m.,* azure, blue; sky-color. — *de Hollande;* Dutch blue. *Pierre d'*—; azure-stone.

azuré, -e, *adj.,* azure, sky-colored. *La voûte* —*e;* the azure skies.

azurer, *v.a.,* to paint azure color, to blue.

azurin, -e, *adj.,* azure. *n.m.,* blue-butterfly.

azyme, *adj.,* azymous, unleavened.

azyme, *n.m.,* azym, unleavened bread. *Fête des* —*s;* feast of unleavened bread.

azymite, *n.m.,* Azymite.

B

b, *n.m.,* the second letter of the alphabet, *b.* *Etre marqué au* —; to be either one-eyed, hunch-backed, or lame (*borgne, bossu, boiteux*). *Ne parler que par* b *ou par* f; never to speak without swearing.

baba, *n.m.,* bun, plum-cake.

babel, *n.f.,* Babel, uproar, disorder. *Tour de* —; tower of Babel. *C'est une vraie tour de* —, *c'est une* —; it is a perfect tower of Babel, uproar.

babeurre, *n.m.,* buttermilk.

babiche, *n.f.,* **babichon,** *n.m.,* lap-dog.

****babil,** *n.m.,* chatter, prating, talk, gabbling, tattle, prattle. *Il nous étourdit par son* —; he bewilders us with his chattering.

****babillage,** *n.m.,* chit-chat, tittle-tattle, prattle, babbling, twaddle.

****babillard,** *n.m.,* **-e,** *n.f.,* chatterer, babbler, tattler; blab, blabber; (orni.) nettle-creeper. *C'est un franc* —; he is a regular babbler. *Ne vous fiez pas à cet homme-là, c'est un* —; don't trust that man, he is a great blab.

****babillard, -e,** *adj.,* babbling, talkative, chattering.

****babillement,** *n.m.,* talkativeness, loquacity, garrulity.

****babiller,** *v.n.,* to prate, to tattle, to gossip.

babine, *n.f.,* lip (of animals) ; chop. *Il s'en lèche les —s ;* he is smacking his lips over it.

babiole, *n.f.,* bauble, gewgaw, toy, knick-knack, plaything, trifle, trinket.

bâbord, *n.m.,* (nav.) port.

bâbord, *adv.,* larboard ; aport.

bâbordais, *n.m.,* (nav.) larboard-watch.

babouche, *n.f.,* Turkish slipper.

babouin, *n.m.,* baboon, monkey (of a child). *Faire baiser le — à quelqu'un ;* to make any one eat humble pie.

babouine, *n.f.,* little fool, little hussy ; lip. *V.* **babine.**

babouiner, *v.n.,* (fam.) to play the buffoon.

bac, *n.m.,* ferry, ferry-boat.

baccalauréat, *n.m.,* bachelorship, bachelor's degree.

bacchanal (-ka-), *n.m.,* racket, uproar. *Faire —;* to make a racket, to kick up a great row.

bacchanale (-ka-), *n.f.,* noisy drinking-bout, revel, debauch.

☉**bacchanaliser** (-ka-), *v.n.,* to revel, to riot.

bacchante (-kant), *n.f.,* bacchante, termagant.

baccharis (-ka-ris), **-ide,** *n.f.,* baccharis, ploughman's spikenard.

baccifère, *adj.,* bacciferous, berry-producing.

bacha, *n.m.* *V.* **pacha.**

bâche, *n.f.,* cart tilt ; hot-bed frame ; tank, cistern ; awning, tarpaulin (of a wagon).

☉**bachelette,** *n.f.,* young girl, maid, lass, damsel.

bachelier, *n.m.,* bachelor of a university.

bâcher, *v.a.,* to tilt, to cover (a cart).

bachique, *adj.,* bacchic, jovial, drunken.

bachon, *n.m.,* wooden pail.

bachot, *n.m.,* wherry, small ferry-boat ; (fam.) bachelor's degree.

bachotage, *n.m.,* ferry-man's business.

bachoteur, *n.m.,* ferry-man.

bachotier, *n.m.,* crammer.

bacile, *n.m.,* (bot.) sea-fennel.

bacillaire, *n.m.,* pyramidal feldspar, scapolite.

bâclage, *n.m.,* line of boats (in a port) ; (fig.) patching, hasty, scamped work.

bâclé, -e, *part.,* barred, fastened, scamped.

bâcler, *v.a.,* to bar or chain, to close, to fasten (a door, a window, a boat, a harbour) ; to do hastily, to polish off ; to scamp (work).

badaud, *n.m.,* -e, *n.f.,* ninny, booby ; gazer, lounger, idler ; cockney.

badaudage, *n.m,* cockneyism.

badauder, *v.n.,* to lounge, to saunter, to loiter.

badauderie, *n.f.,* foolery, silliness, simplicity, lounging, sauntering.

baderne, *n.f.,* (nav.) dolphin, paunch, fender (of ship).

badian, *n.m.,* or **badiane,** *n.f.,* aniseed-tree.

badigeon (-jon), *n.m.,* badigeon, stone-color, whitewash.

badigeonnage (-jo-naj), *n.m.,* painting stone-color ; smearing, making up, daub.

badigeonner (-jo-né), *v.a.,* to paint with stone-color, to whitewash, to daub.

badigeonneur (-jo-neur), *n.m.,* whitewasher, colorer, dauber.

badin, -e, *adj. n.,* waggish, jocular, playful, roguish ; sportive, droll, comical. *Il a l'humeur —e ;* he is of a sportive humor. *Air —;* playful air. *Style —;* playful style. *C'est un vrai —;* he is a regular banterer, a wag ; joker, jester.

badinage, *n.m.,* sport, play, jest ; foolery, playfulness, jocularity, trifle. *Ceci n'est point du —;* this is no foolery. *Il se prête volontiers au —;* he has no objection to a little trifling. *Finissez votre —;* have done with your fooling. *Ce n'est pour lui qu'un —;* it is mere child's play for him.

badine, *n.f.,* switch ; *pl.,* small tongs.

badiner, *v.n.,* to trifle, to dally, to play, to toy, to sport ; to flaunt. *Il ne badine pas ;* he is not joking. *En badinant ;* in fun, by way of a joke. *La dentelle est trop tendue, il faut qu'elle badine un peu ;* the lace is too tight, it must wave about a little. *On ne badine pas avec l'amour ;* love is not to be trifled with.

badinerie, *n.f.,* silly stuff, foolery, trifling.

bafouer, *v.a.,* to scout, to scoff at, to baffle. *On l'a bafoué ;* he was scouted. *Il s'est fait —;* he got scoffed at.

bâfre, *n.f.,* (pop.) guzzling, blow out, gorge.

bâfrer, *v.n.,* (l. ex.) to guzzle, to eat greedily, to have a blow out, a grand feed.

bâfreu-r, *n.m.,* **-se,** *n.f.,* (l. ex.) guzzler, glutton.

bagace. *V.* **bagasse.**

bagage, *n.m.,* luggage, baggage. *Nous avons laissé notre — en arrière ;* we have left our luggage behind. *Plier trousser —;* to pack off. *Il a plié —;* he has taken his last journey (died). *Quel est le — de cet auteur ?* what works has this author written ? *— littéraire ;* literary knowledge.

bagarre, *n.f.,* squabble, scuffle, fray, brawl ; crowd, crush. *Se trouver dans une —;* to get into a fray. *Se tirer d'une —;* to get out of a scuffle.

bagasse, *n.f.,* bagasse, cane trash ; hussy, drab, slut.

bagatelle, *n.f.,* bauble, trash, trinket, trifle, nonsense, mere nothing. *Table de —;* bagatelle table. *Il ne s'amuse qu'à des —s ;* he trifles away his time. *S'amuser à une —;* to trifle away time. *Bagatelles que tout cela ;* that is all stuff and nonsense.

*****bagne,** *n.m.,* convict-prison, hulks.

bagnole, *n.f.,* horse-box (on railways).

☉*****bagnolette,** *n.f.,* a head-dress.

bague (bag), *n.f.,* ring. *— gravée en cachet ;* seal-ring. *—s et joyaux ;* jewels and ornaments. *Course de —;* running at the ring. *Jeu de —;* roundabout. *— au doigt ;* (fig.) clear gain, sinecure, good thing.

baguenaude (bag-nôd), *n.f.,* bladder-nut, trifle.

baguenauder (bag-nô-), *v.n.,* to mind trifles, to trifle time away, to fiddle-faddle.

baguenaudier (bag-nô-), *n.m.,* bladder-nut-tree, bastard senna tree ; trifler ; ring-puzzle.

baguer (ba-ghé), *v.a.,* to baste, to stitch ; (hort.) to ring.

bagues, *n.f. pl.,* (l. u.) luggage.

baguette (ba-ghèt), *n.f.,* switch, rod, ramrod, drum-stick, small stick, wand ; *pl.,* (milit.) gauntlet ; (arch.) baguet. *Ce cheval obéit à la —;* that horse obeys the switch. *— à gant ;* glove-stick. *—s de tambour ;* drum-sticks. *Coup de —;* beat of the drum. *— de fusée volante ;* stick of a rocket. *— d'or ;* golden stick. *— d'huissier ;* usher's rod. *— divinatoire ;* conjuror's wand. *Commander à la —;* to command magisterially. *Passer par les —s ;* to run the gauntlet. *Mener à la —;* to rule with a rod of iron.

baguier (ba-ghié), *n.m.,* casket for rings.

bah, *int.,* pooh, pshaw, nonsense, fudge.

bahut, *n.m.,* trunk, chest, press. *En —;* rounded, convex.

bahuter, *v.n.,* to roister, to kick up a row.

bahutier, *n.m.,* trunk-maker.

bai, -e, *adj.,* bay. *Un cheval —;* a bay horse. *— châtain ;* chestnut. *— miroité ;* dapple-bay. *— clair ;* light-bay. *— doré ;* yellow-bun.

baie, *n.f.,* bay, gulf, road ; (arch.) bay ; (bot.) berry ; ☉humbug, trick. *Donner une — à quelqu'un ;* to humbug one.

baignade, *n.f.,* bath, bathing ; bathing-place.

*****baigné, -e,** *part.,* bathed, weltering ; (geog.) washed. *On l'a trouvé — dans son sang ;* he was found weltering in his blood. *Des yeux —s de larmes ;* eyes bathed in tears. *Etre — de sueur ;* to be in a bath of perspiration.

*baigner, *v.a.*, to bathe, to give a bath, to wash, to lave, to water. *Faire — les chevaux ;* to take horses to the water.

se baigner, *v.r.*, to bathe, to wash ; to welter (in blood).

*baigner, *v.n.*, to soak ; to steep.

*baigneu-r, *n.m.*, -se, *n.f.*, bather, bath-keeper.

⊙*baignoir, *n.m.*, bathing-place.

*baignoire, *n.f.*, bathing-tub, bath ; corner box (thea.). *Voiture —;* bathing-machine.

*bail, *n.m.*, (baux) lease. — *à ferme ;* lease of ground. — *à long terme ;* long lease. *Donner à —;* to lease. *Passer un —;* to draw up a lease. *Rompre, résilier, un —;* to break, to throw up, a lease. *Cela n'est pas de mon —;* I did not bargain for that.

*baille, *n.f.*, (nav.) half tub. — *de sonde ;* bucket (for sounding). — *à brac ;* tar-pail, or kid.

*bâillement, *n.m.*, yawning, yawn ; (gram. ; l.u.) hiatus.

*bâiller, *v.n.*, to yawn, to gape ; to open (fissures) ; to be on the jar, to gape (of doors). *On bâille souvent en voyant bâiller les autres ;* yawning is catching. *Bâiller de sommeil ;* to yawn with drowsiness.

⊙*bailler, *v.a.*, to give, to deliver. — *à ferme ;* to let, to lease, to farm out. *Vous me la baillez belle ;* you are humbugging me.

*baillet, *adj.*, (of horses) sorrel.

⊙*bailleul, *n.m.*, bone-setter. *V.* rebouteur.

*baill-eur, *n.m.*, -euse, *n.f.*, yawner ; gaper. *Un bon — en fait bâiller deux ;* yawning is catching.

baill-eur, *n.m.*, -eresse, *n.f.*, one who leases, lessor. *Un — de fonds ;* money-lender, sleeping partner.

*bailli, *n.m.*, bailiff.

*bailliage, *n.m.*, bailiwick.

*bailliag-er, -ère, *adj.*, of a bailiwick.

*baillive, *n.f.*, bailiff's wife.

bâillon, *n.m.*, gag, muzzle ; bribe.

*bâillonner, *v.a.*, to stop the mouth of, to gag, to muzzle ; to wedge up (a door).

bain, *n.m.*, bath ; bathing-tub ; *pl.*, baths, bathing establishment, bathing place, bathing room, waters. — *de mer ;* salt water bath. — *à domicile ;* bath at home. — *de siège ;* hip bath. — *de vapeur ;* vapor bath. — *de pieds ;* foot bath. *La chambre de —;* the bath-room. *L'ordre du —;* the Order of the Bath.

bain-marie, *n.m.* *Cuire au —;* to cook in a vessel immersed in boiling water.

baïonnette, *n.f.*, bayonet. — *au bout du fusil ;* with fixed bayonets. —*s au canon !* fix bayonets ! *Croiser la —;* to cross bayonets. *Charger à la —;* to charge with fixed bayonets. *Enlever un poste à la —;* to carry a post at the point of the bayonet.

baïram or beiram, *n.m.*, Baïram (Turkish feast).

⊙baisemain, *n.m.*, kissing (of hands) ; compliments. [culation.

baisement, *n.m.*, kissing of feet ; (geom.) os-

baiser, *v.a.*, to kiss.

baiser, *n.m.*, kiss, salute. *Un — de Judas ;* a treacherous kiss.

baiseu-r, *n.m.*, -se, *n.f.*, kisser.

baisoter, *v.a.*, to be always kissing.

baisse, *n.f.*, fall, abatement, decline, falling off. *En —;* (com.) falling. *Jouer à la —;* to bear, to speculate on a fall.

baissé, -e, *part.*, down, let down, lowered. *Il marchait les yeux —s ;* he walked with downcast eyes. *Se retirer tête —e ;* to sneak away. *Donner tête —e dans le piège ;* to fall headlong into the snare.

baisser, *v.a.*, to let down, to lower, to bring down, to hang down ; to droop ; (nav.) to lower, to strike. *Elle baissa son voile ;* she let down

her veil. — *le rideau ;* to drop the curtain. — *la visière d'un casque ;* to lower the beaver of a helmet. — *le drapeau ;* to lower the colors. — *pavillon ;* to strike one's flag ; to knock under to one. — *les yeux ;* to cast one's eyes down. — *la tête ;* to hold, to hang down, to droop one's head. — *l'oreille ;* to look confused.

baisser, *v.n.*, to lower, to wear, to break, to fail, to decay ; to go down ; to ebb ; to be on the decline, on the wane ; to flag, to droop ; to fall. *Le jour baisse ;* night is coming on. *Ce vieillard baisse ;* this old man is breaking up. *Sa vue commence à —;* his sight begins to fail. *Il baisse à vue d'œil ;* he is visibly sinking. *Son génie baisse ;* his genius is on the decline. *Ce malade baisse ;* the patient is losing strength. *Les actions baissent ;* there is a fall in the shares. *Les fonds baissent ;* the funds are falling.

se baisser, *v.r.*, to stoop ; to bow down, to be lowered. *Il n'a qu'à — pour en prendre ;* he has only to pick and choose.

baissier, *n.m.*, bear, operator for a fall.

baissière, *n.f.*, bottom of a cask ; (agri.) hollow, puddle.

baisure, *n.f.*, kissing-crust.

⊙bajoire, *n.f.*, double-faced coin.

bajoue, *n.f.*, hog's cheek ; chap.

bajoyer, *n.m.*, lateral wall, facing.

bal, *n.m.*, ball, dance. — *masqué ;* masked ball. — *paré ;* fancy dress-ball. — *bourgeois ;* private ball. — *champêtre ;* country ball. — *costumé ;* fancy dress ball. *Donner le — à quelqu'un ;* to make one dance for it. *Mettre le — en train ;* to set things going. *Mettre une carte au —;* to stake money upon a card.

baladin, *n.m.*, -e, *n.f.*, mountebank, juggler, buffoon, merry-andrew.

baladinage, *n.m.*, buffoonery, nonsense.

balafre, *n.f.*, gash, slash, cut ; scar.

balafrer, *v.a.*, to gash, to slash.

balai, *n.m.*, broom, brush, besom. — *de jonc ;* carpet-broom. — *de crin ;* hair-broom. — *de plume ;* duster. — *à laver ;* mop. *Manche à —;* broom-stick. *Donner un coup de —;* to sweep up. *Rôtir le —;* to play one's pranks, to lead a fast life. *Il n'est rien tel que — neuf ;* a new broom sweeps clean.

balais, *adj.*, balas. *Un rubis —;* a balas ruby.

balance, *n.f.*, balance, scales, pair of scales ; balance (of an account) ; balance-sheet ; (astron.) Libra. — *romaine ;* steelyard. *Trait de la —;* turn of the scale. — *juste ;* good scales. *Arrêter une —;* to agree a balance. *Réaliser une —;* to withdraw a balance. *Faire pencher la —;* to turn the scale. *Mettre en —;* to balance. *Ses droits peuvent-ils entrer en — avec les miens ?* can his claims be weighed in the same scale with mine ? *Etre en —;* to be irresolute. *Cela tient l'esprit en —;* that makes one irresolute.

balancé, *n.m.*, (dance) setting to one's partner.

balancelle, *n.f.*, (nav.) felucca.

balancement (-män), *n.m.*, balancing, poising ; rocking, see-saw, fluctuation, wavering.

balancer, *v.a.*, to balance, to poise ; to swing, to wave, to weigh, to counterbalance, to rock, to square (accounts). — *un javelot ;* to poise a javelin. — *les avantages et les inconvénients ;* to weigh the advantages and disadvantages. — *les pertes par le gain ;* to balance the loss by the profit. *Ses vertus balancent tous ses vices ;* his virtues outweigh all his vices. — *la victoire ;* to keep the victory in doubt. — *un compte ;* to balance an account.

balancer, *v.n.*, to balance, to hesitate, to be in suspense, to waver, to fluctuate, to demur. *Il balança s'il accepterait la place qu'on lui offrait ;* he hesitated whether he should accept the situation offered him. *Il y a consenti sans*

—; he consented to it without hesitating. *Il n'y a pas à —*; there is no room for hesitation.

se balancer, *v.r.*, to swing, to rock. *Cette femme se balance trop en marchant*; that woman swings too much as she walks. *Un oiseau qui se balance dans l'air*; a bird hovering in the air.

balancier, *n.m.*, scale-maker; pendulum; balance; (coin.) coining-engine; balancing-pole. *Le — d'une horloge*; the pendulum of a clock. *Le — d'un tourne-broche*; the flyer of a roasting jack. *Le — d'une machine à vapeur*; the beam of a steam-engine. *Le — transversal d'une machine à vapeur*; cross-beam of an engine.

balancine, *n.f.*, (nav.) lift.

balançoire, *n.f.*, see-saw; swing. (fig.) *Quelle —!* what a cram!

balane, *n.m.*, (conch.) acorn-shell.

balauste, *n.f.*, balausta, wild pomegranate.

balaustier, *n.m.*, wild pomegranate tree.

balayage, **balayement**, *n.m.*, sweeping.

balayer, *v.a.*, to sweep, to scour. *Sa robe balaie la terre*; her gown sweeps the ground. *Le vent balaie la plaine*; the wind sweeps the plain. *— les mers*; to scour the seas.

balayeu-r, *n.m.*, **-se**, *n.f.*, scavenger, sweeper.

balayures, *n.f. pl.*, sweepings. *— de mer*; sea-weed washed on shore; drift-weed.

balbutiement (-sî-mān), *n.m.*, stuttering, stammering, lisping.

balbutier (-cié), *v.a.* and *n.*, to lisp, to stammer, to mumble. *Un enfant qui commence à —*; a child beginning to lisp. *Elle balbutia quelques mots*; she stammered out a few words. *— un compliment*; to stammer out a compliment. *Il ne fit que — son rôle*; he did nothing but mumble his part.

balbuzard, *n.m.*, bald-buzzard, osprey.

balcon, *n.m.*, balcony.

baldaquin, *n.m.*, baldachin; canopy, tester.

baleine, *n.f.*, whale, whale-bone. *Barbe de —*; whale-bone. *Huile de —*; whale oil. *La pêche de la —*; the whale fishery. *Blanc de —*; spermaceti.

baleiné, **-e**, *adj.*, stiffened with whalebone. *Un corset —*; whalebone stays.

baleineau, *n.m.*, young whale.

baleinier, *n.m.*, *adj.*, whaler.

baleinière, *n.f.*, whale-boat.

balestron, *n.m.*, (nav.) sprit.

⊙**balèvre**, *n.f.*, under lip; (arch.) jutting or projection of one stone beyond another.

ball, *n.m.* V. **pali.**

balisage, *n.m.*, (nav.) establishing of buoys, of beacons.

balise, *n.f.*, (nav.) sea-mark, buoy, beacon; (bot.) the fruit of the shot, canna-seed.

baliser, *v.a.*, (nav.) to buoy, to erect beacons.

baliseur, *n.m.*, person who sets up beacons, superintendent of towing-paths.

balisier, *n.m.*, (bot.) shot, American reed.

baliste, *n.f.*, war-machine, ballista; (ich.) file-fish, trigger-fish.

balistique, *n.f.*, ballistics. *adj.*, ballistic.

balivage, *n.m.*, staddling.

baliveau, *n.m.*, staddle.

baliverne, *n.f.*, nonsense, humbug, stuff. *Il vous conte des —s*; he talks nonsense, tells you cock and bull stories.

baliverner, *v.n.*, to trifle, to talk idly, to fiddle-faddle.

ballade, *n.f.*, ballad.

ballage, *n.m.*, (metal) balling.

ballant, *adj.*, waving, swinging, dangling. *Il va les bras —s*; he swings his arms in walking.

ballast, *n.m.*, (railways) ballasting.

balle, *n.f.*, ball; bullet, shot; husk of rice; bale, pack; (print.) ball. *A vous la —*; it is your turn. *Juger la —*; to foresee the end. *Prendre la — à la volée*; to hit the ball in the

air. *Prendre la — au bond*; to take the ball at the rebound; to seize the opportunity; to take time by the forelock. *Enfants de la —*; children following the business of their father. *C'est un enfant de la —*; he is his father's son. *Renvoyer la —*; to return the ball, to give tit for tat, to turn the tables on. *Fusil chargé à —*; a musket loaded with ball. *—s ramées*; chainshot. *— morte*; spent ball. *À —s franches*; free firing. *— au camp*; rounders. *Marchandise de —*; common, pack wares.

⊙**baller**, *v.n.*, to hop, to skip, to dance.

ballet, *n.m.*, ballet.

ballon, *n.m.*, balloon; football. *Envoyer un — d'essai*; to send out a feeler.

ballonné, **-e**, *adj.*, distended, swollen.

ballonnement (-mān), *n.m.*, (med.) swelling.

ballonnier, *n.m.*, football or balloon maker.

ballot, *n.m.*, bale, package, pack. *Voilà votre —*; that is exactly what you want, the very thing for you.

ballote, *n.f.*, (bot.) horehound.

ballotin, *n.m.*, small parcel, packet.

ballottade, *n.f.*, (man.) ballotade.

ballottage, *n.m.*, balloting.

⊙**ballotte**, *n.f.*, ballot; bucket. V. **boule.**

ballottement (-mān), *n.m.*, tossing, shaking; voting by ballot.

ballotter, *v.a.*, to toss, to toss about; to keep in suspense, to bandy (a tennis-ball); to debate; to ballot. *— quelqu'un*; to toss any one from pillar to post.

ballotter, *v.n.*, to shake, to rattle. *Cette porte ballotte*; that door shakes.

balnéaire, *adj.*, watering, bathing. *Ville —*; watering place.

balourd, *n.m.*, **-e**, *n.f.*, numskull, dunce.

balourd, **-e**, *adj.*, dull, heavy, thick-headed.

balourdise, *n.f.*, stupidity, doltishness; stupid thing, gross blunder.

balsamier, *n.m.* V. **baumier.**

balsamine (-za-), *n.f.*, balsamine.

balsamique (-za-), *adj.*, balsamic, balmy.

balsamite (-za-). V. **tanaisie.**

balustrade, *n.f.*, balustrade.

balustre, *n.m.*, a baluster, hand-rail.

balustrer, *v.a.*, to rail in, fence in, surround with balusters.

balzan, *adj.*, (man.) white-footed, trammeled.

balzane, *n.f.*, (man.) whitefoot, white spot, blaze.

bambin, *n.m.*, baby, brat, bantling.

bambochade, *n.f.*, (paint.) grotesque picture, caricature.

bamboche, *n.f.*, (pop.) puppet show; bit of a thing (person); drinking bout, spree; young bamboo, bamboo-cane. *Faire une —*; to have a spree. *Faire des —s*; to lead a disorderly life.

bambocheu-r, *n.m.*, **-se**, *n.f.*, (pop.) libertine.

bambou, *n.m.*, bamboo-cane, bamboo.

ban, *n.m.*, ban; public proclamation; banishment. *—s, pl.*, banns (of matrimony). *Dispense de —s*; marriage license. *Mettre au —*; to send to Coventry. *Rompre son —*; to break one's ban. *Entre au —*; to be under the ban.

banal, **-e**, *adj.*, common; commonplace; mercenary. *Expression —e*; vulgar, commonplace expression.

banalité, *n.f.*, vulgarity, a commonplace, a trite expression.

banane, *n.f.*, banana.

bananier, *n.m.*, banana-tree.

banc (ban), *n.m.*, bench, seat, settle; pew; reef, shoal, bank; bed; dock, bar. *Un — à dos*, a bench with a back to it. *Un — de gazon*; a turf seat. *— d'église*; church seat, pew. *— de l'œuvre*; churchwardens' pew. *Il est encore sur les —s*; he is still at college. *Échouer sur un — de sable*; to run aground on a sand bank. *Un — de corail*; a coral reef. *Un — de harengs*; a shoal of herrings. *Un — d'huîtres ;* a bed of oysters. *— de pierre ;* layer, bed, of stone. *Etre au — des accusés ;* to be in the dock. *— des témoins ;* witness-box.

bancal, -e, *adj.,* bandy-legged.

⊙**bancelle,** *n.f.,* long narrow form, seat.

banche, *n.f.,* sunken ridge.

banco, *adj.,* banco (a term used in exchange business. *Faire — ;* to hold all the money staked.

bancroche, *adj.* V. **bancal.**

bandage, *n.m.,* (surg.) bandage; application of bandages; belt; truss ; tire (of wheels) ; hoop, (of guns) ; spring. *— herniaire ;* truss. *Délier un — ;* to undo a bandage.

bandagiste, *n.m.,* truss-maker.

bande, *n.f.,* band, belt, strip ; company ; gang; set of people, crew; flight; troop; (her.) bend; (arch.) fascia, string; (anat.) tract. *— de papier ;* a slip of paper, wrapper. *La — d'une selle ;* the side bar of a saddle. *La — d'un billard ;* the cushion of a billiard-table. *Une — de voleurs ;* a gang of thieves. *Ces oiseaux vont par —s ;* those birds go in companies. *Faire — à part ;* to keep apart. *Donner à la — ;* (nav.) to heel. *Demi— ;* parliament-heel of a ship. *Sous — ;* under wrapper.

bandé, -e, *part.,* bandaged, taut, stretched ; (her.) bendy.

bandeau, *n.m.,* headband, fillet, frontlet, bandage; veil, mist; (arch.) string-course. *Avoir un — sur les yeux ;* to be blindfolded. *En—x ;* (of the hair) plain.

bandelette, *n.f.,* little band, string, fillet; (surg.) fascia ; (arch.) bandelet.

bander, *v. a.,* to bind up; to tighten, to bend; to bandy (at tennis) ; (arch.) to lay the stones of an arch. *— une plaie ;* to bind up a wound. *— la caisse ;* to run away. *Se — la tête ;* to bind up one's head. *Se — les yeux ;* to blindfold one's self.

bander, *v.n.,* to be stretched, tight, taut.

⊙*se* **bander,** *v.r.,* to oppose, to resist.

bandereau (ban-dro), *n.m.,* trumpet-sling.

banderole (ban-drol), *n.f.,* banderole, streamer, pennant; shoulder-belt.

bandière, *n.f. Front de — ;* front line of battle ; ⊙banner, flag.

bandit, *n.m.,* robber, vagabond, bandit, ruffian.

⊙**bandoulier,** *n.m.,* highwayman; mountaineer.

bandoulière, *n.f.,* shoulder-belt, bandoleer ; (phot.) sling-case. *Porter la — ;* to be a game-keeper. *En — ;* slung over the shoulder.

bandure, *n.f.,* (bot.) pitcher-plant.

bang, *n.m.,* (bot.) bang.

banian, *n.m.,* Banian (idolater in India).

banlieue, *n.f.,* suburbs, outskirts (of a town).

bannatte or **bannasse,** *n.f.,* tallow sieve or strainer.

banne, *n.f.,* awning, tilt ; tarpaulin; hamper (of boats).

banneau, *n.m.,* small hamper, fruit basket.

banner, *v.a.,* to cover with a tilt.

banneret (-rè), *adj.,* banneret. *Chevalier — ;* knight banneret.

banneton, *n.m.,* basket, (fishing) cauf.

bannette, *n.f.,* small hamper.

banni, -e, *part.,* banished, outlawed.

bannière, *n.f.,* banner, standard, flag, colors, streamer. *Se ranger sous la — de quelqu'un ;* to side with any one. *Aller au-devant de quelqu'un avec croix et — ;* to give one a handsome reception.

bannir, *v.a.,* to banish, to expel, to dismiss ; to drive away, to exclude, reject.

bannissable, *adj.,* deserving banishment.

bannissement (-mān), *n.m.,* banishment.

banque, *n.f.,* bank, banking business; (print. office) wages, pay-day. *Carnet de — ;* bank book. *Mandat de la — ;* bank-post-bill. *Succursale de — ;* branch bank. *Compte de — ;* bank account.

Assignation de — ; bank transfer. *Mettre à la — ;* to put in the bank. *Faire la — ;* to be a banker. *Action de la — ;* bank-stock. *Billet de — de cinq livres ,* a five-pound bank-note. *Avoir un compte en — ;* to have an account open at the bank. *Faire sauter la — ;* to break the bank.

banqueroute (ban-kroot), *n.f.,* bankruptcy. *— frauduleuse ;* frandulent bankruptcy. *Faire — ;* to be bankrupt. *Faire — à quelqu'un ;* to break one's word. *Faire — à l'honneur ;* to forfeit one's honor.

banqueroutier, *n.m.,* **-ère,** *n.f.,* bankrupt.

banquet, *n.m.,* banquet, feast.

banqueter, *v.n.,* to banquet, to feast.

banquette, *n.f.,* bench; (fort.) banquette; outside (of a coach) ; footway (of a road). *Jouer devant les —s ;* (theat.) to play to empty benches.

banquier, *n.m.,* money-agent, banker.

banquise, *n.f.,* ice-belt, ice-floe ; bank (of fog).

bans, *n.m.pl.,* (hunt.) litter for dogs.

bantam, *n.m.,* bantam.

banvin, *n.m.,* (feudal law) right to sell wine.

baobab, *n.m.,* (bot.) baobab.

bapaume, *n.f.,* (nav.). *En — ;* at a standstill.

baptême (ba-têm), *n.m.,* baptism, christening. *Nom de — ;* Christian name. *Extrait de — ;* certificate of baptism. *Recevoir le — ;* to be baptized. *Tenir un enfant sur les fonts de — ;* to stand godfather or godmother to a child. *Le — du tropique ;* the ceremony of crossing the line, ducking at sea.

baptiser (ba-ti-zé), *v.a.,* to baptize, to christen. *— des cloches ;* to consecrate bells. *— un vaisseau ;* to christen a ship. *— quelqu'un ;* to give one a nickname. *— son vin ;* to dilute one's wine.

baptismal, -e (ba-tis-mal), *adj.,* baptismal.

baptistaire (ba-tis-tèr), *adj.,* of baptism. *Registre — ;* parish register. *Extrait — ;* certificate of baptism.

baptiste (ba-tist), *n.m.,* baptist.

baptistère (ba-tis-tèr), *n.m.,* baptistery.

baquet, *n.m.,* tub, trough, bucket.

bar, *n.m.,* (ich.) umbrina ; (pisc.) bass; bar.

baragouin, *n.m.,* gibberish, jargon, lingo. *Je ne comprends pas son — ;* I don't understand his gibberish.

baragouinage, *n.m.,* gibberish ; rigmarole.

baragouiner, *v.n.,* to talk gibberish ; to gabble. *Comme ces étrangers baragouinent ;* how these foreigners do gabble, jabber.

baragouiner, *v.a.,* to sputter out. *— un discours ;* to sputter out a speech. *— une langue ;* to mangle a language.

baragouineu-r, *n.m.,* **-se,** *n.f.,* jabberer.

baraque, *n.f.,* barrack, hut ; shed, shanty ; booth (at fairs); hovel.

baraquement, *n.m.,* (milit.) hutting.

baraquer, *v.a.,* to make barracks ; to hut.

se **baraquer,** *v.r.,* (milit.) to make huts.

baraterie, *n.f.,* (nav.) barratry.

barattage, *n.m.,* churning.

baratte, *n.f.,* churn.

baratter, *v.a.,* to churn.

barbacane, *n.f.,* (fort.) barbacan ; outlet.

⊙**barbacole,** *n.m.,* pedagogue, schoolmaster.

barbare, *adj.,* savage, merciless, barbarous, rude ; barbarian.

barbare, *n.m.,* barbarian.

barbarement (-mān), *adv.,* barbarously.

barbaresque, *adj.,* of Barbary.

barbarie, *n.f.,* barbarity, rudeness, savageness, cruelty. *Commettre une — ;* to commit a piece of barbarity. *— de langage, de style ;* crudeness of language, of style.

barbarisme, *n.m.,* (gram.) barbarism.

barbe, *n.f.,* beard ; whiskers (of cats, dogs, &c.) ; (vet.) barbel ; lappet (of caps) : (arts) rough edge ; beard (of corn, barley, &c.) ; gills (of cocks) ; wattle (of fish). *Jours de — ;* shaving days. *— bleue ;* blue beard. *Sainte— ;*

(nav.) gun-room. *Jeune* —; beardless boy. *Vieille* —; old man, graybeard. *Se faire la* —; to shave one's self. *Se faire faire la* —; to get one's self shaved. *Je le lui dirai à sa* —; I'll tell it him to his face. *Faire la* — *à quelqu'un;* to beard any one, to show who is master. *Rire dans sa* —; to laugh in one's sleeve. *La* — *d'une plume;* the feather of a quill. *Mouiller en* —; (nav.) to come with two anchors ahead. — *d'une coiffe;* pinner. — *de-bouc;* (bot.) goat's beard, tragopogon. — *-de-Jupiter;* Jupiter's beard. — *de-chèvre;* meadow sweet. — *de-moine;* dodder. — *-de-capucin;* bleached dandelion, endive.

barbe, *n.m.,* barb, Barbary horse.

barbes, *n.f.pl.,* lappets, pinners.

barbé, -e, *adj.,* (her.) barbed, bearded; (bot.) barbated.

barbeau, *n.m.,* (ich.) barbel; (bot.) bluebottle.

barbelé, -e, *adj.,* bearded, barbed. *Flèche* —*e;* barbed arrow.

barbet, *n.m.,* **-te,** *n.f.,* water-spaniel. *Ce* — *va bien à l'eau;* that spaniel takes the water well. *Etre crotté comme un* —; to be as dirty as you like.

barbette, *n.f.,* (milit.) barbette. *Tirer en* —; to fire in barbe, in barbette. *Coucher à la* —; to sleep on the floor.

barbeyer, *v.a.,* (nav.) to shiver.

barbiche, *n.f.,* billy-goat beard.

barbichon, *n.m.,* shaggy spaniel puppy.

barbier, *n.m.,* barber, shaver.

barbifier, *v.a.,* (fam.) to shave.

*****barbillon,** *n.m.,* a little barbel; gill (of a cock); wattle (of a fish, a turkey).

*****barbillons,** *n.m.pl.,* (vet.) barbles.

barbon, *n.m.,* graybeard, dotard; (bot.) sweet rush. — *odorant;* lemon grass.

barbote, *n.f.,* (ich.) eel-pout, loach, groundling.

barboter, *v.n.,* to dabble, to paddle, to splash about; (nav.) to shiver.

barboteur, *n.m.,* tame duck.

barboteuse, *n.f.,* (l. ex.) dirty drab; streetwalker.

barbotière, *n.f.,* duck-pond; trough.

barbotine, *n.f.,* (bot.) wormseed.

*****barbouillage,** *n.m.,* daub, daubing; scrawl; rigmarole, twaddle.

*****barbouillé, -e,** *part.,* daubed, besmeared.

*****barbouiller,** *v.a.,* to daub, to besmear; to soil, to dirty, to blot; to scrawl, to scribble; to slur; to stammer, to splutter out; to mumble; to stumble, to flounder; to bungle. *Il lui a barbouillé le visage;* he has besmeared his face for him. *On l'a tout barbouillé d'encre;* they have daubed him all over with ink. — *un plancher;* to daub a floor. *Il n'écrit pas, il barbouille;* he does not write, he scrawls. *Il ne peint pas, il barbouille;* he does not paint, he daubs. — *un compliment;* to stammer out a compliment. *Qu'est-ce qu'il barbouille?* what is he mumbling? — *un récit;* to make a bungle of a story. — *une feuille;* (print.) to slur a sheet.

*****se barbouiller,** *v.r.,* to besmear, to injure one's character.

*****barbouilleur,** *n.m.,* dauber, scribbler; mumbler, babbler.

barbu, -e, *adj.,* bearded.

barbu, *n.m.,* (orni.) barbet.

barbue, *n.f.,* (ich.) brill.

barcarolle, *n.f.,* barcarolle.

⊙**barce** or **berche,** *n.f.,* a small cannon.

barcelonnette, *n.f.,* child's cradle, swing-cot.

bard, *n.m.,* hand-barrow.

bardane, *n.f.,* (bot.) bur, burdock.

barde, *n.f.,* barb (iron armor for horses); rasher of bacon.

barde, *n.m.,* bard, poet.

bardé, -e, *part.,* barded; covered with a thin slice of bacon, larded. *Un cheval* — *et caparaçonné;* a horse barded and caparisoned. *Chapon* —; larded capon.

bardeau, *n.m.,* shingle (board); (bot.) mealytree; (print.) fount-case.

bardelle, *n.f.,* pack-saddle.

barder, *v.a.,* to cover with thin slices of bacon, to lard; to barb a horse; to remove stones, wood, &c., on a handbarrow.

bardeur, *n.m.,* stone-carrier.

bardis, *n.m.,* (nav.) water-board.

bardit, *n.m.,* (antiq.) Germanic war song.

bardot, *n.m.,* small mule, pack-mule; drudge, butt, laughing-stock.

barège, *n.m.,* barege.

barème, *n.m.,* ready reckoner.

baret, *n.m.,* roaring of an elephant.

bareter, *v.n.,* to roar like an elephant.

barge, *n.f.,* (orni.) godwit; (nav.) a barge; hay-mow, wood-pile.

barguette (-ghèt), *n.f.,* ferry-boat.

*****barguignage** (-ghi-gnaj), *n.m.,* (fam.) hesitation, haggling, wavering, higgling, dilly-dallying.

*****barguigner** (-ghi-gné), *v.n.,* to be irresolute, to haggle, to waver, to shilly-shally.

*****barguigneu-r,** *n.m.,* **-se,** *n.f.,* haggler.

barigel, *n.m.,* (Italian) chief-constable.

baril (-ri), *n.m.,* barrel, cask, tub, keg.

*****barille,** *n.f.,* barilla.

*****barillet,** *n.m.,* rundlet; box; barrel of a watch, (of locks) drum.

bariolage, *n.m.,* variegation, odd medley of colors, motley.

barioler, *v.a.,* to streak with several colors, to variegate, to checker, to dapple.

bariquaut, *n.m.* V. **barriquaut.**

baritel, *n.m.,* winding engine. — *à chevaux;* horse-whim, whim-gin.

barlong, -ue, *adj.,* of unequal length.

barnabite, *n.m.,* monk, barnabite-friar.

barnache, *n.f.,* (orni.) barnacle.

baromètre, *n.m.,* barometer, weather-glass. *Le* — *est au beau temps;* the barometer is at set fair.

barométrique, *adj.,* barometrical.

baron, *n.m.,* baron.

baronnage, *n.m.,* baronage.

baronne, *n.f.,* baroness.

baronnet, *n.m.,* baronet. *Chevalier* —; knight baronet.

baronnial, -e, *adj.,* baronial.

baronnie, *n.f.,* barony.

baroque, *adj.,* rough, irregular, uncouth, odd, singular, strange.

barque, *n.f.,* bark, boat, craft; barge. — *de pêcheur;* fishing boat. *Conduire la* —; to steer the boat. *Il conduit bien sa* —; he is getting on very well. *Il sait bien conduire sa* —; he knows how to manage his affairs. *Patron de* —; barge-master.

barquée, *n.f.,* boatful of any goods or stores.

barquerolle, *n.f.,* small barge.

barrage, *n.m.,* toll-bar; barrier; dam; weir.

barrager, *n.m.,* toll-gatherer.

barras, *n.m.* V. **galipot.**

barre, *n.f.,* bar (of metal or wood); cross-bar; railing; bolt; division; lever, crow; dash, cross; (nav.) helm, tiller, bar; stripe; (mus.) bar; bar (of courts of judicature, public assemblies). *Avoir* —*s sur quelqu'un;* to have the advantage over any one. *Jouer aux* —*s;* to play at base (a game). — *sous le vent!* (nav.) helm alee! (man.) —*s;* bars. *Tirer la* —; to close the list. *Je ne fais que toucher* —*s;* I am off again immediately.

barré, *part.* V. **dent.**

barreau, *n.m.,* bar (for closing); bar (place reserved for barristers); lawyers, barristers;

splat (of chairs). *Fréquenter le —;* to attend the courts. *Suivre le —;* to be a barrister. *Etre reçu, admis au —;* to be called to the bar.

barrer, *v.a.,* to bar; to bar up; to fence up; to obstruct, to thwart; to stop up; to cancel; to dash over; to cross off; (her.) to bar; (vet.) to knit fast (a vein). (fig.) *— quelqu'un;* to throw obstacles in any one's way.

barrette, *n.f.,* man's cap; cardinal's cap.

barricade, *n.f.,* barricade.

barricader, *v.a.,* to barricade, to obstruct.

barrière, *n.f.,* rail, bar, barrier, stile; starting post.

barriquaut, *n.m.,* keg.

barrique, *n.f.,* large barrel or cask, hogshead.

barrir, *v.n.,* to trumpet (of elephants).

barrot, *n.m.,* (nav.) beam.

barroté, -e, *adj.,* (of a vessel) full to the beams.

barroter, *v.a.,* (nav.) to load (a vessel).

barrotin, *n.m.,* (nav.) lodge (across deck beam).

bartavelle, *n.f.,* red partridge.

baryte, *n.f.,* baryta.

baryton, *n.m.,* (mus.) baritone; (Greek gram.) barytone.

bas, -se, *adj.,* not high, low; shallow; vile, mean, despicable; abject, sordid; low, lower; inferior. *La marée est —se;* it is low water. *—se mer;* low water. *Une rivière —se;* a shallow river. *Les eaux sont —ses chez lui;* he is hard pushed for money. *Des sentiments —;* mean sentiments. *Une —se flatterie;* mean flattery. *Avoir l'âme —se;* to have a sordid soul. *Le — peuple;* the mob, the common people. *Parler d'un ton —;* to speak in a low voice. *Avoir le cœur haut et la fortune —e;* to have more spirit than fortune. *Avoir la vue —se;* to be short-sighted. *Une messe —se;* a low mass. *— étage;* lower story. *Une —se-fosse;* a dungeon. *Ce — monde;* this lower world. *Les Pays-Bas;* the Netherlands. *Le Bas-Rhin;* the Lower Rhine. *La Basse-Saxe;* Lower Saxony. *Les — officiers;* the inferior officers. *J'ai acheté cela à — prix;* I bought that at a very low price. *Les —ses cartes;* the small cards. *—se naissance;* mean birth. *Le — bout d'une chose;* the lower end of a thing. *La —se latinité;* low Latin. *Faire prendre à quelqu'un un ton plus —;* to make any one lower his tone. *Faire main —se sur;* to pillage, plunder, lay hands upon. *A porte —se, passant courbé;* one must bow to circumstances; the low door suits the shrunken frame.

bas, *adv.,* down, low. *A —!* down with. *A — le tyran!* down with the tyrant! *A — les ministres!* down with the ministers! *Au plus —;* at the very lowest. *Bien —;* very low. *En —;* below, down stairs. *Etre à —;* to be ruined. *Etre —percé;* to be short of, to be run aground for money. *Chapeaux —!* hats off! *Jeter —;* to throw down. *Ici- —;* here below. *Là- —;* over there, over the way, yonder. *Le malade est encore bien —;* the patient is still very weak. *Mettre —;* (of animals) to bring forth, to whelp, to foal, to cub, to lamb, to pup, to kitten; to lay down; to take off. *Parler —;* to speak low. *Regarder, traiter, quelqu'un du haut en —;* to look at, to treat any one contemptuously. *Tenir —;* to keep in submission, to keep under.

bas, *n.m.,* lower part; bottom; foot (of a thing); small (of the leg). *Le — du visage;* the lower part of the face. *Le — de l'escalier;* the foot of the stairs. *Il y a du haut et du — dans la vie;* there are ups and downs in life. *Etre au —;* to be low (of liquids in casks). *Sa voix est belle dans le —;* (mus.) his voice is excellent in the lower notes.

bas, *n.m.,* stocking. *— bleu;* blue-stocking (literary woman). *— à côtes, à jour;* ribbed, open-worked, stocking. *— de laine, de soie;*

woolen, silk, stocking. *Cela vous va comme un — de soie;* it fits you like a glove.

basalte, *n.m.,* basalt.

basaltique, *adj.,* basaltic.

basane, *n.f.,* sheep-leather.

basané, -e, *adj.,* tawny, sun-burnt, swarthy.

bas-bord, *n.m.,* (*n.p.*). (nav.) *V.* **bâbord.**

bascule, *n.f.,* see-saw; weighing-machine; plyer (of a draw-bridge); reciprocating motion; rocker (of cradles); lever. *Chaise à —;* rocking-chair. *Faire la —;* to see-saw. *Fusil à —;* breech-loading gun. *Pont à —;* weigh-bridge.

basculer, *v.n.,* to see-saw, to tip off (to fall).

bas-dessus, *n.m.,* (————) (mus.) low treble.

base, *n.f.,* base, basis, bottom, foundation; ground-work, ground-plot; foot, stock, radix (of logarithms). *La — d'un système;* the basis of a system. *— des fondations;* (engineering) footing.

baselle, *n.f.,* (bot.) basella.

baser, *v.a.,* to found, to fix, to base, to ground, to rest, to settle.

se **baser,** *v.r.,* to be fixed; to be grounded; to be founded; to depend, to rely.

bas-fond, *n.m.,* (———*s*) flat, hollow, bottom; (nav.) shoal, shallow, shallow water.

basilaire, *adj.,* (anat.) basilar.

basilic, *n.m.,* (bot.) basil, sweet basil; (erpetology) basilisk, cockatrice.

basilicon, or **basilicum,** *n.m.,* ointment, basilicon.

basilique, *n.f.,* (anat., arch.) basilic, basilica.

basilique, *adj.,* (anat.) basilical.

basiliques, *n.f.pl.,* Basilic Constitutions.

basin, *n.m.,* dimity.

basique, *adj.,* (chem.) basic.

bas-métier, *n.m.,* (———*s*) (manu.) handframe.

⊙**basoche,** *n.f.,* basoche (corporation of lawyers).

basque, *n.m.f.,* Biscayan; Basqu (nation and language).

basque, *n.f.,* flap, skirt, tail, of a garment. *Etre toujours pendu à la — de quelqu'un;* to be always after any one, pestering anybody.

basquine, *n.f.,* skirt.

bas-relief, *n.m.,* (———*s*) (sculpt.) basso-relievo, bas-relief.

basse, *n.f.,* (mus.) bass, bass-string. *— continue;* thorough-bass. *Contre-—;* double-bass.

basse, *n.f.,* (nav.) shallow, flat, shoal, ridge of rocks, sand-bank, breaker.

basse-contre, *n.f.,* (—*s*-—) (mus.) bass-counter, lower tenor.

basse-cour, *n.f.,* (—*s*-—*s*), inner court, poultry-yard, back-yard.

basse-étoffe, *n.f.,* (*n.p.*) mixture of lead and pewter.

basse-fosse, *n.f.,* (—*s*-—*s*) dungeon.

basse-marche, *n.f.,* (*n.f.*.) treadle (for weaving).

bassement (bâs-mān), *adv.,* meanly, pitifully, poorly, despicably, vilely, sordidly. *Il s'exprime —;* he expresses himself vulgarly. *Penser —;* to have ignoble thoughts.

bassesse, *n.f.,* baseness, meanness, vileness, littleness, villany, servileness; mean, sordid, action. *Avec —;* meanly. *Faire une —;* to do a base action.

basset, *n.m.,* (mam.) terrier; basset-hound.

basset, -te, *adj.,* of low stature.

****basse-taille,** *n.f.,* (—*s*-—*s*) (mus.) bass, (sculpt.) bas-relief. *V.* **baryton** and **bas-relief.**

bassette, *n.f.,* basset (game at cards).

basse-voile, *n.f.,* (—*s*-—*s*) (nav.) lower sail of a ship.

bassin, *n.m.,* basin, valley, hollow; pond; (anat.) pelvis; scale (balance); (nav.) dock. *Droit de —;* dock-due. *Le — d'un port;* the basin of a harbor; wet dock. *Les —s d'une* *balance ;* the scales of a balance. *Cracher au —;* (fig.) to contribute, to fork out. *Mettre dans le —;* (nav.) to dock. *— à flot;* floating dock. *— d'échouage,* or *— de radoub;* dry dock.

bassine, *n.f.,* deep, wide pan.

bassiner, *v.a.,* to warm (a bed); to bathe (with warm lotions), to foment, to steep; to water.

bassinet, *n.m.,* pan, fire-pan (of fire-arms); (bot.) crowfoot; (anat.) calyx.

bassinoire, *n.f.,* warming-pan.

bassiot, *n.m.,* small tub (used by distillers).

basson, *n.m.,* (mus.) bassoon; bassoonist.

baste, *n.m.,* basto (cards).

⊙**baster,** *v.n.,* to suffice. Only employed in: *Baste pour cela ;* well, so be it, let that pass. *Baste !* pooh! nonsense!

⊙**basterne,** *n.f.,* basterna (cart drawn by oxen).

bastide, *n.f.,* block house, country-house, villa (in the south of France).

*****bastille,** *n.f.,* Bastille; fortress.

*****bastillé, -e,** *adj.,* (her.) having inverted battlements.

bastingage, *n.m.,* (nav.) barricading, netting.

bastingue (-ghe), *n.f.,* quarter-netting.

bastinguer, *v.a.,* (nav.) to barricade.

se **bastinguer** (-ghé), *v.r.,* (nav.) to barricade, to put up the netting.

bastion, *n.m.,* bastion.

bastionné, -e (-tio-né), *adj.,* having bastions.

bastionner, *v.a.,* to bastion, to fortify.

bastonnade, *n.f.,* bastinade, bastinado, drubbing.

bastringue (-ghe), *n.m.,* public-house ball; (pop.) uproar, row, shindy.

bastude, *n.f.,* fishing-net (used in the South).

bas-ventre, *n.m.,* (—-—*s*) lower part of the abdomen.

⊙**bat** (bate), *n.m.,* tail of a fish ; (nav.) barrel.

bât (bā), *n.m.,* pack-saddle. *Un cheval de —;* a pack-horse; (fig.) stupid person. *Vous ne savez pas où le — le blesse;* you know not where the shoe pinches him.

bataclan, *n.m.,* uproar, row, shindy. *Et tout le —;* and the rest of it.

*****bataille,** *n.f.,* battle, fight, engagement; battle array; beggar-my-neighbor. *— rangée;* pitched battle. *Ranger une armée en —;* to draw up an army in battle-array. *Cheval de —;* war-horse. *Livrer —,* or *donner —;* to give battle. *Livrer — pour quelqu'un;* to take up the cudgels for any one. *C'est son cheval de —;* it is his sheet-anchor *or* stronghold.

*****batailler,** *v.n.,* to battle, to fight; to struggle hard.

*****batailleu-r, -se,** *adj.,* combative, pugnacious, quarrelsome; disputatious.

*****bataillon,** *n.m.,* battalion; (fig.) great number, host, regiment. *—s, pl.,* army. *Chef de —;* major.

bâtard, -e, *adj.,* bastard, base-born, illegitimate, spurious; mongrel; inclined (of writing). *Chien —;* mongrel. *Fruits —s;* spurious fruits. *Porte —e;* small gateway.

bâtard, *n.m.,* -e, *n.f.,* bastard, natural child.

batardeau, *n.m.,* coffer-dam.

bâtardière, *n.f.,* nursery of grafted trees.

bâtardise, *n.f.,* bastardy, spuriousness.

⊙**batate** (bot.). *V.* **patate.**

batavique, *adj. V.* **larme.**

batayole, *n.f.,* (nav.) stanchion.

bâté, -e, *part.,* saddled with a pack. *Il n'y a point d'âne plus mal — que celui du commun;* what is everybody's business is always badly done.

bateau, *n.m.,* boat, barge, bark; body of a coach. *— à vapeur;* steamer, steamboat. *— d'agrément;* pleasure-boat. *—non ponté;* open boat. *— pêcheur;* fishing-boat. *— délesteur;* ballast-boat, lighter. *Porter —;* (of rivers) to

to be navigable. *— lavoir, à lessive;* washer-woman's boat. *— de passage;* ferry-boat. *—feu;* light-ship. *Arriver en trois —x;* to come with great fuss ; in great state.

batelage (-laj), *n.m.,* juggling, juggler's trick, legerdemain ; boating.

batelée (-lée), *n.f.,* boat-load, boatful of people ; crowd, flock.

batelet (-lè), *n.m.,* a little boat.

bateleu-r, *n.m.,* **-se,** *n.f.,* juggler, buffoon, mountebank, merry-andrew, vaulter, rope-dancer.

bateli-er, *n.m.,* **-ère,** *n.f.,* waterman, ferry-man, boatman.

bâter, *v.a.,* to load with a pack-saddle.

bâti, *n.m.,* basting, tacking (of garments).

bâti, -e, *part.,* built. *Un homme bien —;* a well-built man.

bâtier (-tié), *n.m.,* pack-saddle maker.

batifolage, *n.m.,* romping.

batifoler, *v.n.,* to play, to romp.

batifoleur, *n.m.,* (l.u.) romp.

bâtiment, *n.m.,* building, pile, structure, edifice, ship, vessel. *— marchand;* merchant vessel. *— balise;* beacon-ship, light-ship. *— parlementaire;* (nav.) flag of truce. *Emplacement d'un —;* site of a building. *— qui menace ruine;* building ready to fall.

bâtir, *v.a.,* to build, to raise, to erect, to rear up; to found; to trump up, to tack, to baste (linen, cloth). *C'est — en l'air;* it is building castles in the air. *— sur le devant* (triv.); to grow bulky.

bâtisse, *n.f.,* building, construction (in masonry).

bâtisseur, *n.m.,* (b.s.) builder; wretched builder.

batiste, *n.f.,* cambric. *— de coton;* imitation muslin. *—de France;* French muslin.

bâton, *n.m.,* stick, staff, cudgel, cane, walking-staff, perch, truncheon; straight stroke (writing). *— de canelle;* roll of cinnamon. *— de commandement;* staff of command. *— de pavillon;* flag-staff. *Donner des coups de — à quelqu'un;* to cudgel any one. *Il l'a menacé du —;* he threatened to cane him. *— à deux bouts;* quarter-staff. *Tour du —;* by-profit. *Faire une chose à —s rompus;* to do a thing by fits and starts. *Aller à cheval sur un —;* to ride on a stick. *Faire mourir sous le —;* to beat to death. *Jeter des —s dans les roues;* (fig.) to put spokes in anybody's wheels, to raise obstacles. *Sauter le —;* to do anything in spite of one's self. *Tour du —;* perquisites, pickings.

bâtonnat, *n.m.,* the presidentship of the order of French advocates.

bâtonner, *v.a.,* to cudgel, to cane, to bastinade; to cross out.

bâtonnet, *n.m.,* cat, tip-cat (boys' game).

bâtonnier, *n.m.,* staff-bearer; president of the order of French advocates.

bâtonniste, *n.m.,* cudgel-player.

battage, *n.m.,* threshing (grain); striking (metal).

battant, *n.m.,* clapper (of bells); leaf (of a table or door); fly (of a flag).

battant, *adj.,* at work; beating, pelting; (nav.) ready for battle (of a ship). *Porte —e;* swing-door. *Tout — neuf;* brand-new. *Mener quelqu'un tambour —;* to carry it with a high hand over any one. *Par une pluie —e;* in pelting rain.

battant-l'œil, *n.m.,* (—), morning-cap.

batte, *n.f.,* wooden sabre; beater; washing-board; (gard.) turf-beetle. *— à beurre;* churn-staff.

battellement (-mān), *n.m.,* house-eaves.

battement (-mān), *n.m.,* clapping (of hands); stamping (of feet); flapping (of wings); beating (of the heart); shuffling (of cards); (horl.) beat.

batte-queue, *n.m.,* wag-tail.

batterie (-rî), *n.f.*, fight; battery; scuffle; lock (of fire-arms); beating (of the drum); broadside (of a ship). *Dresser une —;* to erect a battery. *— de cuisine;* kitchen utensils. *— électrique;* electric battery.

batteur, *n.m.*, beater. *—d'or;* goldbeater. *— en grange;* (agri.) thrasher. *—de pavé;* idler, lounger, loafer.

batteuse, *n.f.*, (agri.) thrashing-machine.

battoir, *n.m.*, beetle (of washerwomen); battle-door, racket.

battologie, *n.f.*, tautology.

battologique, *adj.*, tautological.

battre, *v.a.*, to beat, to strike, to bang, to thrash, to whip (a horse); to shuffle (cards); to gammon; to flag (of a sail against a mast). (agri.) *— en grange;* to thrash. *— un noyer;* to thrash a walnut-tree. *—du beurre;* to churn milk. *— monnaie;* to coin money; (fig.) to raise money. *— le fusil;* to strike a light. *— en retraite;* to beat a retreat. *— quelqu'un de ses propres armes;* to foil a man with his own weapons. *— la mesure;* to beat time. *— les cartes;* to shuffle the cards. *—le pavé;* to loaf about. *— la semelle;* to beat the hoof, to be upon the tramp. *— le bois;* to beat the wood for game. *—la campagne;* to rave, to talk, nonsense; to beat about the bush.

se **battre,** *v.r.*, to fight, to combat, to scuffle. *Se — à qui aura quelque chose;* to scramble for something.

battre, *v.n.*, to beat, to pant, to throb; to be loose (of a horse-shoe). *Le pouls lui bat fort;* his pulse beats fast. *Le cœur me bat;* my heart beats. *Le fer de ce cheval bat;* the shoe of that horse is loose. *— des mains;* to applaud. *— de l'aile;* to flutter. *— froid à quelqu'un;* to give any one the cold shoulder.

battu, -e, *part.*, beaten, fought.

battue, *n.f.*, (hunt.) battue, beat.

batture, *n.f.*, gold-lacquering; (nav.) flat, shallow.

bau, *n.m.*, (nav.) beam. *Demi- —;* half-beam. *Maître —;* midship-beam. *Faux —;* orlop beam.

baud, *n.m.*, stag-hound.

baudet, *n.m.*, ass; sawyer's trestle; donkey.

baudir, *v.a.*, (hunt.) to cheer the pack.

baudrier, *n.m.*, baldrick, shoulder-belt, belt.

baudroie, *n.f.*, (ich.) sea-devil, frog-fish.

baudruche, *n.f.*, gold-beater's skin.

bauge, *n.f.*, lair of a wild boar; dirty hovel; (mas.) pugging-mortar.

baume, *n.m.*, balm; balsam; balm-mint. *Je n'ai pas de foi dans son —;* I have no faith in his plan, promises.

baumier, *n.m.*, balm-tree.

bauque, *or* **baugue,** *n.f.*, grass-wrack.

bauquière, *n.f.*, (nav.) clamp.

bavard, -e, *adj.*, prating, talkative, loquacious, babbling.

bavard, *n.m.*, *-e, n.f.*, prater, babbler, chatterer.

bavardage, *n.m.*, babbling, prattling, garrulity.

bavarder, *v.n.*, to babble, to prattle, to blab, to jabber.

bavarderie, *n.f.*, babbling, prating, garrulity, loquacity.

bavardin, -e (l.u.). *V.* **bavard.**

bavardiner, *v.n.*, (l.u.) to talk; to prate, to prattle.

bavardise, *n.f.*, (l.u.) babbling, prating.

bavaroise, *n.f.*, bavaroise (an infusion of tea or milk and some syrup).

bave, *n.f.*, drivel, slaver, dribble; foam; slime.

baver, *v.n.*, to drivel, to slabber, to slaver, to dribble.

bavette, *n.f.*, bib, slabbering-bib. *Tailler des —s;* to gossip.

baveu-x, -se, *adj.*, driveling, slabbering.

baveu-x, *n.m.*, *-se. n.f.*, driveler, dribbler.

baveuse, *n.f.*, (ich.) blenny.

bavoché, -e, *part.*, (engr.) uneven, smeary.

bavocher, *v.a.*, (engr.) to render uneven, to smear.

bavochure, *n.f.*, unevenness, smearing.

bavolet, *n.m.*, rustic head-gear.

bavure, *n.f.*, seam (in molding); blister (on pipes).

bayadèra, *n.f.*, Bayadere (dancing-girl).

bayart, *n.m.*, hand-barrow.

baye. *V.* **baie.**

⊙**bayer,** *v.n.*, to gape, to hanker after. *—après les richesses;* to hanker after riches. *— aux corneilles;* to stand gaping in the air.

bayette, *n.f.*, baize.

⊙**bayeu-r,** *n.m.*, *-se, n.f.*, gaper, starer.

bayonnette. *V.* **baïonnette.**

bazar, *n.m.*, bazaar, hovel, concern.

bazat, *n.m.*, Jerusalem cotton, bazat.

bdellium (-om), *n.m.*, gum resin.

béant, -e, *adj.*, gaping, yawning, wide open. *Gouffre —;* open pit, yawning chasm. *Bouche -e;* gaping mouth, all agape.

béat, *n.m.*, *-e, n.f.*, devout person; (b.s.) sanctimonious individual.

béat, -e, *adj.*, (b.s.) sanctimonious.

béatement, *adv.*, sanctimoniously.

béatification, *n.f.*, beatification.

béatifier, *v.a.*, to beatify.

béatifique, *adj.*, beatifical, blissful.

*****béatilles,** *n.f.pl.*, tit-bits, dainties.

béatitude, *n.f.*, beatitude, blessedness.

beau *or* **bel, belle,** *adj.*, [*bel* before nouns singular beginning with a vowel or *h* mute], beautiful, fine, lovely, handsome; fair; smart, spruce; glorious; lofty, noble; seemly, becoming. *Une belle journée;* a fine day. *C'est un beau parleur;* he is a fine-spoken man. *Se faire beau;* to make one's self smart. *Comme vous voilà beau aujourd'hui!* how spruce you are to-day! *Une belle femme;* a handsome woman. *De beaux traits;* handsome features. *Un beau teint;* a fair complexion. *Le beau sexe;* the fair sex. *Le temps se met au beau;* the weather is clearing up. *A beau jeu, beau retour;* one good turn deserves another. *Donner beau jeu à quelqu'un;* to give any one good cards, to give any one fair play. *Avoir beau jeu;* to have good cards, to have fair play. *Prendre sa belle;* to seize the opportunity. *Faire un beau coup;* to make a lucky hit. *Une belle âme;* a lofty soul. *Il fait beau se promener aujourd'hui;* it is fine weather for walking to-day. *Il en fait de belles;* he is going on at a fine rate, playing fine tricks. *Il m'en a compté de belles;* he told me a lot of lies. *Il m'en a compté de belles sur votre compte;* he abused you right and left to me. *Belle demande!* a fine request to make! *Il l'a échappé belle;* he has had a narrow escape of it. *Charles le Bel;* (of France) Charles the Fair. *Philippe le Bel;* (of France) Philip the Fair. *Philippe le Beau;* (of Spain) Philip the Handsome. *Le beau monde;* the fashionable world. *Mourir de sa belle mort;* to die a natural death. *Au beau milieu;* in the very middle. *La belle plume fait le bel oiseau;* fine feathers make fine birds. *Déchirer à belles dents;* to criticize mercilessly, to rend any one. *Il fera beau quand j'y retournerai;* it will be a long day before I go there again. *Etre dans de beaux draps;* to be in a pretty pickle.

beau, bel, belle, *adv.*, *De plus belle;* with renewed ardor, worse than ever. *Tout beau;* gently, not so fast. *Avoir beau faire;* to try in vain. *J'ai beau faire;* it is in vain that I try. *Avoir beau dire;* to speak in vain. *J'ai beau dire;* it is useless for me to speak. *Bel et bien;* entirely, quite, altogether. *Bel et bon;* all very fine. *Voir tout en beau;* to see everything through rose-colored spectacles. *Faire le beau ;* (of dogs) to beg. *Jouer la belle ;* to play the rubber.

beau, *n.m.,* **belle,** *n.f.,* beauty ; beau, belle ; charmer.

beaucoup, *adv.,* many, much ; a great many, a great deal ; deeply ; considerably ; far. *Avoir — d'argent ;* to have much money. *Avoir — d'enfants ;* to have many children. *Il a — de patience ;* he has a great deal of patience. *A — près ;* by a great deal ; near. *Il n'est pas à — près aussi riche qu'un tel ;* he is not nearly so rich as so-and-so. *Il s'intéresse — à votre affaire ;* he is deeply interested in your case. *De — ;* by far. *Vous l'emportez de — sur lui ;* you are far superior to him. *Vous le surpassez de — ;* you are far beyond him. *Il s'en faut de — ;* he is very far from. *Il s'en faut de — que son ouvrage soit achevé ;* his work is very far from being finished. *A — moins ;* for much less. *— de bruit pour rien ;* much ado about nothing.

beau-fils, *n.m.,* (—*x*—) son-in-law.

beau-frère, *n.m.,* (—*x*—*s*) brother-in-law.

beau-père, *n.m.,* (—*x*—*s*) father-in-law.

beaupré, *n.m.,* (nav.) bowsprit.　　　[feint.

beau-semblant, *n.m.,* (—*x*—*s*) pretense,

beauté, *n.f.,* beauty ; fineness, comeliness, prettiness, loveliness, elegance, agreeableness, neatness. *Tache de — ;* beauty-spot. *Etre dans toute sa — ;* to be in one's prime, at the height of one's beauty. *Conserver sa — ;* to preserve, to keep up, one's beauty. *Avoir un — pour ;* to be sweet upon.

bébé, *n.m.,* baby, baby-doll.

bec, *n.m.,* beak ; bill, nib, rostrum ; burner ; lamp ; snout ; spout ; socket ; mouth-piece. *Le — de certains poissons ;* the snout of some fishes. *Le — d'une aiguière ;* the spout of an ewer. *Le — d'une plume ;* the nib of a pen. *—de lampe ;* socket of a lamp. *— de gaz ;* gas-burner. *— d'une ancre ;* bill of an anchor. *—de-lièvre,* (—*s*—) harelip. *Blanc—,* (—*s*—*s*) greenhorn ; youngster. *—en-ciseaux,* (—*s*—) (orni.) cutwater. *Coups de — ;* pecking. *Donner des coups de — ;* to peck. *Percer à coups de — ;* to peck through. *Coup de— ;* wipe, taunt. *Tour de — ;* kiss, buss. *Causer — à — ;* to have a private talk with. *Avoir le — bien effilé ;* to have one's tongue well hung. *Elle n'a que le — ;* she is all tongue. *Avoir le — gelé ;* to be tongue-tied. *Avoir — et ongles ;* to have teeth and nails. *Faire le — à quelqu'un ;* to give one his cue. *Faire le petit — ;* to mince. *Tenir quelqu'un le — dans l'eau ;* to keep in suspense. *S'humecter le — ;* to wet one's whistle. *Se prendre de — avec quelqu'un ;* to have a quarrel with any one. *Mener quelqu'un par le — ;* to lead any one by the nose. *Passer la plume par le — ;* to frustrate, to balk. *Se laisser passer la plume par le — ;* to let one's self be taken in.

bécabunga, or **beccabunga,** *n.m.,* (bot.) beccabunga, brook-lime.

*****bec-à-cuiller,** *n.m.,* (—*s*—) (orni.) spoonbill.

bécard or **beccard,** *n.m.,* female salmon.

bécane, *n.f.,* bike, bicycle.

bécarre, *n.m.* and *adj.,* (mus.) natural.

bécasse, *n.f.,* woodcock ; idiot. *Brider la — ;* to cozen any one. *C'est une — ;* she is a goose.

bécasseau, *n.m.,* young woodcock ; dunlin, sand-piper.

bécassine, *n.f.,* (orni.) snipe.

bec-courbé, *n.m.,* (—*s*—*s*). *V.* **avocette.**

bec-croisé, *n.m.,* (—*s*—*s*) (orni.) crossbill.

bec-d'âne (bé-da-n), *n.m.,* (—*s*—) mortise-chisel.

bec-de-corbin, *n.m.,* (—*s*—) bill-head ; (nav.) ripping-iron.　　　[stork's bill (bot.).

bec-de-grue, *n.m.,* (—*s*—) crane's bill,

bec-de-lièvre, *n.m.,* (—*s*—) harelip ; harelipped person.

becfigue, *n.m.,* (orni.) fig-pecker.

bec-fin, *n.m.,* (—*s*—*s*) (orni.) warbler.

béchamel, *n.f.,* (cook.) cream-sauce.

bécharu, *n.m.,* (orni.) flamingo.

bêche, *n.f.,* grafting-tool ; spade.

bêcher, *v.a.,* to dig.

béchique, *adj.,* (med.) bechic, cough-relieving.

bec-jaune, (—*s*—*s*). *V.* **béjaune.**

becqué, *adj.,* (her.) beaked.

becquée or **béquée,** *n.f.,* a billful. *Donner la — à un oiseau ;* to feed a bird.

becqueter or **béqueter,** *v.a.,* to peck.

se **becqueter** or **béqueter,** *v.r.,* to peck one another ; to beak ; to bill.

bécune, *n.f.,* (ich.) trumpet-fish, sea-snipe.

bedaine, *n.f.,* (jest.) paunch. *Remplir, farcir sa — ;* to stuff one's belly.

bédane, *n.m.,* mortise-chisel, paring-chisel.

bedeau, *n.m.,* beadle.

bédégar, *n.m.,* (phar.) bedeguar.

bedon, *n.m.,* ⊙ tabret, drum. *adj.,* barrel-bellied.

bédouin, *n.m.* and *adj.,* Bedouin.

bée, *adj.,* open at one end (of casks).

bée, *n.f.,* mill-dam. *V.* **abée.**

béer. *V.* **bayer.**

beffroi, *n.m.,* belfry ; watch-tower ; steeple ; alarm-bell.

bégaiement or **bégayement** (-ghê-mān), *n.m.,* stammering, faltering.

bégayer, *v.n.,* to stammer ; to lisp ; to falter.

bégayer, *v.a.,* to stammer out, to stutter, to lisp.

bégu, -ë, *adj.,* (of a horse) that does not mark age, counter-marked.

bègue (bèg), *adj.,* stammering, stuttering.

bègue, *n.m.f.,* stammerer, stutterer.

bégueule (-gheul), *n.f.,* prude, proud minx.

bégueule, *adj.,* prudish, squeamish, strait-laced.

bégueulerie (-gheul-rî), *n.f.,* prudery, affected austerity, squeamishness.

béguin (-ghin), *n.m.,* hood, child's cap ; beguin, monk, beghard. *Avoir un — pour ;* to be sweet upon.

béguine, *n.f.,* beguine ; (b.s.) affectedly devout person ; nun.　　　[affected devotion.

béguinage (-ghi-) *n.m.,* convent of beguins ;

bégum (-gom), *n.f.,* begum.

béhémoth, *n.m.,* behemoth, hippopotamus.

béhen (-hène), *n.m.,* (bot.) behen.

beige, *adj.,* (of wool) natural, undyed.

beige, *n.f.,* unbleached serge.

*****beignet,** *n.m.,* fritter.

beiram. *V.* **bairam.**

béjaune, *n.m.,* (falconry) eyas, nias ; ninny ; blunder, silliness, mistake. *Montrer à quelqu'un son — ;* to show any one his ignorance. *Payer son — ;* to pay one's footing.

bel, *adj.m. V.* **beau.**

bélandre, *n.f.,* (nav.) bilander.

bêlant, -e, *adj.,* bleating.

bélée, *n.f.,* (nav.) white hawser.

bêlement (-mān), *n.m.,* bleating of sheep.

bélemnite, *n.f.,* (foss.) belemnite.

bêler, *v.n.,* to bleat. *Brebis qui bêle perd sa goulée ;* (prov.) too much talk, no dinner.

belette, *n.f.,* weasel, fitchet.

beige, *n.m.f.* and *adj.,* Belgian.

belgique, *adj.,* Belgic.

belic, belif, or **bellif,** *n.m.,* (her.) gules.

bélier, *n.m.,* ram ; battering-ram ; Aries (one of the signs of the zodiac).

bélière, *n.f.,* sheep-bell, clapper-bell.

bélitre, *n.m.,* rascal, scoundrel, ragamuffin.

belladone, *n.f.,* belladonna, deadly nightshade.

bellâtre, *n.m.,* insipid beauty ; fop, coxcomb. *adj.,* beauish, foppish.

belle, *n.f. V.* **beau.**

belle, *adj. V.* **beau.**

belle-dame, *n.f.,* (—*s*—*s*). *V.* **arroche.**

belle-de-jour, *n.f.*, (—*s*—) convolvulus, yellow day-lily.

belle-de-nuit, *n.f.*, (—*s*—) marvel of Peru.

belle-d'un-jour, *n.f.*, (—*s*—) (bot.) yellow day-lily.

belle-fille, *n.f.*, (—*s*—*s*) daughter-in-law; step-daughter.

bellement (-mān), *adv.*, (l.u.) softly.

belle-mère, *n.f.*, (—*s*—*s*) mother-in-law; step-mother.

belles-lettres, *n.f.pl.*, (*n.s.*) polite literature, belles-lettres.

belle-sœur, *n.f.*, (—*s*—*s*) sister-in-law; step-sister.

belligérant, -e (bel-li-), *n.* and *adj.*, belligerent, engaged in war.

belligérer, *v.n.*, to make war.

belliqueu-x, -se (bel-li-), *adj.*, warlike, martial, valiant; bellicose, quarrelsome.

bellissime, *adj.*, (l.u.) extremely fine.

bellot, -te, *adj.*, pretty, neat, natty.

beluge, *n.m.*, (ich.) beluga.

belvéder (-dère), *or* **belvédère**, *n.m.*, turret, terrace, belvidere.

belzébuth, *n.m.*, Beelzebub.

bémol, *n.m.*, (mus.) flat, bemol.

bémol, *adj.*, flat.

bémoliser, *v.a.*, (mus.) to mark with a flat.

ben (bène), *n.m.*, (bot., pharm.) ben; ben-nut. *Noix de* —; ben-nut, oil-nut.

bénarde, *n.f.*, mortise dead-lock. *Serrure* —; opening and shutting on both sides. *Clé* —; solid-key, pin-key.

bénédicité, *n.m.*, grace (before meals).

bénédictin, *n.m.*, **-e**, *n.f.*, *adj.*, Benedictine.

bénédiction, *n.f.*, consecration, benediction, blessing, benison. *La — d'une église;* the consecration of a church. *Pays de* —; country of plenty. *Maison de* —; house of piety. *Combler de —s;* to load with blessings. *Donner la* —; to bless. *Quelle* —*!* what a blessing! *En* —; blessed, held sacred.

bénéfice, *n.m.*, benefice, living; benefit, advantage, profit; privilege. *A* —; (com.) at a premium. — *brut;* gross profit. — *net;* net profit. — *à charge d'âmes;* a living with care of souls. *Il faut prendre le —avec les charges;* we must take it for better or worse. *Avoir une représentation à* —; (thea.) to take a benefit.

⊙**bénéficence**, *n.f.*, beneficence, favor.

bénéficiaire, *adj.* *Héritier* —; heir liable to no debts above the value of the assets.

bénéficiaire, *n.m.f.*, beneficiary, recipient; (thea.) person who takes a benefit.

bénéficial, -e, *adj.*, beneficiary (of livings).

bénéficier, *n.m.*, beneficed clergyman, incumbent.

bénéficier, *v.a.*, to extract metal from its ore.

bénéficier, *v.n.*, (com.) to get, to gain, to profit by.

benêt, *n.* and *adj. m.*, booby, fool, simpleton; silly.

⊙**bénévole**, *adj.*, gentle, kind, kindly. *Lecteur* —; kind, gentle, reader.

bénévolement (-mān), *adv.*, out of good will.

bengali (bin-), *n.m.*, Bengalee; (orni.) bengalee.

béni, -e, *part.*, blessed, praised. *V.* **bénit**.

****bénignement**, *adv.*, benignly, kindly, graciously.

****bénignité**, *n.f.*, benignity, graciousness, kindness.

****béni-n, -gne**, *adj.*, benign, kind, gentle, good-natured, placid; (med.) mild.

bénir, *v.a.*, to bless, to praise; to wish well; to hallow; to consecrate. *Dieu vous bénisse,* God bless you.

bénit, -e, *part.*, hallowed, consecrated. *Du pain* —; consecrated bread. *De l'eau—e;* holy-water. *Eau —e de cour;* empty promises.

bénitier (-tié), *n.m.*, holy-water basin; fount.

benjamin (bin-), *n.m.*, favorite, youngest child.

benjoin (bin-), *n.m.*, benjamin, benzoin, asa-dulcis.

benoîte, *n.f.*, (bot.) herb-bennet, avens.

benzine, *n.f.*, benzine.

benzoate (bin-), *n.m.*, (chem.) benzoate.

benzoïque (bin-), *adj.*, (chem.) benzoic.

****béquillard**, *n.m.*, (pop.) old cripple.

****béquille**, *n.f.*, crutch, crutch-stick; (agri.) spud; (nav.) shore.

****béquiller**, *v.n.*, to walk on crutches.

****béquiller**, *v.a.*, (gard.) to dig weeds up with a spud; (nav.) to shore up.

ber (bère), *n.m.*, (nav.) cradle.

berbère, *n.m.* and *f.*, Berber.

berbéris, *n.m.*, (bot.) barberry.

****bercail**, *n.m.*, (*n.p.*) sheepfold, fold.

berce, *n.f.*, (bot.) cow-parsnip.

berceau, *n.m.*, cradle; place of one's infancy; arbor, bower; (arch.) vault; (nav.) cradle; (fig.) source, origin, infancy.

bercelle, *n.f.*, pincers (used by enamelers).

bercelonnette, *n.f.* *V.* **barcelonnette**.

bercement, *n.m.*, rocking, lulling; deception, delusion.

bercer, *v.a.*, to rock, to lull asleep; to lull, to amuse, to feed with hope; to delude, to flatter. *se bercer*, *v.r.*, to delude one's self, to feed on, to cradle. *Il se berce de vaines espérances;* he deludes himself with vain hopes. *Le diable le berce;* he is always on the rack. *J'ai été bercé de cela;* I have heard that from my cradle.

berceuse, *n.f.*, rocker; rocking-chair.

béret, *n.m.*, cap; Tam o' Shanter.

bergame, *n.f.*, bergamot.

bergamote, *n.f.*, odoriforous citron; bergamot (pear); comfit box.

berge, *n.f.*, steep bank of a river; bluff.

berger, *n.m.*, shepherd; swain, lover. *L'heure du* —; the happy, favorable, moment.

bergère, *n.f.*, shepherdess; nymph, lass; (fig.) easy-chair.

bergerette, *n.f.*, little shepherdess, country lass; (ornith.) wagtail.

bergerie, *n.f.*, sheepfold, pen; *pl.*, pastorals.

bergeronnette, *n.f.*, young shepherdess, lass; (orni.) dish-washer, wagtail.

béril, *n.m.* *V.* **béryl**.

berle, *n.f.*, smallage, water-parsnip.

berline, *n.f.*, traveling-coach, berlin.

berlingot, *n.m.*, chariot resembling a berlin, sort of gig.

berloque *or* **breloque**, *n.f.*, (milit.) dinner-drum, breakfast-drum. (fig.) *Battre la* —; to talk at random.

berlue, *n.f.*, dimness of sight, dazzling. *Avoir la* —; to be dim-sighted; (fig.) to be blind, not to ee further than one's nose.

berme, *n.f.*, (fort.) berme.

bermudienne (-di-è-n), *n.f.*, (bot.) bermu-diana.

bernable, *adj.*, deserving to be laughed at, ridiculous.

bernacle, *n.f.* *V.* **barnacle**.

bernardin, *n.m.*, **-e**, *n.f.*, bernardine (monk, nun).

berne, *n.f.*, tossing in a blanket; banter. *En* —; (nav.) awaft. *Mettre le pavillon en* —; to set up the flag at half-mast.

bernement, *n.m.* *V.* **berne**.

berner, *v.a.*, to toss in a blanket; to ridicule, to make a fool of, to deride, to laugh at.

berneur, *n.m.*, chaffer, banterer, sneerer.

bernique, *int.*, (pop.) no use; not a bit of it, no go. *Je croyais le trouver chez lui, mais* — I thought I should find him in the house, but the bird had flown!

berniquet, *n.m.*, (pop.) bran-basket. Only

used in the expressions : *Etre au —;* to be reduced to beggary. *Mettre quelqu'un au —;* to reduce any one to beggary.

bernous, *n.m.*, bernous, hooded cloak.

berret, *n.m.* V. **béret.**

béryl, *n.m.*, beryl.

besace, *n.f.*, wallet. *Etre à la —;* to be reduced to beggary. *Mettre à la —;* to bring one to beggary.

besacier, *n.m.*, one who carries a wallet, a beggar.

besaigre, *adj.*, (of wine) sourish, tartish. *Tourner au —;* to turn sour.

besant, *n.m.*, (her.) bezant ; (antiq.) byzant.

besas, beset, *n.m.*, (trictrac) ambs-ace.

besi, *n.m.*, a species of pear.

⊙**besicles**, *n.f. pl.*, spectacles ; barnacles.

bésigue, *n.m.*, besique or bézique (a card game).

*besogne**, *n.f.*, work, business, labor, job, piece of work. *Mettre la main à la —;* to set to work. *Mettre quelqu'un à la —;* to set any one to work. *Vous avez fait là une belle —;* you have made a pretty mess of it. *Aimer — faite;* to hate work. *S'endormir sur la —;* to be slack about one's work. *Tailler de la — à quelqu'un;* to cut out work for, to give trouble to, any one. *Etre accablé de —;* to be over head and ears in work. *Abattre de la —;* to get through a lot of work. *Aller vite en —;* to act quickly; not to mince matters.

⊙**besogner**, *v.n.*, to work, to labor.

*besogneu-x, -se**, *adj.*, necessitous, needy.

besoin, *n.m.*, need, want, occasion, emergency; distress, necessity, requirement. *Avoir — de quelque chose;* to want something. *Je n'en ai pas —;* I have no occasion for it. *J'en ai plus — que vous;* I want it more than you do. *Il est dans le —;* he is in distress. *N'avoir — de rien;* to want nothing. *Au —;* at a pinch, in case of need. *Il l'a assisté dans le —;* he was a friend to him in his distress. *Autant qu'il est —;* as much as is needful. *Il n'est pas — de, il n'est pas — que;* it is not necessary to, there is no occasion for. *Pour subvenir à ses —s;* to supply one's wants. *On connaît les amis au —;* a friend in need is a friend indeed.

besson, -ne, *adj. n.*, twin.

bestiaire, *n.m.*, (antiq.) gladiator, bestiarius ; fable-book.

bestial, -e, *adj.*, beastly, bestial, brutish.

bestialement (-măn), *adv.*, bestially, brutally, like a beast.

bestialité (-tia-), *n.f.*, bestiality.

bestiasse (-tias), *n.f.*, dolt, simpleton, ass.

bestiaux (-tiô), *n.m.* (plural of **bétail**) cattle.

bestiole (-tiol), *n.f.*, (l.u.) little animal ; poor fool.

bêta, *n. m.*, **bêtasse**, *n. f.*, blockhead, simpleton, fool. *C'est un gros —;* he is a stupid fellow.

*bétail**, *n.m.*, (bestiaux) cattle. *Gros —;* horned cattle. *Menu —;* small cattle.

bête, *n.f.*, beast, brute, dumb creature, beast ; fool, blockhead, stupid creature, fool ; beast (game at cards). *— à laine;* sheep. *— à cornes;* horned beast. *— de somme;* beast of burden. *— brute;* brute beast. *— de la Vierge;* lady-bird. *Une bonne —;* a good-natured fool. *C'est une — maligne —;* he is a spiteful animal. *C'est ma — noire;* he, she, it, is my pet aversion. *Faire la —;* to play the fool, to stand in one's own light. *Remonter sur sa —;* to get on one's legs again. *Morte la —, mort le venin;* dead men tell no tales.

bête, *adj.*, silly, stupid, foolish, nonsensical. *Il est — à manger du foin;* he is a perfect idiot. *Pas si —;* not such a fool, not so green !

bétel, *n.m.*, (bot.) betel.

bêtement (-măn), *adv.*, like a fool, foolishly, stupidly,

---

bêtise, *n.f.*, silliness, stupidity, tomfoolery, silly thing, absurdity. *C'est sa — qui l'a perdu;* his stupidity was the ruin of him. *Il a fait une —;* he did a stupid thing. *Quelle — !* what an absurdity ! *Il a dit une —;* he said a silly thing. *Il ne dit que des —s;* he talks nothing but nonsense. *C'est de la —;* it's all nonsense. *Faire des —s;* to play pranks.

bétoine, *n.f.*, (bot.) betony.

bétoire, *n.m.*, drain-pit, drain-hole.

béton, *n.m.*, beton, concrete.

bette, *n.f.*, (bot.) beet.

betterave (-rav), *n.f.*, beet, beet-root, mangold-wurzel.

bétyle, *n.f.*, (myth.) idol-stone.

beuglement, *n.m.*, bellowing, lowing.

beugler, *v.n.*, to bellow, to low. *Il se mit à —;* he began to roar like a bull.

beurre, *n.m.*, butter. *— fondu;* butter melted. *Pot de —;* jar of butter. *Pot à —;* butter-jar. *— noir;* brown butter. *Faire son —;* to make nice pickings. *Promettre plus de — que de pain;* to promise more than one can perform. *On ne peut manier le — qu'on ne se graisse les doigts;* you cannot touch pitch without soiling your fingers.

beurré, *n.m.*, butter-pear.

beurrée, *n.f.*, slice of bread and butter.

beurrer, *v.a.*, to butter.

beurrerie (beur-rî), *n.f.*, butter-dairy.

beurrier, *n.m.*, butter-dish.

beurri-er, *n.m.*, **-ère**, *n.f.*, butter-man, butter-woman. *Il n'est bon que pour la beurrière;* (of a book) it is only fit for the cheesemonger's shop.

bévue, *n.f.*, blunder, oversight, mistake. *Une — grossière;* an egregious mistake. *Faiseur de —s;* blunderer.

bey, *n.m.*, bey.

bezet, *n.m.* V. **besas.**

bézoard, *n.m.*, (phar.) bezoar.

bezole, *n.m.*, (ich.) bezola.

b-fa-si, (mus.) B ; (vocal mus.) si.

biais, *n.m.*, bias, slope ; slant, sloping, askew ; way, manner, shift, subterfuge. *Couper une étoffe de —;* to cut on the bias, cross. *Prendre une affaire du bon —, du mauvais —;* to go the right, the wrong, way to work. *User de —;* use subterfuges.

biaisement (-măn), *n.m.*, sloping, slanting, (b.s.) to shift, evasion.

biaiser, *v.n.*, to slope, to slant, to lean ; to use shifts, evasions. *C'est un homme qui biaise;* he is a shuffler.

biaiseur, *n.m.*, shuffler, shifter.

biangulaire, *adj.*, biangulated.

bibelot, *n.m.*, bauble, trinket, nicknack, gewgaw.

biberon, *n.m.*, the lip of a cruet; feeding-bottle. *Elever un enfant au —;* to bring up a child by hand.

biberon, -ne, *n.m.* and *n.f.*, tippler, toper.

bible, *n.f.*, Bible.

bibliographe, *n.m.*, bibliographer.

bibliographie, *n.f.*, bibliography.

bibliographique, *adj.*, bibliographical.

bibliolithe, *n.f.*, bibliolite.

bibliomane, *n.m.*, bibliomaniac.

bibliomanie, *n.f.*, bibliomania.

bibliophile, *n.m.*, lover of books.

bibliopole, *n.m.*, bibliopole, bibliopolist.

bibliothécaire, *n.m.*, librarian, library-keeper.

bibliothèque, *n.f.*, library ; book-case, book-shelves. *C'est une — vivante;* he is a walking library.

biblique, *adj.*, biblical.

bibliste, *n.m.*, biblist.

bibus, *n.m.*, trifle. *Des raisons de —;* paltry reasons.

bicarbonate, *n.m.,* (chem.) bicarbonate.

biceps (-sèps), *n.m.,* (anat.) biceps.

⊙**bicêtre,** *n.m.,* mad-house. (The French Bedlam.)

biche, *n.f.,* hind; roe. *A pied de —;* clawfooted.

bichette, *n.f.,* little dear, love (child).

bichon, *n.m.,* **-ne,** *n.f.,* lap-dog; little dear, love.

bichonner, *v.a.,* to curl.

se **bichonner,** *v.r.,* to curl one's hair.

biconcave, *adj.,* bi-concave.

bicoque, *n.f.,* little paltry town; hut, hovel.

bicorne, *adj.,* bicornered, two-horned.

bicornu, *-e, adj.,* bicornous.

bicuspidé, *-e, adj.,* (bot.) having two points, bicuspid.

bidenté, *-e, adj.,* bidental.

bidet, *n.m.,* pony, nag; bidet (bath).

bidon, *n.m.,* can; camp-kettle; canteen.

bief (bié), *or* **biez** (bié), *n.m.,* mill-course, mill-race; reach (canals).

bielle, *n.f.,* crank, connecting-rod.

bien (bi-in), *n.m.,* good, benefit, welfare, well-being, blessing; gift; boon, mercy; endowment; estate; property; gains; *pl.,* good things; goods; chattels. *Le souverain —;* the sovereign good. *Les —s de la terre;* the good things of the earth. *Rendre le — pour le mal;* to render good for evil. *Cela ne fait ni — ni mal;* that does neither good nor harm. *Cela fait du —;* that does one good. *Dire du — de quelqu'un;* to speak well of any one. *Grand — vous fasse;* much good may it do you. *Un homme de —;* an honest, virtuous man. *Les gens de —;* good men. *En tout — et tout honneur;* with honorable intentions. *— clair et liquide;* unencumbered estate. *— embarrassé;* encumbered estate. *— engagé, hypothéqué;* mortgaged estate. *Avoir du — au soleil;* to have landed property. *Avoir du — mal acquis;* to have ill-gotten gains. *Dépenser, manger son —;* to spend one's fortune. *Le — public;* public weal. *Abondance de —s ne nuit pas;* store is no sore. *Mener à —;* to bring to a successful issue. *Le mieux est l'ennemi du —;* leave well alone. *Périr corps et —s;* (of ships) to go down with all hands. *Séparation de corps et de —s;* judicial separation (a mensâ et thoro).

bien (bi-in), *adv.,* well; right; proper, properly; finely; in a fine plight, pickle, mess; comfortable; well off; on good terms; in favor; good-looking; much; certainly; truly; indeed; quite; full; completely; formally; clearly; expressly; very; far; very much; very well; many; great many; a great deal. *Il se conduit —;* he behaves well. *Il se porte —;* he is well. *Il parle — français;* he speaks French well. *Assez —;* pretty well. *Fort —;* very well. *Passablement —;* tolerably well. *Ils sont fort — ensemble;* they are on very good terms. *On est fort — ici;* this is a very comfortable place. *Je suis très — ici;* I am quite comfortable here. *Cette femme est —;* that woman is good-looking. *Cette jeune personne se tient —;* that young lady has a good carriage. *— trouvé;* cleverly thought of. *C'est —;* that's right. *Tout va —;* all's right. *Je me trouve — de ce nouveau régime;* I am all the better for this new diet. *Il est — dans ses affaires;* he is well to do. *Nous voilà —;* we are in a fine pickle. *Voilà — du bruit pour un rien;* here is a mighty deal of stir about nothing. *Il y avait — du monde;* there were many people. *Il est déjà — loin;* he is very far off by this time. *Vous êtes — bon;* you are very kind. *— mieux;* far better. *Il a été — attrapé;* he has been finely caught. *Il a été — battu;* he has been soundly beaten. *J'en ai — assez de tout ce monde;* I am heartily sick of all these people. *Il y a — dix lieues d'ici;* it is fully ten leagues away. *Je l'ai — pensé;* I thought so. *Je vous l'avais — dit;* I

told you so. *Il y a — là de quoi plaisanter!* a fine matter truly for joking! *Auriez-vous — l'assurance de le nier?* would you really be bold enough to deny it? *C'est être — prompt;* this is being rather hasty. *Je le savais —, je m'en doutais —;* I knew as much, I suspected as much. *— lui a pris de;* it was well for him he did so. *Je le veux —;* I have no objection. *Voulez-vous — me donner son adresse?* would you be so good as to give me his address? *Regardez-moi —;* look at me steadfastly.

bien-aimé, *-e, adj. & n.m.f.,* (—-s) beloved, well-beloved, darling, dear, lief.

bien-dire, *n.m.,* (n.p.) (fam.) fine speaking. *Le bien faire vaut mieux que le —;* to act well is better than to talk well. *Etre sur son —;* to be on one's best behavior.

bien-disant, *-e, adj.,* (—-s) well-spoken.

bien-être, *n.m.,* (n.p.) well-being, welfare, comfort, comforts. *Tout le monde cherche son —;* every one looks after his own comforts.

bienfaisance, *n.f.,* beneficence, bounty, munificence. *Société de —;* benevolent society. *Œuvre de —;* charity.

bienfaisant, *-e, adj.,* beneficent, kind, gracious, bountiful, munificent.

bienfait, *n.m.,* good term, good office, kindness, benefit, favor, pleasure, courtesy. *Combler de —s;* to load with favors. *On oublie plus tôt les —s que les injures;* services are sooner forgotten than injuries. *Un — n'est jamais perdu;* a kindness is never thrown away.

bienfait-eur, *n.m.,* **-rice,** *n.f.,* benefactor, benefactress, patron.

bien-fonds, *n.m.,* (—-s—) landed property.

bienheureu-x, *-se, adj.,* happy, fortunate, blest, blissful; blessed.

biennal, *-e* (bi-èn-nal), *adj.,* biennial.

bien que, *conj.,* though, although. *Bien qu'il le sache, il n'en parle pas;* although he knows it, he says nothing about it. *Si —;* so that.

bienséance, *n.f.,* decency, decorum, propriety, seemliness; conveniency; manners. *Garder la —, les —s;* to observe decorum.

bienséant, *-e, adj.,* decent, becoming, fitting, seemly, beseeming, decorous, fit.

⊙**bien-tenant,** *n.m.,* **-e,** *n.f.,* (—-s) (jur.) person in possession.

bientôt, *adv.,* soon, ere long, shortly. *A —!* good-bye for the present.

***bienveillance,** *n.f.,* benevolence, good-will, protection, favor, friendliness, kindness. *Gagner la — de quelqu'un;* to win any one's good will.

***bienveillant,** *-e, adj.,* benevolent, kind, friendly, well-wishing.

bienvenir, *v.n.* Only used in the expression: *Se faire —;* to ingratiate one's self into any one's favor.

bienvenu, *-e* (bi-in-vnu), *adj.,* welcome. *C'est un homme qui est — partout;* he is welcome everywhere. *Soyez le —;* be welcome.

bienvenue, *n.f.,* welcome; footing. *Payer sa —;* to pay one's footing. *Souhaiter la — à (quelqu'un);* to greet (any one).

⊙**bienvoulu,** *-e, adj.,* beloved, loved.

bière, *n.f.,* beer. *Petite —;* small beer. *Débit de —;* ale-house. *Ce n'est pas de la petite —;* it is no joke.

bière, *n.f.,* coffin, bier.

bièvre, *n.m.,* beaver, castor.

biez, *n.m. V.* **bief.**

biffer, *v.a.,* to cancel, to strike off; to run the pen through; to blot out.

bifide, *adj.,* (bot.) bifid.

biflore, *adj.,* (bot.) biflorous.

bifolié, *-e, adj.,* (bot.) two-leaved.

bifteck, *n.m.,* beefsteak (*Châteaubriand*); rump-steak. *— d'ours;* bear-steak (A. Dumas).

bifurcation, *n.f.,* bifurcation.

bifurqué, -e, *adj.,* bifurcated, forked.

se bifurquer, *v.r.,* to be forked, bifurcated.

bigame, *adj.,* guilty of bigamy.

bigame, *n.m.f.,* bigamist.

bigamie, *n.f.,* bigamy.

bigarade, *n.f.,* Seville orange.

bigaradier, *n.m.,* Seville orange-tree.

bigarré, e, *adj.,* (b.s.) party-colored, motley, streaked.

bigarreau, *n.m.,* bigaroon (cherry).

bigarreautier, *n.m.,* bigarreautier, bigaroon-tree.

bigarrer, *v.a.,* to checker, to streak, to make motley, party color.

bigarrure, *n.f.,* medley, mixture.

bigéminé, -e, *adj.,* bigeminate.

bigle, *adj.,* (l.u.) squint-eyed.

bigler, *v.n.,* (l.u.) to squint.

*bignonie, *n.f.,* trumpet-flower.

bigorne, *n.f.,* beaked anvil, bickern.

bigorneau, *n.m.,* periwinkle.

bigot, -e, *n.f.,* bigot; devotee; hypocrite.

bigot, -e, *adj.,* bigoted.

bigoterie (-trî), *n.f.,* bigotry. *Donner dans la —;* to turn bigot.

bigotisme, *n.m.,* bigotry.

bigoudis, *n.m.,* curling pin, roller.

bigourneau. *V.* **bigorneau.**

bigue (big.) *n.f.,* (nav.) sheers.

bihoreau, *n.m.,* night heron.

bijon, *n.m.,* (l.u.). *V.* **térébenthine.**

bijou, *n.m.,* jewel, trinket. *Cet enfant est son —;* that child is his darling. *Venez, mon —;* come, darling.

bijouterie (-trî), *n.f.,* jewelry.

bijouti-er, *n.m.,* **-ère,** *n.f.,* jeweler.

bijugué, -e, (-ghé), *adj.,* bijugous.

bilabié, -e, *adj.,* (bot.) bilabiate.

bilan, *n.m.,* (com.) balance-sheet; schedule. *Déposer son —;* to stop payment; to become bankrupt.

bilatéral, -e, *adj.,* bilateral; (jur.) reciprocal.

bilboquet, *n.m.,* cup and ball; curling-pipe. *C'est un véritable —;* he is a giddy-headed fellow.

bile, *n.f.,* bile; gall, anger, spleen. *Échauffer la — à quelqu'un;* to provoke any one's anger. *Décharger sa —;* to vent one's anger. *Ne pas se faire de —;* to take things easily.

biliaire, *adj.,* (med.) biliary.

bilieu-x, -se, *adj.,* bilious; choleric, passionate, angry. *Au teint —;* bilious looking.

bilingue, *adj.,* double-tongued, bilingual.

bill, *n.m.,* (—s) bill (projet de loi).

*billard, *n.m.,* billiards; billiard-table; billiard-room.

*billarder, *v.n.,* to strike a ball twice; to strike the two balls together.

*bille, *n.f.,* billiard-ball; marble taw (to play with); a log, balk (of timber). *Faire une —;* to hole a ball.

*billebaude, *n.f.,* hurly-burly, confusion. *A la —;* in confusion, in disorder.

*billet, *n.m.,* note, letter; bill, hand-bill; ticket, label; promissory note; billet (for quartering soldiers); note of hand; circular letter. *— à vue, à ordre;* bill payable at sight, to order. *— payable à présentation;* bill payable on demand. *— de complaisance;* accommodation bill. *— véreux;* unsafe bill. *— échu;* bill due. *Faire les fonds d'un —;* to provide for a bill. *J'en ai fait mon —;* I gave my promissory note for it. *— de banque;* bank-note. *— à porteur;* to bearer. *— à ordre;* to order. *—doux;* love-letter. *— d'entrée;* entrance-ticket. *—blanc;* a blank. *— de logement;* billet. *— d'aller;* single ticket. *— d'aller et retour;* return ticket.

*billeté, -e, *adj.,* ticketed; labeled; (her.) billeted.

*billeter, *v.a.,* to ticket, to label; to billet.

*billette, *n.f.,* notice to pay toll; (her.) billet.

*billevesée, *n.f.,* idle story, foolish trash, crochet, stuff, nonsense.

billion, *n.m.,* one thousand millions.

*billon, *n.m.,* base coin; place where base coin is received (to be melted); (agri.) ridge. *Monnaie de —;* copper money.

*billonnage, *n.m.,* dealing in base coin; (of land) ridging.

⊙***billonnement** (bi-io-n-mān), *n.m.,* debasing coin.

⊙***billonner,** *v.a.,* to debase coin, to circulate debased coin; (agri.) to ridge.

⊙***billonneur,** *n.m.,* debaser, utterer of debased coin.

*billot, *n.m.,* block, log; clog (for animals).

bilobé, -e, *adj.,* (bot.) bilobate.

biloculaire, *adj.,* (bot.) bilocular.

bimane, *n.m.* and *adj.,* (zool.) bimanous.

bimbelot (bim-blo), *n.m.,* plaything, toy.

bimbeloterie (bim-blo-trî), *n.f.,* playthings, toy trade.

bimbelotier (bim-blo-), *n.m.,* toyman.

binage, *n.m.,* plowing, second dressing; saying mass twice in a day.

binaire, *adj.,* binary.

binard, *n.m.,* wagon, trolley, truck.

biné, -e, *adj.,* binated.

biner, *v.a.* and *v.n.,* (agri.) to dig again, to dress a second time; to say two masses in a day.

binet, *n.m.,* save-all. *Faire —;* to be miserly.

binette, *n.f.,* hoe; face, phiz. *Quelle —! what a face, to be sure!*

binocle, *n.m.,* double eye-glass; binocle.

binoculaire, *adj.,* binocular.

binôme, *n.m.,* (alg.) binomial.

biographe, *n.m.,* biographer.

biographie, *n.f.,* biography.

biographique, *adj.,* biographical.

biologie, *n.f.,* biology.

biologique, *adj.,* biological.

bipédal, -e, *adj.,* bipedal.

bipède, *n.m.,* biped. *— antérieur;* (man.) fore limbs of a horse. *—postérieur;* hind limbs.

bipède, *adj.,* two-legged, bipedal.

bipenne, *n.f.,* two-edged ax.

biquadratique (-koua-), *adj.,* (alg.) biquadratic.

bique, *n.f.,* she-goat; pony, nag; jade.

biquet, *n.m.,* kid; assay scales.

birème, *n.f.,* bireme.

biribi, *n.m.,* biribi (a game of chance); back lining (of a shoe); punishment regiment in Algeria.

birloir, *n.m.,* window-catch holder.

bis (bi), **-e,** *adj.,* brown; tawny, swarthy. *Du pain —;* brown bread. *A — à blanc;* anyhow. [encore.

bis (bîss), *int.,* twice; encore. *Crier —;* to

bisaïeul, *n.m.,* great-grandfather.

bisaïeule, *n.f.,* great-grandmother.

bisaille, *n.f.,* whole meal; field pea.

bisannuel, -le, *adj.,* (bot.) biennial.

*bisbille, *n.f.,* quarrel, bickering, jangling.

biscaïen (i-in), *n.m.,* long-barreled musket; grapeshot ball.

biscaïen, -ne, *adj.,* ⊙ long-barreled (of guns).

bischof *or* **bishof,** *n.m.,* bishop (liquor).

biscornu, -e, *adj.,* outlandish, odd, queer.

biscotin, *n.m.,* sweet biscuit.

biscuit, *n.m.,* biscuit, sea-bread; hard kind of brick; semi-vitrified porcelain. *S'embarquer sans —;* to embark on an enterprise unprepared. *— à la cuiller;* Savoy biscuit.

bise, *n.f.,* north wind, cold wind; blast.

biseau, *n.m.,* (cook.) kissing-crust; beveling; basil; (carp.) feather edge; (print.) side-stick.

biseauter, v.a., to bevel ; to cheat in gambling. *Cartes biseautées ;* corner-bent cards.

biser, v.n., to blacken, to get brown (of seeds).

biser, v.a., (dye.) to dye a stuff over again.

biset, n.m., rock-dove or pigeon ; coarse gray cloth ; national guard on duty in private clothes.

bisette, n.f., footing lace ; (orni.) sea-duck.

bismuth, n.m., bismuth, tin-glass.

bison, n.m., (mam.) bison.

bisonne, n.f., gray cloth used for lining.

bisquain, n.m., sheep's skin with the wool on.

bisque, n.f., (cook.) bisk soup, cullis ; odds (at tennis). *Avoir quinze et — sur la partie ;* to have the odds in one's favor.

bisquer, v.n., (fam.) to be vexed, to be riled. *Faire — ;* to vex, plague, rile.

bissac, n.m., wallet ; (fig.) beggary.

bissection, n.f., (geom.) bisection.

bisser, v.a., to encore.

bissexe, adj., bisexous, bisexual.

bissexte, n.m., bissextile.

bissextil, -e, adj., bissextile. *Année —;* leap-year.

bissexuel, -le, adj., (bot.) bisexous, bisexual.

bissus (-sus), n.m. V. **byssus**.

☉**bistoquet**, n.m., billiard-mace.

bistorte, n.f., (bot.) bistort, snake-weed.

bistouri, n.m., (surg.) bistoury, knife.

bistourné, -e, adj., twisted, crooked.

bistourner, v.a., to twist.

bistre, n.m., (paint.) bister.

bistré, -e, adj., color of bister ; swarthy, dusky, tawny. *Teint —;* swarthy complexion.

bistreu-x, -se, adj., of bister.

biterné, -e, adj., (bot.) biternate.

bitord, bitors, n.m., (nav.) twine, spun-yarn.

bitte, n.f., (nav.) bitt.

bitter, v.a., (nav.) to bitt (a cable).

bitton, n.m., (nav.) timber-head.

bitume, n.m., bitumen.

bituminer, v.a., to bituminate.

bitumineu-x, -se, adj., bituminous.

bivalve, adj., bivalvular.

bivalve, n.m., bivalve.

bivouac or **bivac**, n.m., bivouac.

bivouaquer or **bivaquer**, v.n., to bivouac.

bizarre, adj., odd, fantastical, singular, strange, whimsical, extravagant, out of the way.

bizarre, n.m. V. **bizarrerie**.

bizarrement, adv., oddly, fantistically, whimsically, queerly, strangely.

bizarrerie (-rar-rî), n.f., caprice, extravagance, whim, singularity, oddness.

blafard, -e, adj., dim, dull, wan, lurid. *Lumière —e ;* dim, lurid light.

blague (blag), n.f., tobacco-pouch ; (pop.) fudge, humbug ; hoax. *La bonne — !* what a joke !

blaguer (-ghé), v.a. and n., (pop.) to hoax, to humbug ; to draw the long bow.

blagueur (-gheur), n.m., (pop.) hoaxer, humbug.

blaireau, n.m., badger, shaving-brush.

blâmable, adj., blamable, faulty, culpable.

blâme, n.m., blame, reproach, obloquy, disapprobation, reprehension. *Action digne de — ;* blameable action. *Déverser le — sur ;* to cast the blame on. *Eviter le — ;* to avoid being blamed. *Donner le — à quelqu'un ;* to blame any one. *Rejeter le — sur ;* to throw the blame on. *Tout le — en tombe sur lui ;* all the blame falls upon him.

blâmer, v.a., to blame, to censure, to disapprove, to find fault with. *On ne saurait le — ;* he cannot be blamed.

blanc, -he (blan, blansh), adj., white ; clean ; hoar, hoary ; (print.) open (of type) ; blank (of verses). *— comme neige ;* as white as snow. *Gelée —he ;* hoar frost. *Vers —s ;* blank verse. *C'est bonnet —, et — bonnet ;* it is six of one and half a dozen of the other. *Rouge soir et — matin, c'est la journée du pèlerin ;* evening red and morning gray sets the traveler on his way. *Du linge — ;* clean linen. *Passer une nuit —che ;* to have a sleepless night.

blanc, n.m., white, blank. *—seing ;* blank signature. *Le — de l'œil ;* the white of the eye. *— d'Espagne ;* whiting. *— de baleine ;* spermaceti. *— de céruse ;* ceruse. *— de plomb ;* white lead. *— de chaux ;* whitewash. *— de volaille ;* breast of a fowl. *De but en — ;* bluntly. *Dire tantôt —, tantôt noir ;* to say first one thing, then another. *Se manger le — des yeux ;* to look daggers at one another. *Ligne de — ;* (print.) white line. *Tirage en — ;* (print.) working the white paper. *Tirer en — ;* (print.) to work the white paper. *En — ;* left blank. *Le — ;* the target.

blanc-bec, n.m., (—s—s) beardless youth, youngster ; (b.s.) greenhorn.

***blanchaille**, n.f., fry, small fish, white-bait.

blanchâtre, adj., whitish, somewhat white.

blanche, n.f., minim (in music).

blanchement (blansh-mān), adv., (l. u.) cleanly, neatly.

blancher, n.m., tanner (of small skins).

blancherie, n.f. V. **blanchisserie**.

blanchet, n.m., strainer ; (print.) blanket.

blancheur, n.f., whiteness ; hoariness, cleanliness ; light ; purity, innocence, virtue.

blanchiment, n.m., bleaching, blanching, washing. *Le — de l'argent ;* the washing of silver. *Mettre des chandelles au — ;* to bleach candles.

blanchir, v.a., to whiten, to make white ; to whitewash ; to wash, to bleach, to make clean ; to blanch ; to boil off, to scald (fruits, greens) ; (print.) to white over ; to plane, to rough down. *— un plafond ;* to whitewash a ceiling. *— des toiles ;* to bleach linen. *— les flans ;* (coin.) to blanch planchets. *— du linge ;* to wash linen. *On me blanchit ;* they find me in washing. *On blanchit aujourd'hui chez nous ;* this is washingday with us. *— un ais ;* to plane a board. *— à neuf ;* to clear-starch.

blanchir, v.n., to whiten, to grow white, to foam. *Il commence à — ;* he is getting gray. *Tête de fou ne blanchit jamais ;* a fool's head is never gray.

se blanchir, v.r., to whiten, to wash.

blanchissage, n.m., washing. *— de fin* or *à neuf ;* clear-starching.

blanchissant, -e, adj., that whitens, grows white, foaming.

blanchisserie (-shis-rî), n.f., bleaching-house, laundry.

blanchisseur, n.m., washerman, bleacher.

blanchisseuse, n.f., washerwoman, laundress. *— de fin ;* clear-starcher.

blanc-manger, n.m., (—s—s) (cook.) blancmange.

blanc-seing, n.m., (—s—s) signature in blank.

blanque, n.f., lottery, lucky bag (of articles).

blanquette, n.f., blanket (pear) ; blanquette (wine) ; ragout with white sauce ; (bot.) cornsalad ; (ich.) white-bait. V. **blanchaille**.

blaque, n.f. V. **blague**.

blaser, v.a., to blunt, to pall ; to cloy, to sicken, to surfeit. *Il est blasé sur les plaisirs ;* he has lost all sense of enjoyment. *Il est blasé sur tout ;* he is sick of everything.

se blaser, v.r., to be palled, surfeited, used up.

blason, n.m., heraldry, blazon, blazonry ; coat of arms.

blasonner, v.a., to blazon ; (fam.) to criticize, to traduce, to blacken.

blasphémat-eur, n.m., **-rice**, n.f., blasphemer

blasphématoire, adj., blasphemous.

blasphème, n.m., blasphemy.

blasphémer, *v.a.*, to blaspheme.

blasphémer, *v.n.*, to blaspheme, to curse.

blatier, *n.m.*, corn-chandler, dealer in corn.

blatte, *n.f.*, (ent.) mill-moth. — *d'Amérique;* cockroach. *V.* **cafard.**

blaude, *n.f. V.* **blouse.**

blé, *n.m.*, wheat, corn; grain. — *-froment;* wheat. — *-seigle;* rye. *Grands —s;* wheat and rye. *Petits —;* oats, barley. — *méteil;* wheat and rye. — *de Turquie;* Indian corn. — *noir,* — *sarrasin;* buckwheat. — *barbu;* stiff wheat. *Du — en herbe;* corn in the blade. *Serrer du —;* to house corn. *Manger son — en herbe;* to spend one's money before one has it. *Facteur en —;* corn-factor. *Halle au —;* corn exchange.

bleime, *n.f.*, (vet.) bleyme.

blême, *adj.*, sallow, pale, ghastly, wan.

blêmir, *v.n.*, to turn or grow pale.

blende, *n.f.*, (min.) mock ore; blende.

blennie (blè-nî), *n.f.*, (ich.) blenny.

blennorrhée (blèn-no-rée), *n.f.*, blennorrhœa, gleet.

blésement, *n.m.*, lisping.

bléser, *v.n.*, to lisp.

blessant, *-e*, *adj.*, offensive, shocking.

blessé, *-e*, *part.*, wounded, hurt, diseased.

blesser, *v.a.*, to wound, to cut, to hurt, to pinch, to offend, to injure, to grate, to fret, to wring, to shock, to gall. *Cela me blesse;* that hurts me. *Mes souliers me blessent;* my shoes pinch me. *Cette phrase blesse l'oreille;* that sentence grates upon the ear. — *la vue;* to offend the eye. — *les oreilles chastes;* to offend chaste ears. — *l'honneur de quelqu'un;* to wound any one's honor. — *les convenances;* to offend against propriety.

se **blesser**, *v.r.*, to hurt or cut one's self; to take offense.

blessure, *n.f.*, wound, cut, hurt. *Les —s faites à l'honneur;* the wounds inflicted upon one's honor. *Gratification pour —;* (milit.) smart-money. *Coups et —s;* aggravated assault.

blet, *-te*, *adj.*, (fruit) soft, sleepy. *Poire blette;* sleepy pear.

blète or **blette**, *n.f.*, (bot.) blite, strawberry-spinach; kind of amaranth, flower-gentle.

bleu, *-e*, *adj.*, (—s) blue. *Avoir les yeux —s;* to be blue-eyed. *Cordon —;* first-rate cook. *Conte —;* tale of a tub, fairy tale. *Il m'a battu tout —;* he has beaten me black and blue.

bleu, *n.m.*, (—s) blue, blueness. — *de Prusse;* Prussian blue. — *d'azur;* smalt. — *de cobalt;* cobalt blue. — *de ciel;* sky blue. *Petit —;* bad, sourish wine.

bleuâtre, *adj.*, bluish, somewhat blue.

bleuet, *n.m. V.* **bluet.**

bleuette, *n.f. V.* **bluette.**

bleuir, *v.a.*, to make blue, to blue.

blindage, *n.m.*, sheeting, iron-plating, armor-plating; (milit.) poling.

blinder, *v.a.*, to sheet, to plate; (milit.) to cover with blinds.

blindes, *n.f. pl.*, (fort.) blinds.

bloc, *n.m.*, lump, bulk, mass; block, log; stocks. *Acheter en —;* to buy in a lump.

blocage, *n.m.*, rubble.

blocage, *n.m.*, (print.) turned letter, turning.

*****blocaille**, *n.f.*, (mas.) rubble-stone; pebble-work.

blockhaus (blok-hôs), *n.m.*, (—) blockhouse.

blocus, *n.m.*, (—) (milit.) investment; (nav.) blockade. *Lever le —;* to raise the blockade.

blond, *-e*, *adj.*, flaxen, fair, light. *Des cheveux —s;* light hair. *Un homme —;* a fair man. *Il est délicat et —;* he is a dainty spark, difficult to please.

blond, *n.m.*, *-e*, *n.f.*, fair, light color; fair person. — *ardent;* sandy color. — *cendré;* light yellow. — *doré;* golden. *Courtiser la brune et la —e;* to make love to a number of women.

blonde, *n.f.*, blond, blond-lace.

blondier, *n.m.*, blonde-lace maker.

blondin, *n.m.*, *-e*, *n.f.*, a fair-complexioned person; spark. *Un beau —;* a fine young spark.

blondir, *v.n.*, to grow light or fair.

blondissant, *-e*, *adj.*, yellowish, golden.

bloqué, *n.m.*, ball holed (at billiards).

bloquer, *v.a.*, to blockade; to block up, to fill up (cavities in walls with mortar); (print.) to turn; to hole a ball (billiards).

se **blottir**, *v.r.*, to squat, to cower, to crouch, to lie close to the ground.

blouse, *n.f.*, pocket (of a billiard-table); smock-frock; blouse; pinafore.

blouser, *v.a.*, to hole (at billiards); to cheat. *Il m'a blousé;* he has cheated me.

se **blouser**, *v.r.*, to hole one's own ball; to blunder; to be in the wrong box.

bluet, *n.m.*, (bot.) bluebottle, corn-flower; (orni.) bluebird, kingfisher.

bluette, *n.f.*, spark, flash, flake of fire; (lit.) literary trifle; smart production.

blutage, *n.m.*, bolting, sifting (of flour).

bluteau or **blutoir**, *n.m.*, bolter, bolting-mill.

bluter, *v.a.*, to bolt, to sift (meal).

bluterie (-trî), *n.f.*, bolting-room.

boa, *n.m.*, (—s) (erpetology) boa; fur tippet.

bobèche, *n.f.*, sconce; socket (of a candle-stick).

bobine, *n.f.*, bobbin; spool, reel.

bobiner, *v.a.*, to wind on a bobbin, to spool.

bobineuse, *n.f.*, winder.

bobo, *n.m.*, hurt, sore. *Avoir —;* to have a slight ailment.

bocage, *n.m.*, grove, coppice.

bocag-er, *-ère*, *adj.*, of groves, shady.

bocal, *n.m.*, short-necked bottle; glass bowl; large phial; carboy mouthpiece.

bocard, *n.m.*, metal.) stamper, crushing-mill.

bocardage, *n.m.*, (metal.) crushing, pounding, stamping.

bocarder, *v.a.*, (metal.) to stamp, to pound.

bock, *n.m.*, glass of beer.

bodruche. *V.* **baudruche.**

bœuf, *n.m.*, ox, bull; beef. *Troupeau de —s;* drove of oxen. *Accoupler, découpler, les —s;* to yoke, to unyoke, oxen. *Du — à la mode;* a-la-mode beef. *Un —;* a dull-pated, heavy fellow. *Mettre la charrue devant les —s;* to put the cart before the horse. *Le — gras;* the fatted ox, prize ox.

bœufs (beû), *n.m. pl.*, oxen.

boghei (-gay), *n.m.*, (—s) light gig, buggy.

bogue (bog), *n.f.*, chestnut-bur.

bohé or **bohea**, *n.* and *adj. m.*, bohea tea.

bohème, *n.m.f.*, **bohémien**, *n.m.*, *-ne*, *n.f.*, gipsy, bohemian, tramp.

boiard, *n.m. V.* **boyard.**

boire (buvant, bu), *v.a.*, to drink, to imbibe; to absorb. — *un affront;* to pocket an affront. — *le calice jusqu'à la lie;* to drain the cup to the dregs. *Qui fait la folie, la boit;* as you brew, so you must drink.

boire, *v.n.*, to drink, to tipple; to blot, to be puckered (of needle-work). — *à la ronde;* glasses round. — *à la santé de quelqu'un;* to drink any one's health. *C'est un homme qui boit;* he is a drunkard. — *à longs traits;* to drink long draughts. — *sec;* to drink hard, neat. — *comme un trou;* to drink like a fish. *A —;* some drink. *Ce papier boit;* this paper blots. *Qui a bu, boira;* habit is second nature. *Le vin est tiré, il faut le —;* in for a penny, in for a pound.

boire, *n.m.*, drink, drinking. *Le — et le manger;* eating and drinking. *Elle lui apprête son*

— et son manger; she prepares his meals for him.

bois, *n.m.,* wood, forest; timber; horns (of a deer, &c.); cross (of Christ); bedstead; stock (of a gun); staff (of a lance). *Un — de haute futaie;* a wood of lofty trees. *Un — taillis;* a copse. *— mort sur pied;* dead wood. *Mort—;* wood of little value, such as hawthorn, bramble, &c. *La lisière d'un —;* the skirt, edge of a wood. *La faim chasse le loup du —;* hunger will break through stone walls. *— puant;* bean trefoil. *— de rose;* tulipwood. *— de gaiac;* lignum vitæ. *— de Sainte-Lucie;* Mahaleb. *— de palissandre;* violet ebony. *— sur pied;* standing wood. *— d'équarrissage;* square timber. *— en grume;* round timber. *Le fil du —;* the grain of the wood. *— de sciage;* sawn timber. *— de refend;* cleft timber. *— chablis;* wind-fallen wood. *— de charpente;* timber, straight timber. *— de charronnage;* wheelwrights' timber. *— de construction pour la marine;* ship timber. *— de chauffage;* firewood. *— flotté;* floated wood. *— d'araignée;* crow-foot. *Faire du —;* to get wood. *Une voie de —;* load of wood. *Un train de —;* a float of wood. *Il ne sait plus de quel — faire flèche;* he does not know which way to turn, what to be at. *Je sais de quel — il se chauffe;* I know what metal he is made of. *Il est du — dont on fait les flûtes;* he will chime in with anything. *Trouver visage de —;* to find no one at home. *Un — de lit;* a bedstead. *Le — tortu fait le feu droit;* the end justifies the means.

boisage, *n.m.,* wood-work.

boisé, -e, *adj.,* woody, abounding with wood, wooded. *Chambre —e;* wainscoted room.

boisement, *n.m.,* planting land with trees, timbering, afforestation.

boiser, *v.a.,* to put woodwork to; to timber.

boiserie (boaz-rî), *n.f.,* wainscot, wainscoting.

boiseu-x, -se, *adj.,* woody, ligneous.

boisseau, *n.m.,* bushel.

boisselée (boas-lée), *n.f.,* a bushelful.

boisselier, *n.m.,* cooper, bushel-maker.

boissellerie (boa-sèl-rî), *n. f.,* cooperage, bushel-making.

boisson, *n.f.,* drink, beverage, drinking, drunkenness. *Être adonné à la —;* to be addicted to drinking. *Être pris de —;* to be intoxicated.

boite, *n.f.,* ripeness, maturity of wine. *En —;* matured.

boîte, *n.f.,* box; case (of a watch, a rudder). *— de montre;* watch-case. *— à poudre;* powder-box. *— à savon;* soap-tray. *— à thé;* tea-caddy. *— aux lettres;* letter-box.

boîte, *n.f.,* foot-soreness (of cattle).

boitement (boat-mān), *n.m.,* halting, limping.

boiter, *v.n.,* to be lame, to walk lame, to limp, to halt, to hobble. *— d'un pied;* to walk lame of one foot. *En boitant;* limpingly.

boiterie (boa-trî), *n.f.,* (vet.) halting.

boiteu-x, -se, *n.* and *adj.,* lame person; lame, halt, hobbling; limping. *Le Diable —;* the Devil on two sticks. *Attendre le —;* to bide one's time. *Il ne faut pas clocher devant les —;* you must not remind people of their infirmities.

boîtier, *n.m.,* surgeon's case of instruments.

bol, *n.m.,* a large pill, bolus; (min.) bole; bowl, basin, finger-glass.

bolaire, *adj.,* (min.) bolary.

bolet, *n.m.,* (bot.) boletus.

bolide, *n.m.,* (astron.) bolis, fire-ball.

bolus, *n.m.* V. **bol.**

bombance, *n.f.,* feasting, junketing. *Faire —;* to feast.

bombarde, *n.f.* bomb-ketch, bomb-vessel; (mus.) organ-stop.

bombardement, *n.m.,* bombardment.

bombarder, *v.a.,* to bombard.

bombardier, *n.m.,* bombardier.

◉**bombasin,** *n.m.,* bombazine.

bombe, *n.f.,* bomb-shell, ball. *La — a crevé en l'air;* the bomb has burst in the air. *Voûte à l'épreuve de la —;* bomb-proof vault. *Gare la —! look out for squalls!

bombé, -e, *adj.,* arched; barreled; convex.

bombement (-mān), *n.m.,* swelling, bulging out, convexity.

bomber, *v.a.,* to cause anything to bulge, to jut, to swell out, to arch, to curve, to barrel (of roads).

bomber, *v.n.,* to bulge, to jut out.

bomberie (bon-brî), *n.f.,* shell-foundry, bomb-foundry.

bombeur, *n.m.,* maker of convex glasses.

bombonne, *n.f.,* big can, drum.

bombyx, *n.m.,* (ent.) bombyx, silkworm.

bomerie (bôm-rî), *n.f.,* (com.) bottomry.

bon, -ne, *adj.,* good, kind; favorable; fine, convenient, advantageous, profitable, proper; safe, solvent; full; silly, foolish; wholesome; easy, good-natured. *—! good! C'est—;* all right, very good. *Cela ne présage rien de —;* that bodes no good. *En — état;* sound. *—ne foi;* plain dealing, uprightness. *—sens;* sensibleness. *Faire—ne chère;* to live well. *A— appétit il ne faut point de sauce;* a good appetite needs no sauce. *Une —ne fois;* once for all. *Vous êtes trop —;* you are too kind. *C'est une —ne personne;* she is a good creature. *— à prendre;* worth taking. *— à boire;* good to drink. *A quoi — tant de peines?* what is the use of so much trouble? *—ne nourriture;* wholesome food. *Voilà ce qu'il y a de—;* that's one comfort. *Prendre quelque chose en —ne part;* to take a thing well. *Les — comptes font les —amis;* short reckonings make long friends. *Tout lui est —;* all is fish that comes to his net. *C'est une —ne tête;* he has a good head-piece. *A — jour, —ne œuvre;* the better the day, the better the deed. *De—ne heure;* early. *Il est encore de —ne heure;* it is still early. *A la —ne heure!* good! well done! that's something like. *Se donner du — temps;* to divert one's self. *Trouver—;* to approve, to like. *Sentir —;* to have a good smell. *Tenir—;* to hold out. *Il ne fait pas — avoir affaire à lui;* it is dangerous to meddle with him. *La lui garder —ne;* to owe any one a grudge. *Être homme à —nes fortunes;* to be a lady-killer. *Il y va de —ne foi;* he plays fair and square. *Si — vous semble;* if you think proper. *Vous êtes — vous!* I like you! *De — cœur;* heartily. *De—ne foi;* sincerely. *La faire courte et—ne;* to have a short but merry life. *Que vous êtes—!* how silly you are! *Tout de —;* in earnest. *A quelque chose malheur est —;* it's an ill wind that blows good to no one. *Faire—ne mine à mauvais jeu;* to put a good face upon matters. *A — vin, point d'enseigne;* good wine needs no bush. *Une—ne fuite vaut mieux qu'une mauvaise attente;* discretion is the better part of valor.

bon, *n.m.,* good quality, what is good in a thing; the best, the fun of a thing; voucher, check, bond. *Il a cela de — qu'il ne ment jamais;* he has this good quality, that he never tells a lie. *Le — de l'histoire;* the cream of the story.

bon, *int.,* well, good, right.

bonace, *n.f.,* (nav.) calm, smooth sea; lull.

bonasse, *adj.,* simple, foolish; silly, credulous; soft, complying.

bonbon, *n.m.,* bonbon, sweetmeat, comfit.

bonbonnière, *n.f.,* sweetmeat box; snug little house.

bon-chrétien (-kré-), *n.m.,* (—s. —s) Bartlett [pear.

bond, *n.m.,* bound, skip, gambol; caper, leap, jump. *Faire un—;* to make a bound. *Second —;* rebound. *Prendre la balle au—;* to catch the ball at the bound; to seize time by the forelock. *Il m'a fait faux —*; he has given me the slip. *Il s'élança d'un — par-dessus la muraille ;* he cleared the wall at a bound. *Par sauts et par —s ;* by leaps and bounds. *Il ne va que par sauts et par —s ;* he only works by fits and starts. *Tant de — que de volée ;* anyhow, *or* by hook or by crook.

bondé, -e, *adj.,* quite full, full to the bung.

bonde, *n.f.,* sluice ; bung, bung-hole.

bonder, *v.a.,* (nav.) to lade full, to fill.

bondir, *v.n.,* to bounce, to bound, to rebound ; to caper, to skip, to frisk. *Il bondissait de rage ;* he bounded with rage. *Cela fait — le cœur ;* that makes one's heart leap.

bondissant, -e, *adj.,* bounding, skipping, frisking.

bondissement (-mān), *n.m.,* bouncing, bounding, skipping, frisking.

bondon, *n.m.,* bung ; bunghole.

bondonner, *v.a.,* to bung, to stop with a bung, to close up.

bondonnière, *n.f.,* bung-borer (tool).

bonduc, *n.m.,* (bot.) nickar-tree.

bon-henri, *n.m.,* (—) (bot.) all-good, English mercury.

bonheur (bo-neur), *n.m.,* happiness, prosperity, felicity, welfare, blessing, good fortune, good luck, chance, happy thing. *Envier le — d'autrui ;* to envy another's prosperity. *Le — de l'Etat ;* the welfare of the state. *Faire le — de quelqu'un ;* to delight any one. *Avoir du — ;* to be lucky. *Etre en — ;* to be fortunate. *Par — ;* luckily. *Porter — ;* to bring good luck. *Jouer de — ;* to be lucky, in luck's way. *Au petit — ;* happen what may, I will chance it.

bonhomie (bo-no-mi), *n.f.,* good nature, easy humor, simplicity, credulity.

bonhomme (bo-nom), *n.m.,* (bonshommes) simple, good-natured man ; old codger. *Vieux — ;* old fellow, old buffer, fogy. *Petit — ;* little fellow.

⊙**bonhommeau,** *n.m.* *V.* **bonhomme.**

boni, *n.m.,* (—s) (fin.) bonus.

boniface, *adj.,* simple, artless.

bonification, *n.f.,* amelioration, improvement; (com.) allowance.

bonifier, *v.a.,* to better, to improve, to ameliorate ; to make up, to make good.

boniment, *n.m.,* quack's show, puff ; humbug, clap-trap speech.

bonisseur, *n.m.,* showman's puffer ; speech.

bonjour, *n.m.,* good morning, good day, compliments. *Je vous souhaite le — ;* I wish you good morning.

bonne, *n.f.,* nursery-maid ; lady's-maid ; good friend ; fine story. *— à,* or *pour, tout faire ;* maid of all work.

bonneau, *n.m.,* (nav.) buoy of an anchor.

bonne-dame, *n.f.,* (—s—s). *V.* **arroche.**

bonnement (bo-n-mān), *adv.,* plainly, simply, honestly, truly, merely.

bonnet, *n.m.,* cap. *— de laine ;* woolen cap. *— de nuit ;* night-cap. *Gros — ;* big wig, person of importance. *Opiner du — ;* to adopt the opinion of another ; to vote blindly. *Triste comme un — de nuit ;* as dull as ditch water. *Jeter son — par-dessus les moulins ;* to throw off all restraint ; to be reckless. *Avoir la tête près du — ;* to be hot-headed. *Ce sont deux têtes dans un — ;* they are hand and glove together. *C'est — blanc et blanc — ;* it is six of one and half a dozen of the other. *Prendre sous son — ;* to invent, make up a tale. *Y jeter son — ;* to give it up.

bonnetade, *n.f.,* capping, half-capping (jest).

⊙**bonneter,** *v.a.,* to cap, to doff one's hat (jest) ; to cringe.

bonneterie (bo-n-trî), *n.f.,* hosiery business.

bonneteur, *n.m.,* (l.u.) cringer, card-sharper.

bonnetier (bo-n-tié), *n.m.,* hosier.

bonnette, *n.f.,* (fort.) bonnet ; (nav.) studding sail; (of a telescope or camera) cap.

bonsoir, *n.m.,* good evening, good night ; not if I know it. *— et bonne nuit !* a good night's rest to you !

bonté, *n.f.,* goodness, excellence, kindness, attention, good-heartedness, favor. *Abuser de la — de quelqu'un ;* to take advantage of any one's goodness. *Avoir la — de ;* to be so good as to.

bonze, *n.m.,* bonze (Buddhist priest).

⊙*boquillon,** *n.m.,* woodman, feller of wood.

boracique, *adj.* *V.* **borique.**

borax (-raks), *n.m.,* borax.

borborygme, *n.m.,* (med.) borborygm, rumbling.

bord, *n.m.,* shore ; bank, strand, side, margin; brink, edge, brim, skirt ; rim, border, extremity; hem, edging, lace ; (nav.) board ; (nav.) broadside ; (nav.) tack. *Le — de la mer ;* the seashore. *Le — d'une rivière ;* the bank of a river. *Le — d'un précipice ;* the brink of a precipice. *Le — d'une table ;* the edge of a table. *Le — d'un chapeau ;* the rim of a hat. *Le — d'un bateau ;* the side of a boat. *Le — d'une robe ;* the skirt of a gown. *J'ai son nom sur le — des lèvres ;* I have his name on the tip of my tongue. *A pleins —s ;* full to the brim. *J'allai à son — ;* I went aboard his ship. *Coucher à — ;* to sleep on board ship. *Tourner, changer, virer, de — ;* to tack about, to veer. *Courir même que l'ennemi ;* to stand on the same tack with the enemy. *— au large ;* standing off shore. *— à terre ;* standing in shore. *— à — ;* alongside.

bordage, *n.m.,* (nav.) planking, plank, poling, bulwarks.

bordé, *n.m.,* hem, edging, bordering.

bordeaux, *n.m.,* claret, Bordeaux wine.

bordée, *n.f.,* (nav.) broadside ; volley ; salvo; stretch, tack. *Lâcher, or tirer, une — ;* to fire a broadside. *Une — d'injures ;* a shower of abuse. *Courir des —s ;* to tack about.

bordel, *n.m.,* (l. ex.) brothel.

bordelais, -e, *n.m.f.* and *adj.,* of Bordeaux.

bordement, *n.m.,* edge.

border, *v.a.,* to edge, to hem, to skirt, to bind, to lace, to border ; (nav.) to gather (the sheets); to plank ; to lay (a deck) ; to tuck up (bed-clothes) ; to line (a road). *Les soldats bordent la côte ;* soldiers line the coast. *— les côtés d'un vaisseau ;* to plank a ship. *— les ponts ;* to lay a ship's decks. *— une écoute ;* to tally a sheet. *Borde au vent !* haul aft the sheets.

bordereau, *n.m.,* (com.) account, memorandum, note.

bordi-er, -ère, *adj.,* (nav.) lop-sided.

bordier, *n.m.,* lop-sided ship.

bordigue (-dig), *n.f.,* crawl (for taking fish).

bordure, *n.f.,* frame, edge, edging ; border, curb ; rim ; (nav.) foot.

bore, *n.m.,* (chem.) boron.

boréal, -e, *adj.,* boreal, northern.

borée, *n.m.,* Boreas, North-wind.

*****borgne,** *n.* and *adj.,* one-eyed person ; blind of one eye ; one-eyed ; dark, obscure, paltry. *Changer son cheval — contre un aveugle ;* to change for the worse. *Au royaume des aveugles les —s sont rois ;* among the blind, the one-eyed is king.

*****borgnesse,** *n.f.,* (pop.) one-eyed woman.

borique, *adj.,* (chem.) boracic.

bornage, *n.m.,* settling bounds, fixing limits.

borne, *n.f.,* landmark ; boundary, limit, confine ; bounds ; mile-stone, spur-post. *Mettre des —s à son ambition ;* to set bounds to one's ambition. *Cela passe toutes les —s ;* that is going beyond all bounds. *Etre planté là comme une — ;* to stand there like a post.

borné, -e, *part.,* bounded, limited, confined ; narrow, mean, small ; shallow. *Esprit fort — ;* narrow mind.

borne-fontaine, *n.f.*, (—*s*—*s*) water-post.

borner, *v.a.*, to set landmarks; to bound, to set bounds to, to limit, to circumscribe, to restrict, to terminate, to confine. — *son ambition*; to set bounds to one's ambition.

se **borner**, *v.r.*, to keep within bounds, to restrain one's self. *Il faut se — à cela*; we must be content with that, or not go beyond that.

bornous (-noos), *n.m.*, *V.* **bernous**.

bornoyer, *v.a.*, to place, to set marks in, to look with one eye at.

bosan, *n.m.*, bosa (Turkish beverage).

bosel, *n.m.*, (arch.) torus.

bosphore, *n.m.*, Bosphorus.

bosquet, *n.m.*, grove, thicket.

bossage, *n.m.*, (arch.) bossage, embossment, relief.

bosse, *n.f.*, hunch, hump; bump; bruise; knob, protuberance, lump; bunch; boss; embossment; (sculp.) relievo, relief, embossment; (paint.) bust; boss (at tennis). *Ne demander que plaie et —*; to think of nothing but mischief or fighting. *Ouvrage relevé en —*; embossed piece of work. *Ouvrage de demi —*; figure in half-relief. *Donner dans la —*; to fall into the snare, to be duped, to be caught. *Travailler en —*; to emboss.

bosselage (bos-laj), *n.m.*, embossing.

bosselé, -e, *adj.*, bruised (metal); (bot.) bunched; embossed.

bosseler (bos-lé), *v.a.*, to dent; to emboss.

bosselure (bos-lur), *n.f.*, embossment.

bosser, *v.a.*, (nav.) to stopper.

bossette, *n.f.*, (arch., man.) boss, stud.

bossoir, *n.m.*, (nav.) cat-head; bow.

bossu, -e, *n.* and *adj.*, hunchback; hunchbacked, humpbacked, deformed, uneven, crooked, tortuous. — *par-devant*; pigeon-breasted. *Rire comme un —*; to split one's sides with laughter.

bossuer, *v.a.*, to bruise, to dent, to batter.

se **bossuer**, *v.r.*, to get bruised, dented.

bostangi, *n.m.*, (—*s*) soldier of the Turkish militia.

boston, *n.m.*, boston (game at cards).

bostrychite (-kit), *n.f.*, (min.) bostrychite.

bot, *adj.*, club-footed. *Pied —*; (subst.) club-foot. *C'est un pied —*; he is club-footed.

bot, *n.m.*, Dutch-boat.

botanique, *n.f.*, botany.

botanique, *adj.*, botanical.

botaniste, *n.m.*, botanist.

botargue, *n.f. V.* **boutargue**.

botte, *n.f.*, boot (man's only); Wellington boot; bunch, bundle, truss; (fenc.) pass, thrust, lunge; step of a coach; cask; clod of dirt or snow; wine vessel, butt. —*s à genouillère*; jack-boots. —*s à l'écuyère*; top-boots. *Souliers* —*s*; Blucher boots. —*s retroussées*, —*s à revers*; top-boots. —*s de sept lieues*; ogre's boots. —*s fines*; dress boots. *Tirant de —*; boot-strap. *Tige de —*; boot-leg. *Tire —*; boot-jack. *Mettre du foin dans ses —*; to feather one's nest. *A propos de —s*; about nothing. *Graisser ses —*; to prepare for a journey, for death. *Décrotter, cirer, des —s*; to clean, to polish, boots. *Une — d'asperges*; a bundle of asparagus. *Une — de foin*; a truss of hay. *Porter une — à quelqu'un*; (fenc.) to make a pass, a lunge, at one. *Parer une —*; to parry a pass. *Il lui a porté une vilaine —*; he served him a very scurvy trick.

botté, -e, *adj.*, booted, with boots on.

bottelage (bo-tlaj), *n.m.*, tying up in bundles.

botteler (bo-tlé), *v.a.*, to put up in bundles.

botteleur (bo-tleur), *n.m.*, (agri.) binder, bandster.

botter, *v.a.*, to make, to supply any one with, boots; to boot anybody. *Ce bottier botte bien, mal;* this bootmaker makes boots well, badly. (fam.) *Cela me botte;* that suits me down to the ground.

se **botter**, *v.r.*, to put one's boots on; to get one's shoes clogged with dirt; to ball (of horses); (milit.) to boot. *Cet homme se botte bien, mal;* this man wears well made, badly made, boots.

bottier, *n.m.*, bootmaker, shoemaker.

bottine, *n.f.*, half-boot; lady's boot.

boubie, *n.f.*, (orni.) booby, gannet.

bouc, *n.m.*, he-goat; goat-skin; pulley. — *émissaire;* scape-goat.

boucage, *n.m.*, (bot.) burnet saxifrage.

boucan, *n.m.*, a place to smoke-dry in.

boucaner, *v.a.*, to smoke (meat, hides).

boucaner, *v.n.*, to smoke-dry; to hunt wild bulls for their hides.

boucanier, *n.m.*, buccaneer, bucanier; free-booter; buccaneer's musket.

boucaro, *n.m.*, boucaro, red clay.

boucassin, *n.m.*, lining.

boucaut, *n.m.*, cask, hogshead.

bouche, *n.f.*, mouth; lips; tongue; muzzle (of a cannon); voice; victuals; eating, living; cooks (of a sovereign); mouth, opening, aperture (of canals, rivers); plug-hole, fire-plug. *Dépense de —;* household expenses. *Munitions de —;* provisions. — *à —;* face to face. — *béante;* open-mouthed. *De —;* by word of mouth. *Être sur sa —;* to be given to gluttony. *Que l'imposture ne souille point votre —;* let not falsehood sully your lips. — *close;* keep it to yourself; mum's the word! *Il dit cela de —, mais le cœur n'y touche;* he says one thing and thinks another. *Fermer la — à quelqu'un;* to stop any one's mouth. *Il dit tout ce qui lui vient à la —;* he says whatever comes uppermost. *Faire la petite —;* to be difficult to please, dainty. *Elle n'en fait point la fine —;* she does not mince it. *Faire la — en cœur;* to screw up one's mouth, to look captivating. *Cela rend la — amère;* that leaves a bitter taste in the mouth. *Garder une chose pour la bonne —;* to keep a tit-bit till the last. *Cela fait venir l'eau à la —;* that makes one's mouth water. *Prendre sur sa —;* to stint one's self. *Selon ta bourse, gouverne ta —;* you must cut your coat according to your cloth. *Il arrive bien des choses entre la — et le morceau;* there is many a slip between the cup and the lip. *Cheval qui a bonne —;* hard-feeding horse. *Un cheval qui n'a ni — ni éperon;* a horse that obeys neither bridle nor spur. *Un homme fort en —;* a man that out-talks everybody. *Il y en avait à — que veux-tu;* there was enough and to spare.

bouchée, *n.f.*, mouthful. *Ne faire qu'une — de quelqu'un;* to make but a mouthful of any one, to beat any one with ease.

bouche-nez, *n.m.*, stench-trap.

boucher, *v.a.*, to stop, stuff, choke up; to obstruct. — *une bouteille;* to cork a bottle. — *un tonneau;* to bung a barrel. — *la vue d'un voisin;* to obstruct a neighbor's view. *Se — les oreilles;* to stop one's ears. *Se — le nez;* to hold one's nose. — *un trou;* to stop up a gap, to pay a debt.

boucher, *n.m.*, butcher. — *en gros;* carcass-butcher.

bouchère, *n.f.*, a butcher's wife, woman keeping a butcher's shop.

boucherie (boo-shrî), *n.f.*, shambles, butchery, market; slaughter, carnage, massacre.

bouche-trou, *n.m.*, (—*s*) a stop-gap.

bouchoir, *n.m.*, oven-door, lid, stopper.

bouchon, *n.m.*, cork, stopper; ⊙darling; wisp (of straw, &c.); packet (of linen); pot-house. *Frotter un cheval avec un — de paille;* to rub down a horse with a wisp of straw. — *de-cabaret;* tavern-bush (kind of game).

bouchonner, *v.a.*, to rub down (a horse).

bouchonnier, *n.m.*, corkcutter.

bouchot, *n.m.*, fishing-hurdles; mussel-bed.

bouchure, *n.f.*, quickset hedge.

boucle, *n.f.*, buckle; ring; curl, ringlet, lock; (arch.) knocker; (nav.) staple, ring. *Des —s d'oreilles;* ear-rings. *Mettre une perruque en —s;* to curl a wig. *Mettre en —;* to put in irons.

bouclé, -e, *part.*, buckled, curled. *Cheveux —s;* curly hair.

boucler, *v.a.*, to buckle; to put a ring to; to curl (hair); (hunt.) to ferret out.

se **boucler**, *v.r.*, to curl one's hair.

boucler, *v.n.*, to curl, to put out, bulge.

bouclier, *n.m.*, buckler, shield; defense, protection; (ich.) lump-fish. *Levée de —s;* rising in arms; insurrection.

⊙**boucon**, *n.m.*, (l. ex.) poisoned drink or dish.

bouddhique, *adj.*, Buddhistic.

bouddhisme, *n.m.*, Buddhism.

bouddhiste, *n.m.* and *f.*, Buddhist.

bouder, *v.n.*, to pout, to look sour, to sulk; to pout at; not to be able to play (dominoes); (hort.) to be stunted.

se **bouder**, *v.r.*, to be sulky with, to be cool, towards each other.

bouderie (bou-drî), *n. f.*, pouting, sulking, sulkiness.

boudeu-r, -se, *adj.*, sulky, sullen.

boudeu-r, *n.m.*, **-se**, *n.f.*, person who sulks.

boudin, *n.m.*, black pudding; (nav.) pudding; (arch.) torus; saddle-bag, cloak-bag; spring (of a coach); long curl; sausage-finger.

boudinage, *n.m.*, slubbing, roving.

boudine, *n.f.*, (glass-making) bunt, knot.

boudineu-r, *n.m.*, **-se**, *n.f.*, rover, slubber.

boudini-er, *n.m.*, **ère**, *n.f.*, black-pudding-maker.

boudinoir, *n.m.*, roving-machine.

boudoir, *n.m.*, boudoir, lady's private-room.

boue, *n.f.*, dirt, mire, mud; filth; meanness; sordidness; sediment (of ink). *Je n'en fais pas plus de cas que de la — de mes souliers;* I don't value it more than the dirt on my shoes. *Une âme de —;* a mean soul. *Tirer quelqu'un de la —;* to raise any one from the dunghill. *Traîner quelqu'un dans la —;* to load any one with abuse.

bouée, *n.f.*, (nav.) buoy. *— de sauvetage;* life-buoy.

boueur, *n.m.*, scavenger, dustman.

boueu-x, -se, *adj.*, dirty, miry; muddy; foul. *Chemin —;* dirty road. *Ecriture —se;* thick writing.

bouffant, -e, *adj.*, puffed.

⊙**bouffante**, *n.f.*, hoop, farthingale.

bouffarde, *n.f.*, (pop.) short pipe. *Téter or fumer sa —;* to have a whiff, to blow one's cloud.

bouffe, *n.m.*, buffoon. *pl.*, Italian opera (in Paris). *Aller aux —s;* to go to the Italian opera.

bouffée, *n.f.*, puff, gust, blast, whiff; fit. *Par —s;* by fits and starts.

bouffer, *v.n.*, to puff, to swell, to rise, to bulge.

bouffer, *v.a.*, to blow (meat).

bouffette, *n.f.*, bow (ribbon), ear-knot.

bouffi, -e, *adj.*, puffed up, swollen, inflated. *Des joues —es;* puffed out cheeks. *— d'orgueil;* puffed up with pride. *Ange —;* chubby child.

bouffir, *v.a.*, to puff up, to swell, to bloat.

bouffissure, *n.f.*, swelling, puffing up; turgidness, bombast.

bouffon, *n.m.*, buffoon, jester, clown; merry-andrew, jack-pudding, droll. *Un mauvais —;* a sorry jester. *Faire le —;* to play the buffoon.

bouffon, -ne, *adj.*, jocose, facetious, comical.

bouffonner, *v.n.*, to be jocose, full of jests; to play the buffoon.

bouffonnerie (-fo-n-rî), *n.f.*, buffoonery, drollery, jesting.

bouge, *n.m.*, little closet, hole, wretched den, hovel; bulge of a cask.

bougeoir (-joar), *n.m.*, flat candlestick, chamber-candlestick; taper-stand.

bougeotte, *n.f.*, pigeon-hole.

bouger, *v.n.*, to stir, to budge, to wag, to fidget. *Il ne bouge de cette maison;* he is always at that house.

bougie, *n.f.*, candle, wax-candle, wax-light; (surg.) bougie.

bougier, *v.a.*, to wax.

bougonner, *v.n.*, to grumble, to scold, to jaw, to mum.

bougran, *n.m.*, buckram.

bougre, *n.m.*, blackguard; fellow. *Bon —;* good sort of fellow. *Mauvais —;* nasty fellow, ugly customer.

*****bouillabaisse**, *n.f.*, Provençal fish-soup with garlic, &c.; mish-mash.

*****bouillant, -e**, *adj.*, boiling, boiling-hot, scalding-hot, piping-hot; hot, fiery, hasty, eager, fierce, hot-headed. *Jeunesse —e;* fiery youth. *— de colère;* boiling with anger. *— d'impatience;* burning with impatience.

*****bouille**, *n.f.*, fishing-pole.

*****bouiller**, *v.a.*, to stir the water with a pole.

*****bouillerie**, *n.f.*, boilery.

*****bouilleur**, *n.m.*, boiler-tube (of an engine).

*****bouilli**, *n.m.*, boiled beef, bouilli.

*****bouillie**, *n.f.*, pap (for infants); pulp (to make paper). *Faire de la — pour les chats;* fruitless labor, profitless undertaking.

*****bouillir**, *v.n.*, to boil, to simmer. *Faire — à demi;* to parboil. *— à gros bouillons;* to boil fast. *— à petits bouillons;* to boil gently; to simmer. *Cela sert à faire — la marmite;* that helps to make the pot poil.

*****bouillir**, *v.a.*, to boil. Only used in the popular and figurative expression : *— du lait à quelqu'un;* to say something very pleasant to somebody.

*****bouilloire**, *n.f.*, boiler, kettle.

*****bouillon**, *n.m.*, broth; bubble, ripple, bubbling; ebullition, transport; puff (of a lady's dress). *— en tablette;* portable broth, meat-tablet. *— de poulet;* chicken broth. *— de veau;* veal-broth. *— coupé;* broth diluted with water. *Prendre un —;* to take some broth. *Boire un —;* to swallow a mouthful (in bathing); to meet with a loss. *— pointu;* clyster. *L'eau sort de la roche à gros —s;* the water comes gushing out of the rock. *Un — d'eau;* a bubbling fountain.

*****bouillon-blanc**, *n.m.*, (—s-—s) mullein, cow's-lung-wort.

*****bouillonnant, -e**, *adj.*, bubbling, gurgling.

*****bouillonnement** (-io-n-mān), *n.m.*, bubbling up, spouting or gushing out; ebullition, effervescence, agitation.

*****bouillonner**, *v.n.*, to bubble, to gush out, to boil, to boil over.

bouillonner, *v.a.*, to put puffs to. *— une robe;* to put puffs to a dress.

*****bouillotte**, *n.f.*, foot-warmer.

*****bouillotte**, *n.f.*, bouillotte (game at cards).

bouin, *n.m.*, (dy.) head of silk.

bouis, *n.m.*, glazing-stick.

boujaron, *n.m.*, tot, about half a gill (nav.).

boulaie, *n.f.*, (l.u.) birch plantation.

boulang-er, *n.m.*, **-ère**, *n.f.*, baker; baker's wife.

boulanger, *v.a.*, to make bread. *Du pain bien boulangé;* well-made bread.

boulanger, *v.n.*, to bake.

boulangerie (-lan-jrî), *n.f.*, baking, bakers' business; bakehouse.

boule, *n.f.*, bowl, ball, pate, head, noddle, sconce. *Il est rond comme une —;* he is as round as a ball. *Un jeu de —;* a bowling-green. *Jouer à la —;* to play at bowls. *Avoir la —;* to play first. *Boule-de-neige,* (—s-—) (bot.) snow-ball. *— d'eau chaude;* hot water bottle. ⊙*A la — vue;* in haste, carelessly. *— ;* (for voting) ballot. (pop.) *Perdre la —;* to lose one's head.

bouleau, n.m., birch, birch-tree.

bouledogue, n.m., bull-dog.

bouler, v.n., to swell, to pout (of pigeons).

boulet, n.m., bullet, ball; fetlock-joint (of a horse); (man.) boulet. *Un — de canon;* a cannon-ball. *Un coup de —;* a cannon-shot. *— rouge;* red-hot ball. *— ramé;* chain-shot, bar-shot. *Condamner au —;* (milit.) to condemn to chain and ball. *Tirer à —s rouges sur quelqu'un;* to load any one with abuse.

bouleté, -e, adj., (vet.) upright on fetlock-joint. *V.* **juché**.

boulette, n.f., forced-meat ball; pellet, paper-bullet, blunder. *Faire des —s;* to commit blunders.

bouleux, n.m., thick-set horse; heavy hack; drudge. *Un bon —;* a plodding man, a drudge.

boulevard or **boulevart** (bool-var), n.m., bulwark, rampart; boulevard.

bouleversement (bool-vers-mān), n.m., destruction, ruin; overthrow; overthrowing; overturning; commotion, confusion, disorder.

bouleverser (bool-vèr-) v.a., to overthrow; to throw down, to subvert; to agitate, to trouble, to throw into commotion; to upset; to unsettle, to unhinge, to convulse. *Cela m'a tout bouleversé;* it has quite unhinged me.

⊙à la **boule vue**, adv. *V.* **boule**.

boulier, n.m., bag-net (fishing).

boulimie, n.f., (med.) bulimy.

boulimique, adj., bulimic.

boulin, n.m., pigeon-hole; (mas.) pigeon-cove; putlog. *Trous de —;* scaffolding-holes.

bouline, n.f., (nav.) bowline, gantlet. *Aller à la —;* to sail close to the wind; to tack about. *Courir la —;* to run the gantlet.

bouliner, v.n., to sail close to the wind.

bouliner, v.a., to haul to windward. *— une voile;* to haul a sail to windward.

boulingrin, n.m., bowling-green, grass-plot.

boulinier, n.m., (nav.) *Un bon —;* a ship that sails well to windward.

bouloir, n.m., (mas.) larry, pole.

boulon, n.m., bolt, large iron pin.

boulonnement, n.m., bolting, pinning.

boulonner, v.a., to pin, to fasten with iron pins, to bolt.

boulot, -te, adj., fat, dumpy, squatty.

boulotter, v.n., to jog along.

⊙**bouque**, n.f., channel, strait, mouth, passage.

⊙**bouquer**, v.a. and n., to kiss forcibly; to yield, to truckle.

bouquet, n.m., bunch, cluster, tuft; nosegay, bouquet, posy; birth-day ode, sonnet; birth-d y present; flavor, aroma (of wine). *Un — de plumes;* a plume of feathers. *Un — de pierreries;* a sprig of jewels. *Un — de bois;* a cluster of trees. *Fleur qui vient en —s;* flower that grows in bunches. *— de fusées;* bunch of rockets. *Réserver une chose pour le —;* to keep a thing for the last. *Et maintenant, pour le —!* and now, to cap the story!

bouquetier (book-tié), n.m., flower-vase.

bouquetière, n.f., flower-girl.

bouquetin, n.m., wild goat, ibex.

bouquin, n.m., old he-goat; buck-hare; old book. *Mauvais —;* worthless book; (of pipes) mouth-piece.

bouquiner, v.n., to buck, to couple (of hares); to hunt after, to read, old books.

bouquinerie (-ki-n-ri), n.f., old-book trade.

bouquineur, n.m., lover of old books, book-fancier.

bouquiniste, n.m., dealer in old books.

bouracan, n.m., a sort of camlet, barracan.

bouracanier, n.m., barracan maker.

bourbe, n.f., mire, mud, dirt.

bourbeux, -se, adj., miry, muddy, sloughy, sloshy.

bourbier, n.m., slough, puddle, mire, mud;

lurch, plunge, scrape, danger. *Il s'est mis dans le —;* he has got himself into a scrape.

*****bourbillon**, n.m., core (of an abscess).

bourcette. *V.* **mâche**.

bourdaine, or **bourgène**, n.f., black alder.

bourdalou, n.m., hat-band; sort of chamber-pot.

bourde, n.f., fib, sham, humbug, lie. *Donner une — à quelqu'un;* to tell any one a fib.

bourder, v.n., to fib, to sham, to humbug.

bourdeur, n.m., fibber, shammer.

*****bourdillon**, n.m., stave-wood (for casks).

bourdon, n.m., drone; pilgrim's staff; great bell; (mus.) drone; humble-bee; great bell; (print.) out, omission.

bourdonnant, -e, adj., humming, buzzing.

bourdonnement (-mān), n.m., buzz, buzzing; hum, humming; murmur; tinkling noise.

bourdonner, v.n., to buzz, to hum, to murmur.

bourdonner, v.a., to hum; to bore; to pester.

bourdonnet, n.m., (surg.) dossil.

bourdonneur, n.m., humming-bird, colibri.

bourg, n.m., borough, market-town.

bourgade, n.f., small market-town, straggling village.

bourgène, n.f. *V.* **bourdaine**.

bourgeois, n.m., -e, n.f., (-joâ, -joaz), burgess, citizen, townsman, commoner; master, mistress, owner of a merchant-ship; contractor. *Un bon —;* a substantial citizen. *Un petit —;* a humble citizen. *Etre en —;* (of officers) to be dressed in plain clothes.

bourgeois, -e, adj., middle-class; belonging to, or becoming, a citizen, citizenlike; private; plain; common. *Famille —e;* good middle-class family. *Avoir l'air —, les manières —es;* to be common in one's gait and manners. *Cuisine —e;* plain, homely cooking. *Pension —;* private boarding-house. *Comédie —e;* private theatricals.

bourgeoisement (-joaz-mān), adv., citizen-like, humbly; vulgarly.

bourgeoisie (-joa-zî), n.f., middle-class, citizenship, citizens. *Droit de —;* freedom of a city. *Haute —;* upper middle-class, gentry. *Caution —;* good security.

bourgeon (boor-jon), n.m., bud, gem; shoot; pimple.

bourgeonnant, -e, adj., budding.

bourgeonné, -e, part., budded, pimpled.

bourgeonnement (-jo-n-mān), n.m., budding, budding-time.

bourgeonner (-jo-né), v.n., to bud, to shoot, to put forth young shoots; to break out in pimples.

bourgeonnier (-jo-nié), n.m., (orni.) bullfinch.

bourgmestre, n.m., burgomaster.

*****bourgogne**, n.m., Burgundy wine.

bourgépine (-ghé-), n.f., (bot.) buckthorn.

*****bourguignon, -ne** (-ghi-), n. and adj., Burgundian, of Burgundy.

bourlet, n.m. *V.* **bourrelet**.

bournous. *V.* **bernous**.

bourrache, n.f., (bot.) borage.

bourrade, n.f., blow with a musket butt; beating, home-thrust; taunt; (hunt.) snapping.

bourras, n.m. *V.* **bure**.

bourrasque, n.f., squall; relapse; fresh attack (of a disease); vexation; caprice; fit of anger, of ill-humor.

bourre, n.f., hair, fluff (of animals); stuff, trash; flock (of wool); floss (of silk); wad (of fire-arms); kind of down (on the buds of trees). *Lit de —;* flock-bed.

bourreau, n.m., hangman, executioner; tormentor, tyrant, butcher. *Un — d'argent;* a spendthrift.

bourrée, n.f., brushwood, chatwood; small fagot; boree (dance).

bourreler (boor-), *v.a.*, to torment, to sting; to torture, to rack, to goad.

bourrelet *or* **bourlet**, *n.m.*, pad; cushion; sand-bag; swelling (about the loins); padded cap; (of horses) collar.

bourrelier (boor-), *n.m.*, harness-maker.

bourrelle, -ment, *n.m.*, torment, torture.

bourrellerie (boo-rèl-rî), *n.f.*, business of a harness-maker.

bourrer, *v.a.*, to ram; to thrash; to abuse; to stuff, to wad; to cram with food; ⊙ to nonplus; (hunt.) to snap. — *de coups*; to give a sound thrashing to.

se **bourrer**, *v.r.*, to cram one's self with food; to abuse each other.

bourrer, *v.n.*, (of horses) to bolt.

bourriche, *n.f.*, game-basket.

bourrique, *n.f.*, she-ass; ignorant, stupid person.

bourriquet, *n.m.*, ass's colt; hand-barrow; windlass; mason's horse.

bourriquier, -ère, *n.m.f.*, donkey-driver.

bourrir, *v.n.*, to whir (of partridges).

bourroir, *n.m.*, tamping-bar.

bourru, -e, *adj.*, cross, morose, peevish, crabbed, moody, wayward, surly, snappish; unfermented.

bourse, *n.f.*, purse; hair-bag; purse-net; saddle-bag; scholarship; foundation; (anat.) sac; (bot.) wrapper; (surg.) suspensory bandage; (com.) exchange. *Coupeur de* —; cutthroat. *Avoir la* —; to keep the money. *Faire* — *commune*; to live in common. *Faire* — *à part*; to keep one's own money. *La* — *ou la vie!* your money or your life! *Aller à la* —; to go to the Exchange, to go on 'Change. *Loger le diable en sa* —; to be penniless. *Avoir toujours la* — *à la main*; to be always dipping into one's purse. *Sans* — *délier*; without expense.

bourses, *n.f.pl.*, scrotum.

boursette, *n.f.*, small purse.

boursicaut, *n.m.*, small purse; small sum.

boursier, *n.m.*, purse-maker; foundation scholar; exhibitioner.

***boursiller**, *v.n.*, to club together; to fork out.

bourson, *n.m.*, fob, little pocket.

boursouflage, *n.m.*, bombast, fustian.

boursouflé, -e, *adj.*, bloated; bombastic, inflated, turgid. *Style* —; turgid style.

boursoufler, *v.a.*, to bloat, to make turgid, to puff up.

boursouflure, *n.f.*, bloatedness (face); turgidness (style).

bousage, *n.m.*, dunging.

bousard, *or* **bouzard**, *n.m.*, deer's ball.

bousculade *or* **bousculement** (boos-kul-măn), *n.m.*, jostling, hustling; bullying.

bousculer (boos-) *v.a.*, to turn upside down, to throw into disorder; to jostle, to hustle, to squeeze.

bouse (booz), *n.f.*, cow-dung.

***bousillage**, *n.m.*, mud-wall; mud-walling; bungling piece of work.

***bousiller**, *v.a.*, to make a mud-wall; to bungle, to botch.

***bousilleu-r**, *n.m.*, **-se**, *n.f.*, mud-wall builder, bungler, botcher.

bousin, *n.m.*, the soft crust of freestone; (l.ex.) row, shindy.

boussole, *n.f.*, sea compass, compass; mariner's needle; guide, direction.

boustrophédon, *n.m.*, (antiq.) boustrophedon.

bout, *n.m.*, end, extremity, tip; top, point; bit; nipple; muzzle, ferrule; fag-end. *Le* — *des doigts;* the finger-ends. *Savoir une chose sur le* — *des doigts;* to have a thing at one's finger's ends, to know it perfectly. *Brûler la*

chandelle par les deux — *s;* to burn the candle at both ends, to be a bad manager. *Le bas* —; the lower end. *Le* — *de la langue;* the tip of the tongue. *Le* — *de la mamelle;* the nipple of the breast. — *s de manches;* false sleeves. — *s d'aile;* pinions. *Bâton à deux* — *s;* quarter staff. *Au* — *d'une heure de conversation;* after an hour's conversation. *Tenir le haut* —; to get the upper hand. *Se tenir sur le* — *des pieds;* to stand on tip-toe. *Patience, nous ne sommes pas au* —; have patience, we have not done yet. *Tirer un coup de pistolet à* — *portant;* to fire off a pistol point-blank. *Rire du* — *des dents des lèvres;* to laugh in a forced manner. *Un* — *de ruban;* a bit of ribbon. *Il est économe de* — *s de chandelle;* he is penny wise and pound foolish. *Mettre la patience de quelqu'un à* —; to exhaust any one's patience. *Pousser quelqu'un à* —; to drive any one to extremities. *Venir à* — *de;* to succeed, to get through anything. *On ne saurait venir à* — *de cet enfant;* this child cannot be managed. *A tout* — *de champ;* at every turn. *Au* — *du compte;* after all; upon the whole. *D'un* — *à l'autre;* from beginning to end. *Au* — *de l'aune faut le drap;* the last straw breaks the camel's back. *Jusqu'au* — *des ongles;* to one's finger-tips. *Laisser voir le* — *de l'oreille;* to reveal one's true character. — *rimé. V.* **bout-rimé.**

boutade, *n.f.*, (boo-) whim, fit, start, caprice, frolic, freak. *Par* — *s;* by fits and starts.

boutant, *adj.*, (arch.) supporting. *Arc* —; buttress.

boutargue *or* **botargue**, *n.f.*, botargo.

bout-dehors, (—*s*—). *V.* **boute-hors.**

bouté, -e, *adj.*, (man.) straight-legged. *Cheval* —; straight-legged horse.

boute-en-train, *n.m.*, (—) stallion kept with mares; bird piper. *Etre le* —; to be the life and soul of the company.

boutefeu, *n.m.*, (artil.) linstock; incendiary, firebrand.

⊙**boute-hors**, *n.m.*, (—) (nav.) boom; outrigger; good command of words. *Jouer au* —; to try to oust one another, to play at beggar my neighbor.

***bouteille**, *n.f.*, bottle; bottleful; bubble; bottle case. *Boucher une* —; to cork a bottle. *Déboucher une* —; to uncork a bottle. *Mise en* —; bottling. *Faire sauter le bouchon d'une* —; to crack a bottle (instead of uncorking it). *N'avoir rien vu que par le trou d'une* —; to know nothing of the world.

⊙***bouteiller. *V.* **boutillier.**

***bouteilles**, *n.f.pl.*, (nav.) round house.

⊙**bouter**, *v.a.*, to pare, to flesh, to put.

bouter, *v.n.*, (of wine) to become ropy.

bouterolle (boo-trol), *n.f.*, chape (of a scabbard).

boute-selle, *n.m.*, (— — *s*) (milit.) signal to saddle.

⊙**boute-tout-cuire**, *n.m.*, (—) (fam.) a spendall, glutton.

bouteuse, *n.f.*, pin-sticker.

bouteux, *n.m.*, putting-net, shrimp-net.

⊙***boutillier**, *n.m.*, cup-bearer.

boutique, *n.f.*, shop; merchandise of a shop; tools; implements; well for fish. *Garçon de* —; shop-boy. *Demoiselle de* —; shopgirl. *Cela vient de votre* —; that is your doing. — *bien fournie;* a well-stocked shop. *Il a vendu toute sa* —; he has left off business, or disposed of his business.

boutiqu-ier (boo-), *n.m.*, **-ière**, *n.f.*, tradesman, shopkeeper; vulgar fellow. *adj.*, shoppy.

boutis, *n.m.*, (hunt.) rooting-place.

boutisse (boo-), *n.f.*, (mas.) header, bondstone.

boutoir, *n.m.*, snout of a wild boar; buttress; parer; currier's knife. *Coup de* —; rough answer; disagreeable proposal; stunner.

bouton, n.m., button; stud; bud; nipple; pimple; gem; knob; sight (of a gun); (chem.) button. — *à queue;* shank button. — *d'or;* buttercup. *Le — d'une serrure;* the knob, button of a lock. *Serrer le — à quelqu'un;* to keep a tight hand over; to press hard upon.

boutonné, -e, part., buttoned, pimpled; (fig.) reserved. *Nez —;* nose full of red pimples. *C'est un homme —;* he is very reserved.

boutonnement (-mān), n.m., budding, buttoning.

boutonner, v.a., to button; (fenc.) to touch.

se **boutonner**, v.r., to button one's coat.

boutonner, v.n., to bud, to button.

boutonnerie (boo-to-n-rî), n.f., button-trade.

⊙**boutonnet**, n.m., little bud, button, gem.

boutonnier, n.m., button-maker.

boutonnière, n.f., button-hole; (fig.) cut, gash.

bout-rimé, n.m., poetry made on given rhymes.

bouts-rimeur, n.m., (— - —s) person who fills up given rhymes.

*****bout-saigneux**, n.m., (—s— —) scrag-end.

bouture, n.f., (hort.) slip; cutting.

bouvart or **bouveau**, n.m., young bull.

bouverie (boo-vrî), n.f., ox-stall.

bouvet, n.m., joiner's grooving-plane.

bouvi-er, n.m., **-ère**, n.f., cowherd, drover, ox-drover; (fig.) churl.

*****bouvillon**, n.m., young bullock, steer.

*****bouvreuil**, n.m., (boo-) bullfinch.

bovine, adj., bovine. *Peste —;* cattle plague.

boxe, n.f., boxing.

boxer, v.n., to box.

se **boxer**, v.r., to box.

boxeur, n.m., boxer. *Combat de —s;* boxing-match.

boyard, n.m., boyard (Russian nobleman).

boyau, n.m., bowel, gut, cat-gut; (hort.) branch; hose, pipe. *Corde à —;* catgut. — *de tranchée;* branch of a trench (fort.) *Descente de —x;* rupture.

boyauderie, n.f., gut-works.

boyaudier, n.m., gutspinner.

brabançon, -ne, adj., Brabantine.

brabant, n.m., Belgian plow.

bracelet (bra-slè), n.m., armlet, bracelet, bangle.

brachial, -e (-kî-), adj., (anat.) brachial.

brachygraphie (-kî-), n.f., brachygraphy.

brachylogie (-kî-) n.f., (rhet.) brachylogy.

braconnage, n.m., poaching.

braconner, v.n., to poach, to steal game.

braconnier, n.m., poacher.

bractée, n.f., (bot.) bract, bractea.

bractéifère, adj., (bot.) bracteate.

bractélé, -e, adj. V. **bractéifère**.

brague (brag), n.f., (nav.) breeching. pl., breeches.

braguette, n.f. V. **brayette**.

brahmane, brahme, n.m., Brahmin.

brahmanique, adj., Braminical.

brahmanisme, n.m., Braminism.

brai, n.m., resin, rosin, pitch.

braie, n.f., napkin, clout; (nav.) coat. pl., breeches, trousers. *S'en tirer les —s nettes;* to get off unharmed, to get clear off.

*****braillard**, n.m., **-e**, n.f., bawler, brawler, squaller.

*****braillard, -e**, adj., brawling, squalling; obstreperous.

braillement, n.m., squalling.

*****brailler**, v.n., to bawl, to be noisy.

brailleu-r, -se, adj. and n. V. **braillard**.

braiment, n.m., braying of an ass.

braire, v.n., to bray; (fig.) to cry, to whine.

braise, n.f., live coals; embers, burning coal. *Il l'a donné chaud comme —;* he blurted it all out. *Tomber de la poêle dans la —;* from the frying-pan into the fire. *Passer sur une chose comme un chat sur la —;* to pass lightly over a subject; to skip over.

braiser, v.a., (cook.) to bake, to braise.

braiser, n.m., brazier.

braisière, n.f., oven.

brame. V. **brahmane**.

bramement, n.m., (hunt.) belling.

bramer, v.n., (of deer) to bell.

bramin or **bramine**, n.m. V. **brahmane**.

⊙**bran**, n.m., bran; (pop.) excrement. — *de son;* coarse bran; sawdust. — *de judas;* freckles.

bran ! int. (l. ex.) — *de lui !* a fig for him !

brancard, n.m., stretcher, litter, hand-barrow; shaft (of a cart).

brancardier, n.m., (milit.) ambulance-man, litter-bearer.

branchage, n.m., branches, boughs; horns.

branche, n.f., branch, bough, stick, arm; pin-wire; part, division; (arch.) branch; side (of a ladder); branch (of a family); (bot.) grain. *A —s ;* branched. *Sauter de — en —;* to go from one thing to another. *Jeune —;* twig. — *s gourmandes;* proud wood. *S'accrocher à toutes les —s;* to try every possible means, whether fair or foul. *Être comme l'oiseau sur la —;* to be unsettled.

⊙**brancher**, v.a., to hang on a tree.

brancher, v.n., (hunt.) to perch, to roost; to branch off.

branche-ursine, or **branc-ursine**, n.f., (—) (bot.) brank-ursine.

branchial, -e, adj., (ich.) branchial. *Opercule —;* gill-cover.

branchier, adj. m., brancher, percher.

branchies (-shî), n.f. pl., fish-gills.

branchu, -e, adj., ramous, forked, bifurcated; two-horned.

brandade, n.f., ragout (of cod).

brande, n.f., heath, heather.

brandebourg, n.m., gimp, braid; facing.

⊙**brandevin**, n.m., wine-brandy.

*****brandillement**, n.m., tossing, swinging.

*****brandiller**, v.a., to swing, to shake to and fro.

***se brandiller**, v.r., to swing.

*****brandilloire**, n.f., swing, see-saw; (agri.) swing-plough.

brandir, v.a., to brandish, to swing; to flourish; (carp.) to pin.

brandon, n.m., torch, wisp of lighted straw; fire-brand, flake of fire. — *de discorde;* cause of discord.

brandonner, v.a., to place brands in to mark the seizure of a field. [tottering.

branlant, -e, adj., shaking, loose; wagging,

branle, n.m., jogging, push, shake, swing, tossing, motion, shaking; peal; sort of dance, brawl; hammock; (nav.) hammock. *Être en —;* to be in motion. *Donner le —;* to set going. *Mener le —;* to lead the dance.

branle-bas, n.m., (—) (nav.) clearing, for action. *Faire le —;* to clear the decks. — *l* up all hammocks !

branlement (branl-mān), n.m., jogging; shaking, swinging; tottering.

branle-queue, n.m., (—) (orni.) wag-tail; dish-washer.

branler, v.a., to jog, to wag, to move, to shake, to brandish.

se **branler**, v.r., to move.

branler, v.n., to shake, to jog, to totter, to rock; to stir, to move, to wag; to give way, to waver. — *dans le manche;* to shake in the handle, to be unsteady, irresolute, to be shaky. *Tout ce qui branle ne tombe pas;* a creaking gate hangs long, or threatened men live long.

branloire, n.f., see-saw; swing.

braque, n.m., brach-hound; a hare-brained fellow; mad-cap.

⊙**braquemart**, n.m., cutlass; broadsword.

braquement (brak-mān), *n.m.*, pointing (of ordnance).

braquer, *v.a.*, to set, to turn, to level, to point. — *un canon;* to level a cannon. — *une lunette;* to point a telescope.

bras, *n.m.*, arm; power; sconce (candelabrum); arm (of anchors, capstans, levers, seats); brace (of yards); handle; shaft (of litters); (mec.) side rod; arm (of a horse); claw (of a crawfish). *Etre blessé au* —; to be wounded in the arm. *Il a le* — *en écharpe;* he has his arm in a sling. *Recevoir quelqu'un à* — *ouverts;* to receive any one with open arms. *Demeurer les* — *croisés;* to stand with folded arms. *A pleins* —; by armfuls. *Un* — *de mer;* an arm of the sea. *A force de* —; by strength of arms. *Ne vivre que de ses* —; to live by the labor of one's hands. *Avoir quelqu'un sur les* —; to have any one to maintain. *Avoir de grandes affaires sur les* —; to have great concerns in hand. *J'ai sur les* — *un puissant ennemi;* I have to do with a powerful enemy. *Les* — *m'en sont tombés;* I was struck dumb with surprise. *Se jeter entre les* — *de quelqu'un;* to fly to any one for protection. *Tendre les* — *à quelqu'un;* to offer one's aid to any one. *Moulin à* —; handmill. *Les* — *de la mort;* the jaws of death. *A tour de* —; with all one's might. *A* —*-le-corps;* in one's arms. *Saisir quelqu'un à* —*-le-corps;* to seize any one round the body. *— dessus* — *dessous;* arm in arm. *Avoir les* — *longs;* to have great influence. *En prendre long comme le* —; to take an ell; to impose upon.

braser, *v.a.*, to braze, to solder.

brasier, *n.m.*, quick clear fire; red-hot fire; brazier, furnace.

*brasillement (-mān), *n.m.*, (n.v.) glittering, glancing, sparkling of the sea.

*brasiller, *v.a.*, to sparkle (of the sea).

brasque, *n.f.*, brasque (cement made of clay and charcoal dust).

brasquer, *v.a.*, to cover with brasque.

brassage, *n.m.*, stirring up; mashing; brewing; (coin.) mixing.

brassard, *n.m.*, brace (armor), armlet, armguard.

brasse, *n.f.*, (nav.) fathom, six feet, stroke. *Pain de* —; a twenty or twenty-five pound loaf.

brassée, *n.f.*, armful; stroke (swimming).

brasser, *v.a.*, to brew, to mash; to stir; to hatch, to work, to plot.

brasserie, *n.f.*, brewery, brewhouse.

brasseu-r, *n.m.*, -**se**, *n.f.*, brewer.

brasseyage, *n.m.*, (nav.) bracing.

brassiage, *n.m.*, (nav.) sounding.

brassière, *n.f.*, shoulder-strap, brace, bodice with shoulder straps; restraint. *Etre en* —*s;* to be under restraint.

brassin, *n.m.*, brewing tub; mash-tub; boiling (quantity boiled or brewed).

brassoir, *n.m.*, (metal.) stirring-stick.

brasure, *n.f.*, brazing, soldering.

bravache, *n.m.*, bully, swaggerer, blusterer.

bravade, *n.f.*, bravado, boast, bluster.

brave, *adj.*, brave, gallant, true; smart, fine, spruce; honest; good, kind. — *capitaine;* gallant captain. *Il est* — *comme l'épée qu'il porte;* he is as true as steel. *Il n'est* — *qu'en paroles;* he is only brave as far as words go. *Un homme* —; an honest man. *Vous voilà bien* — *aujourd'hui;* how smart you are to-day. *C'est un* — *homme;* he is an honest, worthy fellow. *C'est un* — *garçon;* he is a capital fellow; a brick.

brave, *n.m.*, brave or courageous man; (b.s.) ruffian, bully. *Faux* —; blustering bully. *Faire le* —; to play the bully. — *à trois poils;* hardfighter; man of real courage, right down plucky, regular game. *En* —; bravely, gallantly.

bravement (-mān), *adv.*, bravely, stoutly, valiantly, manfully; skillfully, finely.

braver, *v.a.*, to defy, to set at defiance, to bid defiance, to dare, to beard, to face, to brave. — *les autorités;* to set the authorities at defiance. — *la mort;* to face death.

braverie (-vrî), *n.f.*, boasting; finery, fine clothes.

bravo, *n.m.*, (bravi *or* bravos) bravo, hurrah; hired assassin; applause.

bravo! *adv.*, bravo! well done! capital!

bravoure, *n.f.*, bravery, courage, manhood, gallantry; (mus.) bravura. *Il a fait preuve de* —; he has given proofs of courage.

brayer (bra-ié), *n.m.*, (surg.) truss, bandage.

brayer (brè-ié), *v.a.*, (nav.) to pay over.

brayette (bra-iète), *n.f.*, flap (of trousers); (bot.) cowslip.

brayon (bra-ion), *n.m.*, trap (for vermin).

break (brèke), *n.m.*, (—*s*) break (carriage).

bréant *or* **bruant**, *n.m.*, (orni.) bunting, yellow-hammer.

brebis, *n.f.*, ewe; sheep. *pl.*, flock. — *égarée;* stray sheep. *Troupeau de* —; flock of sheep. *Une* — *galeuse;* a scabby sheep. *Mener paître les* —; to lead the sheep to pasture. *Il ne faut qu'une* — *galeuse pour gâter tout un troupeau;* one scabby sheep will taint a whole flock. *Qui se fait* —, *le loup le mange;* daub yourself with honey, and you'll never want for flies. *A* — *tondue, Dieu mesure le vent;* God tempers the wind to the shorn lamb. *Faire un repas de* —; to eat a dry meal. *La* — *galeuse;* the black sheep. — *comptées, le loup les mange;* we must watch as well as count.

brèche, *n.f.*, breach, flaw, rupture, hiatus; notch, gap. *Battre en* —; to batter in, to breach. *Monter à la* —; to mount the breach. *La* — *d'un couteau;* the notch of a knife. *Faire* — *à un pâté;* to make a gap in a pie. *C'est une* — *à l'honneur;* it is a breach of honor.

brèche, *n.f.*, (min.) breccia.

brèche-dent, *adj.*, (—) that has lost a front tooth or two; broken-mouthed.

brèche-dent, *n.m.f.*, (—) person who has lost a front tooth.

brechet, *n.m.*, breastbone, brisket.

bredi-breda, *adv.*, (fam.) hastily.

bredindin, *n.m.*, (nav.) garnet.

brédissure, *n.f.*, (med.) locked jaw.

*bredouillage, *n.m.*, jabbering, sputtering.

*bredouille, *n.f.*, (trictrac) lurch. *Jouer* —; to play lurches. *Sortir* —; to go away as one came. *Revenir* —; to return with an empty bag (of sportsmen). *Se coucher* —; to go to bed supperless.

*bredouillement, *n.m.*, stuttering, stammering, faltering.

*bredouiller, *v.n.*, to stammer, to stutter, to falter.

*bredouilleu-r, *n.m.*, -**se**, *n.f.*, stammerer, stutterer.

br-ef, -ève, *adj.*, brief, short, concise, succinct. *Une réponse brève;* a brief reply. *Avoir le parler* —; to be a man of few words.

bref, *adv.*, in a few words; in short, in fine, to be short.

bref, *n.m.*, brief (pope's pastoral letter); church calendar.

brège, *n.f.*, salmon-net, close-net.

bregin, *n.m.*, close-net.

*bréhaigne, *adj.*, barren, sterile.

*bréhaigne, *n.f.*, (pop.) barren, sterile woman.

brelan, *n.m.*, brelan (game at cards); pairroyal; gaming-house. *Tenir* —; to keep a gaming-house.

brelander, *v.n.*, to gamble, to be a gamester.

brelandi-er, *n.m.*, -**ère**, *n.f.*, gamester, gambler.

brelique-breloque, *adv.*, at random; higgledy-piggledy; slap-dash.

brelle, *n.f.*, raft, float of wood.

breloque, *n.f.,* charm, gewgaw, toy, trinket. *V.* **berloque.**

⊙**breluche,** *n.f.,* drugget, linsey-woolsey.

brème, *n.f.,* (ich.) bream.

breneu-x, -se, *adj.,* (l.ex.) dirty, soiled.

brequin, *n.m.,* wimble, bit of a wimble.

brésil, *n.m.,* Brazil-wood.

*****brésiller,** *v.a.,* to break small, to cut small; to dye with Brazil-wood.

*****brésillet,** *n.m.,* Brazil or Jamaica-wood.

breste, *n.f.,* catching birds with lime.

*****brétailler,** *v.n.,* (b.s.) to tilt, to fight.

*****brétailleur,** *n.m.,* (b.s.) bruiser, bully.

bretaudé, -e, *adj.,* crop-eared.

bretauder, *v.a.,* to crop badly (animals).

bretelle, *n.f.,* strap; brace. *En avoir jusqu'aux —s;* to be over head and ears in trouble.

breton, -ne, *adj.* and *n.m.f.,* of Brittany.

brette, *n.f.,* (jest.) long sword, rapier.

bretté, -e, *adj.,* matched, indented, jagged.

bretteler, *v.a.,* (arch.) to indent.

bretter, *v.a.,* (arch.) to indent.

bretteur, *n.m.,* bully, fighter.

bretture, *n.f.,* teeth, notches (in tools).

*****breuil,** *n.m.,* inclosed copse, thicket.

breuvage, *n.m.,* beverage, potion, draught, liquor, drink; (vet.) drench.

brève, *n.f.,* short syllable; (mus.) short note.

brevet, *n.m.,* warrant, brevet; (milit.) commission; patent; license (of printers). — *d'apprentissage;* indentures.

breveté, -e (brèv-), *part.,* patented.

breveté, *n.m.,* **-e,** *n.f.,* patentee.

breveter (brèv-), *v.a.,* to patent, to license.

bréviaire, *n.m.,* breviary.

brévité, *n.f.,* (gram.) shortness (of syllables).

bribe, *n.f.,* hunch. *pl.,* scraps, bits; odd ends.

bric-à-brac, *n.m.,* (—) odds and ends; old stores; curios. *Marchand de —;* dealer in old iron, old pictures, old stores, curios.

brick, *n.m.,* (nav.) brig.

bricole, *n.f.,* breast-collar of a horse; rebound of a ball (at tennis); back stroke (at billiards); strap; (nav.) pitching, rolling. *De* or *par —;* indirectly, unfairly, by a fluke.

bricoler, *v.n.,* (billiards, tennis) to hit a back stroke; (fig.) to cadge, to dodge, to shuffle.

bride, *n.f.,* bridle, reins, check, curb; string (of a woman's cap, bonnet); loop (for a button); (surg.) frenum. *Mettre la — à un cheval;* to put a bridle upon a horse. *Tenir la — haute à un cheval;* to keep a tight rein. *Lui tenir la — courte;* to shorten the rein. *Lâcher la —;* to give rein, to give head. *Courir à toute —, à — abattue;* to run at full speed. *Tourner —;* to turn back. *Tenir quelqu'un en —;* to keep any one within bounds, to curb. *A cheval donné on ne regarde pas à la —;* one does not look a gift-horse in the mouth. *Laisser* or *mettre la — sur le cou;* to give head entirely; (fig.) to let any one have his own way.

bridé, -e, *part.,* bridled. *Oison —;* silly creature.

brider, *v.a.,* to bridle; to tie fast, to fasten; to restrain, to curb, to keep under; to check. — *l'ancre;* (nav.) to shoe the anchor. — *ses désirs;* to curb one's desires. — *son cheval par la queue;* to begin at the wrong end. *Mon habit me bride sous les bras;* my coat is too tight under the arms.

bridon, *n.m.,* snaffle-bridle.

brie, *n.f.,* rolling-pin. *Fromage de Brie;* Brie cheese.

bri-ef, -ève, *adj.,* short, brief, curt.

brièvement (-èv-mān), *adv.,* briefly, succinctly, in short.

brièveté (-èv-té), *n.f.,* brevity, shortness, briefness, conciseness, succinctness.

brigade, *n.f.,* (milit.) brigade gang, troop, body.

brigadier, *n.m.,* corporal (of cavalry); sergeant (of police); (nav.) bowman.

brigand, *n.m.,* brigand, highwayman, robber; ruffian, thief.

brigandage, *n.m.,* robbery, brigandage, plunder.

brigandeau, *n.m.,* cheat, rogue, knave.

brigander, *v.n.,* to rob, to plunder.

brigandine, *n.f.,* coat of mail, brigandine.

brigantin, *n.m.,* brigantine, brig.

brigantine, *n.f.,* small brigantine.

*****brignole,** *n.f.,* French plum.

brigue (brig), *n.f.,* intrigue, bribery; canvassing; cabal, faction.

briguer (-ghé), *v.a.,* to canvass for, to solicit, to seek, to court, to stand for, to seek, to aspire to.

brigueur (-gheur), *n.m.,* canvasser, solicitor.

*****brillamment** (-mān), *adv.,* brilliantly, in a brilliant manner; in brilliant fashion.

*****brillant, -e,** *adj.,* brilliant, shining, sparkling, glittering, bright, showy, effulgent, beaming, radiant; robust, blooming (of health). *Esprit —;* sparkling wit. —*s appas, charmes —s;* dazzling charms. *Affaire —e;* (milit.) famous action.

*****brillant,** *n.m.,* brilliancy, brightness, splendor, radiancy, refulgence, resplendency, luster; brilliant (diamond).

*****brillanté, -e,** *adj.,* cut into a brilliant. *n.m.,* diaper, damask.

*****brillanter,** *v.a.,* to cut into a brilliant. —*son style;* (fig.) to load it with false ornaments.

*****briller,** *v.n.,* to shine, to glitter, to sparkle, to glisten, to be bright, sparkling; to play, to blaze, to dawn, to lighten, to flourish, to gleam, to glare. *Tout ce qui — n'est pas or;* all that glitters is not gold.

brimbale, *n.f.,* brake, handle of a pump.

brimbaler, *v.n.,* (fam., l.u.) to ring, to swing, to toss.

brimborion, *n.m.,* nicknack, bauble, gewgaw.

brin, *n.m.,* blade, slip, slender stalk; sprig, shoot; bit, jot. *Un — de romarin;* a sprig of rosemary. *Un beau — de bois;* a fine straight piece of timber. *Un beau — d'homme;* a tall well-set youth. *Beau — de fille;* fine slip of a girl. *Un — de paille;* a straw. *Un — de fil;* a bit of thread. *Il n'y en a —;* there is none at all. *Un — de feu;* a bit of fire. *De,* or *en, —;* (of wood) unhewn.

brinde, *n.f.,* health, toast. *Porter des —s;* to drink toasts. *Etre dans les —s;* to be drunk, tipsy.

*****brindille,** *n.f.,* sprig, twig.

bringuebale, *n.f. V.* **brimbale.**

brio, *n.m.,* dash, spirit, pluck, go; raciness, vivacity.

brioche, *n.f.,* bun, cake; mistake, blunder.

brion, *n.m.,* (bot.) tree-moss.

*****briquaillon,** *n.m.,* brickbat.

brique, *n.f.,* brick. — *anglaise;* Bath brick.

briquet, *n.m.,* steel, flint, tinder-box; short saber, dirk; (dog) beagle, harrier. *Battre le —;* to strike a light. — *pneumatique;* fire syringe. *Pierre à —;* flint.

briquetage (brik-taj), *n.m.,* brick-work; imitation brick-work.

briqueté (brik-), *part.,* bricked; brick-like.

briqueter (brik-), *v.a.,* to brick; to imitate brick-work.

briqueterie (brik-trî), *n.f.,* brick-field, brick-making.

briqueteur (brik-teur), *n.m.,* bricklayer.

briquetier (brik-tié), *n.m.,* brick-maker.

briquette, *n.f.,* compressed, patent fuel.

bris, *n.m.,* (jur.) breaking open (of doors, prisons); wreckage, fragment; rigging (the market).

brisant, *n.m.,* breaker, breakwater.

*****briscambille,** *n.f. V.* **brusquembille.**

brise, *n.f.,* breeze. — *carabinée;* stiff gale.

brisé, -e, *part.,* broken to pieces; harassed, fatigued; folding; (her.) rompu. *Lit* —; folding-bed. *Chaise —e;* folding-chair. *Porte —e;* folding-door.

⊙**brise-cou,** *n.m.,* (—) break-neck pace; (man.) rough-rider. *V.* **casse-cou.**

brise-eau, *n.m.,* (—) breakwater.

brisée, *n.f.,* fan-joint (of umbrellas).

brisées, *n.f. pl.,* boughs cut off; footsteps, wake, shoes, heels, ground. *Marcher sur les — de quelqu'un;* to follow in any one's footsteps. *Aller sur les — de quelqu'un;* to walk in any one's shoes, to poach on any one's preserves. *Reprendre ses —;* to retrace one's steps.

brise-glace, *n.m.,* (—, *or* — — —*s*) ice-breaker; starling (of a bridge).

brise-lames, *n.m.,* (—) breakwater.

brisement (briz-mãn), *n.m.,* breaking, dashing (of waves); heartrending; contrition.

brise-pierre, *n.m.,* (—) (surg.) stone-crusher.

briser, *v.a.,* to break to pieces, to dash to pieces; to flaw, to burst, to crack, to knock off, to shatter, to shiver, to snap, to crush, to crash; to bruise. *Être brisé;* to feel sore all over.

briser, *v.n.,* (nav.) to break, to dash. *Brisons-là;* let us say no more on the subject; enough! *se* **briser,** *v.r.,* to break, to be dashed to pieces; to fold up.

brise-raison, *n.m.,* (—) wrong-headed person.

brise-scellé, *n.m.,* (— — —*s*) (l.u.) seal-breaker.

brise-tout, *n.m.,* (—) person that breaks everything; rough, clumsy fellow.

briseur, *n.m.,* (l.u.) one who breaks anything. *—d'images;* image-breaker, iconoclast.

briseuse, *n.f.,* breaker, breaker-engine.

brise-vent, *n.m.,* (—, *or* — — —*s*) (gard.) screen.

brisoir, *n.m.,* brake (for flax).

brisque, *n.f.,* a card game; trump.

brisure, *n.f.,* break, folding-point; catch, fastening; (her.) rebatement.

britannique, *adj.,* British, Britannic.

broc (brô), *n.m.,* large jug; pot, spit. *De bric et de —;* anyhow; by hook or by crook. *Manger de la viande de — en bouche;* to have one's meat hot from the spit.

brocantage, *n.m.,* dealing in second-hand goods, broker's business; bartering.

brocanter, *v.n.,* to deal in second-hand goods; to exchange, to barter.

brocanteu-r, *n.m.,* **-se,** *n.f.,* a dealer in second-hand goods; broker.

brocard, *n.m.,* taunt, jeer; joke, scoff; lampoon.

brocarder, *v.a.,* to taunt, to jest, to jeer.

brocardeu-r, *n.m.,* **-se,** *n.f.,* scoffer, jeerer.

brocart, *n.m.,* brocade.

brocatelle, *n.f.,* brocatel; (min.) brocate.

brochage, *n.m.,* stitching (books).

brochant, *part.* (her.) — *sur le tout;* over all.

broche, *n.f.,* spit; needle to knit with; spindle; skewer; spigot, peg (of casks); gudgeon (of locks); tusk (of wild boars); brooch (jewel); iron-pin. *Mettre la viande à la —;* to spit the meat.

broché, -e, *adj.,* stitched (books); embossed (linen); figured (stuffs).

brochée, *n.f.,* spitful, rod full of candles.

brocher, *v.a.,* to stitch (a book); to figure (stuffs); to emboss (linen); to knit (stockings); to strike (a nail into a horse's foot); to do things in a hurry, to dispatch. *— une comédie,* etc.; to polish off a comedy, etc.

brochet, *n.m.,* pike, jack.

brocheter (brosh-té), *v.a.,* (cook.) to skewer.

brocheton (brosh-ton), *n.m.,* small pike, pickerel.

brochette, *n.f.,* little skewer; meat (roasted on skewers); pin. *Elever des oiseaux à la —;* to feed birds by hand. *Enfant élevé à la —;* child brought up with great care.

brocheu-r, *n.m.,* **-se,** *n.f.,* knitter; book-stitcher.

brochoir, *n.m.,* smith's shoeing-hammer.

brochure, *n.f.,* stitching; book stitched and covered with a wrapper; pamphlet, tract.

brocoli, *n.m.,* broccoli.

brodé, -e, *part.,* embroidered.

brodequin (brod-kin), *n.m.,* buskin, sock; half-boot, laced-boot (generally of women and children). *Chausser le —;* to go on the comic stage.

broder, *v.a.,* to embroider; to adorn, to embellish a story, to exaggerate, to amplify.

broderie (bro-drî), *n.f.,* embroidery; embellishment; exaggeration, amplification.

brodeu-r, *n.m.,* **-se,** *n.f.,* embroiderer. — *mécanique;* embroidering machine.

brodoir, *n.m.,* bobbin, frame.

broie, *n.f.,* brake (for hemp).

broiement (broa-mãn), *n.m.,* grinding, powdering, pounding, pulverization.

brome, *n.m.,* (chem.) brome.

bromure, *n.m.,* (chem.) bromide.

bronchade, *n.f.,* stumbling, tripping.

bronchement (bronsh-mãn), *n.m.,* (l.u.) flinching, stumbling. *V.* **bronchade.**

broncher, *v.n.,* to stumble, to trip, to reel; to blunder, to falter, to fail, to flinch. *Il n'y a si bon cheval qui ne bronche;* it is a good horse that never stumbles.

bronches, *n.f. pl.,* (anat.) bronchi, bronchiæ, bronchial tubes.

bronchies, *n.f. pl. V.* **branchies.**

bronchique, *adj.,* (anat.) bronchial.

bronchite, *n.f.,* (med.) bronchitis.

bronchotomie (-ko-), *n.f.,* (surg.) bronchotomy.

bronze, *n.m.,* bronze; bronze-figure, medal; (fig.) iron (insensibility), impudence, brass. *Un cœur de —;* a heart of iron, steel.

bronzer, *v.a.,* to bronze, to paint in bronze color; to tan (face). *— un canon de fusil;* to bronze the barrel of a musket. *Bronzé par le hâle;* sunburnt, tanned by the sun.

broquart, *n.m.,* (hunt.) brocket.

broquette, *n.f.,* tin tack, small nail.

⊙**brossailles.** *V.* **broussailles.**

brosse, *n.f.,* brush; painter's brush. — *à dents;* tooth-brush. — *à habits;* clothes-brush. (fig.) brush-wood, cover.

brossée, *n.f.,* (fam.) brushing; drubbing, thrashing.

brosser, *v.a.,* to brush, to rub with a brush. *se* **brosser,** *v.r.,* to brush one's self.

brosser, *v.n.,* to run through woods or bushes; to scour.

brosserie (bros-rî), *n.f.,* brushmaking business; brush manufactory.

brosseur, *n.m.,* (milit.) an officer's servant.

brossier, *n.m.,* brushmaker; brusher.

brou, *n.m.,* husk, peel, shell (of walnuts). *— de noix;* walnut brandy.

brouée, *n.f.,* fog, mist, drizzle, blight.

brouet, *n.m.,* thin broth, porridge. — *noir;* black broth.   [chair.

brouette, *n.f.,* wheelbarrow; barrow; bath-

brouetter, *v.a.,* to wheel in a barrow.

brouetteur, *n.m.,* bath-chairman.

brouettier, *n.m.,* barrow man.

brouhaha, *n.m.,* hubbub, uproar, hurly-burly.

*brouillamini, *n.m.,* confusion; disorder.

*brouillard, *n.m.,* fog, mist, haze, damp; (com.) waste-book. *Un — épais;* a dense fog. *Je n'y vois que du —;* I am muddled.

*brouillard, *adj.,* blotting. *Du papier —;* blotting paper.

*brouillasser, *v. imp.,* to drizzle. *Il brouillasse;* it is drizzling.

*brouille, *n.f.,* quarrel, falling out, misunderstanding, disagreement, discord, broil. *Etre en*

— *avec;* to be on bad terms with, to disagree
with.

*brouillé, -e, *part.*, jumbled, at variance. *Des
œufs —s;* buttered or scrambled eggs. *Nous
sommes —s;* we have fallen out. *Un teint —;*
a mottled complexion. *Etre — avec la justice;*
to be in the clutches of the law. [bling.

*brouillement, *n.m.*, mixing together, jum-
*brouiller, *v.a.*, to throw into confusion, to
mix together, to blend, to stir up, to shake, to
jumble, to shuffle, to confound; to set at variance; to embroil, to confuse; to puzzle. — *deux
personnes l'une avec l'autre;* to set two people
at variance. *Vous me brouillez;* you put me out.
se*brouiller, *v.r.*, to be out, to put one's self
out, to confound one's self; to fall out with any
one. *Le temps se brouille;* the weather is spoil-
ing. *Se — avec la justice;* to fall foul of the
law, to fall into the clutches of the law.

*brouiller, *v.n.*, to blunder, to mar.

*brouillerie (broo-), *n.f.*, misunderstanding,
disagreement, coolness, variance.

*brouillon, *n.m.*, rough draft, rough copy;
waste-book.

*brouillon, *n.m.*, -ne, *n.f.*, blunderer, bungler,
mar-all, mar-plot.

*brouillon, -ne, *adj.*, mischief-making; blundering.

brouir, *v.a.*, to blight, to blast, to nip, to
parch.

brouissure, *n.f.*, blight, scorching.

*broussailles, *n.f. pl.*, bushes, brushwood,
brambles.

brousse, *n.f.*, brushwood, undergrowth.

broussin, *n.m.*, excrescence from a tree.

brout, *n.m.*, browse.

broutant, -e, *adj.*, browsing.

broutement, *n.m.*, browsing.

brouter, *v.a.n.*, to browse, graze. *L'herbe
sera bien courte s'il ne trouve de quoi —;* the
grass must be very short, if he cannot get a bite.

broutilles, *n.f. pl.*, sprigs, small-wood, chatwood; (fig.) trinkets, nicknacks.

brouture, *n.f.*, browsing.

broyer, *v.a.*, to grind, to pound, to beat meal,
to bruise; to break (hemp). — *l'encre;* (print.) to
bray the ink. — *du noir;* to be in a brown study.

broyeur, *n.m.*, grinder, pounder, hemp or
flax-breaker.

⊙broyon, *n.m.*, brayer (for printer's ink).

bru, *n.f.*, daughter-in-law.

bruant, *n.m.*, (orni.) yellow-hammer.

brucelle, *n. f.*, (bot.) brownwort; *pl.*,
tweezers.

*brugnon, *n.m.*, nectarine.

bruine, *n.f.*, small drizzling rain.

• bruiner, *v. imp.*, to drizzle.

bruire, *v.n.*, to rustle, to rattle; (of the wind)
to roar, to sough.

bruissement (-mān), *n.m.*, rustling noise,
rattling, roaring; whirring, (of the wind) soughing.

bruit, *n.m.*, noise, bustle, din, racket, creaking, knocking, sound, clamor, buzz; quarrel,
dispute; fame, name, reputation; report, talk;
rumor. — *d'une arme à feu;* report of a fire-
arm. *Faire un — sourd;* to rumble, to hum. *Au
— des cloches,* or *du canon;* at the ringing of the
bells, the roar of the guns. *On le fit entrer sans
—;* he was let in noiselessly. *Cet événement fait
du —;* that affair is making a great noise. *Ils
ont eu du —ensemble;* they came to high words.
Il s'est répandu un —; a rumor has spread.
Un faux —; a false report. *Il court un —; it is
reported. *Il n'est — que de;* there's no talk but
of. *Grand — petite besogne;* great cry, little
wool.

brûlable, *adj.*, (l.u.) fit to be burnt.

brûlant, -e, *adj.*, burning, scorching, hot,
burning hot, torrid; eager, earnest, ardent.

brûlé, *n.m.*, burning. *Cela sent le —;* that
smells of burning.

brûlé, -e, *part.*, burnt.

brûle-gueule, *n.m.*, (—) short pipe.

brûlement (-mān), *n.m.*, burning.

à brûle-pourpoint, *adv.*, (of shooting) close to;
point-blank; to one's face, in one's teeth; unreservedly. *adj.*, irrefutable. *Un argument —;*
an irrefutable argument.

brûler, *v.a.*, to burn, to consume by fire, to
cauterize; to parch, to scorch, to blast, to scar,
to swelter. — *de fond en comble;* to burn to
the ground. — *la cervelle à quelqu'un;* to blow
any one's brains out. *Son style brûle le papier;*
his style is full of fire. — *de l'encens devant
quelqu'un;* to flatter any one excessively. —
une étape; to pass a halting-place without stopping. — *le pavé;* to dash along at full tilt. —
ses vaisseaux; not to go back.

brûler, *v.n.*, to burn, to be on fire; to be all
in a flame. *Les mains lui brûlent;* his hands
burn. *Je brûle de vous revoir;* I am impatient, longing to see you again. — *d'un feu
lent;* to be consumed by degrees.

se brûler, *v.r.*, to burn one's self, to be burnt, to
scorch. *Venir se — à la chandelle;* to burn
one's wings at the candle. — *la cervelle;* to
blow one's brains out. — *les doigts;* to burn
one's fingers.

brûlerie, *n.f.*, (l.u.) burning; brandy-distillery.

brûle-tout, *n.m.*, (—) save all.

brûleur, *n.m.*, incendiary, firer; (fig.)
blackguard.

brûloir, *n.m.*, brûloire, *n.f.*, burner, roaster.

brûlot, *n.m.*, fire-ship; firebrand, incendiary.

brûlure, *n.f.*, burn, scald, scalding.

brumaire, *n.m.*, Brumaire, second month of
the calendar of the first French republic, from
Oct. 23rd to Nov. 21st.

brumal, -e, *adj.*, (l.u.) brumal, winterly,
wintry.

brume, *n.f.*, fog, haze, mist.

brumeu-x, -se, *adj.*, foggy, hazy, misty.

brun, -e, *adj.*, brown, dark, dun, dusk;
gloomy, sad. *Il commence à faire —;* it is beginning to be dusk.

brun, *n.m.*, brown; dark person. — *châtain;*
chestnut brown. — *clair;* light brown. —
foncé; dun-colored.

brunâtre, *adj.*, brownish.

brune, *n.f.*, dusk (of the evening); dark woman, dark girl.

brunelle, *n.f.*, (bot.) self-heal.

brunet, -te, *adj.*, brownish.

brunette, *n.f.*, dark woman, dark girl; ⊙love
ballad.

bruni, *n.m.*, (tech.) burnish.

brunir, *v.a.*, to brown, to make brown, to
darken; to burnish.

se brunir, *v.r.*, to turn dark or brown.

brunir, *v.n.*, to turn brown.

brunissage, *n.m.*, burnishing.

brunisseu-r, *n.m.*, -se, *n.f.*, one who bur-
nishes, burnisher.

brunissoir, *n.m.*, burnisher (tool).

brunissure, *n.f.*, burnishing; browning.

brusque, *adj.*, blunt, abrupt, rough, gruff,
short-crusted, sudden, unexpected.

*brusquembille, *n.f.*, game at cards.

brusquement, *adv.*, bluntly, abruptly, roughly, hastily, gruffly.

brusquer, *v.a.*, to offend; to treat roughly,
bluntly, to be sharp with any one. *Il brusque
tout le monde;* he is abrupt with everybody. —
une chose; to do a thing in haste. — *l'aventure;*
to decide at once. — *la fortune;* to tempt fortune.

brusquerie, *n.m.*, bluntness; abruptness,
roughness, gruffness; suddenness, hastiness.

brut (brut), -e, *adj.*, rough, raw, crude, unpolished, unhewn, coarse, unfashioned; clownish, awkward; rude, ill-bred. *Diamant —;* rough diamond. *Sucre —;* brown sugar. *Bête —e;* (fam.) brute beast. *Produit —;* gross produce; gross returns. *Vin —;* unadulterated wine.

brut (brut), *adv.,* (com.) gross.

brutal, -e, *adj.,* brutal, brutish, surly, bearish, churlish, cynical.

brutal, *n.m.,* brute.

brutalement (-tal-mān), *adv.,* brutally, brutishly, rudely, churlishly.

brutaliser, *v.a.,* to bully; to use one brutally.

brutalité, *n.f.,* brutality, brutishness; outrageous language. *Dire des —s à quelqu'un ;* to abuse any one in a brutal manner.

brute, *n.f.,* brute, beast; brutal person.

bruyamment (bru-ia-mān), *adv.,* noisily, loudly, clamorously.

bruyant, -e (bru-iān, -te), *adj.,* noisy, blustering, clamorous, clattering, loud.

bruyère (bru-ièr), *n.f.,* heath, sweet-heather. *Coq de —;* grouse.

bryon, *n.m. V.* **brion.**

bryone, *n.f.,* (bot.) bryony.

buanderie (-drî), *n.f.,* wash-house, laundry.

buandi-er, *n.m.,* **-ère,** *n.f.,* bleacher; washerman, washerwoman.

bubale, *n.m.,* species of buffalo.

bube, *n.f.,* pimple, blotch.

bubon, *n.m.,* (med.) bubo.

bubonocèle, *n.m.,* (med.) bubonocele.

bucarde, *n.m.,* (conch.) heart-shell, cockle.

buccal, -e, *adj.,* buccal.

buccin (buk-sin), *n.m.,* (conch.) whelk; (mus.) bass-trombone.

buccinateur, *n.m.,* (anat.) buccinator.

bucentaure, *n.m.,* Bucentaur.

bucéphale, *n.m.,* Bucephalus (Alexander's [horse].

bûche, *n.f.,* billet, chump of wood, lump of coal, log; dull-pated fellow, blockhead.

bûcher, *n.m.,* wood-house; funeral-pile, pyre, stake.

bûcher, *v.a.,* (carp.) to rough-hew, to cut down; (fig.) to fag at, to work hard, to drudge.

bûcheron (bûsh-ron), *n.m.,* woodcutter.

bûchette, *n.f.,* stick of dry wood.

bucoliaste, *n.m.,* bucolic, writer of bucolics.

bucolique, *adj.,* bucolic. *—s, n.f. pl.,* bucolics; (fam.) rattle-traps.

budget, *n.m.,* budget. *Le — de l'Etat ;* the state budget. *Le — de la marine ;* the naval estimates. *Le — de la guerre ;* the army estimates. *Le — d'un ménage ;* household expenses.

budgétaire, *adj.,* pertaining, relating, to the budget.

buée, *n.f.,* ⊙lye, washing in lye; steam, reek.

buffet, *n.m.,* cupboard, sideboard; refreshment-room; service (of plate). *— d'orgues ;* organ-case.

buffle, *n.m.,* buffalo; buff-leather; buff.

buffleterie (-fle-trî), *n.f.,* belts, straps, &c., (of a soldier).

buffletin, *n.m.,* young buffalo.

bufonite, *n.f.,* (foss.) bufonite.

bugle, *n.f.,* (bot.) bugle.

buglosse, *n.f.,* (bot.) bugloss.

bugrane, *n.f.,* (bot.) rest-harrow.

buhotier, *n.m.,* shrimp-net.

buie, *n.f.,* pitcher, jug.

buire, *n.f.,* vase, jug, beaker, flagon.

buis, *n.m.,* box; box-tree, box-wood. *— piquant ;* butcher's broom.

buissaie, *n.f.,* grove of box-trees.

buisson, *n.m.,* bush, thicket. *— ardent ;* (bot.) evergreen thorn. *Trouver — creux ;* to find the birds flown.

buissonner, *v.n.,* (bot.) to bush.

buissonneu-x, -se, *adj.,* bushy, woody.

buissonni-er, -ère, *adj.* Only used in the expressions: *Lapins buissonniers ;* thicket-rabbits. *Faire l'école buissonnière ;* to play the truant.

bulbe, *n.f.,* (bot.) bulb.

bulbe, *n.m.,* (anat.) bulb.

bulbeu-x, -se, *adj.,* bulbous.

bulbifère, *adj.,* (bot.) bulbiferous.

bullaire (-lèr), *n.m.,* collection of papal bulls.

bulle, *n.f.,* bubble; (med.) bubble, blister; (metal.) bead. *— d'eau ;* water-bubble. *— d'air ;* air-bubble. [golden bull.

bulle, *n.f.,* pope's bull. *La — d'or ;* the **bulle,** *adj.,* whity-brown (of paper). *Papier —;* whity-brown paper.

bullé, -e, *adj.,* authentic; by pope's bull.

bulletin, *n.m.,* paper, circular, voting paper; (milit.) bulletin; bulletin, official report. *— de bagages ;* luggage-ticket.

bunium, *n.m.,* earth-nut; pig-nut.

buphthalme, *n.m.,* (bot.) ox-eye.

buplèvre, *n.m.,* (bot.) hare's-ear.

bupreste, *n.m.,* (ent.) burn-cow; golden beetle.

buraliste, *n.m.,* office-keeper, clerk; money-taker.

burat, *n.m.,* drugget; bunting.

buratine, *n.f.,* poplin.

bure, *n.f.,* drugget; fustian, rough serge (of monk's dress), baize; (min.) shaft, pit-hole.

bureau, *n.m.,* bureau, writing-table, desk; office; board, bench (in a court of judicature); committee; court (personages). *— de tabac ;* tobacconist's shop. *Chef de —;* head clerk; chief of a department. *Déposer sur le —;* (parliament) to lay upon the table. *Payer à — ouvert ;* (com.) to pay on demand. *Prendre l'air du —;* to see how matters stand; to call in at the office. *Vent du —;* aspect of affairs. *— de placement ;* registry office for servants, etc.

⊙**bureau,** *n.m.,* drugget.

bureaucrate, *n.m.,* bureaucrat, clerk in a public office; red-tapist.

bureaucratie, *n.f.,* bureaucracy, red-tapeism.

burette, *n.f.,* cruet; vase, flagon; (bicycle) oil-can.

burgau, *n.m.,* **burgaudine,** *n.f.,* burgau; burgau mother of pearl.

burgrave, *n.m.,* Burgrave.

burgraviat, *n.m.,* Burgraviate.

burin, *n.m.,* graver, graving-tool; (fig.) pen.

buriner, *v.a.,* to engrave.

burlesque, *adj.,* burlesque, merry, comical, jocose, jocular, ludicrous. *Vers —s ;* doggerel verses.

burlesque, *n.m.,* burlesque.

burlesquement, *adv.,* comically, ludicrously, in a jocose way.

burnous, *n.m. V.* **bernous.**

bursal, -e, *adj.,* fiscal.

busard, *n.m.,* (orni.) buzzard; (fig.) blockhead, dolt.

busc, *n.m.,* busk (of stays); mitre (of locks).

buse, *n.f.,* (orni.) buzzard; (fig.) blockhead. *On ne saurait faire d'une — un épervier ;* one cannot make a silk purse out of a sow's ear.

busqué, *part.,* busked; curved, arched.

busquer, *v.a.,* to put a busk in; (of skirts) to shorten, to draw up.

se **busquer,** *v.r.,* to wear a busk.

⊙**busquière,** *n.f.,* busk-case.

busserole, *n.f.,* (bot.) whortle-berry.

buste, *n.m.,* (sculpt.) bust; head and shoulders. *Portrait en —;* half-length portrait.

but, *n.m.,* mark; object, end, aim, purpose, design, view; goal. *Viser au —;* to aim at the mark. *Le — de ses désirs ;* the object of his desires. *Se proposer un —;* to have an object in view. *Arriver le premier au —;* to be the first to reach the goal. *— à —;* without any odds, evens. *Jouer — à —;* to play even. *De — en blanc ;* bluntly, without any preamble; point-blank.

butant, *adj.* V. **boutant**.

bute, *n.f.*, farrier's knife.

butée, *n.f.*, (arch.) abutment-pier. V. **butée**.

buter, *v.n.*, to hit the mark; to stumble; to aim at. *Ce cheval bute à chaque pas;* that horse stumbles at every step.

buter, *v.a.*, (gard.) to earth up; (arch.) to prop up. *— un mur;* to prop a wall with a buttress. *— un arbre;* to heap up earth round the root of a tree. *— du céleri;* to earth up celery. **se buter**, *v.r.*, to be bent on; to stick to; to contradict, to oppose.

butin, *n.m.*, booty, pillage, spoils, prize, plunder.

butiner, *v.n.*, to spoil, to pillage, to plunder, to get booty, to pilfer; to collect, to gather.

butiner, *v.a.*, (fig.) to pilfer.

butome, *n.m.*, (bot.) flowering rush; water-gladiole.

butor, *n.m.*, (orni.) bittern; churl, dull fellow.

butorde, *n.f.*, coarse, pig-headed woman.

butte, *n.f.*, rising ground, ridge, knoll, mound, bank. *Etre en — à;* to be exposed to.

buttée, *n.f.* V. **butée**.

butter, *v.a.*, (gard.) to earth up.

butter, *v.n.* V. **buter**.

buttoir, *n.m.*, ridging-plow; buttress; (rail.) buffer-stop; catch-peg.

butyreu-x, -se, *adj.*, butyrous; buttery.

buvable, *adj.*, drinkable, fit to drink.

buvard, *n.m.*, blotting-case, blotting-pad. *Papier —;* blotting paper.

buvetier (buv-tié), *n.m.*, keeper of a tavern.

buvette, *n.f.*, refreshment-room, tap-room, shades, public house.

buveu-r, *n.m.*, **-se**, *n.f.*, drinker; toper.

buvoter, *v.n.*, to sip, to tipple.

bysse, *n.m.* V. **byssus**.

byssus, *n.m.*, (bot., antiq.) byssus.

byzantin, -e, *adj.*, Byzantine style.

C

C, *n.m.*, the third letter of the alphabet, *c*.

c., (ab.) (com.) *compte;* account.

c' (contraction of *ce*, and used only before the verb *être*), this, it.

ça, *adv.*, here. *— et là;* here and there, up and down, to and fro.

ça, *int.*, now. *— voyons!* now, let us see! *Or — commençons!* come, begin !

ça, *pron.*, (for *cela*) that. *Donnez-moi —;* give me that. *Comme —;* like that; so. *Comment vous portez-vous? comme ci comme —;* how do you do? only so-so.

cabalant, -e, *adj.*, caballing.

cabale, *n.f.*, cabal; cabala.

cabaler, *v.n.*, to cabal, to plot.

cabaleur, *n.m.*, caballer, intriguer.

cabaliste, *n.m.*, cabalist.

cabalistique, *adj.*, cabalistic.

caban, *n.m.*, cloak with a hood.

cabanage, *n.m.*, camp, hutting.

cabane, *n.f.*, cot, hut, shed, cabin, cottage ; flat-bottomed boat on the Loire.

cabaner, *v.a.*, (nav.) to capsize (a boat).

cabaner, *v.n.*, (nav.) to capsize.

cabanon, *n.m.*, cell (prison).

cabaret, *n.m.*, wine-shop, tavern, pot-house; china tea- or coffee-service, liqueur-service, tray; (bot.) asarum. *Pilier de —;* tavern haunter, tippler. *— borgne;* pot-house.

cabareti-er, *n.m.*, **-ère**, *n.f.*, publican, tavern-keeper.

cabas, *n.m.*, basket; cottage bonnet · wicker-work carriage, rumbling-carriage.

⊙**cabasset**, *n.m.*, helmet.

cabéliau, *n.m.*, (ich.) keeling.

cabestan, *n.m.*, capstan, capstern, hand-winch. *Grand —;* main capstan. *—volant;* crab. *Envoyer un homme au —;* to send a man to the capstan (to be punished).

***cabillaud**, *n.m.*, (ich.) cod (live cod).

cabine, *n.f.*, (nav.) cabin.

cabinet, *n.m.*, closet, study, cabinet; practice (of a professional man); summer-house; office (of an attorney, a barrister); cabinet, cabinet-council. *— de lecture;* reading-room. *— de toilette;* dressing-room. *— de bains;* bath-room. *— d'aisance;* water-closet. *Affaires de —;* chamber practice (of lawyers).

câble, *n.m.*, cable. *Filer du —;* (nav.) to pay out, to veer more cable; (fig.) to spin out the time. *— de remorque;* tow-cable. *Bitter le —;* to bit the cable. *Maître —;* sheet-cable. *— d'affourche;* small bower-cable. *— de touée;* stream-cable.

câblé, *n.m.*, thick cord.

câblé, -e, *adj.*, (arch.) cabled, twisted.

câbleau or **câblot**, *n.m.*, cablet, small cable ; mooring-rope, painter.

câblée, *n.f.*, cable's length.

câbler, *v.a.*, to twist threads into a cord; to make ropes or cables.

cabliau, *n.m.* V. **cabillaud**.

cablogramme, *n.m.*, cablegram.

caboche, *n.f.*, pate, noddle, nob; head-piece, hobnail. *Grosse —;* logger-head. *Etre bonne —;* to have a good head-piece.

cabochon, *n.m.*, polished but uncut precious stone; (tech.) fancy brass nail.

cabochon, *adj.*, (of stones) polished only, but uncut.

cabosse, *n.f.*, cacao pod.

cabot, *n.m.*, (ich.) bull-head. V. **chabot**.

cabotage, *n.m.*, coasting, coasting-trade. *Vaisseau de —;* coasting-vessel.

caboter, *v.n.*, to coast.

caboteur, *n.m.*, coaster.

cabotier, *n.m.*, coasting-vessel.

cabotin, *n.m.*, (b.s.) strolling player; low comedian.

cabre, *n.f.*, gin; (nav.) sheers.

se cabrer, *v.r.*, to prance, to rear, to rise up; to fly into a passion; to be refractory. *Faire se — un cheval;* to make a horse rear.

cabrer, *v.a.*, to provoke any one, to make any one fly into a passion; to offend, to shock.

cabri, *n.m.*, kid.

cabriole, *n.f.*, caper; (man.) cabriole.

cabrioler, *v.n.*, to caper, to cut capers.

cabriolet, *n.m.*, cabriolet, cab, gig. *— à pompe;* curricle. *Place de —;* cab-stand.

cabrioleur, *n.m.*, caperer.

cabus, *adj.*, (of cabbages) headed.

caca, *n.m.*, child's excrement. *Faire —;* to do one's excrement.   [mull.

cacade, *n.f.*, (l.u.) (l.ex.) mess, mistake, failure,

cacao, *n.m.*, cacao, chocolate-nut.

cacaotier or **cacaoyer**, *n.m.*, cacao-tree.

cacaoyère, *n.f.*, cacao-plantation.

cacatois, *n.m.*, (nav.) royal, mast-top.

cacatois or **kakatoès**, *n.m.*, (orni.) cockatoo.

caccaber, *v.n.*, to cry (of partridges).

cachalot, *n.m.*, cachalot; spermaceti-whale.

cache, *n.f.*, hiding-place; (hunt.) stake-net.

caché, -e, *part.*, hid, hidden. *Ressorts —s;* hidden, secret springs. *N'avoir rien de — pour quelqu'un;* to keep nothing secret from anyone, to have no secrets for. *Jeu —;* underhand game.

cache-cache, *n.m.*, (n.p.) hide and seek.

cachectique (shèk-), *adj.*, (med.) cachetic.

cache-entrée, *n.m.*, (—, *or* - — -*s*) drop (of a key-hole).

cachement (kash-mān), *n.m.*, (l.u.) concealing, hiding.

cachemire, *n.m.*, cashmere.

cache-nez, n.m., muffler, comforter.

*cache-peigne, n.m., (—, or — —s) head-ornament to conceal the comb.

cacher, v.a., to hide, to secrete, to conceal, to disguise, to lurk ; to abscond. *Cachez votre jeu ;* hide your cards. — *son jeu ;* to hide, to mask, one's play. — *son nom, son âge ;* to conceal one's name, one's age. — *sa vie ;* to lead a secluded life.

se **cacher**, v.r., to hide, to secrete one's self ; to lurk ; to abscond.

cachet, n.m., seal (of private individuals) ; stamp ; ticket. *Lettre de —;* lettre-de-cachet, (arbitrary warrant of imprisonment). — *de chiffres, d'armes ;* seal with a cipher, with a coat of arms. — *volant ;* flying seal. *Courir le —;* to give private lessons in town, to go about teaching. *Son style a un — particulier ;* his style has a certain stamp, characteristic, character all its own.

cacheté, -e, part., sealed. *Soumissions —es ;* sealed tenders.

cacheter (kash-té), v.a., to seal, to seal up. *Cire à —;* sealing-wax. *Pain à —;* wafer.

cachette, n.f., hiding-place. *En —;* secretly, by stealth.

cacheur, -se, n.m.f., sneak, sly-boots.

cachexie (-shè-ksi), n.f., (med.) cachexy.

cachot, n.m., dungeon ; (milit.) black hole.

cachotte, n.f., tobacco-pipe without a heel.

cachotterie (-sho-trî), n.f., mysterious ways, secret practice (about trifles).

cachotti-er, n.m., **-ère**, n.f., mysterious, sly.

cachou, n.m., cachou.

cacique, n.m., cazique or cacique (Indian chief).

cacis. V. cassis.

cacochyme (-shim), adj., (med.) cachochymic.

cacochymie (-shi-), n.f., (med.) cacochymy.

cacoèthe, adj., (med.) (ulcers) malignant, incurable.

cacographie, n.f., cacography.

cacolet, n.m., mule-litter, pannier. *En —;* on panniered mules.

cacologie, n.f., cacology.

cacophonie, n.f., cacophony.

cacotrophie, n.f., (med.) cacotrophy.

cactier or **cactus**, n.m., (bot.) torch-thistle, cactus.

cadastral, -e, adj., referring to the register of lands ; pertaining to real estate.

cadastre, n.m., register of the survey of lands.

cadastrer, v.a., to survey.

cadavéreu-x, -se, adj., cadaverous, wan, ghastly.

cadavérique, adj., (anat.) of a dead body.

cadavre, n.m., corpse, dead body. *C'est un — ambulant ;* he is a walking ghost.

cadeau, n.m., present, gift. *Faire — de ;* to make a present of.

cadédis (-diss), int., zounds, faith !

cadenas (-nâ), n.m., padlock ; clasp, snap. — *à secret ;* secret padlock. *Enfermer sous —;* to padlock.

cadenasser, v.a., to padlock ; to clasp.

cadence, n.f., time (in dancing) ; (mus.) quivering, shake ; (man., harmony) cadence. *Aller en —;* to keep time.

cadencé, -e, part., cadenced, numbered, harmonious.

cadencer, v.a., to cadence, to harmonize ; (mus.) to time, to shake, to trill.

cadène, n.f., (l.u.) chain ; chain-gang (of convicts).

cadenette (-nett), n.f., hair-cue, tress (of hair).

cadet, -te, adj., younger, junior (of two). *Branche —te ;* younger branch.

cadet, n.m., (milit.) cadet ; younger brother ; younger son ; junior (of two), (fam.) young

fellow. *C'est un jeune — de haut appétit ;* he is an extravagant young gentleman.

cadette, n.f., younger sister, younger daughter ; paving stone ; long billiard cue.

cadi, n.m., cadi (Turkish judge).

cadis, n.m., sort of woolen serge.

cadisé, n.m., kind of drugget.

cadmie, n.f., (chem., metal.) oxide of zinc.

cadmium, n.m., cadmium.

cadogan, n.m. V. **catogan**.

cadole, n.f., latch, little bolt.

cadran, n.m., dial-plate, dial.

cadrat, n.m., (print.) quadrat. — *creux ;* quotation.

cadratin, n.m., (print.) M quadrat. *Demi —;* N quadrat.

cadrature, n.f., (horl.) movement ; dial-work.

cadre, n.m., frame (for a picture) ; (nav. milit.) ; list of officers ; framework ; skeleton ; limits. *Etre sur les —;* (nav.) to be on the sick list.

cadrer, v.n., to agree, to square with, to tally ; to suit, to fit in with.

cadrille, n.f., check, square.

cadriller, v.a., to rule (in squares), to checker.

cadu-c, -que, adj., decrepit ; broken-down ; decayed, crazy ; lapsed, null, void (of legacies) ; (bot.) deciduous. *Age —;* decrepit old age. *Devenir —;* to decay. *Legs —;* lapsed legacy (barred by limitation). *Le mal —;* the falling sickness, epilepsy.

caducée, n.m., caduceus, Mercury's wand ; tipstaff.

caducité, n.f., caducity ; decay, decline.

cæcum (sékom), n.m., (anat.) cæcum.

cafard, -e, adj., hypocritical, sanctimonious.

cafard, n.m., **-e**, n.f., canter, hypocrite ; telltale ; humbug, sneak.

cafard, n.m., (ent.) cockroach. V. **blatte**.

cafarderie, n.f., cant, hypocrisy, false devotion.

cafardise, n.f., (l.u.) piece of hypocrisy ; cant.

café, n.m., coffee ; coffee-house ; coffee (berry). *Tasse de —;* cup of coffee. *Rôtir, moudre, prendre, du —;* to roast, to grind, to drink, coffee. — *au lait ;* coffee with milk. — *à la crème ;* coffee with cream. — *chantant ;* music-hall.

caféier, n.m. V. **cafier**.

caféière, n.f., coffee-plantation.

cafetan, or **caftan**, n.m., caftan (Turkish garment).

cafetier, n.m., coffee-house keeper.

cafetière, n.f., coffee-pot.

cafier, or **caféier**, n.m., coffee-tree.

cafre, n.m.f., Caffre.

cage, n.f., cage ; coop (for fowls) ; (tech.) frame ; casing, housing. *Mettre un homme en —;* to put a man in prison, or under lock and key. *La belle — ne nourrit pas l'oiseau ;* all is not gold that glitters.

cagée, n.f., cage-full.

*cagnard, -e, adj., lazy, skulking, slothful.

*cagnard, n.m., **-e**, n.f., lazy-bones, skulker. *C'est un —;* he is a skulker, loafer.

*cagnarder, v.n., to loaf.

*cagnardise, n.f., laziness, slothfulness, skulking.

*cagne, n.f., (l.u.) slut.

*cagneu-x, -se, adj., knock-kneed, splayfooted.

cagot, -e, adj., (fam.) bigoted, hypocritical.

cagot, n.m., **-e**, n.f., (fam.) bigot.

cagoterie, n.f., (fam.) affected devotion, hypocrisy, bigotry.

cagotisme, n.m., (fam.) bigotry, false devotion.

cagoule, n.f., a monk's cloak.

cague, n.f., Dutch sloop.

cahier, n.m., paper-book ; copy-book ; quarter of a quire of paper ; book (manuscript) ; sheet.

—des charges; specifications. *—des frais;* bill of costs.

cahin-caha, *adv.,* (fam.) so-so, lamely, poorly, slowly, reluctantly.

cahot, *n.m.,* jerk; jolt of a coach.

cahotage, cahotement, *n.m.,* jolting, jerking.

cahotant, -e, *adj.,* rough, jolting.

cahoter, *v.n.,* to jolt, to toss about.

cahoter, *v.a.,* to jolt, to jog, to jerk.

cahute, *n.f.,* hut, crib, hovel; (nav.) small cabin.

caïc *or* **caique,** *n.m.,* yawl, long-boat, levantine-boat.

calche, *n.f.,* (nav.) ketch.

caïd, *n.m.,* (—s) Arab military chief or judge.

caïeu, *n.m.,* (hort.) sucker, off-shoot.

*caille,** *n.f.,* (orni.) quail.

caillé, *adj.,* curdled, clotted.

*caillé,** *n.m.,* curdled milk, curds.

*caillebot,** *n.m.,* guelder-rose.

*caillebotis,** *n.m.,* (nav.) grating of the hatches.

*caillebotté, -e,** *part.,* curdled.

*caillebotte,** *n.f.,* mass of curds.

*caillebotter,** *v.n.,* to curdle.

*caille-lait,** *n.m.,* (—) (bot.) cheese-rennet.

*caillement,** *n.m.,* curdling, coagulating.

*cailler,** *v.a.,* to curdle, to clot, to curd.

se cailler, *v.r.,* to coagulate, to turn to curds.

*cailletage,** *n.m.,* gossiping, idle talk, tittle-tattle.

*cailleteau,** *n.m.,* young quail.

*cailleter,** *v.n.,* to gossip, to chatter.

*caillette,** *n.f.,* rennet; gossip; chatterer.

*caillot,** *n.m.,* clot of blood; coagulum.

*caillotis,** *n.m.,* kelp (ashes of seaweed).

*caillot-rosat,** *n.m.,* (—s—s) a kind of pear.

*caillou,** *n.m.,* flint, flint-stone, pebble.

*cailloutage,** *n.m.,* stoning, graveling, ballasting; flint-ware, pebble-work.

*caillouter,** *v.a.,* to macadamize, to gravel, to ballast.

*caillouteu-x, -se,** *adj.,* pebbly, flinty.

*cafeffloutis,** *n.m.,* broken stones, gravel; broken flint.

caïmacan, *n.m.,* caimacan (a Turkish officer).

caïman, *n.m.,* American crocodile, caiman.

caimand. *V.* **quémand.**

caimander. *V.* **quémander.**

caimandeu-r, -se. *V.* **quémandeur.**

caïque, *n.m.* *V.* **caïc.**

caisse, *n.f.,* case, box, chest, trunk; coffer, till; cash-room, counting-house; cylinder (of a drum); (anat.) drum (of the ear); body (of a coach); pay-office. *—de médicaments,* medicine chest. *— militaire;* military chest. *La — du régiment;* the regimental chest. *Avoir tant d'argent en —;* to have so much money in hand. *Les —s de l'Etat;* the coffers of the state. *Livre de —;* cash-book. *Tenir la —;* to keep the cash. *—de secours mutuels;* sick-fund. *—des pensions;* pension fund. *Faire la—;* to make up the cash account. *— d'amortissement;* sinking fund. *—d'épargne;* savings-bank. *— d'escompte;* discounting bank. *Grosse —;* big drum. *Battre la —;* to beat the drum. *Bander la —;* to brace the drum. *Tenir la —;* to act as cashier. (jest.) *Sauver la —;* to run off with the till.

caissier, *n.m.,* treasurer, cashier.

caisson, *n.m.,* (milit.), ammunition wagon, caisson, chest; (nav.) locker; (arch.) coffer; compartment ceiling; sunk-panel; (artil.) limber. *Les—s des vivres;* the provision wagons. *— à poudre;* powder-chest.

cajoler, *v.a.,* to cajole, to coax, to wheedle.

cajolerie, *n.f.,* cajolery, coaxing, wheedling.

cajoleu-r, *n.m.,* **-se,** *n.f.,* cajoler, coaxer, wheedler.

cal, *n.m.,* callosity; (med.) callus.

calade, *n.f.,* (man.) calade; descent, slope.

calage, *n.m.,* wedging, lowering, sinking.

calaison, *n.f.,* load water line; sea-gauge.

calambour, *n.m.,* calambac (wood).

calamendrier, *n.m.,* (bot.) common wall-germander.

calament, *n.m.,* (min. bot.) calamint.

calaminaire, *adj.,* (l.u.) belonging to calamine.

calamine, *n.f.,* (min.) calamine.

calamite, *n.f.,* (min.) calamite.

calamité, *n.f.,* calamity, distress.

calamiteu-x, -se, *adj.,* distressful, calamitous.

calandrage, *n.m.,* calendering, hot-pressing, mangling. [(orni.) calandra.

calandre, *n.f.,* (ent.) weevil; mangle, calender;

calandrer, *v.a.,* to calender, to press, to smooth, to mangle.

calandreur, *n.m.,* mangler, calenderer.

calangue, *n.f.,* (nav.) creek, cove.

calao, *n.m.,* (orni.) horn-bill.

calatrava, *n.f.,* a Spanish military order.

calcaire, *adj.,* calcareous.

calcaire, *n.m.,* limestone.

calcanéum (-om), *n.m.,* (anat.) calcaneum, os calcis, heel-bone.

calcédoine, *n.f.,* (min.) chalcedony.

calcédonieu-x, -se, *adj.,* chalcedonic.

calcin, *n.m.,* calcined glass.

calcinable, *adj.,* calcinable.

calcination, *n.f.,* calcination.

calciner, *v.a.,* to calcine, to burn.

se calciner, *v.r.,* to calcine.

calcis, *n.m.,* (orni.) night-hawk.

calcite. *V.* **chalcite.**

calcium (-om), *n.m.,* calcium.

calcographie, *n.f.,* calcography.

calcul, *n.m.,* calculation, ciphering, arithmetic, computation, reckoning, counting, estimate, forecast; design, selfish motive; (med.) calculus; stone in the bladder. *— différentiel;* differential calculus. *—approximatif;* rough calculation. *Il apprend le —;* he learns arithmetic. *De — fait;* everything included.

calculable, *adj.,* computable, calculable.

calculant, -e, *adj.,* calculating, reckoning; designing.

calculateur, *adj.,* calculating.

calculateur, *n.m.,* calculator, reckoner, accountant; schemer.

calculatoire, *adj.,* calculatory.

calculer, *v.a.,* to calculate, to compute, to reckon, to estimate; to forecast, to contrive, to devise; to determine.

calculeu-x, -se, *adj.,* (med.) calculous.

calculeu-x, *n.m.,* **-se,** *n.f.,* person affected with calculus.

cale, *n.f.,* (nav.) hold (of a ship); wedge, prop; ducking, keel-hauling (punishment); (tech.) block, quay. *— de construction;* stocks. *— de magasin, d'un quai;* slip. *A fond de —;* at the bottom of the hold. *Eau de —;* bilge water. *Donner la — à un matelot;* to give a sailor a ducking. *—sèche;* dry ducking. *Etre à fond de —;* (fam.) to be hard up, to be at the end of one's resources.

calebasse, *n.f.,* (bot.) calabash; gourd; (fig. & fam.) pate, nob, noddle.

calebassier, *n.m.,* calabash tree.

calèche, *n.f.,* calash; barouche, open carriage.

caleçon, *n.m.,* drawers, pair of drawers.

caleçonnier, *n.m.,* one who makes drawers.

calédonien, -ne, *n.* and *adj.,* Caledonian.

caléfacteur, *n.m.,* cooking apparatus, kitchener, cooking-stove.

caléfaction, *n.f.,* calefaction, heating.

calembour, *n.m.,* pun.

calembouriste, *n.m.,* a punster.

calembredaine, *n.f.,* fib, fetch, quibble, subterfuge.

calencar, *n.m.,* a kind of Indian chintz.

calence, *n.f.,* want of work. *En —;* out of work.

calender (-dèr), *n.m.*, kind of dervis.

calendes, *n.f.pl.*, (antiq.) calends ; convocation of the country clergy. *Renvoyer aux — grecques ;* to put off till doomsday.

calendrier, *n.m.*, calendar, almanac. *Vieux —;* the old calendar (old style). *Nouveau —, — grégorien ;* the new, the Gregorian, calendar.

calenture, *n.f.*, (med.) calenture.

calepied, *n.m.*, toe-clip (bicycle).

calepin, *n.m.*, note-book, memorandum-book.

caler, *v.a.*, (nav.) to lower, to strike ; to support, to wedge up. *— les voiles ;* to strike sail. *Cale tout !* let go amain ! *— la voile ;* to yield, to sing small.

caler, *v.n.*, to have more or less draught, to sink. *Ce navire cale trop ;* that ship draws too much water. *—;* (at marbles) to knuckle down. *—;* (school) to keep away from.

calfait, *n.m.*, (nav.) calking iron.

calfat, *n.m.*, (nav.) calker.

calfatage, *n.m.*, (nav.) calking.

calfater, *v.a.*, (nav.) to calk.

calfatin, *n.m.*, (nav.) calker's boy.

calfeutrage, *n.m.*, stopping of chinks.

calfeutrer, *v.a.*, to stop up the chinks, to make air tight.

se **calfeutrer**, *v.r.*, to be stopped up (of chinks); to be made air tight.

calibre, *n.m.*, caliber, bore (of a gun) ; caliber, size (of a bullet); diameter of a body ; kind, sort, stamp ; caliber.

calibrer, *v.a.*, to give the caliber to, to take the caliber of ; to proportion.

calice, *n.m.*, chalice, communion-cup ; (bot.) calyx, flower-cup ; grief, sacrifice. *Boire le — jusqu'à la lie ;* to drink the cup to the dregs. *Boire, avaler, le — ;* to swallow the pill.

calicinal, -e, *adj.*, (bot.) calycinal, calycine.

calicot, *n.m.*, calico ; counter-jumper.

califat, *n.m.*, califate, caliphate, kalifate.

calife, *n.m.*, calif, caliph, kalif.

à califourchon, *adv.*, astride, astraddle.

califourchon, *n.m.*, hobby. *C'est son —;* it is his hobby.

câlin, *n.m.*, -e, *n.f.*, wheedler, cajoler. *C'est une petite —e ;* she is a little wheedler.

câlin, -e, *adj.*, wheedling, cajoling, caressing, coaxing, fondling. *Cet homme a l'air —;* that man has a wheedling look about him. [dle.

câliner, *v.a.*, to fondle, to cajole, to whee-
se **câliner**, *v.r.*, to coddle one's self, to take one's ease, to give one's self up to indolence, to nurse one's self.

câlinerie, *n.f.*, wheedling, cajolery, fondling, caressing.

caliorne, *n.f.*, (nav.) winding-tackle.

calleu-x, -se, *adj.*, callous, hard, horny.

calligraphe, *n.m.*, caligraphist, good penman.

calligraphie, *n.f.*, caligraphy, calligraphy, penmanship.

calligraphique, *adj.*, caligraphic.

callisthénie, *n.f.*, calisthenics.

callosité (kal-lo-), *n.f.*, callousness ; callosity.

calmande, *n.f.*, calamanco ; woolen stuff ; (ich.) whiff.

calmant, *n.m.*, (med.) composing draught ; anodyne, sedative.

calmant, -e, *adj.*, anodyne, calming, soothing.

calmar, *n.m.*, ○pen-case ; (ich.) calamary.

calme, *adj.*, still, quiet, serene, calm ; dispassionate, unruffled, composed, collected ; (com.) dull.

calme, *n.m.*, stillness, calmness, tranquillity, quiet, calm, composure. *— plat ;* (nav.) dead calm.

se **calmer**, *v.r.*, to become calm, to calm one's self ; to compose one's self ; to get appeased, to blow over, to subside, to abate.

calmer, *v.a.*, to still, to quiet, to appease, to allay, to pacify, to calm, to soothe.

calmer, *v.n.*, (nav.) to lull, to fall to a calm. *Le vent calme ;* the wind is dropping.

calmie, *n.f.*, (nav.) lull.

calomel *or* **calomélas**, *n.m.*, calomel.

calomniat-eur, *n.m.*, -**rice**, *n.f.*, calumniator, slanderer.

calomnie, *n.f.*, calumny, slander.

calomnier, *v.a.*, to calumniate, to slander.

calomnieusement (-eûz-mān), *adv.*, calumniously, slanderously.

calomnieu-x, -**se**, *adj.*, calumnious, slanderous.

calonière, *n.f.*, (pop.) pop-gun. *V.* **canonnière**.

calorifère, *n.m.*, hot-air stove or pipe.

calorimètre, *n.m.*, calorimeter.

calorifique, *adj.*, calorific.

calorique, *n.m.*, caloric, heat.

calotte, *n.f.*, calotte, smoking-cap ; skull-cap (of priests) ; (surg.) head-piece ; (anat.) pan (of the brain) ; (arch.) calotte ; box on the ears ; cap of valve (mech.). *La — rouge d'un cardinal ;* the red calotte of a cardinal. *Donner des —s à ;* to box any one's ears.

calotter, *v.a.*, to box the ears of.

calottier, *n.m.*, calotte-maker ; cap-maker.

caloyer, *n.m.*, caloyer (Greek monk).

calque, *n.m.*, tracing, calquing ; imitation copy.

calquer, *v.a.*, to counter-draw, to trace ; to copy, to imitate closely. *— à la pointe ;* to trace with a point. *— à la vitre ;* to counter-draw on glass.

calquoir, *n.m.*, tracing-point.

calumet, *n.m.*, pipe, calumet.

calus (-luss), *n.m.*, callus ; callousness ; callosity ; (med.) callus.

calvaire, *n.m.*, mount Calvary ; a calvary.

calvanier, *n.m.*, (agri.) day-laborer, stacker.

calville, *n.m.*, calville (apple).

calvinien, -**ne** (-i-in, -i-è-n), *adj.*, Calvinistic.

calvinisme, *n.m.*, Calvinism.

calviniste, *n.m.*, Calvinist.

calviniste, *adj.*, Calvinistic.

calvitie (-sî), *n.f.*, baldness. *— des paupières ;* loss of the eye-lashes.

camaïeu, *n.f.*, cameo ; (paint.) camaieu ; cameo brooch ; monotonous play.

****camail** (-s) hood, capuchin, cardinal (garment) ; bishop's purple ornament worn over the rochet.

camaldule, *n.m.*, monk of the Order of St. Benedict.

camarade, *n. m. f.*, comrade, fellow, mate, chum ; female companion ; playmate, play-fellow ; fellow-laborer ; fellow-servant. *— de collège ;* college companion. *— de classe ;* school-fellow. *— de lit ;* bed-fellow. *— de voyage ;* fellow-traveler. *— de malheur ;* fellow-sufferer. *— de chambre ;* chum.

camaraderie, *n.f.*, companionship, intimacy, close friendship ; coterie, clique ; party spirit.

camard, -e, *adj.*, flat-nosed, snub ; flat.

camard, *n.m.*, -e, *n.f.*, flat-nosed person. *La —e ;* (pop.) death.

****camarilla**, *n.f.*, camarilla (a coterie).

camarine, *n.f.*, (bot.) crow-berry.

cambiste, *n.m.*, cambist.

cambouis, *n.m.*, coom, cart-grease.

cambre, *n.f.*, cambering, curving, arching.

cambré, -e, *part.*, bent, cambering, having a fall (in the back) ; arched, well-set. *Pont de navire —;* cambering deck.

cambrer, *v.a.*, to bend, to curve, to arch. *— la forme d'un soulier ;* to give the bend to a last, to block (boots).

se **cambrer**, *v.r.*, to camber ; to take a sweep ; to warp ; to draw one's self up (by throwing the chest forward).

****cambrillon**, *n.m.*, stiffener (of a shoe).

cambrioleu-r, -se, *n.m.f.,* house-thief ; house-breaker ; burglar.

cambriolage, *n.m.,* house-entering, house-breaking ; burglary.

cambrure, *n.f.,* bend, flexure, incurvation, arch, curve.

cambuse, *n.f.,* (nav.) store-room.

cambusier, *n.m.,* (nav.) steward's mate, store-keeper.

came, *n.f.,* (conch.) chama ; heart-cockle ; (tech.) peg-cam ; cog. *V.* **chame.**

camée, *n.m.,* a cameo.

camélée, *n.f.,* (bot.) widow-wail.

caméléon, *n.m.,* chameleon.

caméléopard, *n.m.,* camelopard.

camélia *or* **camellia,** *n.m.,* (bot.) camelia.

cameline, *n.f.,* (bot.) camelina, gold of pleasure.

camelot (-lô), *n.m.,* (stuff) camlet ; cheap Jack, peddler, hawker ; (of newspapers) news-boy, paper-boy.

camelote (-lott), *n.f.,* worthless merchandise, trash, stuff ; bosh.

camelotine, *n.f.,* a sort of camlet.

camérier, *n.m.,* chamberlain (of the pope).

camériste, *n.f.,* maid of honor ; waiting-woman, lady's maid ; chambermaid.

camerlingat, *n.m.,* camerlingate (at Rome).

camerlingue, *n.m.,* camerlingo (papal officer).

camion, *n.m.,* minikin-pin ; little cart ; truck ; dray, wagon ; (paint.) kettle.

camionnage, *n.m.,* carting, carriage (in a dray).

camionneur, *n.m.,* drayman.

⊙**camisade,** *n.f.,* (milit.) night attack, camisade.

camisard, *n.m.,* Camisard (French Calvinist).

camisole, *n.f.,* petticoat bodice. — *de force ;* strait waistcoat *or* jacket.

*****camomille,** *n.f.,* camomile.

camouflet, *n.m.,* whiff of smoke (in the face) ; affront, snub ; rap over the knuckles.

camp (kān), *n.m.,* camp ; (fig.) army, party. *Lever le* — ; to break up the camp. *Prendre le* — ; to pack off.

*****campagnard, -e,** *adj.,* rustic, countrified, rural.

*****campagnard,** *n.m., -e, n.f.,* countryman, peasant ; clodhopper, clown. *C'est une* — *e ;* she is a hoyden.

*****campagne,** *n.f.,* country, fields, plain ; seat, estate, country-house ; field, campaign ; (nav.) voyage, cruise. *Gens de la* — ; peasantry. *Comédiens de* — ; strolling players. *En pleine or rase* — ; in the open country, plain. *Battre la* — ; to scour the country ; to wander about ; to be delirious ; to blunder, to bungle. *Les armées sont en* — ; the armies have taken the field. *Pièces de* — ; field pieces. *Faire une* — ; to make a campaign. *Ouvrir la* — ; to open the campaign. *Tenir la* — ; to keep the field. *Mettre ses amis en* — ; to set one's friends to work. — *de croisière ;* cruising voyage. *Etre à la* — ; to be in the country. *Etre en* — ; to be in the field ; to be at work ; to be out (not at home). *La* — *de Rome ;* the campagna. *Parties de* — ; picnics.

*****campagnol,** *n.m.,* field-mouse.

campane, *n.f.,* (arch.) bell ; (sculp.) ornament with fringe and tassels.

campanelle *or* **campanette,** *n.f.,* bell-flower, Canterbury-bell.

campanile, *n. m.,* (arch.) campanile, bell-tower.

campanule, *n.f.,* campanula, bell-flower. — *gantelée ;* throat-wort. — *raiponce ;* rampion bell-flower. — *à feuilles rondes ;* hare-bell.

campanulé, -e, *adj.,* campanulate, bell-shaped.

campé, -e, *part.,* encamped ; (fig.) well set up. *Bien* — *sur ses jambes ;* firmly planted on his legs.

campêche, *n.m.,* (bot.) campeachy wood, logwood, blood-wood.

campement (kānp-mān), *n.m.,* (milit.) encampment, encamping ; camp detachment. *Matériel de* — ; camping apparatus. *Effets de* — ; camping baggage.

camper, *v.n.,* to encamp, to pitch tents. *Faire* — *son armée ;* to encamp one's army.

camper, *v.a.,* to camp, to seat, to fix, to stand before, to clap down. — *là quelqu'un ;* to leave any one in the lurch.

se camper, *v.r.,* to stand before, to sit down, to clap one's self down. *Il se campa dans un fauteuil ;* he sat himself down in an arm-chair. — *devant une glace ;* to stand bravely before a mirror.

⊙**camphorata,** *n.f. V.* **camphrée.**

camphre, *n.m.,* camphor.

camphré, -e, *adj.,* camphorate, camphorated.

camphrée, *n.f.,* camphorosma.

camphrier, *n.m.,* (bot.) camphor-tree.

campine, *n.m.,* fine fat pullet.

campos, *n.m.,* play-day, holiday, relaxation. *Les écoliers demandent* — ; the boys ask for a holiday. *Prendre* — ; to take a holiday.

camus, -e, *adj.,* flat-nosed ; disappointed ; baulked ; dumbfounded. *Un vilain* — ; an ugly flat-nosed fellow. *La* — *e ;* (pop.) death, grim death.

*****canaille,** *n.f.,* rabble, riff-raff, mob ; scum ; scoundrel ; noisy children, brats. *Hors d'ici,* — *! begone, you scoundrel ! Vile* — ; miserable scum. *Ces* — *s de domestiques ;* these rascally servants !

canaillerie, *n.f.,* blackguardism.

canal, *n.m.,* canal, pipe ; conduit, duct ; drain ; tube ; spout ; watercourse (of water-mills) ; channel, bed, strait ; (arch.) fluting, means. *Creuser un* — ; to dig a canal. *Ce pays est tout coupé de canaux ;* that country is quite intersected with canals. — *latéral,* — *de dérivation ;* lateral drain. — *de cheminée ;* chimney-flue. — *d'irrigation ;* trench for irrigation. — *thoracique ;* thoracic duct. — *de larmier ;* (arch.) channel of a coping. *Il est le* — *de toutes les grâces ;* all favors come through him. *Faire* — ; to cross a strait. [rowed.

canaliculé, -e, *adj.,* (bot.) channeled, furrowed.

canalisation, *n.f.,* canalization.

canaliser, *v.a.,* to establish canals, to intersect with canals.

canamelle, *n.f.,* (bot.) sugar-cane ; reed.

canapé, *n.m.,* sofa, couch.

canaque, *adj.,* Kanaka, wild, savage.

canard, *n.m.,* drake, duck ; hoax ; water-spaniel. — *privé ;* tame duck. — *ordinaire ;* mallard. *Dire des* — *s à ;* to hoax. *Cet homme est un* — *privé ;* that man is a sort of decoy-duck.

canard, -e, *adj.,* for ducks. *Bâtiment* — ; vessel that pitches. *Chien* — ; water-spaniel.

canardeau, *n.m.,* young duck.

canarder, *v.a.,* to shoot from under a shelter ; to hoax, to gammon.

canarder, *v.n.,* (nav.) to pitch (of a ship) ; (mus.) to goose.

⊙**canardier,** *n.m.,* wild-duck shooter ; hoaxer.

canardière, *n.f.,* place for catching wild-ducks ; loop-hole (to shoot through) ; duck-gun ; decoy-pond.

canari, *n.m.,* canary, canary-bird ; flat.

cancan, *n.m.,* tittle-tattle ; scandal ; tale-bearing ; noise ; indecent dance. *Faire des* — *s ;* to tittle-tattle, to invent scandalous stories.

cancaner, *v.n.,* to tattle, to invent scandalous stories ; to dance the cancan.

cancani-er, *n.m., -ère, n.f.,* lover of tittle-tattle.

cancer (-sèr), *n.m.*, (med., astron.) cancer.

cancéreu-x, -se, *adj.*, (med.) cancerous.

cancre, *n.m.*, crab, cray-fish; miser; dunce (at school).

cancrelat, *n.m.*, cockroach.

candélabre, *n.m.*, candelabrum, sconce.

candeur, *n.f.*, openness of heart, frankness, candor, ingenuousness.

candi, *n.m.*, sugar-candy, candy.

candi, -e, *adj.*, candied.

candidat, *n.m.*, candidate.

candidature, *n.f.*, candidature.

candide, *adj.*, fair, open, frank, candid, ingenuous, sincere.

candidement (-mān), *adv.*, openly, frankly, candidly.

se **candir,** *v.r.*, to candy. *Faire se* —; to candy.

cane, *n.f.*, female duck.

canéficier, *n.m.*, cassia-tree. *V.* **casse.**

canepetière, *n.f.*, (orni.) lesser bustard.

canepin (ka-n-pin), *n.m.*, kid skin (for gloves).

caner, *v.n.*, to shirk danger, to funk, to show the white feather.

caner, *v.a.*, to leave undone, shirk.

canescent, -e, *adj.*, (bot.) canescent.

caneter, *v.n.*, to waddle.

caneton (ka-n-ton), *n.m.*, young duck, duckling.

canette, *n.f.*, small duck, young duck; (her.) duck without legs; a measure for beer; (pop.) marbles.

canevas (ka-n-vâ), *n.m.*, canvas; sail-cloth; sketch, rough draught; (mus.) canvas. *Tracer son* —; to prepare one's ground-work. *Faire le* — *d'une comédie ;* to sketch out, to compose the skeleton of a play.

canezou, *n.m.*, woman's jacket.

⊙**cangrène,** *n.f. V.* **gangrène.**

cangue, *n.f.*, a kind of pillory used in China.

caniche, *n.m.f.*, poodle-dog, water-spaniel.

caniculaire, *adj.*, canicular. *Les jours* —*s;* the dog-days.

canicule, *n.f.*, dog-days; (astron.) canicule; dog-star.

canif, *n.m.*, penknife.

canin, -e, *adj.*, canine. *Dent* —*e ;* canine tooth. *Lettre* —*e ;* the letter R.

caniveau, *n.m.*, (arch.) channel-stone.

cannage, *n.m.*, (l.u.) cane-work ; caning.

cannaie, *n.f.*, cane-brake, cane-field.

canne, *n.f.*, walking-stick ; long measure; cane, reed; glassblower's pipe. — *à sucre ;* sugar-cane. — *à épée ;* sword-stick. — *à vent ;* air-gun.

canneberge (-bèrj), *n.f.*, cranberry, moor-berry.

cannelas (-lâ), *n.m.*, cinnamon, candied cinnamon.

canneler, *v.a.*, to flute, to channel, to groove.

cannelle, *n.f.*, cinnamon bark. — *blanche ;* canella.

cannelle *or* **cannette,** *n.f.*, spigot; tap, cock.

cannelier, *n.m.*, cinnamon-tree.

cannelon (ka-n-lon), *n.m.*, fluted mold (for ices).

cannelure, *n.f.*, channeling, fluting, grooving. — *à côtes ;* fluting with intervals. — *avec rudentures ;* fluting enriched with cables. — *à vive arête ;* fluting without intervals. —*s plates ;* square fluting.

cannequin, *n.m.*, sort of cotton stuff.

*****cannetille,** *n.f.*, wire-ribbon.

cannibale (can-ni-bal), *n.m.*, man-eater, cannibal.

cannibalisme, *n.m.*, cannibalism ; ferocity.

canon, *n.m.*, cannon, gun ; cylinder, tube, pipe ; barrel (of a gun, of a quill) ; (ecc.) canon law, rule ; catalogue of saints ; (mus.) canon ; (print.) canon ; (man.) canon-bit; leg (of trousers). *L'âme d'un* —; the chamber of a cannon.

La lumière, la culasse, le recul, d'un —; the touch-hole, the breech, the recoil, of a cannon. *L'affût d'un* — ; a gun-carriage. *Enclouer un* —; to spike a gun. *Une pièce de* —; a piece of ordnance. *Gros* —; (print.) canon. *Petit* —; (print.) two-line English. — *de dix livres ;* ten-pounder. *Un coup de* —; a cannon-shot. *De la poudre à* —; gunpowder. *Etre à portée de* —; to be within cannon-shot. *Etre hors de portée de* —; to be beyond cannon range. — *de retraite;* (milit.) gun-fire ; (nav.) stern-chaser. — *démarré ;* cannon drawn in to be loaded. — *rayé ;* rifled gun. *A* — *rayé ;* rifled, rifle-barreled. — *renforcé ;* cannon whose breech is thicker than its bore. — *d'un soufflet ;* nose, nozzle pipe of a pair of bellows. — *de gouttière ;* spout of a gutter. *Les* —*s d'un concile ;* the canons of a council. *Ecole de droit* —; school of canon law. — *des Ecritures ;* the sacred canon. *Le* — *de la messe ;* the canon of the mass. — *enluminé ;* illuminated canon.

canonial, -e, *adj.*, canonical.

canonicat, *n.m.*, canonry, canonship, prebend ; (fig.) sinecure.

canonicité, *n.f.*, canonicity.

canonique, *adj.*, canonical.

canoniquement (-mān), *adv.*, canonically.

canonisation, *n.f.*, canonization.

canoniser, *v.a.*, to canonize.

canoniste, *n.m.*, canonist.

canonnade, *n.f.*, cannonading, cannonade.

canonnage, *n.m.*, gunnery.

canonner, *v.a.*, to attack with heavy artillery, to cannonade.

se **canonner,** *v.r.*, to cannonade.

canonnier, *n.m.*, gunner.

canonnière, *n.f.*, *adj.*, ⊙ loop-hole ; tent ; tilt ; drain-hole ; pop-gun. —, *or chaloupe* — (nav.) ; gun-boat.

canot, *n.m.*, ship's-boat, cutter, yawl. — *de sauvetage ;* life-boat.

canotage, *n.m.*, boating, aquatics.

canotier, *n.m.*, rower, oarsman ; boat-keeper ; bargeman ; straw hat.

cantabile (-lé), *n.m.*, (mus.) cantabile.

cantal, *n.m.*, cantal (sort of cheese).

cantalabre, *n.m.*, door-case, casing.

cantaloup, *n.m.*, musk-melon.

cantate, *n.f.*, (mus.) cantata.

*****cantatille,** *n.f.*, cantatilla.

cantatrice, *n.f.*, eminent singer.

cantharide, *n.f.*, (ent.) cantharis, Spanish fly ; (pharm.) (*pl.*) cantharides.

canthus, *n.m.*, (anat.) canthus, corner of the eye.

cantilène, *n.f.*, (mus.) cantilena, melody.

cantine, *n.f.*, bottle-case ; (milit.) canteen.

cantini-er, *n.m.*, -**ère,** *n.f.*, sutler, canteen-woman.

cantique, *n.m.*, song, canticle, hymn.

canton, *n.m.*, canton, district ; (her.) canton.

cantonade, *n.f.*, (theat.) wings. *Parler à la* —; to speak to an actor off the stage ; (fig.) to speak to empty benches.

cantonal, -e, *adj.*, cantonal.

cantonné, -e, *adj.*, (arch., her., milit.) cantoned.

cantonnement (-to-n-mān), *n.m.*, (milit.), cantonment.

cantonner, *v.a.*, (milit.) to canton.

se **cantonner,** *v.r.*, to take up a position, quarters, abode ; to fortify one's self.

cantonner, *v.n.*, (milit.) to be cantoned.

cantonnier, *n.m.*, road-man ; (rail.) plate-layer ; signal-man.

cantonnière, *n.f.*, signal-woman ; valance.

canule, *n.f.*, clyster-pipe, injection tube ; faucet, quill ; (fig.) bore, plague.

canzone, *n.f.*, (mus.) canzone.

caolin, *n.m. V.* **kaolin.**

caoutchouc, *n.m.*, caoutchouc, India-rubber; (bot.) gum-tree.

cap, *n.m.*, cape, headland, point, promontory, foreland; (nav.) head. *Doubler un* —; to double a cape. *Où est le* — ? (nav.) how is her head? *Mettre le — sur;* to steer for. *Avoir le — au large;* to stand off. *De pied en* —; from top to toe.

capable, *adj.*, able, fit, capable; calctlated to, apt to. *Il est — de vous desservir;* he is capable of doing you an ill office. *Il est — de tout;* he is capable of any thing. *C'est un homme* —; he is a clever man. *Avoir l'air* —; to put on a conceited, bumptious, knowing look. *Faire le* —; to affect capability, to look as if you were in the know. *Prendre un air* —; to assume a knowing look.

capablement, *adv.*, (l.u.) ably, skillfully.

capacité, *n.f.*, (extent, size, capaciousness; ability, capacity; (nav.) bulk, burden, tonnage. *Manquer de* —; to lack capacity.

caparaçon, *n.m.*, caparison, trappings.

caparaçonner, *v.a.*, to caparison (a horse).

cape, *n.f.*, cloak with a hood; riding-hood; cape; (nav.) try-sail. *Rire sous* —; to laugh in one's sleeve. *N'avoir que la — et l'épée;* to be titled, but penniless. *Roman de — et d'épée;* romantic, melodramatic story. *Etre à la* —; (nav.) to try, to be lying to. *A la — !* bring to!

capéer, *v.n.*, (nav.) to lie to.

capelan, *n.m.*, beggarly priest; (ich.) caplin.

capelet, *n.m.*, (vet.) capped hock.

capeline, *n.f.*, hood; (of armor) capeline.

capendu, *n.m.*, capender (apple).

caperon. *V.* capron.

capharnaüm, *n.m.*, (—s) (fig. fam.) place of confusion; Babel, bear-garden.

capillaire (-pil-lèr), *adj.*, capillary.

capillaire, *n.m.*, (anat.) capillary; (bot.) maiden-hair; Venus's-hair. *Sirop de* —; capillaire.

capillarité, *n.f.*, (phys.) capillarity, capillary attraction or repulsion.

capilotade, *n.f.*, hash, ragout; thrashing, drubbing; slandering. *Mettre quelqu'un en* —; to beat black and blue.

capitaine, *n.m.*, captain. — *d'infanterie;* infantry captain. — *de cavalerie;* captain of cavalry. — *de vaisseau;* post-captain. — *au long cours;* captain of a trading vessel (going to foreign parts). — *de pavillon;* flag-captain. — *d'armes;* master-at-arms. — *de port;* harbor-master. *Grade de* —; captaincy.

capitainerie, *n.f.*, captaincy.

capital, -e, *adj.*, capital, main, chief, leading, important. *Les sept péchés capitaux;* the seven capital sins. *Peine —e;* capital punishment.

capital, *n.m.*, capital; principal; stock. *Mettre un — à fonds perdu;* to sink a capital. *Rembourser le* —; to reimburse the principal.

capitale, *n.f.*, capital, chief city; capital letter.

capitalisation, *n.f.*, capitalization.

capitaliser, *v.a.*, to capitalize. *Se* —, *v.r.*, to be capitalized.

capitaliste, *n.m.*, capitalist, moneyed man.

capitan, *n.m.*, braggadocio, swaggerer, bully.

capitane, *n.f.*, (nav.) admiral's galley.

capitan-pacha, *n.m.*, (—s—s) Turkish admiral.

capitation, *n.f.*, capitation, poll-tax.

capiteu-x, -se, *adj.*, heady, strong. *Bière —se;* strong beer. *Vin* —; heavy wine.

capitole, *n.m.*, Capitol (of Rome, of the United States).

capitolin, *adj.*, capitoline.

capiton, *n.m.*, (com.) cappadine.

capitonner, *v.a.*, to stuff, to pad (arm-chairs, &c.); to tuft, to button.

⊙**capitoul**, *n.m.*, capitoul (alderman, town-councillor at Toulouse).

⊙**capitoulat**, *n.m.*, capitoulship.

capitulaire, *adj.*, capitulary.

capitulaire, *n.m.*, capitular, capitulary.

capitulairement (-lèr-mān), *adv.*, capitularly.

capitulant, *adj.*, capitulary.

capitulant, *n.m.*, capitular, capitulary.

capitulation, *n.f.*, capitulation; convention, compromise. *Amener à une* —; to bring to terms. — *de conscience;* a conscientious compromise.

capitule, *n.m.*, capitule (part of the Liturgy).

capituler, *v.n.*, to capitulate, to compound. — *avec sa conscience;* to compound with one's conscience, to silence it by concessions.

caplan, (ich.). *V.* capelan.

capon, *n.m.*, mean fellow, sneak; cheat, coward; (nav.) cat-tackle. *Poulie de* —; cat-block.

caponner, *v.n.*, to trick, to cheat; to be cowardly, to hang back.

caponner, *v.a.*, (nav.) to cat (the anchor).

caponnière, *n.f.*, (fort.) rifle-pit.

caporal, *n.m.*, corporal; (of tobacco) sort of "shag."

capot, *n.m.*, (nav.) hood (of ladders).

capot, *adj.*, capot (at cards); silly. *Faire* —; to capot, to win all the tricks, to beat hollow. *Etre* —; to have lost all the tricks; (fig.) to look foolish; to be balked. *Faire* —; (nav.) to capsize, to upset.

capote, *n.f.*, large cloak with a hood; (soldier's) great-coat; capuchin, hood, mantle.

capraire, *n.f.*, (bot.) goat-weed, capraria.

câpre, *n.f.*, (bot.) caper.

capricant *or* **caprisant**, *adj.*, (med.) bounding, unequal (of the pulse).

caprice, *n.m.*, caprice, whim, humor, freak; fit, flight, sally; (mus.) caprice. *Les —s de la mode;* the caprices, freaks of fashion. *Les —s de la fortune;* the fickleness of fortune. *Composer de* —; to compose when the spirit moves, when the fit is on.

capricieusement (-mān), *adv.*, capriciously, fantastically, whimsically.

capricieu-x, -se, *adj.*, capricious, whimsical, fickle, freakish, skittish.

capricorne, *n.m.*, (astron.) Capricorn; (ent.) capricorn-beetle.

câprier, *n.m.*, (bot.) caper-bush.

caprification, *n.f.*, caprification.

caprifiguier (-ghié), *n.m.*, wild fig-tree.

capripède, *n.m.*, goat-footed; satyr.

capron *or* **caperon**, *n.m.*, the hautbois-strawberry.

capronier, *n.m.*, the hautbois-strawberry plant.

capselle, *n.f.*, (bot.) cassweed; shepherd's pouch.

capsulaire, *adj.* (bot.) capsulary; (anat.) capsular.

capsule, *n.f.*, (bot.) capsule, pod; (anat.) capsula; percussion, cap (of fire-arms).

⊙**captal**, **x.m.**, chief, lord.

captateur, *n.m.*, (jur.) inveigler (one who uses undue influence).

captation, *n.f.*, inveigling, undue influence, captation.

captatoire, *n.f.*, inveigling.

capter, *v.a.*, to court, to coax, to win by bribery. — *la bienveillance de quelqu'un;* to curry the favor of any one. — *les suffrages;* to bribe, to win unfairly, to get by bribery.

captieusement (-sieūz-mān), *adv.*, captiously, insidiously, cunningly, deceitfully.

captieu-x, -se (-cieu-), *adj.*, captious, insidious.

capti-f, -ve, *adj.*, captive.

capti-f, *n.m.*, **-ve**, *n.f.*, captive.

captiver, *v.a.*, to captivate, to charm, to enslave; to bring under. *—l'attention;* to captivate attention. *La beauté qui le captive;* the beauty that enslaves him. *— la bienveillance;* to win any one's favor.

se **captiver,** *v.r.*, to lay a restraint upon oneself; to cling to (tenaciously); (fig.) to cringe, to fawn upon.

captivité, *n.f.*, captivity, bondage. *Racheter de —;* to ransom from captivity.

capture, *n.f.*, capture, seizure; prize, booty.

capturer, *v.a.*, to capture; to apprehend, to arrest.

capuce, *n.f.,* or **capuchon,** *n.m.*, hood, cowl.

capuchonné, -e, *adj.*, hooded.

capuchonner, *v.n.*, (man.) to arch the neck (of a horse).

capucin, *n.m.,* **-e,** *n.f.*, capuchin friar, capuchin nun. *Tomber comme des —s de cartes;* to tumble over one another.

capucinade, *n.f.*, stupid sermon.

capucine, *n.f.*, (bot.) nasturtium; (nav.) standard; band (of a soldier's musket).

capucinière, *n.f.*, (b.s.) capuchin friary.

capulet, *n.m.*, hood, cap.

caput-mortuum, *n.m.*, (chem.) caput-mortuum; worthless remains.

caquage, *n.m.*, dressing and curing of herrings; barreling (of powder).

caque, *n.f.*, keg, barrel. *La — sent toujours le hareng;* what is bred in the bone will never come out of the flesh.

caquer, *v.a.*, to cure; to barrel.

caquet, *n.m.*, cackle (of geese, &c.); tittletattle, idle talk, gossip, scandal. *Avoir bien du —;* to be a chatter-box. *Rabattre, rabaisser, le — à quelqu'un;* to take anyone down a peg or two. *— bon bec;* dame prattler.

caquetage (kak-taj), *n.m.*, tattling, cackling.

caquète, *n.f.*, carp-tub.

caqueter (kak-té), *v.n.*, to cackle, to chatter, to gossip, to babble.

caqueterie (kak-trî), *n.f.*, babbling, prattling, gossiping.

caqueteu-r, *n.m.,* **-se,** *n.f.*, prattler, tattler, idle prater, gossip.

caqueur, *n.m.*, fish-curer.

car, *conj.*, for, because, as.

carabé, *n.m.*, yellow, amber.

carabin, *n.m.*, saw-bones, medical student.

carabinade, *n.f.*, (l.u.) (student's, soldier's) trick; discharge of carbines.

carabinage, *n.m.*, rifling.

carabine, *n.f.*, carbine, rifle.

carabiné, -e, *adj.*, rifled; (nav.) stiff (of the wind).

⊙**carabiner,** *v.n.*, to skirmish.

carabiner, *v.a.*, to rifle a gun-barrel.

carabinier, *n.m.*, carabineer, rifleman.

caraco, *n.m.*, woman's jacket.

caracole, *n.f.*, (man.) circling caracole. *En —;* winding.

caracoler, *v.n.*, to caracole, to circle.

caracouler, *v.n.*, to coo. *V.* **roucouler.**

caractère, *n.m.*, character, letter, type, print; hand-writing; stamp, badge, mark, dignity, temper, humor, spirit, expression; aspect; (arith.) digit; charm, spell. *— lisible;* legible print. *Beaux —s;* fine type. *Le — d'un auteur;* the stamp of an author. *Un homme d'un bon —;* a good-natured man. *Ne pas démentir son —* to act up to one's character. *Il est sorti de son —;* he lost his temper. *Avoir, montrer, du —;* to have spirit, to show spirit. *C'est un homme à —;* he is a spirited, determined man.

caractériser, *v.a.*, to characterize, describe, define, mark, distinguish.

caractéristique, *adj.*, characteristic.

caractéristique, *n.f.*, (gram. math.) characteristic; (logarithms) index.

carafe, *n.f.*, decanter, flagon, water-bottle.

carafon, *n.m.*, cooler; small decanter; quarter bottle.

*****caragne,** *n.f.*, aromatic resin, caranna.

caraïte, *n.m.*, caraite (Jewish sectarian).

carambolage, *n.m.*, (billiards) cannon; (pop.) affray, shindy; (fig.) rebound (against).

caramboler, *v.n.*, (billiards) to cannon.

caramboleur, *n.m.*, good cannon-player.

caramel, *n.m.*, burnt sugar, caramel. *— au beurre;* butter-scotch, tōffee.

carapace, *n.f.*, turtle-shell, carapace.

carapat, *n.m.*, oil of palma Christi.

caraque, *n. f.*, carack (Portuguese Indiaman). **caracas,** *n.m.*, cocoa.

carat, *n.m.*, (gold) carat; small diamonds sold by weight.

caratch, *n.m.* (n.p.), tribute.

caravane, *n.f.*, caravan, convoy. *Marcher en —;* to walk in a band. *Faire ses —s;* to lead a dissipated life.

caravanier, *n.m.*, leader of caravan.

*****caravansérail,** *n.m.*, a caravansary (inn).

caravanséraskier, *n.m.*, keeper of a caravansary.

caravelle, *n.f.*, caravel (Portuguese boat).

carbatine, *n.f.*, green hide, skin.

carbazotique, *adj.*, (chem.) carbazotic.

carbonarisme, *n.m.*, carbonarism.

carbonaro, *n.m.*, carbonaro.

carbonate, *n.m.*, (chem.) carbonate.

⊙**carboncle.** *V.* **escarboucle; furoncle; rubis.**

carbone, *n.m.*, (chem.) carbon.

carboné, -e, *adj.*, carbonated.

carboneu-x, -se, *adj.*, (chem.) carbonaceous.

carbonique, *adj.*, carbonic.

carbonisation, *n.f.*, carbonization.

carboniser, *v.a.*, to carbonize.

carbonnade, *n.f.*, (cook.) carbonade.

carburateur, *n.m.*, carburettor (motor).

carbure, *n.m.*, (chem.) carburet, carbide.

carburé, -e, *adj.*, (chem.) carbureted.

carcajou, *n.m.*, American badger.

carcan, *n.m.*, iron collar; carcan (pillory); carcanet (collar of jewels).

carcasse, *n.f.*, carcass, skeleton, bones; (arch.) shell, framework; body; fish-basket.

carcinomateu-x, -se, *adj.*, (med.) carcinomatous.

carcinome, *n.m.*, (med.) carcinoma.

cardage, *n.m.*, act of carding, carding.

cardamine, *n. f.*, (bot.) land-cress, **lady's** smock.

cardamome, *n.m.*, (bot.) cardamom.

cardasse, *n.f.*, (bot.) nopal.

carde, *n.f.*, chard (stalk in the leaves of some plants); card (instrument for combing wool or flax); carding machine.

cardée, *n.f.*, quantity carded.

carde-poirée, *n.f.*, (bot.) chard of beet.

carder, *v.a.*, to card, to comb. *Se —;* to be carded.

cardère, *n.f.*, (bot.) teasel.

carderie, *n.f.*, carding-house; card-manufactory.

cardeu-r, *n.m.,* **-se,** *n.f.*, carder, wool-comber.

cardiaire, *adj.* (zool.) *Ver —;* a parasite bred in the heart. (bot.) *V.* **cardère; chardon à foulon.**

cardialgie, *n.f.*, cardialgy, heartburn.

cardiologie, *n.f.*, cardiology.

cardiaque, *n.m.*, (med.) cardiac.

cardiaque, *adj.*, (med. anat.) cardiac.

cardier, *n.m.*, wool card-maker.

cardinal, *adj.*, cardinal, chief, principal, first.

cardinal, *n.m.*, cardinal; (orni.) cardinal.

cardinalat, *n.m.*, cardinalate, cardinalship.

cardinale, *n.f.*, (bot.) cardinal flower.

cardine, *n.f.*, (ich.) flat-fish, whiff.

cardon, *n.m.*, (bot.) cardoon.

cardonnette, n.f. V. **chardonnette.**

carême, n.m., Lent, Lent-sermons. *Faire le* —; to keep Lent. *Provisions de* —; fish and vegetables. *Cela vient comme marée en* —; that comes in the very nick of time. *Face de* —; pale or wan face. *Arriver comme mars en* —; to be sure to happen; to come like clock-work. *Arriver comme marée en* —; to come in the nick of time.

carême-prenant, n. *m.,* (—*s*—*s*) carnival time; Shrove Tuesday; masker; reveler.

carénage, n.m., careening.

carence, n.f., (jur.) absence of assets, insolvency. *Procès-verbal de* —; declaration of insolvency.

carène, n.f., (nav.) keel; bottom, careen; (bot.) keel. *Demi-* —; (nav.) parliament-heel. *En* —; keel-shaped.

caréné, -e, adj., (bot.) keeled, keel-shaped.

caréner, v.a., (nav.) to careen.

caressant, -e, adj., caressing, endearing, fond, tender; fawning.

caresse, n.f., caress, endearment. *Il ne faut pas se fier aux* —*s de la fortune;* we must not trust to the smiles of fortune.

caressé, -e, part., caressed; polished, finished off, chiseled. *Ces tableaux sont très* —*s;* these pictures have a peculiar richness of finish.

caresser, v.a., to caress, to fondle, to stroke; to fawn upon, to make much of, to flatter, to cajole, to wheedle. — *l'orgueil de quelqu'un;* to pamper any one's pride. — *une chimère;* to cherish, to hug, a visionary scheme.

caret, n.m., rope-maker's reel; (erpetology) tortoise. *Fil de* —; rope-yarn.

carex (-rèks), n.m., (bot.) carex.

cargaison, n.f., cargo, ship-load, freight.

cargue (karg), n.f., (nav.) brail.

carguer (-ghé), v.a., (nav.) to brail up, to clew up. — *une voile;* to clew up a sail.

cargueur (-gheur), n.m., (nav.) reefer; top-block.

cariatide, n.f., (arch.) caryatide.

caribou, n.m., (mam.) caribou.

caricature, n.f., caricature.

caricaturer, v.a., to caricature, to ridicule.

caricaturiste, n.m., caricaturist.

carie, n.f., brown rust; fire-blast; (med.) caries, decay.

carier, v.a., to make carious, to rot. *se* **carier,** v.r., to grow carious, rotten. *Dent cariée;* carious tooth.

***carillon,** n. m., chime, peal; musical bells, chimes; clutter, racket. *A double* —; soundly, lustily. *Le* — *des verres;* the jingling of glasses.

***carillonnement,** n.m., chiming, jingling.

***carillonner,** v. n., to chime; to ring the changes; to jingle, to clatter.

***carillonneur,** n.m., chimer, bell-ringer; change-ringer.

carlette, n.f., square slate.

carlin, n.m., carlin (Italian coin); pug-dog.

carline, n.f., (bot.) carline-thistle.

carlingue (-linghe), n.f., (nav.) carline, carling. — *de cabestan;* keelson, step.

carliste, n.m.f., Carlist (partisan of Charles).

carliste, adj., Carlist.

carlovingien, -ne (-in, -é-n), n. and adj., Carlovingian.

***carmagnole,** n.f., carmagnole (jacket); carmagnole (revolutionary song and dance).

carmagnole, n.m., violent Jacobin.

carme, n.m., Carmelite friar, white friar. —*s déchaussés;* barefooted Carmelites. *Eau des* —*s;* carmelite water.

carme, n.m., (tric-trac) two fours.

carmeline, n.f. carmeline wool.

carmélite, n.f. and adj., Carmelite nun.

carmin, n.m., carmine.

carminati-f, -ve, adj., (med.) carminative.

carminati-f, n.m., (med.) carminative.

carnage, n.m., carnage, slaughter, butchery destruction, havoc.

carnassi-er, -ère, adj., carnivorous, flesh-eating.

carnassier, n.m., feline animal; flesh-eater.

carnassière, n.f., game-bag.

carnation, n.f., carnation, flesh-tint, flesh-color, complexion.

carnaval, n.m., a carnival; guy.

carne, n.f., corner, edge (of a table, &c.).

carné, -e, adj., of a carnation color.

carnet, n.m., note-book, memorandum-book. — *d'échéances;* bill-book. — *de chèques;* check book.

carnier, n.m. V. **carnassière.**

carnification, n.f., (med.) carnification.

se **carnifier,** v.r., (med.) to carnify.

carnivore, adj., carnivorous.

carnosité, n.f., carnosity.

***carogne,** n.f., (l. ex.) hag, jade, impudent slut.

carolus (-lus), n.m., carolus (old French coin).

caronade, n.f., (artil.) carronade.

caroncule, n.f., (anat., bot.) caruncle.

carotide, adj., (anat.) carotid.

carotide, n.f., (anat.) carotid.

carotidien, adj. m., (anat.) carotid. *Canal* —; carotid canal.

carotique, adj., (med.) comatose.

carotte, n.f., carrot. — *de tabac;* roll of tobacco. (fig.) *Quelle* —*!* what a chouse!

carotter, v.n., to live on little; to play low; to chouse, to diddle.

carotti-er, n.m., -ère, n.f., (triv.) V. **carotteur.**

carotteu-r, n.m., **-se,** n.f., timid player; petty jobber; cheat, trickster.

caroube or **carouge,** n.f., (bot.) carob-bean.

caroubier, n.m., carob-tree, St. John's bread tree.

carouble, n.f., skeleton-key.

caroubleur, n.m., house-breaker.

carpe, n.f., (ich.) carp. *Saut de* —; somerset. *Faire la* — *pâmée;* to sham fainting. *Muet comme une* —; dumb as an oyster.

carpe, n.m., (anat.) wrist.

carpeau, n.m., small carp.

carpien, -ne (-in, -é-n) adj., (anat.) carpal.

***carpillon,** n.m., (ich.) young carp.

carquois, n.m., quiver. *Il a vidé son* —; he has shot his bolt.

carrare, n.m., Carrara marble.

carre, n.f., back and shoulders (of any one). *La* — *d'un chapeau;* the crown of a hat. *La* — *d'un habit;* the part of a coat from the waist upwards. *La* — *d'un soulier;* the square toe of a shoe. *Un homme d'une bonne* —; a broad-shouldered man. *Lame à trois* —*s;* three-edged sword.

carré, n.m., square; landing, floor; printing demy (of paper). *Un* — *de tulipes;* a square bed of tulips. *Un* — *d'eau;* a square sheet of water. — *de toilette;* dressing-case. — *des officiers;* ward-room.

carré, -e, adj., square, quadratic; well-set, well-knit; plain, straightforward; demy (of paper); (rhet.) flowing. *Partie* —*e;* party of four (two men and two women).

carreau, n.m., (med.) tabes mesenteriea.

carreau, n.m., square; lozenge; square tile or brick; small flag-stone; ground, floor; pane (of glass); cushion, hassock; tailor's goose; diamond (at cards); (gard.) bed, square; (arch.) stretcher; rubber (file); ⊙ square-headed arrow, cross-arrow. *Brochet* —; very large pike. *Tomber sur le* —; to fall on the floor. *Coucher sur le* —; to sleep on the floor. *Jeter quelqu'un sur le;* to send any one sprawling upon the ground. *Rester sur le* —; to be killed on the spot. *Étoffes à* —*x;* stuff checks. *C'est un valet de* —; he is a contemptible fellow.

carrefour, *n.m.,* cross-way or street, cross-road, quadrant, crowded thoroughfare. *Les* —*s d'une ville;* the public places of a town. — *des auteurs;* Grub-street. *Langage de* —; low, vulgar language; Billingsgate. *Orateur de* —; stump-orator.

carrelage, *n.m.,* tile-flooring, brick-paving.

carreler, *v.a.,* to pave (a floor) with square tiles, bricks, stones; to cobble.

carrelet, *n.m.,* (ich.) flounder; square net; shoemaker's awl.

carrelette, *n.f.,* flat file.

carreleur, *n.m.,* floor-tiler, brick-pavior; tramping cobbler.

carrelier, *n.m.,* a tile-maker.

carrelure, *n.f.,* new-soling of shoes.

carrément, *adv.,* squarely; plainly; straight-forwardly. *Couper* —; to cut square. *Tracer un plan* —; to draw a plan square.

carrer, *v.a.,* to square.

se **carrer,** *v.r.,* to strut, to stalk; to double one's stake (at *bouillotte* — a card game). *Se* — *dans son fauteuil;* to sit in state.

carrick, *n.m.,* box-coat, cape; gig.

carrier, *n.m.,* a quarry-man.

carrière, *n.f.,* race-ground, course, &c.; career, race; course; scope; play, vent; quarry. *Le bout de la* —; the goal. *Parcourir la* —; to run round, to run over the course. *Donner* — *à son imagination;* to give scope, free vent to one's imagination. *Se donner* —; to throw off all re-straint. *Donner* — *à un cheval;* to give a horse his head. — *de marbre;* marble quarry.

carriole, *n.f.,* covered cart, jaunting car, pleasure-van; wretched carriage.

carrossable, *n.f.,* (of roads) practicable for carriages. *Route* —; carriage road.

carrosse, *n.m.,* four-wheeled carriage, coach. — *de remise;* livery-coach, — *de louage;* hack-ney-coach. *Mener un* —; to drive a carriage. *Aller en* —; to ride in a coach. *Rouler* —; to keep a carriage; to live in grand style.

carrossée, *n.f.,* coachful, carriageful.

carrosserie, *n.f.,* coach-making; coach-build-ing.

carrossier, *n.m.,* coachmaker, carriage-builder; coach-horse.

carrousel, *n.m.,* tournament; roundabout.

⊙**carrousse,** *n.f.,*carouse. *Faire* —; to carouse, to drink hard.

carrure, *n.f.,* breadth of shoulders.

cartahu, *n.m.,* (nav.) whip; girt-line. *Poulie de* —; single block.

cartayer, *v.n.,* to avoid ruts.

carte, *n.f.,* pasteboard; card, postcard; label, ticket; map, chart; bill; bill of fare; account. *Un jeu de* —*s;* a pack of cards. *Les basses* —*s;* the small cards. —*s préparées;* marked cards. *Donner les* —*s;* to deal. *Battre les* —; to shuf-fle. *Faire des tours de* —; to play tricks with cards. *Mettre aux* —*s;* to pay the card money. *Château de* —*s;* gingerbread *or* jerry-built house. *Brouiller les* —*s;* to sow discord. *Voir le des-sous des* —*s;* to be in the secret; "in the Know." *Avoir* — *blanche;* to have full power. *Tirer les* —*s;* to tell fortunes (with cards). — *de géo-graphie;* map, chart. *Faire la* — *d'un pays;* to map out a country. — *topographique;* topo-graphical chart. — *marine;* sea-chart. *Perdre la* —; to lose one's wits. *Dîner à la* —; to dine from the bill of fare.

cartel, *n.m.,* challenge, cartel; dial-case, clock; frieze-panel, frame; (milit., nav.) cartel. — *d'armoiries;* (her.) shield.

carterie, *n.f.,* card-making, card-factory.

carteron, *n.m. V.* **quarteron.**

cartésianisme, *n.m.,* Cartesian philosophy.

cartésien, -ne (-in, -è-n), *adj.,* Cartesian.

carthaginois, -e, *n.* and *adj.,* Carthaginian.

carthame, *n.m.,* (bot.) carthamus, safflower.

cartier, *n.m.,* playing-card maker.

cartilage, *n.m.,* (anat.) cartilage, gristle.

cartilagineu-x,-se, *adj.,* cartilaginous, gristly.

cartisane, *n.f.,* foil-card. *Dentelle à* —; vellum-lace.

cartomancie, *n.f.,* cartomancy.

cartomancien, *n.m.,* -ne, *n.f.,* fortune-teller (by cards).

carton, *n.m.,* pasteboard; (paint.) cartoon; bandbox; case; hat-box; bonnet-box; (print.) four-page cancel. — *lissé;* glazed pasteboard. — *de pâté;* mill board. *Les* —*s de Raphaël;* the cartoons of Raphael. — *de dessins;* portfolio of drawings.

cartonnage, *n.m.,* (book-bind.) boarding.

cartonné, -e, *adj.,* (book-bind.) in boards.

cartonner, *v.a.,* to put in boards.

cartonnerie, *n.f.,* pasteboard manufactory.

cartonneu-r, *n.m.,* -se, *n.f.,* binder, boarder (of books).

cartonnier, *n.m.,* pasteboard-maker, seller.

carton-pierre, *n.m.,* (*n.p.*), statuary paste-board.

cartouche, *n.m.,* escutcheon, shield, ring; (arch.) cartouch, modillion.

cartouche, *n.f.,* cartouch, case-shot, canister-shot (of cannon); cartridge.

cartouchier, *n.m.,* (nav.) cartridge-box, *or* pouch.

cartouchière, *n.f.,* cartridge-box.

cartulaire, *n.m.,* cartulary.

carus, *n.m.,* (med.) deep coma.

carvi, *n.m.,* (bot.) caraway; caraway-seed.

caryatide. *V.* **cariatide.**

caryophyllée, *adj.,f.,* (bot.) caryophyllous.

caryophyllées, *n.f. pl.,* caryophyllæ.

caryophylloïde, *n.f.,* caryophilloid.

cas, *n.m.,* case, event, esteem, value; needs, concern; (jur., math., gram., med.) case. *Un* — *pendable;* a hanging matter. *Un* — *imprévu;* an unforeseen case. *Un tout en* —; sunshade. *Au* —, *en* — *que cela soit;* in case it should turn out to be. *Auquel* —; in which case. *Le* — *échéant;* if such should be the case; in that case. *En tel* —, *en pareil* —; in such a case. *Hors le* —; unless, except, save. *C'est le* — *de parler;* it is the time to speak out. *Faire grand* — *de quel-qu'un;* to have a great esteem for any one, to value highly. *Faire peu de* —; to make light of. *En tout* —; at all events, however. *En* — *de besoin;* in case of need. *C'est le* — *ou jamais;* it is now or never. *Il n'est pas dans le* — *de vous nuire;* he is not in a position to harm you. *C'est bien le* — *de le dire;* you may indeed well say so. *Un en* —; a snack (in case of need).

casani-er, -ère, *n.* and *adj.,* domestic person; domestic, retired, stay at home, home-bird.

casaque, *n.f.,* great coat, cassock. *Tourner* —; to change sides, to rat.

casaquin, *n.m.,* short gown, jacket.

cascade, *n.f.,* cascade, waterfall; leap, bound. *Un discours plein de* —*s;* a jumbled, jerky speech.

cascarille, *n.f.,* cascarilla.

cascatelle, *n.f.,* cascade (of Tivoli).

case, *n.f.,* division; cabin, dwelling-place, small house, hut; box (for animals); pigeon-hole, compartment; point (backgammon); square (chess, draughts); (nav.) berth.

casé, -e, *part.,* placed. *Le voilà* —; he is provided for.

caséeu-x, -se, *adj.,* caseous, cheesy.

casemate (kaz-mat), *n.f.,* (fort.) casemate; dungeon, cell.

casematé, -e, *adj.,* casemated.

caser, *v.n.,* (backgammon) to make a point.

caser, *v.a.,* to place, to find a place for, to provide for; to arrange, put in order.

se **caser**, *v.r.*, to take up one's abode, one's quarters, to get settled.

caserne, *n.f.*, barracks. — *de pompiers ;* fire-brigade station. *Intendant de —;* barrack-master.

casernement, *n.m.*, quartering in barracks.

caserner, *v.a.*, to quarter in barracks.

caserner, *v.n.*, to be in barracks.

casier, *n.m.*, set of pigeon-holes ; rack, ledger-rack.

***casilleux**, *adj. m.*, brittle.

casimir, *n.m.*, kerseymere cloth.

casino, *n.m.*, casino, club.

casoar, *n.m.*, (orni.) cassowary.

casque, *n.m.*, helmet, casque, head-piece ; (bot.) hood ; (her.) helmet, casque ; (conch.) helmet-shell.

casquette, *n.f.*, cap (of a man or boy).

cassable, *adj.*, breakable.

cassade, *n.f.*, sham, flam ; lie, fib, cheat.

cassage, *n.m.*, breakage.

***cassaille**, *n.f.*, the breaking up (of ground).

cassant, -e, *adj.*, brittle, apt to break ; (of a man) abrupt, bluff, gruff.

cassation, *n.f.*, breaking ; (jur.) annulment, repeal, quashing. *Se pourvoir en —;* to lodge an appeal. *Cour de —;* the highest court of appeal in France.

cassave, *n.f.*, cassava.

casse, *n.f.*, (bot.) cassia ; (print.) case ; (com.) breakage ; ⊙ (milit.) cashiering, dismissal. — *aromatique ;* bastard cinnamon. *Cet officier mérite la —;* that officer deserves to be dismissed the service. *Haut de —;* (print.) upper-case. *Bas de —;* (print.) lower-case. *Apprendre la —;* to learn the boxes.

casseau, *n.m.*, (print.) half-case.

casse-cou, *n.m.*, (—, *or* — —*s*) break-neck ; (man.) rough-rider.

casse-lunettes, *n.m.*, (*plur. —*) (bot.) eye-bright.

casse-mottes, *n.m.*, (*plur. —*) (agri.) clod-breaker.

casse-noisettes, *n.m.*, (*plur. —*) nut-crackers.

casse-noix, *n.m.*, (—) nut-crackers ; (orni.) nut-hatch.

casser, *v.a.*, to break ; to crack ; to cashier ; to waste ; to wear out ; to annul ; to rescind ; to shiver (a mast). *Qui casse les verres les paie or Il faut payer les pots cassés ;* you must stand the racket. — *un jugement ;* to reverse a judgment. *Cassé de vieillesse ;* worn out with old age. *Voix cassée ;* broken voice. *Vous me cassez la tête ;* you bore me to death. — *aux gages ;* to dismiss, to discharge.

se **casser**, *v.r.*, to break ; to break down ; to wear out ; to snap. *Se — la tête ;* to break one's head ; to puzzle one's brains. *Se — le cou ;* to break one's neck. *Se — la jambe ;* to break one's leg.

casser, *v.n.*, to break. *A tout —;* with a vengeance ; at break-neck speed.

casserole, *n.f.*, saucepan, stewpan.

casse-tête, *n.m.*, (—) tomahawk ; puzzle-brain ; heady wine ; din, noise. *Quel —!* what a din !]

cassetin, *n.m.*, (print.) box.

cassette, *n.f.*, casket ; cash-box. *La — du roi ;* the King's privy purse.

casseu-r, *n.m.*, **-se**, *n.f.*, breaker, smasher. *C'est un grand — de raquettes ;* he is a real matador. *Un — d'assiettes ;* a quarrelsome fellow, blusterer, bully.

cassier, *n.m.*, cassia-tree.

cassine, *n.f.*, (milit.) cassine ; country-box ; badly-kept house ; stall, booth.

cassiopée, *n.f.*, (astron.) Cassiopeia.

cassis (kä-sis), *n.m.*, black currant ; black currant-tree ; black-currant ratafia (liquor).

cassolette, *n.f.*, perfuming pan ; scent-box,

fragrant smell ; (b.s.) stench, odor. *Quelle —! what a perfume !*

casson, *n.m.*, fragment of plate-glass ; lump.

cassonade, *n.f.*, moist sugar.

cassure, *n.f.*, broken place ; break, crack, snap ; fracture ; (nav.) hogging.

***castagnette**, *n.f.*, castanet.

caste, *n.f.*, caste.

⊙**castel**, *n.m.*, castle.

***castillan, -e**, *n.* and *adj.*, Castilian.

***castille**, *n.f.*, altercation, bickering, strife.

***castine**, *n.f.*, (metal.) flux.

castor, *n.m.*, (mam.) castor, beaver ; beaver hat ; tile.

castoréum (-om), *n.m.*, (phar.) castoreum.

castorine, *n.f.*, castorine.

castramétation, *n.f.*, castrametation.

castrat, *n.m.*, castrato, castrate.

castration, *n.f.*, castration.

casualité, *n.f.*, (l.u.) casualty, fortuitousness.

casuel, -le, *adj.*, casual, contingent, precarious, fortuitous, accidental.

casuel, *n.m.*, perquisites, extra salary ; fees. *Le — d'une cure ;* surplice fees.

casuellement (-män), *adv.*, casually, accidentally, by chance, fortuitously.

casuiste, *n.m.*, casuist.

catachrèse (-krèz), *n.f.*, (rhet.) catachresis.

cataclysme, *n.m.*, cataclysm, deluge, flood ; (fig.) disaster, overthrow.

catacois. *V.* **cacatois**.

catacombes, *n.f.pl.*, catacombs.

catacoustique, *n.f.*, catacoustics.

catadioptrique, *n.f.*, catadioptrics.

catadioptrique, *adj.*, catadioptrical.

⊙**catadoupe** *or* **catadupe**, *n.f.*, catadupa, cataract, waterfall.

catafalque, *n.m.*, catafalque ; bed of state.

cataire, *adj.*, of a cat, cat-like. *Frémissement* — (med.) ; thrill, purring tremor, of the heart.

cataire, *n.f.*, (bot.) catmint, catnip.

catalan, -e, *n.* and *adj.*, Catalonian.

catalecte *or* **catalectique**, *adj.*, (poet.) catalectic.

catalectes, *n.m. pl.*, (lit.) catalectics.

catalepsie, *n.f.*, catalepsy.

cataleptique, *adj.*, cataleptic.

catalogue (-log), *n.m.*, list, enumeration, catalogue.

cataloguer (-ghé), *v.a.*, to catalogue.

catalpa, *n.m.*, (bot.) catalpa.

cataplasme, *n.m.*, cataplasm, poultice.

catapuce, *n.f.*, (bot.) caper-spurge.

catapulte, *n.f.*, (antiq.) catapult.

cataracte, *n.f.*, cataract ; waterfall ; (med.) cataract.

cataracté, -e, *adj.*, (med.) afflicted with a cataract.

se **cataracter**, *v.r.*, to have an incipient cataract.

catarrhal, -e, *adj.*, (med.) catarrhal.

catarrhe, *n.m.*, catarrh, cold. — *d'été ;* hay-fever.

catarrheu-x, -se, *adj.*, (med.) catarrhous.

catastrophe, *n.f.*, catastrophe, calamity.

catéchiser, *v.a.*, to catechise ; to reason with ; to lecture ; to give anyone his cue ; to coach up.

catéchisme, *n.m.*, catechism. *Faire le — à quelqu'un ;* to give anyone his cue.

catéchiste, *n.m.*, catechist.

catéchuménat (-ku-), *n.m.*, catechumenate.

catéchumène (-ku-), *n.m.f.*, catechumen.

catégorie, *n.f.*, category, predicament.

catégorique, *adj.*, categorical, proper, explicit.

catégoriquement (-rik-män), *adv.*, categorically, to the purpose.

catégoriser, *v.a.*, to class.

⊙**caterve**, *n.f.*, troop, band.

cathartine, *n.f.*, cathartine.

cathartique, *n.m.* and *adj.*, cathartic, purgative.

ex **cathédra**, with high authority.

cathédrale, *n.* and *adj. f.*, cathedral; cathedral church.

cathédrant, *n.m.*, president (over a thesis).

cathérétique, *adj.*, (pharm.) caustic.

cathéter (-tèr), *n.m.*, (surg.) catheter.

cathétérisme, *n.m.*, (surg.) catheterism.

catholicisme, *n.m.*, Catholicism.

catholicité, *n.f.*, Catholicity; Catholic countries.

catholicon, *n.m.*, (phar.) catholicon.

catholique, *adj.*, Catholic, moral, orthodox. *Cela n'est pas —;* that is not orthodox.

catholique, *n.m.f.*, Catholic. *Un — à gros grains;* a lax Catholic.

catholiquement (-măn), *adv.*, in a catholic way.

cati, *n.m.*, pressing, gloss, lustre.

cati, *adj.*, pressed.

en **catimini**, *adv.*, slily, stealthily.

catin, *n.f.*, (l.ex.) harlot, strumpet.

catir, *v.a.*, to give a gloss to. *— à chaud;* to hot-press. *— à froid;* to cold-press.

catissage, *n.m.*, glossing, pressing.

catisseur, *n.m.*, presser.

catmarin, *n.m.*, (ornith.) red-throated diver.

catodon, *n.m.*, catodon, a species of whale.

catogan *or* **cadogan**, *n.m.*, club of hair.

catoptrique, *n.f.*, catoptrics.

catoptromancie, *n.f.*, catoptromancy.

caucasique, *adj.*, (geog.) Caucasian.

cauchemar (kosh-mar), *n.m.*, nightmare, incubus. *Il donn lc —;* he tires one to death.

caucher, *n.m.*, vellum-mold.

cauchois, -e, *adj.*, of Caux.

caudataire, *n.m.*, the train-bearer.

caudé, -e, *adj.*, (her.) caudated, tailed.

⊙**caudebec**, *n.m.*, woolen French hat.

caudex (kô-dèks), *n.m.*, stem of a tree.

caudicule, *n.f.*, (bot.) caudicle.

caudines, *adj.f.pl.*, caudine.

caulicoles, *n.f.pl.*, (arch.) caulicole.

caulinaire, *adj.*, (bot.) cauline.

cauris, *n.m.*, cowry.

causal, -e, *adj.*, causal.

causalité, *n.f.*, causality.

causant, -e, *adj.*, chatty, talkative.

causati-f, -ve, *adj.*, (gram.) causative.

causation, *n.f.*, causation.

causativement, *adv.*, causatively.

cause, *n.f.*, cause; grounds, motive; subject; case, trial, brief. *—s éloignées;* remote causes. *Prendre fait et — pour quelqu'un;* to espouse any one's cause; to side with; to stand by. *—appelée, remise;* cause called in court, put off. *—embrouillée, douteuse;* intricate, doubtful case. *Donner gain de — à;* to decide in favor of. *Avoir gain de —;* to gain the day. *Etre hors de —;* not to be concerned in a law-suit. *Mettre hors de —;* to dismiss the parties (to a suit); (fig.) to free from blame; to put out of the question. *Etre condamné sans connaissance de —;* to be cast without a hearing. *Ses héritiers ou ayants —;* his heirs or assigns. *Un avocat sans —;* a briefless barrister. *Parler avec connaissance de —;* to speak from a knowledge of the case. *Etre la —innocente,* or *involontaire, d'un accident;* to be the harmless, *or* involuntary, cause of an accident. *Il ne le fera pas, et pour —;* he won't do it, and for a very good reason. *A ces —s;* (jur.) these reasons moving us thereunto. *A — de;* for the sake of, on account of, because of, for. *A — de quoi?* why? wherefore? for what reason? *A — que;* because.

causer, *v.a.*, to cause, to be the cause of, to occasion, to give rise to.

causer, *v.n.*, to chat, to talk, to prate. *— de choses et d'autres;* to talk of one thing and another. *— de la pluie et du beau temps;* to talk about the weather. *—littérature, voyages;* to talk about literature, travels. *Vous aurez causé;* you have been babbling.

causerie (kôz-rî), *n.f.*, talk, chat, gossip.

causette, *n.f.*, chit-chat. *Faire la —;* to have a chat.

causou-r, -se, *adj.*, talkative, chatty.

causeu-r, *n.m.*, **-se**, *n.f.*, talker, conversationalist.

causeuse, *n.f.*, small sofa, settee.

causticité, *n.f.*, causticity.

caustique, *adj.*, biting, cutting, caustic.

caustique, *n.m.*, caustic, biting, cutting.

caustique, *n.f.*, (geom., phys.) caustic curve.

caustiquement, *adv.*, caustically, cuttingly.

cauteleusement (kôt-leûz-măn), *adv.*, craftily, slyly.

cauteleu-x, -se (kôt-leû), *adj.*, cunning, crafty.

cautère, *n.m.*, (med.) issue, cautery; (vet.) firing-iron. *Panser un —;* to dress a cautery. *Pois à —;* issue peas.

⊙**cautérétique**. *V.* **cathérétique**.

cautérisation, *n.f.*, cauterization.

cautériser, *v.a.*, to cauterize, to sear, to burn.

caution, *n.f.*, surety, security, bail, pledge. *— légale;* common bail. *— solvable;* special bail. *Un homme sujet à —;* a man not to be trusted.

cautionné, -e, *part.*, bailed; (of things) suspicious, doubtful.

cautionnement (kô-sio-n-măn), *n.m.*, bailing, bail, caution-money; security.

cautionner, *v.a.*, to stand bail for any one, to stand surety for.

cavage, *n.m.*, hollowing out, digging; cellarage.

cavalcade, *n.f.*, ride, cavalcado.

⊙**cavalcadour**, *n.m.*, riding-master, equerry, master of the horse.

cavale, *n.f.*, mare, steed.

cavalerie (ka-val-rî), *n.f.*, cavalry, horse.

cavalier, *n.m.*, horseman; rider, cavalier; trooper; gentleman, gallant; (dancing) partner; knight (at chess); (fort.) cavalier; (man.) rider; (mec.) spoil-bank. *Servir de — à une dame;* to escort a lady.

cavali-er, -ère, *adj.*, cavalier, free, proud, haughty, unceremonious.

cavalièrement (-măn), *adv.*, cavalierly, bluntly, unceremoniously.

cavatine, *n.f.*, (mus.) cavatina.

cave, *n.f.*, cellar, vault, cellarage; boot (of a coach); case of bottles, cellaret; (cards) pool, stock. *Rat de —;* twisted taper. *Rats de —;* excisemen.

cave, *adj.*, hollow, sunken. *Œil —;* hollow eye. *Lune —;* lunar month of 29 days. *Année —;* lunar year (353 days).

caveau, *n.m.*, small cellar; vault (in a church).

cavecé, -e, *adj.*, with a black head (of a roan horse or mare). *Cheval rouan — de noir;* roan horse with a black head.

caveçon, *n.m.*, (man.) cavezon, curb. *Il a besoin de —;* he wants curbing.

cavée, *n.f.*, (hunt.) hollow way.

caver, *v.a.*, to hollow, to make hollow, to scoop out, to dig under; to hollow (running); to stake (at play). *— au plus fort;* to play deep; to carry things to extremes.

se **caver**, *v.r.*, to become hollow or sunken; to stake.

caverne, *n.f.*, cavern; cave, hollow, den.

caverneu-x, -se, *adj.*, hollow, sepulchral; (anat.) cavernous, spongy. *Voix —se;* hollow voice.

cavet, *n.m.*, (arch.) cavetto.

caviar, *n.m.*, (cook.) caviar, caviare.

cavillation (-vil-la-), *n.f.*, sophistry, cavil, cavilling.

caviste, *n.m.*, cellarer, cellar man.

cavité, *n.f.,* cavity, hollow.

ce, cet, *m.,* **cette,** *f.,* **ces,** *pl.,* demonst. adj., this, these; that, those. *Ce livre;* this *or* that book. *Ce héros;* this *or* that hero. *Cet arbre;* this *or* that tree. *Cet homme;* this *or* that man. *Cette femme;* this *or* that woman. *Ces livres;* these *or* those books. *Ce livre-ci;* this book. *Ce livre-là;* that book.

ce, demonst. pron., he, she, it; they. *J'aime votre frère, c'est un bon ami;* I love your brother, he is a good friend. *Lisez Racine et Boileau, ce sont de grands poètes;* read Racine and Boileau, they are great poets.

ce (for *cela*), it, that; he, she, they. *C'est fait;* it is done. *C'est fort bien fait;* that's very well done. *C'en est fait de moi;* it is all up with me. *C'en est fait;* it is all over, it is done. *C'est bien fait;* it serves him right. *Et ce, pour cause;* and this for a good reason. *Je lui ai dit telle chose, et ce pour le persuader de le faire;* I told him such a thing, and it was to persuade him to do it. *Qui est-ce?* who is he? *Qui était-ce?* who was it? *Qui sera-ce?* who will it be? *Qui est-ce qui arrive là?* who is coming there? *Est-ce moi?* is it I? *Est-ce lui?* is it he? *Est-ce nous qu'il menace?* is it towards us his threats are directed? *Est-ce eux que vous prétendez soumettre?* is it they you pretend to subdue? *Sont-ce les Anglais?* is it the English? *C'est vous qu'on demande;* it is you who are wanted. *Ce sont eux que j'ai vus;* it is they I have seen. *Sont-ce là les dames que vous attendiez?* are these the ladies you expected? *Oui, ces ont elles;* yes, they are. *C'était eux, ce furent eux, ce sera nous, ce sera vous autres, ce sera eux, ce serait eux;* it was they, &c. *Qu'est-ce?* what is that? *Qu'est-ce que je vois là-bas?* what do I see yonder? *Sont-ce là vos raisons?* are those your reasons? *Est-ce là votre carrosse?* is that your coach? *Oui, ce l'est;* yes, it is. *Sont-ce là vos chevaux?* are these your horses? *Oui, ce les sont;* yes, they are. *Quel jour est-ce aujourd'hui?* what day is it to-day? *C'est jeudi;* it is Thursday. *Quand sera-ce?* when will it be? *Ce sera pour demain;* it will be for to-morrow.

ce qui, que, dont, à quoi; that, which, what, of what, to what, *Je ne sais ce que nous deviendrons;* I do not know what will become of us. *Ce qui se passe;* what happens. *Ce que je vous dit;* what I tell you. *Faites ce dont je vous ai parlé;* do what I told you of. *Ce qui réussit est toujours approuvé;* what meets with success always meets with approbation. *C'est ce que je disais;* it is what I said. *Ce que j'ai vu de beau;* the fine things I saw. *Tout ce qu'on fait de mauvais;* all the mischief that is done. *Savez-vous à quoi il pense?* do you know what he is thinking of?

ce qui *or* **ce que,** serve for two verbs, the latter of which, when *ce* begins the sentence, is governed by *ce:* if the latter verb is *être,* followed by *que* or *de, ce* must be repeated before it. *Ce que je crains, c'est d'être surpris;* what I fear is to be surprised. *Ce qu'il demande, c'est une pension;* what he asks for is a pension. [But *ce* cannot be repeated when *être* is followed by an adjective.] *Ce qu'on vous a dit est vrai;* what you have been told is true. *Ce qu'on vous a dit, ce sont des contes;* what you have been told are mere idle tales. *C'était un grand capitaine que César;* Cæsar was a great captain. *Sont-ce les richesses qui vous rendront heureux?* can riches make you happy? *C'est moi qu'on veut perdre;* I am the man they wish to ruin. *C'est à vous que je parle;* it is to you I speak. *C'est d'elle que je parle;* it is of her that I speak. *C'est là que je les attends;* there I shall have them. *C'est un bonheur que d'avoir échappé;* it is good luck to have escaped. *C'était à vous de parler;* it was your duty to speak. *C'était à vous à par-*

ler; it was your turn to speak. *Si c'était à refaire;* if it were to be done again. *C'est à qui parlera;* they vie with one another as to who shall speak. *C'était à qui s'offrirait;* they vied with one another as to who would offer himself. *Ce serait pour moi un grand plaisir;* it would give me great pleasure. *Ce n'est pas qu'il la craigne, mais il aime la paix;* not that he fears her, but he loves peace. *Ces malheureux ne savent ce que c'est que la vertu;* these wretches know not what virtue is. *C'est-à-dire;* that is to say. *Ce n'est pas à dire que;* it does not follow that. *C'est pourquoi;* therefore, wherefore, for which reason. *C'est que;* you must know; I must tell you. *Ce que c'est que de nous!* what poor mortals we are.

céans, *adv.,* within, here within, in this house, home. *Maître de—;* master of the house. *Il dînera—;* he will dine at home.

ceci, demonst. pron., this. *Que veut dire—?* what does this mean? *C'est—, c'est cela;* it is first one thing and then another.

cécité, *n.f.,* blindness. *Frapper de—;* to strike blind.

cédant, *n.m.,* **-e,** *n.f.,* (jur.) grantor; assignor, transferrer.

cédant, -e, *adj.,* that assigns, transfers; that grants.

céder, *v.a.,* to give, to give up, to yield, to transfer; to sell, to part with, to make over. *— le pas à quelqu'un;* to give precedence to any one. *— le haut du pavé;* to give the wall.

céder, *v.n.,* to give way, to give; to submit; to give in. *Il faut—;* we must submit. *— à son penchant;* to give way to one's inclinations. *Je lui cède en tout;* I give in to him in everything. *Ne le—à personne;* to yield to no one; to be second to none. *La porte céda;* the door gave way.

*****cédille,** *n.f.* (gram.) cedilla.

cédrat, *n.m.,* (bot.) (tree) cedrate, lemon-tree; (fruit) lemon.

cédratier, *n.m.,* (bot.) cedrate, lemon-tree.

cèdre, *n.m.,* cedar; cedar of Lebanon.

cédrie, *n.f.,* cedrie, cedar-resin.

cédule, *n.f.,* (jur.) cedule, schedule, memorandum, notice; note of hand.

ceindre (ceignant, ceint), *v.a.,* to enclose, to encompass, to surround, to bind; to fence; to gird on, to put on, to encircle. *Une corde lui ceignait les reins;* his loins were girt with a cord. *— le diadème;* to put on the diadem.

se ceindre, *v.r.,* to bind round one; to encircle one's brow with anything.

ceintrage, *n.m.,* (nav.) frapping, swifting (of rigging).

ceintrer, *v.a.,* (nav.) to frap, to gird. *—un vaisseau;* to frap a ship.

ceinture, *n.f.,* sash, girdle, belt; waist-band, waist-ribbon; the waist; enclosure, circle; (arch.) cincture (of a column), molding; (nav.) swifter. *Bonne renommée vaut mieux que — dorée;* a good name is better than riches. *— de deuil;* funeral hangings. *Chemin de fer de—;* circular railway.

ceinturé, -e, *adj.,* confined, girt; wearing a sash.

ceinturer, *v.a.,* to girdle, to girt.

ceinturier, *n.m.,* girdle-maker, belt-maker.

ceinturon, *n.m.,* belt, sword-belt.

cela, demonst. pron., that. *— est vrai;* that is true. *Comment —?* how so? *C'est—;* that's it. *Ce n'est pas—;* that 's not it, that will not do. *N'est-ce que—?* is that all? *Comme—;* so so. *Il est comme—;* it is his way, it is just like him. *C'est — même;* that 's the very thing. *Par — même;* for that very reason. *Pour — oui;* most certainly. *Pour — non;* certainly not.

céladon, *adj., m.,* sea-green (color). *Ruban —;* sea-green ribbon.

céladon, *n.m.*, sea-green (color) ; sentimental lover ; old beau.

célébrant, *n.m.*, officiating priest at mass.

célébration, *n.f.*, solemn performance, celebration.

célèbre, *adj.*, celebrated, famous, renowned ; eminent, distinguished.

célébrer, *v.a.*, to praise, to extol, to sing, to solemnize ; to glorify, to celebrate, to record.

célébrité, *n.f.*, celebrity ; fame.

celer or **céler**, *v.a.*, to conceal, to keep close or secret, to secrete. *Se faire* —; *to say* ``not at home.''

céleri (sèl-ri), *n.m.*, celery. *Botte de* —; bundle of celery.

célérité, *n.f.*, celerity, rapidity, dispatch, speed.

céleste, *adj.*, celestial, heavenly, divine. *Bleu* —; sky-blue. *La colère* —; the anger of heaven.

célestin, *n.m.*, celestin (monk — *moine*).

céliaque, *adj.*, (anat.) cœliac.

célibat, *n.m.*, celibacy, single life; single state. *Femme, homme, dans le* —; single woman, single man.

célibataire, *n.m.*, single man, bachelor.

celle, *demonst. pron. ;* she, that. *V.* **celui**.

⊙**celle**, *n.f.*, cell (of a hermit).

cellér-ier, *n.m.*, -**ière**, *n.f.*, cellarer.

cellier, *n.m.*, cellar, store-room.

cellulaire, *adj.*, cellular.

cellule, *n.f.*, cell, partition; cell (of honey).

celluleu-x, **-se**, *adj.*, cellular.

célosie, *n.f.*, (bot.) cock's-comb; coxcomb.

celte, *n.m.*, Celt.

celtique, *adj.*, Celtic.

celtique, *n.m.*, Celtic language.

celui, *m.*, **celle**, *f.*, **ceux**, **celles**, *pl.*, *demonst. pron.*, he, him; she, her, they, them; that, those. *Ceux qui ont vécu avant nous ;* those who lived before us.

celui-ci, **celle-ci**, *sing.*, **ceux-ci**, **celles-ci**, *pl.*, *demonst. pron. ;* this, these.

celui-là, **celle-là**, *sing.*, **ceux-là**, **celles-là**, *pl.*, *demonst. pron. ;* that, those. *Aimez-vous mieux celui-ci ?* do you like this best ? *Celui-là n'est pas si beau ;* that one is not so fine. *Celui-ci est meilleur que celui-là ;* this is better than that. [*Celui-ci* relates to an object near the speaker; *celui-là*, to an object distant from him; or after two nouns already expressed, *celui-ci* refers to the last, *celui-là* to the first mentioned.]

cément, *n.m.*, cement.

cémentation, *n.f.*, cementation.

cémentatoire, *adj.*, cementatory.

cémenter, *v.a.*, to cement.

cénacle, *n.m.*, (antiq.) guest-chamber (where the Lord's supper was taken) ; (fig.) club, literary coterie.

cendre, *n.f.*, ashes ; embers ; cinder ; dust, ashes (of the dead). *C'est un feu qui couve sous la* —; it is a smoldering fire. *La* —, *les* —*s des morts ;* the ashes of the dead.

cendres, *n.f. pl.*, ashes. — *ardentes ;* live embers. — *qui couvent ;* smoldering ashes. *Le mercredi des* —; Ash-Wednesday. *Mettre en* —; to lay in ashes. *Renaître de ses* —; to rise from one's ashes.

cendré, **-e**, *adj.*, ashy. *Gris* —; ashy gray, pale gray. *Lumière* —; earth-shine.

cendrée, *n.f.*, small shot.

cendreu-x, **-se**, *adj.*, ashy, full of, or covered with, ashes.

cendrer, *v.a.*, to paint ash-gray, to ash.

cendrier, *n.m.*, ash-pan, cinder-pail ; ash-hole ; ash-tray.

***cendrille**, *n.f.*, (orni.) tomtit.

cène, *n.f.*, the Lord's supper, communion.

cenelle, *n.f.*, (bot.) haw.

cénobite, *n.m.*, cenobite, monk.

cénobitique, *adj.*, cenobitical.

cénotaphe, *n.m.*, cenotaph.

cens (sâns), *n.m.*, cense, quit-rent ; census, franchise, rating.

censable, *adj.*, owner of quit-rent. *Seigneur* —; lord of the manor.

⊙**cense**, *n.f.*, farm, fee-farm.

censé, **-e**, *adj.*, accounted, deemed, reputed, supposed, pretended. *Il est — être ;* he is supposed to be.

censéable, *adj.*, liable to quit-rent.

censeur, *n.m.*, censor ; censurer ; critic ; censor of the press ; examiner of plays ; proctor.

⊙**censier**, *adj. m.*, of quit-rent.

censi-er, *n.m.*, -**ère**, *n.f.*, farmer ; rent-roll.

censitaire, *n.m.*, copy-holder.

censive, *n.f.*, quit-rent, manor.

censorial, **-o**, *adj.*, censorial.

censuel, **-le**, *adj.*, feudal, of quit-rent.

censurable, *adj.*, censurable.

censure, *n.f.*, censorship ; censure, criticism ; reproof ; ecclesiastical censure ; the censors.

censurer, *v.a.*, to find fault with ; to blame, to censure, to condemn.

cent, *adj.*, hundred, cent. — *un ans ;* one hundred and one years. *Cinq pour* —; five per cent. *Je vous le donne en* —; it's 100 to 1 against your guessing it. [*Cent* takes the sign of the plural, if preceded and multiplied, but not followed, by a number: *trois cents ; trois cent cinquante.*] *Les* — *Jours ;* the Hundred days (from March 20th to end of June, 1815).

centaine, *n.f.*, a hundred ; a hundred, or so ; thread that ties up a skein. *V.* **sentène**.

centaure, *n.m.*, (myth., astron.) centaur.

centaurée, *n.f.*, (bot.) centaury.

centenaire, *adj.*, centenary, secular, of a hundred years' standing, centennial.

centenaire, *n.m.f.*, centenarian.

centenier, *n.m.*, centurion (in the Channel Isles) ; sergeant of police.

centésimal, **-e**, *adj.*, centesimal.

centiare, *n.m.*, the hundredth part of an are (square yard 1.1960).

centième, *adj.*, hundredth.

centième, *n.m.*, the hundredth part.

centigrade, *adj.*, centigrade.

centigramme, *n.m.*, the hundredth part of a gram (grain 0.1543).

centilitre, *n.m.*, the hundredth part of a liter (cubic inch 0.61028).

centime, *n.m.*, the hundredth part of a franc (cent 0.193).

centimètre, *n.m.*, the hundredth part of a meter (inch 0.39371).

centinode, *n.f.*, centinody, knot-grass.

centipède, *adj.*, centipedal ; *n.m.*, centipede.

centon, *n.m.*, (lit.) cento.

central, **-e**, *adj.*, central, chief, head.

centralisat-eur, **-rice**, *adj.*, centralizing.

centralisation, *n.f.*, centralization.

centraliser, *v.a.*, to centralize.

se **centraliser**, *v.r.*, to become centralized.

centre, *n.m.*, center, middle. *Chaque chose tend à son* —; everything converged to its center. *Etre dans son* —; to be in one's element.

centrifuge, *adj.*, centrifugal.

centripète, *adj.*, centripetal.

centrisque, *n.m.*, (ich.) centriscus, trumpet-fish.

cent-suisse, *n.m.*, one of the hundred that formed the body-guard to the king of France. *Les* —*s ;* the hundred Swiss guards.

centumvir, *n.m.*, centumvir.

centumviral, **-e**, *adj.*, centumviral.

centumvirat, *n.m.*, centumvirate.

centuple, *n.m.*, centuple, hundred-fold.

centuple, *adj.*, a hundred-fold.

centupler, *v.a.*, to increase a hundred-fold, to centuple.

centuriateur, *n.m.*, (ecc. lit.) centuriator.

centurie, *n.f.*, (antiq., ecc.) century; hundred (territorial division).

centurion, *n.m.*, centurion.

cep, *n.m.*, vine-stock, vine-stalk, vine-plant.

cépage, *n.m.*, vine-slip, vines. *Les —s de la Bourgogne;* the vines of Burgundy.

cèpe, *n.m.*, (bot.) esculent boletus.

cépée, *n.f.*, (agri.) tuft of shoots from the same stump; (hunt.) young wood; a wood of one or two years' growth.

cependant, *adv.*, in the mean time, meanwhile; however, nevertheless; yet, still.

cependant, *conj.*, yet, and yet.

céphalalgie, *n.f.*, cephalalgy, headache.

céphalée, *n.f.*, (med.) headache.

céphalique, *adj.*, (med.) cephalic.

céphalète, *n.f.*, (med.) cephalitis.

céphée, *n.m.* (astron.) Cepheus.

cérame, *n.f.*, Greek vase.

céramique, *adj.*, ceramic, fictile.

céramique, *n.f.*, fictile art, molding.

céraste, *n.m.*, cerastes, horned viper.

cérat, *n.m.*, ointment, salve.

cerbère, *n.m.*, (myth.) Cerberus.

cerce, *n.f.*, hoop, band, binding.

cerceau, *n.m.*, hoop, ring; hoop-net; pinion-quill. *Faire courir un —;* to trundle a hoop.

cercelle, *n.f.*, water-fowl, teal.

cerclage, *n.m.*, hooping (of casks, &c.).

cercle, *n.m.*, circle, sphere, round, ring, orb, hoop; club, company; binding-hoop. *Un quart d' —;* a quadrant. *Un demi-cercle;* a semicircle. *Décrire, former, un —;* to describe, to form, a circle. *— vicieux;* arguing in a circle; begging the question.

cercler, *v.a.*, to bind with hoops, to hoop.

cerclier, *n.m.*, hoop-maker.

*cercueil (-keu-), *n.m.*, coffin; (fig.) grave, tomb. *— de bois;* shell. *Mettre au —;* to bring to the grave.

céréale, *adj.*, cereal, corn.

céréales, *n.f. pl.*, corn, grain, corn crops, cerealia. *Commerce des —;* corn-trade, breadstuffs.

cérébral, -e, *adj.*, cerebral, brain. *Fièvre —e;* brain fever.

cérébrite, *n.f.*, (med.) inflammation of the brain.

cérémonial, *n. m.*, ceremonial; ceremony, ceremonies, etiquette, state.

cérémoniaire, *n.m.*, master of the ceremonies.

cérémonie, *n.f.*, ceremony; (biblical) ceremonial; fuss, ado. *Visite de —;* formal visit. *Faire des —s;* to stand upon ceremonies. *En grande —;* in state.

cérémonieu-x, -se, *adj.*, ceremonious, formal, precise.

cérès, *n.f.*, (myth., astron.) Ceres; (fig.) harvest, corn.

cerf (sèr), *n.m.*, stag, hart, deer. *— commun;* red-deer. *Un bois de —;* the horns of a stag. *Corne de —;* hartshorn.

*cerfeuil, *n.m.*, (bot.) chervil. *— musqué;* sweet cicely.

cerf-volant (sèrvo-) *n.m.*, (—s- —s) (ent.) stag-beetle, bull-fly; kite, paper-kite.

cerisaie, *n.f.*, cherry-orchard.

cerise, *n.f.*, cherry; (of coffee) berry.

cerise, *n.m.*, cherry-color, cerise.

cerisier, *n.m.*, (bot.) cherry-tree, cherry-wood.

cerne, *n.m.*, (bot.) ring.

cerneau, *n.m.*, kernel of a green walnut; green walnut.

cerner, *v.a.*, to cut or dig round (a tree); to surround, to encompass, to hem in; to take the kernel out of green walnuts; (arch.) to gird; (milit.) to invest. *Des yeux cernés;* eyes with dark circles round them.

cérocome, *n.m.*, (ent.) cerocoma.

céroxyle, *n.m.*, (bot.) wax-palm, wax-tree.

cerre, *n.m.*, bitter-oak.

certain, -e, *adj.*, certain, sure, positive, undoubted; resolved, fixed, determined; some, certain. *C'est un homme d'un — mérite;* he is a man of some merit. *A —es époques de l'année;* at certain periods of the year. *Dans —s cas;* in certain cases. *Un — personnage;* a certain personage.

certain, *n.m.*, certainty; certain; (exchange language) certain price. *Il ne faut pas quitter le — pour l'incertain;* we must not quit a certainty for an uncertainty.

certainement (-mān), *adv.*, certainly, assuredly, without fail, indeed, surely, infallibly.

certes, *adv.*, indeed, most certainly.

certificat, *n.m.*, certificate, testimonial. *— de vie;* attestation, affidavit of existence.

certificateur, *n.m.*, (jur.) certifier, voucher.

certification, *n.f.*, certifying, vouching; witnessing.

certifier, *v.a.*, to certify, to testify, to attest, to aver. *— une caution;* to guarantee that bail is valid. *— véritable;* to witness (a signature).

certitude, *n.f.*, certitude, certainty; assurance, steadiness. *Avoir la —;* to be certain.

cérumen (-mèn), *n.m.*, cerumen, ear-wax.

cérumineu-x, -se, *adj.*, waxy, ceruminous.

céruse, *n.f.*, ceruse, white lead.

cervaison, *n.f.*, (hunt.) stag-season.

cerveau, *n. m.*, brain; mind; intelligence. *Rhume de —;* cold in the head. *— brûlé;* disordered brain. *Avoir le — creux;* to be crack-brained, visionary. *Etre pris du —;* to have a cold in one's head. *Se brûler le —;* to blow out one's brains.

cervelas, *n.m.*, saveloy, Bologna sausage.

cervelet, *n.m.*, (anat.) cerebellum.

cervelle, *n.f.*, brains; head; mind; pith (of palm-trees). *Se brûler la —;* to blow out one's brains. *Cela lui tourne la —;* that turns his head. *Se creuser la —;* to puzzle one's brains. *Tenir en —;* to keep in suspense.

cervical, -e, *adj.*, (anat.) cervical.

cervier. *V.* **loup-cervier.**

cervoise, *n.f.*, a sort of beer, ale.

césar, *n.m.*, Cæsar; emperor, prince, conqueror.

césarien, -ne (-è-n), *adj.*, Cesarean.

césarisme, *n.m.*, Cæsarism.

cessant, -e, *adj.*, ceasing. *Toute affaire —e;* to the suspension of all other business.

cessation, *n.f.*, cessation, suspension, intermission, discontinuance, stoppage.

cesse, *n.f.*, ceasing, intermission, rest, respite. *Parler sans —;* to talk for ever.

cesser, *v.n.*, to cease, to leave off, to forbear, to discontinue, to give over, to be at an end, to have done, to intermit, to end. *Il ne cesse de pleurer;* he never leaves off crying. *Faire —;* to put a stop to, *or* an end to.

cesser, *v.a.*, to cease, to leave off; to intermit; to break off. *— ses payments;* (com.) to stop payment.

cessible, *adj.*, (jur., com.) transferable, assignable.

cession, *n.f.*, transfer, assignment (of property); yielding up, relinquishment; surrender.

cessionnaire, *n.m.*, grantee; assignee, transferee.

ceste, *n.m.*, (antiq., myth.) cestus, gauntlet; whirl-bat.

césure, *n.f.*, cesura, pause, rest.

cet, cette. *V.* **ce.**

cétacé, -e, *adj.*, cetaceous.

cétacé, *n.m.*, cetaceous animal.

cétérac, *n.m.*, (bot.) ceterach.

cétine, *n.f.*, pure spermaceti, cetine.

cétoine, *n.f.*, (ent.) floral-beetle.

chable, *n.m.*, rope, tackle, tow-line.

chabler, *v.a.*, to fasten a cable to a piece of

timber; to lash, to fasten to a cable. — *les noyers*; to knock down walnuts with a pole.

chableur, *n.m.*, water-bailiff.

chablis, *n.m.*, wind-fallen wood, dead-wood; chablis (white wine).

chaboisseau, *n.m.*, sea-scorpion.

chabot, *n.m.*, (ich.) miller's-thumb, bull-head.

chabraque, *n.f.* V. **schabraque**.

chacal, *n.m.*, jackal.

chaconne, *n.f.*, chacone (dance tune).

chacun, **-e**, *pron.*, everyone, each. — *veut être heureux*; everybody wishes to be happy. — *en parle*; everybody speaks of it. *Rendre à* — *ce qui lui appartient*; to return everyone his own. — *vit à sa guise*; everyone lives as he likes. — *le sien, n'est pas trop*; everyone his own. — *a sa marotte*; every man has his hobby. — *pour soi*; everyone for himself. — *à son tour*; each in his turn. *Ils s'en retournèrent — chez eux*; each of them returned to his own home. *Vous danserez — à votre tour*; you will dance each in your turn. *Ils auront — leur part*; each of them will have his share. *Donnez à — sa part*; give everyone his share. *Tous les membres ont voté — selon ses instructions*; every member voted according to his instructions.

⊙**chacunière**, *n.m.*, one's own house.

chafouin, **-e**, *adj.*, sorry, mean-looking, pitiful, scrubby-looking.

chafouin, *n.m.*, **-e**, *n.f.*, pitiful object; poor wretch.

chagrin, *n.m.*, sorrow, grief, vexation, trouble, concern, regret; fretfulness, peevishness, chagrin; shagreen (leather). *Mourir de* — ; to die of a broken heart. *Demi* — , half-bound.

chagrin, **-e**, *adj.*, gloomy, melancholy, sad, dull, fretful, peevish, waspish, discontented, sullen, cross, morose.

chagrinant, **-e**, *adj.*, sorrowful, sad; vexatious, provoking, troublesome.

⊙**chagrinement** (-mān), *adv.*, sorrowfully; peevishly, fretfully.

chagriner, *v.a.*, to render gloomy, to grieve, to vex, to afflict, to cross, to trouble, to perplex, to disquiet; to shagreen (skins).

se **chagriner**, *v.r.*, to fret, to vex one's self, to grieve, to take on.

chagrinier, *n.m.*, shagreen-maker.

chahut, *n.m.*, vulgar dance; row, shindy.

chahuter, *v.n.*, to make a row, kick up a shindy.

chai, *n.m.*, wine store (above ground).

chaîne, *n.f.*, chain, shackle, cord; galleys, chain of galley-slaves; belting-course (for walls); bonds, bondage; drag-chain (of canals); warp (weaving); drag-chain (of canals); warp chain; (dancing) right and left. — *longue*; watch guard. — *de gilet*; Albert chain. — *de sûreté*; coupling-chain. *Charger quelqu'un de* —*s*; to load with fetters. — *de montagnes*; long ridge of mountains. *La — des idées*; the chain of ideas. *Attacher avec des* —*s*; to chain up. *Tendre des* —*s*; to lay chains across. *A la* — ; chained up. *Faire la* — (in a fire); to form in line; to pass buckets from hand to hand.

chaînetier (shên-tié), *n.m.*, chain-maker.

chaînette, *n.f.*, little chain; (arch.) catenary arch.

chaînon, *n.m.*, link.

chair, *n.f.*, flesh, meat; skin (of a person). *pl.*, (paint.) flesh. — *vive*; quick flesh. — *morte*; dead skin. — *ferme, molle*; firm, soft, flesh. —*s baveuses*; (med.) proud flesh. — *blanche*; white meat. — *noire*; game. — *de poule*; goose-flesh, (med.) *cutis anseris. J'en ai la —de poule*; I shudder at the thought, it makes my flesh creep. *Un morceau de* — ; a piece of meat. *La — d'un poisson*; the fleshy part of a fish. *Couleur de* — ; flesh-color. *Convoitises de la* — ; the lusts of the flesh. *Le Verbe s'est*

fait — ; the Word was made flesh. *La résurrection de la* — ; the resurrection of the body. *Pester entre cuir et* — ; to keep one's ill humor to one's self. *Hacher menu comme — à pâté*; to make mince meat of. *Ni — ni poisson*; neither fish, flesh nor fowl. *En — et en os*; in flesh and blood.

chaire, *n.f.*, pulpit; professorship; desk (in churches); bishop's throne. *Monter en* — ; to mount the pulpit. — *apostolique*; apostolic see. — *curule*; curule chair. — *de droit*; professorship of law.

chaise, *n.f.*, chair, seat; (carp.) timber-work, frame; curb; chaise (carriage). — *à dos*; high-backed chair. — *de paille*; straw-bottomed chair. — *percée*; close-stool. — *brisée*; folding chair. — *à deux chevaux*; chaise and pair. — *à bascule*; rocking-chair. — *à porteurs*; sedan-chair. — *longue*; lounging-chair; couch.

chaisier, *n.m.*, chair-maker; **chaisière**, *n.f.*, chair-letter.

chako, *n.m.* V. **shako**.

chaland, *n.m.*, **-e**, *n.f.*, customer, purchaser.

chaland, *n.m.*, (nav.) lighter, barge.

chalandeau, *n.m.*, lighterman, bargeman.

⊙**chalandise**, *n.f.*, custom.

chalastique (ka-), *adj.*, (med.) chalastic.

chalcédoine. V. **calcédoine**.

chalcite (kalsit), *n.m.*, (chem.) chalcite.

chalcographe (kal-), *n.m.*, chalcographer, engraver on brass.

chalcographie (kal-), *n.f.*, chalcography, engraving on brass; engraving establishment; printing-office (of the pope).

chaldaïque (kal-), *adj.*, Chaldaic.

chaldéen, **-ne** (-in, -è-n), *adj.* V. **chaldaïque**.

chaldéen, *n.m.*, **-ne**, *n.f.*, Chaldean.

chaldéen, *n.m.*, Chaldaic, Chaldean.

châle, *n.m.*, shawl.

châlet, *n.m.*, cheese-house, Swiss cottage.

chaleur, *n.f.*, heat, glow; fervency, zeal, ardor; warmth; (phys.) caloric. *Son style manque de* — ; his style lacks warmth. *Les grandes* —*s*; the hot season; the height of summer. *Sentir de la* — ; to feel warm.

chaleureu-x, **-se**, *adj.*, warm, ardent; glowing; spirited, vehement.

⊙**châlit**, *n.m.*, bedstead.

⊙**chaloir**, *v. imp.*, to care for, to matter. *Il ne m'en chaut*; I don't care, it matters not to me. *Peu m'en chaut*; it signifies little to me.

chalon, *n.m.*, drag, drag-net.

chaloupe, *n.f.*, (nav.) ship's boat, long boat, launch. — *canonnière*; gun-boat.

chalumeau, *n.m.*, stalk of corn; straw; pipe, reed; blow-pipe; shawm.

chalumet, *n.m.*, top (of a pipe).

chalut, *n.m.*, drag-net, trawl.

chalybé, **-e** (ka-), *adj.*, chalybeate.

chamade, *n.f.*, (milit.) parley, chamade. *Battre la* — ; to sound a parley; to surrender, to yield.

*****chamailler**, *v.n.*, to bicker, to squabble, to wrangle.

*****se* **chamailler**, *v.r.*, to squabble, to wrangle. — *des dents*; to feed, to stuff.

*****chamaillis**, *n.m.*, fray, squabble, uproar, wrangle.

charmarre, *n.f.*, smock-frock; lace, embroidery.

chamarrer, *v.a.*, to lace, to trim with lace, to bedizen; to load with ridicule.

chamarrure, *n.f.*, trimming, lacing, bedizening.

chambellan (-bel-lān), *n.m.*, chamberlain.

chambourin, *n.m.*, strass.

chambranle, *n.m.*, (carp.) chambranle; casing of a chimney, door-case, window-frame. — *de cheminée*; mantel-shelf.

chambre, *n.f.*, chamber, room; lodging, apartment; House (of parliament); (metal.)

bead, chaplet; (opt.) camera, chamber; (artil.) chamber; (nav.) cabin; honey-comb (of cannon). — *ardente*; ardent chamber (history of France). — *claire*; light room; (opt.) camera lucida. — *haute*; House of Lords. — *à coucher*; bedchamber. — *garnie*; furnished lodging. *Femme de —*; chambermaid. *Robe de —*; dressing-gown. *Garder la —*; to keep one's room. *Convoquer les —s*; to convoke parliament. *Avoir des —s à louer dans la tête*; to be rather empty-headed, to be a visionary. *Arrêter, louer, une —*; to hire, to secure a room. *Faire une —*; to do (clean) a room.

chambré, -e, *adj.*, (of fire-arms) chambered, provided with a powder-chamber; honeycombed (of cannon).

chambrée, *n.f.*, persons sleeping in one room; (thea.) house; mess, barrack-room (of soldiers).

chambrelan, *n.m.*, (pop., l.u.) workman who works in his own room; single-room lodger.

⊙**chambrer**, *v.n.*, to chum together.

se **chambrer**, *v.r.*, to become honeycombed.

chambrer, *v.a.*, to keep anyone confined either by force or art; to take one aside in a company; to chamber (of guns).

chambrette, *n.f.*, little room.

⊙**chambrier**, *n.m.*, chamberlain.

chambrière, *n.f.*, chamber-maid; (man.) horse-whip.

chame *or* **came**, *n.f.*, (conch.) chama; muscle, heart-cockle.

chameau, *n.m.*, camel; (fig.) heavy fellow. *Rejeter le moucheron et avaler le —*; to strain at a gnat, and swallow a camel.

chamelier, *n.m.*, camel-driver.

chamelle, *n.f.*, female camel.

chamelon (sham-lon), *n.m.*, young camel.

chamois, *n.m.*, chamois, shamoy, wild goat; shammy; shammy-leather; chamois leather.

chamois, *adj.*, buff, drab.

chamoiser, *v.a.*, to shamoy.

se **chamoiser**, *v.r.*, to be shamoyed.

chamoiserie, *n.f.*, chamois factory; chamois leather.

chamoiseur, *n.m.*, shamoy-dresser.

champ (shan), *n.m.*, field, piece of ground; career; opportunity, scope; matter, theme, subject; compass, space; (her.) field. *A tout bout de —*; every moment. *A travers —s*; over hedge and ditch, across country. — *de bataille*; field of battle. — *de courses*; race-course. — *de repos*; the churchyard, God's acre. — *clos*; lists (for combat). *Sur-le- —*; at once, immediately. *Battre aux —s*; (milit.) to beat a salute. *Donner la clef des —s*; to give anyone his liberty. *Etre aux —s*; to be in the country; (fig.) to be in a passion. *Courir les —s*; to run about the country. *Prendre la clef des —s*; to take to one's heels; to bolt. *Il est fou à courir les —s*; he is as mad as a march hare. *Etre aux —s*; not to know where one is.

*****champagne**, *n.m.*, champagne. — *frappé*; iced champagne. — *mousseux*; sparkling champagne. — *non mousseux*; still champagne. *Fine —*; liqueur brandy.

*****champagniser**, *v.a.*, to turn into champagne.

champart, *n.m.*, (feudality) field-rent paid in kind to the lord.

champarter, *v.a.*, to exercise the right of levying field-rent in kind.

champarteur, *n.m.*, bailiff charged to collect field-rent in kind.

⊙**champeaux**, *n.m. pl.*, grass fields.

champenois, *n.m.*, -e, *n.f.*, native of Champagne.

champenois, -e, *adj.*, of Champagne.

champêtre, *adj.*, rural, rustic, country-like, sylvan. *Garde —*; keeper.

*****champignon**, *n.m.*, mushroom, toadstool; waster, thief (in a candle); bonnet-stand, peg; (arch.) cap.

*****champignonnière**, *n.f.*, mushroom-bed.

champion, *n.m.*, champion, chieftain; combatant.

championnat, *n.m.*, championship.

champlure, *n.f.*, frost-bite (of a vine); taphole (of a cask).

chance, *n.f.*, hazard (at dice); chance, luck, good luck, good fortune; risk. *Courir la —*; to run the risk. *Etre en —*; to be lucky, or in luck's way. *Souhaiter bonne — à quelqu'un*; to wish any one good luck. *Il n'est — qui ne retourne*; luck will change.

chancelant, -e, *adj.*, staggering, tottering, unsettled; unsteady, irresolute, wavering.

chanceler, *v.n.*, to stagger, to totter, to reel, to falter, to waver, to be unsteady.

chancelier, *n.m.*, chancellor. *Grand —*; high chancellor.

chancelière, *n.f.*, chancellor's wife; footmuff.

chancellement (-mān), *n.m.*, reeling, tottering, staggering, unsteadiness.

chancellerie (-sèl-rî), *n.f.*, chancellor's house, office, chancellery. *Grande —*; office of the great seal. *Petite —*; office of the privy seal.

chanceux-x, -se, *adj.*, lucky, fortunate; uncertain, doubtful (of things).

chancir, *v.n.*, to grow musty, moldy.

chancissure, *n.f.*, mustiness, moldiness.

chancre, *n.m.*, (agri., bot., vet.) canker; (med.) chancre.

chancreux-x, -se, *adj.*, cancerous, cankered; (med.) chancrous.

chandeleur (shand-lēur), *n.f.*, Candlemas.

chandelier, *n.m.*, candlestick; chandler; tallowchandler; (nav.) crotch. — *à manche*; flat candlestick. — *de mineur*; miner's crowbar. *Etre placé sur le —*; to occupy a conspicuous position.

chandelière, *n.f.*, tallow-chandler (woman).

chandelle, *n.f.*, candle, tallow-candle; light. — *plongée*; dip-candle. — *de glace*; icicle. — *de veille*; rush-light. *Moucher la —*; to snuff the candle. *Eteindre la —*; to put out the candle. *Souffler la —*; to blow out the candle. *Travailler à la —*; to work by candle-light. *Brûler la — par les deux bouts*; to burn the candle at both ends. *Le jeu n'en vaut pas la —*; it is not worth one's while. *S'en aller comme une —*; to go off like the snuff of a candle. *Voir trente-six —s*; to be stunned; to see the stars by daylight. *C'est une économie de bouts de —*; that is penny wise and pound foolish. *Il vous doit une belle —*; he ought to be very grateful to you.

chandellerie, *n.f.*, candle-factory.

chanfrein, *n.m.*, forehead (of a horse); chanfrin (armor for a horse's head); (arch.) chamfer, chamfret; (zool.) chaffron.

chanfreiner, *v.a.*, (arch.) to chamfer, to rabbet; (carp.) to cant, to edge.

change, *n.m.*, exchange (barter); (com.) exchange; money-change; agio; (fig.) wrong scent. *Lettres de —*; letters of exchange. *Agent de —*; stock-broker. — *commun*; average exchange. — *direct*; direct exchange. — *extérieur*; foreign exchange. — *du jour*; current exchange. *Commerce de —*; exchange business. *Cote de —*; current rate of exchange. *Fausse lettre de —*; forged bill. *Lettre de — sur l'étranger*; foreign bill of exchange. *Le — est au pair*; the exchange is at par. *Première de —*; first of exchange. *Seconde de —*; second of exchange. *Seule de —*; sole of exchange. *Au — de*; at the rate of exchange of. *Bureau de — de monnaie*; exchange office. *Donner le — à quelqu'un*; to put any one on the wrong scent. *Rendre le — à quelqu'un*;

to give a Roland for an Oliver, *or* tit for tat; to pay back in one's own coin. *Tirer une lettre de — sur quelqu'un;* to draw a bill on anyone.

changeant, -e (-jän, -t), *adj.,* changeable, fickle, unsteady, variable, inconstant, unstable, unsettled (of the weather).

changement (shanj-män), *n.m.,* change, alteration, changing, variation, mutation; (jur.) amendment. *Amener un —;* to bring about a change. *— à vue;* scene-shifting. *— de voie;* shunting.

changeoter (-jo-té), *v.n.,* (fam., l.u.) to change often.

changer, *v.a.,* to change, to exchange; to alter, to turn, to commute, to convert, to transform. *se changer,* *v.r.,* to be changed, converted; to alter, to change.

changer, *v.n.,* to change, to alter. *— de logis, de demeure,* to shift one's quarters, to remove. *— d'avis;* to alter one's mind. *— de chemise;* to change one's shirt. *— d'habits;* to change clothes. *— de voie* (rail.); to shunt.

changeur, *n.m.,* money-changer.

chanoine, *n.m.,* canon.

chanoinesse, *n.f.,* canoness.

⊙**chanoinie,** *n.f.,* canonry, canonship.

chanson, *n.f.,* song, ballad; ditty; (fig.) idle story, stuff, trash. *Refrain d'une —;* chorus of a song. *C'est toujours la même —;* it is the same thing over and over again; it is always harping on the same string. *Voilà bien une autre —;* that is another story altogether. *—s que tout cela!* all idle stories! *—s!* humbug, stuff!

chansonner, *v.a.,* (b.s.) to lampoon.

chansonnette, *n.f.,* little song, ditty.

chansonneur, *n.m.,* lampooner.

chansonnier, *n.m.,* ballad-writer; song-book.

chansonnière, *n.f.,* song-writer (woman).

chant, *n.m.,* singing, strain, song; air; lay, ditty, melody; chant, hymn, book. *Plain —;* plain chant, canto fermo. *Le — du coq;* the crowing of the cock. *— funèbre;* dirge.

chantable, *adj.,* fit to be sung, worth singing.

chantage, *n.m.,* extortion of hush money; blackmailing.

chantant, -e, *adj.,* tunable, easily sung, easily set to music; musical, harmonious.

chanteau, *n.m.,* hunch of bread; bit of stuff.

chantepleure (shant-pleur), *n.f.,* funnel with a rose; gully-hole.

chantepleurer, *v.a.,* to tread (grapes).

chanter, *v.n.,* to sing, to chant; to chirp, to warble, to crow; (fam.) to say too much. *Ce criminel a chanté à la question;* (fam.) that prisoner let the cat out of the bag. *— juste, agréablement, passablement;* to sing true, agreeably, tolerably. *— faux;* to sing out of tune. *— à livre ouvert;* to sing at sight. *C'est comme si vous chantiez;* it is as if you were talking to the wind. *L'alouette chante;* the lark carols. *Le coq chante;* the cock crows. *La cigale chante;* the grasshopper chirps. *— sur tous les tons;* to ring the changes on. *Tel chante qui ne rit pas;* the heart may be sad though the face be gay. *Je lui ai chanté sa gamme;* I lectured him finely. *— à faire pitié;* to sing wretchedly.

chanter, *v.a.,* to sing, to chant; to extol, to praise; to celebrate; to warble; to talk, to tell, stuff. *— victoire;* to cry victory, to crow over a victory. *Que me chantez-vous là?* what stuff are you telling me now? *Se —;* to be sung.

chanterelle (shän-trél), *n.f.,* first string of a violin, &c.; decoy-bird; musical-bottle.

chanteu-r, -se, *adj.,* singing (of birds).

chanteur, *n.m.,* singer, vocalist; songster (of birds). *— des rues;* ballad-singer; extortioner.

chanteuse, *n.f.,* singer, street-singer, vocalist.

chantier (-tié), *n.m.,* timber-yard, wood-yard; stone-yard; dock-yard; stand, block, stocks;

shop, shed. *L'ouvrage est sur le —;* the work is begun or in hand.

****chantignole,** *n.f.,* (carp.) wooden block; bracket.

chantonner, *a.n.,* to hum, to hum a tune.

⊙**chantonnerie** (to-n-rî), *n.f.,* humming, drawling.

chantournage, *n.m.,* cutting in profile.

chantourné, *n.m.,* head-piece of a bedstead.

chantourner, *v.a.,* to cut in profile.

chantre, *n.m.,* singer, chorister, chanter; precentor, lay-clerk; songster, songstress (of birds). *Les —s des bois;* the feathered songsters.

chantrerie, *n.f.,* precentorship.

chanvre, *n.m.,* hemp.

chanvrier, *n.m.,* hemp-dresser, dealer in hemp.

chanvrière, *n.f.,* hemp-field.

chaos (kaô), *n.m.,* chaos, confusion, disorder.

chaotique, *adj.,* chaotic.

chape, *n.f.,* cope (church garment); (arch.) cope. *Disputer de la — à l'évêque;* to dispute about what does not concern one.

chapeau, *n.m.,* hat; bonnet; wreath of flowers (for a bride); (carp.) hand-piece; (bot.) cap; pileus (of a mushroom). *— à grand bord;* broad-brimmed hat. *— à petit bord;* narrow-brimmed hat. *— à haute forme;* tall-hat, top-hat. *— d'évêque;* (bot.) barrenwort. *— chinois;* (milit. mus.) Chinese bells. *— de paille d'Italie;* Leghorn hat. *La carre d'un —;* the crown of a hat. *— à cornes;* three-cornered hat. *Ôter son —;* to take off one's hat. *— bas;* hat in hand. *—x bas!* hats off. *— de paille;* straw hat. *— de velours;* velvet bonnet. *Le bord, la passe, la forme d'un —;* the border, the front, the shape of a hat. *— de fleurs;* garland of flowers. *Frère —;* assistant-brother (monk). *Enfoncer son —;* to pull one's hat over one's eyes; to screw up one's courage. *Il y a eu bien des —x de reste;* there were many men killed. *Il n'y avait pas un seul —;* there wasn't a single man there.

⊙**chape-chute,** *n.f.,* windfall, lucky hit.

⊙**chape-chuter,** *v.n.,* to make a slight noise.

chapelain (shap-lin), *n.m.,* chaplain.

chapeler (sha-plé), *v.a.,* to rasp (bread).

chapelet (cha-plè), *n.m.,* chaplet, rosary, beads, bead-roll; (man., arch.) chaplet; beads (in brandy). *Dire son —;* to tell one's beads. *Défiler son —;* to say all one has to say; to empty one's budget. *Il n'a pas gagné cela en disant son —;* he did not get that for nothing.

chapeli-er, -ère, *n.m.f.,* hatter, hat manufacturer.

chapelle, *n.f.,* chapel; church plate, living; vault of an oven. *Faire —;* (nav.) to broach to, to chapel the ship. *Maître de —;* precentor. *— ardente;* lights round a coffin. *Pour la petite — s'il vous plaît;* please remember the grotto. *Tenir —;* to attend divine service in state.

chapellenie (sha-pèl-nî), *n.f.,* chaplainship, chaplaincy.

chapellerie (sha-pèl-rî), *n.f.,* hat-making; hat-trade.

chapelure (sha-plur), *n.f.,* bread; raspings; grated bread.

chaperon (sha-pron), *n.m.,* chaperon, hood; shoulder-knot; chaperon; coping of a wall; holster-cap.

chaperonner, *v.a.,* to cope a wall; to chaperon (a young girl); to hood (a hawk).

chapier, *n.m.,* priest with a cope, cope-maker.

chapiteau, *n.m.,* (arch.) capital; crest; top; (of a press, mirror, &c.); head of a still; cap (of a fusee).

chapitre, *n.m.,* chapter (of a book, of knights, of a cathedral); chapter; chapter-house; subject, matter of discourse, head. *En voilà assez sur ce —;* that is quite enough on that score. *Avoir voix au* —; to have interest at the board. *Passons sur ce* —; let us waive the subject.

chapitrer, *v.a.,* to reprimand, to rebuke, to lecture any one.

chapon, *n.m.,* capon; sop in broth; crust of bread rubbed with garlic. *Le vol du* —; certain extent of ground about a country-seat. *Avoir les mains faites en* — *rôti;* to have crooked fingers; to be light-fingered. *Qui* — *mange* — *lui vient;* money begets money.

chaponneau, *n.m.,* (l.u.) young capon.

chaponner, *v.a.,* to capon.

chaponnière, *n.f.,* stew-pan (for capons).

chaque, *adj.,* each, every. —*pays a ses coutumes;* every country has its customs. *A* —*jour suffit sa peine;* sufficient for the day is the evil thereof.

char, *n.m.,* car, chariot. —*funèbre;* hearse. — *à bancs;* wagonette, jaunting car. — *de triomphe;* triumphal car.

charabia, *n.m.,* gibberish, gabble.

charade, *n.f.,* charade.

charançon, *n.m.,* snout, beetle, weevil.

charançonné, -e, *adj.,* (of corn) weeviled.

charbon, *n.m.,* coal; embers; charcoal; carbuncle; (agri.) black rust; (med.) anthrax. — *de bois;* charcoal. — *de terre;* coal. *Etre sur les* —*s;* to be on thorns. *Mine à* —; coal-mine.

charbonnage, *n.m.,* (l.u.) coal-mining.

charbonnée, *n.f.,* short rib of beef.

charbonner, *v.a.,* to char; to black with coal; to besmut.

se **charbonner,** *v.r.,* to be charred, to burn black, to smolder.

charbonnerie (-bo-n-rî), *n.f.,* coal-store.

charbonneu-x, -se, *adj.,* (med.) carbuncled.

charbonnier, *n.m.,* charcoal-burner, coal-seller, coal-man; coal-shed, coal-hole; (ich.) coal-fish; (nav.) collier. *Le* — *est maître chez lui* or *chez soi;* a man's house is his castle.

charbonnière, *n.f.,* charcoal-kiln; coal-seller; coal-man's wife; (orni.) titmouse.

***charbouiller,** *v.a.,* (agri.) to blight.

charbucle, *n.f.,* (agri.) blight (in corn).

charcuter, *v.a.,* to chop up (meat); to hack, to mangle.

charcuterie (-ku-trî), *n.f.,* pork-butcher's meat; pork-butcher's business; dressed pork.

charcuti-er, *n.m.,* -**ère,** *n.f.,* (-tié, -ti-èr), pork-butcher.

chardon, *n.m.,* thistle; spike (on a wall). — *aux ânes;* cotton-thistle. —*à foulon;* teasel. — *étoilé;* star-thistle.

chardonner, *v.a.,* to teasel (cloth).

chardonneret (-do-n-rè), *n.m.,* (orni.) goldfinch; painted-lady, butterfly.

chardonnette or **cardonnette,** *n.f.,* prickly artichoke.

chardonnière, *n.f.,* thistle-waste.

charge, *n.f.,* load, lading, freight, pack; tax, expense; burden, clog; charge; accusation, imputation, indictment; post; place; office, employment; order, command, commission; custody, care; charge, onset; charge (of a gun); (vet., paint., jur.) charge; exaggeration, caricature. *Femme de* —; housekeeper. *Etre à* — *à quelqu'un;* to be a burden upon any one. *Cela est à ma* —; I have to pay for that. *Il faut prendre le bénéfice avec les* —*s;* we must take the good with the bad. *Faire une* —; (milit.) to charge. *Se démettre de sa* —; to resign one's place or office. *On a donné trop de* — *à ce mur;* this wall has been overloaded. *Sonner la* —; to sound the charge. *Revenir à la* —; to make a new attempt. *A la* — *de, à la* — *que;* upon condition that, provided that. *Prendre* —; to take in cargo. *Rompre* —; to break bulk.

chargé, -e, *part.,* loaded, burdened; (print.)

foul (of proofs). *Dés* —*s;* loaded dice; registered (of a letter). *Le temps est* —; the weather is overcast. — *d'affaires;* chargé d'affaires, envoy. — *de cours;* assistant-lecturer; professor; substitute.

chargeant, -e (-jän, -t), *adj.,* clogging, heavy.

chargement, *n.m.,* cargo, lading, freight, shipment; bill of lading; shipment.

charger, *v.a.,* to load, to saddle, to lade, to freight, to charge; to burden, to clog, to overburthen, to encumber; to impute, to lay a thing to any one's charge; to charge with, to command, to give a thing in charge, to trust with; to charge, to fall upon, to make an onset on; to load (a gun); to fill (pipe); to set down; to lay on; (paint.) to overcharge, to exaggerate. — *un fusil;* to load a gun. — *toutes les voiles;* to clap on all sails. — *une lettre;* to register a letter.

se **charger,** *v.r.,* to take charge, to charge one's self; to become overcast (of the weather); to burden one's self, to saddle one's self with.

charger, *v.n.,* to load; to exaggerate, to lay it on.

chargeur, *n.m.,* loader, ship-porter; (nav.) gunner.

⊙**charier.** *V.* **charrier.**

chariot, *n.m.,* wagon, cart, truck, trolley, wain. (astron.) *Le grand* —; Charles' wain; Ursa Major. *Le petit* —; Ursa Minor.

charitable, *adj.,* charitable.

charitablement, *adv.,* charitably.

charité, *n.f.,* charity, love, benevolence; alms, almsgiving. *Faire la* —; to give alms. *Demander la* —; to beg. — *bien ordonnée commence par soi-même;* charity begins at home. *Sœur de* —; sister of mercy. *La* —, *s'il vous plaît!* a penny, kind gentleman, if you please.

charivari, *n.m.,* rough music, hubbub, clatter, noise, shindy.

charivariser, *v.a.,* to give rough music; to kick up a row.

charivariseur, charivarieur, or **charivariste,** *n.m.,* mock-musican; rioter, roysterer.

charlatan, *n.m.,* mountebank, quack, charlatan, empiric, wheedler.

charlatane, *n.f.,* wheedler.

charlataner, *v.a.,* to gull, to wheedle, to cajole.

charlatanerie, *n.f.,* quackery, charlatanery, juggling.

charlatanesque, *adj.,* quackish.

charlatanisme, *n.m.,* quackery, charlatanism, charlatanry.

charlemagne, *n.m.,* (fig.) short broadsword. *Faire* —; to leave off a winner.

charlot, *n.m.,* curlew. — *de plage;* sea-lark.

charlotte, *n.f.,* (cook.) charlotte.

charmant, -e, *adj.,* charming, delightful, pleasing, lovely.

charme, *n.m.,* charm, spell, enchantment; attraction, delight; (bot.) horn-beam, yoke-elm. *Cela vous va comme un* —; that fits you perfectly, splendidly, to a tee. *Se porter comme un* —; to be in perfect health. *Sous le* —; under the spell.

charmer, *v.a.,* to charm, to enchant, to bewitch, to fascinate; to captivate, to please, to delight, to beguile, to while away. *Je suis charmé de vous voir;* I am delighted to see you.

charmeur, *n.m.,* (l.u.) charmer, enchanter.

charmeuse, *n.f.,* (l.u.) bewitching woman, enchantress.

***charmille,** *n.f.,* horn-beam, yoke-elm; hedge of yoke-elm trees; bower, arbor.

charmoie, *n.f.,* grove of hornbeam or yoke-elm trees.

charnel, -le, *adj.,* carnal, sensual.

charnellement (-män), *adv.,* carnally.

charnier, *n.m.,* charnel-house; ⊙larder.

charnière, n.f., hinge, joint.

charnu, -e, adj., fleshy, plump; brawny, carneous.

charnure, n.f., flesh, skin.

*__charogne__, n.f., carrion; (fig.) blackguard.

charpente, n.f., timber-work, carpenter's work; frame, frame-work. *Bois de —;* timber.

charpenter, v.a., to square timber; to hack, to mangle.

charpenterie (-pän-trî), n.f., carpentry; carpenter's work, carpenter's trade; timberwork; timber-yard (of dock-yards).

charpentier (-tié), n.m., carpenter; (whalefishery) whale-cutter.

charpi, n.m., cooper's block.

charpie, n.f., lint. *En —;* (of meat) boiled to rags.

charrée, n.f., buck-ashes; lye.

charretée (shar-tée), n.f., cart-load.

charretier (shar-tié), n.m., carman, carter, wagoner; plow-boy, plowman. *Il n'y a si bon — qui ne verse;* it's a good horse that never stumbles. *Jurer comme un — embourbé;* to swear like a trooper.

charreti-er, -ère, adj., passable for carts, &c. *Chemin —;* cart-road. *Voie —ère;* track (space between the two wheels of a cart).

charrette, n.f., cart. *— à bras;* hand-cart. *— à ressorts;* spring-cart. *Train de —;* skeleton-cart. *Mettre la — devant les bœufs;* to put the cart before the horse. *Mieux vaut être cheval que —;* better lead than be led. *C'est un avaleur de —s ferrées;* he is a great brag.

charriage, n.m., cartage.

charrier, v.a., to cart, to bring in a cart; to drift; (med.) to be loaded with.

charrier, v.n., to drift (of ice), scud (of clouds). *La rivière charrie;* the river is filled with drift-ice. *— droit;* to behave properly; to do what is right.

charrier, n.m., bucking-cloth.

charroi, n.m., carting, wagonage.

charron, n.m., wheelwright.

charronnage, n.m., wheelwright's work.

charroyer, v.a., to cart (heavy things).

charrue, n.f., plow. *Mettre la — devant les bœufs;* to put the cart before the horse. *Passer la — sur;* to plow. *Tirer la —;* to drudge, work hard.

charte, n.f., charter; policy; title-deeds. *La grande —;* Magna Charta.

charte partie, n.f., (—s —s) (com.) charter-party.

chartographe, n.m., chartographer.

chartographique, adj., chartographic.

chartographie, n.f., chartography; mapping.

⊙**charton** or **charreton**, n.m., carter, coachman.

⊙**chartre**, n.f., charter (old document).

⊙**chartre**, n.f., prison; consumption. *Tenir quelqu'un en — privée;* to detain anyone illegally.

chartreuse, n.f., Carthusian convent; Carthusian nun; isolated country-house; (cook.) mixed vegetables. *Liqueur —;* (cordial).

chartreux, n.m., Carthusian friar, cat of a bluish gray.

chartrier, n.m., charter-house; charter-room, muniment-room; keeper of charters.

chartron, n.m. *Faire* or *former le —;* to stand in a row near the footlights.

charybde, n.m., Charybdis. *Tomber de — en Scylla;* to fall from the frying-pan into the fire.

chas, n.m., eye (of a needle); weaver's starch; (tech.) plumb rule.

châsse, n.f., reliquary; shrine; frame; handle (of lancets); cheek (of a balance).

chassé, n.m., chasse, a step in dancing.

chasse, n.f., chase, hunt, hunting, chasing, pursuit; game; (mus.) chasse; play (of machinery). *— à courre;* coursing, hunting. *— au tir;* shooting. *— au vol, — aux oiseaux;* fowling. *— aux flambeaux;* bat fowling. *Un garde —;* a game-keeper. *Prendre —* (nav.); to sheer off. *Donner —;* to pursue. *Soutenir —;* to maintain a running fight.

chasse-avant, n.m., (—) overseer, foreman.

chasse-chien, n.m., (—, or — — —s) beadle; keeper employed to drive away dogs.

chasse-coquins, n.m., (—, or — — —s) beggar-driver, beadle.

chasse-cousins, n.m., (—, or — — —s) paltry dinner, bad wine; cold shoulder, poor reception.

chassé-croisé, n.m., (—s —s) (dancing) chassé-croisé; (fig.) a change of office or situation.

chasse-ennui, n.m., (—) an exhilarant, stimulant.

chasselas (shas-la), n.m., grapes, chasselas.

chasse-marée, n.m., (—) fish-cart; driver of a fish-cart; lugger.

chasse-mouches, n.m., (—) fly-flap; fly-net.

chasse-mulet, n.m., (—, or — — —s) miller's man.

chasse-neige, n.m., snow-plow.

chasse-pierres, n.m., (—) (railways) guard-iron, cow-catcher; catapult.

*__chasse-poignée__, n.m., (—, or — — —s) cutler's tool, driver.

chassepot, n.m., name of the rifle in use in the French army until 1871.

chasser, v.a., to hunt, to chase, to pursue; to beat (gold); to turn out, to expel; to drive, to drive forward. *— un clou;* to drive in a nail. *— un domestique;* to turn away, to discharge, a servant. *Qui deux choses chasse, ni l'une ni l'autre ne prend;* (prov.) between two stools one falls to the ground. *— le mauvais air;* to ventilate. *Ne pas — deux lièvres à la fois;* not to have too many irons in the fire. *Un clou chasse l'autre;* one idea drives away another. *— la terre;* (nav.) to approach, to reconnoiter, the coast.

chasser, v.n., to shoot; to hunt; to roll along easily; to drive (of clouds); (print.) to drive out. *— au fusil;* to shoot. *— aux perdrix;* to shoot partridges. *— aux lions;* to hunt lions. *— sur son ancre;* (nav.) to drag the anchor. *— à courre;* to hunt, to course. *— au faucon;* to hawk. *— de race;* (prov.) to be a chip of the old block. *— aux blancs moineaux;* to lose one's time in running after impossibilities.

chasseresse (shas-rès), n.f., huntress.

chasse-roue, n.m., (—, or — — —s) spur-post; guard-iron.

chasseu-r, n.m., **-se**, n.f., hunter, sportsman; huntsman, gamekeeper; chasseur (footman); light infantry soldier; ship that chases another. *—s à cheval;* (milit.) light cavalry.

chassie, n.f., gum of the eye.

chassieu-x, -se, adj., blear-eyed.

châssis, n.m., (print.) chase; window-sash frame. *Fenêtre à —;* sash-window. *— dormant;* the fixed part of a window-frame. *— de jardin, de couche;* garden-frame; glass-frame. (motor) chassis. *—presse;* (phot.) printing-frame.

chassoir, n.m., cooper's tool, driver; (tech.) drift.

chaste, adj., chaste, continent, honest, modest, pure, virtuous; (style) neat, correct, terse.

chastement, adv., chastely, honestly, purely, virtuously. [nence, purity.

chasteté, n.f., chastity, chasteness, conti-

chasuble, n.f., chasuble.

chasublier, n.m., maker of chasubles.

chat, n.m., **-te**, n.f., cat; darling, dear; searcher (to examine cannons); plumb-rule; (nav.) cat. *Petit —;* kitten. *Herbe aux —s;* cat's-mint. *— musqué;* civet, musk-cat. *— cervier;* lynx. *— bon aux souris;* good mouser. *—*

à neuf queues ; cat-o'-nine-tails. *Votre chatte est pleine ;* your cat is with kitten. *A bon — bon rat ;* set a thief to catch a thief ; tit for tat ; diamond cut diamond. *— échaudé craint l'eau froide ;* a burnt child dreads the fire. *La nuit tous les —s sont gris ;* when candles are away all cats are grey. *Il n'y a pas là de quoi fouetter un — ;* it is a mere trifle. *N'éveillez pas le — qui dort ;* let sleeping dogs lie. *Acheter — en poche ;* to buy a pig in a poke. *Se servir du patte du — pour tirer les marrons du feu ;* to make a cat's-paw of anyone. *Il n'y a pas un — ;* there is not a living soul there. *Le — parti, les souris dansent ;* when the cat 's away the mice will play. *Comme — sur braise ;* like a cat on hot bricks. *Œil-de— ;* calf's snout, snapdragon. *Patte-de— ;* ground-ivy. *Pied-de— ;* cat's-foot, ale-hoof, tune-hoof. *Sabbat de —, musique de — ;* caterwauling. *Mon petit — ;* (term of endearment) my dear, my darling. *Appeler un — un — ;* to call a spade a spade, not to mince matters. *Avoir un — dans la gorge ;* to have a phlegm in one's throat (of singers). *Nous avons d'autres —s à fouetter ;* we have other fish to fry. *— en poche ;* a pig in a poke. *Bailler le — par les pattes ;* to bell the cat. *Ces gens vivent comme chien et — ;* these people live like cat and dog. *Emporter le — ;* to go away without paying one's reckoning, to take French leave.

*châtaigne, *n.f.,* chestnut. *— amère ;* horse-chestnut. *— d'eau ;* water-caltrops.

*châtaigneraie, *n.f.,* chestnut grove.

*châtaignier, *n.m.,* chestnut-tree or wood.

châtain, *adj.,* chestnut, nut-brown, auburn. *— clair ;* light auburn.

chataire, *n.f.* V. **cataire.**

château, *n.m.,* castle, fort, citadel ; country-seat, mansion, palace. *— fort ;* fortress. *— seigneurial ;* baronial-hall. *Faire des —x en Espagne ;* to build castles in the air. *— de carte ;* house of cards. *— d'eau ;* water-works, artificial fountain.

châteaubriand, *n.m.,* fillet-steak.

châtelain (shâ-tlin), *n.m.,* **-e,** *n.f.* and *adj.,* lord, lady, of a manor, squire.

châtelé, -e, *adj.,* (her.) turreted.

⊙**châtelet** (shâ-tlè), *n.m.,* small castle ; a former prison or law-courts at Paris.

⊙**châtellenie,** *n.f.,* castellany, castle-ward.

⊙**chatepeleuse,** *n.f.,* curculio, weevil.

chat-huant (sha-uàn), *n.m.,* (—s—s) owl, screech-owl, horn-owl.

châtiable, *adj.,* chastisable, punishable.

châtier (-tié), *v.a.,* to chastise, to correct, to punish, to scourge, to flog ; (c. rel.) to chasten. *Qui aime bien, châtie bien ;* spare the rod and spoil the child. *— une pièce de vers ;* to polish a piece of poetry.

chatière (-ti-èr), *n.f.,* cat's hole ; cat-trap.

châtiment, *n. m.,* chastisement, correction, punishment, castigation ; (c. rel.) chastening.

chatoiement or **chatoîment,** *n.m.,* chatoyment, sparkling, glistening, play of colors.

chaton, *n.m.,* kitten ; bezel (of a ring) ; outward husk or cup of the nut ; (bot.) catkin ; case of a watch.

*chatouillement, *n.m.,* tickling ; titillation.

*chatouiller, *v.a.,* to tickle, to titillate ; to please, to gratify ; to flatter ; to touch a horse lightly with the spur.

se **chatouiller,** *v.r.,* to tickle oneself ; to excite oneself to gayety, good humor).

*chatouilleu-x, -se, *adj.,* ticklish, delicate, nice ; touchy.   [ing (of colors).

chatoyant, -e, *adj.,* chatoyant, shot, glisten-

chatoyer, *v.n.,* to be chatoyant, to glisten ; to play (of colors) ; (of style) to be florid.

chat-pard, *n.m.,* (—s—s) mountain-cat.

châtré, *n.m.,* eunuch. *Voix de — ;* shrill voice.

---

châtré, -e, *adj.,* emasculate, castrated.

châtrer, *v.a.,* to castrate ; to expurgate ; to take away the honey and wax from a bee-hive; to lop, prune ; (fig.) to mutilate, to curtail, to retrench ; (vet.) to geld. *— une truie ;* to spay a sow. *— des cotrets ;* to take sticks from fagots of wood. *— les tiges de tabac ;* to top tobacco-plants.

se **châtrer,** *v.r.,* to castrate oneself ; to be mutilated (of books, plays, &c.).

châtreur, *n.m.,* gelder.

châtrure, *n.f.,* castrating ; gelding.

chatte, *n.f.,* she-cat. *V.* **chat.**

chattée, *n.f.,* litter of kittens.

chattemite, *n. f.,* demure-looking person ; hypocrite, dissembler.

chatter, *v.n.,* to kitten.

chatterie, *n.f.,* playfulness ; hypocritical caress ; daintiness ; pretty or coaxing way.

chaud, -e, *adj.,* hot, warm, burning, glowing ; ardent ; fervent, fervid, fierce ; zealous, eager ; coaxing, hasty, hot-headed, passionate ; proud (of animals). *Fièvre —e ;* violent fever. *Pleurer à —es larmes ;* to cry bitterly. *Tomber de fièvre en — mal ;* to fall out of the frying-pan into the fire. *Faire — ;* to be warm (of weather). *Avoir la tête —e ;* to be passionate. *Tout — ;* quite hot. *Il faut battre le fer pendant qu'il est — ;* (prov.) strike while the iron is hot ; make hay while the sun shines. *Cet ouvrage est tout — ;* this work is quite new. *Ne trouver rien de trop — ni de trop froid ;* to wish to have everything. *La donner bien —e ;* to excite unnecessarily great alarm. *Etre — de vin ;* (fam.) to be a little sprung. *L'action fut —e ;* (milit.) the engagement was a warm one. *Manger —, boire — ;* to eat, drink, warm things.

chaud, *n.m.,* heat, warmth. *Il fait — ;* it is hot. *Il fait grand — ;* it is very hot. *Avoir — ;* to be hot. *Souffrir le — et le froid ;* to endure heat and cold. *Cela ne fait ni — ni froid ;* that is immaterial, of no importance ; that is neither here nor there. *Souffler le — et le froid ;* to blow hot and cold in the same breath. *Cela ne lui fait ni — ni froid ;* that is quite indifferent to him.

chaud, *adv.,* hot, warm.

chaude, *n.f.,* (metal.) heating. *Battre la — ;* to beat whilst the metal is hot. *A la — ;* in the first heat of passion, on the spur of the moment.

⊙**chaudeau,** *n.m.,* caudle ; egg-flip.

chaudelait, *n.m.,* batter-pudding.

chaudement (shôd-màn), *adv.,* warmly, briskly, quickly, eagerly, fiercely, hotly.

chaud-froid, *n.m.,* fancy dish (eaten cold).

chaudier, *v. n.,* (hunt.) (of bitches) to be proud ; to couple.

chaudière, *n.f.,* copper, large kettle ; boiler (of a steam-engine).

chaudret or **chauderet,** *n.m.,* (gold-beating) mould of about one thousand leaves.

chaudron, *n.m.,* large kettle, boiler, caldron.

chaudronnée, *n.f.,* caldronful, kettleful.

chaudronnerie, *n.f.,* coppersmith's trade, copper wares, brazier's wares.

chaudronni-er, *n.m.,* **-ère,** *n.f.,* brazier, coppersmith. *— de campagne ;* tinker.

chauffage, *n.m.,* fuel, firewood, firing ; right of cutting firewood ; (nav.) breaming.

chauffe, *n.f.,* (metal.) furnace.

chauffe-assiettes, *n.m.,* (—) plate-warmer.

chauffe-chemise, *n.m.,* (—, or —-—s) or

chauffe-linge, *n.m.,* (—) clothes-horse, linen-warmer.

chauffe-cire, *n.m.,* (—) (pers.) chafe-wax.

chauffe-lit, *n.m.,* (—, or —-—s) bed-warmer.

chauffe-pieds, *n.m.,* (—) foot-warmer.

chauffer, *v.a.,* to heat, to warm ; to excite. *— un vaisseau ;* (nav.) to bream a ship. *— un poste ;* (milit.) to keep up a sharp fire on a post. *— quelqu'un ;* to pay any one off.

se **chauffer**, v.r., to warm one's self. *Ne pas se — du même bois*; not to be of the same way of thinking. *Savoir de quel bois on se chauffe*; to know what stuff anyone is made of.

chauffer, v.n., to be heating, to grow hot; to be urgent, pressing; (of a steam engine) to get up steam. *Ce n'est pas pour vous que le four chauffe*; there is nothing for you.

chaufferette (shô-frèt), n.f., foot-warmer (in the house); chafing-dish.

chaufferie, n.f., chafery, stoke-hole.

chauffeur, n.m., fireman, stoker, chauffeur; bellows-blower; (fig.) braggart, humbug.

chauffoir, n.m., warming-place; warm cloth; heater.

chauffure, n.f., flaw (in iron or steel).

chaufour, n.m., lime-kiln.

chaufournier, n.m., lime-burner.

chaulage, n.m., (agri.) liming.

chauler, v.a., to lime; to steep wheat in lime-water previous to sowing it.

chaulier, n.m., lime-burner.

chaumage, n.m., stubble-cutting; time at which stubble is cut.

chaume, n.m., stubble; stubble-field; thatch; (bot.) culm, haulm. *Etre né sous le —*; to be born in a cottage. *Couvreur en —*; thatcher. *Couvrir de —*; to thatch. *Plein de —*; stubbly.

chaumer, v.a. and n., to cut stubble.

chaumière, n.f., thatched house, cottage, cot

chaumine, n.f., small cottage, hut.

chaussant, -e, adj., (l.u.) easy to put on, fitting (leg or foot).

chausse, n.f., stocking, hose; shoulder-knot; straining-bag, filter. *— d'aisances*; waste-pipe of a water-closet.

chaussé, -e, part., shod. *Bien —*; well-shod, nicely booted. *Ils sont chaussés au même point*; they get on capitally.

chaussée, n.f., causeway; bank, highway. *Au rez de —*; level with the ground. *J'habite la rez-de-chaussée*; I live on the ground-floor.

chausse-pied, n.m., (— — —s) shoe-horn; (fig.) help, assistance.

chausser, v.a., to put on (shoes, boots, stockings); to make shoes; to get firmly fixed into one's head; to suit; (man.) to put one's feet too far forward in the stirrups. *— le cothurne*; to put on the buskin, go on the tragic stage; to write in an inflated style. *— le brodequin*; to put on the sock, go on the comic stage; to compose, to act comedy. *Les cordonniers sont les plus mal chaussés*; nobody is worse shod than the shoe-maker's wife. *— des arbres*; to earth up trees. *— une opinion*; to be wedded to an opinion. *Cet homme n'est pas aisé à chausser*; (fam. and fig.) that man is not easily persuaded.

se **chausser**, v.r., to put on one's shoes, boots, stockings; to become strongly wedded to an opinion.

chausser, v.n., to make boots or shoes, to wear shoes. *Ils chaussent au même point*; they wear shoes of the same size; (fig.) they are of the same stamp.

chausses, n.f. pl., breeches, small-clothes, trowsers. *— à tuyaux d'orgue*; trunk hose. *Ne pas avoir de —*; to be very poor. *Avoir la clef de ses —*; to be one's own master. *Laisser ses — quelque part*; to leave one's bones somewhere, to die. *Tirer ses —*; to scamper away. *Elle porte les —*; she wears the breeches.

chaussetier (shôs-tié), n.m., hosier.

chausse-trape, n.f., (— — —s) (milit.) caltrop; snare, trap; (bot.) star-thistle.

chaussette, n.f., sock; under-stocking; anklet.

chausson, n.m., sock; under-stocking; pump; light shoe (worn when playing rackets, or when fencing); list-shoe; puff-paste; fruit-tart.

chaussure, n.f., foot-gear, shoes, slippers, boots, pumps. *Il a trouvé — à son pied*; he has

found what he wanted; he has met with his match.

chauve, adj., bald, baldpated.

chauve-souris, n.f., (—s —) bat, flitter-mouse.

⊙**chauveté** (shôv-té), n.f., baldness, calvity.

chauvir, v.n., to prick up the ears (of horses, asses, mules).

chaux, n.f., lime; limestone; (chem.) calx, lime. *— éteinte*; slaked lime. *— vive*; quick-lime. *Pierre à —*; limestone. *Donner un blanc de —*; (mas.) to give a coat of whitewash. *Etre fait à — et à ciment*, or *à — et à mortier*; to be well and solidly done.

chavirement, n.m., capsizing, upsetting.

chavirer, v.n., to capsize, to upset.

chavirer, v.a., to turn upside down; to turn inside out.

chebec, n.m., (nav.) xebec.

chef, n.m., chief, head, commander, conductor, master, principal, ringleader, foreman (of a jury); fag-end (of a piece of linen); (nav.) end of a cable; (med.) tail of a bandage. *En —*; in chief. *— de bureau*; senior clerk. *— de cabinet*; head of a department. *— d'état-major*; chief of the staff. *— d'état major-général*; quarter-master-general. *— de musique*; band-master. *— d'orchestre*; musical-director. *— de parti*; party-leader. *— de pièce*; captain of a gun. *— de rayon*; (com.) head of a department. *— de train*; railway guard. *— de famille*; head of a house. *— de cuisine*; master-cook. *— d'accusation*; count of indictment, charge. *Faire quelque chose de son —*; to do a thing on one's own responsibility. *De son —*; in one's own right.

chef-d'œuvre (shè-deuvr), n.m., (—s —) trial piece; master-piece; master-stroke.

⊙**chefecier.** *V.* **chevecier.**

chef-lieu, n.m., (—s —x) chief residence; head-quarters, chief town; county-town.

chégros, n.m., shoemaker's thread or end, cobbler's-ends, wax end.

cheik or **scheik**, n.m., sheik.

chéiroptère (ké-). *V.* **chiroptère.**

chélidoine (ké-), n.f., (bot.) celandine, swallow-wort.

chélone (ké-), n.f., (bot.) chelone, snake-head, shell-flower.

chélonée (ké-), n.f., sea-tortoise.

chélonite (ké-), n.f., chelonite.

⊙se **chêmer**, v.r., to fall away, to waste, to pine.

chemin, n.m., way, road, path, track; means; course; (nav.) way; (railways) line, road. *Grand —*; highway, high-road. *Voleur de grands —s*; highwayman. *— passant*; much frequented thoroughfare. *—s vicinaux, communaux*; village, parochial roads. *— de traverse*; cross-road. *— détourné*; out of the way road. *— de fer*; railway, railroad. *— de fer à rail plat*; tramroad. *— de service*; (railways) attendant path. *Embranchement de — de fer*; branch railway. *Le — de l'hôpital*; the way to the work-house. *— couvert*; (fort.) covered way, corridor. *— de halage*; towing-path. *A mi —*; half-way. *—faisant*; on the way. *— de velours*; the primrose way. *Le — des écoliers*; the longest way. *Se mettre en —*; to begin a journey. *Rebrousser —*; to go back. *Etre toujours par voie et par —*; to be always gadding about. *Aller toujours son —*; to pursue one's point. *Aller son petit bonhomme de —*; to jog along quietly. *Passez votre —*; go your way. *Tout — mène à Rome*; there are more ways to heaven than one. *Ce jeune homme fera son —*; this young man will make his way. *N'y pas aller par quatre —s*; not to beat about the bush. *Qui trop se hâte, reste en —*; slow and sure wins the race. *— de Saint-Jacques*; (astron.) milky-way. *Faire voir du —*; to give trouble.

chemineau, n.m., portable stove; tramp.

cheminée, n.f., chimney; fire-place; mantel-shelf; nipple (of a percussion gun). *Tuyau de* —; chimney-flue. *Ramoneur de* —; chimney-sweep. *Corps de* —; chimney-stack. *Sous le manteau de la* —; secretly (*sub rosâ*). *Il faut faire une croix à la* —; we must chalk that up. *Se chauffer à la* — *du roi René;* to warm one's self in the sun.

cheminement, n.m., (milit.) approach, progress (of siege operations).

cheminer, v.n., to walk, to go; to proceed leisurely; to be well connected (of things). *Ce poème chemine bien;* the various parts of this poem are well connected.

chemise, n.f., shirt, shift, chemise; (fort., mas.) chemise; coat (of a mold); wrapper, cover, envelope; case. — *blanche;* clean shirt. — *de nuit;* night-gown; night-shirt. — *de mailles;* coat of mail. *Vendre jusqu'à sa* —; to sell the shirt off one's back. *Passer une* —; to put on a shirt. *La peau est plus proche que la* —; my shirt, but nearer is my skin. *En manches de* —; in shirt-sleeves. *Le temps de mettre une* —; just time to dress.

chemiser, v.a., to coat.

chemiserie, n.f., shirt-warehouse; shirt-making; shirts.

chemisette, n.f., light under-waistcoat; shirt-front; dicky; chemisette. *Corps de* —; habit-shirt.

chemisi-er, n.m., -**ère**, n.f., shirt-maker.

chênaie, n.f., oak-plantation.

chenal, n.m., channel, watercourse (of harbors, &c.); (geog.) track; gutter (of roofs).

chenaler, v.n., (nav.) to sail through a channel.

chenapan, n.m., (pop.) vagabond, good for nothing wretch, scamp, blackguard.

chêne, n.m., (bot.) oak. *De* —; oaken. — *vert;* evergreen-oak. — *liège;* cork-tree.

chêneau, n.m., young oak.

chéneau, n.m., gutter (of roofs).

chenet, n.m., andiron, fire-dog.

chênette, n.f., (bot.) germander. — *amère;* wall germander.

chènevière, n.f., hemp-field.

chènevis (shèn-vi), n.m., hemp-seed.

chènevotte, n.f., boon, stalk (of hemp).

chènevotter, v.n., (agri.) to shoot weak wood.

chenil (-ni), n.m., dog-kennel; dirty hovel; kennel of hounds.

*****chenille**, n.f., caterpillar, worm; kind of silk cord; kind of dressing-gown; evil doer; bore (troublesome person). — *velue;* hairy caterpillar. — *rase;* naked caterpillar. *Laid comme une* —; as ugly as a toad.

*****chenillette**, n.f., (bot.) caterpillar.

chénopode (ké-), n.m., (bot.) all-good.

chenu, -e, adj., hoary, hoar-back; gray-headed.

cheptel (shĕ-tèl), n.m., (jur.) lease of cattle; cattle leased out.

chèque, n.m., check; cheque. — *barré;* crossed cheque.

ch-er, -ère, adj., dear, beloved; dear, costly, expensive. *Rendre* —; to endear. *Il fait* — *vivre à Paris;* living is dear in Paris.

cher, adv., dear, dearly. *Acheté, payé* —; dear bought. *Je le lui ferai payer plus* — *qu'au marché;* I will make him pay dearly for it. *Faire payer trop* —; to ask too much for.

cher., ab. for Chevalier.

chercher, v.a., to seek, to look for, to search, to be in quest of; to endeavor, to cast about for, to attempt, to try to find. *Que cherchez-vous?* what are you looking for? *Aller* —; to go and bring, to go and fetch, to go for. *Je viendrai vous* —; I will come for you. *Envoyer* —; to send for. *Il est allé* — *son cheval;* he has gone to fetch his horse. *Allez me* — *la lettre;* go and

bring me the letter. — *noise,* — *querelle à;* to pick a quarrel with. — *quelqu'un par mer et par terre;* to look for any one high and low. — *des yeux;* to look for. — *midi à quatorze heures;* to seek for difficulties where there are none; (prov.) to look for a knot in a bulrush. *Le bien cherche le bien;* money begets money; money flies to money; deep calls to deep.

chercheu-r, n.m., -**se**, n.f., seeker, searcher, inquirer. — *de franches lippées;* spunger.

chère, n.f., cheer, entertainment, fare; reception. *Bonne* —; junketing. *Homme de bonne* —; a man who likes good living. *Faire bonne* —; to live well. *Faire maigre* —; to live poorly. *Ne savoir quelle* — *faire à quelqu'un;* not to know how to welcome any one enough. *Il n'est* — *que d'appétit;* hunger is the best sauce. *Il n'est* — *que de vilain;* there is nothing like a miser's feast. *Faire* — *de prince à quelqu'un;* treat any one sumptuously. [high price.

chèrement, adv., dearly, tenderly; dear, at a

chéri, -e, part., beloved, cherished.

chérif, n.m., (—s) cherif (Arabian prince).

chérir, v.a., to love dearly, to cherish; to hug.

chérissable, adj., deserving, worthy of love.

cherté, n.f., dearness, high price, dearth.

chérubin, n.m., cherub.

chervis, n.m., (bot.) skirret.

chéti-f, -ve, adj., lean, thin, pitiful, piteous, puny; sorry, bad, mean, wretched.

chétivement (-tiv-măn), adv., meanly, pitifully, sorrily, poorly, penuriously; feebly.

cheulard, n.m., lout, gaby.

cheval, n.m., horse, nag; horse-flesh; (astron.) horse. — *de frise;* cheval de frise. — *fondu;* saddle my nag (game). — *marin;* sea-horse. — *de rivière;* river-horse. *Fer à* —; horse-shoe. — *gris pommelé, truité, aubère, rouan, poil de souris, isabelle, soupe au lait;* dapple-gray, trout-colored, fleabitten-gray, roan, mouse-colored, light dun, cream-colored, horse. *Petit* —; nag, pony. — *de parade, de bataille;* prancer, charger. — *de selle, de chasse, de trait;* saddle-horse, hunter, draught-horse. — *de brancard, de main, à deux mains;* shaft-horse, led-horse, saddle and shaft-horse. — *de bât;* pack-horse; lout, booby. — *de course, d'amble;* race-horse, nag. — *de Barbarie* or *Barbe;* barb. — *entier;* — *hongre;* entire horse, stone-horse; gelding. — *à bascule;* rocking-horse. — *simulé;* (fowling) stalking-horse. — *de bois;* (milit.) horse (for punishment). — *de charrue, de labour;* plow-horse. — *de conduite;* led horse. — *de gauche;* near-side horse. — *sous la main;* off-side horse. — *de louage;* horse for hire, livery horse. — *à une main;* horse for riding or driving only. — *à deux mains, à deux fins, à toutes mains;* horse for riding and driving. — *de race, de pur sang;* blood-horse. — *au vert;* grass-horse. — *qui a beaucoup d'action;* high stepper. *Chevaux de frise;* (milit.) chevaux de frise. *Case, wagon, pour les chevaux;* horse-box. *Chair de* —; horse-flesh. *L'art de monter à* —; horsemanship. *Aller à* —; to ride. *A* —*!* to horse! *Etre à* —; to be on horseback. *Etre à* — *sur un bâton;* to ride a stick. *Il est le* — *de bât;* he is the drudge. *Travail de* —; hard work. *Brider son* — *par la queue;* to begin at the wrong end. *Parler à* —; to speak magisterially, severely. *Etre mal à* —; to be in a quandary. *Monter sur ses grands chevaux;* to ride the high horse. *A* — *donné il ne faut point regarder à la bride;* one must not look a gift horse in the mouth. *Il n'est si bon* — *qui ne bronche;* 'tis a good horse that never stumbles. *Huile de* —; horse-grease. *Etre à* — *sur l'étiquette;* to be a stickler for etiquette. *Changer son* — *borgne contre un aveugle;* to make a bad bargain; to change for the worse. *L'œil du maître engraisse le* —; matters prosper under the master's eye.

chevalement, *n.m.,* (arch.) prop, stay, shore.

chevaler, *v.a.,* to prop, to shore up.

chevaler, *v.n.,* to run about, to run up and down.

chevaleresque, *adj.,* chivalrous, knightly.

chevalerie, *n.f.,* knighthood, chivalry. — *errante;* knight-errantry.

chevalet, *n.m.,* wooden horse (instrument of torture); bridge (of a stringed instrument); easel; the gallows of a printing-press; horse for scraping hides on; sawing-trestle or horse; buttress, prop, shore; clothes-horse; cross-beam (of a dormer window); pyrotechnist's horse or rack; (nav.) roller (to pass the cables from one place to another). *Tableau de* —; (paint.) easel-piece.

chevalier, *n.m.,* knight; cavalier; knight (at chess); (orni.) sandpiper. *Armer quelqu'un* —; to dub any one a knight. — *d'honneur;* the first gentleman-usher to the queen. *Le* — *du guet;* formerly the captain of the night watch at Paris. — *de l'arquebuse;* one of the artillery-company. — *errant;* knight-errant. — *d'industrie;* one that lives by his wits, sharper, swindler. — *de la coupe;* tavern-knight. *Se faire le* — *de quelqu'un;* to stand up for any one. — *de Saint-Louis;* knight of St. Louis. — *de la légion d'honneur;* knight of the legion of honor. — *rouge;* (orni.) red-shank.

chevalière, *n.f.,* knight's lady; signet-ring.

chevaline, *adj.,* equine, of horses.

chevalis, *n.m.,* passage, canal (cut in the bed of a river).

⊙**chevance,** *n.f.,* goods and chattels, substance.

chevane, *n.f.,* (pisc.) chub, cheven.

chevauchage, *n.m.,* (print.) riding.

chevauchant, -e, *adj.,* (bot.) equitant.

chevauchée, *n.f.,* circuit, progress; riding.

chevauchement (-vôsh-mān), *n.m.,* (of bones) overlapping.

chevaucher, *v.n.,* to ride, to be astride; (nav.) to ride, to cross; (carp.) to overlap; (print. and surg.) to ride.

chevaucher, *v.a.* — *le vent;* to beat up against the wind.

chevaucheur, *n.m.,* rider, horseman.

⊙à **chevauchons,** *adv.,* astraddle.

chevau-léger, *n.m.,* light-horseman. — *-s;* light cavalry.

chevêche, *n.f.,* white owl, owlet, church owl.

chevecier, *n.m.,* dean (of certain chapters).

chevelé, -e, *adj.* (her.) (of the hair) crined.

cheveline (shěv-), *n.f.,* coral club-top.

chevelu, -e (shěve-), *adj.,* long-haired, hairy; (bot.) fibrous; (of literature) romantic. *Comète* — *e;* haired comet. *Cuir* —; scalp.

chevelu, *n.m.,* (bot.) chevelure; beard of the root.

chevelure (shěv-), *n.f.,* hair, head of hair; scalp. *La* — *de Bérénice;* (constellation) Berenice's hair (Coma Berenices).

chever, *v.a.,* (gold.) to hollow out.

chevet, *n.m.,* pillow; bolster; the head (of a bed); bedside; (nav.) cushion, bag. *Droit de* —; sort of fee or present. *Le* — *d'une église;* apsis of a church. *Trouver quelque chose sous son* —; to dream of anything. *C'est son épée de* —; he is his trusty councilor.

chevêtre, *n.m.,* halter; (carp.) binding-joist; (surg.) bandage to support the lower jaw.

cheveu, *n.m.,* hair. *Les* — *x;* the hair of the head. — *x de Vénus;* (bot.) maiden-hair. *Tresse de* — *x;* plait of hair. — *x roux;* sandy hair. — *x d'ébène;* raven locks. — *x épars;* disheveled locks. — *x postiches;* false hair. *Je désire me faire couper les* — *x;* I want to have my hair cut. *Raser les* — *x;* to shave the head. *Se prendre aux* — *x;* to take one another by the hair. *Cela fait dresser les* — *x sur la tête;* that makes one's hair stand on end. *Prendre l'occasion aux* — *x;*

to take time by the forelock. *En* — *x;* bareheaded (wearing nothing on one's head). *Tiré par les* — *x;* far-fetched.

*chevillage,** *n.m.,* pegging, bolting.

chevillard, *n.m.,* carcass-butcher, meat-salesman.

*cheville,** *n.f.,* peg, pin; bolt; plug; botch, stop-gap; (poet.) line or word of necessity; (nav.) iron bolt; branch (of a deer's head). *Trouver à chaque trou une* —; to find a peg for every hole. — *ouvrière;* pole-bolt of a coach; principal agent, mainspring of a party, of an affair. *La* — *du pied;* the ankle-bone. — *à goujon;* common bolt. — *à goupille;* forelock bolt. — *à bouche et à croc;* bolt with ring and hook. — *à tête de diamant;* square-headed bolt. — *à pointe perdue;* short drove-bolt. — *d'affût;* gun-carriage bolt. — *à cosse;* fender-bolt. *Vous ne lui allez pas à la* —; you are a pigmy compared with him; no match for him. *A la* —; by the carcass, or half carcass.

*chevillé, -e,** *adj.,* (her.) branched.

*cheviller,** *v.a.,* to peg or pin; to fasten with a peg; (dy.) to wring. *Des vers chevillés;* botched verses. *Il a l'âme chevillée dans le corps;* he has nine lives.

*chevillette,** *n.f.,* key or peg (of a bookbinder's sewing press).

*chevillon,** *n.m.,* turner's peg.

*chevillot,** *n.m.,* (nav.) toggle, belaying-pin.

*chevillure,** *n.f.,* branches of a deer's head.

chèvre, *n.f.,* she-goat, nanny-goat; (mec.) crab, gin; crane; (astron.) capella. *Enter en pied de* —; to graft slopeways. *Barbe-de-*—; (bot.) jew's beard. — *à musc;* musk goat, Thibet musk. *Avoir la* —, *prendre la* —; to take offense. *Ménager la* — *et le chou;* to run with the hare and hold with the hounds. *Où la* — *est attachée il faut qu'elle broute;* one must bow to circumstances.

chevreau, *n.m.,* kid; kid (skin).

*chèvrefouille,** *n.m.,* honeysuckle. — *des bois;* woodbine.

chèvre-pied or **chèvre-pieds,** *adj.,* (of satyrs) goat-footed.

chevrette, *n.f.,* roe, doe; shrimp, prawn; syrup-pot; little andiron or fire dog.

*chevreuil,** *n.m.,* roebuck, roe-deer; venison.

chevri-er, *n.m.,* **-ère,** *n.f.,* goat-herd.

*chevrillard,** *n.m.,* young roebuck.

chevron, *n.m.,* rafter; stripe (on a soldier's sleeve; (nav.) scantling, long wedge; (her.) chevron. — *de long pan;* long rafter. — *s de croupe;* hips. — *s cintrés;* arched rafters. — *s de remplage;* joists. *Mettre les* — *s à la batterie;* to apply the wedges to the trucks.

chevronné, -e, *adj.,* (her.) chevroned.

⊙**chevrotage,** *n.m.,* goat-fee.

chevrotain, *n.m.,* chevrotain.

chevrotant, -e, *adj.,* quivering, tremulous.

chevrotement (-mān), *n.m.,* tremulous motion, trembling, quivering of the voice.

chevroter, *v.n.,* to kid; to sing or speak in a tremulous voice.

chevrotin, *n.m.,* kid leather.

chevrotine, *n.f.,* buck-shot.

chez (shé), *prep.,* at, to, in, one's house; at the house of; at, to, the native place of; in, with; among. *J'ai été* — *vous;* I have been at your house. *Chacun est maître* — *soi;* every man is master in his own house. *Je viens de* — *vous;* I come from your house. *J'ai passé par* — *vous;* I called at your house in passing. *Je viens de* — *ma mère;* I come from my mother's. *C'est* — *lui une habitude;* it a habit with him. *Avoir un* — *soi;* to have a home of one's own. *Il n'y a pas de petit* — *soi;* home is home, be it ever so homely.

chiaoux, *n.m.,* Turkish officer, messenger.

chiasse, *n.f.,* dross, scum ; dung (of flies).

chibouque, n.f., chibouk (Turkish pipe).

chic, n.m., tact, effect, knack, style (paint.). Il a du —; there is something stylish about him.

chicambaut, n.m., (nav.) bumkin, luff-block.

chicane, n.f., cavil, evasion, quibble; chicanery, pettifogging, caviling, quibbling; the quirks of the law; wrangling. Gens de —; pettifoggers. Chercher — à quelqu'un; to pick a trumpery quarrel with any one.

chicaner, v.n., to chicane, to cavil, to quibble, to use tricks, to quarrel with; to use quirks, shifts; to wrangle, to perplex. — le vent; (nav.) to hug the wind.

chicanerie (shi-), n.f., chicanery; quibbling, caviling.

chicaneu-r, n.m., -**se**, n.f., **chicani-er**, n.m., -**ère**, n.f., and adj., chicaner, caviler, pettifogger, wrangler; litigious, caviling, wrangling.

chicard, -**e**, adj., (pop.) swellish.

chiche, adj., niggardly, penurious, stingy, scurvy, shabby, scanty, sordid, sparing, parsimonious, niggard. Pois —s; chick-peas, dwarf-peas.

chichement (shish-mān), adv., niggardly, penuriously, stingily, parsimoniously.

⊙**chicheté**, n.f., niggardliness, covetousness, penuriousness.

chicon, n.m., cos-lettuce; heart (of).

chicoracé, -**e**, adj., endive-like, chicoraceous.

chicoracée, n.f., (bot.) chicoraceous plant.

chicorée, n.f., succory, endive, chicory.

chicot, n.m., small broken piece of wood; stump (of teeth); stub, stump (of trees). — du Canada; bonduc.

chicoter, v.n., (pop.) to wrangle, to trifle, to split hairs.

chicotin, n.m., orpine, rosewort, rose-root, livelong; juice of bitter apple. Amer comme —; as bitter as gall.

chie-en-lit, n.m., (—) merry-andrew, masker, jack-pudding.

chien, n.m., -**ne**, n.f. (-ln, -è-n), dog, bitch; cock (of a gun or pistol). — babillard; (hunt.) liar. — caniche; poodle-dog; poodle; water-dog. — volant; tailless bat. Grand —; dog-star. — de pure race; true-bred dog. — métis; half-bred dog; mongrel. Cette chienne est pleine; that bitch is with pup. — d'arrêt; pointer. — couchant; setter; toad-eater; lick-spittle. — courant; beagle. — turc; Barbary, Turkish dog. — d'attache; ban-dog. — de basse-cour; house-dog. — de berger; shepherd's dog. — de boucher; mastiff. — de ferme; house-dog. — marin, — de mer; (ich.) dog-fish, hound-fish. — de race; thorough-bred dog. — pour le renard; fox-hound. — pour le sanglier; boar-hound. — du grand Saint-Bernard; Alpine mastiff. — de Terre-neuve; Newfoundland dog. — terrier; terrier. Une meute de —s; a pack of hounds. Un petit —, un jeune —; a puppy, a whelp. — de salon; lap-dog. Chasser au — d'arrêt; to shoot over dogs. Donner lâcher les —s; to let loose, cast off, the dogs. Jeter sa langue aux —s; to give it up (of a riddle). C'est Saint Roch et son —; they are like Darby and Joan; they are inseparable. Hâler les —s; to set on the dogs. Rompre les—s; to call off the dogs. Etre comme un — à l'attache; to be like a galley-slave. Faire le — couchant; to creep and crouch and truckle. Mener une vie de —; to lead a dog's life. Bons —s chassent de race; like father, like son; cat after kind. Entre — et loup; in the dusk of the evening. Ils s'accordent comme — et chat; they agree like cat and dog. Leurs —s ne chassent pas ensemble; they don't agree together. Qui m'aime, aime mon —; love me, love my dog. — qui aboie ne mord pas; his bark is worse than his bite. — hargneux a toujours l'oreille déchirée; quarrelsome curs have dirty

coats. Qui veut noyer son — l'accuse de la rage; give your dog a bad name, and hang him. Un — regarde bien un évêque; a cat may look at a king. C'est le — du jardinier; it is the dog in the manger. Autant vaut être mordu d'un — que d'une chienne; as well be hanged for a sheep as a lamb. Etre reçu comme un — dans un jeu de quilles; to be as welcome as a dog at a wedding.

chien de mer or **chien marin**, n.m., (ich.) dog-fish, hound-fish.

chiendent, n.m., dog-grass, quitch-grass, couch-grass. — fossile; amianthus.

chiennée, n.f., a litter of pups.

chienner (shiè-), v.n., to whelp, to pup.

chiffe, n.f., poor stuff; rags.

chiffon, n.m., rag, scrap; trinket, frippery. Mon petit —; you little darling.

chiffonnage, n.m., (paint.) rumpled drapery; rumpling, crumpling, tumbling.

chiffonne, adj. f., (gard.) puny, useless. Branche —; puny, stunted, branch.

chiffonner, v.a., to rumple, to wrinkle, to crumple, to tumble, to ruffle, to tease, to vex.

chiffonni-er, n.m., -**ère**, n.f., rag-picker.

chiffonni-er, n.m., or -**ère**, n.f., chiffonier.

chiffre, n.m., figure, number; total amount; cipher; flourish of letters, monogram; digit. — périodique; (arith.) figure of the recurring period. Ecrire en —; to write in cipher.

chiffrer, v.n., to cipher, to mark, to write in cipher.

chiffrer, v.a., to cipher, to foot up; to figure, to number (of music).

chiffreur, n.m., reckoner.

***chignon**, n.m., nape (of the neck); hair twisted behind, chignon.

chimère, n.f., (myth.) chimera; myth, idle fancy, vain imagination; (conch., ich.) chimera.

chimérique, adj., chimerical, visionary, fantastical.

chimériquement, adv., chimerically.

chimie, n.f., chemistry.

chimique, adj. chemical.

chimiste, n.m., chemist.

chimpanzé, n.m., (zool.) chimpanzee.

china, n.m., (bot.) China-root. V. **squine**.

chinchilla, n.m., (mam.) chinchilla.

chiner, v.a., (manu.) to color, to dye.

chinois, -**e**, n. and adj., Chinese.

chinoiserie, n.f., Chinese ornament; knick-knack; folly, farce, joke.

chiourme, n.f., convict-gang.

chiper, v.a., to pilfer, to crib, to prig, to bag.

chipie, n.f., affected, mincing, peevish woman; prude.

chipoter, v.n., to dally, to trifle, to dispute about trifles; to higgle; to haggle.

chipoti-er, n.m., -**ère**, n.f., trifler, dallier, shuffler; higgler, haggler.

chique, n.f., quid of tobacco; (ent.) chegre, chegoe, chigre; marble (to play with).

chiquenaude (shik-nôd), n.f., fillip.

chiquenauder, v.a., to fillip.

chiquer, v.n., to chew tobacco; to eat heartily; (paint.) to dash off.

chiquet, n.m., driblet, bit; shred. Un — de vin; a drop of wine. — à —; bit by bit.

chiragre (ki-), n.f., chiragra.

⊙**chirimoya**, n.f., custard-apple.

chirographaire (ki-), adj., on note of hand.

chirologie (ki-), n.f., chirology.

chiromancie (ki-), n.f., chiromancy, palmistry.

chiromancien (ki-), n.m., chiromancer.

chirone, n.f., (bot.) centaury.

chiroptère (ki-), n.m., (mam.) cheiropter, bat.

chirurgical, -**e**, adj., surgical.

chirurgie, n.f., surgery.

chirurgien (-in), n.m., surgeon. Aide-—, (—s-—s) assistant surgeon.

chirurgique, *adj.*, surgical.

chiste (kist), *n.m.*, (surg.) cyst.

chiure, *n.f.*, fly-blow. *Marqué de —s de mouches*; fly-bitten. *Faire des —s de mouches sur*; to fly-blow.

chlamyde (kla-), *n.f.*, chlamys.

chlorate (klo-), *n.m.*, (chem.) chlorate.

chlore (klor), *n.m.*, (chem.) chlorine; (bot.) yellow-wort.

chloré, -e (klo-), *adj.*, chloruretted.

chlorhydrate (klo-), *n.m.*, (chem.) hydrochlorate.

chlorhydrique (klo-), *adj.*, (chem.) hydrochloric, muriatic.

chloride (klo-), *n.m.*, (chem.) a combination of chlorine with a simple substance, chloride.

chlorique (klo-), *adj.*, (chem.) chloric.

chloroforme (klo-), *n.m.*, chloroform.

chloroformer, *v.a.*, to administer chloroform.

chloromètre (klo-), *n.m.*, chlorometer.

chlorométrie (klo-), *n.f.*, chlorometry.

chlorose (klo-rōz), *n.f.*, (med.) chlorosis, green sickness; (bot.) etiolation.

chlorotique (klo-), *adj.*, chlorotic.

chlorure (klo-), *n.m.*, chloride.

choc, *n.m.*, shock, clashing, encounter; brunt; collision, disaster, blow. *Soutenir le —*; to stand the shock.

chocolat, *n.m.*, chocolate. *Bâton de —*; stick of chocolate.

chocolati-er, *n.m.*, **-ère**, *n.f.*, chocolate-maker; chocolate-dealer.

chocolatière (-ti-èr), *n.f.*, chocolate-pot.

chœur (keur), *n.m.*, choir, chorus. *Enfant de —*; choir boy, chorister. *Chanter en —*; to sing in chorus.

choir (chu), *v.n.*, to fall.

choisir, *v.a.*, to choose, to make choice of; to pitch upon, to pick out; to nominate; to single out, to select. *Il n'y a point à —*; there is no choice left. *Se —*; to choose for one's self.

choix (shoâ), *n.m.*, choice, choosing, option, selection, distinction, discernment. *Par —*; from choice. *Sans —*; indifferently. *Au —*; all at one price. *Avoir le — forcé*; to have Hobson's choice.

cholagogue (ko-la-gog), *n.m.*, (med.) cholagogue.

cholédoque, *adj.*, (anat.) biliary, hepatic. *Canal —*; hepatic duct.

choléra-morbus (ko-), *n.m.*, (n.p.) cholera-morbus. *Faux —*; cholerine.

cholérine (ko-), *n.f.* cholerine.

cholérique, *n.m.f.*, (med.) person affected with cholera; cholera patient. *adj.*, choleric, bilious.

choliambe (ko-), *n.m.*, choliambic verse.

chômable, *adj.*, to be kept as a holiday.

chômage, *n.m.*, stoppage; want of work; cessation from work; enforced idleness; respite. *Le — d'un moulin*; the standing still of a mill.

chômer, *v.a.*, to abstain, to cease, from work on a particular day, to rest. *C'est un saint qu'on ne chôme pas*; he is in no great repute.

chômer, *v.n.*, to want work, to be at a standstill; (agri.) to lie fallow. *Il chôme de besogne*; he is out of work. *— de quelque chose*; to stand in need of a thing.

*chondrille (kon-), *n.f.*, (bot.) gum-succory; wall-lettuce.

chondrologie, *n.f.*, chondrology.

chope, *n.f.*, large beer-glass; mug of beer.

⊙**chopine**, *n.f.*, pint (a measure nearly equal to an English pint).

chopiner, *v.n.*, to tipple.

chopper, *v.n.*, to stumble, to trip up; to blunder.

choquant, -e, *adj.*, rude, offensive; shocking; unpleasant, disagreeable, improper.

choquer, *v.a.*, to shock, to strike, to dash against, to clash with; to offend, to give offense, to shock, to disgust, to displease, to grate upon; (nav.) to surge.

se choquer, *v.r.*, to take offense; to come into collision with.

choquer, *v.n.*, to strike glasses; to be offensive; to hurt any one's feelings; to be shocking.

choral (ko-), *adj.*, choral. *n.m.*, chant.

chorée (ko-), *n.m.*, (poet.) choreus.

chorée (ko-), *n.f.*, chorea, St. Vitus' dance.

chorège (ko-), *n.m.*, (antiq.) choragus.

chorégraphe (ko-) *n.m.*, choragrapher.

chorégraphie (ko-), *n.f.*, choregraphy.

chorégraphique (ko-), *adj.*, choregraphical.

chorévêque (ko-), *n.m.*, chorepiscopus.

choriambe (ko-ri-ănb), *n.m.*, (poet.) choriamb.

chorion (ko-), *n.m.*, (anat.) chorion.

choriste (ko-), *n.m.*, chorister; chorus singer (thea.).

chorographie (ko-), *n.f.*, chorography.

chorographique (ko-), *adj.*, chorographical.

choroïde (ko-), *n.f.*, *adj.*, (anat.) choroid.

chorus (ko-rûss) *n.m.*, chorus. *Faire —*; to sing the chorus, to join in; to chime in; to applaud, to approve, to agree.

chose, *n.f.*, thing; matter, business, affair, deed; reality, action; (jur.) chattels. *Ce n'est pas grand —*; 'tis no great matter. *Quelque — de beau*; something fine. *Peu de —*; a mere trifle, nothing. *La — publique*; the commonwealth, common weal. *Etre tout —*; (pop.) to be out of sorts. *Rester tout —*; to remain confused. *C'est tout autre —*; that is quite another thing. *Dites bien des — de ma part à votre frère*; remember me to your brother. *Bien des — chez vous*; kind regards at home. *Monsieur —*; Mr. "what's his name." *—s de la mer* (nav.); wreckage; flotage, flotsam (jur.).

chou, *n.m.*, cabbage; colewort; puff-paste; kale; darling, dear; bow, rosette. *— cabus*; headed-cabbage. *— marin*; sea-kale, wort, sea-cabbage. *— pommé*; white-headed cabbage. *— non pommé*; bore-kale, brown-kale. *Filet à —*; cabbage-net. *Rejet de —*; cabbage-sprout. *Pomme de —*; cabbage-head. *Tige, trognon, de —*; cabbage-stalk. *— crépu*; Scotch kale. *— de Milan*; savoy. *—x verts, jeunes —x*; sprouts. *—x blancs*; white-heart cabbages. *—x brocolis*; broccoli. *— oléifère*; colza. *— de chien*; dog's cabbage. *—palmiste*, (*—x—s*) palm-cabbage. *— navet*, (*—x—s*) rape-colewort. *—rave*, (*—x—s*) turnip-cabbage. *—! —là!* *—pille!* (hunt.) at it! go it! *Des —x et des raves*; ducks and drakes. *— pour —*; taking one thing and another. *Il en fait ses —x gras*; he feathers his nest with it. *Il s'entend à cela comme à ramer des —x*; he knows nothing at all about it. *Aller planter ses —x*; to retire into private life. *Mon petit —*; my little darling. *Bête comme un —*; as stupid as an owl.

chouan, *n.m.*, brown owl, royalist insurgent (French Revolution).

chouanner, *v.n.*, to carry on a guérilla warfare (after the manner of the Chouans).

chouannerie, *n.f.*, the party of the Chouans; Vendean royalists.

chouant, *n.m.*, a sort of owl.

choucas, *n.m.*, or **chouchette**, *n.f.*, jackdaw.

choucroute, *n.f.*, sour-krout, sauer-kraut.

chouette, *n.f.*, screech-owl. *adj.*, capital, excellent, stunning. *Faire la —*; (piquet) to play alone against two.

chouettement, *adv.*, (pop.) capitally, famously.

chou-fleur, *n.m.*, (*—x—s*) cauliflower.

*chou-pille, *n.m.*, (*—*) shooting-dog.

chouquet, *n.m.*, (nav.) block, moor's-head, cap of the mast-head.

chou-rave, *n.m.*, (*—x—s*) turnip-cabbage.

choyer, *v.a.*, to take great care of, to be fond of, to pamper, to fondle, to pet, to make much of, to cocker-up.

se **choyer**, *v.r.*, to pamper one's self.

chrématologie (kré-), *n.f.*, (l.u.) chrematology.

chrématologique (kré-), *adj.*, chrematological.

chrême (krem), *n.m.*, chrism, holy oil.

chrémeau (kré-), *n.m.*, chrism-cloth.

chrestomathie (kres-to-ma-ci), *n.f.*, chrestomathy, select extracts.

chrétien, -ne (kre-ti-in, -ti-è-n), *n.* and *adj.*, Christian.

chrétiennement (kré-tien-mān), *adv.*, Christianly, Christian-like.

chrétienté (kré-ti-in-té), *n.f.*, Christendom. *Marcher sur la* —; (fam.) to wear shoes and stockings in holes.

chrismal (kri-), *n.m.*, chrismatory.

chrismation, *n.f.*, chrismation.

le **christ** (krist), *n.m.*, Christ, crucifix. *Jésus Christ* (jé-zu-kri); Jesus Christ. [*Christ* without *Jésus* is never used in French without *le.*]

christe (krist), *n.f.*, (bot.) crithmum, samphire, sea-fennel. — *marine*; crithmum, samphire, sea-fennel.

christianiser (kris-), *v.a.*, to Christianize.

christianisme (kris-tia-nism), *n.m.*, Christianity.

christiaque (kris-tiak), *adj.*, Christian.

chromate (kro-), *n.m.*, (chem.) chromate.

chromatique (kro-), *adj.*, (chem. and mus.) chromatic.

chromatique, *n.f.*, (mus., paint.) chromatics.

chromatiquement, *adv.*, (mus.) chromatically.

chrome (krôm), *n.m.*, chromium.

chromique, *adj.*, (chem.) chromic.

chromolithographie, *n.f.*, chromo-lithography.

chronicité (kro-), *n.f.*, (med.) chronicity.

chronique (kro-), *n.f.*, chronicle, history; summary, reports. — *scandaleuse;* tittle-tattle, scandalous reports.

chronique, *adj.*, (med.) chronic.

chroniqueur (kro-), *n.m.*, chronicler.

chronogramme (kro-), *n.m.*, chronogram.

chronographe (kro-), *n.m.*, chronographer.

chronographie (kro-), *n.f.*, chronography.

chronologie (kro-), *n.f.*, chronology.

chronologique (kro-), *adj.*, chronological.

chronologiste (kro-), *n.m.*, chronologer.

⊙**chronologue** (kro-), *n.m.*, chronologer.

chronomètre (kro-), *n.m.*, chronometer.

chrysalide (kri-), *n.m.*, aurelia, chrysalis, nympha; pupa; pupe; grub.

chrysanthème (kri-), *n.m.*, chrysanthemum; ox-eye daisy; marigold.

chrysite (kri-), *n.f.*, chrysite, touch-stone.

chrysobate (kri-), *n.f.*, chrysobates.

chrysobéril (kri-), *n.m.*, chrysober.

chrysocale (kri-), *n.m.*, an alloy of copper and zinc, resembling gold; pinchbeck.

chrysocolle (kri-), *n.f.*, chrysocolla, borax.

chrysocome (kri-), *n.f.*, (bot.) chrysocoma, goldylocks.

chrysogonum (kri-), *n.m.*, moth-mullein, red turnip.

chrysolithe (kri-), *n.f.*, chrysolite.

chrysophris (kri-), *n.m.*, (ich.) gilt-head.

chrysoprase (kri-), *n.f.*, chrysoprase.

⊙**chrysulée** (kri-), (chem.) *n.f.*, chrysulea, aqua regia.

chu, -e, *part.* (of *choir*), fallen.

⊙**chucheter**, *v.n.*, to whisper; to twitter.

chuchotement, *n.m.*, whispering, whisper, rustling.

chuchoter, *v.n.* and *a.*, to whisper.

chuchoterie (sho-trî), *n.f.*, whispering.

chuchoteu-r, *n.m.*, -**se**, *n.f.*, whisperer.

chut (shut), *int.*, hush!

chute, *n.f.*, fall, tumble; decline; falling, overthrow, lapse, downfall, descension, decay; catastrophe, disaster; failure, miscarriage. — *d'eau;* waterfall, cataract. *La* — *du jour;* the close of day. — *d'eau;* waterfall, watercourse. — *d'une voile;* (nav.) depth of a sail; drop (of the principal square sails). — *de courants;* setting of the tides.

chuter, *v.n.*, (thea.) to fail, to be damned.

chyle, *n.m.*, chyle.

chyleu-x, -se, *adj.*, chylous.

chylifère, *adj.*, (anat.) chyliferous.

chylification, *n.f.*, chyliaction, chylification.

chylose, *n.f.*, chylification.

chyme, *n.m.*, chyme.

chymification, *n.f.*, chymification.

ci, *adv.*, here. *Celui*— *est meilleur que celui-là;* this is better than that. *Cet homme*— ; this man. —*dessus, —devant;* above, before, heretofore, ex, former. *Par*— *par-là;* here and there, up and down; off and on. —*après;* hereafter. —*dessous;* below. —*contre;* opposite. *Entre* — *et demain;* between this time and to-morrow. *Entre* — *et là;* between this and then. (French Revolution) *Un* —-*devant noble, un* —-*devant;* an ex-noble, royalist. *Les* —-*devant nobles, les* —-*devant;* the royalists, the aristocracy.

cibagé, *n.m.*, an Indian pine, cibage.

cibaudière, *n.f.*, sort of fishing-net.

cible, *n.f.*, mark to be shot at, target.

ciboire, *n.m.*, a sacred vase, pyx; (arch.) ciborium, canopy.

ciboule, *n.f.*, scallion, green onion; eschalot.

ciboulette, *n.f.*, (bot.) chive. *V.* **civette**.

cicatrice, *n.f.*, scar, seam, mark.

cicatricule, *n.f.*, cicatricule, eye or thread; (of an egg) small scar.

cicatrisant, -e, *adj.*, cicatrizing.

cicatrisant, *v.a.*, to mark with a scar, to scar; to cicatrize; to close, heal up.

se **cicatriser**, *v.r.*, to be cicatrized, to skin over, to heal up.

ciccus, *n.m.*, a species of grasshopper; a species of wild-goose; ciccus.

cicéro, *n.m.*, (print.) pica. — *gros œil;* pica. — *petit œil;* small pica.

cicérole, *n.f.*, chick-pea.

cicéron, *n.m.*, Cicero.

cicérone, *n.m.*, cicerone.

cicéronien, -ne (-in, -è-n), *adj.*, Ciceronian.

⊙**cicisbée**. *V.* **sigisbée**.

ciclamor, *n.m.* *V.* **orle**.

cicutaire, *n.f.*, cicuta, water-hemlock.

cid (sid), *n.m.*, cid (chief, commander).

cidre, *n.m.*, cider. *Gros* —; strong cider. —*paré;* old cider. —*piquant;* rough cider.

cie, (ab.) Co. (for Company).

ciel (siel), *n.m.*, (cieux) heaven, the heavens, the firmament, the sky; paradise. *Grâces au* —; thanks be to heaven, to God. *C'est un coup du* —; it is a judgment of heaven. *O—! O* heavens! *Juste* —! good heavens! great god! *Du* —; heavenly. *Arc-en*— (—*s*—); rainbow. *Remuer* — *et terre;* to leave no stone unturned.

ciel, *n.m.*, (ciels) tester of a bed; (c. rel.) the canopy which is carried over the host; sky (paint.); the roof of a quarry; air, climate. *Un beau* —; a fine climate. *L'Italie est sous un des plus beaux* —*s de l'Europe;* Italy has one of the finest climates in Europe.

cierge, *n.m.*, wax-taper, church candle, wax-light. — *du Pérou;* torch thistle. — *pascal;* Easter cierge. —*s d'eau;* water-jets. *Droit comme un* —; as stiff as a poker.

ciergé, -e, *adj.*, (nav.) stiff.

ciergier, *n.m.*, wax-chandler.

cigale, n.f., cicada, grasshopper. — *de rivière;* water-grasshopper. — *de mer;* shrimp.

cigare, n.m., cigar.

cigarette, n.f., cigarette.

*****cigogne,** n.f., (orni.) stork. — *à sac;* hurgil. *Bec de* —; (bot.) crane's bill. *Conte à la* —, or *conte de la* —; absurd and improbable story.

*****cigogneau,** n.m., (fam.) a young stork.

ciguë (si-gû), n.f., hemlock. — *vireuse,* or — *d'eau;* water-hemlock, cow-bane.

cil, n.m., eye-lash; (bot.) lash, hair.

ciliaire, adj., ciliary.

cilice, n.m., hair-cloth.

cilié, -e, adj., (bot.) ciliated, lashed.

*****cillement.** n.m., twinkle, winking.

*****ciller,** v.a., to wink, to twinkle; (hawking) to seel.

*****ciller,** v.n., to wink; to twinkle.

*****cillo,** n.m., (med.) winker.

cimaise, n.f., cyma, ogee.

cimbalaire, n.f. V. **cymbalaire.**

cime, n.f., top, summit, peak; height; (bot.) cyme, summit. *En* —; (bot.) cymose.

ciment, n.m., cement.

cimenter, v.a., to cement; to confirm, to strengthen, to consolidate.

cimentier (-tié), n.m., (tech.) cement-maker.

cimeterre (sim-tèr), n.m., scimeter, falchion, sword.

cimetière (sim-tièr), n.m., church-yard, burying-ground, cemetery.

cimier, n.m., buttock, round of beef; crest of a head-piece; apex. — *de cerf;* haunch of venison.

cimolée, n.f., cimolite; cimolian earth; cutler's dust.

cimolée or **cimolie,** adj.f., cimolian.

cinabre, n.m., cinnabar.

cincenelle, n.f., tow-line.

cinchonine, n.f., cinchonia, cinchonine.

cincle, n.m., (orni.) water-ouzel, dipper.

cinéraire, adj., cinerary.

cinéraire, n.f., (bot.) cineraria.

cinération, n.f., cineration.

cinglage, n.m., ⊙run of a ship in twenty-four hours, ship's course, sailing; (metal.) shingling.

cingler, v.n., to sail before the wind, to scud along.

cingler, v.a., to lash; (metal.) to shingle.

cinglerie, n.f., shingling-house.

cinnamome, n.m., cinnamon.

cinq (sînk), adj., five.

cinq, n.m., a five; cinque (at games).

cinquantaine, n.f., some fifty; half a hundred.

cinquante, adj., fifty.

⊙**cinquantenier,** n.m., captain of fifty men.

cinquantième (-ti-èm), adj., fiftieth.

cinquantième, n.m., fiftieth part.

cinquième, adj., fifth.

cinquième, n.m., fifth part; pupil on the fifth form. n.f., the fifth form in colleges and public schools.

cinquièmement, adv., fifthly.

cintrage, n.m., arching, curving.

cintre, n.m., arch, semi-circle; curve; (carp.) center-bit. *Cette cave est en* —; that cellar is built arch-wise. — *surbaissé;* elliptical arch; adj., (fig.) low, flattened. *A plein* —; semi-circular.

cintrer, v.a., to arch, to build in the form of an arch, to curve.

cioutat, n.m., cioutat (a kind of grape).

cipaye, n.m., Sepoy.

cipolin, n.m., cipollino, cipolin marble.

cippe, n.m., cippus (column).

cirage, n.m., waxing; blacking; (paint.) cameo with a yellow ground.

circée, n.f., (bot.) enchanter's nightshade.

circompolaire, adj., circumpolar.

circoncire, v.a., to circumcise.

circoncis, n.m., one who is circumcised.

circonciseur, n.m., circumcisor

circoncision, n.f., circumcision.

circonférence, n.f., circumference.

circonflexe, n.m. and adj., circumflex accent; circumflex.

circonlocution, n.f., circumlocution.

circonscription, n.f., circumscription, bound; division, district.

circonscrire, v.a., to circumscribe, to encircle, to enclose, to limit, to stint.

circonspect, -e (-pé, -pèkt), adj., circumspect, wary, guarded, discreet, cautious.

circonspection, n.f., circumspection, wariness, caution. *Avec* —; cautiously.

circonstance, n.f., circumstance, occasion; occurrence, event, conjuncture, case. — *aggravante;* aggravation. *De* —; required by or adapted to circumstances. *Suivant les* —*s;* as the case may be. *Dans les* —*s critiques;* on critical occasions, or in emergencies.

circonstancier, v.a., to state circumstantially; to tell, to detail, to particularize.

circonvallation (-val-la-), n.f., circumvallation.

circonvenir, v.a., to circumvent, to deceive, to impose upon; to over-reach.

circonvention, n.f., circumvention, over-reaching. *User de* —; to circumvent.

circonvoisin, -e, adj., circumjacent, neighbouring, adjoining.

circonvolution, n.f., circumvolution.

circuit, n.m., circuit; roundabout road; circumlocution.

circulaire, adj., circular, round.

circulaire, n.f., circular.

circulairement (-lèr-mān), adv., circularly.

circulant, -e, adj., circulating.

circulation, n.f., circulation; currency; issue; traffic. *Mettre en* —; to issue (money).

circulatoire, adj., circulatory, circulating.

circuler, v.n., to circulate; to pass from hand to hand; to spread. *Faire* —; to make people move on. *Circulez, Messieurs!* move on, please!

circumnavigateur (-kom-), n.m., circumnavigator.

circumnavigation (-kom-), n.f., circumnavigation.

cire, n.f., wax; beeswax; wax-light. — *à cacheter,* or — *d'Espagne;* sealing-wax.

cirer, v.a., to wax, to black (boots). *Se* —; to be waxed. *Se* — *les bottes;* to clean one's boots.

cirier, n.m., wax-chandler; wax-maker; (bot.) candle-berry, wax-tree.

ciron, n.m., (ent.) flesh-worm, mite.

cirque, n.m., circus.

cirre, n.m., (bot.) tendril; (zool.) cirrus.

cirreu-x, -se, adj., ending in a cirrus.

cirrhose, n.f., (med.) cirrhosis.

cirrus, n.m., cirrus, curl-cloud; mare's tail.

cirsakas, n.m. V. **sirsacas.**

cirse, n.m., (bot.) horse-thistle. — *des champs;* way-thistle, field-thistle.

cirsion, n.f., (bot.) cirsium, gentle-thistle.

cirsocèle, n.f., (med.) cirsocele.

cirure, n.f., prepared wax.

*****cisaille,** n.f., (coin.) clippings or shearings of metals; pl., shears.

*****cisailler,** v.a., (coin.) to mark, to clip.

cisalpin, -e, adj., Cisalpine.

ciseau, n.m., chisel. — *d'orfèvre;* graver.

ciseaux, n.m. pl., scissors. — *de jardinier;* shears. — *de tailleur;* shears. — *boutonnés* (surg.); probe-scissors. — *mousses* (surg.); blunt-pointed scissors.

ciseler (siz-lé), v.a., to chisel, to chase, to carve, to emboss, to sculpture.

ciselet (siz-lè), n.m., graver; chasing tool.

ciseleur (siz-leur), n.m., chaser; carver; sculptor.

ciselure (siz-lur), *n.f.*, chasing, sculpture, carving; chased work, carved work, sculpturing.

cisoires, *n.f. pl.*, bench-shears.

cissite, *n.f.*, aetites, eagle-stone.

cissoïdai, -e, *adj.*, cissoid.

cissoïde, *n.f.*, (geom.) cissoid.

ciste, *n.m.*, (antiq.) basket; **(arch.)** cist; (bot.) cistus, rock-rose.

cistophore, *n.f.*, (antiq.) cistophora, cane-phora.

cistophore, *n.m.*, (antiq.) cistophorus.

citadelle, *n.f.*, citadel, fortress, castle.

citadin, *n.m.*, **-e,** *n.f.*, citizen, burgess; (b.s.) cit; cockney.

citadine, *n.f.*, hackney-coach, fly.

citateur, *n.m.*, quoter; book containing a collection of quotations.

citation, *n.f.*, citation, quotation, quoting; summons. *Se faire délivrer une —;* to take out a summons. *Lancer une —;* (jur.) to issue a summons.

cité, *n.f.*, city; town. *La céleste —;* the heavenly city. *Droits de —;* the rights of a citizen; freedom (of a city); citizenship.

citer, *v.a.*, to cite, to quote; to name; to summon; to subpœna.

citérieur, -e, *adj.*, citerior, hither.

citerne, *n.f.*, cistern, reservoir, tank.

citerneau, *n.m.*, small cistern or tank.

cithare, *n.f.*, (antiq.) cithara; zither.

citli, *n.m.*, tapeti, Brazilian rabbit.

citole, *n.m.* a musical instrument, dulcimer.

citoyen, *n.m.*, **-ne,** *n.f.* (-in, -è-n), citizen, free-man of a city, patriot.

citragon, *n.m.*, balm-mint.

citrate, *n.m.*, (chem.) citrate. [yellow.

citrin, -e, *adj.*, citrine, lemon-colored, pale

citrique, *adj.*, citric.

citron, *n.m.*, citron, lemon; lime; lemon-color. *adj.*, lemon-colored.

citronnade, *n.f.*, lemon-squash.

citronnat, *n.m.*, candied lemon-peel; sugar-plum with lemon-peel in it.

citronné, -e, *adj.*, lemon-flavored.

citronnelle, *n.f.*, balm-mint, garden-mint, citron-water.

citronnier, *n.m.*, lemon-tree; citron-tree.

****citrouille,** *n.f.*, pumpkin, gourd.

⊙**civadière,** *n.f.*, (nav.) sprit-sail.

cive *or* **civette,** *n.f.*, (bot.) chive.

civet, *n.m.* *— de lièvre;* stewed or jugged hare.

civette, *n.f.*, (mam.) civet-cat; civet; (bot.) chive.

civière, *n.f.*, hand-barrow; litter, stretcher.

civil, -e, *adj.*, relating to the community in general; private, plain; civil, courteous, well-bred, gallant. *Requête —e;* bill of review. *Partie —e;* the public prosecutor. *Droit —;* (jur.) common law.

civil, *n.m.*, civil, civil service.

civilement (-măn), *adv.*, civilly; courteously, politely. *Mort —;* dead in law.

civilisable, *adj.*, civilizable.

civilisat-eur, -rice, *adj.*, civilizing.

civilisation, *n.f.*, civilization.

civiliser, *v.a.*, to civilize.

se **civiliser,** *v.r.*, to become civilized.

civilité, *n.f.*, civility, good manners, good breeding, politeness, courtesy, manners; compliment, courteousness. *Il n'a pas lu la — puérile et honnête;* he never learned politeness. *Mes —s à Monsieur votre frère;* my compliments to your brother. *Il est de la —, il est de — de;* it is but common civility to.

civique, *adj.*, civic.

civisme, *n.m.*, civism.

clabaud, *n.m.*, (hunt.) liar; (b.s.) babbler, bawler, ranter.

clabaudage, *n.m.*, barking, baying; clamor, bawling.

clabaudement, *n.m.*, peg-peg (i. e., of a wooden leg).

clabauder, *v.n.*, to give tongue (falsely); to clamor, to bawl out.

clabauderie (-bo-drî), *n.f.*, clamor, bawling; ranting, abuse; tall-talk, brawl.

clabaudeu-r, *n.m.*, **-se,** *n.f.*, brawler, clamorer, scold.

claie, *n.f.*, wattle, hurdle; (of a sieve) screen. *Passer à la —;* to screen.

clair, -e, *adj.*, clear, bright, relucent, shining, luminous; light, lightsome, light-colored; transparent; pure, limpid; thin; plain, manifest, evident, obvious, intelligible, visible. *C'est — comme jour;* it is as plain as a pike-staff. *Etoffe —e;* thin, flimsy stuff. *Lait —;* whey; (of eggs) addled, barren.

clair, *n.m.*, light, clearness; (paint.) light. *Il fait — de lune;* it is moonlight. *Vin tiré au —;* racked wine. *Tirer au —;* to bottle off; to clari y, to fine.

clair, *adv.*, clearly, plain, plainly. *Parler — et net;* to speak out plainly, openly; not to mince matters. *N'y pas voir —;* not to see; (fig.) not to understand. *Arbres — semés;* sparse, thinly scattered trees.

clairçage, *n.m.*, decoloring (of sugar).

clairçer, *v.a.*, to decolor; (sugar) to clarify.

claire, *n.f.*, burnt bones; sugar-boiler.

clairée, *n.f.*, clarified sugar.

clairement (klèr-măn), *adv.*, clearly, plainly, distinctly, evidently, intelligibly.

clairet, *adj.*, (of wines) palish, lightish.

clairet, *n.m.*, precious stone that is too pale; pale wine; clairet (an infusion of wine, honey, sugar, and aromatic plants).

clairette, *n.f.*, a kind of grape.

claire-voie, *n.f.*, (—s—s) opening (in a garden wall); lattice, wicket; (nav.) sky-light. *A —;* in open work. *Semer à —;* to sow thin.

clairière, *n.f.*, glade; thin part (in linen).

clair-obscur, *n.m.*, (—s—s) (paint.) chiaro-oscuro, clare-obscure, light and shade; mezzo-tint.

clairon, *n.m.*, clarion, trumpet, bugle; (nav.) rift (in a cloud).

clairsemé, -e, *adj.*, thin, thinly sown, scarce, scattered.

clairvoyance, *n.f.*, sharpness, acuteness, perspicacity; clear-sightedness; clairvoyance.

clairvoyant, -e, *adj.*, clear-sighted, discerning, sharp, acute; clairvoyant.

clameur, *n.f.*, clamor, outcry.

clamponnier, *n.m.*, long pasterned horse.

clan, *n.m.*, clan. *Chef de —;* chieftain of a clan. *Membre d'un —;* clansman.

clandestin, -e, *adj.*, clandestine, secret, underhand.

clandestine, *n.f.*, (bot.) broom-rape, mother-wort.

clandestinement (-ti-n-măn), *adv.*, clandestinely, privately, underhandedly.

clandestinité, *n.f.*, clandestineness, secrecy.

clape, *n.f.*, (mec.) sluice.

clapet, *n.m.*, valve, clapper, clack.

clapier, *n.m.*, burrow; hutch.

clapir, *v.n.*, to squeak (of rabbits).

se **clapir,** *v.r.*, to hide in a hole, to squat, to cower.

clapotage, *n.m.*, rippling, plashing; (nav.) chopping.

clapoter, *v.n.*, to ripple, to plash, to chop.

clapoteu-x, -se, *adj.*, rippling, choppy, plashing; rough.

clapotis, *n.m.* *V.* clapotage.

clappement (klap-măn), *n.m.*, clacking, smacking (of the tongue against the palate).

clapper, *v.n.*, to clack, to smack.

claque, *n.f.*, flap, slap, smack; claque (paid

clappers at theaters). *pl.*, clogs, galoches. *Chapeau à —*; cocked hat. *Face à —s*; sneering face, *i. e.*, which you would like to slap.

claque, *n.m.*, opera hat, crush hat.

claquebc s, *n.m.*, (mus.) musical sticks.

claquedent, *n.m.*, (l.u.) poor half-starved wretch, beggar; boaster.

claquement (klak-mān), *n.m.*, clapping, clap; snapping (of the fingers); cracking (of whips); chattering (of the teeth).

claquemurer, *v.a.*, to immure, to coop up, shut up, confine, imprison.

se **claquemurer**, *v.r.*, to shut one's self up.

*****claque-oreille**, *n.m.*, (— - —s) (pop.) flop hat, slouch hat.

claquer, *v.n.*, to snap, to crack; to clap, to smack, to clack. *Faire —*; to crack (a whip), to snap (one's fingers); to smack (one's tongue). *— des mains*; to clap. *— des dents*; to chatter. (fig.) *Faire — son fouet*; to boast; (fam.) to die, to kick the bucket.

claquer, *v.a.*, to slap, to crack, to smack; (fig.) to applaud.

claquet, *n.m.*, mill-clapper.

claquette, *n.f.*, clapper, rattle.

claqueur, *n.m.*, clapper.

clarification, *n.f.*, clarification, clarifying, fining.

clarificatoire, *adj.*, clarifying.

clarifier, *v.a.*, to clarify, to purify, to fine.

se **clarifier**, *v.r.*, to clarify, to get clarified, to settle.

clarine, *n.f.*, little bell (for cattle).

clarinette, *n.f.*, (mus.) clarinet, clarionet.

clarté, *n.f.*, light, splendor, clearness, transparency, limpidity, brightness; perspicuity.

classe, *n.f.*, class, order, rank; tribe; form (in a school); school-room, school-time. *pl.*, school-days. *En —*; in school. *Basses —s*; junior classes. *Hautes —s, —s supérieures*; upper classes (of schools). *Il a fait toutes ses —s*; he has gone through all the forms. *L'ouverture, or la rentrée, des —s*; the reopening of the schools. *Hautes —s*; higher classes (of society); (nav.) enrollment.

classement (klas-mān), *n.m.*, classing, classification.

classer, *v.a.*, to class, to sort; (nav.) to enroll.

classeur, *n.m.*, portfolio, sorter.

classicisme, *n.m.*, classicism.

classification, *n.f.*, classification.

classifier, *v.a.*, to classify.

classique, *adj.*, classic, academical; standard (of authors, books).

classique, *n.m.*, classic.

clatir, *v.n.*, (hunt.) to blab (of dogs).

claude, *n.m.* and *adj.*, (fam.) simpleton, fool, dolt; doltish; silly.

claudication, *n.f.*, claudication, lameness, limping.

claudicant, -e, *adj.*, lame, limping.

clause, *n.f.*, clause, condition, stipulation.

claustral, -e, *adj.*, claustral; monastic.

clavaire, *n.f.*, (bot.) club-top.

clavé, -e, *adj.*, (bot.) club-like.

claveau, *n.m.*, rot, scab (of the sheep); (arch.) key or arch-stone.

clavecin (klav-sin), *n.m.*, harpsichord.

claveciniste, *n.m.f.*, harpsichord-player.

clavelé, -e, *adj.*, (vet.) affected with rot.

clavelée, *n.f.*, rot, scab.

clavette, *n.f.*, (tech.) peg, cotter-pin; key, catch, latch.

clavicule, *n.f.*, clavicle, collar-bone.

claviculé, -e, *adj.*, (zool.) having a collar-bone.

clavier, *n.m.*, key-board, key-frame; key-ring.

claviforme, *adj.*, (bot.) clavate, club-shaped.

clayer, *n.m.*, hurdle.

clayère, *n.f.*, oyster-bed; breeding-ground.

claymore, *n.f.*, claymore.

clayon, *n.m.*, small hurdle, stand (for cheese)

clayonnage, *n.m.*, wicker; basket-work.

clef (klé), *n.f.*, key; plug (of cocks); (arch.) crown; fid (of masts); (nav.) hitch; (mus.) clef, tuning-key. *Un trousseau de —s*; a bunch of keys. *— de voûte*; keystone of a vault. *Fermer une porte à —*; to lock a door. *La grammaire est la — des sciences*; grammar is the key to the sciences. *Mettre la — sur la fosse*; to relinquish an inheritance. *Mettre la — sous la porte*; to run away from one's creditors; to bolt. *La — est à la porte*; the key is in the door.

clématite, *n.f.*, (bot.) clematis, climber.

clémence, *n.f.*, clemency, mercy, forgiveness, leniency.

clément, -e, *adj.*, clement, merciful, lenient; mild (of the weather).

clémentines, *n.f. pl.*, Clementines (the constitutions of Clement the Fifth).

clenche or **clenchette**, *n.f.*, thumb-lift of a latch; (mus.) clef.

clephte, *n.m.*, free Greek mountaineer.

clepsydre, *n.f.* clepsydra, water-clock.

clerc (klèr), *n.m.*, clerk, clergyman; scholar. *Petit —*; junior clerk. *Maître —*; head-clerk. *Pas de —*; blunder. *Ce n'est pas un grand —*; he is no great scholar.

clergé, *n.m.*, clergy.

clérical, -e, *adj.*, clerical.

cléricalement (-kal-mān), *adv.*, clerically.

cléricalisme, *n.m.*, clericalism.

cléricature, *n.f.*, clerkship, apprenticeship, articles; ministry, holy orders.

cléristère, *n.m.*, (arch.) clearstory, clerestory.

clic-clac, *n.m.*, cracking (of a whip).

clichage, *n.m.*, stereotyping, casting.

cliché, *n.m.*, stereotype plate; (photo.) negative; (sculp.) cast.

clicher, *v.a.*, to stereotype.

clicheur, *n.m.*, stereotyper.

client, *n.m.*, **-e**, *adj.*, client (of lawyers); patient (of physicians); customer (of tradesmen).

clientèle, *n.f.*, clients; practice (of physicians); (Rom. antiq.) protection, patronage, business; custom (of tradesmen); connection. *Se faire une —*; to form a connection.

clifoire, *n.f.*, squirt (toy).

*****clignement**, *n.m.*, winking, blinking, wink.

⊙*****cligne-musette**, *n.f.*, (*n.p.*) hide and seek.

*****cligner**, *v.a.*, to blink, to wink, to twinkle.

*****clignotant, -e**, *adj.*, winking, blinking.

*****clignotement** (kli-gnot-mān), *n.m.*, winking, twinkling, blinking.

*****clignoter**, *v.n.*, to wink, to twinkle, to blink.

climat, *n.m.*, climate, clime.

climatérique, *adj.*, climacteric, climatic.

climatérique, *n.f.*, climacteric, climatic. *La grande —*; the great climacteric.

climax (-maks), *n.m.*, (l.u.) (rhet.) climax.

clin, *n.m.*, wink (of an eye); (archit.) louvre-boarding; (nav.) clincher-work. *A —*; clincher-built. *Faire un — d'œil à quelqu'un*; to wink at any one. *En un — d'œil*; in the twinkling of an eye, in an instant, in a trice.

*****clincaille**, **clincaillerie**, **clincaillier**. *V.* quincaille, quincaillerie, quincaillier.

clinique, *adj.*, clinic, clinical.

clinique, *n.f.*, clinical surgery, clinical medicine, or lectures.

clinquant, *n.m.*, tinsel; glitter; affectation; foil.

clinquanter, *v.a.*, to cover with tinsel.

clique, *n.f.*, set, coterie, party; clique. *Emporter ses —s et ses claques*; to pack bag and baggage, to be off.

cliquet, *n.m.*, click; catch.

cliqueter (klik-té), *v.n.*, to clack, to click.

cliquetis (klik-tî), *n.m.*, clanking of arms, clash ; clatter ; rattling, jingle.

cliquettes (kli-kèt), *n.f. pl.*, snappers, bones.

clisse, *n.f.*, wicker-mat ; (surg.) splint.

clissé, -e, *adj.*, cased in wicker.

clitoris (-rî), *n.m.*, (anat.) clitoris.

clivage, *n.m.*, (min.) cleavage.

cliver, *v.a.*, to cleave (diamonds). *Se* — ; to be cleft.

cloaque, *n.m.*, sink ; cess-pool, sewer ; filthy hole ; (anat.) cloaca.

cloche, *n.f.*, bell ; blister (on the hands, feet) ; cover, dish-cover ; (cook.) stew-pan ; (gard.) bell-glass, hand-glass ; (chem., phys.) receiver. — *de plongeur ;* diving-bell ; (nav.) barrel (of a capstan). *Tinter les —s ;* to toll the bells. *Qui n'entend qu'une — n'entend qu'un son ;* one should hear both sides of a question.

clochement (klosh-mān), *n.m.*, hobbling, halting, limping ; lameness.

cloche-pied, *n.m.*, *(n.p.)* hopping on one leg. *A —* ; upon one foot, hopping. *Aller à —* ; to hop.

clocher, *n.m.*, steeple, belfry, parish. *Course au —* ; steeple-chase. *Avoir la maladie du —* ; to be homesick. *Il n'a jamais quitté son — de vue ;* he has never been out of his parish. *Esprit de —* ; narrowmindedness ; prejudice, short-sightedness.

clocher, *v.n.*, to halt, to limp, to hobble. — *du pied droit ;* to limp with the right foot. *Raissonnement qui cloche ;* lame argument. *Il y a quelque chose qui cloche ;* there 's something wrong somewhere ; a hitch somewhere.

clocher, *v.a.*, (gard.) to cover with a glass-bell.

clocheton, *n.m.*, little steeple, bell-turret.

clochette, *n.f.*, small bell, hand-bell ; (bot.) bell-flower.

cloison, *n.f.*, partition (of boards or masonry), division, compartment ; (anat., bot.) partition ; (nav.) bulkhead.

cloisonnage, *n.m.*, partition-work, wains-coting.

cloisonné, -e, *adj.*, (bot.) valved ; (conch.) chambered, wainscoted.

cloisonner, *v.a.*, to partition.

cloître, *n.m.*, cloister ; close ; monastery.

cloîtré, -e, *adj.*, cloistered (of a person).

cloîtrer, *v.a.*, to shut up in a cloister, to cloister, to immure.

cloîtrier, *n.m.*, cloister monk.

clopin-clopant, *adv.*, limpingly, haltingly ; hobbling along.

clopiner, *v.n.*, to limp, to halt, to hobble.

cloporte, *n.m.*, (ent.) multiped, woodlouse.

cloque, *n.f.*, blister ; (agri.) brown rust.

clore, *v.a.*, to inclose, to fence, to shut in ; to end, to finish, to conclude ; to close (accounts, discussions, a session).

clore, *v.n.*, to close, to shut.

clos, -e, *part.*, closed, tight, shut, sealed. *A huis —* ; with closed doors. *Bouche — e ;* mum's the word. *Champ —* ; lists. *Ce sont lettres —es ;* it 's a secret. *— et couvert ;* wind and water tight.

clos, *n.m.*, close ; inclosure, field. *— de vigne ;* vineyard.

closeau, *n.m.*, small garden.

closerie, *n.f.*, small farm ; bit of land.

clossement, *n.m.* V. **gloussement**.

closser, *v.n.* V. **glousser**.

clôture, *n.f.*, inclosure, fence ; seclusion (of nuns) ; closing, close, (parl.) closure, proroguing. *Mettre une —* ; to inclose.

clôturer, *v.a.*, (jur., parliament) to close, to prorogue.

clou, *n.m.*, nail, hobnail, spike ; stud ; (med.) carbuncle, boil ; clove. — *à crochet ;* tenter-hook. *—s à vis ;* clincher-nails. *Enfoncer un*

— ; to drive a nail. *River le — à quelqu'un ;* to clinch any one's argument. *Cela ne vaut pas un — ;* that's not worth a straw, a rap ; (lit., a tin-tack). *Un — chasse l'autre ;* one idea drives away another.

clouage, clouement, *n.m.*, nailing ; nail-work.

clouer, *v.a.*, to nail ; to fix ; to rivet ; to detain, to confine.

se **clouer**, *v.r.*, to buckle to ; to be nailed (of a thing).

clouter, *v.a.*, to adorn with nails, to stud.

clouterie (-trî), *n.f.*, nail manufactory, nail-trade.

cloutier (-tié), *n.m.*, nail-maker, nail-dealer.

cloutière, *n.f.*, anvil for making nails.

clovisse, *n.m.*, (conch.) winkle.

cloyère, *n.f.*, oyster-basket.

club, *n.m.*, club, assembly.

clubiste, *n.m.f.*, member of a club.

clysoir, *n.m.*, clyster-pipe.

⊙**clystère**, *n.m.*, injection, clyster, enema.

clystériser, *v.a.*, (jest.) to give clysters.

cnique (knik), *n.m.*, (bot.) horse-thistle.

co (prefix used in composition, signifying *with, conjointly*), co.

coaccusé, *n.m.*, **-e**, *n.f.*, fellow-prisoner ; co-respondent.

coacquéreur, *n.m.*, co-purchaser, co-buyer ; joint buyer.

coacti-f, -ve, *adj.*, coactive, coercive.

coaction, *n.f.*, coaction.

coadjut-eur, *n.m.*, **-trice**, *n.f.*, coadjutor, coadjutrix.

coadjutorerie (-torirî), *n.f.*, coadjutorship.

coadné, -e, *adj.*, (bot.) joined, coadunate.

coadunation, *n.f.*, coadunation.

coagulant, -e, *adj.*, coagulative.

coagulation, *n.f.*, coagulation, congealing.

coaguler, *v.a.*, to coagulate, to congeal.

se **coaguler**, *v.r.*, to coagulate, to congeal.

coagulum (-lom), *n.m.*, (chem.) coagulum.

coalescence, *n.f.*, coalescence.

coalescent, -e, *adj.*, coalescent.

se **coaliser**, *v.r.*, to coalesce, to league, to unite, to combine.

coalition, *n.f.*, coalition.

coassement (ko-as-mān), *n.m.*, croaking (of frogs).

coasser, *v.n.*, to croak (of frogs).

coassocié, *n.m.*, (com.) co-partner, fellow-partner.

coati, *n.m.*, (mam.) coati.

cobalt, *n.m.*, (min.) cobalt.

cobaye, *n.m.*, guinea-pig.

cobéa, *n.m.*, (bot.) cobæa.

cobelligérant, -e, *adj.*, cobelligerent.

cobit, *n.m.*, (ich.) cobitis, loach.

cobourgeois, *n.m.*, co-partner in a ship.

cobra-capello, *n.m.*, (—) hooded-snake, spectacle-snake.

coca, *n.m.*, (bot.) coca, erythroxylon coca.

***cocagne**, *n.f.*, feast, treat ; the land of milk and honey. *Mât de —* ; greasy pole. *Pays de —* ; the land of plenty.

cocarde, *n.f.*, cockade, ear-knot.

cocasse, *adj.*, (pop.) odd, laughable, ridiculous, comical, droll.

cocasserie, *n.f.*, drollery, caricature.

cocatrix, *n.f.*, cockatrice.

coccifère, *adj.*, (bot.) cocciferous.

coccinelle, *n.f.*, (ent.) lady-bird, lady-cow.

coccoloba, *n.m.* (—), (bot.) grape-tree.

coccyx (kok-sis), *n.m.*, (anat.) coccyx.

⊙**coche**, *n.m.*, barge ; coach. *— d'eau ;* tow-barge. *Manquer le —* ; to let slip the opportunity. *C'est la mouche du —* ; he is a busy-body. *Le siége du —* ; the coachman's box.

coche, *n.f.*, notch, score ; sow, she-pig. *Faire une —* ; to notch.

*cochenillage, n.m., cochineal.

*cochenille (kosh-), n.f., cochineal.

*cocheniller, v.a., to dye with cochineal.

*cochenillier, n.m., cochineal-fig, nopal.

cocher, n.m., coachman, driver; (astron.) Auriga. — de fiacre, de cabriolet; hackney coachman, cabman.

cocher, v.n., to tread (of birds).

côcher, v.a., to notch.

cochère, adj.f., for carriages. Porte —; carriage-entrance, gateway.

cochet, n.m., young cock.

cochevis (kosh-vi), n.m., tufted or crested lark.

cochléaria (-klé-), n.m., (bot.) cochlearia, scurvy-grass.

cochon, n.m., hog, pig, boar, porker; (metal.) pig, dross. — de lait; sucking-pig. — d'Inde or de Barbarie; Guinea-pig. C'est un —; he is a dirty fellow. Avoir gardé les —s ensemble; to be hail fellows well met.

cochonnée, n.f., litter (of pigs).

cochonner, v.n., to farrow, to pig.

cochonner, v.a., to do a thing in a slovenly manner, to botch.

cochonnerie (ko-sho-n-rî), n.f., nastiness, filth; beastliness, beastly or blackguard action or language, obscenity; trash, rubbish.

cochonnet, n.m., young pig; die with twelve sides; jack (at bowls).

coco, n.m., cocoa, cocoa-nut; liquorice-water; (fam.) chap, fellow, darling; horse, nag.

cocon, n.m., cocoon.

cocorico. See coquerico.

cocorli, n.m., (orni.) dunlin; purr; sea-lark.

cocotier (-tié), n.m., cocoa-tree.

cocréancier, n.m., joint-creditor.

cocrète, n.f., (bot.) yellow-rattle. — des prés; lousewort.

coction, n.f., coction, boiling.

cocu, n.m., (l.ex.) cuckold.

cocuage, n.m., (l.ex.) cuckoldom.

cocufier, v.a., (l.ex.) to cuckold.

code, n.m., code, digest, collection of laws; law; (phar.) pharmacopœia.

codébit-eur, n.m., -rice, n.f., joint-debtor.

codécimateur, n.m., fellow tithe-owner. [tiff.

codemandeur, n.m., co-plaintiff, joint-plain-

codétenteur, n.m., joint-holder.

codétenu, -e, n.m. and f., fellow-prisoner.

codex (-deks), n.m., pharmacopœia.

codicillaire, adj., contained in a codicil.

codicille, n.m., codicil.

codification, n.f., codification.

codifier, v.a., to codify.

*codille, n.m., codille (at the game of ombre).

codonataire, n.m.f., joint donor or donee.

cœcum. V. cæcum.

coefficient, n.m., (alg.) coefficient.

coégal, -e, adj., coequal.

coégalité, n.f., coequality.

coemption, n.f., coemption.

coéquation, n.f., assessment of taxes.

coercible, adj., coercible.

coerciti-f, -ve, adj., coercive.

coercition, n.f., coercion.

coéternel, -le, adj., coeternal.

coéternité, n.f., coeternity.

cœur (keur), n.m., heart, mind, soul; courage, spirit, spiritedness, mettle; stomach; core; depth; hearts (cards); middle, midst. Mal au —; sickness. Serrement de —; heartpang. Du fond de son —; from the bottom of one's heart. Au — dur; hard-hearted. De —; with one's whole heart, with all one's might. A vous de —; affectionately yours. Avoir le — contrit; to be of a contrite heart. Le — lui saigne; his heart bleeds. Avoir à — prendre à —; to have at heart. Cela lui tient au —; he has set his heart upon it. Avoir quelque chose sur le —; to have

something on one's mind. Le — me le disait bien, my heart misgave me. Si le — vous en dit; if you feel inclined. Il a le — au métier; he loves his business. Il a le — porté à cela; he is bent upon it. Avoir le — tendre; to be tender-hearted. Il a le — bien placé; his heart is in the right place. Il n'a point de —; he has no spirit. Sans —; heartless. Avoir le — bas; to be mean-spirited. Avoir le — sur les lèvres; to be open-hearted. Soulèvement de —; rising of the stomach. J'ai mal au —; I feel sick. Avoir le — mort; to be sick at heart. Ouvrir, décharger, son — à quelqu'un; to unbosom one's self to any one. En avoir le — net; to know the rights of any thing. Au — de l'hiver; in the depth of winter. A contre- —; against one's will, reluctantly, against the grain. De bon —; heartily. De grand —; gladly, willingly, with pleasure. De tout mon —; with all my heart. De gaîté de —; in sheer wantonness. A — joie; to one's heart's content. Par —; by heart. Dîner par —; to dine with Duke Humphrey (i.e., to go without dinner). Tant que le — me battra; to the last drop of my blood. Tenir au —; to stick in one's throat. Avoir le — brisé; to be broken-hearted. Avoir le — fendu; to be cut to the heart. Loin des yeux loin du —; out of sight, out of mind. Avoir le — gros; to be ready, to cry, to have one's heart full. C'est un crève —; it is a heart-rending thing. Mettre du — au ventre à quelqu'un; to give heart to any one. Faire contre fortune bon —; to put a good face upon matters.

coexistant, -e, adj., co-existent.

coexistence, n.f., co-existence.

coexister, v.n., to co-exist.

coffre, n.m., chest, trunk, coffer; (hunt.) carcase; drum (of a mill); (print.) coffin. — de sûreté; strong box. — de bord; sea-chest. Elle est belle au —; she has golden charms (i.e. is rich). Un — fort, (—s—s) a strong box. Avoir le — bon; to be strong chested.

coffrer, v.a., (fam.) to imprison, lock up.

coffret, n.m., little chest or trunk, casket.

coffretier (-tié), n.m., trunk-maker.

cofidéjusseur, n.m., joint surety.

*cognasse, n.f., wild quince.

*cognassier, n.m., wild quince-tree.

cognat, n.m., cognate.

cognation, n.f., cognation.

*cognée, n.f., ax, hatchet. Mettre la — à l'arbre; to lay the ax to the tree; to begin an enterprise. Aller au bois sans —; to go to sea without biscuit (i.e. to be unprepared). Jeter le manche après la —; to give a thing up in despair.

*cogne-tétu, n.m., (—, or —-—s) (pop.) great worker, little doer; fussy-do-nothing.

*cogner, v.a., to knock in, to drive in, to bump.

*se cogner, v.r., to knock up against, to hit, to strike one's self.

cogniti-f, -ve, adj., (philos.) cognitive.

*cognoir, n.m., (print.) shooting-stick.

cohabitation, n.f., cohabitation.

cohabiter, v.n., to cohabit.

cohérence, n.f., coherency.

cohérent, -e, adj., coherent.

cohériter, v.n., to inherit conjointly.

cohériti-er, n.m., -ère, n.f., co-heir, co-heiress.

cohésion, n.f., cohesion.

cohobation, n.f., (chem.) cohobation.

cohober, v.a., (chem.) to cohobate.

cohorte, n.f., cohort, band, crew, troop, horde, gang.

cohue, n.f., rout, mob, crush, tumultuous crowd, clamorous multitude; (fig.) court of justice.

coi, -te, adj., quiet, still, snug.

coiffe, n.f., head-dress; caul, hood (of children); skull-cap; net; (bot.) galla. — *de chapeau;* lining of a hat.

coiffer, *v.a.,* to put (anything) on one's head; to dress the hair; to infatuate; to throw at any one's head; to make tipsy; (hunt.) to take by the ears; (nav.) to back; to cap (bottles); (arch.) to cap. *Etre bien coiffé;* to have one's hair well dressed; to have a hat that becomes one. *Enfant né coiffé;* child born with a caul upon its head. *Il est né coiffé;* he was born to fortune or with a silver spoon in his mouth. — *sainte Catherine;* to remain an old maid. *Du vin coiffé;* mixed wine. — *une bouteille;* to cap a bottle. *Chien bien coiffé;* dog with a handsome head and long ears. *Cette femme coiffe son mari;* that woman deceives her husband. *Il est coiffé de cette femme;* he is bewitched, smitten with that woman. — *une voile;* to back a sail.

se **coiffer,** *v.r.,* to wear (on one's head); to dress one's hair; to get intoxicated; to be infatuated with; (nav.) to be laid aback. *Se — de faux cheveux;* to wear false hair. *Se — en cheveux;* to wear no cap.

coiffer, *v.n.,* to dress hair; to become; to suit; (nav.) to be laid aback.

coiffeu-r, *n.m.,* **-se,** *n.f.,* hairdresser.

coiffure, *n.f.,* head-dress, style of arranging the hair.

coin, *n.m.,* corner, angle, nook, coin; (coin.) stamp; (railways) pin; (print.) quoin; clock (of stockings); (tech.) gad; (mec.) wedge. *Il n'a pas bougé du — du feu;* he has never been from home. *Etre marqué au —;* to bear the stamp of. *Frappé au bon —;* of the right sort, excellent in every way. *Il mourra au — d'un bois (d'une laie);* he will die destitute. *—s et recoins;* cricks and corners, nooks and crannies. *Jouer aux quatre —s;* to play puss in the corner.

coinçage, *n.m.,* wedging, keying.

coincer, *v.a.,* to wedge.

coïncidence, *n.f.,* coincidence.

coïncident, *adj.,* coincident.

coïncider, *v.n.,* to coincide, to be coincident.

coïndication, *n.f.,* (med.) coindication.

coing (coin), *n.m.,* quince.

coïntéressé, *n.m.,* associate, partner having a joint interest with another.

coïon or **couillon,** *n.m.,* (l.ex.) dastard, coward.

coïonner or **couillonner,** *v.a.,* (l.ex.) to use one scurvily, to make a fool of one; to call one a coward.

coïonner or **couillonner,** *v.n.,* (l.ex.) to joke, to gammon, to humbug.

coïonnerie (ko-io-n-rî) or **couillonnerie, couillonnade,** *n.f.,* (l.ex.) dastardliness, a mean, low action; gammon, humbug.

coït, *n.m.,* coition, copulation.

coïte, *n.f.* *V.* **couette.**

cojouissance, *n.f.,* joint use.

coke, *n.m.,* coke.

col, *n.m.,* neck (of the body); cravat; neck (of bottles, of mountains); pad, stiffener; collar. *Faux —;* collar. — *droit;* stand-up collar. — *de cravate;* stiffener. — *de la vessie, de la matrice;* neck of the bladder, of the womb.

colarin, *n.m.,* (arch.) gorgerin.

colas, *n.m.,* booby, fool.

colature, *n.f.,* (pharm.) colature, straining.

colback, *n.m.,* colback, busby.

colchique, *n.m.,* meadow-saffron, colchicum.

colcotar, *n.m.,* (chem.) colcothar.

colégataire, *n.m.,* co-legatee.

coléoptère, *adj.,* coleopterous. *n.m.,* coleopter, beetle.

coléoptères, *n.m.pl.,* coleoptera.

colère, *n.f.,* passion, anger, wrath, rage, fury. *Accès de —;* fit of passion. *Etre en —;* to be angry. *Se mettre en —;* to fly into a passion.

colère, *adj.,* passionate, hasty, choleric.

colérique, *adj.,* choleric, irascible, passionate.

coliart, *n.m.,* (ich.) skate.

colibri, *n.m.,* humming-bird.

colicitant, *n.m.,* (jur.) co-vendor.

colifichet, *n.m.,* knick-knack, gew-gaw, trifle, bauble, trumpery, toy, bird-cake.

colimaçon, *n.m.,* snail.

colin, *n.m.,* (ich.) coal-fish.

*****colin-maillard,** *n.m.,* (*n.p.*) blindman's-buff; blindman (at blindman's buff).

colin-tampon, *n.m.,* (*n.p.*) a Swiss beating of drum. *Je m'en moque comme de —;* (pop.) I do not care a fig about it.

colique, *n.f.,* colic, griping; stomach-ache. *pl.,* after-pains. — *saturnine;* painter's colic.

colis, *n.m.,* package, parcel, bale, case, article.

colisée, *n.m.,* Coliseum; Colosseum.

collaborat-eur, *n.m.,* **-rice,** *n.f.,* (kol-la-), fellow-laborer, assistant, associate, contributor.

collaboration (kol-la-), *n.f.,* assistance, contribution, coöperation.

collaborer, *v.n.,* to work together, to coöperate.

collage, *n.m.,* pasting, gluing, sizing (of paper); paper-hanging.

collant, -e, *adj.,* sticky, tight, close-fitting.

collants, *n.m. pl.,* tights.

collapsus (-sus), *n.m.,* (med.) collapse.

collataire (kol-la-tè-r), *n.m.,* one who has been collated to a benefice.

collatéral, -e (kol-la-), *adj.,* collateral.

collatéral, *n.m.,* (jur.) collateral.

⊙**collatérale,** *n.f.,* aisle (of churches).

collatéralement, *adv.,* (jur.) collaterally.

collateur (kol-la-), *n.m.,* collator.

collati-f, -ve (kol-la-), *adj.,* collative.

collation (kol-la-cion), *n.f.,* collation.

collation (ko-la-cion), *n.f.,* collation, light repast; (eccl.) advowson-gift.

collationner (kol-la-cio-né), *v.a.,* to collate, to compare.

collationner (ko-la-cio-né), *v.n.,* to make a light repast; to take a collation.

colle, *n.f.,* paste, glue; sham, fib, bouncer, cracker. — *forte;* glue. — *à bouche;* mouth-glue. — *de poisson;* isinglass.

collecte (kol-lèkt), *n.f.,* gathering; collection (of money); collect (prayer).

collecteur (kol-lèk-teur), *n.m.,* collector, tax-gatherer.

collecti-f, -ve (kol-lèk-), *adj.,* collective.

collectif (kol-lèk-), *n.m.,* collective noun.

collection (kol-lèk-cion), *n.f.,* collection; set, file.

collectionner (kol-lèk-cio-né), *v.a.,* to collect, to make collections of things.

collectionneu-r (kol-lèk-cio-), *n.m.,* **-se,** *n.f.,* collector.

collectivement (kol-lèk-tiv-mān), *adv.,* collectively.

collège, *n.m.,* college, grammar-school. — *électoral;* assembly of electors; constituency.

collégial, -e, *adj.,* collegial; collegiate. *Eglise —e;* a collegiate church.

collégiale, *n.f.,* collegiate church.

collégialement, *adv.,* scholastically.

collégien (-ji-in), *n.m.,* collegian, school-boy.

collègue (kol-lég), *n.m.,* colleague.

collement, *n.m.,* (med.) cohesion, adhesion.

coller, *v.a.,* to paste, to glue; to size; to stick together; to clear (with isinglass); to stump (embarrass any one); to plow (at exam.); to hang (paper). *Etre collé;* to be close up against the cushion (at billiards). *J'ai été collé;* I was plowed.

se **coller,** *v.r.,* to stick to; to cake; to apply closely to; (at billiards) to be right up against the cushion.

coller, *v.n.,* to stick, to adhere; to fit tight

(of clothes). *Ce pantalon colle bien;* those trousers fit nicely.

collerette (kol-rèt), *n.f.*, collar (for ladies); (bot.) involucrum; (tech.) flange.

collet, *n.m.*, collar (of a gown, coat); cape; bands (for the neck); neck (of teeth); (hunt.) snare; crown (of anchors); (tech.) collet; clergyman. — *montant;* stand-up collar. — *rabattu;* turned-down collar. *Petit* —; one of the cloth, young clergyman. — *monté;* buckram collar. *Un* — *monté;* a stuck-up, strait-laced, prudish person. — *de mouton;* neck of mutton. *Prendre, saisir, quelqu'un au* — ; to collar any one. *Prêter le* — *à quelqu'un;* to cope with any one, to try one's strength with any one. *Tendre un* —; to set a snare.

colleter (kol-té), *v.a.*, to collar any one, to seize any one by the neck.

se **colleter,** *v.r.*, to collar each other; to lay hold of each other by the collar, to grapple with, to wrestle.

colleter, *v.n.*, to set snares (for game).

colleteur, *n.m.*, gin-setter; (pop.) wrangler, fighter.

colleur, *n.m.*, paper-hanger; gluer; paster; bill-sticker; sizer.

collier, *n.m.*, collar; ring (mark round the neck of certain animals); bow (of spurs); (arch., tech.) collar; necklace. *Cheval de* —; draught-horse. — *de force;* training collar. — *de misère;* drudgery. *Donner un coup de* —; to make a strenuous effort. *Etre franc du* —; never to shirk one's work; to be always in earnest; (of a horse) to work well.

⊙**colliger,** *v.a.*, to collect, to cull.

colline, *n.f.*, hill, hillock. *La double* —; Parnassus. *Gagner la* —; to take to one's heels. *Le penchant d'une* —; the declivity of a hill; a hill-slope.

colliquati-f, -ve (kol-li-koua-), *adj.*, (med.) colliquative.

colliquation (kol-li-koua-), *n.f.*, (med.) colliquation, melting.

collision (kol-li-), *n.f.*, collision.

collocation (kol-lo-) *n.f.*, collocation; setting in order, rank. — *de l'argent;* investing of money.

collodion, *n.m.*, collodion.

colloque (kol-lok), *n.m.*, colloquy, conference, dialogue.

colloquer (kol-lo-ké), *v.a.*, to rank, to place in order; to place. *v.n.*, to colloquize.

colluder (kol-lu-dé), *v.n.*, to collude.

collusion (kol-lu-zion), *n.f.*, collusion, prevarication. *User de* —; to prevaricate.

collusoire (kol-lu-zoar), *adj.*, collusory, collusive.

collusoirement (kol-lu-zoar-mān), *adv.*, collusively.

collyre, *n.m.*, (med.) collyrium, eye-salve.

colmatage (kol-), *n.m.*, (agri.) warping (of land).

colmate, *n.m.*, warp, warped land.

colmater, *v.a.*, to warp (land).

colombage, *n.m.*, (carp.) stud-work, joists.

colombe, *n.f.*, dove; (carp.) joist, upright.

colombier, *n. m.*, dove-cot, pigeon-house; (print.) pigeon-hole, gap. *Faire venir les pigeons au* —; to draw customers to the shop. *Grand* —; atlas paper.

colombin, -e, *adj.*, columbine, dove-color.

colombin, *n.m.*, (min.) lead ore; (orni.) stock-dove.

colombine, *n.f.*, pigeon-dung, fowls'-dung; (bot.) columbine.

colombo, *n.m.*, (bot.) calumba, colombo.

colon, *n. m.*, colonist, planter; cultivator; West Indian settler.

côlon, *n.m.*, (anat.) colon.

colonel, *n.m.*, colonel. *Grade de* —; colonelcy.

colonelle, *n.f.* and *adj.*, ⊙ colonel's company; colonel's wife.

colonial, -e, *adj.*, colonial.

colonie, *n.f.*, colony, settlement.

colonisation, *n.f.*, colonizing, colonization.

coloniser, *v.a.*, to establish a colony, to colonize.

colonnade, *n.f.*, (arch.) colonnade.

colonne, *n.f.*, column, pillar; bed-post; row (of units, tens); (milit., nav., phys., print., arch.) column. — *cannelée;* fluted column. — *plaquée;* pilaster. — *torse;* wreathed column.

colonnette, *n.f.*, little column.

colophane, *n.f.*, black rosin, colophony.

coloquinte, *n.f.*, colocynth; bitter apple.

colorant, -e, *adj.*, coloring.

coloration, *n.f.*, coloration.

coloré, -e, *part.*, colored. *Vin* —; deep-colored wine. *Teint* —; ruddy complexion.

colorer, *v.a.*, to color, to dye; to varnish; to color (to give a false appearance to).

se **colorer,** *v.r.*, to color (of a thing).

coloriage, *n.m.*, (paint.) coloring.

colorier, *v.r.*, to color, to illuminate.

coloris, *n.m.*, color, hue; (paint.) coloring.

coloriste, *n.m.*, colorer; colorist.

colossal, -e, *adj.*, colossal, of giant proportions.

colosse, *n.m.*, colossus, giant.

colostrum, *n.m.*, (n.p.) (med.) colostrum.

colportage, *n.m.*, hawking; peddling; peddlery; book-stall trade.

colporter, *v.a.*, to hawk about; to retail; to spread. — *une nouvelle;* to retail a piece of news.

colporteur, *n.m.*, hawker, peddler; spreader of news.

coltis, *n.m.*, (nav.) beak-head.

colure, *n.m.*, (astron., geog.) colure.

columelle, *n.f.*, (bot.) columella.

colza, *n.m.*, colza, rape, rape-seed.

coma, *n.m.*, (med.) coma.

comateu-x, -se, *adj.*, comatose.

combat (kon-ba), *n.m.*, combat, fight, battle; fighting; contest, action, engagement, struggle; strife, warring. — *singulier;* single combat. — *à outrance;* mortal combat. — *égal;* drawn battle. — *simulé;* sham fight. *Au fort du* —; in the thick of the fight. *Etre hors de* —; to be disabled. *Mettre hors de* —; to disable. *Faire branle-bas de* —; (nav.) to clear for action.

combattable, *adj.*, combatable.

combattant, *n.m.*, combatant, fighting man, champion; (orni.) ruff.

combattre, *v.a.*, to fight, to combat; to wage war against, to battle with, to dispute, to contest, to strive against. — *une opinion;* to combat an opinion.

se **combattre,** *v.r.*, to combat; to contend with each other.

combattre, *v.n.*, to fight, to combat, to war, to contend, to vie with one another, to struggle. — *de politesse;* to vie with one another in politeness.

⊙**combe,** *n.f.*, valley.

combien (kon-bi-in), *adv.*, how much, how many; how; how far; how long; what. *En* — *de temps?* in how long? — *y a-t-il depuis cela?* how long is it since then? — *cela vaut-il?* what is that worth? *A* — *évaluez-vous cela?* What price do you put upon that?

combinaison, *n.f.*, combination; contrivance; ingenuity; management; calculation.

combinat-eur, -rice, *n.f.*, combiner, contriver.

combiné, -e, *part.*, united; (chem.) combined.

combiner, *v.a.*, to combine, to contrive.

se **combiner,** *v.r.*, to combine, to be contrived.

comble, *n.m.*, heaping (of measure); consummation; fulfillment; zenith; acme; summit, height, top, complement. *pl.* roof, roof-timbers. *Ferme des* —*s ;* (carp.) framing of a roof. *De fond en* —; from top to bottom. *Ruiné de fond en* —; utterly ruined. *La mesure est au* —; the measure is full. *Pour* — *de gloire ;* to complete his glory. *Pour* — *de malheur ;* to crown all ; to cap our misfortune. *Au* — *de ;* at the height of. *Mettre le* — *à ;* to complete, to crown.

comble, *adj.,* heaped up full to the top. *Salle* —; house full, packed.

combleau, *n.m.,* (nil.) gun-tackle.

comblement, *n.m.,* filling up, heaping up.

combler, *v.a.,* to heap, to heap up, to make up, to fill up, to crown ; to cover (deficit) ; to complete ; to overwhelm. — *de faveurs ;* to load with favors.

comblète, *n.f.,* (hunt.) cleft (of a deer's foot).

combrière, *n.f.,* tunny net.

combuger, *v.a.,* to rinse out (casks).

comburant, -e, *adj.,* (chem.) burning.

combustible, *adj.,* combustible.

combustible, *n.m.,* fuel, firing ; (chem.) combustible.

combustibilité, *n.f.,* combustibility.

combustion (kon-bus-tion), *n.f.,* combustion, conflagration, flame ; (fig.) tumult, uproar.

comédie, *n.f.,* comedy, play ; play-house, theatre ; shamming, farce ; players ; play-book. *Donner la* — ; to make people laugh ; to be the laughing-stock. *Jouer une* — ; to act a play. *Le sujet, l'intrigue, le dénouement, d'une* — ; the subject, plot, upshot, of a comedy.

comédien, *n.m.,* -**ne,** *n.f.* (di-in, di-è-n), comedian, actor, actress, player ; hypocrite, dissembler. *Troupe de* —*s ;* company of actors. —*s ambulants ;* strolling players.

comestible, *adj.,* eatable ; edible.

comestible, *n.m.,* eatable. *pl.,* eatables, provisions, victuals.

cométaire, *adj.,* cometary.

comète, *n.f.,* comet ; kind of game at cards ; satin ribbon ; peculiar kind of firework. — *chevelue ;* haired comet. — *barbue ;* bearded comet. — *à queue ;* tailed comet. *Vin de la* —; wine of the year 1811.

cométographie, *n.f.,* cometography.

comices, *n.f. pl.,* (antiq.) comitia.

comicial, -e, *adj.,* comitial.

comifère, *adj.,* (bot.) comose.

comique, *adj.,* comical, ludicrous, laughable, funny. *Le genre* —; comedy. *Acteur* —; comic actor.

comique, *n.m.,* the comic art, comedy ; comical part or side ; comic actor *or* author *or* singer. *Avoir du* — *dans la figure ;* to have a comical face.

comiquement (-màn), *adv.,* comically, humorously.

☉**comite** *or* **come,** *n.m.,* overseer of a crew of galley-slaves, warder.

comité, *n.m.,* meeting of a few persons ; small party ; committee, board. — *permanent ;* standing committee. *La chambre formée en* —; a committee of the whole house. *Petit* —; a small party ; select few. *En petit* — ; among ourselves. *Dîner en petit* —; to have a small dinner party of intimate friends. — *de lecture ;* a committee for deciding upon the performance of new plays.

comma, *n.m.,* (print.) colon ; (mus.) comma.

command, *n.m.,* (jur.) purchaser ; principal.

commandant, *adj.,* (milit., nav.) commanding ; (fig.) imposing, dictatorial.

commandant, *n.m.,* (milit., nav.) commandant, major. — *de place ;* governor (of a fortified town). — *de la marine ;* flag-officer. — *d'une escadre ;* commodore. *Bien, mon* —*!* very well, major.

commande, *n.f.,* order. *Ouvrage de* —; work done to order. *Marchandise de* —; goods

bespoken. *Sur* —; to order. *Maladie de* —; feigned sickness. *Louanges de* —; forced praise.

commandement, *n.m.,* command, order ; word of command ; manner of commanding ; writ, order ; commandment, precept, law, rule, injunction. *Il a tout à son* —; he has all things at command. *Être de* —; to be prescribed *or* ordered. *Secrétaire des* —*s ;* private secretary (to a prince).

commander, *v.a.,* to command, to order, to govern ; to have the command of ; to bespeak ; to overlook. *Cette tour commande la ville ;* that tower overlooks the town.

commander, *v.n.,* to command, to rule ; to direct ; to order, to bid ; (milit., nav.) to give the word of command. — *à ses passions ;* to master one's passions. — *à la route* (nav.); to shape a ship's course.

se **commander,** *v.r.,* to control oneself.

commanderie (ko-màn-drî), *n.f.,* commandery.

commandeur, *n.m.,* commander (in orders of knighthood).

commanditaire, *n.m.,* sleeping partner.

commandite, *n.f.,* limited joint-stock company.

commanditer, *v.a.,* to finance a commercial undertaking, to become a sleeping partner.

comme, *adv.,* as, like ; so ; almost, nearly ; as it were, as if ; how, in what way ; so much. — *aussi ;* (jur.) and likewise. *Faites* — *lui ;* do like him. — *ci* — *cela ;* so so, indifferently. *Il est* — *mort ;* he is almost dead. *La lumière est* — *l'une des couleurs ;* light is, as it were, one of the colors. — *vous me traitez ;* how badly you treat me. *Vous voyez* — *il travaille ;* you see how hard he works. — *quoi ;* as how.

comme, *conj.,* as, seeing that, since, because.

commémoraison, *n.f.,* (c.rel.) commemoration, remembrance, mention, of a saint.

commémorati-f, -ve, *adj.,* commemorative.

commémoration (kom-mé-), *n.f.,* (c.rel.) commemoration. *La* — *des morts ;* commemoration of the dead ; All-Souls'-Day. *Faire* — *de quelqu'un ;* (fam.) to make mention of any one.

commémorer, *v.a.,* (neologism) to commemorate, to remember, to recollect.

commençant, *n.m.,* -**e,** *n.f.,* beginner, novice, tyro.

commencement (ko-màns-màn), *n.m.,* beginning, commencement ; setting in. *Au* —; in the beginning, at first. *Les* —*s sont toujours difficiles ;* beginnings are always difficult.

commencer, *v.a.,* to begin, to commence ; to initiate, to impart the first principles to. — *quelqu'un ;* to initiate, to begin with anyone. — *un cheval ;* to begin training a horse.

commencer, *v.n.,* to commence, begin. *Lorsqu'il commença de parler ;* when he began speaking. *Cet enfant commence à parler ;* this child begins to speak. [*Commencer de* indicates an action which will have an ending ; *commencer à* indicates an action which will go on progressing.] *N'a pas fait qui commence ;* the beginning is not every thing. *A moitié fait qui commence bien ;* a good beginning is half the battle.

commendataire, *adj.,* (canon law) commendatory.

commende, *n.f.,* (canon law) commendam.

commender, *v.a.,* to give in commendam.

commensal, *n.m.,* -**e,** *n.f.,* habitual guest ; boarder ; officer admitted to the royal table. *Être* — *d'une maison ;* to be habitually a guest in a house. *Être commensaux ;* to be companions at meals.

commensalité, *n.f.,* right of admission to the royal table.

commensurabilité, *n.f.,* (math.) commensurableness, commensurability.

commensurable, *adj.,* (math.) commensurable.

commensuration, *n.f.,* (math.) commensuration.

comment, *adv.,* how, in what manner; why, wherefore; what ! indeed ! — *cela?* how is that? — *faire?* what is to be done ? How can it be helped ? — *! vous voulez le faire;* what ! you wish to do it !

comment, *n.m.,* the reason, the why and the wherefore. *Savoir le pourquoi et le —;* to know the why and the wherefore.

commentaire, *n.m.,* commentary, comment, exposition; remark, observation. *Point de —!* (fam.) no impertinent remarks !

commentateur, *n.m.,* commentator, annotator.

commenter, *v.a.,* to comment, to criticise, to explain, expound, annotate.

commenter, *v.n.,* to criticise; to comment upon.

commérage, *n.m.,* gossiping; gossip, tittle-tattle.

commerçable, *adj.,* negotiable.

commerçant, *n.m.,* trader, merchant, tradesman.

commerçant, -e, *adj.,* commercial, mercantile; trading.

commerce, *n.m.,* commerce, trade, trading, traffic; intercourse, communication, correspondence, acquaintance, communion, conversation ; a game at cards. — *des colonies,* — *avec les colonies;* colonial trade. *Affaires de —;* mercantile affairs. *Femme de —;* tradeswoman. *Fond de —;* business, stock. *Etre dans le —;* to be in business, in trade. — *en gros;* wholesale trade. — *en détail;* retail trade. *Il fait un gros —;* he drives a roaring trade. *Chambre de —;* chamber of commerce. — *de galanterie;* intrigue. *Lier — avec quelqu'un;* to establish a correspondence with anyone. *Liez — avec lui;* get acquainted with him. *Etre d'un — sûr;* to be a person to be depended upon.

commercer, *v.n.,* to trade, to drive a trade, to traffic in.

commercial, -e, *adj.,* commercial.

commercialement, *adv.,* commercially.

commère, *n.f.,* godmother; gossip; friend, body. *Cet homme est une vraie —;* that man is a regular gossip. *C'est une fameuse —;* (fam.) she is a bold, cunning woman, not easily discouraged. *Tout se fait par compère et par —;* all is done by favor.

commérer, *v.n.,* to gossip; to tittle-tattle.

commettage, *n.m.,* (nav.) laying of ropes and cables.

commettant, *n.m.,* constituent; employer; principal; (jur.) warrantor. *Corps de —s;* constituents, constituency.

commettre, *v.a.,* to commit, to perpetrate; to appoint, to delegate, to constitute, to commission, to empower; to commit to any one's charge, to intrust, to trust with, to confide ; to expose; to embroil; to set by the ears, to make mischief between ; (nav.) to lay.

se **commettre,** *v.r.,* to commit oneself; to expose oneself, to trust oneself.

commination, *n.f.,* (rhet.) commination.

comminatoire, *adj.,* (jur.) comminatory.

comminuti-f, -ve, *adj.,* comminutive.

comminution, *n.f.,* comminution.

commis, -e, *part.,* committed, appointed, entrusted, exposed ; (nav.) laid.

commis, *n.m.,* clerk ; book-keeper ; shopman. *Premier —;* head clerk. — *marchand;* merchant's clerk. — *voyageur;* commercial traveler, bagman. — *aux vivres;* (nav.) steward. — *d'administration;* accountant. — *de boutique, de magasin;* shopman, counter jumper.

commise, *n.f.,* (feudal jur.) forfeit, escheat; female-clerk, counterwoman.

commisération (kom-mi-zi-), *n.f.,* commiseration.

commissaire, *n.m.,* commissary; commissioner ; manager ; trustee ; (of a vessel) purser. — *des guerres;* commissary. — *des vivres;* commissary of stores. — *adjoint;* deputy commissioner. — *des pauvres;* member of a charitable board. — *aux saisies réelles;* sequestrator. — *de police;* superintendent of police. — *priseur,* (—*s* —*s*) auctioneer, appraiser.

commissariat, *n.m.,* commissaryship, trusteeship ; (milit.) commissariat.

commission, *n.f.,* commission, trust, charge; commission-trade; errand; mandate, warrant; the holding a trust for a time only ; a committee. *Il est allé en —;* he is gone on an errand. *Obtenir — d'un juge;* to obtain a judge's warrant. — *rogatoire;* writ of inquiry. — *d'enquête;* committee of inquiry. *Maison de —;* agency-office. *Membre d'une —;* committee-man. *En —;* (nav.) in commission. *En —;* (com.) on sale or return. *Faire des —s;* to run errands or to obtain orders.

commissionnaire, *n.m.,* messenger; porter, carrier, errand-boy; agent. — *de vente;* salesman. — *de roulage;* carrier, wagon office-keeper. — *chargeur;* freight agent. — *expéditeur;* shipping-agent.

commissionner, *v.a.,* to empower, to commission.

commissoire, *adj.,* (jur.) binding.

commissure, *n.f.,* (anat.) commissure.

commissural, -e, *adj.,* commissural.

committimus, *n.m.,* (n.p.) (jur.) *Lettres de —;* chancery order appointing the court which is to take cognizance of an action.

committitur, *n.m.,* (n.p.), (jur.) order of the president of a court of justice appointing a judge to hold an inquiry.

commodat, *n.m.,* (jur.) gratuitous loan (to be repaid in kind); bailment.

commode, *adj.,* commodious, convenient, favorable, serviceable, handy ; comfortable ; agreeable, easy ; good-natured, accommodating. *Une maison —;* a comfortable house. *Il n'est pas —;* he is not accommodating, not easy, to get on with.

commode, *n.f.,* chest of drawers, drawers.

commodément, *adv.,* commodiously, conveniently, comfortably, suitably, easily.

commodité, *n.f.,* convenience, accommodation ; ⊙conveyance; comfort, ease. —*s;* water-closet.

commodore, *n.m.,* (nav.) commodore.

commotion, *n.f.,* commotion; shock ; (med.) concussion (of the brain).

commuable, *adj.,* commutable.

commuer, *v.a.,* (jur.) to commute.

commun, -e, *adj.,* common ; usual, ordinary, every day; mean, vulgar. *Le sens —;* common sense. *Je n'ai rien de — avec lui;* I have nothing in common with him. *A frais —s;* jointly. *Faire bourse —e;* to have one common stock or purse. *Lieux —s;* common places. *Le droit —;* common law. *D'une — voix;* unanimously. *Une voix —e;* a vulgar voice. *Le bruit —;* current report. *Cette terre vaut tant de revenu année —e;* that land yields so much a year on an average. *Peu —;* uncommon, rare, unusual.

commun, *n.m.,* the generality ; commonalty; common people, the vulgar, the mob. *Vivre sur le —;* to spunge. *L'âne du — est toujours le plus mal bâté;* matters of public concern are commonly neglected. *Le — des hommes;* the generality of men. *Le — des martyrs;* the common herd. —*s;* servants, or domestic offices, out-buildings.

communal, -e, *adj.,* parochial ; parish ; communal.

communauté, *n.f.,* community, society ; communion ; corporation — *de biens;* community of property (between husband and wife); (jur.) communion.

communaux, *n.m.pl.*, (jur.) pasture grounds, common.

commune, *n.f.*, commune (inhabitants); parish, township (in France); town-hall. *La chambre des —s;* the House of Commons. *Le maire d'une —;* the mayor of a district. *Assemblée de la —;* vestry.

communément, *adv.*, commonly, usually, generally.

communiant, *n.m.*, -**e**, *n.f.*, communicant.

communicabilité, *n.f.*, communicability.

communicable, *adj.*, communicable.

communicati-f, -**ve**, *adj.*, communicative.

communication, *n.f.*, intercourse, communication. —*de pièces;* (jur.) production of documents. *En — avec;* open to (mec.). *De —;* communicating, connecting.

communicativement, *adv.*, communicatively.

communier, *v.n.*, to communicate, to receive the sacrament.

communier, *v.a.*, to give the communion.

communion, *n.f.*, communion, fellowship; sacrament. *Faire sa première —;* to receive the sacrament for the first time; to be confirmed.

communiqué, *n.m.*, official communication, statement.

communiquer, *v.a.*, to communicate, to impart; to show, to tell, to acquaint.

se **communiquer**, *v.r.*, to be communicative, to communicate with; to spread (of places). *Vous vous communiquez trop;* you are too communicative.

communiquer, *v.n.*, to hold or keep up a correspondence with.

communisme, *n.m.*, communism.

communiste, *n.m.f.*, communist.

commutati-f, -**ve**, *adj.*, (jur.) commutative.

commutation, *n.f.*, (jur.) commutation.

comocladie, *n.f.*, (bot.) maiden-plum, comocladia.

compacité, *n.f.*, (phys.) compactness, density.

compact, -**e**, *adj.*, compact, close, serried; (phys.) dense, solid.

*compagne, *n.f.*, female companion; consort, partner; helpmate; playmate; (of animals) mate. *Fidèle —;* faithful attendant.

*compagnie, *n.f.*, society, company; (com.) company; (hunt.) covey; levy, troop. — *ordonnancée;* chartered company. — *de commerce;* trading company. *Il n'y a pas si bonne — qui ne se sépare;* the best of friends must part. *Sa maison est le rendez-vous de la bonne —;* his house is the resort of fashionable people. *Dame de —;* lady's companion. *Etre de bonne —;* to be well-bred. *Aller en —;* to go together. *Tenir — à quelqu'un;* to keep any one company. *Fausser — à quelqu'un;* to desert any one, to give the slip to any one. *Une — de perdrix;* a covey of partridges. *Vous me traitez comme si j'étais —;* you treat me as if I were somebody. *Former une —;* to establish a company. *Règle de —;* fellowship. *Une — d'infanterie;* a company of foot. *Une — de cavalerie;* a troop of horse. — *franche;* independent company.

*compagnon, *n.m.*, companion, fellow, associate, co-mate, consort, mate, partner; journeyman, playfellow, playmate; droll fellow. *— d'école, d'étude;* schoolfellow. — *de table;* messmate. — *de jeu;* playfellow. — *de taverne;* pot-companion. — *d'armes;* companion in arms. *Joyeux —;* jolly fellow, jolly dog. *Traiter de pair à —;* to go cheek by jowl; to be " hail fellow well met " to anyone.

*compagnonnage, *n.m.*, journeymanship, trades-union, time of service.

comparabilité, *n.f.*, comparableness.

comparable, *adj.*, comparable, to be compared.

comparaison, *n.f.*, comparison; simile, similitude. *Toute — cloche;* comparisons are odious. *Il n'y a point de — de vous à lui;* there is no comparison between you and him. *Ce n'est qu'un ignorant en — d'un tel;* he is a mere ignoramus in comparison with such a one. *Par — à, or avec, ce que j'ai fait;* in comparison to, or with, what I have done.

comparaître, *v.n.*, to appear (before a tribunal).

comparant, -**e**, *n.m.f.* and *adj.*, person appearing in court on a summons; appearer.

comparati-f, -**ve**, *adj.*, comparative.

comparatif, *n.m.*, (gram.) comparative, comparative degree.

comparativement (-măn), *adv.*, comparatively.

comparer, *v.a.*, to compare. *Se —;* to be compared.

⊙**comparoir**, *v.n.*, (jur.) to appear.

comparse, *n.m.*, (thea.) supernumerary, figurant, figurante.

compartiment, *n.m.*, compartment, division.

compartimenté, -**e**, *adj.*, with compartments.

comparution, *n.f.*, (jur.) appearance.

compas, *n.m.*, pair of compasses, compass. — *à trois branches;* triangular compasses. — *à pointes changeantes;* draught compasses. — *de réduction;* proportional compasses. — *de variation;* azimuth compass. *Faire toutes choses par règle et par —,* to do everything by rule and compass. *Il a le — dans l'œil;* he has a good eye for distances, or he has a sure eye.

compassé, -**e**, *adj.*, formal, stiff, starched.

compassement (-păs-măn), *n.m.*, compassing, (fig.) stiffness, starchedness.

compasser, *v.a.*, to measure with compasses; to proportion; to regulate; to weigh; to consider. *Un homme bien compassé;* a formal, affected man.

compassion, *n.f.*, compassion, pity, mercy. *Avoir — de quelqu'un, avoir de la — pour quelqu'un;* to take compassion on any one, to have compassion for any one.

compatibilité, *n.f.*, compatibility.

compatible, *adj.*, compatible, consistent. *Son humeur n'est pas — avec la mienne;* his temper does not agree with mine.

compatir, *v.n.*, to sympathize with, to compassionate, to commiserate, to pity; to agree, to be compatible with.

compatissance, *n.f.*, pity, sympathy.

compatissant, -**e**, *adj.*, compassionate, tender, pitying, feeling.

compatriote. *n.m.f.*, compatriot, fellow-countryman, fellow-countrywoman.

compendieusement, *adv.*, in brief, compendiously.

compendium (kon-pin-di-om), *n.m.*, compendium, abridgment, summary.

compensable, *adj.*, that may be compensated, compensable.

compensateur, *n.m.*, (horl.) compensating balance. — *magnétique;* magnetic compensator (to indicate the deviations of the mariner's compass).

compensat-eur, -**rice**, *adj.*, (horl.) compensative, compensating. *Pendule —;* compensating pendulum.

compensation, *n.f.*, compensation, amends, reparation, satisfaction; set-off. *Faire —;* to compensate, to make amends for.

compensatoire, *adj.*, compensatory.

compenser, *v.a.*, to counter-balance, to set against; to compensate, to make up for. *Rien ne compense la perte de l'honneur;* nothing can make up for the loss of honor.

se **compenser**, *v.r.*, to compensate each other; to be balanced, to be set off against; to be counteracted by.

compérage, *n.m.*, compaternity ; cheating, trickery, collusion.

compère, *n.m.*, godfather ; gossip ; crony ; pal ; confederate of a quack. *Un bon* — ; a good companion, fellow. *Un rusé* — ; a sly old blade. *Par* — *et par commère ;* by favor and interest.

compère-loriot, *n.m.*, (—*s*- —*s*) (orni.) gold-hammer, goldfinch, loriot, stye (on the eye).

compétemment (kon-pé-ta-mān), *adv.*, (l.u.) competently.

compétence, *n.f.*, competency, cognizance ; competition ; department, sphere, province. *Cela n'est pas de votre* — ; that is beyond your province.

compétent, -e, *adj.*, sufficient, suitable, requisite ; due ; (jur.) cognizant ; competent. *C'est un juge* — ; he is a competent judge. *Vous n'êtes pas* — *pour cela ;* you are not fit for that.

compéter, *v.n.*, (jur.) to belong ; to be due ; to be cognizable.

compétit-eur, *n.m.*, **-rice**, *n.f.*, competitor, competitress, candidate.

compétition, *n.f.*, competition, rivalry, strife.

compilateur, *n.m.*, compiler.

compilation, *n.f.*, compilation.

compiler, *v.a.*, to compile.

complainte, *n.f.*, complaint (jur.) ; lament, complaint, lamentation, moan, plaint, wailing ; plaintive ballad.

complaire, *v.n.*, to humor, to please, to gratify, to comply with the wishes (of) ; to condescend to.

se **complaire**, *v.r.*, to delight in ; to admire one's self.

complaisamment (-zam-an), *adv.*, complaisantly, obligingly.

complaisance, *n.f.*, kindness, goodness ; complaisance, complacency ; (com.) accommodation. —*s ;* love, affection. *Abuser de la* — *de quelqu'un ;* to abuse any one's goodness. *Faire une chose par* — ; to do a thing out of kindness.

complaisant, -e, *adj.*, complaisant, affable, civil, obliging ; kind.

complaisant, *n.m.*, **-e**, *n.f.*, over-civil person, fawner ; go-between.

complant, *n.m.*, (agri.) plantation, vineyard.

complément, *n.m.*, complement, completion, supplement ; objective case.

complémentaire, *adj.*, complementary, completing.

compl-et, -ète, *adj.*, complete, full, total, whole, perfect. *Un habillement* — ; a complete suit of clothes. *Œuvres* —*ètes ;* complete works.

complet, *n.m.*, complement, full number. *Être au* — ; to be full. *Au grand* — ; quite full ; all present.

complètement (kon-plet-mān), *adv.*, completely, thoroughly, entirely, wholly ; utterly.

complètement, *n.m.*, finishing, completion.

compléter, *v.a.*, to complete, to perfect ; to fill up, make up.

compléti-f, -ve, *adj.*, (gram.) completive.

complexe, *adj.*, complex ; complicated.

complexion, *n.f.*, constitution ; disposition, complexion, humor, temper, inclination.

complexionné, -e, *adj.*, constituted ; inclined.

complexité, *n.f.*, complexity.

complication, *n.f.*, intricacy, complication.

complice, *n.m.f.* and *adj.*, accomplice, accessory, privy to ; a party to.

complicité, *n.f.*, complicity, participation.

complies, *n.f.pl.*, (c. rel.) compline.

compliment, *n.m.*, compliment. *pl.*, congratulations. *Faire* — *à quelqu'un ;* to compliment any one. *Faites-lui mes* —*s ;* give him, her, my compliments. *Mes* —*s chez vous ;* remember me to all at home. *Je vous en fais mon* — ; I wish you joy. *Rengainer son* — ; to stop short, not to go on with. *Sans* — ; really, sincerely.

complimenter, *v.a.*, to compliment, to congratulate.

complimenteu-r, *n.m.*, **-se**, *n.f.*, complimenter.

complimenteu-r, -se, *adj.*, complimentary.

compliqué, -e, *adj.*, complicated, intricate.

compliquer, *v.a.*, to render intricate, to complicate, to entangle.

se **compliquer**, *v.r.*, to become complicated.

complot, *n.m.*, plot, conspiracy.

comploter, *v.a.*, to plot.

comploteur, *n.m.*, plotter, schemer.

componction, *n.f.*, compunction, contrition, remorse.

componé, -e, *adj.*, (her.) compony.

⊙**comportement**, *n.m.*, demeanor, comportment.

comporter, *v.a.*, to permit, to allow, to admit of. *Le temps le comporte ;* the times require it.

se **comporter**, *v.r.*, to behave, to behave one's self ; to act ; to manage. *Se* — *mal ;* to misbehave. *Il se comportera mieux à l'avenir ;* he will behave better for the future.

composant, *n.m.*, (chem.) component.

composante, *n.f.*, (math.) component.

composé, -e, *adj.*, composed, compound ; complicate ; affected, stiff. *Un mot* — ; a compound word. *Il a l'air extrêmement sérieux et* — ; he looks very grave and formal. *Air* — ; stiff, starched air.

composé, *n.m.*, compound.

composée, *n.f.*, (bot.) composite flower.

composer, *v.a.*, to compose, form, create, compound, make, fashion, adjust, regulate. — *sa mine ;* to adjust one's looks. *Il faut savoir se* — *selon le temps, selon les lieux ;* one must regulate one's self according to time and place. — *des almanachs ;* to indulge in chimerical dreams. — *un papier d'examen ;* to write out an examination paper.

composer, *v.n.*, to compound, to compromise, to make up, to adjust ; to capitulate. *Il a composé avec ses créanciers ;* he has compounded with his creditors.

composeur, *n.m.*, scribbler, paltry writer.

composite, *adj.*, (arch.) composite.

composite, *n.m.*, composite order.

compositeur, *n.m.*, composer (of music) ; (jur.) compounder ; (print.) compositor. *Amiable* — ; (jur.) compounder, friendly arbitrator.

composition, *n.f.*, composition, construction, composing, written examination ; theme, agreement, settlement ; capitulation. *Venir à* — ; to come to an agreement. *Un homme de* — ; an easy, tractable person. *Faire bonne* — ; to grant advantageous terms. *Il est de difficile* — ; he is hard to deal with. *Se rendre par* — ; to surrender upon terms. *Entrer en* — ; to enter into terms of composition.

compost, *n.m.*, (agri.) compost.

composter, *v.a.*, (agri.) to compost.

composteur, *n.m.*, (print.) composing-stick.

compote, *n.f.*, compote, stewed fruit, stew. —*de pigeons ;* stewed pigeons. *Avoir l'œil en* —; to have a black eye. *Avoir les yeux en* — ; to have a pair of black eyes.

compotier (-tié), *n.m.*, shallow dish for stewed fruit.

compréhensibilité, *n.f.*, comprehensibility.

compréhensible, *adj.*, comprehensible, conceivable, intelligible.

compréhensi-f, -ve, *adj.*, comprehensive.

compréhension, *n.f.*, comprehension, apprehension, understanding, intelligence.

compréhensivité, *n.f.*, comprehensiveness, faculty of comprehending.

comprendre, *v.a.*, to comprehend, to include, to comprise, to contain, to understand, to conceive. *Je comprends fort bien ce que vous* *me dites ;* I understand very well what you say to me. *— mal ;* to misunderstand. *A ce que je comprends ;* by what I understand. *Je ne le comprends pas ;* I do not know what to make of him.

compresse, *n.f.,* (surg.) compress, bolster, pledget. *—fenêtrée ;* perforated compress.

compressibilité, *n.f.,* compressibility.

compressible, *adj.,* compressible.

compressi-f, -ve, *adj.,* (surg.) compressive.

compression, *n.f.,* compression, squeezing, condensation ; (surg.) astriction.

comprimable, *adj.,* compressible.

comprimé, -e, *part.,* (bot.) compressed, flat, condensed ; put down, kept under.

comprimer, *v.a.,* to compress, to condense ; to quell ; to put down, to keep down, to restrain, to check, to curb.

compris, -e, *adj., part.,* understood, included. *Y —;* inclusive of, including. *Non —;* not including, exclusive of, without.

compromettant, *adj.,* injurious, dangerous, compromising ; incriminating, damaging ; disreputable.

compromettre, *v.n.,* to compromise, to implicate ; to put to arbitration, to consent to a reference, to refer to the arbitrament of one or more arbitrators.

compromettre, *v.a.,* to expose, to commit, to compromise, to jeopardize, to imperil, to endanger. *— son autorité, sa dignité ;* to imperil one's authority or character.

se **compromettre**, *v.r.,* to implicate, to compromise, oneself.

compromis, *n.m.,* mutual agreement, compromise. *Mettre en —;* to submit to arbitration.

compromissaire, *n.m.,* arbitrator, referee.

compromissionnaire, *adj.,* by compromise.

comptabilité (kon-ta-), *n.f.,* accounts, bookkeeping. *Il entend bien la —;* he has a thorough knowledge of accounts.

comptable (kon-tabl), *adj.,* accountable, responsible. *Agent —;* accountant ; responsible agent ; (nav.) paymaster. *Nous sommes —s de nos talents à la patrie ;* we are accountable to our country for our talents.

comptable, *n.m.,* accountant ; responsible agent.

comptant (kon-tän), *n.m.,* ready money, cash. *Au —;* (com.) for cash. *Payer —;* to pay ready money. *Avoir du —;* to be well provided with cash. *Voilà tout mon —;* here is all my cash.

comptant, *adj.,* (of money) ready ; (of payment) in cash ; (com.) prompt.

compte (kont), *n.m.,* account, reckoning, calculation, score ; due, rate ; question ; statement, report ; profit ; benefit ; esteem, value, regard. *Avez-vous votre —?* have you got the right amount ? *Je n'ai pas mon —;* I have not my due. *De — fait ;* altogether, on computation. *— rond ;* even money. *— borgne ;* odd money. *A —;* on account. *A bon —;* cheaply, at a small cost. *Livre de —;* book of accounts. *Roue de —;* (horl.) notch-wheel. *Chambre des —s ;* chamber of accounts. *Auditeur des —s ;* auditor of the exchequer. *Arrêter, solder, un —, des —s ;* to settle accounts. *Arrêté de —;* account agreed upon, statement of account. *Pour solde de —;* in full of all demands. *Faire rendre —;* to call to account. *Rendre —;* to give an account. *Avoir un — en banque ;* to have money at a banker's. *Mettre en ligne de —;* to pass to account. *Valider un —;* to verify an account. *Ouïr un —;* to audit an account. *Arrêter un —;* to strike a balance. *Il y a un reliquat de —à solder ;* there is a balance still owing. *Tenir —;* to keep an account. *Ne tenir n. — ni mesure ;* to leave all at sixes and sevens. *A bon —;* at a cheap rate. *Etre de bon —;* to be fair

in one's dealings. *Faire —;* to depend upon, to expect, to intend. *Il n'y a pas trouvé son —;* he did not find what he expected *or* that it paid. *Ils sont bien loin de —;* they are a long way out. *Vous m'en rendrez —;* you shall answer for it. *Il faut lui rendre — de tout ;* we must account to him for everything. *Faire le — de ;* to suit, to do well. *Je prends cela sur mon —;* I will be responsible for that. *On ne sait à quoi s'en tenir sur son —;* we do not know what to think of him. *A ce —là ;* at that rate. *Les bons —s font les bons amis ;* short reckonings make long friends. *Faire — d'une personne ;* to value a person. *Il n'en fait aucun —;* he slights him. *Au bout du —;* when all is said and done. *En fin de —;* in the end. *Se rendre — de ;* to get a clear idea of. *Erreur n'est pas —;* errors excepted.

compte-pas, *n.m.,* (—) odometer, pedometer ; surveying-wheel. *V.* **odomètre**.

compter (kon-té), *v.a.,* to count, to reckon, to number, to calculate, to compute ; to include ; to charge ; to settle accounts. *— ses pas ;* to walk slowly. *Marcher à pas comptés ;* to walk with measured steps.

compter, *v.n.,* to reckon, to calculate ; to intend, to purpose ; to think, to expect. *Quand comptez vous partir?* when do you purpose setting out ? *Je compte le voir demain ;* I expect to see him to-morrow. *— sur ;* to depend upon, to rely upon, to count upon ; to anticipate, to expect. *Comptez que ;* remember that. *Comptez dessus ;* depend upon it. *A — de ;* from, reckoning from. *Qui compte sans son hôte compte deux fois ;* he who reckons without his host, must reckon again.

compte rendu, *n.m.,* return, report, statement.

compteur (kon-teur), *n.m.,* counter, accountant, computer ; (mach.) tell-tale ; (tech.) meter. *— kilométrique ;* cyclometer.

comptoir (kon-toâr), *n.m.,* counter ; counting-house ; factory, settlement ; bar (of a public house, &c.). *Dame de —;* shopwoman ; barmaid. *Garçon de —;* barman, barkeeper.

compulser, *v.a.,* to look through a register ; to examine, in virtue of a judge's order.

compulsoire, *n.m.,* (jur.) examination of papers in virtue of a judge's order.

comput (kon-put), *n.m.,* computation.

computation, *n.f.,* computation.

computiste, *n.m.,* computer, computist.

comtal, -e, *adj.,* belonging to an earl or a countess.

comtat, *n.m.,* county (of Avignon, *or* Venaissin).

comte, *n.m.,* count ; earl.

comté, *n.m.,* county ; earldom, shire.

comtesse, *n.f.,* countess.

concasser, *v.a.,* to pound, to bruise, to crush.

concasseur, *n.m.,* bruising, *or* crushing, mill ; (tech.) steam-roller.

concaténation, *n.f.,* concatenation.

concave, *adj.,* concave.

concavité, *n.f.,* concaveness, concave, concavity.

concavo-concave, *adj.,* concavo-concave.

concavo-convexe, *adj.,* concavo-convex.

concédant, *n.m.,* grantor.

concéder, *v.a.,* to grant, to yield, to allow.

se **concéder**, *v.r.,* to be granted, allowed.

concentration, *n.f.,* concentration.

concentré, -e, *part.,* concentrated ; concentred ; close, silent, reserved, close-tongued. *Un homme toujours —;* a thoughtful man ; a man who is not communicative. *Haine —e ;* suppressed hatred.

concentrer, *v.a.,* to concentrate ; to dissemble, to repress, to smother. *— sa fureur ;* to dissemble one's rage.

se **concentrer**, *v.r.*, to concentrate, to meet in one centre; to centre; to retire within one's self.

concentrique, *adj.*, concentric.

concentriquement, *adv.*, concentrically.

concept (kon-sèpt), *n.m.*, (log.) concept.

conceptible, *adj.*, conceivable.

coecepti-f, -ve, *adj.*, conceptive.

conception, *n.f.*, conception; apprehension; thought, notion, understanding; wit, conceit. *Il a la* — *vive, facile, dure;* he is quick, easy, dull, of apprehension. *Vous n'avez pas de* — *comment* . . . ; you have no idea how . . .

concernant, *prep.*, concerning, relating to, touching, about, in reference to.

concerner, *v.a.*, to relate or belong to, to concern, to regard.

concert, *n.m.*, concert; harmony; unanimity, concord. — *spirituel ;* oratorio. — *de louanges;* chorus of praises. *De* —; by mutual consent. *Agir de* —; to act in concert. *Faire une chose de* —; to go hand in hand in a business.

concertant, -e, *adj.*, in concert (mus.). *Symphonie* —*e;* symphony performed in concert by two or three or more instruments.

concertant, *n.m.*, **-e**, *n.f.*, performer in a concert.

concerté, -e, *adj.*, concerted, planned; contrived; affected; studied; starched.

concerter, *v.a.*, to contrive, to concert; to plan, to devise ; ⊙to practise for a concert.

se **concerter**, *v.r.*, to plan together, to concert; to lay ones' heads together ; to deliberate.

concerto, *n.m.*, (—*s*) concerto.

concesseur, *n.m.*, grantor.

concession, *n.f.*, concession, grant, privilege.

concessionnaire, *n.m.*, grantee. — *d'un privilège ;* patentee.

concetti, *n.m.pl.*, (*n.s.*) witty conceits; affected wit.

concevable, *adj.*, conceivable, imaginable.

concevoir, *v.a.*, to apprehend, to imagine, to understand, to perceive, to take, to comprehend; to word, to express ; to conceive ; to become pregnant. *Elle est hors d'âge de* —; she is past child-bearing.

conche, *n.f.*, (tech.) brine-pit.

conchoïdal, -e (-ko-), *adj.*, (geom.) conchoidal.

conchoïde (-ko-), *n.f.*, (geom.) conchoid.

conchologie, *n.f.*, conchology.

conchologique, *adj* conchological.

conchologiste, *n.m.*, conchologist.

conchyte (-kit), *n.f.*, conchite.

concierge, *n. m. f.*, house-porter, portress ; door-keeper, hall-porter.

conciergerie, *n.f.*, place of porter or door-keeper ; porter's lodge. *Conciergerie ;* a prison in Paris.

concile, *n.m.*, an assembly of prelates and doctors, council ; decrees and decisions of a council.

conciliable, *adj.*, reconcilable.

conciliabule, *n.m.*, conventicle, cabal, secret meeting. — *en plein air ;* field conventicle.

conciliaire, *adj.*, of or belonging to a council.

conciliairement, *adj.*, in council.

conciliant, -e, *adj.*, conciliating, reconciling, conciliatory.

conciliat-eur, *n.m.*, **-rice**, *n.f.*, conciliator ; reconciler.

conciliat-eur, -rice, *adj.*, conciliatory, conciliating.

conciliation, *n.f.*, conciliation ; reconciliation.

conciliatoire, *adj.*, conciliatory.

concilier, *v.a.*, to reconcile, to conciliate, to accord ; to gain, to win, to procure.

se **concilier**, *v.r.*, to conciliate, to gain, to win, to ingratiate one's self. *Se* — *les esprits ;* to gain people's good will.

concis, -e, *adj.*, concise, brief, short.

concision, *n.f.*, brevity, conciseness.

concitoyen, *n.m.*, **-ne**, *n.f.* (-in, -è-n), fellow-citizen ; fellow-townsman or townswoman.

conclave, *n.m.*, assembly of cardinals ; conclave.

conclaviste, *n.m.*, conclavist.

concluant, -e, *adj.*, conclusive, decisive.

conclure, *v.a.*, to conclude, to finish ; to infer from; to move. *Qu'en voulez-vous* —*?* what do you infer from that ?

conclure, *v.n.*, to conclude, to infer; to think, to judge. *Cette raison ne conclut pas ;* this reason proves nothing. — *criminellement contre quelqu'un ;* to bring any one in guilty.

conclusi-f, -ve, *adj.*, conclusive.

conclusion, *n.f.*, final decision, conclusion ; end, issue ; inference.

concoct-eur, -rice, *adj.*, concoctive.

concoction, *n.f.*, concoction.

concombre, *n.m.*, (bot.) cucumber. — *sauvage ;* horse cucumber.

concomitance, *n.f.*, concomitance.

concomitant, -e, *adj.*, concomitant.

concordance, *n.f.*, concordance, agreement; concord.

concordant, *n.m.*, (mus.) baritone.

concordant, *adj.*, (mus.) concordant.

concordat, *n.m.*, concordat, compact, agreement; composition; bankrupt's certificate. *Bénéfice de* — ; (jur.) benefit of the insolvent act. *Sans* — ; (jur.) uncertificated (of bankrupts).

concordataire, *n.m.*, certificated bankrupt.

concorde, *n.f.*, concord, good understanding, agreement, harmony. *Mettre la* — *entre des ennemis ;* to reconcile enemies.

concorder, *v.n.*, to live in concord, to agree, to concur.

concourant, -e, *adj.*, concurrent.

concourir, *v.n.*, to concur, to conspire, to contribute to, to cooperate in ; to compete for; to unite ; to meet. *Tout concourt à ma ruine ;* all things conspire to my ruin. *Etre admis à* —; to be allowed to compete. *Ces deux hommes ont concouru pour le prix ;* these two men competed for the prize.

concours, *n.m.*, concurrence, cooperation, assistance ; concourse ; meeting ; match, tournament ; competition ; competitive examination. *Son* — *m'a été fort utile ;* his cooperation has been very useful to me. *Se présenter au* —; to compete for.

concr-et, -ète, *adj.*, (arith., log.) concrete ; (math.) applicate.

concret, *n.m.*, (log.) concrete.

concrétion, *n.f.*, concretion.

concubinage, *n.m.*, concubinage.

concubinaire, *n.m.*, one who keeps a concubine.

concubine, *n.f.*, concubine.

concupiscence, *n.f.*, concupiscence, lust.

concupiscent, -e, *adj.*, concupiscent, libidinous.

concupiscible, *adj.*, concupiscible.

concurremment (-kur-ra-măn), *adv.*, concurrently, in concurrence; jointly, together.

concurrence (kon-kur-rans), *n. f.*, competition, rivalry, opposition. *Jusqu'à* — *de;* to the amount of, to the extent of. *Faire* — *à ;* to compete with, to oppose.

concurrent, *n.m.*, **-e**, *n.f.*, competitor, rival, opponent.

concussion, *n. f.*, extortion, embezzlement, peculation. *User de* —; to be guilty of bribery.

concussionnaire, *n.m.*, extortioner, peculator, embezzler.

concussionnaire, *adj.*, guilty of peculation, of bribery, extortion.

condamnable (-da-na-), *adj.*, condemnable, blamable, criminal.

condamnation (-da-na-), *n.f.*, condemnation, judgment, sentence. *Subir sa* —; to undergo one's sentence. *Subir* —; to accept a sentence (without appeal). — *par défaut*; judgment by default. *Passer* —; to pass sentence; to confess oneself in the wrong.

condamné, *n.m.*, **-e**, *n.f.* (kon-da-né), condemned, convict.

condamner (kon-da-né), *v.a.*, to condemn, to sentence; to blame, to censure; to block up (doors, windows); to give over (patients). — *à une amende;* to fine. — *d'avance;* to prejudge.

condensabilité, *n.f.*, condensability.

condensable, *adj.*, condensable.

condensateur, *n.m.*, (phys.) condenser.

condensation, *n.f.*, condensation.

condenser, *v.a.*, (phys.) to condense. — *de nouveau;* to recondense. *Machine à* —; condensing-engine.

se **condenser**, *v.r.*, (phys.) to condense, to be condensed.

condenseur, *n.m.*, (mec.) condenser.

condescendance, *n.f.*, condescension, compliance. *Acte de* —; act of condescension, condescendence.

condescendant, -e, *adj.*, condescending, complying.

condescendre, *v.n.*, to condescend, to comply, to yield, to stoop to.

condiment, *n.m.*, condiment.

condisciple, *n.m.*, school-fellow.

condit, *n.m.*, (pharm.) confection.

condition, *n.f.*, condition, circumstances, nature; quality, figure, rank, fortune; station; situation, place; offer, terms; (silk manu.) drying-room. *Améliorer sa* —; to better one's circumstances. *Les gens de* —; people of fashion. *Etre de* —; to be well born. *Etre de basse* —; to be low born. *Chacun doit vivre selon sa* —; every one ought to live according to his station. *Toutes les —s ont leurs désagréments;* every condition has its own drawbacks. *Il est dans une bonne* —; he has a good place. — *provisionnelle;* proviso. *Sans* —; without a proviso. *Ils se sont rendus à des —s honorables;* they surrendered upon honorable terms. *A* —, *sous* —; on condition. *Vendre sous* —; to sell on approval. *A* — *que;* on condition, provided that. *En* —; in service (of servants).

conditionné, -e *adj.*, made up, conditioned (with *bien* or *mal*); sound; downright; egregious; tipsy, tight; in a pretty state.

conditionnel, -le, *adj.*, conditional; (jur.) provisory.

conditionnel, *n.m.*, (gram.) conditional.

conditionnellement, *adv.*, conditionally, on condition.

conditionnement, *n.m.*, drying (of silk).

conditionner, *v.a.*, (com.) to put into good condition, to make up; to dry (of silk).

condoléance, *n.f.*, condolence. *Faire ses compliments de* — *à quelqu'un;* to pay a visit of condolence to anyone.

condoma, *n.m.*, a species of antelope.

condor, *n.m.*, (orni.) condor.

conduct-eur, *n.m.*, **-rice**, *n.f.*, conductor, conductress, leader, guide; driver. — *de train;* guard.

conduct-eur, -rice, *adj.*, leading; (phys.) conducting.

conductibilité, *n.f.*, conductibility.

conductible, *adj.*, conductible.

conduction, *n.f.*, (phys.) conduction; (civic law) hiring.

conduire (conduisant, conduit), *v.a.*, to conduct, to lead, to guide, to convey, to carry, to bring, to take; to go along with, to accompany, to attend, to escort; to have the command of; to govern, to rule, to direct, to manage. *Conduisez monsieur à sa chambre;* show the gentleman to his room. — *un troupeau;* to drive a flock. — *une affaire;* to manage a business. — *un jeune homme;* to train or bring up a youth. — *la conscience de quelqu'un;* to direct any one's conscience. — *un bâtiment, un travail;* to be surveyor of a building, to have the direction of a work. *Savoir* — *sa barque;* to play one's cards well.

se **conduire**, *v.r.*, to conduct, to behave oneself; to guide, to govern, oneself; to find one's way.

conduire, *v.n.*, to conduct, to lead to; to drive. *Ce chemin conduit à la ville;* this road leads to the town. — *à grandes guides;* to drive four-in-hand. *L'art de* —; the art of driving.

conduit, *n.m.*, conduit, duct, passage, pipe; tube, canal. — *auditif;* auditory passage. — *acoustique;* speaking-pipe. — *de vent;* (mach.) blast-pipe.

conduite, *n.f.*, conduct, leading; management, charge, direction, administration; behavior, demeanor, deportment; guidance, prudence, discretion; water-pipes; (nav.) conduct-money; (mus.) port (of the voice). *Tuyau de* —; delivery pipe. *Se charger de la* — *d'une affaire;* to undertake the management of a business. *La* — *d'une pièce de théâtre;* the disposition, arrangement, of a drama. — *régulière;* orderly conduct. *Avoir de la* —; to be well-behaved. *Manquer de* —; to misconduct oneself, to be ill-behaved. *Faire la* — *à quelqu'un;* to see anyone off; to attend anyone to the grave.

condupliqué, *adj.*, (bot.) (of leaves) conduplicated.

condyle, *n.m.*, (anat.) condyle.

condyloïde, *adj.*, condyloid.

cône, *n.m.*, cone; (opt.) pencil; (bot.) strobile. *En* —; conical.

⊙**confabulateur**, *n.m.*, story-teller, conversationalist.

⊙**confabulation**, *n.f.*, confabulation.

⊙**confabuler**, *v.n.*, to confabulate, to chat.

confection, *n.f.*, confection, making up; ready made clothes; electuary; execution, completion. *La* — *du chyle;* the formation of the chyle. *La* — *d'un inventaire;* the completing an inventory. *Maison de* —; dress-making establishment.

confectionné, -e, *adj.*, made, manufactured, ready-made.

confectionner, *v.a.*, to manufacture, to make, to finish.

confectionneu-r, *n.m.*, **-se**, *n.f.*, maker, finisher (of wearing apparel), clothier, outfitter.

confédérati-f, -ve, *adj.*, confederative.

confédération, *n.f.*, confederation, confederacy.

confédéré, -e, *n.* and *adj.*, confederate, associate, federate, accomplice.

se **confédérer**, *v.r.*, to confederate, to unite, to combine.

conférence, *n.f.*, conference; lecture; comparison, collation. *Maître de* —; lecturer, professor.

conférencier, *n.m.*, lecturer.

conférer, *v.a.*, to compare, to collate, to confer, to bestow, to grant. — *un auteur avec un autre;* to collate two authors.

conférer, *v.n.*, to consult together, to confer; to bestow, to grant; (print.) to revise.

conferve, *n.f.*, (bot.) conferva, hair-weed.

confesse, *n.*, (c. rel.) confession (to a priest). [This noun has no gender, is always accompanied by *à* or *de*, and *never* by any article.] *Aller à* —; to go to confession.

confesser, *v.a.*, to confess; to acknowledge, to avow, to own, to admit. *C'est le diable à* —; it is terribly hard, or very hard lines.

se **confesser**, *v.r.*, to confess one's sins, to confess (to a priest). *Se* — *au renard;* to betray oneself.

confesseur, *n.m.*, confessor ; father confessor.

confession, *n.f.*, confession, acknowledgment, avowal. *Donner à quelqu'un le bon Dieu sans —;* to trust any one with untold gold.

confessionnal, *n.m.*, confessional.

confiance, *n.f.*, confidence, reliance, trust, dependence, assurance ; self-conceit. *Avoir de la — en quelqu'un;* to repose confidence in any one. *Donner sa — à quelqu'un;* to confide in any one. *Homme de —;* confidential man of business. *Une personne de —;* a trustworthy person. *Cela donne de la —;* that inspires confidence.

confiant, -e, *adj.*, confident, unsuspecting, sanguine; self-conceited.

confidemment (-da-mān), *adv.*, in confidence, confidentially.

confidence, *n.f.*, confidence, secrecy, secret, disclosure; trust (of benefices). *Etre dans la — de quelqu'un;* to be in any one's confidence. *Il était dans la —;* he was in the secret. *Un échange de —s;* an exchange of secrets. *Faire une — à quelqu'un;* to tell a secret to any one; to take any one into one's confidence. *Faire une — fausse;* to make a pretended disclosure. *Tenir un bénéfice en —;* to hold a living in trust.

confident, n.m., -e, *n.f.,* confident, confidant, confidante.

confidentiaire (-ci-), *n.m.*, one who holds a living in trust.

confidentiel, -le (-ci-), *adj.*, confidential.

confidentiellement (-ci-), *adv.*, confidentially.

confier, *v.a.*, to confide, to intrust, to commit to; to tell in confidence.

se **confier**, *v.r.*, to trust in; to place reliance on; to unbosom one's self to. *Se — en ses forces;* to trust to one's own strength. *Je me confie à vous;* I trust you.

configuration, *n.f.*, configuration, form, shape.

configurer, *v.a.*, (l.u.) to configurate, to form, to shape.

confinement, *n.m.*, (jur.) confinement, imprisonment.

confiner, *v.n.*, to border upon; to confine, to limit, to adjoin.

confiner, *v.a.*, to confine, to imprison.

se **confiner**, *v.r.*, to confine, to limit one's self.

confinité, *n.f.*, confinity, contiguity.

confins, *n.m.pl.*, confines, borders, limits. *Aux — de la terre;* at the ends of the earth.

confire (consisant, confit), *v.a.*, to preserve, to candy, to pickle. *Confit en dévotion;* extremely devout. *— une peau;* to soak a skin. *C'est un homme confit;* he is done for. *Se —;* to be preserved.

confirmati-f, -ve, *adj.*, confirmatory.

confirmation, *n.f.*, confirmation, ratification, sanction. *Cela a besoin de —;* that requires confirmation.

confirmer, *v.a.*, to confirm, to ratify, to sanction. *— quelqu'un;* (l.ex.) to give any one a slap in the face.

se **confirmer**, *v.r.*, to be confirmed.

confiscable, *adj.*, confiscable, forfeitable, liable to forfeiture.

confiscant, *adj.*, (jur.) confiscating.

confiscation, *n.f.*, confiscation, forfeiture.

confiserie, *n.f.*, confectionery, confectioner's shop.

confiseur, n.m., -se, *n.f.*, confectioner.

confisquer, *v.a.*, to confiscate, to forfeit, to impound.

confite, *part., adj.*, preserved, pickled.

confiteor, *n.m.*, (—) confiteor. *Dire son —;* to acknowledge one's fault.

confiture, *n.f.*, preserve, jam.

confituri-er, n.m., -ère, *n.f.*, dealer in preserves, confectioner; preserve-maker.

conflagration, *n.f.*, conflagration.

conflit, *n.m.*, contention, strife, contest, rivalry, conflict, collision, encounter; jarring, clashing.

confluent, *n.m.*, (geog.) confluence, junction, conflux.

confluent, -e, *adj.*, (med.) confluent. *Petite verolé —e;* confluent small-pox.

confluer, *v.n.*, to be confluent.

confondre, *v.a.*, to confound, to confuse; to blend, to mix, to mingle; to amaze, to astound, to abash.

se **confondre**, *v.r.*, to be confounded, to blend, to mingle, to be lost in.

conformation, *n.f.*, conformation.

conforme, *adj.*, conformable, congenial, consonant, consistent. *Pour copie —;* a true copy, conformable to the original.

conformé, -e, *adj.*, formed, shaped.

conformément, *adv.*, suitably, conformably, agreeably.

conformer, *v.a.*, to conform.

se **conformer**, *v.r.*, to conform one's self, to follow, to comply with. *Se — aux circonstances;* to conform to circumstances.

conformiste, *n.m.f.*, conformist.

conformité, *n.f.*, likeness, agreement, conformity, compliance. *En —;* conformably, in compliance with, agreeably to.

confort, *n.m.*, comfort, ease; ⊙help, succour.

confortable, *adj.*, consolatory, comfortable.

confortable, *n.m.*, comfort, ease.

confortant, -e, *or* **confortati-f, -ve**, *adj.*, strengthening, comforting.

confortatif, *n.m.*, (med.) corroborant.

confortation, *n.f.*, (l.u.) strengthening.

conforter, *v.a.*, to comfort; (med.) to strengthen; to console.

confraternité, *n.f.*, fraternity, brotherhood, fellowship.

confrère, *n.m.*, colleague; fellow-member; contemporary, brother-magistrate, etc.

confrérie, *n.f.*, brotherhood, confraternity.

confrication, *n.f.*, (pharm.) confrication.

confrontation, *n.f.*, confrontation; comparing, collation (of writings).

confronter, *v.a.*, to confront, to stand face to face; to compare, to collate. *— la copie à l'original;* to compare the copy with the original.

confus, -e, *adj.*, vague, indistinct, ashamed, abashed, crestfallen, confused; obscure, dim, faint. *Bruit —;* confused rumor.

confusément, *adv.*, confusedly, vaguely, dimly.

confusion, *n.f.*, confusion; disorder, disturbance, trouble; shame, blush. *Mettre tout en —;* to disturb everything. *En —;* in disorder, disorderly.

confutation, *n.f.*, confutation; refutation.

confuter, *v.a.*, to disprove, to confute, to refute.

congé, *n.m.*, (milit.) leave; liberty, permission; discharge, dismissal; warning, notice (to quit); holiday; congé; permit; (nav.) pass, clearance; (arch.) apophysis; escape; (milit.) furlough. *Prendre —;* to take one's leave. *Jour de —;* holiday. *En —;* on leave, on furlough.

congéable, *adj.*, dismissable, dischargeable; (jur.) held under tenancy at will.

congédier, *v.a.*, to discharge, to dismiss, to pay off; to disband, to break up.

congélable, *adj.*, congealable.

congélateur, *n.m.*, refrigerator, freezing machine.

congélation, *n.f.*, congelation, congealing; (mas.) rock-work; icicle (on sculptures).

congeler, *v.a.*, to congeal, to freeze; to coagulate.

se **congeler**, *v.r.*, to congeal, to freeze; to coagulate.

congénère, *adj.*, congener, congenerous.
congénital, -e, *adj.*, congenital.
congestion (-jès-tion), *n.f.*, congestion.
congiaire, *n.m.*, (antiq.) subsidy.
conglobation, *n.f.*, (rhet.) conglobation.
⊙**conglobé, -e**, *adj.*, conglobate; (anat.) lymphatic ; globate, globated.
conglomérat, *n.m.*, (geol.) conglomerate.
conglomération, *n.f.*, conglomeration.
conglomérer, *v.a.*, to conglomerate.
conglutinant, -e, *adj.*, conglutinant.
conglutinati-f, -ve, *adj.*, conglutinative.
conglutination, *n.f.*, conglutination.
conglutiner, *v.a.*, to glue together ; to thicken, to conglutinate.
congratulation, *n.f.*, congratulation.
congratulatoire, *adj.*, congratulatory.
congratuler, *v.a.*, (jest.) to congratulate, to felicitate.

congre, *n.m.*, conger ; conger-eel.
congréer, *v.a.*, (nav.) to worm (a cable).
congréganiste, *n.m.f.*, congregationalist.
congrégation, *n.f.*, fraternity, congregation ; brotherhood. — *des fidèles ;* whole body of any church.
congrès, *n.m.*, congress.
congrier, *n.m.*, stake-net.
congru, -e, *adj.*, suitable, consistent, agreeable to, congruous, proper. *Portion —e ;* suitable allowance.
congruité, *n.f.*, congruity, consistency, propriety.
congrûment, *adv.*, congruously, properly.
conicine, *n.f.*, (chem.) conia.
conifère, *adj.*, coniferous.
coniforme, *adj.*, coniform.
conique, *adj.*, conical.
coniques, *n.f.pl.*, conics, conic sections.
conite, *n.m.*, (min.) conite.
conjectural, -e, *adj.*, conjectural.
conjecturalement (-ral-mãn), *adv.*, conjecturally.
conjecture, *n.f.*, guess, conjecture, surmise.
conjecturer, *v.a.*, to conjecture, to guess, to surmise.
conjoindre, *v.a.*, to conjoin, to join, to unite, to connect.
conjoint, -e, *part.*, conjoined, joined, united. *Les futurs —s ;* the bride and bridegroom that are to be. *Feuilles —es ;* (bot.) conjugate leaves. *Règle —e ;* (arith.) chain-rule.
conjointement (kon-joint-mãn), *adv.*, conjointly, unitedly.
conjoncti-f, -ve, *adj.*, conjunctive.
conjonction, *n.f.*, conjunction ; union, connection ; coition.
conjonctive, *n.f.*, (anat.) conjunctiva.
conjonctivement, *adv.*, conjunctively.
conjoncture, *n.f.*, conjuncture, juncture.
conjugaison, *n.f.*, (gram., anat.) conjugation.
conjugal, -e, *adj.*, conjugal.
conjugalement (-gal-mãn), *adv.*, conjugally.
conjugati-f, -ve, *adj.*, (gram.) conjugative, relating to conjugation.
conjuguer (-ghé), *v.a.*, (gram.) to conjugate.
se **conjuguer**, *v.r.*, to be conjugated.
conjungo, *n.m.*, (jest.) wedding, marriage ; (diplom.) writing without stops or space.
conjurateur, *n.m.*, plotter, conspirator ; conjurer.
conjuration, *n.f.*, conspiracy, plot ; conjuration, exorcism. *pl.*, entreaties.
conjuré, n.m., conspirator, plotter.
conjuré, -e, *part.*, confederate, sworn.
conjurer, *v.a.*, to implore ; to conspire, to plot ; to swear ; to raise evil spirits, to exorcise, to conjure, to ward off, to avert. *Il trouva moyen de — la tempête ;* he found a way of warding off the storm.

connaissable, *adj.*, (l.u.) recognisable, easily known.
connaissance, *n.f.*, knowledge ; acquaintance ; intercourse ; senses, consciousness ; learning, understanding ; (hunt.) the print of a stag's foot on the ground. *pl.*, knowledge, attainments, acquirements. *La — du bien et du mal ;* the knowledge of good and evil. *Prendre — d'une chose ;* to take note of a thing. *Prendre — d'une cause ;* to take cognizance of a case. *Parler en — de cause, agir avec — de cause ;* to speak knowingly, to proceed upon a thorough knowledge of the matter. *Faire — avec quelqu'un ;* to form the acquaintance of any one. *Être en pays de — ;* to be among friends. *Ses —s sont très-bornées ;* his knowledge is very limited.
connaissants, *adj. m.pl.*, (jur.) skilled ; well acquainted with.
connaissement (-nès-mãn), *n.m.*, (com.) bill of lading.
connaisseu-r, *n.m.*, **-se**, *n.f.*, *adj.*, connoisseur, one skilled in a thing.
connaisseu-r, -se, *adj.*, judge, good judge, connoisseur.
connaître (connaissant, connu), *v.a.*, to know, to be aware of, to perceive ; to understand, to be versed in anything ; to be acquainted with ; to experience, to discern, to distinguish. *Je le connais de vue ;* I know him by sight. *Faire — ;* to make it appear, to prove, to reveal, to make known. *Se faire — ;* to make one's self known. *Je le ferai — ;* I will show him up. *Dès qu'il est question d'intérêt, il ne connaît plus personne ;* in matters of interest, everybody is a stranger to him. *Je ne connais que cela ;* that's all I can say, all I know. *— à fond ;* to know thoroughly. *Connaissez-vous cet homme-là ?* are you acquainted with that man ? *— quelque chose à quelqu'un ;* to know that a person has or possesses.
se **connaître**, *v.r.*, to know one's self ; to know each other ; (of things) to be known. *Connais-toi, toi-même ;* know thyself. *Il ne se connaît pas ;* he is out of his senses. *Se — en quelque chose ;* to understand a thing, to be a judge of a thing. *Ne pas se — de joie ;* to be beside one's self with joy. *Je m'y connais ;* I understand all about it, I know what it all means.
connaître, *v.n.*, to know ; to have cognizance, to take cognizance (of).
conné, -e (ko-n-né), *adj.*, (bot.) connate.
connecti-f, -ve, *adj.*, (bot.) connective.
connétable, *n.m.*, high constable, mayor.
connétable, *n.f.*, high constable's wife.
connétablie, *n.f.*, the court and jurisdiction of the high constable ; residence of the high constable.
connexe (ko-n-nèks), *adj.*, (jur.) connected.
connexion (ko-n-nèk-sion), *n.f.*, connection, affinity.
connexité (ko-n-nèk-si-té), *n.f.*, connection, connexity.
connivence (ko-n-ni-), *n.f.*, connivance.
connivent, -e (ko-n-ni-), *adj.*, (anat., bot.) connivent.
conniver (ko-n-ni-), *v.n.*, to connive.
connu, n.m., known ; that which is known.
connu, -e, *part.*, known, understood. *Il est — comme le loup blanc ;* he is known by everybody. *Il gagne à être — ;* he improves on acquaintance. *Connu !* that's an old story. *En chiffres —s ;* in plain figures.
conoïdal, *adj.*, (bot.) conoidal.
conoïde, *n.m.*, (anat., geom.) conoid.
conoïde, *adj.*, (anat., geom.) conoidical.
conque, *n.f.*, conch, sea-shell ; (anat.) concha, pavilion of the ear.
conquérant, *n.m.*, conqueror ; (fam.) lady-killer.
conquérant, -e, *adj.*, conquering.

conquérir (conquérant, conquis), *v.a.*, to conquer, to subdue; to gain, to obtain, to win over.

conquêt, *n.m.*, (jur.) acquisition, acquired property. —*s*; property (acquired by two married people).

conquête, *n.f.*, conquest, acquisition; success, winning of favors.

consacrant, *adj.*, consecrating, officiating.

consacrant, *n.m.*, consecrator, officiant.

consacrer, *v.a.*, to consecrate; to dedicate, to devote; to hallow, to sanctify; to sanction, to perpetuate; to appropriate, to give. — *son temps à* ; to devote one's time to.

se **consacrer**, *v.r.*, to devote one's self.

consanguin, -e (-ghin, -ghi-n), *n.* and *adj.*, (jur.) on the father's side. *Frère* —, *sœur* —*e* ; half-brother, half-sister, on the father's side. *Les* —*s* ; half-brothers and sisters on the father's side.

consanguinité (-gu-i-), *n.f.*, consanguinity.

conscience, *n.f.*, conscience, perception, consciousness, sentiment; (print.) work paid by the day; the compositors paid by the day. *Cri de* —; qualm of conscience. — *nette* ; clear conscience. *Remords de* —; remorse, sting of conscience. *Se faire un cas de* — *d'une chose* ; to make a matter of conscience of anything. *Avoir la* — *de* ; to be conscious of. *Il a la* — *large* ; he is not over scrupulous. *La main sur la* —; candidly, sincerely. *Il a dit tout ce qu'il avait sur la* —; he has opened his mind without reserve. *Transiger avec sa* —; to compound with one's conscience. *En* —; conscientiously; in conscience; indeed, candidly.

consciencieusement, *adv.*, conscientiously.

consciencieu-x, -**se**, *adj.*, conscientious.

conscient, -e, *adj.*, (philo.) conscious.

conscription, *n.f.*, (milit.) conscription; enlistment; enrolling.

conscriptionnel, -**le**, *adj.*, relating to the conscription, enlistment.

conscrit, *adj.*, conscript. *Père* —; Roman senator.

conscrit, *n.m.*, conscript, recruit, raw soldier; freshman; novice, greenhorn.

consécrateur, *n.m.*, consecrator.

consécration, *n.f.*, consecration, dedication; ordination; sanction.

consécuti-f, -**ve**, *adj.*, consecutive; following.

consécutivement (-tiv-mān), *adv.*, consecutively.

conseigle, *n.m.*, meslin (mixture of rye and wheat or oats).

*****conseil**, *n.m.*, counsel, advice; council; council-board; board; resolution, course, determination; counselor, adviser. — *de commerce* ; board of trade. — *municipal* ; town-council. — *des ministres* ; cabinet-council. — *de révision* ; military board of appeal. *Il ne prend* — *que de sa tête* ; he does everything by himself, without consulting any one. *La nuit porte* —; sleep upon it. — *de guerre* ; court-martial, council of war. — *de famille* ; family council; commission of lunacy. *A parti pris pas de* — ; advice is useless to a man who has made up his mind.

*****conseiller**, *v.a.*, to advise, to counsel, to give advice.

*****conseill-er**, *n.m.*, -**ère**, *n.f.*, counselor, adviser; councilor; puisne justice; judge.

*****conseilleur**, *n.m.*, adviser; officious person.

consentant, -e, *adj.*, consenting, willing.

consentement (kon-sant-mān), *n.m.*, consent, assent.

consentir, *v.n.*, to consent, to agree to, to acquiesce ; to assent to ; (nav.) to spring, to break (of masts). *Qui ne dit mot consent* ; silence gives consent.

*****conséquemment** (-ka-mān), *adv.*, consequently, accordingly, conformably.

conséquence, *n.f.*, consequence, sequel ;

event, issue; inference; movement, importance; weight, deduction. *Tirer une* —; to draw an inference. *Prévoir les* —*s d'une démarche* ; to foresee the consequences of a measure. *Cela tire à* —; that will be a precedent. *De peu de* —; of no consequence, insignificant. *C'est un homme sans* —; he is a person of no consequence. *Faire l'homme de* —; to set up for a man of consequence. *Une affaire de nulle* —; an affair of no moment. *En* —; accordingly. *En* — *de vos ordres* ; according to your orders. *Cela ne tire pas à* —; that is of no importance.

conséquent, -e, *adj.*, just, rational, consistent, coherent.

conséquent, *n.m.*, (log., math.) consequent. *Par* —; consequently, in consequence.

conservat-eur, *n.m.*, -**rice**, *n.f.*, *adj.*, preserver, guardian, keeper; conservative. — *des chasses* ; ranger. — *des eaux et forêts* ; commissioner of woods and forests.

conservatif, -**ve**, *adj.*, preservative.

conservation, *n.f.*, preservation; conservation, registration (of mortgages).

conservatoire, *n.m.*, academy of music and school of elocution; Magdalen asylum; museum; (of objects of art).

conservatoire, *adj.*, conservative, conservatory, preservative.

conserve, *n.f.*, preserve; pickle; (nav.) consort; (phar.) conserve. *pl.*, preservers (spectacles). *Deux vaisseaux vont de* —; two ships keep company together. —*s au vin aigre* ; pickles.

conservé, -e, *part.*, preserved. *Ce tableau est bien* —; this painting is well preserved. *Etre bien* —; to bear one's age well ; to be hale and hearty.

conserver, *v.a.*, to preserve, to keep; to maintain. *Une vie réglée conserve et fortifie la santé* ; a regular life preserves and strengthens health.

se **conserver**, *v.r.*, to be preserved ; to preserve one's self; to keep (of meat, etc.) ; to bear one's age well. *Son teint s'est bien conservé* ; her complexion wears well. *Conservez-vous* ; take care of yourself.

considérable, *adj.*, considerable, notable, eminent, illustrious, important. *Peu* —; of little importance.

considérablement, *adv.*, considerably.

considérant, *n.m.*, (jur.) preamble ; recital.

considération, *n.f.*, consideration, attention ; account, regard, stake ; note, respect, esteem. *Cela mérite* — ; that requires consideration. *C'est à votre* — *qu'il l'a fait* ; it is out of regard for you that he did it. *Faire entrer en* — ; to take into consideration. *N'avoir aucune* — *pour les gens* ; to have no regard for people. *Il n'a nulle* — *dans le monde* ; he is held in no esteem whatever. *Un homme de* — ; a man of note. *En* — *de* ; in consideration of, out of regard for, for the sake of.

considérément, *adv.*, considerately, prudently, thoughtfully.

considérer, *v.a.*, to consider, to take into consideration, to look at, to view, to gaze upon, to regard, to behold, to contemplate; to pay regard to ; to have a consideration for, to value, to esteem, to respect, to look up to ; to mind, to look to ; to look upon. *Tout bien considéré* ; all things considered. — *une chose en elle-même* ; to look at a thing in itself. *Il faut bien* — *les choses avant de s'engager* ; you must look before you leap.

se **considérer**, *v.r.*, to esteem one's self; to look to one's self ; to be considered.

*****consignataire**, *n.m.f.*, trustee, depositary ; (com.) consignee.

*****consignat-eur**, *n.m.*, -**rice**, *n.f.*, (com.) consignor.

*consignation, *n.f.*, consignment, deposit; lodgment (banking); (jur.) consignation. *Caisse des dépôts et —s;* deposit bank. *Ces marchandises sont à la — d'un tel;* these goods are consigned to so and so.

*consigne, *n.f.*, (milit.) orders, pass-word; instructions; cloak-room (at stations). *Manquer à la —;* to disregard orders. *Forcer la —;* to force a sentry, to infringe orders. *Lever la —;* to revoke orders; to release from confinement.

*consigner, *v.a.*, to deposit; to record, to enter, to note down, to register; to refuse admittance; to keep in; (com.) to consign. *Je l'ai consigné à ma porte;* I have left orders not to admit him.

consistance, *n.f.*, consistency, consistence; firmness; stability; credit, consideration; (jur.) matter. *Le temps n'a point de —;* the weather is unsettled. *C'est un esprit qui n'a point de —;* he is a person of no consistency. *Cette nouvelle prend de la —;* the news is gaining ground.

consistant, -e, *adj.*, consisting of; firm, fixed, solid, compact.

consister, *v.n.*, to be composed of, to consist. *Le tout consiste à savoir;* the main point is to know. *Son revenu consiste en rentes;* his revenue consists of property in the funds.

consistoire, *n.m.*, consistory:

consistorial, -e, *adj.*, consistorial.

consistorialement, *adv.*, in a consistory.

consolable, *adj.*, consolable.

consolant, -e, *adj.*, consoling, comforting, consolatory.

consolat-eur, *n.m.*, **-rice**, *n.f.*, comforter, consoler.

consolat-eur, -rice, *adj.*, consoling; consolatory.

consolation, *n.f.*, consolation, comfort, solace.

consolatoire, *adj.*, consolatory.

console, *n.f.*, (arch.) console, bracket-table; pier-table; corbel.

consoler, *v.a.*, to console, to solace, to comfort.

se consoler, *v.r.*, to be consoled, to be comforted; to solace, to console oneself.

consolidant, *n.m.* and *adj.*, (med., surg.) consolidant.

consolidation, *n.f.*, consolidation, funding.

consolidement, *n.m.*, act of consolidating, consolidation.

consolider, *v.a.*, to consolidate, to strengthen.

se consolider, *v.r.*, to consolidate, to grow firm.

consolidés, *n.m. pl.*, consolidated funds, consols.

consommable, *adj.*, consumable.

consommateur, *n.m.*, consumer, eater, drinker; (theol.) perfecter.

consommation, *n.f.*, consummation; consumption; drinks, refreshments. *Voulez-vous jouer les —s?* shall we play for the drinks?

consommé, *n.m.*, broth, gravy-soup, beef-tea.

consommé, -e, *part.*, consumed, used; consummated; consummate; profound; accomplished.

consommer, *v.a.*, to consummate, to complete, to perfect, to finish, to accomplish; to consume, to use.

⊙**consompti-f, -ve**, *adj.*, (med.) consumptive, in a decline.

⊙**consomptif**, *n.m.*, (med., surg.) caustic.

consomption, *n.f.*, consumption; destruction; (med.) atrophy, decline. *Être atteint de —;* to be in a decline.

consonnance, *n.f.*, consonance, consonancy; concord.

consonnant, -e, *adj.*, consonant.

consonne, *n.f.*, consonant.

consorts, *n.m. pl.*, consorts; (jur.) associates, people connected together, having the same interest; (b. s.) confederates.

consoude, *n.f.*, (bot.) comfrey, consound.

conspirant, -e, *adj.*, (mec.) conspiring.

conspirateur, *n.m.*, conspirator.

conspiration, *n.f.*, conspiracy, plot. *La — des poudres;* the gunpowder-plot.

conspirer, *v.a.* and *n.*, to conspire, to agree together, to concur, to combine; to plot. *Tout conspire à me ruiner;* everything conspires to my ruin. *— la ruine de l'État;* to plot the ruin of the State.

conspuer, *v.a.*, to spit upon; to despise, to flout, to spurn, to hiss.

constable, *n.m.*, constable.

constabulaire, *adj.*, constabulary.

constamment (-sta-măn), *adv.*, with constancy, steadily, perseveringly; constantly.

constance, *n.f.*, constancy; perseverance; steadiness, steadfastness; firmness, persistence.

constant, -e, *adj.*, constant, unshaken; steadfast, persevering, unvarying, invariable; steady, lasting; certain, unquestionable. *Il est — que;* it is an established fact that.

constante, *n.f.*, (alg.) constant quantity.

constatation, *n.f.*, authentication; ascertaining, verification; declaration.

constater, *v.a.*, to prove, to verify, to establish undeniably, to testify to; to ascertain, to state, to declare.

constellation (-stèl-la-), *n.f.*, constellation.

constellé, -e, (-stèl-lé), *adj.*, constellated; studded.

consteller, *v.a.*, to constellate, to dot, to strew, to stud.

consternation, *n.f.*, consternation, dismay.

consterner, *v.a.*, to strike with consternation; to astound, to amaze, to dismay, to dishearten.

constipation, *n.f.*, constipation, costiveness.

constipé, -e, *adj.*, costive, constipated.

constiper, *v.a.*, to constipate, to bind.

constituant, -e, *adj.*, constituent; giving a power of attorney.

constituant, *n.m.*, member of the Constituent Assembly (French hist.).

constituante, *n.f.*, Constituent Assembly (French hist.).

constituer, *v.a.*, to constitute, to establish, to make; to place, to put, to organize; to raise to an office or dignity; to settle, to assign; to give into custody. *Qui vous a constitué juge?* who made you judge in the matter? *— quelqu'un prisonnier;* to commit anyone to prison. *— une rente;* to settle an annuity. *— un précédent;* to establish a precedent.

se constituer, *v.r.*, to constitute oneself, to form oneself into. *Se — prisonnier;* to give oneself up.

constituti-f, -ve, *adj.*, constitutive.

constitution, *n.f.*, constitution, establishment, formation, composition; temper, temperament; settlement of an annuity; declaration of appointment.

constitutionnalité, *n.f.*, constitutionality.

constitutionnellement (-nèl-măn), *adv.*, constitutionally.

constitutionnalisme, *n.m.*, constitutionalist.

constitutionnel, -le, *adj.*, constitutional.

constricteur, *n.m.*, (anat.) constrictor.

constriction, *n.f.*, constriction, contraction, compression; (med.) astriction.

constricti-f, -ve, *adj.*, (med.) constringent.

constringent, -e, *adj.*, constringent.

constructeur, *n.m.*, constructor, builder; shipbuilder, shipwright.

construction, *n.f.*, act of building; arrangement and connection of words in a sentence; construction; building, erection; structure; shipbuilding. *Faire de nouvelles —s;* to erect new buildings. *La — d'une carte géographique;* the construction of a map. *Faire la — d'une phrase;* to construct a phrase. *Vaisseau de —*

française; French-built ship. *En* —; building, (nav.) on the stocks. *De* —; building, build.

constructivité, *n.f.*, (phrenology) constructiveness.

construire (construisant, construit), *v.a.*, to construct, to build, to erect, to rear up, to frame; to arrange; (gram.) to construct. *De* —; building. *En* —; in course of erection; (of ships) on the stocks.

consubstantialité (-sia-), *n.f.*, consubstantiality.

consubstantiation (-sia-), *n.f.*, consubstantiation.

consubstantiel, -le, (-sièl), *adj.*, consubstantial.

consubstantiellement (-sièl-măn), *adv.*, consubstantially.

consul, *n.m.*, consul.

consulaire, *adj.*, consular. *Personnage* —; an ex-consul.

consulairement (-lèr-măn), *adv.*, consularly; by consuls.

consulat, *n.m.*, consulate; consulship.

consultant, *adj.m.*, consulting. *Avocat* —; chamber-counselor. *Médecin* —; consulting physician.

consultant. *n.m.*, consulter; person consulted.

consultati-f, -ve, *adj.*, consultative, deliberative. *Avoir voix* —*ve;* to have the right of discussion without that of voting.

consultation, *n.f.*, consultation; conference; opinion, advice.

consulter, *v.a.*, to consult, to advise with, to take advice of, to deliberate, to confer. — *un avocat;* to take counsel's opinion. — *une affaire;* to examine into an affair. — *son chevet;* to consult one's pillow. *Ils consultèrent ensemble;* they laid their heads together. *Il en veut* — *avec ses amis;* he wishes to confer with his friends about it.

se **consulter**, *v.r.*, to consider, to reflect, to deliberate; to be consulted. *La voix de la raison ne se consulte jamais;* the voice of reason is never listened to.

consulteur, *n.m.*, counselor, adviser.

consumant, -e, *adj.*, consuming, devouring, burning.

consumer, *v.a.*, to consume; to destroy; to wear out or away; to squander, to waste, to spend. *Le temps consume toutes choses;* time wears out everything. *Cette maladie le consume;* that disease is wearing him to nothing.

se **consumer**, *v.r.*, to decay, to waste away, to wear out; to ruin one's self; to undermine one's health; to waste one's strength. *Il se consume d'ennui;* he is wasting away with weariness. *Se* — *de douleur;* to pine away with grief.

contabescence, *n.f.*, (med.) consumption.

contabescent, -e, *adj.*, (med.) consumptive.

contact (-takt), *n.m.*, contact, connection, touch; (mining) nip (of the roof or wall).

contagieu-x, -se, *adj.*, contagious, catching; infectious.

contagion, *n.f.*, contagion, infection. — *de mœurs;* corruption of manners. *La* — *du vice;* the infection of vice.

*****contaille**, *adj.f.*, floss. *Soie* —; floretta, refuse, floss-silk.

contamination, *n.f.*, contamination.

contaminer, *v.a.*, to contaminate.

conte, *n.m.*, story, tale, falsehood, fib, nonsense. — *s de fées;* fairy tales. *Réciter un* —; to tell a story. — *en l'air;* improbable story, fiction. — *fait à plaisir;* made-up story. — *gras;* smutty, lascivious story. — *de bonne femme,* — *à dormir debout,* — *bleu,* — *borgne;* idle, silly story; old woman's tale. *Il brode un peu le* —; he **exaggerates** the story a little (*i.e.,*

improves upon it. *Ce sont des* —*s;* it is only a joke. *C'est un grand faiseur de* —*s;* he is a great fibber, a great story-teller.

contemplat-eur, *n.m.*, **-rice**, *n.f.*, contemplator.

contemplati-f, -ve, *adj.*, contemplative.

contemplation, *n.f.*, contemplation, meditation, reflection; admiration.

contempler, *v.a.*, to contemplate, to behold, to survey, to view, to gaze on.

contempler, *v.n.*, to contemplate, to meditate, to reflect.

contemporain, -e, *adj.*, contemporary, contemporaneous.

contemporain, *n.m.*, **-e**, *n.f.*, contemporary.

contemporanéité, *n.f.*, contemporaneity, contemporariness.

contempt-eur, **-rice**, *adj.*, contemptuous, scornful, insolent, disdainful.

contempt-eur, *n.m.*, **-rice**, *n.f.*, contemner, despiser, scorner.

⊙**contemptible**, *adj.*, contemptible, despicable, mean.

contenance (cont-nans), *n.f.*, capacity, capaciousness; contents; countenance, posture, look, air, bearing, attitude, deportment; (nav.) burden. — *fière;* haughty air. — *assurée;* bold look. — *ridicule;* ridiculous carriage. — *étudiée;* studied deportment. *Il n'a point de* —; he does not know which way to turn. *Perdre* —; to be abashed, out of countenance. *Faire perdre* —; to put out of countenance. *Servir de* —; to keep one in countenance. *Porter quelque chose par* —; to carry a thing to keep one's self in countenance. *Un éventail sert de* —; a fan keeps one in countenance. *Faire bonne* —; to keep one's countenance; to show spirit or resolution. *Se donner une* —; to keep one's self in countenance. *Ne savoir quelle* — *prendre;* not to know what to do with one's self.

contenant, *n.m.*, holder, container.

contenant, -e, *adj.*, holding, containing.

contendant, -e, *adj.*, contending. *Les parties* —*es;* the contending parties, the candidates.

contendant, *n.m.*, contender.

contenir (con-tnir), *v.a.*, to contain; to comprise; to hold; to include; to comprehend; to confine; to keep in, to keep within, to restrain; to repress; to hold or keep in check or awe, to rule, to bridle; to dam. *Les gardes avaient peine à* — *la foule;* the guards could with difficulty keep back the crowd. *On ne saurait le* —; there is no keeping him within bounds.

se **contenir**, *v.r.*, to keep within bounds, to be moderate; to abstain from, to refrain from, to forego; to refrain, to forbear; to contain one's self; to curb one's passions; to keep one's temper.

content, -e, *adj.*, content, contented; satisfied, pleased, glad, gratified. *Il est* — *de sa condition;* he is contented with his lot. *Avoir le visage* —; to look pleased. *Etre* —; to be willing, to be satisfied. *Etre* — *de quelqu'un;* to be pleased with any one. *Il est bien* — *de lui-même;* he has a great idea of himself.

content, *n.m.* *Tout son* —; one's fill; all one wants, as much as one likes.

contentement (kon-tant-măn), *n.m.*, content, contentment, satisfaction; comfort, pleasure; blessing. — *passe richesse;* enough is as good as a feast.

contenter, *v.a.*, to content, to give satisfaction, to satisfy; to please, to gratify, to indulge, to humor. *On ne saurait* — *tout le monde;* one cannot please every body.

se **contenter**, *v.r.*, to indulge or gratify one's self; to be satisfied with; to content one's self with, to be content with; to take up with; to rest satisfied with. *Je me contente d'une honnête médiocrité;* I am satisfied with a moderate competence. *Contentez-vous de cela;* be content with that.

contentieusement (-si-euz-mān), *adv.*, contentiously, litigiously.

contentieu-x, -se, *adj.*, litigious, in litigation, in dispute, contestable, contended for; controvertible, disputable; contentious, quarrelsome. *Esprit —;* quarrelsome fellow.

contentieux, *n.m.*, debatable matters, affairs in litigation; disputed claims. *Bureau du —;* office for the settlement of disputed claims. *Agent du —;* solicitor.

contentif, *adj.m.*, (surg.) (bandages) retentive, binding.

contention, *n.f.,* contention, contest, debate, strife; eagerness; vehemence, intenseness, heat; (surg.) keeping reduced (of fractures). *— d'esprit;* intense application of mind.

contenu, *n.m.*, contents; enclosure; tenor, terms.

conter, *v.a.*, to tell, to relate. *— des fagots;* to tell idle stories. *En —;* to romance, to tell fibs. *En — de belles, — des sornettes;* to tell what is untrue, to hoax, to humbug, to deceive. *En — à une femme, lui — des douceurs, lui — fleurettes;* to talk soft nonsense to a woman. *S'en faire* or *s'en laisser —;* to listen to soft nonsense.

conter, *v.n.,* to relate, to tell a story. *Il conte bien;* he tells a story well.

conterie, *n.f.,* coarse glass-ware.

contestable, *adj.*, contestable, debatable, controvertible.

contestablement, *adj.*, contestably.

contestant, -e, *adj.*, contending.

contestant, *n.m.,* **-e,** *n.f.,* contesting party, litigant.

contestation, *n.f.,* contestation, contest, dispute, debate; strife, variance, wrangling, bickering; litigation. *En —;* at issue; at variance, at odds. *Hors de toute —;* beyond all contestation, dispute.

⊙**conteste,** *n.m.,* contestation, contest, dispute. *Sans —;* indisputably. *V.* **sans contredit.**

contester, *v.a.*, to contest, to dispute; to deny, to contend, to debate. *Il me conteste ma qualité;* he calls my rank in question. *On lui conteste cette terre;* his right to that estate is disputed. *Se —;* to be contested, to be denied.

conteu-r, *n.m.,* **-se,** *n.f.,* story-teller, tale-teller, one who tells or relates stories or tales, narrator, teller; romancer, fibber.

conteu-r, -se, *adj.*, fond of telling tales.

contexte, *n.m.,* context; text (of a deed).

contexture, *n.f.,* contexture (of the muscles, &c.); texture (of a stuff).

contigu, -ë, *adj.*, contiguous, adjoining. *Ces deux provinces sont —ës;* these two provinces border on each other. *Mon champ est — à la forêt;* my field is bounded by the forest.

contiguïté, *n.f.,* contiguity.

continence, *n.f.,* continency, chastity.

continent, *n.m.,* continent, mainland.

continent, -e, *adj.*, sober, temperate, chaste, continent; (med.) continent, continuous, unremitting. *Fièvre —e;* incessant fever.

continental, -e, *adj.*, continental.

contingence, *n.f.,* contingency, casualty.

contingent, *n.m.,* contingent, quota.

contingent, -e, *adj.*, casual, contingent, accidental.

continu, *n.m.,* (philos.) that which is divisible, matter, body, space.

continu, -e, *adj.*, continuous, uninterrupted; continual, continued; unintermitting, incessant. *Basse —e;* (mus.) thorough-bass.

continuateur, *n.m.,* continuator, continuer.

continuation, *n.f.,* continuation; (jur.) continuance.

⊙ *à la* **continue,** *adv.*, in process of time, in the long run.

continuel, -le, *adj.*, continual, uninterrupted, endless, perpetual.

continuellement (-el-mān), *adv.*, continually, uninterruptedly, constantly; endlessly, perpetually.

continuer, *v.a.*, to continue; to proceed with; to go on with; to persevere; to lengthen, to prolong; to extend.

continuer, *v.n.,* to continue, to keep on, to go on with, to run on to, to extend, to continue the work of. *Continuez, je vous prie;* pray go on. *Continuez à bien faire, et vous vous en trouverez bien;* continue to do well, and you will find the benefit of it.

se **continuer,** *v.r.*, to be continued, to last; to be prolonged.

continuité, *n.f.,* continuity; continuance. *Solution de —;* solution of continuity.

continûment, *adv.*, unremittingly; without cessation; (jur.) continually, continuously.

contondant, -e, *adj.*, (surg.) bruising, contusing; (instruments) blunt.

contorniate, *adj.*, (of medals) contourniated.

contorsion, *n.f.,* contortion, distortion; grimace.

contour, *n.m.*, circuit, circumference; contour, outline; (carp.) curtail; (mas.) quirk.

contourné, -e, *adj.*, outlined; spiral; twisted; distorted; deformed; ill-shaped.

contournement, *n.m.,* outlining; twisting; winding, rounding, convolution.

contourner, *v.a.*, to outline, to give the proper contour to; to distort, to twist, to deform; to twine round, to twist round; to turn around, to wind round; to round.

se **contourner,** *v.r.*, to grow crooked, to become bent, twisted, deformed.

contourneuse, *n.f.,* shaping-machine.

contractant, -e, *adj.*, contracting. *Partie —e;* contracting party; (jur.) covenanter.

contractant, *n.m.,* **-e,** *n.f.,* contractor, stipulator; (jur.) covenanter.

contracté, -e, *part.*, (gram.) contracted, shortened.

contracter, *v.a.*, to contract; to covenant, to stipulate, to bargain, to make a contract; to shrink, to straiten; to shorten, to abridge; to acquire, to get; to catch. *— de bonnes habitudes;* to acquire good habits.

se **contracter,** *v.r.*, to contract, to shrink up, to straiten; to shorten.

contracter, *v.n.,* to contract, make a contract.

contracti-f, -ve, *adj.*, (med.) contractive.

contractile, *adj.*, contractile.

contractilité, *n.f.,* contractility, contractibility.

contraction, *n.f.,* contraction.

contractuel, -le, *adj.*, (jur.) stipulated, agreed upon, done by contract.

contracture, *n.f.,* (arch.) diminution; (med.) contraction; (physiology) contraction.

contradicteur, *n.m.,* contradictor, gainsayer; (jur.) adversary, opposer, opponent.

contradiction, *n.f.,* contradiction, denial; opposition; inconsistency; discrepancy; (jur.) claim of adverse title. *Esprit de —;* spirit of contradiction.

contradictoire, *adj.*, contradictory; inconsistent, conflicting. *Jugement —;* judgment after the hearing of all parties concerned.

contradictoirement (-toar-mān), *adv.*, contradictorily; inconsistently.

***contraignable,** *adj.*, (jur.) compellable, constrainable. *— par corps;* attachable, liable to arrest.

***contraignant, -e** *adj.*, compelling, compulsive; troublesome.

contraindre (contraignant, contraint), *v.a.*,

to constrain, to compel, to force, to make, to drive, to necessitate, to impel, to oblige by force ; to put a constraint upon ; to restrain ; to squeeze, to pinch, to cramp, to straiten ; (jur.) to attach, to arrest for debt.

se contraindre, *v.r.*, to constrain oneself, to refrain, to forbear.

contraint, -e, *adj.*, forced, stiff, unnatural, affected ; cramped, constrained.

contrainte, *n.f.*, constraint, compulsion, coercion ; restraint. *Parler sans* — ; to speak freely. *Avec* — ; restrainedly. — *par corps* ; arrest for debt. *Jugement de* — *par corps* ; capias.

contraire, *adj.*, contrary, opposite, adverse ; repugnant, inconsistent ; opposed, against ; hurtful, bad, prejudicial, not good for. *Le vin vous est* — ; wine is bad for you.

contraire, *n.m.*, contrary, opposite, reverse. *Au* — ; on the contrary, on the other hand. *Tout au* —, *bien au* — ; quite the contrary, quite the reverse. *Aller au* — *d'une chose, d'une personne ;* to go or speak against a thing, a person.

contrairement (kon-trer-män), *adv.*, contrarily, contrary.

contralte, *n.m.* *V.* **contralto.**

contraltiste, *n.m.f.*, contralto singer.

contralto, *n.m.*, (—) (mus.) contralto, counter-tenor.

contrapontiste, *n.m.*, (mus.) contrapuntist.

contrariant, -e, *adj.*, provoking, annoying, vexatious ; disappointing.

contrarier, *v.a.*, to contradict, to gainsay ; to disappoint, to thwart, to counteract, to baffle, to oppose, to annoy, to vex. *Etre contrarié par les vents ;* to be wind-bound.

contrariété, *n.f.*, contrariety, contradiction ; cross, vexation, annoyance, impediment, hindrance, difficulty, obstacle ; disappointment. *Quelle* — *!* how annoying !

contrastant, -e, *adj.*, contrasting.

contraste, *n.m.*, contrast, opposition.

contraster, *v.a.*, to contrast.

contraster, *v.n.*, (paint.) to contrast ; to put in contrast, to form a contrast, to set off by opposition.

contrat, *n.m.*, contract, deed, instrument, articles, indenture ; agreement, bargain. *Minute d'un* — ; draft of a deed. *Un* — *en bonne forme ;* a contract in due form. *Dresser un* — ; to draw up a deed. *Passer un* — ; to sign and seal a deed. — *à la grosse ;* (nav.) bottomry ; bottomry-bond.

contravention, *n.f.*, contravention, infraction.

contre, *prep.*, against ; contrary to ; by, near, close, close by. — *le bon sens ;* contrary to common sense. *A* —*-cœur ;* repugnantly, reluctantly. *Aller* — *vent et marée ;* to sail against wind and tide. *Se fâcher* — *quelqu'un ;* to be angry with anyone. *Se battre* — *quelqu'un ;* to fight against anyone. *Par* — ; as a set-off. *Pour et* — ; for and against, pro and con.

contre, *adv.*, near, close up against, against. *Tout* —; close by, close up against ; quite close, near. *Ci*— ; opposite ; in the margin.

contre, *n.m.*, con (the opposite of *pro*) ; against ; the opposite side of the question. *Savoir le pour et le* — ; to know the long and short of a matter, or the pro and the con.

contre-allée, *n.f.*, (— — — *s*) side-walk ; side-alley.

contre-amiral, *n.m.*, (— *-amiraux*) rear-admiral ; rear-admiral's flag-ship.

contre-appel, *n.m.*, (— — — *s*) (fenc.) caveating ; second roll call ; check-roll.

contre-approches, *n.f.pl.*, (*n.s.*) (fort.) counter-approaches.

contre-attaques, *n.f.pl.*, (*n. s.*) (milit.) counterworks.

contre-balancer, *v.a.*, to counterbalance, to counterpoise ; to countervail.

se contre-balancer, *v.r.*, to counterbalance one another, to be counterbalanced, to be equipoised.

contrebande, *n.f.*, contraband goods, smuggled goods ; smuggling. *Un homme de* — ; an obnoxious fellow, a black sheep. *Faire la* — ; to smuggle, to deal in smuggled goods.

contre-bandé, -e, *adj.*, (her.) counter-barred.

contrebandier, *n.m.*, smuggler, contrabandist.

contre-barré, -e, *adj.*, (— — —*s*) (her.) counterbended.

en contre-bas, *adv.*, (arch.) downwards.

contrebasse, *n.f.*, (mus.) double-bass.

contrebassiste, *n.m.*, (mus.) double-bass player.

contre-basson, *n.m.*, (— — —*s*) (mus.) double bassoon ; double bassoon-player.

contre-batterie, *n.f.*, (— — —*s*) cross-battery, counter-battery ; counter-plot.

à contre-biais, *adv.*, contrariwise, the wrong way ; the other way.

à contre-bord, *adv.*, (nav.) *Les deux vaisseaux courent à* — ; the two vessels are running aboard of each other ; on a contrary tack.

contre-boutant, *n.m.*, (— — —*s*) counterfort ; butment ; buttress.

contre-bouter, *v.a.*, to buttress ; to support with a raking shore or but ; to shore up.

contre-brasser, *v.a.*, (nav.) to brace about the yards ; to counterbrace.

contre-calquer, *v.a.*, to counter-draw.

contre-capion, *n.m.*, (— — —*s*). — *de poupe ;* the false post of a row-galley, — *de proue ;* the stemson of a galley.

contrecarrer, *v.a.*, to thwart, to oppose.

contre-caution, *n.f.*, (jur.) counter-surety ; counter-bond.

contre-charme, *n.m.*, (— — —*s*) counter-charm.

contre-châssis, *n.m.*, (—) outer-sash ; double-sash.

contre-chef, *n.m.*, (— — —*s*) foreman.

contre-civadière, *n.f.*, (— — —*s*) (nav.) bowsprit topsail.

contre-clef, *n.f.*, (— — —*s*) (arch.) second stone in the crown of an arch.

contre-cœur, *n.m.*, (— — —*s*) chimney-back. *À* — ; reluctantly, against the grain.

contre-coup, *n.m.*, (— — —*s*) rebound ; counter-blow ; consequence, result, effect. *Par* —; as a consequence.

contre-courant, *n.m.*, (— — —*s*) counter-current.

contredanse, *n.f.*, quadrille.

contre-déclaration, *n.f.*, (— — —*s*) counter-declaration.

contre-dégagement, *n.m.*, (— — —*s*) (fenc.) double.

contre-dégager, *v.n.a.*, (fenc.) to double.

contre-digue, *n.f.*, (— — —*s*) embankment, dike (for the strengthening of another).

contredire, *v.a.*, to contradict, to gainsay ; to be inconsistent with ; (jur.) to confute, to disprove, to answer ; (hunt.) to reclaim.

se contredire, *v.r.*, to contradict oneself, to contradict one another ; to be inconsistent with, to be contradictory to.

contredisant, -e, *adj.*, contradicting.

contredisant, *n.m.*, respondent, contradicter.

contredit, *n.m.*, answer, reply, contradiction ; (jur.) objection, rejoinder. *Cela est sans* — ; that is beyond all dispute. *Sans* — ; incontestably, safely, beyond a doubt. *On peut dire sans crainte d'être* — ; it may safely be pronounced (Macaulay).

contrée, *n.f.*, country, region, district.

*contre-écaille, *n.f.*, (— — —*s*) the reverse side of a shell.

contre-écart, *n.m.,* (— - —*s*) (her.) counter-quarter.

contre-écarteler, *v.a.,* (her.) to counter-quarter.

contre-échange, *n.m.,* (— - —*s*) mutual exchange.

contre-enquête, *n.f.,* (— - —*s*) counter-inquiry.

contre-épaulette, *n.f.,* (—-—*s*) epaulet without fringe.

contre-épreuve, *n.f.,* (—-—*s*) counter-proof; spiritless copy, feeble imitation; counter-verification.

contre-épreuver, *v.a.,* (engr.) to take a counter-proof. *Se* —; to be counter-proved.

contre-espalier, *n.m.,* (—-—*s*) espalier facing another (with a walk between).

contre-expertise, *n.f.,* (— - —*s*) counter-valuation *or* survey.

contre-étais, *n.m. pl.,* (nav.) back-stay.

contre-étambot, *n.m.,* (nav.) false stern-post.

contre-étrave, *n.f.,* (— - —*s*) (nav.) apron.

contrefaçon, *n.f.,* counterfeiting, counterfeit, pirating, forgery, infringement; spurious copy or edition.

contrefacteur, *n.m.,* counterfeiter (of coin); forger (of bills); infringer (of patents).

contrefaction, *n.f.,* act of forging, counterfeiting, forgery.

contrefaire, *v.a.,* to counterfeit, to imitate, to copy; to mimic, to ape; to pirate; to disguise, to disfigure; to deform.

se **contrefaire,** *v.r.,* to dissemble, to sham.

contrefaiseur, *n.m.,* mimicker, imitator.

contrefait, -e, *part.,* counterfeit, deformed. *Un homme tout* —; a deformed man.

contre-fanon, *n.m.,* (— - —*s*) (nav.) vertical lines.

contre-fenêtre, *n.f.,* (— - —*s*) inside-sash, shutter.

contre-fente, *n.f.,* (— - —*s*) (surg.) contra-fissure, counter-cleft.

contre-feu, *n.m.,* back of a fire-place.

contre-fiche, *n.f.,* (— - —*s*) (carp.) brace, strut.

contre-fil, *n.m.,* (*n.p.*) the opposite direction. *Le — de l'eau;* up river, up stream. *A* —; backwards; against the stream; against the grain; the wrong way.

contre-finesse, *n.f.,* (— - —*s*) counter-trick; counter-cunning; trick for trick.

contre-foc, *n.m.,* (— - —*s*) fore-top stay-sail.

contrefort, *n.m.,* counterfort, buttress, pillar, pier; (geol.) lesser chain; stiffener (of boots).

contre-fossé, *n.m.,* (— - —*s*) counter-drain; (fort.) advance-fosse.

contre-fracture, *n.f.,* (—-—*s*) (surg.) contra-fissure.

contre-fruit, *n.m.,* (— - —*s*) (arch.) overspan.

contre-fugue, *n.f.,* (mus.) counterfugue.

contre-gage, *n.m.,* (—-—*s*) double security, pledge.

contre-gager, *v.a.,* to take security, to take a pledge.

contre-garde, *n.f.,* (— - —*s*) counterguard.

⊙**contre-garde,** *n.m.,* (— - —*s*) deputy warden of the mint.

contre-hacher, *v.a.,* (engr.) to counter- *or* cross-hatch.

contre-hachure, *n.f.,* (— - —*s*) counter- *or* cross-hatching.

contre-hâtier (-tié), *n.m.,* (— - —*s*) kitchen fire-dog, spit-rack.

en **contre-haut,** *adv.,* (arch.) upwards.

contre-indication, *n.f.,* (— - —*s*) (med.) contra-indication.

contre-indiquer, *v.a.,* (med.) to contra-indicate.

contre-issant, -e, *adj.,* (— - —*s*) (her.) counter-salient.

contre-jauger, *v.a.,* (carp.) to fit a mortise to a tenon, to countergauge.

contre-jour, *n.m.,* (—-—*s*) counter-light, false-light. *A* —; in a false light.

contre-jumelles, *n. f. pl.,* (*n. s.*) channel stones.

contre-lames, *n.f. pl.,* (*n.s.*) (gauze-making) counter-lams.

contre-latte, *n.f.,* (— - —*s*) counter-lath.

contre-latter, *v.a.,* to counter-lath.

contre-lattoir, *n. m.,* (— - —*s*) lath-holder, clincher.

contre-lettre, *n.f.,* (— - —*s*) (jur.) defeasance, counter-deed.

*****contre-maille,** *n.f.,* (—-—*s*) double-mesh net.

*****contre-mailler,** *v.a.,* to double-mesh.

contremaître, *n.m.,* first mate, boatswain's mate; overseer; foreman.

contremandement, *n.m.,* counter-order, countermand.

contremander, *v.a.,* to countermand.

contremarche, *n.f.,* counter-march; (carp.) rise.

contremarcher, *v.n.,* to counter-march.

contre-marée, *n.f.,* (— - —*s*) under back-water *or* counter-tide.

contremarque, *n.f.,* countermark; check (thea.). [bishop.

contremarquer, *v.a.,* to countermark; to

contre-mine, *n.f.,* (— - —*s*) countermine.

contre-miner, *v.a.,* to countermine.

contre-mineur, *n.m.,* (—-—*s*) counterminer.

⊙**contre-mont,** *adv.,* upwards; up-hill; up-stream.

contre-mot, *n.m.,* (—-—*s*) (milit.) countersign.

contre-mouvement, *n.m.,* (—-—*s*) counter-movement.

contre-mur, *n.m.,* (— - —*s*) (fort.) counter-mure, outer wall.

contre-murer, *v.a.,* (fort.) to countermure, to double-wall.

contre-opposition, *n.f.,* (—-—*s*) counter-opposition.

contre-ordre, *n.m.,* (—-—*s*) counter-order.

contre-ouverture, *n.f.,* (—-—*s*) counter-opening.

contre-partie, *n.f.,* (—-—*s*) counterpart; opposite; contrary; (mus.) counterpart.

contrepédaler, *v.n.,* to back-pedal (bicycles).

contre-peser, *v.a.,* to counter-balance.

contre-pied, *n.m.,* (*n.p.*) (hunt.) back-scent; the reverse. *Les chiens avaient pris le* —; the dogs had taken the wrong back-scent. *Il prend toujours le — de ce qu'on dit;* he always misconstrues what is said. *A — de;* contrary to, against.

contre-planche, *n.f.,* (—-—*s*) counter-plate.

contre-platine, *n.f.,* (—-—*s*) screw-piece.

contre-poids, *n.m.,* (—) counterpoise, counterbalance; balancing-pole; equilibrium.

contre-poil, *n.m.,* (*n.p.*) wrong way of the hair *or* of the nap. *A* —; against the grain. *Prendre une affaire à* —; to take a thing in a wrong sense. *Prendre quelqu'un à* —; to shock, to offend, any one.

contre-poinçon, *n.m.,* (—-—*s*) clincher, die (instrument).

contre-poinçonner, *v.a.,* to stamp with a die.

contrepoint, *n.m.* (mus.), counterpoint; (nav.) double-rope attached to the clew of a sail.

contre-pointer, *v.a.,* to quilt on both sides; to contradict, to run counter to; (artil.) to point cannon against cannon. — *du canon;* to direct a battery against another battery.

contrepoison, *n.m.,* antidote, counter-poison.

contre-porte, *n.f.,* (—-—*s*) double-door, baize-door.

contre-poser, *v.a.,* (com.) to set down wrong, to misplace.

contre-position, *n.f.,* (—-—*s*) contra-position.

contre-projet, *n.m.,* (— - —*s*) counter-plan.

contre-promesse, *n.f.*, (— —*s*) (jur.) counter-bond.

contre-proposition, *n.f.*, (— —*s*) counter-proposal; reply, retort.

contre-queue d'aronde, *n.f.*, (— —*s*) (fort.) counter-swallowtail.

*****contre-quille**, *n.f.*, (— —*s*) (nav.) keelson.

contre-rail, *n.m.*, (— —*s*) guard- *or* check-rail.

contre-retable, *n.m.*, (— —*s*) back of the altar-piece.

contre-révolution, *n.f.*, (— —*s*) counter-revolution.

contre-révolutionnaire, *adj.*, (— —*s*) counter-revolutionary.

contre-révolutionnaire, *n.m.*, (— —*s*) counter-revolutionist.

contre-révolutionner, *v.a.*, to effect a counter-revolution.

contre-ronde, *n.f.*, (— —*s*) (milit.) counter round.

contre-ruse, *n.f.*, (— —*s*) counter-trick, counter-plot.

contre-sabord, *n.m.*, (— —*s*) (nav.) port-lid.

à **contre-saison**, *adv.*, out of season; unseasonable; ill-timed.

contre-salut, *n.m.*, (— —*s*) (nav.) answer to a salute.

contre-sanglon, *n.m.*, (— —*s*) girth-leather, strap.

contrescarpe, *n.f.*, (fort.) counterscarp.

contrescarper, *v.a.*, to counterscarp.

contre-scel, *n.m.*, (— —*s*) counter-seal.

contre-sceller, *v.a.*, to counter-seal.

contreseing, *n.m.*, counter-signature, counter-sign.

contresens, *n.m.*, contrary sense, contrary meaning; wrong construction; mistranslation; wrong meaning; false reading; wrong side (of stuffs). *Faire un* —; to mistranslate, to misinterpret, to misconceive. *A* —; in a wrong way, on the wrong side. *Employer une étoffe à* —; to make up a stuff on the wrong side.

*****contre-signal**, *n.m.*, (— *-signaux*) counter-signal.

*****contresignataire**, *n.m.*, countersigner.

*****contresigner**, *v.a.*, to countersign.

*****contre-taille**, *n.f.*, (— —*s*) (com.) counter-tally. *pl.*, (engr.) cross-lines, cross-cut.

contretemps, *n.m.*, untoward accident, disappointment; mischance, mishap; (man.) counter-time; (mus.) syncopation. *A* —; unseasonably, at the wrong time; (mus.) out of time; with syncopation. [terrace.

contre-terrasse, *n.f.*, (— —*s*) (her.) lower

contre-tirer, *v.a.*, to counterdraw, to trace; to counterprove. [stroyer.

contre-torpilleur, *n.m.*, torpedo boat de-

contre-tranchée, *n.f.*, (— —*s*) (fort.) counter-trench.

contrevairé, *-e*, *adj.*, (her.) countervairy.

à **contre-val**, *adv.*, downhill, downward, downstream.

contrevallation, *n.f.*, (fort.) contravallation.

à **contre-vapeur**, *adv.*, backward; back.

contrevenant, *n.m.*, *-e*, *n.f.*, contravener, infringer, offender, transgressor.

contrevenir, *v.n.*, to infringe, to act contrary to; to disobey; to violate; to transgress.

contrevent, *n. m.*, window-shutter, outside shutter.

contre-vérité, *n.f.*, (— —*s*) irony; mock praise, antiphrasis.

contre-visite, *n.f.*, (— —*s*) second search.

contre-voile d'étai, *n.f.*, (nav.) middle stay-sail.

contribuable, *n.m.f.*, tax-payer; rate-payer. *adj.*, taxable; rateable.

contribuer, *v.n.*, to contribute, to conduce, to help on, to tend. — *au succès de*; to contribute

to the success of. *Il y a contribué*; he has contributed to it. *On a fait* — *tout le pays*; the whole country was laid under contribution.

contributi-f, -ve, *adj.*, contributive.

contribution, *n.f.*, contribution; tax; share, part, portion; (com.) average. —*s directes*; direct or assessed taxes. —*s indirectes*; indirect taxes. *Mettre à* —; to lay under contribution, to put in requisition.

contributoire, *adj.*, what has to be paid. *Portion* —; amount to be paid, assessment.

contributoirement, *adv.*, contributorily.

contrister, *v.a.*, to grieve, to vex, to sadden, to pain.

contrit, -e, *adj.*, contrite, penitent; afflicted, grieved.

contrition, *n.f.*, contrition.

contrôlage, *n.m.*, controlling, control; hall-marking, stamping.

contrôle, *n.m.*, control, controller's office; (thea.) check-taker's office; roll, list; stamp, plate-mark, assay-mark, hall-mark (on gold and silver); stamp-office; (milit.) muster-roll; control, censure; register, registry-duty. *Porter quelqu'un sur le* — ; to place any one's name on the rolls. *Rayer quelqu'un des* —*s*; to strike any one off the rolls.

contrôler, *v.a.*, to register, to put upon the rolls; to check, to verify, to examine; to control; to censure, to criticise upon; to stamp, to hall-mark. — *de la vaisselle*; to mark plate.

contrôleu-r, *n.m.*, *-se*, *n.f.*, controller, superintendent, surveyor (of taxes); censurer, critic, fault-finder; (thea.) check-taker, ticket-collector.

controuver, *v.a.*, to forge, to fabricate; to invent, to counterfeit, to feign.

controversable, *adj.*, that may be disputed; controvertible, controversial.

controverse, *n.f.*, controversy, discussion, disputation, dispute. *Ouvrage de* —; polemics.

controversé, -e, *adj.*, controverted; debated, argued pro and con, disputed.

controverser, *v.a.*, to controvert, to dispute, to discuss.

controversiste, *n.m.*, controvertist, disputant, controversialist.

contumace, *n.f.*, contumacy, non-appearance, default, contempt of court; contumaciousness, obstinacy, perverseness. *Condamner par* —; to sentence by default. *Purger la* —; to plead against a judgment given in default.

contumace, *n.m.* and *f.*, (jur.) defaulter, one in contumacy.

contumace, *adj.*, contumacious; (fig.) rebellious.

contumacer, *v.a.*, (l.u.) (criminal law) to judge or try by default. *Se laisser* —; to let judgment go by default.

contumax, *adj.*, (l.u.) contumacious.

contumax, *n.m.*, one guilty of contumacy (canon law).

contus, -e, *adj.*, bruised, contused.

contusion, *n.f.*, contusion, bruise.

contusionné, -e, *adj.*, (surg.) bruised.

contusionner, *v.a.*, to contuse, to bruise.

convaincant, -e, *adj.*, convincing.

convaincre, *v.a.*, to convince; to persuade, to satisfy; to convict.

se **convaincre**, *v.r.*, to convince one's self, to be convinced; to satisfy, or to persuade one's self.

convaincu, -e, *part.*, convinced, convicted; sincere, earnest, of conviction.

convalescence, *n.f.*, convalescence. *En pleine* —; quite convalescent.

convalescent, -e, *adj.*, convalescent.

convalescent, *n.m.*, *-e*, *n.f.*, convalescent person.

convallaire, *n.f.*, convallary, lily of the valley. *V.* **muguet**.

convenable (conv-nabl), *adj.*, suitable, fit, proper, convenient, apposite, consonant; seasonable; adequate, conformable, accordant, agreeable; meet, seemly, becoming, beseeming; befitting, expedient; fitting. *Peu* —; indecorous, unfit. *Juger* —; to deem proper.

convenablement, *adv.*, suitably, fitly, becomingly, decently, worthily, duly, expediently, advisably.

convenance, *n.f.*, fitness, proportion, harmony; seasonableness (of time), decency, propriety, expediency; seemliness, convenience. *pl.*, propriety, decorum, good manners. *Mariage de* —; marriage for money and position. *Blesser les* —*s*; to offend against propriety. *Braver les* —*s*; to set all decorum at defiance. *Manquer de* — *envers quelqu'un*; to be guilty of a breach of good manners towards any one.

⊙**convenant, -e**, *adj.* V. **convenable**.

convenir, *v.n.*, to agree; to admit, to own, to acknowledge; to suit, to fit, to match, to serve one's turn; to be proper for; to become; to be suitable; to be fit, expedient, convenient, meet, proper. *Je suis convenu d'y aller ;* I have agreed to go there. *Cette maison m'a convenu ;* the house suited me. *Il convient que vous y alliez ;* it is proper you should go there.

se **convenir**, *v.r.*, to suit each other, to agree.

conventicule, *n.m.*, conventicle.

convention, *n.f.*, convention, agreement, covenant, treaty. *pl.*, conditions, articles, agreement. *Je m'en tiens à la* —; I stand by the agreement. *Membre de la* — *nationale ;* member of the National Convention (French hist.). *De* —; conventional.

conventionnel, -le, *adj.*, conventional.

conventionnel, *n.m.*, member of the National Convention (French hist.).

conventionnellement, *adv.*, by agreement.

conventualité, *n.f.*, monastic life.

conventuel, -le, *adj.*, conventual.

conventuel, *n.m.*, conventual.

conventuellement, *adv.*, conventually.

convergence, *n.f.*, convergence.

convergent, -e, *adj.*, convergent, converging.

converger, *v.n.*, to tend to one point, to converge.

convers, -e, *adj.*, lay. *Frère* —, *sœur* —*e ;* convert; lay brother or sister.

convers, *n.m.*, (ich.) young shad.

conversation, *n.f.*, conversation, converse, talk, discourse. *Par où entamer la* — *?* how shall we begin the conversation? *S'emparer de la* —; to monopolize the conversation. *Etre à la* —; to be attending to the conversation. *Laisser tomber la* —; to drop the conversation.

converse, *n.* and *adj.f.*, (log.) converse; (math.) inverted. *Proposition* —; (log.) converse proposition. *Proposition* —; (math.) inverted proposition.

converser, *v.n.*, to converse, to talk; to discourse, to commune; (milit.) to wheel about.

conversible, *adj.*, convertible.

conversion, *n.f.*, conversion; transformation; change; converting, changing; (milit.) wheeling. *Quart de* —; (milit.) wheel of the quarter circle. *Faire une* —; to wheel.

converso, *n.m.*, (nav.) main deck; poop.

converti, *n.m.*, -e, *n.f.*, convert. — *au lit de la mort ;* clinical convert.

convertible, *adj.*, (theol., fin.) convertible.

convertir, *v.a.*, to convert; to change, to turn; to make a convert; to bring over, to turn, to transform.

se **convertir**, *v.r.*, to be converted, to turn, to be made a convert.

convertissable, *adj.*, (fin., theol.) convertible.

convertissement (-măn), *n.m.*, conversion.

convertisseur, *n.m.*, converter.

convexe, *adj.*, convex.

convexité, *n.f.*, convexity.

convexo-concave, *adj.*, convexo-concave.

convexo-convexe, *adj.*, convexo-convex.

conviction, *n.f.*, conviction, convincing proof. *Agir par* —; to act from conviction. *Avoir la* — *intime ;* to be thoroughly convinced; to be quite sure.

convictionnel, -le, *adj.*, convictive.

convictionnellement, *adv.*, (l.u.) convictively.

convié, *n.m.*, -e, *n.f.*, guest, one invited.

il **convient**, *v.imp.*, it is fit, expedient, convenient, becoming, meet. V. **convenir**.

convier, *v.a.*, to invite, to bid; to request the company of any one; to incite, to urge. — *à un dîner ;* to invite to dinner.

convive, *n.m.f.*, guest. *C'est un bon* —; he is a good table companion.

convivialité, *n.f.*, conviviality.

convocable, *adj.*, (very l.u.) convocable.

convocation, *n.f.*, convocation, requisition, summons.

convoi, *n.m.*, funeral procession ; funeral ; (milit., nav.) convoy ; (railways) train. V. **train**. — *de grande vitesse ;* fast train. — *de petite vitesse,* — *de marchandises ;* freight train. — *direct ;* express train. — *omnibus ;* slow train. — *de voyageurs ;* passenger train. — *parcourant toute la ligne ;* through train. — *funèbre ;* funeral procession. *Etre du* —; to be at the funeral. *En* —; (nav.) with convoy.

convoiement, *n.m.*, (milit., nav.) convoying, convoy.

⊙**convoitable**, *adj.*, covetable, desirable.

convoiter, *v.a.*, to covet, to hanker after, to conceive a violent passion for, to lust after.

convoiteur, *n.m.*, -**se**, *n.f.*, coveter.

⊙**convoiteu-x, -se**, *adj.*, covetous, lusting after.

convoitise, *n.f.*, covetousness, eager desire; lust.

convol, *n.m.*, (jur.) second or re-marriage.

convoler, *v.n.*, to marry again. — *en secondes, troisièmes, noces ;* to marry a second, a third, time.

convoluté, -e, *adj.*, (bot.) convoluted.

convoluti-f, -ve, *adj.*, curling (of leaves).

convolve, *n.m.*, (bot.) convolvulus.

convoquer, *v.a.*, to convoke, to convene, to summon, to assemble, to call together.

convoyer, *v.a.*, (milit., nav.) to convoy.

convoyeur, *n.* and *adj.m.*, (nav.) convoy (ship).

convulsé, -e, *adj.*, (med.) convulsed.

convulser, *v.a.*, to convulse. *Se* —; to be or become convulsed.

convulsibilité, *n.f.*, (med.) liability to convulsion.

convulsi-f, -ve, *adj.*, convulsive.

convulsion, *n.f.*, convulsion. *Donner des* —*s ;* to throw into convulsions. *Tomber en* —*s ;* to be seized with convulsions.

convulsionnaire, *adj.*, subject to convulsions.

convulsionnaire, *n.m.f.*, convulsionary.

convulsionner, *v.a.*, (med.) to convulse, to produce convulsions.

convulsivement, *adv.*, convulsively.

conyze, *n.f.*, (bot.) conyza, flea-bane.

coobligation, *n.f.*, joint obligation.

coobligé, *n.m.*, joint bondsman.

coopérant, -e, *adj.*, co-operating, concurring.

coopérat-eur, *n.m.*, -**rice**, *n.f.*, co-operator, fellow-laborer, fellow-workman.

coopérat-eur -**rice**, *adj.*, (l.u.) co-operating.

coopérati-f, -ve, *adj.*, co-operative.

coopération, *n.f.*, concurrence, co-operation.

coopérer, *v.n.*, to co-operate, to concur.

cooptation, *n.f.*, co-optation.

coopter, *v.a.*, to co-optate.

coordination, *n.f.*, arrangement, disposition, co-ordination.

coordonnée, *n.f.*, (geom.) co-ordinate.

coordonner, *v.a.*, to co-ordinate; to arrange, to dispose.

copahu, *n.m.*, copaiba, copaiva.

copaïer *or* **copayer**, *n.m.*, copaiba tree.

copal, *n.m.*, copal.

copartageant, -e (-jän, -te), *n.* and *adj.*, joint-sharer; having a joint share.

copeau, *n.m.*, chip, shaving (of wood). *Des —x;* shavings. *Vin de —x;* rape-wine.

copeck, *n.m.*, (—s). *V.* **kopeck.**

copermutant, *n.m.*, one who exchanges with another, permuter.

copermutation, *n.f.*, the act of exchanging, permutation.

copermuter, *v.a.*, to permute, to exchange.

copernicien, -ne (-in, -èn), *adj.*, Copernician.

cophte *or* **copte**, *n.m.* and *adj.*, Copt; Coptic. *Un moine —;* a Coptic monk. *La langue —;* the Coptic language.

copie, *n.f.*, copy, image, transcript; exercise; imitation; task; (print.) copy. *— figurée;* fac-simile. *— au net;* fair copy. *Pour — conforme;* a true copy.

copier, *v.a.*, to copy; to imitate; to mimic, to take off, to ape.

se copier, *v.r.*, to be always the same; to copy or repeat one's self.

copieusement (ko-pieûz-män), *adv.*, copiously, abundantly, heartily (of eating).

copieu-x, -se, *adj.*, copious, plentiful, hearty. *Un homme — en paroles;* a man of many words.

copiste, *n.m.*, copier, transcriber, copyist, imitator; mere copier.

copreneur, *n.m.*, co-lessee, joint-tenant.

coprévenu, *n.m.* *V.* **coaccusé.**

copropriétaire, *n.m.f.*, joint-proprietor.

copropriété, *n.f.*, joint property.

copte, *n.m.* *V.* **cophte.**

copter, *v.a.*, to toll.

coptique, *adj.*, Coptic.

copulati-f, -ve, *adj.*, copulative.

copulation, *n.f.*, copulation.

copule, *n.f.*, (log.) copula.

coq, *n.m.*, cock, rooster; weathercock; (horl.) cock. *— d'Inde;* turkey-cock. *— de bruyère;* grouse. *— à queue fourchue;* black cock. *— de combat;* game-cock. *— des bois;* wood-cock. *— de montre;* cock of a watch. *— des jardins;* costmary. *— du village,* — *de la paroisse;* cock of the walk. *Joute de —s;* cock-fight. *Faire jouter des —s;* to make cocks fight. *Au chant du —;* at cock-crow. *Etre comme un — en pâte;* to live in clover. *Etre rouge comme un —;* to have a face like a biffin apple; to be as red as a turkey-cock.

coq, *n.m.*, (nav.) cook.

coq-à-l'âne, *n.m.*, (—) idle discourse, nonsense, cock-and-bull story. *Il fait toujours des —;* he is always talking nonsense.

coqualin, *n.m.*, striped squirrel.

coquard, *n.m.*, mongrel pheasant; (fam.) old cock, old beau.

coquâtre, *n.m.*, (orni.) half-gelded cock.

coque, *n.f.*, shell (of eggs, walnuts, snails); pearl-shell; (nav.) hull; (conch.) cockle. *Des œufs à la —;* boiled eggs. *— du Levant;* Indian berry. *Je ne donnerai pas une — de noix de toutes ses promesses;* I would not give a straw for all his promises.

coquecigrue, *n.f.*, sea-stork, sea-locust; idle story, stuff; fiddle-faddle. *A la venue des —s;* never, or once in a blue moon.

coquelicot, *n.m.*, wild-poppy, corn-poppy.

coquelourde, *n.f.*, Pasque-flower, Flora's-bell.

coqueluche (ko-klush), *n.f.*, ⊙ hood; favorite, reigning fancy; rage, whooping-cough. *Il est*

est *la — des femmes;* he is a great favorite with women.

⊙**coquelucher**, *v.n.*, to have the whooping-cough.

⊙**coquelunchon**, *n.m.*, (jest.) hood of a monk's cloak, cowl.

coquemar (kok-mär), *n.m.*, pipkin, boiler, kettle, skillet.

coquereau, *n.m.*, (nav.) hoy, lighter.

coqueret, *n.m.*, or **coquerelle**, *n.f.*, winter-cherry.

coquerico, *n.m.*, cock-a-doodle-doo.

coquerie, *n.f.*, (nav.) caboose.

coqueriquer, *v.n.*, (l.u.) (pers.) to crow.

coqueron, *n.m.*, (nav.) cook-room.

coquet, -te, *adj.*, coquettish, pretty, stylish; smart, natty.

coquet, *n.m.*, jilt, flirt; cock-boat.

coqueter (kok-té), *v.n.*, (l.u.) to coquet, to flirt; to play the lady-killer; to paddle a boat, to scull.

coquetier (kok-tié), *n.m.*, poulterer; egg-merchant; egg-cup.

coquette, *n.f.*, coquette, flirt, jilt. *Faire la —;* to coquet.

coquetterie (ko-kè-trî), *n.f.*, coquetry; affectation (in dress); love of dress; flirtation; finicalness. *Une — d'expressions;* far-fetched expressions.

***coquillage**, *n.m.*, shell-fish; shells; shell-work.

***coquillart**, *n.m.*, bed of shells and stones.

***coquille**, *n.f.*, shell (of fruit, of animals); (print.) wrong letter; thumb (of a latch); footboard (of coach-box); post demy, small post (paper); under-part of a staircase; (anat.) concha. *pl.*, wares of little value. *— de Sainte Jacques;* scallop. *— de beurre;* pat of butter. *Rentrer dans sa —;* to draw in one's horns. *A qui vendez-vous vos —s;* it is of no use trying to do me. *Il fait bien valoir ses —s;* he praises his goods, and no mistake.

coquiller, *v.n.*, (of bread) to swell; to crumple, to curl up.

***coquilleu-x**, -se, *adj.*, shelly.

***coquillier**, *n.m.*, collection of shells; cabinet of shells.

***coquilli-er**, -ère, *adj.*, conchiferous.

coquin, -e, *adj.*, idle, debauched; free and easy; roguish, rascally.

coquin, *n.m.*, knave, rascal, rogue, scamp. *Tour de —;* knavish trick.

coquine, *n.f.*, slut, hussy, jade.

coquinerie (ko-ki-n-rî), *n.f.*, knavery, rascally trick, roguery.

cor, *n.m.*, corn; horn, hunting-horn. *Avoir des —s aux pieds;* to have corns on one's feet. *A — et à cri;* with horn and voice; with hue and cry; with might and main.

coracoïde, *adj.*, (anat.) coracoid.

***corail**, *n.m.*, coral. *Des lèvres de —;* rosy lips.

***coraillère**, *n.f.*, (nav.) coral-fishing boat.

***corailleur**, *n.m.*, coral-diver, coral-fisher.

***corailleur**, *adj.*, of coral fishing. *Bateau —;* coral-fisher's boat.

⊙**corallin**, -e, *adj.*, red like coral, coralline.

coralline, *n.f.*, (zool.) coralline; (nav.) *V.* **coraillère.**

coralloïde, *adj.*, coralloid.

coralloïde, *n.m.*, coralloid.

coran, *n.m.*, Koran.

corbeau, *n.m.*, crow; raven; (arch.) corbel, bracket; (astron.) corvus; (nav.) grappling-iron.

***corbeille**, *n.f.*, flat, wide basket; (arch.) corbel; (fort.) corbeil; clump (of trees); wedding presents. *Une — de fleurs;* a basket of flowers. *— de mariage* or *de noces;* wedding presents; (on change) reserved enclosure, change.

***corbeillée**, *n.f.*, basketful.

corbigeau, *n.m.* ⊙*V.* **courlis.**

5

*corbillard, *n.m.*, hearse.

*corbillat, *n.m.*, young raven.

*corbillon, *n.m.*, small basket; crambo.

⊙**corbin**, *n.m.*, (orni.) crow. *V.* **bec-de-corbin**.

corbine, *n.f.*, (orni.) carrion-crow.

corbleu ! *int.* By the Powers! Zounds! By Jove! Hang it!

corbusée, *n.f.*, (orni.) black-neb.

corcelet, *n.m.* *V.* **corselet**.

corceron, *n. m.*, (pisc.) float.

cordage, *n.m.*, cordage, cord, rope, rigging; the measuring of wood by the cord. *— de rechange ;* spare ropes.

cordat, *n.m.*, packing-cloth.

corde, *n.f.*, cord, rope; line; twist, twine, string; (mus.) chord; tone, note; concord; span (of an arch); laniard (of buoys); thread (of cloth); hanging (death by); gallows. *— à danser ;* dancing-rope. *Danseur de —;* rope-dancer. *— à boyau ;* cat-gut. *Echelle de —;* rope-ladder. *Une — de bois ;* a cord of wood. *Ne touchez point cette — là ;* do not harp upon that string. *Toucher la grosse —;* to hit the main point of the question. *Instrument à —s ;* stringed instrument. *— de violon ;* fiddle-string. *Flatter la —;* to play with delicacy. *Avoir deux —s à son arc ;* to have two strings to one's bow. *Son habit montre la —;* his coat is threadbare. *Cela est usé jusqu'à la —;* that is thoroughly hackneyed. *Friser la —;* narrowly to escape hanging. *Il y va de la —;* it is a hanging matter. *Filer sa —;* to go the way of the gallows. *Avoir de la — de pendu ;* to have the devil's own luck. *Tenir la —;* to lead. *Passer à fleur de —;* to only just succeed (of a thing). *Etre au bout de sa —;* to be at the end of one's tether.

cordé, -e, *part.*, twisted, corded.

cordé, -e, *adj.*, (bot.) cordated, heart-shaped.

cordeau, *n.m.*, line, cord. *Au —;* in a straight line.

cordeler, *v.a.*, to twist, to twine; to wreathe.

cordelette, *n.f.*, small cord; string.

cordelier, *n.m.*, cordelier; Franciscan friar; gray-friar.

cordelière, *n.f.*, Franciscan nun; cordelier's girdle; (arch.) twisted fillet.

cordelle, *n.f.*, (nav.) tow-line, tow-rope.

corder, *v.a.*, to cord; to bind with a cord. *v.n.*, (pop.) to cotton; to agree. *— du bois ;* to measure wood by the cord.

se **corder**, *v.r.*, to be corded; to get stringy.

corderie, *n.f.*, rope-walk, rope-yard; rope-making; (nav.) boatswain's store-room.

cordial, -e, *adj.*, cordial, hearty, sincere.

cordial, *n.m.*, cordial.

cordialement (kor-dial-măn), *adv.*, cordially, heartily, sincerely.

cordialité, *n.f.*, cordiality; heartiness; hearty affection.

cordier, *n.m.*, rope-maker; (of violins) tail-piece.

cordiforme, *adj.*, cordiform, heart-shaped.

cordon, *n.m.*, twist, string; check-string (of carriages); cord; fillet, thread, ribbon; order; girdle; plinth, edging of stone; (milit., fort., arch.) cordon; (anat.) funis; edge (of coins); door-rope. *— ombilical ;* umbilical cord. *— de chapeau ;* hat-band. *— de sonnette ;* bell pull. *Un — bleu ;* a knight of the Holy Ghost. *— bleu ;* blue-ribbon; a first-rate cook. *Un — rouge ;* a knight of the order of St. Louis. *Tirer le —;* to pull the string; to be a house-porter. *Le —, s'il vous plaît ;* open the door, please.

cordonnage, *n.m.*, (coin) milling; edging.

cordonner, *v.a.*, to twist, to twine; to braid; (of coins) to line, to mill, to edge.

cordonnerie, *n.f.*, shoemaking, the trade of a shoemaker; shoe-place.

cordonnet, *n.m.*, twist; edging, milling (of coins—*de pièces de monnaie*).

cordonnier, *n.m.*, cordwainer; shoemaker. *— pour femmes ;* ladies' shoemaker.

corée, *n.m.*, (poet.) choreus, trochee. *V.* **chorée**.

corégence, *n.f.*, co-regency.

corégent, *n.m.*, -e, *n.f.*, co-regent.

coreligionnaire, *n.m.f.*, co-religionist.

coriace, *adj.*, tough, ropy, leathery, stringy; niggardly. *Un homme —;* a close-fisted fellow.

coriacé, -e, *adj.*, coriaceous.

coriaire, *adj.*, fit for tanning. *n.f.* (bot.) *V.* **corroyère**.

coriambe, *n.m.*, (poet.) choriambus.

coriandre, *n.f.*, (bot.) coriander.

corindon, *n.m.*, (min.) corundum, adamantine spar.

corinthien, -ne (-in, -e-n), *adj.*, Corinthian.

corinthien, *n.m.*, **-ne**, *n.f.*, Corinthian.

coris, *n.m.* *V.* **cauris**.

corlieu, corlis, *n.m.*, curlew.

corme, *n.f.*, (bot.) service *or* sorb-apple.

cormier, *n.m.*, (bot.) service-tree.

cormoran, *n.m.*, sea-raven, cormorant.

cornac, *n.m.*, elephant driver, cornac; showman; chaperon, mentor.

cornage, *n.m.*, (vet.) roaring (of horses).

cornaline, *n.f.*, cornelian stone.

cornard, *adj.*, (pop., l.ex.) roaring (of horses).

cornard, *n.m.*, (pop., l.ex.) cornuto, cuckold.

cornardise, *n.f.*, (pop., l.ex.) cuckoldom.

corne, *n.f.*, horn, hoof; corner; shoe-horn; dog's ear (on books, leaves); (nav.) gaff, throat; outside rind (of animals' feet); cap of the Doge of Venice. *Bête à —s ;* horned beast. *Essence de — de cerf ;* spirits of hartshorn. *Faire les —s à quelqu'un ;* to snap one's fingers at any one. *Montrer les —s ;* to show one's teeth. *Lever les cornes ;* to hold up one's head again. *Les —s d'un bonnet carré ;* the corners of a square cap. *Chapeau à trois —s ;* three-cornered hat. *Les —s de la lune ;* the horns of the moon. *Les —s de l'autel ;* the horns of the altar. *— d'abondance ;* cornucopia, horn of plenty. *Faire une — à une carte de visite ;* to turn down the corner of a visiting-card. *Faire des —s à un livre ;* to dog's-ear a book.

corné, -e, *adj.*, corneous, horny.

corneau, *n.m.*, (hunt.) cross between a mastiff and a hound.

cornée, *n.f.*, (anat.) cornea.

cornéenne, *n.f.*, horn-stone.

*corneille, *n.f.*, carrion-crow, rook, daw. *— emmantelée ;* hooded-rook. *Bayer aux —s ;* to stare about vacantly. *Il y va comme une — qui abat des noix ;* he goes at it tooth and nail, *or* rashly, slapdash, headlong.

cornement, *n.m.*, tingling of the ears.

cornemuse, *n.f.*, bagpipe. *Joueur de —;* bag-piper.

cornéole, *n.f.*, (bot.) dyer's weed.

corner, *v.n.*, to blow, to wind or sound a horn; to gore; (man.) to wheeze; to tingle (of the ears); to be tainted (of meat). *Les oreilles me cornent ;* my ears tingle.

corner, *v.a.*, to blare out, to blurt out, to trumpet. *Il a corné cela par toute la ville ;* he has trumpeted it through the whole town. *— quelque chose aux oreilles de quelqu'un ;* to din a thing into any one's ears.

cornet, *n.m.*, horn, ear-trumpet; ink-horn; dice-box; paper cone; (conch.) cornet. *— de postillon ;* post-boy's horn. *— à bouquin ;* cow-herd's horn. *— à piston ;* cornet.

cornette, *n.f.*, head-dress, cornet, mob-cap; cornetcy; (nav.) broad pennant.

⊙**cornette**, *n.m.*, (milit.) cornet.

corneur, *n.m.*, horn-blower.

corneur, *adj.*, (vet.) wheezing, roaring.

corniche, *n.f.*, (arch.) cornice.

cornichon, *n.m.*, little horn; gherkin; (fig. and fam.) greenhorn, ninny, flat, muff.

cornicule, *n.f.*, small horn, cornicle.

corniculé, -e, *adj.*, corniculate, horned.

corni-er, -ère, *adj.*, corner; at the angle. *Pilastre —*; corner-column.

cornière, *n.f.*, corner gutter; (print.) corner iron; T iron; (nav.) fashion-piece.

cornifle, *n.m.*, (bot.) horn-wort.

*****cornillas**, *n.m.*, young rook.

corniste, *n.m.*, cornist, player upon the horn.

*****cornouille**, *n.f.*, dogberry.

*****cornouiller**, *n.m.*, dogberry-tree, cornel-tree.

cornu, -e, *adj.*, horned; angular, cornered; (fig.) extravagant, absurd.

cornue, *n.f.*, (chem.) retort.

corollaire, *n.m.*, corollary.

corolle, *n.f.*, (bot.) corol, corolla.

corollifère, *adj.*, corollated, bearing a corolla.

coronaire, *adj.*, (anat.) coronary.

coronal, -e, *adj.*, (anat.) coronal.

coronal, *n.m.*, (anat.) coronal.

coroner (-nèr), *n.m.*, (—s) coroner.

*****coronille**, *n.f.*, (bot.) coronilla.

coronoïde, *adj.*, (anat.) coronoid.

coronope, *n. m.*, (bot.) wart-cress. *— de ruelle;* crow's-foot.

corossol, *n.m.*, (bot.) custard-apple. *— des marais;* cork-wood.

corossolier, *n.m.*, (bot.) anona, custard-apple tree.

corporal, *n.m.*, (c. rel.) corporal, communion cloth.

corporalité, *n.f.*, corporality.

corporation, *n.f.*, corporation, corporate body.

corporéité, *n.f.*, corporeity.

corporel, -le, *adj.*, corporal, corporeal, bodily.

corporellement (-mãn), *adv.*, corporally, bodily.

corporifier, *v.a.*, to embody, to form into a body.

corps (kor), *n.m.*, body; person; fellow; creature; substance, thickness, consistence; company, society, commonalty, college; main point; barrel (of pumps); caudex (of roots); (of wine, of writing, of sovereigns, of musical instruments, of wearing apparel) body; corps; set of men; (print.) depth, body, of a letter; shell (of a house, a pulley). *— mort;* dead body. *— morts;* (nav.) moorings. *— glorieux;* glorified body. *Un drôle de —*; a queer fellow, a queer fish. *Se tuer le — et l'âme;* to work one's self to death. *Répondre — pour —*; to be answerable for a person. *Faire — neuf;* to take a new lease of life. *Il fait bon marché de son —*; he makes himself very cheap; he exposes himself unnecessarily to danger. *Il faut voir ce que cet homme a dans le —*; we must see what stuff this man is made of. *Enlever un homme comme un — saint;* (prov.) to kidnap a man. *Gagner son pain à la sueur de son —*; to earn one's bread by the sweat of one's brow. *Tomber rudement sur le — à quelqu'un;* to speak in offensive terms of any one. *Etre séparés — et biens;* to be separated (mensã et thoro). *C'est un pauvre —*; he is a poor weak fellow. *C'est un — de fer que cet homme;* that man is made of iron. *Passer son épée au travers du — à quelqu'un;* to run any one through the body. *Il a le diable au —*; he is a devil of a fellow. *— de bâtiment;* main building. *— de logis;* detached building. *— de cheminée;* chimney-stack. *Le — du délit;* substance, main proof, of an offense (*corpus delicti*). *Un vin qui a du —*; a full-bodied wine. *Prendre du —*; to grow stout, fat. *Le — du clergé;* the body of the clergy. *Les — de métiers;* the trades' companies. *Ils font — à part;* they are a separate body. *Esprit de —*; spirit

of party; brotherhood in arms. *Un — d'infanterie;* a body of foot-soldiers. *Garde du —*; a life-guard. *Un — de garde;* a guard-house; watch-house; round-house. *— à —*; hand to hand. *A — perdu;* headlong; desperately. *A bras-le-corps;* by the waist. *Saisir quelqu'un à bras-le —*; to seize any one round the waist. *N'avoir rien dans le —*; to have taken no food; to be a person of no pluck. *A son — défendant;* reluctantly, in one's own defense. *Le vaisseau a sombré — et biens;* the vessel foundered with all hands.

corpulence, *n.f.*, corpulence, corpulency; stoutness. *Un homme de petite —*; a stoutish man.

corpulent, -e, *adj.*, corpulent, stout.

corpusculaire, *adj.*, corpuscular.

corpuscule, *n.m.*, corpuscule or corpuscle.

corpusculiste, *n.m.*, corpuscularian.

correct (-rèct), **-e**, *adj.*, accurate, correct, right.

correctement, *adv.*, correctly, accurately, rightly, right.

correcteur, *n. m.*, corrector, emendator; (print.) reader. *Père —*; superior of a convent.

correcti-f, -ve, *adj.*, corrective.

correctif, *n.m.*, corrective.

correction, *n.f.*, correction; correctness, accuracy; alteration; reprimand; reproof; (print.) reading, correcting. *Maison de —*; house of correction, reformatory.

correctionnel, -le, *adj.*, correctional (of misdemeanors); punishable; reformatory. *Tribunal de police —le;* police-court.

correctionnellement, *adv.*, by way of correction; before the magistrate; for misdemeanors.

correctivement (-tiv-mãn), *adv.*, correctively, as a corrective.

correctoire, *n.m.*, book of penance, formulary.

correctrice, *n.f.*, lady superior of a convent of Minimi nuns.

corrégidor, *n.m.*, corregidor (Sp. magistrate).

corrélati-f, -ve, *adj.*, correlative.

corrélati-f, *n.m.*, **-ve**, *n.f.*, correlative.

corrélation, *n.f.*, correlation.

correspondance, *n.f.*, correspondence, intercourse; connection, relation; conformity, harmony. *Etre en — avec quelqu'un;* to correspond with any one. *Entretenir une — avec quelqu'un;* to keep up a correspondence with any one. *Voiture de —*; correspondence-coach; railway-omnibus. *Service de —*; cross-post.

correspondant, -e, *adj.*, correspondent, corresponding.

correspondant, *n.m.*, correspondent, corresponding member; parents' representative.

correspondre, *v.n.*, to correspond, to communicate, to be in correspondence with; to agree, to suit, to harmonize.

corridor, *n.m.*, lobby, corridor, gallery, passage. *Cette porte donne sur le —*; this door opens out into the gallery or passage.

corrigé, *n.m.*, corrected copy; key (book).

corrigeant, -e (-jãn, -t), *adj.*, correcting.

corriger, *v.a.*, to correct; to rectify; to repair; to amend; to reclaim; to reprove; to reprehend, to chide, to chastise. *— des épreuves;* (print.) to correct proofs.

se **corriger**, *v.r.*, to correct one's self, to amend, to reform, to be reformed. *Elle s'est bien corrigée de cela;* she has quite broken herself of that.

corrigible, *adj.*, corrigible.

corroborant, -e (kor-ro-), *adj.*, (med.) corroborant.

corroborant, *n.m.*, (med.) corroborant.

corroborati-f, -ve (kor-ro-), *adj.*, (med.) corroborative.

corroboratif (kor-ro-), *n.m.*, (med.) corroborative.

corroboration (kor-ro-), *n.f.*, (med.) corroboration, strengthening.

corroborer (kor-ro-), *v.a.*, to strengthen, to corroborate.

corrodant, -e, *adj.*, corroding. *n.m.*, corrodent.

corroder (kor-ro-dé), *v.a.*, to corrode.

corroi, *n.m.*, currying of leather ; (mas.) claying, puddling.

corroirie, *n.f.*, (tech.) currier's shop, currying.

corrompre, *v.a.*, to corrupt ; to adulterate, to spoil ; to infect ; to taint ; to vitiate ; to pervert ; to bribe. *Les mauvaises compagnies corrompent les bonnes mœurs ;* evil communications corrupt good manners. *— des témoins ;* to bribe witnesses. *Se laisser — ;* to take a bribe.

se **corrompre**, *v.r.*, to grow corrupt ; to become tainted, to fester.

corrompu, -e, *part.*, corrupted ; bribed ; spoiled ; unsound. *Homme — ;* debauchee. *Mœurs —es ;* dissolute manners.

corrosi-f, -ve (kor-rô-), *adj.*, corrosive.

corrosif, *n.m.*, corrosive.

corrosion (kor-rô-zion), *n.f.*, corrosion.

corroyer, *v.a.*, to curry (leather) ; to prepare clay for puddling ; to puddle ; to beat up. *— du bois ;* to plane wood. *— du fer ;* to hammer iron. *— du sable ;* to roll sand.

corroyère, *n.f.*, (bot.) sumac.

corroyeur, *n.m.*, currier.

corrugateur, *n.m.*, (anat.) corrugator.

corrugation, *n.f.*, corrugation, wrinkling.

corrupt-eur, *n.m.*, **-rice**, *n.f.*, (kor-rup-), corrupter, seducer, spoiler ; briber.

corrupt-eur, -rice, *adj.*, corrupting, perverting, corrupt, infectious.

corruptibilité (kor-rup-), *n.f.*, corruptibility.

corruptible (kor-rup-), *adj.*, corruptible.

corruption (kor-rup-), *n.f.*, corruption ; taint, putridity, rottenness ; depravity, perversity, defilement ; bribery.

cors, *n.m. pl.*, (hunt.) horns ; branches. *Un cerf dix — ;* a full-grown stag.

corsage, *n.m.*, trunk, bust, chest (of the body) ; bodice, body (of a dress). *— de dessous ;* petticoat bodice.

corsaire, *n.m.*, privateer, commander of a privateer ; corsair, rover ; shark, Jew. *A — — et demi ;* set a thief to catch a thief.

corsé, *adj.*, rich, full-bodied, having body (of wine) ; (fam.) strong, thick, stout ; substantial, copious ; plentiful.

corse, *n.m.f.* and *adj.*, Corsican.

corselet, *n.m.*, corselet.

corser, *v.n.*, to fit (of stays). *v.a.*, (fig.) to thicken, to complicate.

se **corser**, *v.r.*, to put one's stays on ; (fig.) to acquire strength ; to grow serious.

corset, *n.m.*, corset, stays ; bodice ; (surg.) bandage.

corseti-er, *n.m.*, **-ère**, *n.f.*, (-tié, -ti-èr), corsetmaker, stay-maker.

cortège, *n.m.*, train, retinue, cortege ; procession ; attendants.   [ment.]

cortès (-tèss), *n.f.pl.*, Cortes (Spanish Parlia-

cortical, -e, *adj.*, (bot., anat.) cortical.

cortiqueu-x, -se, *adj.*, (bot.) corticose.

coruscation, *n.f.*, coruscation.

corvéable, *adj.*, (feudalism) liable to forced labor.

corvéable, *n.m.*, one liable to forced labor.

corvée, *n.f.*, (feudalism) statute-labor ; duty, service, fatigue duty done by soldiers ; toil ; drudgery ; bore. *Quelle — !* what a bore !

corvette, *n.f.*, corvette, sloop of war.

corybante, *n.m.*, priest of Cybele.

corybantique, *adj.*, corybantic. *—s, n.f. pl.*, feasts in honor of Cybele.

corymbe, *n.m.*, (bot.) cluster, corymb.

corymbé, -e, *adj.*, (bot.) corymbiate.

corymbeu-x, se, *adj.*, (bot.) corymbose.

corymbifère, *adj.*, (bot.) corymbiferous. *—s ; n.f.pl.*, corymbiferous plants.

coryphée, *n.m.*, corypheus ; leader, chief ; principal man ; (theat.) chorus-master.

coryza, *n.m.*, (med.) coryza, cold in the head.

cosaque, *n.m.*, Cossack.

cosaque, *n.f.*, Cossack dance. *Je veux te faire danser une — ;* (pop.) I 'll let you have a taste of the stick.

cosécante, *n.f.*, (geom.) co-secant.

*coseigneur, *n.m.*, joint lord of a manor.

coseigneurie, *n.f.*, joint lordship.

cosinus (-si-nûs), *n.m.*, (geom.) co-sine.

cosmétique, *n.m.* and *adj.*, cosmetic.

cosmétique, *n.f.*, art of using cosmetics.

cosmique, *adj.*, (astron.) cosmical.

cosmiquement, *adv.*, (astron.) cosmically.

cosmogonie, *n.f.*, cosmogony.

cosmogonique, *adj.*, cosmogonical.

cosmographe, *n.m.*, cosmographer.

cosmographie, *n.f.*, cosmography.

cosmographique, *adj.*, cosmographical.

cosmolabe, *n.m.*, (astron.) cosmolabe.

cosmologie, *n.f.*, cosmology.

cosmologique, *adj.*, cosmological.

cosmologiste or **cosmologue**, *n.m.*, cosmologist.

cosmopolite, *n.m.*, cosmopolite.

cosmopolite, *adj.*, cosmopolitan.

cosmopolitisme, *n.m.*, cosmopolitism.

cosmorama, *n.m.*, cosmorama.

cosse, *n.f.*, cod, shell, husk, pod ; (nav.) thimble.

cosser, *v.n.*, (of rams) to butt.

cosson, *n.m.*, (ent.) weevil ; (agri.) new shoot of a vine.

cossu, -e, *adj.*, husked, podded ; substantial, warm, wealthy, rich. *En conter de —es ;* to tell spicy tales. *Un homme — ;* a monied man.

costal, -e, *adj.*, costal.   [side-lights.

costières, *n.f. pl.*, (theat.) grooves for the

costume, *n.m.*, garb, uniform ; manners, usages ; costume, dress. *Grand — ;* full dress. *Petit — ;* undress. *— de soirée ;* evening-dress. *— tailleur ;* tailor-made dress.

costumer, *v.a.*, to dress in fancy dress.

se **costumer**, *v.r.*, to dress one's self up ; to dress in fancy dress.

costumier, *n.m.*, costumer, dealer in fancy dress clothes.

cotangente, *n.f.*, (geom.) co-tangent.

cote, *n.f.*, letter, number, figure (to indicate the order) ; (com.) quotation ; quota, share, price, price-list. *Faire une — mal taillée ;* to make a clumsy compromise.

côte, *n.f.*, rib (of the body, of cloth, of fruit) ; (arch., bot., manu.), rib ; (agri.) edge ; hill, declivity ; shore, sea-coast. *— d'aloyau ;* wing-rib. *Fausses —s ;* short ribs. *Se casser une — ;* to break a rib. *Rompre les —s à quelqu'un ;* to break anyone's bones. *Mesurer les —s à quelqu'un ;* to thrash anyone. *Se mettre à la — ;* (nav.) to run aground, ashore. *Ranger la — ;* to coast. *Raser la — ;* to sail along, to hug, the shore. *— à — ;* side by side. *Le long de la — ;* along the hill or the shore. *— de fer ;* (hist.) iron-side.

côté, *n.m.*, side ; broadside ; way, manner ; flank ; part ; slice. *Il a un point de — ;* he has got a stitch in his side. *Le — faible ;* the weak side. *Mettre une bouteille, un tonneau, sur le — ;* to empty a bottle, a cask. *De tous —s ;* on all sides. *— de première ;* (print.) outer form. *— de seconde ;* inner form. *De mon — ;* for my own part. *Ils sont parents du — maternel ;* they are related on the mother's side. *Il est du — gauche ;* he is a natural child. *Se ranger du —*

de quelqu'un; to side with anyone. *De quel —êtes-vous?* whom do you side with? *Il se met du — du plus fort;* he takes the strongest side. *A — de;* by, near. *Etre à — de la question;* to be beside the question. *Donner à —;* to miss. *De —;* sideways, aslant, askew, obliquely, aside. *D'à —;* adjoining, next house. *Une vue de —;* a side-view. *Regarder de —;* to look askance. *Mettre une chose de —;* to lay by. *De — et d'autre;* up and down, here and there, on all sides, in every direction. *C'est son — faible;* it is his weak side. *S'asseoir à — de quelqu'un;* to sit down by the side of any one. *Se tenir les —s de rire;* to shake one's sides with laughing. *De l'autre —;* in the next room. *Mettre les rieurs de son —;* to turn the laugh against any one. *Etre sur le —;* to be on one's back, ill.

coteau, *n.m.*, declivity, slope; little hill, hillock, rising ground.

côtelette (kot-let), *n.f.*, chop, cutlet. *Une — de mouton;* a mutton chop. *Des —s de veau;* veal cutlets. *— de porc frais;* pork chop. *Des —s;* mutton chop whiskers.

cotenanci-er, -ère, *n.m.f.*, co-tenant.

coter, *v.a.*, to number; to quote, to fix, to price. *Se —;* to be quoted, to be priced. *— le cours des effets publics;* to quote the price of stocks.

coterie (ko-trî), *n.f.*, coterie, set, club; circle, gang.

cothurne, *n.m.*, buskin. *Chausser le —;* to put on the buskin (play in tragedy).

cothurné, -e, *adj.*, (antiq.) cothurnated.

côtier (-tié), *adj., n.m.*, coasting; coasting-pilot.

côtière (-ti-èr), *n.f.*, (gard.) border, sloping bed; (nav.) (l.u.) coasts, coast-line.

***cotignac** (-gna), *n.m.*, quiddany, marmalade of quinces.

***cotillon**, *n. m.*, under-petticoat; cotillon (dance). *Il aime le —;* he is fond of women. *Régime du —;* petticoat government.

cotir, *v.a.*, (fruit) to bruise, to damage.

cotisation, *n.f.*, clubbing, subscription; assessment, quota, share.

cotiser, *v.a.*, to assess, to rate.

se **cotiser**, *v.r.*, to rate, to assess; to unite, to club together; to get up a subscription; to subscribe.

cotissure, *n.f.*, (fruit) damage, bruising.

coton, *n.m.*, cotton; down (of fruit and hair on the face). *— épluché;* picked cotton. *— brut;* raw cotton. *— plat;* darning cotton. *— à tricoter;* knitting cotton. *— de couleur;* colored cotton. *Bobine de —;* reel of cotton. *Echeveau de —;* skein of cotton. *Balle de —;* bale of cotton. *Toile de —;* cotton cloth. *Il jette un vilain —;* he is going to the dogs. *Il jette, il file, un mauvais —;* he is in a bad way. *Mettre dans du —;* to coddle, to nurse, to indulge. *Elever dans du —;* to molly-coddle; to bring up delicately.

cotonnade, *n.f.*, cotton cloth, cotton-check.

cotonné, -e, *part.*, woolly (of hair); wadded, padded; covered with, full of, cotton.

cotonner, *v.a.*, to fill, to stuff with, cotton; to pad.

se **cotonner**, *v.r.*, to be covered with down, to become downy; to cotton, to nap, to become mealy (of vegetables). *Les artichauts, les radis se cotonnent;* artichokes, radishes grow pithy or spongy.

cotonner, *v.n.*, to cotton, to nap.

cotonneu-x, -se, *adj.*, pithy, spongy, mealy; (bot.) downy, cottony (of style); spun out, lax, diffuse.

cotonnier, *n.m.*, cotton-tree.

cotonni-er, -ère, *adj.*, cotton, of cotton.

cotonnière, *n.f.*, (bot.) cotton-weed; cud-weed.

cotonnine, *n.f.*, cotton sail-cloth.

côtoyer, *v.a.*, to go by the side of, to skirt; (nav.) to coast, to coast along; to keep close to, to hug the shore.

cotret, *n.m.*, fagot, stick. *Il est sec comme un —;* he is as thin as a lath. *De l'huile de —;* stirrup oil; (fig.) cudgeling.

cottage, *n.m.*, cottage.

cotte, *n. f.*, petticoat, jacket; coat. *— d'armes;* coat of arms. *— de mailles;* coat of mail. *— morte;* estate (of a deceased monk).

cotte, *n.m.*, (ich.) bull-head. *— chabot;* sea-scorpion.

cotut-eur, *n.m.*, **-rice**, *n.f.*, joint-guardian.

cotylédon, *n.m.*, (anat., bot.) cotyledon.

cotylédoné, -e, *adj.*, (bot.) cotyledonous.

cotylier, *n.m.*, (bot.) cotyledon, navel-wort.

cotyloïde, *adj.*, (anat.) cotyloid.

cou, *n.m.*, neck. *— de travers;* wry-neck. *Sauter, se jeter, au — de quelqu'un;* to fall on a person's neck. *Se casser le —;* to break one's neck. *Couper le — à;* to cut the neck of. *Rompre le — à;* to break the neck of. *Prendre ses jambes à son —;* to take to one's heels. *— de pied;* instep.

couard, *n.m.*, (fam.) coward, dastard.

couard, -e, *adj.*, (fam.) coward, cowardly.

couardement, *adv.*, (fam.) in a cowardly manner.

couarder, *v.n.*, (fam.) to act in a cowardly manner.

couardise, *n.f.*, (fam.) cowardice.

coucal, *n.m.*, pheasant-cuckoo.

couchage, *n.m.*, bedding (for the army); act of lying in bed; price of a bed, night's lodging.

couchant, *adj.*, lying; setting. *Un chien —;* a setter. *Faire le chien —;* to crawl and cringe. *Soleil —;* setting sun.

couchant, *n.m.*, west; wane, decline.

couche, *n.f.*, bed; bedstead; confinement, childbed, lying-in; delivery, birth; swaddling-clothes, diaper; layer, stratum, row; (gard.) hot-bed, bed; (mining) seam; layer, stratum, coat (of varnish, colour); stake (at play). *La — nuptiale;* the nuptial bed. *Pendant ses —s;* during her confinement. *Elle est morte en —s;* she died in childbed. *Etre en, faire ses, —s;* to be confined, to lie-in. *Heureuse —;* good delivery. *Fausse —;* miscarriage. *Partager la — de quelqu'un;* to share any one's bed.

couché, -e, *part.*, put to bed, in bed, gone to bed, lying down, flat down, recumbent, jacent; (her.) couchant.

couchée, *n.f.*, resting-place; sleeping place; bed; night's lodging.

coucher, *v.a.*, to put to bed; to lay down; to lay low; to lodge; to knock down; to incline; to lay on; ⊙ to stake. *— quelqu'un en joue;* to take aim at anyone, to cover anyone. *— en joue;* to aim at, to cover. ⊙ *— gros;* to play deep. *— par écrit;* to write down, take down, enter.

se **coucher**, *v.r.*, to go to bed; to lay one's self down, to lie down, to lie flat; to set; to go down. *Allez vous —;* go to bed. *Il n'est pas encore temps d'aller se —;* it is not bed-time yet. *Se — comme les poules;* to go to bed with the sun (i.e., very early). *Comme on fait son lit, on se couche;* as you make your bed, so you must lie. *Allez vous —;* (fam.) get along with you; stuff and nonsense. *Le soleil se couche;* the sun is setting.

coucher, *v.n.*, to lie, to sleep, to pass the night; to lie down, to rest. *— au cabaret;* to sleep at a public-house. *— à la belle étoile;* to sleep in the open air. *— sur la dure;* to sleep upon bare boards or on the ground. *— tout habillé;* to sleep with one's clothes on.

coucher, *n.m.*, bed-time, going to bed; sleeping; setting (of the sun). *C'est l'heure de son*

—; it is his bed-time. *Le petit —;* the king's select circle whilst preparing for bed.

couchette, *n.f.,* bedstead, small bed, crib.

coucheu-r, *n.m.,* **-se,** *n.f.,* bed-fellow. *Mauvais* —; nasty customer; cross-grained person. *Bon* —; easy-going fellow.

couchis, *n.m.,* layer, stratum; bolster.

couci-couci, *adv.,* (fam.) so so, middling, indifferently.

coucou, *n.m.,* cuckoo; barren strawberry-plant; Dutch clock; coach, omnibus; one-horse chaise; (bot.) cowslip, daffodil.

coude, *n.m.,* elbow; bend, angle; winding; turning, turn; knee (of machinery); neck (of a bayonet). *Donner des coups de —;* to elbow. *Hausser le —;* to drink hard, to fuddle.

coudé, -e, *part.,* bent, elbowed, cranked.

coudée, *n.f.,* arm's length; cubit. *Avoir les —s franches;* to have elbow room, full play, scope, freedom.

cou-de-pied, *n.m.,* (*—s-—*) instep.

couder, *v.a.,* to bend, to make an elbow.

se **couder,** *v.r.,* to elbow, to form an elbow.

coudoyer, *v.a.,* to elbow, to jostle.

se **coudoyer,** *v.r.,* to elbow, to jostle, one another.

coudraie, *n.f.,* hazel-copse; filbert-orchard.

coudran, *n.m.,* (nav.) tar. *V.* **goudron.**

coudranner, *v.a.,* (nav.) to soak cords in tar.

coudre, *n.m.,* nut-tree, hazel-tree. *V.* **coudrier.**

coudre (cousant, cousu), *v.a.,* to sew, to stitch; to tack; (fig.) to add, to connect, to unite. — *à;* to stitch *or* sew to. — *du linge;* to sew linen. — *à grands points;* to take long stitches.

⊙**coudrette,** *n.f.,* hazel-copse.

coudrier, *n.m.,* hazel-tree.

couenne (kooa-n), *n.f.,* rind, pig-skin; (med.) buff; birth-mark, mole.

couenneu-x, -se (kooah-), *adj.,* (med.) containing buff. *Angine —se ;* diphtheria.

couette, *n.f.,* little-tail; tuft; sea-gull; ⊙ feather-bed; (mec.) socket.

coufique, *adj.,* (philol.) cufic.

cougourde, *n.f.,* (bot.) bottle-gourd.

couguar (-gar), *n.m.,* (mam.) cougar.

couillon, *n.m.,* coward, funk; fool, muff.

couillonnade, *n.f.,* gammon, humbug, bosh.

couillonner, *v.a.,* to gammon, to humbug, to bamboozle; to funk, to shirk.

coulage, *n.m.,* leakage, waste; melting, casting.

coulamment (koo-la-män), *adv.,* fluently, freely, readily. *Il parle —;* he talks fluently.

coulant, -e, *adj.,* flowing; fluent; smooth; easy, accommodating; slip (of knots). *Style —;* easy, fluent style. *Nœud —;* noose.

coulant, *n.m.,* slide, slider, runner; neck-jewel; slide (of an umbrella).

coulé, *n.m.,* (mus.) slur; slide (dance); cast (founding); (paint.) first wash; (billiards) following stroke.

coulée, *n.f.,* running, flowing, flow; (of writing) running-hand; tapping (metal); (hunt.) track path. *Trou de —;* (metal.) tap-hole.

coulement (kool-män), *n.m.,* running, flow (of liquids).

couler, *v.n.,* to flow, to run; to glide, to glide along; to pour, to stream; to trickle, to drop; to leak, to run out; to ooze out; to glide away, to fly away, to slip; to slide away, to go down; (founding) to run through the mold; to gutter; to touch lightly upon; to be shed, to be split. *Se laisser — jusqu'à terre;* to slide down to the ground. *Faire —;* to shed. *L'échelle va —;* the ladder will slip. *L'encre ne coule pas;* the ink does not run freely. *Le nez lui coule;* his nose runs. *La chandelle coule;* the candle gutters. *Les larmes lui coulent des yeux;* tears

are flowing from his eyes. — *sur un fait;* to glide *or* slur over a fact. — *bas, à fond;* to founder, to sink.

couler, *v.a.,* to cast; to strain; to slip in; to pass (time); (mus.) to slur; to run down; to do for; to scald (linen); to fall off, to drop; to sink; to run smooth, to flow. — *une statue;* to cast a statue. — *une glace;* to cast a plate of glass. — *un vaisseau à fond;* to sink a ship. — *un pas;* to pass smoothly over a step (in dancing).

se **couler,** *v.r.,* to slip, to creep, to steal, to slide; (of metals) to be cast.

couleur, *n.f.,* color, paint; favor (ribbon); coloring; appearance; suit (at cards). *—s aigres;* harsh colors. *—s amies;* blending colors. — *éclatante;* striking color. — *tranchante;* glaring color. — *solide;* fast color. — *de feu;* flame color. — *de rose;* rose color. *Pâles —s;* (med.) chlorosis, green sickness. — *locale;* local coloring. — *voyante;* showy color. — *à l'huile;* oil color. *—s passantes;* fading colors. *Diversifier, mêler, assortir, les —s;* to vary, to blend, to match, colors. *Juger d'une chose comme un aveugle des —s;* to talk of a subject without knowing anything about it. *Voir tout — de rose;* to see the bright side of things. *Les hommes de —;* men of color, mulattoes. *Lampes de —;* variegated lamps. *Reprendre —;* to be in favor again; to appear in society again. *Changer de —;* to change color. *La — lui monta au visage;* the color came into his face. *Ce rôti a bien pris —;* that roast meat is nicely browned. *L'affaire prend —;* the matter is looking better, or is taking a turn. *De quelle — tourne-t-il ?* what are trumps? *Donner de la —;* to follow suit. *Prendre —;* (lansquenet) to stake and cut the cards. *Appliquer les —s;* to lay on the colors. *Adoucir, amortir, les —s;* to soften, to deaden, colors. *Rehausser les —s;* to heighten colors. *Peindre à pleines —s;* to paint with a full brush. *Mettre en —;* (paint.) to stain. *Style sans —;* colorless style. *Prendre —;* to assume a character; (of persons) to take a side. *Il l'a trompé sous — d'amitié;* he deceived him under a show of friendship. *Sous — de;* under the pretext of.

couleuvre, *n.f.,* adder; (fig.) mortification, vexation, bitter pill. *Faire avaler des —s à quelqu'un;* to put all sorts of indignities upon a person.

couleuvreau, *n.m.,* young adder.

couleuvrée, *n.f.,* (bot.) bryony.

couleuvrine, *n.f.,* culverin; aspic. *Etre sous la — d'un autre;* to be dependent on another. *Etre sous la — d'une place;* to be within reach of a fort.

coulis, *adj. m.* Vent —; wind that comes through cracks and chinks, draught of air.

coulis, *n.m.,* (cook.) cullis, gravy, jelly; (mas.) grout, solder.

coulisse, *n.f.,* groove; sliding board; running-string; rib (presses); (print.) galley; (theat.) side-scene, wing; behind the scenes; shutter, door; (exchange language) coulisse (unauthorised part of the exchange); bucket shop; frequenters of the coulisse; outside brokers. — *d'arbalète;* chase of a cross-bow. *Propos de —s;* green-room talk. *Faire les yeux en —;* to look askance.

coulissé, -e, *adj.,* grooved.

coulisseau, *n.m.,* slide, slide-block, wooden groove for beds with castors; guide (engineering).

coulissier, *n.m.,* stock-jobber; outside broker; green-room frequenter.

couloir, *n.m.,* skimming-dish, strainer; (arch.) passage, lobby. ⊙ — *de la bile;* biliary duct.

couloire, *n.f.,* colander, sieve, strainer.

coulpe, *n.f.*, (rel.) sin, fault. *J'en dis ma* —; I confess and repent.

coulure, *n.f.*, running (metal); falling off, dropping off (fruit).

coumarine, *n.f.*, (chem.) coumarine.

coup (koo), *n.m.*, blow, thump, knock, stroke, hit, stab, thrust, lash; crack (of a whip); beat (of a drum); draught (liquids); clap (of thunder); (artil.) charge; move (at chess, draughts); (fenc.) thrust; gust (of wind); throw (at dice); shot, report (of fire-arms); butt (of rams); time; trick; event; aim; attempt; act; action; deed; kick; push. *pl.*, knocking. — *amorti*; spent shot. *Grand* —; hard blow; last cast. *Porter un* —; to deal a blow. *Petit* —; pat; sip (of liquids). *Heureux* —; lucky hit. — *monté*; got-up affair. — *mortel*, — *de mort*; death-blow. — *de maître*; master-stroke. — *de jarnac*; treacherous, unexpected blow. — *de tête*; act of desperation, freak. — *de partie*; decisive blow. — *de poing*; blow with the fist, fisticuff. — *de coude*; nudge. *un* — *de revers*; back-stroke; backhander. *Donner des* —*s de pied*; to kick. — *de massue*; blow with a club, stunning blow; thunder-stroke. — *de bâton*; blow with a stick; cudgeling. *Donner des* —*s de bâton à quelqu'un*; to cudgel any one. *Donner un* — *d'épée*; to deal a sword thrust. — *de fleuret*; pass. *Donner des* —*s de fouet*; to lash. — *de dent*; bite. *Au or sur le* — *de trois heures*; when the clock strikes three. *Un* — *de sifflet*; a whistle. *Donnez-vous un* — *de peigne*; comb yourself. — *de foudre*; thunderbolt. — *de sang*; apoplectic fit; congestion of the brain. — *de soleil*; sunstroke. — *d'air*; cold in the head or chest. *Le* — *de grâce*; the coup-de-grace, the finishing stroke. *C'est comme un* — *d'épée dans l'eau*; it is like beating the air. *Un* — *de bec or de patte*; a piece of slander; sarcastic remark. *Assommer quelqu'un de* —*s*, *rouer quelqu'un de* —*s*; to beat in a cruel manner. — *d'assommoir*; overwhelming, stunning blow. *Détourner le* —; to ward off the blow. *Faire son* —; to succeed. *Manquer son* —; to fail. — *perdu*; random shot. *Donner un* — *de chapeau*; to take off one's hat. *Faire d'une pierre deux* —*s*; to kill two birds with one stone. *Flanquer des* —*s à quelqu'un*; to give any one a thrashing. *Sans* — *férir*; without striking a blow, without firing a shot. *Porter* —; to hit home. *Encore un* —; once more, again; one more blow. *Encore un* — *je vous dis*; once more I tell you. *D'un seul* —; at one blow; at one swoop. *A* — *perdu*; in vain. *Sous le* — *de*; under the threat of. — *sur* —; one after another, without stopping, in succession. *Pour le* —; this time, for once. *Après* —; too late. *A tous* —*s*; at every turn, every moment. *Du premier* —; at the first, at once. *Tout à* —; all of a sudden, suddenly. *Tout d'un* —; at once, all at once. *A* — *sûr*; certainly, to a certainty, unquestionably. *Il a reçu un* — *de fusil*; he received a gun-shot wound. — *de canon à l'eau*; shot between wind and water. — *de partance*; (nav.) farewell gun; signal for departure. *Un* — *de vent*; a squall. — *de main*; (milit.) coup-de-main, surprise, sudden, unexpected, desperate, attack. *Donner un* — *de main à quelqu'un*; to give any one a helping hand. *Donner un* — *d'épaule à quelqu'un*; to give any one a lift. *Donner un* — *de collier*; to put one's shoulder to the wheel. *Frapper les grands* —*s*; to resort to decisive measures. *Asséner un* —; to deal a blow. — *d'œil*; glance, look. *Jeter un* — *d'œil sur*; to take a peep at. *Avoir le* — *d'œil juste*; to have a carpenter's eye. *Au premier* — *d'œil*; at first sight. *Cette démarche a porté* —; this step has taken effect. *Un* — *de bonheur*; a lucky hit. *Un* — *de malheur*; an unlucky hit. — *d'étourdi*; rash act. — *de désespoir*; desperate attempt.

— *d'essai*; first attempt. — *d'éclat*; striking act, brilliant exploit. — *d'état*; violent measure, exercise or abuse of authority; revolution, state-stroke. — *d'autorité*; act of authority. *Par un* — *de hasard*; by a mere chance. — *de bonheur*; lucky chance. — *imprévu*; unexpected accident. — *du ciel*; providential stroke. —*s et blessures*; (jur.) cutting and maiming. — *de théâtre*; unexpected event; clap-trap. *Il a fait le* —; he has done the deed. *Un* —; once. *Il a encore trois* —*s à jouer*; he has still three shots. *Tirer un* —; to fire a shot. *Porter un* — *fourré à quelqu'un*; to do anyone an ill turn, to strike a blow in the dark. *C'est un* — *qui porte*; that is a home-thrust. *Le* — *vaut l'argent*; it is worth trying. *Buvez encore un* —; drink once more. *Boire un grand* —; to take a long draught. *Buvons un* — *ensemble*; let us have a drink together. *Boire un* — *de trop*; to have a drop too much. *Tuer quelqu'un à* —*s de bâton*; to beat anyone to death. *Faire les cent* —*s*; to run riot. *Etre aux cent* —*s*; to be at one's wits' end; not to know which way to turn.

coupable, *adj.*, culpable, guilty, at fault, sinful, criminal. *Déclarer quelqu'un* —; to bring any one in guilty. *Se déclarer* —, *non* —; to plead guilty, not guilty.

coupable, *n.m.f.*, guilty person; culprit.

coupage, *n.m.*, cutting; diluting (of wine).

coupant, *n.m.*, edge (of a sword). — *de l'ongle du sanglier*; the edge of a wild boar's foot (hunt.).

coupant, -e, *adj.*, cutting, sharp.

coupe, *n.f.*, cutting; chopping; felling (of wood); wood felled; cut (style); cut (place); the cut end; felling; a fall of timber; cup; chalice; quaffing-bowl; (arch.) section, plan, slope; division; (astron.) Crater; calice; cup; (theol.) wine; cutting (at cards). *La* — *des cheveux*; hair-cutting. *La* — *des pierres*; stone-cutting. *Mettre en* —; to mark for cutting. — *réglée*; annual cutting; regular contribution. *La* — *d'un bois taillis se fait tous les neuf ans*; coppice wood is felled every ninth year. *Mettre en* —; to cut down periodically (of forests); (fig.) to lay under regular contribution. *Il a la* — *malheureuse*; he has a very unlucky hand at cutting. *Etre sous la* — *de quelqu'un*; to play first (at cards); (fig.) to be in anyone's power. *Boire la* — *jusqu'à la lie*; to drink the cup of bitterness to the dregs. *Il y a loin de la* — *aux lèvres*; there's many a slip between the cup and the lips. — *d'un ouvrage*; division of a work into parts. *La* — *et liaison des scènes*; the division and connection of the scenes. *La* — *des vers*; the division of the verses. *Boire dans une* —; to drink out of a cup.

coupé, *n.m.*, coupee (step in dancing); brougham; front part of a French diligence. — *lit*; sleeping car.

coupé, -e, *part.*, cut, short, laconic. *Un pays* —; a country intersected with rivers, canals, &c. *Un style* —; a laconic style. *Du lait* —; milk and water. *Du vin* — *d'eau*; wine and water.

coupe-asperges, *n.m.*, (—) (hort.) asparagus-knife.

☉**coupeau**, *n.m.*, top of a hill; cop.

coupe-bourgeons, *n.m.*, (plur. —) vine-grub.

coupe-cercle, *n.m.*, (— — —*s*) round-punch (for cutting out pasteboard).

coupe-cors, *n.m.*, (—) corn-cutter.

coupe-fils, *n.m.*, pliers.

coupe-gorge, *n.m.*, (—) cut-throat place; nest of swindlers; the dealer turning up his own card first (lansquenet).

coupe-jarret, *n.m.*, (— — —*s*) cut-throat, assassin, ruffian. [cutter.]

coupe-légumes, *n.m.*, (plur. —) vegetable-

coupellation (-pel-la-), *n.f.*, (chem.) cupellation; testing (metal).

coupelle, *n.f.*, cupel. *Argent de* —; purest silver. *Essai à la* —; cupellation. *Mettre à la* —; to submit to cupellation; to put to the test.

coupeller, *v.a.*, to test (metals).

***coupe-paille**, *n.m.*, (—) chaff-cutter.

coupe-pâte, *n.m.*, (—) dough-knife.

couper, *v.a.*, to cut; to cut off, to dock, to lop, to strike off; to cut down; to cut out; to clip, to pare, to cut away, to geld; to cross, to get before; to dilute (milk, wine, with water); (milit.) to intercept; to divide, to intersect, to interrupt; to hinder; to impede, to get before; to strike; to geld; to cut up, to carve; to amputate; to chop. — *menu*; to mince. — *un habit*; to cut out a coat. — *par tranches*; to slice, to cut into slices. *Les sanglots lui coupent la voix;* her sobs stifle her utterance. — *la bourse à quelqu'un;* to pick any one's pocket. — *le cours d'une rivière;* to interrupt the course of a river. — *les vivres à une armée;* to intercept the provisions of an army. — *la parole à quelqu'un;* to interrupt any one. *Pour* — *court;* to be brief, in short. — *le chemin à quelqu'un;* to stop any one's way. — *la ligne;* (milit.) to break through the line. — *le sifflet à quelqu'un;* (pop.) to cut anyone's throat. — *les vivres à quelqu'un;* to stop anyone's allowance — *un cheveu en quatre;* to split hairs. — *le câble;* to take the decisive step. — *l'herbe sous le pied;* (fig.) to supplant anyone; to lay by the heels. — *bras et jambes;* (fig.) to dumfound. — *chemin à un incendie, à un maladie;* to stop the progress of a fire, of a disease.

se couper, *v.r.*, to cut oneself; to be chafed; to cut; to wear out; to burst; to crack; to intersect, to intersect one another; to cross; to contradict oneself, to falter, to equivocate. *Se* — *la gorge;* to cut one's throat. *Se* — *la main;* to cut one's hand. *Ce cuire s'est coupé;* this leather has burst.

couper, *v.n.*, to cut, to cut in (at cards); to chop. *A qui à* —? whose cut is it? — *dans le vif;* to cut to the quick. — *court à quelqu'un;* to cut any one short. — *par le plus court;* to take the shortest way.

coupe-racines, *n.m.*, (*plur.* —) (agri.) root-cutter.

couperet (koo-prè), *n.m.*, chopper, enameler's file.

couperose (koo-prôz), *n.f.*, copperas; (med.) stone-pock. — *verte;* green vitriol. — *blanche;* white vitriol. — *bleue;* blue vitriol.

couperosé, -e (koo-prô-zé), *adj.*, blotched, pimpled.

coupe-tête, *n.m.*, (n.p.) leap-frog.

coupeu-r, *n.m.*, -**se**, *n.f.*, cutter; player (lansquenet). — *de bourses;* pickpocket, cut-purse.

coupeur d'eau, *n.m.*, (orni.) cut-water.

couplage, *n.m.*, coupling; one of the sixteen parts composing a float of wood; pair of boats.

couple, *n.f.*, couple (two things of the same kind); (of game) brace. *Une* — *de bœufs;* a yoke of oxen. *Une* — *de perdrix;* a brace of partridges.

couple, *n.m.*, couple (two beings acting in concert); pair (of animals, male and female); (nav.) frame. *C'est un* — *bien assorti;* they are a well-matched couple. *Un* — *de chevaux;* a pair of horses. *Maître* —; midship-frame. —*s de remplissage;* (nav.) filling timber. — *de balancement;* balance timbers. *Par* —*s;* in pairs.

coupler, *v.a.*, to couple, to link.

couplet, *n.m.*, couplet; verse; song; tirade; hinge.

coupleter, *v.a.*, to write a song.

⊙**coupletier**, *n.m.*, song writer.

coupoir, *n.m.*, cutter (sharp instrument); blade; knife; (print.) lead-cutter; (foundry) dressing-bench.

coupole, *n.f.*, spherical vault; cupola.

coupon, *n.m.*, remnant; coupon, dividend warrant, cheque; (com.) part (of shares); (theat.) ticket.

coupure, *n.f.*, cutting; cut, slit, incision; suppression, erasion; (milit.) entrenchment, ditch behind a breach; (banking term) small note, bond, coupon. *J'ai une* — *au doigt;* I have a cut on my finger.

cour, *n.f.*, court (of a prince); court (of justice); love-suit, courtship; yard, court, courtyard. *Basse-*, —(*-s — -s*) back-yard, poultry-yard. — *d'entrée;* entrance-court, front-court. — *de derrière;* back-court. — *de récréation;* playground. *Les gens de la* —; courtiers. *Eau bénite de* —; empty promises. *C'est la* — *du roi Pétaud;* it is Bedlam broken loose. *Faire la* — *à une dame;* to court a lady. *Faire un doigt de* —; to show some attention to. *Mettre hors de* —; to nonsuit.

courable, *adj.*, (hunt.) that may be hunted.

courage, *n.m.*, courage, daring; spirit, mettle, fearlessness; fortitude, greatness of soul; heart, zeal; passion, temper. *Prendre* —; to be of good heart, to pluck up courage. *Manquer de* —; to be wanting in courage. *Perdre* —; to be discouraged. *Tenir or prendre son* — *à deux mains;* to summon up all one's courage. *Je n'ai pas le* — *de le lui refuser;* I have not the heart to refuse it him. —*!* come! take courage! cheer up!

courageousement (-jeûz-mãn), *adv.*, courageously, bravely, valiantly, gallantly, fearlessly, resolutely.

courageu-x, -se, *adj.*, courageous, daring, gallant, valiant, brave, fearless.

couramment (koo-ra-mãn), *adv.*, fluently, readily, off-hand. *Il lit* —; he reads fluently.

courant, -e, *adj.*, current, running, present; ordinary; fair, middling (of goods); lineal (of measures). *Le mois* —; the present month. *Monnaie* —*e;* current coin. *Le prix* —; the current price. *Compte* —; account current. *Ecriture* —*e;* running-hand.

courant, *n.m.*, current, stream, tide; course, routine; present price; present month, instant. *Le* — *du marché;* the market price. *Le* — *des affaires;* the course of affairs. *Etre au* — *des nouvelles;* to know the news of the day. *Tenir quelqu'un au* — *de;* (com.) to keep any one constantly advised of. *Se mettre au* — *de;* to acquaint one's self with. *Fin* —; (com.) at the end of the present month. *En* —; cursorily, in haste. *Je vous tiendrai au* — *;* I'll let you know; I'll keep you informed.

courante, *n.f.*, courant (a kind of dance); running-hand (of writing); (l. ex.) looseness, relaxation.

courbage, *n.m.*, bending, curving.

***courbaril**, *n.m.*, locust-tree. *Bois de* —; locust-wood.

courbatu, -e, *adj.*, (vet.) foundered; knocked up; stiff in the joints; (med.) affected with lumbago. *Je me sens tout* —; I feel stiff and bruised all over.

courbature, *n.f.*, (vet.) foundering, lameness; (med.) stiffness in the back and limbs, lumbago.

courbaturer, *v.a.*, to knock up; to make any one feel stiff all over. *Se* —; to knock oneself up; to get knocked up.

courbe, *adj.*, curved, bent, crooked.

courbe, *n.f.*, curve (nav., carp.) knee; (vet.) curb; turn (in a road).

courbement, *n.m.*, bending.

⊙**courbément**, *adv.*, curvedly, crookedly.

courber, *v.a.*, to bend, to warp, to make crooked, to curve, to incurvate; (tech.) to sag, to bow down, to weigh down. *Courbé de vieillesse;* bent with age. *Se tenir courbé;* to stoop.

se **courber**, v.r., to bend, to bow ; to stoop ; to bow down.

courber, v.n., to bow, to bend.

courbet, n.m., bill-hook ; bow of a pack-saddle.

courbette, n.f., (man.) curvet ; cringing, bowing and scraping. Il fait des —s ; he bows and scrapes and cringes.

courbetter, v.n., (man.) to curvet.

courbure, n.f., curve, curvature, bending, curvation, bend ; (tech.) sagging.

*coureailler, v.n., to cry like a quail.

*courcaillet, n.m., cry of the quail ; quail-pipe.

courcive, n.f. V. **coursive**.

courçon, n.m., (artil.) iron hoop, band.

coureau, n.m., strait, channel ; yawl.

courée, n.f., or **courai**, n.m., (nav.) stuff to pay a ship's bottom, grading.

coureur, n.m., runner, racer ; courser, hunter ; light-porter ; running footman ; groom ; gadder ; rambler, rover, stroller ; inconstant lover ; rake, libertine ; (milit.) skirmisher ; scout. — de sermons ; sermon hunter. — de nuit ; man who keeps late hours. — de cachets ; visiting tutor, master.

coureuse, n.f., gadder, street-walker. — de cachets ; visiting or daily governess.

coure-vite or **court-vite**, n.m., (—) (orni.) courser.

courge, n.f., gourd, pumpkin ; yoke (to carry pails). — à la moelle ; squash.

courir (courant, couru), v.n., to run ; to hasten ; to hunt, to run after ; to ramble, to gad abroad, to run about, to rove, to run up and down ; to flow, to stream ; to run on ; to run along, to extend, to stretch ; to prevail, to be prevalent, to be about, abroad ; to go round ; to be current, to circulate, to be reported ; (nav.) to sail. — à toutes jambes ; to run as fast as possible ; at the top of one's speed. — à bride abattue ; to ride full gallop. — après ; to run after. Devancer en courant ; to outrun. — çà et là ; to run about, up and down ; to gad about. L'année qui court ; the present year. Au temps, par le temps, qui court ; as times go now-adays. La monnaie qui court ; current money. La mode qui court ; the prevailing fashion. Le bruit court qu'il est mort ; there is a report that he is dead. Il court bien des maladies ; there is much illness about. — à l'autre bord ; (nav.) to stand upon the other tack. — au large ; to stand off. — à sa perte ; to hasten to one's ruin. — à l'hôpital ; to be ruining one's self. — aux armes ; to fly to arms. — sur le marché de quelqu'un ; to outbid any one. — à sa fin ; to draw to an end. Faire — des bruits ; to spread reports. Faire — une santé ; to make a toast go round.

courir, v.a., to run after, to pursue ; to travel over ; to hunt ; to frequent ; to infest ; to expose one's self, to run, to take. — les rues ; to run about the streets. — la pretantaine ; to gad about. — les bals, les théâtres ; to frequent balls, theatres. — le pays ; to rove, to stroll about. — le monde ; to travel. Être fou à — les rues or les champs ; to be as mad as a March hare. — la poste ; to do a thing precipitately. — sa vingtième année ; to be in one's twentieth year. — le plat pays, la mer ; to be a pirate. — le même lièvre ; to be engaged in the same pursuit, — même fortune ; to be in the same boat.

courlieu or **courlis**, n.m., (orni.) curlew.

couronne, n.f., crown, coronet ; wreath ; (anat., arch., astron., conch., hort., hunt.) crown ; crown (of the teeth) ; crown (a coin) ; (vet.) coronet ; (fort.) crown work ; (of paper) large foolscap ; (of a lamp) chimney-holder. — civique ; civic crown. — d'épines ; crown of thorns. La — du martyre ; the crown of martyrdom. Décerner une — ; to award a wreath. — impériale ; (bot.) crown-imperial. — de pieu ;

head of a stake. — des blés ; rose-campion. Domaine de la — ; crown-lands. C'est le plus beau fleuron de sa — ; it is the brightest jewel in his crown. Traiter de — à — ; to treat as from sovereign to sovereign. — matrimoniale ; (hist. of Scotland) matrimonial crown.

couronné, -e, part., crowned, capped ; encompassed ; (vet.) broken-kneed ; (arch.) Arbre — ; tree the top of which is withering. Cheval — ; broken-kneed horse.

couronnement (koo-ro-n-mān), n.m., crowning, coronation ; completion ; crowning, coping (of walls) ; cap (of blocks) ; (nav.) taffrail of a ship.

couronner, v.a., to crown ; to decree a crown ; to award a prize ; to wreath ; (arch.) to cap. — de fleurs ; to crown with flowers. La fin couronne l'œuvre ; all 's well that ends well.

se **couronner**, v.r., to be crowned, to wear a crown ; to begin to wither at the top (of trees) ; to be broken-kneed, to come down (of a horse).

couronnure, n.f., crown (on a stag's head).

courre, n.m., (hunt.) starting-place ; hunting or coursing country.

courre, v.a., (hunt.) to run ; to hunt. Laisser — ; to slip the hounds.

courrier, n.m., courier, post, post-boy ; messenger. — de la malle ; mail-cart driver. Jour de — ; post-day. Par le — de ce jour ; by to-day's post. Par le retour du or par retour de — ; by return of post. L'heure du — ; post-time. Faire son — ; to write one's letters. Lire or dépouiller son — ; to read one's letters.

courrière, n.f., (l.u.) wanderer ; forerunner, harbinger ; messenger.

courroi, n.m., roller, tenter (used by dyers).

courroie, n.f., strap, thong ; belt, band. Allonger la — ; to make the most of one's money. Serrer la — à quelqu'un ; to curtail any one's allowance. Lâcher la — ; to give rein, to give rope.

courroucer, v.a., to provoke to anger, to incense ; to irritate. Flots courroucés ; angry waves.

se **courroucer**, v.r., to become angry.

courroux, n.m., wrath, anger, rage. Être en — ; to be angry.

courroyage, n.m., tentering.

courroyer, v.a., to tenter, to stretch stuffs just dyed.

courroyeur, n.m., one who stretches stuffs just dyed.

cours, n.m., course, stream, current, running, vent, scope ; public drive ; vogue ; currency (of coin) ; progress ; continuation ; term, space ; lectures, course of lectures ; (com.) market price ; (nav.) voyage. Donner un libre — à sa fureur ; to give full vent to one's anger. Le — du soleil est d'orient en occident ; the course of the sun is from east to west. Ce bruit a eu — ; the rumor was current. Donner — à ; to give currency to. Salle de — ; lecture-room. Faire un — ; to give a course of lectures. Suivre un — ; to attend a course of lectures. Ce jeune homme a fini ses — ; this young man has finished his studies. — d'eau ; stream ; watercourse. — de ventre ; looseness of the bowels. Avoir son — ; to take its course (of a disease). — légal ; legal tender. Dernier — ; closing price. Premier — ; opening price. Obtenir le — ; (com.) to command a price. Voyage de long — ; ocean travel ; voyage to foreign parts.

course, n.f., race, running ; run ; career ; tilt ; coursing, hunting, chase ; cruise, cruising, incursion, privateering ; journey, walk ; excursion, jaunt ; round, call, errand ; tour ; fare ; course ; (nav.) cruise ; length of the stroke (of a piece of machinery). Il est léger à la — ; he is a swift runner. Surpasser à la — ; to outrun. — de bague ; running at the ring. — de chevaux ;

horse-race. *Champ de* —; race-course. — *au clocher;* steeple-chase. *Une* — *à pied;* a footrace. — *de chars;* chariot-race. — *de haies;* hurdle-race. *Aller en* —; to go upon a cruise. *Vaisseau armé en* —; ship armed for cruising, privateer. *Etre en* —; to be out. *Faire des* —*s;* to go on errands, to pay calls. *Faire une* —*à cheval;* to take a ride. *Faire une* —*à pied;* to walk out on foot. *Prendre un fiacre à la* —; to take a hackney coach by the drive. *Lutte à la* —; foot-match.

coursier, *n.m.,* charger, steed ; (nav.) bow, bow-chase ; float-board.

coursive, *n.f.,* (nav.) waist; passage ; halfdeck.

courson, *n.m.,* shoot cut down to three or four eyes ; vine-shoot.

court, -e, *adj.,* short ; scanty; brief, concise, curt, succinct ; narrow ; limited. *Etre* — *d'argent;* to be short of money. *Avoir la vue* —*e;* to be near-sighted. *Il est revenu avec sa* —*e honte;* he came back unsuccessful. *Il veut la faire* —*e et bonne;* he wishes to have a short but a merry life.

court, *n.m.,* the shortest way. *Savoir le* — *et le long d'une affaire;* to know the long and the short of an affair. *Prendre le plus* —; to take the shortest way.

court, *adv.,* short. *S'arrêter tout* —; to stop short. *Tourner* —; to turn short. *Pour le plus* —; to be short. *Couper* — *à quelqu'un;* to cut any one short. *Demeurer tout* —; to stop short. *Tenir quelqu'un de* —; to keep anyone under. *Tout* —; only that, and no more. *A* — *de;* short of.

courtage, *n.m.,* (com.) business of a broker ; brokerage, commission. — *de change;* billbrokerage. *Faire le* —; to carry on the business of a broker.

courtaud, -e, *adj.,* thick-set, dumpy ; docked, crop-eared (of dogs, horses). *Etriller quelqu'un en chien;* to give any one a good licking.

courtaud, *n.m.,* -**e,** *n.f.,* short, thick-set person. — *de boutique;* shop drudge, counterjumper. [In the latter sense, *courtaud* is not used in the feminine.]

courtauder, *v.a.,* to dock, to crop (horses, &c.).

*****court-bouillon,** *n.m.,* (—*s*-—*s*) a wine sauce to boil fish in.

court-bouton, *n. m.,* (—*s*-—*s*) peg (of a plow).

courte-botte, *n.m.,* (—*s*-—*s*) shrimp of a fellow.

courte-boule, *n.f.,* short bowls.

courte-haleine, *n.f.,* shortness of breath, asthma.

courtement, *adv.,* (l.u.) shortly, briefly.

*****courte-paille,** *n.f.,* cut (wisp of straw). *Tirer à la* —; to draw cuts, lots.

courtepointe, *n.f.,* counterpane, quilt.

courtepointier (-tié), *n.m.,* quilt-maker.

courtier, *v.a.,* to buy and sell as a broker, to act as a commission agent.

courtier (-tié), *n.m.,* broker ; agent. — *de change;* bill-broker, money-broker. — *non breveté,* — *marron;* unlicensed broker. — *maritime;* ship-broker. — *pour les denrées coloniales;* colonial broker. — *d'assurances, d'actions;* insurance, share, broker. — *pour les sucres;* sugar-broker. — *de mariage;* matrimonial agent. — *electoral;* electioneering agent ; canvasser.

courtière, *n.f.,* matrimonial agent, go-between.

courtil, *n.m.,* croft (small field).

courtilière, *n.f.,* mole-cricket.

*****courtille,** *n.f.,* tea-gardens.

courtine, *n.f.,* (fort.) curtain.

courtisan, *n.m.,* courtier.

courtisane, *n.f.,* courtesan.

courtisanerie, *n.f.,* court flattery; toadyism.

courtisanesque, *adj.,* courtier-like.

courtiser, *v.a.,* to court, to pay court to, to woo, to flatter. — *une femme;* to make love to a woman.

court-jointé, -e, *adj.,* (— -—*s*) short-jointed.

court-mancher, *v.a.,* (cook.) to skewer.

court-monté, -e, *adj.,* low-backed (of horses).

courtois, -e, *adj.,* courteous, polite, wellbred. *Armes* —*es;* blunt arms.

courtoisement (-toaz-mān), *adv.,* in a courteous manner, courteously.

courtoisie, *n.f.,* courteousness, courtesy, kindness, good turn.

à **courts jours,** *adv.,* having a few days to run (of bills). *Lettre de change à* —; bill which has but a few days to run.

court-vêtu, -e, *adj.,* (—-—*s*) in short petticoats.

court-vite, *n.m.,* (—). *V.* **coure-vite.**

couscous, *n.m.,* (n.p.) couscous (Arabian dish).

couseuse, *n.f.,* sewer, stitcher (of books).

cousin, *n.m.,* -**e,** *n.f.,* cousin; friend, crony. — *germain;* first cousin, cousin german. — *au troisième degré;* third cousin.

cousin, *n.m.,* (ent.) gnat.

cousinage, *n.m.,* relationship of cousins, relation, kindred.

cousiner, *v.a.,* to call cousin.

se **cousiner,** *v.r.,* to call one another cousin.

cousiner, *v.n.,* to sponge, to live on others, to be friends, cronies.

cousinerie, (koo-zi-n-rî), *n.f.,* host of cousins.

cousinière, *n.f.,* gnat-veil, mosquito-net.

cousoir, *n.m.,* (book-bind.) sewing-press.

coussin, *n.m.,* cushion, hassock; pad ; (min., surg.) bolster. — *de mire;* bed of a cannon.

coussinet, *n.m.,* small cushion; pad ; iron wedge; (surg.) bolster; (arch.) cushion ; (railways) chair; pillion (of saddles); (bot.) whortleberry; cranberry.

cousu, -e, *part.,* sewed, stitched; seamed; closed. *Ses finesses sont cousues de fil blanc;* his tricks are very shallow. *Bouche cousue;* mum's the word. *Etre* — *d'argent;* to be rolling in money.

coût, *n.m.,* (jur.) cost, charge; price, expense.

coûtant, *adj.,* of the cost. *Prix* —; prime cost.

couteau, *n.m.,* knife; ⊙short sword, dagger. — *à découper,* — *à dépecer,* carving-knife. *A* —*x tirés;* at daggers drawn — *pliant;* claspknife. — *à ressort;* spring-knife. — *à deux tranchants;* two-edged knife. *Planche à* — *x;* knife-board. *Donner un coup de* — *à quelqu'un;* to stab anyone with a knife. *Aiguiser ses* —*x;* to prepare for the engagement. — *poignard;* dagger-knife. *Ils en sont à* —*x tirés;* they are at daggers drawn.

coutelas (koo-tlâ), *n.m.,* cutlass.

coutelier (-lié), *n.m.,* cutler.

coutelière, *n.f.,* knife-case; cutler's wife.

coutellerie (koo-tèl-rî), *n.f.,* cutler's shop; cutlery, cutler's ware.

coûter, *v.n.,* to cost; to stand in; to be expensive; to be painful, troublesome, mortifying; to be an effort, a trial. *Il lui en coûte beaucoup de dire cela;* it is very painful to him to say that. *L'argent ne lui coûte rien;* he knows not the value of money. *Que coûte-t-il de souhaiter?* there is nothing so easy as wishing. *Tout lui coûte;* everything is an effort to him. *Coûte que coûte;* come what may; at any price. *Rien ne lui coûte;* he spares no trouble; he sticks at nothing.

coûter, *v.a.,* to cost. *Cela lui coûta la vie;* that cost her her life, or him his life.

coûteusement, *adv.,* expensively.

coûteu-x, -se, *adj.,* expensive, costly.

coutier (-tié), *n.m.,* tick-maker.

coutil (koo-ti), *n.m.,* ticking, duck. *Fil de* —; drill.

coutre, *n.m.,* plow - share, coulter ; (nav.) cutter.

coutrier, *n.m.,* subsoil-plow.

coutume, *n.f.,* custom ; habit ; practice, usage; ⊙tax; collection of customs. *Selon ma* —; according to my custom. *Comme de* —; as usual. *Avoir — de ;* to be accustomed to. *Une fois n'est pas* —; once does not constitute a habit; one swallow does not make a summer.

coutumi-er, -ère, *adj.,* common, ordinary, customary; accustomed, used; wonted, habitual. *Pays* —; country governed by common law. *Il est — du fait ;* it is not the first time he has done it; he is an old offender, an old hand.

⊙**coutumier,** *n.m.,* customary (book of common law).

couture, *n.f.,* seam; sewing, stitching; scar. *Rabattre les —s ;* to flatten the seams. *Ils ont été battus à plate —;* they were beaten hollow. *— ouverte ;* (nav.) open seam.

couturer, *v.a.,* to seam. *Il a le visage couturé ;* his face is seamed, scarred.

couturier, *n.* and *adj. m.,* (anat.) sartorious muscle ; tailor's muscle ; sempster, sewer ; ladies' tailor.

couturière, *n.f.,* dressmaker, seamstress, needle-woman.

couvage, *n.m.,* brooding, sitting.

couvain, *n.m.,* eggs of bees, or of bugs ; breeding-cells, etc.

couvaison, *n.f.,* brooding-time, sitting.

couvée, *n.f.,* nest of eggs; brood, covey ; (b.s.) generation, progeny. *D'une* —; at one brood.

couvent, *n.m.,* convent, monastery, nunnery.

couver, *v.a.,* to sit on, to hatch; to brood on, to incubate, to brood, to brew. *— quelqu'un des yeux ;* to look tenderly at anyone ; to devour with one's eyes; to gloat over. *— de mauvais desseins ;* to brew evil designs. *— une maladie ;* to be sickening for an illness.

se **couver,** *v.r.,* to brood, to sit, to lie hid, to hatch.

couver, *v.n.,* to brood, to sit, to lie hid; to lurk; to smolder; to prepare secretly.

couvercle, *n.m.,* cover, lid ; (tech.) cap, shutter.

couverseau, *n.m.,* drum-cover (of a mill).

couvert, *n. m.,* dinner things; breakfast things; cover (plate, spoon, knife, and fork); case (containing a spoon, knife, and fork); shelter; covert, shady place, thicket; cover, wrapper. *Mettre le* —; to lay the cloth. *Oter le* —; to remove the cloth, to clear the table. *Donner le — à quelqu'un ;* to shelter anyone. *Table de dix —s ;* table laid for ten. *Un — de plus ;* another knife and fork.

couvert, -e, *part.,* covered; (fort.) covered, hid, hidden, secret; close, concealed; cloudy, overcast (of the weather); obscure, ambiguous (of words); clad, deep-colored (of wine). — *de plaies ;* covered with sores. *Il est toujours bien* —; he is always well clothed. *Mots —s ;* ambiguous words. *A mots —s ;* in innuendoes. *Pays* —; woody country. *Chemin* —; (fort.) covert-way. *Lieu* —; shady place. *Temps* —; cloudy weather. *A* —; under cover; sheltered, secure. *Se mettre à* —; to shelter one's self. *Etre à* —; to have good security, to be safe.

couverte, *n.f.,* glaze, glazing.

⊙**couvertement,** *adv.,* covertly, secretly.

couverture, *n.f.,* cover (of a book); wrapper; coverlet, counterpane, quilt, bed-clothes ; blanketing; rug, cloak, blind ; (com.) guaranty, security. *— de laine ;* blanket. *— de cheval ;* horse-cloth. *— piquée ;* quilt. *— de selle ;* saddle-cloth. *Faire la* —; to turn down the bed.

couverturier, *n.m.,* blanket-maker.

couvet, *n.m.,* earthenware foot-stove.

couveuse, *n.f.,* brooding-hen.

couvi, *adj.,* addle, addled. *Œuf* —; rotten egg.

couvoir, *n.m.,* incubator.

couvre-chef, *n. m.,* (———*s*) covering for the head, headgear, head-dress, kerchief.

couvre-feu, *n.m.,* (—) curfew, curfew-bell; fire-cover, fire-plate.

couvre-lumière, *n.m.,* (———*s*) (artil.) apron.

couvre-pieds, *n.m.,* (—) foot-coverlet.

couvre-plat, *n.m.,* (— - —*s*) dish-cover.

couvreur, *n.m.,* tiler, slater. *— en ardoise ;* slater. *— en chaume ;* thatcher. *— en tuiles ;* tiler.

couvrir (couvrant, couvert), *v.a.,* to cover; to envelop; to wrap up; to muffle up; (com., milit.) to cover; (of horse) to serve, to leap; to excuse, to palliate; to defray (expenses); to overflow, to overspread; to overrun; to protect; to copulate; to cloak, to keep secret, to disguise. *— un toit ;* to roof. *— de honte ;* to load with shame. *— sa faute ;* to palliate one's fault. *Un bon général doit savoir — sa marche ;* a good general should know how to conceal his march.

se **couvrir,** *v.r.,* to cover oneself, to put on one's hat, to be covered ; to cover *or* defend oneself ; to conceal oneself ; to get under cover ; to be overcast (of the weather) ; to reimburse oneself. *Couvrez-vous ;* put your hat on. *Le temps se couvre ;* the weather is becoming overcast.

covenant (kov-nän), *n.m.,* covenant.

covenantaire, *n.m.,* covenanter.

covendeu-r, *n.m.,* **-se,** *n.f.,* joint-vendor.

cowpox, *n.m.,* cow-pox.

coxal, *adj.,* (anat.) of the hip, coxal, iliac.

crabe, *n.m.,* crab.

crabier, *n.m.,* crab-eater.

crac, *int.,* creaking noise, crack, pop ! *—! le voilà parti ;* he was off in the twinkling of an eye ! *or* before you could say Jack Robinson ! *Monsieur de* —; Baron Munchausen.

crachat, *n.m.,* spittle, expectoration ; slight materials (of buildings); star, grand cross.

crachement (krash-män), *n.m.,* spitting. *— de sang ;* spitting of blood.

craché, -e, *part.adj. Tout* —, *toute* —*e ;* the very image of; the dead spit of.

cracher, *v.a.,* to spit, to spit out, to utter, to come out with; to come down with, to fork out (money). *— du coton ;* (pop.) to have a thirst on.

cracher, *v.n.,* to spit, to sputter (of speech, of pens). *— au bassin ;* to contribute. *— au nez, au visage, de quelqu'un ;* to spit in anyone's face. *— en l'air ;* to be hoist with one's own petard. *C'est à — dessus ;* it is a mean, despicable thing.

cracheu-r, *n.m.,* **-se,** *n.f.,* spitter.

crachoir, *n.m.,* spittoon.

crachotement, *n.m.,* frequent spitting.

crachoter, *v.n.,* to spit often.

craie, *n.f.,* chalk. *Marquer avec de la* —; to chalk.

craïer, *n.m.,* (nav.) pole-masted vessel.

craillement, *n.m.,* cawing (of crows).

crailler, *v.n.,* to caw.

craindre (craignant, craint), *v.a.,* to fear, to apprehend; to be afraid of, to dread, to stand in awe *or* fear of; to be afraid; to dislike; to be unable to bear. *Il craint d'être découvert ;* he is afraid of being discovered. *Il craint que sa femme ne meure ;* he fears his wife will die. *Je ne crains pas de le dire ;* I do not hesitate to say so. *Ces arbres craignent le froid ;* these trees dread the cold. *Se faire — de quelqu'un ;* to be held in dread by anyone. *A* —; to be feared; dangerous; to be avoided.

crainte, *n.f.*, fear, dread, awe, apprehension. *Retenir quelqu'un par la —;* to keep any one in awe. *Sans —;* fearlessly. *Avec —;* fearfully, in terror, in dread. *— de, de — de;* for fear of. *De — que;* for fear of; for fear that, lest. *De — d'être surpris;* for fear of being surprised. *De — qu'il ne le fasse;* lest he should do it.

crainti-f, -ve, *adj.*, fearful, apprehensive, timid, timorous, cowardly.

craintivement, *adv.*, fearfully, timorously.

*cramaillèr, *n.m.*, (horl.) notch-wheel.

crambe *or* **crambé**, *n.m.*, (bot.) colza, sea kale.

cramoisi, *n.m.*, crimson.

cramoisi, -e, *adj.*, crimson; red, scarlet.

crampe, *n.f.*, cramp; cramp-fish, numb-fish; (nav.) cramp-iron; hook of a block. *Avoir des —s d'estomac;* griping; cramping. *Tirer sa —;* (pop.) to bolt, to run away.

crampon, *n.m.*, (bot.) fulcrum, prop; (farriery) calkin; (hort.) climbing-spur; (mach.) click; cramp-iron, cramp-hook; hold-fast; grappling iron; brace. *— de fer à cheval;* frost-nails of a horseshoe.

cramponné, -e, *part.*, clinging to; (her.) having half a potence at both ends, cramponée; (farriery) with calkins.

cramponner, *v.a.*, to cramp, to fasten with a cramp-iron. *— un cheval;* to shoe a horse with frost-nails, calkins.

se cramponner, *v.r.*, to cling, to hold fast, to fasten to anything; to cling like grim death to.

cramponnet, *n.m.*, little cramp-iron, tack, loop. *— de targette;* lock staple.

cran, *n.m.*, notch; cog; (bot.) scurvy-grass, cochlearia, horse-radish; (print.) nick; (vet.) notch, ridge. *D'un —;* by a notch. *Baisser d'un —;* to take a peg lower. *Monter d'un —;* to rise a peg higher.

crâne, *n.m.*, skull, brain-pan, cranium; (pop.) madcap, swaggerer, blusterer. *adj.*, bold, brave; famous, capital, spicy.

crânement, *adv.*, swaggeringly; capitally, in style, famously, fearlessly, unblushingly.

crânerie (crâ-n-rî), *n.f.*, (pop.) swaggering, blustering, vaporing.

crangon, *n.m.*, shrimp.

craniologie *or* **cranologie**, *n.f.*, craniology.

craniologique, *adj.*, craniological.

craniologiste, *n.m.*, craniologist.

craniomètre, *n.m.*, craniometer.

craniométrie, *n.f.*, craniometry.

craniométrique, *adj.*, craniometrical.

cranioscopie, *n.f.*, cranioscopy.

cranologie, *n.f.* *V.* **craniologie**.

cranson, *n.m.*, scurvy-grass. *— rustique;* horse-radish.

crapaud, *n.m.*, toad; urchin, brat, fellow; low-seat chair; (artil.) mortar-carriage; (vet.) crepane, maltworm. *La bave d'un —;* toad-spittle. *C'est un vilain —;* he is a mean, despicable fellow. *Il est chargé d'argent comme un — de plumes;* all the money he has he can put in his eye. *— de gouvernail;* (nav.) goose-neck. *— de mer;* toad-fish; hog-fish. *— pêcheur;* fishing frog. *— volant;* churn-owl. *— de timon;* pole-end (of a carriage).

*crapaudaille, *n.f.*, a gang of vagabonds, riff-raff. *V.* **crépodaille**.

crapaudière, *n.f.*, toad-hole; (fig.) low, swampy place.

crapaudine, *n.f.*, (min.) bufonite, toad-stone, wolf's-tooth; leaden grating; valve of an escape pipe; (vet.) crepane, crack; (bot.) sideritis, iron-wort; (mec.) socket. *A la —;* cut open and broiled; spatch-cocked.

crapelet, *n.m.*, young toad; toadlet.

crapone, *n.f.*, (horl.) square flat file.

crapoussin, *n.m., -e, n.f.*, scrubby little man *or* woman, dwarf, bloated little shrimp.

crapule, *n.f.*, low vulgar debauchery; intemperance; gluttony, drunkenness; low, debauched people; blackguards.

crapuler, *v.n.*, to live in vice, to fuddle or drink hard, to give one's self up to all sorts of low debauchery.

crapuleusement, *adv.*, dissolutely.

crapuleu-x, -se, *adj.*, drunken, intemperate, vulgar, debauched; grossly vicious, dissolute.

craque, *n.f.*, fib, humbug, fudge, bouncer. *int.*, crack, bang.

craquelé, -e *adj.*, crackled, fissured (of china).

craqueler, *v.n.*, to crack; to crackle (of china).

craquelin (kra-klin), *n.m.*, cracknel.

craquelot (kra-klo), *n.m.*, red-herring.

craqueloti-er, *n.m.*, **-ère** (kra-klo-tièr), *n.f.*, herring-curer.

craquelure, *n.f.*, fissure, crack (in china).

craquement (krak-mān), *n.m.*, crack, cracking noise, crunching; crepitation, creaking, snapping (of trees, boughs). *Un — de dents;* a chattering of the teeth.

craquer, *v.n.*, to creak, to crunch, to crack, to crackle, to snap; to chatter (of the teeth); to tell a lie, to boast; to draw the long bow. *Faire — ses doigts;* to make one's fingers snap.

craquerie, *n.f.*, cracking, boasting, drawing the long bow, fiction, story, fib, fudge.

craquètement, *n.m.*, crackling; gabbling (of the stork and other birds).

craqueter (kra-kté), *v.n.*, to crackle, to crepitate; to gabble (of some birds). *Le laurier craquète au feu;* laurel crackles in the fire.

craquette, *n.f.*, notch (of a tailor); scum (on melted butter).

craqueu-r, *n.m.*, **-se**, *n.f.*, noisy, boasting fellow; bouncer, braggart.

crase, *n.f.*, (gram.) crasis, contraction of two syllables into one; (med.) crasis.

crasiologie, *n.f.*, crasiology.

crassane, *n.f.*, cresane (a sort of pear).

crasse, *n.f.*, dirt, filth, scurf; squalor; niggardliness, stinginess; coat of filth, layer of dirt; rusticity, bad manners; (of coals) ashes, cinders. *— de la tête;* dandruff. *La — des métaux;* the dross, scum, scale, of metals.

crasse, *adj.*, gross, thick, coarse, crass. *Une ignorance —;* gross *or* crass ignorance.

crasser, *v.a.*, to foul, to dirty (of fire-arms).

se crasser, *v.r.*, to become foul (of fire-arms).

crasseu-x, -se, *adj.*, dirty, filthy, nasty, squalid, rusty; sordid, stingy, mean. *Cheveux —;* greasy hair.

crasseu-x, *n.m.*, **-se**, *n.f.*, sloven, slut; niggard, miser, skinflint. *Un —;* a filthy fellow.

crassule, *n.f.*, (bot.) crassula.

cratère, *n.m.*, (geol.) crater; (antiq.) bowl, cup; (astron.) Crater, Cup.

craticulation, *n.f.*, (paint.) squaring.

craticuler, *v.a.*, (paint.) to square. *V.* **graticuler**.

cratirites, *n.f. pl.*, wild Grecian figs.

craupécherot *or* **corbeau pêcheur**, *n.m.*, (orni.) bald-buzzard, osprey, fishing-eagle.

cravache, *n.f.*, horsewhip, riding-whip.

cravan, *n.m.*, (orni.) brent-barnacle, brand-goose, brent.

cravate, *n.f.*, cravat, neck-tie, neckcloth, neckerchief; (of curtains) band. *— d'un drapeau;* knot of a flagstaff. *— longue;* scarf.

cravate, *n.m.*, Croat; Croatian horse. *Régiment de —s;* formerly regiment of light cavalry; regiment of Croats. *adj.*, Croatian. *Cheval —;* Croatian horse.

cravater, *v.a.*, to put any one's neck-tie on for him; to go round the neck; to fit.

se cravater, *v.r.*, to put on one's neck-tie.

crayère, *n.f.*, chalk-pit.

crayeu-x, -se, *adj.*, chalky.

crayon, *n.m.*, chalk ; pencil ; pencil drawing ; portrait in crayons ; description of a person, manner, style ; sketch, rough-draft, outline. — *noir ;* blacklead-pencil. — *d'ardoise ;* slate-pencil. — *de pastel ;* pastel, crayon. *Affûter un —, donner une pointe à un —;* to point a pencil. *Au —;* in pencil.

crayonner, *v.a.*, to draw with a pencil ; to sketch rudely or imperfectly ; to sketch, to trace the outline, to chalk, to delineate ; to paint badly.

crayonneur, *n.m.*, (b.s.) dauber.

crayonneu-x, -se, *adj.*, chalky.

cré, *adj.*, abbreviation of *sacré.*

créadier, *n.m.*, sort of drag-net.

créance, *n.f.*, credence, credit, trust, belief ; debt, money owing ; influence ; (hunt.) command. *Lettres de —;* letter of credence, credentials. *Lettre de —;* letter of credit. *Donner — à une chose ;* to give credit to a thing. *Chien de bonne —;* dog well in hand. *Oiseau de peu de —;* (hawking) bird that will not come back to its master.

créanci-er, *n.m.,* **-ère,** *n.f.,* creditor ; (jur.) covenantee, obligee. — *hypothécaire ;* mortgagee. — *importun ;* dun.

créat, *n.m.,* (man.) riding-master's assistant.

créateur, *n.m.,* creator, maker.

créat-eur, -rice, *adj.*, creative, creating, inventive. *Il a le génie —;* he has an inventive genius.

créatine, *n.f.,* (chem.) creatine.

création, *n. f.,* creation ; production ; foundation ; establishment.

créature, *n.f.,* creature ; thing ; dependant, tool.

⊙**crébèbe,** *n.m. V.* **cubèbe.**

crécelle, *n.f.,* rattle.

crécerelle, *n.f.,* (orni.) kestrel, windhover.

crèche, *n.f.,* crèche, manger, crib ; day-nursery ; foundling-hospital ; (arch.) starling.

crédence, *n.f.,* credence, credence-table ; buttery, pantry, safe.

crédencier, *n.m.,* pantler, clerk of the buttery, buttery-keeper.

crédibilité, *n.f.,* credibility.

crédit, *n.m.,* credit ; trust ; authority, interest, influence, patronage, sway, power ; repute, esteem, name, vogue, favor, request. *Lettre de —;* letter of credit. *Faire —, vendre, donner, à —;* to credit, to give trust, to give credit. *Ouvrir un — à quelqu'un ;* to open an account with any one. *Il a bon —;* his credit is good. *Avoir — en banque ;* to have funds in the bank. *Faire — de la main à la bourse ;* to trust no farther than one can see. — *est mort ;* old Trust is dead. *Cela l'a mis en —;* that brought him into repute. *Etre en grand —;* to be in high repute. *A —;* on credit, on trust ; to no purpose ; gratuitously, without proof, without ground, at random. *Avoir du —;* to have influence.

créditer, *v.a.,* to trust ; to enter upon the credit side (of an account), to credit. *Etre crédité sur une ville ;* to have letters of credit on a town.

créditeur, *n.m.,* creditor.

créditeur, *adj. Compte —;* creditor's account.

credo, *n.m.,* (—) creed, belief.

crédule, *adj.,* credulous, easy of belief.

crédulement, *adv.,* with credulity, credulously.

crédulité, *n.f.,* credulity.

créer, *v.a.,* to create ; to invent ; to imagine ; to produce ; to beget ; to appoint ; to establish. — *un chevalier ;* to dub a knight. — *une rente ;* to invest funds for an annuity. *Se — des moyens ;* to find means. *Se — des ressources ;* to find resources.

*****crémaillère,** *n.f.,* hook, pot-hanger, pot-hook ; (horl.) rack ; (tech.) rack, toothed rack. *La —*

d'une cric ; the rack of a screw-jack. *Chaise à —;* spring-back chair. *Pendre la —;* to give a house-warming. *Aller pendre la —;* to go to a house-warming.

*****crémaillon,** *n.m.,* small pot-hook.

crémaster, *n.* and *adj. m.,* (anat.) cremaster.

crémation, *n.f.,* cremation.

crème, *n.f.,* cream ; the best part of a thing, the cream. — *fouettée ;* whipt cream. *Fromage à la —;* cream-cheese. — *de tartre ;* cream of tartar. *Pot à —;* cream-jug.

crément, *n.m.,* (gram.) increase (of a word).

crémer, *v.n.,* to cream, to gather cream.

crémerie, *n.f.,* milk-shop, dairy.

crémeu-x, -se, *adj.,* creamy.

crémi-er, *n.m.,* **-ère,** *n.f.,* milkman, milk-woman ; dairy man or woman. *f.,* cream-jug, milk-jug.

*****crémillée,** *n.f.,* ward (of a lock).

crémone, *n.m.,* a Cremona violin.

crémone, *n.f.,* window-fastening, spring.

crénage, *n.m.,* (letter-founding) kerning.

créné, -e, *adj.,* (bot.) crenated, indented.

créneau, *n.m.,* battlement ; embrasure ; loop-hole.

crénelage, *n.m.,* (coin.) milling.

crénelé, -e, *part. adj.,* (her.) embattled ; loop-holed ; indented, notched ; (of wheels) cogged ; (of coins) milled ; (bot.) denticulated, crenated.

créneler (kré-n-lé), *v.a.,* to embattle ; to loop-hole ; to indent, to notch. — *une roue ;* to tooth, to cog, a wheel. — *une pièce de monnaie ;* to mill a piece of money.

crénelure (kré-n-lur), *n.f.,* crenelation ; notching ; (anat.) indentation ; (bot.) crenature ; crenel.

créner, *v.a.,* (type-founding) to kern.

crénerie, *n.f.,* (type-founding) kerning.

crénilabre, *n.m.,* (ich.) gold-finny.

crénom, *int.,* by George ! by Jove ! hang it !

crénon, *n.m.,* first splitting of a block of slate.

crénulé, -e, *adj.,* notched, indentated ; crenulate.

crénure, *n.f.,* (print.) hole in the bar of a frame.

créole, *n.m.f.,* Creole ; West Indian.

créosote, *n.f.,* (chem.) creosote.

crépage, *n.m.,* glossing of crape ; crisping.

crêpe, *n.m.,* crape ; (fig.) vail. *Il porte un — à son chapeau ;* he wears a crape hat-band. — *crêpé ;* crisped crape. — *lisse ;* smooth crape.

crêpe, *n.f.,* pancake.

crêper, *v.a.,* to crisp, to crape, to frizzle. *Cheveux crêpés ;* frizzed hair.

crépi, *n.m.,* rough-cast, parget.

*saint-***crépin,** *n.m.,* Saint Crispin ; kit (of a journeyman shoemaker). *Perdre son saint-—;* to lose one's all.

crépine, *n.f.,* fringe (woven on the top) ; caul covering the bowels of sheep. *A —;* fringy.

crépir, *v.a.,* to parget, to rough-cast, to plaster. — *le cuir ;* to work leather in grain, to pummel a hide on the flesh side. — *le crin ;* to crisp hair.

crépissage, *n.m.,* (mas.) plastering, pargeting, rough-casting. [ing ; parget.

crépissement, *n.m.,* pargeting, rough-cast-

crépissure, *n.f.,* pargeting, rough-casting.

crépitant, -e, *adj.,* crepitating, crackling.

crépitation, *n.f.,* or **crépitement,** *n.m.,* crepitation, crackling.

crépodaille or **crapaudaille,** *n.f.,* thin crape, gauze-crape. [hair-pad.

crépon, *n.m.,* crepon, frizette, rouge-puff,

crépu, -e, *adj.,* crisped, frizzled, crisp, crispy, woolly. *Les nègres ont les cheveux —s ;* negroes have woolly hair.

crépusculaire, *adj.*, crepuscular. *Lumière* —; twilight.

crépuscule, *n.m.*, crepuscule, twilight; dawn. — *du soir*; owl-light, twilight.

créque, *n.f.*, sloe.

créquier, *n.m.*, sloe tree.

cresane, *n.f.* *V.* **crassane**.

crescendo, *adv.*, (mus.) crescendo.

créseau, *n.m.*, species of woolen stuff, kersey.

cresserelle, *n.f.* *V.* **crécerelle**.

cresson, *n.m.*, cress, cresses, water-cress. — *alénois, de jardin;* dittander; garden-cress. — *doré;* golden saxifrage. — *des prés;* lady's smock. — *sauvage;* water-plantain. — *de rivière;* water-rocket.

cressonnière, *n.f.*, cress-bed.

crésus, *n.m.*, (—) very rich man. *C'est un* —; he is a very Crœsus.

crétacé, -e, *adj.*, cretaceous.

crête, *n.f.*, crest, tuft, comb of a cock *or* hen; top-knot; (anat.) ridge; (arch.) ridge; top; bank; coping. — *de morue,* head-piece (of a cod). *Lever la* —; to be conceited; to hold one's head high. *Baisser la* —; to come down a peg. *Rabaisser la* — *à quelqu'un;* to bring anyone down a peg. — *d'un fossé;* bank on the side of a ditch. — *d'une montagne;* ridge of a mountain. — *d'une grosse vague;* crest of a billow. — *marine;* samphire. — *de coq;* cock's-comb; hog's-ear shell. *Crête-de-coq,* (—*s*—) louse-wort.

crêté, -e, *adj.*, crested, tufted.

crêteler, *v.n.*, (of hens) to cackle.

crétin, *n.m.*, (med.) cretin; idiot, dunce. *C'est un* —; he is a dunce.

crétiniser, *v.a.*, to brutalize, to brutify, to make an idiot of.

se **crétiniser**, *v.r.*, to become brutified; to become stupid.

crétinisme, *n.m.*, cretinism, idiocy.

crétique, *adj.*, cretic.

crétois, -e, *n.* and *adj.*, Cretan.

cretonne, *n.f.*, fine linen, long-cloth, cretonne.

cretons, *n.m.pl.*, residuum of melted tallow and kitchen-stuff; graves. — *de lard;* scrapings.

creusage, *n.m.*, deepening, hollowing; plowing; digging.

creusement (kreuz-măn), *n.m.*, (l.u.) digging; excavation, hollowing, deepening.

creuser, *v.a.*, to dig, to delve; to hollow, to make hollow, to excavate, to scoop out; to sink, to deepen. — *la terre;* to dig the ground. — *un fossé;* to dig a ditch. — *un puits;* to sink a well. — *une question;* to examine a question thoroughly.

se **creuser**, *v.r.*, to become hollow. *Se* — *le cerveau;* to rack one's brain.

creuser, *v.n.*, to dig. — *sous terre;* to dig underground. — *bien avant;* to dig deep.

creuset, *n.m.*, crucible, melting-pot; (chem.) test, trial. *Passer par le* —; to assay, to refine.

creux, *n.m.*, hollow, cavity; pit, hole, chasm; gutter, delve; mold; mortar, trough; pit of the stomach. — *planté d'arbres;* dell planted with trees. — *profond dans une mine;* groove in a mine. *Le* — *de la main;* the hollow of the hand. *Il a un bon* —; he has a fine bass voice. — *d'un vaisseau* (nav.); depth of a ship's hold. — *d'une voile;* cavity of a sail (which retains the wind).

creu-x, -se, *adj.*, hollow, cavernous; deep; empty, unsubstantial, airy, fantastical, chimerical, extravagant. *Des yeux* —; eyes sunk in the head. *Avoir les joues* —*ses;* to have hollow cheeks. *Il a le ventre* —; his belly is empty. *Un fossé* — *de trois pieds;* a ditch three feet deep. *Esprit* —; *cerveau* —; cracked-brain, empty head. *Pensées —ses;* airy notions. *Viande* —*se;* frothy, unsubstantial food. *Songer* —; to be in a brown study.

*crevaille, *n.f.*, guzzling, gormandizing, stuffing; tuck out, blow out.

crevaison, *n.m.*, puncture (bicycle).

crevasse, *n.f.*, crevice, chink, rift, crack; gap, cranny; (vet.) malt-worm, cratches. *Des* —*s aux mains;* chaps.   [to make cracks.

crevasser, *v.a.*, to split, to crack; to chap; *se* **crevasser**, *v.r.*, to crack, to split, to gape, to become chapped.

crevé, -e, *n.m.*, *-e,* *n.f.*, (l.ex.) very fat man; bloated fellow. *Petit* —; fast young fellow; one used up, done up.

crevé, *n.m.*, opening, slash (in sleeves).

crève-cœur, *n.m.*, (—) heart-break, heart-breaking thing, heart-sore; heart-rending thing.

crever, *v.a.*, to burst, to break, to split, to crack, to rift, to tear, to rend; to stave in; to cram any one with victuals. — *une botte;* to burst a boot. — *les yeux à quelqu'un;* to put out any one's eyes. — *un cheval;* to kill a horse. *Cela vous crève les yeux;* that lies under your very nose (i.e., is obvious, self-evident).

crever, *v.n.*, to burst; to die, to perish. *C'est une médecine à faire* — *un cheval;* this medicine is enough to kill a horse. — *de graisse;* to be extremely fat. — *de chaud;* to be dying with heat. — *de rire;* to split one's sides with laughing. — *de faim;* to be dying with hunger. — *d'orgueil;* to be bursting with pride. — *de biens;* to wallow in wealth.

se **crever**, *v.r.*, to burst; to kill oneself. *Se* — *de boire et de manger;* to cram or stuff till one is ready to burst. *Se* — *de travail;* to overwork oneself.

crevet, *n.m.*, stay-lace with tags at both ends.

crevette, *n.f.*, prawn, shrimp.

cri, *n.m.*, cry; scream; screaming; roar, roaring; bawling, howling, yell, yelling, outcry, clamor; whine, whining; squeak, squeaking; opinion. — *de joie,* — *d'allégresse;* shout, shouting, hallooing, huzza, acclamation. — *aigre, aigu, perçant;* scream, shriek, squeak, shrill cry. *Les* —*s des femmes;* the squalling of women. — *de guerre;* watchword. — *d'armes;* (her.) motto. *Jeter un* —, *faire des* —*s, pousser un* —; to utter a cry, to cry out lustily; to raise an outcry; to complain loudly. *Demander à grands* —*s;* to demand with a loud voice. *Je poussai un grand* —; I shrieked out. *Jeter les hauts* —*s;* to cry out. *Le* — *de la nature;* the voice of nature. *Donner du* — *à la soie;* to sulphur silk. *A cor et à* —*s;* with hue and cry. *Il n'y a qu'un* — *sur son compte;* there is only one opinion about him.

criage, *n.m.*, public crying.

*criaillement, *n.m.*, act of wrangling; brawling; (of geese) gabbling.

*criailler, *v.n.*, to bawl, to brawl, to cry, to clamor; to scold, to chide; (of geese) to gabble.

*criaillerie, *n.f.*, brawling, clamoring, scolding, wrangling.

*criailleu-r, *n.m.*, *-se,* *n.f.*, brawler, bawler, wrangler; shrew, scold.

criant, -e, *adj.*, crying; glaring, shocking, shameful; noisy. *Injustice* —*e;* crying, daring injustice.

criard, -e, *adj.*, crying, bawling, squalling, noisy; brawling, clamorous, scolding; (paint.) discordant; shrill. *Dettes* —*es;* dribbling or small debts. *Voix* —*e;* shrill voice.

criard, *n.m.*, *-e,* *n.f.*, brawler, clamorer; scold, shrew.

criarde, *n.f.*, thick gummed cloth; varnished cloth.

criblage, *n.m.*, sifting.

crible, *n.m.*, sieve; riddle. *Percé comme un* —; as full of holes as a sieve; riddled.

cribler, *v.a.*, to sift, to riddle; to scan, to examine; to pepper (a person). — *de coups;* to shoot, run, or stab through and through. *Criblé* *de mitraille ;* riddled with shot. *Criblé de dettes ;* over head and ears in debt.

cribleu-r, *n.m.,* **-se,** *n.f.,* sifter.

cribleu-x, -se, *adj.,* (anat.) pierced like a sieve, sieve-like.

criblier, *n.m.,* sieve-maker.

criblure, *n.f.,* siftings.

cribration, *n.f.,* (chem.) cribration.

cribriforme, *adj.,* cribriform.

cric (krî), *n.m.,* lifting-jack, screw-jack, hand-screw ; little ratchet-wheel on which the braces of carriages are fixed. — *à baril ;* tilting-jack.

cric-crac (krik-krak), (onomatopœia) imitation of the creaking noise produced by breaking or tearing.

cricoïde, *n.m.* and *adj.,* (anat.) cricoid.

cri-cri, *n.m.,* (— —*s*) (pop.) (ent.) cricket ; (ornith.) bunting.

crid (krid), *n.m.* *V.* **criss.**

criée, *n.f.,* proclamation of sale ; auction. *Sa maison est en —;* his house is to be sold by auction. *Audience des —s ;* auction mart. *A la —;* by auction.

crier, *v.n.,* to cry, to cry out, to halloo, to shout, to bawl ; to scream, to shriek, to screech ; to squall, to clamor ; to squeak ; to call out ; to whine, to pule ; to complain loudly, to brawl, to exclaim ; to scold ; to huzza, to talk loudly ; to gabble (of geese) ; to screech (of owls) ; to troat (of deer) ; to chirp (of grasshoppers and other insects) ; to groan (of roe-bucks) ; to creak (of doors). — *aux armes ;* to cry to arms. — *au secours ;* to call out for help. — *au meurtre ;* to cry out murder. — *au voleur ;* to cry out thief. — *au feu ;* to cry out fire. — *à l'injustice ;* to exclaim against an injustice. — *au scandale ;* to inveigh against a scandal. — *gare ;* to cry out beware ! take care. — *misère ;* to plead poverty. — *miséricorde ;* to cry for mercy. — *famine ;* to cry out famine. — *à tue-tête, comme un perdu ;* to cry out ; to shriek at the top of one's voice or as loud as one can. — *bien fort ;* to cry out lustily. *Les boyaux lui crient ;* his bowels rumble. *Il crie avant qu'on l'écorche ;* he cries before he is hurt. *Tout le monde crie contre cela ;* everybody cries out against it.

crier, *v.a.,* to proclaim ; to cry ; to hawk ; to put up for sale ; to publish, to blazon. *Cet enfant est perdu, il faut le faire —;* the child is lost, we must have him cried. *Faites — ce paquet de livres ;* put up this lot of books.

crierie (kri-rî), *n.f.,* bawling, clamor ; wrangling ; scolding, brawling.

crieu-r, *n.m.,* **-se,** *n.f.,* bawling man or woman, squaller, bawler ; crier ; auctioneer ; hawker. — *public ;* town-crier.

crime, *n.m.,* crime ; sin, transgression, offense, felony ; guilt, guiltiness, wickedness, sinfulness. — *d'Etat ;* treason. — *de lèse-majesté ;* high treason. — *capital ;* capital offense, crime ; (jur.) felony. — *dénaturé ;* unnatural crime. — *abominable ;* base, foul crime. — *qualifié ;* indictable offense. *Faire un — à quelqu'un de ;* to impute as a crime to any one. *Etre porté au —;* to be prone to crime. *Endurci dans le —;* hardened in crime.

criminaliser, *v.a.,* to remove a cause from a civil to a criminal court.

criminaliste, *n.m²,* writer on criminal law.

criminalité, *n.f.,* criminality.

criminel, -le, *adj.,* criminal, felonious, guilty, unlawful. *Juge —;* a judge that tries criminal cases. *Chambre —le, cour —le ;* criminal court.

criminel, *n.m²,* **-le,** *n.f.,* criminal, culprit, offender, felon. — , *n.m.,* criminal affair, proceedings before a criminal court. — *d'état ;* state criminal. *Au —;* in criminal matters, criminally.

criminellement (-nèl-mān), *adv.,* criminally, culpably, guiltily.

crin, *n.m.,* hair (of the mane and tail of the

horse and other animals) ; horse-hair ; abrupt termination of a metallic vein. *Un sommier or matelas de —;* horse-hair mattress. *Se prendre aux —s ;* to seize one another by the hair. *A tous —s ;* with flowing mane and tail ; (fig.) a zealous, indefatigable worker.

crinal, *n.m.,* (surg.) Anel's probe.

crincrin, *n.m.,* (onomatopœia), screeching fiddle ; scraper ; scraping (of fiddles).

crinier, *n.m.,* horse-hair worker, chair stuffer.

crinière, *n.f.,* lion's mane, horse's mane. *Vilaine —;* ugly head of hair ; shock.

crinoline, *n.f.,* crinoline.

crinon, *n.m.,* crinodes. (*pl.*)

criocère *or* **porte-croix,** (—) *n.m.,* (ent.) crioceris.

crique, *n.f.,* creek, cove ; flaw, crack.

criquer, *v.n.,* to crack, to chink (of metals).

criquet, *n.m.,* bad horse, tit ; little man ; (ent.) gryllus, locust.

crise, *n.f.,* crisis ; fit, convulsion. *L'affaire est dans sa —;* the matter is come to a crisis. — *de nerfs ;* fit of hysteria.

crispation, *n.f.,* crispation, shriveling ; thrilling sensation. *Donner des —s à quelqu'un ;* to put any one on thorns.

crisper, *v.a.,* to shrivel, to contract, to make shrink ; to thrill, to make thrill, to thrill through ; to irritate (the nerves) ; to give any one the fidgets, to fidget.

se **crisper,** *v.r.,* to shrivel, to shrivel up.

crispin, *n.m.,* valet (in Molière's comedies). *C'est un —;* he looks like a valet. *Jouer les —s ;* (thea.) to perform the parts of valets.

criss, *n.m.,* creese, Malay dagger.

crissement, *n.m.,* grating of the teeth.

crisser, *v.n.,* to grate (of the teeth).

cristal, *n.m.,* (*cristaux*) crystal. *pl.,* crystal ware, cut glass dishes. — *de roche ;* rock crystal. — *de mine ;* quartz. — *de l'eau ;* the limpidity of water. *Le Palais de —;* the Crystal Palace.

cristallerie (-tèl-rî), *n.f.,* glass-cutting ; crystal manufactory ; glass-house, glassworks.

cristallier, *n.m.,* glass-cutter.

cristallière, *n.f.,* crystal mine.

cristallin, -e, *adj.,* crystalline ; pellucid.

cristallin, *n.m.,* (anat.) crystalline lens ; (astron.) crystalline heaven.

⊙**cristallin,** *n.m.,* colored transparent crystals.

cristallisable, *adj.,* crystallizable.

cristallisant, -e, *adj.,* (chem.) crystallizing.

cristallisation, *n.f.,* crystallizing, crystallization.

cristalliser, *v.a.* and *n.,* to crystallize ; to be converted into crystal. — *la soie ;* to let the alum settle upon the silk.

se **cristalliser,** *v.r.,* to crystallize ; to candy.

cristallisoir, *n.m.,* crystallizing-pan, crystallizer.

cristallographie, *n.f.,* crystallography.

cristalloïde, *n.f.,* crystalloid membranous capsule containing the crystalline lens of the eye.

cristallotechnie (-tèk-nî), *n.f.,* art of crystallizing salts.

cristallotomie, *n.f.,* the art of cutting crystals.

criste-marine, *n.f.* *V.* **passe-pierre.**

criterium (-om), *n.m.,* criterion, standard, test ; touchstone. *L'évidence est le — de la vérité ;* evidence is the criterion of truth.

critiquable, *adj.,* that may be criticised, censurable ; exceptionable.

critique, *n.m.,* critic ; censurer, censorious person, carper. — *fâcheux ;* fault-finder.

critique, *n.f.,* criticism, censure ; science of criticism, critique ; critical taste. *La —;* the critics. *Faire de la —;* to write criticisms. *Faire la — d'un ouvrage ;* to criticise, to review, a work.

critique, *adj.*, critical; censorious, carping; censuring; alarming; ticklish; momentous. *Humeur* —; censorious temper. *Signes* —*s*; critical symptoms. *Pouls* —; alarming pulse.

critiquer, *v.a.*, to criticise, to examine; to censure, to reflect on, to blame, to find fault with.

critiqueur, -se, *n.m.f.*, criticiser, fault-finder, carper.

croassement (kro-as-mān), *n.m.*, croak, croaking, cawing (of crows).

croasser, *v.n.*, to croak, to caw (of crows).

croate, *n.m.f.* and *adj.*, Croatian.

croc (krô), *n.m.*, hook; crook, grapnel, drag; fang, tusk; canine tooth; dog-tooth; tooth; (l. u.) curling moustache; (nav.) boat-hook. — *de batelier*; waterman's pole. — *de candelette*; hook of the forecastle. — *à trois branches*; grapnel with three hooks. — *de capon*; cat-hook. — *de palan*; tackle-hook. *Mettre, pendre, au* —; to put, to lay, on the shelf, to lay by. *Mettre les armes au* —; to give up the army. *Moustaches en* —; curling moustache.

croc (krock), *n.m.*, crackling, crackling noise. *Faire* — *sous la dent*; to crackle under the teeth.

croc-en-jambe (kro-kān-), *n.m.*, (—*s*—) trip up; Cornish hug; dirty trick. *Donner un* — *à quelqu'un*; to trip up anyone's heels; to supplant anyone, to play anyone a dirty trick.

croche, *adj.*, crooked, bent. *Avoir la main* —; (fig.) to be grasping.

croche, *n.f.*, (mus.) quaver. *Double* —; semiquaver. *Triple* —; demi-semiquaver. *Quadruple* —; hemi-demi-semiquaver. *Chanter par* —; to semiquaver.

crocher, *v.a.*, to hook; to crook (card-teeth). — *l'organeau d'une ancre*; to fish up the anchor by the ring. *Se* —; to have a set-to; to come to blows.

crocher, *v.n.*, (agri.) to produce, to bear. *Les arbres crochent bien*; the trees are full of bearers.

croches, *n.f. pl.*, smith's tongs.

crochet, *n.m.*, hook; steelyard; two-pronged hoe; turn (on a road); (surg.) key, crotchet; (erpetology) fang; (arch.) crocket; (anat.) dog-tooth, canine tooth; (dental surg.) wire; ⊙heart-breaker (of curls). *pl.*, fangs, tusks; crotchets; braces. — *d'une porte*; hasp, clasp. *Clou à* —; tenter-hook. *Des ouvrages au* —; crotchet-work. *Un* — *de diamants*; a crotchet of diamonds. — *de chiffonnier*; stick with a hook at the end, used by rag-gatherers. *Un* — *de serrurier*; a pick-lock. — *d'arbre*; bearer. *Broder au* —; to crochet. — *de porte-faix*; porter's knot. *Être sur les* —*s de quelqu'un*; to live at another person's expense. *Je suis ici sur mes* —*s*; I live here upon my own hook. — *d'armes*; (nav.) hooks to support the small arms in a cabin. — *de retraite*; eye-bolts in the train of a gun-carriage. — *de bittes*; hooks to fasten the cross-piece to the bits. — *d'épontilles*; hasps of the stanchions between decks.

crochetable, *adj.*, (of locks) pickable.

crochetage (krosh-taj), *n.m.*, porterage, lock-picking. [do crochet-work.

crocheter (krosh-té), *v.a.*, to pick a lock, to *se crocheter*, *v.r.*, (pop.) to fight (like black-guards).

crocheteur, *n.m.*, porter, street-porter. *Injures de* —; billingsgate abuse. — *de serrure*; picklock, housebreaker.

crochetier (-tié), *n.m.*, hook-maker, clasp-maker; maker of porters' knots.

crocheton, *n.m.*, small hooks; crotchets.

crochu, *n.m.*, a tool to bend card-teeth.

crochu, -e, *adj.*, crooked, hooked. *Il a les mains* —*es*; he is light-fingered.

crocodile, *n.m.*, crocodile. — *d'Amérique*;

American crocodile, alligator. *Larmes de* —; hypocritical tears.

crocodiléen, *n.m.*, crocodilian.

crocus (-kus), *n.m.*, crocus, saffron.

croiler *or* **croler**, *v.n.*, (hawking) to scour.

croire (croyant, cru), *v.a.*, to believe, to credit, to give credit to; to have faith in, to trust to, to place reliance on; to be advised, persuaded; to think; to deem; to presume, to be of opinion. *Je le crois bien*; I really believe it. *Je n'en crois rien*; I don't believe a word of it. *Il le croit bonnement*; he fairly believes it. *Il ne croit point*; he has no belief. — *une chose trop légèrement*; to believe something too easily. — *conseil*; to be advised. *A l'en croire, tout est perdu*; if he is to be believed, all is lost. *J'en crois à peine mes yeux*; I can hardly believe my eyes. *S'il faut en* — *les apparences*; if appearances are to be trusted. *Je crois pouvoir le faire*; I think I can do it. *Croyez-vous qu'il le fasse?* do you think he will do it? *Je crois qu'il le fera*; I think he will do it. *Croyez-vous qu'il le fera?* do you think he will do it? *Je ne le crois pas*; I do not think he will. *Il est à* — *qu'il le veut ainsi*; it is to be presumed that he will have it so.

croire, *v.n.*, to believe, to have faith in, to be a believer; to trust; to credit; to be of opinion; to think; to consider. — *en Dieu*; to believe in God. — *aux revenants*; to believe in ghosts. — *aux miracles*; to believe in miracles. *Je crois bien*; I should think so! no wonder! *Je crois que non*; I believe not. *C'est à ne pas y* —; it is past belief.

se **croire**, *v.r.*, to think or believe one's self, to consider one's self; to be believed, to be credible. *Cet homme se croit habile*; that man thinks himself skillful. *Cela peut se* —; it is credible. *Il s'en croit beaucoup*; he thinks a great deal of himself. *Il se croit tout permis*; he thinks he may do anything.

croisade, *n.f.*, crusade; (astron.) Southern Cross, Crosier.

croisé, -e, *part.*, crossed; cross (of the breeds of animals); twilled, double-milled (of cloth); (min.) promiscuous. *Serge* —*e*; kersey. *Demeurer, se tenir, les bras* —*s*; to sit with folded arms, to do nothing. *Avoir les jambes* —*es*; to sit cross-legged. *Feux* —*s*; cross fire. *Rimes* —*s*; alternate rhymes.

croisé, *n.m.*, Crusader; twill; crossing (a step in dancing). *Chassé* —; (fig.) change of places.

croisée, *n.f.*, window; casement, sash; (arch.) cross-aisle, transept; (print.) cross. — *cintrée*; arched window. —*s d'ogives*; pointed arches. — *de l'ancre*; cross of the anchor.

croisement (croaz-mān), *n.m.*, act of crossing; crossing; cross-breeding (of animals).

croiser, *v.a.*, to cross, to lay across or cross-wise, to set across, to cross out, to strike out, to efface; to thwart; to cross (breeds of animals). — *quelqu'un*; to cross one in his designs. *Des races croisées*; mixed breeds. *Je l'ai croisé dans la rue*; I passed him in the street.

croiser, *v.n.*, to lap over; to cruise. — *sur une côte*; to cruise along a coast.

se **croiser**, *v.r.*, to cross each other, to be crossed, to lie athwart each other; to intersect each other; to thwart one another; to take up the cross, to engage in the holy war. *Ces deux courriers se sont croisés*; these two messengers passed each other on the way.

croisette, *n.f.*, crosswort; (her.) cresslet; (nav.) pin or bolt used as a fid to a flag-staff. — *noire, grosse* —; (bot.) cheese-rennet, ladies' bed-straw.

croiseur, *n.m.*, cruiser.

croisière, *n.f.*, (nav.) cruise, cruising squadron; cruising latitude; sort of tool to mark sea-biscuit ; (railways) intersection of two lines, siding.

***croisille**, *n.f.*, cross-piece.

***croisillon**, *n.m.*, cross-bar ; sash-bar.

croissance, *n.f.*, growth, increase ; vegetation. — *entière ;* full growth. *Arrêter dans sa* —; to stunt the growth of. *Avoir pris toute sa* —; to be full-grown.

croissant, *n.m.*, crescent, the moon in her increase ; short bout (of a violin); pruning-hook ; hedge-bill, hedging-bill ; (ich.) moon-fish ; curtain-pin (in the form of a crescent). *En* —; lunated. *Les cornes du* —; the horns of the crescent. *L'empire du* —; the Crescent. — *de cheminée ;* chimney-hook. — *de pic or de gui ;* (nav.) throat *or* jaw of the gaff.

croissant, -e, *adj.*, growing, increasing.

croisure, *n.f.*, the length of the yards (of a ship); coat-staves ; crossing, mill (in stuffs) ; (poet.) intermixture, mingling.

croît, *n.m.*, increase (from breeding) ; growth.

croître (croissant, crû), *v.n.*, to grow, to wax, to grow up, to grow tall, to spring up ; to augment, to increase ; to lengthen ; to swell *or* swell out, to be swollen ; to multiply, to be multiplied *or* increased ; to be grown ; to sprout, to shoot. — *trop rapidement ;* to outgrow, to overgrow. *Les jours commencent à* —; the days begin to lengthen, to draw out. *Elle ne fait que* — *et embellir ;* she grows handsomer every day.

croix, *n.f.*, cross mark ; rood ; affliction, trouble, tribulation ; star ; (coin.) cross ; (print.) dagger ; (her.) cross. *Sainte* —; holy rood. *Les bras d'une* —; the bars of a cross. *Mettre quelque chose en* —; to put a thing cross-wise. *Avoir les jambes en* —; to sit cross-legged. *Faire le signe de la* —; to cross one's self. *On est allé au-devant de lui avec la* — *et la bannière ;* they went to meet him with cross and banner, with great ceremony. *Il faut faire une* — *à la cheminée ;* we must make a cross on the chimney, we must score that up. *Jouer à* — *et à pile ;* to play at head and tail, at pitch and toss. — *de par Dieu, de Jésus ;* cross-row, criss-cross-row, primer, horn-book, alphabet. — *de Saint André or de Bourgogne ;* St. Andrew's-cross, saltier (her.). — *de Saint Antoine ;* St. Anthony's-cross. — *de Lorraine ;* cross with two bars. *Grand*—; knight grand-cross. *Croix de chevalier ;* (bot.) caltrops, tribulus. — *de Jérusalem ;* (bot.) lychnis Chalcedonica. — *sur les câbles ;* (nav.) cross in the hawse. *Mettre les vergues en* —; to square the yards. — *du Sud,* — *australe* (astron.); Southern Cross, Crosier.

cromlech, *n.m.*, (—*s*) cromlech.

cromorne, *n.f.*, (mus.) krumhorn, cremona.

crône, *n.m.*, (nav.) wheel-crane (on a wharf).

croquade, *n.f.*, (paint.) rough sketch.

croquant, *n.m.*, poor wretch, fellow ; countryman ; gristle. *pl.*, name given to French peasants who rebelled under Henri IV and Louis XIII.

croquant, -e, *adj.*, crisp, crackling, short, craunching. *Biscuit* —; hard biscuit. *Caractère* —; crispness.

croquante, *n.f.*, crisp-tart; almond-cake. *à la* **croque-au-sel**, *adv.*, with salt only; (fig.) as easily as possible.

croque-abeilles, *n.m.*, titmouse.

croque en bouche, *n.m.*, crisp sweetmeat; crisp cake.

⊙**croque-lardon**, *n.m.f.*, (— — —*s*) lick-spittle ; (l. ex.) lick-dish, spunger; dinner-hunter.

croque-mitaine, *n.m.*, (— — —*s*) old bogey, black bogey, bugbear.

croque-mort, *n.m.*, (— — —*s*) undertaker's man.

croque-note, *n.m.*, (— — —*s*) sorry musician, scraper, strummer; crochet-monger.

croquer, *v.n.*, to crackle between the teeth, to craunch, to scrunch. *Etre gentil à* —; to be as pretty as you like.

croquer, *v.a.*, to craunch ; to devour, to eat hastily ; to make the first sketch or rough draught of a drawing or picture, to sketch; to filch, to pilfer; (nav.) to hook *or* grapple anything. *Il n'a fait que* — *ce poème ;* he has only written a sketch of the poem. — *le mar-mot ;* to dance attendance.

croque-sol, *n.m.*, (— — —*s*). *V.* **croque-note**.

croquet, *n.m.*, crisp biscuit.

croquette, *n.f.*, (cook.) croquette.

croqueur, *n.m.*, devourer, gormandizer, glutton; (l.ex.) greedy-gut, greedy-guts.

***croquignole**, *n.f.*, fillip; cracknel.

***croquignoler**, *v.a.*, to fillip.

croquis, *n.m.*, (paint.) rough draft, outline, sketch. *Cahier de* —; sketch-book. *Faire le* — *d'une figure ;* to sketch a figure.

crosse, *n.f.*, (of bishops) crosier; (of muskets) but-end; bat (to play with); cricket (game). *Jouer à la* —; to play at cricket.

crossé, -e, *adj.*, crosiered. *Un abbé* — *et mitré ;* a crosiered and mitred abbot.

crosser, *v.a.*, to beat; to scold; to treat any one with contempt; to strike a ball with a bat.

crosser, *v.n.*, to play at cricket; to bat.

crossette, *n.f.*, (agri.) layer; (arch.) return, ear, elbow, ancone.

crosseur, *n.m.*, cricket-player, cricketer, hockey-player.

***crossillon**, *n.m.*, the curled end of the crosier.

crotale, *n.m.*, (antiq.) crotalum; (zool.) rattle-snake.

crotaphite, *adj., n.m.*, (anat.) crotaphite.

crotte, *n.f.*, dirt, mud, mire; dung. *Il fait bien de la* —; it is very dirty. *Etre dans la* —; to be in a state of squalid misery. —*s de brebis ;* treadles of sheep. —*s de lapins ;* crotels of a rabbit. — *de renard ;* scumber.

crotté, -e, *part.*, dirty, muddy, squalid; wretched, sorry. — *comme un barbet ;* as dirty as a pig. *Un poète* —; a paltry poet. *Il fait bien* — *dans les rues ;* the streets are very dirty. — *jusqu'à l'échine ;* with mud up to the eyes; draggle-tailed.

crotter, *v.a.*, to dirt, to dirty, to bemire; to daggle, to draggle, to bedraggle; to splash, to spatter, to bespatter. *Se* —; to dirty one's self; to get dirty; to draggle.

crottin, *n.m.*, dung (of horses, sheep, etc.).

crou, *n.m.*, (geol.) sandy, clayey soil.

crouchaut, *n.m.*, crotch, floor-timbers of a boat or ship.

croulant, -e, *adj.*, sinking, crumbling, ready to fall, tottering; tumbledown.

croulement (krool-mān), *n.m.*, sinking, falling in or down (of a building); ruin.

crouler, *v.n.*, to sink, to give way, to fall, to fall in, to crumble, to ruin; to go to ruin.

crouler, *v.a.*, (nav.) to launch; (hunt.) to wag (said of stags when they are frightened). *Le cerf croule la queue ;* the stag wags his tail.

⊙*se* **crouler**, *v.r.*, to fail in an enterprise; (fig.) to sink.

crouli-er, -**ère**, *adj.*, quaggy, boggy, swampy, moving, shifting (of land).

croup (kroop), *n.m.*, (med.) croup.

croupade, *n.f.*, (man.) croupade.

croupal, -e, *adj.*, pertaining to the croup; croupal.

croupe, *n.f.*, croup, crupper, the buttocks (of a horse), rump; top *or* brow of a hill; (arch.) hip-roof; body (of an edifice). *Cheval à* — *de mulet ;* narrow-rumped horse. *Etre, aller, monter, en* —; to ride behind another. — *d'église ;* half-cylinder roof. *En* —; behind.

croupé, -e, *adj.,* with a rump, crupper. *Cheval bien —;* horse with a fine crupper.

⊙ *à* **croupeton,** *adv.,* squatting.

croupi, -e, *adj.,* stagnant, putrid, ditch (water). *De l'eau —e;* stagnant water, ditch-water.

croupiader, *v.n.,* to cast anchor by the stern-cable.

croupier, *n.m.,* croupier (at a gaming-table); partner (of a gambler).

croupière, *n.f.,* saddle-tie, crupper; (nav.) stern-cable, stern-fast. *Tailler des —s à quelqu'un;* to cut out work for anyone; (milit.) to put to flight. *Mouiller en —;* to cast anchor by the stern.

croupion, *n.m.,* rump. *Parlement —;* the Rump Parliament.

croupir, *v.n.,* to stagnate; to lie, to wallow, to be sunk in. *— dans le vice;* to wallow in sin. *— dans l'oisiveté;* in idleness.

croupissant, -e, *adj.,* standing, stagnating, putrescent.

croupissement, *n.m.,* standing still, stagnation, putrefaction.

croupon, *n.m.,* square hide, butt.

croustade, *n.f.,* dish prepared with crusts.

croustillant, -e, *adj.,* crisp, crusty.

*****croustille,** *n.f.,* little crust, crust.

*****croustiller,** *v.n.,* to bite, eat, *or* gnaw a crust, to munch.

*****croustilleusement,** *adv.,* (fam., l.u.) comically, with mirth, pleasantly; smuttily.

*****croustilleu-x, -se,** *adj.,* (fam., l.u.) droll, funny; smutty. *Des contes —x;* smutty tales.

croûte, *n.f.,* crust; cake; coarse painting, daub; (med.) scab, scurf. *La — de dessous;* the under-crust. *Casser une — avec quelqu'un;* to take a crust with any one. *Ne manger que des —s;* to fare badly.

croûté, -e, *adj.,* crusted, caked, crusty.

croûtelette (kroo-tlèt), *n.f.,* little crust.

se **croûter,** *v.r.,* to cake, to crust.

croûtier (-tié), *n.m.,* picture-broker, dealer in daubs *or* coarse paintings; dauber.

croûton, *n.m.,* small crust; wretched dauber; (cook.) sippet.

croyable, *adj.,* credible, believable, to be believed *or* credited; like, likely; reliable. *Cela n'est pas —;* that is not likely.

croyance, *n.f.,* belief, creed, faith, persuasion; opinion; trust, credit. *Fausse —;* misbelief. *La — des chrétiens;* the belief of the Christians. *La — des juifs;* the Jewish creed. *Cela passe toute —;* that surpasses all belief.

croyant, *n.m.,* **-e,** *n.f.,* believer. *Les vrais —s;* true believers.

cru, *n.m.,* growth; invention; making, fabrication. *Boire du vin de son —;* to drink wine of one's own growth. *Vin du —;* wine of the country. *Des fruits d'un bon —;* fruit of a good soil. *Cela n'est pas de son —;* that thing is not of his own invention.

cru, -e, *adj.,* raw, crude, uncooked; indigestible; unwrought, hard, blunt, harsh, coarse, rough; indecent, smutty, obscene, bawdy; undigested, unconcocted; stiff. *Tout —;* quite raw. *Cuir —;* undressed leather. *Soie —e;* raw silk. *Métal —;* raw metal, ore. *Eau —e;* hard water. *Couleur —e;* stiff color. *Une lumière —e;* a hard light.

à **cru,** *adv.,* on the bare skin, next the skin. *Botté or chaussé à —;* wearing boots without stockings. *Monter à cheval à —;* to ride a horse bare-backed.

cruauté, *n.f.,* cruelty, hardship. *User de —;* to be guilty of cruelty.

cruche, *n.f.,* pitcher, jar, jug; stupid person, blockhead, booby, lout, dolt. *Tant va la — à l'eau qu'à la fin elle se casse;* the pitcher goes to the well once too often.

cruchée, *n.f.,* pitcherful, jugful, jarful.

crucherie, *n.f.,* (fam.) stupidity, silliness. *Vous ne dites que des —s;* you only talk utter nonsense.

cruchette, *n.f. V.* **cruchon.**

cruchon, *n.m.,* little pitcher.

crucial, -e, *adj.,* crucial, cross-like.

crucifère, *n.f.* and *adj.,* (bot.) cruciferous plant; cruciferous. *pl.,* cruciferæ.

crucifiement *or* **crucifiment** (-mãn), *n.m.,* crucifixion.

crucifier, *v.a.,* to crucify.

crucifix (-fi), *n.m.,* crucifix, cross. *Mangeur de —;* great bigot. *Galerie du —;* rood-loft. *Faire le demi —;* (pop.) to beg.

crucifixion, *n.f.,* crucifixion.

cruciforme, *adj.,* cross-shaped, cross-like, cruciform.

crudité, *n.f.,* crudity, crudeness, rawness; coarse expression; offensive, harsh words; (paint.) stiffness, crudeness; (of water) hardness.

crue, *n.f.,* rise, swelling; growth, growing; increase, flood, inundation. *La — des eaux;* the swelling of the waters. *— de mer;* surge of the sea. *Cet arbre a pris toute sa —;* that tree has attained its full growth.

cruel, -le, *adj.,* cruel, merciless, pitiless, ruthless, hard-hearted; relentless, remorseless; sanguinary, murderous, bloodthirsty; hard, inflexible, flinty; grievous, sad, tormenting. *Il fait le —;* he acts a cruel part. *Elle n'est pas —le;* she is not hard-hearted.

cruel, *n.m.,* **-le,** *n.f.,* cruel one.

cruellement (-èl-mãn), *adv.,* cruelly, barbarously; unmercifully, mercilessly, pitilessly, ruthlessly, grievously, severely, sorely.

⊙ **cruentation,** *n.f.,* (med.) cruentation.

crûment, *adv.,* bluntly, coarsely, roughly inconsiderately, crudely.

cruor, *n.m.,* (physiology) cruor.

crural, -e, *adj.,* (anat.) crural.

crustacé, -e, *adj.,* crustaceous.

crustacé, *n.m.,* crustacean.

cruzade, *n.f.,* cruzado, cruzade (Portugues, coin).

crypte, *n.f.,* crypt. *n.m.,* (bot., anat.) crypt.

cryptogame, *n.f.,* (bot.) aphrodite, cryptogam.

cryptogame, *adj.,* (bot.) cryptogamous.

cryptogamie, *n.f.,* (bot.) cryptogamia.

cryptographie, *n.f.,* cryptography.

cryptographique, *adj.,* cryptographical.

crypto-portique, *n.m.,* (— —s) (arch.) cryptoporticus.

crystal. *V.* **cristal.**

c-sol-ut, *n.m.,* (mus.) c. *Cet air est en —;* this tune is in c.

ct (ab. of **courant**), inst. (instant).

cte (ab. of **comte**), earl.

ctesse (ab. of **comtesse**), countess.

cu, *n.m.,* (very l. ex.) *V.* **cul.**

cubage, *n.m., or* **cubature,** *n.f.,* cubature.

cubation, *n.f.,* cubature.

cube, *n.m.,* (geom., arith.) cube. *Le — de deux est huit;* the cube of 2 is 8.

cube, *adj.,* (arith., geom.) cubic.

cubèbe, *n.m.,* cubeba.

cuber, *v.a.,* (geom., arith.) to cube.

cubilot, *n.m.,* (metal.) cupola.

cubique, *adj.,* (arith., geom.) cubic, cubical. *Racine —;* cube root.

cubital, -e, *adj.,* (anat.) cubital, ulnar.

cubitus (-tus), *n.m.,* (anat.) cubitus.

cuboïde, *n.m.,* (anat.) cuboid.

cucubale, *n.m.,* (bot.) cucubalus, berry-bearing campion.

cucuje, *n.m.,* (zool.) corn-beetle, luminous-beetle.

cucurbitacé, -e, *adj.,* cucurbitaceous.

cucurbitacée, *n.f.,* (bot.) cucurbitaceous plant. *pl.,* cucurbitaceæ.

cucurbite, *n.f.*, (chem.) cucurbit.

cueillage (keu-iaj), *n.m.*, act of gathering, picking.

*****cueille** (keu), *n.f.*, (agri.) gathering of fruit; (nav.) width of sail-cloth.

*****cueillette** (keu-iet), *n.f.*, gathering; crop; nutting (fruit) ; (nav.) mixed cargo ; collection of money for the poor.

*****cueilleu-r** (keu-ieur), *n.m.*, **-se**, *n.f.*, gatherer.

*****cueillir** (keu-), (cueillant, cueilli, je cueille), *v.a.*, to cull, to pick, to pluck; to gather; to take up; (nav.) to coil. — *des fleurs;* to pluck flowers. — *des lauriers;* to gather laurels.

*****cueilloir** (keu-), *n.m.*, fruit-basket.

cuider, *n.m.*, fruit-basket.

cuiller or **cuillère** (ku-lièr), *n.f.*, spoon. — *à soupe;* soup-ladle. — *à café;* tea-spoon. — *à bouche;* table-spoon. — *à dessert;* dessert-spoon. — *à ragoût;* gravy-ladle. *Élever à la* —*;* to bring up by hand.

*****cuillerée** (ku-), *n.f.*, spoonful, ladleful. *Grande* — or — *à bouche;* tablespoonful. *Petite* — or — *à café;* teaspoonful.

*****cuilleriste**, *n.m.*, spoon maker.

*****cuilleron**, *n.m.*, bowl of a spoon.

cuir, *n.m.*, hide, skin, leather; strop; slip of the tongue, *i.e.*, pronouncing *s* for *t*, and vice versa, at the end of words, or using these letters unnecessarily; as : *Il est sorti zhier, j'étaità la campagne*, for *Il est sorti hier, j'étais à la campagne.* —*s bruts;* raw hides. —*s apprêtés;* dressed hides. — *à rasoir* or *à repasser;* razor-strop. *Faire du* — *d'autrui large courroie;* to make free with other people's money. *Tanner le* — *à quelqu'un;* to give any one a hiding. *Pester entre* — *et chair;* to fume inwardly. *Faire des* —*s en parlant;* to pronounce final *s* instead of final *t*, and vice versa; or to sound *s* or *t* when there is none at the end of words, i.e. : to drop one's *h*'s. — *de Russie;* Russian leather.

cuirasse, *n.f.*, cuirass, breast-plate, armor-plate, shell. — *à l'épreuve du mousquet;* ball-proof cuirass. *Le défaut de la* —*;* the extremity of or break in the armor, vulnerable part. *On lui a trouvé le défaut de la* —*;* we have found his weak side. *Endosser la* —*;* to turn soldier.

cuirassé, -e, *adj.*, armed with a cuirass, armor-plated, iron-cased ; ready armed ; hardened; secret, close. *Il est* — *;* he is prepared for anything, he is incapable of feeling remorse. *Vaisseau* —*;* iron-clad ship, iron-clad.

cuirassement, *n.m.*, armor-plating.

cuirasser, *v.a.*, to arm with a cuirass ; to iron-plate (nav.); to steel, to harden, to season. *se* **cuirasser**, *v.r.*, to put on a cuirass; to harden or fortify one's self.

cuirassier, *n.m.*, cuirassier.

cuire (cuisant, cuit), *v.a.*, to cook, to do; to boil; to bake; to roast; to broil, to grill; to dress, to prepare; to stew; to burn (of the sun); to ripen; (physiology) to concoct, to digest. — *la viande;* to do the meat. — *trop;* to overdo. — *des briques;* to burn bricks. — *à l'eau;* to boil. *Faire* — *des œufs;* to boil eggs.

cuire, *v.n.*, to be cooked, to be done; to be burned; to bake; to broil; to boil; to smart, to burn. *La main me cuit;* my hand smarts. *Vous viendrez* — *à mon four;* you will want me some day, and then I shall be even with you. *Il vous en cuira;* you shall smart for it.

cuirer, *v.a.*, to cover in leather.

cuisage, *n.m.*, burning ; charring.

cuisant, -e, *adj.*, easy to cook ; sharp, smarting ; piercing, exquisite; severe; poignant. *Douleur* —*e;* violent pain.

cuisier, *n.m.*, brick-burner.

cuisine, *n.f.*, kitchen ; cookery ; the cooks ; spice-box ; fare, living ; (nav.) cuddy, caboose, galley. — *bourgeoise;* plain living; homely fare. *Graisses de* —*;* kitchen stuff. *Être chargé de*

— *;* to be monstrously fat. *Faire la* —*;* to cook, to dress victuals. *Chef de* — *;* master-cook. *Aide de* —*;* under-cook. *Fille de* — *;* kitchen-maid.

cuisiner, *v.n.*, to cook, to dress victuals.

cuisinier, *n.m.*, cook, man-cook.

cuisinière, *n.f.*, cook, woman-cook ; Dutch oven, meat-screen.

cuissard, *n.m.*, cuish (armor) ; (surg.) thigh-piece.

cuisse, *n.f.*, thigh ; (of meat) rump ; leg (of poultry).

cuisse-madame, *n.f.*, (— -*s*) sort of pear.

cuisson, *n.f.*, dressing (of victuals) ; cooking (baking, boiling, roasting, &c.) ; smart (pain). *Ressentir une* — *;* to feel a smarting pain.

cuissot, *n.m.*, haunch (of venison).

cuistre, *n.m.*, college-fag; college-scout; vulgar, pedantic fellow.

cuit, -e, *part.*, cooked, done, roasted, boiled, baked ; (fig.) done for, dished. *Cela est trop* —*;* that is done too much, overdone (of meat). — *au four ;* baked. — *à point ;* done to a turn.

cuite, *n.f.*, baking ; burning (of bricks, etc.); (manu.) boiling.

cuivre, *n.m.*, copper, brass. — *jaune;* brass. — *rouge;* copper. — *vierge;* native copper. — *battu;* wrought copper. — *fondu;* cast copper. — *en barres;* bar copper. — *en planches;* sheet copper. *Fonte de* — *;* pig copper. —*s;* brass instruments.

cuivré, -e, *adj.*, copper-colored ; (fig.) ringing, clear, sonorous.

cuivrer, *v.a.*, to cover with sheet copper, to copper.

cuivrerie, *n.f.*, copper wares, brass-wares.

cuivreu-x, -se, *adj.*, coppery.

cul (ku), *n.m.*, (very l. ex.) breech ; backside ; posterior; rump; bottom ; tail (of carts); top; cylinder head (mech.). — *par-dessus tête;* head over heels. *Donner du pied au* — *à quelqu'un;* to kick any one. *Être à* — *;* not to know what to do. *Faire le* — *de poule;* to pout. — *de basse-fosse;* dungeon. — *-de-jatte*, (—*s*—) cripple (seated on a wooden bowl). — *-de-lampe*, (—*s*—) (arch.) bracket, pendant; (print.) tail-piece. — *de porc*, (nav.) wall-knot. — *-de-sac*, (—*s*—) blind alley. — *-de-four*, (—*s*—) (arch.) demi-cupola. — *-blanc*, (—*s*—*s*) (orni.) wheat-ear, white-tail, fallow-chat, fallow-finch ; snipe.

culasse, *n.f.*, breech (of a cannon, musket, etc.); pavilion (of diamonds).

culbutant, *n.m.*, (orni.) tumbler.

culbute, *n.f.*, somersault ; ruin, failure, bankruptcy ; fall, tumble, somersault. *Faire la* — *;* to turn a somersault. *Au bout du fossé la* — *;* look before you leap.

culbuter, *v.a.*, to throw down, to throw down headlong ; to overthrow, to ruin, to upset ; to make any one, anything, tumble down ; to do for. *Cette entreprise l'a culbuté;* this enterprise has ruined him.

culbuter, *v.n.*, to fall head over heels.

culbutis, *n.m.*, confused heap; jumble.

culée, *n.f.*, abutment (of bridges); tail (of a hide); (nav.) stern-way.

culer, *v.n.*, to fall astern, to make stern-way; to veer (of the wind). *Scier à* — *;* to back water.

culeron, *n.m.*, (sadlery) crupper-loop.

culière, *n.f.*, gutter-stone, kennel-stone, breech of harness, hind girth.

culinaire, *adj.*, culinary.

culmifère, *adj.*, (bot.) culmiferous.

culminant, *adj.*, culminating ; prominent. *Point* — *;* culminating point, top, summit.

culmination, *n.f.*, culmination.

culminer, *v.n.*, (astron.) to culminate.

culot, *n.m.*, youngest bird (of a brood); youngest (of a family), last born; youngest member of a society; bottom (of lamps, crucibles, etc.); residuum. *Le — d'une pipe;* black at the bottom of a pipe-plug.

culotte, *n.f.,* small clothes, breeches ; rump (of an ox, a pigeon). *— de bœuf;* rump of beef. *— de peau;* leather breeches ; (fig.) old retired officer.

culotter, *v.a.,* to breech, to put in breeches ; to color (pipe).

se **culotter,** *v.r.,* to put on one's breeches ; to get colored (pipe).

culottier, *n.m.,* breeches-maker.

⊙**culottin,** *n. m.,* newly-breeched boy ; tight breeches.

culpabilité, *n.f.,* guilt ; culpability.

culte, *n.m.,* creed ; religion ; worship ; adoration ; veneration, honor, love, respect, cultivation. *Rendre un — à;* to worship.

cultivable, *adj.,* cultivable, arable.

cultivat-eur, *n.m.,* -**rice,** *n.f.,* husbandman, farmer, grower, agriculturist.

cultivat-eur, -**rice,** *adj.,* agricultural.

cultivation, *n.f.,* cultivation.

cultiver, *v.a.,* to cultivate; to till; to improve; to inform ; to exercise, to practice; to cultivate the acquaintance of.

culture, *n.f.,* culture ; cultivation ; tillage, husbandry ; growth ; education, improvement. *Etre sans —;* to be *or* lie fallow. *La petite —;* farming on a small scale ; raising of poultry, etc.

cumin, *n.m.,* (bot.) cumin. *— des prés;* caraway seed.

cumul, *n.m.,* accumulation, junction ; plurality of offices *or* places, pluralism. [man.

cumulard, *n.m.,* (fam. b. s.) pluralist, place-

cumulati-f, -**ve,** *adj.,* accumulative.

cumulativement (-tiv-mān), *adv.,* by accumulation.

cumuler, *v.a.,* to accumulate, to cumulate.

cumuler, *v.n.,* to be a pluralist of offices, to hold several offices.

se **cumuler,** *v.r.,* to be held at the same time.

cunéaire, *adj.,* cuneate, cuneated.

cunéiforme, *adj.,* cuneiform.

cunette, *n.f.,* (fort.) cunette.

cupide, *adj.,* covetous, greedy, grasping.

cupidité, *n.f.,* cupidity ; covetousness ; concupiscence, lust.

cupidon, *n.m.,* (myth.) Cupid, Love. *Vieux —;* old beau.

cupulaire, *adj.,* cup-shaped.

cupule, *n.f.,* (bot.) cupule ; cup (of acorns).

curabilité, *n.f.,* curableness.

curable, *adj.,* that may be healed, curable.

curaçao (ku-ra-so), *n.m.,* Curaçoa.

curage, *n.m.,* cleansing, cleaning (of harbors, sewers, &c.) ; (bot.) water-pepper.

curare, *n.m.,* curare, arrow-poison.

curatelle, *n.f.,* guardianship, trusteeship.

curat-eur, *n.m.,* -**rice,** *n.f.,* curator, curatrix, trustee ; committee.

curati-f, -**ve,** *adj.,* curative.

curatif, *n.m.,* curative agent.

curation, *n.f.,* (med.) treatment.

curcuma, *n.m.,* (bot.) curcuma, turmeric.

cure, *n.f.,* cure, healing; living, benefice, parsonage, rectory; ⊙ care. *N'en avoir —;* to pay no heed to.

curé, *n.m.,* rector, vicar. *C'est Gros Jean qui en remontre à son —;* the clerk wants to teach the parson. *Monsieur le —;* your re erence.

cure-dents, *n.m.,* (— — —) tooth-pick.

curée, *n.f.,* (hunt.) quarry; (fig.) prey, booty; feast ; scramble. *Mettre en —;* to flesh the dogs, to feed them. *Les chiens sont en —;* the dogs are being fed.

cure-langue, *n.m.,* (— - —s) tongue-scrape.

curement, *n.m.,* cleansing, cleaning (of harbors, sewers).

cure-môle, *n.m.,* (— - —s) dredging-machine.

*****cure-oreilles,** *n.m.,* (— - —) ear-pick.

cure-pieds, *n.m.,* (— - - —) horse-picker ; hoof-pick.

curer, *v.a.,* to cleanse, to clean out (harbors, sewers); to pick (the teeth, the ears). *Se — les dents;* to pick one's teeth.

curette, *n.f.,* scraper, scoop.

cureur, *n.m.,* cleanser (of harbors, sewers).

curial, -**e,** *adj.,* vicarial, rectorial. *Maison —e;* parsonage-house.

curiale, *n.m.,* (antiq.) member of the curia.

curie, *n.f.,* ward; (antiq.) curia.

curieusement (-euz-mān), *adv.,* curiously, inquisitively; carefully; minutely.

curieu-x, -**se,** *adj.,* curious ; inquisitive ; prying ; fond of ; careful ; nice ; particular ; rare, singular. *Il est — de tableaux;* he is fond of pictures.

curieu-x, *n.m.,* -**se,** *n.f.,* inquisitive person, spectator, looker-on ; virtuoso ; curious fact. *Le — de la chose est ;* the curious part of the thing is.

curion, *n.m.,* (antiq.) curio.

curiosité, *n. f.,* curiosity ; inquisitiveness ; rarity ; care ; taste for. *Par —;* out of curiosity.

curoir, *n.m.,* plow-scraper.

curseur, *n.m.,* (math.) cursor, slider, slide, index.

cursi-f, -**ve,** *adj.,* cursive ; running ; cursory.

cursivement, *adv.,* cursorily.

curule, *adj.,* curule. *Chaise —;* curule chair.

curure, *n.f.,* dirt, sewage.

curvati-f, -**ve,** *adj.,* (bot.) slightly curved.

*****curviligne,** *adj.,* curvilineal.

curvirostre, *adj.,* (orni.) curvirostral, hook-billed.

cuscute, *n.f.,* (bot.) dodder.

cuspide, *n.f.,* cuspis, cusp.

cuspidé, -**e,** *adj.,* (bot.) cuspidate.

cussoné, -**e,** *adj.,* (tech.) worm-eaten, weeviled.

custode, *n.f.,* pyx-cover ; curtain of the high altar ; holster-cap; ⊙ curtain. *Sous la —;* in private.

custode, *n.m.,* warden, keeper, curator.

cutané, -**e,** *adj.,* cutaneous.

cuticule, *n.f.,* (anat., bot.) cuticle.

cutter (-tèr), *n.m.,* (—s) (nav.) cutter.

cuvage, *n.m.,* (tech.) fermenting (of wine); place where wine is fermented.

cuve, *n.f.,* tub, vat, copper. *— de brasseur;* brewing-vat. *— matière;* mash-tub. *Fossé à fond de cuve;* (fort.) flat-bottomed ditch. *A fond de —;* (fig.) thoroughly, exhaustively. *— de bain;* bathing-tub.

cuveau, *n.m.,* small vat, small tub ; (min.) corf, cage, kiddle-outright.

cuvée, *n.f.,* tubful ; vatful; (fam.) sort, kind, quality. *En voici d'une autre —;* here's one of another sort for you.

cuvelage (kuv-laj), *n.m.,* lining, casing; tubbing (mines).

cuveler (kuv-lé), *v.a.,* to tub (mines); to line, to case.

cuver, *v.n.,* to work, to ferment, to settle.

cuver, *v.a.,* to appease ; to calm ; to sleep off the effects of wine. *— son vin;* to sleep one's self sober.

cuvette, *n.f.,* wash-hand basin ; basin, cistern (of barometers, steam-engines); (fort.) cuvette. *Montre à —:* capped watch.

cuvier, *n.m.,* wash-tub.

cyame, *n.m.,* (ent.) whale-louse.

cyanate, *n.m.,* (chem.) cyanate.

cyanhydrique, *adj.,* (chem.) hydrocyanic, prussic.

cyanogène, *n.m.,* (chem.) cyanogen.

cyanomètre, *n.m.,* (phys.) cyanometer.

cyanure, *n.m.,* (chem.) cyanide.

cyathe, *n.m.,* (antiq.) cyathus.

cyclamen (-me-n), *n.m.*, (bot.) cyclamen, sow-bread.

cycle, *n.m.*, cycle; (liter.) period.

cyclique, *adj.*, cyclical.

cycloïdal, -e, *adj.*, cycloidal.

cycloïde, *n.f.*, (geom.) cycloid.

cyclométrie, *n.f.*, cyclometry.

cyclone, *n.m.*, tornado.

cyclope, *n.m.*, Cyclops.

cyclopéen, -ne (-in, -è-n), *adj.*, cyclopean.

*cygne, *n.m.*, swan. *Jeune* —; cygnet. (fig.) *Le* — *Thébain ;* Pindar. *Le* — *de Mantoue ;* Virgil. *Le* — *de Cambrai ;* Fénelon.

cylindracé, -e, *adj.*, (bot.) cylindraceous.

cylindrage, *n.m.*, mangling (of linen).

cylindre, *n.m.*, cylinder; roller; garden-roller; mangle, calender; barrel; rundle. *Passer au* —; to pass through the mangle.

cylindrer, *v.a.*, to calender; to roll. — *les allées d'un jardin ;* to roll the paths of a garden.

cylindrique, *adj.*, cylindric.

cylindroïde, *n.m.*, cylindroid.

cymaise, *n.f.* *V.* **cimaise.**

cymbalaire, *n.f.*, ivy-leaved toad-flax.

cymbale, *n.f.*, cymbal.

cymbalier, *n.m.*, cymbal-player.

cymbiforme, *adj.*, (bot.) cymbiform.

cyme, *n.m.*, (bot.) cyme. *V.* **cime.**

cymrique, *n.m.* and *adj.*, Kymric.

cynanche *or* **cynancie**, *n.f.*, (med.) cynanche.

cynanque, *n.m.*, (bot.) dog's-bane.

cynégétique, *n.f.*, cynegetics. *adj.*, relating to hunting and dogs.

cynips, *n.m.*, (ent.) cynips.

cynique, *adj.*, cynical, snarling, snappish; impudent, barefaced, indecent.

cynique, *n.m.*, cynic.

cynisme, *n.m.*, cynicism.

cynocéphale, *n.m.*, (zool.) cynocephalus.

cynoglosse, *n.f.*, (bot.) cynoglossum, hound's-tongue.

cynorrhodon, *n.m.*, (bot.) hip.

cynosure, *n.f.*, (bot.) cynosurus; (astron.) Cynosure, Little Bear.

cyprès, *n.m.*, cypress, cypress-tree; cypress-wood.

cyprière, *n.f.*, cypress-grove.

cypripède, *n.m.*, (bot.) lady's-slipper.

cyrénaïque, *adj.*, cyrenaic. *n.m.*, cyrenaic philosopher.

cyrillien *or* **cyrillique**, *adj.* *Alphabet* —; the Slavonic alphabet invented in the 9th century by St. Cyrillus.

cystique, *adj.*, (anat.) cystic.

cystite, *n.f.*, (med.) cystitis.

cystocèle, *n.f.*, (med.) cystocele.

cystotome, *n.m.*, (surg.) an instrument to cut into the bladder.

cystotomie, *n.f.*, cystotomy.

cytarexylon, *n.m.*, (bot.) fiddle-wood.

cytise, *n.m.*, (bot.) cytisus, bean-trefoil.

cyzicène, *n.m.*, (Grec. antiq.) guest-chamber.

czar (gzar), *n.m.*, czar.

czarien, -ne (-in, -è-n), *adj.*, of the czar.

czarine, *n.f.*, czarina.

czarowitz, *n.m.*, czarowitz.

D

d, *n.m.*, the fourth letter of the alphabet, *d.*

d', ab. of **de**.

dà, *particle*, truly, indeed. *Oui-dà ;* yes, for-sooth. *Nenni-dà*, *non-dà ;* no, indeed; no, for-sooth.

da-capo, *adv.*, (mus.) da capo   [grass.

dactyle, *n.m.*, (poet.) dactyl ; (bot.) orchard-

dactylographe, *n.m.*, type-writer, typist.

dactylographie, *n.f.*, dactylography, type-writing.

dactylique, *adj.*, dactylic.

dactylologie, *n.f.*, dactylology.

dactyloptère, *adj.*, (ich.) finger-finned.

dactyloptère, *n.m.*, dactylopterus, flying-fish.

dada, *n.m.*, horse, cock-horse; hobby, hobby-horse. *Aller à* —; to ride a cock-horse. *Être sur son* —; to indulge in one's hobby.

dadais, *n.m.*, booby, clown, ninny.

⊙**dagorne**, *n.f.*, one-horned cow; hag.

dague (dag), *n.f.*, dagger, dirk. *pl.*, tusks (of a wild boar); first horns (of a two-year old deer).

daguer (da-ghé), *v.a.*, to stab; (hunt.) to rut.

daguerréotype (da-ghér-), *n.m.*, daguerreo-type.

daguet (da-ghé), *n.m.*, (hunt.) brocket, pricket.

dahlia, *n.m.*, dahlia.

*daigner, *v.n.*, to deign, to be graciously pleased, to condescend, to vouchsafe.

*d'ailleurs. *V.* ailleurs.

daim (din), *n.m.*, deer, fallow-deer; buck.

daine (dèn *or* di-n), *n.f.*, doe.

daintiers (-tié), *n.m. pl.*, (hunt.) dowcets.

dais, *n.m.*, canopy; dais, platform.

dalème, *n.f.*, self-consuming stove.

dallage, *n.m.*, paving with flag-stones, flag-ging.

dalle, *n.f.*, slab; flag, flag-stone; sink-stone; slice (of fish).

daller, *v.a.*, to pave with flag-stones, to flag.

dalmatique, *n.f.*, dalmatic, tunic.

dalot, *n.m.*, (nav.) scupper-hole, scupper.

daltonisme, *n.m.*, (med.) color-blindness.

⊙**dam**, *n.m.*, hurt, injury. *A son, votre, leur* —; to his, your, their injury.

damage, *n.m.*, puddling, ramming.

damas, *n.m.*, damask; (bot.) damson; Damas-cus blade.

damasquiner, *v.a.*, to damaskene, to emboss; to frost (cutlery).

damasquinerie (-ki-n-rî), *n.f.*, damaskening.

damasquineur, *n.m.*, damaskener, one who damaskenes.

damasquinure, *n.f.*, damaskened work; em-bossing.

damassé, *n.m.*, damask linen, damask cloth.

damasser, *v.a.*, to damask.

damasserie (da-mas-rî), *n.f.*, damask linen manufactory.

damasseur, *n.m.*, damask weaver.

damassin, *n.m.*, figured linen cloth, diaper.

damassure, *n.f.*, damasking (of linen).

dame, *n.f.*, lady; married lady; nun; dame; man, draught (backgammon); (draughts) draught, man, king, queen; queen (cards, chess); dam, rammer; (nav.) rowlock. —*s de France ;* prin-cesses of the royal family of France. — *d'hon-neur ;* maid of honor, bridesmaid. *Elle fait la* —; she sets up for a lady. *Notre*—; Our Lady. *Ma chère* —; my dear madam. *Jouer aux* —*s ;* to play at draughts. *Aller à* —; (at draughts) to make a king. *Aller à* —; (at chess) to make a queen; — *s seules ;* ladies' compartment.

dame, *int.*, by our lady ! well ! forsooth ! well, you see ! — *! c'est juste ;* well, you see ! it is right.

dame-jeanne, *n.f.*, (—*s*—*s*) demijohn, car-boy.

damer, *v.a.*, to crown (a man at draughts); to queen; (arch.) to allow half a foot for sloping; to ram. — *le pion à quelqu'un ;* to outdo, outwit any one; to be more than a match for.

dameret, *adj. m.*, (l.u.) foppish.

dameret, *n.m.*, lady's man, spark, beau.

damier, *n.m.*, draught-board.

damnable (dä-nabl), *adj.*, damnable.

damnablement (dä-na-), *adv.*, damnably.

damnation (dä-na-), *n.f.*, damnation.

damné, -e (dä-né), *part.*, damned.

damné, -e (dä-né), *n.m.*, soul damned. *Les* —*s ;* the damned. *Souffrir comme un* —; to suffer horribly. *C'est l'âme —e du ministre ;* he is the tool of the minister (i.e., does his dirty work for him).

damner (dâ-né), *v.a.*, to damn.

se **damner** (dâ-né), *v.r.*, to damn one's self.

⊙**damoiseau,** *n.m.*, beau, fop, spark; young page.

⊙**damoiseau.** *V.* **damoiseau.**

⊙**damoiselle,** *n.f.*, damsel.

danché, -e, *adj.*, (her.) indented.

dandin, *n.m.*, ninny.

dandinement (-di-n-mān), *n.m.*, jogging, waddling; swinging, slouching.

dandiner, *v.a.*, to dandle, to rock.

dandiner, *v.n.*, to swing (of bells); to waddle, to slouch.

se **dandiner,** *v.r.*, to waddle; to twist (one's body) about; to strut, to slouch; to dilly-dally, to dally.

dandy, *n.m.*, dandy.

dandysme, *n.m.*, dandyism.

danger, *n.m.*, danger, peril, risk, hazard, jeopardy. *Braver les —s ;* to brave dangers. *Affronter les —s ;* to face dangers. *Etre en — de ;* to be in danger of.

dangereusement (danj-reuz-mān), *adv.*, dangerously.

dangereu-x, se, *adj.*, dangerous.

danois, -e, *adj.*, Danish.

danois, *n.m.*, **-e,** *n.f.*, Dane.

danois, *n.m.*, Danish; dane (dog).

dans, *prep.*, in, within, into; with, according to, formerly. *Il fait cela — le dessein de s'établir ;* he does so with the intention of establishing himself. *J'ai beaucoup travaillé — le temps ;* I used to study a good deal formerly.

dansant, -e, *adj.*, dancing. *Soirée —e ;* dancing party, evening party.

danse, *n.f.*, dance, dancing; beating, hiding. *Aimer la —;* to like dancing. *— de corde ;* rope-dancing. *Il a une — contrainte ;* he has a stiff way of dancing. *Donner une — à quelqu'un ;* to give any one a drubbing. *Entrer en —;* to join the dance. *— de St. Guy ;* St. Vitus's dance.

danser, *v.n.*, to dance. *— en mesure ;* to keep time in dancing. *Faire — quelqu'un ;* to lead any one a dance. *Il ne sait sur quel pied —;* he does not know which way to turn. *Il en dansera en l'air ;* he will swing for it. *Se —;* to be danced.

danser, *v.a.*, to dance. *— un menuet ;* to dance a minuet.

danseu-r, *n.m.*, **-se,** *n.f.*, dancer, ballet-girl. *— de corde ;* rope-dancer.

dansotter, *v.n.*, to dance a little, to skip, to hop, to dance stiffly.

danubien, -ne (-in, -è-n), *adj.*, Danubian.

daphné, *n.m.*, (bot.) daphne.

darce, *n.f. V.* **darse.**

dard, *n.m.*, dart; sting; (bot.) pistil. *Le — d'une abeille ;* the sting of a bee; (pisc.) dace.

darder, *v.a.*, to dart; to shoot forth, to beam, to hurl; to spear, to harpoon. *Le soleil darde ses rayons ;* the sun darts forth his rays.

⊙**dardeur,** *n.m.*, shooter, dart-flinger.

dardillon, *n.m.*, barb (of a fish-hook).

dariole, *n.f.*, cream-cake.

darne, *n.f.*, slice of fish.

darse, *n.f.*, (nav.) wet-dock.

dartre, *n.f.*, skin disease; eruption (of the skin); blotch, tetter; herpes. *— farineuse ;* pityriasis, dandriff.

dartreu-x, -se, *adj.*, herpetic, scurfy, scabby.

dartreu-x, *n.m.*, **-se,** *n.f.*, person affected with skin disease; scabby fellow.

dataire, *n.m.*, datary (chancery officer of Rome).

date, *n.f.*, date, period. *A courte —;* short-dated. *A longue —;* long-dated. *Prendre —;* to fix a day. *Je suis le premier en —;* I have the priority. *En — de ;* under date of, bearing

the date. *D'ancienne,* or *de vieille, de longue —;* of long standing, long since.

dater, *v.a.*, to date.

dater, *v.n.*, to date; to date from; to form a period; to reckon. *— de loin ;* to date far back; to happen long ago. *A — de ;* reckoning from. *Se —;* to be dated.

daterie (da-trî), *n.f.*, datary's office.

datif, *n.m.*, (gram.) dative, dative case.

dati-f, -ve, *adj.*, (jur.) dative. *Tutelle —ve ;* dative guardianship.

dation, *n.f.*, (jur.) giving. *— en payement ;* giving in payment.

datisme, *n.m.*, tautology.

datte, *n.f.*, (bot.) date.

dattier, *n.m.*, date-tree.

datura, *n.m.*, (bot.) datura stramonium, thorn-apple.

daube, *n.f.*, (cook.) stew, daube.

dauber, *v.a.*, (pop.) to cuff, to drub; (fig.) to banter; to jeer.

daubeur, *n.m.*, jeerer, banterer, sneerer.

daubière, *n.f.*, long stew-pan.

dauphin, *n.m.*, (ich.) dolphin; dauphin (eldest son of the kings of France).

dauphine, *n.f.*, dauphiness.

dauphinelle, *n.f.*, (bot.) lark-spur.

daurade, *n.f.*, (ich.) gilt head.

d'autant. *V.* **autant.**

davantage, *adv.*, more; longer, further. *Pas —;* no more. *Je n'en dirai pas —;* I shall say no more. *Je n'en sais pas —;* I know nothing more about it. *Ne restez pas —;* do not stay any longer.

davier, *n.m.*, dentist's forceps; (nav.) davit.

de, *prep.*, of, from, by, with, in, upon, out of, some, any, for, at, to. *Un plat d'argent ;* a silver dish. *De Paris à Londres ;* from Paris to London. *De près, de loin ;* near, afar. *Faire de son mieux ;* to do one's best. *Vivre de fruits et de légumes ;* to live on fruit and vegetables. *Sauter de joie ;* to leap for joy. *Se moquer de quelqu'un ;* to laugh at any one. *Il y eut cent hommes de tués ;* there were a hundred men killed. *Il n'y a personne de blessé ;* there is no one wounded. *Plus d'effets et moins de paroles ;* more deeds and fewer words. *Quelque chose de bon ;* something good. *Indigne de vivre ;* unworthy to live. *Le désir d'apprendre ;* the wish to learn. *Avoir besoin d'argent ;* to be in want of money. *Qu'est-ce que de nous !* what poor creatures we are ! *L'un d'entre eux ;* one of them. *D'après l'original ;* from the original. *De chez vous ;* from your house. *De par le roi ;* in the king's name. *De ce que ;* because. *Les hommes d'à-présent* or *d'aujourd'hui ;* the men of the day. *Un coup de bâton ;* a blow with a stick. *Trait de plume ;* dash of the pen. *Un coup de fusil ;* a shot. *Signe de tête ;* nod. *Leçons de danse ;* lessons in dancing. *Un enfant d'un bon naturel ;* a good-natured child. *Une lame d'épée ;* a sword-blade. *Une prise de tabac ;* a pinch of snuff. *Un collier de perles ;* a pearl necklace. *Etre d'un repas ;* to make one at a banquet. *N'avez-vous point d'enfants ?* have you no children ? *Etre —;* to be one of a party. [*De* is changed into *d'* before a vowel or silent *h.*]

dé, *n.m.*, die (for playing); thimble; (arch.) coin, block, dado; (nav.) cock (of blocks); (coin.) die. *— fermé ;* woman's thimble. *— ouvert ;* tailor's thimble. *Jouer au —s ;* to play at dice. *—s pipés ;* cogged or loaded dice. *Avoir le —;* to be one's turn to play. *Flatter le —;* to slide the dice; to soften a thing down. *A vous le —;* now it is your turn, your throw. *Le — en est jeté ;* the die is cast. *Tenir le — de la conversation ;* to engross the conversation.

déalbation, *n.f.*, (chem.) dealbation.

débâchage, *n.m.*, untilting, uncovering.

débâcher, *v.a.*, to uncover, to untilt.

débâclage, n.m., clearing, opening (of a port).

débâcle, n.f., breaking up (of the ice); clearing (of a harbor); (fig.) overthrow, shock, downfall, collapse, disaster.

débâclement, n.m., breaking up of the ice.

débâcler, v.n., to break up (of the ice).

débâcler, v.a., to clear (a harbor); to unbar (doors). — les bateaux; to clear the harbor of boats. — une porte, une fenêtre; to unbar a door, a window.

débâcleur, n.m., water or port-bailiff.

débagouler, v.n., (l.ex.) to spew, to puke.

débagouler, v.a., (l.ex.) (fig.) to launch into abuse; to insult, to abuse any one foully.

débagouleur, n.m., (l.ex.) scurrilous, foul-mouthed blabber.

déballage, n.m., unpacking (goods exposed for sale, show).

déballer, v.a., to unpack.

à la **débandade**, adv., in confusion, helter-skelter, at sixes and sevens. Mettre tout à la —; to put everything in confusion.

à la **débandade**, n.f., rout, stampede; breaking the ranks.

debandement (dé-band-mān), n.m., disbanding; (milit.) leaving the ranks.

débander, v.a., to unbind; to unbend, to loosen. — un pistolet; to uncock a pistol. — quelqu'un; to take off the handkerchief tied over any one's eyes.

se **débander**, v.r., to slacken or grow loose, to relax; to disband; to get uncocked (of fire-arms); to grow milder (of the weather). — l'esprit; to relax one's mind.

débanquer, v.a., to break the bank (at play).

débaptiser (dé-ba-ti-zé), v.a., to change the name of. Il jugea à propos de se —; he thought proper to change his name.

***débarbouiller**, v.a., to clean, to make clean, to wash the face.

se **débarbouiller**, v.r., to wash one's face; to extricate one's self.

débarcadère, n.m., landing, landing-place, wharf, terminus, station (of railways).

débardage, n.m., unlading (of wood).

débarder, v.a., to unlade wood; to clear a wood of the trees which have been felled in it.

débardeur, n.m., lumper; workman who breaks up boats; wharf-porter; lighterman; docker.

débarqué, n.m., -e, n.f., person landing. Un nouveau —; one just come to town; a raw countryman. [ment.

débarquement, n.m., landing, disembark-

débarquer, v.a., to disembark, to land, to unship.

débarquer, v.n., to land. Nous débarquâmes en tel endroit; we went ashore at such a place. Au —; on landing.

débarras, n.m., riddance, disencumbrance. Bon —! a good riddance! Chambre de —; lumber-room.

débarrassé, -e, part., disembarrassed; rid of, released from.

débarrassement, n.m., (l.u.) disembarrassment, clearance, riddance; extrication.

débarrasser, v.a., to clear, to clear away, to disencumber, to rid, to free, to disentangle, to disembarrass; to extricate.

se **débarrasser**, v.r., to disentangle, to extricate one's self from, to rid one's self of, to shake off; to get clear, to get clear of; to clear, to be cleared (of the road, the way).

débarrer, v.a., to unbar.

débat, n.m., debate, dispute, discussion, strife, contest. pl., debates; pleading, summing up. Vider un —; to settle a dispute. A eux le —; let them settle it between them.

débatelage, n.m., unlading of boats.

débateler, v.a., to unlade boats.

débâter, v.a., to unsaddle; to take off a pack-saddle.

débâtir, v.a., to pull down; to unbaste, to untack (of garments).

débattre, v.a., to debate, to discuss, to argue.

se **débattre**, v.r., to struggle, to strive, to flounder, to writhe; to dispute; to be debated.

débauche, n.f., debauch; debauchery; lewdness, dissoluteness. Aimer la —; to be fond of reveling.

débauché, n.m., debauchee, rake.

débaucher, v.a., to debauch; to entice away; to take away.

se **débaucher**, v.r., to become debauched; to be led away from one's occupations.

débaucheu-r, n.m., -se, n.f., debaucher, seducer.

débet, n.m., debit, balance of an account. Etre or rester en —; to owe a balance.

débiffé, -e, part., discomposed, disordered, out of order. Visage —; haggard countenance.

débiffer, v.a., to debilitate, to disorder, to enfeeble, to put out of sorts. Etre tout débiffé; to be quite out of sorts.

débile, adj., weakly, weak, feeble. Avoir le cerveau —; to have weak brains. Mémoire —; weak memory.

débilement (dé-bil-mān), adv., feebly, weakly.

débilitant, n.m., (med.) debilitant.

débilitant, -e, adj., (med.) debilitating, weakening.

débilitation, n.f., debilitation, enfeebling.

débilité, n.f., debility, weakness.

débiliter, v.a., to debilitate, to enfeeble.

***débillardement**, n.m., (carp.) cutting diagonally.

***débillarder**, v.a., (carp.) to cut diagonally.

***débiller**, v.a., to loosen horses.

débine, n.f., difficulties, poverty, straits, embarrassment, mess, beggary. Il est tombé dans la —; he has fallen into poverty.

débit, n.m., sale, traffic; market; retail shop; license to sell; delivery, utterance; debit side (book-keeping); (mus.) recitative. Marchandise de bon —; goods that have a ready sale. — de tabac; tobacconist's shop. Porter au — de quelqu'un; to debit any one with. Il a un beau —; he has a fine delivery.

débitage, n.m., cutting up (of stones, timber).

débitant, n.m., -e, n.f., retailer, dealer. — en détail, en gros; retail, wholesale, dealer.

débiter, v.a., to sell; to retail; to give out, to spread, to report, to utter; to debit; to cut up (wood, stone). — en gros, en détail; to sell, wholesale, by retail. — son rôle; to recite one's part. — des nouvelles; to spread news.

débit-eur, n.m., -rice, n.f., debtor; seller, retailer; (jur.) obligor. Etre — de; to be in debt to.

débiteur, adj.m., debtor. Compte —; debtor's account.

débiteu-r, n.m., -se, n.f., prattler, newsmonger. C'est une grande —se de mensonges; she is a regular fib-teller.

débitter, v.a., (nav.) to unbitt (a cable).

déblai, n.m., cutting, clearing; excavating, excavation; rubbish; riddance. Etre en —; to have been excavated.

déblaiement, déblayement, n.m., clearing, clearing away; clearance; freeing; cutting, digging.

déblatérer, v.n., to speak against; to rail at.

déblayer, v.a., to clear away; to clear.

déblocage, n.m., (print.) turning letters.

déblocus, n.m., raising the blockade of.

débloquer, v.a., to raise a blockade; (print.) to turn letters.

déboire, n.m., after-taste; vexation; mortification; disappointment.

déboisement, *n.m.*, clearing *or* denudation of trees, forests.

déboiser, *v.a.*, to clear *or* denude.

se **déboiser**, *v.r.*, to become denuded.

déboitement (dé-boat-măn), *n.m.*, disjointing, dislocation.

déboîter, *v.a.*, to put out of joint, to dislocate, to disjoint.

se **déboîter**, *v.r.*, to be dislocated, to become disjointed.

débonder, *v.a.*, to take the bung out of ; to loosen, to unbind. — *un étang ;* to open the sluice of a pond.

se **débonder**, *v.r.*, to gush, to sluice out, to break out *or* open, to burst forth, to escape out of the bung-hole ; to be relaxed (of a person).

débonder, *v.n.*, to escape through the bung-hole ; to escape through the sluice of a pond ; to gush out.

débondonnement, *n.m.*, unbunging.

débondonner, *v.a.*, to take out the bung.

débonnaire, *adj.*, good-natured ; compliant, gentle, easy-tempered.

débonnairement, *adv.*, compliantly, easily.

⊙**débonnaireté**, *n.f.*, compliance, meekness.

débord, *n.m.*, edge (of a coin) ; ⊙overflowing ; ⊙(med.) defluxion.

débordé, -e, *adj.*, overflowed ; lewd, dissolute, debauched.

débordement, *n.m.*, overflowing, breaking out, inundation, irruption ; (fig.) dissoluteness, debauchery, lewdness ; torrent, flood ; (med.) overflow.

déborder, *v.n.*, to overflow, to run over ; to project, to bag, to jut out ; (nav.) to get clear, to sheer off. *La doublure déborde ;* the lining bags. *Cette maison déborde ;* that house juts out.

déborder, *v.a.*, to take off the border ; to outrun ; to go beyond ; (milit.) to outflank ; to edge (plumber's business).

se **déborder**, *v.r.*, to overflow ; to break, to burst, forth.

débordoir, *n.m.*, edging-tool (of a plumber).

débosseler (dé-bos-lé), *v.a.*, to take the bruises, the dents, out of.

débotté, *n.m.*, with boots off.

débotter, *v.a.*, to pull off boots.

se **débotter**, *v.r.*, to pull off one's boots.

débouché, *n.m.*, opening, expedient ; outlet, issue ; (com.) market, sale ; water-way.

débouchement (de-boosh-măn), *n.m.*, uncorking, unstopping, outlet ; debouching ; market, sale ; disemboguement.

déboucher, *v.a.*, to open ; to clear ; to uncork.

déboucher, *v.n.*, to pass out ; to fall into (rivers) ; (milit.) to debouch ; to relieve the bowels ; to expand the mind. *Au — du défilé ;* on coming out of the defile.

débouchoir, *n.m.*, lapidary's tool.

déboucler, *v.a.*, to unbuckle, to uncurl. — *une jument ;* to unring a mare.

***débouilli**, *n.m.*, (dy.) boiling.

***débouillir**, *v.a.*, (dy.) to boil.

déboulonner, *v.a.*, (tech.) to unbolt, to unpin.

débouquement (dé-book-măn), *n.m.*, (nav.) narrow channel ; disemboguement.

débouquer, *v.n.*, (nav.) to disembogue.

débourbage, *n.m.*, (metal.) trunking.

débourber, *v.a.*, to cleanse ; to take the mud away ; (metal.) to trunk. — *une voiture ;* to draw a carriage out of the mire.

débourgeoiser, *v.a.*, to polish, to make a lady *or* gentleman of.

se **débourgeoiser**, *v.r.*, to become polished.

débourrement (dé-boor-măn), *n.m.*, taking off the fleece.

débourrer, *v.a.*, (man.) to break in ; to worm (fire-arms) ; to empty (a pipe) ; to polish (a person). — *un jeune homme ;* to form *or* polish

a young man. — *un cheval ;* to break in a horse ; to take the fleece off.

⊙**débours**, *n.m.*, disbursement, sum laid out.

déboursé, *n.m.*, money laid out, disbursement, outlay.

déboursement, *n.m.*, disbursement, outlay, expenditure.

débourser, *v.a.*, to disburse, to expend, to lay out.

debout, *adv.*, upright, on end ; up ; standing ; in existence (of things) ; ahead (of the wind). *Il se tient —;* he is standing up. *Etre —;* to be up, to be stirring. *Allons, —, il est déjà grand jour ;* come, get up, it is broad daylight. *Un conte à dormir —;* rigmarole. *Avoir le vent —;* to have the wind ahead *or* a head wind.

débouté, *n.m.*, (jur.) dismission, setting aside, nonsuit.

débouter, *v.a.*, (jur.) to overrule, to reject, to non-suit. *Il a été débouté de sa demande ;* his demand was rejected ; he was non-suited.

déboutonné, -e, *part.*, unbuttoned.

déboutonner, *v.a.*, to unbutton.

se **déboutonner**, *v.r.*, to unbutton one's self ; to unbosom one's self.

***débraillé, -e**, *part.*, open-breasted, loosely dressed, untidy, in disorder. *Tout —;* all untidy. [disorder ; license, licentiousness.

débraillement *or* **débraillé**, *n.m.*, untidiness,

*se **débrailler**, *v.r.*, to uncover one's breast, to become untidy, disordered.

débrayage, *n.m.*, disengaging gear (motor).

débrayer, *v. n.*, to throw out of gear, to disengage.

***débredouiller**, *v.a.*, *se —*, *v.r.*, to save the lurch (backgammon).

débridement (dé-brid-măn), *n.m.*, unbridling ; despatching, hurrying over ; (surg.) relieving constriction by incision.

débrider, *v.a.*, to unbridle ; to despatch, to hurry ; (surg.) to remove constriction by incision.

débrider, *v.n.*, to unbridle one's horse ; to halt ; to stop *Sans —;* without stopping ; at a stretch. [rubbish.

débris, *n.m.*, remains, wreck, ruins ; waste ;

débrochage, *n.m.*, unstitching ; unspitting.

débrocher, *v.a.*, to unstitch, to unspit.

***débrouillement**, *n.m.*, disentangling, unravelling.

***débrouiller**, *v.a.*, to disentangle, to unravel, to clear up, to explain.

se **débrouiller**, *v.r.*, to unravel ; to be disentangled, to be cleared up. (gems).

débrutir, *v.a.*, to clear off the rough ; to polish

débrutissement (-tis-măn), *n.m.*, rough-polishing (of gems).

débucher, *v.n.*, (hunt.) to start.

débucher, *v.a.*, (hunt.) to dislodge, to start.

débucher, *n.m.*, (hunt.) start. *Il se trouva au —;* he was present at the start.

débusquement, *n.m.*, driving out ; dislodging ; ousting.

débusquer, *v.a.*, to turn out, to oust to expel ; (hunt.) to start, to dislodge.

début, *n.m.*, lead, first cast, *or* throw ; outset ; debut ; first appearance ; beginning. *Voilà un beau —;* that is a fine beginning.

débutant, -e, *n.f.*, actor, actress, appearing for the first time ; beginner.

débuter, *v.n.*, to lead, to play first ; to begin ; to open ; to set out ; to make one's first appearance. *Il a mal débuté dans le monde ;* he made a bad beginning in life.

débuter, *v.a.*, to drive from the jack (at bowls) ; to drive from the mark (at cards).

deçà, *prep.*, this side of. *En —, de —, par —, la rivière ;* this side of the river. *En — de la rivière ;* on this side of the river.

deçà, *adv.*, here, on this side. — *et delà ;* here

and there, this and that side, up and down. *Jambe —, jambe delà;* one leg this side, the other that. *De —, par —, en —;* this side.

déca (particle used in French weights and measures) deca (ten times the unit).

décachetable, *adj.*, to be unsealed, opened.

décachetage, *n.m.*, unsealing, opening.

décacheter (dé-kash-té), *v.a.*, to unseal, to open; to break open, to break the seal of.

décadaire, *adj.*, having ten days, decadal.

décade, *n.f.*, decade.

décadenasser, *v.a.*, to unpadlock.

décadence, *n.f.*, decay, decline, wane, downfall.

décadi, *n.m.*, decadi (the tenth day of a decade in the calendar of the first French Republic).

décaèdre, *adj.*, decahedral.

décaèdre, *n.m.*, (geom.) decahedron.

décagone, *n.m.*, (fort., geom.) decagon.

décagone, *adj.*, decangular, decagonal.

décagramme, *n. m.*, decagram (5'64 drams avoirdupois).

décaissage, *n.m.*, uncasing, unpacking.

décaisser, *v.a.*, to take out of its box, to unpack.

décalage, *n.m.*, unwedging.

décaler, *v.a.*, to unwedge.

décalitre, *n.m.*, decalitre (2'2009 gallons).

décalogue, *n.m.*, Decalogue.

décalquer, *v.a.*, to transfer a tracing.

décaméron, *n.m.*, decameron.

décamètre, *n.m.*, decameter (32'808992 feet).

décampement (dé-kanp-măn), *n.m.*, (milit.) decampment.

décamper, *v.n.*, (milit.) to decamp; to move off, to walk off; to pack off, to bolt, to levant.

décanat, *n.m.*, deanery, deanship.

décandrie, *n.f.*, (bot.) decandria.

décantation, *n.f.*, (chem.) decantation.

décanter, *v.a.*, (chem.) to decant, to pour off gently.

décanteur, *n.m.*, (chem., pharm.) decanter.

décapage, *n.m.*, cleaning, scraping (metal).

décaper, *v.n.*, (nav.) to double a cape.

décaper, *v.a.*, to clean, to scrape (metal).

décapétalé, *-e*, *adj.*, (bot.) having ten petals.

décaphylle, *adj.*, (bot.) having ten leaves.

décapitation, *n.f.*, decapitation, beheading.

décapiter, *v.a.*, to behead, to decapitate.

décapode, *adj.*, ten-footed, decapodal.

décapole, *n.f.*, Decapolis.

décarrelage, *n.m.*, unpaving.

décarreler (dé-kar-lé), *v.a.*, to take up a floor, to unpave.

décastère, *n.m.*, decastere (13'1 cubic yards).

décastyle, *n.m.*, (arch.) decastyle.

décasyllabe, *adj.*, decasyllabic.

décatir, *v.a.*, to sponge woolen cloth.

se **décatir**, *v.r.*, (of cloth) to lose its gloss.

décatissage, *n.m.*, sponging.

décatisseur, *n.m.*, sponger.

décavé, *-e*, *adj.*, having lost one's stake, ruined, beggared, lost in reputation.

décaver, *v.a.*, to win the whole of one of the players' stakes; to ruin, to beggar.

décédé, *-e*, *part.*, deceased, dead.

décédé, *n.m.*, *-e*, *n.f.*, deceased; person deceased.

décéder, *v.n.*, to die, to expire, to decease.

déceindre, *v.a.*, to ungird, to loose a girdle.

décèlement (-sèl-măn), *n.m.*, disclosure, betrayal.

déceler, *v.a.*, to disclose, to reveal, to betray.

se **déceler**, *v.r.*, to betray one's self.

déceleu-r, *n.m.*, *-se*, *n.f.*, betrayer, revealer.

décembre, *n.m.*, December.

décemment (dé-sa-măn), *adv.*, in a decent manner, decently.

décemvir (-sèm-), *n.m.*, decemvir.

décemviral, *-e*, *adj.*, decemviral.

décemvirat, *n.m.*, decemvirate.

décence, *n.f.*, decency, propriety.

décennal, *-e* (-sèn-nal), *adj.*, decennial.

décent, *-e*, *adj.*, decent, becoming.

décentralisation, *n.f.*, decentralization.

décentraliser, *v.a.*, decentralize.

décepti-f, *-ve*, *adj.*, deceptive.

déception, *n.f.*, deception, deceit, fraud.

décerner, *v.a.*, to decree, to enact; to award, to bestow, to issue (a summons). — *un mandat d'amener;* to issue a writ of arrest. *Se —;* to be awarded, to be decreed, etc.

décès, *n.m.*, decease, demise, death.

décevable, *adj.*, deceivable.

décevant, *-e*, *adj.*, deceptive.

décevoir, *v.a.*, to deceive, to disappoint.

déchaînement (-shèn-măn), *n.m.*, unbridling; letting loose (passions); fury, rage, violence, exasperation, inveighing, invective.

déchaîner, *v.a.*, to unchain; to let loose, to turn loose, to exasperate.

se **déchaîner**, *v.r.*, to break loose, to free one's self from one's chains, to burst upon; to run riot; to inveigh.

déchalement, *n.m.*, lying dry; ebbing, far out.

déchaler, *v.a.n.*, to leave bare or dry; to lie dry; to ebb far out.

déchanter, *v.n.*, to change one's tone, to lower one's pretensions, to sing another tune. *Je le ferai —;* I'll make him sing small.

déchaperonné, *-e*, *adj.*, (of a wall) dismantled of its coping.

déchaperonner, *v.a.*, to unhood, to uncope.

décharge, *n.f.*, unloading, unlading; lumber-room; discharge; release; relief; exoneration; (jur.) defense; shower of blows; (mil.) volley, round. *Pièce de —;* lumber-room. *Table de —;* dinner-wagon. *Témoin à —;* witness for the defense. *Entendre les témoins à charge et à —;* to hear witnesses for and against.

déchargement, *n.m.*, unloading, unlading.

décharger, *v.a.*, to unload, to unlade, to empty, to vent; to disburden, to lighten; to discharge; to release, to set free; to exonerate; (hort.) to prime; to dismiss. — *sa conscience;* to clear one's conscience. — *son cœur à quelqu'un;* to open one's heart to any one. — *son fusil sur quelqu'un;* to discharge one's musket at any one. — *sa bile, sa colère, sur quelqu'un;* to vent one's bile, to wreak one's anger, upon any one. — *un accusé;* to exculpate, to discharge an accused person. *Il a été déchargé de toute accusation;* he was entirely exculpated.

se **décharger**, *v.r.*, to be unloaded, to discharge itself (liquids); to disembogue (rivers); to free one's self; to give vent to; to go off of itself (of a gun); to change, to fade (of colors); to lay the blame. *Se — d'une faute sur quelqu'un;* to shift the blame on any one.

décharger, *v.n.*, to unload; to unlade; to come off (of ink).

déchargeur, *n.m.*, unloader, wharf-porter, heaver, lumper.

décharné, *-e*, *part.*, fleshless; lean, thin, spare; emaciated; (of style) bald, meager, poor. *Visage —;* gaunt face. *Style —;* bald style.

décharnement, *n.m.*, emaciation; leanness; poverty; (of style) baldness.

décharner, *v.a.*, to strip off the flesh; to impoverish, to make lean, to emaciate; to render meager, naked.

⊙**décharpir**, to tear into rags; to part, to separate (fighters).

déchasser, *v.a.*, (turnery) to drive out pegs; *v.n.*, (dancing) to slide to the left.

déchaumage, *n.m.*, (agri.) digging up the stubble; plowing up the stubble.

déchaumer, *v.a.*, to plow up the stubble; to break up fallow land.

déchaussé, -e, adj., bare-footed.

déchaussement (-shôs-mān), n.m., pulling off (shoes or stockings), laying bare; baring (of teeth); shrinking, lancing of the gums.

déchausser, v.a., to pull off shoes and stockings; to lay bare (trees, teeth, buildings).

se **déchausser,** v.r., to take off one's shoes and stockings; to become bare (of the teeth).

déchaussoir, n.m., gum-lancet.

déchaux, adj.m., barefooted (of friars). C'est un pied —; he is a low poverty-stricken fellow. A peine de —; under pain of forfeiture.

dèche, n.f., (pop.) destitution, beggary. En —; out of pocket.

déchéance, n.f., (jur.) forfeiture; fall, decay.

déchet, n.m., (com.) loss, waste.

décheux, -se, adj., needy, beggarly.

déchevelé, -e, part., disheveled.

décheveler (-shĕ-vlé), v.a., to dishevel. V. **écheveler**

déchevêtrer, v.a., to take the halter off, to unhalter; to disentangle, to release.

se **déchevêtrer,** v.r., to get its halter off; to break from its halter.

*****décheviller,** v.a., to unpeg, to unpin.

déchiffrable, adj., capable of being deciphered, legible, intelligible.

déchiffrement, n.m., deciphering; reading or playing at sight.

déchiffrer, v.a., to decipher; to unravel; to make clear; to read or play at sight.

se **déchiffrer,** v.r., to be deciphered, to be unraveled.

déchiffreur, n.m., decipherer; player at sight.

déchiqueté, -e, part., (bot.) laciniate; jagged. Feuille —e; jagged leaf.

déchiqueter (dé-shik-té), v.a., to cut, to slash, to mangle; to cut in long pieces; to pink.

déchiqueteur (-shik-teur), n.m., cutter, slasher, or ripper.

⊙**déchiqueture** (-shik-tur), n.f., slashing, cutting, pinking.

déchirage, n.m., ripping up, breaking up, of a ship's planks. Bois de —; old ship-timber.

déchirant, -e, adj., heart-rending, harrowing, piercing; excruciating.

déchiré, -e, part., torn, rent, ragged, tattered. Etre tout —; to be all in rags. Chien hargneux a toujours l'oreille —e; snarling dogs have always sore ears.

déchirement (-shir-mān), n.m., rending, tearing; (surg.) laceration. pl., (fig.) intestine broils. — d'entrailles; excruciating pain in the bowels. —s de cœur; anguish of heart.

déchirer, v.a., to tear, to rend, to lacerate; to bespatter, to revile, to defame. — une plaie; to tear open a wound. — à coups de fouet; to lash to pieces. — quelqu'un à belles dents; to pull any one to pieces. — l'oreille; to grate on the ear. — de vieux vaisseaux; to rip up old vessels. — la cartouche; to bite the cartridge. Etre déchiré de remords; to be tortured with remorse. — son prochain; to slander one's neighbor.

se **déchirer,** v.r., to tear, to be torn, to be rent; to vilify, to abuse, to defame, each other. Ce papier se déchire très facilement; this paper tears very easily. Je sentis mon cœur —; I felt my heart breaking.

déchireu-r, n.m., **-se,** n.f., tearer, render; breaker up, ripper up (of boats, ships).

déchirure, n.f., rent, tear, break.

déchoir (déchu), v.n., to decay, to fall off, to decline; to forfeit, to lose; (nav.) not to keep the right course. — de son rang; to fall from one's rank. Il est fort déchu de sa réputation; he is greatly fallen in reputation. — de ses espérances; to be less sanguine in one's hopes. Etre

déchu d'un droit; to have forfeited a claim. Commencer à —; to begin to fall away.

déchouement, n.m., the floating of a stranded ship.

déchouer, v.a., to get off, to set afloat.

déchristianiser, v.a., to unchristianize.

se **déchristianiser,** v.r., to lose the character of Christian, to fall away from Christianity.

déchu, -e, part., decayed, sunk, fallen. Ange —; fallen angel.

déci, particle used in French weights and measures, deci (one-tenth of the unit).

décidé, -e, adj., decided, determined, resolved, resolute; confident.

décidément, adv., decidedly, positively; actually, really; on consideration.

⊙**décidence,** n.f., the falling of the womb.

décider, v.a., to decide, to determine, to settle, to induce, to persuade.

décider, v.n., to decide, to determine. Que le sort décide entre nous; let fortune determine between us. Cet événement décida de mon sort; that event decided my fate.

se **décider,** v.r., to decide, to determine, to resolve, to make up one's mind; to be decided, to be settled. La victoire s'est décidée en faveur de nos armes; victory favored our arms. Tout se décidait par intérêt; everything was decided by interest.

décidu, -e, adj., (bot.) deciduous.

décigramme, n.m., decigram (15·4325 grain).

décilitre, n.m., deciliter (0·176 pint).

déciller. V. **dessiller.**

décimable, adj., tithable.

décimal, -e, adj., decimal.

décimateur, n.m., tithe-owner.

décimation, n.f., decimation.

décime, n.m., decime, tenth part of a franc; war-tax.

décimer, v.a., to decimate (to punish every tenth soldier); to destroy, to thin, to sweep off, to carry off; to annihilate.

décimètre, n.m., decimeter (3·937 inches).

décimo, adv., tenthly.

décintrement, n.m., (arch.) removing the centerings (of walls).

décintrer, v.a., (arch.) to remove the centers from an arch.

décintroir, n.m., (tech.) cutting-hammer.

décirer, v.a., to take the wax off. Se —; to become unwaxed; to lose its wax.

décisi-f, -ve, adj., decisive, conclusive; positive, peremptory. C'est un homme —; he is a positive man. Prendre un ton —; to assume a peremptory tone.

décision, n.f., decision; determination; resolution. Une — de droit; a decision in law.

décisivement (-ziv-mān), adv., decisively, peremptorily, positively.

décisoire, adj., (jur.) decisory.

décistère, n.m., decistere (3·53 cubic feet).

déciviliser, v.a., to uncivilize.

déclamateur, n.m., declaimer, stump-orator. Ce n'est qu'un —; he is a mere ranter.

déclamateur, adj., declamatory, stilted, bombastic. Style —; high-flown style.

déclamation, n.f., declamation, elocution; manner, art of reciting, declaiming; abuse, invective. — oratoire, théâtrale; oratorical, theatrical elocution. Professeur de —; teacher of elocution. Il s'est livré à des —s contre sa partie adverse; he indulged in invectives against his adversary.

déclamatoire, adj., declamatory.

déclamer, v.a., to declaim; to recite; to spout, to mouth (out).

déclamer, v.n., to declaim; to recite; to spout, to rant, to inveigh.

déclarat-eur, n.m., **-rice,** n.f., declarer.

déclarati-f, -ve, adj., declaratory.

déclaration, *n.f.*, declaration, proclamation; disclosure; notification; (jur.) schedule; statute (of bankruptcy); (jur.) affidavit; verdict (of juries). — *d'entrée, de sortie;* declaration of goods (at the custom-house) on entering, on leaving the town.

déclaratoire, *adj.*, declaratory.

déclaré, -e, *adj.*, declared; open; avowed; acknowledged; recognized. *Ennemi* —; declared *or* avowed enemy.

déclarer, *v.a.*, to declare, to make known; to proclaim; to certify; to denounce; to find (guilty, not guilty). — *sa volonté;* to make known one's will.

se **déclarer**, *v.r.*, to declare, to be declared, to break out, to speak one's mind; to declare oneself, itself; to set in (of the weather). *La petite vérole s'est déclarée;* small-pox has broken out.

déclasser, *v.a.*, to alter the classing of; to undervalue, to depreciate; to strike off the rolls; to dismiss from the service.

déclaveter, *v.n.*, to get loose (of gearing).

déclencher, *v.a.*, to unlatch a door, to lift up the latch, to unhook, to loosen.

déclic, *n.m.*, (mec.) click; trigger, catch; monkey (of a pile-driver).

déclimater, *v.a.*, to declimatize.

déclin, *n.m.*, decline, decay; wane (of the moon); ebb; close; main-spring (of fire-arms). *L'hiver est sur son* —; winter is drawing to a close. *Le jour à son* —; twilight.

déclinable, *adj.*, (gram.) declinable.

déclinaison, *n.f.*, (gram.) declension; (astron., phys.) declination. — *de la boussole;* variation of the compass. — *d'un cadran;* declination of a dial.

déclinant, -e, *adj.*, declining. *Cadran* —; declining dial.

déclinatoire, *adj.*, declinatory. *Exception* —; exception.

déclinatoire, *n.m.*, (jur.) declinatory plea, exception.

décliner, *v.n.*, to decline; to be on the wane, to fall off; to refuse to entertain. *Ses forces déclinent beaucoup;* his strength is fast declining. *Ce malade décline tous les jours;* the patient is falling away every day.

décliner, *v.a.*, (gram.) to decline; to state. — *son nom;* to state one's name. — *une juridiction;* to decline, to except to, the jurisdiction of a court of law.

déclive, *adj.*, declivous, sloping; (surg.) dependent.

déclivité, *n.f.*, declivity, slope.

décloîtrer, *v.a.*, to withdraw from a convent, to uncloister; to secularize.

se **décloîtrer**, *v.r.*, to leave the cloister; to return to the world; to unfrock oneself.

déclore, *v.a.*, to unclose, to throw open.

déclos, -e, *part.*, unclosed; open.

déclôture, *n.f.*, unclosing, opening.

déclouer, *v.a.*, to unnail.

décochement (-kosh-mān), *n.m.*, discharge, darting (of arrows, shafts); shooting.

décocher, *v.a.*, to discharge, to let fly (arrows); to let fly; to bring out; to dart.

décoction, *n.f.*, (pharm.) decoction.

*****décognoir**, *n.m.*, (print.) shooting-stick.

décoiffer, *v.a.*, to take off a head-dress, to undress the hair; to take the sealing-wax off the cork of a bottle. — *St. Pierre pour coiffer St. Paul;* to rob Peter to pay Paul.

se **décoiffer**, *v.r.*, to undo one's head-dress, to take off one's cap. *Cet enfant se décoiffe tous jours;* that child is constantly pulling off its cap.

décoinçage, *n.m.*, unwedging; (rail.) unkeying, unlocking.

décoincer, *v.a.*, to unwedge; (rail.) to unkey.

se **décoincer**, *v.r.*, to get unwedged.

décollation, *n.m.*, decollation, beheading.

décollement (-kol-mān), *n.m.*, ungluing, unpasting, coming off.

décoller, *v.a.*, to behead; to unglue, to deglutinate; to come off the cushion (at billiards).

se **décoller**, *v.r.*, to unglue, to get unglued, to come off (the cushion).

décolleté, -e, *part.*, in a low dress; (of dresses) low; (fig.) broad, free, licentious.

décolleter (-kol-té), *v.a.*, to uncover the neck.

se **décolleter**, *v.r.*, to bare one's shoulders; to wear a low dress.

décolleter, *v.n.*, to leave the neck bare.

décoloration, *n.f.*, discoloration.

décoloré, -e, *part.*, discolored, faded; (fig.) (of style) tame, colorless.

décolorer, *v.a.*, to discolor, to take away the color of, to change from the natural hue of.

se **décolorer**, *v.r.*, to lose one's *or* its color; to become discolored, to fade. *Ces roses se décolorent;* these roses are losing their color.

décombler, *v.a.*, to empty.

décombrer, *v.a.*, to clear away rubbish from, to clear.

décombres, *n.m.pl.*, rubbish, ruins.

décommander, *v.a.*, to countermand.

se **décommander**, *v.r.*, to be countermanded.

décompléter, *v.a.*, to render incomplete.

décomposable, *adj.*, decomposable; decompoundable.

décomposé, -e, *part.*, decomposed; decomposite. *Un visage* —; a distorted countenance.

décomposer, *v.a.*, to decompose, to discompose, to distort; to decompound. *La terreur décompose le visage;* terror distorts the face.

se **décomposer**, *v.r.*, to decompose, to become decomposed; to be distorted.

décomposition, *n.f.*, decomposition, analysis; discomposition.

décompte (dé-kont), *n.m.*, deduction; allowance; deficiency; drawback; disappointment. *Trouver du* —; to be disappointed.

décompter (dé-kon-té), *v.a.*, to deduct; to reckon off.

décompter, *v.n.*, to reckon off; to be disappointed; to lose one's illusions.

déconcerté, -e, *adj.*, disconcerted.

déconcerter, *v.a.*, to disconcert, to confuse, to foil, to baffle.

se **déconcerter**, *v.r.*, to be disconcerted or put out; to be confused.

déconclure, *v.a.*, to annul, to break off.

déconfire, *v.a.*, to discomfit; to nonplus; to do for.

déconfiture, *n.f.*, discomfiture; havoc; overthrow, break-down; (jur.) insolvency.

déconfort, *n.m.*, discomfort, sorrow, distress.

déconforter, *v.a.*, to discomfort, to grieve, to distress.

*****déconseiller**, *v.a.*, to dissuade.

déconsidération, *n.f.*, disrepute; disesteem, discredit.

déconsidéré, -e, *adj.*, sunk into disrepute, discredited.

déconsidérer, *v.a.*, to bring into disrepute, to discredit.

se **déconsidérer**, *v.r.*, to fall, to sink, into disrepute.

déconstruire, *v.a.*, to take to pieces; to unbuild, to demolish, to pull down; to decompose; (gram.) to construct badly. — *des vers;* to turn verse into prose.

décontenancé, -e, *part.*, out of countenance, abashed.

décontenancer, *v.a.*, to abash, to put out of countenance.

se **décontenancer**, *v.r.*, to be put out of countenance, to be abashed.

déconvenue, *n.f.*, discomfiture, disaster, mishap, failure.

décor, *n.m.*, decoration, ornamental painting;

(paint.) graining. *pl.*, (theat.) scenery. — *en bois ;* graining in imitation of wood. *Peintre en —s ;* grainer.

décorateur, *n.m.*, ornamental painter, decorator; scene-painter; grainer.

décorati-f, -ve, *adj.*, decorative, ornamental.

décoration, *n.f.*, decoration, embellishment; star; star of the order of the Legion of Honor. *pl.*, scenery. *Porter une* —; to wear the star of an order.

décorder, *v.a.*, to untwist, to untwine.

décoré, -e, *part.*, knighted; decorated; wearing the insignia of some order of knighthood.

décoré, *n.m.*, knight; knight of the Legion of Honor.

décorer, *v.a.*, to decorate, to ornament, to adorn; to dignify; to trim; to set off; to confer (titles, honors); to confer the knighthood of the Legion of Honor; to paint. — *d'un ordre ;* to confer an order. *Se* — *d'un titre ;* to assume a title.

décorner, *v.a.*, to unhorn. — *un livre ;* to undo the dog's ear of. — *une carte ;* to turn the corner of.

décortication, *n.f.*, stripping off bark, decortication; pulping, husking, barking.

décortiquer, *v.a.*, to decorticate, to bark, to husk.

décorum (-rom), *n.m.*, decorum, propriety, decency. *Observer le* —; to observe proprieties. *C'est pour garder le* —; it is for decency's sake. *Blesser le* —; to offend against the laws of decorum.

découcher, *v.n.*, to sleep out; to stay out all night.

découcher, *v.a.*, to turn out of bed.

découdre, *v.a.*, to unsew, to unstitch, to rip up. *se* **découdre**, *v.r.*, to come unsewed, unstitched.

découdre, *v.n.*, to contend. *Ils veulent en* —; they are bent on coming to blows, or fighting it out.

découlant, -e, *adj.*, flowing, running.

découlement (-kool-mān), *n.m.*, flowing, running, dropping, trickling.

découler, *v.n.*, to trickle, to flow, to run; to spring from, to proceed. *La sueur découlait de son visage ;* the perspiration was running down his face. *C'est de Dieu que les grâces découlent ;* all blessings flow from God.

découpage, *n.m.*, (tech.) cutting out, carving out. — *à l'emporte-pièce ;* punching.

découpé, -e, *part.*, (paint.) cut out; (bot.) cut; standing out, defined, sharp, clear (of a landscape).

découpé, *n.m.*, (hort.) mingled bed, parterre.

découper, *v.a.*, to cut into pieces, into shreds; to cut up, to carve; to pink, to slash; to cut out. — *un poulet ;* to carve a fowl. — *une jupe ;* to slash a petticoat. — *des figures ;* to cut out figures.

se **découper**, *v.r.*, to stand out, to show up against.

découpeu-r, *n.m.*, **-se**, *n.f.*, carver, pinker, cutter.

découple *or* **découpler**, *n.m.*, (hunt.) uncoupling, unleashing of dogs.

découplé, -e, *part.*, uncoupled; strapping. *C'est un gaillard bien* —; he is a strapping fellow. *Une fille bien —e ;* a well-set girl.

découpler, *v.a.*, to uncouple, to unleash, to let loose.

découpoir, *n.m.*, (tech.) punch, stamping-machine, stamping press; butler's tray.

découpure, *n.f.*, cutting out, pinking, work cut out; cut paper-work.

décourageant, -e (-jān, -t), *adj.*, discouraging, disheartening.

découragement (-raj-mān), *n.m.*, discouragement; despondency. *Tomber dans le* —; to become discouraged.

décourager, *v.a.*, to discourage, to dishearten, to daunt, to deter.

se **décourager**, *v.r.*, to be discouraged, disheartened. *Il y a de quoi se* —; it is enough to dishearten one.

décourant, -e, *adj.* *V.* **décurrent**.

décourber, *v.a.*, to unyoke barge horses; to unbend, to straighten.

découronner, *v.a.*, to discrown, to lay bare. — *une hauteur,* to sweep the top of a hill (of troops).

décours, *n.m.*, decrease; wane (of the moon).

décousu, -e, *part.*, *adj.*, unsewed, unstitched, ripped; (of style, etc.) desultory, loose, unconnected. *Style* —; desultory style. *Des idées —es ;* unconnected ideas.

décousure, *n.f.*, seam-rent; (hunt.) gash (by a wild boar).

découvert, -e, *part.*, uncovered, detected, plain; discovered, open; unguarded; undecked (of boats). *Une allée —e ;* an open walk. *Un pays* —; an open country. *A* —; in the open, exposed to the fire of the enemy; unprotected; barefaced; (com.) overdrawn. *Être à* —; (com.) to have no security, to be unsecured; to be overdrawn.

découvert, *n.m.*, (com.) uncovered balance, overdraft, deficit.

découverte, *n.f.*, discovery, detection; (nav.) lookout; (milit.) reconnoitering. *Aller à la* —; to scout. *Envoyer à la — de ;* to send to reconnoiter.

découvreur, *n.m.*, discoverer.

découvrir, *v.a.*, to uncover, to expose, to lay bare, to bare, to unmuffle, to unroof; to see, to spy out, to discover, to disclose; to unveil; to find out, to descry, to discern; to detect. — *les racines d'un arbre ;* to lay bare the roots of a tree. — *son jeu ;* to show one's cards; to betray oneself. *Je lui ai découvert mon cœur ;* I opened my heart to him. — *une mine d'or ;* to discover a gold mine. — *le pot aux roses ;* to find out the intrigue, the mystery.

se **découvrir**, *v.r.*, to uncover oneself, to unbosom oneself; to expose oneself; to be detected; to make oneself known, to betray oneself; to clear up (of the sky).

décramponner, *v.a.*, to uncramp, to loosen.

se **décramponner**, *v.r.*, to let go one's hold.

décrasse-peigne, *n.m.*, comb-cleaner, combbrush.

décrasser, *v.a.*, to take off the dirt, to clean, to scour, to polish. — *la tête ;* to clean the head. *Il faut — ce jeune homme ;* that young man requires brushing up.

se **décrasser**, *v.r.*, to wash, to clean oneself; to polish oneself, to become polished.

décréditement (-dit-mān), *n.m.*, discrediting, discredit; disrepute.

décréditer, *v.a.*, to discredit, to disgrace, to bring into discredit *or* disrepute.

se **décréditer**, *v.r.*, to sink into discredit, to lose one's credit *or* reputation.

décrépi, -e, *adj.*, unplastered.

décrépir, *v.a.*, (mas.) to unplaster.

décrépissage, *n.m.*, (mas.) unplastering.

décrépit, -e, *adj.*, decrepit, broken-down.

décrépitation, *n.f.*, decrepitation, crackling.

décrépiter, *v.n.*, to decrepitate, to crackle.

décrépitude, *n.f.*, decrepitude.

décret, *n.m.*, decree, fiat, order, enactment; ⊙(jur.) writ; order in council.

décrétale, *n.f.*, decretal.

décréter, *v.a.*, to decree, to order, to enact; ⊙(jur.) to issue a writ against.

décreusage, *n.m.*, ungumming (of silk).

décreuser, *v.a.*, to ungum.

décri, *n.m.*, crying down, prohibition ; disrepute, discredit.

décrier, *v.a.*, to decry, to cry down, to run down ; to discredit, to bring into disrepute.

se **décrier**, *v.r.*, to bring one's self into disrepute; to cry one another down.

décrire, *v.a.*, to describe, to trace, to draw.

se **décrire**, *v.a.*, to be described.

décrocher, *v.a.*, to unhook, to take down.

se **décrocher**, *v.r.*, to become unhooked.

décroire, *v.a.*, to disbelieve, to discredit.

décroisement, *n.m.*, uncrossing.

décroiser, *v.a.*, to uncross.

décroissance, *n.f.* V. **décroissement**.

décroissant, -e, *adj.*, decreasing, diminishing; decrescent; (math.) descending.

décroissement (-kroas-mān), *n.m.*, decrease, diminution, wane.

décroître, *v.n.*, to decrease, to diminish, to wane ; to draw in (of days) ; to come down (in life).

décrottage, *n.m.*, cleaning of boots, trowsers.

décrotter, *v.a.*, to rub off the dirt, to clean, to brush off.

se **décrotter**, *v.r.*, to clean or brush one's self.

décrotteur, *n.m.*, shoe-boy, shoe-black.

décrottoir, *n.m.*, a scraper (for shoes).

décrottoire, *n.f.*, shoe-brush, hard brush.

décrue, *n.f.*, decrease ; fall (of water). *La crue et la — de l'eau ;* the rise and fall of water.

décruer, *v.a.*, (dy.) to scour (silk).

décrûment, *n.m.*, (dy.) scouring.

décrusement or **décrusage**, *n.m.*, (dy.) ungumming.

décruser, *v.a.*, to ungum.

déçu, -e, *part.*, deceived; frustrated.

décuire, *v.a.*, to thin (syrup). *Ce sirop est trop épais, il faut le — ;* this syrup is too thick, it must be thinned.

déculassement, *n.m.*, unbreeching.

déculasser, *v.a.*, to unbreech (a gun).

décuple, *adj.*, tenfold, decuple.

décuple, *n.m.*, decuple, tenfold. *Il a gagné le — de ce qu'il avait avancé ;* he has gained ten times as much as he laid out.

décupler, *v.a.*, to increase tenfold.

décurie, *n.f.*, (antiq.) decury.

décurion, *n.m.*, (antiq.) decurion.

décurrent, -e, *adj.*, (bot.) decurrent.

décursi-f, -**ve**, *adj.*, decursive.

décussation, *n.f.*, decussation.

décuvage, *n.m.*, or **décuvaison**, *n.f.*, tunning (of wine).

décuver, *v.a.*, to tun.

***dédaigner**, *v.a.*, to disdain, to scorn, to despise, to slight, to disregard, to turn up one's nose at.

***dédaigneusement** (-eûz-mān), *adv.*, disdainfully, scornfully.

***dédaigneu-x**, -**se**, *adj.*, disdainful, scornful; regardless, careless of. *Faire le — ;* to turn up one's nose at.

dédain, *n.m.*, disdain, scorn, disregard. *Prendre en — ;* to conceive a dislike for.

dédale, *n.m.*, labyrinth, maze.

dédamer, *v.n.*, to displace a man (at draughts). *v.a.*, to uncrown a king.

dedans, *adv.*, within, in; inside. *Il est là-dedans ;* he is within. *En — ;* on the inside, within. *Sa porte était fermée en — ;* his door was fastened inside. *Donner — ;* to fall into the trap. *Etre — ;* to be in for it. *Mettre quelqu'un — ;* to take any one in. *Se mettre — ;* to get taken in, to get into a scrape. *De — ;* from within. *Par — ;* within, inside. *Etre tout en — ;* to be uncommunicative, reticent, close.

dedans, *n.m.*, inside ; interior. *Du — au dehors ;* from within outwards. *Au — et au dehors ;* at home and abroad.

dédicace, *n.f.*, dedication, consecration ; inscription.

dédicatoire, *adj.*, dedicatory.

dédier, *v.a.*, to dedicate, to consecrate ; to devote ; to inscribe.

dédire, *v.a.*, to gainsay, to unsay, to contradict, to disown.

se **dédire**, *v.r.*, to recant, to retract, to unsay what one has said; to go back from one's word, to recede. *Se — de sa promesse ;* to revoke one's promise. *Il ne peut s'en — ;* he cannot go back on it *or* back out of it.

dédit, *n.m.*, unsaying ; forfeit, forfeiture; retraction; deed stipulating forfeiture. *Au — de ;* on the forfeiture of. *Avoir son dit et son — ;* to say yes one day and no the next.

dédommagement (-maj-mān), *n.m.*, indemnification; compensation, damages, amends, indemnity.

dédommager, *v.a.*, to indemnify, to make amends, to make good; to compensate, to make up for.

se **dédommager**, *v.r.*, to indemnify one's self, to recoup one's self.

dédorer, *v.a.*, to ungild. *Jeunesse dédorée ;* degenerate youth.

se **dédorer**, *v.r.*, to lose its gilt (of metal, etc.).

dédoublé, *n.m.*, diluted alcohol.

dédoublement or **dédoublage**, *n.m.*, dividing into two; unlining; diluting.

dédoubler, *v.a.*, to take out the lining; to divide into two; to dilute; (nav.) to unsheath (a vessel). *— une pierre ;* to cut a stone into two parts lengthwise.

se **dédoubler**, *v.r.*, to become unlined, to be unfolded ; to be divided into two ; to be diluted; (nav.) to be unsheathed.

déduction, *n.f.*, deduction; set off; inference; taking from, defalcation; (obsol.) enumeration, recital.

déduire (déduisant, déduit), *v.a.*, to take from, to deduct, to subtract; to draw from, to deduce, to infer.

⊙**déduit**, *n.m.*, amusement, pleasure, pastime.

déesse, *n.f.*, goddess, female deity.

défâcher, *v.a.*, to pacify.

se **défâcher**, *v.r.*, to be pacified or pleased again, to cool down ; to cease to be angry. *S'il est fâché, qu'il se défâche ;* if he is angry, let him cool down again.

défaçonner, *v.a.*, to put out of shape; to spoil any one's manners.

se **défaçonner**, *v.r.*, to get out of shape ; to lose one's good manners.

***défaillance**, *n.f.*, fainting fit, swoon ; exhaustion; extinction (of a family); ⊙ (chem.) deliquescence. *Tomber en — ;* to fall into a swoon; (jur.) default.

***défaillant**, *n.m.*, -e, *n.f.*, (jur.) defaulter.

***défaillant**, -e, *adj.*, falling off; decaying ; without heirs; weak, feeble; faltering, unsteady.

***défaillir**, *v.n.*, to grow faint and weak, to fail, to sink ; to decay ; to swoon, to faint away. *Ses forces défaillent tous les jours ;* his strength fails him every day. *Il se sent — ;* he feels himself sinking. *Je me sentis — ;* I felt I was going to faint.

défaire, *v.a.*, to undo, to unmake ; to take asunder ; to unpin ; to unrip ; to unknit; to make away with ; to defeat, to rout ; to eclipse, to obscure ; to emaciate, to make lean, to waste; to discompose, to alter; to free, to deliver, to rid. *— une malle ;* to unpack a trunk. *— un nœud ;* to untie a knot. *Sa maladie l'a bien défait ;* his illness has given him a worn appearance. *Défaites-moi de cet importun ;* rid me of that troublesome fellow. *— un marché,* *un mariage ;* to annul, break off, a bargain, a marriage.

se **défaire**, *v.r.*, to rid one's self, to get rid of, to get quit of, to ease one's self of, to make away, to forsake, to leave off ; to come undone, to become loose; to lose strength and quality (of wine). *Se — de son ennemi ;* to dispatch one's enemy. *Se — d'un vice ;* to throw off a vice.

Se — d'une mauvaise habitude; to break one's self of a bad habit. *Défaites-vous de vos préjugés;* shake off your prejudices. *Se — de sa marchandise;* to sell off one's wares. *Se — d'un bénéfice;* to give up a living. *Se — d'un cheval;* to part with a horse. *Se — d'un domestique;* to discharge a servant. *Ce vin se défait;* this wine is losing its flavor.

défait, -e, *part.*, undone, defeated; meager, lean, wasted; pale; worn out, wan.

défaite, *n.f.*, defeat, overthrow; (com.) sale; evasion, shift, put-off, sham, pretense. *Ces marchandises-là sont de bonne —;* those goods command a ready sale. *La — est ingénieuse;* that is an ingenious evasion. *C'est une —;* that is a mere put-off.

défalcation, *n.f.*, defalcation, deduction.

défalquer, *v.a.*, to take off, to defalcate, to deduct.

défausser, *v.a.*, to straighten.

se **défausser**, *v.r.*, (at cards) to get rid of useless cards, or to play a card of another suit.

défaut, *n.m.*, defect; fault; flaw, blemish; want; shortcoming; default. *Chacun a ses —s;* every one has his defects. *Il n'y a personne sans —;* there is no man but has his faults. *Cette pièce de porcelaine a un —;* there is a flaw in that piece of china. *Le — de blé, de subsistances;* want of corn, of victuals. *C'est là le — de la cuirasse;* that's his weak point. *Condamner par —;* to cast for non-appearance. *Jugement par —;* judgment by default. *Les chiens sont en —;* the hounds have lost the scent. *Trouver quelqu'un en —;* to find any one at fault. *Mettre quelqu'un en —;* to baffle, to foil any one, to throw off the scent. *Au —, à — de;* in default of, for want of. *Faire —;* to be wanting; to fail; to be missed.

défaveur, *n.f.*, disfavor, disgrace, discredit.

défavorable, *adj.*, unfavorable, disparaging.

défavorablement, *adv.*, unfavorably; disparagingly.

défécation, *n.f.*, (pharm.) defecation. *Matière à —;* temper (of sugar).

défecti-f, -ve, *adj.*, (gram.) defective.

défection, *n.f.*, defection, falling off, disloyalty.

défectivité, *n.f.*, (gram.) defectiveness.

défectueusement (-éûz-măn), *adv.*, defectively.

défectueu-x, -se, *adj.*, defective, imperfect.

défectuosité, *n.f.*, defect, imperfection, flaw.

défendable, *adj.*, defensible, tenable.

défendant, *part.*, defending. *Il l'a tué à son corps —;* he killed him in self-defense. *Faire une chose à son corps —;* to do a thing reluctantly, in self-defense.

défende-ur, *n.m.*, **-resse**, *n.f.*, (jur.) defendant; respondent.

défendre, *v.a.*, to defend, to protect; to shelter, to shield, to support, to uphold, to vindicate; to forbid, to prohibit. *— son ami;* to defend one's friend. *On a défendu le port des armes;* the carrying of arms is prohibited. *La raison nous défend de faire une injustice;* reason forbids us to do an injustice. *— sa maison à quelqu'un;* to forbid any one the house.

défendre, *v.n.*, (jur.) to defend. *Il a été condamné faute de —;* he was cast for want of being defended; (nav.) to fend off.

se **défendre**, *v.r.*, to defend one's self; to excuse one's self from doing a thing; to clear one's self; to deny a thing; to keep, to shield one's self from; to help, to forbear. *Cet accusé a voulu se — lui-même;* that prisoner wanted to conduct his own defense. *Il ne peut se — de tant de reproches;* he cannot clear himself from so many imputations. *Ne pas s'en — ;* to acknowledge, admit anything. *Je ne m'en défends pas;* I admit it, own it.

défens, *n.m.*, (forestry) defense (of forests).

défendures, *n.f.pl.*, hurdles, fences.

défense, *n.f.*, defense, protection; prohibition, interdiction; apology, vindication, justification; warning, notice; task; (nav.) fender; skid; boom. *pl.*, (fort.) outwork, defense; tusk, fang (of boars); tusk (elephants). *Se mettre en —;* to stand upon one's defense. *Etre hors de —;* not to be in a condition to defend one's self. *Bois en —;* a wood so far grown that cattle may be let into it without danger to the trees. *Cordes de —;* fenders of junk or old cable. *Faire —;* to forbid, to prohibit. *Preuves alléguées pour la — d'une cause;* plea. *Donner ses —s;* to answer. *Arrêt de —;* decree to suspend the execution of a former decree. *Armé, muni, de —s;* tusked, fanged (of boars, elephants). *— d'entrer;* no admittance except on business. *— de fumer;* no smoking allowed. *— d'uriner;* commit no nuisance.

défenseur, *n.m.*, defender, supporter, vindicator, advocate; defender, counsel. *Un — nommé d'office;* a defender appointed by the court.

défensi-f, -ve, *adj.*, defensive.

défensive, *n.f.*, safeguard, defensive. *Se tenir sur la —;* to stand upon the defensive.

déféquer, *v.a.*, to defecate.

déférant, -e, *adj.*, complying, condescending, yielding.

déférence, *n.f.*, deference, regard, respect.

déférent, *adj. m.*, deferent. *Cercle —;* (anc. astron.) deferent. *Canal —;* (anat.) deferent.

déférer, *v.a.*, to confer, to bestow; to tender, to inform against. *— le serment à quelqu'un;* to tender an oath to, to bring before any one, to put any one on his oath. *— quelqu'un en justice;* to impeach any one in court. *— quelqu'un à l'inquisition;* to report any one to the inquisition.

déférer, *v.n.*, to defer, to yield, to comply, to condescend. *— aux sentiments des autres;* to defer to the sentiments of others. *— à quelqu'un;* to pay deference to one.

déferler, *v.a.*, (nav.) to unfurl.

déferler, *v.n.*, to break into foam, to roll in (of the sea). *La lame déferle;* the wave bursts into foam, rolls in shore.

déferrer, *v.a.*, to unshoe (a horse); to nonplus, to confound.

se **déferrer**, *v.r.*, to come off, to fall off, to lose a shoe; to be nonplused or confounded. *Mon lacet se déferre;* the tag is coming off my lace.

défet, *n.m.*, waste sheet (in bookselling).

****défeuillaison**, *n.f.*, defoliation.

****défeuiller**, *v.a.*, to take off the leaves. *Le vent a défeuillé les arbres;* the wind has blown off the leaves.

se **défeuiller**, *v.r.*, to lose, to shed their leaves (of trees). *Les arbres se défeuillent;* the trees are losing, shedding their leaves.

défi, *n.m.*, defiance, challenge. *Un cartel de —;* a written challenge. *Envoyer un — à quelqu'un;* to send any one a challenge. *Je lui ai fait un — aux échecs;* I challenged him to a game at chess. *Mettre au —;* to set at defiance.

défiance, *n.f.*, distrust, mistrust; diffidence, caution. *Concevoir de la —;* to entertain distrust. *Etre dans la —;* to have one's misgivings. *Une sotte — le retient;* he is held back by a foolish diffidence.

défiant, -e, *adj.*, distrustful, mistrustful, suspicious.

déficient, -e, *adj.*, (arith.) deficient.

déficit (-sit), *n.m.*, deficit, deficiency. *Combler le —;* to make up the deficit.

défier, *v.a.*, to defy, to challenge; to brave, to face, to dare; to set at defiance. *— quelqu'un au trictrac;* to challenge any one to play at backgammon. *— les dangers;* to face dangers. *Il ne faut jamais — un fou;* never bid defiance to a madman, *Je vous défie de m'en donner la preuve ;* I defy you to give me a proof of it.

défier, *v.n.*, (nav.) to bear off, to fend.

se défier, *v.r.*, to defy, to challenge, each other ; to distrust, to mistrust ; to suspect. *Je me défie de cet homme ;* I distrust that man. *Se — de ses forces ;* to distrust one's own strength. *Se — de soi-même ;* to distrust one's self.

défigurement, *n.m.*, disfigurement ; defacement.

défigurer, *v.a.*, to disfigure, to mar, to distort, to spoil. *La petite vérole l'a tout défiguré ;* the small-pox has quite disfigured him. *— la vérité ;* to distort the truth.

se défigurer, *v.r.*, to disfigure one's self, to become disfigured, to become deformed.

défilade, *n.f.*, filing past ; going off *or* past ; marching past.

défilé, *n.m.*, defile, narrow pass ; strait, difficulty ; (milit.) defiling, filing off *or* past, marching past. *Je ne vois aucun moyen de sortir de ce — ;* I see no way of getting out of this difficulty.

défilement, *n.m.*, filing off, marching past *or* going past ; (fort.) defilading.

défiler, *v.a.*, to unstring, to unthread ; to untwist. *— des perles ;* to unstring pearls. *— son chapelet ;* to say all one has to say (on a subject). *Elle a défilé son chapelet ;* she has given up devotion. *Le chapelet se défile ;* the association is falling to pieces. *— un ouvrage ;* (fort.) to defilade.

défiler, *v.n.*, to defile, to file off, march past, go past. *Les soldats ne pouvaient — que deux à deux ;* the soldiers could only go past two by two.

défiler, *n.m.*, (milit., l.u.) filing off, marching past.

défini, *n.m.*, the definite.

défini, *-e*, *part.*, determined, definite, defined. *Nombre — ;* definite number.

définir, *v.a.*, to define, to determine ; to decide ; to explain, to describe. *— une personne ;* to give an idea of a person. *Se — ;* to be defined, to be determined, to be made out.

définissable, *adj.*, definable.

définisseur, *n.m.*, definer.

définiteur, *n.m.*, definitor (in convents).

définiti-f, -ve, *adj.*, definitive, final ; ultimate, eventual, peremptory, positive. *En —ve ;* definitively, after all, in short. *En —ve, que voulez-vous ?* in a word, what do you want ?

définition, *n.f.*, definition ; decision, determination. *Faire une — ;* to give a definition.

définitivement (-tiv-mān), *adv.*, definitively, positively, decidedly, ultimately, eventually.

définitoire, *n.m.*, chapter (of monks).

déflagration, *n.f.*, (chem.) deflagration.

défléchi, -e, *adj.*, turned aside, deflected.

défléchir, *v.n.*, to turn from *or* aside, to deflect.

se défléchir, *v.r.*, to deflect.

déflegmation, *n.f.*, (chem.) dephlegmation.

déflegmer, *v.a.*, (chem.) to dephlegmate.

défleuraison, *n.f.*, fall of the blossom.

défleurir, *v.n.*, to shed blossoms.

défleurir, *v.a.*, to nip or strip off blossoms ; to take off the bloom of fruit (by handling it).

déflexion, *n.f.*, (phys.) deviation, deflection.

défloration, *n.f.*, defloration.

déflorer, *v.a.*, to deflour, to deflower. *— un sujet ;* to take the freshness off a subject.

⊙défluer, *v.n.*, (astrol.) to flow, to recede.

défonçage, *n. m.*, (agri.) subsoil plowing ; trenching.

défoncé, -e, *part.*, broken, battered in. *Chemin — ;* broken road.

défoncement (-fons-mān), *n.m.*, (tech.) staving in, beating in of the head of casks ; (agri.) digging up ; deep plowing.

défoncer, *v.a.*, to stave in (a cask) ; to bilge ; to cut up ; to knock in (the head of a cask). *— un terrain ;* to dig up, to trench ground. *— une peau ;* to dip a hide. *— un chapeau ;* to batter in a hat.

se défoncer, *v.r.*, to give way at the bottom ; to break up (of roads) ; to get cut up.

déformation, *n.f.*, deformation.

déformé, -e, *adj.*, deformed, out of shape.

déformer, *v.a.*, to put out of form, to throw out of shape.

se déformer, *v.r.*, to lose the proper form or shape, to get out of shape. *Sa taille se déforme ;* her figure is losing its shape, its litheness.

défortifier, *v.a.*, to dismantle.

se défortifier, *v.r.*, to get dismantled.

défouetter, *v.a.*, (book-bind.) to untie.

défournement, *n.m.*, drawing out of the oven.

défourner, *v.a.*, to draw out of an oven. *— le pain,* to draw the batch.

défourrer, *v.a.*, (nav.) to unwrap, to take off the envelope.

défrai, *n.m.*, (pop.) defraying, settling expenses.

défraîchi, *adj.*, no longer fresh ; faded.

défraîchir, *v.a.*, to destroy, to take off, the brilliancy, gloss, *or* freshness of a thing.

se défraîchir, *v.r.*, to lose its brilliancy, freshness.

défranciser, *v.a.*, to unfrenchify.

défrayement, *n.m.*, defraying.

défrayer, *v.a.*, to defray, to bear, the cost of ; to amuse ; to be the laughing-stock of. *— la compagnie ;* to be the laughing-stock of the company.

défrayeur, *n.m.*, defrayer.

défrichage *or* **défrichement** (-frish-mān), *n.m.*, clearing, grubbing up ; land so cleared. *Faire le — d'un terrain ;* to clear a piece of ground. *Ce — est en plein rapport cette année ;* this piece of cleared land is in full bearing this year.

défriché, *adj.*, cleared (of land).

défricher, *v.a.*, to clear, to grub up ; to unravel (l.u.). *— un champ ;* to clear a field.

défricheur, *n.m.*, clearer, digger.

défrisement (-friz-mān), *n.m.*, uncurling.

défriser, *v.a.*, to uncurl, to put out of curl ; (pop.) to disappoint, to ruffle.

se défriser, *v.r.*, to uncurl, come out of curl.

défroncement, *n.m.*, unplaiting, unfolding.

défroncer, *v.a.*, to undo gathers, folds, or plaits ; to unknit (the brows). *— le sourcil ;* to smooth one's brow.

défroque, *n.f.*, old clothes ; old things, effects ; cast-off clothes.

défroquer, *v.a.*, to unfrock.

se défroquer, *v.r.*, to forsake, to renounce one's order (of monks).

défruiter, *v.a.*, to strip of its fruit.

défuner, *v.a.*, (nav.) to strip (a mast).

défunt, -e, *adj.*, defunct, deceased, late. *Les enfants du — ;* the deceased's children.

dégagé, -e, *part.*, disengaged ; redeemed (of a pledge) ; flippant ; bold ; easy ; slender, graceful. *Chambre —e ;* room that has a back-door. *Escalier — ;* back stairs. *Taille —e ;* free, easy figure (pers.). *Air — ;* free, easy way or manner.

dégagement (-gaj-mān), *n.m.*, redeeming, disengagement, clearance ; (fenc.) disengaging ; release, liberation, discharge. *Le — d'effets déposés au mont-de-piété ;* the redeeming of articles at the pawnbroker's. *Le — de sa parole ;* the calling in of one's word. *Le — de la voie publique ;* the clearing of the street. *Le — de la poitrine ;* the easing of the chest. *Escalier de — ;* private staircase. *Tuyau de — ;* waste pipe.

dégager, *v.a.*, to redeem ; to take out of pawn ; to free, to clear, to disengage, to extricate, to disentangle, to separate; to evolve; to deliver, to rescue. — *sa parole;* to redeem one's word; to withdraw one's word. — *quelqu'un de sa parole;* to release any one from his word. — *une porte;* to clear a doorway. — *la tête, la poitrine;* to ease, relieve, *or* lighten the head, the chest. *Il l'a dégagé de ses ennemis;* he rescued him from his enemies. *Je le dégageai de ses liens;* I freed him from his bonds. — *le fer;* (fenc.) to disengage. *Cet habit dégage la taille;* that coat shows off the figure to advantage. — *les cheveux;* to disentangle the hair.

se **dégager**, *v.r.,* to be cleared from; to extricate, to disengage, to free, to disentangle, to loose one's self; to break loose; to get away, to get clear; (chem.) to be evolved.

dégaine, *n.f.,* (fam.) awkwardness; ridiculous manners, deportment, awkward gait, &c. *Quelle —! * what a figure for you.

dégainer, *n.m.,* unsheathing, drawing (of a sword). *Etre brave jusqu'au —;* to be brave till it comes to the push.

dégainer, *v.a.,* to draw, to unsheath one's sword; to fork out.

dégaineur, *n.m.,* fighter, bully, quarrelsome fellow, professed duelist.

dégaler, *v.a.,* to pick clean (of skins).

dégalonner, *v.a.,* to unlace, unstrip.

déganter, *v.a.,* to pull off gloves.

se **déganter**, *v.r.,* to take off one's gloves.

dégarni, -e, *adj.,* unfinished; bare, naked; empty.

dégarnir, *v.a.,* to untrim, to unfurnish, to strip; to thin; to uncover; to dismantle. — *une chambre, une maison;* to unfurnish a room, a house. — *le cabestan;* (nav.) to unring the capstan. — *un vaisseau de ses agrès;* to strip a vessel of its rigging. — *un arbre;* to thin a tree. — *une robe;* to untrim a gown.

se **dégarnir**, *v.r.,* to strip one's self; to empty, become empty; to grow thin; to lose; to part with; to wear lighter clothes. *Sa tête se dégarnit;* his hair is growing thin. *La salle se dégarnit;* the house is getting empty. *Il ne faut pas trop se hâter de se —;* people should not be in too great a hurry to put on lighter clothing.

dégasconner, *v.a.,* to teach a Gascon to speak good French, to acquire French manners, &c.

se **dégasconner**, *v.r.,* to lose the Gascon accent.

dégât, *n. m.,* havoc, damage, depredation, waste, ravage. *La grêle a fait un grand —;* the hail has caused great havoc. *Faire le —;* to ravage.

dégauchi, -e, *adj.,* planed, smoothed, straightened.

dégauchir, *v.a.,* to smooth, to plane, to level, to straighten; to form, to polish. — *un jeune homme;* to polish a young man.

dégauchissage *or* **dégauchissement** (-shismān), *n. m.,* planing, straightening, leveling, smoothing.

dégazer, *v.a.,* (chem.) to free from gas.

dégazonnement, *n.m.,* unturfing.

dégazonner, *v.a.,* to unturf.

dégel, *n.m.,* thaw. *Avoir du —;* to have a thaw. *Etre au —;* to be thawing (of the weather). *Le vent est au —;* the wind will bring on a thaw.

dégeler (dé-jlé), *v.a.n.,* to thaw.

se **dégeler**, *v.r.,* to thaw.

⊙**dégénérat-eur, -rice,** *adj.,* degenerating.

dégénération, *n.f.,* degeneration; degeneracy, deterioration.

dégénérér, *v.n.,* to decline, to degenerate, to fall away (from). — *de ses ancêtres;* to degenerate from one's ancestors.

dégénérescence, *n.f.,* (med.). *V.* **dégénération.**

dégénérescent, -e, *adj.,* degenerating.

dégingandé, -e, *adj.,* tottering; awkward;

gawky; swinging in one's gait; clumsy; illformed; unconnected; disjointed.

se **dégingander**, *v.r.,* to get out of shape; to swing about.

dégîter, *v.a.,* (hunt.) to dislodge, to start.

dégluer, *v.a.,* to take off the bird-lime; to unglue.

se **dégluer**, *v.r.,* to get rid of bird-lime; to get unglued *or* cleared (of the eyes).

déglutition, *n.f.,* deglutition, swallowing.

*dégobiller**, *v.a.,* (l.ex.) to bring up; to puke, to spew, to vomit, to throw up.

*dégobillis**, *n.m.,* (l.ex.) vomit, spew.

dégoiser, *v.a.n.,* ⊙ to chirp, to twitter; to rattle; to blab out; to chatter; to prattle. *En dégoise-t-elle!* how she does rattle on, to be sure! *Il a dégoisé tout ce qu'il sait;* he blabbed out all he knew.

dégommage, *n.m.,* ungumming.

dégommer, *v.a.,* (dy.) to wash out the gum; (pop.) to turn out of office; to oust; to kill.

dégonder, *v.a.,* to unhinge, to take from its hinge.

se **dégonder**, *v.r.,* to come unhinged, to come off its hinges.

dégonflement, *n.m.,* subsiding, falling, collapsing; reduction.

dégonfler, *v.a.,* to cause a thing to collapse, to reduce a swelling; to discharge the gas from a balloon.

se **dégonfler**, *v.r.,* to go down, to be reduced, to subside, to unbosom one's self.

dégor, *n.m.,* a discharging tube.

dégorgement, *n.m.,* breaking out, overflowing; unstopping; outfall, outflow. — *d'un tuyau;* cleansing, unstopping of a pipe.

dégorgeoir (-joar), *n.m.,* priming-iron, ventbit (for guns); outlet, issue; spout.

dégorger, *v.a.,* to clear, to open; to cleanse, to scour.

dégorger, *v.n.,* to discharge one's self, to overflow. *Faire —;* to purge (fish); (fig.) to make any one stump up.

se **dégorger**, *v.r.,* to discharge, to empty itself; to get unstopped, to get clear.

dégoter, *v.a.,* (pop.) to knock down; to oust, to displace, to push off.

dégourdi, -e, *adj.,* quick, sharp, acute, shrewd (pers.); tepid (water). *C'est un homme bien —;* he is a shrewd fellow.

dégourdi, *n.m., -e,* *n.f.,* quick, sharp, acute, shrewd man *or* boy; pert, forward woman *or* girl.

dégourdir, *v.a.,* to quicken, to revive; to sharpen, to render shrewd; to polish. — *ses jambes;* to stretch one's limbs. *Faire — de l'eau;* to take the chill off water. — *un jeune homme;* to polish a young man.

se **dégourdir**, *v.r.,* to remove the numbness from; to lose the numbness of; to stretch one's self; to become sharp, polished, shrewd; to brighten up.

dégourdissement (-dis-mān), *n.m.,* removal of numbness; return of circulation; quickening, reviving.

dégoût, *n. m.,* disgust, disrelish, loathing; dislike, distaste; mortification. *Il lui a pris du — pour la viande;* he has taken a dislike to meat. *Avoir du — pour la vie;* to be disgusted with life. *On lui a donné bien des —s;* they made him swallow many a bitter pill.

dégoûtant, -e, *adj.,* disgusting, loathsome, distasteful, nauseous, sickening; unpleasant, disheartening. *Plaie —;* disgusting sore.

dégoûté, -e, *n.* and *adj.,* fastidious person, fastidious. *Faire le —;* to be squeamish, fastidious. *C'est un bon —;* he likes good things. *Vous n'êtes pas —!* you're not at all particular! I should rather think so!

dégoûter, *v.a.,* to disgust; to put out of

conceit. *Cela est bien fait pour — quelqu'un du métier ;* that is well calculated to disgust any one with the trade. *Il est dégoûté de la vie ;* he is disgusted with life.

se dégoûter, *v.r.,* to take a disgust, a dislike, a distaste to ; to nauseate, to dislike, to lose courage, to be disheartened.

dégouttant, -e, *adj.,* dropping, dripping.

dégouttement, *n. m.,* dripping, falling in drops.

dégoutter, *v.n.,* to drop, to trickle, to drip, to dribble. *La sueur lui dégouttait du front ;* the perspiration was rolling off his forehead. *Faire — du beurre sur de la viande ;* to drip butter upon meat.

dégradant, -e, *adj.,* degrading, debasing.

dégradation, *n.f.,* degradation ; (mil.) cashiering, drumming out ; damage, dilapidation ; (jur.) waste ; (paint.) diminution of light and shade.

dégrader, *v.a.,* to debase, to degrade, to deface, to strip ; (paint.) to diminish the light and shade ; to damage, to dilapidate ; (mil.) to cashier, to drum out. *— un bois, une maison ;* to damage a wood, a house. *Le temps a dégradé ce monument ;* time has defaced that monument.

se dégrader, *v.r.,* to degrade, to debase, to disgrace one's self ; to become damaged, defaced, dilapidated ; (jur.) to waste.

dégrafer, *v.a.,* to unclasp, to unhook.

se dégrafer, *v.r.,* to become unhooked, unfastened (of garments) ; to unbutton, unhook, unfasten one's clothes.

dégraissage or **dégraissement,** *n.m.,* cleaning, scouring.

dégraisser, *v. a.,* to scour, to remove greasy stains ; to fleece any one ; to impoverish land, to carry off the soil ; (carp.) to beard, to thin ; (cook.) to remove fat. *— un bouillon ;* to skim the fat off broth. *— un habit ;* to clean a coat. *La poudre dégraisse les cheveux ;* powder cleans the hair. *Terre à —;* fuller's earth. *Les ravines dégraissent les terres ;* torrents impoverish land (by carrying off the soil).

dégraisseur, *n.m.,* scourer, cleaner.

dégraissis, *n.m.,* scourings.

dégraissoir, *n.m.,* scraper.

dégravoiement or **dégravoiment,** *n. m.,* (arch.) baring, laying bare (by water).

dégravoyer, *v.a.,* (arch.) to wash away, to bare, to lay bare (of water).

degré, *n.m.,* step, stair, staircase ; stage, grade, gradation ; degree, point, extent, pitch ; (astron., geol., gram., math., phys.) degree ; (of universities) degree. *A un très haut —;* to a very great extent. *Par — s ;* gradually. *Au suprême —;* in the highest degree.

dégréement, *n.m.,* (nav.) unrigging.

dégréer, *v.a.,* (nav.) to unrig. *— un mât ;* to strip a mast.

dégrèvement (-grèv-mān), *n.m.,* reduction, relief ; disencumbrance ; redemption.

dégrever, *v.a.,* to diminish, to reduce (a tax) ; to disencumber, to free, to redeem.

dégringolade, *n.f.,* fall, tumble.

dégringoler, *v.n.,* to run down, to tumble down ; to topple down or over ; to go from bad to worse ; to go to the dogs.

dégrisement (-griz-mān), *n.m.,* (fam.) sobering, getting sober ; cooling down.

dégriser, *v.a.,* to sober ; to cool, to bring to one's senses.

se dégriser, *v.r.,* to sober down ; to come to one's senses ; to cool down ; to lose one's illusions.

dégrossage, *n.m.,* drawing fine ; (wire-drawing) reducing, thinning.

dégrosser, *v.a.,* to reduce ; to thin (ingots).

dégrossi, *n.m.,* (arts) roughing, rough-hewing, roughing down ; dressing, drawing.

dégrossir, *v.a.,* to chip, to chip off the grosser parts ; to rough-hew, to hew down ; to clear up,

to unravel ; to make a rough sketch of. *— un bloc de marbre ;* to chip a block of marble.

dégrossissage, *n.m.,* (arts) roughing, roughhewing ; roughening down ; (carp.) dressing, trimming.

*déguenillé, -e (dég-ni-lé), *n.m.f.* and *adj.,* tatterdemalion, ragged person ; tattered, ragged, in rags. *Un grand —;* a big tatterdemalion. *Quelle est cette petite —e?* who is that little girl in rags and tatters? *Elle était toute —e ;* she was in rags and tatters. *Un habit —;* a ragged coat.

déguerpir, *v.a.,* (jur.) to quit, to give up.

déguerpir (-ghèr-), *v.n.,* to pack off, to move off ; to be gone. *Je le ferai bien —;* I'll make him pack off. *— au plus vite ;* to be gone as fast as possible.

déguerpissement (-ghèr-pis-mān), *n.m.,* (jur.) quitting ; yielding, giving over, departure, removal.

dégueuler (-gheu-), *v.n.,* (l.ex.) to spew, to vomit.

*déguignonner (-ghi-), *v.a.,* to change illluck, to bring better luck to.

déguisement (-ghiz-mān), *n.m.,* concealment, disguise. *Parlez sans —;* speak openly.

déguisable, *adj.,* disguisable, concealable.

déguiser (-ghi-), *v.a.,* to disguise, to conceal, to hide. *On le déguisa en femme ;* they disguised him as a woman.

se déguiser, *v.r.,* to disguise one's self ; to conceal from one's self.

dégustateur, *n.m.,* taster (of wines).

dégustation, *n.f.,* tasting (of wines).

déguster, *v.a.,* to taste (wines) ; to sip. *Se —;* to be tasted, to be sipped.

déhaler, *v.n.,* (nav.) to tow out or back out.

déhâler, *v.a.,* to take off sun-burns.

se déhâler, *v.r.,* to clear one's complexion.

déhanché, -e, *adj.,* hipped, hipshot ; (fig.) ungainly. *n.m.f.,* hipshot person ; ungainly man, woman or girl.

déhanchement, *n.m.,* swinging about ; twisting about.

se déhancher, *v.r.,* to waddle, to swing about, to twist one's body about.

déharnachement (-nash-mān), *n.m.,* unharnessing.

déharnacher, *v.a.,* to unharness.

déhiscence, *n.f.,* (bot.) dehiscence.

déhiscent, -e, *adj.,* (bot.) dehiscent.

déhonté, -e, *adj.,* shameless, unabashed, *C'est un homme —;* he is a man destitute of shame.

dehors (dĕ-or), *adv.,* out, without, out of doors, abroad, externally ; (nav.) out, at sea. *En —;* without, outside. *Au —;* outwardly. *De —;* from without. *Au dedans et au —;* at home and abroad. *Mettre quelqu'un —;* to turn any one out of doors.

dehors, *n.m.,* outside, exterior. *pl.,* appearances ; (fort.) outworks ; dependencies, approaches, grounds (of a house). *Sauver les —;* to save appearances.

déhortatoire, *adj.,* dehortatory.

déicide, *n.m.,* deicide.

déification, *n.f.,* deification.

déifier, *v.a.,* to deify.

déisme, *n.m.,* deism.

déiste, *n.m.,* deist.

déiste, *adj.,* deistical.

déité, *n.f.,* deity, god, goddess, divinity.

déjà, *adv.,* already, before, yet. *Pas — si ;* not so very, not so great. *Pas — tant ;* not so very much.

déjection, *n.f.,* (med.) dejection ; ejection, evacuation.

déjeté, -e, *part., adj.,* warped, sprung.

se déjeter, *v.r.,* to warp (of wood) ; (med.) to deviate.

déjettement (dé-jèt-mān), *n.m.*, warping; deviation.

déjeuner *or* **déjeuné**, *n.m.*, breakfast, breakfast-service. — *à la fourchette;* meat breakfast. *Second* —; luncheon. *Un* — *de porcelaine;* a porcelain breakfast-service.

déjeuner, *v.n.*, to breakfast.

déjoindre, *v.a.*, to disjoin, to disunite, to sever.

se **déjoindre**, *v.r.*, to become disjoined, to separate, to part, to come apart.

déjouer, *v.a.*, to baffle, to frustrate, to foil. — *un projet;* to baffle a project. — *quelqu'un;* to baffle any one, to foil any one.

déjouer, *v.n.*, (fam.) to play badly; (nav.) to wave, to flutter (of the flag).

déjucher, *v.n.a.*, to unroost, to come down from the roost. *Je vous ferai bien* — *de là;* I will make you come down from there.

déjuger, *v.a.*, to judge differently.

se **déjuger**, *v.r.*, to change, to reverse one's opinion.

delà, *prep.*, beyond; farther than, on the other side of. *Au* —, *de* —, *par* —, *en* —; beyond, further on, upwards. *Deçà et* —; right and left; all about. *Jambe deçà, jambe* —; one leg this side, the other that side.

délabré, **-e**, *part.*, tattered, in rags, shabby, seedy; (of things) tumbledown, ramshackle. *Une santé* —; shattered health. *Un navire* —; a dismantled vessel. *Terre* —; land gone to waste. *Un estomac* —; a disordered stomach. *Être* —; to be all in tatters.

délabrement, *n.m.*, ruin, decay, dilapidation; shabbiness, raggedness.

délabrer, *v.a.*, to shatter, to ruin, to pull to pieces, to destroy, to tear to tatters.

se **délabrer**, *v.r.*, to fall to tatters, to pieces, to go to ruin; to decay. *Tous mes meubles se délabrent;* all my furniture is going to wrack and ruin.

délacer, *v.a.*, to unlace. — *un corset;* to unlace stays.

se **délacer**, *v.r.*, to unlace one's self; to come undone (of stays, strings, etc.).

délai, *n.m.*, delay, extension of time, reprieve. *User de* —s; to put off, to procrastinate. *Dans un* — *de;* within (a given time).

délaiement, *n.m.*, diluting.

délaissé, **-e**, *part.*, abandoned, forlorn, forsaken, friendless. *Des orphelins* —s; helpless orphans.

délaissement (-lès-mān), *n.m.*, destitution, forlornness, helplessness, desertion; (jur.) abandonment to a mortgagee.

délaisser, *v.a.*, to forsake, to abandon; to cast off, to desert, to leave; to relinquish. *Se* —; to give up one's property (in favor of another).

délardement, *n.m.*, (arch.) unlarding; splay, slope, beveling, chamfering.

délarder, *v.a.*, (arch.) to unlard, to splay, to bevel, to chamfer.

délassement (-lâs-mān), *n.m.*, remission of attention *or* application, relaxation; repose, recreation, diversion.

délasser, *v.a.*, to refresh, to relax, to divert. *Le sommeil vous délasse;* sleep refreshes one. *Un changement d'occupation délasse l'esprit;* a change of occupation relaxes the mind.

se **délasser**, *v.r.*, to refresh one's self, to rest.

délat-eur, *n.m.*, **-rice**, *n.f.*, informer, denouncer, accuser.

délation, *n.f.*, information, denunciation, informing.

délatter, *v.a.*, to unlath.

délavage, *n.m.*, diluting of color (in drawing and water-color painting); soaking.

délavé, **-e**, *adj.*, weak, pale, dim (of gems); diluted (of colors).

délaver, *v.a.*, to dilute color (in drawing

and water-color painting); to soak, imbibe with water.

se **délaver**, *v.r.*, to become soaked, imbibed with water; to lose color.

délayable, *adj.*, dilutable.

délayage, *n.m.*, diluting, dilution.

délayant, *n.m.*, (med.) diluent.

délayant, **-e**, *adj.*, (med.) diluent.

délayement (-lè-i-mān), *n.m.*, diluting.

délayer, *v.a.*, to dilute; to temper (lime); to spin out.

deleatur, *n.m.*, (—) (print.) dele.

délectable, *adj.*, delicious, delectable, delightful.

délectablement, *adv.*, deliciously, delightfully.

délectation, *n.f.*, delectation, delight, gratification.

délecter, *v.a.*, (l.u.) to delight.

se **délecter**, *v.r.*, to take delight. *Se* — *à l'étude;* to delight in study.

délégant *or* **délégateur**, *n.m.*, **-e**, **-trice**, *n.f.*, delegator.

délégataire, *n.m.f.*, delegatee.

délégation, *n.f.*, delegation, assignment; proxy.

délégatoire, *adj.*, delegatory.

délégué (-ghé), *n.m.*, delegate, deputy; proxy.

délégué, **-e**, *adj.*, delegated.

déléguer (-ghé), *v.a.*, to delegate; to assign. — *son autorité;* to delegate one's authority.

se **déléguer**, *v.r.*, to be delegated, assigned.

délestage, *n.m.*, (nav.) unballasting.

délester, *v.a.*, to unballast.

délesteur, *n.m.*, (nav.) ballast-heaver, ballast-lighter.

délétère, *adj.*, deleterious.

délibérant, **-e**, *adj.*, deliberative.

délibérati-f, **-ve**, *adj.*, deliberative.

délibération, *n.f.*, deliberation; resolution. *Mettre en* —; to bring under deliberation.

délibéré, **-e**, *adj.*, deliberate, bold, decided, resolute. *Marcher d'un pas* —; to walk resolutely. *De propos* —; with set purpose, designedly, purposely.

délibéré, *n.m.*, (jur.) deliberation.

délibérément, *adv.*, deliberately, boldly, resolutely.

délibérer, *v.n.*, to deliberate; to determine, to resolve. *Il n'y a pas lieu à* —; there is no occasion for deliberating. *Il en sera délibéré;* it shall be taken into consideration.

délicat, **-e**, *adj.*, delicate, weak, dainty, nice, touchy, fastidious, ticklish. *Vous êtes bien* —; you are very fastidious. *Faire le* —; to be fastidious. *Affaire* —*e;* ticklish affair. *Il est* — *sur le point d'honneur;* he is very tender on points of honor. *Il est* — *sur le manger;* he is very dainty.

délicatement (-kat-mān), *adv.*, delicately, daintily, tenderly. *Peu* —; indelicately.

⊙**délicater**, *v.a.*, to cocker, to fondle, to pamper. *V.* **dorloter**.

se **délicater**, *v.r.*, to nurse one's self, to indulge one's self.

délicatesse, *n.f.*, delicacy; tenderness; daintiness, scrupulousness, refinement; nicety (of language); ticklishness; squeamishness; considerateness. *pl.*, dainties. *Les* —s *d'une langue;* the niceties of a language. *Avoir une grande* — *de conscience;* to have a very scrupulous conscience. *Ce serait une* — *de votre part;* it would be very nice of you.

délice, *n.m. sing.;* **délices**, *n.f. pl.*, delight, pleasure; deliciousness. *Goûter les* —s *de la vie;* to enjoy the delights of life. *Faire ses* —s *d'une chose;* to delight in a thing. *Je faisais les* —s *de ma mère;* I was my mother's darling.

délicieusement (-eûz-mān), *adv.*, deliciously, delightfully.

délicieu-x, -se, *adj.,* delicious, delightful; capital. *Cette histoire est —se;* that's a capital story.

se **délicoter,** *v.r.,* (man.) to slip the halter.

délictueux, -se, *adj.,* (jur.) unlawful, felonious.

délié, -e, *adj.,* untied, loose; small, thin; light, easy, flowing (of style); slender, slim; cunning. *Avoir l'esprit —;* to be quick, shrewd. *Avoir la langue —e;* to have a voluble, glib tongue.

délié, *n.m.,* (penmanship) thin stroke, upstroke.

délier, *v.a.,* to unbind; to untie; to liberate, to release, to absolve. *— quelqu'un d'un serment;* to free any one from an oath. *On l'a délié de ses vœux;* he was liberated from his vows.

se **délier,** *v.r.,* to come untied, to get unfastened; to get loose.

délimitation, *n.f.,* settling the limits, fixing the boundaries.

délimiter, *v.a.,* to settle the boundaries, fix the limits.

délinéation, *n.f.,* delineation.

délinéer, *v.a.,* to delineate.

délinquant, *n.m., -e, n.f.,* delinquent, offender.

⊙**délinquer,** *v.n.,* (jur.) to offend, to trespass.

déliot, *n.m.,* finger-stall, thumb-stall.

déliquescence (-kès-sänss), *n.f.,* (chem.) deliquescence.

déliquescent, -e, *adj.,* (chem.) deliquescent.

deliquium (-kui-om), *n.m.,* (chem.) deliquium.

délirant, -e, *n.* and *adj.,* (med.) one who is delirious; delirious, frenzied, frantic; maddening, rapturous.

délire, *n.m.,* delirium, frenzy, folly, deliriousness. *Avoir le —;* to rave. *Tomber en —;* to become delirious.

délirer, *v.n.,* to be delirious, to rave, to wander.

delirium tremens (de-li-riom tré-mïnss), *n.m.,* (*n.p.*) (med.) delirium tremens.

délissage, *n.m.,* roughing, ruffling; sorting (of rags).

délisser, *v.a.,* to rough, ruffle, sort.

délisseur, -se, *n.m.f.,* sorter (of rags).

délit, *n.m.,* misdemeanor, delinquency, offense; (mas.) wrong bed (of stone). *En flagrant —;* in the very act.

déliter, *v.a.,* (mas.) to surbed (stones).

se **déliter,** *v.r.,* to break in the grain; to cleave; to scale off.

délitescence (-tès-säns), *n.f.,* (med.) delitescence.

délivrance, *n.f.,* deliverance, delivery; rescue, relief.

délivre, *n.m.,* (anat.) after-birth; heam (of animals).

délivrer, *v.a.,* to deliver, to release, to set free; to rid of, to hand over. *— de prison;* to release from prison. *— de la marchandise;* to deliver goods. *Se faire —;* to obtain, to take out.

se **délivrer,** *v.r.,* to deliver one's self, to free one's self.

délivreur, *n.m.,* deliverer; rescuer; (man.) ostler; groom; (techn.) one of the two drums of a cotton-machine.

délogement (-loj-män), *n.m.,* removal; change of quarters, departure, decamping.

déloger, *v.n.,* to remove, to quit, to go from one's house; to go away, to march off. *— sans tambour ni trompette;* to march off in silence, to steal away; to decamp quietly, to bolt in the night.

déloger, *v.a.,* to turn out (of house); to oust; to drive away; (milit.) to dislodge.

délové, *adj.,* (nav.) uncoiled (of rope).

délover, *v.a.,* (nav.) to uncoil.

déloyal, -e, *adj.,* disloyal, false, treacherous, unfair.

déloyalement (dé-loa-yal-män), *adv.,* disloyally, treacherously.

déloyauté, *n.f.,* dishonesty, perfidiousness, treachery.

delta, *n.m.,* (geog.) delta.

deltoïde, *adj.,* (anat., bot.) deltoid.

déluge, *n.m.,* deluge, flood. *Un — de larmes;* a flood of tears. *Un — de paroles;* a torrent of words.

déluré, -e, *adj.,* wide-awake, sharp.

délustrer, *v.a.,* to take off the luster, the gloss of.

déluter, *v.a.,* to unlute.

démagogie, *n.f.,* demagogism.

démagogique, *adj.,* demagogic, demagogical.

démagogue (-gog), *n.m.f.,* demagogue.

démaigrir, *v.n.,* (jest.) to recover flesh.

démaigrir, *v.a.,* (arch.) to thin.

démailler, *v.a.,* to undo the meshes of.

se **démailler,** *v.r.,* to become undone.

***démailloter,** *v.a.,* to unswathe.

demain, *adv.,* to-morrow. *— matin;* to-morrow morning. *— soir;* to-morrow night. *Après —;* the day after to-morrow. *A — les affaires!* we will talk of business another day!

demain, *n.m.,* to-morrow. *Avec lui c'est toujours —;* he is always putting off, procrastinating.

démanché, -e, *adj.,* off the handle; (fig.) ungainly, loose, dislocated, unconnected, disjointed.

démanché, *n.m.,* an ungainly fellow; (mus.) shift.

démanchement (-mansh-män), *n.m.,* taking off (a handle); unhafting; (mus.) shift.

démancher, *v.a.,* to take off the handle, to unhaft.

se **démancher,** *v.r.,* to lose its handle; to go wrong; (mus.) to shift.

démancher, *v.n.,* (nav.) to get out of the channel; (mus.) to shift.

demande, *n.f.,* question, query, request, petition; demand, suit, inquiry; (com.) order, proposal; (mus.) subject of a fugue. *Faire sa — par écrit;* to present one's request in writing. *Appuyer une —;* to second a request. *A sotte — point de réponse;* a silly question needs no answer.

demander, *v.a.,* to ask, to beg, to request, to solicit, to sue for, to demand; (jur.) to pray; to desire; to wish, to want; to ask for, to call for; to inquire after; to require; (com.) to order. *Faire —;* to ask for. *— l'aumône;* to ask for alms. *— son pain;* to beg one's bread. *Que demandez-vous?* what do you want? *N'est-il venu personne me —?* has nobody called for me? *On vous demande;* you are wanted. *Cela demande une explication;* that requires an explanation. *On demande;* wanted. *Ne pas — mieux;* to ask for nothing better; to be only too glad; to be most happy to.

demander, *v.n.,* to ask, to beg; to wish, to request; to require, to demand.

se **demander,** *v.r.,* to ask one's self, to wonder.

demandeu-r, *n.m., -se, n.f.,* asker; applicant. *A beau — beau refuseur;* diamond cut diamond.

demande-ur, *n.m.,* **-resse,** *n.f.,* (jur.) demandant, plaintiff.

démangeaison (-jè-zon), *n.f.,* itching; longing. *Avoir une grande — de parler;* to be dying to talk.

démanger, *v.n.,* to itch; to long. *La tête me démange;* my head itches. *Les pieds lui démangent;* he longs to go out.

démanteler (-man-tlé), *v.a.,* (milit.) to dismantle.

démantellement (tèl-män), *n.m.,* (fort., milit.) dismantling.

démantibuler, *v.a.*, to break, to dislocate; to put out of order.

démarcation, *n.f.*, demarcation. *Ligne de* —; line of demarcation.

démarche, *n.f.*, gait, walk; proceeding, measure; step, course; application, overture. — *noble; noble* bearing. *Faire une* —; to take a step; to make an application. *On observe toutes ses* —*s ;* all his steps are dogged.

démarier, *v.a.*, to annul a marriage.

se **démarier**, *v.r.*, to get unmarried.

démarquer, *v.a.*, to unmark.

démarquer, *v.n.*, to lose the mark of its age (of a horse).

démarrage, *n.m.*, unmooring.

démarrer, *v.a.*, to unmoor. — *un cordage ;* to unbend a rope.

démarrer, *v.n.*, to leave, to slip her moorings (of a ship); to move, to stir, to get away.

démasquer, *v.a.*, to unmask; to show up. — *une batterie ;* to unmask a battery.

se **démasquer**, *v.r.*, to unmask, to take off one's mask. *Il s'est démasqué ;* he has pulled off his mask.

démâtage, *n.m.*, (nav.) dismasting.

démâter, *v.a.*, to dismast.

démâter, *v.n.*, to lose her masts (of a ship).

démêlage, *n.m.*, combing (of wool).

démêlé, *n.m.*, strife, contest, contention, quarrel. *Leur* — *est fini ;* their difference is at an end.

démêler, *v.a.*, to disentangle, to separate; to contest; to distinguish; to discern, to clear up, to penetrate, to fathom, to unravel, to extricate; to untwist, to unfold; to comb out. *Avoir à* — *avec ;* to have to do with. *Je ne veux rien avoir à* — *avec lui ;* I will have nothing to do with him. — *le vrai d'avec le faux ;* to distinguish truth from falsehood.

se **démêler**, *v.r.*, to be unraveled; to be disentangled, to extricate one's self; to get clear of, to comb one's hair.

démêloir, *n.m.*, large tooth-comb.

démembrement, *n.m.*, dismemberment; dismembered part.

démembrer, *v.a.*, to tear limb from limb; to dismember, to disjoint.

déménagement (-naj-mān), *n.m.*, household removal, removing, change of residence. *Voiture de* —; furniture van.

déménager, *v.a.*, to remove one's furniture.

déménager, *v.n.*, to remove (to change one's residence. *Sa raison déménage ;* he is getting childish.

déménageur, *n.m.*, furniture-remover.

démence, *n.f.*, insanity, madness, lunacy, mental aberration. *Tomber en* —; to become insane.

se **démener**, *v.r.*, to stir, to struggle, to make a great fuss, to strive hard, to toil and moil. *Se* — *avec vigueur ;* to struggle vigorously.

démenti, *n.m.*, lie; flat contradiction, disappointment. *Donner un* — *à quelqu'un ;* to give any one the lie. *Vous en aurez le* —; you will get the worst of it, to be worsted.

démentir, *v.a.*, to give the lie to, to contradict; to deny; to belie, to refute. *Démentirez-vous votre signature ?* will you deny your signature ? — *sa gloire ;* to belie one's fame. *Ses actions démentent ses discours ;* his actions belie his language.

se **démentir**, *v.r.*, to contradict one's self; to belie one's self; to fall off, to flag, to give way. *Cet ouvrage se dément un peu vers la fin ;* this work falls off, flags, a little towards the end.

démérite, *n.m.*, demerit.

démériter, *v.n.*, to demerit. *Je n'ai point démérité de vous, auprès de vous ;* I have done nothing to forfeit your esteem.

démesuré, -e, *adj.*, huge, immoderate; inor-

dinate, unbounded, excessive. *Il a une envie — e de vous voir ;* he is dying to see you.

démesurément, *adv.*, immoderately, inordinately, excessively, hugely.

démettre, *v.a.*, to put out of joint, to dislocate; to dismiss; to turn out; (jur.) to overrule, to nonsuit.

se **démettre**, *v.r.*, to be put out of joint; to resign, to throw up (an appointment). *Il s'est démis le poignet ;* he has dislocated his wrist. *Se* — *de son emploi ;* to resign one's position.

démeublement, *n.m.*, unfurnishing; absence of furniture.

démeubler, *v.a.*, to unfurnish, to strip of furniture.

demeurant, *n.m.*, remainder, residue. *au* **demeurant**, *adv.*, in other respects; after all, otherwise.

demeurant, -e, *adj.*, (jur.) dwelling, living, abiding.

demeure, *n.f.*, abode, home, dwelling, lodgings; stay; (jur.) delay. *Changer sa* — *de* —; to change one's lodgings. *En* —; behindhand; in arrears. *Mettre en* —; (jur.) to summon, to compel, to lay under the necessity. *Etre à* —; to be a fixture, stationary. *Cela n'est pas à* —; that is only temporary. *Péril en la* —; danger in delay.

demeurer, *v.n.*, to live, to lodge, to reside; to continue, to remain, to rest; to stay; to stand, to stop. — *à la campagne ;* to live in the country. — *en arrière ;* to stay behind. — *sur son appétit ;* not to fully satisfy one's appetite. *Où en êtes-vous demeuré ?* where did you leave off ? *Demeurons-en là ;* let us keep to that, let us stop there. *La victoire nous est demeurée ;* victory remained with us. — *d'accord ;* to agree.

demi, *n.m.*, (arith.) half. *Deux demies font un entier ;* two halves make a whole.

demi, -e, *adj.*, half. *Un demi-pied ;* half a foot. *Demi-soupir ;* (mus.) quaver rest. *Un pied et* —; a foot and a half. *Une demi-heure ;* half an hour. *Une heure et* —*e ;* an hour and a half. *Entendre à demi-mot ;* (— — -*s*) to take in any one's meaning at once. *Demi-cercle*, (— — -*s*) semi-circle. *En demi-cercle ;* semi-circular. *Demi-dieu*, (— — -*x*) demi-god. *A fourbe, fourbe et* —; set a thief to catch a thief. *N'en pas faire à* —; not to stop half-way; to go right through with.

demi, *adv.*, half. *Il est à* —*-fou ;* he is half mad. *Faire les choses à* —; to do things by halves.

demie, *n.f.*, the half-hour.

démieller, *v.a.*, to take the honey off.

demi-bain, *n.m.*, hip-bath.

demi-fleuron, *n.m.*, (— — -*s*). *V.* fleuron.

demi-fortune, *n.f.*, (— — -*s*) four-wheeled one-horse carriage.

demi-jour, *n.m.*, twilight.

demi-lune, *n.f.*, (— — —) (fort.) crescent, half-moon.

⊙**demi-métal**, *n.m.*, semi-metal.

demi-mot, *n.m.*, hint.

demi-pension, *n.f.*, half-board, partial-board.

demi-setier, *n.m.*, (— — -*s*) half a pint English.

demi-solde, *n.f.*, (*n.p.*) half-pay. *Officier en* —; half-pay officer.

démission, *n.f.*, resignation. *Donner sa* —; to send in one's resignation, to resign. *Offrir sa* —; to tender one's resignation.

démissionnaire, *n.m.f.*, resigner. *Il est* —; he has resigned his position.

démissionnaire, *adj.*, who has resigned, thrown up (his commission), vacated his seat.

démissionner, *v.n.*, to resign.

démitrer, *v.a.*, (lu.) to unmitre.

démobiliser, *v.a.*, to demobilize.

démocrate, *n.m.f.*, democrat.

démocratie, n.f., democracy.

démocratique, adj., democratic.

démocratiquement, adv., democratically.

démocratiser, v.a.n., to democratize.

se **démocratiser**, v.r., to become democratized.

démodé, -e, adj., out of fashion, antiquated, old-fashioned.

demoiselle, n.f., young lady; unmarried lady; young girl; gentlewoman; hot water-bottle; dragon-fly; (orni.) Numidian crane; paving-beetle.

démolir, v.a., to demolish, to pull down, to subvert, to overthrow, to destroy. Je l'ai démoli; I floored him.

démolisseur, n.m., demolisher, subverter.

démolition, n.f., demolition. pl., old building materials. Par suite de —s; because of the pulling down of the building.

démon, n.m., devil, fiend; demon; genius. Petit —; little demon (child). Faire le —; to play the devil. Quel — vous agite? what evil spirit torments you?

démonétisation, n.f., withdrawal from circulation (of money); calling in.

démonétiser, v.a., to withdraw from circulation; to call in (money).

démoniaque, adj., demoniacal, demoniac.

démoniaque, n.m.f., demoniac, demon, devil.

démonographe, n.m., demonographer.

démonographie, n.f., demonology.

démonologie, n.f., demonology.

démonomanie, n.f., demonomania.

démonstrateur, n.m., demonstrator, lecturer.

démonstrati-f, -ve, adj., demonstrative.

démonstration, n.f., demonstration, proof.

démonstrativement (-tiv-mān), adv., demonstratively.

démontable, adj., that can be taken to pieces.

démontage, n.m., taking to pieces.

démonter, v.a., to dismount, to unhorse; to nonplus, to baffle; to alter (one's countenance); to take to pieces, to undo; (nav.) to supersede, to unship. — le gouvernail; to unship the rudder. — un capitaine; to supersede a captain.

se **démonter**, v.r., that may be taken to pieces (of machinery); to lose one's countenance; to be unhinged; to be nonplused or disconcerted; to be getting out of order or out of gear (of machinery); to become impaired (of the health).

démontrable, adj., demonstrable.

démontrer, v.a., to demonstrate, to prove.

démoralisat-eur, -rice, adj., corrupting, demoralizing.

démoralisation, n.f., demoralization.

démoraliser, v.a., to demoralize.

⊙**démoraliseur**, n.m., corrupter.

démordre, v.n., to let go one's hold; to depart. to desist, to retract, to yield. Faire — quelqu'un; to make one change his resolution. Il n'en démordra pas; he will not abate an inch, he will stick to.

démotique, adj., demotic.

démoucheter, v.a., to take off the button of a foil. to uncap.

se **démoucheter**, v.r., to become uncapped.

demoulage, n.m., taking from the mold.

démouler, v.a., to take from the mold.

démunir, v.a., to strip a place of ammunition; to deprive; to leave unprovided.

se **démunir**, v.r., to deprive one's self, to part with; to leave one's self unprovided for.

démurer, v.a., to unwall, to open.

démuseler (-muz-lé), v.a., to unmuzzle.

dénaire, adj., denary.

dénanti, -e, adj., unsecured, unprovided; stripped, bare.

dénantir, v.a., to deprive of security.

se **dénantir**, v.r., to give up securities, to part with.

dénationaliser, v.a., to denationalize.

dénatter, v.a., to unmat.

dénaturalisation, n.f., denaturalization.

dénaturaliser, v.a., to denaturalize.

dénaturation, n.f., (chem.) debasement, misrepresentation; perversion, sophistication.

dénaturé, -e, adj., unnatural, barbarous, cruel.

dénaturer, v.a., to alter the nature of; to deface, to disfigure; to change, to misrepresent, to pervert, to distort; (chem.) to debase.

dendrite (din-), n.f., (min.) dendrite.

dendroïde (din-), adj., (bot.) dendroid.

dénégation, n.f., denial; (law) traverse.

dénégatoire, adj., (law) traversing.

déni, n.m., (jur.) denial, refusal. — de justice; refusal of justice.

déniaisé, -e, adj., sharpened, who has had his eyes opened, cunning. Un homme —; a cunning, crafty man.

déniaiser, v.a., to sharpen the wits of; to cheat, to take in, to dupe, to open the eyes of.

se **déniaiser**, v.r., to learn wit, to become sharp, to grow cunning.

déniché, -e, part., gone, flown. Les oiseaux sont —s; the birds have flown.

dénicher, v.a., to take out of its nest; to turn out; to hunt out; to find out. — une statue; to take a statue out of its niche.

dénicher, v.n., to forsake its nest (of a bird); to hasten away; to make off, to run away. Allons, il faut —; come, be off with you.

dénicheur, n.m., birds'-nester. Un — de merles; sharper. Un — de fauvettes; fortune-hunter; lady-killer.

denier, n.m., (antiq.) denarius; denier; money; farthing; mite; cash, funds; rate of interest; (pharm.) scruple; old French copper coin worth 1-13th of a farthing; (coin.) weight of a little above 1¼ grammes. — à Dieu; earnest money. A beaux —s comptants; in cash, in ready money. Les —s publics; the public money. ⊙Au — vingt-cinq; four per cent. Le — de Saint Pierre; Peter's pence. Le — de la veuve; the widow's mite. Cet homme n'a pas un — vaillant; that man is not worth a farthing. Rendre compte à livres sous et —s; to account to the uttermost farthing.

dénier, v.a., to deny, to refuse. Se —; to be denied; to deny one's self.

dénigrant, adj., disparaging.

dénigrement, n.m., vilifying, disparagement.

dénigrer, v.a., to disparage, to traduce, to vilify.

dénombrement, n.m., enumeration, census, list.

dénombrer, v.a., to number, to enumerate.

dénominateur, n.m., (arith.) denominator.

dénominati-f, -ve, adj., denominative.

dénomination, n.f., denomination, name.

dénominer, v.a., (jur.) to denominate, to mention by name.

dénoncer, v.a., to denounce, to inform against, to impeach, to announce, to lodge information against; to give notice, to proclaim, to declare.

dénonciat-eur, n.m., -**rice**, n.f., denunciator, informer, accuser.

dénonciation, n.f., denunciation, denouncement, declaration, intimation.

⊙**dénotation**, n.f., denotation.

dénoter, v.a., to describe; to denote, to betoken.

dénouement or **dénoûment**, n.m., event, issue; denouement, catastrophe, unraveling; undoing, ending (of a play).

dénouer, v.a., to untie, to loose; to give elasticity; to solve (difficulties); to unravel (plots).

se **dénouer**, v.r., to untie, to unravel, to unfold, to clear up. Sa langue s'est dénouée à la fin; he has spoken out at last.

denrée, n.f., commodity, wares, provisions.

Il vend bien sa —; he makes the most of his talents.

dense, *adj.*, dense, close, thick.

densité, *n.f.*, density, thickness.

dent, *n.f.*, tooth; notch; cog; prong. —*s de lait ;* first teeth. —*s de sagesse ;* wisdom teeth. —*s d'en haut ;* upper teeth. —*s d'en bas ;* lower teeth. *Faire ses* —*s ;* to cut one's teeth. *Les* —*s percent à cet enfant ;* that child is cutting his teeth. *Les* —*s lui claquent ;* his teeth chatter. *Serrer les* —*s ;* to set the teeth. *Grincer des* —*s ;* to gnash the teeth. *Une* — *qui branle ;* a loose tooth. *Le mal de* —*s ;* the toothache. *Avoir mal aux* —*s ;* to have a toothache. *Les* —*s lui tombent ;* he is losing his teeth. *L'alvéole d'une* —; the socket of a tooth. *Se curer les* —*s ;* to pick one's teeth. *Le fruit vert agace les* —*s ;* green fruit sets the teeth on edge. *Une vieille sans* —; a toothless hag. *Armé jusqu'aux* —*s ;* armed to the teeth. *N'avoir pas de quoi mettre sous la* —; not to have a morsel to put in one's mouth. *Avoir une* — *contre quelqu'un ;* to have an old grudge against one. *Déchirer à belles* —*s ;* to tear to pieces, to rend any one. *Chacun lui donne un coup de* —; every one has a fling at him. *Etre sur les* —*s ;* to be tired out, done up. *Montrer les* —*s à quelqu'un ;* to show one's teeth to any one. *Ne pas desserrer les* —*s ;* not to open one's lips. *Parler entre ses* —*s ;* to speak betwixt one's teeth. *Parler des grosses* —*s ;* to talk big. *Prendre le mors aux* —*s ;* to run away (of horses); to be earnest in business. *Rire du bout des* —*s ;* to sham a laugh, to pretend to laugh. *Murmurer entre ses* —*s ;* to mutter to one's self. *C'est vouloir prendre la lune avec les* —*s ;* it is aiming at impossibilities. *Les* —*s d'une roue ;* the cogs of a wheel. *Ce couteau a des* —*s ;* that knife is notched. *Manger du bout des* —*s ;* to eat with no appetite, to play with one's food. *Avoir les* —*s bien longues ;* to be very hungry.

dentaire, *adj.*, dental.

dentaire, *n.f.*, (bot.) dentaria, toothwort.

dental, -e, *adj.*, (gram.) dental.

dentale, *n.m.*, (conch.) dentalium, dental, tooth-shell.

dentale, *n.f.*, (gram.) dental.

dent-de-lion, *n.m.*, (—*s*——) dandelion.

denté, -e, *adj.*, toothed; (bot.) dentated. *Roue* —*e ;* cogged wheel. *Feuille* —*e en scie ;* serrated leaf.

dentée, *n.f.*, bite from a hound; rip (of a tusk)

denrelaire, *n.f.*, (bot.) lead-wort.

dentelé, -e (dănt-lé), *adj.*, notched, jagged, denticulated, toothed, indented.

dentelé, *n.m.*, (anat.) denticulated muscle.

denteler, *v.a.*, to indent, to notch, to jag, to tooth, to cog.

dentelle, *n.f.*, lace, lace-work. *Manchettes à* —; lace ruffles.

dentelli-er, *n.m.*, **-ère,** *n.f.*, lace-man, lace-woman, lace-maker.

dentelure (dăn-tlur), *n.f.*, jagging, notching, denticulation, indenting.

denticulé, -e, *adj.*, (bot.) denticulated, indented.

denticules, *n.m.pl.*, (arch.) denticles.

dentier (-tié), *n.m.*, set of teeth (natural or artificial).

dentifrice, *n.m.*, dentifrice. *adj.*, good for the teeth. *Poudre* —; tooth-powder.

dentiste, *n.m.*, dentist.

dentisterie, *n.f.*, dentistry.

dentition, *n.f.*, dentition, cutting of teeth.

denture, *n.f.*, set of teeth; (horl.) teeth range.

dénudation, *n.f.*, denudation.

dénuder, *v.a.*, to denude; to lay bare; to strip.

dénué, -e, *adj.*, destitute; void; devoid. —*de*

support ; bereft of support. — *d'esprit ;* devoid of wit.

dénuement or **dénûment,** *n.m.*, destitution, deprivation, penury, want.

dénuer, *v.a.*, to strip, to leave destitute.

se **dénuer,** *v.r.*, to strip one's self; to leave one's self destitute.

dépaillage, *n.m.*, unbottoming (of chairs).

dépailler, *v.a.*, to unbottom.

se **dépailler,** *v.r.*, to lose its straw-seat.

dépaissance, *n.f.*, pasturage, high pasture ground.

dépalissage, *n.m.*, (hort.) unpaling.

dépalisser, *v.a.*, to unpale.

dépaqueter (dé-pak-té), *v.a.*, to unpack.

dépareillé, -e, *adj.*, unmatched, imperfect, odd.

***dépareiller,** *v.a.*, to unmatch, to spoil the pair of, to render incomplete. — *des gants ;* to unmatch gloves. *Livres dépareillés ;* odd goods.

déparer, *v.a.*, to undress (altars); to strip; to disfigure, to take away the beauty; to disparage.

déparier, *v.a.*, to take away one (of a pair); to separate.

déparler, *v.n.*, to cease talking, to talk nonsense.

déparquer, *v.a.*, to unpen (of oysters) ; to unbed.

départ, *n.m.*, departure, setting out; (chem.) parting; (metal.), departure. *Etre sur son* —; to be on the eve of setting out.

départager, *v.a.*, to settle by a casting vote. — *les voix, les suffrages ;* to give a casting-vote.

département, *n.m.*, distribution; department; line, business (province or business assigned to a particular person). *Les* —*s de la France ;* the departments of France. — *des affaires étrangères ;* foreign-office. — *de l'intérieur ;* home-office. *Cela n'est pas de son* —; that does not lie in his province.

départemental, -e, *adj.*, departmental.

départir, *v.a.*, to distribute, to divide, to endow, to bestow, to allot, to grant.

se **départir,** *v.r.*, to depart, to desist, to swerve, to deviate. *Il s'est départi de sa demande ;* he has desisted from his demand. *Se* — *de son devoir ;* to swerve from one's duty.

dépassement, *n.m.*, over-extension, excess.

dépasser, *v.a.*, to go beyond; to exceed, to surpass; to outsail; to overreach, to overstep; to be higher or taller; to draw out (ribbons). — *ses pouvoirs ;* to exceed one's powers. *Il me dépasse de trois pouces ;* he is taller than I am by three inches.

dépâtissage, *n.m.*, sorting (of type).

dépâtisser, *v.a.*, (print.) to sort and distribute (type).

dépavage, *n.m.*, unpaving.

dépaver, *v.a.*, to unpave, to take up the pavement.

dépaysé, -e, *part.*, away from home, out of one's element. *Se trouver — dans une société ;* to feel out of one's element.

dépayser (-pè-i-zé), *v.a.*, to take, to send from home; to remove; to put out; to put on a wrong scent.

se **dépayser,** *v.r.*, to leave one's home; to go abroad; to get out of one's element.

dépècement (-pès-măn), *n.m.*, cutting up, cutting in pieces, carving, breaking up, tearing up; dismemberment; eating away (of the sea).

dépecer (dép-sé), *v.a.*, to cut up, to carve, to cut in pieces; to dismember; to eat away. — *une volaille ;* to cut up a fowl. — *de la viande ;* to carve meat.

dépeceur, *n.m.*, carver, cutter, meat-dresser.

dépêche, *n.f.*, dispatch (letter on affairs of state); (com.) correspondence, mail, telegram. *Les* —*s ;* the post-bag. *Faire les* —*s ;* to make up the dispatches, the mails.

à **dépêche-compagnon**, adv., hurriedly, carelessly. *Travailler à —;* to hurry over one's work. *Se battre à —;* to give no quarter in fighting.

se **dépêcher**, v.r., to make haste, to look sharp. *Dépêchez-vous ;* make haste.

dépêcher, v.a., to send off dispatches, a courier, a messenger; to dispatch; to be quick, to do things quickly, to hasten ; to make way for any one, to kill.

dépêcher, v.n., to dispatch, to hurry off, to send off a courier, or messenger, in haste. *On a dépêché à Vienne;* a courier has been sent to Vienna.

dépeçoir, n.m., chopping-knife.

dépeindre, v.a., to depict; to describe; to portray; to paint; to represent.

dépelotonner, v.a., to unwind.

se **dépelotonner**, v.r., to become unwound.

****dépenaillé**, -e, adj., (fam.) tattered, ragged, in rags; ill-clad; slatternly; emaciated.

****dépenaillement**, n. m., raggedness; faded appearance (of the face).

dépendamment (-da-mān), adv., (l.u.) dependently.

dépendance, n.f., dependence; appendage; out-house; offices; out-building. *Etre dans la — de quelqu'un ;* to be dependent on any one. *Tenir quelqu'un dans la —;* to keep any one in a state of dependancy.

dépendant, -e, adj., dependent. *En —;* (nav.) edging off.

dépendre, v.a., to take down; to unhang.

dépendre, v.n., to depend; to be dependent; to rest. *Cela dépend de moi ;* that depends on, rests with, me.

dépens, n.m. pl., expense, cost. *Vivre aux — d'autrui;* to live at other people's expense. *Faire la guerre à ses —;* to play a losing game. *Il a gagné son procès avec —;* (jur.) he gained his lawsuit with costs.

dépense, n.f., expense; expenditure; outlay, waste, flow; steward's office; pantry. *pl.,* supplies. *Comité des —s;* committee of supplies. *De folles —s;* extravagant expense. *—s de bouche;* living expenses. *La — du ménage;* household expense. *Sa — excède ses revenus;* his expenditure exceeds his income. *Ne pas plaindre la —;* not to spare expense. *Faire de la —;* to spend money. *Faire la —;* to do the housekeeping. *Aimer la —;* to like spending money.

dépenser, v.a., to spend; to expend; to consume; (b.s.) to waste. *Il aime à —;* he is fond of spending. *Se —;* to be spent.

dépensi-er, -ère, n., adj., extravagant person, spendthrift; extravagant.

dépensier, n.m., burser; (nav.) purser's steward.

déperdition, n.f., deperdition, loss, waste; (med.) discharge.

dépérir, v.n., to perish, to decline, to pine away, to waste, to wither, to dwindle, to waste away, to decay, to go to ruin.

dépérissement (-ris-mān), n.m., wasting away, decay, withering, falling away.

dépersuader, v.a., to dissuade.

dépêtrer, v.a., to disentangle, to extricate, to disengage, to clear, to free.

se **dépêtrer**, v.r., to get out of; to rid one's self of, to get clear of.

dépeuplement, n.m., depopulation; thinning (of forests).

dépeupler, v.a., to unpeople, to depopulate, to unstock, to thin. *— un colombier;* to unstock a pigeon-house. *— une forêt;* to thin a forest.

se **dépeupler**, v.r., to be depopulated, to be unstocked.

dépiécer, v.a. V. **dépecer**.

dépilage, n.m., taking off the hair or the fleece (of hides).

dépilati-f, **-ve**, adj., depilatory.

dépilation, n.f., depilation.

dépilatoire, n.m., depilatory.

se **dépiler**, v.r., to lose the hair (of animals).

dépiquage, n.m.. (agri.) treading out (corn, etc.).

dépiquer, v.a., to unquilt, to unstitch; to cheer up. *— quelqu'un ;* to cheer any one; to put any one in a better humor; (gard.) to transplant.

se **dépiquer**, v.r., to recover one's good humor; to recoup one's self.

dépister, v.a., (hunt.) to track; to ferret out, to hunt out; to throw off the scent.

dépit, n.m., spite, vexation. *Avoir du —;* to be vexed. *Il pleurait de —;* he wept for vexation. *Faire quelque chose par —;* to do a thing out of spite. *En — de;* in spite of. *Ecrire en — du bon sens;* to write nonsense.

dépiter, v.a., to vex, to spite.

se **dépiter**, v.r., to be vexed, to be in a pet, to get out of temper.

déplacé, -e, part., displaced, misplaced, ill-timed, unbecoming. *Discours —;* uncalled for speech.

déplacement (dé-plas-mān), n.m., displacement, change of place; removal.

déplacer, v.a., to displace, to misplace, to remove, to change.

se **déplacer**, v.r., to change one's place, to leave one's place, one's residence; (of things) to be displaced.

déplaire, v.n., to displease, to offend; to incur the displeasure of any one; to be unpleasant, disagreeable, to give offense. *Ne vous en déplaise ;* with your leave, if you don't mind. *N'en déplaise à ;* with all due deference to.

se **déplaire**, v.r., to dislike, to be displeased with, to displease each other; not to thrive (of animals, plants). *Je ne me déplairais pas ici ;* I should not dislike living here. *Les troupeaux se déplaisent dans ce lieu-là;* the flocks do not thrive in that place.

déplaisance, n.f., dislike, aversion.

déplaisant, -e, adj., unpleasant, disagreeable, annoying, obnoxious.

déplaisir, n.m., displeasure, dislike, annoyance, grief, sorrow, trouble, affliction.

déplantage, n.m., or **déplantation**, n.f., displanting.

déplanter, v.a., to displant.

déplantoir, n.m., (gard.) trowel.

déplâtrage, n.m., unplastering.

déplâtrer, v.a., (mas.) to unplaster.

dépleurer, v.n., to cease weeping.

déplier, v.a., to unfold, to open ; to lay out, display (goods).

déplissage, n.m., unplaiting.

déplisser, v.a., to unplait.

se **déplisser**, v.r., to come out of plait.

déploiement or **déploiment** (dé-ploa-mān), n.m., display, unfolding ; (milit.) deployment.

déplombage, n.m., unstopping ; unsealing.

déplomber, v. a., to unlead, to unload (a stick); to unstop (a tooth).

déplorable, adj., deplorable, lamentable, wretched.

déplorablement, adv., deplorably, lamentably, wretchedly.

déplorer, v.a., to deplore, to bewail, to lament, to mourn ; to regret.

déployé, -e, adj., unfolded, displayed, open. *Voguer à voiles —es ;* (nav.) to be under full sail. *A gorge —e ;* at the top of one's voice, lustily, with all one's might.

déployer, v.a., to unfold, to unroll, to unfurl, to set out, to display, to open, to show, to stretch, to spread ; (milit.) to deploy. *— les voiles ;* to spread the sails. — *toute son éloquence ;* **to** put forth all one's eloquence.

se **déployer,** *v.r.,* to unroll, to display one's self ; (milit.) to deploy.

déplumé, -e, *adj.,* unplumed, unfeathered.

déplumer, *v.a.,* to unplume, to deprive of feathers; to pluck; to pick.

se **déplumer,** *v.r.,* to molt, to shed feathers.

dépocher, *v.a.n.,* to take out of one's pocket ; to fork out, stump up.

dépolir, *v.a.,* to take off the polish. — *du verre ;* to rough glass. *Le feu dépolit le marbre ;* fire takes the polish off marble.

dépolissage, *n.m.,* (of glass) roughing.

déponent, *adj., n.m.,* (gram.) deponent.

dépopulariser, *v.a.,* to render unpopular.

se **dépopulariser,** *v.r.,* to become unpopular.

dépopulation, *n.m.,* depopulation.

déport, *n.m.,* delay; (jur.) challenging one's self ; (on change) backwardation.

déportation, *n.f.,* deportation (transportation), exile, banishment.

déporté, *n.m.,* person sentenced to deportation ; transport, convict.   [doings.

déportements, *n.m.pl.,* misconduct; evil-

déporter, *v.a.,* to deport, to transport for life ; to banish, to exile.

se **déporter,** *v.r.,* to desist from. *Se — de ses prétentions ;* ω withdraw one's claims.

déposant, -e, *adj.,* depositing; giving evidence.

déposant, *n.m., -e, n.f.,* deponent ; witness ; bailer.

déposer, *v.a.,* to lay down ; to lay aside ; to strip, to divest, to depose ; to deposit ; to give evidence ; to lodge (a complaint). *On le déposa de sa charge ;* he was removed from office. — *son bilan ;* to file one's schedule.

déposer, *v.n.,* to settle, to leave a sediment (of liquids) ; to give evidence.

dépositaire, *n.m.,* depositary, trustee, guardian ; consignee.

déposition, *n.f.,* deposition, deprivation ; deposing ; evidence. *La — porte que ;* the evidence says that.

déposséder, *v.a.,* to dispossess, to oust.

dépossesseur, *n.m.,* dispossessor.

dépossession, *n.f.,* dispossession, deprivation.

déposter, *v. a.,* to drive from a post, to dislodge.

dépôt, *n.m.,* depositing, deposit, trust ; lodgment (of money); depository, warehouse ; depot, agency ; sediment, settling. — *de mendicité ;* poorhouse, workhouse. *Faire un —;* to make a deposit. *En —;* as a deposit in trust ; (com.) on sale.

dépotage, *n.m.,* decanting.

dépoter, *v.a.,* to take out of a pot; to decant.

dépotoir, *n.m.,* general deposit of night-soil.

dépoudrer, *v.a.,* to unpowder.

se **dépoudrer,** *v.r.,* to unpowder one's hair.

***dépouille,** *n.f.,* spoil; slough, skin, hide; wardrobe (of persons deceased); remains ; spoils, booty ; crop ; exuviæ. — *mortelle ;* mortal remains. *La — d'un serpent ;* the slough of a serpent. *L'âme quitta sa — mortelle ;* the soul forsook its earthly tenement. *Il a laissé sa — à un tel ;* he left his wardrobe to such a one. —*s opimes ;* spolia opima. *Il s'enrichit des —s d'autrui ;* he enriches himself with the spoils of others.

***dépouillé, -e,** *part.,* stripped; naked. *Jouer au roi —;* (fig. and fam.) to compass the ruin of any one.

***dépouillement** (dé-poo-i-mān), *n.m.,* spoliation ; despoiling ; privation; scrutiny (of a ballot-box); abstract (of an account). *Au —du scrutin ;* on the counting of the votes.

***dépouiller,** *v.a.,* to unclothe; to strip; to skin, to lay bare; to despoil, to deprive ; to throw off ; to cast off (of insects); to lay aside ; to gather

(crops) ; to inspect (a ballot-box) ; to present an abstract (of accounts). — *ses vêtements ;* to throw off one's clothes. — *une anguille ;* to skin an eel.

se ***dépouiller,** *v.r.,* to shed its skin (of insects and animals); to molt ; to divest one's self of, to strip one's self of ; to throw off ; to dispense with ; to renounce.

dépouilleur, *n.m.,* teller (of votes by ballot).

dépourvoir, *v.a.,* to leave unprovided or destitute.

se **dépourvoir,** *v.r.,* to leave one's self unprovided. *Se — d'argent ;* to leave one's self without cash.

dépourvu, -e, *adj.,* destitute, unprovided, devoid. *Au —;* unawares. *Pris au —;* caught napping.

dépravation, *n.f.,* depravity, depravement ; depravation.

dépravé, -e, *adj.,* vitiated, depraved. *Goût —;* depraved taste.

dépraver, *v.a.,* to vitiate, to deprave.

se **dépraver,** *v.r.,* to become vitiated, depraved. *Son goût se déprave ;* his taste is becoming vitiated.

déprécati-f, -ve, *adj.,* (theol.) deprecatory.

déprécation, *n.f.,* deprecation.

dépréciat-eur, *n.m.,* **-rice,** *n.f.,* depreciator.

dépréciation, *n.f.,* depreciation.

déprécier, *v.a.,* to depreciate, to undervalue, to slight ; to run down, to disparage ; to underrate.

se **déprécier,** *v.r.,* to depreciate one's self ; (of things) to fall in value.

déprédat-eur, *n.m.,* **-rice,** *n.f.,* depredator.

déprédat-eur, -rice, *adj.,* predatory.

déprédation, *n.f.,* plundering, depredation, malversation.

dépréder, *v.a.,* (l.u.) to depredate, to plunder.

déprendre, *v.a.,* to loosen, to part.

se **déprendre,** *v.r.,* to get detached or loose ; to give up, to renounce.

dépression, *n.f.,* hollow, depression, falling in; (astron., anat., surg.) depression.

déprier, *v.a.,* to disinvite.

déprimer, *v.a.,* to press down, to depress ; to underrate.

se **déprimer,** *v.a.,* to be flattened, depressed.

déprisant, -e, *adj.,* depreciating.

dépriser, *v.a.,* to undervalue, to underrate; to disparage.

de profundis (-fon-dis), *n.m.,* (c. rel.) de profundis.

dépuceler, *v.a.,* to deflower.

depuis, *adv.,* since, afterwards, ever after, since that time. *Je ne l'ai point vu —;* I have not seen him since.

depuis, *prep.,* since, from, after, for the last. — *la création du monde ;* since the creation of the world. — *peu ;* lately. — *quand ?* how long since ? — *deux ans ;* two years since. — *longtemps ;* for a long time. — *ce temps-là ;* ever after; since then. — *quelque temps ;* for some time.

depuis que, *conj.,* since. — — *vous êtes parti ;* since you went away.

dépurati-f, -ve, *adj.,* depurative.

dépuration, *n.f.,* depuration.

dépuratoire, *adj.,* depuratory.

dépurer, *v.a.,* to depurate.

députation, *n.f.,* deputation; deputyship.

député, *n.m.,* deputy, delegate; M.P.

députer, *v.a.,* to depute, to send.

députer, *v.n.,* to send a deputation.

déracinement (-si-n-mān), *n.m.,* rooting up, eradication.

déraciner, *v.a.,* to root up, to pluck up, to pull up by the root, to eradicate, extirpate. — *un cor ;* to cut out a corn. — *un mal ;* to eradicate an evil.

se **déraciner**, v.r., to unroot, to be torn up by the roots.

dérader, v.n., (nav.) to be driven out to sea.

déraidir, v.a., to unstiffen, to make pliant, to soften.

se **déraidir**, v.r., to grow pliant, soft, supple.

***déraillement**, n.m., running off the rails.

***dérailler**, v.n., to run off the rails, to leave the metals.

***dérailler**, v.a., to throw off the rails.

déraison, n.f., unreasonableness, folly, irrationality, preposterousness.

déraisonnable, adj., senseless, unreasonable, void of reason, preposterous.

déraisonnablement, adv., unreasonably, irrationally, preposterously.

déraisonnement, n.m., irrational talk.

déraisonner, v.n., to reason falsely, to talk nonsense, to talk irrationally.

dérangé, -e, adj., out of order, deranged, crazy ; unwell, out of sorts. Estomac — ; disordered stomach.

dérangement (dé-rānj-mān), n.m., derangement, discomposure, trouble, embarrassment ; disorder, disturbance.

déranger, v.a., to derange, to put out of its place, out of order, to displace ; to discompose ; to disconcert, to incommode, to put out of sorts, to unsettle, to disturb, to upset. Cela m'a tout dérangé ; that has quite disconcerted me. La moindre chose le dérange ; the least thing in the world unsettles or upsets him.

se **déranger**, v.r., to be deranged ; to get out of order ; to be unwell ; to trouble or disturb oneself ; to misconduct oneself ; to lead a disorderly life.

déraper, v.n., (nav.) to get atrip ; to sideslip (of bicycles). L'ancre a dérapé ; the anchor is atrip. Faire— une ancre ; to trip an anchor.

déraper, v.a., to pick (grapes) from the bunch.

dératé, -e, adj., deprived of spleen, lively ; cunning, sharp. Courir comme un — ; to go like a shot ; to run like a greyhound.   [spleen.

dérater, v.a., to take out, to extract, the

derby, n.m., derby.

derechef, adv., over again, afresh, anew, again.

déréglé, -e, adj., irregular, intemperate ; exorbitant ; unruly ; dissolute, profligate, lawless. Vie —e ; irregular life. Appétit — ; immoderate appetite. Imagination —e ; disordered imagination. Désirs —s ; inordinate desires. Une conduite —e ; disorderly conduct.

déréglement, n.m., intemperateness ; irregularity ; unruliness, riot, disorder ; dissoluteness, licentiousness, profligacy. Vivre dans le — ; to lead a disorderly life.

déréglément, adv., disorderly, inordinately, intemperately, dissolutely, loosely.

dérégler, v.a., to put out of order, to disorder.

se **dérégler**, v.r., to be out of order, to be deranged ; to lead a disorderly life.

dérêner, v.n., to unrein, to unbridle.

dérider, v.a., to unwrinkle, to take away the wrinkles, to smooth, to clear, to cheer up. La joie déride le front ; joy smooths the brow.

se **dérider**, v.r., to unbend one's brow ; to cheer up ; to relax, to unbend.

dérimer, v.a., to turn verse into prose.

dérision, n.f., derision, mockery, ridicule. Par — ; out of ridicule. Tourner tout en — ; to turn everything into ridicule.

dérisoire, adj., derisive, derisory, mocking.

dérivati-f, -ve, adj., derivative.

dérivatif, n.m., derivative, counter-irritant.

dérivation, n.f., derivation.

dérive, n.f., drift, lee-way. En or A la — ; adrift. Avoir belle — ; (nav.) to have good searoom.

dérivé, -e, adj., derivative ; drifted.

dérivé, n.m., (gram.) derivative.

dériver, v.n., to be derived ; to get clear of the shore ; (nav.) to drift ; to derive, to proceed from. Faire — ; to derive.

dériver, v.a., to derive ; to divert, turn off (of rivers).

derme, n.m., (anat.) derma.

derni-er, -ère, adj., last ; highest, greatest, vilest, meanest ; youngest (of a family of children) ; (mus.) closing. En — lieu ; in the last place. En — ressort ; as a last appeal. Rendre le — soupir ; to breathe one's last. C'est la —e lettre qu'il ait écrite ; it is the last letter he wrote. Mettre la —e main à quelque chose ; to put the finishing touch to anything. Une affaire de la —e importance ; an affair of the greatest importance. Arriver au — degré ; to arrive at the highest degree. Cela est du — ridicule ; that is ridiculous to a degree. Aux —s les bons morceaux ; last come, best served.

derni-er, n.m., -ère, n.f., last ; end of the gallery (tennis). Le — des hommes ; the vilest of men. Jusqu'au — ; to the last. Dernier-né, (—s—s) last born male child.

dernièrement, adv., lately, of late, latterly, recently.

dérobé, -e, part., stolen, hidden, secret, concealed ; spare, leisure (of time) ; (arch.) private. Escalier — ; private staircase. Fèves —es ; beans taken out of their skins. A la —e ; by stealth, clandestinely. S'en aller à la —e ; to steal away, to slip out. Heures —es ; leisure hours.

dérober, v.a., to rob, to steal, to pilfer, to plunder, to purloin ; to conceal, to hide, to protect, to screen, to shelter ; to shell (beans). — quelqu'un à la justice ; to screen anyone from justice.

se **dérober**, v.r., to steal away, to escape, to disappear, to avoid, to shun. Il s'est dérobé ; he has stolen away. Se — à la justice ; to fly from justice. Le vaisseau se déroba bientôt à la vue ; the ship was soon lost to view.

dérochage, n.m., scouring (of metals).

dérocher, v.a., to scour (of metals).

dérogation, n.f., derogation.

dérogatoire, adj., derogatory.

dérogeance, n.f., forfeiture (of nobility).

dérogeant, -e (-jänt, -t), adj., derogatory.

déroger, v.n., to derogate ; to take away, to detract ; to condescend ; to stoop. — à l'usage établi ; to act contrary to established custom. — à la noblesse ; to forfeit one's nobility.

⊙**déroidir**. V. déraidir.

dérougir, v.a., to take off the redness.

se **dérougir**, v.r., to lose its redness.

dérougir, v.n., to lose its redness.

***dérouillement**, n.m., removal of rust.

***dérouiller**, v.a., to remove the rust, to polish, to brighten up.

se **dérouiller**, v.r., to lose its rust ; to rub off the rust ; to polish up ; to read up a subject. L'esprit se dérouille dans le grand monde ; good company rubs the rust off one's mind.

déroulement (dé-rool-mān), n.m., unrolling ; production of the evolute (of curves).

dérouler, v.a., to unroll ; to spread out, to display ; (geom.) to produce the evolute. — les merveilles de la création ; to unfold the wonders of creation.

se **dérouler**, v.r., to unroll, to unfold ; to display itself ; to spread out ; to open to the view ; (of the waves) to roll in.

déroute, n.f., rout, defeat, overthrow, ruin ; failure, disorder, confusion. Mettre une armée en — ; to rout an army. Mettre quelqu'un en — ; to confuse, to nonplus, to silence anyone. En pleine — ; in full flight. Ses affaires sont en — ; he is in a bad way (financially).

dérouter, v.a., to embarrass, to bewilder ; to

disconcert, to perplex ; to baffle, to foil. *Je suis tout dérouté ;* I am quite out of my latitude.

derrière, *prep.,* behind, behind one's back. *Laisser loin — soi ;* to leave far behind one. *Regardez — vous ;* look behind you.

derrière, *adv.,* behind. *Par — ;* from behind. *Porte de — ;* back-door ; (fig.) evasion.

derrière, *n.m.,* hind, hinder part ; posteriors ; tail-board (of a cart) ; breech. *Etre logé sur le — ;* to lodge at the back of the house. *Montrer le — ;* to turn tail, to show the white feather.

derviche or **dervis,** *n.m.,* dervis.

des, *art.pl.,* of the ; from the. V. **de.**

dès, *prep.,* from, since, as early as. *— le point du jour ;* from break of day. *— le berceau ;* from the cradle. *— à présent ;* from this moment, forthwith, henceforth. *— lors ;* from that time.

dès que, *conj.,* when, as soon as ; since. *Dès qu'il parut ;* as soon as he appeared. *— — (for du moment que) vous le souhaitez ;* since you wish it.

désabonnement, *n.m.,* withdrawal of subscription.

se **désabonner,** *v.r.,* to withdraw one's subscription (from a newspaper or periodical).

désabuser, *v.a.,* to disabuse, to undeceive.

se **désabuser,** *v.r.,* to undeceive one's self. *Désabusez-vous ;* undeceive yourself.

désaccord, *n.m.,* disagreement ; (mus.) discord. *Etre en — ;* to be at variance. *Etre en — avec soi-même ;* to be inconsistent with one's self.

désaccorder, *v.a.,* to untune, to set at variance.

se **désaccorder,** *v.r.,* to get out of tune.

désaccouplement, *n.m.,* uncoupling.

désaccoupler, *v.a.,* to uncouple.

se **désaccoupler,** *v.r.,* to uncouple, to get uncoupled ; to come asunder.

désaccoutumance, *n.f.,* want of custom.

désaccoutumer, *v.a.,* to disaccustom.

se **désaccoutumer,** *v.r.,* to break one's self of, to lose the habit of. *Se — de faire une chose ;* to leave off doing a thing.

désachalandage, *n.m.,* loss of custom.

désachalander, *v.a.,* to take away the customers, to drive away customers.

désaffection, *n.f.,* disaffection.

désaffectionner, *v.a.,* to lose affection, to cause any one to lose affection.

se **désaffectionner,** *v.r.,* to lose affection.

désaffourcher, *v.a.,* (nav.) to unmoor or heave up an anchor.

désaffubler, *v.a.,* to unmuffle.

désagencement, *n.m.,* throwing out of gear.

désagencer, *v.a.,* to throw out of gear, to disarrange, to disorder.

désagréable, *adj.,* disagreeable, unpleasant ; unacceptable ; uncomfortable ; obnoxious ; unsightly ; distasteful. *Cela est — à voir ;* that is displeasing to the sight.

désagréablement, *adv.,* disagreeably, unpleasantly ; unacceptably ; uncomfortably ; obnoxiously.

désagréer, *v.a.,* to displease. *Cela ne me désagrée pas ;* I do not dislike that.

⊙**désagréer,** *v.a.,* to unrig. V. **dégréer.**

désagrégation, *n.f.,* disaggregation.

désagréger, *v.a.,* to disaggregate.

se **désagréger,** *v.r.,* to become disaggregated, to break away, to be rent asunder.

désagrément, *n.m.,* disagreeableness ; unpleasantness, defect ; blemish ; annoyance, discomfort, vexation..

désajustement, *n.m.,* disarrangement ; disorder.

désajuster, *v.a.,* to derange, to disarrange, to disturb, to put out of order, to disorder.

se **désajuster,** *v.r.,* to become disarranged or disturbed, to get out of order. *Sa coiffure s'est désajustée ;* her hair has become disarranged.

désalignement, *n.m.,* (milit.) breaking line, out of line.

désaligner, *v.a.,* (milit.) to break the line.

se **désaligner,** *v.r.,* (milit.) to fall out of line.

désallier, *v.a.,* to disunite (allies).

se **désallier,** *v.r.,* to break off an alliance.

désaltérant, -e, *adj.,* thirst-quenching.

désaltérer, *v.a.,* to quench the thirst, to refresh.

se **désaltérer,** *v.r.,* to quench one's thirst.

désamorcer, *v.a.,* to uncap (fire-arms).

⊙**désancrer,** *v.n.,* to weigh anchor.

*****désappareiller.** V. **dépareiller.**

désapparier, *v.a.,* to unpair (birds).

désappointement (-point-mān), *n.m.,* disappointment.

désappointer, *v.a.,* to disappoint ; ⊙ to strike soldiers off the rolls ; to unstitch.

désapprendre, *v.a.,* to unlearn, to forget.

désapprobat-eur, *n.m.,* **-rice,** *n.f.,* censurer, fault-finder.

désapprobat-eur, -rice, *adj.,* disapproving, censuring, carping. *Un geste — ;* a gesture of disapprobation.

désapprobation, *n.f.,* disapprobation, disapproval.

désappropriation, *n.f.,* renunciation (of property).

se **désapproprier,** *v.r.,* to renounce (property).

désapprouver, *v.a.,* to disapprove of, to blame.

désarborer, *v.a.,* (nav.) to strike, to haul down.

désarçonner, *v.a.,* to dismount, to unsaddle, to unhorse, to pull off ; to baffle, to nonplus, to floor, to silence.

désargenter, *v.a.,* to unsilver, to drain of money. *Ces emplettes m'ont désargenté ;* these purchases have emptied my purse.

se **désargenter,** *v.r.,* to become unsilvered, to lose its plating, to spend all one's money.

désarmé, -e, *part.,* disarmed, unarmed.

désarmement, *n.m.,* disarming, disarmament ; (nav.) laying up.

désarmer, *v.a.,* to disarm, to unarm, to appease, to calm ; to foil ; to uncock (a gun) ; (nav.) to unship (oars) ; to lay up, to dismantle. *Ses pleurs me désarmèrent ;* her tears disarmed me. *— la colère de quelqu'un ;* to appease any one's anger. *— un vaisseau ;* to dismantle a ship, to lay her up ; to pay off the officers and crew.

désarmer, *v.n.,* to disarm ; (nav.) to be dismantled, to be paid off.

désarrimer, *v.a.,* (nav.) to alter or shift the stowage in the hold.

désarroi, *n.m.,* disorder, disarray, confusion, hurly-burly.

désarticulation, *n.f.,* (surg.) amputation (in a joint).

désarticuler, *v.a.,* to disjoint.

désassemblage, *n.m.,* disjoining.

désassembler, *v.a.,* to take to pieces, to separate.

désassocier, *v.a.,* to dissociate.

désassorti, -e, *adj.,* unmatched, ill-sorted ; jarring, unsuitable.

désassortiment, *n.m.,* unmatching; bad assortment ; unpairing.

désassortir, *v.a.,* to unmatch ; to unstock.

désastre, *n.m.,* disaster, break-down ; failure.

désastreusement (-treūz-mān), *adv.,* disastrously.

désastreu-x, -se, *adj.,* disastrous, very sad. *C'est — ;* it is sad in the extreme.

désavantage, *n.m.,* disadvantage ; detriment, prejudice. *L'affaire a tourné à leur — ;* the business turned out to their detriment, or badly for them. *Parler au — de quelqu'un ;* to speak disparagingly of any one.

désavantager, v.a., to deprive of an advantage, to disadvantage, to prejudice.

désavantageusement (-jeuz-mān), adv., disadvantageously, disparagingly.

désavantageu-x, -se, adj., disadvantageous, detrimental, prejudicial.

désaveu, n.m., disavowal, denial ; recantation. Il fait le — de cette action ; he disowns that action.

désaveugler, v.a., to undeceive, to open the eyes of.

désavouer, v.a., to disown, to disclaim, to disavow, to deny ; to retract, to recant. — sa signature ; to repudiate or deny one's signature. Cette mère a désavoué son enfant ; that mother has disowned her child.

descellement, n.m., (mas.) loosening, unsealing.

desceller, v.a., to unseal ; (mas.) to loosen. se **desceller**, v.r., to become unloosened or unsealed ; to get loose.

descendance, n.f., descent, lineage, pedigree, birth, extraction.

descendant, -e, adj., descending, going down ; (milit.) coming off duty.

descendant, n.m., -e, n.f., descendant, offspring, progeny.

descendant, n.m., (l.u.) ebb-tide.

descendre, v.n., to descend ; to go down ; to go down stairs ; to come, to step, to get down ; to alight ; to stay, to put up ; to fall ; to reach ; to come from ; (nav.) to land ; to ebb, to subside. Descendez vite ; make haste and come down. — de cheval ; to dismount. — de voiture ; to get out of, or to alight from, a carriage. — d'un bateau ; to get out of or off a boat. — dans un puits ; to go down into a well. La marée descend ; the tide is ebbing. — dans sa conscience ; to examine one's conscience. Il descendit à l'hôtel ; he put up at the hotel. Nous descendîmes dans une île ; we landed on an island. Il vaut mieux monter que —; it is better to rise than to fall.

descendre, v.a., to descend, to take down, to bring, to let down ; to go, to come, to get down ; to set down ; to land. Descendez ce tableau ; take that picture down. Où vous descendrai-je ? where shall I set you down ? — la garde ; to come off guard. Faire —; to bring down, to fetch down, to let down, to send down ; to lower, to sink.

descente, n.f., descent ; going down ; taking down ; subsiding (of waters) ; dismounting ; disembarkment ; (fin.) run ; declivity ; irruption ; rupture, hernia ; (milit.) coming off guard. La justice a fait une — chez lui ; the police have searched his house. — de lit ; bedside carpet, rug.

descriptible, adj., describable.

descripti-f, -ve, adj., descriptive.

description, n.f., description, inventory.

desdits, m.pl., **desdites**, f.pl., from the said.

déséchouer, v.a., (nav.) to get afloat ; to get off.

désemballage, n.m., unpacking. V. **déballage**.

désemballer, v.a., to unpack. On a désemballé les marchandises ; the goods have been unpacked.

désembarquement, n.m., disembarkation, landing. V. **débarquement**.

désembarquer, v.a., to disembark, to land ; to unship, to unlade.

désembellir, v.n., to lose one's or its beauty.

désemboîter, v.a., to disjoint ; to put out of socket ; to dislocate. se **désemboîter**, v.r., to become disjointed.

désembourber, v.a., to draw out of the mire. se **désembourber**, v.r., to get out of the mire.

désemparer, v.n., to quit, to go away. Sans —; on the spot, at once, without intermission.

désemparer, v.a., to quit, to clear out, to dislodge ; (nav.) to disable. — un vaisseau ; to disable a ship.

désempenné (dé-zan-pèn-né), adj., stripped of its feathers.

désempeser, v.a., to unstarch. se **désempeser**, v.r., to become unstarched, limp.

désemplir, v.a., to make less full, to diminish the contents of. — un tonneau ; to part empty a cask. se **désemplir**, v.r., to become less full. Ma bourse se désemplit ; my purse is getting low.

désemplir, v.n., to grow empty, to become less full. Sa maison ne désemplit point ; his house is always full of company.

désempoissonner, v.a., to unstock (a pond).

désenchantement (-shānt-mān), n.m., disenchantment.

désenchanter, v.a., to disenchant. se **désenchanter**, v.r., to become disenchanted.

désenchanteur, -eresse, adj., disenchanting.

désenchâsser, v.a., to unset (jewels).

désenclaver, v.a., to disenclose (land).

désenclouer, v.a., to take out a nail, to unnail. — un canon ; to unspike a cannon. — un cheval ; to take a nail out of a horse's foot.

désencombrement, n.m., disencumbrance ; dispersing.

désencombrer, v.a., to disencumber ; to clear.

désenfiler, v.a., to unthread, to unstring. se **désenfiler**, v.r., to come unthreaded or unstrung.

désenfler, v.a., to reduce the swelling. se **désenfler**, v.r., to become less swollen.

désenfler, v.n., to become less swollen ; to cease to be swollen.

désenflure, n.f., diminution, disappearance of a swelling.

désengrener, v.a., to throw out of gear.

désenivrer, v.a., to sober, to make sober again. Il ne désenivre pas ; he is always drunk. se **désenivrer**, v.r., to get sober again, to recover, to be cured of. Se — en dormant ; to sleep oneself sober.

désenlaidir, v.a., to render less ugly. se **désenlaidir**, v.r., to become less ugly.

désennui, n.m., amusement, recreation, diversion, distraction.

désennuyer, v.a., to enliven ; to cheer, to divert, to amuse. se **désennuyer**, v.r., to find amusement ; to divert oneself, to kill time.

désenrayer, v.a., to unlock or unskid.

désenrayer, v.n., to unskid.

désenrhumer, v.a., to cure of a cold. v.n. Ne pas —; to be never without a cold. se **désenrhumer**, v.r., to cure, get rid of, one's cold.

désenrôlement, n.m., (milit.) discharge.

désenrôler, v.a., to discharge.

désenrouer, v.a., to cure of hoarseness.

désenrouer, v.n. Ne pas —; to be always hoarse. se **désenrouer**, v.r., to cure one's hoarseness.

désensabler, v.a., to get out of the mud or sand.

désensevelir (-sĕv-lir), v.a., to unwrap ; to unshroud ; to exhume.

désensevelissement, n.m., unshrouding ; exhumation, disinterment.

désensorceler, v.a., to unbewitch.

désensorcellement, n.m., unbewitching.

désentêter, v.a., to cure of obstinacy ; to drive out of the head. se **désentêter**, v.r., to be cured of obstinacy or infatuation. Il ne peut se — de cette opinion ; he cannot get that opinion out of his head.

désentortiller, v.a., to untwist; to clear; to unravel.

désentraver, v.a., to unfetter, to untangle.

désenverguer (-ghé), v.a., to unbend (sails).

désert, -e, adj., desert, solitary, wild, waste, unfrequented; abandoned, deserted.

désert, n.m., desert, solitary place, waste, wilderness. Prêcher au —; to speak to the wind.

déserter, v.a., to desert, to abandon, to forsake, to quit, to leave. — les drapeaux ; to desert one's colors.

déserter, v.n., to desert, to leave. — à l'ennemi ; to go over to the enemy.

déserteur, n.m., deserter.

désertion, n.f., desertion.

désespérance, n.f., despair.

désespérant, -e, adj., desperate, hopeless, discouraging, disheartening; distressing; provoking; matchless.

désespéré, -e, part., hopeless, desperate; disconsolate, despondent, disheartened.

désespéré, n.m., -e, n.f., madman, madwoman; person in despair. Se battre en —; to fight desperately. Agir en —; to behave like a madman.

désespérément, adv., desperately, despairingly; hopelessly.

désespérer, v.n., to despair, to despond, to give up all hope. — de quelqu'un, de quelque chose ; to despair of any one, of anything ; to give up any one, anything, for lost.

désespérer, v.a., to drive to despair; to dishearten; to dispirit; to distress, to torment.

se **désespérer**, v.r., to be in despair, to give way to despair, to despond.

désespoir, n.m., despair; hopelessness, desperation, despondency; grief, affliction. Etre au—; to be in despair, distress; to be vexed, grieved. Mettre au — ; to drive to despair; to vex extremely. Tomber dans le — ; to sink into despair. De — ; through despair. En — de cause; as a last resource, shift.

****déshabillé** (dé-za-), n.m., dishabille, undress. — du matin ; morning dress or wrapper.

****déshabiller** (dé-za-), v.a., to undress, to strip, to disrobe.

se ****déshabiller** (dé-za-), v.r., to undress one's self.

déshabité, -e (dé-za-), adj., uninhabited, deserted.

déshabituer (dé-za-), v.a., to unaccustom, to break of.

se **déshabituer** (dé-za-), v.r., to unaccustom one's self; to break one's self. Se — d'une chose; to leave off doing a thing.

déshérence (dé-zé-), n.f., (jur.) escheat.

déshéritement (dé-za-), n.m., disinheritance.

déshériter (dé-zé-), v.a., to disinherit.

désheurer (dé-zeu-), v.a., (fam., l.u.) to derange the hours of, to disturb.

se **désheurer** (dé-zeu-), v.r., (fam., l.u.) to change one's hours ; to disturb one's self; (of clocks) to strike one time and mark another; to strike wrong.

déshonnête (dé-zo-), adj., immodest, indecent, shameful; dishonest.

déshonnêtement (dé-zo-nêt-mān), adv., indecently, immodestly, shamefully; dishonestly.

déshonnêteté (dé-zo-nêt-té), n.f., (l.u.) indecency, immodesty; dishonesty.

déshonneur (dé-zo-), n.m., dishonor ; disgrace, shame, discredit. Il a mis le comble à son — ; he has put the finishing stroke to his dishonor. Faire — à quelqu'un ; to disgrace any one. ⊙ C'est me prier de mon — ; that is asking me to dishonor myself. Tenir à — ; to look upon as dishonorable.

déshonorable (dé-zo-), adj., dishonorable, disgraceful.

déshonorablement (dé-zo-), adv., dishonorably.

déshonorant, -e (dé-zo-), adj., dishonorable, disgraceful, shameful.

déshonorer (dé-zo-), v.a., to dishonor, to bring to shame, to bring shame upon, to disgrace, to tarnish, to disparage.

se **déshonorer** (dé-zo-), v.r., to dishonor one's self, to disgrace one's self.   [tum.

desideratum, n.m., (desiderata, pl.), desidera-

****désignati-f, -ve** (desiderata, pl.), adj., indicative.

****désignation**, n.f., designation, indication ; nomination, choice, election.

****désigné, -e**, part., appointed, indicated, prescribed. A l'heure —e ; at the appointed hour.

****désigner**, v.a., to designate, to describe; to denote, to betoken; to appoint, to fix; to assign, to elect, to nominate, to choose, to point out; to name, to call.

désillusion, n.f., **désillusionnement**, n.m., disillusion ; disappointment.

désillusionner, v.a., to undeceive, to disillusionize, to disappoint.

désincorporer, v.a., to disincorporate, to separate, to disunite, to disembody.

désinence, n.f., (gram.) termination, ending.

désinfatuer, v.a., to disabuse, to undeceive, to dispel the infatuation of.

se **désinfatuer**, v.r., to cease to be infatuated.

désinfectant, adj., disinfecting.

désinfectant, n.m., disinfectant.

désinfecter, v.a., to disinfect, to purify.

se **désinfecter**, v.r., to become disinfected.

désinfection, n.f., disinfection, fumigation.

désintéressé, -e, adj., uninterested; disinterested; unselfish, impartial, unbiased; indemnified.

désintéressement (-rès-mān), n.m., impartiality; indifference; disinterestedness, self-denial.

désintéressément, adv., (l.u.) disinterestedly.

désintéresser, v.a., to indemnify; to buy out the interest of; to refund, to repay.

****désinterligner**, v.a., (print.) to unlead.

désinvestir, v.a., (law) to devest; to deprive, to divest; (mil.) to raise the siege of.

désinviter, v.a., to recall an invitation.

désinvolte, adj., free, easy, unconstrained.

désinvolture, n.f., easy or graceful bearing or gait; ease, gracefulness.

désir, n.m., desire, wish; longing. — déréglé ; inordinate desire. Au gré de ses —s ; agreeably to his wishes. Brûler du — de ; to long to do.

désirable, adj., desirable.

désirer, v.a., to desire, to wish for, to long for, to want. Que désirez-vous de moi ? what do you want of or with me ? Cet ouvrage ne laisse rien à — ; this work is most satisfactory in all respects. A — ; desirable. Cela laisse à — ; there is room for improvement.

désireu-x, -se, adj., desirous, anxious, eager (to).

désistement, n.m., desistance, (law) nonsuit.

se **désister**, v.r., to desist from, to give over, to abandon, to renounce, (jur.) to waive.

dès lors, adv. V. **dès**.

desman, n.m., (zool.) musk-rat.

désobéir, v.n., to refuse to obey; to disobey.

désobéissance, n.f., disobedience; undutifulness; (jur.) contumacy.

désobéissant, -e, adj., disobedient; undutiful.

désobligeamment (-ja-mān), adv., disobligingly; unkindly.

désobligeance, n.f., unkindness; lack of complaisance.

désobligeant, -e (-jān, -t), adj., disobliging ; unkind; uncivil.

désobligeante (-jant), n.f., carriage for two.

désobliger, v.a., to disoblige; to displease.

désobstruant, -e, adj., (med.) deobstruent.

désobstruant, n.m., (med.) deobstruent.

désobstructi-f, -ve, adj., (med.) deobstruent.

désobstructi-f, *n.m.*, (med.) deobstruent.

désobstruer, *v.a.*, to clear from obstruction, to free, to deobstruct.

désoccupation, *n.f.*, inactivity, want of employment, leisure. *V.* **désœuvrement**.

désoccupé, -e, *adj.*, unemployed, unoccupied; at leisure; idle.

désœuvré, -e, *adj.*, unoccupied, idle, unemployed. *Etre* —; to be unemployed. *Le temps pèse aux gens —s;* time hangs heavily on the hands of idlers.

désœuvrement, *n.m.*, want of occupation, idleness.

désolant, -e, *adj.*, disheartening, grievous, afflicting, distressing, dispiriting; mortifying, provoking, unbearable, tiresome.

désolateur, *n.m.*, spoiler, ravager, destroyer. *adj.*, desolating, ravaging, destructive.

désolation, *n.f.*, desolation, disconsolateness, affliction, grief, vexation.

désolé, -e, *part.*, afflicted, disconsolate, broken-hearted, in great distress; very sorry; grieved. *Je suis —, mais il n'est impossible de venir;* I am very sorry, but I cannot possibly come.

désoler, *v.a.*, to desolate, to lay waste, to waste, to devastate; to afflict, to grieve, to make disconsolate, to drive mad; to vex; to pester, to harass, to annoy, to torment. *La mort de son ami le désole;* the death of his friend cuts him to the quick. *Ce retard me désole;* this delay vexes me.

se désoler, *v.r.*, to grieve, to give one's self up to affliction, to pine with grief, to be disconsolate.

désopilant, -e, *adj.*, funny, laughable, side-splitting; (med.) deobstruent.

désopilant, *n.m.*, (med.) deobstruent.

désopilati-f, -ve, *adj.*, (med.) deobstruent, opening.

désopilation, *n.f.*, (med.) deobstruction, clearance.

désopiler, *v.a.*, (med.) to deobstruct, to clear. *Cela désopile la rate;* that dispels the spleen.

se désopiler, *v.r.*, to brighten up, to cheer up.

désordonné, -e, *adj.*, disorderly; dissolute, unruly, inordinate; immoderate, extravagant. *Appétit —;* immoderate appetite.

désordonnément, *adv.*, disorderly, irregularly; inordinately, immoderately, excessively.

désordonner, *v.a.*, to disorder, to disturb.

se désordonner, *v.r.*, to become disordered.

désordre, *n.m.*, disorder, confusion; licentiousness; disorderly life; riot, debauchery; discomposure, perturbation; variance, dissension, discord; disturbance; devastation. *Vivre dans le —;* to lead a riotous life. *Il a l'esprit en —;* his mind is in a state of perturbation. *Les passions mettent le — dans l'âme;* the passions discompose the soul. *Faire cesser le —;* to put an end to the disturbance. *En —;* in disorder.

désorganisat-eur, -rice, *n.* and *adj.*, disorganizer; disorganizing.

désorganisation, *n.f.*, disorganization.

désorganiser, *v.a.*, to disorganize.

se désorganiser, *v.r.*, to become disorganized.

désorienter, *v.a.*, to put any one out of his reckoning; to lead astray; to mislead; to bewilder; to put out, to disconcert, to put out of countenance. *Etre désorienté;* to lose one's way or one's bearings; to be out of one's element or of one's reckoning. *Notre guide était tout à fait désorienté;* our guide was quite out of his reckoning.

désormais, *adv.*, henceforth, hereafter, from this time.

désossement (dé-zos-mān), *n.m.*, boning.

désosser, *v.a.*, to bone. *Une dinde désossée;* a boned turkey.

se désosser, *v.r.*, to become disjointed.

désourdir (dé-zoor-), *v.a.*, (l.u.) to unweave; to unravel.

désoxydation, *n.f.*, (chem.) disoxidation, deoxidation.

désoxyder, *v.a.*, (chem.) to disoxidate, to deoxidate.

se désoxyder, *v.r.*, to disoxidate, to deoxidize; to become deoxidized.

désoxygénation, *n.f.*, (chem.) disoxygenation.

désoxygéner, *v.a.*, (chem.) to disoxygenate.

se désoxygéner, *v.r.*, to become disoxygenated.

despote, *n.m.*, despot.

despotique, *adj.*, despotic, despotical.

despotiquement (-tik-mān), *adv.*, despotically.

despotisme, *n.m.*, despotism.

despumation, *n.f.*, (chem.) despumation.

despumer, *v.a.*, (chem.) to despumate, to skim.

desquamation (-koua-), *n.f.*, desquamation.

dessabler, *v.a.*, to clear of sand.

dessaboté, -e, *adj.*, unhoofed (of horses).

dessaisir, *v.a.*, to dispossess.

se dessaisir, *v.r.*, to deprive one's self of, to give up, to part with.

dessaisissement (-zis-mān), *n.m.*, parting with, cession, abandonment.

dessaisonner, *v.a.*, (agri.) to change the rotation of crops; to grow out of season.

dessalé, -e, *part.*, unsalted, soaked; sharp, cunning.

dessalé, *n.m.*, **-e**, *n.f.*, sharp fellow, sharp woman, knowing person.

dessalement, *n.m.*, clearing of salt, soaking.

dessaler, *v.a.*, to remove salt from meat; to soak.

se dessaler, *v.r.*, to become less salt.

dessangler, *v.a.*, to ungirth, to loosen the girth.

desséchant, -e, *adj.*, drying.

desséché, -e, *part.*, dried up; desiccated. *Des ossements —s;* dried bones. *Des marais —s;* drained marshes.

desséchement (-sésh-mān), *n.m.*, drying up, drainage, dryness; emaciation.

dessécher, *v.a.*, to dry, to dry up; to parch; to drain; to wither; to waste, to emaciate.

se dessécher, *v.r.*, to dry up, to become dry; to be drained; to wither; to waste away.

dessein, *n.m.*, design, intention, intent; resolution; plan, scheme, purpose, view. *Le — en est formé;* the resolution is taken. *Cacher son —;* to hide one's purpose. *Former le — de faire une chose;* to intend to do a thing. *Changer de —;* to alter one's mind. *Avoir — de;* to intend. *Avoir de grands —s;* to have great views. *De prémédité;* of set purpose. *A —;* designedly, on purpose, intentionally. *A bon —;* with a good intention. *A — de;* in order to, with the object of. *A — que;* that, to the end that. *Sans —;* undesignedly, unintentionally.

desseller, *v.a.*, to unsaddle.

dessemelé, -e, *adj.*, without soles, soleless.

dessemeler, *v.a.*, to take soles off, to wear out the soles of.

desserre, *n.f.*, (l.u.) loosening. *Etre dur à la —;* to be close-fisted.

desserrer, *v.a.*, to loosen, to slacken; to relax, to open; (print.) to unlock. *Je n'ai pas desserré les dents;* I never opened my lips, never said a word.

se desserrer, *v.r.*, to get loose, to loosen.

dessert, *n.m.*, dessert.

desserte, *n.f.*, leavings; ecclesiastical functions, officiating; connection; service. *Chemin de —;* connecting road.

dessertir, *v.a.*, to unset (gems).

desservant, *n.m.*, curate, officiating minister, worker.

desservir, v.a., to take away, to clear the table, to remove the cloth; to do an ill office; to officiate (of clergyman). *Il vous a desservi auprès du ministre;* he has done you an ill turn with the minister.

dessiccati-f, -ve, adj., desiccative, desiccant.

dessiccatif, n.m., desiccative, desiccant.

dessiccation, n.f., desiccation.

dessiller, v.a., to open (eyes). — *les yeux à quelqu'un;* to undeceive any one.

se **dessiller**, v.r., to become opened.

dessin, n.m., drawing; design, sketch; pattern; draught, plan; (mus.) arrangement. — *lavé;* washed drawing. — *colorié;* colored drawing. — *haché;* hatched drawing. — *lithographié;* lithographic drawing. — *à la craie;* chalk drawing. *Cette étoffe est d'un joli* —; this stuff is of a pretty pattern. — *à main levée;* free-hand drawing.

dessinateur, n.m., draughtsman; designer, pattern-drawer.

dessiné, -e, part., drawn. *Une figure bien* —*e;* a well-drawn face. *Un jardin bien* —; a garden well laid out.

dessiner, v.a., to draw, to design, to sketch, to delineate; to set off, to mark, to indicate; to lay out. — *au crayon;* to draw with a pencil. — *de fantaisie, d'après nature, d'après la bosse;* to draw from fancy, from nature, from the bust. *Un vêtement qui dessine bien les formes;* a dress that sets off the figure to advantage.

se **dessiner**, v.r., to be delineated, to be visible, to appear; to assume a form, to be formed, to be conspicuous; to display one's figure to advantage; to stand out, to show prominently. *Une terre se dessine dans la brume;* land is visible through the mist.

dessolement, n.m., altering the rotation of crops.

dessoler, v.a., (agri.) to unsole (animals); to take off the sole; to change the rotation of crops.

dessouder, v.a., to unsolder.

se **dessouder**, v.r., to get unsoldered.

dessoudure, n.f., unsoldering.

dessoufrage, n.m., desulphuration.

dessoufrer, v.a., to desulphurate. [sober.

dessoûler, v.a., (pop.) to sober, to make

dessoûler, v.n., to get sober again. *Il ne dessoûl pas;* he is always on the drink.

se **dessoûler**, v.r., (pop.) to get sober again.

dessous, adv., under, underneath, below. *Ci*—; underneath, below. *En* —; underneath; downward; (fig.) sly, artful.

dessous, prep., under, underneath, beneath. *Je l'ai cherché dessus et* — *la table;* I have looked for it upon and under the table.

dessous, n.m., lower part; under side; wrong side; worst; lee (of the wind). *Le* — *du vent;* (nav.) leeward. *Avoir le* —; to be worsted, to have the worst of it. *Au*— —; below; under; beneath. *Je suis logé au*— *de lui;* I lodge below him. *Cet emploi est au*— *de lui;* that employment is beneath him. *Par*— —; under, beneath. *Là*—; there, under there. *Voir le* — *des cartes;* to be in the secret; in the know; to have been behind the scenes. *Jusqu'au troisième* —; very deep. — *de bras;* dress-preserver.

dessus, adv., on, upon, over; uppermost. *Il n'est ni* — *ni dessous;* it is neither on nor under. *Sens* — *dessous;* upside down, topsy-turvy. *Au*—; above; upwards. *Ci*—; above. *Voyez ci*—; see above. *En*—; on the upper *or* right side; in the upper part, above; at the top; uppermost. *Cela est noir en* — *et blanc en dessous;* it is black on the upper side, and white underneath. *Là*—; on it, on that, on there; to, on, about, this subject; upon this head; on which, thereupon, saying this, with these words. *Passons la* —; let us dismiss the subject. *Vous*

pouvez compter là— —; you may rely upon that. *Par*— —; above; over; more, over and above. *Il sauta par*— —; he jumped over.

dessus, prep., on, upon. *Otez cela de* — *la table;* take that off the table. *Cela est au*— *de ses forces;* that is beyond his strength. *Cet homme est au*— *de la calomnie;* this man is out of the reach of slander. *Il sauta par*— *la barrière;* he leaped over the gate. *Par*— *tout;* above all. *Il a des affaires par*— *les yeux;* he is over head and ears in business. *Par*— *le marché;* into the bargain.

dessus, n.m., top, the upper part; upper side, right side; upper hand, advantage; (mus.) treble. *Le* — *de la tête;* the crown of the head. *Le* — *de la main;* the back of the hand. *Le* — *d'un livre;* the cover of a book. — *de fauteuil;* antimacassar. — *de marbre;* marble-top. — *de porte;* panel-frieze. — *de toilette;* toilet cover. *Avoir* or *prendre le* —; to gain the ascendancy, the upper hand. *Le* — *du vent;* (nav.) the weather-gauge. *Etre au*— *du vent;* to be to windward, leeward. *Bas*— (—); second treble.

destin, n.m., destiny, doom, fate; career. *On ne peut fuir son* —; no one can escape his destiny.

destinataire, n.m.f., (com.) consignee; (post.) addressee; receiver, recipient.

destination, n.f., destination; intention, object, end. *A* — *de;* addressed to; (nav.) bound for.

destiné, -e, part., destined, born. *Il est* — *au barreau;* he is destined for the law. *Il était* — *à périr de cette manière;* he was doomed to perish in this way.

destinée, n.f., fate, destiny; doom; career. *Remplir ses* —*s;* to fulfil one's destiny. *Finir sa* —; to terminate one's career.

destiner, v.a., to destine, to intend, to design, to purpose; to doom. *A qui destine-t-on un si riche présent ?* for whom is so rich a present intended ?

se **destiner**, v.r., to be destined, intended. *Il se destine au barreau;* he intends to follow the profession of the law.

destituable, adj., removable from office.

destitué, -e, adj., destitute, devoid; cashiered, removed. — *de bon sens;* devoid of sense.

destituer, v.a., to dismiss, to turn out, to discharge, to remove (from office); to cashier.

destitution, n.f., dismissal, removal.

⊙**destrier**, n.m., steed, charger, war-horse.

destruct-eur, n.m., **-rice**, n.f., destroyer; ravager, spoiler. *Les soldats sont de grands* —*s;* soldiers are great spoilers.

destruct-eur, **-rice**, adj., destructive, destroying, deadly, ruinous; subversive.

destructibilité, n.f., destructibility.

destructi-f, -ve, adj., destructive, destroying.

destruction, n.f., destruction.

désuétude (-su-), n.f., disuse, desuetude. *Tomber dans la* —; to fall into disuse; to become obsolete (of words).

désunion, n.f., disunion, disjunction.

désunir, v.a., to disunite, to disjoin, to part, to separate.

se **désunir**, v.r., to disunite, to come asunder, to divide, to fall out.

désusité, -e, adj., obsolete, out of use; exploded.

détachage, n.m., cleaning, scouring; removal of spots.

détachement (dé-tash-măn), n.m., indifference; (milit.) detachment, draught. — *de tout intérêt;* disinterestedness.

détacher, v.a., to detach, to disengage, to loosen, to untie, to unbind, to unfasten; to undo; to separate, to cut off; to give (a blow); (milit.) to draught, to tell off; to take out stains, to clean. — *une épingle;* to take out a pin. — *un* *ruban ;* to loosen a ribbon. — *une agrafe ;* to undo a clasp. — *un soufflet à quelqu'un ;* to give any one a box on the ear. *Morceaux détachés ;* extracts.

se **détacher,** *v.r.,* to become loosened, unfastened; to get loose ; to come undone; to be detached; to disengage one's self; to break away *or* off; to come off *or* away; to wean one's self of. *Se — d'une femme ;* to break off acquaintance with a woman. *Se — du jeu ;* to leave off gambling.

détacheu-r, *n.m.,* **-se,** *n.f.,* scourer, cleaner.

***detail,** *n.m.,* detail, small matter, trifle, mere nothing; retail; particular, circumstance. *Vendre en —;* to sell by retail. *Je n'ai omis aucun des —s ;* I omitted none of the circumstances. *En —;* minutely, piece-meal; bit by bit.

***détaillant,** *n.m.,* **-e,** *n.f.,* retailer, publican.

***détailler,** *v.a.,* to cut in pieces; to retail; to sell by retail; to detail, to relate minutely.

se **détailler,** *v.r.,* to be cut up, to be related minutely; to be retailed.

détailleu-r, *n.m.,* **-se,** *n.f.,* retailer.

détalage, *n.m.,* taking out of harness, unharnessing.

détaler, *v.a.,* to take in goods ; to pack up.

détaler, *v.n.,* to take in goods; to shut up shop; to scamper away; to take one's self off.

détalinguer (-ghé), *v.n.,* (nav.) to unbend (a cable).

détaper, *v.a.,* to take out the tampion (of a gun).

déteindre, *v.a.,* to take out the dye *or* color.

déteindre, *v.n.,* to lose color, to fade; to come off (of colors). *Cette étoffe déteint beaucoup ;* this stuff fades very much.

se **déteindre,** *v.r.,* to lose color ; to fade ; to come off (of colors).

dételage, *n.m.,* taking out of harness, unharnessing.

dételer (dé-tlé), *v.a.,* to unharness, to take out of harness, to unyoke.

détendoir, *n.m.,* stretcher, unstretcher (weaving).

détendre, *v.a.,* to unbend, to slacken, to relax, to loosen, to take down, to unhang. — *un arc ;* to unbend a bow. — *son esprit ;* to relax one's mind. — *une tapisserie ;* to take down a set of hangings. — *une tente ;* to strike a tent.

se **détendre,** *v.r.,* to unbend, to slacken; to take relaxation, repose; to become easier ; to become milder (of weather).

détendre, *v.n.,* to take down, to unhang (tapestry); to strike (tents).

détenir (dé-tnir), *v.a.,* to detain, to withhold, to keep back, to confine. — *quelqu'un en prison ;* to keep in prison.

détente, *n.f.,* unbending, relaxing; trigger (of a gun); (horl.) detent, stop. *Machine à —;* expansion-engine. *A la —;* in pulling the trigger. *Lâcher la —;* to pull the trigger. *Etre dur à la —;* (fig. and fam.) to be close-fisted.

détent-eur, *n.m.,* **-rice,** *n.f.,* holder, detainer.

***détentillon,** *n.m.,* (horl.) detent, *or* stop, of the minute-hand.

détention, *n.f.,* detention, imprisonment.

détenu, -e, *part.,* detained, withheld. — *en prison ;* kept in prison. — *prisonnier ;* kept a prisoner. *Etre — pour dettes ;* to be in prison for debt.

détenu, *n.m.,* **-e,** *n.f.,* prisoner, convict.

détergent, -e, *adj.,* (med.) detergent.

déterger, *v.a.,* (med.) to deterge; to absterge, to cleanse. — *une plaie ;* to cleanse a wound.

détérioration, *n.f.,* deterioration, debasement; wear and tear.

détériorer, *v.a.,* to deteriorate, to impair, to make worse.

se **détériorer,** *v.r.,* to deteriorate; to become defaced, to become debased; to become the worse for wear.

déterminable, *adj.,* determinable.

déterminant, -e, *adj.,* determinative, decisive, conclusive.

déterminati-f, -ve, *adj.,* (gram.) determinative.

déterminatif, *n.m.,* (gram.) determinative word.

détermination, *n.f.,* determination, resolution, decision, settled purpose.

déterminé, -e, *part.,* determined, decided; fixed; resolved on; caused; determinate; ascertained. *Un sens —;* a determinate signification. *Il est — à tout ;* he is ready for anything.

déterminé, -e, *adj.,* determined, bold, steady, resolute.

déterminé, *n.m.,* desperate fellow, resolute man. *Un petit —;* a froward, ungovernable child.

déterminément, *adv.,* absolutely, positively, determinately, expressly, precisely; boldly, resolutely.

déterminer, *v.a.,* to determine, to decide, to settle, to fix; to ascertain; to resolve; to take a resolution; to fix the meaning; to lead to, to cause, to bring on *or* about. *C'est moi qui l'ai déterminé à cela ;* it was I who made him take that resolve.

se **déterminer,** *v.r.,* to resolve ; to determine ; to be determined. *Je ne puis me — à rien ;* I cannot resolve upon anything.

déterminisme, *n.m.,* (philos.) determinism.

déterré, *n.m.,* person dug up. *Avoir l'air d'un —;* to look like one risen from the dead. *Il a l'air d'un —;* he is as pale as a ghost.

déterrer, *v.a.,* to dig up; to disinter, to take up ; to find, to discover, to bring to light, to ferret out, to rout out; to unkennel (foxes) ; to unearth (hunt.).

déterreur, *n.m.,* hunter out, ferreter. — *de saints ;* discoverer of the names of saints.

détersi-f, -ve, *adj.,* (med.) detersive, abstergent, cleansing.

détersif, *n.m.,* (med.) detergent, detersive.

détestable, *adj.,* detestable, hateful, abominable, odious ; wretchedly bad, wretched. *J'ai une plume —;* I have a wretchedly bad pen.

détestablement, *adv.,* detestably, abominably, hatefully.

détestation, *n.f.,* detestation, abhorrence.

détester, *v.a.,* to detest, to hate, to abhor ; to dislike.

détester, *v.n.,* (l.u.) to blaspheme. *Ne faire que jurer et —;* to do nothing but curse and swear.

détiarer, *v.a.,* to discrown.

détignonner, *v.a.,* to tear the hair of.

détirer, *v.a.,* to draw out, to stretch, to wiredraw. — *une étoffe ;* to pull out a stuff. — *des cuirs ;* to stretch hides.

détiser, *v.a.,* to rake out (the fire); to still, to quell.

détisser, *v.a.,* to unweave.

se **détisser,** *v.r.,* to get unwoven.

détitrer, *v.a.,* to distitle, to deprive of (a title).

détonant, *adj.,* detonating.

détonation, *n.f.,* detonation, report. *A —;* detonating.

détoner, *v.n.,* to detonate.

détonneler, *v.a.,* to draw out of a cask.

détonner, *v.n.,* to be out of tune, to play *or* sing out of tune; to talk nonsense.

détordage, *n.m.,* untwisting, picking.

détordre, *v.a.,* to untwist, to unwring.

se **détordre,** *v.r.,* to come untwisted.

détorquer, *v.a.,* to distort, to misrepresent. — *un passage ;* to distort the meaning of a passage.

détors, -e, *adj.,* untwisted.

⊙**détorse,** *n.f.* V. **entorse.**

*détortiller, *v.a.*, to untwist; to unravel.
se détortiller, *v.r.*, to become untwisted; to be unraveled.

détouper, *v.a.*, to unstop, to take out the bung, to clear of brambles; to take the tow out of.

*détoupillonner, *v.a.*, to prune (orange-trees).

détour, *n.m.*, winding, turning; roundabout way, circuitous road; shift, evasion, trick, subterfuge, dodge. *Le — d'une rue;* the turning of a street. *Les —s d'un bois;* the windings and turnings of a wood. *Quel — vous avez fait!* what a roundabout way you have come! *Je connais ses tours et ses —s;* I know all his evasions and subterfuges. *Etre sans —;* to be sincere, straightforward. *User de —s;* to resort to shifts and evasions.

détourné, -e, *part.*, turned away; retired; indirect, oblique. *Des chemins —s;* by-ways. *Voie —e;* indirect means.

détournement, *n.m.*, turning away, turning aside; embezzlement. *— de mineur;* (law) abduction of a minor.

détourner, *v.a.*, to turn away, to turn aside, to lead astray, to turn off, to lead off, out of; to divert, to avert, to drive or keep back, to estrange; to secrete; to convey away, to embezzle, to appropriate; to deter, to dissuade. *— la vue;* to turn the eyes away. *— un coup;* to avert a blow. *On l'accuse d'avoir détourné ces fonds;* he is accused of having converted these funds to his own use. *Cela me détourne de mes occupations;* that draws me away from my business.

se détourner, *v.r.*, to turn away; to turn aside; to go out of the way, to swerve. *Se — de son chemin;* to go out of one's way. *Se — de son devoir;* to swerve from one's duty. *Se — de son travail;* to leave one's work.

détourner, *v.n.*, to turn, to turn off.

détourn-eur, -euse, *n.m.f.*, shoplifter.

détracter, *v.a.*, (l.u.) to detract, to traduce, to slander, to speak ill of, to backbite.

détract-eur, *n.m.*, **-rice**, *n.f.*, detracter, slanderer, traducer.

detracteur, *adj.m.*, detractive, detracting.

détraction, *n.f.*, detraction.

détranger, *v.a.*, (hort.) to drive away (insects).

détraquer, *v.a.*, to spoil a horse's paces, to throw a horse out of his paces; to disorder, to put out of order; to throw into confusion; to lead astray.

se détraquer, *v.r.*, to lose its paces (of a horse); to be out of order, to be disordered; to go astray. *Cette montre se détraque;* this watch is out of order. *Sa tête se détraque;* his brain is disordered. *Un cheval qui se détraque;* a horse that loses his paces.

détrempe, *n.f.*, distemper, painting in distemper. *Une —;* a sketch in distemper. *Un mariage en —;* an irregular union. *Ouvrage —;* a poor copy of another work.

détremper, *v.a.*, to dilute, to dissolve, to moisten, to weaken; to enervate. *— des couleurs;* to dilute colors. *— de la farine avec des œufs;* to beat up flour with eggs. *— de l'acier;* to soften steel.

détresse, *n.f.*, distress, sorrow, grief, trouble, anguish. *J'eus pitié de sa —;* I took compassion on his sorrow.

détresser, *v.a.*, to unweave, to unplait.

se détresser, *v.r.*, to become unwoven, etc.

détriment, *n.m.*, detriment; injury, prejudice; (geol.) remains. *Au — de;* to the prejudice of.

détritage, *n.m.*, crushing.

détriter, *v.a.*, to crush.

détrition, *n.f.*, detrition.

détritoir, *n.m.*, crushing-mill.

détritus (-tûs), *n.m.*, detritus, residue, refuse.

détroit, *n.m.*, (geog.) strait; sound, narrows; firth; (British) channel.

détromper, *v.a.*, to undeceive.

se détromper, *v.r.*, to be undeceived; to undeceive one's self.

détrônement (dé-trô-n-mān), *n.m.*, dethronement.

détrôner, *v.a.*, to dethrone.

détrôneur, *n.m.*, dethroner.

détrousser, *v.a.*, to untuck, to let down; to rifle, to rob. *— les voyageurs;* to plunder travelers.

⊙**détrousseur**, *n.m.*, highwayman, robber.

détruire (détruisant, détruit), *v.a.*, to destroy, to ruin, to pull down, to exterminate, to subvert, to do away with, to put to death, to break up. *— une ville de fond en comble;* to raze a town to the ground. *— une armée;* to overthrow an army. *— la santé;* to ruin the health. *— radicalement;* to eradicate.

se détruire, *v.r.*, to fall to ruin, to decay; to destroy each other, to neutralize one another; to destroy one's self, to make away with one's self.

dette, *n.f.*, debt, score; obligation, promise, pledge, duty. *— hypothécaire;* debt upon mortgage. *—s actives;* book-debts, assets. *—s passives;* debts, liabilities. *—s criardes;* petty debts. *Contracter, faire, des —s;* to contract debts, to run into debt. *Etre accablé, perdu, criblé, de —s;* to be over head and ears in debt.

*deuil, *n.m.*, mourning, grief, sorrow, gloom, mournful aspect; black; mourners; time of mourning. *Habit de —;* mourning. *Grand —;* deep mourning. *Petit* or *demi —;* half mourning. *Personne qui mène le —;* chief mourner. *Voiture de —;* mourning coach. *Suivre le —;* to be one of the mourners. *Porter le —, être en —;* to be in, to put on, mourning. *Prendre le —;* to go into mourning. *Faire prendre le — à;* to put into mourning. *Faire son — d'une chose;* to resign one's self to the loss of anything.

deutéro-canonique, *adj.*, deuterocanonical.

deutéronome, *n.m.*, Deuteronomy.

deux, *adj.*, two, both, second. *— à —;* two by two. *— fois;* twice. *— fois autant;* twice as much, twice as many. *De — jours en — jours;* every two days. *De — jours l'un;* every other day. *Regarder quelqu'un entre — yeux;* to stare at any one. *Piquer des —;* to clap spurs to one's horse. *Tous — ;* both, both together. *Tous les — ;* both. *Henri — ;* Henry the second. *N'en faire ni un ni — ;* to decide at once. *Maintenant à nous — ;* now I am ready for you; now we'll have it out together.

deux, *n.m.*, two; second; (cards, dice) deuce. *Le — du mois;* the second of the month. *On peut faire cela à — ;* two can play at that game.

deuxième (deu-zièm), *adj.*, second, other.

deuxièmement (-zièm-mān), *adv.*, secondly.

deux-points, *n.m.*, (—) (gram.) colon.

dévalement, *n.m.*, sloping, slope; letting-down, lowering.

⊙**dévaler**, *v.a.*, to let down; to descend, to go or come down. *— les degrés;* to go down the stairs. *— du vin à la cave;* to let wine down into the cellar.

⊙**dévaler**, *v.n.*, to descend, to slope, to go down, to come down (stream).

dévalisement, *n.m.*, rifling, robbing, stripping, plunder.

dévaliser, *v.a.*, to rifle, to strip, to rob, to plunder.

dévalis-eur, -euse, *n.m.f.*, robber, plunderer.

devancer, *v.a.*, to precede, to go before; to get before, to outrun, to outwalk, to outstrip; to take the place of; to have the precedence; to be beforehand, to forestall, to get the start of; to anticipate; to go beyond, to surpass, to outdo. *— à cheval;* to outride. *Son génie a devancé son siècle;* his genius has outrun his century. *J'allais vous voir, mais vous m'avez devancé;* I was going to see you, but you are beforehand with me. *Avoir de l'argent — soi;* to have money at or in hand.

devanci-er, *n.m.,* **-ère,** *n.f.,* predecessor. *pl.,* ancestors, forefathers.

devant, *prep.,* before; in front of, over against, opposite to; (nav.) ahead of. *Regarder — soi;* to look before one; look ahead. *Otez-vous de — mon jour;* get out of my light. *Otez-vous de — moi;* stand out of my sight. *Ils passent par — chez nous;* they pass our door. *Il marchait — moi;* he walked before, in front of, me. *Quand il fut — ses juges;* when he was in the presence of his judges. *Par-— notaire;* in the presence of a notary (*i. e.,* a legal form). *Tout — l'église;* just opposite the church.

devant, *adv.,* before; (nav.) ahead. *Passez —;* go before. *Le train de — d'une voiture;* the forewheels of a coach. *Les jambes de —;* the forelegs. *Sens — derrière;* hind part foremost.

devant, *n.m.,* front, the fore-part. *Il est logé sur le —;* he lodges in the front. *Un — de cheminée;* a chimney-board. *— d'autel;* frontal (panel in front of an altar). *Prendre le —;* to set out before; to get before. *Prendre les — s;* to forestall, to be first in the field. *Aller, venir, envoyer, au-— de quelqu'un;* to go, to come, to send, to meet any one; (fig.) to meet half-way; to provide for or against; to meet, to encounter, to oppose, to obviate. *Aller au-— d'une chose;* to prevent anything. *Aller au-— des désirs de quelqu'un;* to anticipate anyone's wishes. *Ci-—;* before, formerly, heretofore, late. *Les premiers vont —;* first come, first served. *Un ci-—;* an ex-noble.

devantier (-tié), *n.m.,* (fam., l.u.) apron.

devantière (-ti-èr), *n.f.,* riding petticoat.

devanture, *n.f.,* front (of buildings). *— de boutique;* shop-front.

dévastat-eur, *n.m.,* **-rice,** *n.f.,* destroyer, despoiler, desolater, ravager.

dévastat-eur, **-rice,** *adj.,* devastating, desolating, destructive.

dévastation, *n.f.,* devastation; ravage; havoc.

dévaster, *v.a.,* to devastate, to lay waste, to desolate, to make desolate, to spoil, to ravage.

déveine, *n.f.,* change of luck (from good to bad); reverses, run of ill-luck. *Quelle — !* what ill-luck !

développable, *adj.,* susceptible of development.

développante (dév-lo-pant), *n.f.,* (geom.) evolvent; involute.

développée, *n.f.,* (geom.) evolute.

développement (dév-lop-mãn), *n.m.,* unfolding, opening; development, growth, progress; elucidation; display; clearing up; (geom.) evolution.

développer (dév-lo-pé), *v.a.,* to open, to unwrap; to unfold; to develop, to expand; to display, to expound, to elucidate, to lay open, to explain; to clear up, to unravel; (arch.) to trace upon a plan. *— le plan d'un ouvrage;* to explain the plan of a work. *— un système;* to expound a system.

se **développer,** *v.r.,* to expand; to unfold itself, to display itself, to be unfolded *or* displayed; to be cleared up, to be unraveled; to extend itself, to spread out, to stretch out *or* forth, to be stretched out. *Les bourgeons commencent à se —;* the buds are beginning to expand. *Cet enfant se développe;* that child is growing. *La raison se développe;* reason is asserting itself.

devenir (dĕ-vnir), *v.n.,* to become, to grow, to get, to turn; to become of, to come to. *— homme de bien;* to become a good man. *Ces fruits deviennent rouges en mûrissant;* those fruits turn red when ripening. *Cela commence à — fatigant;* that begins to grow tiresome. *— à rien;* to come to nothing. *Que deviendrai-je?* what will become of me? *Qu'est devenu votre*

frère? what has become of your brother? *Je ne sais ce qu'il est devenu;* I don't know what has become of him. *Que voulez-vous — ?* what profession do you intend to follow, what do you intend to be? *Je ne sais plus que —;* I don't know which way to turn. *Faire — fou;* to drive one mad.

déventer, *v.a.,* (nav.) to take the wind out (of sails).

dévergondage, *n.m.,* open profligacy; shamelessness; barefaced impudence; dissoluteness.

dévergondé, -e, *n.* and *adj.,* rake; harlot; brazen-faced, lewd, shameless, impudent.

dévergonder, *v.a.,* to render shameless, licentious; to render dissolute.

se **dévergonder,** *v.r.,* to become shamelessly dissolute and licentious; to lose all feeling of shame; to run riot.

déverguer (-ghé), *v.a.,* to unbend the sails.

déverrouillement, *n.m.,* unbolting.

*****déverrouiller,** *v.a.,* to unbolt.

devers, *prep.,* ⊙towards, about, near. *Par —;* in one's possession; (jur.) before. *Il vient de — ces pays-là;* he comes from somewhere about those parts. *Il a les papiers par — lui;* he is possessed of the papers. *Par — la loi;* in the eyes of the law.

dévers, -e, *adj.,* (arts) bending, jutting out, leaning. *Ce mur est —;* that wall juts out.

dévers, *n.m.,* (tech.) inclination.

déversement, *n.m.,* inclination, bending, warping; pouring, flowing; discharge, overflow.

déverser, *v.n.,* to bend, to lean, to jut out, to warp; (com.) to throw upon the market.

déverser, *v.a.,* to bend, to incline; to throw, to cast; to divert (of water). *— une pièce de bois;* to bend a piece of wood. *— le mépris;* to throw contempt (upon any one).

se **déverser,** *v.r.,* to incline, to lean, to bend, to warp; to fall into, to empty (of rivers, canals, etc.).

déversoir, *n.m.,* weir; dam (of a river).

dévêtement, *n.m.,* stripping.

dévêtir, *v.a.,* to undress, to strip of clothes; (jur.) to divest.

se **dévêtir,** *v.r.,* to take off one's clothes, to undress, to strip, to leave off part of one's clothes; to give up, to divest oneself. *Se — d'un héritage;* to give up an inheritance.

dévêtissement (-tis-mãn), *n.m.,* (jur.) giving up, divestiture.

déviation, *n.f.,* deviation, curvature.

dévidage, *n.m.,* winding, reeling off.

dévider, *v.a.,* to wind (into skeins).

dévideu-r, *n.m.,* **-se,** *n.f.,* winder, reeler.

dévidoir, *n.m.,* reel, skein-winder.

dévier, *v.n.,* to swerve; to deviate; to glance off.

se **dévier,** *v.r.,* to deviate, to swerve. *— de son chemin;* to deviate from one's road.

devin, *n.m.,* **-eresse,** *n.f.,* diviner, augur, soothsayer. *Serpent —;* boa-constrictor.

deviner, *v.a.,* to divine, to foretell, to predict; to guess, to guess at. *Devinez ce que j'ai fait;* guess what I have done. *Cela se devine;* it is easily imaginable; you can see it at a glance. *— une énigme;* to guess an enigma. *En devinant;* at a guess.

se **deviner,** *v.r.,* to understand each other.

devinette, *n.f.,* puzzle, poser, riddle.

devineu-r, *n.m.,* **-se,** *n.f.,* guesser.

dévirer, *v.a.,* (nav.) to heave back.

⊙**devis,** *n.m.,* talk, chat.

devis, *n.m.,* (com.) estimate, specification. *Donner un —;* to give in an estimate.

dévisager, *v.a.,* to disfigure, to scratch the face of; (pop.) to stare out of countenance, to look up and down.

se **dévisager,** *v.r.,* to disfigure one another; to scratch each other's faces; (pop.) to stare each other out of countenance, to look each other up and down.

devise, *n.f.*, device, emblem; motto, posy. *La — d'une bague;* the posy of a ring.

deviser, *v.n.*, (fam.) to chat, to talk.

dévissage, dévissement, *n.m.*, unscrewing.

dévisser, *v.a.*, to unscrew.

se **dévisser**, *v.r.*, to become unscrewed.

dévoiement (dé-voa-mân), *n.m.*, looseness, relaxation; (arch.) inclination, slope.

dévoilement (-voal-mân), *n.m.*, unveiling, disclosing, unraveling.

dévoiler, *v.a.*, to unveil; to discover, to uncover; to unravel; to absolve from vows.

se **dévoiler**, *v.r.*, to betray one's self, to be unveiled, to be disclosed, to be revealed.

dévoîment, *n.m.* V. **dévoiement**.

devoir, *n.m.*, duty; task, exercise. *pl.*, lessons. *S'acquitter de son —;* to perform one's duty. *Être à son —;* to be at one's post. *Rentrer dans son —;* to return to one's duty. *— pascal;* Easter communion. *—s seigneuriaux;* manorial fees. *Se faire un — de;* to make a point of. *Se mettre en — de faire une chose;* to set about doing a thing, to prepare to do. *J'irai vous rendre mes —s;* I shall go and pay my respects to you. *Les derniers —s;* funeral rites.

devoir, *v.a.*, to owe, to be in debt; to be bound to; to have to; must. *— une somme d'argent à quelqu'un;* to owe a sum of money to any one. *Il doit au tiers et au quart;* he owes money right and left. *Qui a terme ne doit rien;* no one need pay before a debt is due. *Fais ce que dois, advienne que pourra;* do your duty, come what may. *Dussé-je;* were I to, though I should. *Il doit partir dans peu de jours;* he is to set out in a few days. *Je dois parler sur ce sujet;* I am to speak on that subject. *Je lui dois tous mes maux;* I owe all my misfortunes to him. *Il ne devrait pas abandonner ses parents;* he ought not to forsake his parents. *Vous auriez dû vous conduire autrement;* you should have behaved otherwise. *Nous devons obéir aux lois;* we must obey the laws. *La campagne doit être belle maintenant;* the country must be beautiful now. *Il devait partir ce matin;* he was to have set out this morning. *Tous les hommes doivent mourir;* all men must die. *Il a dû,* or *avait dû, quitter Londres ce matin;* he must have, or was to have, left London this morning.

se **devoir**, *v.r.*, to owe one's self; to owe it to one's self. *Se — à sa patrie, à sa famille;* to owe one's self to one's country, to one's family. *On se doit d'être honorable;* a man owes it to himself to be honorable. *Cela ne se doit pas;* that is not right; that must, or should, not be done.

dévole, *n.f.*, having no trick (at cards).

dévoler, *v.n.*, to lose all the tricks.

dévolu, -e, *adj.*, devolved upon, vested in, fallen to, escheated. *Terre —e à la couronne;* an escheat.

dévolu, *n.m.*, (ecc.) devolution, lapse of right; claim, choice. *Un bénéfice tombé en —;* a benefice fallen into lapse of right. *Une dame jeta un — sur lui;* a lady cast a spell over him. *J'ai jeté mon — sur cela;* I have fixed my choice upon that.

dévolution, *n.f.*, (jur.) devolution; escheat.

dévonien, -ne, *adj.*, (geol.) devonian.

dévorant, -e, *adj.*, devouring; ravenous; consuming; wasting. *Estomac, appétit, —;* ravenous hunger, ravenous appetite. *Un mal —;* a wasting disease. *Soif —e;* burning thirst. *Climat —;* wasting climate.

dévorateur, *n.m.*, devourer, destroyer.

dévorer, *v.a.*, to devour, to eat up; to prey upon, to destroy, to suppress, to squander, to consume; to gaze at eagerly; to pore over; to swallow, to conquer, to master; to pocket. *La faim le dévore;* he is almost dying of hunger.

Il a dévoré tout son bien; he has squandered away all his fortune. *Il est dévoré d'ambition;* he is consumed with ambition. *— sa douleur;* to stifle one's sorrow. *— un affront;* to brook or pocket an affront. *— les livres;* to pore over, to read, books greedily. *— quelqu'un des yeux;* to gaze at eagerly, to stare at, to gloat over.

dévoreu-r, *n.m.*, **-se**, *n.f.*, devourer, glutton. *— de livres;* book-worm.

dévot, -e, *adj.*, devout, godly, pious, holy; saintly. *Avoir l'air —;* to have a sanctified look.

dévot, *n.m.*, **-e**, *n.f.*, devout person; (b.s.) devotee, saint, bigot. *Ne vous y fiez pas, c'est un faux —;* put no trust in him, he is a bigot.

dévotement (dé-vot-mân), *adv.*, devoutly, piously.

dévotieux, -se (-ci-), *adj.*, devout.

dévotion, *n.f.*, devotion, piety, religion; godliness; disposal, service, command; devoutness; devotedness. *Faire ses —s;* to perform one's devotions; to receive the sacrament. *Tout ce qu'il a est à ma —;* all he has is at my disposal. *Il n'est de — que de jeune prêtre;* new brooms sweep clean.

dévouement (dé-voo-mân), *n.m.*, devotion, devotedness; self-sacrifice; attachment; zeal.

dévouer, *v.a.*, to devote; to dedicate; to consecrate; to consign. *Il lui est entièrement dévoué;* he is entirely devoted to him. *— quelqu'un au mépris;* to consign any one to contempt. *Votre bien, votre tout dévoué;* yours most truly or sincerely.

se **dévouer**, *v.r.*, to devote one's self, to dedicate one's self. *Se — à la patrie;* to sacrifice one's self to one's country.

dévoyé, *n.adj.*, misled; stray sheep; wanderer from the fold.

dévoyer, *v.a.*, to mislead, to lead astray; (arch.) to place obliquely; to cause a looseness (in the bowels).

se **dévoyer**, *v.r.*, ⊙ to lose one's way; (arch.) to be placed obliquely; (rel.) to go astray.

dextérité, *n.f.*, dexterity, adroitness, cleverness, skill.

dextre, *adj.*, right-handed; (her.) dexter.

⊙**dextre**, *n.f.*, the right hand.

⊙**dextrement**, *adv.*, dexterously.

dextrine, *n.f.*, (chem.) dextrine.

dey, *n.m.*, dey.

dia! *int.*, hoi (to make horses turn to the left). *Il n'entend ni à — ni à hurhau;* there is no making him hear reason. *L'un tire à — et l'autre à hurhau;* they pull different ways.

diabase, *n.f.*, (min.) green-stone.

diabète, *n.m.*, (med.) diabetes.

diabétique, *adj.*, diabetic.

diable (diâbl), *n.m.*, devil; hell; wayward child; deuce; truck, drag. *Un ragoût à la —;* a wretchedly bad dish. *Les —s sont déchaînés;* hell has broken loose. *Va au —;* go to the devil. *Un bon —;* a good-natured fellow. *Un méchant —;* a mischievous dog. *Un pauvre —;* a poor wretch. *Le — s'en mêle;* the devil is in it. *Le — t'emporte;* the devil take you. *Quel — d'homme est-ce là?* what devil of a fellow is this? *C'est là le —;* there's the rub. *C'est une — d'affaire;* it is a confounded business. *Cela ne vaut pas le —;* that is not worth a straw, a rap. *Il a le — au corps;* the devil is in him. *Brûler une chandelle au —;* to hold a candle to the devil. *Faire le — contre quelqu'un;* to play the devil with any one. *Faire le — à quatre;* to play the devil; to play all sorts of tricks. *Tirer le — par la queue;* to be hard up. *Il n'est pas si — qu'il est noir;* the devil is not so black as he is painted. *Au — ! the devil take it. *Allé au —;* gone to the devil. *Au — vert;* a devil of a way. *C'est le — à confesser;* it is terribly hard to do. *Loger le — dans sa bourse;* to be penniless. *La beauté du —;* youth and freshness. *Le — bat sa femme et marie sa fille ;* it rains and shines at the same time. *— de mer ;* sea-cormorant, sea-devil.

diable ! *int.,* the devil, the deuce, confound it ! hang it ! *Comment —!* how the devil ! *Que — avez-vous ?* what the devil is the matter with you ? *A quoi — s'amuse-t-il ?* what the deuce is he about ? *De quoi — se mêle-t-il ?* why the deuce does he meddle ?

diablement, *adv.,* devilishly, devilish.

diablerie, *n.f.,* witchcraft ; jugglery ; devilry (of children) ; piece of devilry. *Il y a quelque — là-dessous ;* there is some jugglery in all that.

diablesse, *n.f.,* shrew, vixen ; she-devil. *Une bonne —;* a good-natured creature. *Une pauvre —;* a poor wretch.

diablotin, *n. m.,* imp, little devil ; troublesome imp ; chocolate lozenge ; (nav.) mizzen-top, stay-sail.

diabolique, *adj.,* diabolical, devilish.

diaboliquement (-lik-mān), *adv.,* diabolically, devilishly.

diachylon or **diachylum,** *n.m.,* diachylon, diachylum.

diaco, *n.m.,* deacon or chaplain in the order of Malta.

diacode, *n.m.,* diacodium.

diacommatique, *n.f.,* (mus.) the raising of a note to lead to a transition.

diaconal, -e, *adj.,* diaconal.

diaconat, *n.m.,* diaconate, deaconry, deacon's orders.

diaconesse, *n.f.,* deaconess.

diaconie, *n.f.,* deaconry, almonry.

diacoustique, *n.f.,* diacoustics.

diacre, *n.m.,* deacon.

diadelphie, *n.f.,* (bot.) diadelphia.

diadelphique, *adj.,* (bot.) diadelphian.

diadème, *n.m.,* diadem, crown.

diaggot, *n.m.,* birch-oil.

diagnostic, *n.m.,* (med.) diagnostic.

diagnostique, *adj.,* (med.) diagnostics.

diagnostiquer, *v.a.,* to diagnose.

diagonal, -e, *adj.,* diagonal.

diagonale, *n.f.,* (geom.) diagonal.

diagonalement (-nal-mān), *adv.,* diagonally.

diagramme, *n.m.,* (geom.) diagram.

diagraphe, *n.m.,* diagraph.

dialecte, *n.m.,* dialect.

dialecticien (-in), *n.m.,* dialectician.

dialectique, *n.f.,* dialectics, logic.

dialectique, *adj.,* dialectic, dialectical.

dialectiquement (-tik-mān), *adv.,* dialectically.

dialogique, *adj.,* dialogistic, dialogistical.

dialogisme, *n.m.,* dialogism.

dialogiste, *n.m.,* writer of dialogues, dialogist.

dialogue (-log), *n.m.,* dialogue.

dialoguer (-ghé), *v.a.,* to make several persons speak in character ; (mus.) to make two or more voices, or two or more instruments, reply to each other ; to put in the form of a dialogue.

dialoguer (-ghé), *v.n.,* to compose dialogues ; to speak, to talk ; to converse familiarly with, to chat with, to carry on a dialogue.

dialogueur, *n.m.,* dialogue-writer, dialogist.

diamant, *n.m.,* diamond ; (nav.) crown, throat (of anchors) ; (horl.) jewel. *— taillé ;* cut diamond. *— brut ;* rough diamond. *— de nature ;* diamond unfit for the wheel. *—s de la couronne ;* crown jewels. *— de première eau ;* diamond of the first water. *Monter un —;* to set a diamond. *— de vitrier ;* glazier's diamond.

diamantaire, *adj.,* of diamond brilliancy.

diamantaire, *n.m.,* diamond-cutter.

diamanter, *v.a.,* to set with diamonds ; to render sparkling ; to tinsel, to frost.

diamantifère, *adj.,* diamondiferous.

diamétral, -e, *adj.,* diametrical.

diamétralement (-tral-mān), *adv.,* diametrically. *Sentiments — opposés ;* sentiments diametrically opposed to each other.

diamètre, *n. m.,* diameter. *Demi-diamètre ;* semi-diameter.

diandrie, *n.f.,* (bot.) diandria.

diandrique, *adj.,* (bot.) having two stamens.

diane, *n.f.,* (nav.) morning-gun ; (milit.) reveille, the beat of drum at day-break.

diantre, *n.m.,* the deuce. *Au — soit l'imbécile !* the deuce take the fool !

diantre, *int.,* the deuce ! the dickens !

diantrement, *adv.,* deucedly ; confoundedly.

diapalme, *n.m.,* (pharm.) a kind of ointment.

diapason, *n.m.,* (mus.) pitch, diapason ; tuning-fork.

diapédèse, *n.m.,* (med.) diapedesis.

diaphane, *adj.,* diaphanous, transparent, translucent.

diaphanéité, *n.f.,* diaphaneity, transparency.

diaphorèse, *n.f.,* (med.) diaphoresis.

diaphorétique, *adj.,* (med.) diaphoretic.

diaphragmatique, *adj.,* (anat.) diaphragmatic.

diaphragme, *n.m.,* diaphragm, midriff ; partition with an opening through it; body (of a building).

diaphragmite, *n.f.,* (med.) diaphragmatitis.

diaphtore, *n.f.,* (med.) corruption of the aliments in the stomach; corruption of the fœtus in the womb.

diapré, -e, *adj.,* diapered, variegated, diversified. *Un nez —;* a nose covered with red pimples.

diapré, *n.m.,* diaper-work.

diaprer, *v.a.,* to variegate, to diaper.

se **diaprer,** *v.r.,* to become diapered, to become variegated.

diaprun, *n.m.,* (pharm.) lenitive electuary, confection of senna.

diaprure, *n.f.,* variegation.

diarrhée, *n.f.,* (med.) diarrhœa.

diarthrose, *n.f.,* (anat.) diarthrosis.

diascordium (-om), *n.m.,* (pharm.) diascordium.

diastase, *n.f.,* (surg.) diastasis.

diastole, *n.f.,* (physiology) diastole.

diastrophie, *n.f.,* (surg.) the displacing of the muscles, with or without luxation.

diastyle, *n.m.,* (arch.) diastyle.

diatessaron, *n.m.,* (mus.) diatessaron.

diathèse, *n.f.,* (med.) diathesis.

diatonique, *adj.,* (mus.) diatonic.

diatoniquement, *adv.,* in a diatonic scale, diatonically.

diatragacanthe, *n.m.,* (pharm.) tragacanth powder.

diatribe, *n. f.,* sharp criticism, dissertation, castigation, diatribe.

dicacité, *n.f.,* waggery, causticity.

dichorée (-ko-), *n.m.,* (Latin, Grec. poet.) dichoreus, dichoree.

dichotome (-ko-), *adj.,* (bot.) dichotomous.

dichotomie (-ko-), *n.f.,* (astron.) dichotomy.

dicotylédone, *n.f.,* (bot.) dicotyledon.

dicotylédone, *adj.,* (bot.) dicotyledonous.

dictame, *n.m.,* (bot.) dittany ; (fig.) balm, remedy. *— blanc ;* fraxinella, bastard dittany. *— faux ;* bastard dittany. *Origan —, — de Crète ;* dittany of Crete ; Cretan marum.

dictamen (-mèn), *n.m.,* dictate, suggestion, consciousness.

dictateur, *n.m.,* dictator.

dictatorial, -e, *adj.,* dictatorial.

dictature, *n.f.,* dictatorship.

dictée, *n.f.,* act of dictating, dictation. *Ecrire sous la —;* to write from dictation.

dicter, *v.a.,* to dictate, to indite; to prompt; to suggest; to prescribe.

diction, *n.f.*, diction, elocution, phraseology, style; delivery.

dictionnaire, *n.m.*, dictionary. — *vivant;* walking dictionary. *A coups de —;* by constant reference to the dictionary; labored. — *de pronociation;* pronouncing dictionary. — *de mots obscurs;* glossary. — *de géographie;* geographical dictionary, gazetteer. — *de marine;* dictionary of naval terms.

dicton, *n.m.*, saying, common saying, byword, saw, proverb; (l.u.) sarcasm.

dictum (-tom), *n.m.*, (jur.) purview of an act or decree.

didactique, *adj.*, didactic.

didactique, *n.m.*, didactic order; didactic language.

didactique, *n.f.*, didactic art.

didactiquement, *adv.*, didactically.

didactyle, *adj.*, didactylous.

dideau, *n.m.*, crossing-net.

didelphe, *n.m. adj.*, (zool.) didelphys; didelphic.

didyme, *adj.*, (bot.) didymous.

didynamie, *n.f.*, (bot.) didynamia.

dièdre, *adj.*, (geom.) dihedral.

diel, *n.m.*, a kind of French fuller's earth.

diérèse, *n.f.*, (gram.) diæresis.

dièse, *n.f.*, (mus.) diesis, sharp.

diésé, -e, *adj.*, (mus.) marked with a diesis, sharp.

diéser, *v.a.*, (mus.) to mark a note to be played sharp; to play a note sharp.

diète, *n.f.*, diet, regimen; diet (an assembly of the states of Germany). *Faire —;* to diet one's self, to live moderately.

diététique, *adj.*, (med.) dietetical.

diététique, *n.f.*, (med.) dietetics.

diététiste, *n.m.*, (med.) dietetist.

diétine, *n.f.*, local diet; cantonal convention, dietine.

dieu, *n.m.*, God. — *tout-puissant;* Almighty God. *Le — des armées;* the Lord of Hosts. *Le bon —;* God Almighty; the host. *Croire en —;* to believe in God. *Porter le bon — à un malade;* to carry the host to a sick person. *La Fête-Dieu;* Corpus Christi-day. *Un homme de —;* a godly man. *Un Hôtel-Dieu,* (—s—) a hospital. — *vous bénisse;* God bless you. *S'il plaît à —, avec l'aide de —, — aidant;* God willing, God helping. — *le veuille, plût à —;* God grant it, would to God. — *m'en garde, — m'en préserve, à — ne plaise;* God forbid. — *merci, grâces à —;* thank God. *Bon —! mon —! good* God! good heavens! dear me! goodness me! *Jurer ses grands dieux;* to swear by all that is sacred. *Au nom de —;* in God's name. *Pour l'amour de —;* for God's sake, out of charity, for charity's sake. *Les dieux du paganisme;* the heathen gods. — *! grand —! good* God!

dieudonné, *n.m.*, heaven-sent, heaven-born. *A la grâce de —;* In God's name! As the Lord directs.

diffamant, -e, *adj.*, defamatory, libelous, slanderous.

diffamat-eur, *n.m.*, **-rice,** *n.f.*, defamer, detractor, slanderer, libeler, calumniator.

diffamation, *n.f.*, defamation, aspersion, calumny, slandering, libeling, traducing. — *verbale;* (jur.) slander.

diffamatoire, *adj.*, defamatory, libelous, slanderous.

diffamer, *v.a.*, to defame, to slander, to traduce.

différemment (di-fé-ra-mān), *adv.*, differently.

différence, *n.f.*, odds; difference, disagreement; diversity, disproportion, contrast, disparity. — *marquée;* material difference. — *notable;* wide difference. — *du tirant d'eau;* (nav.) difference in the draught of water. — *en moins;* difference against. — *en plus;* difference in favor of. *Avec cette — que;* except that. *A la — de;* contrary to.

différencier, *v.a.*, to make a difference, to distinguish; (math.) to differentiate.

différend, *n.m.*, difference, quarrel, dispute; difference (of value). *Avoir un — avec quelqu'un;* to be at variance with any one. *Partager le —;* to split the difference.

différent, -e, *adj.*, different, dissimilar, unlike, various, divers, distinct, sundry, opposite, contrary. — *l'un de l'autre;* unlike. *A des degrés —s;* in different degrees.

différentiel, -le, *adj.*, (math.) differential. *Calcul —,* differential calculus.

différentielle, *n.f.*, (math.) differential.

différentier, *v.a.*, (math.) to differentiate.

différer, *v.a.*, to defer, to delay, to put off, to postpone, to adjourn. *Ce qui est différé n'est pas perdu;* what is put off is not lost.

différer, *v.n.*, to defer, to put off, to delay. *se différer,* *v.r.*, to be put off, delayed.

différer, *v.n.*, to differ, to be unlike, to be different; to disagree.

difficile, *adj.*, difficult, hard, trying; nice; particular; willful, skittish (of horses). *Un homme —;* a man hard to please. *Temps —s;* hard times. *De — accès;* hard to get at. *Il est — sur les aliments;* he is fastidious as regards his meals. *Faire le —;* to be difficult to please, to be squeamish.

difficilement (-sil-mān), *adv.*, with difficulty, with much ado, with great pains, not easily.

difficulté, *n.f.*, difficulty; objection; obstacle, hindrance, impediment; cross, rub; misunderstanding, quarrel. *Cela ne souffre point de —;* that admits of no difficulty. — *de respirer;* shortness of breath. *Faire des —s;* to raise objections. *Faire — de quelque chose;* to scruple about anything. *Trancher la —;* to decide peremptorily. *Avoir des —s;* to have crosses. *Il y a entre eux quelque —;* there is some tiff between them. *Sans —;* undoubtedly, without doubt.

difficultueu-x, -se, *adj.*, squeamish, fidgety, never satisfied; hard to please.

diffluence, *n.f.*, diffluence.

diffluent, -e, *adj.*, diffluent.

diffluer, *v.n.*, to spread diffusely.

difforme, *adj.*, deformed, ill-favored, misshapen, ugly.

difformer, *v.a.*, to deform, to deface (coins).

difformité, *n.f.*, deformity, ugliness.

diffraction, *n.f.*, (opt.) diffraction.

diffus, -e, *adj.*, diffuse, prolix, wordy, verbose, long-winded.

diffusément, *adv.*, diffusely, verbosely, wordily.

diffusion, *n.f.*, diffusion; diffusiveness; prolixity, vagueness, wordiness, verbosity. — *de style;* prolixity of style.

digastrique, *adj.*, (anat.) digastric.

digérer, *v.a.*, to digest; to examine, to discuss, to scan, to set in order; to bear, to brook, to stomach, to put up with, to suffer. — *de la viande;* to digest meat. *Non digéré;* undigested. *Bien —;* to thoroughly master. *Il ne peut — cet affront;* he cannot brook or swallow that affront.

digérer, *v.n.*, (chem.) to digest.

digeste, *n.m.*, digest.

digesteur, *n.m.*, (chem) digester.

digesti-f, -ve, *adj.*, digestive.

digestif, *n.m.*, (med.) digestive.

digestion (-tion), *n.f.*, digestion. *Cela aide à la —;* that aids digestion. *Cette entreprise est de dure —;* this is a laborious enterprise.

digital, -e, *adj.*, digital.

digitale, *n.f.*, (bot.) foxglove, digitalis.

digitaline, *n.f.*, (chem.) digitaline.

digité, -e, adj., (bot.) digitated, finger-like, fingered.

digitigrade, n.m., (mam.) digitigrade.

diglyphe, n.m., (arch.) diglyph.

*****digne,** adj., deserving, worthy; dignified. Un — homme; a worthy man. Un — magistrat; an upright magistrate. — de foi; deserving of credit. Cela est — de lui; that's just like him. Il était — d'un meilleur sort; he deserved a better fate.

*****dignement,** adv., worthily, deservedly, justly, according to one's deserts; handsomely, properly, suitably, with dignity. Il s'acquitte — de sa charge; he performs the duties of his office in a worthy manner.

dignifier, v.a., to dignify, to elevate, to enhance.

*****dignitaire,** n.m., dignitary.

*****dignité,** n.f., dignity; stateliness, power. Il soutient la — de son rang; he maintains the dignity of his station. Eire constitué en —; to be raised to power. Parvenir aux —s; to attain to honors. Faire de la —; to assume an air of (offended) dignity.

digon, n.m., pole, flag-yard; gaff.

digresser, v.n., to depart from the main subject, to digress.

digressi-f, -ve, adj., digressive.

digression, n.f., digression. Faire des —s; to wander away from one's subject.

digressivement, adv., digressively.

digue (dig), n.f., dike, dam, mound, embankment, bank; bound, obstacle; bulwark, security.

diguement (dig-män), n.m., embankment, causeway (ports).

diguer (-ghé), v.a., to dam, to dike, to embark; to spur.

digyne, adj., (bot.) digynous (having two pistils).

digynie, n.f., (bot.) digynia.

dilacération, n.f., tearing or rending, dilaceration, laceration.

⊙**dilaniat-eur, -rice,** adj., dilaniating, lacerating, rending.

dilapidat-eur, n.m., **-rice,** n.f., dilapidator, squanderer.

dilapidat-eur, -rice, adj., wasteful, extravagant.

dilapidation, n.f., dilapidation, waste, embezzlement.

dilapider, v.a., to dilapidate, to waste, to squander; to embezzle.

dilatabilité, n.f., (phys.) dilatability.

dilatable, adj., (phys.) dilatable, expansible.

dilatant, n.m., (surg.) dilating body, agent, instrument.

dilatateur, n.m., (surg.) dilator. adj., dilating.

dilatation, n.f., dilatation, expansion, distension; (surg.) enlargement, stretching. La — d'une plaie; the dilatation of a sore.

dilatatoire, n.m. V. **dilatateur.**

dilater, v.a., to dilate, to enlarge, to widen; to distend, to expand. La joie dilate le cœur; joy gladdens the heart.

se **dilater,** v.a., to dilate, to be dilated; to be distended.

dilatoire, adj., dilatory.

dilection, n.f., love, charity (episcopal).

dilemme (di-lem), n.m., dilemma.

dilettante (di-let-tan-t), n. m. f., (dilettanti) dilettante.

dilettantisme (-lèt-tan-), n.m., dilettantism.

diligemment (-ja-män), adv., diligently, speedily, promptly, expeditiously.

diligence, n.f., diligence, speed, despatch; stage-coach, summary of a lecture; (jur.) suit, proceedings; vigilance, care. Bureau des —s; coach-office. Aller en —; to go with speed;

to go by coach. User de —; to use despatch. A la — d'un tel; (jur.) at the suit of such a one. Voyager par la — d'Adam; to go on shanks' mare.

diligent, -e, adj., diligent, quick; sedulous, assiduous, mindful, active, watchful.

diligenter, v.a., to hasten, to forward, to urge on, to be quick.

se **diligenter,** v.r., to make haste, to use diligence, to be quick.

diligenter, v.n., to hasten, to be quick.

dilogie, n.f., duo-drama (i.e., in two parts).

diluer, v.a., to dilute.

dilution, n.f., dilution.

diluvien, -ne (-in, -ène), adj., diluvian.

diluvium (-viome), n.m., (geol.) diluvium.

dimable, adj., tithable.

dimanche, n.m., Sunday, Sabbath, the Lord's-day. Le — de Pâques; Easter Sunday. Le — des Rameaux; Palm-Sunday. Le — gras; Shrove Sunday. Tel qui rit vendredi — pleurera; laugh to-day and cry to-morrow, i.e., laughter is akin to tears. (Racine.)

dime, n.f., tithe.

dimée, n.f., tithing.

dimension, n.f., dimension.

dimer, v.a., to tithe, to levy tithes. — dans un champ; to tithe a field. — au pressoir; to tithe wine in the press.

dimer, v.n., to have a right to tithe.

dimeur, n.m., tithe-gatherer.

diminuer, v.a., to diminish, to lessen, to shorten, to reduce, to retrench, to curtail, to impair, to abate, to slacken.

diminuer, v.n., to diminish, to lessen, to decrease, to abate, to fall, to go down (in price).

diminuti-f, -ve, adj., diminutive.

diminutif, n.m., diminutive.

diminution, n.f., diminution; abridgment, curtailing, reduction, abatement; diminishing, lessening. — de dépenses; curtailment of expenses; tapering (of columns).

dimissoire, n.m., (ecc.) dimissory letter.

dimissorial, -e, adj., (ecc.) dimissory.

dinanderie (di-nan-drî), n.f., brass wares.

dinandier, n.m., brazier.

dinatoire, adj., relating to dinner. Déjeuner —; lunch-dinner.

dinde, n.f., turkey-hen.

dindon, n.m., turkey-cock; (person) goose. C'est un franc —; he is a thorough goose.

dindonneau, n.m., young turkey; poult.

dindonni-er, n.m., **-ère,** n.f., turkey-keeper.

dîné, or **diner,** n.m., dinner, dinner-party. L'heure du —; dinner-time.

⊙**dinée,** n.f., dinner (at an inn) or on the road.

diner, v.n., to dine, to be at dinner. Prier quelqu'un de —; to ask anyone to stay to dinner. Prier à —; to invite to dine. — par cœur; to go dinnerless. — de; to dine off. Son assiette dine pour lui; though he dines out, still he pays.

dinette, n.f., treat, feast, doll's dinner. Faire la —; to play at dinners.

dineur, n.m., diner; eater.

dinosaurien, n.m., (foss.) dinosaurian.

dinothérium (-té-ri-ome), n.m., (—s) (foss.) dinotherium.

diocésain, -e, adj., diocesan.

diocésain, n.m., **-e,** n.f., inhabitant of a diocese.

diocèse, n.m., diocese.

dicecie (di-é-sî), n.f., (bot.) dicecia.

dioïque, adj., (bot.) dicecian.

dionée, n.f., (bot.) dionæa, catch-fly plant.

dionysiaque, adj., (antiq.) concerning Bacchus, of Bacchus.

dionysiaques or **dionysies,** n.f.pl., (antiq.) Dionysia.

dioptrique, n.f., (opt.) dioptrics.

dioptrique, adj., dioptrical.

diorama, n.m., diorama.

diorite, n.m., (geol.) green-stone.

diphtongue (-tong), n.f., diphthong.

diploé, n.m., (anat.) diploe.

diplomate, n.m., diplomatist.

diplomate, adj., diplomatic.

diplomatie, n.f., diplomacy.

diplomatique, n.f., diplomatics.

diplomatique, adj., diplomatic.

diplomatiquement (-tik-măn), adv., diplomatically.

diplomatiste, n.m., diplomatist.

diplôme, n.m., diploma.

diplopie, n.f., double vision, diplopia.

dipode, adj., having two feet or two fins.

diptère, adj., (arch., ent.) dipteral.

diptère, n.m., dipteral insect. pl., diptera.

diptyque, n.m., (antiq.) diptych.

dire (disant, dit), v.a., to tell, to say, to speak, to state, to write, to relate ; to think ; to believe ; to express ; to name, to decree. — d'avance ; to say beforehand. — entre les dents ; to mutter between one's teeth. Dites votre avis ; give your opinion. Dis-je ; said I. On dit ; it is said. On le dit parti ; he is said to have left. — du bien ou du mal de quelqu'un ; to speak well or ill of anyone. — des injures à quelqu'un ; to call any one names. — des duretés ; to say harsh things. — quelque chose à l'oreille ; to whisper anything. Si le cœur vous en dit ; if you feel so minded. Le cœur vous en dit-il ? are you agreeable or game ? Pour tout — ; in a word. Pour mieux — ; or rather. Soit dit entre nous ; between ourselves. Cela va sans — ; that is understood, that goes without saying, of course, that is a matter of course. C'est-à-dire ; that is to say. Pour ainsi — ; so to speak. Ce n'est pas à — que ; it does not follow that. Est-ce à — que ? does it follow that ? Que veut — cela ? qu'est-ce que cela veut — ? what is the meaning of that ? — la messe ; to say mass. Je ne sais que — de tout cela ; I do not know what to think of all that. Faire — à quelqu'un ; to make any one say ; to send word to anyone. Tout est dit ; all is over ; there 's an end of it. Cela ne dit rien ; that is nothing to the point. Cela soit dit en passant ; but that by the way. C'est tout — ; I need n't say more ! Cela vous plaît à — ; you are pleased to say so. Quand je vous le disais ; or je vous le disais bien ; or je vous l'avais bien dit ; did n't I tell you so ! or, what did I tell you. Trouver à — ; to find amiss, to find fault.

se **dire**, v r., to call oneself, to style oneself, to give oneself out as ; to be called ; to be said.

dire, n.m., what one says, saying, words, statement ; (jur.) allegation. Le — du défendeur ; the statement of the defendant. Au — de tout le monde ; according to what everybody says ; by all accounts. Le bien-dire ; elegance of speech. Se fier pour quelque chose au — des autres or d'autrui ; to take anything upon trust.

direct (di-rèkt), -e, adj., direct, straight, immediate ; direct, assessed (of taxes). En ligne —e ; in a straight line. — (rail.) express, through. Par train — ; by express, through train.

directe, n.f., (feudal jur.) lordship.

directement, adv., directly, straightforwardly ; point-blank, home. Aller — à son but ; to go straight to one's goal. — contraire ; quite contrary. — en face ; just opposite.

direct-eur, n.m., **-rice**, n.f., director, manager, superintendent, overseer, conductor ; directress, conductress ; warden, master, principal. — de la monnaie ; master of the mint. — général des postes, postmaster general.

direction, n.f., direction, management, directorship ; director's house or office ; (math.) bearing ; (mining) stretch ; bearing. Avoir la — ; to preside. — de créanciers ; meeting of creditors.

Biens en — ; goods placed under the control of assignees.

directoire, n.m., directory, rubric ; guide ; the supreme executive council of France in 1795.

directorat, n.m., directorship, directorate.

directorial, -e, adj., directorial.

dirigeant, -e (-jän, -t), adj., directing, leading, acting.

diriger, v.a., to direct ; to guide, to conduct, to manage ; to steer, to govern; (of troops) to forward, send off, despatch. — des poursuites contre ; to take proceedings against.

se **diriger**, v.r., to direct one's steps, to go towards ; to make for ; to take pattern from ; to direct, to govern, one's self ; (nav.) to stand in.

dirimant, -e, adj., (canon law) invalidating. Empêchement — ; an impediment that invalidates a marriage.

dirimer, v.a., to invalidate, to annul.

discale, n.f., (com.) tret, tare, shrinkage.

discaler, v.n., (com.) to tare, to diminish.

discernement, n.m., distinction ; discernment, judgment, discrimination. Age de — ; years of discretion.

discerner, v.a., to discern, to distinguish, to know, to discriminate. — le vrai du faux ; to distinguish truth from untruth.

disciple, n.m., disciple, pupil, scholar, follower.

disciplinable, adj., disciplinable, governable, tractable.

discipline, n.f., discipline, education, training; castigation, scourge. Donner la — ; to chastise.

discipliner, v.a., to discipline ; to chastise, to scourge.

se **discipliner**, v.r., to be formed to discipline ; to scourge one's self.

discobole, n.m., (antiq.) discobolus.

discoïde, adj., (conch.) discoidal, discoid.

discontinu, -e, adj., discontinuous.

discontinuation, n.f., discontinuance, discontinuation.

discontinuer, v.a., to discontinue, to interrupt, to leave off, to suspend, to give over.

discontinuer, v.n., to discontinue, to cease, to leave off.

discontinuité, n.f., discontinuity, discontinuance, discontinuation.

disconvenable, adj., unsuitable, improper.

disconvenablement, adv., improperly, unsuitably.

disconvenance, n.f., incongruity, discrepancy, disagreement, unsuitableness ; dissimilarity, dissimilitude ; disproportion, difference, inequality.

disconvenir, v.n., to deny, to disown ; not to suit, to disagree with. Il ne disconvient pas du fait ; he does not deny the fact.

discord, n.m., discord, dissension.

discord, adj. m. (mus.) out of tune, jarring, discordant.

discordance, n.f., discordancy, disagreement, discrepancy ; (mus.) inconsonancy ; dissonance.

discordant, -e. adj., discordant, jarring, dissonant, harsh, out of tune ; untunable, tuneless, unmusical ; disagreeing, inharmonious, incongruous.

discorde, n.f., discord, disagreement, variance, disunion, dissension, strife. Pomme de — ; bone of contention.

discorder, v.n., (mus.) to be out of tune, to be discordant, inconsonant ; to jar.

discoureu-r, n.m., **-se**, n.f., talker ; babbler, chatterer, twaddler. Quel ennuyeux — ! what a chattering bore !

discourir, v.n., to discourse, to descant on, to reason about.

discours, n.m., discourse ; speech, oration, address ; subject. Les parties du — ; the parts of speech. — oratoire ; set speech. — en l'air ; idle talk. C'est un bon — ; it is a good speech.

Faire un —; to make a speech, to deliver an address, an oration. *Tenir des* —; to say things.

discourtois, -e, *adj.,* discourteous, unmannerly; uncivil.

discourtoisement, *adv.,* discourteously.

discourtoisie, *n.f.,* discourtesy, unmannerliness, incivility.

discrédit, *n.m.,* discredit, disrepute, disgrace.

discréditer, *v.a.,* to discredit; to bring into discredit, into disrepute; to bring discredit on.

discr-et, -ète, *adj.,* discreet, considerate, cautious, prudent; wary, circumspect; reserved, secret, close; shy.

discrètement, *adv.,* discreetly, cautiously, circumspectly, warily, prudently, reservedly.

discrétion, *n.f.,* circumspection, prudence; discretion, reserve, wariness; reservedness, discreetness. *L'âge de* —; years of discretion. *Agir, parler avec* —; to act or speak warily. *Vivre à* —; (milit.) to have free quarters. *Se rendre à* —; to surrender at discretion. *Avoir du pain à* —; to have bread ad libitum.

discrétionnaire, *adj.,* discretionary.

discrétoire, *n.m.,* council-room; council.

disculpation, *n.f.,* exculpation.

disculper, *v.a.,* to exculpate, to vindicate, to clear, to exonerate.

discursi-f, -ve, *adj.,* discursive.

⊙**discussi-f, -ve,** *adj.,* (med.) discutient.

discussion, *n.f.,* discussion, debate; altercation, strife, wrangling, dispute; (jur.) seizure and sale (of the property of a debtor). — *de biens;* (jur.) distraint, execution. *Sans division ni* —; jointly and severally.

discutable, *adj.,* debatable, disputable, contestable.

discuter, *v.a.,* to discuss, to debate, to argue; to examine, to canvass, to inquire into; to scan, to sift, to search into. — *un point de droit;* to discuss an article of law. — *les biens d'un débiteur;* to distrain the goods of a debtor.

disert, -e, *adj.,* copious, fluent, eloquent.

disertement, *adv.,* copiously, profusely, fluently, fully.

disette, *n.f.,* scarcity, dearth, want; poverty, penury.

⊙**disetteu-x, -se,** *adj.,* needy, necessitous.

diseu-r, *n.m., -se, n.f.,* teller, speaker, talker. — *de bonne aventure;* fortune-teller. — *de bons mots;* jester. — *de nouvelles;* newsmonger. — *de riens;* idle talker. *Un beau* —; a fine talker.

disgrâce, *n.f.,* disgrace, disfavor; misfortune, affliction; reverse, downfall.

disgracié, -e, *part.,* out of favor. — *de la nature;* deformed, disfigured, ill-favored.

disgracier, *v.a.,* to disgrace, to put out of favor.

disgracieusement, *adv.,* awkwardly, ungracefully, unhandsomely.

disgracieu-x, -se, *adj.,* ungraceful, uncomely, uncouth, ungracious; disagreeable; unpleasant, awkward.

disgrégation, *n.f.,* (opt.) disgregation; separation. *V.* **désagrégation.**

disjoindre, *v.a.,* to disjoin, to disunite.

se **disjoindre,** *v.r.,* to come apart or asunder.

disjoncti-f, -ve, *adj.,* (gram.) disjunctive.

disjonction, *n.f.,* disjunction, separation; (jur.) severance.

disjonctive, *n.f.,* (gram.) disjunctive.

dislocation, *n.f.,* dislocation, dismemberment, luxation. *Il y a* —; the bone is out of joint. *La— d'une armée;* the breaking up of an army.

disloquer, *v.a.,* to dislocate, to dismember, to disjoint, to put out of joint; to take to pieces (machine); (milit.) to break up (an army).

dispache, *n.f.,* (insur.) assessment.

dispacheur, *n.m.,* nautical assessor.

disparaître, *v.n.,* to vanish; to vanish out of sight; to get out of the way; to elope; to abscond; to disappear.

disparate, *n.f.,* incongruity, dissimilarity.

disparate, *adj.,* incongruous, dissimilar, disparate; unlike, ill-matched.

disparité, *n.f.,* disparity, dissimilarity.

disparition, *n.f.,* disappearance.

dispendieu-x, -se, *adj.,* expensive; costly.

dispensaire, *n.m.,* (med.) pharmacopœia; dispensary.

dispensat-eur, *n.m. -rice, n.f.,* dispenser.

dispensation, *n.f.,* dispensation, distribution.

dispense, *n.f.,* dispensation, exemption, permission, license.

dispenser, *v.a.,* to exempt; to dispense with; to dispense, to bestow. *Dispensez-moi de faire cela;* excuse me from doing that. *Le soleil dispense à tous sa lumière;* the sun bestows or sheds his light upon all.

se **dispenser,** *v.r.,* to dispense with; to exempt or excuse oneself from; to spare oneself; to be distributed.

disperser, *v.a.,* to disperse; to scatter, to dispel, to break up.

se **disperser,** *v.r.,* to disperse; to be dispersed, to spread about, to be scattered, to dispel.

dispersion, *n.f.,* dispersion, dispersing, scattering, breaking up.

dispondée, *n.m.,* (poet.) dispondee.

disponibilité, *n.f.,* (jur.) power of disposal (of property); (milit.) state of being unattached. *Etre en* —; (milit.) to be unattached. *Fonds en* —; disposable funds.

disponible, *adj.,* free, disposable, available, unoccupied, disengaged, vacant. *n.m.,* goods in bond.

dispos, *adj. m.,* active, nimble, cheerful, well, hearty.

disposé, -e, *part.,* disposed, inclined; ready; prepared; apt, liable. *Un homme bien — pour quelqu'un;* a man well disposed towards any one. *Mal* —; ill-disposed.

disposer, *v.a.,* to dispose, to order, to lay out; to prepare, to make ready, to fit; to incline, to prevail upon; to have at command.

se **disposer,** *v.r.,* to dispose oneself, to be disposed; to get ready, to prepare; to array oneself; to be about to.

disposer, *v.n.,* to dispose of; to prescribe, to ordain, to order, to make over; (com.) to draw a bill. *Vous pouvez — de moi;* you may draw upon me. *L'homme propose et Dieu dispose;* man proposes and God disposes. *Disposez de moi;* make what use you like of me.

⊙**dispositi-f, -ve,** *adj.,* preparatory.

dispositif, *n.m.,* (jur.) purview, terms (of an act, decree, etc.). *Le — d'un arrêt;* the purview or terms of a decree.

disposition, *n.f.,* disposition, arrangement; order; provision; disposal; service; tendency; inclination, aptness; humor; mind, resolution; habit. *Les —s d'une loi;* the provisions of a law. — *testamentaire;* (jur.) will, bequest, devise. *Il a des gens à sa* —; he has people at his disposal. *Il a de très bonnes —s pour vous;* he is very well disposed towards you. *Etre en bonne* —; to enjoy good health; to be very fit. *Cela est à votre* —; that is at your service.

disproportion, *n.f.,* disproportion.

disproportionné, -e, *adj.,* disproportionate.

disproportionnel, -le, *adj.,* disproportional.

disproportionnellement (-nèl-mãn), *adv.,* disproportionally.

disputable, *adj.,* disputable, controvertible, contestable, debatable; doubtful.

*****disputailler,** *v.n.,* to wrangle about trifles.

*****disputaillerie,** *n.f.,* wrangling, squabbling, bickering.

*****disputailleur,** *n.m.,* caviler, wrangler.

disputant, *n.m.,* disputant.

dispute, n.f., discussion, disputation, dispute, contest, wrangle, wrangling.

disputer, v.n., to discuss; to argue, to dispute; to contend, to contest, to wrangle. — *contre quelqu'un;* to dispute with any one. *Le — à;* to vie with. — *sur un point de droit;* to discuss a point of law. *De quoi dispute-t-on?* what is the matter under discussion? — *de;* to contend for.

disputer, v.a., to contend for, to dispute, to call in question; to fight for. *Il lui dispute le pas;* he contends with him for precedence. — *le passage à quelqu'un;* to oppose any one's passage.

se disputer, v.r., to dispute; to contend for; to wrangle.

disputeu-r, -se, n. and *adj.*, wrangler, disputant; disputatious, quarrelsome.

disqualifier, v.a., to disqualify.

disque, n.m., disc, quoit; (bot.) discus.

disquisition, n.f., disquisition.

disruption, n.f., disruption.

dissecteur, n.m., dissector.

dissection, n.f., dissection. — *des nerfs;* neurotomy.

dissemblable, adj., dissimilar, unlike, different.

dissemblablement, adv., dissimilarly.

dissemblance, n.f., dissimilitude, dissimilarity, difference.

dissembler, v.n., to differ, to be unlike.

dissémination, n.f., dissemination; (bot.) semination; scattering (of seeds).

disséminer, v.a., to disseminate, to scatter.

dissension, n.f., dissension, discord, disunion; strife, feud.

dissentiment, n.m., dissent, disagreement.

dissentir, v.n., to dissent.

disséquer, v.a., (surg.) to dissect; to analyze.

disséqueur, n.m., (iron.) dissector. *V.* **dissecteur**.

dissertat-eur, n.m., **-rice**, n.f., dissertator.

dissertati-f, -ve, adj., dissertative, disquisitive.

dissertation, n.f., dissertation, treatise (in schools); composition, essay.

disserter, v.n., to dissert. — *sur un point d'histoire;* to expatiate on a point of history.

dissidence, n.f., scission, dissidence, difference of opinion, dissent.

dissident, -e, n. and adj., dissident, dissenter; dissentient, dissident, dissenting.

dissimilaire, adj., dissimilar, different, unlike.

dissimilitude, n.f., dissimilitude, difference, unlikeness.

dissimulat-eur, n.m., **-rice**, n.f., dissembler, hypocrite.

dissimulation, n.f., dissimulation, dissembling; double-dealing. *User de —;* to dissemble. — *de naissance;* concealment of birth.

dissimulé, -e, n. and adj., dissembler; dissembling, double-faced, artful. *Homme profondément —;* man extremely double-faced. *Caractère —;* artful disposition.

dissimuler, v.a., to dissemble, to conceal, to hide; to play the hypocrite; to feign to take no notice of; to pretend not to do. — *sa haine;* to dissemble one's hatred. — *une injure;* to take no notice of an insult.

se dissimuler, v.r., to conceal; to be concealed or suppressed or hid.

dissimuler, v.n., to dissemble. *Il dissimula qu'il s'en fût aperçu;* he pretended not to have perceived it.

dissipat-eur, -rice, n. and adj., squanderer, spendthrift, prodigal, waster; lavish, wasteful, extravagant.

dissipation, n.f., dissipation, wasting; waste; recreation, relaxation, diversion. *Vivre dans la —;* to lead a dissipated life.

dissiper, v.a., to dissipate, to scatter, to dispel, to disperse; to consume, to waste, to squander or fritter away, to spend; to recreate, to divert, to relax. — *les factions;* to quell factions. — *son bien;* to squander away one's wealth.

se dissiper, v.r., to divert, recreate, or relax one's self; to be dispersed, dispelled, or dissipated; to vanish, to pass away; to clear off.

dissolu, -e, adj., dissolute, profligate, lewd, loose, licentious.

dissolubilité, n.f., dissolubility.

dissoluble, adj., dissoluble, dissolvable.

dissolument, adv., dissolutely, loosely, lewdly, licentiously, riotously.

⊙**dissoluti-f, -ve**, adj. *V.* **dissolvant**.

dissolution, n.f., dissolution; solution; dissoluteness, looseness of manners, licentiousness, lewdness; riot. — *des simples;* dissolution of herbs. *La — d'un mariage;* the annulling of a marriage. — *de société;* dissolution of partnership.

dissolvant, n.m., dissolvent, resolvent, solvent. *L'eau est un grand —;* water is a powerful dissolvent.

dissolvant, -e, adj., dissolvent, resolvent, solvent.

dissonance, n.f., (mus.) dissonance, discord.

dissonant, -e, adj., dissonant, discordant, jarring.

dissoner, v.n., (mus.) to make discord, to jar, to be discordant or dissonant.

dissoudre (dissolvant, dissous), v.a., to dissolve; to break, to break up. — *un mariage;* to annul a marriage.

se dissoudre, v.r., to dissolve, to be dissolved, to melt; to break up.

dissou-s, -te, part., dissolved, broken up.

dissuader, v.a., to dissuade, to advise to the contrary.

dissuasi-f, -ve, adj., dissuasive.

dissuasion, n.f., dissuasion.

dissyllabe, adj., (gram.) dissyllabic.

dissyllabe, n.m., (gram.) dissyllable.

dissyllabique, adj., dissyllabic.

distance, n.f., distance. *Tenir à —;* to keep at a distance. *Garder sa —;* to keep one's distance.

distancé, -e, part., distanced.

distancer, v.a., to distance, to outdo.

distant, -e, adj., distant, remote, far off.

distendre, v.a., (med.) to distend.

se distendre, v.r., (med.) to be distended.

distension, n.f., (med.) distension, tension.

distillable, adj., distillable.

distillateur, n.m., distiller.

distillation, n.f., distillation.

distillatoire, adj., distillatory.

distiller, v.a., to distill; to discharge, to vent. — *deux fois;* to rectify. — *son esprit sur quelque chose;* to puzzle one's brains over a thing. — *son venin sur quelqu'un;* to vent one's spite upon any one.

distiller, v.n., to drop, to distill, to drizzle, to trickle; to be discharged, to be vented.

distillerie (-til-rî), n.f., distillery, still-house.

distinct (-tinct), **-e**, adj., distinct, different; separate; plain; clear.

distinctement, adv., distinctly, clearly, plainly.

distincti-f, -ve, adj., distinctive, distinguishing, characteristic. *Caractère —, marque —ve;* characteristic.

distinction, n.f., distinction, division; difference; eminence, superiority. *Sans —;* promiscuously, indiscriminately. *Faire — de l'ami et de l'ennemi;* to distinguish between a friend and a foe. *Un homme de —;* a man of refinement

Défaut de —; want of distinction. *Par* —; for distinction, for distinction's sake.

distingué, -e, *adj.,* distinguished, eminent, conspicuous; gentlemanly; ladylike; genteel. *Naissance* —*e;* high birth.

distinguer (-ghé), *v.a.,* to discern, to distinguish; to make a distinction, to discriminate; to make eminent, to single out; to honor; to take notice of, to treat with marks of distinction.

se **distinguer,** *v.r.,* to distinguish *or* signalize one's self, to make oneself eminent; to be distinguished *or* conspicuous, to gain distinction. *Il se distingue par ses talents;* he is conspicuous for his talents.

distique, *n.m.,* distich, couplet.

distique, *adj.,* (bot.) having flowers *or* leaves in double and opposite rows.

distordre, *v.a.,* (med.) to distort, to sprain. *Se* —, *v.r.,* to become distorted.

distors, -e, *adj.,* distorted.

distorsion, *n.f.,* distortion, sprain.

distraction, *n.f.,* separation, subtraction; abstraction, absence of mind, wandering, heedlessness, inattention; recreation, diversion, relief. — *de dépens;* (jur.) awarding of expenses. *A t-on fait* — *des dépens;* have costs been allowed? *Il est sujet à des* —*s;* he is subject to fits of absence of mind. *Par* —; inadvertently; by way of amusement.

distraire, *v.a.,* to separate, to subtract; to call off, to take off, to divert from, to distract, to disturb; to divert; to entertain; to turn from; to deprive. *La moindre chose le distrait;* the least thing diverts his attention. — *des études;* to disturb from study.

se **distraire,** *v.r.,* to divert one's attention; to be disturbed; to divert oneself, to amuse oneself, to take some relaxation.

distrait, -e, *adj.,* absent-minded; heedless, wandering, distracted, vacant. *Un homme* —; an absent-minded man. *Air* —, *regards* —*s;* absent air, vacant looks.

distrait, *n.m.,* absent-minded man.

distrayant, -e, *adj.,* diverting, pleasing, entertaining.

distribuable, *adj.,* distributable.

distribuer, *v.a.,* to distribute, to divide, to deal out, to portion out, to serve out; to dispose, lay out, arrange; (print.) to distribute; (theat.) to cast, to allot. — *des aumônes;* to distribute alms. — *un appartement;* to lay out a suite of rooms.

distributaire, *n.m.f.,* recipient, receiver, sharer.

distribut-eur, *n.m.,* **-rice,** *n.f.,* distributer, bestower, dispenser. — *des vivres;* (nav.) purser's steward, purser's mate.

distributi-f, -ve, *adj.,* distributive.

distribution, *n.f.,* distribution; division; laying out, disposition; delivery (of letters by post); (print.) distribution; (theat.) cast. *Ordre de* —; roll of creditors (for dividends). *La* — *de cet appartement est commode;* this suite of rooms is conveniently laid out.

distributivement (-tiv-mān), *adv.,* distributively.

district (-trik), *n.m.,* district; (fig.) province, jurisdiction.

dit, *n.m.,* maxim; saying; ☉ fable, tale. *Les* —*s et faits des anciens;* the acts and sayings of the ancients. *Avoir son* — *et son dédit;* to be able to say and unsay.

dit, -e, *part.,* said, spoken; surnamed, alias, called. *Ce qui fut* — *fut fait;* he made his words good. *Aussitôt* —, *aussitôt fait;* no sooner said than done. *Susdit;* above-mentioned. *Autrement* —; in other words. *Cela* —; thereupon. *Se le tenir pour* —; to take it for granted.

dithyrambe, *n.m.,* dithyramb; dithyrambic, dithyrambus.

dithyrambique, *adj.,* dithyrambic.

dito, *adv.,* (com.) Do (ditto).

diton, *n.m.,* (mus.) ditone.

ditriglyphe, *n.m.,* (arch.) ditriglyph.

diurétique, *n.m.,* and *adj.,* (med.) diuretic.

diurnal, *n.m.,* (c. rel.) diurnal, daily prayer-book.

diurne, *adj.,* (astron., med., ent.) diurnal, daily.

diurne, *n.m.,* (ent.) diurnal insect. —*s;* diurna.

divagant, *adj.,* wandering, rambling.

divagat-eur, -rice, *n.* and *adj.,* desultory, rambling speaker; desultory, rambling.

divagation, *n.f.,* divagation; wandering, rambling, disconnected, straying; (jur.) straying (of animals). *Se perdre dans les* —*s;* to lose sight of the question.

divaguer (-ghé), *v.n.,* to be incoherent (either in writing or speaking), to ramble, to stray, to wander, to rave; to digress, to wander from the question; to go astray; to stray (of cattle).

divan, *n.m.,* divan, sofa.

divarication, *n.f.,* (med.) divarication.

divariqué, -e, *adj.,* (bot.) straggling.

☉**dive,** *adj.,* divine. *s.f.,* goddess, diva.

divergence, *n.f.,* divergence, divergency; difference of opinion.

divergent, -e, *adj.,* divergent; different; (bot.) spreading.

diverger, *v.n.,* to diverge; to branch off; to spread.

divers, -e, *adj.,* diverse, various, different, multifarious, miscellaneous; divers, sundry, several.

divers, *n.m.pl.,* (com.) sundries.

diversement, *adv.,* diversely, variously, differently.

diversifier, *v.a.,* to diversify, to variegate, to vary. — *l'entretien;* to give variety to the conversation.

se **diversifier,** *v.r.,* to be varied, diversified.

diversion, *n.f.,* diversion.

diversité, *n.f.,* diversity, variety, difference.

divertir, *v.a.,* to divert; to embezzle, to convert to one's own use, to make away with, to convey away; to amuse, to recreate, to delight, to exhilarate. — *des fonds;* to misapply funds. *Deniers divertis;* embezzled money.

se **divertir,** *v.r.,* to amuse oneself, to make merry, to divert *or* recreate oneself; to be diverted *or* amused, to be merry; to make sport with. *Divertissez-vous bien;* enjoy yourself.

divertissant, -e, *adj.,* diverting, entertaining, amusing.

divertissement (-tis-mān), *n.m.,* diversion, pastime, relaxation; amusement; entertainment; purloining, embezzlement. *Une comédie avec des* —*s;* a farcical comedy. — *de deniers;* embezzling of money.

dividende, *n.m.,* dividend. — *arriéré;* unclaimed dividend. *Faire un* —; (com.) to declare a dividend.

divin, -e, *adj.,* divine; godlike; heavenly; admirable, exquisite. *L'office* —; divine service. *Ouvrage* —; most admirable work. *Beauté* —*e;* heavenly beauty.

divinat-eur, *n.m.,* **-rice,** *n.f.,* diviner. *adj.,* prophetic, divining, foreseeing.

divination, *n.f.,* divination. — *par le feu;* pyromancy.

divinatoire, *adj.,* divinatory; divining.

divinement (di-vi-n-mān), *adv.,* divinely, admirably, exquisitely.

diviniser, *v.a.,* to deify; to laud to the skies.

divinité, *n.f.,* Divinity, Godhead, deity. *Adorer la* —; to worship the Divinity. *C'est une* — *que cette femme;* that woman is an angel.

divis, *n.m.,* (l.u.) division, share. *Posséder par* —; to possess a portion of.

divise, *n.f.*, (her.) narrow band.

diviser, *v.a.*, to divide; to parcel out; to part, to portion out; to disunite, to set at variance. — *le tout en ses parties;* to divide the whole into its parts.

se **diviser**, *v.r.*, to divide; to be divided; to be split into parts; to be disunited; to be at variance.

diviseur, *n.m.*, (arith.) divisor; divider.

diviseur, *adj.m.*, divisive, dividing.

divisibilité, *n.f.*, divisibility.

divisible, *adj.*, divisible.

division, *n.f.*, division; partition; dividing; (math., print., rhet., milit., parliament) division; (nav.) squadron. *Etre en* —; to be at variance.

divisionnaire, *adj.*, divisional; divisionary, of a division.

divorce, *n.m.*, divorce; variance. *Faire* — *avec sa femme;* to divorce one's wife. *Faire* —; to renounce. *Ils sont dans un continuel* —; they are always at variance.

divorcer, *v.n.*, to be divorced. *Elle a divorcé d'avec lui;* she has been divorced from him.

divulgation, *n.f.*, divulgence; revelation; publishing.

divulguer (-ghé), *v.a.*, to divulge, to blaze abroad, to reveal, to publish *or* make public.

dix, *adj.*, ten, tenth. *Innocent* —; Innocent the tenth.

dix, *n.m.*, ten; tenth.

dix-huit, *adj.*, eighteen, eighteenth.

dix-huit, *n.m.*, eighteen, eighteenth.

dix-huitième, *adj.*, eighteenth.

dixième (-zièm), *adj.*, tenth. *Le — jour;* the tenth day. *La — fois;* the tenth time.

dixième, *n.m.*, tenth.

dixième, *n.f.*, (mus.) tenth.

dixièmement (di-zièm-mān), *adv.*, tenthly.

dixme, *n.f. V.* **dîme**.

dix-neuf, *adj.*, nineteen, nineteenth.

dix-neuf, *n.m.*, nineteen, nineteenth.

dix-neuvième, *adj.*, nineteenth.

dix-neuvième, *n.m.*, nineteenth.

dix-sept, *adj.*, seventeen, seventeenth.

dix-sept, *n.m.*, seventeen, seventeenth.

dix-septième, *adj.*, seventeenth.

dix-septième, *n.m.*, seventeenth.

dizain, *n.m.*, decastich; (c.rel.) rosary consisting of ten beads; ten packs (of cards); set of ten.

dizaine, *n.f.*, some ten. *Il y avait une — de personnes;* there were ten or twelve people.

dizeau, *n.m.*, shock of wheat (consisting of ten sheaves); ten trusses of hay.

⊙**dizenier** *or* **dizainier**, *n.m.*, tithing-man.

djinn, *n.m.*, (—*s*) (Arabian myth.) imp, evil spirit, demon. *Les* —*s;* swarm of demons.

d.m. (ab. for Docteur Médecin), M.D.

do, *n.m.*, (mus.) c; do, ut.

docile, *adj.*, docile, tractable, submissive, yielding, manageable.

docilement (do-sil-mān), *adv.*, with docility, submissively.

docilité, *n.f.*, docility, tractableness, manageableness; obedience.

docimasie *or* **docimastique**, *n.f.*, (metal.) docimacy.

docimastique, *adj.*, docimastic.

dock, *n.m.*, dock; bonded warehouse.

docte, *adj.*, erudite, learned.

doctement, *adv.*, learnedly, in a learned manner; pedantically.

docteur, *n.m.*, doctor. — *en théologie, en droit, en médecine;* doctor of divinity, of laws, of medicine.

doctissime, *adj.*, most learned.

doctoral, -e, *adj.*, doctoral.

doctoralement, *adv.*, doctorally.

doctorat, *n.m.*, doctorate, doctor's degree.

doctorerie (-tor-rî), *n.f.*, examination for the degree of D.D.

doctoresse, *n.f.*, (jest.) doctoress.

doctrinaire, *n.m.*, lay brother; doctrinaire. *adj.*, lay, stiff, formal, pedantic.

doctrinairement, *adv.*, stiffly, formally, systematically.

doctrinal, -e, *adj.*, doctrinal.

doctrine, *n.f.*, doctrine.

document, *n.m.*, document, title, title-deed, charter, certificate.

dodécaèdre, *n.m.*, (geom.) dodecahedron.

dodécagone, *n.m.*, (geom.) dodecagon.

dodécagone, *adj.*, twelve-angled.

dodécastyle, *adj.*, dodecastyle.

dodelinement, *n.m.*, rocking, swinging; dandling, fondling.

dodinage, *n.m.*, shaking up, stirring (of wine).

dodiner *or* **dodeliner**, *v.a.*, to rock; to swing, to fondle, to dandle.

dodiner, *v.n.*, (horl., ˈl.u.) to oscillate, to vibrate.

se **dodiner**, *v.r.*, to nurse oneself, to coddle oneself.

dodo, *n.m.*, (fam.) by-by, lullaby; sleep, bed. *Aller à* —; to go to bed, to go to sleep.

dodo, *n.m.*, (pop.) (orni.) dodo. *V.* **dronte**.

dodu, -e, *adj.*, plump.

dogaresse, *n.f.*, the wife of a doge.

dogat, *n.m.*, dogate.

doge, *n.m.*, doge.

dogmatique, *adj.*, dogmatic.

dogmatique, *n.f.*, dogmatics.

dogmatiquement (-tik-mān), *adv.*, dogmatically.

dogmatiser, *v.n.*, to dogmatize.

dogmatiseur, *n.m.*, dogmatizer.

dogmatiste, *n.m.*, dogmatist.

dogme, *n.m.*, dogma, tenet, doctrine.

dogre, *n.m.*, Dutch dogger, dogger-boat.

dogue (dog), *n.m.*, mastiff, house-dog; bull-dog.

doguin, *n.m.*, -ne, *n.f.*, (-ghin, -ghi-n), pug-dog, pug.

doigt (doa), *n.m.*, finger; toe; hand; digit. *Les cinq* —*s de la main;* the five fingers of the hand. *Un — du pied;* a toe. *Donner sur les* —*s;* to give a rap on the knuckles. *Etre à deux* —*s de sa ruine;* to be upon the brink of ruin. *Savoir quelque chose sur le bout du* —; to have a thing at one's fingers' ends. *Mon petit* — *me l'a dit;* a little bird told me so. *Se mordre les* —*s de quelque chose;* to repent of a thing. *Il est à deux* —*s de la mort;* he is at death's door. *J'en mettrais le* — *au feu;* I would lay my life upon it. *Etre servi au* — *et à l'œil;* to be served at a nod. *On le montre au* —; he is pointed at. *Vous avez mis le* — *dessus;* you have hit the nail on the head. *Un* — *de vin;* a toothful of wine. *S'en lécher les* —*s;* to lick one's lips; to gloat over anything. *Il lui obéit au* — *et à l'œil;* he is at his beck and call. *Y mettre les quatre* —*s et le pouce;* to eat greedily; to do a thing clumsily. *Etre comme les deux* —*s de la main;* to be hand and glove together; to be inseparable.

doigter (doa-té), *v.a.n.*, (mus.) to finger.

doigter, *n.m.*, (mus.) fingering.

doigtier (doa-tié), *n.m.*, finger-stall, thumb-stall, thimble.

doit, *n.m.*, (com.) Dr. (debtor). — *et avoir:* Dr. and Cr.

doitée, *n.f.*, bit of thread.

dol, *n.m.*, (jur.) deceit, fraud.

dolabelle, *n.f.*, small hatchet.

dolabre, *n.f.*, dowel-ax.

dolage, *n.m.*, adzing, planing.

dolce (dol-cé), *adv.*, (mus.) dolce.

doléance, *n.f.*, complaint, lamentation; grievance. *Faire, conter, ses* —*s;* to tell one's griefs, to pour out one's troubles.

dolemment (do-la-mān), *adv.*, mournfully, wofully, dolefully.

dolent, -e, *adj.*, doleful, woful, piteous, mournful; whining.

doler, *v.a.*, to smooth with the adz; to plane; to pare.

doliman, *n.m.*, dolman.

dollar, *n.m.*, dollar.

dolman, *n.m.*, shell-jacket; hussar's pelisse.

dolmen, *n.m.*, (—s) dolmen, cromlech.

doloir, *n.m.*, paring-knife, parer.

doloire, *n.f.*, adz; chip-ax.

dolomie *or* **dolomite,** *n.f.*, (min.) dolomite.

dom, *n.m.*, dom ; don. *V.* **don.**

domaine, *n.m.*, domain; estate, demesne, possession, property; department, province, compass, sphere. *Le — de la couronne;* the crownlands. *Cela n'est point de mon —;* that is not in my province. *Tomber dans le — du public;* to become public property.

domanial, -e, *adj.*, demesnial, domanial.

domanialiser, *v.a.*, to annex to, to include in (a domain).

dôme, *n.m.*, (arch.) dome, cupola; principal church, canopy; round top. *— de verdure;* verdant arch.

domerie, *n.f.*, an abbey.

domestication, *n.f.*, domestication.

domesticité, *n.f.*, domesticity, the being in service; domestic servants; domesticated state.

domestique, *adj.*, domestic, homely, homebred; menial; tame; domesticated.

domestique, *n.m.*, servant, domestic; servants, domestics (of a house); household; home. *Il a changé tout son —;* he has changed all his servants. *Il aime son —;* he is fond of his home. *— de place;* guide. *— à,* or *pour, tout faire;* general servant.

domestique, *n.f.*, woman-servant, maid-servant, servant. *— pour tout faire;* maid, servant, of all-work.

domestiquement (-tik-mān), *adv.*, servantlike, menially.

domestiquer, *v.a.*, to domesticate, to tame. *Se —;* to become domesticated.

domicile, *n.m.*, domicile, abode, residence. *— politique;* political residence. *— civil;* ordinary residence, dwelling. *A —;* at one's own house, *or* at people's houses, at home. *— légal;* settlement, legal settlement. *De l'eau à —;* water brought to the house. *Elire —,* or *faire élection de —;* to choose one's residence; to settle down.

domiciliaire, *adj.*, domiciliary. *Faire une visite — chez quelqu'un;* to search anyone's house.

domicilié, -e, *adj.*, resident, domiciled. *Il est —;* he is settled, he has taken a house.

se **domicilier,** *v.r.*, to settle down, to dwell in a place.

dominance, *n.f.*, preponderance, dominance, rule.

dominant, -e, *adj.*, dominant, predominant, reigning, prevalent. *Passion —e;* ruling passion. *Goût —;* reigning taste. *La religion —e;* the established religion.

dominante, *n.f.*, (mus.) dominant. *Dans le mode d'ut, sol est la —, et fa la sous-dominante;* in the key of c, ɢ is the dominant, ꜰ the subdominant.

dominat-eur, -rice, *n.* and *adj.*, dominator, ruler, tyrant; ruling, governing, dominant, domineering, arrogant.

domination, *n.f.*, domination; dominion, rule, sway.

dominer, *v.n.*, to rule, to bear rule *or* sway, to have the mastery; to dominate, to preponderate, to prevail; to domineer, to lord it; to rise above; to command a view of, to look over, to tower above; to command; to predominate.

Il faut que la raison domine sur les passions; reason must prevail over the passions. *Sa tête domine au-dessus de la foule;* his head rises above the crowd. *Cette tour domine sur tous les environs;* that tower overlooks all the surrounding country.

dominer, *v.a.*, to rule, to govern, to sway, to prevail over, to domineer over; to rise above, to command a view of; to command, to keep in subjection. *La citadelle domine la ville;* the citadel commands the town.

dominicain, *n.m.*, Dominican, Dominican friar.

dominicain, -e, *adj.*, Dominican.

dominicaine, *n.f.*, Dominican nun.

dominical, -e, *adj.*, dominical. *Lettre —e;* dominical letter. *L'oraison —e;* the Lord's prayer.

dominicale, *n.f.*, Sunday sermon.

domino, *n.m.*, domino. *En —;* in a domino. *Jouer aux —s;* to play at dominoes. *Faire —;* to play out, to win.

dominoterie, *n.f.*, stained papers.

dominotier (-tié), *n.m.*, paper-stainer; dealer in stained papers.

dommage, *n.m.*, damage, injury, hurt, detriment, loss; harm. *Cela me porte —;* that is a loss to me. *Faire du —;* to do harm. *C'est —;* it is a pity. *—s et intérêts, —s-intérêts;* (jur.) damages.

dommageable (-jabl), *adj.*, hurtful, prejudicial, injurious.

domptable (don-tabl), *adj.*, tameable; governable, manageable.

dompter (don-té), *v.a.*, to subdue, to subjugate, to quell, to tame. *— ses passions;* to overcome one's passions. *— des animaux;* to tame animals. *— un cheval;* to break in a horse.

se **dompter,** *v.r.*, to quell, to overcome one's passions.

dompteur (don-teur), *n.m.*, subduer; tamer; breaker in; vanquisher.

dompte-venin, *n.m.*, (—) (bot.) swallowwort.

don, *n.m.*, gift, donation, present, endowment; knack, talent. *Les —s du ciel;* the gifts of heaven. *—s de la nature;* natural endowments. *— gratuit;* free gift. *Le — de la parole;* the gift of speech. *Il a le — de plaire;* he has the knack of pleasing.

don, *n.m.*, don.

dona, *n.f.*, (—s) dona, donna.

donataire, *n.m.f.*, donee.

donat-eur, *n.m.*, **-rice,** *n.f.*, donor, giver.

donation, *n.f.*, donation, free gift; deed of gift. *—s de la couronne;* grants of the crown. *Faire — de ses biens;* to make over one's property by deed of gift.

donatisme, *n.m.*, Donatism.

donatiste, *n. m.*, Donatist.

donc, *conj.*, therefore; accordingly, hence; then, consequently; eh, of course, to be sure. *Répondez —;* answer, I tell you. *Qu'ai-je fait?* whatever have I done?

dondon, *n.f.*, (fam., b. s.) plump, jolly, fresh-colored woman *or* girl.

donjon, *n.m.*, keep, turret, castle-keep; dungeon; pavilion.

donjonné, -e, *adj.*, turreted.

donnant, -e, *adj.*, generous. *Il n'est pas —;* he is not generous. *— donnant;* give and take, tit for tat.

donne, *n.f.*, deal (at cards).

donné, -e, *part.*, given.

donnée, *n.f.*, *sing.*, **données,** *n.f. pl.*, datum, data, principles, facts admitted *or* known; notion, idea, information; (math.) known quantity, datum; theme of a play, a poem, etc.

donner, *v.a.*, to give, to bestow, to present with, to make a present of; to give away; to cause ; to grant, to confer upon ; to ascribe ; to deal (at cards) ; to wish (good day, etc.) ; to devote ; (com.) to sell, to let have. — *en échange ;* to give in exchange. — *tort à quelqu'un ;* to blame any one. — *sa fille en mariage ;* to give one's daughter in marriage. *Qui donne tôt, donne deux fois ;* he gives twice who gives in a trice. — *la vie ;* to grant, to spare life. — *le bonjour à quelqu'un ;* to wish any one good day. — *un soufflet à quelqu'un ;* to box any one's ears. — *rendez-vous ;* to appoint a place of meeting. — *quittance ;* to give a receipt. — *le branle à une affaire ;* to set an affair going. — *le ton ;* to set the fashion. — *la chasse ;* to pursue. — *sa parole ;* to give one's word. — *du chagrin ;* to vex. — *de la peine ;* to trouble. — *les mains à une chose ;* to give one's consent to a thing. — *de l'altesse à quelqu'un ;* to "style" or "dub" any one highness. — *une baie ;* to humbug. — *sa voix, son suffrage ;* to give one's vote, one's suffrage. — *gain de cause ;* to decide in favor of. *Donnez des sièges ;* bring chairs. *Il en donne à tout le monde ;* he makes a fool of everybody. *Je donne beaucoup au hasard ;* I attribute a good deal to chance. *Donner à boire ;* to give to drink. *Donnez-nous à manger ;* give us something to eat. — *à penser, à réflechir ;* to set thinking, to give food for reflection. *C'est à vous à* — ; it is your turn to deal. *En* — *à quelqu'un ;* to beat, to maul, any one ; to cheat a:y one, to take any one in.

se **donner,** *v.r.,* to give one's self; to wre ; to take place (of battles) ; to get ; to a... to attach, one's self ; to give one's self c... — *à quelqu'un ;* to abandon, to devote o... to any one. *Se* — *la peine de ;* to ta... the trouble to. *Se* — *des airs ;* to give one's se... airs. *Se* — *de la tête contre les murs ;* to run one's head against a stone wall. *S'en* — *à cœur joie ;* to indulge one's self to one's heart's content; to take one's fill of anything.

donner, *v.n.,* to give, to give away ; to addict one's self ; to give one's self up; to get into the head (of liquor) ; to hit, to strike; (milit.) to charge; to be engaged, to attack (of troops) ; to deal ; to yield, to bear, to produce ; to look out ; to look into, to overlook. — *contre un banc de sable ;* to strike on a sand-bank. *Mes fenêtres donnent sur la rue ;* my windows look out into the street. — *à penser à quelqu'un ;* to set any one thinking. — *à parler ;* to furnish matter for talk. — *dedans ;* to fall into a snare. — *dans une embuscade ;* to fall into an ambuscade. — *dans le piège,* or *dans le panneau ;* to fall into the snare. *Le soleil donne dans ma chambre ;* the sun shines into my room. *Ce vin donne dans la tête ;* that wine gets up into one's head. *Le régiment a donné ;* the regiment is in action, is under fire.

donneu-r, *n.m.,* **-se,** *n.f.,* giver, donor. *Il n'est pas* — ; he is not fond of giving; he is close-fisted. — *d'eau bénite de cour ;* man of promises only.

don quichotte, *n.m.,* (— —*s*) Don Quixote, madcap ; lanky fellow.

don quichottisme, *n.m.,* (*n.p.*) quixotism.

dont, *pron.,* whose, whereof, of which, of whom, for whom, etc. *Dieu* — *nous admirons les œuvres ;* God whose works we admire. *Ce* — *il s'agit ;* the business in hand. *L'affaire* — *je vous ai parlé ;* the business I spoke to you about.

donte, *n.f.,* body (of a lute).

donzelle, *n.f.,* damsel, wench.

dorade, *n.f.,* (astron., ich.) dorado, swordfish.

doradille, *n.f. V.* **cétérac.**

doré, -e, *part.,* gilt, gilt over, gilded, golden. *Langue* —*e ;* silver tongue; winning, deceitful tongue. — *sur tranche ;* gilt-edged *or* with gilt edges.

dorée, *n.f.,* (ich.) doree, John-Dory ; slice of bread and jam.

dorénavant, *adv.,* henceforth, hereafter, for the future, from this time forward.

dorer, *v.a.,* to gild, to gild over. — *un pâté ;* to glaze a pie with the yolk of eggs. — *la pilule ;* to gild the pill.

se **dorer,** *v.r.,* to gild ; to assume a golden hue *or* tinge.

doreu-r, *n.m.,* **-se,** *n.f.,* gilder.

dorien (-in), *n.* and *adj. m.,* Dorian ; Doric.

dorine, *n.f.,* (bot.) golden saxifrage.

dorique, *n.m.* and *adj.,* Doric.

doris, *n.f.,* (conch.) doris (a sort of mollusk).

dorloter, *v.a.,* to cocker, to fondle, to pamper ; to coddle, to pet, to make much of.

se **dorloter,** *v.r.,* to coddle one's self ; to indulge one's self.

dormant, -e, *adj.,* sleeping, dormant, stagnant; (com.) dull ; unemployed (of money). *Eau* —*e ;* stagnant water. *Manœuvre* —*e ;* (nav.) standing part of a tackle. *Châssis* —; fixed sash.

dormant, *n.m.,* (tech., carp.) dormant, dormer, sleeper, post, fixed frame ; epergne.

dormeu-r, *n.m.,* **-se,** *n.f.,* (pers.) sleeper ; sluggard.

dormeuse, *n.f.,* easy traveling carriage; lounging chair.

*****dormille,** *n.f.,* (ich.) loac..

dormir (dormant, dormi), *v.n.,* to sleep, to be asleep ; to be supine ; to be still ; to be dormant (of money) ; to be stagnant (of water) ; to do nothing. — *d'un bon sommeil, d'un bon somme ;* to sleep soundly. — *trop longtemps ;* to oversleep one's self. — *la grasse matinée ;* to lie late in bed. — *tout debout ;* not to be able to keep one's eyes open. *Qui dort, dîne ;* sleeping is as good as eating. *Il dort comme une marmotte* or *comme un sabot ;* he sleeps like a top. *Il n'y a point de pire eau que l'eau qui dort ;* still waters run deep. — *sur les deux oreilles ;* to sleep soundly. *Qui a renommée de se lever matin peut* — *jusqu'à midi ;* a good reputation covers a multitude of sins. *Ce sont des contes à* — *de bout ;* they are old wives' tales (i. e., tedious, nonsensical).

dormir, *n.m.,* sleep.

dormiti-f, -ve, *adj.,* soporific, somniferous. *Une potion* —*ve ;* a sleeping draught.

dormitif, *n.m.,* dormitive. *L'opium est un dangereux* —; opium is a dangerous sleeping-draught.

doronic, *n.m.,* (bot.) doronicum, leopard's-bane.

dorsal, -e, *adj.,* dorsal.

dorsténie, *n.f.,* (bot.) dorstenia, contrayerva.

dortoir, *n.m.,* dormitory.

dorure, *n.f.,* gilding ; glazing (of pastry).

dos, *n.m.,* back, rear, top, ridge. *Sur le* —; upon the back, pickaback. — *courbé, voûté ;* bent back. *L'épine du* — ; the spine, backbone. — *d'une montagne ;* ridge of a mountain. *Avoir quelqu'un sur le* — ; to be saddled with somebody. *Tourner le* — ; to take to flight. *Tourner le* — *à quelqu'un ;* to turn one's back on *or* to forsake any one. *Avoir bon* — ; to have a strong back. *Faire le gros* — ; to set up its back (of a cat) ; to give one's self airs. — *d'âne ;* shelving ridge. *En* — *d'âne ;* with a shelving ridge. *Le juge les renvoya* — *à* — ; the judge non-suited them both. *En avoir plein le* — ; to be sick and tired of anything. *Se mettre le juge à* — ; to make an enemy of the judge, or to set the judge against one.

dosable, *adj.,* measurable.

dosage, *n.m.,* (chem., pharm.) dosing, proportioning; quantitative analysis.

dose, *n.f.,* dose ; quantity, portion.

doser, *v.a.,* to dose, to proportion.

dossier, *n.m.,* back (of a seat) ; brief (of a barrister) ; bundle of papers. — *d'un lit ;* headboard of a bed, back-board (of a boat).

dossière, n.f., back-band, ridge-band (of harness); back-plate (of a cuirass).

dot (dot), n.f., marriage portion; dowry. La — d'une religieuse; what a nun pays for being admitted into a nunnery. Coureur de —s; fortune-hunter.

dotal, -e, adj., dotal, concerning dowry.

dotation, n.f., endowment, dotation.

doter, v.a., to endow, to give a portion, to give a dowry. — une église; to endow a church.

douaire, n.m., jointure, dower, marriage-settlement. Il lui a assigné dix mille livres de —; he has settled ten thousand francs upon her.

douairi-er, -ère, adj., dowager.

douairière, n.f., dowager; jointress.

douane, n.f., custom-house, custom-duty, duty. Préposé à la —; custom-house officer. Conseil des —s; board of customs. Droit de —; customs duty.

douaner, v.a., to clear goods at the customhouse; to pass through the custom-house.

douanier, n.m., custom-house officer; tide-waiter.

douani-er, -ère, adj., relating to the customhouse, of customs.

doublage, n.m., lining, plating; (nav.) sheathing. — de cuivre; copper-sheathing; (print.) double.

double, adj., double, duplicate; twofold, twice as much, twice as many; strong (of quality); double, deceitful, arrant; downright, regular. Partie —; (com.) double entry. C'est un — coquin; he is a downright, arrant scoundrel.

double, n.m., double; duplicate, replica; counterpart (of a deed), double-faced; (theat.) substitute, understudy; an old French coin worth two deniers; (mus.) a turn. Plus du—; more than the double. Mettre une chose en —; to double a thing. Jouer quitte ou —; to play double or quits. Parier — contre simple; to bet two to one.

double, adv., double. Voir —; to see double.

doublé, n.m., (billiards) doublet.

doubleau, n.m., (carp.) binding joist. V. arc-doubleau.

à double emploi, adv., for a double purpose.

doublement, n.m., doubling.

doublement, adv., doubly, in a double manner.

doubler, v.a., to double; to line (clothes); (arch.) to fur; (milit., nav., print., theat.) to double; to sheathe (a ship). — le pas; to go faster.

doublet, n.m., (billiards, jewelry, trictrac) doublet; (linguistics) doublets.

doublette, n.f., coupler (of organs).

doubleu-r, -se, n.f., doubler.

doublon, n.m., doubloon, Spanish pistole; (print.) double. [derstudy.

doublure, n.f., lining; (theat.) substitute, un-

douce-amère, n.f., (—s—s) woody nightshade, bitter-sweet.

douceâtre, adj., sweetish.

doucement (doos-màn), adv., slowly, leisurely; gently, softly, tenderly, quietly; blandly; peaceably, calmly, smoothly, placidly; mildly; melodiously; meekly; patiently; comfortably; indifferently, not very well, so so. Aller tout —; to be so so.

doucerette, n.f., bland-looking creature.

doucereu-x, -se, adj., sweetish, mawkish; mealy-mouthed.

doucet, -te, adj., demure, mild, affected. Faire le —; to look demure.

doucette, n.f., (bot.) corn salad, lamb's lettuce, Venus's looking-glass.

doucettement (-sèt-màn), adv., (pop.) gently, softly, only so so. Il va tout —; he's only so so.

douceur, n.f., sweetness; fragrance; softness;

mildness; kindness, good-nature; melodiousness, harmony; mellowness; calmness; smoothness; peacefulness; meekness, gentleness; sweet thing; delight, pleasure, comfort; douceur. Employer la — ; to use gentle means. Prendre quelqu'un par la — ; to treat anyone with kindness. Goûter les —s de la vie; to taste the comforts of life. Les —s de la société; the delights of society. Plus fait — que violence; kindness does more than harshness.

douche, n.f., douche, shower-bath.

doucher, v.a., to give a douche, a shower-bath.

doucine, n.f., (arch.) doucine; (carp.) molding-plane.

doucir, v.a., to polish (looking-glasses).

doucissage, n.m., polishing.

douelle, n.f., (arch.) archivolt, curve; stave (of a cask).

douer, v.a., to endow, to bestow upon, to favor.

*douille, n.f., socket, hose, pipe; case or shell (of cartridges).

*douillet, -te, n. and adj., effeminate, delicate person; soft, downy; nice; tender; effeminate; delicate. C'est un —; he loves to indulge himself.

*douillette, n.f., wadded dress, wadded great coat.

*douillettement (doo-lèt-màn), adv., softly, tenderly, delicately, effeminately.

douleur, n.f., pain; ache; soreness; anguish, pang, grief, sorrow, affliction; woe. — aiguë; acute pain.

⊙ se **douloir**, v.r., to grieve, to wail, to lament.

douloureusement (-reûz-màn), adv., grievously.

douloureu-x, -se, adj., painful, tender, smarting, sore; grievous, afflicting, sorrowful; sad. Cri —; mournful cry.

doupion, n.m., double cocoon; coarse, raw silk.

doute, n.m., doubt; scruple, fear, dubiousness; apprehension, misgiving, distrust. Mettre en —; to call in question. Faire naître des —s; to give rise to misgivings. Jeter des —s dans l'esprit; to fill the mind with distrust. Sans —; without doubt, no doubt, doubtless, unquestionably, to be sure. Sans — que; no doubt that. Cela ne fait aucun —; there is no doubt about it.

douter, v.a., to doubt, to question, to hesitate, to suspect, to scruple. Il doute de tout; he doubts everything. Je doute que cela soit; I doubt whether it be so. Je doute qu'il veuille le faire; I doubt whether he will do it. Je ne doute pas qu'il ne le fasse; I do not doubt but that he will do it. Ne — de rien; to be over confident, credulous.

se **douter**, v.r., to suspect, to surmise, to conjecture; to distrust, to mistrust, to fear. Je m'en doutais bien; I thought as much. Je me doutais qu'il viendrait; I suspected he would come. Pouvais-je me — qu'il dût venir sitôt? could I imagine that he was to come so soon? Ne se — de rien; to suspect nothing; to be unconscious of what is going on.

douteur (doo-), n.m., doubter.

douteusement (doo-teûz-màn), adv., doubtfully.

douteu-x, -se, adj., doubtful, dubious, ambiguous, questionable. D'une manière —se; doubtfully. Il est — qu'il le fasse; it is doubtful whether he will do it.

douvain, n.m., stave-wood.

douve, n.f., stave; trench, moat; salt-marsh; (bot.) spearwort.

dou-x, -ce, adj., sweet; soft, smooth; easy; gentle, mild; fragrant, agreeable, comfortable, charming, pleasant; harmonious; peaceful, calm; unfermented; fresh (of water); mellow. *Eau —ce;* fresh water, soft water. *Poisson d'eau —ce;* fresh-water fish. *Senteur —ce;* sweet smell. *Une taille douce;* a copper-plate. *Un billet —;* a love-letter. *Faire les yeux —;* to cast amorous glances. *Il fait bien —;* the weather is very mild. *—ce rêverie;* sweet musing. *Mener une vie —ce;* to lead an easy, agreeable life. *Un — sourire;* a gracious smile. *Il est — comme un agneau;* he is as gentle as a lamb.

doux, *adv.,* gently; submissively. *Filer —;* to knuckle under; to eat humble pie. *Tout —;* softly, gently.

douzaine, *n.f.,* dozen. *Une demi —;* half a dozen. *A la —, Par —;* by the dozen. *C'est un poète à la —;* he is a sorry poet, a rhyming hack.

douze, *adj.,* twelve, twelfth. *Les —signes du zodiaque;* the twelve signs of the zodiac. *Charles —;* Charles the twelfth. *C'est le — aujourd'hui;* to-day is the twelfth.

douze, *n.m.,* twelve, twelfth. *Le —du mois;* the twelfth instant. *Un in— ;* a duodecimo.

douzième, *n.m.* and *adj.,* twelfth.

douzièmement, *adv.,* twelfthly, in the twelfth place.

*****douzil,** *n.m.,* spigot, peg.

doxologie, *n.f.,* doxology.

doyen, *n.m.,* dean; senior, oldest member.

doyenné (doa-ié-né), *n.m.,* deanship, deanery; dean's-pear.

drachme (drakm), *n.f.,* drachma; dram.

dracocéphale, *n.m.,* (bot.) dragon's-head.

draconien, -ne (-in, è-n), *adj.,* draconian.

draconte, *n.m.,* (bot.) dragon's-wort.

dragage, *n.m.,* dragging (of a river).

dragée, *n.f.,* comfit, sugar-plum, sugar-almond; small shot. *—s lissées;* plain sugar-plums. *Grosse —;* buck-shot. *Avaler la —;* to swallow the pill. *Tenir la — haute à quelqu'un;* to keep in suspense; to make a person pay dearly for.

drageoir (dra-jo-ar), *n.m.,* comfit-dish.

dragon (-jon), *n.m.,* (bot.) shoot, sucker.

drageonner (-jo-né), *v.n.,* to put forth shoots *or* suckers.

dragme. *V.* **drachme.**

dragoman. *V.* **drogman.**

dragon, *n.m.,* dragon; vixen; (astron., erpetology) Draco. *— ailé;* flying dragon. *Sa femme est un vrai —;* his wife is a regular termagant *or* virago. *— de vertu;* great prude.

dragon, *n.m.,* dragoon.

dragonnade, *n.f.,* dragonnade.

dragonne, *n.f.,* sword-knot; violent woman. *A la —;* cavalierly, unceremoniously; with a high hand.

dragonner, *v.a.,* (l.u.) to dragoon; to worry. *se* **dragonner,** *v.r.,* (l.u.) to worry oneself.

dragonnier, *n.m.,* dragon-tree.

draguage (-gaj), *n.m.* *V.* **dragage.**

drague (drag), *n.f.,* dredge, dredger; dredging-machine, dredge-net; grains (of malt).

draguer (-ghé), *v.a.,* to drag, to dredge. — *une ancre;* to sweep the bottom for a lost anchor.

draguette (-ghèt), *n.f.,* small dredge *or* drag-net.

dragueur (-gheur), *n.m.,* dredger.

drain, *n.m.,* drain, draining-pipe.

drainage, *n.m.,* drainage.

draine, *n.f.,* (orni.) missel, missel-thrush.

drainer, *v.a.,* to drain.

dramatique, *adj.,* dramatic.

dramatique, *n.m.,* drama, dramatic style.

dramatiser, *v.a.,* to dramatize.

dramatiste, *n.m.f.,* (l.u.) dramatist.

dramaturge, *n.m.f.,* dramatist, [Often used ironically.]

drame, *n.m.,* drama.

drap (dra), *n.m.,* cloth, sheet, pall. — *fin;* superfine cloth, broadcloth. *Gros —;* coarse cloth. *Etre dans de beaux —s;* to be in a fine mess *or* pickle. — *mortuaire;* pall. *Tailler en plein —;* to have abundance of means at command. *Il voudrait avoir le — et l'argent;* he would like to have his cake and eat it.

drapé, -e, *part.,* covered, clothed; hung with black; (bot.) thick, close; woolen. — *à l'antique;* clothed after the antique.

drapeau, *n.m.,* flag, standard, ensign, streamer, colors; rag. *Se ranger sous les —x de;* to serve under, to espouse the cause of. *Sous les —x;* serving in the army.

draper, *v.a.,* to cover with cloth; to hang (a carriage) with black; to arrange, to ornament with drapery; (paint., sculpt.) to give drapery to; (fig.) to censure, to reflect on. *se* **draper,** *v.r.,* to wrap one's self up; (fig.) to make a show of; to parade; to assume an air of importance.

draperie (drap-rî), *n.f.,* drapery, woolen cloths; cloth-trade, cloth-making.

drap-ier, *n.m.,* **-ère,** *n.f.,* draper, woolen-draper, clothier.

drapière, *n.f.,* packing-pin *or* skewer.

drastique, *n.m.* and *adj.,* (med.) drastic.

drave, *n.f.,* (bot.) whitlow-grass.

drawback, *n.m.,* (—s) drawback.

drayage, *n.m.,* fleshing (of hides).

drayer, *v.a.,* to flesh (hides).

drayoire, *n.f.,* fleshing-knife.

drayure, *n.f.,* fleshings (of hides).

drèche, *n.f.,* malt; malt-grains. *Four à —;* malt-kiln. *Faiseur de —;* maltster.

drelin, *n.m.,* (onomatopœia) tinkling, jingling.

dressage, *n.m.,* training (of horses).

dresse, *n.f.,* underlay (of shoes).

dresser, *v.a.,* to erect, to straighten, to make straight; to raise, to set up; to hold upright; to spread; to lay (a snare); to pitch (camp); to trim (a boat); to lay out, to arrange; to make out (accounts); to draw up (a report); to prick up (the ears); to train (animals). *— la tête;* to raise the head. *Cheval qui dresse les oreilles;* a horse that pricks up his ears. *— des statues;* to erect statues. *— un lit;* to put up a bed. *— une tente;* to pitch, to set up, a tent. *— un buffet;* to lay out a sideboard. *— un piège;* to lay a trap. *— un plan;* to draw up a plan. *— des arbres;* to dress trees. *— un cheval;* to train a horse. *— quelqu'un;* to form anyone. *Dresse la chaloupe!* trim the boat! *— la barre du gouvernail;* to right the helm. *se* **dresser,** *v.r.,* to stand on end (of the hair); to stand erect; to rear; to form oneself; to be trained.

dresser, *v.n.,* to stand on end. *Les cheveux lui dressèrent sur la tête;* his hair stood on end.

dressoir, *n.m.,* dresser; sideboard.

*****drille,** *n.m.,* ⊙soldier; fellow. *Un bon —;* a jolly fellow. *Un pauvre —;* a poor wretch.

*****drilles,** *n.f.pl.,* rags; oakum (for paper).

drisse, *n.f.,* (nav.) halyard; yard-rope; gear.

drogman, *n.m.,* dragoman.

drogue (drog), *n.f.,* drug; rubbish; stuff; drogue (a card game). *N'être que de la —;* to be nothing but trash, rubbish. [doctor.

droguer (-ghé), *v.a.,* to drug, to physic; to *se* **droguer,** *v.r.,* to physic, *or* doctor, oneself.

droguer, *v.n.,* to play at drogue; (pop.) to dance attendance.

droguerie (dro-grî), *n.f.,* drugs, drug-trade.

droguet (-ghè), *n.m.,* drugget.

droguetier (-ghè-tié), *n.m.,* drugget-weaver.

droguier (-ghié), *n.m.,* medicine-chest.

droguiste (-ghist), *n.m.f.,* druggist.

droit, -e, *adj.,* straight, right, plumb; direct; upright, erect; just, righteous; stand-up (collars). *Ligne —e;* straight line. *En —e ligne;*

in a straight line. *Remettre quelqu'un dans le — chemin;* to put any one in the right way again. *Tenir la tête —e;* to hold one's head upright, erect. *Il est — comme un cierge;* he is as straight as an arrow. *Le côté —;* the right-hand side. *Un col —;* a stand-up collar.

droit, *n.m.,* right; equity; law; authority; claim, title; fee; due (tax); duty, custom-duty. *Les —s de l'hospitalité;* the rights of hospitality. *Jouir de ses —s;* to enjoy one's rights. *Faire — à chacun;* to do every one justice. *Le — des gens;* the law of nations. *Renoncer à ses —s;* to give up one's right. *Faire — à la demande de quelqu'un;* to accede to any one's request. *Faire son —;* to study for the law. *—d'aînesse;* birthright, primogenitureship. *— de péage;* toll. *A bon —;* with good reason. *Donner — à;* to entitle. *Y avoir —;* to have a right to.

droit, *adv.,* straight, straight on, directly; honestly, uprightly. *A tort ou à —;* right or wrong. *A qui de —;* whom it may concern. *Allez tout —;* go straight on. *Aller — au but;* to go straight to the mark. *— comme ça;* (nav.) right on.

droite, *n.f.,* right hand, right; right side; right-hand side. *A —;* on the right. *Prendre la —;* to turn to the right. *Tourner à —;* to turn to the right.

droitement (droat-mān), *adv.,* uprightly, sincerely; rightly, straightforwardly, judiciously.

droitier, -ère (-tié, -tiè-r), *adj.,* right-handed.

droiture, *n.f.,* uprightness, integrity, equity, honesty, rectitude. *En —;* directly, in a direct manner.

drolatique, *adj.,* amusing, laughable, pleasant, comical, facetious; broad, licentious.

drôle, *adj.,* droll, jocose, ludicrous; comical, strange, funny, curious, odd, queer. *Un — de corps;* a queer fellow, an odd fish.

drôle, *n.m.,* rogue; rascal, blackguard; scoundrel; sharp fellow.

drôlement (drôl-mān), *adv.,* comically, facetiously, jocosely.

drôlerie (drôl-rī), *n.f.,* drollery, droll thing.

drôlesse, *n.f.,* wench, jade; hussy.

dromadaire, *n.m.,* dromedary.

drome, *n.f.,* float, raft.

dronte, *n.m.,* (orni.) dodo.

drosère, *n.f.,* (bot.) sundew.

drosse, *n.f.,* (nav.) truss, rope.

drosser, *v.n.,* to drive or drift ashore; to drift.

drouine, *n.f.,* tinker's sack.

drouineur or **drouinier,** *n.m.,* tinker.

droussage, *n.m.,* carding and oiling (wool).

drousser, *v.a.,* to card and oil (wool).

droussette, *n.f.,* large card for wool.

drousseur, *n.m.,* carder, wool-comber.

dru, -e, *adj.,* fledged (of birds); brisk, lively, smart; close-planted, thick-set.

dru, *adv.,* thick, thickly, fast, hard. *Les balles tombaient — comme grêle* or *comme mouches;* the bullets fell as thick as hail.

druide, *n.m.,* druid.

druidesse, *n.f.,* druidess.

druidique, *adj.,* druidical.

druidisme, *n.m.,* druidism.

drupacé, -e, *adj.,* (bot.) drupaceous.

drupe, *n.m.,* (bot.) drupe.

dryade, *n.f.,* Dryad; (bot.) dryas.

du, *art.m.,* (contraction of *de le*) of the, from the, by the; some, any.

dû, *n.m.,* due, what is owed, what is owing; duty. *A chacun son —;* give the devil his due.

dû, due, *part.* (of devoir), due, owed. *J'aurais — faire cela;* I ought to have done that.

dualisme, *n.m.,* dualism.

dualiste, *n.m.f.,* dualist, manichean.

dualité, *n.f.,* duality.

dubitati-f, -ve, *adj.,* dubitative.

dubitation, *n.f.,* dubitation, doubt.

duc, *n.m.,* duke; (orni.) horn-owl. *Grand- —,* (—s—s) grand-duke; great horn-owl.

ducal, -e, *adj.,* ducal. *Grand- —,* (—-ducaux) grand-ducal.

ducat, *n.m.,* ducat.

ducaton, *n.m.,* ducatoon.

duché, *n.m.,* dukedom, duchy.

duchesse, *n.f.,* duchess; a kind of sofa; a kind of pear. *Lit à la —;* four-post bedstead.

ducroire, *n.m.,* (com.) del credere.

ductile, *adj.,* ductile.

ductilité, *n.f.,* ductility.

dudit, *adj.m.,* of or from the said.

*****duègne,** *n.f.,* duenna.

duel, *n.m.,* duel; struggle; (gram.) dual number. *Appeler en —;* to challenge.

duelliste, *n.m.,* duelist.

⊙**duire,** *v.n.,* to suit, to fit.

duite, *n.f.,* wool of cloth, weft, woof.

dulcification, *n.f.,* dulcification.

dulcifier, *v.a.,* to dulcify.

dulcinée, *n.f.,* dulcinea, sweetheart.

dulie, *n.f.,* dulia (worship of saints).

dûment, *adv.,* duly.

dune, *n.f.,* down; sand-drift, sand-hill.

dunette, *n.f.,* (nav.) poop.

dunkerque, *n.m.,* whatnot, cabinet.

duo, *n.m.,* (—s) (mus.) duo, duet, duetto.

duodécimal, -e, *adj.,* duodecimal.

duodénal, -e, *adj.,* duodenal.

duodénum (-nom), *n.m.,* (anat.) duodenum.

duodi, *n.m.,* duodi (second day of the decade in the calendar of the first French Republic).

dupe, *n.f.,* dupe; gull.

duper, *v.a.,* to dupe, to deceive, to gull, to take in.

duperie (du-prī), *n.f.,* dupery, trickery; trick, take-in, sell.

dupeu-r, *n.m.,* **-se,** *n.f.,* cheat, trickster.

duplicata, *n.m.,* (—) duplicate.

duplication, *n.f.,* duplication.

duplicature, *n.f.,* (anat.) duplicature.

duplicité, *n.f.,* duplicity; double-dealing, deceit.

⊙**duplique,** *n.f.,* (jur.) rejoinder, rebutter.

⊙**dupliquer,** *v.n.,* (jur.) to rejoin, to put in a rejoinder.

duquel, *pron.,* of which, from which. *V.* **lequel** and **dont.**

dur, -e, *adj.,* hard; tough; obdurate, harsh, merciless, unkind, unfeeling, hard-hearted. *Il a les traits —s;* his features are hard. *Le regard —;* a harsh look. *Des vers —s;* harsh verses. *Un esprit —;* a dull understanding. *Marchandise —e à la vente;* goods of slow sale. *Avoir l'oreille —e;* to be dull of hearing. *Le temps est —;* the weather is severe. *Tableau —;* stiff painting; harsh painting.

dur, *adv.,* hardly; firmly. *Il entend —;* he is hard of hearing.

durabilité, *n.f.,* durableness.

durable, *adj.,* durable, lasting, solid.

durablement, *adv.,* durably, lastingly.

duracine, *n.f.,* sort of peach; duracine.

durant, *prep.,* during. *— sa vie, sa vie —e* or *durant* (Littré); during his lifetime.

dur-bec, *n.m.,* (—s—s) (orni.) hawfinch.

durcir, *v.a.,* to harden, to make hard, to make tough; to indurate.

se **durcir,** *v.r.,* to harden, to indurate, to grow hard.

durcir, *v.n.,* to harden, to become hard; to stiffen; to indurate.

durcissement (-sis-mān), *n.m.,* hardening, stiffening; induration.

dure, *n.f.,* bare ground; bare floor, bare board. *Coucher sur la —;* to sleep on the ground, on the bare floor.

durée, *n.f.,* duration, continuance. *Etre de longue —e;* to be durable.

durement (dur-män), *adv.*, hard; hardly, harshly, sharply, roughly, rigorously.

dure-mère, *n.f.*, (n.p.) (anat.) dura mater.

durer, *v.n.*, to last, to continue; to remain; to endure; to stand, to subsist. *Une étoffe qui dure;* a stuff that wears well. *Le temps lui dure;* time hangs heavy upon him. *Ne pouvoir — en place;* to be unable to sit still. *Faire vie qui dure;* to take care of one's money, to think of the morrow. *Ne pouvoir — dans sa peau;* to be ready to jump out of one's skin.

duret, -te, *adj.*, (l.u.) somewhat hard, rather tough, toughish.

dureté (dur-té), *n.f.*, hardness, toughness; harshness, austerity, unkindness; stiffness. *La — du fer;* the hardness of iron. *Avoir une — d'oreille;* to be hard of hearing. *La — de son regard;* the sternness of his look. *— de cœur;* hard-heartedness.

duretés, *n.f.pl.*, harsh, offensive words.

***durillon**, *n.m.*, callosity, hard skin; corn.

⊙**durillonner,** *v.n.*, to become hard.

se **durillonner,** *v.r.*, to become covered with warts, callosities.

duriuscule, *adj.*, (jest.) somewhat hard, tough, hardish.

duumvir (du-om-), *n.m.*, duumvir.

duumvirat, *n.m.*, duumvirate.

duvet, *n.m.*, down; wool, nap.

duveté, -e (duv-té), *adj.*, (of birds) downy.

duveteu-x, -se, *adj.*, (of fruit) downy.

dynamètre, *n.m.*, dynameter.

dynamique, *n.f.*, dynamics.

dynamique, *adj.*, dynamical.

dynamisme, *n.m.*, name given to the doctrine of Newton.

dynamite, *n.f.*, dynamite.

dynamomètre, *n.m.*, dynamometer.

dynaste, *n.m.*, (antiq.) kinglet.

dynastie, *n.f.*, dynasty.

dynastique, *adj.*, dynastic.

dyscole, *adj.*, (l.u.) who departs from an established opinion; difficult to live with.

dyscrasie, *n.f.*, (med.) dyscrasy.

dysenterie (dis-sant-rí), *n.f.*, dysentery.

dysentérique, *adj.*, dysenteric.

dysopie, *n.f.*, (med.) dysopsy, dysopsia.

dysorexie, *n.f.*, dysorexy.

dyspepsie, *n.f.*, dyspepsia.

dysphagie, *n.f.*, dysphagia.

dysphonie, *n.f.*, dysphony.

dysphorie, *n.f.*, dysphoria.

dyspnée, *n.f.*, dyspnœa.

dysurie, *n.f.*, dysury.

dytique, *n.m.*, (ornith.) diver; water-beetle.

E

e, *n.m.*, the fifth letter of the alphabet, e.

e, abbreviation of *Eminence, Excellence.*

eau, *n.f.*, water; rain, stream, river, pond, flood; perspiration; tea (of herbs); liquid; wash. *pl.*, (nav.) track, wake; luster, gloss; watering-place. *— bénite;* holy water. *— douce;* fresh water, soft water. *— dure;* hard water. *— de mer;* sea-water. *— saumâtre;* brackish water. *— mère;* mother-water (chem.). *— de source;* spring-water. *— courante;* running water. *— morte;* still water. *— panée;* toast and water. *Morte- —,* (n.p.) neap-tide. *— forte,* (n.p.) aqua fortis. *Grandes —x;* high flood (of rivers). *Grandes —x de Versailles;* fountains in full play. *Cure d'—x;* water cure. *Hautes —x;* high water. *— bénite de cour;* empty promises, blarney, soft sawder. *— dormante;* stagnant water. *Aller aux —x;* to go to a watering-place. *Porter de l'— à la mer;* to carry coals to Newcastle. *Ils se ressemblent comme deux gouttes d'—;* they are as like as two peas. *Il n'est*

pire — que celle qui dort; still waters run deep. *Cela s'en est allé en — de boudin;* that came to nothing at all. *Aller à l'—;* to take the water (of a dog). *Un jet d'—;* a water-spout, fountain. *Une pièce d'—, une nappe d'—;* a sheet of water; an artificial lake. *—x jaillissantes;* gushing waters. *Passer l'—;* to cross the water. *Au bord de l'—;* at the water's edge. *Nager entre deux —x;* to swim under water; to waver between two parties. *A fleur d'—;* on a level with the water. *Faire venir l'— au moulin;* to bring grist to the mill. *Mettre de l'— dans son vin;* to come down a peg or two. *Pêcher en — trouble;* to fish in troubled water. *Cela fait venir l'— à la bouche;* that makes one's mouth water. *Lancer un navire à l'—;* to launch a ship. *Faire de l'—;* (nav.) to water, to take in fresh water. *Faire une voie d'—;* to spring a leak. *— de-vie, (—x- —) brandy. *— de rose;* rose-water. *— d'arquebusade;* arquebusade water. *Il tombe de l'—;* it is raining. *Il est tout en —;* he is in a bath of perspiration. *Suer sang et —;* to toil and moil. *Donner — à un drap;* to give a gloss to a piece of cloth. *Maître des —x et forêts;* ranger of the woods and forests. *—x-fortes;* etchings, collection of etchings. *L'— va toujours au moulin;* money begets money. *Tout va à vau l'—;* all is going to wreck and ruin. *Les —x sont basses chez lui;* he is hard up. *Une goutte d'— suffit pour faire déborder un vase plein;* the last straw breaks the camel's back. *D'ici là il passera bien de l'— sous le pont;* it will be a long time before that happens.

ébahi, -e, *adj.*, wondering, aghast, dumfounded.

*s'*ébahir,** *v.r.*, to wonder at, to be amazed, to be aghast.

ébahissement (-is-män), *n.m.*, wonderment, amazement, astonishment.

ébarbage, *n.m.*, (arts) paring, paring away; (engr.) edging off; scraping.

ébarber, *v.a.*, to pare, to strip (quills); (engr.) to edge off, to scrape; to edge a dash off.

ébarboir, *n.m.*, (arts) parer, scraper.

ébat, *n.m.*, (fam.) diversion, pastime, sport, gambol, frolic. *Prendre ses —s;* to disport oneself.

ébattement (é-bat-män), *n.m.*, balancing (of a vehicle); (jest.) diversion, pastime, sport, gambol.

*s'*ébattre,** *v.r.*, to sport, to take one's pleasure, to gambol, to frolic.

ébaubi, -e, *adj.*, (fam., jest.) amazed, astonished, dumfounded.

ébauchage, *n.m.*, sketching.

ébauche, *n.f.*, sketch, rough draught, drawing, outline.

ébaucher, *v.a.*, to make the first draught, to draw an outline of, to sketch, to rough-hew; to delineate; (mas.) to boast.

ébaucheur, *adj.*, (tech.) roughing.

ébauchoir, *n.m.*, (sculp.) boasting-tool; mortise chisel.

⊙*s'*ébaudir,** *v.r.*, (jest.) to frolic, to frisk, to skip about.

⊙**ébaudissement,** *n.m.*, frollicking.

ebbe or **èbe,** *n.m.*, (nav.) ebb, reflux, low water.

ébène, *n.f.*, ebony, ebony work. *Des cheveux d'—;* raven locks.

ébéner, *v.a.*, to ebonize.

ébénier, *n.m.*, ebony-tree. *Faux —;* laburnum.

ébéniste, *n.m.*, cabinet-maker.

ébénisterie, *n.f.*, cabinet-work.

⊙**éberner,** *v.a.* *V.* **ébrener.**

éblouir, *v.a.*, to dazzle; to fascinate. *Le soleil nous éblouit;* the sun dazzles us. *S'—;* to be dazzled, fascinated.

éblouissant, -e, *adj.*, dazzling, resplendent.

éblouissement (-is-măn), *n.m.*, dazzling ; (fig.) dizziness ; fascination, charm.

éborgnage, *n.m.*, nipping off of buds.

*__**éborgner**__, *v.a.*, to blind of one eye, to put out an eye ; to nip the buds off.

*__s'__**éborgner**, *v.r.*, to make oneself blind of one eye.

ébouage, *n.m.*, scavenging.

ébouer, *v.a.*, to scavenge.

éboueur, *n.m.*, road-scraper, scavenger.

ébouillanter, *v.a.*, to scald.

*__**ébouillir**__, *v.n.*, to boil down, to boil away. *Cette sauce est trop ébouillie ;* that sauce has boiled away too much.

éboulement (é-bool-măn), *n.m.*, falling in, falling down, landslip, sinking. — *de terre ;* landslip.

ébouler, *v.n.*, to fall in, to fall down, to sink.

*__s'__**ébouler**, *v.r.*, to fall in, to fall down, to sink. *Ce rempart s'éboule ;* the rampart is falling in.

éboulis, *n.m.*, rubbish, fallen ground.

ébourgeonnement (-jo-n-măn), *n.m.*, (hort.) nipping of the buds, disbudding.

ébourgeonner (-jo-né), *v.a.*, (hort.) to nip off the buds.

ébourgeonnoir, *n.m.*, nipping-knife.

ébouriffé, -e, *adj.*, disordered, ruffled, in disorder ; in a flutter. *Elle arriva tout —e ;* she came in with her hair all ruffled. *Qu'avez-vous donc ? vous voilà tout —* ; what is the matter with you ? you are all of a flutter.

ébousiner, *v.a.*, (mas.) to clean off.

ébraisoir, *n.m.*, furnace-shovel.

ébranché, -e, *adj.*, lopped, trimmed, pruned.

ébranchement (é-bransh-măn), *n.m.*, (hort.) pruning, lopping, trimming.

ébrancher, *v.a.*, (hort.) to prune, to lop, to trim.

ébranlement (é-branl-măn), *n.m.*, shock, concussion, shaking ; perturbation, disturbance, trouble.

ébranler, *v.a.*, to shake, to move ; to disturb. *Les vents ont ébranlé cette maison ;* the winds have shaken that house. — *la résolution de quelqu'un ;* to shake any one's resolution. *Sa fidélité ne fut jamais ébranlée ;* his fidelity was never shaken.

*__s'__**ébranler**, *v.r.*, to shake, to be shaken, to be disturbed ; (milit.) to move, to get under way, to be set in motion. *Quand les deux armées s'ébranlèrent ;* when the two armies moved forward. *La voiture s'ébranla ;* the coach got under way.

ébrasement (é-brăz-măn), *n.m.*, (arch.) splaying.

ébraser, *v.a.*, (arch.) to splay.

ébrèchement, *n.m.*, notching.

ébrécher, *v.a.*, to notch, to jag, to indent, to impair. *Ses folles dépenses ont ébréché sa fortune ;* his extravagant living has made a gap in his fortune.

*__s'__**ébrécher**, *v.r.*, to be notched, to break off a piece (of one's tooth).

ébrener, *v.a.*, (l. ex.) to clean (a child).

ébriété, *n.f.*, ebriety, inebriety.

⊙*__**ébrillade**__. *n.f.* (man.) jerk (with the bridle).

ébrouement, *n.m.*, sneezing, snorting.

ébrouer, *v.a.*, (dy.) to wash ; to shell or husk.

*__s'__**ébrouer**, *v.r.*, (man.) to snort ; to sneeze.

ébruiter, *v.a.*, to make known, to spread about.

*__s'__**ébruiter**, *v.r.*, to be made known, to be noised abroad.

ébrun, *n.m.*, horned rye.

ébuard, *n.m.*, wooden wedge.

ébullition, *n.f.*, boiling, ebullition.

écachement, *n.m.*, bruising, crushing.

écacher, *v.a.*, to crush, to squash, to squeeze flat. *Nez écaché ;* flat nose.

*__**écaille**__, *n.f.*, scale ; shell ; chipping (porcelain). *Des —s d'huître ;* oyster-shells. *Peigne d'—* ; tortoise-shell comb.

*__**écaillé, -e**__, *adj.*, scaly.

*__**écaill-er**__, *n.m.*, **-ère**, *n.f.*, oyster-man, oyster-woman.

*__**écailler**__, *v.a.*, to scale.

*__s'__**écailler**, *v.r.*, to peel off, to scale, to scale off ; to chip off.

*__**écailleu-x, -se**__, *adj.*, scaly, squamous.

écale, *n.f.*, shell (of peas) ; hull, husk (of nuts). — *de noix ;* walnut-shell.

écaler, *v.a.*, to shell (beans, peas) ; to hull, to husk (almonds, nuts).

*__s'__**écaler**, *v.r.*, to shell, to be shelled.

*__**écarbouiller**__, *v.a.*, (pop.) to crush, to squash.

écarlate, *n.f.*, and *adj.*, scarlet.

écarlatine. V. **scarlatine**.

*__**écarquillement**__ (-măn), *n.m.*, (fam.) opening wide, spreading out (of one's eyes, legs).

*__**écarquiller**__, *v.a.*, (fam.) to open, to spread out, to open wide. — *les jambes ;* to spread out one's legs. — *les yeux ;* to open wide, to strain one's eyes.

écart, *n.m.*, step aside, digression, swerving, error ; mistake, fault, deviation ; (man.) strain ; (at écarté) cards rejected. *Il fit un — pour éviter le coup ;* he stepped aside to avoid the blow. *Faire un —* ; to step aside. *Faire un — dans un discours ;* to make a digression in a speech. *Les —s de l'imagination ;* the flights of the imagination. *Ce cheval s'est donné un —* ; that horse has strained itself. *Les —s de la jeunesse ;* the errors of youth. *Faire son —* ; to discard. *À l'—* ; aside, apart, by one's self, in solitude, in a lonely place. *Mettre à l'—* ; to put by, to lay aside. *Il le prit à l'—* ; he took him aside. *Se mettre, se tenir, à l'—* ; to keep aloof, to stand aside. *Laisser à l'—* ; to leave aside, to shun, to omit.

écarté, *n.m.*, ecarté (cards).

écarté, *part.*, remote, lonely, secluded.

écartelé, -e, *adj.*, quartered, torn to pieces ; (her.) quartered.

écartèlement, *n.m.*, tearing to pieces, quartering.

écarteler, *v.a.*, to quarter, to tear to pieces ; (her.) to quarter.

écartelure, *n.f.*, (her.) quartering.

écartement, *n.m.*, putting aside ; removal, scattering, spreading ; separation ; (surg.) diastasis.

écarter, *v.a.n.*, to set aside, to remove ; to waive ; to pass over ; to dispel ; to widen ; to divert ; to keep from ; to disperse, to scatter, to avert ; to discard. — *une mauvaise pensée ;* to dismiss an evil thought. — *un coup ;* to ward off a blow.

*__s'__**écarter**, *v.r.*, to turn aside ; to deviate ; to err, to stray ; to ramble ; to swerve ; to remove, to make way. *S'— de son sujet ;* to stray from one's subject. *S'— de son chemin ;* to go out of one's way. *S'— de son devoir ;* to swerve from one's duty. *La foule s'écarta ;* the crowd made way.

*__**écartillement**__, *n.m.* V. **écarquillement**.

*__**écartiller**__, *v.a.* V. **écarquiller**.

ecce homo (èk-sé-), *n.m.*, (—) ecce homo ; (fig.) thin, pale person.

ecchymose (é-ki-), *n.f.*, (med.) ecchymosis.

ecchymosé (é-ki-), *adj.*, being in a state of ecchymosis, bruised.

ecclésiaste, *n.m.*, Ecclesiastes.

ecclésiastique, *adj.*, ecclesiastic, clerical.

ecclésiastique, *n.m.*, clergyman, priest, ecclesiastic.

ecclésiastiquement (-tik-măn), *adv.*, ecclesiastically.

écervelé, -e, *adj.*, hare-brained, mad-brained, rash, giddy. *Une tête —e ;* a mad-cap.

écervelé, *n.m.*, **-e**, *n.f.*, mad-cap ; hare-brained person. *C'est un —* ; he is not to be relied upon.

échafaud, n.m., scaffold; (arch.) stage; stand; gallows. — de service; temporary stage.

échafaudage, n.m., scaffolding, great preparations; display.

échafauder, v.n., to scaffold, to erect scaffolding; to pile up; to shore up.

échafauder, v.a., to make great preparations for a work; ⊙ to pillory.

s'échafauder, v.r., to be piled up; to be shored up; (fig.) to raise one's self, to support one's self, to find supporters.

échalas, n.m., prop for a vine; vine-stick; hop-pole. C'est un —; he is as thin as a lath.

échalassement, n.m., (hort.) propping.

échalasser, v.a., to prop vines, etc.

échalier, n.m., fence, hurdle, stile.

échalote, n.f., shallot, eschalot.

échampir, v.a., (house paint) to set off. V. réchampir.

échancré, -e, part., hollowed out, indented; (bot.) emarginated; sloped.

échancrer, v.a., to slope, to hollow out, to indent.

échancrure, n.f., hollowing, sloping, slope, indentation; cut, opening.

échange, n.m., exchange, barter. Un — de compliments; an exchange of compliments. Libre —; free-trade.

échangeable (-jabl), adj., exchangeable.

échanger, v.a., to exchange, to barter, to interchange. — une propriété contre une autre; to exchange one property for another.

échangiste (libre), n.m., free-trader.

échanson, n.m., cup-bearer.

échansonnerie (-so-n-rî), n.f., cup-bearers of a prince; a king's wine-cellars.

*échantillon, n.m., sample, pattern, specimen; tally; (nav.) scantling; (tech.) gauge.

*échantillonnage, n.m., sampling; gauging.

*échantillonner, v.a., to sample, to gauge.

échanvrer, v.a., to hatchel.

échanvroir, n.m., hackle.

échappade, n.f., (engr.) slip, escapade.

échappatoire, n.f., shift, subterfuge, creep-hole, put-off, evasion.

échappé, -e, n.f., a person who has made his or her escape, a runaway; a horse of mongrel or cross breed. Un — des galères; an escaped convict. Un — des petites-maisons; a madman, a crack-brained fellow.

échappée, n.f., prank; sally, snatch; (arch.) rounding off; space for carriages to turn in. Faire quelque chose par —s; to do a thing by snatches, by fits and starts. — de vue; vista. — de lumière; (paint.) accidental light. A l'—; by stealth.

échappement, n.m., (horl.) escape, escapement. — à recul; recoil-escapement. — à repos; dead-beat escapement. — à ancre; anchor or lever escapement. — de la vapeur; (mec.) puff.

échapper, v.n. to escape, to make one's escape, to get away, to get out of, to avoid, to shun, to fly, to break out. Laisser —; to overlook, to pass over, to let pass. Faire — un prisonnier; to favor a prisoner's escape. — au naufrage; to escape shipwreck. — du naufrage; to escape from the wreck. Cela m'est échappé; that has slipped my memory. Cela m'a échappé; it escaped me (i. e. I did not know of it), or I said it inadvertently. Laisser — l'occasion; to let slip an opportunity. Laisser — un mot; to drop a word. [When échapper means to avoid, to be preserved, it requires the preposition à: On échappe à l'orage. When it means to steal away, to leave a place, it requires the preposition de: On échappe de prison.]

échapper, v.a., to escape, to avoid; (man.) to put to the greatest speed. L'— belle; to have a narrow escape. — le danger; to avoid danger. — la côte; to escape stranding.

s'échapper, v.r., to get loose, to get away, to escape, to steal away, to slip away; to vanish, to disappear; to forget one's self. Il s'est échappé jusqu'à dire; he forgot himself so far as to say.

écharbot, n.m., (bot.) water-chestnut, water-caltrop.

écharde, n.f., prick, prickle (of a thistle); splinter; (piscat.) stickleback.

échardonnage, n.m., clearing of thistles.

échardonner, v.a., to clear of thistles.

échardonnoir, n.m., weed-hook.

écharner, v.a., to excarnate; to flesh.

écharnoir, n.m., fleshing-knife.

écharnure, n.f., scrapings or parings of hides.

écharpe, n.f., scarf; sash; arm-sling; (nav.) shell of a pulley or block; (engineering) surface-table; water-table; (her.) scarp. Changer d'—; to be a turncoat, to change sides, to rat. Avoir le bras en —; to have one's arm in a sling. Le canon tire en —; the cannon fires slanting. Coup d'épée en —; slanting cut. Avoir l'esprit en —; to be heedless, absent, inattentive. En —; over the shoulder.

écharper, v.a., to slash, to cut; to cut to pieces, to hack. Il lui a écharpé le visage; he gave him a slash across the face. — un régiment; to cut a regiment to pieces.

échars, -e, adj., (coins) light; below the legal standard. Vents —; (nav.) shifting winds, light and variable winds.

écharser, v.n., (nav.) to veer, to shift about, to change often. ⊙ v.a., to lower the standard of coins.

échasse, n.f., (orni.) stilt-bird. — à manteau noir; long-legged plover.

échasse, n.f., stilt; tressel, trussel (of stages); upher. — d'échafaud; upher, scaffolding-pole. Il est toujours monté sur des —s; he is always on stilts, in buckram.　[bird; —s, grallae.

échassier, n.m., (orni.) long-legged wading

échauboulé, -e, adj., (med.) full of pimples.

échauboulure, n.f., (med.) pimple, blotch, rash, pustule.

échaudage, n.m., lime-wash; lime-washing.

échaudé, n.m., simnel, cracknel. — au beurre; simnel with butter.

échaudé, -e, part., scalded. Chat — craint l'eau froide; a burnt child dreads the fire.

échauder, v.a., to scald.

s'échauder, v.r., to burn one's self; to burn one's fingers. Il s'y est échaudé; he burnt his fingers in that business.

échaudis, n.m., (nav.) triangular shape.

échaudoir, n.m., scalding-house; scalding-tub.

échauffaison, n.f., (med.) overheating, eruption, rash.

échauffant, -e, adj., heating, binding.

échauffe, n.f., heap. Mettre les peaux en —; to heap the hides.

échauffé, n.m., odor (caused by excessive heat). Sentir l'—; to have or exhale a hot smell.

échauffée, n.f., first operation of salt-makers in warming their oven.

échauffement (é-shôf-mān), n.m., heating; over-excitement.

échauffer, v.a., to warm, to heat, to overheat; to excite, to inflame, to irritate, to anger; to vex. Echauffez la chambre; warm the room. Les épices échauffent le sang; spices heat the blood. Cela lui échauffe la bile; that provokes him.

s'échauffer, v.r., to grow warm, to overheat one's self; to grow angry, to fly into a passion, to chafe, to fume. La chambre s'échauffe; the room is getting warm. Il s'est échauffé à marcher; walking has made him warm. La querelle s'échauffe; the quarrel is running high.

Le jeu s'échauffe ; they are playing deep. *S'— sur la voie ;* (hunt.) to follow the chase eagerly.

échauffourée, *n.f.,* a rash, headlong, or blundering enterprise ; skirmish, affray ; blunder.

échauffure, *n.f.,* red pimple, rash.

échauguette (-ghèt), *n.f.,* (milit.) watch-box, watch-tower.

échauler, *v.a.* V. **chauler.**

échaux, *n.m.pl.,* channels, furrows, watercourse, drains.

échéable, *adj.,* falling due, payable.

échéance, *n.f.,* falling due, expiration, maturity. *— commune ;* average maturity. *— prochaine ;* nearly due. *A courte —;* at a short date, short-dated. *A longue —;* at a long date ; long-dated. *Jusqu'à l'—;* until maturity, till due. *Payer une lettre de change à l'—;* to pay a bill of exchange at maturity.

échéant, *part.,* falling due. *Le cas —;* if such should be the case ; in that case.

échec, *n.m.,* check, repulse, defeat ; blow ; loss. *Donner —;* to check. *— et mat ;* checkmate. *Etre — et mat ;* to be checkmated. *Il a souffert un grand —;* he has suffered a dreadful blow. *Tenir un homme en —;* to have a man under one's thumb. *Tenir une armée en —;* to keep an army at bay.

échecs (é-shè), *n.m.pl.,* chess ; board and set of chess-men ; chess-men. *Jouer aux —;* to play at chess.

échelette, *n.f.,* rack (for pack-saddles, carts) ; (orni.) wall-creeper.

échelier, *n.m.,* peg-ladder.

échelle, *n.f.,* ladder ; ladder-staircase ; scale ; degree ; (nav.) quarter-deck ladder. *— brisée ;* folding-ladder. *— de siège ;* scaling-ladder. *— de corde ;* rope-ladder. *— do meunier ;* trapladder. *— à incendie ;* fire-ladder, fire-escape. *— de jardin ou de tapissier ;* pair of steps. *— de dunette ;* poop-ladder. *— de commandement ;* accommodation-ladder. *— campanaire ;* bellfounder's diapason. *—s du Levant ;* sea-ports in the Levant. *Faire la courte —;* to mount upon one another's shoulders. *Faire à quelqu'un la courte —;* to give a lift to any one ; to help any one through. *Sentir l'—;* to deserve hanging. *Après lui il faut tirer l'—;* he has left nothing to be done, *or* you cannot go one better.

échelon (ésh-lon), *n.m.,* round, rung, step (of a ladder) ; step, stepping-stone ; (milit.) echelon. *Descendre d'un —;* to come down a step. *Marcher en —s ;* to march in echelons.

échelonner, *v.a.,* to draw up in echelons ; to arrange according to gradation. *— un corps d'infanterie ;* to draw up a body of infantry in echelons.

s'échelonner, *v.r.,* to be graduated ; to rise gradually ; to be arranged *or* drawn up in echelons.

échenal *or* **écheneau,** *n.m.,* gutter, basin.

*****échenillage,** *n.m.,* clearing, ridding of caterpillars.

*****écheniller** (ésh-ni-), *v.a.,* to rid plants of caterpillars.

*****échenilleur,** *n.m.,* caterpillar-destroyer : (ornith.) caterpillar-eater.

*****échenilloir,** *n.m.,* averruncator.

écheno. V. **échenal.**

écheoir. V. **échoir.**

écheveau (ésh-vo), *n.m.,* hank, skein. *Dévider un —;* to reel, to wind off, a skein.

échevelé, -e (é-shèv-lé), *adj.,* disheveled ; whose hair hangs loose ; disordered ; romantic, extravagant.

échevette, *n.f.,* small skein.

échevin (ésh-vin), *n.m.,* sheriff, alderman.

échevinage, *n.m.,* shrievalty, sheriffdom, sheriffship.

échidné (é-kid-), *n.m.,* (zool.) echidna.

échi-f, -ve, *adj.,* (hunt.) voracious, greedy.

échiffe *or* **échiffre,** *n.m.,* (arch.) partition-wall (of a staircase).

*****échignole,** *n.f.,* (tech.) button-maker's spindle.

*****échillon,** *n.m.,* waterspout.

échimose, *n.f.* V. **ecchymose.**

échine, *n.f.,* spine, backbone, chine ; (arch.) echinus, ovolo. *Une maigre —;* a thin, lank person. *Crotté jusqu'à l'—;* bespattered, *or* splashed, up to the neck (with mud).

échiné, *part.,* *adj.,* broken-backed ; belabored ; beaten to death ; tired out.

échinée, *n.f.,* (cook.) chine, chine-piece.

échiner, *v.a.,* to break the back, to kill, to murder ; to beat unmercifully ; to knock up, to tire out.

s'échiner, *v.r.,* to knock one's self up with work ; to work one's self to death ; (of things) to get used up.

échinite (é-ki-), *n.m.,* (foss.) petrified sea-hedgehog, echinite.

échinope (é-ki-), *n.m.,* (bot.) echinops, globe-thistle.

échinophore (é-ki-), *n.f.* and *adj.,* (bot.) prickly samphire ; echinophora ; (conch.) unival-vular shell.

échioïde (é-ki-), *n.m.* (bot.). V. **vipérine.**

échiqueté, -e (é-shik-té), *adj.,* checkered ; (her.) checky.

échiquier, *n.m.,* chess-board ; exchequer ; square net. *Ouvrage fait en —;* checkerwork. *En —;* in squares ; (nav.) in bow and quarter line.

écho (é-ko), *n.m.,* echo. *Le jeu des —s ;* echo-stop (in organs). *—s de lumière ;* (paint.) reverberations of light.

échoir (échéant, échu), *v.n.,* to expire, to fall due, to be out, to lapse, to devolve ; to chance, to happen, to fall, to fall out ; to fall to. *Le premier payement doit — à Noël ;* the first payment falls due at Christmas. *Cette lettre de change est échue ;* that bill of exchange is due. *A —;* (of bills) running, not due. *Cela lui est échu en partage ;* that fell to his lot. *Si le cas y échoit, s'il y échet, le cas échéant ;* the case occurring ; in such a case.

échomètre (é-ko-), *n.m.,* echometer.

échométrie (é-ko-), *n.f.,* echometry.

échoppage, *n.m.,* edging, scorping.

échoppe, *n.f.,* booth, stall ; round *or* flat graver ; scalper ; scorper, burin.

échopper, *v.a.,* to scorp, to edge.

échoppi-er, -ère, *n.m.* and *f.,* stall-keeper.

échouage, *n.m.,* (nav.) beaching, stranding. *Lieu d'—;* place proper for running a vessel aground.

échouement, *n.m.,* running aground, stranding.

échouer, *v.n.,* to run aground *or* on shore, to cast away, to run against, to hit, to strand, to be stranded ; to miscarry, to fail, to be disappointed. *La frégate échoua contre un rocher ;* the frigate struck upon a rock. *— dans un examen ;* to fail, to be plowed.

échouer, *v.n.,* (nav.) to strand, to run aground.

écimer, *v.a.,* to top, to pollard (trees).

éclaboussement, *n.m.,* splashing, bespattering.

éclabousser, *v.a.,* to splash, to bespatter.

éclaboussure, *n.f.,* splash ; (nav.) spoondrift.

éclair, *n.m.,* lightning, flash of lightning, sort of chocolate cake ; (chem.) shine. *—s de chaleur ;* heat-lightning. *Il a passé comme un —;* he shot by like lightning. *Faire des —s ;* to lighten.

éclairage, *n.m.,* lighting, illumination. *— au gaz ;* gas-lighting, gas-light. *Gaz d'—;* illuminating gas, ethylene.

éclaircie, *n.f.,* glade, vista ; opening, rift (in clouds, etc.).

éclaircir, *v.a.*, to clear, to brighten ; to clarify ; to thin, to make thin ; to clear up, to elucidate, to illustrate, to explain, to throw a light on. *Cet auteur éclaircit bien des vérités ;* that author illustrates many truths. *— une difficulté ;* to clear up a difficulty. *Le temps éclaircit la vérité ;* time brings truth to light. *— quelqu'un ;* to enlighten any one, to instruct, to inform, any one. *Il faut l'en —;* he must be informed of it. *— une peau ;* to gloss a skin.

s'éclaircir, *v.r.*, to clear, to brighten, to become clear or bright, to grow light ; to be solved, to be explained, to be elucidated. *Le temps s'éclaircit ;* the weather is clearing up. *Son teint commence à s'—;* her complexion is becoming clearer. *S'— d'une chose ;* to inquire about or into a business, to inform one's self about anything, to clear up a matter. *Il faut s'— sur cette affaire ;* that affair must be cleared up.

éclaircissement (-sis-män), *n.m.*, clearing up, explanation, illustration, elucidation, solution ; hint, light, discovery, insight. *Avoir un —, en venir à un — avec quelqu'un ;* to have an explanation, to come to an explanation, with any one.

éclaire, *n.f.*, (bot.) celandine. *La grande —;* swallow-wort, tetter-wort. *La petite —;* crowfoot, pilewort.

éclairé, -e, *adj.* and *part.*, lighted ; enlightened ; judicious ; intelligent, clear-sighted.

éclairer, *v.a.*, to light, to give light to; to illuminate ; to carry a light before, to show a light to; to enlighten, to instruct; to observe, to watch; (milit.) to reconnoiter ; (paint.) to throw light in, to put light in. *Eclairez monsieur ;* show a light to the gentleman. *Les bonnes lectures éclairent l'esprit ;* the reading of good books enlightens the mind. *Il faut l'— de près ;* he must be watched closely. *— une question ;* to throw light upon a question.

s'éclairer, *v.r.*, to become enlightened ; to instruct, enlighten, one another.

éclairer, *v.n.*, to sparkle, to shine, to brighten, to glitter. *v. imp.*, to lighten. *Il éclaire ;* it lightens.

éclaireur, *n.m.*, (milit.) scout. *Aller en —;* (milit.) to scout.

éclamé, *adj.*, broken-legged ; broken-winged.

éclanche, *n.f.*, shoulder of mutton.

éclancher, *v.a.*, to unrumple (stuffs).

éclat, *n.m.*, shiver; splinter (of wood, stone, brick); brightness, refulgence, radiancy, resplendency, glitter, effulgence ; clap, crash, noise ; lustre, pomp, richness, magnificence, glory, gaudiness (of colors); rumor, uproar. *Un — de pierre ;* a fragment of stone. *Un — de bombe ;* a splinter of a shell. *On ne saurait soutenir l'— du soleil ;* there is no bearing the glare of the sun. *L'— des yeux ;* the brilliancy of the eyes. *L'— et la pompe de son style ;* the splendor and pomp of his style. *Un — de-rire ;* a burst of laughter. *Un grand — de voix ;* a loud shout. *Action d'—;* splendid achievement ; brilliant action. *Des personnes d'—;* eminent persons. *Cette action a fait —;* that action has made a great deal of noise. *Voler en —s ;* to be shivered, to fly into a thousand pieces.

éclatant, -e, *adj.*, bright, sparkling, glittering, brilliant, radiant, dazzling, striking, gorgeous, effulgent, shining, signal, glorious ; piercing, loud, shrill. *Tout — de lumière ;* all radiant with light. *Son —;* shrill sound. *Bruit —;* crash. *Actions —es ;* brilliant exploits. *Vengeance —e ;* signal vengeance.

éclater, *v.n.*, to split, to shiver, to break in pieces, to burst ; to crack, to clap ; to cry out, to exclaim against, to fly into, to break out or forth; to blaze out ; to shine, to sparkle, to glitter, to flash, to irradiate. *Une bombe éclate en tombant ;* a bomb bursts on falling. *Le tonnerre*

vient d'—; there has just been a clap of thunder. *— de rire ;* to burst out laughing. *— en injures ;* to burst forth into abuse. *L'incendie éclata pendant la nuit ;* the fire broke out during the night. *Faire —;* to shiver, to shatter ; to splinter; to snap, to burst, to cause to explode ; to vent, to give vent to ; to brighten, to blaze forth; to show, to discover, to make appear.

s'éclater, *v.r.*, to split, to shiver, to fly into fragments, to burst.

éclectique, *n.m.* and *adj.*, eclectic.

éclectisme, *n.m.*, eclecticism.

écli, *n.m.*, (nav.) splinter.

éclié, -e, *adj.*, splintered, sprung (of masts, etc.).

éclipse, *n.f.*, eclipse, disappearance; absence. *Faire une —;* to vanish, to disappear.

éclipser, *v.a.*, to eclipse ; to throw into the shade.

s'éclipser, *v.r.*, to be eclipsed *or* darkened, to disappear, to vanish. *Il s'éclipsa tout d'un coup ;* he suddenly disappeared.

écliptique, *n.f.* and *adj.*, (astron.) ecliptic.

éclisse, *n.f.*, (surg.) splint ; splinter ; cheese-wattle ; stand ; rib, side-piece (of violins, pails, tubs, casks, etc.)

éclisser, *v.a.*, (surg.) to splint.

églogue, *n.f.* *V.* **églogue**.

éclopé, -e, *n.* and *adj.*, cripple, halt ; footsore, lame, badly hurt. *Il est tout —;* he is quite lame.

écloper, *v.a.*, to lame ; to make lame ; footsore. *S'—,* *v.r.*, to become lame, footsore.

éclore, *v.n.*, to hatch ; to blow, to open ; to break, to dawn. *Les poulets commencent à —;* the chickens are beginning to pierce the shell. *Faire — des oiseaux ;* to hatch birds ; (fig.) to bring to light, to usher in ; to give birth to, to produce, to bring out ; to blow, open.

éclosion, *n.f.*, hatching ; blowing, opening.

écluse, *n.f.*, lock, guard-lock, sluice, dam, mill-dam, wear, weir, flood-gate. *— de moulin ;* mill-gate. *— à sas ;* lift-lock. *— à vannes ;* sliding flood-gate. *Déversoir à —;* weir. *— à marée montante ;* tide-gate.

éclusée, *n.f.*, sluice-full of water ; lockage.

écluser, *v.a.*, to build locks ; to take a boat through a lock.

éclusier, *n.m.*, sluice-man, lock-keeper.

écobuage, *n.m.*, (agri.) weeding, burning of weeds.

écobue, *n.f.*, weeder, turfing iron.

écobuer, *v.a.*, to weed a field and burn the weeds.

écœurement, *n.m.*, disgust ; sickening ; anguish of heart.

écœurer, *v.a.*, to disgust; to sicken ; (fig.) to shock ; to dishearten.

écofrai *or* **écofroi**, *n.m.*, (tech.) cutting-board.

écoinçon *or* **écoinson**, *n.m.*, (mas., carp.) diagonal, angle-tie ; angle stuff-bead ; (carp.) jamb (of doors) ; (carp.) reveal (of windows).

écolage, *n.m.*, schooling.

écolâtre, *n.m.*, (theol.) doctor, teacher.

école, *n.f.*, school ; college ; scholastic philosophy ; sect ; training, practice ; blunder. *Petite —;* day-school. *Maître d'—;* schoolmaster. *Camarade d'—;* schoolfellow. *— de droit ;* law-school. *— de marine ;* naval school. *— d'équitation ;* *— de natation ;* riding-school, swimming-school. *— communale ;* parish-school. *Cela sent l'—;* that savors of pedantry. *Faire —;* to be at the head of a school *or* sect ; *or* to be fundamental (of a doctrine) ; to found a school (of art, literature). *Dire les nouvelles de l'—;* to tell tales out of school. *Faire l'— buissonnière ;* to play truant. *Faire une —;* (backgammon) to blunder in pegging one's points. *Envoyer à l'—;* to peg. *Faire une —;* to commit a stupid blunder. *Basse —;*

ordinary horsemanship. *Haute* —; high horse-manship.

écoli-er, *n.m.*, **-ère**, *n.f.*, schoolboy, school-girl, pupil, scholar, learner, a tyro. *En* —; boy-like. *Prendre le chemin des* —*s ;* to go a round-about way; to loiter. *Ce n'est qu'un* —; he is but a novice. *Tour d'*—; schoolboy trick. *Papier* —; exercise-paper.

écolleter, *v.a.*, to cut off, to round off.

éconduire, *v.a.*, to show out; to bow out; to dismiss; to put off, to refuse, to deny. *Il nous éconduit poliment ;* he gives us a polite refusal.

économat, *n.m.*, stewardship; bursarship; bursary; steward's *or* bursar's office.

économe, *adj.*, economical, saving, thrifty. *C'est une femme* —; she is a thrifty woman. *Etre* — *de louanges ;* to be sparing of praise.

économe, *n.m.f.*, steward, housekeeper, man-ager, economist, purser, bursar, treasurer (of col-leges, hospitals).

économie, *n.f.*, economy; thrift. *Vivre avec* —; to live economically. *Faire des* —*s ;* to put by money, to save money. *L'*— *de l'univers ;* the disposition of the universe. *L'*— *du corps humain ;* the harmony of the human body. *L'*—*d'un discours ;* the management *or* disposition of a speech. *Il n'y a pas de petites* —*s ;* a penny saved is a penny earned, *or* take care of the pence, etc.

économique, *adj.*, economic, economical, cheap. *Ménage* —; economical housekeeping. [*Economique* is applied to things only: as, *four-neau* —; fuel-saving stove.]

économique, *n.f.*, economics.

économiquement (-mik-mān), *adv.*, economi-cally.

économiser, *v.a.*, to economize, to save, to put by, to husband. — *ses forces ;* to husband one's strength.

économiste, *n.m.*, economist.

écope, *n.f.*, (nav.) scoop, skeet, ladle.

écorce, *n.f.*, bark, rind; peel; shell; outside, surface. *Oter l'*—; to peel. *Cet homme n'a que l'*—; he is but a superficial, a shallow man. *Juger du bois par l'*—; to judge of the inside by the outside. *Entre l'arbre et l'*— *il ne faut pas mettre le doigt ;* you should not interfere in other people's quarrels.

écorcement *or* **écorçage**, *n.m.*, barking, strip-ping (of trees).

écorcer, *v.a.*, to bark, to strip, to peel.

écorché, *n.m.*, (paint.) figure without skin (for the study of the muscles).

à écorche-cul, *adv.*, (l.ex.) sliding on the ground; against the grain, unwillingly. *V. à* **rebrousse-poil.**

écorchée, *n.f.*, (conch.) conus (striated cone). *A l'*—; in lots *or* small parcels.

écorchement, *n.m.*, excoriation; flaying, skin-ning.

écorcher, *v.a.*, to flay, to skin; to gall, to peel off, to rub off the bark; to take off the skin; to fleece. — *l'anguille par la queue ;* to begin at the wrong end. *Cela écorche les oreilles ;* that grates on one's ears. *Ce procureur écorchait ses clients ;* that attorney fleeced his clients. — *le français ;* to speak broken French, to mur-der the French language. *Jamais beau parler n'écorcha la langue ;* civility costs nothing. *Il crie avant qu'on l'écorche ;* he cries out before he is hurt.

s'écorcher, *v.r.*, to tear off one's skin, to get skinned, to gall *or* be galled; (fig.) to speak ill of *or* disparage one's self.

écorcherie, *n.f.*, knacker's yard; inn in which travelers are fleeced; expensive place; fleecing.

écorcheur, *n.m.*, knacker; flayer; fleecer.

écorchure, *n.f.*, scratch, excoriation; slight wound.

écorner, *v.a.*, to break the horns, the corners,

of; to dog's ear; to curtail, to impair, to lessen, to diminish. *Il fait un vent à* — *un bœuf ;* it is blowing great guns.

écorniffer, *v.a.*, to sponge upon, to hang on.

écorniflerie, *n.f.*, sponging, hanging on.

écornifleu-r, *n.m.*, **-se**, *n.f.*, sponger, hanger-on.

écornure, *n.f.*, corner broken off, breaking at the edges, chipping.

écossais, **-e**, *n.* and *adj.*, Scotsman, Scots-woman; Scottish.

écossaise, *n.f.*, Scotch plaid, plaid-stuff.

écosser, *v.a.*, to shell, to husk (peas *or* beans).

écosseu-r, *n.m.*, **-se**, *n.f.*, sheller.

écot, *n.m.*, share (of a reckoning); reckoning; score; quota; company; stump (of a tree). *Payez votre* —; pay your share. *Parlez à votre* —; speak to your own company; mind your own business. *De tous* —*s ;* meddling with every-thing.

écotage, *n.m.*, stemming (of tobacco).

écôter, *v.a.*, to stem.

*****écouailles**, *n.f.pl.*, coarsest wool, tail wool.

écoulement (é-kool-mān), *n.m.*, flowing, run-ning, draining; (com.) sale, output, outlet. *L'*— *de l'eau ;* the flowing of water. *L'*— *de nos pro-duits ;* the sale of our commodities.

écouler, *v.a.*, to pour away; (com.) to drain; to sell.

s'écouler, *v.r.*, to run *or* flow away; to pass away, to glide away; to slip away; (com.) to go off. *L'eau s'écoule ;* water flows away. *L'ar-gent s'écoule ;* money slips away. *Le temps s'écoule ;* time passes away. *Ces marchandises s'écoulent vite ;* these goods sell fast, *or* go off well, *or* have a good sale, *or* command a ready sale.

écourgeon. *V.* **escourgeon.**

écourter, *v.a.*, to shorten, to dock, to crop; to curtail. — *un chien ;* to crop a dog. *Cheval écourté ;* cropped horse. *Nez écourté ;* snub-nose.

écoutant, **-e**, *n.* and *adj.*, listener, hearer; listening, attending. *Avocat* —; briefless bar-rister.

écoute, *n.f.*, hiding-place for listening; (nav.) sheet, main-sheet (cordage). *Etre aux* —*s ;* to be on the watch, on the look-out; to eavesdrop. *Entre deux* —*s ;* both sheets aft.

écouter, *v.a.*, to listen; to hearken; to give hearing; to hear; to pay attention to; to mind. — *à la porte ;* to listen at the door. — *les avis de quelqu'un ;* to listen to any one's advice. — *raison ;* to listen to reason. *Ecoutez ;* hark ye, look here, come! *Il n'écoute personne ;* he heeds nobody. *Ne l'écoutez pas !* never mind him! *Se faire* —; to obtain a hearing, to enforce obedience.

s'écouter, *v.r.*, to like to hear one's self; to be over careful of one's self; to indulge one's self. *Il s'écoute trop ;* he nurses himself too much.

écouteu-r, *n.m.*, **-se**, *n.f.*, listener. *C'est un* — *aux portes ;* he is an eaves-dropper.

écouteux, *adj.*, skittish, jibbing (of horses).

*****écoutille**, *n.f.*, (nav.) hatchway. *Fermer les* —*s ;* to close the hatches.

écoutoir, *n.m.*, ear-trumpet.

*****écouvillon**, *n.m.*, scovel (of ovens); swab; mop; sponge (of a cannon).

*****écouvillonner**, *v.a.*, to sweep; to mop; to sponge (of a cannon).

écran, *n.m.*, screen; hand-screen; fire-screen. — *de toilette ;* splash-guard. — *en bannière ;* banner screen.

écrasage, *n.m.*, crushing; bruising.

écrasant, **-e**, *adj.*, crushing; humiliating; exorbitant, excessive; overwhelming; ruinous.

écrasé, **-e**, *part.*, crushed, ruined. *Nez* —; flat nose. *Taille* —*e ;* squat figure (pers.).

écrasement (é-krâz-mān), *n.m.*, crushing; crush; bruising; squashing; overwhelming; destruction, ruin.

écraser, *v.a.*, to crush; to bruise; to weigh down, to overburden, to overwhelm; to bear down; to run over; to ruin; to squash. — *des groseilles;* to squash gooseberries. *J'ai manqué d'être écrasé par un carrosse;* I was near being run over by a coach. *Être écrasé de travail;* to be overwhelmed with work. — *d'impôts;* to overburden with taxes. — *ses rivaux;* to crush one's rivals.

écraseur, *n.m.*, crusher, bruiser; steam-roller.

écrelet, *n.m.*, gingerbread, nut.

écrémer, *v.a.*, to take off the cream, to skim; to take the best of.

écrémoire, *n.f.*, skimmer; milk-skimmer.

écrêter, *v.a.*, to sweep off the top of a work, to dismantle with shot; to cut off the comb of a cock.

écrevisse, *n.f.*, crayfish; (astron.) Cancer. *Une — de mer;* a crawfish. *Rouge comme une —;* as red as a boiled lobster.

s'écrier, *v.r.*, to cry out, to exclaim. *V. s'ex-clamer.*

*écrille, *n.f.*, grate (of a fish-pond).

écrin, *n.m.*, casket, jewel-box *or* case.

écrire (écrivant, écrit), *v.a.*, to write; to spell; to pen, to set down, to write word; to write to ask. — *quelque chose sur un registre;* to enter anything in a register. *Papier à —;* writing-paper. — *que;* to write to say that, to state that.

s'écrire, *v.r.*, to sign one's self, to write one's name; to be written, to be spelled; to write to each other.

écrit, *n.m.*, writing, written agreement; pamphlet. *Mot d'—;* short note; line; word. *Met-tre, coucher, par —;* to set anything down in writing.

écrit, -e, *part.*, writ, written, fated. *Cela était — au ciel;* that was written above. *Il est — que je ne gagnerai jamais;* I am fated never to win. *C'etait —;* it was bound to happen.

écriteau, *n.m.*, bill (poster); board; sign-board.

écritoire, *n.f.*, ink-horn; inkstand. — *porta-tive;* pocket inkstand.

écriture, *n.f.*, writing, hand, handwriting; scripture. *pl.* accounts, papers, documents, lawyer's bills. — *coulée;* secretary-hand, running-hand. *Mauvaise —;* scrawl. *L'Écriture sainte;* the Holy Scriptures, the Bible. *Commis aux —s;* copying clerk.

écriturer, *v.n.*, to do copying work.

écriturier, ère, *n.m.f.*, copying-clerk, copyist.

*écrivailler, *v.a.*, to scribble.

*écrivaillerie, *n.f.*, scribbling.

*écrivailleur, *n.m.* *V.* **écrivassier**.

*écrivain, *n.m.*, writer, author; writing-master; captain's clerk. — *public;* public scrivener, petition writer.

écrivassier, *n.m.*, (in the Channel Isles) solicitor; scrivener.

écriveu-r, -se, *adj.*, fond of *or* always writing, scribbling.

écrou, *n.m.*, screw nut; female screw; jail- *or* gaol-entry. *Livre, registre, d'—;* jail- *or* gaol-book.

écrouelle, *n.f.*, freshwater shrimp.

écrouelles, *n.f.pl.*, king's evil; scrofula.

écrouelleu-x, -se, *adj.* and *n.*, scrofulous; person affected with the king's evil.

écrouer, *v.a.*, to enter in the jail- *or* gaol-book; to imprison; to lock up.

écroues, *n.f.pl.*, bills of expense of the royal kitchen.

écrouir, *v.a.*, to hard-hammer (metal).

écrouissement, écrouissage, *n.m.*, hammer-hardening.

écroulé, -e, *part.*, fallen down, overthrown. *Un mur —;* a fallen wall. *Un empire —;* an overthrown empire.

écroulement (é-krool-mān), *n.m.*, falling in, falling down, crumbling down; wreck, ruin.

s'écrouler, *v.r.*, to fall in, to fall down, to fall to pieces; to break down; to collapse; to perish. *Cet édifice vint à s'—;* that building fell down. *La terre s'écroula;* the ground gave way. *Faire s'—;* to pull *or* bring down.

écroûter, *v.a.*, to cut off the crust. *S' —;* to lose its crust (of bread).

écru, -e, *adj.*, unbleached, raw. *Fil —, soie —e;* raw thread, raw silk. *Toile —e;* brown holland.

écrues, *n.f.pl.*, wood of new and spontaneous growth.

ectropion, *n.m.*, (med.) eversion of the eyelids.

⊙**ectype**, *n.f.*, ectype.

écu, *n.m.*, shield; ⊙crown, an obsolete French coin; ⊙half a crown; money, cash; copy-paper. *Amasser des —s;* to hoard up money. *C'est le père aux —s;* he is a moneyed man.

écuage, *n.m.*, scutage, land-tax.

écubier, *n.m.*, (nav.) hawse-hole.

*écueil (ékeu-i), *n.m.*, reef, rock; sand-bank; breaker; peril, danger; obstacle; stumbling-block. *Donner sur un —;* to strike against a rock. *Le monde est plein d'—s;* the world is full of dangers.

écuelle, *n.f.*, porringer, bowl, basin. *Laver les —s;* to wash the dishes. *Des lavures d'—s;* dish-water, hog-wash. *Etre propre comme une — de chat;* to be filthy, very dirty.

écuellée, *n.f.*, porringer-full, bowl-full.

écuisser, *v.a.*, to thin (trees at the foot).

éculer, *v.a.*, to tread down at heel.

s'éculer, *v.r.*, to wear down at the heel.

écumage, *n.m.*, skimming; scumming.

écumant, -e, *adj.*, foaming; frothy, seething.

écume, *n.f.*, froth, foam; scum, dross; dregs; slag; lather. *L'— de la mer;* the foam of the sea. *L'— de certains métaux;* the dross of certain metals. *L'— d'un cheval;* the foam of a horse. *Jeter de l'—;* to foam. — *de mer;* white talc; meerschaum; sea-ware.

écuménicité, *n.f.* *V.* **œcuménicité**.

écuménique, *adj.* *V.* **œcuménique**.

écuméniquement, *adv.* *V.* **œcuménique-ment**.

écumer, *v.n.*, to foam, to froth. *La mer écume;* the sea foams. *Il écumait de rage;* he was foaming with rage.

écumer, *v.a.*, to skim; to pick up; to gather, to collect, rake up. — *le pot;* to skim the pot. — *les marmites;* to be a sponger. — *les mers;* to scour the seas.

écumeur, *n.m.*, skimmer, collector; parasite, plagiarist. — *de marmites;* sponger, hanger-on. — *de mer;* sea-robber, sea-rover.

écumeu-x, -se, *adj.*, frothy, foaming.

écumoire, *n.f.*, skimmer, scummer.

écurage, *n.m.*, scouring, cleaning.

écurer, *v.a.*, to scour, to cleanse. — *de la vaisselle;* to scour dishes.

*écureuil, *n.m.*, squirrel.

écureu-r, *n.m.*, **-se**, *n.f.*, scourer of kitchen utensils. — *de puits;* well-cleanser.

écurie, *n.f.*, stable; stabling; mews; stud; equipage. *Valet d'—;* stable-boy, groom, ostler.

écusson, *n.m.*, escutcheon; shield, coat of arms; (arch.) knob; (hort., nav.) escutcheon.

écussonner, *v.a.*, (hort.) to bud.

écussonnoir, *n.m.*, (hort.) budding-knife.

écuyer, *n.m.*, esquire, squire; equerry; riding-master; rider; wall hand-rail (of a staircase). *Il est bon —;* he is a good horseman. — *tran-chant;* carver. — *de cuisine;* head cook; house-steward. *Grand —;* master of the horse.

écuyère, *n.f.*, horsewoman, female equestrian performer. *A l'—*; in riding fashion. *Bottes à l'—*; top boots, riding boots.

eczéma, *n.m.*, (*n.p.*) (med.) eczema.

edda, *n.f.*, (*—s*) edda.

éden (é-dè-n), *n.m.*, Eden.

édenté, -e, *adj.*, toothless; (fig.) broken, edentate. *Vieille —e;* toothless hag. *Un peigne —;* a broken-toothed comb.

édenter, *v.a.*, to wear out, to break the teeth of objects such as combs, saws, etc.; to deprive of one's teeth; to cause any one to lose his teeth. *La vieillesse nous édente;* old age causes us to lose our teeth.

s'édenter, *v.r.*, to lose its *or* one's teeth.

édentés, *n.m.pl.*, (zool.) edentata.

édicter, *v.a.*, to enact, to decree. *Peines édictées par la loi;* penalties enacted by law.

édicule, *n.f.*, small edifice, pavilion, kiosk.

édifiant, -e, *adj.*, edifying.

édificateur, *n.m.*, (l.u.) builder, constructor.

édification, *n.f.*, building, erection; edification. [ture, fabric.

édifice, *n.m.*, edifice, building, pile; struc-

édifier, *v.a.*, to build, to erect, to construct; to edify, to improve, to instruct, to enlighten, to satisfy. *Il m'a édifié sur son compte;* he told me all about him.

édile, *n.m.*, edile.

édilité, *n.f.*, edileship.

édit, *n.m.*, edict, decree.

éditer, *v.a.*, to publish, to edit (of books).

éditeur, *n.m.*, publisher.

édition, *n.f.*, edition.

édredon, *n.m.*, eider-down; eider-down quilt.

éducat-eur, -rice, *n.* educator; teacher; educationalist. *adj.* educative, instructing.

éducatif, -ve, *adj.*, educative.

éducation, *n.f.*, education; breeding, rearing (of animals); training; manners. *Faire l'— d'un jeune homme;* to educate a young man. *Tenir une maison d'— de demoiselles;* to keep a boarding school for young ladies. *Il n'a point d'—;* he has no breeding.

édulcoration, *n.f.*, edulcoration; sweetening.

édulcorer, *v.a.*, (pharm.) to edulcorate, to sweeten.

éduquer, *v.a.*, (pop.) to bring up, to educate, children.

éfaufiler, *v.a.*, to reeve out (of textile fabrics).

effaçable, *adj.*, effaceable.

effaçage, *n.m.*, effacing; erasing.

effacement, *n.m.*, effacing, effacement; obliteration, blotting out; disappearance; humility, self-effacement; throwing back (of the shoulders). *Homme d'—;* man of retiring manner.

effacer, *v.a.*, to efface, to expunge; to wear out; to rub out; to strike out; to blot out; to scrape out, to scratch out; to wash away, to obliterate; to eclipse, to throw into the shade; to throw back (the shoulders); to surpass, to excel, to outdo. *— ses péchés par ses larmes;* to wash out one's sins by one's tears.

s'effacer, *v.r.*, to get obliterated; to wash out; to wear away; to keep in the background; to draw aside; to give way; to straighten one's self; to throw one's self well back. *Il s'effaça pour éviter le coup;* he drew aside to avoid the blow.

effaceu-r, -se, *n.m.f.*, eraser.

effaçure, *n.f.*, blot, blotting out, obliteration, erasure.

effaner, *v.a.*, (agri.) to strip of leaves.

effaré, -e, *part.*, wild; scared; bewildered. *Un visage —;* a haggard, scared countenance.

effaroment, *n.m.*, bewilderment, distraction, terror, affright.

effarer, *v.a.*, to terrify, to scare.

s'effarer, *v.r.*, to be scared, to take fright.

effarouchant, -e, *adj.*, terrifying, startling.

effarouchement, *n.m.*, scare, fright, affright, alarm, umbrage.

effaroucher, *v.a.*, to scare away; to startle, to shock, to give umbrage.

s'effaroucher, *v.r.*, to be scared, to be startled, to take umbrage or alarm; to take fright.

effecti-f, -ve, *adj.*, effective, real, positive; (com.) in cash. *C'est un homme —;* he is a man of his word.

effectif, *n.m.*, (milit.) effective force; strength.

effection, *n.f.*, (geom.) effection.

effectivement (-tiv-mān), *adv.*, in effect, really, actually, indeed, in fact; and to be sure; yes, so it is.

effectuer, *v.a.*, to effect, to execute, to accomplish; to carry out; to bring about; to work out.

s'effectuer, *v.r.*, to be effected, executed, accomplished; to take place; to take effect; to be carried out.

effémination, *n.f.*, effeminacy.

efféminé, -e, *adj.*, effeminate, womanish. *Air —;* effeminate look.

efféminer, *v.a.*, to effeminate, to enervate.

effendi *or* **efendi** (è-fān-di), *n.m.*, effendi (Turkish title).

effervescence, *n.f.*, effervescence; excitement; ferment.

effervescent, -e, *adj.*, effervescent, effervescing; excited, excitable.

effet, *n.m.*, effect, consequence, result; performance, intent, execution; purpose; power (mec.); bill of exchange, bill. *pl.*, goods; luggage; movables, chattels; funds; stocks. *Produire de l'—;* to make an impression. *Ces choses-là font un vilain —;* those things look bad. *Souscrire un —;* to sign a bill. *— à échoir;* running bill. *Faire les fonds d'un —;* to provide for a bill. *Faire-honneur à un —;* to honor a bill. *A double —;* double acting (mec.). *En —;* in reality, indeed. *Pour cet —;* to that end, for that purpose. *A l'— de;* to the end that, with a view to. *A quel —?* to what purpose? to what end? *A —;* sensational, clap-trap. *Cela me fait cet —;* it seems so to me. *Faire de l'—;* to make a show; to be showy. *Faire l'— de;* to make one think of; to put one in mind. *— rétrograde;* (at billiards) screwing back. *— contraire;* screw. *— de côté;* side.

*effeuillaison, *n.f.*, fall of the leaves.

*effeuillement, *n.m.*, stripping off the leaves; defoliation.

*effeuiller, *v.a.*, to strip of leaves, to pluck; to pick to pieces (a flower).

*s'effeuiller, *v.r.*, to lose *or* shed its leaves (of a tree, a flower). *Les roses s'effeuillent;* the roses are shedding their leaves.

efficace, *adj.*, efficacious, effectual, effective.

efficace, *n.f.*, efficacy, efficiency, virtue.

efficacement (-kas-mān), *adv.*, efficaciously, efficiently, effectually.

efficacité, *n.f.*, efficacy, efficiency.

efficient, -e, *adj.*, efficient.

effigie, *n.f.*, effigy. *Pendre en —;* to hang in effigy.

effigier, *v.a.*, to make an effigy of.

effilé, *n.m.*, fringe.

effilé, -e, *adj.*, slender, slim; sharp, fine, tapering. *Avoir la taille —e;* to have a thin, slender figure.

effiler, *v.a.*, to unweave, to ravel out, to unravel; to thin (the hair); (hunt.) to tire out the dogs.

s'effiler, *v.r.*, to ravel, to ravel out, to fray out; to taper.

effiloche, *n.f.*, untwisted silk, light refuse silk.

effilocher *or* **effiloquer**, *v.a.*, to ravel out, to undo.

effiloque, *n.f.* *V.* **effiloche**.

effilure, n.f., raveled thread.

efflanqué, -e, adj., lean, thin, lank, raw-boned; meager. Style —; meager style.

efflanquer, v.a., to make lean, to emaciate.

effleurer, v.a., to take the surface off; to pick, to pluck (flowers); to skim over, to skim the surface of, to glance at; to grace, to touch upon, to dip into.

effleurir, v.a., (chem.) to effloresce.

s'effleurir, v.r., to effloresce.

efflorescence, n.f., efflorescence.

efflorescent, -e, adj., efflorescent.

effluence, n.f., (phys.) effluence.

effluent, -e, adj., (phys.) effluent.

effluve, n.m., effluvium. pl., effluvia.

effondrement, n.m., (agri.) digging deep; trenching; falling in, sinking.

effondrer, v.a., (agri.) to dig deep, to break in, to weigh down, to sink. — une volaille; to draw a fowl. — du poisson; to gut fish.

s'effondrer, v.r., to fall in; to give way.

*effondrilles, n.f.pl., grounds, sediment, dregs.

s'efforcer, v.r., to strain, to strive, to make an effort, to exert one's self; to struggle, to endeavor, to attempt.

effort, n.m., effort, exertion, endeavor; force, strength; (nav., vet.) strain, weight; stress. L'— de l'eau a rompu cette digue; the force of the water has broken down that dyke. Ce cheval a un —; that horse is strained. Faire un — sur soi-même; to do one's self violence, to strive to overcome one's repugnance. Se donner un —; to overstrain one's self, to sprain one's back.

effraction, n.f., breaking, breaking open, house-breaking. Vol avec —; burglary.

effraie, n.f., white barn-owl; screech-owl.

s'effranger, v.n., to become unraveled, to fray at the edges.

effrayant, -e, adj., frightful, fearful, dread-ful, terrific; appalling; grim, hideous.

effrayé, -e, part., afraid, daunted, dismayed.

effrayer, v.a., to fright, to frighten, to alarm, to terrify, to dismay.

s'effrayer, v.r., to be frightened, to be startled, to take fright, to take alarm. Il s'effraie de peu de chose; he is soon frightened.

effréné, -e, adj., unbridled, unrestrained, un-ruly; lawless; wild; frantic. Passions —es; unbridled passions. [tion (of land).]

effritement, n.m., crumbling to dust; exhaus-

effriter, v.a., (agri.) to exhaust (land).

s'effriter, v.r., (agri.) to become exhausted; to crumble to dust.

effroi, n.m., fright, terror, consternation; dread, dismay. Porter partout l'—; to carry consternation everywhere.

effronté, -e, n. and adj., shameless, brazen-faced person; shameless, bold, brazen-faced.

effrontément, adv., impudently, boldly, shamelessly.

effronterie, (é-front-rî), n.f., effrontery, bold-ness, impudence, shamelessness. Il est plein d'—; he is full of impudence. Il a eu l'— de me menacer; he had the effrontery to threaten me. Payer d'—; to brazen a thing out.

effroyable, adj., frightful, dreadful, horrid, horrible, awful; downright; shocking; prodi-gious. Elle est d'une laideur —; she is fright-fully ugly.

effroyablement, adv., frightfully, horribly, dreadfully, awfully; shockingly. Elle est — laide; she is frightfully ugly.

effusion, n.f., effusion, pouring out, overflow-ing, shedding. [riage.

éfourceau, n.m., two-wheeled timber-car-

égagropile, n.m., (vet.) wool-ball.

égal, -e, adj., equal, uniform, like, alike; even, level, same. Tout lui est —; it is all one to him. Une humeur —e; an even temper.

Cela m'est —; it is all the same to me. C'est —, si j'avais su; never mind, if I had only known.

égal, n.m., -e, n.f., equal. A l'— de; in com-parison of, as much as, equal to. Traiter d'—; to treat as one's equal. Sans —; matchless. D'— à —; between equals; on equal terms.

également (é-gal-măn), adv., equally, alike, impartially, uniformly; also, likewise, too.

égaler, v.a., to equal, to make even, level; to come up to, to match, to emulate; to compare, to parallel.

s'égaler, v.r., to render one's self equal; to compare one's self to.

égalisation, n.f., equalization.

égaliser, v.a., to equalize, to make level; to square accounts. — un terrain; to level a piece of ground. S'—; to find its own level.

égalitaire, adj., based on equality, or on equal rights; leveling.

égalité, n.f., (geom.) equality, parity; even-ness, uniformity; congruity. A — de mérite; where there is equality of merit. — d'âme; equanimity.

égard, n.m., regard, consideration, respect; deference, attentions. Avoir —; to pay regard. Avoir — à quelque chose; to be regardful of any-thing. Avoir des —s pour; to have considera-tion for, to pay regard, deference to. Eu — à; considering. Eu — à la qualité; considering the quality. Avoir de grands —s pour quelqu'un; to show great deference to any one. Par — pour; out of regard for. Par — pour vous; for your sake. A l'— de; respecting; with regard to. A cet —; in this respect. A tous —s; in all respects.

égaré, -e, part., strayed; misguided, misled, roving, wild; mislaid; disordered, distracted, bewildered. Brebis —es; lost sheep.

égarement (é-gar-măn), n.m., straying, losing one's way; mistake, error; wildness (of the look); disorder, ill-conduct, excess, frenzy, be-wilderment. — d'esprit; mental alienation.

égarer, v.a., to mislead, to misguide; to be-wilder; to impair (intellect); to lead astray, to lead into error; to mislay. — quelque chose; to mislay anything.

s'égarer, v.r., to lose one's way, to stray; to err; to mistake; to be led into error; to go astray; to ramble; to lose one's self. Il s'est égaré de son chemin; he has lost his way. Il s'égara dans la forêt; he lost himself in the forest.

égarotté, -e, adj., (man.) wither-wrung.

égayer, v.a., to enliven, to divert, to make cheerful, to lighten, to raise (the spirits), to cheer, to cheer up; to thin (trees). — un ap-partement; to make an apartment lighter.

s'égayer, v.r., to make merry, to be merry, to divert one's self, to sport, to cheer up. Il faut vous —; you must cheer up. Nous nous égayâmes à ses dépens; we made merry at his expense.

égide, n.f., Ægis (shield of Jupiter, of Pallas); shield, buckler, breast-plate; protector. Il me sert d'—; he is my protector. Sous son —; under his ægis; under his protection.

égilops (-lops), n.m., (med.) egilops.

églantier (-tié), n.m., (bot.) eglantine, wood-bine, hip-tree, brier, dog-brier. — odorant; sweet-brier.

églantine, n.f., (bot.) (flower) eglantine, hip, dog-rose, sweet-brier, woodbine.

églefin, n.m., (ich.) haddock.

église, n.f., church; chimney cowl; cowl. L'— anglicane; the church of England. Un homme d'—; a churchman, a clergyman. Gueux comme un rat d'—; as poor as a church mouse.

églogue (-log), n.f., eclogue.

⊙**égoïser**, v.n., to egotize.

égoïsme, *n.m.*, egotism, selfishness ; (philos.) egoism.

égoïste, *adj.*, egotistic ; selfish, egoistic.

égoïste, *n.m.f.*, egotist ; (philos.) egoist. *C'est un* — ; he is an egotist.

égopode, *n.m.*, (bot.) gout-weed, goutwort.

égorger, *v.a.*, to cut the throat of, to slaughter, to butcher, to kill.

égorgeur, *n.m.*, slaughterer, murderer.

*s'égosiller, *v.r.*, to make one's throat sore, to make one's self hoarse (with speaking) ; to bawl out, to strain one's voice.

égotisme, *n.m.*, (ant.) egotism.

égotiste, *n.m.*, (ant.) (l.u.) egotist.

égout, *n.m.*, running or falling of water ; sink, drain, sewer ; eaves, projecting roof. — *collecteur ;* main-sewer.

égoutier, *n.m.*, sewer-man.

égouttage, *n.m.*, drainage ; draining, dripping.

égoutter, *v.n.*, to drain, to drip.

égoutter, *v.a.*, to drain, to let drop.

s'égoutter, *v.r.*, to drop, to drain.

égouttoir, *n.m.*, drainer, plate-rack.

égoutture, *n.f.*, drainings, drippings.

égrain *or* **égrin**, *n.m.*, seedling pear *or* apple tree.

égrainer. *V.* **égrener**.

s'égrainer. *V.* **s'égrener**.

égrappage, *n.m.*, picking (of grapes, currants, etc.).

égrapper, *v.a.*, to pick (grapes, currants, etc.) from the bunch.

égrappoir, *n.m.*, grape-picker (instr.).

*égratigner, *v.a.*, to scratch, to claw ; (paint.) to stencil. *S'il ne mord pas, il égratigne ;* if he does not bite he scratches.

*égratigneu-r, *n.m.*, **-se**, *n.f.*, scratcher ; (paint.) stenciler.

*égratignure, *n.f.*, scratch ; slight wound. *Il ne saurait souffrir la moindre* — ; he cannot bear the least thing *or* hurt.

*égravillonner, *v.a.*, to ablaqueate.

égrefin, *n.m. V.* **églefin**.

égrenage, *n.m.*, shelling, husking (grains) ; picking (grapes) ; (arts) ginning.

égrener, *v.a.*, to shell, to husk (grain) ; to pick from the bunch (grapes) ; (arts) to gin.

s'égrener, *v.r.*, to shell (of grain) ; to fall from the stalk ; to shed seeds.

*égrillard, -e, *adj.*, sprightly, brisk, lively ; free, broad.

*égrilloir, *n.m.*, weir, grate (to keep the fish in a pond).

égrisée, *n.f.*, diamond-dust.

égriser, *v.a.*, to clean, to rough-down, to cut (diamonds).

égrisoir, *n.m.*, diamond-dust box.

égrugeoir (-joàr), *n.m.*, mortar.

égruger, *v.a.*, to pound, to bruise. — *du sel ;* to pound salt.

égueulé, *n.m.*, **-e**, *n.f. adj.*, (égheulé), broken-mouthed ; (pop.) vulgar, foul-mouthed person.

égueulement (é-gheul-mǎn), *n.m.*, (artil.) breaking at the mouth of a cannon.

égueuler (égheulé), *v.a.*, to break off the mouth *or* neck (of glass and other vessels).

s'égueuler, *v.r.*, to bawl till one's throat is sore ; (artil.) to break at the mouth (of a gun).

égyptien (-si-in, -si-èn), *adj.*, Egyptian.

égyptien, *n.m.*, **-ne**, *n.f.*, Egyptian ; gipsy.

eh, *int.*, ah ! well ! — *bien !* well ! — *bien, soit ;* well, be it so.

éhanché, -e, *adj. V.* **déhanché**.

éherber, *v.a. V.* **sarcler**.

éhonté, -e, *adj.*, shameless, brazen-faced.

éhouper, *v.a.*, to lop off the top (of a tree).

eider, *n.m.*, (—*s*) (orni.) eider, eider-duck.

éjaculateur, *adj.*, (anat.) ejaculatory.

éjaculation, *n.f.*, throwing out with force, discharge ; ejaculation (fervent prayer).

⊙**éjaculatoire**, *adj. V.* **éjaculateur**.

éjaculer, *v.a.*, (anat.) to throw out, to ejaculate, to discharge.

éjarrer, *v.a.*, to remove the coarse hairs (from furs).

éject-eur, -rice, *adj.* ejecting. *Tuyau* — ; discharge pipe.

élaboration, *n.f.*, elaboration.

élaboré, -e, *adj.*, elaborate, wrought, labored.

élaborer, *v.a.*, to elaborate, to work out.

élagage, *n.m.*, (hort.) lopping ; branches lopped off.

élaguer (-ghé), *v.a.*, to lop, to prune ; to curtail, to cut down, to cut out. *Elaguez ces détails inutiles ;* cut out those useless particulars.

élagueur, *n.m.*, (hort.) pruner.

élan, *n.m.*, start, spring ; dash, rush ; sally, flight, glow, soaring ; burst, outburst, transport ; (mam.) elk, moose-deer. *Par —s ;* by starts. *Prendre un* — ; to take a spring, a flight.

élancé, -e, *adj.*, slender, slim, thin, lank.

élancement (é-lǎns-mǎn), *n.m.*, shooting, twitch, twinge. *pl.*, transports.

élancer, *v.a.*, (l.u.) to launch, to dart, to shoot.

s'élancer, *v.r.*, to bound, to shoot, to shoot *or* to spring forth, to dart forth, to rush, to dash, to spring ; to take one's flight. *Il s'élança sur son cheval ;* he leapt *or* sprang on horseback. *Il s'élança sur l'ennemi ;* he rushed upon the enemy. *S'— sur quelqu'un ;* to spring upon any one. *Mon âme s'élança vers Dieu ;* my soul soared up to God.

élancer, *v.n.*, to shoot, to twitch (of pain).

élanion, *n.m.*, (orni.) kite. — *martinet ;* swallow-tailed kite.

élargir, *v.a.*, to stretch, to widen, to make wider, to let out ; to enlarge, to release, to set at liberty. — *un habit ;* to let out a coat. — *ses quartiers ;* to extend one's quarters. — *un compas ;* to open a pair of compasses. — *un prisonnier ;* to set a prisoner at liberty.

s'élargir, *v.r.*, to widen, to become wider ; to enlarge ; to stretch ; to enlarge one's estate ; to set one's self free.

élargissement (-jis-mǎn), *n.m.*, widening, enlarging ; release, discharge (from prison).

élargissure, *n.f.*, piece let in ; eking-piece.

élasticité, *n.f.*, elasticity, springiness.

élastique, *adj.*, elastic, springy.

élastique, *n.f.*, india-rubber ; elastic-net ; spring-side.

élatine, *n.f.*, (bot.) water-wort.

élavé, *adj.*, (hunt.) soft and discolored.

elbeuf, *n.m.*, Elbeuf-cloth.

eldorado, *n.m.*, (—*s*) El Dorado.

éléatique, *n.m.*, *adj.*, eleatic.

élécteur, *n.m.*, elector.

électi-f, -ve, *adj.*, elective.

élection, *n.f.*, election, return, polling ; choice, appointment. *Temps, lieu d'* — ; (surg.) most favorable time, place, for performing an operation. *Solliciter des suffrages aux —s ;* to solicit votes at elections. *Aux —s générales ;* at the general election.

électoral, -e, *adj.*, electoral, elective. *Priver du droit* — ; to disfranchise.

électorat, *n.m.*, electorate.

électrice, *n.f.*, Elector's consort, Electress.

électricité, *n.f.*, electricity.

électrique, *adj.*, electric. *Secousse* — ; electric shock. *Conducteur* — ; electric conductor.

électrisable, *adj.*, electrifiable.

électrisant, -e, *adj.*, electrifying.

électrisation, *n.f.*, electrification.

électriser, *v.a.*, to electrify.

s'électriser, *v.r.*, to be electrified, to electrify.

électro-aimant, *n.m.*, (—*—s*) electro-magnet,

électro-chimie, *n.f.*, (*n.p.*) electro-chemistry.

électro-dynamique, *n.f.*, (*n.p.*) electro-dynamics.

électro-magnétisme, *n.m.*, (*n.p.*) electro-magnetism.

électromètre, *n.m.*, (phys.) electrometer.

électro-négati-f, -ve, *adj.*, electro-negative.

électrophore, *n.m.*, (phys.) electrophorus.

électro-positi-f, -ve, *adj.*, electro-positive.

électroscope, *n.m.*, (phys.) electroscope.

électuaire, *n.m.*, electuary.

élégamment (-ga-mȧn), *adv.*, elegantly, stylishly.

élégance, *n.f.*, elegance, style.

élégant, -e, *n.* and *adj.*, gentleman, lady, of fashion; swell, exquisite; elegant, fashionable, stylish.

élégiaque, *adj.*, elegiac.

élégiaque, *n.m.*, elegist.

élégie, *n.f.*, elegy.

élément, *n.m.*, element, hobby, favorite pastime; component part. *La chasse est son* — ; hunting is his hobby. *Etre dans son* — ; to be quite at home (in anything).

élémentaire, *adj.*, elementary, elemental.

élémi, *n.m.*, (pharm.) elemi.

éléphant, *n.m.*, elephant.

éléphantiasis (-tia-zis), *n.f.*, (med.) elephantiasis.

éléphantin, -e, *adj.*, elephantine.

élevage, *n.m.*, (agri.) breeding, raising, rearing (of cattle).

élévateur, *adj., n.m.*, (anat.) elevator, elevatory; raising, lifting.

élévation, *n.f.*, elevation, lifting up, raising; rising ground, height, eminence; (persp.) view; exaltation; greatness; (of soul); nobleness; (c. rel.) elevation of the host; rise (of prices); raised plan. *Il lui doit son* — ; he is indebted to him for his promotion. *Il a beaucoup d'* — ; he possesses great elevation of mind. — *dans le style ;* loftiness of style. — *de côté ;* side view (of a building).

élévatoire, *n.m.*, (surg.) elevator.

élève, *n.m.f., part.*, pupil, scholar; student; (nav.) midshipman. — *maître* (m.), *maîtresse* (f.); pupil-teacher, pupil, governess. — *en chambre ;* parlor boarder.

élève, *n.f.*, (agri.) breeding (of cattle).

élevé (él-vé), **-e**, *part.*, raised, grand; heroic, eminent, stately, lofty; high (of prices); exalted. *C'est un jeune homme bien* — ; he is a very well-bred youth.

élever (él-vé), *v.a.*, to raise, to raise up, to exalt, to lift up; to cast up; to ennoble; to erect, to rear up, to set up; to augment, to increase; to run up (of accounts); to bring up, to breed; to rear ; to educate, to train up, to nurse, to foster. — *quelqu'un jusqu'aux nues ;* to extol any one to the skies. — *la voix ;* to raise one's voice. *J'ai pris de la peine à* — *ces plantes ;* I took some trouble to raise those plants.

s'élever, *v.r.*, to arise, to break out; to ascend, to mount, to go up, to run up; to amount; to be elevated; to increase, to augment ; to run up (of accounts); to be started. *Une tempête s'éleva ;* a storm arose. *Il s'éleva une querelle ;* a quarrel broke out. *Les vapeurs s'élèvent de la terre ;* vapors rise from the earth. *Celui qui s'élève sera abaissé ;* he who exalts himself shall be humbled. *Les vagues s'élevèrent hautes et menaçantes ;* the waves rolled high and threatening.

éleveur (él-veur), *n.m.*, elevator; cattle-breeder, grazier.

élevure (él-vur), *n.f.*, pimple, blotch, blain.

elfe, *n.m.*, elf (fairy).

élider, *v.a.*, (gram.) to cut off, to elide.

s'élider, *v.r.*, to be elided, to be cut off. *Cette lettre s'élide ;* that letter is elided.

éligibilité, *n.f.*, eligibility, fitness.

éligible, *adj.*, eligible, fit.

s'élimer, *v.r.*, to wear out, to rub out.

élimination, *n.f.*, elimination, dismissal, expulsion; removal, rejection.

éliminer, *v.a.*, to eliminate, to strike out *or* off, to expel, to discard, to dismiss, to remove; to delete.

élingue (é-ling), *n.f.*, (nav.) sling, strop.

élinguer (-ghé), *v.a.*, (nav.) to sling.

élire, *v.a.*, to elect, to choose, to return, to appoint, to designate. — *domicile ;* to take up one's abode.

élision, *n.f.*, elision.

élite, *n.f.*, choice, pick, select few, flower, prime. *L'* — *de l'armée ;* the pick of the army. *J'ai eu l'* — *de ses livres ;* I have had the pick of his books. *D'* — ; picked, crack.

élixir, *n.m.*, elixir.

elle, *pron.*, she, her, it ; **elles**, *pl.*, they, them. *Je parle d'* — ; I speak of her. *Je reviens à* — ; I return to her. *Je lui parle ;* I am speaking to her. *Je les lui donne à elle-même ;* I give them to her, place them in her own hands. *Je les vois,* —*s et leur frère ;* I see them and their brother.

ellébore, *n.m.*, (bot.) hellebore. — *noir ;* Christmas-thorn, black hellebore. *Avoir besoin d'* — ; not to be in one's right senses.

elléborine, *n.f.*, (bot.) helleborine, bastard hellebore.

ellipse (è-lips), *n.f.*, (gram., geom.) ellipsis; ellipse.

ellipsoïdal, -e, *adj.*, ellipsoidal.

ellipsoïde, *n.m.*, (geom.) ellipsoid.

ellipticité, *n.f.*, ellipticity.

elliptique, *adj.*, elliptical.

elliptiquement, *adv.*, elliptically.

elme (Feu Saint), *n.m.*, corposant, Castor and Pollux.

élocution, *n.f.*, elocution.

éloge, *n.m.*, eulogium, eulogy, panegyric, encomium, praise, commendation. *Digne d'* — ; praiseworthy. *Faire soi-même son* — ; to sound one's own praises. *Faire l'* — *d'un auteur ;* to speak in praise of an author. — *funèbre ;* funeral oration.

élogieu-x, -se, *adj.*, full of praise, eulogistic, flattering.

élogiste, *n.m.f.*, (ant.) eulogist, writer of panegyrics.

****éloigné, -e**, *part.*, removed, distant, wide, remote, far; absent, foreign. *Temps* —*s ;* distant times. *Cause* —*e ;* remote cause. *Il est fort* — *de le croire ;* he is far from believing it. *Se tenir* — ; to keep away, to stand aloof. *D'une manière* —*e ;* distantly.

****éloignement**, *n.m.*, removal, removing; distance, remoteness; retirement; aversion, dislike; estrangement, unwillingness. *On voit Paris dans l'* — ; Paris is seen in the distance. *Avoir de l'* — *pour le travail ;* to have an aversion for work.

****éloigner**, *v.a.*, to remove, to put away, to send away ; to dismiss; to discard ; to repudiate ; to remove further ; to waive ; to avert ; to banish; to drive away ; to put off, to delay, to retard ; to alienate, to estrange ; to indispose. — *un sujet ;* to waive a subject. — *les soupçons ;* to discard suspicion. — *quelqu'un de ;* to indispose any one (towards). — *quelqu'un de son pays ;* to send any one away from his country. *Eloignez de vous ces mauvaises pensées ;* dismiss such evil thoughts.

*s****éloigner**, *v.r.*, to go away, to remove, to recede ; to forsake ; to withdraw ; to ramble ; to digress ; to swerve ; to deviate ; to be different, to differ from, to dislike; (paint.) to appear in the distance; to be alienated, to be wanting, to fall off, to fail. *Ne vous éloignez pas ;* don't go far. *S'* — *de son devoir ;* to deviate from one's duty. *S'* — *de son sujet ;* to digress from one's subject. *Cette* *opinion s'éloigne de la mienne;* that opinion differs from mine.

élongation, *n.f.*, elongation ; digression.

élonger, *v.a.*, (nav.) to sheer off, to lay alongside of, to run out a warp.

éloquemment (-ka-màn), *adv.*, eloquently.

éloquence, *n.f.*, eloquence, oratory. — *de la tribune;* parliamentary eloquence.

éloquent, **-e**, *adj.*, eloquent.

élu, *n.m.*, **-e**, *n.f.*, (person) elected, chosen, elect.

élu, **-e**, *part.*, elected, chosen, elect, appointed, designated, returned.

élucidation, *n.f.*, elucidation.

élucider, *v.a.*, to elucidate.

élucubration, *n.f.*, lucubration.

élucubrer, *v.a.n.*, to lucubrate.

éludable, *adj.*, evadible, eludible.

éluder, *v.a.*, to elude, to evade.

élyme, *n.m.*, (bot.) elymus, lyme-grass.

élysée, *n. m.*, (myth.) Elysium. *L'Elysée;* the residence (in Paris) of the President of the Republic.

élysée, *adj.*, Elysian. *Les champs —s;* the Elysian Fields.

élyséen, **-ne** (-in, -è-n), *adj.*, Elysian.

élysiens (-în), *adj. m. pl.*, (myth.) Elysian.

élytre, *n.m.*, (ent.) elytron, wing-shell.

elzévir, *n.m.*, Elzevir (edition).

elzévirien, **-ne**, *adj.*, elzevirian, Elzevir.

émaciation, *n.f.*, emaciation.

émacié, **-e**, *adj.*, emaciated.

*****émail**, *n.m.*, enamel ; (her.) tincture ; (fig. gloss, brilliancy. — *de Hollande;* Dutch blue. *Peindre en —;* to enamel. *Peinture en —;* enameling, enameled picture. *Peintre en —;* enameler.

*****émailler**, *v.a.*, to enamel ; (fig.) to adorn, to embellish, to stud, to strew ; to covet.

*****émailleur**, *n.m.*, enameler.

*****émaillure**, *n.f.*, enameling.

émanation, *n.f.*, emanation.

émancipation, *n.f.*, emancipation.

émanciper, *v.a.*, to emancipate.

*s'***émanciper**, *v.r.*, to gain one's liberty, to free one's self ; to take too much liberty, to get too free, to go beyond bounds, to forget one's self, to play pranks. *Vous vous émancipez trop;* you are getting rather too free.

émaner, *v.n.*, to emanate.

émargement, *n.m.*, writing on the margin ; marginal note ; signature on the margin.

émarger, *v.a.*, to write, to sign, on the margin ; to receipt ; (fig.) to draw one's salary ; (tech.) to diminish the breadth of the margin of engravings, etc.

émarginé, **-e**, *adj.*, (bot.) emarginate.

émasculation, *n.f.*, emasculation.

émasculer, *v.a.*, to emasculate.

embabouiner, *v.a.*, (fam., l.u.) to wheedle ; to gammon.

emballage, *n.m.*, packing up, packing ; package. *Toile d'—;* packing-canvas, pack-cloth.

emballer, *v.a.*, to pack up ; to wrap up ; to pack off ; (fam. jest.) to send away, to pack off (any one), to look at, to quod.

emballeur, *n.m.*, packer ; (pop.) bragger, bobby, policeman.

embander, *v.a.*, to tie up ; to swathe.

embarcadère, *n.m.*, terminus ; wharf ; pier ; steps, landing-stage.

embarcation, *n.f.*, small boat, craft ; crew, passengers.

embardée, *n.f.*, (nav.) yaw, lurch.

embarder, *v.a.* and *n.*, (nav.) to yaw, to lurch.

embargo, *n.m.*, embargo. *Lever l'—;* to take off an embargo. *Mettre un — sur;* to lay an embargo on.

*****embarillé**, **-e**, *adj.*, barreled up.

*****embariller**, *v.a.*, to barrel, to barrel up.

embarquement, *n.m.*, embarkation, embarking, shipping, shipment.

embarquer, *v.a.*, to embark, to ship, to put on ship-board ; to take on board ; to see off. *On l'a embarqué dans une méchante affaire;* he has been drawn into some bad business.

*s'***embarquer**, *v.r.*, to embark, to go on board, to take shipping ; to put to sea, to sail, to set out ; to engage.

embarras, *n.m.*, incumbrance, hindrance, impediment ; embarrassment, difficulty, trouble, intricacy, fuss ; perplexity, puzzle ; (med.) derangement. *Cet homme fait bien de l'—;* that man makes a great fuss. *Etre dans l'—;* to be in difficulties. *Se mettre dans l'—;* to get into trouble, into a scrape. *Je suis dans l'—;* I am at a loss. *Ce n'est pas l'—;* that 's easy enough ; I see no objection. *Avoir l'— du choix;* to have too much to choose from. — *de voitures;* block of carriages.

embarrassant, **-e**, *adj.*, embarrassing, puzzling, awkward ; perplexing, encumbering, cumbersome, troublesome.

embarrassé, **-e**, *part.*, embarrassed, entangled, perplexed, obstructed, constrained ; out of countenance. *Etre —;* to be at a loss.

embarrasser, *v.a.*, to embarrass, to hamper, to encumber, to obstruct ; to clog, to trouble, to confound, to puzzle ; to come amiss to, to inconvenience, to incommode ; to insnare. *Etre embarrassé de sa personne;* not to know what to do with one's self. *Que cela ne vous embarrasse point;* do not trouble yourself about that. *Cette question l'a embarrassé;* that question puzzled him. *Il est embarrassé de répondre;* he is at a loss for an answer. — *une rue;* to obstruct a street.

*s'***embarrasser**, *v.r.*, to entangle one's self, to be embarrassed, entangled ; to be solicitous about, to concern one's self with ; (med.) to be affected. *Il ne s'embarrasse de rien;* nothing ever troubles him. *Sa langue s'embarrasse;* his tongue begins to falter ; his speech is impeded.

embasement, *n.m.*, (arch.) continuous base ; basement.

embastillement, *n.m.*, imprisoning ; surrounding with forts.

embastiller, *v.a.*, to imprison ; to surround with forts.

embatage, *n.f.*, casing, tiring of wheels.

⊙*****embatailler**, *v.a.*, to embattle.

embâter, *v.a.*, to put on a pack-saddle ; to saddle, to encumber. *On l'a embâté d'une affaire bien désagréable;* they have saddled him with a very disagreeable job.

embâtonner, *v.a.*, (l. u.) to arm with a cudgel.

embattés, *n.m.pl.*, periodical winds.

embattoir, *n.m.*, shoeing pit (for wheels).

embattre, *v.a.*, to case, to tire (a wheel).

embauchage, *n.m.*, hiring, engaging (workmen) ; tampering, gaining over, enticing away ; enlisting, recruiting.

embaucher, *v.a.*, to hire, to engage (workmen) ; to entice away, to tamper with ; to enlist, to recruit.

embaucheur, *n.m.*, hirer ; recruiting-officer ; recruiter, crimp.

embauchoir, *n.m.*, boot-tree ; boot-last.

embaumement (an-bôm-màn), *n.m.*, embalming.

embaumer, *v.a.*, to embalm ; to perfume, to scent. *v.n.*, to smell very sweet.

embaumeur, *n.m.*, embalmer.

embecquer, *v.a.*, to feed (a bird) ; to bait (a hook).

embéguiner (-ghi-), *v. a.*, to muffle up ; to infatuate, to bewitch.

*s'***embéguiner**, *v. r.*, to be infatuated, to be bewitched, to become bigoted.

embelle, *n.f.*, (nav.) waist.

embellie, *n.f.*, (nav.) lull, momentary calm; favorable change; clearing.

embellir, *v.a.*, to embellish, to beautify; to adorn, to decorate, to set off. — *un conte;* to embellish a tale.

*s'***embellir**, *v.r.*, to grow beautiful, to improve in beauty, to grow handsome.

embellir, *v.n.*, to beautify, to grow handsomer. *Elle ne fait que croître et* — *;* she grows taller and handsomer every day.

embellissement (-lis-mān), *n.m.*, embellishment, improvement, adornment.

embérize, *n.f.*, (zool.) bunting.

*s'***emberlucoquer**, *v.r.*, (fam.) to be taken with, to be wedded to.

*****embesogné**, **-e**, *adj.*, (fam., jest.) busy, busily engaged.

embêtement, *n.m.*, (triv.) annoyance, bother; nuisance, bore.

embêter, *v.a.*, (triv.) to stupefy, to stultify, to besot; to annoy, to plague; to tease, to torment, to rile; to worry; to aggravate, to bore.

*s'***embêter**, *v.r.*, (triv.) to feel dull, bored.

emblaison, *n.f.*, seed-time, sowing-time.

emblavage, *n.m.*, (agri.) wheat-sowing.

emblaver, *v.a.*, to sow with corn.

emblavure, *n.f.*, land sown with corn.

*d'***emblée**, *adv.*, at the first, in a trice; at the first onset; at the first trial; there and then; straight off the reel.

emblématique, *adj.*, emblematical.

emblème, *n.m.*, emblem. *Etre l'*— *de;* to be emblematical of.

emboire, *v.a.*, to imbibe; (sculp.) to coat (with oil or wax).

*s'***emboire**, *v.r.*, (paint.) to get dull or flat; to dry in.

emboîtement (ān-boat-mān), *n.m.*, fitting in, jointing, clamping.

emboîter, *v.a.*, to joint; to set (bones); to clamp, to fit, to fit in. — *le pas;* (milit.) to lock up.

*s'***emboîter**, *v.r.*, to fit, to fit in.

emboîture, *n.f.*, socket, clamp; (pottery) collar. *L'*— *des os;* the juncture of the bones.

embolie, *n.f.*, (med.) embolism.

embolisme, *n.m.*, embolism.

embolismique, *adj.*, embolismic, embolismal.

embonpoint, *n.m.*, plumpness, corpulence, stoutness, obesity. *Prendre de l'*— *;* to get stout, to pick up flesh. *Perdre son* — *;* to fall away, to lose flesh.

emboquer, *v.a.*, to feed, to cram food down.

*s'***emboquer**, *v.r.*, to cram food down one another's throat.

embordurer, *v.a.*, (l.u.) to put in a frame, to frame.

embossage, *n.m.*, (nav.) bringing the broadside to bear.

embosser, *v.a.*, (nav.) to bring the broadside to bear.

*s'***embosser**, *v.r.*, (nav.) to be brought to bear (broadside on).

embouché, **-e**, *part.*, entered (of boats); prompted, tutored. *Etre mal* — *;* to be foulmouthed, impertinent.

emboucher, *v.a.*, to put to one's mouth (wind instruments); to prompt; to bit (a horse). *Il l'a bien embouché;* he gave him a good prompting.

*s'***emboucher**, *v.r.*, (of rivers) to fall into; to empty, to discharge itself.

embouchoir, *n.m.*, boot-tree; mouth-piece (of instruments).

embouchure, *n.f.*, mouth-piece (of wind instruments); mouth (of a river, of a harbor); out-fall (engineering).

embouer, *v.a.*, (pop.) to cover with mud; to bemire; to vilify.

embouquement, *n.m.*, (nav.) entrance to a strait.

embouquer, *v.n.*, (nav.) to enter a strait.

embourbé, **-e**, *part.*, stuck fast (in the mud). *Il jure comme un charretier* — *;* he swears like a trooper.

embourber, *v.a.*, to put in the mire; to bemire. — *quelqu'un dans une mauvaise affaire;* to get any one into a troublesome business.

*s'***embourber**, *v.r.*, to sink in the mud, to stick in the mire; to be bemired; to be involved (in any trouble).

embourrer. *V.* **rembourrer**.

embourser, *v.a.*, to put into one's purse; to receive; to pocket.

embout, *n.m.*, ferrule.

embouter, *v.a.*, to ferrule, to tip.

emboutir, *v.a.*, (gold.) to scoop out; (coppersmith's work) to beat out; (arch.) to sheet; to stamp; to plate; to tip.

embranchement, *n.m.*, branch, branching off; branch-road; branch-line, junction (rail.).

embrancher, *v.a.*, (carp.) to put together; to join.

*s'***embrancher**, *v.r.*, to branch off; to branch (of roads); to abut, to join.

embrasé, **-e**, *part.*, in flames, on fire; glowing, aglow, in a glow.

embrasement (an-brâz-mān), *n.m.*, conflagration, burning; combustion; kindling.

embraser, *v.a.*, to fire, to set on fire, to kindle, to inflame. *La guerre a embrasé toute l'Europe;* war has set all Europe ablaze.

*s'***embraser**, *v.r.*, to kindle, to take fire, to glow, to be aglow, to be inflamed. *Cette matière s'embrase facilement;* that stuff easily catches fire.

embrassade, *n.f.*, embrace, hug, kissing, kiss.

embrasse, *n.f.*, curtain-loop, curtain-band.

embrassé, **-e**, *part.*, embraced. *Ils se tenaient* — *s;* they remained locked in each other's arms.

embrassement (an-bras-mān), *n.m.*, embrace.

embrasser, *v.a.*, to embrace, to clasp; to kiss; to encompass, to encircle, to comprehend, to comprise, to take in, to include; to seize, to avail one's self of, to undertake. *Qui trop embrasse, mal étreint;* grasp all, lose all. — *la querelle de quelqu'un;* to espouse any one's quarrel. — *une occasion;* to seize, to avail one's self of, an opportunity.

*s'***embrasser**, *v.r.*, to embrace, or to kiss, one another. [embracer, kisser.

embrasseu-r, *n.m.*, **-se**, *n.f.*, (fam., l. u.)

embrassure, *n.f.*, band of iron, binder.

embrasure, *n.f.*, embrasure; recess.

embrayage, *n.m.*, connecting (of wheels); coupling gear (motor).

embrayer, *v.a.*, to engage, to connect (man.).

embrelage, *n.m.*, lashing.

embreler, *v.a.*, to lash (a wagon load).

embrener, *v.a.*, (l. ex.) to dirty, to soil. *S'*— *dans quelque affaire;* to entangle one's self in a dirty piece of business.

embrèvement, *n.f.*, (carp.) mortise, franking.

embrever, *v.a.*, (carp.) to mortise, to frank, to join.

embrigadement, *n. m.*, (milit.) brigading; enlisting, recruiting.

embrigader, *v.a.*, (milit.) to brigade; to form into brigades.

embrocation, *n.f.*, embrocation.

embrochement, *n.m.*, spitting (of meat).

embrocher, *v.a.*, to spit, to put upon the spit. — *quelqu'un;* to run any one through the body.

embroucher, *v.a.*, to overlap, overlay (tiles, etc.).

*****embrouillé**, **-e**, *part.*, perplexed, intricate; entangled, obscure.

*****embrouillement** (an-brou-i-mān), *n. m.*, embroiling, confusion, intricacy, perplexity.

***embrouiller**, v.a., to embroil, to confuse, to confound, to jumble up ; to perplex, to obscure. s'**embrouiller**, v.r., to become intricate or entangled ; to get confused ; (fam.) to get fuddled, muddled. [blunderer.

embrouilleu-r, n.m., **-se**, n.f., mar-plot ;

embroussaillé, **-é**, adj., covered with brushwood, bushy, matted, intricate.

embruiné, **-e**, adj., (agri.) spoilt by drizzle.

embrumé, **-e**, adj., foggy, misty, hazy.

embrumer, v.a., to overcast, to cover with fog or mist. S'—; to be covered with fog, to get misty, hazy.

embrun, n.m., (nav.) spray.

embrunir, v.a., to brown.

embryogénie, n.f., embryogeny.

embryographie, n.f., embryography.

embryologie, n.f., embryology.

embryon, n.f., embryo ; (bot.) germ ; little bit of a man ; dwarf, shrimp.

embryonnaire, adj., embryonic.

embu, **-e**, part. of **emboire**, soaked in, dried in.

embu, n.m., (paint.) dulness, flatness (of pictures).

embûche, n.f., snare, ambush. Dresser des —s ; to lay snares.

embûcher, v.a., to begin cutting (trees) ; to drive back, to covert (hunt.). S'— ; to return to covert.

embuscade, n.f., ambuscade ; ambush ; lurking-place, snare. Etre, Se mettre, Se tenir, en —; to lie or be lying in wait, in ambush.

embusquer, v.a., to ambuscade, to post. s'**embusquer**, v.r., to lay in ambuscade, to lie in wait.

émender, v.a., to amend, to correct.

émeraude (é-mrôd), n.f., emerald. [gence.

émergence, n.f., (phys.) emersion, emer-

émergent, adj., (phys.) emergent.

émerger, v.n., to emerge, to rise out.

émeri (é-mri), n.m., (min.) emery. Bouché à l'— ; with a ground stopper.

***émerillon**, n.m., whirl (for weaving) ; (nav.) swivel-hook.

***émerillon**, n.m., (orni.) stone-falcon, merlin.

***émerillonné**, **-e**, adj., brisk, sprightly, wideawake, lively.

émerisé, **-e**, adj. Papier —; emery paper. Toile —e ; emery cloth.

émérite, adj., emeritus ; retired, pensioned, superannuated ; practised, adept.

émersion, n.f., emersion.

émérus, n.m., (bot.) bastard-senna, colutea.

***émerveillement**, n.m., wonder, astonishment.

***émerveiller**, v.a., to astonish, to amaze. s'**émerveiller**, v.r., to marvel, to wonder, to be astonished.

émétique, n.m., adj., emetic, puke, vomit ; emetical.

émétiser, v.a., (pharm.) to add emetic to a mixture ; to treat with emetics.

émettre, v.a., to put in circulation, to utter ; to emit, to issue, to give out, to put forth, to express.

émeu, n.m., (zool.) emu.

émeute, n.f., riot, disturbance, commotion, uproar, tumult ; rising, mutiny. Chef d'— ; ringleader.

émeuter, v.a., to rouse, to stir up, to excite.

émeutier (-tié), n.m., rioter.

émier, v.a. V. **émietter**.

émiettement, n.m., crumbling.

émietter, v.a., to crumble. s'**émietter**, v.r., to crumble.

émigrant, **-e**, n. and adj., emigrant ; emigrating.

émigration, n.f., emigration, migration.

émigré, n.m., **-e**, n.f., emigrant ; refugee.

émigrer, v.n., to emigrate ; to migrate.

émincé, n.m., (cook.) mince ; thin slices.

émincer, v.a., to mince (meat).

éminemment (-na-mān), adv., eminently, in a high degree.

éminence, n.f., eminence ; elevation, rising ground, height.

éminent, **-e**, adj., eminent, high, lofty, conspicuous.

éminentissime, adj., most eminent.

émir, n.m., Ameer, Emir.

émissaire, n.m., emissary ; (tech.) overflow pipe, overflow channel. Bouc — ; scape-goat.

émission, n.f., emission, issue, uttering, putting into circulation.

emmagasinage, n.m., warehousing.

emmagasiner, v.a., to warehouse, to store.

emmaigrir, v.a. V. **amaigrir**.

***emmaillotement**, n.m., swaddling, swathing.

***emmailloter**, v.a., to swaddle, to swathe, to bind up in swaddling clothes.

emmanchement (an-mansh-mān), n.m., (paint., sculpt.) joining, hafting, helving ; putting a handle.

emmancher, v.a., to put a handle to, to haft, to helve ; to begin, to set about. Affaire mal emmanchée ; ill-managed affair. s'**emmancher**, v.r., to fit in, to be begun ; to be done. Cela ne s'emmanche pas ainsi ; that is not the way to set to work.

emmancheur, n.m., (nav.) to enter the channel.

emmancheur, n.m., handle-maker.

emmanchure, n.f., arm-hole.

emmannequiner, v.a., to put in hampers ; to basket (plants).

emmantelé, **-e**, adj., covered with a cloak ; (fort.) ⊙fortified. Corneille —e ; hooded-crow ⊙**emmanteler**, v.a., (fort.) to wall-round.

emmariné, **-e**, adj., accustomed to the sea.

emmariner, v.a., to man (a ship) ; to accustom to the sea. s'**emmariner**, v.r., to be manned (of a ship) ; to get accustomed to the sea.

emmêlé, **-e**, adj., entangled.

emmêler, v.a. to entangle. s'**emmêler**, v.r., to get entangled.

emménagement (an-mé-naj-mān), n.m., removal, installation. pl., (nav.) internal arrangements, accommodation.

emménager, v.n., to move in. s'**emménager**, v.r., to move in.

emménagogue, n.m. and adj., (med.) emmenagogue.

emmener (an-mné), v.a., to carry away, to take away, to lead away, to fetch away, to convey away. Il l'a emmené dans sa voiture ; he took him away in his carriage. Emmenez-le ! off with him !

emmenotter, v.a., to handcuff, to manacle.

emmeuler, v.a., to stack hay.

emmiellé, **-e**, adj., honeyed, sweet, soft. Paroles —es ; honeyed words.

emmieller, v.a., to honey ; to sweeten with honey ; to cajole.

emmiellure, n.f., (vet.) a resolvent plaster.

emmitonner, v.a., to wrap up ; to wheedle, to coax.

emmitoufler, v.a., to muffle up.

emmortaiser, v.a., to mortise, to set in a mortise. s'**emmortaiser**, v.r., to mortise.

emmotté, **-e**, adj., (of roots of trees) covered with soil.

emmuseler, v.a., to muzzle.

émoi, n.m., emotion, anxiety, flutter, ferment. Mettre en —; to put in a flutter, a ferment. Etre en —; to be agitated or in a ferment.

émollient, **-e**, adj., emollient, softening.

émollient, n.m., emollient.

émolument, n.m., emolument, fee, perquisite. pl. salary.

émolumentaire, adj., emolumental.

émolumenter, *v. n.*, to profit; to get fees, perquisites.

émonctoire, *n.m.*, (med.) emunctory.

émondage, *n.m.*, pruning, lopping, trimming.

émonde, *n.f.*, dung (of birds of prey).

émonder, *v.a.*, to prune, to lop.

émondes, *n.f.pl.*, branches lopped off; trash, refuse.

émondeu-r, *n.m.*, **-se**, *n.f.*, pruner, trimmer, dresser.

émorfiler, *v.a.*, to beard off; to blunt.

émotion, *n.f.*, emotion; stir, commotion.

émottage, *n.m.*, clod-crushing.

émotter, *v.a.*, (agri.) to break clods of earth.

émottoir, *n.m.*, (agri.) roller, clod-breaker.

émoucher, *v.a.*, to drive flies away; to clear of flies.

émouchet, *n.m.*, sparrow-hawk. *Donner l'— à une peau;* to soak a hide.

émouchette, *n.f.*, fly-net (for horses).

émoucheu-r, *n.m.*, **-se**, *n.f.*, (pers.) fly-fanner.

émouchoir, *n.m.*, fly-flap.

émoudre, *v.a.*, to whet, to grind, to sharpen. *— des couteaux;* to grind knives. *Faire — des ciseaux;* to have scissors ground.

émouleur, *n.m.*, knife-grinder.

émoulu, -e, *part.*, ground. *Frais — de;* fresh from, just come from. *Il est frais — du collège;* he is fresh from college. *Combattre à fer —;* to fight with sharp weapons.

émoussage, *n.m.*, (agri.) emuscation.

émoussé, -e, *part.*, blunt; dull. *Un esprit —;* a dull mind. *Des sens —s;* deadened senses. *État —;* bluntness.

émousser, *v.a.*, to make blunt; to take off the edge; to dull; to take the moss off trees; to deaden. *— un rasoir;* to take the edge off a razor.

s'émousser, *v.r.*, to get blunt; to become dull; to be, to become, deadened *or* blunted. *La pointe de ce couteau s'est émoussée;* the point of this knife is blunted.

émoussoir, *n.m.*, moss-scraper.

*****émoustillé, -e**, *adj.*, brisk, sprightly.

*****émoustiller**, *v.a.*, to exhilarate, to put into spirits. *S'—;* to bestir one's self; to look alive.

émouvant, *adj.*, touching, moving, affecting, stirring.

émouvoir, *v.a.*, to move, to stir up; to agitate, to provoke; to rouse; to raise; to affect, to touch. *Il sait l'art d'— les passions;* he knows how to stir up the passions. *Il est ému de crainte;* he is moved with fear. *— une sédition;* to raise a sedition.

s'émouvoir, *v.r.*, to rise; to be roused; to be stirred up. *Il s'émut à la vue du péril;* he was troubled at the sight of the danger. *Il s'émeut de rien;* the least thing upsets him.

*****empaillage**, *n.m.*, stuffing (animals).

*****empaillement**, *n.m.*, bottoming (with straw); stuffing (animals).

*****empaillé, -e**, *part.*, stuffed.

*****empailler**, *v.a.*, to pack in straw; to stuff (birds); to straw bottom. *— des ballots;* to pack up bales in straw. *— une plante;* to wrap straw round a plant.

*****empailleu-r**, *n.m.*, **-se**, *n.f.*, chair-mender; bird-stuffer.

empalement (an-pal-mān), *n.m.*, impalement; (tech.) paddle-door, shuttle.

empaler, *v.a.*, to impale.

empan, *n.m.*, span.

empanacher, *v.a.*, to plume, to adorn with a plume. *— un casque;* to adorn a helmet.

empanner, *v.a.*, (nav.) to bring to. *v.n.*, to tie to.

empaquetage, *n.m.*, packing.

empaqueter (an-pak-té), *v.a.*, to pack up, to make up into a bundle, to do up.

s'empaqueter, *v.r.*, to wrap up. *Il s'empaqueta dans son manteau;* he wrapped himself up in his cloak.

s'emparer, *v.r.*, to possess one's self of; to make one's self master of; to take possession of, to seize, to secure; to engross (conversation); to master. *S'— d'un héritage;* to seize upon an inheritance.

empâtement, *n.m.*, stickiness, clamminess; cramming (of poultry); (surg.) puffiness.

empâter, *v.a.*, to make clammy, sticky; to cram (fowls); (paint.) to impaste. *Cela m'a empâté les mains;* that has made my fingers sticky. *Face empâtée;* pudding face.

empattement, *n.m.*, footing, foundation, base, basement; (tech.) platform (of a crane); (nav.) splicing.

empaumer, *v.a.*, to grasp; to take possession of; to gain over; (at tennis) to strike with the palm of the hand *or* with a bat. *— la voie;* (hunt.) to catch the scent.

empaumure, *n.f.*, top-antlers; palm-piece of a glove.

empeau, *n.m.*, (hort.) flute-grafting.

empêchable, *adj.*, preventable.

empêché, -e, *part.*, hindered, at a loss. *Etre — de sa personne;* to be greatly embarrassed. *Faire l'—;* to affect to be busy.

empêchement (an-pêsh-mān), *n. m.*, hindrance, obstacle, impediment, opposition, obstruction, difficulty; objection. *Lever tous les —s;* to remove all obstacles. *Apporter de l'— à quelque chose;* to throw impediments in the way of anything. *Je n'y mets point d'—;* I do not oppose it.

empêcher, *v.a.*, to oppose, to prevent; to hinder, to obstruct, to impede, to put a stop to. *— un mariage;* to oppose a marriage. *Cette muraille empêche la vue;* this wall obstructs the view. *Cela n'empêcha pas qu'il ne le fît;* that did not prevent him from doing it (i. e., he did it all the same). *Il m'empêche de travailler;* he hinders me from working. *L'un n'empêche pas l'autre;* the one does not bar the other. *Cela n'empêche pas que;* and yet, for all that.

s'empêcher, *v.r.*, to forbear, to refrain from, to keep from, to abstain. *Il ne saurait s'— de médire;* he cannot keep from slandering. *Je ne saurais m'empêcher de le faire;* I cannot help doing it.

*****empeigne**, *n.f.*, upper leather; vamp.

empellement, *n.m.*, sluice, dam.

empennelage, *n.m.*, backing an anchor.

empenneler, *v.a.*, to back an anchor.

empennelle, *n.f.*, small anchor; kedge.

empenner, *v.a.*, to feather arrows.

empenoir, *n.m.*, lock-chisel.

empereur, *n.m.*, emperor.

empesage, *n.m.*, starching.

empesé, -e, *part.*, starched; (of style) stiff, formal.

empeser, *v.a.*, to starch; (nav.) to wet (sails). *— un jabot;* to starch a frill. *S'—;* to be starched.

empeseu-r, *n.m.*, **-se**, *n.f.*, starcher.

empester, *v.a.*, to infect, to taint. *v.n.*, to stink horribly.

empêtré, -e, *part.*, entangled.

empêtrer, *v.a.*, to entangle, to embarrass, to hamper, to saddle, to fetter. *— quelqu'un dans une mauvaise affaire;* to involve any one in a disagreeable business.

s'empêtrer, *v.r.*, to become entangled, hampered, embarrassed.

emphase, *n.f.*, magniloquence, pomposity; emphasis, stress.

emphatique, *adj.*, bombastic, affected; emphatic.

emphatiquement (-tik-mān), *adv.*, bombastically, pompously, emphatically.

emphractique, *n.m.adj.*, (pharm.) emphractic.

emphysème, *n.m.*, (med.) emphysema.

emphytéose, *n.f.*, long lease, feudal holding.

emphytéote, *n.m.*, tenant on a long lease.

emphytéotique, *adj.*, emphyteutic. *Bail* —; very long lease. *Redevance* —; ground-rent.

empiècement, *n.m.*, yoke (of blouse).

empierrement, *n.m.*, stoning, metalling, ballasting ; broken stones ; metaled road.

empierrer, *v.a.*, to stone, to metal (roads).

empiètement, *n.m.*, encroaching, encroachment ; infringement ; trespass.

empiéter, *v.a.*, to encroach, to make encroachments, to intrench upon, to invade, to usurp.

empiéter, *v.n.*, to encroach. *La mer empiète sur la côte;* the sea encroaches upon the coast. *Il empiète sur mes droits;* he encroaches upon my rights.

empiffrer, *v.a.*, to cram, to stuff.

*s'***empiffrer**, *v.r.*, to cram, to stuff.

empile, *n.f.*, (pisc.) gut-line.

empilement, *n.m.*, piling ; stacking.

empiler, *v.a.*, to pile up ; to stack ; to bin ; to fasten (hook).

empileur, *n.m.*, stacker.

empirance, *n.f.*, damage (to goods in transit).

empire, *n.m.*, empire, sovereignty ; authority ; reign ; sway, dominion, command, ascendency ; dominions. *Bas*——; Lower Empire. *L'humide* —; (poet.) the sea. — *d'Occident, d'Orient;* the Western, the Eastern, Empire. *Vous avez un* — *absolu sur moi;* you have absolute command over me. *Avoir de l'* — *sur quelqu'un;* to sway any one. *Traiter quelqu'un avec* —; to treat one imperiously, with haughtiness. *Avoir de l'* — *sur soi;* to have control over one's passions. *Se disputer l'*—; to contend for sovereignty.

empirée, *n.m.* V. **empyrée**.

empirement, *n.m.*, aggravation.

empirer, *v.a.*, to make worse.

empirer, *v.n.*, to grow worse. *Sa maladie empire chaque jour;* his illness gets worse every day. *La chose empira,* matters grew worse.

empirique, *adj.*, empiric, empirical.

empirique, *n.m.*, empiric.

empiriquement, *adv.*, empirically.

empirisme, *n.m.*, empiricism.

emplacement (an-plas-mān), *n. m.*, site, ground, piece of ground, place, spot.

emplanture, *n.f.*, (nav.) step (of a mast).

emplastration, *n.f.*, (hort.) budding.

emplastrer, *v.a.*, to bud.

emplâtre, *n.m.*, plaster, salve, ointment ; helpless creature. *Mettre un* — *à;* (med.) to put a plaster on. *Mettre un* — *à une affaire;* to patch up a business. *C'est un véritable* —; he is fit for nothing.

emplette, *n.f.*, purchase. *Faire* — *de quelque chose;* to purchase anything. *Faire des* —*s;* to go shopping.

emplir, *v.a.*, to fill, to fill up.

*s'***emplir**, *v.r.*, to fill ; to be filled.

emploi, *n.m.*, employ, employment ; situation, place, post ; entry (of accounts) ; (theat.) line of business ; (fin.) appropriation. — *abusif;* misemployment. *Faux* —; false item. *Faire un bon* — *de son temps;* to make a good use of one's time. *Double* —; useless repetition. *Donner de l'*—; to give employment. *Sans* —; out of employment. [employé, official.

employé, *n.m.*, clerk, person employed.

employer, *v.a.*, to employ, to use, to make use of ; to bestow ; to devote ; to spend ; to lay out, to invest. *Bien* — *son temps;* to employ one's time well. — *son temps à l'étude;* to spend one's time in study. — *une phrase;* to use a phrase. — *mal;* to misemploy. — *le vert et le sec;* to leave no stone unturned. *Je l'ai*

employé à cela; I set him to work on that. — *une somme en recette;* (com.) to enter a sum as received.

*s'***employer**, *v.r.*, to employ, to exert, one's self ; to use one's interest. — *pour quelqu'un;* to use one's interest in any one's favor.

emplumer, *v.a.*, (mus.) to feather, to fledge ; to quill. — *un clavecin;* to quill a harpsichord.

*s'***emplumer**, *v.r.*, to become fledged ; to feather one's nest ; (pop.) to pick up flesh. *Il s'est bien emplumé dans cette maison;* he feathered his nest well in that house.

empocher, *v.a.*, (fam.) to pocket. *Il empoche tout ce qu'il gagne;* he pockets all his winnings.

empoignement, *n. m.*, grasping ; capture, arrest.

*****empoigner**, *v.a.*, to grasp, to seize, to lay hold of ; to take up, to take into custody. *Cela est trop gros, on ne saurait l'*—; that is too thick, it is impossible to grasp it. *Je vous ferai* —; I shall have you taken up.

*s'***empoigner**, *v.r.*, to lay hold of each other. *Ils se sont empoignés;* they laid hold of each other, they had a set-to.

empointer, *v.a.*, to stitch ; to point (pins, needles).

empointeur, *n.m.*, stitcher ; pointer.

empois, *n.m.*, starch.

empoisonné, -e, *part.*, poisoned ; poisonous.

empoisonnement (-poâ-zo-n-mān), *n.m.*, poisoning.

empoisonner, *v.a.*, to poison ; to infect ; to mar, to corrupt ; to embitter, to envenom. *Ces maximes sont capables d'*— *la jeunesse;* these maxims are calculated to corrupt the young.

*s'***empoisonner**, *v.r.*, to poison one's self.

empoisonneu-r, *n. m.*, -**se**, *n. f.*, poisoner, corrupter ; wretched cook.

empoisser, *v.a.* V. **poisser**.

empoissonnement (-poâ-so-n-mān), *n.m.*, stocking with fish.

empoissonner, *v.a.*, to stock with fish.

emporté, -e, *adj.*, fiery, passionate, hasty, hot, hot-headed ; runaway ; unmanageable.

emportement, *n.m.*, transport ; passion, fit of passion ; hastiness ; outburst ; anger, rage ; frenzy, violence.

emporte-pièce, *n.m.*, punch (instrument) ; puncher ; cutting-out machine ; fly-press ; sarcastic person ; virulent satirist. *C'est une réponse à l'*—; it is a very cutting answer.

emporter, *v.a.*, to carry away, to take away, to sweep away, to convey away ; to remove (stains) ; to carry off (kill) ; to entail, to involve ; to gain, to obtain ; to blow off ; to burn. *Le vent a emporté mon chapeau;* the wind has blown my hat off. *Cette maladie l'a emporté;* that illness carried him off. — *de haute lutte;* to carry with a high hand. *L'*—*sur;* to prevail ; to have the advantage, to get the better of, to carry the day ; to preponderate, to overcome, to outweigh, to surpass. *L'amour l'emporte souvent sur la raison;* love often gets the better of reason. *Il l'a emporté sur tous ses concurrents;* he triumphed over all his competitors. *Cette considération l'emporte sur toutes les autres;* that consideration outweighs every other. — *ses cliques et ses claques;* to pack up bag and baggage. — *la pièce;* to strike home.

*s'***emporter**, *v.r.*, to fly into a passion ; to declaim, to inveigh against ; to rail at ; to run away (of horses). — *contre le vice;* to declaim against vice. — *comme une soupe au lait;* to take fire like gunpowder.

empotage, *n.m.*, potting.

empoter, *v.a.*, (hort.) to inclose in pots, to pot.

empourpré, -e, *adj.*, purple, purpled, empurpled.

empourprer, *v.a.*, *s'*—, *v.r.*, to purple.

empreindre, *v.a.*, to imprint, to stamp; to mark; to impress; to tincture. *S'—*, to become tinged.

empreinte, *n.f.*, mark, stamp, print, impression; (paint.) first coat. *L'— d'un cachet ;* the stamp of a seal. *Son ouvrage porte l'— de son esprit ;* his work bears the stamp of his mind. *Marqué à l'— de ;* bearing the stamp of.

empressé, -e, *adj.,* active; assiduous; officious; eager, earnest. *Il paraît fort — auprès d'elle ;* he appears markedly attentive to her. *Des soins empressés ;* assiduous attentions. *Faire l'— ;* to put one's self forward.

empressement (an-près̀s-mān), *n.m.,* eagerness, earnestness; assiduous attention; alacrity, promptness, haste, hurry. *Avec — ;* eagerly, earnestly, cheerfully, industriously. *Il a beaucoup d'— à vous servir ;* he is very anxious to serve you. *Trop d'— ;* overforwardness.

s'empresser, *v.r.,* to hasten, to be eager (to), to be earnest, forward, to be ardent, to flock, to crowd, to press forward. *S'— de parler ;* to hasten to speak.

emprisonnement (-zo-n-mān), *n.m.,* imprisonment, confinement, custody. *— cellulaire ;* solitary confinement.

emprisonner, *v.a.,* to imprison, to confine.

emprunt, *n.m.,* borrowing, loan. *Il est toujours aux —s ;* he is always borrowing. *Argent d'— ;* borrowed money. *Une beauté d'— ;* an artificial beauty. *Faire un — ;* to contract a loan.

emprunter, *v.a.,* to borrow. *— de l'argent à quelqu'un ;* to borrow money of any one. *Nom emprunté ;* assumed name. *Air emprunté ;* an embarrassed look. *Ne choisit pas qui emprunte ;* beggars cannot be choosers.

emprunteu-r, -se, *n.* and *adj.,* borrower; borrowing, prone to borrow; not original.

empuantir, *v.a.,* to cause an ill smell, to infect.

s'empuantir, *v.r.,* to stink, to have a bad odor.

empuantissement (-tis-mān), *n.m.,* stench.

empyème, *n.m.,* (med.) empyema.

empyrée, *n.m.* and *adj.,* the empyrean; empyreal.

empyreumatique, *adj.,* empyreumatical.

empyreume, *n.m.,* empyreuma.

ému, -e, *part.,* moved, affected. *Fort — ;* much affected.

émulat-eur, *n.m.,* **-rice,** *n.f.,* (l.u.) emulator, rival, imitator.

⊙**émulati-f, -ve,** *adj.,* emulative.

émulation, *n.f.,* emulation; rivalry.

émule, *n.m.,* rival, competitor, emulator.

émulgent, -e, *adj.,* (anat.) emulgent.

émulsi-f, -ve, *adj.,* emulsive.

émulsion, *n.f.,* emulsion.

émulsionner, *v.a.,* to mix an emulsion with.

émyde, *n.f.,* marsh-tortoise.

en, *prep.,* in, into, within, on, to, at, like, in the form of, as a, out of, by, for. *Je l'ai mise — pension ;* I have sent her to a boarding-school. *— haut ;* above, upstairs. *— bas ;* below, downstairs. *— avant ;* forward. *— arrière ;* backward, behind. *— dedans ;* within. *— dehors ;* without. *Aller — France ;* to go to France. *En tout temps ;* at all times. *— hiver ;* in winter. *Etre — bonne santé ;* to be in good health. *— nourrice ;* out at nurse. *— prière ;* at prayers. *Vivre — roi ;* to live like a king. *Agir — furieux ;* to act as a madman. *Etre — robe de chambre ;* to be in one's dressing-gown. *— dépit de lui ;* in spite of him. *De plus — plus ;* more and more. *Voir — songe ;* to see in a dream. *Il l'aborda — riant ;* he came up to her with a smile. *— passant ;* by the way. *— colère ;* in a passion. *— guerre ;* at war. *— paix ;* at peace. *Tomber — décadence ;* to fall

into decay. *— trois jours ;* in three days. *Etre — ville ;* to be out.

en, *pron., m.f. sing.* and *pl.,* of him, of her, of it, its, of them, their; from him, from her, from it, from them; by him, by her, by it, by them; about him, about her, about it, about them; thence, from thence; some of it, any. *Avez-vous de l'argent ?* have you any money ? *J'— ai ;* I have some. *Vous — parlez toujours ;* you are always speaking of him, of it. *Il — est mort un ;* one of them is dead. *J'— suis bien aise ;* I am very glad of it. *J'— suis fâché ;* I am sorry for it. *J'— suis surpris ;* I wonder at it. *Qu'— dites-vous ?* what do you say to it ? *Je n'— ai point ;* I have none. *— voulez-vous ?* will you have any ? *Donnez m'— ;* give me some. *C'est un bœuf, j'— vois les cornes ;* it is an ox, I see its horns. *Si vous voulez voir de beaux tableaux, il — a ;* if you wish to see fine pictures, he has some. *Il — est des femmes comme des enfants ;* it is with women as with children. *Il — est de cela comme de la plupart des choses ;* it is with that as with most other things. *Après cela ils — vinrent aux mains ;* after that they came to blows. *— vouloir à quelqu'un ;* to have a grudge against any one. *S'— aller ;* to go away. *S'— retourner ;* to return. *C'— est fait ;* it is all over. *Il s'— faut de beaucoup ;* you are a long way off. *Il ne sait où il — est ;* he knows not how far he has got. *Il — tient ;* he is caught. *Voulez-vous — être ?* will you make one of us ? *Parlez-lui— ;* speak to him of it. *Il veut — découdre ;* he wants to fight it out.

énallage, *n.f.,* (gram.) enallage.

s'énamourer, *v.r.,* to fall in love (with).

énarrer, *v.a.,* to relate in detail.

enarrhement, *n.m.*   V. **arrhement**.

enarrher, *v.a.*   V. **arrher**.

énarthrose, *n.f.,* (anat.) enarthrosis.

en-belle, *n.f.,* (nav.) direct fire. *adj.,* direct. *adv.,* directly, fairly.

encablure, *n.f.,* (nav.) cable's length.

encadré, -e, *part.,* framed.

encadrement, *n.m.,* framing, frame; (mil.) enlistment.

encadrer, *v.a.,* to frame, to encircle; to introduce, to insert. *Faire — un tableau ;* to have a picture framed. *S'—, v.r.,* to be introduced, inserted, inclosed; to fit in.

encadreur, *n.m.,* picture-frame maker.

encager, *v.a.,* to cage, to put in a cage.

encaissage, *n.m.,* incasing; (hort.) tubbing.

encaisse, *n.f.,* (fin., com.) cash in hand, cashbalance, metallic reserve.

encaissé, -e, *part.,* incased; embanked; sunk, hollow. *Cette rivière est —e ;* that river flows between high banks.

encaissement (ān-kès-mān), *n.m.,* packing in cases; packing; putting in boxes; embankment ; (fin.) collection. *Sauf — ;* when paid, if paid.

encaisser, *v.a.,* to incase, to pack; to put in a box; to embank; to collect; to encash, to receive; (fin.) to collect; to lay down a bed (to roads).

encan, *n.m.,* auction, public sale. *Vente à l'— ;* sale by public auction. *Mettre à l'— ;* to put up for sale. *Vendre à l'— ;* to sell by auction.

*****encanailler,** *v.a.,* to degrade; to lower by mixing with low company.

*****s'encanailler,** *v.r.,* to keep low company; to lose caste. *Gardez-vous de vous encanailler ;* beware of keeping low company.

encapuchonné, -e, *part.,* cowled, hooded.

encapuchonner, *v.a.,* to put on a cowl.

s'encapuchonner, *v.r.,* to wear a cowl ; to put on a cowl ; (man.) to arch the neck (of horses).

encaquement, *n.m.,* packing ; barreling.

encaquer, *v.a.,* to barrel ; to cram full up.

encaqu-eur, *n.m.*, **-euse**, *n.f.*, packer.

encarter, *v.a.*, (print.) to insert as a cancel.

*s'***encarter**, *v.r.*, to be inserted as a cancel.

en-cas, *n.m.*, (—) sunshade (large enough to be used as an umbrella); collation kept ready in case of need.

encastelé, -e, *adj.*, hoof-bound (of a horse).

*s'***encasteler**, *v.r.*, to be hoof-bound.

encastelure, *n.f.*, contracted heels.

encastrement, *n.m.*, fitting; fitting in.

encastrer, *v.a.*, to fit, to fit in.

*s'***encastrer**, *v.r.*, to fit, to fit in.

encaustique, *n.f.* and *adj.*, (paint.) encaustic, furniture-paste.

encavement (ān-kav-mān), *n.m.*, storing (in cellar).

encaver, *v.a.*, to put *or* store in a cellar.

encaveur, *n.m.*, cellar-man.

enceindre, *v. a.*, to inclose, to encircle, to encompass, to surround. — *de murailles;* to inclose with walls.

enceinte, *adj. f.*, pregnant ; with child ; enceinte.

enceinte, *n.f.*, circuit, circumference ; inclosure, precincts ; place ; (fort.) enceinte. *Mur d'—;* inclosure wall. *Mur d'—;* wall of circumvallation. *Dans cette —;* within these walls.

encens, *n.m.*, incense, frankincense ; fragrance ; homage ; praise ; flattery. *Brûler de l'— sur les autels;* to burn incense on the altars. *Donner de l'— à quelqu'un;* to flatter any one.

encensement (an-sāns-mān), *n.m.*, incensing ; praising, praise ; flattery.

encenser, *v.a.*, to incense, to perfume with frankincense ; to flatter, to pay homage to.

encenseur, *n.m.*, burner of incense ; flatterer.

encensier, *n.m.*, rosemary.

encensoir, *n.m.*, censer, perfuming-pan ; (astron.) Ara ; (fig.) ecclesiastical power. *Mettre la main à l'—;* to meddle with ecclesiastical affairs. *Donner de l'— par le nez, casser le nez à coups d'—;* to flatter fulsomely.

encéphale, *n.m.*, encephalon (brain).

encéphalique, *adj.*, (anat.) encephalic.

encéphalite, *n.f.*, inflammation of the brain.

encéphalocèle, *n.f.*, encephalocele, hernia of the brain.

enchaînement (ān-shèn-mān), *n.m.*, chaining, linking ; concatenation, chain, series, connection.

enchaîner, *v.a.*, to chain up, to chain, to bind in chains, to chain down, to detain, to restrain ; to captivate ; to link, to connect.

*s'***enchaîner**, *v.r.*, to link, to be connected.

enchaînure, *n.f.*, (tech.) chain ; chain-work ; connection.

enchanteler (ān-shān-tlé), *v.a.*, to arrange timber in a yard ; to set (casks) on gawntrees.

enchantement (ān-shān-tmān), *n.m.*, enchantment, charm, delight ; magic, witchcraft. *Par —;* by enchantment. *Il est dans l'—;* he is delighted.

enchanter, *v.a.*, to enchant, to bewitch, to fascinate, to charm, to gratify. *Je suis enchanté de vous voir;* I am delighted to see you.

enchante-ur, -resse, *n.* and *adj.*, enchanter, enchantress, bewitcher, charmer, enchanting, bewitching. *Voix —resse;* enchanting voice.

enchaper, *v.a.*, to hook, to fasten ; to case, to inclose one cask in another.

enchaperonner, *v.a.*, to hood (a hawk).

encharner, *v.a.*, to put hinges to.

enchâsser, *v.a.*, to enchase, to enshrine ; to insert ; to introduce ; to set. — *dans de l'or ;* to set in gold. — *un diamant;* to set a diamond. — *une anecdote dans un discours;* to introduce an anecdote into a speech.

enchâssure, *n.f.*, setting ; insertion ; introduction.

enchausser, *v.a.*, (gard.) to earth up.

enchaux, *n.m.*, lime-wash.

enchère, *n.f.*, bidding (at an auction) ; auction. *Vente à l'—, aux —s;* sale by auction. *Couvrir une —;* to make a higher bid. *Vendre à l'—, aux —s;* to sell by auction. *Folle —;* bidding for what one cannot pay. *Mettre aux —s;* to bring to the hammer ; to put up to auction. *Payer la folle —;* to pay dear for one's rashness. *Il est à l'—;* he is to be bought by the highest bidder. — *au rabais;* a Dutch auction.

enchérir, *v.a.*, to bid for, to outbid, to overbid; to raise (prices).

enchérir, *v.n.*, to bid, to outbid ; (fig.) to surpass, to outdo, to go further; to rise (in price). *La volaille a enchéri;* poultry has risen in price.

enchérissement (-ris-mān), *n.m.*, rise, increase, advance in price.

enchérisseur, *n.m.*, bidder (at an auction).

enchevalement, *n.m.*, propping, underpinning (of a house).

enchevauchure, *n.f.*, (tech.) lapping over.

enchevêtré, -e, *part.*, entangled ; confused ; in a tangle, mixed up.

enchevêtrement, *n.m.*, entanglement ; confusion.

enchevêtrer, *v.a.*, to halter ; to entangle, to confuse.

*s'***enchevêtrer**, *v.r.*, to get a foot entangled in the halter ; to get entangled ; to get confused, embarrassed.

enchevêtrure, *n.f.*, (carp.) binding ; (vet.) halter-cast.

enchifrené, -e, *part.*, stuffed up (of the nose). *Je suis tout —;* my nose is all stuffed up.

enchifrènement (-èn-mān), *n.m.*, stuffing up (of the nose) ; snuffles.

*s'***enchifrener**, *v.a.*, to get a cold in the head.

enchiridion (-ki-), *n.m.*, (antiq.) manual, enchiridion.

enhymose (-ki-), *n.f.*, (med.) cutaneous hyperæmia.

enclave, *n.f.*, piece of inclosed land ; boundary, limit ; recess (of a lock on a river).

enclavé, -e, *part.*, inclosed.

enclavement (an-klav-mān), *n.m.*, inclosing.

enclaver, *v.a.*, to inclose ; to hem in, to wedge in.

*s'***enclaver**, *v.r.*, to be inclosed (in other land).

enclin, -e, *adj.*, inclined, prone, addicted, apt, given to.

encliquetage, *n.m.*, (tech.) catch.

encliqueter, *v.a.*, to cog with a catch.

enclitique, *n.f.*, (gram.) enclitic.

encloîtrer, *v.a.*, to cloister.

enclore, *v.a.*, to inclose, to fence or take in.

enclos, *n. m.*, inclosure, close ; paddock ; orchard.

enclouage, *n.m.*, spiking.

enclouer, *v.a.*, to prick animals (in shoeing); to spike (a gun).

encloure, *n.f.*, prick (in shoeing, etc.); difficulty, obstacle, hitch.

enclume, *n.f.*, anvil ; (anat.) incus. *Billot d'—;* anvil-block. *Etre entre le marteau et l'—;* to be between the devil and the deep sea. *Remettre sur l'—;* to remodel. *Il frappe toujours sur la même —;* he is always harping on the same string.

enclumeau *or* **enclumot**, *n.m.*, hand-anvil.

encoche, *n.f.*, notch (on a tally, etc.).

encocher, *v.a.*, to notch. — *une flèche;* to fit an arrow in the bow.

encoffrer, *v.n.*, to put in a coffer ; to lay up ; to bag, to cage, to quod.

***encoignure** *or* **encognure** (an-ko-gnur), *n.f.*, corner ; angle (of a street) ; corner-piece.

encollage, *n.m.*, sizing.

encoller, *v.a.*, to size.

encolure, *n.f.*, neck and shoulders of a horse; (b.s.) appearance, looks (of a person).

encombrant, *adj.*, bulky, cumbering, encumbering, cumbersome.

encombre, *n.m.*, accident, impediment, hindrance, obstacle.

encombrement, *n.m.*, obstruction, stoppage; crowding, crowd.

encombrer, *v.a.*, to obstruct, to encumber, to embarrass, to block up; to throng.

à l'encontre, *prep.*, counter, against. *Aller à l'— de quelque chose;* to run counter to a thing.

encorbellement (-bèl-mãn), *n.m.*, (arch.) corbeling, projecting.

encore, *adv.*, yet, still, more, again; once more; further; moreover; besides, however. *Il n'est pas — venu;* he is not yet come. *A sept heures j'attendais —;* at seven o'clock I was still waiting. *— ?* what, again? *Outre l'argent, on lui donna — un cheval;* besides the money, he had, moreover, a horse given him. *— s'il voulait m'envoyer dire;* if, only, he would send me word. *Vous servez-vous — de ce livre?* are you still using that book? *Il est — plus riche que son frère;* he is still richer than his brother. *Quoi — ?* what else? *— moins;* still less. *Prenez — un verre de vin;* take another glass of wine. *— une fois je vous dis;* I tell you once more. *Hier —;* only yesterday.

encore, *conj.*, even, yet. *— que;* though, although.

encorné, -e, *adj.*, horned, tossed.

encorner, *v.a.*, to horn; to gore; to toss.

encourageant, -e, *adj.*, encouraging, cheering, inspiriting.

encouragement (-raj-mãn), *n.m.*, encouragement, incitement, incentive; countenance, support.

encourager, *v.a.*, to encourage, to stimulate; to contenance, to support, to be a promoter of.

s'encourager, *v.r.*, to encourage each other.

encourir, *v.a.*, to incur, to draw down upon one's self, to fall under. *— le mépris de tout le monde;* to draw down general contempt upon one's self.

encouture, *n.f.*, (nav.) clincher-work.

encrage, *n.m.*, (print.) inking.

encrassement, *n.m.*, fouling (of fire-arms).

encrasser, *v.a.*, to make dirty, to dirty; to foul.

s'encrasser, *v.r.*, to get foul *or* greasy, to become dirty; to lower one's self; to become foul.

encre, *n.f.*, ink. *— à écrire;* writing ink. *— d'imprimerie;* printing ink. *— de Chine;* Indian ink. *C'est la bouteille à l'—;* there's no seeing through that. *Tacher d'—;* to ink. *Ecrire de bonne — à quelqu'un;* to write in strong terms to any one. *Etre dans la bouteille à l'—;* to be in the secret.

encrêper, *v.a.*, to cover with crape.

s'encrêper, *v.r.*, to put on crape.

encrer, *v.a.*, (print.) to ink. *v.n.*, to take the ink.

encrier, *n.m.*, inkstand, ink-horn; (print.) ink-trough. *Table d'—;* (print.) ink-table.

encroué, *adj.*, entangled (of trees).

encroûté, -e, *part.*, covered with a crust; rusty; full of prejudices.

encroûter, *v.a.*, to crust; to plaster a wall.

s'encroûter, *v.r.*, to crust, to get hard, to become heavy; to become stupid, rusty.

encuirasser, *v.a.*, to cover with a cuirass.

s'encuirasser, *v.r.*, to put on one's cuirass; to get covered with dirt; to become hardened.

enculasser, *v.a.*, to breech (a gun).

encuvement (ãn-kuv-mãn), **encuvage**, *n.m.*, tubbing.

encuver, *v.a.*, to put into a vat, to tub.

encyclique, *n.f.* and *adj.*, encyclical letter; encyclical.

encyclopédie, *n.f.*, encyclopædia.

encyclopédique, *adj.*, encyclopedic.

encyclopédiste, *n.m.*, encyclopedist.

endécagone, *n.m.* and *adj.*, (geom.) hendecagon.

endémique, *adj.*, endemical, endemic.

endenté, -e, *adj.*, indented; furnished with teeth.

endenter, *v.a.*, (carp.) to indent; to cog, to tooth, to supply with teeth.

endetter, *v.a.*, to cause to run into debt; to get a person into debt.

s'endetter, *v.r.*, to run into debt, to contract debts.

endêvé, -e, *n.* and *adj.*, (fam., l.u.) irritable, passionate person; impatient, irritable, passionate.

endêver, *v.n.*, to fume, to be vexed. *Faire — quelqu'un;* to vex any one; to drive any one mad.

endiablé, -e, *adj.*, possessed; devilish; wicked, horrible.

endiablé, *n.m.*, **-e**, *n.f.*, person possessed. *C'est un —;* he is like one possessed.

endiabler, *v.n.*, to be furious. *Faire —;* to torment, to plague to death; to render furious.

endiguement, **endigage**, *n.m.*, damming in; damming up.

endiguer (-ghé), *v.a.*, to dam in; to dam up; to embank.

endimanché, -e, *adj.*, dressed in Sunday best; with all one's finery on.

s'endimancher, *v.r.*, to put on one's Sunday clothes.

endive, *n.f.*, endive.

endoctriner, *v.a.*, to indoctrinate, to teach; to give his cue (to any one).

endoctrineur, *n.m.*, teacher; prompter.

endolori, -e, *adj.*, painful, aching, sore.

s'endolorir, *v.r.*, to make sore, tender; to ache, to become sore.

endolorissement, *n.m.*, pain, aching, soreness.

endommagement (-maj-mãn), *n.m.*, loss, injury.

endommager, *v.a.*, to damage, to injure.

s'endommager, *v.r.*, to be damaged; to become deteriorated.

endormeur, *n.m.*, cajoler, wheedler, flatterer, coaxer.

endormi, -e, *part.*, asleep, sleeping; sleepy, drowsy, sluggish; benumbed. *J'ai la jambe —e;* my leg is benumbed.

endormi, *n.m.*, **-e**, *n.f.*, sleepy person; sleepy head; person asleep. *Faire l'—;* to sham sleep.

endormir, *v.a.*, to lull asleep, to send to sleep; to rock to sleep; to wheedle, to amuse, to deceive; to benumb, to lull. *Endormez cet enfant;* rock that child to sleep. *Sa conversation vous endort;* his conversation sends you to sleep. *Cela m'a endormi la jambe;* that has benumbed my leg.

s'endormir, *v.r.*, to fall asleep, to go to sleep, to slumber; to be lulled into security. *S'— du sommeil de la tombe;* to sleep the sleep of death. *S'— dans le vice;* to be steeped in vice. *Il s'est endormi sur cette affaire;* he was wanting in vigilance in that business. *S'— sur le rôti;* to let slip the favorable opportunity.

endos, *n.m.*, (com.) endorsement.

endosmose, *n.f.*, (phys.) endosmose.

endosse, *n.f.*, (fam.) trouble; burden.

endossement (ãn-dôsmãn), *n.m.*, (com.) endorsement. *V.* **endos**, which is more frequently used.

endosser, *v.a.*, to put on one's back; to buckle on; to put on; to don; to saddle; (com.) to indorse. *— une lettre de change;* to indorse a bill of exchange. *— le harnais;* to put on the harness.

endosseur, n.m., (com.) indorser.

endroit, n.m., place, spot, part, passage ; point ; right side (of a stuff). Son plus bel — ; any one's, any thing's, best side. — faible ; weak point. — sensible ; sensitive point. A l'— de ; with regard, or with respect, to. A deux — s ; reversible (of stuffs).

enduire (enduisant, enduit), v.a., to do over, to lay over, to coat, to smear. — une muraille de plâtre ; to do a wall over with plaster.

enduit, n.m., coat, coating, layer ; glaze, glazing ; varnish ; polish.

endurant, -e, adj., patient, enduring ; tolerant. Peu — ; impatient of injury.

endurci, -e, part., hardened, obdurate, inured, callous. Un cheval — aux coups ; a horse inured to blows. Pécheur — ; hardened sinner.

endurci, n.m., -e, n.f., hardened sinner.

endurcir, v.a., to harden, to make hard, to toughen, to inure ; to render obdurate, to steel ; to indurate ; to render callous. Le travail endurcit le corps ; labor hardens the body. L'avarice avait endurci son cœur ; avarice had steeled his heart.

s'endurcir, v.r., to harden ; to grow hard ; to be steeled ; to become callous ; to indurate.

endurcissement (-sis-mān), n.m., hardness ; hardness of heart, obduracy ; callousness.

endurer, v.a., to endure, to bear ; to suffer, to undergo ; to allow, to put up with, to permit.

énéide, n.f., Eneid, Æneid.

énéorème, n.m., (med.) eneorema.

énergie, n.f., force, energy, strength, force, vigor, power. Avec — ; with energy. Sans — ; of no energy.

énergique, adj., energetic, energetical, strong, vigorous, forcible. Remède — ; powerful remedy.

énergiquement (-jik-mān), adv., energetically, vigorously, strenuously.

énergumène, n.m.f., demoniac ; fanatic ; desperado.

énervation, n.f., or **énervement,** n.m., enervation.

énerver, v.a., to enervate, to unnerve.

s'énerver, v.r., to become enervated or unnerved.

enfaîteau, n.m., (mas.) ridge-tile, gutter-tile.

enfaîtement (ān-fêt-mān), n.m., (arch.) ridge-lead.

enfaîter, v.a., to ridge a house.

enfance, n.f., infancy, childhood ; childishness, puerility, dotage ; childish action. Première — ; earliest infancy. Dès mon — ; from my infancy. Sortir de l'— ; to emerge from childhood. Etre en — ; to be in one's dotage. Tomber en — ; to become childish.

enfant, n.m.f., child ; infant ; native ; (jur.) issue. — adoptif ; adopted child. L'— prodigue ; the prodigal son. L'— à naître ; the child unborn. — trouvé ; foundling. — naturel ; natural child. Un — de famille ; a young gentleman. — de la balle ; child that follows his father's profession, or chip of the old block. Un — à la mamelle ; an infant at the breast. Un — mort-né ; a still-born child. Discours d'— ; childish language. — de chœur ; chorister. Les — s perdus ; (milit.) the forlorn hope. Faire l'— ; to play the child ; to behave like a child. C'est bien l'— de sa mère ; he is a chip of the old block. En travail d'— ; in labor. C'est un bon — ; he is a good child, he is a good fellow. Les — s de France ; the children of the King of France, the children of the eldest son of the King of France. Petits enfants ; little children. Petits-enfants ; grandchildren.

enfantement (ān-fān-tmān), n.m., childbirth.

enfanter, v.a., to bear, to bring forth ; to produce ; to beget ; to bring to light ; to give birth to.

*****enfantillage,** n.m., child's play, childishness.

enfantin, -e, adj., infantine, childish.

enfariner, v.a., to flour, to sprinkle with flour. Etre enfariné de quelque science ; to have a smattering of some science. Etre enfariné d'une mauvaise doctrine ; to be prepossessed in favor of a bad doctrine. Il est venu nous dire cela la gueule enfarinée ; (triv.) he came, full of stupid confidence, to tell us that.

enfer (an-fèr), n.m., hell ; infernal, or lower, regions. Au fond de l'— ; in the depths of hell. Les peines de l'— ; the torments of hell. L'— s'est déchaîné contre moi ; hell is let loose against me. Tison d'— ; hell-hound. Un feu d'— ; a scathing fire.

enfermé, n.m., close, confined air. Sentir l'— ; to smell close.

enfermer, v.a., to shut, to shut in ; to shut up ; to lock up ; to inclose ; to coop up, to conceal ; to comprehend, to comprise. C'est un homme à — ; that man ought to be confined in a mad-house. — à clef ; to keep under lock and key. — un parc de murailles ; to wall in a park.

s'enfermer, v.r., to lock one's self up, to seclude one's self ; to lock, to lock up (of a thing).

enferrer, v.a., to run any one through with a sword, etc. ; to transfix.

s'enferrer, v.r., to run one's self through with a sword, etc. ; (fig.) to injure one's self ; to fall into a snare ; to get into a fix.

enficeler, v.a., to tie with a string.

enfièvrement, n.m., feverishness.

enfilade, n.f., suite (of chambers) ; string (of phrases) ; (milit.) enfilade. D'— ; raking (fire).

enfiler, v.a., to thread, to string ; to pierce, to run any one through with a sword, etc. ; to engage in ; to slip on ; (milit.) to enfilade. — une aiguille ; to thread a needle. — des perles ; to string pearls ; to lose one's time. — un discours ; to begin a long-winded speech. — un homme ; to run a man through the body.

s'enfiler, v.r., to be run through, to be pierced ; to get engaged or involved in.

enfileur, n.m., header (in pin-making) ; prattler ; (pop.) cheat, wheedler.

enfin, adv., in fine, finally, at length, in short, after all, at last, lastly.

enflammé, -e, part., on fire, in flames, ignited ; kindled.

enflammer, v.a., to set on fire, to fire, to set in a blaze, to kindle ; to inflame ; to heat ; to incense, to provoke.

s'enflammer, v.r., to take fire, to be kindled, to be inflamed, to blaze ; to be ablaze ; to be incensed ; to ignite. On vit tout le vaisseau s'— ; they saw the whole ship ablaze or break into flames.

enflé, -e, part., swelled, inflated, puffed up, bloated ; (lit.) bombastic, turgid, high-flown.

enfle-bœuf, n.m., golden-beetle. [shrouds.

enflécher, v.n., (nav.) to go up into the

enfléchure, n.f., shroud, ratline.

enfler, v.a., to swell, to swell out, to blow out, to bloat ; to puff up, to distend, to elate, to excite ; to inflate. Le vent enflait nos voiles ; the wind swelled our sails.

s'enfler, v.r., to swell, to grow turgid. La voile s'enfle ; the sail swells out. S'— d'orgueil ; to be puffed up with pride.

enflure, n.f., bloatedness, swelling ; (fig.) bombast, turgidness. — du style ; turgidness of style.

enfoncé, -e, part., broken open, sunken. Des yeux enfoncés ; sunken eyes. — ! (pop.) dished ! done for !

enfoncement (ān-fons-mān), n.m., sinking, sinking down ; breaking in ; recess ; (paint.) background.

enfoncer, v.a., to sink, to sink to the bottom ;

to drive in; to break in; to outwit, to surpass; to ruin, to blow up, to dish, to diddle. — *un clou dans la muraille ;* to drive a nail into the wall. — *son chapeau ;* to pull one's hat over one's eyes. — *un bataillon ;* to break through a battalion.

s'**enfoncer**, *v.r.*, to sink, to sink down; to break down ; to bury one's self in ; to plunge ; to fail, to make a mess of. *S'— dans un bois ;* to dive into a wood. *Cet homme s'enfonce dans l'étude ;* that man buries himself in study. *S'— dans la débauche ;* to plunge into debauchery.

enfoncer, *v.n.*, to sink.

enfonceur, *n.m.*, one who breaks in or through anything ; (fig.) cheat, diddler. — *de portes ouvertes ;* braggart.

enfonçure, *n.f.*, cavity, hole, hollow ; boards (of a bedstead) ; bottom pieces (of casks).

enforcir, *v.a.*, to strengthen.

s'**enforcir**, *v.r.*, to gather strength ; to grow stronger.

enforcir, *v.n.*, to gather strength, to get strength.

enformer, *v.a.*, to put on the block ; to block (hats).

enfouir, *v.a.*, to hide or bury in the ground, to cover with earth.

enfouissement (ān-foo-is-mān), *n.m.*, burying, hiding in the ground.

enfouisseu-r, *n.m.*, **-se**, *n.f.*, burier.

enfourcher, *v.a.*, to bestride, to straddle ; to pierce with a pitchfork.

enfourchure, *n.f.*, fork, crotch ; (hunt.) forked head (of a stag).

enfourner, *v.a.*, to put in the oven. *Bien —, mal — ;* to make a good, a bad, beginning.

enfournée, *n.f.*, putting in the oven or kiln.

s'**enfourner**, *v.r.*, to get into a difficult road, into a blind alley, into a scrape.

enfreindre (enfreignant, enfreint), *v.a.*, to infringe, to break, to violate. — *un traité ;* to infringe a treaty. — *les lois ;* to transgress the laws.

enfroquer, *v.a.*, (b.s.) to make (any one) turn monk or friar.

s'**enfroquer**, *v.r.*, (b.s.) to turn monk.

s'**enfuir**, *v.r.*, to run away, to flee, to take flight, to escape ; to run off ; to elope ; to run out, to leak. *Ils s'étaient enfuis de prison ;* they had made their escape from prison. *La bouteille s'enfuit ;* the bottle leaks.

enfumé, -e, *part.*, smoked, smoky.

enfumer, *v.a.*, to smoke, to fill with smoke, to smoke out. — *un renard ;* to smoke out a fox.

enfutage, *n.m.*, casking.

enfutailler, *v.a.*, to cask, to barrel, to tun.

engagé, *n.m.*, enlisted soldier.

engagé, -e, *part.*, engaged, enlisted ; (nav.) in action, water-logged. *La clef est —e dans la serrure ;* the key sticks in the lock. *Vaisseau — ;* water-logged ship.

engageant, -e (-jān-t), *adj.*, engaging, winning, pleasing, taking, winsome. *Il a des manières —es ;* he has winning manners.

engageantes, *n.f.pl.*, short under-sleeves with lace cuffs.

engagement (ān-gaj-mān), *n.m.*, engagement, pledging, pawning ; engagement (promise) ; enlisting ; (milit.) bounty ; (milit.) action. *pl.*, (com.) liabilities. *Entrer dans un — ;* to enter into an engagement. *Manquer à un — ;* to fail to keep an engagement.

engager, *v.a.*, to pawn, to pledge ; to engage, to induce, to invite, to persuade, to urge ; (milit.) to enlist ; to hire ; to bind ; (b.s.) to involve ; to unite, to compel. — *ses meubles ;* to pledge one's furniture. *Cela ne vous engage à rien ;* that binds you to nothing. — *quelqu'un dans une mauvaise affaire ;* to entangle any one in a bad business. — *le combat ;* to begin the action.

— *un soldat ;* to enlist a soldier. — *une clef dans une serrure ;* to entangle a key in a lock.

s'**engager**, *v.r.*, to engage one's self, to be a security, to promise, to take upon one's self, to undertake, to bind one's self ; to hire one's self ; to enlist ; to entangle one's self, to get involved. *S'— pour un ami ;* to stand security for a friend. *S'— dans une mauvaise affaire ;* to get involved in a bad business. *Le combat ne tarda pas à s'— ;* the battle soon began.

⊙**engagiste**, *n.m.*, tenant (of crown lands).

engainer, *v.a.*, to sheathe ; to case ; to put up (of swords).

enganter, *v.a.*, (nav.) to come up with, to overtake, to overreach ; to entrap, to cajole, to insnare.

engazonner, *v.a.*, to turf ; to cover with turf.

engeance (an-jāns), *n.f.*, breed, brood (animal) ; (b.s.) race (pers.). *Des poules d'une grande — ;* hens of a large breed. *Maudite — ;* cursed race. *Quelle — !* what a lot or set !

engeancer, *v.a.*, to embarrass ; to saddle (with).

engelure (an-jlur), *n.f.*, chilblain.

engendrer, *v.a.*, to beget, to engender, to generate, to procreate ; to breed, to spawn ; (fig.) to produce, to give rise, to occasion. *Ne pas — la mélancolie ;* to be of a very gay disposition. *Le mauvais air engendre des maladies ;* bad air breeds diseases. *La familiarité engendre le mépris ;* familiarity begets contempt.

s'**engendrer**, *v.r.*, to be bred, engendered ; to breed, to be produced, generated.

engeoler, *v.a. V.* **enjôler**.

engeoleur, *n.m. V.* **enjôleur**.

engerber, *v.a.*, to sheaf, to bind, to heap up.

engin, *n.m.*, machine, engine ; snare, gin, net ; hoist (of a mill).

englober, *v.a.*, to unite ; to put, to throw, together.

engloutir, *v.a.*, to swallow up, to devour ; to ingulf ; to absorb ; to dissipate, to squander away ; to run through.

s'**engloutir**, *v.r.*, to be swallowed up, to be ingulfed.

engloutissement, *n.m.*, ingulfing, swallowing up, sinking.

engloutisseu-r, -se, *n.m.f.* and *adj.*, swallower, devourer ; devouring.

engluer, *v.a.*, to lime, to daub with bird-lime ; (fig.) to take in.

s'**engluer**, *v.r.*, to be caught, to stick in bird-lime ; to be caught, to be taken in (pers.).

engonoé, -e, *adj.*, awkward, ungainly.

engoncement, *n.m.*, awkward appearance.

engoncer, *v.a.*, to cramp, to disfigure, to give an awkward appearance to.

engorgement, *n.m.*, obstruction, stopping up, congestion.

engorger, *v.a.*, to obstruct, to block up, to choke up, to stop up ; (med.) to congest.

s'**engorger**, *v.r.*, to be obstructed, choked up ; (med.) to be congested.

engoué, -e, *adj.*, infatuated with ; wrapped up in ; obstructed, choked.

engouement or **engoûment** (ān-goo-mān), *n.m.*, infatuation ; (med. vet.) obstruction. *On ne saurait le faire revenir de son — ;* it is impossible to cure him of his infatuation.

engouer, *v.a.*, to obstruct the throat ; to infatuate.

s'**engouer**, *v.r.*, to obstruct one's throat ; to be obstructed ; to be infatuated. *S'— d'une femme ;* to be wrapped up in a woman.

engouffrer, *v.a.*, to ingulf, to swallow up.

s'**engouffrer**, *v.r.*, to be ingulfed ; to blow hard ; to rush (of the wind in a narrow passage) ; to run into. *Le vent s'engouffre dans la cheminée ;* the wind rushes into the chimney. *Que de fortunes se sont engouffrées dans cette entreprise !* how many fortunes have been swallowed up in that enterprise !

engoulé, -e, adj., gobbled up; (her.) engoulee.

engouler, v.a., to swallow up, to gobble up.

engoulevent (ān-gool-vān), n.m., (orni.) fern-owl; goat-sucker.

engourdi, -e, adj., torpid, benumbed, dull.

engourdir, v.a., to benumb, to make torpid; to dull, to make languid, to enervate. Le froid engourdit les mains; cold benumbs one's hands. L'oisiveté engourdit l'esprit; idleness benumbs the mind.

s'engourdir, v.r., to get benumbed; to become torpid, enervated, enfeebled.

engourdissement (ān-goor-dis-mān), n.m., numbness, torpor, enervation. Avoir un — au bras; to have a numbness in the arm. Tirer quelqu'un de son —; to rouse any one from his torpor.

engrainer, v.a., to feed with grain; to fill the mill-hopper.

engrais, n.m., rich pasture; fatting; manure, soil. Mettre des bœufs à l'—; to put oxen to fatten.

engraissement (ān-grès-mān), n.m., fattening; corpulence.

engraisser, v.a., to fatten, to cram (poultry); to manure. — des bestiaux; to fatten cattle.

engraisser, v.n., to become corpulent, to fatten; to thrive.

s'engraisser, v.r., to fatten, to grow fat, stout; to grow rich; to grow thick or ropy. S'— des misères publiques; to fatten on public misery.

engranger, v.a., (agri.) to get in, to house, to store.

engravement (ān-grav-mān), n.m., (nav.) stranding.

engraver, v.a., to run aground, to strand; (nav.) to place, to hide, things in the ballast.

engraver, v.n., s'—, v.r., (nav.) to get embedded in the sand.

engrêlé, -e, adj., (of lace) purled; (her.) engrailed.

engrêler, v.a., (her.) to engrail; to purl.

engrêlure, n.f., purl; (her.) engrailing.

engrenage, n.m., gear, gearing (mec.). A —; serrated. Roue d'—; brake-wheel.

engrener, v.a., to put corn (in the mill-hopper); to feed with corn; to throw into gear, to engage (mec.).

s'engrener, v.r., to work into each other (of toothed wheels); to be put in gear. Ces roues s'engrènent bien; these wheels work well into each other.

engrener, v.n., to put corn (into the mill-hopper); to work into each other (of toothed wheels); to begin. Il a bien engrené; he has begun well.

engrenure, n.f., toothing, cogging.

engrosser, v.a., (l.ex.) to make pregnant, to get with child. v.n., to be with child.

s'engrumeler, v.r., to clot, to coagulate.

***enguenillé, -e** (ăng-), part., tattered.

***enguenillier,** v.a., to clothe in tatters.

***s'enguenillier,** v.r., to be clothed in tatters.

enhardir, v.a., to embolden, to encourage. Ce succès l'avait enhardi; that success had emboldened him.

s'enhardir, v.r., to make bold, to grow bold. Il s'est enhardi à parler en public; he made bold to speak in public.

enharmonique, adj., (mus.) enharmonic.

enharnachement, n.m., harnessing, trappings.

enharnacher, v.a., to harness; to rig out, to deck out, to accoutre. Vous voilà plaisamment enharnaché; you are oddly accoutred.

enherber, v.a., to turn into pasture land.

énieller, v.a., to clear of corn-cockles.

énigmatique, adj., enigmatical.

énigmatiquement (-tik-mān), adv., enigmatically.

énigme, n.f., enigma, riddle. Deviner une —; to guess a riddle. Vous parlez par —s; you speak in riddles. Proposer une —; to put a riddle. Mot d'une —; answer to a riddle.

enivrant, -e, adj., intoxicating.

enivré, -e, part., intoxicated.

enivrement, n.m., intoxication.

enivrer, v.a., to inebriate, to intoxicate; to elate. La bière enivre comme le vin; beer intoxicates as well as wine. La prospérité nous enivre; prosperity elates us.

s'enivrer, v.r., to get intoxicated; to be elated (with). Il s'est enivré à ce repas; he got intoxicated at that dinner. S'— d'espérance; to be elated with hope. S'— de son vin; to drink alone and to excess; to have too good an opinion of one's self.

enjabler, v.a., to bottom or head (a cask).

enjaler, v.a., (nav.) to stock (an anchor).

enjambée, n.f., stride. Faire de grandes —s, to take long strides.

enjambement (ān-jān-bmān), n.m., (poet.) running of the sense into the next line; over-lapping; encroaching.

enjamber, v.n., to stride; to project, to encroach upon; (poet.) to overlap, to encroach.

enjamber, v.a., to stride over, to skip or leap over.

enjaveler, v.a., (agri.) to sheaf.

enjeu, n.m., stake (at play). Retirer son —; to withdraw one's stake; to declare off.

enjoindre, v.a., to enjoin, to charge, to direct, to command, to prescribe. Dieu nous enjoint d'observer ses lois; God commands us to observe his laws. Il lui est enjoint de; he is directed to.

enjôlement, n.m., wheedling, coaxing, inveigling.

enjôler, v.a., to coax, to wheedle, to inveigle.

enjôleu-r, n.m., -se, n.f., wheedler, coaxer.

enjolivement (-liv-mān), n.m., embellishment, decoration, ornament, set-off, flourish.

enjoliver, v.a., to embellish, to adorn, to set off, to ornament, to beautify.

enjoliveur, n.m., (b.s.) embellisher.

enjolivure, n.f., set-off, ornament, embellishment.

enjoué, -e, adj., playful, sprightly; lively, sportive. Il a l'humeur —e; he is of a playful disposition. Il écrit d'un style —; he writes in a sportive style.

enjouement or **enjoûment** (ān-joo-mān), n.m., playfulness, sportiveness, sprightliness, liveliness, humor. Avec —; playfully.

enkysté, -e, adj., (med.) encysted.

s'enkyster, v.r., to become encysted.

enlacement (ān-las-mān), n.m., lacing, entwining; interweaving, entanglement.

enlacer, v.a., to lace; to entwine; to twist; to interlace; to clasp; to interweave. — quelqu'un dans ses bras; to clasp in one's arms.

s'enlacer, v.r., to entwine; to twist; to be interlaced.

enlaidir, v.a., to make ugly, to disfigure.

enlaidir, v.n., to grow ugly, to be disfigured.

enlaidissement (-dis-mān), n.m., ugliness; disfigurement.

enlèvement (ān-lèv-mān), n.m., carrying off; removal; carrying off forcibly, kidnaping; abduction; translation (to heaven); buying up, monopoly. L'— des Sabines; the rape of the Sabines.

enlever, v.a., to lift, to raise; to carry, to carry off; to carry away; to rescue; to pick out; to carry away forcibly, to kidnap; to take off, to clear away, to remove; to sweep off; to charm, to delight, to burn (the mouth). On lui a enlevé sa femme; his wife has been carried off. On lui *a enlevé ses meubles ;* his furniture has been removed. *Enlevez cela de dessus la table ;* take that off the ___ble. — *une place ;* (milit.) to carry a town. — *la peau ;* to flay the skin. *La mort l'a enlevé à la fleur de son âge ;* death carried him off in his prime. — *des taches ;* to take out stains. — *tous les prix ;* to carry off all the prizes. *Cela enlève la bouche ;* that burns the mouth. *Enlevé !* carried ! done ! *Se faire — par ;* to elope with.

s'**enlever**, v.r., to rise, to be lifted; to come off, to peel off; to come out; to go off (of goods on sale); to get into a passion.

enleveur, n.m., kidnaper, abductor, ravisher.

enlier, v.a., (mas.) to bond, to bind (stones).

enlisement, n.m., ingulfing, swallowing up (in sand).

s'**enliser**, v.r., to be ingulfed, swallowed up.

enluminer, v.a., to color, to illuminate, to flush (the complexion); (lit.) to overload with ornaments. *Visage enluminé ;* flushed or red face.

s'**enluminer**, v.r., to rouge, to paint. *S'— la trogne* (triv.); to get a red nose (from drinking).

enlumineu-r, n.m., **-se**, n.f., map or print colorer; illuminator.

enluminure, n.f., coloring; colored print; tinsel.

ennéagone (è-n-né-), n.m., (geom.) enneagon.

ennéagonal, adj., nonagon, enneagonal.

ennéandrie (è-n-né-), n.f., (bot.) enneandria.

ennemi, n.m., **-e**, n.f., (è-n-mi) enemy, foe; thing prejudicial. — *déclaré ;* open or avowed enemy. *C'est autant de pris sur l'— ;* it is so much gained from the enemy. *Il n'y a pas de petit — ;* every enemy is to be feared.

ennemi, **-e**, adj., hostile, inimical; injurious; adverse, contrary, hurtful, prejudicial; (paint.) unfriendly. *La fortune — e ;* adverse fortune. *L'armée — e ;* the enemy.

ennoblir, v.a., to ennoble, to dignify, to exalt.

s'**ennoblir**, v.r., to be ennobled, exalted. *S'— de ;* to be proud of, to rejoice at.

ennui, n.m., tediousness, weariness; tedium, spleen, vexation, boredom; tiresome thing; nuisance. *Quel — !* what a nuisance !

ennuyant, **-e**, adj., annoying, tedious, irksome, tiresome. *Cela est fort — ;* that is very tiresome. *Temps — ;* trying weather.

ennuyer, v.a., to tire, to weary, to be tiresome, to be tedious, to tease, to annoy, to bother, to vex, to bore. *Cela m'ennuie ;* that annoys me. *Cela m'ennuie à la mort ;* that bores me to death.

s'**ennuyer**, v.r., to be wearied, to have a bad time of it, to tire one's self, to feel dull, to be bored. *Il s'ennuie de tout ;* he wearies of everything.

ennuyeusement (ăn-nui-ieŭz-măn), adv., tediously, irksomely.

ennuyeu-x, **-se**, n. and adj., tiresome person, bore; tedious, wearisome, dull, tiresome; annoying, provoking, vexing. *Livre — ;* dull, tedious book.

énoncé, n.m., statement; (geom.) enunciation, assertion, declaration, terms.

énoncer, v.a., to state, to express, to declare, to utter, to word, to enunciate.

s'**énoncer**, v.r., to express one's self; to be expressed. *Il s'énonce bien ;* he expresses himself well. *Il n'a pas le don de s'— ;* he has not the gift of expressing himself clearly.

énonciati-f, **-ve**, adj., enunciative, enunciatory.

énonciation, n.f., enunciation, delivery, utterance; statement; expression, wording.

***enorgueillir** (ăn-nor-ghĕ-yir), v.a., to make proud, to elevate, to puff up.

*s'**enorgueillir** (ăn-nor-ghĕ-yir), v.r., to grow proud of, to be puffed up, to become elated, to glory in, to pride one's self upon.

énorme, adj., enormous, huge, atrocious, heinous. *Crime — ;* heinous crime.

énormément, adv., enormously, hugely, immensely, beyond measure.

énormité, n.f., enormousness, hugeness, vastness; enormity, atrocity, heinousness.

énouage, n.m., burling, picking.

énouer, v.a., to pick cloth; to burl.

⊙**enquérant**, **-e**, adj., inquisitive, prying.

s'**enquérir** (s'enquérant, enquis), v.r., to inquire, to ask, to make inquiries. *Il faut s'— de la vérité du fait ;* we must inquire into the truth of the matter.

enquête, n.f., inquiry, inquest; investigation, examination, commission. — *en matière criminelle ;* criminal investigation. *Ordonner une — ;* to direct an inquiry to be made ; to appoint a commission of inquiry.

⊙s'**enquêter**, v.r., to inquire, to care for.

enraciné, **-e**, adj., rooted, inveterate, deep seated.

enraciner, v.a., to root, to implant. *Des préjugés enracinés ;* inveterate prejudices.

s'**enraciner**, v.r., to take root, to become rooted. *Il ne faut pas laisser s'— les maux ;* evils must not be allowed to take root.

enragé, **-e**, part., mad, rabid, desperate, raging, enraged ; obstinate, determined. *Manger de la vache — ;* to know hard times; to undergo great hardships. *Un chien — ;* a mad dog.

enragé, n.m., madman.

enrageant, **-e** (-jăn, -t), adj., vexing, maddening.

enrager, v.n., to be mad, to run mad, to go mad, to be enraged, to fume; to stamp with rage. *Faire — ;* to madden. — *contre quelqu'un ;* to be enraged against any one. *Il n'enrage pas pour mentir ;* he makes light of telling lies.

enraiement or **enrayement**, n.m., putting on the drag, skidding ; locking.

enrayer, v.a., to put spokes to ; to skid (a wheel), to put on the drag; to apply the brake; (agri.) to plow the first furrow ; (fig.) to stop; to keep down, to moderate, to stem.

enrayer, v.n., to put on the drag, to skid (of a wheel); (fig.) to keep down, to moderate, to check.

enrayure, n.f., drag, skid ; lock-chain.

enrégimenter, v.a., to embody, to form into regiments; to enroll.

enregistrable, adj., registrable.

enregistré, **-e**, adj., registered, recorded.

enregistrement, n.m., registering, registry, entry, enrollment. *Faire l'— ;* to register.

enregistrer, v.a., to register, to enter in a register, to enroll, to record.

enregistreur, n.m., registrar.

enrêner, v.a., to rein in, to tie by the reins.

enrênoire, n.f., peg for tying reins.

enrhumer, v.a., to give a cold to any one. *Je suis enrhumé ;* I have a cold. *Être enrhumé du cerveau ;* to have a cold in the head.

s'**enrhumer**, v.r., to catch cold.

enrichi, n.m., **-e**, n.f., upstart.

enrichir, v.a., to enrich, to make rich; to adorn, to embellish; to store. — *son esprit ;* to enrich one's mind.

s'**enrichir**, v.r., to enrich one's self with, to grow rich, to thrive; to be stored. *S'— des dépouilles d'autrui ;* to thrive on the spoils of others.

enrichissement (-shis-măn), n.m., enriching, embellishment, adornment.

enrôlement (ăn-rôl-măn), n.m., enlisting, enlistment, enrollment.

enrôler, v.a., to enlist, to enroll.

s'**enrôler**, v.r., to enroll one's self, to enlist.

enroué, **-e**, adj., hoarse, husky.

enrouement or **enroûment** (ăn-roo-măn), n.m., hoarseness, huskiness.

enrouer, *v.a.*, to make hoarse.

s'enrouer, *v.r.*, to become, to get, hoarse, husky.

*****enrouiller**, *v.a.*, to rust, to make rusty. *L'humidité enrouille le fer ;* damp rusts iron.

s'enrouiller, *v.r.*, to grow, to get rusty.

enroulement (ăn-rool-măn), *n.m.*, rolling up; (arch.) scroll.

enrouler, *v.a.*, to roll, to roll up, to twist, to coil.

s'enrouler, *v.r.*, to roll one's self up ; to roll up; to twist round.

enrubanner, *v.a.*, to deck out with ribbons.

s'enrubanner, *v.r.*, to deck one's self out with ribbons ; to adorn one's self too much.

enrue, *n.f.*, large furrow.

ensablement, *n.m.*, sand-bank ; ballasting.

ensabler, *v.a.*, to run aground, to strand ; to cover with sand ; to ballast.

s'ensabler, *v.r.*, to run aground ; to sink in sand ; to be blocked up with sand.

ensacher, *v.a.*, to bag.

ensaisinement, *n.m.*, (feudal law) acknowledging a purchaser of land as a tenant.

ensaisiner, *v.a.*, to put in possession of property; (feudal law) to acknowledge a purchaser ol land as a tenant. [with blood.

ensanglanter, *v.a.*, to make bloody, to stain

enseignable, *adj.*, teachable.

*****enseignant**, -e, *adj.*, teaching. *Corps* — ; university ; body of teachers ; staff.

*****enseigne**, *n.f.*, mark, sign, sign-board ; ensign (flag) ; ⊙ensigncy ; streamer (flag). *n.m.*, ensign (officer), standard-bearer. — *de vaisseau ;* sub-lieutenant. *A bonnes* —*s ;* deservedly ; on sure grounds. *Etre logé à même* — ; to be in the same predicament. *A telles* —*s que ;* so much so that ; as proof. *A bon vin point d'* — ; good wine needs no bush.

*****enseignement** (ăn-sègn-măn), *n.m.*, pre-cept, instruction, teaching, teaching profession; tuition ; lesson. ⊙*pl.*, (jur.) proof. *Il est dans l'*— ; he is a teacher, a master.

*****enseigner**, *v.a.*, to teach, to teach how to, to instruct ; to show, to inform, to direct to. *En-seignez-nous le chemin ;* show us the way. *En-seignez-nous la maison ;* direct us to the house.

ensellé, -e, *adj.*, saddle-backed.

ensemble, *adv.*, together, conjointly, at the same time. *Mêler* — ; to mix together. *Ils ne sont pas bien* — ; they are not friends.

ensemble, *n.m.*, whole, general effect ; mass ; uniformity ; harmony. *Tout cela forme un assez bel* — ; all that forms a respectable whole. *Morceau d'* — ; a concerted piece of music ; part music. *Le tout* — ; the whole, the general effect. *Mouvement d'* — ; combined movement.

ensemencement (ăns-măns-măn), *n. m.*, (agri.) sowing.

ensemencer, *v.a.*, to sow. *S'* — ; to be sowed.

enserrer, *v.a.*, ⊙ to contain, to inclose; to lock up; to encompass, to hem in ; (gard.) to put into a greenhouse.

ensevelir (ăn-sĕ-vlir), *v.a.*, to shroud, to put in a shroud ; to bury ; to swallow up, to entomb, to ingulf ; to engross ; to absorb. — *les morts ;* to bury the dead. *Etre enseveli dans le chagrin ;* to be absorbed in grief.

s'ensevelir, *v.r.*, to be buried ; to bury one's self.

ensevelissement (ăn-sĕ-vlis-măn), *n.m.*, put-ting in a shroud ; burying, burial.

ensevelisseu-r, *n.m.*, -**se**, *n.f.*, layer-out.

ensiforme, *adj.*, ensiform, sword-shaped.

ensoleillé, -e, *adj.*, sunny, bathed in sunshine.

ensorceler, *v.a.*, to bewitch. *Cette femme l'a ensorcelé ;* that woman has bewitched him.

ensorceleu-r, *n.m.*, -**se**, *n.f.*, bewitcher. *adj.*, bewitching.

ensorcellement (-sèl-măn), *n.m.*, bewitch-ment.

ensoufrer, *v.a.*, to dip in brimstone.

ensuite, *adv.*, after, afterwards, then; in the next place; what then ? what next ? what of that ! well ! *Vous irez là* —; you will go there afterwards. — *il me dit;* then he told me. *Et* —? what then?

ensuite, *prep.*, after (old). — *de cela;* after that. — *de quoi;* after which.

⊙**ensuivant**, *adj.*, following. *V.* **suivant**.

s'ensuivre, *v.r.*, to follow, to result, to ensue, to spring, to proceed. *Il s'ensuit que vous avez tort;* it follows that you are in the wrong. *Il ne s'ensuit pas que j'aie tort;* it does not follow that I am wrong. *De grands malheurs s'ensuivirent;* great misfortunes resulted from it. [This verb is only used in the third person, singular and plural.]

entablement, *n.m.*, (arch.) entablature; en-tablement; tablet.

s'entabler, *v.r.*, (man.) to entable.

entacher, *v.a.*, to taint, to infect; to sully, to tarnish.

*****entaille**, *n.f.*, notch, gash; (carp.) mortise ; groove.

*****entailler**, *v.a.*, to notch; to cut away.

*****entaillure**, *n.f.*, notch.

entame, *n.f.*, first cut, first *or* outside slice (of a loaf).

entamer, *v.a.*, to make an incision, to cut, to make the first cut; to broach, to begin; to break into ; (milit.) to break through; (b.s.) to encroach upon; (b.s.) to impair; to injure; to prevail upon. — *la peau;* to cut the skin. — *un pain;* to begin a loaf. — *d'un coup de dent,* to bite into. — *une matière, un sujet;* to begin, to broach a subject. — *la réputation de quelqu'un ;* to injure any one's reputation.

entamure, *n.f.*, cut; first cut; incision; graz-ing; opening, beginning.

entassement (ăn-tăs-măn), *n.m.*, heap, accu-mulation, pile; crowding.

entasser, *v.a.*, to heap, to heap up, to pile up; to hoard, to hoard up; to accumulate ; to cram; to huddle, to pack together. — *des écus;* to hoard up money. *Personne entassée;* thick-set person.

entasseur, *n.m.*, hoarder, heaper.

ente, *n.f.*, graft, block, tree bearing a graft ; (paint.) handle (of a brush).

entement, *n.m.*, grafting; joining.

entendement (ăn-tand-măn), *n.m.*, under-standing; judgment, head, sense.

entendeur, *n.m.*, hearer, understander. *A bon* — *demi-mot suffit* or *a bon* — *salut ;* a word to the wise is sufficient.

entendre, *v.a.*, to hear ; to understand ; to know; to expect, to require, to intend; to mean, to think proper. *A vous* — ; according to you. *J'ai entendu dire ;* I heard some people say. *Il n'est pire sourd que celui qui ne veut pas* — ; none so deaf as those who won't hear. — *les témoins ;* to hear the witnesses. *Il entend un peu l'anglais ;* he understands English a little. — *mal ;* to misunderstand. *Entendons-nous ;* let us come to a right understanding. — *à demi-mot ;* to take the hint. *Donner à* — ; to intimate, to hint. *Ne pas* — *malice ;* to mean no harm. *Il a fait allusion à votre disgrâce, mais sans y* — *malice ;* he alluded to your mis-hap, but he did not mean any harm. — *raison ;* to listen to reason. — *raillerie ;* to take a joke. *Il n'entend pas raillerie ;* he cannot take a joke. *Il n'entend pas la raillerie ;* he is no hand at jokes. — *la messe,* — *les vêpres ;* to attend mass, vespers. *Il entend bien son métier ;* he knows his trade very well. *Cet homme n'entend rien aux affaires ;* that man knows nothing about business. *Qu'entendez-vous par là ?* what do you mean by that ? *Chacun fait comme il l'en-tend ;* everybody does as he thinks proper.

s'**entendre**, v.r., to hear one another; to understand one another; to be heard; to be understood; to act in concert with, to have a secret understanding with; to come to an arrangement with; to come to terms with; to agree with, to be on good terms with; to be skillful in; to be a judge of. *Le bruit est si grand qu'on ne s'entend pas;* there is so much noise that we cannot hear one another speak. *Le canon de Waterloo s'entendait à dix lieues du champ de bataille;* the cannon of Waterloo were heard at a distance of ten leagues from the field of battle. *On l'accuse de s'— avec l'ennemi;* he is accused of acting in concert with the enemy. *S'— à une chose;* to be skillful in a thing. *Il ne s'entend pas mal à cela;* he is pretty well up in that. *S'— en une chose;* to understand how to do a thing. *Il s'entend en musique;* he understands music. *Je m'entends bien;* I know very well what I mean. *Ils s'entendent pour me nuire;* they have laid their heads together to injure me. *Ils s'entendent comme larrons en foire;* they are as thick as thieves. *Cela s'entend* or *cela s'entend bien;* let it be understood; of course, as a matter of course, to be sure.

entendre, v.n., to hear, to hear of; to approve of, to consent to; to listen to. — *dur;* — *de corne;* to be hard of hearing; to misunderstand. — *clair;* to be quick of hearing. *Ne savoir auquel —;* not to know whom to listen to, to which to attend to first. *Il n'entend pas de cette oreille-là;* he is deaf on that side, or he does not see it in that light. *J'entends que vous restiez avec moi;* I expect you to remain with me.

entendu, -e, adj., heard; understood; agreed; arranged; managed; intelligent, skillful. *Un homme bien — aux affaires;* a man well up in business matters. *Faire l'—;* to put on a knowing look. — *!* all right, agreed. *C'est —;* that's a bargain, that's settled.

enténébrer, v.a., to involve in darkness; to wrap in darkness, in night.

entente, n.f., meaning; skill, judgment, understanding, agreement; harmony. *Mots à double —;* ambiguous words, with a double meaning. *L'— est au diseur;* everybody understands his own meaning best. *L'— du coloris;* skill in coloring.

enter, v.a., to graft, to ingraft. — *de nouveau;* to regraft. — *en écusson;* to bud, to ineye.

entérinement (-ri-n-mān), n.m., judicial ratification, confirmation.

entériner, v.a., to ratify, to confirm.

entérique, adj., (med.) enteric.

entérite, n.f., (med.) enteritis.

enterrement (ān-tèr-mān), n. m., burial, funeral, interment. *Billet d'—;* invitation to a funeral. *Etre prié à un —;* to be invited to a funeral.

enterrer, v.a., to bury, to inter, to inhume; to survive, to eclipse, to surpass; to end, to terminate; to sink (of money). — *son secret;* to bury one's secret. *Molière a enterré tous ses devanciers;* Molière threw all his predecessors into the shade. — *la synagogue avec honneur;* to terminate an affair with honor.

s'**enterrer,** v.r., to bury one's self; to see no company (or to go with his head to the ground (of a horse).

enterreur, n.m., burier; (zool.) sexton-beetle.

en-tête, n.m., (— -s) heading; head; headline. — *de facture;* bill-head.

entêté, -e, n.m.f. and adj., stubborn person; obstinate, wayward, self-willed, stubborn; infatuated. — *comme un âne;* as stubborn as a mule. *Il est — de cette femme;* he is infatuated with that woman.

entêtement (ān-tê-tmān), n.m., stubbornness,

waywardness; obstinacy; infatuation. *Son — le perdra;* his stubbornness will be his ruin.

entêter, v.a., to affect the head, to make giddy, to intoxicate; to prepossess, to infatuate, to render vain; to head (pins). *Vin qui entête;* heady wine. *Les louanges nous entêtent;* praises are apt to make us conceited.

s'**entêter,** v.r., to become stubborn, wayward, obstinate; to be infatuated with, to take a strong fancy to, to be bent upon; to do a thing at any price.

entêteu-r, n.m., **-se,** n.f., header (of pins).

enthousiasme, n.m., enthusiasm, rapture, ecstasy.

enthousiasmer, v.a., to enrapture, to render enthusiastic. *Il est enthousiasmé de cette musique;* he is in raptures with that music.

s'**enthousiasmer,** v.r., to become enthusiastic; to be in raptures.

enthousiaste, n.m.f., enthusiast.

enthousiaste, adj., enthusiastic.

enthymème, n.m., (log.) enthymeme.

entiché, -e, part., (l.u.) infected (fruit); tainted, marred; infatuated with, wedded to; overfond of, overpartial to. *Fruit —;* spoiled fruit.

enticher, v.a., to taint, to infect; to infatuate. *Vous l'avez entiché de ce système;* you have infatuated him with that system.

s'**enticher,** v.r., to become infected; infatuated with; wedded to. *Il s'est entiché de cette femme;* that woman has bewitched him.

enti-er, -ère (-tié, -tiè-r), adj., entire, whole, complete, total; obstinate, positive, self-willed; (arith.) integral. *Une —e soumission;* complete submission. *Cheval —;* stone-horse, stallion, entire horse. *Pain —;* whole loaf. *Nombre —;* (arith.) integer. *Il est très —;* he is very self-willed or obstinate.

entier (-tié), n.m., entireness; (arith.) integral. *En son —;* at full length; in full, bodily, wholly.

entièrement (ān-tièr-mān), adv., entirely, wholly. — *ruiné;* utterly ruined.

entité, n.f., (philos.) entity.

entoilage, n.m., F. ing; pasting or mounting on canvas.

entoiler, v.a., to line; to mount upon canvas.

entoir, n.m., (hort.) grafting-knife.

entomologie, n.f., entomology.

entomologique, adj., entomological.

entomologiste, n.m., entomologist.

entonnem t (ān-to-n-mān), n.m., tunning, barreling, casking.

s'**entonner,** v.r., (of the wind) to rush into, to blow down. *Le vent s'entonne dans la cheminée;* the wind blows down the chimney.

entonner, v.a., to tun, to barrel, to put into casks (mus.) to begin to sing; to intonate, to strik up; to celebrate, to quaff. *Il entonne bien;* (pop.) he drinks hard. — *une chanson à boire;* to strike up a drinking song.

entonnerie n-to-n-rî), n.f., place where beer is barreled.

entonnoir, n.m., funnel; (anat.) funnel. *Fleurs en —;* funnel-shaped flowers; (fig. and pop.) tippler, hard-drinker, toper.

entorse, n.f., sprain; strain, twist, shock. *Il s'est donné une — au pied;* he has sprained his foot.

***entortillage,** n.m., entanglement, intricacy, obscurity; subterfuge; circumlocution, equivocation; involved or obscure discourse.

***entortillé, -e,** part., twined, wound about; twisted; (of style) involved, obscure.

***entortillement,** n.m., winding, twining, twisting, entanglement; intricacy, obscurity. *L'— d'un serpent;* the twisting of a serpent.

***entortiller,** v.a., to wrap, to roll round, to wind, to coil; to twist, to distort; to get round.

to get the better of. *Laissez-moi tranquille, vous m'entortillez;* (pop.) leave me alone, you bother me.

s'entortiller, *v.r.,* to twist round, to wind round; to twine.

entour, *n.m.,* [always employed in the plural, save in the adverbial expression : *A l'*— ; around]. —*s;* environs, adjacent parts ; persons around one. *Prendre les —s;* to gain over to one's interest the persons around any one.

entourage, *n.m.,* frame ; setting, mounting, (of jewelry) : confidants, advisers, friends, servants, relations, circle, attendants.

entourer, *v. a.,* to inclose, to surround, to encompass ; to hem round. — *une ville de murailles;* to encompass a town with walls. *Entouré de terre;* land-locked. — *quelqu'un de soins;* to lavish attentions upon any one.

entournure, *n.f.,* arm-hole ; sloping (of sleeves).

en-tout-cas, *n.m.,* (—) sun-shade.

s'entr'accorder, *v.r.,* to agree together.

s'entr'accuser, *v.r.,* to accuse one another.

entr'acte, *n. m.,* (— — —s) (thea.) interval (between the acts); interlude, intermede. *Dans l'*—; between the acts. *Faire de longs —s;* to have long intervals, waits.

s'entr'admirer, *v.r.,* to admire one another.

s'entr'aider, *v.r.,* to help, to aid, one another.

*entrailles, *n.f. pl.,* entrails, bowels, intestines, inward parts ; feelings, tenderness, heart; pity. *Elle a pour moi des — de mère;* she has a motherly affection for me. *Cet acteur a des —s;* this actor has feeling.

s'entr'aimer, *v.r.,* to love one another.

entrain, *n.m.,* warmth ; heartiness ; spirit, spirits ; animation ; life ; go.

entraînant, -e, *adj.,* that carries away, captivating, inspiriting, seductive. *Un style* —; a captivating style. *Eloquence —e;* winning eloquence.

entrainement (ān-trè-n-mān), *n.m.,* impulse, sway, prevalence ; rapture, enthusiasm ; temptation, allurement ; training (of horses for races).

entraîner, *v.a.,* to carry away, to sweep off ; to hurry away, to hurry along; to draw, to drag after, to bring, to win, to gain, over; to drag away, along; to entail, to involve; to train (race-horses). — *les cœurs ;* to win all hearts. — *quelqu'un dans l'erreur ;* to lead any one into error. *La guerre entraîne après elle bien des maux ;* war drags after it many evils.

entraîneur, *n.m.,* horse-trainer.

entrait, *n.m.,* (carp.) tie-beam.

entrant, -e, *adj.,* ingoing, incoming, insinuating ; entering office. *Les conseillers —s ;* the newly appointed councilors.

entrant, *n.,* person coming in. *Les —s et les sortants ;* the outgoers and incomers.

s'entr'appeler, *v.r.,* to call one another.

entrave, *n.f.,* clog, hindrance, obstacle, impediment, shackle, fetter. *pl.,* horse-lock; trammels, fetters.

entraver, *v.a.,* to shackle, to clog ; to fetter, to trammel ; to hinder, to impede, to thwart. — *un cheval ;* to shackle a horse.

entravon, *n.m.,* cutting-boot (on a horse's fetlock).

s'entr'avertir, *v.r.,* to give one another notice, to warn one another.

entre, *prep.,* between, betwixt ; among, amongst, with ; in, of, into. — *le ciel et la terre;* between heaven and earth. *Regarder quelqu'un — les deux yeux ;* to stare at any one. — *chien et loup ;* between lights, at dusk. *Ils résolurent — eux;* they resolved among themselves. — *autres ;* among others. *Je le mettrai — vos mains ;* I will deliver it into your hands. *Cela soit dit — nous;* that is between ourselves.

*entre-bâillé, -e, *adj.,* ajar, half open.

entre-bâillement, *n.m.,* part-opening.

*entre-bâiller, *v.a.,* to half open.

s'entre-baiser, *v.r.,* to kiss one another.

s'entre-battre, *v.r.,* to beat one another, to fight together.

s'entre-blesser, *v.r.,* to wound one another.

entrechat, *n.m.,* (dancing) caper, entrechat.

s'entre-chercher, *v.r.,* to seek one another, to look for one another.

entrechoquement, *n.m.,* clash ; clashing; conflict.

s'entre-choquer, *v.r.,* to knock, to clash, to beat, to dash, against one another ; to interfere, to thwart each other.

s'entre-clore, *v.r.,* to half-close.

entre-colonne, *n.f.,* (— —s) or **entre-colonnement,** *n.m.,* (— — —s) (arch.) intercolumniation.

s'entre-connaître, *v.r.,* to know each other.

entrecôte, *n.m.,* (cook.) piece off the ribs.

s'entrecouder, *v.r.,* to elbow one another.

entre-coupe, *n.f.,* (— — —s), (arch.) turning-space.

entrecoupement, *n.m.,* intersection ; cutting ; crossing ; faltering.

entrecoupé, -e, *part.,* broken (of words).

entrecouper, *v.a.,* to traverse, to cross, to intersect ; to stop, to interrupt, to break off.

s'entrecouper, *v.r.,* to cut *or* cross one another ; to interrupt one another; to intersect; (vet.) to hit *or* chafe one leg against the other.

entrecroisement, *n.m.,* intersection, crossing.

s'entre-croiser, *v.r.,* to cross one another, to intersect.

s'entre-déchirer, *v.r.,* to tear one another to pieces.

s'entre-défaire, *v.r.,* to defeat one another.

s'entre-détruire, *v.r.,* to destroy one another.

entre-deux, *n.m.,* (—) intermediate space ; partition ; cut ; (cook.) middle pier-piece (of a cod) ; insertion (lace) ; (nav.) trough of the sea.

entre-deux, *adv.,* (l.u.) betwixt and between.

s'entre-dévorer, *v.r.,* to devour one another ; to ruin one another.

s'entre-dire, *v.r.,* to tell one another. *S'— des injures ;* to call one another names.

s'entre-donner, *v.r.,* to give one another.

entrée, *n.f.,* entry, entrance ; mouth ; entering, coming in; reception ; beginning ; introduction, inlet ; (cook.) first-course, side-dish; admission-money, entrance-money ; custom-duty ; entrée (dancing). *L'— d'un port;* the mouth of a harbor. — *et sortie d'un acteur ;* entrance and exit of an actor. *Avoir ses —s ;* to have free admission *or* access to, to be on the free-list of a theatre. *Droit d'*— ; custom-duty. *Payer l'*—; to pay a town-due ; (custom-house) to pay duty. *Tuyau d'*—; (tech.) inlet-pipe. ⊙*D'*—; at first, at the first.

s'entre-fâcher, *v.r.,* to anger one another.

entrefaites, *n.f. pl.,* interval, meantime. *Dans ces* —, *Sur ces* —; meanwhile.

entre-filet, *n.m.,* a short paragraph, note.

s'entre-fouetter, *v.r.,* to whip *or* lash one another.

s'entre-frapper, *v.r.,* to strike one another.

entregent, *n.m.,* (fam.) shrewdness, address, tact. *Cet homme fera son chemin, il a de l'*—; that man will get on, he possesses tact.

s'entr'égorger, *v.r.,* to cut each other's throat ; to kill one another.

s'entre-haïr, *v.r.,* to hate each other.

s'entre-heurter, *v.r.,* to knock *or* beat one against the other.

entre-jambes, fork ; knee-hole.

entrelacement (-las-mān), *n.m.,* interweaving, wreathing, blending, intertwining.

entrelacer, *v.a.,* to interlace, to intertwine, to interweave, to wreathe, to weave, to braid; to plash; to wattle. *Des branches entrelacées;* interwoven branches.

s'entrelacer, *v.r.,* to entwine, to twist, to wreathe.

entrelacs (-lâ), *n.m.,* ciphers; flourishes; interlaced ornaments; (arch., paint.) twine.

entrelardé, -e, *part.,* interlarded, streaky.

entrelarder, *v. a.,* to interlard; to insert between.

entre-large, *adj.,* (com.) of middle width.

***entre-ligne,** *n.m.,* (— — —s) space between lines, interlineation; (print.) space-line, lead.

s'entre-louer, *v.r.,* to praise one another, to laud one another.

entre-luire, *v.n.,* to glimmer.

s'entremanger, *v.r.,* to eat one another.

entremêlement, *n.m.,* intermixing; intermixture.

entremêler, *v.a.,* to intermingle, to intermix.

s'entremêler, *v.r.,* to intermingle, to intermix; to meddle. *Des nuances qui s'entremêlent;* shades (of color) which are blended together.

s'entre-mesurer, *v.r.,* to measure each other.

entremets (-mè), *n. m.,* (cook.) side - dish, entremets.

entremetteu-r, *n.m.,* **-se,** *n.f.,* go-between, manager, mediator; procurer; procuress.

s'entremettre, *v.r.,* to interpose, to interfere, to intermeddle, to meddle.

entremise, *n.f.,* interposition, mediation, intervention, interference, mediation, agency; (nav.) carling. *Par l'— de la presse;* through the medium of the press. *Par son —;* thanks to him.

s'entre-mordre, *v.r.,* to bite one another.

s'entr'empêcher, *v.r.,* to hinder, to thwart, one another.

entre-nœud, *n.m.,* (— — —s) (bot.) internode.

entrenouer, *v.a.,* to interknot.

s'entre-nuire, *v. r.,* to hurt one another, to injure each other.

s'entre-pardonner, *v.r.,* to pardon one another.

s'entre-parler, *v.r.,* to speak to one another, to talk together.

entrepas, *n.m.,* (man.) amble, ambling pace.

s'entre-percer, *v.r.,* to run each other through, to pierce each other.

***s'entre-piller,** *v.r.,* to plunder one another.

***entre-pointillé, -e,** *adj.,* (engr.) composed of line and dotted engraving.

entrepont, *n.m.,* (nav.) between decks, orlop deck. *Dans les —;* between decks.

entreposage, *n.m.,* bonding, warehousing.

entreposer, *v.a.,* to bond, to put in bond; to store, to warehouse.

entreposeur, *n.m.,* bonded-warehouse-keeper; warehouse-keeper.

entrepositaire, *n.m.,* bonder.

entrepôt, *n.m.,* mart, free port, emporium; bond; bonded warehouse; store. *— fictif;* town warehouse. *— réel;* king's warehouse, queen's warehouse, bonded warehouse. *Mutation d'—;* removal to another warehouse; removal of bonded goods. *Port à l'—;* bonded port; warehousing port. *En —;* in bond. *Faire une mutation d'—;* to remove goods to another warehouse. *Mettre en —;* to bond. *Réintégrer dans l'—;* to rewarehouse.

s'entre-pousser, *v.r.,* to push each other.

entreprenable, *adj.,* undertakable.

entreprenant, -e *adj.,* enterprising, adventurous, venturesome; daring, bold, pushing, encroaching.

entreprendre, *v.a.,* to undertake, to attempt, to take in hand, to take upon one's self; to contract for, to contract to; to adventure, to offer, to venture; to trouble. *— quelqu'un;* to set on any one, to fall foul of any one to banter or jeer any one.

entreprendre, *v.n.,* to encroach on, to infringe upon; to undertake.

entrepreneur, *n.m.,* master - builder; contractor. *— de diligences;* coach proprietor. *— de maçonnerie;* master-mason. *— de pompes funèbres;* undertaker.

entrepreneuse, *n.f.,* maker.

entrepris, -e, *adj.,* crippled, impotent; disconcerted. *Il est — d'un bras;* he has lost the use of an arm.

entreprise, *n.f.,* enterprise, undertaking, attempt, venture; usurpation, violence; contract; (com.) concern, establishment, com.any. *A —;* by contract. *Par —;* by contract. *Ouvrage à l'—;* work by contract. *— par masse de travaux;* contract by the lump. *Il échoue dans ses —s;* he fails in his undertakings. *— générale des messageries;* general coach and conveyance office. *Tenter l'—;* to make the attempt.

s'entre-produire, *v.r.,* to produce each other.

s'entre-quereller, *v.r.,* to quarrel with each other.

entrer, *v.n.,* to enter, to come in, to go in, to get in, to walk in, to march in, to drop in, to step in; to pierce, to run into; (astron.) to house; (nav.) to let in; to enter (book-keeping). *— bien avant;* to penetrate far. *— une seconde fois;* to re-enter. *Faire —;* to show in, to usher in, to send in. *Faire — un vaisseau dans un bassin;* to dock a ship. *— dans le monde;* to go out into the world or into society. *— en possession;* to take possession. *— au service de quelqu'un;* to enter any one's service. *— en maison;* to go into service. *— en religion;* to become a monk or a nun. *— dans sa vingtième année;* to enter on one's twentieth year. *— en jeu;* to come into play. *Vous n'entrez pas dans ma pensée;* you mistake my meaning. *— dans les intérêts de quelqu'un;* to side with any one. *— dans les goûts;* to be of any one's taste. *— en danse;* to begin to dance. *Faire — quelque chose dans un discours;* to introduce something into a speech. *Il y entre pour un cinquième;* he has a fifth share in the enterprise. *Cet article n'entre pour rien dans mes demandes;* this article has nothing to do with my demands. *On ne saurait lui rien faire — dans la tête;* there is no driving anything into his head. *On n'entre pas ici;* no admittance here.

entre-rails, *n.m.,* (rail.) gauge, four-foot way.

s'entre-regarder, *v.r.,* to look at, to stare at one another.

s'entre-regretter, *v.r.,* to regret each other.

s'entre-répondre, *v.r.,* to answer one another.

entre-sabords, *n.m.,* (nav.) between ports.

s'entre-saluer, *v.r.,* to salute one another.

s'entre-secourir, *v.a.,* to help, to succor, one another.

entresol, *n.m.,* mezzanine, entresol (suite of low rooms between the ground floor and the first floor).

entre-sourcils, *n.m.,* (—) space between the eyebrows.

s'entre-soutenir, *v.r.,* to support one another.

s'entre-souvenir, *v.r.,* to half remember.

s'entre-suivre, *v.r.,* to follow each other, to succeed each other.

***entretaille,** *n.f.,* (engr.) interline; (dancing) change of foot.

***s'entre-tailler.** *V. s'entrecouper* (vet.).

***entretaillure,** *n.f.,* (vet.) cutting, crepance.

s'entre-talonner, *v.r.,* to tread on each other's heels; to follow each other closely.

entre-temps, *n.m.,* (—) interval. *Dans l'—;* meanwhile.

entretenir (än-trè-tnir), *v.a.,* to hold, to hold together, to keep up; to keep in repair, to keep in good order; to keep, to preserve, to maintain, to support, to feed; to cherish; to converse, to talk with; to entertain. *— les chemins;* to keep the roads in repair. — *la paix ;* to maintain peace.

.**s'entretenir**, *v.r.*, to hold together, to keep up; to be sustained, to be maintained, to be supported, to be kept up; to maintain, to keep, to support one's self ; to subsist; to converse with, to discourse with, to commune with, to talk to. *S'— avec quelqu'un ;* to talk with any one. *S'— par lettres ;* to converse by letters. *S'— de quelqu'un ;* to speak of any one. *Il s'entretient du jeu ;* he lives by gambling. *S'— avec soi-même ;* to meditate, to reflect.

entretenu, -e, *part.* of **entretenir**. *Femme —e ;* kept woman, mistress.

entretien (-ti-in), *n.m.*, maintenance, keeping, living, livelihood; keeping in repair; conversation, discourse, talk ; communication, conference. *Faire l'— du public ;* to be the talk of the parish. *Un homme d'un agréable — ;* a man of agreeable conversation.

entre-tisser, *v.a.*, to interweave.

entre-tissu, -e, *adj.*, interwoven.

entretoile, *n.f.*, insertion; open-work.

entretoise, *n.f.*, (carp.) tie-beam, cross-bar; cross-piece; transom.

s'entre-toucher, *v.r.*, to touch one another.

s'entre-tuer, *v.r.*, to kill each other.

s'entre-vendre, *v.r.*, to sell to each other; to sell each other, to betray each other.

entre-voie, *n.f.*, (— — —s) (rail.) the six-foot way.

entrevoir, *v.a.*, to have *or* catch a glimpse of, to only just see, to discover a little of; to have an imperfect notion of, to foresee. *— quelqu'un ;* to have a glimpse of any one. *J'entrevois de grands obstacles ;* I foresee great difficulties. *Laisser —;* to show, to discover, to disclose.

s'entrevoir, *v.r.*, to have a meeting, interview, conference; to see, to visit, each other.

entrevous, *n.m.*, (carp.) interjoist.

entrevoûter, *v.a.*, to plaster between joists.

entrevue, *n.f.*, interview, meeting.

***entr'paillé, -e**, *adj.*, (l.ex.) big-bellied.

s'entr'obliger, *v.r.*, to oblige each other.

entr'ouïr, *v.a.*, (l.u.) to hear imperfectly.

entr'ouvert, -e, *part.*, partly open, ajar; gaping, yawning ; (man.) strained shoulder.

entr'ouverture, *n.f.*, (vet.) shoulder strain.

entr'ouvrir, *v.a.*, to open a little, to half-open. *— une porte ;* to half-open; to set a door ajar.

s'entr'ouvrir, *v.r.*, to open, to gape, to yawn; to be ajar.

s'entr'user, *v.r.*, to wear each other out.

enture, *n.f.*, (gard.) incision, cut (for grafting).

énumérateur, *n.m.*, enumerator.

énumérati-f, -ve, *adj.*, enumerative.

énumération, *n.f.*, enumeration. [reckon.

énumérer, *v.a.*, to enumerate, to count, to

envahir, *v. a.*, to invade, to overrun, to spread over, to overgrow; to encroach upon, to usurp.

envahissant, -e, *adj.*, invading, encroaching.

envahissement (-is-mān), *n.m.*, overrunning, invasion, encroachment, usurpation.

envahisseur, *n.m.*, invader. *adj.*, invading, encroaching; silting (of sand).

envaser, *v.a.*, to fill up, to choke with mud.

s'envaser, *v.r.*, (nav.) to stick fast in the mud; to become filled up and choked with mud ; to silt up (of sand, etc.).

enveloppe (ān-vlop), *n.f.*, wrapper, cover, covering; envelope; exterior; disguise; (anat.) coat; casing (of cylinders); tunic (of the eye); (fort.) envelope; (mec.) case, casing; (tech.) cage ; (metal.) moid. *— de voyage ;* hold-all. *Ecrire sous l'— de quelqu'un ;* to write under another person's cover.

enveloppé, -e, *part.*, enveloped, surrounded ; ambiguous, equivocal; confused; muddled. *Etre*

— dans un désastre ; to be involved in a misfortune.

enveloppement (ānv-lop-mān), *n.m.*, enveloping, surrounding; wrapping up, envelopment.

envelopper, *v.a.*, to envelop, to wrap up, to cover, to fold up, to do up, to put up ; to muffle; to beset, to inclose, to environ, to hem in, to surround ; to involve, to implicate ; to disguise. *— quelque chose de papier ;* to wrap anything up in paper. *— l'ennemi ;* to hem in the enemy.

s'envelopper, *v.r.*, to cover *or* wrap one's self up, to envelop one's self, to muffle one's self up; to involve one's self.

envenimer, *v.a.*, to poison, to envenom, to irritate, to inflame, to exasperate. *— une plaie ;* to irritate a wound. *Il l'a envenimé contre moi ;* he has exasperated him against me.

s'envenimer, *v.r.*, to be envenomed ; to fester, to rankle.

enverger, *v.a.*, to garnish with little willow branches.

enverguer (-ghé), *v.a.*, (nav.) to bend a sail to the yards.

envergure, *n.f.*, unfolding; (nav.) extent of sail upon the yards; length of a yard; spread of a bird's wings when extended. *D'— ;* from tip to tip.

envers (ān-vèr), *prep.*, towards, to. *Je vous défendrai — et contre tous ;* I will defend you against all men *or* against the whole world.

envers, *n.m.*, wrong side, reverse side, back. *A l'— ;* on the wrong side; inside out. *Il a l'esprit à l'— ;* he is wrong-headed, crack-brained, beside himself.

à l'envi, *adv.*, in emulation of one another, emulously vying with one another. *A l'— l'un de l'autre ;* in emulation of one another. *Ils travaillent à l'— l'un de l'autre ;* they vie with each other as to who shall work most.

enviable, *adj.*, enviable, to be envied.

envie, *n.f.*, envy, enviousness; wish, desire, longing, hankering, inclination; birth-mark; hangnail. *L'— le dévore ;* he is eaten up with envy. *Sécher d'— ;* to pine away with envy. *Faire —;* to be tempting. *Porter — à quelqu'un ;* to envy any one. *Avoir — de ;* to have a mind to. *J'ai grande — d'aller la voir ;* I have a great mind to go and see her. *— de dormir ;* sleepiness, drowsiness. *On lui en a donné — ;* they have set him all agog upon it. *L'— lui en est passée ;* his longing is over. *Il m'en a ôté l'— ;* he has put me out of conceit with it. *Passer son — de quelque chose ;* to satisfy one's longing for anything. *Il a une — au visage ;* he has a birth-mark on his face. *Il ne fait — à personne ;* no one envies him.

envié, -e, *part.*, envied. *Il est — de tout le monde ;* he is envied by everybody.

⊙***envieilli, -e**, *adj.*, inveterate, long-established, old, of long standing; hardened. *V.* **enduroi, invétéré.**

⊙***envieillir**, *v.a.*, to make one look old. *V.* **vieillir.**

envier, *v.a.*, to envy, to be envious of, to grudge ; to desire, to long for, to wish for. *Je ne lui envie point sa bonne fortune ;* I do not envy him his good fortune.

envieu-x, -se, *adj.*, envious, jealous. *Se faire des — ;* to excite envy.

enviné, -e, *adj.*, smelling of wine. *Ce baril est — ;* that cask smells of wine.

environ, *adv.*, about, nearly, thereabouts.

environnant, -e, *adj.*, surrounding.

environner, *v.a.*, to surround ; to stand round ; to encompass, to beset ; to environ ; to encircle, to inclose. *— d'une balustrade ;* to inclose with a rail. *Les gardes qui environnaient le prince ;* the guards who stood round the prince. *L'éclat qui l'environne ;* the splendor which surrounds him.

environs, *n.m.pl.*, environs; vicinity, neighborhood; country round.

envisager, *v.a.*, to look, to stare, in the face, to eye, to face; to consider, to view, to look upon, to look at. — *de sang froid le péril ;* to look danger in the face.

envoi, *n.m.*, sending; thing sent, present, packet, parcel, package, goods forwarded; goods to be forwarded; (lit.) envoy; (nav.) order to put the helm alee. *Compléter un —;* to make up a parcel. *Faire un —;* to send off a parcel *or* package. *Lettre d'—;* letter of advice.

s'envoiler, *v.r.*, (metal.) to warp, to bend.

envoisiné, -e, *adj.*, surrounded by neighbors.

er.voisiner, *v.a.*, to surround with neighbors.

s'envoler, *v.r.*, to fly away, to take wing; to be carried off (by the wind); to disappear, to vanish. *L'oiseau s'est envolé ;* the bird has flown.

envoûtement, *n.m.*, magical charm.

envoûter, *v.a.*, to cast a spell on any one.

envoyé, *n.m.*, envoy ; deputy, delegate ; messenger. *L'— de Dieu ;* the messenger of God.

envoyer, *v.a.*, to send, to forward, to dispatch; to transmit. *Je vous envoie mon domestique ;* I send you my servant. *— chercher ;* to send for. *— au diable, — à tous les diables ;* to send to the devil. *— paître, — promener ;* to send off, to send about one's business ; to send any one off with a flea in his ear. *— dire ;* to send word. — *en prison ;* to commit to prison. *Envoie !* (nav.) bout-ship ! *S'— ;* to send to each other; to be sent.

envoyeur, *n.m.*, sender. *adj.m.*, (post-office) dispatching. *Bureau —;* dispatching office.

éolien, -ne, (-li-in, -liè-n), *adj.*, Eolian, Eolic. *Harpe —e ;* Eolian harp.

éolien, *n.m.*, Eolic (dialect).

éolipyle, *n.m.*, (phys.) æolipile (smoke-driving apparatus).

éolique, *adj.*, Eolic, Eolian.

épacte, *n.f.*, (astron.) epact.

***épagneul**, *n.m.*, -e, *n.f.*, spaniel.

épais, -se, *adj.*, thick, big; heavy, dull, gross. *Mur — de deux pieds ;* wall two feet thick. *Brouillard —;* thick fog. *Ignorance —se ;* gross ignorance. *Un homme —;* a blockhead. *Avoir la langue —se ;* to speak thick. *Des cheveux —;* thick hair.

épais, *n.m.*, thickness ; thick part.

épais, *adv.*, thick, thickly. *Semer —;* to sow thick.

épaisseur, *n.f.*, thickness ; depth ; density ; dullness.

épaissir, *v.a.*, to thicken, to make thick.

s'épaissir, *v.r.*, to become thick, to get thick, to grow thick ; to become big, to grow large ; to become heavy *or* dull. *Sa langue s'épaissit ;* he is beginning to speak thick.

épaissir, *v.n.*, to thicken, to become thick; to get stout, to grow stout, to become stout.

épaississement (-sis-mān), *n.m.*, thickening, thickness.

épamprage *or* **épamprement**, *n.m.*, lopping off ; pruning ; feeding off (of a corn-field).

épamprer, *v.a.*, to lop off, *or* to prune, a vine; to feed off.

épanchement (é-pānsh-mān), *n.m.*, pouring out, shedding; overflowing, effusion. — *de cœur ;* opening of one's heart.

épancher, *v.a.*, to pour out, to spill; to shed; to open. — *son cœur ;* to open one's heart.

s'épancher, *v.r.*, to be discharged, poured out, to escape; to open one's heart, to unbosom one's self.

épanchoir, *n.m.*, outlet, drain.

épandre, *v.a.*, to pour out, to scatter, to strew, to throw here and there. *V.* **répandre**.

s'épandre, *v.r.*, to spread out, to be scattered, to flow.

épanorthose, *n.f.*, (rhet.) epanorthosis.

épanoui, -e, *adj.*, blown, full-blown; cheerful, jolly, beaming.

épanouir, *v.a.*, to expand, to smooth, to brighten up, to gladden. — *la rate ;* to make merry, to drive away the spleen.

s'épanouir, *v.r.*, (of flowers) to blow, to expand, to open ; to brighten up. *Son visage s'épanouit ;* his face brightened up.

épanouissement (-noo-is-mān), *n.m.*, blowing, opening (of flowers) ; (bot.) expansion.

éparcet, *n.m.* *V.* **esparcet, esparcette**.

s'éparer, *v.r.*, (man.) to jerk, to fling out ; to kick. *V.* **ruer**.

***épargnant, -e**, *adj.*, sparing, saving, economical ; parsimonious.

***épargne**, *n.f.*, economy, saving, thrift, sparingness ; ⊙treasury. — *mesquine ;* shabby saving. *Avec —;* sparingly. *Aller à l'—, user d'—;* to save, to be saving. *Il vit de ses —s ;* he lives on his savings. *Aller à l'— des mots ;* to be sparing of words. *Caisse d'—* or *caisse d'— et de prévoyance ;* savings-bank. *Tailler,* or *graver, en —;* (engr.) to reserve.

***épargner**, *v.a.*, to save, to lay up, to lay by, to spare, to husband, to economize ; to spare (any one). — *son bien ;* to save one's wealth. *On ne lui épargne pas l'argent ;* they allow him plenty of money. *Ne m'épargnez pas ;* do not spare me.

s'*épargner, *v.r.*, to spare one's self ; to spare one another.

***épargner**, *v.n.*, to economize, to be saving, to be sparing. — *sur sa toilette ;* to save in dress.

***éparpillement**, *n.m.*, scattering, dispersing, dispersion.

***éparpiller**, *v.a.*, to scatter, to strew about, to spread, to throw here and there, to disperse ; to fritter away, to squander. — *ses troupes ;* to scatter one's troops.

épars, -e, *adj.*, scattered, dispersed, straggling, sparse ; (of hair) disheveled ; thin (of plants).

éparvin *or* **épervin**, *n.m.*, (vet.) spavin. — *osseux, — sec ;* blood-spavin ; string-halt.

épaté, -e, *adj.*, broad-footed ; wide ; with the foot broken off (of glasses); flat (of noses) ; (pop.) amazed, dumfounded.

épatement, *n.m.*, amazement.

épater, *v.a.*, to break the foot off (a glass) ; to flatten ; to widen; (pop.) to amaze, to dumfound.

s'épater, *v.r.*, to sprawl ; to get broken (of glass).

épaulard, *n.m.*, (ich.) grampus, ork.

épaule, *n.f.*, shoulder ; start (of wheels). *Des —s larges ;* broad shoulders. *Hausser les —s ;* to shrug one's shoulders. *Faire hausser les —s à quelqu'un ;* to make any one shrug his shoulders. *Plier les —s ;* to put up with. *Prêter l'— à quelqu'un ;* to back up any one. *Donner un coup d'— à ;* to help any one ; to give any one a lift. *Faire une chose par-dessus l'— ;* to leave a thing undone ; to do a thing over the left. *Porter sur les —s ;* (fig.) to be heartily sick of. *Marcher des —s ;* to slouch. *L'— d'un bastion ;* the flank of a bastion. *—s d'un vaisseau ;* bows of a ship.

épaulée, *n.f.*, push (with the shoulders); (cook.) fore-quarter of mutton without the shoulder. *—s ;* shouldering. *Faire une chose par —s ;* to do a thing by fits and starts.

épaulement (é-pôl-mān), *n.m.*, a shoulderpiece, covert ; shoulder ; (fort.) epaulement, demi-bastion, breastwork.

épauler, *v.a.*, to break the shoulder, to splay; to help, to back, to countenance, to bring to the shoulder, to prop; to press to the shoulder (of rifles). — *des troupes ;* to cover troops. *Bête épaulée ;* animal with a sprained shoulder ; (fig., fam.) a perfect fool ; a dishonored woman.

épaulette, *n.f.*, shoulder-strap; shoulder-piece; epaulet. — *à gros grains*, — *à graine d'épinards;* (milit.) epaulet with large bullion worn by field and general officers.

épave, *adj.*, (jur.) stray, strayed.

épave, *n.f.*, wreck; (jur.) waif; stray; estray. — *s maritimes*, — *s de mer;* wreck, wreckage.

épeautre, *n.m.f.*, spelt, great barley; wheat.

épée, *n.f.*, sword; (fig.) brand, steel; swordsman. *Charger l'*— *à la main;* to charge sword in hand. *Un homme d'*—; a swordsman, a soldier. *Mettre l'*— *à la main;* to draw one's sword. *Se battre à l'*—; to fight with swords. *Passer l'*— *au travers du corps;* to run a man through the body. *Presser quelqu'un l'*— *dans les reins;* to press any one close, hard. *Une* — *vierge;* a sword that has never been fleshed or drawn. *N'avoir que la cape et l'*—; to have nothing but one's nobility; to have no other fortune but one's sword. *Il est brave comme l'*— *qu'il porte;* he is true to the backbone. *L'*— *use le fourreau;* the sword wears out the scabbard. *C'est un coup d'*— *dans l'eau;* it is beating the air. *Passer au fil de l'*—; to put to the edge of the sword, to put to the sword. *Etre, en être, aux* —*s et aux couteaux;* to be at daggers drawn. *Jouer de l'*— *à deux talons;* to take to one's heels. *Son* — *est trop courte;* his arm is not long enough. *C'est son* — *de chevet;* he is his bosom friend, his constant companion; (fig.) his favorite theme; his hobby. — *de mer;* (ich.) sword-fish.

épeiche, *n.f.*, (orni.) golden oriole, witwall.

épeler (é-plé), *v.a.*, to spell. *Epelez ce mot;* spell that word. — *mal;* to misspell.

épellation, *n.f.*, naming the letters of a word, spelling.

épenthèse, *n.f.*, (gram.) epenthesis.

épenthétique, *adj.*, (gram.) epenthetical.

éperdu, -e, *adj.*, distracted, bewildered, aghast. *Tout* — *d'amour;* quite distraught with love.

éperdument, *adv.*, distractedly, passionately, desperately.

éperlan, *n.m.*, (ich.) smelt, sparling.

éperon (épron), *n.m.*, spur; wrinkle, crow's foot; gaffle (of game cocks); (arch.) buttress, counterfort; (nav.) head of a ship; cutwater, ram; (fort.) spur. *Donner de l'*— *à un cheval;* to clap spurs to a horse. *Chausser les* —*s;* to put on spurs. *Cheval qui n'a ni bouche ni* —; horse that obeys neither rein nor spur. *Il a besoin d'*—*s;* he wants spurring on. *Chausser les* — *à quelqu'un;* to put spurs on any one.

éperonné, -e (é-pro-né), *adj.*, spurred; wrinkled. *Elle a les yeux* —*s;* she has wrinkles about her eyes.

éperonner, *v.a.*, to spur; to spur on; to urge forward; to wrinkle.

éperonnerie, *n.f.*, spur-making, spur-trade.

éperonnier, *n.m.*, spur-maker; Indian peacock.

éperonnière, *n.f.*, spur-leather; (bot.) lark-spur.

épervier, *n.m.*, (orni.) hawk, sparrow-hawk; cast-net.

épervière, *n.f.*, (bot.) hawkweed.

épervin, *n.m.* V. **éparvin**.

éphèdre, *n.m.*, shrubby horse-tail, sea-grass.

éphélide, *n.f.*, (med.) sun-burn; freckle.

éphémère, *adj.*, ephemeral.

éphémère, *n.f.*, ephemera, day-fly.

éphémérides, *n.f.pl.*, ephemerides.

éphod (é-fod), *n.m.*, (Jewish antiq.) ephod.

éphore, *n.m.*, (Grec. antiq.) ephor.

épi, *n.m.*, ear of corn; awn. — *bien garni;* well-filled ear. — *de cheveux;* tuft of hair, topknot. — *de diamants;* cluster of diamonds. — *d'eau;* pond-weed. — *de faîte;* (arch.) top of the crown-post. *Assembler en* —; to scarf.

épice, *n.f.*, spice. *pl.*, ⊙judges' fees. *Pain d'*—; gingerbread. *Fine* —; sharp fellow, knowing blade. *Dans les petits sacs sont les bonnes* —*s;* little and good, or small parcels hold fine wares (pers.). *Herbe aux* —*s;* allspice.

épicé, -e, *adj.*, spiced, spicy; hot, seasoned.

épicène, *adj.*, (gram.) epicene.

épicer, *v.a.*, to spice; ⊙(of judges) to charge too high fees.

épicerie (é-pi-srî), *n.f.*, spices, grocery; grocery-business. *Petite* —; chandlery.

épichérème (-ké-), *n.m.*, (log.) epichirema.

épici-er, *n.m.*, **-ère**, grocer; vulgar fellow. *Il faut envoyer ce livre à l'*—; this book must go to the butter-shop.

épicrâne, *n.m.*, (anat.) epicranium.

épicurien, -ne (-i-in, -iè-n), *n.* and *adj.*, epicure; epicurean.

épicurisme, *n.m.*, epicureanism, epicurism.

épicycle, *n.m.*, (astron.) epicycle.

épicycloïde, *n.f.*, (geom.) epicycloid.

épidémie, *n.f.*, epidemic.

épidémique, *adj.*, epidemic, epidemical.

épidendre, *n.m.*, (bot.) epidendrum.

épiderme, *n.m.*, epidermis, cuticle, scarfskin.

épidermique, *adj.*, (anat.) epidermic, epidermical.

épididyme, *n.m.*, (anat.) epididymis.

épié, -e, *part.*, eared, awny, awned.

épier, *v.n.*, to ear, to shoot into ears.

épier, *v.a.*, to watch, to be a spy upon, to pry into. *Il épie ce que vous faites;* he is a spy upon your actions. *On épie vos démarches;* your steps are being dogged. *S'*—; to watch one another.

épierrement, *n.m.*, clearing land of stones.

épierrer, *v.a.*, to clear away stones.

épieu, *n.m.*, boar-spear, javelin, stake.

épieu-r, -se, *n.m.f.*, watcher, spier, eavesdropper; Paul Pry.

épigastre, *n.m.*, (anat.) epigastrium.

épigastrique, *adj.*, (anat.) epigastric.

épiglotte, *n.f.*, (anat.) epiglottis.

épigrammatique, *adj.*, epigrammatic, epigrammatical.

épigrammatiquement, *adv.*, epigrammatically.

épigrammatiser, *v.n.*, to write epigrams.

épigrammatiste, *n.m.*, epigrammatist.

épigramme, *n.f.*, epigram.

épigraphe, *n.f.*, epigraph.

épigraphie, *n.f.*, epigraphics, epigraphy.

épigraphique, *adj.*, pertaining to epigraphy.

épigyne, *adj.*, (bot.) epigynous.

épilatoire, *adj.*, depilatory.

épilepsie, *n.f.*, (med.) epilepsy. *Attaque d'*—; epileptic fit, fit of epilepsy.

épileptique, *n.m.f.*, and *adj.*, epileptic; epileptical.

épiler, *v.a.*, to depilate.

s'épiler, *v.r.*, to pluck out one's gray hairs.

épileu-r, -se, *n.f.*, depilator (pers.).

*épillet, *n.m.*, (bot.) spikelet.

épilobe, *n.m.*, (bot.) willow-herb.

épilogue (-log), *n.m.*, epilogue.

épiloguer (-ghé), *v.n.*, to carp at, to censure, to criticise, to find fault with, to split hairs. *Il épilogue sur tout;* he finds fault with everything.

épiloguer, *v.a.*, to criticise, to find fault with, to carp at.

épilogueur (-gheur), *n.m.*, critic, fault-finder, carper. *adj.*, fault-finding, carping.

épiloir, *n.m.*, tweezers.

épinaie, *n.f.*, brake, thicket, thorn-bush.

épinard (-när), *n.m.*, (bot.) spinach. *pl.*, (cook.) spinach greens. — *fraise;* strawberry-blite, strawberry-spinach. — *sauvage;* all-good. *Epaulettes à graine d'*—*s;* epaulets with large bullion.

épine, *n.f.*, thorn; prickle; spine; rub, obstacle, difficulty; bristling point (metal.). — *blanche;* hawthorn; barberry. — *dorsale, du dos;* spine; backbone. *Noble* —; hawthorn. — *noire,* German acacia; blackthorn, sloe. *Avoir une — au pied;* to have a thorn in one's side. *Tirer à quelqu'un une — du pied;* to get some one over a difficulty. *Etre sur les —s, sur des —s,* to be on pins and needles, or on thorns. *Il n'y a pas de roses sans —s;* no rose without a thorn, no joy without alloy. *Les —s de la chicane;* the thorny points of the law.

épines, *n.f.pl.*, (metal.) bristling points.

épinette, *n.f.*, (mus.) spinet; (bot.) North American fir-tree.

épineu-x, -se, *adj.*, thorny, prickly; knotty, ticklish, intricate. *Arbres* —; thorny trees. *Pomme —se;* (bot.) stramony, thorn-apple. *Question —se,* ticklish question.

épine-vinette, *n.f.*, barberry, barberry.

épingle, *n.f.*, pin, scarf-pin, breast-pin. —*s;* pin-money, gratuity, douceur. *Attacher avec une —;* to pin. *Il est toujours tiré à quatre —s;* he is always as neat as hands can make him; he always looks as if he had just stepped out of a bandbox, or is always dressed up to the nine. *Tirer son — du jeu;* to get out of a scrape, to back out of anything. *A coups d'—s;* inch by inch; by pin-pricks. — *à cheveux;* hairpin. *Oter les —s;* to unpin.

épinglé, *adj.*, pinned; corded, terry. *Velours* —; light terry velvet.

épingler, *v.a.*, to pin, to prick, to clean.

épinglette, *n.f.*, (artil.) priming-iron; priming-wire; (mining) piercer; (tech.) pricker.

épingli-er, -ère, *n.m., -ère*, *n.f.*, pin-maker.

épinière, *adj.f.*, (anat.) spinal. *Moelle* —; spinal marrow.

épiniers, *n.m.pl.*, (hunt.) brake, thicket.

épinoche, *n.f.m.*, (com.) best coffee. *f.*, (Ich.) stickleback.

épiphanie, *n.f.*, Epiphany.

épiphonème, *n.m.*, (rhet.) epiphonema.

épiphora, *n.m.*, (med.) epiphora, watery eye.

épiphyse, *n.f.*, (anat.) epiphysis.

épiploon, *n.m.*, (anat.) epiploon.

épique, *adj.*, epic.

épiscopal, -e, *adj.*, episcopal.

épiscopal, *n.m.*, episcopalian.

épiscopalement, *adv.*, episcopally.

épiscopat, *n.m.*, episcopate, episcopacy.

épiscopaux, *n.m.pl.*, Episcopalians.

épisode, *n.m.*, episode.

épisodique, *adj.*, episodical.

épispastique, *n.m., adj.*, (med.) epispastic.

épisperme, *n.m.*, (bot.) seed-coat, episperm, aril, arillus.

épisser, *v.a.*, (nav.) to splice.

épissoir, *n.m.*, (nav.) fid, splicing-fid; marlinspike.

épissure, *n.f.*, (nav.) splice.

épistolaire, *adj.*, epistolary.

épistolaire, *n.m.*, letter-writer.

épistoli-er, -ère, *n.f.*, letter-writer; (c. rel.) lectionary.

épistolographe, *n.m.*, Greek *or* Latin letter-writer.

épistyle, *n.m.*, (arch.) epistyle.

épitaphe, *n.f.*, epitaph.

épitase, *n.f.*, (dramatic lit.) epitasis.

épithalame, *n.m.*, epithalamium, nuptial song.

épithème, *n.m.*, (pharm.) epithem.

épithète, *n.f.*, epithet.

épitoge, *n.f.*, hood; shoulder-knot; cassock.

épitomé, *n.m.*, epitome; compendium; abridgment.

épître, *n.f.*, epistle, letter, missive. — *dédicatoire;* dedicatory epistle. *Le côté de l'—;* the right-hand side of the altar.

épitrope, *n.f.*, (rhet.) epitrope.

épizootie (-ti), *n.f.*, epizooty.

épizootique, *adj.*, epizootic. *Maladie* —; epizootic distemper.

*****éplaigner**, *v.a.*, (manu.) to raise the nap of the cloth, to tease, to teasel.

éplaigneur, *n.m.*, cloth-dresser, teaseler.

éploré, -e, *adj.*, in tears, weeping, disconsolate, distressed.

éployé, -e, *adj.*, (her.) spread (of the eagle)

épluchage, *n.m.*, (manu.) picking.

épluchement (é-plush-mān), *n.m.*, cleaning, picking.

éplucher, *v.a.*, to pick, to clean, to sift; to examine minutely. — *la vie de quelqu'un;* to examine minutely into any one's life. — *un ouvrage;* to examine a work minutely, *or* to pick any work to pieces.

s'éplucher, *v.r.*, to clean itself (of certain animals); (fig.) to examine one's self.

éplucheu-r, *n.m., -se*, *n.f.*, picker; faultfinder; hair-splitter.

éplucheuse, *n.f.*, picker (instrument).

épluchoir, *n.m.*, paring-knife.

épluchures, *n.f.pl.*, parings, pickings, orts, refuse.

épode, *n.f.*, epode.

épointé, -e, *adj.*, without a point, blunt-topped; (of a dog) with a broken thigh; (of a horse) hip-shot.

épointement, *n.m.*, bluntness.

épointer, *v.a.*, to break off the point, to blunt.

s'épointer, *v.r.*, to have its point broken off.

*****épointillage**, *n.m.*, (tech.) burling.

*****épointiller**, *v.a.*, (tech.) to burl (cloth).

épointure, *n.f.*, (of horses, etc.) hip-shot.

épois, *n.m.pl.*, trochings (of a deer).

éponge, *n.f.*, sponge. *Passer l'— sur quelque action;* to say no more about, *or* to forget, an action. *Presser l'—;* to squeeze the sponge; to exact too much. *Il boit comme une —;* he drinks like a fish.

éponger, *v.a.*, to sponge; to sponge up; to mop.

épongier, *n.m.*, (l.u.) spongeman.

*****épontille**, *n.f.*, (nav.) stanchion, prop.

*****épontiller**, *v.a.*, to prop, to shore.

éponyme, *n.m.* and *adj.*, (antiq.) eponym; eponymous.

épopée, *n.f.*, epopee; epic poem.

époque, *n.f.*, epoch; period, time, date; era. *Faire* —; to mark an era. *Dès cette* —; from that time. *A l'— de;* at the time of.

époucé, -e, *adj.*, thumbless.

époudrer, *v.a.*, (l.u.) to dust. *V.* **épous-seter**.

épouffé, -e, *adj.*, (fam.) out of breath.

s'épouffer, *v.r.*, to steal away, to scamper off; to get out of breath from laughing. *V.* **pouffer**.

*****épouiller**, *v.a.*, (l.ex.) to louse; to clean of lice.

*****s'épouiller**, *v.r.*, (l.ex.) to louse one's self.

époularder, *v.a.*, to pick, to clean (tobacco).

époulin, espolin, *or* **espoulin**, *n.m.*, (manu.) small shuttle, spool.

époumoner, *v.a.*, to tire the lungs of; to exhaust.

s'époumoner, *v.r.*, to tire one's lungs; (fig.) to vociferate, to shout one's self hoarse.

épousailles, *n.f.pl.*, espousals, nuptials.

épouse, *n.f.*, spouse, bride, wife, consort.

épousé, -e, *part.*, married, wedded.

épousée, *n.f.*, bride, wife.

épouser, *v.a.*, to marry, to take in marriage, to wed, to espouse, to embrace, to take up. — *une héritière;* to marry an heiress. — *les intérêts d'autrui;* to espouse the interests of others.

s'épouser, *v.r.*, to marry each other.

épouseur, n.m., marrying man; intended husband.

époussetage, n.m., dusting.

épousseter (é-pous-té), v.a., to dust, to wipe off the dust; to beat the dust out of; to leather, to dust (beat). — *quelqu'un ;* to dust any one's jacket for him.

s'épousseter, v.r., to wipe the dust off one's self.

époussette, n.f., dusting-rag, duster.

épouti, n.m., orts (in cloth).

époutieuse (-tieuz), n.f., picker, cleaner, burler (of cloth).

époutir, v.a., to pick, to clean (cloth).

épouvantable, adj., frightful, dreadful, tremendous, shocking, horrible; appalling. *A un degré —;* to a frightful degree.

épouvantablement, adv., frightfully, dreadfully, tremendously.

***épouvantail**, n.m., scare-crow; bugbear; (orni.) sea-swallow. *C'est un — de chenevière ;* she is a perfect scarecrow.

épouvante, n.f., terror, dismay, affright. *Porter l'— dans le pays ennemi ;* to spread terror in the enemy's country. *L'— les a pris;* they were seized with dismay. *Frapper d'—;* to dismay, to affright.

épouvantement, n.m., terror, affright.

épouvanter, v.a., to terrify, to frighten, to appall, to scare.

s'épouvanter, v.r., to be frightened or terrified; to take fright.

époux, n.m., spouse, husband, bridegroom. pl., husband and wife. *Futur —;* intended husband.

épreindre (épreignant, épreint), v.a., to squeeze out, to press, to express.

épreinte, n.f., tenesmus ; straining ; (fig.) pressure (chiefly used in pl.).

s'éprendre, v.r., to become enamored of; to fall in love with.

épreuve, n.f., trial, proof, test, ordeal, examination; (print.) proof, revise. *J'en ai fait l'—;* I have tried it, made a trial of it. *Passer par de rudes —s ;* to go through hard trials. *Mettre à l'—;* to make a trial of, to put to the test. *A l'— du feu;* fire-proof. *A l'— des balles ;* ball-proof. *A l'— de l'eau ;* waterproof. *A toute —;* trusty, well-tried, faithful, devoted. *Courage à toute —;* courage proof against everything. *— judiciaire ;* ordeal. *Temps d'—;* probation. *— chargée ;* (print.) foul proof. *— peu chargée ;* (print.) clean proof. *Corriger une —;* (print.) to correct a proof. *Première — d'auteur ;* (print.) reader's proof. *Seconde — d'auteur ;* (print.) revise. *Troisième — d'auteur ;* (print.) second revise. *— avant la lettre ;* (engr.) proof before letters. *Tirer une —;* (print.) to pull a proof.

épris, -e, adj., in love, taken with, smitten, charmed with. *Il en est —;* he is smitten with her.

éprouver, v.a., to try, to prove; to put to the proof; to feel, to experience, to meet with; to go through. *— la fidélité de quelqu'un ;* to try any one's fidelity. *— une douleur ;* to feel a pain. *— des malheurs ;* to meet with misfortunes. *— un canon ;* to test a cannon. *S'— à ;* to try one's hand at.

éprouvette, n.f., gauge; steam-gauge; test-glass; eprouvette (for testing gunpowder).

sel d'epsom, n.m., Epsom salts.

eptacorde, n.m. *V.* **heptacorde.**

eptagone, n.m. *V.* **heptagone.**

épucer, v.a., to catch the fleas of; to clear of fleas.

s'épucer, v.r., to catch one's fleas.

épuisable, adj., exhaustible.

épuisé, -e, part., exhausted; drained; spent; worn out; used up; threadbare; out of print; done

up. *Terre —e ;* exhausted ground. *L'édition est épuisée ;* the book is out of print.

épuisement (é-puiz-mān), n.m., draining; draining off; exhaustion. *L'— des finances ;* the low state of the finances. *Tuyau d'—;* exhausting-pipe.

épuiser, v.a., to exhaust, to spend, to drain, to use up; to eat up, to consume. *— une matière ;* to exhaust a subject. *Leurs ressources étaient épuisées ;* their resources were exhausted.

s'épuiser, v.r., to be exhausted, to waste, to wear out, to exhaust one's self ; to sell off, to get out of print.

épuisette, n.f., scoop, hand-net, landing-net.

épulide or **épulie**, n.f., (surg.) epulis.

épulons, n.m.pl., (antiq.) epulones.

épulotique, n.m. and adj., (pharm.) epulotic.

⊙**épurati-f, -ve**, adj., depurating; purifying; refining.

épuration, n.f., purification, purifying, refining, refinement. *— du sang;* purifying of the blood.

épuratoire, adj., purifying.

épure, n.f., (arch.) diagram, draught, working-drawing (of a building).

épurement, n.m., purifying.

épurer, v.a., to purify, to clear, to clarify, to refine; to purge. *— de l'eau bourbeuse ;* to clear muddy water. *— de l'or ;* to refine gold.

s'épurer, v.r., to be purified, to grow finer, more refined (of style, language).

épurge, n.f., (bot.) caper-spurge.

équarrir, v.a., (tech.) to square; to cut up.

équarrissage, n.m., (carp.) squareness; squaring; scantling; flaying and cutting up (horses). *Dix pouces d'—;* ten inches square. *Bois d'—;* squared timber. *Clos d'—;* knacker's yard.

équarrissement, n.m., (tech.) squaring.

équarrisseur, n.m., knacker.

équarrissoir, n.m., rimer; knacker's knife.

équateur (é-koua-), n.m., equator, equinoctial line; (country) Ecuador.

équation (é-koua-), n.f., (alg.) equation. *— du premier degré ;* (alg.) simple equation. *Poser une —;* to state an equation. *Montre à —;* chronometer.

équatorial, -e (é-koua-), adj., equatorial. n.m., equatorial telescope (instrument).

équerre, n.f., set square; square rule. *Dresser à l'—;* to square. *A fausse —;* out of square; bevel. *Courbe à —;* (nav.) square knee.

équerrer, v.a., to square, to bevel.

équestre (é-kuèstr) adj., equestrian.

équiangle (é-kui-) adj., (geom.) equiangular.

équidifférent, -e (é-kui-), adj., equidifferent.

équidistant, -e (é-kui-), adj., (geom.) equidistant.

équilatéral, -e (é-kui-), adj., (geom.) equilateral.

équilatère (é-kui-), adj., (l.u.) (geom.) equilateral.

équilboquet, n.m., mortise-gauge.

équilibre, n.m., equilibrium, equipoise, poise, balance. *Mettre en —;* to poise. *Faire l'—;* to make things equal. *Perdre l'—;* to lose one's equilibrium, one's balance.

équilibrer, v.a., to poise; to place in equilibrium. *S'—;* to balance (of things).

équilibriste, n.m.f., acrobat.

équille, n.f., (pisc.) sand-eel.

équinoxe, n.m., equinox. *Vents d'—;* equinoctial wind.

équinoxial, -e, adj., equinoctial. *Ligne —e ;* equinoctial line.

équipage, n.m., equipage, carriage; turnout; equipment; dress; gear, tackle, implements; plight; crew. *Avoir son —, rouler —;* to keep one's carriage. *Etre dans un triste —;* to be badly equipped. *Etre en triste —;* to be in a sad plight. *— de Jean de Paris ;* brilliant equipage.

— de Bohême; sorry equipage. Maître d'—; (nav.) boatswain.

équipe, n.f., (nav.) train of boats; manning; set, gang (of workmen). Chef d'—; foreman. Homme d'—; boatman, oarsman, porter. Faire l'—; to manage; to man (a boat).

équipée, n.f., prank; freak, frolic.

équipement (é-kip-măn), n.m., outfit, fitting out, equipment, accouterment; manning. Petit —; kit.

équiper, v.a., to equip, to fit out, to stock, to furnish, to man; to ill-treat, to pay out. — une flotte; to fit out a fleet.

s'équiper, v.r., to fit one's self out; to dress up; to titivate one's self; to rig one's self out.

équipet, n.m., (nav.) locker.

équipollence, n.f., (l.u.) equipollence.

⊙**équipollent**, n.m., equipollent, equivalent. A l'—; in proportion.

équipollent, -e, adj., equipollent, equivalent.

⊙**équipoller**, v.a., to be equivalent, to be of the like value; to balance.

équipondérance (é-kui-), n.f., equiponderance.

équitable, adj., equitable, upright, just, fair.

équitablement, adv., equitably, justly, fairly.

équitant, -e (é-kui-), adj., (bot.) (of leaves) equitant.

équitation (é-kui-), n.f., equitation, riding, horsemanship.

équité, n.f., equity, justice.

équivalemment (-la-măn), adv., (l.u.) equivalently.

équivalence, n.f., equivalence.

équivalent, -e, adj., equivalent.

équivalent, n.m., equivalent.

équivaloir, v.n., to be equivalent, to be tantamount to.

équivalve, adj., (conch.) equivalve.

équivoque, adj., equivocal, ambiguous, doubtful, uncertain. Un homme —; a man of doubtful character.

équivoque, n.f., equivocation; ambiguity; evasion, shuffling; (paint.) defect, fault. User d'—s; to equivocate.

équivoquer, v.n., to equivocate, to speak ambiguously, to quibble, to shuffle.

s'équivoquer, v.r., to use one word for another, to make a slip, to be mistaken.

érable, n.m., maple, maple-tree. — blanc; sycamore. — à sucre; sugar-maple. — moucheté; birds'-eye maple.

éradicati-f, -ve, adj., eradicative.

éradication, n.f., eradication.

érafler, v.a., to scratch slightly, to graze.

éraflure, n.f., slight s ratch, graze.

*+**éraillé, -e**, part., frayed, fretted; bloodshot (of the eyes); nav.) (of ables and ropes) chafed, galled ; (of the voice) rough, hoarse, husky.

*+**éraillement**, n.m., (med.) eversion f the eyelids; fraying, fretting, unweaving; huskiness, hoarseness.

*+**érailler**, v.a., to fray, to fret, to unweave.

*+**s'érailler**, v.r., t fray; (nav.) to chafe; to become bloodshot (of the eyes); to become husky, hoarse (of the voice). La gaze est sujette à s'—; gauze is apt to fray.

*+**éraillure**, n.f., fret, fraying; chafing, gall.

ératé, -e, part., spleened; sprightly, lively, gay, arch, shrewd. Un petit garçon —; a sprightly little boy.

érater, v.a., to pull out the spleen; to spleen.

s'érater, v.r., to run one's self out of breath, to lose one's breath through running.

ère, n.f., era, epoch.

érèbe, n.m., (myth.) Erebus.

érecteur, n.m. and adj., (anat.) erector (muscle).

érectile, adj., (anat.) erectile.

érection, n.f., erection, erecting; establishment, raising.

éreinter, v.a., to break any one's back; to tire out, to knock up, to do up; to beat unmercifully (fig.); to cut to pieces; to lash with satire; to slay.

s'éreinter, v.r., to break one's back, to tire one's self out, to be knocked up; to drudge, to toil and moil.

érémitique, adj., hermitical, eremitical.

érésipélateu-x, -se, adj., (med.) erysipelatous.

érésipèle, n.m., (med.) erysipelas, St. Anthony's fire; (vet.) wild-fire.

éréthisme, n.m., (med.) erethismus.

ergastule, n.f., (Rom. antiq.) slaves' prison.

ergo, conj., (log.) ergo; then, therefore. — glu, — gluc; (fam., jest.) ergo, nothing at all; and what then.

ergot, n.m., spur (of certain birds); (agri.) ergot, spur; (pharm.) ergota, horn-seed; (nav.) taggle; dew-claw (of a dog); (vet.) ergot. Monter sur ses — s; to ride the high horse. Etre sur ses — s; to keep one's distance; to be standoffish. — de coq; cock's-spur.

ergotage, n.m. V. ergoterie.

ergoté, -e, adj., spurred, having a dew-claw (of a dog). Un coq bien —; a well-spurred cock. Seigle —; spurred rye.

ergoter, v.n., to cavil, to wrangle, to chop logic. Il ergote sur tout; he finds fault with everything.

ergoterie (èr-go-trî), n.f., caviling; quibbling, quibble.

ergoteu-r, n.m., **-se**, n.f., caviler, quibbler.

ergotisme, n.m., caviling, quibbling, quibble; (med.) ergotism.

éridan, n.m., (astron.) Eridanus.

ériger, v.a., to erect, to raise, to rear, to set up, to institute.

s'ériger, v.r., to erect one's self into; to set up for, to pose as, to pretend to be; to be erected, raised, built. S'— en censeur public; to set up for a public censor.

*+**érigne** or **érine**, n.f., (surg.) hook.

érigone, n.f., (astron.) Virgo.

ermin, n.m., customs duty (in the Levant).

erminette or **herminette**, n.f., (carp.) adz.

ermitage, n.m., hermitage.

ermite, n.m., hermit, recluse. Pâtes d'—; dry walnuts.

érodé, -e, adj., (tech.) eroded, gnawed.

érosi-f, -ve, adj., erosive.

érosion, n.f., erosion.

érotique, adj., erotic.

érotomanie, n.f., erotomania, nymphomania.

erpétologie, n.f., erpetology.

errant, -e (èr-răn, -t), adj., wandering, lost, fugitive, roving, errant; rambling. Chevalier —; knight-errant. Le juif —; the wandering Jew.

errant, n.m., lost sheep.

errata (èr-ra-ta), n.m., (—) errata.

erratique, adj., (med., astron.) erratic.

erratum, n.m., (—) erratum. V. errata.

erre, n.f., course, way; (nav.) way (of a ship). pl., track (of a stag). Aller grand'—; to go very fast. Marcher sur les —s de quelqu'un; to tread in any one's footsteps.

errements (èr-măn), n.m.pl., traces, track, manner, way, proceedings; vagaries, follies. Reprendre les anciens — d'une affaire or suivre les vieux —; to fall into the old track again.

errer (èr-ré), v.n., to wander, to ramble, to stray, to range, to rove, to stroll, to roll; to err. to mistake, to be mistaken, to go astray. — partout; to ramble about. — çà et là; to ramble about, to stroll up and down, to wander to and fro. Aller errant; to wander up and down.

erreur (èr-reur), n.f., error, illusion, mistake, blunder. Sauf —; errors excepted. Etre dans l'—; to be mistaken. Tirer quelqu'un de son—s to convince any one of his error. —*! not a bit of it* ! — *n'est pas compte ;* misreckoning is no payment.

errhin, *n.m.,* (med.) errhine.

errhin, -e, *adj.,* (med.) errhine.

erroné, -e (èr-ro-né), *adj.,* erroneous, mistaken, false, unsound, untrue.

erronément, *adv.,* erroneously.

ers (èr), *n.m.,* tare, vetch, lentil.

erse, *n.f.,* (nav.) iron cringle. —*s de poulies ;* block-strops.

erse, *adj.,* Erse (Gaelic, Irish, Scotch).

erseau, *n.m.,* cringle.

érubescent, -e, *adj.,* erubescent, reddening.

érucage, érucago, *or* **érucague** (-kag), *n.f.,* (bot.) rocket.

éructation, *n.f.,* eructation, belching.

éructer, *v.a.,* (l.u.) to eructate, to belch.

érudit, -e, *adj.,* erudite, learned.

érudit, *n.m.,* scholar, learned man.

érudition, *n.f.,* learning, erudition, scholarship.

érugin'eu-x, -se, *adj.,* eruginous.

erupti-f, -ve, *adj.,* (med.) eruptive.

éruption, *n.f.,* act of breaking forth, eruption; cutting (of teeth).

érysipélateu-x, -se, *adj.* V. **érésipélateux.**

érysipèle, *n.m.* V. **érésipèle.**

ès, *art.,* (contraction of *en les*), in, of ; (before certain names of towns) *Saint-Germain — Laye. Maître — arts ;* master of arts.

escabeau, *n.m.,* stool.

escabelle, *n.f.,* stool. *Déranger les —s à ;* (fig.) to upset (any one's) calculations ; to baffle or foil (any one).

escache, *n.f.,* scatch, bit (for horses).

escadre, *n.f.,* (nav.) squadron, fleet. *Chef d'—;* commodore ; flag-officer.

*escadrille,** *n.f.,* (nav.) small squadron, flotilla.

escadron, *n.m.,* (milit.) squadron (of horse). *Chef d'—;* major.

escadronner, *v.n.,* to manœuvre (of cavalry).

escalade, *n.f.,* scaling (a wall) ; (milit.) escalade.

escalader, *v.a.,* to scale, to climb over ; (milit.) to escalade. *S'—;* to be scaled.

escale, *n.f.,* (nav.) putting in, calling. *Faire — dans un port ;* to put into a port, to touch at, to call at (a port).

escalier, *n.m.,* staircase, stairs, flight of stairs, steps. — *en limaçon ;* winding staircase. — *dérobé ;* private staircase. — *de commandement ;* (nav.) companion-ladder.

escalin, *n.m.,* Dutch (sixpenny piece).

escalope, *n.f.,* split-bean ; (pisc.) scallop ; (cook.) a kind of stew.

escamotage, *n.m.,* juggling, sleight of hand ; legerdemain ; prigging, filching.

escamote, *n.f.,* juggler's ball.

escamoter, *v.a.,* to juggle, to juggle away ; to pilfer, to shuffle out off, to ease of. *On lui a escamoté sa bourse ;* they eased him of his purse.

escamoteur, *n.m.,* juggler, conjurer ; fleecer, pilferer ; pickpocket.

escamper, *v.n.,* to scamper away.

escampette, *n.f.,* scampering. *Il a pris de la poudre d'—;* he has scampered away.

escapade, *n.f.,* prank, freak, spree, frolic, lark. *Faire une —;* to have a lark.

escape, *n.f.,* (arch.) scape.

*escarbille,** *n.f.,* coal cinder, clinker.

escarbot, *n.m.,* (ent.) horn-beetle.

escarboucle, *n.f.,* (min.) carbuncle.

escarcelle, *n.f.,* (jest.) purse, money-bag. *Il a rempli son —;* he has filled his purse.

escargot, *n.m.,* snail, edible snail.

escarmouche, *n.f.,* skirmish ; brush. — *de route ;* (milit.) running fight. *Aller à l'—;* to go out skirmishing ; (fig.) caviling, bickering.

escarmoucher, *v.n.,* to skirmish ; (fig.) to cavil, to bicker.

escarmoucheur, *n.m.,* skirmisher ; caviler.

escarole, *n.f.,* (bot.) endive.

escarotique, *n.m. and adj.,* (med.) escharotic, caustic.

escarpe, *n.f.,* (fort.) scarp, escarp.

escarpé, -e, *adj.,* steep, precipitous, rugged, cragged ; (nav.) bluffy.

escarpement, *n.m.,* (fort.) escarpment, steepness.

escarper, *v.a.,* to cut steep *or* vertically ; (milit.) to escarp ; (fig.) to do for.

escarpin, *n.m.,* pump (shoe). *Jouer de l'—;* to run away, to take to one's heels, to bolt.

escarpolette, *n.f.,* swing, see-saw. *Il a la tête à l'—;* he is a hare-brained fellow.

escarre, *n.f.,* (med.) eschar ; slough ; ☉(fig.) gap.

escaveçade, *n.f.,* (man.) jerk (with the cavesson).

escient, *n.m.,* (l.u.) knowledge. *A son —;* to his knowledge, wittingly. *A bon —;* in good earnest ; wittingly, knowingly.

esclaire, *n.m.,* (hawking) bird of prey.

esclandre, *n.m.,* fracas, uproar ; scandal, exposure, scene. *Faire —;* to make a scene, to cause an uproar.

esclavage, *n.m.,* slavery ; bondage ; thralldom ; inthrallment ; drudgery. *Réduire à l'—;* to enslave, to reduce to slavery.

esclave, *n.m.,f.,* slave ; bondman ; drudge. *Commandeur d'—s ;* slave-driver. *Propriétaire d'—s ;* slave-owner. *On est — dans cette maison ;* one is a very drudge in that house (*i.e.* the work is endless in).

esclave, *adj.,* slavish. *Avoir une âme —;* to have a slavish, base disposition.

escobard, *n.m.,* equivocator, shuffler.

escobarder, *v.n.,* to equivocate, to prevaricate, to shuffle.

escobarderie, *n.f.,* prevarication, shuffling, subterfuge.

☉**escoffion,** *n.m.,* cap, hair-net.

escogriffe, *n.m.,* sharper, shark, sponger ; tall, lank, ungainly fellow.

escompte (ès-cont), *n.m.,* discount. *A —;* at a discount. *Faire l'—;* to discount.

escompter (ès-conté), *v.a.,* to discount, to cash ; (fig.) to anticipate, to forestall. — *un billet, un effet ;* to cash a bill.

escompteur (ès-kon-teur), *n.m.,* (com.) discounter.

escope, *n.f.* V. **écope.**

escopette, *n.f.,* carbine.

escopetterie, *n.f.,* volley of carbines, etc.

escopettier, *n.m.,* rifleman.

escorte, *n.f.,* escort ; (nav.) convoy (fig.) ; retinue, train, attendants. *Servir d'— à ;* to serve as an escort to, to guard. *Bâtiment d'—;* convoy-ship.

escorter, *v.n.,* to escort ; to accompany, to attend. — *la caisse militaire ;* to escort the military chest.

escot, *n.m.,* kind of serge ; (nav.) skeet.

escouade, *n.f.,* (milit.) squad ; gang.

escourgée, *n.f.,* scourge ; lash ; lashing.

escourgeon (-jon), *n.m.,* winter-barley.

escousse, *n.f.,* (l.u.) spring, run, start. *Prendre son —;* to take one's spring.

escrime, *n.f.,* fencing. *Salle d'—;* fencing-school. *Être hors d'—;* to be put off one's guard ; to be at one's wits' end.

escrimer, *v.n.,* to fence ; to spar ; to have a trial of skill.

s'escrimer, *v.r.,* to strive ; to try ; to dabble in ; to have some knowledge of. *Il s'escrime toujours, mais rien n'y fait ;* he keeps on pegging away, but nothing comes of it.

escrimeur, *n.m.,* fencer.

escroc (ès-krô), *n.m.*, sharper, swindler, blackleg.

escroquer, *v.a.*, to swindle, to cheat.

escroquerie (ès-kro-krî), *n.f.*, swindling, swindle, cheating.

escroqueu-r, *n.m.*, **-se**, *n.f.*, cheat, swindler.

escubac. *V.* **scubac**.

esculape, *n.m.*, (—*s*) Æsculapius; (fam.) a clever physician.

esculent, -e, *adj.*, (l.u.) edible, eatable, esculent.

escurial, *n.m.*, Escurial.

ésope, *n.m.*, (—*s*) Æsop; (fam.) hunchback. *C'est un —;* he is a hunchback.

ésotérique, *adj.*, esoteric.

espace, *n.m.*, space, room, place, volume. —*s imaginaires;* imaginary space. *Court — de temps;* short space of time.

espace, *n.f.*, (print.) space.

espacement (ès-pas-mān), *n.m.*, (arch.) interval, interspace, spread; (print.) spacing.

espacer, *v.a.*, to leave a space between; to separate, to place apart; to plant at regular intervals; (print.) to space.

espade, *n.f.*, tewing-beetle (for hemp).

espader, *v.a.*, to tew hemp.

espadeur, *n.m.*, hemp-beater.

espadon, *n.m.*, espadon, broadsword; two-handed sword; (ich.) swordfish.

espadonner, *v.n.*, to fight with the broadsword.

espadot, *n.m.*, boat-hook.

espadrille, *n.f.*, bathing shoe, sandal.

*****espagnol, -e**, *n.* and *adj.*, Spaniard; Spanish. *La langue —e;* the Spanish tongue.

*****espagnol**, *n.m.*, Spanish (language).

*****espagnolette**, *n.f.*, baize; French window fastening.

espalier, *n.m.*, (hort.) espalier; fruit-wall; (nav.) stroke-oar. *Venir en —;* to grow on an espalier.

espalmer, *v.a.*, (nav.) to grave.

esparcet, *n.m.*, **esparcette**, *n.f.*, French honeysuckle; esparcet; sainfoin.

espargoute, *n.f.* *V.* **spergule**.

espars, *n.m.pl.*, (nav.) spars.

espèce, *n.f.*, species, kind, sort; nature; breed; case at issue, case in point, (jur.) case. *pl.*, specie, ready money, hard cash; (theol.) element. *L'— humaine;* mankind. *Payer en —s;* to pay in cash. —*s sonnantes;* hard cash, cash down.

espérance, *n.f.*, hope, confidence, trust, expectation. *Dans l'—;* in expectation. *Se nourrir d'—;* to feed on hope. *Vivre d'—;* to live on hope. *Répondre à ses —s;* to answer one's expectations.

espérer, *v.a.*, to hope, to hope for, to expect; to trust. *Il espère une meilleure fortune;* he hopes for a better fortune. *Je n'espère plus rien;* I have no further hopes.

espérer, *v.n.*, to hope, to hope for, to be hopeful of; to put one's trust in. *J'espère bien;* I hope so indeed. *En voilà une, j'espère;* that's one, if you like.

espiègle, *n.m.f.* and *adj.*, frolicsome child; frolicsome, waggish, arch, roguish.

espièglerie, *n.f.*, frolic, roguish *or* playful trick, waggishness.

espingole, *n.f.*, blunderbuss.

espion, *n.m.*, **-ne**, *n.f.*, spy; (at races) touter.

espionnage, *n.m.*, espionage; spy system, spying.

espionner, *v.a.*, to spy, to pry into.

esplanade, *n.f.*, esplanade, parade.

espoir, *n.m.*, hope, expectance. *Avoir l'— de;* to be in hopes of. *Mettre son — dans;* to set one's hopes on. *Sans —;* hopeless.

espolin, *n.m.* *V.* **époullin**.

esponton, *n.m.*, spontoon, half-pike.

espouleur, *n.m.* *V.* **époulleur**.

espoulin, *n.m.* *V.* **époullin**.

espringale, *n.f.*, springal (a kind of sling).

esprit, *n.m.*, spirit, soul, ghost, shade; mind, sense, understanding, wit, intellect; humor, disposition, temper, character; meaning; spirit, spirituous liquor; (gram.) breathing. — *malin —;* evil spirit, fiend. — *follet;* goblin. *Dieu est un —;* God is a spirit. *Le Saint—*, *l'—Saint;* the Holy Ghost. — *doux;* (Grec. gram.) soft breathing. — *rude;* (Grec. gram.) hard breathing. — *borné, étroit;* narrow intellect. — *dérangé;* disordered mind. — *de corps;* fellow-feeling, brotherhood. — *d'ordre;* orderliness, management. — *de suite;* consistency. — *de parti;* party spirit. *Cultiver l'—;* to cultivate the mind. *Un homme d'—;* a man of parts, a sensible man, a man of wit. *Un ouvrage d'—;* a work of talent. *Un bel —;* a wit. *Un — fort;* a free-thinker. — *présent;* ready wit. *S'alambiquer l'—;* to puzzle one's brains. *Un homme à l'— étroit;* a narrow-minded man. *Aliéner l'— de quelqu'un;* to drive any one mad. *Avoir l'— sain;* to be of sound mind. *Avoir de l'—;* to be intelligent, to be witty, to be sensible. *Avoir l'— aux talons;* to shine at the wrong end, to go a wool-gathering. *Avoir l'— bien fait;* to be good-tempered. *Faire de l'—;* to play the wit. *Faire revenir l'— à quelqu'un;* to bring any one to his senses. *Faire revenir quelqu'un à l'— de;* to recall to any one, *or* remind any one of. *Où avait-il l'— quand?* where were his wits when? *what was he thinking of, when? Vous n'avez pas saisi l'— de cet auteur;* you have not understood the meaning of that author. *Reprendre ses —s;* to recover one's senses; to come to one's self. *Ne pas avoir l'— tranquille;* to be uneasy in one's mind. *Remettre les —s;* to quiet people's minds. *Rendre l'—;* to give up the ghost. *Venir dans l'—;* to come into one's mind. *Passer pour un homme d'—;* to pass for a wit. *Les grands —s se rencontrent;* great wits jump together (i.e., when two people say the same thing together). —*s animaux;* animal spirits. *L'— court les rues;* wit is a drug in the market.

esprité, -e, *adj.*, intelligent, clever, witty.

esprot, *n.m.*, sprat.

esquicher, *v.n.*, *s'—*, *v.r.*, (reversis) to play a low card in order not to win a trick. *S'—;* (fig.) to answer evasively, to back out of.

esquif, *n.m.*, skiff.

*****esquille**, *n.f.*, splinter (of a bone).

esquinancie, *n.f.*, quinsy.

esquine, *n.f.*, (man.) horse's loins; (bot.) China-root. *Un cheval fort d'—;* a horse strong in his loins. (bot.) *V.* **squine**.

esquipot, *n.m.*, (fam.) money-box.

esquisse, *n.f.*, sketch, outline, rough drawing; rough-draft; plan. *Cahier d'—s;* sketch-book. *Faire l'— de;* to make a sketch of. *L'— d'un poème;* the sketch of a poem.

esquisser, *v.a.*, (paint.) to sketch, to outline.

esquiver, *v.a.*, to shun, to avoid, to elude.

s'esquiver, *v.r.*, to escape, to slip away, to steal away, to give the slip, to make off.

esquiver, *v.n.*, to slip away, to make off; to avoid.

essai, *n.m.*, trial, essay, attempt, endeavor; sample; experiment; testing, assaying (metal.). *Donner, prendre, à l'—;* to give, to take, on trial. *Faire son coup d'—;* to make one's first attempt. *Faire l'— de;* to make a trial of. — *sur la peinture;* essay on painting. *Faire l'— de l'or;* to assay gold. *Pour —;* by way of trial.

essaim (è-sin), *n.m.*, swarm; bevy, host.

essaimer, *v.n.*, to swarm. *Cette ruche a essaimé;* that hive has swarmed.

essanger, *v.a.*, to soak, to scour (dirty linen).

essarder, v.a., (nav.) to mop, to swab. [lands].

essartement, n.m., grubbing, clearing (of

essarter, v.a., to clear, to grub; to assart.

essaver, v.a., to drain.

essayage, n.m., trying-on (of clothes).

essayer, v.a., to try; to essay, to attempt, to make a trial of; to assay. — de l'or; to assay gold. — une chose; to try a thing.

s'**essayer**, v.r., to try one's strength or one's skill, to make attempts, to try one's hand. Il s'est essayé à peindre; he has tried his hand at painting.

essayer, v.n., to try, to attempt, to make a trial. Essayez de le persuader; try to persuade him. — de marcher; to try to walk.

essayerie, n.f., assay-office (of the mint).

essayeur, n.m., assayer.

essayiste, n.m.f., essayist.

esse, n.f., S; linch-pin (of the axle-tree of a coach); fore-lock (of a gun-carriage).

esseigler, v.a., to clear of rye.

esselier, n.m., (man.) brace.

esséminer, v.a., (l.u.) to disperse; to scatter.

essence, n.f., essence; substance; species (of trees); benzene; (of roses) otto, attar. — de romarin; essence of rosemary. — de la vie; heart's blood.

essénien, n.m., Essene.

essentiel, -le (-cièl), adj., essential, material. C'est là le point — ; that is the main point.

essentiel (-cièl), n.m., essential, essential point, main point, main thing. [materially.

essentiellement (-sièl-män), adv., essentially,

essette, n.f., hammer-axe. [doned.

esseulé, -e, adj., (fam., l. u.) solitary, aban-

essieu, n.m., axle-tree; pin (of a block). écartement des —x; wheel base (motor).

essor, n.m., flight; soaring, soar; strain; swing, play, scope, impulse, impulsion. Donner l'— à; to give wings to, to give scope to. L'— du génie; the soaring of genius. Prendre son —; to take one's flight.

essorant, -e, adj., (her.) soaring. Un oiseau —; (her.) a soaring bird.

essorer, v.a., to hang in the air in order to dry.

s'**essorer**, v.r., to soar aloft.

essoreu-r, -se, n.m.f., dryer. n.f., drying machine.

*****essoriller**, v.a., to cut the ears (of a dog); to crop short (hair); to crop a dog.

essoufflé, -e, part., breathless; out of breath. Etre tout — ; to be quite out of breath.

essoufflement, n.m., panting, breathlessness.

essouffler, v.a., to put out of breath; to wind (horses). S'—, v.r., to put one's self out of breath; to get or be out of breath.

essui, n.m., drying-closet, drying-house.

essuie-main, n.m., (—, or ——s) towel.

essuie-pieds, n.m., mat, door-mat.

essuie-plume, n.m., (—, or ——s) pen-wiper.

essuyage, n.m., wiping.

essuyer, v.a., to wipe, to wipe off, to wipe away, to wipe dry; to sustain, to support, to bear, to endure, to go through, to undergo. — les larmes de quelqu'un; to console any one. — des affronts; to endure affronts. — un refus or un revers; to meet with a refusal or a check.

s'**essuyer**, v.r., to dry one's self. S'— les mains, la figure; to wipe one's hands, one's face.

est (èst), n.m., east. D'—; eastern, easterly. Un vent d'—; an easterly wind. A l'—; to the east, eastward. Vers l'—; eastward.

estacade, n.f., stockade; boom (of a harbor).

estafette, n.f., courier, express messenger; (milit.) estafette.

estafier, n.m., (b.s.) tall footman, flunkey, livery servant; lanky Jack; hector, bully.

estafilade, n.f., cut (in the face), gash, slash; rent (in clothes).

estafilader, v.a., to slash, to cut, to gash.

estagnon, n.m., a copper bottle.

estame, n.f., worsted, knitted worsted.

estamet, n.m., coarse, woolen fabric.

estaminet, n.m., coffee-house; smoking divan; shades; tap-room.

estampage, n.m., stamping (metal.).

estampe, n.f., print, engraving, cut; stamp. Magasin d'—s; print-shop; (tech.) stamping-machine, punch.

estamper, v.a., to stamp; to punch, to brand.

estampeur, n.m., stamper. adj., stamping.

estampillage, n.m., stamping, marking.

*****estampille**, n.f., stamp, mark, trade-mark.

*****estampiller**, v.a., to stamp, to mark.

estanc, adj.m., (nav.) water-tight, well-found. Un navire — ; (nav.) a well-found ship.

estance, n.f., (nav.) stanchion.

ester, v.n., (jur.) to appear in court, to plead (before justice).

estère, n.f., straw mat; creek, cove.

esteuble, n.f., stubble. V. **éteule**.

esthétique, n.f., æsthetics.

esthétique, adj., æsthetical.

estimable, adj., estimable.

estimateur, n.m., appraiser, appreciator, valuer.

estimatif, adj., estimative. Etat — ; estimate.

estimation, n.f., estimation, appraising, valuation, estimate. Faire une — de; to appraise, to estimate.

estime, n.f., esteem, regard, estimation; (nav.) reckoning. Avoir de l'— pour; to hold in esteem. Etre perdu d'— et de réputation; to have lost one's reputation, and the esteem of every one.

estimer, v.a., to estimate, to value; to rate, to assess; to esteem, to regard, to prize, to consider, to deem, to account. — des meubles; to value furniture. — trop; to overrate.

s'**estimer**, v.r., to esteem, or to prize, one's self; to set a value on one's self; to consider one's self; to esteem one another.

estival, -e, adj., estival, summer.

estivation, n.f., (bot.) estivation; (zool.) torpor.

estive, n.f., (nav.) trimming, stowing (cargo).

estiver, v.a., (nav.) to stow, to trim, to press the cargo down; to turn cattle out to grass during summer.

estoc, n.m., tuck (sword); point of a sword; trunk, stock (of trees); (nav.) ledge, rock, shelf. Frapper d'— et de taille; to cut and thrust, or to lay about (recklessly). Parler d'— et de taille; to talk at random. Dites-vous cela de votre — ? do you say that of yourself? is it original? Etre réduit à blanc — ; to be done up or reduced to nothing. A blanc — ; (agri.) to the root.

estocade, n.f., (fenc.) stoccado, stoccade, thrust, lunge; unexpected attack.

estocader, v.n., (fenc.) to thrust, to make passes, to lunge.

estomac (-ma), n.m., stomach; breast; chest. Avoir mal à l'— ; to have a stomach-ache. Ardeur d'— ; heartburn. Soulever l'— ; to turn the stomach. Tiraillements d'— ; twitching pains in the stomach. Le creux de l'— ; the pit of the stomach.

s'**estomaquer**, v.r., (fam.) to take offense; not to be able to brook anything; to exhaust one's self by speaking. Il s'est estomaqué; he is put out.

estompage, n.m., (draw.) stumping.

estompe, n.f., stump. Dessin à l'— ; stump-drawing.

estomper, v.a., to stump; to shade off.

estouffade, n.f. V. **étouffée**.

estrade, n.f., platform, stand, stage. ⊙Battre l'— ; to scout; to be on the tramp. Batteurs d'— ; ⊙scouts; (fam.) strollers, trampers, vagrants.

estragon, n.m., (bot.) tarragon.

⊙**estramaçon**, n.m., two-edged sword. *Coup d'—* ; cut with the edge of a sword.

estramaçonner, v.r., (jest., l.u.) to strike with the edge of a sword, to cut, to slash.

estrapade, n.f., strappado ; gibbet used for the strappado ; (man.) estrapade. *Se donner l'—* ; to torture one's brains.

estrapader, v.a., to give the strappado, to torture.

estrapasser, v.a., (man.) to overwork, to over-ride.

estraper, v.a., to mow (stubble).

estrope, n.f., (nav.) strop.

estroper, v.a., (nav.) to strop.

estropiat, n.m., (fam.) cripple ; beggar.

estropié, -e, n.m., -e, n.f., cripple.

estropié, -e, part., crippled, lame ; disabled. *Etre — d'un bras ;* to have an arm disabled. *Passage —;* mutilated passage.

estropier, v.a., to cripple, to lame, to maim, to disable ; to mangle, to murder, to spoil, to mutilate. *— un passage ;* to mutilate a passage. *— un rôle ;* (theat.) to murder a part.

estuaire, n.m., (geog.) estuary.

esturgeon (-jon), n.m., (ich.) sturgeon.

esule, n.f., (bot.) esula.

et (é), conj., and. *—...—;* both...and ; then, thereupon. *— vous — moi ;* both you and I. [The final *t* of *et* is never pronounced.]

établage, n.m., stabling.

étable, n.f., stable (for oxen, sheep, goats) ; stall ; cattle-shed ; cattle-house ; pig-sty, hog-sty, sty. *S'aborder de franche —;* (nav.) to run right into one another, to run foul of one another.

établer, v.a., to put in a stable, to stable.

établi, n.m., bench (joiner's) ; shop-board, counter (tailor's).

établi, -e, part., established ; settled, laid down.

établir, v.a., to establish, to set, to fix, to erect, to set up, to set up in business ; to insti-tute, to found, to aver, to make good, to lay down (statements) ; to assert ; to prove, to make out, to show ; to induct ; to strike (balance) ; to impose (a tax). *— sa fille ;* to settle one's daugh-ter. *— un fait ;* to state a fact ; to make it good. *— par des exemples ;* to prove, to make good, by examples.

*s'***établir**, v.r., to establish one's self, to fix one's residence, to take up one's residence ; to settle down, to settle (marry) ; to set up shop ; to set up in business, to set up for one's self, to set up. *Il est venu s'— en France ;* he came to settle in France. *Il songe à s'—;* he is thinking of settling down.

établissement (-blis-mān), n.m., establish-ment, establishing, settlement ; setting up, fixing, placing, erecting ; proving, making out, showing ; imposition (of taxes) ; settling ; setting up in busi-ness ; (nav.) tide-table. *L'— d'un fait ;* the stating, proving of a fact. *Les hôpitaux sont des —s très-utiles ;* hospitals are highly useful institu-tions. *L'— de ses enfants ;* the settling of one's children. *Frais de premier —;* first expenses. *Dans l'—;* on the premises.

étage, n.m., story, floor ; flight (of stairs) ; (geol., mining) layer, stratum. *Il demeure au troisième —;* he lives on the third floor. *Il y a des hommes d'esprit de tout — ;* there are wits of every degree. *C'est un sot à triple —;* he is a consummate fool. *Avoir un menton à double —;* to have a double chin. *De bas —;* of low degree ; low birth.

étagé, -e, part., adj., rising tier upon tier ; tapered, tapering.

étager, v.a., to taper ; to dispose in tiers. *S'—;* to rise tier upon tier ; to taper.

étagère, n.f., what-not, shelves.

étague (é-tag), n.f., (nav.) hoisting the yards.

étai, n.m., stay, shore ; prop, strut. *— de misaine ;* (nav.) fore-stay. *—d'artimon ;* (nav.) mizzen-stay. *— du grand mât ;* (nav.) main-stay.

étaie, n.f., (her.) chevronel.

⊙**étaiement**, n.m., propping, staying, shoring, supporting, bearing up. *V.* **étayement.**

étaim (é-tin), n.m., fine carded wool.

étain, n.m., tin ; pewter. *— fin ;* pure tin. *— commun ;* block tin. *— métallique ;* white tin. *— oxydé ;* tin-stone. *— en feuilles ;* tin-foil. *— de glace ;* tin-glass.

étal, n.m., stall ; butcher's stall ; butcher's shop.

étalage, n.m., laying out, exposing of goods for sale ; goods exposed for sale ; shop-window ; window ; stallage ; finery, fine clothes ; showing off, ostentatious display, show. *Cela n'est bon qu'à servir d'—;* that will only serve for show. *Faire — de son esprit ;* to parade one's wit. *Faire de l'—;* to make a show, to show off.

étalagiste, n.m., stall-keeper, window-dresser.

étale, adj., (nav.) still ; slack (of the water) ; settled, steady (of the wind). *Mer —;* slack water, tide.

étalé, -e, part., spread out, unfolded, dis-played.

étaler, v.a., to expose for sale ; to put in the shop-window ; to spread, to spread out ; to show, to set forth, to display, to parade, to make a show or parade of, to show off.

*s'***étaler**, v.r., to be exposed for sale ; to be hung up in the window ; to be displayed, to be spread out ; to stretch one's self out, to sprawl ; to show one's self off, to show off. *S'— sur l'herbe ;* to stretch one's self at full length on the grass.

étalier, n.m., journeyman-butcher.

étalinguer (-ghé), v.a., (nav.) to clinch.

étalingure, n.f., (nav.) clinch, bend (of a cable).

étalon, n.m., stallion ; standard (of weight and measures). *D'—;* standard. *— de haras ;* stud-horse.

étalonnage or **étalonnement**, n.m., stamp-ing (of weights, etc.) ; gauging.

étalonner, v.a., to stamp ; to gauge.

étalonneur, n.m., inspector of weights and measures.

étamage, n.m., tinning ; quicksilvering, silver-ing ; plating.

étambot (formerly étambord), n.m., (nav.) stern-post.

étambrai, n.m., (nav.) partner (of a mast, etc.).

étamer, v.a., to tin ; to plate (glass) ; to foli-ate, to quicksilver.

étameur, n.m., tinman ; silverer.

étamine, n.f., stamin ; tammy ; sieve ; strainer, colander ; bolting-cloth ; bolter ; bunting ; (bot.) stamen, male organ, thrum. *Passer par l'—;* to sift. *Il a passé par l'—;* he has been strictly examined.

étaminé, -e, adj., (bot.) stamened.

étamineuse, adj. f., (bot.) having stamina, but no petals or leaves.

étaminier, n.m., stamin-maker.

étamper, v.a., to punch (horse-shoes).

étampure, n.f., the holes of a horse-shoe.

étamure, n.f., melted tin, tinning, material for tinning.

étanche, adj., water-tight ; air-tight ; steam-tight.

étanché, part., stopped (of a leak).

étanchement (é-tānsh-mān), n.m., stanch-ing ; stopping ; quenching ; slaking. *L'— du sang ;* the stopping of blood.

étancher, v.a., to stanch ; to stop ; to slake, to quench. *— le sang ;* to stop the blood. *— la soif ;* to quench the thirst. *— un vaisseau-* (nav.) to free a ship of water.

étançon, *n.m.*, prop, stay, supporter, shore; (nav.) stanchion.

étançonner, *v.a.*, to prop, to underprop, to stay, to support, to shore.

étanfiche, *n.f.*, quarry-stratum.

étang, *n.m.*, pond, fish-pond; pool. *Peupler un —;* to stock a pond. *Pêcher un —;* to drag a pond.

étape, *n.f.*, store-house; rations; forage; halting place; stage. *Brûler l'—;* to pass through without stopping.

étapier, *n.m.*, (milit.) distributor of rations.

état, *n. m.*, state; commonweal, commonwealth; case, condition; position, circumstance, plight, predicament, account, statement, return; list, register, inventory, estimate; establishment; calling, profession, station; office. *pl.*, dominions; (med.) acme; (milit.) list, musterroll. *Mettre hors d'— de;* to put it out of any one's power to. *Il est en— de payer;* he is able to pay, he is in a position to pay. *En quelque — que soit l'affaire;* however the matter may stand. *De son —;* by profession, by trade. *Se mettre en— de défense;* to put one's self in a state of defense. *Mettre en —;* to enable, to prepare for. *Tenir une chose en —;* to keep a thing ready; to keep a thing in its place. *Tenir en —;* to keep in suspense. *Faire peu d'— de;* to have a poor opinion of. *L'—-major*, (—*s*— *s*) (milit.) staff, staff-office. —*s-généraux;* states-general. — *de comptes;* statement of accounts. *Tenir un grand —;* to keep a large establishment. *Ministre, secrétaire, d'—;* minister, secretary, of state. *Coup d'—;* stroke of state policy. *Homme d'—;* statesman. *Affaires d'—;* state affairs. *Raison d'—;* state policy. *Les —s-Unis d'Amérique;* the United States of North America. *Remettre en —;* to set right again.

étau, *n.m.*, vice. *Les mâchoires de l'—;* the chops of the vice. — *à main;* hand-vice.

étayement (-tê-mān), *n.m.*, staying, shoring, bearing up, propping, supporting.

étayer, *v.a.*, to stay, to prop, to bear up, to support, to shore.

etc., *conj.*, (ab. of *et cætera*) etc.

et cætera, *conj.*, *et cætera*.

été, *n.m.*, summer; prime (of life). — *chaud, brûlant;* warm, scorching, summer. *Au milieu de l'—;* in the middle of summer. *Etre dans son —;* to be in one's prime.

***éteigneu-r**, *n.m.*, -**se**, *n.f.*, (pers.) extinguisher.

***éteignoir**, *n.m.*, extinguisher (instrument).

éteindre (*éteignant, éteint), *v.a.*, to put out, to extinguish, to quench, to appease; to exterminate, to destroy, to obliterate; to soften (colors); to wear out; to liquidate (a debt); to strike out. *Eteignez la chandelle;* put out the candle. — *de la chaux;* to slake lime. — *la soif;* to quench the thirst. — *une pension;* to buy up, to redeem, an annuity. — *une obligation;* to cancel an obligation. — *le souvenir de;* to obliterate the recollection of. — *une couleur;* to soften down a color.

s'éteindre, *v.r.*, to be extinguished, to be put out, quenched; to go out to die away, to die out; to decrease, to diminish, to be diminished; to be slaked (of lime). *Le feu s'éteint;* the fire is going out. *Cette maison va s'—;* that family will soon die out, will soon be extinct.

éteint, -e, *part.*, put out, extinguished, out, extinct. *Mon feu est —;* my fire is out. *Elle a la voix —e;* her voice is scarcely audible. *Des yeux —s;* dull eyes.

étendage, *n.m.*, lines to hang things to dry upon; drying-room.

étendard, *n.m.*, standard, colors, banner, flag. *Arborer, déployer, planter, un —;* to hoist, to display, to plant, a standard. *Lever l'— de la révolte;* to raise the standard of rebellion.

étendeuse, *n.f.*, (spinning) stretcher.

étendoir, *n.m.*, drying-room; (print.) peel.

étendre, *v.a.*, to spread, to stretch, to expand, to distend; to lay out; to lengthen, to prolong, to draw out; to lay dead, to kill one on the spot; to enlarge, to extend, to widen; to wire-draw; to lay on (colors); to overthrow, to throw down. — *du beurre sur du pain;* to spread butter upon bread. — *son armée;* to extend one's army. — *du linge;* to lay out linen. — *le bras;* to stretch out one's arm. — *les ailes;* to spread the wings. — *son commerce;* to extend one's trade.

s'étendre, *v.r.*, to stretch one's self out, to sprawl; to reach, to extend; to expatiate, to dwell; to lengthen, to grow out; to draw out, to launch. *Il s'étendit tout de son long sur l'herbe;* he laid himself at full length upon the grass. *Aussi loin que la vue peut s'—;* as far as the eye can reach. *S'— sur un sujet;* to expatiate, to dwell, upon a subject.

étendu, -**e**, *part.*, stretched, spread, extended. *Du linge — sur l'herbe;* linen laid out on the grass. *Un empire fort —;* a widely extended empire. *La vue est ici fort —e;* the view here is very extensive. *Des connaissances —es;* extensive knowledge. *Il a une voix très —e;* he has great compass of voice. *C'est un esprit fort —;* he is a man of vast intellect.

étendue, *n.f.*, extent, extensiveness, expanse; compass, length. *Dans toute son —;* to the full. *La vaste — des mers;* the wide expanse of ocean. *Grande — de voix;* great compass of voice.

éternel, -**le**, *adj.*, eternal, everlasting, everenduring, endless, ever-living. *Le Père —;* God Almighty.

éternel, *n.m.*, Eternal, God; Everlasting.

éternelle, *n.f.* V. **immortelle**.

éternellement (-nèl-mān) *adv.*, eternally, to all eternity, everlastingly; forever, perpetually; incessantly, continually, for evermore.

éterniser, *v.a.*, to perpetuate. — *son nom;* to immortalize one's name.

s'éterniser, *v.r.*, to be perpetuated, to be rendered eternal.

éternité, *n.f.*, eternity, everlastingness. *De toute —;* from all eternity.

éternue, *n.f.*, (bot.) florin, sneezewort.

éternuement or **éternûment**, *n.m.*, sneezing, sneeze.

éternuer, *v.n.*, to sneeze.

éternueu-r, *n.m.*, -**se**, *n.f.*, sneezer.

étésien, *adj.*, etesian.

étêtement (é-têt-mān), *n.m.*, pollarding, topping.

étêter, *v.a.*, (hort.) to top, to pollard; to take off the heads of (nails, pins).

⊙**éteuf** (é-teu), *n.m.*, ball (at tennis).

éteule or **esteuble**, *n.f.*, stubble.

éther (é-tèr), *n.m.*, ether.

éthéré, -**e**, *adj.*, ethereal.

éthérifier, *v.a.*, to etherealize; to etherize.

s'éthérifier, *v.r.*, to become etherized.

éthérisation, *n.f.*, (chem.) etherification.

éthériser, *v.a.*, (chem.) to etherealize; (med.) to produce insensibility by means of ether.

éthiopien, *n.m.*, -**ne**, *n.f.*, Ethiopian.

éthique, *n.f.*, ethics, morals.

éthique, *adj.*, ethic, ethical.

ethmoïdal, -**e**, *adj.*, (anat.) ethmoidal. *L'os —;* ethmoidal bone.

ethmoïde, *n.m.*, (anat.) ethmoid.

ethnarchie, *n.f.*, ethnarchy.

ethnarque, *n.m.*, ethnarch.

ethnique, *adj.*, ethnic, ethnical.

ethnographe, *n.m.*, ethnologist.

ethnographie, *n.f.*, ethnography.

ethnographique, *adj.*, ethnographical.

ethnologie, *n.f.*, ethnology, ethnography.

ethnologue, *n.m.*, ethnologist, ethnographer.

ethnologique, *adj.*, ethnologic, ethnological.

éthologie, *n.f.*, ethology.

éthologique, *adj.*, ethologic.

éthopée, *n.f.*, description of human passions and manners.

étiage (é-tiaj), *n.m.*, low-water mark.

étier (é-tié), *n.m.*, ditch (for conveying sea-water to a salt-marsh).

étincelant, -e (é-tin-slän, -t), *adj.*, sparkling, glittering, flashing, twinkling, glistening.

étinceler (é-tin-slé), *v.n.*, to sparkle, to flash, to gleam, to twinkle, to glitter. *Les yeux lui étincellent de colère;* his eyes are flashing with anger. *Cet ouvrage étincelle d'esprit;* that work sparkles with wit.

étincelette, *n.f.*, little spark.

étincelle, *n.f.*, spark, flash of fire. *Jeter des —s;* to throw out sparks. *Il n'a pas une — de bon sens;* he is utterly devoid of good sense.

étincellement (-sèl-män), *n.m.*, sparkling, twinkling, glistening, scintillation.

étiolement (é-tiol-män), *n.m.*, etiolation, branching; sickliness (of plants); (med.) chlorosis; paleness, emaciation.

étiolé, -e, *adj.*, *part.*, etiolated; pale, wan, emaciated; sickly.

étioler, *v.a.*, to etiolate (plants).

s'étioler, *v.r.*, to etiolate, to blanch; (pers.) to be weakened, to grow enfeebled; (of plants) to waste away; to wither.

étiologie, *n.f.*, (med.) etiology.

étique, *adj.*, hectic; consumptive; lean, lank, emaciated.

étiqueter (é-tik-té), *v.a.*, to label, to ticket.

étiquette, *n.f.*, ticket, label; etiquette. *Condamner sur l'— du sac;* to condemn without examining, or to condemn on appearances. *Tenir à l'—;* to be particular; to stand on ceremony.

étirage, *n.m.*, stretching; wire-drawing.

étire, *n.f.*, stretching-iron (of curriers).

étirer, *v.a.*, to stretch; (tech.) to lengthen, to wire-draw.

s'étirer, *v.r.*, to stretch out one's limbs.

étisie, *n.f.*, consumption, decline.

étoffe, *n.f.*, stuff; cloth, material; condition, quality, worth. *pl.*, stuffs; (print.) wear and tear, plant. *— drapée;* woolen cloth. *Il y a de l'— chez lui;* he has got some stuff in him.

étoffé, -e, *adj.*, stuffed, lined; upholstered (of furniture); comfortably off; stout, full-bodied; substantial. *Discours bien —;* well-arranged speech; speech full of capital things. *Maison bien —e;* well-furnished house. *Homme bien —;* man in good circumstances.

étoffer, *v.a.*, to stuff, to line, to furnish with materials; to upholster.

étoile, *n.f.*, star; (man.) blaze; center (of walks in parks); star-wheel, fate, destiny; asterisk; (print., fort.) star. *A la lumière des —s;* by starlight. *— polaire;* polar-star. *— tombante, filante;* shooting star. *— de mer;* starfish. *Coucher à la belle —;* to sleep in the open air. *Né sous une mauvaise —;* born under an unlucky star. *Voir des —s en plein midi;* to "see stars."

étoilé, -e, *adj.*, starry; full of stars, studded. *La voûte —e;* the spangled vault. *Bouteille —e;* starred bottle (cracked).

étoiler, *v.a.*, to star, to stud with stars; to crack; to blaze; to mark with a star.

s'étoiler, *v.r.*, to star, to crack; to become studded with stars.

étole, *n.f.*, (c.rel.) stole.

étonnamment (é-to-na-män), *adv.*, astonishingly, wonderfully, amazingly.

étonnant, -e, *adj.*, astonishing, surprising, wonderful, marvelous, amazing.

étonné, -e, *part.*, astonished. *Etre — de;* to be astonished at. *Faire, jouer l'—;* to feign astonishment.

étonnement (é-ton-män), *n.m.*, astonishment, amazement; admiration, wonder; fright, terror; ⊙shock. *Frapper d'—;* to strike with amazement. *Remplir d'—;* to fill with astonishment. *Je ne reviens pas de mon —;* I cannot recover from my astonishment. *Tout le monde est dans l'—;* every body is amazed. *A l'— de tout le monde;* to the astonishment of everybody.

étonner, *v.a.*, to astonish, to amaze, to startle, to stagger; to astound, to stun. *Je suis étonné qu'il ne m'en ait rien dit;* I wonder he said nothing about it to me.

s'étonner, *v.r.*, to be astonished, to be amazed, to wonder. *Il ne s'étonne de rien;* he is astonished at nothing.

étouffade, *n.f.* V. **étouffée**.

étouffant, -e, *adj.*, suffocating; sultry, close, sweltering. *Chaleur —e;* sweltering heat.

étouffé, -e, *part.*, suffocated, stifled; suppressed; concealed; stamped out.

étouffée, *n.f.*, (cook.) estoufade.

étouffement (é-toof-män), *n.m.*, suffocation, stifling.

étouffer, *v.a.*, to suffocate, to choke, to throttle, to smother, to stifle, to suppress; to hush up; to deaden (sound). *Les mauvaises herbes étouffent le blé;* weeds choke the corn. *— une affaire;* to hush up an affair. *— une révolte;* to suppress a revolt. *— la voix;* to drown the voice.

étouffer, *v.n.*, to be choking, to be choked; to be suffocated; to swelter. *On étouffe ici;* there is no breathing here. *— de rire;* to choke with laughter.

étouffoir, *n.m.*, cinder-pail; extinguisher (for charcoal); damper (piano).

étoupe, *n.f.*, tow, oakum. *Mettre le feu aux —s;* to add fuel to the flame; to fan. *— goudronnée;* tarred oakum.

étoupement, *n.m.*, stopping, stuffing; (nav.) calking.

étouper, *v.a.*, to stop (with tow *or* oakum); (nav.) to calk. *S'— les oreilles;* to stop one's ears with cotton-wool.

étoupier, -ère, *n.m.f.*, oakum-picker.

*****étoupille**, *n.f.*, (artil.) quick-match; tube.

*****étoupiller**, *v.a.*, (artil.) to prime.

*****étoupillon**, *n.m.*, (artil.) toppin.

étoupin, *n.m.*, wad, wadding.

étourdeau, *n.m.*, young capon.

étourderie, *n.f.*, giddiness, heedlessness, thoughtlessness, giddy act, blunder. *Il fait toujours des —s;* he is always committing some thoughtless act or other.

étourdi, -e, *adj.*, stunned; giddy, dizzy, thoughtless, heedless; giddy-headed.

étourdi, *n.m.*, **-e**, *n.f.*, rattle-head, mad-cap, romp. *C'est une —e;* she is a giddy creature. *A l'—e;* giddily, heedlessly, rashly. *Jeter à l'—e;* to blurt out.

étourdiment, *adv.*, inconsiderately, heedlessly, thoughtlessly.

étourdir, *v.a.*, to stun, to deafen, to make dizzy, to make giddy; to astound; to din; to assuage (pain); to parboil. *— la grosse faim;* to take the edge off one's appetite. *— de la viande;* to partly cook meat. *— de l'eau;* to take the chill off of the water.

s'étourdir, *v.r.*, to divert one's thoughts; to be preoccupied; to try to forget. *Il s'étourdit sur son chagrin;* he tries to forget his grief.

étourdissant, -e, *adj.*, stunning, deafening, astounding.

étourdissement (-dis-män), *n.m.*, stunning, dizziness, giddiness; amazement; stupefaction; stupor; shock. *Il a des —s;* he is subject to attacks of giddiness. *Le premier — passé;* when the first shock was over.

étourneau, *n.m.*, (orni.) starling; giddy fellow; flea-bitten horse.

étourneau, *adj.*, flea-bitten (of horses).

étrange, *adj.*, strange, odd, queer, novel; uncouth. *Chose* —! strange! strange to say! *C'est une personne bien* —; she is a very queer sort of a person.

étrangement (é-tranj-mān), *adv.*, strangely, queerly; terribly.

étrang-er, **-ère**, *adj.*, strange; foreign; unknown; irrelevant; outlandish. *Ministre des affaires* —ères; minister for foreign affairs. *Être* — *à une science*; to be unacquainted with a science. *Un fait* — *à la cause*; a fact unconnected with or foreign to the case. *Corps* —; extraneous body. *Une langue* —e; a foreign language.

étrang-er, *n.m.*, **-ère**, *n.f.*, foreigner, stranger, alien, outsider; foreign parts. *C'est un* —; he is a foreigner. *A l'* —; abroad. *Passer à l'* —; to go abroad.

⊙**étranger**, *v.a.*, to estrange, to drive away. s'**étranger**, *v.r.*, (hunt.) to desert a country, to disappear from (of game).

étrangeté (é-tranj-té), *n.f.*, strangeness; oddness, queerness.

⊙**étranglant, -e**, *adj.*, strangling; overwhelming, amazing; decisive.

étranglé, -e, *part.*, scanty, too narrow. *Discours* —; speech too much compressed.

étranglo-loup, *n.m.*, (—) (bot.) true-love.

étranglement, *n.m.*, strangling; garotting; (med.) strangulation; stricture.

étrangler, *v.a.*, to strangle, to throttle, to choke, to stifle; to make too little, too narrow, to make scanty, to compress, to confine, to scant, to slur over. *Cet habit est étranglé*; that coat is too scanty. — *une affaire*; to slur over a business.

s'**étrangler**, *v.r.*, to strangle one's self.

étrangler, *v.n.*, to be choked, to be strangled.

étrangleur, -se, *n.m.f.*, garotter, strangler.

***étranguillon** (-ghi-ion), *n.m.*, (vet.) strangles. *Poire* —; choke-pear.

étrape, *n.f.*, small sickle (for stubble).

étraper, *v.a.*, to cut stubble.

étraquer, *v.n.*, (hunt.) to track (on the snow).

étrave, *n.f.*, (nav.) stem.

être (étant, été), *v.n.*, to be, to exist; to belong; to have; to stand; to take part in; to come; to go; to lie; to prove to be; to turn out to be. — *en bonne santé*; to be in good health. — *fatigué*; to be tired. — *à quelque chose*; to be doing anything. *Y* —; to be at home; to have hit it. *En* — *là*; to have come to that. *J'y suis*; I have it. *Je suis des vôtres*; I shall join your party. *Je n'en suis plus*; I cry off. *Il n'en est rien*; such is not the case, it is nothing of the sort. — *sage*; (of children) to be good. — *bien avec quelqu'un*; to be on good terms with any one. — *mal avec quelqu'un*; to be on bad terms with any one. — *de moitié*; to go halves. *Eh bien, soit*; well, let it be so. *Ainsi soit-il*; so be it. *Ce tableau est du Poussin*; this picture is by Poussin. *Il est de Paris*; he is a native of Paris. *Cet enfant est à moi*; that child belongs to me. *Cela n'est pas*; it is not so. *C'est que*; the fact is, the truth is. *Si ce n'est que*; except that. *N'eût été que*; had it not been for. *Il en sera de nous comme des autres*; it will be with us as with others. *Ce sont eux qui*; it is they who. *Je suis à vous dans un moment*; I shall be at your service, with you, in a moment. *Cette fois ça y est*; now for it! Done this time, and no mistake! *Qu'est-ce que c'est*? what is it? *C'est à vous de parler*; it is for you to speak. *C'est à vous à parler*; it is your turn to speak. *Où en êtes-vous?* where are you? how far have you got? *Je ne sais pas où j'en suis*; I do not know how I am situated, I do not know what I am about. *Il est à présumer*; it is to be presumed. *Il n'est pas en moi de l'éviter*; it does not depend upon me to avoid it. *En êtes-vous encore là?* do you still believe that? *Il en sera ce qu'il plaira à Dieu*; it will be as God pleases. *J'en serai de moitié*; I will go halves in it. *J'y suis pour un tiers*; I am in for a third share. *Je n'en suis plus*; I have declared off. *Je n'y suis pour rien*; I have no hand in the matter. *C'en est fait de lui*; it is all over with him. *Voilà où nous en sommes*; such is our present situation. *Il ne sait où il en est*; he does not know where he is. *Que sera-ce de?* what will become of? *Vous y êtes*; you have hit it. *Cela n'en est pas*; that does not belong to it. *Je suis tout à vous*; I am entirely at your service. *Si j'étais de or Si j'étais que de vous*; (fam.) were I in your place. *Je n'y suis pour personne*; I am at home to no one. *Madame n'y est pas*; my mistress is not at home. *Quoi qu'il en soit*; at all events, be that as it may. *En* — *pour son argent*; to lose one's money over anything. *J'en suis pour mes frais*; I have lost my time and money. *En* — *pour vingt francs*; to be in for it to the tune of twenty francs. — *à l'étroit*; to be cramped for room. *On ne peut pas* — *et avoir été*; you can't have your cake and eat it.

être, *n.m.*, being, existence; trunk (of a tree). *Les* —*s d'une maison*; the parts, ins and outs of a house. *Non* —; nonentity. *Bien*— —; welfare, comforts of life. *Il sait tous les* —*s de cette maison*; he knows all the ways of that house. *Couper à blanc* —; (of trees) to cut down to the root.

étrécir, *v.r.* V. **rétrécir**.

s'**étrécir**, *v.r.* V. **se rétrécir**.

étrécissement (-sis-mān), *n.m.* V. **rétrécissement**.

étrécissure, *n.f.* V. **rétrécissure**.

étreindre (étreignant, étreint), *v.a.*, to bind, to tie, to tie up; to press, to clasp.

étreinte, *n.f.*, knot; clasping, pressing; embrace. *De douces* —*s*; sweet embraces.

étrenne (é-trè-n), *n.f.*, handsel. *pl.*, New Year's gift.

étrenner (é-trè-né), *v.a.*, to give a New Year's gift, to give a Christmas-box; to handsel; to try or put on for the first time; to buy the first lot.

***étrésillon**, *n.m.*, prop, stay, support.

***étrésillonner**, *v.a.*, to prop, to stay.

étrier, *n.m.*, stirrup; iron-hook; (surg.) stirrup-bandage; strap. *Il est ferme sur ses* —*s*; he has a firm seat in the saddle. *Vin or coup de l'* —; stirrup-cup. *Il a toujours le pied à l'* —; he is never out of the saddle. *Courir à franc* —; to ride full speed. *Faire perdre les* —*s à quelqu'un*; to put any one out of countenance. *Tenir l'* — *à*; to give a lift to.

étrière, *n.f.*, stirrup-bar; spring-bar.

***étrille**, *n.f.*, curry-comb.

***étriller**, *v.a.*, to curry, to comb (a horse); to fleece; to give a thrashing to; to drub.

étriper, *v.a.*, to gut (animal). *Aller à* — *cheval*; to ride a horse at breakneck speed.

étriqué, -e, *adj.*, scanty; narrow; curtailed. *Habits* —*s*; scanty clothes, coat.

étrivière, *n.f.*, stirrup-leather. *Donner les* —*s à quelqu'un*; to give any one a thrashing. *Allonger l'* —; to raise fresh difficulties; to cause further delay.

étroit, -e, *adj.*, narrow, tight, strait, close; intimate; limited, confined; scanty, small. *Habit* —; tight coat. *Esprit* —; narrow mind. *Etre dans une* —*e amitié avec quelqu'un*; to be on the most intimate terms with any one. *A l'* —; narrowly. *Etre à l'* —; to be pinched, to be poor, to be badly off for room. *Vivre à l'* —; to live sparingly.

étroitement (é-troat-mān), *adv.*, closely,

tightly, narrowly; intimately, sparingly. — *uni;* closely united.

étroitesse, *n.f.,* narrowness; straitness; tightness, closeness. — *d'esprit;* narrow-mindedness.

étronçonner, *v.a.,* to lop off.

étrusque, *adj.,* Etruscan.

étude, *n.f.,* study; (in colleges) school-room, time of study; examination; survey; rehearsal; (paint.) academy figure; office, chambers, practice (of attorneys); disguise, art, affectation. *pl.,* education. *Cabinet d'—;* study. *Maître d'—;* usher. *Avoir de l'—;* to be a man of attainment. *Je me fais une — de;* I make it a study to. *Il a fait ses —s;* he has finished his education. *Il a fait de bonnes —s;* he has had a good education. *Etre sans —;* to have no education. *A l'—;* (of plans) being considered, under consideration; (of plays) in rehearsal.

étudiant, *n.m.,* student, undergraduate. — *en droit;* law student. — *en médecine;* medical student.

étudié, -e, *part.,* studied, affected, far-fetched. *Langage —;* studied language. *Tableau fort —;* elaborate piece of painting.

étudier, *v.n.,* to study; to learn; to practise (music); to examine; to survey.

étudier, *v.a.,* to study; to practise (music). — *la nature;* to study nature. — *son rôle;* to study one's part. — *un discours;* to study a speech.

s'étudier, *v.r.,* to study, to make it one's study, to school one's self.

étudiole, *n.f.,* paper-case.

étui, *n.m.,* case, box; sheath, wing-sheath; needle-case. — *de chapeau;* hat-box.

étuve, *n.f.,* sweating-room; (manu.) stove, drying stove.

étuvée, *n.f.,* stewed meat.

étuvement (é-tuv-măn),*n.m.,* bathing, fomenting (of a wound).

étuver, *v.a.,* to bathe, to foment; (cook.) to stew.

☉**étuviste,** *n.m.,* bath-keeper.

étymologie, *n.f.,* etymology.

étymologique, *adj.,* etymological.

étymologiquement, *adv.,* etymologically.

étymologiser, *v.n.,* to etymologize.

étymologiste, *n.m.,* etymologist.

eubages, *n.m.pl.,* Gaulish Druids.

eucharistie (eu-ka-ris-tî), *n.f.,* Eucharist.

eucharistique, *adj.,* eucharistical.

eucologe, *n.m.,* euchology.

eucraisie, *n.f.,* (med.) eucrasy.

eudiomètre, *n.m.,* eudiometer.

eudiométrie, *n.f.,* eudiometry.

eudiométrique, *adj.,* eudiometric.

eufraise, *n.f.,* (bot.) euphrasy, eyebright.

euh, *int.,* aha! oh! Euh! Euh! so, so.

eulogie, *n.f.,* ☉ (rel.) consecrated bread. *pl.,* (Grec. rel.) broken remnants of the host.

euménide, *n.f.,* (myth.) Fury.

eunuque, *n.m.,* eunuch.

eupatoire, *n.f.,* (bot.) eupatory.

euphémique, *adj.,* euphemistic.

euphémisme, *n.m.,* euphemism.

euphonie, *n.f.,* euphony.

euphonique, *adj.,* euphonical.

euphorbe, *n.m.,* (bot.) euphorbia, spurge, (pharm.) euphorbium.

euphorbiacées, *n.f.pl.,* (bot.) euphorbiaceæ.

européen, -ne (-in, è-n), *n.* and *adj.,* European.

eurythmie, *n.f.,* eurythmy.

eustache, *n.m.,* cheap clasp-knife, whittle.

eustyle, *n.m.,* (arch.) eustyle.

eutychéen or **eutychien,** *n.m.,* eutychian.

eux, *pron.m.pl.,* they; them. — *-mêmes;* themselves. *Entre —;* between them.

évacuant, -e, *adj.,* (med.) evacuant.

évacuant, *n.m.,* (med.) evacuant.

évacuati-f, -ve, *adj.,* (med., l.u.) evacuant.

évacuation, *n.f.,* evacuation; ejection. *L'— d'une place;* the evacuation of a fortress *or* town.

évacuer, *v.a.,* to evacuate; to throw off, to eject, to clear. — *les humeurs;* to throw off the humours. *Faites — la salle;* clear the room. — *une place;* to evacuate a place.

s'évader, *v.r.,* to make one's escape, to escape, to break loose; to get away.

évagation, *n.f.,* evagation.

évaluable, *adj.,* ratable, appraisable.

évaluation, *n.f.,* valuation, estimate. *L'— d'une perte;* the estimate of a loss.

évaluer, *v.a.,* to value, to estimate, to rate.

évangélique, *adj.,* evangelical.

évangéliquement (-lik-măn), *adv.,* evangelically.

évangéliser, *v.a.,* to evangelize, to preach the Gospel to.

évangéliser, *v.n.,* to evangelize, to preach the Gospel.

évangéliste, *n.m.,* Evangelist.

évangile, *n.m.,* Gospel. *Côté de l'—;* left-hand side of the altar. *Prêcher l'—;* to preach the Gospel. *Il croit cela comme l'—;* he takes that for Gospel. *Prendre tout pour paroles d'—;* to take all for Gospel. *L'— du jour;* the current news; (rel.) the gospel for the day.

évanoui, -e, *adj.,* in a swoon; insensible, unconscious, senseless; vanished, dispelled, gone.

s'évanouir, *v.r.,* to faint, to swoon, to swoon away; to vanish, to disappear, to fade away. *Cette nouvelle l'a fait s'—;* that news made her swoon.

évanouissement (-noo-is-măn), *n.m.,* swoon, swooning away, fainting fit, syncope, disappearance. *Revenir d'un —;* to recover from a swoon.

évaporable, *adj.,* evaporable.

évaporati-f, -ve, *adj.,* causing evaporation.

évaporation, *n.f.,* evaporation; giddiness, thoughtlessness.

évaporatoire, *adj.,* evaporating.

évaporé, -e, *n.* and *adj.,* giddy, thoughtless person; evaporate, evaporated. *Un jeune homme —;* a giddy-brained youth.

évaporer, *v.a.,* to evaporate, to give vent, to pour out in words. — *son chagrin;* to give vent to one's grief.

s'évaporer, *v.r.,* to evaporate; to get giddy, heedless. *Il commence à s'—;* his conduct is becoming irregular.

évasé, *part.,* widened; bell-shaped; bell-mouthed. *Nez —;* nose with wide nostrils.

évasement (é-vâz-măn), *n.m.,* width, widening (at the mouth of a vase, etc.); (arch.) splay.

évaser, *v.a.,* to widen (an opening); to spread, to extend; (arch.) to splay. — *un tuyau;* to widen a pipe. — *un arbre;* to extend a tree. *S'—,* to be widened; to extend, to spread.

évasi-f, -ve, *adj.,* evasive.

évasion, *n.f.,* escape, flight, elopement.

évasivement, *adv.,* evasively.

évasure, *n.f.,* opening; splay.

évêché, *n. m.,* bishopric; episcopate, see; bishop's palace.

évection, *n.f.,* (astron.) evection.

*****éveil,** *n.m.,* (l.u.) awakening; (fig.) warning, hint, alert; alarm; suspicion; awaking, rousing. *En —;* on one's guard; on the watch. *Donner l'—;* to warn.

*****éveillé, -e,** *adj.,* awake, brisk, lively, sprightly; sharp, smart, intelligent. *Elle est fort —e;* she is very sprightly.

*****éveiller,** *v.a.,* to awake, to awaken, to wake, to rouse, to excite, to enliven. — *les soupçons;* to arouse suspicion.

*****s'éveiller,** *v.r.,* to awake, to wake up; to get

animated. *Elle s'est éveillée en sursaut ;* she awoke with a start.

éveilleu-r, -se, *n.m.f.,* awakener ; rouser.

événement (é-vén-män), *n.m.,* event, occurrence ; emergency ; issue, end, result. *A tout —;* at all events ; to provide for emergencies. *En cas d'—;* upon an emergency.

évent, *n.m.,* flatness, vapidness, deadness ; open air ; vent-hole ; air-hole ; (artil.) windage. *Sentir l'—;* to smell vapid. *Avoir la tête à l'—;* to be thoughtless, hare-brained, scatter-brained.

éventable, *adj.,* liable to go flat.

*** éventail,** *n.m.,* fan. *Fenêtre en —;* fan-light.

*** éventailliste,** *n.m.f.,* fan-maker.

éventaire, *n.m.,* flat basket.

éventé, -e, *part.,* fanned, aired, flat, dead ; giddy, thoughtless. *Vin —;* dead, flat wine. *Un homme —;* a giddy, scatter-brained man.

éventer, *v.a.,* to fan, to winnow (corn) ; to air ; to deaden ; to let (wine) get flat ; to injure by exposure to the air ; to discover (a mine) ; to divulge, to get wind of ; to let out (a secret) ; to discover.

s'éventer, *v.r.,* to fan one's self, to evaporate, to pall, to become flat ; to be divulged ; to get abroad ; to get wind.

éventoir, *n.m.,* fire-fan.

éventrer, *v.a.,* to embowel, to disembowel, to eviscerate, to gut (fish) ; to rip up, to break open ; to open (a pie).

s'éventrer, *v.r.,* to rip open one's bowels.

éventualité, *n.f.,* uncertainty, contingency, eventuality.

éventuel, -le, *adj.,* eventual, contingent, uncertain.

éventuel, *n.m.,* extra-grant, capitation-fee.

éventuellement (-tuèl-män), *adv.,* eventually, contingently.

éventure, *n.f.,* crack, flaw.

évêque, *n.m.,* bishop. *— in partibus ;* bishop in partibus. *Devenir d'— meunier ;* to descend from peer to peasant. *Un chien regarde bien un —;* a cat may look at a king.

éversif, -ve, *adj.,* eversive ; subversive.

éversion, *n.f.,* eversion, overthrow.

s'évertuer, *v.r.,* to struggle, to strive, to exert or bestir one's self ; to move heaven and earth. *Je m'évertue à le faire ;* I do all I can to accomplish it.

éviction, *n.f.,* (jur.) eviction, ejectment.

évidement, *n.m.,* scooping out, hollowing ; groove, hollow.

évidemment (-da-män), *adv.,* evidently, obviously, plainly, clearly.

évidence, *n.f.,* evidence, obviousness, plainness, clearness. *Mettre en —;* to make conspicuous, to make prominent. *Etre en —;* to be conspicuous. *Se rendre à l'—;* to be convinced ; to submit to.

évident, -e, *adj.,* evident, plain, clear, obvious.

évider, *v.a.,* to hollow, to groove, to scoop out ; to stamp, to pink ; to unstarch.

évidoir, *n.m.,* hollowing-bit, borer.

évidure, *n.f.,* (tech.). *V.* **évidement.**

évier, *n.m.,* sink, sink-stone.

évincer, *v.a.,* to evict, to eject ; to oust. *Il a été évincé ;* he was turned out.

évitable, *adj.,* avoidable ; evitable.

évitage, *n.m.,* (nav.) swinging ; swinging-room.

évitée, *n.f.,* (nav.) swinging berth, swinging-room. *Le vaisseau fait son —;* the ship is swinging round *or* to. *Avoir son —;* to have a wide berth.

évitement (é-vit-män), *n.m.,* (railways) siding, shunting. *Gare, voie, d'—;* siding.

éviter, *v.a.,* to shun, to avoid, to evade, to eschew ; to elude, to escape, to save. *— les périls ;* to avoid dangers. *— les mauvaises compagnies ;* to shun bad company. *— la peine ;* to save trouble.

s'éviter, *v.r.,* to avoid each other ; to spare one's self ; (of things) to be avoided.

éviter, *v.n.,* (nav.) to swing. *— au vent ;* to stem the wind. *— à la marée ;* to stem the tide.

évocable, *adj.,* (jur.) removable.

évocation, *n.f.,* evocation, raising up ; (jur.) removal.

évocatoire, *adj.,* (jur.) for removal (from one court to another).

évoluer, *v.n.,* (nav., milit.) (l.u.) to perform evolutions ; to evolve, to revolve.

évolution, *n.f.,* evolution.

évolutionnaire, *adj.,* (milit., nav.) evolutionary.

évoquer, *v.a.,* to evoke, to raise up, to conjure up ; to call up. *— à un tribunal supérieur* (jur.) to remove to a superior court.

évulsion, *n.f.,* (tech.) evulsion.

ex (èks), (prefix) ex.

ex abrupto, *adv.,* suddenly, unexpectedly.

exacerbation, *n.f.,* (med.) exacerbation.

exact, -e (ég-zakt), *adj.,* exact, accurate, correct, precise, punctual ; close. *—e analyse ;* close analysis. *Les sciences —es ;* the exact sciences. *— à ;* exact in.

exactement, *adv.,* exactly, punctually, accurately ; correctly, precisely.

exacteur, *n.m.,* exactor, extortioner.

exaction, *n.f.,* exaction, extortion.

exactitude, *n.f.,* exactness, punctuality, exactitude ; correctness, accuracy, precision, closeness. *Agir avec —;* to be punctual.

exaèdre, *n.m.* and *adj. V.* **hexaèdre.**

exagérati-f, -ve, *adj.,* exaggeratory ; given to exaggeration.

exagération, *n.f.,* exaggeration, amplification ; overrating ; aggravation.

exagérer, *v.a.,* to exaggerate, to magnify.

exagone, *n.m.* and *adj. V.* **hexagone.**

exaltation, *n.f.,* exaltation, exalting.

exalté, -e, *n.* and *part.,* enthusiast, fanatic ; person over-excited ; exalted, elated ; over-excited, heated, feverish.

exaltor, *v.a.,* to exalt, to extol, to magnify, to glorify, to cry up ; to excite, to elate, to inflame, to over-excite ; (chem.) to exalt, to purify.

s'exalter, *v.r.,* to become excited, elated, to rise, to be exalted ; to be over-excited ; to extol, to magnify ; to cry up one another.

examen (-min), *n.m.,* examination, investigation, survey ; inspection, scrutiny. *— préliminaire ;* little-go. *Jury d'—;* board of examiners. *Faire l'— d'un livre ;* to examine a book. *Après mûr —;* after mature examination. *— de conscience ;* self-examination. *Se préparer à un —;* to prepare for an examination. *Libre —;* free thinking.

examinat-eur, *n.m.,* **-rice,** *n.f.,* examiner. *— supérieur pour les mathématiques ;* (universities) moderator. *— adjoint ;* assistant-examiner.

examiné, -e, *part.,* examined.

examiner, *v.a.,* to examine, to inquire into, to inspect, to survey, to look at ; to weigh, to discuss, to consider, to explore. *— à fond ;* to sift thoroughly. *— rapidement ;* to glance over, to run over.

s'examiner, *v.r.,* to examine, to search one's self ; to examine one's own conscience ; to examine, *or* to observe, one another attentively.

exanthémateu-x, -se, *adj.,* (med.) exanthematous.

exanthématique, *adj.,* (med.) exanthematic.

exanthème, *n.m.,* (med.) exanthema.

exarchat (-ka), *n.m.,* exarchate.

exarque, *n.m.,* exarch,

exaspérant, -e, *adj.*, exasperating, aggravating.

exaspération, *n.f.*, exasperation, aggravation; acme.

exaspéré, -e, *part.*, exasperated, enraged, incensed.

exaspérer, *v.a.*, to exasperate, to enrage, to incense, to inflame.

s'exaspérer, *v.r.*, to become, *or* get, *or* grow exasperated, enraged, incensed.

exaucement (ég-zôs-mān), *n.m.*, granting, hearing (of prayers).

exaucer, *v.a.*, to hearken to, to hear favorably; to grant. *Dieu exauce les prières des humbles;* God gives an ear to the prayers of the humble.

excavateur, *n.m.*, excavator.

excavation, *n.f.*, excavation, excavating.

excaver, *v.a.*, to excavate, to hollow out.

excédant, -e, *adj.*, exceeding; tiresome, unbearable.

excédent, *n.m.*, overplus; surplus; overweight; (arith.) excess, difference.

excéder, *v.a.*, to exceed, to go beyond; to wear out, to tire out. *Il a excédé son pouvoir;* he has exceeded his power. — *quelqu'un de coups;* to beat and bruise any one unmercifully.

s'excéder, *v.r.*, to be worn out; to wear out; to weary, to tire, one's self out. *S'— de débauches;* to wear one's self out with debauchery. *S'— de travail;* to overwork one's self; to work too hard.

excellemment (èk-sè-la-mān), *adv.*, excellently, surpassingly.

excellence, *n.f.*, excellence, excellency. *Par —;* preeminently, above all. *Votre —;* your Excellency. *Donner de l'—;* (fam.) to call any one Excellency.

excellent, -e, *adj.*, excellent; delightful; delicious.

excellentissime, *adj.*, most excellent.

exceller, *v.n.*, to excel, to be eminent, to transcend, to be transcendent, to surpass.

excentricité, *n.f.*, eccentricity.

excentrique, *adj.*, eccentric, odd.

excentrique, *n.m.*, (mec.) eccentric-wheel.

excepté, *prep.*, except, excepting, save, but. *— que;* except that.

excepter, *v.a.*, to except. *S' —;* to be excepted.

exception, *n.f.*, exception; (jur.) exception; (jur.) plea; (jur.) bar. *— déclinatoire;* (jur.) plea against the jurisdiction. *— péremptoire;* (jur.) demurrer. *— d'incompétence;* (jur.) foreign plea. *— tirée de l'aveu or des actes de la partie;* estoppel. *A l'— de;* with the exception of, except, excepting. *D'—;* exceptional.

exceptionnel, -le, *adj.*, exceptional.

excès, *n.m.*, excess, abuse, waste; intemperance, riot, debauchery; (jur.) ill-usage, outrage, violence; (geom., arith.) excess, difference. *A l'—, avec —, jusqu'à l'—;* to excess, excessively, immoderately. *Faire des —;* to commit excesses, to be guilty of excesses.

excessif, -ve, *adj.*, excessive, extreme, extravagant; exorbitant; intemperate.

excessivement (-siv-mān), *adv.*, excessively, to excess.

exciper, *v.n.*, (jur.) to plead *or* to allege an exception.

excipient, *n.m.*, (pharm.) excipient.

excise, *n.f.*, excise; excise-office.

exciser, *v.a.*, (surg.) to amputate, to cut off.

excision, *n.f.*, (surg.) excision, cutting off.

excitabilité, *n.f.*, excitability.

excitable, *adj.*, excitable.

excitant, -e, *adj.*, (med.) exciting.

excitant, *n.m.*, (med.) excitant.

excitat-eur, *n.m.*, **-rice,** *n.f.*, exciter.

excitatif, -ve, *adj.*, excitative.

excitation, *n.f.*, exciting, excitation, excitement, inciting.

excitement (èk-sit-mān), *n.m.*, (med.) excitement.

exciter, *v.a.*, to excite, to provoke, to stir up, to cause, to inspire, to arouse, to rouse; to urge, to stimulate, to encourage, to inspirit, to animate, to quicken, to instigate, to prompt, to spur; to inflame, to irritate. — *un chien contre quelqu'un;* to set a dog at any one.

s'exciter, *v.r.*, to excite, to animate, to encourage one's self; to animate, to encourage one another; to be excited.

exclamatif, -ve, *adj.*, exclamative; (gram.) of exclamation.

exclamation, *n.f.*, exclamation. *Point d'—;* note of exclamation.

s'exclamer, *v.r.*, to exclaim, to cry out, to clamor; to protest.

exclure, *v.a.*, to exclude, to debar, to shut out; to keep from, to bar, to leave out.

exclusif, -ve, *adj.*, exclusive.

exclusion, *n.f.*, exclusion.

exclusivement (-ziv-mān), *adv.*, exclusively.

excommunicateur, *n.m.*, excommunicator. *adj.*, excommunicating.

excommunication, *n.f.*, excommunication.

excommunié, -e, *n.m.f.*, excommunicated. *Avoir un visage d'—;* to look pale and wretched.

excommunier, *v.a.*, to excommunicate.

excoriation, *n.f.*, (surg.) excoriation, barking.

excorier, *v.a.*, (surg.) to excoriate.

excrément, *n.m.*, excrement. — *de la terre;* scum of the earth.

excrémenteu-x, -se, *or* **excrémentiel, -le,** *or* **excrémentitiel, -le,** *adj.*, excrementitious, excremental, excrementitial.

excréteur *or* **excrétoire,** *adj. m.*, (physiology) excretory, excretive.

excrétion, *n.f.*, (physiology) excretion.

excroissance, *n.f.*, excrescence, excrescency; fungus.

excursion, *n.f.*, excursion, inroad; digression, ramble; trip. *En —;* for an outing. *Faire une —;* to make an excursion, to take a trip.

excursionniste, *n.m.f.*, excursionist, tourist.

excusable, *adj.*, excusable, pardonable, venial; (jur.) by misadventure (homicide).

⊙**excusation,** *n.f.*, (jur.) excusation, plea.

excuse, *n.f.*, excuse, apology; (jur.) plea, excusation. *Faire des —s;* to apologize. *Faites —! excuse me!* I beg your pardon! *Je vous fais —;* I beg your pardon.

excuser, *v.a.*, to excuse, to exculpate, to pardon; to bear with; to apologize for. *Il l'a excusé auprès du roi;* he has apologized for him to the king. *On doit — les fautes de la jeunesse;* one must bear with the errors of youth.

s'excuser, *v.r.*, to excuse, to exculpate one's self; to throw the blame on; to decline; to apologize, to make an apology. *Le capitaine s'est excusé sur son lieutenant;* the captain cast the blame upon his lieutenant. *S'— de faire une chose;* to decline doing a thing. *Qui s'excuse, s'accuse;* a guilty conscience needs no accuser.

exeat (èg-zé-at), *n.m.*, exeat; pass, leave (to go out of one diocese into another). *Donner à quelqu'un son —;* to send off, to discard, to dismiss, any one. *Donner un — à;* to give any one leave to go out.

exécrable, *adj.*, execrable, deplorable.

exécrablement, *adv.*, execrably, deplorably.

exécration, *n.f.*, execration. *Il est en — à tout le monde;* he is held in abhorrence by everybody.

exécratoire, *adj.*, execratory.

exécrer, *v.a.*, to execrate, to hold in execration *or* in detestation.

exécutable, *adj.*, feasible, practicable.

exécutant, n.m., (mus.) performer, player.

exécuter, v.a., to execute, to perform; to accomplish, to carry out, to achieve, to fulfill ; (jur.) to distrain ; (jur.) to serve ; to put to death. *J'exécuterai ce que j'ai promis ;* I shall perform what I promised. *— un arrêt ;* to carry out a sentence.

s'exécuter, v.r., to be performed, to be done, to take place ; to sell off (one's property for the benefit of creditors); to sacrifice one's self ; to yield, to comply, to submit. *Allons, exécutez-vous ;* come, do the needful.

exécut-eur, n.m., **-rice**, n.f., executor, executrix ; executioner, hangman. *— testamentaire ;* executor, executrix. *Livrer à l'—;* to deliver over to the executioner.

exécuti-f, **-ve**, adj., executive. n.m., the Executive.

exécution, n.f., execution, accomplishment, performance, achievement, fulfillment. *Mettre des ordres à — ;* to execute orders. *Mettre à — ;* to carry out. *L'— de ce travail ne répond pas au plan ;* the execution of this work does not come up to the plan. *L'— d'un morceau de musique ;* the performance of a piece of music. *Homme d'— ;* resolute, bold, enterprising, practical man. *Ordre d'— ;* (of a criminal) death-warrant, warrant for execution. *Procéder à l'— ;* to carry out an execution.

exécutoire, n.m. and adj., (jur.) writ of execution ; executory.

exèdre, n.m., (arch.) exedra.

exégèse, n.f., exegesis.

exégétique, adj., exegetical.

exemplaire, adj., exemplary.

exemplaire, n.m., model, pattern ; copy (of printed books, engravings); specimen. *J'ai trois —s de ce livre-là ;* I have three copies of that book. *J'ai un bel — de cette médaille ;* I have a fine copy of that medal.

exemplairement (-plèr-mān), adv., exemplarily, in an exemplary manner.

exemple, n.m., example, pattern ; precedent, parallel, instance ; copy, copy-slip. *Proposer un — ;* to offer an example. *Ne vous réglez pas sur son — ;* do not follow in his footsteps. *Faire un — de quelqu'un ;* to make an example of any one. *Prendre — sur quelqu'un ;* to be guided by any one. *Il n'y en a point d'— ;* there is no precedent for it, there is no example of such a thing. *Donnez-m'en un — ;* give me an instance. *Citer un — ;* to quote an instance. *Prêcher d'— ;* to practice what one preaches. *Un dictionnaire sans —s est un squelette ;* a dictionary without examples is a mere skeleton. *A l'— de ;* in imitation of. *Par — ;* for instance, for example ; indeed ! bless me ! upon my word ! upon my honor ! only fancy ! the idea ! *Par —, voilà qui est fort !* well now, I like that ! *Sans — ;* extraordinary, unexampled, unparalleled.

exempt, **-e** (èg-zān, -t), adj., exempt, exempted, free from.

exempt, n.m., ecclesiastic exempted from the jurisdiction of the ordinary. *— de police ;* police officer ; constable.

exempter (èg-zan-té), v.a., to exempt, to free ; to dispense, to excuse, to exonerate.

s'exempter, v.r., to exempt one's self from, to dispense with.

exemption (èg-zānp-sion), n.f., exemption, exoneration, immunity ; dispensation. *Lettre d'— des droits de douane ;* (com.) bill of sufferance.

exequatur (-koua-), n.m., (—) exequatur.

exercer, v.a., to exercise, to train up ; to perform, to practice, to exert ; to fill an office ; to follow, to carry on (a trade or profession) ; (milit.) to drill. *— des soldats ;* to drill soldiers. *— sa mémoire ;* to exercise one's memory. *— la patience de quelqu'un ;* to try any one's patience.

— l'hospitalité ; to practice hospitality. *— la médecine ;* to practice medicine.

s'exercer, v.r., to exercise, to practice ; to exercise, to train, one's self ; to exert one's self ; to try one's hand at.

exercer, v.n., to practice ; to visit (manufacturers and others who sell excisable articles). *Avocat qui n'exerce plus ;* retired barrister.

exercice, n.m., exercise, practice, use ; work, labor ; trouble, fatigue ; inspection (of an officer of the indirect taxes) ; (administration) receipts and expenditure during a certain time ; (milit.) drill ; drilling. *Entrer en — ;* to commence one's duties. *Sortir d'— ;* to finish one's term of service. *L'— d'une profession ;* the exercise of a profession. *Faire l'— ;* to exercise, to drill. *Faire faire l'— à des soldats ;* to drill, to train, soldiers. *Subir l'— ;* to be drilled. *Prendre de l'— ;* to take exercise. *Se tenir en — ;* to keep one's self in practice. *— à feu ;* rifle, carbine exercise. *— de piété ;* practice of piety.

exérèse, n.f., (surg.) extraction, amputation, cutting off.

exergue (èg-zèrg), n.m., exergue.

exfoliati-f, **-ve**, adj., (surg., pharm.) exfoliative.

exfoliation, n.f., (surg.) exfoliation.

s'exfolier, v.r., to exfoliate.

exfumer, v.a., (paint.) to soften.

exhalaison, n.f., exhalation, effluvium.

exhalant, n.m. and adj., (anat.) exhaling vessel ; exhaling.

exhalation, n.f., exhalation.

exhalatoire, adj., evaporating. n.m., evaporating-vessel.

exhaler, v.a., to send forth, to exhale ; to give forth, to breathe ; to vent ; to give vent to ; to emit. *Ces fleurs exhalent une douce odeur ;* these flowers emit a sweet smell. *— sa colère ;* to give vent to one's anger.

s'exhaler, v.r., to be emitted, to be exhaled ; to give vent to, to indulge in. *S'— en plaintes, en menaces ;* to give vent to complaints, to indulge in threats.

exhaussement (èg-zôs-mān), n.m., (arch.) height ; raising up, mound.

exhausser, v.a., (arch.) to raise, to raise up, to run up, to make higher. *S'— ;* to be raised ; to raise one's self.

exhérédation, n.f., (jur.) disinheriting, exheredation, disinheritance.

exhéréder, v.a., (jur.) to exheredate, to disinherit.

exhiber, v.a., to exhibit, to produce, to show. *— ses papiers, son passeport ;* to produce one's papers, one's passport.

exhibition, n.f., (jur.) exhibition, producing, exhibiting.

exhibitoire, adj., exhibitory, prohibitive.

exhilarant, **-e**, adj., exhilarating.

exhortati-f, **-ve**, adj., exhortative.

exhortation, n.f., exhortation.

exhortatoire, adj., exhortatory.

exhorter, v.a., to exhort, to admonish.

exhumation, n.f., exhumation, disinterment.

exhumer, v.a., to exhume, to dig out ; to disinter ; to bring to light ; to rake up.

exigeant, **-e** (-jān-t), adj., unreasonable, overparticular, too exacting ; troublesome, hard to please.

exigence, n.f., unreasonableness ; unreasonable claim or demand ; exigency, exigence. *Selon l'— du cas ;* as occasion shall require.

exiger, v.a., to exact, to require, to demand, to enforce. *— des égards ;* to enforce respect. *— le payement d'une dette ;* to exact the payment of a debt.

exigibilité, n.f., exigibility.

exigible, adj., exigible, demandable.

exigu, **-ë**, adj., scanty, slender, slight, small.

exiguité, *n.f.*, scantiness, slenderness, slightness, smallness.

exil, *n.m.*, exile, banishment. *Envoyer en* —; to banish.

exilé, *n.m.*, -e, *n.f.*, exile, refugee.

exiler, *v.a.*, to exile, to banish.

s'exiler, *v.r.*, to exile one's self; to withdraw, to seclude, one's self. *Il s'est exilé du monde;* he has withdrawn from the world.

exinanition, *n.f.*, exhaustion.

existant, -e, *adj.*, existing, in being, existent, extant; in force.

existence, *n.f.*, existence, being, subsistence; living. *pl.,* (com.) stock on hand. *Mettre un terme à son* —; to put an end to one's existence.

exister, *v.n.*, to exist; to be in existence, to live; to be extant; to subsist. *Cette dette n'existe plus;* this debt is extinct. *Les ouvrages qui existent;* the works which are extant.

exocet, *n.m.,* (ich.) exocœtus, flying fish.

exode, *n.m.,* Exodus; exode.

exomphale, *n.f.,* (surg.) exomphalos.

exonération, *n.f.,* exoneration; freedom from blame.

exonérer, *v.a.,* to exonerate, to discharge, to free from.

exophtalmie, *n.f.,* exophthalmia.

exophtalmique, *adj.,* exophthalmic.

exorable, *adj.,* exorable.

exorbitamment (-ta-mān), *adv.,* exorbitantly, excessively, extravagantly.

exorbitant, -e, *adj.,* extravagant, exorbitant, excessive.

exorciser, *v.a.,* to exorcise, to put out (devils); to conjure.

exorcisme, *n.m.,* exorcism.

exorciste, *n.m.,* exorcist, exorciser.

exorde, *n.m.,* exordium, commencement; beginning.

exosmose, *n.f.,* (phys.) exosmose, exosmosis.

exostose, *n.f.,* (med., bot.) exostosis.

s'exostoser, *v.r.,* (surg.) to form in exostosis.

exotérique, *adj.,* exoteric; vulgar.

exotique, *adj.,* exotic, foreign; outlandish.

expansibilité, *n.f.,* expansibility.

expansible, *adj.,* expansible, expansive.

expansi-f, -ve, *adj.,* expansive; unreserved, open-hearted, overflowing.

expansion, *n.f.,* expansion, unreservedness; opening out. *Avoir de l'*—; to be open, unreserved, communicative.

expatriation, *n.f.,* expatriation; self-banishment.

expatrier, *v.a.,* to expatriate; to send into banishment.

s'expatrier, *v.r.,* to expatriate one's self; to leave one's native country.

expectance, *n.f.,* expectancy.

expectant, -e, *adj.,* expectant.

expectant, *n.m.,* (med.) expectant.

expectati-f, -ve, *adj.,* expectant.

expectative, *n.f.,* expectation, hopes, prospect; (jur.) expectancy. *Il est dans l'*—; he is in expectation. *Avoir l'*— *de quelque chose;* to look forward to the possession of anything.

expectorant, -e, *adj.,* expectorant.

expectorant, *n.m.,* expectorant.

expectoration, *n.f.,* expectoration; sputa.

expectorer, *v.a.,* to expectorate, to spit.

expédient, *n.m.,* expedient; shift; ☉(jur.) compromise. *Homme d'—s;* man full of expedients, *or* full of resource. *En être aux —s;* to be reduced to expedients *or* to shifts. *Son dernier* —; one's last shift.

expédient, *adj.m.,* expedient, fit, meet, proper, advisable.

expédier, *v.a.,* to dispatch, to perform, to send off; to forward; to knock off, to clear off; to clear (at the custom-house); to draw up. — *des marchandises;* to forward goods. — *un*

acte; to draw up a deed. — *des troupes;* to send off troops.

expéditeur, *n.m.,* sender, commission-agent; (nav.) shipper.

expéditi-f, -ve, *adj.,* expeditious, quick.

expédition, *n.f.,* expedition, dispatch; sending, shipment; copy (of a deed); clearance (at the custom-house). *pl.,* dispatches. *Faire l'*— *de;* (com.) to forward. *Le courrier attend ses* —*s;* the courier is waiting for his dispatches. *Homme d'*—; sharp man of business.

expéditionnaire, *adj.,* expeditionary.

expéditionnaire, *n.m.,* sender, shipper; commission-agent, copying-clerk, forwarding-clerk.

expérience, *n.f.,* experience; trial, experiment. *Faire une* —; to make an experiment. *Des* —*s de chimie;* experiments in chemistry. *Je sais cela par* —; I know that by experience. *Parler par* —; to speak from experience.

expérimental, -e, *adj.,* experimental.

expérimentateur, *n.m.,* experimentalist.

expérimenté, -e, *adj.,* experienced.

expérimenter, *v.a.,* to experiment, to try by use, to test; to experience.

expert, -e, *adj.,* expert, skillful, well versed in.

expert, *n.m.,* appraiser, valuer; surveyor; expert.

expertement, *adv.,* expertly, skillfully.

expertise, *n.f.,* survey, valuation, assessment (of specially appointed surveyors); report (of survey), appraisement, arbitration. *Faire une* —; to make a survey.

expertiser, *v.a.,* to make a survey; to appraise, to value, to assess.

expiation, *n.f.,* expiation, atonement, satisfaction. *En* — *de;* as an atonement for. *Faire* — *de;* to make an atonement for.

expiatoire, *adj.,* expiatory. *Sacrifice* —; sin-offering.

expier, *v.a.,* to expiate, to atone for; to make reparation for.

expirant, -e, *adj.,* expiring, dying; faint, inaudible.

expirateur, *adj.m.,* (anat.) expiratory.

expiration, *n.f.,* expiration.

expirer, *v.n.,* to expire; to breathe one's last; to die away; to come to an end, to run out. *Mon bail a expiré hier;* my lease was up yesterday.

expirer, *v.a.,* to breathe out; to exhale, to expire.

expléti-f, -ve, *adj.,* (gram.) expletive.

explétif, *n.m.,* (gram.) expletive.

explicable, *adj.,* explicable, explainable.

explicateur, *n.m.,* explainer, cicerone, guide.

explicati-f, -ve, *adj.,* explicative, explanatory.

explication, *n.f.,* explanation, explication, interpretation; construing; meaning. *Avoir une* — *avec;* to have an explanation with. *Cela demande* —; that requires an explanation.

explicite, *adj.,* explicit, clear; express.

explicitement (-cit-mān), *adv.,* explicitly; clearly.

expliquer, *v.a.,* to explain, to express, to declare, to account for; to teach, to expound; to construe, to illustrate. *Expliquez-moi ce que cela signifie;* explain to me what that means. — *une énigme;* to solve a riddle. — *une doctrine;* to expound a doctrine.

s'expliquer, *v.r.,* to explain one's self; to have an explanation; to be explained; to be accounted for; to be made manifest.

expliqueur, *n.m.,* explainer.

exploit, *n.m.,* exploit, achievement, feat, deed; (jur.) writ, process. *Dresser un* —; to draw up a writ. *Signifier un* —; to serve a writ.

exploitabilité, *n.f.,* workableness.

exploitable, *adj.,* workable, that may be turned to account; improvable; (jur.) distrainable. *Cette mine est encore* —; that mine may still be worked.

exploitant, *n.m.*, worker (of mines); farmer, grower. *adj.*, *huissier* —; (jur.) process server.

exploitation, *n.f.*, working; improving (lands); cultivation (of wood); employing, using; taking advantage of, cheating. — *d'un champ;* (agri.) cultivation of a field. — *par compartiments;* (mining) panel-work. — *par grande taille;* long-work. — *rurale;* farming. *Matér'el d'*—; working-stock. *En* —; being worked; in activity. *Mettre en* —; to work. — *de l'homme par l'homme;* profiting by the labor of others; sweating system.

exploiter, *v.a.*, to work; to improve; to cultivate for sale; to use; to make the most of. — *une mine;* to work a mine; to take advantage of, to impose upon. — *un bois;* to cultivate a wood for sale. — *une place;* to make the most of a situation. — *la curiosité publique;* to speculate upon public curiosity. *Cet homme m'a exploité;* that man has cheated *or* taken advantage of me.

☉**exploiter**, *v.n.*, to serve writs.

*s'***exploiter**, *v.r.*, to be worked, to take advantage one of the other.

exploiteur, *n.m.*, (b.s.) person who takes advantage (of others), who works, who uses (others); sweater.

explorable, *adj.*, explorable.

explorateur, *n.m.*, explorer.

explorat-eur, -rice, *adj.*, exploratory.

exploration, *n.f.*, exploration.

explorer, *v.a.*, to explore. *S'* —; to be explored.

explosible, *adj.*, explosive.

explosi-f, -ve, *adj.*, explosive.

explosion, *n.f.*, explosion; bursting, blowing up; outbreak, outburst. *Faire* —; to explode; to burst out, to break out.

exponentiel, -le, *adj.*, (alg.) exponential.

exportateur, *n.m.*, exporter.

exportation, *n.f.*, exportation, export.

exporter, *v.a.*, to export. *S'*—; to be exported.

exposant, *n.m.*, **-e**, *n.f.*, exhibitor; (jur.) petitioner; (math.) exponent, index.

exposé, *n.m.*, statement; account, outline; (jur.) recital. *Faire un* —; to draw up a statement. — *des motifs;* explanatory statement.

exposé, -e, *part.* and *adj.*, exposed, on view; situated; having a certain aspect; uncovered; liable; abandoned.

exposer, *v.a.*, to expose, to expose to view, to show, to exhibit; to endanger, to hazard, to venture, to render liable, to make liable, to lay open; to state, to set forth; to expound, to explain, to abandon. — *en vente;* to expose for sale. — *sa vie;* to venture one's life. — *ses sentiments;* to state one's sentiments. — *un système;* to unfold a system. — *un corps mort sur un lit de parade;* to lay out a dead body in state.

*s'***exposer**, *v.r.*, to expose one's self; to be exposed, to be liable, to lay one's self open, to lie open. *Il s'expose à la risée de tout le monde;* he makes himself the laughing-stock of everybody.

exposer, *v.n.*, to explain; to exhibit. *Je ne connais personne qui expose mieux;* I know no one who can explain a thing better. *Ce peintre n'a pas encore exposé;* that painter has not yet exhibited.

exposition, *n.f.*, exhibition, exposing; exposure; lying-in-state (of dead bodies); situation; aspect, statement, explanation. *La grande* —; the Great Exhibition. *Maison dans une* — *agréable;* house with a pleasant aspect. *Faire une fidèle* — *de toutes ses raisons;* to give a faithful account of all one's reasons.

exprès, -se, *adj.*, express, positive; plain, clear, distinct. *La loi est* —*se sur ce point;* the law is positive on that point.

exprès, *n.m.*, express (messenger).

exprès, *adv.*, expressly, purposely, on purpose. *Il semble fait* — *pour cela;* he seems to be cut out for it. *C'est un fait* —; it is done on purpose.

express, *n.m.* and *adj.*, (railways) express, express train. *Le train* —; the express train.

expressément, *adv.*, expressly, positively; clearly, distinctly.

expressi-f, -ve, *adj.*, expressive.

expression, *n.f.*, expression, expressiveness, utterance. *Son regard est plein d'*—; his look is full of expression. — *imaginaire;* (alg.) imaginary, impossible, binomial. *La plus simple* —; (math.) the lowest terms. *Réduire à la plus simple* —; to reduce to the lowest terms.

exprimable, *adj.*, expressible.

exprimer, *v.a.*, to express, to press out, to squeeze out; to be expressive of; to declare, to utter, to tell; to word. — *le suc d'une plante;* to squeeze the juice out of a plant.

*s'***exprimer**, *v.r.*, to express one's self; to be expressed.

ex professo, *adv.*, ex professo.

expropriation, *n.f.*, (jur.) expropriation, dispossession. — *forcée;* compulsory dispossession. *Jury d'*—; (jur.) valuation jury.

exproprier, *v.a.*, (jur.) to dispossess; to expropriate.

expulser, *v.a.*, to expel, to thrust out, to turn out, to eject, to drive out, to put out.

expulseur, *adj.*, expelling.

expulsi-f, -ve, *adj.*, (med.) expulsive.

expulsion, *n.f.*, expulsion, extrusion; (jur.) ejection; ejectment.

expurgatoire, *adj.*, expurgatory. *Index* —; expurgatory index.

expurger, *v.a.*, to expurgate, to remove, to cancel, to amend.

exquis, -e, *adj.*, exquisite, nice, refined; choice, select. *Vin* —; delicious wine. *Avoir un goût* —; to have an exquisite taste.

exquis, *n.m.*, exquisiteness.

exquisement (-kiz-măn), *adv.*, exquisitely.

exsangue, exsanguin, -e, *adj.*, bloodless, anæmic; weak, feeble, spiritless.

exsiccation, *n.f.*, (chem.) exsiccation; dryness.

exsuccion, *n.f.*, exsuction.

exsudation, *n. f.*, exsudation, exudation; sweat; oozing out; perspiration.

exsuder, *v.n.*, to exude, to perspire; to ooze out.

☉**extant, -e**, *adj.*, (jur.) existing.

extase, *n.f.*, ecstasy, trance; rapture. *Tomber en* —; to be entranced; to fall into ecstacy or in a trance.

*s'***extasier**, *v.r.*, to be enraptured, to go into raptures; to be struck with admiration.

extatique, *adj.*, ecstatic, rapturous.

extenseur, *n.m.* and *adj.*, (anat.) extensor.

extensibilité, *n.f.*, extensibility, expansion.

extensible, *adj.*, extensible, tensible; tensile.

extensi-f, -ve, *adj.*, extending, expanding.

extension, *n.f.*, extension; tension, strain; extent; span.

in **extenso**, *adv.* *V.* **in extenso**.

exténuation, *n.f.*, extenuation, exhaustion, debility.

exténuer, *v.n.*, to extenuate, to enfeeble, to weaken, to debilitate. *Sa maladie l'a fort exténué;* his illness has weakened him very much.

extérieur, -e, *adj.*, exterior, external, outward, outer, outside; foreign.

extérieur, *n.m.*, exterior, outside appearance; foreign countries, abroad. *Les nouvelles de l'*—; news from abroad. *A l'intérieur et à l'*—; at home and abroad.

extérieurement (-eur-măn), *adv.*, externally, outwardly.

exterminat-eur, -rice, n. and adj., destroyer, exterminator; exterminating, destroying.

exterminati-f, -ve, adj., exterminating.

extermination, n.f., extermination.

exterminer, v.a., to exterminate, to destroy, to annihilate.

externat, n.m., day-school.

externe, adj., external, exterior, outward, outdoor.

externe, n. m., day-scholar; (of hospitals) dresser.

extinction, n.f., extinction, extinguishment; destruction; abolition; appeasement; redemption (of annuities); liquidation, settlement (of debts); quelling, suppression (of disturbances); extermination; quenching; slaking (of lime). — *des racines;* (alg., arith.) evolution. — *de voix;* loss of voice. *A l'—* *des feux, des bougies;* (at auctions) by inch of candle. *Jusqu'à — de chaleur naturelle;* till one is exhausted.

extinguible, adv., extinguishable.

extirpateur, n. m., extirpator, destroyer; (agri.) weeder; weeding-tool, spud.

extirpation, n.f., excision, extirpation; uprooting, destruction, weeding up.

extirper, v.a., to extirpate, to root out, to pull up, to exterminate, to cut off. — *un cancer;* to cut out a cancer.

extorquer, v.a., to extort, to wrest, to worm out of.

extorqueu-r, -se, n.m.f., extortioner.

extorsion, n.f., extortion.

extra, n. m., (—) extra, something extra. *C'était ma fête et nous avons fait un —, un peu d'—;* it was my birthday, so we had something extra, something out of the common. *Plat d'—;* extra dish.

extractible, adj., extractible.

extractif, n.m., (chem.) extractive, extract.

extracti-f, -ve, adj., extractive.

extraction, n.f., extraction; origin, descent, lineage. *L'— d'une dent;* the drawing of a tooth. *De basse —;* of low birth, of humble parentage.

extrader, v.a., to extradite; to surrender.

extradition, n.f., extradition.

extrados, n.m., (arch.) extrados.

extradossé, -e, adj., (arch.) extra-dossed.

extraire (extrayant, extrait), v.a., to extract, to draw, to take out; to make extracts from; to select; to abridge; to take from one prison to another. — *un livre;* to make an abridgment of a book.

extrait, n. m., extract; selection; epitome; spirit; abstract; docket. — *de naissance, de baptême, de mariage;* certificate of birth, baptism, marriage. — *mortuaire;* certificate of death. — *authentique;* certified copy of a document.

extrajudiciaire, adj., extrajudicial.

extrajudiciairement, adv., extrajudicially.

extra-muros (-rôs), adv., outside the walls (of a city, assembly).

extraordinaire, adj., extraordinary, unusual; uncommon, out of the way; singular, odd, queer; enormous. *Il n'y a rien d'— à cela;* there is nothing extraordinary in that. *Question —;* rack (torture). *Visage —;* odd face.

extraordinaire, n.m., extraordinariness, extraordinary thing, uncommon thing. *L'— c'est que . . . ;* the extraordinary part of it is . . .

extraordinairement (-nèr-mān), adv., extraordinarily, unusually; oddly, enormously. *Procéder — contre quelqu'un;* (jur.) to prosecute any one criminally.

extrapassé, -e, part., (paint.) beyond natural limits. *V.* strapassé.

extrapasser, v.a., (paint.). *V.* strapasser.

extravagamment (-ga-mān), adv., extravagantly, unreasonably.

extravagance, n.f., extravagance, folly, wildness; mad action. *J'ai pitié de son —;* I pity his folly. *Il a dit mille —s;* he said a thousand extravagant things.

extravagant, -e, n. and adj., extravagant, wild person; extravagant, wild. *C'est un —;* he is a mad fellow.

extravagante, n.f., (c.rel.) extravagant, papal constitution. *Les —s;* the decretals.

extravaguer (-ghé), v.n., to talk wildly, to rave, to talk like a madman.

extravasation or **extravasion,** n.f., (med.) extravasation; effusion (of blood).

extravasé, -e, adj., extravasated; let out. *Sang —;* extravasated blood.

s'extravaser, v.r., to be extravasated.

extrême, adj., extreme, utmost, excessive.

extrême, n.m., extreme, utmost, point. *Jusqu'à l'—, à l'—;* to an extreme. *Il se jette dans les —s;* he runs into extremes. *Les —s se touchent;* extremes meet.

extrêmement (èks-trêm-mān), adv., extremely; immensely, enormously; exceedingly.

extrême-onction, n.f., (n.p.) (c.rel.) extreme unction.

in extremis (i-nèks-tré-mîs), adv., (jur.) at the point of death.

extrémité, n.f., extremity, extreme; excess; last moment; end, tip; verge, border, brink. *A l'—;* to extremity, at a push; without resource; dying. *Passer d'une — à l'autre;* to pass from one extreme to another. *Pousser à la dernière —;* to drive to extremities. *A toute —;* at the worst.

extrinsèque, adj., extrinsic. *Valeur — des mœnnaies;* value assigned to coins independently of their actual weight.

exubérance, n.f., exuberance, luxuriance.

exubérant, -e, adj., exuberant, luxuriant.

exubérer, v.n., to exuberate; to abound; to luxuriate.

exulcérati-f, -ve, adj., (med.) producing ulcers; exulcerative.

exulcération, n.f., (med.) exulceration.

exulcérer, v.a., (med.) to exulcerate.

exultation, n.f., exultation, rapture, great joy.

exutoire, n.m., (med.) exutory, issue.

ex-voto, n.m., (—) votive offering.

F

f, n.m.f., the sixth letter of the alphabet, f. *Les F et les B;* oaths, swearing.

fa, n.m., (mus.) fa; **F.** *Clef de —;* bass, bass-clef.

fabagelle, n.f., **fabago,** n.m., (bot.) fabago, bean-caper.

fable, n.f., fable, story; untruth; tale; mythology; laughing-stock, by-word. *Etre la — de tout le monde;* to be the laughing-stock or byword of everybody.

fabliau, n.m., ancient tale in verse.

fablier, n.m., fabulist; book of fables.

fabricant, n.m., manufacturer, maker.

fabricateur, n.m., (b.s.) fabricator, maker; coiner, forger. — *de fausse monnaie;* coiner of base money. — *de nouvelles;* forger of news.

fabrication, n.f., fabrication, manufacture, making, make; forgery; coining. *La — d'un faux acte;* the forging of a deed.

fabricien (-si-in) or **fabricier,** n.m., vestryman.

fabrique, n.f., building (of churches); vestryboard; making, fabrication; (manu.) works; manufactory; factory; forging. *Marchandises de —;* goods of inferior quality. *Prix de —;* cost, or manufacturer's, price. *Marque de —;* trade-mark. *C'est de sa —;* (fig.) that is pure invention on his part.

fabriquer, *v.a.*, to manufacture ; to fabricate ; to coin (money) ; to forge. *Se* —; to be manufactured.

fabuleusement (-leûz-mān), *adv.*, fabulously; incredibly.

fabuleu-x, -se, *adj.*, fabulous, fictitious, extraordinary ; incredible.

fabuliste, *n.m.*, fabulist.

façade, *n.f.*, front, face (of an edifice) ; frontage ; façade.

face, *n.f.*, front ; fore-part (of a building) ; face ; state ; aspect, appearance ; countenance ; surface ; turn (of affairs). *Une* — *réjouie ;* a jolly face. *Faire* — *à ;* to face ; to fulfill ; to meet. *A la* — *de ;* in the presence of ; before. *En* — *de ;* in the face of ; opposite. *De* —; in front ; abreast of ; full face. *Vu de* —; seen in front ; taking a front view ; seen from the front. *Donner sur la* — *à quelqu'un ;* to give any one a slap in the face. — *de réprouvé ;* sinister-looking countenance. — *de carême ;* pale face. *Faire volte-* —; to face about. *Faire* — *à ses affaires ;* to meet one's engagements. *Les affaires ont bien changé de* —; things have taken quite another turn. — *à* —; face to face. *De prime* —; at first. *Jouer à pile ou* —; to play pitch and toss ; at heads or tails.

facé, -e, *adj.*, (l.u.) faced. *Un homme bien* —; a full- or good-faced man.

facétie (-ci), *n.f.*, facetiousness, jest, joke, witty saying. *Recueil de* —*s ;* facetiæ.

facétieusement (-sieñz-mān), *adv.*, facetiously, jestingly ; jocosely.

facétieu-x, -se (-ci-), *adj.*, facetious, jocular, humorous. *n.m.*, jester, joker.

facette, *n.f.*, facet, face. *Diamant taillé à* —*s ;* diamond cut facet-wise.

facetté, -e, *part.*, faceted.

facetter, *v.a.*, to cut with facets.

fâché, -e, *adj.*, (contre) angry, displeased; (de) sorry, vexed. *Il est* — *de vous avoir offensé ;* he is sorry he has offended you. *Etre* — *contre quelqu'un ;* to be angry with any one. *Etre* — *d'un malheur ;* to be sorry for a misfortune. *Etre* — *avec ;* to be on bad terms with.

fâcher, *v.a.*, to anger, to make angry, to offend, to vex, to displease. (*imp.* l.u.). *Il me fâche d'être forcé de vous dire ;* I am sorry to be obliged to tell you. *Soit dit sans vous* —; with all due deference.

se **fâcher**, *v.r.*, to be *or* get angry, to get into a passion, to be offended. *Ne vous fâchez pas ;* do not take offence.

fâcherie (fâ-shri), *n.f.*, angry feeling, disagreement, quarrel, vexation.

fâcheusement, *adv.*, unpleasantly, inopportunely, disagreeably ; grievously, sadly ; awkwardly.

fâcheu-x, -se, *adj.*, grievous, sad, troublesome, vexatious ; difficult ; cross, peevish. *C'est un* — *personnage ;* he is a troublesome personage. *Il est* — *que vous n'ayez pas été averti à temps ;* it is a pity that you were not told in time.

fâcheux, *n.m.*, troublesome, unkind person, or fellow, pesterer, intruder, bore. *Le* — *de l'affaire ;* the worst of the matter.

facial, -e, *adj.*, (anat.) facial. *Angle* —; facial angle.

faciès (fa-siès), *n.m.*, (med.) facial expression.

facile, *adj.*, facile, easy ; yielding, complying ; voluble ; weak ; flowing, fluent, ready. *Un homme de* — *accès ;* a man easy of access. *Style* —; easy, fluent style. *Un homme* —; a man of an easy temper. *Tout cela est plus* — *à dire qu'à faire ;* all that is easier said than done.

facilement (fa-sil-mān), *adv.*, easily, readily, yieldingly ; fluently.

facilité, *n.f.*, facility, ease, easiness, readiness; fluency ; quickness ; (com.) accommodation. *pl.*,

(com.) easy terms. *Il a une grande* — *à parler ;* he has great fluency of speech.

faciliter, *v.a.*, to facilitate, to make easy.

façon, *n.f.*, make ; making, workmanship; shape, fashion ; (agri.) dressing ; way, manner ; look, appearance, mien ; compliment ; affectation ; ceremony ; attention. *pl.*, ceremony. *A la* — *de ;* after the manner of. *De cette* —; in this manner. *La* — *d'un habit ;* the make, the cut, of a coat. *Prendre à* —; to make up ladies', gentlemen's, own materials. *Tailleur à* —; tailor who makes up your own materials. *Donner à* —; to put out to make. *C'est sa* — *de penser ;* it is his way of thinking. *De* — *ou d'autre ;* somehow or other, somehow. *En aucune* —; by no means, in no wise. *De quelque* — *que ce soit ;* anyhow. *De toute* —; at any rate. *Un homme de bonne* —; a good-looking man. *Cela n'a ni mine ni* —; that has neither grace nor shape. *En donner de la bonne* — *à quelqu'un ;* to give a good hiding or talking to. *S'en donner de la bonne* —; to go on at a fine rate ; to refuse one's self nothing. *Faire des* —*s ;* to be ceremonious. *Un homme plein de* —*s ;* a ceremonious man. *Point de* —*s ;* no ceremony. *Sans* —*s ;* without ceremony. *Pourquoi faites-vous tant de* —*s ?* why do you stand so much on ceremony ? *De* — *que ;* in such a way as, so that. *Payer la* —; to pay the piper. *De sa* —; of his own invention.

faconde, *n.f.*, (fam.) talkativeness, loquacity ; fluency. *Avoir de la* —; to have the gift of the gab, eloquence.

façonné, -e, *part.*, figured (of stuffs); wrought.

façonnage *or* **façonnement**, *n.m.*, fashioning, shaping, making.

façonner, *v.a.*, to make, to make up, to fashion, to figure, to form, to adorn, to embellish, to work, to polish; to accustom, to use.

se **façonner**, *v.r.*, to become used *or* accustomed to; to become polished.

façonner, *v.n.*, (fam.) to be ceremonious ; to stand on ceremony.

façonnerie (fa-so-n-rî), *n.f.*, figuring (of stuffs).

façonni-er, -ère, *adj.*, ceremonious, precise, formal, affected.

fac-similaire, *adj.*, fac-similar, exactly copied.

fac-similé, *n.m.*, facsimile.

fac-similé, *part.*, copied exactly.

fac-similer, *v.a.* to facsimile ; to copy exactly.

factage, *n.m.*, porterage, carriage ; goods *or* parcels delivery.

facteur, *n.m.*, maker; agent, assistant; (arith., com.) factor ; postman, letter-carrier ; railway porter ; (fig.) factor, element, agent. — *de pianos ;* pianoforte-maker. — *d'orgues ;* organ-builder.

factice, *adj.*, factitious, artificial, unnatural, forced, got up ; (of words) unauthorized.

facticement (-tis-mān), *adv.*, factitiously, in a factitious manner.

factieu-x, -se, *adj.*, factious, mutinous, seditious.

factieux, *n.m.*, factionist, rebel ; sedition-monger.

faction, *n.f.*, faction; sentry, watch, duty of a sentinel. *Etre en* —, *faire* —; to be on duty. *Entrer en* —; to go on duty. *Relever de* —; to relieve sentry.

factionnaire, *n.m.*, sentinel, sentry.

factorage, *n.m.*, (com.) factorage.

factorerie (-tor-rî), *n.f.*, (com.) factory.

factotum, *n.m.*, (—*s*) factotum ; do-all.

factrice, *n.f.*, (com.) female agent, factor.

factum (-tom), *n.m.*, (—*s*) (jur.) statement (of a cause).

facture, *n.f.*, composition, workmanship (of

music, verse); (com.) bill of parcels; invoice, bill; (of organs) building. *Tête de* —; bill-head. *Livre de* —*s;* invoice-book. *Faire une* —; to make out an invoice.

facturer, *v.a.,* to invoice.

facturier, *n.m.,* invoice-book; invoice-clerk.

facule, *n.f.,* (astron.) facula.

facultati-f, -ve, *adj.,* optional, discretionary; (com.) blank (of credit). *Bref* —; pope's license.

faculté, *n.f.,* faculty, ability, propriety, power, virtue, quality; talent; option; right. *pl.,* faculties, means, property. —*s intellectuelles;* mind, intellectual faculties. *Il a la* — *de parler en public;* he has a talent for public speaking. *Les* —*s de l'esprit;* the powers of the mind.

fadaise, *n.f.,* trifle, stuff, fiddle-faddle, silliness, silly thing; nonsense, twaddle. —*s que tout cela !* Tom-foolery!

fadasse, *adj.,* insipid, dull; mawkish, sickening; pale, insignificant.

fade, *adj.,* insipid, unsavory, tasteless, heavy, dull; pointless, tame; flat, stale.

fadement, *adv.,* heavily, dully, spiritlessly, insipidly; mawkishly; tastelessly.

fadeur, *n.f.,* insipidity, insipidness, unsavoriness, tastelessness; silliness; pointlessness; tameness.

fagot, *n.m.,* fagot, bundle; idle story; former convict; ticket of leave. *Ame d'un* —; small sticks of a fagot. *Bois de* —; bavin. *Il y a* —*s et* —*s;* there are men and men; or all men or things are not alike. *Sentir le* —; to be suspected of heresy. *Conter des* —*s;* to tell idle stories. *Prendre un air de* —; to warm one's self. *Etre habillé comme un* —; to be dressed in a slovenly, slatternly manner.

fagotage, *n.m.,* fagot-making, fagot-wood, chatwood; brushwood.

fagoté, -e, *part.,* dressed in a slovenly manner. *Comme le voilà* —; how slovenly dressed he is, or what a fright he looks.

fagoter, *v.a.,* to fagot, to make into fagots; to jumble together; to dress in a slovenly manner, to dress like a fright. *Peut-on* — *ainsi un enfant ?* how can people make such a fright of a child?

se **fagoter,** *v.r.,* to dress one's self in a slovenly manner, to dress like a fright. *Cette femme semble prendre à tâche de se* —; that woman seems to do her best to make a fright of herself.

fagoteur, *n.m.,* fagot-maker; bungler; scribbler.

fagotin, *n.m.,* small fagot; monkey dressed up (in man's clothes); clown, merry-andrew, sorry-jester (of a quack).

fagoue, *n.f.,* pancreas; sweetbread (of veal).

⊙**faguenas** (fag-nā), *n.m.,* rank smell.

faible, *adj.,* weak, feeble, faint, deficient; helpless; backward; light (coin.); small (of number); (mus.) thin. *Homme* —; weak man. — *de corps et d'esprit;* weak in body and mind. *Le plus* — *est toujours écrasé;* the weakest goes to the wall. *Le côté* — *d'une chose;* the weak side of a thing.

faible, *n.m.,* weak person; weak side, weak part, weakness; backward boy or girl; blind side, foible; failing; partiality. *Avoir du* — *pour;* to have a partiality for. *Je le tiens par son* —; I have got him by his blind or weak side.

faiblement, *adv.,* weakly, faintly, feebly; slenderly, poorly; helplessly.

faiblesse, *n.f.,* weakness, feebleness, faintness, fainting fit, swoon; slenderness, deficiency, backwardness; thinness, poorness; defect; foible, partiality; lightness (coin.); invalidity. *Avoir de la* — *pour quelqu'un ;* to be partial to any one. *Sentir de la* —; to feel faint. *Tomber en* —; to swoon away, to be seized with a fainting fit. *Il lui a pris une* —; she, he, was

seized with a fainting fit. *Avoir de fréquentes* —*s;* to be subject to fainting fits. *Une femme qui a eu une* —; a woman that has made a slip, a mistake.

faiblir, *v.n.,* to become weak; to abate; to slacken, to flag, to give way, to yield, to relax.

faïence, *n.f.,* crockery; earthenware; crockery-ware; faïence; delft-ware. — *anglaise;* blue, yellow, crockery-ware; earthenware. — *fine;* china.

faïencé, -e, *adj.,* cracked. *V.* **fêlé** —, *n.m.,* imitation ware.

faïencerie (fa-ian-srî), *n.f.,* crockery-ware factory; earthenware factory; crockery-ware.

faïenci-er, *n.m.,* -**ère,** *n.f.,* dealer in crockery-ware, crockery-ware man or woman.

faille, n.f., (geol.) out-throw, excavation; faul... Flemish gros grain silk; female head-dress used in Flanders.

failli, n.m., -**e,** *n.f.,* bankrupt; insolvent.

faillibilité, n.f., liability to err, fallibility.

faillible, adj., liable to err, fallible.

faillir, v.n., to err, to miss; to fail; to trespass; to transgress; to mistake, to be mistaken; to be extinct; to be on the point of, to be well nigh; to be near, on the point of; to be a bankrupt. *Il a failli;* he missed his aim. *Les plus doctes sont sujets à* —; the most learned are liable to be mistaken. *Jouer à coup faillant ;* to take the place of him who misses. *Le cœur me faut ;* I am ready to faint. *J'irai sans* —; I will go without fail. *Il a failli tomber;* he was near falling. *Il s'en faut beaucoup, il s'en faut de beaucoup;* very far from it; a long way out. *Peu s'en faut ;* very near. *Tant s'en faut;* far from it. *V.* **falloir.**

faillite, n.f., bankruptcy, failure, insolvency. *Etre en* —; to be a bankrupt. *Faire* —; to fail, to become bankrupt. *Actif d'une* —; assets in a bankruptcy. — *frauduleuse;* fraudulent bankruptcy. *Syndical de* —; commission in bankruptcy. *Déclaration de* —; declaration of insolvency.

faim (fin), *n.f.,* hunger, appetite; (fig.) thirst. *Avoir* —; to be hungry. *Mourir de* —; to be starving, to be dying with hunger. — *canine ;* rabid hunger. *Apaiser la* — *de quelqu'un ;* to stay any one's hunger. *Etourdir la* —; to take the edge off one's appetite. *Un meurt-de* —; a starveling. *Faire mourir de* —; to starve out. *Réduire par la* —; to starve out. *Se laisser mourir de* —; to starve one's self to death. *La* — *chasse le loup hors du bois ;* hunger will break through stone walls. — *insatiable des richesses ;* insatiable thirst for riches.

faim-valle, *n.f.,* (n.p.) (vet.) hungry-evil (in horses).

faine, *n.f.,* (bot.) beech-mast, beechnut.

fainéant, -e, *n.* and *adj.,* sluggard, loiterer, skulker; idle, lazy, slothful, sluggish.

fainéanter, *v.n.,* to be idle, to be indolent, to loaf.

fainéantise, *n.f.,* idleness, laziness, slothfulness, sloth; loafing.

faire (faisant, fait), *v.a.,* to make, to do; to create, to bear, to exert; to construct, to frame; to coin; to counterfeit; to work, to effect, to perform; to celebrate; to hold (festivals); to play (a game); to play off (tricks); to prosecute (studies); to raise (troops); to have (children); (nav.) to make for, to set (sail); to receive, to take in (a supply); to build (nests); to offer up (prayers); to carry on (a trade); to compose (books); to take (a ride, a walk); to follow (profession); to inflict (injuries); to pay (attention); to oblige; to practice, to transact, to commit, to perpetrate; to exercise, to discharge; to fashion, to form, to improve; to use, to accustom, to inure, to train up; to act, to personate, to affect, to set up for, to sham, to counterfeit ; to wage ; to lay (eggs) ; to charge for, to sell ; to be ; to render ; to give out, to tell ; to cause ; to get ; to bring ; to bid, to order. — to be done. *Avoir beaucoup à —, avoir fort à — ;* to have a great deal to do. *Donner fort à à quelqu'un ;* to give any one a great deal of trouble. *Cela fera tout aussi bien ;* that will do just as well. *Se laisser — ;* to offer no resistance, to submit to anything. *N'avoir rien à — ;* to have nothing to do. *Faites ce que vous voudrez, c'est le moindre de mes soucis ;* do your worst, I care not. *Qu'y — ?* what is to be done ? *— des enfants ;* to have children. *— et dire sont deux ;* saying and doing are different things. *Cet écolier a-t-il fait son thème ?* has that boy done his exercise ? *— sa besogne ;* to do one's work. *— tous ses efforts, tout son possible ;* to do one's utmost. *A tout — ;* fit for everything ; of all work. *Bonne à tout — ;* maid of all work. *Etre à tout — ;* to be fit for anything. *— du bien, du mal ;* to do good, harm. *— une bonne œuvre ;* to do a good work. *— la charité ;* to give alms, to do good. *— l'aumône ;* to give alms. *— un mauvais coup ;* to do a bad action. *— une sottise ;* to do a foolish thing. *— des bassesses ;* to behave meanly. *— son devoir ;* to do one's duty. *— son apprentissage ;* to serve one's apprenticeship. *— un tour de jardin ;* to take a turn in the garden. *— le tour du jardin ;* to walk round the garden. *— une promenade ;* to take a walk. *— une lieue à pied ;* to walk a league. *Il fait bien ses affaires ;* he is getting on well. *— une chambre ;* to clean a room. *— la couverture ;* to turn down the bed. *— les foins ;* to make hay. *— la moisson ;* to get in the harvest. *Que ferez vous de votre fils ?* what will you do with your son ? *Il est fait au chaud et au froid ;* he is used to heat and cold. *Les affaires font les hommes ;* business makes men. *Que faites-vous aujourd'hui ?* what are you going to do to-day ? *Je n'ai rien à faire ;* I have nothing to do. *Je n'ai que — de lui ;* I do not want him. *Je n'ai que — de lui ni de ses visites ;* I want neither him nor his visits. *— la revue d'une armée ;* to review an army. *— des recrues ;* to recruit. *— la médecine ;* to practice medicine. *— des armes ;* to fence. *— de grandes affaires ;* to carry on a large trade. *la cuisine ;* to dress meat, to cook. *— un métier ;* to carry on a trade. *Il ne sait pas — son métier ;* he does not know his trade. *— le roi ;* to personate the king. *— l'amant ;* to act the lover. *— le savant ;* to set up for a learned man. *Elle ne fait œuvre de ses dix doigts ;* she never does a thing. *— le malade ;* to sham illness. *— la sourde oreille ;* to pretend to be deaf, to turn a deaf ear. *— mine de, — semblant de ;* to feign, to pretend. *Il faisait semblant de n'en rien savoir ;* he pretended to know nothing about it. *Que voulez-vous que j'y fasse ?* what can I do, how can I help it ? *Ce petit garçon fait le mutin ;* that little boy is refractory. *Cela fait toutes mes délices ;* that is my greatest delight. *On le faisait mort ;* they made him out to be dead. *Faites-le entrer ;* bid him come in, show him in. *Il le fit mettre à mort ;* he had him put to death. *Je le lui ai fait avoir ;* I have procured it for him. *— bâtir ;* to have built. *— aller une machine ;* to set a machine going. *— venir ;* to send for. *— dire une leçon à quelqu'un ;* to hear any one say his lesson. *Cela fait beaucoup ;* that makes a great difference. *Cela ne fait rien ;* that makes no difference. *— entendre à quelqu'un ;* to give any one to understand, to hint to any one. *— voir ;* to show. *— connaître ;* to make known. *— savoir ;* to inform. *Faites-moi savoir de vos nouvelles ;* let me hear from you. *— accueil ;* to welcome. *— affront ;* to insult. *— attention ;* to pay attention, to mind, to heed. *— banqueroute ;* to go bankrupt. *— bonne chère ;* to live well. *— bonne*

mine à quelque chose ; to put a good face on anything. *— carême ;* to keep Lent. *— cas de ;* to value, to have a good opinion of. *— peu de cas de ;* to make light of. *Ne — cas que de l'argent ;* to value nothing but money. *— compassion ;* to raise compassion. *— une confidence à quelqu'un ;* to intrust a secret to any one. *— conscience ;* to scruple. *— don ;* to make a donation, a present of. *— envie ;* to raise envy, to make envious. *— feu ;* to fire. *— front ;* to face. *— montre de ;* to make a show of. *— de l'eau ;* (nav.) to take in fresh water. *— du bois, du biscuit ;* (nav.) to furnish with wood, with biscuit. *— eau ;* (nav.) to make water, to leak. *— force de voiles ;* to crowd all sail. *— voile ;* (nav.) to make for, to set sail. *Je ne ferai rien de la sorte ;* I shall do nothing of the kind. *Je ne puis qu'y — ;* I cannot help it. *On ne saurait qu'y — ;* it cannot be helped. *Si — se peut ;* if possible. *— son chemin ;* to get on (in life). *Ne — qu'un ;* to be hand and glove together. *— la saint lundi ;* to do no work on Mondays. *— des siennes ;* to be at one's old tricks. *N'en — rien ;* to do nothing of the sort. *— à sa guise ;* to do as one likes. *Pour bien — ;* by rights, properly.

se **faire**, *v.r.,* to be done, to be made ; to happen ; to take place ; to be ; to grow ; to become ; to be used to, to accustom one's self to ; to give one's self out as ; to set up for ; to pretend. *Quelle idée vous faites-vous de cet homme-là ?* what is your idea of that man ? *Si cela peut se — ;* if that can be done. *Je me suis fait au bruit de la rue ;* I have got accustomed to the noise of the street. *Se — à la fatigue ;* to inure one's self to fatigue. *Se — à tout ;* to accustom one's self to everything. *Se — médecin ;* to become a doctor. *Il se fait plus riche qu'il ne l'est ;* he gives himself out for being richer than he is. *Se — des amis ;* to make one's self friends. *Se — aimer ;* to make one's self beloved. *Se — voir ;* to show one's self. *Se — saigner ;* to get one's self bled. *Se — mal ;* to hurt one's self. *Comment cela se fait-il ?* how is that ? *Il peut se — que ;* it is possible that. *Il pourrait se — que ;* it might happen that. *Se — un devoir de ;* to make it a duty or a point to. *Il se fait tard ;* it is getting late. *Paris ne s'est pas fait en un jour ;* Rome was not built in a day. *Se — la main ;* to get one's hand in. *Se — vieux, vieille ;* to be getting old, to age. *Se — jour ;* to force one's way through. *Se — une tête ;* to alter one's features. *Cela se fait maintenant ;* that is the fashion now. *Cela ne se fait pas ;* that is not done ; that is not the custom.

faire, *v.n.,* to do, to make ; to act ; to mean, to signify ; to look ; to deal (at cards) ; to be ; to fit ; to arrange, to manage. *— pour quelqu'un ;* to supply any one's place, to act for any one. *— bien ;* to do right. *— mal ;* to do wrong. *Il n'en veut — qu'à sa tête ;* he will only do as he pleases. *C'est à — à vous ;* you are well able to do it. *C'est bien à — à vous de ;* does it become you to ? *C'est à — à moi de lui parler ;* it is my business to speak to him. *Il ne fait que sortir et rentrer ;* he does nothing but go out and in. *Il ne fait que de sortir ;* he has only just gone out. *Qu'est-ce que cela fait là ?* what does that do there ? *Qu'est-ce que cela fait ?* what does that matter ? *Qu'est-ce que cela vous fait ?* what is that to you ? *Cela ne me fait rien ;* that is nothing to me. *Ces deux choses font fort bien ensemble ;* these two things go very well together. *L'or fait bien avec le vert ;* gold looks very well upon green. *Faites qu'il soit content ;* see that he is satisfied. *Faites en sorte que je vous voie ;* manage so that I may see you ; contrive to let me see you. *Rien n'y faisait ;* nothing would do. *Il fait chaud ;* it is hot. *Il fait froid ;* it is cold. *Il fait beau ;* it is fine. *Quel temps fait-il ?* what sort of weather is it ?

Quel temps il fait ! what weather, to be sure ! *Il fait cher vivre à Londres;* living is dear in London. *Il fait bon ici;* it is comfortable, nice, pleasant here. *A qui à — ?* whose deal is it ? *Je viens de —;* I have just dealt.

faire, *n.m.*, doing, making, execution; (fine arts) manner, style ; (com.) goods, articles.

faisable, *adj.*, practicable, allowable, feasible.

faisan, *n.m.*, **faisane**, *n.f.*, pheasant. *Une poule —e;* a hen-pheasant. *Coq —;* cock-pheasant. *— noir, de montagne;* black-cock.

faisances, *n.f.pl.*, dues over and above the rent. *— valoir;* farm cultivation, land under cultivation.

faisandeau, *n.m.*, young pheasant.

faisandé, -e, *part.*, gamy, high.

faisander, *v.a.*, to keep game till it is high. *se* **faisander**, *v.r.*, to get gamy, or high.

faisanderie (-drî), *n.f.*, pheasantry.

faisandier, *n.m.*, pheasant-breeder.

faisant, -e, *adj.*, acting, doing. *n.m.*, doer.

faisceau, *n.m.*, bundle ; sheaf (of arrows) ; (anat.) fasciculus ; pile (of arms) ; (arch.) cluster ; (opt.) pencil ; (fig.) union, alliance, number. *pl.*, (antiq.) fasces. *— d'armes;* pile of arms. *Mettre les armes en —x;* to pile arms. *En —;* in a bundle or bundles ; (arch.) clustered. *— de rayons;* (opt.) pencil of rays.

faiseu-r, *n.m.*, **-se**, *n.f.*, maker ; (b.s.) swindler ; monger, doer. *— de vers;* versifier, poetaster. *— de systèmes;* system-monger. *Mangez de ce pâté, c'est d'un bon —;* try a piece of this pie, it is made by a first-rate hand. *Les grands diseurs ne sont pas les —s;* great talkers are little doers. *— d'affaires;* promoter, jobber. *— de tours;* mountebank. *— d'embarras;* fussy person.

fait, *n.m.*, fact, act, deed, doing ; case ; matter, business ; event, occurrence ; point, point in question ; what suits ; share. *C'est un — bien constaté;* it is a well-known fact. *Par le — seul;* by the mere fact. *Par le seul —;* by the simple fact, ipso facto. *Prendre quelqu'un sur le —;* to catch any one in the very act. *Prendre — et cause pour quelqu'un;* to take any one's part, to side with any one. *Voies de —;* violence, assault. *Pour venir au —;* to come to the point. *Au —;* in fact, in point of fact. *Etre au — de;* to be acquainted with ; to be aware of. *Il est au — de cette affaire;* he is well acquainted with that affair. *C'est un — à part;* that is another matter. *De —;* indeed, certainly. *Il est de — que;* it is a fact that, *or* it is notorious that. *Les hauts —s d'un guerrier;* the exploits of a warrior. *Voilà mon —;* that is just what I want. *Mettre en —;* to lay down as a fact. *Etre sûr de son —;* to be sure of anything, to be sure of what one states. *C'est votre —;* that just suits you. *Dire à quelqu'un son —;* to tell any one what you think of him. *Au — et au prendre;* at a scratch or pinch, when it comes to the scratch. *—s et dits;* doings and sayings. *En venir au — et au prendre;* to come to the scratch. *Se mettre au — de;* to acquaint one's self with. *Trouver le — de quelqu'un;* to find what any one wants. *Donner son — à quelqu'un;* to pay any one out. *Mettre quelqu'un au —;* to acquaint any one with the point in question. *Tout à —;* entirely, completely, quite. *Si —;* yes, yes indeed, *or* yes, though. *Vous n'y êtes pas allé. Si —;* you did not go there. Yes, I did ; yes, indeed I did. *— à part;* exceptional case.

fait, -e, *part.*, made, done, shaped ; organized ; fit, qualified ; calculated, intended, settled, ended, over; accustomed to, grown, full grown, grown up. *Ce qui est —, est —;* what is done, cannot be undone. *Un homme —;* a grown-up man. *De compte —;* upon computation. *Comme le voilà —!* how ill he looks !

Tenez cela pour —; consider it done. *Cela vaut —;* that is as good as done. *C'est — de lui;* he is undone. *C'en est — de;* it is all over *or* up with. *Ce qui est — n'est pas à faire;* what is done is done. *Aussitôt dit, aussitôt —;* no sooner said than done. *Tout —;* ready made, cut and dry. *C'est bien —;* it serves him, her, you, them, right. *Est-ce — ?* have you done ? is it done ? *C'est un grand pas de —;* it is a great step forward. *C'est comme un — exprès;* it seems done on purpose. *Cela est — pour moi, cela semble — pour moi; cela n'est — que pour moi;* such things happen to me alone, such is my luck. *Travailler à prix —;* to work by the piece.

faitage, *n.m.*, ridge-piece ; roofing.

faîte, *n.m.*, top, summit, pinnacle ; zenith ; height ; ridge, coping (of building). *Le — des grandeurs;* the pinnacle of greatness. *— de cheminée;* chimney-top.

fait exprès, *n.m.*, thing done on purpose *or* intentionally.

faitière (-tièr), *adj.*, of the ridge. *Tuile —;* ridge-tile, pantile. *Lucarnes —s;* sky-lights.

faitière, *n.f.*, ridge-tile, pantile.

faix (fê), *n.m.*, weight, burden, load. *Plier sous le —;* to sink under the weight *or* burden.

fakir, *n.m.*, fakir (Mahommedan friar).

falaise, *n.f.*, cliff. *Les blanches —s d'Albion;* the white cliffs of England.

falaiser, *v.n.*, to dash against the cliffs (of waves).

falbala, *n.m.*, furbelow, flounce ; finery.

falcade, *n.f.*, (man.) falcade.

falciforme, *adj.*, (bot.) falcate, falcated.

fale, *n.f.*, crop (of a bird).

fallacieusement (fal-la-sieuz-mān), *adv.*, fallaciously, falsely.

fallacieu-x, -se (fal-la-), *adj.*, fallacious, false.

falloir, *v.imp.*, must, should, ought ; to be necessary, requisite ; to be obliged ; to need, to stand in need of, to want. *Ce qu'il faut;* what is wanted *or* necessary. *Il faut le faire;* it must be done. *Il faut que je fasse cela;* I must do that. *Il faut que j'y aille;* I must go there. *Il fallait venir plus tôt;* you ought to have come sooner. *Il faudra le satisfaire;* you will have to satisfy him. *Il aurait fallu s'y prendre ainsi;* you should have gone to work in this way. *Faut-il le demander ?* need you ask ? *Il fallait voir comme il était content;* you should have seen how pleased he was. *Je ne sais ce qu'il lui faut;* I do not know what he wants. *Il me le faut;* I must have it. *Il me faut de l'argent;* I must have some money. *J'en ai plus qu'il ne m'en faut;* I have more than I want. *Combien vous en faut-il?* how much do you want ? *Que lui faut-il pour sa peine?* how much must he have for his trouble ? *Faites cela comme il faut;* do that properly, well. *Il fait ce qu'il faut;* he does what is requisite. *Des gens comme il faut;* well-bred people. *Un homme comme il faut;* a gentlemanly man. *C'est l'homme qu'il faut;* he is the very man for the place *or* for the work. *Il se vante de ne pas me craindre, il faudra voir!* he boasts that he does not fear me, but wait a bit ! *Il me menace d'un procès, c'est ce qu'il faudra voir!* he threatens me with an action, but we shall see about it !

s'en **falloir**, *v.r.*, to be wanting; to be far ; to fall short; to be near, to be on the point. *Il s'en fallut de peu que je ne fusse écrasé;* I was near being run over. *Peu s'en est fallu que je ne mourusse;* I was near dying *or* within an ace of dying. *Il s'en faut de beaucoup que la somme y soit;* the sum is far from being complete. *Il s'en faut de beaucoup que l'un ait autant de mérite que l'autre;* the one is far from possessing as much merit as the other. *Il s'en faut de beaucoup;* very far from it. *Vous croyez m'avoir* *tout payé; mais il s'en faut de beaucoup;* you imagine you have squared with me; but you are a long way out. *Il s'en faut de peu qu'il ne soit aussi grand que son frère;* he is nearly as tall as his brother. *Tant s'en faut que;* so far from, far from it. *Tant s'en faut qu'il consente qu'au contraire il fera tout pour l'empêcher;* he is so far from consenting that he will, on the contrary, do all he can to prevent it. *Tant s'en faut qu'au contraire;* (fam., jest.) on the contrary, quite the reverse. [When *s'en falloir* is preceded by a negative, or accompanied by a word having a negative sense, as *peu, guère, presque, rien,* or if the phrase implies doubt, or has an interrogative meaning, the dependent clause is accompanied by the negation *ne;* but when *s'en falloir* is neither preceded by a negative, nor accompanied by any of the above words, the dependent clause does not take the negative particle.]

falot, *n.m.,* lantern, torch; fire-pot, cresset.

falot, -e, *adj.,* comical, droll, laughable, funny, queer.

falotement, *adv.,* comically, amusingly, ludicrously, grotesquely.

falourde, *n.f.,* bundle of fire-wood; (orni.) sea-swallow.

falquer, *v.n.,* (man.) to make falcades.

falques, *n.f.pl.,* (man.) falcade; (nav.) washboard; weather-board.

falsifiable, *adj.,* falsifiable; adulterable.

falsificateur, *n.m.,* falsifier; debaser.

falsification, *n.f.,* falsification, adulteration, debasement.

falsifié, -e, *adj.,* adulterated, falsified.

falsifier, *v.a.,* to falsify, to alter (texts); to adulterate, to debase. *— les métaux;* to adulterate metals. *— de la monnaie;* to debase coin.

falun, *n.m.,* falun, shell-marl.

faluner, *v.a.,* to manure with shell-marl.

falunière, *n.f.,* falun pit, shell-marl pit.

famé, -e, *adj.,* famed. *Bien —;* of good repute. *Homme mal —;* man of ill-repute.

famélique, *n.m.f.* and *adj.,* starveling; starving, famishing. *Auteur —;* starving author. *Il a bien l'air d'un —;* he looks like a poor starving wretch.

fameu-x, -se, *adj.,* famous, famed, celebrated, renowned, notorious, first-rate, capital; (iron.) precious. *— imbécile;* precious fool. *— voleur;* notorious thief.

familiariser, *v.a.,* to accustom to, to familiarize.

se **familiariser** (avec), *v.r.,* to familiarize one's self with; to make one's self familiar with, to grow familiar; to accustom one's self to; to grow tame.

familiarité, *n.f.,* familiarity, familiar terms; intimacy. *pl.,* liberties. *Vivre sur le pied de la plus grande —;* to be on the most familiar terms.

famili-er, -ère, *adj.,* familiar, free, intimate, unconstrained, homely; tame.

famili-er, *n.m.,* **-ère,** *n.f.,* familiar. *C'est un des —s du prince;* he is one of the prince's favorite companions.

familièrement (-măn), *adv.,* familiarly.

***famille,** *n.f.,* family, kindred, kin; race, tribe, parentage. *Être chargé de —;* to have a large family. *Il a un air de —;* there is a family likeness about him. *Affaires de —;* domestic concerns. *Chef de —;* head of a family. *En —;* at home. *Fils de —;* gentleman's son.

famine, *n.f.,* famine, dearth. *Crier — sur un tas de blé;* to plead poverty though rolling in riches. *Prendre par la —;* to starve out, to reduce by famine.

fanage, *n.m.,* (agri.) tossing, tedding of hay; haymaker's pay; leaves of a plant.

fanaison, *n.f.* V. **fenaison**.

fanal, *n.m.,* lantern of a ship; signal-light, watch-light, beacon.

fanariote, *n.m.f.* V. **phanariote**.

fanatique, *n.m.f.* and *adj.,* fanatic, bigot, enthusiast; fanatical, bigoted.

fanatiser, *v.a.,* to fanaticize.

fanatisme, *n.m.,* fanaticism, bigotry.

fanchon, *n.m.,* kerchief (for the head).

fandango, *n.m.,* fandango (Spanish dance).

fane, *n.f.,* leaf-top; envelope (of a flower). *—s, pl.,* fallen leaves; dead leaves.

fané, -e, *adj.,* faded, withered.

faner, *v.a.,* to toss, to ted hay; to make fade, to tarnish.

se **faner,** *v.r.,* to fade, to fade away, to droop, to wither, to tarnish. *Cette femme commence à se —;* that woman begins to fall off.

faneu-r, *n.m.,* **-se,** *n.f.,* haymaker.

faneuse, *n.f.,* hay-making machine.

fanfan, *n.m.f.,* darling, duck, ducky (child).

fanfare, *n.f.,* flourish, flourish of trumpets, brass-band. *Sonner une —;* to strike up a flourish.

fanfaron, *adj.m.,* blustering, swaggering, bragging, boasting.

fanfaron, *n.m.,* blusterer; swaggerer; boaster, braggart. *Faire le —;* to play the braggart.

fanfaronnade, *n.f.,* blustering, bragging, boasting.

fanfaronnerie (-ro-n-rî), *n.f.,* blustering, swaggering, bragging, boasting.

fanfreluche, *n.f.,* bauble, gewgaw, tinsel.

fange, *n.f.,* mire, mud, dirt; vileness; degradation; debasement.

fangeu-x, -se, *adj.,* miry, muddy, dirty.

fanion, *n.m.,* (milit.) V. **fanon**.

fanon, *n.m.,* dewlap (of oxen); fetlock (of horses); fin (of whales); (c.rel.) pendant (of a bishop's miter); (milit.) pennon.

fanons, *n.m.pl.,* (surg.) bandages.

fantaisie, *n.f.,* imagination; fancy; whim, caprice, crotchet, odd fancy; conceit; liking; (mus.) fantasia. *Il a eu la — d'aller voyager;* he has taken it into his head to travel. *Vivre à sa —;* to live as one likes. *Cela est-il à votre —?* is that to your liking? *Il lui prit — d'aller le voir;* she suddenly made up her mind to pay him a visit. *Par —;* out of pure whim. *Objets de —;* fancy articles. *Avoir une —;* to fancy. *Avoir des —s;* to be fanciful.

fantaisiste, *n.m.f.,* whimsical painter *or* writer; humorist.

fantasmagorie, *n.f.,* phantasmagoria, dissolving view.

fantasmagorique, *adj.,* phantasmagorical.

fantasmagoriquement, *adv.,* phantasmagorically.

fantasque, *adj.,* fantastic, fantastical, fanciful, whimsical, queer; strange, odd.

fantasquement, *adv.,* (l.u.) fantastically, fancifully, whimsically, oddly.

fantassin, *n.m.,* foot-soldier.

fantastique, *adj.,* fantastic, fantastical, fanciful, chimerical.

fantastiquement (-tik-măn), *adv.,* fantastically.

fantoccini (făn-tot-shee-nee), *n.m.pl.,* fantoccini (puppets).

fantoche, *n.m.,* puppet. *adj.,* odd, queer.

fantôme, *n.m.,* phantom, specter, ghost.

fanum (fa-nom), *n.m.,* (—) (antiq.) fane.

faon (făn), *n.m.,* doe, fawn.

faonner (fa-né), *v.n.,* to fawn (as a deer).

faquin, *n.m.,* scoundrel, mean rascal, puppy.

faquinerie (fa-ki-n-rî), *n.f.,* rascally action, rascally meanness; scoundrelism.

faquir, *n.m.* V. **fakir**.

farandole, *n.f.,* farandole (Provençal dance).

faraud, *n.m.,* a vulgar fop; snob, swell.

farce, *n.f.,* (cook.) stuffing, forced meat;

farce (thea.); drollery; tomfoolery; practical joke; waggish trick, prank. *Tirez le rideau, la — est jouée;* let down the curtain, the farce is ended. *Faire une — à quelqu'un;* to play any one a trick. *Faire ses —s;* to sow one's wild oats.

farceur, *n.m.,* farce player; droll person; dog (pers.), rogue, practical joker; humbug. *Faire le —;* to play the fool.

farci, -e, *adj., part.,* stuffed; crammed, filled with.

farcin, *n.m.,* (vet.) farcin, farcy.

farcineu-x, -se, *adj.,* affected with farcy.

farcir, *v.a.,* to stuff, to cram, to fill.

se **farcir,** *v.r.,* to stuff, to cram, to be filled.

farcissure, *n.f.,* (cook.) stuffing.

fard, *n.m.,* paint, rouge; varnish; disguise, dissimulation. *Parlez-moi sans — ;* speak to me without disguise. *Se mettre du — à la figure;* to paint, to rouge one's face. *Sans —;* plainly, frankly.

fardage, *n.m.,* (nav.) dunnage.

fardé, -e, *part.,* painted.

fardeau, *n.m.,* burden, load, weight; mash (for brewing); mass (mining). *Imposer un — à quelqu'un;* to put a burden upon any one. *S'imposer un —;* to take a burden upon one's self.

farder, *v.a.,* to paint (the face); (fig.) to varnish, to gloss over.

se **farder,** *v.r.,* to paint one's face, to paint.

farder, *v.n.,* to sink, to give way; (nav.) to swell out (of sails). *Ce mur commence à —;* this wall is beginning to sink,

fardier, *n.m.,* truck, trolley; dray (for stones).

*****farfouiller,** *v.a.* and *n.,* to rummage.

faribole, *n.f.,* idle story, trifle.

farinacé, -e, *adj.,* farinaceous.

farine, *n.f.,* flour, meal; farina. *Fleur de —;* flour. *Folle —;* mill-dust. *Marchand de —;* flour-dealer. *Gens de même —;* birds of a feather. *Donner dans la —;* (paint.) to paint in a wishy-washy manner. *D'un sac à charbon il ne saurait sortir de blanche —;* (prov.) what can you expect from a pig but a grunt? or you can't make a silk purse out of a sow's ear.

fariner, *v.a.,* to flour, to meal.

farinet, *n.m.,* one-faced die.

farineu-x, -se, *adj.,* white with flour; mealy, farinaceous.

farinier, *n.m.,* flour-dealer.

farinière, *n.f.,* meal-tub, flour-bin.

farlouse, *n.f.,* (orni.) titlark, titling.

far-niente, *n.m.,* (*n.p.*) far-niente, doing nothing, pleasant idleness, repose.

faro, *n.m.,* faro (Belgian beer).

farouch *or* **farouche,** *n.m.,* (agri.) clover, clover grass.

farouche, *adj.,* wild; fierce; sullen; unsociable; shy. *Regard —;* fierce look. *Cette femme est bien —;* that woman is very shy.

farrago, *n.m.,* farrago.

fasce, *n.f.,* (her.) fesse.

fascé, -e, *adj.,* (her.) fessy.

fascia, *n.m.,* (anat.) fascia.

fasciculaire, *adj.,* (bot.) fascicular.

fascicule, *n.m.,* (bot.) fascicle, small bundle (of plants, herbs); part (number of a work).

fasciculé, -e, *adj.,* (bot.) fasciculate, fasciculated.

fascié, -e, *adj.,* fasciated.

fascinage, *n.m.,* (fort.) fascine work; the making of fascines.

fascinat-eur, -rice, *adj.,* fascinating.

fascination, *n.f.,* fascination.

fascine, *n.f.,* (fort.) fascine; fagot, hurdle, bavin.

fasciner, *v.a.,* to fascinate.

faséole, *n.f.,* phasel, kidney-bean.

fashion, *n.f.,* fashion; fashionable world.

fashionable, *n.m.f.,* and *adj.,* fashionable; beau, belle; swell.

fasier, *v.n.,* (nav.) (of sails) to shiver. *Mettre à —;* (nav.) to spill.

faste, *n.m.,* (*n.p.*) pomp, ostentation, display, vain show, pageantry.

fastes, *n.m.pl.,* fasti, annals; records.

fastidieusement (-euz-mān), *adv.,* tediously, irksomely.

fastidieu-x, -se, *adj.,* irksome, tedious, wearisome, tiresome, dull.

fastigié, -e, *adj.,* fastigiate, fastigiated.

fastueusement (-euz-mān), *adv.,* magnificently, ostentatiously, pompously, splendidly, gorgeously.

fastueu-x, -se, *adj.,* ostentatious, pompous, gorgeous, showy; sumptuous; stately.

fat (fat), *n.* and *adj. m.,* fop, coxcomb; foppish. *En —;* foppishly. *C'est un —;* he is a coxcomb.

fatal, -e, *adj.,* fatal; inevitable. *Terme —;* (jur.) expiration of a delay. *Ces remèdes ont été —s au malade;* those remedies proved fatal to the patient.

fatalement (fa-tal-mān), *adv.,* fatally; inevitably.

fatalisme, *n.m.,* fatalism.

fataliste, *n.m.f.,* fatalist.

fatalité, *n.f.,* fatality.

fatidique, *adj.,* fatidical.

fatigant, -e, *adj.,* fatiguing, toilsome, irksome, wearisome, tiresome, tedious.

fatigue, *n.f.,* fatigue, toil, hardship, weariness. *Excéder de —;* to wear out with fatigue, to tire out. *Un homme de —;* a man capable of resisting fatigue. *Supporter la —;* to stand fatigue. *Rompre à la —;* to accustom to fatigue. *Tomber de —;* to be worn out with fatigue.

fatigué, -e, *part.,* fatigued, jaded; (paint.) overworked. *Des chevaux —s;* jaded horses.

fatiguer (-ghé), *v.a.,* to fatigue, to tire, to weary, to harass, to tease; (paint.) to overwork. *La lecture fatigue la vue;* reading fatigues the sight. *— un champ;* to impoverish a field. *— une salade;* to mix a salad.

se **fatiguer,** *v.r.,* to fatigue one's self; to tire one's self out; to be jaded; to tire.

fatiguer, *v.n.,* to tire; to be fatiguing; (nav.) to work. *— à l'ancre;* (nav.) to ride hard. *Ne pas — à l'ancre;* (nav.) to ride easy. *Ne pas — à cheval;* (man.) to ride easy.

fatras, *n.m.,* rubbish, trash, stuff, medley, litter, confusion; balderdash.

fatrassier, *n.m.,* untidy person.

fatuité, *n.f.,* fatuity, self-conceit, foppishness. *Quelle — !* what a piece of impertinence !

faubert, *n.m.,* (nav.) swab, mop.

fauberter, *v.a.,* (nav.) to swab, to mop.

fauberteur, *n.m.,* (nav.) swabber.

faubourg (fô-boor), *n.m.,* outskirt, suburb, slums. *Le — Saint-Germain ne l'entendait pas ainsi;* the old French aristocracy did not see it in that light.

faubourien, -ne (-iin, -è-n), *adj.,* suburban; low.

faubourien, *n.m.,* dweller in a suburb.

fauchage, *n.m.,* mowing.

fauchaison, *n.f.,* mowing-time.

fauchard, *n.m.,* sickle.

fauche, *n.f.,* mowing; mowing-time.

fauchée, *n.f.,* day's mowing.

faucher, *v.a.,* to reap, to mow, to cut down.

faucher, *v.n.,* (man.) to throw the fore-legs sideways in walking (of a horse).

fauchet, *n.m.,* hay-rake.

fauchette, *n.f.,* (gard.) small hedge-knife, border-shears.

faucheur, *n.m.,* mower, reaper; field-spider.

faucheur *or* **faucheux,** *n.m.,* field-spider.

*****faucille,** *n.f.,* sickle, reaping-hook.

*faucillon, n.m., bill-hook.

faucon, n.m., (orni.) falcon; hawk.

fauconneau, n.m., ⊙ (artil.) falconet; (orni.) young hawk.

fauconnerie (fô-co-n-rî), n.f., falconry, hawking.

fauconnier, n.m., falconer. *Monter à cheval en* —; to mount a horse on the off-side.

fauconnière, n.f., hawking-pouch, saddle-bag.

faufiler, v.a., to tack, to baste (needle-work).

se faufiler, v.r., to insinuate one's self, to ingratiate one's self; to intrude one's self; to curry favor with. *Il se faufile partout;* he intrudes himself everywhere.

faulx, n.f. V. **faux**.

faune, n.m., (myth.) faun.

faune, n.f., (zool.) fauna.

faussaire, n.m.f., forger. *Poursuivre comme* —; to prosecute for forgery.

faussement (fôs-mān), adv., falsely, erroneously, wrongfully, untruly.

fausser, v.a., to bend; to warp; to strain; to falsify; to pervert; to violate, to break; (mus.) to put out of tune; to strain (a lock, a key). — *une cuirasse;* to indent a cuirass. — *sa parole;* to violate one's word. — *compagnie à quelqu'un;* to give any one the slip.

se fausser, v.r., to bend; to be warped or perverted.

fausset, n.m., spigot, peg; (mus.) falsetto. *Chanter en* —; to sing in falsetto. *Trou de* —; vent-hole.

fausseté (fôs-té), n.f., falsity, falseness, falsehood, duplicity, insincerity, deceitfulness, treachery.

faute, n.f., fault, mistake, error; want, scarcity, dearth. *A* — *de;* (jur.) in default of. *Faire une* —; to make a mistake. *Ne pas se faire* — *de;* not to be sparing of; to deny one's self nothing. *Relever une* —; to point out a mistake. *Surprendre quelqu'un en* —; to find any one at fault. *A qui la* —? whose fault is it? — *de;* for want of. — *d'orthographe;* wrong spelling. — *d'inattention;* slip. — *d'impression;* misprint. *Ne vous en faites pas* —; do not spare it. *Il est mort - de secours;* he died for want of help. *Sans* —; without fail. — *de mieux;* for want of something better. *Rien ne vous fera* —; you will want for nothing.

*fauteuil, n.m., arm-chair; chair (speaker's, president's seat); academic chair (of the French Academy). — *à la Voltaire;* reclining arm-chair. *Occuper le* —; to fill the chair.

faut-eur, n.m., -**rice**, n.f., abettor, favorer, fomentor. *Etre* — *de;* to abet. *Les* —*s d'un crime;* the abettors of a crime.

-fauti-f, -**ve**, adj., faulty; at fault; defective, incorrect.

fauve, adj., fawn-colored, tawny. *Bêtes* —*s;* fallow-deer, stag, etc.; wild beasts.

fauve, n.m.sing., (hunt.) deer, fallow-deer. *Chasser le* —; to haunt wild animals.

fauveau, n.m., fawn-colored ox.

fauvette, n.f., (orni.) warbler. *Petite* —; garden-warbler, redwing. — *babillarde;* white-throat. — *à tête noire;* blackcap.

faux (fô), n.f., scythe; (anat.) falx.

fau-x, -**sse**, adj., false, untrue, erroneous, wrong; spurious; unsound; base, counterfeit; artificial; fictitious, mock, sham, pretended; insincere, double, treacherous, deceitful; (mus.) out of tune; forged. *Acte* —; (jur.) forgery. — *témoin;* false witness. *Chose* —*sse;* untruth. —*sse doctrine;* erroneous doctrine. —*sse monnaie;* counterfeit money. — *brave;* braggadocio, swaggerer. —*sse démarche;* wrong step. *Voix* —*sse;* voice out of tune. — *brillant;* tinsel. —*sse équerre;* bevel. —*sse fenêtre;* blank or sham window. — *comme un*

jeton; false as Judas. *Faire* — *bond;* not to keep an engagement. *Faire* —*sse route;* to take the wrong road; to be on the wrong track. *Faire un* — *pas;* to stumble; (fig.) to make a slip.

faux, n.m., falsehood, forgery; false. *Discerner le vrai d'avec le* —; to discern truth from falsehood. *Crime de* —; crime of forgery. *Un* —; a forgery. *Commettre un* —; to commit a forgery. *Poursuivre pour* —; to prosecute for forgery. *Arguer de* —; to accuse, to tax, as false. *S'inscrire en* — *contre une chose;* to deny the truth of an assertion.

faux, adv., erroneously, falsely, wrongfully; (mus.) out of tune. *Il chante* —; he sings out of tune. *A* —; falsely, unjustly. *Etre accusé à* —; to be accused unjustly. *Porter à* —; (arch.) to be out of perpendicular, not to be upright. *Cette poutre porte à* —; that post is out of the perpendicular.

faux-fuyant, n.m., (———*s*) by-place; subterfuge, evasion, creep-hole.

favelotte, n.f., horse-bean.

faveur, n.f., favor, boon; interest; vogue; grace; ribbon. *A la* — *de;* by favor of, under cover of. *En* — *de;* in behalf of, in favor of. *Etre en* —; to be in favor, in vogue. *Prendre* —; to get or come into favor, into vogue. *Mettre en* —; to bring into favor, into vogue.

favonette, n.f., everlasting pea.

favorable, adj., favorable, propitious; fair. *Le ciel vous soit* —! heaven befriend you!

favorablement, adj., favorably, propitiously.

favori, -te, n. and adj., favorite.

favori, n.m., whisker.

favoriser, v.a., to favor, to befriend, to countenance; to aid, to assist; to endow; to protect; to promote, to further, to facilitate.

favoritisme, n.m., favoritism.

fayard (fa-iar), n.m., (bot.) (pop.) beech.

fayence, n.f. V. **faïence**, etc.

⊙**féage**, n.m., feoffment.

⊙**féal, -e**, adj., trusty, faithful.

⊙**féal**, n.m., trusty, faithful friend. *A nos amis et féaux;* to our trusty and well-beloved friends.

⊙**féauté**, n.f., fealty.

fébricitant, -e, n. and adj., (med.) feverish; fever-patient.

fébrifuge, n.m. and adj., antifebrile.

fébrile, adj., febrile, feverish.

fécal, -o, adj., fecal. *Matière* —; feces, excrement.

fèces, n.f.pl., (pharm.) sediment; (med.) feces.

fécial, n.m. and adj., (Rom. antiq.) fecial.

fécond, -e, adj., fecund, fruitful, prolific; copious, abundant, fertile, rich, teeming, voluminous. *Mine* —*e;* rich mine. *Avoir l'esprit* —; to have a fertile imagination. *Etre* — *en;* to teem with.

fécondant, -e, adj., fertilizing, genial.

fécondation, n.f., fecundation, inpregnation; fructification; fertilization.

féconder, v.a., to fecundate, to impregnate; to make fruitful, to fertilize.

fécondité, n.f., fecundity, fruitfulness, fertility.

fécule, n.f., fecula.

féculence, n.f., feculency.

féculent, -e, adj., feculent.

féculerie, n.f., manufactory of fecula.

fédéral, -e, adj., federal.

fédéraliser, v.a., (neologism) to make federate. *Se* —, v.r., to federalize.

fédéralisme, n.m., federalism.

fédéraliste, n.m., federalist.

fédérati-f, ve, adj., federate, federative. *Alliance* —*ve;* federative alliance.

fédération, n.f., federation, alliance.

fédéré, -e, n. and adj., federate, ally.

se **fédérer,** *v.r.*, to federate ; to combine ; to band together ; to take united action.

fée, *n.f.*, fairy ; fay. *Comme une —* ; fairy-like. *C'est la — Carabosse ;* she 's an old hag.

féerie, *n.f.*, fairy scene, enchantment ; fairy-land.

féerique, *adj.*, fairy-like ; enchanting, wonderful, marvelous, magical.

feindre (feignant, feint), *v.a.*, to feign, to dissemble, to disguise, to pretend, to imagine, to sham. *— une maladie ;* to sham illness.

feindre, *v.n.*, to feign, to sham. *Il possède l'art de —* ; he is an adept in the art of dissembling.

feint, -e, *part.*, feigned, make-believe, pretended, sham. *Amitié —e ;* pretended friendship.

feinte, *n.f.*, feint ; pretense, dissimulation ; artifice ; invention ; (mus.) accidental ; (print.) friar ; (pisc.) shad. *User de —* ; to dissemble. *Il fit une —* ; (fenc.) he made a feint. *Sans —* ; frankly.

feintier, *n.m.*, shad-net.

⊙**feintise,** *n.f.*, feint, pretense, sham.

feld-maréchal, *n.m.*, field-marshal.

feldspath, *n.m.*, (min.) feldspar, feldspath.

feldspathique, *adj.*, (min.) feldspathic.

fêlé, -e, *part.*, cracked (of glass) ; (pers.) crack-brained ; delicate (of the chest). *C'est un cerveau —* ; he is a hare-brained fellow. *Les pots —s sont ceux qui durent le plus ;* threatened men live longest.

fêler, *v.a.*, to crack (glass).

se **fêler,** *v.r.*, to crack or get cracked (of glass).

félicitation, *n.f.*, felicitation, congratulation. *Lettre de —* ; letter of congratulation.

félicité, *n.f.*, felicity, bliss, happiness.

féliciter, *v.a.*, to congratulate, to felicitate, to wish joy.

se **féliciter,** *v.r.*, to congratulate one's self, to be pleased or satisfied.

félin, -e, *adj.*, feline.

fellah, *n.m.*, (—*s*) fellah (Egyptian peasant).

félon, -ne, *n.* and *adj.*, (l.u.) traitor ; felon ; felonious.

félonie, *n.f.*, (feudalism) felony, disloyalty, treason.

felouque, *n.f.*, (nav.) felucca (boat).

fêlure, *n.f.*, crack, chink, fissure.

femelle, *n.f.* and *adj.*, female ; she, hen. [Applied *only* to animals except in a bad sense.] (pers.) loose woman, creature.

féminin, -e, *adj.*, feminine, female, womanish, woman-like, effeminate. *Genre —* ; feminine gender. *Sexe —e ;* female sex.

féminin, *n.m.*, (gram.) feminine.

féminiser, *v.a.*, (gram.) to make feminine, to render effeminate.

femme (famme), *n.f.*, woman ; wife, married woman, attendant ; lady. *Une — auteur ;* an authoress. *Mari et —* ; man and wife. *Une — sage ;* a well-conducted woman. *Une sage —* ; a midwife. *— de chambre ;* waiting-woman, lady's maid. *— de charge ;* housekeeper. *— de journée, —de ménage ;* char-woman. *— en puissance de mari* or *— couverte ;* (jur.) feme-covert. *Avoir —* ; to have a wife. *Avoir — et enfants ;* to have a wife and children. *Prendre —* ; to take a wife. *Bonne —* ; good, obliging woman ; old woman ; simple, superstitious woman.

femmelette (fa-mlèt), *n.f.*, silly, weak woman ; effeminate man.

fémoral, -e, *adj.*, (anat.) femoral.

fémur, *n.m.*, (anat.) femur, thigh-bone ; (vet.) hurl-bone. *Tête du —* ; head or apophysis of the femur.

fenaison, *n.f.*, hay-time, hay-harvest ; hay-making.

fendage, *n.m.*, splitting, cleaving.

fendant, *n.m.*, hector, bully. *Faire le —* ; to play the bully.

fenderie (fan-drî), *n.f.*, slitting (of iron into rods) ; slitting-mill.

fendeur, *n.m.*, cleaver, slitter, splitter. *— de roues,* wheel-cutter.

*se **fendiller,** *v.r.*, to slit ; to chink ; to crack.

fendoir, *n.m.*, cleaver ; chopper.

fendre, *v.a.*, to cleave, to split, to rive, to crack, to cut open, to rend, to rip ; to break ; to burst. *— du bois ;* to cleave wood. *Un navire qui fend l'eau ;* a ship that plows the sea. *— les airs ;* to cleave the air. *— la presse ;* to break through the crowd.

se **fendre,** *v.r.*, to cleave, to burst asunder, to split, to slit ; to chap, to chink, to rive, to gape ; (fenc.) to lunge.

fendre, *v.n.*, to be ready to split ; to break, to burst. *La tête me fend ;* my head is ready to split.

fendu, -e, *part.*, cleft, split, cloven. *Bien —* ; long-legged. *Des yeux bien —s ;* large, well-shaped eyes.

fêne, *n.f.* *V.* **faîne.**

fenestré, -e, *adj.* *V.* **fenêtré.**

fenêtrage, *n.m.*, fenestration, windows, lights.

fenêtre, *n.f.*, window, casement ; (anat.) aperture. *— à châssis ;* sash-window. *— en baie, en saillie ;* bay, bow, window ; (Gothic arch.) oriel-window, oriel. *— à coulisse, en guillotine ;* sash-window. *— en éventail ;* fan-light. *— en ogive ;* (arch.) Gothic window. *Condamner une —* ; to block up a window. *Fausse —* ; sham or blind window. *Regarder par la —* ; to look out of the window. *Jeter par la —* ; to throw out of the window, to be a spendthrift, to squander one's money.

fenêtré, -e, *adj.*, windowed ; fenestrated.

***fenil,** *n.m.*, hayloft.

***fenouil,** *n.m.*, fennel ; fennel-seed. *— puant,* anet. *— de mer ;* sea-samphire. *— de porc ;* sulphur-wort, hog's-fennel.

***fenouillet,** *n.m.*, (bot.) fennel-apple.

***fenouillette,** *n.f.*, fennel-apple ; fennel-water.

fente, *n.f.*, slit, chink, cleft, chap, flaw ; gap, cranny, crevice ; (min.) rent ; cleavage ; (nav.) spring ; (dress) placket hole.

fenton, *n.m.*, iron-cramp, iron-tie.

fenugrec, *n.m.*, (bot.) fenugreek.

féodal, -e, *adj.*, feudal.

féodalement, *adv.*, feudally.

féodalité, *n.f.*, feudality, feudalism.

fer (fèr), *n.m.*, iron ; head, point ; sword, brand, steel ; tag ; (nav.) spindle (of vanes). *pl.*, iron-work ; irons, chains, fetters. *— battu ;* wrought-iron. *— fondu ;* cast-iron. *— impur ;* iron-ore. *— doux ;* soft iron. *— aigre ;* brittle iron. *— laminé ;* rolled iron. *— oligiste, spéculaire ;* (min.) iron-glance. *— rouverin ;* red-scar iron. *— de carillon ;* bar-iron. *Le — d'une pique ;* the head of a pike. *— de lacet, — d'aiguillette ;* tag of a lace. *Le — et le feu ;* fire and sword. *— en barres ;* bar-iron. *— à cheval ;* horse-shoe ; (fort.) horse-shoe ; (man.) horse-shoe bat. *— à marquer ;* marking-iron. *— dur ;* hard iron. *— à cheval cramponné, — à cheval relevé ;* horse-shoe with calkins. *— de fenderie ;* slit iron. *— de fonte ;* cast iron. *— à glace ;* frost shoe. *— de lance ;* (arch.) stanchion. *— à repasser ;* iron, box-iron, flat-iron. *— à souder ;* soldering-iron. *Bande, pièce, de —* ; (tech.) strap. *Bois de —* ; iron-wood. *Fil de —* ; wire, iron-wire. *Fonte de —* ; cast iron. *Limaille de —* ; iron dust, iron filings. *Marchand de —* ; dealer in iron, ironmonger. *Mine de —* ; (min.) iron-ore. *Minerai de —* ; iron-ore ; iron-stone. *Ouvrage en —* ; iron-work. *Scorie de —* ; iron-dross. *Usine de —* ; iron-works. *A tête de —* ; strong-headed, resolute, determined. *— d'arc-boutant ;* (nav.) goose-neck of a boom. *— de gaffe ;* (nav.) boat-hook. *— à calfat, — de* *calfat ;* calker's iron, calking-iron. *Petits —s ;* punches (book-bind.). *Avoir toujours quelque — qui cloche ;* to have always some screw loose. *Il y a quelque — qui cloche ;* there 's a hitch somewhere. *Battre le — ;* to fence, to tilt. *Battre le — pendant qu'il est chaud ;* to strike the iron while it is hot, to make hay while the sun shines. *Etre aux —s, être dans les —s ;* to be fettered, bound, to be in chains ; to be in prison, in captivity. *Etre condamné à cinq ans de —s ;* (milit.) to be condemned to five years' imprisonment. *Employer le — et le feu ;* to use the knife and cautery ; to employ violent means. *Etre un corps de — ;* to be made of iron. *Mettre les —s au feu ;* to put the irons into the fire, to fall to work. *Porter le — et la flamme dans ;* to ravage with fire and sword. *Tomber les quatre —s en l'air ;* to fall upon one's back, to be struck all of a heap. *Ne tenir ni à — ni à clou ;* to be badly fastened, badly arranged. *Cela ne vaut pas les quatre —s d'un chien ;* that is not worth a fig, a straw, a rap. *Cet enfant userait du — ;* that child would wear out nails. *Etre sur le — ;* (nav.) to be at anchor. *Notre navire était depuis trois jours sur le — ;* our ship had been lying at anchor for three days.

fer (cheptel de), *n.m.* V. **cheptel.**

fer-blanc, *n.m.,* (*—s—s*) tin, tin-plate, latten.

ferblanterie, *n.f.,* tin-ware.

ferblantier (-tié), *n.m.,* tinman.

fer-chaud, *n.m.,* (*n.p.*) (med.) cardialgia, heartburn, pyrosis.

féret, *n.m.* (min.) hematite.

férial, -e, *adj.,* (ecc.) ferial (of the days).

férie, *n.f.,* day of rest, holiday ; (antiq.) (*pl.*) feriæ ; (ecc.) feria.

férié, -e, *adj.,* of holidays. *Jour — ;* holiday, general holiday.

⊙**férir,** *v.a.,* to strike. *Sans coup — ;* without striking a blow [only *now* used in this expression].

ferlage, *n.m.,* (nav.) furling.

ferler, *v.a.,* (nav.) to furl.

fermage, *n.m.,* rent (of a farm) ; farming, leasing ; rent ; (jur.) rent-charge. *Refus de payer le — ;* denial of rent.

fermant, -e, *adj.,* closing (with lock and key).

ferme, *n.f.,* farm, farm-house, homestead ; farming ; letting out on lease. *— école ;* agricultural college ; (carp.) trussed girder ; main couple ; truss ; (carp.) rib (of centerings, roofs) ; (thea.) set-piece. *— triangulaire ;* (carp.) truss. *Emplacement de — ;* farmstead. *Régisseur de — ;* farm-bailiff. *Maîtresses —s ;* (carp.) principal rafters bearing on the girders. *—s de remplage ;* (carp.) middle rafters. *Prendre à — ;* to farm. *Donner, bailler, à — ;* to let, to farm, to farm out. *Monter une — ;* to stock a farm. *Bail à — ;* lease of ground.

ferme, *adj.,* firm, steady, fast ; fixed, steadfast ; strong, stout ; stiff ; unshaken, constant, resolute. *Etre — à cheval ;* to sit firm in the saddle. *D'un ton — ;* in a decided tone. *Avoir le poignet — ;* to have a strong wrist.

ferme, *adv.,* firmly, fast, hard. *Frapper — ;* to strike hard. *Tenir — ;* to hold fast.

ferme ! *int.,* cheer up ! courage ! go it !

fermement, *adv.,* firmly, steadily, fixedly, steadfastly, strongly, stoutly.

ferment, *n.m.,* ferment ; leaven ; yeast.

fermentable, *adj.,* fermentable.

fermentati-f, -ve, *adj.,* fermentative.

fermentation, *n.f.,* fermentation, working ; (fig.) ferment.

fermenter, *v.a.,* to ferment, to rise, to work. *La pâte fermente ;* the dough is rising.

fermentescible, *adj.,* fermentable.

fermer, *v.a.,* to shut, to shut up, to fasten, to close, to close up ; to encompass ; to inclose. — *la porte au nez de quelqu'un ;* to shut the door in any one's face. — *la porte à clef ;* to lock the door. — *la porte à double tour ;* to double-lock the door. — *la porte au verrou ;* to bolt the door. — *un robinet ;* to stop a cock. — *la marche ;* to bring up the rear. — *de haies ;* to hedge in. — *de palissades ;* to rail in, fence in. *— de murs ;* to wall in. — *les yeux sur quelque chose ;* to wink at anything. — *les yeux à la lumière ;* to shut one's eyes to the truth. — *l'oreille aux médisances ;* to ignore slander. — *la bouche à quelqu'un ;* to stop any one's mouth. — *boutique ;* to shut up shop. — *les yeux à or de quelqu'un ;* to close the eyes of any one (in death). — *l'écurie quand les chevaux sont partis ;* (prov.) to shut the stable when the steed is out.

se **fermer,** *v.r.,* to shut, to shut up, to close, to be closed, to be inclosed, to be encompassed. *Cette plaie se fermera bientôt ;* that wound will soon close up.

fermer, *v.n.,* to shut, to be shut.

fermeté, *n.f.,* firmness ; constancy, steadiness, stability ; vigor, resolution.

fermeture, *n.f.,* closing, shutting ; (carp., locksmith) fastening. *A la — des chambres ;* at the end of the session (parliament).

fermeur, *n.m.,* (anat.) closer.

fermier, *n.m.,* husbandman, farmer ; tenant. — *général ;* farmer-general (of revenues). — *à bail ;* tenant-farmer.

fermière, *n.f.,* farmer's wife.

fermoir, *n.m.,* clasp, snap.

fermure, *n.f.* V. **fermeture** (nav.).

féroce, *adj.,* ferocious, fierce, savage. *Bête — ;* wild beast.

férocement, *adv.,* ferociously.

férocité, *n.f.,* ferocity, fierceness.

*****ferraille,** *n.f.,* old iron, scrap iron.

*****ferrailler,** *v.n.,* to forge, to hammer ; to dabble in fencing ; to fence badly ; (b.s.) to fight (with swords) ; to wrangle.

*****ferrailleur,** *n.m.,* dealer in old iron ; fighter (with a sword) ; wrangler.

ferrandinier, *n.m.,* silk-weaver.

ferrant, *adj.* *Maréchal — ;* farrier ; shoesmith.

ferré, -e, *part.,* shod ; metaled ; stoned ; ferruginous ; chalybeate (of water) ; skilled, versed in, thoroughly up in. *Chemin — ;* metaled road. *Eau —e ;* chalybeate water. — *à glace ;* roughshod ; skilled in. *Voie —e ;* railroad.

ferrement (fèr-mãn), *n.m.,* iron tool ; ironing ; putting the irons on (convicts). *pl.,* iron-work, iron fitting.

ferrer, *v.a.,* to bind, to hoop, with iron. — *une canne ;* to put a ferrule on, to tip, a cane. — *un lacet ;* to tag a lace. — *un cheval ;* to shoe a horse. — *à glace ;* to rough-shoe.

ferret, *n.m.,* tag (of a lace). *Je ne voudrais pas en donner un — d'aiguillette ;* I would not give a fig, a rush, for it.

ferreur, *n.m.,* tagger (of laces).

ferrière, *n.f.,* tool-bag (of farriers).

ferrifère, *adj.,* ferriferous.

ferron, *n.m.,* dealer in bar-iron.

ferronnerie (fé-ro-n-ri), *n.f.,* iron-store ; iron-foundry ; ironmongery.

ferronni-er, *n.m.,* **-ère,** *n.f.,* ironmonger.

ferronnière, *n.f.,* coronet ; lady's head-dress.

ferrugineux, *adj., n.m.,* (pharm.) iron, steel.

ferrugineu-x, -se, *adj.,* ferruginous. *Eau —se ;* chalybeate water.

ferrure, *n.f.,* iron-work ; iron binding ; shoeing (animal) ; pelt, pelting (of boots).

fertile, *adj.,* fertile, fruitful, teeming.

fertilement (-til-mãn), *adv.,* fertilely, abundantly, fruitfully, plenteously.

fertilisable, *adj.,* that can be fertilized.

fertilisant, -e, *adj.,* fertilizing.

fertilisation, n.f., fertilization.

fertiliser, v.a., to fertilize, to manure.

fertilité, n.f., fertility, fruitfulness.

féru, -e, part., smitten; stung to the quick.

férule, n.f., ferule, rod; stroke, cut; (bot.) ferula, giant-fennel.

fervemment (-va-mān), adv., fervently.

fervent, -e, adj., fervent.

ferveur, n.f., fervor, fervency.

fescennin, -e, adj., (antiq.) Fescennine.

fesse, n.f., buttock, breech, rump, bottom. —s; rump, bottom; (nav.) tuck.

fesse-cahier, n.m., (— or —-—s) quill driver; literary hack.

fessée, n.f., whipping, flogging.

fesse-mathieu, n.m., (—-—x) miser, old hunks, skinflint, close-fist, pinch-fist.

fesser, v.a., to whip; to flog, to spank. — le cahier; to drive the quill, to be a literary hack.

fesseu-r, n.m., **-se,** n.f., whipper, flogger.

fessier, n.m., breech, bottom; (anat.) gluteal.

fessi-er, -ère, adj., (anat.) gluteal.

fessu, -e, adj., (pop.) large-breeched.

festin, n.m., feast, banquet, entertainment. Faire —, faire un —; to feast, to banquet. Salle de —; banqueting hall. Pour tout —; as only fare.

festiner, v.a., (jest.) to feast, to entertain.

festiner, v.n., (jest.) to banquet, to feast, to make merry.

festival, n.m., festival (musical).

feston, n.m., festoon; scallop.

festonner, v.a., to festoon; to scallop.

festoyer, v.a., to entertain; to feast.

fête, n.f., holiday, festival; saint's day; festivity; feast, merry-making. — carillonnée; high jinks; great holiday. — patronale; patron saint's day. Jour de sa —; one's saint's day; one's birthday. Un jour de —; a holiday. —s mobiles; moveable feasts. — légale; bank holiday. Troubler la —; to mar the pleasure (of the company). Trouble —; mar- or kill-joy, wet blanket. Faire — à quelqu'un; to make any one welcome. Se faire de —; to intermeddle. Se faire une — de, se faire — de; to look forward with pleasure to. Payer sa —; to keep one's birthday or saint's day. Ce n'est pas tous les jours —; Christmas comes but once a year.

fête-dieu, n.f., (n.p.) Corpus Christi.

fêter, v.a., to keep holiday, to keep, to celebrate, to observe, as a holiday; to entertain, to feast. — quelqu'un; to receive any one with open arms; to make any one very welcome. C'est un saint qu'on ne fête pas; he is a person without credit or authority.

fetfa, n.m., fetwah (decision of a mufti).

fétiche, n.m., fetich.

fétichisme, n.m., feticism, fetichism.

fétide, adj., fetid, rank, offensive.

fétidité, n.f., fetidness, offensiveness.

fétoyer, v.a. V. **festoyer.**

fétu, n.m., straw, wisp; (fig.) pin; rap. Tirer au court —; to draw lots, to draw cuts. Cela ne vaut pas un —; that is not worth a fig or rap. Un cogne —; a fussy person.

fétu-en-cul, n.m., (—). V. **paille-en-queue.**

fétus, n.m. V. **fœtus.**

feu, n.m., fire, burning, conflagration, combustion; fire-place; chimney; set of fire-irons; family, household, house; light, signal-light, torch-light; brunt (of fire-arms); brilliancy, luster; heat, ardor, flame, passion; vivacity, spirit; animation, mettle; liveliness, sprightliness; (feudalism) hearth; (milit.) firing; (vet.) fire; (theat.) extra pay. — follet; ignis fatuus, Jack-o'-lantern, will-o'-the-wisp. — grisou; fire-damp. — de joie; bonfire. Mettre le — à une chose; to set a thing on fire. Prendre l'air du —; to warm one's self. Se tenir au coin du —; to keep in the chimney-

corner. Mettre le pot au —; to set the dinner going. Couleur de —; flame-color. — grégeois; Greek fire. — Saint-Elme; corposant, Castor and Pollux. — Saint-Antoine; St. Anthony's fire. Il n'a jamais vu le —; he has never smelt gunpowder. Mettre tout à — et à sang; to put everything to fire and sword. Brûler un homme à petit —; to kill a man by inches. C'est le — et l'eau; they are as opposite as fire and water. J'en mettrais ma main au —; I would stake my life upon it. Il n'y a point de — sans fumée; there is no smoke without fire. Se jeter dans le — pour éviter la fumée; to jump from the frying-pan into the fire. Il y a tant de —x dans ce village; there are so many chimneys, so many families, in this village. Garniture de —; set of fire-irons. N'avoir ni — ni lieu; to have neither house nor home. Le — dont il brûle; the flame that consumes him. Ce vin a trop de —; that wine is too fiery. Il prend — aisément; he takes fire easily. Il jette — et flamme; he frets and fumes. Il a jeté tout son —; he has spent all his fire. — bien nourri, — bien servi; (milit.) galling, well-sustained fire. — rasant; (milit.) flank fire. — coulant; (milit.) running-fire. Triste —, — triste; dull fire. — vif; (milit.) brisk fire. — d'artifice; fireworks. —x de Bengale; blue-lights. — de cheminée; chimney on fire. — d'enfer; scorching, scathing fire. Boîte à —; coal-box (locomotive). Bouche à —; piece of ordnance. Coffre à —; (nav.) fire-chest. Coup de —; shot; shot-wound. Fer à donner le —, fer à mettre le —; cauterizing iron. Lance à —; match. A l'épreuve du —; fire-proof. Sous le — de; upon the spur of the. Activer le —; to stir the fire. Attiser le —; to poke the fire. Cesser le —; (milit.) to leave off firing or to cease fire. Condamner au —; to condemn to the stake. Crier au —; to cry fire! Donner le — à; (vet.) to sear. Faire —; (milit.) to fire. Faire du —; to make a fire. Courir comme au —; to run after eagerly. Faire — qui dure; to husband one's property; to take care of one's health. Faux —; flash in the pan. Faire faux —; to miss fire, to flash in the pan. Faire long —; to hang fire; to be protracted; to miscarry. Faire — des quatre pieds; to strain every nerve. Jeter ses premiers —x; to sow one's wild oats. Jeter de l'huile sur le —; to add fuel to the flame. Se jeter dans le — pour quelqu'un, se mettre au — pour quelqu'un; to go through fire and water for any one. Jouer avec le —; to play with edged tools. Mettre le — au four; to heat the oven. Mettre le — sous le ventre à quelqu'un; to urge any one to do a thing. Donner le — trop chaud, trop ardent, à la viande; to roast meat before too fierce a fire. Montrer une chose au —; to dry anything by the fire; to warm anything through by the fire. Soutenir le —; (milit.) to stand fire. Soutenir un —; (milit.) to keep up a fire. Ne voir que du — à quelque chose; to be dazzled by anything, not to make it out. Le — a pris à la maison; the house has caught fire. Le — lui sort par les yeux; his eyes flash fire. Feu! (milit.) fire! Il n'est — que de bois vert; none are so active as the young. Il ne faut pas jouer avec le —; one should not play with edged tools.

feu, -e, adj., late, the late deceased, defunct. Le — roi; the late king. La —e reine, — la reine; the late queen. — les princes, les —s princes; the late princes.

feudataire, n.m.f., adj., feudatory.

feudiste, n.m. and adj., feodist.

*****feuillage,** n.m., foliage, leaves, leafage; (bot.) frond; frondescence.

*****feuillaison,** n.f., (bot.) foliation.

*****feuillant,** n.m., feuillant, monk.

*****feuillantine,** n.f., feuillantine (nun); (cook.) a kind of puff-paste.

*feuillard, *n.m.*, hoop-wood.

*feuille, *n.f.*, leaf; sheet (of paper, metal); paper, newspaper, journal; foil (of mirrors); way-bill (of public coaches, etc.); list; veneer (cabinet-making). *pl.*, (arch.) foils; foliation; feathering. *L'aisselle d'une* —; the axil of a leaf. *Trembler comme la* —; to shake like an aspen-leaf. *Vin de deux —s;* wine two years old. *— de papier;* sheet of paper. *— volante;* loose sheet; flying sheet. *— de décharge, — de rebut;* (print.) waste-sheet. *— à plaquer;* veneer. *— morte;* sere leaf. *— hebdomadaire;* weekly paper. *— quoti-dienne;* daily newspaper. *— de route;* way-bill; (milit.) route of the road.

*feuillé, -e, *adj.*, (her.) leafy; (bot.) foliate.

*feuillé, *n.m.*, (paint.) foliage, leafage.

*feuillée, *n.f.*, bower, green arbor, foliage.

*feuille-morte, *n.m.*, feuillemort.

*feuille-morte, *adj. invariable*, feuillemort (of a yellow brown color).

*feuiller, *v.n.*, to come into leaf; (paint.) to paint the foliage of a picture.

*feuilleret, *n.m.*, fillister, fillister-plane.

*feuillet, *n.m.*, leaf (two pages of a book); (com.) folio; (mam.) fech; (min.) thin plate; (bot.) gill, gills. *— à poing;* hand-saw. *Tournez le* —; turn over the leaf. *— refait;* (print.) cancel. *Faire une corne à un* —; to turn down a leaf.

*feuilletage (feu-l-taj), *n.m.*, puff-paste, flaky paste.

*feuilleté, -e, *part.*, (min.) foliated. *Gâteau* —; flaky-puff; buttered-roll.

*feuilleter (feu-l-té), *v.a.*, to turn over, to peruse, to run over; to thumb.

*se feuilleter, *v.r.*, (min.) to split into thin plates; to be thumbed (of books).

*feuilletis, *n.m.*, the cutting edge (of diamonds).

*feuilleton (feu-i-ton), *n.m.*, feuilleton (the bottom part of journals devoted to literary articles, critiques, etc.); fly-sheet; (parl.) list (of petitions).

*feuilletoniste, *n.m.f.*, writer of feuilletons.

*feuillette, *n.f.*, quarter-cask.

*feuillu, -e, *adj.*, leafy; (bot.) folious.

*feuillure, *n.f.*, (carp.) cheek (of a door), rabbet.

feurre, *n.m.*, straw (for chair bottoms).

feutier, *n.m.*, fire-attendant.

feutrabilité, *n.f.*, felting quality.

feutrage, *n.m.*, felting.

feutre, *n.m.*, felt; hat; tile; (saddlery) packing.

feutrer, *v.a.*, to felt; to pad; to pack.

feutrier, *n.m.*, felt-maker.

feutrière, *n.f.*, felt-cloth.

fève, *n.f.*, bean; broad bean; berry; chrysalis (of silk-worms); (vet.) lampas. *—s de haricot;* kidney-beans. *—s de marais;* broad beans. *— de Tonka;* Tonquin bean. *Roi de la* —; twelfth-night king. *Rendre — pour pois;* to give tit for tat. *Donner un pois pour avoir une* —; to give a sprat to catch a herring. *Trouver la — au gâteau;* to hit the mark; to make a lucky discovery.

féverole (fèv-rol), *n.f.*, horse-bean; dried kidney-bean; bean.

févier, *n.m.*, (bot.) three-horned acacia, honey-locust, etc., genus gleditschia.

février, *n.m.*, February.

fez, *n.m.*, (—) fez (worn by Turks).

fi! *int.*, fie! fie. *— donc;* fie! for shame. *Faire — d'une chose;* to turn up one's nose at anything.

fiacre, *n.m.*, hackney-coach; cab. *Place de —s;* cab-stand. *Cocher de* —; cabman.

*fiançailles, *n.f. pl.*, betrothal, engagement.

fiancé, *n.m.*, -e, *n.f.*, betrothed.

fiancer, *v.a.*, to betroth, to affiance. *Se* —; to become engaged.

fibre, *n.f.*, fiber, filament; (fig.) feeling.

fibreu-x, -se, *adj.*, fibrous, fibrose; stringy.

*fibrille, *n.f.*, (anat.) fibril.

*fibrilleu-x, -se, *adj.*, fibrillous.

fibrine, *n.f.*, (chem.) fibrine.

fic, *n.m.*, (med.) ficus; tumor.

ficelé, -e, *part.*, tied, tied up; (pop.) dressed; dressed out. *Comme le voilà* —! what a guy he looks!

ficeler (fi-slé), *v.a.*, to bind, to tie, with string; to do up, to dress up. *— de fil de fer;* to wire.

ficeleur, -se, *n.m.f.*, packer.

ficelier, *n.m.*, reel, roller (for string).

ficelle, *n.f.*, pack-thread, twine, string; dodge; stage-trick. *Montrer la* —; to betray the secret motive.

fichant, -e, *adj.*, (fort.) darting. *Feu* —; darting, plunging fire; (fig.) annoying.

fiche, *n.f.*, hook, peg, pin (for a hinge); fish (at cards). *— de consolation;* small compensation; sop.

fiché, -e, *part.*, driven in; (her.) fitchee. *Aller se faire* —; to go and be hanged. *Envoyer faire* —; to send to the deuce.

ficher, *v.a.*, (past part., fiché, fichu), to drive in, to thrust in, to fasten in; (mas.) to pin up; (pop.) to give in a rude manner; to throw aside. *— un clou;* to drive in a nail. (fam.) *— le, or son, camp;* to decamp, to run away; to be off. *Je vous en fiche!* Is it though! Would you though!

se ficher, *v.r.*, (pop.) to throw one's self down, on, ete.; to laugh at, to make game of.

ficheron, *n.m.*, iron-pin.

fichet, *n.m.*, ivory peg (to mark with).

fichoir, *n. m.*, peg, clothes-peg.

fichtre! *int.*, (pop.) the deuce! the devil; hang it! confound it!

fichu, *n.m.*, neckerchief. *Corps de* —; habit-shirt.

fichu, -e, *part.* (pop.) pitiful; deuced; done for; thrown aside; dressed, got up. *Comme le voilà* —! what a guy he looks!

fichure, *n.f.*, harpoon.

ficiforme, *adj.*, fig-shaped.

ficoïde, *n.f.*, (bot.) ice-plant.

⊙fictice, *adj.* V. fictif.

ficti-f, -ve, *adj.*, supposed, fictitious, imaginary.

fiction, *n.f.*, fiction, figment; fabrication; fable.

fictionnaire, *adj.*, fictitious, founded on fiction.

fictivement (-tiv-mān), *adv.*, fictitiously.

fidéicommis, *n.m.*, (jur.) trust.

fidéicommissaire, *n.m.*, (jur.) trustee.

fidéjusseur, *n.m.*, (jur.) surety; guarantor.

fidéjussion, *n.f.* V. cautionnement.

fidèle, *adj.*, loyal, true, trusty, faithful, exact, accurate, safe, sure. *Traducteur* —; correct or accurate translator. *Copie* —; exact copy. *Mémoire* —; retentive or good memory.

fidèle, *n.m.f.*, faithful friend. *pl.*, (rel.) believers; worshipers; congregation.

fidèlement (fi-dèl-mān), *adv.*, faithfully, truly, loyally, trustily; accurately, exactly.

fidélité, *n.f.*, fidelity, faithfulness, loyalty, fealty; secrecy; exactness, accuracy; retentiveness (of the memory); (jur.) allegiance. *— éprouvée;* tried fidelity. *Prêter serment de* —; to take an oath of fidelity.

fiduciaire, *n.m.*, (jur.) fiduciary. *Circulation* —; paper currency. *Monnaie* —; paper-money.

fiduciaire, *adj.*, (jur.) in trust.

fief (fièf), *n.m.*, fee, fief. *Franc* —; free-hold.

fieffé, -e, *adj.*, (fam., pop.) arrant, downright, regular. *Fripon* —; arrant knave.

fieffer, *v.a.*, to enfeoff, to invest with a fee.

fiel, *n.m.*, gall; hatred, bitterness, rancor, spleen. *Vésicule du* —; gall-bladder. *Amer* *comme* —; as bitter as gall. *Un homme plein de* —; a man full of malice. *Il a vomi tout son* —; he has vented all his spleen.

fiente, *n.f.*, dung. *Appliquer un banc de* —; (manu.) to dung.

fienter, *v.a.*, to dung.

fier, *v.a.*, to trust, intrust.

se **fier** (à), *v.r.*, to trust to; to rely, to depend upon; to put one's trust in. *Je me fie à vous;* I trust to you. *Je me fie sur vous;* I depend on you. *Fiez-vous-y;* (iron.) do not trust to that. *Bien fou qui s'y fie;* more fool he who relies upon it.

fi-er (fi-èr), **-ère**, *adj.*, proud, high-spirited, haughty, stout, bold; (her.) fierce, extreme, remarkable; famous, fine, capital. *Il est — comme Artaban;* he is as proud as Lucifer. *J'ai fait un — déjeuner* or *dîner;* I have had a capital breakfast, dinner; I have dined like a lord.

fier-à-bras, *n.m.*, (—) bully, hector, braggart.

fièrement (fièr-mān), *adv.*, proudly, arrogantly, haughtily, soundly, stoutly, boldly; (pop.) preciously, finely, famously.

fierté, *n.f.*, pride, haughtiness, arrogance; boldness, dignity. *Rabaisser, rabattre, la — de quelqu'un;* to bring down, to humble, any one's pride.

fièvre, *n.f.*, fever, feverishness, ague, restlessness, excitement; heat. *pl.*, (med.) ague. — *ardente;* burning fever. — *d'hôpital;* typhus fever; gaol fever. — *hectique;* hectic fever. — *intermittente;* intermittent fever, ague. — *lente;* low fever; hectic. — *de lait;* milk fever. — *tierce;* tertian fever. — *tremblante;* ague. — *de cheval;* violent fever. *Accès de* —; fit of fever; fit of the ague. *Trembler la* —; to shake with fever. *Sortir de* —; to recover from a fever. *Donner la* —; to put in a fever. *Tomber de — en chaud mal;* to fall from the frying-pan into the fire. *Que la — le serre!* plague take him! plague on him! *Avoir la* —; to be feverish.

fiévreu-x, **-se**, *adj.*, feverish; liable to fever; full of fever; restless.

fiévreux, *n.m.*, fever-patient. *Salle des* —; fever-ward.

fiévrotte, *n.f.*, slight fever.

fifre, *n.m.*, fife; fifer.

fifrer, *v.n.*, to fife.

figaro, *n.m.*, barber; go-between; knavish valet.

figement (fij-mān), *n.m.*, congealing, congealment, coagulation, curdling.

figer, *v.a.*, to congeal, to coagulate, to curdle, to curd.

se **figer**, *v.r.*, to congeal, to coagulate, to curdle, to curd.

figue (fig), *n.f.*, (bot.) fig. *Moitié —, moitié raisin;* so so; not quite the thing; half well, half ill. *Faire la — à;* to despise, to treat with contumely; to brave, to defy.

figuerie (fi-grî), *n.f.*, fig-ground.

figuier (fi-ghié), *n.m.*, fig-tree; (orni.) fig-eater. — *d'Adam, — des banians;* (bot.) banian, banian-tree. — *d'Inde;* opuntia, Indian fig-tree.

⊙**figuline**, *n.f.*, pot, vase (of earthenware).

figurabilité, *n.f.*, figurability.

figurant, *n.m.*, **-e**, *n.f.*, (theat.) figurant (dancer), supernumerary, super.

figurati-f, **-ve**, *adj.*, figurative, typical.

figurative, *n.f.*, (Grec. gram.) characteristic.

figurativement (-tiv-mān), *adv.*, figuratively.

figure, *n.f.*, figure, form, shape; countenance, face, appearance, show; court-card, diagram; representation; symbol, type; (mus.) figured passage. *Faire* —; to make, to cut, a figure. *A la* —; to one's face, in one's teeth. *Etre bien de* —; to be good-looking. *Etre mal de* —; to be ill-looking.

figuré, *n.m.*, (gram.) figurative sense.

figuré, **-e**, *part.*, figured; figurative; (mus.) figured; (math.) figural. *Sens* —; figurative meaning.

figurément, *adv.*, figuratively.

figurer, *v.a.*, to figure, to represent, to typify.

se **figurer**, *v.r.*, to imagine, to fancy, to picture to one's self. *Figurez-vous que;* would you believe that. *Se figure-t-il que . . . ?* does he imagine for a moment that . . . ?

figurer, *v.n.*, to look well, to match, to suit; to make, to cut, a figure; to flourish, to dance in figures; (theat.) to be a supernumerary.

figurine, *n.f.*, (paint.) little figure, miniature figure; postage stamp.

figuriste, *n.m.*, figurist.

fil, *n.m.*, thread, wire; yarn; edge; grain; chain, string, series; crack, flaw (in marble, stone); stream, current (of water). — *de caret;* rope-yarn. — *retors;* twine. — *à voile;* sail-twine. — *d'emballage;* pack-thread. — *à plomb;* plumb-line, plumb-rule. — *de la bonne Vierge;* air-thread, gossamer. — *d'archal, — de fer;* iron wire. — *de laiton;* brass wire. — *d'Ecosse;* cotton. *Le — d'une épée;* the edge of a sword. — *d'Ariane;* Ariadne's thread; clew. *Grillage en — métallique;* wire-work. *A — fin;* fine-grained (of wood). *A gros —;* coarse-grained. *Aller de — en aiguille;* to go from point to point; minutely. *Aller contre le —;* to go against the stream; to go against the grain. *Aller de droit* —; to go straightforwardly. *Avoir du — à retordre;* to have work cut out for one. *Donner du — à retordre à quelqu'un;* to give no end of trouble to any one, to annoy any one. *Donner le — à;* to whet, to sharpen, to put an edge on. *Faire un —;* to spin a yarn. *Mettre, passer, au fil de l'épée;* to put to the edge of the sword. *Oter lc — de;* to take the edge off. *Suivre le — de l'eau* or *du courant;* to go with the stream. *Ne tenir qu'à un —;* to hang upon a thread. *A toile ourdie Dieu envoie le —;* make a beginning; God will provide for the ending. *Finesses cousues de — blanc;* tricks easily found out.

filage, *n.m.*, spinning; (bot.) cotton-rose; cud-weed.

filagramme. *V.* **filigrane**.

filaire, *n.f.*, (ent.) filaria.

filament, *n.m.*, filament, thread; fiber.

filamenteu-x, **-se**, *adj.*, thready, stringy.

filandière, *n.f.*, spinster, spinner. *Les sœurs —s;* the fates, the fatal sisters.

filandres, *n.f.pl.*, gossamer, air-threads; strings (of leguminous plants).

filandreu-x, **-se**, *adj.*, stringy, thready.

filant, **-e**, *adj.*, flowing, ropy; (of stars) shooting.

filasse, *n.f.*, harl, tow (of flax, hemp).

filassi-er, *n.m.*, **-ère**, *n.f.*, flax-dresser.

filateur, *n.m.*, mill-owner; spinner.

filatrice, *n.f.*, (tech.) silk-winder (pers.).

filature, *n.f.*, spinning; spinning-mill; rope-walk.

file, *n.f.*, row, rank, file. *Ranger par* —; to draw up in file. *Chef de* —; front-rank man. *Par — à droite, à gauche!* right or left wheel! *A la* —; one after another.

filé, *n.m.*, thread (of gold or silver).

filer, *v.a.*, to spin; to conduct, to carry on; to spin out; (nav.) to veer. *Machine à* —; spinning-machine. — *sa corde;* to go the way to the gallows. — *le parfait amour;* to be all love and sentiment.

filer, *v.n.*, to rope; (milit.) to file; (of cats) to purr; to shoot (of ships, of stars); to flare (of lights); to cut one's stick, to take one's self off. *Il faut* —; we must be off. *Allons, filez;* come, make yourself scarce. *Ce sirop file;* this sirup is ropy. — *doux;* to be all submission, to put up with an insult, to pocket an affront; to sing small. *Du temps que Berthe filait;* in the good old times. — *à l'anglaise;* to leave without saying good-bye.

filerie (fi-lrî), *n.f.*, rope-walk; wire-drawing; wire-mill.

filet, *n.m.*, string, filament, small thread; fiber; (bot.) fillet; chine; (arch.) bead (of liquor); dash, drop; streak; gleam; streamlet; bed-molding; runner (of strawberries); (anat.) frenum; (print.) rule; string (of the tongue); (man.) bridoon; snaffle-bridle; net; snare; rack (rail). — *d'or;* fillet of gold. *Un — de vin-aigre;* a dash of vinegar. *Avoir le —;* to be tongue-tied. *Il n'a pas le —;* he has a well-oiled tongue. *Avoir le — coupé;* to have a glib tongue. — *d'une vis;* thread of a screw. *Prendre au —;* to catch in a net. *Faiseur de —s;* net-maker. *Faire tomber dans un —;* to ensnare. *Coup de —;* cast of a net; haul. — *de voix;* thin voice.

fileur, *n.m.*, spinner; wire-drawer. — *de cartes;* card-sharper.

fileuse, *n.f.*, spinner, spinster.

filial, -e *adj.*, filial.

filialement (-al-mān), *adv.*, filially.

filiation, *n.f.*, filiation; (fig.) connection.

filière, *n.f.*, draw-plate; screw-plate; (carp.) purlin; string, series; ordeal.

filiforme, *adj.*, (bot.) filiform; thread-shaped.

filigrane, *n.m.*, filigrane, filigree-work; filigree; water-mark (in paper).

filin, *n.m.*, (nav.) cordage.

filipendule, *n.f.*, (bot.) dropwort.

*fille, *n.f.*, girl, female, lass, maiden; daughter; servant-maid; spinster; offspring. *Petite- —;* grand-daughter. *Arrière-petite- —;* great grand-daughter. *Belle- —;* daughter-in-law; step-daughter. — *s d'honneur;* maids of honor. *Vieille —;* old maid. — *de chambre;* chamber-maid. — *de service;* housemaid. — *de bou-tique;* shop-girl. — *de joie;* prostitute. *Rester —;* to be an old maid. — *à marier;* marriage-able daughter.

*fillette, *n.f.*, lass, young girl.

*filleul, *n.m.*, godson, godchild.

*filleule, *n.f.*, goddaughter.

filoche, *n.f.*, net-work.

filon, *n.m.*, metallic vein, lode.

filoselle, *n.f.*, floss-silk.

filou, *n.m.*, pickpocket, sharper, thief.

filouter, *v.a.*, to pickpocket, to steal; to cheat, to swindle; to chisel.

filouterie (fi-lout-rî), *n.f.*, picking pockets, swindling; cheating, filching.

fils (fiss), *n.m.*, son, child, offspring, lad, boy, fellow. *Petit- —;* grandson. *Arrière-petit- —;* great grandson. *Beau- —;* son-in-law; step-son. — *de famille;* gentleman's son; nobleman. *Etre bien — de son père;* to be a chip of the old block. — *de ses œuvres;* self-made man. *Il est bon —;* he is a good or an easy-going fellow.

filterie, *n.f.*, twine factory.

filtrage, *n.m.*, filtering, straining.

filtrant, -e, *adj.*, filtering, straining.

filtration, *n.f.*, filtration, filtering, straining, percolation.

filtre, *n.m.*, filter; filtering-machine; philter, love potion. *V.* **philtre.**

filtrer, *v.a.*, to filter, to strain; to percolate. *Pierre à —;* filtering-stone.

se filtrer, *v.r.*, to filter, to be filtered.

filure, *n.f.*, spinning.

fin, *n.f.*, end, close, conclusion, termination, issue, expiration, aim, design, view, object, in-tention. *Mettre — à;* to put an end to. *Tirer à sa —;* to be drawing to an end. *Etre à sa —;* to be at one's last shift. *La — couronne l'œuvre;* all is well that ends well. *Aller, ten-dre, à ses —s;* to pursue one's point. — *de*

non-recevoir; (jur.) plea to bar; exception. *A ces —s;* for this, for that, end. *Mener à bonne —;* to bring to an end, to succeed in. *Cheval à toute —;* horse fitted to ride and drive. *A telle — que de raison;* at any rate, for such purpose as may be required. *A la —;* at last, at length, in the end, in the long run. *A la — des —s vous voilà;* at last you have come! *Qui veut la — veut les moyens;* where there's a will there's a way. *Savoir le fort et le — de son art;* to know every trick of the trade. — *de siècle,* *adj.*, up to date.

fin, -e *adj.*, fine, thin, refined; acute, ingen-ious; delicate, polite; shrewd, cunning, sly; small (of handwriting). —*es herbes;* sweet or savory herbs. *Diamants —s;* gems, precious stones. *Des traits —s;* delicate features. *Il a l'oreille —e;* he has a quick ear. *Un — voilier;* a swift sailer. *Avoir le nez —;* to have a good nose, to be far-sighted. *C'est un — matois;* he is a knowing fellow. *Le — mot;* the main point, gist. *Je n'entends pas le — mot de tout cela;* I don't see the force of that. *Plus — que lui n'est pas bête;* he who can take him in is no fool. *Du — fond;* from the very depths of.

fin, *n.m.*, sharp fellow, keen fellow; gist, main point; (metal.) pure metal. *Savoir le fort et le — de quelque chose;* to know the long and the short of anything. — *contre — n'est pas bon à faire doublure,* or, —, — *et demi;* diamond cut diamond. *Jouer au plus —;* to finesse; to vie in cunning. *Ecrire en —;* to write small hand.

final, -e *adj.*, final, last, ultimate.

finale, *n.m.*, (mus.) finale. *n.f.*, (gram.) last syllable.

finalement (fi-nal-mān), *adv.*, finally, lastly.

finalité, *n.f.*, finality.

finance, *n.f.*, cash, ready money; finance, financiers. *pl.*, finances; exchequer, treasury. *Projet de loi de —;* bill of supply.

financer, *v.n.*, to lay out money; to come down with one's own money.

financier, *n.m.*, financier.

financi-er, -ère, *adj.*, financial.

finasser, *v.n.*, to shuffle, to finesse.

finasserie (fi-na-srî), *n.f.*, finesse, petty trick-ery; shirking.

finasseu-r, *n. m.*, **-se,** *n. f.*, artful dodger.

finaud, -e *n.* and *adj.*, sly, artful, cunning person, sly-boots; sly, artful.

finement (fi-n-mān), *adv.*, artfully, slyly, delicately, ingeniously, shrewdly; archly.

finesse, *n.f.*, fineness; delicacy; ingenuity; finesse, artifice, craftiness, slyness, craft, shrewd-ness. *User de —;* to display cunning. *Faire — d'une chose;* to make a secret of a thing. *Entendre — à une chose;* to put a malicious construction *or* interpretation on a thing. *Des —s cousues de fil blanc;* artifices easily seen through.

finet, -te, *adj.*, (l.u.) sly, subtle, cunning.

finette, *n.f.*, thin stuff, tissue, flannelette.

fini, -e *part.*, finished, ended, complete. *C'est une affaire —e;* it is a settled matter.

fini, *n.m.*, finish, high finish; finite, perfection. *Donner le — à;* to finish off, or to put the finish-ing touch to. *Le — et l'infini;* the finite and the infinite.

finir, *v.a.*, to finish, to complete, to end, to terminate; to finish off; to put an end to; to complete, to perfect; to cease, to leave off.

finir, *v.n.*, to finish; to terminate, to con-clude; to be at an end, to be over; to expire. *En — avec;* to put an end to. *Il ne finira jamais;* he will never stop. *A n'en plus —;* without end, endless. *Cela n'en finit pas —;* there's no end to it. *As-tu fini!* (pop.) have you done! *Finissez donc!* do be quiet! *Voulez-vous finir?* will you be quiet?

finissage, *n.m.*, finishing off.

finisseu-r, *n.m.*, **-se**, finisher.

finnois, **-e**, *n.* and *adj.*, Finn; Finnish.

fiole, *n.f.*, vial.

fion, *n.m.*, (pop.) finishing touch, knack; fugue.

fioritures, *n.f.pl.*, (mus.) grace-notes.

firmament, *n.m.*, firmament.

firman, *n.m.*, firman.

fisc, *n.m.*, public treasury, fisc.

fiscal, **-e**, *adj.*, fiscal, financial.

fiscalité, *n.f.*, (b.s.) fiscal laws, matters.

fissipare, *adj.*, (zool., bot.) fissiparous.

fissipède, *n.m.* and *adj.*, fissiped.

fissirostre, *adj.*, (orni.) fissirostral.

fissirostres, *n.m.pl.*, (orni.) fissirostres.

fissure, *n.f.*, fissure, cleft; crack, rent.

se **fissurer**, to become fissured.

fiston, *n.m.*, (fam.) boy, lad, young one.

fistulaire, *adj.*, fistular, fistuliform.

fistule, *n.f.*, fistula.

fistuleu-x, **-se**, *adj.*, fistulous; fistular.

fixation, *n.f.*, fixation; appointing, fixing, rating, assessment.

fixe, *n.m.*, fixed, firm, steady, fast, set; appointed, regular; settled weather. *Traitement* —; regular salary. *Les* —*s*; (astron.) fixed stars; (chem.) fixed bodies.

fixe, *adj.*, fixed, settled, steady, certain, stationary, regular. *Prix* —; set price. (milit.) —*!* eyes front! steady!

fixé, *n.m.*, oil-painting protected by glass.

fixement, *adv.*, fixedly, wistfully, hard; steadily; in the face.

fixer, *v.a.*, to fix, to fasten, to stick; to settle; to determine, to appoint; to attract, to gaze on; to stare at. —*un jour;* to appoint a day. *les regards de quelqu'un;* attract any one's attention. *Je suis fixé sur son compte;* I have got his measure; I know all about him.

se **fixer**, *v.r.*, to fix, to be fixed, to settle down, to be settled, to elect domicile; to live. *Se* — *à quelque chose;* to settle upon anything.

fixité, *n.f.*, fixity, fixedness, stability.

fla, *n.m.*, double beat of the drum.

flabelliforme, *adj.*, (bot.) fan-shaped.

flac, *int.*, slap, bang.

flaccidité, *n.f.*, flabbiness, flaccidity.

flache, *n.f.*, hole in the pavement; plash, puddle, pool; (carp.) flaw.

flacon, *n.m.*, flagon; flask; vial; smelling bottle.

flafla, *n.m.*, claptrap, show, dash.

flagellant, *n.m.*, flagellant.

flagellation, *n.f.*, flagellation, scourging, lashing, whipping, flogging.

flageller (fla-jèl-lé), *v.a.*, to flagellate, to scourge, to lash, to flog, to whip.

flagelliforme, *adj.*, whip-shaped.

flageoler, *v.n.*, to tremble, to shake.

flageolet (fla-jo-lè), *n.m.*, flageolet; spindle-leg; dwarf kidney-bean.

flagorner, *v.a.*, to flatter servilely; to fawn upon, to toady to.

flagornerie, *n.f.*, sycophancy, base flattery.

flagorneu-r, *n.m.*, **-se**, *n.f.*, sycophant, toady.

flagrant, **-e**, *adj.*, flagrant, gross. *En* — *délit;* in the very act.

flair, *n.m.*, (hunt.) scent. *Il a le* —; he knows how to find out things.

flairer, *v.a.*, to smell, to scent, to detect; to find out. — *quelque chose;* to smell a rat.

flaireur, *n.m.*, (l.u.) smeller. — *de cuisine;* sponger; smell-feast.

flamand, **-e**, *n.* and *adj.*, Fleming; Flemish.

flamant, *n.m.*, (orni.) flamingo.

flambant, **-e**, *adj.*, blazing, flaming; flash; (her.) flaming. — *neuf;* brand-new.

flambard, **-e**, *adj.*, (pop.) bright, flashy.

flambard, *n.m.*, sword with a waving blade; (nav.) fishing smack.

flambe, *n.f.*, (bot.) common iris.

flambé, **-e**, *adj.*, singed; ruined, done for. *Il est* —; he is done for. *Mon argent est* —; my money is lost.

flambeau, *n.m.*, link, taper, torch; candlestick; light, luminary. *Porte-* —, (—*-*—*x*) link-boy. *Les* —*x de la nuit;* the stars. *A la lumière des* —*x;* by torch-light.

flamber, *v.a.*, to singe, to fumigate; to inflame, to fire. — *une volaille;* to singe a fowl.

flamber, *v.n.*, to blaze, to flame, to flare.

flamberge, *n.f.*, (jest.) sword. *Mettre* — *au vent;* to draw one's sword. — *au vent;* with drawn sword.

flambergeant, *n.m.*, curlew.

flamboiement, *n.m.*, flaming, blazing; flare.

flamboyant, **-e**, *adj.*, flaming, blazing; gleaming, glistening; (her.) flamboyant.

flamboyer, *v.n.*, to flame, to blaze, to flare; to flash.

flamine, *n.m.*, (antiq.) flamen.

flamme, *n.f.*, flame, blaze, fire, glow, luster; ardor; passion; (nav.) pendant; (vet.) fleam. *Ce feu ne fait point de* —; that fire does not blaze. *Jeter de la* —; to flame. *Jeter feu et* —; to fret and fume.

flammèche, *n.f.*, flake of fire; spark.

flammerole, *n.f.*, fire-drake; will o' the wisp.

flammette, *n.f.*, (vet.) fleam; little flame.

flan, *n.m.*, custard; a blank coin.

flanc (flan), *n.m.*, flank, side; entrails; womb, bosom; (nav.) breast. *Se battre les* —*s;* to exert one's self (to no purpose). *Par le* — *droit;* (milit.) to the right about. *Prêter le* — *à;* to lay one's self open to. *Etre sur le* —; (pop.) to be laid up; to be on one's back.

flanchet, *n.m.*, flank of beef or of cod.

flanconade, *n.f.*, (fenc.) flanconade.

flandrin, *n.m.*, tall lanky fellow.

flanelle, *n.f.*, flannel.

flâner, *v.a.*, to lounge, to saunter, to stroll, to loaf.

flânerie (flâ-n-rî), *n.f.*, lounging; lounge; stroll; sauntering; loafing.

flâneu-r, *n.m.*, **-se**, *n.f.*, lounger, stroller, saunterer; loafer.

flanquant, **-e**, *adj.*, (fort.) flanking.

flanquement (flank-mān), *n.m.*, (fort.) flanking.

flanquer, *v.a.*, (arch., fort.) to flank; to defend, to secure, to guard; to deal (a blow); to strike; to throw; to toss, to fling, to pitch. — *un soufflet à quelqu'un;* to box any one's ears. — *à la porte;* to bundle out. *Je lui ai flanqué une pile;* (triv.) I gave him a sound licking.

se **flanquer**, *v.r.*, to throw one's self down *or* in; to fall down; to poke, to intrude; to give one's self *or* each other.

flaque, *n.f.*, small pool, puddle.

flaquée, *n.f.*, dash (of water); dab.

flaquer, *v.a.*, (l.u.) to dash (water, etc.).

flasque, *adj.*, lank, slack, limp, feeble, weak, flabby.

flasque, *n.m.*, cheek (of gun-carriages).

flasque, *n.f.*, flask, powder-flask.

flatir, *v.a.*, (coin.) to flatten.

flatoir, *n.m.*, (coin.) flattening-hammer.

flâtrer, *v.a.*, to fire; to cauterize (dogs, etc.).

flatter, *v.a.*, to flatter, to tickle; to gloss over; to cajole; to deceive, to delude; to caress, to endear, to make much of; to stroke, to coax, to fawn; to smooth; to touch gently; to run one's fingers over. *Elle aime à s'entendre* —; she likes to be flattered. *Un portrait flatté;* a flattering likeness. *La musique flatte l'oreille;* music soothes the ear. *Le chien flatte son maître;* the dog fawns upon his master.

se **flatter**, *v.r.*, to flatter one's self, to deceive, to delude one's self; to hope, to trust, to expect.

flatterie (fla-trî), *n.f.*, flattery, adulation.

flatteu-r, -se, adj., flattering, complimentary; fawning; gratifying, pleasing; eulogistic.

flatteu-r, n.m., -se, n.f., flatterer.

flatteusement (-teuz-măn), adv., flatteringly.

flatuleu-x, -se, adj., flatulent, windy.

flatulence, n.f., flatulence, wind.

flatulent, -e, adj., flatulent, windy.

flatuosité, n.f., flatulency.

fléau, n.m., (agri.) flail; scourge, plague; beam (of a balance); iron bar (to fasten folding gates).

flèche, n.f., arrow, dart, shaft; (astron.) sagitta; spire; (tric-trac) point; tandem (of driving); (nav.) pole; perch (of carriages); (fort.) bonnet; (arch.) rise. *Tirer une* —; to let fly an arrow. *Faire — de tout bois*; to leave no stone unturned. *Il ne sait plus de quel bois faire* —; he does not know which way to turn, he is at his wit's end. *— de lard*; flitch of bacon.

fléchier, n.m., arrow-maker.

fléchière, n.f., (bot.) arrow-head.

fléchir, v.a., to bend, to bow; to move, to melt; to persuade, to touch, to soften. *Se laisser* —; to relent, to give in, to consent.

fléchir, v.n., to bend, to bow, to yield, to give way, to stagger, to waver.

fléchissable, adj., flexible, pliant.

fléchissement (-shis-măn), n.m., bending, giving way.

fléchisseur, n. and adj. m., (anat.) flexor.

flegmasie, n.f. V. **phlegmasie.**

flegmatique or **phlegmatique,** adj., (med.) phlegmatic, cold, dull, sluggish, phlegmatic (of the mind). n., cold, dull, phlegmatic person.

flegme or **phlegme,** n.m., phlegm, coldness.

flegmon, n.m. V. **phlegmon.**

flegmoneu-x, -se, adj. V. **phlegmoneux.**

flétan, flételet, or **flétau,** n.m., (ich.) halibut.

flétrir, v.a., to wither, to dry up, to cause to fade, to blight, to blast; to tarnish, to blemish, to brand, to disgrace, to stain, to dishonor, to stigmatize.

se flétrir, v.r., to fade, to wither, to tarnish; to dishonor one's self; to be branded, to be stigmatized.

flétrissant, -e, adj., dishonoring, blighting.

flétrissure, n.f., fading, decaying, withering; blemish, blot, brand, discredit, disgrace; stigma.

flette, n.f., flat-bottomed boat.

fleur, n.f., flower, bloom, blossom; choice, best, pick; flourish; (pharm.) flour. *— de farine*; best flour, whites. *—s d'arbre*; blossoms of a tree. *Etre dans la — de son âge*; to be in the prime of life. *Etre dans toute sa* —; to be in its prime (of a thing). *Avoir la — d'une chose*; to have the best of a thing. *Semer de —s*; to strew with flowers. *—s blanches*; whites, fluor-albus. *A — de*; even with, level with. *A — de terre*; even with the ground. *Fine* —; pick, flower. *A —s*; flowery, flowered. *Yeux à — de tête*; goggle or prominent eyes. *Entrer en* —; to flower, bloom. *A — d'eau*; between wind and water.

fleurage, n.m., pollard.

fleuraison or **floraison,** n.f., efflorescence, blowing-time, flowering season.

fleur de lis, n.f., fleur-de-lis.

fleurdelisé, -e, part., marked with a fleur-de-lis.

fleurdeliser, v.a., to mark with a fleur-de-lis.

fleuré, adj., (her.) flowery, flowered.

fleurer, v.n., to smell, to exhale. *Cela fleure bon*; that smells nice. (pop.) *for* **flairer,** or **sentir.**

fleuret, n.m., silk ferret; (fenc.) foil.

fleureter. V. **flirter.**

fleurette, n.f., little flower, floweret; amorous discourse, gallant speech. *Conter* —; to talk sweet nonsense, to make love to,

fleuri, -e, part., flowery, florid, agreeable. *Teint* —; florid complexion. *Ecrire d'une manière* —; to write in a florid style.

fleurir, v.n., to flower, to blow; to bloom, to blossom; to thrive, to be in repute, to flourish, to prosper. *Cet arbre fleurissait tous les ans deux fois*; this tree blossomed twice every year. *Cet auteur florissait sous le règne de*; that author flourished under the reign of. *Les arts et les sciences florissaient alors*; arts and sciences flourished then.

fleurir, v.a., to ornament with flowers.

se fleurir, v.r., to adorn one's self with flowers.

fleurissant, -e, adj., blossoming, blooming.

fleuriste, n.m.f., florist, floriculturist; artificial-flower-maker; (in compound words) flower. *Jardinier* —; flower-gardener, nursery-man. *Jardin* —; flower-garden.

fleuron, n.m., flower-work (paint., etc.); jewel, ornament; (print.) tail-piece. *C'est le plus beau — de sa couronne*; it is the brightest jewel in his crown.

fleuronné, -e, adj., (bot.) having florets; (paleography) ornamented. (her.) V. **fleuré.**

fleuve, n.m., river (which falls into the sea), stream; (myth., paint., sculpt.) river-god. *Le bord d'un* —; the bank of a river. *L'embouchure d'un* —; the mouth of a river.

flexibilité, n.f., flexibility, flexibleness, pliancy, suppleness.

flexible, adj., flexible, pliable, pliant, supple.

flexion, n.f., flexion, bending.

flexueu-x, -se, adj., (bot.) flexuous.

flexuosité, n.f., (bot.) flexuosity.

flibot, n.m., (nav.) fly-boat.

flibustier (-tié), n.m., buccaneer, freebooter.

flic-flac, n.m., crack of the whip; flick-flack.

flint-glass, n.m., flint-glass.

flirter, v.n., to flirt.

floc, n.m., flock; tuft, tassel.

floche, n.f., rag; flock. adj., shaggy. *Soie* —; floss-silk.

flocon, n.m., flake; flock, tuft. *Un — de laine*; a flock of wool. *Il tombait de la neige à gros —s*; snow fell in great flakes.

floconneux, -se, adj., flaky.

flonflon, n.m., tol-de-rol (chorus).

floraison, n.f. V. **flouraison.**

floral, -e, adj., (bot.) floral. *Jeux floraux*; floral games. [Flora.

flore, n.f., (bot.) anthology, flora; (myth.)

floréal, n.m., Floreal (the eighth month of the calendar of the first French republic, from April 20th to May 19th).

florence, n.m., sarcenet.

florencé, -e, adj., (her.) flowery.

florentin, -e, n. and adj., Florentine.

florentine, n.f., florentine.

florès (-rès), adv., figure, dash. *Faire* —; to make a show, to cut a dash.

florifère, adj., (bot.) floriferous.

florin, n.m., florin.

florissant, -e, adj., prosperous, flourishing.

floriste, n.m., florist.

flosculeu-x, -se, adj., (bot.) floscular, flosculous.

floss, n.m., (metal.) floss.

flot, n.m., wave, billow, flood, surge; tide, flood-tide; crowd (of persons); stream, torrent. *Les —s de la mer*; the waves of the sea. *Le bruit des —s*; the roaring of the waves. *Mettre un vaisseau à* —; to set a ship afloat. *Etre à* —; to be afloat. *A —s*; in streams, in torrents; in crowds. *Demi* —; half-flood, half-tide. *— et jusant*; flood and ebb.

flottable, adj., navigable (for rafts).

flottage, n.m., floating of wood, rafting.

flottaison, n.f., flotation (nav.). *Ligne de* —; load water-line or mark.

flottant, n.m., (of hydraulic wheels) float.

flottant, -e, adj., floating, flowing; irresolute, wavering, fluctuating.

flotte, n.f., fleet; navy, shipping, cable-buoy; (fishing) float.

flotté, -e, part., floated. Bois —; float-wood.

flottement (flot-mān), n.m., floating; wavering, irresolution; (milit.) undulation.

flotter, v.n., to float, to waft; to be irresolute, to fluctuate, to waver. Faire — du bois; to float wood. v.a., (nav.) to ease off, to slacken (cable).

flotteron, n.m., small float.

flotteur, n.m., raftsman; (nav.) cable-buoy; water-gauge.

***flottille,** n.f., flotilla.

flou, n.m., (paint.) softness; delicacy of touch.

flou, adj., (paint.) light and soft.

flou, adv., (paint.) lightly.

flouer, v.a., to cheat; to diddle out of.

flouerie (flou-rî), n.f., cheating, swindling.

floueur, n.m., sharper, cheat, gull-catcher.

flou-flou, n.m., (—) rustling, rustle of silk.

fluant, -e, adj., liquid, flowing, flimsy, unresisting, transient; badly sized (of paper).

fluate, n.m., (chem.) fluate, fluoride.

fluaté, -e, adj., fluoride of. Chaux —e; fluoride of lime.

fluctuant, adj., fluctuating.

fluctuation, n.f., fluctuation.

fluctueu-x, -se, adj., fluctuating, agitated, boisterous.

fluer, v.n., to flow, to run.

fluet, -te, adj., thin, spare, lean, slender, lank.

flueurs, n.f.pl., (med.) fluor-albus, whites.

fluide, adj., liquid, flowing, fluid.

fluide, n.m., fluid.

fluidité, n.f., fluidity, fluidness.

fluor, n.m., (chem.) fluorine; (min.) fluor; fluor-spar. Spath —; fluor, fluor-spar.

fluorine, n.f., (chem.) fluorine; (min.) fluoride.

flûte, n.f., (nav.) flute; (mus.) flute; French roll, tall glass (for champagne). Jouer de la —; to play the flute. — allemande, traversière; German flute. Petite —; piccolo. Ce qui vient de la — s'en retourne au tambour; lightly come, lightly go. Ajuster ses —s; to tune one's pipes; to prepare one's measures. Accordez vos —s; settle it between you.

flûté, -e, adj., soft, fluted, fluty; piping; squeaky.

flûteau, n.m., child's whistle; (bot.) water-plantain.

flûter, v.n., to flute, to pipe; to drink hard; to tipple.

flûteu-r, n.m., **-se,** n.f., (b.s.) player on the flute, piper, (fam.) toper, tippler.

flûtiste, n.m., flutist, flute-player.

fluvial, -e, adj., fluvial.

fluviatile, adj., fluviatile, fluviatic.

flux (flu), n.m., flux, flow, influx, flood; stream, rising; (at cards) flush. — de sang; bloody flux. — de ventre; dysentery.

fluxion, n.f., inflammation; swelling. pl., (math.) fluxions. Une — de poitrine; inflammation of the lungs.

fluxionnaire, adj., (l.u.) subject to inflammation.

foarre, foerre, fouarre, n.m., straw (of oats).

foc, n.m., (nav.) jib, stay-sail. Grand —; standing-jib. Petit —; fore stay-sail. Bâton de —; jib-boom.

focal, adj., focal.

foène, n.f., eel-spear.

fœtus (fé-tus), n.m., fœtus.

foi, n.f., faith, belief; fidelity, honor; trust; credit, evidence; proof, testimony; (milit.) parole; fealty. N'avoir ni — ni loi; to regard neither law nor gospel, or to be utterly reckless, unprincipled. Ma —! really! faith! to be sure!

I declare! Fausser sa —; to break one's faith. — de gentilhomme; as I am a gentleman, on the word or honor of a gentleman. Garder sa —; to keep one's faith. Manquer à sa —; to break one's faith. Bonne —; good faith, honesty, plain-dealing. Mauvaise —; dishonesty, unfairness, false play. Profession de —; creed, belief. Un homme de bonne —; an honest man. Ajouter — à quelque chose; to give credit to anything. Avez-vous — à ces contes-là? do you believe such stories? En — de quoi; in testimony whereof. De bonne —; sincerely, honestly, uprightly, in earnest. Agir de bonne —; to act fairly. Faire — de; to testify, to prove, to be evidence of.

foible. V. **faible.**

foie, n.m., liver. Maladie de —; liver-complaint. Pâté de — gras; goose liver pie.

foin, n.m., hay, grass. Meule de —; haystack or rick; (of artichokes) choke. Grenier à —; hayloft. Faire les —s; to make hay. Mettre du — dans ses bottes; to feather one's nest. Avoir du — dans ses bottes; to be well off.

foire, n.f., (l. ex.) diarrhœa; fair (market); fairing. La — n'est pas sur le pont; there is no occasion to be in such a hurry. Ils s'entendent comme larrons en —; they are hand and glove together.

foirer, v.n., (l.ex.) to have diarrhœa; (fig.) to show the white feather.

foireu-x, -se, adj., (l.ex.) lax, relaxed. n., one who has diarrhœa. Avoir la mine —se; to look pale, sick.

fois, n.f., time, occasion (repetition). Une — par an; once a year. Deux — par semaine; twice a week. Plusieurs —; several times. De — à autre; from time to time. Une autre —; another time. Une — pour toutes; once for all. Une — autant; as much again. A la —, tout à la —; all together, all at once. Autant de — que, toutes les — que; as often as. Une — n'est pas coutume; once does not constitute a habit. A plusieurs —; repeatedly. Y regarder à deux —; to look twice (before doing anything). N'en pas faire à deux —; not to hesitate a moment. Trois — trois; three times three.

foison, n.f., plenty, abundance. A —; plentifully, abundantly; in crowds.

foisonner, v.n., to abound; to increase; to swarm (of animals).

fol, -le, adj., V. **fou.**

folâtre, adj., sportive, frolicsome, playful; wanton.

folâtrer, v.n., to play, to sport, to toy, to romp, to frolic. En folâtrant; sportively, wantonly.

folâtrerie, n.f., frolic, prank, gambol, toying, wanton trick.

foliacé, -e, adj., foliaceous.

foliaire, adj., of leaf, of leaves.

foliation, n.f., (arch.) feathering; (bot.) foliation.

folichon, -ne, n. and adj., wag, frolicsome person; gamesome, wanton, sportive, fresh, frolicsome. Un petit —; a little wag.

folie, n.f., madness, folly, distraction, lunacy, frenzy; piece of folly, foolery, foolishness, mania, hobby; country-seat. Un accès de —; a fit of madness. Faire des —s; to squander money; to carry on. Qui fait la — la boit; as you brew, so you must drink. Aimer à la —; to love to distraction. A la —; madly, passionately.

folié, -e, adj., foliated.

folio, n.m., folio. Un in- —, (—) a folio book. — recto; first page. — verso; second page.

foliole, n.f., (bot.) foliole.

follement (fol-mān), adv., madly, foolishly, dotingly, extravagantly, distractedly.

follet, -te, adj., wanton, playful, frolicsome, waggish; downy (of hair). Poil —; down. Feu

—; ignis fatuus, will-o'-the-wisp, jack-a-lantern. *Esprit* —; sprite, goblin, hobgoblin.

follet, *n.m.,* goblin, sprite, elf.

folliculaire, *n.m.,* (b.s.) pamphleteer.

follicule, *n.m.,* follicle.

follicule, *n.f.,* (pharm.) pod (of senna).

fomentation, *n.f.,* fomentation.

fomenter, *v.a.,* to foment, to feed. — *des troubles;* to excite troubles. — *une querelle;* to stir up a quarrel.

foncé, -e, *adj.,* dark, deep (of color); bottomed (of chairs *or* casks); (meta.) moneyed; well versed in.

foncement (fons-mān), *n. m.,* sinking (of wells).

foncer, *v.a.,* to bottom (a cask); to sink (wells); to deepen (of colors). *v.n.,* to dash, to rush upon; to supply funds. *Foncez!* charge down! *Se* —, *v.r.,* (of color) to deepen; (pop.) to be getting tipsy.

foncet, *n.m.,* barge-boat.

fonceur, *n.m.,* sinker (of wells).

fonci-er, -ère, *adj.,* landed; ⊙ deep-seated, thorough. *Contribution* —*ère;* land-tax. *Propriétaire* —; land owner. *Rente* —*ère;* ground rent.

foncièrement (-sièr-mān), *adv.,* thoroughly, completely; at the bottom; in the main.

fonction, *n.f.,* functions, office. *pl.,* functions, duty, office; working, action. *Entrer en* —; to enter upon one's duties *or* upon office. *Faire ses* —*s;* to perform one's duties. *Sortir de* —; to retire from office. *En* —; acting, at work.

fonctionnaire, *n. m.,* functionary, officer, office-holder, official.

fonctionnel, -le, *adj.,* functional.

fonctionnement, *n. m.,* acting, operating, working, action.

fonctionner, *v.n.,* to work, to act, to operate.

fond, *n.m.,* bottom, end, lower end, ground; groundwork; foundation; depth; center, heart, further end, most remote part, main point; basis; essential part, essence, gist; (paint.) background. *pl.,* (print.) inner margin; (thea.) back-scene; (mining underground) recess; (nav.) flooring (of a cap, crown, caul). *Sans* —; bottomless. *Tomber au* —; to fall to the bottom. *Le* — *d'un carrosse;* the back of a coach. — *de lit;* wooden bottom of a bed. *Dans le* —; at bottom, in reality. *Le* — *d'un bois;* the heart of a forest. *Il faut venir au* —; we must get to the bottom. *Voir le* — *du sac;* to search, probe, a thing to the bottom. *Velours à* — *d'or;* velvet with a gold ground. *Des arbres occupent le* — *du tableau;* trees occupy the background of the picture. *Le* — *d'un miroir;* the back of a looking-glass. *Bas*—, (—-—*s*) deep water. *Haut*—, (—-—*s*) shallow water. *Perdre* —; to get out of one's depth. *Prendre* —; to touch bottom. *Donner* —; (nav.) to cast anchor. *Couler à* —; (nav.) to sink, to run down. *A* — *de cale;* in the bottom of the hold. *A* —; thoroughly, fully, to the bottom, perfectly. *Fin* —; lowest depth, very depths of, innermost recesses; farthest end, extremity, ends of. *Il possède cette science à* —; he is a thorough master of that science. *Au* —; in the main, at bottom. *De* — *en comble;* wholly, from top to bottom, irretrievably. *Il est ruiné de* — *en comble;* he is utterly ruined. *Faire* — *sur;* (fig.) to rely, to depend on.

fondage, *n.m.,* casting, smelting, melting.

fondamental, -e, *adj.,* fundamental, essential, radical.

fondamentalement (-tal-mān), *adv.,* fundamentally, essentially, radically.

fondant, -e, *adj.,* melting, dissolving. *Tableau* —; dissolving view. *Poire* —*e;* melting, over-ripe pear.

fondant, *n.m.,* flux (melting); sweetmeat.

fondat-eur, *n.m.,* **-rice,** *n.f.,* founder, foundress.

fondation, *n.f.,* foundation; groundwork; basis, bed; bottoming (of roads); endowment, establishment. *La* — *d'une colonie;* the establishment of a colony.

fondé, *n.m.,* proxy. — *de pouvoirs, de procuration;* private attorney; agent acting under power of attorney, legal representative.

fondé, -e, *adj.,* founded, well-founded; authentic, strong; (fin.) consolidated. *Etre* — *à;* to have a right to, to have authority to, to be justified in. *Etre* — *en droit;* to have a just cause.

fondement (fond-mān), *n. m.,* foundation; groundwork; basis; ground, cause. *Jeter les* —*s de la paix;* to lay the foundations of peace. *Ce bruit est sans* —; that report is without foundation. *Dénué de* —; groundless.

fonder, *v.a.,* to lay the foundation, to build, to erect, to found; to ground, to base, to rest; to establish; to justify; to endow. — *un empire;* to lay the foundation of an empire.

se fonder, *v.r.,* to rely, to rest upon, to be grounded, to be founded. *Se* — *sur l'analogie;* to be founded upon analogy.

fonderie (fon-drī), *n.f.,* foundry, foundery, founding; melting-house, smelting-house. — *de caractères;* letter-foundry, type-foundry.

fondeur, *n.m.,* founder, melter; smelter (of ore). — *en caractères;* letter-founder, type-founder.

fondis, *n.m.,* giving way, sinking, settling.

fondoir, *n.m.,* melting-house.

fondre, *v.a.,* to melt, to dissolve, to cast; (paint.) to soften; to blend. — *une cloche;* to cast a bell.

se fondre, *v.r.,* to melt; to dissolve; to blend, to coalesce; to be cast; to be merged, to be fused; to diminish, to disappear suddenly, to melt away.

fondre, *v.n.,* to melt down; to melt away; to dissolve; to burst (into tears); to dart, to pounce upon; to make a stoop (of birds); to fall away, to vanish. *Il fondît sur lui;* he pounced upon him. — *en larmes;* to burst into tears.

fondrière, *n.f.,* bog, quagmire, slough, gully.

***fondrilles,** *n.f. pl.,* grounds, sediment, dregs. *V.* **effondrilles.**

fonds (fōn), *n.m.,* land, soil, ground; landed property; funds, stock, capital, principal, cash, ready money; stock in trade, business; subject, matter. *pl.,* funds, stocks. *Article de* —; leading article. *Biens*—; landed property. *Acheter des* —; to put money in the funds. *Mettre de l'argent à* — *perdus;* to sink money (in an annuity). *Spéculer sur les* —*publics;* to speculate in the public funds. *Céder son* —; to give up one's business. *Etre en* —; to be in cash. *Faire rentrer des* —; to get in money. *Ce marchand a vendu son* —; that tradesman has sold his business. *Un* — *inépuisable de science;* an inexhaustible mine of knowledge. — *secrets;* service-fund, service-money. — *d'amortissement;* sinking fund.

fondue, *n.f.,* (cook.) dish made of cheese and eggs.

fonger, *v.n.,* to blot (of paper).

fongible, *adj.,* (jur.) fungible.

fongosité, *n.f.,* (med.) fungus.

fongueu-x, -se (-gheū, -z), *adj.,* (med.) fungous, proud.

fongus (-gus), *n.m.,* (med.) fungus.

fontaine, *n.f.,* fountain; spring; cistern; tap, cock, plug; (for tea) urn. *De l'eau de* —; spring water. *Il a été à la* — *de Jouvence;* he has renewed his youth. *Il ne faut jamais dire:* " —, *je ne boirai pas de ton eau*"; we must never say, " I shall never need that," *or* " such a thing will never happen."

fontainier. *V.* **fontenier.**

fontanelle, *n.f.,* (anat.) fontanel.

⊙**fontange,** *n.f.,* topknot (ribbon).

fonte, *n.f.,* melting, casting, cast; cast-iron; brass; smelting; (print.) font, fount; holster (of saddles. *Fer de* — *or* — *de fer;* cast-iron. *Jeter en* —; to cast. *Métal de* —; gun-metal; brass.

fontenier, *n.m.*, fountain-maker; turncock.

fonticule, *n.m.*, (surg.) issue.

fonts (fōn), *n.m. pl.*, font. *Tenir quelqu'un sur les* —; to stand godfather, godmother, to any one.

for, *n.m.*, (l.u.) tribunal, conscience. — *extérieur;* temporal jurisdiction of the church. — *intérieur;* spiritual jurisdiction; inner conscience.

forage, *n.m.*, boring; drilling; wine dues.

forain, -e, *adj.*, foreign, alien, outlandish, traveling, itinerant. *Marchand* —; hawker, peddler. *Rade* —*e;* (nav.) open roadstead. *Spectacle* —; traveling show. *Marchand* —; pork-salesman. *Chemin* —; carriage road. *Propriétaire* —; absentee landlord.

foraminé, *adj.*, foraminous.

forban, *n.m.*, pirate, sea-robber, corsair.

forçage, *n.m.* (coin.) overweight.

forçat, *n.m.*, galley-slave, convict.

force, *n.f.*, strength, might, force; forcibleness, power, authority; violence, constraint, necessity; command, vigor, energy, efficacy; fortitude, resolution; skill, cleverness, proficiency; (nav.) press (of sail). *pl.*, troops, forces. *Les —s lui manquent;* his strength is failing him. *Frapper de toute sa* —; to strike with all one's might. *Etre à bout de* —*s;* to be done up. *Mettre des —s sur pied;* to raise forces. *Assembler ses* —*s;* to muster one's forces. *Les —s de terre;* land forces. *La — de la vérité;* the power of truth. *Céder à la — majeure;* to yield to superior force. *Dans toute la — du terme;* in every sense of the word. *De gré ou de* —; whether you like it or no. — *est restée à la loi;* order was restored. *User de* —, *employer la* —; to use forcible means. *Faire — de voiles;* to crowd all sail. *Faire — de rames;* to row with all one's might. *Maison de* —; house of correction, bridewell. *Il n'a ni — ni vertu;* he has neither valor nor virtue. *A — de;* by dint of. *De* —; a match for. *De — à;* strong enough to; equal to. *A — de bras;* by strength of arm. *A — d'argent;* with large sums of money. *De* —, *par* —; forcibly, by force, by forcible means. *A toute* —; absolutely, by all means, at all hazards. *Travailler à* —; to work hard. — *me fut de;* I was compelled to.

force, *adv.*, much, a great quantity of, a great deal of; many, a great many, any number of. *Je leur fis — compliments;* I paid them any number of compliments. — *gens;* any number of people.

forcé, -e, *part.*, forced, unnatural, strained, far-fetched; (man.) overreached; compulsory, unavoidable. *C'est* —; it is inevitable; it must happen. *Vent* —; (nav.) violent, boisterous wind.

forcément, *adv.*, forcibly, by force, compulsorily; necessarily; inevitably.

forcement, *n.m.*, forcing, compelling, compulsion; rape. — *de recette;* compulsion to refund.

forcené, -e, *n.* and *adj.*, madman, mad-woman; furious, frantic, mad, passionate, infuriated; enraged.

forceps (-séps), *n.m.*, (surg.) forceps.

forcer, *v.a.*, to force, to compel, to constrain; to impel; to break open, to wrench, to wrest, to bend, to break through; to run down (hunt.). — *une porte;* to break open a door. — *une clef;* to force a key. — *un cheval;* to override or overdo a horse. — *la nature;* to force or outrage nature. — *sa voix;* to strain one's voice, — *les voiles;* to crowd all sail. — *les rames;* to ply the oars. — *le pas;* to quicken one's pace.

se **torcer**, *v.r.*, to strain, to strain one's self; to do violence to one's feelings.

forcerie, *n.f.*, forcing house.

forces, *n.f.pl.*, shears.

forcet, *n.m.*, whip-cord.

forclore, *v.a.*, (jur.) to foreclose, to estop.

forclusion, *n.f.*, (jur.) foreclosure, foreclosing, estoppel.

foré, -e, *part.*, bored, drilled; piped (of keys).

forer, *v.a.*, to bore, to drill, to perforate, to pierce.

forestier, *n.m.*, ranger, keeper, forester.

foresti-er, -**ère**, *adj.*, forest, pertaining to forests. *Enlever au régime des lois —ères;* to disafforest. *Garde* —; forest-ranger, forester.

forêt, *n.f.*, forest, forest-land, woodland; roof-timber; den of thieves, shock (of hair). *Conversion en* —; afforestation. *Convertir en* —; to afforest. *Déclarer ne plus être* —; to disafforest. *Une — de cheveux;* a great shock of hair.

foret, *n.m.*, gimlet, borer, drill.

forfaire, *v.n.*, to fail in one's duty; to trespass, to transgress; to prevaricate; to be false to. *Il a forfait à l'honneur;* he has been false to honor.

forfaire, *v.a.*, to forfeit (fief).

forfait, *n.m.*, forfeit, crime, offense, transgression; contract. *Entreprendre à* —; to contract for, to take by the job. *A* —; in the lump; on speculation.

forfaiture, *n.f.*, forfeiture; prevarication.

forfanterie (-fan-trî), *n.f.*, romancing, bragging, puffing, boasting.

forficule, *n.f.*, (ent.) earwig.

forge, *n.f.*, forge, smithy; farmer's shop; blacksmith's shop. *pl.*, iron-works. *Grosse* —; large forge. — *de campagne;* (milit.) traveling forge. *Maître de* —; iron-master.

forgeable (-jabl), *adj.*, forgeable.

forger, *v.a.*, to forge, to hammer; to invent, to fabricate, to contrive, to forge, to coin. — *des nouvelles;* to fabricate news. — *des mots;* to coin words. *Fer forgé;* wrought iron.

se **forger**, *v.r.*, to create, to imagine, to conjure up, to fancy.

forgerie, *n.f.*, iron-works.

forgeron, *n.m.*, smith, blacksmith. *En forgeant on devient* —; practice makes perfect.

forgeur, *n.m.*, forger, hammerman, contriver, inventor, fabricator.

forhuer or **forhuir**, *v.n.*, (hunt.) to blow, to wind (a horn); to recall the hounds; to recheat.

forjet, *n.m.*, jutting out (of a wall).

forjeter, *v.n.*, (arch.) to jut out.

forlancer, *v.a.*, (hunt.) to dislodge, to start (game).

forlonger, *v.a.*, to spin out, to lengthen, to protract. *v.n.*, to get ahead (of a stag).

se **forlonger**, *v.r.*, to be spun out, to be drawn out; (hunt.) to run a length; to get ahead. *Le cerf s'était forlongé;* the stag had got ahead.

formaliser, *v.a.*, to offend, to shock.

se **formaliser**, *v.r.*, to take exception to, *or* offense at, to feel offended.

formalisme, *n.m.*, formalism.

formaliste, *adj.*, formal, precise, ceremonious. *Il est trop* —; he is too precise.

formaliste, *n.m.*, formalist.

formalité, *n.f.*, formality, form, ceremony. *Défaut de* —, *manque de* —; (jur.) informality.

formariage, *n.m.*, (feudal-law) marriage between serfs belonging each to a different lord.

format, *n.m.*, form, size, shape (of a book).

format-eur, -**rice**, *adj.*, formative, creative.

formation, *n.f.*, formation.

forme, *n.f.*, form, shape, figure, make; mode, mold, frame; body (of a hat); mold (in paper-making); (print.) form; seat; stall (of a choir); bed of gravel; (vet.) ring-bone; (nav.) dock. — *de soulier;* last of a shoe. *Mettre des souliers en* —; to put shoes on the last. — *de chapeau;* hat block. *Sans autre — de procès;* without any further formality. *En* —; formally. — *de* *procédure ;* law proceeding, procedure. *En la — qui suit ;* as follows. *Argument en — ;* formal argument. *Pour la — ;* for form's sake. *— brisée ;* stretchers. *Dans les —s ; en bonne — ;* in due form, in order.

formé, -e, *adj. & part.,* formed ; full-grown, mature, matured ; set (of fruit).

formel, -le, *adj.,* formal, express, precise, plain, explicit.

formellement (-mèl-mān), *adv.,* formally, expressly, precisely, strictly.

former, *v.a.,* to form, to frame, to fashion, to compose, to make up, to bring up, to cut out, to mold, to season ; (jur.) to array (a panel). *— une difficulté ;* to raise a difficulty. *— une plainte ;* to lodge a complaint. *— un jeune homme ;* to train up a youth.

se former, *v.r.,* to be made, formed ; to be bred, to form, to take, to assume a form, to take shape, to improve ; to resolve one's self into (a committee, etc.). *— une idée de quelque chose ;* to form an idea of anything. *Il se formera avec le temps ;* he will become polished or improve with time.

formica-leo, *n.m.,* (—) myrmeleon, ant-lion.

formicant, *adj.,* (med.) (of the pulse) weak and frequent.

formication, *n.f.,* (med.) formication.

formidable, *adj.,* formidable, dreadful, frightful ; tremendous, fearful.

formier, *n.m.,* last-maker.

formique, *adj.,* (chem.) formic.

formuer, *v.a.,* (hawking) to mew.

formulaire, *n.m.,* formulary.

formule, *n.f.,* formula, form ; prescription. *— d'algèbre ;* algebraic formula.

formuler, *v.a.,* (med.) to write a prescription in due form ; to detail, to state ; (jur.) to draw up in due form, to formulate ; (alg.) to reduce to a formula. *Se — ;* to be drawn up.

fornicat-eur, *n.m.,* **-rice,** *n.f.,* fornicator.

fornication, *n.f.,* fornication.

forniquer, *v.n.,* to fornicate.

forpaître or **forpaiser,** *v.n.,* (hunt.) to feed at a distance from the covert.

⊙**fors,** *prep.,* save, except, but.

forsenant, *adj.,* (hunt.) eager after game.

fort, -e, *adj.,* strong, stout, powerful, violent, plentiful, copious ; severe (of illness) ; sturdy, robust, lusty, hardy, able-bodied, vigorous, able ; hard, painful, difficult ; skillful, clever ; high (of wind) ; heavy (of ground, of rain). *Avoir la tête —e, l'esprit — ;* to be strong minded. *Un esprit — ;* a free-thinker. *Un coffre — ;* a strong box, a safe. *Colle —e ;* glue. *Terre—e ;* heavy ground. *Place —e ;* stronghold. *Expression —e ;* telling expression. *— de poids ;* overweight, too heavy. *A plus —e raison ;* so much the more or all the more reason. *Le plus — en est fait ;* the worst is over. *Etre — aux échecs ;* to play at chess very well. *Se faire — de ;* to undertake, to take upon one's self to, to feel confident of being able to. *Se porter — pour quelqu'un ;* to answer for any one. *Trouver plus — que soi ;* to meet with more than one's match. *C'est plus — que moi ;* I cannot help it. *C'est trop —, c'est par trop — ;* it is too bad. *Voilà qui est — ;* come ! I like that.

fort, *n.m.,* strongest part of a thing ; thickest part (of a wood) ; stronghold, fort ; strength, skill ; depth, heat, height ; center. *Le — d'une affaire ;* the main point of a business. *La raison du — est toujours la meilleure ;* might is right. *La critique est son —;* criticism is his forte. *Dans le — de* or *au — de l'hiver ;* in the depth of winter. *Dans le — sa colère ;* in the height of his passion. *Dans le — du combat ;* in the heat of the fight. *Au — de la tempête ;* in the height of the storm. *— de la halle ;* market-porter. *Le — portant le faible,* or *du — au*

faible ; one thing with another ; on an average. *Connaître,* or *savoir, le — et le faible de ;* to know the ins and outs of. *Le plus — est fait ;* the worst is over, or the most difficult part is done.

fort, *adv.,* very very much, highly, extremely, vastly, exceedingly ; hard, forcibly. *— bien ;* very well. *Bien — ;* very hard, or very loud. *— et ferme ;* resolutely ; for all one is worth. *Il pleut — ;* it is raining fast. *Frapper — ;* to strike hard.

forte, *adv.,* (mus.) forte.

fortement, *adv.,* strongly, vigorously, with force, stoutly, forcibly, much ; exceedingly.

forteresse (for-très), *n.f.,* fortress, stronghold.

°**fortifiant, -e,** *adj.,* strengthening, fortifying, invigorating, bracing.

fortifiant, *n.m.,* (med.) tonic.

fortification, *n.f.,* fortification ; redoubt.

fortifier, *v.a.,* to fortify, to strengthen, to invigorate, to brace ; to corroborate, to confirm. *Le bon vin fortifie l'estomac ;* good wine is strengthening.

se fortifier, *v.r.,* to fortify one's self, to gather strength, to grow strong ; to make one's self a proficient ; to gain proficiency ; to make one's self better acquainted ; to become skilled.

fortin, *n.m.,* (milit.) fortlet, little fort.

à fortiori (-cio-), *adv.,* à fortiori, much more.

fortitrer, *v.n.,* (hunt.) to avoid the dogs.

fortitude, *n.f.,* fortitude.

fortrait, -e, *adj.,* (of horses) overworked, spent.

fortraiture, *n.f.,* overfatigue (of a horse).

fortuit, -e, *adj.,* fortuitous, casual. *Cas — ;* mere chance or accident.

fortuitement (-tu-it-mān), *adv.,* fortuitously, casually, accidentally, by chance.

fortune, *n.f.,* fortune, chance, risk, hazard, wealth, luck, success, property ; (myth.) Fortune. *La — lui sourit ;* fortune smiles upon him. *Avoir de la — ;* to possess property, to be rich. *Artisan de sa — ;* architect of one's own fortune. *La — du pot ;* pot-luck. *Bonne — ;* good luck, good fortune, windfall. *Mauvaise — ;* ill-fortune, ill-luck. *Courir après la — ;* to hunt after riches. *Brusquer la — ;* to tempt fortune. *Faire — ;* to make a fortune. *Etre en — ;* to be lucky, to be in luck's way. *Manger sa — ;* to squander one's fortune. *Il faut faire contre mauvaise — bon cœur ;* we must put a good face upon matters. *De — ;* enriched, self-made. *Homme à bonnes —s ;* lady-killer ; intriguer. *— de mer ;* sea risks. *Demi — ;* one-horse carriage.

fortuné, -e, *adj.,* fortunate, lucky ; happy.

forum (fo-rom), *n.m.,* (antiq.) forum.

forure, *n.f.,* bore, hole drilled.

fosse, *n.f.,* hole, pit, den, grave ; (hort.) trench ; cesspool, pipe ; (of the nose) chamber. *Basse— ;* dungeon. *Avoir un pied dans la — ;* to have one foot in the grave. *— de céleri ;* celery-trench. *— à fumier ;* dung-hole. *— aux lions ;* lion's den ; (nav.) boatswain's store-room. *Mettre dans la — ;* to lay in the grave. *Mettre la clé sur la — ;* to waive one's right of inheritance.

fossé, *n.m.,* ditch, drain ; (fort.) moat, fosse. *Mourir au bord d'un — ;* to die in a ditch. *Sauter le — ;* to pass the Rubicon, to cast the die. *Ce qui tombe dans le — c'est pour les soldats ;* "findings is keepings."

fossette, *n.f.,* dimple ; (play) chuck-farthing ; pit of the stomach.

fossile, *n.m.* and *adj.,* fossil.

fossoyage, *n.m.,* ditching ; grave-digging.

fossoyer, *v.n.,* to ditch, to dig a trench round.

fossoyeur, *n.m.,* ditcher, grave-digger ; sexton.

fou or **fol, folle,** *adj.,* mad, foolish, wild, insane, senseless, frolicsome ; playful ; excessively fond; distracting (of pain); excessive. *Un fol espoir;* a foolish hope. *Devenir —;* to go mad. *Être — de;* to be mad for; to be passionately fond of. *Que vous êtes — !* how foolish you are ! *— à lier;* raving, mad.

fou, *n.m.,* **folle,** *n.f.,* madman, madwoman; madcap; mad-brain; jester, fool; bishop (at chess); (orni.) booby. *Maison de —s;* lunatic asylum. *Faire le —;* to play the fool. *Plus on est de —s, plus on rit;* the more the merrier. *Qui ne sait pas être — n'est pas sage;* it takes a wise man to make a fool.

fouace, *n.f.,* buttered roll; hearth-cake.

fouage, *n.m.,* hearth-money, hearth-penny.

*****fouaille,** *n.f.,* (hunt.) quarry.

*****fouailler,** *v.a.,* to lash, to whip.

foudre, *n.f.,* thunder, thunder-bolt, lightning. *Coup de —;* clap of thunder. *La — est tombée sur;* a thunderbolt fell on. *Lancer la —;* to hurl the thunderbolt. *Être tué par la —;* to be killed by lightning.

foudre, *n.m.,* thunderbolt; great orator; great warrior, captain, hero; a large cask, a tun. *Un — de guerre;* a great captain.

foudroiement *or* **foudroîment** (foo-droa-mǎn), *n.m.,* thunder-striking, crushing; overwhelming.

foudroyant, -e, *adj.,* terrible, crushing, dreadful; fulminating, thundering; withering.

foudroyer, *v.a.,* to thunder-strike; to batter with cannon and mortars; to riddle with shot; to fulminate, to blast; to crush, to overwhelm, to ruin, to confound.

fouée, *n.f.,* bat-fowling; oven-fire; fagot.

fouenne, *n.f. V.* **faine.**

fouet, *n.m.,* whip, horsewhip, lash; whipcord; whipping; whisk; cat, cat-o'-nine-tails. *— à blancs d'œufs;* egg-whisk. *Faire claquer un —;* to crack a whip. *Faire claquer son —;* to sound one's own trumpet. *Donner le — à quelqu'un;* to whip any one. *Donner des coups de — à;* to whip. *Se faire donner le —;* to get whipped. *Poulie à —;* (nav.) tail-block. *Coup de —;* sudden contraction of muscles of leg.

fouetté, -e, *part.,* whipped; streaked (of flowers and fruit). *De la crème —e;* whipped cream. *Tulipe —e;* streaked tulip.

fouette-queue, *n.m.,* star-lizard.

fouetter, *v.a.,* to whip, to horsewhip, to lash, to scourge, to flog; to whisk; to flick; to toss off, to quaff; (nav.) to lash; (nav.) to flap back against the masts (of sails). *Il n'y a pas là de quoi — un chat;* it is a mere trifle. *Il a bien d'autres chiens à —;* he has other fish to fry. *Fouette ! cocher;* whip up *or* faster, coachman.

fouetter, *v.a.* and *n.,* to cut (of the wind); to beat *or* patter against (of hail, rain, snow); to sweep (of cannon).

fouetteur, *n.m.,* flogger, whipper.

fougade *or* **fougasse,** *n.f.,* (milit.) fougade.

fouger, *v.n.,* (hunt.) to grub (of wild boars).

fougeraie (fou-jrè), *n.f.,* fern-plot *or* brake.

fougère, *n.f.,* (bot.) fern; brake; (fig.) drinking glass. *— aquatique, fleurie, royale;* flowering fern, king's fern. *— impériale, femelle;* brake. *— musquée;* sweet fern.

fougon, *n.m.,* (nav.) cook's galley, caboose.

fougue (foug), *n.f.,* fury, passion, transport, heat, ardor, fire, spirit, spiritedness, mettle; (nav.) mizzen-top. *Dans la — de la colère;* in the heat of passion. *La — de la jeunesse;* the impetuosity of youth. *Un cheval qui a trop de —;* a horse that has too much mettle.

fougueu-x, -se (-gheû, -z), *adj.,* fiery, hot, hasty, impetuous, ardent, spirited, animated, passionate, mettlesome, high-mettled. *Cheval —;* spirited horse.

*****fouille,** *n.f.,* excavating; excavation; digging. *Faire des —s;* to excavate, to make excavations.

*****fouille-au-pot,** *n.m.,* (—) (l. ex.) scullion, turnspit.

*****fouiller,** *v.a.,* to excavate, to dig; to search, to pry into, to rummage; to ransack, to probe to the bottom; to think out; (paint., sculpt.) to sink. *— une mine;* to work a mine. *— quelqu'un;* to search any one.

*se **fouiller,** *v.r.,* to search one's pockets, to feel in one's pockets; to search one another.

*****fouiller,** *v.n.,* to dig, to search, to rummage, to ransack. *— dans sa mémoire;* to ransack one's brain.

*****fouillis,** *n.m.,* confusion, medley; jumble, litter, mess; confused mass (of foliage).

fouine, *n.f.,* (mam.) martin, beech-martin; martlet; (agri.) pitchfork, fork; (fishing) gig, fishgig, fizgig, gaff.

fouiner, *v.n.,* to sneak away, to steal away, to slink off, to steal off.

fouir, *v.a.,* to dig, to delve.

fouissement (foo-is-mǎn), *n.m.,* digging.

foulage, *n.m.,* (manu.) fulling.

foulant, -e, *adj.,* pressing down. *Pompe —e;* forcing-pump.

foulard, *n.m.,* silk handkerchief; scarf.

foule, *n.f.,* crowd, throng, multitude, concourse, mob, press, shoal, ry, herd, common herd; (manu.) fulling. *Venir en —;* to flock, to throng together. *Entrer en —;* to crowd in. *La — des draps;* (manu.) the fulling of cloth. *Sortir de la —; se tirer de la —;* to rise above the common herd. *En —;* in crowds. *Faire —;* to crowd round.

foulé, -e, *part.,* trodden down, trampled upon, oppressed; (manu.) milled.

foulée, *n.f.,* pile (of skins); tread (of steps). *pl.,* (hunt.) foiling, fusee, slot; (man.) appui.

fouler, *v.a.,* to tread, to trample on, to trample down, to grind down, to oppress; to gall (animal); to sprain; (agri.) to jam; (manu.) to full; (manu.) to mill; (hunt.) to beat (a wood). *— la vendange;* to press the grapes. *— aux pieds;* to trample under foot. *— du drap;* to full cloth. *— un chapeau;* to work a hat. *— un cheval;* to override a horse.

*se **fouler,** *v.r.,* to sprain one's self. *— le pied;* to sprain one's foot. *Ne pas se —;* (fig.) to take things easy.

fouler, *v.n.,* (print.) to press.

foulerie (foo-lrî), *n.f.,* fullery.

fouleur, *n.m.,* wine-presser; fuller.

fouloir, *n.m.,* (manu.) beater; (artil.) rammer; sponge-rod; tobacco-plug; plugger.

fouloire, *n.f.,* (manu.) fulling-board.

foulon, *n.m.,* fuller. *Chardon à —;* (bot.) teasel, fuller's thistle. *Moulin à —;* fulling-mill. *Terre à —;* fuller's earth.

foulonnier, *n.m.,* fuller.

foulque, *n.f.,* (orni.) coot.

foulure, *n.f.,* sprain, strain; (manu.) fulling; (manu.) milling. *pl.,* (hunt.) foiling, fusee, slot (of a stag); (vet.) warbles.

four, *n.m.,* oven; bake-house; kidnaping-house, crimping-house; dark room; furnace; kiln; (metal.) hearth; (fig. and fam.) bungle, mull, mess, failure. *Mettre le pain au —;* to put the batch into the oven. *— de campagne;* portable oven. *— à briques;* brick-kiln. *— à chaux;* lime-kiln. *Gueule de —;* kiln-hole. *Des petits —s;* (cook.) small cakes. *Pièces de —;* (cook.) pastry. *Charger le —;* to heat the oven. *Aller au —;* to go to the bake-house. *Ce n'est pas pour vous que le — chauffe;* that is not meant for you. *Vous viendrez cuire à mon —;* you will have need of me some day. *Faire —;* to be unsuccessful, to fail, to be a frost (fam., thea.) *Faire un —;* to commit a blunder.

fourbe, *n.f.,* cheating, imposture, low villainy, knavery.

fourbe, *n.m.f.,* cheat; knave, impostor.

fourbe, *adj.*, deceitful, knavish, crafty.

fourber, *v.a.*, to cheat, to take in, to gull, to impose upon, to trick.

fourberie, *n.f.*, cheating, knavery, imposture, deceit.

fourbir, *v.a.*, to furbish, polish.

fourbisseur, *n.m.*, furbisher; sword-cutler.

fourbissime, *adj.*, most knavish.

fourbissure, *n.f.*, furbishing; rubbing up.

fourbu, -e, *adj.*, (vet.) foundered; diseased in the feet. *Rendre —;* to founder.

fourbure, *n.f.*, foundering; founder in the feet.

fourche, *n.f.*, fork, pitchfork. *—s patibulaires;* forked gibbet. *—s Caudines;* Caudine forks. *Faire la —;* to fork, to branch off. *Faire une chose à la —;* to do a thing anyhow.

fourché, -e, *part.*, forked, split; cloven; (her.) fourchee. *Croix —e;* (her.) cross fourchee.

fourcher, *v.n.*, to fork; to branch off; to trip (of the tongue). *Chemin qui fourche;* road that branches off. *La langue lui a fourché;* his tongue tripped.

se **fourcher**, *v.r.*, to fork, to branch off.

fourcher, *v.a.*, (agri.) to fork.

fourchet, *n.m.*, (vet.) foot-rot.

fourchetée, *n.f.*, forkful.

fourchette, *n.f.*, fork; rest (of a musket); forset (of gloves); sleeve-fish (of a shirt); prop (of carts); wish-bone (of birds); merry-thought. *Les dents d'une —;* the prongs of a fork. *Déjeuner à la —;* meat-breakfast. *— du pied d'un cheval;* the frog of a horse's foot. *— à découper* or *grande —;* carving-fork. *La — de l'estomac;* the breast-bone. *La — d'Adam;* the fingers. *C'est une bonne —;* she is a hearty eater.

fourchon, *n.m.*, prong; fork (of a tree).

fourchu, -e, *adj.*, forked; cloven; furcate. *Barbe —e;* forked beard. *Pied —;* cloven foot. *Chemin —;* road branching off. *Menton —;* indented chin. *N'avoir pas la langue —e;* to be plain-spoken.

fourchure, *n.f.*, furcation-fork.

fourgon, *n.m.*, van, carriage; (milit.) baggage-wagon; poker (of ovens); (railways) van. *La pelle se moque du —;* the pot calls the kettle black.

fourgonner, *v.n.*, to poke the fire (of an oven); to stir, to poke the fire; to poke, to fumble, to rummage.

fourmi, *n.f.*, ant, pismire, emmet. *Avoir des —s dans l'oreille;* to have a tingling in one's ear.

fourmilier, *n.m.*, ant-eater.

fourmilière, *n.f.*, ant-hill, ant-nest; (fig.) swarm; crowd.

***fourmillement**, *n.m.*, tingling; (fig.) swarming, teeming.

***fourmiller**, *v.n.*, to swarm, to abound with, to be full of; to feel a tingling, to tingle.

fournage, *n.m.*, charge for baking.

fournaise, *n.f.*, furnace.

fournaliste, *n.m.*, stove-maker.

fourneau, *n.m.*, stove, cooking-range, kitchener, furnace; (milit.) chamber (mine). *pl.*, (nav.) cook's galley. *— de cuisine;* kitchen stove. *— portatif;* portable stove. *Le — d'une pipe;* the bowl of a pipe. *Haut —;* blast furnace.

fournée, *n.f.*, a batch, baking; kilnful (of bricks); ovenful.

fourni-er, *n.m.*, **-ère**, *n.f.*, oven-keeper; parish-baker.

fournil (-ni), *n.m.*, bakehouse.

fourniment, *n.m.*, ⊙powder-flask, powder-horn; (milit.) belt, shoulder-belt, buffs.

fournir, *v.a.*, to furnish, to provide, to supply, to stock, to store, to procure, to afford; to make up, to complete (a sum of money); to draw a bill; (com.) to meet, to value (on); (fig.) to go over the whole course (of a horse). *— l'armée*

de vivres; to supply the army with provisions. *— des défenses;* to furnish means of defense.

se **fournir**, *v.r.*, to furnish, to supply one's self; to find one's self (in); to deal (with).

fournir, *v.n.*, to contribute, to supply, to be sufficient, to suffice. *— à la dépense;* to bear the expense.

fournissement (-nis-mān), *n.m.*, (com.) share of capital; capital.

fournisseur, *n.m.*, contractor, tradesman, purveyor; (theat.) property-man. *— breveté de;* by appointment to.

fourniture, *n.f.*, furnishing, providing, supplying; supply, provision. *Il fait les —s de la maison;* he supplies the family. *— de salade;* dressing of a salad. *Faire — de;* to supply. *—s de bureau;* stationery, sundries.

fourrage, *n.m.*, fodder, provender; forage; (artil.) wad, wadding; foraging-party. *— vert;* green fodder, grass. *— sec;* dry fodder, hay. *Envoyer au —;* to send out foraging.

fourrager, *v.n.*, to forage; to pilfer, to plunder. *— dans un champ;* to forage in a field. *— au vert;* to forage for grass. *— au sec;* to forage for hay.

fourrager, *v.a.*, to forage, to ravage; to rummage; to rake.

fourragère, *adj.f.*, fit for fodder. *Plantes —s;* plants fit for fodder.

fourrageur, *n.m.*, forager; rummager.

fourré, *n.m.*, thicket; brake, jungle.

fourré, -e, *part.*, furred, interchanged; counter, secret; underhand (of blows); woody (of countries); mixed (of hay, straw); furred (of clothing); plated (of metals); stuffed (cook.). *Bois —;* wood full of thickets and briers. *Pays —;* country full of woods, hedges, etc. *Coup —;* underhand trick, thrust. *Paix —e;* peace suddenly patched up. *Médaille —e;* plated medal. *Langue —e;* savory tongue. *Toile —e;* diaper.

fourreau, *n.m.*, case, scabbard, sheath, cover; child's frock; front fork (of bicycle). *L'épée, or la lame, use le —;* the sword wears out the scabbard; the mind is too active for the body. *Coucher dans son —;* to sleep in one's clothes.

fourrer, *v.a.*, to put, to thrust; to cram, to stuff; to beat, to knock; to line with fur; (nav.) to serve (cables and ropes). *Fourrez cela dans l'armoire;* put that away into the cupboard. *Il fourre du latin dans ses discours;* he stuffs his speeches cram full of Latin. *— quelque chose dans la tête de quelqu'un;* to beat a thing into any one's brains or head. *Il fourre son nez partout;* he pokes his nose everywhere.

se **fourrer**, *v.r.*, to get, to creep, in; to intrude or thrust one's self, to poke one's self in; to wear warm clothing or furs; (nav.) to serve (of cables). *Il se fourre partout;* he pokes his nose in everywhere. *Ne savoir où se —;* not to know where to hide one's self.

fourreur, *n.m.*, furrier.

fourrier, *n.m.*, (obs.) harbinger; (milit.) quartermaster; (nav.) clerk. *Faire le bon —;* to help one's self to the best pieces.

fourrière, *n.f.*, pound, greenyard. *Mettre un cheval en —;* to impound a horse.

fourrure, *n.f.*, fur, furred gown; (her.) vair; (nav.) service. *— de gouttière;* water-way.

fourvoiement (-voa-mān), *n.m.*, (l.u.) going astray, wandering, blunder, mistake; (fig.) error, going the wrong way.

fourvoyer, *v.a.*, to mislead, to lead astray, to lead into error; to baffle, to foil.

se **fourvoyer**, *v.r.*, to go astray, to stray, to lose one's way; to err grossly, to go on the wrong scent.

foustanelle, *n.f.*, fustanelle.

fouteau, *n.m.*, (pop.) beech, beech-tree.

foutelaie, *n.f.*, beech grove or plantation.

foyer, *n.m.*, fire-grate, hearth, fire-box (of an engine); hearthstone; (thea.) lobby, green-room; focus; (of a pipe) bowl; (fig.) seat, hot-bed, source; home. — *des acteurs*; (thea.) green-room. — *du public*; (thea.) lobby, crush-room. *Combattre pour ses —s*; to fight for one's home. *Aimer à garder son —*; to like quiet, to like to lead a secluded life.

frac, *n.m.*, dress coat, dress jacket.

fracas, *n.m.*, crash, noise; din, bustle, fuss. *Avec —*; with a crash. *Faire du — dans le monde*; to make a noise *or* show in the world.

fracasser, *v.a.*, to break to pieces, to shatter, to shiver.

se **fracasser**, *v.r.*, to break to pieces, to be shattered.

fraction, *n.f.*, breaking; fraction; portion; (arith. fraction.

fractionnaire, *adj.*, fractional.

fractionnement, *n.m.*, dividing into fractions.

fractionner, *v.a.*, to divide into fractions.

fracture, *n.f.*, breaking (with violence); rupture; (surg.) fracture.

fracture, *-e*, *adj.*, (surg.) fractured.

fracturer, *v.a.*, (surg.) to fracture.

se **fracturer**, *v.r.*, (surg.) to fracture one's self; to be fractured.

fragiforme, *adj.*, strawberry-shaped.

fragile, *adj.*, fragile; brittle; frail. — *comme du verre*; as brittle as glass. — *l* glass, with care.

fragilité, *n.f.*, fragility; brittleness; frailty.

fragment, *n.m.*, fragment, piece, scrap, particle.

fragmentaire, *adj.*, fragmentary, fragmental.

fragon, *n.m.*, (bot.) butcher's broom.

frai, *n.m.*, spawn, spawning (of fish); fry (young fish); roe, hard roe.

fraichement (frèsh-man), *adv.*, coolly, freshly; coldly; newly, recently, just.

fraicheur, *n.f.*, coolness, freshness, bloom; coldness, dampness; floridness, ruddiness; luster, brilliancy; (nav.) flaw of wind.

fraichir, *v.n.*, to freshen, to begin to blow fresh, to get cool. *Le vent fraichit*; it is beginning to blow.

fraie, *f.*, spawning time.

frairie, *n.f.*, (fam.) merry-making. *Faire —, être en —*; to make merry, to be merry-making.

fra-is, -iche, *adj.*, cool, fresh, coldish; recent, new; youthful; florid, ruddy; newlaid (of eggs). *Temps —*; cool weather. *Eau —iche*; cold water. *Des nouvelles —iches*; fresh news. *Des œufs —*; new-laid eggs. *Du pain —*; new bread. *Plaie toute —iche*; raw wound. *Du saumon —*; fresh salmon. *Un teint —*; a florid complexion.

frais, *n.m.*, cool, coolness, freshness; cool spots; (nav.) gale. *Mettre du vin au —*; to cool wine. *Il fait —*; it is cool. *Prendre le —*; to take the air, to go out for an airing. *Bon —, joli —*; (nav.) fresh gale. *Grand —*; strong gale. *Au —*; in the cool of the evening.

frais, *n.m.pl.*, expense, expenses; charge, charges, cost, outlay. *Faux —*; incidental expenses; (jur.) untaxable costs. *Menus —*; petty expenses. *Les — d'un procès*; the costs of a lawsuit. *Tous —faits*; clear of all charges; all paid. *A grands —*; very expensively. *A peu de —*; at little cost, cheaply. *Constituer quelqu'un en —*; to put any one to expense. *Se mettre en —*; to put one's self to expense. *Recommencer sur nouveaux —*; to begin anew, to begin over again. *A — communs*; jointly, at joint expense. *En être pour ses —*; to have lost one's time and money. *Faire les — de*; to bear the expense of. *Faire ses —*; to cover one's expenses. *Faire dès —*; to go to *or* to incur expense; to take trouble, to make efforts to please.

fraise, *n.f.*, (bot.) strawberry; ruff; (fort.) fraise; (hunt.) start; crow. — *des bois*; wood *or* wild strawberry. — *de veau*; calf's crow.

fraisement (frèz-mān), *n.m.*, (arch.) starlings (of bridges); (fort.) fraising.

fraiser, *v.a.*, to plait, to ruffle; (fort.) to fraise; to knead dough thoroughly.

fraisette, *n.f.*, small ruff.

fraisier, *n.m.*, strawberry-plant.

fraisil (-zi), *n.m.*, coal-dross, breeze.

framboise, *n.f.*, (bot.) raspberry.

framboisé, *-e*, *part.*, flavored with raspberries; having a flavor of raspberries.

framboiser, *v.a.*, to give a raspberry flavor to.

framboisier, *n.m.*, raspberry-bush, raspberry-plant.

framée, *n.f.*, Frankish lance, javelin.

franc (fran), *n.m.*, franc (French coin worth $0.193); (hort.) seedling. *Au marc le —*; at the rate of so much in the dollar.

franc, -he (fran, frānsh), *adj.*, free, unconstrained, exempt from; frank, downright, open, sincere; entire, full; complete; true, real; mere; arrant; staunch, right; very; whole, clear; (paint.) bold. — *de port*; post-paid. *Compagnie —he*; free-company. *Cœur —*; open heart. *Etre — du collier*; to draw freely (of horses); (fig.) to be eager, obliging, honest. *Un — charlatan*; a downright quack. *Une —he coquette*; an arrant jilt. *Avoir son — parler avec*; to speak one's mind, to speak out; not to mince matters. — *Taupins*. *V.* **taupins**.

franc, *adv.*, frankly, freely, plainly, openly, sincerely; clean, quite, completely, entirely.

fran-c, -que, *n.* and *adj.*, Frank; Frankish.

français, -e, *adj.*, French. *La langue —e*; the French tongue. *A la —e*; in the French fashion.

français, *n.m.*, *-e*, *n.f.*, Frenchman, Frenchwoman.

français, *n.m.*, French. *Entendre le —*; to understand French. *Parler —*; to speak French; to call a spade a spade. *En bon —*; in plain terms; like a true Frenchman. *Parler — comme une vache espagnole*; to murder the French language. *Les Français* = le Théâtre Français.

franc-alleu, *n.m.*, (—s—s). *V.* **alleu**.

francatu, *n.m.*, a kind of apple.

de **franc-étable**, *adv.*, (nav.) collision, foul.

franc-fief, *n.m.*, (—s—s) a fief possessed by a commoner.

franc-funin, *n.m.*, (—s—s) (nav.) white hawser.

franchement (frānsh-mān), *adv.*, frankly, freely, openly, plainly, sincerely, unreservedly, ingenuously, boldly; really, frankly speaking. *J'avoue — que*; I readily admit that.

franchir, *v.a.*, to leap, to get over; to clear; to pass, to pass over, to overstep, to go beyond, to break through; to cross, to traverse; to surmount; (nav.) to head (the sea). *Il a franchi le fossé*; he has jumped over the ditch. — *une barrière*; to clear a bar. — *les montagnes*; to cross the mountains. — *les bornes du devoir*; to overstep the bounds of duty. — *le pas*; to take a resolution. — *le mot*; to let out the word. — *une difficulté*; to overcome a difficulty.

franchise, *n.f.*, franchise, exemption, immunity, freedom (of a city); frankness, sincerity, openness, candor, plainness; (paint.) boldness, freedom. *Parler avec —*; to speak frankly. — *du coloris*; (paint.) freedom of coloring. *En — de droit*; duty-free.

franchissable, *adj.*, passable, capable of being crossed.

franchissement, *n.m.*, leap over, leaping.

francisation, *n.f.*, gallicizing; (com.) registering as a French ship.

franciscain, *n.m.*, Franciscan, gray friar.

franciser, *v.a.,* to frenchify, to gallicize.

se **franciser,** *v.r.,* to become French.

francisque, *n.f.,* battle ax.

franc-maçon, *n.m.,* (—s— —s) freemason.

franc-maçonnerie, *n.f.,* (*n.p.*) freemasonry.

franco, *adv.,* free of expense, pre-paid. *Ecrire* —; address, post-paid.

francolin, *n.m.,* (orni.) francolin.

franc-parler, *n.m.,* (*n.p.*) liberty *or* freedom of speech.

franc-quartier, *n.m.,* (—s— —s) (her.) quarter, franc-quarter.

franc-réal, *n.m.,* (—s— —s) sort of pear.

⊙**franc-tenancier,** *n.m.,* (—s— —s) free-holder.

franc-tillac, *n.m.,* (nav.) flush-deck.

franc-tireur, *n.m.,* (—s— —s) (milit.) sharpshooter, skirmisher; volunteer.

frange, *n.f.,* fringe, valance.

frangé, -e, *adj.,* (bot.) fimbriate.

franger, *v.a.,* to fringe, to valance.

franger *or* **frangier,** *n.m.,* fringe-maker.

frangipane, *n.f.,* almond-cake.

frangipanier, *n.m.,* (bot.) red jasmine.

franque, *adj.f.,* Frankish.

franquette, *n.f.,* (l.u.) frankness. *A la bonne* —; frankly, freely, sincerely.

frappant, -e, *adj.,* striking, impressive.

frappe, *n.f.,* (coin.) stamp; set of matrices.

frappé, -e, *part.,* struck; iced (of liquids); strong and close (of cloth); powerful, forcible. — *d'étonnement;* struck with wonder. *Vers bien* —*s;* spirited verses.

frappé, *n.m.,* (mus.) fall (of the foot).

frappe-main, *n.m.,* (*n.p.*) hot-cockle.

frappement (frap-mān), *n.m.,* striking, clapping (of hands).

frapper, *v.a.,* to strike, to smite, to slap, to tap, to hit; to make an impression; to affect, to move; to astonish, to surprise; to frighten; to stamp, to coin; to ice (liquids); (nav.) to seize. — *vivement;* to rap. — *avec le pied;* to stamp. — *légèrement;* to pat. — *la terre du pied;* to stamp one's foot upon the ground. — *monnaie;* to coin money. — *un coup;* to strike a blow.

se **frapper,** *v.r.,* to strike one's self; to strike one another; to be impressed *or* affected; to be filled with gloom *or* dismay.

frapper, *v.n.,* to knock, to strike, to rap. — *à la porte;* to knock at the door. — *juste;* to strike home. *Entendre* —; to hear a knock.

frappeu-r, *n.m.,* -**se,** *n.f.,* beater; striker. *adj.,* striking, rapping. *Esprit* —; spirit-rapper.

frasque, *n.f.,* freak, prank, trick.

frater (-tèr), *n.m.,* surgeon's boy; saw-bones; village barber; (milit., nav.) barber.

fraternel, -le, *adj.,* fraternal, brotherly.

fraternellement (-nèl-mān), *adv.,* fraternally.

fraterniser, *v.n.,* to fraternize.

fraternité, *n.f.,* fraternity, brotherhood.

fratricide (murder), *n.m.,* (pers.) *m.f.,* fratricide. *adj.,* fratricidal.

fraude (frôd), *n.f.,* fraud, deceit, imposition, fraudulency. *En* —; fraudulently. *Faire une* —; to commit a fraud. *Passer en* —; to smuggle.

frauder, *v.a.,* to defraud, to smuggle.

fraudeu-r, *n.m.,* -**se,** *n.f.,* defrauder, smuggler.

frauduleusement (-leûz-mān), *adv.,* fraudulently.

frauduleu-x, -se, *adj.,* fraudulent.

fraxinelle, *n.f.,* fraxinella, white dittany, bastard dittany.

frayer, *v.a.,* to trace out, to open out, to mark out; to rub against, to graze, to brush; to make, to prepare, to show. *Qui n'est pas frayé;* unbeaten, untrodden. *Chemin frayé;* beaten path *or* track. *Le coup n'a fait que* — *sa botte;* the blow only grazed his boot.

se **frayer,** *v.r.,* to open for one's self; to prepare (a way); to carve out.

frayer, *v.n.,* to wear away; to keep company, to frequent, to be on good terms; (of fishes) to milt, to spawn. *Ces deux hommes ne frayent pas ensemble;* these two men do not agree together.

frayère, *n.f.,* spawning-place.

frayeur, *n.f.,* fright, terror, dread, fear. *Etre saisi de* —; to be seized with terror.

frayoir, *n.m.,* (hunt.) fray, rub.

frayure, *n.f.,* (hunt.) rubbing, fraying.

fredaine, *n.f.,* frolic, prank, freak. *Faire des* —*s;* to play pranks; to sow one's wild oats.

fredon, *n.m.,* (mus.) trill, shake; (at cards) pair-royal.

fredonnement (-do-n-mān), *n.m.,* humming.

fredonner, *v.a.* and *n.,* to hum.

fredonneur, -se, *n.m.f.,* hummer.

frégate, *n.f.,* frigate; (orni.) frigate bird.

frégaté, *adj.,* frigate-built.

frégaton, *n.m.,* frigatoon.

frein, *n.m.,* bit, bridle; curb, check; brake; drag, skid, brake (of carriages); (fig.) restraint; (anat.) frenum, ligament. *Ronger son* —; to champ the bit; to fret one's self. *Mettre un* — *à sa langue;* to bridle one's tongue. *Il faut mettre un* — *à sa cruauté;* his cruelty must be curbed. *Serrer le* —; (rail.) to apply, to put on, the brake.

frelampier, *n.m.,* scamp, rascally fellow.

frelatage, *n.m.,* adulteration, sophistication.

frelater, *v.a.,* to adulterate, to sophisticate. *Ce vin est frelaté;* this wine is adulterated. *Ouvrages frelatés;* spurious works.

frelaterie (-la-tri), *n.f.,* sophistication, adulteration. *V.* **frelatage.**

frelateur, *n.m.,* sophisticator, adulterator.

frêle, *adj.,* frail, fragile; faint, weak.

frêler, *v.n.,* to crackle (of hair, feathers).

freloche, *n.f.,* gauze-net, butterfly-net.

frelon, *n.m.,* (ent.) hornet, drone; (bot.) kneeholly.

freluche, *n.f.,* tuft (of silk); hair-thread.

freluquet, *n.m.,* puppy, coxcomb, prig.

frémir, *v.n.,* to shudder, to tremble, to quiver, to shake; to vibrate, to murmur, to rustle, to moan; to simmer. — *de colère;* to tremble with anger. *J'entendais* — *le feuillage;* I heard the leaves rustling.

frémissant, -e, *adj.,* quivering, trembling.

frémissement (-mis-mān), *n.m.,* shudder, shuddering, quivering, trembling; roaring; vibration; murmuring (of water); simmering. — *caire;* (med.) thrill, purring tremor of the heart.

frênaie, *n.f.,* ash-grove.

frêne, *n.m.,* ash, ash-tree.

frénésie, *n.f.,* frenzy, madness, fury.

frénétique, *adj.,* distracted, frantic, raving.

frénétique, *n.m.f.,* raving, distracted person.

fréquemment (-ka-mān), *adv.,* frequently, often.

fréquence, *n.f.,* frequency; quickness (of the pulse).

fréquent, -e, *adj.,* frequent. *Pouls* —; quick pulse.

fréquentati-f, -ve, *adj.,* (gram.) frequentative.

fréquentatif, *n.m.,* (gram.) frequentative.

fréquentation, *n.f.,* frequenting, frequentation; company.

fréquenter, *v.a.,* to frequent, to keep company with, to resort to; to haunt.

fréquenter, *v.n.,* to frequent, to visit often, to associate (with); to converse (with).

frère, *n.m.,* brother; fellow-Christian; friar, monk. — *aîné;* elder brother. — *cadet;* younger brother. —*s jumeaux;* twins. *Demi*— ; half-brother. — *consanguin;* brother by the father's side. — *utérin;* brother by the mother's side. — *de lait;* foster-brother. *Beau*—, (—*x* —*s*) brother-in-law. — *lai,* — *convers;*

lay-brother. — *chapeau;* assistant brother. *Faux* —; false brother, false friend. — *d'armes;* brother in arms. *Il est bon* —; he is a jolly fellow.

frérot, *n.m.,* (fam.) little brother.

fresaie, *n.f.,* (orni.) white-owl, screech-owl. *V.* **effraie**.

fresque, *n.f.,* fresco. *Peindre à* —; to paint in fresco.

fressure, *n.f.,* (cook.) pluck; fry; haslet.

fret (frè), *n.m.,* freight. *Prendre du* —; to take in freight.

fréter, *v.a.,* to charter; to freight.

fréteur, *n.m.,* freighter; charterer.

***frétillant, -e,** *adj.,* frisky, wriggling; fidgety.

***frétillement,** *n.m.,* frisking, wriggling; (fig.) itching, longing.

***frétiller,** *v.n.,* to frisk, to wriggle; (fig.) to itch, to long, to be impatient. *Les pieds lui frétillent;* he is impatient to be off. *La langue lui frétille;* he is longing to speak.

fretin, *n.m.,* small fry, young fish; trash, rubbish.

frettage, *n.m.,* hooping, binding.

frette, *n.f.,* (tech.) iron hoop, band, ring.

fretté, -e, *adj.,* hooped, iron-bound; (her.) fretty.

fretter, *v.a.,* to hoop, to bind.

freux, *n.m.,* rook.

friabilité, *n.f.,* friability.

friable, *adj.,* friable, crisp, short.

friand, -e, *adj.,* dainty, nice, fond of; partial to. *Avoir le goût* —; to have a nice taste. *Un morceau* —; a delicate morsel. *Etre* — *de;* to be fond of, partial to.

friand, *n.m.,* -e, *n.f.,* epicure, dainty person.

friandise, *n.f.,* daintiness, dainty, nicety, tit-bit. *Aimer les* —*s;* to be fond of dainties.

fricandeau, *n.m.,* (cook.) fricandeau; veal-stew.

fricassée, *n.f.,* (cook.) fricassee.

fricasser, *v.a.,* to fricassee; (pop.) to squander away, to waste, to dissipate.

fricasseur, *n.m.,* bad cook; (fig.) spendthrift, rake.

friche, *n.m.,* waste *or* fallow land. *Laisser une terre en* —; to let a piece of ground lie fallow.

fricot, *n.m.,* (pop.) ragout, stew.

fricoter, *v.n.,* (pop.) to feast. *v.a.,* (fig., pop.) to squander.

fricoteur, *n.m.,* (pop.) feaster; fast liver; (milit.) marauder.

friction, *n.f.,* friction, rubbing. *Gants à* —*s;* flesh-gloves.

frictionner, *v.a.,* (med.) to rub.

se **frictionner,** *v.r.,* (med.) to rub one's self.

frictionneu-r, -se, *n.m.f.,* professional rubber.

frigidité, *n.f.,* frigidity.

frigorifique, *adj.,* frigorific.

frileu-x, -se, *adj.,* chilly; (pop.) funky, cowardly.

frileux, *n.m.,* chilly person; (pop.) coward, funk.

frileuse, *n.f.,* lady's warm cap.

frimaire, *n.m.,* Frimaire, the third month of the calendar of the first French republic, from November 21st to December 20th.

frimas, *n.m.,* rime, hoar-frost. *Saison des* —; the wintry season.

frime, *n.f.,* (triv.) show, pretense, joke, fun of the thing. *Il n'en a fait que la* —; he only made a show of it, it was all pretense.

fringale, *n.f.,* (fam.) sudden pang of hunger. *Avoir la* —; to feel hungry all of a sudden.

fringant, -e, *adj.,* brisk, nimble, frisky; smart, dapper. *Cheval* —; frisky horse.

fringuer (-ghé), *v.n.,* to frisk; to skip.

friolerie (frio-lrî), *n.f.,* dainty.

friolet, *n.m.,* sort of pear.

fripe, *n.f.,* rag; scrap; eatable.

friper, *v.a.,* to rumple; to spoil, to wear out; (pop.) to gobble down, to eat greedily, to devour; (pop.) to waste, to dissipate, to squander.

se **friper,** *v.r.,* to get rumpled.

friperie (fri-prî), *n.f.,* frippery, old clothes; old clothes' trade; rag-fair. *Se jeter, tomber, sur la* — *de quelqu'un;* to fall foul of any one.

fripe-sauce, *n.m.,* (—) (l.ex.) greedy-guts, glutton; bad cook.

fripi-er, *n.m.,* -**ère,** *n.f.,* dealer in old clothes, furniture-broker.

fripon, -ne, *adj.,* knavish, roguish, rascally.

fripon, *n.m.,* -**ne,** *n.f.,* knave, rogue, cheat, swindler; rascal. *Un tour de* —; a knavish trick.

friponneau, *n.m.,* little rogue, rascal, cheat.

friponner, *v.a.* and *n.,* to cheat; to pilfer.

friponnerie (-po-n-rî), *n.f.,* knavish trick, roguishness, knavery.

friquet, *n.m.,* tree-sparrow; (utensil) slice.

frire, *v.a.* and *n.,* to fry. *Il n'y a rien à* —; (pop.) there is nothing to eat, there is nothing to be gained. *Il n'a plus de quoi* —; he is quite ruined.

frisage, *n.m.,* curling, rolling; lattice-work, trellis.

frise, *n.f.,* (arch., paint., sculpt.) frieze; dreadnought. *Cheval de* —; (fort.) cheval-de-frise.

friser, *v.a.,* to curl, to frizz (hair), to crisp; to graze, to glance upon, to touch lightly, to approach, to border upon. *Elle frise la quarantaine;* she is close upon forty.

se **friser,** *v.r.,* to curl, to curl one's hair; to fall into curl.

friser, *v.n.,* to curl; (print.) to slur.

frisotter, *v.a.,* (b.s.) to be curled, to frizzle.

se **frisotter,** *v.r.,* (b.s.) to be curled, to frizzle one's self.

frisquette, *n.f.,* (print.) frisket.

frisson, *n.m.,* shivering, cold fit; chill; shudder, thrill. *Avoir le* —; to have the shivers. *Cela donne le* —; that makes one shudder.

frissonnant, *adj.,* shuddering, shivering.

frissonnement (-so-n-mān), *n.m.,* shivering, shudder, flutter.

frissonner, *v.n.,* to shiver, to shudder; to quake, to tremble.

frisure, *n.f.,* curling, crisping; curls.

frit, -e, *part.,* (pop.) ruined, undone. *Il est* —; he is done for. *Tout est* —; all is over.

fritillaire, *n.f.,* (bot.) fritillary.

fritte, *n.f.,* (glass-making) frit.

friture, *n.f.,* frying; thing fried; fried fish; butter for frying.

frivole, *adj.,* frivolous, trifling, shallow, futile.

frivolité, *n.f.,* frivolity, frivolousness; (needle-work) tatting.

froc, *n.m.,* frock, garment (of monks). *Prendre le* —; to turn monk. *Jeter le* — *aux orties;* to throw off the cowl; to give up one's profession.

frocaille, *n.f.,* (b.s.) monks.

frocard, *n.m.,* (b.s.) monk.

froid, *n.m.,* cold, coldness, chilliness, frigidity; unconcern; lukewarmness, dullness; gravity, reserve. *Transir de* —; to benumb with cold. *Il est tout raide de* —; he is quite stiff with cold. *Avoir* —; to be cold. *Mourir de* —; to be perished with cold. *Grelotter de* —; to shiver with cold. *Prendre* —; to catch cold. *Il y a du* — *entre eux;* there is a coolness between them. *Les grands* —*s;* extreme cold; depth of winter. *A* —; coldly; in cold blood.

froid, -e, *adj.,* cold, frigid, lifeless; lukewarm, cool, indifferent, dispassionate, dull; reserved, distant. *Temps* —; cold weather. — *comme glace;* as cold as ice. — *aux yeux;*

want of pluck, funk. *Un homme —;* a cold sort of man. *Un homme de sang- —;* a cool-headed man. *Battre — à quelqu'un;* to give any one the cold shoulder. *N'avoir pas — aux yeux;* not to be afraid of one's shadow, to be game, plucky.

froidement (froad-mān), *adv.*, coldly, frigidly, lukewarmly, dispassionately, lifelessly.

froideur, *n.f.,* coldness, chilliness ; lukewarmness, indifference, coolness.

froidure, *n.f.,* coldness (of the weather); cold; (fig.) winter.

froissement (froas-mān), *n.m.,* bruising, rumpling, crumpling ; (fig.) clashing ; hurt, slight, affront ; annoyance, vexation.

froisser, *v.a.,* to bruise, to strike, to dash, to clash with ; to rumple, to crumple ; to gall, to offend, to hurt, to wound. *Je ne voudrais pas le —;* I should not like to hurt his feelings.

se froisser, *v.r.,* to take offense.

froissure, *n.f.,* bruise, rumple, crumple.

frôlement (frôl-mān), *n.m.,* grazing, rustling, rustle ; contact, touch.

frôler, *v.a.,* to graze, to touch slightly in passing ; to brush past ; to rub (seeds) in one's hands.

se frôler, *v.r.,* to graze, to touch one another, to rub up against, to brush past.

fromage, *n.m.,* cheese. *— mou ;* soft cheese. *— à la crême ;* cream-cheese. *— de cochon ;* brawn.

fromag-er, *n.m.,* **-ère,** *n.f.,* cheesemonger.

fromager, *n.m.,* cheese-mold ; (bot.) silk-cotton-tree.

fromagerie (-ma-jrī), *n.f.,* cheese-dairy, cheese-trade.

fromageu-x, -se, *adj.,* cheesy.

froment, *n.m.,* wheat. *De —;* wheaten.

fromentacé, -e, *adj.,* (bot.) frumentaceous.

fromental, *n.m.,* rye-grass ; oat-grass.

fronce, *n.f.,* (needle-work) gather ; (paper) crease.

froncement (frons-mān), *n.m.,* contraction, knitting (of the brows) ; frowning ; frown ; pursing ; gathering.

froncer, *v.a.,* to contract (the brow) ; to knit, to wrinkle ; to purse (the lips) ; to gather (needle-work).

se froncer, *v.r.,* to contract, to pucker, to wrinkle ; to grow dark (of the brow).

froncis, *n.m.,* gathering, fold.

frondaison, *n.f.,* (bot.) foliation, foliage.

fronde, *n.f.,* sling ; (surg.) bandage ; (wars of the) Fronde (French hist.).

frondée, *n.f.,* sling-shot.

fronder, *v.a.,* to sling ; to fling ; to blame, to censure ; to reflect upon, to find fault with.

fronderie (fron-drī), *n.f.,* (French hist.) riot of the Fronde ; riot, disturbance.

frondeur, *n.m.,* slinger ; censurer, fault-finder, critic ; rioter.

front, *n.m.,* forehead, brow, face, front ; boldness, impudence, brass. *La jeunesse au —riant ;* youth with its smiling face. *— d'airain ;* brazen-face. *Le — d'un bâtiment ;* the front of a building. *De —;* in front, abreast. *Faire — à ;* to face.

frontal, *n.m.,* frontal ; frontal bone ; (surg.) head-bandage.

frontal, -e, *adj.,* (anat.) frontal.

fronteau, *n.m.,* frontlet ; frontal ; (nav.) breast-work.

frontière (-ti-èr), *n.f.,* frontier, border, confine, limit.

frontispice, *n.m.,* frontispiece.

fronton, *n.m.,* (arch.) pediment, fronton ; (nav.) poop-rail.

frottage, *n.m.,* rubbing ; polishing, waxing.

frottée, *n.f.,* (pop.) a drubbing.

frottement (frot-mān), *n.m.,* rubbing, friction.

frotter, *v.a.,* to rub ; to polish, to wax, to dry-rub ; to bang, to pommel, to warm (the ear) of. *Se faire —;* to get a drubbing.

se frotter, *v.r.,* to rub one's self ; to provoke (any one) ; to come in contact with ; to meddle (with anything). *Se — les yeux ;* to rub one's eyes. *Ne vous y frottez pas ;* do not meddle with it. *Ne vous frottez pas à lui ;* do not provoke him. *Qui s'y frotte s'y pique ;* meddle, and smart for it.

frotter, *v.n.,* to rub.

frotteur, *n.m.,* rubber, dry-rubber, scrubber, floor-polisher.

frottis, *n.m.,* (paint.) light touch.

frottoir, *n.m.,* rubbing-cloth, razor-cloth, rough-towel, scrubber.

frouer, *v.n.,* to pipe, to call (birds).

frou-frou, *n.m.,* (— -—s) rustling of silk, etc.

froufrouter, *v.n.,* to rustle.

fructidor, *n.m.,* Fructidor, the twelfth month of the calendar of the first French republic, from August 18th to September 16th.

fructifère, *adj.,* (bot.) fructiferous, fruit.

fructification, *n.f.,* fructification.

fructifier, *v.n.,* to be fruitful, to fructify, to bear fruit, to thrive, to prosper.

fructueusement (-eúz-mān), *adj.,* fruitfully, profitably. [itable.

fructueu-x, -se, *adj.,* fruitful ; fertile, pro-

frugal, -e, *adj.,* frugal, sparing.

frugalement (-gal-mān), *adv.,* frugally.

frugalité, *n.f.,* frugality ; thrift.

frugivore, *adj.,* frugivorous.

fruit, *n.m.,* fruit ; dessert ; offspring ; advantage, benefit, profit ; utility ; effect, result ; (mas.) batter. *— hâtif ;* early fruit. *— indigène ;* native fruit. *— tardif ;* late fruit. *— à noyau ;* stone fruit. *— à pépin ;* kernel fruit. *Avec —;* profitably. *— sec ;* (school) blockhead, dunce. *Tirer du — de ;* to derive benefit from.

fruité, -e, *adj.,* (her.) fructed.

fruiterie (frui-trī), *n.f.,* fruit-loft, fruit-trade.

fruiti-er, -ère, *adj.,* fruit, fruit-bearing. *Arbre —;* fruit-tree. *Jardin —;* orchard, fruit garden.

fruiti-er, *n.m.,* **-ère,** *n.f.,* fruiterer, green-grocer ; fruit-woman

fruition, *n.f.,* fruition, enjoyment.

frusquin, *n.m.,* (triv.) one's all. *Son saint —;* one's all ; all one's toggery.

fruste, *adj.,* worn, defaced, corroded (of coins). *n.m.,* defaced effigy.

frustratoire, *adj.,* frustratory.

frustrer, *v.a.,* to defraud, to frustrate, to disappoint, to baulk, to foil ; to baffle. *Il a frustré ses créanciers ;* he has defrauded his creditors.

fuchsia, *n.m.,* fuchsia.

fuchsine, *n.f.,* (chem.) fuchsine, an aniline red dye.

fucus (-kus), *n.m.,* (bot.) fucus, wrack, sea-wrack.

fugace, *adj.,* fugitive ; flying ; fleeting ; transient.

fugiti-f, -ve, *adj.,* fugitive, gliding, flitting ; transient, fleeting, short-lived. *Des plaisirs —s ;* transient pleasures.

fugiti-f, *n.m.,* **-ve,** *n.f.,* fugitive, runaway, wanderer.

fugue (fug), *n.f.,* (mus.) fugue ; wild prank, lark. *Faire une —;* to take to one's heels ; to have a lark.

fuie, *n.f.,* small pigeon-house, coop.

fuir (fuyant, fui), *v.n.,* to flee, to fly ; to run away ; to elude, to shun, to avoid, to eschew ; to shift about ; to leak ; (paint.) to appear at a distance ; to recede. *Ce tonneau fuit ;* this cask leaks.

fuir, *v.a.,* to fly, to avoid, to shrink from.

se fuir, *n.f.,* to fly from one's self ; to shun, to avoid one another.

fuite, *n.f.,* flight, running away.

shunning; evasion, shift, subterfuge; running out, leakage. *Prendre la* —; to run away. *Mettre en* —; to put to flight.

fulgurant, *adj.*, (meteorology) attended with lightning; flashing, vivid, sharp.

fulguration, *n.f.*, (chem.) fulguration; lightning.

fulgurite, *n.m.*, (phys.) fulgurite.

fuligineu-x, -se, *adj.*, fuliginous.

fuliginosité, *n.f.*, fuliginosity.

fulmicoton, *n.m.*, (chem.) gun-cotton.

fulminant, -e, *adj.*, fulminant, fulminating.

fulminate, *n.m.*, (chem.) fulminate.

fulmination, *n.f.*, fulmination.

fulminer, *v.n.*, to storm, to thunder; (chem.) to fulminate, to explode.

fulminer, *v.a.*, (ecc.) to fulminate, to issue forth.

fulminique, *adj.*, (chem.) fulminic.

fumable, *adj.*, smokable.

fumade, *n.f.*, dunging.

fumage, *n.m.*, lacquering (of silver wire).

fumant, -e, *adj.*, smoking, reeking, fuming.

fumé, -e, *adj.*, smoked, manured; (fig. and pop.) done for.

fumé, *n.m.*, (engr.) smoke-proof.

fumée, *n.f.*, smoke; fume, reek; vanity; phantom, bubble; dream, vain hope. *pl.*, (hunt.) fumet, dung of deer; fumes. *Des tourbillons de* —; volumes of smoke. *S'exhaler en* —; to evaporate in smoke. *Il n'y a point de* — *sans feu*; there is no smoke without fire.

fumer, *v.n.*, to smoke; to reek, to steam; to fret and fume.

fumer, *v.a.*, to smoke, to smoke-dry; (agri.) to dung, to manure. — *des jambons*; to smoke hams. — *un champ*; to dung a field.

fumerolle, *n.f.*, fumarole.

fumeron (fu-mron), *n.m.*, half-burnt charcoal.

fumet, *n.m.*, flavor (of meat), bouquet (of wines); raciness; (hunt.) scent. *Ce vin a un bon* —; that wine has a fine flavor or bouquet.

fumeterre (fum-tèr), *n.f.*, (bot.) fumitory, fumiter.

fumeur, *n.m.*, smoker.

fumeu-x, -se, *adj.*, fumous, fumy.

fumier, *n.m.*, manure, dung, muck; dunghill; trash, rubbish. *Mourir sur un* —; to die in a ditch.

fumifuge, *adj.*, smoke-expelling.

fumigation, *n.f.*, fumigation.

fumigatoire, *adj.*, (med.) fumigating.

fumiger, *v.a.*, to fumigate.

fumiste, *n.m.*, chimney-doctor or curer; chimney-builder.

fumivore, *n.m. and adj.*, smoke-consumer; smoke-consuming.

fumoir, *n.m.*, (tech.) smoking-shed, smoking-house; (in a private house) smoking-room or smoke-room.   [manuring,

fumure, *n.f.*, (agri.) dressing; dunging,

funambule, *adj.*, funambulatory.

funambule, *n.m.*, funambulist, rope-dancer.

fune, *n.f.*, (nav.) rope, line; (pisc.) drag-rope.

funèbre, *adj.*, funeral, funereal, mournful, melancholy, dismal, ominous.

*funérailles, *n.f.pl.*, funeral, obsequies.

funéraire, *adj.*, funeral, funereal.

funeste, *adj.*, fatal; melancholy; baneful, disastrous, distressing; deadly.

funestement, *adv.*, fatally, disastrously.

funiculaire, *n.m.*, cable railway.

fungus (fon-gus), *n.m.* V. **fongus**.

funicule, *n.m.*, (bot.) funiculus, funicle.

funin, *n.m.*, (nav.) white hawser.

fur, *n.m.* *A* — *et à mesure, au* — *et à mesure*; in proportion, gradually as, as fast as. *On le paye au* — *et à mesure de l'ouvrage*; he is paid in proportion to the quantity of work done.

furet, *n.m.*, ferret. *Chasser au* —; to hunt

with a ferret. *C'est un* —; he is a ferreter or a Paul Pry.

fureter (fur-té), *v.n.*, to ferret, to ferret out, to search out, to rummage.

fureter, *v.a.*, to ferret out, to hunt after news, to be on the lookout for.

fureteur (fur-teur), *n.m.*, ferreter, Paul Pry; pryer. — *de nouvelles*; news-hunter.

fureur, *n.f.*, fury, madness, rage, wildness; mania, frenzy, passion. *Quand il entre en* —; when he gets into a fury. *Lorsque la* — *le prend*; when he is seized with a fit of passion. *Cette actrice fait* —; that actress is quite the rage. *Etre transporté de* —; to be transported with rage. *Il a la* — *du jeu*; he has a passion for gambling. *Avec* —; furiously.

furfuracé, -e, *adj.*, furfuraceous; scurvy.

furibond, -e, *n. and adj.*, furious, raging, wild; furious-looking.

furibonder, *v.n.*, to be in a rage, to fume.

furie, *n.f.*, fury, rage, heat, height; (myth.) Fury. *Entrer en* —, *se mettre en* —; to get into a rage. *Dans la* — *du combat*; in the heat of the battle. *C'est une* —; she is a very fury, or a termagant.

furieusement (-eûz-mān), *adv.*, furiously; prodigiously, with a vengeance.

furieu-x, -se, *adj.*, furious, mad, enraged, raging, fierce, savage, impetuous; monstrous, confounded, tremendous.

furin, *n.m.*, deep water, open sea, high seas.

furolles, *n.f. pl.*, fiery exhalations.

furoncle, *n.m.*, (med.) furuncle, boil; gathering; (vet.) ambury.

furti-f, -ve, *adj.*, furtive, stealthy, secret. *Entrer d'un pas* —; to steal in.

furtivement (-tiv-mān), *adv.*, furtively, stealthily, y stealth, secretly.

fusain, *n.m.*, (bot.) prickwood, spindle-tree; (for drawing) charcoal.

fusarolle, *n.f.*, (arch.) fusarole.

fuseau, *n.m.*, spindle, bobbin; distaff. *Jambes de* —; spindle legs.

fusée, *n.f.*, spindleful, bobbinful; (vet.) splint, splinter; (surg.) fistula; (artil., her., horl.) fusee; rocket; (of oars) dolphin; barrel (of a kitchen-jack). — *d'amorce*; (artil.) tube. — *courante*; line-rocket or sky-rocket. — *porte amarre*; (nav.) life-saving apparatus. *Avoir une* — *à démêler avec quelqu'un*; to have a bone to pick with anyone. *Une* — *volante*; a sky-rocket.

fuséen, -ne, *n.m.*, (artil.) rocket-gunner.

fuselé, -e, *adj.*, slender, tapering, spindle-shaped.

fuser, *v.n.*, to expand, to spread (insensibly); to liquefy, to dissolve, to meet; (fig.) to unite.

fusibilité, *n.f.*, fusibility.

fusible, *adj.*, fusible.

fusiforme, *adj.*, (bot.) spindle-shaped, fusiform.

fusil (-zi), *n.m.*, steel (to strike a light; to sharpen knives); tinder-box; musket, gun. *Pierre à* —; flint. *Il fut tué d'un coup de* —; he was killed by a musket shot. *Un coup de* —; a gun-shot, musket shot, report of a gun. — *à deux coups*; double-barreled gun. — *de chasse*; fowling-piece. — *de munition*; musket. — *à piston*; percussion-gun. — *à vent*; air-gun. — *à aiguille*; needle-gun. *Canon de* —; gun-barrel. *Portée de* —; musket range. *A portée de* —; within musket range.

fusilier, *n.m.*, fusileer.

*fusillade, *n.f.*, discharge or volley of musketry, firing, shooting.

*fusiller, *v.a.*, to shoot (down); to execute (mil.). *se fusiller*, *v.r.*, to fire at each other.

fusion, *n.f.*, fusion, melting; coalition; blending.

fusionnement, *n.m.*, amalgamation, fusion; coalescence, union.

fusionner, *v.a.* and *n.*, to unite, to amalgamate; to blend. *Se* —, *v.r.*, to coalesce.

fustet, *n.m.*, smoke-tree, Venetian sumach, fustic.

fustigation, *n.f.*, fustigation, whipping, flogging.

fustiger, *v.a.*, to flog, to scourge, to whip.

fût, *n.m.*, stock (of a gun or pistol); shaft (of a column); cask; barrel (of a drum); case (of an organ).

futaie, *n.f.*, forest of high, lofty trees; forest trees. *Demi-* —; forest of half-grown trees. *Haute* —; forest of full-grown trees. *Arbre de haute* —; full-grown forest trees. *Bois de haute* —; wood of full-grown forest trees, timber-trees, timber.

*****futaille**, *n.f.*, small cask, barrel. *— en botte;* barrel-staves.

futaine, *n.f.*, fustian.

futé, -e, *adj.*, sharp, cunning, sly.

futée, *n.f.*, joiner's putty.

futile, *adj.*, futile, frivolous, trifling.

futilité, *n.f.*, futility, trifle; frivolity.

futur, -e, *adj.*, future.

futur, *n.m.*, **-e**, *n.f.*, intended (husband, wife). *Sa —e;* his intended wife.

futur, *n.m.*, futurity; (gram.) future.

futurition, *n.f.*, futurition.

fuyant, -e, *adj.*, flying, fleeting; fleeing, retreating; receding (of the forehead); fading (of colors); (paint.) tapering. *Echelle —e;* tapering scale.

fuyard, *n.m.*, **-e**, *n.f.*, *adj.*, fugitive, runaway.

G

g, *n.m.*, the seventh letter of the alphabet, g.

gaban, *n.m.* V. **caban**.

gabarage, *n.m.*, lighterage.

gabare, *n.f.*, lighter, flat-bottomed barge, store-ship, transport-ship.

gabari or **gabarit**, *n.m.*, mold, model, build (of a ship); (rail.) carriage-gage.

gabarier, *n.m.*, lighterman; master of a store-ship.

⊙**gabatine**, *n.f.*, flam, humbug, hoax. *Donner de la — à quelqu'un;* to bamboozle any one.

gabegie, *n.f.*, (pop.) fraud, deceit.

gabelage (ga-blaj), *n. m.*, drysalting time; excise mark.

gabeler (ga-blé), *v.a.*, to dry (salt).

gabeleur (ga-bleur), *n.m.*, salt-dryer.

gabelle, *n.f.*, gabel, salt-tax, duty on salt. *Frauder la* —; to defraud the excise.

gabet, *n.m.*, vane.

gabier, *n.m.*, (nav.) top-man.

gabion, *n.m.*, (fort.) gabion.

gabionnade, *n.f.*, (milit.) gabionade.

gabionner, *v.a.*, (fort.) to cover with gabions.

gâche, *n.m.*, staple, wall-hook.

gâcher, *v.a.*, to mix mortar; to rinse; (fig.) to bungle, to make a mess of, to botch; to sell under price.

gâchette, *n.f.*, staple, spring (of a lock); follower (of a firelock).

gâcheur, *n. m.*, mason's laborer; bungler; one who sells under price (fig.). *C'est un* —; he is a bungler, a botcher.

gâcheu-x, -se, *adj.*, splashy, sloppy. *Chemin* —; sloppy road.

gâchis, *n.m.*, slop, mess, pickle, hash. *Faire du — de;* to make a hash of, to make a mess of. *Etre dans le* —, *avoir du* —; to be in a mess, in a pickle.

gade, *n.m.*, (ich.) codfish.

gadelle, *n.f.*, red-currant.

gadellier, *n.m.*, red-currant bush.

gadoïde, *n.m.*, (ich.) codfish.

gadouard, *n.m.*, nightman, scavenger.

gadoue, *n.f.*, filth, night-soil, sewage matter; (pop.) trollop.

gaélique, *n.m.* and *adj.*, Gaelic.

gaffe, *n.f.*, (nav.) gaff, boat-hook.

gaffeau, *n.m.*, small boat-hook.

gaffer, *v.a.*, (nav.) to hook.

gage, *n.m.*, pawn, pledge; security, deposit; token, testimony; stake, forfeit (play); (jur.) lien. *—s;* wages, hire, pay; (fig.) assurance, promise, proof. *Prêter sur —s;* to lend money on pawned articles. *Prêteur sur —s;* pawn-broker. *Mettre en* —; to pawn. *Donner en* —; to pawn. *Retirer un* —; to redeem a pledge. *Jouer aux —s;* to play at forfeits. *Casser aux —s;* to dismiss from service, to discharge, to cashier. *A —s;* hired, paid. *Prendre à —s;* to hire.

gager, *v.a.*, to hire; to lay, to lay a wager, to hold a wager, to bet, to stake; to pay wages to, to pay; (fig.) to predict, to be almost certain. *— avec quelqu'un, contre quelqu'un;* to lay a wager with, against any one. *— le double contre le simple;* to bet two to one. *— sa vie;* to stake one's life. *Gage que si, gage que non;* I bet it is, I bet it is not.

gagerie (gaj-rî), *n.f.* V. **saisie**.

gageu-r, *n.m.*, **-se**, *n.f.* V. **parieur**.

gageure (ga-jur), *n.f.*, bet, wager, stake, stakes. *Faire une* —; to lay a wager. *Soutenir la* —; to stick to a thing, to maintain one's ground, opinion. *La — est la preuve des sots;* betting marks the fool.

gagiste, *adj.*, (jur.) by pledge. *Créancier* —; pledgee, bailee.

gagiste, *n.m.*, hireling; (thea.) supernumerary; (jur.) pledgee, bailee.

*****gagnage**, *n.m.*, pasturage, pasture-land.

*****gagnant**, *n.m.*, **-e**, *n.f.*, winner.

*****gagnant, -e**, *adj.*, winning.

*****gagne-deniers**, *n.m.*, (——*s*), laborer, laboring man, day-laborer.

*****gagne-pain**, *n.m.*, (—) bread-winner; means of subsistence, livelihood, daily bread.

*****gagne-petit**, *n.m.*, (—) knife-grinder.

gagné, -e, *adj.*, gained, won. *Donner* —; to give in, to own one's self beaten. *Avoir ville —e;* to carry the day, to gain one's point. *Crier ville —e;* to make sure of success; to cry victory (before it is won).

*****gagner**, *v.a.*, to gain, to make; to earn, to get; to win; to prevail upon; to gain over, to bribe; to allure, to attract, to entice; to carry, to make one's self master of; to prepossess; to deserve; to seize, to come over; to reach, to overtake, to get to, to come to, to arrive at; to catch. *— sa vie avec peine;* to work hard for one's living. *Vous n'y gagnerez rien;* you will gain nothing by it. *— une bataille;* to gain a battle. *— un pari;* to win a bet. *— la partie;* to win the game. *— son procès;* to win one's case. *Je n'ai pu — cela sur lui;* I could not prevail upon him to do that. *— quelqu'un;* to win any one's money (at play). *— quelqu'un;* to draw, to win, any one over. *—la contrescarpe;* to carry the counterscarp. *J'y gagnai une pleurésie;* I caught pleurisy there. *— un rhume;* to catch a cold. *La faim me gagne;* I am beginning to feel hungry. *La nuit nous gagnera;* night will overtake us. *— le logis;* to reach home. *— du chemin, — du pays;* to gain ground; to get forward, to get on. *— du temps;* to gain time. *— du pied, — les champs;* to run away, to reach the open. *— le devant;* to get the start. *— quelqu'un de vitesse;* to get the start of any one; to be beforehand with any one. *— le dessus;* to get the better of. *— un vaisseau;* to gain ground on a ship. *— la volonté d'un cheval;* to break, to subdue, a horse.

*****se gagner**, *v.r.*, to gain, to earn, to make, to acquire; to be catching, to be contagious.

*****gagner**, *v.n.*, to gain, to make, to earn, to get,

to reach; to win (at cards, in a lottery). — à
être connu; to improve upon acquaintance. Qui
épargne gagne; a penny saved is a penny earned.

*gagneu-r, n.m., **-se**, n.f., winner, gainer.

gai, -e, adj., gay, merry, lively, exhilarating,
mirthful, cheerful; blithe, buxom, gladsome,
pleasant; (of colors) gaudy, bright, vivid; (mus.)
allegro. Vert —; light green. Temps —; exhilarating weather. Il a le vin —; he is very
merry in his cups. — comme un pinson; as gay
as a lark, as merry as a grig. Etre fort —; to be
in excellent spirits. Il est — comme un bonnet
de nuit; he is as dull as ditch-water.

gai, adv., (l.u.) gaily, merrily.

gaiac, n.m., (bot.) guaiac, guaiacum, holy-
wood, wood of life; Indian wood. Bois de —;
lignum-vitæ; (bot.) lignum-vitæ tree. Gomme,
or résine, de —; guaiacum.

gaiement or **gaîment** (ghè-mān), adv., gaily,
merrily, cheerfully, cheerily, briskly, blithely,
jovially, laughingly; willingly, heartily.

gaieté or **gaîté**, n.f., gayety, merriment,
mirth, glee; cheerfulness, blitheness, merriness,
mirthfulness, joviality, sportiveness, good humor; youthful frolic. Cheval qui a de la —;
(man.) mettlesome horse. De — de cœur; wantonly, out of sheer wantonness. Etre en —;
to be sprung.

*gaillard, -e, adj., joyful, joyous, jovial, jolly,
merry, lively; blithe, buxom, light-hearted; libertine, wanton; broad; tipsy; sprung (half-
tipsy); cool, fresh (of the wind). Nous étions
tous un peu —s; we were all rather sprung.
Vent —; cool wind.

gaillard, n.m., lively, merry, jovial fellow;
fellow, blade, jolly dog. Gros —; great big fellow. Petit —; sly dog. — résolu; determined
dog.

gaillard, n.m., (nav.) castle. — d'arrière;
quarter-deck. — d'avant; forecastle. Sur le
— d'avant; before the mast.

*gaillarde, n.f., gaillard (dance); wanton;
(print.) bourgeois.

*gaillardement, adv., joyously, merrily,
blithely; boldly, briskly.

*gaillardise, n.f., sprightliness, liveliness,
mirth, jollity; broad, free, wanton language.
Dire des —s; to make use of free, wanton language.

*gaillet, n.m., (bot.) V. caille-lait.

gain, n.m., gain, profit, emolument, lucre;
winning, gaining. — net; clear gain, net profit.
—s nuptiaux, —s de survie; (jur.) whatever is
left to the survivor (husband or wife). Amour
du —; love of lucre. — de jeu; winnings. Tirer
du — de; to profit by. Vivre de son —; to live
by one's winnings. Avoir — de cause; to carry
the day, to win. Donner — de cause à; to yield
to any one. Se retirer sur son —; to retire upon
one's winnings.

gaine, n.f., scabbard, sheath; (of a clock) case;
(bot.) ochrea; (archi.) terminal; (nav.) canvas-
edging. — de pavillon; canvas edging of an
ensign.

gainerie, n.f., sheath-making.

gainier, n.m., sheath-maker, scabbard-maker;
(bot.) judas-tree.

gaîté. V. gaieté.

gala, n.m., gala. Habits de —, full, or court,
dress.

galactomètre, n.m., lactometer.

galamment (ga-la-mān), adv., gracefully;
with gallantry, courteously, in a courtly manner;
handsomely, genteelly; gallantly, bravely, nobly.

galane, n.f., (bot.) tortoise-flower.

galanga, n.m., (bot.) galangale, galanga.

galant, -e, adj., honest, upright; civil; liberal, generous; gallant, courteous; fine, flattering,
complimentary, genteel. C'est un — homme; he
is a man of honor. Un homme —; a courteous,

polite man, ladies' man. Un billet —; a love-
letter. Humeur —e; gay humor. En — homme;
like a gentleman, gallantly. Manières —es;
gallant manners. Femme —e; courtesan, gay
woman.

galant, n.m., gallant, wooer, sweetheart,
suitor, lover; sharp fellow. Faire le —; to court
the ladies. Un vert galant; a dashing ladies'
man, a devoted admirer of the fair sex. —
d'hiver; (bot.) snow-drop.

galanterie (ga-lan-trî), n.f., politeness, gal-
lantry (towards the ladies), flattering, courteous
compliment; present; intrigue, love affair;
(med.) syphilis. Dire des —s; to flirt with. Ce
n'est qu'une —; it is but a mere compliment.

galantin, n.m., dangler, beau.

galantine, n.f., galantine; (bot.) snow-drop.
— perce-neige; snow-drop.

⊙**galantiser**, v.a., to dangle after.

⊙se **galantiser**, v.r., to admire one's self.

galaxie, n.f., (astron.) Galaxy, Milky-Way.

galbanum (-non n.m., (bot.) galbanum.
Donner du — à quelqu'un; to raise false hopes.

galbe, n.m., (arch.) graceful sweep; entasis;
swelling; outline, curve, sweep (of the face).

gale, n.f., itch; scab; mange; scurf (of vegetables, fruit). Etre méchant comme la —; to be
very spiteful. N'avoir pas la — aux dents; to be
a glutton.

galé, n.m., gale, sweet-willow, Dutch myrtle.

galéace or **galéasse**, n.f., (nav.) galeas.

galée, n.f., (print.) galley. Coulisse de —;
galley-slice.

galéga, n.m., (bot.) galega, goat's rue.

galène, n.f., (min.) galena. — de fer; wolfram. Fausse —; mock-lead.

galénique, adj., (med.) galenic, galenical.

galénisme, n.m., (med.) galenism.

galéniste, n.m., (med.) galenist.

galéobdolan, n.m., (bot.) yellow archangel.

galéopsis, n.m., (bot.) galeopsis; stinking
dead-nettle, blind-nettle.

se **galer**, v.r., (pop.) to scratch, or to rub, one's
self. v.a., to scratch, to claw.

galère, n.f., galley, row-galley; organ-builder's plane; Spanish wagon. Etre condamné aux
—s; to be condemned to the galleys. Tenir —;
to maintain a galley. Vogue la —; happen or
come what may. Qu'allait-il faire dans cette —?
what business had he there or whatever induced
him to get into that scrape? C'est une vraie —;
it is frightful drudgery.

galerie (ga-lrî), n.f., gallery, lobby, corridor;
(fig.) spectators, lookers on, company; (nav.) stern
gallery, balcony; passage; (mec.) foot-board;
(mining) level, drift, creep-hole; (thea.) gallery;
(furniture) beading, rim; (for curtains) cornice. Petite —; (arch.) heading. — principale; (arch.) body-range (of vaults); (mining)
foot-board. — d'allongement; (mining) main
level. — d'écoulement; (engineering) drainage,
drain-gallery; (mining) adit; offtake; drift;
thirl. — du faux pont; (nav.) gangway. —
en saillie; (arch.) bartizan. Faire —; to look
on (at balls); to be a wall-flower. — de tableaux;
picture-gallery.

galérien (-ri-in), n.m., galley-slave, convict.

galerne, n.f., (nav.) northwesterly wind.

galet, n.m., shuffle-board; pebble, shingle;
shingly beach; gravel; (locksmith's work) roller.

galetas (gal-tâ), n.m., garret, attic; hole, hovel.

galette, n.f., broad thin cake; sea-biscuit.
Plat comme une —; flat as a pancake.

galeu-x, -se, adj., itchy; scabby; mangy;
scurfy (of plants, trees). Chien —; mangy dog.
Brebis —se; scabby sheep. Arbre —; scurfy
tree. Qui se sent — se gratte; (prov.) if the cap
fits, wear it.

galeu-x, n.m., **-se**, n.f., mangy fellow.

galhauban, n.m., (nav.) back-stay. Rides

de —s; laniards of the back-stays. *—s volants;* preventer back-stays.

galimafrée, *n.f.*, (cook.) hotch-potch, hash, mishmash.

galimatias (-tiâ), *n.m.*, fustian, nonsense; balderdash, rigmarole, gibberish.

galion, *n.m.*, (nav.) galleon.

galiote, *n.f.*, galliot; half-galley, bark, boat, ketch, tub; (bot.) bennet. *— à bombes;* bomb-ketch. *— de Hollande;* track-scout.

galipot, *n.m.*, white resin.

galipoter, *v.a.*, (nav.) to pitch.

galle, *n.f.*, oak-apple, gall. *Noix de —;* gall-nut. *—s de chêne;* oak galls.

gallerie, *n.f.*, bee-moth.

gallican, -e (gal-li-), *adj.*, Gallican, French.

gallicanisme, *n.m.*, Gallicanism.

gallicisme (gal-li-), *n.m.*, gallicism.

gallinacé, -e, *adj.*, (orni.) gallinaceous.

gallinacés (gal-li-), *n.m.pl.*, (orni.) gallinaceæ.

galline, *n.f.*, (ich.) sapphirine garnet; swallow-fish; tub-fish.

gallique (gal-lik), *adj.m.*, (chem.) gallic. *Acide —;* gallic acid; (geog.) Gallic.

gallois, -e, *adj.*, Welsh.

gallois, *n.m.*, **-e**, *n.f.*, Welshman; Welsh-woman.

gallois, *n.m.*, Welsh language.

gallon, *n.m.*, (measure of capacity) gallon.

galoche, *n.f.*, galosh, clog; (nav.) clamp. *Un menton de —;* a long-pointed chin. *— de fer;* (nav.) hanging clamp.

galon, *n.m.*, galoon, lace, gimp; grocer's round box, officers' stripes.

galonner, *v.a.*, to lace, to adorn with gold or silver-lace. *Habit galonné;* laced coat.

galonnier, *n.m.*, gold-lace maker; silver-lace maker.

galop (ga-lô), *n.m.*, gallop, galloping; (dance) gallop; (pop.) scolding, reprimand. *Petit —;* hand gallop. *— raccourci, demi —;* canter. *Grand —* or *— de charge;* full gallop.

galopade, *n.f.*, galloping; gallop; (fam.) blowing up.

galopant, -e, *adj.*, galloping.

galoper, *v.n.*, to gallop; to run on; to run about; to dance the gallop. *Faire — un cheval;* to make a horse gallop.

galoper, *v.a.*, to gallop; to pursue; to run after; to seize upon.

galopin, *n.m.*, errand boy; young scoundrel; blackguard; rogue, imp.

⊙**galoubet**, *n.m.*, (mus.) tabor-pipe.

galuchat, *n.m.*, dog-fish skin; shark-skin.

galurin, *n.m.*, hat, tile (slang).

galvanique, *adj.*, galvanic. *Pile —;* galvanic battery, galvanic trough.

galvaniser, *v.a.*, to galvanize.

galvanisme, *n.m.*, galvanism.

galvanomètre, *n.m.*, galvanometer.

galvanoplastie, *n.f.*, electrotype. [to spoil.

galvauder, *v.a.*, to abuse; to scold; to mess,

gamache, *n.f.*, spatterdash, legging; (orni.) black cap.

gambade, *n.f.*, skip, gambol; blarney. *Payer en —s;* to pay in excuses.

gambader, *v.n.*, to gambol, to skip, to romp, to frisk.

gambette, *n.f.*, (orni.) red-shank.

gambier, *n.m.*, iron bar; gambier.

*****gambiller**, *v.n.*, to kick about, to fidget.

gambit, *n.m.*, (at chess) gambit.

gamelle, *n.f.*, (milit., nav.) porringer, platter, bowl, basin, mess. *Camarade de —;* messmate. *Manger à la même —;* to eat out of the same dish, to mess together.

gamin, *n.m.*, boy, lad, urchin, street-arab, chit; blackguard, idle boy, cub, brat.

gamine, *n.f.*, little girl, hoyden, chit of a girl; saucy baggage; hussy.

gamme, *n.f.*, (mus.) gamut, scale; (fig.) comprehension, tone; dressing. *— chromatique;* chromatic scale. *Etre hors de —;* to be off the hinges. *Changer de —;* to alter one's tone, to turn over a new leaf. *Chanter la — à quelqu'un;* to lecture any one soundly. *Mettre quelqu'un hors de —;* to put any one out, to disconcert any one. *Je lui ai répondu sur la même —;* I answered him in the same tone.

ganache, *n.f.*, lower jaw (of a horse); lout, dolt, booby, blockhead.

ganga, *n.m.*, (orni.) sand-grouse.

ganglion, *n.m.*, (surg.) ganglion; spavin.

ganglionnaire, *adj.*, (anat.) ganglionary.

gangrène, *n.f.*, gangrene, mortification; (fig.) corruption, canker.

gangrené, -e, *adj.*, gangrened, mortified; cankered, corrupt.

gangrener, *v.a.*, to gangrene, to mortify. *Se —, v.r.*, to become gangrened, to be mortified; to gangrene; (fig.) to canker.

gangreneu-x, -se, *adj.*, (med.) gangrenous, cankered.

gangue (gang), *n.f.*, gangue, vein-stone.

ganivet, *n.m.*, small penknife; (surg.) small knife.

gannaliser, *v.a.*, to embalm.

gannet, *n.m.*, (orni.) wagel.

gano (ombre), let me have the deal, "I have the king."

ganse, *n.f.*, knot, bobbin; edging, braid, gimp; cord, twist; loop (of diamonds). *— de soie;* silk-cord.

gant, *n.m.*, glove, gauntlet, gantlet. *— bourré;* fencing-glove; (fig.) merit, credit, honor. *— de Notre-Dame;* (bot.) throatwort. *Baguette à —s;* glove-stick. *Souple comme un —;* as soft as a glove. *L'amitié passe le —;* excuse my glove. *Jeter le —;* to throw down the gauntlet, to challenge. *Ramasser, relever, le —;* to take up the gauntlet, to accept the challenge. *Aller à quelqu'un comme un —;* to fit any one like a glove; to suit any one to a T. *Se donner les —s;* to attribute to one's self the success, the merit (of a thing). *Il s'en donne les —s;* he takes the credit of it.

gantelée, *n.f.*, (bot.) foxglove, throatwort. *Campanule —;* throatwort.

gantelet (gan-tlè), *n.m.*, gauntlet; (tech.) hand-leather; (surg.) glove-bandage.

ganter, *v.a.*, to glove, to fit with gloves; to fit (of gloves). *Cela me gante;* that suits me down to the ground.

se **ganter**, *v.r.*, to put on one's gloves, to get one's gloves (at so and so's).

ganterie (gan-trî), *n.f.*, glove-making; glove trade.

gant-ier, *n.m.*, **-ière**, *n.f.* (-tier, -ti-èr), glover.

garage, *n.m.*, (railways) shunting; (on rivers, canals) putting into wet dock; garage. *Voie de —;* siding.

garançage, *n.m.*, (dy.) madder dyeing.

garance, *n.f.*, (bot.) madder, madder-root. *Petite —;* squinancy. *—robée;* barked madder.

garancer, *v.a.*, (dy.) to madder.

garanceur, *n.m.*, (dy.) madder-dyer.

garancière, *n.f.*, madder-ground.

garant, *n.m.*, **-e**, *n.f.*, guarantee; surety, security; voucher; warrantor; (nav.) tackle-fall. *Se rendre —*, or *se porter —;* to warrant, to vouch for. *J'en suis —;* I answer for it, vouch for it.

garanti, *n.m.*, **-e**, *n.f.*, warrantee.

garantie (-tî), *n.f.*, warranty; guaranty; warranting, guaranteeing; making good; security, voucher, pledge. *— accessoire;* (jur.) collateral security. *Sous —*, (—-—s) counterbound. *— de droit;* (jur.) implied warranty. *Etre — à quelqu'un de quelque chose;* to pledge one's self to any one for anything.

garantir, *v.a.,* to guarantee; to warrant; to vouch for; to insure; to make good, to indemnify; to keep from; to protect, to defend, to shelter, to shield, to guard. *Je lui ai garanti le fait;* I vouched for the fact (to him). *Je ne vous le garantis pas;* I will not warrant it you. *— quelqu'un de toutes poursuites;* to secure any one against all demands. *— du froid;* to keep from cold.

se **garantir,** *v.r.,* to secure one's self, to preserve one's self, to shelter one's self; to keep one's self from; to keep clear of, to steer clear of.

garat, *n.m.,* sort of calico.

garbure, *n.f.,* (cook.) sort of thick porridge.

garce, *n.f.,* strumpet, bitch, beast.

garcette, *n.f.,* (nav.) gasket, rope's end, sinnet; cat-o'-nine-tails, cat.

garçon, *n.m.,* boy, lad; bachelor; journeyman, man; shop-boy, shopman; porter, officeporter; waiter; groom; (nav.) younker. *C'est un vieux —;* he is an old bachelor. *Faire le mauvais —;* to hector, to bluster. *Faire le beau —;* to riot, to lead a dissipated life. *Brave —;* worthy fellow; trump; dear fellow; good fellow. *Premier —;* foreman. *— tailleur;* journeyman tailor. *Vous voilà joli — !* a pretty fellow you make!

garçonner, *v.n.,* to hoiden, to romp.

garçonnet, *n.m.,* little boy.

garçonnière, *n.f.,* romp, tom-boy, hoiden; bachelor's rooms.

garde, *n.f.,* keeping; defence; watching; guard; watch; nurse; custody, charge, ward (of a lock); fly-leaf (of books); low card (at cards); (fenc.) ward, guard; (nav.) anchorwatch; care, heed. *Avoir la — d'un poste;* to have the defense of a post. *— avancée;* advance-guard. *Faire la —, être de —;* to be on guard. *Monter la —;* to mount guard. *Monter une — à quelqu'un;* to rate soundly. *Descendre la —;* to come off guard. *Relever la —;* to relieve guard. *La — montante;* the relieving guard. *La — descendante;* the coming off guard. *Officier de —;* officer on guard. *—s du corps;* life-guards. *Un corps de —;* a guardhouse. *— à vous;* attention, look out. *Faire bonne —;* to keep good watch. *d'enfants;* nurse. *Avoir en —;* to have in one's keeping. *Donner en — à quelqu'un;* to commit to any one's keeping. *Dieu vous ait en sa sainte —;* God have you in his holy keeping! *Se tenir en —;* to be upon one's guard. *Il a toujours — à carreau;* he is always guarded against, ready for every emergency. *Fruit de —;* fruit that will keep. *Prenez — à cela;* take care of that. *Prenez — de tomber;* take care not to fall. *Prendre —;* to mind. *Il prend — à un sou;* he looks at a penny. *Ne prenez pas — à moi;* do not mind me. *Il m'offense sans y prendre —;* he offends me without meaning it. *Se donner de — de quelqu'un, de quelque chose;* to be on one's guard against any one, anything. *S'en donner jusqu'à la —;* to go the whole hog. *Etre hors de —;* to be completely ignorant of an affair. *N'avoir — de faire une chose;* to be far from doing a thing; not to be fool enough to do a thing; to be unable to do a thing. *Mon chien est de bonne —;* mine is a good watch-dog. *Il n'a — de tromper, il est trop honnête homme;* he is too honest to think of cheating. *Il n'a — de venir;* he will take care to keep away. *Je n'ai — d'y aller;* I am not such a fool as to go there. *Nous n'avons — d'en douter;* far be it from us to doubt it. *Etre sur ses —s; se tenir sur ses —s;* to be upon one's guard. *A la — !* guard, guard! watch, watch!

garde, *n.m.,* keeper, warden, warder; guard, attendant; watchman. *— des sceaux;* keeper of the seals. *— des rôles; — des archives;* master of the rolls. *— national;* national guard. *— du commerce;* sheriff's officer, bailiff. *— de nuit;*

watchman. *— du corps;* life-guardsman. *Les —s du corps;* the life-guards.

garde-barrière, *n.m.f.,* (—, *or* —s—s) gatekeeper.

garde-bois, *n.m.,* (—, *or* —s—) wood-steward.

garde-boutique, *n.m.,* (—, *or* —-—s) unsaleable goods, old shopkeeper.

garde-cendre, *n.m.,* (—, *or* —-—s) fender.

garde-champêtre, *n.m.,* (—s-—s) keeper.

garde-chasse, *n.m.,* (—, *or* —s—s) gamekeeper.

garde-chevron, *n.m.,* (—-—s) barge-board, verge-board.

garde-chiourme, *n.m.,* (—, *or* —s—) overseer of convict-gangs; warder.

garde-corps, *n.m.,* (—) rail, hand-rail; (nav.) life-line; swifter (of capstans).

garde-côte, *n.m.,* (—s-—s) cruiser, guardship. —; coast-guard.

garde-crotte, *n.m.,* (—) splash-board.

garde-éclusier, *n.m.,* lock-keeper.

garde-essieu, *n.m.,* axle-guard.

garde-étalon, *n.m.,* (—, *or* —s-—s) stallionkeeper.

garde-feu, *n.m.,* (—, *or* —-—x) fire-guard; fender; match-tub.

garde-forestier, *n.m.,* (—s-—s) forester.

garde-fous, *n.m.,* (—-—s) parapet (of bridges, quays); rail, hand-rail, railings; (nav.) lifeline; swifter (of capstans).

garde-frein, *n.m.,* (—s-—s) brakesman.

garde-ligne, *n.m.,* watchman.

garde-magasin, *n.m.,* (—, *or* —s-—s) warehouse-keeper, warehouseman, store-keeper.

garde-malade, *n.m.f.,* (—, *or* —s-—s) nurse, sick nurse, attendant.

garde-manche, *n.m.,* (—-—s) half-sleeve.

garde-manger, *n.m.,* (—) buttery, larder, pantry; safe.

garde-marteau, *n.m.,* (—, *or* —s-—x) (forestry) hammer-keeper.

garde-meuble, *n.m.,* (—, *or* —-—s) storeroom, repository, lumber-room.

garde-nappe, *n.m.,* (—, *or* —-—s) tablemat.

garde-national, *n.m.,* (—s-nationaux) national guard, militiaman.

garde-nationale, *n.f.,* (—s-—s) national guard, militia.

garde-note, *n.m.,* (—s-—s) notary.

garde-pêche, *n.m.,* (—, *or* —s-—s) riverkeeper, water-bailiff.

garde-port, *n.m.,* harbor-master.

garder, *v.a.,* to keep, to preserve; to lay up, to lay by, to save; to tend, to take care of, to look after, to look to, to nurse; to guard, to protect, to defend; to observe; to keep down, to keep on (one's stomach). *Je garde cela pour moi;* I keep that for myself. *Gardez votre place;* keep your place. *— la chambre;* to keep one's room. *— la maison;* to take care of the house. *— un secret;* to keep a secret. *En donner à —;* to impose upon. *Je la lui garde bonne;* I have a rod in pickle for him. *— les bestiaux;* to tend cattle. *— les enjeux;* to keep the stakes. *— le mulet;* to dance attendance. *Dieu m'en garde;* God forbid, heaven preserve me from it! *— la bienséance;* to observe decency. *— son ban;* to complete one's period of exile. *— un malade;* to nurse a sick person. *— à vue;* not to lose sight of. *— sa dignité, son rang;* to maintain, to uphold, one's dignity, one's rank. *— sous clef;* to keep locked up. *— une médecine;* to keep a dose of medicine down.

se **garder,** *v.r.,* to keep; to keep down, to keep in; to beware; to take care not to; to abstain from, to refrain; to guard. *Gardez-vous bien de faire cela;* take care not to do that. *Gardez-vous d'ennemis;* beware of enemies. *Gardez-vous en* *bien;* do nothing of the kind. *Ce fruit ne peut se — longtemps;* this fruit cannot keep, cannot be kept, long. *Il faut savoir se — à carreau;* we must always be prepared for emergencies.

garde-robe, *n.m.,* (—--*s*) apron (to preserve).

garde-robe, *n.f.,* (—--*s*) wardrobe; water-closet, privy; (bot.) southern-wood.

garde-roues, *n.m.,* paddle-box.

garde-temps, *n.m.,* (—) time-piece, chronometer.

gardeu-r, *n m.,* **-se,** *n.f.,* keeper; herd; swineherd.

garde-vaisselle, *n.m.,* (—, *or* —*s*—) gentleman of the ewry, yeoman of the scullery.

garde-vente, *n.m.,* (—, *or* —*s*—) wood-merchant's agent.

garde-vue, *n.m.,* (—) screen, lamp-shade.

gardien, *n.m.,* **-ne,** *n.f.* (-in, -è-n), guardian; keeper; door-keeper; trustee; warden (prison); (jur.) bailiff's man, broker's man; superior (of a Franciscan convent. *— de la sainte barbe;* (nav.) gunner's mate. *— de la fosse aux lions;* boatswain's mate.

gardien, -ne, *adj.,* tutelary, guardian.

gardon, *n.m.,* (ich.) roach.

gare ! *int.,* make way; take care; look out; beware ! *— de là !* clear the way there ! *— là !* look out there ! *— de devant !* make way before ! *— l'eau ! — l'eau là-bas !* take care below ! *— le fouet ! — le bâton !* beware of the rod ! beware of the stick ! *Crier —!* to give warning.

gare, *n.f.,* wet-dock, basin; (railways) platform, terminus, station. *— d'arrivée, — de départ;* arrival, departure-platform. *— d'évitement;* (railways) siding, shunting line, loop line. *Chef de —;* (railways) station-master.

garenne (ga-rè-n), *n.f.,* warren. *— forcée, privée;* inclosed warren.

garennier, *n.m.,* warrener, warren-keeper.

garer, *v.a.,* to secure, to moor, to fasten; (rail.) to shunt. *— un bateau;* to dock a boat.

se **garer,** *v.r.,* to keep in shore (of boats); (rail.) to be shunted; to keep out of the way, to get out of the way of. *Il faut se — d'un fou;* we must get out of the way of a madman.

gargantua, *n.m.,* (—*s*) a glutton.

gargariser, *v.a.,* to gargle, to gargarize.

se **gargariser,** *v.r.,* to gargle one's throat.

gargarisme, *n.m.,* gargle; gargling.

gargotage, *n.m.,* ill-dressed victuals.

gargote, *n.f.,* cheap eating-house; cook-shop, pot-house.

gargoter, *v.n.,* to frequent pot-houses; to tipple; to cook wretchedly.

gargoti-er, *n.m.,* **-ère,** *n.f.* (-tié, -ti-èr), low pot-house keeper; publican; bad cook.

*****gargouille,** *n.f.,* gargoyle, water-spout; gutter-spout; (tech.) drain-pipe.

*****gargouillement,** *n.m.,* rumbling, rattling (of water in the stomach).

gargouiller, *v.n.,* to rattle, to rumble, to dabble, to paddle.

gargouillette, *n.f.,* water-jug.

*****gargouillis,** *n.m.,* gurgling (of water).

gargousse, *n.f.,* cannon-cartridge. *Papier à —;* cartridge-paper.

gargoussier, *n.m.,* (nav.) cartridge-box.

garigue, *n.f.,* (l.u.) waste-land, waste.

garnement, *n.m.,* good-for-nothing fellow, scapegrace, scamp, rascal.

garni, *n.m.,* furnished lodgings. *Loueur, loueuse en —;* lodging-house keeper. *Être en —, loger en —;* to live in furnished apartments.

garni, -e, *part.,* garnished; furnished, trimmed. *Maçonnerie —e;* masonry filled up (in the middle). *Chambres —es;* furnished rooms.

garnir, *v.a.,* to furnish, to provide, to stock; to ornament, to trim, to garnish, to adorn; to line, to fill, to occupy, to mount; (nav.) to rig; to quilt; to serve; (fish.) to bait. *— une maison;*

to furnish a house. *— une boutique;* to stock a shop. *— une chemise;* to trim a shirt. *— une robe;* to trim a gown; to line a gown.

se **garnir,** *v.r.,* to furnish one's self; to provide one's self with; to stock one's self; to fill, to be filled; to protect one's self.

garnisaire, *n.m.,* bailiff's man.

garnison, *n.f.,* garrison; (jur.) bailiff's men. *Troupes en —;* garrisoned troops.

garnissage, *n. m.,* trimming (of clothes); facing. *Bois de —;* facing-board.

garnisseu-r, *n.m.,* **-se,** *n.f.,* trimmer.

garniture, *n.f.,* furniture, trimming; garnish, garnishing; lining; ornaments, set; (nav.) rigging. *La —* d'une chemise;* the trimming of a shirt. *La — d'une épée;* sword ornaments. *Une — de diamants;* a set of diamonds. *— de cheminée;* set of chimney ornaments. *— de foyer;* set of fire-irons. *— de rideau;* valance. *— de toilette;* toilet-set.

garou, *n.m.,* (bot.) spurge-flax. *V.* **loup-garou.**

garrot, *n.m.,* (vet.) withers; bending lever; (surg.) tourniquet; packing-stick. *Cheval blessé sur le —;* (vet.) horse wither-wrung; (fig.) injured in one's reputation.

garrotte, *n.f.,* garrote, strangulation.

garrotter, *v.a.,* to bind, to tie down; to pinion; to handcuff; to garrote *or* strangle (in Spain).

garrulité, *n.f.,* (l.u.) garrulity, loquacity.

gars, *n.m.,* lad, stripling, younker fellow.

garus, *n.m.,* Garus (elixir).

gas, *n.m. V.* **gars.**

gascon, -ne, *adj.,* Gascon.

gascon, *n.m.,* **-ne,** *n.f.,* Gascon; boaster, braggart.

gascon, *n.m.,* Gascon language.

gasconisme, *n.m.,* Gasconism.

gasconnade, *n.f.,* gasconade, boast, brag.

gasconner, *v.n.,* to speak Gascon, to speak with a Gascon accent; to gasconade, to brag.

*****gaspillage,** *n.m.,* disorder; waste, wasting, squandering.

*****gaspiller,** *v.a.,* to confuse, to throw into disorder; to waste, to lavish, to squander, to consume, to fritter away. *— son temps;* to waste one's time. *— son argent;* to squander, to fritter away one's money.

*****gaspilleu-r,** *n.m.,* **-se,** *n.f.,* waster, squanderer, spendthrift.

gaster (-tèr), *n.m.,* (med.) stomach.

gastéropodes, *n.m. pl.,* (zool.) gasteropods.

gastralgie, *n.f.,* (med.) gastralgia.

gastriloque, *n.m.,* (l.u.). *V.* **ventriloque.**

gastrique, *adj.,* gastric, of the stomach.

gastrite, *n.f.,* gastritis.

gastro, a prefix from Gr., gastro.

gastrologie, *n.f.,* gastrology.

gastronome, *n.m.,* gastronomist.

gastronomie, *n.f.,* gastronomy.

gastronomique, *adj.,* gastronomic.

gastroraphie, *n.f.,* (surg.) gastroraphy.

gastrotomie, *n.f.,* (surg.) gastrotomy.

gât, *n.m.,* (nav.) landing; steps, stairs.

gatan, *n.m.,* razor-fish.

gâté, -e, *adj., part.,* spoiled, damaged, tainted. *Viande —e;* tainted meat. *Enfant —;* spoiled child.

gâteau, *n.m.,* cake; honey-comb; (surg.) pledget. *— des rois;* Twelfth-night cake. *— de miel;* honey-comb. *Avoir part au —;* to share in the booty, to have a finger in the pie. *Partager le —;* to go halves.

gâte-enfants, *n.m.f.,* (—) spoiler of children.

gâte-maison, *n.m.f.,* too good a servant.

gâte-métier, *n.m.f.,* (—, *or* —--*s*) person who spoils a trade; underseller.

gâte-papier, *n.m.f.,* (—) scribbler, paltry writer.

gâte-pâte, *n.m.f.*, (—) bad pastry-cook, bad baker ; (fig.) bungler, botcher.

gâter, *v.a.*, to spoil, to damage, to hurt, to injure, to impair, to mar ; to taint, to corrupt, to deprave, to make worse. *La grêle a gâté les vignes ;* the hail has damaged the vines. *Le soleil gâte la viande ;* the sun taints meat. — *du papier ;* to waste *or* blot paper, to scribble. *se gâter, v.r.,* to taint, to spoil ; to be spoiled, to become corrupt ; to break up (of weather). *Ce vin commence à se — ;* that wine is beginning to spoil. *Le temps se gâte ;* the weather is breaking up.

gâterie (gâ-trî), *n.f.*, excessive humoring ; foolish indulgence.

gâte-sauce, *n.m.*, (—, *or* — -—*s*) scullion ; (b.s.) bad cook.

gâte-tout, *n.m.f.*, (—) spoil-all, mar-all.

gâteu-r, *n.m.*, **-se**, *n.f.*, spoiler, waster.

gâteuse, *n.f.*, ulster.

gâteu-x, *n.m.*, **-se**, *n.f.*, idiot (one who has lost control over the excretory organs).

gatte, *n.f.*, (nav.) manger.

gattilier, *n.m.*, (bot.) chaste-tree, vitex.

gauche (gôsh), *adj.*, left ; crooked ; clumsy, awkward. *Le côté —;* the left side. *La main —;* the left hand. *Un air —;* an awkward air. *Des manières —s ;* clumsy manners.

gauche, *n.f.*, left-hand ; left-hand side ; left side ; (milit.) left wing, left flank, left wheel. *A —;* on the left, to the left. *Tournez à — ;* turn to the left. *Donner à — ;* to be in the wrong box.

gauchement (gôsh-mān), *adv.*, awkwardly, uncouthly, clumsily.

gauch-er, -ère, *n.* and *adj.,* left-handed person ; left-handed.

gaucherie (gô-shrî), *n.f.*, awkwardness, clumsiness ; clumsy action ; blunder.

gauchir, *v.n.*, to turn aside, to step aside, to flinch ; to become warped ; (fig.) to dodge, to prevaricate.

gauchir, *v.a.*, to warp ; to pervert. *se gauchir, v.r.,* to warp.

gauchissement, *n.m.*, (carp.) warping.

gaudage, *n.m.*, dyeing with weld.

gaude, *n.f.*, (bot.) dyer's-weed ; weld. *pl.*, hasty-pudding ; hominy.

se gaudir, v.r., to rejoice ; to make merry, to make fun *or* game of.

gaudissard, *n.m.*, bagman ; wag.

gaudisserie, *n.f.*, waggishness ; broad humor ; joke, jest.

gaudriole, *n.f.*, broad joke, coarse joke.

⊙**gaudron**, *n.m.* V. **godron**.

gaudronné, -e, *adj.*, (bot.) repand.

gaufrage, *n.m.*, goffering.

gaufre, *n.f.*, honey-comb ; waffle (thin cake) ; victim ; dupe.

gaufrer, *v.a.*, to goffer, to crimp, to emboss, to plait, to flute. *Fer à —;* goffering iron.

gaufreu-r, *n.m.*, **-se**, *n.f.*, gofferer.

gaufrier, *n.m.*, waffle-iron, goffer-iron.

gaufrure, *n.f.*, goffering.

gaule, *n.f.*, pole ; switch, rod, staff.

gauler, *v.a.*, to beat trees with a long pole, to knock down (fruit).

gaulette, *n.f.*, small switch, small pole.

gaulis, *n.m.*, small wood, chip-wood ; copse, coppice.

gaulois, -e, *adj.*, Gaulish, Gallic ; (fig.) old-fashioned.

gaulois, *n.m.*, **-e**, *n.f.*, Gaul ; plain talker.

gaulois, *n.m.*, Gallic language. *C'est du — ;* (fig.) it is an old-fashioned expression.

gaupe, *n.f.*, slut, trollop.

se gausser, v.r., (pop.) to banter, to jeer, to make game of. *Il se gausse de tout le monde ;* he makes game of everybody. V. **gosser**.

gausserie (gô-srî), *n.f.*, bantering, banter.

gausseu-r, *n.m.*, **-se**, *n.f.*, banterer.

gausseu-r, -se, *adj.*, bantering, mocking.

gavauche, *n.m.*, (nav.) disorder, confusion.

gave, *n.m.*, torrent, mountain stream (in the Pyrenees).

gaver, *v.a.*, (pop.) to cram, to gorge (with food). *Se —, v.r.*, to cram one's self with food, to gorge.

gavion *or* **gaviot**, *n.m.*, (pop.) throat.

gavotte, *n.f.*, gavotte (kind of dance).

gayac, *n.m.* V. **gaïac**.

gaz (gâz), *n.m.*, gas, gas-light, gas-lighting ; (med.) flatus, wind. — *étouffant ;* choke-damp. *Eclairage au — ;* lighting with gas. *Un conduit de — ;* a gas-pipe. *Bec de —;* gas-burner. *Jet de —;* jet of gas. *Usine à —;* gas-works. *Fermer le bec de —;* to turn off the gas. *Ouvrir le bec de —;* to turn on the gas. *Réservoir de —;* gas-holder. *Au —;* by gas-light. *Lustre à —;* gasalier. *Compteur à —;* gas-meter.

gaze, *n.f.*, gauze, vail, gloss.

gazé, -e, *adj.*, vailed, softened, toned down. *n.m.*, hawthorn-butterfly.

gazéifier, *v.a.*, (chem.) to gasify.

se gazéifier, v.r., to gasify.

gazéiforme, *adj.*, (chem.) gasiform.

gazelle, *n.f.*, gazelle.

gazer, *v.a.*, to cover with gauze ; to gloss over, to tone down.

gazette, *n.f.*, gazette ; newspaper ; (fig.) news-monger, blab.

gazeu-x, -se, *adj.*, (chem.) gaseous ; aerated. *Limonade —se ;* effervescing lemonade.

gazier, *n.m.f.*, gauze-maker. *m.*, gas-fitter.

gazomètre, *n.m.*, gasometer.

gazométrie, *n.f.*, gasometry.

gazon, *n.m.*, grass ; turf ; sward, grass-plot ; lawn ; (fort.) gazon. *Parterre de —;* grass-plot. *Abonder en —;* to abound in grass.

gazonnant, *adj.*, (gard.) producing grass.

gazonnement *or* **gazonnage** (ga-zo-n-mān), *n.m.*, turfing.

gazonner, *v.a.*, to cover with turf, to turf.

*****gazouillement**, *n.m.*, chirping, warbling (of birds) ; purling, bubbling (of a brook) ; prattle.

*****gazouiller**, *v.n.*, to chirp, to warble ; to prattle ; to twitter ; to lisp ; to murmur. *Cet enfant commence à — ;* that child begins to prattle.

gazouillis, *n.m.*, warbling, twitter.

geai (jè), *n.m.*, (orni.) jay.

géant, *n.m.*, **-e**, *n.f.*, giant, giantess. *Aller à pas de — ;* to stride like a giant.

géant, -e, *adj.*, gigantic.

gecko, *n.m.*, (zool.) gecko.

géhenne (-è-n), *n.f.*, gehenna, hell.

geindre (geignant, geint), *v.n.*, to whine, to moan ; to complain.

gélatine, *n.f.*, gelatine.

gélatineu-x, -se, *adj.*, gelatinous.

gélatinifier, *v.a.*, to gelatinate.

se gélatinifier, v.r., to gelatinate.

gelé, -e, *part.*, frozen, frost-bitten. *Il a le bec —;* he is tongue-tied. *Je suis —;* I am quite frozen. *La rivière a —;* the river is frozen. *Les doigts lui ont —;* his fingers were frozen.

gelée, *n.f.*, frost ; (cook.) jelly. — *blanche ;* white frost, hoar-frost. — *de groseille ;* currant jelly.

geler, *v.a.*, to freeze.

se geler, v.r., to freeze.

geler, *v.n.*, to freeze. *Il gèle ;* it freezes. *Il gèle à pierre fendre ;* it is freezing very hard.

géli-f, -ve, *adj.*, split, cracked by frost.

⊙**geline**, *n.f.*, hen, fat hen.

gelinotte, *n.f.*, young fat pullet, barn-door fowl. — *des bois ;* hazel-hen.

gélivure, *n.f.*, crack (caused by frost).

gémeaux, *n.m.pl.*, (astron.) Gemini, the Twins ; (agri.) meadows mowed twice a year.

géminé, -e, *adj.*, (bot.) geminate, double ; (jur.) reiterated.

gémir, *v.n.*, to groan, to moan, to sigh ; to lament, to bewail ; to grieve ; to repine. — *de douleur ;* to groan with pain. — *sous le joug ;* to groan under the yoke. *Je gémis de votre erreur ;* I bewail your error. *Faire — la presse ;* to print away ; to keep the press going.

gémissant, -e, *adj.*, moaning, lamenting.

gémissement (gé-mis-mān), *n.m.*, groan, moan, wail ; complaint, lamentation ; groaning, moaning, bewailing. *Pousser un —;* to utter a groan.

gemmation (jèm-ma-), *n.f.*, gemmation ; budding.

gemme, -e, *adj.*, of gems. *Des pierres —s;* gems. *Sel —;* rock-salt.

gemme, *n.f.*, (bot.) gem ; leaf-bud ; (min.) gem.

gemmer, *v.n.*, to bud, to germinate.

gemmer, *v.a.*, to tap a tree (for resin).

gemmiforme, *adj.*, (bot.) bud-shaped.

gemmipare (jèm-mi-), *adj.*, gemmiparous.

gémonies, *n.f.pl.*, (antiq.) gemoniæ. (fig.) pillory, gibbet.

génal, *adj.*, (anat.) of the cheeks.

gênant, -e, *adj.*, troublesome, embarrassing, uneasy, difficult ; incommodious, awkward ; inconvenient.

gencive, *n.f.*, gum (of the teeth).

gendarme, *n.m.*, (armed) policeman ; ⊙ man-at-arms; constable; gendarme ; virago (woman) ; (b. s.) thief-taker; flaw (in a diamond). *pl.*, sparks. *C'est un vrai —;* she is a regular termagant.

⊙**gendarmer**, *v.a.*, to dragoon.

se **gendarmer**, *v.r.*, to resist, to struggle ; to fly into a passion ; to get into a rage.

gendarmerie, *n. f.*, gendarmerie (armed) police ; constabulary (French horse and foot police).

gendarmeux, -se, *adj.*, flawy, spotty.

gendre, *n.m.*, son-in-law.

gêne, *n.f.*, ⊙rack, torture ; constraint, difficulty, uneasiness ; inconvenience, annoyance, difficulty, trouble ; torment; narrow circumstances ; embarrassment, pecuniary difficulty, straits, penury. *Etre à la —;* to be uneasy, uncomfortable. *Sans —;* unconstrained, unrestrained, free, familiar, offhand ; at home. *Mettre à la —;* to put any one to trouble. *Se mettre l'esprit à la —;* to rack one's brains. *Etre sans —;* to be free and easy. *Se donner de la — pour quelqꝏe chose ;* to make one's self uneasy about anything. *Connaître la —;* to know what want is. *Où il y a de la — il n'y a pas de plaisir ;* there's nothing like making one's self at home.

gêné, -e, *part.*, constrained, uneasy ; short of cash. *Air —;* constrained air. *N'être pas —;* to be too free, too familiar. *Il est plus gênant que —;* he doesn't mind being unpleasant to others.

généalogie, *n.f.*, genealogy ; pedigree.

généalogique, *adj.*, genealogical.

généalogiste, *n.m.*, genealogist.

génépi *or* **génipi**, *n.m.*, (bot.) artemisia ; Alpine wormwood.

gêner, *v.a.*, to impede, to obstruct ; to thwart; to trouble, to inconvenience, to incommode, to be in the way of any one ; to put restraint upon ; to disturb, to embarrass, to annoy ; to cramp, to pinch, to hurt. *Ce soulier me gêne ;* this shoe pinches me. *La présence de cet homme me gênait ;* the presence of that man annoyed me. *Il me gêne dans mes projets ;* he thwarts me in my plans. *Est ce que je vous gêne ?* am I in your way ?

se **gêner**, *v.r.*, to constrain one's self, to put one's self out of the way, to put one's self to inconvenience. *On ne doit pas se — entre amis ;* there is no need of ceremony among friends. *Ne*

pas se —; not to hesitate, not to mince matters. *Ne vous gênez pas ;* don't stand upon ceremony ; make yourself quite at home.

général, *n.m.*, (log., milit.) general. — *de brigade ;* brigadier-general. — *de division ;* lieutenant-general ; major-general. *En —;* in general, generally.

général, -e, *adj.*, general.

généralat, *n.m.*, generalship.

générale, *n.f.*, (milit.) fire-drum, general.

généralement (-ral-mān), *adv.*, generally, in general.

généralisat-eur, -rice, *adj.*, generalizing.

généralisation, *n.f.*, generalization.

généraliser, *v.a.*, to generalize.

généralissime, *n.m.*, generalissimo, commander-in-chief.

généralité, *n.f.*, generality.

générat-eur, -rice, *adj.*, generating, generative, genial.

générat-eur, -rice, *n.f.*, generator.

générati-f, -ve, *adj.*, generative.

génération, *n.f.*, generation, descent, production ; genesis. *De — en —;* from generation to generation.

généreusement (-reûz-mān), *adv.*, generously, bountifully, munificently ; stoutly, bravely.

généreu-x, -se, *adj.*, generous, noble ; liberal, benevolent, bountiful ; courageous.

générique, *adj.*, generic.

générosité, *n.f.*, generosity, liberality, benevolence.

genèse, *n.f.*, Genesis.

genestrolle, *n.f.*, (bot.) dyer's-broom, greenweed.

genêt, *n.m.*, (bot.) broom. — *épineux. V.* ajonc.

genet, *n.m.*, jennet ; Spanish horse. [poem.

généthliaque, *n.m.*, genethliac, birthday

généthliaque, *adj.*, genethliacal.

genêtière, *n.f.*, broom-field.

genêtrelle, *n.f.*, greenweed.

genette, *n.f.*, (mam.) genet, ring-curb-bit, civet ; (bot.) genista.

à la **genette**, *adv.*, with short stirrups.

génevois, -e, *n.* and *adj.*, Genevese.

genévrette, *n.f.*, juniper wine.

genévrier, *n.m.*, juniper-tree.

géniculé, -e, *adj.*, (bot.) geniculated.

génie, *n.m.*, genius ; spirit; nature ; bent, talent ; (milit.) engineers. *Suivre son —;* to follow the bent of one's genius. *Le — d'une langue ;* the genius of a language. *Le corps du —;* (milit.) the engineers. *Soldat du —;* sapper and miner. *Garde du —;* barrack-master.

genièvre, *n.m.*, juniper-berry ; juniper-tree; gin.

génisse, *n.f.*, heifer.

génital, -e, *adj.*, genital.

géniteur, *n.m.*, (b.s.) generator.

génitif, *n.m.*, (gram.) genitive. *Au —;* in the genitive case.

⊙**géniture**, *n.f.*, (jest.) offspring.

génois, -e, *n.* and *adj.*, Genoese.

genope, *n.f.*, (nav.) seizing, lashing, belaying.

genoper, *v.a.*, (nav.) to seize, to lash, to belay.

genou, *n.m.*, knee ; (nav.) lower futtock ; (mec.) ball and socket. — *de —à —;* to be on one's knees. *Se mettre à —x ;* to kneel. *Tenir un enfant sur ses —x ;* to hold a child on one's lap. *Fléchir le —;* to bend the knee. *Tomber aux —x de quelqu'un ;* to fall at any one's feet. — *de la rame ;* arm of an oar.

*****genouillère**, *n.f.*, knee-piece (of armor) ; top (of a boot) ; knee-cap ; pulley-piece.

génovéfain, *n.m.*, canon of St. Geneviève.

genre, *n.m.*, genus ; species ; kind, sort ; fashion, taste ; style, manner ; course, line ; airs, affectation, mannerism, attitudinizing; gender; (paint.) genre. *Le* — *humain;* mankind. *Un* — *de vie;* a course of life. *Il a un* — *qui lui est propre;* he has a style peculiar to himself. *Le* — *tragique;* tragedy. *Le* — *comique;* comedy. *De bon* —; gentlemanly, ladylike. *De mauvais* —; ungentlemanly, unladylike.

gens (jän), *n.m.*, people, persons, folk, men, hands; domestics, servants, attendants. *Ce sont des* — *fort dangereux, de fort dangereuses* —; they are very dangerous people. *Des* — *fins, de fines* —; cunning folk. *Tous les* — *de bien;* all honest people. *Tous les habiles* —; all clever people. *Toutes les vieilles* —; all old people. *Les petites* —; humble people. — *de lettres;* men of letters. — *de guerre;* soldiers. — *d'église;* churchmen. — *d'affaires;* men of business. *Le droit des* —; the law of nations. *Il y a* — *et* —; there are people of all sorts. *Les vieilles* — *sont prudents;* old people are prudent. *A* — *de village trompette de bois;* rough tools for rough work. [*Gens* requires all adjectives that follow it to be in the *masculine,* and all those that precede it to be in the *feminine.* The masculine, however, is used before *gens,* when the word *tous* alone precedes it, or when *tous* is accompanied by an adjective having the same termination for both genders. When *gens* more particularly refers to men, as in the expressions, *gens de lettres, gens de loi,* etc., the adjectives that precede *gens* are also put in the masculine.]

gent, *n.f.,* (jest.) nation, people, race, tribe. *La* — *marécageuse;* the marshy tribe.

gentiane, *n.f.,* (bot.) gentian.

gentianelle, *n.f.,* (bot.) gentianella.

gentil (-ti), *n.* and *adj.m.,* Gentile.

gentil, **-le**, *adj.,* pretty, nice, amiable; graceful, pleasing; (iron.) ridiculous, pretty, fine. *Un* — *métier!* a fine occupation, indeed! *Un* — *enfant;* a pretty, amiable child.

gentil, *n.m.,* **-le**, *n.f.,* pretty person. *Faire le* —; to affect graceful manners.

*gentilhomme (-ti-iom), *n.m.,* (*gentilshommes*) (-ti-zom), nobleman, gentleman. — *à lièvre;* poor country squire.

*gentilhommerie (-ti-io-mrî), *n.f.,* nobility, gentry, gentility.

*gentilhommière (-ti-io-mièr), *n.f.,* small country-seat.

gentilité, *n.f.,* or **gentilisme**, *n.m.,* Gentile nations; heathenism.

*gentilâtre, *n.m.,* lordling; squireen.

*gentillesse, *n.f.,* prettiness, gracefulness; pretty thing, pretty thought; (b.s.) pretty trick; fine trick. *Voilà de vos* —*s;* these are some of your fine tricks.

gentillet, **-te**, *adj.,* rather nice; rather pretty.

gentiment, *adv.,* prettily, gracefully; (iron.) nicely, like a good boy or girl.

génuflexion, *n.f.,* genuflexion, kneeling.

géocentrique, *adj.,* (astron.) geocentric.

géodésie, *n.f.,* geodesy.

géodésique, *adj.,* geodesical.

géognosie, *n.f.,* geognosy.

géognostique, *adj.,* geognostic.

géogonie, *n.f.,* geogony.

géogonique, *adj.,* geogony.

géographe, *n.m.,* geographer. *Ingénieur-* —; (—*s*—*s*) geographical engineer.

géographie, *n.f.,* geography. *Cartes de* —; (geographical) maps.

géographique, *adj.,* geographical.

géographiquement, *adv.,* geographically.

geôlage (jô-), *n.m.,* gaol fee.

geôle (jôl), *n.f.,* gaol, jail, prison.

geôlier (jô-lié), *n.m.,* gaoler, jailer.

geôlière, *n.f.,* gaoler's wife.

géologie, *n.f.,* geology.

géologique, *adj.,* geological.

géologue (-log), *n.m.,* geologist.

géomance *or* **géomancie**, *n.f.,* geomancy.

géomancien (-ci-in), *n.m.,* geomancer.

géométral, **-e**, *adj.,* geometrical. *Plan* —; ground-plan.

géométralement (-tral-män), *adv.,* geometrically.

géomètre, *n.m.,* geometrician, geometer.

géométrie, *n.f.,* geometry.

géométrique, *adj.,* geometrical.

géométriquement (-trik-män), *adv.,* geometrically.

géoponique, *adj.,* geoponic.

géorama, *n.m.,* georama.

géorgien, **-ne**, *n.* and *adj.,* Georgian.

géorgique, *adj.,* Georgic.

géorgiques, *n.f.pl.,* Vergil's Georgics.

géoscopie, *n.f.,* geoscopy.

gérance, *n.f.,* management; managership; editorship.

géranium (-om), *n.m.,* (bot.) geranium.

gérant, *n.m.,* manager, conductor; (com.) principal; responsible editor. — *à bord;* (nav.) ship's husband.

gerbe, *n.f.,* sheaf; bundle, lot.

gerbée, *n.f.,* bundle of straw (unthrashed).

gerber, *v.a.,* to make up, to bind into sheaves. — *des tonneaux;* to pile casks upon each other.

gerbier, *n.m.,* corn-stack.

gerbière, *n.f.,* harvest-wagon.

gerbillon, *n.m.,* small sheaf.

gerboise, *n.f.,* (mam.) jumping mouse.

gerce, *n.f.,* (ent.) (pop.) tinea, clothes-moth; chap, crack.

gercer, *v.a.,* to chap; to crack. *Le froid gerce les lèvres;* cold weather chaps the lips. *se* **gercer**, *v.r.,* to chap, to crack.

gercer, *v.n.,* to chap, to crack.

gerçure, *n.f.,* chap; crack; chink, cleft.

gérer, *v.a.,* to manage, to administer, to conduct.

gerfaut, *n.m.,* (orni.) gerfalcon.

germain, **-e**, *adj.,* german, first. *Cousin* —, *cousine* —*e;* cousin-german, first-cousin. *Issu de* —; second-cousin. *Il a le* — *sur moi;* he is cousin-german to my father, to my mother.

germain, *n.m.,* -**e**, *n.f.,* (jur.) brother, sister (of the whole blood).

germain, **-e**, *n.* and *adj.,* German (native of ancient Germany).

germandrée, *n.f.,* (bot.) germander.

germanique, *adj.,* Germanic.

germanisme, *n.m.,* germanism.

germe, *n.m.,* germ; bud; seed; sprout, shoot; (bot.) ovarium. *Pousser des* —*s;* to sprout.

germer, *v.n.,* to shoot, to spring up, to sprout, to bud. *Le blé commence à* —; the corn is beginning to spring up.

germinal, **-e**, *adj.,* germinal.

germinal, *n.m.,* Germinal, the seventh month of the calendar of the first French republic, from March 21st to April 19th.

germinatif, **-ve**, *adj.,* germinal.

germination, *n.f.,* (bot.) germination.

germoir, *n.m.,* malt-house.

géroflier, *n.m.,* clove-tree.

gérondif, *n.m.,* (gram.) gerund.

géronte, *n.m.,* (—*s*) silly old man, old dotard.

gerzeau, *n.m.,* (bot.) (pop.) fennel-flower.

gésier, *n.m.,* gizzard; pannel (of a hawk).

☉**gésir**, *v.n.,* to lie. *Ci-gît;* here lies. *C'est là que gît le lièvre;* there's the rub; that's the main point.

gesse, *n.f.,* (bot.) vetch.

gestation, *n.f.,* gestation. [Pope's sedan chair.

gestatoire, *adj.,* gestatory. *Chaise* —;

geste, *n.m.,* gesture; action; movement, sign. *Faire des* —*s;* to gesticulate.

geste, *n.f.,* (old French literature). *Chanson de* —; heroic poem.

⊙**gestes**, *n.m.pl.*, great deeds, heroic achievements, exploits.

gesticulat-eur, *n.m.*, **-rice**, *n.f.*, gesticulator.

gesticulation, *n.f.*, gesticulation.

gesticuler, *v.n.*, to gesticulate.

gestion, *n.f.*, management, administration, conduct.

geyser, *n.m.*, (—*s*) geyser.

giaour, *n.m.*, (—*s*) giaour.

gibbeu-x, **-se**, *adj.*, gibbous, convex.

gibbon, *n.m.*, (mam.) gibbon, ape.

gibbosité, *n.f.*, gibbosity, gibbousness, hunch.

gibecière (ji-bsièr), *n.f.*, game-bag; pouch, bag, poke; juggler's pocket. *Tours de* —; leger-de-main, or sleight of hand tricks.

gibelet, *n.m.*, gimlet, borer. *Il a un coup de* —; he is cracked.

gibelin, *n.m.*, (Italian hist.) Ghibelline.

gibelotte, *n.f.*, (cook.) rabbit-stew.

giberne, *n.f.*, cartridge-box.

gibet, *n.m.*, gibbet, gallows.

gibier, *n.m.*, game. — *à plume*; feathered game. *Gros* —; forest game. *Menu* —; small game. — *dérobé*; poached game. — *de galère*, — *de potence*, — *de grève*; Newgate-bird, jail-bird, gallows-bird, gallows-swinger. *Pièce de* —; head of game. *Ce n'est pas là votre* —; that is no affair of yours. *Ce n'est pas de son* —; that is not his fancy; that is beyond his capacity.

giboulée, *n.f.*, shower, hail-shower. — *de mars*; April shower.

giboyer, *v.n.*, to go out shooting; to hunt, to shoot; to poach.

giboyeur, *n.m.*, fowler, sportsman; dealer in game.

giboyeu-x, **-se**, *adj.*, full of game.

gibus, *n.m.*, crush-hat; opera-hat, top-hat.

gifle, *n.f.*, slap in the face; box on the ear.

gifler, *v.a.*, to slap in the face; to box the ears of.

gigantesque, *adj.*, gigantic, colossal.

gigogne, *n.f.* *Mère* —; woman with many children. *La mère* —; the old woman who lived "in a shoe."

gigot, *n.m.*, leg of mutton. *pl.*, (man.) hind legs of a horse; legs, shanks (of persons). *Etendre ses* —*s*; to stretch one's legs. *Des manches à* —; leg of mutton sleeves.

gigotté, **-e**, *adj.*, strong-limbed.

gigotter, *v.n.*, to kick about; (fig.) to fidget, to dance, to cut capers.

gigue (jig), *n.f.*, shank; jig.

gilet, *n.m.*, waistcoat, vest. — *de flanelle*; flannel waistcoat. — *d'armes*; fencing-jacket. — *de force*; strait-jacket. — *de sauvetage*; life-jacket. *Donner un* — *à*; (fencing) to beat outright.

gileti-er, *n.m.*, **-ère**, *n.f.*, waistcoat maker.

gille, *n.m.*, clown, ninny, simpleton; large fishing-net. *Faire* —; to run away, to become bankrupt.

gimblette, *n.f.*, ring-biscuit, jam-roll.

gingas, *n.m.*, ticking, tick.

gingembre, *n.m.*, (bot.) ginger.

gingeolier, *n.m.*, (bot.) lote, jujube-tree.

ginglyme, *n.m.*, hinge, joint; (anat.) hinge-joint.

ginguet, **-te** (-ghè, -ghèt), *adj.*, weak, sorry, worthless, short, scanty. *Habit* —; scanty coat. *Esprit, style* —; frivolous mind, frivolous style.

ginguet, *n.m.*, weak or thin wine, bad wine.

ginseng, *n.m.*, (pharm.) ginseng.

gipsy, *n.m.f.*, (*gipsies*) gipsy.

girafe, *n.f.*, (mam.) giraffe, camelopard.

girande, *n.f.*, girande (cluster of water-jets); bouquet (fireworks).

girandole, *n.f.*, girandole, branched candle-stick; (of gems) sprig; (fireworks) girandole; (bot.) whorl.

girasol, *n.m.*, (min.) girasol.

giration, *n.f.*, gyration.

giratoire, *adj.*, gyral, gyratory.

giraumon *or* **giraumont**, *n.m.*, (bot.) pumpkin.

girofle, *n.m.*, (bot.) clove. *Un clou de* —; a clove. *Griffe de* —; clove-stalk.

giroflée, *n.f.*, gilliflower, stock. — *jaune*; wallflower. *Une* — *à cinq feuilles*; (pop.) slap in the face.

giroflée, *adj.*, of clove. *Cannelle* —; (com.) clove-bark.

giroflier, *n.m.*, (bot.) clove-tree.

girolle, *n.f.*, edible agaric.

giron, *n.m.*, lap; (arch.) tread (of a step); (her.) gyron. *Le* — *de l'église*; the bosom, pale, of the Church.

gironde, *n.f.*, (French hist.) Girondist party.

girondin, *n.m.*, (French hist.) Girondist.

gironné, *adj.*, rounded; (her.) gyronny.

girouette, *n.f.*, weathercock, vane. — *à fumée*; smoke-disperser. *Fer de* —; spindle of a vane. *C'est une* —; he is a mere weathercock, a mere time-server.

gisant, **-e**, *adj.*, lying (ill, dead); stretched. *Meule* —*e*; bed, nether millstone.

gisement (jiz-mān), *n.m.*, (nav.) bearing; (min.) layer, bed. —*s houillers*; coal-measures.

gisent, *third person pl. present indicative of old verb gésir*; lie, are lying.

gît, *third person sing. present indicative of old verb gésir*; lies (sick, dead). *Son cadavre* — *sur la terre*; his body lies on the ground. *Ci* —; here lies.

gitan-o, *n.m.*, **-a**, *n.f.*, (—*s*) Spanish gipsy.

gîte, *n.m.*, home, lodging-place, refuge, shelter; lodging, resting-place, quarters; nether millstone; form, seat (of hares); (mining) layer, stratum, bed, deposit. *Un lièvre va toujours mourir au* —; a person likes to come home to die. *Dernier* —; long home; (of beef) round. — *à la noix*; silver-side.

gîter, *v.a.*, to lodge, to house, to put up, to shelter.

se **gîter**, *v.r.*, to lodge, to sleep; to shelter one's self, to take up one's abode.

givre, *n.m.*, hoar-frost, rime.

givre, *n.f.*, (her.) serpent; wyvern.

givré, **-e**, *adj.*, rimy, white with frost.

glabre, *adj.*, (bot.) glabrous, smooth, without down.

glaçage, *n.m.*, (tech.) frosting, glazing.

glaçant, **-e**, *adj.*, freezing; icy, chilling.

glace, *n.f.*, ice; glass, plate-glass; looking-glass; (carriage) window; flaw (in a diamond); frost-work. *Banc de* —; field of ice. *Clarté de la* —; ice-blink. *Montagne de* —; iceberg. *Froid comme* —; as cold as ice. *Mettre du vin à la* — *or frapper de* —; to ice wine. *Champagne frappé de* —; iced champagne. *Boire à la* —; to drink iced water. *Rompre la* —; to break the ice. *Prendre une* —; to take an ice. *Baisser les* —*s*; to lower the windows (of a carriage).

glacé, **-e**, *part.*, frozen, frosted, iced; freezing, nipping, biting, icy; chilling, cold, icy-cold, clay-cold; (of stuffs) shot, shot-colored.

glacée, *n.f.*, (bot.) ice-plant. *V.* **glaciale**.

glacer, *v.a.*, to freeze, to ice; to freeze up, to congeal, to chill; to strike, to overpower, to paralyze; to glaze; to frost; to hide the seams (of a garment). *Ce récit nous glaça d'horreur*; this story struck us dumb with horror. — *des confitures*; to ice sweetmeats. — *de la viande*; to glaze meat. — *une doublure*; to stitch down a lining. — *la soie*; (dy.) to alum silk.

se **glacer**, *v.r.*, to freeze, to chill; to become weak, to grow feeble.

glacer, *v.n.*, to freeze.

glacerie, *n.f.*, ice-making; ice manufactory; looking-glass manufactory; coffee-house.

glaceu-r, *n.m.*, **-se**, *n.f.*, glazer.

glaceu-x, -se, *adj.*, having flaws, flawy (of gems).

glaciaire, *adj.*, (geol.) of glaciers, glacial. *Période* — ; ice period.

glacial, -e, *adj.*, frozen, glacial, icy, frigid. *Air* — ; nipping air. *Vent* — ; biting wind. *Mine* —*e;* frigid countenance. *Mer* —*e, océan* — ; (geog.) Frozen Sea, Arctic Ocean.

glaciale, *n.f.*, (bot.) ice-plant.

glacier, *n.m.*, glacier; field of ice; coffee-house keeper; dealer in ice; confectioner.

glacière, *n.f.*, ice-house; freezing-machine; field of ice.

glacis, *n.m.*, (paint.) glazing; (fort.) glacis; (arch.) slope, sloping bank, weathering; (needle-work) serging.

glaçon, *n.m.*, icicle, piece of ice, floe. *Petit* — ; icicle.

glaçure, *n.f.*, glazing.

gladiateur, *n.m.*, gladiator.

glaïeul, *n.m.*, (bot.) gladiole, sword-grass, corn-flag, iris. — *puant;* spurgewort, stinking gladwin. — *des marais;* gladwin iris.

glaire, *n.f.*, glair, white of egg.

glairer, *v.a.*, to glair.

glaireu-x, -se, *adj.*, glairy.

glaise, *n.f.*, clay; potter's earth.

glaise, *adj.*, loamy, clayey. *Terre* — ; loam, clay.

glaiser, *v.a.*, to loam, to marl. — *des terres;* to marl land.

glaiseu-x, -se, *adj.*, clayey, marly, loamy.

glaisière, *n.f.*, marl-pit, clay-pit.

glaive, *n.m.*, sword; blade, steel. *Puissance du* — ; power of the sword; power of life and death.

glanage, *n.m.*, gleaning.

gland, *n.m.*, acorn; tassel; (anat.) glans. — *de mer;* (conch.) acorn-barnacle, acorn-shell. — *de terre;* (bot.) earth-nut.

glande, *n.f.*, (anat.) gland; kernel. *Endurcissement des* —*s;* scirrhosity. — *lymphatique;* lymphatic gland.

glandé, -e, *adj.*, (vet.) glandered; (her.) acorned.

glandée, *n.f.*, pannage (duty); crop of acorns.

glandulaire, *adj.* *V.* **glanduleux.**

glandule, *n.f.*, (anat.) glandule.

glanduleu-x, -se, *adj.*, glandulous, glandular.

glandulifère, *adj.*, (anat.) glanduliferous.

glane, *n.f.*, gleaning. *Faire* — ; to glean. — *d'oignons;* rope of onions. — *de poires;* bunch of pears ; (of straw) wisp.

glaner, *v.a.* and *n.*, to glean.

glaneu-r, *n.m.*, **-se,** *n.f.*, gleaner.

glanure, *n.f.*, gleanings.

glapir, *v.n.*, to yelp (of puppies and foxes) ; to screech, to scream, to squeak (of persons).

glapissant, -e, *adj.*, (of puppies and foxes) yelping; shrill; screeching, screaming, squeaking.

glapissement (-pis-mān), *n.m.*, yelping ; screeching, scream, squeaking.

glas, *n.m.*, knell; passing-bell, tolling. — *funèbre;* funeral-knell, death-bell. *Sonner le* — ; to ring the knell, to toll the knell.

glaucome, *n.m.*, (med.) glaucoma.

glauque, *adj.*, glaucous.

glèbe, *n.f.*, glebe, ground, land, earth, soil. *Être attaché à la* — ; to be bound to the soil.

gléchome (-kom), *n.m.*, ground-ivy.

glène, *n.f.*, (anat.) glene, socket ; (nav.) coil ; (fish.) basket.

gléner, *v.a.*, (nav.) to coil.

glénoïdal, -e, *adj.*, (anat.) glenoid. *Cavité* —*e de l'omoplate;* glenoid cavity of the scapula.

glénoïde, *adj.*, (anat.) glenoid.

glénoïdien, -ne (-in, -è-n), *adj.*, (anat.) glenoid.

glette, *n.f.*, (metal.) litharge ; dross.

glissade, *n.f.*, sliding, slide ; slipping ; slip ; (dancing) glissade. *Faire une* — ; to have a slide ; to make a slip.

glissant, -e, *adj.*, slippery; (fig.) ticklish, delicate, tender. *Il fait* — ; it is slippery walking. *Pas* — ; dangerous step, ticklish affair. *Terrain* — ; slippery, tender ground.

glissé, *n.m.*, (dancing) glisse ; slide.

glissement (glis-mān), *n.m.*, slipping; sliding ; gliding.

glisser, *v.n.*, to slip, to slip over ; to slide ; to glance over ; to slur over ; to make little or no impression ; to glance ; to pass (over). *L'échelle glissa;* the ladder slipped. — *sur la glace;* to slide. *Cela m'a glissé des mains;* that slipped through my fingers. *Glissons là-dessus;* let us pass over that.

glisser, *v.a.*, to slip, to slip in ; to slide, to slide in ; to insinuate, to introduce. *Il glissa sa main dans ma poche;* he slipped his hand into my pocket.

se **glisser,** *v.r.*, to slip, to slide, to creep in, to steal in ; to insinuate one's self.

glisseur, *n.m.*, slider.

glissoire, *n.f.*, slide.

globe, *n.m.*, globe, sphere, orb, glass-shade. — *de feu;* fire-ball.

globeu-x, -se, *adj.*, round.

in **globo.** *V.* **in globo.**

globulaire, *n.f.*, globularia, globe-daisy.

globulaire, *adj.*, globular.

globule, *n.m.*, globule.

globuleu-x, -se, *adj.*, globulous, globular, globous.

gloire, *n.f.*, glory, fame, honor ; glorification; halo ; vanity, pride ; boast, boasting. *Être la* — *de;* to be the glory of. *Se faire une* — *de quelque chose;* to glory in anything ; to pride one's self upon. *Mettre sa* — *à;* to glory in.

gloria, *n.m.*, (—) coffee (with brandy in it).

gloriette, *n.f.*, pavilion, summer-house.

glorieusement (-euz-mān), *adv.*, gloriously, honorably.

glorieu-x, -se, *adj.*, glorious, honorable; (rel.) glorified, blessed ; vainglorious, conceited, self-conceited ; proud.

glorieu-x, *n.m.*, **-se,** *n.f.*, braggart, boaster ; vainglorious person. *Faire le* — ; to be a braggart.

glorification, *n.f.*, glorification.

glorifier, *v.a.*, to glorify, to give glory to ; to honor.

se **glorifier,** *v.r.*, to glory in, to boast.

gloriole, *n.f.*, vainglory, vanity. *C'est la* — *qui les tient;* they are eaten up with vanity.

glose (glōz), *n.f.*, gloss; glozing ; comment; carping ; criticism ; parody.

gloser, *v.a.*, to gloss ; to gloze, to criticise, to carp at, to find fault with.

gloser, *v.n.*, to carp at, to find fault with.

gloseu-r, *n.m.*, **-se,** *n.f.*, carper ; fault-finder.

glossaire, *n.m.*, glossary, vocabulary.

glossateur, *n.m.*, glossarist.

glossite, *n.f.*, (med.) glossotis.

glossographe, *n.m.*, glossographer.

glossographie, *n.f.*, glossography.

glossologie, *n.f.*, glossology.

glossopètre, *n.m.*, (geol.) glossopetra.

glotte, *n.f.*, (anat.) glottis.

glouglou, *n.m.*, gurgling, gurgle ; (of turkeys) gobble.

glouglouter, *v.n.*, to gurgle ; (of a turkey) to gobble.

gloume, *n.m.* *V.* **glume.**

gloussement (glous-mān), *n.m.*, clucking ; cluck, chuckle.

glousser, *v.n.*, to cluck ; to chuckle.

glouteron (glou-tron), *n.m.*, (bot.) burdock.

glouton, -ne, *adj.*, gluttonous, greedy.

glouton, *n.m.*, **-ne,** *n.f.*, glutton.

gloutonnement (-to-n-män), adv., gluttonously, greedily, ravenously.

gloutonnerie (-to-n-rî), n.f., gluttony, greediness.

glu, n.f., bird-lime, lime.

gluant, -e, adj., glutinous, sticky, slimy; adhesive.

gluau, n.m., lime-twig. *Tendre des —x*; to set lime-twigs.

glucose, n.f., (chem.) glucose, glycose.

gluer, v.a., to lime ; to make sticky.

glui, n.m., barley straw.

glume, n.f., (bot.) glume, husk.

gluten (-tèn), n.m., gluten.

glutinati-f, -ve, adj., agglutinative.

glutination, n.f. V. **agglutination**.

glutineu-x, -se, adj., glutinous, viscous.

glutinosité, n.f., glutinosity, glutinousness, viscidity ; stickiness.

glycérine, n.f., glycerine.

glycine, n.f., (bot.) glycin, a Chinese plant.

glyconien or **glyconique**, adj., glyconian.

glycose, n.f. V. **glucose**.

glyphe, n.m., (arch.) glyph.

glyptique, n.f., glyptics.

glyptographie, n.f., glyptography.

gnaphale, n.m., (bot.) cudweed, everlasting.

gneiss, n.m., (min.) gneiss.

gnome, n.m., gnome.

gnomide, n.f., gnome.

gnomique, adj., gnomical, sententious.

gnomon, n.m., gnomon, pin of a dial.

gnomonique, n.f., gnomonics, dialing.

gnose, n.f., (theol.) gnosis ; (philos.) gnosticism.

gnosticisme, n.m., gnosticism.

gnostiques, n.m.pl., gnostics.

tout de **go**, adv., freely, by itself, easily, unceremoniously.

gobbe, n.f., poisoned ball (for a dog) ; fattening ball (for poultry) ; wool-ball (in sheep).

gobelet (go-blè), n.m., goblet, mug, drinking-cup ; juggler's box ; buttery (of palaces). *Officier du —*; officer of the buttery. *Joueur de —*; juggler ; thimble-rigger. *Tour de —*; juggler's trick.

gobelin (go-blin), n.m., goblin, evil spirit.

gobelins, n.m.pl., Gobelins (manufacture of tapestry at Paris).

gobelotter (go-blo-té), v.n., to tipple.

gobeloterie, n.f., tippling.

gobeloteur, n.m.f., tippler.

gobe-mouches, n.m., (—) (orni.) fly-catcher ; (bot.) fly-trap ; simpleton ; gull ; trifler, ninny.

gober, v.a., to gulp down, to swallow; to swallow down, to believe easily; to nab; to lay hold of ; to put up with; to pocket. *Il gobe des mouches;* he trifles away his time. *Je ne vais pas — cela;* I am not going to swallow that. *— le morceau;* to swallow the bait, to be caught, taken in.

goberge, n.f., cross bar (of a bedstead); handle (of a joiner's press) ; (pisc.) large cod.

se **goberger**, v.r., to enjoy one's self ; to take one's ease, to lounge.

gobet, n.m., gobbet. *Prendre au —*; to nab.

gobetage, n.m., (mas.) pointing, stopping.

gobeter (gob-té), v.a., (mas.) to point.

gobeur, n.m., swallower, gobbler, gulper; gull (person).

gobin, n.m., (fam., l.u.) a little hunchback.

godage, n.m., bagging, puckering (of a coat).

*godaille, n.f., tippling, drinking.

*godailler, v.n., to tipple.

*godailleur, n.m., tippler.

godelureau, n.m., popinjay, coxcomb, fop.

godenot, n.m., puppet, juggler's puppet; (b.s.) ill-shaped man, punch.

goder, v.n., to crease; to bag (of clothes) ; to pucker (of needle-work).

godet, n.m., small cup ; horn (for drinking) ; calyx (of a flower); cup (of a lamp).

godiche, n. and adj., simpleton, ninny ; clumsy; spoony.

godichon, -ne, n. and adj., silly, simple; clumsy, gawky, ninny, booby.

*godille, n.f., (nav.) scull.

*godiller, v.n., (nav.) to scull.

*godilleur, n.m., (nav.) sculler.

godiveau, n.m., (cook.) force-meat pie.

godron, n.m., ⊙ plait; (arch.) godroon.

godronner, v.a., ⊙ to plait round ; to godroon.

goéland, n.m., (orni.) gull; sea-gull.

goélette, n.f., (nav.) schooner.

goémon, n.m., sea-wrack ; sea-weed.

goétie (-ci), n.f., goety, sorcery.

⊙**goffe**, adj., ill-shaped, awkward.

*gogaille, n.f., (pop.) merry-making.

gogo, n.m., gull, gudgeon, simpleton.

à **gogo**, adv., in clover. *Etre à —*; to live in clover.

goguenard, -e (gog-nâr), adj., bantering, jeering, jovial, merry.

goguenard, n.m., -e, n.f., banterer, jeerer, chaffer.

goguenarder (gog-nar-dé), v.n., to jeer, to banter, to chaff; to crack jokes.

goguenarderie, n.f., jeering, jeer, bantering.

goguettes, n.f.pl., merry story, merry saying; pleasure-party. *Etre en —*; to be in a merry mood. *Chanter — à quelqu'un;* to abuse any one.

goinfre, n.m., gormandizer.

goinfrer, v.n., to gormandize.

goinfrerie, n.f., gormandizing.

goitre, n.m., goitre, wen ; (bot.) struma.

goitreu-x, -se, adj., goitrous. (orni.) pelican.

goitreu-x, n.m., -se, n.f., goitrous person ;

golfe, n.m., gulf, bay ; firth, frith.

gommage, n.m., gumming.

gomme, n.f., gum ; (med.) gummatum. — *arabique;* gum arabic. *—gutte*, (—s- —s) gamboge. — *élastique;* india-rubber, caoutchouc.

gommer, v.a., to gum.

gomme-résine, n.f., (—s- —s) gum-resin.

gommeu-x, -se, adj., gummous, gummy.

gommeux, n.m. *Petit —*; fop, coxcomb.

gommier, n.m., gum-tree.

gomphose, n.f., (anat.) gomphosis.

gond, n.m., hinge (for doors) ; pintle (of a rudder). *Hors des —s;* unhinged ; (fig.) enraged, beside one's self. *Cela me fait sortir des —s;* that exasperates me.

gondole, n.f., gondola; car (of a balloon); eye-cup ; eye bath.

gondoler, v.n., (tech.) to warp (of wood). *se — (pop.)* to shake with laughter.

gondolier, n.m., gondolier.

gonfalon or **gonfanon**, n.m., gonfalon.

gonfalonier, n.m., gonfalonier.

gonflement, n.m., swelling; tumidness; inflation, filling ; distension.

gonfler, v.a., to swell, to puff up, to inflate, to fill out, to fill with wind. *Des yeux gonflés;* swollen eyes.

se **gonfler**, v.r., to swell, to swell up, to fill out, to be swollen ; to increase, to distend.

gonfler, v.n., to swell, to swell up.

gong, n.m., (—s) gong.

gonin, n.m., knave, rogue, rascal. *Maître —;* knowing card, artful dodger.

goniomètre, n.m., goniometer.

goniométrie, n.f., goniometry.

gonne, n.f., sea-cask, tar-barrel.

gonorrhée, n.f., gonorrhœa.

gord, n.m., bow-net; fishing weir.

gordien (-di-in), adj.m., Gordian

gordius (-us), n.m., hair-worm, gordius.

goret, n.m., (jest.) young pig; (fig.) dirty fellow ; (of hatters, etc.) foreman ; (nav.) hog.

goreter, *v.a.,* (nav.) to hog.

gorge, *n.f.,* throat, gullet; neck and shoulders (of a woman); breast, bosom, neck; mouth, orifice; defile, strait, narrow pass; (arch., fort.) gorge; groove (of a pulley); roller (of maps). *Un mal de —;* a sore throat. *Avoir mal à la —;* to have a sore throat. *A pleine —;* at the top of one's voice. *Couper la — à quelqu'un;* to cut any one's throat; to ruin any one. *Prendre quelqu'un à la —;* to seize any one by the throat. *Rire à — déployée;* to split one's sides with laughter. *Rendre —;* to disgorge, to refund, to stump up. *Faire des —s chaudes de quelque chose;* to ridicule, to laugh, at anything, to chuckle over. *Cette fumée prend à la —;* this smoke nearly chokes one.

gorge-de-pigeon, *adj. invariable,* iridescent, shot (of colors).

gorge-de-pigeon, *n.m.,* (n.p.) shot-color.

gorgée, *n.f.,* draught; mouthful, gulp, sip.

gorger, *v.a.,* to gorge; to cram; to swell.

se gorger, *v.r.,* to gorge one's self.

gorgeret, *n.m.,* (surg.) gorget, gorgeret.

gorgerette, *n.f.,* gorget; lady's ruffle; capstring (of children); (ornith.) black-cap.

gorgerin, *n.m.,* neck-piece (armor); (arch.) gorgerin.

gorgone, *n.f.,* (myth.) Gorgon; (zool.) gorgonia.

***gorille,** *n.m.,* (mam.) gorilla.

gosier, *n.m.,* throat, gullet, voice; (anat.) fauces. *Coup de —;* (mus.) breath. *Avoir le — sec;* to be always thirsty. *S'humecter le —;* to wet one's whistle.

gossampin, *n.m.,* silk-cotton-tree.

gosse, *n.m.,* brat, urchin. *n.f.,* flam, bad joke.

gothique, *adj.,* pertaining to the Goths, Gothic. *Ecriture —;* black letter.

gothique, *n.f.,* (print.) old English.

gouache, *n.f.,* body-color; painting.

gouailler, *v.a.,* (pop.) to chaff, to tease.

gouailleu-r, *n.m.,* **-se,** *n.f.,* chaffer, joker, teaser.

goudron, *n.m.,* tar.

goudronnage, *n.m.,* tarring.

goudronner, *v.a.,* to tar. *Eau goudronnée;* tar-water. *Toile goudronnée;* tarpaulin.

goudronnerie (-dro-n-rî), *n.f.,* tar-works.

gouet, *n.m.,* (bot.) arum, cuckoo-pintle.

gouffre, *n.m.,* gulf, abyss, pit; whirlpool.

gouge, *n.f.,* gouge.

gouger, *v.a.,* to gouge.

gougette, *n.f.,* small gouge.

gouin, *n.m.,* slovenly sailor.

gouine, *n.f.,* (pop.) street-walker.

goujat, *n.m.,* soldier's servant, camp-follower; hodman; blackguard; snob; vulgar fellow; bungler. *— de vaisseau;* powder monkey.

goujon, *n.m.,* gudgeon. *Avaler le —;* to swallow the bait; to fall into the snare.

goule, *n.f.,* ghoul.

goulée, *n.f.,* (pop.) mouthful.

goulet, *n.m.,* narrow entrance to a harbor, inlet, mouth, neck.

goulette, *n.f., V.* **goulotte.**

gouliafre, *n.m.,* (pop.) glutton.

goulot, *n.m.,* neck (of a bottle).

goulotte, *n.f.,* water-channel.

goulu, -e, *adj.,* gluttonous, greedy.

goulu, *n.m.,* **-e,** *n.f.,* glutton, greedy person.

goulûment, *adv.,* gluttonously, greedily.

goum, *n.m.,* (—*s*) (milit.) contingent (in Algeria).

***goupille,** *n.f.,* (tech.) pin; peg; bolt.

***goupiller,** *v.a.,* (tech.) to pin, to bolt.

***goupillon,** *n.m.,* aspersorium; aspergill; holy-water sprinkler; bottle-brush.

***goupillonner,** *v.a.,* to cleanse with a bottle-brush.

gourbi, *n.m.,* (—*s*) hut, cabin.

gourd, -e, *adj.,* benumbed.

gourde, *n.f.,* (bot.) gourd; calabash; wicker bottle, flask; piaster (a coin).

gourdin, *n.m.,* cudgel, club, stick; (nav.) rope's end.

gourdiner, *v.a.,* (pop.) to cudgel.

goure, *n.f.,* adulterated drug; (fig.) take-in.

gourer, *v.a.,* (pop.) to adulterate drugs; to cheat, to take in.

goureur, *n.m.,* adulterator of drugs; cheat, trickster.

gourgandine, *n.f.,* (pop.) street-walker, strumpet.

gourgane, *n.f.,* broad bean, bean.

gourgouran, *n.m.,* Indian silk stuff.

gourmade, *n.f.,* punch, cuff, fisticuff.

gourmand, -e, *adj.,* gluttonous, greedy.

gourmand, *n.m.,* **-e,** *n.f.,* glutton, epicure.

gourmander, *v.a.,* to chide, to reprimand, to reprove harshly; to check, to curb; (cook.) to lard; (of trees) to prune.

gourmandise, *n.f.,* gluttony, greediness.

gourme, *n.f.,* (med.) ringworm of the scalp; (vet.) glanders. *Jet r sa —;* to have a running at the nose (of a horse); to have a rash (of children); to sow one's wild oats (of a young man).

gourmé, -e, *part.,* curbed; stiff, formal, solemn, grave.

gourmer, *v.a.,* to curb (a horse); to box, to thump, to pommel.

se gourmer, *v.r.,* to thump, to pommel one another.

gourmet, *n.m.,* connoisseur in wines; epicure; judge of.

gourmette, *n.f.,* (man.) curb, curb-chain. *Lâcher la — à quelqu'un;* to give any one more scope.

gournable, *n.f.,* (nav.) treenail *or* trenail.

gournabler, *v.a.,* (nav.) to treenail.

goussant *or* **goussaut,** *n.m.,* thick-set horse.

gousse, *n.f.,* pod, husk. *— d'ail;* clove of garlic.

gousset, *n.m.,* fob; arm-pit; smell from ditto; (obs.) purse; gusset (of a shirt); (carp.) brace. *Vider un —;* to pick a pocket.

goût, *n.m.,* taste, savor, relish; smell; inclination, liking; style, manner, fashion. *Avoir du — pour;* to like, to have a liking for, to be fond of. *Avoir le — de;* to taste of. *Avoir le — difficile;* to be difficult to please, to be nice, particular. *Relever le —;* to give a relish to. *Avoir le — dépravé;* to have one's palate out of order. *Cela plaît au —;* that is pleasing to the taste. *Avoir bon —;* to taste nice. *Viande de haut —;* highly-seasoned meat. *Ce pain a un — de noisette;* that bread tastes of nuts. *Être de son —;* to be palatable; to hit one's fancy. *C'est un critique plein de —;* he is a critic of great taste. *Chacun à son —;* every one to his liking. *Prendre — à une chose;* to take a liking to a thing. *Trouver une chose à son —;* to find a thing to one's liking, to approve of, to be partial to. *Il ne faut point disputer des —s;* there's no accounting for tastes. *De bon —;* in good taste. *De mauvais —;* in bad taste, vulgar. *Ces vers sont dans le — de Racine;* these verses are in the style of Racine. *Faire une chose par —;* to do a thing from taste. *Cela est-il de votre —?* is that to your taste? *Satisfaire ses —s;* to satisfy one's tastes. *Chacun son —;* tastes differ.

goûter, *v.a.,* to taste, to relish; to like, to approve of, to appreciate; to enjoy, to delight in; to try; to smell. *Voulez-vous — notre vin?* will you taste our wine? *Ce prédicateur est bien goûté;* that preacher is very much liked. *— les plaisirs de la table;* to enjoy the pleasures of the table. *— le repos;* to enjoy repose.

se goûter, *v.r.,* to be tasted; to be relished; to

like each other. *Une sauce doit toujours se —; a sauce ought always to be tasted.

goûter, *v.n.*, to taste; to smell; to lunch; to try, to make a trial of; to approve of. *Goûtez de ce vin;* try this wine.

goûter, *n.m.*, lunch, light refreshments.

goutte, *n.f.*, drop, small quantity; dram; jot; (arch., pharm.) drop; (med.) gout. — *à —;* drop by drop. *Mère —;* unpressed wine. *Boire la —;* to have a drop (of liquor). *Boire une —;* to have a nip. *Ils se ressemblent comme deux —s d'eau;* they are as like as two peas. — *scia-tique;* sciatica, hip-gout. — *vague;* wandering gout. — *militaire;* gleet. *Accès de —;* attack of the gout. *Etre travaillé de la —;* to suffer from gout. — *à — on emplit la cuve;* many a mickle makes a muckle. *Payer la —;* to stand a drink. *C'est une — d'eau dans la mer;* it is a drop in the ocean.

goutte, *adv.*, (l.u.) in the least, at all. *Il ne voit —;* he does not see at all or a wink. *N'y voir —;* not to make it out at all. *N'entendre —;* not to hear at all; not to understand in the least.

gouttelette (gou-tlèt), *n.f.*, small drop.

goutteu-x, -se, *adj.*, gouty.

goutteu-x, *n.m.*, **-se**, *n.f.*, gouty person.

gouttière, *n.f.*, gutter of a roof, shoot; spout (for rain-water); cornice (of a carriage); fore-edge (of a book); (anat.) groove. *pl.*, (nav.) water-way. — *de plomb;* leaden spout.

gouvernable, *adj.*, governable.

*****gouvernail**, *n.m.*, rudder, helm. *Tenir le —;* to be at the helm; (of a bicycle) hand-bar.

gouvernance, *n.f.*, governorship, tutorship.

gouvernant, -e, *adj.*, governing, ruling.

gouvernant, *n.m.*, governor, ruler. *Les —s;* those who govern.

gouvernante, *n.f.*, governor's wife; gover-ness; housekeeper (to a single man).

gouverne, *n.f.*, guidance, guide, direction, rule. *Je vous dis cela pour votre —;* I tell you that for your guidance. *Aviron de —;* stern-oar.

gouvernement, *n.m.*, government, rule, sway; management; governorship; government-house; (nav.) steering. *En son —;* under his management.

gouvernemental, -e, *adj.*, of the govern-ment.

gouverner, *v.a.*, to govern, to rule, to com-mand, to manage, to direct, to regulate, to look to, to take care of; to husband; to bring up (children); to breed (animals); (nav.) to steer; to rein up (a horse). — *un ménage;* to direct a household. — *quelqu'un;* to rule any one. — *un vaisseau;* to steer a ship. *C'est lui qui.gouverne la barque;* he is the life and soul of the business. *Il gouverne bien sa barque;* he knows how to manage his affairs, or to feather his nest, or to make money.

se **gouverner**, *v.r.*, to govern one's self; to behave one's self; to be governed; to manage one's own affairs.

gouverner, *v.n.*, to govern, to rule; to manage; (nav.) to steer, to answer the helm.

gouverneur, *n.m.*, governor, ruler, tutor, manager.

goyave, *n.f.*, (bot.) guava (fruit).

goyavier, *n.m.*, (bot.) guava (tree).

grabat, *n.m.*, pallet, truckle-bed. *Sur le —;* on a sick-bed; very ill; laid up; (fig.) to be wretchedly poor.

grabataire, *n.* and *adj.*, bedridden.

grabeau, *n.m.*, fragments, siftings, waste, refuse.

grabuge, *n.m.*, (triv.) wrangling, quarrel, squabble, brawl.

grâce, *n.f.*, grace; favor, pardon; mercy, indulgence; forgiveness; gracefulness, elegance, charm. *pl.*, thanks; (myth.) Graces. *Accor-*

der une —; to grant a favor. *De — !* for mercy's sake! pray! I pray you! *Bonnes —s;* good graces; head curtains (of a bed). *Actions de —;* thanksgiving. *A la — de;* at the mercy of. *A la — de Dieu!* in God's hands! (fam.) anyhow, higgledy-piggledy. *Demander — à;* to ask par-don of, to crave quarter of. *Faire une — à quel-qu'un;* to do any one a favor. *Faire — à quel-qu'un;* to forgive any one; to pardon any one. *Faire — de;* to spare. *Se mettre dans les bonnes —s de quelqu'un;* to get into any one's good graces. *Rentrer en —;* to get into favor again. *Il est dans les bonnes —s du roi;* he is in the king's good graces. *Perdre les bonnes —s de quelqu'un;* to lose any one's good graces. *Trou-ver — devant quelqu'un;* to find favor in any one's sight. *Demander or prier en —;* to ask as a favor, to entreat. *L'an de —;* the year of grace, in the year of our Lord. *Rendre —s au ciel;* to return thanks to heaven. *Dire ses —s;* to say grace. — *à Dieu;* thank God. *Je vous rends —;* I thank you. *Sans —;* graceless. *Avec —;* gracefully. *Faire une chose de bonne —;* to do a thing with a good grace; readily. *De mauvaise —;* reluctantly, grudgingly. *Sacri-fier aux —s;* to sacrifice to the Graces.

graciable, *adj.*, (jur.) pardonable.

gracier, *v.a.*, (jur.) to pardon.

gracieusement (-eûz-mān), *adv.*, graciously, kindly, gracefully.

gracieuseté, *n.f.*, graciousness; kindness, courtesy (act of); acknowledgment, gratuity. *Ce serait une — de votre part;* it would be an act of kindness on your part.

gracieu-x, -se, *adj.*, graceful, pleasant, cour-teous, gracious, kind, obliging, civil.

gracilité, *n.f.*, gracility; slimness, slender-ness.

gradation, *n.f.*, gradation; degrees; climax. — *inverse;* anti-climax.

grade, *n.m.*, grade, rank; degree; step, title. *Monter en —;* to be promoted.

gradé, *adj.m.*, (mil.) with an inferior rank.

grader, *v.a.*, to confer a grade or rank on.

gradin, *n.m.*, step; shelf; bench; tier. *pl.*, benches rising one above the other, tiers. *Sur les —s;* (fig.) at school.

graduation, *n.f.*, graduation; drying-house.

gradué, *n.m.*, graduate (of a university).

gradué, -e, *adj.*, *part.*, graduated, progres-sive. *Cours de thèmes —s;* progressive course of exercises.

graduel, -le, *adj.*, gradual.

graduel, *n.m.*, (c. rel.) gradual.

graduellement (-èl-mān), *adv.*, gradually.

graduer, *v.a.*, to graduate; to proportion; to increase regularly. *Se faire —;* to graduate, to take a degree.

graffite, *n.m.*, drawing.

*****graillement**, *n.m.*, hoarseness, huskiness.

*****grailler**, *v.n.*, (hunt.) to recall the hounds.

*****graillon**, *n.m.*, broken meat; remnants, burned meat scraps; smell of burnt meat or fat. *Marie —;* slattern, slut.

*****graillonner**, *v.n.*, to smell of burnt meat or fat.

*****graillonneu-r**, *n.m.*, **-se**, *n.f.*, (l.ex.) gobber; dealer in broken meats; (f.) bad cook.

grain, *n.m.*, grain, berry, bead; jot, bit, par-ticle; squall. *Gros —s;* wheat and rye, winter corn. *Menus —s;* spring corn. *Un — de rai-sin;* a grape. — *de chapelet;* bead of a chaplet. *Un rosaire à gros —s;* a rosary of large beads. *Un — de sel;* a grain of salt. *Il n'a pas un — de bon sens;* he has not a grain of sense. *Un — de folie;* a touch of madness. *Etre dans le —;* to be on the road to fortune. *Poules de —;* corn-fed pullets. *Catholique à gros —s;* lax Catholic. — *de beauté;* mole, beauty spot. *Essuyer un —;* to be overtaken by a squall. *V.* **rafale**.

graine, *n.f.*, seed; berry; set (persons); eggs

(of silkworms). *Monter en —*; to run to seed. *C'est une mauvaise —*; he is a bad lot. — *d'Avignon;* French berry. — *de lin;* linseed. — *de vers à soie;* silkworm's eggs. — *de niais;* bait for fools. *C'est de la — de niais;* why, a fool would not be taken in by it. *Monter en —;* (fig.) to run to seed; to be growing an old maid.

grainer, *v.n.* V. **grener.**

grainetis (grè-n-tï), *n.m.*, (coin.) punch, puncheon.

graini-er or **grainetier,** *n.m.*, **-ère,** *n.f.*, seedsman, seedswoman, corn-chandler.

graissage, *n.m.*, greasing; grease.

graisse, *n.f.*, fat, fatness; grease; (pharm.) tallow. — *de rôti;* dripping. — *de cuisine;* kitchen-stuff. — *de rognon;* suet. *Tourner à la —;* (of wine) to get ropy.

graisser, *v.a.*, to grease; to make greasy; to make dirty; to lubricate, to oil. — *la patte à quelqu'un;* to give any one a sop, to fee, to tip. — *ses bottes;* (pop.) to prepare for a journey, to prepare for kingdom come.

graisser, *v.n.*, to get ropy (of wine).

graisserie, *n.f.*, grease-trade or shop.

graisseu-x, -se, *adj.*, greasy; fatty.

graissier, *n.m.*, grease-merchant.

gralle, *n.m.*, (orni.) grallic, wading-bird. V. **échassier.**

grallipède, *adj.*, grallatory, long-legged.

gramen (-mèn), *n.m.*, gramineous plant.

graminée, *adj.f.*, gramineous.

graminée, *n.f.*, gramineous plant.

graminiforme, *adj.*, graminifolious.

grammaire, *n.f.*, grammar. — *raisonnée;* analytical grammar.

grammairien, *n.m.*, **-ne,** *n.f.* (-in, -è-n), grammarian.

grammatical, -e, *adj.*, grammatical. *Correction—e;* good grammar.

grammaticalement (-kal-mān), *adv.*, grammatically.

grammatiste, *n.m.*, grammatist.

gramme, *n.m.*, gramme (15+432 grains troy).

grand, -e, *adj.*, great, large; high, lofty, tall; wide; big, grown-up; capacious; huge; grand, noble, stately, majestic; broad (of daylight). *Homme —;* tall man. — *homme;* great man. *Une —e personne;* a grown-up person. *Les blés sont déjà —s;* the corn is already high. *Il fut — dans l'adversité;* he bore up well in adversity. *Un — personnage;* a great personage. *Il n'a pas — argent;* he has not much money. *Le — prêtre;* the high-priest. *Le — monde;* the fashionable world. *J'ai eu grand'peur;* I was greatly frightened. *La grand'messe,* (—*—s*) high mass. *Grand'garde,* (—*—s*) (milit.) outpost. *—es eaux;* floods, or (fig.) the fountains at Versailles in full play. *Voleur de — chemin;* highwayman. *Le — ressort;* the main-spring. *Il est — jour;* it is broad daylight. — *livre;* ledger. — *livre de la dette publique,* —*-livre;* list of the creditors of the State.

grand, *n.m.*, grandee; nobleness, grandeur, grandness, great things. *pl.,* the great, great people; (at school) the big boys. *Trancher du —;* to carry it with a high hand. *Du petit au —;* comparing little things with great ones. *Promesse de — n'est pas héritage;* put not your faith in the promises of the great. *En —;* on a large scale; in grand style; (paint.) at full length (portraits).

grand-duc, *n.m.*, (—*s——s*) grand-duke.

grand-ducal, *adj.m.* (— *-ducaux*), **grand-ducale,** *adj.f.,* (—*—s*) of a grand-duke.

grandelet, -te (gran-dlè, -t), *adj.*, biggish, pretty tall.

grandement (gran-dmān), *adv.*, grandly, nobly; greatly, vastly, highly, extremely, largely, very much; handsomely.

grandesse, *n.f.*, grandeeship.

grandeur, *n.f.*, size; height; length; breadth; bulk, bulkiness; greatness, largeness, magnitude, hugeness, bigness; tallness; might; grandeur, nobleness; (titles) grace, highness. *Ils sont de même —;* they are of the same size. *De — naturelle;* life-size. *Il a un air de — qui impose;* he has an air of grandeur that commands respect. — *d'âme;* magnanimity. *Regarder quelqu'un du haut de sa —;* to look down upon any one. *Ma "—" ne va pas jusqu'à cette planche;* my "highness" cannot reach up to that shelf (V. Hugo).

grandiose, *adj.*, grand, imposing.

grandiose, *n.m.*, grandeur.

grandir, *v.n.*, to grow; to grow up, to spring up; to grow tall, to grow big; to increase, to magnify, to give importance to. — *trop pour ses habits;* to grow out of one's clothes.

se grandir, *v.r.*, to make one's self appear taller; to become taller, to grow taller; to grow; to become greater, to raise one's self, to rise.

grandissement, *n.m.*, growth, increase, rise.

grandissime, *adj.*, very great, very large.

grand'mère, *n.f.*, (—*·—s*) grandmother.

grand-oncle, *n.m.*, (—*s——s*) great-uncle.

grand-père, *n.m.*, (—*s——s*) grandfather, grandsire.

grand'tante, *n.f.*, (—*·——s*) great-aunt.

grand-vizir, *n.m.*, grand-vizier.

grange, *n.f.*, barn. *Batteur en —;* thrasher.

granit (-nit), *n.m.*, (min.), granite.

granitelle, *adj.*, (min.) granitoid.

granitique, *adj.*, (min.) granitic.

granivore, *adj.*, granivorous.

granulaire, *adj.*, (min.) granular.

granulation, *n.f.*, granulation.

granule, *n.m.*, (bot.) granule.

granulé, -e, *part.*, granulated, granular.

se granuler, *v.r.*, to granulate.

granuleu-x, -se, *adj.*, granulous, granular, granulated.

graphique, *adj.*, graphic, graphical. *Représentation —;* (math.) scheme.

graphiquement, *adv.*, graphically.

graphite, *n.m.*, (min.) graphite; plumbago.

graphomètre, *n.m.*, (math.) graphometer.

grapin, *n.m.* V. **grappin.**

grappe, *n.f.*, bunch (of grapes, currants); cluster (of fruit); (artil.) grape, grapeshot; (vet.) grape, wart. *Mordre à la —;* to bite at the hook, to swallow the bait. *Croître en —;* to cluster.

*grappillage,** *n.m.*, gleaning, pickings.

*grappiller,** *v.a.* and *n.*, to glean grapes; to glean; to gain a trifle, to make a little profit.

*grappilleu-r,** *n.m.*, **-se,** *n.f.*, grape-gleaner; gleaner; petty extortioner.

*grappillon,** *n.m.*, little bunch of grapes.

grappin, *n.m.*, (nav.) grapple, grappling, grappling-iron, hook; toasting-fork. — *à main;* hand grapple. — *de brûlot;* fire grappling. *Jeter le — sur quelqu'un;* to get any one into one's clutches.

grappu, -e, *adj.*, loaded with bunches.

gras, -se, *adj.*, fat, fleshy, plump, full of fat, corpulent, obese; greasy, oily, unctuous; rich; broad, indecent; (paint.) thick; (print.) thick-faced (of letters). — *comme un moine;* as fat as butter. *Dormir la — matinée;* to sleep all the morning; to get up late. *Il en fait ses choux —;* he feathers his nest with it. *Ce cheval a la vue —se;* this horse is dim-sighted. *Cette sauce est trop —se;* this gravy is too rich. *Soupe —se;* meat soup. *Dîner —;* meat dinner. *Du vin —;* thick, ropy wine. *De l'encre —se;* thick ink. *Terre —se;* heavy, clayey soil. *Terres —ses;* rich land. *Du son —;* fine bran. *Jour —;* meat-day. *Les jours —;* shrove days, shrove-tide. *Avoir la langue —se;* to speak thick. *Temps —;* hazy weather. *Cette comédie* *est trop —se ;* this comedy is too broad. *Le pavé est —;* the pavement is slippery. *Cet homme n'en est pas plus —;* this man is none the better for it.

gras, *n.m.,* fat, fat part, fleshy part; meat; meat diet; calf (of the leg). *Faire —, manger —;* to eat meat.

gras-cuit, *adv.,* (of bread) heavy.

gras-double, *n.m.,* (— — —s) tripe.

gras-fondu, *n.m.,* (n.p.) or **gras-fondure,** *n.f.,* (n.p.) (vet.) molten grease.

gras-mollet, *n.m.,* (— — —s) (ich.) lump-fish.

grassement (grâs-mān), *adv.,* plentifully, largely, liberally ; comfortably. *Payer —;* to pay generously. *Vivre —;* to live comfortably, to live well.

grasset, -te, *adj.,* fattish, pretty fat, pretty plump ; (of meat) thin flank.

grasset, *n.m.,* (vet.) stifle; stifle-joint.

grassette, *n.f.,* (bot.) butterwort, sanicle.

grasseyement, *n.m.,* burring, rolling of r's.

grasseyer, *v.n.,* to burr; to roll one's r's.

***grassouillet, -te,** *adj.,* plump.

grat (gra), *n.m.,* place scratched by fowls.

grateron, *n.m.,* (bot.) scratch-weed ; goose-grass ; cleavers.

graticuler, *v.n.,* (paint.) to square.

gratification, *n.f.,* gratuity, reward, encouragement ; present.

gratifier, *v.a.,* to confer on, to bestow on; to favor ; to attribute, to ascribe. *— quelqu'un de ses bévues ;* to father one's blunders upon somebody else. *— quelqu'un d'un coup de poing ;* to favor any one with a hiding.

gratin, *n.m.,* burnt part; scraping. *Au —;* (cook.) dressed with bread crumbs.

gratiné, -e, *adj.,* burnt; browned.

gratiole (-ci-), *n.f.,* (bot.) gratiola, hyssop. *— officinale ;* hedge-hyssop.

gratis (gra-tis), *adv.,* gratis, for nothing, gratuitously ; free of cost.

gratis, *n.m.,* exemption from cost; free gift.

gratitude, *n.f.,* gratitude, thankfulness.

gratte, *n.f.,* (nav.) scraper. *— double ;* double-headed scraper.

gratté, -e, *part.,* scratched.

gratte-bosse, *n.f.,* (—) scratch-brush.

gratte-bosser, *v.a.,* to scratch with the brush in gilding.

gratte-cul, *n.m.,* (— — —s) (bot.) canker, dog-rose. *Il n'est point de si belle rose qui ne devienne —;* all beauty is subject to decay.

gratte-langue, *n.m.,* (— — —s) tongue-scraper.

gratteleu-x, -se (gra-tleû, -z), *adj.,* itchy.

grattelle, *n.f.,* (med.) rash, itching.

gratte-navire, *n.m.,* (— — —s) ship-scraper.

gratte-papier, *n.m.,* (—, or — — —s) scribbling drudge, quill driver.

gratter, *v.a.,* to scratch, to scrape, to claw, to dig, to paw. *Trop — cuit, trop parler nuit ;* the least said the soonest mended. *— quelqu'un où il lui démange ;* to talk of a thing that pleases any one. *— le papier ;* to drive the quill.

se gratter, *v.r.,* to scratch one's self; to scrape one's self. *Qui se sent galeux se gratte ;* let him whom the cap fits wear it.

grattoir, *n.m.,* scratching-knife, scraper, eraser.

gratton, *n.m.,* (bot.). *V.* **grateron.**

gratuit, -e, *adj.,* gratuitous, free. *Supposition —e ;* gratuitous supposition.

gratuité, *n.f.,* gratuity, free gift.

gratuitement (-tī-tmān), *adv.,* gratuitously ; free, for nothing ; groundlessly.

grauwacke, *n.f.,* (geol., min.) graywacke, greywacke ; grit-rock.

gravatier (-tié), *n.m.,* rubbish-carter.

gravati-f, -ve, *adj.,* (med.) dull, heavy.

gravats (-vâ), *n.m.pl. V.* **gravois.**

grave, *adj.,* heavy ; grave, serious, solemn,

sedate, demure, sober ; weighty, of importance ; dangerous ; low, deep, hollow, (mus.) flat. *Contenance, mine, —;* solemn look. *Blessure —;* dangerous wound. *Note —;* low note. *Ton —;* deep tone. *Accent —;* grave accent.

grave, *n.m.,* gravity ; heavy body. *Passer du — au gai ;* to pass from the grave to the gay. *Chute des —s ;* (phys.) descent of bodies.

grave, *n.f.,* beach, strand in Newfoundland.

gravé, -e, *part.,* engraved. *Etre — de petite vérole ;* to be pitted with small-pox; to be pock-marked.

gravelage, *n.m.,* graveling.

gravelée (gra-vlée), *adj.f.,* crude. *Cendre —;* pearl ash.

graveleu-x, -se (gra-vleû, -z), *adj.,* troubled with gravel ; gravelly, sandy, gritty ; obscene, smutty. *Terroir —;* gravelly soil. *Fruit —;* stony fruit. *Crayon —;* gritty pencil.

graveleux, *n.m.,* (med.) person affected with gravel.

gravelle, *n.f.,* (med.) gravel.

gravelure (gra-vlur), *n.f.,* obscenity, broadness, ribaldry, smut, smuttiness.

gravement (gra-vmān), *adv.,* gravely, seriously, solemnly, soberly ; grievously ; (mus.) deeply.

graver, *v.a.,* to engrave ; to grave ; to impress, to imprint. *— à l'eau-forte ;* to etch. *— en creux ;* (engr.) to sink. *— au burin ;* to engrave. *se graver,* *v.r.,* to be engraved ; to be graven, to be impressed, imprinted. *Se — quelque chose dans l'esprit ;* to impress anything on one's mind.

graveur, *n.m.,* engraver. *— à l'eau-forte ;* etcher.

gravier, *n.m.,* gravel, grit. *pl.,* (med.) gravel. *Couvrir de —;* to gravel.

gravière, *n.f.,* gravel pit; (agri.) vetch and lentils ; (orni.) plover.

gravimètre, *n.m.,* (phys.) gravimeter.

gravir, *v.a. and n.,* to clamber, to clamber up, to climb, to climb up, to scale, to ascend.

gravitation, *n.f.,* (phys.) gravitation.

gravité, *n.f.,* gravity ; seriousness, solemnity, demureness, sedateness, graveness ; weight, importance, (mus.) flatness, lowness. *Centre de —;* centre of gravity. *— de son ;* deepness of sound.

graviter, *v.n.,* (phys.) to gravitate.

gravois, *n.m., pl.,* coarse plaster, mortar ; rubbish (of plaster). *Enlever les —;* to carry away the rubbish.

gravure, *n.f.,* engraving, graving, cut, print. *— sur pierre ;* stone-engraving. *— au burin ;* stroke-engraving. *— en creux ;* die-sinking ; intaglio. *— en taille-douce ;* copperplate-engraving. *— au trait ;* line-engraving. *— sur acier ;* steel engraving. *— sur bois ;* wood-engraving. *— en caractères d'imprimerie ;* letter-engraving. *— en pierres fines ;* seal-engraving ; engraving on precious stones.

gré, *n.m.,* will, wish ; liking, pleasure ; mind, taste, inclination ; accord, consent. *De bon —;* willingly. *De mauvais —,* or *contre son —;* unwillingly, against the grain. *Il y est allé de son —;* he went of his own accord. *Cela est-il à votre —?* is that to your liking ? *Elle est assez à mon —;* I like her well enough. *Bon — mal —,* or *de — ou de force;* whether one will or no, willing or unwilling, willy nilly, nolens volens. *Au — des flots;* at the mercy of the waves. *Ses crins flottaient au — du vent;* his mane waved in the wind. *Prendre, avoir, recevoir en —;* to take in good part, to approve of. *Prendre en —;* to receive with resignation; to take a liking to. *Savoir —, bon —, beaucoup de —, à quelqu'un de quelque chose;* to be thankful to any one for anything. *Savoir mauvais — à quelqu'un de quelque chose;* not to thank any one for anything *or* to resent interference. *Je lui en sais* *bon* —; I am deeply grateful to him. *Plein* —; free-will, own free-will. *Vendre de — à* —; to sell by private contract.

gréage, *n.m.,* (nav.) rigging.

grèbe, *n.m.,* (orni.) grebe. *— huppé;* great-crested grebe.

grec, -que, *adj.,* Greek, Grecian.

grec, *n.m.,* **-que,** *n.f.,* Greek, Grecian. *m.,* miser; sharper, black-leg, cheat. *Etre — en quelque chose;* to be a dab at anything.

grec, *n.m.,* Greek language. *C'est du — pour moi;* that is Greek, Hebrew, to me.

gréciser, *v.a.,* to hellenize.

grécisme, *n.m.,* grecism.

gréciste, *n.m.,* Grecian; Hellenist, Greek scholar.

grecque, *n.f.,* Greek woman, Grecian woman; (arch.) fret, fret-work; bookbinder's saw; saw. *Ornr de —s;* (arch.) to fret. *Orné d'une —;* (arch.) fretted.

grecquer, *v.a.,* (bookbind.) to saw-bind.

gredin, *n.m.,* **-e,** *n.f.,* villain, scamp, scoundrel, blackguard; lapdog; slut.

gredinerie (-di-n-rî), *n.f.,* blackguardism, villainy, rascality.

gréement, *n.m.,* (nav.) rigging. *V.* **agrès.**

gréer, *v.a.,* (nav.) to rig.

gréeur, *n.m.,* (nav.) rigger.

greffe, *n.m.,* (jur.) registry, record-office; registrar's office, clerk's office.

greffe, *n.f.,* graft, grafting, engraftment. *— à l'anglaise;* whip-grafting. *— par approche;* graft by approach. *— en couronne;* crown-graft. *— en écusson;* shield-graft; graft by gems; budding. *— en fente;* chink-graft, cleft-graft, shoulder-graft. *— en flûte;* flute-graft. *Lever une —;* to take a graft.

greffer, *v.a.,* to graft.

greffeur, *n.m.,* grafter.

greffier, *n.m.,* registrar, **recorder, clerk of the court.**

greffoir, *n.m.,* grafting-knife.

grégaire, *adj.,* gregarious.

grège, *adj.,* raw (of silk).

grégeois (-joâ), *adj.,* only used in *Feu* —; Greek fire; wild fire.

grégorien, -ne (-in, -è-n), *adj.,* Gregorian.

⊙**grègues** (grèg), *n.f.,* breeches. *Tirer ses —s;* to run away, to cut one's sticks, to take to one's heels.

grêle, *n.m.,* highest note (of a horn).

grêle, *n.f.,* hail, hail-storm; (of the eyelid), stye. *Grain de —;* hailstone. *— de coups;* shower of blows.

grêle, *adj.,* slender, slim, lank; shrill. *Des jambes —s;* spindle legs. *Voix —;* shrill voice. *Intestins —s;* (anat.) small intestines.

grêlé, -e, *part.,* ravaged by hail; pock-marked, pitted with small-pox. *Cet homme a été —;* that man has suffered great losses. *Un homme —;* a man pitted with small-pox.

grêler, *v. imp.,* to hail. *Il grêle;* it hails.

grêler, *v.a.,* to ravage by hail, to ruin.

grêlet, *n.m.,* granite hammer.

grêlet, -te, *adj.,* thinnish, puny.

grelin, *n.m.,* (nav.) warp; stream-cable; (ich.) coal-fish. *— en queue de rat;* pointed stream-cable.

grêlon, *n.m.,* large hail-stone.

grelot, *n.m.,* little bell ' hawk bell, rattle. *Attacher le —;* to bell the cat (to take the first step in a difficult enterprise). *Trembler le —;* to tremble, to shake (till one's teeth chatter).

grelotter, *v.n.,* to quake, to shiver.

greluchon, *n.m.,* favored lover.

grément or **gréement,** *n.m.,* (nav.) rigging.

grémial, *n.m.,* (c. rel.) gremial, (eccl.) bishop's apron.

grémil, *n.m.,* (bot.) gromwell, gromil.

***grémillet,** *n.m.,* (bot.) scorpion-grass, scorpion's tail.

grenade, *n.f.,* pomegranate; (milit.) grenade.

grenadier, *n.m.,* pomegranate-tree; pomegranate; (milit.) grenadier. *— sauvage;* (bot.) wild pomegranate. *Jurer comme un —;* to swear like a trooper. *C'est un —, c'est un vrai —;* she is a regular termagant.

grenadière, *n.f.,* ⊙grenade-pouch; upper band (of a rifle). *Mettre son fusil à la —;* (milit.) to sling one's musket.

***grenadille,** *n.f.,* (bot.) grenadilla, passion-flower.

grenadin, *n.m.,* (cook.) small fricandeau.

grenadine, *n.f.,* grenadine (silk).

***grenaille,** *n.f.,* granulated metal; **refuse corn.**

***grenailler,** *v.a.,* to granulate.

***se grenailler,** *v.r.,* to granulate.

grenat, *n.m.,* (min.) garnet; great humming-bird; dried lemon-peel. *Couleur —;* garnet-red.

grené, *n.m.,* (engr.) stippling, blending.

greneler, *v.a.,* to grain (leather).

grener, *v.n.,* to seed, to run to seed; to produce seed.

grener, *v.a.,* to granulate, to corn; to grain (leather); (engr.) to stipple. *— de la poudre à canon;* to corn gunpowder.

grèneterie (grè-n-trî), *n.f.,* seed trade.

grèneti-er, *n.m.,* **-ère,** *n.f.* (grè-n-tié), seedsman; seedswoman.

grènetis (grè-n-tî), *n.m.,* milling, milled edge; milling punch, stamp.

grenettes, *n.f.pl.,* Avignon-berry, French-berry.

grenier, *n.m.,* granary, corn-loft, loft, cock-loft; garret; (nav.) floor-ceiling (of a ship). *— au foin;* hayloft. *En —;* in the granary, in store; (nav.) in bulk, unpacked. *Aller du — à la cave, de la cave au —;* to talk in a disjointed way, to tell a long rigmarole, to write up and down hill. *Charger en —;* (nav.) to load in bulk.

***grenouille,** *n.f.,* frog; (print.) frog.

***grenouillère,** *n.f.,* place full of frogs; marshy place; fen; (b.s.) damp, unhealthy house.

***grenouillet,** *n.m.,* (bot.) Solomon's seal, knee-grass.

***grenouillette,** *n.f.,* (med.) ranula; (bot.) buttercup; frogbit. *V.* **ranule.**

grenu, *adj.,* seedy, full of corn; granulous. *Epi bien —;* ear very full of corn. *Cuir bien —;* leather that has a good grain. *Huile —e;* clotted oil. *Marbre —;* grained marble.

grès, *n.m.,* sandstone; stoneware; (min.) grit, grit-stone, grit-rock. *— à bâtir;* free-stone. *— des rémouleurs;* grindstone.

⊙ **gréseu-x, -se,** *adj.,* sandy, gritty.

grésière, *n.f.,* sandstone quarry.

***grésil,** *n.m.,* sleet.

***grésillement,** *n.m.,* shriveling, shriveling up; wrinkling, pattering, crackling (as parchment does in the fire); shriveled state; chirping (of crickets).

***grésiller,** *v.imp.,* to sleet, to patter, to crackle.

***grésiller,** *v.a.,* to shrivel, to shrivel up, to wrinkle, to chirp (of crickets).

gresserie (grè-srî), *n.f.,* sandstone, grit, free-stone; stoneware; sandstone quarry.

grève, *n.f.,* strand; Grève (a square at Paris, where capital punishments formerly took place); strike of workmen. *Faire or se mettre en —;* to strike, to go out on strike (of workmen). *En —;* on strike.

grevé, *n.m.,* (jur.) heir of entail.

grever, *v.a.,* to wrong, to injure; to burden; to encumber (with debt, etc.). *Un pays grevé d'impôts;* a country burdened with taxes. *Terre grevée d'hypothèques;* estate encumbered with mortgages. *Terre non grevée;* unencumbered estate.

grianneau, n.m., young heath-cock; young grouse.

griblette, n.f., (cook.) hash of broiled meat.

*****gribouillage,** n.m., scrawl; daub (paint.).

*****gribouille,** n.m., simpleton, blockhead.

*****gribouiller,** v.a., to scrawl, to scribble (writing); to daub (paint.).

*****gribouillette,** n.f., scramble, scrambling. Attraper quelque chose à la —; to scramble for anything. À la —; negligently; carelessly; higgledy-piggledy.

gribouilleur, -se, n.m.f., scrawler, scribbler. adj., scrawling, scribbling, daubing.

gribouri, n.m., (zool.) vine-grub.

grièche, adj., (l.u.) prickly. Ortie- —(—s——s); sting-nettle. Pie- —(—s——s); shrew, scold, vixen.

grief (gri-èf), n.m., grievance, wrong, injury; complaint. Faire un —à quelqu'un; to do any one an injury. Redresser un —; to redress an injury. —s, —s et contredits; (jur.) plea.

grièvement (-èv-mān), adv., grievously, sorely, gravely, greatly, sadly, badly.

grièveté (-èv-té), n.f., enormity, gravity, heinousness.

griffade, n.f., clawing, scratch.

griffe, n.f., claw; fang; pounce, talon; grasp; (gard.) bulb; stamped facsimile of a signature; (tech.) catch; music-pen. Je suis sous ses —s; I am in his clutches. Donner un coup de — à quelqu'un; to do any one an ill office; to speak ill of any one. Apposer sa — à; to put one's signature to.

griffer, v.a., (falconry) to take with the claws, to claw; to scratch (of cats); (pop.) to clutch, to grab.

griffon, n.m., griffin, griffon (also a kind of water dog).

griffonnage, n.m., scrawl, scrawling, scribbling, scribble.

griffonner, v.a., to scrawl; to scribble.

griffonneu-r, n.m., **-se,** n.f., scrawler, scribbler.

*****grignon,** n.m., hard crust; residuum.

*****grignoter,** v.a., to nibble; to get pickings.

*****grignotis** (-ti), n.m., (engr.) crispness.

grigou, n.m., beggarly fellow, miserable wretch; sordid miser.

gril (gri), n.m., gridiron. Etre sur le —; to be upon thorns, to be in a mess; to be on tenter hooks.

*****grillade,** n.f., grilling, grill; broil; toast. Mettre à la —; to broil.

*****grillage,** n.m., grilling, broiling, toasting; light iron railing; wire lattice; wire guard; (metal.) roasting. — de bois; (arch.) frame of timber.

grillager, v.a., to lattice, to grate, to wire; to inclose with lattice work.

*****grille,** n.f., grate; grating; railing; gate (garden). — de fer; iron railing.

grille-pain, n.m., toasting-fork.

*****griller,** v.a., to inclose with iron rails; to rail in; to grate; (cook.) to broil, to grill, to toast; (metal.) to roast; to scorch (of the sun).

*****se griller,** v.r., to be scorched; to be parched; to be roasted.

*****griller,** v.n., (cook.) to broil; (fig.) to be on thorns, in hot water.

*****grillet,** n.m., or *****grillette,** n.f., (her.) hawk's bell.

*****grilleté, -e,** adj., (her., falconry) belled.

*****grilletier** (-tié), n.m., grate-maker.

*****grillon,** n.m., (ent.) cricket. — domestique; house-cricket. —-taupe (—s——s), taupe—(—s——s); fen-cricket, mole-cricket.

*****grillotter,** v.n., to chirp (like the cricket).

grimaçant, -e, adj., grimacing, grinning, (fig.) gaping, ill-fitting (of shoes).

grimace, n.f., grimace, wry face; humbug,

cant; pin-cushion, wafer-box. Faire la —; to make faces. Faire des —s à quelqu'un; to make faces at any one, to grin at any one. Faire la —; to be disgusted, not to like it. Cet habit fait la —; that coat puckers.

grimacer, v.n., to make faces, wry faces; to grin; to simper, to mince; to sham; to pucker.

grimacerie (-ma-srî), n.f., (l.u.) grimaces; grinning.

grimaci-er, -ère, adj. and n., grimacing; simpering; dissembling; canting, finical, mincing; simperer; dissembler, hypocrite, humbug.

grimaud, -e, adj., (l.u.) (of children) cross, ill-tempered, peevish.

grimaud, n.m., urchin, brat, dunce; scribbler, sorry writer, pedant.

grime, n.m., ⊙brat; (thea.) old man, old fogy. Il joue les —s; (thea.) he plays old men's parts.

se grimer, v.r., (thea.) to paint, to make up, to play old men, old women's parts, duennas, etc.

grimoire, n.m., conjuring book, black-book; obscure language; illegible scrawl. Il sait le —; he knows what he is about. C'est du — pour lui; it is Greek to him.

grimpant, -e, adj., (bot.) climbing.

grimpart, n.m., (orni.) nut-hatch.

grimper, v.n., to climb, to climb up, to clamber up, to creep up (of plants).

grimpereau, n.m. V. **grimpart.**

grimpeurs, n.m.pl., (orni.) climbers.

grincement (grins-man), n.m., gnashing, grinding (of the teeth); grating.

grincer, v.a., to gnash (the teeth); to grate. Faire — les dents; to make the teeth grate, to set the teeth on edge.

grincer, v.n., to grind; to gnash; to grate. — des dents; to grind one's teeth. La porte grinça sur ses gonds rouillés; the door grated on its rusty hinges.

grincheu-x, -se, adj., ill-tempered, peevish, crabbed, surly.

gringalet, n.m., weak, puny man, bit of a fellow, stripling, nobody.

gringolé, -e, adj., (her.) snake-headed.

gringotter, v.n., to twitter; to hum.

gringotter, v.a., to hum a tune badly.

gringuenaude, n.f., (l.ex.) dirt, filth.

griot, n.m., (of meal or flour) seconds.

griotte, n.f., marble with red and brown spots; morella cherry.

griottier, n.m., (bot.) egriot-tree, morella tree.

grippe, n.f., (l.u.) fancy, whim; hobby; crotchet, dislike; (med.) influenza. Prendre quelqu'un en —, se prendre de — contre quelqu'un; to take a dislike to any one. — argent; money-grubber.

grippé, part., (med.) shrunk, contracted (of the face); (of persons) ill with influenza.

grippeminaud (grip-minô), n. m., grimalkin (of a cat).

gripper, v.a., to gripe, to clutch, to seize, to snatch up; to nab; to crib.

se gripper, v.r., to shrivel; to take a dislike to.

grippe-sou, n.m., (—, or —-—s) pinch-penny; curmudgeon.

gris, -e, adj., gray; gray-headed; tipsy, fuddled. Cheveux —; gray hair. Lettres —es; (print.) flourished letters. Temps —; raw, dull, cloudy weather. Faire mine —e à quelqu'un; to look black at any one. Papier —; brown paper. En voir de —es; to have an unpleasant time of it. En faire voir de —es à; to lead any one a dance.

gris, n.m., gray. — cendré; ash-gray. — pommelé; dappled gray. — brun; drab.

gris-gris, n.m., amulet.

*****grisaille,** n.f., cameo with a gray ground; hair partly gray.

*****grisailler,** v.a., to paint gray.

*****grisailler,** v.n., (of hair) to turn gray.

grisâtre, adj., grayish.

griser, v.a., to give a gray tint to; to make tipsy, to fuddle.

se **griser**, v.r., to be intoxicated, to get tipsy, to be fuddled.

griser, v.n., (dy.) to turn gray.

griset, n.m., (orni.) young goldfinch.

grisette, n.f., gray gown, russet gown; (orni.) white-throat; grisette, gay work girl.

grisoller, v.n., to warble, to carol (of the lark).

grison, -ne, adj., gray, gray-haired, gray-headed.

grison, n.m., gray-beard (old man); donkey, ass (person); footman in gray livery; private agent; detective.

grisonnant, adj., getting gray.

grisonner, v.n., to grow gray (of hair).

grisou, n.m., (mining) fire-damp.

grive, n.f., (orni.) thrush. Il est soûl comme une —; he is as drunk as a fiddler. Faute de —s on mange des merles; half a loaf is better than no bread.

grivelé, -e (gri-vlé), adj., speckled.

griveler, v.a.n., to pilfer, to filch.

⊙**griveleur**, n.m., pilferer.

grivois, -e, adj., jolly; broad, obscene. Conte —; broad story.

grivois, n.m., jolly dog.

grivoise, n.f., jolly wench.

grog, n.m., grog — américain; hot punch.

*****grognard, -e**, adj., grumbling, growling.

*****grognard**, n.m., -e, n.f., grumbler, growler; veteran of the first French Empire.

*****grognement**, n.m., grunt, grunting, growling, grumbling.

*****grogner**, v.n., to grunt, to growl, to grumble.

*****grogneu-r, -se**, adj. and n., grumbling, growling; grumbler, growler.

*****grognon**, adj. m.f., grumbling, growling.

*****grognon**, n.m.f., grumbler, growler.

groin, n.m., snout (of a hog).

groisil, n.m., broken or pounded glass.

grolle, n.f., (orni.) rook.

groller, v.n., to croak, to grumble.

grommeler (grom-lé), v.n., to grumble, to mutter; to grunt.

grondant, -e, adj., scolding; roaring, rumbling.

grondement, n.m., rumbling, roaring, growling; snarl, snarling; roaring, peal.

gronder, v.n., to growl, to grumble, to mutter; to snarl, to rumble, to roar, to peal.

gronder, v.a., to chide, to scold, to reprimand.

gronderie (-drî), n.f., scolding, chiding.

grondeu-r, -se, adj., grumbling, scolding.

grondeu-r, -se, n.f., scold; grumbler.

grondin, n.m., (ich.) red gurnet.

groneau, n.m., gray gurnet.

groom, n.m., (—s) groom, buttons, tiger.

gros, -se, adj., large, big, great, bulky; pregnant, with child; loud (of laughter); dark (of color); rough (of the voice); heavy (of cavalry); coarse, thick; rich, substantial; foul, bad, heavy (of the weather); high. — bon sens; plain common sense. — mots; oaths, high words. —se somme d'argent; large sum of money. — drap; coarse cloth. — souliers; thick shoes. — rhume; bad cold. —se viande; butcher's meat. — lourdaud; blockhead. Un — marchand; a substantial tradesman. — bonnet; big - wig. — temps; foul, rough, heavy weather. La mer est —se; the sea runs high. Une —se femme; a stout woman. Une femme —se; a pregnant woman. Toucher la grosse corde; to come to the main point. Jouer — jeu; to play high. A la —se; roughly; (com.) on bottomry.

gros, n.m., large part; bulk, mass; main body (of an army); large hand (writing); (com.) wholesale. Vendre en —; to sell wholesale. En — et en détail; wholesale and retail. Faire le — de la besogne; to do the heavy work.

gros, adv., much. Gagner —; to earn, to win much, a great deal.

gros-bec, n.m., (— - —s) (orni.) grosbeak.

gros canon, n.m., (print.) French canon.

*****groseille**, n.f., — à grappes; red currant, white currant. — à maquereau, — verte; gooseberry.

*****groseillier**, n.m., red-currant-tree, white-currant-tree; gooseberry-bush. — noir; (l.u.) black-currant-tree. V. cassis.

*****groseillon**, n.m., small currant.

gros-jean, n.m., (— - —s) a vulgar fellow, a countryman, mere nobody. Etre — comme devant; to be as you were (i.e., no better off). — en remontre à son curé; (prov.) to teach one's grandmother how to suck eggs.

grosse, n.f., gross (twelve dozen); large hand (writing); bottomry; (jur.) copy. Contrat à la —; bottomry bond. Prêt à la —; bottomry loan.

grossement, adv., grossly, coarsely.

grosserie (grô-srî), n.f., ironmongery; wholesale. Il ne fait que la —; he is a wholesale dealer only.

grossesse, n.f., pregnancy.

grosseur, n.f., bigness, largeness, hugeness, size, bulk; swelling.

grossi-er, -ère, adj., coarse, thick; homely, plain, common; clumsy, rough, rude; unpolished, uncivilized; unmannerly, scurrilous; churlish, unpolite, uncouth, boorish. Des meubles —s; clumsy furniture. Mœurs —ères; unpolished manners. Vous êtes bien —; you are very unmannerly. Il m'aborda d'un air —; he accosted me rudely. Erreur —ère; gross mistake.

grossièrement (-sièr-mān), adv., coarsely, rudely, roughly, uncouthly, boorishly, unmannerly, scurrilously; churlishly; grossly, indecently.

grossièreté (-sièr-té), n.f., coarseness, grossness; rudeness, clownishness, roughness, incivility, bluntness, unmannerliness; coarse language, scurrility; clumsiness, awkwardness; churlishness. Il lui a dit des —s; he said rude things to him.

grossir, v.a., to make bigger, greater; to enlarge, to augment, to increase; to swell, to swell out; to magnify.

se **grossir**, v.r., to grow bigger, larger; to increase in size; to increase, to augment, to be increased; to swell; to magnify.

grossir, v.n., to get big, large; to grow stout; to magnify; to enlarge; to swell out.

grossissant, adj., magnifying. Verre —; magnifying glass.

grossissement (-sis-mān), n.m., magnifying, enlargement, increase; exaggeration.

grosso-modo, adv., summarily, generally, roughly.

grossoyer, v.a., to engross, to copy in a large hand.

grotesque, n.m. and adj., grotesque; grotesque figure; grotesque dancer; clown.

grotesquement, adv., grotesquely.

grotte, n.f., grotto, grot; crypt.

*****grouillant, -e**, adj., (pop.) stirring, moving about; swarming, crawling. Tout — de vermine, crawling with vermin.

*****grouillement** (groo-), n.m., (pop.) rumbling (of the intestines); rattling; stirring, swarming.

*****grouiller**, v.n., (pop.) to stir, to move; to rumble (of the intestines); to shake (the head with old age); to swarm. Le ventre me grouille; my belly rumbles. La tête lui grouille; his head shakes. Cela grouille de vermine; that is alive with vermin.

group (groop), *n.m.*, (com.) sealed bag of specie.

groupe, *n.m.*, group, cluster, clump (of trees); crowd, flock, (print.) heading.

groupement, *n.m.*, grouping.

grouper, *v.a.*, to group.

se **grouper**, *v.r.*, to form into groups, to be grouped, to gather, to collect.

grouper, *v.n.*, (paint.) to group.

gruau, *n.m.*, oat-meal; gruel, groats; (tech.) small crane. *Farine de* —; groats. *Pain de* —; finest wheaten bread.

grue, *n.f.*, (orni., tech.) crane; (astron.) Grus; simpleton, goose. *Faire le pied de* —; to dance attendance.

⊙**gruerie**, *n.f.*, wood-mote.

grugeon, *n.m.*, lump (of sugar).

gruger, *v.a.*, to craunch, to eat, to eat up, to devour. — *du sucre;* to craunch sugar.

grugerie, *n.f.*, craunching.

grugeur, *n.m.*, squanderer, sponger, parasite.

grume, *n.f.*, bark. *En* —; with the bark on.

grumeau, *n.m.*, clod, clot, lump.

se **grumeler**, *v.r.*, to clot.

grumeleu-x, **-se** (gru-mleû, -z), *adj.*, clotted, grumous, rugged, rough. *Sang* —; clotted blood. *Poires* —*ses;* rough pears.

gruyer, *n.m.*, a justice in eyre.

gruy-er, **-ère**, *adj.*, of the crane. *Faucon* —; hawk trained to fly the crane. *Faisan* —; crane pheasant. ⊙*Seigneur* —; lord having certain rights on the woods of his vassals.

gruyère, *n.m.*, Gruyere cheese.

guano (gooa-no), *n.m.*, guano.

gué (ghé), *n.m.*, ford. *Passer une rivière à* —; to ford a river. *Sonder le* —; to probe the ford; (fig.) to sound a person.

guéable (ghé-), *adj.*, fordable.

guèbre, *n.m.* *V.* **gaure**.

guédasse, *n.f.*, weed-ash.

guède (ghèd), *n.f.*, (dy.) woad, dyer's-woad, pastel.

guéder (ghé-dé), *v.a.*, to dye with woad; ⊙to cram, to stuff (with food).

⊙*se* **guéder**, *v.r.*, to cram one's self with food.

guéer (ghéé), *v.a.*, to ford. — *un cheval;* to water a horse. — *du linge;* to wash linen (in a river). *Se* —, *v.r.*, to be forded.

guelfe, *n.m.*, (Italian hist.) Guelph.

***guenille** (ghé-), *n.f.*, rag,tatter; rubbish, trifle, trumpery, thing.

***guenilleu-x**, **-se**, *adj.*, tattered, ragged, in rags; rubbishy, trumpery, worthless.

***guenillon** (ghè-), *n.m.*, little rag; scrap.

guenipe (ghè-), *n.f.*, slut, trollop; drab.

guenon (ghè-), *n.f.*, (mam.) monkey; she-monkey; fright, ugly woman; strumpet.

guenuche (ghè-), *n.f.*, young she-monkey. — *coiffée;* over-dressed woman; ape in petticoats.

guépard, *n.m.*, (mam.) cheetah.

guêpe (ghêp), *n.f.*, (ent.) wasp. — *-frelon* (—*s*—*s*); hornet. *Mouche-* — (—*s*—*s*); wasp-fly. *Taille de* —; very slender waist. *Nid de* —; wasps' nest.

guêpier, *n.m.*, wasps' nest; (orni.) bee-eater; scrape, difficulty. *Donner, tomber, dans un* —; to get into a scrape.

⊙**guerdon** (ghèr-), *n.m.*, guerdon, recompense, reward, meed.

⊙**guerdonner**, *v.a.*, to requite, to reward, to recompense.

guère or **guères** (ghèr), *adv.*, but little, not much, not very; not long; hardly, scarcely, very few. *N'avoir* — *d'argent;* to have but little money. *Il n'est* — *sage;* he is not very wise. *Il ne tardera* — *à venir;* it will not be long before he comes *or* he will soon come. *Il ne s'en faut* — *plus;* it wants but little. *N'avoir* — *plus;* to have little more. *N'avoir* — *moins;* to

have little less. *Je ne le vois* —; I hardly ever see him.

guéret (ghé-rè), *n.m.*, (agri.) land unsown; fallow-land. *pl.*, (poet.) fields.

guéridon (ghé-), *n.m.*, gueridon, round table, centre table, loo-table, stand; (nav.) scoop.

guérilla (ghé-) *n.f.*, guerilla.

guérilla, *n.m.*, guerilla-soldier.

guérir (ghé-), *v.a.*, to heal, to cure. — *la fièvre;* to cure a fever. — *quelqu'un d'une erreur;* to rid any one of an error. *Cela ne me guérira de rien;* that will be of no use to me.

se **guérir**, *v.r.*, to recover, to be cured, to heal, to be healed, to recover one's health, to mend; to get rid, to be rid of. *Se* — *de ses préventions;* to get rid of one's prejudices. *Médecin, guéris-toi toi-même;* physician, heal thyself.

guérir, *v.n.*, to heal, to heal up; to recover, to be cured; to get rid, to be rid. *On ne guérit point de la peur;* fear admits of no cure.

guérison (ghé-), *n.f.*, recovery, healing, cure. *Il lui doit sa* —; he owes his recovery to him.

guérissable, *adj.*, curable.

guérisseu-r, *n.m.*, **-se**, *n.f.*, (b.s.) healer, curer.

guérite (ghé-), *n.f.*, sentry-box; turret, watch-tower. *Gagner la* —; to take to one's heels, to make off.

guerre (ghèr), *n.f.*, war; warfare; strife, dissension, contest. — *à mort;* war to the knife. — *de plume;* paper warfare. *Vaisseau de* —; man-of-war. *Petite* —; sham fight; war on a small scale. *Cri de* —; war-cry. *Foudre de* —; great warrior *or* general. *Gens de* —; military men. *Place de* —; fortified town, fortress. *Nom de* —; nickname; assumed name. *Aller à la petite* —; to go out pillaging. *Faire la* — *avec;* to serve with, to be a fellow-soldier. *Faire la* — *à ses passions;* to struggle against one's passions. *Faire la* — *à;* to be at war with. *Il lui en fit la* —; he found fault with him for it. *Faire la* — *à l'œil;* to be on the look-out for opportunities. *Faire bonne* — *à quelqu'un;* to deal fairly with any one. *De bonne* —; by fair play, by fair means. *A la* — *comme à la* —; one must take things as they come. *Qui terre a,* — *a;* much coin, much care. *Moitié* —, *moitié marchandise;* armed (of ships); (fig.) half-willingly, half-compulsorily. *Faire une chose de* — *lasse;* to do a thing against one's will, after long resistance. *En* —; at variance.

guerri-er, **-ère**, *n.* and *adj.*, warrior; female warrior; warlike; martial.

guerroyant, **-e**, *adj.*, martial, combative, pugnacious.

guerroyer, *v.n.*, to make war, to wage war, to war.

guerroyeur, *n.m.*, man fond of fighting.

guet (ghè), *n.m.*, watch; watching sentinel. — *de nuit;* patrol, night-watch. *Mot du* —; watchword. *Maison du* —; round-house. *Crier au* —; to call the watch. *Etre au* —, *avoir l'œil au* —, *l'oreille au* —; to be on the watch, to be on the look-out. *Ce chien est de très bon* —; this is a very good watch-dog. *Se donner le mot du* —; to act in concert. *Faire le* —; to watch, to keep watch; to look out, to be on the look-out. *Au* —; on the watch, on the look-out.

guet-apens (ghè-ta-pän), *n.m.*, (—*s*—) ambush, ambuscade; willful injury; lying in wait. *De* —; by lying in wait. *Dresser un* — *à;* to waylay.

guêtre (ghê-tr), *n.f.*, gaiter. *Grande* —; legging. *Tirer ses* —*s;* to run away; to hook it. *Laisser ses* —*s quelque part;* to leave one's bones somewhere.

guêtré, **-e**, *adj.*, gaitered.

guêtrer, *v.a.*, to put on gaiters, to gaiter.

se **guêtrer**, *v.r.*, to put on one's gaiters.

guêtrier, *n.m.*, gaiter-maker.

guetter (ghé-té), *v.a.*, to lie in wait for, to watch for, to be upon the watch for ; to dog the footsteps of, to watch ; to wait for, to await.

guetteur, *n.m.*, (nav.) signal-man, lookout-man. [gully-hole.

gueulard (gheu-lar), *n.m.*, furnace-mouth ;
gueulard, *n.m.*, **-e**, *n.f.*, (pop.) brawler, bawler ; glutton. *adj.*, (of horses) hard-mouthed.

gueule (gheul), *n.f.*, mouth (of an animal) ;
jaws, chops. — *renversée ;* (arch.) ogive. *A — dépourvue de dents ;* (ich.) leather-mouthed. *En — ;* (bot.) labiated. *La — d'un chien ;* the mouth of a dog. — *de canon ;* muzzle of a gun. *La—d'un sac ;* the mouth of a sack. *Mettre quelqu'un à la — du loup ;* to put any one in the clutches of his enemy. — *fraîche ;* (triv.) person always ready to eat. *Homme fort en — ;* (triv.) abusive man ; great gabbler. *Femme trop forte en — ;* (triv.) ill-tongued woman. *Fine — ;* (fam.) epicure, judge of good living. *Il n'a que de la — ;* (triv.) he is all talk. *Donner sur la — à quelqu'un ;* (triv.) to give any one a dressing. *Il est venu la — enfarinée ;* (triv.) he came blundering and full of confidence. *Il a la — pavée ;* (triv.) his throat must be paved. *Il a la — morte ;* (triv.) he is down in the mouth.

gueule-de-loup, *n.f.*, cowl, chimney cowl ; (—*s*—) (bot.) snapdragon, calf's snout.

gueulée, *n.f.*, (l.ex.) large mouthful ; indecent expression.

gueuler (gheu-lé), *v.n.*, (pop.) to bawl, to squall, to clamor, to mouth.

gueuler, *v.a.*, (hunt.) to take up, to seize.

gueules, *n.m.*, (her.) gules. *Porter des — ;* to bear gules. [low set, rabble, riffraff.

*****gueusaille** (gheu-), *n.f.*, parcel of beggars,

gueusailler, *v.n.*, to beg, to loaf, to go begging.

gueusant, **-e** (gheu-), *adj.*, begging, mumping.

gueusard, *n.m.*, beggar, scoundrel, black-guard, ragamuffin, loafer.

gueuse (gheuz), *n.f.*, pig-iron ; beggar ; bad woman, wench, hussy.

gueuser, *v.a.* and *n.*, (fam.) to beg ; to clamour for. — *des encens ;* to clamour after praise.

gueuserie (gheû-zrî), *n.f.*, beggary, beggarliness ; trash ; poverty, mendicity, villainy.

gueuset, *n.m.*, pig-iron.

gueu-x, **-se**, *adj.*, poor, beggarly, wretched, destitute. — *comme un rat d'église ;* as poor as a church-mouse.

gueux, *n.m.*, beggar ; knave, rascal, ragamuffin, scoundrel. *Tas de — ;* pack of scoundrels.— *revêtu ;* upstart, beggar on horseback.

gui (ghi), *n.m.*, mistletoe ; (nav.) main-boom (of a sloop, of a brig).

guibre (ghi-br), *n. f.*, (nav.) cut-water.

guichet (ghi-shè), *n.m.*, wicket ; grating ; door ; shutter, small window. *A remettre au — ;* to be handed in over the counter.

guichetier (ghish-tié), *n.m.*, turnkey.

guide (ghid), *n.m.*, guide ; guide-book ; text-book ; (milit.) fugleman.

guide, *n.f.*, rein (of a bridle). *Conduire à grandes —s ;* to drive four-in-hand. *Mener la vie à grandes —s ;* to live in grand style, a very fast life.

guide-âne, *n.m.*, (—, or — - -*s*) guide-book.

guide-chaîne, *n.m.*, (—, or — - -*s*) (horl.) guard, ratchet.

guide-main, *n.m.*, (—, or — - -*s*) (of the piano-forte) chiroplast, hand-guide.

guider (ghi-dé), *v.a.*, to guide, to lead, to conduct ; to direct ; to actuate ; (nav.) to steer.

guidon (ghi-), *n. m.*, (milit.) field-colors, guidon ; (of fire-arms) sight ; (of writings) reference, marks ; (nav.) broad pendant ; (mus.) direction ; handle-bar. — *de renvoi ;* reference.

guifette (ghi-), *n.f.*, (orni.) sea-swallow.

*****guignard** (ghi-), *n.m.*, (orni.) dotterel.

*****guigne** (ghi-), *n.f.*, black-heart cherry ; (fam. and fig. ill-luck.

*****guigner** (ghi-), *v.a.*, (fam.) to wink at, to ogle, to peer at ; to covet ; to peep at ; to have in view, to have a design upon. — *une charge ;* to have an eye to some post.

*****guigner**, *v.n.*, to leer, to peer, to ogle.

*****guignette** (ghi-), *n.f.*, (orni.) common sand-piper.

*****guignier** (ghi-), *n.m.*, black-heart cherry-tree.

guignol, *n.m.*, puppet-show ; Punch and Judy show.

*****guignon** (ghi-), *n.m.*, (fam.) bad luck, ill-luck. *Avoir du — ;* to be unlucky. *Etre en — ;* to have a run of ill-luck.

guignonnant, **-e**, *adj.*, provoking.

guigue (gig), *n.f.*, (nav.) gig.

*****guildive** (ghi-), *n.f.*, (l.u.) tafia, rum.

*****guillage** (ghi-), *n.m.*, working, fermentation (of beer).

*****guilaume** (ghi-), *n.m.*, rabbet plane.

*****guilledin** (ghi-), *n.m.*, gelding.

*****guilledou** (ghi-), *n.m.*, (pop.) places of ill-fame. *Courir le — ;* to frequent places of ill-fame.

*****guillemet** (ghi-), *n. m.*, (print.) inverted comma.

*****guillemeter**, *v.a.*, to put between inverted commas.

*****guillemot** (ghi-), *n.m.*, (orni.) guillemot.

guiller, *v.n.*, to work, to ferment (of beer).

*****guilleret**, **-te** (ghi-), *adj.*, sprightly, gay, lively, dapper. *Il a l'air — ;* he has a sprightly air.

*****guilleri** (ghi-), *n.m.*, chirping (of sparrows).

guillet, *n.m.*, tip cat (game).

*****guillocher** (ghi-), *v.a.*, (arch.) to engine-turn.

*****guillochis** (ghi-), *n.m.*, (arch.) engine-turning.

*****guillotine** (ghi-), *n.f.*, guillotine.

*****guillotiné**, *n.m.*, **-e**, *n.f.*, person guillotined ; executed.

*****guillotinement**, *n.m.*, guillotining.

*****guillotiner**, *v.a.*, to guillotine, to behead.

guimauve (ghi-), *n.f.*, marsh-mallow.

*****guimaux** (ghi-), *n.m.pl.*, meadows mowed twice a year.

guimbarde (ghin-), *n.f.*, wagon, van ; jew's-harp ; rickety old coach.

guimpe (ghinp), *n.f.*, stomacher, chemisette ; veil (for nuns).

guinard, *n.m.*, (ich.) red gurnet.

guindage (ghin-), *n.m.*, (nav.) hoisting.

guindant (ghin-), *n.m.*, (nav.) hoist (of flags).

guinde, *n.f.*, **guinda**, **guindeau**, *n.m.*, (nav.) windlass, hoist.

guindé, **-e**, *part.*, stiff, strained, forced, unnatural ; (of style) stilted, formal. *Cet homme est toujours — ;* that man is always as stiff as a poker.

guinder (ghin-dé), *v.a.*, to hoist, to strain, to force ; (nav.) to hoist up (masts) ; (of style) to strain, to force.

se guinder, *v.r.*, to be strained ; to be forced, to bridle up.

guinderesse (ghin-drès), *n.f.*, (nav.) top-rope.

guinderie (ghin-drî), *n.f.*, constraint, stiffness.

guinée (ghi-), *n.f.*, guinea ; long cloth.

guingan (ghin-), *n.m.*, gingham.

guingois (ghin-ghoa), *n.m.*, crookedness. *De — ;* awry, cross-grained. *Marcher tout de — ;* to walk crookedly. *Avoir l'esprit de — ;* to be cross-grained.

guinguette (ghin-ghèt), *n.f.*, road-side inn ; tea-garden.

guiorant, **-e**, *adj.*, squeaking.

guiorer (ghi-), *v.n.*, (of mice) to squeak.

guipon (ghi-), *n.m.*, (nav.) mop.

guipure (ghi-), *n.f.*, guipure-lace.

guirlande (ghir-), *n.f.*, garland, wreath ; girdle (of jewels) ; (arch.) belt (of a column).

guise (ghiz), *n.f.*, manner, way ; fancy, humor. *En — de* ; by way of. *Chacun vit à sa —* ; everybody lives as he likes. *Faire à sa —* ; to do as one likes ; to have one's own way.

guitardin (ghi-), *n.m.*, (bot.) fiddle-wood.

guitare (ghi-), *n.f.*, guitar. *Jouer, pincer, de la —* ; to play the guitar.

guitariste, *n.m.f.*, guitarist, guitar-player.

guiterne (ghi-), *n.f.*, (nav.) prop.

guit-guit (ghi-ghi), *n.m.*, (—s——s) a variety of humming-birds.

guiton (ghi-), *n.m.*, (nav.) dog-watch.

guivre, *n.f.* V. **givre**.

gulf-stream, *n.m.*, (*n.p.*) (geog.) Gulf-Stream.

gumène, *n.f.*, (her.) cable (of an anchor).

gustatif, *adj.m.*, (anat.) (of nerves) gustatory, hypoglossal.

gustation, *n.f.*, tasting, gustation.

gutta-percha (-ka), *n.f.*, (*n.p.*) gutta-percha.

gutte. V. **gomme**.

guttier, *n.m.*, (bot.) gamboge-tree.

guttifères, *n.m.pl.*, (bot.) guttiferæ.

guttiforme, *adj.*, drop-shaped.

guttural, -e (gut-tu-), *adj.*, guttural.

gutturale, *n.f.*, guttural.

gymnase (jim-nâz), *n.m.*, gymnasium.

gymnaste, *n.m.*, gymnast.

gymnastique, *n.f.*, gymnastics.

gymnastique, *adj.*, gymnastic.

gymnique, *adj.*, gymnic.

gymnique, *n.f.*, gymnic.

gymnosophiste, *n.m.*, gymnosophist.

gymnosperme, *adj.*, (bot.) gymnospermous.

gymnospermie, *n.f.*, (bot.) gymnospermia.

gymnote, *n.m.*, gymnotus. *— électrique ;* electric eel.

gynandre, *adj.*, (bot.) gynandrous.

gynandrie, *n.f.*, (bot.) gynandria.

gynécée, *n.m.*, women's apartment, gyneceum, gynæceum.

gynécocratie (-ci), *n.f.*, gynæcocracy, petticoat government.

gynécocratique, *adj.*, of a gynæcocracy.

gypaète, *n.m.*, (orni.) griffin, bearded vulture, lammergeier.

gypse, *n.m.*, gypsum, parget ; plaster of Paris.

gypseu-x, -se, *adj.*, gypseous.

gyratoire, *adj.* V. **giratoire**.

gyromancie, *n.f.*, gyromancy.

gyroselle, *n.f.*, (bot.) Virginian cowslip.

gyrovague, *n.m.*, wandering monk ; tramp.

H

[All words in which the *h* is aspirated, are marked thus †.]

h, *n.m.f.*, the eighth letter of the alphabet, h.

†ha ! *int.*, ah ! ha !

habeas corpus, *n.m.*, (*n.p.*) habeas-corpus.

habile, *adj.*, able, clever, skillful ; expert, sharp, quick ; qualified ; capable ; knowing, cunning ; (nav.) able-bodied. *— dans les affaires ;* skillful in business.

habilement (a-bil-mān), *adv.*, cleverly, skillfully, ably ; dexterously ; knowingly.

habileté (a-bil-té), *n.f.*, ability, skill, cleverness, skillfulness, artfulness, sharpness.

habilissime, *adj.*, very clever, very skillful.

habilitation, *n.f.*, (jur.) habilitation, qualification, aptitude.

habilité, *n.f.*, (jur.) competency, qualification.

*habiliter, *v.a.*, (jur.) to qualify.

*habillage, *n.m.*, (cook.) trussing poultry.

habillant, -e, *adj.*, dressy, nice, rich.

habillé, -e, *part.*, dressed, clothed, clad, decked out.

*habillement, *n.m.*, clothes, clothing, dress, wearing apparel, attire. *— complet ;* complete suit of clothes.

*habiller, *v.a.*, to dress, to clothe ; to make clothes for ; to wrap up ; to become ; to fit ; (cook.) to prepare. *Ce tailleur m'habille ;* that tailor makes my clothes, works for me. *Il habille bien ;* he works well. *Cette étoffe vous habille bien ;* that stuff becomes you very well. *— une pensée en vers ;* to clothe a thought in verse. *— de la volaille ;* to draw and truss fowls. *— du poisson ;* to gut and scale fish. *— du cuir ;* to dress leather.

s'habiller, *v.r.*, to dress one's self ; to have one's clothes made ; to find one's own clothes ; to abuse each other. *Cet homme s'habille bien ;* that man dresses well.

habilleu-r, *n.m.*, **-se**, *n.f.*, (thea.) dresser ; skin-dresser.

habit, *n.m.*, garment, dress, apparel, garb ; coat, dress coat. *pl.*, clothes, wearing apparel. *— bourgeois ;* private clothes. *— complet ;* suit of clothes. *— habillé ;* dress coat, full dress, evening dress. *— galonné ;* laced-coat. *— de cheval ;* riding-coat. *— s de deuil ;* mourning. *Porter un — râpé ;* to wear a shabby, seedy coat. *L'— ne fait pas le moine ;* it is not the cowl that makes the friar ; it is not the coat that makes the man. *Prendre l'— ;* to become a monk *or* (of a nun) to take the veil.

habitabilité, *n.f.*, habitableness ; habitability.

habitable, *adj.*, inhabitable, habitable.

habitacle, *n.m.*, ☉ habitation, abode, dwelling ; (nav.) binnacle.

habitant, *n.m.*, **-e**, *n.f.*, inhabitant, resident, inmate ; occupant, occupier ; denizen. *Les —s des bois ;* the denizens of the woods.

habitat, *n.m.*, (zoöl.) habitat.

habitation, *n.f.*, habitation, residence, abode, tenement, dwelling-place ; place of abode ; plantation, settlement (in a colony) ; (zool., bot.) habitat, haunt. *Maison d'— ;* (jur.) dwelling-house.

habiter, *v.a.*, to inhabit, to dwell in, to live in, to reside in, to frequent. *— un lieu ;* to live in a place.

habiter, *v.n.*, to inhabit ; to dwell in ; to reside in ; (jur.) to cohabit.

habitude, *n.f.*, habit, custom, use ; practice, wont ; (b.s.) trick. *Il n'en fait pas une habitude ;* he does not make a custom of it. *L'— est une autre nature ;* use is a second nature. *Faire quelque chose par — ;* to do a thing from habit. *Faire perdre une vilaine — à quelqu'un ;* to break any one of a bad habit, of a nasty trick. *D'— ;* usual, habitual ; usually, generally.

habitué, -e, *part.*, used, accustomed.

habitué, *n.m.*, **-e**, *n.f.*, frequenter, customer. *Les —s d'un café ;* the regular customers of a tavern. *Ce monsieur est un de nos —s ;* that gentleman is one of our regular customers.

habituel, -le, *adj.*, habitual, customary, usual.

habituellement (-èl-mān), *adv.*, habitually, customarily, usually.

habituer, *v.a.*, to use, to accustom to habituate, to inure. *— les jeunes gens à la fatigue ;* to inure young men to fatigue.

s'habituer, *v.r.*, to accustom, to inure, one's self. *Je m'y habituerai ;* I shall get used to it. *S'— au climat ;* to get inured to the climate.

†hâbler, *v.n.*, to brag, to boast, to draw the long-bow.

†hâblerie, *n.f.*, bragging, boasting, drawing the long-bow.

†hâbleu-r, *n.m.*, **-se**, *n.f.*, bragger, boaster.

†hache, *n.f.*, ax, hatchet. *— d'armes ;* battle-ax, pole ax. *Fait à coups de — ;* clumsily made, roughly done. *— d'abordage ;* boarding-hatchet.

†haché, -e, *adj.*, (style) abrupt, irregular, desultory.

*†hache-paille, n.m., (—) chaff-cutter.

†hacher, v.a., to chop, to hew, to hack, to cut to pieces; (engr.) to hatch; (cook.) to hash, to mince; (drawing) to tint. — *en morceaux;* to cut to pieces. — *quelqu'un menu comme chair à pâté;* to make mince-meat of any one.

†hachereau (ha-shrô), n.m., little ax, hatchet.

†hachette, n.f., hacking-knife, hatchet.

†hachis, n.m., (cook.) minced meat, hash.

†hachisch, n.m. (n.p.), hashish.

†hachoir, n.m., chopping-board; chopping-knife; chaff-cutter.

†hachure, n.f., (engr.) hatching.

†hagard, -e, adj., haggard, wild.

hagiographe, n.m., hagiographer.

hagiographe, adj., hagiographic.

hagiographie, n.f., hagiography.

hagiologique, adj., hagiological.

†haha! n.m., ha-ha, haw-haw.

†hahé! int., (hunt.) tally-ho!

†hai! int., hey! well! indeed! bless me!

†haie, n.f., hedge, hedgerow; beam of a plow; row, line. — *vive;* quickset hedge. *Se ranger en* —; to form a line. *Fermer d'une* —; to hedge in. *Border la* —; to line a road (with troops).

†haïe! int., (carter's cry) gee ho!

*†haillon, n.m., rag, rags, tatters.

†haine, n.f., hate, hatred; spite, aversion, dislike; grudge. *Avoir de la* — *pour, avoir en* —; to hate. *Porter de la* — *à;* to feel hatred towards.

†haineusement, adv., hatefully, spitefully.

†haineu-x, -se, adj., hateful, malignant, spiteful.

†haïr, v.a., to hate, to detest, to loathe. — *cordialement;* to hate heartily. — *comme la peste,* — *à la mort;* to feel a deadly hatred towards.

†haire, n.f., hair-shirt.

†haïssable, adj., hateful, odious.

†halage, n.m., towage, towing. *Chemin de* —; towing-path.

†halbran, n.m., young wild-duck.

†halbrené, -e, adj., ragged feathered (of a bird); ragged, in a sad light.

†halbrener, v.n., to shoot wild ducks.

hale, n.m., tow-line, tow-rope. — *bas;* (nav.) down-haul.

†hâle, n.m., heat of the sun; sunburn; scorching heat; tanned complexion. *Le* — *fane tout;* the heat of the sun dries up everything; (agri.) drying wind.

†hâlé, -e, part., sun-burnt; swarthy; tanned.

haleine, n.f., breath, wind. *Perdre l'* —; to get out of breath. *Reprendre* —; to recover one's breath. *Courir à perte d'* —; to run until one is out of breath. *Phrases à perte d'* —; long-winded sentences. *Tout d'une* —; in the same breath. *Un ouvrage de longue* —; a long-winded work. *Tenir en* —; to keep on the alert. *Tenir les gens en* —; to keep the ball rolling.

halenée, n.f., smell, breath, whiff.

halener, v.a., to breathe; (hunt.) to get scent of.

†haler, v.a., (nav.) to haul, to heave; to set, to excite. — *un bateau à la cordelle;* to tow a boat. — *un bâtiment;* to track a vessel. — *le vent;* to haul the wind. — *un chien sur quelqu'un;* to set a dog at any one.

†hâler, v.a., to tan, to burn (of the sun). *se* **†hâler**, v.r., to become sun-burnt.

†haletant, -e, adj., out of breath, panting, puffing.

†haleter (hal-té), v.n., to blow, to puff, to pant or gasp for breath.

†haleur, n.m., tracker, hauler.

halieutiques, n.m.pl., halieutics.

halitueu-x, -se, adj., (med.) halituous.

†hallage, n.m., market-dues.

hallali, n.m., (stag-hunting) whoop; flourish of the horn at the death.

†halle, n.f., market; market-place. *Langage des* —*s;* Billingsgate (language). *Dames de la* —; market women. *Aller à la* —; to go to market. — *aux blés;* corn-exchange. *Fort de la* —; market-porter.

†hallebarde (hal-bard), n.f., halberd. *Pleuvoir or tomber des* —*s;* to rain cats and dogs.

†hallebardier, n.m., halberdier.

†hallier, n.m., thicket; partridge-net; market-keeper.

hallucination (hal-lu-), n.f., hallucination, delusion.

halluciné, -e, adj. and n., (med.) hallucinated; (fig.) deluded.

halluciner, v.a., to hallucinate, to delude.

†halo, n.m., halo.

†hâloir, n.m., drying-room (for hemp).

†halot, n.m., rabbit burrow.

†halochimie, n.f., (chem.) of the preparation of salts.

†halte, n.f., halt; stand, stop; halting-place; resting-place. *Faire* —; to halt. — *la!* hold! stop there! that won't do!

haltères, n.m., dumb-bells; (of insects) poisers.

halurgie, n.f., making or extracting salts.

†hamac, n.m., hammock. *Haut les* —*s;* (nav.) up all hammocks. — *à l'anglaise;* (nav.) cot.

hamadryade, n.f., (myth.) Hamadryad, wood-nymph.

†hameau, n.m., hamlet.

hameçon (am-son), n.m., hook, fish-hook; bait. *Mordre à l'* —; to take the bait.

hameçonné, -e, adj., hooked.

⊙hameçonner, v.a., to hook; to take in.

†hampe, n.f., staff (of a lance, etc., etc.); handle (of a brush); flower-stalk.

†han, n.m., heave (of a workman striking a heavy blow.

†hanap, n.m., goblet; bowl.

†hanche, n.f., hip, haunch; (nav.) quarter. *Les poings sur les* —*s;* with his or her arms akimbo.

hanchoan, n.m., Brazilian buzzard.

†hanebane, n.f. V. **jusquiame**.

†hangar, n.m., outhouse, shed, cart-shed, cart-house.

†hanneton (ha-n-ton), n.m., may-bug, cock-chafer; (fig.) thoughtless, giddy person.

†hanovrien, -ne (-in, -è-n), adj., Hanoverian.

†hanovrien, n.m., -ne, n.f., Hanoverian.

†hanscrit, n.m. V. **sanscrit**.

†hanse, n.f., Hanse-Towns. *La* — *Teutonique;* the Hanse-Towns.

hanséatique or **anséatique**, adj., Hanseatic.

†hansière, n.f., (nav.) hawser. V. **haussière**.

†hanter, v.a., to haunt; to frequent, to resort to; to associate with. *Dis-moi qui tu hantes et je te dirai qui tu es;* tell me the company you keep, and I will tell you what you are; birds of a feather flock together.

†hanter, v.n., to frequent. —*chez quelqu'un;* to be a visitor at any one's house.

†hantise, n.f., (b.s.) intercourse, intimacy.

†happe, n.f., axle-tree bed (of carriages); cramp-iron.

†happe-chair, n.m., (—) grasp-all; torment, dun.

†happelourde (ha-ploord), n.f., paste, imitation stone; well-dressed fool.

†happer, v.a., to snap, to snap up; to catch, to lay hold of, to nab.

†haquenée (ha-knée), n.f., ambling nag; ill-made, ungainly woman. *Aller sur la* — *des cordeliers;* to trudge along on foot; to ride on shank's mare.

†haquet (ha-kè), n.m., dray.

†**haquetier** (hak-tié), *n.m.*, drayman.

†**harangue**, *n.f.*, harangue, speech, address, oration. *La tribune aux — s;* the rostrum.

†**haranguer** (-ghé), *v.a.*, to harangue.

†**haranguer**, *v.n.*, to harangue, to hold forth, to speechify.

†**harangueu-r** (-gheur), *n.m.*, **-se**, *n.f.*, haranguer, orator; speech-maker, speechifier.

†**haras**, *n.m.*, stud, breeding-stud. (orni.) *V.* **ara**.

†**harasse**, *n.f.*, crate.

†**harasser**, *v.a.*, to harass, to tire out, to weary, to overtire, to jade.

†**harceler**, *v.a.*, to harass, to torment; to gall. *— l'ennemi;* to harass the enemy.

†**harcellement**, *n.m.*, harassing, tormenting.

†**harde**, *n.f.*, herd (of deer); leash (for dogs).

†**harder**, *v.a.*, (hunt.) to leash dogs.

†**hardes**, *n.f.pl.*, wearing apparel, attire, clothes, belongings, traps.

†**hardi, -e**, *adj.*, bold, daring, fearless, intrepid, impudent. *Air —;* impudent look. *Manières —es;* forward manners. *Ce musicien a le jeu —;* this musician has a bold touch. *(interj.)* *hardi!* go it!

†**hardiesse**, *n.f.*, boldness, hardihood, daring, fearlessness; assurance; impudence, audacity. *Avoir la — de dire;* to have the boldness to say. *Il y a beaucoup de — dans ce dessin;* there is great boldness in this drawing. *— de style, d'expression;* boldness of style, of expression.

†**hardiment**, *adv.*, boldly, fearlessly, daringly, impudently. *Marcher — à l'ennemi;* to march boldly against the enemy.

†**hare!** *int.*, (hunt.) halloo!

†**harem** (ha-rèm), *n.m.*, harem.

†**hareng** (ha-ran), *n.m.*, herring. *— frais;* fresh herring. *— saur;* red herring. *La caque sent toujours le —;* what is bred in the bone will never come out of the flesh.

†**harengaison** (ghè-zon), *n.f.*, herring-season; catch *or* take of herrings.

†**harengère**, *n.f.*, herring-woman; fish-woman; fish-fag.

†**harengerie** (ha-ran-jrî), *n.f.*, herring-market.

†**harenguet** (-ghè), *n.m.*, (ich.) herring-cob, sprat.

⊙*†**hargnerie**, *n.f.*, squabbling, wrangling.

*†**hargneu-x, -se**, *adj.*, cross; cross-grained; snappish; peevish, surly, crusty; snarling; vicious (of horses). *Chien —;* snarling dog; quarrelsome fellow.

†**haricot**, *n.m.*, kidney-bean. *— de mouton;* (cook.) haricot mutton; Irish stew. *—s verts;* French beans. *—s d'Espagne;* scarlet runners.

†**haridelle**, *n.f.*, jade, hack, sorry horse; lanky, gawky woman.

†**harle**, *n.m.*, (orni.) merganser.

harmonica, *n.m.*, harmonica; musical glasses.

harmonie, *n.f.*, harmony; unison, concord; union; keeping; (mus.) harmonics. *Avec —;* harmoniously. *En —;* in time, in keeping. *Sans —;* inharmonious, unmusical.

harmonier, *v.a.* *V.* **harmoniser**.

*s'***harmonier**, *v.r.* *V.* **s'harmoniser**.

harmonieusement (-euz-màn), *adv.*, harmoniously, musically.

harmonieu-x, -se, *adj.*, harmonious, musical, sweet, melodious; friendly, blending (of colors).

harmonique, *n.m.* and *adj.*, harmonics; harmonic, harmonical.

harmoniquement (-nik-màn), *adv.*, harmoniously.

harmoniser, *v.a.*, to harmonize.

*s'***harmoniser**, *v.r.*, to harmonize.

harmoniste, *n.m.*, harmonist.

harmonium, *n.m.*, (mus.) harmonium.

†**harnachement** (har-nash-màn), *n.m.*, harness; harnessing; trappings.

†**harnacher**, *v.a.*, to harness, to rig out.

harnacheur, *n.m.*, harness-maker, dealer; harnessing groom.

harnais *or* **harnois**, *n.m.*, harness; horse-trappings, trappings, armor, equipment. *En-dosser le —;* to don the uniform. *Cheval de —;* draught-horse. *Blanchir sous le —;* to grow gray in the service.

†**haro**, *n.m.*, hue and cry. *—! shame!* out upon! *Crier — sur;* to raise an outcry.

†**harpagon**, *n.m.*, miser, skinflint.

*se†**harpailler**, *v.r.*, to wrangle, to squabble.

†**harpaye**, *n.f.*, (orni.) moor-buzzard, marsh-harrier.

†**harpe**, *n.f.*, harp; (conch.) harp-shell. *Pincer de la —;* to play the harp. *— éolienne;* Eolian harp.

†**harpé, -e**, *adj.*, harp-shaped, well-shaped (of greyhounds).

†**harpeau**, *n m.*, (nav.) grappling-iron.

†**harpège**, *n.m.* *V.* **arpège**.

†**harpéger**, *v.n.* *V.* **arpéger**.

†**harper**, *v.a.*, to gripe, to grapple, to grasp, to clutch. *v.n.*, (man.) to raise the legs without bending them.

*se†**harper**, *v.r.*, to grapple one another.

†**harpie**, *n.f.*, harpy; vixen, shrew.

†**harpin**, *n.m.*, boat-hook; carbuncle.

harpiste, *n.m.f.*, harpist.

†**harpon**, *n.m.*, harpoon, spear; fish-spear.

†**harponner**, *v.a.*, to harpoon, to spear.

†**harponneur**, *n.m.*, harpooner.

†**hart**, *n.f.*, withe, fagot-band; rope, halter. *C'est un homme qui mérite la —;* he is a man who deserves hanging *or* hanging is too good for him. *Sous peine de la —;* under pain of death.

haruspice, *n.m.* *V.* **aruspice**.

†**hasard**, *n.m.*, chance, accident, casualty, hazard, risk, danger, peril. *Jeu de —;* game of chance. *Coup de —;* lucky chance, stroke. *Une chose de —;* a second-hand article. *Au —;* at random, at a venture. *A tout —;* at all events. *A tous —s;* at all risks. *Par —;* by chance, accidentally. *S'abandonner au —;* to rely solely upon chance. *Jeter quelque chose au —;* to leave anything to chance. *Courir le —;* to run the risk. *Un coup de —;* a stroke of luck. *Est-ce que par — il ne viendrait pas?* he surely does n't mean not to come! *Corriger le —;* to assist fortune; to cheat at cards.

†**hasardé, -e**, *part.*, hazarded, ventured, bold, free; (cook.) tainted, stale.

†**hasarder**, *v.a.*, to hazard, to risk, to venture, to expose; to run the risk.

*se†**hasarder**, *v.r.*, to hazard, to venture, to risk. *Se — à faire une chose;* to venture to do a thing.

†**hasardeusement** (-deûz-màn), *adv.*, hazardously.

†**hasardeu-x, -se**, *adj.*, hazardous, venturesome, unsafe, dangerous, perilous.

†**haschisch**, *n.m.* (n.p.). *V.* **hachisch**.

†**hase**, *n.f.*, doe-rabbit, doe-hare.

†**hast**, *n.m.*, staff. *Arme d'—;* long-hafted weapon.

hastaire, *n.m.*, (antiq.) spearman.

†**haste**, *n.f.*, (antiq.) spear, spike.

†**hasté, -e**, *adj.*, (bot.) hastated.

†**hastiforme**, *adj.*, (bot.) halberd-shaped.

†**hâte**, *n.f.*, hurry; haste. *En —;* in haste, hastily. *En toute —;* with all possible speed. *A la —;* in a hurry, in haste. *Avoir —;* to be in a hurry; to long to; to be anxious to. *Faire une chose à la —;* to do a thing in a hurry. *S'éloigner à la —;* to hasten away. *Revenir en toute —;* to hasten back. *Trop de — gâte tout;* more haste, less speed.

†**hâtelet** (hâ-tlè), *n.m.*, small skewer.

†**hâter**, *v.a.*, to hasten, to forward, to expedite; to hurry, to hurry on; to hurry over; to push on, to force (fruit). *Ouvrage hâté, ouvrage gâté;* haste makes waste.

se†**hâter**, v.r., to make haste, to hurry, to hurry one's self. *Hâtez-vous de partir;* make haste and get away.

†**hâtier** (hâ-tié), n.m., spit-rest.

†**hâti-f, -ve**, adj., forward; precocious, premature; (hort.) early. *Fruit —;* early fruit.

†**hâtiveau**, n.m., (hort.) hasty pear; early pea.

†**hâtivement** (hâ-ti-vmän), adv., (hort.) early, prematurely.

†**hâtiveté** (hâ-tiv-té), n.f., earliness, forwardness.

†**haubans**, n.m.pl., (nav.) shrouds. *Grands —;* main-shrouds. *— de misaine;* fore-shrouds.

†**haubergeon**, n.m., small hauberk.

†**haubert**, n.m., hauberk.

†**hausse**, n.f., (com.) rise, advance; (print.) overlay; block (for raising anything); (of a rifle) backsight. *A la —;* (com.) on the advance. *Etre en —;* to be rising. *Jouer à la —;* (com.) to speculate on a rise. *Joueur à la —;* bull. *— d'archet;* nut of a fiddle-bow.

†**hausse-col**, n.m., (— — —s) gorget, neck-piece.

†**haussement** (hôs-män), n.m., raising, lifting, rising; shrugging.

†**hausser**, v.a., to raise, to raise up, to lift up; to increase; to shrug; (com.) to advance. *—les épaules;* to shrug one's shoulders. *— la voix;* to raise one's voice. *— les gages;* to raise the wages. *— le coude;* to drink hard.

se†**hausser**, v.r., to be raised; to rise, to raise one's self; to clear up (of the weather); to increase; (com.) to rise. *Se — sur la pointe des pieds;* to stand upon tip-toe.

†**hausser**, v.n., to rise; to get higher; to increase. *La rivière a bien haussé;* the river has risen very much. *Le change hausse;* the rate of exchange is rising. *Les actions haussent;* the price of shares is rising. *La rente hausse;* the funds are going up.

†**haussier**, n.m., bull, operator for a rise.

haussière. *V.* **aussière** and **hansière**.

†**haut, -e**, adj., high; tall; lofty, chief, principal ; upper ; grand, important, eminent; haughty ; elevated ; loud (of sound). *Au plus— degré;* in the highest degree. *Les —es régions de l'air;* the upper regions of the air. *Le — mal;* epilepsy. *Il a juré, la main —e;* he swore with uplifted hand. *Marcher la tête —e;* to walk with head erect. *Il peut aller partout la tête —e;* he can hold up his head anywhere. *La marée, la mer, est —e;* it is high water, high tide. *Gagner la —e mer;* to put out to sea. *Vaisseau de — bord;* ship of the line, man of war. *Avoir la voix —e;* to have a loud voice. *Lire à —e voix;* to read aloud. *Crier à —e voix;* to cry out loudly. *Pousser les —s cris;* to complain loudly, to raise an outcry. *Prendre le — ton;* to assume a high tone. *Une personne de — rang;* a person of high rank. *—e estime;* great esteem. *—s faits;* great deeds, exploits, doughty deeds. *Voici bien du — style;* this is lofty style with a vengeance. *Crime de —e trahison;* crime of high treason. *— en couleur;* of a ruddy complexion. *Le — commerce;* the higher branches of commerce, finance. *Messe —e;* high mass. *La chambre —e;* the upper house. *Le —Canada;* Upper Canada. *Le — bout de la table;* the upper end of the table. *Viande de — goût;* high-seasoned meat. *Jeune cadet de — appétit;* extravagant young fellow. *Les —es cartes;* the court-cards. *Tenir la bride —e à quelqu'un;* to keep a tight hand over any one.

†**haut**, n.m., height; top; summit; upper part; (mus.) high notes. *Le — d'une rue;* the upper end of a street. *Le — d'une page;* the top of a page. *Il est en —;* he is upstairs. *Je demeure dans une chambre d'en —;* I live in an upper room. *De — en bas;* from top to bottom. *D'en —;* from above. *Tomber de son —;* to fall flat down; to be thunderstruck. *Il y a du — et du bas dans la vie;* there are ups and downs in life. *Le — d'un clocher;* the top of a steeple. *Regarder quelqu'un de — en bas;* to eye any one from head to foot; to look down upon any one. *Traiter quelqu'un de — en bas;* to treat any one with contempt. *Cette maison a quarante pieds de —;* this house is forty feet high. *Il a deux mètres de —;* it is six feet high.

†**haut**, adv., high; loud; aloud, loudly. *Montez plus —;* go up higher. *Ainsi qu'il a été dit plus —;* as has already been said. *Reprendre les choses de plus —;* to begin farther back. *Parlez plus —;* speak louder. *Tout —;* aloud. *Parler —;* to speak aloud, to speak out. *— le pied;* off with you; let us be off at once. *Faire — le pied;* to vanish, to disappear; to run away. *Renvoyer des chevaux — le pied;* to send horses away bare-backed. *— la main;* with a high hand; offhand; in a high-handed manner. *Mener un cheval — la main;* to hold a tight rein on a horse.

⊙†**haut-à-bas**, n.m., (—) hawker, peddler.

†**haut-à-haut**, n.m., (—) (hunt.) halloo.

†**hautain, -e**, adj., haughty, supercilious, proud.

†**hautainement** (hô-tè-n-män), adv., haughtily, superciliously, proudly.

†**hautbois** (hô-boâ), n.m., hautboy; oboe; oboe-player.

⊙†**haut-de-chausses** or **haut-de-chausse**, n.m., (—s— —, or —s— —s) small-clothes; trunk-hose; breeches.

†**haute-contre**, n.f., (—s— —) (mus.) counter-tenor.

†**haute lisse**, n.f., tapestry hangings.

†**hautement** (hô-tman), adv., aloud, boldly, resolutely, stoutly, proudly.

†**haute paye**, n.f., extra pay.

†**hautesse**, n.f., highness (the Sultan's title).

⊙†**haute-taille**, n.f., (—s— —s) (mus.) upper-tenor.

†**hauteur**, n.f., height, altitude, hill ; rising ground, eminence; depth; elevation; firmness, haughtiness, arrogance. *La — d'une montagne;* the height of a hill. *Mur à — d'appui;* wall breast-high. *La — d'un bataillon;* the depth of a battalion. *La — d'un astre;* the altitude of a star. *Prendre la — du soleil;* to take the sun's altitude. *Etre à la — d'une île;* (nav.) to be off an island. *La — de ses conceptions;* the loftiness of his ideas. *Etre à la — de quelqu'un;* to be a match for any one. *Etre à la — du siècle;* to keep pace with the age. *Etre à la — d'une tâche;* to be equal to any task. *Parler avec —;* to speak haughtily. *Avec —;* imperiously, haughtily. *De toute sa —;* at its or his full height.

†**haut-fond**, n.m., (—s— —s) (nav.) shoal.

†**haut-fourneau**, n.m., (—) blast-furnace.

†**haut-le-corps**, n.m., (—) skip, start, bound. *Il fit un — en nous voyant venir;* he started as he saw us coming.

†**haut-le-pied**, n.m., (—) scoundrel, tramp, loafer.

†**haut-pendu**, n.m., (nav.) scud, squall.

†**hautur-ier, -ière**, adj., of the high seas.

†**hauturier**, n.m., sea-pilot.

†**havane**, n.f., Havana. *n.m.*, Havana cigar.

†**hâve**, adj., pale, wan; emaciated.

†**haveron** (ha-vron), n.m., wild oats.

†**havir**, v.a., to scorch (meat).

†**havir**, v.n., to scorch, to burn (of meat).

se †**havir**, v.r., to scorch, to burn (of meat).

†**havrais, -e**, adj., of Havre, native of Havre.

†**havre**, n.m., haven, harbor, port, tidal harbor.

†**havresac**, n.m., knapsack, wallet; haversack.

†**hé!** int., ho! ah ! hey ! I say !

⊙†**heaume** (hôm), n.m., helm, helmet; (nav.) tiller, bar.

hebdomadaire, adj., weekly.

hebdomadier, *n.m.*, one on duty for a week (in convents and chapters).

héberge, *n.f.*, (jur.) point of disjunction, break.

hébergement, *n.m.*, lodging; harboring.

héberger, *v.a.*, to lodge, to entertain, to harbor.

hébété, *n.m.*, -e, *n.f.*, dolt, blockhead.

hébéter, *v.a.*, to stupefy, to besot; to dull.

hébétude, *n.f.*, idiocy.

hébraïque, *adj.*, Hebrew, Hebraic.

hébraïquement, *adv.*, Hebraically.

hébraïsant, *n.m.*, Hebraist.

hébraïsme, *n.m.*, Hebraism.

hébreu, *n.* and *adj.m.*, Hebrew; Hebraic.

hécatombe, *n.f.*, hecatomb. [perches).

hectare, *n.m.*, hectare (2 acres, 1 rood, 35

hectique, *adj.*, (med.) hectic.

hectisie, *n.f.*, (med.) consumption.

hectogramme, *n.m.*, hectogram (3·527 oz. avoirdupois).

hectolitre, *n.m.*, hectoliter (22·009668 imperial gallons).

hectomètre, *n.m.*, hectometer (328·08992 British statute feet).

hégémonie, *n.f.*, hegemony.

hégire, *n.f.*, hegira (Mahometan era).

heiduque, *n.m.*, Hungarian foot-soldier.

hein ! *int.*, hey ! what !

hélas ! *int.*, alas ! ah !

†**héler**, *v.a.*, (nav.) to hail, to speak (a ship) ; to hail, to call (any one).

hélianthe, *n.m.*, (bot.) helianthus, sunflower.

hélianthème, *n.m.*, (bot.) helianthemum, rock-rose.

héliaque, *adj.*, (astron.) heliacal.

héliastes, *n.m.pl.*, (antiq.) heliasts.

hélice, *n.f.*, screw. *Vapeur à* —; screw-steamer. *En* —; spiral, winding. *Propulseur à* —; screw-propeller.

hélicon, *n.m.*, Helicon.

héliocentrique, *adj.*, heliocentric.

héliographie, *n.f.*, heliography.

héliographique, *adj.*, heliographic.

héliomètre, *n.m.*, heliometer.

hélioscope, *n.m.*, helioscope.

héliotrope, *n.m.*, (bot.) heliotrope ; sun-flower ; (min.) heliotrope, blood-stone.

hélix, *n.m.*, (anat.) helix.

hellébore, *n.m.* V. **ellébore**.

helléborine, *n.f.* V. **elléborine**.

hellènes (èl-lè-n), *n.m.pl.*, Hellenes.

hellénique, *adj.*, Hellenic.

hellénisme, *n m.*, Hellenism.

helléniste, *n.m.*, *adj.*, Hellenist.

helminthe, *n.m.*, (zool., med.) intestinal worm.

helminthologie, *n.f.*, helminthology.

helvétique, *adj.*, Helvetic, Swiss.

†**hem !** *int.*, hem !

hématite, *n.f.*, (min.) hematite.

hématocèle, *n.f.*, (surg.) hematocele.

hématologie, *n.f.*, hematology.

hématose, *n.f.*, hæmatosis, sanguification.

hématurie, *n.f.*, (med.) hæmaturia.

hémérocalle, *n.f.*, (bot.) hemerocallis.

hémi, a prefix from Greek ἡμί, half, semi.

⊙**hémicoptère**, *n.m.* V. **phénicoptère**.

hémicycle, *n.m.*, hemicycle.

hémine, *n.f.*, (antiq.) hemina, cotyla (about half a pint).

hémiplégie or **hémiplexie**, *n.f.*, (med.) hemiplegy, hemiplegia.

hémiptère, *n.m.*, (ent.) hemipter.

hémiptère, *adj.*, hemipteral.

hémisphère, *n.m.*, hemisphere.

hémisphérique, *adj.*, hemispheric.

hémistiche, *n.m.*, hemistich (half of a twelve-syllabled verse).

hémoptoïque, **hémoptypique**, *adj.*, (med.) spitting blood.

hémoptysie, *n.f.*, hæmoptysis.

hémorragie, *n.f.*, hemorrhage.

hémorroïdal, -e, *adj.*, hemorrhoidal.

hémorroïdale, *n. f.*, (anat.) hemorrhoidal artery.

hémorroïdes, *n.f.pl.*, hemorrhoids, piles.

hémostatique, *adj.*, (med.) styptic.

hendécagone, *n.m.*, (geom.) hendecagon.

hendécasyllabe, *n.m.*, hendecasyllable.

†**hennir** (ha-), *v.n.*, to neigh.

†**hennissement** (ha-), *n.m.*, neighing.

henriade (**La**) Voltaire's epic poem.

hépatique, *adj.*, hepatic.

hépatique, *n.f.*, (bot.) liverwort.

hépatite, *n.f.*, hepatitis, inflammation of the liver; (min.) hepatite, liver-stone.

heptacorde, *n.m.*, heptachord.

heptagonal, -e, *adj.*, heptagonal.

heptagone, *n.m.* and *adj.*, heptagon; heptagonal.

heptaméron, *n.m.*, heptameron.

heptandre, *adj.*, heptandrian.

heptandrie, *n.f.*, heptandria.

heptangulaire, *adj.*, heptangular.

heptaphylle, *adj.*, (bot.) heptaphyllous.

heptarchie, *n.f.*, heptarchy.

heptarchique, *adj.*, heptarchic.

héraldique, *adj.*, heraldic.

†**héraut**, *n.m.*, herald.

herbacé, -e, *adj.*, (bot.) herbaceous.

herbage, *n.m.*, herbage, grass, pasture, pasture-ground; meadow land.

herbager, *n.m.*, grazier.

herbe, *n.f.*, herb, grass, wort, weed ; blade : plant, root. *Brin d'* —; blade of grass. —*s potagères* ; pot-herbs. — *marine* ; sea-weed. — *militaire* ; milfoil. — *de la Saint-Jean*; ground-ivy. —*de Saint-Jean* ; mugwort. *Bouillon aux* —*s* ; herb soup. *Mettre un cheval à l'* —; to put a horse out to grass. *Blé en* —; corn in the blade. *Mauvaises* —*s* ; weeds. — *à l'ambassadeur, à la reine (tabac)*; snuff, tobacco. — *aux charpentiers, à la coupure (millefeuille)* ; milfoil. — *aux chats (marum)* ; cat-thyme. — *aux chantres (vélar)* ; hedge-mustard, hedge-garlic. — *aux cuillers (cochléaria)* ; scurvy-grass, cochlearia. — *aux écus (nummulaire)* ; money-wort. — *aux gueux (clématite)* ; clematis, climber, ladies' bower. — *aux Patagons (hydrocotyle)* ; hydrocotyle. — *au pauvre homme (gratiole)* ; hyssop. —*aux perles (grémil)* ; gromwell, gromil. — *du siège (scrofulaire)* ; figwort. —*aux verrues (héliotrope)* ; heliotrope. *Mauvaise* — *croît toujours* ; ill weeds grow apace. *Manger son blé en* —; to spend one's money before one gets it. *Couper l'* — *sous le pied à quelqu'un ;* to supplant any one, to oust any one; to cut any one out; to take the wind out of anybody's sails. *C'est un docteur en* — ; he is a doctor in embryo. *Il a marché sur quelque mauvaise* —; he has got out of bed the wrong way. *L'* — *sera courte s'il ne trouve à brouter* ; he will pick up a living somehow.

***herbeiller**, *v.n.*, (hunt.) to graze.

herber, *v.a.*, to lay on the grass. — *de la toile ;* to grass-bleach.

herberie, *n.f.*, bleaching-ground.

herbette, *n.f.*, (poet.) short grass ; sward.

herbeu-x, -**se**, *adj.*, grassy, herbous.

herbier, *n.m.*, herbal, herbarium, collection of plants.

herbière, *n.f.*, herb-woman ; (man.) grass-cutter.

herbivore, *adj.*, herbivorous.

herbivore, *n.m.*, herbivorous animal.

herborisation, *n.f.*, herborization, herborizing, herborizing excursion.

herboriser, *v.n.*, to herborize.

herboriseur, *n.m.*, collector of plants.

herboriste, *n.m.f.*, herbalist, herborist, dealer in medicinal herbs.

herboristerie, n.f., herb trade, herbalist's shop.

herbu, -e, adj., grassy; covered with grass.

hercotectonique, n.f., art of fortification.

hercule, n.m., (astron.) Hercules, man of herculean strength.

herculéen, -ne (-in, -èn), adj., Herculean.

†**hère**, n.m., sorry fellow, poor wretch; poor devil, wight; game at cards.

héréditaire, adj., hereditary.

héréditairement, adv., hereditarily.

hérédité, n.f., heirship, right of inheritance; succession; hereditary right; inheritance; heredity.

hérésiarque, n.m., heresiarch.

hérésie, n.f., heresy. Il ne fera point d'—; he will not set the Thames on fire.

héréticité, n.f., heretical nature or tendency.

hérétique, n.m.f. and adj., heretic; heretical.

†**hérissé, -e**, adj., rough, shaggy, on end, bristling with; (bot.) hairy, prickly, covered with, full of, studded with, armed with, defended by; (of a person) crabbed, cross, peevish. Cheveux —s, poil —; shaggy hair or mane.

†**hérissement**, n.m., bristling; shagginess.

†**hérisser**, v.a., to bristle, to bristle up, to erect; to arm; to lard. Le lion hérisse sa crinière; the lion bristles up his mane. Les piquants qui hérissent la tige du rosier; the prickles that arm the stalk of a rose-bush. — son style de néologismes; to lard one's style with neologisms. — un mur; (man.) to roughcast a wall. se†**hérisser**, v.r., to stand on end, to stand erect; to bristle, to bristle up; to be bristling with, to be armed; to be covered, to be studded (with).

†**hérisser**, v.n., to bristle, to bristle up; to be full of, to be loaded with.

†**hérisson**, n.m., (mam.) hedgehog, urchin; (fort.) herisson; canting-wheel; sprocket-wheel; sprocket; rag-wheel; spur-wheel. Jeune —; (mam.) hedgepig. — de mer; (ich.) sea-hedgehog; sea-urchin; (fig.) cross-grained person.

hérisson, -ne, adj., cross-grained, crabbed.

†**hérissonné, -e**, adj., (her.) crouching.

héritage, n.m., heritage, inheritance, heirdom, estate, patrimony; legacy. —s libres; (jur.) fee-simple. —s substitués; (jur.) fee-tail. Faire un —; to inherit property.

hériter, v.n., to inherit, to be heir; to succeed.

hériter, v.a., to inherit.

hériti-er, n.m., -ère, n.f. (-tié, ti-èr), heir, heiress, inheritor. — institué, testamentaire; (jur.) heir under a will; devisee. — naturel; (jur.) heir of one's body. — par substitution; heir of entail. — légitime; lawful heir. — universel; sole heir. — présomptif; heir-apparent. Il est — de son oncle; he is heir to his uncle.

hermaphrodisme, n.m., hermaphrodism.

hermaphrodite, n.m. and adj., hermaphrodite; hermaphroditic.

hermeline, n.f., (her.) sable.

herméneutique, n.f., and adj., hermeneutics; hermeneutic, hermeneutical.

hermès (èr-mès), n.m., (sculpt.) Hermes, bust of Mercury.

hermétique, adj., hermetic, close, hermetical. Science —; hermetical science. Colonne —; (sculpt.) column with a bust (for capitals).

hermétiquement (-tik-mān), adv., hermetically, closely.

hermine, n.f., (mam.) ermine; hermine; winter-weasel; (her.) ermine; ermine (fur). — d'été; (mam.) stoat.

herminé, -e, adj., (her.) ermined.

herminette, n.f., (carp.) adz. — courbée; hollow adz.

hermitage, n.m., hermitage.

hermite or **ermite**, n.m., hermit.

†**herniaire**, adj. hernial. Bandage —; truss.

†**herniaire**, n.f., (bot.) rupture-wort.

†**hernie**, n.f., hernia, rupture.

†**herniole**, n.f., (bot.) rupture-wort.

†**hernute**, n.m.pl., Moravian brother.

hérodiens (-in), n.m., (Bibl. hist.) Herodians.

héroï-comique, adj., heroi-comic; mock-heroic; serio-comic.

héroïde, n.f., heroic epistle.

héroïne, n.f., heroine.

héroïque, adj., heroic; (med.) powerful. Temps —s; heroic ages.

héroïquement (-ik-mān), adv., heroically.

héroïsme, n.m., heroism.

†**héron**, n.m., heron. — crabier; crab-eater. Masse de —; heron plume.

†**héronneau**, n.m., young heron.

†**héronner**, v.n., (hawking) to fly the heron.

†**héronni-er, -ère**, adj., heron-like; thin, lank, spare; (hawking) trained to fly the heron.

†**héronnière**, n.f., heronry.

†**héros** (-rô), n.m., hero.

herpès, n.m., (med.) herpes, tetters.

herpétique, adj., (med.) herpetic.

herque, n.f., iron rake.

†**hersage**, n.m., (agri.) harrowing of a field.

†**herschel**, n.m., (astron.) Georgium Sidus, Herschel, Uranus.

†**herse**, n.f., harrow; (fort.) portcullis, herse; candlestick (used in Catholic churches); (nav.) iron cringle; (bot.) caltrop.

†**hersé, -e**, part. and adj., (agri.) harrowed; (her.) with a herse.

†**herser**, v.a., (agri.) to harrow.

†**herseur**, n.m., harrower.

hésitation, n.f., hesitation; faltering.

hésitant, -e, adj., hesitating, wavering, undecided, stammering.

hésiter, v.n., to hesitate, to falter, to hum and haw; to pause; to stop, to waver; to be doubtful; to hang back, to demur. Faire —; to stagger. Sans —; unhesitatingly.

hétéroclite, adj., (gram.) heteroclite, anomalous; eccentric, odd, whimsical, uncouth. Manières —s; eccentric manners. Visage —; odd face. Bâtiment —; irregular building.

hétérodoxe, adj., heterodox.

hétérodoxie, n.f., heterodoxy.

hétérogène, adj., heterogeneous, dissimilar, incongruous.

hétérogénéité, n.f., heterogeneity, heterogeneousness.

hétérosciens (-si-in), n.m. pl., (geog.) Heteroscians.

hetman, n.m., hetman (general of cossacks).

†**hêtre**, n.m., beech, beech-tree.

heu, n.m., (nav.) hoy.

heu! int., alas! lackaday! hey! ah! aye!

☉**heur**, n.m., luck, good fortune, chance. Il n'y a qu'heur et malheur en ce monde; chance is everything (what's one man's meat is another man's poison).

heure, n.f., hour; o'clock; time, time of day; moment, moments; appointment. pl., primer (prayer-book). Belle —; pleasant time of day. La belle — pour arriver! what a nice time to come! — indue; late hour. Une bonne, grande —; a good, a full, hour. — dernière, grande —; last moments. — marquée, désignée, dite; appointed hour. — suprême; dying hour, hour of death, last or supreme moments. —s en sus; after-hours, over-time (of workmen). Ami, homme, de toutes les —s; friend who is always welcome, friend always ready to oblige. Livre d'—s; (c. rel.) prayer-book. Une paire d'—s; a primer. Un mauvais quart d'—; a bad time. Quart d'— de Rabelais; paying time, settling time, trying time. J'y serai dans une —; I will be there within an hour. Quelle — est-il? what o'clock is it? Il est une — et demie; it is half-past one. Sur les une —; about one o'clock.

L'horloge a sonné deux —s; the clock has struck two. *Chercher midi à quatorze —s;* to create difficulties where there are none; to look for grapes on thorns. *Mettre une montre à l'—;* to set a watch. *Il est l'— de dîner;* it is dinner-time. *A l'— qu'il faut;* in due time. *Vous venez à l'— qu'il fallait;* you come in the very nick of time. *Je le ferai à mes —s perdues;* I will do it in my leisure hours. *Faites le sur l'—;* do it this very moment. *Donner —;* to fix an hour; to make an appointment. *L'— du berger;* the propitious hour for lovers. *De bonne —;* betimes, early, soon. *Venez de meilleure —;* come sooner. *A cette —, à l'— qu'il est;* now, at present, nowadays; by this time. *Pour l'—;* at present. *Tout à l'—;* by-and-by, presently; not long ago, just now. *D'une — à l'autre;* from one moment, from one minute, to the other. *D'— à autre;* now and then. *D'— en —;* hourly, every hour, every moment. *A la bonne —;* well done! that 's something like! *Les Heures;* (myth.) the Hours (*Horæ*).

heureusement (eu-reûz-mān), *adv.,* happily, luckily; successfully, fortunately, prosperously; by good luck; well.

heureu-x, -se, *adj.,* happy; blessed, blissful; lucky, fortunate; successful; prosperous, favorable, auspicious; pleasing, prepossessing; good; excellent, rare; happy, pleased, delighted. *Une —se vieillesse;* a happy old age. *Il est né —;* he was born lucky. *Des couches —ses;* a happy delivery (of a woman). *Une physionomie —se;* a pleasing countenance. *Etre —;* to be lucky. *— au jeu;* lucky at play. *Il est — d'avoir eu votre protection;* he was lucky to find you there. *L'— de la chose c'est que;* the luckiest part of the thing was that.

†**heurt,** *n.m.,* collision; blow; shock, knock.

heurté, *adj.,* (of style) abrupt, harsh, jerky.

†**heurtement,** *n.m.,* hiatus; collision; shock; jar, jingling; clash.

†**heurter,** *v.a.,* to run up against, to knock up against, to strike against, to hit against; to hit, to strike; to come across, to meet; to run foul of; to jostle; to shock; to go counter to, to hurt, to offend, to disoblige; to jar with; (paint.) to color hard. *— quelqu'un;* to run against any one. *Ce vaisseau a heurté l'autre;* this ship ran foul of the other. *— les préjugés de;* to shock the prejudices of. *Dessin heurté,* drawing roughly colored.

se†**heurter,** *v.r.,* to strike, to hit, one's self; to strike against one another, to run foul of each other; to come across one another; to come into collision; to jostle one another; to clash. *Se — à la tête;* to strike one's head. *Les boucs se heurtent de leurs têtes;* goats butt at one another with their heads.

†**heurter,** *v.n.,* to strike, to knock, to hit; to dash, to knock (at a door).

⊙†**heurtoir,** *n.m.,* top-stone, flapper; (obs.) knocker; (arch.) lock-sill; (fort.) hurter.

hexacorde, *n.m.,* (mus.) hexachord.

hexaèdre, *n.m.* and *adj.,* (geom.) hexahedron; hexahedral.

hexagonal, -e, *adj.,* hexagonal.

hexagone, *n.m.* and *adj.,* (geom.) hexagon; hexagonal.

hexamètre, *n.m.,* hexameter.

hexandre, *adj.,* (bot.) hexandrous.

hexandrie, *n.f.,* (bot.) hexandria.

hexaples, *n.m.pl.,* (theol.) Hexapla.

hiatus (ia-tus), *n.m.,* hiatus.

hibernant, -e, *adj.,* hibernating.

hibernation, *n.f.,* hibernation.

hiberner, *v.n.,* to hibernate.

†**hibou,** *n.m.,* owl; (pers.) moper, owl. *— commun;* (orni.) long-eared owl. *— scops;* (orni.) scops-eared owl. *Faire le —;* to mope like an owl.

†**hic,** *n.m.,* knot, difficulty, rub. *Voilà le —;* there 's the rub.

hidalgo, *n.m.,* hidalgo; Spanish knight.

†**hideusement** (-deûz-mān), *adv.,* hideously, frightfully, horribly, dreadfully, shockingly.

†**hideu-x, -se,** *adj.,* hideous, frightful, horrible, dreadful, shocking.

†**hie,** *n.f.,* beetle, paving-beetle, rammer (of paviers). *Battre à la —;* to ram.

hièble, *n.f.,* (bot.) danewort, dwarf-elder.

hiémal, -e, *adj.,* wintery, hyemal. *Plantes —es,* winter-plants.

†**hiement** (hî-mān), *n.m.,* grating, creaking (of machines); ramming.

hier (i-ièr), *adv.,* yesterday. *— matin;* yesterday morning. *— soir* or *au soir;* last night, last evening. *Avant—;* the day before yesterday. *La nuit d'—;* yesternight, yesternight. *Homme d'—;* upstart. *Etre né d'—;* to have no experience.

†**hier** (hi-é), *v.a.* and *n.,* to ram; (of machines) to creak, to grate.

†**hiérarchie,** *n.f.,* hierarchy.

†**hiérarchique,** *adj.,* hierarchical.

†**hiérarchiquement** (-shik-mān), *adv.,* hierarchically.

†**hiérarque,** *n.m.,* hierarch.

hiératique, *adj.,* hieratic. [glyphic.

hiéroglyphe. *n.m.,* (antiq.) hieroglyph, hiero-

hiéroglyphique, *adj.,* hieroglyphical, hieroglyphic.

hiéroglyphiquement (-fik-mān), *adv.,* hieroglyphically.

hiéronique, *n.m.,* conqueror in the sacred games.

hiéronymite, *n.m.,* hieronymite (monk of the Spanish order of the Hieronymites).

hiérophante, *n.m.,* (Grec. antiq.) hierophant.

hilaire, *n.m.,* hilary.

hilarant, -e, *adj.,* exhilarating, enlivening, cheerful. *Gaz —;* (chem.) laughing gas.

hilarité, *n.f.,* hilarity; cheerfulness; mirth, laughter, merriment.

†**hile,** *n.m.,* (bot.) hilum, hile.

hindoustani, *n.m.,* (n.p.), *adj.,* (philology) hindustani.

hippiatrique, *n.f.,* (vet.) hippiatry.

hippique, *adj.,* hippic.

hippocampe, *n.m.,* (myth., zool.) hippocampus, hippocamp, sea-horse.

hippocentaure, *n.m.,* (antiq.) hippocentaur.

hippocras (-krâs). *V.* **hypocras.**

hippocratique, *adj.,* hippocratic.

hippocrène, *n.f.,* (myth.) Hippocrene.

hippodrome, *n.m.,* hippodrome, circus, amphitheater; race-course.

hippodromie, *n.f.,* horse-racing.

hippogriffe, *n.m.,* hippogriff, winged horse.

hippolithe, *n.f.,* (vet.) hippolith.

hippomane, *n.m.,* hippomane.

hippopotame, *n.m.,* hippopotamus, river-horse, sea-horse.

hirondelle, *n.f.,* (orni.) swallow. *— domestique, — de cheminée;* house-swallow. *— rustique, — de fenêtre;* martin. *— de rivière; — de rivage;* sand-martin. *— de mer;* sea-gull; (ich.) swallow-fish; tub-fish; tub. *Pierre d'—;* swallow-stone; cab, conveyance. *Une — ne fait pas le printemps;* one swallow does not make a spring.

hirsute, *adj.,* hirsute, hairy.

hispide, *adj.,* (bot.) hispid, strigous.

hispidité, *n.f.,* (bot.) hispidity, strigosity.

†**hisser,** *v.a.,* to hoist, to lift, to heave, to heave up, to raise, to haul up; to haul out (sails); to sway up (yards). *— promptement;* (nav.) to trice.

se†**hisser,** *v.r.,* to raise *or* lift one's self up, to get up.

histiologie, *n.f.* *V.* **histologie.**

histoire, n.f., history, tale, story, narration ; long rigmarole ; idle story, untruth, falsehood, concern, trifle, small matter. — *faite à plaisir ;* a trumped up story. *Faiseur d'—s ;* story-teller. *Peintre d'—* ; historical painter. *Tableau d'—* ; historical picture, history piece. *C'est une autre —* ; that is quite another story, or a horse of another color. *Voilà bien des —s ;* what a fuss you make about it. *— de ;* only to ; merely for the sake of. *— de rire ;* for the laugh or fun of the thing. *Le plus beau de l'—c'était ;* the best of it was.

histologie, n.f., histology.

⊙**historial, -e**, adj., historical.

historien (-ri-in), n.m., historian.

historier, v.a., to embellish, to ornament, to adorn, to flourish.

historiette, n.f., little story ; short tale.

historiographe, n.m., historiographer.

historique, adj., historical. *Cela est —* ; that is a fact.

historique, n.m., historical account.

historiquement (-rik-mān), adv., historically.

histrion, n.m., histrion, actor, stage-player ; player ; (b.s.) mountebank.

histrionique, adj., histrionic.

histrionner, v.n., (jest.) to act, to perform plays, to play.

hiver (i-vèr), n.m., winter. *— doux ;* mild winter. *— rude ;* severe winter. *Cœur de l'—* ; mid-winter, depth of winter. *Queue de l'—* ; latter end of winter. *Au cœur, au milieu, au plus fort, de l'—* ; in the depth of winter.

hivernage, n.m., winter, winter time ; wintering place ; (agri.) winter-plowing, winter-fodder.

hivernal, -e, adj., (l.u.) wintry, hibernal.

hiverner, v.n., to winter.

hiverner, v.a., (agri.) to winter-fallow.

s'hiverner, v.r., to inure one's self to cold ; to winter, to hibernate, to pass the winter.

†**ho !** int., ho ! hoa ! oh ! hoy ! (nav.) ahoy !

†**hobereau** (ho-brō), n.m., (orni.) hobby ; country squire ; squireen.

†**hoc**, n.m., hock (game at cards). *Cela lui est —* ; he is sure of that, that will be his. *Etre —* ; to be taken.

†**hoca**, n.m., hoca (game of chance).

†**hoche**, n.f., (of tallies) notch.

†**hochement** (hosh-mān), n.m., shaking, tossing, wagging (of the head).

†**hochepied**, n.m., heron-hawk.

†**hochepot**, n.m., (cook.) hodge-podge, hotch-potch.

†**hochequeue**, n.m., (orni.) nut-hatch, wagtail.

†**hocher**, v.a., to jog, to shake, to wag, to toss ; to jag, to notch. *— la tête ;* to shake one's head.

†**hocher**, v.n., (man.) to jerk the bit.

†**hochet**, n.m., coral, rattle (for children) ; toy, bauble, plaything. *Il y a des —s pour tout âge ;* every age has its hobby.

*†**hogner**, v.n., (l.u. pop.) to grumble, to growl.

†**hoirs**, n.m.pl., (jur.) heirs.

hoirie, n.f., (jur.) inheritance.

†**hola !** int., holla ! hoa ! (nav.) holloa ! ho, there ! stop !

†**holà**, n.m., stop ; end. *Mettre le —* ; to put a stop to (a quarrel).

†**hôlement**, n.m., hooting (of owls).

†**hôler**, v.n., to hoot.

†**hollandais, -e**, n.m.f. and adj., Dutchman ; Dutchwoman ; Dutch.

†**hollandais**, n.m., Dutch language.

†**hollandé, -e**, adj., dressed (of quills). *Batiste —e ;* strong thick cambric.

†**hollander**, v.a., to dress (quills).

holocauste, n.m., holocaust, burnt-offering ; sacrifice.

holographe, adj. *V.* **olographe.**

holothurie, n.f., holothuria, trepang.

†**hom !** int., hum ! humph !

†**homard**, n.m., (ich.) lobster. *— femelle ;* hen lobster. *— mâle ;* cock lobster.

hombre, n.m., (game at cards) ombre.

homélie, n.f., homily ; sermon.

homéopathe, n.m. and adj., (med.) homeopathist.

homéopathie, n.f., (med.) homeopathy.

homéopathique, adj., homeopathic.

homérique, adj., Homeric.

homicide, n.m., homicide ; manslaughter ; manslayer, murderer. *—involontaire ;* manslaughter. *—volontaire ;* willful murder. *— commandé par la légitime défense ;* (jur.) chance-medley. *— non qualifié crime ni délit ;* (jur.) justifiable homicide. *— par imprudence ;* homicide by misadventure.

homicide, adj., murderous, homicidal. *Des yeux —s ;* killing eyes.

hommage, n.m., homage, respect ; service ; acknowledgment, token, gift, testimony. *pl.*, respects, homage. *Faire — à quelqu'un ;* to do homage to any one. *Rendre — à la vérité ;* to do homage to truth. *Rendre ses —s à quelqu'un ;* to pay one's respects to any one. *— de reconnaissance ;* token of gratitude. *Avec les —s de l'auteur ;* with the author's compliments.

hommagé, -e, adj., held by homage.

hommager, n.m., homager.

hommasse, adj., masculine (of women).

homme, n.m., man ; (triv., pop.) husband, old man. *Dieu créa l'— à son image ;* God created man after his own image. *— d'église, d'épée, de lettres, d'état ;* churchman, military man, literary man, statesman. *— du monde ;* man of the world. *C'est un — marqué a l'A ;* he is an excellent man ; he is the soul of honor. *Le roi des —s ;* the king of good fellows. *C'est un — à pendre, or un — de sac et de corde ;* he is a man who deserves hanging. *C'est un pauvre —* ; he is a poor sort of a man. *C'est un — pauvre ;* he is a poor man. *Bon —* ; good, virtuous man ; good-natured, simple, easy-going man ; old fellow ; old codger. *— bon ;* kind-hearted, good, virtuous man. *Brave —* ; worthy man ; good fellow, good chap. *— brave ;* brave, daring man. *— de paille ;* man-of-straw. *— de cœur ;* man of feeling, spirit ; courageous man. *Un — comme il faut ;* a gentleman. *— d'hier ;* upstart, novice. *— d'affaires ;* business man. *— de journée ;* day-laborer. *— de cour ;* courtier. *— de robe ;* lawyer. *— de bois ;* (man.) fagot ; dumb-jockey. *— à tout faire ;* jack of all trades. *— des bois ;* (mam.) wild man, baboon. *Enlèvement d'—* ; (jur.) man-stealing. *Herbe à pauvre —* ; (bot.) hedge-hyssop. *La perle des —s ;* (fam.) a very trump of a man, a trump. *Il n'y a tête d'— qui ose ;* no man alive, no man living, would dare. *C'est un — que cet —là ;* he is a man every inch of him. *C'est le dernier des —s ;* he is the worst of men, the greatest villain alive. *Il n'est pas — à faire de ces choses là ;* he is not the sort of man to act like this. *C'est un — à ménager ;* he is a man to be considered. *Voilà mon —* ; that is the man for my money or for me. *Il a trouvé son —* ; he has found his match.

⊙**hommeau** or **hommelet**, n.m., little man, bit of a man.

homme-dieu, n.m., (n.p.) Man-God.

homocentrique, adj., (astron.) homocentric.

homogène, adj., homogeneous.

homogénéité, n.f., homogeneity, homogeneousness.

homologati-f, -ve, adj., homologative, affirmative.

homologation, n.f., (jur.) confirmation, approval, homologation.

homologue (-log), adj., (geom.) homologous, similar, like.

homologuer (-ghé), *v.a.*, (jur.) to confirm, to homologate.

homoncule *or* **homuncule**, *n.m.*, (fam.) little man.

homonyme, *adj.*, homonymous.

homonyme, *n.m.f.*, homonym; namesake.

homonymie, *n.f.*, homonymy.

homophonie, *n.f.*, homophony.

honchets, *n.m.pl.* V. **jonchets**.

†**hongre**, *n.m.* and *adj.*, (vet.) gelding; gelded; emasculated. —, *cheval* —; gelding.

†**hongré**, *part.*, gelded, gelt.

†**hongrer**, *v.a.*, to geld (a horse).

†**hongrois, -e**, *n.* and *adj.*, Hungarian.

†**hongrois**, *n.m.*, Hungarian language.

†**hongroyeur**, *n.m.*, tanner of Hungary leather; saddler's currier.

honnête, *adj.*, honest, upright, virtuous, becoming, seemly, decent, modest, decorous; handsome; genteel; suitable, proper, befitting, civil, kind, courteous, polite, moderate, reasonable. *Un — homme ;* an honest man. *Une — femme ;* a virtuous woman. *— garçon ;* honest fellow. *Récompense —;* handsome reward. *Prétexte —;* fair pretense. *Prix —;* reasonable price. *— aisance or fortune —;* decent competency. *Un homme —;* a civil man. *Cet habit est encore —;* this coat is still respectable.

honnête, *n.m.*, honesty, probity.

honnêtement, *adv.*, honestly, uprightly, honorably, virtuously ; becomingly, decently, modestly, decorously, handsomely, genteelly; suitably, properly, befittingly; civilly, kindly, courteously, politely, handsomely (liberally); moderately, reasonably.

honnêteté (o-nêt-té), *n.f.*, honesty, probity, uprightness, integrity; modesty, decency; chastity, virtue; propriety, fitness, suitableness, decorum; laudableness, praiseworthiness, respectability, decorum; politeness, courtesy, kindness. *Blesser les règles de l'—;* to offend against the rules of propriety. *Faire une — à quelqu'un ;* to be civil, courteous, polite to any one. *— ne coûte pas ;* politeness costs nothing.

honneur, *n.m.*, honor; credit; respect, love; court-card, honor (at cards). —*s ;* regalia (crown jewels). *Affaire d'—;* affair of honor. *Chevalier d'—;* gentleman in waiting. *Croix d'—;* cross of the Legion of Honor. *Dame d'—;* lady of honor ; lady in waiting. *Fille d'—;* maid of honor. *Demoiselle d'—;* bride's-maid. *Garçon d'—;* bride's-man, best man. *Membre de la Légion d'—;* member of the Legion of Honor. *Parole d'—;* word of honor. *Parole d'—! or ma parole d'—!* upon my honor ! *Partie d'—;* rubber (at cards) ; conquering game. *D'—;* honorable ; honorary. *Non en homme d'—;* dishonorably ; ungentlemanlike, ungentlemanly. *En —;* in honor, in request. *Sauf votre —;* saving your presence. *Etre en —;* to be honored ; to be in favor, in request. *Faire — à ;* to do credit to, to be an honor to; (com.) to honor, to meet (bills). *Faire — à ses affaires ;* to meet one's engagements. *Faire à quelqu'un l'— de quelque chose ;* to ascribe the honor of anything to any one. *Faire les —s ;* to do the honors. *Se faire — de quelque chose ;* to consider, to esteem, anything an honor ; to take a pride in anything ; to glory in ; to take credit for anything. *Faire réparation d'—;* to make an apology. *Ne jouer que l'—, ne jouer que pour l'—;* to play for love. *Piquer d'—;* to put a man on his mettle. *Prendre iout au point d'—;* to be too nice, too delicate on a point of honor. *En sortir à son —, en sortir avec —;* to come off with honor. *Tenir à — de ;* to esteem it an honor to. *S'en tirer avec —;* to come off with honor. *D'—, sur mon —;* upon my honor. *Foi d'homme d'—;* as I am a man of honor. *A tout seigneur, tout —;* give

honor where honor is due. *Vous me faites —,* you honor me. *Briguer les —s ;* to seek honors. *Un homme d'— n'a que sa parole ;* an honest man's word is as good as his bond. *En tout bien, tout —;* with nothing but honorable intentions.

†**honni**, *part.*, dishonored, disgraced. *— soit qui mal y pense ;* evil be to him who evil thinks.

†**honnir**, *v.a.*, to dishonor, to disgrace, to brand, to cover with shame, to treat with contempt.

honorabilité, *n.f.*, honorableness, respectability.

honorable, *adj.*, honorable ; respectable, creditable, reputable ; proper, suitable.

honorablement, *adv.*, honorably ; respectably, creditably ; properly, suitably ; nobly, sumptuously, splendidly.

honoraire, *adj.*, honorary, titular, titulary.

honoraire, *n.m.*, fee; salary; stipend. *Les —s d'un avocat ;* a barrister's fee.

honorée, *n.f.*, (com.) letter, favor. *Votre —;* your favor.

honorer, *v.a.*, to honor, to pay honor to ; to do credit to, to be an honor to.

s'honorer, *v.r.*, to acquire honor ; to do one's self honor ; to think, to consider, to deem, to esteem it an honor ; to glory in, *or* pride one's self upon ; to take a pride in.

ad **honores** (-rès), *adv.*, (l.u.) honorary, *ad honorem.*

honorifique, *adj.*, titular, honorary.

†**honte**, *n.f.*, shame ; disgrace, reproach, scandal, infamy; confusion. *Mauvaise —;* bashfulness. *Sans —;* shameless, unblushing; shamelessly, unblushingly. *Avoir — de faire une mauvaise action ;* to be ashamed of doing a bad action. *Rougir de —;* to blush for very shame. *Faire — à quelqu'un ;* to make any one feel ashamed ; (but also :) *Nous lui avons fait —;* he was ashamed of us. *Vous me faites —;* I am ashamed of you. *Faire la — de ;* to be a disgrace to. *Il est la — de sa famille ;* he is a disgrace to his family. *Revenir avec sa courte —;* to return without success ; to return affronted, balked, unsuccessful. *Avoir toute — bue ;* to be lost to all shame, to all sense of shame. *Perdre toute —;* to lose all shame, all sense of shame. *Regarder comme une —;* to look upon, to hold, as a disgrace. *Que — ne vous fasse dommage ;* (prov.) don't be ashamed to do what is right.

†**honteusement** (-teûz-màn), *adv.*, shamefully, disgracefully, ignominiously, infamously, scandalously.

†**honteux, -se**, *adj.*, ashamed ; bashful, shy ; shameful, disgraceful, scandalous, disreputable, discreditable. *Il a l'air —;* he has a bashful look. *Pauvres —;* modest poor. *Une conduite —se ;* disgraceful conduct. *Les parties —ses ;* the secret parts, pudenda. *Morceau —;* last piece in the dish (at table). *Il n'y que les — qui perdent ;* a close mouth catches no flies, or nothing ask, nothing have. *Jamais — n'eut belle amie ;* faint heart never won fair lady.

hôpital, *n.m.*, hospital ; alms-house, poor-house. *— ambulant ;* field-hospital. *Vaisseau— (—x-hôpitaux) ;* hospital-ship. *Aller à l'—;* to go to the workhouse ; to go to the dogs. *Prendre le chemin de l'—;* to be on the high-road to ruin ; to go the way to the workhouse. *Mettre à l'—;* (fig.) to ruin, to beggar any one.

†**hoquet**, *n.m.*, hiccough, hiccup. *— de la mort ;* death-rattle. *Avoir le —;* to have the hiccoughs, the hiccups. *Faire passer le —;* to stop the hiccoughs, the hiccups.

†**hoqueton** (hok-ton), *n.m.*, jacket (short coat or cassock) ; yeoman of the guard.

horaire, *adj.*, horary, horal ; *n.*, time-table.

†**horde**, *n.f.*, horde.

hordéiforme, *adj.*, barley-shaped.

⊙†**horion**, n.m., (jest.) bang, thump, violent blow.

horizon, n.m., horizon. *A l'*—; on the horizon. *Monter sur l'*—; (astron.) to ascend. *Le croissant de la lune, qui venait de s'envoler de l'*—; the crescent moon in her upward flight from the horizon (V. Hugo).

horizontal, -e, adj., horizontal.

horizontalement (-tal-män), adv., horizontally.

horloge, n.f., clock; time-keeper; (nav.) glass. — *d'eau;* clepsydra. — *marine;* chronometer. — *solaire;* sun-dial. *Monter une* —; to wind up a clock. — *de sable;* hour-glass. — *de la mort;* (insect) death-watch. —*qui marche huit jours;* eight-day clock.

horloger, n.m., clockmaker, watchmaker.

horlogère, n.f., clockmaker's wife, watch-maker's wife.

horlogerie (-lo-jrî), n.f., watchmaking, clock-making; clock-work; horology.

hormis, prep., except, excepting, but, save, saving.

horographie, n.f., horography.

horoscope, n.m., horoscope. *Tirer l'* — *de quelqu'un;* to cast any one's nativity; to predict the fate of. *Faire tirer son* —; to have one's fortune told.

horreur (or-reur), n.f., horror, dread, detestation, abomination; awe; enormity; fright (very ugly person). *Etre saisi d'* —; to be seized with horror. *J'ai* — *d'y penser;* I dread to think of it. *Une belle* —; an awful spectacle, sight. *Inspirer l'* — *du vice;* to inspire a horror for vice. *Avoir* — *de* or *avoir en* —; to have a horror of; to hold in abomination, in detestation. *Faire* — *à;* to horrify, to disgust. *On m'a dit des* —*s de cet homme là;* I have been told shocking things about that man.

horrible (or-ribl), adj., horrible, horrid, hideous, frightful, shocking, dreadful, fearful. *Il fait un temps* —; it is shocking weather.

horriblement (or-ri-), adv., horribly, horridly, shockingly, hideously, frightfully.

horripilation (or-ri-), n.f., (med.) horripilation.

†**hors**, prep., out; beyond; past; but, except, save. — *de saison;* out of season. — *de doute;* without question, beyond doubt. — *de prix;* extremely dear, priceless. — *de combat;* disabled. *Je suis tout* — *de moi;* I am quite beside myself. —*d'ici!* away with you, out of my sight! — *cela, nous sommes d'accord;* beyond that, or in other respects, we agree.

†**hors-d'œuvre**, n.m., (—) out-work, out-building; digression; episode; (cook.) side-dish.

hortensia, n.m., (bot.) hortensia, hydrangea.

horticole, adj., horticultural.

horticulteur, n.m., horticulturist.

horticultural, -e, adj., horticultural.

horticulture, n.f., horticulture. *Exposition d'*—; flower-show.

hosanna (o-za-n-na), n.m., (—s) Hosanna.

hospice, n.m., hospital, refuge; alms-house; (in the Alps) convent, monastery. — *des enfants trouvés;* foundling hospital. — *des aliénés;* lunatic asylum.

hospitali-er, -ère, adj., hospitable.

hospitali-er, n.m., -**ère**, n.f., hospitaler.

hospitalièrement, adv., hospitably.

hospitalité, n.f., hospitality.

hospodar, n.m., hospodar.

hostie, n.f., (Jewish antiq.) offering; victim, sacrifice; (c. rel.) host, consecrated wafer.

hostile, adj., hostile, inimical, adverse.

hostilement (os-til-män), adv., hostilely, adversely.

hostilité, n.f., hostility; enmity.

hôte, n.m., host; landlord, innkeeper, publican; guest; lodger; traveler; inhabitant, occu-

pant, occupier. *Table d'*—; table d'hôte, ordinary. *Qui compte sans son* — *compte deux fois;* he who reckons without his host must reckon again.

hôtel, n.m., town mansion, large house; hotel, inn. — *de ville;* town-hall. — *des monnaies;* mint. *L'*—*-Dieu;* the chief hospital of a town. *Maître d'*—; steward. *Descendre à l'*—; to put up at an inn, at an hotel. *Etre à l'*—; to stay, to lodge, at an hotel, at an inn. — *des Postes;* General Post-Office. — *des ventes;* auction mart. — *meublé* or *garni;* furnished lodgings or apartments, lodging-house.

hôteli-er, n.m., -**ère**, n.f., innkeeper, host, hostess, landlord, landlady, of an inn.

hôtellerie (-tè-lrî), n.f., inn, hotel, hostelry.

hôtesse, n.f., hostess; landlady of an inn, guest, visitor, lodger.

†**hotte**, n.f., dosser, basket (carried on the back); basket funnel.

†**hottée**, n.f., basketful.

†**hottentot**, n.m., -**e**, n.f., Hottentot.

†**hottereau** or †**hotteret**, n.m., garden-basket.

†**hotteu-r**, n.m., -**se**, n.f., basket-carrier.

†**houache** or **houaiche**, n.f., or **ouaiche**, n.m., (nav.) wake, track (of a ship). *V.* **sillage**.

†**houblon**, n.m., hop. — *sauvage;* wild hop, hedge-hop. *Four à* —; hop-kiln. *Perche à* —; hop-hole.

†**houblonner**, v.a., n., to hop.

†**houblonnière**, n.f., hop-ground, hop-garden, hop-field, hop-yard.

†**houcre**, n.m. *V.* **hourque**.

†**houe**, n.f., (agri.) hoe.

†**houement**, n.m. hoeing.

†**houer**, v.a. and n., to hoe, to dig.

*†**houille**, n.f., pit-coal, coal, sea-coal. — *flambante;* inflammable coal, open-burning coal. — *grasse;* smith-coal, cannel-coal. — *maigre;* uninflammable coal, close-burning coal. — *schisteuse;* slate-coal. — *sèche;* glance-coal; (min.) culm. — *de moyenne grosseur;* cob-coal. *Bateau pour le transport de la* —; coal-barge. *Chargeur de* —; coal-whipper. *Dépôt de* —; coal-depot, coal-wharf, coal-store. *Mine de* —; coal-mine, coal-pit. *Exploiter une mine de* —; to work a coal-mine.

*†**houill-er, -ère**, adj., coal, coaly. *Terrains* —*s;* coal-fields. *Exploiter un terrain* —; to work a coal-field. *Gisements* —*s;* coal-measures or beds.

*†**houillère**, n.f., coal-mine, colliery, coal-pit. *Exploitant de* —; coal-master. *Propriétaire de* —; coal-owner, coal proprietor.

*†**houilleur**, n.m., collier, coal-miner.

*†**houilleu-x, -se**, adj., containing coal, coaly.

†**houlan**, n.m., (—s). *V.* **uhlan**.

†**houle**, n.f., (nav.) billow, surge, swell; skillet, iron pot.

†**houlette**, n.f., crook, sheep-hook; crosier; trowel; spatula.

†**houleu-x, -se**, adj., (nav.) swelling. *Mer* —*se;* rough, rolling sea.

†**houlque**, n.f. *V.* **houque**.

†**houp!** (hoop), int., (hunt.) holla! — *là;* gee up!

†**houper**, v.a., (hunt.) to hoop; to shout.

se **houper**, v.r., to shout to each other.

†**houppe**, n.f., tuft; top-knot; tassel. — *à poudrer;* powder-puff.

†**houppé, -e**, adj., (bot.) tufted, crested.

†**houppée**, n.f., (nav.) crest, foam (of a wave).

†**houppelande** (hoo-pland), n.f., overcoat (great coat).

†**houpper**, v.a., to tuft. — *de la laine;* to tuft, to comb (wool).

†**houque**, n.f., (bot.) feather-grass.

†**houra**, int. *V.* **hourra**.

*†**hourailler**, v.n., (hunt.) to hunt with bad hounds.

*†houraillis, *n.m.*, (hunt.) pack of good-for-nothing hounds.

†hourdage, *n.m.*, rough-walling, pugging.

†hourder, *v.a.*, to rough-work, to rough-wall, to pug.

†hourdi, *n.m.*, (nav.) wing-transom.

†hourdis, *n.m.* V. **hourdage**.

†houret, *n.m.*, (hunt.) bad hound.

†houri, *n.f.*, houri.

†hourque, *n.f.*, (nav.) hooker.

†hourra, *n.m.*, (—s) hurrah, hurray.

†hourvari, *n.m.*, (hunt.) cry to call back the dogs; uproar, din, tumult, crash and thunder (of battle).

†housard, *n.m.* V. **hussard**.

†houseaux, *n.m.pl.*, spatterdashes, leggings. *Laisser ses* —; (fig.) to leave one's bones, to die, to kick the bucket.

*†houspiller, *v.a.*, to pull, to touse, to worry, to mob, to tug, to maul; to abuse, to cut up, to rate.

*se †houspiller, *v.r.*, to tug, to maul, to worry each other; to wrangle.

†houssage, *n.m.*, dusting, sweeping (with a feather-broom).

†houssaie, *n.f.*, holly-grove.

†houssard, *n.m.* V. **hussard**.

†housse, *n.f.*, housing, horse-cloth; saddle-cloth, hammer-cloth; cover (for a bed, &c).

†houssé, -e, *adj.*, (her.) clothed (of a horse).

†housser, *v.a.*, to dust, to sweep.

†houssine, *n.f.*, switch.

†houssiner, *v.a.*, to switch; to beat, to thrash.

†houssoir, *n.m.*, whisk; birch-broom; feather-broom.

†housson, *n.m.*, (bot.) knee-holly, butcher's-broom.

†houx, *n.m.*, holly, holly-tree. —*frelon* (——s), *petit* —; butcher's-broom.

†hoyau, *n.m.*, mattock; pickax.

⊙*†huaille, *n.f.*, mob, rabble.

†huard, *n.m.*, ospray, osprey, sea-eagle.

hubert, *n.m.*, (insect) vine-fretter.

se hubir, *v.r.*, to bristle up (of cats).

†hublot or **hulot**, *n.m.*, (nav.) small port-hole.

†huche, *n.f.*, pan, kneading-trough; trough; bin-hopper (of a mill). — *au pain* ; bread-pan.

†hucher, *v.a.*, (hunt.) to whistle. *Se* —, to whistle to each other.

†hue ! *int.*, gee ! gee up ! to the right.

†huée, *n.f.*, shouting, shout; hooting.

†huer, *v.a.* and *n.*, to shout after, to hoot at; to hoot.

†huette, *n.f.* V. **hulotte**.

†huguenot, -e (hug-no, -t), *n.* and *adj.*, Huguenot.

†huguenote, *n.f.*, kitchen-stove (in earthenware); pipkin. *Des œufs à la* —; eggs cooked in mutton gravy.

†huguenotisme, *n.m.*, (l.u.) Huguenotism.

†huhau ! *int.*, gee up ! to the right ! V. **hue**.

huilage, *n.m.*, oiling.

huile, *n.f.*, oil. — *douce ;* sweet oil. — *rance ;* rancid oil. — *de ricin ;* castor-oil. — *de navette ;* rape-oil. — *de lin ;* linseed-oil. — *de baleine ;* train-oil, whale oil. — *comestible ;* salad-oil. — *à brûler ;* lamp-oil. — *de cotret ;* stirrup oil (thrashing). — *de bras*, — *de coude*, — *de poignet ;* elbow grease, thews and sinews. — *de pied de bœuf ;* neat's foot oil. *A l'* —; with oil. *Cet ouvrage sent l'* —; that work smells of the lamp. *Jeter de l'* — *sur*, or *dans*, *le feu ;* to add fuel to the flame. *Tache d'* —; oil-stain; (fig.) irremediable evil, lasting shame.

huiler, *v.a.*, to oil; to anoint with oil; to grease.

huilerie, *n.f.*, oil-works, oil-shop.

huileu-x, -se, *adj.*, oily, greasy.

huilier, *n.m.*, cruet-stand.

huilière, *n.f.*, (nav.) oil-pitcher.

⊙huis, *n.m.*, door. *A* — *clos ;* with closed doors, in private, in camerâ.

huisserie (ui-srî), *n.f.*, door-frame.

huissier, *n.m.*, usher; door-keeper; tipstaff, sheriff's officer, bailiff; gentleman-usher. — *audiencier ;* crier of the court.

†huit (*huit*, before a vowel, a silent *h*, and at the end of the phrase; *hui* before a word beginning with a consonant, when *huit* qualifies it), *adj.*, eight; eighth. *Dans* — *jours*, *d'aujourd'hui en* — ; this day week. *Il y a eu hier* — *jours ;* yesterday week. *Il y a eu Dimanche* — *jours ;* last Sunday week.

†huit, *n.m.*, eight; eighth. *Le* — *du mois ;* the eighth of the month.

†huitain, *n.m.*, stanza of eight lines.

†huitaine, *n.f.*, eight days. *Dans la* —; in the course of the week.

†huitième (hui-ti-èm), *adj.*, eighth.

†huitième, *n.m.*, eighth.

†huitième, *n.f.*, eighth class, eighth form (or *first* form in England).

†huitièmement, *adv.*, eighthly.

huître, *n.f.*, oyster; (fig.) blockhead, dunce. — *marinée ;* pickled oyster. — *à l'écaille ;* oyster in the shell. *Cloyère d'* —*s ;* basket of twenty-six dozen of oysters. *Frai d'* —*s ;* oyster-brood. *C'est une* — *à l'écaille ;* he is a blockhead.

huitrier, *n.m.*, (orni.) oyster-catcher.

huitrière, *n.f.*, oyster-bed.

†hulan, *n.m.*, (—s). V. **uhlan**.

†hulotte, *n.f.*, owlet, wood-owl.

humain, -e, *adj.*, human; humane, benevolent. *Le genre* —; mankind.

humain, *n.m.*, human being, man.

humainement, *adv.*, humanly; humanely.

humaniser, *v.a.*, to humanize, to civilize; to soften, to mollify.

s'humaniser, *v.r.*, to become humanized; to comply with, to come down to the intellectual level of others.

humaniste, *n.m.*, humanist.

humanitaire, *adj.* and *n.m.*, humanitarian.

humanité, *n.f.*, humanity; human nature; mankind. *pl.*, humanities, classical studies.

humble, *adj.*, humble; lowly, meek, modest.

humblement, *adv.*, humbly; meekly.

humectant, -e, *adj.*, refreshing, moistening, emollient.

humectant, *n.m.*, humectant; (med.) emollient.

humectation, *n.f.*, moistening, wetting.

humecter, *v.a.*, to wet, to moisten, to damp, to refresh.

s'humecter, *v.r.*, to be moistened; to refresh one's self. *S'* — *le gosier ;* to wet one's whistle.

†humer, *v.a.*, to inhale, to suck in, to sniff. — *l'air ;* to inhale th~ air.

huméral, -e, *adj.*, (anat.) humeral.

humérus (-rûs), *n.m.*, (anat.) humerus.

humeur, *n.f.*, humor; temper, disposition, turn of mind, mood, caprice, fancy, whim; ill-humor. —*s froides ;* king's evil, scrofula. — *noire ;* spleen. *Elle a l'* — *gaie ;* she is of a cheerful disposition. *Etre d'* — *à* or *etre en* — *de faire quelque chose ;* to be in a mood to do anything. *Etre de bonne* — ; to be in a good humor or temper. *Etre de mauvaise* —; to be out of temper. *Avoir de l'* — ; to be out of temper. *Avec* —; peevishly, crossly, ill-humoredly. *Prendre de l'* — ; to get out of temper.

humide, *n.* and *adj.*, moisture, humidity; humid, watery; damp, wet, moist, liquid.

humidement (u-mid-mǎn), *adv.*, (l.u.) in a damp place.

humidité, *n.f.*, humidity, dampness, moisture, wateriness, wetness.

humiliant, -e, *adj.*, humiliating, degrading.

humiliation, *n.f.*, humiliation, abasement, degradation.

humilier, *v.a.*, to humble, to humiliate, to take down, to bring down, to abase.

s'**humilier**, *v.r.*, to humble, to humiliate, to abase, one's self.

humilité, *n.f.*, humility, humbleness, meekness, lowliness.

humoral, -e, *adj.*, (med.) humoral.

humorisme, *n.m.*, (med.) humoralism.

humoriste, *adj.*, peevish, ill-tempered ; humoristic.

humoriste, *n.m.*, ill-tempered, peevish person; humorist ; (med.) humoralist.

humoristique, *adj.*, humoristic.

humus (u-mûs), *n.m.*, soil, mold.

†**hun**, *n.m.*, Hun.

†**hune**, *n.f.*, (nav.) top. *La grande* — ; the main-top. *La* — *de misaine ;* the fore-top. *La* — *d'artimon ;* the mizzen-top.

†**hunier**, *n.m.*, top-sail. *Le grand* — ; the main top-sail. *Le petit* — ; the fore top-sail.

†**huppe**, *n.f.*, (orni.) peewit ; lapwing ; tuft, topknot.

†**huppé, -e**, *adj.*, tufted, crested (of birds) ; (fam.) crack, best, well off, smartly dressed. *Des plus* —*s ;* of the highest, smartest. *Les plus* —*s y sont pris;* (prov.) the most cunning are deceived.

†**hure**, *n.f.*, head (of a wild boar). — *de saumon ;* jowl of a salmon. *Vilaine* — ; mop; shock of hair.

†**hurhau!** *int.*, gee ! gee ho ! *V.* **hue.**

†**hurlement**, *n.m.*, howl, howling, roar ; yell, yelling, shriek, scream.

†**hurler**, *v.n.*, to howl, to yell ; to roar, to bellow, to shout, to scream. *Hurler avec les loups;* to do as others do.

†**hurleur**, *n.m.*, howler.

†**hurluberlu**, *n.m.*, (jest.) giddy goose, harebrained person, harum-scarum. *En* — ; thoughtlessly, inconsiderately.

†**hussard**, *n.m.*, hussar.

à la †**hussarde**, *adv.*, like hussars ; by rapine, by pillage. *Bottes à la* — ; riding-boots.

†**hutte**, *n.f.*, hut, cottage, shed, shanty.

se†**hutter**, *v.r.*, to make a hut, to lodge in.

hyacinthe, *n.f.*, (bot., min.) hyacinth.

hyades, *n.f.pl.*, (astron.) Hyades.

hyalin, -e, *adj.*, hyaline.

hyalode, *adj.*, of the color of glass.

hybride, *n.m.* and *adj.*, hybrid, mongrel.

hydr, hydro, prefix from Greek ὕδωρ.

hydragogue (-gog), *n.m.*, (med.) hydragogue.

hydrate, *n.m.*, (chem.) hydrate.

hydraté, *adj.*, (chem.) hydrated.

hydraulique, *n.f.* and *adj.*, hydraulics ; hydraulic. *Bélier* — ; (phys.) water-ram. *Ouvrages* —*s ;* water-works. *Puissance* — ; water-power.

hydre, *n.f.*, hydra.

hydrocèle, *nf.*, hydrocele.

hydrocéphale, *n.f.*, hydrocephalus.

hydrochlorate, *n.m.*, (chem.) hydrochlorate.

hydrochlorique, *adj.*, (chem.) hydrochloric.

hydrocotyle, *n.f.*, (bot.) hydrocotyle.

hydrodynamique, *n.f.* and *adj.*, hydrodynamics ; hydrodynamic.

hydrogène, *n.m.*, (chem.) hydrogen.

hydrogéné, -e, *adj.*, (chem.) hydrogenated, combined with hydrogen.

hydrogéner, *v.a.*, to hydrogenize.

hydrographe, *n.m.*, hydrographer.

hydrographie, *n.f.*, hydrography.

hydrographique, *adj.*, hydrographical.

hydrolithe, *n.f.*, hydrolite.

hydrologie, *n.f.*, hydrology.

hydromancie, *n.f.*, hydromancy.

hydromel, *n.m.*, hydromel, mead. — *vineux ;* metheglin, mead.

hydromètre, *n.m.*, hydrometer.

hydrométrie, *n.f.*, hydrometry.

hydrométrique, *adj.*, hydrometrical.

hydrophane, *n.f.*, (min.) hydrophane.

hydrophobe, *n.m.f.* and *adj.*, hydrophobiac.

hydrophobie, *n.f.*, hydrophobia.

hydropique, *n.m.f.* and *adj.*, dropsical person ; dropsical.

hydropisie, *n.f.*, dropsy.

hydropneumatique, *adj.*, hydropneumatic.

hydroscope, *n.m.*, hydroscope ; bletonist.

hydroscopie, *n.f.*, hydroscopy, bletonism.

hydrostatique, *n.f.* and *adj.*, hydrostatics ; hydrostatical.

hydrosulfate or **hydrosulfure**, *n.m.*, (chem.) hydrosulphate, hydrosulphuret.

hydrosulfurique, *adj.*, hydrosulphuric.

hydrothérapie, *n.f.*, (med.) hydropathy.

hydrothérapique, *adj.*, hydropathic.

hydrothorax (-raks), *n.m.*, hydrothorax.

hydrotique, *adj.*, hydrotic.

hydrure, *n.m.*, (chem.) hydruret.

hyémal, -e, *adj.* *V.* **hiémal.**

hyémation, *n.f.*, hyemation.

hyène, *n.f.*, hyena.

hygiène, *n.f.*, hygiene.

hygiénique, *adj.*, hygienic.

hygrologie, *n.f.*, (med.) hygrology.

hygromètre, *n.m.*, hygrometer.

hygrométrie, *n.f.*, hygrometry.

hygrométrique, *adj.*, hygrometrical.

hymen (i-mèn) or **hyménée**, *n.m.*, Hymen; marriage, wedlock.

hymen, *n.m.*, (anat.) hymen.

hyménoptère, *n.m.* and *adj.*, hymenopter ; hymenopteral.

hymnaire, *n.m.*, hymn-book, hymnal.

hymne, *n.m.*, hymn (patriotic).

hymne, *n.f.*, hymn (sung in churches). *Recueil d'* —*s ;* hymn-book.

hyoïde, *n.m.* and *adj.*, (anat.) hyoid bone, tongue-bone ; hyoid.

hypallage, *n.f.*, (gram.) hypallage.

hyperbate, *n.f.*, (gram.) hyperbaton.

hyperbole, *n.f.*, (rhet.) hyperbole ; exaggeration ; (math.) hyperbola.

hyperbolique, *adj.*, hyperbolic ; hyperbolical.

hyperboliquement (-lik-mãn), *adv.*, hyperbolically.

hyperborée or **hyperboréen, -ne** (-in, -èn), *adj.*, hyperborean.

hyperboréens, *n.m.pl.*, (Grec. antiq.) Hyperboreans.

hypercatalectique, *adj.*, hypercatalectic.

hypercritique, *n.m.*, hypercritic. *adj.*, hypercritical.

hyperdulie, *n.f.*, hyperdulia (worship of the Virgin Mary).

hypertrophie, *n.f.*, (med.) hypertrophy.

hypertrophié, *adj.*, (of the heart) enlarged.

hypèthre, *n.m.*, (arch.) hypæthron. *adj.*, hypæthral (i.e., uncovered (of temples)).

hypnotique, *adj.*, (med.) hypnotic.

hypocondre, *n.m.*, (anat.) hypochondrium.

hypocondriaque or **hypocondre**, *n.m.f.* and *adj.*, (med.) hypochondriac, hypochondriacal.

hypocondrie, *n.f.*, hypochondriasis, spleen.

hypocras, *n.m.*, hippocras.

hypocrisie, *n.f.*, hypocrisy. *Avec* — ; hypocritically.

hypocrite, *n.m.f.* and *adj.*, hypocrite ; hypocritical.

hypocritement, *adv.*, hypocritically.

hypogastre, *n.m.*, (anat.) hypogastrium.

hypogastrique, *adj.*, hypogastric.

hypogée, *n.m.*, (arch.) hypogeum.

hypoglosse, *n.m.* and *adj.*, (anat.) hypoglossal nerves ; hypoglossal, under the tongue.

hypoglottide, *n.f.*, (pharm.) a lozenge.

hypophylle, *adj.*, (bot.) hypophyllous.

hypopyon, *n.m.*, hypopium.

hypostase, *n.f.*, (theol.) hypostasis.

hypostatique, *adj.*, (theol.) hypostatical.

hypostatiquement (-tik-mān), *adv.*, hypostatically.

hypostyle, *adj.*, *n.m.*, (arch.) hypostyle.

hypoténuse, *n.f.*, (geom.) hypothenuse.

hypothécaire, *adj.*, on mortgage. *Créancier* —; mortgagee.

hypothécairement (-kèr-mān), *adv.*, by *or* with mortgage.

hypothèque, *n.f.*, mortgage. *Créancier sur* —; mortgagee. *Débiteur sur* —; mortgager. *Donner en* —; to give as a mortgage. *Eteindre, purger, une* —; to pay off a mortgage.

hypothéquer, *v.a.*, to mortgage. *Il est bien hypothéqué;* (fig.) he is very infirm.

hypothèse, *n.f.*, hypothesis, supposition. *Par* —; by supposition.

hypothétique, *adj.*, hypothetical.

hypothétiquement (-tik-mān), *adv.*, hypothetically.

hypotypose, *n.f.*, (rhet.) hypotyposis.

hypsomètre, *n.m.*, hypsometer.

hypsométrie, *n.f.*, altimetry, hypsometry.

hysope, *n.f.*, (bot.) hyssop.

hystérie, *n.f.*, hysteria, hysterics.

hystérique, *adj.*, *n.m.f.*, hysteric, hysterical.

hystérite, *n.f.*, (med.) hysteritis.

hystérocèle, *n.f.*, (med.) hysterocele.

hystérologie, *n.f.*, (rhet.) hysterology, hysteron-proteron.

hystéromanie, *n.f.*, (med.) hysteromania.

hystéromètre, *n.m.*, (surg.) hysterometer.

hystérotome, *n.m.*, (surg.) hysterotome.

hystérotomie, *n.f.*, (surg.) hysterotomy.

I

i, *n.m.*, the ninth letter of the alphabet, i. *Il met les points sur les* —; he is very particular, very precise, *or* punctilious.

iambe, *n.m.*, (poet.) iambus, iambic.

iambique, *adj.*, iambic.

ibid, ab. of *ibidem*.

ibidem (-dèm), *adv.*, ibidem, ibídem, the same.

ibis (i-bis), *n.m.*, (orni.) ibis.

icaque, *n.f.*, cocoa-plum.

icaquier, *n.m.*, cocoa-plum tree.

⊙**icel-ui**, *m.*, **-le**, *f.*, *pron.*, (jur.) this; that.

ichneumon, *n.m.*, (mam., ent.) ichneumon; ichneumon-fly.

ichnographie (ik-no-), *n.f.*, ichnography, ground-plan.

ichnographique, *adj.*, ichnographic.

ichor (i-kor), *n.m.*, (med.) ichor.

ichoreu-x, -se, *adj.*, (med.) ichorous.

ichtyocolle (ik-ti-), *n.f.*, isinglass, fish-glue.

ichtyographie, *n.f.*, ichthyography.

ichtyographique, *adj.*, ichthyographic.

ichtyolithe, *n.m.*, ichthyolite.

ichtyologie, *n.f.*, ichthyology.

ichtyologique, *adj.*, ichthyological.

ichtyologiste, *n.m.*, ichthyologist.

ichtyophage, *n.m.f. adj.*, ichthyophagist; ichthyophagous.

ichtyosaure, *n.m.*, (geol.) ichthyosaurus.

ici, *adv.*, here, hither, in this place; now. *Il a passé par* —; he passed this way. *Venez* —; come here. *D'—;* hence. *D'— à deux jours;* within two days. *D'— là;* from here to there; between this and then. — *près;* hard by. *Par* —; through here, this way. — *bas;* here below. *Jusqu'* —; till now, up to this time, hitherto; down to here. *C'est* —; this is the place; here we are.

icoglan, *n.m.*, page of the Sultan.

iconoclaste. *n.m.*, iconoclast.

iconographe, *n.m.*, iconographer.

iconographie, *n.f.*, iconography.

iconographique, *adj.*, iconographical.

iconolâtre, *n.m.*, iconolater, image-worshiper.

iconolâtrie, *n.f.*, iconolatry, image-worship.

iconologie, *n.f.*, iconology.

iconostase, *n.f.*, iconostasis.

icosaèdre, *n.m.*, (geom.) icosahedron.

icosandre, *adj.*, icosandrous.

icosandrie, *n.f.*, (bot.) icosandria.

ictère, *n.m.*, (med.) icterus, jaundice.

ictérique, *adj.*, icteric, jaundiced.

id, ab. of *idem*.

ide, *n.m.*, (ich.) ide; (piquet) name of each of the two tricks played to decide a bet.

ides, *n.f.pl.*, ides.

idéal, -e, *adj.*, ideal, vain, imaginary, visionary.

idéal, *n.m.*, ideal. *Le beau* —; the beauideal, ideal beauty, *or* perfection.

idéalement, *adv.*, ideally.

idéaliser, *v.a.*, to idealize. *S'* —; to become idealized.

idéalisme, *n.m.*, idealism.

idéaliste, *n.m.*, idealist.

idée, *n.f.*, idea, notion, perception; plan; hint; conceit, fancy; sketch, outline; mind, head; thought; meaning, opinion, taste; reason; invention; imagination; just a taste. *Selon nos —s;* according to our notions. *En* —; in imagination, in fancy. *Il me vient à l'* —; it occurs to me. *Avoir une* —; to have an idea. *N'avoir pas d'— de;* to have no notion of. *Se faire une* —; to form an idea. *Il me revient en* —, *à l'* —, *que* . . . ; it recurs to me that. *Changer d'* —; to alter one's mind. *Se mettre dans l'* —; to take it into one's head. *Oter une chose de l'— de quelqu'un;* to get a thing out of any one's head. *Donner une — d'ail à quelque chose;* to give just a taste of garlic to anything. *On ne peut lui ôter cela de l'* —; one cannot get that out of his head. *Il me vient une* —; an idea strikes me. *Perdre l'— de;* to lose all recollection of. — *creuse;* empty notion. — *fixe;* fixed idea. — *plaisante;* odd conceit. *J'ai* —; I rather think. *A-t-on* — *!* what an idea! *Quelle* — *!* well! I never.

idem (i-dèm), *adv.*, idem, ditto.

identification, *n.f.*, identification.

identifier, *v.a.*, to identify.

s'identifier, *v.r.*, to identify one's self, to become indentified; to identify.

identique, *adj.*, identical, the same.

identiquement (-tik-mān), *adv.*, identically.

identité, *n.f.*, identity, sameness.

idéographie, *n.f.*, ideography.

idéographique, *adj.*, ideographic.

idéologie, *n.f.*, ideology.

idéologique, *adj.*, ideological.

idéologue, *n.m.*, ideologist.

idio-électrique, *adj.*, idio-electric.

idiomatique, *adj.*, idiomatic.

idiome, *n.m.*, idiom, dialect, language.

idiopathie, *n.f.*, (med.) idiopathy; (philos.) inclination.

idiopathique, *adj.*, idiopathic.

idiosyncrasie, *n.f.*, idiosyncrasy.

idiot, -e, *n.m.f. and adj.*, idiot, natural fool; fool; idiotic, absurd, foolish. *C'est — ce que vous faites là;* there is no common sense in that. *C'est du dernier* —; it is the height of absurdity.

idiotie (-ci), *n.f.*, (med.) idiocy, idiotcy, imbecility.

idiotisme, *n.m.*, (gram.) idiom, idiotism; (med.) idiocy, idiotcy.

idolâtre, *n.m. and adj.*, idolater; idolatrous. *Elle est — de ses enfants;* she dotes on her children.

idolâtrer, *v.n.*, to worship idols.

idolâtrer, *v.a.*, to idolize, to be extremely fond of, to dote upon. *Il idolâtre cette femme;* he idolizes that woman.

idolâtrie, *n.f.*, idolatry. *Il l'aime à l'* —; he idolizes her, *or* loves her to madness.

idolâtrique, *adj.* idolatrous.

idole, *n.f.*, idol. *C'est une vraie —;* she is nothing but a wax doll. *Il se tient là comme une —;* he stands there like a statue. *Faire son — de;* to idolize.

idylle, *n.f.*, idyl, idyll.

if, *n.m.*, yew, yew-tree; lamp stand.

*****igname**, *n.f.*, Indian potato; yam.

*****ignare**, *n.m.* and *adj.*, dunce, ignoramus; illiterate, ignorant.

igné, -e (ig-né), *adj.*, igneous.

ignescence, *n.f.*, ignescence.

ignicole (ig-ni), *n.m.* and *adj.*, ignicolist, fire-worshiping; fire-worshiper.

ignition (ig-ni-), *n.f.*, ignition. *Entrer en —;* to ignite.

ignivome, *adj.*, vomiting-fire.

ignivore (ig-ni), *adj.*, ignivorous, fire-eating.

*****ignobilité**, *n.f.*, ignobleness, baseness, vileness.

*****ignoble**, *adj.*, ignoble, vile, mean, disgraceful, base; beastly, filthy.

*****ignoblement**, *adv.*, ignobly, vilely, basely.

*****ignominie**, *n.f.*, ignominy; disgrace, dishonor.

*****ignominieusement** (-eûz-mān), *adv.*, ignominiously.

*****ignominieu-x, -se**, *adj.*, ignominious.

*****ignoramment** (-ra-mān) *adv.*, ignorantly, unknowingly.

*****ignorance**, *n.f.*, ignorance; error, mistake, blunder. — *crasse;* sordid or gross ignorance. *Par —;* from ignorance. *Être dans l'— de;* to be ignorant of. *Prétendre cause d'—;* to plead ignorance. *Croupir dans l'—;* to wallow in ignorance.

*****ignorant, -e**, *n.* and *adj.*, ignoramus, ignorant person; ignorant, illiterate, unlearned; unacquainted with.

*****ignorantin**, *n.m.* and *adj.*, ignorant. *—s, frerès —s;* lay-brothers (teachers of the poor).

*****ignorantissime**, *adj.*, most ignorant.

*****ignoré, -e**, *part.*, unknown; concealed, forgotten.

*****ignorer**, *v.a.*, to be ignorant of, not to know, to be unacquainted with; not to be aware of. *J'ignorais qu'il fût arrivé;* I was not aware he had arrived. *Ne pas —;* to know, to be aware of.

*****s'ignorer**, *v.r.*, not to know one's self; to be ignorant of one's own capabilities.

iguane, *n.m.*, (zool.) iguana.

il, *pron. m.*, he; it, there; *pl.* **ils**, they. — *me parle;* he speaks to me. — *fait froid;* it is cold. — *y a des gens;* there are persons, people. — *s'éleva un murmure;* a murmur arose.

île, *n.f.*, island, isle. *Les Îles;* the Antilles, (also formerly a province of France containing the capital, Paris.) *—s sous le vent;* Leeward Islands. *—s du vent;* Windward Islands. *L'— de France;* Mauritius.

iléon or **ileum**, *n.m.*, (anat.) ileum.

iles, *n.m.pl.*, (anat.) ilia, flanks. *Os des —;* os ilium, hip-bone.

ilet, *n.m.* *V.* **ilot**.

iléus (-ûs), *n.m.*, (med.) ileus; iliac passion.

iliade, *n.f.*, Iliad.

iliaque, *adj.*, (anat.) iliac.

ilion or **ilium**, *n.m.*, (anat.) coxa, haunch-bone; (hist.) Ilium, Troy.

illégal, -e (il-lé), *adj.*, illegal, unlawful.

illégalement (il-lé-gal-mān), *adv.*, illegally, unlawfully.

illégalité (il-lé-), *n.f.*, illegality, unlawfulness.

illégitime (il-lé), *adj.*, illegitimate; unlawful, unjust; spurious.

illégitimement (il-lé-), *adv.*, illegitimately, unlawfully.

illégitimité (il-lé-), *n.f.*, illegitimacy, unlawfulness, spuriousness.

illettré, -e (il-lè), *adj.*, illiterate, unlettered.

illibéral, -e (il-li-), *adj.*, illiberal; mean; mechanical (of artisans).

illibéralement (il-li-), *adv.*, illiberally; meanly.

illibéralité, *n.f.*, illiberality, meanness.

illicite (il-li-), *adj.*, illicit, unlawful.

illicitement (il-li-cit-mān), *adv.*, illicitly, unlawfully.

illimitable (il-li-), *adj.*, illimitable.

illimité, -e (il-li-), *adj.*, unlimited, unbounded, boundless.

illisibilité, *n.f.*, illegibility.

illisible, (il-li-), *adj.*, illegible.

illisiblement (il-li-), *adv.*, illegibly.

illogicité (il-lo-), *n.f.*, illogicalness.

illogique (il-lo-), *adj.*, illogical.

illogiquement (il-lo-jik-mān), *adv.*, illogically.

illuminant, *n.m.* and *adj.*, illuminant; illuminating.

illuminateur (il-lu-), *n.m.* and *adj.*, illuminator; illuminating, enlightening.

illuminati-f, -ve (il-lu-), *adj.*, illuminative.

illumination (il-lu-), *n.f.*, illumination.

illuminé, -e (il-lu-), *adj.*, illuminated, enlightened.

illuminé, *n.m.*, -e, *n.f.*, visionary, fanatic.

illuminer (il-lu-), *v.a.*, to illuminate; to illumine; to light up; to enlighten the mind. *S'—;* to become illuminated; to brighten up, to beam.

illuminisme (il-lu-), *n.m.*, illuminism.

illusion (il-lu-), *n.f.*, illusion, self-deception, self-delusion, delusion; fallacy; chimera; phantom. *Se faire — à soi-même;* to deceive, to delude one's self. *Être dans l'—;* to be laboring under a delusion.

illusionner, *v.a.*, to delude; to deceive *S'—;* to delude, to deceive one's self.

illusoire (il-lu-), *adj.*, illusive, illusory, delusive.

illusoirement (il-lu-zoar-mān), *adv.*, illusively, fallaciously.

illustration (il-lus-), *n.f.*, illustration, illustriousness; celebrity, renown; illustrious man; explanation; elucidation. *C'est une des —s de la France;* he is one of the glories of France.

illustre (il-lu-), *adj.*, illustrious, famous, renowned, eminent.

illustre, *n.m.*, illustrious man, worthy.

illustrer (il-lu-), *v.a.*, to illustrate; to do honor to; to give luster to; to render illustrious; to illuminate; to explain; to make clear.

s'illustrer, *v.r.*, to render one's self illustrious; to become illustrious.

illustrissime (il-lu-), *adj.*, most illustrious.

îlot, *n.m.*, islet; eyot; block, cluster (of houses).

ilote, *n.m.*, helot, slave.

ilotisme, *n.m.*, helotism.

image, *n.f.*, image, likeness, resemblance; picture, statue. *Être sage comme une —;* to be as good as gold.

imag-er, *n.m.*, -ère, *n.f.*, image-vendor.

imager, *v.a.*, to picture; to adorn with images.

imagerie (i-ma-jrî), *n.f.*, image-trade.

imaginable, *adj.*, imaginable.

imaginaire, *adj.*, imaginary, visionary, fancied, unreal; (math.) imaginary, impossible. *Espaces —s;* imaginary realms.

imaginati-f, -ve, *adj.*, imaginative.

imagination, *n.f.*, imagination, conception, fancy, conceit; thought; invention. *C'est une effet de l'—;* it is all fancy. *Se faire des —s;* to fancy all sorts of things.

imaginative, *n.f.*, imagination, fancy, imaginative faculty.

imaginer, *v.a.*, to imagine, to conceive, to contrive; to fancy, to think, to believe, to suppose; to contrive, to devise.

s'imaginer, *v.r.*, to imagine one's self, to imagine, to think, to fancy, to believe, to conceive. *Imaginez-vous;* just fancy.

iman, *n.m.*, iman (Mohammedan priest).

imbécile, *adj.*, imbecile, foolish, silly, simple.

imbécile, *n.m.f.*, idiot, fool, simpleton, ninny.

imbécilement (-sil-mān), *adv.*, foolishly, stupidly.

imbécillité, *n.f.*, imbecility, idiotcy; stupidity, foolishness.

imberbe, *adj.*, beardless; raw, green.

imberbe, *n.m.*, beardless boy.

imbiber, *v.a.*, to imbibe; to imbue; to soak; to steep, to take in, to drink in.

s'imbiber, *v.r.*, to imbibe, to soak.

imbibition, *n.f.*, imbibition.

imbrication, *n.f.*, over-lapping.

imbricé, -e, *adj.*, imbricated, overlapping.

imbrim (in-bri-m), *n.m.*, (orni.) loon, great diver.

imbriqué, -e, *adj.*, (bot.) imbricated, overlapping.

***imbroglio** (-bro-lio), *n.m.*, (—s) imbroglio, confusion, intricacy, perplexity.

imbu, -e, *adj.*, (de) imbued, impressed (with), tinctured.

imbuvable, *adj.*, undrinkable.

imitable, *adj.*, imitable.

imitat-eur, -rice, *adj.*, imitative.

imitat-eur, *n.m.*, -rice, *n.f.*, imitator.

imitati-f, -ve, *adj.*, imitative. *Les arts —s ;* the imitative arts.

imitation, *n.f.*, imitation. *A l'— de ;* in imitation of.

imiter, *v.a.*, to imitate, to copy, to mimic, to take off, to take pattern upon; to resemble.

immaculé, -e (im-ma-), *adj.*, immaculate, spotless.

immanent, -e (im-ma-), *adj.*, immanent; inherent.

immangeable (im-man-jabl), *adj.*, uneatable.

immanquable (im-man-), *adj.*, infallible, certain, sure.

immanquablement (im-man-), *adv.*, infallibly, certainly, without fail.

immarcescible (im-mar-), *adj.*, incorruptible, unfading.

immatérialisme (im-ma-), *n.m.*, immaterialism.

immatérialiste (im-ma-), *n.m.*, immaterialist.

immatérialité (im-ma-), *n.f.*, immateriality.

immatériel, -le (im-ma-), *adj.*, immaterial, incorporeal.

immatériellement (im-ma-té-rièl-mān), *adv.*, immaterially, incorporeally.

immatriculation (im-ma-), *n.f.*, matriculation.

immatricule (im-ma-), *n.f.*, (jur.) matriculation; registering.

immatriculé, -e (im-ma-), *adj.*, registered, matriculated.

immatriculer (im-ma-), *v.a.*, to matriculate; to register. *Se faire —;* to get one's name entered.

immédiat, -e (im-mé-), *adj.*, immediate.

immédiatement (im-mé-diat-mān), *adv.*, immediately; directly.

immémorial, -e (im-mé-), *adj.*, immemorial.

immémorialement (im-mé-) *adv.*, immemorially.

immense (im-māns), *adj.*, immense, infinite, boundless; enormous, huge; prodigious.

immensément (im-mān-), *adv.*, immensely.

immensité (im-mān-), *n.f.*, immensity, boundlessness; boundless space.

· **immensurable** (im-mān-), *adj.*, immensurable.

immerger (im-mèr-), *v.a.*, to immerge, to immerse, to plunge, to dip. *S'—;* to be immerged, to plunge.

immérité, -e (im-mé-), *adj.*, undeserved, unmerited, uncalled for.

immersi-f, -ve (im-mèr-), *adj.*, by immersion.

immersion (im-mèr-), *n.f.*, immersion.

immesurable, *adj.*, immeasurable.

immesuré, -e, *adj.*, unmeasured.

imméthodique, *adj.*, unmethodical.

immeuble (im-meu-bl), *adj.*, (jur.) real.

immeuble, *n.m.*, estate, real estate, landed estate; realty; fixture.

immigrant (im-mi-), *n.m.*, -e, *n.f.*, immigrant.

immigration (im-mi-), *n.f.*, immigration.

immigrer (im-mi-), *v.n.*, to immigrate.

imminence (im-mi-), *n.f.*, imminence, impendency.

imminent, -e (im-mi-), *adj.*, imminent, impending.

s'immiscer (si-mi-sé), *v.r.*, to interfere, to take upon one's self; to meddle with; (jur.) to enter upon (possession). *S'— dans les affaires des autres;* to meddle with other people's business.

immiscibilité (im-mis-), *n.f.*, immiscibility.

immiscible (im-mis-), *adj.*, immiscible.

immission (im-mi-), *n.f.*, immission.

immixtion (im-miks-tion), *n.f.*, blending; (jur.) entering on possession; uncalled for, unwarrantable interference.

immobile (im-mo-), *adj.*, immovable, motionless; unshaken, stable, firm.

immobilement, *adv.*, immovably.

immobili-er, -ère (im-mo-), *adj.*, real (of estate). *Société —ère;* building society.

⊙**immobilier**, *n.m.*, landed property.

immobilisation (im-mo-), *n.f.*, (jur.) conversion of property into real estate.

immobiliser (im-mo-), *v.a.*, to convert into real estate; to realize.

immobilité (im-mo-), *n.f.*, immobility, immovability.

immodération, *n.f.*, immoderation.

immodéré, -e (im-mo-), *adj.*, immoderate, intemperate, excessive, violent.

immodérément (im-mo-), *adv.*, immoderately, intemperately, excessively.

immodeste (im-mo-), *adj.*, immodest, indecent.

immodestement (im-mo-), *adv.*, immodestly, indecently.

immodestie (im-mo-dès-tî), *n.f.*, immodesty, indecency.

immolateur (im-mo-), *n.m.* and *adj.*, immolator, sacrificer; immolating, sacrificing.

immolation (im-mo-), *n.f.*, immolation, sacrifice.

immoler (im-mo-lé), *v.a.*, to immolate, to sacrifice, to slay; (fig.) to laugh at, to ridicule.

s'immoler, *v.r.*, to immolate, to sacrifice one's self; to sacrifice one's feelings; to stand ridicule. *S'— pour sa patrie;* to sacrifice one's self for one's country. *Il s'est immolé de bonne grâce;* he stood the joke very well.

immonde (im-mond), *adj.*, unclean, impure.

immondices (im-mon-), *n.f.pl.*, filth, dirt; (Bibl.) uncleanliness, impurity.

immondicité (im-mon-), *n.f.*, (Bibl.) uncleanness.

immoral, -e (im-mo-), *adj.*, immoral.

immoralité (im-mo-), *n.f.*, immorality.

immortaliser (im-mor-), *v.a.*, to immortalize.

s'immortaliser, *v.r.*, to immortalize one's self.

immortalité (im-mor-), *n.f.*, immortality.

immortel, -le (im-mor-), *adj.*, immortal, everlasting.

immortel, *n.m.*, -le, *n.f.*, immortal.

immortelle, *n.f.*, (bot.) everlasting.

immortellement, *adv.*, immortally.

immortification (im-mor-), *n.f.*, (theol.) immortification.

immortifié, -e (im-mor-), *adj.*, unmortified.

immuable (im-mu-), *adj.*, immutable, unalterable, unchangeable.

immuablement (im-mu-), *adv.*, immutably, unalterably, unchangeably.

immunité (im-mu-), *n.f.*, immunity.
immutabilité (im-mu-), *n.f.*, immutability, unchangeableness.
impact, *n.m.*, (mech.) impact.
impair, -e, *adj.*, odd, uneven.
impairement (in-pèr-mān), *adv.*, (math.) unevenly, oddly.
impalpabilité, *n.f.*, impalpability.
impalpable, *adj.*, impalpable.
impanation, *n.f.*, (theol.) impanation.
impané, -e, *adj.*, impanate.
impardonnable, *adj.*, unpardonable.
impardonnablement, *adv.*, unpardonably.
imparfait, -e, *adj.*, imperfect, unfinished, incomplete; defective.
imparfait, *n.m.*, (gram.) imperfect, imperfect tense.
imparfaitement (-fèt-mān), *adv.*, imperfectly.
imparisyllabique, *adj.*, (gram.) imparisyllabic.
imparité, *n.f.*, inequality, imparity.
impartageable (-jabl), *adj.*, indivisible.
impartial, -e, *adj.*, impartial.
impartialement (-sial-mān), *adv.*, impartially.
impartialité, *n.f.*, impartiality.
impasse, *n.f.*, blind alley (street *or* court with only one entrance); inextricable difficulty, dead-lock, dilemma; (at whist) finesse.
impassibilité, *n.f.*, impassibility, impassiveness.
impassible, *adj.*, impassible, impassive, undisturbed, unmoved.
impassiblement, *adv.*, impassively, undisturbedly.
impastation, *n.f.*, (mas.) impastation.
impatiemment (-sia-mān), *adv.*, impatiently, eagerly.
impatience, *n.f.*, impatience; restlessness, eagerness; longing. *L'— dans les douleurs;* impatience under suffering. *Donner des —s;* to put out of all patience. *Etre dans l'— de faire une chose;* to be impatient, eager to do a thing, to long to do.
impatient, -e, *adj.*, impatient; anxious, restless, eager.
impatientant, -e, *adj.*, provoking, vexing.
impatienter, *v.a.*, to make impatient, to tire any one's patience, to put out of patience; to provoke.
*s'***impatienter**, *v.r.*, to lose one's patience, to become *or* grow impatient; to fret, to worry.
*s'***impatroniser**, *v.r.*, (b.s.) to assume *or* usurp authority; to get a footing; to set up as a master.
impayable, *adj.*, invaluable, matchless, priceless; inimitable, exceedingly funny, capital, extraordinary; unheard of.
impayé, -e, *adj.*, unpaid.
impeccabilité (in-pèk-ka-), *n.f.*, impeccability.
impeccable, *adj.*, impeccable.
impénétrabilité, *n.f.*, impenetrability, imperviousness.
impénétrable, *adj.*, impenetrable, impervious; unfathomable, inscrutable. *Un homme —;* a very close man.
impénétrablement, *adv.*, impenetrably.
impénitence, *n.f.*, impenitence. *Mourir dans l'—;* to die impenitent.
impénitent, -e, *n.* and *adj.*, impenitent.
impenses, *n.f.pl.*, (jur.) expenses (for repairs, improvements).
impérati-f, -ve, *adj.*, imperative. *Prendre un ton —;* to assume an imperative tone.
impératif, *n.m.*, (gram.) imperative.
impérativement (-tiv-mān), *adv.*, imperatively.
impératoire, *n.f.*, (bot.) masterwort.

impératrice, *n.f.*, empress.
imperceptible, *adj.*, imperceptible.
imperceptiblement, *adv.*, imperceptibly.
imperdable, *adj.*, (of law-suits, of games) that cannot be lost.
imperfectibilité, *n.f.*, imperfectibility.
imperfectible, *adj.*, imperfectible.
imperfection, *n.f.*, imperfection.
imperforation, *n.f.*, (med.) imperforation.
imperforé, -e, *adj.*, (med.) imperforated.
impérial, -e, *adj.*, imperial.
impériale, *n.f.*, roof, outside (of a coach); all-fours (cards); imperial serge; (bot.) imperial; melon pompion; imperial (under the lip).
impérialement (-al-mān), *adv.*, imperially.
impérialiste, *n.m.*, imperialist.
impériaux, *n.m.pl.*, imperialists.
impérieusement (-eûz-mān), *adv.*, imperiously.
impérieu-x, -se, *adj.*, imperious, haughty, supercilious, domineering; lordly.
impérissabilité, *n.f.*, imperishableness.
impérissable, *adj.*, imperishable.
impérissablement, *adv.*, imperishably.
impéritie (-ci), *n.f.*, incapacity; unskillfulness, ignorance.
imperméabilité, *n.f.*, impermeability.
imperméable, *adj.*, impermeable, impervious. *— à l'air;* air-tight. *— à l'eau;* waterproof.
impermutabilité, *n.f.*, (phys.) impermutability.
impermutable, *adj.*, that is not permutable.
impersonnalité, *n.f.*, (philos.) impersonality.
impersonnel, -le, *adj.*, impersonal.
impersonnel, *n.m.*, (gram.) impersonal verb.
impersonnellement (-nèl-mān), *adv.*, (gram.) impersonally.
impersuadé, -e, *adj.*, unpersuaded.
impersuasible, *adj.*, impersuasible.
impertinemment (-na-mān), *adv.*, impertinently, insolently; sillily, foolishly, nonsensically, pertly.
impertinence, *n.f.*, impertinence, insolence, sauciness; rudeness; silliness, offensive thing.
impertinent, -e, *n.* and *adj.*, impertinent person, saucy person, sauce-box; impertinent, saucy, insolent, pert.
imperturbabilité, *n.f.*, imperturbability.
imperturbable, *adj.*, imperturbable.
imperturbablement, *adv.*, imperturbably.
impétigo, *n.m.*, (med.) impetigo, ringworm.
impétrable, *adj.*, (jur.) impetrable, obtainable.
impétrant, *n.m.*, -e, *n.f.*, (jur.) grantee; candidate (successful); graduate, recipient.
impétration, *n.f.*, (jur.) impetration.
impétrer, *v.a.*, (jur.) to impetrate, to obtain.
impétueusement (-eûz-mān), *adv.*, impetuously, vehemently, violently, forcibly.
impétueu-x, -se, *adj.*, impetuous, vehement, violent, boisterous; headlong.
impétuosité, *n.f.*, impetuosity, impetuousness; force, vehemence, impetus, boisterousness.
impie, *adj.*, impious, ungodly, reprobate.
impie, *n.m.f.*, impious man, impious woman, ungodly person, reprobate, infidel.
impiété, *n.f.*, impiety, ungodliness.
impitoyable, *adj.*, pitiless, unpitying; merciless, unmerciful; ruthless, unrelenting, unsparing.
impitoyablement, *adv.*, pitilessly, mercilessly, unmercifully; ruthlessly, unrelentingly, unsparingly.
implacabilité, *n.f.*, implacability, implacableness.
implacable, *adj.*, implacable.
implacablement, *adv.*, implacably.
implantation, *n.f.*, implantation.
implanter, *v.a.*, to implant; to plant.
*s'***implanter**, *v.r.*, to be planted, to be fixed, to be lodged, to take root.

implexe, *adj.*, implex, intricate.

implication, *n.f.*, implication, involving, entangling; contradiction.

implicite, *adj.*, implicit; tacit, implied.

implicitement (-sit-măn), *adv.*, implicitly, tacitly.

impliquer, *v.a.*, to implicate, to involve, to entangle; to imply, to infer.

impliquer, *v.n.*, to involve contradiction.

implorat-eur.-rice, *n.m.f.* and *adj.*, implorer, imploring, supplicant.

imploration, *n.f.*, supplication, imploration.

implorer, *v.a.*, to implore, to call upon, to crave, to supplicate, to beg, to entreat, to beseech, to call for.

impoli, **-e**, *adj.*, impolite, unpolite, uncourteous, uncivil, rude, coarse.

impoliment, *adv.*, unpolitely, uncourteously, uncivilly, rudely.

impolitesse, *n.f.*, impoliteness, unpoliteness, incivility, rudeness; impolite thing, rudeness. *Faire une — à quelqu'un ;* to behave rudely to any one.

impolitique, *adj.*, impolitic.

impolitiquement (-tik-măn), *adv.*, unwisely.

impondérabilité, *n.f.*, (phys.) imponderability.

impondérable, *adj.*, (phys.) imponderable, imponderous.

impopulaire, *adj.*, unpopular.

impopulairement (-lèr-măn), *adv.*, unpopularly.

impopularité, *n.f.*, unpopularity.

imporeu-x, -se, *adj.*, imporous.

imporosité, *n.f.*, imporosity.

importable, *adj.*, (com.) importable.

importance, *n.f.*, importance, consequence, moment; consideration, weight, consequentialness. *D'—;* of consequence, of moment; consequentially; soundly, sharply, thoroughly. *Corriger quelqu'un d'—;* to punish any one soundly. *De la dernière —;* of the greatest or of the highest importance. *Avoir de l'—;* to be of importance, of moment, of consequence. *Homme d'—;* man of consequence. *Se donner des airs d'—;* to give one's self consequential airs. *Faire l'homme d'—;* to set up for a man of importance, to presume.

important, **-e**, *adj.*, important, of consequence, of moment; momentous, weighty. *Question —e;* weighty question. *Un homme —;* a man of note, of influence. *Peu —;* immaterial, of little consequence.

important, *n.m.*, essential, chief, point; consequential man. *Faire l'—;* to set up for a man of importance; to give one's self an air of importance.

importateur, *n.m.*, (com.) importer.

importation, *n.f.*, importation; (com.) imports.

importer, *v.imp.*, to import, to be of moment, to be of consequence, to concern; to matter, to signify. *Il n'importe pas;* it is no matter, it matters not, it is of no consequence, it does not matter, it does not signify. *N'importe;* no matter, never mind. *Que m'importe?* what matters it to me? *Que vous importe?* of what consequence is it to you? *Qu'importe?* what does it matter? *Peu importe;* it does not much matter. *Venez n'importe quand;* come when you like; no matter when. *N'importe comment;* any how, no matter how.

importer, *v.a.*, (com.) to import; (fig.) to import, to introduce. *— des expressions étrangères;* to introduce foreign expressions.

importun, **-e**, *n.m.f.* and *adj.*, tiresome person, troublesome person, intruder, bore, hanger-on, dun ; importunate, troublesome, tiresome ; obtrusive, irksome, inconvenient. *Visite —e;* obtrusive visit. *Etre —;* to intrude; to be troublesome.

importunément, *adv.*, (l.u.) importunely, obtrusively.

importuner, *v.a.*, to importune, to pester, to trouble, to annoy, to plague, to incommode ; to tease. *— ses débiteurs;* to dun one's debtors.

importunité, *n.f.*, importunity.

imposable, *adj.*, taxable.

imposant, **-e**, *adj.*, imposing, commanding, striking; stately. *Attitude —e;* commanding attitude.

imposer, *v.a.*, to force upon ; to lay on (of hands) ; to set ; to lay upon, to lay to any one's charge ; to impose, to enjoin, to prescribe ; to give, to confer, to lay ; to tax ; to charge, to impute ; to thrust upon, to force upon ; (print.) to impose. *C'est au vainqueur d'— la loi aux vaincus;* it is for the conqueror to prescribe laws for the conquered. *— des peines ;* to inflict punishment. *— silence;* to impose silence. *— des droits;* to levy duties. *— un pays;* to tax a country. *— un nom;* to give a name. *Je ne prétends pas vous — mon opinion;* I don't pretend to force my opinion upon you.

s'imposer, *v.r.*, to obtrude, to be obtrusive, to obtrude one's self ; to impose a tax upon one's self. *S'en —;* to deceive one's self.

imposer, *v.n.*, to awe, to overawe, to keep in awe. *C'est un homme dont la présence impose;* he is a man whose presence overawes one. *Sa mine impose;* his looks command respect, veneration. *En —;* to deceive. *En — à quelqu'un;* to impose upon any one ; to overawe, to deceive.

imposition, *n.f.*, imposition ; tax ; impost ; assessment ; (print.) imposition. *— des mains;* laying on of hands. *— d'un tribut;* imposition of a tribute. *— d'une peine;* infliction of a punishment. *Lever les —s;* to levy taxes.

impossibilité, *n.f.*, impossibility. *Etre de toute —;* to be utterly impossible. *Se trouver dans l'— de faire quelque chose;* to find it impossible to do a thing.

impossible, *n.m.*, impossibilities ; a great deal. *Je ne puis pas faire l'—;* I cannot do impossibilities. *A l'— nul n'est tenu;* there is no doing impossibilities ; there is no flying without wings. *Gagner l'—;* to gain enormously, or a great deal. *Chercher l'—, vouloir trouver l'—;* to attempt the impossible. *Viser l'—;* to aim at impossibilities.

impossible, *adj.*, impossible, fabulous, outrageous ; out of the way ; out of the question ; out of all reason ; unacceptable, most absurd.

imposte, *n.f.*, (arch.) impost, molding, fanlight. *[—s;* false oracles.

imposteur, *adj.*, deceitful, false. *Des oracles*

imposteur, *n.m.*, impostor, cheat.

imposture, *n.f.*, imposture, deception, falsehood, fallacy, illusion.

impôt, *n.m.*, tax, duty ; impost. *— sur les feux;* hearth-money. *— sur chaque tête* or *— sur les personnes;* poll-tax. *Lever des —s;* to levy taxes. *Percevoir les —s;* to collect the taxes. *— personnel et mobilier;* house-tax. *L'assiette de l' —;* the assessment of the taxes. *— sur le revenu;* income-tax.

impotence, *n.f.*, (med.) impotence ; weakness.

impotent, **-e**, *adj.*, (med.) impotent, infirm.

impraticabilité, *n.f.*, impracticability.

impraticable, *adj.*, impracticable ; untractable, unmanageable ; uninhabitable, impassable ; impossible, not to be done. *L'humidité rend cette chambre — pendant l'hiver ;* the damp renders this room uninhabitable during the winter. *Des chemins —s;* impassable roads.

imprécation, *n.f.*, imprecation, curse. *Faire des —s;* to curse. *Charger d'—s;* to load with imprecations, with curses.

imprécatoire, *adj.*, imprecatory.

*****imprégnation**, *n.f.*, impregnation.

*****imprégner**, *v.a.*, to impregnate.

*s'imprégner, *v.r.*, to become impregnated.
imprenable, *adj.*, impregnable.
imprescriptibilité, *n.f.*, imprescriptibility, indefeasibility.
imprescriptible, *adj.*, indefeasible.
impresses, *adj.pl.* V. **intentionnelles**.
impressi-f, **-ve**, *adj.*, impressive, striking.
impression, *n.f.*, impression; impress, mark, trace; issue, edition; print; printing; (paint.) priming. *Faute d'—*; misprint. *L'— d'un sceau;* the impression of a seal. *Frais d'—*; printing expenses. *Etre susceptible d'—*; to be impressible. *Etre à l'—*; to be in the printer's hands; to be in the press.
impressionnable, *adj.*, impressionable, sensitive; impressive; excitable, nervous.
impressionner, *v.a.*, to impress, to make an impression on; to move, to affect.
imprévoyance, *n.f.*, want of foresight, improvidence.
imprévoyant, **-e**, *adj.*, wanting foresight, improvident.
imprévu, **-e**, *adj.*, unforeseen, unexpected, unthought of, unlooked for, unhoped for.
imprimable, *adj.*, fit to be printed.
imprimé, *n.m.*, printed book, printed paper, printed document; (post.) book-packet. *pl.*, book-post.
imprimer, *v.a.*, to imprint, to impress, to stamp, to print, to implant, to instill; to give (motion); (paint.) to prime. *Se faire —;* to appear in print. *S'—;* to be printed; to be impressed, to be stamped.
imprimerie (in-pri-mrî), *n.f.*, printing; printing-office, printing establishment.
imprimeur, *n.m.*, printer; pressman. *— en taille-douce;* copper-plate printer. *— litho-graphe;* lithographic printer.
imprimure, *n.f.*, (paint.) priming.
improbabilité, *n.f.*, improbability, unlikelihood.
improbable, *adj.*, improbable, unlikely.
improbablement, *adv.*, improbably.
improbance, *n.f.*, (jur.) inconclusiveness.
improbant, **-e**, *adj.*, (jur.) inconclusive.
improbat-eur, **-rice**, *n.* and *adj.* V. **désap-probateur**.
improbation, *n.f.* V. **désapprobation**.
improbe, *adj.*, dishonest.
improbité, *n.f.*, improbity, dishonesty.
improductibilité, *n.f.*, unproductiveness.
improductible, *adj.*, unproducible.
improducti-f, **-ve**. *adj.*, unproductive.
improductivement (-tiv-mān), *adv.*, unproductively.
impromptu, *n.m.*, (—, or —*s*) impromptu.
impromptu, **-e**, *adj.*, impromptu, extemporary, extempore, unprepared.
impropice, *adj.*, unpropitious.
impropre, *adj.*, improper, wrong, unfit for. *Terme —;* wrong expression.
improprement, *adv.*, improperly.
impropriété, *n.f.*, impropriety (of language); (fig.) unfitness.
improuver, *v.a.*, to disapprove, to blame.
improvisat-eur, *n.m.*, **-rice**, *n.f.*, improvisator, extemporary speaker, extemporizer.
improvisation, *n.f.*, improvisation, extemporaneous speaking; (mus.) voluntary.
improviser, *v.a.*, to improvise, to produce extempore, to make extempore.
improviser, *v.n.*, to extemporize, to speak extempore.
à l'improviste, *adv.*, all of a sudden, suddenly, unawares, unexpectedly; aback. *Prendre à l'—;* to catch any one unawares or napping.
imprudemment (-da-mān), *adv.*, imprudently, unadvisedly, indiscreetly, incautiously.
imprudence, *n.f.*, imprudence, unadvisedness; indiscretion, imprudent act, folly. *Faire une*

—; to do an imprudent thing. *Commettre une* —; to be guilty of an indiscretion.
imprudent, **-e**, *n.m.f.* and *adj.*, imprudent, foolhardy person; imprudent, unadvised, unwise, incautious.
impubère, *adj.*, impuberal.
impuberté, *n.f.*, impuberty.
impubliable, *adj.*, unpublishable.
impudemment (-da-mān), *adv.*, impudently, audaciously, shamelessly.
impudence, *n.f.*, impudence, audaciousness, shamelessness; impudent thing, impudent conduct, piece of impudence.
impudent, **-e**, *n.m.f.* and *adj.*, impudent person, shameless person, brazen-face; impudent, saucy, shameless, brazen-faced.
impudeur, *n.f.*, immodesty, indecency, wantonness.
impudicité, *n.f.*, impudicity, immodesty, unchasteness, lewdness, lasciviousness, lewd act.
impudique, *adj.*, unchaste, lewd, immodest, impure.
impudiquement (-dik-mān), *adv.*, immodestly, unchastely, lewdly, lustfully, impurely.
impuissance, *n.f.*, impotence, impotency; inability, incapacity, powerlessness.
impuissant, **-e**, *adj.*, impotent; powerless, unable.
impulsi-f, **-ve**, *adj.*, impulsive.
impulsion, *n.f.*, impulsion, impulse; impetus; suggestion. *Par —;* by impulse. *Donner l'— à;* to give an impetus to.
impunément, *adv.*, with impunity.
impuni, **-e**, *adj.*, unpunished. *Laisser un affront —;* to put up with an affront, *or* to let an affront go unpunished.
impunité, *n.f.*, impunity.
impur, **-e**, *adj.*, impure, unchaste, immodest, unclean.
impurement (in-pur-mān), *adv.*, impurely, immodestly.
impureté (in-pur-té), *n.f.*, impurity, immodesty, obscenity.
imputabilité, *n.f.*, imputability.
imputable, *adj.*, imputable, attributable; to be deducted, chargeable.
imputati-f, **-ve**, *adj.*, imputative.
imputation, *n.f.*, imputation; charge, deduction.
imputer, *v.a.*, to impute, to attribute, to ascribe to, to charge with; to deduct. *— à crime;* to impute, to charge as a crime. *On vous imputera cela à négligence;* it will be put down to your negligence. *— une somme payée sur le principal;* to deduct a payment on account from the principal.
s'imputer, *v.r.*, to be attributed, imputed, to be put down to; to attribute to one's self. *La faute ne peut s'— qu'à votre imprudence;* the fault can only be put down to your imprudence.
imputrescible, *adj.*, imputrescible.
in (prefix used in composition as a particle of negation, as in *infini*; it is also used as an augmentative prefix, as in *incorporer*), in, un. [Before *b*, *m*, *p*, *in* is changed into *im;* and before *l* and *r*, into *il* and *ir*. When *in* comes before a consonant, as in *insu*, it has the nasal sound; but when placed before a vowel, as in *inégal*, it is sounded like *in* in English; and when coming before *n*, it has also the sound of the English *in*, as in *innocent*.]
inabordable, *adj.*, inaccessible, unapproachable.
inabordé, **-e**, *adj.*, unvisited, unapproached.
inabrité, **-e**, *adj.*, unsheltered, open.
inabrogé, **-e**, *adj.*, unrepealed.
in-absou-s, **-te**, *adj.*, unabsolved, unforgiven.
inabstinence, *n.f.*, intemperance.
inacceptable, *adj.*, unacceptable.
inaccessibilité, *n.f.*, inaccessibility.

inaccessible, *adj.*, inaccessible, unapproachable, unattainable.

inaccommodable, *adj.*, irreconcilable, that cannot be made up.

inaccomplissement, *n.m.*, unaccomplishment.

inaccord, *n.m.*, (gram.) want of concord.

inaccordable, *adj.*, unallowable ; irreconcilable; inadmissible, ungrantable ; untunable.

inaccostable, *adj.*, (l.u.) inaccessible. *C'est un homme —* ; he is not to be approached.

inaccoutumé, -e, *adj.*, unaccustomed, uncustomary, unwonted, unusual.

inacheté, -e, *adj.*, (l.u.) unbought.

inachevé, -e (i-nash-vé), *adj.*, unfinished, uncompleted, incomplete.

inacquérable, *adj.*, unacquirable.

inacti-f, -ve, *adj.*, inactive, inert, out of employment.

inaction, *n.f.*, inaction, indolence, inertness.

inactivement (-tiv-mān), *adv.*, inactively.

inactivité, *n.f.*, inactivity.

inadéquat, -e, (-koua, -t), *adj.*, (philos.) inadequate, incomplete.

inadhérent, -e, *adj.*, not adherent.

inadmissibilité, *n.f.*, inadmissibility.

inadmissible, *adj.*, inadmissible.

inadmission, *n.f.*, non-admission.

inadouci, -e, *adj.*, unsoftened, unmitigated.

inadvertance, *n.f.*, inadvertence, inadvertency, oversight. *Par —* ; from inadvertence, inadvertently, by an oversight.

inaliénabilité, *n.f.*, indefeasibility.

inaliénable, *adj.*, inalienable, indefeasible ; untransferable.

inaliéné, -e, *adj.*, unalienated.

inalliable, *adj.*, that cannot be alloyed, that cannot be combined, incompatible.

inalpin, -e, *adj.*, situated in the Alps. *V.* alpestre.

inaltérabilité, *n.f.*, inalterability, unchangeableness.

inaltérable, *adj.*, inalterable, unalterable, unchangeable, invariable.

inamical, -e, *adj.*, unfriendly.

inamicalement (-kal-mān), *adv.*, in an unfriendly manner.

inamissibilité, *n.f.*, (theol.) inamissibility.

inamissible, *adj.*, (theol.) inamissible (that cannot be lost).

inamovibilité, *n.f.*, irremovability.

inamovible, *adj.*, irremovable, permanent.

inanimation, *n.f.*, want of animation.

inanimé, -e, *adj.*, inanimate, lifeless ; spiritless.

inanité, *n.f.*, (fig.) inanity, emptiness.

inanition, *n.f.*, inanition. *Mourir d' —* ; to die from inanition, from starvation. *Tomber d' —* ; to faint for want of food.

inapaisable, *adj.*, unappeasable.

inapaisé, -e, *adj.*, unappeased.

inapercevable, *adj.*, imperceptible, unperceivable.

inaperçu, -e, *adj.*, unperceived, unobserved.

inapparent, *adj.*, unapparent.

inappauvri, -e, *adj.*, unimpoverished.

inappétence, *n.f.*, (med.) inappetence, inappetency, want of appetite.

inapplicabilité, *n.f.*, inapplicability.

inapplicable, *adj.*, inapplicable.

inapplication, *n.f.*, inapplication.

inappliqué, -e, *adj.*, inattentive, heedless, unmindful.

inappréciable, *adj.*, inappreciable ; inestimable, invaluable.

inappréciablement, *adv.*, inappreciably.

inapprécié, -e, *adj.*, unappreciated.

inapprêté, -e, *adj.*, unprepared, undressed, uncooked.

inapprivoisable, *adj.*, untamable.

inapte, *adj.*, (l.u.) inapt, unfit, unqualified.

inaptitude, *n.f.*, inaptitude, inaptness, unfitness, disqualification.

inarticulé, -e, *adj.*, inarticulate.

☉**inartificiel**, -le, *adj.*, artless, real, true.

☉**inartificiellement**, *adj.*, artlessly, really, truly.

inassermenté, *adj.*, unsworn.

inasservi, -e, *adj.*, unenslaved ; unsubdued.

inassiégeable, *adj.*, unbesiegeable.

inassignable, *adj.*, not assignable.

inassisté, -e, *adj.*, unassisted.

inassorti, -e, *adj.*, ill-assorted.

inassoupi, -e, *adj.*, sleepless.

inassouvi, -e, *adj.*, unsatiated.

inattaquable, *adj.*, unassailable, (fig.) unimpeachable, irreproachable, unobjectionable.

inattendu, -e, *adj.*, unexpected, unforeseen, unhoped for.

inattenti-f, -ve, *adj.*, inattentive, unmindful.

inattention, *n.f.*, inattention.

inaugural, -e, *adj.*, inaugural, opening.

inaugurat-eur, -rice, *n.m.f.*, inaugurator.

inauguration, *n.f.*, inauguration, opening.

inaugurer, *v.a.*, to inaugurate, to open.

inavouable, *adj.*, unavowable.

inca, *n.m.*, Inca (of Peru).

incalculable, *adj.*, incalculable, innumerable, countless, numberless.

incalculablement, *adv.*, incalculably.

incamération, *n.f.*, incameration.

incamérer, *v.a.*, to unite (pope-lands).

incandescence, *n.f.*, incandescence, white heat, burning, ardor.

incandescent, -e, *adj.*, incandescent.

incantation, *n.f.*, incantation.

incapable, *adj.*, incapable ; unable, unfit, incompetent, inefficient. *C'est un homme —* ; he is a man of no capacity. *Rendre —* ; to incapacitate.

incapacité, *n.f.*, incapacity, incapability, inability, unfitness, incompetence, disability, disablement, disqualification. *Frapper d' —* ; to incapacitate. *Etre frappé d' —* ; to be under a disqualification.

incarcération, *n.f.*, incarceration.

incarcérer, *v.a.*, to incarcerate, to imprison.

incarnadin, -e, *adj.*, flesh-colored, rosy.

incarnadin, *n.m.*, carnation-color.

incarnat, -e, *adj.*, rosy, flesh-colored.

incarnat, *n.m.*, carnation ; flesh-color.

incarnation, *n.f.*, incarnation ; (of nails) ingrowing.

incarné, -e, *adj.*, incarnate.

s'incarner, *v.r.*, to become incarnate ; (of nails) to grown in.

incartade, *n.f.*, thoughtless insult, outburst ; prank, folly, freak ; quarrel.

incassable, *adj.*, unbreakable.

incendiaire, *n.m.f.* and *adj.*, incendiary.

incendie, *n.m.*, fire, burning, conflagration. *— par malveillance* or *prémédité* ; incendiary fire, arson. *Appareil de sauvetage pour les —s ;* fire escape. *Arrêter un —* ; to get a fire under.

incendié, *n.m.*, -e, *n.f.*, sufferer by fire. *adj.*, burnt, gutted.

incendier, *v.a.*, to burn, to burn down ; to set fire to. *S' —* ; to set one's house on fire.

incertain, -e, *adj.*, uncertain, questionable ; unsettled, unsteady, inconstant ; faint, vague.

incertain, *n.m.*, what is uncertain, uncertainty ; feeling of uncertainty.

incertainement, *adv.*, (l.u.) doubtfully.

incertifié, -e, *adj.*, uncertified.

incertitude, *n.f.*, uncertainty ; unsteadiness, fickleness, doubt, suspense ; instability ; incertitude. *L' — du temps ;* the unsettled state of the weather.

incessamment (-sa-mān), *adv.*, immediately, directly, shortly, at once ; incessantly.

incessant, -e, *adj.,* incessant.
incessible, *adj.,* inalienable.
inceste, *n.m.,* incest, incestuous person.
inceste, *adj.,* incestuous.
incestueusement (-euz-mān), *adv.,* incestuously.
incestueu-x, -se, *n.m.f.* and *adj.,* incestuous person ; incestuous.
inchantable, *adj.,* unsingable.
incharitable, *adj.,* (l.u.) uncharitable.
inchasteté, *n.f.,* unchastity.
inchoati-f, -ve (-ko-), *adj.,* and *n.m.* (gram.) inchoative, inceptive ; inchoative verb.
incidemment (-da-mān), *adv.,* incidentally.
incidence, *n.f.,* incidence, incidency.
incident, *n.m.,* incident, occurrence ; (b.s., jur.) difficulty, cavil.
incident, -e, *adj.,* incidental, incident.
incidentaire, *n.m.,* (l.u.) caviler.
incidenter, *v.n.,* (jur.) to raise difficulties ; (b.s.) to start objections.
incinération, *n.f.,* incineration.
incinérer, *v.a.,* to incinerate.
incirconcis, -e, *adj.,* uncircumcised.
incirconcis, *n.m.,* (Bibl.) uncircumcised man. *Les —* ; the Gentiles.
incirconcision, *n.f.,* (fig. only) uncircumcision.
incise, *n.f.,* (gram.) incidental, parenthetic clause.
incisé, -e, *adj.,* incised, cut, gashed, notched.
inciser, *v.a.,* to incise, to make an incision, to notch, to gash ; (hort.) to tap (a tree).
incisi-f, -ve, *adj.,* incisive ; (fig.) sharp, cutting. *Dents —ves ;* incisors.
incisivement, *adv.,* cuttingly, sharply.
incision, *n.f.,* incision.
incisive, *n.f.,* incisive tooth ; incisor.
incitant, -e, *adj.,* (med.) inciting, stimulating.
incitant, *n.m.,* (med.) incitant, stimulant.
incitat-eur, *n.m.,* **-rice,** *n.f.,* inciter. *adj.,* inciting.
incitatif, -ve, *adj.,* inciting.
incitation, *n.f.,* incitement, incentive, instigation ; (med.) stimulus.
inciter, *v.a.,* to incite ; to excite ; to instigate, to induce.
incivil, -e, *adj.,* uncivil, unmannerly.
incivilement (-vil-mān), *adv.,* uncivilly, unmannerly.
incivilité, *n.f.,* incivility.
incivique, *adj.,* unpatriotic.
incivisme, *n.m.,* want of patriotism.
inclémence, *n.f.,* inclemency.
inclément, -e, *adj.,* inclement.
inclinaison, *n.f.,* inclination, incline, gradient, slope.
inclinant, -e, *adj.,* inclined, sloping.
inclination, *n.f.,* inclination, bow, stooping ; nodding, bias ; proneness, propensity ; attachment, passion. *Par —* ; from inclination. *Mariage d'—* ; love-match.
incliner, *v.a.,* to incline, to slope ; to stoop ; to bow ; to bend ; (fig.) to dispose, to turn.
s'incliner, *v.r.,* to incline ; to bow, to bend, to bow down ; (geol.) to dip, to tilt, to lower, to depress.
incliner, *v.n.,* to incline, to lean, to be disposed to, to be inclined to.
inclure, *v.a.,* to include, to inclose, to insert, to contain.
inclus, -e, *adj.,* inclosed, included. *Ci —* ; herein inclosed, sent herewith. *Mettre ci —* ; to inclose. *Trouver ci —* ; to find inclosed.
incluse, *n.f.,* an inclosed letter ; inclosed.
inclusi-f, -ve, *adj.,* inclusive ; inclosing.
inclusivement (-ziv-mān), *adv.,* inclusively.
incoercible, *adj.,* incoercible.
*****incognito,** *adv.,* incognito, incognita.

*****incognito,** *n.m.,* incognito. *Garder l'—* ; to preserve one's incognito.
incohérence, *n.f.,* incoherence.
incohérent, -e, *adj.,* incoherent.
incolore, *adj.,* colorless.
incombant, -e, *adj.,* incumbent.
incomber, *v.n.,* to be incumbent on any one ; to be a duty, to devolve upon.
incombustibilité, *n.f.,* incombustibility.
incombustible, *adj.,* incombustible.
incommensurabilité, *n.f.,* incommensurability.
incommensurable, *adj.,* incommensurable.
incommode, *adj.,* inconvenient, unhandy, incommodious ; importunate, annoying, disagreeable, troublesome, tiresome.
incommodé, -e, *part.,* indisposed, unwell, poorly ; distressed (of ships). *Être —* ; to be indisposed. *Un vaisseau —* ; a ship in distress.
incommodément, *adv.,* incommodiously, inconveniently ; uncomfortably.
incommoder, *v.a.,* to incommode, to inconvenience, to trouble ; to disturb, to annoy ; to embarrass, to impair ; to disagree with. *Si cela ne vous incommode pas ;* if it be no trouble to you. *J'ai peur de vous —* ; I am afraid of troubling you.
s'incommoder, *v.r.,* to inconvenience one's self.
incommodité, *n.f.,* inconvenience, incommodiousness, trouble, annoyance ; discomfort, indisposition, infirmity ; distress (of a ship). *Signal d'—* ; (nav.) signal of distress.
incommuable, *adj.,* incommutable.
incommunicable, *adj.,* incommunicable.
incommutabilité, *n.f.,* incommutability.
incommutable, *adj.,* (jur.) incommutable.
incommutablement, *adv.,* (jur.) incommutably.
incomparable, *adj.,* incomparable, matchless, unequaled, peerless.
incomparablement, *adv.,* incomparably.
incompatibilité, *n.f.,* incompatibility, inconsistency.
incompatible, *adj.,* incompatible, inconsistent, incongruous, unsuitable.
incompatiblement, *adv.,* incompatibly, inconsistently.
incompétemment (-ta-mān), *adv.,* incompetently.
incompétence, *n.f.,* incompetence, incompetency.
incompétent, -e, *adj.,* incompetent.
incomplaisance, *n.f.,* want of kindness ; unkindness.
incompl-et, -ète, *adj.,* incomplete, imperfect.
incomplètement (-plèt-mān), *adv.,* incompletely, imperfectly.
incomplexe, *adj.,* incomplex.
incompréhensibilité, *n.f.,* incomprehensibility.
incompréhensible, *adj.,* incomprehensible, unintelligible, inscrutable.
incompréhensiblement, *adv.,* incomprehensibly.
incompressibilité, *n.f.,* incompressibility.
incompressible, *adj.,* incompressible.
incompris, -e, *adj.,* not understood ; unappreciated.
inconcevable, *adj.,* inconceivable ; strange, wonderful, singular, odd ; extraordinary.
inconcevablement, *adv.,* inconceivably.
inconciliable, *adj.,* irreconcilable.
inconciliablement, *adv.,* irreconcilably.
inconclu, -e, *adj.,* unconcluded.
inconcluant, -e, *adj.,* inconclusive.
inconduite, *n.f.,* misconduct.
incongelable, *adj.,* uncongealable.
incongru, -e, *adj.,* incongruous ; unfit, unseemly, indecorous.

incongruité, n.f., incongruity; impropriety, unseemliness; indecency.

incongrûment, adv., incongruously, improperly, in an unseemly manner, indecorously.

inconnu, -e, adj., unknown.

inconnu, n.m., **-e,** n.f., unknown person; stranger.

inconnu, n.m., (n.p.) the unknown, that which is unknown.

inconnue, n.f., (math.) unknown quantity.

inconquis, -e, adj., unconquered.

inconscience, n.f., unconsciousness.

inconscient, adj., unconscious.

inconséquemment, adv., inconsistently.

inconséquence, n.f., inconsistency.

inconséquent, -e, adj. and n.m.f., inconsistent; inconsistent person.

inconsidération, n.f., inconsiderateness.

inconsidéré, -e, adj., inconsiderate, thoughtless, incautious.

inconsidérément, adv., inconsiderately, thoughtlessly, incautiously.

inconsistance, n.f., inconsistency.

inconsistant, adj., inconsistent.

inconsolable, adj., inconsolable, disconsolate.

inconsolablement, adv., inconsolably; disconsolately.

inconsolé, adj., unconsoled, uncomforted.

inconsommé, -e, adj., not consummated; unconsumed.

inconstamment, adv., inconstantly, unsteadily.

inconstance, n.f., inconstancy, fickleness, unsteadiness; changeableness, instability. L'— d'un amant; the fickleness of a lover. L'— du temps; the changeableness of the weather.

inconstant, -e, adj., inconstant, fickle, wavering, changeable; variable, unsettled, unsteady.

inconstant, -e, n.m.f. L'—, l'—e; the fickle man, the fickle woman.

inconstitutionnalité, n.f., unconstitutionality.

inconstitutionnel, -le, adj., unconstitutional.

inconstitutionnellement (-nèl-mãn), adv., unconstitutionally.

incontestable, adj., incontestable, indisputable, unquestionable.

incontestablement, adv., incontestably, indisputably, unquestionably.

incontesté, -e, adj., uncontested, uncontradicted; unquestioned, undisputed.

incontinence, n.f., incontinency.

incontinent, -e, adj., incontinent, unchaste.

incontinent, adv., (l.u.) at once, directly, immediately; forthwith.

incontinu, -e, adj., uncontinuous.

incontinuité, n.f., incontinuity.

incontrôlable, adj., uncontrollable.

incontroversable, adj., incontrovertible.

inconvenable, adj., unbecoming, unsuitable; unseemly.

inconvenablement, adv., unbecomingly.

inconvenance, n.f., impropriety, indecorousness, indecorum; unseemliness. Quelle —! how very improper!

inconvenant, -e, adj., improper, unbecoming, unseemly.

inconvénient, n.m., inconvenience, disadvantage; untoward incident; ill consequence, harm, trouble, objection. Je ne vois pas d'— à cela; I see no objection to that.

inconverti, -e, adj., unconverted.

inconvertible, adj., unconvertible.

incorporalité, n.f., incorporeality.

incorporation, n.f., incorporation.

incorporéité, n.f., incorporeity.

incorporel, -le, adj., incorporeal.

incorporer, v.a., to incorporate; to embody; to fuse. — un régiment dans un autre; to embody one regiment into another.

s'incorporer, v.r., to incorporate, to be embodied; to unite with; to be blended.

incorrect, -e, adj., incorrect, wrong, erroneous.

incorrectement, adv., incorrectly, inaccurately, wrongly.

incorrection, n.f., incorrectness, inaccuracy.

incorrigibilité, n.f., incorrigibility.

incorrigible, adj., incorrigible, irreclaimable.

incorrigiblement, adv., incorrigibly.

incorrompu, -e, adj., (l.u.) incorrupt, pure.

incorruptibilité, n.f., incorruptibility.

incorruptible, adj., incorruptible.

incorruption, n.f., incorruption.

incrassant, -e, adj., (med.) incrassating, nutritive.

incrassant, n.m., (med.) nutritive.

inorédibilité, n.f., incredibility.

incrédule, adj., incredulous, unbelieving.

incrédule, n.m.f., unbeliever; infidel.

incrédulité, n.f., incredulity; unbelief.

incréé, -e, adj., increate, increated.

incriminable, adj., incriminable, impeachable.

incrimination, n.f., (jur.) incrimination; charge, accusation.

incriminer, v.a., to incriminate, to accuse, to charge, to impeach.

incroyable, adj., incredible, past belief.

incroyable, n.m., French dandy (1795-1799).

incroyablement, adv., incredibly.

incroyance, n.f., unbelief.

incroyant, n.m., unbeliever.

incrustation, n.f., incrustation.

incruster, v.a., to incrust, to inlay.

s'incruster, v.r., to become incrusted.

incubation, n.f., incubation.

incube, n.m., incubus.

incuit, n.m., underdone part of roast meat.

incuit, -e, adj., underdone (of roast meat).

inculpable, adj., (jur.) chargeable.

inculpation, n.f., inculpation.

inculpé, n.m., **-e,** n.f., (jur.) prisoner, accused.

inculper, v.a., to accuse, to inculpate.

inculquer, v.a., to inculcate, to impress.

s'inculquer, v.r., to be inculcated or impressed.

inculte, adj., uncultivated; untilled, unplowed, waste; unpolished, rude. Terres —s; waste lands.

incultivable, adj., uncultivable.

incultivé, -e, adj., uncultivated.

inculture, n.f., (l.u.) inculture, want of culture.

incunable, n.m. and adj., old, early; early printed book.

incurabilité, n.f., incurability.

incurable, n.m.f. and adj., incurable. Les —s; hospital for incurables.

incurablement, adv., incurably.

incurie, n.f., carelessness, thoughtlessness; heedlessness; negligence.

incurieusement, adv., incuriously.

incurieu-x, -se, adj., incurious.

incuriosité, n.f., incuriosity.

incursion, n.f., incursion, inroad, irruption; (fig.) excursion.

incuse, adj. and n.f., badly or imperfectly struck medal.

inde, n.m., (dy.) indigo, indigo-blue.

***indébrouillable,** adj., inextricable, inexplicable, that cannot be unraveled.

indécemment, adv., indecently.

indécence, n.f., indecency; obscenity.

indécent, -e, adj., indecent; obscene.

indéchiffrable, adj., undecipherable, illegible, inexplicable; (fig.) obscure, intricate.

indéchirable, adj., untearable.

indéchiré, -e, adj., untorn.

indécis, -e, adj., undecided, doubtful; indeterminate, undefined, faint, **vague** ; wavering. *Il était —* ; he was wavering.

indécision, *n.f.,* indecision, irresolution ; wavering ; indistinctness.

indéclinabilité, *n.f.,* indeclinableness.

indéclinable, *adj.,* (gram.) indeclinable.

indécomposable, *adj.,* indecomposable.

indécousable, *adj.,* unsewable.

indécrit, -e, *adj.,* nondescript.

indécrottable, *adj.,* (pop.) uncleanable, unpolishable, rude, incorrigible, unteachable ; intractable.

indéfectibilité, *n.f.,* indefectibility.

indéfectible, *adj.,* indefectible.

indéfendable, *adj.,* indefensible, untenable.

indéfini, -e, *adj.,* indefinite, unlimited.

indéfiniment, *adv.,* indefinitely.

indéfinissable, *adj.,* indefinable, undefinable, unaccountable ; nondescript.

indéformable, *adj.,* that cannot be put out of shape.

indéfrichable, *adj.,* (of land) unclearable.

indéfriché, -e, *adj.,* uncleared, uncultivated.

indélébile, *adj.,* indelible, ineffaceable.

indélébilité, *n.f.,* indelibility.

indélibéré, -e, *adj.,* indeliberate.

indélicat, -e, *adj.,* indelicate ; unhandsome ; unbecoming ; unscrupulous.

indélicatement (-ka-tmän), *adv.,* indelicately, unhandsomely, unbecomingly.

indélicatesse, *n.f.,* indelicacy ; unhandsomeness.

indemne (in-dèm-n), *adj.,* (jur.) indemnified. *Rendre —* ; to indemnify.

indemnisation, *n.f.,* indemnification.

indemniser (in-dèm-ni-zé), *v.a.,* to indemnify ; to recoup ; to make good.

s'indemniser, *v.r.,* to indemnify one's self ; to recoup one's self.

indemnité, *n.f.,* indemnity.

indémontrable, *adj.,* undemonstrable.

indémontré, -e, *adj.,* undemonstrated.

indéniable, *adj.,* undeniable ; unquestionable ; obvious, self-evident.

indépendamment (-ḍa-män), *adv.,* independently.

indépendance, *n.f.,* independence.

indépendant, -e, *adj.,* independent.

indépendant, *n.m.,* Independent.

indéracinable, *adj.,* ineradicable.

indescriptible, *adj.,* indescribable.

indescriptiblement, *adv.,* indescribably.

indésirable, *adj.,* undesirable.

indestituable, *adj.,* irremovable.

indestructibilité, *n.f.,* indestructibility.

indestructible, *adj.,* indestructible.

indéterminable, *adj.,* indeterminable.

indétermination, *n.f.,* indetermination, irresolution.

indéterminé, -e, *adj.,* indeterminate, unlimited.

indéterminément, *adv.,* indeterminately.

indevinable, *adj.,* unguessable.

indévot, -e, *n.m.f.* and *adj.,* irreligious.

indévotement, *adv.,* irreverently.

indévotion, *n.f.,* irreligion.

index (in-dèks), *n.m.,* index, table of contents ; forefinger. *— expurgatoire ;* expurgatory index. *Mettre à l'—* ; to prohibit. *Etre à l'—* ; to be forbidden.

indicateur, *adj.,* indicating, indicatory.

indicateur, *n.m.,* indicator, gauge, guide ; (anat.) index ; railway guide, time-table. *Doigt —* ; forefinger.

indicatif, *n.m.,* (gram.) indicative mood.

indicati-f, -ve, *adj.,* indicative.

indication, *n.f.,* indication, information ; sign, mark, proof, declaration.

indice, *n.m.,* indication, indicator, sign, mark, token, symptom ; clew.

indicible, *adj.,* inexpressible, unspeakable, ineffable, unutterable.

indiciblement, *adv.,* unspeakably, ineffably, unutterably ; inexpressibly.

indiction, *n.f.,* indiction, convocation, prescription.

indicule, *n.m.,* (l.u.) slight indication.

indien, -ne (-in, -è-n), *n.m.f.* and *adj.,* Indian.

indienne, *n.f.,* printed calico, printed cotton, print.

indienneur, *n.m.,* calico-printer.

indifféremment (-ra-män), *adv.,* indifferently, indiscriminately ; equally, alike.

indifférence, *n.f.,* indifference, unconcern.

indifférent, -e, *adj.,* indifferent ; unconcerned ; immaterial ; (pers.) cold, unmindful, indolent, insensible. *Il lui est — de sortir ou de rester ;* it is the same to him whether he goes out or not. *Cela m'est parfaitement —* ; I don't mind which it is, *or* it is quite immaterial to me.

indifférent, *n.m., -e, n.f.,* indifferent person (one who is neither a friend nor an enemy). *Faire l'—* ; to feign indifference.

indigénat, *n.m.,* denizenship ; naturalization (in Poland).

indigence, *n.f.,* indigence, poverty, need.

indigène, *n.m.f.* and *adj.,* indigenous ; native (of a continent).

indigent, -e, *adj.* and *n.,* indigent, needy, necessitous ; poor person.

indigéré, -e, *adj.,* undigested, crude.

indigeste, *adj.,* indigestible, undigested ; crude.

indigestion, *n.f.,* indigestion.

*indignation, *n.f.,* indignation. *Avec —* ; indignantly. *Faire éclater son —* ; to give vent to one's indignation.

*indigne, *adj.,* unworthy, undeserving ; infamous, worthless, scandalous. *— de succéder ;* (jur.) debarred from inheriting.

*indigne, *n.m.,* worthless, infamous wretch ; (jur.) one debarred by law from inheriting.

*indigné, -e, *part.,* indignant, shocked.

*indignement, *adv.,* unworthily, infamously, scandalously.

*indigner, *v.a.,* to render indignant ; to raise the indignation of ; to shock.

*s'indigner, *v.r.,* to be indignant, shocked.

*indignité, *n.f.,* indignity ; unworthiness, worthlessness ; vileness, baseness ; infamy, scandalous thing. *Quelle — !* what a shame ! what a scandalous thing !

indigo, *n.m.,* indigo.

indigoterie, *n.f.,* indigo manufactory.

indigotier (-tié), *n.m.,* indigo-plant.

indiquer, *v.a.,* to indicate, to show, to point out ; to direct to, to inform of, to acquaint with, to appoint, to mention, to name, to recommend, to state, to sketch out. *Voulez-vous m'— le chemin de l'église ?* will you show me the way to the church ? *Au lieu indiqué ;* at the appointed place. *S'—* ; to be indicated.

indirect, -e, *adj.,* indirect ; (of evidence) circumstantial ; (of heirs) collateral.

indirectement, *adj.,* indirectly.

indisciplinable, *adj.,* indisciplinable ; indocile, unruly, ungovernable.

indiscipline, *n.f.,* indiscipline, insubordination.

indiscipliné, -e, *adj.,* undisciplined.

indiscr-et, -ète, *adj.,* indiscreet, inconsiderate, unwary ; inquisitive ; injudicious ; tell-tale, unable to keep a secret. *n.m.f.,* babbler, blabberer.

indiscrètement (-krèt-män), *adv.,* indiscreetly, inconsiderately ; unadvisedly, injudiciously, unguardedly.

indiscrétion, *n.f.,* indiscretion, inconsiderateness, imprudence, unwariness ; piece of indiscretion, indiscreet thing. *Serait-ce une — de ma* *part de demander . . . ?* would it be indiscreet of me to ask . . . ?

indiscutable, *adj.*, incontestable, unquestionable, indisputable.

indispensabilité, *n.f.*, indispensableness.

indispensable, *adj.*, indispensable. *n.m. L'—*; the strict necessities, the indispensable *or* strictly necessary ; the needful.

indispensablement, *adv.*, indispensably.

indisponibilité, *n.f.*, unavailableness.

indisponible, *adj.*, indisposable; unavailable.

indisposé, -e, *adj.*, indisposed, unwell.

indisposer, *v.a.*, to indispose; to render, to make unwell; to disaffect, to disincline, to estrange, to set against. *Je craignais que son intervention ne vous indisposât contre moi ;* I was afraid his interference would set you against me.

s'indisposer, *v.r.*, to be indisposed; to be unwell.

indisposition, *n.f.*, indisposition; disinclination.

indisputable, *adj.*, indisputable.

indissolubilité, *n.f.*, indissolubility.

indissoluble, *adj.*, indissoluble.

indissolublement, *adv.*, indissolubly.

indistinct, -e, *adj.*, indistinct, confused, vague, faint, dim.

indistinctement, *adv.*, indistinctly, indiscriminately ; vaguely, dimly, confusedly.

indistinction, *n.f.*, indistinction, indistinctness.

individu, *n.m.*, individual, self. *Avoir soin de son —*; to take care of one's self, of number one.

individualization, *n.f.*, individualization.

individualizer, *v.a.*, to individualize.

individualisme, *n.m.*, individualism.

individualité, *n.f.*, individuality, entity.

individuel, -le, *adj.*, individual.

individuellement (-duèl-mān), *adv.*, individually.

indivis, -e, *adj.*, (jur.) undivided.

indivis, *n.m.*, (jur.) joint-tenancy. *Par —*; in joint-tenancy.

indivisé, -e, *adj.*, undivided.

indivisément, *adv.*, indivisibly.

indivisibilité, *n.f.*, indivisibility.

indivisible, *adj.*, indivisible.

indivisiblement, *adv.*, indivisibly.

indivision, *n.f.*, joint-possession, copartnership; joint-tenancy.

in-dix-huit, *n.m.* and *adj.*, (—) (print.) decimo-octavo, in eighteen, 18mo.

indocile, *adj.*, indocile, unmanageable.

indocilité, *n.f.*, indocility, untractableness.

indocte, *adj.*, illiterate, ignorant, unlettered.

indo-germanique, *adj.*, Indo-Germanic.

indolemment (-la-mān), *adv.*, indolently.

indolence, *n.f.*, indolence, sloth. *Son — le perdra ;* his indolence will be the death of him.

indolent, -e, *n.* and *adj.*, indolent person; indolent, sluggish, slothful.

indomptable, *adj.*, indomitable; untamable, ungovernable.

indomptablement, *adv.*, indomitably, untamably, ungovernably.

indompté, -e, *adj.*, untamed, wild; uncontrollable; unconquered, unsubdued.

indou, *n.m.* and *adj.*, Hindoo.

in-douze, *n.m.* and *adj.*, (—) (print.) duodecimo, in twelve, 12mo.

indu, -e, *adj.*, undue, unseasonable, late. *Heure —e ;* unseasonable *or* late hour.

indubitable, *adj.*, indubitable, certain, beyond doubt.

indubitablement, *adv.*, indubitably, undoubtedly, unquestionably.

inductif, -ve, *adj.*, inductive.

inductile, *adj.*, inductile.

induction, *n.f.*, (philos.) induction, inference.

induire, (induisant, induit), *v.a.*, to induce, to

lead, to infer. *— en erreur ;* to lead into error. *S'—*; to be inferred.

indulgence, *n.f.*, lenity, leniency, indulgence. *User d'—* (*envers*) ; to show indulgence to. *Avoir de l'—* (*pour*) ; to be indulgent to; to make allowance for.

indulgent, -e, *adj.*, lenient, indulgent, considerate.

indult (in-dult), *n.m.*, indult.

indultaire, *n.m.*, (canon law) incumbent *or* nominee (by virtue of an indult).

indûment, *adv.*, unduly.

induration, *n.f.*, (med.) induration.

induré, *adj.*, (med.) indurated.

s'indurer, *v.r.*, to indurate.

industrialisme, *n.m.*, industrialism.

industrialiste, *n.m.*, industrialist.

industrie, *n.f.*, skill, ingenuity ; business, trade ; manufactures, arts and manufactures ; industry, work. *Vivre d'—* ; to live by one's wits. *Chevalier d'—*; swindler, sharper.

industriel, *n.m.*, manufacturer, commercial man ; tradesman; trader.

industriel, -le, *adj.*, industrial, manufacturing. *Les produits —s ;* the products of arts and manufactures. *Les arts —s ;* the mechanical arts. *Richesses —les ;* commercial wealth.

industrieusement (-eûz-mān), *adv.*, industrially, ingeniously, skillfully.

industrieu-x, -se, *adj.*, ingenious, skillful, industrious.

indut, *n.m.pl.*, assistant priest.

inébranlable, *adj.*, immovable; resolute ; unmoved, unshaken, steady, firm.

inébranlablement, *adv.*, immovably, steadily, resolutely, firmly.

inébriati-f, -ve, *adj.*, inebriating, inebriant.

inédit, -e, *adj.*, inedited, unpublished, new.

ineffabilité, *n.f.*, ineffability, unspeakableness.

ineffable, *adj.*, ineffable, inexpressible, unutterable.

ineffablement, *adv.*, ineffably, unutterably.

ineffaçable, *adj.*, indelible, ineffaceable.

ineffaçablement, *adv.*, indelibly, ineffaceably.

inefficace, *adj.*, inefficacious, ineffective, ineffectual, unavailing.

inefficacement, *adv.*, inefficaciously, inefficiently.

inefficacité, *n.f.*, inefficacy, inefficiency.

inégal, -e, *adj.*, unequal, uneven, rough ; (fig.) disproportioned, ill-matched.

inégalement, *adv.*, unequally, unevenly.

inégalité, *n.f.*, inequality; unevenness, ruggedness, irregularity.

inélégamment, *adv.*, inelegantly.

inélégance, *n.f.*, inelegance.

inélégant, -e, *adj.*, inelegant, unpolished.

inéligibilité, *n.f.*, ineligibility.

inéligible, *adj.*, ineligible.

inéluctable, *adj.*, fatal, inevitable, unavoidable; indisputable, unquestionable, overwhelming.

inéludable, *adj.*, which cannot be set aside *or* evaded.

inénarrable, *adj.*, unspeakable, unutterable, indescribable.

inepte, *adj.*, inept, unfit, foolish, silly.

ineptement, *adv.*, ineptly, foolishly, sillily.

ineptie (-ci), *n.f.*, ineptness, ineptitude, foolishness, absurdity.

inépuisable, *adj.*, inexhaustible.

inépuisablement, *adv.*, inexhaustibly.

inerme, *adj.*, (bot.) inermous, thornless.

inerte, *adj.*, inert, sluggish, inactive, dull.

inertie (-ci), *n.f.*, inertia ; inertness ; indolence, inactivity. *Force d'—* ; vis inertiæ, passive resistance.

inespérable, *adj.*, that cannot be hoped for.

inespéré, -e, *adj.*, unhoped for, unlooked for, unexpected.

inespérément, *adv.,* (l.u.) unexpectedly.

inestimable, *adj.,* inestimable.

inestimé, -e, *adj.,* unesteemed.

inévitable, *adj.,* inevitable, unavoidable.

inévitablement, *adv.,* inevitably, unavoidably.

inexact, -e, *adj.,* inexact, inaccurate.

inexactement, *adv.,* inaccurately, incorrectly.

inexactitude, *n.f.,* inexactness, inaccuracy, incorrectness; unpunctuality.

inexcusable, *adj.,* inexcusable, unjustifiable, unwarrantable.

inexcusablement, *adv.,* inexcusably, unjustifiably.

inexécutable, *adj.,* impracticable.

inexécuté, -e, *adj.,* unexecuted.

inexécution, *n.f.,* inexecution.

inexercé, -e, *adj.,* unexercised, unpractised.

inexigible, *adj.,* not demandable.

inexorable, *adj.,* inexorable, inflexible, unrelenting.

inexorablement, *adv.,* inexorably.

inexpérience, *n.f.,* inexperience.

inexpérimenté, -e, *adj.,* inexperienced, unpracticed; untried.

inexpiable, *adj.,* inexpiable, unatonable.

inexpié, *adj.,* unatoned (for).

inexplicable, *adj.,* inexplicable, unaccountable, singular.

inexplicablement, *adv.,* inexplicably, unaccountably.

inexpliqué, *adj.,* unexplained.

inexploitable, *adj.,* unworkable; uncultivable.

inexploité, *adj.,* (of land) untilled, uncultivated; (mines, &c.) unworked.

inexploré, -e, *adj.,* unexplored.

inexplosible, *adj.,* unexplosive.

inexpressible, *adj.,* unexpressible.

inexpressi-f, -ve, *adj.,* inexpressive, lacking expression.

inexprimable, *adj.,* inexpressible, unutterable, unspeakable.

inexpugnable, *adj.,* inexpugnable, impregnable.

inextensible, *adj.,* inextensible; inextendible.

in extenso (i-nèks-tin-sô), *adv.,* in extenso, fully, at full length.

inextinguible (-gu-i-), *adj.,* inextinguishable, unquenchable. *Soif* —; quenchless thirst.

in extremis, *adv.* *V.* **extremis** (in).

inextricable, *adj.,* inextricable.

inextricablement, *adv.,* inextricably.

*infaillibilité, *n.f.,* infallibility.

*infaillible, *adj.,* infallible.

*infailliblement, *adv.,* infallibly; without fail; unerringly.

infaisable, *adj.,* impracticable; infeasible; not to be done; impossible.

infalsifiable, *adj.,* unfalsifiable.

infamant, -e, *adj.,* infamous, ignominious, degrading. *Peine —e;* degrading punishment.

infâme, *adj.,* infamous, base; squalid, sordid, filthy, nasty. *D'une manière —;* infamously.

infâme, *n.m.f.,* infamous person; wretch, villain.

infamie, *n.f.,* infamy, ignominy; baseness, infamous action.

infant, -e, *n.m., -e,* *n.f.,* Infante; Infanta (Spanish title).

infanterie (in-fan-trî), *n.f.,* infantry, foot.

infanticide, *n.m.f.,* infanticide, child-murderer.

infanticide, *n.m.,* infanticide; child-murder.

infatigabilité, *n.f.,* indefatigableness.

infatigable, *adj.,* indefatigable, untiring, unwearied.

infatigablement, *adv.,* indefatigably, untiringly.

infatuation, *n.f.,* infatuation.

infatuer, *v.a.,* to infatuate, to bewitch.

s'infatuer, *v.r.,* to be infatuated, bewitched.

infécond, -e, *adj.,* infertile, unfruitful, barren, sterile.

infécondité, *n.f.,* infertility, unfruitfulness, barrenness, sterility.

infect (in-fèkt), **-e,** *adj.,* infectious; foul, noisome.

infectant, -e, *adj.,* infecting; tainting; offensive.

infecter, *v.a.,* to infect, to taint, to corrupt, to pollute. *v.n.,* to stink.

infection, *n.f.,* stench; infection; infectious disease. *Foyer d'—;* hotbed of disease; center of infection.

infélicité, *n.f.,* infelicity, unhappiness.

inféodation, *n.f.,* infeudation, infeoffment.

inféoder, *v.a.,* to infeoff; to entail.

s'inféoder, *v.r.,* to be infeoffed *or* entailed.

infère, *adj.,* (bot.) inferior, lower.

inférer, *v.a.,* to infer, to conclude, to deduce.

inférieur, -e, *adj.,* inferior, subordinate, lower, nether; under, petty, below.

inférieur, *n.m.,* inferior, subordinate, subaltern.

inférieurement (-eur-mān), *adv.,* in an inferior manner *or* degree.

infériorité, *n.f.,* inferiority.

informable, *adj.,* unclosable.

infermenté, -e, *adj.,* unfermented.

infernal, -e, *adj.,* infernal, hellish. *Pierre —e;* lunar caustic.

infernalement, *adv.,* infernally.

infertile, *adj.,* infertile, unfruitful; sterile, barren.

infertilisable, *adj.,* infertilizable.

infertilité, *n.f.,* infertility, unfruitfulness, barrenness.

infester, *v.a.,* to infest, to harass, to annoy; to overrun; to haunt.

infidèle, *adj.,* unfaithful, faithless; untrue, unbelieving; false, disloyal.

infidèle, *n.m.f.,* unfaithful person; infidel, unbeliever.

infidèlement, *adv.,* unfaithfully, faithlessly.

infidélité, *n.f.,* infidelity, unbelief, faithlessness, unfaithfulness; dishonesty, deceitfulness; inaccuracy. *Faire des —s à;* to be unfaithful to.

infiltration, *n.f.,* infiltration.

s'infiltrer, *v.r.,* to infiltrate; to percolate; (fig.) to spread, to creep.

infime, *adj.,* (of ranks) lowest.

infimité, *n.f.,* lowest degree, depth; lowest state of abjection; nothingness.

infini, -e, *adj.,* infinite, boundless, endless; numberless; immense.

infini, *n.m.,* (n.p.) infinite. *A l'—;* to infinity, ad infinitum, infinitely; endlessly; indefinitely.

infiniment, *adv.,* infinitely, without end; exceedingly, extremely, very much. *Il a — d'esprit;* he is exceedingly witty. *L'— petit;* the infinitesimal.

infinité, *n.f.,* infinity, infiniteness, infinitude; crowd, host, no end of.

infinitésimal, -e, *adj.,* infinitesimal, infinitely small.

infinitif, *n.m.* and *adj.,* (gram.) infinitive, infinitive mood.

infirmati-f, -ve, *adj.,* annulling, invalidating.

infirmation, *n.f.,* invalidation, annulment.

infirme, *n.m.f.* and *adj.,* invalid; valetudinarian; infirm, weak, feeble, frail, sickly.

infirmer, *v.a.,* to invalidate, to nullify.

infirmerie, *n.f.,* infirmary; sick-ward; sanatorium.

infirmi-er, *n.m.,* **-ère,** *n.f.,* hospital-attendant; hospital-nurse.

infirmité, *n.f.*, infirmity, weakness, failing.

inflammabilité, *n.f.*, inflammability.

inflammable, *adj.*, inflammable.

inflammation, *n.f.*, inflammation.

inflammatoire, *adj.*, inflammatory.

inflation, *n.f.*, (med.) inflation.

infléchi, -e, *adj.*, (opt.) inflected, bent.

infléchir, *v.a.*, (opt.) to inflect, to bend.

s'infléchir, *v.r.*, (opt.) to be inflected.

infléchissable, *adj.*, (of things) inflexible, unbendable.

inflexe, *adj.*, inflected.

inflexibilité, *n.f.*, inflexibility, inexorableness.

inflexible, *adj.*, inflexible; unrelenting, unbending, inexorable.

inflexiblement, *adv.*, inflexibly, inexorably.

inflexion, *n.f.*, inflection; variation.

inflicti-f, -ve, *adj.*, inflictive.

infliction, *n.f.*, infliction.

infliger, *v.a.*, to inflict, to impose.

s'infliger, *v.r.*, to inflict one's self; to impose on one's self. — *des privations;* to impose privations on one's self.

inflorescence, *n.f.*, (bot.) inflorescence.

influence, *n.f.*, influence; sway; power. *Avoir beaucoup d'— sur;* to have great influence over. *Avoir de l'—;* to be influential; to possess influence.

influencer, *v.a.*, to influence, to sway, to bias. *Se laisser —;* to let one's self be biased.

influent, -e, *adj.*, influential.

influenza, *n.f.*, (med.) influenza.

influer, *v.n.*, to influence, to sway; to exert an influence (over); to make an impression.

influx, *n.m.*, (tech.) influx.

influxion, *n.f.*, influxion, influx.

in-folio, *n.m. and adj.*, (—) (print.) folio.

⊙**infondre**, *v.a.*, to infuse.

information, *n.f.*, inquiry; information. *Aller aux —s,* or *prendre des —;* to make inquiries.

informe, *adj.*, unformed; shapeless; misshapen; crude, undigested, imperfect; (jur.) informal. *Etoiles —s;* unformed stars.

informé, *n.m.*, (jur.) investigation, inquiry.

informer, *v.a.*, to inform; to acquaint, to give information, to apprise.

s'informer, *v.r.*, to inquire, to make inquiries; to ask. *Il s'est informé de votre santé;* he inquired after your health.

informer, *v.n.*, (jur.) to inquire into, to investigate. *La justice informe;* proceedings have been taken.

informité, *n.f.*, (philos.) shapelessness.

infortiat, *n.m.*, (n.p.) infortiate (second vol. of Justinian's digest).

infortune, *n.f.*, misfortune, adversity.

infortuné, -e, *n. and adj.*, unfortunate, unhappy, ill-fated, wretched person; unfortunate, unhappy, ill-fated, wretched.

infracteur, *n.m.*, infractor, infringer, breaker, violator.

infraction, *n.f.*, infraction, infringement, breach, violation. *Une — à la loi;* a breach of the law.

infranchissable, *adj.*, insurmountable, insuperable, impassable.

infrangibilité, *n.f.*, infrangibility.

infrangible, *adj.*, infrangible.

infréquenté, -e, *adj.*, unfrequented.

infructueusement, *adv.*, fruitlessly, to no purpose, in vain.

infructueu-x, -se, *adj.*, unfruitful, fruitless, unavailing.

infus, -e, *adj.*, intuitive, inspired; innate, inborn.

infusé, *n.m.*, (med.) infusion.

infuser, *v.a.*, to infuse, to steep. — *à froid;* to make a cold infusion.

s'infuser, *v.r.*, to be infused, to draw, to stand (of tea).

infusibilité, *n.f.*, infusibility.

infusible, *adj.*, unfusible.

infusion, *n.f.*, infusion; intuition.

infusoires, *n.m.pl. and adj.*, (zool.) infusoria; infusorial, infusory.

*****ingagnable**, *adj.*, that cannot be won, that cannot be gained.

ingambe, *adj.*, nimble, brisk, active.

s'ingénier, *v.r.*, to strive, to tax one's ingenuity; to work one's hardest; to work for all one is worth. *Je m'ingénie à le faire;* I work my hardest to accomplish it.

ingénieur, *n.m.*, engineer. — *civil;* civil engineer. — *constructeur de vaisseaux;* master-shipwright, naval architect. *Art de l'—;* engineering. — *des mines;* mining engineer. — *des ponts et chaussées;* civil engineer (under government) for bridges and roads in France. — *géographe,* (—*s*—*s*) geographer. — *-opticien,* (—*s*—*s*) optician.

ingénieusement, *adv.*, ingeniously.

ingénieu-x, -se, *adj.*, ingenious, intelligent, clever, witty. — *à mentir;* practised in the art of falsehood.

ingéniosité, *n.f.*, ingenuity, ingeniousness.

ingénu, -e, *adj.*, ingenuous, frank, open, candid.

ingénu, *n.m.*, -e, *n.f.*, ingenuous person, artless person, simple-minded youth *or* maiden. *Jouer les —s;* (theat.) to play juvenile parts. *Faire l'—;* to affect simplicity.

ingénuité, *n.f.*, ingenuousness, frankness, openness, candidness, simplicity.

ingénument, *adv.*, ingenuously, frankly, openly, candidly.

ingerçable, *adj.*, not liable to crack.

ingérence, *n.f.*, interference, meddling, dabbling.

ingérer, *v.a.*, (phys.) to introduce, to ingest.

s'ingérer, *v.r.*, to meddle with, to interfere, to obtrude. *S'— dans les affaires d'autrui;* to meddle with other people's business.

ingestion (-jès-ti-on), *n.f.*, (phys.) introduction, ingestion.

in globo, *adv.*, in a lump, altogether.

inglorieusement, *adv.*, ingloriously.

inglorieu-x, -se, *adj.*, inglorious.

ingouvernable, *adj.*, ungovernable.

ingrat, -e, *n.m.f. and adj.*, unthankful, ungrateful, ingrate person; ungrateful, ingrate, unthankful, thankless, unprofitable, unfruitful; sterile; unpleasant.

ingratitude, *n.f.*, ingratitude, thanklessness, piece of ingratitude.

ingrédient (-di-ān), *n.m.*, ingredient.

inguéable, *adj.*, unfordable.

inguérissable, *adj.*, incurable.

inguinal, -e (-gu-i-), *adj.*, inguinal.

ingurgitation, *n.f.*, (med.) ingurgitation.

inhabile, *adj.*, unqualified; incapable, unskillful, unfit.

inhabilement, *adv.*, unskillfully.

inhabileté, *n.f.*, inability, unskillfulness, incompetency, incapacity.

inhabilité, *n.f.*, (jur.) incompetency; disability.

inhabitable, *adj.*, uninhabitable, (of homes) untenanted, tenantless.

inhabité, -e, *adj.*, uninhabited.

inhabitude, *n.f.*, want of habit.

inhalation, *n.f.*, inhalation.

inhaler, *v.a.*, to inhale.

inharmonie, *n.f.*, want of harmony.

inharmonieu-x, -se, *adj.*, inharmonious, unmusical.

inhérence, *n.f.*, inherence.

inhérent, -e, *adj.*, inherent.

⊙**inhiber**, *v.a.*, to inhibit, to forbid.

inhibition, *n.f.,* (jur.) inhibition, prohibition.

inhibitoire, *adj.,* inhibitory.

inhonoré, -e, *adj.,* (l.u.) unhonored.

inhospitali-er, -ère, *adj.,* inhospitable; unfriendly, forbidding.

inhospitalièrement, *adv.,* inhospitably.

inhospitalité, *n.f.,* inhospitality.

inhumain, -e, *adj.,* inhuman, cruel.

inhumainement (i-nu-mè-n-män), *adv.,* inhumanly.

inhumanité, *n.f.,* inhumanity, cruelty.

inhumation, *n.f.,* inhumation, interment.

inhumer, *v.a.,* to inhume, to bury, to inter.

inimaginable, *adj.,* unimaginable, incomprehensible, inconceivable.

inimitable, *adj.,* inimitable.

inimitablement, *adj.* inimitably.

inimitié, *n.f.,* enmity, hatred, antipathy, aversion. *Avoir de l'— pour;* to bear enmity **to,** to have an aversion to.

inimprimable, *adj.,* unprintable.

ininflammabilité, *n.f.,* uninflammability.

ininflammable, *adv.,* uninflammable.

inintelligence, *n.f.,* lack of intelligence.

inintelligent, *adj.,* unintelligent.

inintelligible, *adj.,* unintelligible.

inintelligiblement, *adv.,* unintelligibly.

ininterrompu, *adj.,* uninterrupted.

inique, *adj.,* iniquitous; unrighteous.

iniquement (i-nik-män), *adv.,* iniquitously.

iniquité, *n.f.,* iniquity; unrighteousness, sin.

initial, -e, *adj.,* initial.

initiale, *n.f.,* initial.

initiat-eur, *n.m.,* **-rice,** *n.f.,* one who initiates, initiator.

initiati-f, -ve, *adj.,* initiatory, initiative.

initiation, *n.f.,* initiation.

initiative, *n.f.,* initiative. *Prendre l'—;* to take the initiative.

initié, -e, *adj.,* initiated.

initié, *n.m.,* person initiated.

initier, *v.a.,* to initiate, to admit.

injecté, -e, *adj.,* injected; bloodshot, flushed. *Yeux —s de sang;* bloodshot eyes.

injecter, *v.a.,* to inject. *S'—;* to become injected, bloodshot.

injecteur, *n.m.,* injector.

injection, *n.f.,* injection, redness.

injonction, *n.f.,* injunction, order. *Faire — à;* to enjoin.

injouable, *adj.,* unplayable, unactable.

injudicieusement, *adv.,* injudiciously.

injudicieu-x, -se, *adj.,* injudicious.

injure, *n.f.,* insult, injury, wrong. *pl.,* abuse, abusive language, taunt; outrage, slander. *Dire des —s à quelqu'un;* to call any one names, to abuse any one. *Faire — à quelqu'un;* to wrong any one. *Avoir toujours l'— à la bouche;* to be abusive, to be foul-mouthed. *Ils se sont dit mille —s;* they abused one another like pickpockets.

injurier, *v.a.,* to abuse, to call names, to rail at, to insult.

injurieusement (-eûz-män), *adv.,* injuriously, wrongfully, abusively, reproachfully, revilingly.

injurieu-x, -se, *adj.,* injurious, wrongful; reproachful, abusive, offensive, reviling.

injuste, *adj.,* unjust, unfair, wrong, wrongful.

injuste, *n.m.,* what is unjust, wrong; unjust person, wrong-doer.

injustement, *adv.,* unjustly, wrongly, wrongfully, unfairly.

injustice, *n.f.,* injustice; wrong, act of injustice.

injustifiable, *adj.,* unjustifiable.

in naturalibus. *V.* **naturalibus** (in).

innavigable, *adj.,* unnavigable; unseaworthy.

inné, -e, *adj.,* innate, inborn, inbred.

innégociable. *adj.,* (com.) not negotiable.

innocemment (ino-sa-män), *adv.,* innocently, harmlessly; simply, sillily, foolishly.

innocence, *n.f.,* innocence, guiltlessness; harmlessness, inoffensiveness; simplicity, silliness.

innocent, -e, *adj.,* innocent, guiltless, guileless; harmless, inoffensive; simple, silly. *Il a été reconnu —;* he was found not guilty. *Se déclarer —;* to plead not guilty. *Tenir pour —;* to hold guiltless.

innocent, *n.m.,* **-e,** *n.f.,* innocent person; simpleton, idiot. *Tourte d'—s;* pigeon-pie made with young pigeons. *Faire l'—;* to sham innocence.

innocenter, *v.a.,* to acquit.

innocuité, *n.f.,* innocuousness, harmlessness.

innombrable, *adj.,* innumerable, numberless, endless.

innombrablement, *adv.,* innumerably, endlessly.

innominé, *adj.,* (anat.) nameless, unnamed.

innommé, *adj.,* (jur.) unnamed, nameless.

innovat-eur, *n.m.,* **-rice,** *n.f.,* innovator.

innovation, *n.f.,* innovation.

innover, *v.n.,* to innovate, to make innovations.

inobservable, *adj.,* inobservable.

inobservance, *n.f.,* non-observance, inobservance.

inobservation, *n.f.,* non-observance.

inobservé, -e, *adj.,* unobserved, unnoticed, overlooked.

inoccupation, *n.f.,* inoccupation.

inoccupé, -e, *adj.,* unoccupied, unemployed.

in-octavo, *n.m.,* and *adj.,* (—) (print.) octavo, in octavo, 8vo.

inoculateur, *n.m.,* inoculator. *adj.,* inoculating.

inoculation, *n.f.,* inoculation.

inoculer, *v.a.,* (med.) to inoculate.

s'inoculer, *v.r.,* (med.) to inoculate one's self; to be inoculated.

☉**inoculiste,** *n.m.,* partisan of inoculation.

inodore, *adj.,* inodorous, scentless, free from smell. *Cabinet —;* water-closet.

inoffensi-f, -ve, *adj.,* inoffensive.

inoffensivement, *adv.,* inoffensively.

inofficiel, -le, *adj.,* unofficial.

inofficiellement, *adv.,* unofficially.

inofficieu-x, -se, *adj.,* (jur.) inofficious.

inofficiosité, *n.f.,* (jur.) inofficiousness.

inondation, *n.f.,* inundation, overflow, flood, deluge.

inonder, *v.a.,* to inundate, to overflow, to deluge; to overrun, to overspread, to pour into, to overwhelm.

inopérant, -e, *adj.,* inoperative.

inopiné, -e, *adj.,* unforeseen, unexpected, unlooked for, sudden.

inopinément, *adv.,* unawares, unexpectedly, suddenly.

inopportun, -e, *adj.,* inopportune, unseasonable, untimely, ill-timed.

inopportunément, *adv.,* inopportunely.

inopportunité, *n.f.,* inopportuneness, unseasonableness.

inorganique, *adj.,* inorganical.

inosculation, *n.f.,* (anat.) inosculation, anastomosis.

inostensible, *adj.,* inostensible.

inostensiblement, *adv.,* inostensibly.

inoubliable, *adj.,* not to be forgotten.

inoublié, -e, *adj.,* unforgotten, well-remembered.

inouï, -e, *adj.,* unheard of, unprecedented, extraordinary, strange, wonderful.

inoxydable, *adj.,* which cannot be oxygenized.

in pace, *n.m.,* (—) in peace.

in-partibus. *V.* **partibus** (in).

in petto (-pèt-to), *adv.,* in petto, in secret.

in-plano, *n.m.* and *adj.,* (—) (print.) broadside.

in-promptu, *n.m.* *V.* **impromptu.**

inqualifiable, *adj.*, that cannot be qualified; for which no name is too bad.

inquart, *n.m.*, (chem.) quartation.

in-quarto (-kooar-), *n.m.* and *adj.*, (—) (print.) quarto, in quarto, 4to.

inqui-et, -ète, *adj.*, unquiet, anxious, uneasy; restless, fidgety.

inquiétant, -e, *adj.*, alarming, disquieting.

inquiéter, *v.a.*, to make uneasy, to disquiet; to disturb, to trouble, to alarm.

s'inquiéter, *v.r.*, to be anxious, to be uneasy, to make one's self uneasy, to alarm one's self.

inquiétude, *n.f.*, anxiety, uneasiness, disquietude, alarm, fear; solicitude, restlessness; slight pains, uneasy feeling. *Donner de l'— à ;* to make uneasy. *Il est sans — sur l'avenir ;* he is without anxiety about the future. *Soyez sans — là-dessus ;* make yourself easy on that score. *Avoir des —s ;* to be uneasy.

inquisiteur, *n.m.*, inquisitor.

inquisition, *n.f.*, inquisition.

inquisitorial, -e, *adj.*, inquisitorial.

insaisissable, *adj.*, unseizable; imperceptible; (jur.) not distrainable.

insalubre, *adj.*, insalubrious, unhealthy, unwholesome.

insalubrement, *adv.*, insalubriously.

insalubrité, *n.f.*, insalubrity, unhealthiness, unwholesomeness.

insanité, *n.f.*, insanity.

insatiabilité, *n.f.*, insatiability.

insatiable, *adj.*, insatiable.

insatiablement, *adv.*, insatiably.

insciemment, *adv.*, unwittingly, unknowingly.

inscription, *n.f.*, inscription; registry, entry; term (of schools); (fin.) stock-receipt; inscribing. *— hypothécaire ;* registry of mortgage. *— de faux ;* allegation of forgery. *Avoir toutes ses —s ;* (of students) to have kept all one's terms. *Prendre ses —s ;* to enter one's name for the (university) terms.

inscrire, *v.a.*, to inscribe, to enter, to set down; to register; to impanel (jury).

s'inscrire, *v.r.*, to inscribe one's self; to enter one's name. *S'— en faux contre ;* to deny the truth of, to protest against.

inscrutabilité, *n.f.*, inscrutability; unsearchableness.

inscrutable, *adj.*, inscrutable, unfathomable.

inscrutablement, *adv.*, inscrutably.

insécable, *adj.*, insecable, indivisible.

insecte, *n.m.*, insect.

insecticide, *adj.*, insect-destroying.

insectivore, *adj.*, insectivorous.

insécurité, *n.f.*, insecurity.

in-seize, *n.m.* and *adj.*, (—) (print.) sixteen, in sixteen, 16mo.

insensé, -e, *n.m.f.* and *adj.*, insane, madman, madwoman; maniac; unwise person; fool; insane, mad; foolish, senseless.

insensibilité, *n.f.*, insensibility, unconsciousness, unfeelingness.

insensible, *adj.*, insensible, unconscious, unfeeling; hard-hearted; imperceptible.

insensiblement, *adv.*, insensibly, imperceptibly, gradually, by degrees.

inséparabilité, *n.f.*, inseparableness.

inséparable, *adj.*, inseparable.

inséparablement, *adv.*, inseparably.

inséparables, *n.m.f.pl.*, great chums; (orni.) love-birds.

insérer, *v.a.*, to insert, to put in, to wedge in.

insermenté, *adj.*, unsworn.

insertion, *n.f.*, insertion.

insidieusement (-eûz-măn), *adv.*, insidiously.

insidieu-x, -se, *adj.*, insidious.

*****insigne**, *adj.*, signal, high, notorious, arrant, downright. *L'— honneur ;* the high honor.

*****insigne**, *n.m.*, badge, mark. *pl.*, insignia.

*****insignifiance**, *n.f.*, insignificance.

*****insignifiant, -e**, *adj.*, insignificant.

insincère, *adj.*, insincere.

insinuant, -e, *adj.*, insinuating.

insinuatif, -ve, *adj.*, (l.u.) insinuating.

insinuation, *n.f.*, insinuation; hint, innuendo, suggestion, intimation; ⊙ (jur.) registration.

insinuer, *v.a.*, to insinuate; to hint, to suggest; to instill, to intimate.

s'insinuer, *v.r.*, to insinuate, to introduce one's self (in), to creep (into), to worm one's self (into), to steal (into).

insipide, *adj.*, insipid, tasteless, unsavory, dull, flat.

insipidement (-pid-măn), *adv.*, insipidly; dully, heavily.

insipidité, *n.f.*, insipidity, insipidness, unsavoriness, tastelessness; dullness.

insistance, *n.f.*, insistence, insisting, entreaty; urgent request.

insister, *v.n.*, to insist; to persist, to urge, to press, to lay stress (upon). *Il insiste à demander ;* he persists in demanding.

insociabilité, *n.f.*, unsociableness.

insociable, *adj.*, unsociable.

insociablement, *adv.*, unsociably.

insocial, -e, *adj.*, unsocial.

insolation, *n.f.*, insolation; sun-stroke.

insolemment (-la-măn), *adv.*, insolently, impudently, saucily.

insolence, *n.f.*, insolence, impertinence, sauciness, incivility, rudeness.

insolent, -e, *adj.* and *n.*, insolent, rude, pert, saucy, impudent; insolent person.

insolidité, *n.f.*, insolidity.

insolite, *adj.*, unusual, unwonted.

insolitement, *adv.*, unusually.

insolubilité, *n.f.*, insolubility.

insoluble, *adj.*, insoluble.

insolvabilité, *n.f.*, insolvency.

insolvable, *adj.*, insolvent.

insomnie (in-som-nî), *n.f.*, sleeplessness, wakefulness; insomnia. *Heures d'— ;* sleepless nights.

insondable, *adj.*, unfathomable; fathomless.

insouciance, *n.f.*, carelessness, thoughtlessness, heedlessness, listlessness.

insouciant, -e, *adj.*, careless, thoughtless, heedless, listless, indifferent.

insoucieu-x, -se, *adj.*, careless, free from care.

insoumis, *n.m.*, (milit. jur.) defaulting recruit, defaulter.

insoumis, -e, *adj.*, unsubdued, refractory; unruly.

insoumission, *n.f.*, insubordination.

insoutenable, *adj.*, indefensible, insupportable, unbearable, untenable.

inspecter, *v.a.*, to inspect, to survey; to superintend, to supervise.

inspect-eur, *n.m.*, **-rice**, *n.f.*, inspector, superintendent, surveyor.

inspection, *n.f.*, inspection, survey; superintendence; view, sight. *Passer à l'— ;* (milit.) to undergo inspection. *A la première — ;* at first sight. *Faire l'— de ;* to examine, to survey, to inspect.

inspirat-eur, -rice, *adj.* and *n.*, inspiring, suggesting; (anat.) inspiratory; inspirer.

inspirateur, *n.m.*, (anat.) inspiratory muscle.

inspiration, *n.f.*, inspiration, suggestion; inhaling.

inspiré, *n.m.*, **-e**, *n.f.*, person inspired.

inspirer, *v.a.*, to inspire; to breathe; to inhale; (fig.) to suggest, to prompt; to instill; to advise.

instabilité, *n.f.*, instability, fickleness.

instable, *adj.*, unstable, fickle.

installation, *n.f.*, installation; installment; induction (to a living).

installer, *v.a.*, to install, to induct.

s'installer, *v.r.*, to install one's self; to place one's self (in), to settle.

instamment (ins-ta-mān), *adv.*, earnestly, urgently.

instance, *n.f.*, entreaty, solicitation, urgency, earnestness; (jur.) instance. *pl.*, urgency. *Faire de grandes, de vives, —s;* to entreat earnestly. *Avec —;* earnestly. *En —;* (jur.) on the cause-list. *Tribunal de première —;* inferior court.

instant, *n.m.*, instant, moment, trice. *A l'—;* instantly, immediately. *Dans un —;* in an instant. *Je reviens à l'—;* I shall go back immediately.

instant, -e, *adj.*, earnest, pressing, urgent.

instantané, -e, *adj.*, instantaneous.

instantanéité, *n.f.*, instantaneousness.

instantanément, *adv.*, instantaneously.

instar, *adv.*, like. *A l'— de;* like; in imitation of.

instigat-eur, *n.m.*, **-rice**, *n.f.*, instigator, inciter. *adj.*, instigating, inciting.

instigation, *n.f.*, instigation.

instillation (-til-la-), *n.f.*, instillation.

instiller (ins-til-lé), *v.a.*, to instill.

instinct (-tin), *n.m.*, instinct. *D'— or par —;* instinctively.

instincti-f, -ve, *adj.*, instinctive.

instinctivement, *adv.*, instinctively.

institué, *n.m.*, (jur.) tenant in tail.

instituer, *v.a.*, to institute, to establish, to settle, to found, to appoint, to originate. *S'—;* to institute one's self; to be appointed.

institut, *n.m.*, institution, order, institute.

institutes, *n.f.pl.*, (jur.) institutes.

institut-eur, *n.m.*, **-rice**, *n.f.*, institutor, tutor; governess; schoolmaster; schoolmistress.

institution, *n.f.*, institution, establishment; school, seminary; (jur.) settlement. *— de demoiselles;* seminary for young ladies. *Chef d'—;* head of an academy or school. *Maîtresse d'—;* lady-principal.

instructeur, *n.m.* and *adj.*, (milit.) instructor; (l.u.) instructor. *Sergent —;* drill-sergeant. *Juge —;* examining magistrate.

instructi-f, -ve, *adj.*, instructive.

instruction, *n.f.*, instruction; education; information, attainments; lesson; direction; (jur.) inquiry, examination. *Avoir de l'—;* to be well educated. *—s détaillées;* particular instructions. *Sans —;* untaught, uneducated. *Donner des —s;* to give directions. *Juge d'—;* examining magistrate.

instruire (instruisant, instruit), *v.a.*, to instruct, to teach, to inform, to apprise, to acquaint; to train; (jur.) to investigate, to examine, to proceed.

s'instruire, *v.r.*, to instruct, to inform, to improve, one's self; (jur.) to form the subject of an inquiry, to be under examination, to be heard (of a case).

instruisable, *adj.*, (l.u.) teachable.

instruit, -e, *part.*, instructed; informed; learned, well informed, aware.

instrument, *n.m.*, instrument, document; implement, tool; underling. *— tranchant;* edge-tool. *—s aratoires;* agricultural implements. *Servir d'—;* to be instrumental (in).

instrumentaire, *adj.*, (jur.) required by law. *Témoin —;* witness (required by law) to a deed.

instrumental, -e, *adj.*, instrumental.

instrumentation, *n.f.*, (mus.) instrumentation.

instrumenter, *v.n.*, (jur.) to act; to draw up deeds, indentures, etc.; to serve writs; to compose instrumental music.

instrumentiste, *n.m.*, instrumentalist.

à l'insu, *prep.*, unknown to. *A mon —, à votre —;* unknown to me, unknown to you;

unknowingly, unwittingly, unconsciously. *A l'— de son père;* unknown to his father.

insubmersible, *adj.*, unsinkable.

insubordination, *n.f.*, insubordination.

insubordonné, -e, *adj.*, insubordinate.

insuccès, *n.m.*, failure, want of success.

insuffisamment, *adv.*, insufficiently.

insuffisance, *n.f.*, insufficiency, incapacity.

insuffisant, -e, *adj.*, insufficient, inadequate.

insufflation, *n.f.*, insufflation.

insuffler, *v.a.*, (med.) to breathe in.

insulaire, *n.m.f.* and *adj.*, islander; insular; native (of an island).

insularité, *n.f.*, insularity.

insultant, -e, *adj.*, insulting.

insulte, *n.f.*, insult, affront, abuse. *Avec —;* insultingly. *Faire une — à quelqu'un;* to offer an insult to any one. *Supporter une —;* to brook an insult.

insulter, *v.a.n.*, to insult, to affront; to abuse.

insupportable, *adj.*, insupportable, insufferable, intolerable.

insupportablement, *adv.*, insupportably, insufferably, intolerably.

insurgé, -e, *part.*, insurgent; in a state of insurrection.

insurgé, *n.m.*, insurgent, rebel.

insurgence, *n.f.*, insurrection.

s'insurger, *v.r.*, to revolt, to rebel, to rise in insurrection; (fig.) to protest against.

insurmontable, *adj.*, insurmountable, insuperable, invincible.

insurmontablement, *adv.*, insurmountably, insuperably.

insurrection, *n.f.*, insurrection, rising.

insurrectionnel, -le, *adj.*, insurrectionary.

intact (in-takt), **-e**, *adj.*, intact, entire, whole, untouched; unblemished, untainted, irreproachable.

intactile, *adj.*, intangible, intactile.

*intaille, *n.f.*, (engr.) intaglio.

intangibilité, *n.f.*, intangibility.

intangible, *adj.*, intangible, untouchable.

intarissable, *adj.*, inexhaustible, endless; never-failing.

intégral, -e, *adj.*, integral, whole, entire.

intégrale, *n.f.*, (math.) integral, fluent.

intégralement (-gral-mān), *adv.*, integrally, entirely, wholly; in full.

intégralité, *n.f.*, integrality, completeness.

intégrant, -e, *adj.*, integral, integrant.

intégration, *n.f.*, (math.) integration.

intègre, *adj.*, honest, upright, just.

intégrement, *adv.*, honestly, uprightly.

intégrer, *v.a.*, (math.) to integrate.

intégrité, *n.f.*, integrity, uprightness, probity; soundness; entireness.

intellect (in-tèl-lèkt), *n.m.*, intellect, understanding.

intellecti-f, -ve, *adj.*, intellective.

intellectuel, -le, *adj.*, intellectual.

intellectuellement, *adv.*, intellectually.

intelligence (-tèl-li-), *n.f.*, intellect; intelligence; understanding; knowledge; good understanding, harmony; acquaintance, intercourse; correspondence; means of information; spirit, spiritual being; skill, ability. *En bonne — avec;* on good terms with. *Etre d'—;* to be in league with; to go hand in hand. *— étroite;* narrow intellect.

intelligent, -e (-tèl-li-), *adj.*, intelligent, sharp, shrewd, clever, quick.

intelligibilité (-tèl-li-), *n.f.*, intelligibility, intelligibleness.

intelligible (-tèl-li-), *adj.*, intelligible; audible; distinct, clear.

intelligiblement (-tèl-li-), *adv.*, intelligibly, audibly, clearly.

intempéramment (-ra-mān), *adv.*, intemperately, immoderately.

intempérance, n.f., intemperance, insobriety, excess.

intempérant, -e, adj., intemperate.

intempéré, -e, adj., intemperate.

intempérie, n.f., inclemency, intemperance.

intempesti-f, -ve, adj., unseasonable, untimely.

intempestivement, adv., unseasonably.

intenable, adj., untenable.

intendance, n.f., administration, direction, management, superintendence; stewardship; the office, the house, of an intendant; (milit.) commissariat.

intendant, n.m., intendant, steward; commissioner, commissary, comptroller; (milit.) commissary. — de la liste civile; comptroller of the civil list.

intendante, n.f., directress.

intense, adj., intense, violent, severe.

intensité, n.f., intensity, intenseness; violence, severity.

intensivement, adv., intensely.

intenter, v.a., to enter (upon); to bring (against); to commence. — une action à or contre quelqu'un; to bring an action against any one.

intention, n.f., intention; intent, purpose, design; meaning; view. — présumée criminelle; implied malice. A l' — de; on account of. Dans l' — de; with a view to. Sans —; unintentionally. Avec —; on purpose. L' — est réputée pour le fait; the will is as good as the deed. Avoir l' — de; to intend to. A mon —, à votre —, etc.; for my sake, for your sake, etc.; my or your benefit.

intentionné, -e, adj., intentioned, disposed, meaning. Une personne bien —e; a well-intentioned, disposed, or meaning, person.

intentionnel, -le, adj., intentional.

intercadence, n.f., (med.) irregular beating of the pulse.

intercadent, adj., irregular (of the pulse).

intercalaire, adj., intercalary. Jour —; intercalary day. Vers —s; burden (of a song).

intercalation, n.f., intercalation.

intercaler, v.a., to intercalate.

intercéder, v.n., to intercede, to plead with or for.

intercepter, v.a., to intercept.

interception, n.f., (phys.) interception.

intercesseur, n.m., intercessor, interceder.

intercession, n.f., intercession.

intercostal, -e, adj., (anat.) intercostal.

intercurrent, -e, adj., (med.) intercurrent.

intercutané, -e, adj., intercutaneous.

interdiction, n.f., interdiction, inhibition, prohibition; suspension; laying under an interdict; deprivation (of civil rights). Frapper d' —; to lay under an interdict.

interdire, v.a., to interdict, to prohibit, to forbid; to suspend; to amaze, to confound, to dumfound, to stupefy; to nonplus; (jur.) to declare a man non compos mentis. — l'entrée à quelqu'un; to shut any one out or refuse any one admission.

interdit, -e, part., abashed, confused, dumfounded, taken aback.

interdit, n.m., interdict, person interdicted. Mettre en —; to taboo.

intéressant, -e, adj., interesting.

intéressé, -e, part., interested, having an interest (in); selfish.

intéressé, n.m., interested party.

intéresser, v.a., to interest; to concern; to affect; to give a share to; to stake money on; (surg.) to injure. Cela ne vous intéresse en rien; that does not concern or affect you in the least.

s'intéresser, v.r., to take an interest in, to be interested, to be concerned for; to have an interest, to be concerned (in).

intérêt, n.m., interest, concern, share. pl., interest; selfishness. Avoir un — à; to have an interest, a share, in. Il est de mon — de le faire; it is to my interest to do it. Il y va de mon —; my interest is at stake. Favoriser les —s de quelqu'un; to promote any one's interest. C'est l' — qui nous guide; it is interest that guides us. Cet argent porte —; this money bears interest. — composé; compound interest. Prendre — à or se prendre d' — pour; to take interest in.

interférence, n.f., (opt.) interference.

interférer, v.n., (opt.) to interfere.

interfoliacé, -e, adj., interfoliaceous, interleaved.

interfolier, v.a., to interleave.

intérieur, -e, adj., interior, internal, inner, inward; intrinsic; inland.

intérieur, n.m., interior, inside, home, private life. Ministre de l' —; Home Secretary. Dans son —; in private life. Tableau de l' —; scene of home-life. Ville de l' —; inland town. Nous nous avançâmes dans l' —; we went inland.

intérieurement, adv., inwardly, internally.

intérim (-rim), n.m., interim. Dans l' —; in the interim; in the interval, meanwhile.

intérimaire, adj., provisional, temporary.

interjection, n.f., (gram.) interjection; (jur.) lodging (of an appeal).

interjeter, v.a., (jur.) to lodge (an appeal).

*interligne, n.f., (print.) lead.

*interligne, n.m., (mus.) space; space between two written or printed lines.

*interligner, v.a., to space out, to interline; (print.) to lead.

interlinéaire, adj., interlineary.

interlinéation, n.f., interlineation.

interlinéer, v.a., to interline.

interlocut-eur, n.m., **-rice**, n.f., interlocutor, speaker.

interlocution, n.f., interlocution, dialogue.

interlocutoire, n.m. and adj., (jur.) interlocutory decree; interlocutory. Arrêt —; interlocutory judgment or decree.

interlope, adj., interloping, intrusive, contraband; fraudulent, clandestine.

interlope, n.m., interloper, interloping trade, smuggling.

interloquer, v.a., to nonplus; to disconcert; to silence; (fam.) to shut up.

intermaxillaire, adj., (anat.) intermaxillary.

intermède, n.m., interlude; (chem.) intermediate.

intermédiaire, adj., intermediate, intervening; lying between.

intermédiaire, n.m., medium, intermediate agent, middleman. Par l' — de; through the medium of.

intermédiat, -e, adj., intermediate.

interminable, adj., interminable, endless.

intermission, n.f., intermission.

intermittence, n.f., intermission; cessation; intermittent character of.

intermittent, -e, adj., intermittent.

intermonde, n.m., intermundane space.

intermusculaire, adj., (anat.) intermuscular.

internat, n.m., boarding-school; house-surgeoncy (of hospitals).

international, -e, adj., international.

interne, n.m.f., (of schools) boarder; (of hospitals) house-surgeon; clinical clerk.

interne, adj., internal, inward, interior; indoor. Élève —; boarder (in school).

interner, v.a., to shut up, to send into, to confine (in the interior of a country); to intern; to banish, to relegate.

internissable, adj., that cannot be tarnished or sullied.

internonce, n.m., internuncio.

interocéanique, adj., interoceanic.

interoculaire, adj., interocular.

interosseu-x, -se, adj., (anat.) interosseous.

interpellat-eur, *n.m.*, **-rice** (-pèl-la-), *n.f.*, interpellator; questioner.

interpellation (-pèl-la-), *n.f.*, interpellation, summons ; question (in parliament).

interpeller (-pèl-lé), *v.a.*, to summon, to call upon, to require, to challenge, to question, to put a question to.

interpolateur, *n.m.*, interpolator.

interpolation, *n.f.*, interpolation.

interpoler, *v.a.*, to interpolate, to foist, to insert.

interposé, **-e**, *part.*, interposed.

interposer, *v.a.*, to interpose.

*s'*interposer**, *v.r.*, to interpose, to come between.

interposition, *n.f.*, interposition ; intervention.

interprétati-f, **-ve**, *adj.*, interpretative.

interprétation, *n.f.*, interpretation, construction. — *erronée ;* misconstruction. *Donner une mauvaise — à ;* to misconstrue.

interprète, *n.m.*, interpreter, expounder ; expositor, translator.

interpréter, *v.a.*, to interpret, to expound ; to explain, to render, to construe. *S'— ;* to be interpreted.

*****interrègne** (-tèr-rè-), *n.m.*, interregnum.

interrogant, *adj.*, (l.u.) (gram.) interrogative, of interrogation ; questioning, inquisitive. *Point —;* note of interrogation.

interrogat-eur, *n.m.*, **-rice**, *n.f.*, interrogator, questioner, examiner.

interrogati-f, **-ve**, *adj.*, interrogative.

interrogation, *n.f.*, interrogation, question. *Point d'— ;* note of interrogation.

interrogatoire, *n.m.*, examination. *Subir un —;* to undergo an examination. *— contradictoire ;* cross-examination.

interroger, *v.a.*, to interrogate, to question ; to consult, to examine. *— l'histoire ;* to consult history. *— contradictoirement ;* to cross-examine.

*s'*interroger**, *v.r.*, to examine one's self *or* one's conscience ; to question each other.

interroi (-tèr-roa), *n.m.*, (antiq.) regent.

interrompre, *v.a.*, to interrupt, to leave off, to break off ; to stop, to suspend.

*s'*interrompre**, *v.r..* to interrupt one's self, to leave off, to break off.

interrupt-eur, **-rice**, *n.* and *adj.*, interrupter ; interrupting.

interruption, *n.f.*, interruption, discontinuance ; suspension, intermission.

intersection, *n.f.*, intersection.

interstellaire (-stèl-lěr), *adj.*, (astron.) interstellar.

interstice, *n.m.*, interstice, opening, chink.

intertropical, *adj.*, intertropical.

intervalle, *n.m.*, interval, interstice, distance; space, room. *Par —s ;* at intervals.

intervenant, **-e**, *n.* and *adj.*, (jur.) intervening party ; intervening.

intervenir, *v.n.*, to intervene, to interfere ; to interpose ; to happen, to occur. *Faire — ;* to bring, to call, in.

intervention, *n.f.*, intervention, interference.

interversion, *n.f.*, inversion.

intervertir, *v.a.*, to invert, to change, to reverse.

intestable, *adj.*, (jur.) intestable.

intestat, *n.m.* and *adj.*, *invariable*, (jur.) intestate. *Héritier ab — ;* heir of one that dies intestate.

intestin, *n.m.*, intestine, bowel, gut.

intestin, **-e**, *adj.*, intestine, internal, domestic, civil.

intestinal, **-e**, *adj.*, (anat.) intestinal.

intimation, *n.f.*, intimation, notification ; legal notice.

intime, *n.m.f.* and *adj.*, intimate, familiar ; inmost, inward ; deep, secret ; close.

intimé, *n.m.*, **-e**, *n.f.*, (jur.) appellee.

intimement (-tim-mān), *adv.*, intimately ; familiarly, deeply, closely.

intimer, *v.a.*, to notify, to give legal notice of, to give notice of appeal ; to summon, to convoke, to enjoin. *On lui intima l'ordre de partir ;* they notified to him the order to depart.

intimidat-eur, **-rice**, *n.* and *adj.*, intimidator ; intimidating.

intimidation, *n.f.*, intimidation.

intimider, *v.a.*, to intimidate, to threaten ; to frighten, to confuse.

*s'*intimider**, *v.r.*, to be intimidated, to be nervous, to become confused.

intimité, *n.f.*, intimacy, close connection, inmost recesses.

intitulé, **-e**, *part.*, entitled.

intitulé, *n.m.*, title (of deeds, books).

intituler, *v.a.*, to entitle, to call, to name.

*s'*intituler**, *v.r.*, to entitle one's self, to call one's self, to style one's self.

intolérable, *adj.*, intolerable, insufferable.

intolérablement, *adv.*, intolerably, insufferably.

intolérance, *n.f.*, intolerance.

intolérant, **-e**, *adj.*, intolerant.

intolérantisme, *n.m.*, system of intolerance.

intonation, *n.f.*, intonation.

intorsion, *n.f.*, intorsion.

intoxicant, **-e**, *adj.*, poisonous.

intoxication, *n.f.*, (med.) poisoning.

intrados, *n.m.*, *n.f.*, (arch.) intrados (interior part of a vault).

intraduisible, *adj.*, untranslatable.

intraitable, *adj.*, untractable, ungovernable, unmanageable, unruly, difficult ; refractory.

intra-muros, *adv.*, inside a town.

intransigeant, *n.m.*, ultra-republican.

intransiti-f, **-ve** (-zi-), *adj.*, (gram.) intransitive.

intransitivement, *adv.*, intransitively.

intransparence, *n.f.*, intransparency.

intransportable, *adj.*, untransportable.

intrant, *n.m.*, in the University of Paris, the name formerly given to him who appointed the Rector.

intraversable, *adj.*, impassable, not to be crossed.

in-trente-deux, *n.m.* and *adj.*, (—) (print.) in thirty-two ; 32mo.

intrépide, *adj.*, intrepid, dauntless, undaunted, fearless, resolute ; bold.

intrépidement (-pi-dmān), *adv.*, intrepidly, fearlessly.

intrépidité, *n.f.*, intrepidity, dauntlessness, boldness, undauntedness, fearlessness.

intrigant, **-e**, *adj.* and *n.*, intriguing ; intriguer ; trimmer.

intrigue (in-trig), *n.f.*, intrigue ; scrape, difficulty ; plot. *— accessoire ;* under-plot. *Démêler, dénouer, une — ;* to unravel an intrigue, a plot.

intrigué, **-e**, *part.*, puzzled, perplexed.

intriguer (-ghé), *v.a.*, to puzzle, to perplex.

*s'*intriguer**, *v.r.*, to intrigue ; to take pains, to rack one's brains, to strive hard.

intriguer, *v.n.*, to intrigue, to plot.

intrigueu-r, *n.m.*, **-se**, *n.f.*, intriguer, plotter.

intrinsèque, *adj.*, intrinsic, intrinsical.

intrinsèquement (-sèk-mān), *adv.*, intrinsically.

introduct-eur, *n.m.*, **-rice**, *n.f.*, introducer.

introducti-f, **-ve**, *adj.*, (jur.) of the first process, introductory.

introduction, *n.f.*, introduction ; preamble ; (jur.) previous proceedings.

introductoire, *adj.*, introductory, preliminary.

introduire (introduisant, introduit), *v.a.*, **to** introduce, to show in, to bring, to bring in ; to conduct; to put, to put in, to let in. — *adroitement;* to shuffle (anyone) in. — *imperceptiblement;* to slip (anyone) in. — *de force;* to thrust (anyone) in.

s'introduire, *v.r.,* to introduce one's self; to get in, to gain admittance; to enter; to be introduced, to be brought in; to intrude, to intrude one's self. *S'— partout;* to intrude everywhere.

introït (-it), *n.m.,* (c. rel.) introit.

intromission, *n.f.,* (phys.) intromission.

intronisation, *n.f.,* enthroning (of bishops).

introniser, *v.a.,* to install; to enthrone.

introspection, *n.f.,* introspection.

introuvable, *adj.,* undiscoverable, not to be found, unfindable.

introuvé, -e, *part.,* unfound.

intrus, -e, *part.* and *n.,* intruded, obtruded; intruder.

intrusion, *n.f.,* intrusion.

intuitif, -ve, *adj.,* intuitive.

intuition, *n.f.,* intuition.

intuitivement (-ti-vmän), *adv.,* intuitively.

intumescence (-mès-sans), *n.f.,* intumescence.

intumescent, -e, *adj.,* intumescent.

intussusception, *n.f.,* (med., physiology) intussusception, introsusception.

inule, *n.f.,* (bot.) inula.

inuline, *n.f.,* (chem.) inuline.

inusable, *adj.,* that will not wear out; durable, everlasting.

inusité, -e, *adj.,* unused, not in use, obsolete; antiquated; unusual.

inutile, *adj.,* useless, fruitless, profitless; unnecessary; unavailing, unavailable, needless, unserviceable, vain, of no use.

inutilement (-til-män), *adv.,* uselessly, fruitlessly, unprofitably, to no purpose, vainly, needlessly.

inutilisable, *adj.,* that cannot be utilized; worthless, profitless.

inutilisé, -e, *adj.,* unutilized.

inutilité, *n.f.,* inutility, uselessness, fruitlessness, unprofitableness; useless thing.

invacillant, -e, *adj.,* non-flickering, steady.

invagination, *n.f.,* (med.) intussusception, invagination.

invaincu, -e, *adj.,* unvanquished, unconquered.

invalidation, *n.f.,* invalidation.

invalide, *adj.,* invalid; infirm; (milit., nav.) disabled; (jur.) void, not valid, without force, without effect.

invalide, *n.m.* and *f.,* invalid; (milit.) pensioner. — *externe;* out-pensioner. *Hôtel des Invalides;* the Chelsea Hospital of France (i. e., for disabled soldiers *or* sailors).

invalidement (-lid-män), *adv.,* invalidly, without force, without effect.

invalider, *v.a.,* to invalidate, to make void; to vitiate, to annul.

invalidité, *n.f.,* invalidity, nullity.

invariabilité, *n.f.,* invariableness, invariability, unchangeableness, constancy.

invariable, *adj.,* invariable, unchangeable, unalterable. *Mot —;* indeclinable word.

invariablement, *adv.,* invariably, unchangeably, unalterably.

invasion, *n.f.,* invasion; inroad; irruption.

invective, *n.f.,* invective. — *sanglante;* bitter invective.

invectiver, *v.n.,* to inveigh.

invendable, *adj.,* unsalable.

invendu, -e, *adj.,* (com.) unsold.

inventaire, *n.m.,* inventory. *Bénéfice d'—;* (jur.) non-liability to debts beyond assets stated in inventory. *Faire l'— de;* to take the inventory of. *Faire l'— des fonds en magasin;* (com.) to take stock.

inventer, *v.a.,* to invent, to find out, to contrive, to devise; to imagine, to forge, to fabricate. *Il n'a pas inventé la poudre;* he will never set the Thames on fire.

invent-eur, -rice, *n.* and *adj.,* inventor, contriver, deviser.

inventif, -ve, *adj.,* inventive.

invention, *n.f.,* invention, contrivance; ingenuity; device, trick; fiction, untruth, falsehood. *Brevet d'—;* patent. *Vivre d'—;* to live upon one's wits.

inventorier, *v.a.,* to inventory, to draw up an inventory of; to schedule, to catalogue.

inversable, *adj.,* that cannot be upset *or* overturned.

inverse, *adj.,* inverse, inverted. *En raison —;* in inverse ratio. *En sens —;* in the contrary direction. *Etre en raison — de;* to be in inverse ratio to.

inverse, *n.m.,* reverse, contrary. *Faire juste l'—;* to do just the contrary, to do the reverse. *En raison — (de);* in inverse ratio (to). *En sens —;* in a contrary direction.

inversement, *adv.,* inversely.

inversion, *n.f.,* (gram.) inversion.

invertébré, -e, *adj.* and *n.,* invertebrate.

inverti, -e, *adj.,* inversed, reversed.

investigat-eur, -rice, *n.* and *adj.,* investigator, explorer; investigating, searching; scrutinizing, inquiring.

investigation, *n.f.,* investigation, inquiry. *Faire des —s dans;* to make inquiries into.

investir, *v.a.,* to invest; to surround, to block up, to lay siege to; to put in possession.

investissement (-tis-män), *n.m.,* (milit.) investment.

investiture, *n.f.,* investiture.

invétéré, -e, *part.,* inveterate.

s'invétérer, *v.r.,* to grow inveterate, to become inveterate *or* chronic (of disease). *Cette maladie s'est invétérée;* this disorder has become chronic.

invincibilité, *n.f.,* invincibleness.

invincible, *adj.,* invincible, insuperable, unconquerable, insurmountable.

invinciblement, *adv.,* invincibly, insuperably, unconquerably, insurmountably.

in-vingt-quatre, *n.m.* and *adj.,* (—) (print.) in twenty-four, 24mo.

inviolabilité, *n.f.,* inviolability.

inviolable, *adj.,* inviolable, inviolate.

inviolablement, *adv.,* inviolably.

inviolé, -e, *adj.,* inviolate.

invisibilité, *n.f.,* invisibility, invisibleness.

invisible, *adj.,* invisible.

invisiblement, *adv.,* invisibly.

invitation, *n.f.,* invitation.

invitatoire, *n.m.,* (c.rel.) invitatory.

invite, *n.f.,* call for trumps.

invité, -e, *n.f.,* guest.

inviter, *v.a.,* to invite, to bid, to beg, to engage, to urge; to allure, to incite, to attract, to tempt. — *à dîner;* to ask to dinner. *S'—;* to invite each other.

invocation, *n.f.,* invocation.

involontaire, *adj.,* involuntary.

involontairement (-tèr-mä), *adv.,* involuntarily.

involucral, -e, *adj.,* (bot.) involucral.

involucre, *n.m.,* (bot.) involucre; cover, husk.

involuti-f, -ve, *adj.,* (bot.) involute, involuted.

involution, *n.f.,* (jur.) involvement, complication.

invoquer, *v.a.,* to invoke, to call upon, to cry unto, to plead; to appeal to.

invraisemblable, *adj.,* unlikely, improbable.

invraisemblablement, *adv.,* improbably.

invraisemblance, *n.f.,* unlikelihood, improbability; unlikely thing.

invulnérabilité, *n.f.,* invulnerability, invulnerableness.

invulnérable, *adj.*, invulnerable.
invulnérablement, *adv.*, invulnerably.
iode, *n.m.*, (chem.) iodine.
iodé, -e, *adj.*, (chem.) iodized.
iodeux, *adj.*, (chem.) iodous.
iodique, *adj.*, (chem.) iodic.
iodure, *n.m.*, (chem.) ioduret, iodide.
ioduré, -e, *adj.*, (chem.) iodureted, containing an iodide.
ionien, -ne (-in, -è-n), *adj.*, Ionian, Ionic.
ionien, *n.m.*, Ionic.
ionique, *adj.*, Ionic. *L'ordre —*; the Ionic order.
iota, *n.m.*, iota; jot, tittle.
iotacisme, *n.m.*, (gram.) frequent recurrence of the letter i.
ipécacuana, *n.m.*, ipecacuanha.
ipso facto, *adv.*, by the very fact.
iranien, -ne, *adj.*, (philology) iranic.
irascibilité, *n.f.*, irascibility, irritability.
irascible, *adj.*, irascible, irritable.
⊙**ire**, *n.f.*, wrath, anger, ire.
iridium, *n.m.*, (*n.p.*) (chem.) iridium.
iridescence, *n.f.*, iridescence.
iridescent, -e, *adj.*, iridescent.
iris (i-ris), *n.m.*, iris, rainbow; (anat.) iris; (bot.) iris, iris-root, orris. *Pois d'—*; issue-pea. *Poudre d'—*; powdered orris-root.
irisé, -e, *adj.*, rainbow-colored, irised, variegated; iridescent.
irlandais, -e, *n.* and *adj.*, Irishman, Irishwoman; Irish.
irlandais, *n.m.*, Irish language.
ironie, *n.f.*, irony, mockery, raillery.
ironique, *adj.*, ironic, ironical.
ironiquement, *adv.*, ironically, sneeringly.
iroquois, *n.m.*, Iroquois; lout.
irrachetable (ir-rash-tabl), *adj.*, unredeemable.
irradiation (ir-ra-), *n.f.*, irradiation.
irradier (ir-ra-), *v.n.*, to irradiate, to emit rays.
irraisonnable (ir-rè-), *adj.*, irrational.
irraisonnablement (ir-ré-), *adv.*, irrationally.
irrationnel, -le, *adj.*, irrational.
irrationnellement, *adv.*, irrationally.
irréalisable, *adj.*, unrealizable.
irréconciliable (ir-ré), *adj.*, irreconcilable.
irréconciliablement (ir-ré-), *adv.*, irreconcilably.
irréconcilié, -e (ir-ré-), *adj.*, unreconciled.
irrécouvrable, *adj.*, irrecoverable.
irrécusable (ir-ré-), *adj.*, unexceptionable, unobjectionable; undeniable.
irrécusablement, *adv.*, unexceptionably; unobjectionably, undeniably.
irréductibilité (ir-ré-), *n.f.*, irreducibleness.
irréductible (ir-ré-), *adj.*, irreducible.
irréfléchi, -e (ir-ré-), *adj.*, thoughtless, heedless, inconsiderate, unguarded.
irréflexion (ir-ré-) *n.f.*, thoughtlessness, heedlessness, inconsiderateness.
irréformable (ir-ré-), *adj.*, unchangeable, irrevocable; irreclaimable.
irréfragable (ir-ré-), *adj.*, irrefragable, irrefutable.
irréfragablement (ir-ré-), *adv.*, irrefragably, undeniably, irrefutably.
irréfutable (ir-ré-), *adj.*, irrefutable.
irréfuté, *adj.*, unrefuted, not disproved.
irrégularité (ir-ré-), *n.f.*, irregularity.
irréguli-er, -ère (ir-ré-), *adj.*, irregular; (math.) scalene.
irrégulièrement (ir-ré-), *adv.*, irregularly.
irréligieusement (ir-ré-), *adv.*, irreligiously, profanely.
irréligieu-x, -se (ir-ré-), *adj.*, irreligious.
irréligion (ir-ré-), *n.f.*, irreligion.
irrémédiable (ir-ré-), *adj.*, irremediable, not to be remedied, helpless, irretrievable.

irrémédiablement (ir-ré-), *adv.*, irremediably; irrecoverably, irretrievably.
irrémissible (ir-ré-), *adj.*, irremissible, unpardonable.
irrémissiblement (ir-ré-), *adv.*, irremissibly, unpardonably.
irréparable (ir-ré-), *adj.*, irreparable, irretrievable, irrecoverable.
irréparablement (ir-ré-), *adv.*, irreparably, irretrievably, irrecoverably.
irréprehensible (ir-ré), *adj.*, irreprehensible, irreproachable, irreprovable.
irréprehensiblement (ir-ré-), *adv.*, irreprehensibly, irreproachably, irreprovably.
irrépressible, *adj.*, irrepressible.
irréprochable (ir-ré-), *adj.*, irreproachable, irreprovable, unexceptionable.
irréprochablement (ir-ré-), *adv.*, irreproachably, irreprovably, unexceptionably.
irrésistibilité (ir-ré-), *n.f.*, irresistibility.
irrésistible (ir-ré-), *adj.*, irresistible.
irrésistiblement (ir-ré-), *adv.*, irresistibly.
irrésolu, -e (ir-ré-), *adj.*, irresolute, wavering, undetermined; unsolved.
irrésoluble (ir-ré-), *adj.*, irresolvable.
irrésolument (ir-ré-), *adv.*, irresolutely.
irrésolution (ir-ré-), *n.f.*, irresolution, indecision.
irrespectueusement, *adv.*, disrespectfully.
irrespectueu-x, -se, *adj.*, disrespectful.
irrespirable, *adj.*, irrespirable, unbreathable.
irresponsabilité, *n.f.*, irresponsibility.
irresponsable, *adj.*, irresponsible.
irrévéremment (ir-ré-vé-ra-man), *adv.*, irreverently.
irrévérence, *n.f.*, irreverence, disrespect.
irrévérencieu-x, -se, *adj.*, irreverent; disrespectful.
irrévérent, -e, *adj.*, irreverent.
irrévocabilité (ir-ré-), *n.f.*, irrevocableness.
irrévocable, *adj.*, irrevocable.
irrévocablement, *adv.*, irrevocably.
irrévoqué, *adj.*, unrevoked; unrepealed.
irrigable, *adj.*, that can be irrigated.
irrigateur, *n.m.*, watering-engine; garden-engine.
irrigation (ir-ri-), *n.f.*, irrigation.
irriguer, *v.a.*, to irrigate, to water.
irritabilité (ir-ri-), *n.m.*, irritability.
irritable, *adj.*, irritable.
irritant, -e, *adj.*, irritating, provoking; (med.) irritant; (jur.) vital.
irritant, *n.m.*, (med.) irritant.
irritation, *n.f.*, irritation; exasperation, vexation.
irrité, -e, *part.*, irritated, exasperated, excited; angry. *Une mer —e ;* an angry sea.
irriter (ir-ri-té), *v.a.*, to irritate, to incense, to anger, to exasperate; to provoke, to excite, to enrage. *Vous irrites sa colère ;* you provoke his anger. *Il est irrité contre vous ;* he is incensed against you.
s'irriter, *v.r.*, to be irritated; to be angry, provoked, exasperated, incensed.
irroration (ir-ro-), *n.f.*, irroration.
irruption (ir-rup-), *n.f.*, irruption; inroad; overflow, bursting in. *Faire — (dans);* to invade, to make an irruption into; to break in or out.
isabelle, *adj.*, dun- or cream-colored (of horses); dove-colored (of birds).
isabelle, *n.m.*, Isabel; dun (horse); dove-color (birds).
isard, *n.m.*, (mam.) izard (name given in the Pyrenees to the antelope chamois).
ischion (-ki-), *n.m.*, (anat.) ischium.
ischurétique (-ku-), *adj.*, (med.) ischuretic.
ischurie (-ku-), *n.f.*, (med.) ischury, ischuria.
isiaque, *adj.*, pertaining, relating, to Isis.
isinglass, *n.m. V.* **ichtyocolle** and **colle de poisson.**

islam, n.m., islam, religion of Mahomet.

islamisme, n.m., islamism.

islandais, -e, n.m.f., adj., Icelander.

isocèle, adj., (geom.) isosceles.

isochromatique (-kro-), adj., isochromatic.

isochrone (izo-krô-n), adj., isochronal, isochronous.

isochronisme, n.m., isochronism.

isolant, -e, adj., (phys.) insulating. Corps —; insulating body.

isolateur, n.m., insulator.

isolation, n.f., isolation, insulation.

isolé, -e, adj., part., isolated, lonely, solitary; detached, insulated, apart, not contiguous. Lieu —; lonely place or spot.

isolement (i-zol-mān), n.m., loneliness, isolation, solitude. Vivre dans l'—; to live a retired life.

isolément, adv., separately. [to separate.

isoler, v.a., to isolate, to insulate, to detach, s'isoler, v.r., to be isolated, insulated, to shun society.

isoloir, n.m., (phys.) insulator.

isomère, adj., (min. chem.) isomeric.

isotherme, adj., isothermal.

israélite (iz-), n.m.f. and adj., Israelite; Israelitic, Israelitish, Jewish. Un bon —; a plain, simple man.

issu, -e, adj., born, descended, or sprung from.

issue, n.f., issue, egress, outlet; end, event; loophole, escape, refuse grain; offal (of animals). A l'— de; on leaving, after.

isthme, n.m., isthmus.

isthmiques, adj.m.pl., (antiq.) Isthmian. Jeux —; Isthmian games.

ita est, adv., (Lat.) so it is.

itague (i-tag), n.f., (nav.) runner-tie.

italianiser, v.a., to Italianize.

italianisme, n.m., Italianism.

italien, -ne (-in, -è-n), n. and adj., Italian.

italien, n.m., Italian language.

italique, n.m. and adj., italics; italic.

item (i-tem), adv., also; moreover, ditto.

item, n.m., (—) item.

itérati-f, -ve, adj., iterative, repeated.

itération, n.f., iteration, repetition.

itérativement (-tiv-mān), adv., repeatedly.

ithos, n.m., (old) ethics.

itinéraire, n.m. and adj., itinerary, route, walk, round; guide, guide-book. Colonne —; way-post.

itou, adv., (fam.) also, too, likewise.

iule, n.m., (ent.) julus; catkin. V. **jule**.

ive or **ivette**, n.f., (bot.) iva.

ivoire, n.m., ivory; (fig.) whiteness. D'—; ivory. — des dents; bone of the teeth.

ivoirier, n.m., ivory-turner.

ivraie, n.f., darnel, tare, tares; rye-grass. Séparer l'— d'avec le bon grain; to separate the tares from the wheat.

ivre, adj., drunk, inebriated, intoxicated. A moitié —; half-tipsy, half-seas-over. — mort; dead drunk. — de joie; beside one's self with joy. — de sang; drunk with blood, thirsting for blood.

ivresse, n.f., drunkenness, inebriety, inebriation, intoxication; frenzy, rapture, enthusiasm.

*****ivrogne**, n.m. and adj., drunkard; drunken, tipsy, given to drink.

*****ivrogner**, v.n., (pop.) to fuddle, to carouse, to booze, to guzzle, to get drunk.

*****ivrognerie**, n.f., inebriation, drunkenness, intoxication.

*****ivrognesse**, n.f., (pop.) drunkard, drunken woman.

ixia, n.f., (bot.) ixia.

ixion, n.m., (astron.) Ixion.

ixode, n.m., (zoöl.). V. **tique**.

izard, n.m. V. **isard**.

J

j, n.m., the tenth letter of the alphabet, j.

⊙**jà**, adv., already.

jable, n.m., cross-groove (cooper's work).

jabler, v.a., to cross-groove (cooper's work).

jabot, n.m., frill (of a shirt); crop, maw (of a bird). Faire —; to give one's self airs. Se remplir le —; to have a blow-out.

jabotage, n.m., jabbering.

jaboter, v.n., to prattle, to chatter.

jaboteu-r, -se, n.m.f., chatterer, jabberer.

jabotière, n.f., frilling.

jacasse, n.f., (pop.) chatterer, prater, talkative female.

jacasser, v.n., to chatter (of the magpie); (fig.) to prate, to jabber.

jacée, n.f., (bot.) knapweed. — des blés; corn-flower.

jacent, -e, adj., (jur.) in abeyance.

jachère, n.f., fallow, fallow-ground. Terre en —; fallow-land. Etre en —; to be fallow.

jachéré, -e, part., fallowed.

jachérer, v.a., to fallow.

jacinthe or **hyacinthe**, n.f., (bot., min.) hyacinth.

jacobée, n.f., (bot.) ragwort.

jacobin, n.m., jacobin friar, monk; Jacobin (ultra radical of the French revolution).

jacobinisme, n.m., Jacobinism.

jacobite, n.m. and adj., Jacobite.

jaconas, n.m., jaconet.

jacot, n.m. V. **jacquot**.

jacquart, n.m. Métier à la —; Jacquart loom.

jacquerie, n.f., jacquerie; rising of peasants.

jacques, n.m., James. — bonhomme; peasant, Hodge (nickname for French peasants as a class).

jacquot or **jacot**, n.m., gray parrot, poll; pug (monkey).

jactance, n.f., boasting, bragging, boast. Plein de —; boastful.

⊙**se jacter**, v.r., to swagger, to brag.

jaculatoire, adj., ejaculatory, spouting.

jade, n.m., (min.) jade, ax-stone.

jadelle, judelle, n.f., (orni.) coot.

jadis (jă-dîs), adv., of old, in days of yore, formerly. Au temps —; in days of old.

jaguar, n.m., (zool.) jaguar.

jaiet, n.m. V. **jais**.

*****jaillir**, v.n., to spout, to spout out, to gush, to gush out, to spurt out; to spring, to burst out. Faire —; to throw up.

*****jaillissant, -e**, adj., spouting, gushing; springing, bursting.

*****jaillissement**, n.m., spouting out, gushing out, spirting, shooting, flashing.

jais, n.m., jet.

jalage, n.m., (feudalism) duty on wine.

jalap (ja-lap), n.m., jalap.

jale, n.f., large bowl, tureen.

⊙**jalet**, n.m., pebble-stone, pebble. Arc à —; stone-bow.

jalon, n.m., leveling-staff; surveying-staff; offset-staff; landmark; mark; indication.

jalonnement, n.m., (land surveying) staking out; marking out.

jalonner, v.n., to stake out; to place landmarks; to mark out, indicate.

jalonneur, n.m., (milit.) marker.

jalousement, adv., jealously.

jalouser, v.a., to be jealous of, to envy. se **jalouser**, v.r., to be jealous of each other.

jalousie, n.f., jealousy; fear, uneasiness, umbrage; blind, Venetian blind; (bot.) three-colored amaranth, sweet William. Par —; out of jealousy. Donner de la — à quelqu'un; to make any one jealous.

jalou-x, -se, n. and adj., jealous person; jealous; desirous, anxious; inclining on one side (of a carriage, of a ship). — d'acquérir de *la gloire ;* desirous of acquiring glory. — *de plaire ;* anxious to please. *Faire des* —; to excite jealousy.

jamais, *adv.,* never, ever. *Je ne la vois* —; I never see her. *Si* — *je deviens riche ;* if ever I grow rich. *A* —, *pour* —; for ever. *A tout* —; for ever and ever. — *de la vie ;* never, never, I tell you.

jamais, *n.m.,* time without end. *Au grand* —; for ever and ever, to all eternity.

jambage, *n.m.,* jamb (of a door); hanger, down-stroke (in writing).

jambe, *n.f.,* leg ; shank ; (of a glass) stem. — *arquée ;* bow-leg. *Courir à toutes* —*s ;* to run at the top of one's speed. — *en deçà,* — *en delà ;* astride. — *de force ;* principal rafter. —*s de quinze ans ;* young legs. *Avoir des* —*s de quinze ans ;* to be as nimble as ever. *Prendre ses* —*s à son cou ;* to take to one's heels. *Etre haut en* —; to be long-legged. *Cela ne lui rend pas la* — *mieux faite ;* he is no better off for it. *Jouer des* —*s ;* to take to flight, to make off. *Je le ferai par-dessous la* — ; I will do it with the greatest ease. *Avoir les* —*s en manche de veste ;* to be bow-legged.

jambé, -e, *adj.,* legged. *Bien* — ; well made about the legs. *Mal* — ; badly made about the legs.

jambette, *n.f.,* small pocket-knife ; (carp.) jamb.

jambi-er, -ère, *adj.,* (anat.) of the leg. *n.f.,* legging, leg-guard.

jambon, *n.m.,* ham.

jambonneau, *n.m.,* small ham, knuckle.

jan, *n.m.,* (tric-trac) jan, table. — *de retour ;* outer table.

janissaire, *n.m.,* janissary.

jansénisme, *n.m.,* Jansenism.

janséniste, *n.m.* and *adj.,* Jansenist.

jante, *n.f.,* felly, rim (of a wheel), felloe.

janvier, *n.m.,* January.

japon, *n.m.,* Japan-ware.

japonais, -e, *n.m.* and *adj.,* Japanese.

japonais, *n.m.,* Japanese language.

japonner, *v.a.,* to hard-bake (porcelain).

jappement (ja-pmān), *n.m.,* yelping.

japper, *v.n.,* to yelp.

⊙**jaque,** *n.f.,* coat. — *de mailles ;* coat of mail.

jaquemart, *n.m.,* jack of the clock-house.

jaquette, *n.f.,* jacket ; tunic, short petticoats (for boys).

jaquier, *n.m.,* breadfruit-tree.

jarde, *n.f.* V. **jardon.**

jardin, *n.m.,* garden ; (nav.) quarter-gallery. — *d'agrément ;* pleasure *or* flower garden. — *potager ;* kitchen-garden. — *fruitier ;* fruit-garden. — *des plantes ;* botanical, zoölogical gardens. — *anglais ;* ornamental garden, grounds.

jardinage, *n.m.,* gardening ; garden-ground ; garden-stuff.

jardiner, *v.n.,* to garden.

jardinet, *n.m.,* small garden.

jardineuse, *adj.f.,* (of emeralds) spotty.

jardinier, *n.m.,* gardener. — *fleuriste ;* (—*s* — *s*) florist. — *maraîcher ;* kitchen-gardener.

jardini-er, -ère, *adj.,* of the garden. *Plantes* —*eres ;* garden-plants.

jardinière, *n.f.,* gardener's wife ; garden-woman ; low ruffle ; flower-stand ; kind of vegetable soup.

jardon, *n.m.,* *or* **jarde,** *n.f.,* (vet.) curb.

jargon, *n.m.,* jargon, gibberish, lingo ; cant ; (min.) jargoon, jargon, gray *or* brown zircon.

jargonner, *v.a.n.,* to talk jargon, to talk twaddle *or* gibberish.

⊙**jarni !** *int.,* by Heaven ! zounds.

jarousse *or* **jarrosse,** *n.f.,* (bot.) vetch.

jarre, *n.f.,* jar, jug, can.

jarret, *n.m.,* ham, hough, hock ; (arch.) projection. — *de veau ;* knuckle of veal. — *de bœuf ;*

shin of beef. *Couper les* —*s à un cheval ;* to hamstring a horse ; (fig.) leg, legs. *Coupe* —, (— — —*s*) ruffian, bully. *Etre ferme sur ses* —*s ;* to keep one's countenance, to stand unmoved. *Avoir du* — ; to be a good walker, a good dancer. *Tendre le* — ; (fig.) to strut.

jarreté, -e (jar-té), *adj.,* close-hammed, close-hocked ; knock-kneed, gartered ; (arch.) protuberant, projecting.

jarretelle, *n.f.,* stocking suspender.

jarreter, *v.a.,* to garter. *Se* — ; to put garters on, to garter one's self.

jarretière (jar-tièr), *n.f.,* garter. *L'ordre de la* — ; the Order of the Garter. *Ne pas aller à la* — *à quelqu'un ;* not to come up to any one (by a long way).

jars (jâr), *n.m.,* (orni.) gander. *Il entend le* — ; he is no fool ; he knows what 's what ; he is up to snuff.

jas, *n.m.,* (nav.) stock, anchor-stock.

jaser, *v.n.,* to prate, to chatter, to gabble, to chat, to babble, to blab, to tattle. — *comme une pie, comme une pie borgne ;* to chatter like a magpie.

jaserie (jâ-zrî), *n.f.,* prating, chattering ; prate, chatter ; twaddle.

jaseu-r, *n.m.,* **-se,** *n.f.,* prater, chatterer ; chatterbox ; (orni.) chatterer. *Grand* — ; (orni.) Bohemian chatterer, waxwing.

jasmin, *n.m.,* (bot.) jasmine, jessamine.

jaspe, *n.m.,* (min.) jasper.

jaspé, -e, *part.,* jasperated, jasper-like ; marbled, veined ; (of binding) sprinkled.

jasper, *v.a.,* to marble ; (binding) to sprinkle.

jaspure, *n.f.,* marbling ; sprinkling.

jatte, *n.f.,* bowl, platter ; (nav.) manger. *Cul-de-jatte ;* cripple (sitting in a bowl).

jattée, *n.f.,* bowlful, platterful.

jauge (jôj) *n.f.,* gauge ; gauging-rod ; (nav.) tonnage, burden. — *d'eau ;* water-gauge ; (hort.) trench.

jaugeage (jô-jaj), *n.m.,* gauging.

jauger, *v.a.,* to gauge, to measure (the capacity of) ; to take the gauge of ; (nav.) to draw (so many feet of water).

jaugeur, *n.m.,* gauger.

jaunâtre, *adj.,* yellowish.

jaune, *adj.,* yellow. — *comme un coing ;* as yellow as a guinea. [egg.

jaune, *n.m.,* yellow. — *d'œuf ;* yolk of an

jaunet, *n.m.,* buttercup ; bachelor's buttons ; (pop.) yellow-boy, gold coin.

jaunir, *v.a.,* to make yellow, to dye yellow ; (arts) to yellow.

jaunir, *v.n.,* to grow yellow, to turn yellow.

jaunissage, *n.m.,* (arts) yellowing.

jaunissant, -e, *adj.,* turning yellow, yellowing ; ripening.

jaunisse, *n.f.,* jaundice ; (vet.) yellows.

javart, *n.m.,* (vet.) quittor.

javeau, *n.m.,* sand-bank.

javelage, *n.m.,* drying (of corn in the fields).

javeler (ja-vlé), *v.a.,* to lay in loose sheaves.

javeleur (ja-vleur), *n.m.,* harvestman ; binder (into loose sheaves).

javeline (ja-vli-n), *n.f.,* javelin.

javelle, *n.f.,* small sheaf ; small bundle (of corn left to dry). *Eau de* — ; bleaching liquid.

javelot (ja-vlo), *n.m.,* javelin.

je, *pron.,* I. — *dis ;* I say. *Parlé* —*?* do I speak ?

jean (jan), *n.m.,* John, Johnny, fool. *La Saint* — ; midsummer. — *farine ;* merry andrew. — *foutre ;* blackguard.

jeannette (ja-nèt), *n.f.,* spinning-jenny.

jectisses, *adj.f.pl. Terres* — ; made earth, loose soil ; rubbish. *Pierres* — ; (mas.) stones small enough to be placed by hand.

jéhovah, *n.m.,* Jehovah.

jéjunum, *n.m.,* (anat.) jejunum,

jenny, n.f., jenny (cotton-frame).

jérémiade, n.f., jeremiad.

jérose, n.f., (bot.) rose of Jericho.

jésuite, n.m., jesuit. — *de,* or *en, robe courte ;* lay jesuit.

jésuitique, adj., jesuitic, jesuitical.

jésuitisme, n.m., jesuitism.

jésus, n.m., long royal, super royal (paper).

jet (jè), n.m., casting, cast; throwing, throw; shoot, sprout; casting (metal.); (agri.) tiller; jet, gush, spirt (of water); new swarm (of bees). *Le* — *d'un filet ;* the casting of a net. *Un* — *de pierre ;* a stone's throw. — *de lumière ;* ray of light. *Le* — *d'une draperie ;* (paint.) the folds or lay of a drapery. — *d'eau ;* waterspout, fountain. — *d'abeilles ;* swarm of young bees. *D'un seul* — ; at one stroke, born of a single effort. *Faire le* — ; (com., nav.) to throw (goods) overboard. — *de marchandises ;* (nav., com., jur.) jetsam, jettison.

jeté, n.m., jeté (dancing).

jeté, -e, part., cast, thrown. *Le dé, le sort, en est* — ; the die is cast, the thing is resolved upon, the step has been taken.

jetée, n.f., jetty, pier, mole. — *de port ;* jetty-head, pier-head.

jeter, v.a., to throw, to cast, to fling, to hurl; to throw down, to cast down, to fling down; to hurl down; to mold; to lay, to shoot, to shoot out, to shoot forth, to send forth; to disembogue, to empty; to discharge, to suppurate. — *l'ancre ;* to cast anchor. — *un soupir ;* to heave a sigh. — *les fondements d'une maison, d'une fortune ;* to lay the foundation of a house, of a fortune. — *de profondes racines ;* to take deep root. — *les yeux sur quelqu'un ;* to cast one's eyes on any one. — *à la mer ;* (nav.) to throw overboard, to jettison. — *bas ;* (dy.) to take out of the copper. — *une draperie ;* to dispose the drapery (paint.). — *ses cartes ;* to play one's cards. *Ce cheval jette sa gourme ;* that horse has the glanders. — *de l'huile sur le feu ;* to add fuel to the flame. — *son argent par les fenêtres ;* to play ducks and drakes with one's money.

se jeter, v.r., to throw one's self, to cast one's self, to fling one's self ; to fall on, to fall upon (attack) ; to shoot ; to strike out, to launch out ; to be thrown down, to be thrown away ; to disembogue, to fall, to empty one's self (of rivers). *Se* — *sur l'ennemi ;* to rush upon the enemy. *Se* — *au cou de quelqu'un ;* to fall on any one's neck. *Se* — *à corps perdu ;* to rush headlong into.

jeton, n.m., counter, token, brass farthing.

jeu, n.m., play ; sport ; fun ; game ; gaming, gambling ; acting (of actors) ; stake ; (of organs) stop ; (nav.) set ; (nav.) suit ; (mec.) length of stroke ; (tech.) play. — *d'enfant ;* child's play. — *de cartes ;* card game; pack of cards. *Bonheur au* — ; good luck at play. — *de hasard ;* game of chance. *De bon ou de franc* — ; by fair play. *Couper* — ; to leave off playing, to go off with one's winnings. *Tenir le* — *de quelqu'un ;* to play for any one. — *de bourse ;* stock jobbing. *J'ai beau* — ; I have a good hand. *Il a le* — *serré ;* he plays a sure game. *Avoir beau* — ; to have a good chance. *Cacher son* — ; to cover one's designs. *Jouer bien son* — ; to play one's cards well. *Faire bonne mine à mauvais* — ; to put a good face upon matters. *Bon* —. *Bon argent ;* in good earnest. *Le* — *ne vaut pas la chandelle ;* it is not worth the trouble, it is not worth powder and shot. *Se piquer au* — ; to persist in playing. *Mettre au* — ; to stake. *Jouer gros* — ; to play high. *Jouer petit* — ; to play low. *Ils sont à deux de* — ; they are upon even terms; two can play at that game. *Un* — *de quilles ;* a set of nine-pins. — *d'échecs ;* set of chess-men. *Ne me mettez pas au* — ; do not mix me in it. *Cela passe le* — ; that is beyond a joke. *Être à deux de* — ; to be even or quits ; to

be a match for each other. *A beau* — *beau retour ;* one good turn deserves another. *Donner beau à* — ; to play into a person's hands. — *de mains* — *de vilains ;* rough play often ends in tears. *Cela n'est pas du* — ; that was not in the bargain; that is not fair. *Je sais son* — ; I know his way. — *de voiles ;* complete set of sails. — *d'avirons ;* set of oars. *Avoir du* — ; (tech.) to have too much play. — *de mots ;* pun ; quibble, play upon words. — *d'esprit ;* piece of wit, witticism. —*x floraux ;* floral games. — *qui trop dure ne vaut rien ;* too much of a good thing is bad.

jeudi, n.m., Thursday. *Le* — *gras ;* Shrove Thursday. *La semaine des trois* —*s ;* when two Sundays come together (i.e., never). — *Saint ;* Maundy-Thursday.

à jeûn, adv., fasting, on an empty stomach. *Je suis encore à* — ; I have not yet breakfasted. *J'ai pris cela à* — ; I took it on an empty stomach.

jeune, adj., young ; younger, junior ; youthful, recent, new ; early, green. — *homme ;* young man, lad, youngster. —*s gens ;* young men ; young people. — *personne ;* young girl, young lady. — *premier,* — *première ;* (thea.) actor, actress, who takes lovers' parts. *Qui* — *n'apprend, rien ne saura ;* an old dog will learn no tricks.

jeûne, n.m., fasting ; fast, abstinence.

jeunement (jeu-n-mān), adv., (hunt.) just. *Cerf de dix cors* — ; stag just turned ten years.

jeûner, v.n., to fast.

jeunesse, n.f., youth, youthful days ; youthfulness ; young people ; (pop.) lad, lass. *Avoir un air de* — ; to have a youthful look. *J'ai rencontré une* — *fort jolie ;* (pop.) I met a very pretty girl. *Si* — *savait, si vieillesse pouvait ;* if things were to be done twice, all would be wise. *Il faut que* — *se passe ;* boys will be boys.

jeunet, -te, adj., very young.

jeûneu-r, n.m., -**se,** n.f., faster.

*****joaillerie,** n.f., jeweler's trade or business; jewelery, jewels.

*****joailli-er,** n.m., -**ère,** n.f., jeweler.

jobard, n.m., ninny, simpleton, fool.

jobarder, v.a., to gull, to fool, to be fooled.

jobarderie, n.f., silliness, foolery.

jobet, n.m., (metal.) iron wire of a mold.

joc, n.m., stop, standstill (used in speaking of mills). *Mettre le moulin à* — ; to stop the mill.

jockey, n.m., (—s) jockey.

jocko, n.m., (mam.) pongo, black-orang.

jocrisse, n.m., cotquean ; dolt, dupe, simpleton, ninny. *Jouer les* —*s ;* to play silly servants' parts.

joie, n.f., joy, joyfulness ; gladness ; glee, mirth; exultation, delight. *Être ravi, comblé, de* — ; to be overjoyed, to be transported with joy. *Ne pas se sentir de* — ; to be beside one's self with joy, to be unable to contain one's self for joy. *Faire la* — *de quelqu'un, être la* — *de quelqu'un ;* to make any one's delight. *Pleurer de* — ; to weep for joy. *Feu de* — ; bonfire.

*****joignant,** prep., next to, contiguous to, adjoining.

*****joignant, -e,** adj., adjoining, next to, adjacent, contiguous.

joindre (joignant, joint), v.a., to join, to adjoin, to put together, to unite, to combine, to fix together, to connect; to add ; to annex, to join with ; to overtake ; to come up to ; (arch.) to fay. — *les mains ;* to clasp the hands.

se joindre, v.r., to join, to unite, to be joined, to be united, to be combined ; to be adjoining, to be adjacent, to be contiguous ; to be added, to consort, to meet.

joindre, v.n., to join, to meet. *Ces planches ne joignent pas ;* these planks do not join.

joint, n.m., joint ; seam, junction. — *articulé ;* knuckle joint. *Trouver le* — ; to hit upon the best or right way.

joint, -e, *part.*, joined, united, added ; jointed. *Prier quelqu'un à mains —es ;* to beg very hard. *Vous trouverez ci— — copie de sa lettre ;* you will find herewith a copy of his letter. *A pieds —s ;* close-legged.

jointe, -e, *adj.*, jointed. *Cheval long —;* long-jointed horse.

jointée, *n.f.*, double handful.

jointi-f, -ve, *adj.*, (arch.) joined, closed.

jointoiement (-toa-mān), *n.m.*, grouting, pointing (of walls).

jointoyer, *v.a.*, to grout, to point.

jointure, *n.f.*, joint, jointing, articulation.

joli, -e, *adj.*, pretty, pleasing, neat, genteel ; fine, good ; nice, comfortable. *Il est dans un — état ;* he is in a nice state, in a pretty mess.

joli, *n.m.*, a pretty thing ; what is pretty. *Le — de la chose c'est que ;* the best of the thing was that.

joliet, -te, *adj.*, rather pretty.

joliment, *adv.*, prettily, pleasingly ; (b.s.) finely ; extremely, excessively ; (fam.) much, many.

jolite, *n.f.*, violet-stone.

jonc (jon), *n.m.*, rush ; Malacca-cane ; keeper (ring). *— marin ;* sea-rush. *— odorant ;* camel's-hay.

jonchaie, *n.f.*, bed *or* plantation of rushes.

jonché, -e, *part.*, strewed, heaped.

jonchée, *n.f.*, strewing, sprinkling (of flowers); scatterer about. *— de crême ;* cream-cheese.

joncher, *v.a.*, to strew, to heap, to scatter.

jonchets, *n.m.pl.*, spilikins (game).

jonciforme, *adj.*, rush-shaped, rush-like.

jonction, *n.f.*, junction, joining, meeting.

jongler, *v.n.*, to juggle.

jonglerie, *n.f.*, juggling, hocus-pocus. *V.* **escamotage.**

jongleur, *n.m.*, juggler ; (fig.) deceiver, trickster, cheat.

jonque, *n.f.*, junk (Chinese vessel).

***jonquille**, *n.f.*, (bot.) jonquil.

jordonner, *v.n.*, to command, to dictate (loudly) (found in V. Hugo).

joseph, *n.m.* *— papier ;* silver-paper, tissue-paper.

jouable, *adj.*, playable.

jouail, *n.m.* *V.* **jas.**

***jouailler**, *v.n.*, to play for amusement.

joubarbe, *n.f.*, (bot.) sengreen ; house-leek.

joue, *n.f.*, cheek. *Coucher, mettre, en —;* to aim at, to take aim at. *En —!* (milit.) present !

joué, -e, *part.*, played ; mocked, made game of. *On m'a —;* I have been made game of, a fool of. *Pièce touchée, pièce —e ;* (at draughts, etc.) if you touch your piece, you must move it.

jouée, *n.f.*, (arch.) reveal.

jouer, *v.a.*, to play ; to stake ; to move ; to perform, to act ; to feign, to imitate ; to make game of, to deceive. *— une partie ;* to play a game. *Ne — que l'honneur ;* to play for love. *— quelque chose ;* to play for something. *— quelqu'un ;* to make a fool of any one. *— un tour à quelqu'un ;* to play any one a trick. *— une comédie ;* to act a comedy. *— un rôle ;* to play a part. *— la comédie ;* to act a sham part. *— un air sur le violon ;* to play a tune on the violin. *Ce papier joue le velours ;* this paper looks like velvet.

se jouer, *v.r.*, to sport, to play, to make game of, to baffle ; to make light of. *Se — de quelqu'un ;* to make a fool of any one. *La fortune se joue des hommes ;* fortune makes sport of mankind. *Se — à quelqu'un ;* to meddle with any one who is more than one's match.

jouer, *v.n.*, to play, to sport ; to trifle ; to run the risk ; to explode (mine) ; to speculate (on the funds) ; to work, to work loose (mec.). *— aux cartes ;* to play at cards. *A qui à —?* whose turn is it to play ? *C'est à moi à —;* it is my turn to play. *— au volant ;* to play at shuttle-cock. *— à jeu sûr ;* to play without risk. *— au plus sûr ;* to play a safe game. *— au plus fin ;* to vie in cunning with. *— à quitte ou double ;* to play double or quits. *— de son reste ;* to stake one's all. *— de malheur ;* to be unfortunate, to have a run of ill-luck. *— de bonheur ;* to be lucky. *Il joue à se faire tuer ;* he ventures his life. *— du violon ;* to play upon the violin. *Faire —;* to set going. *Ils jouent bien au billard ;* they are good at billiards. *— des talons ;* to take to one's heels. *— des gobelets ;* to juggle. *Ne — que pour l'honneur ;* to play for love.

jouet, *n.m.*, plaything, toy ; laughing-stock ; jest ; sport. *Etre le — de la fortune ;* to be the sport of fortune.

joueu-r, *n.m.*, **-se**, *n.f.*, player ; gamester, gambler. *Mauvais — de violon ;* cat-gut scraper. *Beau —;* good-natured player. *Mauvais —;* bad-tempered player. *— à la baisse ;* (exchange language) bear. *— à la hausse ;* (exchange language) bull.

joufflu, -e, *n.* and *adj.*, chubby, chubby-cheeked person.

joug (joog), *n.m.*, yoke ; bondage, slavery. *Mettre les bœufs au —;* to yoke the oxen. *S'affranchir du —, or secouer le —;* to shake off the yoke. *Briser le —;* to throw off the yoke. *Atteler au —;* to yoke.

jouière *or* **jouillère**, *n.f.*, side-wall (of a lock).

jouir, *v.n.*, to enjoy, to revel in, to possess, to be in possession of. *— de l'embarras de quelqu'un ;* to revel in any one's embarrassment. *Les animaux jouissent de la faculté de ;* animals possess the faculty of. *Il est si occupé qu'on n'en peut — un instant ;* he is so busy that one cannot have a minute's conversation with him. *Faire —;* to give pleasure, to please, to delight ; to put in possession of. *Cela ne vous fait pas —;* that's anything but pleasant.

jouissance, *n.f.*, enjoyment, gratification, satisfaction ; fruition, possession ; (fin.) interest payable ; use (of a garden, house).

jouissant, -e, *adj.*, enjoying, in full possession of.

joujou, *n.m.*, plaything, toy. *Faire —;* to play.

jour, *n.m.*, day, daytime, daylight, light ; gap, opening ; facility, means. *A court —;* short-dated (of bills). *A long —;* long-dated. *A chaque — suffit sa peine ;* sufficient unto the day is the evil thereof. *A la pointe du —;* at break of day. *—s caniculaires ;* dog-days. *Le — et la nuit ;* day and night. *Il commence à faire —;* it begins to be light. *Petit —;* morning twilight. *Il fait —;* it is daylight. *Grand —;* broad daylight. *Le — baisse ; dusk is coming on. A la chute du —;* at nightfall. *Demi —;* twilight, half light. *Il est — chez lui ;* he is up and about. *En plein —;* in broad daylight. *Brûler le —;* to shut out the daylight. *Donner le — à ;* to give birth to. *Voir le —;* to see the light ; to come to light. *Mettre au —;* to bring to light. *Se faire —;* to make one's way. *Tôt ou tard la vérité se fait jour ;* sooner or later truth will out. *Tous les —s ;* every day. *De nos —s ;* in our time, at present. *Un— ou l'autre ;* some day or other. *Du — que ;* since the day when. *Quinze —s ;* a fortnight. *Un — de fête ;* a holiday. *— de l'an ;* new-year's day. *— ouvrier, ouvrable ;* working-day. *— gras ;* flesh-day. *— maigre ;* fish-day. *Les —s gras ;* shrove-tide. *Donner, souhaiter, le bon — à quelqu'un ;* to wish any one good morning, to pay one's respects to any one. *Etre de —;* to be on duty. *Eire à —;* to be up to time, up to date. *Il donne tant par —;* he gives so much a day. *Il me remet de —;* he puts me off from day to day. *Je l'attends de — en —;* I expect him every day.

Mourir plein de —s; to die full of years. *Vivre au — la journée, vivre au — le —;* to live from hand to mouth. *Bon —, bonne œuvre;* the better the day, the better the deed. *A chaque — suffit sa peine;* sufficient for the day is the evil thereof. *Ce n'est pas tous les —s fête;* Christmas comes but once a year. *Faire du — la nuit;* to turn day into night. *C'est le — et la nuit;* they are as different as chalk and cheese. *Le goût du —;* the reigning fashion. *Etre dans son bon —;* (paint.) to be in a good light; (fig.) to be on one's good behavior. *Se mettre à tous les —s;* to make one's self cheap. *L'auteur de vos jours;* the author of your being. *Si je vois — à cela;* if I can see through it. *A —;* open, in open work. *Broderie à —;* embroidery in open-work. *Mettre à —;* to bring up to date. *Prendre —;* to fix a day, to make an appointment. *Donner du —;* to give light; to let light in. *— pour —;* to the very day. *— de réception;* at-home day.

journal, *n.m.,* journal, diary; newspaper; (com.) day-book. *— nautique;* (nav.) log-book. *Tenir un —;* to keep a diary.

journali-er, -ère, *adj.,* daily; diurnal; uncertain, inconstant, fickle, capricious, changeable, not the same every day. *Cette femme est très —e;* this woman varies a great deal in beauty.

journalier, *n.m.,* journeyman, day-laborer.

journalisme, *n.m.,* journalism.

journaliste, *n.m.adj.,* journalist, journalistic.

journée, *n.f.,* day; day's work; day's wages; day's journey; battle, revolution, insurrection. *Toute la —;* all day long. *Travailler à la —;* to work by the day. *Homme de —;* day-laborer. *Femme de —;* charwoman. *A grandes —s;* by forced marches; by long stages. *A petites —s;* by short stages. *La — fut rude;* the battle was stubbornly fought. *Les —s de Juillet,* or *les trois —s;* the July insurrection, 1830 (27th, 28th, 29th July, 1830).

journellement (-nèl-màn), *adv.,* daily, every day.

joute, *n.f.,* joust, just, tilt, lists; match, debate. *— de coqs;* cock-fight.

jouter, *v.n.,* to joust, to tilt; to wrestle, to struggle; to argue, to dispute.

jouteur, *n. m.,* tilter; wrestler; antagonist, adversary.

jouvence, *n.f.,* (l.u.) youth. *Fontaine de Jouvence;* fountain of youth.

jouvenceau, *n.m.,* (jest.) lad, stripling, young fellow.

jouvencelle, *n.f.,* (jest.) lass, young girl, damsel.

jovial, -e, *adj.,* jovial, jocund, joyous, merry.

jovialement (jo-vial-màn), *adv.,* jovially, joyously, boisterously.

jovialité, *n.f.,* mirth, merriment, boisterous mirth.

joyau, *n.m.,* jewel. *—x de la couronne;* crown-jewels.

joyeusement (joa-yeûz-màn), *adv.,* cheerfully, joyfully, merrily.

joyeuseté (joa-yeûz-té), *n.f.,* joyfulness, merriment, joke, jest.

joyeu-x, -se, *adj.,* joyful, merry, cheerful, mirthful; gladsome.

jube, *n.f.,* mane (of a lion or horse).

jubé, *n.m.,* (in churches) rood-loft *or* screen. *Venir à —;* to come to terms, to yield; to knuckle under.

jubée, *n.f.,* (bot.) jubœa, coquito (palm).

jubilaire, *adj.,* of jubilee; (pers.) of fifty years' standing.

jubilant, -e, *adj.,* jubilant, delighted.

jubilation, *n.f.,* jubilation, festivity, rejoicing.

jubilé, *n.m.,* jubilee; golden wedding. *Faire —;* (at play) to mix up the cards (so that there be neither winners nor losers).

jubilé, *adj.,* of fifty years' standing.

jubiler, *v.n.,* to make merry, to exult.

jubis, *n.m.,* raisins.

juc, *n.m.,* roost, perch. *V.* **juchoir.**

juché, -e, *part.,* perched, roosted, roosting. *Cheval —;* (man.) boulet (horse). *V.* **boulet** and **bouleté.**

jucher, *v.n.,* to roost, to perch.

se **jucher,** *v.r.,* to roost, to perch, to perch one's self up.

juchoir, *n.m.,* roosting-place; perch.

judaïque, *adj.,* Judaical, Jewish.

judaïquement (-ik-màn), *adv.,* Judaically.

judaïsant, *adj.,* judaizing.

judaïser, *v.n.,* to judaize.

judaïsme, *n.m.,* Judaism.

judas, *n.m.,* Judas (treacherous person); peep-hole. *Baiser de —;* treacherous kiss. *Poil de —;* carroty, sandy hair. *Marques de —;* freckles. *Point de —;* number 13.

judasserie, *n.f.,* trickery, perfidy.

judelle, *n.f.,* (orni.) coot.

judicature, *n.f.,* judicature, magistracy.

judiciaire, *adj.,* judiciary, judicial, legal, forensic.

judiciaire, *n.f.,* judgment; sagacity; discretion.

judiciairement (-èr-màn), *adv.,* judicially, legally, by authority of justice.

judicieusement (-eûz-màn), *adv.,* judiciously, considerately, discreetly.

judicieu-x, -se, *adj.,* judicious, wise, discreet.

juge, *n.m.,* judge; justice. *— de paix;* justice of the peace. *— du camp;* stickler. *— d'instruction;* police magistrate. *Se constituer en — de;* to constitute one's self a judge of. *De fou — brève sentence;* (proverb) a fool's bolt is soon shot.

jugé, -e, *part.,* judged. *Bien —;* well judged. *Au —,* or *au juger;* at a guess.

jugeable (ju-jabl), *adj.,* amenable to a tribunal, to be tried.

jugement (juj-màn), *n.m.,* judgment, opinion, view; trial, sentence. *— par défaut;* judgment by default. *Mettre quelqu'un en —;* to put any one on his trial, to bring any one up for trial. *Rendre un —;* to deliver judgment. *Rendre un — contre;* to sentence. *Prononcer un —;* to give judgment, to pass sentence. *Subir un —;* to be under sentence. *Passer en —;* to be brought up for trial. *Mettre quelqu'un en —;* to indict any one. *Je me rends à votre —;* I bow to your judgment.

juger, *v.a.,* to judge; to conjecture, to think, to believe, to imagine; to try; to bring to trial; to sentence. *— à propos;* to think proper.

se **juger,** *v.r.,* to judge one's self; to deem, to think, one's self; (jur.) to be tried, to be heard. *Vous en jugez-vous capable?* do you think yourself equal to it? *Cette affaire se jugera demain;* (jur.) this case will be heard, will come on, tomorrow.

juger, *v.n.,* to judge; to pass sentence; to give judgment; to deem, to think. *— sur l'étiquette du sac;* to judge by the label; by appearances. *A en — par;* judging by. *Au —;* at a guess. *— d'autrui par soi-même;* to judge of others by one's self.

juger, *n.m.,* judging, judgment; guessing, guess.

jugeu-r, -se, *n.m.f.,* judger, judge of things.

jugulaire, *adj.,* (anat.) jugular.

jugulaire, *n.f.,* (anat.) jugular vein; chin-strap.

juguler, *v.a.,* to strangle; to torment; to cheat out of; to ruin; to dun.

jui-f, -ve, *n.* and *adj.,* Jew; Jewess; Jewish. *Le — errant;* the wandering Jew.

*****juillet,** *n.m.,* July.

juin, *n.m.,* June.

juiverie (jui-vrí), *n.f.*, jewry (Jews' ward); set of Jews ; Jew's bargain *or* trick.

jujube, *n.m.*, jujube. *Pâte de* —; jujube lozenges.

jujubier, *n.m.*, jujube-tree.

jule, *n.m.*, (ent.) iulus (coin) ; (bot.) catkin.

julep (ju-lèp), *n.m.*, julep.

julien, -ne (-li-in, -è-n), *adj.*, Julian. [soup.

julienne (*n.f.*), (bot.) rocket ; (cook.) vegetable

jumart, *n.m.*, jumart.

jume-au, -lle, *n.* and *adj.*, twin ; (anat.) twin muscles ; twin-born ; twin ; double (fruit). *Des cerises* —*lles;* double-cherries. *Frères* —*aux;* twin brothers.

jumelé, -e, *adj.*, (her.) bar-gemel.

jumeler, *v.a.*, to strengthen with cheeks, to clamp, to join ; to match (things). — *un mât;* (nav.) to fish *or* clamp a mast.

jumelle, *n.f.*, twin. —*s de théâtre;* opera-glass. —*s de campagne;* field-glass ; race-glass ; (carp.) cheeks, side-beams ; (her.) gemel ; (nav.) fish clamp (of masts and yards). —*s de re-change;* (nav.) spare clamps.

jument, *n.f.*, mare.

jungle, *n.f.*, jungle.

junon, *n.f.*, (astron.) Juno.

junte, *n.f.*, junta (Spanish council).

jupe, *n.f.*, petticoat ; skirt, kilt (of a gown). — *trotteur;* walking skirt.

jupiter (-tèr), *n.m.*, (astron.) Jupiter.

jupon, *n.m.*, short petticoat. — *de dessus;* upper-skirt. — *de dessous;* under-petticoat.

jurande, *n.f.*, wardenship (of a company) ; wardens.

jurassique, *adj.*. (geol.) Jurassic.

juratoire, *adj.*, by oath.

juré, -e, *adj.*, sworn.

juré, *n.m.*, juror, juryman ; member of a board of examination. *Récuser un* —; to chal-lenge a juror. *Messieurs les* —*s ;* gentlemen of the jury.

jurement (jur-mān), *n.m.*, oath ; swearing. *Proférer un* —; to utter an oath.

jurer, *v.a.*, to swear, to swear by, to vow ; to take an oath of ; to blaspheme ; to protest, to vow, to promise.

se **jurer,** *v.r.*, to swear to one another. *Nous nous jurâmes une éternelle amitié;* we swore eternal friendship to each other.

jurer, *v.n.*, to swear, to blaspheme ; to con-trast; to jar ; to clash ; not to match (of colors); to squeak *or* screech (of musical instruments) ; to jar, to clash (of sound). *Il ne faut* — *de rien;* we must pin our faith to nothing ; we never can tell. *Il jure comme un charretier,* or *grenadier,* or *païen,* or *crocheteur;* he swears like a trooper.

jureur, *n.m.*, swearer.

juridiction, *n.f.*, jurisdiction ; tribunal ; de-partment, province. *Ce n'est pas de sa* —; it is not in his province.

juridictionnel, -le, *adj.*, jurisdictional.

juridique, *adj.*, legal, juridical, judicial.

juridiquement (-dik-mān), *adv.*, juridically, judicially.

jurisconsulte, *n.m.*, jurisconsult, lawyer.

jurisprudence, *n.f.*, jurisprudence.

juriste, *n.m.*, jurist.

juron, *n.m.*, oath. *Gros* —; tremendous oath. *Lâcher un* —; to rap out an oath.

jury, *n.m.*, jury ; board of examiners, commit-tee. — *mi-parti étranger;* party-jury. *Banc du* —; jury-box. *Chef du* —; foreman of the jury. *Former un tableau, une liste, du* —; to impanel a jury. *Juger par le* —; to try by jury. *Récuser un* —; to challenge a jury. — *de jugement;* petty jury. — *d'accusation;* grand jury.

jus, *n.m.*, juice ; gravy ; liquor. *Plein de* —; juicy.

jusant, *n.m.*, (nav.) ebb, ebb-tide.

jusée, *n.f.*, tan-liquor, tanning infusion.

jusque, jusques (in poet. and st. e.), *prep.*, to, even, as far as, till, until ; down to ; up to ; the very. *Depuis Paris jusqu'à Londres;* from Paris to London. *Jusqu'au ciel;* to the skies. *Depuis le premier jusqu'au dernier;* from the first to the last. *Jusqu'à demain;* till to-morrow. *Jusqu'à quand?* or *Jusques à quand?* how long ? till when ? *Jusqu'à présent;* till now. *Jusqu'ou?* how far ? *Jusqu'ici;* as far as here; till now ; down to here. —*là;* up to that time; up to that point; as far as there. *Jusqu'à ce que;* until. *Jusqu'à ce que cela soit fait;* till it be done. *Il a vendu jusqu'à sa chemise;* he has sold the very shirt off his back. *Il n'est pas jusqu'aux enfants qui ne l'adorent;* the very children adore him.

jusquiame, *n.f.*, henbane.

jussion, *n.f.*, royal command, order.

⊙**justaucorps** (-kor), *n.m.*, jerkin, jacket, vest.

juste, *adj.*, just, equitable, legitimate, lawful, appropriate ; apposite ; right ; upright, right-eous ; true, apt, fit, proper, exact ; tight. — *Dieu !* — *ciel !* good God ! just heaven ! *Un homme* —; a righteous man. *Vos souliers sont trop* —*s;* your shoes are too tight. *Ma montre est* —; my watch is right. *Au plus* — *prix;* at the lowest figure.

juste, *n.m.*, upright man, virtuous man ; what is just. *La science du* —; the knowledge of what is just.

juste, *adv.*, just, exactly, accurately, pre-cisely ; (mus.) true. *Chanter* —; to sing true, in time, in tune. *Il raisonne* —; he reasons closely. *Au* —; exactly, precisely, just. *Comme de* —; rightly enough, of course, naturally. *Tout* —; only just enough.

justement, *adv.*, justly, honestly, precisely, exactly, reasonably.

justesse, *n.f.*, justness, accuracy, exactness; appropriateness, precision, propriety, sense. *Avec* —; with precision ; accurately, appropri-ately.

justice, *n.f.*, justice; righteousness ; probity, integrity ; jurisdiction; fairness; impartiality, reason ; courts of justice; execution; gibbet, gallows. *Faire* — *à;* to do justice to. *Rendre* — *à;* to do justice to. *Rendre la* —; to admin-ister justice. *Se faire* — *à soi-même;* to take the law into one's own hands. *Cour de* —; court of law, of judicature. *Appeler, citer, traduire, poursuivre quelqu'un en* —; to sue at law, to proceed against. *Déni de* —; refusal of justice. *La* — *de paix;* court of the justice of the peace. *Que* — *soit faite;* let execution be done. *Faire* — *de;* to punish, to expose, to be avenged on; to refute, *or* confute; to do away with; to sweep away. *Se faire rendre* —; to obtain justice.

justiciable, *n.m.f.* and *adj.*, person amenable to a tribunal; amenable. *Devenir le* — *de;* to come under the jurisdiction of.

justicier, *v.a.*, to punish corporally ; to exe-cute ; to lash.

justicier, *n.m.*, justiciary ; judge; lover of justice.

justifiable, *adj.*, justifiable ; warrantable.

justifiant, -e, *adj.*, justifying.

justifiablement, *adv.*, warrantably, justifi-ably.

justificati-f, -ve, *adj.*, justificative, documen-tary. *Pièce* —*ve;* proof, voucher, documentary evidence.

justification, *n.f.*, justification, vindication, proof ; (print.) justification, length of line.

justifier, *v.a.*, to justify, to vindicate, to prove, to make good ; (print.) to justify; to clear.

se **justifier,** *v.r.*, to justify, to clear, to vindi-cate, one's self.

justifier, *v.n.*, (print.) to justify.
jute, *n.m.*, jute.
juteu-x, -se, *adj.*, juicy.
juvénile, *adj.*, juvenile, youthful.
juvénilement (-nil-mān), *adv.*, boyishly, childishly, in a juvenile manner.
juvénilité, *n.f.*, youth, youthfulness.
juxtaposer, *v.a.*, to place side by side.
se **juxtaposer**, *v.r.*, to be in juxtaposition.
juxtaposition (juks-ta), *n.f.*, juxtaposition.

K

k, *n.m.*, the eleventh letter of the alphabet, k.
kabak, *n.m.*, public-house (in Russia).
kahouanne, *n.f.*, loggerhead turtle.
kaïmac, *n.m.*, (—*s*) sherbet.
kaiserlick, *n.m.*, imperial, Austrian.
kakatoès, *n.m.*, (orni.) cockatoo. *V.* **cacatois**.
kaléidoscope, *n.m.*, kaleidoscope.
⊙**kalendes**, *n.f.pl. V.* **calendes**, kalends.
kali, *n.m.*, (bot.) kali.
kamichi (-shi), *n.m.*, (orni.) horned-screamer.
kan, *n.m.*, khan.
kandjar *or* **kangiar**, *n.m.*, (—*s*) dagger.
kanguroo *or* **kangourou** (-goo-roo), *n.m.*, (mam.) kangaroo.
kantisme, *n.m.*, Kantism.
kantiste, *n.m.*, Kantist.
kaolin, *n.m.*, porcelain clay ; china-clay.
karabé, *n.m. V.* **carabé**.
karat, *n.m. V.* **carat**.
karata, *n.m.*, (bot.) a variety of aloe.
kari, *n.m.*, a kind of spice.
katakoua, *n.m. V.* **kakatoès**.
keepsake, *n.m.*, keepsake.
képi, *n.m.*, military cap ; cap.
kermès (-mès), *n.m.*, (ent.) kermes ; (chem.) kermes-mineral.
kermesse, *n.f.*, a country fair (in the Netherlands).
kérosène, *n.m.*, kerosene.
ketch, *n.m.*, (nav.) ketch, lugger.
khédive, *n.m.*, (—*s*) Khedive, viceroy of Egypt.
kilo, *n.m.*, (ab. of *kilogramme*) kilo.
kilogramme, *n.m.*, kilogram (2·2055 lbs. avoirdupois).
kilolitre, *n.m.*, kilolitre (220·09668 gallons).
kilomètre, *n.m.*, kilometer (1093·6389 yards).
kilométrique, *adj.*, kilometric.
kilostère, *n.m.*, kilostere (1000 stères).
king, *n.m.*, king (sacred book of the Chinese).
kinine, *n.f. V.* **quinine**.
kino, *n.m.*, (pharm.) kino.
kiosque, *n.m.*, kiosk, news-stall.
kirsch-wasser, *n.m.*, kirschwasser.
klephte, *n.m. V.* **clephte**.
knout (knoot), *n.m.*, knout.
knouter, *v.a.*, to knout.
kola, *n.m.*, kola (bean).
kolao, *n.m.*, high mandarin (in China).
kopeck, *n.m.*, (—*s*) kopeck (Russian coin worth about half a penny).
koran, *n.m.*, Koran. *V.* **coran**.
kouan, *n.m.*, (bot.) cochineal, cochineal-fig.
kremlin (krèm-lin), *n.m.*, Kremlin (the palace of the czars at Moscow).
kreutzer (-zèr), *n.m.*, kreutzer (German coin).
kurtchis, *n.m.pl.*, a Persian cavalry corps.
kymrique, *adj. V.* **cymrique**.
kynancie, *n.f.*, (med.) *V.* **cynancie**.
kyrielle, *n.f.*, litany ; (fig.) string (long list of words); long tedious story.
kyste, *n.m.*, (med.) cyst, cystis.
kystique, *adj.*, (med.) cystic.
kystotome, *n.m.*, (surg.) *V.* **cystotome**.
kystotomie, *n.f.*, (surg.). *V.* **cystotomie**.

L

l, *n.m.f.*, the twelfth letter of the alphabet, l.
l', *art.*, (contraction of *le* and *la*) the. *V.* **le**.
l', *pron.*, (contraction of *le* and *la*) him, her, it.
la, *art.f.*, the. *V.* **le**.
la, *pron.*, her, it. *V.* **le**.
là, *adv.*, there, thither, then (of time). —*bas ;* down there. —*haut ;* above, up there. *Çà et* — ; here and there, up and down, all about. —*dessus ;* on there ; upon that ; thereupon. *Mettez le livre* —*dessus ;* put the book on there. —*dessus, il me dit ;* upon that, *or* thereupon, he said to me. —*dessous ;* under there. — *dedans ;* within. *De* — ; thence, from thence ; from that time, from that cause. *Il n'est pas* — ; he is not there, he is away. *Par* — ; that way. *Jusque—;* till then, till that time ; as far as there. *Ce n'est pas* — *que je vise ;* that is not the thing I am aiming at. *Celui-là, celle-là ;* that. *Ceux-là, celles-là ;* those. — *même ;* in that very place. *D'ici* — ; by that time, in the interval. *C'est* — ; it is *or* was there ; there is, such is ; that's the place. *Ce sont* — ; such are, those are. — *où ;* where, there where.
là là, *int.*, now then ! there ! there now !
là là, *adv.*, so so, indifferently.
la, *n.m.*, (mus.) la ; A. *Prendre le* — ; to tune one's instrument.
labarum (-rom), *n.m.*, labarum (standard).
labbe, *n.f.*, (orni.) skua gull.
labeur, *n.m.*, labor, work, toil ; (print.) book-work. *Terres en* — ; lands under cultivation.
labial, -e, *adj.*, labial. *Offres* —*es ;* (jur.) offer to pay without showing the money.
labiale, *n.f.*, (gram.) labial.
labié, -e, *adj.*, (bot.) labiate, labiated.
labiée, *n.f.*, labiate plant.
labile, *adj.*, labile, bad; slippery, failing; (bot.) deciduous. *Mémoire* — ; failing memory.
laboratoire, *n.m.*, laboratory.
laborieusement (-eûz-mān), *adv.*, laboriously, painfully.
laborieu-x, -se, *adj.*, laborious, industrious, hard-working, assiduous, toilsome, painful.
labour, *n. m.*, plowing, tillage, dressing. *Terres de* — ; plowed lands. *Donner un* — *à une terre ;* to till, to dress, a piece of ground. *Donner un* — *à une vigne ;* to dress a vine. *Bœufs de* — ; yoke-oxen. *Mettre en* — ; to plow.
labourable, *adj.*, arable.
labourage, *n.m.*, tillage, husbandry; plowing, tilling.
labourer, *v.a.*, to plow, to till ; to dig, to turn up ; to rip up ; to rip open ; to toil through.
labourer, *v.n.*, to plow, to till ; to drudge ; to toil and moil ; (nav.) to come home, to drag (of anchors); (of ships) to graze the bottom ; (of horses) to stumble.
laboureur, *n. m.*, husbandman, plowman, tiller.
labre, *n.m.*, rock-fish.
labyrinthe, *n.m.*, labyrinth, maze.
labyrinthique, *adj.*, labyrinthic.
lac, *n.m.*, lake ; (of rupees) lac.
laçage, lacement, *n.m.*, lacing.
lacé, *n.m.*, braid, beading.
lacer, *v.a.*, to lace ; (nav.) to attach; to line (of dogs).
se **lacer**, *v.r.*, to lace one's self.
lacérable, *adj.*, lacerable, tearable.
lacération, *n.f.*, laceration.
lacéré, -e, *part.*, (bot.) lacerate, lacerated.
lacérer, *v.a.*, to lacerate, to tear ; (jur.) to tear up, to destroy.
laceret, *n.m.*, small auger.
lacerne, *n.f.*, (antiq.) lacerna, a kind of cloak worn by the Romans.
laceron, *n.m.*, (bot.) sow-thistle. *V.* **laiteron**.

lacet, *n.m.*, lace ; springe ; braid ; bow-string (to strangle) ; zigzags, windings, turnings of mountain-roads. *pl.*, toils. *Ferrer un* — ; to tag a lace. *Mouvement de* — ; (rail.) oscillation.

lâche, *adj.*, loose, slack, lax ; slothful, sluggish ; faint-hearted ; mean-spirited, dastardly ; cowardly, base, mean, shameful. *Ce nœud est trop* — ; this knot is too loose.

lâche, *n.m.*, coward, craven, dastard.

lâché, -e, *part.*, slackened, loose, loosened.

lâchement (lâsh-mān), *adv.*, sluggishly, slothfully ; loosely, slackly ; dastardly, cowardly, basely.

lâcher, *v.a.*, to slacken, to relax, to loose, to make loose, to loosen ; to let go, to let slip, to cast off, to throw off ; to let out, to unbind ; to let loose, to release ; to utter, to blurt out ; to fire, to discharge ; to turn on. — *la bride à un cheval ;* to loosen the reins of a horse. — *pied,* — *le pied ;* to retreat, to turn tail ; to waver, to be irresolute. — *sa proie ;* to let go one's prey. — *un prisonnier ;* to release a prisoner. — *prise ;* to let go one's hold. — *une arme à feu ;* to fire off a gun. — *un soufflet à quelqu'un ;* to give any one a box on the ear. — *une parole,* — *un mot ;* to let out a word. — *le mot, la parole ;* to speak the word. — *une bordée ;* (nav.) to fire a broad-side.

se lâcher, *v.r.*, to slacken, to grow loose ; to become loose, to slip ; to go off ; to let one's tongue run riot, to let out. *Se* — *d'un cran ;* to give the slip.

lâcher, *v.n.*, to slacken, to grow slack, to become slack, to grow loose, to become loose ; to slip, to go off. *Si le fusil vient à* — ; if the gun happens to go off.

lâcheté (lâsh-té), *n.f.*, cowardice, dastardliness, baseness ; base action ; meanness, act of cowardice.

lâcheur, *n.m.*, raftsman, wood-floater ; (fig.) shabby, mean, cowardly fellow.

lacinié, -e, *adj.*, (bot.) laciniate, laciniated, jagged.

laciniure, *n.f.*, (bot.) jag.

lacis, *n.m.*, net-work ; (anat.) plexus.

lack, *n.m.*, (—*s*) lac, lack. *Un* — *de roupies ;* a lac of rupees (i.e., 100,000).

laconique, *adj.*, laconic, laconical.

laconiquement (-nik-mān), *adv.*, laconically ; briefly, concisely.

laconisme, *n.m.*, laconism, laconicism.

lacrymal, -e, *adj.*, lachrymal. *Sac* — ; (anat.) lachrymal bag.

lacrymatoire, *n.m.*, (Roman antiq.) lachrymatory.

lacrymatoire, *adj.*, (Roman antiq.) lachrymary.

lacs (lâ), *n.m.*, string, rope, tape, bow-string ; gin, springe ; (fig.) noose, toils. — *d'amour ;* love-knot.

lactate, *n.m.*, (chem.) lactate.

lactation, *n.f.*, lactation.

lacté, -e, *adj.*, lacteal, milky, lacteous. *La voie* — *e ;* (astron.) the Milky-Way.

lactescence, *n.f.*, lactescence.

lactescent, -e, *adj.*, (bot.) lactescent.

lactifère, *adj.*, lactiferous.

lactique, *adj.*, (chem.) lactic.

lactomètre, *n.m.*, lactometer. *V.* **galactomètre.**

lactucarium, *n.m.*, (pharm.) lettuce-opium.

lacune, *n.f.*, gap, deficiency, break, omission, hiatu ᵉ ; interruption, blank ; desideratum ; (bot.) air-cell, lacuna.

lacustre, *adj.*, lacustral, lacustrine.

ladanum, *n.m.*, (*n.p.*) ladanum, gum-resin.

ladite, *adj.f.*, the same, the said.

ladre, *adj.*, leprous ; measly (of pigs) ; insensible, unfeeling ; mean, sordid, stingy, scurvy, scaly ; niggardly ; churlish. *Lièvre* — ; fen-hare.

ladre, *n.m.*, **-sse**, *n.f.*, leper ; sordid person ; scurvy person, shabby person, niggard, curmudgeon. *Maison de* — *s ;* lazar-house. *Un vrai* — ; a regular curmudgeon. — *vert ;* sordid fellow, stingy churl.

ladrerie, *n.f.*, leprosy ; measles ; sordid avarice, stinginess, sordidness, scurviness, scaliness ; lazar-house.

lady (lè-di), *n.f.*, (*English*) lady.

lagon, *n.f.*, lagoon.

lagope, *n.m.*, (bot.) hare-foot.

lagopède, *n.m.*, (orni.) ptarmigan.

lagostome, *n.m.*, (anat.) hare-lip.

lagune, *n.f.*, lagune, lagoon.

lai, -e, *adj.*, lay.

lai, *n.m.*, layman ; lay (small poem) ; lay, complaint, lament.

laïc. *V.* **laïque**.

laiche, *n.f.*, (bot.) sedge.

laid, -e, *adj.*, ugly, ill-favored, ill-looking ; plain ; unseemly, unhandsome, unbecoming. — *comme le péché ;* as ugly as sin. *Ce que vous dites là est bien* — ; what you say is very unseemly or improper.

laid, *n.m.*, (the) ugly ; ugly part, ugliness ; ugly side ; naughty boy.

laide, *n.f.*, plain girl ; naughty girl.

laidement, *adv.*, uglily.

laideron (lè-dron), *n.f.*, ugly girl, ugly woman ; ugly creature.

laideur, *n.f.*, ugliness, uncomeliness ; plainness ; deformity ; unseemliness.

laie, *n.f.*, wild sow ; path (in a forest) ; (mech.) stone-cutter's hammer.

lainage, *n.m.*, woolen stuff, woolen goods ; fleece ; teasling.

laine, *n.f.*, wool ; worsted. — *à broder ;* Berlin wool. — *d'agneau ;* lamb's-wool. *Flocon de* — ; flock of wool. *Bêtes à* — ; wool-bearing animals. *Se laisser manger la* — *sur le dos ;* to let one's self be fleeced ; to put up with everything. *De* — ; woolen. *Manger la* — *sur le dos à quelqu'un ;* to fleece, to cheat, any one.

lainer, *v.a.*, to tease, to teasel (wool).

lainerie (lè-n-rî), *n.f.*, woolen goods ; woolens ; place for shearing sheep ; woolen-trade ; wool-market ; teaseling-shop.

laineu-r, *n.m.*, **-se**, *n.f.*, teaseler. *f.,* gig (machine for teaseling wool).

laineu-x, -se, *adj.*, woolly, fleecy ; (bot.) downy, woolly ; lanate, lanated.

laini-er, -ère, *adj.*, of wool, woolen.

lainier, *n.m.*, wool-stapler ; wool-comber, wool-sorter.

laïque, *n.m.* and *adj.*, layman ; lay, laic, laical. *Les* —*s ;* the laity.

lais, *n.m.*, standard-tree ; standard ; alluvion ; accretion.

laisse, *n.f.*, string ; leash ; slip ; (hawking) lune. — *de lévriers ;* leash of greyhounds. *Mener quelqu'un en* — ; to hold any one in leading-strings, to lead any one by the nose. *En* — ; in leash, leashed.

laissées, *n.f.pl.*, dung (of bears, wild boars).

laisser, *v.a.*, to leave, to quit, to desert, to abandon ; to part with ; to leave ; to bequeath ; to suffer, to permit, to let, to allow ; to let alone ; to omit ; to leave off ; to leave out ; to give up. — *tout à l'abandon ;* to leave everything in disorder. — *tout aller ;* to neglect everything. — *tout traîner ;* to let everything lie about in disorder, to keep nothing in its proper place. — *la vie à quelqu'un ;* to spare any one's life. — *quelqu'un en paix, en repos ;* to let any one alone, to let any one be. — *là quelqu'un ;* to leave any one in the lurch, to give up any one. — *là quelque chose ;* to leave off, to discontinue, to give up, any thing. — *quelqu'un pour ce qu'il est ;* to take no notice of, not to mind, a person. *Il y a à prendre et à* — *dans ces choses ;* you must pick and choose among all these things. *Avoir le prendre ou le* —; to have the choice. *A prendre ou à laisser ;* to be taken or left alone; take it or leave it. — *une chose à un certain prix ;* to dispose of a thing for a certain price. *On n'a qu'à le* — *faire ;* he only needs being let alone. *Laissez donc!* stuff, nonsense! *Laissez-moi donc tranquille!* do leave me alone! stuff and nonsense! *Laissez-moi faire ;* leave it *or* him *or* her to me. — *aller ;* to let go. — *sortir ;* to let out. *Cela ne laisse pas que d'être vrai ;* it is true, nevertheless. — *à desirer ;* room for improvement.

se **laisser**, *v.r.*, to allow one's self, to suffer one's self. *Se* — *conduire ;* to let one's self be led. *Se* — *aller à ses passions ;* to give one's self up to one's passions. *Se* — *tomber ;* to let one's self fall. *Se* — *mourir ;* to die. *Se* — *aller à la tentation ;* to give one's self up to temptation. *Se* — *aller à la douleur ;* to abandon one's self to grief. *Se* — *lire ;* to be readable, pleasant to read. *Se* — *manger, se* — *boire ;* to be palatable. *Se* — *faire ;* to offer no resistance. *Se* — *dire ;* to allow one's self to be told. *Se* — *prendre ;* to allow one's self to be taken *or* to allow something to be taken from one.

laisser-aller, *n.m.*, (*n.p.*) ease, freedom, unrestraint, negligence; indulgence, indolence; unconstraint.

laisser-courre, *n.m.*, (*n.p.*) (hunt.) starting-place (where the dogs are loosed).

laisser-faire, laissez faire, *n.m.*, non-intervention, non-interference.

laissez-passer, laisser-passer, *n.m.*, (—) permit, leave, permission, permit for transit.

lait, *n.m.*, milk, milk-duct; white, glair (of eggs). *Fièvre de* —; milk-fever. *Frère de* —; foster-brother. *Sœur de* —; foster-sister. *Cochon de* —; sucking-pig. *Petit* —, (*n.p.*), — *clair ;* whey. — *coupé ;* milk and water. — *de beurre ;* butter-milk. — *de poule ;* mulled egg, egg-flip. — *écrémé ;* skim-milk. *Gros* —; curd. *Etre au* —; to be made with milk ; to be restricted to milk diet. *Vache à* —; dairy-cow, milch cow. *Bouillir du* — *à quelqu'un ;* to please, to pamper, any one. — *de chaux ;* whitewash. *Riz au* —; rice milk.

laitage, *n.m.*, milk food. *Régime de* —; milk diet.

laitance *or* **laite**, *n.f.*, (ich.) milt, melt, soft roe; lime-wash, whitewash.

laité, -e, *adj.*, soft-roed.

laitée, *n.f.*, litter (of a bitch). *V.* **portée**.

laiterie (lè-trî), *n.f.*, dairy ; dairy-room ; dairy-farm, milk-farm.

laiteron (lè-tron), *n.m.*, (bot.) sow-thistle ; hare's-lettuce.

laiteu-x, -se, *adj.*, lacteous, milky.

laitier (-tié), *n.m.*, (metal.) dross; slag, clinkers. — *des volcans ;* fragments of lava.

laitier (-tié), *n.m.*, milkman.

laitière, *n.f.*, milkwoman, milkmaid, dairymaid ; milch cow ; woman with a great deal of milk. *Cette vache est une bonne* — ; this cow gives a great deal of milk.

laitière, *adj.*, milch, yielding milk (of cows). *Vache* —; milch cow.

laiton, *n.m.*, latten, brass. *Fil de* —; brass wire.

laitue, *n.f.*, (bot.) lettuce. — *pommée ;* cabbage-lettuce. — *romaine ;* cos-lettuce. — *de mer ;* oyster-green.

laize, *n.f.*, width (of cloth, etc.).

lakiste, *n.m.*, *adj.*, lakist, lake-poet. —*s ;* lakists, lake school.

là là, *adv.* *V.* **là**.

là là ! *int.* *V.* **là**.

lama, *n.m.*, Lama (of the Tartars).

lama *or* **llama**, *n.m.*, (mam.) lama (goat).

lamanage, *n.m.*, harbor-pilotage.

lamaneur, *n.m.*, harbor-pilot.

lamantin, *n.m.* (zool.) *V.* **lamentin**.

lambdoïde, *adj.*, (anat.) lambdoidal.

lambeau, *n.m.*, rag, tatter ; shred, strip, fragment, scrap ; remains (of flesh) ; bit. *Mettre en* —*s ;* to tear into rags.

lambel, *n.m.*, (her.) label.

lambin, -e, *n.* and *adj.*, loiterer, dawdler; slowcoach, slow, dawdling.

lambiner, *v.n.*, to linger, to loiter, to dawdle, to trifle, to dilly-dally.

lambourde, *n.f.*, (carp.) joist; (mas.) soft stone.

lambourder, *v.a.*, to joist.

lambrequins, *n.m.pl.*, (her.) mantling; (arch.) scallop ; valance, hanging fringe.

lambris, *n.m.*, paneling ; wainscot ; ceiling ; dado, canopy ; (poet. st. e.) mansion, palace; sumptuous decoration of a mansion. — *feint ;* imitation paneling.

lambrissage, *n.m.*, wainscoting, paneling.

lambrisser, *v.a.*, to panel; to wainscot.

lambruche *or* **lambrusque**, *n.f.*, (bot.) wild vine, fox grape.

lame, *n.f.*, plate, sheet (metal.) ; (anat.) lamina; blade ; sword, swordsman ; (nav.) billow, surge, wave ; (pers.) hussy, jade, blade ; (bot.) gill ; wire (of gold, of silver). *Fine* —; sly hussy (of a woman). *Entre deux* —*s ;* in the trough of the sea. *Emporté par une* —; washed away. — *de fond ;* ground-swell. *La* — *use le fourreau ;* the steel wears away the scabbard ; the mind wears out the body. *Bonne* —; good swordsman.

lamé, -e, *adj.*, laminated.

lamelle, *n.f.*, lamella.

lamellé, -e, *adj.* *V.* **lamelleux**.

lamelleu-x, -se (la-mèl-leû), *adj.*, lamellated, lamellar ; scaly.

lamentable, *adj.*, lamentable, woeful ; mournful, rueful, sad, distressing.

lamentablement, *adv.*, lamentably, mournfully, woefully, ruefully.

lamentation, *n.f.*, lamentation, bewailing, wailing ; lament, whining.

lamenter, *v.a.*, to lament, to bewail, to bemoan, to mourn, to mourn over.

se **lamenter**, *v.r.*, to lament, to mourn, to moan, to bewail, to whine.

lamenter, *v.n.*, (l.u.) to lament.

lamentin, *n.m.*, lamantin, sea-cow, sea-maid, mermaid, manatee.

lamie, *n.f.*, (antiq., ent.) lamia; (ich.) white shark.

lamier, *n.m.*, foil-maker; (bot.) dead-nettle ; archangel.

laminage, *n.m.*, (metal.) flattening (of gold) ; rolling.

laminer, *v.a.*, (metal.) to flatten (of gold) ; to roll.

laminerie, *n.f.*, (metal.) rolling - mills. *V.* **laminoir**.

lamineur, *n.m.*, (metal.) flattener, roller.

lamineu-x, -se, *adj.* *V.* **cellulaire**.

laminoir, *n.m.*, (metal.) flattening-mill, rolling-mill.

lampadaire, *n.m.*, lamp-post, sconce; (antiq.) torch-bearer.

lampadiste, *n.m.*, (antiq.) lampadist.

lampadophore, *n.m.*, (antiq.) torch-bearer.

lampas (-pâss), *n.m.*, (vet.) lampas (horse disease); silk damask, figured silk. *S'humecter le* —; to wet one's whistle (pop.).

lampassé, -e, *adj.*, (her.) langued.

lampe, *n.f.*, lamp, light. — *d'Argand ;* Argand lamp. — *d'argent ;* silver lamp. — *de sûreté, — de Davy ;* safety-lamp. — *à esprit de vin ;* spirit-lamp. *Dessous de* —; lamp-stand. *Arranger une* — ; to trim a lamp. *Sentir la* — ; to smell of the lamp, of the midnight oil. *Culs de* —*s ;* (print.) tail-pieces.

lampée, *n.f.*, (pop.) tumblerful, bumper.

lamper, *v.a.* and *n.*, (pop.) to toss off (drink); (of the sea) to phosphoresce, to be phosphorescent.

lamperon (lanp-ron), *n.m.*, wick-holder.

lampette, *n.f.*, (bot.) corn-cockle.

lampion, *n.m.*, grease-pot, illumination-lamp; church-lamp; (pop.) three-cornered hat, cocked hat.

lampiste, *n.m.*, lamp-maker; lamp-lighter.

lampisterie, *n.f.*, lamp-room.

***lamprillon**, *n.m.* V. **lamproyon**.

lamproie, *n.f.*, lamprey.

lamproyon, *n.m.*, young lamprey.

lampsane, *n.f.*, (bot.) nipple-wort.

lampyre, *n.m.*, lampyris, glow-worm.

lançage *or* **lancement**, *n.m.*, darting, throwing; (nav.) launch, launching.

lance, *n.f.*, lance, spear; staff; flagstaff; nozzle (of a fire-hose). *Rompre une — pour quelqu'un ;* to take up the cudgels for any one. *Baisser la — ;* to strike one's flag, to give in.

lancéolaire, *adj.*, (bot.) lanceolate, lanceolated, lance-shaped (of leaves).

lancéolé, -e, *adj.*, (bot.) lanceolate.

lancer, *v.a.*, to dart, to fling, to hurl, to throw, to cast, to launch; to shoot, to shoot forth; to issue (a warrant). *— un javelot ;* to dart a javelin. *— une pierre ;* to fling a stone. *— un regard de colère ;* to dart an angry look. *— des regards ;* to cast looks. *— une flèche ;* to shoot an arrow. *— un cheval ;* to push on a horse. *— un vaisseau ;* to launch a ship. *— un arrêt ;* to issue a warrant or fiat.

se lancer, *v.r.*, to dart, to spring; to rush, to make a rush; to launch; to start; to fly; (fig.) to make a start. *Se — dans les affaires ;* to launch out (into business).

lancer, *v.n.*, (of a ship) to yaw, to sheer.

lancette, *n.f.*, (surg.) lancet. *Donner un coup de — ;* to lance.

lanceur, *n.m.*, pushing fellow. *— d'affaires ;* company promoter, speculator.

lanceuse, *n.f.*, procuress, go-between.

lancier, *n. m.*, (milit.) lancer.

lancière, *n.f.*, waste-gate (of a mill-dam).

lancinant, -e, *adj.*, shooting (of pain).

lançoir, *n.m.*, mill-gate (of water-mills).

landamman, *n.m.*, landamman (Swiss magistrate).

landau, *n.m.*, (*landaus*), landau.

lande, *n.f.*, waste land, moor, heath, common.

landgrave, *n.m.*, landgrave.

landgraviat, *n.m.*, landgraviate.

landgravine, *n.f.*, landgravine.

landier, *n.m.*, kitchen fire-dog, andiron.

landière, *n.f.*, booth, stall (erected on commons).

landwehr, *n.f.*, (*—s*) landwehr.

laneret (la-n-rè), *n.m.*, (orni.) lanneret, shrike.

langage, *n.m.*, language, tongue, speech, diction; talk, words, style, expression. *Changer de — ;* to change one's tone. *Ils tiennent tous le même — ;* they all say the same thing.

lange, *n.m.*, swaddling-cloth. *pl.*, swaddling-clothes, swaddling bands.

langoureusement (-reûz-mān), *adv.*, languishingly.

langoureu-x, -se, *adj.*, pining, languishing, melancholy. *n.m.*, languishing lover.

langouste, *n.f.*, spiny lobster, crawfish.

langue (lāng), *n.f.*, tongue; language; neck, tongue, strip (of land). *Une mauvaise — ;* a slanderous tongue. *C'est une mauvaise — ;* he, she, is a tale-bearer. *Tirer la — ;* to put out one's tongue; (fig.) to be in distress. *Avoir la — liée ;* to be tongue-tied. *Avoir la — bien pendue ;* to have the gift of the gab. *Avoir la — grasse ;* to speak thick. *Avoir la — trop longue ;* not to be able to hold one's tongue. *Avoir un mot sur le bout de la — ;* to have a word on the tip of one's tongue. *La — lui a fourché ;* his, her, tongue tripped. *Prendre — ;* to obtain intelligence of what is going on, to make inquiries. *Coup de — ;* backbiting, sarcasm. *Donner des coups de — à ;* to slander, to cast reflections on. *Jeter sa — aux chiens ;* to give up guessing. *Votre énigme est trop difficile, je jette ma — aux chiens ;* your riddle is too difficult, I give it up. *Beau parler n'écorche point la — ;* civility costs nothing. *— vivante ;* living language. *— morte ;* dead language. *— vulgaire ;* vulgar tongue. *Maître de —s ;* teacher of languages. *Quelle — !* what a tongue he, she has ! *Sa — va toujours ;* his or her tongue never stops. *Faire la — à quelqu'un ;* to give any one his cue.

langue-de-serpent, *n.f.*, (*—s— —*) (bot.) serpent's-tongue, adder's tongue; (geol.) serpent's-tongue, petrified fish teeth.

languette (-ghèt), *n.f.*, tongue, strip, valve; partition (thing shaped like a tongue); key (of musical instruments) ; index (of a balance).

langueur (-gheur), *n.f.*, languidness, languor, weakness, weariness. *pl.*, debility. *Maladie de — ;* lingering illness ; decline.

langueyer (-ghé-ié), *v.a.*, to examine the tongue of a hog. *— des valets ;* (fig.) to pump servants (so as to get at their masters' secrets).

langueyeur (-ghè-ieur), *n.m.*, examiner of hogs' tongues.

languier (-ghiè), *n.m.*, smoked hog's tongue.

languir (-ghir), *v.n.*, to languish, to linger, to pine, to pine away, to droop, to be sickly, to fade; to flag. *— de misère ;* to languish in misery. *— d'amour ;* to pine away for love. *La conversation languit ;* the conversation flags. *Ne nous faites pas — ;* don't keep us waiting ; or out with it.

languissamment (-ghi-sa-mān), *adv.*, languishingly, droopingly, lingeringly.

languissant, -e, *adj.*, languid, languishing, lingering, pining, drooping, sickly, fading ; (com.) dull.

lanice, *adj.*, of wool. *Bourre — ;* flock of wool.

lanier, *n.m.*, (orni.) lanner, lanneret, shrike.

lanière, *n.f.*, thong, lash.

lanifère, *adj.*, lanigerous, laniferous.

lanigère, *adj.* V. **lanifère**.

laniste, *n.m.*, (antiq.) lanista.

lansquenet (lans-kĕ-nè), *n.m.*, lansquenet (card game); German foot soldier.

lantanier, *n.m.*, (bot.) lantana.

lanter, *v.a.*, to emboss, to chase (copper ware).

lanterne, *n.f.*, lantern ; (arch.) lantern, lantern-tower, lantern-light ; spy-place ; (mec.) lantern-wheel; trundle ; assay-balance ; glass-case. *pl.*, fooleries ; idle stories, nonsense. *— sourde ;* dark-lantern. *— magique ;* magic-lantern. *Il veut faire croire que des vessies sont des —s ;* he would have one believe that the moon is made of green cheese. *Mettre à la — ;* to hang up at the lamp-post, to lynch (French revolution). *A la — !* to the lamp-post with him, her, them ! lynch him !

lanterner, *v.n.*, to dally, to trifle, to shuffle, to trifle away one's time ; to be irresolute.

lanterner, *v.a.*, to trifle with, to make a fool of ; to put off ; to bore.

lanternerie, *n.f.*, irresolution ; trifling ; dallying ; shuffling ; nonsense.

lanterni-er, -ère, *n.f.*, trifler, babbler ; (l.u.) lantern-maker, lamplighter.

lantiponnage, *n.m.*, nonsense, stuff, rigmarole, twaddle.

lantiponner, *v.a.n.*, to talk nonsense ; to talk stuff and nonsense to ; to bother any one.

lanturelu *or* **lanturlu**, *adv.*, stuff ! fudge ! fiddle-sticks ! *Il lui a répondu — ;* stuff and nonsense ! he said to him.

lanugineu-x, -se, *adj.*, lanuginous, downy.

lapement, *n.m.*, lapping.

laper, *v.a.n.*, to lap, to lick up.

lapereau (la-prô), *n.m.*, young rabbit.

lapidaire, *n.m.*, lapidary.

lapidation, *n.f.*, lapidation, stoning.

lapider, *v.a.*, to lapidate, to stone to death, to pelt with stones; (fig.) to tear to pieces.

lapidification, *n.f.*, lapidification.

lapidifier, *v.a.*, to lapidify.

se **lapidifier**, *v.r.*, to lapidify, to become lapidified.

lapidifique, *adj.*, lapidific.

lapin, *n.m.*, **-e**, *n.f.*, rabbit, buck-rabbit; doe-rabbit. *Monter en* —; to ride beside the driver, or on the box. — *de clapier;* tame rabbit. — *de garenne;* wild rabbit.

lapis *or* **lapis lazuli** (-pis), *n.m.*, (—) lapis lazuli.

lapon, *n.m.*, **-ne**, *n.f.*, Laplander.

laps (laps), *n.m.*, lapse (of time).

laps, -e, *adj.*, lapsed, fallen. — *et relaps;* fallen back into heresy.

lapsus, *n.m.*, slip (of the tongue). — *calami;* slip of the pen. — *linguæ;* slip of the tongue.

laquais (la-kê), *n.m.*, lackey, footman, flunkey.

laque, *n.f.*, lac, lake. *Gomme* —; gum-lac. — *en bâtons;* stick-lac. — *en grain;* seed-lac.

laque, *n.m.*, lacker. *Vernis* —; japan.

laquelle, *pron.f.*, which, who, that.

laquer, *v.a.*, to lacquer, to varnish, to japan.

laquet, *n.m.*, lakelet, little lake.

laqueu-x, -se, *adj.*, of the nature of lac; lake-colored.

larcin, *n.m.*, larceny; theft, pilfering; robbery; plagiarism. *Faire un* —; to commit a theft. *Faire un doux* —; to steal a kiss.

lard (lâr), *n.m.*, bacon, pork, pig's fat. *Flèche de* —; flitch of bacon. *Tranche de* —; rasher of bacon. *Il fait du* —; he grows fat (by sleeping).

larder, *v.a.*, to lard, to stick; to interlard; to run through, to pierce. — *un discours de citations;* to interlard a speech with quotations. — *de coups d'épée;* to run through with a sword. — *de la viande;* to lard meat.

lardoire, *n.f.*, larding-needle *or* pin.

lardon, *n.m.*, thin slice of bacon; joke, cut, jest, jibe.

lare (lâr), *n.m.*, (myth.) Lar, household god. *pl.*, (fig.) fireside, hearth.

large, *adj.*, broad, wide, large; great, grand; extensive, liberal, ample, generous, easy; lax, loose.

large, *n.m.*, breadth, width; (nav.) offing, open sea. *Porter au* —; (nav.) to bear off from the land. *Au* — *!* keep off! *Gagner le* —; *courir au* —; *prendre le* —; to stand out to sea, to put out to sea. *Pousser au* —; to put off, to push off; to sheer off. *Cette rue a soixante pieds de* —; this street is sixty feet wide. *Au* —; spaciously, abroad, comfortably, at one's ease, well off; (*int.*) keep off! *Etre au* —; to be abroad, to be at one's ease. *Etre logé au* —; to have a great deal of room. *Au long et au* —; in length and width, far and wide. *De long en* —; to and fro; backwards and forwards; up and down.

large, *adv.*, wide; grandly; largely. *Ce cheval va trop* —; that horse goes too wide.

largement, *adv.*, largely, abundantly, amply, fully, plentifully, grandly, liberally.

largesse, *n.f.*, largess, liberality, bounty, munificence, gratuity, fee. *Faire des* —*s;* to be liberal. *Pièces de* —; largess money; dole.

largeur, *n.f.*, breadth, width; wideness, broadness.

larghetto (-ghèt-tô), *adv.*, (mus.) larghetto.

largo, *adv.*, (mus.) largo.

largue (larg), *n.m.*, (l.u.) (nav.) offing, open sea.

largue, *adj.*, (nav.) slack, large; flowing. *Ecoutes* —*s;* (nav.) flowing sheets. *Vent* —; leading wind, side wind, wind on the quarter. *Porter or courir* —; (nav.) to sail large.

larguer (-ghé), *v.a.*, (nav.) to cast off; to let run (ropes); to let out (reefs).

larigot, *n.m.*, ⊙ flute, flageolet. *Boire à tire-* —; to drink hard.

larix (la-riks), *n.m.* V. **mélèze**.

larmaire, *adj.*, (bot.) tear-shaped.

larme, *n.f.*, tear; drop. *Pleurer à chaudes* —*s;* to shed bitter tears; to weep bitterly. *Verser des* —*s;* to shed tears. *Fondre en* —*s;* to melt into tears. *A chaudes* —*s;* bitterly. *Avoir le don des* —*s;* to have tears at command.

larmier, *n.m.*, (arch.) larmier, corona, dripstone; coping; eye-vein (of the horse).

larmières, *n.f.pl.*, *or* **larmiers**, *n.m.pl.*, tear-pit (of the stag).

larmoiement (-moa-mān), *n.m.*, watering of the eyes.

larmoyant, -e, *adj.*, weeping, in tears, lachrymose, whining, whimpering; (fig.) pathetic, tragic.

larmoyer, *v.n.*, to cry, to shed tears, to whine, to whimper; to water (of the eyes).

larmoyeu-r, *n.m.*, **-se**, *n.f.*, weeper, whimperer, whiner.

larron, *n.m.*, thief; (print.) bite; (book-bind.) leaf folded in and not cut. *S'entendre comme* —*s en foire;* to be as thick as thieves. *L'occasion fait le* —; opportunity makes the thief.

larronneau, *n.m.*, little thief; pilferer.

larronnesse, *n.f.*, a female thief.

larve, *n.f.*, (ent.) larva, grub, worm, caterpillar.

larves, *n.f.pl.*, (antiq.) ghosts, specters, hobgoblins.

laryngé, -e, *adj.*, laryngean.

laryngien, -ne (-in, -è-n), *adj.*, laryngean.

laryngite, *n.f.*, (med.) laryngitis.

laryngotomie, *n.f.*, (surg.) laryngotomy.

larynx (la-rinks), *n.m.*, (anat.) larynx.

las ! (lâ) *int.*, alas !

las, -se, *adj.*, tired, weary, fatigued. — *de travailler;* tired of working. *Un* — *d'aller;* a lazy fellow. *Faire quelque chose de guerre* —*se;* to do a thing for the sake of peace and quiet.

lascar, *n.m.*, lascar (East Indian sailor).

lasci-f, -ve, *adj.*, lascivious, lewd, lustful, wanton, lecherous.

lascivement (las-siv-mān), *adv.*, lasciviously, lewdly, wantonly, lecherously.

lasciveté (las-siv-tè), *n.f.*, lasciviousness, lewdness, lust, lustfulness.

laser (-zèr), *n.m.*, (bot.) laserwort.

lassant, -e, *adj.*, tiresome, wearisome, fatiguing, tedious.

lasser, *v.a.*, to tire, to weary, to fatigue, to wear out; to catch with a lasso; to lasso.

lasser, *v.n.*, to be tiring, wearying.

se **lasser**, *v.r.*, to tire, to grow tired, to be fatigued, to be wearied.

lassitude, *n.f.*, lassitude, weariness.

last *or* **laste**, *n.m.*, (com., nav.) last (two tons weight, 4,000 kil.).

lasting (-tingh), *n.m.*, lasting (stuff).

latanier, *n.m.*, fan-palm, latania.

latent, -e, *adj.*, latent, hid, concealed, secret.

latéral, -e, *adj.*, lateral, side.

latéralement (-ral-mān), *adv.*, laterally; sideways.

a **latere.** V. **légat**.

lathyrus, *n.m.*, (bot.) lathyrus.

laticlave, *n.m.*, (antiq.) laticlave.

latin, -e, *adj.*, Latin; (nav.) lateen. *Voile* —*e;* lateen sail. *La langue* —*e;* the Latin language.

latin, *n.m.*, Latin. *Il est au bout de son* —; he is at his wit's end. *Du* — *de cuisine;* dog Latin. *Y perdre son* —; not to be able to make it out.

latiniser, *v.a.*, to latinize.

latinisme, *n.m.*, latinism,

latiniste, n.m., latinist.

latinité, n.f., latinity. *La basse* —; low Latin.

latitude, n.f., latitude; extent; room, space, margin; (fig.) freedom of action; climate.

latitudinaire, adj., latitudinarian.

latomie, n.f., (antiq.) latomia.

latrie, n.f., latria.

latrine, n.f., privy, water-closet.

latte, n.f., lath.

latter, v.a., to lath.

lattis, n.m., lathing, lath-work.

laudanisé, -e, adj., containing laudanum.

laudanum, n.m., laudanum.

laudati-f, -ve, adj., laudatory.

laudes (lôd), n.f.pl., (c. rel.) lauds.

lauréat, adj., laureate. n.m., prizeman.

lauréole, n.f., (bot.) spurge-laurel.

laurier, n.m., laurel, bay-tree; (fig.) glory, honor. —*rose;* oleander, rose-bay. — *tin;* wild laurel. *Couronné de* —*s;* crowned with laurels, glory.

laurose, n.m., (bot.) oleander, rose-bay.

lavable, adj., washable.

lavabo (-bô), n.m., wash-stand.

lavage, n.m., washing; slops; wash; diluting, dilution. *En* —; diluted.

lavanche or **lavange**, n.f. V. **avalanche**.

lavande, n.f., (bot.) lavender. — *commune*, — *officinale;* common lavender.

lavanderie, n.f., (old) laundry, wash-house.

lavandier, n.m., yeoman of the laundry.

lavandière, n.f., (l.u.) laundress, washer-woman; (orni.) wagtail; (local) barge, boat.

lavanèse, n.f., (bot.) goat's-rue.

lavaret, n.m., (ich.) gwiniad, fresh-water herring.

lavasse, n.f., sudden shower of rain (l.u.); sloppy sauce; wash, wish-wash.

lave, n.f., lava.

lavé, e, part., washed, pale, faint. *Couleur* —*e;* (paint.) light color. *Cheval bai* —; light bay horse.

lavement (la-vmän), n.m., (c. rel.) washing; (med.) injection, clyster.

laver, v.a., to wash, to wash off, to cleanse; to wash up; to love, to bathe; to absolve, to declare innocent. — *la tête à quelqu'un;* to blow any one up; to rate any one soundly.

se **laver**, v.r., to wash, to wash one's self. *Se* — *les mains;* to wash one's hands. *Se* — *d'un crime;* to clear one's self of a crime. *Je m'en lave les mains;* I will have nothing to do with it, I wash my hands of the business.

lavette, n.f., dish-cloth, dish-clout.

laveu-r, n.m., **-se**, n.f., washer, scourer. —*se de vaisselle;* scullion, scullery-maid. — *de mines;* buddler. — *de cendres;* metal-refiner.

lavis, n.m., wash, coloring, tinting. *Dessin fait au* —; washed drawing; (engr.) aquatint.

lavoir, n.m., washing-place, wash-house; scullery; (metal.) buddle; rubbing-board.

lavure, n.f., dish-water, hogwash; (gold.) washing. *pl.*, goldsmith's sweepings. — *de vaisselle;* dish-water; (fig.) weak, tasteless broth.

laxati-f, -ve, adj., laxative, opening.

laxatif, n.m., (pharm.) laxative.

laxité, n.m., (med.) laxity, looseness.

layer, v.a., to cut a path through a forest.

layetier (-tié), n.m., box-maker, packing-case maker.

layette, n.f., (old) baby-linen; drawer, box.

layetterie (lè-iè-trî), n.f., box-trade; baby-linen trade.

layeur, n.m., forest-surveyor.

layou, n.m., tail-board (of a van); (hunt.) straight path.

lazaret, n.m., lazaretto, lazar-house.

lazariste, n.m., Lazarite, Lazarist (monk).

lazarone, n.m., (*lazaroni*) lazarone.

lazuli. V. **lapis**.

lazulite, n.m., (min.) lazulite, azure-stone.

lazzi, n.m., (—, or —*s*) piece of buffoonery, jest, joke, pun.

le, art.m., **la**, f., **les**, pl.m.f., the. *La nuit;* in the, during the night. *Le coquin!* what a scoundrel!

le, pron.m., **la**, f., **les**, pl.m.f., him, her, it, them; so. *Je les vois;* I see them. *Je le vois;* I see him, it. *Il l'aime;* he loves him, it. *Je l'aime;* I love her. *Donnez-le-moi;* give it me. *La voici;* here she is. *Je suis enrhumée, mes femmes le sont aussi;* I have got a cold, so have my maids.

lé, n.m., breadth (of linen); tow-path.

lèche, n.f., thin slice. — *cul;* toady, lick-spittle.

léché, -e, part., licked. *Tableau* —; (paint.) labored picture.

à **lèche-doigts**, adv., (l.u.) in small quantities, niggardly, meanly, sparingly, just enough to taste.

lèchefrite (lèsh-frit), n.f., dripping-pan.

lécher, v.a., to lick, to lick up; (paint.) to labor, to polish, to elaborate, to overdo.

se **lécher**, v.r., to lick one's self. *S'en* — *les doigts;* to lick one's chops over it.

lécheu-r, n.m., **-se**, n.f., gormandizer; sponger.

leçon, n.f., lesson; lecture; reading. *Vraie* —; true reading (of a text). —*s publiques;* public lectures. *Il a pris des* —*s d'un tel;* he took lessons from such a one. *Faire la* — *à quelqu'un;* to give any one his cue, to lecture any one, to coach up any one.

lect-eur, n.m., **-rice**, n.f., reader, (old) lecturer, professor. — *bénévole;* gentle reader.

lecture, n.f., reading; perusal. *Il a beaucoup de* —; he is well-read. *Savant par la* —; well-read. *Cabinet de* —; reading-room, circulating library; newsroom.

légal, -e, adj., legal, lawful, legitimate.

légalement (-gal-män), adv., legally, lawfully, legitimately.

légalisation, n.f., (jur.) legalization, authentication.

légaliser, v.a., (jur.) to authenticate, to legalize, to render legal.

légalité, n.f., legality, lawfulness.

légat, n.m., legate. — *à latere;* legate à latere.

légataire, n.m.f., (jur.) legatee. — *universel* or — *à titre universel;* sole or residuary legatee.

légation, n.f., legateship, legation.

légatoire, adj., legatory.

lège, adj., (nav.) light.

légendaire, n.m., legendary.

légende, n.f., legend; inscription, motto, story; legend (of medals).

lég-er, -ère, adj., light; buoyant, easy; fleet, fast; nimble, active; fickle, unsteady, light-headed; feeble, faint, frivolous, trifling, slight, inconsiderate, giddy, thoughtless. *A la* —; thoughtlessly, inconsiderately, carelessly. *Vin* —; light wine. *Etre* — *à la course;* to be fleet of foot. *Cavalerie* —*e;* light-horse. *Avoir la tête* —*e;* to be hare-brained, light-headed. *Une faute* —*e;* a small fault. *Etre vêtu à la* —*e;* to be lightly dressed.

légèrement (lé-jèr-män), adv., lightly, slightly; nimbly, swiftly, cursorily, thoughtlessly.

légèreté (lé-jèr-té), n.f., lightness, nimbleness, swiftness, fickleness, unsteadiness; instability; levity, frivolity, airiness, inconsiderateness, thoughtlessness; slight fault. *La* — *d'un cerf;* the fleetness of a stag.

légiférer, v.n., to legislate.

légion, n.f., legion. — *d'honneur;* Legion of Honor (a French order of knighthood, civil and military). — *de parents;* host of relations.

légionnaire, n.m. and adj., legionary; knight of the Legion of Honor.

législat-eur, -rice, adj. and n., legislating, law-giving, regulating; legislator; legislatrix; law-giver, law-maker.

législati-f, -ve, adj., legislative.

législation, n.f., legislation.

législature, n.f., legislature.

légiste, n.m., legist, civilian.

légitimaire, adj., (jur.) secured by law.

légitimation, n.f., legitimation; legalization; recognition.

légitime, adj., just, lawful, legitimate, rightful, justifiable. Part —; legal share. Enfant —; child born in wedlock.

légitime, n.f., (jur.) lawful portion of a child.

légitimement (-tim-mān), adv., legitimately, lawfully, justly, rightfully, fairly, justifiably.

légitimer, v.a., to legitimate; to justify; to legalize; to recognize. L'ivresse ne légitime aucune mauvaise action; drunkenness does not justify any bad action.

légitimiste, n.m.f., legitimist.

légitimité, n.f., legitimacy, lawfulness, rightfulness, fairness, justifiableness.

legs (lê), n.m., legacy, bequest, gift by will.

léguer (lé-ghé), v.a., to leave, to leave by will, to devise, to bequeath. Se —; to be bequeathed.

légume, n.m., vegetable, pot-herb; pulse; legume, legumen.

légumi-er, -ère, adj., of vegetables. n.m., vegetable-dish, vegetable-garden.

légumineuses, n.f.pl., (bot.) leguminous plants.

légumineu-x, -se, adj., leguminous.

légumineux, n.m.pl., vegetables.

lemme (lèm), n.m., (geom.) lemma.

lemne, n.f., (bot.) lemna, duckweed.

lémures, n.m.pl., (Roman antiq.) lemures.

lémuriens (-in), n.m.pl., (mam.) lemuridæ.

lémuries, n.f.pl., (Roman antiq.) lemuria.

lendemain (lān-dmin), n.m., morrow, next day, day after, following day. Le — de ses noces; the day after one's marriage. Penser au —; to think of the morrow.

lendore, n.m.f., dawdle, humdrum, dawdling person.

lénifier, v.a., (med.) to lenify.

léniti-f, -ve, adj., (med.) lenitive.

lénitif, n.m., (med.) lenitive, emollient.

lent, -e, adj., slow, tardy; remiss; lingering, slack, dull. — à parler; slow of speech. — à payer; slack in one's payments. Fièvre —e; slow fever, low fever.

lente, n.f., (ent.) nit.

lentement (lān-tmān), adv., slowly, tardily, remissly; sluggishly.

lenteur, n.f., slowness, tardiness, remissness.

lenticulaire or **lenticulé, -e,** adj., lenticular, lentiform.

lenticule, n.f., (bot.) duckweed.

lentiforme, adj., lentiform, lenticular.

lentigineu-x, -se, adj., (med.) lentiginous; freckled, freckly.

lentigo, n.m., (med.) lentigo; freckles.

***lentille,** n.f., (bot.) lentil; freckle; lens; pendulum-bob. Visage couvert de —s; face freckled all over.

***lentilleu-x, -se,** adj., (l.u.) freckled.

lentisque, n.m., (bot.) lentisk, mastic-tree.

léonin, -e, adj., leonine.

léonure or **léonurus,** n.m., (bot.) motherwort.

léopard, n.m., leopard.

lépas, n.m., (conch.) limpet, patella.

lépidoptère, n.m. and adj., (ent.) lepidopter, lepidoptera; lepidopterous.

lépisme, n.m., (ent.) book-worm, mite.

lèpre, n.f., leprosy.

lépreu-x, -se, n. and adj., leper; leprous.

léproserie (lé-prô-zrî), n.f., lazar-house.

lepte, n.m., (ent.) leptus. — automnal; wheal-worm.

lequel, pron. m., **laquelle,** f., **lesquels,** pl.m., **lesquelles,** pl.f., who, whom, that, which; (interrogatively) which one, which. Lequel, laquelle, vous plaît davantage? which pleases you best? Lequel, laquelle, préférez-vous? which one do you prefer?

lérot or **liron,** n.m., (mam.) garden-dormouse.

les, definite art. and pers. pr. pl., the; them. V. **le.**

lèse, adj., high-treason. [Only used in connection with some other word.]

lèse-faculté, n.f., (n.p.) (jest.) disregard of a physician's advice.

lèse-humanité, n.f., (n.p.) high-treason against humanity.

lèse-majesté, n.f., (n.p.) high-treason; (jur.) leze-majesty.

lèse-nation, n.f., (n.p.) high-treason against the nation.

léser, v.a., to wrong, to injure, to hurt, to aggrieve.

lésine, n.f., niggardliness; stinginess.

lésiner, v.n., to be niggardly, parsimonious, stingy, mean; to higgle, to haggle.

lésinerie (lé-zi-n-rî), n.f., stinginess, meanness, niggardliness; stingy act.

lésineu-r, -se, adj., niggardly, stingy, mean, parsimonious.

lésion, n.f., wrong, injury; (surg.) lesion, hurt; loss (at play).

lesse, n.f. V. **laisse.**

lessive, n.f., lye-washing, wash; washing; linen washed; (chem.) lixivium. Donner sa — à laver; to give one's dirty linen to be washed. Faire la — du gascon; (prov.) to turn one's shirt or neckerchief when it is dirty. A laver la tête d'un More, on perd sa —; it is useless trying to wash a blackamoor white; or, do what you will, you'll never change him. Faire une —, une forte, une furieuse, —; to sustain a loss, a heavy loss (at play).

lessiver, v.a., to wash (in lye); (chem.) to lixiviate. Se faire —; (fig.) to get beaten; to lose heavily (at play).

lessiveu-r, n.m., **-se,** n.f., lye-washer.

lessiveuse, n.f., lye-washing machine; laundress.

lest (lèst), n.m., (nav.) ballast.

lestage, n.m., (nav.) ballasting.

leste, adj., brisk, nimble, active; clever; unceremonious, unscrupulous; indecorous; improper, free.

lesté, -e, adj., ballasted; (fig.) with well-lined stomach.

lestement, adv., briskly, cleverly; freely; indecorously; improperly.

lester, v.a., (nav.) to ballast.

se **lester,** v.r., to take in ballast; to line one's stomach, to lay in a stock of provisions. Je me suis bien lesté avant de me mettre en route; I made a square meal before setting out.

lesteur, n.m., lighter, ballast-lighter; (pers.) ballast-heaver.

léthargie, n.f., lethargy.

léthargique, adj., lethargic, lethargical.

léthé, n.m., (myth.) Lethe.

léthifère, adj., lethiferous.

lettre, n.f., letter, note, bill; (print.) letter, type. pl., literature, letters. Prendre une chose à la —, au pied de la —; to take a thing literally, in a literal sense, to the letter. Rendre à la —; to render word for word, literally. En toutes —s; at full length, plainly, unmistakeably. — de change; bill of exchange. — de crédit; letter of credit; credentials. —s patentes; letters patent. —de cachet; (French hist.) lettres-de-cachet, arbitrary warrant. —s de marque; letters of mark. — de mer; (nav.) pass. — de *voiture ;* way-bill. *— affranchie ;* paid letter. *— recommandée* or *chargée ;* registered letter. *— refusée, — morte, — au rebut, — tombée en rebut ;* dead letter. *Boîte aux —s ;* letter-box. *Expédition des —s ;* dispatch of letters. *Jeter, mettre, une — à la poste ;* to post a letter. *Ce sont —s closes ;* that is a secret. *Un homme de —s ;* a man of letters. *Les belles—s ;* polite literature. *Gravure avant la — ;* proof engraving.

lettré, -e, *adj.,* lettered, literate, literary. *n.m.,* scholar. *Les —s ;* the literate, literati.

lettrine, *n.f.,* (print.) heading, reference.

leu, *n.m.,* old French for *loup,* wolf; still in use in the expression : *à la queue leu leu ;* one after the other, in a file.

leucorrhée, *n.f.,* (med.) leucorrhœa, whites.

leur, personal pron., to them, them. *Je le — donne ;* I give it to them. *Je — ai dit cela ;* I told them that. *Donnez-le— ;* give it to them.

leur, possessive adj., their. *Le —, la —, les —s,* possess. pron., theirs. *J'aime mieux ma maison que la — ;* I like my house better than theirs. *Je ne veux rien du — ;* I want nothing of theirs.

leurre, *n.m.,* lure; decoy; bait; snare, trap. *Se laisser prendre à un — ;* to be caught in a snare, to swallow a bait.

leurrer, *v.a.,* to lure; to entice, to decoy. *se* **leurrer,** *v.r.,* to be ensnared, entrapped; to delude one's self. *Ces oiseaux ne se leurrent pas facilement ;* these birds are not to be easily trapped.

levage, *n.m.,* raising, lifting.

levain, *n.m.,* leaven, barm, yeast; remains; germ. *Pain sans — ;* unleavened bread.

levant, *n.m.* and *adj.,* East, Levant. *Du — au couchant ;* from east to west; rising, orient.

levantin, -e, *n.* and *adj.,* Levantine.

levantine, *n.f.,* levantine (silk cloth).

lève, *n.f.,* mallet, bat (at mall).

levé, *n.m.,* (mus.) rise (of foot, of hand).

levé, -e, *part.,* lifted up, raised; up, risen (out of bed). *Votre maître est-il — ?* is your master up ?

levée, *n.f.,* gathering, crop(fruits, etc.) ; levying ; raising ; (post-office) collection ; embankment ; causeway, dike ; breaking up, removal, rising, recess ; swell (of the sea) ; trick (at cards) ; (nav.) stanch-sheets. *Faires des —s de soldats ;* to raise soldiers. *— de terre ;* embankment.

lève-gazon, *n.m.,* turfing-iron, turf-cutter.

lever, *v.a.,* to lift, to lift up, to heave, to raise up, to pull up; (hunt.) to start, to flush; to take up, to hold; to remove, to take away; to take out; to gather, to collect; to raise, to levy; to survey, to make a survey. *— les oreilles ;* to prick up one's ears. *— les épaules ;* to shrug one's shoulders. *— la main sur quelqu'un ;* to lift up one's hand against any one. *— le camp ;* to break up the camp. *—quelqu'un ;* to help any one up. *— le masque ;* to throw off the mask. *— un plan ;* to draw, to take a plan ; to survey, to make a survey. *— une assemblée ;* to dissolve a meeting. *A qui se lève matin, Dieu prête la main ;* it is the early bird catches the worm.

se **lever,** *v.r.,* to rise, to get up ; to stand up ; to break up ; to start up ; to make a stand ; (of the sea) to heave. *Il se lève de bon matin ;* he rises early. *Se — précipitamment ;* to start up.

lever, *v.n.,* to come up, to be up (of plants); to spring up, to rise. *Faire — un lièvre ;* to start a hare.

lever, *n.m.,* rising ; levee ; surveying. *Au — du soleil ;* at sunrise. *— des plans ;* land-surveying. *— de rideau ;* curtain raiser.

lever-dieu, *n.m.,* (—) (c. rel.) elevation of the host.

léviathan, *n.m.,* leviathan.

levier, *n.m.,* lever; hand-spike; (horl.) arm;

crowbar. *La force du — ;* the power of the lever. *Le point d'appui d'un — ;* the fulcrum of a lever.

levis, *adj.,* for drawing up. *Pont- — ;* drawbridge.

lévite, *n.m.,* Levite.

lévite, *n.f.,* (l.u.) frock-coat.

lévitique, *n.m.,* Leviticus.

levrauder, *v.a.,* (l.u.) to harass, to pester, to badger.

levraut, *n.m.,* leveret, young hare.

lèvre, *n.f.,* lip. *Je l'ai sur le bord des —s ;* I have it on the tip of my tongue. *Il a le cœur sur les —s ;* his heart is on his lips.

levretté, -e, *adj.,* greyhound-like.

levrette, *n.f.,* greyhound; harrier-bitch.

levretter, *v.a.,* to course (hares).

lévrier, *n.m.,* greyhound, harrier.

levron, *n.m.,* young greyhound, young harrier.

levure, *n.f.,* yeast, barm.

lexicographe, *n.m.,* lexicographer.

lexicographie, *n.f.,* lexicography.

lexicographique, *adj.,* lexicographical.

lexicologie, *n.f.,* lexicology.

lexique, *n.m.,* lexicon, dictionary.

lez, *prep.,* near, by.

lézard, *n.m.,* lizard.

lézarde, *n.f.,* crevice, crack, chink.

lézardé, -e, *adj.,* cracked (of walls).

lézardelle, *n.f.,*(bot.) lizard-tail, female lizard.

lézarder, *v.a.,* to crack (of walls).

se **lézarder,** *v.r.,* to crack, to become cracked.

liais, *n.m.,* lias, building limestone.

liaison, *n.f.,* joining, conjunction ; connection, intimacy ; up-stroke (of writing) ; (mus.) slur, binding-note. *Rompre une — ;* to break off a connection.

liaisonner, *v.a.,* (mas.) to bind (stones).

liane, *n.f.,* (bot.) bind-weed, creeper.

liant, -e, *adj.,* supple, flexible, pliant ; forming connections easily ; affable, mild ; sociable, attractive. *n.m.,* suppleness, pliability, pliancy ; affability, sociability, gentleness.

liard, *n.m.,* liard ($0·0025); half a farthing; (fig.) farthing, stiver, rap, picayune. *Il n'a pas un rouge — ;* he has n't a brass farthing.

liarder, *v.n.,* to contribute in small sums; to pay by farthings ; to haggle.

lias, *n.m.,* (geol.) Lias.

liasique or **liassique,** *adj.,* (geol.) Liassic.

liasse, *n.f.,* bundle, file (of papers).

libage, *n.m.,* (mas.) ashlar. *V.* **moellon.**

libation, *n.f.,* libation, potation. *Faire des —s ;* to offer up libations.

libelle, *n.m.,* libel, lampoon.

libellé, -e, *adj.,* drawn up, specified. *n.m.,* wording ; contents.

libeller (li-bèl-lé), *v.a.,* (jur.) to draw up; to word ; to specify the object of.

libelliste, *n.m.,* libeler.

libellule, *n.f.,* (ent.) libellula, dragon-fly.

liber (li-bèr), *n.m.,* (bot.) liber.

libéral, -e, *adj.,* liberal, generous, bounteous, free-hearted, open-handed.

libéral, *n.m.,* liberal, liberalist.

libéralement (-ral-mān), *adv.,* liberally, bountifully, largely, generously, bounteously.

libéralisme, *n.m.,* liberalism.

libéralité, *n.f.,* liberality ; generosity, open-handedness, bounty.

libérat-eur, *n.m.,* **-rice,** *n.f.,* deliverer, liberator, rescuer.

libérati-f, -ve, *adj.,* freedom-giving, liberating.

libération, *n.f.,* deliverance, rescue, discharge, riddance.

libéré, -e, *part.,* liberated, discharged ; (com.) paid up (of shares). *Forçat — ;* returned convict ; ticket-of-leave man.

libérer, *v.a.*, to discharge, to liberate, to free. **se libérer**, *v.r.*, to be liberated, to be discharged; to pay off one's debts; (com.) to be paid up (of shares).

liberté, *n.f.*, liberty, freedom, facility, ease; license, franchise. *On a rendu la — aux prisonniers ;* the prisoners were restored to liberty. *Mettre en —;* to set at liberty. *En —;* freely.

liberticide, *adj.*, liberticide.

libertin, -e, *adj.*, libertine, licentious, wanton, dissolute, idle.

libertin, *n.m.*, **-e**, *n.f.*, libertine, rake; idler; ⊙free-thinker.

libertinage, *n.m.*, libertinism, debauchery; wildness, wantonness; ⊙irreligion. *Vivre dans le —;* to lead a dissolute life.

libertiner, *v.n.*, to be a libertine, to lead a dissolute life, to be rakish; to be idle (of children).

se libertiner, *v.r.*, to be a libertine ; to play the idler (of children).

libidineux-x, -se, *adj.*, libidinous.

ad **libitum**. *V.* ad libitum.

libouret, *n.m.*, mackerel-fishing line.

libraire, *n.m.*, bookseller. *— éditeur ;* publisher and bookseller.

librairie, *n.f.*, book-trade, bookselling ; bookseller's shop, library, publishing-house.

libration, *n.f.*, (astron.) libration.

libre, *adj.*, free; at liberty; unguarded, unconfined, outdoor; bold, broad ; rid, exempt ; (of paper) unstamped ; (of schools) free, private; (of verse) irregular. *Il a tout son temps —;* all his time is his own. *— à vous de sortir ou de rester ;* stay or go, as you please. *Cette place est —;* that seat is unoccupied. *Avoir le champ —;* to have free scope for action.

libre-échange, *n.m.*, (*n.p.*) free-trade.

libre-échangiste, *n.m.*, (*— —s*) free-trader.

librement, *adv.*, freely, without restraint; boldly. *En user —;* to make free with anything.

librettiste, *n.m.*, (the author of the words of an opera), librettist.

libretto, *n.m.*, (*—s* or *libretti*) words of an opera, libretto.

lice, *n.f.*, lists; field, arena, tilt-yard ; barrier, fence; (tapestry) warp ; (mam.) bitch-hound. *Entrer dans la —, en —;* to enter the lists. *Haute —;* high warp. *Basse —;* low warp.

licence, *n.f.*, license, leave ; permission; liberty, licentiousness ; licentiate's degree.

licencié, *n.m.*, licentiate, B. A.

licenciement (-sî-mǎn), *n.m.*, (milit.) disbanding.

licencier, *v.a.*, to disband (troops).

se licencier, *v.r.*, to grow licentious, to take liberties.

licencieusement (-eûz-mǎn), *adv.*, licentiously, lewdly, dissolutely.

licencieu-x, -se, *adj.*, licentious, dissolute.

licet (-sèt), *n.m.*, (—) (l.u.) permission, leave, permit.

lichen (li-kè-n), *n.m.*, (bot.) lichen, moss.

licitation, *n.f.*, sale by auction of (real estate).

licite, *adj.*, licit, lawful, allowable.

licitement (-sit-mǎn), *adv.*, lawfully, licitly.

liciter, *v.a.*, to sell by auction (real estate).

licol, *n.m.* *V.* licou.

licorne, *n.f.*, unicorn. *— de mer ;* narwhal.

licou, *n.m.*, halter.

licteur, *n.m.*, lictor.

lie, *n.f.*, lees, dregs, grounds ; (fig.) scum, refuse. *Boire jusqu'à la —;* to drink to the dregs. *La — du peuple ;* the scum of the people. ⊙**lie**, *adj.*, merry, gay. *Faire chère —;* to lead a merry life.

lié, -e, *part.*, tied, bound, connected. *Une sauce bien —e ;* a thick sauce. *Partie —e ;* rubber (at cards).

liège, *n.m.*, cork ; cork-tree. *Bouchon de —;* cork.

liéger, *v.a.*, to cork (a net).

liégeu-x, -se, *adj.*, like cork, corky.

lien (li-in), *n.m.*, band, rope, strap. *pl.*, bonds, chains, irons. *Briser, rompre, ses —s ;* to break one's bonds. *— conjugal ;* matrimonial bond.

lienterie, *n.f.*, (med.) lientery.

lientérique, *adj.*, lienteric.

lier, *v.a.*, to bind, to bind down ; to fasten, to tie, to tie down, to tie up ; to join; to thicken ; to link, to connect, to enter into, to engage in. *C'est un fou à —;* he ought to be put into a strait-jacket. *— une sauce ;* to thicken a sauce. *— des notes ;* (mus.) to slur notes. *— commerce avec quelqu'un ;* to establish relations with any one.

se lier, *v.r.*, to bind ; to tie ; to thicken ; to become acquainted with ; to become intimate with ; to form a connection.

lierre, *n.m.*, (bot.) ivy. *— terrestre ;* ground-ivy. *— grimpant ;* tree-ivy.

liesse, *n.f.*, mirth, gayety, merriment.

lieu, *n.m.*, place, spot, ground ; family ; cause, reason, occasion. *pl.*, premises, water-closet. *En tout —;* everywhere. *En aucun —;* nowhere. *En quelque — que ce soit ;* anywhere. *Au — que ;* instead of which, whereas. *En son — et place ;* in one's place. *Se porter sur les —x ;* to go to the spot. *En premier —;* in the first place. *En dernier —;* lastly, alternately. *S'allier en bon —;* to marry into a good family. *— commun ;* commonplace topic, commonplace subject. *Il n'y a pas — de craindre ;* there is no cause to fear. *Vous avez donné — à cela ;* you are the occasion of it. *Donner — à ;* to give rise to. *Il m'a tenu — de père ;* he has been a father to me. *Avoir —;* to take place, to happen. *—x d'aisances ;* water-closet. *Etre au — et place de quelqu'un ;* to represent any one. *Au — de ;* in the place of, instead of, in lieu of. *Au — que ;* whereas, when on the contrary, while. *Y avoir —;* there to be occasion or necessity. *Tenir — de ;* to fill the place of; to do instead of.

lieue, *n.f.*, league (two and a half miles English).

lieur, *n.m.*, binder, hay-trusser.

lieutenance (lieu-tnǎns), *n.f.*, lieutenancy.

lieutenant, *n.m.*, lieutenant. *— en premier, en second ;* first lieutenant, second lieutenant. *Sous —, (— — —s)* ensign, sub-lieutenant.

lièvre, *n.m.*, hare. *Bec-de—, (—s—)* hare-lip. *Il ne faut pas courir deux —s à la fois ;* one must not have too many irons in the fire. *C'est là que gît le —;* that's the main point; there's the rub. *Mémoire de —;* bad, shocking memory.

ligament, *n.m.*, (anat.) ligament.

ligamenteu-x, -se, *adj.*, ligamentous.

ligature, *n.f.*, ligature.

lige, *adj.*, liege. *Fief —;* vassalage.

*****lignage**, *n.m.*, lineage.

*****lignager**, *n.m.*, person of the same descent, kinsman.

*****ligne**, *n.f.*, line ; path, way, range ; swath (of grass). *Etre en première —;* to hold the first rank. *Etre hors de —;* to be out of the line, beyond compare ; out of the common. *— de charge, de flottaison ;* load water-mark, water-line. *Grande —;* (rail.) trunk line. *Il ne fait pas ses —s droites ;* he does not keep his lines straight. *A la —;* a new line, a break. *— à pêcher ;* fishing-line. *Pêcher à la —;* to angle. *Troupe de —;* troops of the line. *En —!* (mil.) fall in ! *Venir en première —;* to rank first.

*****lignée**, *n.f.*, lineage, progeny, offspring, issue.

*****ligner**, *v.a.*, (carp.) to draw lines on.

*****lignerolle**, *n.f.*, (nav.) twine.

*****lignette**, *n.f.*, net, twine.

*****ligneul**, *n.m.*, shoemaker's thread, **wax-end**.

*ligneu-x, -se, adj., (bot.) ligneous, woody.

lignite (lig-nit), n.m., lignite, brown-coal.

ligue (lig), n.f., league ; plot, confederacy.

liguer (ighé), v.a., to unite in a league.

se liguer, v.r., to league, to combine, to band together.

ligueu-r, n.m., **-se,** n.f., leaguer.

ligulé, -e, adj., (bot.) ligulate ; strap-shaped.

lilas, n.m., lilac.

lilas, adj., lilac-colored.

liliacée, n. and adj.f., liliaceous plant ; liliaceous.

lilliputien, -ne, adj., lilliputian.

limace, n.f., slug ; (mec.) Archimedean screw, water-screw.

limaçon, n.m., snail ; (anat.) cochlea. Escalier en — ; winding staircase, corkscrew stairs. — de mer ; cockle.

*limaille, n.f., filings.

limande, n.f., (ich.) dab.

limas, n.m. V. **limace.**

limbe, n.m., limb, border, halo.

limbes, n.m.pl., (theol.) limbo, limbus.

lime, n.f., file ; (bot.) sweet lemon. Les dents d'une — ; the teeth of a file. — douce ; smooth file. — sourde ; dead file.

lime-bois, n.m., wood-fretter.

limer, v.a., to file, to smooth, to finish off.

limeur, n.m., filer.

limier, n.m., bloodhound, police-spy, detective.

liminaire, adj., prefatory.

limitati-f, -ve, adj., limiting.

limitation, n.f., limitation.

limitativement, adv., limitedly, with limitation.

limite, n.f., limit, landmark, boundary, bound, border, extremity, confine.

limité, -e, part., limited.

limiter, v.a., to limit, to bound ; to set bounds to ; to circumscribe, to confine ; to stint.

limitrophe, adj., neighboring, bordering.

limon, n.m., slime, ooze ; clay ; mud ; (bot.) lemon ; shaft (of a carriage) ; string-board, notch-board (of a staircase).

limonade, n.f., lemonade.

limonadi-er, n.m., **-ère,** n.f., maker, seller, of lemonade ; coffee-house keeper.

limoneu-x, -se, adj., muddy, turbid ; slimy.

limonier, n.m., shaft-horse ; (bot.) lemon-tree.

limonière, n.f., wagon with two shafts.

limousin, n.m., bricklayer, mason (because most masons hail from Le Limousin).

limousinage, n.m., rough-walling ; ashlar-work.

limousine, n.f., coarse woolen cloak.

limousiner, v.a., to rough-wall.

limpide, adj., limpid, clear.

limpidité, n.f., limpidness, clearness.

limure, n.f., filing ; filings, polish.

lin, n.m., flax. Graine de — ; linseed. Toile de — ; linen-cloth. — des prés ; cotton-grass.

linacées, n.f.pl. V. **linées.**

linaire, n.f., (bot.) toad-flax.

linceul, n.m., winding-sheet, shroud.

linçoir, n.m., ceiling-joist.

linéaire, adj., linear.

linéal, -e, adj., lineal, in a direct line.

linéament, n.m., trace, lineament, feature, outline.

linées, n.f.pl., (bot.) plants of the flax kind.

linette, n.f., flax-seed.

linge, n.m., linen ; cloth, rag. — propre ; clean linen. Changer de — ; to change one's linen. — à barbe ; shaving-cloth.

ling-er, n.m., **-ère,** n.f., linendraper.

lingère, n.f., keeper of a fancy linen-shop ; seamstress, wardrobe woman.

lingerie (lin-jrî), n.f., linen trade, linen-drapery ; hosiery ; linen-room.

lingot, n.m., ingot, bullion ; (hunt.) slug. Or en — ; gold in bullion.

lingotière (-ti-èr), n.f., ingot-mold.

lingual, -e (-gooal), n.f. and adj., (anat., gram.) lingual.

lingue (lingh), n.f., (ich.) ling.

linguet (-ghè), n.m., (nav.) pawl (of a capstan).

linguiforme (-gooi-), adj., linguiform (like a tongue).

linguiste (-gooist), n.m.f., linguist.

linguistique (-gooistik), n.f., linguistics.

lini-er, -ère, adj., of flax. Industrie —ère ; linen-trade ; flax-spinning.

linière, n.f., flax field.

liniment, n.m., (pharm.) liniment.

linon, n.m., lawn (fine linen).

linot, n.m., (orni.) linnet ; cock-linnet.

linotte, n.f., hen-linnet. C'est une tête de —; he is a hare-brained sort of fellow. Siffler la —; (pop.) to drink hard ; to be in limbo, in quod.

linteau, n.m., (carp.) head-piece, lintel.

lion, n.m., (mam.) lion ; (fig.) lord, dandy, beau ; (astron.) Leo. Jeune — ; lion's cub, whelp, young lion. — marin ; sea-wolf. Dent-de—, (—s—) (bot.) dandelion. Coudre la peau du renard à celle du — ; to combine cunning with strength. C'est l'âne couvert de la peau du —; he is the ass with the lion's skin. C'est un —; he is a dandy.

lionceau, n.m., (mam.) young lion, lion's whelp, cub.

lionne, n.f., (mam.) lioness ; fashionable woman ; gay woman.

lionné, -e, adj., (her.) rampant.

lipogrammatique, adj., lipogrammatic.

lipogrammatiste, n.m., lipogrammatist, letter-dropper.

lipogramme, n.m., lipogram.

lipome, n.m., (med.) adipose wen.

lipothymie, n.f., (med.) lipothymy.

lippe, n.f., pouting-lip, thick lip. Faire sa —, à —, faire une grosse, une vilaine, — ; (fam.) to pout.

⊙lippée, n.f., (fam.) mouthful ; meal, feast. [In the latter sense this word is only used with the adj. franche.] Franche — ; hearty meal, a good square meal (free of cost). Chercheur de franches —s ; sponger, parasite.

lippitude, n.f., (med.) lippitude, blearedness.

lippu, -e, adj., thick-lipped.

liquation (-cooa-), n.f., liquation, eliquation.

liquéfaction, n.f., liquefaction.

liquéfiable, adj., liquefiable.

liquéfier, v.a., to liquefy.

se liquéfier, v.r., to liquefy, to become liquefied.

liquet, n.m., (hort.) small baking pear.

liqueur, n.f., liquid ; liquor, spirits ; liqueur, cordial, juice. Vin de — ; sweet wine. —s fraîches ; refreshing drinks. —s fortes ; spirits, intoxicating drinks. Marchand de —s spiritueuses ; dealer in wines and spirits.

liquidambar, n.m., (bot.) liquid-amber.

liquidateur, n.m., liquidator.

liquidation, n.f., liquidation, settling ; settlement ; winding up.

liquide, adj., liquid, watery, flowing ; clear ; net (of money). La plaine — ; the ocean.

liquide, n.m., liquid, fluid ; spirit, spirituous liquor.

liquide, n.f., (gram.) liquid.

liquider, v.a., to liquidate, to settle, to discharge ; to wind up, to sell off.

se liquider, v.r., to liquidate, to be liquidated, to settle, to discharge one's debts.

liquidité, n.f., liquidity, fluidity.

liquoreu-x, adj., luscious, sweet.

liquoriste, n.m., dealer in liqueurs or spirits.

lire (lisant, lu), v.a., to read, to read of, to peruse, to study. Continuer de — ; to read on. — tout bas ; to read to one's self. — à haute voix ;

to read aloud. — *dans la pensée de quelqu'un ;* to read any one's thoughts.

liron, *n.m.* *V.* **loir** and **lérot.**

lis (lîs), *n.m.,* (bot.) lily. — *asphodèle ;* lily-daffodil ; (fig.) whiteness.

liséré, *n.m.,* stripe ; border, piping.

lisérer, *v.a.,* to border with piping.

liseron (li-zron), *n.m.,* (bot.) bind-weed.

liset, *n.m.* (bot.) *V.* **liseron.**

liseu-r, *n.m.,* **-se,** *n.f.,* reader.

lisibilité, *n.f.,* legibility ; readableness.

lisible, *adj.,* legible, readable.

lisiblement, *adv.,* legibly.

lisière, *n.f.,* list (of cloth): strings, leading-strings ; border, skirt, edge, verge, outskirts. — *de toile ;* selvage of linen-cloth. — *d'un bois ;* edge, verge, of a wood.

lissage, *n.m.,* (tech.) smoothing, glossing ; (nav.) railing, rails.

lisse, *adj.,* smooth, sleek, glossy.

lisse, *n.f.,* smoothness, gloss, hand-rail, hand-railing, barrier, fence ; (nav.) sheer-rails, drift-rails, rib-band ; (tapestry) *V.* **lice.** —*s de porte-haubans ;* sheer-rails. —*s de la rabattue ;* drift-rails. —*s de couronnement ;* upper rails of the stern. —*s de grande rabattue ;* quarter-rails. —*s de l'éperon ;* rails of the head. —*s de bastingage ;* rails of the nettings. —*s des couples ;* rib-bands. — *du fort ;* extreme breadth line. — *des façons ;* floor-rib-band. —*s des œuvres mortes ;* rib-bands of the upper-works. —*s de plat-bord ;* drift-rails. — *de vibord ;* waist-rail. —*s de la herpe ;* rails of the head. — *d'hourdi ;* wing-transom.

lisser, *v.a.,* to smooth, to gloss, to polish.

lisseu-r, *n.m.,* **-se,** *n.f.,* polisher.

lissoir, *n.m.,* polisher (tool).

lissure, *n.f.,* polishing, glazing.

liste, *n.f.,* list, roll, catalogue, schedule. — *civile ;* civil list. — *des jurés ;* (jur.) panel.

listeau, *n.m.,* (nav.) rim.

listel, *n.m.,* (*listeaux*) (arch.) listel, list, fillet.

liston, *n.m.,* (her.) scroll.

lit, *n.m.,* bed; bedstead; layer; stratum; channel, direction, set of a current); (fig.) marriage. — *de plume ;* feather-bed. — *de parade ;* bed of state. — *de repos ;* couch. — *de douleur ;* sick-bed. — *de camp ;* field-bed. — *de mort ;* death-bed. — *de sangle ;* folding-bed. — *volant ;* (nav.) cot, berth. — *à quenouilles,* — *à colonnes ;* four-post bedstead, four-poster. *Quenouille de* —, *colonne de* —; bedpost. *Descente de* —; carpet for the bedside. *Bois de* —; bedstead. *Se mettre au* —; to go to bed. *Garder le* —; to keep one's bed. *Ils font* — *à part ;* they do not sleep together. *Il a des enfants de deux* —*s ;* he has children by two wives. *Ruelle de* —; bed-side. — *de dessous ;* understratum (of a quarry). — *de la mer ;* bed of the sea. — *du vent ;* (nav.) the wind's eye. *Tenir le* — *du vent ;* to sail close to the wind. — *de marée ;* tide-way. — *de justice ;* seat of justice, judicial bench; (Fr. Hist.) king's throne. — *de Procruste ;* the bed of Procrustes ; (fig.) tyrannical custom, rule, law, etc. *Comme on fait son* — *on se couche ;* as you make your bed, so you must lie. *Mourir au* — *d'honneur ;* to die in battle. *Au* —*! ;* (hunt.) tally-ho ! *Au saut du* — or *au sortir du* —; as you are getting up ; in the early morning.

litanie, *n.f.,* litany, prayers ; long-winded story.

liteau, *n.m.,* haunt (of a wolf); stripe (on table napkins); (tech.) bracket, ledge. *A* —*x;* with stripes, striped.

litée, *n.f.,* (hunt.) haunt, lair.

literie, *n.f.,* bedding.

litharge, *n.f.,* (min.) litharge.

lithargé, **-e,** or **lithargyré,** **-e,** *adj.,* adulterated with litharge.

lithiase or **lithiasie,** *n.f.,* (med.) lithiasis.

lithiate, *n.m.,* (chem.) lithiate.

lithine, *n.f.,* (chem.) lithia.

lithoclaste, *n.m.,* (surg.) lithoclast (instrument).

lithocolle, *n.f.,* lithocolla.

lithogénésie, *n.f.,* lithogenesy.

lithographe, *n.m.,* lithographer. *Imprimeur* —; lithographic printer.

lithographie, *n.f.,* lithography ; lithograph ; lithographic printing-office.

lithographier, *v.a.,* to lithograph.

lithographique, *adj.,* lithographic.

lithoïde, *adj.,* lithoidal.

lithologie, *n.f.,* lithology.

lithologue, *n.m.,* lithologist.

lithontriptique or **lithotriptique,** *n.m.* and *adj.,* (med.) lithontriptic.

lithophage, *adj.,* lithophagous.

lithophylle, *n.f.,* lithophyl.

lithophyte, *n.m.,* lithophyte.

lithosperme, *n.m.,* (bot.) lithospermum ; gromil, gromwell.

lithotome, *n.m.,* (surg.) lithotome.

lithotomie, *n.f.,* (surg.) lithotomy.

lithotomique, *adj.,* (surg.) lithotomic.

lithotomiste, *n.m.,* (surg.) lithotomist.

lithotriteur, *n.m.,* (surg.) lithotritor.

lithotritie (-tri-ci), *n.f.,* (surg.) lithotrity.

litière (-tièr), *n.f.,* litter ; stable-litter. *Il est sur la* —; he is in the straw (of a horse) ; he is ill in bed (pers.). *Faire* — *de quelque chose ;* to throw away, to waste, to squander.

litigant, **-e,** *adj.,* litigant.

litige, *n.m.,* litigation, legal dispute, suit at law; (fig.) strife. *En* —; litigated, in dispute.

litigieu-x, **-se,** *adj.,* litigious ; given to law-suits.

litispendance, *n.f.,* (jur.) pendency (of a suit).

litorne, *n.f.,* (orni.) litorn, field-fare.

litote, *n.f.,* (rhet.) litotes.

litre, *n.f.,* black band, with hatchment.

litre, *n.m.,* liter (1.760 pint). *Demi* —; pint.

litron, *n.m.,* litron ; (pop.) reputed quart.

littéraire, *adj.,* literary.

littérairement, *adv.,* literarily.

littéral, **-e,** *adj.,* literal.

littéralement (-ral-mān), *adv.,* literally, word for word, verbatim.

littéralité, *n.f.,* literality, literalness.

littérateur, *n.m.,* literary man, scholar, man of letters.

littérature, *n.f.,* literature, learning.

littoral, **-e,** *adj.,* littoral, of the sea-coast.

littoral, *n.m.,* coast, sea-shore, sea-board.

lituite, *n.m.,* (foss.) lituite.

liturgie, *n.f.,* liturgy.

liturgique, *adj.,* liturgic, liturgical.

liturgiste, *n.m.,* writer on the liturgy.

lituus, *n.m.,* (—) (antiq.) augur's wand.

liure, *n.f.,* cord, cart-rope; (nav.) lashing, gammoning (of the bowsprit).

livarde, *n.f.,* cord; (nav.) sprit. *Voile à* —; sprit-sail.

livarder, *v.a.,* (nav.) to sprit.

livide, *adj.,* livid.

lividité, *n.f.,* lividness.

livrable, *adj.,* (com.) deliverable.

livraison, *n.f.,* delivery (of goods); part, number (of a book). *Prendre de* —; to receive. *Faire* —; to deliver (goods, etc.). *Par* —*s;* in parts, numbers.

livre, *n.m.,* book, register, volume. — *manuscrit, imprimé ;* manuscript, printed book. — *en feuilles ;* book in sheets. — *cartonné ;* book in boards. — *broché ;* stitched book. — *épuisé ;* book out of print. — *de consignations ;* (police) charge-sheet. — *d'occasion ;* second-hand book. — *d'heures ;* (c. rel.) prayer-book, primer. *Collationner un* —; to collate a book. *Mettre un* —

au jour ; to publish a book. *Un dévoreur de —s ;* a bookworm (pers.). *Parler comme un —;* to speak like a book. *Traduire à — ouvert ;* to translate at sight. *Chanter à — ouvert ;* to sing at sight. *— de compte ;* book of accounts. *Grand —;* ledger. *— journal ;* day-book. *— de caisse ;* cash-book. *— d'échéances ;* bill-book. *Teneur de —s ;* book-keeper. *Tenir les —s ;* to keep the books, to keep the accounts. *Grand —, grand — de la dette publique ;* register of the National Debt. *— jaune ;* blue book.

livre, *n.f.,* pound (1 lb., 1 oz., 10 1-4 dr. avoir-dupois); livre (coin); franc. *— sterling ;* pound sterling. *— parisis ;* Paris livre ($0·25). *— tournois ;* Tours livre ($0·21). *A la —;* by the pound. *Dix francs la —;* ten francs a pound.

livrée, *n.f.,* livery; livery-servants. *— de noce ;* wedding-favors. *En —;* in livery. *Gens de —;* footmen, flunkeys. *Grande —;* full livery. *Petite —;* undress livery. *Marchandises à —;* goods to be delivered.

livrer, *v.a.,* to deliver; to deliver up, over; to betray; to give up; to commit, to consign. *— de la marchandise à ;* to deliver goods to. *— bataille ;* to engage, to give battle. *— un assaut ;* to make an assault. *— une place à l'ennemi ;* to deliver up a fortress to the enemy. *— une ville au pillage ;* to give up a town to pillage. *— une bataille ;* to fight a battle.

se **livrer,** *v.r.,* to deliver one's self up, over ; to give one's self up, over ; to surrender one's self; to devote, to dedicate, to apply, one's self to ; to confide (in); to trust one's self to ; to riot in ; to expose one's self to.

livret, *n.m.,* little book ; memorandum-book ; workman's certificate ; time-book ; cabman's license ; depositor's book ; multiplication-table ; book (of the play). *— de batteur d'or ;* gold-beater's mold.

livreur, *n.m.,* deliverer (of goods). *Payez le —;* pay on delivery.

lixiviation, *n.f.,* (chem.) lixiviation.
lixiviel, -le, *adj.,* (chem., pharm.) lixivial.
lixivium (-om), *n.m.,* (chem.) lixivium.
llama, *n.m.* V. **lama.**
lobe, *n.m.,* lobe; lobe of the ear; (arch.) cusp; (arch.) foil.
lobé, -e, *adj.,* (bot.) lobed, lobate.
lobélie, *n.f.,* (bot.) lobelia, cardinal-flower. *— enflée ;* Indian tobacco, emetic weed.
lobiole, *n.f.,* small lobe (in lichens).
lobulaire, *adj.,* lobulary.
lobule, *n.m.,* (anat.) lobule.
local, -e, *adj.,* local.
local, *n.m.,* place, habitation, situation, premises, quarters.
localement, *adv.,* locally.
localisation, *n.f.,* localization.
localiser, *v.a.,* to localize.
se **localiser,** *v.r.,* to become, to be, localized.
localité, *n.f.,* locality, place.
locataire, *n.m.f.,* tenant, lodger ; (jur.) lessee. *— à bail ;* lessee. *Recevoir des —s ;* to take in lodgers. *— en vertu d'un bail ;* lease-holder. *Principal —;* tenant.
locati-f, -ve, *adj.,* tenantable ; of or belonging to the tenant. *Valeur —ve ;* value in rent. *n.m.,* locative (gram.).
location, *n.f.,* letting, letting out ; hiring ; renting ; (jur.) location. *Bureau de —;* box-office. *— de livres ;* letting out of books, lending library, circulating library.
locatis (-tis), *n.m.,* (fam. l.u.) hack, jade.
loch, *n.m.,* (nav.) log. *Table de —;* log-book. *Jeter le —;* to heave the log.
loche, *n.f.,* (ich.) loach, groundling.
locher, *v.n.,* (of a horse's shoe) to be loose, to shake. *Il y a là quelque fer qui loche ;* there is a screw loose somewhere.

lochet, *n.m.* V. **louchet.**
lochial, -e, *adj.,* (med.) lochial.
lochies, *n.f. pl.,* (med.) lochia.
locman, *n.m.,* coasting pilot. V. **lamaneur.**
locomobile, *adj.,* portable, movable.
locomobile, *n.f.,* (agri., manu.) traction engine, (portable) steam-engine.
locomot-eur, -rice, *adj.,* (anat.) of or producing locomotion; locomotive.
locomoti-f, -ve, *adj.,* locomotive.
locomotion, *n.f.,* locomotion.
locomotive, *n.f.,* locomotive, engine, locomotive-engine.
locrenan, *n.m.,* (coarse cloth) lockram.
locuste, *n.f.,* (ent.) locust ; (zool.) shrimp, prawn.
locution, *n.f.,* expression, mode, form of speech ; locution ; term, phrase.
lods, *n.m.pl.,* (feudal law) only used in the expression : *— et ventes ;* lord's due.
lof, *n.m.,* (nav.) loof, luff ; weather side, windward. *Aller au —;* to sail near the wind ; to go to windward. *Etre au —;* to be to windward. *— pour —! * to windward ! *Couple de —;* loof-frame. *Largue le —! * up tacks and sheets ! *Bouter le —;* to trim all sharp. *— tout ! * luff round ! round with her ! *— à la risée ! * ease the ship ! (in blowy weather). *Virer —pour —;* to tack, to veer the ship.
lofer, *v.n.,* (nav.) to luff.
logarithme, *n.m.,* (math.) logarithm.
logarithmique, *adj.,* logarithmic.
logarithmique, *n.f.,* logarithmic curve.
loge, *n.f.,* lodge, hut, box ; booth ; stand, stall ; kennel, cell, den ; cabin, closet ; actor's dressing-room. *— d'un chien ;* dog's kennel. *— du tigre ;* tiger's den. *Ouvreuse de —s ;* box-opener. *— grillée ;* latticed box. *— découverte ;* open box. *Premières —s ;* (thea.) first tier of boxes. *— d'avant scène ;* stage box. *— de face ;* front box. *Tenir une —;* (freemasonry) to hold a lodge.
logeable (lo-jabl), *adj.,* inhabitable, tenantable, fit to live in ; commodious, convenient ; that can be housed.
logement (lo-jmãn), *n.m.,* lodgings ; residence ; dwelling ; house-room ; quarters ; quartering ; (milit.) lodgment ; accommodation ; (nav.) room. *— garni ;* furnished apartments.
loger, *v.n.,* to lodge, to live, to put up. *— chez soi ;* to live at home. *— dans une auberge ;* to put up at an inn. *— à la belle étoile ;* to sleep in the open air. *Ici on loge à pied et à cheval ;* accommodation for man and beast.
loger, *v.a.,* to lodge, to harbor ; to find room for, to take in, to put up, to accommodate ; to house ; to billet, to quarter ; to stable. *— des soldats ;* to quarter soldiers.
se **loger,** *v.r.,* to lodge, to take up one's abode ; to put up ; (fig.) to lodge itself, to fix itself.
logette, *n.f.,* little cabin, little box, little cell.
logeu-r, *n.m.,* **-se,** *n.f.,* lodger. *— en garni ;* lodging-house keeper.
logicien (-in), *n.m.,* logician.
logique, *n.f.* and *adj.,* logic, logical.
logiquement, *adv.,* logically.
logis, *n.m.,* house, dwelling, lodging, lodging-house, inn, home. *Corps de —;* main building. *On m'attend au —;* I am expected at home. *Bon — à pied et à cheval ;* good accommodation for man and horse. *Au —;* at home. *La folle du —;* imagination, fancy.
logographe, *n.m.,* early Greek historian, logographer.
logogriphe, *n.m.,* logogriph, riddle, enigma.
logomachie, *n.f.,* logomachy, war of words.
logos, *n.m.,* (n.p.) (theol.) God the Word ; (in Plato's Philos.) the Creator of all things.
loi, *n.f.,* law, precept, command ; power, dominion, sway ; authority ; rule ; (coin) standard. *Homme de —;* lawyer. *Projet de —;* (parlia-

ment) bill. *Présenter un projet de* —; to bring in a bill. *Rejeter un projet de* —; to throw out a bill. *Hors la* —; outlawed. *Faire* —; to have force of law. *Faire la* —; to command, to dictate (to). *Se faire une* —; to make it a point. *Mettre hors la* —; to outlaw. — *annonaire; V.* **annonaire.**

loin, *adv.,* far, far off, a great way off ; at a distance ; remote, distant. *De — en* —; at great intervals, at long distances from each other. *Au* —; far, far away, far and wide. *De* —; from afar, from a distance, a long way off. *Revenir de* —; to have a narrow squeak (for one's life). *Aller chasser au* —; to go out hunting a great way off. — *du monde ;* far from the world. — *d'ici ;* a great way off. — *d'ici !* be gone! — *des yeux,* — *du cœur ;* out of sight, out of mind. *Bien* — *de ;* instead of ; far from. *Bien* — *que ;* far from, so far from. *Bien* — *que cela soit ;* it is so far from being so.

lointain, -e, *adj.,* remote, far distant. *Pays* —; remote country.

lointain, *n.m.,* distance ; distant prospect. *Le* — *d'un tableau ;* the background of a picture.

loir, *n.m.,* (mam.) dormouse.

loisible, *adj.,* optional, lawful, allowable, right. — *à vous de le faire ;* you have a perfect right to do it.

loisir, *n.m.,* leisure, spare time. *J'ai du* —; I am at leisure. *Etes-vous de* —? are you at leisure ? or are you disengaged ? *A* —; leisurely, at leisure.

lok, *n.m. V.* **looch.**

lollard, *n.m.,* (—*s*) Lollard.

lombaire, *adj.,* (anat.) lumbar.

lombard, *n.m.,* pawnbroker ; pawn-shop. *V.* **mont-de-piété.**

lombard, *n.m.,* **-e,** *n.f.,* Lombard.

lombes, *n.m.pl.,* lumbar region, loins.

lombric, *n.m.,* (ent.) dew-worm, earth-worm, lob-worm.

lombrical, -e, *adj.,* lumbrical.

lomentacé, -e, *adj.,* (bot.) lomentaceous.

lompe, *n.m.,* (ich.) lump-fish, sea-owl.

londonien, -ne, *adj.,* Londoner. *adj.,* Londonish.

londrin, *n.m.,* London cloth.

long, -ue (lōn, lōng), *adj.,* long, slow; tedious; prolonged, lengthened ; diffuse ; drawn out. *Le temps est* — *à qui attend ;* it is weary waiting. — *à manger,* — *à tout ;* slow at meat, slow at everything. *De* —*ue main ;* of long standing.

long, *adv.,* length ; extent. *Cela a dix aunes de* —; that is ten ells in length. *Etre couché, étendu, tout de son* — *;* to lie, to be lying, at full length. *Prendre le plus* — *;* to go the longest way round. *Tout le* —; all along. *Tout au* —; along, at large, in detail, in full. *De* — *en large;* up and down ; to and fro. *En* —; lengthways. *Tirer de* — *;* to scamper away ; (fig.) to put off, to procrastinate.

long, *adv.,* much, a great deal. *En savoir* —; to know what's what. *En savoir trop* —; to know too much.

longanimité, *n.f.,* longanimity, forbearance, long-suffering.

long-courrier, *n.m.,* ocean (going) ship.

longe, *n.f.,* loin ; tether, thong. *Une* — *de veau ;* a loin of veal.

longer, *v.a.,* to go, to walk, to run along; to skirt, to coast along.

longévité, *n.f.,* longevity.

longimétrie, *n.f.,* longimetry.

longitude, *n.f.,* (geog.) longitude. *Prendre les* — *s ;* to take the longitude.

longitudinal, -e, *adj.,* longitudinal.

longitudinalement, *adv.,* longitudinally.

long-jointé, -e, *adj.,* (man.) long-jointed.

long-pan, *n.m.,* roof-length.

longrine *or* **longuerine,** *n.f.,* girder, sleeper.

longtemps (lōn-tān), *adv.,* long, a long while, a great while. *Depuis* —; long since, long ago, long before. *Il y a* — *que je ne l'ai vu ;* I have not seen him for a great while.

longue (long), *n.f.,* long syllable ; length ; course of time. *A la* —; with *or* in time, in the long run.

longuement (long-mān), *adv.,* long, a long time, a great while, at length.

longuet, -te, *adj.,* longish, somewhat long, pretty long, at great length.

longueur (-gheur), *n.f.,* length, extent ; slowness, tediousness, dullness ; prolixity. *Trois pieds de* —; three feet in length. *En* —; lengthwise. *Tirer les choses en* —; to delay, to cause delays ; to cause any affair to drag. *Traîner en* — *;* to drag ; to be protracted ; to suffer delays. *Tirer en* —; to spin out.

longue-vue, *n.f.,* (—*s*—*s*) small telescope ; spy-glass.

looch (lok), *n.m.,* (pharm.) loch; emulsion.

lopin, *n.m.,* (pop.) lump ; bit, morsel, portion, share (of eatables). — *de terre ;* bit of ground.

loquace (-kooa), *adj.,* loquacious, talkative.

loquacement, *adv.,* talkatively, loquaciously.

loquacité (-kooa-), *n.f.,* loquacity, talkativeness.

loque, *n.f.,* rag, tatter.

loquèle (-kuèl), *n.f.,* small talk, gabble.

loquet, *n.m.,* latch; (of a knife) catch, hasp, clasp. — *d'écoutilles ;* (nav.) hoop of the scuttles.

loqueteau (lok-to), *n.m.,* little latch.

loquette, *n.f.,* (pop.) scrap, small bit.

lord, *n.m.,* (—*s*) lord.

lorette, *n.f.,* lorette, gay woman.

*lorgnade, *n.f.,* ogle, side-look, side-glance.

*lorgner, *v.a.,* to leer, to ogle ; to look through an opera-glass ; to quiz ; to have an eye on. — *une charge ;* to have an eye on some post, to covet.

*lorgnette, *n.f.,* opera-glass.

*lorgneu-r, *n.m.,* -se, *n.f.,* ogler.

*lorgnon, *n.m.,* eye-glass, quizzing-glass.

loriot, *n.m.,* (orni.) oriole.

lors, *adv.,* then. *Depuis or dès* —; from that time, since then. — *de ;* at the time of. — *même que ;* even though. *Pour* — ; then, at the time, since then ; so, in that case, therefore.

lorsque, *conj.,* when ; at the time or moment. — *j'arrivai ;* when I arrived.

⊙**los,** *n.m.,* praise.

losange, *n.m.,* (math.) lozenge ; lozenge-molding.

losangé, -e, *adj.,* (math.) in lozenges ; (her.) lozengee, lozenzy.

losanger, *v.a.,* to lozenge.

lot (lō), *n.m.,* lot; portion, share ; prize (in a lottery). *Le* — *qui lui est échu ;* the portion which has fallen to his share. *Le gros* —; the first prize (in a lottery).

loterie (lo-trî), *n.f.,* lottery ; raffle. *Mettre à la* —; to put in the lottery. *Gagner à la* —; to win in the lottery. *Faire une* —; to raffle. *C'est une* — ; (fig.) it is a mere matter of chance.

loti, -e, *part.,* divided into lots ; portioned out. *Le voilà bien* —; he has made a good choice.

lotier (-tié), *n.m.,* (bot.) lotus, lotos.

lotion, *n.f.,* lotion, wash ; ablution.

lotir, *v.a.,* to divide into lots, to share ; to portion out.

lotissage, *n.m.,* (chem.) assaying, averaging.

lotissement (-tis-mān), *n.m.,* dividing into lots, lotting.

loto, *n.m.,* loto (game of chance).

lotophages, *n.m.pl.,* Lotophagi (lotus-eaters).

lotte, *n.f.,* (ich.) lote ; eel-pout.

lotus *or* **lotos** (-tûs, -tôs), *n.m.,* (bot.) lotus, lote.

louable, *adj.*, laudable, praiseworthy, commendable; honest, honorable.

louablement, *adv.*, laudably, commendably, praiseworthily.

louage, *n.m.*, letting out, hire, hiring, renting. *A —;* on hire. *Donner à —;* to let out, to hire. *Prendre à —;* to rent, to hire. *Un cheval de —;* a hired horse.

louange, *n.f.*, praise, commendation, eulogy; glory, credit. *Donner des —s;* to bestow praise.

louanger, *v.a.*, to praise up, to flatter, to laud.

louangeu-r, -se, *n.* and *adj.*, praiser, flatterer, panegyrist; laudatory, eulogistic.

louche, *adj.*, squint-eyed; dubious, doubtful, ambiguous, suspicious, equivocal; not clear; (fig.) (of light) dim, dark; (of weather) foul, thick.

louche, *n.m.*, ambiguity, obscurity; suspicious appearance. *Il y a du — dans sa conduite;* there is something suspicious in his conduct.

louche, *n.f.*, soup-ladle; dipper.

louchée, *n.f.*, ladleful.

loucher, *v.n.*, to squint.

louchet, *n.m.*, flat spade, mattock.

louchettes, *n.f.pl.*, goggles.

loucheu-r, -se, *n.m.f. and adj.*, squinter, squinting.

louer, *v.a.*, to let, to let out, to rent, to hire, to hire out, to lease; to take, to rent. *— une maison à quelqu'un;* to let any one a house. *Maison à —;* house to let.

se **louer**, *v.r.*, to hire one's self out; to be let; to be let for.

louer, *v.a.*, to praise, to commend, to laud, to eulogize, to speak highly of.

se **louer**, *v.r.*, to laud, to praise, one's self; to rejoice at; to be satisfied *or* pleased with. *Se — de quelqu'un;* to be well pleased with any one; to be satisfied with any one. *Qui se loue s'emboue;* self praise is no recommendation.

loueu-r, *n.m.*, **-se**, *n.f.*, hirer, letter out; ⊙praiser, flatterer. *— de voitures;* job-master.

lougre, *n.m.*, lugger.

louis, *n.m.*, louis (an old French coin equal to about $4.60). *— d'or;* louis d'or.

loup (loo), *n.m.*, wolf; (med.) lupus; (com.) stock-jobber; black velvet mask; domino; crowbar; packing stick, burnisher. *Gueule de —;* (bot.) snap-dragon. *Manger comme un —;* to eat ravenously; to devour. *Un saut de —;* a ha-ha; a hedge sunk between slopes. *Entre chien et —;* in the dusk of the evening, at dusk. *Renfermer le — dans la bergerie;* to set the fox to keep the geese. *Crier au —!* to cry wolf. *Marcher à pas de —;* to walk cautiously, stealthily, like a thief. *Mettre quelqu'un à la gueule du —;* to throw any one into the lion's mouth. *Il est connu comme le — blanc;* he is known by everybody. *Quand on parle du — on en voit la queue;* talk of the devil and he is sure to appear. *La faim chasse le — hors du bois;* hunger will break through stone walls. *Il faut hurler avec les —s;* when you are at Rome, you must do as Rome does. *Avoir vu le —;* to have seen the world; to know what 's what. *Qui se fait brebis, le — le mange;* daub yourself with honey and you will never want flies. *Il fait un froid de —;* it is terribly *or* bitter cold. *Tenir le — par les oreilles;* to be in a critical situation. *Les —s ne se mangent pas entre eux;* there is honor among thieves. *Un vieux — de mer;* an old sea dog, an old salt.

loup-cerve, *n.f.*, (*—s—s*) (mam.) she-lynx.

loup-cervier, *n.m.*, (*—s—s*) lynx.

loupe, *n.f.*, magnifying-glass, lens, eye-glass; (med.) wen; (of camels) hump; (house painting) cradle.

loupeu-x, -se, *adj.*, wenny, knobby.

loup-garou, *n.m.*, (*—s—s*) man-wolf; bug-bear; owl, surly dog; churlish fellow.

lourd, -e, *adj.*, heavy; lumpish, unwieldy; dull, clumsy, thick-headed; awkward.

lourdaud, *n.m.*, **-e**, *n.f.*, lubber, lout; blockhead, loggerhead.

lourdement, *adv.*, heavily, plump; clumsily; grossly.

lourderie, *n.f.*, clumsiness; gross blunder.

lourdeur, *n.f.*, heaviness, sluggishness; dullness; weight.

⊙**lourdise**, *n.f.*, gross blunder.

⊙**loure**, *n.f.*, loure (dance).

lourer, *v.a.*, (mus.) to join the notes.

loustic, *n.m.*, wag.

loutre, *n.f.*, otter. *— marine;* sea-otter.

⊙**louvat**, *n.m.*, young wolf. *V.* **louveteau**.

louve, *n.f.*, she-wolf; wanton woman; (tech.) sling.

louver, *v.a.*, (tech.) to sling.

louvet, -te, *adj.*, fox-colored (of horses).

louveteau (loov-to), *n.m.*, young wolf.

louveter (loov-té), *v.n.*, to whelp (of wolves).

louveterie (loov-trî), *n.f.*, wolf-hunt.

louvetier, *n.m.*, wolf-hunter; (formerly) master of the wolf-hounds.

louviers, *n.m.*, Louviers cloth.

louvoyage, *n.m.*, (nav.) tacking about.

louvoyer, *v.n.*, (nav.) to tack about; to ply by boards; (fig.) to manœuvre; to dodge.

louvre, *n.m.*, Louvre (public edifice in Paris); palace, magnificent house.

love, *n.f.*, bar (of soap).

lover, *v.a.*, (nav.) to coil.

loxodromie, *n.f.*, (nav.) loxodromics; rhumb line.

loxodromique, *adj.*, loxodromic.

loyal, -e, *adj.*, honest, loyal, honorable, true, fair, fair-dealing, straightforward, upright; (com.) of good quality, unadulterated. *Un — chevalier;* a true knight.

loyalement (loa-yal-măn), *adv.*, fairly, loyally, honestly, faithfully, uprightly.

loyauté, *n.f.*, loyalty, honesty, honorableness, fairness, fair-dealing, integrity.

loyer, *n.m.*, hire, rent. *Donner à —;* to let. *Prendre une maison à —;* to hire *or* rent a house. *Les —s sont élevés dans ce quartier;* rents are high in this neighborhood.

lozange, *n.f.* *V.* **losange**.

lubie, *n.f.*, crotchet, maggot, whim. *Il lui prend souvent des —s;* he often takes whims into his head. *A —;* crotchety, whimsical.

lubricité, *n.f.*, lubricity, lechery, lewdness.

lubrifier, *v.a.*, to lubricate.

lubrique, *adj.*, lecherous, lewd, lascivious, wanton.

lubriquement (-brik-măn), *adv.*, lasciviously, lecherously, lewdly.

lucarne, *n.f.*, skylight, dormer-window, garret-window.

lucet, *n.m.*, (bot.) whortle-berry.

lucide, *adj.*, lucid, clear.

lucidité, *n.f.*, lucidness, lucidity, clearness.

lucifer (-fèr), *n.m.*, Lucifer.

lucifuge, *adj.*, shunning the light.

luciole, *n.f.*, glow-worm; fire-fly.

lucrati-f, -ve, *adj.*, lucrative.

lucre, *n.m.*, lucre, gain.

lucubrateur, *n.m.*, lucubrator.

lucubration, *n.f.* *V.* **élucubration**.

lucullus, *n.m.*, (—) lucullus, lavish entertainer.

luette, *n.f.*, (anat.) uvula.

lueur, *n.f.*, glimmer, glimmering, light, glimpse, gleam, spark. *— blafarde;* pale glimmer. *Faible —;* faint glimmer. *Une — d'espérance;* a glimpse *or* ray of hope. *Jeter une faible —;* to glimmer.

lugubre, *adj.*, lugubrious, doleful, dismal, mournful.

lugubrement, *adv.*, dolefully, dismally, mournfully.

lui, *personal pron.*, he ; him, to him ; her, to her ; it, to it. *C'est —;* it is he. *Parlez-lui;* speak to him, to her. *Donnez-lui-en;* give him some.

luire (luisant, lui), *v.n.*, to shine, to glitter ; to gleam, to glisten ; to dawn, to appear.

luisant, -o, *adj.*, glistening, glittering, shining, shiny ; glossy, bright, dawning. *Un ver —;* a glow-worm.

luisant, *n.m.*, gloss.

luisante, *n.f.*, (astron.) brilliant star.

luites, *n.f.pl.* (hunt.) *V.* **suites.**

lulunithe, *n.f.*, lulunite (small fossil coral).

lumachelle, *n.f.*, (min.) lumachella, shellmarble.

lumbago (lon-) *n.m.*, lumbago.

lumière, *n.f.*, light, lamp ; daylight, day ; touch-hole (of a fire-arm) ; information ; intelligence, knowledge ; insight, wisdom, sagacity ; luminary ; (paint.) light. *A la — de;* by the light of. *Eteindre une —;* to put out a light. *Mettre en —;* to demonstrate, to bring to light, to elucidate. *Etre privé de la —;* to have lost one's sight. *La — du soleil, du jour;* the light of the sun, of day. *La — de la raison;* the light of reason.

***lumignon,** *n.m.*, snuff (of a candle) ; wick (of a lamp) ; candle end.

luminade, *n.f.* *A la —;* by torchlight.

luminaire, *n.m.*, luminary, light ; lights (of a church). *Le — d'un enterrement;* lights (at a funeral).

luminariste, *n.m.*, lamp-lighter, gas-fitter.

lumineusement (-neūz-mān), *adv.*, luminously.

lumineu-x, -se, *adj.*, luminous.

lunaire, *adj.*, lunar.

lunaire, *n.f.*, (bot.) lunary, moonwort.

lunaison, *n.f.*, lunation.

lunatique, *adj.* and *n.m.f.*, moon-struck ; fantastical, whimsical, moon-struck, fantastical, whimsical person, lunatic.

lundi, *n.m.*, Monday.

lune, *n.f.*, moon ; fit, crotchet, whim ; moments. *— de mer;* (ich.) sun-fish. *La — est dans son plein;* the moon is full. *Pleine —, nouvelle —;* full moon, new moon. *Clair de —;* moonlight. *— rousse;* April moon. *— d'août;* harvest-moon. *— d'eau;* white waterlily. *Vouloir prendre la — avec les dents;* to attempt impossibilities. *Avoir des —s;* to have whims. *Faire un trou à la —;* to decamp, to make a moonlight flitting ; to flee from one's creditors. *Aboyer à la —;* to bay the moon. *La — de miel;* the honeymoon.

luné, *adj.*, mooned.

lunetier, *n.m.*, spectacle-maker ; spectacleseller ; optician.

lunette, *n.f.*, spy-glass, eye-glass ; telescope ; merry-thought, wish-bone (of a fowl) ; seat (of a close-stool, a water-closet) ; (arch., fort., man.) lunette ; rim (of a watch case). *pl.*, spectacles. *— d'approche;* spy-glass, small telescope. *— de poche;* pocket spy-glass. *Porter des —s;* to wear spectacles.

lunetté, -e, *adj.*, spectacled.

luniforme, *adj.*, luniform, moon-shaped.

luni-solaire, *adj.*, lunisolar.

lunule, *n.f.*, (geom.) lune.

lunulé, -e, *adj.*, (bot.) lunulate.

lupanar, *n.m.*, house of ill-fame, bawdy house.

lupercales, *n.f.pl.*, (antiq.) lupercalia.

lupin, *n.m.*, (bot.) lupine.

lupus, *n.m.*, (med.) lupus.

luride, *adj.*, lurid.

luridité, *n.f.*, luridness, lurid hue.

luron, *n.m.*, **-ne,** *n.f.*, jolly fellow, brick, fine fellow, determined fellow ; buxom, bouncing girl.

lusiade, *n.f.*, Lusiad (Camoens' epic poem).

lustrage, *n.m.*, (manu.) lustring.

lustral, -e, *adj.*, lustral.

lustration, *n.f.*, lustration.

lustre, *n.m.*, luster, brilliancy, brightness ; renown, distinction, gloss ; splendor ; candlestick, chandelier ornamented with drops of cut glass ; luster (space of five years).

lustré, -e, *part.*, glossy.

lustrer, *v.a.*, to give a luster, a gloss, to.

lustrine, *n.f.*, lustring (silk stuff).

lustucru, *n.m.*, simpleton, silly Billy, muff, what-do-you-call-him.

lut (lut), *n.m.*, (chem.) luting.

luter, *v.a.*, (chem.) to lute.

luth (lut), *n.m.*, (mus.) lute.

luthéranisme, *n.m.*, Lutheranism.

luthérien, -ne (-in, -è-n), *n.* and *adj.*, Lutheran.

luthier, *n.m.*, lute-maker.

lutin, *n.m.*, hobgoblin, goblin ; sprite ; elf, imp ; lively person, wild child. *Faire le —;* to play the deuce.

lutin, -e, *adj.*, roguish, waggish, wanton, sprightly.

lutiner, *v.a.*, to plague, to tease, to pester.

lutiner, *v.n.*, to tear about, to play the deuce.

lutrin, *n.m.*, lectern, reading-desk, choir.

lutte, *n.f.*, wrestling ; struggle, contest, strife. *S'exercer à la —;* to practice wrestling. *De haute —;* by main force, with a high hand. *De bonne —;* by fair play.

lutter, *v.n.*, to wrestle ; to struggle, to contend, to strive (against), to cope with, to vie with. *— contre la tempête;* to strive against the storm. *— contre la tentation;* to struggle against temptation.

lutteur, *n.m.*, wrestler.

luxation, *n.f.*, (surg.) luxation, dislocation.

luxe, *n.m.*, luxury ; display, splendor, magnificence, exuberance, profusion ; extravagance, excess. *Objets de —;* fancy goods. *C'est du —;* that is unnecessary, superfluous, useless, uncalled for.

luxé, *part.*, luxated, dislocated.

luxer, *v.a.*, (surg.) to luxate, to dislocate.

se **luxer,** *v.r.*, to become luxated.

luxueu-x, -se, *adj.*, magnificent, rich, sumptuous.

luxueusement, *adj.*, luxuriously, sumptuously, richly.

luxure, *n.f.*, lust, lewdness.

luxuriance, *n.f.*, luxuriance.

luxuriant, -e, *adj.*, luxuriant.

luxurieusement, *adv.*, lustfully, lewdly.

luxurieu-x, -se, *adj.*, lustful, lewd, wanton.

luzerne, *n.f.*, lucern, lucern-grass.

luzernière, *n.f.*, lucern field.

lycanthrope, *n.m.*, person affected with lycanthropy.

lycanthropie, *n.f.*, lycanthropy.

lycée, *n.m.*, lyceum, college, high-school, public-school.

lycéen (-in), *n.m.*, collegian, public schoolboy.

lychniée, *n.f.*, (bot.) lychnis.

lyciet, *n.m.*, (bot.) lycium, box-thorn.

lycopode, *n.m.*, (bot.) lycopodium, wolf'sclaw, club-moss.

lycopside, *n.f.*, lycopsis, bugloss.

lydien, -ne, *n.m.f.* and *adj.*, Lydian.

lymphatique, *adj.*, (med.) lymphatic.

lymphe, *n.f.*, (med.) lymph ; (bot.) sap.

lynx (links), *n.m.*, lynx. *Avoir des yeux de —;* to be lynx-eyed.

lyre, *n.f.*, lyre ; (fig.) talent of the poet, poetry ; (astron., anat.) lyra. *Jouer de la —;* to play on the lyre.

lyrique, n. and adj., lyric ; lyrical. Vers—s ; lyrical verses. Poète —; lyrical poet. Théâtre —; opera-house.

lyrisme, n.m., dignified and poetic style ; poetic enthusiasm.

lysimachie, n.f., lysimachia, loose-strife, willow herb. — bleue ; purple loose-strife. — jaune ; willow-herb.

lysimaque, n.f., (bot.) loose-strife.

lythrode, n.f., (min.) lythrode.

M

m (me), n.m., (ème), n.f., the thirteenth letter of the alphabet, m.

m. (abbrev. of Majesté), M., Majesty ; (abbrev. of Monsieur) Mr., Mister.

m', (contraction of Me), me. V. **me**.

ma, possessive adj. f., my. [Mon is used for the feminine before a vowel or h mute.] — chère ; my dear. Mon âme ; my soul. V. **mon**.

mâ, n.m., china grass.

m.a., (abbrev. of Maison Assurée) house insured.

mab, n.f., Mab (queen of the fairies).

mabolo, n.m., date-plum.

macabre, adj., used only in the expression, danse — ; the dance of death.

macadam, n.m., road metal, macadam.

macadamiser, v.a., to macadamize.

macaire, n.m., swindler, cheat.

macaque, n.m., dog-faced monkey, baboon.

macaron, n.m., macaroon.

macaronée, n.f., (poet.) macaronic.

macaroni, n.m., macaroni.

macaronique, adj., (poet.) macaronic.

macédoine, n.f., dish consisting of a medley of fruit or vegetables ; medley, hotch-potch, olio.

macer, v.a. V. **masser**.

macération, n.f., maceration.

macérer, v.a., to macerate ; (fig.) to mortify.

macérer, v.n., (chem.) to soak, to stand.

se **macérer**, to macerate one's body; to be macerated; (fig.) to mortify one's self.

machabées (-ka-), n.m. pl., Maccabees.

mâche, n.f., (bot.) corn-salad, lamb's-lettuce.

mâchecoulis or **mâchicoulis**, n.m., (fort.) machicolation.

mâche-dru, n.m., (—) (pop.) glutton.

mâchefer (mâsh-fèr), n.m., dross of iron, slag, clinkers ; scoria, hammerslag ; offal, puddler's offal.

mâchelièrc, n.f. and adj., jaw-tooth, grinder, of the jaw. Dents —s ; jaw-teeth, grinders.

mâchement, n.m., chewing, munching.

mâchemoure, n.f., ship biscuit dust.

mâcher, v.a., to chew, to masticate, (of a horse) to champ (the bit) ; to eat ravenously. — à vide ; to chew the air ; (fig., fam.) to delude one's self with false expectations. — de haut ; (fam.) to eat without appetite. Il faut lui — tous ses morceaux ; everything must be ready made to his hand. Ne pas — ce qu'on pense ; not to hesitate saying what one feels, not to mince matters, to speak one's mind. On lui avait mâché sa besogne ; the work had been cut and dried for him.

se **mâcher**, v.r., to be chewed.

mâcheu-r, n.m., -se, n.f., high feeder, trencher-man, muncher. — de tabac ; chewer of tobacco.

machiavélique, adj., Machiavelian.

machiavélisme, n.m., Machiavelism.

machiavéliste, n.m., Machiavelian.

mâchicatoire, n.m., masticatory.

mâchicoulis, n.m. V. **mâchecoulis**.

machinal, -e, adj., mechanical, automatic, instinctive.

machinalement, adv., mechanically, instinctively.

machinateur, n.m., machinator, plotter, contriver.

machination, n.f., machination ; plot ; contrivance.

machine, n.f., machine, engine, implement; machinery, piece of mechanism, apparatus, appliance, intrigue, system, plan, plot ; (fam.) so and so, thingummy. — pneumatique ; air-pump. — soufflante ; blowing-machine. — à colonne d'eau ; water pressing engine. — à détente de vapeur ; expansion steam-engine. — à simple effet ; single-acting engine. — à double effet ; double-acting machine. — à basse, à haute, à moyenne pression ; low, high, mean pressure engine. — à vapeur ; steam-engine. — de vingt chevaux ; engine of twenty horse power. — à mâter ; (nav.) shears (for masting ships). La — va bien, fonctionne bien ; the machinery, the engine, works well. — de recours ; pilot-engine. La — ronde ; (poet., fam.) the earth, the Universe. C'est une pure —, ce n'est qu'une —; (of persons without energy) he, she, is a mere machine. — ! (fam.) so and so, or what 's his name.

machiner, v.a., to machinate, to contrive, to plot ; to plan, (coin) to mill, to edge. Il machine votre perte ; he is plotting your ruin.

machiniste, n.m., machinist, engineer, engineman ; (theat.) stage-carpenter, scene-shifter.

mâchoire, n.f., jaw, jawbone. Jouer, s'escrimer, de la — ; to eat with avidity, to guzzle. C'est une vraie —; he is a blockhead. Avoir la — pesante, lourde ; to express one's self awkwardly, with difficulty. — d'étau ; vice chaps.

mâchonner, v.a., to chew with difficulty; to mumble, to munch, to champ (the bit). Que mâchonnez-vous entre vos dents ? what are you mumbling between your teeth ?

mâchonneu-r, -se, n.m.f., mumbler.

mâchure, n.f., defect in the nap (of cloth).

mâchurer, v.a., to daub, to smear, to smudge, to blacken ; (print.) to maculate.

macis, n.m., mace (spice).

m.a.c.l. (initial letters of the words Maison Assurée contre l'Incendie), house insured against fire.

maclage, n.m., mixing of glass (when in the furnace).

macle, n.f., (bot.) water-caltrop ; (min.) macle; sort of net ; (her.) mascle. V. **macre**.

macler, v.a., to mix hard and soft glass together in the furnace.

maçon, n.m., mason, bricklayer; mason, freemason. C'est un vrai —; he is a bungler.

maçonnage, n.m., mason's work, masonry, stone-work.

maçonner, v.a., to do mason's work, masonry ; to plaster; to bungle, to do badly. — une porte ; to wall up a door. Voyez comme il a maçonné cela ; see in what a slovenly manner he has done that.

maçonnerie (-s-on-rî), n.f., masonry, mason's work; stone-work; masonry, free-masonry. — en liaison ; bound masonry. — brute ; ashlar. — de blocaille ; rubber-work. — maillée ; net-work.

maçonnique, adj., masonic.

macquage, n.m., breaking (of hemp).

macque, n.f., tewing beetle.

macquer, v.a., to tew, to break hemp.

macre or **macle**, n.f., (bot.) water-caltrop.

macreuse, n.f., (orni.) black-diver, king-duck. Avoir un sang de —; to have a cold, frigid disposition.

macrocosme, n.m., (philos.) macrocosm.

macroure, adj., (zool.) macrourous, long-tailed ; (bot.) spiked.

maculature, n.f., (print.) macule, waste sheet of printed paper ; coarse brown paper.

macule, *n.f.*, stain, spot; (astron.) macula. *Agneau sans —*; lamb without spot.

maculer, *v.a.*, to blot, to spot, to maculate.

maculer, *v.n.*, (print.) to become maculated, blotted.

madame, *n.f.*, madam, mistress, my lady, ma'am. *Monsieur vaut bien —*; the husband is as good as the wife. *Faire la —*; to give one's self airs, to play the grand lady. *C'est une grosse —*; (pop.) she is a rich lady. *— y est-elle?* is your mistress, *or* Mrs. so and so, at home? *— la duchesse;* your grace. *— votre mère;* your mother. *Jouer à la —*; to play at lords and ladies.

madapolam, *n.m.*, long-cloth.

madéfaction, *n.f.*, (pharm.) madefaction.

madéfier, *v.a.*, (pharm.) to madefy.

madeleine, *n.f.*, (*—s*) tea-cake, bun; early pear; used also in: *pleurer comme une —*; to weep like a Magdalen.

madelonnette (ma-dlo-nèt), *n.f.*, repentant woman. *—s;* Magdalen asylum (for repentant women), female penitentiary.

mademoiselle (mad-moa-zèl), *n.f.*, miss. — *votre sœur;* your sister. — *désire-t-elle attendre?* would you like to wait, Miss?

madère, *n.m.*, Madeira; Madeira wine. *Gâteau au —*; tipsy cake.

madone, *n.f.*, madonna.

madrague (-drag), *n.f.*, (fish) tunny-net.

madras (-drâs), *n.m.*, bandana, Madras necker-chief.

madré, -e, *adj.*, speckled, spotted, mottled; cunning, sly, sharp. *C'est un — compère;* he is a sly fellow, a knowing card.

madré, *n.m.*, -e, *n.f.*, cunning, sharp, sly person. *Un fin —*; a cunning blade.

madrépore, *n.m.*, (polypes) madrepore.

madrier, *n.m.*, (fort.) madrier; piece of timber; joist, plank, board.

madrigal, *n.m.*, madrigal.

madrure, *n.f.*, speckling, spotting; mottling.

maëstral, *n.m.* V. mistral.

mafflé, -e, *or* mafflu, -e, *n.* and *adj.*, (fam., l.u.) chub-cheeked person; chub-cheeked.

magasin, *n.m.*, magazine, warehouse, store-house; shop, store; stock; magazine (serial); basket (of a coach). *— de nouveautés;* linen-draper's shop. *Marchandise en —*; stock. *Le — des jeunes Demoiselles;* the Young Ladies' Magazine. *Garçon de —*; warehouseman or counter-jumper.

magasinage, *n.m.*, warehousing; warehouse-rent. *Droit de —*; store dues.

⊙magasiner, *v.a.* V. emmagasiner.

magasinier, *n.m.*, warehouse-keeper.

magdaléon, *n.m.*, (pharm.) magdaleon.

mage, *n.m.*, magian. *pl.*, magi, wise men of the East.

⊙mage *or* maje, *adj.*, first, chief. Only used in the expression: *juge —*; chief-justice.

magenta, *n.m.* and *adj.*, magenta (color).

magicien, *n.m.*, -ne, *n.f.*, (-in, -è-n), magician.

magie, *n.f.*, magic. — *blanche;* natural magic. — *noire;* black art, witchcraft. *La — du style;* the magic of the style.

magique, *adj.*, magic, magical. *Baguette —*; magic wand. *Lanterne —*; magic-lantern.

magisme, *n.m.*, magianism.

magister (-tèr), *n.m.*, country schoolmaster; pedant, pedagogue; (Scotch) dominie.

magistère, *n.m.*, grand mastership of the order of Malta; ⊙ (chem., pharm.) magistery, magistral.

magistral, -e, *adj.*, magisterial, masterly; authoritative, dictatorial; principal, sovereign. *Remède —*; sovereign remedy. *Parler d'un ton —*; to speak in an authoritative tone. *Ligne —e;* principal outline.

magistralement (-tral-mān), *adv.*, magisterially, in a masterly manner.

magistrat, *n.m.*, magistrate, judge, corporation, municipal council (in some French towns).

magistrature, *n.f.*, magistracy bench. — *assise;* judges, bench. — *debout;* body of public prosecutors. V. parquet.

magnan, *n.m.*, silk-worm.

*magnanerie, *n.f.*, silk-worm nursery.

*magnanier, *n.m.*, silk-worm breeder.

*magnanime, *adj.*, magnanimous, high-minded, noble.

*magnanimement, *adv.*, magnanimously.

*magnanimité, *n.f.*, magnanimity, high-mindedness.

magnat (mag-na), *n.m.*, nobleman, magnate.

*magnésie, *n.f.*, magnesia. *Sulfate de —*; Epsom salts.

magnésium, *n.m.*, (*n.p.*) (chem.) magnesium.

*magnétique, *adj.*, magnetic.

*magnétiser, *v.a.*, to magnetize, to mesmerize.

*magnétiseur, *n.m.*, magnetizer, mesmerist, mesmerizer.

*magnétisme, *n.m.*, magnetism, mesmerism; (fig.) attraction.

magnificat (mag-ni-fi-kat), *n.m.*, magnificat (hymn to the Virgin Mary).

*magnificence, *n.f.*, magnificence, splendor, grandeur; lavishness; largess, bounty.

*magnifico, *n.m.*, magnifico (grandee).

*magnifier, *v.a.*, to magnify, to extol, to exalt, to praise.

*magnifique, *adj.*, magnificent, gorgeous, splendid, grand; ostentatious, vain.

*magnifiquement (-fik-mān), *adv.*, magnificently, gorgeously, splendidly, grandly.

magnolia *or* magnolier (mag-no-), *n.m.*, (bot.) magnolia.

magot, *n.m.*, (mam.) magot; baboon; booby; ill-favored man; grotesque figure (of china); hoard of money, hidden treasure.

mahaleb, *n.m.*, (bot.) mahaleb.

⊙maheutre *or* mahoitre, *n.f.*, sleeve.

⊙maheutre, *n.m.*, Protestant soldier of the 16th century (French hist.).

mahométan, -e, *n.* and *adj.*, Mahometan, Mohammedan.

mahométisme, *n.m.*, Mahometanism, Mohammedanism.

mahonille, *n.f.*, Virginian stock.

mahou, *n.m.*, coarse woolen cloth.

mahratte, *n.m.*, Mahratta.

mai, *n.m.*, May; may-pole. *Bois de —*; (bot.) hawthorn. *Planter le —*; to set up the may-pole. *Plantation de —*; may-pole dance.

maidan, *n.m.*, (*—s*) market-place (in the East).

maie, *n.f.*, (nav.) kneading-trough, bread-pan.

maieur, *n.m.*, (local ex.) mayor.

maigre, *adj.*, meager, lean, thin, spare, slender; poor, sorry, scanty, dry, barren; (of coal) close-burning. — *échine;* bare-bones (pers.). — *comme un hareng;* as lean as a shotten herring, as thin as a lath. *Jours —s;* fish-days. *Repas —*; fish meal. *Soupe —*; herb soup (made without meat). — *chère;* poor living, poor fare. — *repas;* sorry meal. *Sujet —*; barren subject. *Ecriture —*; scraggy handwriting.

maigre, *n.m.*, lean; (ich.) umbrina; any food save meat. *Faire —*; to abstain from meat. *Traiter en —*; to treat to a fish dinner, *or* to give no meat. *En —*; (carp.) sharply, scantily.

maigrelet, -te, *adj.*, thin, thinnish, lean, spare.

maigrement, *adv.*, meagerly, poorly, sorrily, sparingly.

maigret, -te, *adj.*, lean, poor, thin, spare.

maigreur, *n.f.*, leanness, meagerness; slenderness, thinness, sorriness, poorness, spareness, scantiness, barrenness.

maigrir, v.n., to grow lean, to become lean; to grow thin, to become thin; to fall away, to waste away. *Il maigrit à vue d'œil;* he grows perceptibly thinner.

*****mail**, n.m., mallet; mall (game); mall, promenade (place).

*****maille**, n.f., mesh; stitch; ring, link; mail; speck (on the wings of partridges); web (in the eye); haw (in the eyes of animals); doit, stiver. *Cotte de —s;* coat of mail. *Ils ont toujours — à partir ensemble;* they have always a crow to pluck with each other, a bone to pick with one another. *N'avoir ni sou ni —;* not to have a farthing, to have nothing to bless one's self with.

maillé, -e, adj., stitched; mailed; speckled, spotted. *Fer —;* wire-netting.

*****maillechort**, n.m., German silver; nickel silver.

*****mailler**, v.a., to stitch; to lattice, to mail.

se **mailler**, v.r., to grow, *or* get, speckled.

mailler, n.m., pack-horse, sumpter horse.

maillet, n.m., mallet, beetle.

*****mailloche**, n.f., mallet, beetle.

maillon, n.m., stitch, running knot.

*****maillot**, n.m., swaddling-band; swaddling-clothes; (of acrobats) tights, fleshings. *Enfant au —;* child in arms.

*****maillure**, n.f., (hawking) spots, speckles.

main, n.f., hand; handwriting; lead, trick, deal (at cards); hook (at the end of a well-rope); handle; hand-shovel; body-loop (of carriages); paw (of some animals). *— de papier;* quire of paper. *En lever la —;* to take one's oath to anything. *En mettre la — au feu;* to stake one's life on anything. *Mettre l'épée à la —;* to draw one's sword. *Mettre le pain à la — à quelqu'un;* to put any one in the way of making a livelihood. *Donner la — à quelqu'un;* to give one's hand to any one, to assist any one, to give any one a helping hand. *Baiser les —s à quelqu'un;* to kiss any one's hands. *Tendre la —;* to hold out one's hand, to lend a helping hand. *Donner les —s à une chose;* to consent to a thing. *Cheval de —;* led horse. *Cela est sous votre —;* that is under your very nose. *Il est sous sa —;* he is dependent upon him; he is in his power. *Mettre la — sur quelqu'un;* to lay hands upon any one. *Il n'y va pas de — morte;* he strikes hard, he hits with a vengeance. *Tenir la — à quelque chose;* to take anything in hand, to see that a thing is done. *Un coup de —;* (milit.) bold, unexpected attack, surprise; a bold stroke. *Tour de —;* sleight of hand. *En venir aux —s;* to come to blows. *En être aux —s;* to be engaged (of troops). *Faire — basse sur;* to lay violent hands on, to plunder. *Tenir la — haute à quelqu'un;* to keep a tight hand over any one. *Il l'a fait haut la —;* he did it as easily as could be. *Mettre la dernière — à un ouvrage;* to put the finishing stroke to a work. *Battre des —s;* to clap one's hands. *Faire crédit de la — à la bourse;* to trust no further than one can see. *Mettre la — à une chose;* to set one's hand to a thing. *Mettre la — à la pâte;* to put one's shoulder to the wheel. *Faire — basse sur;* to plunder, to kill, to slaughter; to seize, to lay hands on. *Il a la — bonne;* he is very handy. *Mettre la — à l'œuvre;* to set about a work. *Mettre la dernière — à une chose;* to put the finishing touch to anything. *Être en —;* to be in hand, to have in hand. *Avoir la — légère;* to be free with one's hand. *Lâcher la —;* to give the rein, to give head; to give more liberty; to lower one's pretensions. *J'ai toujours l'argent à la —;* I am always laying out money. *Se faire la —;* to keep one's hand in. *Se perdre la —;* to get rusty. *Il en a les —s nettes;* his hands are clean of it. *Je m'en lave les —s;* I wash my hands of it. *J'en mettrais ma — au feu;* I would stake my life on it. *Ils se*

tiennent tous par la —; they go hand in hand together. *Les —s m'en sont tombées;* I was amazed, astounded. *Froides —s, chaudes amours;* cold hand, warm heart. *Avoir la —;* to have the deal, to lead, to play first. *Avoir la — crochue;* to be light-fingered. *De la — à la bouche, se perd souvent la soupe;* there's many a slip between the cup and the lip. *A la —;* in hand, by hand; ready. *Une chambre grande comme la —;* a room not fit to swing a cat in. *A deux —s;* with both hands. *A pleines —s;* largely, liberally, plentifully. *A toutes —s;* fit for anything; (man.) fitted to ride and drive. *A — armée;* by main force. *A la portée de la —;* within reach. *De longue —;* long since, of old standing. *De — en —;* from one to another, from hand to hand. *En un tour de —;* in a trice, in a twinkling. *Sous —;* underhand, clandestinely. *Sous la —;* at hand. *En —;* in hand. *Hors —, hors la —;* off-side. *En — propre;* personally, into one's own hands. *— courante;* (com.) waste-book.

main chaude, n.f., hot cockles (game).

main-d'œuvre, n.f., (—s—) workmanship, handicraft, manual labor, hand labor.

mainette, n.f., (bot.) coral club-top.

main-forte, n.f., (n.p.) assistance, help, aid. *Prêter — à quelqu'un;* to lend a helping hand to any one.

mainlevée, n.f., (jur.) replevin; withdrawal; raised hand.

mainmise, n.f., (jur.) seizure.

mainmortable, adj., (jur.) subject to mortmain.

mainmorte, n.f., (jur.) mortmain.

maint, -e, adj., many. *— homme;* many a man. *—es fois;* many a time.

maintenant (min-tnãn), adv., now, and now, at this time, at present, this moment, nowadays, by this time.

maintenir (min-tnir), v.a., to sustain, to keep together; to maintain, to keep up; to secure; to enforce, to preserve.

se **maintenir**, v.r., to hold out, to stand one's ground, to maintain one's position; to subsist, to last, to be in force; to keep up, to be kept up, to be maintained. *Se — dans les bonnes grâces de;* to keep one's self in the good graces of.

maintenue, n.f., confirmation of; possession.

maintien (-ti-in), n.m., maintenance, preservation; keeping up; carriage, deportment, bearing; attitude, demeanor.

maïolique *or* **majolique**, n.f., old Spanish *or* Italian earthenware, faïence.

mairain, n.m. *V.* **merrain**.

maire, n.m., mayor.

mairie, n.f., mayoralty; town-hall.

mais (mah-is), n.m., maize, Indian wheat.

mais (mè), conj., but; why. *— encore;* but yet. *—, qu'ai-je fait?* why, what have I done? *—, oui;* why, yes; yes, of course. *—, non;* why, no; no, of course. *Je n'en puis —;* I cannot help it; I have nothing to do with it.

maison, n.f., house, household, home, habitation; family, race; (com.) firm. *Le devant, le derrière, d'une —;* the front, the back, of a house. *— de campagne;* country-house, country-seat. *— seigneuriale;* mansion. *— de ville, — commune;* town-hall. *A la —;* at home. *Tenir —;* to keep house. *Faire — nette;* to dismiss all the servants; to make a clean sweep (of servants). *Faire — neuve;* to change all one's servants. *Garder la —;* to keep at home; to be confined to the house. *Petites—s;* mad-house. *— garnie;* furnished house. *— d'éducation;* school, boarding-school. *— de jeu;* gaming-house. *La — du roi;* the king's household.

maisonnée, n.f., whole house *or* family. *Faire des demandes par dessus les —s;* to make most unreasonable demands.

maisonnette, n.f., small house, cottage, lodge.

maître, n.m., master, owner, proprietor, landlord; ruler; instructor, teacher, governor, director; chief, head; (nav.) boatswain. — *d'école*; school-master. — *de pension*; boarding-school, or house, master. — *d'étude*; usher. — *de chapelle*; precentor. — *de conférences*; lecturer. — *de forges*; iron-master. — *Jacques*; factotum; Jack-of-all-work. — *à danser*, — *de danse*; dancing-master. — *d'armes*; fencing-master. — *des hautes œuvres*; executioner. — *ès-arts*; master of arts. — *d'hôtel*; steward, butler, major-domo. *Un petit* —; (—s—s) a beau, a dandy; a fop. — *homme*; superior man. *Se rendre* — *de la conversation*; to monopolize the whole conversation. *Vous êtes le* — *d'y aller*; you are at perfect liberty to go there. *Il a trouvé son* —; he has met with his match. *Tel* —, *tel valet*; like master, like man. *Compter de clerc à* —; to render a minute account. *Heurter en* —; to rap hard. *De main de* —, *en* —; in a masterly manner. — *clerc*; chief clerk (of a lawyer). *Le* — *autel* (—s—s); the high-altar. — *câble*; sheet cable. — *d'équipage*; boatswain (of a ship of war). — *canonnier*; master-gunner. — *du port*; harbor-master. — *de vaisseau*; commander of a merchant-ship. *Ce tableau est d'un grand* —; that picture is by a great master. *Coup de* —; masterly stroke. *Main de* —; masterly hand. *Un* — *gonin*; an arch cheat.

maîtresse, n.f. and adj., sweetheart, lady-love, mistress; teacher, governess; landlady. adj., chief, head, leading, governing; main, consummate. *Petite* —; lady of studied elegance. — *de pension*; school-mistress. — *d'hôtel*; landlady, hotel-keeper. — *femme*; superior woman. — *ancre*; sheet anchor.

maîtrise, n.f., freedom (of a company); precentorship.

maîtriser, v.a., to master, to domineer, to lord it over, to get master of, to get under; to overcome, to subdue, to control, to manage. — *ses passions*; to control one's passions.

majesté, n.f., majesty. *Crime de lèse-* —; high-treason. *Sa* —; His or Her Majesty.

majestueusement (-efiz-mān), adv., majestically.

majestueu-x, -se, adj., majestic.

majeur, n.m., a male of full age, major; (mus.) major mode; middle finger.

majeur, -e, adj., major, greater; superior, main, chief, paramount; important; of age, of full age; (mus.) major. *Force* —*e*; superior force; absolute necessity; "*vis major*."

majeure, n.f., (log.) major; of age (of a woman).

majolique, n.f., majolica.

major, n.m., major. *Etat-* —; (milit.) staff, staff-officers, headquarters. — *de place*; town commandant. *Tambour* —; drum major.

majorat, n.m., entail; entailed estate.

majordome, n.m., major-domo.

majorité, n.f., majority, full age. *Arriver à sa* —; to come of age.

majuscule, n.f. and adj., capital; large, capital letter.

maki, n.m., (mam.) lemur.

makis or **maquis**, n.m., thicket, brushwood, bush (in Corsica).

mal, n.m., evil, ill; harm, hurt, pain, ache, sickness, distemper, complaint; hardship; pity; mischief; misfortune; trouble, difficulty, labor. — *du pays*; homesickness, nostalgia. *Les maux de la vie*; the evils of life. *Rendre le bien pour le* —; to return good for evil. *De deux maux il faut choisir le moindre*; of two evils, choose the least. *Il a eu plus de peur que de* —; he was more frightened than hurt. *Il faut éviter le* —

et faire le bien; do good and shun evil. *Quel* — *y a-t-il à cela?* what harm is there in that? *Induire quelqu'un à* —; to lead any one into evil. *Penser à* —; to mean harm, to meditate evil. *Il a* — *au côté*; he has a pain in his side. *Un* — *de tête*; a headache. *La tête me fait* —; my head aches. — *de dents*; tooth-ache. — *d'yeux*; sore eyes. *Vous me faites* —; you hurt me. *Avoir* — *à*; to have a pain or pains in. *Faire* —; to ache, to be painful, to hurt. *Faire du* — *à*; to injure, to harm, to be injurious to. — *d'aventure*; whitlow. — *de mer*; sea-sickness. — *de cœur*; qualmishness. *En* —; amiss, ill, in a bad sense. *Aux grands maux les grands remèdes*; desperate diseases require desperate remedies. *Tomber de fièvre en chaud* —; to fall out of the frying-pan into the fire. *Dire du* — *de son prochain*; to speak ill of one's neighbor. *Prendre en* —; to take offense at. *Mener or conduire à* —; to bring to a bad end. *Tourner à* —; to end badly; to take a bad turn. *Tourner en* —; to misinterpret; to put a wrong construction on. *Avoir* — *au cœur*; to feel sick. *J'ai* — *à la tête*; I have a headache.

mal, adv., ill, wrong, amiss, badly; uncomfortably; on bad terms. *Il écrit* —; he writes badly. *Cela va* —; things are going badly. *Vous vous y prenez* —; you go the wrong way to work. *Cet habit vous sied* —, or *vous va* —; that coat does not become you. *De* — *en pis*; from bad to worse. *Se trouver* —; to faint; to feel faint. *Mettre* — *avec*; to set at variance with. *Etre* — *dans ses affaires*; to be low in the world. *Etre* — *avec quelqu'un*; to be on bad terms with any one. — *à propos*; improperly, unseasonably. *Pas* —; not badly; not a little, not a few. *Etre fort* —; to be very ill. *Etre au plus* —; to be past recovery. *N'être pas* —; not to be bad-looking. *Trouver* —; to find amiss. *C'est* — *à lui de*; it is wrong of him to.

malachite (-kit), n.f., (min.) malachite.

malacie, n.f., (med.) malacia, depraved appetite.

malacologie, n.f., malacology.

malactique, n.m. and adj., (med.) emollient.

malade, adj., sick, ill, diseased; unwell, poorly, bad, sickly, infirm; affected, attacked. — *à la mort*; sick unto death. *Avoir l'air* —; to look ill. *Bras* —; sore arm. *Ces plantes sont* —*s*; those plants are diseased. *Rendre* —; to make ill.

malade, n.m.f., sick person, sufferer, invalid; patient. pl. sufferers.

maladie, n.f., illness, sickness, malady, disease, complaint, disorder, distemper; passion, fondness, mania. ☉ — *du pays*; homesickness, nostalgia. *Faire une* —; to have an illness. — *noire*; hypochondria.

maladi-f, -ve, adj., sickly, puny, ailing, unhealthy.

maladivement, adv., unhealthily, morbidly.

☉**maladiveté** (-div-té), n.f., sickliness, unhealthiness.

maladministration, n.f., maladministration.

☉**maladrerie**, n.f., hospital for lepers.

maladresse, n.f., awkwardness, clumsiness, unskillfulness, awkward thing, blunder; (fig.) bad shot. — *!* bad shot!

maladroit, -e, n. and adj., awkward person; awkward, clumsy, stupid, unskillful. *Vous êtes un* —*!* what an awkward fellow you are! *C'est une* —*e*; she is an awkward, clumsy woman.

maladroitement (-droat-mān), adv., clumsily, awkwardly.

malaga, n.m., Malaga (wine).

malaguette or **maniguette**, n.f., Guinea-pepper.

malai or **malais, -e**, n. and adj., Malay.

malai, n.m., Malay language.

malaise, n.m., uncomfortableness, uneasiness,

discomfort. *Sentir du* —; to feel uncomfortable. *Etre dans le* —; to be in straitened circumstances.

malaisé, -e, *adj.*, hard, difficult, rough, toilsome; inconvenient; straitened in circumstances, hard up.

malaisément, *adv.*, with difficulty, with trouble.

malandre, *n.f.*, (vet.) malanders; rotten knot (in timber).

malandreu-x, -se, *adj.*, having rotten knots (of wood); (fig. and fam.) sickly, seedy.

malandrin, *n.m.*, brigand, highwayman, robber, ruffian, marauder.

mal-appris, -e, *adj.* and *n.*, unmannerly, illbred; ill-bred person, churl, vulgar fellow.

malart, *n.m.*, wild drake.

malavisé, -e, *adj.*, ill-advised, imprudent, ill-informed, unwise, silly, ill-judged.

malaxer, *v.a.*, (pharm.) to work up.

malbâti, -e, *n.* and *adj.*, ill-favored person; ill-shaped, gawky.

mal-bouché, -e, *adj.*, (vet.) ill-mouthed.

malchance, *n.f.*, ill-luck, mishap, mischance.

⊙**malcontent,** *n.m.*, disaffected man, malcontent. *Les —s*; (French hist.) the Malecontents, name of a party at the court of Charles IX. *Coiffé à la —*; with hair cut short.

⊙**malcontent, -e,** *adj.*, displeased, dissatisfied, discontented, malcontent.

maldisant, -e, *n.* and *adj.*, slanderer; slanderous.

mâle, *n.m.*, male; cock.

mâle, *adj.*, male, manly, manful, vigorous, virile; masculine, he. *Air —*; manliness. *Voix —*; manly voice. *Style —*; vigorous style.

malédiction, *n.f.*, malediction, curse. *Donner sa — à*; to curse.

malefaim (mal-fin), *n.f.*, gnawing hunger.

maléfice, *n.m.*, witchcraft, sorcery.

maléficié, -e, *adj.*, bewitched; (fig.) worn out, broken down, decrepit.

maléfique, *adj.*, (astrol.) malevolent, malignant.

malemort, *n.f.*, tragic death; bad end.

malencontre, *n.f.*, mishap, mischance, untoward accident.

malencontreusement (-treûz-măn), *adv.*, unluckily, untowardly.

malencontreu-x, -se, *adj.*, unlucky, untoward. *Evénement* —; untoward event.

mal-en-point, *adv.*, badly off; in a sorry plight.

malentendu, *n.m.*, misunderstanding, misapprehension; mistake; misconception.

malepeste ! (mal-pèst), *int.*, egad ! plague on it !

mal-être, *n. m.*, (*n. p.*) uncomfortableness, uneasiness, painful sensation.

malévole, *adj.*, (fam. l.u.) malevolent, evildisposed.

malfaçon, *n.f.*, bad work; cheat, trickery.

malfaire, *v.n.*, to do evil; to do mischief; to be mischievous.

malfaisance, *n.f.*, (l.u.) evil-doing, mischief ; (jur.) malfeasance.

malfaisant, -e, *adj.*, malevolent, mischievous, unhealthy ; injurious, prejudicial. *Nourriture —e;* unwholesome food.

malfait, -e, *adj.*, ill-made, ill-shaped, deformed; badly done; ill-advised.

malfaiteur, *n.m.*, malefactor, evil-doer.

malfamé, -e, *adj.*, ill-famed.

malformation, *n.f.*, malformation.

malgracieusement, *adv.*, ungraciously, rudely, uncivilly.

malgracieu-x, -se, *adj.*, rude, ungracious, uncivil, churlish.

malgré, *prep.*, in spite of; notwithstanding, against the will of. *Il l'a fait — moi;* he did

it in spite of me. *— cela;* nevertheless; for all that; yet.

malhabile, *adj.*, unskillful, awkward.

malhabilement, *adv.*, unskillfully, awkwardly.

malhabileté (-bil-té), *n.f.*, unskillfulness, awkwardness.

malherbe, *n.f.*, deadly carrot.

malheur, *n.m.*, misfortune; mischance, mishap; unhappiness, unfortunate thing; calamity; disaster; accident; adversity; poverty; disgrace, woe. *Par* —; unhappily, unluckily. *De* —; unlucky, ill-omened. *Oiseau de* —; bird of illomen. *Avoir du* —; to be unfortunate. *Jouer de* —; to be unlucky. *Etre en* —; to have a run of ill luck. *Porter* —; to bring ill luck. *Il n'y a qu'heur et — en ce monde,* hap and mishap govern the world. *C'est un petit* —; it is but a slight misfortune. *Un — ne vient jamais seul ;* misfortunes never come singly. *A quelque chose — est bon ;* it is an ill wind that blows no one any good. *Quel — !* what a misfortune ! *— à vous !* woe betide you ! *— aux vaincus !* woe to the vanquished ! *Pour comble,* or *pour surcroît de* —; to crown all; as a crowning misfortune.

malheureusement (-reûz-măn), *adv.*, unfortunately, unluckily, unhappily.

malheureu-x, -se, *adj.*, unfortunate, unlucky, unsuccessful, disastrous, fatal, unpleasant, disagreeable; unhappy; miserable, wretched, poor, needy. *Il est né* —; he was born unfortunate. *Il mène une vie fort —se;* he leads a most unhappy life. *Faire une fin —se ;* to come to an unhappy end.

malheureu-x, *n.m.*, **-se,** *n.f.*, unhappy person, wretched being; poor wretch, wretch; naughty child. *Ce — fera une mauvaise fin;* the wretch will come to a bad end. *— !* wretch that you are !

malhonnête, *adj.*, dishonest; impolite; uncivil; rude. *n.m.f.,* rude fellow, saucy baggage.

malhonnêtement (-nêt-măn), *adv.*, dishonestly; unpolitely, rudely, uncivilly.

malhonnêteté (-nêt-té), *n.f.*, impoliteness, rudeness, incivility; rude action; dishonesty, knavery. *Il est d'une — révoltante ;* he is shockingly rude.

malice, *n.f.*, malice, maliciousness, spite; roguishness, archness; prank, waggish thing, roguish thing, trick, dodge.

malicieusement (-eûz-măn), *adv.*, maliciously, malignantly; archly, roguishly, slyly.

malicieu-x, -se, *adj.*, malicious, malignant, mischievous ; roguish, waggish, arch ; spiteful, sly. *Un enfant* —; a roguish child.

*****malignement,** *adv.*, malignantly, maliciously.

*****malignité,** *n.f.*, malignity, malice; maliciousness.

malin, *n.m.*, devil, evil spirit, fiend.

mali-n, *-gne, *adj.*, malicious, mischievous, malignant; waggish, arch, roguish; shrewd, sly, knowing, clever, cunning. *L'esprit* —, le — *esprit ;* the evil one, Satan. *Un regard* —; an arch look. *Il est trop — pour se laisser attraper ;* he is too shrewd to be caught. *Fièvre —gne ;* malignant fever.

mali-n, *n.m.*, *-gne,* *n.f.*, malignant, malicious person; sly, shrewd, acute person; knavish person. *C'est un* —; he is a sly one, a knowing one.

maline, *n.f.*, (nav.) spring-tide.

malines, *n.f.*, Mechlin, Mechlin lace.

malingre, *adj.*, poorly, sickly, weakly, puny.

malintentionné, -e, *n.* and *adj.*, evil-minded person, evil-minded, ill-disposed. *Il est — à votre égard ;* he is ill-disposed towards you.

malique, *adj.*, (chem.) malic.

malitorne, *n.* and *adj.*, awkward, ungainly, dowdy person; awkward, ungainly, gawky, clumsy.

mal-jugé, *n.m.,* (*n.p.*) (jur.) erroneous judgment, error in judgment.

mallard, *n.m.,* small grindstone.

malle, *n.f.,* trunk; peddler's box; mail, mail-coach; mail. *Faire, défaire, sa —;* to pack up, to unpack.

malléabilité (mal-lé-), *n.f.,* malleability.

malléable (mal-lé-), *adj.,* malleable.

malléole, *n.f.,* (anat.) malleolus, ankle-bone.

malle-poste, *n.f.,* (*—s—s*) mail-coach.

malletier (mal-tié), *n.m.,* (l.u.) trunk-maker.

mallette, *n.f.,* small trunk; portmanteau.

mallier, *n.m.,* shaft-horse, wheeler.

malmener, *v.a.,* to use ill, to maltreat, to handle roughly; to bully, to abuse.

malotru, *n.m.,* **-e,** *n.f.,* ill-bred person; uncouth person, lout, boor.

***malpeigné,** *n.m.,* dirty fellow, dirty pig. *adj.,* unkempt.

malplaisant, -e, *adj.,* unpleasant, disagreeable.

malpropre, *adj.,* dirty, slovenly, squalid, untidy; unfit for.

malproprement, *adv.,* dirtily, slovenly, squalidly.

malpropreté, *n.f.,* dirtiness, uncleanliness, slovenliness; dirt, filth.

malsain, -e, *adj.,* unhealthy, sickly; unwholesome, injurious, dangerous; not good for. *Cet air est —;* that air is injurious to, not good for, health.

malséance, *n.f.,* unbecomingness, unseemliness, impropriety.

malséant, -e, *adj.,* unbecoming, unseemly, improper.

malsonnant, -e, *adj.,* ill-sounding, offensive.

malt (malt), *n.m.,* malt.

maltage, *n.m.,* maltage.

malté, -e (*adj.*), malted.

malteur, *n.m.,* maltman, maltster.

maltraiter, *v.a.,* to maltreat; to treat harshly, to use ill, to abuse; to handle roughly; to wrong, to injure.

malvacée, *n.* and *adj.f.,* malvaceous plant; malvaceous.

***malveillance,** *n.f.,* malevolence, ill-will, malice.

***malveillant, -e,** *adj.,* malevolent, malignant, ill-disposed, ill-natured, spiteful.

***malveillant,** *n.m.,* evil-minded person.

malversation, *n.f.,* malversation, malpractice, embezzlement, fraud.

malverser, *v.n.,* to be guilty of malversation, of malpractices; to embezzle.

malvoisie, *n.f.,* Malmsey.

malvoulu, -e, *adj.,* (l.u.) disliked, hated; cut, avoided.

maman, *n.f.,* mamma, mother. *Bonne —, grand'—;* grandmother, granny. *Une grosse —;* a fat woman.

mame (pop.), for **madame.**

mamelle, *n.f.,* breast; teat; udder. *Un enfant à la —;* a child at the breast.

mamelon (ma-mlon), *n.m.,* nipple, teat; dug (of animals); pap (of a mountain).

mamelonné, -e, *adj.,* mammillated.

mamelu, -e (ma-mlu), *adj.,* full-breasted.

mameluk (ma-mlook), *n.m.,* Mameluke.

mamillaire (-mil-lèr), *adj.,* (anat.) mammillary.

mammaire (mam-mèr), *adj.,* (anat.) mammary.

mammalogie (mam-ma-), *n.f.,* mammalogy.

mammalogiste (mam-ma-), *n.m.,* mammalogist.

mammifère (mam-mi-), *n.m.* and *adj.,* mammifer ; mammiferous.

mammiforme (mam-mi-) *adj.,* mammiform.

mammon, *n.m.,* Mammon.

mammouth, *n.m.,* mammoth.

m'amour, (obsolete abbreviation of *ma amour*), my love, lovee. **—s;** marks of love, caresses, soft nothings; wheedling, coaxing. *Faire des —s;* to fawn upon, to coax, to wheedle.

manant, *n.m.,* ⊙peasant ; clown, clodhopper.

***mancenille,** *n.f.,* (bot.) manchineel.

***mancenillier,** *n.m.,* manchineel-tree.

manche, *n.m.,* handle ; neck (of musical instruments). **— à gigot;** bone-holder. **— de gigot;** knuckle-bone (of mutton); finger-board (of a violin); tail (of a plow). **— de couteau;** knife handle. *Il branle dans le —;* he hesitates; he is irresolute. *Jeter le — après la cognée;* to throw the rope after the bucket (*i.e.* to give up in despair).

manche, *n.f.,* sleeve ; (geog.) channel ; (at play) rubber, game, heat ; (nav.) flexible pipe, hose. *Bouts de —;* half-sleeves. *Grandes —s;* pudding-sleeves. *—s pendantes;* hanging-sleeves. **— à —;** even (at play). *Avoir une personne dans sa —;* to have somebody at one's disposal. *C'est une autre paire de —s;* that is quite another thing *or* a horse of another color *or* quite another pair of shoes. *J'ai gagné la première —;* I have won the first game (of the rubber) *or* first heat (racing). **— à vent;** (nav.) windsail.

manchette, *n.f.,* cuff, ruffle ; (print.) side-note.

manchon, *n.m.,* muff.

manchot, -te, *n.m.f.* and *adj.,* one-handed, one-armed person ; one-handed, one-armed. *Il n'est pas —;* he is no fool.

manchot, *n.m.,* (orni.) penguin.

mancienne (-si-èn), *n.f.,* mealy-tree, wayfaring-tree.

mandant, *n.m.,* (jur.) employer ; (com.) principal ; constituent, elector.

mandarin, *n.m.,* mandarin.

mandarine, *n.f.,* mandarin orange.

mandarinier, *n.m.,* (bot.) mandarin orange-tree.

mandat, *n.m.,* (jur.) warrant, mandate, authority, charge, commission ; (com.) draft ; check ; money-order; order. **— de comparution;** summons to appear. **— d'arrêt,** **— d'amener;** warrant. **— de** or **sur la poste;** money order. **— de dépôt;** commitment. **— de perquisition;** search warrant. **— de banque;** bank-post bill.

mandataire, *n.m.,* mandatory; proxy, attorney, representative, agent.

mandater, *v.a.,* to deliver an order for the payment of ; to deliver an order for.

mandement (mān-dmān), *n.m.,* mandate, order, mandamus ; charge (of a bishop).

mander, *v.a.,* to write, to write word, to send word, to send for; to inform, to acquaint, to let know. *Je lui ai mandé de venir ;* I have sent him word to come. *On a mandé le médecin ;* the doctor was sent for.

mandibule, *n.f.,* (anat.) mandible, jaw.

⊙***mandille,** *n.f.,* livery-coat.

mandoline, *n.f.,* mandolin.

mandoliniste, *n.m.,* mandolin-player.

mandore, *n.f.,* mandore (sort of lute).

mandragore, *n.f.,* (bot.) mandrake.

***mandrill,** *n.m.,* (mam.) mandrill, rib-nosed baboon.

mandrin, *n.m.,* mandrel, (tech.) chuck, punch.

manducation, *n.f.,* manducation.

manéage, *n.m.,* (nav.) hand-work, handiwork.

manège, *n.m.,* manege, horsemanship ; riding-school ; manœuvre, by-play, trick, intrigue.

mânes, *n.m.pl.,* manes, shade, ghost, shades.

manet, *n.m.,* drift-net.

maneton, *n.m.,* lever-handle.

manette, *n.f.,* (tech.) handgear ; (hort.) trowel.

manganèse, *n.m.,* manganese.

mangeable (-jabl), *adj.,* eatable, fit to eat.

*mangeaille (-jâ-i), n.f., food (for birds, cats) ; (b.s.) victuals, grub, eatables.

mangeant, -e (-jän, -t), adj., eating. *Etre bien —;* to eat heartily ; to be a hearty eater.

mangeoire (-joâr), n.f., manger, crib.

mangeoter, v.n., to eat little, to pick one's food ; to nibble.

manger, v.a., to eat ; to eat up ; to consume ; to squander away, to run through. *Salle à —;* dining-room. *— son bien;* to squander one's property. *A —;* to eat. *Donner à —;* to give food, to keep an eating-house. *— du bout des doigts;* to pick a bit here and there ; to nibble at one's food. *— des yeux;* to look daggers at. *On mange bien dans cet hôtel;* the cooking is excellent in that hotel. *— ses mots;* to clip one's words. *Les gros poissons mangent les petits;* (fig.) might overcomes right.

se manger, v.r., to eat each other ; to eat each other up ; to hurt each other, to look daggers at one another ; (gram.) to be cut off, elided, not pronounced.

manger, v.n., to eat ; to take one's meals ; to feed. *Il mange dans la main;* he eats out of your hand (of an animal). *Donnez-moi à —;* give me something to eat.

manger, n.m., eating, victuals, food. *Le — et le boire;* eating and drinking.

mangerie (man-jrî), n.f., (pop.) eating ; exaction, extortion, imposition.

mange-tout, n.m., (—) prodigal, spendthrift, squanderer.

mangeu-r, n.m., **-se**, n.f., eater ; great eater ; spendthrift. *Un — de viandes apprêtées;* a lazy fellow. *— de petits enfants;* braggart. *— de livres;* a book-worm.

mangeure (-jur), n.f., place nibbled (by mice), feeding (for boars).

mangle, n.f., (bot.) mangle (fruit).

manglier, n.m., (bot.) mangrove, mangle.

mangonneau, n.m., mangonel (an engine formerly used for throwing stones).

mangoustan, n.m., (bot.) mangostan.

mangouste, n.f., (mam.) ichneumon ; mangostan (fruit).

mangue (mang), n.f., (bot.) mango.

manguier (-ghié), n.m., (bot.) mango-tree.

maniable, adj., easy to be handled, workable ; tractable, manageable, supple, pliable.

maniaque, n.m.f. and adj., maniac. adj., mad, furious, eccentric ; crotchety.

manichéen (-in), **-ne**, n. and adj., Manichean.

manichéisme, n.m., Manicheism.

manichordion (-kor-), n.m., manichord, manicordon.

manicle, n.f. V. **manique**.

manie, n.f., mania, madness, folly, fancy, whim, hobby ; inveterate habit.

maniement or **maniment**, n.m., handling ; wielding ; management, use, conduct, handling of money. *— des armes;* manual exercise. *Le — des deniers;* the management of money.

manier, v.a., to feel, to handle ; to touch ; to use, to wield, to ply, to manage, to govern. *Il sait bien — le ciseau;* he is a fine sculptor. *Au —;* by the touch, by handling. *— une affaire;* to manage a business.

manier, v.n., (man.) to act (of a horse).

manière, n.f., manner, way, fashion, sort, kind ; style, mannerism, affectation, fuss ; attitude. *La — dont je lui ai parlé;* the way in which I spoke to him. *De — ou d'autre;* somehow or other. *Chacun a sa —;* every one has his own way of doing. *— de parler;* mode of speech. *De la bonne —;* handsomely. *Par — d'acquit;* for form's sake. *La — de cet auteur est grande;* that author's style is grand. *De la même —;* in the same manner. *Il a des —s agréables;* he has pleasing manners. *De — que* or *de — à ce que;* so that. *Il est une des plus grandes —s*

du siècle; he is one of the finest stylists of the century.

maniéré, -e, adj., affected, unnatural, forced. *Air —;* affected air.

maniériste, n.m., mannerist.

manieur, n.m., handler, manager.

manifestation, n.f., manifestation.

manifeste, adj., manifest, evident.

manifeste, n.m., manifesto.

manifestement, adv., manifestly.

manifester, v.a., to manifest, to make known, to display, to show. *— sa pensée;* to make known one's thought.

se manifester, v.r., to manifest one's self, to assert one's self, to be made manifest.

manigance, n.f., manœuvre, underhand dealing, intrigue.

manigancer, v.a., to contrive, to plot, to concoct. *Se —;* to be brewing, to be concocted.

maniguette, n.f. V. **malaguette**.

maniguière, n.f., net (for catching eels).

manille, n.f., (at cards) manille ; manilla cheroot.

manioc, manihot, or **manioque**, n.m., (bot.) manioc, cassado, tapioca, cassava.

manipulateur, n.m., manipulator.

manipulation, n.f., manipulation.

manipule, n.m., handful ; (c.rel., antiq., pharm.) maniple.

manipuler, v.a. and n., to manipulate.

manique or **manicle**, n.f., hand-leather.

maniveau, n.m., osier-stand ; punnet.

manivelle, n.f., handle, winch, crank, (fig.) drudgery, daily round. *La — d'un gouvernail;* the whipstaff of a helm.

manne (mâ-n), n.f., manna ; (fig.) balm, gift. *— en larmes;* manna in flakes. *— céleste;* manna from Heaven.

manne (ma-n), n.f., hamper, flat basket. *— d'enfant;* cradle. *— à marée;* fish-crate.

mannequin (ma-n-kin), n.m., hamper ; small hamper ; (paint.) lay-figure, dummy, puppet ; insignificant person. *Figure qui sent le —;* unnatural figure. *C'est un vrai —;* he is a mere automaton.

mannequiné, -e, adj., unnatural. *Ces figures sont —es;* (paint.) those figures are unnatural, smack of the lay-figure.

manœuvre, n.f., handiwork, handcraft, working, manœuvre, move, management, tactics ; (nav.) rope; working (a ship) ; (milit.) drill. *pl.* (nav.) rigging. *—s courantes;* running-rigging. *—s dormantes;* standing-rigging. *Officier qui entend la —;* officer expert in working a ship. *Amarrer une —;* to make a rope fast.

manœuvre, n.m., workman, journeyman-mason, laborer ; bungler ; crafty person. *Ce n'est qu'un —;* he is a mere mechanic. *Travail de —;* manual labor.

manœuvrer, v.a. and n., to manœuvre ; to work (a ship). *— les voiles;* to work the sails. *Faire — des soldats;* to drill soldiers.

manœuvrier, n.m., able seaman ; tactician.

manoir, n.m., manor, mansion, manor-house.

manomètre, n.m., (phys.) manometer.

manométrique, adj., (phys.) manometrical.

manouvrier, n.m., day-laborer, workman, hodman.

manquant, -e, n.m.f. and adj., absentee, defaulter ; missing, absent, wanting, failing, short.

manque, n.m., want, lack, need ; shortcoming, failure, defect ; (riding) stumble. *Il a trouvé dix francs de —;* he found he was ten francs short. *— de;* for want of. *— de touche;* (at billiards) miss.

manqué, -e, part., defective ; abortive, miscarried ; a failure ; spoilt. *Une affaire —e, un coup —;* a failure. *Un poète —;* a would-be poet.

manquement (man-kmän), n.m., omission,

shortcoming, oversight, failure, want, slip, breach.

manquer, v.n., to miss, to fail; to be wanting; to be wanting in respect; to be deficient; to miss fire; to stand in need of; to forfeit, to break; to be insolvent; to be near, to have need; to be out, in want, of; to decay; to miscarry; to give way, to infringe, to disregard, to disappoint. *Arme à feu qui manque;* a fire-arm that misses fire. *Marchand qui a manqué;* bankrupt merchant. *Le cœur lui manque;* her heart fails her. *Les forces lui manquent;* his strength fails him. *Le pied lui a manqué;* his foot slipped. *L'argent lui manque;* he is short of money. *Rien ne vous manquera;* you shall want for nothing. *La poudre leur manque;* they are short of powder. *L'affaire a manqué;* the business has miscarried, the affair has fallen through. — *à son devoir;* to fail in one's duty. — *à sa parole;* to break one's word. — *à un rendez-vous;* to fail to keep an appointment. *Je n'y manquerai pas;* I will not fail. *Il ne manque de rien;* he wants for nothing, or has all he wants. *Il ne manque pas de vanité;* he does not lack vanity. — *de parole;* to fail in one's promise. — *d'argent;* to be in want of money. *Ne manquez pas de vous y trouver;* do not fail to be there. *Il a manqué de tomber;* he was very near falling. — *à quelqu'un,* — *de respect à quelqu'un;* to be disrespectful to or wanting in respect to. *Il manque de tout;* he is destitute of everything. *Vous me manquez;* I miss you. *Je vous manque;* you miss me. *Il ne manquait plus que cela!* was the last straw or that crowns all or what next, I wonder! *La — belle,* (lit. to miss a fine opportunity) to have a narrow escape.

manquer, v.a., to miss, to lose. *Il a manqué son coup;* he has missed his aim. — *une occasion;* to lose an opportunity.

se **manquer,** v.r. to forget what is due to one's self, to be wanting in self-respect, to forget one's honor, to prove false.

mansarde, n.f., attic, garret, roof. *Fenêtre en —;* attic window. *Toit en —;* curb roof.

mansardé, -e, adj., with attics, garrets.

manse, n.f., (feudality) revenue (of abbeys). V. **mense.**

mansuétude, n.f., mildness, meekness, gentleness, forbearance.

mante, n.f., mantle (woman's). — *religieuse;* (ent.) praying mantis.

manteau, n.m., cloak; mantle, train, cape; mask, pretense; (her.) mantling. *S'envelopper de son —;* to wrap one's self up in one's cloak. *Le — royal;* the royal mantle. *Cela se vend sous le —;* that is sold clandestinely. *Garder les — x;* to stand sentinel; to take no share in. — *de cheminée;* mantel-piece.

mantelet (man-tlè), n.m., short cloak; mantlet; (fort.) mantlet. — *s de sabords;* (nav.) port-lid; (of a coach) apron.

mantelle, n.f., hooded crow; the coat of a dog; the hair on its back.

mantelure (man-tlur), n.f. mantling.

*****mantille,** n.f., mantilla.

manuel, -le, adj., manual, portable.

manuel, n.m., manual, hand-book, text-book.

manuellement (-èl-män), adv., from hand to hand, manually.

manufacture, n.f., manufacture, making, make; manufactory; mill, works, factory.

manufacturer, v.a., to manufacture. *Se —;* to be manufactured.

manufacturi-er, -ère, adj., manufacturing.

manufacturier, n.m., manufacturer.

manumission, n.f., manumission.

in **manus,** n.m. V. **in manus.**

manuscrit, -e, adj., manuscript matter.

manuscrit, n.m., manuscript.

manutention, n.f., management, care, making, fabrication; (l.u.) upholding, enforcement; (milit.) bake-house, bakery, bread-making.

manutentionner, v.a., to bake for the army.

mappemonde (map-mond), n.f., map of the world. — *céleste,* planisphere.

maque, n.f. V. **macque.**

maquer, v.a. V. **macquer.**

maquereau (ma-krô), n.m., (ich.) mackerel, (l.ex.) pimp, pander; reddish spot on one's legs; procurer, brothel-keeper.

maquerellage, n.m., (l.ex.) panderism, pimping, procuring.

maquerelle, n.f., (l.ex.) procuress.

maquette, n.f., (sculpt.) small rough model (in clay, wax); (paint.) rough sketch, lay figure.

*****maquignon,** n.m. (b.s.), horse-dealer; horse-jockey; jockey; jobber. — *de charges;* (b.s.) agent for the sale of offices. — *de mariages;* (b.s.) matrimonial agent.

*****maquignonnage,** n.m., (b.s.) horse-dealing; jockeyship; bishoping; underhand work; jobbing.

*****maquignonné, -e,** part., trimmed up for sale, bishoped (of horses).

*****maquignonner,** v.a., (b.s.) to jockey, to trim, to bishop (a horse for sale); to job; to carry on any illicit trade.

*****maquilleur,** n.m., (nav.) mackerel-boat.

maquilleuse, n.f., face-painter, enameler.

maquis, n.m. V. **makis.**

marabout, n.m., marabout (priest); ill-favored man, big-bellied copper kettle; (orni.) marabou-stork feathers; a kind of ribbon.

maraîcher, n.m., market-gardener.

marais, n.m., marsh, fen, bog, swamp, morass; low-lying market-garden ground (Paris). *Dessécher un —;* to drain a marsh. — *salant;* salt-marsh. *Chasse au —;* moor-shooting.

marasca, n.m., (hort.) sour cherry.

marasme, n.m., (med.) marasmus, consumption, atrophy, emaciation.

marasquin, n.m., maraschino.

marâtre, n.f., step-mother; unkind, harsh mother.

maraud, -e, n.f., -e, n.f., scoundrel, rascal, knave; slut, jade.

maraudage, n.m., marauding, freebooting.

*****maraudaille,** n.f., rabble, knave.

maraude, n.f., marauding; (cabmen's slang) crawling, plying for hire.

marauder, v.n., to maraud; to crawl, to ply for hire.

maraudeur, n.m., marauder; crawler.

maravédis, n.m., maravedi (small Spanish coin).

marbre, n.m., marble; marble, slab, stone for grinding colors, etc.; (print.) imposing-stone, slab. *pl.,* works, statues, etc., made of marble; samples of various kinds of marble. *Il est de —;* he is made of stone. — *jaspé,* variegated marble. *Plaque de —;* slab of marble. — *filandreux;* fibrous marble. — *terrasseux;* terrene marble. — *du gouvernail;* (nav.) barrel of the steering-wheel. *Sur le —;* (print.) in type.

marbré, -e, part., adj., marbled. *Du papier —;* marbled, mottled paper.

marbrer, v.a., to marble, to vein, to mottle. *Se —;* to become marbled.

marbrerie, n.f., marble-cutting, marble-work, marble-yard; marble-works.

marbreur, n.m., marbler.

marbrier, n.m., marble-cutter, marble-polisher; marble-grainer, dealer in marble.

marbrière, n.f., marble-quarry.

marbrure, n.f., marbling, marble-graining.

marc (mar), n.m., mark. *Poids de —;* eight-ounce weight. *Au — la livre* or *le franc;* so many cents in the dollar. — *d'or;* a duty paid to the king by the titularies of certain offices.

marc (mar), *n.m.*, residuum (of anything squeezed, boiled, or strained). — *de raisin;* skins, husks of grapes after the last pressing. — *de café;* grounds, grouts of coffee.

marcassin, *n.m.,* young wild boar, grice.

marcassite, *n.f.,* (min.) marcasite.

marceline, *n.f.,* colored silk fabric; (min.) red silicate of manganese.

marchand, *n.m.,* -**e,** *n.f.,* merchant, dealer, tradesman, shopkeeper; hawker, peddler, trader, store-keeper; buyer, customer; bidder (at auctions); (orni.) surf-scoter. — *en gros;* wholesale dealer, merchant. — *en détail;* retail merchant. — *fripier;* second-hand clothes dealer. *Petit* — ; chandler. — *ambulant, forain;* itinerant dealer. *N'est pas — qui toujours gagne;* we must expect to meet with losses sometimes. *Y a-t-il — ?* is there a bidder, does any one bid? (at auctions). *Trouver* —; to find a customer, a purchaser. *C'est un — de soupe;* he's a regular Squeers. *En être le mauvais* —; to get the worst of the bargain.

marchand, -**e,** *adj.,* merchantable, marketable, saleable, vendible; mercantile, trading; navigable (of rivers). *Prix* —; trade price, wholesale price. *Place* —*e;* trading-place. *Vaisseau* —; merchantman, merchant-ship. *Capitaine* —; merchant-captain. *Marine* —*e;* merchant-service; mercantile navy.

marchandage, *n.m.,* task-work, piece-work; bargaining.

marchandailler, *v.n.,* to haggle.

marchande, *n.f.,* tradeswoman. — *lingère;* linen draper. — *d'huîtres;* oyster-woman. — *de modes;* milliner.

marchander, *v.a.,* to ask the price of, to cheapen, to bargain for, to haggle for, to chaffer for; to spare; to hesitate to expose; to grudge, to trouble. *Ne pas — quelqu'un;* not to spare any one, not to mince matters with any one. *Il ne marchande pas sa vie;* he does not hesitate to expose his life.

se **marchander,** *v.r.* to be cheapened, to spare each other.

marchander, *v.n.,* to haggle, to chaffer, to stand haggling, to bargain; to be irresolute, to hesitate.

marchandeur, *n.m.,* task-master, middleman; haggler, bargainer.

marchandise, *n.f.,* merchandise, goods, ware, commodity. *Faire valoir sa* —; to cry up one's goods, to set one's self off. — *qui plaît est à demi-vendue;* please the eye and pick the purse.

marche, *n.f.,* walk; walking; gait, march; progress, journey, course, advance; procession; step, stair; move (at chess, drafts); conduct, arrangement; way of proceeding; military frontier, border; marches, borders, between England and Wales, also between England and Scotland. *Ce vaisseau a une — avantageuse;* that vessel is a fast sailer. *Vaisseau construit pour la* —; ship built to sail very fast or for speed; clipper. *Mettre en* —; to set going. *Faire une fausse* —; to play a false move. *Gagner une — sur;* to steal a march upon. — *d'un poème;* progress of a poem. — *d'escalier;* step of a staircase. — *d'un tour;* treadle of a lathe. — *de deux heures;* two hours' walk or journey. *La — de cet homme a été louche dans l'affaire;* the conduct of that man in the matter has been suspicious. — *militaire,* — *triomphale;* military, triumphal, march. *L'armée est en* —; the army is on the march. *Fermer la* —; to close the procession. *Ouvrir la* —; to lead the way.

marché, *n.m.,* market, market-place; market-time; bargain, purchase, price, rate; sale; agreement, contract, treaty. — *au blé, aux herbes, au poisson;* corn, grass, fish-market. *Bon* —; cheapness. *Conclure un* —; to strike a bargain. *Acheter, vendre, à bon* —; to buy, to sell cheap. *Avoir bon — de;* to easily get the better of. *Faire bon — d'une chose;* to hold anything cheap, not to spare; to think little of. *Mettre le — à la main à quelqu'un;* to offer any one to break off a bargain; to make any one take it or leave it. *Vous n'en serez pas quitte à si bon* —; you shall not get off so easily. *On n'a jamais bon — de mauvaise marchandise;* the best is cheapest. *Il le paiera plus cher qu'au* —; he shall smart for it, he shall repent it or rue it. — *d'or;* excellent bargain, great bargain. *Meilleur* — or *à meilleur* —; cheaper. *C'est un — donné;* it is absolutely given away. *Par-dessus le* —; into the bargain. *Le — tient tous les jours;* the market is held every day. *Cours du* —; market-price. *Est-ce — fait?* is it a bargain?

marche-palier, *n.f.,* landing step.

marchepied (marsh-pié), *n.m.,* stepping-stone; towing-path; foot-board, footstool; step (of a coach, altar). *pl.* (nav.) foot-ropes of the yards. *Servir de* —; to serve as a stepping-stone.

marcher, *v.n.,* to walk, to step; to tread; to go, to travel, to march, to wade; to sail, to run, to ply; to move on, to advance, to progress; to go on; to flow, to run, to rank. — *en avant, en arrière, à reculons;* to walk forward, to walk backward. — *à grands pas, sur la pointe du pied;* to stride along, to walk on tiptoe. — *à quatre pattes;* to go on all-fours. — *à pas de loup;* to walk with stealthy steps. — *sur les traces de quelqu'un;* to follow in any one's footsteps. — *sur les talons de quelqu'un;* to tread on any one's heels. — *sur des épines;* to tread on thorns. — *de front;* to march abreast. — *droit;* to walk straight. *Faire* —; to get along, to set going. *Je le ferai — droit;* I will take care that he behaves well. *Cette montre marche bien;* this watch keeps good time. *Ce navire marche bien;* this vessel sails well or is very fast. — *sur quelque chose;* to tread upon anything. — *égal à;* to be equal to. — *à l'ennemi;* to march against the enemy. — *à tâtons;* to grope or feel one's way.

marcher, *n.m.,* walking, walk; gait, step, pace, treading, tread; ground (on which one walks).

marcher, *v.a.,* (hat-making) to press, to felt, to full, to tread.

marcheu-r, *n.m.,* -**se,** *n.f.,* pedestrian, walker, (nav.) sailer. *Bon* —; (nav.) fast-sailing, swift-sailing, vessel; fast sailer.

marcottage, *n.m.,* (hort.) layering.

marcotte, *n.f.,* (hort.) layer.

marcotter, *v.a.,* (hort.) to layer (vines, etc.).

mardelle. *V.* **margelle.**

mardi, *n.m.,* Tuesday. — *gras;* Shrove-Tuesday. — *saint;* Tuesday before Easter; Tuesday in Passion-week.

mare, *n.f.,* pool, pond; trough (used by cider brewers).

maréage, *n.m.,* hire, pay (for a voyage).

marécage, *n.m.,* marsh, bog, fen, swamp, morass.

marécageu-x, -**se,** *adj.,* marshy, fenny, swampy, boggy. *Pays* —, *terrain* —; marshy land.

maréchal, *n.m.,* farrier, shoeing-smith; marshal, field-marshal. — *des logis;* sergeant-major (in the cavalry). — *ferrant;* farrier. — *vétérinaire;* farrier and veterinary surgeon. — *de camp;* brigadier, brigadier-general. — *de France;* Marshal of France. *Grand* —; grand marshal; earl marshal, lord high steward.

maréchalat, *n.m.,* marshalship.

maréchale, *n.f.,* field-marshal's wife.

maréchalerie, *n.f.,* farriery.

⊙**maréchaussée.** *n.f.,* marshalsea, constabulary; mounted police.

marée, *n.f.,* tide, water, flood; (fresh) sea-fish.

Haute —, *pleine* —; high water. *Basse* —; low water. *De* —; tidal. *Grande* —, — *de vive eau;* spring-tide. — *morte;* neap tide. *La* — *monte;* the tide is coming in. *La* — *descend;* the tide is going down, running out. *Prendre la* —; to take advantage of the tide. — *montante;* flood. — *descendante;* ebb. — *qui porte au vent;* wind-tide. *Aller contre vent et* —; to pursue one's course in spite of all difficulties. *Avoir vent et* —; to sail with wind and tide. *Vendeur de* —; fish-monger. *Cela arrive comme* — *en carême;* that comes like fish in Lent. *Ce qui vient de flot s'en retourne de* —; lightly come, lightly go. *La* — *n'attend personne;* time and tide wait for no man.

marégraphe, *n.m.,* tide-gauge.

marelle, *n.f.,* hopscotch.

maremme, *n.f.,* marshy land on the seashore (in Italy).

marengo (-rin-go), *n.m.,* Oxford gray.

marengo, *n.f.,* (cook.) marengo, fowl fricasseed with mushrooms.

mareyeur, *n.m.,* fish-factor, fish-salesman; fish-carrier.

margarine, *n.f.,* (chem.) margarine.

margarique, *adj.,* (chem.) margaric.

margay, *n.m.,* (mam.) margay, tiger-cat.

marge, *n.f.,* margin (of paper, books); freedom, latitude, scope; time, means. *Ecrire une note en* —; to make a marginal note. *Laisser assez de* — *à quelqu'un;* to give any one sufficient scope. *Nous avons de la* —; we have time enough *or* to spare.

margelle, *n.f.,* curb-stone, edge (of a well).

marger, *v.a.,* (print.) to regulate the margin of, to margin.

margeur, *n.m.,* (print.) layer on.

marginal, -e, *adj.,* marginal.

marginé, -e, *part.,* margined, marginated.

marginer, *v.a.* to margin.

margot, *n.f.,* magpie, mag; talkative woman, chatterbox; dim. of **Marguerite,** Madge, Meg, Peggy.

margotin, *n.m.,* small bundle of fagots.

****margouillet,** *n.m.,* (nav.) bull's eye, wooden thimble.

****margouillis** (-goo-yee), *n.m.,* (fam.) puddle, dirty plash, sludge, slop; (fig.) difficulty; embarrassment. *Laisser quelqu'un dans le* —; to leave any one in the lurch.

margrave, *n.m.f.,* margrave; margravine.

margraviat, *n.m.,* margraviate.

marguerite, *n.f.,* daisy; pearl; (nav.) messenger. *Reine-* —, (—*s*—*s*) China-aster, China-star. *Faire* —; (nav.) to clap a messenger on the cable. *Jeter des* —*s devant les pourceaux;* to cast pearls before swine.

****marguillerie,** *n.f.,* churchwardenship.

****marguillier,** *n.m.,* churchwarden.

mari, *n.m.,* husband, spouse. *Affranchissement de la puissance de* —; (jur.) discoverture. *Etat de la femme en puissance de* —; (jur.) coverture. *En puissance de* —; (jur.) feme covert, under coverture.

mariable, *adj.,* marriageable.

mariage, *n.m.,* marriage, matrimony, wedlock; match; wedding; fortune, portion; union, blending. — *d'inclination;* love match. — *de raison,* — *de convenance;* prudent match, marriage for money (*or* position). — *en détrempe;* pretended marriage, illicit intercourse. — *sous la cheminée;* marriage under the rose. — *de la main gauche;* morganatic marriage. *Contrat de* —; marriage contract. *Promettre en* —; to promise in marriage. *Rechercher une jeune fille en* —; to solicit the hand of a young girl. *Prendre en* —; to take to wife. — *de conscience;* private marriage.

marié, *n.m.,* married man; bridegroom. *pl.,* married people. *Nouveaux* —*s;* newly-married couple.

mariée, *n.f.,* married woman; bride. *Se plaindre que la* — *est trop belle;* to find fault with a good bargain.

marier, *v.a.,* to marry, to give in marriage, to match; to blend; to unite. *Il a fort bien marié sa fille;* he has married his daughter very advantageously. — *la vigne avec l'ormeau;* to marry, or to twine, the vine with the elm. — *des couleurs;* to blend, *or* to combine, colors.

se marier, *v.r.,* to marry, to espouse, to wed, to be married to; to match, to ally, to unite, to blend, to combine, to pair. *Il s'est marié très richement;* he has made a very rich match. *Elle est en âge de se* —; she is of an age to marry.

marie-salope, *n.f.,* (—*s*—*s*) mud-barge.

marieu-r, *n.m.,* **-se,** *n.f.,* match-maker.

marin, -e, *adj.,* marine; seafaring; sea; seagoing; seaworthy. *Avoir le pied* —; to be a good sailor; (fig.) not to be put out of countenance.

marin, *n.m.,* mariner, seaman, seafaring man, sailor. — *d'eau douce;* fresh-water sailor, landlubber.

marinade, *n.f.,* marinade, pickled meat; souse; pickles.

marine, *n.f.,* sea-affairs; sea-service; navigation; marine; navy; naval forces; taste, smell, of the sea; (paint.) sea-piece, seascape. *Officier de* —; naval officer. — *marchande;* mercantile, marine. — *militaire or de l'état;* royal navy. *Soldats, troupes, de la* —; marines. *Terme de* —; sea-term. *Sentir la* —, *or avoir un goût de* —; to taste of the sea.

mariné, -e, *part.,* marinated, pickled; (her.) marine. *Des marchandises* —*es;* merchandise spoiled *or* damaged by the sea.

mariner, *v.a.,* to marinate, to pickle, to souse; (nav.) to jerk.

maringouin, *n.m.,* (ent.) musquito.

marinier, *n.m.,* waterman, bargeman, lighterman; mariner, seaman. *Maître* —; master-bargeman. *Officiers* —*s;* petty officers.

à la **marinière,** *n.f. Nager à la* —; to swim on the side; (cook.) "marinière" fashion.

mariniste, *n.m.,* marine-painter.

marionnette, *n.f.,* puppet, marionette; short woman; frivolous, weak-minded woman. *pl.,* puppet-show.

marital, -e, *adj.,* marital, pertaining to a husband.

maritalement (-tal-mān), *adv.,* maritally, as man and wife, matrimonially.

maritime, *adj.,* maritime, naval; nautical.

maritorne, *n.f.,* ill-made, coarse woman; slattern, slut, dirty woman; (at an inn) maid of all work.

marivaudage, *n.m.,* excessively refined style; mannerism, sentimentalism (writing in the style of Marivaux).

marivauder, *v.n.,* to aim at over-refinement, to write in the style of Marivaux.

marjolaine, *n.f.,* (bot.) sweet marjoram.

☉**marjolet,** *n.m.,* fop, little coxcomb.

marli, *n.m.,* catgut, thread gauze.

****marmaille,** *n.f.,* (fam.) brats, lots of little brats.

marmelade, *n.f.,* marmalade. *Cette viande est en* —; that meat is done to a jelly. *Mettre en* —; to beat to a jelly. *Avoir la mâchoire en* —; to have one's jaw smashed in.

marmenteau, *adj.,* reserved, ornamental (of trees).

marmite, *n.f.,* pot, saucepan, boiler, copper. *Elles servent à faire bouillir la* —; they help to make the pot boil. *Ecumeur de* —; sponger, parasite. *Nez en pied de* —; pug nose. — *à vapeur;* steamer. *La* — *bout dans cette maison;* they live well *or* keep a good table. *La* — *est renversée;* they give no more dinner parties, they see no more company.

☉**marmiteu-x, -se,** *n.* and *adj.,* (fam.) pitiful,

poor wretch; sad, wretched, whimpering, whining, pitiful, seedy.

marmiton, *n.m.*, scullion, kitchen drudge.

marmonner, *v.a.* and *n.* V. **marmotter.**

marmoréen, -ne, *adj.*, marmorean.

marmose, *n.f.*, (mam.) marmose.

marmot, *n.m.*, ⊙ monkey; (mam.) marmoset; puppet, grotesque figure; brat, little chap. *Croquer le —;* to dance attendance, to kick up one's heels, to wait.

marmotte, *n.f.*, brat (little girl); (mam.) marmot; woman's head-dress; (nav.) match-tub. *Dormir comme une —;* to sleep like a top.

marmotter, *v.a.* and *n.*, to mutter, to mumble, to grumble, to growl.

marmouset, *n.m.*, grotesque figure; young monkey (little boy); fire-dog, andiron.

marnage, *n.m.*, (agri.) marling, chalking, claying.

marne, *n.f.*, (agri.) marl, chalk, clay.

marner, *v.a.*, (agri.) to marl, to chalk, to clay.

marneron, *n.m.*, (agri.) marler, marl-digger.

marneu-x, -se, *adj.*, marly.

marnière, *n.f.*, marl-pit, clay-pit, chalk-pit.

maronite, *n.m.f.* and *adj.*, Maronite.

maronner, *v.n.*, (pop.) to grumble, to growl, to croak. *Faire —;* to keep waiting a long time; to tease, to plague.

maroquin, *n.m.*, morocco-leather, roan. *—du Levant;* Turkey-leather.

maroquiner, *v.a.*, to morocco.

maroquinerie (-ki-n-rî), *n.f.*, morocco-leather manufacture.

maroquinier, *n.m.*, morocco-tanner.

marotique, *adj.*, marotic (imitation of Marot's style).

marotisme, *n.m.*, marotism (imitation of Marot's style).

marotte, *n.f.*, fool's bauble, cap and bells; fancy, folly, whim, hobby. *Chacun a sa —;* everybody has his hobby.

maroufle, *n.m.*, ragamuffin; booby, clodhopper, bumpkin, clown, churl.

maroufle, *n.f.*, (paint.) lining-paste.

maroufler, *v.a.*, (paint.) to line.

marquant, -e, *adj.*, conspicuous, striking. *Personne —e;* person of note, of distinction.

marque, *n.f.*, mark, cipher, stamp; (com.) private mark; brand (with a hot iron); badge; trace (of footsteps) print; sign; token; testimony; proof, instance; counter (at play); pit (of the small-pox). *— de fabricant;* manufacturer's mark. *— de la douane;* custom-house stamp. *— d'honneur;* badge of honor. *Homme de —;* man of note. *Donner à quelqu'un une — d'estime;* to give any one a proof of esteem. *Lettres de —;* letters of mark (for seizing vessels). *Ville de —;* coinage-town. *— de beau temps;* signs of fine weather. *Une — qu'il est venu, c'est qu'il a laissé ceci;* a proof that he came, is that he left this. *Faire porter ses —s à quelqu'un;* (fam.) to leave one's mark on any one.

marqué, -e, *part.*, marked, evident, conspicuous, obvious; decided; pronounced; strong, resolute. *— de la petite vérole;* pitted with small-pox. *Homme — au bon coin;* a man of the right stamp. *— à l'A.;* thoroughly reliable, the soul of honor. *Ouvrage — au bon coin;* excellent work. *Attentions —es;* marked attentions. *Il est né —;* he was born with a mark. *Avoir les traits —s;* to have strongly-marked features.

marquer, *v.a.*, to mark, to stamp, to note down; to brand; to stigmatize; to leave marks; to score up; to mark out, to trace out; to mark down, to note; to betoken, to bespeak, to denote; to tell, to mention, to write; to show, to give marks of, to testify, to single out. *— son jeu;* to mark one's points at play. *Je lui ai marqué que;* I wrote to him that. *— à quelqu'un sa reconnaissance;* to show one's gratitude to any

one. *— à quelqu'un ce qu'il doit faire;* to specify to any one what he has to do.

marquer, *v.n.*, to make its appearance, to show (of a thing); to be remarked, to be evident; to be remarkable, distinguished; to set off; to be of note; to show the hour (of sun-dials); to mark, to show age by the teeth (of horses); (fenc.) to make a full pass. *Cela marquerait trop;* (fam.) that would attract too much attention. *Cet homme ne marque point;* that man is in no way remarkable.

marqueter, *v.a.*, to speckle, to spot, to inlay.

marqueterie (-kè-trî), *n.f.*, marquetry, checkered-work, checker-work, inlaid-work, inlaying, mosaic, patchwork.

marqueteur, *n.m.*, inlayer.

marquette, *n.f.*, cake (of virgin wax).

marqueur (-keur), *n.m.*, marker, scorer, tally-keeper.

marquis, *n.m.*, marquis, marquess. *— de Carabas;* (jest.) great landed proprietor. *Faire le —;* to give one's self airs.

marquisat, *n.m.*, marquisate.

marquise, *n.f.*, marchioness; marquee, awning, verandah; settee; waist-buckle.

marquiser, *v.a.*, to style any one a marquis.

se **marquiser,** *v.r.*, to assume the title of marquis.

marquoir, *n.m.*, bodkin.

marraine, *n.f.*, godmother, sponsor.

marre, *n.f.*, mattock, hoe.

⊙**marri, -e,** *adj.*, sorry, grieved, concerned, troubled.

marron, *n.m.*, (bot.) large French chestnut; chestnut; ⊙ large curl tied with a ribbon; cracker (fire-works); (milit.) mark; unlicensed broker; unlicensed printer; (print.) work printed clandestinely; chestnut color. *— d'Inde;* horse-chestnut. *— d'eau;* water-caltrops (fruit). *—s glacés;* candied chestnuts. *Tirer les —s du feu;* to pull the chestnuts out of the fire.

marron, *adj. invariable,* maroon, chestnut-color.

marron, -ne, *adj.*, fugitive, runaway (of slaves); wild (of animals that have been tame); (com.) unlicensed, interloping. *Courtier —;* (com.) unlicensed broker. *Cochon —;* wild hog.

marron, *n.m.*, **-ne,** *n.f.*, runaway slave; maroon; free black slave (of the West Indies).

marronnage, *n.m.*, state of a runaway slave; running away (of slaves); carrying on the business of a broker without a license.

⊙**marronner,** *v.a.*, to curl the hair with curling-tongs.

marronnier, *n.m.*, (bot.) French chestnut-tree, chestnut-tree. *— d'Inde;* horse-chestnut-tree.

marrube, *n.m.*, (bot.) madwort; horehound; bugle-weed.

mars (mars), *n.m.*, March; (chem.) Mars (iron); (astron.) Mars; (fig., poet.) war. *pl.*, seed sown in spring. *Giboulées de —;* April showers. *Champ de —;* (milit.) large drilling ground. *Cela vient comme — en carême;* that comes very seasonably, *or* in the nick of time.

marseillaise, *n.f.*, Marseillaise (French national anthem).

marsouin, *n.m.*, (mam.) porpoise, sea-hog; ugly wretch. *Vilain —;* ugly, disagreeable man.

marsupial, -e, *adj.*, (natural hist.) marsupial.

martagon, *n.m.*, (bot.) martagon, mountain-lily, Turk's-cap.

marte, *n.f.* V. **martre.**

marteau, *n.m.*, hammer, clapper; knocker; (ich.) hammer-fish; hammer-oyster. *Etre entre le — et l'enclume;* to be in an embarrassing position. *— à deux mains;* sledge-hammer. *— d'une arbalète;* cross. *Graisser le —;* to fee the porter. *Avoir un coup de* —; to be somewhat gone in the upper story. *Il faut être enclume ou* —; you must bite *or* be bitten. *N'être pas sujet au coup de* —; to be one's own master.

martel, *n.m.*, ⊙hammer. [Only used in: *Avoir* — *en tête ;* to be very uneasy. *Se mettre* — *en tête ;* to fret one's self to death.]

martelage, *n.m.*, (tech.) hammering ; (of trees) marking.

martelé, -e, *part.*, hammered; (mus.) brilliant and distinct. *Vaisselle* —*e ;* hammered plate. *Vers* —*s ;* labored verses.

marteler, *v.a.*, to hammer ; to torment, to tease, to vex, to strain, to labor. *Il martèle ses vers ;* he labors his verses.

martelet, *n.m.*, little hammer.

marteleur, *n.m.*, hammerman.

martial, -e, *adj.*, martial, warlike, soldierly. *Code* —, *législation* —*e ;* articles of war.

martin, *n.m.*, (orni.) pastor, (kind of starling) *La Saint-* —; Martinmas. — *pêcheur ;* kingfisher.

martiner, *v.a.*, to tilt, to hammer.

martinet, *n.m.*, (orni.) martinet, martlet, swift, sea-martin; flat candlestick, hand-candlestick ; tilt-hammer; cat-o'-nine-tails. — *de pic ;* (nav.) peak-halliards of the mizzen.

martingale, *n.f.*, (nav.) man.) martingale. *Jouer à la* —; to play double or quits.

martinisme, *n.m.*, martinism.

martiniste, *n.m.*, martinist.

martin-pêcheur, *n.m.*, (—*s*—*s*) (orni.) kingfisher.

martin-sec, *n.m.*, (—*s*—*s*) a kind of pear.

martre, *n.f.*, (mam.) marten, sable. — *zibeline ;* sable. *Prendre* — *pour renard ;* to take a cow for a bull.

martyr, *n.m.*, -e, *n.f.*, martyr. *Le commun des* —*s ;* the common herd.

martyre, *n.m.*, martyrdom. *Souffrir le* —; to suffer martyrdom. *Faire souffrir le* — *à quelqu'un ;* to make any one suffer martyrdom.

martyriser, *v.a.*, to make any one suffer martyrdom, to make a martyr of ; to torment ; to torture.

martyrologe, *n.m.*, martyrology.

martyrolog ste, *n.m.*, martyrologist.

marum (-rom), *n.m.*, (bot.) cat-thyme.

mascarade, *n.f.*, masquerade, mask.

mascaret, *n.m.*, eddy of water, violent eddy of the tide, swelling (of waters) ; bar (of harbors).

mascarille, *n.m.*, a delicious kind of mushroom ; the flunkey (of Molière's comedies).

mascaron, *n.m.*, (arch.) mask, grotesque figure.

masculin, -e, *adj.*, masculine, male. *Fief* —; fee in tail male.

masculin, *n.m.*, (gram.) masculine.

masculiniser, *v.a.*, to make masculine. *Se—, v.r.*, to become masculine.

masculinité, *n.f.*, masculineness, masculinity.

masque, *n.m.*, mask ; blind, cloak, pretense ; masker, masquerader, mummer ; face-guard ; (paint.) head; (arch.) mask. *Il a un bon* —; (of actors) his features are expressive. *Lever le* —; to pull off the mask. *Arraches les* —*s ;* to tear off the disguise.

⊙**masque**, *n.f.*, ugly woman ; naughty little girl.

masqué, -e, *part.*, masked; disguised. *Etre toujours* —; to be always close. *Bal* —; masked ball, masquerade.

masquer, *v.a.*, to mask, to conceal, to cloak, to disguise; (milit.) to mask.

se **masquer**, *v.r.*, to be masked, to mask ; to disguise one's self ; (of things) to be disguised.

massacrant, -e, *adj.*, killing ; cross, peevish, surly, dreadful, disagreeable. *Humeur* —*e ;* awful temper.

massacre, *n.m.*, massacre, butchery; slaughter, havoc, waste, squandering; bungler, botcher; (hunt.) head (of a deer newly killed).

massacrer, *v.a.*, to massacre, to butcher, to murder, to slay, to slaughter; to bungle, to botch, to destroy; to hack (meat or poultry). *Cet acteur a massacré son rôle ;* that actor murdered his part. — *des hardes, des meubles ;* to spoil clothes, furniture.

massacreur, *n.m.*, slaughterer, slayer; bungler, botcher.

massage, *n.m.*, shampooing.

masse, *n.f.*, mass, heap, lump; earnings; hoard; stock; mace; butt-end, butt; (jur.) creditors, estate (of bankrupts); (com.) capital stock, capital; (tech.) sledge-hammer. — *des biens ;* (jur.) estate. — *des biens immeubles ;* (jur.) real estate. — *des biens meubles ;* (jur.) personal estate. — *de plume ;* fifty pounds of feathers. — *de héron ;* heron's crest, tuft. — *d'eau ;* typha, reed-mace. *En* —; in a body, in the mass, by the bulk. *Les* —*s ;* the people as a whole, the million, the masses. — *d'armes ;* mace. *Soulever les* —*s ;* to stir up the people.

⊙**masse**, *n.f.*, stake, pool (at play).

massement, *n.m.*, (milit.) massing of troops.

massepain (mas-pin), *n.m.*, marchpane (kind of cake).

masser, *v.a.*, (milit.) to mass troops ; ⊙to stake, to put into the pool (at play); (paint.) to mass; to shampoo.

massette, *n.f.*, (bot.) mace-reed, reed-mace; cat's-tail. — *à larges feuilles ;* great cat's-tail.

masseur, -se, *n.m.f.*, shampooer.

massicot, *n.m.*, (chem.) massicot, masticot ; paper-cutter.

massier, *n.m.*, mace-bearer.

massi-f, -ve, *adj.*, massive, bulky ; lumpish ; massy, solid ; clumsy, heavy, dull. *Figure d'argent* —; figure of solid silver, of massive silver. *Avoir l'esprit* —; to be dull-minded.

massif, *n.m.*, (gard.) group, clump, cluster (of trees, flowers); grove; solid mass, group, block, (of masonry) wall (of an oven); (mas.) solid mass.

massivement (-siv-mān), *adv.*, massively, heavily, solidly; stupidly, dully.

massiveté, *n.f.*, massiveness.

massorah *or* **massore**, *n.f.*, masorah, massora.

massorète, *n.m.*, masorite.

massorétique, *adj.*, massoretic, masoretic.

massue, *n.f.*, club, crowbar. *Coup de* —; dreadful blow, heavy blow, knock-down blow; calamity.

mastic, *n.m.*, mastic; cement; putty; (print.) transposition.

masticage, *n.m.*, cementing, puttying.

mastication, *n.f.*, mastication, chewing.

masticatoire, *n.m.*, (med.) masticatory.

mastigadour, *n.m.*, (vet.) masticador, slabbering-bit (of a bridle).

mastiquer, *v.a.*, to putty ; to cement.

mastiquer, *v.n.*, to masticate.

mastodonte, *n.m.*, (fos.) mastodon.

mastoïde, *adj.*, (anat.) mastoid. *Apophyse* —; mastoid process.

mastoïdien, -ne (-in, -è-n), *adj.*, (anat.) mastoidean.

masturbation, *n.f.*, masturbation, self-pollution.

masturber, *v.a.*, to pollute.

se **masturber**, *v.r.*, to commit self-pollution.

masulipatan, *n.m.*, calico (sort of).

masure, *n.f.*, ruins ; hovel, hut, tumble-down house.

mat (mat), -e, *adj.*, unpolished, dead, dull ; flat, insipid ; heavy, sodden; (chess) mated, checkmated. *Or* —; unpolished gold. *Coloris* —; dim coloring. *Broderie* —*e ;* heavy embroidery.

mat (mat), *n.m.*, (chess) mate ; (tech.) deadening. *Donner, faire, échec et* —; to checkmate.

mât (mâ) n.m., mast; pole. *Le grand —;* the main-mast. *— de perroquet;* top-gallant-mast. *— de beaupré;* bowsprit. *— de misaine;* foremast. *— d'artimon;* mizzen-mast. *Bas — de misaine;* lower fore-mast. *Petit — de hune;* topmast. *— de perroquet de fougue;* mizzen topmast. *— de perruche;* mizzen top-gallant-mast. *— à pible;* pole mast. *— vertical;* mast on end. *—s inclinés vers l'arrière;* masts hanging abaft. *— d'un brin;* mast of one piece of wood only. *— d'assemblage;* made mast. *— forcé;* mast which is sprung. *— jumelé, reclampé, renforcé;* mast fished (in a weak place or opposite any spring). *— de pavillon;* ensign staff. *—s de hune de rechange;* spare top-masts. *—s majeurs;* standing masts. *Aller à —s et à cordes;* to scud under bare poles. *—s venus à bas;* disabled masts. *Caler les —s;* to lower the masts. *Lieu d'un —;* station of a mast. *Mettre,* or *guinder, les —s de hune;* to heave the top-masts on end. *— de fortune;* jury mast. *— de rechange;* spare mast. *— de cocagne;* greasy pole.

matador, n.m., matador; matadore (at play); magnate, big wig.

mâtage, n.m., masting (of a ship).

matamore, n.m., hector, bully.

matasse, n.f., raw silk; raw cotton.

⊙**matassins**, n.m.pl., matachin dance; matachins; (figs.) buffoon.

maté, n.m., (bot.) maté; Paraguay tea.

mâté, -e, adj., (nav.) masted. *— en caravelle;* fitted with pole top-masts. *— en chandelier;* masted upright. *— en frégate;* having bent, inclined, masts. *— en vaisseau;* masted as a ship of the line. *— en fourche;* masted with a gaff. *— à pible;* pole-masted. *— en polacre;* masted with three pole masts and square sails. *— en heu;* masted for a sprit. *— en galère;* masted as a galley. *Haut —, trop —;* over-masted.

matelas (ma-tlâ), n.m., mattress; pad; wadding. *— d'un currosse;* squab, cushion, of a coach. *— de bourre;* flock-bed. *— à air;* air mattress.

matelasser (ma-tla-sé), v.a., to cover with a mattress, to stuff.

matelassi-er, n.m., **-ère**, n.f., mattress-maker.

matelot (ma-tlô), n.m., seaman, sailor; (nav.) consort-ship. *Bon —;* able seaman. *— de première classe;* able-bodied seaman. *— à deniers;* seaman engaged for a specified time. *— à mariage;* seaman engaged for the whole voyage. *Vaisseau —;* good company-keeper.

matelotage (ma-tlo-taj), n.m., seamanship; seaman's wages, pay.

matelote (ma-tlot), n.f., (cook.) matelote, fish-stew. *A la —;* seamanlike, sailor fashion.

mâter, v.a., to mast; to toss up (the oars). *Machine à —;* sheers. *Machine à — flottante;* sheer-hulk.

mater, v.a., to mortify, to harass (with corporal hardships); to bring down, to break down, to curb; to subdue, to conquer; to check-mate. *On a bien maté son orgueil;* his pride has been sadly brought down. *On aura de la peine à la —;* she will take some subduing.

mâtereau, n.m., (nav.) small mast; spar, pole, staff.

matérialiser, v.a., to materialize.

matérialisme, n.m., materialism.

matérialiste, n.m.f. and adj., materialist; materialistic.

matérialité, n.f., materiality.

matériaux, n.m.pl., materials, material.

matériel, -le, adj., material; coarse, gross, rough; massy, heavy, dull. *Il est —;* he is a matter-of-fact man. *Faux —;* (jur.) forgery.

matériel, n.m., materials, stock, working-stock; stores, apparatus, fittings, plant. *— d'une armée;* baggage, ammunition, artillery. *— de*

siège; siege apparatus. *— d'une imprimerie;* printing-office plant.

matériellement (-rièl-mân) adv., materially; coarsely, grossly, roughly.

maternel, -le, adj., maternal, motherly. *Parents —s;* relations on the mother's side. *Langue —le;* mother-tongue.

maternellement (-nèl-mân), adv., maternally.

maternité, n.f., maternity.

mâteur, n.m., (nav.) mast-maker.

mathématicien (-siin), n.m., mathematician.

mathématique, n.f., mathematics. *—s pures;* pure mathematics. *—s mixtes;* mixed mathematics. *Etudier les —;* to study mathematics. [Rarely used in the singular.]

mathématique, adj., mathematical.

mathématiquement (-tik-mân), adv., mathematically.

matière (ma-ti-èr), n.f., matter; substance, stuff, fluid; subject, cause, reason, motive, grounds; theme, contents. *— brute, —première;* raw material. *—s d'or et d'argent;* bullion. *S'élever au-dessus de la —;* to soar above matter. *Donner — à parler;* to give occasion for talking. *En — de;* in point of, in matters of.

matin, n.m., morning, noon, forenoon; prime, dawn. *Demain —;* to-morrow morning. *Se lever de grand —;* to rise very early. *Un beau —;* some fine day, or one fine morning. *Un de ces quatre —s;* one of these fine days.

matin, adv., early, early in the morning. *De grand,* or *de bon, —;* very early.

mâtin, n.m., mastiff; rascal, cur. *Mâtin!* By Jove! *Ce — de;* that scoundrel of, that confounded, that cursed.

matinal, -e, adj., morning; early-rising; early, up early.

matinalement, adv., early.

mâtine, n.f., hussy, wench. *Cette — de;* that confounded, or cursed.

mâtineau, n.m., little mastiff.

matinée, n.f., morning, forenoon, morning's work; morning performance. *Dormir,* or *faire, la grasse —;* to lie in bed late in the morning, to sleep it out.

mâtiner, v.a., to serve (of a mastiff); to abuse, to disparage, to snub.

matines, n.f.pl., matins.

matineu-x, -se, adj. (generally), rising early; early riser (of persons).

matini-er, -ère, adj., morning, of the morning. [Only used in: *l'étoile —ère;* the Morning-Star.]

matir, v.a., to deaden (metals).

matois, -e, adj. and n., cunning, artful, sly, deep; cunning person, sly dog. *C'est un fin —;* he's an artful blade.

matoisement, cunningly, slyly.

matoiserie (ma-toa-zrî), n.f., cunning, slyness.

matou, n.m., tom-cat; ugly person, monkey, curmudgeon.

matras (-trâ), n.m., (chem.) matrass.

matricaire, n.f., (bot.) matricaria, feverfew.

matrice, n.f., matrix, womb; (com.) matrice; (min.) matrix; standard weight, measure, original register.

matrice, adj., mother, principal, primitive, unmixed. *Eglise —;* mother-church. *Langue —;* mother-tongue. *Couleurs —s;* primitive, unmixed colors.

matricide, n.m., matricide.

matriculaire, n.m. and adj., matriculate; matriculated.

matricule, n.f. and adj., register, matricula; matriculation, certificate of matriculation; matriculation. *Registre —;* matriculation book.

matrimonial, -e, adj., matrimonial.

matrone, n.f., matron; ⊙midwife.

matte, n.f., (metal.) matt. *pl.,* clotted milk, curds.

maturati-f, -ve, adj., (med.) maturative.

maturatif, n.m., (med.) maturant.

maturation, n.f., maturation, ripening.

mâture, n.f., masting, masts, mast-store; wood for masts, sheer-hack, sheers.

maturité, n.f., maturity, ripeness, completion; consideration. Avec —; maturely, with consideration.

matutinal, -e, adj., (l.u.) matutinal.

maubèche, n.f., (orni.) knot, sandpiper.

maudire (maudissant, maudit), v.a., to curse, to imprecate, to rue.

maudissable, adj., execrable, detestable.

maudit, -e, part., cursed, accursed, outcast, wretched. — soit le maladroit! deuce take the clumsy fool! — soit . . . .! cursed be . . . ! confound . . . !

maugréer, v.n., to fret and fume, to curse and swear; to grumble.

maupiteu-x, -se, adj. and n., ⊙ cruel, pitiless. Faire le —; to look miserable (without cause).

maure, n.m. V. **more.**

mauresque, adj. V. **moresque.**

mauricaud, adj. V. **moricaud.**

mausolée, n.m., mausoleum.

maussade, adj., sulky, sullen, cross, disagreeable; unpleasant, dull, tedious; awkward; slovenly, clumsy.

maussadement (mô-sad-mān), adv., disagreeably, sullenly, peevishly.

maussaderie (mô-sa-drî), n.f., unpleasantness, sullenness, sulkiness.

mauvais, -e, adj., bad, ill, evil; mischievous, ill-natured; injurious; wrong, amiss; unpleasant; contrary, adverse; (print.) battered (of letters); unhandsome. —e nouvelle; bad news. — livre; mischievous, wretched book. Avoir —e mine; to look ill. Prendre quelque chose en —e part; to take a thing ill, in a bad sense, or in bad part. —e tête; hot-headed person. — sujet; worthless fellow, rascal, scoundrel.

mauvais, n.m., bad. Il faut prendre le bon et le —; one must take the good with the bad.

mauvais, adv., bad, wrong. Sentir —; to have a bad smell. Il fait —; it is bad weather. Trouver — que; to take it ill that.

mauve, n.f., mallow; (orni.) sea-gull, seamew.

mauviette, n.f., lark; field-lark; lath (thin person); poor stick.

mauvis, n.m., (orni.) mavis, redwing, throstle.

maxillaire, adj., pertaining to the jaw, maxillary.

maxime, n.f., maxim. Tenir pour — de; to hold it as a maxim to.

maximum, n.m. (—s), (math.) (maxima), highest, height, maximum; acme; (com.) the highest price.

mayonnaise, n.f., (cook.) mayonnaise.

mazagran, n.m., coffee in a glass (named after the once famous Café Mazagran).

mazette, n.f., tit, poor hack (sorry horse); milksop, poor creature; dull-head, duffer (at games). —! (int.) zounds! you don't say so!

md., (ab. of Marchand) shopkeeper.

mde., (ab. of Marchande) shopkeeper.

me, pron., me; to me or at me. Il — blâme; he blames me. Vous — parlez; you speak to me. — voici; here I am.

meâ-culpâ, n.m., (—) expression taken from the Confiteor. Dire, faire, son —; to repent; to confess one's faults.

méandre, n.m., meander, winding.

méat, n.m., (anat.) meatus, duct, passage.

mécanicien (-in), n.m., mechanician; machinist, mechanic; engine-maker; engine-man; engine-driver. Ingénieur —; mechanical engineer. Serrurier —; manufacturing locksmith.

mécanique, n.f., mechanics; mechanism;

machine, machinery, piece of machinery; brake. Serrer la —; to put on the brake.

mécanique, adj., mechanic, mechanical, machine-made.

mécaniquement (-ni-kmān), adv., mechanically.

mécaniser, v.a., to use as a machine; (pop.) to tease, to plague. — les hommes; to use men as mere machines.

mécanisme, n.m., mechanism, machinery; structure; mechanical parts.

mécène, n.m., Mæcenas (a protector of science, art, and literature).

méchamment (mé-sha-mān), adv., wickedly, spitefully, maliciously, ill-naturedly.

méchanceté (mé-shans-té), n.f., wickedness, spitefulness, mischievousness; crossness, naughtiness, ill-nature; ill-natured thing, ill-natured remark, reflection, slander.

méchant, -e, adj., bad, wretched, worthless; wicked, dishonest; sorry, paltry; wicked, ill-natured; mischievous, malicious; wayward, naughty, unkind; (of a horse) vicious. — homme; wicked man. Il a la mine —e; he has an ill-natured look. Un — poète; a sorry, wretched poet.

méchant, n.m., -e, n.f., wicked person; evil doer, reprobate; naughty child. Faire le —; to be fractious (of a child).

mèche, n.f., wick (of a lamp or candle); tinder; match; screw, bit, auger; worm (of corkscrews, wimbles); (surg.) tent; center-bit; whiplash, lock (of hair). — anglaise; center-bit. Découvrir, éventer, la — ; (milit.) to discover the enemy's match by means of a countermine; to find out the secret of a plot. — de cheveux; lock of hair. Il n'y a pas —; it 's no go; it can't be done. S'il y a —; if it can be managed.

⊙**méchef,** n.m., mischief, mischance; harm.

mécher, v.a., to fumigate with brimstone, to sulphur.

mécompte (mé-kont), n.m., miscalculation; mistake, error; disappointment, drawback. Il a trouvé bien du —; he has experienced great disappointment.

mécompter, v.n., to strike wrong (of clocks). se **mécompter** (mé-kon-tè), v.r., to miscalculate; to be disappointed; to be out in one's reckoning. Il s'est mécompté dans son raisonnement; he is out in his reasoning.

méconium (-om) n.m., (med.) meconium.

méconnaissable, adj., not to be recognized; unrecognizable.

méconnaissance, n.f., unthankfulness, ungratefulness, ingratitude.

méconnaissant, -e, adj., thankless, ungrateful, unmindful.

méconnaître, v.a., not to know again, not to recognize; to disown, to disregard, not to know; to ignore, to slight, not to appreciate. Il méconnaît ses parents; he disowns his relations. se **méconnaître,** v.r., to forget one's self.

méconnu, -e, part., unacknowledged; unrecognized; ignored, disowned, disregarded.

mécontent, -e, adj., dissatisfied, displeased, discontented. Il est — de vous; he is displeased with you. Nous êtes — de tout; you are discontented with everything.

mécontent, n.m., -e, n.f., dissatisfied person; malcontent. C'est un —; he is a discontented man.

mécontentement (-tan-tmān), n.m., discontent, discontentedness, dissatisfaction, displeasure. Donner du — à; to displease.

mécontenter, v.a., to discontent, to dissatisfy, to displease.

mécréance, n.f., infidelity, unbelief, irreligion.

mécréant, n.m., unbeliever, infidel.

mécroire, v.n., to disbelieve.

*médaille, n.f., medal; (arch.) medallion; (of porters) badge, ticket; license. — *d'honneur;* prize-medal. *Chaque — a son revers;* everything has its bright and its dark side. *Le revers de la —;* the dark side of the picture. *Tourner la —;* to turn the tables. *La — est renversée;* the tables are turned.

*médaillé, -e, n.m.f. and adj., with a medal as a reward; (of porters) licensed. n., medalist, prize-winner.

médailleur, n.m., die-sinker.

*médaillier, n.m., cabinet of medals.

*médailliste, n.m.f., medalist.

*médaillon, n.m., medallion; locket.

médecin (mé-dsin), n.m., physician, doctor. *Faire venir le —;* to send for the doctor. *Il est abandonné des —s;* the doctors have given him up. *Docteur médecin;* doctor of medicine. *Un — d'eau douce;* a water-gruel doctor. — *chirurgien;* general practitioner. — *empirique;* quack doctor. *Le temps est un grand —;* time cures all ills or time is the great healer.

médecine (mé-dsi-n), n.f., medicine, physic. *Etudiant en —;* medical student. — *légale;* forensic medicine. — *noire;* black draught.

médeciner (mé-dsi-né), v.a., to physic, to doctor.

se **médeciner**, v.r., to physic, to doctor one's self.

médial, -e, adj., (gram.) medial.

médian, -e, adj., (anat.) mesial, middle.

médianoche, n.m., meat-supper (after midnight).

médiante, n.f., (mus.) mediant.

médiastin, n.m., (anat.) mediastine.

médiat, -e, adj., mediate.

médiatement (mé-dia-tmän), adv., mediately.

médiat-eur, n.m., **-rice**, n.f., mediator, mediatrix. adj., mediatory.

médiation, n.f., mediation.

médiatisation, n.f., mediatization.

médiatiser, v.a., to mediatize.

médical, -e, adj., medical. *Matière —e;* materia medica.

médicament, n.m., medicament.

médicamentaire, adj., concerning medicines.

médicamentation, n.f., doctoring, physicking.

médicamenter, v.a., to physic, to doctor.

se **médicamenter**, v.r., to physic, to doctor one's self.

médicamenteux, -se, adj., medicamental.

médication, n.f., medication.

médicinal, -e, adj., medicinal.

médimne, n.m., (antiq.) medimnus.

médiocre, adj., mediocre, middling, ordinary, moderate, passable, indifferent.

médiocre, n.m., mediocrity.

médiocrement, adv., middlingly, indifferently, tolerably; poorly, hardly, barely.

médiocrité, n.f., mediocrity; moderate competence, moderate fortune, very ordinary performance.

médique, adj., Median.

médionner, v.a., to average; to take the average.

médire, v.n., to slander, to speak ill of, to backbite, to traduce. — *de son prochain;* to speak ill of one's neighbor.

médisance, n.f., slander, scandal, backbiting; piece of slander.

médisant, -e, adj. and n., slanderous, scandalous; slanderer. *Il ne faut pas croire les —s;* slanderers are not to be believed.

méditati-f, -ve, adj. and n., meditative; meditative person.

méditation, n.f., meditation, thought.

méditer, v.a., to meditate, to think over, to consider, to reflect; to contemplate, to plan. — *la ruine de quelqu'un;* to plot any one's ruin.

méditer, v.n., to contemplate. *Passer sa vie à —;* to spend one's life in meditation.

méditerrané, -e, adj., mediterranean, midland, inland. *La mer —e;* the Mediterranean Sea.

méditerranéen, -ne, adj., mediterranean.

médium (-om), n.m., (—s) medium; middle.

médius, n.m., middle-finger.

médullaire (mé-dul-ler), adj., medullary, medullar; (bot.) pithy.

méduse, n.f., (zoöl.) medusa, sea-nettle, jelly-fish.

meeting, n.m., (—s) meeting.

méfaire, v.n., to do evil, to do harm, wrong.

méfait, n.m., misdeed; crime.

méfiance, n.f., mistrust, distrust, suspicion, caution. *La — est mère de la sûreté;* safe bind, safe find.

méfiant, -e, adj., mistrustful, distrustful, suspicious; cautious.

se **méfier (de)**, v.r., to mistrust, to distrust, to suspect; to beware, to mind; to be on one's guard (against).

mégalosaure or **mégalosaurus**, n.m., (foss.) megalosaurus.

mégapode, n.m., jungle-fowl.

mégarde, n.f., inadvertence. *Par —;* inadvertently.

mégathérium, n.m., (—s) (foss.) megatherium.

mégère, n.f., (myth.) Megæra; shrew, vixen, termagant.

mégie, n.f., tawing, leather-dressing.

mégisser, v.a., to taw.

mégisserie (mé-gi-srî), n.f., tawing, leather-dressing.

mégissier, n.m., tawer, leather-dresser.

*meilleur, -e, adj., better, preferable, more comfortable, best. *Le —;* the best.

*meilleur, n.m., best; best wine. *Le — du conte* or *de l'histoire;* the best of the story. *Le — n'en vaut rien;* the bad is the best.

meistre or **mestre**, n.m., (nav.) mast, main mast. *Mât de —;* main mast (of ships with lateen sails).

méjuger, v.n., to misjudge.

se **méjuger**, v.r., to overreach one's self.

mélampyre, n.m., (bot.) cow-wheat.

mélancolie, n.f., melancholy, sadness, melancholia. *Chasser la —;* to drive away the spleen. *Il n'engendre point la —;* he is a merry fellow.

mélancolique, adj., melancholy, dismal, gloomy; sad, dull; stern. *Séjour —;* dismal abode.

mélancoliquement (-lik-män), adv., sadly, gloomily, sorrowfully, mournfully.

mélange, n.m., mixture, mingling, crossing; medley; mash (for brewing). pl., miscellaneous works, miscellanea. *Un bonheur sans —;* unalloyed happiness. *Sans —;* unmixed, unblended; (fig.) pure, unalloyed.

mélanger, v.a., to mix, to mingle, to blend; to cross; to mash, to intermix, to dash.

se **mélanger**, v.r., to mix, to mingle, to blend, to temper; to be mashed.

mélasse, n.f., molasses, treacle.

mêlé, -e, part., mixed; miscellaneous; medley (of verses); irregular; (of rhymes) mixed.

mêlée, n.f., conflict; fray, fight, scramble, squabble; thick of the fight; altercation, dispute, clash.

mêler, v.a., to mingle, to mix, to mix up; to blend; to intersperse, to temper; to put in; to jumble; to bring in, to implicate, to involve; to shuffle (cards); to entangle. — *du fil;* to entangle thread. — *les cartes;* to shuffle the cards. — *une serrure;* to force a lock. *Il est mêlé dans une mauvaise affaire;* he is mixed up in a bad business.

se **mêler**, v.r., to mingle, to be mingled, to be mixed; to tamper; to blend; to trouble one's self about; to intermeddle; to interfere (with, in); to take upon one's self, to presume; to take part in; to dabble in; to set one's self to do; to engage in. *Se — dans la foule;* to mingle with the crowd. *Se — de;* to meddle with, to intermeddle. *Mêlez-vous de vos affaires;* mind your own business. *De quoi vous mêlez-vous?* what business is that of yours? *Se — ensemble;* to commingle.

mélèze, *n.m.,* (bot.) larch, larch-tree.

mélianthe, *n.m.,* (bot.) honey-flower.

mélilot, *n.m.,* (bot.) melilot, sweet-trefoil.

méli-mélo, *n.m.,* (—) (fam.) medley, jumble.

mélinet, *n.m.,* (bot.) honeywort.

mélique, *n.f.adj.,* (bot.) melic grass. *Poésie —;* melic poetry.

mélisse, *n.f.,* (bot.) balm-mint, garden-balm. *Eau de —* or *eau des Carmes;* melissa water.

mellifère, *adj.,* melliferous.

mellifères, *n.m.pl.,* melliferous insects.

mellification, *n.f.,* mellification.

melliflu, -e, *adj.,* mellifluous, honeyed, sweet.

mellifluité, *n.f.,* mellifluence.

mellithe, *n.f.,* honey-stone, mellite.

mélodie, *n.f.,* melody, melodiousness, sweetness, harmony.

mélodieusement (-eûz-mān), *adv.,* melodiously, musically, sweetly.

mélodieu-x, -se, *adj.,* melodious, musical, tuneful.

mélodique, *adj.,* (mus.) melodious.

mélodramatique, *adj.,* melodramatic.

mélodramaturge, *n.m.,* melodramatist.

mélodrame, *n.m.,* melodrama.

mélomane, *n.m.,* melomaniac, person music-mad.

mélomanie, *n.f.,* melomania.

melon, *n.m.,* melon; (fig.) jockey-cap, hunting-cap; (of persons) simpleton, muff, flat. *— musqué;* musk-melon. *— d'eau;* watermelon.

meloné, -e, *adj.,* melon-shaped.

melongène or **mélongène,** *n.f.,* mad-apple, egg-plant.

melonnière, *n.f.,* melon-pit; melon-bed.

mélopée, *n.f.,* (mus.) melopœia.

méloplaste, *n.m.,* (mus.) sounding-board; meloplast.

mémarchure, *n.f.,* sprain (in a horse's leg).

membrane, *n.f.,* (anat.) membrane, film; (orni.) web.

membraneu-x, -se, *adj.,* membranous, filmy.

membre, *n.m.,* member; limb; (nav.) ribtimber.

membré, -e, *adj.,* limbed. *Bien —;* having well-made and well-proportioned limbs.

membru, -e, *adj.,* large-limbed, stout-limbed.

membrure, *n.f.,* limbs, frame; cord (to measure fire-wood); ribs, timbers (of a ship); (carp.) split-board.

même, *adj.,* same; self; very own. *Une seule et — origine;* one and the same origin. *C'est la — chose;* it is all one. *Moi-même;* myself. *Eux-s;* themselves. *C'est la bonté —;* she is goodness itself. *La — chose;* the same thing. *La chose —;* the very thing.

même, *adv.,* even, also, likewise. *Il lui a tout donné, — ses habits;* he has given him everything, even to his clothes. *Les plus sages — le font;* even the wisest do it. *Quand — il me l'aurait dit;* even though he had said it me. *A — de;* in a position to, able to. *Mettre à —;* to enable. *Boire à — la bouteille;* to drink out of the bottle itself. *Vous êtes à — de rendre service à cet homme;* you are in a position to do that man a service. *Il vous a mis à — de le faire;* he has enabled you to do it. *De —;* the same; so; like. *Faites de —;* do the same. *Tout de —;* all the same, in the same manner. *De — que;* in the same manner as, so as, as.

même, *n.m.,* same, same thing. *Cela revient au —;* it comes to the same thing or it is all the same. *Faire au —;* (at billiards) to pocket

straight. *Faire* or *refaire au —;* to take in, to cheat; to give like for like; to pay back in his own coin; to give (any one) as good as he brings.

mêmement, *adv.,* also, even, likewise.

mémento (-min-), *n.m.,* (—s) memento, reminder, hint.

mémoire, *n.f.,* memory, recollection, remembrance; commemoration; fame. *Avoir une — de lièvre;* to have a very short memory. *— fidèle;* retentive memory. *Je n'en ai pas la moindre —;* I have not the slightest recollection of it. *De — d'homme on n'a vu telle chose;* such a thing has not been seen within the memory of man. *Des choses dignes de —;* things worthy of commemoration. *Remettre dans la —, conserver la — de;* to remind, to remember. *Rappeler quelque chose à la — de quelqu'un;* to bring anything to any one's recollection, to remind any one of anything. *En — de;* in memory of. *Réhabiliter la — d'un défunt;* to restore the fair fame of any one. *A la — de;* in memory of. *Si j'ai bonne —;* if I remember rightly.

mémoire, *n.m.,* memorial; memorandum; bill, account. *Dresser un —;* to draw up a memorial. *— acquitté;* bill receipted. *— d'apothicaire;* exorbitant bill.

mémorable, *adj.,* memorable.

mémorandum (-dom), *n.m.,* memorandum; memorandum-book; memorial.

mémorati-f, -ve, *adj.,* (fam.) mindful; recollecting. *Etre — de quelque chose;* to remember anything.

mémorial *n.m.,* memorial; (com.) waste-book.

mémorialiste, *n.m.,* memorialist.

menaçant, -e, *adj.,* menacing, threatening. *D'une manière —e;* threateningly

menace, *n.f.,* menace, threat. *— en l'air;* empty threat. *Paroles de —;* threatening words.

menacer, *v.a.,* to threat, to threaten, to menace; to forebode, to portend; to impend. *— de la main;* to threaten to strike (any one). *L'air nous menace d'un orage;* the air presages a storm *or* there is thunder in the air. *— ruine, — de tomber;* to totter, to be on the point of ruin, to decay, to threaten to fall.

ménade, *n.f. V.* bacchante.

ménage, *n.m.,* housekeeping, household; housewifery house; household goods; family; husbandry, economy, saving. *Toile de —;* home-spun linen. *Liqueurs de —;* home-made wines. *Tenir —, être en —;* to keep house, to be a house-keeper. *Entrer en —;* to begin housekeeping. *Rompre son —;* to leave off housekeeping. *Dépense de —;* household expenses. *— de garçon;* bachelor's household. *Faire bon —;* to live well together. *Pain de —;* household bread. *Toile de —;* homespun cloth. *Femme de —;* charwoman. *Elle entend bien le —;* she is a good house-wife. *Vivre de —;* to live sparingly. *Faire le —;* to do the housework. *Mettre en —;* to settle any one.

ménagement (-na-jmān), *n.m.,* **regard,** respect, consideration; circumspection, caution; discretion; management, conduct.

ménager, *v.a.,* to husband, to manage, to spare, to be sparing, to save, to be saving; **to** take care of, to be careful of, to conduct carefully; to treat with caution, to treat gently, **to** treat kindly, to treat with respect, to humor, **to** bring about; to reserve; to procure; to contrive; to dispose, to arrange, to prepare; to help to. *— son bien;* to husband one's fortune. *— quelqu'un;* to treat any one with respect, consideration. *Je n'ai rien à —;* I have no measures to keep. *Pour — notre faiblesse;* out of compassion for our weakness. *— les termes;* to weigh what one says. *— l'occasion;* to improve the opportunity. *— ses forces;* to spare one's strength. *— ses* *amis;* to forbear being troublesome to one's friends. — *son crédit;* to make the most of one's credit. *Je lui ai ménagé une place;* I helped him to get a situation. — *ses ressources;* to husband one's resources. — *une agréable surprise à;* to prepare, to procure, an agreeable surprise for. — *une étoffe;* to make the most of a stuff. — *un escalier dans un bâtiment;* to contrive a staircase in a house. — *la chèvre et le chou;* to hold with the hare and run with the hounds. *Qui vaut aller loin ménage sa monture;* he who wishes to live long avoids excess.

se **ménager,** *v.r.,* to take care of one's self; to spare one's self; to behave with care, with caution, to conduct one's self cautiously. *Se — avec quelqu'un;* to keep in, to keep on good terms, with any one. *Se — entre deux partis contraires;* to steer a successful course between two adverse parties, and remain friendly with both.

ménager, *v.n.,* to save, to save up. *Il ménage pour ses enfants;* he is saving up for his children.

ménag-er, -ère, *adj.,* thrifty, saving, sparing, provident, frugal.

ménager, *n.m.,* economist; thrifty, saving, frugal, sparing man. *Être bon — du temps;* to husband one's time well.

ménagère, *n.f.,* economical housewife; thrifty, saving, frugal, sparing woman; housewife; housekeeper; (of things) cruet-frame, cruet-stand.

ménagerie (-na-jiî) *n.f.,* menagerie.

mendiant, -e, *n.* and *adj.,* beggar, mendicant; beggar-woman; (c.rel.) mendicant-friar, mendicant. *Les quatre —s;* the four orders of mendicant friars; raisins, figs, almonds, and nuts (at dessert).

mendicité, *n.f.,* beggary, mendicity; beggars; vagrancy. *La — est interdite;* begging is forbidden, *or* no begging allowed.

mendier, *v.a.* and *n.,* to beg; to beg for; (b.s.) to solicit meanly, to implore. *Il mendie son pain;* he begs his bread. — *sa vie;* to live by begging.

mené, -e, *part. adj.,* led. — *par sa femme;* henpecked.

meneau, *n.m.,* (arch.) mullion.

menée, *n.f.,* underhand dealing, secret practice, plot, conspiracy; track. *Suivre la —;* (hunt.) to follow the track.

mener, *v.a.,* to carry, to conduct, to lead, to drive (a carriage), to bring; to direct, to head, to command, to guide, to sway, to influence; to introduce, to take; to take along with; to amuse; to lead about, to manage, to steer; to handle; to humbug, to bamboozle. — *les bêtes aux champs;* to drive the cattle to the fields. — *paître les vaches;* to take, to drive, cows to pasture. — *quelqu'un en prison;* to convey any one to jail. — *un enfant par la lisière;* to have a child in leading-strings. — *quelqu'un à la baguette;* to rule any one with a tight hand. — *tambour battant;* to carry it with a high hand over. — *un grand train;* to make a great show. — *le branle;* to take the lead. *Menez-moi chez le ministre;* introduce me to the minister. — *de front;* to have several things on hand. — *bien sa barque;* to manage one's affairs well.

mener, *v.n.,* to drive; to lead, to conduct, to go. *Ce chemin mène à la ville;* this road leads to the town. *Cela ne mène à rien;* that leads to nothing, that is of no use.

ménestrel, *n.m.,* minstrel.

ménétrier, *n.m.,* village fiddler.

meneur, *n.m.,* driver; agent for wet-nurses; leading man, ringleader.

meneuse, *n.f.,* female agent for wet-nurses, baby-farmer.

menhir, *n. m.,* (—s) (archæology) druidical-stone; menhir (standing-stone).

méniane, *n.f.,* (arch.) verandah, balcony (in Italy).

ménianthe, *n.m.,* (bot.) bog-bean, marsh-tre-foil.

menin, *n.m.,* young nobleman attached to the person of the Dauphin, minion, favorite (French hist.).

méninge, *n.f.,* (anat.) meninges.

méningite, *n.f.,* (med.) meningitis.

ménippée, *adj.* and *n.f.,* of satires in the style of those of the philosopher Menippus. *Satire —, la —;* a satire which appeared in 1593 against the party of the Ligue (French hist.).

ménisperme, *n.m.,* (bot.) menispermum, moon-seed.

ménisque, *n.m.,* (opt.) meniscus.

ménologe, *n.m.,* menology.

menotte, *n.f.,* (fam.) little hand (of a child). *pl.,* handcuffs, manacles. *Mettre les —s à;* to handcuff.

mense, *n.f.,* (of abbeys) income, revenue, stock; ⊙ table, board (food).

mensole, *n.f.,* (archit.) keystone.

mensonge, *n.m.,* lie, falsehood, untruth, story; error, illusion, vanity. *Débiter des —s;* to tell lies. *Tout petit —, — de rien, — de marchand;* white lie.

mensong-er, -ère, *adj.,* lying, untrue, deceitful, false, counterfeit, illusory.

mensongèrement, *adv.,* falsely, deceitfully, untruely; illusively.

menstrue, *n.m.,* (chem.) menstruum.

menstruel, -le, *adj.,* (med.) menstrual. *Flux —;* menses, catamenia.

menstrues, *n.f.,* (physiology) menses, catamenia.

mensuel, -le, *adj.,* monthly.

mensuellement, *adv.,* monthly.

mensurabilité, *n.f.,* mensurability.

mensurable, *adj.,* mensurable.

mental, -e, *adj.,* mental.

mentalement (-tal-măn), *adv.,* mentally.

menterie (man-trî), *n.f.,* story, fib, falsehood, untruth.

menteu-r, -se, *adj.,* lying, false, deceitful.

menteu-r, *n.m.,* **-se,** *n.f.,* liar, story-teller, fibber. *Un — de profession;* a confirmed liar.

menthe, *n.f.,* (bot.) mint. — *aquatique;* water-mint. — *verte;* spearmint. — *poivrée;* peppermint.

mention, *n.f.,* mention, mentioning, naming.

mentionner, *v.a.,* to mention, to make mention of, to name.

mentir (mentant, menti), *v.n.,* to lie, to tell a lie, a story, a falsehood, an untruth; to fib, to speak false. *Gardez-vous bien de —;* beware of lying. *Il en a menti;* he is a liar. *Il n'enrage pas pour —;* he does not stick at a lie. *Se — à soi-même;* to belie one's self. *A beau — qui vient de loin;* (prov.) travelers tell fine tales *or* lie with impunity. *Sans —, à ne point —;* to tell the truth, in fact, indeed, candidly, really.

menton, *n.m.,* chin. — *en galoche;* turned-up chin. — *à double étage;* double chin. — *qui avance;* prominent chin. *Avoir deux —s;* to be double-chinned.

mentonnet, *n.m.,* (mec.) ear, tipper; catch.

mentonni-er, -ère, *adj.,* (anat.) of the chin.

mentonnière, *n.f.,* chin-piece, chin-band, chin-strap; bandage for the chin.

mentor (min-), *n.m.,* mentor, guide, tutor.

menu, -e, *adj.,* small, slender, spare, thin, inconsiderable, petty, minor. *Le — peuple;* the common people, the lower classes. — *plomb;* small shot. — *gibier;* small game. — *bétail;* small cattle. — *s plaisirs;* pocket-money.

menu, *n.m.,* minute detail, particulars. *Le — d'un repas;* the bill of fare. *Un paquet de —;* a bundle of small linen. *Par le —;* minutely, in detail.

menu, *adv.,* small, fine; minutely; with quick and short steps. *Il pleuvait dru et —;*

the rain fell fine and fast. *Marcher, trotter, dru et* —; to walk with short and quick steps.

*menuaille, *n.f.*, small money; fry, small fish; trash.

menuet, *n.m.*, minuet.

menuiser, *v.a.* and *n.*, to do carpenter's work.

menuiserie (-nui-zrî), *n.f.*, joinery, joiner's work; carpentry.

menuisier, *n.m.*, joiner, carpenter and joiner. — *en bâtiments;* house-carpenter.

menuisière, *n.f.*, carpenter's wife.

menuisière, *adj.f.*, (ent.) carpenter. *Abeille* —; carpenter-bee.

ménure, *n.f.*, lyre-bird; lyre-pheasant.

méphitique, *adj.*, mephitic.

méphitisme, *n.m.*, mephitis, mephitism.

méplat, *n.m.*, (paint.) flat, flat part, flattish curve.

méplat, -e, *adj.*, (carp., paint.) flat, flatwise.

se **méprendre**, *v.r.*, to mistake; to make a mistake; to be mistaken; to be under a mistake; to misapprehend; (fig.) to forget one's self, to be wanting in respect. *Vous vous méprenez;* you mistake, you forget yourself. *C'est à ne pas s'y* —; you cannot make a mistake. *C'est son père, à s'y* —; you would easily take him for his father; he is the dead-spit of his father.

mépris, *n.m.*, contempt, scorn, contumely. *pl.*, contumelious language, contemptuous treatment. *Avoir du* — *pour quelqu'un;* to feel contempt for any one. *Au* — *des lois;* in defiance of the laws. *Témoigner du* — *pour;* to evince contempt for. *Tomber dans le* —; to fall into contempt. *La familiarité engendre le* —; familiarity breeds contempt.

méprisable, *adj.*, contemptible, despicable.

méprisablement, *adv.*, despicably.

méprisant, -e, *adj.*, contemptuous, scornful.

méprise, *n.f.*, mistake, oversight, misunderstanding; misapprehension; error. *Lourde* —; gross mistake. *Faire une grande* —; to make a great mistake.

mépriser, *v.a.*, to contemn, to despise, to scorn; to slight; to set at naught; to undervalue; to disregard.

mer (mèr), *n.f.*, sea, deep, ocean, main; tide, water; jar (frequently replenished). *La haute* —; main sea; high sea; high water. — *basse;* shallow sea, low water. *Port de* —; sea-port. *Un coup de* —; (nav.) a sea. *Homme de* —; seafaring man. *Loup de* —; expert seaman, Jack Tar; old salt. *D'outre-* —; beyond the seas. *En pleine* —; on the open sea, on the high seas. *Chercher quelqu'un par* — *et par terre;* to look for any one high and low. *C'est la* — *à boire;* it is an endless task, an impossibility. *Porter de l'eau à la* —; to carry coals to Newcastle. *La* — *est belle;* the sea is smooth. *Tenir la* —; to keep at sea. *Tenir bien la* —; to be a good sea-boat. *Jeter, tomber, à la* —; to throw, to fall, overboard. *Embarquer un coup de* —; to ship a sea. *Gros coup de* —; heavy sea. *Mettre à la* —; to put to sea. *Pouvoir tenir la* —; (nav.) to be seaworthy (of a ship). *En* —; at sea. *Prendre la* —; to go to sea. *Mal de* —; seasickness. *Il y avait beaucoup or pas mal de* —; there was a good sea on. *Écumeur de* —; sea-rover. *Entouré par la* —; sea-girt. *Apporté par* —; sea-borne.

mercadet, *n.m.*, jobber.

mercantile, *adj.*, mercantile, commercial; (fig.) grasping, sordid.

*mercantille, *n.f.*, (l.u.) petty trading; hucksterage.

mercenaire, *adj.*, mercenary, venal.

mercenaire, *n.m.*, mercenary, hireling.

mercenairement (-nèr-mān), *adv.*, mercenarily.

mercerie, *n.f.*, mercery, haberdashery.

merci, *n.f.* (n.p.), mercy, discretion, will, pleasure. *Crier* —; to cry for mercy. *Don*

d'amoureuse —; lady's favors. *Se mettre, or être, à la* — *de quelqu'un;* to be, to place one's self, at any one's mercy, discretion.

merci, *n.m.*, thanks; thank you. *Dieu* —; thank God! *Grand* — *!* much obliged! *Sa* —; (old) thanks to him.

merci, *adv.*, thank you, I have had quite enough, I'd rather not.

merci-er, *n.m.*, **-ère**, *n.f.*, mercer, haberdasher. *Petit* —; haberdasher.

mercredi, *n.m.*, Wednesday. — *des Cendres;* Ash-Wednesday.

mercure, *n.m.*, (astron.) Mercury; quicksilver.

mercuriale, *n.f.*, harangue, lecture, reprimand, curtain lecture, censure, rebuke; rating; averages, average prices of grain; (bot.) mercurialis.

mercuriel, -le, *adj.*, mercurial. *Onguent* —; mercurial ointment.

merde, *n.f.*, dirt, dung; excrements (of man and animals). — *!* you be blowed!

mère, *n.f.*, mother; (of animals) dam; (fig.) cause, source, reason. *Belle-* —, (—s——s) mother-in-law; step-mother. *Grand'* —, (——s), (pop.) —*grand*, (—s—) grandmother. *Dure-* —, (n.p.) dura mater. *Pie-* —, (n.p.) pia mater. *Eau* —; mother water. *L'oisiveté est la* — *de tous les vices;* idleness is the mother of all vices. — *nourrice;* foster-mother. *La* — *patrie;* the mother-country. *Notre* — *commune;* our mother-earth.

mère, *adj.*, mother; chief, primitive. — *goutte;* unpressed wine. *— laine;* fine wool.

méreau, *n.m.*, counter, ticket, check.

mérelle, *n.f.* *V.* **marelle**.

méridien (-in), *n.m.*, meridian.

méridien, -ne, *adj.*, meridian.

méridienne (-di-è-n), *n.f.*, siesta, afternoon nap; meridian line. *Faire la* —; to take an afternoon nap.

méridional, -e, *adj.*, meridional, southern.

méringue (-ringh), *n.f.*, meringue (cake).

mérinos (-nôs), *n.m.*, merino sheep; merino (stuff).

merise, *n.f.*, wild cherry.

merisier, *n.m.*, wild cherry-tree.

méritant, -e, *adj.*, meritorious, worthy, deserving.

mérite, *n.m.*, merit, worth; desert, talent, attainments. *Il sera traité selon ses* — *s;* he shall be dealt with according to his deserts. *Se donner le* — *de quelque chose;* to assume the merit of anything. *Se faire un* — *de;* to make a merit of. *Remplir son* —; to act up to one's reputation.

mériter, *v.a.* and *n.*, to deserve, to merit; to earn; to procure, to gain; to need, to require. *Il mérite d'être récompensé;* he deserves to be rewarded. *Cette nouvelle mérite confirmation;* that news requires confirmation. *Cela ne mérite pas qu'on en parle;* that is not worth mentioning.

mérithalle, *n.m.*, (bot.) internode.

méritoire, *adj.*, meritorious.

méritoirement (-toâr-mān), *adv.*, meritoriously.

merlan, *n.m.*, (ich.) whiting; (b.s.) journeyman hair-dresser.

merle, *n.m.*, (orni.) blackbird. — *aquatique;* water-ouzel. *C'est un fin* —; he is a cunning blade or fellow. *Dénicheur de* — *s;* person not to be trusted. *On ne prend pas les vieux* —*s à la pipée;* old birds are not to be caught with chaff.

merlette, *n.f.*, (her.) martlet, hen blackbird.

merlin, *n.m.*, (nav.) marline; cudgel; cleaver, chopper, pole-ax (tool).

merlon, *n.m.*, (fort.) merlon.

merluche, *n.f.*, (ich.) dried haddock; **stock**-fish; salt-cod.

merlus, *n.m.*, hake; haddock.

merrain, *n.m.,* broad lath, planks, stave-wood, (hunt.) horn (of deer); (cooperage) clap-board.

*merveille, *n.f.,* wonder, marvel, miracle, prodigy. *A* —; admirably done, wonderfully well, capitally. *Faire des* —*s;* to perform wonders. *Promettre monts et* —*s;* to promise wonders. *Mes affaires vont à* —; my affairs are going on admirably, swimmingly. *Se porter à* —; to be in splendid health, to be very fit.

*merveilleuse, *n.f.,* affected lady.

*merveilleusement (-efiz-män), *adv.,* wonderfully, admirably; wonderfully well.

*merveilleu-x, -se, *adj.,* wonderful, wondrous, marvelous; remarkable.

*merveilleux, *n. m.,* wonderful, marvelous part; marvelous, exquisite; coxcomb, swell, dandy, beau.

mes (mè), *adj. m.f.pl.,* my.

mésadvenir *or* **mésavenir,** *v.imp.,* (l.u.) to come to any harm, to turn out ill.

mésair *or* **mézair,** *n.m.,* (man.) prancing.

mésaise, *n.m.,* uncomfortableness, uneasiness.

mésalliance, *n.f.,* misalliance, disparagement, bad match.

mésallier, *v.a.,* to disparage; to marry (beneath one); (fig.) to lower, to degrade.

se **mésallier,** *v.r.,* to disparage one's self; to lower or degrade one's self; to contract a misalliance; to marry beneath one.

mésange, *n.f.,* titmouse, tomtit, tit.

mésangette, *n.f.,* bird trap.

mésarriver *or* **mésavenir,** *v.imp.,* to come to any harm, to happen unluckily, to turn out ill.

mésaventure, *n.f.,* mischance, mishap, misadventure.

mésembryanthème, *n.m.,* (bot.) fig-marigold.

mésentère, *n.m.,* (anat.) mesentery.

mésentérique, *adj.,* (anat.) mesenteric.

mésestime, *n.f.,* bad opinion, disesteem; disfavor, discredit, disrepute.

mésestimer, *v.a.,* to disesteem, to undervalue, to depreciate, to despise.

mésintelligence, *n.f.,* misunderstanding, variance, disagreement.

mésinterprétation, *n.f.,* misinterpretation, misconstruction.

mésinterpréter, *v.a.,* to misinterpret, to misconstrue.

mesmérisme, *n.m.,* mesmerism.

mésoffrir, *v.n.,* to underbid.

mesquin, -e, *adj.,* mean, shabby; paltry, poor, pitiful; niggardly, illiberal.

mesquinement (-ki-n-män), *adv.,* shabbily, meanly.

mesquinerie (-ki-n-rî), *n.f.,* meanness, shabbiness; mean *or* paltry thing; stinginess, paltriness.

mess, *n.f.,* (—) (milit.) mess, officers' table.

message, *n.m.,* message; errand.

messag-er, *n.m.,* **-ère,** *n.f.,* messenger, forerunner, harbinger; carrier. *Les hirondelles sont les* —*ères du printemps;* swallows are the forerunners *or* harbingers of spring.

messagerie (mé-sa-jrî), *n.f.,* stage-coach office; stage-coach, coach, stage; carriage of goods; goods traffic, goods department. —*s liners,* steam packets.

messaline, *n.f.,* dissolute woman, strumpet.

messe, *n.f.,* (c.rel.) mass. — *haute, grand'*— (—*.*—*s*); high mass, grand mass. *Petite* —, — *basse;* low mass. — *des morts,* — *de requiem;* mass for the dead. — *de minuit;* midnight service. — *du Saint Esprit;* invocation. *Livre des* —; prayer-book, church-service. *Près du moutier a* — *le dernier;* the nearer the church, the farther from God.

messéance, *n.f.,* unseemliness, unbecomingness.

messéant, -e, *adj.,* unseemly, unbecoming.

messeigneurs, *n.m.pl.,* my lords.

messeoir (mé-soâr), *v.n.,* to be unbecoming; not to befit, to ill-become.

messidor, *n.m.,* Messidor, the tenth month of the calendar of the first French republic, from June 19th to July 18th.

messie, *n.m.,* Messiah.

messier, *n.m.,* keeper of standing crops, of vineyards.

messieurs (mè-sieû), *n.m.pl.,* gentlemen, Messrs.

messin, -e, *adj.,* native of Metz.

messire jean, *n. m.,* (—*s*—*s*) a variety of pear.

mestre, *n.m.* (nav.). *V.* **meistre.**

⊙**mestre de camp,** *n.m.,* colonel (of a horse or infantry regiment). — *général;* brigadier-general.

⊙**mestre de camp,** *n.f.,* the first company of a regiment.

mesurable, *adj.,* measurable.

mesurage, *n.m.,* measurement, measuring; gauging, surveying, metage.

mesure, *n.f.,* measure, gauge, standard; dimension; (mus.) measure, bar; (fenc.) proper distance; (poet.) meter, measure; bound; extent, limit, compass; moderation, prudence; precaution; decorum; calculation, reckoning; propriety. *Il a comblé la* —; he has heaped up the measure. *Au fur et à* — *que;* in proportion as; according to. *Observer la* —; to keep time. *Battre la* —; to beat time. *Chanter,* or *aller, en* —; to keep time in singing. *Ne point garder de* — *avec une personne;* to have no regard, no consideration, for a person. *Cette idée passe la* — *de son esprit;* that idea is beyond the compass of his intellect. *Outre* —; excessively, beyond measure. *A* — *que;* in proportion as. *A* —; in proportion, accordingly. *A la* —; by measure, on draught. *A* — *que l'un avançait, l'autre reculait;* as one advanced, the other retired. *Vous n'avez qu'à travailler, et on vous paiera à* —; you need only work, and you 'll be paid accordingly. *Sans* —; beyond all measure, immeasurably, unguardedly. *Se mettre en* — *de;* to prepare to do anything, to get ready, to arrange. *Prendre ses* —*s;* to take one's precautions.

mesuré, -e, *part.,* measured, regular; cautious; circumspect, guarded, prudent. *Il est très* — *dans ses discours;* he is very guarded in what he says.

mesurer, *v.a.,* to measure, to gauge; to proportion, to survey, to compare, to consider, to weigh, to examine. — *les autres à son aune;* to measure other people's corn by one's own bushel. *A brebis tondue Dieu mesure le vent;* God tempers the wind to the shorn lamb. — *ses discours;* to be cautious in what one says.

se **mesurer,** *v.r.,* to measure one's self; to be measured; to vie, to contend, to cope with; to try one's strength; to measure swords.

mesureur, *n.m.,* measurer, meter, gauger.

mésusage, *n.m.,* misuse, abuse.

mésuser, *v.n.,* to misuse, to abuse.

métabole, *n.f.,* (rhet.) metabola.

métacarpe, *n.m.,* (anat.) metacarpus.

métacarpien, -ne, *adj.,* metacarpal.

métacentre, *n.m.,* (geom. nav.) metacenter.

métachronisme (-kro-), *n.m.,* metachronism.

métacisme, *n.m.,* metacism.

métairie, *n.f.,* land (held on condition that the landlord shall receive half the produce); small farm, dairy-farm; farmhouse.

métal, *n.m.,* metal, ore. — *vierge;* native ore. — *blanc anglais;* Britannia metal. — *blanc d'Alger;* nickel silver, German silver. — *appliqué sur un autre;* charge. — *précieux;* precious metal.

métalepse, *n.f.,* (rhet.) metalepsis.

métallifère (-tal-li-), *adj.,* metalliferous.

métallique (-tal-lik), *adj.*, metallic.

⊙**métallique**, *n.f.*   *V.* **métallurgie**.

métallisation (-tal-li-), *n.f.*, (chem.) metallisation.

métalliser (-tal-li-), *v.a.*, (chem.) to metallize.

métallographie (-tal-lo-), *n.f.*, metallography.

métalloïde, *n.m.*, (chem.) metalloid.

métallurgie (-tal-lur-), *n.f.*, metallurgy.

métallurgique (-tal-lur-), *adj.*, metallurgic.

métallurgiste (-tal-lur-), *n.m.*, metallurgist.

métamorphique, *adj.*, metamorphic.

métamorphisme, *n.m.*, metamorphism.

métamorphose, *n.f.*, metamorphosis, transformation.

métamorphoser, *v.a.*, to metamorphose, to transform.

se **métamorphoser**, *v.r.*, to metamorphose one's self; to be, *or* become, metamorphosed; to change, to alter; to become changed.

métaphore, *n.f.*, (rhet.) metaphor.

métaphorique, *adj.*, metaphorical.

métaphoriquement (-rik-mān), *adv.*, metaphorically.

métaphrase, *n.f.*, metaphrase.

métaphraste, *n.m.*, metaphrast.

métaphysicien (-in), *n.m.*, metaphysician.

métaphysique, *n.f.*, metaphysics.

métaphysique, *adj.*, metaphysical.

métaphysiquement (-zik-mān), *adv.*, metaphysically.

métaphysiquer, *v.n.*, (fam.) to subtilize.

métaplasme, *n.m.*, (gram.) metaplasm.

métastase, *n.f.*, (med.) metastasis.

métatarse, *n.m.*, (anat.) metatarsus.

métathèse, *n.f.*, (gram.) metathesis.

métayage, *n.m.*, leasing of farms (on condition of giving to the owner half the produce).

métay-er, *n.m.*, **-ère**, *n.f.*, metayer, farmer; small farmer, dairy farmer; (*f.*) farmer's wife.

***méteil**, *n.m.*, meslin, maslin (mixture of wheat and rye). *Passe—*; wheat-rye.

***méteil**, *adj.*, of wheat mixed with rye.

métempsycose, *n.f.*, metempsychosis, transmigration of souls.

métempsycosiste, *n.m.f.*, one who believes in metempsychosis.

métemptose, *n.f.*, (astron.) metemptosis.

météore, *n.m.*, meteor, fire-ball.

météorique, *adj.*, meteoric.

météorisation, *n.f.*, (vet.) wind, flatulence.

météorisé, -e, *adj.*, (med.) flatulent, distended.

météorolithe, *n.m.*, meteorite, aerolite.

météorologie, *n.f.*, meteorology.

météorologique, *adj.*, meteorological.

méthode, *n.f.*, method, system; custom, way. *Cet homme a une étrange —;* that man has a strange way with him.

méthodique, *adj.*, methodical, systematical.

méthodiquement (-dik-mān), *adv.*, methodically, systematically.

méthodisme, *n.m.*, methodism.

méthodiste, *n.m.f.*, methodist.

méticuleusement, *adv.*, fastidiously, minutely, nicely.

méticuleu-x, -se, *adj.*, over-scrupulous, fastidious, nice.

métier (-tié), *n.m.*, trade, handicraft, business, calling, craft, profession; loom, frame; framework. *— à bas;* stocking-frame. *— à tisser;* power frame. *— à broder;* tambour-frame. *— à la main;* hand-loom. *De son —;* by trade, by profession. *Homme de —;* mechanic, handicraftsman. *Avoir le cœur au —;* to have one's heart in anything. *Il n'a pas le cœur au —;* his heart is not in it. *Le — des armes;* the profession of arms. *Il est du —;* he is in the same trade, he belongs to the same fraternity; he is of the craft. *C'est un tour de son —;* that's

a trick of his. *Jouer*, or *servir, un tour de son —;* to play a trick. *Chacun son —, et les vaches sont bien gardées;* every one to his trade. *Faire — de;* to make a trade of. *Faire au —;* to work on a frame. *Corps de —;* corporation, guild. *Sur le —;* (fig.) on the stocks.

méti-f, -ve, *adj.*   *V.* **métis**.

métis (-tîs), *-se*, *n.* and *adj.*, creole, mongrel; of mongrel breed, half-bred, cross-bred; hybrid; mixed. *Toile —se;* union cloth. *Se tenir —;* (fig.) to trim one's sails; to steer a middle course (Montaigne).

métissage, *n.m.*, cross-breeding.

métisser, *v.a.*, to cross (animals).

métonomasie, *n.f.*, metonomasy.

métonymie, *n.f.*, (rhet.) metonymy.

métope, *n.f.*, (arch.) metope.

métoposcopie, *n.f.*, metoposcopy.

métoposcopique, *adj.*, metoposcopical.

mètre, *n.m.*, meter (1.093633 yards); (poet.) meter.

métrer, *v.a.*, to measure (by the meter).

métreur, *n.m.*, (arch.) measurer; appraiser, valuer.

métrique, *n.f.*, scansion, versification.

métrique, *adj.*, metrical.

métrologie, *n.f.*, metrology.

métromane, *n.m.f.*, metromaniac.

métromanie, *n.f.*, metromania.

métropole, *n.f.*, mother country, metropolis, capital, metropolitan see.

métropolitain, -e, *adj.*, metropolitan. *Eglise —e;* mother-church.

métropolitain, *n.m.*, metropolitan, bishop, archbishop; underground railway (in Paris).

métrorrhagie, *n.f.*, (med.) metrorrhagia, uterine hemorrhage.

mets (mê), *n.m.*, dish, food, viands.

mettable, *adj.*, fit to be worn, wearable.

metteur, *n.m.*, putter, layer. *— en œuvre;* setter, mounter (of jewels). *— en pages;* (print.) maker-up, clicker. *— en scène;* getter up (of plays); stage manager. *— au point;* carver.

mettre (mettant, mis), *v.a.*, to put, to put out, to put in, to invest (money); to put on, to wear; to place, to lay, to set; to bring; to reduce, to carry; to employ; to contribute, to devote, to give; to stake, to bid. *— au jour;* to bring to light; to give birth to. *— à jour;* to bring up to date. *— en ordre;* to set in order. *— la charrue devant les bœufs;* to put the cart before the horse. *— des paroles en musique;* to set words to music. *— de la prose en vers;* to turn prose into verse. *— du fard, du rouge;* to paint one's face. *— par écrit;* to put *or* set down in writing. *— une chose au net;* to make a fair copy. *— un habit;* to put on a coat. *— le couvert;* to lay the cloth. *— un officier aux arrêts;* to put an officer under arrest. *— quelqu'un en état de;* to enable any one to. *— une chose en tête à quelqu'un;* to persuade any one to do a thing, to suggest the doing of anything. *— un livre au jour;* to publish a book. *— un vaisseau à l'eau;* to launch a ship. *— quelqu'un à la besace;* to reduce any one to beggary. *— un arrêt à exécution;* to execute a decree. *— bas;* to bring forth, to litter. *— quelqu'un dehors;* to turn any one out of doors. *— quelqu'un au fait;* to inform any one of a thing, of what is going on, of the state of matters. *— quelqu'un à l'amende;* to fine any one. *— quelqu'un à la raison;* to bring any one to reason. *— deux personnes mal ensemble;* to set two persons by the ears. *— une affaire en compromis;* to submit a thing to arbitration. *— quelqu'un en peine;* to make any one uneasy. *— quelqu'un en colère;* to put any one into a passion. *— quelqu'un au désespoir;* to drive any one to despair. *— ordre à ses affaires;* to put one's affairs in order. *Il met son nez partout;* he thrusts his nose everywhere. — *en pages ;* (print.) to make up, to click. — *du sien ;* to contribute something; to invest some money; to make concessions; to meet half way; to give a helping hand. *Mettez cinq cents francs ;* make it a hundred dollars.

se **mettre**, *v.r.*, to put *or* place one's self; to sit down; to stand, to lie down ; to dress; to begin; to set about ; to take to, to apply one's self to, to get into ; to spread, to break out. *Se — à table ;* to sit down to table. *Se — à la fenêtre ;* to place one's self at the window. *Se — en danger ;* to get into danger. *Se — en colère ;* to get into a passion. *Se — sur son quant-à-soi ;* to give one's self airs. *Se — dans le commerce ;* to turn tradesman; to take to trade. *Se — à son aise ;* to take one's ease. *Se — sur les rangs pour une charge ;* to enter as a candidate for a place. *Se — en voyage ;* to set out upon a journey. *Se — en route, en chemin, en marche ;* to start, to go forward, to make a move. *Se — bien ;* to dress well. *Se — mal avec quelqu'un ;* to fall out with any one. *Se — en tête ;* to take it into one's head. *Se — bien avec ;* to get on good terms with. *Se — mal avec ;* to quarrel with, to fall out with. *La peste se mit dans l'armée ;* the plague broke out in the army. *Il se met à tout ;* he turns his hand to everything. *Se — à parler ;* to begin to speak. *S'y —;* to set about it, to turn to, to buckle to.

mettre, *v.n.*, to set, to put. — *en mer ;* to put to sea.

meublant, -e, *adj.*, serving to furnish ; fit for furniture. *Meubles —s ;* movables, household goods.

meuble, *n.m.*, piece of furniture; utensil. *pl.*, furniture, household goods, belongings. — *de famille ;* heirloom. — *à demeure fixe ;* fixture. *Se mettre dans ses —s ;* to furnish apartments of one's own, to set up a house.

meuble, *adj.*, movable; personal. *Biens —s et immeubles ;* personal property. *Terre — ;* light mellow land.

meublé, -e, *part.*, furnished. *Etre bien —;* to have one's house, one's rooms, well furnished. *Avoir la bouche bien —e ;* to have a fine set of teeth.

meubler, *v.a.*, to furnish, to stock, to store. — *sa mémoire ;* to store one's memory. — *une maison ;* to furnish a house. — *une ferme ;* to stock a farm.

se **meubler,** *v.r.*, to get furniture of one's own.

meubler, *v.n.*, to look well, to be ornamental.

meuglement, *n.m.* V. **beuglement.**

meugler, *v.n.* V. **beugler.**

meulard, *n.m.*, large millstone; grindstone.

meule, *n.f.*, millstone; grindstone; burr; base (of a deer's head); (agri.) cock, stack, rick; (ich.) sun-fish. — *inférieure, — gisante ;* nether millstone, bedder. — *supérieure ;* upper millstone, runner. *Pierre à —s ;* burrstone. — *de fromage ;* round flat cheese.

meulerie, *n.f.*, millstone *or* grindstone yard.

meulier, *n.m.*, millstone *or* grindstone maker. *meulière, n.f.* and *adj.*, millstone, burrstone, millstone-quarry. *Pierre — ;* millstone.

meulon, *n.m.*, stubble-stack *or* rick ; cock (of hay); haulm-stack; shock *or* stock (of corn).

meunerie (meũ-n-rî), *n.f.*, miller's trade ; flour mill.

meunier, *n.m.*, miller; (ich.) chub. *Se faire d'évêque — ;* (fig.) to come down in the world.

meunière, *n.f.*, miller's wife ; (orni.) long-tailed titmouse.

meurt de faim, *n.m.*, (—) half-starved wretch.

meurt de soif, *n.m.f.*, drunkard.

meurtre, *n.m.*, murder, manslaughter, homicide; sin, great shame, great pity. *Crier au —;* to cry murder; to complain bitterly. *Au —!* murder !

meurtri, -e, *part.*, bruised, black and blue,

contused. *Il est tout — de coups ;* he is covered with bruises.

meurtri-er, -ère, *n.* and *adj.*, assassin, murderer ; murderess ; murdering, murderous, deadly ; bloody ; killing, homicidal.

meurtrière, *n.f.*, (fort.) loophole.

meurtrir, *v.a.*, to bruise, to contuse, to make black and blue ; (fig.) to supple (leather) ; to soften (colors).

meurtrissure, *n.f.*, bruise, contusion.

meute, *n.f.*, pack (of hounds). *Chef de — ;* whipper-in, leader of the band.

⊙ **mévendre,** *v.a.*, to undersell.

mévente, *n.f.*, ⊙underselling ; (com.) not selling, lack of sale.

mézair, *n.m.* V. **mésair.**

mézéréon, *n.m.*, (bot.) mezereon.

mezzanine, *n.f.*, (arch.) mezzanine.

mezzo-termine, *n.m.*, (—) medium, middle course ; mean.

mezzotinto, *n.m.*, (—) mezzotint.

mgr., (ab. of *Monseigneur*) my lord.

mi, *invariable particle*, mid, middle, half. Joined to the names of the months, or to the word *carême*, it forms with them *feminine* compound nouns which require the article : *la mi-carême ;* Mid-Lent ; *la mi-août ;* the middle of August. It may also be joined to the nouns *corps, jambe, chemin, mur, côte, terme, sucre,* when the compound words thus formed require the preposition *à* and do not admit of the article : *à mi-côte ;* half-way up the hill. *A —chemin ;* half-way. *A —mât ;* half-mast high. *A —jambe ;* half-way up the leg ; past the knees. *A mi-corps ;* up to the waist. V. **mi-parti.**

mi, *n.m.*, (mus.) E, mi.

miasmatique, *adj.*, miasmatic, malarious.

miasme, *n.m.*, miasma, miasm, noxious exhalation.

miaulement (miôl-mãn), *n.m.*, mewing.

miauler, *v.n.*, to mew.

mica, *n.m.*, (min.) mica, glimmer, glist, Muscovy glass.

micacé, -e, *adj.*, micaceous.

micaschiste, *n.m.*, (min.) mica-schist, micaslate.

miche, *n.f.*, round loaf ; small loaf, hunch, lump.

michel, *n.m.*, Michael. *La Saint —,* (*n.f.*) Michaelmas. — *Morin ;* Jack of all trades.

micmac, *n.m.*, secret practice, underhand trick *or* dealing, intrigue ; jobbery, foul-play.

micocoulier, *n.m.*, (bot.) nettle-tree.

microcosme, *n.m.*, microcosm.

micrographie, *n.f.*, micrography.

micromètre, *n.m.*, (astron.) micrometer.

microscope, *n.m.*, microscope ; magnifying-glass. *Voir tout avec un — ;* to exaggerate everything.

microscopique, *adj.*, microscopic, microscopical.

microzoaire, *n.m.*, (zoöl.) microscopic animalcule, infusory.

miction, micturition, *n.f.*, (med.) micturition.

midi, *n.m.*, noon, noonday, noontide, mid-day, twelve o'clock (in the day) ; meridian; south ; southern aspect, southern railway. *A — ;* at noon, at twelve o'clock. *Le — de la vie ;* the meridian of life. *A l'heure de — ;* at the hour of twelve. *Sur le coup de — ;* on the stroke of twelve. — *est sonné ;* it has struck twelve. *Chercher — à quatorze heures ;* to look for knots in a bulrush, to create difficulties where there are none. — *vrai ;* true meridian. — *moyen ;* mean meridian. *Les régions du — ;* the regions of the south.

mie, *n.f.*, crum, crumb ; (very little bit).

mie, *adv.*, (l.u.) not, not a jot, not at all, not in the least.

mie, *n.f.*, (ab. of *amie*) dear, sweet, love ;

nurse. *Ma —;* my darling, my sweet, sweetheart, my love. *Il appelle sa —;* he is calling his nurse.

miel, *n.m.,* honey. *Mouche à —;* honey-bee. *Rayon de —;* honey-comb. *Ruche à —;* bee-hive. ☉*— aérien;* manna. *On prend plus de mouches avec du — qu'avec du vinaigre;* fair means go farther than foul. *La lune de —;* the honey-moon.

miélaison, *n.f.,* honey-time.

miellat, *n.m.,* (bot.) honey-dew.

miellé, -e, *adj.,* honey-colored; honeyed, sweet, bland; covered with honey.

mielleusement (-eûz-mān), *adv.,* sweetly, blandly, honey-like.

mielleu-x, -se, *adj.,* honeyed, fair-spoken; sweet, bland; mawkish. *Paroles —ses;* honeyed words.

mien, -ne (mi-in, mi-è-n), *adj.,* (l.u.) mine. *Un — frère;* a brother of mine. *Le —, la —ne, les —s, les —nes,* (pron.) mine, my own. *Je ne demande que le —;* I only ask for my own. *Les —s;* my friends, my relations. *Faire des siennes;* to play tricks, pranks, *or* follies. [Used as adjective in the singular *only,* and *always* with the indefinite article *un, une.*]

miette, *n.f.,* crumb, bit, particle, morsel. *Ramasser les —s;* to pick up the crumbs. *Mettre en —s;* to crumble.

mieux, *adv.,* better; rather, best, more, more correctly, more properly, more comfortable. *J'aimerais —;* I had rather. *En —;* for the better. *De — en —;* better and better. *Je me porte le — du monde;* I am as well as can be. *Le — que je pourrai;* as well as I can. *Il a fait du — qu'il a pu;* he has done his best. *A qui — —;* in emulation of one another, in eager rivalry. *C'est on ne peut —;* it cannot be better *or* cannot be improved upon. *Disons —;* or rather, to speak more correctly. *Vous feriez —;* you had better. *Valoir —;* to be better, to be worth more. *Faute de —;* for want of something better. *Avoir — que cela;* to have much better *or* dearer than that. *Tant —;* so much the better. *Je ne demande pas —;* nothing would give me greater pleasure.

mieux, *n.m.,* better; best, best thing, best plan; improvement. *Le — est l'ennemi du bien;* let well alone. *Il y a du — dans son état;* he is better. *Faire de son —, faire du — qu'on peut;* to do one's best, to do the best one can. *Au —;* at best; for the best. *Pour le —;* for the best.

mieux, *adj.,* better. *Il n'y a rien de —;* there is nothing better.

mieux-disant, -e, *adj.,* better *or* best spoken; more *or* most eloquent.

mieux-être, *n.m.,* better *or* best condition; improvement in one's condition; increase of comfort.

mieux-faisant, -e, *adj.,* best-acting, most kind, most generous; (hist.) the (best) horse in a tournament.

mièvre, *adj.,* (fam.) arch, roguish; quaint, affected style of writing.

mièvrerie *or* **mièvreté,** *n.f.,* (fam.) roguishness, archness; piece of roguery, prank; affectedness, quaintness in writing.

***mignard, -e,** *adj.,* delicate, pretty; mincing. *Manières —es;* mincing manners.

***mignardement,** *adv.,* delicately, daintily, mincingly.

***mignarder,** *v.a.,* to cocker, to fondle, to cuddle, to indulge. *— un enfant;* to cocker a child. *— son style;* to be over nice in writing. *Se —;* to take great care of one's self.

***mignardise,** *n.f.,* delicacy, delicateness; mincing over nicety; fondling, cockering, cuddling; (bot.) feathered pink.

***mignon, -ne,** *adj.,* delicate, pretty, neat, tiny. *Bouche —ne;* pretty, small mouth. *Pied*

— ; neat foot. Argent —; spare money, pocket-money.

***mignon,** *n.m.,* darling, pet, favorite; minion.

***mignonne,** *n.f.,* darling, fondling, favorite; a kind of pear; (print.) emerald, minion.

***mignonnement,** *adv.,* delicately, finely, nicely.

***mignonnette,** *n.f.,* mignonette (sort of lace); ground pepper; (bot.) feathered pink.

☉*mignoter,** *v.a.,* (fam.) to fondle; to cocker; to cuddle.

☉*se mignoter,** *v.r.,* (fam.) to cocker one's self, to nurse one's self.

☉*mignotise,** *n.f.,* (fam.) blandishment, endearment; caress.

migraine, *n.f.,* sick- *or* nervous headache.

migrat-eur, -rice, *adj.,* migrating, migratory.

migration, *n.f.,* migration.

migratoire, *adj.,* migratory.

mijaurée, *n.f.,* (fam.) affected, finical woman; humbug.

mijoter, *v.a.,* (cook.) to cause to simmer; (fam.) to fondle, to cocker; (fig.) to contrive, to plot, to brew.

*se mijoter,** *v.r.,* (fam.) to cocker one's self, to nurse one's self; (cook.) to boil gently, to simmer.

mikado, *n.m.,* (—s) Mikado.

mil, *adj.,* one thousand. [Used for the *first* thousand in dates of the Christian era only.] *L'an — huit cent cinquante;* the year one thousand eight hundred and fifty.

mil, *n.m.,* (bot.) millet.

milady (-lè-) *n.f.* (*miladies*), my lady.

milan, *n.m.,* (orni.) kite.

milandre, *n.m.,* (ich.) tope.

milaneau, *n.m.,* young kite.

milésiaque, *adj.,* Milesian.

miliaire, *n.f.* and *adj.,* (med., anat.) miliaria; miliary. *Fièvre —;* miliaria, miliary fever.

miliasse, *n.f.,* hominy, hasty-pudding.

milice, *n.f.,* militia; soldiery, soldiers; ☉ war, warfare. *Soldat de la —;* militiaman. *Tirer pour la —;* to ballot for the militia.

milicien (-si-in), *n.m.,* militiaman.

milieu, *n.m.,* middle, midst, heart, center; expedient, medium, mean, way, expedient, second course; sphere, society, company. *Au — de la foule;* in the midst of the crowd. *Au beau —;* in the very middle. *Au — des hommes;* among men. *L'air est le — dans lequel nous vivons;* the air is the medium in which we live. *Il faut savoir garder le juste —;* we must know how to observe the golden mean. *— de salon;* center ottoman.

milieu, *adj.,* middle. [Only used in the expression *le point —;* the middle point.]

militaire, *n.m.* and *adj.,* military man, soldier, military, soldiery; soldierly, soldierlike, warlike, military. *L'art, la discipline, —;* military art, discipline.

militairement (-tèr-mān), *adv.,* militarily.

militant, -e, *adj.,* (theol.) militant. *L'église —e;* the church militant.

militer, *v.n.,* to militate, to make (for *or* against). *Cette raison milite pour moi;* that reason militates in my favor.

mille, *n.m.* and *adj.,* thousand, a thousand, one thousand. *Les — et une nuits;* the thousand and one nights. *On a dit cela — et — fois;* that has been said thousands of times. *Le premier —;* the first thousand. *L'an —;* the year one thousand.

mille, *n.m.,* mile (= 1,608 mètres).

***mille-feuille,** *n.f.,* (—) (bot.) milfoil, yarrow.

mille-fleurs, *n.f.,* (—) all-flower. *Eau de —;* extract of all flowers; (med.) cow-water (taken as a remedy). *Huile de —;* oil of cow-dung. *Rossolis de —;* all-flower cordial.

millénaire (mil-lé-), *adj.,* millenary.

millénaire, *n.m.,* millennium; millenarian.

millénarisme, *n.m.*, millenarianism.

⊙millepède, *n.m.* V. mille-pieds.

mille-pertuis, *n.m.*, (—) (bot.) St.-John's-wort.

mille-pieds, *n.m.*, (—) (ent.) milliped.

millépore, *n.m.*, millepore.

millésime (mil-lé-zi-m), *n.m.*, date, year (of a medal, coin, monument).

*millet, *n.m.*, (bot.) millet grass, millet.

milliaire, *n.m.* and *adj.*, milestone ; miliary. *Borne* —, *pierre* — ; milestone. — *doré* ; (*milliarum aureum*) the milestone set up by Augustus in the Forum.

milliard, *n.m.*, one thousand millions.

milliasse, *n.f.*, (fam.) thousands, swarms (vast number).

millième, *n.m.* and *adj.*, thousandth.

millier, *n.m.*, thousand, thousand-weight. — *de fer* ; thousand-weight of iron. *Un* — *d'arbres* ; a thousand trees. *Des* — *d'arbres* ; thousands of trees. *On en trouve par* —*s* ; they are to be found in thousands.

milligramme, *n.m.*, milligram (French weight; ·0154 grain).

millilitre, *n.m.*, milliliter (French measure ; ·06103 cubic inch).

millimètre, *n.m.*, millimeter (French measure ; ·03937 inch).

million, *n.m.*, million.

millionième, *n.m.* and *adj.*, millionth.

millionnaire, *n.m.f.* and *adj.*, millionaire ; person extremely rich ; worth millions. *C'est un* —, *il est* — ; he is a millionaire, he is worth millions.

millouin or milouin, *n.m.*, (orni.) pochard, canvas-back duck.

milord (-lor), *n.m.*, (*milords*) lord, my lord ; your lordship (French); cab, phaeton (private); (pop.) rich man. *C'est un* — ; he is a nabob.

milréis (-is), *n.m.*, milreis (Portuguese coin).

mime, *n.m.* and *adj.*, (antiq.) mime; mimer; mimic; mimical.

mimer, *v.a.*, to mimic.

mimi, *n.m.f.*, darling, puss, pet, sweetheart.

mimique, *n.f.* and *adj.*, art of imitating, mimicry; mimic, mimical.

mimosa, *n.f.*, (bot.) mimosa (the sensitive-plant). [In botanical language this and all other names of plants ending in *a* are masculine.]

mimule, *n.m.* (bot.) monkey-flower.

minable, *adj.*, (fam.) pitiful, wretched-looking ; seedy, shabby.

minage, *n.m.*, (feudalism) toll-dues, corn-duty.

minaret, *n.m.*, minaret; (mining) shaft.

minauder, *v.n.*, to mince, to simper, to smirk, to be lackadaisical.

minauderie (mi-nô-drî), *n.f.*, affected, lackadaisical manners; lackadaisicalness, simpering, smirking.

minaudi-er, -ère, *adj.* and *n.*, affected, lackadaisical; affected, lackadaisical person.

mince, *adj.*, thin, slender, puny, shallow, poor, slight, scanty ; trivial, vulgar. *Esprit* — ; shallow wit. *C'est un homme bien* — ; he is but a shallow man. *Taille* —; slim *or* slender waist. *Il est d'un* — ; he is as shallow as you like, *or* as they make them.

mine, *n.f.*, look, aspect, mien, appearance ; show; air, figure, style. *Il a la* — *trompeuse* ; he has a deceitful look. — *fière* ; proud look. *Il ne faut pas juger des gens à la* — ; people should not be judged by their looks. *Homme de bonne* — ; good-looking man. *De mauvaise* — ; ill-looking. *Avoir bonne* — ; to look well. *Avoir mauvaise* —; to look ill. *Il a la* — *d'être riche* ; he looks like a rich man. *J'ai bien la* — *de payer vos folies* ; it seems as if I shall have to pay for your follies. *Faire* — *d'être fâché* ; to pretend to be angry. *Faire bonne* — *à quelqu'un* ; to

greet any one pleasantly. *Faire mauvaise* — *à* ; to receive coldly, to look daggers at. *Faire bonne* — *à mauvais jeu* ; to put a good face on matters. *Faire la* — *à quelqu'un* ; to pout at any one. *Faire la* — ; to look displeased. *Payer de* —; to be all outside show.

mine, *n.f.*, mine; ore; source, store; plot, secret; mine (French measure, 78 liters); (Grec.) mina. — *d'or* ; gold-mine. — *de charbon de terre* ; coal-pit. *Le puits de la* — ; the shaft of the mine. — *de plomb* ; lead-mine ; plumbago, black-lead pencil. — *d'argent cornée* ; soft silver-ore. — *d'argent rouge* ; silver-ore (mixed with arsenic and sulphur). — *à bocarder* ; ore rough from the mine. — *élevée* ; upright mine. — *profonde* ; mine with downward lodes. — *sèche* ; hard ore. —*s vives* ; rich mines. *Faire jouer une* — ; (milit.) to spring a mine. *Eventer la* — ; (milit.) to discover and destroy the enemy's mine ; (fig.) to discover the plot ; to baffle any one's designs.

miner, *v.a.*, to mine, to undermine, to sap; to hollow, to waste, to wear away ; to consume, to waste by slow degrees, to impair, to prey upon. — *un bastion* ; (milit.) to mine a bastion. *L'eau mine la pierre* ; water wears away stone. *Cette maladie le mine* ; that disease is wearing him away. *Se* —; to become undermined.

minerai, *n.m.*, ore. — *lavé* ; buddled ore. *Extraire le* — ; to dig out ore. — *brut* ; raw ore.

minéral, *n.m.*, mineral.

minéral, -e, *adj.*, mineral.

minéralisateur, *n.m.*, (chem., min.) mineralizer.

minéralisat-eur, -rice, *adj.*, (chem., min.) mineralizing.

minéralisation, *n.f.*, (chem., min.) mineralization.

minéraliser, *v.a.*, (chem., min.) to mineralize.

minéralogie, *n.f.*, mineralogy.

minéralogique, *adj.*, mineralogical, mineralogic.

minéralogiste, *n.m.*, mineralogist.

⊙minéralogue (-log), *n.m.* V. minéralogiste.

minerve, *n.f.*, (myth.) Minerva ; (fam.) head, brain, brains, reason. *Tirer quelque chose de sa* — ; (fam.) to draw, to get, anything from one's head, from one's brains. *Arbre de* —; (poet.) olive-tree. *Oiseau de* —; (poet.) the owl.

minet, *n.m.*, -te, *n.f.*, puss, kitten.

mineur, *n.m.*, miner, underminer, pitman.

mineur, -e, *adj.*, minor, under age ; minor, less, lesser ; (mus.) minor. *Frère* — ; Minorite, Franciscan.

mineur, *n.m.*, -e, *n.f.*, minor ; (jur.) infant.

mineur, *n.m.*, (mus.) minor mode; (in convents) minor.

mineure, *n.f.*, (log.) minor.

miniature, *n.f.*, miniature. *Portrait en* — ; miniature-portrait. *Peintre en* — ; miniature-painter.

miniaturiste, *n.m.f.*, miniature-painter.

mini-er, -ère, *adj.*, pertaining to mines.

minière, *n.f.*, ore; pit.

à minimâ, *adv.* *Appel à* —; (jur.) appeal by the crown when a sentence is too lenient.

minime, *adj.*, very small, very slender, very trifling, trifling, inconsiderable.

minime, *n.m.*, Minim (monk).

⊙minime, *n.f.*, (mus.) minim.

minimum (-mom), *n.m.*, (—*s*) (math.) (*minima*), minimum, lowest.

ministère, *n.m.*, ministry, agency ; services; administration, department, functions; minister's office; ministration. *Le* — *public* ; public authorities; magistrates. *Cela n'est pas de mon* — ; that does not belong to my office. *Le* — *des affaires étrangères, de l'intérieur, de la guerre* ; the foreign, the home, the war, office.

ministériel, -le, *adj.*, ministerial.

ministériellement (-rièl-màn), *adv.*, ministerially.

ministre, *n.m.*, minister; clergyman, rector, vicar; servant. *Le premier* —; the prime minister, the premier. — *d'état;* minister of state. — *du commerce;* president of the board of trade. *Les* —*s de l'autel;* the priests. — *de la Marine;* first Lord of the Admiralty. — *de l'Intérieur;* the Home Minister. — *des Affaires Etrangères;* the Foreign Minister.

minium (-om), *n.m.*, (n p.) (min.) minium, red lead.

minois, *n.m.*, pretty face, looks, air, appearance.

minon, *n.m.*, puss; kitten.

minoratif, *n.m.*, (med.) laxative, gentle aperient.

minorati-f, -ve, *adj.*, laxative.

minorité, *n.f.*, minority, nonage; (jur.) infancy.

minot, *n.m.*, ⊙minot (French measure, 39 liters); (nav.) bumkin.

minotaure, *n.m.*, (myth.) minotaur.

minoterie, *n.f.*, flour export trade; flour mill, flour store.

minotier, *n.m.*, miller, flour dealer; flour-exporter.

minuit, *n.m.*, midnight, twelve o'clock at night. *En plein* —; at the dead of night, in the middle of the night.

minuscule, *adj.*, (of letters) small, very small.

minuscule, *n.f.*, (print.) small letter.

minute, *n.f.*, minute (of time); moment, instant; small hand (writing); first draught, rough draught, minute, copy; draught; (astron., arch., geom.) minute. *Homme à la* —; punctual man. *Vous êtes toujours à la* —; you are always punctual. *Faire la* — *de;* to make a rough draught of; to take the minutes of. *Sablier de* —; minute-glass. —*!* stop a bit!

minuter, *v.a.*, to draw up, to make a rough draught; to minute down; (l.u.) to design, to intend, to purpose.

minuterie (mi-nu-trî), *n.f.*, (horl.) minute wheel-work; minute-wheels; minutes marked on a dial.

minutie (-ci), *n.f.*, trifle, minutiæ.

minutieusement (-ci-eûz-màn), *adv.*, minutely.

minutieu-x, -se, *adj.*, minute; circumstantial.

mioche, *n.m.f.*, (fam.) brat, urchin.

mi-parti, -e, *adj.*, bipartite, divided into two equal but different parts; half and half. *Les avis ont été* —*s;* the votes were equally divided.

miquelet (mi-klè), *n.m.*, soldier; Spanish bandit.

⊙**miquelot** (mi-klô), *n.m.*, begging-pilgrim. *Faire le* — ; to put on a sanctified, a sanctimonious, air.

mirabelle, *n.f.*, (bot.) mirabelle (plum).

miracle, *n.m.*, miracle, wonder. *A* — ; miraculously, extremely well, wonderfully well. *Faiseur de* —*s;* miracle-monger. *Crier* — ; to cry out wonderful! *Crier au* —; to declare a thing a miracle. *Opérer des* —*s;* to work miracles. *C'est un* — *de beauté;* she or it is wonderfully beautiful. *C'est un* — *de vous voir;* it is a wonder to see you. *Le beau* —*!* not so wonderful after all; *or* why, is that all!

miraculeusement (-leûz-màn), *adv.*, miraculously, wonderfully.

miraculeu-x, -se, *adj.*, miraculous, wonderful, marvelous.

mirage, *n.m.*, mirage; looming; (fig.) shadow, outline, delusion.

mirauder, *v.a.* V. **mirer**.

mire, *n.f.*, (artil.) aim; (of firearms) sight,

foresight. *Prendre sa* — ; to take aim. *Point de* —; aim, point aimed at; object, end, in view.

miré, *adj.*, (hunt.) with tusks curved inwards (of boars).

mirer, *v.a.*, to aim, to take aim, to aim at, to have in view; to look at; to examine; to candle (eggs). — *une place;* to aim at a situation. — *des œufs;* to try eggs (by holding them up to the light).

se mirer, *v.r.*, to look at one's self in a glass; to admire one's self; (of things) to be reflected. *Se* — *dans ses plumes;* to take pride in one's beauty and dress.

mirer, *v.n.*, (nav.) to loom, to appear indistinctly ; (of precious stones) to have but few angles, few facets; to take aim.

mirette, *n.f.*, (bot.) Venus's looking-glass. V. **miroir**.

mirifique, *adj.*, wonderful, marvelous; admirable, splendid.

mirliflore, *n.m.*, exquisite, fop, dandy, coxcomb, spark, beau.

mirlirot, *n.m.*, corruption of **mélilot**, q. v.

mirliton, *n.m.*, reed-pipe; bag-wig; tol-de-rollol.

mirmidon *or* **myrmidon**, *n.m.*, (hist.) Myrmidon; shrimp, pygmy (pers.).

mirobolant, -e, *adj.*, prodigious, wonderful, stupendous.

miroder, *v.a.* V. **mirauder** and **mirer**.

miroir, *n.m.*, mirror, looking-glass, glass; (opt.) mirror, speculum. *Etamer un* — ; to foliate a looking-glass. — *ardent;* burning-mirror. *Des œufs au* —; fried eggs. — *de Vénus;* (bot.) Venus's looking-glass.

miroitant, -e, *adj.*, reflecting (like a mirror), glistening, glittering, shimmering.

miroité, -e, *adj.*, shot, shiny, glittering, glistening ; shimmered ; reflected; (of horses) dapple-bay.

miroitement, *n.m.*, reflection of the light by polished surfaces; flashing, shine, glittering, brilliancy, radiance.

miroiter, *v.n.*, to reflect light, to flash, to shine, to glisten, to glitter, to shimmer ; to radiate. *v.a.*, to reflect, to mirror.

miroiterie (mi-roa-trî), *n.f.*, looking-glass trade *or* business, mirror-trade.

miroiterie, *n.f.*, mirror trade; looking-glass manufactory.

miroitier (-tié), *n.m.*, looking-glass maker.

miroton, *n.m.*, (cook.) miroton, beef collope (with onions) ; (of fruits) stewed.

mise, *part. adj.*, put ; dressed, clad, attired.

misaine, *n.f.*, (nav.) foresail. *Mât de* —; foremast. *Voile de* —; foresail.

misanthrope, *n.m.*, misanthrope, misanthropist, man-hater, hater of mankind.

misanthropie, *n.f.*, misanthropy.

misanthropique, *adj.*, misanthropic; misanthropical.

miscellanées, *n.m.pl.*, miscellanea, miscellany.

mischna, *n.f.* (n.p.), mischna, mishna.

miscibilité, *n.f.*, miscibility.

miscible, *adj.*, miscible ; mixable.

mise, *n.f.*, laying, placing; dress, manner of dressing; deposit, investment, outlay, disbursement; stake; bidding (at auctions); capital, share of capital; (l.u.) circulation (of coin). — *à l'eau;* launch (of a ship). — *hors;* (com.) outlay. *Cet homme est de* —; that man is presentable. *Cette raison n'est pas de* —; that reason will not pass *or* will not hold water. *Cette étoffe n'est pas de* —; that stuff is not worn, is not in fashion, not fashionable. *Avoir une* — *simple;* to dress plainly. *Sa* — *était de cinq francs;* he had staked five francs. — *en possession;* taking possession. — *en accusation;* impeachment, indictment. — *en arrestation;* arrest, apprehension. — *à exécution;* carrying out. — *en jugement;* trial. — *en musique;* setting to music. — *en perce;* tapping (of a cask). — *à prix;* upset price. — *en prévention;* (jur.) commitment. — *en pot;* potting. — *en justice;* bringing into court. — *à terre;* setting or putting down. — *en terre;* burial interment. — *en vigueur;* putting into force. — *en liberté;* enlargement, release, discharge. — *en scène;* (thea.) getting up of a dramatic piece. — *en vente;* putting up for sale. — *en œuvre;* working up (of anything); preparation; employing, using, setting. — *en pages;* (print.) clicking, making-up. — *en train;* setting to work, starting; (print.) making ready. — *en vigueur;* enforcement, putting into force. *De* —; acceptable, admissible.

miser, *v.n.,* (local ex.) to bid (at auctions).

misérable, *adj.,* miserable, wretched; wicked; sorry, worthless.

misérable, *n.m.f.,* wretch, miserable wretch, miscreant. *C'est un* —; he is a villain, a miscreant. *C'est une* —; she is a wretch. *Les —s;* the wretched, the outcasts.

misérablement, *adv.,* miserably, wretchedly; worthlessly, wickedly.

misère, *n.f.,* misery, wretchedness, distress, want; trouble, plague, grievous thing, helplessness; trifle, trifling thing. *Il est mort de faim et de* —; he died of starvation and want. *Prendre le collier de* —; to make one's self a drudge. *La — des membres;* the helplessness of the limbs.

miséréré, *n.m.,* (med.) iliac passion; (c.rel) miserere (51st psalm).

miséricorde, *n.f.,* mercy, tenderness, mercifulness; pardon, quarter, grace, forgiveness, pitifulness; small seat. *Crier* —; to cry for mercy. *Il ne mérite point de* —; he deserves no mercy. *Faire* —; to show mercy. *A tout péché* —; all offenses should be forgiven. —*! il va se tuer;* mercy upon me ! he will kill himself.

miséricordieusement (-eûz-măn), *adv.,* mercifully, compassionately.

miséricordieu-x, -se, *adj.,* merciful, compassionate, forgiving, pitiful.

miss, *n.f.,* (—) miss, young lady.

missel, *n.m.,* missal; mass-book, prayer-book.

mission, *n.f.,* mission. *Envoyer en* —; to send on a mission. *Remplir une* —; to perform a mission.

missionnaire, *n.m.,* missionary.

missive, *n.f.* and *adj.,* missive.

mistigri, *n.m.,* pam, loo (card game).

mistral *or* **maëstral,** *n.m.,* (local ex.) north-west wind (in southern France).

mistress, *n.f.,* (*n.p.*) Mrs.

mitaine, *n.f.,* mitten; (fig.) caution.

mite, *n.f.,* (ent.) mite; maggot; moth; tick.

mité, -e, *adj.,* moth-eaten, mity.

Ⓧ**mithridate,** *n.m.,* (pharm.) mithridate. *Vendeur de* —; quack; braggadocio.

mitigation, *n.f.,* mitigation.

mitigé, -e, *part.,* mitigated. *Peine —e;* modified penalty.

mitiger, *v.a.,* to mitigate, to soften, to make less severe, to modify, to temper, to allay, to assuage, to abate; to qualify.

miton, *n.m.,* woman's long mitten.

mitonnage, *n.m.,* simmering.

mitonner, *v.n.,* to lie soaking or stewing; to soak, to stew, to simmer.

mitonner, *v.a.,* to cocker, to fondle, to cuddle. — *quelqu'un;* to humor any one. — *une affaire;* to prepare an affair gradually. *Il aime qu'on le mitonne;* he likes to be cockered.

se **mitonner,** *v.r.,* to nurse one's self, to cocker one's self; (cook.) to simmer.

mitoyen, -ne (mi-toa-yin, -iè-n), *adj.,* middle; intermediate; midway; joint property. *Mur* —;

party-wall. *Cloison —ne;* partition wall between two rooms.

mitoyenneté(-toa-ie-n-té), *n.f.,* joint property; claims of two neighbors to a wall, hedge, or ditch; party-right.

*****mitraillade,** *n.f.,* discharge, fire of grape-shot.

*****mitraille,** *n.f.,* ☉ old iron, scrap-iron, scrap-metal; grapeshot; case-shot, canister-shot, canister; small change, coppers; (nav.) langrage, langrel-shot. *Charge à* —; case-shot.

mitrailler, *v.a.* and *n.,* to fire grapeshot, to riddle with grapeshot.

mitrailleuse, *n.f.,* (artil.) mitrailleuse, machine gun; Gatling gun.

mitre, *n.f.,* miter; chimney-pot (shaped like a miter).

mitré, -e, *adj.,* mitered.

mitron, *n.m.,* journeyman baker; paper cap.

mitte, *n.f.,* cesspool exhalation; stench; eyesore from ditto.

mixte, *adj.,* mixed; mixt; (bot.) common (of buds).

mixte, *n.m.,* mixed body, compound.

*****mixtiligne,** *adj.,* (geom.) mixtilineal, mixtilinear.

mixtion (miks-ti-on), *n.f.,* (pharm.) mixture.

mixtionner (miks-tio-né), *v.a.,* to mix, to mingle.

mixture, *n.f.,* (pharm.) mixture.

mlle. ab. of *Mademoiselle.*

mm. ab. of *Messieurs.*

mme. ab. of *Madame.*

mnémonique, *adj.,* mnemonic, mnemonical.

mnémonique *or* **mnémotechnie,** *n.f.,* mnemonics, mnemotechny.

mobile, *adj.,* movable; changeable, unsteady, variable; quick, lively, mobile.

mobile, *n.m.,* mover, spring, motive power; a soldier of the militia. *Premier* —; prime mover; *primum mobile;* ringleader. *L'intérêt est le plus grand — des hommes;* interest is the prime mover in human actions.

mobile, *n.f.,* militia.

mobiliaire, *adj.,* movable, personal.

mobili-er, -ère, *adj.,* movable; personal, of personal property. *Succession —ère;* inheritance of personal property.

mobilier, *n.m.,* ☉movables; furniture.

mobilisable,*adj.,*(milit.) that can be mobilized.

mobilisation, *n.f.,* act of making movable; conversion into movables; (milit.) mobilization.

mobiliser, *v.a.,* to convert into movables; (milit.) to draft for active service, to mobilize.

mobilité, *n.f.,* mobility, variableness, inconstancy, unsteadiness, unfixedness, instability, fickleness. — *de caractère;* versatility of disposition.

mocassin, *n.m.,* moccasin (shoe).

modale, *n.f.* and *adj.,* (log.) modal.

modalité, *n.f.,* (log.) modality.

mode, *n.f.,* mode, fashion, vogue; way, custom, manner. *pl.,* millinery. *C'est la dernière* —; it is the newest fashion. *Un habit à la* —; a fashionable coat. *Se mettre à la* —; to dress in the fashion. *Être à la* —; to be in fashion. *Du bœuf à la* —; a-la-mode beef. *Marchande de —s;* milliner. *Tante à la — de Bretagne;* father or mother's first cousin; cousin once removed. *Nièce à la — de Bretagne;* daughter of first cousin.

mode, *n.m.,* (gram., log., mus.) mode, way, manner, mood.

modelage (mo-dlaj), *n.m.,* modeling.

modelé (mo-dlé), *n.m.,* (sculp.) model (imitation). *adj.,* modeled.

modèle, *n.m.,* model, copy, pattern, sample, design. — *d'écriture;* copy-slip. *Conformez-vous au* —; keep to the pattern. *Faire le métier de* —; to serve as a model. — *parfait;* perfect model, paragon.

modeler (mo-dlé), *v.a.*, to model, to form, to shape, to mold.

se **modeler**, *v.r.*, to take for one's pattern, to take pattern by *or* upon. *Il se modèle sur son frère;* he takes pattern by his brother.

modeler, *v.a.*, to model.

modeleur (mo-dleur), *n.m.*, modeler.

modénature, *n.f.*, (arch.) proportion, profile and sweep of a cornice molding.

modérat-eur, *n.m.*, **-rice**, *n.f.*, moderator, moderatrix.

modération, *n.f.*, moderation; abatement, diminution; mitigation.

modéré, -e, *adj.*, moderate, reasonable, temperate.

modérément, *adv.*, moderately, in moderation.

modérer, *v.a.*, to moderate, to abate; to restrain, to restrict; to lessen, to reduce. — *ses passions;* to curb one's passions. — *le zèle de quelqu'un;* to restrain any one's zeal.

se **modérer**, *v.r.*, to moderate, to moderate one's self, to keep one's temper; to restrain one's self. *Le temps s'est modéré;* the weather has become calmer.

moderne, *adj.*, modern. *A la* —; in the modern style.

moderne, *n.m.*, modern, modern style.

moderner, *v.a.*, (arch., l.u.) to modernize.

moderniser, *v.a.*, to modernize.

moderniste, *n.m.*, modernist.

modeste, *adj.*, modest, unassuming, unpretending, quiet, simple, plain, moderate, poor.

modestement, *adv.*, modestly, quietly, simply, plainly.

modestie, *n.f.*, modesty, coyness, simplicity, plainness; moderation.

modicité, *n.f.*, smallness, lowness, moderateness, reasonableness.

modificati-f, -ve, *adj.*, modifying.

modificatif, *n.m.*, (gram.) modifying word.

modification, *n.f.*, modification.

modifier, *v.a.*, to modify, to change, to alter.

se **modifier**, *v.r.*, to become modified.

***modillon**, *n.m.*, (arch.) modillion.

modique, *adj.*, moderate, small.

modiquement (-dik-mǎn), *adv.*, moderately.

modiste, *n.m.f.*, man-milliner; milliner.

modulat-eur, -rice, *n.* and *adj.*, modulating; modulator.

modulation, *n.f.*, modulation.

module, *n.m.*, (arch.) module; (alg.) modulus; diameter (of medals).

moduler, *v.a.* and *n.*, to modulate.

moelle, *n.f.*, marrow, pith; (of the land) fat; medulla. *Os à —;* marrow-bone. — *d'arbre;* pith of a tree. — *épinière;* spinal marrow.

moelleusement, *adv.*, softly, easily, with softness; (paint.) with mellowness.

moelleux, *n.m.*, (paint.) mellowness; softness.

moelleu-x, -se, *adj.*, full of marrow, marrowy; pithy; soft; mellow. *Voix —se;* mellow voice. *Vin —;* mellow wine (full of body and flavor). *Discours —;* pithy discourse.

moellon, *n.m.*, ashlar; rough-stone, ragstone. — *brut;* rubble, sandstone (for grinding mirrors). *Maçonnerie de —;* ashlar-work.

mœurs, *n.f.pl.*, manners, morals, morality; habits, inclinations, ways; customs. *Avoir des —;* to be a man of morals. *N'avoir pas de —;* to be immoral, dissolute. *Un homme sans —;* an unprincipled man. *Les — des animaux;* the habits of animals.

mofette *or* **moufette**, *n.f.*, (l.u.) fire-damp (mines); ⊙(chem.) any poisonous gas; (mam.) mephitic weasel. — *atmosphérique;* azote, azotic gas.

mogol, *n.m.*, Mogul.

mohair, *n.m.*, mohair, stuff.

mohican, *n.m.*, Mohican.

moi, *personal pron.*, I, me, to me. — *! trahir le meilleur de mes amis!* what! I betray my best friend! *C'est —;* it is I. *Venez à —;* come to me. *Quant à —;* as for me. — *même;* myself. *A — ! help!* help! here! here! *Parlez- —;* speak to me. *Donnez-le-—;* give it me. *De vous à —;* between you and me; from you to me.

moi, *n.m.*, self, ego.

moïdore, *n.m.*, moidore (Portuguese coin).

moignet, *n.m.*, long-tailed tit.

***moignon**, *n.m.*, stump (of limbs, tree).

***moinaille**, *n.f.*, (b.s.) monkish crew.

moindre, *adj.*, less, least, shorter, lower, inferior. *Le —;* least, shortest, smallest, lowest; meanest, slightest. *La — chose;* the least thing. *Je n'en ai pas le — souvenir;* I have not the least recollection of it.

moindrement, *adv.*, (old) less, least. *Le — du monde;* in the slightest degree. *Pas le — du monde;* not in the least bit.

moine, *n.m.*, monk, friar; warming-pan, bed-warmer; (print.) friar. — *lai;* lay-monk. *Gras comme un —;* as fat as a pig. *L'habit ne fait pas le —;* it is not the cowl that makes the friar.

moineau, *n.m.*, sparrow. *adj.*, (of horses) cropped. — *franc;* house-sparrow. *Tirer sa poudre aux —x;* to waste one's powder and shot.

moinerie (moa-n-rî), *n.f.*, monkhood, monks.

moinesse, *n.f.*, (jest.) nun.

***moinillon**, *n.m.*, petty monk *or* friar.

moinotin, *n.m.*, (ornith.) coal-tit.

moins, *adv.*, less, under, wanting, to; minus. *Parlez —;* speak less. *En — de;* in less than. *De — en —;* less and less, fewer and fewer. *Rien —;* much less. *Du —;* at least, at any rate, at all events, at the very least. *C'est — que rien;* it is next to nothing. *Ni plus ni —;* neither more nor less. *Il ne s'agit de rien — que de sa vie;* nothing less than his life is at stake. *Il n'est rien — que sage;* he is anything but prudent. *Il n'y a rien de — vrai que cette nouvelle;* no news can be further from the truth than this. *Il est une heure — un quart;* it wants a quarter to one. *A —;* for less. *Vous ne l'aurez pas à —;* you shall not have it for less. *A — de;* for less than; unless. *A — que;* unless. —*value, (—-—s)* inferior value.

moins, *n.m.*, least, less; (alg.) minus. *C'est le — que vous puissiez faire;* it is the least you can do. *Pas le — du monde;* not in the least. *Au —;* at least. *Pour le —;* at least, at the least. *Tout au —;* at the very least. *C'est pour ce soir, au moins!* it is for to-night, mind!

moirage, *n.m.*, (manu.) watering (stuffs), mottling.

moire, *n.f.*, (manu.) watering; moire antique; watered silk.

moiré, -e, *adj.*, (manu.) waved, watered, mottled. *n.m.*, watering. — *de soie;* watered silk. — *de laine;* moreen.

moirer, *v.a.*, (manu.) to water (stuffs), to mottle, to wave. *Se —;* to be watered.

mois, *n.m.*, month; monthly allowance; month's pay. *Au —;* by the month. *Au — de;* in the month of. *Par —;* monthly, so much a month.

moise, *n.f.*, (carp.) couple, brace, binding piece.

moiser, *v.a.*, (carp.) to bridge over, to bind, to couple.

moisi, *n.m.*, moldiness, mustiness.

moisi, -e, *part.*, moldy, musty.

moisir, *v.a.*, to mold, to make moldy, to make musty.

se **moisir**, *v.r.*, to grow moldy, to grow musty.

moisir, *v.n.*, to grow moldy, musty.

moisissure, *n.f.*, moldiness, mustiness.

moissine, *n.f.*, a bundle of vine-branches with the grapes hanging to them.

moisson, *n.f.*, harvest; harvest-time; (poet.)

year. *Fête de la —*; harvest home. *Faire la —*; to cut the corn, to gather in the harvest.

moissonner, *v.a.*, to reap, to cut down, to crop, to mow. *— un champ;* to reap a field. *Se —;* to be reaped.

moissonneu-r, *n.m.,* **-se,** *n.f.,* reaper, harvestman, harvest-woman.

moissonneuse, *n.f.,* (agri.) reaping machine.

moite, *adj.,* moist, damp, clammy.

moiteur, *n.f.,* moisture, dampness.

moitié (-tié), *n.f.,* moiety, half; (fam.) better half, wife. *C'est trop cher de —;* it is too dear by half. *Je l'ai laissé à — chemin;* I left him half way. *Etre,* or *se mettre, de — avec quelqu'un;* to go halves with any one.

moitié, de moitié, à moitié, *adv.,* half, by half.

moka, *n.m.,* mocha. *Du café —;* mocha coffee.

mol, *adj.m.* V. **mou.**

molaire, *n.f.* and *adj.,* molar-tooth, mill-tooth, jaw-tooth; molar.

môle, *n.m.,* mole, jetty-head; pier.

môle, *n.f.,* (med.) mole.

moléculaire, *adj.,* molecular.

molécule, *n.f.,* molecule, particle.

molène, *n.f.,* (bot.) mullen, mullein.

molestation, *n.f.,* molestation, annoyance.

molester, *v.a.,* to molest, to trouble, to vex, to annoy.

molette, *n.f.,* rowel (of a spur); (vet.) windgall; muller (for colors); (of hair) feather; (rope-making) whirl; (hort.) turf-knife, turfing-iron.

molinisme, *n.m.,* molinism.

moliniste, *n.m.,* molinist.

molinosisme, *n.m.,* quietism, Molino's system.

mollah. *n.m.* (—*s*), mollah.

mollasse, *adj.,* flabby, flimsy, sodden.

molle, *n.f.,* (ich.) sun-fish.

molle, *adj.f.* V. **mou.**

mollement (mol-mān), *adv.,* softly, slackly, feebly; indolently, effeminately. *Vivre —;* to lead an effeminate life.

mollesse, *n.f.,* softness, laxity, slackness, tameness, weakness, indolence; effeminacy. *Vivre dans la —;* to live in effeminacy.

mollet, -te, *adj.,* soft; light (of bread). *Des œufs —s;* soft-boiled eggs. *Lit —;* soft bed. *Pain —;* light bread.

mollet, *n.m.,* calf (of the leg).

molletière, *n.f.,* legging.

molleton (mol-ton), *n.m.,* swan-skin.

mollification, *n.f.,* mollification, softening.

mollifier, *v.a.,* to mollify, to soften. *Se —;* to become soft.

mollir, *v.n.,* to soften, to grow soft; to mellow (of fruit); to slacken, to flag, to abate, to faint, to yield, to give way. *Le vent mollit;* the wind is going down. *v.a.,* (nav.) to ease.

mollusque, *n.m.,* mollusk.

molosse, *n.m.,* American bat; watch-dog; (ants) molossus.

moly, *n.m.,* wild garlic.

molybdène, *n.m.,* (min.) molybden, molybdena.

môme, *n.m.,* brat, urchin.

moment, *n.m.,* moment, instant; proper time; occasion, point, interval; (mec.) momentum. *Attendez un —;* stop a moment. *Il a des —s de bonté;* he has fits of kindness. *Voici le — de se décider;* now is the time for decision. *Un —; j'ai à vous parler;* one moment, I want to speak to you. *Au — de;* on the point of, just as. *Au — où, — que;* the instant that; just as. *Du — que;* as soon as, since; the moment that. *Du — que vous le voulez;* since you will have it so. *Je l'attends d'un — à l'autre;* I expect him every moment. *Dans le —;* in a moment, in a minute. *En ce —;* at this moment. *A tout —, à tous —s;* every instant, at every turn. *Par —s;* at times, at intervals.

momentané, -e, *adj.,* momentary.

momentanément, *adv.,* momentarily, for the moment, temporarily, for the time being.

momerie (mô-mrī), *n.f.,* mummery.

momie (mô-), *n.f.,* mummy; dark thin person; old fogy.

momification, *n.f.,* mummification.

momifier, *v.a.,* to mummify. *Se —;* to become mummified; to get very thin.

mon, *possessive adj.m.,* **ma,** *f.,* **mes,** *pl.m.f.,* my. *Mon père, ma mère et mes enfants;* my father, mother, and children. *Mon âme;* my soul. *Mon unique ressource;* my only resource. *Mon bon et digne ami;* my good and worthy friend. [*Mon* is used instead of *ma* (in the feminine) before a vowel or silent *h.*]

monacal, -e, *adj.,* monachal, monkish.

monacalement (-kal-mān), *adv.,* like a monk.

monachisme (-shism), *n.m.,* monachism.

monade, *n.f.,* monad.

monadelphie, *n.f.,* (bot.) monadelphia.

monandrie, *n.f.,* (bot.) monandria.

monarchie (-shi), *n.f.,* monarchy.

monarchique (-shik), *adj.,* monarchical, monarchic.

monarchiquement (-shik-mān), *adv.,* monarchically.

monarchiser (-shi-zé), *v.a.,* to monarchize.

monarchiste (-shist), *n.m.,* monarchist.

monarque, *n.m.,* monarch, lord.

monastère, *n.m.,* monastery, convent.

monastique, *adj.,* monastic, monastical.

monaut, *adj.m.,* one-eared (of animals).

monbin, *n.m.,* (bot.) hog-plum.

monceau, *n.m.,* heap, pile; drift, mass; lot.

mondain, -e, *n.* and *adj.,* worldling; worldly, worldly-minded; mundane; earthly.

mondainement (-dè-n-mān), *adv.,* mundanely, in a worldly way.

mondanité, *n.f.,* worldliness, worldly vanities.

monde, *n.m.,* world, universe; mankind, men; people; company, society, set; servants, retinue, attendants; customers. *Faire le tour du —;* to go round the world. *L'autre —;* the next world. *Dans l'autre —;* hereafter. *Il n'est plus du —;* he is dead. *L'an du —;* in the year of the world. *Il voit beaucoup de —;* he sees a great deal of company. *Peu de —, pas grand —;* few people, not many people. *Avoir du —;* to have company, visitors; to entertain. *Connaître son —;* to know whom one has to deal with. *Le mieux du —;* the best in the world. *Pour tout au —;* for all the world; for anything. *Le beau —;* people of fashion, the fashionable world. *Le petit —;* little people. *Ainsi va le —;* such is the world. *Tout votre — est-il arrivé?* has all your party arrived? *Venir au —;* to come into the world. *C'est vieux comme le —;* it is as old as the hills. *Il y a un — fou;* there is a great crush. *Se moquer du —;* to make fun of people. *C'est le bout du —;* it is the utmost you will get. *Tout le — et son père;* all the world and his wife. *Savoir son —;* to know how to behave.

monde, *adj.,* (rel.) clean.

mondé, -e, *part.,* cleansed. *De l'orge —;* hulled *or* husked barley.

monder, *v.a.,* to cleanse; to hull, to husk (barley).

mondificati-f, -ve, *adj.,* (med.) cleansing.

mondifier, *v.a.,* (med.) to cleanse, to wash.

mondor, *n.m.,* man made of money, rolling in money.

mondrain, *n.m.,* sand-hill, sand-mound.

monétaire, *adj.,* monetary.

monétisation, *n.f.,* making and stamping of money, minting, monetization.

monétiser, *v.a.,* to give currency to paper-money, to monetize.

mongol, -e, *adj.,* mongolian, mogul.

moniteur, *n.m.,* monitor, adviser, prefect (at school); Gazette.

monition, n.f., (ecc.) monition.

monitoire, n.m., adj., (ecc.) monitory.

monitor, n.m., (nav.) monitor.

monitorial, -e, adj., (ecc.) monitory.

monnaie, n.f., coin, money; change; mint; coinage; currency. *Hôtel de la* —; the mint. *Fausse* —; counterfeit coin. *Battre* —; to coin money; to raise money. *Papier* —; paper money. — *de compte;* nominal money. — *courante;* current money, currency. — *faible;* light money. — *légale;* legal tender. — *de singe;* sham coin; soft sawder, blarney. *Petite* —; small change. *Donnez-moi la* — *d'un franc;* give me change for a franc. *Payer en* — *de singe;* to laugh at one's creditors, instead of paying them. *Rappeler la* —; to call in money. *Donner, on rendre, à quelqu'un la* — *de sa pièce;* to pay any one back in his own coin.

monnayage, n.m., coining, minting. *Droit de* —; mintage.

monnayer, v.a., to coin, to mint, to stamp.

monnayeur, n.m., coiner, minter. *Faux* —; coiner of base money; forger.

mono, a prefix from Gr. μόνος.

monocéros, n.m., monoceros, unicorn, narwhal.

monochrome, n.m. and adj., monochrome.

monocle, n.m., (single) eye-glass.

monocorde, n.m., monochord.

monocotylédone, n.f. and adj., (bot.) monocotyledon, endogen; monocotyle, monocotyledonous, endogenous.

monodie, n.f., monody.

monœcie (-nè-sî), n.f., (bot.) monœcia.

monogame, n.m.f. and adj., monogamist; monogamous.

monogamie, n.f., monogamy.

monogrammatique, adj., monogrammatic, monogrammic.

monogramme, n.m., monogram.

monographie, n.f., monography.

monoïque, adj., (bot.) monœcious, monœcian.

monolithe, n.m. and adj., monolith; monolithic, monolithal.

monologue (-log), n.m., monologue; soliloquy.

monomane, n.m.f. and adj., monomaniac; monomaniacal.

monomanie, n.f., monomania.

monôme, n.m., (alg.) monomial.

monomètre, n.m., monometer.

monopétale, adj., (bot.) monopetalous.

monophylle, adj., (bot.) monophyllous.

monopole, n.m., monopoly.

monopoleur, n.m., monopolist.

monopolisa-teur, -trice, n. and adj., monopolizing; monopolizer.

monopolisation, n.f., monopolization.

monopoliser, v.a., to monopolize.

monoptère, adj., (arch.) monopteral.

monorime, adj., (poet.) with but one rhyme, being a monorhyme.

monosépale, adj., (bot.) monosepalous.

monosperme, adj., (bot.) monospermous.

monostique, n.m., monostich.

monosyllabe, n.m. and adj., (gram.) monosyllable; monosyllabic.

monosyllabique, adj., monosyllabic.

monothéisme, n.m., monotheism.

monothéiste, n.m. and adj., monotheist; monotheistic.

monotone, adj., monotonous.

monotonie, n.f., monotony, sameness.

monotriglyphe, n.m., (arch.) monotriglyph.

mons, n.m., ab. of *Monsieur,* sir; master so and so (used in contempt).

*monseigneur, n.m. (*messeigneurs, nosseigneurs*), my lord; your Grace; sir; your Royal or Imperial Highness; (in thieves' slang) jemmy, crowbar.

*monseigneuriser, v.a., (jest.) to style my lord; to break open, to jemmy.

monsieur (meu-sieu), n.m., sir, gentleman; this gentleman, the gentleman; the king of France's eldest brother. — *A.;* Mr. A. *Non,* —; no, sir. — *dit;* the gentleman says; this gentleman says; Mr. (so-and-so) says. *Ce* —; that gentleman; (ironically) that man, that fellow. — *le Président;* Mr. President. — *le maire;* Mr. Mayor. *Faire le* —; to play the fine gentleman. *C'est un vilain* —; he is a nasty fellow. — *veut-il déjeuner?* would you like breakfast, sir? — *votre père;* your father.

monstre, n.m., monster.

monstrueusement (-efiz-mān), adv., monstrously, prodigiously.

monstrueu-x, -se, adj., monstrous, prodigious.

monstruosité, n.f., monstrosity, anomaly.

mont, n.m., mount, mountain. *Le* — *Etna;* mount Etna. *Aller par* —*s et par vaux;* to go up hill and down dale. —*de-piété* (—*s*—); mont-de-piété, pawn-shop, lombard-house. *Commissionnaire au* —*de-piété;* pawnbroker. *Mettre au* —*de-piété;* to pawn. —*s et merveilles;* wonderful things, wonderful tales, wonders.

montage, n.m., carrying up; taking up; (arts) mounting, setting, putting together.

*montagnard, -e, adj., mountain, highland.

*montagnard, n.m., -e, n.f., mountaineer, highlander; democrat of the Convention and of the National Assembly of France, 1793.

*montagne, n.f., mountain; party of the democrats in the Convention and in the National Assembly of France, 1793. *Chaîne de* —*s;* range, ridge, of mountains. *Pays de* —*s;* mountainous, hilly country. *La* — *a enfanté une souris;* the mountain has brought forth a mouse.

*montagneu-x, -se, adj., mountainous, hilly.

montanisme, n.m., montanism.

montaniste, n.m., montanist.

montant, n.m., (of a ladder, etc.) upright; amount, sum total; coming in *or* rising tide; ⊙next for promotion; (carp.) upright, door-post; high flavor, pungency; energy, smartness.

montant, -e, adj., ascending, rising; flowing, coming in; high-necked (of dresses); (milit.) relieving. *Un chemin* —; a hilly road. *La marée* —*e;* the flowing tide. *Une robe* —*e;* a high-necked dress. *La garde* —*e;* (milit.) the relieving guard. *En* —; upward, up-hill. *Aller en* —; to rise; to go up hill.

monte, n.f., (of animals) serving, covering season.

montée, n.f., stair, staircase, pair of stairs; flight; acclivity, ascent; rise, slope; (arch.) height.

monter, v.n., to go up, to come up, to get up, to ascend, to mount, to ride; to rise; to boil up (of liquids); to come in; to grow up, to shoot, to increase; to amount. — *et descendre;* to go up and down. — *sur un arbre;* to climb up a tree. — *à sa chambre;* to go up to one's room. — *à cheval;* to ride. — *en chaire;* to mount the pulpit. *Montez!* come up! up with you! — *sur le Parnasse;* to turn poet. *La marée monte;* the tide is coming in.

monter, v.a., to mount, to carry up, to lift up; to make up; to raise, to prepare; to wind up; to equip, to furnish, to stock; to mount, to ride; to put together; to furnish, to supply. — *une montre;* to wind up a watch. — *un diamant;* to set a diamond. — *sa lyre;* to tune one's lyre. — *le gouvernail;* to hang the rudder. — *un vaisseau;* to have the command of a vessel. — *un canot;* to man a boat. — *la garde;* to mount guard. — *un cheval;* to mount a horse; to train a horse. *Faire* —; to send up, to store up; to take up, to bring up.

se monter, v.r., to amount; to rise; to be *or* to get excited; to supply one's self, to take in a stock, a supply (of).

monteur, *n.m.*, setter, mounter (of jewels).

montfaucon, *n.m.*, (near Paris) the gibbet, the gallows.

montgolfière, *n.f.*, fire-balloon.

monticule, *n.m.*, hillock, knoll.

montie (-tî), *n.f.*, (bot.). *V.* **mouron**.

mont-joie, *n.f.*, (—*s*—) title of the first king at arms in France; ancient war-cry of the French.

⊙**mont-joie**, *n.f.*, (—*s*—) cairn.

montoir, *n.m.*, mounting, riding; horse-block; near side. *Côté du* —; near side. *Côté hors* —; off-side. *Difficile, doux au* —; difficult, easy to mount *or* ride.

montrable, *adj.*, showable, presentable.

montre, *n.f.*, watch; sample; show, pattern, parade; show-case, show-window, exhibition. — *à réveil;* alarum-watch. —*marine;* chronometer. — *à répétition;* repeating-watch, repeater. — *à double boîte;* double-cased watch. — *à savonnette;* hunting-watch. — *détraquée;* watch out of order. *Boîte de* —; watch-case. *Il est une heure à ma* —; it is one o'clock by my watch. *Faire* — *de son esprit;* to show off one's wit. *En* —; prominently; (com.) in the window. *Affiche de* —; show-card.

montrer, *v.a.*, to show, to exhibit, to point out; to teach; to set forth, to intimate. — *une chose au doigt;* to point out a thing. — *la porte à quelqu'un;* to show any one the door. — *quelqu'un du doigt;* to point one's finger at any one. *Se faire* — *du doigt;* to get pointed at. *Cela montre la corde;* that is threadbare.

se **montrer**, *v.r.*, to show one's self; to appear; to prove one's self to be; to look; to turn out.

montreur, *n.m.*, shower, showman.

montueu-x, -se, *adj.*, hilly, mountainous.

monture, *n.f.*, animal for riding; nag; mounting, setting (of gems); head-stall (of a bridle). — *d'un fusil;* stock of a gun. — *d'éperon;* spur leather. *Qui veut aller loin ménage sa* —; (prov.) he who wishes to live long, avoids excess.

monument,*n.m.*, monument; tomb; memorial.

monumental, -e, *adj.*, monumental.

moquable, *adj.*, laughable, ridiculous.

moque, *n.f.*, (local) mug ; (nav.) dead-eye, dead-block. — *à un trou;* heart. — *de civadière de trélingage;* sprit-sail sheet-block.

se **moquer**, *v.r.*, to mock, to jeer, to deride, to make game of, to make fun of, to make a fool of, to ridicule, to laugh at; to set at defiance, to disregard; to jest; to scoff at. *On s'est moqué de lui;* they laughed at him. *Se faire* — *de soi;* to get laughed at. *Je m'en moque;* what do I care. *Je ne m'en moque pas mal;* I don't care a straw. *Vous vous moquez, je pense;* you are in jest, I suppose.

moquerie (mo-krî), *n.f.*, mockery, scoff, scorn, jeer, derision, jest.

moquette, *n.f.*, Wilton carpet; velvet pile; decoy-bird.

moqueu-r, -se, *adj.*, mocking, sneering, scornful, jeering, deriding.

moqueu-r, *n.m.*, **-se**, *n.f.*, derider, mocker, scoffer, quiz, wag. — *d'Amérique;* mockingbird.

*****morailles**, *n.f.pl.*, horse-twitchers.

*****moraillon**, *n.m.*, hasp, clasp.

moraine, *n.f.*, (geol.) moraine.

moral, -e, *adj.*, moral, mental.

moral, *n.m.*, mental faculties, mind; spirit, morale, spirits (of troops, etc.). *Il faut vous remonter le* —; you must cheer up *or* shake off vour depression of spirits.

morale, *n.f.*, ethics ; morals, moral philosophy, morality; rebuke, lecture. *Il faut lui faire une bonne* —; you must give him a good lecture. *Faire de la* —; to moralize, to lecture.

moralement (-ral-mān), *adv.*, morally.

moralisation, *n.f.*, moralization.

moraliser. *v.n.*, to moralize.

moraliseur, *n.m.*, (b.s.) moralizer.

moraliste, *n.m.*, moralist, moralizer.

moralité, *n.f.*, morality, morals; moral reflection; moral sense *or* responsibility.

moraves, *adj.*, Moravian brethren. *V.* **hernutes**.

morbide, *adj.*, (paint., sculpt.) soft, delicate ; (med.) morbid.

morbidesse, *n.f.*, (paint.) morbidezza; suppleness, ease, elegance of attitude, manners, gait; softness, delicacy.

morbifique, *adj.*, morbific.

morbleu ! *int.*, zounds !

morce, *n.f.*, curb-stone, binding-stone.

morceau, *n.m.*, bit, piece, morsel; fragment, snack, mouthful. — *délicat* or *bon* —; tit-bit. *Aimer les bons* —*x;* to love good things. *Il a ses* —*x taillés;* he has just enough to live on *or* he must not go beyond his orders. *Manger un* —; to eat a morsel, a mouthful. — *d'ensemble;* (mus.) concerted piece. *Mettre en* —*x;* to tear to pieces.

morceler, *v.a.*, to parcel, to parcel out, to partition, to cut up; to mangle.

se **morceler**, *v.t.*, to be parceled out.

morcellement (-sèl-man), *n.m.*, dividing into parcels, parceling out, partition, subdivision.

mordache, *n.f.*, rice-chops, tongs; gag.

mordacité, *n.f.*, mordacity, corrosiveness ; virulency, bitterness, sarcasm, causticity.

mordant, -e, *adj.*, biting; cutting, sarcastic, keen, sharp; poignant. *Style* —; sarcastic, cutting style.

mordant, *n.m.*, (dy. gilding) mordant; sarcasm, keenness, point.

mordicant, -e,*adj.*, mordant, corrosive ; biting, acrid, pungent.

mordicus (-kus), *adv.*, tenaciously, stoutly, doggedly.

⊙**mordienne** (-di-èn), *s.f.*, only used in the phrase *A la grosse* —; unceremoniously, bluntly.

mordieu, *int.*, zounds ! s'death !

*****mordiller**, *v.a.*, to nibble, to bite at, to gnaw.

mordoré, -e, *adj.*, reddish brown.

mordorure, *n.f.*, reddish brown (color).

mordre, *v.a.*, to bite, to nibble; to corrode, to gnaw; to carp at, to find fault with. — *la poussière;* to bite the dust. *Chien qui aboie ne mord pas;* barking dogs do not bite.

se **mordre**, *v.r.*, to bite one's self. *Se* — *la langue, les lèvres;* to bite one's tongue, one's lip ; (fig.) to repent, to be annoyed. *S'en* — *les doigts;* to repent of anything.

mordre, *v.n.*, to bite, to nibble; to eat away; to hold fast, to take effect, to take to, to like; to get on with, to come at; to criticize; to censure; (print.) to cover. *Je n'ai jamais pu* — *au Latin;* I was never able to take to Latin. *Il ne saurait y* —; it is beyond his reach; he will never attain to it. — *à l'hameçon;* to take, to snap at, *or* swallow, the bait.

mordu, -e, *adj.*, (bot.) premorse (ending abruptly, as if bitten off).

more, *n.m.*, Moor; blackamoor.

⊙**moreau**, *adj.*, extremely black. *Cheval* —; jet-black horse.

morelle, *n.f.*, (bot.) nightshade.

morène, *n.f.*, (bot.) frogbit.

moresque, *adj.*, Moorish, moresque.

moresque, *n.f.*, morris-dance; (paint.) moresque.

moret *or* **mouret**, *n.m.*, (bot.) whortleberry.

morfil, *n.m.*, wire edge (of knives, of razors); elephant's tusks, (unwrought) ivory.

morfondre, *v.a.*, to chill.

se **morfondre**, *v.r.*, to catch cold, to be chilled; to wait in vain, to dance attendance; (vet.) to morfounder. *La pâte se morfond;* the dough is losing its heat. *Il s'y est morfondu;* he wasted much time over it.

morfondu, -e, adj., chilled, frozen; disappointed, downcast; kept waiting.

morfondure, n.f., (vet.) morfoundering; (old) cold, chill, catarrh.

morganatique, adj., morganatic; left-handed (of marriages).

morgeline, n.f., (bot.) chickweed.

morgue (morg.), n.f., haughty look, haughtiness; arrogance, self-sufficiency, conceit; inspection room (of a prison); morgue, dead-house.

⊙**morguer** (ghé), v.a., to dare, to brave, to defy, to beard.

moribond, -e, adj. and n., moribund, dying, in a dying state; person in a dying state.

moricaud, -e, n. and adj., blackamoor; blackish; nigger.

morigéner, v.a., to school, to reprimand; to form the morals of, to educate.

*****morille,** n.f., (bot.) moril (mushroom).

*****morillon,** n.m., black grape; (orni.) tufted duck; rough emerald.

morio, n.m., (zoöl.) Camberwell beauty, white-edged butterfly.

morion, n.m., morion.

morne, n.m., hill, hillock (West Indies).

morne, adj., dull, gloomy, mournful, dejected, depressed; dreary, dismal, dull.

morné, -e, adj., blunted (of arms).

mornifle, n.f., slap in the face.

morose, adj., morose, sullen, sour, surly, peevish.

morosité, n.f., moroseness, sullenness, surliness.

morphée, n.m., Morpheus. *Etre dans les bras de —;* (fig.) to be asleep. *Les pavots de —;* sleep.

morphine, n.f., morphia.

morpion, n.m., (l.ex.) crab-louse; (pers. pop.) vermin, dirty fellow.

mors, n.m., bit (of a bridle); curb, check, restraint. *Les chevaux prirent le — aux dents;* the horses ran away. *Prendre le — aux dents;* to take fright; to run headlong into pleasure; to fly into a passion; to buckle to, to work in good earnest.

morse, n.m., morse, sea-horse, walrus.

morsure, n.f., bite, biting; sting.

mort, n.f., death, decease; (hunt.) mort. *Avoir la — sur les lèvres;* to look like death. *Avoir la — dans l'âme;* to be sick at heart, to be in despair; to be intensely grieved. *Etre à l'article de la —;* to be at the point of death, at death's door. *Mourir de sa belle —;* to die a natural death. *Mourir de — violente;* to die a violent death. *Mettre à —;* to put to death, to slay, to kill. *Il a la — entre les dents;* he has one foot in the grave. *A —;* mortally, to the death. *Les affres de la —;* the terrors of death. *A la vie, à la —;* forever; in life and death. *La peine de —;* capital punishment.

mort, -e, part., dead, defunct; lifeless, insensible; dormant; stagnant; still, inanimate. *Un enfant —né (———s);* a still-born child. *Une fille —née (———s);* a still-born girl. *Le feu est —;* the fire is out. *Argent —;* money lying dead, idle. *Couleur —e;* faint color. *—e-saison, (———s)* slack season. *—e-eau;* neap tide. *Tête —e;* (chem.) *caput mortuum. Il n'y va pas de main —e;* he strikes hard (i.e. like a blacksmith). *—e la bête, — le venin;* dead men do not bite. *Mort-bois; V. bois. Morte-eau; eau morte; V. eau. Morte-paye; V. paye. Œuvres —es;* (nav.) upper works.

mort, n.m., -e, n.f., dead person, deceased; dead body, corpse. *Enterrer les —s;* to bury the dead. *Le jour des —s;* All Souls'-day. *Faire le —;* to pretend to be dead. *Faire un — or faire une partie du —;* (at cards) to play dummy whist. *Prendre le —;* to take dummy.

mortadelle, n.f., (Italian) sausage.

*****mortaillable,** adj., (feudalism) in bondage.

mortaisage, n.m., mortising.

mortaise, n.f., mortise.

mortaiser, v.v., to mortise.

mortalité, n.f., mortality.

mortel, -le, adj., mortal, deadly; grievous, extreme, excessive; long, tedious.

mortel, n.m., -le, n.f., mortal.

mortellement (-tèl-măn), adv., mortally, deadly, grievously, dreadfully.

mortellerie, n.f., stone-breaking.

mortellier, n.m., stone-breaker.

mortier (-tié), n.m., (artil., mas.) mortar; mortier (cap of the president of a court of justice); mortar (vessel). *Président à —;* chief justice.

mortifère, adj., mortiferous, deadly.

mortifiant, -e, adj., mortifying, humiliating.

mortification, n.f., mortification, humiliation.

mortifier, v.a., to mortify, to vex, to humiliate, to humble, to subdue. *— de la viande;* to make meat tender.

se **mortifier,** v.r., to mortify one's self; to grow tender (of meat).

mort-ivre, adj. V. **ivre mort.**

mortuaire, adj., mortuary. *Drap —;* pall. *Registre —;* death register. *Extrait —;* certificate of death. *Droit —;* burial fee.

morue, n.f., cod, codfish.

morve, n.f., snot, mucus; (vet.) glanders.

morveau, n.m., (l. ex.) thick mucus.

morveu-x, -se, adj., snotty; (vet.) glandered. *Cheval —;* horse that has the glanders. *Qui se sent — se mouche;* (prov.) if the cap fits, wear it.

morveu-x, n.m., -se, n.f., (in contempt) child, brat, urchin; despicable, mean fellow. *Petit — va!* you little scamp, you!

morvolant, n.m., silk mixed with floss.

mosaïque, adj., Mosaic, of, from Moses.

mosaïque, n.f., mosaic, mosaic-work, tessellated pavement.

mosaïste, n.m., mosaist, worker in mosaics.

mosarabe, n.m. V. **mozarabe.**

moscouade, n.f., muscovado (unrefined sugar).

mosquée, n.f., mosque.

mot, n.m., word; expression; saying, sentence; motto; note, line, memorandum; answer (to a riddle); cue, hint, intimation; (mil.) parole, watchword. *A bon entendeur, demi— suffit;* a word to the wise is sufficient. *— usité, — inusité;* word in use, obsolete word. *— à double entente;* ambiguous word, bearing a double interpretation. *Jeu de —s;* play upon words. *— forgé;* coined word. *Gros —s;* high words. *— d'ordre;* watch-word, pass-word. *— de passe;* pass-word. *Trancher le —;* to speak out, to speak one's mind, not to mince matters. *Tenir le —;* to take the bet. *Ne dire —, ne pas souffler —;* not to utter, not to breathe, a word. *Qui ne dit — consent;* silence gives consent. *Donner le — à quelqu'un;* to give any one the word, the cue. *Bon —;* witticism. *— pour rire;* jest, joke. *Il lui a dit un — à l'oreille;* he whispered a word in his ear. *Prendre quelqu'un au —;* to take any one at his word. *Ils se sont donné le —;* they understand one another, they have passed the word round. *— à —, — pour —;* word for word. *En un —;* in a word, in short. *A ces —s;* at those words, so saying. *Avoir le — pour rire;* to be ready with a joke; to be full of fun. *Au bas —;* at the least. *Entendre à demi —;* to take a hint. *C'est mon dernier —;* it is the last concession I can make; I will take nothing less. *Savoir le fin —;* to understand the upshot of anything. *Si c'est là le fin —;* if that is the upshot of, or the last word. *Je vous enverrai un —; I shall send you word, or a reminder. Envoyez-moi un —;* let me know or send me a line.

motacille, *n.f.*, wag-tail.

***motelle**, *n.f.*, (ich.) burbot, rockling.

motet, *n.m.*, (mus.) motet.

moteur, *n.m.*, mover, author; motive power, propeller, contriver; (anat.) motor.

mot-eur, -rice, *adj.*, motive, propelling, driving.

motif, *n.m.*, motive, incentive, incitement; ground, cause; (mus.) subject; (paint.) design, pattern. *Pour quel —?* on what ground? on what score? *Faire valoir les —s;* (jur.) to show cause.

motion, *n.f.*, motion. *Faire, appuyer, faire adopter, une —;* to make, to support, to carry, a motion.

motiver, *v.a.*, to allege, to assign, as a motive; to be the cause of, to justify, to bring about; to lead to. *Se —, v.r.,* to be founded *or* justified.

motte, *n.f.*, clod; ball of earth; turf (fuel); lump, roll (of butter).

se **motter**, *v.r.*, (hunt.) to lurk behind a clod.

motteux, *n.m.*, (orni.) fallow-finch; wheatear.

motu proprio, *adv.*, on one's own impulse, spontaneously, of one's own accord.

motus ! (-tûs), *int.*, mum! silence! not a word!

mou, mol, *adj.m.*, **molle**, *f.*, soft, mellow; weak; slack, feeble, nerveless, flabby; inactive; sluggish; tame, effeminate, careless, luxurious. *Cire molle;* soft wax. *Poires molles;* mellow pears. *Style mou;* nerveless style. *Mer molle;* (nav.) slack water. *[Mol is used in the masc. before a vowel or h mute.]*

mou, *n.m.*, soft; slack (of a rope); lights (of animals).

mouchage, *n.m.*, snuffing (of candles).

mouchard, *n.m.*, *or* **mouche**, (l.u.) *n.f.*, spy, police-spy, informer.

moucharder, *v.a.*, to inform, to spy, to spy upon.

mouche, *n.f.*, fly; patch (on the face); beauty-spot; button (of a foil); (astron.) musca; (of a target) bull's-eye; (nav.) fen-boat; loo (at cards). *Prendre la —;* to take offense easily, to be touchy. *Gober les —s;* to stand gaping. *Faire d'une — un éléphant;* to make a mountain of a molehill. *Quelle — vous a piqué?* why, what's the matter with you? what ails you? what whim have you got into your head? *Des pieds de —s;* scrawl (writing). *—s volantes;* (med.) motes in the eyes. *Faire des pieds de —s;* to write an illegible scrawl. *C'est une fine —;* he, she is a sly dog. *Chiures de —s;* fly-blows. *—guêpe, (—s——s)* (ent.) wasp-fly. *— bleue;* blue-bottle. *— à feu;* fire-fly. *— abeille;* drone. *— à miel;* honey-bee. *On prend plus de —s avec du miel qu'avec du vinaigre;* more is done by kindness than by harshness.

moucher, *v.a.*, to wipe the nose of; to snuff; ⊙(fam.) to spy, to dog. *Mouchez cet enfant;* wipe that child's nose. *— une chandelle;* to snuff a candle.

se **moucher**, *v.r.*, to blow one's nose. *Mouchez-vous;* blow your nose. *Ne pas se — du pied or du coude;* to be up to snuff; to be no fool; to do things in grand style.

moucher, *v.n.*, to clear one's nose.

moucherolle, *n.m.*, (orni.) fly-catcher.

moucheron, *n.m.*, gnat, midge, very small fly; snuff (of a candle).

mouchet, *n.m.*, (orni.) bog-rush.

moucheté, -e, *adj.*, spotted, speckled, flecked. *Cheval —;* dappled, spotted horse. *Fleuret —;* capped foil.

moucheter, *v.a.*, to spot, to speckle, to fleck; to cap (of foils).

mouchettes, *n.f.pl.*, snuffers.

moucheture, *n.f.*, spot, speck, speckle; (surg.) scarification; spottedness, speckledness.

moucheur, *n.m.*, candle-snuffer; nose-blower.

mouchoir, *n.m.*, handkerchief. *— de cou;* neckerchief. *— de poche;* pocket handkerchief. *Jeter le —;* to throw the handkerchief (game). *Elle a refusé le —;* (fig.) she would have nothing to say to him.

mouchure, *n.f.*, snuff (of a candle).

mouçon, *n.f.* V. **mousson**.

moudre (moulant, moulu), *v.a.*, to grind, to mill, to crush. *— du blé;* to grind corn. *— de coups;* to beat soundly. *J'ai le corps tout moulu;* I am bruised all over. *Il viendra — à notre moulin;* he will want us some day.

moue, *n.f.*, pout, pouting; wry face, grimace. *Faire la — à quelqu'un;* to make a wry face at any one. *Faire la —;* to pout.

mouée, *n.f.*, (hunt.) reward, hound's fee.

mouette, *n.f.*, (orni.) gull, sea-mew.

moufette, *n.f.* V. **mofette**.

mouflard, *n.m.*, **-e**, *n.f.*, (pop.) bloated face.

moufle, *n.f.*, (mec.) tackle; tackle-block; fingerless glove, mitten.

mouflé, -e, *adj.*, used only in *poulie —;* single pulley connected with others in a tackle-block.

moufle, *n.m.*, (chem.) muffle.

mouflon, *n.m.*, (zoöl.) moufflon, wild sheep.

mouillade, *n.f.*, wetting.

***mouillage**, *n.m.*, anchorage, roadstead, soaking, wetting, watering. *Être au —;* to be at anchor; to lie or ride at anchor. *Droits de —;* harbor dues; keelage.

***mouillé, -e**, *part.*, wet, watery; (of the letter *l*) liquid; (of ships) moored, anchored. *Poule —e;* milksop (pers.).

***mouille-bouche**, *n.f.*, (— *or* ——*s*) a kind of pear.

***mouiller**, *v.a.*, to wet, to moisten, to steep; to moor (a ship). *— l'ancre;* (nav.) to let go the anchor.

***mouiller**, *v.n.*, (nav.) to anchor, to cast anchor.

***mouillette**, *n.f.*, sippet (to eat with boiled eggs).

***mouilloir**, *n.m.*, water-can (in which women dip their fingers when they spin).

***mouillure**, *n.f.*, wetting, watering, sprinkling.

moujik, *n.m.*, (—*s*) moujik, Russian peasant.

moulage, *n.m.*, molding; grinding, milling; mill-work, machinery of a mill, mill-stone spindle; ⊙measuring (of wood).

moulard, *n.m.*, **moularde**, *n.f.*, grindstone-dust.

moule, *n.m.*, matrix, mold, cast; netting-pin. *— à beurre;* butter-print. *Faire un —;* to take a cast. *Jeter en —;* to cast in a mold. *Cela ne se jette pas en —;* (prov.) that cannot be done easily. *Fait au —;* (fig.) beautifully shaped.

moule, *n.f.*, (conch.) mussel.

moulé, -e, *part., adj.*, molded; cast; printed, shaped, formed. *Lettre —e;* printed letter. *Chandelle —e;* molded candle.

moulé, *n.m.*, (pop.) print, printed letters, type.

mouler, *v.a.*, to cast, to mold, to shape, to form, to print.

se **mouler**, *v.r.*, to mold one's self. *— sur un autre;* to take another for one's model.

mouleur, *n.m.*, molder.

moulin, *n.m.*, mill. *— à blé;* corn-mill. *— à vent;* wind-mill. *— à bras;* hand-mill. *— à eau;* water-mill. *— à vapeur;* steam-mill. *— à café;* coffee-mill. *C'est un — à paroles;* she is a chatterbox. *Faire venir l'eau au —;* to bring grist to the mill. *Jeter son bonnet par dessus les —s;* to throw off all restraint, to be regardless of consequences.

moulinage, *n.m.*, (manu.) grinding, milling; silk-throwing.

mouliner, *v.a.*, to eat away wood (of worms); to throw (silk).

moulinet, *n.m.*, small windlass, capstan; small mill. *Faire le — avec une épée ;* to twirl a sword about.

moulineur or **moulinier**, *n.m.*, silk-thrower.

⊙**moult** (moo), *adv.*, much, very much.

moulu, **-e**, *part.*, ground; bruised.

moulure, *n.f.*, (arch.) molding.

mourant, **-e**, *n.* and *adj.*, dying person; dying, expiring; fading, going down gradually.

mouret, *n.m.* V. **moret**.

mourine, *n.f.*, (ich.) eagle-ray.

mourir (mourant, mort), *v.n.*, to die, to depart this life; to perish, to drop off, to go off, to expire, to stop; to go out (of fire); to be out (at play). *Etre mort au monde ;* to be dead to the world. *— de faim ;* to die of starvation. *to starve. — de soif ;* to be dying with thirst. *— de froid ;* to perish from cold. *— d'envie ;* to long for. *— de chagrin ;* to die of a broken heart. *Il la fera — de chagrin ;* he will break her heart. *— de rire ;* to die with laughter. *C'est un meurt de faim ;* he is a pauper, a starveling. *se* **mourir**, *v.r.*, to be dying; to be dying out (of fire). *Cet homme se meurt ;* this man is dying. [Only used in present and imperfect indicative.]

mouron, *n.m.*, (bot.) pimpernel; chickweed; (ent.) eft.

mourre, *n.f.*, (game) mora; Buck-buck, how many fingers do I hold up?

mousquet, *n.m.*, musket, match-lock.

⊙**mousquetade**, *n.f.*, musket-shot, volley of musketry.

⊙**mousquetaire**, *n.m.*, musketeer. [of musketry.

mousqueterie (-kè-trî), *n.f.*, musketry, volley

mousqueton, *n.m.*, musketoon, carbine; pendant (of a watch-chain).

mousse, *n.f.*, moss; froth, foam; lather, effervescence. *Pierre qui roule n'amasse pas de —;* a rolling stone gathers no moss.

mousse, *n.m.*, cabin-boy, ship-boy.

⊙**mousse**, *adj.*, blunt, dull (of tools).

mousseline (moos-li-n), *n.f.*, muslin.

mousser, *v.n.*, to froth, to foam, to effervesce, to lather. *Faire —;* to froth; to puff.

mousseron (moos-ron), *n.m.*, mushroom.

mousseu-x, -se, *adj.*, foaming, frothy; (of wine) sparkling. *Rose —se ;* moss-rose.

moussoir, *n.m.*, chocolate-stick.

mousson, *n.f.*, monsoon.

moussu, -e, *adj.*, mossy, moss-grown.

moustache, *n.f.*, moustache, mustachio; whisker (of animals). *Relever sa —;* to twirl up one's moustache. *Brûler la — à quelqu'un ;* to fire a pistol in any one's face. *Donner sur la — à quelqu'un ;* to hit any one in the face. *Vieille —;* veteran; old gray-beard.

moustiquaire, *n.f.*, musquito-net.

moustique, *n.m.*, musquito.

moût, *n.m.*, must (wine not fermented); wort.

moutard, *n.m.*, (pop.) brat, youngster.

moutarde, *n.f.*, mustard. *Graine de —;* mustard-seed. *S'amuser à la —;* to trifle one's time away. *Il m'a fait monter la — au nez ;* he made me lose my temper. *C'est de la — après dîner ;* it is a day after the fair.

moutardier, *n.m.*, mustard-pot; mustard-maker; (orni.) black-martin, swift.

⊙**moutier**, *n.m.*, convent, monastery.

mouton, *n.m.*, sheep; mutton; sheep-leather; rammer; beetle, monkey (rammer); (pers.) lamb, ninny, decoy, prison-spy. *pl.* (of the sea) white horses, white-crested waves. *Un troupeau de —s ;* a flock of sheep. *Revenons à nos —s ;* let us return to our subject.

⊙*moutonnaille, *n.f.*, flock of sheep.

moutonné, -e, *adj.*, fleecy, curled; (of the sea) white with foam.

moutonner, *v.a.* and *n.*, to make woolly,

fleecy ; to curl, to frizzle ; (nav.) to foam ; (of a crowd) to rear their heads ; to worm anything out of any one ; to spy upon, to denounce.

moutonneu-x, -se, *adj.*, woolly ; foamy, rough (of waves).

moutonni-er, -ère, *adj.*, fleecy, woolly ; sheep-like, silly.

mouture, *n.f.*, grinding ; charge for grinding ; meslin of wheat, rye, and barley. *Tirer d'un sac deux —s ;* to get a double profit on anything.

mouvance, *n.f.*, (feudalism) tenure.

mouvant, -e, *adj.*, moving, shifting, unstable ; (jur.) depending on ; (her.) issuant ; animated, busy. *Sable —;* quicksand.

mouvement (moov-mān), *n.m.*, movement, motion, progress, advance, march ; move, manœuvre ; fluctuation ; (mus.) time ; (paint.) animation, life, bustle, stir ; spirit ; impulse, emotion, disturbance, commotion ; (horl.) works ; animation, sparkle (of style) ; bursts (of eloquence). *Se donner du —;* to bestir one's self. *— naturel ;* natural impulse. *Faire une chose de son propre —;* to do a thing of one's own accord. *Se mettre en —;* to stir, to start ; (mil.) to move forward, to advance.

mouver, *v.a.*, (gard.) to loosen, to stir.

mouvoir (mouvant, mu), *v.a.*, to move, to stir ; to prompt, to stir up, to actuate ; to excite. *se* **mouvoir**, *v.r.*, to move, to stir, to be moved. *Faire se —;* to set in motion.

moxa, *n.m.*, (surg.) moxa.

moye (moa) *n.f.*, soft part (of stone).

moyen (moa-yin), *n.m.*, means, way, manner ; medium ; power, possibility ; (jur.) plea ; (log.) mean ; (math.) middle term. *pl.* means, resources ; pecuniary circumstances ; abilities, talents ; parts. *Il n'y a pas — de faire cela ;* that is not to be done. *Je n'en ai pas le —;* I have not the ability to do it ; I can't afford it. *Le — de lui parler ?* how can one manage to speak to him ? *Contribuer chacun selon ses —s ;* to contribute each according to his means. *Il a beaucoup de —s ;* he is very clever ; he has plenty of brains. *Voies et —s ;* ways and means. *Au — de ;* by means of, with the help of. *Trouver —;* to find means, to contrive, to manage. *Faire valoir ses —s ;* to make the most of one's talents.

moyen, -ne (moa-yin, -yè-n), *adj.*, mean, middle, middle-sized, average. *Le — âge ;* the Middle Ages. *Terme —, chiffre —;* average, mean, on an average.

moyennant (moa-iè-nān), *prep.*, by means of, with the help of ; in consideration of, in return for.

moyennant que, *conj.*, provided that, on condition that.

moyenne, *n.f.*, average ; (math.) mean, medium ; (writ.) round hand. *— approximative ;* rough average. *Sur une — de ;* at an average of. *En —;* on an average; (of writing) in round hand.

⊙**moyennement** (moa-iè-n-mān), *adv.*, moderately, indifferently.

⊙**moyenner**, *v.a.*, to mediate, to procure, to bring about.

moyer, *v.a.*, to saw (freestone).

moyette, *n.f.*, (agri.) shock, stook.

moyeu, *n.m.*, nave (of a wheel) ; preserved plum ; ⊙yolk of an egg.

mozarabe, *n.m.*, Muzarab.

mozarabe or **mozarabique**, *adj.*, muzarabic.

mr. (ab. of *Monsieur*), Mr., Mister.

m'sieu, *n.m.* (pop. for *Monsieur*), sir, mister.

ms., msc., (ab. of *Manuscrit*), ms., manuscript.

mss (ab. of *Manuscrits*), mss., manuscripts.

muabilité, *n.f.* V. **mutabilité**.

muable, *adj.*, mutable, changeable.

muance, *n.f.*, (mus.) changing a note. *En —;* (of the voice) breaking.

mucate, *n.m.*, mucic acid combined.

à muche-pot, *adv.* *V.* **musse-pot** (à).

mucilage, *n.m.*, mucilage.

mucilagineu-x, -se, *adj.*, mucilaginous.

mucosité, *n.f.*, mucus, phlegm.

mucus (-kus), *n.m.*, mucus.

mue, *n.f.*, molting ; molting season ; cast-skin, slough ; mew, coop (cage). *Etre en* — ; to be molting ; to break (of the voice).

muer, *v.n.*, to molt, to cast its skin, to cast horns ; to mew ; (of the voice) to break, to change. *Ce chien mue ;* that dog is shedding its coat. *Sa voix mue ;* his voice is breaking.

muet, -te, *adj.*, dumb, mute, speechless ; taciturn, secret ; (of maps) in outline ; (of evidence) presumptive, circumstantial ; silent (of letters). *Il est sourd—, sourd et —;* he is deaf and dumb. *La frayeur le rendit —;* terror struck him dumb. *Scène —te ;* dumb show.

muet, *n.m.*, **-te**, *n.f.*, dumb man, dumb woman.

muette, *n.f.*, mew, mews ; hunting-lodge.

muezin, *n.m.*, (—*s*) muezzin.

mufle, *n.m.*, snout, muzzle (of animals) ; face, phiz, mug (of persons). *— de veau ;* (bot.) snap-dragon, calf's snout. *Quel — !* what a face !

mufleau, *n.m.*, (bot.) snap-dragon, calf's snout.

muflier, *n.m.*, (bot.) snap-dragon, calf's snout.

mufti or **muphti**, *n.m.*, (—*s*) mufti.

muge, *n.m.*, (ich.) mullet, gray mullet.

mugir, *v.n.*, to bellow, to low ; to roar, to groan ; to sough (of the wind).

mugissant, -e, *adj.*, bellowing, roaring.

mugissement (-jis-mān), *n.m.*, bellowing, lowing ; roaring ; soughing (of the wind).

⊙**mugot**, *n.m.* *V.* **magot**.

muguet (-ghè), *n.m.*, (bot.) lily of the valley, May-lily ; (med.) thrush ; ⊙(fam.) beau, fop. — *des bois ;* woodruff.

mugueter (mug-té), *v.a.*, (fam., l.u.) to play the gallant, to flirt.

⊙**muid**, *n.m.*, hogshead (measure).

mulasse, *n.f.*, young mule.

mulâtre, *adj.*, mulatto.

mulâtr-e, *n.m.*, **-esse**, *n.f.*, mulatto.

⊙**mulcter**, *v.a.*, (jur.) to fine, to punish ; to vex, to ill-treat.

mule, *n.f.*, slipper ; she-mule. *pl.*, chilblains in the heels, kibes ; (vet.) chaps. *La — du pape ;* the pope's slipper. *Baiser la — du pape ;* to kiss the pope's toe. *Ferrer la —;* to get the market-penny (of servants).

mulet, *n.m.*, he-mule ; (bot., orni.) mule ; working-bee ; (ich.) mullet. *Garder le —;* to be kept waiting, to dance attendance.

muletier (mul-tié), *n.m.*, muleteer.

mulle, *n.m.*, (ich.) surmullet.

⊙**mulle**, *n.f.* *V.* **caillette**.

mulle, *adj.*, (com.) of inferior quality (of madder).

mulot, *n.m.*, field-mouse.

multangulaire, *adj.*, (bot.) multangular.

multangulé, -e, *adj.*, multangular.

multi, a prefix from Latin *multus*.

multicapsulaire, *adj.*, (bot.) multicapsular.

multicolore, *adj.*, of many colors, many-colored.

multifide, *adj.*, (bot.) multifid.

multiflore, *adj.*, (bot.) multiflorous, many-flowered.

multiforme, *adj.*, multiform.

multilatère, *adj.*, multilateral, many-sided.

multiloculaire, *adj.*, (bot.) multilocular.

multinôme, *n.m.*, (l.u.) (alg.) multinominal. *V.* **polynôme**.

multipare, *adj.*, multiparous.

multipartite, *adj.*, (bot.) multipartite.

multipède, *adj.*, multiped.

multiple, *n.m.* and *adj.*, (arith.) multiple.

multipliable, *adj.*, multipliable.

multipliant, *adj.*, multiplying. *n.m.*, multiplying-glass.

multiplicande, *n.m.*, (arith.) multiplicand.

multiplicateur, *n.m.*, (arith.) multiplier.

multiplication, *n.f.*, multiplication. *Table de* —; multiplication table.

multiplicité, *n.f.*, multiplicity.

multiplié, -e, *adj.*, multifarious, multiplied, manifold, repeated, frequent.

multiplier, *v.a.*, to multiply.

se **multiplier**, *v.r.*, to multiply ; to be repeated, to be everywhere.

multiplier, *v.n.*, to multiply.

multitude, *n.f.*, multitude.

multivalve, *n.f.* and *adj.*, multivalve ; multivalvular.

muni, -e, *part.*, supplied, furnished, provided (with) ; possessed (of) ; fortified.

municipal, -e, *adj.*, municipal.

municipal, *n.m.*, municipal officer ; municipal guard. *Conseiller —;* member of the town council. *Musique —e ;* town-band.

municipalité, *n.f.*, municipality.

munificence, *n.f.*, munificence, bounty.

munir, *v.a.*, to provide (with), to supply, to furnish (with) ; to arm, to fortify, to secure.

se **munir**, *v.r.*, to provide one's self, to be provided, to be supplied, to be furnished (with).

munition, *n.f.*, ammunition. *pl.*, military stores, provisions. —*s de bouche ;* provisions. —*s de guerre ;* ammunition.

munitionnaire, *n.m.*, (milit.) contractor ; commissary of stores.

muphti, *n.m.* *V.* **mufti**.

muqueu-x, -se, *adj.*, mucous.

mur, *n.m.*, wall. — *mitoyen ;* partition wall. — *de clôture ;* inclosure-wall. — *d'appui ;* wall breast-high, parapet wall. — *blanc ;* dead wall. *Mettre quelqu'un au pied du —;* to nonplus any one, to drive into a corner.

mûr, -e, *adj.*, ripe, mature, matured ; worn out, shabby (of clothes). *L'âge —;* mature age. *Du vin —;* wine fit fcr drinking.

murage, *n.m.*, walling.

*****muraille**, *n.f.*, thick, high wall ; rampart.

*****muraillement**, *n.m.*, (mas.) walling.

mural, -e, *adj.*, mural.

mûre, *n.f.*, (bot.) mulberry. — *sauvage, — de ronce, — de haie ;* blackberry.

mûrement (mûr-mān), *adv.*, maturely. *J'y ai — réfléchi ;* I have deeply reflected upon it.

murène, *n.f.*, (ich.) muræna.

murer, *v.a.*, to wall ; to wall up ; to brick up ; to immure ; to screen, to veil.

murex (-rèks), *n.m.*, (conch.) murex.

muriate, *n.m.*, (chem.) muriate.

muriatique, *adj.*, (chem.) muriatic. *Acide —;* muriatic acid.

mûrier, *n.m.*, mulberry-tree.

mûrir, *v.n.*, to ripen, to grow ripe, to mature.

mûrir, *v.a.*, to ripen, to mature, to bring to perfection or completeness. *Se —;* to ripen.

murmurant, -e, *adj.*, murmuring, babbling, purling ; muttering, grumbling.

murmurateur, *n.* and *adj.m.*, murmurer, grumbler ; discontented, murmuring, grumbling person.

murmure, *n.m.*, murmur ; murmuring, grumbling, muttering ; whispering ; prattling ; babbling ; purl (of a brook) ; soughing (of the wind).

murmurer, *v.n.*, to murmur, to grumble, to mutter ; to whisper ; to gurgle, to prattle, to purl, to babble, to sough.

murmurer, *v.a.*, to mutter, to whisper. *Que murmurez-vous là ?* what are you muttering there ?

se **murmurer**, *v.r.*, to be whispered, to be whispered about.

muron, n.m., blackberry ; wild raspberry.

murrhin, -e, adj., murrhine.

musagète, adj., (myth.) chief of the Muses (of Apollo).

*****musaraigne**, n.f., (mam.) shrew-mouse.

musard, -e, n. and adj., loiterer, dawdler ; loitering, dawdling.

musarder, v.n., to loiter, to dawdle.

musarderie, n.f., loitering, trifling ; dawdling.

musc or **porte-musc**, n.m., (—) (mam.) musk, musk-deer.

musc, n.m., musk (scent).

muscade, n.f., nutmeg ; juggler's ball. *Noix* —; nutmeg.

muscadet, n.m., muscadet (wine).

muscadier, n.m., nutmeg-tree.

muscadin, n.m., musk-lozenge ; ⊙ beau, dandy, fop, spark.

muscat, n.m. and adj., muscatel, muscadine, muscadel (a kind of grapes, of wine, of pears).

muscatelline, n.f., (bot.) adoxa, moschatel.

muscle, n.m., muscle.

musclé, -e, adj., strongly marked (of the muscles).

musculaire, adj., muscular.

musculature, n.f., (sculpt., paint.) muscularity, muscling.

musculeu-x, -se, adj., muscular, brawny, musculous.

muse, n.f., Muse.

muse, n.f., (hunt.) rutting-time.

museau, n.m., muzzle, snout, nose, face.

musée, n.m., museum. — *de tableaux ;* picture-gallery.

museler (mu-zlé), v.a., to muzzle, to silence, to gag.

muselière, n.f., muzzle.

musellement, n.m., muzzling ; (fig.) gagging, silencing.

muser, v.n., to loiter, to trifle, to moon, to dawdle ; (hunt.) to begin to rut. *Qui refuse muse ;* you may lose by refusing.

muserolle (muz-rol), n.f., nose-band, musrole.

musette, n.f., bagpipe ; tune for ditto ; nose-bag (for horses).

muséum (-om), n.m., (—s) museum.

musical, -e, adj., musical.

musicalement (-kal-mãn), adv., musically.

musicien, n.m., **-ne**, n.f., (-in, -è-n), musician.

musico, n.m., (—s) (in the Netherlands) a low music hall ; gaff ; pot-house.

musicomane, n.m., (l.u.) person extremely fond of music. *V.* **mélomane.**

musicomanie, n.f., (l.u.) passion for music. *V.* **mélomanie.**

musi-f or **mussi-f, -ve**, adj., (chem.) mosaic. *Or* —; mosaic-gold, ormolu.

musique, n.f., music ; band, musicians. *Mettre des vers en* —; to set verses to music. *Etre réglé comme un papier de* —; to be as regular as clockwork. *Nous ferons de la* —; we shall have some music. *La — du regiment ;* the regimental band.

musiquer, v.n., to strum (on the piano).

musoir, n.m., pier-head, jetty-head.

musqué, -e, adj., musked, perfumed ; studied, unnatural ; odd, strange.

musquer, v.a., to perfume with musk, to musk, to scent.

se musquer, v.r., to scent one's self with musk.

à musse-pot, adv., in concealment, secretly. *V.* **à muche-pot.**

⊙**se musser**, v.r., to hide one's self ; to lurk in a corner.

mussulman, -e, n. and adj., Mussulman ; Mahometan, Mohammedan.

mustelle, n.f., (ich.) whistle-fish.

⊙**musurgie**, n.f., (mus.) musurgy.

mutabilité, n.f., mutability, changeableness.

mutation, n.f., mutation, change.

muter, v.a., to sulphur (wine-casks).

mutilat-eur, -rice, n. and adj., mutilator ; mutilating.

mutilation, n.f., mutilation ; maiming ; mangling, garbling.

mutiler, v.a., to mutilate ; to maim ; to disfigure, to garble.

mutin, -e, adj., obstinate, stubborn, unruly, fractious ; riotous, seditious, rebellious.

mutin, n.m., **-e**, n.f., obstinate person ; refractory child ; mutineer, rioter.

mutiné, -e, part., mutinous, riotous. *Peuple* —; riotous people. *Les flots* —s; the raging waves.

se mutiner, v.r., to mutiny, to be refractory, unruly. *Cet enfant se mutine ;* that child is getting unruly.

mutinerie (-ti-n-rî), n.f., mutiny, riot, sedition ; unruliness.

mutisme, n.m., dumbness, speechlessness.

mutualité, n.f., mutuality.

mutuel, -le, adj., mutual, reciprocal. *Société de secours* —s ; benefit or friendly society.

mutuellement (-èl-mãn), adv., mutually, reciprocally.

mutule, n.f., (arch.) mutule.

myélite, n.f., (med.) inflammation of the spinal marrow.

myographie, n.f., myography.

myologie, n.f., myology.

myope, n.m.f. and adj., myope, short-sighted person ; short-sighted.

myope, n.m., (ent.) conops.

myopie, n.f., myopia, myopy, short-sightedness.

myose, n.f., (med.) myosis.

myosotis, n.m., (bot.) myositis, forget-me-not, scorpion-grass.

myosure, n.f., (bot.) mouse-tail.

myotomie, n.f., myotomy.

myriade, n.f., myriad.

myriagramme (-gram), n.m., myriagramme (22·0485 lbs. avoirdupois).

myriamètre, n.m., myriametre (6·2138 miles).

myriapode, n.m., (ent.) myriapod.

myrmidon, n.m. *V.* **mirmidon.**

myrobolan, n.m., (bot.) myrobalan.

myrobolan, -te, adj. *V.* **mirobolant.**

myrobolanier, n.m., myrobalan-tree.

myrrhe, n.f., myrrh.

myrrhis (mir-ris), n.m., (bot.) myrrhis.

myrte, n.m., myrtle.

myrtiforme, adj., myrtiform.

myrtille, n.f., (bot.) bilberry.

mystagogue (-gog), n.m., (antiq.) mystagogue.

mystère, n.m., mystery, secret, secrecy ; fuss, ado ; importance. *Sans autre* —; without further ado. *Approfondir un* —; to probe a mystery. *Mettre du — à ;* to make a mystery of.

mystérieusement (-eûz-mãn), adv., mysteriously.

mystérieu-x, -se, adj., mysterious.

mysticisme, n.m., mysticism.

mysticité, n.f., mysticism.

mystificateur, n.m., hoaxer, mystifier. *adj.* mystifying, hoaxing.

mystification, n.f., hoaxing, hoax, mystification.

mystifier, v.a., to hoax, to mystify.

mystique, adj., mystical, mystic.

mystique, n.m.f., (pers.) mystic.

mystique, n.f., (philos.) the study of spirituality.

mystiquement (-tik-mãn), adv., mystically.

mythe, n.m., myth, fable, fiction.

mythique, adj., mythic, mythical.

mythologie, n.f., mythology.

mythologique, adj., mythological, fabulous.

mythologiste or **mythologue**, n.m., mythologist.

myure, adj., (med.) sinking (of the pulse).

N

n (èn), n.f. (ne), n.m., the fourteenth letter of the alphabet, n.

n' (contraction of Ne), not.

nabab, n.m., nabob.

nababie, n.f., nabobship.

nable, n.m., (nav.) scuttle-hole; plug-stopper.

nabot, n.m., -e, n.f., (jest.) shrimp, manikin; (pers.) dwarf.

nacarat, n.m., nacarat.

nacarat, adj. invariable, nacarat.

nacelle, n.f., wherry, small boat, skiff; (of balloon) car; (arch.) scotia, casement.

nacre, n.f., mother-of-pearl.

nacré, -e, adj., nacreous, pearly.

nadir, n.m., (astron.) nadir.

naevus, n.m., birth-mark, mole.

naffe, n.f., orange-flower. Only used in Eau de —; orange-flower water.

nage, n.f., swimming; rowing, sculling, paddling; (fig.) profuse perspiration, sweat. A la —; swimming, by swimming. Passer la rivière à la —; to swim across the river or to row over. Se jeter à la —; to leap into the water. Etre tout en —; to be in a bath of perspiration. Donner la —; to pull the stroke oar, to give the stroke.

nagée, n.f., (l.u.) stroke in swimming or rowing.

nagement (na-jmän), n.m., swimming, rowing.

nageoire, n.f., fin (of a fish); cork, bladder, float for swimming; board floating in a pail (to keep the water steady).

nageoter, v.n., to swim a little, to swim about.

nager, v.n., to swim; to float; to roll; to welter; (nav.) to row, to paddle, to scull, to pull. Il nage comme un poisson; he swims like a fish. — dans l'opulence; to be rolling in riches. — entre deux eaux; to swim under water; (fig.) to be a trimmer. — dans son sang; to be weltering in one's blood. — à culer; (nav.) to back, to back water.

nageu-r, n.m., -se, n.f., swimmer; (nav.) rower, oarsman.

naguère or **naguères** (na-ghèr), adv., lately, but lately, but now, not long ago.

naïade, n.f., (myth.) naiad, water-nymph.

naï-f, -ve, adj., naïve, native, artless, ingenuous; plain, unaffected, natural; candid; simple. Grâce —ve; native grace. Réponse —ve; ingenuous answer.

naïf, n.m., (lit., paint.) nature without art.

nain (nin), -e (nè-n), n. and adj., dwarf; dwarfish. — jaune; Pope Joan (card game). Arbres —s; dwarf trees. Œuf —; addled egg.

naïre, n.m., Indian chief (Malabar).

naissain, n.m., oyster-spat.

naissance, n.f., birth; nativity; descent, extraction; beginning, dawn, rise. Le lieu de sa —; one's birth-place. Jour de —, anniversaire de la —; birth-day. Etre de haute —; to be high-born. Prendre — de; to be born; to originate in. Donner — à; to give rise to. La — de la poésie; the dawn of poetry.

naissant, -e, adj., newly-born; dawning; budding, rising; infant, in its infancy; beginning, growing, nascent. Une fortune —e; a rising fortune.

naître (naissant, né), v.n., to be born, to come into the world; to originate, to arise; to rise, to dawn, to spring up. Il est né poète; he was born a poet. Cela peut faire — des soupçons; that may give rise to suspicion. Faire —; to call into existence; to create, to produce, to excite, to suggest. Je l'ai vu —; I knew him as a child.

naïvement (-iv-män), adv., ingenuously, plainly, candidly, naïvely, artlessly.

naïveté (-iv-té), n.f., native simplicity, ingenuousness, artlessness; simple thing; naïveté.

nanan, n.m., sweetmeats, goody (childish).

nankin, n.m., nankeen.

nanti, -e, part., stocked, furnished with, holding as security. Etre — de; to hold as a pledge.

nantir, v.a., to give as a pledge, to secure.

se nantir, v.r., to hold as a pledge; to provide one's self (with); to take possession (of); to feather one's nest.

nantissement (-tis-män), n.m., security, pledge, lien.

napée, n.f., (myth.) wood-nymph, mountain-nymph.

napel, n.m., (bot.) monk's-hood.

naphte, n.m., naphtha.

napiforme, adj., (bot.) napiform, turnip-shaped.

napoléon, n.m., napoleon (French gold coin, worth $3.86).

napolitain, -e, n. and adj., Neapolitan.

nappe, n.f., cloth, table-cloth, cover; (hunt.) dead animal's skin; clap-net. — d'eau; sheet of water. Eclair en —; sheet-lightning.

napperon (na-pron), n.m., napkin, slip (small table-cloth).

narcisse, n.m., (bot.) daffodil, narcissus. C'est un —; he is enamored of his person.

narcotine, n.f., narcotine.

narcotique, n.m. and adj., narcotic.

narcotisme, n.m., (med.) narcotism.

nard, n.m., (bot., pharm.) nard; (bot.) spike-nard.

nargue (narg), n.f., pshaw, pish, scorn, disdain, slight, sneer. Dire — de; to snap one's finger at. — de l'amour; a fig for, a plague on, love. Faire — à; to snap one's fingers at.

narguer (-ghé), v.a., to defy, to set at defiance; to beard.

narguilé, n.m., narghileh (Turkish, Persian pipe).

narine, n.f., nostril.

narquois, -e, n. and adj., sharper, swindler; banterer, chaffer, quiz; cunning, sly, chaffing, bantering. Parler —; to talk slang.

narquoisement, adv., cunningly, slyly, sneeringly, banteringly.

narrat-eur, n.m., -rice, n.f., (nar-ra-), narrator, relater.

narrati-f, -ve (nar-ra-), adj., narrative, narratory.

narration (nar-ra-), n.f., narration, narrative.

narré (nar-ré), n.m., narrative, narration, recital, account, story.

narrer (nar-ré), v.a., to narrate, to relate, to tell.

narthex, n.m., (arch.) narthex vestibule.

narval, n.m., (mam.) narwhal, sea-unicorn.

nasal, -e, adj., nasal. Son —; nasal sound.

nasale, n.f., (gram.) nasal.

nasalement, adv., (gram.) with a nasal sound.

nasaliser, v.a., to render nasal, to nasalize.

nasalité, n.f., (gram.) nasal sound.

nasard, n.m., organ-stop (to imitate the human voice).

nasarde, n.f., fillip, rap on the nose.

nasarder, v.a., to fillip, to rap on the nose; to jeer, to banter; to defy, to make game of.

naseau, n.m., nostril (of animals). Un fendeur de —x; a swaggerer, a braggart.

nasi, n.m., President of the Sanhedrim.

***nasillant**, -e, adj., speaking through the nose.

***nasillard**, -e, n. and adj., snuffler, person who speaks through his nose; snuffling, nasal.

***nasillement**, n.m., speaking through the nose, snuffling; twang.

***nasiller**, v.n., to speak through the nose, to snuffle.

*nasilleu-r, *n.m.*, -se, *n.f.*, snuffler.

*nasillonner, *v.n.*, to speak a little through the nose.

nasse, *n.f.*, bow-net, weel, eel-pot. *Il est dans la* —; he is in a scrape.

nasselle, *n.f.*, rush net.

natal, -e, *adj.*, natal, native, vernacular. *Lieu* —; birth-place. *Pays* —; native country. *Jour* —; birthday.

natation, *n.f.*, swimming.

natatoire, *adj.*, swimming, natatory.

nati-f, -ve, *adj.*, native, natural. *Il est — de*; he is a native of (towns). *Or* —; native gold.

natif, *n.m.*, native.

nation, *n.f.*, nation. *La grande* —; France (under Napoleon I.).

national, -e, *adj.*, national, native. *Assemblée* —*e*; national assembly. *Garde* —*e*; national guard (corps). *Garde* —; national guard (man).

nationalement (-nal-măn), *adv.*, nationally.

nationaliser, *v.a.*, to nationalize.

se nationaliser, *v.r.*, to become nationalized.

nationalité, *n.f.*, nationality.

nationaux, *n.m.pl.*, natives, native subjects; countrymen.

nativité, *n.f.*, nativity, birth.

natron *or* natrum, *n.m.*, (min.) natron.

natte, *n.f.*, mat, matting, straw-mat; plait, twist (of hair, silk, &c.).

natter, *v.a.*, to mat; to plait, to plat, to twist.

nattier, *n.m.*, mat-maker; straw-plaiter.

in naturalibus, *adv.*, (fam.) in a state of nakedness, stark naked.

naturalisation, *n.f.*, naturalization.

naturaliser, *v.a.*, to naturalize.

naturalisme, *n.m.*, naturalism, naturalness.

naturaliste, *n.m.f.*, naturalist. *adj.*, naturalistic.

naturalité, *n.f.*, citizenship, denizenship.

nature, *n.f.*, nature; kind; habit, constitution, disposition, temper; life, life-size. *Don de la* —; gift of nature. *L'habitude est une seconde* —; habit is a second nature. *La* — *humaine*; human nature; mankind. *Payer en* —; to pay in kind. *L'art perfectionne la* —; nature is improved by art. *Prendre la* — *pour modèle*; to copy nature. *Dessiner d'après* —; to draw from nature, from life. *De* — *à*; calculated to. *Contre* —; unnatural. *adj.*, *pommes de terre* —; plain boiled potatoes.

naturel, -le, *adj.*, natural, native, inborn, innate, inherent, genial; artless, plain, home-bred. *Enfant* —; illegitimate child.

naturel, *n.m.*, native; nature, naturalness; freedom from affectation, genuineness, simplicity; temper, constitution; feeling; life. *Les* —*s d'un pays*; the natives of a country. — *fort et robuste*; strong constitution. *Un homme d'un mauvais* —, *d'un bon* —; an ill-natured, a good-natured, man. *Au* —; naturally, to the life, life-size; (cook.) cooked plain.

naturellement (-rèl-măn), *adv.*, naturally, by nature; genuinely, sincerely, candidly; plainly, freely, artlessly.

naufrage, *n.m.*, shipwreck, wreck. *Faire* —; to be wrecked *or* shipwrecked.

naufragé, -e, *n.* and *adj.*, castaway; wrecked, shipwrecked.

naufrager, *v.n.*, to be shipwrecked, to suffer shipwreck.

naulage, *n.m.*, freight, fare.

naumachie, *n.f.*, naumachy (spectacle representing a sea-fight).

nauséabond, -e, *adj.*, nauseous, loathsome, disgusting, sickening.

nausée, *n.f.*, nausea, qualm, retching; loathing; disgust.

nautile, *n.m.*, (mol.) nautilus; life-belt.

nautique, *adj.*, nautical, nautic.

nautiquement, *adv.*, nautically.

nautoni-er, *n.m.*, -ère, *n.f.*, (poet.) pilot, mariner.

naval, -e, *adj.*, naval, sea, nautical. *Combat* —; sea-fight.

⊙ navée, *n.f.*, boat-load.

navet, *n.m.*, turnip; (hort.) root.

navetier (nav-tié), *n.m.*, shuttle-maker.

navetière, *n.f.*, turnip-field.

navette, *n.f.*, (ecc.) incense-box; (bot.) rape, rape-seed; netting-needle, shuttle. *Faire la* —; to go to and fro; to wobble. *Huile de* —; rape oil. *Point de* —; lock-stitch.

naviculaire, *adj.*, (anat., bot.) navicular.

navigabilité, *n.f.*, navigableness, seaworthiness.

navigable, *adj.*, navigable, seaworthy.

navigateur, *n.* and *adj.m.*, navigator; seafaring.

navigation, *n.f.*, navigation, voyage, sailing. — *de plaisance*; boating, yachting.

naviguer (-ghé), *v.n.*, to navigate, to sail. — *en pleine mer*; to sail in the open sea.

naviguer (-ghé), *v.a.*, to row, to sail (a boat).

⊙ naville, *n.f.*, small irrigation canal.

navire, *n.m.*, vessel, ship. [Not applied to men-of-war.] *Couler à fond un* —; to sink a ship. *Un* — *marchand*; a merchantman.

navrant, -e, *adj.*, heart-rending, heart-breaking, distressing.

navré, -e, *part.*, broken-hearted, wrung, rent, distressed. *Avoir le cœur* —; to be broken-hearted.

navrer, *v.a.*, to wound, to distress; to rend the heart. *Cela me navre le cœur*; that rends my heart.

nazaréen (-ré-in), *n.m.*, -ne (-ré-è-n), *n.f.*, Nazarite, Nazarene.

n.b., (ab. of *Nota Bene*) N. B., *Nota Bene*.

n.d., (ab. of *Notre Dame*) our Lady.

ne, *adv.*, no, not. *Je* — *veux pas*; I will not. *Cela* — *vaut rien*; that is worth nothing. *Il* — *cesse de gronder*; he does not cease scolding, is always on the scold. *Je n'ose lui parler*; I dare not speak to him. *Je* — *peux me taire*; I cannot remain silent. *Je* — *saurais vous dire*; I cannot tell you. *Vous* — *devez pas*; you must not. *Je crains que cela* — *soit*; I fear that it is so. *Je* — *doute pas que cela ne soit*; I do not doubt it. *A moins que cela* — *soit*; unless that is so. *Il* — *fait que dormir*; he does nothing but sleep. — . . . *que*; only, nothing but. *Il n'a fait que cela*; he only did that. *Il* — *le fera plus*; he will not do it again. [*Ne* is contracted into *n'* before a vowel or a silent *h*.]

né, -e, *part.*, born. — *de la mer*; sea-born. *Bien* —; of good birth, well-disposed. *Nouveau*—, *m.*, (—*s*), *nouveau*—*e*, *f.*, (—*s*) newly-born. *Mort*—, *m.*, (—*s*), *mort*—*e*, *f.*, (—*s*) still-born. *Je suis* — *à Londres*; I was born in London. *Premier* —; first-born.

néanmoins, *adv.*, nevertheless, however, for all that, notwithstanding.

néant, *n.m.*, nothing, naught, nothingness, emptiness, nonentity. *C'est un homme de* —; he is a man of nothing. *Mettre au* —; to annul, to set at naught.

nébride, *n.f.*, fawn-skin (worn at the feast of Bacchus).

nébuleuse, *n.f.*, (astron.) nebula.

nébuleu-x, -se, *adj.*, nebulous, cloudy, misty, hazy; obscure, gloomy.

nébulosité, *n.f.*, nebulosity, obscurity, gloom.

nécessaire, *adj.*, necessary, requisite, needful, unavoidable, indispensable.

nécessaire, *n.m.*, necessaries, needful; dressing-case; work-box; canteen. *Se refuser le* —; to refuse one's self the necessaries of life.

nécessairement (-sèr-măn), *adv.*, necessarily; of course.

nécessitante, *adj.f.*, absolute; (theol.) compulsory.

nécessité, *n.f.*, necessity, exigence ; need, want. — *n'a point de loi ;* necessity knows no law. *Faire de — vertu ;* to make a virtue of necessity. *La — est la mère de l'invention ;* necessity is the mother of invention. *Les —s de la nature ;* the wants of nature. *De —;* of necessity, necessarily.

nécessiter, *v.a.*, to compel, to force ; to necessitate ; to oblige, to imply.

nécessiteu-x, -se, *adj.*, necessitous, needy.

nécessiteux, *n.m.*, pauper.

nec plus ultra, *n.m.*, (*n.p.*) ne plus ultra.

nécrologe, *n.m.*, obituary.

nécrologie, *n.f.*, necrology, obituary.

nécrologique, *adj.*, necrologic, necrological.

nécromance or **nécromancie**, *n.f.*, necromancy.

nécromancien (-ci-in), *n.m.*, **-ne** (-ci-è-n), *n.f.*, necromancer.

nécromant, *n.m.*, necromancer.

nécropole, *n.f.*, necropolis.

nécrose, *n.f.*, (med.) necrosis.

nectaire, *n.m.*, (bot.) nectary, honey-cup.

nectar, *n.m.*, nectar.

nef, *n.f.*, nave (of a church) ; (poet.) ship. *Moulin à — ;* mill built upon a boat.

néfaste, *adj.*, (antiq.) (of solemn festivals) of rest ; inauspicious, of evil omen, unlucky. *Jour — ;* day of mourning.

nèfle, *n.f.*, (bot.) medlar.

néflier, *n.m.*, (bot.) medlar-tree.

négatif, *n.m.*, (photograph), negative.

négati-f, -ve, *adj.*, negative.

négation, *n.f.*, negation, negative.

négative, *n.f.*, negative, refusal.

négativement (-tiv-mān) *adv.*, negatively.

négligé, -e, *part.*, neglected, unnoticed, unheeded, unstudied ; careless, slovenly. *Style — ;* careless style. *Extérieur — ;* slovenly exterior.

négligé, *n.m.*, undress, negligee.

négligeable, *adj.*, (math.) that can be neglected, trifling, unimportant. *Quantité — ;* not important enough to be taken into account, *or* that can be set aside.

négligement (-gli-jmān), *n.m.*, (arts) neglect.

négligemment (-ja-mān), *adv.*, negligently, carelessly.

négligence, *n.f.*, negligence, neglect ; carelessness, oversight.

négligent, -e, *adj.* and *n.*, negligent, neglectful, remiss, careless ; negligent person.

négliger, *v.a.*, to neglect, to omit, to overlook, to slight, to pass over, to disregard, to pass by. *se négliger*, *v.r.*, to neglect one's self, to be negligent *or* careless. *Il commence à — ;* he begins to be careless of his person.

négoce, *n.m.*, trade, traffic, business. *Faire un gros — ;* to carry on a large trade.

négociabilité, *n.f.*, negotiability.

négociable, *adj.*, negotiable, transferable.

négociant, *n.m.*, merchant (wholesale).

négociat-eur, *n.m.*, **-rice**, *n.f.*, negotiator, transactor.

négociation, *n.f.*, negotiation, transaction.

négocier, *v.n.*, to negotiate, to trade.

négocier, *v.a.*, to negotiate ; to be in treaty for. *— un mariage ;* to bring about a marriage. *se négocier*, *v.r.*, to be negotiating *or* negotiated (of a thing).

***négraille**, *n.f.*, negro-race.

nègre, *n.m.*, negro, black. *Travailler comme un — ;* to toil and moil ; to work like a slave.

négrerie, *n.f.*, negro-yard.

négresse, *n.f.*, negress.

négrier, *n.* and *adj.m.*, slave-ship, slaver ; slave-dealer. *Capitaine — ;* captain of a slave-ship. *Bâtiment — ;* slave-ship. *Marchand — ;* slave-dealer.

***négrillon**, *n.m.*, **-ne**, *n.f.*, little negro, negro boy, negro girl.

négromancien, négromant, *n.m.* V. **nécromancien, nécromant**.

neige, *n.f.*, snow ; (bot.) guelder-rose. *De gros flocons de — ;* large flakes of snow. *Amas de — ;* snow-drift. *Boule de — ;* snow-ball. *Il est tombé de la — ;* there has been a fall of snow. *D'une blancheur de — ;* as white as snow.

neiger, *v.imp.*, to snow. *Il neige ;* it snows.

neigeu-x, -se, *adj.*, snowy. *Temps — ;* snowy weather.

nélumbo, *n.m.*, (bot.) nelumbium.

néméen (-in), *adj.m.*, Nemean.

nénies, *n.f.pl.*, (antiq.) funeral dirges.

nenni (na-ni), *adv.*, (fam.) no, not at all. *— -da ;* no, indeed ; certainly not.

nénufar, *n.m.*, nenuphar, water-lily, water-rose.

néo, a prefix from Gr. νέος.

néographe, *n.m.* and *adj.*, neographer.

néographisme, *n.m.*, new way of spelling.

néo-latin, *adj.*, neo-latin (applied to the seven modern languages derived from Latin).

néologie, *n.f.*, neology.

néologique, *adj.*, neological.

néologisme, *n.m.*, neologism.

néologiste, *n.m.*, neologist.

néologue, *n.m.*, (b.s.) neologist.

néophyte, *n.m.f.*, neophyte.

néo-platonicien (-ci-in), **-ne** (-ci-è-n), *n.* and *adj.*, (— — —s) Neoplatonist. *Ecole — ne ;* the Neoplatonist school.

néo-platonisme, *n.m.* (*n.p.*), Neo-Platonism.

néotérique, *adj.*, neoteric.

néphralgie, *n.f.*, nephralgia.

néphrétique, *n.m.* and *adj.*, (med.) nephritic (person affected with renal colic).

néphrétique, *n.f.*, renal colic.

néphrite, *n.f.*, nephritis.

népotisme, *n.m.*, nepotism.

neptune, *n.m.*, (astron., myth.) Neptune ; (fig.) the sea ; (tech.) nautical atlas.

neptunien, -ne, *adj.*, (geol.) neptunian.

nérée, *n.m.*, Nereus. *L'empire de —* (poet.) the sea.

néréide, *n.f.*, (myth.) Nereid.

nerf (nèrf), *n.m.*, nerve, sinew ; fortitude, vigor, strength, stamina ; (bookbind.) cord, slip of tape. *Attaque de —s ;* fit, nervous attack, hysterics. [The *f* is mute in *nerf*, when used in the *pl.*, and in *nerf de bœuf.*] *L'argent est le — de la guerre ;* money is the sinews of war. *Donner sur les —s ;* to make one feel nervous ; to irritate one ; to rack one's nerves. *Manquer de — ;* to be wanting in energy.

nerf-férure, *n.f.*, (— s— —s) (vet.) overreach.

nérite, *n.f.*, (conch.) nerite.

néroli, *n.m.*, neroli.

nerprun, *n.m.*, (bot.) buckthorn.

⊙**nervaison**, *n.f.*, (med.) nervous system.

⊙**nerval, -e**, *adj.*, acting upon the nerves, nervine.

nervé, -e, *part.*, nerved, nervose ; corded.

nerver, *v.a.*, to cover with sinews. *— un livre ;* (bookbind.) to cord a book.

nerveu-x, -se, *adj.*, nervous ; sinewy, brawny, muscular, wiry, vigorous. *Etre — ;* to be nervous. *Bras — ;* sinewy arm.

nervin, *n.* and *adj.m.*, nervine.

nervosité, *n.f.*, nervousness ; nervosity.

nervure, *n.f.*, (arch.) nerve ; (bot.) nerve (of a leaf) ; (bookbind.) slips of tape, cording ; (ent.) nervure ; (carp.) rib, fillet ; (needle-work) piping.

nestor, *n.m.*, (—s) Nestor ; oldest, senior.

nestorianisme, *n.m.*, (ecc. hist.) Nestorianism.

nestorien, -ne (-in, -è-n), *adj.* and *n.*, (ecc. hist.) Nestorian.

net, -te, *adj.*, clean, neat, pure ; clear, fair, empty ; plain, distinct ; easy, perspicuous ; flat, frank, point-blank ; (com.) net. *Une chambre*

—*te;* a clean room. *Un cheval sain et* —*;* a horse warranted sound and free from any defect. *Ce vin est* —*;* that wine is clear. *Une écriture* —*te;* a fair hand. *Avoir la voix* —*te;* to have a clear voice. *Je veux en avoir le cœur* —*;* I will know the rights of it. *Faire maison* —*te;* to clear the house of servants. *Une réponse* —*te;* a plain answer. *Son bien est* —*;* his estate is clear. *Une pensée* —*te;* a clear thought. *Il a l'esprit* —*;* he has a clear understanding. *Avoir les mains* —*tes ;* (fig.) to have clean hands; not to be mixed up in any shady enterprise. *Prix* —*;* trade price. *Bénéfice* —*;* clear profit.

net, *n.m.,* fair copy. *Mettre au* —*;* to make a fair copy.

net, *adv.,* clean, entirely ; plainly, freely, flatly, point-blank, outright. *Il me l'a refusé tout* —*;* he flatly refused me *or* he refused me point-blank.

nettement (nèt-màn), *adv.,* neatly ; cleanly ; clearly ; distinctly, outright ; frankly, plainly, flatly. *Parlez-lui* —*;* speak to him plainly, freely.

netteté (nèt-té), *n.f.,* cleanness, cleanliness ; neatness, clearness, distinctness, sharpness, purity, plainness, blamelessness. *Voir avec* —*;* to see with distinctness. — *dans la voix;* clearness of voice.

nettoiement (né-toa-màn), *n.m.,* cleaning, cleansing, clearing ; scouring, sweeping ; brushing, wiping.

nettoyage, *n.m. V.* **nettoiement.**

nettoyer, *v.a.,* to clean, to cleanse, to make clean, to scour, to wipe, to pick, to free, to clear, to rid (of), to sweep away, to sweep, to free (from); to drive off. — *un habit;* to clean a coat. — *les biens d'une maison;* to pay off the debts of a firm. — *le tapis;* to carry off the stakes ; to sweep the board. — *la tranchée,* (milit.) to drive the besiegers from their trench. — *une maison;* (fig. fam.) to carry off the furniture.

se **nettoyer,** *v.r.,* to clean one's self, to be cleaned. — *les dents;* to clean one's teeth.

neuf, *n.* and *adj.,* nine, ninth. *Un* — *de cœur,* a nine of hearts. [Neuf is pronounced *neu* when it precedes an *adj.* or a *n.* beginning with a consonant or *h* aspirate ; and *neuv,* if the *adj.* or *n.* begins with a vowel or a silent *h.*]

neuf, *n.m.,* new ; something new. *A* —*;* anew, again ; like new. *De* —*;* new. *Habiller de* —*;* to dress in new clothes. *Donnez-nous du* —*;* give us something new. *Il y a du* —*;* something has happened.

neu-f, -ve, *adj.,* new ; raw, green, young, inexperienced. *Maison* —*ve ;* new house. *Faire corps* —*;* to take a new lease of life. *Il est tout* — *dans ce métier;* he is quite new to the business. *Une pensée* —*ve ;* a new thought. *Remettre à* —*;* to do up; to make as good as new *or* equal to new.

neume, *n.m.,* (plain chant) the singing of notes without words on one vowel.

neure, *n.m.,* Dutch herring-boat.

neutralement (-tral-màn), *adv.,* (gram.) neutrally.

neutralisant, *n.m.* and *adj.,* (chem.) neutralizing body ; neutralizing.

neutralisation, *n.f.,* neutralization.

neutraliser, *v.a.,* to neutralize.

se **neutraliser,** *v.r.,* to counteract each other, to become neutralized.

neutralité, *n.f.,* neutrality.

neutre, *n.m.* and *adj.,* neuter ; neutral. *Pavillon* —*;* neutral flag. *Nom* —*;* neuter noun. *Verbe* —*;* neuter *or* intransitive verb. *Sel* —*;* neutral salt.

neuvaine, *n.f.,* (c.rel.) novena, neuvaine (nine days' devotion).

neuvième, *n.m.* and *adj.,* ninth. *Il est le* —*,*

elle est la —*, de sa classe ;* he, she, is the ninth in his, in her, class.

neuvième, *n.f.,* (mus.) ninth.

neuvièmement (-vièm-màn), *adv.,* ninthly.

neveu, *n.m.,* nephew. *pl.,* (poet.) posterity, descendants. *Petit-*—*,* (—*s*—*x*) grandnephew. — *à la mode de Bretagne;* cousin once removed. *Nos* —*x, nos derniers* —*x, nos arrière-*—*x;* our posterity, our children's children.

névralgie, *n.f.,* neuralgia.

névralgique, *adj.,* (med.) neuralgic.

névritique, *n.* and *adj.m.,* (med.) neurotic.

névrographie, *n.f.,* neurology.

névrologie, *n.f.,* neurology.

névroptère, *adj.,* neuropteral, neuropterous.

névroptère, *n.m.,* neuropteran.

névrose, *n.f.,* (med.) nervous affection, nervous disorder, neurose.

névrotomie, *n.f.,* neurotomy.

newtonianisme (neu-), *n.m.,* Newtonianism.

newtonien, -ne (neu-to-ni-in, -è-n), *adj.,* Newtonian.

newtonien, *n.m.,* Newtonian.

nez (né), *n.m.,* nose ; face ; scent (of dogs). — *aquilin ;* aquiline nose. — *retroussé ;* turned-up nose. — *écrasé, épaté ;* flat nose, pug nose. *Il s'est cassé le* —*;* he has broken his nose. *Donner sur le* — *à quelqu'un ;* to strike any one on the nose. *Regarder quelqu'un sous le* —*;* to stare any one in the face. *Ne voir pas plus loin que son* —*;* to see no farther than one's nose. *A vue de* —*;* by rule of thumb. *Avoir bon* —*;* to have a good nose. *Il saigne du* —*;* his nose is bleeding. *Au* — *de quelqu'un ;* to a person's face, under a person's nose. *Rire au* — *de quelqu'un ;* to laugh in any one's face. *Fermer la porte au* — *à quelqu'un ;* to shut the door in any one's face. — *à* —*;* face to face. *Parler du* —*;* to speak through the nose. *Fourrer son* — *dans une affaire ;* to thrust one's nose into any business. *Mener quelqu'un par le* —*;* to lead any one by the nose. *Donner du* — *en terre ;* to fall on one's face; (fig.) to miscarry, to fail. *S'y casser le* —*;* to fail in anything. *Tirer les vers du* — *à quelqu'un ;* to pump any one. *Jeter quelque chose au* — *de quelqu'un ;* to cast a thing in any one's teeth; to twit any one (with). *Il a bon* —*;* he is a sagacious man. *Il a un pied de* —*;* he looks foolish; he is sadly disappointed. *Faire un pied de* — *à ;* to laugh at. *Qui coupe son* — *dégarnit son visage ;* it is an ill bird that fouls his own nest. *Il lui en pend autant au* —*;* he may expect as much.

ni, *conj.,* neither ; nor ; either ; or. *Il n'est* — *bon* — *mauvais ;* it is neither good nor bad. — *moi non plus ;* nor I either.

niable, *adj.,* deniable ; (jur.) traversable.

niais, -e, *n.* and *adj.,* ninny, simpleton ; silly, simple, foolish. *Il a l'air* —*;* he has a silly look.

niaisement (nièz-màn), *adv.,* sillily, foolishly.

niaiser, *v.n.,* to stand trifling, to play the fool, to fiddle-faddle.

niaiserie (-èz-rî), *n.f.,* silliness, foolishness, simplicity ; silly thing, trifle, foolery, nonsense.

niche, *n.f.,* niche, nook, corner ; recess, alcove, retreat ; kennel ; trick, prank. *Faire une* — *à ;* to play a trick upon.

nichée, *n.f.,* nest (of young birds) ; brood; crew, gang, set. *Une* — *de souris ;* a brood of mice.

nicher, *v.a.,* to nestle, to build ; to lodge. *Qui vous a niché là ?* who put you there ?

se **nicher,** *v.r.,* to nestle, to nestle one's self ; to hide one's self ; to put one's self. *Où la vertu va-t-elle se* — *?* who could expect to find virtue there ?

nicher, *v.n.,* to nestle, to build a nest.

nichet, *n.m.,* nest-egg.

nichoir, *n.m.,* breeding-cage.

nickel, *n.m.,* (metal.) nickel.

nicodème, *n.m.*, noodle, booby, nincompoop. *C'est un grand* —; he is a great noodle.

nicotiane (-ci-), *n.f.*, (bot.) nicotiana.

nicotine, *n.f.*, nicotine.

nictation, *n.f.*, nictation, nictitation.

nicter, *v.n.*, (vet.) to nictate.

nictitation, *n.f.* *V.* **nictation**.

nid, *n.m.*, nest; berth, post. *Petit à petit l'oiseau fait son* —; little strokes fell great oaks. *Trouver la pie au* —; to find what one is looking for. *Un* — *à rats;* a hovel, a mere hole. — *d'oiseau;* bird's nest. *A chaque oiseau son* — *est beau;* home is home, be it never so homely. *On n'a plus trouvé que le* —; they found the birds flown.

nidification, *n.f.*, nidification, nest-building.

nidoreu-x, -se, *adj.*, nidorous.

nièce, *n.f.*, niece. *Petite-*—, (*—s-—s*) grand-niece. — *à la mode de Bretagne;* cousin, once removed.

nielle, *n.f.*, smut, blight; (bot.) rose-campion, corn-cockle, fennel-flower.

nielle, *n.m.*, niello, inlaid enamel-work.

nieller, *v.a.*, (agri.) to smut, to blast, to blight; to inlay with enamel-work.

se nieller, *v.r.*, to become smutty, blighted.

nielleur, *n.m.*, (gold.) enameler of niello.

niellure, *n.f.*, (gold.) niello-work.

nier, *v.a.*, to deny, to gainsay, to disown, to deny the existence of; (jur.) to traverse. *Il nie que cela soit;* he denies that it is so.

se nier, *v.r.*, to be denied.

nigaud, -e, *n.* and *adj.*, booby, simpleton, silly fellow; silly, foolish. *Un grand* —; a great booby.

nigaud, *n.m.*, (orni.) booby, gannet.

nigauder, *v.n.*, to play the fool, to trifle.

nigauderie (-gô-drî), *n.f.*, silliness, tomfoolery; foolish trick.

nigelle, *n.f.*, (bot.) fennel-flower.

nihilisme, *n.m.*, nihilism.

nihiliste, *n.m.f.* and *adj.*, nihilist, nihilistic.

nilgaut, *n.m.*, (zoöl.) nylghau (kind of antelope).

*nille, *n.f.*, tendril (of a vine).

nilomètre, *n.m.*, nilometer.

nimbe, *n.m.*, (paint.) nimbus, halo.

nipper, *v.a.*, to fit out, to rig out.

se nipper, *v.r.*, to rig one's self out. *Il s'est bien nippé;* he has rigged himself out very well; he is quite a toff.

nippes, *n.f.pl.*, clothes, apparel; togs, toggery; things; furniture. [Mostly used in the plural.]

nique, *n.f.*, (fam., l.u.) sign of mockery or contempt. *Faire la* — *à quelqu'un;* to mock any one, to make fun of. *Faire la* — *à la fortune;* to despise riches.

nitée, *n.f.* *V.* **nichée**.

nitouche, *n.f.*, demure hypocrite. *Sainte* —; demure-looking person. *Faire la sainte* —; to look as if butter would not melt in one's mouth.

nitrate, *n.m.*, nitrate.

nitre, *n.m.*, niter.

nitreu-x, -se, *adj.*, nitrous.

nitrière, *n.f.*, niter-bed.

nitrification, *n.f.*, nitrification.

se nitrifier, *v.r.*, to nitrify.

nitrique, *adj.*, nitric.

nitrite, *n.m.*, nitrite.

nitrogène, *n.m.* and *adj.*, nitrogen; nitrogenous.

nitroglycérine, *n.f.*, (chem.) nitroglycerine.

nitro-muriatique, *adj.*, nitro-muriatic.

nitrosité, *n.f.*, nitrosity, nitrous quality (of).

nivéal, -e, *adj.*, growing in the snow; snowy.

niveau, *n.m.*, level. — *d'eau;* water-level. — *à bulle d'air;* spirit-level. — *à perpendicule;* plumb-level. *Au* — *de;* on a level with, even with. — *des eaux;* water-mark. *Mettre de* —; to level, to make even.

niveler (ni-vlé), *v.a.*, to make even, to take the level of, to level.

nivellette, *n.f.*, level-indicator.

niveleur (ni-vleur), *n.m.*, leveler.

nivellement (-vèl-măn), *n.m.*, leveling.

nivéole, *n.f.*, (bot.) snow-flake, snow-drop.

nivereau, *n.m.*, or **niverolle**, *n.f.*, snow-bird.

⊙nivet, *n.m.*, (pop.) gratuity, tip, douceur.

nivôse, *n.m.*, Nivôse, fourth month of the calendar of the first French republic, from December 21st or 22d to January 19th or 20th.

nobiliaire, *n.m.*, nobiliary.

nobiliaire, *adj.*, of the nobility, aristocratic.

nobilissime, *adj.*, most noble.

noble, *adj.*, noble, great, high, elevated. *Être de* — *sang;* to be of noble blood. *Il a l'air* —; he has a noble look.

noble, *n.m.*, noble, nobleman.

noblement, *adv.*, nobly, honorably, handsomely. *Vivre* —; to live like a noble.

noblesse, *n.f.*, nobility, rank; nobleness, loftiness. *La haute* —; the higher nobility. *La petite* —; the petty nobility. — *de cœur;* nobleness of heart. — *de style;* loftiness of style.

noce, *n.f.*, wedding, wedding-party; jollification, drinking-bout. *pl.*, marriage, nuptials, wedding. *Habit de* —*s;* wedding suit. *Tant qu'à des* —*s;* (prov. pop.) plentifully, as much as you like. *N'être pas à la* —; not to be enjoying one's self. *Gâteau de* —; bride-cake. *Faire la* —; to go on the spree, on the loose. *Je n'ai jamais été à pareilles* —*s;* I never had such a time of it.

nocer, *v.n.*, to go on the spree, on the loose.

noceu-r, -se, *n.m.f.*, gay dog; gay woman.

nocher, *n.m.*, (poet.) pilot. *Caron, le pâle* —; Charon, the grim ferryman. *Mon* — *face à face;* my pilot face to face (Tennyson).

nocial, *n.m.*, wedding dress.

noctambule, *n.m.f.*, noctambulist, sleep-walker.

noctambulisme, *n.m.*, noctambulism, sleep-walking. [night.

nocturne, *adj.*, nocturnal, nightly, night, of

nocturne, *n.m.*, (rel.) nocturn; (mus.) nocturne.

nocturnement, *adv.*, (l.u.) by night, nocturnally.

⊙nocuité, *n.f.*, noxiousness, culpability.

nodosité, *n.f.*, nodosity; (surg.) node.

nodule, *n.m.*, nodule.

nodus, *n.m.*, (surg.) node.

noël, *n.m.*, Christmas; Yule-tide; Christmas carol. *Les fêtes de* —; the Christmas holidays. *A la fête de* —, *à la* —; at Christmas. *Noël! noël!* Hurrah! hurrah!

nœud (neu), *n.m.*, knot; stress, difficulty, intricacy, knotty point; rub; tie, bond, band, bow; knuckle; knob; node (med., bot., astron., lit.). — *serré;* hard knot. — *coulant;* noose, slip knot. *Un* — *de diamants;* a cluster of diamonds. — *d'amour;* love-knot. *Bois plein de* —*s;* wood full of knots. *Voilà le* — *de l'affaire;* there lies the kernel of the matter; there's the rub. *Resserrer les* —*s de l'amitié;* to tighten the bonds of friendship. *Le* — *de la gorge;* Adam's apple. — *d'une pièce de théâtre;* the knot or plot of a play. —*s d'une planète;* nodes of a planet. — *de bouline;* (nav.) bowline-knot. — *de bois;* (nav.) timber-hitch. *Nous filons douze* —*s par heure;* we are making twelve knots an hour. *Le* — *gordien;* the Gordian knot.

noguet, *n.m.*, large, flat wicker basket.

noie-chien, *n.m.*, shooting-boat.

noir, -e, *adj.*, black; swarthy; foul, dirty; dark, gloomy; black and blue; dismal, dull, gloomy; base, wicked, foul, heinous; brown (of bread). — *comme jais;* black as jet. *Des yeux* —*s;* black eyes. *Blé* —; buckwheat. *Bêtes* —*es;* black game. *Une chambre* —*e;* a dark room. *Un temps* —; gloomy weather. *Il a une* *humeur —e;* he has a fit of the blues. *Des idées —es;* gloomy ideas. *Un — attentat;* a foul crime. *Bête —e;* pet aversion. *Rendre —;* to blacken. *— comme dans un four;* dark as pitch.

noir, *n.m.,* black; negro; (agri.) brown-rust. *— de fumée;* lampblack. *— animal;* charcoal. *— d'ivoire;* ivory-black. *Teindre en —;* to dye black. *Porter le —;* to be in mourning. *En —;* in black. *Broyer du —;* to have the blues.

noirâtre, *adj.,* blackish.

noiraud, -e. *adj.,* dark, swarthy-looking.

noirceur, *n.f.,* blackness; darkness; black spot; heinousness, baseness, atrocity, foulness, treacherous action, foul thing. *La — de son crime;* the heinousness of his crime. *La — de son âme;* the baseness of his soul.

noircir, *v.a.,* to black, to blacken, to make black, to stain, to smut; to sully, to traduce, to asperse, to defame. *Le soleil noircit le teint;* the sun tans the complexion. *— la réputation de quelqu'un;* to sully any one's character.

se **noircir,** *v.r.,* to blacken, to grow black *or* dark; to get *or* turn black; to disgrace one's self. *Se — la barbe;* to blacken one's beard. *Cela s'est noirci à la fumée;* that has turned black in the smoke. *Le temps se noircit;* the weather is beginning to get cloudy.

noircir, *v.n.,* to blacken, to grow black.

noircissure, *n.f.,* smudge, black spot.

noire, *n.f.,* (mus.) crotchet.

noise, *n.f.,* quarrel, squabble, brawl. *Chercher — à quelqu'un;* to pick a quarrel with any one. *Avoir — avec;* to have a quarrel with.

noisetier (noaz-tié), *n.m.,* nut-tree, hazel-tree.

noisette, *n.f.,* nut, hazel-nut.

noix (noa), *n.f.,* walnut, nut; kernel; (of meat) pope's eye; tumbler (of fire-arms); plug (of cocks); grinding-wheel (of coffee-mills). *— de galle;* gall-nut. *Coquille de —;* walnut-shell. *La — du genou;* the knee-cap. *— d'acajou;* cachew-nut. *— muscade;* nutmeg. *— vomique;* nux vomica. *Brou de —;* walnut husk. *— de terre, terre— (—);* earth-nut, pig-nut.

noli me tangere (-mé-tan-jé-ré), *n.m.* (—), (bot.) noli me tangere, touch me not.

nolis *or* **nolisement,** *n.m.,* freight, chartering.

noliser, *v.a.,* to freight, to charter.

nom (non), *n.m.,* name; fame, celebrity; (gram.) noun, title, style. *Un — propre, un — de baptême;* a proper, a christian, name. *Je ne le connais que de —;* I only know him by name. *— de guerre;* assumed name; alias; nickname. *Il nomme les choses par leur —;* he calls a spade a spade. *Au — de;* in the name of. *De —;* in name. *Avoir —;* to be called. *— social or raison sociale;* name of the firm, style. *Décliner son —;* to give in one's name. *Changer de —;* to change one's name. *— collectif;* collective noun. *— substantif, — adjectif;* noun substantive, noun adjective. *— d'une pipe, — d'un tonnerre, — d'un petit bon homme!* By Jingo! By George!

nomade, *n.m.* and *adj.,* nomad; nomadic, wandering, migratory. *Peuples —s;* nomadic tribes.

nomancie, *n.f.,* nomancy.

nomarque, *n.m.,* (antiq.) nomarch.

nombrable, *adj.,* (l.u.) countable, numerable.

nombrant, *adj.,* (math.) abstract.

nombre, *n.m.,* number; numbers; quantity, variety; quorum; harmony. *Mettre au — de;* to number among. *— compétent;* quorum (of members). *Surpasser en —;* to outnumber. *— pair;* even number. *— impair;* odd number. *— premier;* primary number. *Etre du —, au — des savants;* to be one of the learned. *Vous n'êtes pas du —;* you are not one of them. *Dans le —;* among the number. *Il y a du — dans ces*

vers; there is harmony in these verses. *— abstrait, — nombrant;* abstract number. *— concret, — nombré;* concrete number. *— d'or* (astron.); golden number. *N'être pas en —* (of assemblies); not to form a quorum. *Tout fait —;* every little helps.

nombré, -e, *part.,* (math.) concrete; numbered.

nombrer, *v.a.,* to number, to compute, to sum up, to reckon.

nombreu-x, -se, *adj.,* numerous; harmonious, full. *Style —;* harmonious style.

nombril (non-bri), *n.m.,* (anat.) navel, umbilic; (bot.) hilum, eye.

nome, *n.m.,* (antiq.) nome.

nomenclateur, *n.m.,* nomenclator.

nomenclature, *n.f.,* nomenclature.

nominal, -e, *adj.,* nominal. *Appel —;* show of hands; call over.

nominalement, *adv.,* nominally.

nominalisme, *n.m.,* (philos.) nominalism.

nominaliste, *n.m., (nominaux)* (philos.) Nominalist.

nominataire, *n.m.,* (ecc.) nominee, presentee.

nominateur, *n.m.,* (ecc.) nominator, presentor, patron.

nominatif, *n.m.,* (gram.) nominative.

nominati-f, -ve, *adj.,* of names.

nomination, *n.f.,* nomination, appointment; election, advowson; gift. *Etre dans la — de;* to be in the gift of.

nominativement (-tiv-mān), *adv.,* by name.

nommé, -e, *part.,* named, said, appointed; designate, a certain. *Le — Jacques;* one James by name *or* the said James. *A jour —;* on the appointed day. *A point —;* in the nick of time. *Un — Charles;* a certain Charles by name.

nommément, *adv.,* namely; particularly, especially.

nommer, *v.a.,* to name, to call, to give a name; to nominate, to appoint, to elect, to mention. *— quelqu'un son héritier;* to institute any one one's heir.

se **nommer,** *v.r.,* to state one's name; to be called. *Comment se nomme-t-il?* what is his name?

nomothète, *n.m.,* (antiq.) nomothete.

non, *adv.,* no, not. *— pas, s'il vous plaît;* not so, if you please. *Vous ne l'aimez pas, ni moi — plus;* you do not like it, nor I either. *Je crois que —;* I think not. *Je dis que —;* I say no. *—da;* no indeed, certainly not.

non-acceptation, *n.f.,* non-acceptance.

non-activité, *n.f.,* (n.p.) (milit.) being unattached (of officers), non-effective.

nonagénaire, *adj.,* of ninety, ninety years of age. *n.m.f.,* nonagenarian.

nonagésime, *adj.,* nonagesimal.

nonagone, *n.m.,* nonagon.

nonandre, *adj.,* (bot.) having nine stamens.

Ⓢ**nonante,** *adj.,* ninety.

Ⓢ**nonantième,** *adj.,* ninetieth.

nonce, *n.m.,* nuncio.

nonchalamment (-la-mān), *adv.,* carelessly, indolently, heedlessly.

nonchalance, *n.f.,* carelessness, heedlessness, remissness, nonchalance.

nonchalant, -e, *n.* and *adj.,* careless, listless person; careless, heedless, listless, remiss.

nonchaloir, *n.m.,* nonchalance, heedlessness.

nonciature, *n.f.,* nunciature, nuncio's residence.

non-conformiste, *n.m., (——s)* nonconformist.

non-conformité, *n.f.,* (n.p.) nonconformity.

none, *n.f.,* (c.rel.) none; (antiq.) ninth hour (3 o'clock p.m.).

nones, *n.f.pl.,* (antiq.) nones.

non-être, *n.m.,* (n.p.) (philos.) non-entity, non-existence.

nonidi, *n.m.*, nonidi (ninth day of the decade of the calendar of the first French republic).

non-intervention, *n.f.*, (*n.p.*) (pol.) non-intervention.

nonius (-ûs), *n.m.*, (math.) nonius, sliding rule.

non-jouissance, *n.f.*, (*n.p.*) non-enjoyment, non-use.

non-lieu, *n.m.*, (*n.p.*) (jur.) no cause, no ground, to prosecute. *Ordonnance de* —; release, discharge. *Rendre une ordonnance de* —; to throw out a bill (of indictment).

non-moi, *n.m.*, (*n.p.*) (philos.) the non ego, the external world.

nonnain, *n.f.*, (jest.) nun; (pigeon) jacobin.

nonnat, *n.m.*, sand-eel, sand-smelt.

nonne, *n.f.*, nun; (pigeon) bald-head.

nonnerie (no-n-rî), *n.f.*, (jest.) nunnery.

nonnette, *n.f.*, (jest.) young nun, nun; sort of gingerbread; (orni.) osprey. — *cendrée*; marsh-tit.

nonobstant, *prep.*, notwithstanding, in spite of.

nonobstant que, *conj.*, notwithstanding, although.

non-ouvré, -e, *adj.*, (of raw materials) unwrought.

non-pair, *adj.*, not even, odd (of numbers).

*nonpareil, -le, *adj.*, nonpareil, matchless, unparalleled.

*nonpareille, *n.f.*, nonpareil; narrow ribbon; nonpareil, nonesuch (apple, small sugar-plum); (print.) nonpareil.

non-payement, *n.m.*, (——*s*) non-payment.

non plus ultra, *n.m.* V. **nec plus ultra**.

non-prix, *n.m.*, (—) (com.) undervalue.

non-résidence, *n.f.*, (*n.p.*) non-residence.

non-sens, *n.m.*, (—) nonsense.

nonuple, *adj.*, ninefold.

nonupler, *v.a.*, to increase nine times.

non-usage, *n.m.*, (*n.p.*) disuse.

non-valeur, *n.f.*, (——*s*) unproductiveness; (com.) bad debt, worthless bill.

non-vente, *n.f.*, no sale.

⊙**non-vue**, *n.f.*, (*n.p.*) (nav.) misty weather, fog.

nopal, *n.m.*, (—*s*) (bot.) nopal; cochineal-fig.

nord, *n.m.*, North; north-wind; Nord (department of France). —*est*, north-east; north-east wind. —*ouest*; north-west; north-west wind. *Au* — or *vers le* —; northwards. *Faire le* —; to sail northwards. *Chemin de fer du* —; Great Northern (railway) of France.

nord, *adj.* *Pôle* —; North pole.

noria, *n.f.*, (—*s*) (mec.) noria, Persian-wheel; chain-pump.

normal, -e, *adj.*, normal. *Ecole* —*e*; normal school. *Etat* —; healthy state, normal condition.

normale, *n.f.*, (geom.) normal, perpendicular.

normalien, normal-school student.

normand, -e, *adj.*, Norman; equivocal (of answers); feigned (reconciliation). *Réponse* —*e*; ambiguous answer.

normand, *n.m.*, -e, *n.f.*, Norman. *Répondre en* —; to give an evasive answer. *C'est un fin* —; he is a crafty fellow. *C'est répondre en* —; that is giving an evasive answer, that is shuffling.

normander, *v.a.*, (agri.) to clean (corn).

nos, *adj.m.f.pl.*, our.

nosographie, *n.f.*, nosography.

nosologie, *n.f.*, nosology.

nosologiste, *n.m.*, nosologist.

nosseigneurs, *n.m.pl.*, my lords; their lordships.

nostalgie, *n.f.*, nostalgia, home-sickness.

nostoc, *n.m.*, (bot.) nostoch.

nota, *n.m.*, (—) observation, note, remark, marginal note. — *bene*; note carefully.

notabilité, *n.f.*, (com.) respectability; notability; principal person.

notable, *adj.*, notable, remarkable, considerable, of influence. *Faits* —*s*; remarkable doings; remarkable facts.

notable, *n.m.*, principal; (hist. of France) notable; leading man; man of note, notability.

notablement, *adv.*, notably, considerably, principally.

notaire, *n.m.*, notary, solicitor, attorney. — *public*; notary public. *C'est comme si le* — *y avait passé*; it is as good as a bond.

notamment (no-ta-mān), *adv.*, specially, especially, particularly, namely.

notarial, -e, *adj.*, notarial.

notariat, *n.m.*, profession of a notary; notary's business.

notarié, -e, *adj.*, notarial.

notation, *n.f.*, notation.

note, *n.f.*, note, mark, remark, brand; bill; account; minute, memorandum. — *infamante*; brand of infamy. *Chanter sur une autre* —; to change one's tune. *Chanter la* —; to sol-fa. *Bien attaquer la* —; to make a note tell. — *sensible*; leading note.

noter, *v.a.*, to note, to note down; to mark, to brand; to observe, to notice, to take notice; (mus.) to note, to prick. *Notez bien cela*; take good note of that. *Notez bien!* mark you! *Mal noté*; (pers.) ill-famed, of bad reputation. *Cela est à* —; that is worth noting down, worth remembering.

⊙**noteur**, *n.m.*, music copier.

notice, *n.f.*, notice, note; account; sketch; review.

notification, *n.f.*, notification.

notifier, *v.a.*, to notify, to give notice of, to make known.

notion, *n.f.*, notion, idea, knowledge. *pl.* elements, rudiments. *Selon la* — *que j'en ai*; according to my notion of it.

notoire, *adj.*, notorious, well-known, plain.

notoirement (no-toar-mān), *adv.*, notoriously, clearly.

notoriété, *n.f.*, notoriety, evidence; reputation.

notre, *adj.m.f.* (*nos*), our. — *maison*; our house. — *père*; our father. *Nos frères et nos sœurs*; our brothers and sisters. *Nos père et mère*; our father and mother.

nôtre (le), *possessive pron. m.f.* (*nôtres*), ours. *C'est votre ami et le* —; it is your friend and ours. *Le* —; our own, ours. *Les* —*s*; our people, our relations, our friends. *Celui-là est-il des* —*s?* is that man one of our people? *Ne serez-vous pas des* —*s?* won't you make one of us, or join our party? *Voilà leur maison, celle-ci est la* —; that is their house, this one is ours.

notre-dame, *n.f.*, our Lady; festival in honor of our Lady; Notre-Dame (church).

noue, *n.f.*, gutter-lead; pantile; pasture ground; cod-sound.

noué, -e, *part.*, knotted, tied, rickety. *Enfant* —; rickety child; (of fruits) set. *Une pièce de théâtre bien* —*e*; dramatic piece, with a skillfully drawn plot.

nouement (noo-mān), *n.m.*, knotting, tying.

nouer, *v.a.*, to tie, to knot, to join; to get up, to concoct; to twist; to clasp, to form; (nav.) to hitch.

se **nouer**, *v.r.*, to attach, to fasten one's self; to grow rickety; (of fruits) to set.

nouer, *v.n.*, (hort.) to set (of fruit).

nouet, *n.m.*, little bag.

noueur, *n.m.*, tier, binder.

noueu-x, -se, *adj.*, knotty, gnarled, knotted, full of knots, nodose.

nougat, *n.m.*, almond-cake.

nouilles or **noules**, *n.f.pl.*, ribbon vermicelli.

noulet, *n.m.*, gutter; rafter (of a roof).

noumène, *n.m.*, (in Kant's philos.) noumenon.

nourrain, *n.m.*, fry (fish). V. **alevin**.

nourri, -e, *part.*, nourished, fed ; rich, full, copious ; (of fire) well sustained, brisk. *Feu bien —;* very brisk fire. *Une couleur —e ;* (paint.) color thickly laid on. *Blé, grain, bien —;* well-filled corn. *Style —;* copious style.

nourrice, *n.f.*, nurse ; wet-nurse. *Mère —;* foster-mother. *Mettre un enfant en —;* to put a child out to nurse. *Elle dit qu'elle a vingt ans ; et les mois de —;* she says she is twenty ; and the rest !

nourricier, *n.m.*, foster-father, fosterer.

nourrici-er, -ère, *adj.*, nutritive, nutritious. *Père —;* foster-father. *Mère —ère ;* foster-mother.

nourrir, *v.a.*, to nourish, to nurture ; to feed, to keep, to maintain, to sustain ; to suckle, to nurse, to foster, to harbor, to entertain ; to supply ; to bring up, to rear, to keep alive ; to cherish. *Le bois nourrit le feu ;* wood feeds the fire. *La Sicile nourrissait Rome ;* Sicily supplied Rome with provisions. *L'étude nourrit l'esprit ;* study strengthens the understanding. *L'espérance nourrit l'amour ;* hope keeps love alive.

se **nourrir,** *v.r.*, to feed, to live upon, to support one's self upon ; to live, to feed upon, to feast on, to delight in. *Se bien nourrir ;* to live well.

nourrissage, *n.m.*, feeding (of cattle).

nourrissant, -e, *adj.*, nutritive, nourishing.

nourrisseur, *n.m.*, cow-keeper, cattle-feeder ; breeder.

nourrisseur, *adj.*, (tech.) feeding.

nourrisson, *n.m.*, foster-child, nurse-child, nursling, suckling.

nourriture, *n.f.*, nourishment, food, diet, board, maintenance, living, livelihood ; nurture. *Son travail lui procure la —;* his labor brings him in a livelihood. *Faire des —s ;* to breed cattle, fowls, etc.

nous, *personal pron.*, we, us ; to us ; each other. *— disons ;* we say. *Il — aime ;* he loves us. *Vous — parlez ;* you speak to us. *—-mêmes ;* ourselves. *— autres ;* we *or* the like of us ! *— aimons ;* we love each other. *C'est à — à ;* it is our turn to. *C'est à — de ;* it is our duty to.

nouure, *n.f.*, rickets ; (hort.) knotting, setting.

nouveau, nouvel, *adj.m.*, **nouvelle,** *f.*, new, recent, novel, fresh, further ; new-fangled, modern, new-fashioned ; inexperienced, green. *Le nouvel an ;* the new year. *De —le date ;* recently. *De —le mode ;* new-fashioned. *Recommencer sur nouveaux frais ;* to begin anew, or all over again. *Un homme —;* an upstart. *Un habit —;* a coat of a new fashion. *Un nouvel habit ;* a fresh *or* another coat. *— venu ;* newly-come. *Un — venu ;* a new-comer ; *des nouveaux venus ;* new-comers ; *une nouvelle venue ;* new-comer (female) ; *des nouvelles venues ;* new-comers (females). *— débarqué ;* (fig.) person just come up from the country. [Nouvel is used for the *masculine* before a vowel or an *h* mute.]

nouveau, *n.m.*, new, something new. *A —;* on new account. *De —;* anew ; again. *Qu'y a-t-il de —?* what is the news ?

nouveau-né, *n.m.* (*— —s*), **nouveau-née,** *n.f.* (*— —-s*), new-born child.

nouveauté, *n.f.*, newness, novelty ; change, innovation. *pl.*, fancy articles. *Magasin de —s ;* linen-draper's shop. *C'est une — que de vous voir ;* it is quite a change to see you. *Marchand de —s ;* linen-draper. *Haute —;* latest fashion.

nouvelle, *n.f.*, news, tidings, intelligence, account ; novelette ; tale, story. *Quelles sont les —s ?* what is the news ? *Débiter des —s ;* to spread news. *— de basse cour ;* idle rumors. *Envoyer savoir des —s de quelqu'un ;* to send to know how any one is. *Mandez-moi de vos —;* let me hear from you. *Ne faites rien que vous n'ayez de mes —;* do nothing till you hear from me. *Vous aurez de mes —s ;* you shall hear from me. *J'en sais des —;* I know something

about it. *Point de —s, bonnes —s ;* no news is good news. *Recevoir des —s de ;* to hear from. *Avez-vous de ses —?* have you heard from him *or* her ? *Vous m'en direz des —;* you 'll be astonished, delighted, highly pleased with it.

nouvellement (noo-vèl-mān), *adv.*, newly, lately, recently.

nouvelleté (-vèl-té), *n.f.*, (jur.) dispossession, trespass.

nouvelliste, *n.m.*, newsmonger ; novelist.

novale, *n.f.*, land newly broken up. *pl.*, tithes on new land.

novat-eur, -rice, *n.* and *adj.*, innovator ; innovating.

novation, *n.f.*, (jur.) substitution, change.

novelles, *n.f.pl.*, (Roman law) Justinian's constitutions.

novembre, *n.m.*, November.

novice, *adj.*, novice, inexperienced, raw, green, new. *Une main —;* an inexperienced hand.

novice, *n.m.f.*, novice, probationer ; (nav.) apprentice. *Il est encore — dans son métier ;* he is yet but a novice in his trade.

noviciat, *n.m.*, novitiate, novices' quarters ; probationership.

⊙**novissimé,** *adv.*, (fam.) very lately.

noyade (noa-yad), *n.f.*, drowning. *Les noyades ;* (Fr. Hist.) judicial drowning.

noyale *or* **noyalle** (noa-yal), *n.f.*, sailcloth, canvas.

noyau (noa-yô), *n.m.*, stone (of fruit) ; nucleus ; core (of statues, of casts) ; (metal.) core ; noyau (cordial). *— de pêche ;* stone of a peach. *Fruits à —;* stone-fruit.

noyé, -e (noa-yé), *part.* and *n.*, drowned, drowning ; a drowned person.

noyer (noa-yé), *n.m.*, walnut-tree.

noyer (noa-yé), *v.a.*, to drown ; to put under water, to swamp, to ruin, to overwhelm ; to deluge ; (paint.) to mix, to blend, to confuse (colors) ; (tech.) to countersink, to let in.

se **noyer** (noa-yé), *v.r.*, to be *or* get drowned, to drown one's self ; to be plunged (in), to go to ruin. *Se — dans le sang ;* to wallow, to welter in blood. *C'est un homme qui se noie ;* his affairs are going to the bad, *or* he is on the down-grade.

noyon (no-yon ; noa-yon ; né-yon), *n.m.*, scratch, mark (at bowls).

noyure (no-yur ; noa-yur), *n.f.*, countersink (for nails, screws).

nu, -e, *adj.*, naked, bare, uncovered ; plain, open, without disguise, unadorned ; destitute. *Il avait la tête —e, il était nu-tête ;* he was bareheaded. *Aller nu-pieds ;* to go barefoot *or* bare-footed. *Un va-nu-pieds ;* a poor destitute wretch. *Observer quelque chose à l'œil —;* to observe anything with the naked eye. *C'est la vérité toute —e ;* it is the naked truth. *—e propriété ;* (jur.) property without the usufruct of it, reversionary interest. *— propriétaire ;* (jur.) owner without the usufruct of his property. *— comme un ver ;* stark-naked.

nu, *n.m.*, (paint.) nude, nudity ; bare (of a wall). *pl.*, (Bibl.) naked. *A —;* naked, bare, open ; next the skin. *Monter un cheval à —;* to ride a horse barebacked. *Mettre à —;* to lay bare *or* open ; to strip.

nuage, *n.m.*, cloud ; mist ; (fig.) darkness, gloom, shadow, sadness, dejection ; dissension, jar, unpleasantness. *Le ciel est couvert de —s ;* the sky is covered with clouds. *Un — de poussière ;* a cloud of dust.

nuageu-x, -se, *adj.*, cloudy, clouded. *Un ciel —;* a cloudy sky.

nuaison, *n.f.*, (nav.) continuance of a steady set breeze.

nuance, *n.f.*, shade, hue, tint, cast ; difference, distinction ; gradation, degree.

nuancer, *v.a.*, to shade, to variegate, to tint,

to blend. — *des couleurs;* to shade colors. *Se* —; *v.r.,* to be variegated, or shaded.

nubécule, *n.f.,* (med.) nubecula.

nubile, *adj.,* marriageable, nubile.

nubilité, *n.f.,* nubility, marriageable age.

nudité, *n.f.,* nudity, nakedness.

nue, *n.f.,* cloud. *pl.,* skies. *Elever jusqu'aux* —*s;* to extol to the skies. *Se perdre dans les* —*s;* to lose one's self in the clouds. *Sauter aux* —; to jump to the ceiling; to go wild with joy. *Tomber des* —*s;* to fall from the clouds, (fig.) to be amazed.

nuée, *n.f.,* cloud; storm; swarm, host, multitude, flock, shower, flight. *Une* — *de barbares;* a swarm of barbarians. *Une* — *de traits;* a shower of darts.

nuement. *V.* **nûment.**

nuer, *v.a.* *V.* **nuancer.**

nuire (nuisant, nui), *v.n.,* to hurt, to prejudice, to do hurt, to harm, to stand in the way of, to annoy, to wrong; to spoil, to hinder, to be prejudicial to. *Il cherche à me* —; he seeks to do me harm. *Le froid nuit à la santé;* cold is hurtful to health. *Ne pas* —; not to harm; not to hurt; to be harmless; to be of use; to help, to assist.

se **nuire,** *v.r.,* to hurt, to injure, one's self; to hurt, to injure, each other.

nuisible, *adj.,* hurtful, detrimental, prejudicial, injurious, noxious.

nuit, *n.f.,* night, night-time; darkness. *Bonnet de* —; night-cap. *A la* — *tombante;* or *à la tombée de la* —; at nightfall, at dusk. *Passer la* —; to spend the night, to sit up all night. — *close;* nightfall. — *blanche;* sleepless night. — *noire;* pitch-dark. *L'astre des* —*s;* the orb of night. *Il fait* —; it is night, dark. *Il se fait* —; night is coming on. *La* — *de l'ignorance;* the darkness of ignorance. *De* —; by night, in the night-time, nightly. *Effet de* —; (paint.) night piece. *Faites une bonne* —; sleep well. *La* — *porte conseil;* seek advice of your pillow; sleep upon it.

nuitamment (-ta-mǎn), *adv.,* by night, in the night, nightly.

nuitée, *n.f.,* night's lodging; night's work; whole night.

nul, -le, *pron.,* no one, not any, nobody, not one. — *n'ose en approcher;* nobody dares come near him, or it.

nul, -le, *adj.,* no, not any; void, of no force, null, invalid. —*le part;* nowhere. *Sans* — *égard;* without any regard. *Rendre* —; to nullify. *C'est un homme* —; he is a mere cipher.

nulle, *n.f.,* null; (cryptography) graphic sign that is meaningless, superfluous.

nullement (nul-mǎn), *adv.,* not at all, by no means.

nullifier (nul-li-fié), *v.a.,* to nullify.

nullité (nul-li-té), *n.f.,* nullity, incapacity; (jur.) flaw. *La* — *d'un acte;* the nullity of a deed. *Cet homme est d'une parfaite* —; that man is a perfect cipher.

numéraire, *n.m.* and *adj.,* metallic currency, specie, cash; legal (of coin). *Valeur* —; legal value, legal tender.

numéral, -e, *adj.,* numeral.

numérateur, *n.m.,* (arith.) numerator.

numération, *n.f.,* (arith.) numeration.

numérique, *adj.,* numerical.

numériquement (-rik-mǎn), *adv.,* numerically.

numéro, *n.m.,* number; (com.) size; sort, kind, quality. *Donnez-moi le* — *de sa maison;* give me the number of his house. *Voyez le* — *cinq;* see number five. *Il entend le* —; (pop.) he understands his business.

numérotage, *n.m.,* numbering.

numéroter, *v.a.,* to number.

numismate, *n.m.,* numismatist.

numismatique, *adj.,* numismatic.

numismatique, *n.f.,* numismatics.

numismatographie, *n.f.,* numismatography.

nummulaire, *n.f.,* (bot.) moneywort.

nummulite, *n.f.,* nummulite.

nuncupatif, *adj.m.,* nuncupatory, nuncupative. *Testament* —; nuncupative will.

nuptial, -e, *adj.,* nuptial, bridal.

nuque, *n.f.,* nape (of the neck); poll (of horses).

nutation, *n.f.,* (astron., bot.) nutation.

nutriti-f, -ve, *adj.,* nutritive, nutritious, nourishing.

nutrition, *n.f.,* nutrition.

nyotage du Pérou, *n.f.,* (bot.) marvel of Peru, mirabilis.

nyctalope, *n.m.f.,* nyctalops.

nyctalopie, *n.f.,* nyctalopia, nyctalopy.

nymphe, *n.f.,* nymph; (ent.) nymph, grub. *pl.,* (anat.) nymphæ.

nymphéa, *n.m.,* (bot.) nenuphar, white water-lily.

nymphéacées, *n.f.pl.,* (bot.) nymphæaceæ.

nymphée, *n.f.* or *m.,* (antiq.) nymphæum.

nymphomanie, *n.f.,* nymphomania.

nyssa, *n.m.,* tupelo, sour-gum-tree.

O

o, *n.m.,* the fifteenth letter of the alphabet, o.

o. (ab. of Ouest), W., West.

o! *int.,* O! oh! *Les* — *de Noël;* Christmas anthems.

oasis (o-a-zîs), *n.f.,* oasis.

obclavé, -e, *adj.,* (bot.) obovate.

obconique, *adj.,* (bot.) obconic, obconical.

obcordé, -e, *adj.,* (bot.) obcordate.

obédience, *n.f.,* (theol.) permission to leave one convent for another; functions (in a convent); jurisdiction (of the pope); (Bibl.) obedience.

obédiencier, *n.m.,* priest doing duty in another's benefice, obedienciary.

obédientiel, -le (-ci-èl), *adj.,* (ecc.) pertaining, relating to obedience; (Bibl.) obediential.

obéir, *v.n.,* to obey, to comply with, to be obedient; to bend, to yield, to give way, to submit. *Pour* — *à;* in obedience to. *Il faut lui* —; he must be obeyed. *Se faire* —; to make one's self obeyed.

obéissance, *n.f.,* obedience, allegiance; dominion (of princes). *Prêter* — *à un prince;* to yield dominion to a prince. *Etre sous l'* — *de père et mère;* to be under the legal authority of parents. *Etre d'une grande* —; to be very obedient.

obéissant, -e, *adj.,* obedient, docile, dutiful, submissive; pliant, obsequious.

obélisque, *n.m.,* obelisk.

obérer, *v.a.,* to encumber, to run into debt. *C'est un homme fort obéré;* he is greatly in debt. *s'obérer,* *v.r.,* to involve one's self in debt, to become involved.

obèse, *adj.,* obese, corpulent.

obésité, *n.f.,* obesity, corpulence.

obier, *n.m.,* guelder-rose.

obit (o-bit), *n.m.,* (c.rel.) obit.

obituaire, *n.m.* and *adj.,* (c.rel.) obituary.

objecter, *v.a.,* to object, to raise as an objection (to), to reproach (with); to allege (against); to demur (to). *Vous m'objecterez que c'est bien connu;* you will say to me that it is a well-known thing.

objecti-f, -ve, *adj.,* objective.

objectif, *n.m.,* (opt.) object-glass; (philos., milit.) object, objective; aim, end.

objection, *n.f.,* objection. *Aller au-devant d'une* —; to meet an objection. *Je ne vois pas d'objection à ce que cela se fasse;* I see no objection to its being done.

objectivement, *adv.*, objectively.

objectivité, *n.f.*, objectivity.

objet, *n.m.*, object, subject, matter, business; aim, end, view, drift, purport; article. *pl.*, goods. *Un — de risée;* a laughing-stock. *Etre l'— de la conversation;* to be the subject of conversation. *Il n'a pour — que son intérêt;* his only aim is self-interest. *Il vend toutes sortes d'—s;* he deals in all sorts of articles. *—s de première nécessité;* articles of indispensable use.

objurgation, *n.f.*, objurgation.

objurgatoire, *adj.*, objurgatory.

oblat, *n.m.*, ☉ lay monk.

oblation, *n.f.*, oblation, offering.

obligataire, *n.m.*, (com., fin.) bond-holder, debenture-holder.

obligation, *n.f.*, obligation; (com., fin., jur.) bond, debenture, preference share. *Remplir ses —s;* to fulfill one's obligations. *Vous êtes dans l'— de lui répondre;* you are bound to answer him. *Etre dans l'— de;* to be under an obligation to. *Porteur d'—;* (com.) bond-holder, debenture holder.

obligatoire, *adj.*, obligatory, incumbent.

obligatoirement (-tôar-mān), *adv.*, obligatorily, compulsorily.

obligé, *n.m.*, indentures (of apprenticeship).

obligé, *n.m.*, -e, *n.f.*, (jur.) obligor, debtor.

obligé, -e, *part.*, obliged, compelled, bound; necessary, usual. *Je suis — de sortir;* I am obliged to go out.

obligeamment (-ja-mān), *adv.*, obligingly.

obligeance (-jans), *n.f.*, kindness, obligingness.

obligeant, -e, *adj.*, obliging, kind.

obliger, *v.a.*, to oblige, to bind; to compel, to induce; to gratify. *Votre devoir vous y oblige;* you are bound in duty to do it. *— un apprenti;* to bind an apprentice.

s'obliger, *v.r.*, to bind one's self.

obliger, *v.n.*, to impose obligations; to oblige, to favor.

oblique, *adj.*, oblique, slanting; (fig.) indirect, unfair. *Pont —;* oblique-bridge, skew-bridge.

obliquement (o-blik-mān), *adv.*, obliquely, crookedly, indirectly, unfairly, aslant.

obliquer, *v.n.*, to walk in an oblique direction, to slant, to swerve, to turn (to).

obliquité, *n.f.*, obliquity; obliqueness; slant; unfairness.

oblitération, *n.f.*, obliteration.

oblitérer, *v.a.*, to obliterate.

s'oblitérer, *v.r.*, to become obliterated; (l.u.) to fall into disuse, to disappear.

oblong, -ue, *adj.*, oblong.

obole, *n.f.*, obole; (fig.) groat, farthing, stiver; mite, particle. *N'avoir pas une —;* not to be worth a stiver.

obombrer, *v.a.*, (Bibl.) to overshadow.

obreptice, *adj.*, obreptitious.

obrepticement (-tis-mān), *adv.*, by concealing the truth, obreptitiously.

obreption, *n.f.*, concealment of the truth, reticence, obreption.

obscène, *adj.*, obscene.

obscénité, *n.f.*, obscenity, obsceneness.

obscur, -e, *adj.*, obscure, dark, black, gloomy, sombre; (fig.) mean, humble, mysterious. *Il fait —;* it is dark. *Naissance —e;* mean birth. *Couleur —e;* dark color. *Clair-—,* (—s-—s) (paint.) light and shade.

obscurantisme, *n.m.*, obscurantism.

obscurantiste, *n.m.*, anti-educationist.

obscurcir, *v.a.*, to obscure, to darken, to dim, to sully, to tarnish, to throw into the shade. *— la vue;* to dim the sight.

s'obscurcir, *v.r.*, to become obscure, dark; to grow dim. *Le soleil s'obscurcit;* the sun is hidden. *Le ciel s'obscurcit;* the sky is overcast. *Son esprit s'obscurcit;* his intellect or mind is becoming clouded.

obscurcissement (-sis-mān), *n.m.*, obscuration, darkness, dimness.

obscurément, *adv.*, obscurely, confusedly, dimly.

obscurité, *n.f.*, obscurity, gloom, darkness; (fig.) humbleness, meanness, mysteriousness. *A travers l'— de la nuit;* through the darkness of the night.

obsécration, *n.f.*, (rhet.) obsecration.

obséder, *v.a.*, to beset; to importune, to possess (of evil spirits); to torment, to haunt.

obsèques (ob-sèk-), *n.f.pl.*, obsequies, funeral.

obséquieusement, *adv.*, obsequiously.

obséquieu-x, -se, *adj.*, obsequious.

obséquiosité, *n.f.*, obsequiousness.

observable, *adj.*, observable.

observance, *n.f.*, observance.

observantin, *n.m.*, Observant Franciscan.

observat-eur, -rice, *n.* and *adj.*, observer; observant, observing, spy, looker-on. *Un esprit —;* an observing mind.

observation, *n.f.*, observance; observation, remark, hint; (fig.) fulfillment, accomplishment. *Etre en —;* to be on the look-out.

observatoire, *n.m.*, observatory.

observer, *v.a.*, to observe, to mind, to notice; to point out (to); to watch, to keep a watch over; to practice, to fulfill, to perform. *— les lois;* to observe the laws. *Lui avez-vous fait — que?* did you point out to him that? *Faire —;* to remind, to call a person's attention to.

s'observer, *v.r.*, to be circumspect, to be cautious, to look about one's self; to eye one another; to be on one's guard; to keep a check upon one's self.

obsesseur, *adj.*, besetting.

obsession, *n.f.*, besetting, obsession; being possessed of.

obsidiane *or* **obsidienne**, *n.f.*, (min.) obsidian (volcanic glass).

obsidional, -e, *adj.*, obsidional. *Couronne —e;* obsidional crown.

obstacle, *n.m.*, obstacle, bar, hindrance, impediment, obstruction, check, drawback. *Lever un —;* to remove an impediment. *Rencontrer un —;* to meet with an obstacle. *Faire naître un —;* to raise an obstacle.

obstétrical, -e, *adj.*, obstetric, obstetrical.

obstétrique, *n.f.*, obstetrics.

obstination, *n.f.*, obstinacy, pertinacity, stubbornness, willfulness.

obstiné, -e, *adj.*, obstinate; self-willed; stubborn; determined.

obstinément, *adv.*, obstinately, stubbornly, willfully.

obstiner, *v.a.*, to make obstinate.

s'obstiner, *v.r.*, to be obstinate, to be obstinately resolved (upon), to insist (on), to persist (in). *S'— à une chose;* to persist in a thing. *Il s'obstine dans son opinion;* he clings to his opinion.

obstructi-f, -ve, *adj.*, obstructive, obstruent.

obstruction, *n.f.*, obstruction, stoppage.

obstrué, -e, *adj.*, obstructed, stopped.

obstruer, *v.a.*, to obstruct, to stop up; to block up, to bar. *S'—;* to become obstructed, knocked up.

obtempérer, *v.n.*, (jur.) to obey; to submit (to), to comply (with), to fall in (with). *— à un ordre;* to obey an order.

obtenir, *v.a.*, to obtain, to procure, to get, to gain. *— satisfaction d'un outrage;* to obtain satisfaction for an insult. *Faire —;* to get, to procure for (anybody).

s'obtenir, *v.r.*, to be obtained *or* obtainable.

obtention, *n.f.*, obtaining, obtainment, getting; (jur.) purchase.

obturateur, *n.m.*, (anat.) obturator; lid, cover.

obturat-eur, -rice, *adj.*, (anat.) obturator; obturating, covering, stopping; pubic (artery).

obturation, n.f., (surg.) covering, stopping.

obtus, -e, adj., obtuse, dull, blunt. *Angle —;* obtuse angle. *Esprit —;* dull, heavy mind.

obtusangle, adj., obtuse-angular.

obtusangulé, -e, adj., (bot.) obtuse-angled.

obus (o-buz), n.m., (artil.) shell.

obusier, n.m., (artil.) howitzer.

obvenir, v.n., (jur.) to escheat.

obvention, n.f., (ecc.) obvention.

obvers or **obverse**, n.m., obverse.

obvier, v.n., to obviate, to prevent, to hinder. *— à un inconvénient ;* to prevent an inconvenience.

oc, adv., (in Old Provençal) yes. *Langue d'—;* langue d'oc (the language south of the Loire).

oca, n.m., (bot.) oca.

occase, adj., (astron.) occasive (*i.e.* westerly).

occasion, n.f., opportunity, occasion ; cause, reason, behalf, sake ; bargain, job-lot, second-hand. *Il faut attendre l'—;* one must bide one's time. *Profiter d'une —;* to take advantage of, to improve, an opportunity. *En toute —;* on all occasions. *Dans l'—;* as occasion offers, when occasion serves. *Par —;* occasionally ; accidentally. *Je vous l'enverrai par —;* I shall send it you by private hand. *À votre —;* for your sake. *D'—;* accidentally ; second-hand. *Marchandise d'—;* second-hand goods, job-lot.

occasionnel, -le, adj., occasional.

occasionnellement (-nèl-mān), adv., occasionally.

occasionner, v.a., to occasion, to bring on, to cause, to produce.

occident, n.m., West. *D'—;* western.

occidental, -e, adj., occidental, western, westerly. *Les Indes —es;* the West Indies.

occidentaux, n.m.pl., natives, inhabitants, of the western countries.

occipital, -e, adj., occipital.

occiput (-put), n.m., occiput.

⊙**occire**, v.a., to slay, to kill, to do for.

⊙**occis**, part., killed, slain, done for.

⊙**occiseur**, n.m., murderer, killer, slayer.

⊙**occision**, n.f., killing; slaughter.

occlusion, n.f., (med.) closing, shutting up.

occultation, n.f., (astron.) occultation.

occulte, adj., occult, hidden, secret.

occupant, -e, n. and adj., occupant, possessor ; occupier ; occupying, engrossing, taking up ; (jur.) concerned (as attorney).

occupation, n.f., occupation, business, employment, work. *Donner de l'— à quelqu'un ;* to cut out work for any one.

occupé, -e, adj., busy, occupied, engaged.

occuper, v.a., to occupy, to employ ; to take up, to fill; to inhabit. *— une maison ;* to occupy a house. *— la place de quelqu'un ;* to be in any one's place. *Il faut — les jeunes gens;* youth must have occupation.

s'occuper à (habitual) *or de* (particular), v.r., to occupy one's self ; to be busy, to apply one's self, to attend to, to trouble one's self about. *S'— à lire ;* to be busy reading. *Je m'occupe de votre affaire ;* I am looking after or attending to your business.

occuper, v.n., (jur.) to be concerned as attorney, to appear ; to plead.

occurrence (o-kur-rans), n.f., occurrence, emergency.

occurrent, -e, adj., (l.u.) occurring, occurrent.

océan, n.m., ocean; the high seas.

océanide, n.f., (myth.) Oceanide, nymph of the Sea, daughter of the Ocean.

océanique, adj., oceanic.

ocelle, n.m., ocellus.

ocellé, -e, adj., ocellated.

ochlocratie (o-klo-cra-ci), n.f., ochlocracy.

⊙**ochre**, n.f. V. **ocre**.

ocre, n.f., ochre.

ocreu-x, -se, adj., ochry, ochreous.

octaèdre, n.m., (geom.) octahedron.

octaédrique, adj., (geom.) octahedral.

octandre, adj., (bot.) octandrian, octandrous.

octandrie, n.f., (bot.) octandria.

octant, n.m., octant ; quadrant.

⊙**octante**, adj., eighty, fourscore.

⊙**octantième** (-tièm), adj., eightieth.

octarchie (-shi), n.f., octarchy.

octave, n.f., octave; eight.

octavin, n.m., octave-flute.

octavo, adv., eighthly. V. **in-octavo**.

octavon, n.m., -ne, n.f., octoroon, mustee, person one-eighth black.

octidi, n.m., octidi, eighth day of the decade in the calendar of the first French republic.

octil, adj.m., (astron.) octile.

octobre, n.m., October.

octogénaire, n.m.f. and adj., octogenary, octogenarian.

octogone, n.m. and adj., octagon; octagonal.

octostyle, adj., octostyle.

octroi, n.m., grant; concession ; town-dues, toll, duty; octroi, toll-house or office.

octroyer, v.a., to grant, to concede.

octuple, adj., eightfold, octuple.

octupler, v.a., (l.u.) to increase eightfold.

oculaire, adj., ocular. *Témoin —;* eye-witness. *Verre —;* eye-glass.

oculaire, n.m., (opt.) eye-glass, eye-piece, eye-end.

oculairement (-lèr-mān), adv., ocularly.

oculiste, n.m., oculist.

odalisque, n.f., odalisk, odalisque.

ode, n.f., ode.

odelette, n.f., (poet.) odelet.

odéon or **odéum**, n.m., Odeon (name of a theatre in Paris).

odeur, n.f., odor, smell, scent, fragrancy, perfume. *N'être pas en — de sainteté auprès de quelqu'un ;* not to be in the good graces of any one. *En — de sainteté ;* in the Lord; in favor.

odieusement (-eûz-mān), adv., odiously, hatefully.

odieu-x, -se, adj., odious, hateful, loathsome, invidious. *Se rendre —;* to make one's self odious.

odieux, n.m., odium, hatefulness, invidiousness. *L'— de la chose ;* the hateful part of the business.

odomètre, n.m., odometer, pedometer. V. **pédomètre**.

odontalgie, n.f., odontalgia, toothache, odontalgy.

odontalgique, n.m. and adj., odontalgic.

odontoïde, adj., (anat.) odontoid.

odontologie, n.f., (anat.) odontology.

odorant, -e, adj., odoriferous, fragrant, sweet-smelling.

odorat, n.m., smell ; smelling ; sense of smell.

odoriférant, -e, adj., odoriferous, fragrant, sweet-scented or smelling.

odyssée, n.f., Odyssey.

œcuménicité, n.f., œcumenicity.

œcuménique, adj., œcumenical.

œcuméniquement, adv., œcumenically.

œdémateu-x, -se, adj., œdematous.

œdème, n.m., (med.) œdema.

œdipe, n.m., riddle-solver.

œgagre (égagr), n.m., wild goat.

œil (eu-ye), n.m., (yeux) eye, look ; bud ; luster, gloss ; (bot.) ox-eye, daisy ; hole (in bread, cheese) ; (print.) face ; bubble (of soup) ; luster (of precious stones) ; eye (of a needle). *Clin d'—;* twinkle. *En un clin d'—;* in the twinkling of an eye. *Un beau coup d'—;* a fine prospect or view or spectacle. *Le premier coup d'—;* the first glance or sight of. *D'un coup d'—;* at a glance. *Avoir mal aux yeux ;* to have sore eyes. *Regarder quelqu'un du coin de l'—;*

to glance at, to ogle, to leer. *Regarder quelqu'un entre les deux yeux;* to look any one full in the face. *Entre quatre yeux;* in private, between ourselves. *Ouvrir de grands yeux;* to stare, to stare with one's eyes wide open. *Avoir l'— à quelque chose;* to have an eye upon anything, to mind, to attend to. *Avoir l'— sur;* to watch any one, to see to anything. *Suivre de l'—;* to follow with the eye, to watch. *Le soleil me donne dans les yeux;* the sun dazzles my eyes. *La lumière me tire les yeux;* the light hurts my eyes. *Cela lui blesse les yeux;* that is an eyesore to him. *A vue d'—;* visibly. *Donner dans l'— à quelqu'un;* to take any one's fancy. *Avoir le compas dans l'—;* to have a good eye for distances. *Avoir le coup d'—;* to have a carpenter's eye. *Faire les yeux doux;* to look lovingly (at), to cast loving glances (at). *Dévorer quelqu'un des yeux;* to look any one through and through. *S'en battre l'—;* not to care a rap about. *Couver des yeux;* to look lovingly (on). *Dévorer une chose des yeux;* to look upon a thing with greedy eyes. *Cela saute aux yeux;* it is obvious; it is as clear as noonday. *Avoir un bandeau sur les yeux;* to be blindfolded. *Pour vos beaux yeux;* for your pretty face or for nothing. *Je lui ai poché l'—;* I gave him a black eye. *Il a de bons yeux;* he is sharp-sighted. *Il n'a des yeux que pour elle;* he sees nothing but her. *Fermer les yeux sur quelque chose;* to connive at, to wink at anything. *Se mettre le doigt dans l'—;* to delude or flatter one's self. *N'avoir pas froid aux yeux;* not to funk; not to stick at trifles; not to be afraid of one's shadow. *Mais! votre chapeau vous crève les yeux;* why, your hat is staring you in the face. *Avoir les yeux battus;* to have a tired look about the eyes. *Avoir les yeux cernés;* to have dark circles round the eyes. *Des yeux à fleur de tête;* goggle-eyes. *Voir de bon —;* to look favorably (on). *Voir de mauvais —;* to look unfavorably (on).

œil-de-bœuf, *n.m.,* (—s—) bull's eye; round or oval window; ⊙a waiting-room in the royal palace at Versailles.

œil-de-chat, *n.m.,* (—s—) (min.) cat's-eye.

œil-de-perdrix, *n.m.,* (yeux-—) soft corn (on the foot).

œil-de-serpent, *n.m.,* (—s—) (min.) serpentine-stone.

œil-d'or, *n.m.,* (—s—) (ich.) gold-finny.

*œillade,** *n.f.,* glance, ogle, sheep's eye. *Jeter des —s;* to cast glances (at), to ogle.

œillère, *adj.f.,* of the eye. *Dent —;* canine tooth.

*œillère,** *n.f.,* eye-flap, blinker (of a horse); canine tooth.

*œillet,** *n.m.,* (bot.) carnation, pink; (nav.) eye; eyelet; eyelet-hole. *— de poète;* sweet william.

*œilleton,** *n.m.,* (hort.) offset; layer.

*œillette,** *n.f.,* field-poppy.

œnanthe, *n.f.,* (bot.) watery drop-wort.

œnologie, *n.f.,* wine-making.

œnomancie, *n.f.,* (antiq.) œnomancy (divination by wine).

œnomètre, *n.m.,* œnometer (to ascertain the strength of wine).

œnophile, *n.m.,* œnophilist. *Société —,* wine company.

œnophore, *n.m.,* (antiq.) wine vessel, goblet.

œsophage, *n.m.,* œsophagus, gullet.

œsophagien, -ne (-in, -é-n), *adj.,* pertaining to the œsophagus.

œstre, *n.m.,* (ent.) œstrus, gad-fly.

œuf (euf), *n.m.,* (œufs) (eû) *pl. pl.,* roe (of a fish). *—s pochés;* poached eggs. *—s à la coque;* boiled eggs. *—s brouillés;* buttered eggs. *— couvi;* addled egg. *— frais;* new-laid egg. *—s sur le plat, —s au miroir;* fried eggs. *Plein*

comme un —; as full as an egg. *Il tondrait sur un —;* he would skin a flint. *Mettre tous ses —s dans un panier;* to risk all in one enterprise. *Donner un — pour avoir un bœuf,* to give a sprat to catch a herring. *Faire d'un — un bœuf;* to make mountains out of mole-hills.

œuvé, -e, *adj.,* hard-roed (of fish).

œuvre, *n.f.,* work, piece of work; works (of an author); production, performance; deed, act; bezel, setting (of a stone); church-wardens' pew; fabric (fund appropriated for the repairs of a church). *— de piété, — de charité;* act of piety, of charity. *—s pies;* pious works. *Une — de génie;* a work of genius. *La fin couronne l'—;* all 's well that ends well. *A l'— on connaît l'ouvrier;* the workman is known by his work. *A bon jour, bonne —;* the better the day, the better the deed. *Maître des hautes —s;* hangman. *Maître des basses —s;* nightman. *Mettre en —;* to make use of, to work up, to bring to bear; to set (jewelry). *Mettre tout en —;* to leave no stone unturned. *—s inédites;* unpublished works. *—s posthumes;* posthumous works. *—s mêlées;* miscellaneous works, miscellanea.

œuvre, *n.m.,* work; (arch.) clear; works of musicians and engravers; performance; (metal.) argentiferous lead. *Gros —;* outer wall. *Travailler au grand —;* to seek the philosopher's stone. *Dans —;* (arch.) apart, inside; clear, in the clear. *Hors d'—;* (arch.) from out to out. *Sous —;* (mas.) underpinning. *A pied d'—;* at hand, in the neighborhood, near.

œuvrer, *v.a.,* to work.

offensant, -e, *adj.,* offensive, obnoxious, abusive.

offense, *n.f.,* offense, affront, insult, injury, wrong; (jur.) contempt, transgression, trespass. *Demander réparation d'une —;* to demand satisfaction for an offense. *Pardonner les —s;* to forgive offenses. *Expier une —;* to atone for an offense.

offensé, *n.m.,* offended party.

offenser, *v.a.,* to offend, to give offense; to hurt, to injure, to insult, to abuse, to shock; to be offensive to, to offend against. *Le coup lui a offensé le cerveau;* the blow hurt his brain. *—la délicatesse;* to offend against delicacy.

s'offenser, *v.r.,* to be offended, to take exception (to), to take offense (at).

offenseur, *n.m.,* offender.

offensi-f, -ve, *adj.,* offensive (attack).

offensive, *n.f.,* offensive.

offensivement (-siv-mǎn), *adv.,* offensively.

offerte, *n.f.,* or **offertoire,** *n.m.,* (c.rel.) offertory.

office, *n.m.,* office; duty; employment, functions; service, turn; worship. *D'—;* officially, ex-officio. *Avocat nommé d'—;* counsel appointed by the judge. *Faire quelque chose d'—;* to do a thing of one's own accord. *C'est un — d'ami que vous lui avez rendu;* it is a friendly turn you have done him. *Rendre un mauvais — à quelqu'un;* to do any one an ill-turn. *L'— divin;* divine service, church-time. *Livre d'—;* prayer-book. *Exercer un —;* to hold an office. *Le saint-—;* the holy-office, the Inquisition.

office, *n.f.,* servants' hall, pantry, larder, steward's room. *pl.* dependencies of the kitchen.

official, *n.m.,* (ecc.) official.

officialité, *n.f.,* officiality.

officiant, *n.* and *adj. m.,* officiating priest, officiating clergyman; officiating.

officiante, *n.f.,* officiating nun.

officiel, -le, *adj.,* official.

officiellement (-èl-mǎn), *adv.,* officially.

officier, *v.n.,* to officiate; to play one's part; to do one's duty at table, to eat heartily.

officier, *n.m.,* officer; butler, steward. *— de marine;* naval officer. *— général;* general officer, (nav.) flag-officer. *— d'état-major;* staff-officer.

— **supérieur;** field-officer. — **de compagnie;** regimental officer. — **de justice;** law-officer. — **de port;** harbor-master. — **de santé;** medical officer; surgeon. **Sous——;** non-commissioned officer. —**s de la bouche;** king's cooks. —**s du gobelet;** king's butlers.

officieusement (-eûz-mãn), *adv.,* officiously, obligingly.

officieuseté, *n.f.,* officiousness.

officieu-x, -se, *n.* and *adj.,* busy-body; officious, obliging.

officinal, -e, *adj.,* (pharm.) officinal.

officine, *n.f.,* an apothecary's laboratory.

offrande, *n.f.,* offering, present.

offrant, *adj.m.,* bidding. *Au plus — et dernier enchérisseur,* to the highest and last bidder.

offrant, *n.m.,* bidder.

offre, *n.f.,* offer, tender, proposal.

offrir (offrant, offert), *v.a.,* to offer, to propose, to tender; to present; to afford, to give, to yield; to bid. — *un présent;* to offer a present.

s'offrir, *v.r.,* to offer, to propose one's self; to offer. *Si l'occasion s'offre;* if occasion offers.

offuscation, *n.f.,* (astron.) obfuscation (of the sun's rays).

offusquer, *v.a.,* to obscure, to darken, to eclipse, to cloud; to dazzle, to blind; to offend. *Le soleil m'offusque les yeux,* the sun dazzles my eyes. *Cet artiste a un rival qui l'offusque;* that artist has a rival who stands in his light.

s'offusquer, *v.r.,* to become darkened; (fig.) to take offense.

ogival, -e, *adj.,* (arch.) pointed.

ogive, *n.f.,* ogive, pointed arch. *En* —; ogival, pointed.

*ognon, n.m. V. **oignon.**

*ognonnet, n.m. V. **oignonnet.**

*ognonnière, n.f. V. **oignonnière.**

ogre, *n.m.,* ogre. *Il mange comme un* —; he eats like a wolf.

ogresse, *n.f.,* ogress.

oh! *int.,* O! ho!

oïdium, *n.m.,* (*n.p.*) (agri.) oidium, vine-mildew.

oie, *n.f.,* (orni.) goose; simpleton, ninny. *Plume d'—;* goose-quill. — *de mer;* merganser. *Contes de ma mère l'—;* tales of Mother Goose, fairy tales. *Jeu de l'—;* game of goose. *Patte d'—;* goose-foot; (fig.) crow's foot, cross- (of roads).

*oignon, n.m., onion; bulb, bulbous root; bunion; turnip (watch). *Regretter les —s d'Egypte;* to sigh for or hanker after the flesh-pots of Egypt. *Chapelet d'—s;* ropeway of onions. *Un — de tulipe;* a tulip bulb. *Etre en rang d'—;* to be all in a row, in a file. *Se mettre en rang d'—;* to take one's place in a row.

*oignonet, n.m., ognonet (summer pear).

*oignonière, n.f., onion-bed.

oïl, *adv.,* (old French) yes. *Langue d'—;* language spoken north of the Loire.

☉**oille* (o-ye), *n.f.,* (cook.) olio.

oindre (oignant, oint),*v.a.,* to anoint. *Oignez vilain, il vous poindra, Poignez vilain, il vous oindra* (*i.e.* if not oppressed, the churls will become oppressors).

oing (oin), *n.m.,* hog's-grease, cart-grease. *Vieux* —; cart-grease, axle-grease.

oint, *n.m.,* anointed. *L'— du Seigneur;* the Lord's anointed.

oiseau, *n.m.,* bird; creature (pers.); (mas.) fellow, chap, bird, fish, hod. — *de proie;* bird of prey. *Tirer aux* —*x;* to go out fowling. — *moqueur;* mocking-bird. *Chasse aux* —*x;* bird-shooting. *Plan à vue d'—;* bird's-eye view. *Il est comme l'— sur la branche;* he is unsettled; he is always on the move. *La belle cage ne nourrit pas l'—;* a fine cage does not fill a bird's belly. *Petit à petit l'— fait son nid;* little strokes fell great oaks. *Il a battu les buissons, un autre a*

pris l'—; he did the work, another stole the profits. *A tout — son nid est beau;* home is home, be it ever so homely. *A vol d'—;* as the crow flies, in a straight line. — *mouche,* (—*x* —*s*) humming-bird. — *trompette;* (orni.) trumpeter. —*x de passage;* birds of passage. —*x de basse-cour;* fowls, poultry. —*x voyageurs;* migratory birds.

oiseler (oa-zlé), *v.a.,* (hawking) to train a bird.

oiseler, *v.n.,* to catch birds.

oiselet, *n.m.,* little bird.

oiseleur (oa-zleur), *n.m.,* bird-catcher.

oiselier, *n.m.,* bird-seller, dealer in birds.

oisellerie (oa-zèl-rî), *n.f.,* bird-catching; bird-trade.

oiseu-x, -se, *adj.,* indolent, idle, useless, trifling. *Mener une vie —se;* to live in idleness. *Paroles —ses;* idle words.

oisi-f, -ve, *adj.,* idle, unoccupied; uninvested, lying dead (of money).

oisif, *n.m.,* idler.

*oisillon, n.m., young bird, fledgling.

oisiveté (oa-ziv-mãn), *adv.,* idly.

oisiveté (oa-ziv-té), *n.f.,* idleness, indolence, ease; sloth. *Croupir dans l'—;* to be steeped, or to wallow, in indolence.

oison, *n.m.,* gosling; ninny, simpleton.

oléagineu-x, -se, *adj.,* oleaginous, oily.

oléandre, *n.m.,* (bot.) oleander, rose-bay.

oléifère, *adj.,* oil-bearing, oleiferous.

oléine, *n.f.,* (chem.) oleine.

oléique, *adj.* (chem.) oleic.

oléracé, -e, *adj.,* oleraceous.

olfacti-f, -ve, *adj.,* olfactory.

oliban, *n.m.,* (pharm.) olibanum.

olibrius (-ûs) *n.m.,* conceited, obtrusive person.

oliette, *n.f.* V. **œillette.**

oligarchie, *n.f.,* oligarchy.

oligarchique, *adj.,* oligarchical.

oligarque, *n.m.,* partisan of an oligarchy.

oligiste, *adj.,* (min.) oligist.

olim, *n.m.,* (—) statute-book.

olinde, *n.f.,* sword-blade.

olivaie, *n.f.,* olive-grove.

olivaire, *adj.,* olivary.

olivaison, *n.f.,* olive season, crop of olives.

olivâtre, *adj.,* olivaceous, olive-green.

olive, *n.f.,* (bot.) olive; (arch.) olive-molding. *Branche, rameau, d'—;* olive branch.

olivète, *n.f.* (bot.) V. **œillette.**

olivettes, *n.f. pl.,* sort of dance after the olives are gathered.

olivier, *n.m.,* olive-tree, olive, olive wood.

ollaire, *adj.f.,* soft (of stones easy to cut); *Pierre —;* potstone.

olla podrida, *n.f.,* (—) olio; olla podrida, hotch-potch.

ollure, *n.f.,* tanner's leather apron.

olographe, *adj.,* holographic, holographical. *Testament —;* will written in the testator's own hand. V. **holographe.**

olographe, *n.m.,* holograph.

olonier, *n.m.,* (bot.) strawberry-tree; cane-apple.

olympe, *n.m.,* Olympus.

olympiade, *n.f.,* Olympiad.

olympien (-pi-in), **-ne** (-pi-è-n), *adj.,* Olympian.

olympique, *adj.,* Olympic.

ombelle, *n.f.,* (bot.) umbel, cluster of blossoms.

ombellé, -e (on-bèl-lé), *adj.,* (bot.) umbellar, umbellated, umbellate.

ombellifère (-bèl-li-), *n.f.* and *adj.,* (bot.) umbelliferous plant; umbelliferous.

ombellule (on-bèl-lul), *n.f.,* (bot.) umbellet, umbellule.

ombilic, *n.m.,* (anat.) umbilic, umbilicus, navel; (bot.) hilum, umbilicus.

ombilical, -e, *adj.,* umbilic, umbilical. *Cordon* —; umbilical cord, navel.

ombiliqué, -e, *adj.,* (bot.) umbilicate, umbilicated.

ombrage, *n.m.,* shade, umbrage, suspicion, distrust. *Faire* —; to overshadow. *Les* —*s verts;* shade of green foliage. *Donner de l'*— *à;* to give umbrage to. *Tout lui porte* —; he takes unbrage at everything.

ombrager, *v.a.,* to shade; to cover; to hide, to conceal.

ombrageu-x, -se, *adj.,* skittish (of horses); suspicious, distrustful.

ombre, *n.f.,* shade; shadow; spirit; background; gloom; pretense. *S'endormir à l'*— *d'un arbre;* to sleep under the shade of a tree. *Se mettre à l'*—; to get into the shade. *L'*— *suit le corps;* the shadow follows the body. *Couvrir d'*—; to shade. *Les* —*s de la nuit;* the shades of night. *Avoir peur de son* —; to be afraid of one's own shadow. *Faire* — *à quelqu'un;* to eclipse any one, to throw any one into the shade, to give umbrage to any one. *Mettre à l'*—; to put into the shade; to shade; (pop.) to give his quietus to any one. —*s chinoises;* dissolving views. *Couvert d'*—, shady.

ombre, *n.m.,* (ich.) umbra; ombre (card game). — *de rivière;* red charr, grayling. *terre d'***ombre,** *n.f.,* black-ochre, umber.

ombré, -e, *part.,* tinted, shaded.

ombrelle, *n.f.,* parasol.

ombrer, *v.a.,* (drawing, paint.) to tint, to shade.

ombreu-x, -se, *adj.,* shady, cool.

ombromètre, *n.m.,* ombrometer, rain-gauge.

oméga, *n.m.,* omega.

omelette (o-mlèt), *n.f.,* omelet.

omettre, *v.a.,* to omit, to leave out, to pass over, to leave undone.

omission, *n.f.,* omission. *Sauf erreur ou* —; errors excepted.

omnibus, *n.m.,* omnibus; (pers.) general servant, maid of all work.

omnipotence, *n.f.,* omnipotence.

omnipotent, *adj.,* omnipotent.

omniprésence, *n.f.,* omnipresence, ubiquity.

omniprésent, -e, *adj.,* ubiquitous, omnipresent.

omniscience, *n.f.,* omniscience.

omnium (-om), *n.m.,* (fin.) omnium; (turf) consolation stakes.

omnivore, *adj.,* omnivorous.

omoplate, *n.f.,* omoplate, scapula, shoulder-blade.

omphalode, *n.m.,* (bot.) omphalode.

on, *pron.,* one, they, we, you, people, men, it, somebody. — *croirait;* one would think. — *dit;* they say; it is said. — *s'imagine;* people think. — *croit;* it is thought. — *me l'a dit;* I was told so. *Que dira-t-on?* what will people say? *Se moquer du qu'en dira-t-on;* not to care what people say. *Croire sur un* — *dit, sur des* — *dit;* to believe upon hearsay. *Si l'on me croit;* if I am believed.

onagre, *n.m.,* (mam., antiq.) onager; (bot.) œnothera.

onanisme, *n.m.,* onanism.

⊙**onc, onques,** *adv.,* never.

once, *n.f.,* (weight) ounce; (mam.) ounce.

oncial, *n.m.,* (l.u.). *V.* **onciale.**

onciale, *n.* and *adj.f.,* uncial.

oncle, *n.m.,* uncle; (pop.) money-lender, usurer. — *à la mode de Bretagne;* father *or* mother's cousin german.

onction, *n.f.,* unction; anointing; grace, impressiveness. *L'extrême* —; (c. rel.) extreme unction, last sacrament.

onctueusement (-eûz-mān), *adv.,* impressively, unctuously.

onctueu-x, -se, *adj.,* unctuous, oily; impressive, moving. *Une terre* —*se;* fat earth. *Un sermon* —; an impressive *or* moving sermon.

onctuosité, *n.f.,* unctuousness, oiliness.

onde, *n.f.,* wave, billow, surge; watering. *L'*— *amère;* the briny main. *Passer l'*— *noire;* to cross the Stygian lake. *Les* —*s d'un bois veiné;* the waves of a piece of veined wood.

ondé, -e, *adj.,* undulated, watered, curled, grained.

ondée, *n.f.,* shower. *Une forte* —; a sharp, tremendous shower; a downpour.

ondin, *n.m.,* -e, *n.f.,* water-sprite, Undine.

ondoiement (-doa-mān), *n.m.,* undulation, swaying motion, private baptism.

ondoyant, -e, *adj.,* undulating, waving, flowing. *Fumée* —*e;* waving smoke. *Vagues* —*es;* waving, surging, swaying billows.

ondoyer, *v.n.,* to undulate, to rise in billows, to wave; to surge.

ondoyer, *v.a.,* to baptize privately.

ondulant, *adj.,* undulating, waving, flowing.

ondulation, *n.f.,* undulation; waving.

ondulatoire, *adj.,* undulatory.

ondulé, *adj.,* undulate, undulated.

onduler, *v.n.,* to undulate, to wave, to curl.

onduleu-x, -se, *adj.,* undulating, flowing, waving.

onéraire, *adj.,* (jur.) acting, accountable.

onéreu-x, -se, *adj.,* burdensome, onerous, heavy.

ongle, *n.m.,* nail (of fingers, claws); claw; hoof. *Couper, ronger, ses* —*s;* to cut, to gnaw, one's nails. *Coup d'*—*s;* scratch. *Jusqu'au bout des* —*s;* to one's fingers' ends *or* tips; every inch. *Rogner les* —*s à quelqu'un;* to clip any one's wings. *Sur l'*—; perfectly. *Avoir bec et* —*s;* to be armed; to defend one's self tooth and nail.

onglée, *n.f.,* numbness of the fingers (from cold).

onglet, *n.m.,* finger-case; (bot.) aiglet; (engr.) graver; (print.) single leaf cancel. *Assemblage à* —; miter (joinery).

onglette, *n.f.,* (engr.) flat graver.

onglon, *n.m.,* hoof (of ruminants); nail (of tortoises).

onguent (on-gan), *n.m.,* ointment, salve. *Dans les petites boîtes, les bons* —*s;* small parcels hold fine wares.

onguiculé, -e (-gu-i-), *adj.,* unguiculate, unguiculated.

onguiforme (-gu-i-) *adj.,* unguiform.

ongulé, -e, *adj.,* hoofed, ungulate.

onirocritie (-cri-ci) *or* **onirocritique,** *n.f.,* interpretation of dreams, oneiroscopy.

oniromance *or* **oniromancie,** *n.f.,* oneiromancy.

onocrotale, *n.m.,* (orni.) pelican.

onomatopée, *n.f.,* (gram.) onomatopœia.

ontologie, *n.f.,* ontology.

ontologique, *adj.,* ontological.

ontologiste, *n.m.,* ontologist.

onyx (o-niks), *n.m.* and *adj.,* onyx.

onzaine, *n.f.,* about eleven, eleven *or* so; an eleven (at cricket).

onze, *n.m.* and *adj.,* eleven, eleventh. [*Onze, onzième, onzaine,* do not admit of being preceded by *l',* say, therefore, *du onze, au onzième, la onzaine*]. *Le* — *du mois;* the eleventh of the month.

onzième, *n.m.* and *adj.,* eleventh.

onzième, *n.f.,* (mus.) eleventh.

onzièmement (on-zièm-mān), *adv.,* eleventhly, in the eleventh place.

oolithe, *n.m.,* oolite.

oolithique, *adj.,* oolitic.

opacité, *n.f.,* opaqueness, opacity, darkness.

opale, *n.f.,* opal.

opalescence, *n.f.,* opalescence.

opalin, -e, *adj.,* opaline.

s'opaliser, *v.r.,* to opalize, to become opalized.

opaque, *adj.,* opaque.

opéra, *n.m.,* opera, opera-house. *C'est un vrai —;* it is a perfect imbroglio.

opérant, -e, *adj.,* operating.

opérat-eur, *n.m.,* **-rice,** *n.f.,* operator; mountebank, quack.

opérati-f, -ve, *adj.,* operative.

opération, *n.f.,* operation, working, performance ; (fin.) transaction. *Subir une —;* to undergo an operation. *Terminer une —;* to close a transaction.

opératoire, *adj.,* operative. *Médecine —;* surgery.

operculaire, *adj.,* (bot.) operculate, operculated.

opercule, *n.m.,* operculum, cover.

operculé, -e, *adj.,* opercular, operculated.

opérer, *v.a.,* to operate, to effect, to bring about, to perform, to work, to act ; to manage, to contrive. *Se faire —;* to undergo an operation.

opérer, *v.n.,* to work, to operate.

s'opérer, *v.r.,* to take place, to come about, to be brought about.

opérette, *n.f.,* operetta.

opes, *n.m. pl.,* (arch.) opes ; (mas.) scaffold-holes, putlog holes.

ophicléide, *n.m.,* ophicleide.

ophidien, -ne (-di-in, -è-n), *adj.,* ophidian.

ophidiens (-di-in), *n.m. pl.,* ophidians.

ophioglosse, *n.m.,* (bot.) ophioglossum. *V.* **langue-de-serpent.**

ophiologie, *n.f.,* ophiology.

ophiologiste, *n.m.,* ophiologist.

ophite, *n.m.,* (min.) ophite.

ophtalmie, *n.f.,* ophthalmia, ophthalmy.

ophtalmique, *adj.,* ophthalmic.

ophtalmographie, *n.f.,* ophthalmography.

ophtalmologie, *n.f.,* ophthalmology.

ophtalmoscope, *n.m.,* ophthalmoscope.

opiacé, -e, *adj.,* (med.) containing opium.

opiat, *n.m.,* opiate.

opilati-f, -ve, *adj.,* (med.) obstruent.

opilation, *n.f.,* (med.) obstruction.

opiler, *v.a.,* (med.) to obstruct.

opimes, *adj.f.pl.,* opima. *Dépouilles —;* opima spolia.

opinant, *n.m.,* speaker, adviser, voter. *adj.,* speaking, advising.

opiner, *v.n.,* to opine, to speak, to give one's opinion, to be of opinion; to advise, to conclude. *Les juges opinèrent à la mort ;* the judges decided for death. *— du bonnet ;* to vote blindly; to concur entirely; to nod assent.

opineur, *n.m.,* opiner.

opiniâtre, *adj.,* stubborn, obstinate, headstrong, self-willed. *Le combat fut —;* the fight was a stubborn one. *Un mal —;* an obstinate, unyielding disease.

opiniâtre, *n.m.f.,* stubborn person. *Je hais les —s ;* I hate stubborn people.

opiniâtrément, *adv.,* obstinately, stubbornly.

⊙**opiniâtrer,** *v.a.,* to contradict, to tease ; to maintain a thing obstinately, to render obstinate.

s'opiniâtrer, *v.r.,* to be obstinate; to insist upon doing. *Ils s'y sont opiniâtrés ;* they obstinately persisted in it.

opiniâtreté, *n.f.,* obstinacy, stubbornness, self-will. *Il suit son entreprise avec —;* he pursues his scheme with pertinacity.

opinion, *n.f.,* opinion, vote, public opinion. *Chacun motiva son —;* every one gave his reasons for his opinion. *Les —s sont partagées ;* opinions are divided. *Résumer les —s ;* to sum up the opinions. *Aller aux —s ;* to put it to the vote. *Recueillir les —s ;* to collect the votes. *C'est une affaire d'—;* it is a mere matter of opinion. *Il a bonne — de lui-même ;* he has a great opinion of himself.

opisthodome, *n.m.,* (antiq.) opisthodome.

opisthographe, *adj.,* (paleography) written on both sides.

opium (o-piom), *n.m.,* opium.

opobalsamum (-sa-mom), *n.m.,* (pharm.) opobalsam, balm of Gilead.

opodeldoch, *n.m.,* opodeldoc.

opossum (-som), *n.m.,* (mam.) opossum.

opportun, -e, *adj.,* opportune, convenient, seasonable, timely, well-timed, expedient.

opportunément, *adv.,* opportunely, seasonably.

opportunité, *n.f.,* opportuneness, seasonableness, expediency ; opportunity.

opposable, *adj.,* opposable.

opposant, -e, *n.* and *adj.,* opponent, adversary; opposing, opposite, adverse.

opposé, -e, *adj.,* opposite, contrary ; facing; disinclined. *Deux armées —es l'une à l'autre ;* two armies opposed one to the other.

opposé, *n.m.,* opposite, reverse, contrary. *Il est tout l'— de son père ;* he is quite the opposite of his father.

opposer, *v.a.,* to oppose; to put in opposition; (jur.) to place opposite; to compare; to plead, to urge. *— la force à la force ;* to oppose force to force.

s'opposer, *v.r.,* to be opposed, to set one's self against, to resist, to stem, to object, to combat, to stand in the way (of). *S'— à quelque chose :* to be opposed to anything. *Vous vous y opposez ;* you stand in the way.

opposite, *n.m.,* (l.u.) opposite, contrary, reverse. *C'est tout l'— de l'autre ;* it is quite the reverse of the other. *A l'—;* over, against, opposite. *A l'— du camp ;* opposite the camp.

opposition, *n.f.,* opposition, resistance; contrast, contradistinction; (jur.) attachment. *Former — à la publication des bans ;* to forbid the bans. *Le parti de l'—;* the opposition (party). *— d'humeur ;* difference of temper.

oppresser, *v.a.,* to oppress, to depress, to deject. *L'excès de nourriture oppresse l'estomac ;* excess of food oppresses the stomach. *Le chagrin l'oppresse ;* grief depresses him.

oppresseur, *n.m.,* oppressor. *adj.m.,* oppressive.

oppressi-f, -ve, *adj.,* oppressive.

oppression, *n.f.,* oppression.

oppressivement (-siv-mān), *adv.,* oppressively.

opprimant, -e, *adj.,* oppressing.

opprimé, -e, *part.,* oppressed.

opprimer, *v.a.,* to oppress; to overwhelm, to crush. *Malheur à ceux qui oppriment !* woe to the oppressors !

opprobre, *n.m.,* opprobrium, shame, disgrace, reproach. *Etre l'— de sa famille ;* to be the disgrace of one's family.

optati-f, -ve, *adj.,* optative.

optatif, *n.m.,* (gram.) optative.

opter, *v.n.,* to choose, to declare. *Il faut qu'il opte entre ces deux emplois ;* he must choose between (for or against) those two occupations.

opticien (-si-in), *n.m.,* optician.

optimé (-mé), *adv.,* bravo, capital, very well, perfectly well.

optimisme, *n.m.,* optimism.

optimiste, *n.m.f.* and *adj.,* optimist; of optimists.

option, *n.f.,* option, choice. *Avoir l'—;* to have the choice. *Je vous en laisse l'—;* I leave you the choice.

optique, *adj.,* optic, optical. *Le nerf —;* the optic nerve. *Illusion —;* optical illusion.

optique, *n.f.,* optics; perspective. *Les illusions de l'—;* the deceptions of optics. *L'— du théâtre ;* stage illusion.

opulemment (-la-mān), *adv.,* opulently.

opulence, *n.f.,* opulence, wealth, affluence,

riches. *Nager dans l'—;* to be possessed of great wealth; to be rolling in money.

opulent, -e, *adj.,* opulent, wealthy, affluent.

opuntia (o-pon-sia), *n.f.,* (bot.) opuntia, prickly pear.

opuscule, *n.m.,* opuscule, pamphlet, tract.

or, *n.m.,* gold; (her.) or. — *affiné;* refined gold. — *moulu;* ormolu. *Paillettes d'—;* gold spangles. *Vaisselle d'—;* gold plate. — *monnayé;* gold specie. — *vierge;* native gold. *Acheter quelque chose au poids de l'—;* to pay very dear for anything. *Etre tout cousu d'—;* to be rolling in riches. *C'est de l'— en barre;* it is as good as ready money. *Il dit* or *parle d'—;* he talks admirably. *Promettre des monts d'—;* to promise all manner of things. *Tout ce qui reluit n'est pas —;* all is not gold that glitters. *Le nombre d'—;* (astron.) the golden number. *L'âge d'—;* the golden age. *Des jours filés d'— et de soie;* happy days, halcyon days.

or, *conj.,* but, now; well; pray. — *sus, commençons;* now, let us begin. — *çà;* now, well now.

oracle, *n.m.,* oracle. *En —;* like an oracle.

orage, *n.m.,* storm, tempest, thunderstorm; (fig.) tumult, disorder, calamity. *Nous aurons de l'—;* we shall have a storm, or a thunderstorm. *Un — mêlé d'éclairs et de tonnerre;* a storm with thunder and lightning. *Chercher un abri contre l'—;* to seek shelter from the storm. *Le temps est à l'—;* the weather is stormy or threatening. *Laisser passer l'—;* to let the storm blow over. *Les —s des passions;* the tempests of the passions.

orageusement, *adv.,* tempestuously, turbulently, boisterously.

orageu-x, -se, *adj.,* stormy, tempestuous, thundery; agitated, restless. *Une mer —se;* a tempestuous sea. *Saison —se;* stormy season. *Mener une vie —se;* to lead an agitated life.

oraison, *n.f.,* speech; oration; orison, prayer. *Une — funèbre;* a funeral oration. *Faire une —;* to say a prayer. *L'— dominicale;* the Lord's prayer.

oral, *n.m.,* vail (used by the pope, and formerly by women).

oral, -e, *adj.,* oral, verbal, viva voce.

oralement (-al-mān), *adv.,* orally; verbally.

orange, *n.f.,* orange. — *douce;* sweet orange. *Ecorce d'—;* orange-peel. *Rouelle d'—* slice of orange. *Fleur d'—;* orange flower.

orangé, -e, *adj.,* orange-colored.

orangé, *n.m.,* orange-color.

orangeade (-jad), *n.f.,* orangeade.

orangeat (-ja), *n.m.,* candied orange-peel.

oranger, *n.m.,* orange-tree; orange-man.

orangère, *n.f.,* orange-woman.

orangerie (o-ranj-rî), *n.f.,* orange-house; orange-grove, orangery.

orangiste, *n.m.,* orange-grower; orange-man.

orang-outang, *n.m.,* orang-outang.

orateur, *n.m.,* orator, speaker, spokesman. — *éloquent, véhément;* eloquent, vehement, orator.

oratoire, *adj.,* oratorial, oratorical. *Débit —;* oratorical delivery. *Art —;* oratory, art of public speaking.

oratoire, *n.m.,* private chapel; oratory; Oratory (religious order).

oratoirement (-toâr-mān), *adv.,* oratorically.

oratorien (-in), *n.m.,* Oratorian.

oratorio, *n.m.,* (mus.) oratorio.

orbe, *n.m.,* (astron.) orbit; orb. *pl.,* folds, coils (of a serpent); (ich.) orbis, orb-fish.

orbe, *adj.,* (surg.) contusing (of blows).

orbiculaire, *adj.,* orbicular.

orbiculairement (-lèr-mān), *adv.,* orbicularly.

orbiculé, -e, *adj.,* (bot.) orbicular, orbiculate, orbiculated.

orbitaire, *adj.,* (anat.) orbital.

orbite, *n.f.,* (astron.) orbit; (anat.) orbit, socket. *L'— de l'œil;* the socket of the eye.

orcanète, *n.f.,* (bot.) orchanet, alkanet, dyer's-bugloss, dyer's-gromwell.

orchestral (-kès-), *adj.,* orchestral.

orchestration (-kès-), *n.f.,* (mus.) scoring.

orchestre (-kès-) *n.m.,* orchestra; band.

orchestrer (-kès-), *v.a.,* (mus.) to score.

orchidées or **orchide** or **orchie** (-ki-), *n.f.pl.,* (bot.) orchidaceæ, (bot.) orchid, orchis, foolstone, bee-flower, gnat-flower.

ordalie, *n.f.,* ordeal (old form of trial).

ordinaire, *adj.,* ordinary, common, usual, customary. *Le cours — de la nature;* the usual course of nature. *Le train — de la vie;* the ordinary course of life.

ordinaire, *n.m.,* ordinary; ordinary practice; daily fare; (milit.) mess, table, ordinary allowance (of wine). *pl.,* menses. *C'est un homme au-dessus de l'—;* he is above the common run. *A l'—;* as usual. *D'—, pour l'—;* usually, ordinarily.

ordinairement (-nèr-mān), *adv.,* ordinarily, usually, commonly.

ordinal, *adj.m.,* ordinal.

ordinand, *n.m.,* candidate for ordination.

ordinant, *n.m.,* ordaining bishop.

ordination, *n.f.,* ordination.

ordo, *n.m.,* (—) ordo, church-service book; (book regulating the order of the daily service in the church).

ordon, *n.m.,* timber-frame.

ordonnance, *n.f.,* order, ordering, ordonnance, ordinance; disposition, arrangement, regulation; (milit.) orderly; (med.) prescription. *Habits d'—;* regimentals. *Officier d'—;* orderly officer. *Par — de médecin;* acting on a doctor's orders; by order.

ordonnancement, *n.m.,* written order of payment.

ordonnancer, *v.a.,* (fin.) to order the payment of, to pass (in writing); to prescribe, to ordain; to charter.

ordonnateur, *n.m.,* ordainer; orderer.

ordonnat-eur, -rice, *adj.,* ordaining; ordering. *n.m.f.,* orderer, ordainer.

ordonné, -e, *part.,* ordered, prescribed; ordained. *Charité bien —e commence par soi-même;* charity begins at home.

ordonnée, *n.f.,* (geom.) ordinate.

ordonner, *v.a.,* to ordain, to order, to regulate; to direct, to command, to enjoin, (med.) to prescribe; to decree; to confer holy orders. *Il est plus aisé d'— que d'exécuter;* ordering and carrying out are two different things. *Mon devoir me l'ordonne;* my duty commands me to do it, enjoins it (upon me). *Le médecin a ordonné la saignée;* the physician has prescribed bleeding.

ordre, *n.m.,* order, word, command, mandate, warrant, management; class; tribe. *pl.,* holy orders. *Maintenir l'—;* to maintain order, peace. *Traiter les choses par —;* to treat things in their order. *Marcher en — de bataille;* to march in battle array. *Il est le premier créancier en —;* he stands first on the list of creditors. *Cet homme n'a pas d'—;* that man has no system. *Cela n'est pas dans l'—;* that is not in order, not right. *Mot d'—;* watchword, password. *L'ancien — de choses;* the old order of things. *J'y mettrai —;* I shall see to it. *Un esprit du premier —;* an intellect of the highest order. *Du premier —;* of the highest order. *Donner ses —s;* to give one's orders. *Un — par écrit;* a written order. *D'— et pour compte de* (com.) by order and on account of. *Un billet à —;* a bill to order. *De quel — faites-vous cela?* by whose order do you do that? *Prendre les —s;* to go into orders. *Conférer les —s;* to ordain. — *de chevalerie;* order of knighthood. *Mettre à l'— du jour;* (mil.) to mention in the general orders. *En bon*

—; in good order. *Rappeler à l'*—; to call to order. *Passer à l'*— *du jour ;* to pass to the order of the day. *Jusqu'à nouvel* —; until further orders.

ordure, *n.f.,* filth, dirt, dust; excrement; dirty thing. *pl.,* sweepings. *Panier aux* —*s ;* dirt basket.

orduri-er, -ère, *n.* and *adj.,* filthy blackguard; ribald; filthy.

oréade, *n.f.,* (myth.) oread.

⊙**orée,** *n.f.,* border, skirt of a wood *or* forest.

***oreillard, -e,** *adj.,* (of horses) lop-eared.

***oreille,** *n.f.,* ear, hearing; tie (of shoes); fluke (of anchors); earth-board (of plows). *pl.,* ears (of a bale); end-teeth (of combs); dog's ears (of books). *Le tympan de l'* — ; the drum of the ear. *Se boucher les* —*s ;* to stop one's ears. *Avoir mal aux* —*s ;* to have an earache. *Avoir un tintement d'*—*s ;* to have a tingling in one's ears. *Boucle d'* —; ear-ring. *Parler à l'* — *à quelqu'un, dire un mot à l'* — *à quelqu'un ;* to whisper a word to any one ; to say a word in any one's ear. *Prêter l'* — *à ;* to lend an ear to ; to listen ; to give ear. *Faire la sourde* —; to turn a deaf ear. *Echauffer les* —*s à quelqu'un ;* to provoke any one. *Donner sur les* —*s à quelqu'un ;* to box any one's ears. *Avoir la puce à l'*—; to be on the alert. *Se faire tirer l'* —; to require pressing. *Il ne se fait guère tirer l'*—; he does not need much pressing. *Etre endetté par-dessus les* —*s ;* to be over head and ears in debt. *Avoir les* —*s rebattues de quelque chose ;* to be tired of hearing a thing. *Ventre affamé n'a point d'* —*s ;* a hungry belly has no ears. *Avoir l'* — *basse ;* to look downcast, or chopfallen, crestfallen. *Avoir les* —*s chastes ;* to be offended by any gross word. *Il a bonne* —; he has a quick ear. *Il a l'*—*dure ;* he is hard of hearing. *Il a de l'*—; he has a delicate **ear,** *or* an ear for music. *Cela lui entre par une* —*et sort par l'autre ;* that goes in at one ear and out at the other. *Tirer l'* — *à quelqu'un ;* to pull any one's ear. *Dormir sur les deux* —*s ;* to sleep soundly ; to make one's mind quite easy. *N'écouter que d'une* — ; to pay little heed to what is said. *Venir corner à l'* — *de ;* to din (anything) into a person's ears. *Je n'entends pas de cette* — *là ;* I will not listen to that ; I don't see it in that light. *Autant vous en pend à l'* —; you may expect as much.

***oreiller,** *n.m.,* pillow. *Une taie d'*—; a pillowcase.

***oreillère,** *n.f.,* (ent.) earwig ; (armor) earpiece.

***oreillette,** *n.f.,* (anat.) auricle ; (bot., conch., zoöl.) ear; small-ear. —*s du cœur ;* (anat.) auricles of the heart ; (of a cat) ear-lap.

***oreillon,** *n.m.,* part of a helmet covering the ear ; small-ear, handle ; (zoöl.) eminence of the ears of bats ; (med.) mumps [in this sense, generally used in the plural]. *pl.,* (of hides) parings.

orémus (-mus), *n.m.,* (—) oremus, orison (prayer) ; (int.) let us pray !

oréographie, *n.f. V.* **orographie.**

ores *or* **ors,** *adv.,* only used in *d'*— *et déjà ;* from this moment.

orfèvre, *n.m.,* goldsmith, silversmith. — *bijoutier ;* goldsmith and jeweler. *Vous êtes* —, *M. Josse ;* you are in the trade, my dear sir ; that is a bit of special pleading ; that's not disinterested advice.

orfèvrerie, *n.f.,* goldsmith's art, silversmith's trade ; jewelry.

orfévri, -e, *adj.,* wrought (by the goldsmith).

orfraie, *n.f.,* sea-eagle, osprey.

orfroi, *n.m.,* orphrey (fringe of gold).

organdi, *n.m.,* book-muslin.

organe, *n.m.,* organ ; voice, medium, agency ; mouthpiece, spokesman. *L'* — *de la vue ;* the organ of sight. *Cet acteur manque d'* —; that actor has no voice.

organeau, *n.m.,* (nav.) ring, anchor ring.

organique, *n.f.,* (antiq.) instrumental music ; mechanics, machines.

organique, *adj.,* organic.

organisat-eur, -rice, *n.* and *adj.,* organizer ; organizing.

organisation, *n.f.,* organization, formation, arrangement ; constitution, nature, mind.

organisé, -e, *part.,* organized. *Une tête bien* —*e ;* a well-balanced mind.

organiser, *v.a.,* to organize ; to form ; to draw up ; to get up, to arrange.

*s'***organiser,** *v.r.,* to become organized ; to get settled.

organisme, *n.m.,* organism.

organiste, *n.m.,* organist.

organsin, *n.m.,* organzine (silk).

organsinage, *n.m.,* organizining (silk-throwing).

organsiner, *v.a.,* to organzine ; to throw (silk).

orgasme, *n.m.,* (med.) orgasm.

orge, *n.f.* [masculine with the adjectives *mondé* and *perlé*], barley. — *mondé ;* hulled barley. — *perlé ;* pearl barley. *Faire ses* —*s ;* to feather one's nest. *Grossier comme du pain d'* —; as uncivil as you like, *or* as they make them.

orgé, -e, *adj.,* mixed with barley water.

orgeat (or-ja), *n.m.,* orgeat (liquor).

orgelet *or* **orgeolet,** *n.m.,* (med.) stye.

orgie (or-jî), *n.f.,* orgy ; frantic revel ; drunken bout. *pl.,* (antiq.) orgies.

orgue (org), *n.m.,* **orgues,** *n.f.pl.,* (mus.) organ ; (fort.) orgues. *Buffet d'*—*s ;* organ-case. — *de Barbarie ;* barrel-organ. — *portatif ;* street organ. *Point d'* —; organ point. — *de mer ;* organ-pipe coral. *Facteur d'* —*;* organ builder. *Jeu d'* —*s ;* organ stop. — *expressif ;* harmonium.

***orgueil** (or-gheu-), *n.m.,* pride, arrogance; ostentation, boasting. *Etre enflé, bouffi, d'* —; to be puffed up with pride.

orgueilleusement (or-gheu-ieûz-màn), *adv.,* proudly, haughtily, ostentatiously.

orgueilleu-x, -se, *n.* and *adj.,* proud, haughty person ; proud, haughty.

orient, *n.m.,* East, Orient, rising, rise ; water (of pearls). *Les peuples d'* —; the Eastern nations. *L'empire d'*—; the Eastern Empire. *Commerce d'*—; the East India trade. *Grand* —; grand lodge (freemasonry).

oriental, -e, *adj.,* Oriental, Eastern. *Indes* —*es ;* India, East India. *A l'*—*e ;* in Eastern fashion.

orientaliste, *n.m.,* Orientalist.

orientation, *n.f.,* finding the cardinal points ; trimming (of sails).

orientaux, *n.m.pl.,* Orientals ; Eastern nations.

orienté, -e, *part.,* (nav.) set (of sails). *Bien* —; having a good aspect. *Mal* —; in a bad aspect. *Carte bien* —*e ;* map exactly drawn.

orientement (oriant-màn), *n.m.,* (nav.) trim (of sails).

orienter, *v.a.,* to set towards the East ; to give the right aspect to ; (nav.) to trim (sails). — *un cadran ;* to set a quadrant.

*s'***orienter,** *v.r.,* to find out the East ; to take one's bearings ; to ascertain one's position ; to see what one is about. *Laissez-moi m'*— let me see where I am.

orifice, *n.m.,* orifice, aperture, hole.

oriflamme, *n.f.,* oriflamme.

origan, *n.m.,* (bot.) origanum, marjoram.

originaire, *adj.,* originally come from ; native of ; native ; first ; primitive. *Il est* — *d'Italie ;* he is of Italian origin ; he comes from Italy.

originairement (-nèr-màn), *adv.,* originally, primitively.

original, -e, *adj.,* original, first, primitive ; eccentric, queer, odd, peculiar, quaint. *Consulter* l'édition —e ; to consult the original edition. Le texte — ; the original text. C'est un génie — ; he is an original genius. Avoir un caractère —; to have an eccentric character.

original, n.m., original (not the copy) ; strange character ; queer fellow ; character, oddity ; (mam.) elk. C'est un — sans copie ; he is eccentricity itself or personified. Copié sur l'— ; copied from the original.

originalement (-nal-mān), adv., originally, in an original manner ; singularly, oddly.

originalité, n.f., originality ; eccentricity ; oddity, oddness, quaintness.

origine, n.f., origin, fountain, source ; seat ; spring ; derivation ; extraction. L'— d'un mot ; the origin of a word. Il était de basse — ; he was of mean extraction. Dans l'— ; originally. Dès l'— ; from the very beginning, from the very first. Avoir or tirer son — de ; to originate in ; to have one's origin.

originel, -le, adj., original, primitive. Péché — ; original sin.

originellement (-nèl-mān), adv., originally.

*originat, n.m., elk. [In Canada.]

*orillard, -e. V. oreillard.

*orillon, n.m., (fort.) orillon ; (of a plow) mold-board ; (of a porringer) handle. pl., (med.) mumps (for which oreillons is also used).

orin, n.m., (nav.) buoy-rope (of an anchor).

orion, n.m., (astron.) Orion.

oripeau, n.m., orsedew ; Dutch gold ; tinsel ; foil ; faded finery, silver lace.

orle, n.m., (arch.) orle, orlet, orlo ; (her.) orle.

orléans, n.m., light cloth for summer wear.

ormaie or **ormoie**, n.f., elm-grove.

orme, n.m., elm. — tilleul ; wych-elm. Attendre sous l'— ; to wait till doomsday.

ormeau, n.m., young elm.

*ormille, n.f., hedge of young elms.

ormin, n.m., (bot.) annual clary.

ormoie, n.f. V. **ormaie**.

orne, n.m., (bot.) ornus, flowering-ash.

orné, -e, part., adorned, ornamented, decked (with).

ornemaniste or **ornementiste**, n.m., (arch.) ornament-maker.

ornement, n.m., ornament, embellishment ; (mus.) grace-note.

ornemental, adj., ornamental.

ornementation, n.f., ornamentation.

orner, v.a., to adorn, to ornament, to decorate, to grace, to bedeck, to embellish, to deck. Les vertus ornent l'âme ; virtues embellish the soul. — son esprit ; to adorn one's mind.

ornière, n.f., rut (of a road) ; old track, beaten path. Il est retombé dans l'— ; he has fallen back into the old track.

ornithogale, n.m., (bot.) ornithogalum, star-of-Bethlehem.

ornitholithe, n.m., ornitholite.

ornithologie, n.f., ornithology.

ornithologiste or **ornithologue**, n.m., ornithologist.

ornithomance or **ornithomancie**, n.f., ornithomancy.

ornithorynque, n.m., (zoöl.) ornithorhynchus, water-mole.

orobanche, n.f., (bot.) orobanche, broom-rape, strangleweed.

orobe, n.f., (bot.) orobus, bitter-vetch.

orographie, n.f., orography.

orologie, n.f., orology.

oronge, n.f., (bot.) orange-agaric. Fausse — ; amanita muscaria, fly-agaric.

*orpailleur, n.m., gold-finder, gold-seeker.

orphelin, -e, n. and adj., orphan, orphaned.

orphelinat, n.m., orphan-asylum, orphanage.

orphéon, n.m., orpheon, choral society ; choral-singing.

orphéoniste, n.m., choral singer.

orphie, n.f., garfish.

orphique, adj. Orphic.

orphique, n.m., votary of Orpheus.

orphiques, n.f.pl., (antiq.) orgies, feasts in honor of Bacchus.

orpiment, n.m., orpiment.

orpimenter, v.a., to color with orpiment.

orpin, n.m., (bot.) orpine ; (min.) orpiment.

orque, n.m., (ich.) ork. V. **épaulard**.

ors, adv. V. **ores**.

*orseille, n.f., (bot.) orchela ; dyer's moss.

ort, adj. invariable, (com.) gross weight. Peser — ; to weigh gross weight.

*orteil, n.m., toe ; great toe. Se dresser sur ses —s ; to stand on tip-toe.

orthodoxe, adj. orthodox.

orthodoxie, n.f., orthodoxy.

orthodromie, n.f., orthodromy.

orthoépie, n.f., orthoëpy.

orthogonal, -e, adj., orthogonal.

orthogonalement, adv., in a right angle.

orthogone, adj., (geom.) orthogonal.

orthographe, n.f., orthography, spelling. Faute d'— ; mistake in spelling.

orthographie, n.f., (arch., bot., geom., persp.) orthography.

orthographier, v.a. and n., to spell.

orthographique, adj. orthographical, orthographic. Dessin — ; orthographical drawing.

orthographiste, n.m., orthographer.

orthopédie, n.f., orthopædy.

orthopédique, adj., orthopædic.

orthopédiste, n.m., orthopædist.

orthopnée, n.f., orthopnœa.

orthoptère, n.m. and adj., orthopterous insect ; orthopterous.

orthoptères, n.m.pl., orthoptera, orthopterans.

ortie (or-tî), n.f., nettle ; (vet.) rowel. Jeter aux —s ; to throw to the dogs, to cast off. Jeter son froc aux —s ; to be unfrocked (of monks).

ortié, -e, adj., nettled. Fièvre —e ; nettle-rash.

ortive, adj., (astron.) ortive.

ortolan, n.m., (orni.) ortolan.

orvale, n.f., (bot.) clary, orval.

orvet, n.m., (erpetology) slow-worm.

orviétan, n.m., orvietan, nostrum. Marchand d'— ; quack-doctor.

oryctographie, n.f., oryctography.

oryctologie, n.f., oryctology.

oryctologiste or **oryctologue**, n.m., oryctologist.

os (ô), n.m., bone. L'— de la jambe ; the shin-bone. — de l'épaule ; shoulder-blade. — à ronger ; bone to pick ; sop ; nut to crack. Jusqu'à la moelle des — ; to the bones. Elle n'a que la peau et les — ; she is nothing but skin and bones. Rompre les — à quelqu'un ; to beat any one unmercifully. Ne pas faire de vieux — ; not to live long. Être trempé, or percé, jusqu'aux — ; to be wet through or to the skin.

oscillant, -e, adj., oscillating.

oscillation (-sil-la-), n.f., oscillation, vibration, swing.

oscillatoire (-sil-la-), adj., oscillatory.

osciller (os-sil-lé), v.n., to oscillate, to swing, to vibrate, to fluctuate, to waver. — entre deux opinions ; to be undecided, to waver between two opinions.

oscitant, -e, adj., (med.) oscitant, gaping, yawning.

oscitation, n.f., oscitancy, gaping.

oscul-eur, -rice, adj., (geom.) osculatory.

osculation, n.f., (geom.) osculation.

osé, -e, adj., bold, daring ; attempted, ventured.

*oseille, n.f., sorrel.

oser, v.a., to dare, to be so bold as, to venture. Vous n'osez rien ; you won't venture anything.

oser, *v.n.,* to dare, to venture, to presume, to attempt. *Je n'oserais, je n'ose;* I dare not. *Si j'ose le dire;* if I may venture so to speak. *Oserai-je le dire?* can I venture to say it? *Oseriez-vous le blâmer?* would you dare to blame him?

eseraie (ô-zrê), *n.f.,* osier-bed.

osier, *n.m.,* osier, withy, wicker. *Un panier d'—;* a wicker-basket.

osmazôme, *n.f.,* (chem.) osmazome.

osmium, *n.m.* (n.p.), (chem.) osmium.

osmonde, *n.f.,* (bot.) osmund.

ossature, *n.f.,* (anat.) osseous frame-work, skeleton.

osselet (o-slê), *n.m.,* ossicle, small bone ; knuckle-bone ; (vet.) osselet.

ossements (os-mān), *n.m.pl.,* bones (of dead bodies).

osseu-x, -se, *adj.,* bony, osseous.

ossianique, *adj.,* of Ossian.

ossification, *n.f.,* ossification.

ossifier, *v.a.,* to ossify.

*s'***ossifier,** *v.r.,* to become ossified.

ossu, -e, *adj.,* large boned, bony.

ossuaire, *n.m.,* ossuary, charnel-house.

ostéine, *n.f.,* (chem.) osseine (substance extracted from bones).

ostensible, *adj.,* ostensible, visible.

ostensiblement, *adv.,* ostensibly, visibly.

ostensoir *or* **ostensoire,** *n.m.,* (c.rel.) monstrance, remonstrance.

ostentat-eur, -rice, *n.* and *adj.,* ostentatious person ; ostentatious.

ostentation, *n.f.,* ostentation, show, boast. *Faire — de ses richesses;* to parade one's wealth.

ostéocolle, *n.f.,* osteocolla, bone-glue.

ostéocope, *adj.,* of the bones. *Douleur —;* osteocope.

ostéogénie, *n.f.,* osteogeny.

ostéographie, *n.f.,* osteography.

ostéolithe, *n.m.,* petrified bone.

ostéologie, *n.f.,* osteology.

ostéotomie, *n.f.,* osteotomy.

ostracé, -e, *adj.,* ostraceous.

ostraciser, *v.a.,* to ostracize, to banish.

ostracisme, *n.m.,* ostracism, banishment. *Frapper d'—;* to ostracize, to banish.

ostracite, *n.f.,* (foss.) ostracite.

ostréiculteur, *n.m.,* oyster-grower.

ostréiculture, *n.f.,* oyster-culture.

ostrogot, *n.m.,* Ostrogoth ; barbarian, savage, fool.

otage, *n.m.,* hostage, pledge. *En —;* as a hostage.

otalgie, *n.f.,* otalgia, ear-ache.

ôté, *prep.,* except, save, but, barring. *— cela, je ferai tout;* I'll do everything but that.

ôter, *v.a.,* to take away ; to remove ; to deprive ; to take off, to deduct ; to take out ; to pull off ; to set aside ; to rid (of). *Otez cette table de là;* take that table away. *Otez la nappe;* take away the cloth. *Je ne puis m'—cela de la tête;* I can't get that out of my head. *— sa cravate, son manteau, son chapeau, ses souliers;* to take off one's neckcloth, cloak, hat, shoes. *— son gilet;* to pull off one's waistcoat. *— son chapeau à quelqu'un;* to take off one's hat to any one. *On lui a ôté sa place;* they have deprived him of his situation. *Cette eau ôte les taches;* that water removes stains.

*s'***ôter,** *v.r.,* to remove ; to get away ; to be moved, to be taken away, to take one's self off ; to stand out. *Otez-vous de devant mes yeux;* get out of my sight. *Otez-vous du chemin;* stand out of the way. *Ote-toi de là que je m'y mette;* make room for me.

ottoman, -e, *n.* and *adj.,* Ottoman.

ottomane, *n.f.,* ottoman (sofa).

ou, *conj.,* or, either, else, or else. *Mort — vif;* either dead or alive.

où, *adv.,* where, whither ; at which ; in which ; to which ; through which ; when, that. *— suis-je?* where am I? *— en suis-je?* how do matters stand? *— allez-vous?* where are you going? *D'—?* whence? where . . . from. *D'— est-il?* what countryman is he? *D'— savez-vous cela?* how do you know that? *D'— vient que?* how is it that? *Par —?* which way? *L'état — il est;* the condition in which he is. *Le but — il tend;* the end he has in view. *— en êtes vous avec lui?* upon what terms are you with him? *Partout —;* wherever. *Le moment — je vous ai quitté;* the moment when *or* just as I left you. *— en êtes vous de votre travail?* how far have you got with your work ; what progress have you made?

⊙*****ouaille,** *n.f.,* sheep. *pl.,* flock (of a pastor).

ouais! *int.,* heyday! whish! dear me! bless my soul!

ouate, *n.f.,* wadding, padding ; cotton-wool. *Doublé de —;* wadded, lined with wadding.

ouater, *v.a.,* to wad, to pad. *Ouaté;* velvety.

oubli, *n.m.,* forgetfulness, neglect, oblivion ; oversight, inadvertence, omission, slip ; breach. *Mettre en —;* to forget. *Ensevelir dans l'—;* to bury in oblivion. *Tomber dans l'—;* to sink into oblivion, to fall into neglect.

oubliable, *adj.,* liable to be forgotten ; that deserves to be forgotten.

⊙**oubliance,** *n.f.* V. **oubli**

oublie, *n.f.,* a kind of very thin pastry ; wafer.

oublier, *v.a.,* to forget, to be unmindful of ; to omit, to leave out. *— son devoir;* to forget one's duty. *N'oubliez pas les pauvres;* remember the poor. *— une injure;* to forget an injury. *Oublions le passé;* let bygones be bygones.

*s'***oublier,** *v.r.,* to forget one's self ; to neglect one's affairs, to be forgotten. *Les parvenus s'oublient facilement;* upstarts easily forget themselves.

oubliettes, *n.f.pl.,* oubliettes ; (fig.) trapdungeon. *Mettre aux —;* to consign to oblivion.

oublieur, *n.m.,* muffin-man.

oublieu-x, -se, *adj.,* forgetful, oblivious, unmindful.

ouest (ou-èst), *n.m.,* West, westerly, western. *Un vent d'—;* a westerly wind. *A l'—;* westward, in a westerly direction ; westerly (of the wind). *Vents d'—;* westerly winds. *L'Ouest;* (rail) the Great Western of France.

ouf! *int.,* oh!

oui, *adv.,* yes. *— —da;* yes, indeed, willingly. *Il ne m'a répondu ni — ni non;* he gave me no positive answer. *Dire, parier, assurer que —;* to say, to bet, to assure that it is so. *Il a dit que —* or *il a dit —;* he said yes.

oui, *n.m.,* yes. *Dire le grand —;* to marry, to pronounce the fatal word "I will." *Le — et le non;* yes and no. *Pour un — et un non;* for the least thing. *Les — et les non;* the ayes and noes.

ouï, -e, *part.,* heard. *J'ai — dire;* I have heard say. *J'ai — parler de;* I have heard of.

ouï-dire, *n.m.,* (—) hearsay.

ouïe, *n.f.,* hearing. *Avoir l'— bonne;* to be quick of hearing.

ouïe, *n.f.,* hole (of a violin, etc.). *pl.,* gills (of fish).

*****ouillage,** *n.m.,* ullage ; filling up of a cask of wine.

ouiller, *v.a.,* to fill up, to refresh, to add to, to replace in a cask the quantity which has disappeared by leakage, etc.

ouïr, *v.a.,* to hear.

ouistiti, *n.m.,* striated monkey.

ouragan, *n.m.,* hurricane, tornado.

ourdir, *v.a.,* to warp ; to plot, to brew, to hatch, to concoct. *— une toile;* to warp a cloth. *— une trahison;* to plot a treacherous deed. *— un complot;* to hatch a plot.

ourdissage, *n.m.*, warping.

ourdisseu-r, *n.m.*, **-se**, *n.f.*, warper.

ourdissoir, *n.m.*, warp-beam.

ourdissure, *n.f.*, warping.

ourler, *v.a.*, to hem (needle-work). — *à jour ;* to hemstitch.

ourlet, *n.m.*, hem.

ours (oors), *n.m.*, bear. *Un — mal léché ;* an unlicked cub, an ill-bred fellow. *Il ne faut pas vendre la peau de l' — avant qu'on l'ait pris ;* you must not count your chickens before they are hatched. *C'est un —;* he is a bear. *Chasse à l' —;* bear-hunt.

ourse, *n.f.*, she-bear ; (astron.) Ursa. *La grande —;* Ursa Major, the Greater Bear. *La petite —;* Ursa Minor, the Lesser Bear.

oursin, *n.m.*, sea-urchin.

ourson, *n.m.*, bear's cub.

ourvari, *n.m.* *V.* **hourvari**.

outarde, *n.f.*, (orni.) bustard.

outardeau, *n.m.*, (orni.) young bustard.

outil (oo-ti), *n.m.*, tool, implement.

*****outillage**, *n.m.*, stock of tools.

*****outillé, -e**, *adj.*, furnished with tools.

*****outiller**, *v.a.*, to furnish with tools.

outrage, *n.m.*, outrage, gross insult, abuse ; injury. *Souffrir un —;* to brook an outrage. *Faire un — à ;* to commit an outrage upon.

outrageant, -e (-jān, -t), *adj.*, outrageous ; insulting, abusive.

outrager, *v.a.*, to outrage, to insult, to shock, to offend. *— la pudeur ;* to commit an outrage upon decency.

outrageusement (-jeûz-mān), *adv.*, outrageously, insultingly.

outrageu-x, -se, *adj.*, outrageous.

outrance, *n.f.*, extreme ; excess. *A —;* with a vengeance ; to the death. *A toute —;* beyond measure.

outre, *n.f.*, leather bottle.

outre, *adv.*, further, beyond. *Passer —;* to go on, to take no notice of a thing, to pass over ; (jur.) to proceed. *D' — en —;* through and through.

outre, *prep.*, beyond ; besides, in addition to, above. *D'—mer ;* from beyond the seas, across the channel. *— cela ;* besides that.

outre que, *conj.*, besides.

outré, -e, *adj.*, exaggerated, far-fetched ; incensed ; strained, excessive, undue. *Pensée —e ;* extravagant thought. *Des louanges —es ;* excessive praise. *Il est — en tout ;* he is far-fetched in everything.

outrecuidance, *n.f.*, presumption ; overweening conceit.

outrecuidant, -e, *adj.*, overweening, presumptuous, conceited.

⊙**outrecuidé, -e**, *adj.*, presumptuous, overweening.

outrément, *adv.*, (l.u.) excessively, beyond measure.

outremer, *n.m.*, ultra-marine (color).

outrepasse, *n.f.*, extra-cuttings (of wood).

outrepasser, *v.a.*, to go beyond, to exceed, to transgress. *— ses pouvoirs ;* to exceed one's powers.

outrer, *v.a.* and *n.*, to exaggerate, to overdo ; ⊙to overwhelm ; to incense ; to strain. *— un cheval ;* to strain a horse. *C'est un homme qui outre tout ;* he is a man who overdoes everything.

ouvert, -e, *part.*, open, unfortified (of towns). *A livre —;* at sight. *Parler à cœur —;* to speak unreservedly, frankly. *Chanter à livre —;* to sing at sight. *Compte —;* (com.) running account. *A bureau —;* on presentation, on demand.

ouvertement, *adv.*, openly, frankly.

ouverture, *n.f.*, opening ; aperture, chasm, gap, hole, chink ; overture, beginning ; orifice,

means, way ; width (of a door). *L' — était assez large pour qu'il passât ;* the opening was wide enough to enable him to pass. *Faire des —s de paix ;* to make overtures of peace. *L' — était bien belle ;* the overture was very fine. *L' — de la chasse ;* the opening of the shooting season. *— d'esprit ;* quick-wittedness.

ouvrable, *adj.*, working, workable. *Jour —;* working-day, week-day.

ouvrage, *n.m.*, work, piece of work ; performance, workmanship ; job. *— de brique ;* brickwork. *Se mettre à l' —;* to set to work. *— à l'aiguille ;* needle-work.

ouvragé, -e, *adj.*, wrought, worked, figured.

ouvrager, *v.a.*, to work, to figure.

ouvrant, -e, *adj.*, opening. *A jour —;* at break of day, at daybreak.

ouvré, -e, *adj.*, diapered ; wrought.

ouvreau, *n.m.*, side-hole (of furnaces).

ouvrer, *v.a.*, to work ; to diaper ; to coin. *— la monnaie ;* to coin money.

⊙**ouvrer**, *v.n.*, to work.

ouvreu-r, *n.m.*, **-se**, *n.f.*, opener. *—se de loges ;* (thea.) box-keeper.

ouvrier, *n.m.*, workman, artisan ; mechanic, operative, journeyman. *— à la journée ;* day-laborer. *A l'œuvre on connaît l' —;* the workman is known by his work. *Mauvais — n'a jamais bons outils ;* a bad workman always blames his tools.

ouvri-er, -ère, *adj.*, operative, working. *Jour —;* working-day. *La classe —ère ;* the working-classes. *Cheville —ère ;* pole-bolt (of a coach) ; (fig.) prime mover.

ouvrière, *n.f.*, workwoman.

ouvrir (ouvrant, ouvert), *v.a.*, to open, to unclose, to set open ; to sharpen (the appetite) ; to broach (opinion); to subject to. *— la terre ;* to dig open the earth. *Cela ouvre l'appétit ;* that sharpens the appetite. *— son cœur à quelqu'un ;* to unbosom one's self to any one.

s'ouvrir, *v.r.*, to open for one's self, to disclose one's self ; to open one's mind. *S' — un passage* or *un chemin ;* to cut a way for one's self (through). *S' — à quelqu'un ;* to open one's mind to any one.

ouvrir, *v.n.*, to open, to expand, to spread.

ouvroir, *n.m.*, workshop ; work-room.

ovaire, *n.m.*, (anat.) ovary ; (bot.) ovary.

ovalaire, *adj.*, (anat.) oval.

ovale, *n.m.* and *adj.*, oval.

ovariotomie, *n.f.*, (surg.) amputation of a diseased ovary.

ovation, *n.f.*, ovation.

ove, *n.m.*, (arch.) ovolo.

ové, -e, *adj.*, ovate, ovated.

ovicule, *n.m.*, small ovolo.

oviducte, *n.m.*, (anat.) oviduct.

ovine, *adj.*, ovine.

ovipare, *n.m.* and *adj.*, oviparous animal ; oviparous.

ovoïde, *adj.*, ovoid.

ovule, *n.m.*, (physiology) ovule, ovulum.

oxalate, *n.m.*, (chem.) oxalate.

oxalide, *n.f.*, (bot.) oxalis.

oxalique, *adj.*, oxalic.

oxycrat, *n.m.*, oxycrate (beverage).

oxydabilité, *n.f.*, oxidability.

oxydable, *adj.*, oxidable.

oxydation, *n.f.*, oxidation.

oxyde, *n.m.*, (chem.) oxide.

oxyder, *v.a.*, (chem.) to oxidate.

s'oxyder, *v.r.*, to be, to become oxidized.

oxygénable, *adj.*, (chem.) oxygenizable.

oxygénation, *n.f.*, (chem.) oxygenation.

oxygène, *n.m.*, (chem.) oxygen.

oxygéner, *v.a.*, (chem.) to oxygenate.

oxygone, *adj.*, (geom.) oxygonal, oxygonial.

oxymel, *n.m.*, oxymel.

oxyrrhodin, *n.m.*, (pharm.) oxyrrhodine.

oyant, *n.m.*, **-e**, *n.f.*, (jur.) auditor, hearer.

ozène, *n.f.*, ozæna.

ozone, *n.m.*, (chem.) ozone.

ozonisation, *n.f.*, ozonization.

ozonomètre, *n.m.*, ozonometer.

P

p, *n.m.*, the sixteenth letter of the alphabet, p.

p. (initial letter of Père), father (priest).

p. (initial letter of Pour), (com.) per.

paca, *n.m.*, kind of guinea-pig.

pacage, *n.m.*, pasture-land.

pacager, *v.n.*, (jur.) to pasture.

in **pace**, *n.m.* *V.* **in pace**.

pacha, *n.m.* (*—s*), pacha, bashaw.

pachalik (pa-ka-lik), *n.m.* (*—s*), pachalic.

pachyderme, *n.m.* and *adj.*, pachyderm ; pachydermatous.

pacificat-eur, -rice, *n.* and *adj.*, pacificator, pacifier ; pacifying, peace-maker.

pacification, *n.f.*, pacification, peace-making, appeasement ; adjustment.

pacifier, *v.a.*, to pacify, to appease ; to still, to calm. *Se —* ; to become, *or* to be, pacified.

pacifique, *adj.*, pacific, peaceable, peaceful.

pacifiquement (-fik-mān), *adv.*, peacefully, peaceably, quietly.

pacotille, *n.f.*, (com.) venture, pack, bale, trumpery wares ; quantity, stock ; seaman's venture. *Marchandises de —* ; slops ; slop-made, ready-made, cheap, goods ; salework.

pacotiller, *v.n.*, to traffic in, *or* take out, small ventures.

pacotilleur, *n.m.*, small sea-trader.

pacte, *n.m.*, compact, contract, pact, agreement.

pactiser, *v.n.*, to covenant, to make a compact with, to compound (with).

pactole, *n.m.*, Pactolus ; (fig.) a source of great wealth.

padischa, *n.m.*, (*—s*) the Sultan of Turkey.

padou, *n.m.*, ferret, narrow tape.

padouane, *n.f.*, Paduan coin (imitation of an ancient medal).

paf, *int.*, slap ! bang !

se **paffer**, *v.r.*, (pop.) to booze, to get drunk.

pæan (pé-an), *n.m.*, pæan.

pagaie, *n.f.*, paddle (of a canoe). *Aller à la —* ; (nav.) to paddle.

en **pagaie**, *adv.*, hurriedly, in disorder ; in bulk, unpacked.

paganisme, *n.m.*, paganism, heathenism.

pagayer, *v.a.* and *n.*, (nav.) to paddle.

pagayeur, *n.m.*, paddler.

page, *n.m.*, page (person). *Etre hors de —* ; to be one's own master.

page, *n.f.*, page (of a book). *Le haut, le bas, d'une —* ; the top, the bottom, of a page. *Mettre en —s* ; (print.) to make up, to click. *Metteur en —s* ; clicker, maker-up.

pagination, *n.f.*, paging.

paginer, *v.a.*, to page, to folio.

****pagne**, *n.m.*, cotton drawers (negro's).

****pagnon**, *n.m.*, black broadcloth.

pagode, *n.f.*, pagoda. *Manche —* ; wide sleeve.

paie, *n.f.* *V.* **paye**.

paiement *or* **paiment**, *n.m.* *V.* **payement**.

païen, -ne, *n.* and *adj.*, pagan, heathen. *Les dieux des —s* ; the gods of the pagans.

****paillard**, **-e**, *n.* and *adj.*, (l.ex.) wanton, lewd person, rake, boon-companion ; lecherous, lewd, broad, racy.

****paillarder**, *v.n.*, (l.ex.) to practise lewdness, to play the wanton.

****paillardise**, *n.f.*, (l.ex.) lechery, lewdness, wantonness.

****paillasse**, *n.f.*, straw mattress, palliasse ; ticking, tick.

****paillasse**, *n.m.*, clown, merry-andrew.

****paillasson**, *n.m.*, straw-matting ; straw-mat ; mat, door-mat ; window pad.

****paille**, *n.f.*, straw ; chaff ; flaw (of gems, of metals) ; (manu.) chip ; mote. *Menue —* ; chaff. *Brin de —* ; bit of straw. *Botte de —* ; truss or bottle of straw. *Chapeau de —* ; straw-hat. *Couleur —* ; straw-colored. *Homme de —* ; man-of-straw. *Un feu de —* ; straw fire, sudden, short blaze. *Tirer à la courte —* ; to draw lots, to draw cuts. *Rompre la — avec quelqu'un* ; to fall out with any one. *Ce diamant a une —* ; that diamond has a flaw in it. *Mourir sur la —* ; to die a miserable death ; to die in the gutter. *Etre sur la —* ; to be miserably poor. *Cela enlève la —* ; that takes the cake. *Tout, — et blé,* everything, to the last penny.

****paille**, *adj. invariable*, straw-colored.

****paillé, -e**, *adj.*, (her.) diapered ; covered with straw ; flawy (of metals) ; straw-colored.

****paille-en-queue**, *n.m.*, (*—*) tropic-bird, phaeton.

****pailler**, *n.m.*, farm-yard, heap of straw, straw-rick, dunghill. *Chapon de —* ; barn-door capon. *Etre sur son —* ; to be in one's stronghold.

****paill-er, -ère**, *adj.*, of farm-yards.

****paillet**, *adj.*, pale (of red wine).

****pailleter**, *v.a.*, to spangle.

****paillette**, *n.f.*, spangle.

****pailleu-r**, *n.m.*, **-se**, *n.f.*, dealer in straw.

****pailleu-x, -se**, *adj.*, flawy (of metals). *Du fer —* ; flawy iron.

****paillon**, *n.m.*, wisp of straw, large spangle ; bit of solder.

pain, *n.m.*, bread, loaf ; cake (of color, etc.). *Un —* ; a loaf. *Du —* ; some bread. *Un petit —* ; a roll. *— mollet* ; soft bread. *Du — bis* ; brown bread. *Du — frais, du — tendre* ; new bread. *Du — rassis* ; stale bread. *— de munition* ; regulation bread. *— sans levain* ; unleavened bread. *— de ménage* ; home-made bread, household bread. *Manger son — blanc le premier* ; to have the best of one's life first, *or* to have one's happiest days over. *— chapelé* ; rasped bread. *Il sait son — manger* ; he knows how to shift for himself. *Ne pas valoir le — qu'on mange* ; not to be worth one's salt. *— quotidien* ; daily bread. *Mettre à quelqu'un le — à la main* ; to give any one his bread. *Avoir son — cuit* ; to have a competency, to have enough to live on. *Avoir du — sur la planche* ; to have saved money. *— de sucre* ; sugar-loaf. *— de savon* ; cake of soap. *— bénit* ; consecrated bread. *C'est — bénit* ; it serves him right. *C'est un long jour qu'un jour sans —* ; 'tis a long lane that has no turning. *Un — à cacheter* ; a wafer. *— d'épice* ; gingerbread. *Tel grain tel —* ; as you sow, you must mow. *Faire passer le goût du —* ; (fam.) to kill, to do for.

pair, *adj.*, even (of numbers) ; similar. *Non —* ; odd. *— ou non* ; odd or even.

pair, *n.m.*, peer ; equal ; par ; equality ; fellow, equal footing, common level ; (of birds) mate. *Le change est au —* ; the exchange is at par. *Au —* ; at par ; not behindhand (with one's task) ; with board and lodging, but no salary. *Etre jugé par ses —s* ; to be tried by one's peers. *Sans —* ; matchless. *Nous voilà — à —* ; now, we are even. *De —* ; on a par, on an equality. *Aller de — avec quelqu'un* ; to go cheek by jowl with any one. *Marcher de — avec* ; to be on an equal footing with. *Traiter quelqu'un de — à compagnon* ; to be hail-fellow well met with any one. *Hors de —* ; beyond comparison, beyond compare, above the level of others.

paire, *n.f.*, pair, brace, couple. *Une — de bœufs* ; a pair of oxen. *Une — de ciseaux* ; a pair of scissors. *Les deux font la —* ; they are well-matched.

pairement (pèr-mān), *adv.*, (arith.) evenly.

pairesse, *n.f.*, peeress.

pairie, *n.f.*, peerage.

paisible, *adj.*, peaceable, peaceful, quiet, still, calm. *Sommeil —*; peaceful sleep. *Mener une vie —*; to lead a peaceful life.

paisiblement, *adv.*, peaceably, peacefully.

paisson, *n.f.*, pasture (in forests).

paître (paissant, pu), *v.a.* and *n.*, to graze, to feed, to tend. *Mener — des moutons;* to drive sheep to pasture. *Envoyer — quelqu'un;* to send any one about his business. *Allez —;* go about your business.

se paître, *v.r.*, to feed (on).

paix, *n.f.*, peace; quiet; rest, stillness, silence; (c. rel.) osculatory, pax. *Troubler la — de;* to disturb the peace of. *Garder la —;* to keep the peace. — *fourrée, — plâtrée;* hypocritical peace, patched-up peace. *Laissez-moi en —;* let me alone. *Il a fait sa —;* he has made his peace. *Ne donner ni — ni trêve à quelqu'un;* to leave no one any rest. *Donner, laisser, ficher la — à;* to leave any one alone; not to bother any one.

paix ! *int.*, peace ! be quiet !

pal, *n.m.*, (—s, or *paux*) pale, stake (punishment); (her.) pale.

paladin, *n.m.*, paladin, champion, knight-errant. *C'est un vrai —;* he is a perfect knight-errant.

palais, *n.m.*, palace; mansion ; court of justice ; law-courts ; hall ; palate (of the mouth); taste. *Terme de —;* law term. *Style du —, style de —;* law style. — *de justice;* law-courts. *Jour de —;* court day.

palan, *n.m.*, (nav.) tackle, hoisting gear.

palanche, *n.f.*, yoke (for carrying pails).

palançons, *n.m.pl.*, (mas.) props (to support mud-walls till they are dry).

palanque, *n.f.*, (fort.) blindage, blind ; stockade.

palanquer, *v.a.*, to hoist, to haul on a tackle.

palanquin, *n.m.*, palanquin.

palastre, *n.m.*, case (of a lock).

palatale, *n.* and *adj.f.*, (gram.) palatal.

palatin, *-e*, *adj.*, Palatine.

palatin, *n.m.*, Palatine.

palatin, *-e*, *adj.*, (anat.) of the palate.

palatinat, *n m.*, Palatinate.

palatine, *n.f.*, wife of a Palatine; Palatine princess ; fur-tippet; tippet, victorine.

pale, *n.f.*, sluice, flood-gate ; blade (of an oar); paddle-board ; (c. rel.) pall ; (orni.) spoonbill.

pâle, *adj.*, pale, wan, pallid ; ghastly. — *comme la mort;* as pale as death. — *de colère;* pale with rage. *Un peu —;* palish, somewhat pale. *Bleu —;* pale blue. — *s couleurs;* (med.) chlorosis, green-sickness. *Cet ouvrage est d'un style —;* the style of that work is tame or colorless.

paléage, *n.m.*, shoveling.

palée, *n.f.*, row of stakes, of pales.

palefrenier (pal-frê-nié), *n.m.*, groom, ostler.

palefroi (pal-froa), *n.m.*, palfrey.

palémon, *n.m.*, prawn.

paléographe, *n.m.*, paleographer.

paléographie, *n.f.*, paleography (study of ancient writings).

paléontologie, *n.f.*, paleontology.

paléontologique, *adj.*, paleontological.

paléontologiste, *n.m.*, paleontologist.

paléothérium, *n.m.*, (—s) (foss.) paleotherium.

paleron (pa-lron), *n.m.*, shoulder-blade, shoulder-bone.

palestine, *n.f.*, (print.) two-line pica.

palestre, *n.f.*, (antiq.) palestra.

palestrique, *adj.*, (antiq.) palestrian, palestric,

palestrique, *n.f.*, (antiq.) palestra (exercises).

palet, *n.m.*, quoit. *Jouer au —;* to play at quoits.

paletot (pal-to), *n.m.*, paletot ; great coat; overcoat. — *pilote;* pilot-coat. — *sac;* sack-coat.

palette, *n.f.*, battledore, racket, bat; (paint.) pallet ; palette ; (surg.) pallet ; (gilding) pallet ; (horl.) pallet; (tech.) float-board, blade. *Sentir la —;* to smack of the pallet.

palétuvier, *n.m.*, (bot.) mangrove, mangle ; button-tree.

pâleur, *n.f.*, paleness, wanness, tameness, ghastliness. — *mortelle;* deathlike pallor.

pali, *n.m.*, (philol.) Pahli, Pali. *Etudier le —;* to study Pahli, the Pali language.

pâli, *-e*, *adj.*, grown pale.

palier, *n.m.*, landing ; landing-place (of a staircase); stair-head, flat, floor. *Demeurer sur le même —;* to live on the same floor. *Un homme est fort sur son —;* every man is a king in his own house.

palière, *n.f.*, top-stair. *Porte —;* landing-door.

palification, *n.f.*, (engineering) palification, pile-driving.

palimpseste, *n.m.*, palimpsest.

palingénésie, *n.f.*, palingenesia, palingenesy, regeneration.

palinod, *n.m.*, palinod (verses made in honor of the Immaculate Conception of the Blessed Virgin).

palinodie, *n.f.*, palinody, recantation. *Chanter la —;* (fam., fig.) to retract, to recant.

pâlir, *v.n.*, to grow, to turn, to become pale, to grow dim, to pale. *Son étoile pâlit ;* his star is on the wane. — *sur les livres;* to pore over books.

pâlir, *v.a.*, to turn, to make pale; to bleach. *Le vinaigre pâlit les lèvres ;* vinegar bleaches the lips. *Faire —;* to throw into the shade; to pale; to eclipse; to frighten.

palis, *n.m.*, pale, paling; inclosure, fence.

palissade, *n.f.*, palisade, paling ; wooden fence; hedgerow ; (fort.) stockade.

palissader, *v.a.*, to fence with palisades, to palisade; (fort.) to stockade, to line with trees.

palissage, *n.m.*, (hort.) paling or nailing up.

palissandre or **palixandre**, *n.m.*, violet ebony, rosewood.

pâlissant, *adj.*, turning pale, waning.

palisser, *v.a.*, (hort.) to pale up, to train, to nail up.

palisson, *n.m.*, (furriers) softening-iron; softening-board.

paliure, *n.m.*, (bot.) dry hawthorn (for hedges).

palixandre, *n.m.* V. **palissandre**.

palladium (pal-la-diom), *n.m.*, Palladium; (fig.) palladium; (chem.) palladium.

pallas (pal-lâs), *n.f.*, (astron.) Pallas.

palle, *n.f.*, (c.rel.) V. **pale**.

palliati-f, *-ve* (pal-li-), *adj.*, (med.) palliative.

palliatif, *n.m.*, palliative.

palliation (pal-li-), *n.f.*, palliation.

pallier (pal-lié), *v.a.*, to excuse; to palliate, to alleviate, to mitigate.

pallium (pa-li-om), *n.m.*, pallium, pall.

palma-christi, *n.m.*, (—) (bot.). V. **ricin**.

palmaire, *adj.*, (anat.) palmar ; (orni.) webbed.

palmarès, *n.m.*, prize-list, programme (distribution of prizes).

palme, *n.f.*, palm, palm-tree; palm-branch; victory, triumph. *Remporter la —;* to bear away the palm. *La — du martyre;* the crown of martyrdom. *Huile de —;* palm-oil.

palme, *n.m.*, palm, hand's breadth.

palmé, *-e*, *adj.*, palmated; webbed; fin-toed; (bot.) handed.

palmette, *n.f.,* palm-leaf (ornament).
palmier, *n.m.,* palm-tree, palm. — *en éventail;* macaw-tree. — *huileux;* palm-oil-tree. — *du Japon,* — *à sagou;* sago-tree. — *marin;* sea-palm-tree. — *nain;* dwarf-palm.
palmifère, *adj.,* (bot.) palmiferous.
palmipède, *adj.,* (orni.) palmiped, fin-footed, web-footed.
palmipède, *n.m.,* (orni.) palmiped.
palmiste, *n.m.,* (bot.) palmetto, cabbage-tree; (orni.) palm-squirrel.
palmite, *n.m.,* palm-sap.
palombe, *n.f.,* (orni.) wood-pigeon, ring-dove.
palonnier, *n.m.,* whipple-tree; (of a coach) swing-bar, pole.
palot, *n.m.,* (pop.) clown, clod-hopper, boor, bumpkin.
pâlot, -te, *adj.,* palish, rather pale.
palpable, *adj.,* palpable.
palpablement, *adv.,* palpably.
palpe, *n.f.,* (ent.) palp, feeler.
palpébral, -e, *adj.,* (anat.) palpebral.
palper, *v.a.,* to feel, to palp; to feel about; to pocket, to receive. — *de l'argent;* to finger money. — *l'eau;* to dip the oar.
palpitant, -e, *adj.,* palpitating, panting. *Cœur* —; throbbing, beating, heart. *Des membres —s;* quivering limbs.
palpitation, *n.f.,* palpitation; throbbing, throb; beating; quivering, quiver; thrill, flutter, fluttering.
palpiter, *v.n.,* to palpitate, to throb; to pant, to beat; to thrill, to quiver; to flutter. *Le cœur lui palpite;* his heart flutters.
palplanche, *n.f.,* sheeting-pile (mas.).
palsambleu! par la sambleu! *int.,* zounds! forsooth! (an oath peculiar to Louis XI.).
paltoquet, *n.m.,* clown, clownish fellow; nobody.
paludéen, -ne (-dé-in, -dé-è-n), *adj.,* paludal, marshy. *Fièvre —ne;* marsh-fever.
paludier, *n.m.,* salt-maker.
paludière, *n.f.,* salt-marsh.
palus (-lûs), *n.m.,* (geog.) marsh, moor, fen.
palustre, *adj.,* paludal.
pâmer, *v.n.,* to swoon away. *Faire — de rire;* to make any one split his sides with laughing, to make any one die with laughter.
se **pâmer,** *v.r.,* to swoon away, to swoon; to faint, to faint away. *Se — de joie;* to be transported with joy. *Se — de rire;* to be ready to die with laughter, to split one's sides with laughter.
pâmoison, *n.f.,* swoon, fainting fit, rapture. *Tomber en* —; to fall into a swoon, to swoon, to faint away.
pampa, *n.f.,* (— *s* (-pass)), pampas.
pampe, *n.f.,* corn-blade.
pamphlet, *n.m.,* pamphlet.
pamphlétaire, *n.m.,* pamphleteer.
pampiniforme, *adj.,* (anat.) pampiniform.
pamplemousse, *n.f.,* (bot.) shaddock.
pampre, *n.m.,* vine-branch (full of leaves); vine-leaf; (arch.) pampre, vine-branch.
pan, *n.m.,* flap, lappet; skirt; large piece; stretch (of the sky); side, section (of a wall). — *d'un habit;* flap of a coat. — *de muraille;* large section of a wall. — *coupé;* (carp.) cant. *A —s coupés;* (carp.) cantwise. *Tour à six —s;* six-sided, six-fronted, tower.
pan! *int.,* slap! flap! smack!
panacée, *n.f.,* panacea, universal remedy, nostrum.
panache, *n.m.,* plume, bunch of feathers; (bot.) streaks of color (in a flower); cap, top (of a church lamp); (arch.) triangular part of an arch. — *de mer;* amphitrite.
panaché, -e, *part.,* plumed, tufted, striped, streaked, variegated. *Tulipe —e, rose —e;* striped tulip, striped rose. *Glace —e;* (cook.) mixed ice-cream.

panacher, *v.a.,* to plume, to streak, to variegate.
se **panacher,** *v.r.,* to become streaked, to become striped, variegated; to be streaked, to be striped.
panachure, *n.f.,* (of flowers, fruit) variety of colors, variegation; streak.
panade, *n.f.,* (cook.) bread-soup.
se **panader,** *v.r.* V. *se* **pavaner.**
panage, *n.m.,* pannage.
panais, *n.m.,* (bot.) parsnip.
panama, *n.m.,* Panama-hat.
panard, *adj.,* (of a horse) crook-legged.
panarine, *n.f.,* (bot.) whitlowwort.
panaris, *n.m.,* (med.) whitlow.
pancaliers, *n.m.,* (bot.) Pancaliers cabbage.
pancarte, *n.f.,* toll-table; tariff; paper, writing; placard, bill; visitor's book. *De vieilles —s;* old writings.
pancrace, *n.m.,* (antiq.) pancratium. *Docteur* —; champion disputant.
pancréas (-âs), *n.m.,* (anat.) pancreas; sweetbread.
pancréatique, *adj.,* (anat.) pancreatic.
pandanées, *n.f.pl.,* (bot.) pandanaceæ.
pandectes, *n.f.pl.,* (Roman jur.) pandects.
pandémonium (-ni-om), *n.m.,* (— *s*) pandemonium.
pandiculation, *n.f.,* (med.) pandiculation.
pandit, *n.m.,* (— *s*) Pandit, Pundit.
pandore, *n.f.,* Pandora. *La boîte de* —; (fig.) prov.) the source of many evils.
pandour, *n.m.,* pandour (Hungarian soldier); marauder; coarse, brutal man.
pané, -e, *part.,* (cook.) covered with bread crumbs. *De l'eau —e;* toast and water.
panégyrique, *n.m.,* panegyric.
panégyriste, *n.m.,* panegyrist.
paner, *v.a.,* (cook.) to crumb, to cover with bread crumbs.
panerée (pa-n-rée), *n.f.,* basketful, hamperful.
paneterie (pa-n-trî), *n.f.,* pantry; bread-room.
panetier (pa-n-tié), *n.m.,* pantler, storekeeper.
panetière (pa-n-tièr), *n.f.,* bag *or* satchel; pouch; scrip.
pangolin, *n.m.,* (mam.) pangolin, short-tailed manis, ant-eater.
panic, *n.m.,* (bot.) panic, panic-grass.
panicule, *n.f.,* (bot.) panicle.
paniculé, -e, *adj.,* paniculate, panicled.
panier, *n.m.,* basket, hamper, pannier; punnet, pottle; crate, creel; scuttle; beehive made of straw, etc.; hoop-petticoat. — *d'osier;* wicker-basket. — *à claire-voie;* open-worked basket. — *à salade;* basket, chaise; (pop.) prison van. — *roulant;* go-cart. — *au papier;* waste-paper basket. — *à ouvrage;* work-basket. — *percé;* spendthrift. *Adieu —s, il vendanges sont faites;* you come too late, it is all over. *Voûte, à anse de* —; (arch.) elliptical vault. *Le dessus du* —; the pick, the best. *Le dessous du* —; the refuse. *Faire danser l'anser du* —; to cheat one's masters, to take the market-penny.
panification, *n.f.,* panification, bread-making.
panifier, *v.a.,* to make bread.
panique, *n.f.* and *adj.,* panic, sudden fright.
panis (pa-nis), *n.m.,* (bot.) panic-grass.
panne, *n.f.,* shag, plush; fat; (carp.) purlin; face (of a hammer). *Culotte de* —; plush breeches. *En* —; lying to. *Être en* —; (nav.) to lie to. *Mettre en* —; (nav.) to bring to, to heave to. *Se tenir en* —; (nav.) to lie to. *Ce cochon n'a presque point de* —; this pig has scarcely any fat. *Être dans la* —; (pop.) to be hard up, to be in a hole and corner.
panné, *adj.,* (pop.) shabby, seedy, poor, penniless, hard up, needy.
panneau, *n.m.,* square, panel; snare, trap;

pannel (of a saddle). — *de lambris ;* wainscot
panel; (hort.) glass-frame ; (nav.) hatch. — *de
porte ;* panel of a door. *Donner dans le —;* to
fall into the snare.

panneauter, *v.n.,* (hunt.) to set snares, to lay
trap-nets.

pannelle, *n.f.,* (her.) poplar leaf.

panneton (pa-n-ton), *n.m.,* (locksmith's work)
key-bit; catch (of window fastenings); bread-pan.

pannicule, *n.m.,* (anat.) adipose membrane;
cellular tissue.

panonceau, *n.m.,* scutcheon, escutcheon.

panoplie, *n.f.,* panoply; trophy.

panorama, *n.m.,* panorama.

panoramique, *adj.,* panoramic.

pan pan, *onomatopœia,* rat-tat-tat ; bang, slap,
flap.

pansage, *n.m.,* dressing, rubbing, grooming
(of horses).

panse, *n.f.,* paunch, belly; rumen, cud (of
ruminating animals) ; lugger-boat (in V. Hugo).
Grosse —; pot-belly, paunch. *Avoir les yeux
plus grands que la —;* to have eyes bigger than
one's belly. — *d'A ;* oval of an *a. Il n'a pas
fait une — d'A ;* he has done nothing at all, he
has not done a stroke.

pansé, -e, *part.,* dressed. *Il est bien —;* he
has had a square meal, *or* his bellyful.

pansement (pans-măn), *n.m.,* dressing (of
wounds); rubbing, grooming (of a horse). *V.
pansage.*

panser, *v.a.,* to dress (wounds) ; to groom (a
horse).

pansu, -e, *adj.,* pot-bellied, tun-bellied, big-
bellied; bulging.

pantagruélique, *adj.,* Pantagruel; epicurean;
insatiable; sumptuous.

pantagruélisme, *n.m.,* epicurism.

pantagruéliste, *n.m.,* epicure.

pantalon, *n.m.,* pantaloons, pair of pantaloons; trousers, pair of trousers ; pantaloon
(pantomime). — *collant ;* tight trousers.
— *rouge ;* (fig.) French soldier.

pantalonnade, *n.f.,* pantaloon's dance, buffoonery ; false demonstration, make-believe,
humbug.

pantelant, -e (pan-tlăn, -t), *adj.,* panting,
heaving; gasping. *Chair —e ;* quivering flesh.

panteler (pan-tlé), *v.n.,* to gasp for breath, to
pant.

pantenne (-tè-n), *n.f.,* punnet, draw-net.
Vergues en —; (nav.) yards placed obliquely, and
sails badly trimmed. *Vaisseau en —;* ship riding
apeak. *Mettre en —;* to top up.

panthée, *adj.f.,* pantheistic.

panthéisme, *n.m.,* Pantheism.

panthéiste, *n.m.,* pantheist.

panthéistique, *adj.,* pantheistic, pantheistical.

panthéon, *n.m.,* pantheon; (in Paris) Pantheon
(where the great dead are buried), the Westmin-
ster Abbey of France.

panthère, *n.f.,* (mam.) panther.

pantière (-tièr), *n.f.,* (hunt.) draw-net, shoot-
ing-pouch.

pantin, *n.m.,* dancing Jack, puppet; (b.s.)
great gesticulator; trimmer, time-server.

pantographe, *n.m.,* pantograph.

pantographie, *n.f.,* pantography.

pantographique, *adj.,* pantographic, panto-
graphical.

pantoiement, *n.m.,* (hawking) pantess.

pantois, -e, *adj.,* ⊙panting, out of breath ;
short-winded, astonished, stupefied, aghast.

pantomètre, *n.m.,* (geom.) pantometer.

pantomime, *n.m.,* pantomime, pantomimist.

pantomime, *n.f.,* dumb-show ; pantomime.

pantomime, *adj.,* pantomimic.

pantoufle, *n.f.,* slipper, slipper-shoe. *Etre
en —s ;* to be in slippers. *Soulier en —;* slip-shod
shoe, shoe down at heel. *Raisonner comme une*

—; to reason like a jackass. *Fer à —;* panton-
shoe, panton.

pantoufler, *v.n.,* to reason like a jackass.

pantouflerie, *n.f.,* stupid conversation; piece
of nonsense, piece of absurdity.

pantouflier, *n.m.,* slipper-maker.

paon (pan), *n.m.,* (orni.) peacock; (astron.)
Pavo. — *sauvage des Pyrénées ;* ruff, reeve. —
bleu ; peacock-fish. *Queue-de— ;* (min.) iridescent sulphate of copper.

paonne (pa-n), *n.f.,* (orni.) pea-hen.

paonneau (pa-nô), *n.m.,* pea-chick.

papa, *n.m.,* papa, dad. *Bon —;* grandpapa.

papal, -e, *adj.,* papal.

papas (pa-pâ), *n.m.,* pope (Greek priest).

papauté, *n.f.,* papacy, popedom, pontificate.

papavéracées, *n.f.pl.,* (bot.) papaveraceæ.

papaye, *n.f.,* (bot.) papaw (fruit).

papayer, *n.m.,* papaw-tree ; papaw.

pape, *n.m.,* Pope (orni.) papa.

papegai (pap-ghè), *n.m.,* (orni.) popinjay.

papelard (pa-plar), *n.m.,* (fam.) hypocrite.

papelard, -e, *adj.,* (fam.) hypocritical. *Air,
ton, —;* sanctified air, tone.

papelardise (pa-plar-dîz), *n.f.,* (fam.) hypocrisy, sanctimoniousness.

papeline, *n.f.,* poplin.

papelonné, *adj.,* (her.) covered with scales.

paperasse (pap-ras), *n.f.,* old paper; waste
paper ; (b.s.) paper.

paperasser, *v.n.,* to rummage papers ; to
scribble away.

paperassier, *n.m.,* everlasting scribbler ; rummager of old papers.

paperassi-er, -ère, *adj.,* red-tape ; formal.

papesse, *n.f.,* papess. *La — Jeanne ;* Pope
Jean.

papeterie (pap-trî), *n.f.,* paper-mill ; paper-
making ; paper-trade ; paper-manufacture ; paper-
manufactory ; stationery ; stationery box *or* case.
Magasin de —; stationer's shop.

papetier (pap-tié), *n.m.,* paper-maker ; stationer.

papier, *n.m.,* paper. — *à écrire ;* writing-paper.
— *brouillard ;* scribbling-paper. — *à lettres ;*
note-paper. — *gris, goudronné ;* brown paper.
Main de —; quire of paper. *Cahier de —;*
paper-book ; quarter of a quire. — *cassé ;*
outside sheets. — *chantonné ;* wrinkled paper.
— *serpent, — de soie ;* silver-paper. — *dentelle ;* lace-paper. — *blanc ;* white paper, blank
paper. — *collé ;* sized paper. — *non collé ;*
unsized paper. — *mécanique ;* machine-made
paper, machine-paper. — *peint, — teint ;*
stained-paper. — *de verre ;* glass-paper, sand-
paper. — *soufflé, — velouté ;* flock-paper. — *coquille ;* demy paper, post-demy. — *Jésus ;* super-
royal paper, long-royal paper. — *pelure ;* foreign
paper, foreign post-paper. — *ministre ;* petition-
paper. — *buvard ;* blotting-paper. *Couteau à —;*
paper-knife, paper-cutter. — *à calquer ;* tracing-
paper. — *rayé ;* striped paper. — *du Nil ;* papyrus. — *naturel ;* fossil-paper. ⊙*—s-nouvelles ;*
newspapers. — *s de bord ;* (nav.) ship's papers.
Etre bien dans les —s de quelqu'un ; to be in any
one's good books, good graces. *Etre mal dans les
—s de quelqu'un,* to be in any one's bad books.
Rayez cela de vos —s ; strike that out of your
books. *Brouiller, gâter, du —;* to waste, to
spoil paper. ⊙*—journal ;* (com.) day-book.
Payer en —; to pay in bills. — *volant ;* fly-
ing-sheet. — *timbré ;* stamped paper. *—monnaie ;* paper-money.

papilionacé, -e, *or* ***papillonacé, -e,** *adj.,*
(bot.) papilionaceous.

papillaire, *adj.,* (anat.) papillary.

papille, *n.f.,* (anat.) papilla.

***papillon,** *n.m.,* (ent.) butterfly ; butterfly
(pers.); (nav.) sky-sail. — *de nuit ;* moth. — *s
noirs ;* the blues, spleen.

*papillonner, *v.n.*, to flutter about ; to hover ; to trifle, to flirt.

*papillotage, *n.m.*, twinkling (of the eyes) ; putting in paper, in curl-papers (of the hair) ; glitter, tinsel ; (print.) mackling, slurring.

*papillote, *n.f.*, curl-paper ; sweetmeat in paper ; chocolate drop ; spangle (of gold or silver) ; (cook.) paper. *Côtelette en —* ; cutlet fried in paper. *Fer à —s* ; curling-irons.

*papilloter, *v.a.*, to put hair in paper.

*papilloter, *v.n.*, to twinkle, to blink; to dazzle, to be gaudy ; (print.) to slur.

papisme, *n.m.*, papism, popery.

papiste, *n.m.f.*, papist.

papiste, *adj.*, papistic, papistical ; popish.

pappeu-x, -se, *adj.*, (bot.) downy, pappous.

papule, *n.f.*, (med.) papula, pimple.

papyracé, -e, *adj.*, thin and dry like paper ; papyraceous.

papyrus, *n.m.*, (bot.) paper-rush ; papyrus.

pâque, *n.f.*, Passover.

pâque *or* pâques, *n.m.*, Easter. *Quinzaine de —s* ; Passion-week and Easter week. *Semaine de —s* ; Easter-week. In the following expressions *Pâques* is feminine plural : *—s fleuries* ; Palm-Sunday. *—s closes* ; Low-Sunday. *Faire ses —* ; to receive the Sacrament (at Easter).

paquebot (pak-bô), *n.m.*, packet-boat, packet liner ; steamer. *— à vapeur* ; steam-packet. *— de poste* ; mail-packet. *Le — d'Angleterre, d'Espagne* ; the English, the Spanish mail.

pâquerette, *n.f.*, (bot.) daisy, Easter-daisy.

paquet, *n.m.*, bundle, parcel ; packet ; mail ; trick ; mass ; lump (pers.) ; (print.) slip. *Faire un —* ; to make up a parcel. *Faire ses —s* ; to pack up one's traps, to pack up. *Hasarder or risquer le —* ; to chance it ; to take the risk. *Faire ses —s pour l'autre monde* ; to set out for the long journey, to kick the bucket. *Faire un — sur quelqu'un* ; to backbite any one. *Donner un — à quelqu'un* ; to play off a trick on any one. *Donner à quelqu'un son —* ; to give the sack to any one ; to silence any one. *Recevoir son —, recevoir ses —s* ; to be discharged, to be sent to the right-about, to get the sack. *Cette femme est un vrai —* ; that woman is a regular dowdy.

paqueter, *v.a.*, to bundle, to bind up in parcels, to roll up.

paquetier (pak-tié), *n.m.*, (print.) piecehand.

paquette, *n.f.*, (bot.) ox-eye daisy.

paqueur, *n.m.*, salt-fish packer.

pâquis, *n.m.*, feeding-ground ; pasture.

par, *prep.*, by, through, out of, about, into, in, from, for, for the sake of, at, with ; during. *De — le roi* ; in the king's name. *Il a fait cela — crainte* ; he did it from fear, through fear. *Il entra — la porte* ; he entered by the door. *Je compris — là* ; I understood from that. *— passe-temps* ; by way of diversion. *Cela se fait — tout pays* ; that is done in all countries. *— où ?* which way ? *— ici* ; this way. *— là* ; that way. *— deçà* ; this side. *— delà* ; that side. *— dedans* ; within. *— dehors* ; without. *—devers* ; by, with. *—dessus* ; over, above, over and above. *—dessus les maisons* ; above the houses. *—dessous* ; under, underneath. *— devant* ; before, forwards. *— derrière* ; behind, backwards. *— le haut, — en haut* ; towards the top, upwards. *— le bas, — en bas* ; downwards. *Prenez-le — le bras* ; take his arm. *— le passé* ; formerly. *—ci —là* ; here and there ; off and on. *— aventure* ; by chance. *—devant* ; (jur.) in the presence of. *Il a passé — Paris* ; he passed through Paris. *Se promener — les rues* ; to walk about the streets. *Jeter — la fenêtre* ; to throw out of the window. *Il faut en passer — là* ; you must put up with it, you must come to that. *Elle finit — le persuader* ; she, at length, persuaded him. *Distribuer — chapitres* ; to divide into chapters. *Aller — bandes* ; to go in companies. *Couper —*

morceaux ; to cut in pieces, into pieces. *Donner tant — tête* ; to give so much per head. *Une guinée — soldat* ; a guinea each soldier. *— soi-même* ; by one's self, unaided, unassisted.

para, *n.m.*, (—s) para, Turkish coin worth about half a penny.

parabase, *n.f.*, (antiq.) parabasis, (prologue).

parabole, *n.f.*, (geom.) parabola ; parable. *Le —s de Salomon* ; the proverbs of Solomon.

parabolique *adj.*, parabolic, parabolical.

paraboliquemenᵗ (-lik-mān), *adv.*, parabolically.

paracentèse, *n.f.*, (surg.) paracentesis, tapping.

⊙parachèvement, *n.m.*, ending, finishing; completion, last touch.

⊙parachever, *v.a.*, to finish, to end, to complete, to put the finishing touch to.

parachronisme (-kro-), *n.m.*, parachronism.

parachute, *n.m.*, parachute.

paraclet, *n.m.*, (Bibl.) Paraclete, comforter.

parade, *n.f.*, parade ; show, boast ; state, pageant, pageantry ; (fenc.) parade, parrying ; (milit.) parade ; burlesque scenes ; outside shows (at fairs). *Chambre de —* ; state-room. *Lit de —* ; bed of state. *Faire — d'une chose* ; to make a parade, a display, of anything. *Faire —* ; (nav.) to dress a ship with flags. *Ne pas être heureux à la —* ; not to be quick at repartee, to be a bad hand at repartee. *A la —* ; (milit.) on parade. *Habit de —* ; state, court, official dress.

parader, *v.n.*, to parade, to show off ; to cruise. *Faire — un cheval* ; to show off the paces of a horse.

paradigme, *n.m.*, (gram.) paradigm.

paradis, *n.m.*, paradise ; (thea.) upper gallery, gods. *Le — terrestre* ; earthly paradise. *Ce lieu-ci est un vrai —* ; this place is a heaven on earth. *Oiseau de —* ; bird of paradise. *Pomme de —* ; apple of paradise. *Sur ma part du —* ; as I hope to be saved. *Ne pas le porter en —* ; to suffer for anything.

paradisier, *n.m.*, (orni.) bird of paradise.

paradoxal, -e, *adj.*, paradoxical.

paradoxalement, *adv.*, paradoxically.

paradoxe, *n.m.*, paradox.

⊙paradoxe, *adj.*, paradoxical.

paradoxisme, *n.m.*, (rhet.) paradoxy.

parafe *or* paraphe, *n.m.*, flourish (added to one's signature) ; initials and flourish ; paraph, sign manual, signature.

parafer *or* parapher *v.a.*, to put one's flourish, dash, *or* initials to ; to sign.

paraffine, *n.f.*, (chem.) paraffine.

parage, *n.m.*, (nav.) latitude, quarter ; parts, place ; (l.u.) extraction, descent, lineage ; *pl.*, seas. *De haute —* ; of high degree. *Dans ces —s* ; in these seas.

paragoge, *n.f.*, (gram.) paragoge.

paragogique, *adj.*, (gram.) paragogic, paragogical.

paragraphe, *n.m.*, paragraph.

⊙paraguante (-gooant), *n.f.*, present, tip, largesse, douceur.

paraître (paraissant, paru), *v.n.*, to appear, to make one's appearance, to be seen, to be visible ; to make a show, to make some figure ; to seem, to look ; to come out, to be published ; (nav.) to heave in sight. *— en mer* ; to loom. *Commencer à —* ; to appear, to come in sight. *Ces raisons paraissent bonnes* ; these reasons seem to be plausible. *Quand votre ouvrage paraîtra-t-il ?* when will your work be published ? *Chercher à —* ; to endeavour to make an appearance, to cut a figure. *Il n'y a rien qui n'y paraisse* ; that is very evident, very clear. *Faire —* ; to show, to discover, to exhibit. *Il paraît* ; it appears. *Il y paraît* ; there are appearances of it, it is evident. *Il n'y paraît pas* ; one would not have thought it, there are no signs of it. *Il n'y paraît plus;* there is no trace of it. *Vient de* —; just out, just published. *Sans qu'il y paraisse;* without making any show.

paralipse, *n.f.*, (rhet.) paralipsis.

parallactique, *adj.*, (astron.) parallactic.

parallaxe, *n.f.*, (astron.) parallax.

parallèle, *adj.*, (geom.) parallel.

parallèle, *n.f.*, (geom.) parallel; (fort.) parallel.

parallèle, *n.m.*, parallel, comparison, simile; (geog.) parallel, circle of latitude. *Mettre en* —; to draw a parallel between, to compare.

parallèlement, *adv.*, parallelly, in parallel lines; comparatively.

parallélépipède or **parallélipipède**, *n.m.*, (geom.) parallelopiped.

parallélisme, *n.m.*, parallelism.

parallélogrammatique, *adj.*, (geom.) parallelogrammic.

parallélogramme, *n.m.*, (geom.) parallelogram. — *articulé;* (mec.) parallel-joint. — *de Watt;* (mec.) parallel motion.

parallélographe, *n.m.*, parallel-ruler.

paralogisme, *n.m.*, paralogism.

paralysateur, -trice, *adj.n.f.*, paralyzing.

paralyser, *v.a.*, (med.) to paralyze; to render powerless, to paralyze. *Se* —; to become paralyzed, to paralyze each other.

paralysie, *n.f.*, (med.) paralysis, palsy. *Tomber en* —; to have a paralytic stroke. *Attaque de* —; paralytic stroke.

paralytique, *n.m.f.* and *adj.*, paralytic; paralytical, palsied.

paramètre, *n.m.*, (geom.) parameter.

parangon, *n.m.*, ⊙paragon, model; comparison, parallel; (jewelry) flawless stone, paragon. *Gros* —; (print.) double pica. *Petit* —; (print.) paragon. *Cela est sans* —; that is without a parallel, unparalleled. *Faire le* — *d'une chose avec une autre;* to compare one thing with another.

parangon, *adj. invariable*, (jewelry) without defect, perfect, flawless. *Diamant* —; diamond without a flaw.

parangonnage, *n.m.*, (print.) ranging.

parangonner, *v.a.*, ⊙to compare, to make a comparison of; (print.) to adjust, to range.

parant, -e, *adj.*, ornamental, decking, adorning, dressy.

parapet, *n.m.*, parapet, parapet-wall, breastwork.

paraphe, parapher. V. **parafe, parafer**.

paraphernal, -e, *adj.*, (jur.) paraphernal. *Biens paraphernaux;* paraphernal property, paraphernalia.

paraphernaux, *n.m.pl.*, (jur.) paraphernalia, wife's property.

paraphimosis (-zîs), *n.m.*, (surg.) paraphimosis.

paraphrase, *n.f.*, paraphrase; commentary, amplification.

paraphraser, *v.a.* and *n.*, to paraphrase, to comment, to amplify.

paraphraseu-r, *n.m.*, -**se**, *n.f.*, (b.s.) amplifier, paraphraser.

paraphraste, *n.m.*, paraphrast.

paraplégie, *n.f.*, (med.) paraplegia.

parapluie, *n.m.*, umbrella. *Canne (f.)* or *manche (m.) de* —; umbrella-stick.

parasange, *n.f.*, (antiq.) parasang (Persian measure of distance).

parasélène, *n.f.*, (astron.) paraselene.

parasite, *n.m.*, parasite; hanger-on; sycophant.

parasite, *adj.*, parasitic, parasitical; sycophantic; superfluous, redundant. *Plante* —*s;* parasitical plants. *Insectes* —*s;* parasitic insects. *Mots* —*s;* superfluous, redundant words.

parasitisme, *n.m.*, (med.) parasitism.

parasol (-sol), *n.m.*, parasol. *Plante en* —; umbelliferous plant.

paratitlaire, *n.m.*, (jur.) author of paratitla, summaries.

paratitles, *n.m.pl.*, (jur.) paratitla, paratitles, summaries, abridgments.

paratonnerre, *n.m.*, lightning - conductor; (nav.) marine conductor, conductor.

paravent, *n.m.*, screen, folding-screen. *Chinois de* —; guy; grotesque figure. *Comédie de* —; private performances, theatricals.

parbleu ! *int.*, zounds ! forsooth !

parc, *n.m.*, park; pen (for cattle); sheepfold; bed, breeding-ground (of oysters); (artil.) park; warren (for game); (agri.) sheepwalk; (nav.) locker. — *de construction;* shipyard. *Les murailles d'un* —; the walls of a park.

parcage, *n.m.*, folding (of sheep); penning (of cattle).

parcellaire, *adj.*, in or by small portions, in detail. *Cadastre* —; register of lands divided into small portions.

parcellaire, *n.m.*, register of a survey in detail.

parcelle, *n.f.*, particle, portion; driblet, installment. — *du sol;* portion of the soil. *Payer par* —*s;* to pay by installments.

parceller, *v.a.*, to portion or parcel out.

parce que, *conj.*, because, inasmuch as, forasmuch as; why, wherefore.

parchemin, *n.m.*, parchment, skin. *pl.*, titles of nobility; descent, pedigree. *Allonger le* —; to lengthen out deeds uselessly. *Il est fier de ses* —*s;* he is proud of his pedigree.

parcheminerie (-mi-n-rî), *n.f.*, parchment-making; parchment-factory; parchment-trade.

parcheminier, *n.m.*, parchment-maker.

parcimonie, *n.f.*, parsimony, sparingness.

parcimonieusement, *adv.*, parsimoniously, sparingly.

parcimonieu-x, -se, *adj.*, parsimonious, sparing.

parcourir, *v.a.*, to travel over, to go over, to run over, to perambulate ; to scour, to take a survey (of); to look over ; to peruse ; to turn over the leaves (of a book). *Il a parcouru toute l'Asie;* he has travelled all over Asia. — *la ville;* to scour, to look over the town. — *un livre;* to look through a book. *Je l'ai parcouru;* I have read it cursorily.

parcours, *n.m.*, line, distance, length, course, journey; road, way; commonage. *Faire le* — *entre;* to ply between.

pardessus, *n.m.*, overcoat, greatcoat.

pardon, *n.m.*, pardon, forgiveness ; condonation. *pl.*, (c.rel.) indulgences; fair (in Brittany); pilgrimage. *Je vous demande* —; I beg your pardon. — ; excuse me; by your leave.

pardonnable, *adj.*, pardonable, excusable.

pardonné, -e, *part.*, pardoned, forgiven.

pardonner, *v.a.*, to pardon, to forgive, to overlook; to spare, to excuse; to condone ; not to grudge. — *les offenses;* to forgive offenses. — *une erreur à quelqu'un;* to excuse an error in any one. *Pardonnez à ma franchise de vous dire cela;* excuse my frankness in telling you that. *Pardonnez-moi;* pardon me; excuse me.

paréage or **pariage**, *n.m.*, (feudal law) joint possession.

pareaux, *n.m.pl.*, weights (of a fishing net).

parégorique, *n.m.* and *adj.*, (med.) paregoric.

*pareil, -le, *adj.*, like, alike, equal; similar, such, like this, like that, like it. *Je n'ai rien vu de* —; I never saw the like. *Sans* —; peerless, matchless. *C'est un homme sans* —; he has not his match, he has no equal. *Comment pouvez-vous me dire chose* —*le ;* how can you say or tell me such a thing.

pareil, *n.m.f.*, equal, fellow, match. *Il a trouvé son* —; he has found his match. *Fré-*

quentez vos —s ; keep company with your equals.

pareille, *n.f.,* like *or* similar treatment. *Rendre la — à quelqu'un ;* to serve any one the same, to pay any one back in his own coin, to even with any one; to return like for like. *Avoir le —;* to have one like (it), *or* to have the fellow to (it).

*pareillement, *adv.,* similarly ; in the same way, likewise, too.

parélie. *V.* **parhélie.**

parelle, *n.f.,* (bot.) parella, patience.

parement (par-măn), *n.m.,* ornament ; cuff ; facing (of dress); cuff (of sleeves) ; large stick (of a fagot; (arch.) facing ; altar-cloth ; curb-stone.

parementer, *v.a.,* (arch.) to face.

parenchymateu-x, -se, *adj.,* parenchymatous.

parenchyme, *n.m.,* (anat. bot.) parenchyma ; diploe (of leaves).

parénèse, *n.f.,* parenesis.

parénétique, *adj.,* parenetic.

parent, *n.m.,* -**e,** *n.f.,* relation, relative ; kinsman, kinswoman, kin: *pl.,* parents, father and mother ; relatives, relations, connections, kindred. *— paternel ;* relation on the father's side. *— maternel ;* relation on the mother's side. *Un bon ami vaut mieux qu'un —;* a good friend is better than a kinsman. *Grands-—;* grandfather and grandmother. *Proche —;* near relative ; (jur.) next of kin.

⊙**parentage,** *n.m. V.* **parenté.**

parenté, *n.f.,* relationship, consanguinity, kindred ; relations, relatives, kinsfolk, connections, family.

parentèle, *n.f.,* (fam.). *V.* **parenté.**

parenthèse, *n.f.,* parenthesis, digression. *Par —;* by way of parenthesis, by-the-bye, by-the-way. *Entre —s ;* in parenthesis. *Avoir les jambes en —;* (fam.) to be bandy-legged.

parer, *v.a.,* to adorn, to set off (against), to set out, to deck, to embellish; to attire; to trim ; to shelter ; to guard (against) ; to provide (against); to parry, to ward off ; (nav.) to clear ; to pare (horses' hoofs). *— un coup ;* to ward off a blow. *— du cuir ;* to dress leather. *— du cidre ;* to make cider ferment. *— un agneau ;* to dress a lamb. *— un cap ;* (nav.) to clear a cape. *— un câble ;* to clear a cable. *— une ancre ;* to clear an anchor. *— un enfant ;* to dress out a child. *Il est assez paré de sa bonne mine ;* his good looks set him off sufficiently. *— sa marchandise ;* to set off one's goods.

se parer, *v.r.,* to adorn one's self ; to dress ; to dress one's self out ; to screen, to guard one's self; to assume; to make a show, to boast. *Elle se pare d'une manière ridicule ;* she decks herself out in a ridiculous manner.

parer, *v.n.,* (fenc.) to parry ; to screen, to defend ; to guard (against). *— et porter en même temps ;* to parry and thrust at the same time. *On ne peut pas — à tout ;* one can't guard against everything.

parère, *n.m.,* (com.) opinion (of merchants on matters of commerce); (of insurance) report.

parésie, *n.f.,* (med.) slight palsy.

paresse, *n.f.,* idleness, sloth, laziness, indolence ; weakness. *— d'esprit ;* sluggishness of intellect, indolence of mind.

paresser, *v.n.,* to idle, to fritter away one's time, to be idle.

paresseusement (-eŭz-măn), *adv.,* lazily, idly, slothfully.

paresseu-x, -se, *n.* and *adj.,* sluggard, idle, lazy person ; lazy, idle, slothful, sluggish, indolent; (of the stomach) weak; (of the bowels) sluggish.

paresseux, *n.m.,* (mam.) sloth.

pareur, *n.m.,* (tech.) finisher.

parfaire, *v.a.,* to perfect, to complete, to make up, to finish thoroughly.

parfait, -e, *adj.,* perfect, finished ; accomplished, complete, full. *Accord —;* (mus.) perfect chord. *Cela est fait et —;* that is completely finished.

parfait, *n.m.,* perfection ; (gram.) perfect. *Plusque-—;* pluperfect. *Au —;* (gram.) in the perfect.

parfaitement (-fèt-măn), *adv.,* perfectly, completely, exactly, just so, to be sure ; decidedly.

parfilage, *n.m.,* unraveling, threading.

parfiler, *v.a.* and *n.,* to unravel ; to pick out the threads of ; to thread.

parfois, *adv.,* sometimes, occasionally, now and then.

parfond, *n.m.,* ground-net ; ground-tackle.

parfondre, *v.a.,* to fuse (enamel).

se parfondre, *v.r.,* to be fused.

parfournir, *v.a.,* to render complete, to make up.

parfum (-fun), *n.m.,* perfume, odor, scent, fragrance, flavor; bouquet (of wines). *Le — des fleurs ;* the fragrance of flowers.

parfumé, -e, *adj.,* scented, savory, flavored.

parfumer, *v.a.,* to perfume, to sweeten, to scent; to fumigate.

se parfumer, *v.r.,* to use perfumes, to scent one's self.

parfumerie (-fu-mrî), *n.f.,* perfumery.

parfumeu-r, *n.m.,* **-se,** *n.f.,* perfumer.

parfumoir, *n.m.,* perfuming-pan ; fumigator.

parhélie *or* **parélie,** *n.m.,* parhelion, mock-sun.

pari, *n.m.,* bet, wager, stake. *Faire un —;* to lay a bet. *Tenir le —;* to take the bet.

paria, *n.m.,* pariah, outcast.

pariade, *n.f.,* pairing-time (of partridges).

parier, *v.a.,* to bet, to lay a wager, to stake ; to undertake to say, to be almost certain. *Il y a à —;* the odds are. *C'est à — dix contre un ;* it is ten to one. *— pour quelqu'un ;* to back any one. *J'en parierais ma tête ;* I would bet anything, stake my head (upon it).

pariétaire, *n.f.,* (bot.) parietary.

pariétal, *adj.m.,* (anat.) parietal.

pariétal, *n.m.,* (anat.) parietal-bone.

parieur, *n.m.,* wagerer, bettor, betting-man.

paris, *n.m.,* Paris (fig.). *Monsieur de —;* Jack Ketch. *Premier —;* leading article. *Prendre — pour Corbeil, le Pirée pour un homme ;* not to know a hawk from a handsaw.

parisette, *n.f.,* (bot.) paris, true-love.

parisien, -ne, *n.* and *adj.,* Parisian.

parisienne, *n.f.,* (print.) pearl ; Parisienne (patriotic song).

⊙**parisis** (-zîs), *adj.,* of Paris (of coin).

parisyllabique (-sil-la-bik), *adj.,* (gram.) parisyllabic.

parité, *n.f.,* parity, likeness, equality ; comparison, parallel case.

parjure, *n.m.f.* and *adj.,* perjurer ; perjured, forsworn.

parjure, *n.m.,* perjury, false oath.

se parjurer, *v.r.,* to perjure, *or* to forswear, one's self ; to be forsworn.

parlage, *n.m.,* empty talk, prattle, twaddle.

parlant, -e, *adj.,* speaking ; talkative, chatty ; (her.) allusive, canting. *Ce portrait est —;* that is a speaking likeness. *Cet homme est peu —;* that man is not talkative, is very reticent.

parlement, *n.m.,* parliament ; court. *Contraire aux usages du —;* unparliamentary.

parlementaire, *n.m.* and *adj.,* bearer of a flag of truce ; parliamentarian ; parliamentary. *Un vaisseau —;* a cartel-ship.

parlementer, *v.n.,* to parley, to come to a parley, to come to terms.

parler, *v.n.,* to speak, to talk, to commune, to discourse, to converse, to talk about, to mention, to say, to tell. *Façon de —;* mode of speaking, manner of speech. — *à l'oreille ;* to whisper. — *en public ;* to speak in public. — *trop ;* to speak too much. *Sans — de ;* without mentioning, to say nothing of. *Il parle mal de vous ;* he speaks ill of you. *Faire — de soi ;* to get one's self talked about. — *à un sourd ;* to speak to a post. *Cela ne vaut pas la peine d'en — ;* it is not worth mentioning. *Cela parle tout seul ;* the thing speaks for itself. *Il en parle bien à son aise ;* it is easy for him to say so. *Je lui apprendrai à — ;* I will teach him to govern his tongue. *Il trouvera à qui — ;* he will find his match. — *en l'air ;* to talk at random. — *à cheval à quelqu'un ;* to speak imperiously to any one, to dictate to any one. — *de la pluie et du beau temps ;* to talk of indifferent matters. — *d'abondance ;* to speak on the spur of the moment, extempore. *Il a bien fait — de lui ;* he has got himself much talked about. — *en maître ;* to speak peremptorily. *Trop gratter cuit, trop — nuit ;* least said, soonest mended ; speech is silvern, silence is golden. *Sans — de ;* without mentioning, to say nothing of.

parler, *v.a.*, to speak (a language). — *français ;* to speak French. *Il parle bien sa langue ;* he speaks his language well. *Parlez-moi de cela !* now that's something like ! *Ne m'en parlez pas, par exemple !* I can vouch for the truth of it ! *Moi qui vous parle ;* I, my very own self.

se **parler**, *v.r.*, to speak to each other ; to be spoken (of languages). *Elles se parlent des yeux ;* they speak to each other with their eyes.

parler, *n.m.*, speech, utterance, way *or* manner of speaking ; language, accent. *Avoir son franc — ;* to be outspoken ; not to mince matters ; to speak one's mind. *Jamais beau — n'écorche la langue ;* fair words are always the best ; civility costs nothing.

parlerie, *n.f.*, prating, chatter, talkativeness.

parleu-r, *n.m.*, **-se**, *n.f.*, speech-maker, talker. *Un beau — ;* a good speaker.

parli-er, **-ère**, *adj.*, (l.u.) talkative.

parloir, *n.m.*, parlor.

parlote, *n.f.*, resort of gossips ; gossiping club ; debating-society.

parloter, *v.n.*, to chatter, to talk twaddle ; to gossip ; to practice speaking.

parmentière (-tièr) *n.f.*, (bot.) potato.

parmesan, *n.m.*, Parmesan cheese.

parmi, *prep.*, among, amongst, amid, amidst.

parnasse, *n.m.*, Parnassus. *Le — français ;* French poetry, the French poets.

parnassien, **-ne** (-in, -è-n), *adj.*, Parnassian.

parnassien, *n.m.*, (jest.) son of Parnassus, poet.

parodie, *n.f.*, parody.

parodier, *v.a.*, to parody.

parodiste, *n.m.*, author of a parody.

paroi, *n.f.*, wall, partition ; side, casing, outer side ; (anat.) coat, wall. *Les —s d'un vase ;* the inner sides of a vase. *Les —s de l'estomac ;* the coating, the wall of the stomach. *La — d'un rocher ;* the outer side of a rock.

paroisse, *n.f.*, parish, parish-church ; parishioners. *Etre de deux —s ;* not to be fellows (of things).

paroissial, **-e**, *adj.*, parochial, parish.

paroissien (-in), *n.m.*, **-ne** (-è-n), *n.f.*, parishioner.

paroissien, *n.m.*, church-service ; prayer-book. *C'est un pauvre — ;* he is a poor sort of a fellow.

parole, *n.f.*, word ; speech, language ; saying, sentiment ; utterance, voice ; eloquence ; promise ; trust ; (milit.) parole. *Il traîne ses —s ;* he drawls his words. *Il a perdu la — ;* he has lost the use of his tongue. *Porter la — ;* to speak, to be the spokesman. *Adresser la — à quelqu'un ;* to address any one. *Prendre la — ;* to

begin to speak, to address the house, to be speaking ; to have one's turn to speak (in Parliament). *Avoir la — ;* to be allowed to speak ; to be upon one's legs, to be in possession of the House ; to catch the speaker's eye (in Parliament). *Demander la — ;* to request permission to speak ; (parliamentary) to rise to order. *Céder la — ;* to decline speaking, to give up one's turn to speak. *Couper la — à quelqu'un ;* to interrupt any one speaking. *—s mémorables ;* notable sayings. *Il a la — lente ;* his utterance is slow *or* he is slow of utterance. *Il a la — tremblante ;* his voice falters. *La puissance de la — ;* the might of eloquence. *Engager sa — ;* to promise, to pledge one's word. *Tenir —, sa — ;* to keep one's word, to be as good as one's word. *Donner sa — ;* to give one's word. *Dégager sa — ;* to recall one's word. *Se dédire de sa —, manquer de —, or manquer à sa — ;* to go from, to break, one's word. *Il est prisonnier sur — ;* he is a prisoner on parole. *Il est homme de — ;* he is a man of his word. — *d'honneur ;* word of honor. *Ils ont eu des —s ;* words passed between them. *Se prendre de —s ;* to have words. *Un homme d'honneur n'a que sa — ;* an honest man's word is as good as his bond.

paroli, *n.m.*, double stake (at faro, &c.). *Faire — ;* to double. *Rendre le — à quelqu'un ;* to outdo any one.

paronomase, *n.f.*, paronomasia.

paronomasie, *n.f.*, resemblance between words of different languages.

paronychie, *n.f.*, (med.) paronychia, whitlow.

paronyme, *n.m.* and *adj.*, (gram.) paronym ; paronymous.

paronyque, *n.f.*, (bot.) whitlowwort.

parotide, *n.f.* and *adj.*, (anat.) parotid, parotid gland *or* artery ; (med.) parotitis, mumps ; parotid.

parotidien, **-ne** (-in, -è-n), *adj.*, (anat.) parotid.

parotidite, *n.f.*, (med.) parotitis, mumps ; (vet.) vives.

paroxysme, *n.m.*, (med.) paroxysm, fit ; (fig.) height, acme.

parpaing (-pin), *n.m.*, (mas.) perpend-stone.

parque, *n.f.*, (myth.) Fate, fatal sister. *pl.*, Fates.

parquer, *v.a.*, to fold, to pen, to pen up, to inclose ; to surround ; (artil.) to park. — *des bœufs ;* to pen cattle. — *des moutons ;* to fold sheep.

se **parquer**, *v.r.*, to be placed in an inclosure ; (artil.) to be parked ; to be pent up.

parquer, *v.n.*, to be penned, to be penned up (of cattle) ; (artil.) to be parked.

parquet, *n.m.*, bar (of a court of justice) ; office of the public prosecutor ; body of magistrates ; wood flooring (of rooms) ; back (of a looking-glass) ; (nav.) locker. — *à boulets ;* (nav.) shot-locker.

parquetage, *n.m.*, flooring ; inlaid-flooring.

parqueter, *v.a.*, to floor, to inlay.

parqueterie (-kè-tri), *n.f.*, parquetry, inlaid flooring.

parqueteur, *n.m.*, floor-layer.

parrain, *n.m.*, godfather, sponsor ; introducer ; ⊙second (in a duel).

parricide, *n.m.* and *adj.*, parricide ; matricide ; parricidal ; matricidal ; murderous.

parse *or* **parsi**, *n.m.* and *adj.*, Parsee.

parsemer, *v.a.*, to strew, to spread, to sprinkle ; to intersperse, to stud, to dot, to spangle. — *un chemin de fleurs ;* to strew a path with flowers. *Le ciel est parsemé d'étoiles ;* the sky is studded with stars.

part, *n.f.*, share, part, portion ; concern, interest ; part, side, concern. *Voilà votre — ;* voici la mienne ;* there is your share, here is mine. *Etre de — avec quelqu'un ;* to go shares with any one. *Faire la — à quelqu'un ;* to give any one his share. *Faire la — du feu ;* to circumscribe the fire ; (fig.) to allow for necessary losses. *Entrer en — avec quelqu'un ;* to go shares with any one. *Mettre de — ;* to give a share (in a business) ; to take in as partner. *Avoir — à quelque affaire ;* to have a share in any business. *Avoir — au gâteau ;* to share in the profits of anything, to have a finger in the pie. *Prendre — à ;* to participate in, to be a party to. *Faire part de quelque chose à quelqu'un ;* to give any one a share of anything ; to apprise any one of anything. *Billets de faire —;* circular letters to announce a birth, a death, &c. *Faire la — des accidents ;* to make allowance for accidents. *Prendre en bonne — ;* to take in a good sense. *Prendre en mauvaise — ;* to take amiss. *Je le sais de bonne — ;* I have it from a good source ; I know it on good authority. *Dites-lui de ma — ;* tell him from me. *Saluez-le de ma — ;* remember me to him. *Je prends cela de la — d'où il vient ;* I take it from whence it comes. *Je vais quelque — ;* I am going somewhere. *On ne le trouve nulle — ;* he is not to be found anywhere. *Autre — ;* somewhere else. *Nulle — ;* nowhere. *En quelque — que ;* wherever. *D'une — il considérait que ;* on one side he considered that. *De — et d'autre, de toutes —s ;* on either side, on all sides. *De — en —;* through and through. *A — ;* apart, aside. *Mettre à — ;* to set apart. *Il le tira à — ;* he took him aside. *C'est un fait à — ;* that is a particular case. *Raillerie à — ;* in good earnest, joking aside.

part (part), *n.m.,* (jur.) parturition, delivery ; child, infant, birth.

partage, *n.m.,* share, lot, portion ; apportionment ; partition ; sharing, distribution, division. *— égal ;* equal division. *Faire le — du butin ;* to divide the spoils. *La prudence est le — des vieillards ;* prudence is proper to old age. *Faire le — de ;* to divide. *Etre le — de ;* to be the lot of. *Tomber,* or *échoir, en — à ;* to fall to the lot of.

partageable (-jabl), *adj.,* divisible into shares.

partageant (-jān), *n.m.,* (jur.) sharer.

partager, *v.a.,* to share ; to give a share ; to divide, to parcel, to portion, to distribute ; to partake of, to participate in, to take part in. *Partagez cela entre vous ;* divide that between you. *— le butin ;* to share the spoils. *Les avis se trouvent partagés ;* the votes are divided. *Il faut — le différend ;* we must split the difference. *Je partage votre joie ;* I participate in, or share, or am a sharer in, your joy.

se **partager,** *v.r.,* to divide, to be divided, to part ; to divide one's time *or* affection, etc., between.

partager, *v.n.,* to share, to receive a share. *Il est bien partagé ;* the fates have been kind to him, *or* his bread is well buttered.

partance, *n.f.,* (nav.) sailing, departure. *Coup de — ;* signal for sailing ; sailing-gun. *En —;* on the point of sailing, *or* about to sail.

partant, *adv.,* consequently, hence ; therefore, and therefore, thus.

partenaire, *n.m.f.,* partner (at cards *or* dancing).

parterre, *n.m.,* flower-bed, garden-plot ; (thea.) pit ; audience, public. *Réjouir le — ;* to please the audience. *Aller au — ;* to go into the pit.

parthe, *n.* and *adj.,* parthian.

parthénogénèse, *n.f.,* (ent.) parthenogenesis.

parthénon, *n.m.,* Parthenon.

parti, *n.m.,* party, side, part, cause ; resolution, choice, ways, means, expedient, course, method ; offer, condition ; use, advantage ; calling, profession ; (milit.) detachment ; match (marriage). *Chef de — ;* leader of a party.

Entrer dans un — ; to join a party. *Etre du bon —;* to be on the right side. *Etre du — de ;* to be on the side of. *Prendre le — de quelqu'un ;* to take any one's part, to side with any one. *Homme de — ;* party man. *Esprit de — ;* party spirit. *Il a pris son — ;* he has made up his mind. *J'ai pris le — de me taire ;* I chose to be silent. *C'est un — pris ;* it is a foregone conclusion, a fixed determination. *A — pris, point de conseil ;* when a man's mind is made up, advice is useless. *Voilà le — qu'il nous faut prendre ;* this is what we must do *or* the course we must take. *C'est le — le plus court ;* that is the shortest way. *C'est un bon — ;* it is a very good offer. *Faire un mauvais — à quelqu'un ;* to do harm to any one. *Il cherche à tirer — de tout ;* he endeavors to turn everything to account. *Il a épousé un bon — ;* he has made a good match. *Tirer le meilleur — de quelque chose ;* to make the best of anything. *En prendre son — ;* to resign one's self to anything (to the inevitable). *De — pris ;* deliberately. *Tirer — de ;* to make the best of ; to turn to account. *C'est un — pris chez lui ;* he *will* do it.

partiaire (-ci-èr), *adj.,* (jur.) farmer who gives a portion of the produce of the land for rent.

partial, -e (-ci-al), *adj.,* partial, biased.

partialement (-cial-mān), *adv.,* partially, with partiality.

se **partialiser** (-cia-li-), *v.r.,* to be partial *or* biased.

partialité (-cia-li-), *n.f.,* partiality, bias.

in **partibus,** *adv.,* in partibus. *Un évêque in —;* a bishop in partibus.

participant, -e, *adj.,* participating.

participant, *n.m., -e,* *n.f.,* participant, sharer.

participation, *n.f.,* participation, privity, share ; knowledge. *La — aux droits ;* the participation of rights. *Cela s'est fait sans ma — ;* that was done without my knowledge.

participe, *n.m.,* (gram.) participle.

participer, *v.n.,* to partake (of), to participate, to share, to have a share in, to be a party to. *Je participe à votre douleur ;* I take part in *or* share your sorrow. *Le mulet participe du cheval et de l'âne ;* the mule partakes of both the horse and the ass.

particulariser, *v.a.,* to particularize.

particularisme, *n.m.,* (rel. pol.) particularism.

particulariste, *n.m.,* (pol.) particularist.

particularité, *n.f.,* particular, particularity ; peculiarity, circumstance.

particule, *n.f.,* particle.

particuli-er, -ère, *adj.,* particular, peculiar, private ; circumstantial, singular, appropriate, special ; specific ; express. *L'intérêt — doit céder à l'intérêt général ;* private interest must give way to public interest. *On lui a donné une chambre —ère ;* they gave him a private room. *Le cas est fort — ;* the case is altogether singular. *Il a un talent — ;* he has a peculiar talent.

particulier, *n.m.,* particular individual, private individual, civilian ; (pop.) fellow. *Ce n'est qu'un simple — ;* he is only a private individual. *Que nous veut ce — ?* what does that fellow want with us ? *En — ;* in particular, in private. *Etre en son — ;* to be in one's own room. *Il faut le voir en — ;* you must see him privately. *En mon — ;* as for me.

particulièrement (-lièr-mān), *adv.,* particularly, peculiarly, especially.

partie (-tî), *n.f.,* part, match, game ; project, plan, scheme ; line of business ; client, adversary ; (com.) parcel ; ☉(bookkeeping) entry ; (play) game ; party ; contracting party. *pl.* pudenda. *Air à quatre —s ;* tune in four parts. *Tenir bien sa — ;* to act one's part well. *Vous en êtes en — cause ;* you are partly the cause of it. *Faire une — de piquet ;* to play a game at piquet. *— nulle ;* drawn game. *— liée ;* rubber, (racing) heats. — *d'honneur ;* conqueror. — *de plaisir ;* pleasure trip. — *publique ;* public prosecutor, crown. *C'est — remise ;* the pleasure is only deferred. *Un coup de —;* masterly stroke, decisive blow. *La — n'est pas égale;* it is not an equal match. *Quitter la —;* to give up, to throw up the game. *Voulez-vous être de la —?* will you be one of us? *Lier une —;* to make up or fix up a party (for amusement). *— carrée ;* pleasure party consisting of two gentlemen and two ladies. *— fine ;* select party or few friends. — *intéressée ;* party concerned. *Avoir affaire à forte —;* to have to deal with more than one's match. *Qui n'entend qu'une — n'entend rien ;* he who hears one side only, hears nothing. — *double ;* (bookkeeping) double entry. *— simple ;* (bookkeeping) single entry. *En —;* partly, in part. *En grand —;* in a great measure. *— bien, — mal ;* partly well, partly ill. *Prendre à —;* to take to task. *Se porter — contre ;* (jur.) to appear against.

partiel, -le (-ci-èl), *adj.,* partial.

partiellement (-cièl-män), *adv.,* partially, by instalments ; in part.

partir (partant, parti), *v.n.,* to set out, to start, to go, to go away, to depart ; to be off, to spring (of birds) ; to come, to proceed ; to flow from ; to go off (of firearms). *— du port ;* to sail from the harbor. *Faire —;* to send off, to dispatch (troops). *Il part comme l'éclair ;* he is off like lightning. *Faire — un lièvre ;* to start a hare. *— d'un éclat de rire ;* to burst into a fit of laughter. *— comme un trait ;* to dart off like an arrow. *La bombe part du mortier ;* the bomb is shot from the mortar. *Cela part d'un bon cœur ;* that flows from a good heart. *A — de ;* from, beginning from, reckoning from. *A — du règne ;* from the reign of. *A — d'aujourd'hui ;* from this day forward ; from to-day.

partir, *v.a.,* to part, to divide. [Only used in : *Ils ont toujours maille à —;* they are always squabbling.] *Avoir maille à — avec ;* to have a bone to pick with.

partir, *n.m.,* (man.) start ; going, leaving.

partisan, *n.m.,* partisan.

partiti-f, -ve, *adj.,* (gram.) partitive.

partition, *n.f.,* partition, division ; (mus.) score.

partner, *n.m.f.,* (—s). *V.* **partenaire.**

partout, *adv.,* everywhere, all over, on all sides. *— où ;* wherever.

parturition, *n.f.,* (med.) parturition.

paru, -e, *adj.,* appeared, published, out.

parure, *n.f.,* attire, dress, finery, ornament. *— de diamants ;* set of diamonds. *Meubles de même —;* furniture that matches.

parvenir, *v.n.,* to attain, to arrive, to come, to get (at), to reach, to succeed, to rise, to get on, to make one's way ; to reach the ears of. *— à ses fins ;* to attain one's ends. *Faire —;* to forward, to send to any one.

parvenu, -e *part.,* arrived, reached.

parvenu, *n.m.,* parvenu, upstart.

parvis, *n.m.,* parvis, open space (in front of a church) ; outer sanctuary, cathedral court ; (poet.) inclosure, hall, temple.

pas, *n.m.,* step, pace ; footstep, walk, gait ; progress, precedence ; pains, trouble, labor ; threshold, passage ; passage (of arms). *Marcher d'un — léger ;* to walk with a light step. *Il le suit — à —;* he follows him step by step. *A petits —;* slowly ; with short steps. *Il n'y a qu'un —;* it is but a step from here. *Il marche à grands —;* he takes long strides. *Marcher à — comptés ;* to walk very slowly. *Faire un — en arrière ;* to draw back a little. *Aller, marcher, à — de loup ;* to go softly, stealthily, without noise. *Retourner sur ses —;* to go back, to retrace one's steps. *Aller à — mesurés ;* to proceed with circumspection. *Au*

—; walking, at a walking pace ; in time. *Faire un faux —;* to make a false step. *— de clerc ;* blunder. *Avoir le —;* to have precedence (of). *De ce —;* directly, at once. *Mettre un cheval au —;* to walk a horse, to rein in a horse (to a foot pace). *Mettre au —;* to discipline ; to bring any one into line ; to recall any one to his duty, to put any one on his good behavior. *— accéléré ;* (milit.) quick time, quick march. *— redoublé ;* (milit.) double quick time. *Marcher sur les — de quelqu'un ;* to tread in any one's footsteps. *Se tirer d'un mauvais —;* to get out of a scrape. *Sauter le —;* to take a resolution ; (fam.) to kick the bucket. *— d'une vis ;* furrow of a screw. *— de fusée ;* (horl.) turn of a fusee. *Aller au —;* to walk (of a horse). *Y aller de ce —;* to go (anywhere) directly, at once. *Ce n'est que le premier — qui coûte,* in everything the beginning is the difficulty.

pas, *adv.,* no ; not, not any. *— un ;* not one. *Je ne veux —;* I will not. *— du tout ;* not at all. *Presque —;* scarcely any. *Je n'ai — de livre ;* I have no book.

pascal, -e, *adj.,* paschal.

pas-d'âne, *n.m.,* (—) sharp bridle-bit ; basket-hilt (of a sword) ; (bot.) colt's-foot.

pasigraphie, *n.f.,* pasigraphy.

pasquin, *n.m.,* pasquin.

pasquinade, *n.f.,* pasquinade, lampoon.

⊙**pasquiniser,** *v.a.,* to lampoon, to satirize.

passable, *adj.,* passable, tolerable, middling, decent.

passablement, *adv.,* passably, tolerably, indifferently, middlingly.

passade, *n.f.,* passing, short stay ; (fig.) passing fancy, temporary connection ; (man.) passade, ducking. *Je ne suis que de — à Paris ;* I am only making a short stay in Paris.

passage, *n.m.,* passage ; arcade ; thoroughfare, crossing ; transition, transit ; passage-money ; toll ; lane, court ; gateway, archway. *Oiseaux de —;* birds of passage. *— à niveau* (railways) ; level crossing. *Otez-vous du —;* stand out of the way. *Se faire — or s'ouvrir un —;* to make, to cut, one's way through. *Attendre,* or *guetter, au —;* to lie in wait for, to waylay, to wait for any one on his way. *Barrer le —;* to bar, to stand in the way. *Céder le —;* to let pass first. *Livrer — à ;* to make way for.

passager, *v.a.* and *n.,* (man.) to passage. *— un cheval ;* to passage a horse.

passag-er, -ère, *adj.,* passing, transient, transitory, fugitive, fleeting, short-lived, momentary ; migratory.

passag-er, *n.m.,* **-ère,** *n.f.,* passenger ; person passing through ; traveler ; passer-by.

passagèrement (-jèr-män), *adv.,* transiently, for a moment.

passant, *n.m.,* passenger, passer-by ; wayfarer, traveler.

passant, -e, *adj.,* open, much frequented ; (of colors) fading. *Un chemin —;* a much frequented thoroughfare. *Une rue —e ;* a much frequented street. *En —;* going along ; on the way ; (fig.) by the way. *Disons le en —;* let us say so by the way.

passation, *n.f.,* (jur.) drawing up a title-deed, a contract, passing (of contracts).

passavant, *n.m.,* pass, permit (of the custom-house) ; (nav.) gangway.

passe, *n.f.,* pass, situation, state, case ; (print.) overplus ; (fenc.) pass, passado, thrust ; port (at billiards) ; channel, passage (of harbors, of rivers) ; odd money ; stake (at play) ; (geog.) track. *Etre en — d'avoir quelque emploi ;* to be in a fair way to procure employment. *Il est en fort belle —;* he has a very fine prospect before him.

passe, *adv.,* well, let it be so. *— encore pour cela ;* well, well, let that be too ; well and good.

passé, -e, *part.,* past, gone, over; dead, vanished; faded, worn, out of use; withered. *Il a trente ans — s;* he is over thirty. *La pluie est —e;* the rain is over.

passé, *n.m.,* past, past life, time past, things past; (gram.) past tense.

passé, *prep.,* except; after.

passe-campane, *n.f.,* (—) (vet.) capellet.

passe-carreau, *n.m.,* (— —x) sleeve-board.

passe-cheval, *n.m.,* horse ferry-boat.

passe-debout, *n.m.,* (—) permit for transit.

passe-dix, *n.m.,* (—) passage (play).

passe-droit, *n.m.,* (— — s) favor; injustice, wrong.

passée, *n.f.,* (hunt.) flight, passage (of woodcocks). *Tuer des bécasses à la —;* to shoot woodcocks as they fly by.

passe-fleur, *n.f.,* (— — s) (bot.) a species of anemone.

passéger, *v.n.* V. **passager.**

passe-lacet, *n.m.,* (— — s) bodkin.

passement (pâs-mān), *n.m.,* lace (of gold, silk, etc., for clothes or furniture).

passementer (pâs-man-té), *v.a.,* to lace (clothes, furniture).

passementerie (pâs-man-trî), *n.f.,* lace, lacemaking, lace-trade.

passementi-er (-tié), *n.m.,* **-ère** (-tièr), *n.f.,* lace-maker, lace-man, lace-woman.

***passe-méteil,** *n.m.,* meslin (mixture of wheat and rye).

passe-parole, *n.m.,* (—) (milit.) pass-parole.

passe-partout, *n.m.,* (—) master-key, passkey, latch-key; (engr.) passe-partout; (print.) factotum; compass-saw. *L'argent est un bon —;* money opens most doors.

passe-passe, *n.m.,* (—) sleight of hand. *Tour de —;* legerdemain; hocus-pocus.

passe-pied, *n.m.,* (— — s) passe-pied (dance).

passe-pierre, *n.f.,* (—, *or* — — s), samphire, sea-samphire.

passepoil, *n.m.,* piping (for clothes).

passe-pomme, *n.f.,* jenneting.

passeport, *n.m.,* passport; pass; (fig.) recommendation.

passer, *v.n.,* to pass, to pass on, to pass along, to pass away; to die, to expire; to pass for, to be considered; to pass muster; to fade (of flowers). *Cette fleur va passer;* that flower is faded. — *en sautant;* to skip over. — *par;* to pass through. *Laisser —;* to overlook. *Il a passé par la ville;* he passed through the town. *Passez par ici;* come this way. — *outre;* to go beyond; (fig.) to move the previous question. *Il a passé par de rudes épreuves;* he has gone through severe trials. *Mes beaux jours sont passés;* my best days are over. *La fantaisie m'en est passée;* I have no desire for it now. *Faire —;* to let in, to admit; to pass on, to pass off; to hand round, to forward; to infuse, to instill; to while away (of time). *Faire — un mal;* to cure an illness. *Il passera un jour par mes mains;* some day or other he will fall into my hands. *Cela est passé en proverbe;* that has become a proverb. *Il faut en — par là;* we must submit, there is no way out of it; it must be borne, *or* endured. *Il faut y —;* we must go through it. *Il ne lui passe rien;* he forgives him nothing. — *chez;* to call on. *Je passerai chez vous demain;* I will call on you to-morrow. *Cela m'a passé de l'esprit;* that has slipped my memory. *Il a été passé par les armes;* he was shot. — *pour;* to pass for, to be considered *or* thought. *On ne passe pas;* no thoroughfare. *J'en passe: . . . et des meilleures;* I pass over some of the most valid reasons; I om¹t some, and they are not to be despised. *Passons au déluge;* granted; let 's come to the point, if you don't mind. *Passons!* I will not insist.

passer, *v.a.,* to pass, to cross, to go over; to ferry across; to slip, to exceed, to surpass; to utter (base coin); to strain (liquids); to run (tape); to put on (wearing apparel); to dress (skins, stuffs); to omit, to leave out; to allow, to grant, to pardon, to waive. — *la rivière;* to cross the river. — *la rivière à la nage;* to swim across the river. *Passez votre chemin;* go your way. — *son habit;* to put on one's coat. *Je n'y entends rien, cela me passe;* I can't make it out, it is beyond my comprehension; that beats me. — *son temps à se divertir;* to spend one's time in amusement. — *son envie d'une chose;* to gratify one's desire for a thing. — *sous silence;* to take no notice of. *Passez cet endroit;* pass over that place. *Passez moi cet article;* pass me that article. — *condamnation sur soi-même;* to pass sentence on one's self. — *une obligation;* to enter into a bond. — *un soldat par les baguettes;* to make a soldier run the gauntlet. — *tout le monde au fil de l'épée;* to put everybody to the sword. *Voulez-vous me — cela?* will you hand, pass, me that?

se **passer,** *v.r.,* to pass, to pass away; to fade; to decay, to fall off; to happen; to be satisfied; to forbear, to do without, to dispense with, to make shift. *L'occasion se passe;* the opportunity is slipping away. *Je dois l'avertir de tout ce qui se passe;* I must inform him of everything that happens. *Il se passe de peu;* he is satisfied with little. *Il ne saurait se — de vin;* he cannot do without, or dispense with, wine.

passerage, *n.f.,* (bot.) pepperwort.

passereau (pâ-srō), *n.m.,* (orni.) sparrow.

passerelle (pâ-srèl), *n.f.,* foot-bridge; (nav.) gangway.

passerine (pâ-sri-n), *n.f.,* (bot.) sparrowwort.

passerinette (pâ-sri-nèt), *n.f.,* (orni.) redwing.

passe-rose, *n.f.,* (— — s) (bot.) hollyhock.

passe-temps, *n.m.,* (—) pastime.

passeur, *n.m.,* ferry-man.

passe-velours, *n.m.,* (—) (bot.) coxcomb, flower-gentle.

passe-vin (pâs-vin), *n.m.,* (—) wine-strainer.

⊙**passe-volant,** *n.m.,* (— — s) interloper, intruder; (milit.) fagot.

passibilité, *n.f.,* passibility.

passible, *adj.,* passible; liable (to); punishable (by).

passi-f, -ve, *adj.,* passive. *Dette —ve;* debt.

passif, *n.m.,* (gram.) passive; (com.) liabilities, debts.

passiflore, *n.f.,* (bot.) granadilla, passionflower.

passion, *n.f.,* passion; love; fondness; prejudice; passing bell; Passion sermon. *Commander à ses — s;* to curb one's passions. *Déclarer sa —;* to declare one's love. *Il n'a — des médailles;* he thinks of nothing but medals. *De —, avec —;* passionately.

passionné, -e, *adj.,* passionate, impassioned, passionately fond of, doting on. *Amant —;* passionate lover. *Il est — pour la gloire;* he thinks of nothing but glory.

passionnément, *adv.,* passionately, fondly.

passionner, *v.a.,* to impassion, to interest deeply.

se **passionner,** *v.r.,* to be impassioned, to become enamored, to have a strong desire for; to take a deep interest in. *Vous vous passionnez trop;* you are too ardent or impetuous.

passivement (-siv-mān), *adj.,* passively.

passiveté *or* **passivité,** *n.f.,* passiveness.

passoire, *n.f.,* colander, strainer.

pastel, *n.m.,* pastel; crayon; (bot.) woad, dyer's woad.

pastenade, *n.f.,* (bot.) parsnip.

pastèque, *n.f.,* water-melon.

pasteur, *n.m.,* pastor, minister; clergyman; shepherd.

pastiche, *n.m.*, (paint.) pasticcio; imitation (of an author); (mus.) medley.

*****pastille**, *n.f.*, lozenge.

pastisson, *n.m.* *V.* **pâtisson**.

pastoral, -e, *adj.*, pastoral.

pastorale, *n.f.*, pastoral.

pastoralement (-ral-mān), *adv.*, pastorally.

pastoureau, *n.m.*, little shepherd boy.

pastourelle, *n.f.*, shepherd girl; (dance) pastourelle.

pat (pat), *n.m.*, stalemate (at chess).

patache, *n.f.*, (nav.) patache; coach, public conveyance; rickety old coach.

patagon, *n.m.*, patacoon (Spanish coin).

pataquès (-kèss), *n.m.*, (fam.) fault which consists in sounding a *t* for an *s*, and an *s* for a *t*; dreadful slip.

patarafe, *n.f.*, scrawl; flourish, dash.

patard, *n.m.*, farthing, doit.

patarin, *n.m.* *V.* **albigeois** and **vaudois**.

patate, *n.f.*, (bot.) sweet potato; potato; "tater."

patati, patata, *int.*, tut, tut! pooh! pooh!

patatras! *int.*, crack! thump! slap! bang!

pataud, *n.m.*, pup with large paws; (fig.) lout, clumsy fellow. *Etre à nage —;* to be in clover.

pataud, -e, *adj.*, (pers.) ill made, clumsy, awkward.

patauger, *v.n.*, to splash, to flounder about; to become entangled, embarrassed; to make a mess of.

patchouli, *n.m.*, patchouli.

pate, *n.f.* *V.* **patte**.

pâte, *n.f.*, paste, dough; constitution, temper; kind, sort; (print.) pie, pi. *— brisée;* short paste. *— feuilletée;* puff paste. *— croquante;* crisp paste. *Mettre la main à la —;* to do a thing one's self; to set to work one's self; to lend a helping hand. *C'est une bonne — d'homme;* he is a good-natured fellow. *Une bonne — de femme;* a good-natured woman.

pâté, *n.m.*, pie, pasty; blot (of ink); block (of buildings); (print.) pie, pi. *Un — de venaison;* a venison pasty. *Faire le —;* to pack the cards (at play). *Un gros —;* a plump chub-faced child. *Faire un —;* to make a blot. *Petit —;* patty.

pâtée, *n.f.*, paste (to fatten poultry); mess (for dogs or cats).

patelin (pa-tlin), *n.m.*, (fam.) wheedler.

patelin, -e, *adj.*, (fam.) wheedling. *Air —;* wheedling look.

patelinage (pa-tli-), *n.m.*, (fam.) wheedling.

pateliner (pa-tli-), *v.n.*, (fam.) to wheedle.

pateliner, *v.a.*, (fam.) to manage adroitly.

patelineu-r, *n.m.*, **-se**, *n.f.*, (fam.) wheedler.

patelle, *n.f.*, patella; (conch.) limpet.

patemment (-ta-), *adv.*, evidently, obviously, publicly.

patène, *n.f.*, (c.rel.) paten, patin.

patenôtre (pa-tnôtr), *n.f.*, paternoster; Lord's prayer. *pl.*, (pop.) beads of a rosary.

☉**patenôtrier**, *n.m.*, bead-maker.

patent, -e, *adj.*, patent; obvious, manifest. *Lettres —es;* letters patent.

patentable, *adj.*, licensable.

patente, *n.f.*, license (for the exercise of a trade); (nav.) bill of health. *— nette;* clean bill. *— brute;* foul bill.

patenté, -e, *n.* and *adj.*, licensed dealer; licensed.

patenter, *v.a.*, to license.

pater (pa-tèr), *n.m.*, (—) Lord's prayer, paternoster; great bead (of a chaplet).

patère, *n.f.*, window-screw; clothes peg; curtain rest, curtain hook.

☉**paterne**, *adj.*, (jest.) fatherly, paternal.

paternel, -le (-ti-), *adj.*, paternal, fatherly. *Parents —s;* relations on the father's side. *Bénédiction*

—le; father's blessing. *Amour —;* fatherly love.

paternellement (-nèl-mān), *adv.*, paternally, fatherly.

paternité, *n.f.*, paternity, fathership.

pâteu-x, -se, *adj.*, doughy, clammy, sticky; milky (of gems); muddy (of roads). *Chemin —;* muddy road.

pathétique, *adj.*, pathetic, affecting, moving, touching.

pathétique, *n.m.*, pathos.

pathétiquement (-tik-mān), *adv.*, pathetically.

pathognomonique, *adj.*, pathognomonic.

pathologie, *n.f.*, pathology.

pathologique, *adj.*, pathologic.

pathologiste, *n.m.*, pathologist.

pathos (pa-tôs), *n.m.*, (b. s.) bathos, bombast, fustian, rant.

patibulaire, *adj.*, patibulary (gallows, hanging). *n.*, gallows, gibbet.

patiemment (pa-sia-mān), *adv.*, patiently, with patience.

patience, *n.f.*, patience, endurance, forbearance; button-cleaner; puzzle (game). *Un jeu de —;* a puzzle. *Avoir de la —;* to have patience. *Etre à bout de —;* to be out of patience, to lose patience. *Prendre son mal en —;* to bear one's misfortune patiently. *Perdre —;* to lose patience. *Perdre toute —;* to lose all patience. *Prendre —;* to have patience, to bide one's time. *Prendre en —;* to bear patiently.

patience, *n.f.*, (bot.) patience, dock.

patient, -e, *adj.*, patient, enduring, forbearing.

patient, *n.m.*, sufferer; patient; culprit (about to be executed).

patienter, *v.n.*, to have or take patience, to bide one's time.

patin, *n.m.*, skate; sill (of a stair-case); clump (of boots); patten, clog, snow-shoe.

patine, *n.f.*, patina, verd-antique (fine rust on medals).

patiner, *v.n.*, to skate; (of wheels) to slide.

patiner, *v.a.*, to handle, to fumble, to paw; (l.ex.) to feel about.

patineu-r, *n.m.*, **-se**, *n.f.*, skater.

patineur, *n.m.*, (l.ex.) handler, fumbler.

patio, *n.m.*, court (Spanish).

pâtir, *v.n.*, to suffer; to drudge; to toil. *Vous en pâtirez;* you 'll suffer for it, you 'll rue it.

pâtis, *n.m.*, pasture-ground.

pâtisser, *v.n.*, to make pastry.

pâtisserie (pâ-ti-srî), *n.f.*, pastry; pastry-business.

pâtissi-er, *n.m.*, **-ère**, *n.f.*, pastry-cook.

pâtissoire, *n.f.*, pastry-board, pastry-table.

pâtisson, *n.m.*, (bot.) squash-melon.

patois, *n.m.*, patois, dialect; jargon; lingo; rigmarole.

pâton, *n.m.*, bolus (for fattening poultry).

patraque, *n.f.*, rubbish, trumpery thing; bad watch; (pers.) broken-down, worn out, poor stick; gimcrack.

pâtre, *n.m.*, herdsman, shepherd.

ad **patres** (pa-très), *adv.*, (triv.) to kingdom come. *Envoyer quelqu'un ad —;* to knock any one on the head, to kill.

patriarcal, -e, *adj.*, patriarchal.

patriarcat, *n.m.*, patriarchate, patriarchship.

patriarche, *n.m.*, patriarch.

patrice, *n.m.*, patrician.

patriciat, *n.m.*, dignity of a patrician; order of patricians; patriciate.

patricien, -ne (-in, -è-n), *n.* and *adj.*, patrician.

patrie, *n.f.*, native country, native land, home, fatherland; birth-place.

patrimoine, *n.m.*, patrimony, inheritance.

patrimonial, -e, *adj.*, patrimonial.

patriote, *n.m.f.* and *adj.*, patriot; patriotic.

patriotique, *adj.*, patriotic.

patriotiquement (-tik-mān), *adv.*, like a patriot, patriotically.

patriotisme, *n.m.*, patriotism.

⊙**patrociner**, *v.n.*, (jest.) to argue; to lecture, to talk.

patron, *n.m.*, patron; patron saint; master (of a house); master, employer; (fam.) governor; principal; (nav.) coxswain; master (of slaves); (canon law) advowee; pattern, model; (tech.) templet. — *d'un vaisseau marchand* ; master of a merchantman. — *de chaloupe ;* coxswain of a longboat. *Je veux parler au —* ; I want to speak to the principal, to the governor. *Faire un —* ; to take a pattern. *Dès — minette ;* from cockcrow.

patronage, *n.m.*, patronage; pattern-work; advowson.

patronal, -e, *adj.*, patronal. *Fête —e ;* patron saint's day.

patronat, *n.m.*, (Rom. hist.) protection, patronizing; patronate; employment of labor.

⊙**patroniser**, *v.a.*, to patronize.

⊙**dès le patron-jaquet, dès le patron-minet**, *adv.*, very early, at daybreak.

patronne, *n.f.*, patroness; female guardian saint; employer, mistress.

patronner, *v.n.*, to patronize, to take the pattern of; to stencil.

patronner, *v.a.*, to patronize.

patronnesse, *adj.f.*, patronizing, supporting. *Dame —* ; lady who gives her patronage.

patronymique, *adj.*, patronymic.

*****patrouillage**, *n.m.*, (l.u.) mess, paddling.

*****patrouille**, *n.f.*, patrol. *Faire la —* ; to patrol. *— grise ;* night-patrol.

*****patrouiller**, *v.n.*, (pop.) to paddle, to puddle, mess about; (milit.) to patrol.

*****patrouiller**, *v.a.*, (pop.) to spoil things (by messing them about).

*****patrouillis**, *n.m.*, mess, puddle.

patte, *n.f.*, paw (of animals); flap (of pockets); foot (of birds, of glasses); leg (of an insect). — *de chien ;* dog's paw. — *d'oie ;* foot of a goose. — *de collet ;* shoulder-strap. *Des —s d'araignée ;* spider's legs. — *d'écrevisse ;* claws of a crayfish, fluke (of anchors); (tech.) cramp, hook, holdfast. *Marcher à quatre —s ;* to go on all fours. *Passer sous la — de quelqu'un ;* to fall into any one's clutches. *Mettre la — sur quelqu'un ;* to lay hands upon any one. *Donner un coup de — à quelqu'un ;* to slang any one in (his presence or absence). *Graisser la — à quelqu'un ;* to give any one a sop, to fee any one. —*s de mouches ;* scrawl. *Faire — de velours ;* to cajole, to flatter; to touch softly.

patte-d'oie, *n.f.*, (—s—) (bot.) goose-foot; intersection of several roads; crow's foot.

⊙**patte-pelu**, *n.m.*, (—s—s), **patte-pelue**, *n.f.*, (—s) wolf in sheep's clothing; hypocrite.

pattu, -e, *adj.*, rough-footed; heavy, large-pawed.

pâturage, *n.m.*, pasture, pasture-ground, grazing.

pâture, *n.f.*, food, pasturage. *Servir de — à ;* to become the prey (of). *Vaine —* ; common. *Droit de vaine —* ; common of pasture.

pâturer, *v.n.*, to pasture, to graze, to feed.

pâtureur, *n.m.*, (milit.) pastor, pasturer.

paturin, *n.m.*, (bot.) meadow-grass. — *comprimé ;* wire-grass.

pâturon, *n.m.*, pastern (of a horse).

paucité, *n.f.*, (l.u.) paucity.

paulette, *n.f.*, tax (formerly paid for permission to dispose of one's office).

paulo-post-futur, *n.m.*, (gram.) paulo-post-future.

paulownia, *n.m.*, (bot.) paulownia.

paume, *n.f.*, palm (of the hand); tennis rackets (game). *Longue —* ; lawn-tennis. *Jeu de —* ; tennis, tennis court, racket court.

paumelle, *n.f.*, sort of barley; hand-leather, hand-guard.

paumer, *v.a.*, (pop.) to give a punch, to slap, to smack; to grab, to nab.

paumier, *n.m.*, tennis-court keeper.

paumoyer, *v.a.*, (nav.) to underrun (cables).

paumure, *n.f.*, top-antlers.

paupérisme, *n.m.*, pauperism.

paupière, *n.f.*, eyelid; eyelash; (fig.) eye, eyes. *Fermer la —* ; to shut one's eyes; to sleep; to die.

pause, *n.f.*, pause, stop, rest, stand; (mus.) rest, semi-breve rest.

pauser, *v.a.*, (mus.) to pause, to make a pause.

pauvre, *adj.*, poor, needy, wretched, destitute; paltry, sorry, scanty; mean, beggarly. *Une langue —* ; a poor language. *Un sujet —* ; a barren subject. *Le — homme !* poor silly fellow ! — *d'esprit ;* poor in spirit; weak-headed. *Un homme —* ; a poor man. *C'est un — poète ;* he is a wretched poet. *Un — hère, un — diable ;* a poor devil.

pauvre, *n.m.*, poor person, poor man, pauper, beggar. —*s honteux ;* poor people who are ashamed to beg. *Aux —s la besace ;* the back is made for the burden.

pauvrement, *adv.*, poorly, wretchedly.

pauvresse, *n.f.*, poor woman, beggar-woman, beggar-girl.

pauvret, *n.m.*, **-te**, *n.f.*, poor creature, poor thing.

pauvreté, *n.f.*, poverty, indigence, need; sorry thing, wretchedness. — *n'est pas vice ;* poverty is no crime. *Dire des —* ; to deal in platitudes.

pavage, *n.m.*, pavement, paving.

pavane, *n.f.*, pavan (dance).

se **pavaner**, *v.r.*, to strut, to strut along; to stalk proudly; to flaunt.

pavé, *n.m.*, paving-stone; pavement; paved road; road-way, street, streets. *Etre sur le —* ; to be without a home; to be on the streets. *Battre le —* ; to idle or lounge about town. *Tâter le —* ; not to walk firmly. *Le haut du —* ; the wall side. *Tenir le haut du —* ; to hold the first rank. *Brûler le —* ; to drive like the wind, to tear along the road. *Etre sur le — du roi ;* to be on the king's highway. *Mettre sur le —* ; to turn into the streets; to turn out of the house; to turn out of employment. *Les pavés le disent ;* the thing is in every one's mouth.

pavement (pav-mān), *n.m.*, paving; pavement.

paver, *v.a.*, to pave.

pavesade, *n.f.*, (nav.) pavisade.

paveur, *n.m.*, pavier, pavior.

pavie, *n.m.*, cling-stone peach.

*****pavillon**, *n.m.*, pavilion, summer-house; wing, outhouse, lodge; tent, flag, standard; (c.rel.) veil of the tabernacle; bell (of a trumpet). *Amener son —* ; to strike her flag (of a ship). — *blanc ;* flag of truce. — *de poupe ;* ensign. *Hisser le —* ; to hoist the flag. *Baisser —* ; to yield, to give in, to surrender. *Vaisseau —* ; flag-ship.

pavois, *n.m.*, shield; (nav.) armor.

pavoisement, *n.m.*, (nav.) dressing with flags.

pavoiser, *v.a.*, (nav.) to adorn with flags; to dress.

pavot, *n.m.*, (bot.) poppy.

payable, *adj.*, payable.

payant, -e, *adj.*, paying. *Carte —e ;* bill (at an eating-house). *Billet —* ; paid ticket.

payant, *n.m.*, *-e*, *n.f.*, payer, person who pays.

paye (pè-ye), *n.f.*, pay, salary; wages; (fam.) paymaster. *Une bonne —* ; a good paymaster. *Morte— (—s— —s) ;* old servant kept and paid without doing any work; defaulting tax-payer. *Haute —* ; (milit.) extra pay for good conduct stripes.

payement (pè-mān), *n.m.*, payment. *Jour de* — ; pay-day. *Non-——, (——-s)* non-payment.

payen, -ne, *adj.* V. **païen**.

payer, *v.a.*, to pay, to pay for, to pay off, to pay away, to recompense, to reward, to requite ; to expiate, to atone for, to satisfy, to indemnify. *— trop ;* to overpay. *— argent comptant ;* to pay cash down. *Se faire — ;* to get paid, to get one's money. *Qui répond paye ;* the bail must pay. *— quelqu'un d'ingratitude ;* to reward any one with ingratitude. *— de belles paroles ;* to pay with fine speeches. *— le tribut à la nature ;* to pay the debt of nature. *— en même monnaie ;* to pay in like coin. *— les violons ;* to pay the piper. *— d'effronterie ;* to brazen it out. *— d'audace ;* to face it out. *Il me la payera ;* he shall pay for it ; I'll be revenged on him for it. *Vous en payerez la folle enchère ;* you shall pay dear for your rashness. *— de sa personne ;* to expose one's self to danger ; to risk one's skin ; (fig.) to exert one's self. *Etre payé pour savoir ;* to know a thing to one's cost. *Ce n'est pas payé ;* (at billiards, etc.), that's hard lines (when a stroke has just been missed).

se payer, *v.r.*, to be satisfied ; to be bought, to treat one's self to. *Se — de raisons ;* to be satisfied with reasons. *Cela ne peut pas se — ;* that cannot be bought, that cannot be had for money. *Je ne me paye pas de mauvaises raisons ;* nothing but good reasons will satisfy me. *Je me paierai un habit neuf ;* I shall treat myself to a new coat.

payeu-r, *n.m.*, **-se**, *n.f.*, paymaster ; payer.

pays (pè-yee), *n.m.*, country, fatherland, birthplace, native place, home ; part of the country, place, district ; (pop.) fellow-countryman. *Gagner du — ;* to get on, to make progress. *Courir le — ;* to ramble, to rove about. *Battre le —;* to wander about ; (mil.) to scour the country. *Etre en — de connaissance ;* to be among friends. *Savoir la carte du — ;* to know one's ground, one's people. *— perdu ;* out-of-the-way place, waste, desert. *— natal ;* native country. *De quel — êtes-vous ?* what countryman are you ? *Avoir le mal du — ;* to be homesick. *Nul n'est prophète en son — ;* no man is a prophet in his own country. *Il est bien de son — ;* he is very simple, very credulous. *A vue de — ;* at first sight, by guess. *Faire voir du — à quelqu'un ;* to lead any one a dance. *— ruiné vaut mieux que — perdu ;* half a loaf is better than no bread.

paysage (pè-i-zaj), *n.m.*, landscape, scenery ; landscape-painting.

paysag-er, -ère, *adj.*, rustic, country.

paysagiste (pè-i-za-jist), *n.m.*, landscape-painter.

paysan (pè-i-zan), *n.m.*, **-ne** (-za-n), *n.f.*, countryman ; countrywoman ; peasant, rustic.

paysannerie (pè-i-za-n-rî), *n.f.*, rusticity, country manners.

payse, *n.f.*, (pop.) fellow countrywoman.

péage, *n.m.*, toll, due ; toll-house.

péager, *n.m.*, toll-gatherer.

peau, *n.f.*, skin, hide, fell, peel ; rind, pelt, fur ; (fig., fam.) person. *— d'oignons ;* onion-peel. *— de fruit ;* skin of fruit. *Oter la — ;* to peel. *Contes de — d'âne ;* nursery tales, fairy tales. *Etre dans la — de quelqu'un ;* to be in any one's shoes. *Il ne faut pas vendre la — de l'ours avant de l'avoir tué ;* do not count your chickens before they are hatched. *— de soie ;* Japanese silk.

peausserie (pô-srî), *n.f.*, peltry ; skinner's trade.

peaussier (pô-sié), *n.m.*, skinner, skin-dresser.

peaussier, *adj.*, (anat.) cutaneous (muscle).

pébrine, *n.f.*, disease (in silk-worms).

pec, *adj.*, newly salted (of herrings).

pécari, *n.m.*, peccary, Mexican boar.

peccable (pèk-kabl), *adj.*, peccable, faulty.

*peccadille, *n.f.*, peccadillo, slight offense.

⊙**peccant, -e** (pèk-kān, -t), *adj.*, (med.) morbid, not healthy, peccant.

peccata, *n.m.*, **(—)** (pop.) an ass ; fool, dolt, blockhead.

peccavi (pèk-ka-vi), *n.m.*, **(—)** peccavi.

pêche, *n.f.*, (bot.) peach. *— hâtive ;* early peach. *— tardive ;* late peach.

pêche, *n.f.*, fishing, angling. *La — à la ligne ;* angling. *Aller à la — ;* to go out fishing. *Ligne de — ;* fishing line.

péché, *n.m.*, sin, trespass, transgression. *— originel ;* original sin. *— mignon ;* besetting sin. *— grave ;* heinous sin. *— irrémissible ;* unpardonable sin. *Racheter ses —s ;* to redeem one's sins. *A tout — miséricorde ;* there is mercy for every sin. *Rechercher les vieux —s de quelqu'un ;* to rake up the old sins of any one. *Etre laide comme les sept —s capitaux ;* to be as ugly as sin. *Se dire les sept —s mortels ;* to abuse one another mercilessly. *— avoué est à demi pardonné ;* a fault confessed is half redressed.

pécher, *v.n.*, to sin, to transgress, to trespass ; to offend ; to err ; to be deficient, to fail. *— contre la bienséance ;* to offend against decency. *Ce n'est pas par là qu'il pèche ;* that is not his failing.

pêcher, *v.a.* and *n.*, to fish, to angle, to fish for, to fish up, to drag out ; to find, to pick up. *— à la ligne ;* to angle for, with rod and line. *— un étang ;* to draw a pond. *— en eau trouble ;* to fish in troubled waters. *— au plat ;* to pick into the dish. *Où avez-vous pêché cela ?* where did you pick that up *or* where did you get hold of that ?

pêcher, *n.m.*, peach-tree.

pêcheresse (pé-shrès), *n.f.* V. **pécheur**.

pêcherie (pê-shrî), *n.f.*, fishing-place ; fishery, fish-pond.

péche-ur, *n.m.*, **-resse**, *n.f.*, sinner.

pêcheu-r, *n.m.*, **-se**, *n.f.*, fisher, angler, fisherman, fisherwoman. *— à la ligne ;* angler. *Ligne de — ;* fishing-line.

pêcheu-r, *adj.*, fishing.

pécore, *n.f.*, stupid creature, blockhead, animal, creature.

pecque, *n.f.*, silly, conceited woman *or* girl.

pectiné, -e, *adj.*, pectinal, comb-shaped.

pectoral, -e, *adj.*, pectoral.

pectoral, *n.m.*, breast-plate ; (med.) pectoral.

péculat, *n.m.*, peculation, embezzlement. *Etre coupable de — ;* to peculate.

péculateur, *n.m.*, (l.u.) peculator.

pécule, *n.m.*, savings, earnings, hoard.

⊙**pécune**, *n.f.*, ready money, cash, tin.

pécuniaire, *adj.*, pecuniary.

pécunieu-x, -se, *adj.*, moneyed.

pédagogie, *n.f.*, pedagogy.

pédagogique, *adj.*, pedagogical.

pédagogue, *n.m.*, pedagogue.

pédale, *n.f.*, pedal ; treadle ; foot-board.

⊙**pédané**, *adj.*, formerly said of judges who tried cases standing up.

pédant, -e, *n.* and *adj.*, pedant ; pedantic.

⊙**pédanter**, *v.n.* V. **pédantiser**.

pédanterie (pé-dan-trî), *n.f.*, pedantry.

pédantesque, *adj.*, pedantic.

pédantesquement, *adv.*, pedantically.

pédantiser, *v.n.*, to act, *or* play, the pedant.

pédantisme, *n.f.*, pedantry.

pédéraste, *n.m.*, pederast.

pédérastie, *n.f.*, pederasty.

pédestre, *adj.*, pedestrian, on foot.

pédestrement, *adv.*, on foot. *Aller — ;* to go on foot.

pédicelle, *n.m.*, (bot.) pedicle, pedicel.

pédiculaire, *adj.*, pedicular.

pédiculaire, *n.f.*, (bot.) pedicularis, louse-wort.

pédicule, *n.m.,* (bot.) pedicel; (med.) neck.

pédiculé, -e, *adj.,* pedicellate.

pédicure, *n.m.f.,* corn-cutter ; chiropodist.

pédiforme, *adj.,* foot-shaped.

pédiluve, *n.m.,* (med.) pediluvium, foot-bath.

pédimane, *n.m.* and *adj.,* (mam.) pedimane ; pedimanous.

pédomètre, *n.m.,* pedometer.

pédon, *n.m.,* courier on foot, runner.

pédonculaire, *adj.,* (bot.) peduncular.

pédoncule, *n.m.,* (bot.) peduncle, flower-stalk.

pédonculé, -e, *adj.,* (bot.) pedunculate.

pégase, *n.m.,* Pegasus.

pègle, *n.f.,* pitch (from wood).

pègre, *n.m.,* thief. *n.f.,* light-fingered gentry.

*****peignage,** *n.m.,* combing, wool-combing.

*****peigne,** *n.m.,* comb ; (paint.) graining-tool. *— fin ;* small-tooth comb. *— à démêler ;* large-tooth comb. *Etre sale comme un —;* to be as dirty as you like.

*****peigné, -e,** *part.,* combed ; (fig.) elaborate, labored. *Un jardin bien —;* a well-kept garden. *Un mal —* or *un malpeigné ;* a dirty, slovenly, ill-dressed fellow.

peignée, *n.f.,* cardful (of wool).

*****peigner,** *v.a.,* to comb, to card ; (pop.) to beat, to drub; to polish (style).

se **peigner,** *v.r.,* to comb one's self ; (pop.) to beat one another.

peignerie, *n.f.,* comb manufactory; comb-trade.

*****peigneu-r,** *n.m.,* **-se,** *n.f.,* (manu.) comber.

*****peignier,** *n.m.,* comb-maker.

*****peignoir,** *n.m.,* dressing-gown, wrapper; bathing-gown.

*****peignures,** *n.f.pl.,* combings.

peindre (peignant, peint), *v.a.,* to paint, to portray ; to describe, to depict; to draw, to represent; to express. *— d'après nature;* to paint from nature. *à l'huile;* to paint in oils. *— l'histoire;* to paint historical subjects. *— le portrait;* to take likenesses, to paint portraits. *Se faire —;* to sit for one's portrait. *Fait à —;* very handsome. *Il nous a peint sa détresse;* he described his distress to us.

se **peindre,** *v.r.,* to paint one's self; to be represented, to be expressed *or* described, to be depicted. *La douleur se peignait sur son visage;* grief was depicted on his face.

peine, *n.f.,* punishment, penalty, pain; affliction, grief, sorrow, misery; uneasiness, trouble, anxiety, labor ; pains ; reluctance. *Sous les —s de droit;* on pain of being punished according to law. *Partager les —s de quelqu'un;* to share any one's troubles. *Il n'y a que des —s dans la vie;* the world is full of sorrow. *Cela fait — à voir;* it hurts one to see it. *A chaque jour suffit sa —;* sufficient for the day is the evil thereof. *Je suis en — de savoir ce qu'il deviendra;* I am at a loss to know what will become of him. *Faire de la — à quelqu'un;* to pain any one. *Etre dans la —;* to be in trouble. *Se mettre en — de;* to trouble one's self about. *Je voudrais vous épargner cette —;* I would willingly spare you that trouble. *Cela n'en vaut pas la —;* it is not worth while. *Il a de la — à parler;* he is scarcely able to speak. *Il a de la — à marcher;* he can scarcely walk. *Il a eu beau coup de — à en venir à bout;* he had much trouble to bring it about, to get through it. *J'ai — à le croire;* I can hardly believe it. *Un homme de —;* a laborer. *Ce n'est pas la —;* it is not worth while. *A —;* hardly, scarce, scarcely. *A — sait-il lire;* he can hardly read. *A grand' —;* with great trouble, with much difficulty. *Mourir à la —;* to die in harness or to work one's self to death.

peiné, -e, *part.,* pained, grieved ; labored,

elaborate, stiff. *Un ouvrage —;* a labored piece of work.

peiner, *v.a.,* to pain, to make uneasy, to put to trouble ; to fatigue, to labor.

se **peiner,** *v.r.,* to take pains; to grieve, to fret.

peiner, *v.n.,* to labor, to toil; to be reluctant, to be loath.

peint, -e, *part.,* painted, drawn. *Toiles —es;* printed calicoes.

peintre, *n.m.,* painter. *— de paysage;* landscape painter. *Un — en bâtiments;* a house-painter.

peinturage, *n.m.,* painting (on wood); daub.

peinture, *n.f.,* painting ; paint ; picture, portraiture; description, appearance; painters' work; colors. *— à l'huile;* oil-painting. *— en détrempe;* distemper-painting. *— en mosaïque;* mosaic-painting. *En —;* in painting, in appearance.

peinturer, *v.a.,* (l.u.) to paint (with one color only); to daub.

peintureur, *n.m.,* bad painter, dauber. *V.* **barbouilleur.**

pékin, *n.m.,* pekin (textile fabric); (fig.) civilian, snob. *C'est un mauvais —;* he's a nasty fellow.

pelade, *n.f.,* alopecy, alopecia, scurf.

pelage, *n.m.,* coat, fur (color of).

pélagianisme, *n.m.,* pelagianism, Pelagius' tenets.

pélagien, -ne (-in, -è-n), *adj.,* pelagian.

pélagique, *adj.,* pelagic (of the sea).

pélamide, *n.f.,* (ich.) pelamis.

pelard (pe-lar), *adj.,* barked (of wood).

pélasgique, *adj.,* pelasgian.

pelé, *n.m.,* bald-pated man ; ragamuffin. *n'y avait que quatre —s et un tondu;* there was nothing but the rag, tag, and bobtail. *adj.,* bald; bare, naked ; threadbare, napless.

pêle, *n.m. V.* **pêne.**

pêle-mêle, *adv.,* pell-mell, confusedly, helter-skelter.

pêle-mêle, *n.m.,* pell-mell, disorder, jumble, confusion.

peler, *v.a.,* to strip of hair, to make bald ; to pare, to skin, to peel, to scald (pigs). *— un cochon de lait;* to scald a sucking pig. *— un arbre;* to peel a tree. *— des amandes;* to peel almonds.

se **peler,** *v.r.,* to come off (of the hair) ; to peel off.

peler, *v.n.,* to peel off (of the skin).

pèlerin (pèl-rin), *n.m.,* **-e** (-ri-n), *n.f.,* pilgrim, traveler ; hypocrite, dissembler.

pèlerin, *n.m.,* (orni.) peregrine falcon.

pèlerinage (pel-ri-), *n.m.,* pilgrimage. *Aller en —;* to go on a pilgrimage.

pèlerine (pèl-ri-n), *n.f.,* tippet, cape.

pélican, *n.m.,* pelican ; (tech.) holdfast.

pelin, *n.m.,* lime-pit (for hides).

pelisse, *n.f.,* pelisse.

pellage, *n.m.,* shoveling.

pellagre, *n.f.,* (med.) pellagra.

pelle, *n.f.,* shovel, scoop, spade; (of an oar) blade ; (of lock-gates) paddle. *La — se moque du fourgon;* the pot calls the kettle black. *Oter avec la —;* to shovel out. *Remuer à la —;* to shovel. *Remuer l'argent à la —;* (fig.) to have heaps, loads of money.

pellée, pellerée, pelletée (pèl-rée, pèl-tée), *n.f.,* shovelful.

pelleron (pèl-ron), *n.m.,* baker's peel.

pelleterie (pèl-tri), *n.f.,* furriery; peltry.

pelleti-er, *n.m.,* **-ère,** *n.f.,* furrier.

pelleversage, *n.m.,* spade-tilling.

pellicule (pèl-li-kul), *n.f.,* pellicle.

pellucide (pel-lu-), *adj.,* (phys.) pellucid.

pellucidité, *n.f.,* pellucidness, clearness.

pelotage, *n.m.,* winding skeins into balls; pack of vigonia wool; loose play (at billiards, etc.)

pelote (plot), n.f., pin-cushion; clew, ball of thread; pellet; blaze (on a horse's forehead). — *de neige;* snow-ball. *Faire sa —;* to feather one's nest.

peloter (plo-té), v.a., to make up into a ball; to throw balls; to bang, to cuff, to beat; to hoard, to save.

se **peloter**, v.r., to roll round; to roll one's self up; to bang each other about; to dispute.

peloter, v.n., (at tennis) to knock the ball about.

peloton (plo-ton), n.m., ball, knot, group, cluster; lump (of fat); (milit.) half-company; tennis-ball; group, knot (of people). *Ils entraient par —s;* they entered by groups. *Se mettre en —;* to roll one's self up like a ball. *Feu de —;* volley-firing, platoon-firing.

pelotonner (plo-to-né), v.a., to wind into balls, to put up into balls.

se **pelotonner**, v.r., to gather into knots, into groups; to gather into a round mass; to roll one's self up.

pelouse (plooz) n.f., lawn, greensward; grass-plot.

pelu, -e, adj., hairy. [Only used in **patte-pelu,** which see.]

peluche (plush), n.f., shag, plush, cotton and woolen drugget.

peluché, -e, adj., shaggy.

pelucher (plu-shé), v.n., to become shaggy, to wear rough.

pelure (plur), n.f., paring, peel, rind.

pelvien, -ne (-in, -è-n), adj., (anat.) pelvic.

pemphigus, n.m., (med.) pemphigus.

***penaille,** n.f., rags; (b.s.) monks.

***penaillerie,** n.f., rags; set of ragamuffins; (b.s.) monks.

***penaillon,** n.m., rag; monk.

pénal, -e, adj., penal.

pénalité, n.f., penal system; penalty; penal enactment.

penard, n.m., old fox (pers.), old libertine.

pénates, n.m.pl., (antiq.) penates, household gods; fireside, home.

penaud, -e, n. and adj., abashed, sheepish person; abashed, sheepish, chopfallen, crestfallen.

penchant, n.m., slope, declivity; inclination, acclivity, decline, propensity, bent, tendency, taste. *Le — d'une montagne;* the slope of a mountain. *Suivre son — or se laisser aller à son —;* to follow one's bent.

penchant, -e, adj., shelving, sloping, declining, leaning.

penchement (pansh-mān), n.m., inclination, leaning, bending, stoop, stooping.

pencher, v.a., to incline, to lean, to bend, to stoop. — *la tête;* to bend the head. — *un vase;* to incline a vase.

se **pencher,** v.r., to bend, to bend over, to stoop, to tilt, to slope, to be inclined. *Se — sur le bord d'un précipice;* to bend over the brink of a precipice.

pencher, v.n., to lean; to slope, to incline, to be disposed. *Il penche vers le nord;* it leans to the north. — *vers la clémence;* to lean to mercy. — *vers or — du côté de;* to incline towards, to lean the side of.

pendable, adj., deserving hanging, abominable. *Cas —;* hanging matter. *Un tour —;* an abominable trick.

pendaison, n.f., hanging (on the gallows).

pendant, prep., during.

pendant que, conj., whilst, while.

pendant, n.m., thing pendent, thing hanging; counterpart, pendant, fellow; frog (of a sword-belt). — *d'oreille;* ear-ring. *Il faut un — à ce tableau;* this picture needs a fellow. *C'est son —;* he is his counterpart.

pendant, -e, adj., pendent, hanging, pending, depending; standing (of crops). *Oreilles —es;*

hanging ears. *Marcher les bras —s;* to walk with one's arms dangling. *Le procès est —;* the cause is pending.

pendard, n.m., -e, n.f., rascal, rogue, scoundrel; jade.

pendeloque (pan-dlok), n.f., ear-drop; pendant, drop.

pendentif, n.m., (arch.) pendentive.

penderie (pen-dri), n.f., ⊙hanging (putting to death); (tech.) drying-house.

pendeur, n.m., hangman, executioner; (nav.) pennant (rope), span.

***pendiller,** v.n., to hang loose, to dangle, to swing.

pendre, v.a., to hang, to hang up, to suspend. — *de la viande au croc;* to hang up meat on a hook. — *des voleurs;* to hang robbers. *Il ne vaut pas la corde pour le —;* he is not worth hanging. *Il dit pis que — de vous;* he says all kinds of things of you.

se **pendre,** v.r., to hang one's self.

pendre, v.n., to hang, to hang up, to hang down, to be suspended, to dangle, to droop, to sag. *Les joues lui pendent;* his cheeks are flabby. *Autant lui en pend à l'oreille;* he may expect a like treatment, *or* to be served in the same way. *Il a dit pis que — de vous;* he said everything that was bad of you *or* he abused you right and left.

pendu, n.m., one that has been hanged. *Il est sec comme un —;* he is as thin as a lath. *Avoir de la corde de — dans sa poche;* to have the devil's own luck.

pendu, -e, part., hanged, hung. *Aussitôt pris, aussitôt —;* no sooner said than done. *Il est toujours — à ses côtés;* he is always dangling after her. *Avoir la langue bien —e;* to have a well-oiled tongue.

pendule, n.f., (horl.) time-piece, chimney clock, ornamental clock. — *détraquée;* clock out of order. *Remonter une —;* to wind up a clock. — *de voyage;* carriage-clock.

pendule, n.m., pendulum.

penduliste, n.m., clock-case maker.

pêne, n.m., bolt (of a lock); lock-bolt.

pénétrabilité, n.f., penetrability.

pénétrable, adj., penetrable.

pénétrant, -e, adj., penetrating, piercing, keen, insinuating, acute, searching, impressive. *Il fait un froid —;* it is piercingly cold.

pénétratif, -ve, adj., (l.u.) penetrating.

pénétration, n.f., penetration, acuteness, shrewdness; sagacity. *Avoir une grande — d'esprit;* to have great acuteness of mind.

pénétré, -e, part., penetrated. — *de douleur;* grieved to the heart, cut to the quick.

pénétrer, v.a., to penetrate, to go through, to enter, to pierce; to pervade; to fathom; to impress; to imbue; to see through; to affect, to move. — *quelqu'un;* to see through any one. *Son état m'a pénétré;* his situation deeply moved me.

se **pénétrer,** v.r., to penetrate each other; to impress one's self, to convince one's self; to impress one's mind.

pénétrer, v.n., to penetrate; to pervade; to pierce, to get in. *Il pénétra bien avant dans le pays;* he went a great way into the country *or* he explored the interior.

pénible, adj., painful, laborious; troublesome, difficult, hard.

péniblement, adv., painfully, laboriously.

péniche, n.f., (nav.) pinnace.

pénicillé, -e, adj., (anat.) pencil-shaped.

pénil, n.m., (anat.) mons veneris.

péninsulaire, adj., peninsular.

péninsule, n.f., peninsula.

pénitence, n.f., penitence, repentance, penance, punishment, disgrace. *Faire — de ses péchés;* to do penance for one's sins. *Faire —;* to fare poorly. *Mettre un enfant en —;* to punish a child. *Il est en —;* he is in disgrace.

pénitencerie (-tän-srî), *n.f.*, penitentiary's court; penitentiary (office).

pénitencier, *n.m.*, reformatory; penitentiary.

pénitent, -e, *n.* and *adj.*, penitent, repentant. *Pécheur —;* contrite sinner.

pénitentiaire (-ci-èr), *adj.*, penitentiary, penal. *Maison —;* penitentiary.

pénitenti-aux (-ci-ô), **-elles** (-ci-èl), *adj.pl.*, penitential. *Psaumes —;* penitential psalms.

pénitentiel (-ci-èl), *n.m.*, penitential.

pennage, *n.m.*, plumage (hawking).

penne (pè-n), *n.f.*, beam-feather (of a hawk); feather; (orni.) feather of the tail *or* wing; (nav.) peak of a mizzen *or* lateen sail.

penné, *adj.*, (bot.) pennate, pennated.

penniforme, *adj.*, penniform.

pennon (pè-n-non), *n.m.*, pennon.

pénombre, *n.f.*, penumbra; (fig.) darkness, obscurity, twilight, semi-darkness; subdued light.

penon, *n.m.*, (nav.) dog-vane.

pensant, -e, *adj.*, thinking. *Bien —;* right-thinking, well-disposed, right-minded. *Mal —;* evil-thinking, evil-disposed.

pensée, *n.f.*, thought, opinion, sentiment, idea, conception; mind, belief, opinion; design; notion; meaning; sketch, first draught; (bot.) pansy, heart's-ease. *— ultérieure;* after-thought. *S'accoutumer à la — de la mort;* to accustom one's self to the idea of death. *Parler contre sa —;* to speak against one's conviction, opinion. *Entrer dans la — de quelqu'un;* to gather any one's meaning, to follow any one's reasoning *or* train of thought. *Lire dans la — de quelqu'un;* to read any one's thoughts. *Cela m'est venu dans la —;* that came into my mind. *S'entretenir avec ses —s;* to hold converse with one's self.

penser, *v. n.*, to think, to believe, to imagine; to reflect, to meditate, to deem, to be of opinion; to hope; to be on the point, to be near, to have like; to take heed, to take care. *L'homme pense;* man is a thinking being. *— à quelque chose;* to think of anything. *Il est venu sans qu'on y pensât;* he came unexpectedly. *C'est un homme qui pense bien;* he is a man who thinks well. *Il l'a fait sans y —;* he did it unwittingly. *A quoi pensez-vous, de faire cela?* what do you mean by doing that? *— à mal;* to have some ill design, to mean harm. *Il pensait à me surprendre;* he thought to surprise me. *Il a pensé mourir;* he nearly lost his life. *J'ai pensé tomber;* I was near falling. *A ce que je pense;* to my mind, in my mind, in my opinion. *Façon de —;* way of thinking. *— à soi;* look to one's self, to take care of one's self. *Faire —;* to remind. *Cela donne bien à —;* that is very suggestive, *or* food for reflection. *Pensez donc!* just think of it! just imagine!

penser, *v.a.*, to think, to think of. *Il ne dit jamais ce qu'il pense;* he never says what he thinks. *— du bien de;* to think well of. *— à quelque chose pour faire réussir une affaire;* to think of something to bring a matter to a successful issue. *Que pensez-vous de cela?* what think you of that? *Pensez à moi;* think of me. *Que pensez-vous de lui?* what is your opinion of him?

penser, *n.m.*, inward reasoning, thought.

penseur, *n.m.* and *adj.*, thinker; thinking, reflecting, thoughtful.

pensi-f, -ve, *adj.*, pensive, thoughtful.

pension, *n.f.*, pension, annuity, allowance, payment; board; board and lodging; boarding-house; boarding-school; livery (of horses); (milit.) mess. *Prendre quelqu'un en —;* to receive any one as a boarder. *Se mettre en —;* to go to a boarding-house. *— bourgeoise;* family boarding-house. *Mettre ses chevaux en —;* to put one's horses out at livery. *Mettre son fils en —;* to place one's son at a boarding-school. *— de demoiselles;* young ladies' boarding-school, seminary for young ladies. *— de jeunes gens;* boarding-school for young gentlemen, seminary for young gentlemen. *— de retraite;* retiring pension. *Obtenir une —;* to obtain a pension. *— viagère;* life-annuity. *Demi- —;* board.

pensionnaire, *n.m.f.*, boarder; pensioner; pensionary (in Holland). *Demi- —;* day-boarder. *Prendre des —s;* to take in boarders.

pensionnat, *n.m.*, boarding-school.

pensionner, *v.a.*, to pension, to grant a pension to.

pensum (pin-som), *n.m.*, (—s) imposition, extra task (at school). *Donner pour — to* give as an extra task.

pent, penta, prefix from Gr. πέντε.

pentacorde, *n.m.*, (mus.) pentachord.

pentagone, *n.m.* and *adj.*, (geom., fort.) pentagon; pentagonal.

pentamètre, *n.m.* and *adj.*, pentameter.

pentandrie, *n.f.*, (bot.) pentandria.

pentaphylle, *adj.*, (bot.) pentaphyllous.

pentateuque, *n.m.*, (Bible) Pentateuch.

pente, *n.f.*, declivity, inclination, slope, descent; acclivity, ascent; incline, gradient; pitch (of roofs); valance (of a bed); (nav.) sides (of an awning); propensity, bent, turn. *Le terrain va en —;* the ground shelves down. *Aller en —;* to slope, to shelve, to incline. *Avoir de la —;* to have a natural propensity for pleasure.

pentecôte (pant-kôt), *n.f.*, Whitsuntide, Pentecost. *Dimanche de la —;* Whitsunday.

pentière (-tièr), *n.f.* V. **pantière**.

penture, *n.f.*, iron-work, iron-brace; (tech.) hinge. *— de sabords;* (nav.) googings of the port-lids. *—s en fer à cheval;* scuttle-hinges.

pénultième (-ti-em), *adj.*, last but one; (gram.) penultimate.

pénultième, *n.f.*, (gram.) penult, penultima.

pénurie, *n.f.*, penury, want, scarcity, dearth.

péone, *n.f.* V. **pivoine** (bot.).

péotte, *n.f.*, peotta, large gondola.

péperin, *n.m.*, peperine (volcanic stone).

pépie, *n.f.*, pip, roup (disease of birds); (fig.) thirst. *Elle n'a point la —;* she is not tongue-tied. *Il a la —;* he is for ever drinking; he is always dry.

pépier, *v.n.*, to chirp, to pip.

pépin, *n.m.*, (bot.) kernel, pip, stone. *— de raisin;* grapestone.

pépinière, *n.f.*, (hort.) nursery.

pépiniériste, *n.m.*, nursery-man.

pépite, *n.f.*, (min.) nugget.

péplon *or* **péplum,** *n.m.*, (antiq.) peplus (lady's cloak).

pepsine, *n.f.*, (chem. pharm.) pepsine.

péquin, *n.m.*, civilian, snob.

percale, *n.f.*, cambric; muslin.

percaline, *n.f.*, glazed calico; (bookbind.) cloth.

perçant, -e, *adj.*, piercing, sharp, keen, shrill, acute. *Froid —;* piercing cold. *Vent —;* sharp, keen wind. *Des yeux —s;* sharp, piercing eyes. *Des cris —s;* piercing cries. *Voix —e;* shrill voice.

perce, *n.f.*, piercer, borer, drill. *en perce, adv.*, broached, tapped. *Mettre en —;* to prick, to pierce. *Mettre du vin en —;* to broach a cask of wine.

percé, -e, *part.*, pierced, bored, in holes; out at elbows. *Habit —;* coat in holes. *Avoir le cœur —;* to be struck to the heart. *Maison bien —e;* well-lighted house. *Paysage bien —;* broad, well-opened out landscape. *Chaise —e;* close-stool. *Il est bas —;* he is low in cash. *Fruits —s de vers;* worm-eaten fruits. *C'est un panier —;* money burns his pocket, he is a spendthrift.

perce-bois, *n.m.*, (—) (ent.) borer, wood-borer; death-watch.

percée, *n.f.*, *or* **percé,** *n.m.*, opening, cutting (in a wood), vista, glade. *Faire une — dans;* to hew a passage through.

*perce-feuille, *n.f.,* (——*s*) (bot.) thorough-wax, hare's ear.

perce-forêt, *n.m.,* (——*s*) (fam., l.u.) keen sportsman.

perce-lettre, *n.m.,* (——*s*) bodkin (for piercing paper).

percement, *n.m.,* piercing, opening; cutting, boring; perforation.

perce-mousse, *n.f.,* or **perce-neige,** *n.f.,* (—) (bot.) snow-drop.

*perce-oreille, *n.m.,* (——*s*) (ent.) earwig.

perce-pierre, *n.f.,* (——*s*) V. **passe-pierre.**

percepteur, *n.m.,* collector (of taxes); gatherer. — *des impôts;* tax-gatherer, collector.

perceptibilité, *n.f.,* perceptibility, liability to collection (as taxes).

perceptible, *adj.,* collectible; perceptible, perceivable.

perceptiblement, *adv.,* perceptibly.

perception, *n.f.,* the faculty of perceiving, perception; gathering, collecting; receipt; collectorship; collector's office.

percer, *v.a.,* to bore, to drill, to pierce, to tap, to broach, to open; to penetrate, to see through; to thrill; to lance; (engineering) to tunnel; to wet through (of rain). — *avec un foret;* to drill, to pierce. — *d'outre en outre;* to run through and through. — *un ais;* to bore a plank. — *un tonneau;* to tap a cask. — *un escadron;* to cut a passage through a squadron. — *avec le bec;* to peck through. — *d'un coup d'épée;* to run through the body. — *l'avenir;* to dive into the future. *Les os lui percent la peau;* his bones are coming through his skin. — *un abcès;* to lance, to open an abscess. — *une forêt;* to open up, or to make a road through, a forest. — *une porte dans un mur;* to open a door in a wall.

se percer, *v.r.,* to bore, to be bored; to pierce one's self, to be pierced.

percer, *v.n.,* to pierce, to pierce through, to break, to break through, to come out, to come through, to open; to appear, to peep out, to peep forth, to transpire; to show one's self, to discover one's self, to manifest one's self; to rise, to make one's way, to get on; to make one's way through a crowd. *Les dents vont bientôt à cet enfant;* that child's teeth will soon come through, that child will soon cut his teeth. *Cette tumeur percera d'elle-même;* that tumor will break, burst, of itself. — *par son mérite;* to rise, or to make one's way, by one's merit. *Si compacte que soit la foule, perçons toujours;* however dense the crowd may be, let us break through all the same.

perces, *n.f.pl.,* holes of wind instruments.

perce-roche, *n.f.,* (zoöl.) terebella.

perceur, *n.m.,* borer.

percevoir, *v.a.,* to receive, to gather, to levy, to collect (taxes); (philos.) to perceive.

perche, *n.f.,* perch, pole; perch (measure); (hunt.) horns; (ich.) perch. — *commune;* barse. *Petite* —; cole-perch. *Grande* —; (pers.) walking rushlight, lanky person.

perché, *n.m.,* perched, perched up, roosting. *Au* —; when perched, when roosting.

percher, *v.n.,* to perch.

se percher, *v.r.,* to perch one's self, to perch, to roost.

percheronne, *n.m.f.,* horse or mare (native of la Perche).

perchette, *n.f.,* pole, prop, stay.

percheur, *n.m.* and *adj.,* perching, roosting; percher (ornith.) titlark.

perchlorure, *n.m.,* (chem.) bichloride, perchloride.

perchoir, *n.m.,* roost.

perclus, -e, *adj.,* (med.) crippled, impotent. *Avoir le cerveau* —; to be wanting in sense, in judgment.

perçoir, *n.m.,* piercer (to tap casks).

perçu, -e, *part.,* collected.

percussion, *n.f.,* percussion, reverberation.

percutant, -e, *adj.,* (artil.) percussion. *Fusée* —; percussion-fuse.

percuter, *v.a.,* to percuss.

perdable, *adj.,* losable.

perdant, -e, *n.* and *adj.,* loser; losing.

perdition, *n.f.,* waste, wreck, ruin; perdition, destruction. *S'en aller en* —; to go to ruin, to go to wrack and ruin. *Flotte de* —; accursed fleet. *En* —; (of ships) sinking, in great distress.

perdre, *v.a.,* to lose, to be deprived of, to be out of pocket; to waste, to ruin, to be the ruin of, to undo, to corrupt, to debauch; to spoil; (nav.) to carry away; (nav.) to cast away; (tech.) to discharge (water). — *la santé;* to lose one's health. — *la raison;* to lose one's reason, mind. — *haleine;* to lose one's breath. — *la tête, la carte;* to lose one's wits, one's head. — *une gageure;* to lose a wager. — *quelqu'un de réputation;* to defame any one. — *l'occasion;* to lose the opportunity. — *une chose de vue;* to lose sight of a thing. *Ses débauches le perdront;* his debauchery will be the ruin of him. *L'inondation a perdu les blés;* the floods have spoilt the crops. *Y* — *son latin;* not to be able to make it out.

se perdre, *v.r.,* to be lost, to lose one's self, to lose one's way, to stray; to be cast away; to have a rambling way of arguing; to be nonplused; to disappear, to fall into disuse; to ruin one's self; to go to ruin, to go to wrack and ruin; to spoil, to be spoilt; to get bewildered; to be at a loss; (nav.) to be carried away; (nav.) to be cast away; to hole one's own ball (at billiards). *Je m'y perds;* I am getting bewildered; I cannot make head or tail of it. *Se* — *d'honneur;* to disgrace one's self.

perdre, *v.n.,* to lose, to be a loser, to be out of pocket; (nav.) to ebb. *La marée perd;* the tide is ebbing.

perdreau, *n.m.,* (orni.) young partridge.

perdrigon, *n.m.,* Perdrigon-plum.

perdrix, *n.f.,* (orni.) partridge. — *grise;* common partridge. — *rouge;* red-legged partridge. *Couple de* —; brace of partridges. *Œil de* —; soft corn.

perdu, -e, *part.,* lost, ruined, wasted; bewildered; undermined; spoilt; stray, forlorn, obsolete, out of use. — *de dettes;* over head and ears in debt. — *de réputation;* ruined in reputation. *Courir, crier, comme un* —; to run, to cry, like a madman. *Un de* — *deux de retrouvés;* there's as good fish in the sea as ever was caught or when one door shuts another opens. *C'est du bien* —; it is casting pearls before swine. *Tirer à coups* —*s;* to shoot at random. *Pays* —; out-of-the-way, deserted country. *A corps* —; headlong, desperately. *Heures* —*es;* spare time, leisure hours. *Un bienfait n'est jamais* —; a good action never remains unrewarded. *Enfants* —*s* or sentinelle —*e;* (milit.) forlorn hope. *Salle des pas* —*s;* outer hall, waiting hall (courts of law).

père, *n.m.,* father, parent; sire; man, fellow. — *de famille;* father of a family. *Nos* —*s;* our forefathers. — *s du désert;* old anchorites. *Le saint-* —; le très saint- —, notre saint- —, notre très saint- —, le — *des fidèles,* le — *des Chrétiens;* (c.rel.) the pope. — *spirituel;* father confessor. *Beau-* —, (—*x-* —*s*) father-in-law; step-father. — *nourricier;* foster-father. — *la joie;* frank, gay, hearty fellow. — *aux écus;* man with a great deal of money. *De* — *en fils;* from father to son, from sire to son. — *noble;* (thea.) heavy father, old man. *Dormir,* or *s'endormir, avec ses* — *s;* to sleep with one's fathers. *Petit* —; dada, papa. *De* —; fatherly, paternal.

pérégrination, *n.f.,* peregrination.

péregrinité, n.f., (jur.) alienage, alienism, alienship.

péremption, n.f., (jur.) limitation, nonsuit.

péremptoire, adj., peremptory.

péremptoirement (-tôar-mān), adv., peremptorily.

⊙**pérennial**, -**e** (-rè-n-nial), adj., perennial.

pérennité, n.f., perpetuity.

péréquation, n.f., assessment, equal distribution.

perfectibilité, n.f., perfectibility.

perfectible, adj., perfectible.

perfection, n.f., perfection, completeness. Le plus haut degré de — ; the acme of perfection. La — en personne; perfection personified, the pink of perfection. En — ; to perfection.

perfectionnement (-sio-n-mān), n.m., improvement, perfecting, finishing. Leçons de — ; finishing lessons.

perfectionner, v.a., to perfect, to bring to perfection ; to improve ; to improve upon. — ce que les autres ont inventé ; to improve on the inventions of others.

se **perfectionner**, v.r., to perfect one's self ; to improve one's self ; to improve.

perfide, n.m.f. and adj., perfidious, treacherous, false, false-hearted person ; perfidious, treacherous, false. Le — m'a trahi; the perfidious man betrayed me.

perfidement (-fid-mān), adv., perfidiously, falsely, treacherously, basely.

perfidie, n.f., perfidy, perfidiousness ; treachery ; false-heartedness, treacherousness; treacherous action, treacherous thing. Faire une — ; to commit an act of perfidy.

perfolié, -**e**, adj., (bot.) perfoliate, perfoliated.

perforage, n.m., boring ; perforation.

perforant, -**e**, adj., perforating ; perforative.

perforateur, n.m., (tech.) perforator.

perforati-f, -**ve**, adj., (surg.) perforative.

perforation, n.f., perforation.

perforer, v.a., to perforate, to bore.

péri, n.m., peri (Persian fairy).

périanthe, n.m., (bot.) perianth, perianthium.

périapte, n.m., periapt.

péribole, n.m., (arch.) peribolus.

péricarde, n.m., (anat.) pericardium.

péricardite, n.f., (med.) pericarditis.

péricarpe, n.m., (bot.) seed-vessel, pericarp.

périchondre, n.m., (anat.) perichondrium.

péricliter, v.n., to be in danger, in jeopardy ; to threaten to fall (of building).

péricrâne, n.m., (anat.) pericranium.

péridot, n.m., chrysolite, peridot, olivine.

péridrome, n.m., (arch.) peridrome.

périgée, n.m. and adj., (astron.) perigee, perigeum ; in its perigee.

périgourdin, -**e**, adj., of Perigord. n., native of Perigord.

périgueux(-gheû), n.m., (min.) Perigord stone.

périhélie, n.m. and adj., (astron.) perihelion, perihelium ; in its perihelion.

*****péril**, n.m., peril, danger, jeopardy, hazard, risk. Au — de ma vie ; at the hazard of my life. Etre en — de ta vie ; to be in danger of one's life. Prendre une affaire à ses risques et —s ; to run the risk of anything ; to take all the risks. Mettre en — ; to endanger, to put in jeopardy.

*****périlleusement**, adv., perilously, dangerously, hazardously.

*****périlleu-x**, -**se**, adj., perilous, dangerous, hazardous.

périmer, v.n., (jur.) to be barred by limitation, to pass out of date ; to lapse, to drop.

périmètre, n.m., (geom.) perimeter.

périnéal, -**e**, adj., perinæal.

périnée, n.m., (anat.) perinæum.

période, n.f., stage, period (revolution) ; (med.) period ; (astron.) period ; (chron.) period ;

(gram.) period, sentence ; (mus.) phrase. — lunaire ; lunar period. — bien arrondie ; well-rounded period. — embarrassée ; involved period.

période, n.m., pitch, summit, degree, acme, period. Long — de temps ; long period of time.

périodicité, n.f., periodicity.

périodique, adj., periodic, periodical ; (arith.) recurring, circulating. Fraction — ; (arith.) circulating, recurring decimal, repetend. Fraction — composée ; (arith.) mixed circulating decimal. Style — ; full style.

périodiquement (-dik-mān), adv., periodically.

périoste, n.m., (anat.) periosteum.

périostose, n.f., (med.) periostitis.

péripatéticien, -**ne** (-ci-in, -è-n), n. and adj., Peripatetic.

péripatétisme, n.m., Peripateticism.

péripétie (-pé-ci), n.f., sudden turn of fortune ; revolution, vicissitude ; (thea.) catastrophe, event, incident.

périphérie, n.f., (geom.) periphery.

périphrase, n.f., periphrasis, periphrase, circumlocution.

périphraser, v.n., to periphrase, to talk in a roundabout way, to express by circumlocution.

périple, n.m., (ancient geog.) periplus.

péripneumonie, n.f., (med.) peripneumonia, peripneumony.

périptère, n.m. and adj., (arch.) periptery ; peripteral.

périr, v.n., to perish, to decay, to die, to be lost, to be destroyed, to sink, to fall off ; (jur.) to be barred by limitation. — de froid ; to perish with cold. — corps et biens ; (of ships) to be lost with all hands. Tôt ou tard les méchants périssent malheureusement ; sooner or later the wicked come to an untimely end. Faire — une armée ; to destroy an army. L'instance est périe ; (jur.) the suit is barred by limitation. Faire — ; to put to death ; to do away with.

périsciens (-si-in), n.m.pl., (geog.) Periscians, Periscii.

périssable, adj., perishable.

périssoire, n.f., canoe.

péristaltique, adj., (med.) peristaltic.

péristole, n.f., (physiolog.) the peristaltic motion (of the intestines).

péristyle, n.m. and adj., (arch.) peristyle ; ornamented with a peristyle.

périsystole, n.f., (physiolog.) perisystole.

péritoine, n.m., (anat.) peritoneum.

péritonite, n.f., (med.) peritonitis.

perkale, perkaline. V. **percale, percaline**.

perlasse, n.f., pearlash.

perle, n.f., pearl ; bead, beading (of bracelets, necklaces); best ; (print.) pearl; (arch.) bead ; (pharm.) pearl. Nacre de — ; mother of pearl. — baroque ; irregular pearl. — tube ; bugle. Jeter des —s devant les pourceaux ; to cast pearls before swine. —s fines ; native, real pearls. Semence de —s ; the smallest pearls. Herbe aux —s ; gromwell, gromil. C'est la — des hommes ; he is the best of men. Nous ne sommes pas ici pour enfiler des —s ; we are not here to pick straws, or to trifle our time away. Faire la — ; to froth, to froth up (of brandy).

perlé, -**e**, adj., pearled, set with pearls ; pearly, beady ; boiled twice (of sugar) ; (her.) pearled ; (mus.) brilliant and delicate. Bouillon — ; pearly broth. Orge — ; pearl-barley.

perler, v.n., to pearl, to bead, to form globules. v.a., to pearl ; to give a finish to ; to polish.

se **perler**, v.r., to be, or to become, pearled.

perli-er, -**ère**, adj., of pearl. Huître —ère ; pearl-oyster.

perlière, n.f., (bot.) cudweed.

perlimpinpin, n.m., used only in : poudre de — ; quack powder ; nostrum (pop.).

perlon, *n.m.*, (ich.) swallow-fish, sapphirine-gurnet, tub-fish.

perlure, *n.f.*, (hunt.) curling (of horns).

permanence, *n.f.*, permanence, permanency. *Armée en* —; standing army. *L'assemblée s'est déclarée en* —; the assembly declared its sittings permanent. *En* —; permanently.

permanent, **-e**, *adj.*, permanent, lasting; (mec.) constant.

perméabilité, *n.f.*, permeability, perviousness.

perméable, *adj.*, permeable, pervious.

permettre, *v.a.*, to permit, to allow, to suffer, to give leave, to let, to enable, to afford. *Permettez-moi de vous dire ;* allow me to tell you, let me tell you. *Permettez !* allow me ! excuse me ! *se permettre*, *v.r.*, to permit, to allow, to suffer one's self (to); to indulge; to indulge one's self; to take the liberty (of); to take upon one's self (to), to assume, to dare.

permis, **-e**, *part.*, lawful, permitted, allowed; justifiable. *S'il m'est — de le dire ;* if I may say so. *A vous — de* or *— à vous de ;* you may if you like. *S'il m'est — de ;* if I may, if I may be allowed. *Est-il — d'entrer ?* may I come in ?

permis, *n.m.*, permit, license, pass ; leave. *— de chasse ;* shooting-license. *— de circulation* (rail.) pass. *— de séjour ;* permission to reside.

permission, *n.f.*, permission, consent, allowance, leave, permit. *Avec votre — ;* by your leave. *Abuser de la — ;* to go beyond bounds. *Prendre la — sous son bonnet ;* to take French leave.

permixtion (-miks-ti-on), *n.f.*, permixtion.

permutabilité, *n.f.*, commutability, permutability.

permutable, *adj.*, (gram.) commutable.

permutant, *n.m.*, permuter.

permutation, *n.f.*, permutation, commutation, exchange, change. *— de consonnes ;* transposition of consonants.

permuter, *v.a.*, to exchange, to permute, to commute, to transpose. *se permuter*, *v.r.*, (gram.) to be permuted, *or* exchanged, *or* transposed.

pernicieusement (-euz-mān), *adv.*, perniciously, mischievously, hurtfully, injuriously, prejudicially.

pernicieu-x, **-se**, *adj.*, pernicious, mischievous, hurtful, injurious, prejudicial. *— à la santé ;* pernicious to health.

péroné, *n.m.*, (anat.) fibula (small bone of the leg).

péronnelle, *n.f.*, hussy, saucy baggage, gossip; silly, talkative woman.

péroraison, *n.f.*, peroration.

pérorer, *v.n.*, to harangue ; to hold forth; to speechify.

péroreur, *n.m.*, haranguer, speechifier.

pérot, *n.m.*, sapling (of the age of two cuttings).

pérou, *n.m.*, Peru. *Ce n'est pas le — ;* it is no great thing, no great haul.

péroxyde, *n.m.*, (chem.) peroxide.

perpendiculaire, *n.f.* and *adj.*, perpendicular. *Abaisser une — ;* to let fall a perpendicular. *Elever une — ;* to raise a perpendicular.

perpendiculairement (-lèr-mān), *adv.*, perpendicularly.

perpendicularité, *n.f.*, perpendicularity.

perpendicule, *n.m.*, (l.u.) plumb-line, perpendicle.

perpétration, *n.f.*, (jur.) perpetration.

perpétrer, *v.a.*, (jur.) to perpetrate, to commit.

perpétuation, *n.f.*, perpetuation.

perpétuel, **-le**, *adj.*, perpetual, permanent, never-ceasing, endless, for life.

perpétuellement (-èl-mān), *adv.*, perpetually, everlastingly.

perpétuer, *v.a.*, to perpetuate. *se perpétuer*, *v.r.*, to be perpetuated, to last, to endure, to continue.

perpétuité, *n.f.*, perpetuity. *A —* ; forever; for life. *Condamner aux travaux forcés à — ;* to sentence to penal servitude for life.

perplexe, *adj.*, perplexed, embarrassed, irresolute ; perplexing.

perplexité, *n.f.*, perplexity, embarrassment.

perquisition, *n.f.*, perquisition, search; investigation. *Mandat de — ;* search-warrant. *Lancer un mandat de — ;* to issue a search-warrant.

perré, *n.m.*, (arch.) water-wing; (of the sea) pebbly shore, shingly beach.

perrin-dandin, *n.m.*, an ignorant, greedy judge.

perron, *n.m.*, flight of steps (before a house) ; outside landing ; (arch.) perron.

perroquet, *n.m.*, (orni.) parrot ; parrot (pers.) ; (nav.) top-gallant sail, gallant. *Parler comme un — ;* to talk like a parrot.

perruche, *n.f.*, she-parrot ; perroquet; (nav.) mizzen top-gallant sail.

perruque, *n.f.*, wig, periwig, peruke, pig-tail ; mop, shock. *— à nœuds ;* bobwig, bobtail-wig. *Tête à — ;* barber's block; prejudiced old man.

perruquier, *n.m.*, wig-maker, peruke-maker; hair-dresser ; barber.

perruquière, *n.f.*, barber's wife.

⊙**pers**, **-e**, *adj.*, blue ; bluish.

persan, **-e**, *n.* and *adj.*, Persian.

persan, *n.m.*, Persian language.

persane, *n.f.*, Persian woman.

perse, *n.f.*, (geog.) Persia ; Persian woman ; chintz.

perse, *n.m.*, (ancient hist.) Persian.

persécutant, **-e**, *adj.*, troublesome, teasing.

persécuter, *v.a.*, to persecute, to trouble, to importune, to tease ; to bore, to dun.

persécut-eur, **-rice**, *n.* and *adj.*, persecutor, troublesome man *or* woman ; persecuting, importunate, troublesome.

persécution, *n.f.*, persecution, annoyance, importunity.

persée, *n.m.*, (astron.) Perseus.

persévéramment (-ra-mān), *adv.*, perseveringly.

persévérance, *n.f.*, perseverance, steadiness, industry.

persévérant, **-e**, *adj.*, persevering, steady, industrious.

persévérer, *v.n.*, to persevere, to be steadfast, to persist in one's opinion. *— dans un dessein ;* to persevere in a design.

persicaire, *n.f.*, (bot.) water-pepper.

persicot, *n.m.*, persicot (cordial).

persienne, *n.f.*, shutter-blind, Venetian shutter. *— fixe ;* louver window.

persiflage, *n.m.*, quizzing, bantering, banter, chaffing, chaff.

persifler, *v.a.*, to quiz, to rally, to banter, to chaff.

persifleur, *n.m.*, banterer, quiz. *adj.*, quizzing, bantering, chaffing.

persil, *n.m.*, (bot.) parsley. *— d'âne ;* beaked parsley. *— des marais ;* sium angustifolium *or* marsh-parsley.

*persillade, *n.f.*, (cook.) beef dressed with vinegar and parsley.

*persillé, **-e**, *adj.*, spotted ; blue-moldy (of cheese).

persique, *adj.*, (arch.) Persian, Persic.

persistance, *n.f.*, persistence, persistency.

persistant, **-e**, *adj.*, (bot.) persistent, persisting.

persister, *v.n.*, to persist (in), to keep to. *Il persiste à nier ;* he persists in denying. *Il persiste dans son sentiment ;* he maintains his opinion.

personnage, n.m., personage, person, great person, somebody ; (theat.) character, part. C'est un sot —; he is a silly, ignorant fellow. Il joue bien son —; he plays his part well. Je connais le —; I know the fellow. Voilà un plaisant — l what an absurd fellow l Tapisserie à —s ; figured tapestry.

personnalité, n.f., personal feeling; self-love, selfishness, egotism ; personality ; personal remark.

personnat, n.m., sort of benefice.

personne, n.f., person, man, woman, child, female ; own self ; exterior, appearance; (gram., theol.) person. Jeune —; young lady, young girl. Parlant à sa —; (jur.) speaking to him in person. Les —s de condition ; people of fashion. Sans acception de —s ; without respect of persons. Il est bien fait de sa —; he has a handsome person or exterior. J'y étais en —; I was there in person. Avoir soin de sa —; to take care of one's self. Il aime sa —; he loves his dear self. Payer de sa —; to expose one's self to danger; to be in the thick of the fight or fray ; (fig.) to exert one's self. A la première, seconde, troisième —; (gram.) in the first, second, third, person. C'est la bonté en —; he (or she) is kindness itself.

personne, pron.m., nobody, no man, none, no one ; anybody, any one. Il n'y a — à la maison ; there is nobody at home. Je doute que — y réussisse ; I doubt whether any one will or would succeed in it.

personnée, n. and adj.f., (bot.) personate, masked flower; personate, masked.

personnel, -le, adj., personal ; selfish.

personnel, n.m., ⊙personal character ; staff, (all the persons composing any establishment); staff of servants, officials, hands ; (milit., nav.) personnel.

personnellement (-nèl-màn), adv., personally.

personnification, n.f., personification, personation.

personnifier, v.a., to personify ; to impersonate.

perspecti-f, -ve, adj., perspective.

perspective, n.f., perspective, view; prospect, distance, vista, opening. — aérienne ; aerial perspective. Cela borne la —; that bounds the prospect. — riante; delightful prospect. Il a la — d'une grande fortune; he has a large fortune in prospect. En —; in the distance; in prospect, in expectation.

perspicace, adj., perspicacious.

perspicacité, n.f., perspicacity.

perspicuité, n.f., perspicuity.

persuader, v.a., to persuade, to make to believe, to convince, to satisfy; to imagine. J'en suis persuadé ; I am convinced of it.

se persuader, v.r., to persuade, to convince one's self ; to be persuaded, to imagine.

persuader, v.n., to persuade, to convince.

persuasible, adj., persuasible, persuadable.

persuasi-f, -ve, adj., persuasive ; persuading, convincing, clinching.

persuasion, n.f., persuasion, conviction, belief, opinion. L'éloquence a pour but la —; the object of eloquence is to persuade. Agir à la — d'un autre; to act by (the) persuasion of another.

persuasivement, adv., persuasively.

perte, n.f., loss, losings ; ruin, waste, wastefulness ; fall, doom. A —; at a loss ; (med.) flooding. Faire une —; to meet with a loss. Etre en —; to be a loser. Courir à sa —; to go to one's ruin, to one's doom. — de temps ; waste of time. La — du Rhône; (geog.) place where the Rhone disappears beneath the rocks. Vendre à —; to sell at a loss. En pure —; to no purpose, uselessly, in vain. A — de vue ; as far as the eye can reach. Je suis en —; I am a loser by it.

pertinacité, n.f., pertinacity.

pertinemment (-na-màn), adv., pertinently.

pertinence, n.f., pertinency.

pertinent, -e, adj., pertinent.

pertuis, n.m., (geog.) straits ; sluice, narrow opening in a flood-gate.

pertuisane, n.f., partisan, halberd.

pertuisanier, n.m., halberdier ; warder.

perturbat-eur, -rice, n. and adj., disturber ; disturbing.

perturbation, n.f., perturbation, disturbance, commotion.

pervenche, n.f., (bot.) periwinkle.

pervers, -e, adj., perverse, froward, untoward, wicked.

pervers, n.m., perverse, froward person ; wrong-doer.

perversion, n.f., perversion.

perversité, n.f., perversity, perverseness, frowardness, untowardness.

pervertir, v.a., to pervert, to be pervertive of, to be a perverter of. Se —; to be perverted.

pervertissable, adj., pervertible.

pervertissement (-tis-màn), n.m., perversion, corruption.

pervertisseur, n.m., perverter, corrupter.

pesade, n.f., (man.) pesade.

pesage, n.m., weighing ; weighing-room, saddling-room.

pesamment (pĕ-za-màn), adv., heavily, ponderously, weightily, lumpishly; slowly.

pesant, -e, adj., heavy, ponderous, weighty ; unwieldy, lumpish ; cumbersome; sluggish, slow; full weight. Fardeau —; heavy burden. Cheval — à 'a main ; hard-mouthed horse. Il a la main —e ; he has a heavy hand. Il a l'esprit —; he is dull-minded. Joug —; heavy yoke. Un louis d'or —; a louis d'or of the full weight.

pesant, n.m., weight. Il vaut son — d'or ; he is worth his weight in gold.

pesant, adv., weight, in weight.

pesanteur, n.f., weight, heaviness, weightiness ; sluggishness, dullness, slowness, unwieldiness ; ponderosity, ponderousness ; (phys.) force of gravity, gravity. — de tête ; heaviness in the head. — d'esprit ; dullness of mind.

pesée, n.f., weighing ; all that is weighed at once. Faire une —; to weigh.

pèse-acide, n.m., acetometer.

pèse-lait, n.m., lactometer.

pèse-lettres, n.m., letter-weigher, letter-scales.

pèse-liqueur, n.m., (—, or —-s) hydrometer.

peser, v.a., to weigh ; to ponder, to consider, to estimate. — les raisons de quelqu'un ; to weigh any one's arguments. — ses paroles ; to weigh one's words.

peser, v.n., to weigh, to be of weight, to be heavy ; to hang upon ; to bear upon; to lean, to lie heavy ; to be a burden; to dwell upon. Viande qui pèse sur l'estomac ; meat that lies heavy upon the stomach. Cela me pèse sur le cœur; that lies heavy upon my heart. — sur un levier; to bear upon a lever.

pesette, n.f., assay-scales.

peseur, n.m., weigher.

peson, n.m., steelyard.

pessaire, n.m., (med.) pessary.

pesse, n.f., (bot.) mare's tail.

pessimisme, n.m., pessimism.

pessimiste, n.m., pessimist.

peste, n.f., plague, pestilence, pest, torment, bore, nuisance; stench. La flatterie est la — des cours; flattery is the plague of courts. — soit du fou ! plague on the fool ! — soit de ! out upon !

peste, adj., sly, arch.

peste ! *int.*, plague on it ! the deuce ! by Jove ! hang it ! bless me ! indeed !

pester, *v.n.*, to inveigh against, to bluster, to storm, to rave. *Il peste contre ses juges ;* he rails, (swears) at his judges. — *entre chair et cuir ;* to fret and fume in secret.

pestifère, *adj.*, (l.u.) pestiferous, pestilential.

pestiféré, *-e*, *n.* and *adj.*, person infected with the plague ; plague-stricken.

pestilence, *n.f.*, pestilence.

pestilent, *-e*, *adj.*, pestilential.

pestilentiel, *-le* (-ci-èl), *adj.*, pestilential, infectious, contagious.

pet, *n.m.*, (lex.) fart, wind. *Un — de nonne ;* apple-fritter.

pétale, *n.m.*, (bot.) petal, flower-leaf.

pétalé, *-e*, *adj.*, (bot.) petalous, petaled.

pétalisme, *n.m.*, (antiq.) petalism.

pétalite, *n.f.*, petalite.

pétaloïde, *adj.*, petaloid.

pétarade, *n.f.*, (of animals) farting ; trumpeting with the mouth ; cracking ; noise of crackers.

pétard, *n. m.*, (milit.) petard ; (fireworks) cracker.

pétarder, *v.a.*, to blow up with a petard.

pétardier, *n.m.*, one who makes petards.

pétase, *n.m.*, (antiq.) petasus ; broad-brimmed hat.

pétaud, *n.m. C'est la cour du roi —;* it is Bedlam broken loose ; Dover court.

pétaudière, *n.f.*, bear-garden, tumultuous assembly.

pétéchial, *-e*, *adj.*, (med.) petechial. *Fièvre —e ;* petechial fever.

pétéchies, *n.f.pl.*, (med.) petechiæ.

pet-en-l'air, *n.m.*, (—) man's short morning gown.

péter, *v.n.*, (lex.) to burst ; to break, to snap ; to crackle, to crack ; to bounce ; to fart, to break wind ; (of fire-arms) to explode, to burst.

péteu-r, *n.m.*, *-se*, *n.f.*, (lex.) sorry fellow, milksop.

*****pétillant**, *-e*, *adj.*, crackling, sparkling.

*****pétillement**, *n.m.*, crackling, sparkling.

*****pétiller**, *v.n.*, to crackle ; to sparkle ; to long to do a thing, to be eager to. *Son ouvrage pétille d'esprit ;* his work sparkles with wit. *Ses yeux pétillent ;* his eyes sparkle. — *d'impatience ;* to boil over with impatience.

pétiolaire (-ci-), *adj.*, (bot.) petiolary.

pétiole (-ci-), *n.m.*, (bot.) petiole, leaf-stalk.

pétiolé, *-e* (-ci-), *adj.*, (bot.) petiolate.

petiot, *-e*, *n.* and *adj.*, tiny, wee ; little fellow, little one ; darling.

petit, *-e*, *adj.*, little, small, diminutive, short, unimportant, petty, slight, trifling ; light ; faint ; grand (of one's children's children). — *fils* (—*s*—) ; grandson. *Un — homme ;* a little man. *Un homme — ;* a mean man. *Un — roi ;* a petty king. *Le — peuple ;* the common people. *Le — monde ;* the common people. — *e guerre. V. guerre.* — *collet ;* young clergyman. *-e vérole ;* small-pox. *De la —e bière ;* small-beer. — *à — ;* by degrees. — *maître,* (—*s*—*s*) coxcomb. *-e-maîtresse,* (—*s*—*s*) belle ; vain, foppish woman. *— à — l'oiseau fait son nid ;* small strokes fell great oaks. *Les —s ruisseaux font les grandes rivières ;* many a little makes a mickle. *En —, au — pied ;* in miniature, on a small scale. *En — pays ;* in a small way. *Etre aux —s soins pour ;* to be all attention to. — *mercier — panier ;* (prov.) small positions for small brains.

petit, *n.m.*, *-e*, *n.f.*, little child ; little one ; dear, darling ; young one ; whelp, pup, kitten, cub. *Les petits ;* (at school) the junior boys. *Les —s d'une chienne ;* the pups of a bitch. *Les —s d'une truie ;* the litter of a sow. *Faire des —s ;* to bring forth young ones. *Pauvre — ;* poor little fellow or chap.

petitement (pĕtit-mān), *adv.*, in a small way ; little ; slenderly, meanly, poorly. *Il est logé — ;* he has modest lodgings, he is cramped for room.

petite-oie, *n.f.*, (n.p.) (cook.) giblets ; ⊙stockings, gloves, hat and other minor parts of clothing ; ⊙minor tokens of love.

petitesse, *n.f.*, smallness, littleness, shortness, insignificance ; meanness, shabbiness ; shallowness, narrowness. — *d'âme ;* meanness of soul. — *d'esprit ;* narrowness of mind. *C'est une — de sa part ;* it is a piece of meanness on his part.

petit-gris, *n.m.*, (—*s*—) minever, Siberian squirrel.

pétition, *n.f.*, petition, memorial, request. *Faire une — ;* to draw up, to address, a petition. *Faire présenter une — ;* to petition, to memorialize. — *de principe ;* (log.) petitio principii, begging the question.

pétitionnaire, *n.m.f.*, petitioner, applicant.

pétitionnement, *n.m.*, petitioning, memorializing.

pétitionner, *v.n.*, to make a request, to petition, to memorialize.

pétitoire, *adj.*, (jur.) petitory (claiming the right of property in real estate).

pétitoire, *n.m.*, (jur.) claim of ownership.

peton, *n.m.*, foot (of children) ; tiny foot.

pétoncle, *n.m.*, (conch.) scallop.

pétreau, *n.m.*, (gard.) sucker (of a tree).

pétrée, *adj. f.*, (geog.) stony. [Only used in *Arabie — ;* Arabia Petræa.]

pétrel, *n.m.*, (orni.) petrel.

pétreu-x, *-se*, *adj.*, (anat.) stone-like ; rocky, stony.

pétri, *-e*, *part.*, kneaded. *C'est un homme tout — de salpêtre ;* he is a passionate *or* violent-tempered man. — *d'ignorance ;* steeped in ignorance.

pétrifiant, *-e*, *adj.*, petrifying.

pétrification, *n.f.*, petrifaction, petrification.

pétrifier, *v.a.*, to petrify.

se **pétrifier**, *v.r.*, to petrify, to turn into stone.

pétrin, *n.m.*, kneading-trough ; scrape, hobble, pickle ; hot-water. *Se mettre dans le — ;* to get into hot-water, into a scrape. *Un — impossible ;* terrible, indescribable disorder, confusion.

pétrir, *v.a.*, to knead, to mold, to form.

pétrissable, *adj.*, that can be kneaded ; (fig.) yielding, pliant, submissive, obedient, easily led.

pétrissage, *n.m.*, kneading, working, forming.

pétrisseur, *n.m.*, *-se*, *n.f.*, kneader, journeyman-baker. — *mécanique ;* kneading machine.

pétrole, *n.m.*, petroleum, rock-oil.

pétroleu-r, *n.m.*, *-se*, *n.f.*, miscreant who commits arson by means of petroleum (as in France under the Commune).

pétrosilex (-lèks), *n.m.*, (min.) petrosilex.

in **petto** (i-n pèt-to), *adv.*, in petto, secretly, inwardly.

pétulamment (-la-mān), *adv.*, petulantly.

pétulance, *n.f.*, petulance, petulancy.

pétulant, *-e*, *adj.*, petulant ; saucy, frisky.

⊙**petun**, *n.m.*, tobacco, snuff.

⊙**petuner**, *v.n.*, to take snuff ; to smoke.

pétunia, *n.m.*, (bot.) petunia.

pétunsé *or* **pétunzé**, *n.m.*, petunse, china-stone.

peu, *adv.*, little, not much, few, not many. — *ou point ;* little or nothing. *Ni — ni point ;* none at all. — *d'argent ;* little money. — *d'hommes ;* few men. — *aimable ;* not very amiable. *Fort — ;* very little. *Quelque — ;* a little. *Si — que ;* however little. *Si — que rien ;* next to nothing. *Tant soit — ;* ever so little. — *à — ;* by degrees. *Dans —, dans — de temps ;* in a little *or* short time. *Dans — de jours ;* in a few days. *A — près, à — de chose près ;* nearly about, within a trifle. *Attendez un — ;* wait a little. *Imaginez un — !* just fancy ! *Pour — que ;* if only . . . if at all . . . if . . . ever so little.

peu, *n.m.*, little, few. *Le — que je vaux;* the little (that) I am worth. *Encore un —;* a little longer; a little more. *Se contenter de —;* to be contented with little. *Vivre de —;* to live on next to nothing.

peulvan *or* **peulven**, *n.m.*, (archæol.) menhir.

peuplade, *n.f.*, colony; tribe; horde.

peuple, *adj.*, (l.u.) vulgar, common.

peuplé, -e, *adj.*, peopled; stocked; planted (with); filled (with).

peuple, *n.m.*, people, nation, race, tribe; multitude, crowd, citizens, working classes, lower classes; vulgar; fry (fish); sucker (of a plant); ⊙ (bot.) poplar; (techn.) deal-wood. *Le menu —, le bas —, le petit —;* the common people. *La lie du —;* the scum of the people. *Mettre du — dans un étang;* to stock a pond with fry.

peuplement, *n.m.*, peopling; stocking a poultry-yard, a pond; planting new trees.

peupler, *v.a.*, to people, to populate; to stock with inhabitants; to stock with animals; to plant, to propagate; to breed.

se **peupler**, *v.r.*, to become peopled.

peupler, *v.n.*, to multiply; to breed.

peuplier, *n.m.*, poplar.

peur, *n.f.*, fear, fright; dread, terror. *Avoir —;* to be afraid. *Avoir grand'peur;* to be in great fear. *Mourir de —;* to be frightened to death, to die of fright. *Faire — à quelqu'un;* to frighten any one. *Sans —;* fearless. *En être quitte pour la —;* to get off with the fright; to be merely frightened. *Avoir — de son ombre;* to be afraid of one's shadow. *Etre mis à faire —;* to look a fright. *Avoir plus de — que de mal;* to be more frightened than hurt. *De — de;* for fear of. *De — que;* lest, for fear that. *De — qu'il ne le sache;* lest he should know it.

peureu-x, -se, *adj.*, fearful, timid, timorous.

peut-être, *adv.*, perhaps, may be, perchance, peradventure. *— viendra-t-il, — qu'il viendra;* perhaps he will come. *— que oui;* perhaps so.

peut-être, *n.m.*, perhaps, supposition. *Il n'y a pas de —;* there is no perhaps in the matter.

phaéton, *n.m.*, phaeton; (fam.) Jehu, driver.

phagédénique, *adj.*, (med.) phagedenic.

phagédénisme, *n.m.*, (med.) phagedena.

phalange, *n.f.*, phalanx, battalion, band; force, host; (anat.) phalanx.

phalanger, *n.m.*, (mam.) phalanger.

phalangite, *n.m.*, soldier of a phalanx.

phalanstère, *n.m.*, phalanstery.

phalanstérien, -ne (-in, -è-n), *n.* and *adj.*, phalansterian.

phalaris (-ris), *n.m.*, (bot.) phalaris, canary grass.

phalarope, *n.m.*, (orni.) phalarope.

phalène, *n.f.*, (ent.) moth.

phaleuce *or* **phaleuque**, *n.m.* and *adj.*, (Gr. and Lat. poet.) hendecasyllable; hendecasyllabic.

phallique, *adj.*, phallic.

phanérogame, *n.f.* and *adj.*, (bot.) phanerogamic plant; phanerogamous.

phantaisie, *n.f.* V. **fantaisie**.

phantasmagorie, *n.f.* V. **fantasmagorie**.

phantasmagorique, *adj.* V. **fantasmagorique**.

pharaon, *n.m.*, Pharaoh.

pharaon, *n.m.*, faro, pharaon (card game).

pharaonique, *adj.*, Pharaonic.

phare, *n.m.*, light-house, beacon, beacon-light. *— flottant;* light-ship.

*****pharillon**, *n.m.*, lantern (used by fishermen to attract fish at night).

pharisaïque, *adj.*, Pharisaic, Pharisaical.

pharisaïsme, *n.m.*, Pharisaism.

pharisien (-zi-in), *n.m.*, -ne (-zi-è-n), *n.f.*, Pharisee.

pharmaceutique, *n.f.* and *adj.*, pharmaceutics; pharmaceutical.

pharmacie, *n.f.*, pharmacy; chemist's shop;

apothecary's shop, apothecary's business; medicine chest; dispensary. *— domestique;* medicine chest.

pharmacien (-in), *n.m.*, apothecary; chemist and druggist.

pharmacologie, *n.f.*, pharmacology.

pharmacologique, *adj.*, relating to pharmacology.

pharmacopée, *n.f.*, pharmacopœia.

pharmacopole, *n.m.*, (jest.) pharmacopolist; vendor of drugs.

pharyngite, *n.f.*, (med.) pharyngitis.

pharynx, *n.m.*, pharynx.

phase, *n.f.*, phase, phasis; aspect; stage, period, turn.

phaséole, *n.f.* V. **faséole**.

phébé, *n.f.*, (poet.) the moon.

phébus (-bûs), *n.m.*, (myth.) Phœbus; (fig.) ranter, fine talker; bombast, fustian. *Parler —;* to talk fustian, to rant. *Donner dans le —;* to write fustian.

phénicien, -ne (-ci-in, -ci-è-n), *n.* and *adj.*, Phœnician.

phénicoptère, *n.m.*, (orni.) phenicopter, flamingo.

phénique, *adj.*, (chem.) carbolic, phenic.

phénix (fé-niks), *n.m.*, phenix, fabulous bird; (astron.) Phenix. *C'est un —;* he is a very marvel.

phénol, *n.m.*, phenol.

phénoménal, -e, *adj.*, phenomenal.

phénomène, *n.m.*, phenomenon. *C'est un — que de vous voir ici;* it is quite a miracle, a wonder, to see you here.

phil- *or* **philo-**, a prefix from Gr. φίλος.

philanthrope, *n.m.*, philanthropist.

philanthropie, *n.f.*, philanthropy.

philanthropique, *adj.*, philanthropic.

philharmonique, *adj.*, philharmonic.

philhellène, *n.m.f.*, philhellenist.

philinte, *n.m.*, (fig.) everybody's friend.

philippique, *n.f.*, philippic.

philistin, *n.m.*, philistine; (fig.) snob, cockney, vulgar fellow.

phillyrée, *n.f.*, (bot.) phillyrea.

philologie, *n.f.*, philology.

philologique, *adj.*, philological.

philologue, *n.m.*, philologist.

philomathique, *adj.*, philomathic.

philomèle, *n.f.*, (poet.) philomela (the nightingale).

philosophale, *adj.f.*, philosopher's. *Pierre —;* philosopher's stone.

philosophe, *n.m.*, philosopher.

philosopher, *v.n.*, to philosophize.

philosophie, *n.f.*, philosophy; (print.) small pica; sixth form (in French public-schools).

philosophique, *adj.*, philosophical.

philosophiquement (-fik-mān), *adv.*, philosophically.

philosophisme, *n.m.*, philosophism.

philosophiste, *n.m.*, philosophist.

philotechnique (-tèk-nik), *adj.*, philotechnic.

philtre, *n.m.*, philter.

phimosis (-zis), *n.m.*, (med.) phimosis.

phlébite, *n.f.*, (med.) phlebitic.

phlébotome, *n.m.*, (surg.) lancet (for bleeding).

phlébotomie, *n.f.*, phlebotomy.

phlébotomiser, *v.a.*, to phlebotomize.

phlébotomiste, *n.m.*, phlebotomist.

phlegmagogue, *adj.*, expectorant.

phlegmasie, *n.f.*, phlegmasy.

phlegmatique, *adj.* V. **flegmatique**.

phlegme, *n.m.* V. **flegme**.

phlegmon, *n.m.*, (med.) phlegmon.

phlegmoneu-x, -se, *adj.*, (med.) phlegmonous.

⊙**phlogistique**, *n.m.*, (chem.) phlogiston.

phlogose, *n.f.*, (med.) inflammation.

phlox, *n.m.*, (bot.) phlox.

phlyctène, *n.f.*, (med.) bulla, blister.

phœnicure, *n.m.*, (orni.) red-start, red-tail.

pholade, *n.f.*, (conch.) pholas.

phonétique, *adj.*, phonetic.

phonique, *n.f.* and *adj.*, phonics ; phonic.

phonograph, *n.m.*, phonograph ; (pers.) phonographer.

phonographie, *n.f.*, phonography.

phonographique, *adj.*, phonographical.

phonolithe, *n.m.*, (min.) phonolite.

phonologie, *n.f.*, phonology.

phonomètre, *n.m.*, (phys.) phonometer (to measure the intensity of sound).

phoque, *n.m.*, (mam.) phoca, seal, sea-dog.

phormion or **phormione**, *n.m.*, (bot.) phormium.

phosphate, *n.m.*, (chem.) phosphate.

phosphite, *n.m.*, (chem.) phosphite.

phosphore, *n.m.*, phosphorus.

phosphorescence, *n.f.*, phosphorescence.

phosphorescent, -e, *adj.*, phosphorescent.

phosphoreux, *adj.*, phosphorous.

phosphorique, *adj.*, phosphoric.

phosphure, *n.m.*, phosphuret.

phosphuré, -e, *adj.*, phosphureted.

photographe, *n.m.*, photographist, photographer.

photographie, *n.f.*, photography, photograph.

photographier, *v.a.*, to photograph.

photographique, *adj.*, photographic.

photolithographie, *n.f.*, photolithography.

photomètre, *n.m.*, (phys.) photometer.

photométrie, *n.f.*, photometry.

photométrique, *adj.*, photometric.

photophobie, *n.f.*, (med.) photophobia.

photosphère, *n.f.*, (astron.) photosphere.

phrasaire, *n.m.*, phrase-book.

phrase, *n.f.*, phrase, sentence, affected style, empty talk, twaddle. — *faite ;* idiomatic phrase. *Faire des — s ;* to talk in set phrases. — *toute faite ;* common-place, common topic. *Membre de — ;* clause.

phrasé, -e, *part.adj.*, phrased.

phraséologie, *n.f.*, phraseology.

phraser, *v.a* and *n.*, (mus.) to mark the phrases ; to form phrases, to phrase.

phraseur or **phrasier**, *n.m.*, (fam.) phraseologist ; prolix, verbose, tedious writer *or* talker, twaddler ; bombastic writer.

phrénésie, phrénétique. *V.* **frénésie, frénétique.**

phrénique, *adj.*, (anat.) phrenic.

phrénologie, *n.f.*, phrenology.

phrénologique, *adj.*, phrenologic.

phrénologiste or **phrénologue**, *n.m.*, phrenologist.

phrygien, -ne, *adj.*, phrygian. *Bonnet — ;* phrygian cap (the cap of Liberty). *Mode — ;* (mus.) warlike music (in use among the ancient Greeks).

phtiriasis, *n.f.*, (med.) pedicular disease.

phtisie, *n.f.*, (med.) phthisis, consumption. *Être atteint de la — ;* to be in consumption, to be consumptive.

phtisique, *n.m.f.* and *adj.*, consumptive person, person in consumption ; phthisical, consumptive.

phylactère, *n.m.*, phylactery.

phylarque, *n.m.*, (antiq.) phylarch.

phyllithe, *n.m.*, phyllite.

phylloxera, *n.m.*, (—) (ent., agri.) phylloxera.

physicien (-in), *n.m.*, natural philosopher.

physico-mathématique, *adj.*, physico-mathematical.

physiocrate, *n.m.*, economist (one who believes that wealth is founded upon agriculture).

physiognomonie, *n.f.*, physiognomy (art).

physiognomonique, *adj.*, physiognomic.

physiographe, *n.m.*, physiographer,

physiographie, *n.f.*, physiography.

physiographique, *adj.*, physiographical.

physiologie, *n.f.*, physiology.

physiologique, *adj.*, physiological.

physiologiste, *n.m.*, physiologist.

physionomie, *n.f.*, physiognomy, countenance, aspect, look ; physiognomy (art).

physionomiste, *n.m.*, physiognomist.

physique, *n.f.*, physics, natural philosophy.

physique, *adj.*, physical, material, bodily ; absolute, real.

physique, *n.m.*, physique, natural constitution of a man ; outward appearance.

physiquement (fi-zik-mān), *adv.*, physically, bodily.

phytographie, *n.f.*, phytography.

phytolithe, *n.m.*, phytolite, petrified plant.

phytologie, *n.f.*, phytology.

piaculaire, *adj.*, expiatory.

⊙**piaffe**, *n.f.*, ostentation ; show, dash.

piaffer, *v.n.*, (man.) to paw the ground, to prance (of horses) ; ⊙to make a show, to cut a dash.

piaffeur, *n.m.* and *adj.*, pawer, prancer, pawing the ground (of horses) ; (fig.) showy *or* dashy person.

*piailler, *v.n.*, to bawl, to squall, to scold ; to rant. *Des enfants qui piaillent toujours ;* children constantly screaming, squalling brats.

*piaillerie, *n.f.*, bawling, squalling.

*piailleu-r, *n.m.*, **-se**, *n.f.*, scold ; squaller, bawler, bawling man or woman.

pian, *n.m.*, (med.) yaws.

pianino, *n.m.*, (—s) upright piano.

pianissimo, *adv.*, very softly.

pianiste, *n.m.f.*, pianist.

piano, *adv.*, (mus.) piano, softly.

piano (—*s*) or **piano-forte** (—*s*—) or **forte-piano** (—*-—s*), *n.m.*, piano-forte. — *à queue ;* grand piano. — *carré ;* square piano, cottage piano. — *droit ;* upright or cottage piano. *Jouer du — ;* to play on the piano.

piast or **piaste**, *n.m.*, Polish nobleman.

piastre, *n.f.*, piaster (coin).

piaulard, piauleur, *n.m.*, puler, whiner.

piaulement, *n.m.*, whining, puling.

piauler, *v.n.*, to pule, to whine ; (of chickens) to pip.

pible, *n.m.*, (nav.) pole. *Mât à — ;* pole-mast.

pic, *n.m.*, pick, pickax ; (nav.) gaff ; (orni.) woodpecker ; peak (of a mountain) ; pique (at the game of piquet). *A — ;* perpendicularly ; (nav.) apeak ; (pop.) just in time.

pica, *n.m.*, (med.) pica.

picador, *n.m.*, (—s) picador.

picard, -e, *n.* and *adj.*, Picardian ; (fig.) cunning, cautious fellow ; artful dodger.

picholine, *n.* and *adj.f.*, pickled olive ; pickled.

⊙**picorée**, *n.f.*, marauding, pilfering, plundering. *Aller à la — ;* to go a plundering, to go out marauding.

picorer, *v.n.*, ⊙to go out marauding, plundering ; (fig.) to plagiarize, to crib.

picoreur, *n.m.*, ⊙marauder ; plagiarist, cribber.

picot, *n.m.*, splinter (of wood) ; purl (of lace).

picoté, -e, *part.*, pricked, marked. *Il est — de petite vérole ;* he is pitted with small-pox.

picotelle, *n.f.*, (orni.) nut-hatch.

picotement (pi-kot-mān), *n.m.*, pricking, tingling, itching.

picoter, *v.a.*, to prick, to tingle ; to provoke, to tease ; to peck (of birds) ; (man.) to touch (gently) with the spur.

se picoter, *v.r.*, to tease, to irritate, to torment, one another.

picoterie (pi-ko-trī), *n.f.*, (fam.) teasing, bickering.

picotin, *n.m.*, peck (of oats).

picrate, *n.m.*, (chem.) carbazotate, picrate.

picrique, *adj.*, (chem.) carbazotic, picric.

pic-vert, *n.m.*, (*—s—s*). V. **pivert**.

pie, *n.f.*, (orni.) magpie, pie. *—grièche*, (*—s—s*) shrike; shrew, vixen. *Elle jase comme une —;* she chatters like a magpie. *Il croit avoir trouvé la — au nid;* he thinks he has made a great discovery; he has found a mare's nest.

pie, *adj.*, (l.u.) pious, charitable; (of horses) piebald.

pièce, *n.f.*, piece, length, fragment, trick; play, performance; document, paper; head (of cattle, of poultry, game); apartment; puncheon, cask (of oil, wine, etc.); piece of ordnance, cannon; document; joint (of cooked meat). *Mettre en —s;* to pull, to tear, to pieces. *Etre armé de toutes —s;* to be armed at all points. *Faire de toutes —s;* to do a thing entirely, to carry anything through. *Emporter la —;* to sting to the quick, to strike home. *Rassemblage de —s;* patchwork. *— de vin;* puncheon of wine. *En —;* in the cask, in the wood. *— d'eau;* sheet of water. *Une — d'artillerie;* a piece of ordnance. *—s de campagne;* field-pieces. *—s de batterie;* heavy ordnance. *— de théâtre;* play. *Etre bien près de ses —s;* to have very little money. *Tout d'une —;* all of a piece; (of persons) bolt upright. *Jouer une — à quelqu'un;* to play any one a trick. *Accommoder, habiller de toutes —s;* to abuse soundly, to rate, to treat ill, to fall foul of. *Travailler à l'emporte —;* to work by fits and starts, feverishly, to scamp work. *Une bonne —;* a cunning blade. *Donner la —;* to tip. *— de résistance;* principal dish, joint. *— justificative;* voucher. *— de conviction;* material, circumstantial evidence. *— à —;* bit by bit. *Tant la —;* so much a piece, a cask. *Travailler à ses —s;* to work by the job.

piécette, *n.f.*, small Spanish silver coin, peseta.

pied (pié), *n.m.*, foot; footing; track; leg (of furniture); bottom, ground; pace, slip, track; stalk (of plants). *Les doigts du —;* the toes. *— bot;* club-foot, club-footed. *Avoir des cors aux —s;* to have corns on one's feet. *Le cou-de-—,* (*—s—*) the instep. *Marcher sur la pointe du —;* to walk on tip-top. *Un coup de —;* a kick. *Donner des coups de— à;* to kick. *Aller à —;* to go on foot. *Sur —;* on foot, standing, astir, sitting up. *Taper du —;* to stamp. *Marcher —s nus;* to walk barefooted. *Mettre sous ses —;* to trample upon. *Les —s de devant;* the fore-feet. *Petits —s,* (—) small fowl, small game. *— plat, plat —;* flat foot; (fig.) knave, mean rascal. *— poudreux;* vagabond, rascal, scoundrel. *Une coutume qui prend —;* a custom that is gaining ground. *Perdre —;* to get out of one's depth. *Avoir —;* not to be out of one's depth. *—et poings liés;* tied hand and foot. *Lâcher —;* to give way, to fall back. *Prendre — sur quelque chose;* to take anything as a precedent. *Ne savoir sur quel — danser;* not to know which way to turn. *Sauter à —s joints;* to jump upon; (fig.) to ride rough-shod over. *Tenir le — sur la gorge de quelqu'un;* to attempt to force any one to do anything. *Tenir — à boule;* to stick to one's work. *Couper l'herbe sous le — à quelqu'un;* to supplant any one. *Il a été sur — toute la nuit;* he has been up all night. *De — en cap;* cap-a-pie, from head to foot. *Haut le —;* be off with you; let us be off at once! *Faire haut le —;* to vanish, to disappear; to run away. *Haut-le—,* (—) (fam.) a man with no fixed residence; a scoundrel. *Renvoyer des chevaux haut le —;* to send horses away without saddles or harness. *Au — de la lettre;* strictly speaking, literally. *Si vous lui donnez un —, il en prendra quatre;* give him an inch and he'll take an ell. *Il a trouvé chaussure à son —;* he has found just

what he wanted; he has met with his match. *Il s'est tiré une épine du —;* he pulled a thorn out of his foot; (fig.) he has got out of a difficulty. *Etre en —;* to be in the exercise of one's functions. *De — ferme;* without stirring, firmly. *De plain —;* on a level with. *Etre assis au — d'un arbre;* to be seated at the foot of a tree. *Un — de céleri;* a stick of celery. *Le — du lit;* the foot of the bed. *Le — d'une table;* the leg of a table. *— de mât;* heel of a mast. *Cela a tant de — de long;* that is so many feet long. *— à —;* step by step; by degrees. *Sur le — de;* at the rate of. *D'arrache —;* without intermission, without stopping. *Au petit —;* on a small scale. *Faire des —s et des mains pour;* to do one's utmost (to), to leave no stone unturned (to). *Sur le — où en sont les choses;* as matters stand. *Avoir bon —, bon œil;* to be hale and hearty. *Mettre quelqu'un à —;* to dismiss a functionary; to deprive a cabman of his license. *Ne pas se moucher du —;* to give one's self airs; to be no fool. *Sécher sur —;* to pine away. *La mort l'a pris au — levé;* death took him without warning, unawares. *Aller du — comme un chat maigre;* to be a capital walker.

pied-à-terre, *n.m.*, (—) temporary lodging; country-box; shooting lodge.

pied-d'alouette, *n.m.*, (*—s—*) (bot.) larkspur.

pied-de-coq, *n.m.*, (*—s—*) (bot.) cock's-foot-grass.

pied-de-lion, *n.m.*, (*—s—*) (bot.) lion's-foot.

pied-de-poule, *n.m.*, (*—s—*) (bot.) crow-foot.

pied-de-veau, *n.m.*, (*—s—*) calf's foot; (bot.) cuckoo-pint, wake-robin.

pied-d'oiseau, *n.m.*, (*—s—*) (bot.) bird's-foot.

pied-droit, *n.m.*, (*—s—s*) (arch.) pier; pied droit, upright, pillar.

piédestal, *n.m.*, (arch.) pedestal.

pied-fort, *n.m.*, (*—s—*) (coin.) a gold, silver, or copper coin (thicker than others).

piédouche, *n.m.*, (arch.) piedouche, small pedestal for a bust, a vase, etc.

piège, *n.m.*, snare, trap, decoy. *Tendre, dresser, un —;* to set a snare. *Prendre au —;* to catch in a trap. *Il a donné, il est tombé, dans le —;* he fell into the snare.

pie-grièche, *n.f.*, (*—s—s*) (orni.) shrike; (pers.) shrew.

pie-mère, *n.f.*, (*n.p.*) (anat.) pia mater.

*****pierraille**, *n.f.*, broken stone.

pierre, *n.f.*, stone, flint; (fig.) steel, rock; gem; (med.) calculus. *— de taille;* freestone. *— à aiguiser;* grindstone. *— précieuse;* gem, precious stone. *— fausse;* paste. *— à fusil;* flint. *— à cautère;* potential cautery. *— d'achoppement;* stumbling-block. *— de touche;* touchstone. *Première —;* foundation-stone. *La — philosophale;* the philosopher's stone. *Il gèle à — fendre;* it is freezing extremely hard. *Jeter la — à quelqu'un;* to attack any one (in words). *Jeter des —s dans le jardin de quelqu'un;* to throw out insinuations against any one. *— d'attente;* (mas.) toothing; (fig.) stepping-stone. *— angulaire;* corner-stone. *— d'évier;* gutter-stone, kitchen-sink. *— milliaire;* mile-stone. *Faire d'une — deux coups;* to kill two birds with one stone. *— qui roule n'amasse pas de mousse;* a rolling stone gathers no moss. *Faire rire un tas de —;* to make a cat laugh.

pierrée, *n.f.*, (engineering) rubble drain.

pierreries (pièr-rî), *n.f.pl.*, jewels, precious stones.

pierrette, *n.f.*, little stone, pebble; (orni.) hen-sparrow.

pierreu-x, -se, *n.* and *adj.*, stony, flinty, gritty, gravely; calculous.

pierrier, *n.m.*, stone drain, swivel-gun.

pierrot, *n.m.*, house-sparrow; clown, merry-andrew.

pierrures, *n.f.pl.*, (hunt.) pearls; bur (of deer).

piété, *n.f.*, piety, godliness; love, affection.

piéter, *v.n.*, ⊙ to set against. — *l'étrave, l'étambord, le gouvernail;* (nav.) to mark the numbers of feet on the stem, on the stern-post, on the rudder.

⊙**se piéter**, *v.r.*, to resist, to set one's self against.

piétinement (-ti-n-mān), *n.m.*, moving of feet; stamping, trampling.

piétiner, *v.n.*, to stamp, to move one's feet about. — *de colère;* to stamp with rage.

piétiner, *v.a.*, to tread, or to trample, under foot, to trample on.

piétisme, *n.m.*, pietism.

piétiste, *n.m.*, pietist.

piéton, *n.m.*, **-ne**, *n.f.*, pedestrian, foot-passenger; rural postman.

piètre, *adj.*, (fam.) shabby, wretched; pitiful. *n.*, vagabond, tramp, loafer.

piètrement, *adv.*, (fam.) pitifully, wretchedly, shabbily.

piètrerie, *n.f.*, (l.u.) shabby thing, wretched stuff.

piette, *n.f.*, (orni.) weasel-coot.

pieu, *n.m.*, stake, pile, post, pale.

pieusement (pi-eûz-mān), *adv.*, piously, devoutly, religiously; implicitly, obediently; reverently.

pieuvre, *n.f.*, (mol.) octopus, poulp, cat-o'-nine tails.

pieu-x, **-se**, *adj.*, pious, godly, religious, holy.

pif, *n.m.*, bottle-nose, nozzle. — *paf;* (int.) slap! bang!

piffre, *n.m.*, **-sse**, *n.f.*, (l.ex.) stout person; glutton.

se piffrer, *v.r.*, (l.ex.) to eat greedily, or to excess.

pigamon, *n.m.*, meadow-rue.

pigeon (-jon), *n.m.*, pigeon, dove; dupe, gull. — *culbutant;* tumbler. — *à grosse gorge;* pouter, cropper. — *ramier;* wood-pigeon. — *voyageur* or *messager;* carrier-pigeon. *Des* — *s à la crapaudine;* broiled pigeons. *Gorge de* — ; shot-colored (of silks).

pigeonneau (-jo-no), *n.m.*, young pigeon.

pigeonnier (-jo-nié), *n.m.*, pigeon-house, dove-cot.

pigment, *n.m.*, (anat.) pigment.

***pigne**, *n.f.*, (metal.) pena gold, pena silver; (bot.) kernel of the fir-apple.

***pignocher**, *v.n.*, to eat without appetite, to pick here and there; to nibble at food.

***pignon**, *n.m.*, gable end, gable (of a house); kernel (of a fir-apple); (mec.) pinion. *Avoir* — *sur rue;* to have a house of one's own.

pignorati-f, **-ve**, *adj.*, (jur.) with power of redemption.

pilaire, *adj.*, pilous, pilose, hairy.

pilastre, *n.m.*, (arch.) pilaster.

pilau, *n.m.*, pilaff (stewed rice).

pile, *n.f.*, pile, heap; pier (of a bridge); mole (mas.); (arch.) tambour; (of coins) reverse, pile. *Mettre* en — ; to pile up. — *de cuivre;* pile of weights. — *voltaïque*, — *de Volta*, — *galvanique;* voltaic, galvanic battery. — *ou face, croix ou* — ; head or tail, man or woman. *Jouer à* — *ou face*, or *à croix ou* — ; to play at heads or tails, to toss. *N'avoir ni croix ni* — ; to be penniless, destitute.

pile-culée, *n.f.*, (—*s* — *s*) abutment-pier.

piler, *v.a.*, to pound, to crash, to powder.

pileur, *n.m.*, pounder, beater.

pileu-x, **-se**, *adj.* V. **pilaire**.

pilier, *n.m.*, pillar, column, post; (pers.) support, supporter, fixture; constant frequenter; stump (leg). — *de cabaret;* tavern-

haunter, regular tippler. — *butant;* butting pillar. — *de carrière;* pillar, support of a quarry.

***pillage**, *n.m.*, pillage, plunder, pilfering, plundering. *Livrer au* — ; to give up to plunder. *Tout y est au* — ; everything is at the mercy of any one, can be had for the taking.

***pillard**, **-e**, *n.* and *adj.*, pillager, plunderer; pillaging, plundering.

***piller**, *v.a.*, to pillage, to plunder, to ransack; to purloin, to pilfer; to attack (of dogs). — *une ville;* to plunder a town. *Ce chien pille tous les autres chiens;* that dog attacks, or flies at, all the other dogs. *Pille! Pille!* seize him! seize him!

***pillerie**, *n.f.*, pillage, plunder, pilfer, extortion.

***pilleur**, *n.m.*, pillager, plunderer, pilferer.

pilon, *n.m.*, pestle; stamper. *Mettre au* — ; to tear up (books).

pilonnage, *n.m.*, (tech.) pugging; pounding, stamping, milling.

pilonner, *v.a.*, (tech.) to pug; to pound, to mill, to stamp.

pilori, *n.m.*, pillory. *Mettre quelqu'un au* — ; (fig.) to defame anybody.

pilorier, *v.a.*, to pillory, to put in the pillory, to slander, to libel, to asperse.

piloris, *n.m.*, (mam.) musk-rat.

piloselle, *n.f.*, (bot.) mouse-ear.

pilot (pi-lô), *n.m.*, (tech.) heap of salt; pile, stake of timber.

pilotage, *n.m.*, pile-driving; piling; (nav.) piloting.

pilote, *n.m.*, pilot, guide. — *côtier;* coasting pilot. — *lamaneur;* coasting, harbor, river pilot. — *hauturier;* sea pilot.

piloter, *v.a.* and *n.*, (tech.) to pile, to drive piles in.

piloter, *v.a.*, (nav.) to pilot; (fig., fam.) to pilot, to guide, to serve as a guide.

pilotin, *n.m.*, (nav.) pilot's apprentice.

pilotis, *n.m.*, piling, pile-work; stilt.

pilule, *n.f.*, (pharm.) pill. *Dorer la* — ; to gild the pill.

pilulier, *n.m.*, pill-machine.

pilum, *n.m.*, (—) (antiq.) pilum (Roman antiq.).

pimbêche, *n.f.*, impertinent woman, saucy baggage. *Quelle* — *!* what a minx!

piment, *n.m.*, pimento, capsicum, all-spice.

pimpant, **-e**, *adj.*, natty, tidy; fine, spruce, smart, stylish.

pimprenelle, *n.f.*, (bot.) pimpernel, burnet. — *d'Afrique;* honey-flower.

pin, *n.m.*, (bot.) pine-tree, pine, Scotch fir. *Pomme de* — ; fir-cone; fir-nut; fir-apple.

pinace, *n.f.* V. **pinasse**.

pinacle, *n.m.*, pinnacle. *Mettre quelqu'un sur le* — ; to praise any one to the skies. *Il est sur le* — ; he is as high as he can go.

pinale, *n.f.*, pine-plantation.

pinasse or **pinace**, *n.f.*, (nav.) pinnace.

pinastre, *n.m.*, (bot.) pinaster.

pinçard, *adj.*, wearing the shoe at the toe (of a horse).

pince, *n.f.*, pliers, nippers; tongs; hold; gripe; crow, crowbar (lever); sharp-pointed fold (in garments); toe (of a horse's foot); claw (of a lobster); edge (of a deer's hoof); (surg.) forceps. *Petites* —*s;* tweezers. —*s à sucre;* sugar-tongs. —*s d'un cheval;* horse's fore-teeth. — *d'un fer à cheval;* front of a horse-shoe. *Prendre une bûche avec la* — ; to take up a log with the tongs. *Etre menacé de la* —, *craindre la* — ; to be in danger of being arrested, to fear arrest. *Gare la* — *!* mind you are not sent to prison! *Avoir la* — *forte, la* — *rude;* to have a good gripe.

pincé, **-e**, *adj.*, pinched; affected, stiff, prim; thin; tight. — *!* caught! found out! taken in!

pinceau, *n.m.,* pencil, brush. *Trait, coup, de* — ; dash, stroke, of the pencil. *Avoir un beau* — ; (paint.) to have a fine touch. — *à barbe;* shaving brush.

pincée, *n.f.,* pinch.

pincelier, *n.m.,* (paint.) dip-cup, smutch-pot.

*****pince-maille,** *n.m.,* (—, *or* — — —*s*) pinchpenny, skinflint, screw.

pincement, *n.m.,* (agri.) pinching, nipping off of the heads of buds.

pince-nez, *n.m.,* (—) double eye-glass, folding eye-glass; folder.

pincer, *v.a.,* to pinch, to press, to hold fast, to gripe, to bite ; to nip, to nip off ; to rally, to reproach ; to surprise, to catch ; to play (the guitar, harp) ; (nav.) to hug. — *les petits bourgeons d'un arbre;* to nip off the small buds of a tree. — *de la harpe;* to play upon the harp. — *quelqu'un;* to give any one a nip. *Il pince en riant;* he can nip and laugh. — *le vent;* (nav.) to hug *or* haul close to the wind. *Se faire* — ; to get caught, to get found out, taken in.

se **pincer,** *v.r.,* to pinch one's self.

pincer, *v.n.,* to pinch, to rally, to reproach ; to play (the guitar, harp) ; (man.) to spur gently.

pince-sans-rire, *n.m.,* (—) sly, malicious person ; dry joker.

pincette, *n.f., or* **pincettes,** *n.f.pl.,* tongs, tweezers, nippers. *On ne le toucherait pas avec des* — *s ;* a person would not touch him with a pair of tongs.

pinchina, *n.m.,* thick, coarse woolen cloth.

pinçon, *n.m.,* pinch (mark).

pinçure, *n.f.,* pinching, pinch ; crease.

pindarique, *adj.,* pindaric.

pindariser, *v.n.,* to speak affectedly ; to talk fustian, bombast ; to write fustian, bombast.

pindariseur, *n.m.,* ranter, talker of fustian, bombast ; writer of fustian, bombast.

pinde, *n.m.,* Pindus ; (fig.) poets, poetry.

pinéal, -e, *adj.,* (anat.) pineal.

pineau, *n.m.,* black Burgundy grape.

pingouin *or* **pinguin,** *n.m.,* (orni.) penguin ; auk.

pingre, *n.m. and adj.,* (pop.) miser, skinflint ; avaricious, mean, stingy, close-fisted.

pinne *or* **pinne marine,** *n.f.,* (mol.) pinna.

pinné, -e, *adj.,* (bot.) pinnate, pinnated.

pinnule, *n.f.,* pinnule, sight-vane (of instruments).

pinque, *n.f.,* (nav.) pink.

pinson, *n.m.,* (orni.) finch ; chaffinch. *Gai comme un* — ; as gay as a lark, as merry as a grig.

pintade, *n.f.,* (orni.) Guinea-fowl, pearl-hen.

pintadeau, *n.m.,* Guinea-chick.

pinte, *n.f.,* pint (obsolete measure).

pinter, *v.n.,* to tipple, to guzzle.

piochage, *n.m.,* digging, working, fagging.

pioche, *n.f.,* pickax, mattock.

piocher, *v.a.,* to dig.

piocher, *v.n.,* to dig ; to fag, to work hard, to study hard ; to fight.

piocheur, *n.m.,* digger ; hard-working student ; fag, sweater.

pioler. *V.* **piauler.**

pion, *n.m.,* pawn (at chess) ; man (at draughts) ; man without property *or* resources ; usher (in a school). *Damer le* — *à quelqu'un;* to outdo any one.

pionce, *n.f.,* nap, snooze, forty winks.

pioncer, *v.n.,* to snooze, to have a nap, to have forty winks.

pionceur, *n.m.,* snoozer, heavy sleeper.

pione, *n.f. V.* **pivoine** (bot.).

pionner, *v.n.,* to take pawns (at chess).

pionnier, *n.m.,* pioneer.

piot (piô), *n.m.,* (pop.) wine.

piote, *n.f.,* a species of gondola.

pioupiou (pioo-), *n.m.,* (—*s*) (pop.) foot-soldier, tommy, worm-crusher.

pipe, *n.f.,* pipe, tobacco-pipe ; pipe (cask).

pipeau, *n.m.,* pipe, oaten pipe, reed-pipe, shepherd's pipe ; bird-call ; limed twig ; snare.

pipée, *n.f.,* bird-catching (with a bird-call) ; (fig.) deceit, trickery. *Prendre à la* — ; to catch with a bird-call ; (fig.) to cozen, to take in.

piper, *v.a.,* to catch birds with a bird-call ; to deceive, to trick ; to dupe, to cheat ; to prepare (cards) ; to load, to cog (dice).

piperesse, (st.e.) *fem.* of **pipeur,** *q. v.*

⊙**piperie** (pi-prî), *n.f.,* cheating (at play) ; deceit, trickery.

pipeu-r, -se, *n. and adj.,* cheat, trickster (at play) ; cheat, deceiver ; cheating, deceitful.

pipi, *n.m.,* (triv.) urine, water. *Faire* — ; to piddle.

pipi *or* **pitpit,** *n.m.,* (orni.) titling, titlark, pipit.

pipoir, *n.m.,* owl-call.

piquamment, *adv.,* piquantly, smartly.

piquant, -e, *adj.,* prickly, stinging ; sharp, pungent ; biting, nipping ; cutting, keen ; lively, piquant, pointed, smart. *De la moutarde* —*e;* hot mustard. *Froid* — ; biting cold. *Des mots* —*s ;* pointed words, cutting words. *Il a une conversation* —*e ;* his conversation is very smart. *Elle a l'air* — ; she has a lively, attractive, pleasing appearance.

piquant, *n.m.,* prickle ; quill (of porcupines) ; pungency, pith, point, fun, cream ; piquancy. *Le* — *de la chose;* the point, fun, or cream of the thing.

pique, *n.f.,* pike (weapon) ; pique, grudge, spite, quarrel. *Bois de* — ; pikestaff. *Demi-* — ; short pike. *Etre à cent* —*s de;* to be miles off in guessing. *Etre à cent* —*s au-dessus, au-dessous, de quelqu'un, de quelque chose;* to be far above, below, any one *or* anything. *Petite* — ; slight pique, quarrel, tiff. *Par* — ; out of pique or out of spite.

pique, *n.m.,* spade (at cards). *As de* — ; (fig.) parson's *or* pope's nose.

piqué, -e, *part.,* quilted ; larded. *Jupon* — ; quilted petticoat. *Poulet* — ; larded chicken. *Cela n'est pas* — *des vers;* it is a smart bit of work *or* it is not to be sneezed at.

piqué, *n.m.,* quilting. *Goût de* — ; (of wine) sourish taste, tartness.

pique-assiette, *n.m.,* (—, *or* — — —*s*) spunger ; dinner-hunter ; trencher-friend.

pique-bœuf, *n.m.,* (—, *or* — — —*s*) cattle-drover ; (orni.) buphaga, beef-eater.

pique-nique, *n.m.,* (— — —*s*) picnic. *Faire un* — ; to have a picnic.

piquer, *v.a.,* to prick ; to prod ; to goad ; to sting ; to puncture ; to bite ; to quilt ; to stitch ; to lard ; to stick ; to prick off, to mark off ; to be piquant ; to excite, to stimulate, to urge on, to goad on ; to pique, to gall, to nettle ; to spur ; (surg.) to puncture. — *les absents;* to prick off the absent. — *d'honneur;* to put on (his *or* her) mettle. — *des bœufs;* to goad oxen. *Quelle mouche le pique?* what has put him into a passion ? what 's up with him ? — *une jupe;* to quilt a petticoat. — *de la viande;* to lard meat. — *un cheval;* to spur a horse. — *la curiosité de quelqu'un;* to excite or rouse any one's curiosity. *Il en fut piqué;* he was nettled at it. — *une tête;* to take a header. — *un soleil;* (fam.) to get very red.

se **piquer,** *v.r.,* to prick one's self, to sting one's self ; to be offended, to be nettled, to feel affronted, to be piqued ; to pride one's self, to plume one's self, to pique one's self, to take a pride in ; to turn sour ; to become spotted. *Se* — *d'honneur;* to make it a point of honor ; to think one's self bound in honor. *Se* — *au jeu;* to persist in playing although losing. *Ce papier se pique;* this paper is becoming spotted, covered with spots. *Ce vin se pique;* this wine is turning sour. *Se — de rien;* to take offense at the least thing.

piquer, *v.n.,* to sting; to be piquant; (man.) to spur. *— des deux;* to spur a horse (with both heels); to put spurs to one's horse; to gallop off at full speed; (fig. fam.) to go very fast; to strive hard.

piquet, *n.m.,* picket, peg, stake; (milit.) picket; piquet (card game); cluster of flowers (on a bonnet). *Etre au —;* to be standing up in a corner (as a punishment in schools). *Etre de —;* (milit.) to be on picket duty. *Planter le —;* to pitch the tents, to take up one's quarters. *Lever le —;* to strike the tents; to decamp. *Aller planter le — chez quelqu'un;* to take up one's quarters with any one.

piqueté, -e, *adj.,* spotted, dotted.

piqueter, *v.a.,* to set or mark with stakes or pickets; to fix. [wine.

piquette, *n.f.,* rape wine; sour wine; thin

piqueur, *n.m.,* outrider; marker who notes down the names of persons absent; (cook.) one who lards (meat); (man.) stud-groom; (hunt.) whipper-in, huntsman. *— d'assiettes;* spunger. *— d'écurie;* head-groom. *— de vins;* wine-taster.

piqueu-r, *n.m., -se, n.f.,* stitcher.

piquier, *n.m.,* pikeman.

piqûre, *n.f.,* pricking, prick, sting, puncture; worm-hole; (needlework) quilting, stitching; (vet.) warbles.

pirate, *n.m.,* pirate, corsair, buccaneer; extortioner.

pirater, *v.n.,* to pirate, to exercise piracy, to commit piracy.

piraterie (pi-ra-trî), *n.f.,* piracy; act of piracy; extortion.

pire, *adj. and n.m.,* worse, worst. *Le remède est — que le mal;* the remedy is worse than the disease. *Le —;* the worst. *Il n'y a — sourd que celui qui ne veut pas entendre;* none so deaf as those who won't hear. *Il n'y a — eau que l'eau qui dort;* still waters run deep.

piriforme, *adj.,* (anat.) pear-shaped.

pirogue (pi-rog), *n.f.,* pirogue, canoe, jolly boat.

pirole, *n.f.,* (bot.) wintergreen.

pirouette, *n.f.,* pirouette; rapid whirling round; whirligig; subterfuge.

pirouetter, *v.n.,* to pirouette; to whirl about or round.

pirrhonien, -ne, *adj. V.* pyrrhonien.

pirrhonisme, *n.m. V.* pyrrhonisme.

pis, *n.m.,* udder, dug (of cows, etc.).

pis, *adv. and n.m.,* worse, worst. *Le — qui puisse arriver;* the worst that can happen. *Mettre quelqu'un au —;* to bid any one do his worst. *De mal en —;* from bad to worse. *De — en —;* worse and worse. *Qui — est;* what is worse. *Mettre les choses au —;* to suppose the worst.

pis aller, *n.m.,* worst; last shift, last resource; makeshift; compensation. *Au — —;* at the worst; let the worst come to the worst. *C'est votre — —;* it is your last shift, your last resource. *C'est un —;* it is a makeshift.

piscicole, *adj.,* piscicultural.

pisciculteur, *n.m.,* pisciculturist.

pisciculture, *n.f.,* pisciculture, fish culture.

pisciforme, *adj.,* pisciform, fish-shaped.

piscine, *n.f.,* piscina.

piscivore, *adj.,* piscivorous.

pisé, *n.m.,* pisé (mas.).

pissasphalte, *n.m.,* pissasphalt.

pissat, *n.m.,* piss, urine.

pissement (pis-mãn), *n.m.,* pissing.

pissenlit, *n.m.,* (bot.) dandelion; pissabed.

pisser, *v.a. and n.,* to piss; to make water.

pisseu-r, *n.m., -se, n.f.,* pisser.

pissoir, *n.m.,* public urinal.

pissoter, *v.n.,* to piss often.

pissotière, *n.f.,* public urinal; paltry fountain.

pistache, *n.f.,* pistachio, pistachio-nut.

pistachier, *n.m.,* pistachio-tree.

piste, *n.f.,* track, course, race-course, footprints, trace, trail. *Suivre quelqu'un à la —;* to follow on the track of any one. *Suivre un lièvre à la —;* to follow the scent of a hare.

pistia, *n.m.,* (bot.) water-lettuce.

pistil, *n.m.,* (bot.) pistil.

pistole, *n.f.,* pistole (gold coin of Spain); lock-up (for remanded prisoners). *Il est cousu de —s;* he is rolling in riches, or made of money.

pistolet, *n.m.,* pistol. *Un coup de —;* a pistol-shot. *Tirer un coup de —;* to fire off a pistol. *— d'arçon;* horse-pistol. *Quel drôle de —!* (fig. and fam.) what a funny sort of fellow !

piston, *n.m.,* sucker, bucket (of a pump); piston. *Fusil à —;* percussion-gun. *Tige de —;* piston-rod. *Cornet à —;* cornet.

pitance, *n.f.,* pittance, allowance (of food); dole; daily subsistence. *Maigre —;* short allowance. *Aller à la —;* to go to market.

pitaud, *n.m., -e, n.f.,* clown, lubber, lout.

pite, *n.f.,* (bot.) agave, pitahemp.

piteusement (pi-teûz-mãn), *adv.,* piteously, woefully, sadly.

piteu-x, -se, *adj.,* piteous, pitiable, woeful. *Faire —se mine;* to look the picture of misery. *Faire —se chère;* to fare badly.

pitié, *n.f.,* pity, compassion; mercy; contempt, disdain. *Emouvoir la — de quelqu'un;* to move any one's pity. *D'un œil de —;* with an eye of pity. *Il vaut mieux faire envie que —;* better be envied than pitied. *C'est grande —, c'est grand —;* it is a great pity. *Vos menaces me font —;* your threats excite my disdain (i.e., I despise your threats). *A faire —;* pitifully, wretchedly. *Regarder quelqu'un en —;* to take pity on, or despise, any one. *Par —;* for pity's sake; out of pity. *Il me fait —;* I pity him or I despise him.

piton, *n.m.,* screw-ring, staple; (geog.) peak.

pitoyable, *adj.,* pitiful, pitiable, piteous; compassionate; contemptible, wretched.

pitoyablement, *adv.,* pitifully, piteously; wretchedly.

pittoresque (pit-to-rèsk), *adj.,* picturesque, graphic. *n.m.,* picturesque, picturesqueness.

pittoresquement (pit-to-rèsk-mãn), *adv.,* picturesquely, in a picturesque manner.

pitre, *n.m.,* clown.

pituitaire, *adj.,* pituitary.

pituite, *n.f.,* pituite, phlegm, mucus.

pituiteu-x, -se, *adj.,* pituitous, phlegmatic.

pivert, *n.m.,* (orni.) green woodpecker.

pivine, *n.f.,* ash-gull.

pivite, *n.f.,* peewit, lapwing.

pivoine, *n.m.,* (orni.) bullfinch, gnat-snapper.

pivoine, *n.f.,* (bot.) pæony, peony.

pivot, *n.m.,* pin, spindle, pivot, hinge; (hort.) tap-root. *— de meule de moulin;* spindle of a mill.

pivotant, -e, *adj.,* (bot.) tap-rooted. *Racine —e;* (bot.) tap-root.

pivoter, *v.n.,* to turn on a pivot, to revolve upon, to turn.

pizzicato, *n.m. and adv.,* (mus.) pizzicato.

placabilité, *n.f.,* placableness, placability.

placable, *adj.,* placable.

plaçable, *adj.,* placeable, saleable.

placage, *n.m.,* plating (metal.); veneering (of wood); patchwork.

plaçage, *n.m.,* stalling (of animals); placing.

placard, *n.m.,* placard, poster, bill; (print.) slip; cupboard (in a wall); (carp.) door-leap. *Porte en —;* panel-door.

placarder, *v.a.,* to placard, to post up. *— un avis au public;* to post up a public notice; (fig.) to libel; to expose, to show up.

place, *n.f.,* place, room, seat, spot, ground; post, employment, office, town, stronghold;

fortress; square; room, stead. *Retenir des —s;* to secure seats. *Mettre chaque chose à sa —;* to put each thing in its place. *Faire — à qui qu'un;* to make room for any one. *Sur —;* on the spot, on the premises. *En —!* in your places, take your seats! *Sur la —;* upon the spot; (com.) in the market; on change. *Il ne saurait demeurer en —;* he can never stand still. *Mettez-vous à ma —;* put yourself in my place. *Si j'étais à votre —;* if I were in your place. *— de confiance;* place of trust. *Un homme en —;* a man in office. *— d'armes;* place of arms, stronghold, square, parade-ground. *— de guerre, — forte;* fortress, stronghold. *La — n'est plus tenable;* it is no longer possible to remain. *Demeurer,* or *rester, sur la —;* to be left dead on the spot, on the field. *Qui va à la chasse, perd sa —;* if you leave your place, you lose it. *— de fiacres;* hackney-coach stand. *Une voiture de —;* a hackney-coach. *La tête, la fin, de la —;* the top, the bottom, of the stand. *Avoir crédit sur la —;* (com.) to have credit (in the market, on change). *— marchande;* place good for trade, trading town. *Se faire —;* to make one's way. *Faire la —;* (com.) to solicit orders, to canvass. *—!* make room! make way!

placé, -e, *part.,* placed. *Il est bien —;* he has a good place, situation. *Il a le cœur bien —;* his heart is in the right place. *Cela n'est pas bien —;* that is ill-timed. *Haut —;* in a high position.

placement (plas-mān), *n.m.,* placing; (com.) sale; putting out, investing, investment (money). *Bureau de —;* intelligence-office; registry-office (for servants).

placenta (-sin-ta), *n.m.,* (anat., bot.) placenta.

placentaire, *adj.,* placentary, placental.

placer, *n.m.,* (—s) (gold digging) placer.

placer, *v.a.,* to place, to put, to seat, to get a situation for, to find a place for; to introduce (goods); to dispose, to set, to invest, to deposit, to lodge. *— de l'argent à la banque;* to lodge money in the bank. *— de l'argent sur l'État;* to invest money in the funds. *Il place bien ce qu'il dit;* what he says is to the purpose. *— quel-qu'un;* to get any one a place.

se placer, *v.r.,* to place one's self; to obtain a situation; to be sold, to sell.

placet, *n.m.,* petition.

placeu-r, *n.m.,* **-se,** *n.f.,* placer; registry office keeper.

placide, *adj.,* placid, calm, unruffled.

placidement, *adv.,* placidly, calmly.

placidité, *n.f.,* placidity, placidness; calmness.

placi-er, *n.m.,* **-ère,** *n.f.,* outdoor clerk, under-letter (of standings); (com.) town traveler, agent.

plafond, *n.m.,* ceiling. *— en voussure;* cove, coving. *— en corniche;* soffit.

plafonnage, *n.m.,* ceiling (action, work).

plafonner, *v.a.,* to ceil, to make a ceiling.

plafonneur, *n.m.,* plasterer.

plagal, *adj.,* (mus.) plagal.

plage, *n.f.,* beach, strand, shore, seashore. *— de sable;* sandy beach. *Vaisseau jeté sur la —;* ship stranded on the beach.

plagiaire, *n.m.,* plagiarist.

plagiat, *n.m.,* plagiarism.

⊙**plaid,** *n.m.,* plea, pleading, hearing. *Être sage au retour des —s;* to be wise after the event. *Chefs—s;* chief-pleas (court of).

plaid (plè), *n.m.,* plaid, traveling rug.

plaidable, *adj.,* pleadable.

plaidant, *adj.,* pleading, litigant. *Avocat —;* barrister, pleader.

plaider, *v.a.,* to plead, to argue, to allege; to intercede (for); to be at law, to litigate. *— quel-qu'un;* to sue any one at law. *— le faux pour savoir le vrai;* to allege what is false to get at the truth. *Plaidez ma cause;* intercede for me.

plaider, *v.n.,* to plead; to be at law, to go to law. *Se —,* *v.r.,* to be pleaded or argued. *La cause se plaide aujourd'hui;* the case comes on for hearing to-day.

plaideu-r, *n.m.,* **-se,** *n.f.,* litigant, suitor.

plaidoirie, *n.f.,* barrister's, counsel's speech; address. *pl.,* pleadings.

plaidoyer, *n.m.,* speech for the defense, counsel's address. *pl.* pleadings.

plaie, *n.f.,* wound; plague, evil. *Panser une —;* to dress a sore or wound. *— enveni-mée;* rankling sore. *Mettre le doigt sur la —;* to point out the evil. *Ne demander que — et bosse;* to be bent on quarreling, to be always ready for a row.

plaignant, -e, *n.* and *adj.,* (jur.) complainant, plaintiff, prosecutor; complaining.

plain, -e, *adj.,* plain, even, flat, level. *En —e campagne;* in open country. *Chambres de —-pied, —-pied (—);* rooms on one floor. *—chant, (n.p.)* plain chant. *Cela va de — pied;* that comes as a matter of course; it is all plain sailing.

plaindre (plaignant, plaint), *v.a.,* to pity, to compassionate, to commiserate; to grudge. *Je vous plains;* I pity you. *Il est à —;* he is to be pitied. *— sa peine;* to grudge one's pains. *— le pain qu'ils mangent;* to grudge the very bread they eat. *Il ne plaint rien à ses enfants;* he begrudges his children nothing.

se plaindre, *v.r.,* to complain, to groan, to moan; to grudge one's self. *J'ai bien lieu de me plaindre de vous;* I have good reason to complain of you. *— en justice;* to lodge a complaint in court.

plaine, *n.f.,* plain, level, lea, common, heath.

plainte, *n.f.,* complaint, action, plaint; groan-ing, lamentation; wailing. *Porter —;* to lodge a complaint.

plainti-f, -ve, *adj.,* plaintive, querulous, com-plaining, doleful, mournful, sad.

plaintivement (-tiv-mān), *adv.,* plaintively, mournfully, dolefully, sadly.

plaire (plaisant, plu), *v.n.,* to please, to be agreeable; to delight, to suit. *— à quelqu'un;* to please any one. *Cela vous plaît à dire;* you are pleased to say so. *Plaît-il?* what do you say; beg pardon! *Je ferai ce qu'il vous plaira;* I will do what you please. *Il ne me plaît pas que vous y alliez;* I do not like your going there. *Si cela ne vous plaît pas;* if you are averse to it. *Plût à Dieu;* would to God. *A Dieu ne plaise;* God forbid.

se plaire, *v.r.,* to delight in, to take pleasure in; to like, to love; to be pleased with, to take to; to flatter one's self; to thrive. *Il se plaît à faire du mal;* he delights in doing mischief.

plaisamment (plè-za-mān), *adv.,* humorously, pleasantly; ludicrously, laughably, amusingly.

plaisance, *n.f.,* pleasure. *Maison de —;* villa, country seat. *Bateau de —;* pleasure boat. *Lieu de —;* pleasant retreat.

plaisant, -e, *adj.,* pleasant; humorous, ludi-crous, amusing, droll, funny, comical, pretty; odd, strange; singular, curious. *C'est le plus — homme du monde;* he is the most amusing fellow alive. *Ce sont de —es gens;* (iron.) they are impertinent people. *Il vous a fait un — régal;* he entertained you right royally. *C'est un — personnage;* he is a ridiculous fellow.

plaisant, *n.m.,* jester; humor, fun, ludi-crousness. *Il fait le —;* he tries to be funny. *Un mauvais —;* a sorry jester, a humbug. *Le — de l'aventure;* the laughable part of the adventure.

plaisanter, *v.a.,* to joke, to banter, to jeer, to make fun of.

plaisanter, *v.n.,* to jest, to joke, to make merry. *Il plaisante sur tout;* he jests about everything. *C'est un homme qui ne plaisante pas;*

he is not a man to be trifled with. *Il ne plaisante pas là-dessus;* he is in downright earnest in the matter. *En plaisantant;* in jest, by way of a joke, jestingly.

plaisanterie (plè-zan-trî), *n.f.*, pleasantry, jesting, joking, jest, joke; mockery; mere farce. — *de bon ton, de mauvais ton;* genteel, vulgar, pleasantry. — *légère, piquante;* light, pointed, pleasantry. *Cela est dit par* —; that is said in jest, by way of a joke. — *à part;* jesting aside. *Il sait manier, il manie bien, la* —; he is a good hand at a joke. *Une bonne plaisanterie mérite les honneurs du bis;* a good story will bear repetition.

plaisir, *n.m.*, pleasure, delight, joy; recreation, diversion, sport, entertainment; will, consent, approbation; favor, courtesy, kindness, good turn. *Se faire un — de;* to take pleasure in, to be pleased to. *Se faire un — de son devoir;* to delight in doing one's duty. *Prendre — à quelque chose;* to delight in anything. *Cela fait — à voir;* that is a pleasant sight. *Nul — sans peine;* no joy without alloy. *La peine passe le* —; the pain exceeds the pleasure. *Partie de* —; pleasure party, picnic. *Jouer pour le —, pour son* —; to play for love, for diversion. *Menus —s;* pocket-money. *Faites-moi le* —; do me the favor. *A* —; carefully; at one's ease; gratuitously; designedly. *Un conte fait ou inventé à* —; a made-up story, a gratuitous tale, a lie. *Par* —; for pastime, for sport; (fam., l.u.) by way of trial. *Au* —! good-bye! *Faire* —; to give pleasure, to oblige; to be pleasing.

plan, *n.m.*, plane; plan, draught, design, model; scheme, project; ground, perspective. — *incliné;* inclined plane. *Premier* —; foreground. *Arrière-*—, (——*s*) (paint.) background. — *d'arrimage;* (nav.) tier. — *de niveau;* datum line. — *horizontal;* groundplan. *Lever de —s;* surveying. *Faire le — de;* to survey. — *à vue d'oiseau;* bird's-eye view. — *en relief;* plan in relief. *Lever un* —; to take a plan of. *Faire l'élévation d'un* —; to give a raised plan of. *Réléguer au second* —; to put into the background.

plan, -e, *adj.*, even, plain, level, flat.

planche, *n.f.*, board, plank; (engr.) plate; (gard.) bed, border. — *s d'un bateau;* planks, ribs, of a boat. — *à bouteilles;* bottle-rack. *Faire la* —; to float on one's back. *Monter sur les —s;* to tread the boards. *S'appuyer sur une — pourrie;* to lean upon a rotten staff. *Faire la — aux autres;* to show others the way. — *à débarquer;* gangway of a boat. — *de salut;* sheet anchor. *Jour de* —; (com.) working day.

planchéiage, *n.m.*, boarding, planking, flooring.

planchéier, *v.a.*, to plank, to floor, to board (with planks).

planchéieur, *n.m.*, floor-layer.

plancher, *n.m.*, floor; ceiling; (nav.) stage. — *parqueté;* inlaid, wooden floor. — *carrelé;* brick, stone floor. *Frotter un* —; to scrub, or polish, a floor. *Le — des vaches;* dry land, terrâ firma. *Sauter au* —; to jump to the ceiling; (fig.) to be driven mad.

planchette, *n.f.*, little board; (math.) plane table.

plançon or **plantard**, *n.m.*, sapling; slip, twig, shoot (of willow, etc.).

plane, *n.m.* V. **platane**.

plane, *n.f.*, draw-knife; turning chisel; spoke-shave.

planer, *v.n.*, to hover, to tower; to soar; to look down (from on high). *Un milan qui plane;* a kite hovering. — *sur les difficultés;* to soar above difficulties (i.e., to overcome them).

planer, *v.a.*, to make smooth, to plane, to planish. — *un morceau de bois;* to plane a piece of wood. — *le cuivre;* to beat copper

smooth. — *une peau;* to strip the wool off a skin.

planétaire, *adj.*, planetary.

planétaire, *n.m.*, planetarium, orrery.

planète, *n.f.*, planet, star.

planeur, *n.m.*, (manu.) planisher.

planimétrie, *n.f.*, (geom.) planimetry.

planisphère, *n.m.*, planisphere.

in **plano**, *adv.* V. **in plano**.

plant, *n.m.*, set, twig, plant, young plant, slip, plantation, grove. *En* —; standing; (fig.) in the lurch. — *de vigne;* slip of vine. *Jeune* —; vineyard newly set; plantation of young trees. *Rester en* —; to remain standing. *Laisser en* —; to give the slip to; to leave in the lurch. *Mettre en* —; (pop.) to pawn.

plantage, *n.m.*, planting; plantation.

plantain, *n.m.*, (bot.) plantain.

plantard, *n.m.* V. **plançon**.

plantation, *n.f.*, planting; plantation.

plante, *n.f.*, sole of the foot; (bot.) plant. — *ligneuse;* ligneous plant. — *fibreuse;* fibrous plant. — *herbacée;* herbaceous plant. *Le jardin des —s;* the botanical garden, zoölogical gardens. — *s marines;* marine plants. — *s parasites;* parasitical plants. — *s à tuyau;* culmiferous plants.

planter, *v.a.* and *n.*, to plant; to set, to fix, to drive in; to set up, to erect; to lay out, to give the slip to, to leave in the lurch. — *des oignons, des pois;* to plant onions, peas. — *des bornes;* to set bounds. — *le piquet en quelque lieu;* to take up one's quarters in any place. — *là quelqu'un;* to leave any one in the lurch, to give any one the slip. — *au nez de;* to cast in the teeth of; to tell point-blank. *Maison bien plantée;* house well seated, *or* in a pleasant, commanding position. *Cheveux bien plantés;* hair well set up. *se* **planter**, *v.r.*, to be planted; to place one's self; to station one's self; to settle.

planteur, *n.m.*, planter.

plantigrade, *n.m.* and *adj.*, plantigrade.

plantoir, *n.m.*, dibble, planting-tool.

planton, *n.m.*, (milit.) orderly. *Etre de* —; to be on duty.

plantule, *n.f.*, (bot.) plantule.

plantureusement (-reûz-mān), *adv.*, (fam.) plentifully, copiously, abundantly, luxuriantly.

plantureu-x, -se, *adj.*, plentiful, copious; abundant.

planure, *n.f.*, shavings (of wood).

plaque, *n.f.*, plate; slab; patch, veneer; badge, star. — *de fonte;* plate of cast iron. — *de porte-faix;* badge of a porter. — *tournante;* (railways) turning plate.

plaqué, *n.m.*, plated metal, electro-plate.

plaqué, -e, *part.*, plated.

plaqueminier, *n.m.*, (bot.) ebony-tree.

plaquer, *v.a.*, to plate; to lay on, to veneer. — *du bois;* to veneer wood. — *des bijoux;* to plate jewels.

plaquette, *n.f.*, small thinly bound book; a small copper coin, small plate, board, slab.

plaqueur, *n.m.*, veneerer; plater.

plaquis, *n.m.*, incrustation.

plasticité, *n.f.*, plasticity.

plastique, *n.f.* and *adj.*, plastic art; plastic.

plastron, *n.m.*, breast-plate; (fenc.) plastron; fencing-pad; drill-plate; laughing-stock, butt.

plastronner, *v.a.*, to put a plastron on any one, to cover or protect with a breast-pad.

se **plastronner**, *v.r.*, to put on a breast-pad, to plastron one's self.

plat, *n.m.*, dish; plate; collection-plate; (nav.) mess; sheet (of glass); flat side (of anything). — *d'argent;* silver dish. — *de la main;* back of the hand. — *apprêté;* made dish. *réchauffé;* warmed-up dish. — *à barbe;* shaving dish. *Camarade de* —; messmate. — *de l'équipage;* (nav.) mess (for seven men). *Servir* *un — de son métier;* to give a specimen of one's work. *C'est un — de son métier;* this is one of his tricks. *— s de balance;* scales of a balance. *Des coups de — d'épée;* strokes with the flat of a sword. *Donner du — de la langue;* to flatter, to coax, to wheedle; to talk blarney. *Mettre les pieds dans le —;* to put one's foot in it. *Mettre les petits —s dans les grands;* to spare neither money nor trouble to receive a person.

plat, -e, *adj.,* flat; dull, insipid, spiritless, pointless, low, shallow, empty; (of the hair) straight, lank; (of rhymes) consecutive. *Un pays —;* a flat country. *Cheveux —s;* straight hair. *Elle a la physionomie —e;* she has an unmeaning countenance. *Vin —;* flat wine. *Cheval —;* lank horse. *Avoir le ventre —;* to have an empty belly. *Sa bourse est bien —e;* his purse is very low. *Son armée a été battue à —e couture;* his army was utterly routed. *Un pied —, un — pied;* a worthless fellow. *Un style —;* a flat, spiritless, pointless style. *C'est un — personnage;* he is a dull fellow. *A —;* flat. *A — ventre;* flat on the ground, flat on one's face.

platane, *n.m.,* plane-tree, platane.

plat-bord, *n.m.,* (—s—s) (nav.) gunwale, gunnel, port-last. *Lisses de —;* drift-rails.

plateau, *n.m.,* wooden scale; waiter, tray, tea-tray; upland, table-land. *— à découper;* butler's tray. *— de carafe;* decanter-stand.

plate-bande, *n.f.,* (—s—s) (arch., hort.) plat-band; border plot, flower-bed. *— de baie;* lintel of a door *or* window.

platée, *n.f.,* (arch.) massive foundation under the whole area of the building; dishful.

plate-forme, *n.f.,* (—s—s) platform. *— de batterie;* platform of a battery. *— de fondation;* (carp.) sleepers.

plate-longe, *n.f.,* (—s—s) kicking-strap; leading-rein.

platement (plat-măn), *adv.,* flatly, dully, plainly, without spirit.

plateur, *n.f.,* (jest., l.u.) flatness.

platinage, *n.m.,* whitening (of copper).

platine, *n.f.,* linen-dryer; (print.) platine; lock (of firearms); (tech.) plate. *—s de montre;* plates of a watch. *— de serrure;* plate of a lock.

platine, *n.m.,* (metal.) platinum.

platise, *n.f.,* (l.u.) dull, senseless writing *or* words, platitudes.

platitude, *n.f.,* platitude, dullness; flatness.

platonicien, -ne (-si-in, -si-èn), *n.* and *adj.,* Platonist; Platonic.

platonique, *adj.,* Platonic.

platonisme, *n.m.,* Platonism.

plâtrage, *n.m.,* plaster-work, plastering; unsolid work.

plâtras, *n.m.,* old plaster-work; rubbish; piece of dried mortar.

plâtre, *n.m.,* plaster; (b.s.) paint (on the face). *Enduire de —;* to coat with plaster. *— cuit;* calcined plaster. *Battre quelqu'un comme —;* to beat any one to a jelly. *Essuyer les —s;* to live in a newly built house (therefore damp).

plâtré, -e, *part.,* plastered. *Visage —;* painted face. *Paix —e;* patched-up peace.

plâtrer, *v.a.,* to plaster; to patch up, to piece up; (agri.) to manure with plaster.

se plâtrer, *v.r.,* (b.s.) to paint one's self. *Elle se plâtre;* (b.s.) she paints her face; she makes up.

plâtreu-x, -se, *adj.,* chalky.

plâtrier, *n.m.,* plasterer.

plâtrière, *n.f.,* chalk-pit, plaster-quarry.

plausibilité, *n.f.,* plausibleness, plausibility.

plausible, *adj.,* plausible.

plausiblement, *adv.,* plausibly.

plèbe, *n.f.,* common people.

plébéien, -ne (-in, -è-n), *n.* and *adj.,* plebeian.

plébiscite, *n.m.,* plebiscite.

pléiade, *n.f.,* **pléiades,** *n.f.pl.,* Pleiades (the seven stars).

plein, -e, *adj.,* full, filled, replete; copious; solid (of doors); entire, whole, thorough, complete. *Rivière —e de poissons;* river well stocked with fish. *Livre — d'érudition;* book stored with learning. *Homme — d'esprit;* man full of wit. *— comme un œuf;* as full as an egg; (fam.) chock-full. *—e lune;* full moon. *Une chienne —e;* a bitch with young. *—e récolte;* plentiful crop. *A —es voiles;* all sails set. *Arbre en — vent;* tree in the open air. *Etre en — mer;* to be out at sea, in the open sea. *En —e rue;* in the middle of the street. *En — jour;* in broad daylight. *En — midi;* at high noon. *En —e nuit;* in the dead of night. *En —e paix;* in the midst of peace. *En — classe;* before the whole class. *En — été;* in the height of summer. *En — hiver;* in the heart of winter. *Avoir le cœur —;* to have one's heart full. *Donner à —e main, à —es mains;* to give, to bestow, largely, freely. *Porter —;* (nav.) to keep the sails full. *Battre son —;* to be in full swing (of balls, parties); to be high (of the tide).

plein, *n.m.,* full part; plenum. *Dans le —;* in the middle. *A pur et à —;* fully, to the full, entirely.

plein, *adv.,* full. *— les deux mains;* both hands full. *En —;* fully, entirely; right in. *A pur et à —;* altogether, completely. *Tout —;* a great many, numbers, very many.

pleinement, *adv.,* fully, entirely, to the full.

plénière, *adj.f.,* plenary; full, complete. *Indulgence —;* plenary indulgence. *Cour —;* plenary court.

plénipotentiaire, *n.m.* and *adj.,* plenipotentiary.

plénitude, *n.f.,* plenitude, fullness.

pléonasme, *n.m.,* pleonasm.

pléonastique, *adj.,* pleonastic.

plésiosaure, *n.m.,* (foss.) plesiosaur, plesiosaurus.

plet, *n.m.,* (nav.) coil.

pléthore, *n.f.,* plethora.

pléthorique, *adj.,* plethoric.

pleu-pleu *or* **plui-plui,** *n.m.,* (—) green woodpecker.

pleur, *n.m.,* (poet.) lament. *Un — éternel;* a never-ending lament (V. Hugo). *pl.,* tears.

pleurant, -e, *adj.,* weeping, crying.

pleurard, *n.m.,* puling, squalling child; blubberer.

pleure, *n.f.,* (anat.). *V.* **plèvre.**

pleure-misère, *n.m.,* (—) grumbler; curmudgeon.

pleurer, *v.n.,* to cry, to weep over, to shed tears, to bewail; to mourn; to run (of the eyes). *— comme un enfant;* to cry like a child. *— amèrement;* to weep bitterly. *— à chaudes larmes;* to shed bitter tears. *— de joie;* to weep for joy. *— à volonté;* to cry at will. *— sur quelqu'un;* to weep over any one.

pleurer, *v.a.,* to weep, to bewail; to lament; to mourn; to deplore the loss (of); to grudge.

pleurésie, *n.f.,* pleurisy.

pleurétique, *adj.,* pleuritic.

pleureu-r, *n.m.,* **-se,** *n.f.,* weeper; mourner.

pleureur, *n.m.,* (mam.) weeper, sapajou.

pleureu-r, -se, *adj.,* weeping, crying, mournful, tearful. *Saule —;* weeping willow.

pleureuses, *n.f.pl.,* weeping bands.

pleureu-x, -se, *adj.,* weeping, crying.

pleurnichement (-nish-măn), *n.m.,* whine, whining.

pleurnicher, *v.n.,* to snivel, to whimper, to whine.

pleurnicherie (-ni-shrî), *n.f.,* whining.

pleurnicheu-r, *n.m.,* **-se,** *n.f.,* whimperer, suiveler.

pleuronecte, *n.m.*, (ich.) pleuronectes.

pleuropneumonie, *n.f.*, (med.) pleuro-pneu-monia.

pleurs, *n.m.pl.*, tears ; crying, weeping ; bleeding (of a vine). *Essuyer ses —* ; to dry one's tears. *to shed tears. Essuyer ses —* ; to dry one's tears.

pleutre, *n.m.*, coward ; contemptible fellow.

pleuvoir (pleuvant, plu), *v.imp.*, to rain. *Il pleut à verse* ; it is pouring with rain. *— à petites gouttes* ; to drizzle. *— des hallebardes* ; to rain cats and dogs. *L'argent y pleut* ; it rains riches there. *— à seaux* ; to rain in torrents. *Comme s'il en pleuvait* ; in quantities, a great quantity, in shoals, in torrents. *Faire —* ; to shower down upon ; to pour, send in or down.

plèvre, *n.f.*, (anat.) pleura.

plexus (plèk-sus), *n.m.*, (anat.) plexus.

pleyon, *n.m.*, osier-tie.

pli, *n.m.*, plait, fold, bend, wrinkle, rumple ; tuck, coil ; undulation, depression, wave ; cover, letter, envelope, message, crease. *Cet habit ne fait pas un —* ; that coat has not a wrinkle in it. *Sous le même —* ; under the same cover. *Fouiller dans tous les —s et replis, sonder tous les —s et replis, du cœur* ; to search into the innermost recesses of the heart. *Un faux —* ; a crease (in stuffs). *Il a pris son —* ; he has taken his bent, decided upon his course (of action). *Avoir des —s au front* ; to have wrinkles on one's forehead. *Le — du bras* ; the bend of the arm. *Un — de terrain* ; an undulation or depression of the ground. *Cela ne fera pas un —* ; there will not be the slightest difficulty, all will go as on wheels. *Prendre un mauvais —* ; to get into bad habits.

pliable, *adj.*, pliable, pliant, bending, flexible, supple.

pliage, *n.m.*, folding.

pliant, -e, *adj.*, pliant, pliable, bending, flexible, supple. *Siège —* ; a folding-stool.

pliant, *n.m.*, folding-stool, fold-stool.

plica, *n.m.*, (med.). V. **plique**.

plicatile, *adj.*, (bot.) plicate, twining.

pliciforme, *adj.*, in the form of a fold.

plie, *n.f.*, (ich.) plaice.

plié, -e, *part.*, folded.

plié, *n.m.*, bend of the knee in dancing.

pliement (plî-mān), *n.m.*, act of folding.

plier, *v.a.*, to fold, to fold up ; to bend ; to bring under. *— une lettre* ; to fold a letter. *— du linge* ; to fold up linen. *— les voiles* ; to furl the sails. *— bagage* ; to decamp, to pack or make off. *— son esprit aux volontés d'autrui* ; to bend one's mind, to yield to the will of others.

se plier, *v.r.*, to be folded, bent ; to bow, to bend. *Je ne saurais me — à cela* ; I cannot stoop to that.

plier, *v.n.*, to bend ; to yield ; to give way. *Faire — un arc* ; to bend a bow. *Il vaut mieux — que rompre* ; better bend than break. *— sous l'autorité de quelqu'un* ; to yield to any one's authority. *L'infanterie plia* ; the infantry gave way.

plieu-r, *n.m.*, **-se**, *n.f.*, folder.

plinthe, *n.f.*, (arch.) plinth.

plioir, *n.m.*, folding-knife ; paper-folder.

plique, *n.f.*, (med.) plica.

plissé, *n.m.*, kilting, plaits ; wrinkling.

plissement (plis-mān), *n.m.*, folding ; plaiting, doubling over ; undulation (of waves).

plisser, *v.a.*, to plait ; to kilt, to wrinkle.

se plisser, *v.r.*, to form plaits ; to be plaited, or wrinkled, to pucker.

plissure, *n.f.*, plaiting.

ploc, *n.m.*, (nav.) sheathing hair, cow-hair.

ploiement, *n.m.*, folding.

plomb (plon), *n.m.*, lead, shot ; plumb-line, plummet ; custom-house seal ; sink. *De —* ; (fig.) heavy ; (of clouds or sky) gray, leaden, of a leaden hue. *Menu —* ; small shot. *— en saumon* ; pig-lead. *Jeter son — sur quelque chose* ; to have an eye upon anything. *Mine de —* ; black-lead pencil, lead. *— dans la tête* ; (fig.) ballast. *A —* ; perpendicularly, directly ; vertically ; right, or sheer, down. *Sous les —s* ; under the leads. *Tomber à —* ; to plumb ; to fall vertically.

plombage, *n.m.*, leading, lead work ; plumbing.

plombagine, *n.f.*, plumbago, black-lead.

plombé, -e, *part.*, leaded ; (fig.) of a leaden hue, leaden-colored ; (of sticks) loaded. *Dent —e* ; tooth that has been stopped. *Il a le teint —* ; he has a livid complexion.

plomber, *v.a.*, to lead ; to load, to seal, to stop, to mark or stamp with lead ; to stop (a tooth) ; to plumb. *— le faîte d'un toit* ; to lead the ridge of a roof. *— un mur* ; to plumb a wall. *Se —* ; to assume a leaden hue.

plomberie (plon-brî), *n.f.*, plumbery ; lead-making ; lead-manufactory ; lead-works.

plombeur, *n.m.*, (custom-house) stamper, *Rouleau —* ; field roller.

plombeu-x, -se, *adj.*, leady, leaden.

plombier, *n.m.*, plumber.

plombifère, *adj.*, plumbiferous.

plongé, -e, *part.*, immersed ; dipped (of candles) ; sunk (in despair) ; weltering (in blood). *Chandelle —e* ; dip candle.

plongeant, -e (-jān, -t), *adj.*, plunging. *Vue —e* ; view from a height. *Feu —* ; plunging fire (coming from above) ; raking fire.

plongée, *n.f.*, (fort.) glacis, slope.

plongement (plonj-mān), *n.m.*, plunging ; dipping ; dip ; (the sea) pitching.

plongeon (-jon), *n.m.*, (orni.) diver ; loon ; dive, diving. *Faire le —* ; to dive ; to duck ; (fig.) to flinch ; to back out of.

plonger, *v.a.*, to plunge, to dip, to immerse ; to throw, to involve. *— quelqu'un dans la douleur* ; to plunge any one into grief.

se plonger, *v.r.*, to be plunged.

plonger, *v.n.*, to dive, to dip ; to duck ; to take a downward direction ; to welter ; to pitch (of ships).

plongeur, *n.m.*, plunger, diver. *Cloche de, or à, —* ; diving-bell.

plongeur, *adj.*, (hydr.) plunging, diving.

ploquer, *v.a.*, (nav.) to felt (a ship's bottom) ; to sheath with hair.

ployable, *adj.*, pliable, easy to bend ; flexible.

ployer, *v.a.*, to bend, to bow ; to fold up.

se ployer, *v.r.*, to be bent, to be folded ; to bend, to give way.

ployer, *v.n.*, to bend ; to yield, to submit ; to give way.

pluche. V. **peluche**.

pluie, *n.f.*, rain ; downpour ; shower, abundance of. *Un jour de —* ; a rainy day. *Il tombe de la —* ; it is raining. *Petite — abat grand vent* ; a little rain lays a great dust. *Après la —, le beau temps* ; every cloud has its silver lining. *— battante* ; pelting rain. *Le temps est à la —* ; it looks like rain. *Faire la — et le beau temps* ; to be absolute master, to rule the roost. *Parler de la — et du beau temps* ; to talk of indifferent things. *Une — de fleurs* ; flowers in abundance.

plui-plui, *n.m.*. V. **pleu-pleu**.

plumage, *n.m.*, plumage, feathers.

*plumail, *n.m.*, feather-broom. V. **plumet** or **plumeau**.

plumasseau, *n.m.*, quill (for harpsichords) ; feather (of arrows) ; (surg.) pledget ; feather-broom, duster.

plumasserie (-ma-srî), *n.f.*, feather-trade.

plumassier, *n.m.*, feather-merchant (dresser, or seller).

plume, *n.f.*, feather, plume, quill, pen. *— d'acier* ; steel pen. *Tailler une —* ; to mend, to cut a pen. *Mettre la main à la —* ; to take pen in hand. *Se laisser aller au courant de la —* ; to write off-hand. — *de corbeau;* crow-quill. *La belle— fait le bel oiseau;* fine feathers make fine birds. *Il est au poil et à la — ;* he is fit for anything; fit as a fiddle. *Il y a laissé de ses —s;* he has been stripped of his feathers. *Passer la — par le bec à quelqu'un;* to baffle any one. *La fente d'une —;* the slit of a pen. *Le bec d'une —;* the nib of a pen. *Une bonne —;* a good penman. *Jeter la — au vent;* to allow chance to decide. *Guerre de —;* paper warfare. *Une — à son chapeau;* a feather in one's cap.

plumeau, *n.m.,* feather-broom, duster ; penstand.

plumée, *n.f.,* penful (of ink); plucking goosefeathers ; plucking.

plumer, *v.a.,* to pluck, to plume ; to fleece. *— une volaille;* to pluck a fowl. *— quelqu'un;* to fleece any one; (in rowing) to feather. *— la poule sans la faire crier;* to fleece the sheep without making it bleat.

plumet, *n.m.,* plume, ostrich feather ; feather broom.

plumetis (plum-tî), *n.m.,* feather-stitch.

plumeu-x, -se, *adj.,* (bot.) plumous, feathery.

plumipède, *n.m.,* plumiped.

plumiste, *n.m.,* artist in feathers.

plumitif, *n.m.,* (jur.) minute-book ; (fam.) penman, clerk, scratch-paper.

plum-pudding, *n.m.* (—*—s*). *V.* **pouding.**

plumule, *n.f.,* (bot.) plumule.

plupart, *n.f.,* most, most part, the greatest part ; generality, majority (of); most people. *La — du monde prétend;* most people say. *La — de ses amis l'abandonnèrent;* most of his friends forsook him. *La — écrivent;* most people write. *Pour la —;* mostly. *Les hommes sont pour la — intéressés;* the generality of men are selfish. *La — du temps;* generally, mostly, in most cases.

pluralité, *n.f.,* plurality.

pluriel, -le, *adj.,* (gram.) plural.

pluriel, *n.m.,* (gram.) plural.

plus, *adv.,* more, over, most ; also, moreover ; further ; besides ; item ; plus ; no more, not any more, no longer, not again ; never again. *— savant que lui;* more learned than he. *Il a — d'argent que moi;* he has more money than I. *Il m'en coûte — qu'a vous;* it costs me more than it does you (to have to say it, etc.). *Il a — de vingt ans;* he is more than twenty. *Nous sommes — qu'à moitié persuadés;* we are more than half convinced. *Je n'y retournerai — ;* I will go there no more. *— je la vois, — je la hais;* the more I see her, the more I hate her. *— loin;* further. *— près, de — près;* nearer. *— de larmes;* no more tears. *N'avoir — rien;* to have nothing left. *Il y a — ;* what is more. *Il y en a tant et —;* there is enough and to spare. *Au —, tout au —;* at most, at the most. *Il a tout au — trente ans;* he is thirty at most. *De —;* besides, moreover, aga'n, furthermore, nay. *De —, il faut remarquer;* we must observe besides. *D'autant —;* the more so. *De — en —;* more and more. *Il s'enrichit de — en —;* he grows richer and richer every day. *Ni — ni moins;* neither more nor less. *Vous avez beau dire, il n'en sera ni — ni moins;* you may talk as much as you please, it will be so. *— ou moins;* more or less, thereabout. *Qui —, qui moins;* some more, some less. *Sans — différer;* without furt! er delay. *Sans — de façon;* without any more ado. *— tard, — loin, — près;* later, farther, nearer. *Qui — est;* what is more. *N'être — ;* to be no more. *Deux fois — ;* twice as much. *Deux fois de — ;* twice more. *Je n'ai — qu'à;* it only remains for me to.

plus, *n.m.,* more ; most. *Le — que je puisse faire;* the most I can do.

plusieurs, *pron.* and *adj.,* *m.f.pl.,* several, some.

plus-pétition, *n.f.,* (*n.p.*) (jur.) exorbitant demand.

plus-que-parfait (plus-kĕ-par-fè), *n.m.* (*n.p.*) (gram.) pluperfect tense.

plus-value, *n.f.,* (—*—s*) (fin.) superior value.

plutocratie, *n.f.,* plutocracy.

plutonique, *adj.,* (geol.) plutonic.

plutôt, *adv.,* rather, sooner, in preference to. *— mourir que faire une lâcheté;* rather die than do a dishonorable thing. *Voyez —;* look, or see, for yourself !

pluvial, *n.m.,* (c. rel.) pluvial.

pluvial, *adj.,* of rain, rainy. *Eau —e;* rainwater.

pluvier, *n.m.,* plover.

pluvieu-x, -se, *adj.,* rainy, showery, wet. *Un jour —;* a rainy day.

pluviomètre, *n.m.,* pluviometer, rain-gauge, udometer.

pluviôse, *n.m.,* Pluviose, fifth month of the calendar of the first French republic, from January 20th to February 18th or 19th.

pneumatique, *n.f.* and *adj.,* pneumatics ; pneumatic. *Machine — ;* air-pump.

pneumatocèle, *n.f.,* (med.) pneumatocele.

pneumatologie, *n.f.,* pneumatology.

pneumatose, *n.f.* (med.) pneumatosis.

pneumonie, *n.f.,* pneumonia.

pneumonique, *n.m.f.* and *adj.,* (med.) pneumonic.

pochade, *n.f.,* (paint.) rough sketch ; (pop.) set to, mauling.

poche, *n.f.,* pocket ; pouch ; sack ; bag ; rabbit-net ; purse-net ; small fiddle ; crop (of a bird) ; sack (of an abscess, etc.) ; (needlework) pucker ; wrinkle (in clothes) ; kit (of a violin). *Fouiller dans ses —s;* to search one's pockets. *Un mouchoir de —;* a pocket handkerchief. *Mettre en — ;* to pocket. *Jouer de la —;* to come down with the money. *Acheter chat en — ;* to buy a pig in a poke. *Argent de —;* pocket-money. *Connaître comme sa — ;* to know perfectly.

poché, -e, *part.,* blotted (of writing) ; poached (of eggs) ; black (of the eyes). *Des œufs —s;* poached eggs. *Avoir les yeux —s au beurre noir;* to have one's eyes black and blue.

pocher, *v.a.,* to poach ; to bruise. *— les yeux à quelqu'un;* to give any one a pair of black eyes. *Se faire — les yeux;* to get one's eyes blacked.

pochet, *n.m.,* nose-bag.

pocheter (posh-té), *v.a.,* to keep in one's pocket.

pocheter, *v.n.,* to be kept in one's pocket.

pochette, *n.f.,* ☉pocket ; net (for rabbits) ; small fiddle, kit.

podagraire, *n.f.,* (bot.) goatweed, goutwort.

podagre, *n.f.,* podagra, gout in the feet.

podagre, *n.m.f.* and *adj.,* gouty person ; afflicted with the gout, gouty, podagrical.

podestat, *n.m.,* podesta (magistrate in Italy).

podosperme, *n.m.,* (bot.) funiculus.

poêle, *n.f.,* frying-pan. *Tomber de la — dans le feu;* to jump out of the frying-pan into the fire.

poêle *or* **poile,** *n.m.,* stove.

poêle, *n.m.,* pall (at a funeral) ; (c. rel.) canopy.

poêlée, *n.f.,* panful.

poêlette, *n.f.,* small pan.

poêlier, *n.m.,* stove-maker.

poêlon, *n.m.,* saucepan (small).

poêlonnée, *n.f.,* saucepanful.

poème, *n.m.,* poem.

poésie, *n.f.,* poetry ; poesy.

poète, *n.m.,* poet ; poetess. *Méchant —;* wretched poet, poetaster. *— lauréat;* poet laureate. *Elle est —;* she is a poetess.

poétereau (po-é-trô), *n.m.,* poetaster ; rhymester.

poétesse, *n.f.,* (l.u.) poetess.

poétique, *n.f.* and *adj.,* poetics ; poetical.

poétiquement (-tik-mān), *adv.*, poetically.

poétiser, *v.n.*, ⊙ to versify, to poetize; to make poetical.

poids (poâ), *n.m.*, weight; heaviness; gravity; burden, load; moment, importance, consequence, consideration. *Le — d'un fardeau;* the weight of a burden. *Cela est de —;* that is full weight. *Un — de dix livres;* a ten-pound weight. *Avoir du —;* to weigh; (fig.) to be influential, to have influence. *Faire bon —;* to give good weight. *Vendre une chose au — de l'or;* to sell a thing extremely dear. *Le — des affaires;* the burden of affairs.

*poignant, -e, *adj.*, poignant; acute, keen; stinging; painful, sad.

*poignard, *n.m.*, poniard, dagger. *Coup de —;* stab. *Ce fut un coup de — pour elle;* she was cut to the quick by it, it was a crushing blow for her.

*poignarder, *v.a.*, to poniard, to stab, to wound, to grieve to the heart; to kill.

se poignarder, *v.r.*, to stab one's self.

poigne, *n.f.*, (pop.) grasp, gripe, clutch; (fig.) strength, vigor.

*poignée, *n.f.*, handful; handle; hilt (of swords); bunch (of keys); shake (of the hand). *A —s;* by handfuls. *Jeter de l'argent à —;* to throw money about like shells. *Prendre à —;* to grasp tightly.

*poignet, *n.m.*, wrist; wrist-band (of linen); cuff (of a gown).

poil, *n.m.*, hair (of animals); hair (of persons other than that of the head); wool (of some animals); beard; nap (of cloth, of hats); color (of horses); (bot.) bristle, wool; (fig.) boldness, courage, resolution. *— de chèvre;* goat's hair, mohair. *— follet;* down; soft hair. *— de drap;* nap of cloth. *Monter un cheval à —;* to ride a horse bareback. *Il y a laissé de son —;* he was pretty well fleeced there. *Etre au — et à la plume;* to be fit for anything. *Faire le — à un cheval;* to trim a horse; (fig.) to outdo, to cut out. *De quel — est ce cheval?* what is the color of that horse? *— bai;* bay. *Reprendre du — à la bête;* to be at it again; to begin again. *Chercher du — aux œufs;* to split hairs.

poile, *n.m.* V. **poêle**.

poilu, -e, *adj.*, hairy, shaggy; (bot.) bristly, pilose.

*poincillade, *n.f.*, (bot.) (Barbadoes) flower-fence.

poinçon, *n.m.*, punch, puncheon; bodkin; stiletto, awl, pointer; stamp, die; puncheon (cask); (carp.) king-post; stamp (of coins).

poinçonnage, *n.m.*, stamping.

poinçonner, *v.a.*, to stamp.

poinçonneur, -se, *n.m.*, stamper, puncher. *n.f.*, stamping machine.

poindre, *v.n.*, to peep, to dawn, to break; to appear, to begin. *Le jour commençait à —;* day was beginning to break. *Le poil commence à lui — au menton;* his beard is beginning to grow.

poindre, *v.a.*, (l.u.) to sting. *Oignez vilain, il vous poindra; poignez vilain, il vous oindra;* save a thief from the gallows and he will cut your throat. *Quel taon vous point?* why, what's the matter with you? (lit., what gnat has stung you).

poing, *n.m.*, fist, hand. *Coup de —;* punch, cuff. *Se battre à coups de —;* to fight with fisti-cuffs. *Fermer le —;* to clinch, clench one's fist. *A — fermé;* with clinched, clenched fist. *Faire le coup de — avec quelqu'un;* to have a set-to with any one. *Il sait faire le coup de —;* he knows how to box. *Pieds et —s liés;* bound hand and foot.

point, *adv.*, no, not; not at all; none (*more emphatic than* **pas**). *Je ne l'ai — vu;* I have not seen him. *Il n'a — d'argent;* he has no money at all. *— du tout;* not at all. *— d'amitié*

sans vertu; there can be no friendship without virtue.

point, *n.m.*, point; dot, mark; full stop; period; speck; hole (of a strap, etc.); break (of day); (needlework) stitch; moment, difficulty, state, case, terms; place, quarter; (nav.) tack (of the sheets). *— de côté;* pain in the side, stitch. *Un —;* full stop. *— et virgule;* semi-colon. *Deux—s;* colon. *— d'interrogation;* note of interrogation. *— d'admiration, — d'ex-clamation;* note of exclamation. *Lettre de deux —s;* (print.) two-line letter. *Il ne met jamais de — sur les i;* he never dots his i's. *Mettre les —s sur les i;* to dot one's i's; to be very punctilious, to mind one's P's and Q's. *—* (mus.) pause. *— d'appui;* fulcrum. *— d'An-gleterre;* Brussels point (lace). *Faire venir quelqu'un à son —;* to bring any one over to one's views. *Il fut sur le — d'être tué;* he was very near being killed. *A —;* in the nick of time. *A — nommé;* at the appointed time. *Tout vient à — à qui sait attendre;* patience and time bring everything to pass, *or* all comes to him who knows how to wait. *Un — fait à temps en sauve mille;* a stitch in time saves nine. *L'affaire est réduite à ce —;* the matter has come to this point *or* pitch. *Au plus haut —;* to the highest pitch. *Au dernier —;* in the highest degree. *C'est un — arrêté;* it is a thing agreed upon. *Avoir un — de côté;* to have a stitch in one's side. *Faire un — à;* (needlework) to put a stitch in. *— de vue;* point of view, prospect; (fig.) light, sight, opinion. *— du vent;* (nav.) tack. *— d'honneur;* point of honor. *De tout —;* in every respect, entirely. *De — en —;* exactly, in particular, in detail. *—s cardinaux;* cardinal points. *— du compas;* point of the compass. *Rendre des — à;* to be more than a match for, to give odds (at a game). *Faute d'un —;* for a trifle. *La viande est cuite à —;* the meat is done to a turn.

pointage, *n.m.*, (artil., nav.) pointing, level-ing.

pointal, *n.m.*, (carp.) prop, girder.

pointe, *n.f.*, point (sharp end); (print.) bod-kin; pungency, tartness, sharpness; witticism; tack, tin-tack (nail, rivet, French nail); etching-needle; head (of an arrow, of a lance); (fenc.) small sword; (agri., geog.) point. *La — d'une épée;* the point of a sword. *— d'une plume;* nib of a pen. *La — du jour;* the break, the dawn, of day. *Marcher sur la — du pied;* to walk on tiptoe. *Tourner la — du pied en dehors;* to turn one's toes out. *Tailler en —;* to cut point-wise. *Se terminer en —;* to end in a point. *Faire une —;* (milit.) to deviate from the line; (fig.) to turn aside. *Pousser sa —;* to pursue one's point, to persist (in); to go on (with). *Avoir une — de vin;* to be slightly excited, flustered. *— d'une épigramme;* point of an epigram. *Faire la —;* (man.) to rear. *— de terre;* foreland.

pointé, -e, *adj.*, pointed.

pointement (point-mān), *n.m.*, (artil.) point-ing, leveling.

pointer, *v.a.*, to pierce, to stick; to stab; to prick, to mark; to point; to dot; to sharpen; (print.) to register. *— la carte;* (nav.) to point the chart. *— un canon;* to point a cannon.

pointer, *v.n.*, to point, to dot; to spring up, to soar, to fly high; to keep, to appear, to come out; (man.) to rear.

pointeur, *n.m.*, pointer, marker, checker; (artil.) artillery-man (who points the gun).

*pointillage, *n.m.*, (engr.) dotting, stippling.

*pointillé, *n.m.*, (engr.) dotting, stippling.

*pointille, *n.f.*, trifle, trifling point; bickering, cavil (about a trifling subject).

*pointiller, *v.n.*, to dot, to stipple; to cavil, to carp at,

*pointiller, v.a., to nettle, to tease.

*pointillerie, n.f., bickering, caviling, hairsplitting.

*pointilleu-x, -se, adj., caviling, particular, punctilious, captious. Un critique — ; a carping critic.

pointu, -e, adj., pointed, sharp, sharp-pointed, peaked. Chapeau — ; sugar-loaf hat.

pointure, n.f., (print.) point ; (of shoes) size.

poire, n.f., (bot.) pear; weight (of a steelyard). — d'angoisse ; choke-pear. Entre la — et le fromage ; at dessert. — à poudre ; powderhorn, powder-flask. Garder une — pour la soif ; to lay up something for a rainy day. —s secrètes ; pear-bit (of a bridle). — de Messire Jean ; a kind of very sweet pear.

poiré, n.m., perry.

poireau or **porreau,** n.m., (bot.) leek ; (vet.) wart.

poirée, n.f., (bot.) white beet.

poirier, n.m., pear-tree.

pois, n.m., (bot.) pea, peas, pease. Cosse de — ; pea-cod. — rames ; branch peas. — carrés ; marrow-fats. — chiches ; chick-peas; dwarf peas. — cassés ; split peas. — verts or petits — ; green peas. Il donne un — pour avoir une fève ; he gives a sprat to catch a herring.

poison, n.m., poison, venom.

poissard, -e, adj., vulgar, low. Style — ; Billingsgate style.

poissarde, n.f., fishwoman, fish-fag ; low or vulgar woman.

poisser, v.a., to pitch, to do over with pitch; to make sticky.

poisseu-x, -se, adj., pitchy, gluey, sticky.

poisson, n.m., fish ; half a gill. pl., (astron.) Pisces. — de mer, de rivière ; sea-fish, river-fish. Colle de — ; isinglass. — d'avril ; April fool. — rouge ; gold-fish. — juif ; hammer-fish. Donner un — d'avril à quelqu'un ; to make an April fool of any one. Être comme un — sur la paille ; to be like a fish out of water.

*poissonnaille, n.f., small fish or fry.

poissonnerie (-so-n-rî), n.f., fish-market.

poissonneu-x, -se, adj., abounding in fish, full of fish.

poissonnier, n.m., fishmonger, fish-salesman.

poissonnière, n.f., fishmonger (woman) ; fishkettle.

poitrail, n.m., breast (of a horse) ; breastpiece (of harness) ; (arch.) breast-summer.

poitrinaire, n.m.f. and adj., consumptive.

poitrine, n.f., chest, breast, lungs ; brisket. Maladie de — ;consumption. Une fluxion de — ; inflammation of the lungs. Il a bonne — ; he has good lungs.

poivrade, n.f., pepper sauce.

poivre, n.m., pepper. — en grains ; whole pepper. — de la Jamaïque ; all-spice, Jamaicapepper. — et sel ; (of the beard) grizzly.

poivrer, v.a., to pepper, to put pepper in ; (of a bill) to lay it on, to fleece.

poivrier, n.m., pepper-plant ; pepper-box.

poivrière, n.f., spice-box ; pepper-box ; (fort.) sentry-box.

poix, n.f., pitch ; shoemakers' wax. Cela tient comme — ; that sticks like pitch.

polacre or **polaque,** n.f., (nav.) polacca, polacre.

⊙**polacre** or **polaque,** n.m., Polack (Polish).

polaire, adj., polar. Etoile — ; polar star.

polarisation, n.f., polarization.

polariser, v.a., to polarize.

polarité, n.f., (phys.) polarity.

polatouche, n.m., flying-squirrel.

polder (pol-dèr), n.m., polder (tract of low land reclaimed from the sea by means of high embankments, in Holland and Belgium).

pôle, n.m., (astron., geog.) pole. — arctique ; arctic pole. — antarctique ; antarctic pole. —s de l'aimant ; magnetic poles.

polémarque, n.m., (antiq.) polemarch.

polémique, n.f. and adj., polemics, controversy, disputation; polemic, polemical.

polémoscope, n.m., polemoscope.

polenta, n.f., (n.p.) a sort of pap.

poli, -e, adj., polished, bright, glossy, smooth; polite, civil ; refined.

poli, n.m., polish, finish, gloss.

police, n.f., police ; police-regulations ; (fig.) polity, government ; (print.) font; policy (of insurance). Commissaire de — ; commissary or inspector of police. Espion de — ; police-spy. Être mandé à la police ; to be sent for to the police-office. Faire la — d'une salle ; to keep order in a hall. Faire la — des rues ; to keep the streets clear. Salle de — ; (milit.) guardroom. Bonnet de — ; foraging-cap. Tribunal de — ; police-court.

policement, n.m., civilizing.

policer, v.a., to establish a regular government; to civilize, to polish, to refine.

polichinelle, n.m., punch, buffoon ; merryandrew.

poli-couteaux, n.m., knife-cleaner.

poliment, adv., politely.

polir, v.a., to polish, to polish up, to brighten, to burnish ; to make polite, to civilize, to refine. — un discours ; to polish a discourse. — une langue ; to polish a language.

se polir, v.r., to polish (of a thing); to become refined (of people).

polissage, n.m., polishing, finishing.

polisseu-r, n.m., **-se,** n.f., polisher.

polissoir, n m., polisher (tool).

polissoire, n.f., shining-brush.

polisson, n.m., blackguard ; low fellow, ragamuffin ; scamp ; mischievous child.

polisson, -ne, adj., mischievous, idle, blackguard, rude.

polissonne, n.f., gadabout (girl who runs about the streets).

polissonner, v.n., to play the blackguard, to crack broad jokes ; (of children) to run about the streets.

polissonnerie (-so-n-rî), n.f., blackguardism, blackguard trick, broad, smutty joke.

polissure, n.f., polishing.

politesse, n.f., politeness, civility, good breeding, polite thing, kindness, attention, compliment. Faire une — ; to do a polite thing. Ce serait une — de votre part de ; it would be kind of you to.

politicien, n.m., politician.

politique, adj., political, politic, prudent, wise.

politique, n.m., politician, statesman. C'est un rusé — ; he is a crafty politician.

politique, n.f., policy ; politics, statecraft ; prudence. Etudier la — ; to study politics. Parler — ; to talk politics. — extérieure ; foreign politics ; foreign policy.

politiquement (-tik-màn), adv., politically, (fig.) shrewdly.

politiquer, v.n., (fam.) to talk politics, to meddle with politics.

polka, n.f., polka.

polker, v.n., to dance the polka.

poll, n.m., (n.p.) (pol.) poll.

pollen (pol-lè-n), n.m., (bot.) pollen.

pollicitation (pol-li-), n.f. (jur.) pollicitation.

pollué, -e (pol-lué) adj., polluted, defiled.

polluer (pol-lué), v.a., to pollute, to defile, to profane.

se polluer, v.r., to pollute one's self.

pollution (pol-lu-), n.f., pollution, profanation.

polonais, -e, adj., Polish.

polonais, n.m., Pole ; Polonese, Polish (language).

polonaise, *n.f.*, polonaise (dress, dance, tune).
poltron, -ne, *n.* and *adj.*, coward, poltroon, skulker; cowardly, dastardly, chicken-hearted.
poltronnerie (-tro-n-rī), *n.f.*, cowardice, poltroonery, cowardly action.
poly-, a prefix from Gr. πολύς.
polyacoustique, *adj.*, polyacoustic.
polyadelphie, *n.f.*, polyadelphia.
polyandrie, *n.f.* (bot.) polyandria.
polyarchie, *n.f.*, polyarchy.
polychreste, *adj.*, (pharm.) polycrest.
polychrome, *adj.*, (tech.) of many colors.
polyèdre, *n.m.*, (geom.) polyhedron.
polygala *or* **polygale**, *n.m.*, (bot.) polygala, milkwort.
polygame, *n.m.f.* and *adj.*, polygamist; polygamous.
polygamie, *n.f.*, polygamy; (bot.) polygamia.
polygarchie, *n.f.* *V.* **polyarchie.**
polyglotte, *n.m.f.* and *adj.*, polyglot.
polygone, *n.m.* and *adj.*, (fort., geom.) polygon; ordnance-yard, practice-ground; polygonal.
polygraphe, *n.m.*, polygraph (instrument for multiplying copies of a writing); manifold writer.
polygraphie, *n.f.*, polygraphy.
polygynie, *n.f.*, polygynia.
polymathie, *n.f.*, polymathy (knowledge of many arts and sciences).
polymathique, *adj.*, polymathic.
polymorphe, *adj.*, polymorphous.
polymorphisme, *n.m.*, polymorphy.
polynôme, *n.m.*, (alg.) polynome, polynomial.
polype, *n.m.*, polyp, polypus. — *du nez* ; polypus (in the nose).
polypétale, *adj.*, (bot.) polypetalous.
polypeu-x, -se, *adj.*, (med.) polypous.
polyphone, *adj.*, polyphonic.
polyphylle, *adj.*, polyphyllous.
polypier, *n.m.*, polypier, coral.
polypode, *n.m.*, (bot.) polypody.
polyptique, *n.m.*, (feudality) register of rents, taxes.
polyscope, *n.m.*, polyscope.
polyspaste, *n.m.*, polyspast.
polysperme, *adj.*, polyspermous.
polystyle, *adj.*, (arch.) polystyle.
polysyllabe, *n.m.* and *adj.*, polysyllable; polysyllabic, polysyllabical.
polysyllabique, *adj.*, polysyllabic, polysyllabical.
polytechnicien, *n.m.*, cadet of the Paris Polytechnic School.
polytechnique (-tèk-nïk), *adj.*, polytechnic. *Ecole* — ; Polytechnic School (French national military and civil-service academy).
polythéisme, *n.m.*, polytheism.
polythéiste, *n.m.* and *adj.*, polytheist; polytheistic, polytheistical.
polytric, *n.m.*, (bot.) golden maiden-hair, hair-moss.
pomifère, *adj.*, pomiferous.
pommade, *n.f.*, pomatum (for the hair); lip-salve; (man.) vault, vaulting.
pommader, *v.a.*, to pomade.
pomme, *n.f.*, apple; ball, knob; head (of a cabbage, of a lettuce, of a walking-stick). — *sauvage;* crab, crab-apple. — *d'Adam;* Adam's apple. — *de discorde;* apple of discord, bone of contention. — *d'amour;* tomato. — *de terre;* potato. — *de chêne;* oak-apple. — *de coloquinte;* bitter-apple. — *de pin;* pineapple; fir-apple. — *de choux, de laitue;* head of a cabbage, of a lettuce. — *de canne;* head or handle of a cane. — *de lit;* ball at the top of a bed-post. —*s de pavillon;* (nav.) trucks of the ensign-staff. —*s de girouette;* (nav.) acorns of the vanes.
⊙**pommé**, *n.m.*, cider.
pommé, -e, *part.*, grown to a round head, cabbaged ; (fig., fam.) complete, downright. *Laitue* —*e;* cabbage-lettuce. *Un fou* — ; a downright fool. *Une sottise* —*e;* an egregious blunder.

pommeau, *n.m.*, pummel (of saddles, swords).
pommelé, -e, *adj.*, dappled, mottled ; cloudy (with dappled clouds). *Cheval gris-* — ; dapple-gray horse.
se **pommeler** (po-m-lé), *v.r.*, to become dappled. *Le ciel s'est pommelé;* the sky has become dappled.
pommelle, *n.f.*, roller-bolt (of carriages); grating (of pipes); drain-pipe; strainer.
pommer, *v.n.*, (hort.) to cabbage, to grow to a round head.
pommeraie (po-mrè), *n.f.*, apple-orchard.
pommette, *n.f.*, pommel, knob, ball ; cheek-bone.
pommier, *n.m.*, apple-tree; apple-roaster.
pomoyer, *v.n.*, (nav.) to underrun (cables).
pompe, *n.f.*, pomp ; splendor ; ceremony, state; dignity, majesty. *Marcher en grande* — ; to march in great state. — *funèbre;* funeral pomp. — *du style;* loftiness of style. *Entrepreneur de* —*s funèbres;* undertaker.
pompe, *n.f.*, pump. *Piston d'une* — ; plug, sucker, of a pump. — *à feu;* steam-pump. — *aspirante;* suction-pump. — *à incendie;* fire-engine. — *à vapeur;* steam-pump or engine. — *d'arrosement;* watering-engine, garden engine. —*s funèbres;* funerals, burials. *La* —*est haute;* the pump sucks. *La* —*se décharge;* the pump has lost water. — *à bière;* beer-engine. *A la* —; on draught. *A la* —! (nav.) pump ship, ho !
pomper, *v.n.*, to pump.
pomper, *v.a.*, to pump, to suck up. — *l'humidité;* to suck up the moisture.
pompeusement (-peūz-mān), *adv.*, pompously, with great pomp.
pompeu-x, -se, *adj.*, pompous, stately, lofty. *Style, discours* — ; lofty style, speech.
pompier, *n.m.*, fireman ; pump-maker.
pompon, *n.m.*, top-knot (of horses) ; ear-knot; (milit.) tuft.
pomponné, -e, *part.*, decked out, tricked out.
pomponner, *v.a.*, (fam.) to ornament, to deck out, to dress. — *son style;* to trick out one's style.
se **pomponner**, *v.r.*, (fam.) to dress one's self up.
⊙**ponant**, *n.m.*, west; western ocean (in contradistinction to the Mediterranean).
ponçage, *n.m.*, pumicing ; pouncing.
ponce, *n.f.*, Pontius ; pumice ; (drawing) pounce. *Pierre* —; pumice-stone.
ponceau, *n.m.*, (bot.) corn-poppy ; culvert ; archway ; one-arched bridge ; red color, poppy-color, flame-color.
ponceau, *adj.*, poppy-colored.
poncer, *v.a.*, to pumice ; (drawing) to pounce. — *de la vaisselle;* to rub plate with pumice-stone.
ponceu-x, -se, *adj.*, pumiceous.
poncif, *n.m.* *V.* **poncis.**
poncire, *n.m.*, poncire lemon.
poncis, *n.m.*, (drawing, engr.) pounced drawing.
ponction, *n.f.*, (surg.) puncture, tapping.
ponctionner, *v.a.*, (med.) to tap, to puncture.
ponctualité, *n.f.* punctuality.
ponctuation, *n.f.*, punctuation; vowel-pointing.
ponctué, -e, *part.*, punctuated, dotted. *Plante* —*e;* dotted plant. *Ligne* —*e;* dotted line.
ponctuel, -le, *adj.*, punctual, exact.
ponctuellement (-èl-mān), *adv.*, punctually, exactly.
ponctuer, *v.a.*, to punctuate, to point.
pondage, *n.m.*, poundage (duty per pound).
pondérabilité, *n.f.*, ponderability.
pondérable, *adj.*, ponderable.
pondération, *n.f.*, (phys.) ponderation ; poising, balancing.
pondérer, *v.a.*, to poise, to balance.

pondeuse, *n.f.*, layer; laying (of hens).

pondre, *v.a.*, to lay eggs.

poney, *n.m.*, pony.

pongo, *n.m.*, (mam.) pongo, black orang.

pont, *n.m.*, bridge; deck (of a ship); flap (of trousers). — *levis*, (—*s*—) drawbridge. — *tournant* ; swing - bridge. — *dormant* ; fixed bridge. — *suspendu* ; suspension - bridge. — *tube* ; tubular bridge. — *à bascule* ; weigh-bridge. *Faire un — d'or à quelqu'un* ; to make great pecuniary concessions to any one. — *aux ânes* ; asses' bridge (the 47th proposition in France, instead of the 5th in America). *La foire n'est pas sur le —* ; (prov.) there is no need to be in such a hurry. *Les —s et chaussées* ; department of roads and bridges. — *volant* ; (nav.) hanging stage. *Premier —* ; lower deck. *Second —* ; upper deck of a two-decker. *Troisième —* ; upper deck of a three-decker. *Faux —* ; spar-deck. — *arqué* ; cambered deck. — *coupé* ; half-deck. *Entre —* ; orlop deck, between decks. *Équipage de —* ; pontoon train. *Se porter comme le Pont Neuf* ; to be in splendid health; to be as fit as a fiddle. *C'est vieux comme le Pont Neuf* ; it is as old as the hills *or* Queen Anne is dead.

pont-aqueduc, *n.m.*, (—*s*—*s*) aqueduct-bridge.

ponte, *n.f.*, laying of eggs.

ponte, *n.m.*, punter (cards); (ombre) ponto, the ace of hearts *or* diamonds.

ponté, -e, *adj.*, decked (of a ship).

ponter, *v.n.*, (play) to punt.

pontet, *n.m.*, trigger-guard; saddle-tree.

pontife, *n.m.*, pontiff. *Le souverain —* ; the sovereign pontiff, the pope.

pontifical, *n.m.*, pontifical.

pontifical, -e, *adj.*, pontifical.

pontificalement (-kal-män), *adv.*, pontifically.

pontificat, *n.m.*, pontificate.

pontin, *adj.*, Pontine. *Les marais —s* ; the Pontine marshes (between Rome and Naples).

pont-levis, *n.m.*, (—*s*—) drawbridge; flap (of trousers); (man.) pontlevis.

pont-neuf, *n.m.*, (—*s*—*s*) street-ballad, popular song.

ponton, *n.m.*, pontoon, bridge of boats; hulk; convict-ship.

pontonage, *n.m.*, bridge-toll; hire of a ferry-boat; pontage.

pontonnier, *n.m.*, toll-collector; (milit.) pontonier.

portuseau, *n.m.*, water-line (in paper).

pope, *n.m.*, pope (priest of the Greek church).

popeline, *n.f.*, poplin.

poplité, -e, *adj.*, (anat.) popliteal.

populace, *n.f.*, populace, mob, rabble.

populaci-er, -ère, *adj.*, low, vulgar.

populaire, *adj.*, popular, vulgar. *n.m.*, populace, rabble.

populairement (-lèr-män), *adv.*, popularly.

populariser, *v.a.*, to popularize, to make popular.

se **populariser**, *v.r.*, to make one's self popular.

popularité, *n.f.*, popularity.

population, *n.f.*, population.

populeu-x, -se, *adj.*, populous.

populo, *n.m.*, (—*s*) (jest.) plump little boy, chubby-cheeks.

poracé, -e, *adj.*, (med.) porraceous.

porc (pork), *n.m.*, hog, pig, pork; porker; swine. — *marin* ; porpoise. *Soie de —* ; hog's bristles. *Gardeur de —s* ; swine-herd. — *frais* ; pork. *Côtelette de —* ; pork-chop. [The final *c* of *porc* is silent before words beginning with a consonant.]

porcelaine, *n.f.*, porcelain, china, chinaware ; china vase *or* vases. *Terre à —* ; china-clay.

porcelainier, *n.m.*, workman in a porcelain manufactory, china manufacturer.

porcelet, *n.m.*, young pig; porket; (insect) wood-louse.

porc-épic (por-ké-pik), *n.m.*, (—*s*—*s*) porcupine.

porchaison, *n.f.*, wild-boar season.

porche, *n.m.*, porch, portal.

porch-er, *n.m.*, -**ère**, *n.f.*, swineherd.

porcherie, *n.f.*, pig-sty, piggery.

porcine, *adj.f.*, porcine.

pore, *n.m.*, pore.

poreu-x, -se, *adj.*, having pores, porous.

porisme, *n.m.*, (geom.) porism; (antiq.) corollary.

porosité, *n.f.*, porosity.

porphyre, *n.m.*, (min.) porphyry; (pharm.) slab (for grinding).

porphyrisation, *n.f.*, grinding (with a muller), pulverization.

porphyriser, *v.a.*, to grind; to porphyrize; to pound, to powder; to pulverize.

porque, *n.f.*, sow; (nav.) rider. — *de fond* ; floor-riders. *Allonges de —* ; futtock-riders. *Aiguillettes de —* ; upper futtock-riders.

porracé, -e, *adj.* V. **poracé.**

porreau, *n.m.* V. **poireau.**

porrection, *n.f.*, (c. rel.) presentation of the instruments.

porrigo, *n.m.*, (med.) porrigo, ring-worm.

port, *n.m.*, port, haven, harbor, sea-port town; wharf, quay; postage, carriage (of parcels); aspect; presence, bearing, gait, portliness; (nav.) burden; (mus.) grace-note, portamento. — *de mer* ; sea-port. — *de toutes marées* ; deep-water harbor. — *à marée* ; tidal harbor. — *marchand* ; commercial harbor. — *de guerre* ; naval harbor *or* station. *Franc de —* ; prepaid, carriage paid. *Prendre —, surgir au —* ; to come into harbor, to land; to attain one's end, to come to an anchor. *Arriver à bon —* ; to come safe into harbor; to arrive safely; (fig.) to end happily. *Faire naufrage au —* ; to be wrecked in port. — *de lettre* ; postage. — *payé* ; post-paid. *Permis de — d'armes* ; license to carry arms. — *d'armes* ; gun-license. — *de voix* ; (voc. mus.) portamento-voice. *Elle a un — de reine* ; her walk is that of a queen. *Le — d'une plante* ; (bot.) the aspect of a plant. — *permis* ; (nav.) weight of luggage (free on board ship to officers, sailors, and passengers). *Conduire,* or *mener, à bon —* ; (fig.) to bring to a successful issue.

portable, *adj.*, that can be worn, wearable; portable, payable (at).

portage, *n.m.*, portage (at water-falls in America); conveyance, porterage. V. **port**. *permis* (nav.), under **port**. *Faire —* ; to carry a boat overland (at waterfalls).

*****portail**, *n.m.*, front gate, west-door (of a church); door-way, portal.

portant, -e, *adj.*, bearing, carrying. *L'un — l'autre* ; one with another, one carrying the other. *Il est bien —* ; he is in good health. *Tirer sur quelqu'un à bout —* ; to shoot at any one quite close, *or* point-blank.

portati-f, -ve, *adj.*, portable.

porte, *adj.*, (anat.) portal. *Veine —* ; portal vein.

porte, *n.f.*, gate, gateway, door-way, door; door-step, threshold; eye (for hooks); defile (of mountains); the Sublime Porte. *Les —s d'une ville* ; the gates of a town. —*s d'enfilade* ; suite of doors. — *d'entrée* ; entrance door, street door, front door. — *de sortie* ; exit door, side door, back door. — *à —* ; next door to each other. — *cochère* ; courtyard-gate. — *à deux battants* ; folding-doors. — *battante* ; baize-door. — *vitrée* ; glass door. —*croisée*, (—*s*—*s*) terrace, *or* garden, glass door. *Mettre quelqu'un à la —* ; to turn any one out of doors. *Fermer la — au nez de quelqu'un* ; to shut the door in any one's face. — *de derrière* ; back door; (fig.)

shift. *Prendre la* — ; to take to the door. *Refuser la* — ; to refuse admittance. *A —s ouvrantes ;* at the opening of the gates. *A — close ;* with closed doors. *—s d'un bassin ;* gates of a dock. *La — ottomane ;* the Ottoman, the Sublime Porte. *Faire défendre sa — à ;* not to be at home to.

porté, -e, *part.,* carried, inclined, prone, disposed ; (of shadows) projected. *Il est — par la loi que ;* the law provides that. *Il est — à médire ;* he is prone to backbiting.

porté, *n.m.,* wear ; appearance, style, look.

porte-affiches, *n.m.,* advertising board ; (man) sandwich-man.

*****porte-aiguille,** *n.m.,* (—) (surg.) needle-holder ; (—, or ——s) needle-case.

porte-allumettes, *n.m.,* (—) match-box.

porte-amarre, *n.m.,* life-saving apparatus, line rocket.

⊙**porte-arquebuse,** *n.m.,* (—) king's gun-bearer.

porte-assiette, *n.m.,* (—, or ——s) plate-stand.

⊙**porte-auge,** *n.m.,* (—) hodman, mason's laborer.

porte-baguette, *n.m.,* (—) pipe (of muskets, pistols).

porte-baïonnette, *n.m.,* (—, or -—s) bayonet-belt.

porte-balle, *n.m.,* peddler, packman.

porte-barres, *n.m.,* (—) pole-ring.

porte-bonheur, *n.m.,* bearer of good tidings ; bangle.

porte-bossoir, *n.m.,* (——s) (nav.) supporter of the cat-head.

porte-bouquet, *n.m.,* bouquet-holder.

porte-bouteilles, *n.m.,* wine-rack, wine-bin.

porte-carabine, *n.m.,* (—) carbine-swivel.

porte-carafe, *n.m.,* decanter stand.

porte-cartes, *n.m.,* (—) card-rack, card-case.

porte-chape, *n.m.,* cope-bearer.

porte-cierge, *n.m.,* taper-bearer.

porte-choux, *n.m.,* market-gardener's horse.

porte-cigare, *n.m.,* (—) cigar-holder.

porte-cigares, *n.m.,* (—) cigar-case.

porte-clefs, *n.m.,* (—) turnkey ; (mus.) keyboard, key-ring.

porte-collet, *n.m.,* pad, stiffener (for collars).

porte-coquetiers, *n.m.,* egg-stand.

porte-crayons, *n.m.,* pencil-case.

porte-croix, *n.m.,* (—) cross-bearer.

porte-crosse, *n.m.,* (—) crosier-bearer ; (milit.) carbine-bucket.

porte-cure-dent, *n.m.,* (——s) tooth-pick case *or* holder.

porte-dieu, *n.m.,* (—) (c. rel.) viaticum-bearer.

porte-drapeau, *n.m.,* (—) (milit.) ensign-bearer, ensign, color-sergeant.

portée, *n.f.,* brood, litter ; reach (of the hand, arm) ; reach (of the mind) ; capacity, compass ; comprehension ; import (extent of signification) ; shot (of a missile weapon) ; (artil.) range ; (arch.) pitch ; bearing ; resting-point ; (mus.) staff, stave. *Hors de la — du canon ;* beyond cannon range. *A or à la — du fusil ;* within gun-shot range. *Cela n'est pas à ma —;* that is not within my reach. *Etre à la — de la voix de quelqu'un ;* to be within hearing, within call. *A — de trait ;* within bow-shot. *Cet ouvrage n'est pas à ma —;* that work is not within my compass, is beyond me. *Cela passe ma — ;* that is beyond my comprehension, I cannot make it out, I fail to understand. *Se mettre à la — de quelqu'un ;* to come down to the level of any one. *Esprit d'une haute — ;* an intellect of great range of thought. *La — d'un raisonnement ;* the scope or bearing of an argument.

⊙**porte-enseigne,** *n.m.,* (—) standard-bearer.

porte-épée, *n.m.,* (—) sword-bearer ; sword-belt, sword-hanger.

porte-éperon, *n.m.,* (—, or -—s) spur-strap.

porte-étendard, *n.m.,* (—) standard-bearer ; cornet.

porte-étrier, *n.m.,* (—) stirrup-strap.

porte-étrivière, *n.m.,* stirrup-bar.

*****porte-éventail,** *n.m.,* (—) fan-carrier.

portefaix, *n.m.,* porter, street-porter.

porte-fer, *n.m.,* (—) horse-shoe case, iron-stand.

*****portefeuille,** *n.m.,* portfolio ; pocket-book ; (pol.) office, portfolio, bill-case. *Tout son bien est en — ;* all his property is invested in bills. *Cet auteur a plusieurs ouvrages en — ;* that author has several works in manuscript, or lying by. *Courir le — ;* to go office-hunting. *En — ;* (com.) (of bills) in hand.

porte-flambeau, *n.m.,* (— or ——x) light-bearer ; torch-bearer ; linkman.

porte-fleurs, *n.m.,* flower-stand.

porte-fouet, *n.m.,* whip-socket ; whip-holder.

porte-fourchette, *n.m.,* (—, or ——s) knife-rest.

porte-fromage, *n.m.,* (—) cheese-tray or stand.

porte-fût, *n.m.,* cask-stand. [box.

porte-gargousse, *n.m.,* (—) (nav.) cartridge-

porte-giberne, *n.m.,* (mil.) pouch-belt.

porte-hache, *n.m.,* (milit.) axe-case ; axe-bearer.

porte-haubans, *n.m.,* (—) (nav.) chain-wale.

porte-huilier, *n.m.,* (—) cruet-stand.

porte-lanterne, *n.m.,* lantern-fly ; lamp-bracket (bicycles).

porte-lettres, *n.m.,* (—) letter-case.

porte-liqueurs, *n.m.,* (—) liquor-frame.

porte-livre, *n.m.,* book-prop.

porte-lof, *n.m.,* (—, or ——s) (nav.) bumkin.

porte-malheur, *n.m.,* (—) ill omen, bearer of ill-luck.

porte-malle, *n.m.,* (—). *V.* **porte-balle.**

portemanteau, *n.m.,* portmanteau ; coat-peg ; coat-stand ; coat-rail.

porte-masse, *n.m.,* mace-bearer.

porte-mèche, *n.m.,* (—) wick-holder ; (surg.) tent-probe.

portement, *n.m.,* (paint.) carrying, bearing. *— de croix ;* carrying the cross.

porte-mitre, *n.m.,* (—) miter-bearer.

porte-monnaie, *n.m.,* (—) purse, flat purse.

porte-montre, *n.m.,* (—) watch-stand.

porte-montres, *n.m.,* (—) show-case (for watches).

porte-mors, *n.m.,* (—) heading-rein, check-piece.

porte-mouchettes, *n.m.,* (—) snuffer-tray.

porte-mousqueton, *n.m.,* (—) carbine-swivel, hook.

porte-musc, *n.m.,* (—). *V.* **musc** (mam.).

porte-musique, *n.m.,* music-stand ; canter-bury.

porte-objet, *n.m.,* (—, or ——s) object-holder, slide.

porte-page, *n.m.,* (—) (print.) page-paper.

porte-parapluies, *n.m.,* (—) umbrella-stand.

porte-parole, *n.m.,* mouthpiece, spokesman.

porte-peigne, *n.m.,* comb-bag, comb-case.

porte-pièce, *n.m.,* (—, or ——s) shoemaker's punch.

porte-pierre, *n.m.,* (—) (surg.) caustic-case.

porte-pipe, *n.m.,* (—) pipe-case.

porte-plume, *n.m.,* (—, or ——s) pen-holder.

porte-plumes, *n.m.,* (—) pen-case.

porte-queue, *n.m.,* (—, or ——s) train-bearer. *Grand — ;* (orni.) swallow-tail butterfly.

porte-queues, *n.m.,* (—) (billiards) cue-rack.

porter (-tèr), *n.m.,* porter (beer).

porter, *v.a.,* to carry, to bear ; to bring ; to support ; to wear, to have on ; to convey, to declare, to express, to measure ; to bring forth, to yield ; to produce ; to declare, to manifest, to induce, to prompt, to impel, to urge, to prevail, to excite, to persuade, to contain, to import, to hit, to strike, to take effect, to tell. — *un fardeau;* to carry a burden. *L'un portant l'autre;* one with another, upon an average. *Vous en porterez le péché;* the sin will lie at your door. *Il ne porte jamais d'argent sur lui;* he never carries money about him. — *un habit;* to wear a coat. — *le deuil;* to be in mourning. — *perruque;* to wear a wig. — *ses cheveux;* to wear one's own hair. — *une bague au doigt;* to wear a ring on one's finger. *Il a porté la livrée;* he has worn a livery, he has been a servant. *Elle porte la culotte;* she wears the breeches or the gray mare is the better horse. — *l'épée;* to wear a sword. — *les armes;* to carry arms, to shoulder arms. — *la tête haute;* to carry one's head high. — *le bras en écharpe;* to carry one's arm in a sling. — *aux nues;* to laud to the skies. — *son pied en dedans;* to walk with the feet turned in. — (*le nez*) *au vent;* to toss (the head) in the air; (of a horse) its nose in the wind. *Le* — *haut;* to carry it with a high hand. — *la main à l'épée;* to lay one's hand upon one's sword. — *une botte;* (fenc.) to make a thrust. *Porter coup;* to strike home *or* to tell. — *ses vues bien haut;* to have great aspirations. *Somme qui porte intérêt;* sum that yields *or* bears interest. *Il en portera la peine;* he will suffer for it. *Vin qui porte bien l'eau;* wine that bears being watered. *Ils l'ont porté à la vengeance;* they have excited him to revenge. *Etre porté à la vertu;* to be inclined to virtue. *L'ordre du roi ne porte pas cela;* the king's order does not convey as much. *L'arrêt porte condamnation;* the sentence carries condemnation with it. *La déclaration porte que;* the declaration stipulates that. — *amitié à quelqu'un;* to bear any one friendship. — *respect;* to respect. — *envie;* to envy. — *bonheur;* to bring good luck. — *préjudice;* to be prejudicial to. — *témoignage;* to bear witness. — *son jugement sur quelque chose;* to pass judgment upon anything. — *une santé;* to propose a toast, to drink to the health of.

se **porter,** *v.r.,* to be, to do (of health) ; to tend, to incline ; to be inclined, to be disposed ; to be worn ; to proceed ; to repair ; to move ; to stand forth ; to be prone, to resort, to flock (to); to turn, to be directed. *Comment vous portezvous?* how do you do ? *Se* — *bien;* to be well, in good health. *Ne pas se* — *bien;* to be unwell. — *sur les lieux;* to repair to the place. *Cette pièce réussit, la foule s'y porte;* the piece has caught on, crowds go to see it. *Il se porte au bien;* he is well disposed. *Il s'est porté à cela lui-même;* he took to that of his own accord. *Se* — *fort pour quelqu'un;* to answer for any one, to stand security for any one. *Portez-vous bien!* good health ! take care of yourself.

porter, *v.n.,* to bear, to rest, to lie ; (artil., man.) to carry ; (nav.) to stand, to bear off ; (her.) to bear ; to aim at ; to hit, to take effect ; to reach ; to bear young, to be with young (of animals). *Le carrosse porte sur la flèche;* the coach bears upon the pole. *Un raisonnement qui porte à faux;* an inconclusive argument, a remark not to the point. *Tous les coups que l'on tire ne portent pas;* all shots fired do not carry home, *or* hit the mark. *Ce vin porte à la tête;* that wine goes to the head. *Sa vue porte loin;* his eye reaches far. — *au nord-ouest;* to stand to the north-west. *Les voiles portent;* the sails are full. — *gueules;* (her.) to bear gules.

porte-respect, *n.m.,* (—) weapon carried in self-defence ; life-preserver ; mark of dignity ; person of an imposing exterior.

porte-rideau, *n.m.,* (——*x*) curtain-pole.

porte-rôtie, *n.m.,* (——*s*) toast-stand, toast-rack.

porte-scie, *n.m.,* (—, *or* ——*s*) (ent.) saw-fly. *Insectes* — · saw-flies.

porte-serviettes, *n.m.,* towel-horse.

porte-tapisserie, *n.m.,* (—) tapestry frame.

porte-trait, *n.m.,* (—, *or* ——*s*) trace-strap, trace-robin.

porteu-r, *n.m.,* -**se,** *n.f.,* porter, carrier, heaver ; bearer ; (com.) holder. *Le* — *d'une lettre;* the bearer of a letter. *Payable au* — ; payable to bearer. *Cheval* — ; near-side horse. — *de chaise;* chairman.

porte-vent, *n.m.,* (—) (mus.) wind-trunk (of organs).

porte-verge, *n.m.,* (—, *or* ——*s*) verger, beadle.

porte-vergue, *n.f.,* (—) (nav.) iron-horse.

porte-vis, *n.m.,* (—) screw-piece.

porte-voix, *n.m.,* (—) speaking-trumpet.

portier (-tié), *n.m.,* porter, door-keeper.

portière (-ti-èr), *n.f.,* curtain (before a door) ; carriage-door ; portress.

portière, *adj.,* of an age to bear (of cows).

portion, *n.f.,* portion, part, share ; allowance, pittance. — *de nourriture;* allowance of food. *Diminuer la* — *de quelqu'un;* to curtail any one's allowance.

portioncule, *n.f.,* (l.u.) a small portion.

portique, *n.m.,* portico, doorway ; porch.

portor, *n.m.,* portor (black marble).

⊙**portraire,** *v.a.,* to portray, to depict, to paint.

portrait, *n.m.,* portrait, likeness, picture, image, description. *Peintre de* —*s;* portrait painter. — *en grand;* full size portrait. — *à l'huile;* portrait in oils. — *en pied;* full length portrait. — *flatté;* flattering portrait. — *chargé;* caricature.

portraitiste, *n.m.f.,* portrait-painter.

portraiture, *n.f.,* ⊙ portraiture ; portrait-painting. *Livre de* — ; (paint.) drawing-book.

portugais, *n.m.,* Portuguese (language).

portugais, -e, *n.* and *adj.,* Portuguese.

portulan, *n.m.,* (nav.) a book (of sea-ports).

posage, *n.m.,* laying ; laying down ; (of bells, etc.) putting up.

pose, *n.f.,* laying, setting, laying down on ; posture, attitude ; show, sham, make-believe ; hanging (of bells) ; stationing, posting (of sentries). — *de la première pierre;* laying of the foundation stone.

posé, -e, *part.,* laid, set, poised, bearing, resting, leaning. *Cela* —, *il s'ensuit que;* this being granted, it follows that. *Un homme bien* — *dans le monde;* a man in a good position, a man of standing.

posé, -e, *adj.,* sedate, staid, sober, grave.

posément, *adv.,* sedately, staidly.

poser, *v.a.,* to place, to set, to lay down ; to suppose, to admit, to grant ; to post up ; to hang, to put up (bells) ; (mus.) to pitch ; (arith.) to put down ; to pose (at dominoes). — *le pied;* to set foot. *Posez votre paquet;* lay down your bundle. — *l'arme à terre;* to ground arms. — *les armes;* to lay down one's arms. — *une figure;* to put a figure in the proper position. — *la première pierre d'un édifice;* to lay the first stone of an edifice. — *à sec;* to lay down dry. — *à cru;* to erect timber framework on the bare ground. — *à plat;* to lay down flat. — *une sonnette;* to hang a bell. — *des gardes;* to post guards. — *en fait;* to lay down as a fact. — *une question;* to put a question. *Posons que cela soit;* let us suppose it to be so. *Il pose bien sa voix;* he gives his voice the proper pitch. *se* **poser,** *v.r.,* to place, perch, pitch, settle one's self ; to assume an attitude, to set up (for) ; to pitch (of birds).

poser, *v.n.,* to bear, to rest, to lean ; to take a posture, to stand, to dance attendance, to wait, to sit for one's portrait, to attitudinize.

poseur, *n.m.,* one who lays down stones, etc. ;

setter, layer ; (rail.) plate-layer. —*de sonnettes ;* bell-hanger.

poseu-r, *n.m.*, **-se**, *n.f.*, one who gives himself airs ; a prig, a snob.

positi-f, **-ve**, *adj.*, positive, certain, practical ; certain, sure, matter-of-fact. *Ce fait est —;* it is a positive fact. *Un esprit —;* a practical mind. *C'est un homme —;* he is a matter-of-fact man. *Elle ne m'avait rien promis de —;* she had made me no positive *or* definite promise. *C'est —!* it 's a fact !

positif, *n.m.*, positive reality, certainty, fact ; (gram.) positive.

position, *n.f.*, position, situation, status, standing ; posture ; stand, place ; station of life, case, state ; circumstances. *— embarrassante ;* involved circumstances. *Fausse —;* (arith.) false position. *Dans une bonne —;* well off. *Dans une — peu élevée ;* in a small, *or* inferior, position. *Etre en — de ;* to be able to. *Quelle est sa —?* how is he circumstanced ?

positivement (-tiv-măn), *adv.*, positively, exactly, expressly, explicitly.

positivisme, *n.m.*, (philos.) positivism.

positiviste, *n.m.*, (philos.) positivist, follower of positivism.

pospolite, *n.f.*, pospolite (Polish nobility).

possédé, *n.m.*, **-e**, *n.f.*, person possessed, madman, maniac. *Un homme — du démon ;* a man possessed of the devil. *Il se démène comme un —;* he lays about him like a madman.

posséder, *v.a.*, to possess, to be possessed of, to be master of, to be conversant with, to enjoy, to own, to hold, to have, to be worth (of a person) ; to be acquainted with. *— un emploi ;* to hold a situation. *Les vertus qu'il possède ;* the virtues he is possessed of. *L'ambition le possède ;* he is eaten up with ambition. *Le diable le possède ;* the devil is in him. *Bien — une langue ;* to be thorough master of a language. *Bien — son sujet ;* to have a thorough command of one's subject.

se **posséder**, *v.r.*, to command one's temper, to command one's self, to master one's passions, to contain one's self. *Ne point se —;* to be beside one's self. *Il ne se possède pas de joie ;* he is beside himself with joy.

possesseur, *n.m.*, possessor, owner, master ; occupant, occupier. *— légitime ;* lawful possessor.

possessif, *n.m.* and *adj.*, (gram.) possessive case ; possessive.

possession, *n.f.*, possession, occupation, right, privilege. *Mettre en —;* to give possession, to invest. *— antérieure ;* preoccupancy. *Prise de —;* taking possession. *— injuste ;* wrongful possession. *Etre en — de ;* to be able to, to have the right *or* privilege (of).

possessoire, *adj.*, (jur.) possessory. *Action —;* possessory action.

possessoire, *n.m.*, (jur.) possession (of real property).

posset, *n.m.*, posset.

possibilité, *n.f.*, possibility.

possible, *adj.*, possible. *Il est — de le faire ;* it is possible to do it. *Il est — qu'il le fasse ;* he may possibly do it. *Venez le plus tôt —;* come as early as you can.

possible, *n.m.*, possibility, utmost. *Faire tout son —;* to do one's utmost. *Je ferai tout mon —;* I 'll do whatever lies in my power, *or* the best I can, *or* all I can. *Au —;* amazingly, to a degree. *C'est —;* very likely, that may be. *Pas —!* you don't say so !

postal, **-e**, *adj.*, postal, of the post.

postalement, *adv.*, by post.

postcommunion, *n.f.*, (c. rel.) post-communion.

postdate, *n.f.*, (l.u.) postdate.

postdater, *v.a.*, to postdate.

poste, *n.m.*, post ; guard-house, station ; station-house ; place, employment ; (nav.) berth ; station (of a ship). *— de chirurgiens ;* surgeons' berth. *— des malades ;* cockpit. *— de combat ;* quarters. *— d'un vaisseau ;* station of a ship in a fleet. *Etre à — fixe dans un lieu ;* to be stationed in a place, to reside on the spot ; (fig.) to be a fixture. *Etre à son —;* to be at one's post.

poste, *n.f.*, post, post-house ; post-stage ; post-office ; mail ; buck-shot. *Aller en —;* to travel post. *Courir,* or *aller, la —;* to ride *or* travel post ; to go post-haste, very fast. *Chevaux de —;* post-horses. *— aux chevaux ;* post-house. *— aux lettres ;* letter-post, pillar post. *Bureau de —;* post-office. *— pour —;* by return of post. *Maître de —;* postmaster. *Relais de —;* post-stage. *— restante ;* till called for. *Directeur des —s ;* postmaster general. *Grande —;* General Post-office. *Petite —;* district post-office ; receiving house.

posté, **-e**, *part.*, placed, stationed.

postel, *n.m.*, teasel, kind of thistle (used in cloth manufactories).

poster, *v.a.*, to station, to place, to post.

postérieur, **-e**, *adj.*, posterior, subsequent, later ; future.

postérieur, *n.m.*, posteriors.

postérieurement (-eur-măn), *adv.*, subsequently, after, since.

à postériori, *adv.*, (log.) a posteriori (from the effect to the cause) ; *or* from what follows.

postériorité, *n.f.*, posteriority.

postérité, *n.f.*, posterity, issue. *En appeler à la —;* to appeal to posterity. *Transmettre son nom à la — la plus reculée ;* to transmit, *or* hand down, one's name to the remotest posterity. *Passer à la —;* to be handed down to posterity.

postface, *n.f.*, address (placed at the end of a work), after-address.

○**postfixe**, *n.m.*, (gram.) postfix, termination.

posthume, *n.m.* and *adj.*, posthumous child ; posthumous. *Œuvres —s ;* posthumous works. *Un fils —;* a posthumous son. *C'est un —;* he is a posthumous child.

postiche, *adj.*, superadded ; false, misplaced ; false, artificial, sham, mock ; (milit.) provisional acting. *Dents —s ;* false teeth. *Cheveux —s ;* false hair. *Caporal —;* acting corporal.

*****postillon**, *n.m.*, postilion ; post-boy ; (back-gammon) mark above the half.

postposer, *v.a.*, ○to put after ; (book-bind.) to transpose.

postpositi-f, **-ve**, *adj.*, (gram.) postpositive.

postposition, *n.f.*, postposition.

postscénium, *n.m.*, (—) postscenium.

post-scriptum (-tom), *n.m.*, (—) postscript.

postulance, *n.f.*, application, candidature.

postulant, *n.m.*, **-e**, *n.f.*, postulant, candidate, applicant.

postulat, *n.m.*, postulate.

postulation, *n.f.*, conducting a suit, *or* cause ; (canon law) application for a dispensation.

postulatum, *n.m.*, (*postulata*) (philos.) postulate. *V.* **postulat.**

postuler, *v.a.*, to solicit ; to apply for, to be a candidate for ; (ecc.) to apply for a dispensation. *— une place ;* to apply for a place.

postuler, *v.n.*, to conduct a suit, to plead.

posture, *n.f.*, posture, attitude, situation, condition.

pot, *n.m.*, pot, jug ; tankard, can, jar ; (stationery) foolscap ; ○pot, morion, helmet. *Mettre en —;* to pot. *— de chambre ;* chamber-pot. *Bête comme un —;* as stupid as an owl. *Mettre le — sur le feu ;* to put the pot on the fire. *Prendre la fortune du —;* to take pot-luck. *— pourri ;* hotch-potch ; jar filled with all sorts of flowers ; medley, jumble, olio. *— à feu ;* (artil.) fireball, cresset, fire-pot. *—au-feu ;* (—) meat to boil (to make soup) ; broth ; (fig.)

bread and butter, bread and cheese. — *à l'eau;* water-jug. — *au lait;* milk-can. *Tourner autour du* —; to beat about the bush. *Gare le* — *au noir;* beware of the danger. *Découvrir le* — *aux roses;* to find out the secret, to lay bare the mystery. *Il en payera les* —*s cassés;* he will pay for the damage, stand the racket. *C'est le* — *de terre contre le* — *de fer;* it is the earthen pot against the iron pot (*i.e.*, the weak against the strong). *Un* — *fêlé dure longtemps;* threatened men live long. *Il n'y a si méchant* — *qui ne trouve son couvercle;* every Jack has his Jill. *Être à* — *et à rôt avec;* to be great pals with *or* to be very thick with.

potable, *adj.,* drinkable.

potage, *n.m.,* porridge, soup. — *aux herbes;* vegetable soup. *Il ne trouva que cela pour tout* —; that's all he found. *Pour tout* —; in all, all told.

potager, *n.m.,* kitchen-stove; kitchen-garden; soup-pan.

potag-er, -ère, *adj.,* culinary, cooking. *Herbes, or plantes, —ères;* pot-herbs. *Jardin* —; kitchen-garden.

potamot, *n.m.,* (bot.) pond-weed.

potasse, *n.f.,* potash. — *d'Amérique;* pearl-ash.

potassium (-siom), *n.m.,* potassium.

pot-de-vin, *n.m.,* (— *s* —) gratuity; premium; good-will; bonus; bribe; tip.

pote, *adj.,* (fam.) big, swollen, sore (of the hand).

poteau, *n.m.,* post, stake, pillar. — *cornier;* corner-post. — *indicateur* or *guide;* finger-post; sign-post. — *d'enseigne;* sign-post. — *d'arrivée;* winning-post. — *de départ;* starting-post.

potée, *n.f.,* potful; houseful *or* swarm (of children); putty (of tin); (metal.) molding, luting loam. — *d'étain;* putty-powder. — *d'émeri;* emery dust.

potelé, -e (po-tlé), *adj.,* plump, fat, chubby.

potelet (po-tlè), *n.m.,* (carp.) strut; prop.

potence, *n.f.,* gallows, gibbet; bracket; prop; crutch (shaped in the form of a T); sliding rule for measuring the height of men and horses; (nav.) gallowsbit; (horl.) potence. *Gibier de* —; Newgate or jail bird.

potentat, *n.m.,* potentate.

potentiel, -le, (-ci-èl), *adj.,* (med., gram.) potential.

potentiellement (-ci-èl-), *adv.,* potentially.

*potentille, *n.f.,* (bot.) cinque-foil.

poterie (-trî), *n.f.,* pottery, earthenware. — *de grès;* stoneware.

poterne, *n.f.,* (fort.) postern.

potiche, *n.f.,* China or Japan vase.

potier (-tié), *n.m.,* potter. *Terre à* —; potter's clay. — *d'étain;* pewterer.

potin, *n.m.,* pinchbeck; (fam.) gossip, tittle-tattle.

potion, *n.f.,* (med.) potion, draught.

potiron, *n.m.,* pumpkin.

⊙potron-jaquet or **potron-minet,** *n.m.* V. **patron-jaquet.**

pou, *n.m.,* louse. *Des* —*x;* lice.

pouacre, *n.m.* and *adj.,* (pop.) niggardly; nasty fellow; filthy; nasty.

pouah! *int.,* faugh! ugh!

pouce, *n.m.,* thumb; inch. *Il s'en mordra les* —*s;* he will rue it, or regret it. *Serrer les* —*s à quelqu'un;* to wrest a secret from any one. *Mettre les* —*s;* to give in; to knuckle under. *Manger sur le* —; to have a snack.

poucet, *n.m.,* small thumb. *Le petit* —; Tom Thumb.

poucettes, *n.f.pl.,* manacles (for the thumbs).

poucier, *n.m.,* thumb-stall.

pou-de-soie, *n.m.* (— *x* —), *or* **poult-de-soie,** *n.m.,* (— *s* —) (silk) paduasoy; stout silk.

pouding, *n.m.,* pudding.

poudingue (-dingh), *n.m.,* pudding-stone.

poudre, *n.f.,* dust, sand; powder; gunpowder. — *d'or;* gold dust. *Sucre en* —; castor sugar. *Réduire en* —; to pulverize. *Jeter de la* — *aux yeux de quelqu'un;* to throw dust into the eyes of any one, to impose on any one. *Du tabac en* —; snuff. — *de chasse;* shooting-powder. *Du café en* —; ground coffee. — *à canon;* gunpowder. *La soute aux* —*s;* (nav.) the powder magazine. *Les* —*s;* the powder magazine. *Il n'a pas inventé la* —; he is no conjurer; he will never set the Thames on fire. *Mettre le feu aux* —*s;* (fig.) to fan the flame.

poudrer, *v.a.,* to powder, to pounce, to sprinkle. *se* **poudrer,** *v.r.,* to powder one's hair.

poudrerie, *n.f.,* gunpowder factory.

poudrette, *n.f.,* dried night soil. *Faire la* —; (of fowls) to roll in the dust.

poudreu-x, -se, *adj.,* dusty, powdery. *C'est un* — *pied* —; he is a vagabond, a tramp.

poudrier, *n.m.,* sand-box, pounce-box; gun-powder-maker.

poudrière, *n.f.,* powder-mill; powder magazine; sand-box.

poudroyer, *v.a.,* to fill, *or* cover, with dust. *v.n.,* to rise (of the dust); to be dusty (of roads).

pouf, *n.m.,* puff; puffery, hoax; ottoman seat; centre ottoman. *Faiseur de* —*s;* (fig.) puffer; boaster, charlatan. *Faire des* —*s;* to disappear without paying one's debts.

pouf, *adv.,* plump, bang. *A* —; (pop.) on tick, on credit.

pouf, *adj. invariable,* crumbling (of stones).

pouffer, *v.n.,* to puff. Only used in — *de rire;* to burst out laughing.

poufferie, *n.f.,* puffery.

pouffiste, *n.m.,* puffer.

*pouillé, *n.m.,* register of benefices.

*pouiller, *v.a.,* (pop.) to rail at, to abuse.

*se pouiller, *v.r.,* (pop.) to abuse each other.

*pouilles, *n.f.pl.,* abuse, abusive language. *Il m'a chanté* —; he abused me.

*pouilleu-x, -se, *n.* and *adj.,* lousy person; beggarly fellow; lousy, wretched, mean.

*pouillot, *n.m.,* (orni.) pewet.

*poulailler, *n.m.,* hen-house, poultry-house; poultry-cart; (of persons) poulterer, poultry salesman.

poulain, *n.m.,* foal, colt; (med.) bubo.

poulaine, *n.f.,* (nav.) figure-head.

poulan, *n.m.,* (at cards) pool.

poularde, *n.f.,* fat pullet; capon.

poule, *n.f.,* hen; fowl; pool (play). *Jeune* —; pullet. — *d'Inde;* turkey-hen. — *d'eau;* moor-hen. *Faire venir la chair de* —; to make one's flesh creep, to make one shudder. *Plumer la* — *sans la faire crier;* to make any one disgorge without any fuss. — *mouillée;* milk-sop (pers.).

poulet, *n.m.,* chicken; love-letter; (stationery) fancy note-paper.

poulette, *n.f.,* young hen, pullet lass. *A la* —; with white sauce.

⊙poulevrin. V. **pulvérin.**

pouliche, *n.f.,* filly, foal.

poulie, *n.f.,* pulley; (nav.) block.

poulier, *v.a.,* to hoist, to lift up, with a pulley.

poulierie, *n.f.,* block-shed; block-manufacture; block-manufactory.

poulieur, *n.m.,* block-maker.

⊙poulin, *n.m.* V. **poulain, pouliche.**

pouliner, *v.n.,* to foal (of mares).

poulinière, *n.f. Jument* —; brood mare

pouliot, *n.m.,* (bot.) penny-royal.

poulpe, *n.m.,* (mol.) octopus, devil-fish.

pouls (poo), *n.m.,* pulse. — *déréglé;* irregular pulse. — *faible;* low pulse. — *élevé;* high pulse. — *formicant;* small, weak and frequent pulse. *Se tâter le* —; to feel one's own pulse;

(fig.) to gauge one's strength. *Tâter le — à quelqu'un;* to feel any one's pulse. *Le — lui bat;* his pulse beats.

poult-de-soie, *n.m.* (—s—). V. **pou-de-soie.**

poumon, *n.m.,* lung, lungs.

poupard, *n.m.,* (triv.) babe, baby, baby-doll.

poupart, *n.m.,* large edible crab.

poupe, *n.f.,* poop, stern. *A — carrée;* square-sterned. *A — étroite;* vertical-sterned. *Vent en —;* stern-wind. *Mettre vent en —;* to bear away before the wind. *Mouiller en —;* to moor by the stern. *Avoir le vent en —;* to sail before the wind; (fig.) to be in luck's way.

poupée, *n.f.,* doll; puppet; (arch.) poppy-head; (hort.) crown-graft; bunch of hemp *or* flax tied to the distaff. *Enter en —;* (hort.) to graft in the bark.

poupin, -e, *n.* and *adj.,* (fam.) fop, beau, dandy, belle; smart, spruce, dashy.

poupon, *n.m., n.f.,* plump, chub-cheeked baby, boy, girl. *Ma —ne;* my darling.

pour, *prep.,* for; on account of; in order; towards; to; though, notwithstanding. — *toujours,* —*jamais;* for ever. — *le moins;* at least. — *cet effet;* therefore, for this purpose. — *ainsi dire;* as it were, so to speak. *Il fera cela —vous;* he will do that for your sake. *On l'a laissé — mort;* he was left for dead. — *qui me prenez-vous?* whom do you take me for? *Je le tiens — mon ami;* I take him to be, *or* consider him, my friend. — *moi;* for my part, as for me. — *ce qui est de moi, j'y consens;* for my part I consent to it. *Comme —;* as if, as much as (to). — *ce qui est de;* as regards, as for.

pour, *n.m.,* for, pro. *Les — et les contre;* the pros and cons.

pourboire, *n.m.,* drink-money; tip. *Demander un —;* to ask for something (over and above the legal fare).

pourceau, *n.m.,* hog, pig, swine. *Etable à —x;* hog-sty. — *de mer;* sea-hog, porpoise. *C'est un vrai —;* he is a perfect beast.

pour-cent, *n.m.,* percentage.

pourchasser, *v.a.,* to pursue, to seek eagerly; to chase; to dun, to badger.

pourfendeur, *n.m.,* (l.u.) killer; swaggerer, bully, — *de géants;* giant-killer, braggadocio.

pourfendre, *v.a.,* (fam.) to cleave asunder, to cleave; to kill outright.

pourir, *v.n.* V. **pourrir.**

pourissage *or* **pourrissage,** *n.m.,* (tech.) retting.

pourissoir *or* **pourrissoir,** *n.m.,* (tech.) retting vat.

pouriture, *n.f.* V. **pourriture.**

pourlécher, *v.a.,* (l.u.) to lick all over; (fig.) to polish, to labor.

se pourlécher, *v.r.,* (fam.) to lick one's chops; (fig.) to gloat over (in anticipation).

pour lors, *adv.,* then, after that; at that time; henceforward.

pourparler, *n.m.,* parley, conference. *Entrer en —s;* to enter into negotiations; to discuss.

pour peu que, *conj.,* ever so little, however little; if only.

pourpier, *n.m.,* (bot.) purslain.

pourpoint, *n.m.,* doublet. *A brûle-—;* quite close; point-blank. *Mettre quelqu'un en —;* to ruin any one. *Se mettre en —;* to be ready to fight. *Un argument à brûle —;* a convincing, irresistible argument. *Donner à quelqu'un un —de pierre;* to clap any one into prison.

pourpre, *n.m.,* purple; (med.) purples; (her.) purpure.

pourpre, *adj.,* purple.

pourpre, *n.f.,* purple (stuff); purple-dye; purple-fish; (fig.) sovereign dignity; cardinalate. *Porter la —;* to wear the purple. *Etre né dans la —;* to be born in a palace, in the purple.

pourpré, -e, *adj.,* purpled, purple. *Fièvre —e;* purpura, petichial fever.

pourprier, *n.m.,* (mol.) purpura.

⊙**pourpris,** *n.m.,* inclosure; abode, home.

pour que, *conj.,* in order that, so that, to.

pourquoi, *adv.,* why, wherefore. — *cela?* why so? — *pas?* why not?

pourquoi, *conj.,* why, for what, upon what account; for what reason. *Demandez-moi —;* I don't know why (*i.e.* I should like to know why). *C'est —;* therefore.

pourquoi, *n.m.,* the reason why; the why and the wherefore. *Je voudrais bien savoir le —;* I would fain know the why and the wherefore.

pourri, *n.m.,* rottenness, rotten part.

pourri, -e, *part.,* rotten. — *de cuisson;* done to rags. *Pomme —e;* rotten apple. *Pierre —e;* rotten stone.

pourrir, *v.n.,* to rot, to grow rotten; to perish.

pourrir, *v.a.,* to rot, to make rotten; to mature (of a cold), to ripen.

se pourrir, *v.r.,* to get rotten.

pourrissage, *n.m.* V. **pourissage.**

pourrissant, -e, *adj.,* rotting.

pourrissoir, *n.m.* V. **pourissoir.**

pourriture, *n.f.,* rot, rottenness, putrefaction, decay; (agri.) brown rust; (vet.) rot.

poursuite, *n.f.,* pursuit, chase; prosecution; persecution; (jur.) suit, action, proceedings. *Intenter des —s;* (jur.) to institute proceedings, to take proceedings.

poursuivable, *adj.,* actionable.

poursuivant, *n.m.,* candidate; suitor, wooer; (jur.) prosecutor, plaintiff. — *d'armes;* pursuivant at arms.

poursuivant, *adj.,* pursuing; (jur.) suing, prosecuting.

poursuivre, *v.a.,* to pursue, to hunt, to chase; to endeavor to obtain, to seek for; to go on (with), to proceed (with), to follow up; to persecute, to annoy, to beset; to haunt; (jur.) to sue; (jur.) to prosecute, to action. — *quelqu'un en justice;* to prosecute any one at law. — *l'ennemi;* to pursue the enemy. — *un procès;* to carry on a lawsuit. — *une charge;* to endeavor to obtain a post. — *une pension;* to solicit a pension. — *son discours;* to proceed with one's speech. — *son chemin;* to proceed on one's way, to pursue one's road, to go on one's way.

se poursuivre, *v.r.,* to pursue one another, to be pursued, to be continued; (jur.) to be sued; to be prosecuted.

poursuivre, *v.n.,* to pursue, to continue. *Poursuivez!* go on!

pourtant, *adv.,* however, howsoever, yet, still, for all that, notwithstanding, though, nevertheless.

pourtour, *n.m.,* periphery, circumference, circuit; pit-tier (in a theatre).

pourvoi, *n.m.,* (jur.) appeal (for reversal of judgment), application. — *en grâce;* petition for mercy.

pourvoir, *v.n.,* to see to, to look to; to attend to; to provide (for), to supply, to make provision for; to nominate, to appoint. *Pourvoyez à cette affaire;* see to that business. — *à sa subsistance;* to provide for one's living. — *à un bénéfice;* to prefer to a living, to appoint, to nominate to a living.

pourvoir, *v.a.,* to invest with, to put in possession of; to provide, to supply, to furnish, to stock; to endow. — *une place de vivres;* to victual a garrison. *Ce père a bien pourvu tous ses enfants;* that father has made a handsome provision for all his children.

se pourvoir, *v.r.,* to provide one's self; to apply, to sue, to make application for. *Se — en justice;* to sue at law. *Se — par appel;* to enter an appeal. *Se — en cassation;* to appeal for a reversal of judgment. *Se — en grâce;* to petition for mercy.

⊙**pourvoirie**, *n.f.*, provision-store.

pourvoyant, *adj.*, providing, provident.

pourvoyeur, *n.m.*, purveyor, provider, caterer; (fig.) go-between.

pourvoyeuse, *n.f.*, procuress.

pourvu que, *conj.*, provided that; provided; it is to be hoped that, let us hope that. — *vous le fassiez;* provided you do it.

pousse, *n.f.*, shoot, sprout; (vet.) heaves, shortness of breath, broken wind (in horses); asthma; ⊙bum-bailiffs (sheriff's officers); bitterness (a disease in wines); choke-damp (in mines).

poussé, -e, *part.*, pushed. *Ce cheval est — de nourriture;* this horse has been fed too much. *Du vin —;* turbid, diseased wine.

pousse-café, *n.m.*, liqueur (after coffee).

⊙**pousse-cul**, *n.m.*, (—, *or —-—s*) bum-bailiff.

poussée, *n.f.*, pushing, thrusting; push, thrust (of arches); press (of business). *Donner la — à quelqu'un;* to follow up any one closely. *Faire une belle —;* (fam., iron.) to do a mighty fine thing. *Donner une — à;* to give a push to.

pousse-pieds, *n.m.* (—). *V.* **anatife**.

pousser, *v.a.*, to push, to give a push to, to thrust, to give a thrust to, to shove, to shove on, to drive, to drive on, to impel; to strike, to throw, to hit; to carry on, to extend, to forward; to send forth, to shoot forth, to put out, to put forth (of plants); to urge, to stir up, to provoke, to impel, to incite, to instigate; to bring forward, to assist forward, to help on; to utter (a groan), to heave, to fetch (a sigh). — *en avant;* to push on. — *dehors;* to thrust out. — *un cheval;* to urge on a horse. — *le temps avec l'épaule;* (prov.) to endeavor to gain time. — *la porte au nez de quelqu'un;* to slam the door in any one's face. — *le dé;* to throw the dice. — *une botte;* (fenc.) to make a thrust. — *un mur plus loin;* to carry a wall further on. — *un raisonnement trop loin;* to carry an argument too far. — *à bout;* to provoke beyond endurance. — *une affaire à bout;* to carry a thing to a successful issue *or* to go through with anything. — *une tranchée;* to carry forward a trench. — *des cris;* to utter cries. — *des soupirs;* to heave sighs. *Vous me poussez trop;* you urge me too far. *C'est un tel qui l'a poussé;* it was so and so who egged him on. — *sa pointe;* to pursue one's point. *On l'a poussé à se battre;* they set him on to fight. — *quelqu'un de questions;* to badger, to ply any one with questions. *Les arbres commencent à — des boutons,* the trees are beginning to put forth buds.

se **pousser**, *v.r.*, to push forward, to push one's self forward, to be pushed forward, to be pushed, to be carried; to push forward one another. *Se — de nourriture;* to eat too much.

pousser, *v.n.*, to sprout, to sprout forth, to shoot, to shoot forth (of plants); to be broken-winded (of horses); to grow (of the hair, nails); to push forward, to push on, to go on; to bulge, to jut out. *Les blés poussent déjà;* the corn is already coming up. *Ce mur pousse en dehors;* this wall bulges outwards. *Poussons jusqu'à la forêt;* let us push forward, *or* on, as far as the forest.

poussette, *n.f.*, pushpin (game).

pousseu-r, *n.m.*, **-se**, *n.f.*, pusher, shover; utterer (of sighs).

poussier, *n.m.*, coal-dust; gunpowder-dust; turf-dust.

poussière, *n.f.*, dust, powder; (bot.) pollen, male-seed; (of water) spray. *Nuage de —;* cloud of dust. — *de la mer;* spray. *Réduire en —;* to reduce to dust. *Jeter de la — aux yeux de quelqu'un;* to throw dust into any one's eyes. *Tirer quelqu'un de la —;* to raise any one from the depths of poverty. *Il fait de la —;* it is dusty, the roads are dusty.

poussiéreu-x, -se, *adj.*, dusty.

poussif, *n.m.*, (pop.) pursy fellow *or* creature.

poussi-f, -ve, *adj.*, (pop.) pursy; (vet.) short-winded, broken-winded.

poussin, *n.m.*, chick, young chicken. — *qui ne fait que d'éclore;* chick just out of its shell.

poussinière, *n.f.*, chick-room, chicken-coop; (pop.) (astron.) Pleiades.

poussoir, *n.m.*, (horl.) pusher; driver (dentistry).

poussolane. *V.* **pouzzolane**.

poutre, *n.f.*, beam; girder; mote (in the eye).

poutrelle, *n.f.*, small beam; (carp.) stop-plank.

pouvoir (pouvant, pu), *v.n.*, to be able, can, may, to have power, to be allowed, to be possible. — *marcher;* to be able to walk. *Je ne puis vous répondre;* I cannot answer you. *N'en — plus;* to be worn out, to be completely exhausted, to be tired out, to be done up. *N'en — mais, ne — mais d'une chose;* (fam.) to have had no share (in), nothing to do (with) anything. *Pouvait-il mais de cela?* could he possibly help that? *Puisse-t-il réussir;* may he succeed. *Il peut arriver que;* it may happen that. *Il pourrait survenir une circonstance qui changeât la face des choses;* some circumstance might arise which would change the whole face of matters. *Je n'y puis rien;* I cannot help it. *Je puis ne pas le faire;* I may not do it. *Je ne puis pas le faire;* I cannot do it. *Il peut se faire or il se peut faire que;* it may happen that; it may be possible for me to. *Vous avez pu voir;* you may have seen. *Vous n'avez pas pu voir;* you cannot have seen. *Vous avez pu ne pas voir;* you may not have seen. *Il peut, or pourrait, avoir vingt ans;* he may, *or* might, be twenty. *Cela se pourrait bien;* it might be so; it is not at all unlikely. *Cela pourrait bien être;* it might be so. *Il se pourrait bien que;* it might be, it might happen that. *Il pourrait se faire que;* it is not at all unlikely that. *Pouvez-vous bien! how can you!* *Autant que faire se peut;* as far as it is possible. *On ne peut plus;* exceedingly, extremely, etc.

pouvoir, *v.a.*, can do, to be able to do; to have power. *Je ne puis rien à cela;* I can do nothing in that business. *Vous pouvez tout sur lui;* you have great power over him. *Je ne crois pas le —;* I do not think I can do it.

se **pouvoir**, *v.r.imp.*, to be possible, may be, can be. *Cela se peut;* that may be, that is possible. *Il se pourrait que;* it might happen that. *Cela ne se peut pas;* that is impossible.

pouvoir, *n.m.*, power; sway, authority, might, force, command, government; executive power. *Il est en son — de;* he has it in his power to. *Avoir une chose en son —;* to have a thing in one's possession. *Etre fondé de —s;* to have a power of attorney. *Il a plein — de;* he has full powers to. *Abuser de son —;* to abuse one's power. *Avoir un —;* (jur.) to have a power of attorney, a letter of attorney.

pouzzolane *or* **pozzolane**, *n.f.*, (—s) pozzalana, puzzolana, pozzuolana.

pp., ab. of the word *Pères,* fathers (of the church).

pragmatique, *n.f.* and *adj.*, pragmatic sanction; pragmatic.

prairial, *n.m.*, Prairial, ninth month of the calendar of the first French republic, from May 20th to June 18th.

prairie, *n.f.*, meadow, grass-land, grass-field, prairie, savannah. —*s artificielles;* grounds sown with grass, clover.

praline, *n.f.*, burnt almond.

praliner, *v.a.*, to burn with sugar (like burnt almonds); to crystallize.

prame, *n.f.*, (nav.) pram, dingy (Norwegian boat).

praticabilité, *n.f.*, practicability.

praticable, *adj.*, practicable, feasible, possible ; passable (of roads); accessible, real. *Si la chose est —;* if the thing be practicable. *Les chemins ne sont pas —s ;* the roads are not passable. *Porte —, fenêtre —;* (thea.) real door, real window.

praticables, *n. m. pl.*, (thea.) real (not painted) objects.

praticien (-si-in), *n.m.* and *adj.*, practitioner; (sculpt.) figure-carver; practicing. *Médecin —;* practicing physician.

pratiquant, -e, *adj.* and *n.*, church-goer, communicant.

pratique, *n.f.*, practice, practical part, observance, usage, habit; dealing, doing, customer, custom ; practice (of attorneys, notaries, physicians) ; Punch's whistle, squeaker ; underhand dealing, secret practice ; (nav.) pratique. *Mettre en —;* to put into practice, to practice. *Faire de sourdes —s ;* to carry on clandestine, underhand dealings. *— basse, première —;* he is a good customer. *Donner — à un vaisseau ;* (nav.) to admit a vessel to pratique. *Cet avoué entend bien la —;* that attorney is well versed in the practice of the law. *Terme de —;* law-term. *Obtenir,* or *recevoir, —;* (nav.) to take pratique.

pratique, *adj.*, pertaining to practice, practical, experienced. *Etre — d'un lieu ;* (nav.) to be a good pilot for a place.

pratiquement (-tik-mān), *adv.*, practically.

pratiquer, *v.a.*, to practice, to exercise; to frequent, to converse with, to keep company with ; to tamper with, to suborn, to bribe, to obtain, to procure; (arch.) to contrive, to let in. *— la médecine ;* to practice as a doctor. *Se garder de — les méchants ;* to avoid associating with the wicked. *— un chemin ;* to open a road. *— un trou ;* to make, to contrive, to let in, a hole. *— des intelligences ;* to get intelligence. *— des témoins ;* to suborn witnesses.

se **pratiquer**, *v.r.*, to be in use, to be practiced, to be customary, to open *or* make for one's self (a way). *Cela ne se pratique point ;* that is not usual; such things are not done.

pratiquer, *v.n.*, to practice, to exercise, to frequent, to associate with ; to obtain, to open ; to build, to contrive ; to arrange ; (nav.) to have free intercourse.

pré, *n.m.*, meadow, small mead ; paddock ; ground (to fight a duel). *Se trouver sur le —;* to be upon the ground.

préadamites, *n.m.pl.*, preadamites.

préalable, *adj.*, preliminary ; previous.

préalable, *n.m.*, necessary preliminary ; preliminary. *Au —;* previously, first of all.

préalablement, *adv.*, previously, first.

préambule, *n.m.*, preamble, preface. *Point de —;* no preface, please ! go straight to the point.

préau, *n.m.*, yard, paddock, green; close (of a cathedral) ; courtyard (of a convent *or* prison).

prébende, *n.f.*, prebend, prebendaryship.

prébendé, -e, *adj.*, in possession of a prebend ; prebendal.

prébendier, *n.m.*, prebendary.

précaire, *adj.*, *n.m.*, precarious ; uncertain ; precarious tenure.

précairement (-kèr-mān), *adv.*, precariously.

précaution, *n.f.*, precaution ; caution, care. *Prendre des —s auprès de quelqu'un ;* to proceed warily with any one. *User de —;* to use caution.

précautionner, *v.a.*, to warn, to caution.

se **précautionner**, *v.r.*, to be cautious, to guard against, to take precautions. *Se — contre la chaleur ;* to guard against the heat.

précédemment (-da-mān), *adv.*, before, previously.

précédent, -e, *adj.*, precedent, former, preceding, previous.

précédent, *n.m.*, something done *or* said previously ; precedent.

précéder, *v.a.*, to precede, to go before, to go first; to have *or* take precedence (of). *Il était précédé par, il était précédé de ;* he was preceded by.

préceinte, *n.f.*, (nav.) wale, bend, rib-band. *— basse, première —, seconde —;* main wale. *Troisième et quatrième —;* channel-wale.

précepte, *n.m.*, precept, rule.

précepteur, *n.m.*, tutor, private tutor, preceptor, teacher, master.

préceptoral, -e, *adj.*, preceptorial.

préceptorat, *n.m.*, preceptorship, tutorship.

précession, *n.f.*, (astron.) precession.

prêche, *n.m.*, sermon (Protestant); Protestant church, meeting-house. *Quitter le —;* to cease to be a Protestant ; to turn Catholic.

prêcher, *v.a.*, to preach, to hold forth, to preach up, to extol, to praise, to keep telling, to repeat. *— la parole de Dieu ;* to preach the word of God. *Ne — que malheur et misère ;* to be always complaining of the hardness of the times. *— les fidèles ;* to exhort the faithful. *— toujours la même chose ;* to be always repeating the same thing. *— dans le désert ;* to preach to empty benches ; (fig.) to convince no one. *Chacun prêche pour son saint ;* every one has an eye to his own interest, *or* looks after number one. *— ses exploits ;* to extol, to boast, of one's exploits.

prêcher, *v.n.*, to preach. *— d'exemple ;* to set the example, to practice what one preaches. *— sur la vendange ;* to preach over one's cups. *On a beau — à qui n'a cœur de bien faire ;* to reprove a fool is but labor lost.

prêcheu-r, *n.m.*, **-se,** *n.f.*, (fam.) preacher, sermonizer. *Frère —;* Dominican friar.

prêcheuse, *n.f.*, conceited woman ; prude ; euphuist.

précieusement (-efiz-mān), *adv.*, preciously, carefully ; (paint.) very elaborately.

précieu-x, -se, *adj.*, precious, costly, valuable ; affected, finical, precise, over-nice. *C'est un document des plus —;* it is a most valuable document. *Tableau d'un fini —;* picture of exquisite, *or* elaborate, finish.

précieux, *n.m.*, affectation, affectedness ; affected man.

préciosité, *n.f.*, (l.u.) affectation, affectedness ; euphuism.

précipice, *n.m.*, precipice. *On l'a tiré du —;* he has been rescued from destruction.

⊙**précipitable**, *adj.*, (chem.) precipitable.

précipitamment (-ta-mān), *adv.*, precipitately, hurriedly, rashly, precipitously, headlong.

précipitant, *n.m.*, (chem.) precipitant.

précipitation, *n.f.*, precipitation, haste, hurry ; (chem.) precipitation.

précipité, -e, *part.*, precipitated, hurled ; precipitate ; rash, hasty, sudden. *— de haut en bas ;* hurled headlong from top to bottom. *Course —e ;* hasty flight. *Marcher à pas —s ;* to walk with hurried steps. *Départ —;* sudden departure.

précipité, *n.m.*, (chem.) precipitate.

précipiter, *v.a.*, to precipitate, to throw, to hurl, to dash down ; to hurry on, to hasten ; to plunge ; (chem.) to precipitate. *— sa retraite ;* to hasten one's retreat. *— ses pas ;* to quicken one's steps.

se **précipiter**, *v.r.*, to precipitate one's self ; to rush forward, to dash forth ; to spring forth, to dart, to hurl one's self (down), to run. *Se — sur quelqu'un ;* to rush upon any one.

préciput, *n.m.*, preference legacy ; jointure.

précis, *n.m.*, summary, abstract, compendium, epitome.

précis, -e, *adj.*, precise, distinct, exact, strict, formal, terse, concise, fixed, just. *Venir à* *l'heure —e;* to come exactly at the appointed time. *Prendre des mesures —es;* to take just or strict measures.

précisément, *adv.,* precisely, exactly, quite, just; just so.

préciser, *v.a.,* to state precisely, to specify, to fix, to determine.

précision, *n.f.,* precision, preciseness.

précité, *adj.,* (jur.) above-mentioned, aforesaid.

précoce, *adj.,* precocious, early, forward; premature. *Fruit —;* early fruit. *Un esprit —;* a precocious mind.

précocité, *n.f.,* precociousness, precocity.

précompte, *n.m.,* previous deduction.

précompter (-kon-té), *v.a.,* to deduct beforehand or previously.

préconçu, -e, *adj.,* preconceived.

préconisation, *n.f.,* preconization, commendation; praise.

préconiser, *v.a.,* to extol, to cry up, to praise, to recommend; to preconize, to sanction the appointment of.

préconnaissance, *n.f.,* foreknowledge.

préconnaître, *v.a.,* to foreknow.

précordial, -e, *adj.,* (anat.) præcordial.

précurseur, *n.m.,* forerunner, precursor, harbinger, herald. *adj.,* premonitory.

prédécéder, *v.n.,* to die first, to predecease.

prédécès, *n.m.,* predecease.

prédécesseur, *n.m.,* predecessor.

prédestinateur, *n.m.,* predestinator.

prédestinatien (-si-in), *n.m.* and *adj.,* predestinarian.

prédestination, *n.f.,* predestination. *— à la grâce;* predestination to be saved.

prédestiné, -e, *n.* and *adj.,* one of the elect; elect, predestinated. *Avoir un visage de —;* to have a happy-looking face.

prédestiner, *v.a.,* to predestinate, to foredoom.

prédéterminant, *adj.,* (theol.)predetermining.

prédétermination, *n.f.,* predetermination.

prédéterminer, *v.a.,* to predetermine.

prédial, -e, *adj.,* predial. *Des rentes —es;* ground-rents.

prédicable, *adj.,* (log.) predicable.

prédicament, *n.m.,* (log.) predicament.

prédicant, *n.m.,* (b.s.) Protestant preacher.

prédicat, *n.m.,* (log., gram.) predicate.

prédicateur, *n.m.,* preacher, divine, teacher.

prédication, *n.f.,* preaching.

prédiction, *n.f.,* prediction, forecast.

prédilection, *n.f.,* predilection, partiality, preference. *De —;* favorite.

prédire, *v.a.,* to predict, to foretell, to forebode; to presage, to forecast.

prédisposant, -e, *adj.,* (med.) predisposing.

prédisposer, *v.a.,* (med.) to predispose.

prédisposition, *n.f.,* (med.) predisposition, tendency.

prédominance, *n.f.,* predominance, prevalence.

prédominant, -e, *adj.,* predominant, prevalent, prevailing.

prédominer, *v.n.,* to predominate, to prevail.

prééminence, *n.f.,* pre-eminence.

prééminent, -e, *adj.,* pre-eminent.

préempter, *v.a.,* to preempt, to buy beforehand.

préemption, *n.f.,* preemption.

préétablir, *v.a.,* to preestablish.

préexistant, -e, *adj.,* pre-existent, pre-existing.

préexistence, *n.f.,* pre-existence.

préexister, *v.n.,* to pre-exist.

préface, *n.f.,* preface, preamble, exordium, introduction.

préfectoral, *adj.,* pertaining, relating to a French prefect; prefectorial.

préfecture, *n.f.,* prefectship, prefecture; prefect's house, prefect's offices. *— de police;* headquarters (of the police); Scotland yard.

préférable, *adj.,* preferable.

préférablement, *adv.,* preferably.

préférence, *n.f.,* preference. *De —;* in preference.

préférer, *v.a.,* to prefer, to choose.

préfet, *n.m.,* (Rom. antiq.) prefect; chief administrator of each department in France. *— des études;* vice-principal (of schools). *— de police;* chief commissioner of police. *— maritime;* naval commander-in-chief (of a district).

préfète, *n.f.,* " préfet's " wife.

préfinir, *v.a.,* (jur.) to fix a term, or a delay, to limit, to prearrange, to appoint.

préfix (-fiks), **-e,** *adj.,* (jur.) prefixed, appointed.

préfixe, *n.m.* and *adj.,* (gram.) prefix; prefixed.

préfixion, *n.f.,* (jur.) settled time, prefixion.

préfloraison, *n.f.,* (bot.) prefloration.

préfoliation, *n.f.,* (bot.) foliation, vernation.

⊙**prégnation,** *n.f.,* gestation (of animals).

préhensible, *adv.,* prehensible.

préhensile, *adj.,* prehensile.

préhension, *n.f.,* prehension.

préhistorique, *adj.,* pre-historic, pre-historical.

préjudice, *n.m.,* prejudice, hurt, wrong, detriment, injury, loss, damage. *Il a obtenu cela à mon —;* he obtained that to my prejudice, or to my detriment. *Cela vous portera —;* that will be detrimental to you. *Au — de;* to the detriment of. *Sans — de mes droits;* without prejudice to my claims.

préjudiciable, *adj.,* prejudicial, detrimental, injurious, hurtful.

préjudiciaux, *adj.m.pl.* *Frais —;* (jur.) previous costs.

préjudiciel, -le, *adj.,* (jur.) interlocutory. *Question —le;* interlocutory question (to be decided previous to the principal action).

préjudicier, *v.n.,* to prejudice, to do prejudice (to), to be prejudicial, to be detrimental (to), to hurt, to injure.

préjugé, *n.m.,* presumption, appearance, prejudice; (jur.) precedent. *Exempt de —s;* free from prejudices. *Homme sans —;* unprejudiced man. *Se défaire de ses —s d'enfance;* to rid one's self of one's early prejudices. *Dissiper les —s;* to remove prejudices.

préjuger, *v.a.,* to prejudge; to conjecture; to foresee, to guess (at); (jur.) to give an interlocutory judgment.

prélart or **prélat,** *n.m.,* (nav.) tarpaulin.

se **prélasser,** *v.r.,* to strut, to stalk (past), to parade, to make a great show; to loll, to lounge; to take one's ease.

prélat, *n.m.,* prelate; (nav.) *V.* **prélart.**

⊙**prélation,** *n.f.,* preference, prelation.

prélature, *n.f.,* prelacy, episcopacy.

prèle or **presle,** *n.f.,* (bot.) horsetail, shavegrass.

prélegs (-lè), *n.m.,* preference, legacy.

préléguer (-ghé), *v.a.* to give as a preference-legacy.

prêler, *v.a.,* to rub with horsetail.

prélèvement (-lèv-màn), *n.m.,* previous deduction, levying.

prélever (prél-vé), *v.a.,* to deduct, to take off first, to levy. *Se —;* to be deducted previously, to be levied.

préliminaire, *n.m.* and *adj.,* preliminary.

préliminairement, *adv.,* preliminarily.

prélire, *v.a.,* (print.) to read a first time.

prélude, *n.m.,* prelude.

préluder, *v.n.,* to prelude, to flourish, to play a prelude. *— à une chose par une autre;* to make one thing a prelude to another.

prématuré, -e, *adj.,* premature, untimely.
prématurément, *adv.,* prematurely.
prématurité, *n.f.,* prematureness, prematurity.

préméditation, *n.f.,* premeditation, malice aforethought; (jur.) malice prepense. *Avec —;* designedly, willfully; with malice aforethought.
prémédité, -e, *pavt.,* premeditated.
préméditer, *v.a.,* to premeditate. *Se —;* to be premeditated.

prémices, *n.f.pl.,* first-fruits; (fig.) beginning.
premi-er, -ère, *adj.,* first; foremost; opening; premier; chief, principal; former, ancient, old, primitive, primeval; early prime; (of materials) raw. *Nos —s parents;* our first parents. *Les —s temps du monde;* the early ages of the world. *Au — abord;* at first view, or sight. *— en date;* senior. *En — lieu;* in the first place. ☉*— -pris;* wretched-looking man. *Il a l'air d'un —-pris;* he looks wretched. *— venu;* first comer; no matter who. *—-né, (—s—-s)* first-born. *En — e;* in a first-class carriage. *Les —es;* first tier boxes *or* dress-circle; first-class cabin *or* saloon cabin. *Matière —e;* raw material. *Les —s vont devant;* first come, first served.

premier, *n.m.,* former; first; first floor; chief, head, leader. *Jeune —,* m., *jeune —ère,* f., V. **jeune.** *Il demeure au —;* he lives on the first floor.
premièrement (-mièr-mān), *adv.,* first, firstly, in the first place.
prémisses, *n.f.pl.,* (log.) premises.
prémonitoire, *adj.,* (med.) premonitory.
prémontrés, *n.m.pl.,* Premontrants, a regular order of canons of Prémontré in Picardy (France).
prémotion, *n.f.,* (theol.) premotion.
prémunir, *v.a.,* to forewarn, to caution, to provide; to fortify, *or* secure, beforehand.
se prémunir, *v.r.,* to provide, to be provided; to strengthen, to fortify one's self (against). *Se — contre le froid;* to fortify one's self against the cold.
prenable, *adj.,* to be taken, pregnable; seizable; expugnable; corruptible.
prenant, -e, *adj.,* receiving (of a person); having to receive money; prehensile. *Queue —e;* prehensile tail. *Partie —e;* payee.
prendre (prenant, pris), *v.a.,* to take; to take up; to lay hold of; to seize; to accept; to apprehend; to fetch; to assume; to contract; to pick out; to snatch; to catch (a cold); to take root; to freeze (of rivers, etc.); to turn, to curdle (of milk); to ignite, to begin to burn; to act, to succeed; to imbibe; to call for (any one); to attack (of diseases); to collect (votes); to contract (diseases, engagements); to help one's self to. *— garde;* to take heed. *— parti pour quelqu'un;* to take any one's part, to side with any one. *— feu;* to take *or* catch fire. *— son parti;* to make up one's mind. *— les armes;* to take up arms. *— une ville d'assaut;* to take a town by storm. *— médecine;* to take physic. *— du tabac;* to take snuff. *— congé de quelqu'un;* to take leave of any one. *— la rue à droite;* to take the street on the right. *— le plus court;* to go the shortest way. *— les devants;* to go on before. *— bien son temps;* to hit the time well, to choose the right moment. *— naissance;* to take its rise (of things). *— fait et cause pour quelqu'un;* to take any one's part, to undertake any one's defense, to side with any one. *— quelqu'un sur le fait;* to catch any one in the act. *— exemple sur quelqu'un;* to model one's self on any one. *— avis de quelqu'un;* to take any one's advice. *— les avis;* to collect the votes. *— intérêt, — part à;* to take part in, to be a party to, to be concerned in, to be a partaker of, to be interested in. *— l'air;* to take an airing. *— bien le sens d'un auteur;* to catch an author's meaning. *Vous prenez mal mes paroles;* you misconstrue my words. *— une chose en bonne part;* to take a thing well, in good part. *— les choses de travers;* to take things amiss, the wrong way. *— bien,* or *mal, une affaire;* to go the right, or the wrong, way to work in anything. *— sur son sommeil;* to encroach upon one's sleep. *— les choses comme elles viennent;* to take things as they come. *— l'occasion aux cheveux;* to take time by the forelock. *— pour dit;* to take for granted. *A tout —;* upon the whole, in the main. *— le chemin de l'hopitâl;* to be on the high road to ruin. *Ne savoir pas — quelqu'un;* not to know how to deal with any one. *Il en a pris sa bonne part;* he has had his fair share of it. *Il m'a pris en amitié;* he has taken a liking to me. *Je vous y prends;* now I have caught you (at it). *Ça ne prend pas;* (fam.) that 's no go; it does n't catch on. *Si la curiosité me prend d'y aller;* if curiosity prompts, or impels, me to go there. *L'envie lui prit d'y aller;* he took a sudden fancy to go (there). *Il prend beaucoup sur lui;* he assumes much, he takes much upon himself. *Cela prend forme;* that is beginning to take shape. *Je sors d'en —;* (fam.) I 'd rather be excused; I have just had one (i.e., a drink), or just bought some (of things). *Qu'est-ce qui vous prend?* what 's up now? *C'est autant de pris sur l'ennemi;* it is so much snatched from the fire. *Ce qui est bon à — est bon à rendre;* what is worth taking is worth keeping. *Bien lui en prit;* it was lucky for him he did. *— terre;* (nav.) to land. *— le vent;* (nav.) to sail near the wind. *— le large;* (nav.) to stand out to sea, to cross the bar.

se prendre, *v.r.,* to be taken, to be caught; to catch, to cling; to freeze, to congeal (of liquids); to begin; to go to work. *Le sirop se prendra bientôt;* the syrup will soon coagulate, or set. *Se — à pleurer;* to begin to cry. *Se bien — à une chose;* to go the right way to work. *De la manière dont il s'y prend;* by the way he goes to work. *Se — d'amitié pour quelqu'un;* to take a liking to any one. *Se — de paroles avec quelqu'un;* to have high words with any one. *S'en — à;* to blame, to lay the blame on. *S'en — à quelqu'un;* to lay the blame at any one's door. *Se — de vin;* to get tipsy. *Prenez-vous en à vous-même;* you have only yourself to thank for it.

prendre, *v.n.,* to take, to turn; to take root; to congeal, to freeze; to succeed; to burn up, to begin to burn; to curdle (of milk). *Il lui en prendra mal;* it will be the worse for him. *Il lui prit une fièvre;* he was attacked by fever. *La Seine a pris cet hiver là;* the Seine was frozen over that winter.

prendre, *n.m.,* act of taking. *Au fait et au —;* at the scratch, when it comes to the scratch.

preneu-r, *n.m.,* **-se,** *n.f.,* taker; lessee; (of animals) catcher; (com.) purchaser, buyer.
preneur, *adj.m.,* catching, capturing; (nav.) that takes a prize.
prénom (-non), *n.m.,* Christian name; prenomen.
prénommé, -e, *adj.part.,* above-named, aforesaid.
prénommer, *v.a.,* to prenominate, to forename.
prénotion, *n.f.,* prenotion, surmise, conjecture.
préoccupation, *n.f.,* preoccupation, prepossession of the mind; thought; anxiety; prejudice.
préoccupé, -e, *part.,* preoccupied, absorbed; prejudiced, biased; thoughtful, anxious.
préoccuper, *v.a.,* to engross, to engage, to preoccupy the mind, to prepossess, to prejudice, to bias; to absorb, to trouble.

préopinant, *n.m.*, **-e**, *n.f.*, previous speaker; last speaker.

préopiner, *v.n.*, to vote before another, to express one's opinion first.

préordination, *n.f.*, preordination.

préordonner, *v.a.*, to preordain, to predetermine.

préparant, *adj.*, (anat.) spermatic. *Vaisseaux —s;* spermatic duct.

préparateur, *n.m.*, preparer, dresser; assistant; private tutor, crammer.

préparatif, *n.m.*, preparation. *—s de guerre, de voyage;* war preparations, preparations for a journey.

préparation, *n.f.*, preparation. *— chimique;* chemical preparation. *Sans —;* extempore.

préparatoire, *n.m.* and *adj.*, preparative, preliminary, preparatory.

préparer, *v.a.*, to prepare, to dispose, to fit; to provide; to make ready; to dress; (agri.) to till; (fig.) to break (news) to. *— les voies à quelqu'un;* to pave the way for any one.

se **préparer**, *v.r.*, to prepare for one's self, to prepare one's self, to get ready. *Se — pour un voyage;* to get ready for a journey. *Se — au combat;* to prepare for battle. *Préparez-vous à le recevoir;* prepare to meet him. *Voilà un orage qui se prépare;* there is a storm brewing.

prépondérance, *n.f.*, preponderance, sway.

prépondérant, **-e**, *adj.*, preponderant, prevailing; convincing. *Voix —e;* casting-vote.

préposé, *n.m.*, custom, *or* excise, officer; overseer, superintendent.

préposer, *v.a.*, to set (over), to charge (with), to intrust (to); to appoint, to commit; to put forward, to set up; to depute.

prépositi-f, **-ve**, *adj.*, (gram.) prepositive.

préposition, *n.f.*, (gram.) preposition.

prépuce, *n.m.*, prepuce, foreskin.

prérogative, *n.f.*, prerogative, privilege; attribute.

près, *prep.*, by, near, nigh, close to, hard by, nearly; almost, about; on the point; in comparison. *S'asseoir — de quelqu'un;* to sit by any one. *Il demeure ici —;* he lives close by. *De —;* close, near; closely, intimately. *Combattre de —;* to fight hand to hand. *Suivre de —;* to follow on the heels of. *A cela —;* save that, with that exception; nevertheless, for all that. *A beaucoup —;* by a great deal, nothing near. *Tout —;* very near. *A peu —;* pretty near, nearly so, thereabouts. *A peu de chose —;* within a trifle. *Au plus —;* to the nearest place; (nav.) close to the wind. *De — et de loin;* far and nigh.

présage, *n.m.*, presage, omen, foreboding. *Un oiseau de sinistre —;* a bird of evil omen.

présager, *v.a.*, to presage, to forebode, to portend, to conjecture.

se **présager**, *v.r.*, to be foreboded, to be presaged.

pré-salé, *n.m.*, (*—s- —s*) salt-marsh-fed (mutton).

presbyopie, *n.f.*, (opt.) presbyopy, presbyopia, far-sightedness, long sight.

presbyte, *n.m.f.* and *adj.*, presbyte; far-sighted person; presbyopic; long-sighted. *Vue —;* long sight.

presbytéral, **-e**, *adj.*, priestly. *Maison —e;* parsonage, vicarage.

presbytéranisme, *n.m.* V. **presbytérianisme**.

presbytère, *n.m.*, parsonage, parsonage-house, vicarage; ⊙presbytery.

presbytérianisme, *n.m.*, presbyterianism.

presbytérien, **-ne** (-ri-in, -ri-èn), *n.* and *adj.*, presbyterian.

presbytie (-ci), *n.f.*, (opt.) presbyopy, far- *or* long-sightedness, presbyopia.

prescience, *n.f.*, prescience, foreknowledge, foresight.

prescriptible, *adj.*, prescriptible.

prescription, *n.f.*, (jur.) limitation; prescription, precept. *Interruption de la —;* (jur.) bar to a limitation. *Etabli par —;* prescriptive. *Se perdre par —;* (jur.) to be lost by limitation. *—s médicales;* medical prescriptions.

prescrire, *v.a.*, to prescribe, to direct, to order, to enjoin, to set; (jur.) to bar. *— des lois;* to prescribe laws. *— un régime;* to prescribe a diet.

se **prescrire**, *v.r.*, to prescribe to one's self, to be prescribed; (jur.) to be lost by limitation.

prescrire, *v.n.*, to bar by limitation.

préséance (pré-séans), *n.f.*, precedence. *Avoir la — sur;* to take precedence of.

présence, *n.f.*, presence, attendance, sight, view. *Faire acte de —;* to put in an appearance. *Mettre en —;* to bring face to face. *En — de;* in presence of, in view of. *En ma —;* before me. *Deux armées en —;* two armies facing each other. *— d'esprit;* presence of mind.

présent, *n.m.*, present, present time; present, gift; (gram.) present, present tense. *Donner en —;* to give as a present. *Faire — de;* to make a present of. *Dès à —;* from this time. *A —;* at present. *Pour le —;* for the present, for the nonce. *Jusqu'à —;* till now.

présent, **-e**, *adj.*, present! here! *Etre —;* to be present, to stand by.

présentable, *adj.*, presentable, fit to be seen.

présentat-eur, *n.m.*, **-rice**, *n.f.*, presenter (to benefices); introducer.

présentation, *n.f.*, presentation, presentment, introduction. *A —;* (com.) on presentation, on demand. *En retard de —;* (com.) overdue.

présente, *n.f.*, present letter. *pl.* (jur.) presents.

présentement (-zant-mān), *adv.*, now, at present.

présenter, *v.a.*, to present, to offer, to hold out, to show, to turn, to expose, to bring forward, to introduce. *— ses lettres de créance;* to present one's credentials. *— les armes;* to present arms. *— une personne à une autre;* to introduce one person to another. *— à quelqu'un ses respects;* to pay one's respects to any one.

se **présenter**, *v.r.*, to present one's self, to appear, to come forward, to offer one's self, to offer itself; to occur. *Il s'est présenté à moi;* he presented himself before me. *Cet homme se présente bien;* that man has a good address. *La chose se présente bien;* the thing looks well, *or* promises well. *Il se présenta une difficulté;* a difficulty occurred, *or* arose.

présenter, *v.n.*, (nav.) to stem. *— au vent;* to head to the wind.

présenteur, *n.m.*, (l.u.) presenter.

préservat-eur, **-rice**, *adj.*, preservative. *n.m.* and *f.*, preserver.

préservati-f, **-ve**, *adj.*, preservative.

préservatif, *n.m.*, preservative.

préservation, *n.f.*, preservation.

préserver, *v.a.*, to preserve, to defend, to keep. *Le ciel m'en préserve!* heaven forbid!

se **préserver**, *v.r.*, to preserve one's self, to guard against, to keep off. *Se — d'une maladie;* to stall off a disease.

présidence, *n.f.*, presidency, chairmanship.

président, *n.m.*, president, chairman; presiding judge; speaker (of the House of Commons). *— d'âge;* president by seniority.

présidente, *n.f.*, lady president; president's wife.

présider, *v.a.*, to preside, to preside (over), to be president (of), to be chairman (of). *— une réunion;* to preside over a meeting.

présider, *v.n.*, to preside, to be president *or* chairman; to be in the chair; to direct. *— à une assemblée;* to preside over an assembly. —

à la direction d'un ouvrage; to have the management of a work.

présides, *n.m.pl.,* Spanish penal colonies.

présompti-f, -ve, *adj.,* presumptive, apparent, presumed (of heirs). *Héritier —;* heir-apparent.

présomption, *n.f.,* presumption, presumptuousness, self-conceite.

présomptueusement (-eûz-mān), *adv.,* presumptuously.

présomptueu-x, -se, *adj., n.,* presumptuous, presuming, self-conceited. *Jeune —!* presumptuous youth!

presque, *adv.,* almost, nearly, all but. *Un ouvrage — achevé;* a work nearly finished. *Je ne l'ai — pas vu;* I scarcely saw him at all. — *jamais;* hardly ever. — *plus de;* scarcely any left. — *rien;* hardly anything.

presqu'île, *n.f.,* (— — — *s*) peninsula.

⊙**presqu'ombre,** *n.f.* V. **pénombre.**

pressage, *n.m.,* pressing.

pressamment (-sa-mān), *adv.,* pressingly, earnestly, urgently.

pressant, -e, *adj.,* pressing, urgent, earnest, importunate, vigorous; acute (of pain).

presse, *n.f.,* press (newspapers, machine); printing-press, haste, hurry; pressure, crowd, throng; impress (forcing men into the service); press-gang; urgency; (bot.) a clingstone peach. — *à copier;* copying-machine. — *d'imprimerie;* printing-press. — *à satiner;* hot-press, cold-press. *Fendre la —;* to force one's way through the crowd. *Cet ouvrage est sous —;* this work is in the press. *Mettre sous —;* to send to press, to go to press. *Il n'y a pas de —;* there 's no hurry. *Il n'y a pas —;* there 's no crowd.

pressé, -e, *adj.,* in haste, in a hurry; urgent, immediate; eager, anxious, very busy; close, serried, thick; condensed, brief, concise. *Vous êtes bien —;* you are in a great hurry. *Cela n'est pas —;* there 's no hurry for that. *Je suis très —;* I am very busy.

pressée, *n.f.,* pressful; pressing, pressure.

pressement, *n.m.,* pressing, compression.

pressément, *adv.,* (l.u.) hurriedly, hastily.

pressentiment, *n.m.,* presentiment, misgiving, foreboding.

pressentir, *v.a.,* to have a presentiment of; to foresee; to anticipate; to ascertain the intentions of; to sound. — *quelqu'un;* to sound any one. *Il faut le —;* we must sound him. *Se —,* to be foreseen.

presse-papiers, *n.m.,* (—) paper-weight.

presser, *v.a.,* to press, to squeeze, to clasp; to pull (trigger); to crowd, to throng; to hasten, to hurry; to urge, to be pressing with, to importune; to be hard upon; to exaggerate; to impress (sailors). — *une éponge;* to squeeze a sponge. *On pressa si fort les ennemis;* they pressed so hard upon the enemy. — *vivement un siège;* to carry on a siege vigorously. — *une entreprise;* to push an enterprise with vigor. *Il pressa son départ;* he hastened his departure. — *la détente;* to pull the trigger.

se presser, *v.r.,* to press, to press close, to squeeze; to crowd; to be in a hurry, to make haste, to hurry. *Se — de faire une chose;* to make haste to do a thing. *Pressons-nous;* let us make haste.

presser, *v.n.,* to be urgent; to be acute (of pain). *Rien ne presse,* or *il n'y a rien qui presse;* there is no hurry.

presseur, *n.m.,* presser.

pressier, *n.m.,* (print.) pressman.

pression, *n.f.,* pressure, pressing. *Machine à vapeur à haute —, à moyenne —, à basse —;* steam-engine of high pressure, of mean pressure, of low pressure.

pressis, *n.m.,* (l.u.) gravy, juice.

pressoir, *n.m.,* press; press-room; wine-press, cider-press; press-house.

pressurage, *n.m.,* (of fruit) pressing.

pressurer, *v.a.,* to press (grapes or apples); to squeeze; to grind down, to oppress. — *une orange;* to squeeze an orange. — *la bourse de quelqu'un;* to drain any one's purse. *Il ne songe qu'à vous —;* his only thought is to drain you of money.

pressureur, *n.m.,* presser (of fruit).

prestance, *n.f.,* commanding appearance, bearing, carriage, deportment; good presence.

prestant, *n.m.,* diapason (of an organ).

prestation, *n.f.,* taking (of an oath); prestation (payment in kind).

preste, *adj.,* agile, nimble, quick, smart, sharp. *C'est un homme — et habile;* he is a clever, smart fellow.

preste, *adv.,* presto, quick, sharp.

prestement, *adv.,* nimbly, quickly.

prestesse, *n.f.,* agility, quickness, nimbleness.

prestidigitateur, *n.m.,* conjurer, juggler.

prestidigitation, *n.f.,* jugglery, legerdemain.

prestige, *n.m.,* enchantment, fascination; deception, illusion; magic spell; prestige.

prestigieu-x, -se, *adj.,* enchanting, bewitching, illusive.

prestimonie, *n.f.,* (canon law) prestimony.

presto, *adv.,* (mus.) presto.

prestolet, *n.m.,* priestling.

présumable, *adj.,* presumable, supposable.

présumé, *part. adj.,* presumed, supposed, conjectured, reputed.

présumer, *v.a.,* to presume, to conjecture, to suppose. — *trop de quelqu'un;* to presume too much upon any one. — *trop de soi;* to be too assuming. *Il est à —;* it is to be supposed.

présupposer (-su-pô-zé), *v.a.,* to presuppose.

présupposition, *n.m.,* presupposition.

présure, *n.f.,* rennet (for curdling milk).

prêt, *n.m.,* loan; (milit.) advance-pay.

prêt, -e, *adj.,* ready, in readiness, prepared, willing. *Tenir —;* to keep ready. *Tenez-vous — à partir;* be ready to start.

prêtable, *adj.,* lendable.

pretantaine, *n.f. Courir la —;* to gad about.

prêté, -e, *part.,* lent.

prêté, *n.m.,* (l.u.) thing lent. *C'est un — rendu;* it is but tit for tat.

prétendant, *n.m., -e,* *n.f.,* claimant, candidate; suitor, wooer; pretender (to the throne).

prétendre, *v.a.,* to claim, to lay claim to, to pretend to. *Que prétendent ces misérables?* what do these wretches lay claim to, or mean?

prétendre, *v.n.,* to lay claim to; to pretend, to mean; to maintain. *Je prétends que mon droit est incontestable;* I maintain that my claim is incontestable. *Je prétends vous traiter comme mon propre fils* (Racine); I mean (intend) to treat you as my own son.

prétendu, -e, *adj.,* pretended, feigned, sham, so-called; said to be, would be. *C'est un — bel esprit;* he is a would-be wit.

prétendu, *n.m., -e,* *n.f.,* intended, future husband, future wife. *Voilà mon —;* that is my intended.

prête-nom, *n.m.,* (— — *s*) one that lends his name to another; dummy.

pretentaine, *n.f.* V. **pretantaine.**

prétentieu-x, -se, *adj.,* assuming, pretentious, affected, stilted (of style).

prétention, *n.f.,* pretension, claim, intention, wish, expectation. *Venir à bout de ses —s;* to make good one's claims. *Sa — est mal fondée;* his demand is groundless. *Il a des —s à l'esprit;* he thinks he is, or claims to be, witty. *C'est un homme sans —s;* he is a man of no pretensions. *Se désister d'une —;* to relinquish a claim.

prêter, *v.a.,* to lend, to impart, to give rise to, to attribute, to ascribe, to father; to take (oath). — *de l'argent à intérêt;* to lend money on interest. — *secours;* to lend a helping hand. —

main-forte à quelqu'un; to assist any one, to come to any one's assistance. — *l'oreille;* to give ear (to), to listen. — *serment;* to take the oath. — *foi et hommage;* to take an oath of allegiance. — *le collet à quelqu'un;* to try one's strength with any one. — *le flanc;* to expose one's self. — *à la petite semaine;* to make short loans at a high rate of interest.

se **prêter,** *v.r.,* to give way (to); to lend one's self, or itself (to); to indulge; to humor; to countenance, to favor.

prêter, *v.n.,* to lend; to give a hold to; to afford matter for; to stretch (of a thing). *Ce cuir-là prête comme un gant;* that leather stretches like a glove. *Donner un prêté pour un rendu;* to give a Roland for an Oliver.

prêter, *n.m.,* loan. *C'est un — à ne jamais rendre;* it is a loan never to be repaid.

prétérit (-rit), *n.m.,* (gram.) preterit.

prétérition, *n.f.,* (rhet.) preterition; pretermission.

prétermission, *n.f.* V. **prétérition.**

prêteu-r, *n.m.,* **-se,** *n.f.,* lender. — *sur gages;* pawnbroker. *adj.,* given to lending, of a lending disposition.

préteur, *n.m.,* (antiq.) pretor, prætor.

prétexte, *n.m.,* pretext, pretense; plea. — *spécieux;* plausible pretense. *Faux — ;* false pretense. *Sous — de le secourir;* under pretense of assisting him.

prétexte, *n.* and *adj.f.,* (Rom. antiq.) prætexta, tunic.

prétexter, *v.a.,* to pretend, to feign, to affect, to sham; to allege, to plead.

pretintaille, *n.f.,* furbelow; (fig.) accessory, appendage, incidental profit.

pretintailler, *v.a.,* to tinsel, to trim (a dress).

prétoire, *n.m.,* (antiq.) pretorium.

prétorien, -ne (-in, -è-n), *adj.,* (antiq.) pretorian.

prétorien, *n.m.,* (antiq.) pretorian guard.

***prêtraille,** *n.f.,* (b.s.) priesthood; parsons.

prêtre, *n.m.,* priest, clergyman; parson. *Il s'est fait — ;* he has taken orders. — *habitué;* an unpaid supernumerary priest. *Grand — ;* high priest.

prêtresse, *n.f.,* priestess.

prêtrise, *n.f.,* priesthood.

préture, *n.f.,* pretorship.

preuve, *n.f.,* proof, evidence, testimony, token, mark; (com.) proof-sample; proof (of spirits). *En venir à la — ;* to come to the proof. *Faire — de noblesse;* to give proof of nobility; to uphold the honor of one's house. *Il a fait ses —s;* he has given proofs of his capacity. *Faire — de courage;* to show, or approve, one's self a man of courage. *Servir de — ;* to serve as a proof. *—s induites des circonstances;* (jur.) circumstantial evidence.

preux, *n.* and *adj.m.,* valiant knight, gallant knight; worthy; gallant, doughty, valiant, stout, worthy.

prévaloir, *v.n.,* to prevail, to stand. *La faveur prévaut souvent sur le mérite;* favor frequently prevails over merit.

se **prévaloir,** *v.r.,* to take advantage, to avail one's self; to boast of, to pride one's self upon; to glory in. *Se — de sa naissance;* to take advantage of, or to glory in, one's birth.

prévaricateur, *n.m.,* prevaricator; betrayer of any one's trust.

prévaricat-eur, -rice, *adj.,* prevaricating.

prévarication, *n.f.,* prevarication; breach of trust. [one's trust.

prévariquer, *v.n.,* to prevaricate, to betray

prévenance (pré-vnans), *n.f.,* kindness, kind attention.

prévenant, -e, *adj.,* prepossessing; engaging; ready to oblige, attentive, obliging, kind. *Il a un air — ;* he has a prepossessing look.

prévenir (pré-vnir), *v.a.,* to go before, to precede, to come before, to be beforehand with, to get the start of, to anticipate; to forestall ; to prevent, to hinder; to prepossess, to prejudice; to predispose, to bias, to inform, to warn; to caution, to give notice; to let know. — *le mal;* to prevent evil. — *les objections;* to forestall objections. — *les besoins de quelqu'un;* to anticipate any one's wants. *Il m'a fait — de son arrivée;* he sent to tell me of his arrival. *On vous en avait prévenu;* you had had information of it, *or* you had been informed of it.

se **prévenir,** *v.r.,* to be prepossessed, to be prejudiced, to anticipate each other. *Se — en faveur de quelqu'un;* to take a liking to any one.

préventi-f, -ve, *adj.,* preventive.

prévention, *n.f.,* prepossession, prejudice, bias; suspicion, presumption; prevention; accusation; (jur.) prosecution; (jur.) commitment. *Donner des —s contre soi;* to raise prejudices against one's self. *Vaincre les —s de quelqu'un;* to overcome any one's prejudices. *Etat de — ;* (jur.) commitment. *Etre en état de — ;* (jur.) to be committed for trial.

préventivement, *adv.,* by way of prevention; (jur.) while awaiting trial, on suspicion.

prévenu, -e, *n.f.,* (jur.) prisoner (before trial), the accused, the prisoner (at the bar).

prévision, *n.f.,* prevision; forecast; foreknowledge; conjecture.

prévoir, *v.a.,* to foresee; to conjecture; to expect, to anticipate, to provide (for *or* against); to meet. *Il faut tout — ;* we must provide against everything, against all eventualities.

prévôt, *n.m.,* provost; (nav.) marshal. *Grand —, grand — de l'armée;* (milit.) provost-marshal. — *de salle d'armes;* fencing-master's assistant. — *des marchands;* (old) mayor of Paris.

prévôtal, -e, *adj.,* relating, pertaining to a provost.

prévôtalement (-tal-mān), *adv.,* by a provost-court.

prévôté, *n.f.,* provostship.

prévoyance, *n.f.,* foresight, forethought, prudence, caution. *Rien n'échappe à sa — ;* nothing escapes his foresight.

prévoyant, -e, *adj.,* provident, prudent, careful, cautious.

priapée, *n.f.,* obscene picture; obscene poem.

priapisme, *n.m.,* (med.) priapism.

prié, *n.m.,* **-e,** *n.f.,* person invited, guest.

prie-dieu, *n.m.,* (—) praying-desk; devotion chair; faldstool.

prier, *v.a.* and *n.,* to pray; to entreat, to beseech, to call upon, to beg (of), to implore, to supplicate, to request; to invite, to bid. — *quelqu'un d'une grâce;* to request a favor of any one. *Il m'a prié de l'accompagner;* he begged of me to accompany him. *On m'a prié de le faire;* I have been requested to do it. *Je vous en prie;* I beg of you. — *à dîner;* to invite to dinner. — *de dîner;* to press any one to stay to dinner. *Se faire — or aimer à se faire — ;* to require pressing.

prière, *n.f.,* prayer, suit, request, entreaty, desire, invitation; petition. *Instante — ;* earnest prayer. *Faire une — à quelqu'un;* to make a request to any one. *Etre en — ;* to be at prayers. *Faire une chose à la — de quelqu'un;* to do a thing at any one's request, at any one's entreaty. *Dire ses —s, faire sa —, faire ses —s;* to say one's prayers. — *de faire renvoyer la lettre!* will you kindly send back the letter!

prieur, *n.m.,* prior (superior of a convent).

prieure, *n.f.,* prioress.

prieuré, *n.m.,* priory.

prima donna, *n.f.,* (*prime donne*) the chief singer (in an opera).

primage, *n.m.,* (com.) primage (allowance paid to the captain of a ship).

primaire, *adj.*, primary. *Ecole* —; elementary school.

primat, *n.m.*, primate, metropolitan.

primatial, -e (-ci-al), *adj.*, primatial, primatical.

primatie (-ma-cî), *n.f.*, primacy, primateship.

primauté, *n.f.*, primacy, supremacy, priority; preeminence; the lead (at cards, dice). *Gagner quelqu'un de* —; to anticipate any one, to be beforehand with any one.

prime, *adj.*, (alg.) accented. *b', b* —; b', b accented.

prime, *n.f.*, premium, bounty; bonus, prize; (c.rel.) prime (first canonical hour succeeding lauds; (fenc.) prime; primero (card game); (com.) prime wool; (jewelry) pebble; (exchange language) agio; (customs) drawback. *A* —; at a premium. *Réponse des —s;* (com.) option.

de **prime abord**, *adv.*, at first.

de **prime face**, *adv.*, at first, *prima facie.*

primer, *v.n.*, to play first, to lead (at play); to take the lead, to beat, to override, to excel, to surpass; to go before everything. *Il prime en tout;* he excels in everything. *Les affaires priment tout;* business before everything else.

primer, *v.a.*, to surpass, to excel; to go before everything; to give a prize (at an agricultural show). *Il prime tous les autres;* he excels all the others.

de **prime-saut**, *adv.*, suddenly; off-hand, spontaneously; all at once, at the first effort.

prime-sauti-er, -ère, *adj.*, quick (of thought), ready-witted; impulsive, off-handed; thoughtless, inconsiderate, heedless. *Les Français ont, en général, l'esprit —;* the French are, in general, ready-witted.

primeur, *n.f.*, first of the season (of vegetables, fruit, flowers, wine); early fruit; early vegetables; early flower; early sentiment, first love; freshness, bloom; earliest communication. *Les fruits sont chers dans la* —; fruit is dear in the early part of the season, fruit is dear when it first comes in. *Certains vins ne sont pas bons dans la* —; certain wines are not good when they are new. *Servir à table un plat de —s;* to serve up a dish of early vegetables. *Je vous en donnerai la* —; you will be the first to get the news.

primevère, *n.f.*, primrose, cowslip, oxlip.

primicériat, *n.m.*, dignity, office of primicerius, dean (in some churches).

primicier, *n.m.*, local dean.

primidi, *n.m.*, Primidi (first day of the decade in the calendar of the first French republic).

primipare, *adj.*, primiparous.

primiti-f, -ve, *adj.*, primitive, primeval, primogenial, original; native, aboriginal; (gram.) primitive, original.

primitif, *n.m.*, (gram.) primitive.

primitivement (-tiv-mān), *adv.*, primitively, originally.

primitivité, *n.f.*, primitiveness.

primo, *adv.*, firstly, first, in the first place.

primogéniture, *n.f.*, primogeniture.

primordial, -e, *adj.*, primordial.

primordialement (-al-mān), *adv.*, primordially.

primulacées, *n.f. pl.*, (bot.) primulaceæ.

prince, *n.m.*, prince. *— royal;* crown prince. *Etre bon* —; (fam.) to be a good fellow (easygoing, good-natured). *Vivre en* —; to live like a prince. *Dîner de* —; princely dinner.

princeps (-sèps), *adj. invariable*, (print.) earliest, first, original (edition).

princerie (prin-srî), *n.f.*, (local) deanery.

princesse, *n.f.*, princess. *Oui, ma* —; (fam.) yes, my charmer.

princi-er, -ère, *adj.*, princely, like a prince.

princier, *n.m.*, primicerius, first dignitary. *V.* **primicier.**

principal, -e, *adj.*, principal, chief, main; leading, capital, senior, superior; (astron.) primary.

principal, *n.m.*, principal, chief thing, principal point, chief point, material point; principal, capital (money); principal, head-master; (jur.) principal cause of action. *Pour vous, le — est que vous ayez soin de votre santé;* the main thing for you is to take care of your health. *Payer le — et l'intérêt;* to pay both principal and interest.

principalat, *n.m.*, head-mastership, principalship.

principalement (-pal-mān), *adv.*, principally, chiefly.

⊙**principalité**, *n.f. V.* **principalat.**

principat, *n.m.*, princedom.

principauté, *n.f.*, principality, princedom.

principe, *n.m.*, beginning, source, outset, origin, motive, cause, principle. *pl.*, principles, rudiments. *Dès le* —; from the very origin. *Etablir, poser, un* —; to establish, to lay down, a principle. *Partir d'un* —; to start from a principle. *Homme sans —s;* unprincipled man. *L'amour-propre est le — de presque toutes nos actions;* self-love is the motive of almost all our actions.

principion, principule, *n.m.*, petty prince, princelet.

printani-er, -ère, *adj.*, spring, spring-like, vernal; youthful; early. *Fleurs —ères;* springflowers; cowslips. *Etoffes —ères;* spring materials, or stuffs; spring goods. *Potage —;* spring-soup (with early vegetables).

printemps (-tān), *n.m.*, spring, spring-time; prime, bloom. *Le — de la vie;* the morning of life. *Dans le — de sa vie;* in the prime of one's days. *Au — de ses jours;* in the bloom of one's youth.

à priori, *adv.*, à priori (*i.e.* from what precedes).

priorité, *n.f.*, priority.

pris, -e, *part.*, taken, caught, seized, congealed, curdled, frozen, frozen over; stuffed up (of the nose). *Homme bien — dans sa taille;* well-set man. *Cet homme est — de vin;* that man is the worse for liquor. *La rivière a — dans la nuit; — dans les glaces;* ice-bound.

prisable, *adj.*, estimable, valuable.

prise, *n.f.*, taking, capture; prize; hold, handle, purchase; quarrel; dose; pinch. *pl.*, fighting, close quarters. *La — d'une ville;* the taking of a town. *— de possession;* taking possession. *— de possession d'un bénéfice;* induction to a living. *— d'habit;* (c. rel.) taking the habit, *or* the veil. *Décret de — de corps;* writ of arrest. *Part de —;* prize-money. *Amariner une* —; to man a prize. *Etre de bonne* —; to be a lawful prize. *Lâcher* —; to let go one's hold. *Donner — à la critique;* to lay one's self open to criticism, to expose one's self to criticism, to afford matter for criticism. *Donner — sur soi à son ennemi;* to give one's enemy a hold over one. *— de tabac;* pinch of snuff. *En venir aux —s;* to grapple with one another, to come to blows. *Les deux chiens sont aux —s;* the two dogs are fighting. *Etre aux —s avec la mauvaise fortune;* to be struggling with, *or* against, adversity. *Etre aux —s avec la mort;* to be on the point of death, *or* at death's door; to be in great danger. *Mettre aux —s;* to set (together) by the ears.

prisée, *n.f.*, estimate, appraisement, valuation. *Faire la —;* to make an estimate of.

priser, *v.a.*, to prize, to rate, to value, to set a high price on, to appraise, to estimate; to esteem, to have an esteem for.

se **priser**, *v.r.*, to be valued, to be esteemed; to set a high value on one's self.

priser, *v.a. and n.*, to take snuff.

priseu-r, *n.m.*, **-se**, *n.f.*, snuff-taker.

priseur, *adj.*, who appraises. *Commissaire —* ; appraiser, auctioneer. *Expert — assermenté ;* sworn appraiser.

prismatique, *adj.*, prismatic.

prisme, *n.m.*, prism.

prismoïde, *n.m.* and *adj.*, prismoid ; prismoidal.

prison, *n.f.*, prison, gaol, jail ; imprisonment, confinement. *S'échapper de —* ; to break out of prison. *— d'état ;* state prison. *Etre dans la — de saint Crépin ;* to wear shoes which pinch. *Envoyer en —* ; to send to prison.

prisonni-er, *n.m.*, **-ère**, *n.f.*, prisoner. *— d'état ;* state-prisoner.

privati-f, -ve, *adj.*, (gram.) privative ; (jur.) in severalty.

privation, *n.f.*, privation, deprivation, want, need, bereavement, loss ; hardship. *Vivre de —s ;* to lead a life of privation. *Etre dans la —* ; to be in want. *La — de la vue ;* the loss of sight.

privativement (-tiv-măn), *adv.*, exclusively.

privauté, *n.f.*, extreme familiarity, liberty. *Prendre des —s ;* to take liberties.

privé, -e, *part.*, deprived. *Corps — de vie ;* lifeless body. *Homme — de sa raison ;* man deprived of his reason.

privé, -e, *adj.*, private ; tame (animal) ; privy, intimate, free. *Vie —* ; private life. *De son autorité —e ;* of one's own authority.

⊙**privément**, *adv.*, familiarly, intimately.

priver, *v.a.*, to deprive, to debar ; to bereave ; to tame (animal). *— quelqu'un de ses biens ;* to deprive any one of his property. *Je ne veux pas vous — de cela ;* I won't rob you of that.

se priver, *v.r.*, to deprive, or debar, one's self ; to stint, *or* deny, one's self ; to abstain (from).

privilège, *n.m.*, privilege, exemption, immunity ; grant, favor ; (jur.) preference ; (thea.) license ; franchise, prerogative, right. *Accorder un — à ;* to grant a privilege to ; to license (printers). *Priver de ses —s ;* to deprive any one of his privileges ; to disfranchise. *Atteinte portée aux —s ;* breach of privilege. *Les —s de la noblesse ;* the privileges of the nobility.

privilégié, -e, *adj.*, privileged, exempt ; (thea.) licensed ; (jur.) entitled to preference (of creditors) ; (of shares) preference, preferential. *Lieu —* ; privileged place. *C'est un être —* ; he is a privileged, *or* favored, being.

privilégié, *n.m.*, privileged person.

privilégier, *v.a.*, to grant a privilege, to privilege, to license.

prix, *n.m.*, price, cost, value, worth, terms ; return, premium ; estimation ; reward ; prize. *— fait ;* settled price. *Mettre un — à ;* to set a price upon. *— excessif ;* extravagant price. *Juste —* ; moderate price. *— de fabrique ;* manufacturer's price. *Une chose de —* ; a thing of great value. *Hors de —* ; extravagantly dear. *De —* ; precious, valuable. *Une chose qui n'a point de —* ; a thing that is invaluable, beyond all price. *Vendre à tout —* ; to sell at any price, at any cost. *Mettre la tête d'un homme à —* ; to set a price upon a man's head. *— fixe ;* (com.) net price, no abatement. *A tout — or à quelque — que ce soit ;* cost what it will. *La vertu trouve son — en elle-même ;* virtue is its own reward. *Remporter le —* ; to carry off the prize. *Au — de ;* at the cost of, in comparison with. *A vil —* ; under price, dirt-cheap. *— courant ;* (com.) current price, market price. *— coûtant ;* cost price. *A — d'argent ;* for money. *N'avoir pas de —* ; to be invaluable, *or* priceless ; *also*, to be valueless.

probabilisme, *n.m.*, probabilism.

probabilité, *n.f.*, probability, likelihood.

probable, *adj.*, probable, likely, credible. *Cela est bien peu —* ; that is anything but probable.

probablement, *adv.*, probably, likely.

probante, *adj.f.*, probatory (of documents) ; convincing, conclusive (arguments). *En forme —* ; in an authentic form. *Raison —* ; convincing reason.

probation, *n.f.*, probation.

probatique, *adj.*, only used in *piscine —* (the reservoir near the Temple in which Hebrew Priests washed the animals that were to be sacrificed).

⊙**probatoire**, *adj.*, probatory.

probe, *adj.*, honest, upright ; of probity. *Homme —* ; man of probity.

probité, *n.f.*, probity, honesty, integrity, uprightness. *— éprouvée ;* tried probity.

problématique, *adj.*, problematical.

problématiquement (-tik-măn), *adv.*, problematically.

problème, *n.m.*, problem, question. *Poser un —* ; to state a problem. *Résoudre un —* ; to solve a problem. *C'est un —* ; it is a question.

proboscide, *n.f.*, (natural hist., her.) proboscis.

proboscidiens, *n.m.pl.*, (zool.) proboscidians, proboscideæ.

procédé, *n.m.*, behavior, proceeding, way of acting ; dealing, conduct ; (billiards) cue-tip ; process, operation. *pl.*, delicate, gentlemanly manners, fair dealings. *Je n'aime pas ces —s ;* I don't like that way of acting, I dislike those manners. *Manquer aux —s ;* to behave in an unhandsome manner. *C'est un homme à —s ;* he is a gentlemanly man, *or* a man of fair dealings. *— chimique ;* chemical process.

procéder, *v.n.*, to proceed, to go on ; to come from ; to arise (from), to originate (in) ; to behave, to conduct one's self ; (jur.) to proceed. *— criminellement contre quelqu'un ;* to proceed (criminally) against any one. *Cela procède bien ;* that is going on very well.

procédure, *n.f.*, (jur.) proceedings ; practice, procedure, process.

procès, *n.m.*, lawsuit, suit, action, trial, process. *Etre en —* ; to be at law. *Intenter un —, faire un —, à quelqu'un ;* to bring an action against any one, to institute proceedings against any one. *Gagner son —* ; to gain one's suit, *or* case. *Perdre son —* ; to lose one's case. *Faire le — à quelqu'un ;* to try any one, to bring any one to trial ; to call any one to account, to find fault with, to censure. *Sans autre forme de —* ; without more ado, without further formality.

processi-f, -ve, *adj.*, litigious.

procession, *n.f.*, procession.

processionnal, *n.m.*, (c.rel.) processional.

processionnel, -le, *adj.*, processional.

processionnellement (-nèl-măn), *adv.*, in procession.

procès-verbal, *n.m.*, (*— -verbaux*) (authentic written minute, *or* report, of an official act *or* proceeding) ; proceedings, official report, information against ; (parl.) journal, minute of proceedings.

prochain, -e, *adj.*, near, nearest, next, approaching, near at hand, nigh, approximate, proximate ; (com.) proximo. *Village —* ; neighboring village. *Le mois —* ; next month. *La semaine —e ;* next week. *Son départ est —* ; his departure is nigh at hand, *or* imminent. *Fin —e ;* approaching end. *Fin —* ; (com.) at the end of next month.

prochain, *n.m.*, neighbor, fellow-creature.

prochainement (-shé-n-măn), *adv.*, in a short time, shortly, soon.

prochaineté, *n.f.*, nearness, proximity.

proche, *adj.*, near, next, near at hand, neighboring, nigh, approaching. *La ville la plus —* ; the nearest town. *— parent ;* near relation.

proche, *prep.*, near, nigh.

proche, *adv.*, near, nigh. *De — en —* ; from

place to place ; gradually, one after another. *Le choléra s'étendit rapidement de — en —;* the cholera spread rapidly from place to place.

proches, *n.m.pl.,* near relations, near relatives ; relations, relatives, kinsmen, kin, kindred.

prochronisme, *n.m.,* prochronism.

procidence, *n.f.,* (med.) prolapsus.

proclamateur, *n.m.,* proclaimer, proclaiming.

proclamation, *n.f.,* proclamation.

proclamer, *v.a.,* to proclaim, to cry out, to give out, to announce, to trumpet forth; to publish, to declare.

proclitique, *n.m.* and *adj.,* (gram.) unaccented word; unaccented.

proclive, *adj.,* inclined.

proclivité, *n.f.,* proclivity.

procombant, -e, *adj.,* (bot.) procumbent.

proconsul, *n.m.,* (Roman hist.) proconsul.

proconsulaire, *adj.,* (Roman hist.) proconsular.

proconsulat, *n.m.,* (Roman hist.) proconsulship.

procréateur, *adj.,* procreative, procreating.

procréation, *n.f.,* procreation.

procréer, *v.a.,* to procreate, to beget.

procurateur, *n.m.,* procurator, proxy.

procuratie (-ci), *n.f.,* procuracy (at Venice); procurator's palace.

procuration, *n.f.,* procuration, power of attorney, letter of attorney, warrant of attorney; proxy (deed).

procuratrice, *n.f.* *V.* **procureur.**

procurer, *v.a.,* to procure, to obtain, to help to, to get. *— une charge à quelqu'un ;* to procure, to obtain, to get, a post for any one.

se **procurer,** *v.r.,* to procure, to obtain, to get for one's self; to be procured, to be obtained, to be procurable. *Se — de l'argent ;* to obtain money. *Ce poisson se procure très-difficilement ;* this sort of fish is hard to get.

procur-eur, *n.m.,* **-atrice,** *n.f.,* proxy. *Agir par —;* to act by proxy.

procureur, *n.m.,* ⊙ solicitor, attorney, procurator. ⊙ *— fiscal ;* (feudalism) lord's attorney; purveyor (of monastic orders). *— général ;* Attorney General. *— du roi, — imperial, — de la république ;* public prosecutor.

procureuse, *n.f.,* procuress; bawd.

prodigalement (-gal-mān), *adv.,* prodigally, extravagantly, lavishly, profusely.

prodigalité, *n.f.,* prodigality, profusion, extravagance, lavishness.

prodige, *n.m.,* prodigy, wonder, marvel.

prodigieusement (-efiz-mān), *adv.,* prodigiously, wonderfully, wondrously, marvelously, stupendously.

prodigieu-x, -se, *adj.,* prodigious, wondrous, wonderful, marvelous, vast, stupendous.

prodigue, *adj.,* prodigal, profuse, lavish, wasteful. *L'enfant —;* the prodigal son.

prodigue, *n.m.f.,* prodigal, spendthrift, squanderer.

prodiguer (-ghé), *v.a.,* to lavish, to waste, to squander away, to be prodigal of, to be lavish of, to throw away. *— sa vie ;* to expose one's life.

se **prodiguer,** *v.r.,* to be lavished, to be thrown away; to expose one's self.

prodrome, *n.m.,* introduction, preface ; (med.) premonitory symptoms.

product-eur, -rice, *adj.,* productive, producing.

producteur, *n.m.,* (polit. econ.) producer.

productibilité, *n.f.,* producibleness.

productible, *adj.,* producible.

producti-f, -ve, *adj.,* productive.

production, *n.f.,* act of producing, production; (jur.) exhibition (of deeds); (jur.) deeds exhibited; (anat.) process, growth.

productivement, *adv.,* productively.

productivité, *n.f.,* productiveness.

produire (produisant, produit), *v.a.,* to produce, to bring forth; to bear, to yield, to be worth; to be productive of, to be the cause of; to breed, to generate, to show, to exhibit, to adduce ; to make known. *— des titres ;* to show title-deeds. *— des témoins ;* to bring forward witnesses. *Cette charge produit dix mille francs par an ;* this office, or post, is worth four hundred a year. *La guerre produit de grands maux ;* war is productive of, *or* begets, great evils. *— un jeune homme dans le monde ;* to introduce a young man into society ; to bring out, *or* make known, a young man.

se **produire,** *v.r.,* to introduce one's self, to put one's self forward, to make one's way; to be produced, *or* brought forth; to occur, to happen, to manifest itself.

produire, *v.n.,* (jur.) to deliver particulars, to show title-deeds.

produit, *n.m.,* produce, product, yield ; production, exhibit; (arith. geom.) product, proceeds. *Il vit du — de sa terre ;* he lives on the produce of his land. *—s agricoles ;* agricultural produce. *— chimique ;* chemical product. *— net ;* (com.) net proceeds.

proème, *n.m.,* proem, preface, prelude, introduction.

proéminence, *n.f.,* prominence, protuberance, projection.

proéminent, -e, *adj.,* prominent, protuberant.

profanateur, *n m.,* profaner.

profanation, *n.f.,* profanation.

profane, *adj.,* profane, secular, unworthy.

profane, *n.m.f.,* profane person, unlearned person; outsider, black sheep; the vulgar herd.

profaner, *v.a.,* to profane, to defile, to pollute ; to desecrate. *C'est — le talent que de faire cela ;* it is a profanation of talent to do that.

proférer, *v.a.,* to utter, to speak; to pronounce. *Se —;* to be uttered.

prof-ès, -esse, *n.* and *adj.,* professed friar; professed nun ; professed.

professer, *v.a.,* to profess, to make a profession of ; to exercise, to practice, to teach, to be a professor of, to lecture on. *— le plus grand respect pour quelqu'un ;* to profess the greatest respect for any one. *— une science ;* to teach a science. *— un métier ;* to practise a trade, to exercise a calling.

professer, *v.a.* and *n.,* to be a professor, to be a lecturer; to lecture, to teach.

professeur, *n.m.,* professor; teacher ; lecturer ; practicer (of an art or calling). *Chaire de —;* professorship. *— en droit ;* professor of law.

profession, *n.f.,* profession, declaration; profession (occupation), calling ; trade, business. *Il fait — de bel esprit ;* he sets up for a wit. *De quelle — est-il ?* what is his profession ? *Dévot de —;* professed bigot.

professionnel, -le, *adj.,* professional.

ex **professo,** *adv.,* ex professo ; thoroughly ; in a professional manner.

professoral, -e, *adj.,* professorial.

professorat, *n.m.,* professorship, lectureship; teaching.

profil, *n.m.,* profile, side face; side-view ; section, outline ; (drawing) section. *Un visage de —;* a face in profile.

profiler, *v.a.,* to profile ; to represent in profile, to show in profile. *Se —;* to appear in profile ; to stand out.

profit, *n.m.,* profit, gain, emolument, benefit, utility ; improvement, progress ; use. *Au — de ;* for the benefit of, for the use of, in support of, in aid of. *— net ;* clear profit. *Il ne m'en revient aucun —;* I get nothing by it. *Mettre tout à —;* to turn everything to the best advantage ; to turn everything to account. *Faire son — de ;* to make a profit by ; to make the best of, to avail one's self of. *Tirer du — de;* to profit by. *—s éventuels;* perquisites.

profitable, *adj.,* profitable; advantageous.

profiter, *v.n.,* to profit, to gain; to benefit, to avail one's self; to improve. *— sur des marchandises;* to profit by goods. *Faire — son argent;* to lay out one's money advantageously. *— des bons avis;* to profit by good advice. *— de l'occasion;* to avail one's self of, to improve, the opportunity. *Les biens mal acquis ne profitent point;* ill gotten goods never go far, *or* never serve. *— en sagesse;* to improve in wisdom. *C'est un terrain où rien ne profite;* it is a soil where nothing thrives.

profond, -e, *adj.,* deep, profound; wide, vast, extensive; sound; downright, consummate; heavy (of sighs); dark (of the night). *Un — sommeil;* a sound sleep. *—e révérence;* low bow, low courtesy. *Science —e;* profound learning. *Puits —;* deep well. *Un savant —;* a profound scholar. *Un — penseur;* a profound thinker. *Un — scélérat;* a consummate villain. *Nuit —e;* dark night, pitch dark.

profond, *n.m.,* depth, abyss.

profondément, *adv.,* deep, deeply, profoundly, widely, greatly, soundly, fast. *Saluer —;* to bow low. *Dormir —;* to sleep soundly.

profondeur, *n.f.,* depth; profoundness, profundity; penetration; extent.

profus, -e, *adj.,* profuse.

profusément, *adv.,* profusely.

profusion, *n.f.,* profusion, profuseness. *Donner avec —;* to give profusely, lavishly. *A —;* in profusion.

Ⓖ**progéniture,** *n.f.,* (jest.) progeny, offspring.

prognathe, *adj.,* (ethnology) prognathous.

prognathisme, *n.m.,* (ethnology) the being prognathous.

prognostic, *n.m.* *V.* **pronostic.**

prognostique, *adj.,* (med.) prognostic.

programme, *n.m.,* programme, bill, list, syllabus. *— de spectacle;* play-bill.

progrès, *n.m.,* progress; course, advancement, improvement, proficiency, furtherance, rise. *— d'une maladie;* progress of a disease. *Il a fait de grands —s;* he has greatly improved, he has made great progress.

progresser, *v.n.,* to progress, to improve.

progressi-f, -ve, *adj.,* progressive.

progression. *n.f.,* progression.

progressiste, *n.m.,* progressist, liberal, radical.

progressivement (-siv-măn), *adv.,* progressively, by degrees.

prohiber, *v.a.,* to forbid, to interdict, to prohibit.

prohibiti-f, -ve, *adj.,* prohibitive, prohibitory.

prohibition, *n.f.,* prohibition, interdiction.

prohibitionniste, *n.m.,* (com.) prohibitionist.

proie, *n.f.,* prey, prize, booty. *Oiseaux de —;* birds of prey. *Etre en — à la douleur;* to be a prey to grief. *Etre ardent à la —;* to be eager after booty. *Partager la —;* to divide the spoil. *Etre en — à ses valets;* to be pilfered by one's own servants.

projectile, *n.m.* and *adj.,* projectile.

projection, *n.f.,* projection.

projecture, *n.f.,* (arch.) projecture, projection.

projet, *n.m.,* project, scheme, design, plan, contemplation, idea, first sketch; rough draft. *Former,* or *concevoir, un —;* to form, *or* to contrive, a scheme. *Homme à —s;* schemer.

projeter (proj-té), *v.a.,* to project, to plan, to contrive, to scheme; to contemplate, to intend; to project, to throw out, to cast forward; to project, to delineate. *— d'aller à la campagne;* to contemplate going into the country. *La terre projette son ombre;* the earth throws forward its shadow.

se **projeter,** *v.r.,* to project, to jut out, to shoot out, to be prominent, to stand out.

projeter, *v.n.,* to form projects.

projeteu-r, *n.m.,* **-se,** *n.f.,* projector, person full of projects; schemer.

prolapsus, *n.m.,* (med.) prolapsus, prolapse. *— de la luette;* prolapse of the uvula.

prolégomènes, *n.m.pl.,* prolegomena (prefatory matter).

prolepse, *n.f.,* (rhet.) prolepsis.

proleptique, *adj.,* (med.) proleptic, proleptical.

prolétaire, *n.m.* and *adj.,* proletary; proletarian.

prolétariat, *n.m.,* proletariat, pauperism.

prolifère, *adj.,* (bot.) proliferous.

prolifique, *adj.,* prolific.

prolixe, *adj.,* prolix, tedious, diffuse, verbose.

prolixement, *adv.,* prolixly, diffusely.

prolixité, *n.f.,* prolixity, diffuseness.

prologue (-log), *n.m.,* prologue.

prolongation, *n.f.,* prolongation, protraction, delay.

prolonge, *n.f.,* (artil.) binding rope, lashing; (artil.) small ammunition-wagon.

prolongement (-lonj-măn), *n.m.,* prolongation, continuation, extension.

prolonger, *v.a.,* to prolong, to lengthen, to continue, to extend, to protract, to lengthen out, to draw out; (geom.) to produce; (nav.) to bring alongside; to sail along. *— un trève;* to prolong a truce. *— un quai;* to prolong a quay. *— le temps;* to spin out the time. *— le terme d'un payement;* to extend the time for payment.

se **prolonger,** *v.r.,* to be prolonged; to extend, to be continued. *Les débats se sont prolongés fort avant dans la nuit;* the debate was continued far into the night.

promenade (pro-mnad), *n.f.,* walking, walk; airing; walk, promenade (place); ambulatory, drive, excursion, pleasure-trip. *— à pied;* walk. *— à cheval;* ride (on horseback). *— en voiture;* drive, airing. *— en bateau;* row, sail. *Faire une —;* to take a walk, to go for a walk. *Faire une — en voiture;* to take a drive, to go for a drive. *La — est belle aujourd'hui;* it is beautiful weather for a walk. *C'était une vraie —;* it was a real pleasure-trip.

se **promener** (pro-mné), *v.r.,* to walk, to take a walk, to go for a walk, to promenade; to wander, to ramble. *Se — à cheval;* to ride, to take a ride, to go out riding. *Se — en voiture;* to take a drive, to drive out. *Se — sur l'eau;* to go on the water; to go for a row; to go for a sail. *Du haut de Montmartre la vue se promène sur toute la ville de Paris;* from the top of Montmartre the eye wanders over all the city of Paris. *Envoyer quelqu'un se —;* to send any one packing, *or* about his business. *Qu'il aille se —;* let him go to Bath. *Allez vous —;* go about your business. *En se promenant;* slowly; leisurely.

promener, *v.a.,* to take out for a walk, to take out walking; to take, to take out, for an airing, for a drive; to take, to take out, for a ride; to take out (animal); to turn (one's eyes, looks); to run one's eyes over; to scan, to survey; to lead about, to take about. *— sa vue sur une assemblée;* to survey an assembly. *— quelqu'un;* to bandy any one about.

promeneu-r, *n.m.,* **-se,** *n.f.,* walker, pedestrian; rider, person taking a ride; person taking a drive; (fig.) humbug.

promenoir, *n.m.,* walk, place for walking; covered walk or gallery.

promesse, *n.f.,* promise, word; promissory note, note of hand. *Tenir sa —;* to keep one's promise. *Satisfaire à sa —;* to be as good as one's word. *Vendre avec — de garantir;* to warrant the quality of one's goods.

promettant, *n.m.,* (jur.) promisor, obligor.

prometteu-r, *n.m.,* **-se,** *n.f.,* promiser.

promettre, *v.a.*, to promise, to forebode. *Il m'a promis de venir;* he promised me that he would come. — *et tenir sont deux;* it is one thing to promise, another to perform. *Voilà un temps qui promet un orage;* this weather forebodes a storm.

se promettre, *v.r.*, to promise one's self; to purpose, to resolve, to intend; to expect, to hope, to promise each other; to be promised.

promettre, *v.n.*, to promise, to be promising, to bid fair. *Ce jeune homme promet beaucoup;* that is a very promising young man.

prominence, *n.f.*, prominence.

prominent, -e, *adj.*, prominent.

prominer, *v.n.*, to rise above; to be prominent.

promis, -e, *part.,* promised, intended, engaged. *La terre —e;* the promised land. *Chose —e, chose due;* promises should be kept. *Un —, n.,* an intended, a lover.

promiscuité, *n.f.*, promiscuousness.

promission, *n.f.*, (Bib.) promise. *La terre de —;* the land of promise.

promontoire, *n.m.*, (geog.) promontory, headland.

promoteur, *n.m.*, promoter. *adj.*, promoting, inducing.

promotion, *n.f.*, promotion, preferment.

promouvoir, *v.a.*, to promote, to prefer, to raise, to advance.

prompt, -e (prŏn, prŏnt), *adj.*, prompt, quick, active, ready; sudden, speedy, swift; hasty, passionate. *—e réponse;* quick answer. *Il a la repartie —e;* he is quick at repartee. *Il est à servir ses amis;* he is ever ready to serve his friends. *Avoir l'esprit —;* to have a quick understanding, to be very sharp.

promptement (prŏn-tmän), *adv.*, promptly, quickly, readily, suddenly, speedily, swiftly; hastily, passionately.

promptitude (prŏn-ti-tud), *n.f.*, promptitude, speed, speediness; quickness, readiness, suddenness, swiftness; hastiness, passion.

promulgation, *n.f.*, promulgation.

promulguer (-ghé), *v.a.*, to promulgate. *Se —;* to be promulgated.

pronaos, *n.m.*, (—) (arch., antiq.) pronaos.

pronateur, *n.* and *adj.m.*, (anat.) pronator.

pronation, *n.f.*, (anat.) pronation.

prône, *n.m.*, (c.rel.) sermon (after or before mass); lecture, rebuke, sermon.

prôner, *v.a.*, to cry up, to extol, to preach up, to commend, to praise, to set forth; to preach to, to lecture; to sermonize; (l.u.) to preach.

prôner, *v.n.*, to lecture, to remonstrate.

prôneur, *n.m.*, (l.u.) preacher.

prôneu-r, *n.m.*, **-se**, *n.f.*, puffer, trumpeter; lecturer, preacher, rebuker.

pronom (-non), *n.m.*, (gram.) pronoun.

pronominal, -e, *adj.*, pronominal.

pronominalement (-nal-män), *adv.*, (gram.) pronominally.

prononçable, *adj.*, pronounceable.

prononcé, *n.m.*, (jur.) judgment delivered, sentence, decree.

prononcé, -e, *adj.*, pronounced, decided, decisive, marked; (paint., sculpt.) prominent. *Les muscles en sont bien —s;* the muscles are very prominent. *Caractère —;* decided character. *Goût —;* decided taste. *Fortement —;* strongly marked.

prononcer, *v.a.*, to pronounce, to articulate, to utter, to say, to speak, to give utterance to; to give; to deliver; to make; to declare; (jur.) to find, to give in; (paint.) to delineate strongly, to bring out, to give prominence to. *— un discours;* to deliver a discourse, to make a speech. *— une sentence;* (jur.) to pass sentence.

se prononcer, *v.r.*, to pronounce one's self, to

declare one's self, to speak out, to express one's sentiments; to show one's self, to manifest one's self; to be pronounced; to be marked; to become evident.

prononcer, *v.n.*, to pronounce; to declare one's sentiment, to decide with authority.

prononciation, *n.f.*, pronunciation; utterance, delivering, delivery. — *d'une sentence;* passing sentence. — *nette, distincte;* clear, distinct pronunciation. — *vicieuse, locale;* vicious, local pronunciation. *Il a la — belle;* he has a fine utterance, or delivery.

pronostic, *n.m.*, prognostic, prognostication; (med.) prognostic, prognosis.

pronostiquer, *v.a.*, to prognosticate.

pronostiqueur, *n.m.*, prognosticator.

propagande, *n.f.*, propaganda.

propagandiste, *n.m.*, propagandist.

propagateur, *n. m.*, propagator, **spreader**. *adj.*, propagating, spreading.

propagation, *n.f.*, propagation, spread, spreading, diffusion. *La — d'une maladie;* the spread of a disease. *La — des connaissances;* the diffusion of knowledge.

propager, *v.a.*, to propagate, to spread, to spread abroad, to diffuse.

se propager, *v.r.*, to be propagated, to be diffused, to be spread abroad; to propagate, to spread.

propension, *n.f.*, propensity, tendency, inclination, bent, disposition.

prophète, *n.m.*, prophet, seer. *Personne n'est — dans son pays;* no man is a prophet in his own country.

prophétesse, *n.f.*, prophetess.

prophétie (-cî), *n.f.*, prophecy, prophesying.

prophétique, *adj.*, prophetic, prophetical.

prophétiquement (-tik-män), *adv.*, prophetically.

prophétiser, *v.a.*, to prophesy, to foretell.

prophylactique, *adj.*, (med.) prophylactical, prophylactic.

prophylactique *or* **prophylaxie**, *n.f.*, (med.) the science of prophylactic medicine.

propice, *adj.*, propitious, favorable, kind. *Le ciel soit — à ses vœux;* heaven favor his wishes. *Rendre —;* to render propitious, to propitiate.

propitiation, *n.f.*, propitiation.

propitiatoire, *n. m.* and *adj.*, propitiatory, mercy-seat; propitiatory.

propitier, *v.a.*, to propitiate.

propolis (-lis), *n.f.*, propolis.

proportion, *n.f.*, proportion, relation, ratio, due share; suitableness. — *gardée;* in proportion. *A —;* proportionable, proportional, proportionably, proportionately, proportionally. *A de —;* in proportion to.

proportionnalité, *n.f.*, proportionality, proportionateness.

proportionné, -e, *adj.*, proportioned; suited.

proportionnel, -le, *adj.*, proportional.

proportionnelle, *n.f.*, (math.) proportional.

proportionnellement (-nèl-män), *adv.*, proportionably, proportionately.

proportionnément, *adv.*, proportionally, proportionately, in proportion to.

proportionner, *v.a.*, to proportion, to adjust, to fit, to accommodate, to adapt, *or* to adjust; to suit. — *sa dépense à son revenu;* to suit one's expenditure to one's revenue, to cut one's cloth according to one's measure.

se proportionner, *v.r.*, to be proportioned; to proportion one's self, to suit one's self.

propos, *n.m.*, discourse, talk, words; purpose, resolution, design. *pl.*, idle remarks, tittle-tattle, talk. *Changeons de —;* let us talk of something else. — *de table;* table-talk. — *interrompu;* desultory talk. *Je me moque des —;* what do I care for people's tattle! *Jeter des — d'accommodement;* to hint at reconciliation. *A —, adj.*, seasonable, proper, fit, to the purpose,

A —, adv., seasonably, opportunely, pertinently, by the way, talking of that, now I come to think of it. *Venir fort à —;* to come in the nick of time. *Elle fait chaque chose à —;* she does everything at the proper time. *Mal à —;* ill-timed, unseasonable, unseasonably. *Hors de —;* unseasonably; not to the purpose, impertinent, impertinently. *A —, j'ai oublié de vous dire l'autre jour;* now I think of it, I forgot to tell you the other day. *Il s'est fâché à — de rien;* he got angry for nothing at all. *Il est venu me quereller à — de bottes;* he came to quarrel with me for no earthly reason. *A quel — ?* what about? *A — de quoi ?* for what reason? why? *A tout —;* at every turn, ever and anon. *A — de;* with respect to. *A —, n.,* fitness, expediency, appositeness, pertinence; design. *L'à — fait le mérite;* seasonableness gives everything its price. *De — délibéré;* of set purpose. *Juger à —;* to think proper. *Il est à — de;* it is expedient to.

proposable, *adj.,* that can be proposed, proposable.

proposant, *n.m.,* (French protestant) student in divinity.

proposant, *adj.m.,* (c.rel.) proposing.

proposer, *v.a.,* to propose, to offer, to propound, to move, to make a motion; to designate, to set up, to state, to move. *— un sujet à traiter;* to propose a subject for writing upon. *— une question;* to propound a question. *— quelqu'un pour exemple;* to set up anybody as a pattern.

se **proposer,** *v.r.,* to propose one's self, to offer one's self; to be proposed, to be offered; to propose, to purpose, to intend, to have in view.

proposer, *v.n.,* to propose. *L'homme propose et Dieu dispose;* man proposes and God disposes.

proposeur, *n.m.,* proposer, propounder.

proposition, *n.f.,* proposition; motion; proposal, offer. *Pain de —;* show-bread *or* shewbread. *Faire des —s à quelqu'un;* to make proposals to any one.

propre, *adj.,* own; very, same, self-same, very same; adapted, appropriate, calculated, fit, fitted; qualified, proper, suitable; clean; neat, tidy; nice; accurate, right, correct. *C'est son — fils;* it is his own son. *En main —;* in one's own hands. *Amour —, (—s—s)* self-love, conceit. *Nom —;* proper name. *Ce sont ses —s paroles;* they are his very words. *Termes —s;* proper, *or* correct, expressions. *Il est — à tout;* he is fit for anything. *Le mot —;* the proper *or* right word. *Il est toujours fort —;* he is always very neat. *Avoir une écriture —;* to write a neat hand.

propre, *n.m.,* characteristic, attribute; peculiar quality, property, part; (gram.) proper sense, literal sense; (jur.) real estate, real property; (c.rel.) particular prayers. *Le — des oiseaux est de voler;* it is in the nature of birds to fly. *Avoir en —;* to own. *N'avoir rien en —;* to have no property. *Posséder en —;* to possess in one's own right. *Le — et le figuré;* the literal and figurative sense. *Prendre un mot au —;* to use a word in its literal sense. *C'est du — !* what a dirty action! what a nasty thing!

proprement, *adv.,* properly, correctly, rightly; literally; cleanly; neatly, tidily. *— dit;* properly called, properly so called. *A — parler;* properly speaking. *S'habiller —;* to dress neatly.

propret, -te, *adj.,* spruce, neat, tidy, natty.

propreté, *n.f.,* cleanness, cleanliness; spruceness, neatness, niceness.

propréteur, *n.m.,* (Roman hist.) propretor.

propriétaire, *n.m.f.,* owner; proprietor; proprietress; landlord; landlady; freeholder, esquire, man of independent means. *Nu —;* (jur.) owner without the usufruct of his property.

propriété, *n.f.,* property; ownership; estate; peculiar quality, essential faculty; propriety, correctness (of words, terms). *pl.,* lands, estates. *— littéraire;* copyright. *Nue —;* (jur.) property without the usufruct of it, reversionary interest. *Doter quelqu'un d'une —;* to settle an estate upon any one. *Violer la —;* to trespass.

propulser, *v.a.,* to propel.

propulseur, *n.m.,* (tech.) propeller. *— à hélice;* screw-propeller.

propulsion, *n.f.,* propulsion.

propylée, *n.m.pl.,* (arch.) propylæum.

prorata, *n.m.,* proportion. *Au — de;* pro rata, in proportion.

prorogati-f, -ve, *adj.,* prorogative.

prorogation, *n.f.,* prolongation; adjournment; prorogation (of parliament).

proroger, *v.a.,* to prolong time, to protract, to adjourn, to delay; to prorogue (parliament).

prosaïque, *adj.,* prosaic, prosy; dull, tedious, matter of fact.

prosaïquement, *adv.,* prosaically, dully, unpoetically, tediously, coldly.

prosaïser, *v.n.,* to write prose, to vulgarize.

prosaïsme, *n.m.,* prosaism; (fig.) prosiness, dullness, monotony, vulgarity. *Le — de la vie;* the monotony of life.

prosateur, *n.m.,* prose-writer, prosaist.

proscénium (-sé-ni-om), *n.m.,* (antiq.) proscenium.

proscripteur, *n.m.,* proscriber, banisher.

proscription, *n.f.,* proscription, outlawry.

proscrire, *v.a.,* (proscrivant, proscrit), to proscribe, to outlaw; to expel, to banish; to taboo. *Se —;* to be proscribed, to proscribe each other.

proscrit, *n.m., -e, n.f.,* proscribed person, exile, outlaw, refugee, outcast. *Figure de —;* disagreeable face, displeasing face.

prose, *n.f.,* prose; (c.rel.) prose. *Mettre en —;* to turn into prose.

prosecteur, *n.m.,* (anat.) prosector.

prosélyte, *n.m.f.,* proselyte.

prosélytisme, *n.m.,* proselytism.

prosodie, *n.f.,* (gram.) prosody.

prosodique, *adj.,* prosodial, prosodical.

prosopopée, *n.f.,* (rhet.) prosopopœia.

prospectus (-tus), *n.m.,* prospectus; handbill.

prospère, *adj.,* prosperous, thriving; propitious, favorable.

prospérer, *v.n.,* to prosper, to be prosperous, to be successful, to thrive, to speed.

prospérité, *n.f.,* prosperity, success, well-being. *Quel visage de — !* what a happy, cheerful face! how well you look!

prostate, *n.f.,* (anat.) prostate, prostate gland.

prostatique, *adj.,* (anat.) prostatic.

prosternation, *n.f.,* prostration, obeisance.

prosternement, *n.m.,* prostration.

prosterner, *v.a.,* to prostrate.

se **prosterner,** *v.r.,* to prostrate one's self, to fall down, to bow one's head; to bow low.

prosthèse, *n.f.,* (gram.) prosthesis; (surg. l.u.) prosthesis. *V.* **prothèse.**

prostituée, *n.f.,* prostitute.

prostituer, *v.a.,* to prostitute.

se **prostituer,** *v.r.,* to prostitute one's self.

prostitution, *n.f.,* prostitution.

prostration, *n.f.,* prostration.

prostyle, *n.m.* and *adj.,* (arch.) prostyle.

protagoniste, *n.m.,* (theat.) principal character, protagonist.

protase, *n.f.,* protasis.

protatique, *adj.,* protatic.

prote, *n.m.,* (print.) overseer; (iron.) reader.

protect-eur, -rice, *n.* and *adj.,* protector, protectress, patron, patroness, patronizer, fosterer; protective, patronizing, fostering. *Société —rice des animaux;* society for the prevention of cruelty to animals.

protection, *n.f.*, protection, defense; support, patronage, influence, favor, countenance; (nav.) shelter, cover.

protectionniste, *n.m. and adj.*, (com.) protectionist.

protectorat, *n.m.*, protectorate, protectorship.

protée, *n.m.*, Proteus.

protégé, *n.m.*, -e, *n.f.*, favorite, dependant; protégé; protégée.

protéger, *v.a.*, to protect, to defend, to shield, to shelter; to patronize, to countenance, to favor. — *contre le mal;* to shield from harm.

protestant, -e, *n. and adj.*, Protestant.

protestantisme, *n.m.*, Protestantism.

protestation, *n.f.*, protestation, protest. *d'amitié;* profession of friendship. *Faire insérer une — dans le procès-verbal;* to enter a protest.

protester, *v.a.*, to protest; to vow. *Je vous le proteste sur mon honneur;* I swear to you on my honor. — *une lettre de change;* to protest a bill of exchange. *Se —;* to be protested.

protester, *v.n.*, to protest. — *de nullité;* to protest against the validity of a deed.

protêt, *n.m.*, (com.) protest. — *faute de payement;* protest for non-payment. *Faire signifier un —;* to give notice of a protest.

prothèse, *n.f.*, (surg.) prothesis. — *dentaire;* setting of artificial teeth.

proto, a prefix from Gr. πρῶτος.

protocarbure, *n.m.*, (chem.) carburet.

protochlorure, *n.m.*, (chem.) protochloride.

protocole, *n.m.*, protocol; formulary, preamble.

protonotaire, *n.m.*, protonotary.

prototype, *n.m.*, prototype, model.

protoxyde, *n.m.*, (chem.) protoxide.

protubérance, *n.f.*, (anat.) protuberance.

protubérant, *adj.*, protuberant.

protuteur, *n.m.*, (jur.) person acting as guardian.

⊙**prou**, *adv.*, enough, much. *Ni peu ni —;* neither little nor much. *Peu ou —;* little or much.

proue, *n.f.*, (nav. and poetic) prow, stem.

prouesse, *n.f.*, prowess, valor; performance; (iron.) feat of valor.

prouvable, *adj.*, provable.

prouver, *v.a.*, to prove, to show; to make good, to substantiate; to be a proof of, to give proof of, to verify.

provéditeur, *n.m.*, (Ital.) proveditore.

provenance (pro-vnâns), *n.f.*, (com.) production, origin, source, growth; produce, goods. *En —;* proceeding, coming (from).

provenant, -e (pro-vnan, -t), *adj.*, proceeding, accruing, arising.

provençal, -e, *n. and adj.*, Provençal.

provende, *n.f.*, (l.u.) provision; (agri.) provender, provisions, victuals.

provenir (pro-vnir), *v.n.*, to spring, to accrue, to issue, to proceed, to result (from); to come, to arise (from).

proverbe, *n.m.*, proverb, saying. *Devenir —, passer en —;* to become a proverb, to become proverbial.

proverbial, -e, *adj.*, proverbial.

proverbialement (-al-mân), *adv.*, proverbially.

providence, *n.f.*, Providence (of God).

providentiel, -le, *adj.*, providential.

*****provignement**, *n.m.*, layering of vines; (of words) pruning (Ronsard).

*****provigner**, *v.a.*, to layer vines.

*****provigner**, *v.n.*, (agri.) to increase; ⊙to multiply, to increase.

provin, *n.m.*, layer (of a vine).

province, *n.f.*, province, shire, county. *Les gens de —;* country people. *En —;* in the country, in the provinces. *Il a encore l'air de —;* he has still a countrified air.

provincial, *n.m.*, provincial, country person; superior of a monastic fraternity.

provincial, -e, *n. and adj.*, provincial, country, country-like. *Manières —es;* country manners.

provincialat, *n.m.*, provincialship (of convents).

provincialisme, *n.m.*, (gram.) provincialism.

proviseur, *n.m.*, head-master, principal of a (government) college.

provision, *n.f.*, provision, stock, store, supply; (fam.) hoard; (com.) stock on hand; provisional maintenance. *Par —;* provisionally, in the mean time. *Faire ses —s;* to provide one's self with necessaries. *Faire sa — de bois, de charbon;* to take in, to lay in, one's stock of wood, of coal, of fuel. *—s de bouche;* provisions. *—s de guerre;* ammunition. *Aller à la —;* to go marketing. *Faire — de;* to get in a supply of. *Faire la — d'une lettre de change;* (com.) to provide for a bill of exchange.

provisionnel, -le, *adj.*, provisional.

provisionnellement (-nèl-mân), *adv.*, provisionally.

provisoire, *n.m.*, provisional state.

provisoire, *adj.*, provisional, temporary.

provisoirement (-zoar-mân), *adv.*, provisionally, temporarily; in the mean time.

provisorat, *n.m.*, head-mastership, principalship.

provocant, *adj.*, provoking, provocative; exciting, defiant, instigating.

provocat-eur, -rice, *n. and adj.*, provoker; instigator, abettor, aggressor; provoking, instigating, abetting. *Agent —;* hired plotter, hireling.

provocation, *n.f.*, provocation, instigation. — *en duel;* challenge to fight.

provoquer, *v.a.*, to provoke, to incense, to call forth, to promote; to instigate; to challenge. — *des applaudissements;* to call forth applause. — *en duel;* to challenge. — *au sommeil;* to invite to sleep.

proxénète, *n.m.*, (com.) ⊙ broker; pimp, pander; go-between.

proximité, *n.f.*, proximity, nearness, near relationship. *Le théâtre est à sa —;* the theater is in his neighborhood. *Il y a — de sang entre vous et moi;* you and I are nearly related by the ties of blood. *A — de;* within a short distance of, in the neighborhood of.

proyer, *n.m.*, (orni.) common bunting.

prrr! *int.*, not I! not a bit of it! don't you wish you may get it! whistle for it!

prude, *n.f. and adj.*, prude; prudish.

prudemment (-da-mân), *adv.*, prudently, discreetly, wisely, cautiously.

prudence, *n.f.*, prudence; discretion.

prudent, -e, *adj.*, prudent, cautious, discreet.

pruderie (pru-drî), *n.f.*, prudery.

⊙**prud'homie**, *n.f.*, uprightness, integrity, probity; (com.) trade-arbitration.

prud'homme, *n.m.*, skillful or able person (in an art or trade); expert; ⊙ upright, honest man. *Conseil des —s;* council of experts.

pruine, *n.f.*, bloom (of fruits).

pruiné, *adj.*, covered with bloom (of fruits).

prune, *n.f.*, plum. — *de Brignoles;* prunello. — *de Monsieur;* Orleans plum. — *sauvage;* skeg. — *de mirabelle;* mirabelle plum. — *de reine-Claude;* greengage. — *de Damas;* damson. *Couleur —;* violet color. *Ce n'est pas pour des —s;* (fig.) it is not for nothing.

pruneau, *n.m.*, prune, dried plum; French plum.

prunelaie (pru-n-lè), *n.f.*, plum-orchard.

prunelle, *n.f.*, (bot.) sloe, bullace; (woolen stuff) prunella, prunello; (anat.) pupil, apple (of the eye), eye-ball. *Jouer de la —;* to cast sheep's eyes, to ogle, to leer.

prunellier, n.m., (bot.) sloe-tree, bullace-tree.

prunier, n.m., (bot.) plum-tree.

prurigineu-x, -se, adj., (med.) pruriginous.

prurit, n.m., (med.) prurience, pruriency, pruritus, itching.

prusse, n.f. Pour le roi de —; to no purpose, in vain, for nothing.

prussiate, n.m., (chem.) prussiate.

prussien, -ne (-in, -è-n), n. and adj., Prussian.

prussique, adj., (chem.) prussic. Acide —; prussic acid.

prytane, n.m., (Grec. antiq.) prytanis. pl., prytanes.

prytanée, n.m., (Grec. antiq.) prytaneum.

p.s., initial letters of postscriptum, P.S., postscript.

psalmiste, n.m., psalmist.

psalmodie, n.f., psalmody; sing-song.

psalmodier, v.n. and a., to recite, to chant, psalms; to read, to recite in a sing-song manner.

psaltérion, n.m., (mus.) psaltery.

psammite, n.m., (min.) psammite, graywacke or greywacke.

psaume, n.m., psalm.

psautier (-tié), n.m., psalter, psalm-book; (c. rel.) chaplet of 150 beads; nun's veil.

pseudo, a prefix from Gr. ψεῦδος.

pseudonyme, adj., pseudonymous; under an assumed name. n.m., pseudonym, nom de plume; alias.

psora or **psore**, n.f., (med.) psora, itch.

psorique, adj., (med.) psoric, itchy.

psyché, n.f., (myth.) Psyche; Psyche-glass, cheval-glass.

psychique, adj., psychical.

psychologie (-ko-), n.f., psychology.

psychologique (-ko-), adj., psychologic, psychological.

psychologiste or **psychologue** (-ko-), n.m., psychologist.

psylle, n.m., snake-charmer.

ptérodactyle, n.m., (foss.) pterodactyl.

ptyalisme, n.m., (med.) ptyalism.

puamment (pu-a-măn), adv., stinkingly; grossly, impudently; (fig., fam.) impudently, in a barefaced manner.

puant, -e, adj., stinking; impudent, barefaced. Devenir —; to begin to stink. Mensonge —, impudent lie. — menteur; impudent liar.

puant, n.m., (pop.) stinkard.

puanteur, n.f., stink, stench, offensive smell.

pubère, adj., pubescent, of puberty.

puberté, n.f., puberty.

pubescence, n.f., (bot.) pubescence, down.

pubescent, -e, adj., (bot.) pubescent, downy.

pubien, -ne (-in, -è-n), adj., (anat.) pubic.

pubis, n.m. and adj., (anat.) of pubis; pubic. Os —; os pubis, pubic bone, share-bone; pubes.

publi-c, -que, adj., public; notorious. Rendre —; to make public, to publish; (of women) on the town, loose, fast. La chose — que; the common weal. La partie — que; the crown, the public prosecutor.

public, n.m., public. En —; publicly.

publicain, n.m., (Rom. antiq.) publican; (fig.) extortioner.

publicateur, n.m., (jur.) publisher.

publication, n.f., publication; publishing, proclamation.

publiciste, n.m., publicist.

publicité, n.f., publicity, notoriety; advertising, advertisements.

publier, v.a., to publish, to make public, to proclaim, to celebrate, to trumpet forth, to bring out, to issue. — quelque chose sur les toits; to proclaim anything from the house-tops, to trumpet forth anything. — une ordonnance; to issue an ordonnance.

publiquement (-blik-măn), adv., publicly, in public.

puce, n.f., (ent.) flea. Herbe aux —s; fleabane, fleawort. — d'eau; water-beetle. — de mer; psyllus marinus. — de terre; earthpuceron. Avoir la — à l'oreille; to have a flea in one's ear, to be uneasy, anxious. Mettre à quelqu'un la — à l'oreille; to give any one cause for uneasiness.

puce, adj., puce, puce-colored.

puceau, n.m., chaste youth; (iron.) spoony, simpleton.

pucelage (pu-slaj), n.m., (l.ex.) maidenhead, virginity; (mol.) cowry; (bot.) periwinkle.

pucelle, n.f., (fam.) maid, maiden, virgin; (ich.) shad. La — d'Orléans; the maid of Orleans (Joan of Arc).

puceron (pu-sron), n.m., (ent.) plant-louse; green-fly.

puddlage, n.m., (metal.) puddling.

puddler (-dlé), v.a., (metal.) to puddle.

puddleur, n.m., (metal.) puddler.

pudeur, n.f., bashfulness, shame; modesty, decency; discretion, reserve. — virginale; virgin bashfulness.

pudibond, -e, adj., bashful, modest.

pudicité, n.f., modesty, pudicity, chastity.

pudique, adj., chaste, modest, bashful.

pudiquement (-dik-măn), adv., chastely, purely.

puer, v.n. and a., to stink, to have an offensive smell; to smell of; to stink of; to be full of conceit. Il pue le vin; he stinks, or smells, very strong of wine.

puéril, -e, adj., juvenile, boyish; puerile, childish.

puérilement (-ril-măn), adv., puerilely, childishly.

puérilité, n.f., puerility, childishness.

puerpéral, -e, adj., puerperal.

puff (puf, peuf), n.m., exaggerated statement, puff. Faire le —; to puff.

puffin, n.m., (orni.) puffin.

pugilat, n.m., pugilism, boxing.

pugiliste, n.m., pugilist, boxer.

puine, n.m., (forestry) wood of little value. V. mort-bois under **bois**.

puiné, -e, n.m. and adj., younger brother; younger sister; younger.

puis, adv., then, afterwards, after that, next, besides. Et —; and besides, and then. Et — ? what then? what next? well?

puisage, n.m., drawing water, drawing up.

puisard, n.m., cesspool; sink; dip-well; (mining) sump, water-sump.

puisatier, n.m., well-sinker.

puiser, v.a., to draw, to fetch up, to take, to borrow; to imbibe; to let in. — de l'eau à la rivière; to draw water out of the river. — à la source; to go to the fountain-head. — des opinions; to imbibe opinions.

puiser, v.n., to draw, to borrow, to take; (nav.) to make water. C'est un auteur qui puise partout; he is an author who borrows from all quarters.

puisque, conj., since, seeing, seeing that, inasmuch as.

puissamment (-sa-măn), adv., powerfully, forcibly, potently; extremely, very. Il est — riche; he is exceedingly rich.

puissance, n.f., power; dominion, sway, empire; ability, force; faculty; influence; influential man; virtue, quality, property; (mining) thickness (of layers or lodes); (mec.) power; horsepower. Toute—, (n.p.) omnipotence, almighty power. Haute—; high-mightiness (title). Cette femme est en — de mari; that woman is under the control of her husband. Soumettre à sa —; to bring under one's dominion. Traiter de — à —; to treat on equal terms. — motrice; moving power. Les grandes —s; the great powers.

puissant, -e, adj., powerful, potent, mighty;

forcible, strong, lusty, stout, corpulent; wealthy, rich. — *prince;* mighty prince. *Famille —e;* influential family. *Le Tout- —,* (n.p.) the Almighty. *Il est tout- — auprès de lui;* he can get him to do anything.

puits (puï), *n.m.,* well, hole for water; pit, shaft; well-hole (of staircases); (nav.) well-room. *— commun;* public well. *— à pompe;* pump-well. *— à roue; — à poulie;* draw-well. *— arté-sien;* artesian well. *— perdu;* drain-well, blind-well. *— de mine;* shaft of a mine. *— d'aérage;* air-shaft. *— d'abondance;* (fig.) an inexhaustible mine. *C'est un — de science;* he is extremely learned; he is a walking dictionary, a living encyclopædia. *La vérité est au fond d'un —;* truth lies at the bottom of a well (*i.e.,* has to be sought out).

pullulation, *n.f.,* rapid increase, swarming.

pulluler (pul-lu-), *v.n.,* to increase, to multiply, to pullulate, to swarm.

pulmonaire, *adj.,* (anat., med.) pulmonary. *Phthisie —;* pulmonary disease, consumption.

pulmonaire, *n.f.,* (bot.) pulmonaria, pulmonary. *Grande —;* lungwort; sage of Jerusalem, Jerusalem cowslip. *— des Français;* golden lungwort. *— de chêne;* liverwort.

pulmonie, *n.f. V.* **pneumonie.**

pulmonique, *n.m.f. and adj.,* consumptive.

pulpation, *n.f.,* (pharm.) reducing to pulp, pulpation.

pulpe, *n.f.,* pulp; pap. *— cérébrale;* (anat.) cerebral substance.

pulper, *v.a.,* (pharm.) to reduce to pulp.

pulpeu-x, -se, *adj.,* (bot.) pulpous, pulpy.

pulsati-f, -ve, *adj.,* (med.) pulsative, pulsatory.

***pulsatille,** *n.f.,* (bot.) pasque-flower, pulsatilla.

pulsation, *n.f.,* beating of the pulse, pulsation; (phys.) pulse.

pulvérat-eur, -rice, *n. and adj.,* (zoöl.) pulverulent.

pulvérescence, *n.f.,* pulverulence.

pulvérescent, -e, *adj.,* pulverulent.

pulvérin, *n.m.,* priming powder; priming powder-horn; mist, spray (from waterfalls).

pulvérisable, *adj.,* pulverizable.

pulvérisateur, *n.m.,* pulverizer. *adj.,* pulverizing.

pulvérisation, *n.f.,* pulverization.

pulvériser, *v.a.,* to reduce to powder, to grind to dust, to pulverize; to annihilate; to reduce to atoms.

pulvérulent, -e, *adj.,* (bot.) pulverulent; easy to reduce into powder.

puma, *n.m.,* puma, cougar (American lion).

pumicin, *n.m.,* palm-oil.

punais, -e, *adj.,* affected with ozæna.

punaise, *n.f.,* bug; (ent.) bug; B-flat. *Couvain de —s;* nest of bugs.

punaisie, *n.f.,* ozæna.

punch (ponsh), *n.m.,* punch (beverage). *Offrir un — à quelqu'un;* to entertain any one.

punique, *adj.,* punic.

punir, *v.a.,* to punish, to chastise, to avenge. *Puni de mort;* punished with death.

punissable, *adj.,* punishable.

punisseur, *n.m. and adj.,* avenger, punisher; avenging, punishing.

punition, *n.f.,* punishment. *Par —;* as a punishment.

pupillaire (-pil-lèr), *adj.,* pupillary.

pupillarité (-pil-la-), *n.f.,* (jur.l.u.) nonage, minority.

pupille, *n.m.f.,* ward, pupil (under a guardian).

pupille, *n.f.,* pupil, apple of the eye.

pupitre, *n.m.,* desk, writing-desk; reading-desk.

pur, -e, *adj.,* pure, genuine, unadulterated;

unspotted, innocent, chaste, spotless; clean, clear, unmingled, unalloyed; mere, sheer, down-right, neat (of liquor). *Une lumière —e;* a clear light. *Un ciel —;* a clear, cloudless sky. *Etre en état de —e nature;* to be stark naked. *Du vin —;* wine without water, pure wine. *Obligation —e et simple;* unconditional, unqualified, absolute obligation. *C'est la —e vérité;* it is the plain, unvarnished truth. *Par —e bonté;* out of sheer kindness. *—e sottise;* downright nonsense. *Ce fruit est du poison tout —;* that fruit is downright poison. *Félicité —e;* unalloyed happiness. *Une réputation —e;* an untarnished reputation. *Une gloire —e;* unsullied glory. *Un trait —, un dessin —;* (drawing) a clean stroke, a clean drawing. *A — et à plein;* unreservedly, entirely. *En —e perte;* in vain, to no purpo: ..

puraau, *n.m.,* part uncovered (of slates, tiles).

purée, *n.f.,* thick soup; pea-soup; mashed potatoes.

purement (pur-mān), *adv.,* purely, genuinely, merely, only; innocently. *— et simplement;* unconditionally: merely.

pureté (pur-té), *n.f.,* pureness, purity, gentleness, innocence; chastity.

purgati-f, -ve, *adj.,* purgative, purging.

purgatif, *n.m.,* purgative.

purgation, *n.f.,* purgative, purge.

purgatoire, *n.m.,* purgatory.

purge, *n.f.,* ☉purge, cleansing. *— d'hypothèques;* (jur.) paying off of a mortgage.

purger, *v.a.,* to purge, to purge away; to cleanse, to purify, to clear, to refine. *— un malade;* to purge a sick person. *— son bien de dettes;* to clear one's estate of mortgages.

se **purger,** *v.r.,* to purge one's self, to purify one's self.

purifiant, -e, *adj.,* purifying, cleansing.

purificateur, *n.m.,* purificator.

purification, *n.f.,* purification.

purificatoire, *n.m.,* (c.rel) purificatory.

purifier, *v.a.,* to purify, to cleanse; to refine; to try (metal). *— le langage;* to refine the language.

se **purifier,** *v.r.,* to purify one's self, to purify, to refine.

puriforme, *adj.,* (med.) puriform.

purin, *n.m.,* (agri.) liquid manure.

purisme, *n.m.,* purism.

puriste, *n.m.,* purist.

puritain, -e, *n. and adj.,* Puritan.

puritanisme, *n.m.,* Puritanism.

purpurin, -e, *adj.,* purplish.

purpurine, *n.f.,* purple, bronze.

purulence, *n.f.,* purulence, purulency.

purulent, -e, *adj.,* purulent.

pus, *n.m.,* (med.) pus, matter.

pusillanime (-zil-la-), *adj.,* pusillanimous, faint-hearted, chicken-hearted, cowardly.

pusillanimité (-zil-la-), *n.f.,* pusillanimity, faint-heartedness, cowardice.

pustule, *n.f.,* pustule, pimple, blotch, blain; (bot.) blister.

pustulé, -e, *adj.,* (bot.) blistered.

pustuleu-x, -se, *adj.,* pustulous.

putain, *n.f.,* (l.ex.) street-walker, prostitute, strumpet.

putasserie, *n.f.,* whoredom; whoring, wenching.

putassier, *n.m.,* (l.ex.) one who frequents prostitutes, whoremonger.

putati-f, -ve, *adj.,* putative, reputed, supposed.

putativement, *adv.,* reputedly, putatively.

putois, *n.m.,* polecat.

putréfaction, *n.m.,* putrefaction.

putréfait, -e, *adj.,* (l.u.) putrefied.

putréfié, -e, *part.,* putrefied.

putréfier, *v.a.,* to putrefy.

se **putréfier**, *v.r.*, to putrefy.
putrescible, *adj.*, putrefiable.
putride, *adj.*, (med.) putrid.
putridité, *n.f.*, putridity.
pygargue, *n.m.*, erne, sea-eagle.
pygmée, *n.m.*, pygmy, dwarf.
pylône, *n.m.*, (antiq. arch.) porch (of Egyptian temples).
pylore, *n.m.*, (anat.) pylorus.
pyloride, *n.f.*, bivalve shell.
pylorique, *adj.*, (anat.) pyloric.
pyracanthe, *n.f.*, (bot.) pyracanth.
pyrale, *n.f.*, (ent.) pyralis.
pyramidal, **-e**, *adj.*, pyramidal, pyramidic, pyramidical.
pyramidalement (-dal-mān), *adv.*, pyramidally, pyramidically.
pyramide, *n.f.*, pyramid.
pyramider, *v.n.*, to rise like a pyramid ; to tower, to taper.
pyrée, *n.m.*, fire-altar.
pyrèthre, *n.m.*, (bot.) Spanish camomile, feverfew.
pyrétologie, *n.m.*, pyretology.
pyriforme, *adj.* *V.* **piriforme**.
pyrique, *adj.*, pyrotechnic, pyrotechnical.
pyrite, *n.f.*, (min.) pyrites.
pyriteu-x, -se, *adj.*, (min.) pyritic, pyritical.
pyrolâtrie, *n.f.*, the worship of fire, pyrolatry.
****pyroligneux**, *adj.*, pyrolignous.
pyrologie, *n.f.*, pyrology.
pyromancie, *n.f.*, pyromancy.
pyromètre, *n.m.*, pyrometer.
pyrophore, *n.m.*, pyrophorus.
pyroscaphe, *n.m.*, (nav.) steamer, steamboat.
pyrosis, *n.f.*, (med.) pyrosis, water brash.
pyrotechnie (-tèk-), *n.f.*, pyrotechnics, pyrotechny.
pyrotechnique (-tèk-), *adj.*, pyrotechnic, pyrotechnical.
pyroxène, *n.m.*, (min.) pyroxene.
pyrrhique, *adj.*, Pyrrhic.
pyrrhique, *n.m.*, (poet.) Pyrrhic.
pyrrhique, *n.f.*, (antiq.) Pyrrhic (dance).
pyrrhonien, **-ne** (-in, -è-n), *n.* and *adj.*, Pyrrhonist, Pyrrhonean ; Pyrrhonic.
pyrrhonisme, *n.m.*, Pyrrhonism.
pythagoricien, **-ne** (-in, -é-n), *n.* and *adj.*, Pythagorean ; Pythagoric, Pythagorical.
pythagorique, *adj.*, Pythagoric, Pythagorical.
pythagorisme, *n.m.*, Pythagorism.
pythie, *n.f.*, (antiq.) the Pythia (priestess of Apollo).
pythien (-tiin), *adj.*, Pythian.
pythique, *adj.*, Pythian.
pythiques, *n.f.pl.*, Pindarus' odes.
python, *n.m.*, (zool.) python, rock-snake.
pythonisse, *n.f.*, (antiq.) pythoness ; witch.

Q

q, *n.m.*, the seventeenth letter of the alphabet, q.
qu', contraction of *Que*.
quacre, *n.m.* *V.* **quaker**.
quadernes (kooa-dèrn), *n.m.pl.*, two fours (backgammon).
quadragénaire (kooa-), *n.* and *adj.*, person forty years old ; of forty years of age ; of forty.
quadragésimal, **-e** (kooa-), *adj.*, quadragesimal.
quadragésime (kooa-), *n.f.*, Quadragesima (Sunday).
quadrangle (kooa-), *n.m.*, quadrangle.
quadrangulaire (kooa-), *adj.*, quadrangular, four-cornered.
quadrangulé, **-e** (kooa-), *adj.*, quadrangular.
⊙**quadrat**, *adj.* (astrolog.) quadrate. — *aspect ;* quartile. *V.* **quadrature**.

quadrat, *n.m.*, (print.) quadrat. *V.* **cadrat**.
quadrateur, *n.m.*, squarer of the circle.
quadratin, *n.m.*, (print.) M quadrat. *Demi-*— ; (print.) N quadrat. *V.* **cadratin**.
quadratique (kooa-) *adj.*, quadratic.
quadratoriste, *n.m.*, fresco-painter.
quadratrice (kooa-), *n.f.*, (geom.) quadratrix.
quadrature (kooa-), *n.f.*, (astron., geom.) quadrature ; (astrolog.) quartile ; (paint.) fresco-painting.
quadrature, *n.f.*, (horl.) movement, dial-work. *V.* **cadrature**.
quadriailé, *adj.*, four-winged.
quadricapsulaire (kooa-), *adj.*, (bot.) quadricapsular.
quadricorne (kooa-), *adj.*, quadricornous.
quadridenté, **-e** (kooa-), *adj.*, (bot.) quadridentate.
quadriennal. *V.* **quatriennal**.
quadrifide (kooa-), *adj.*, (bot.) quadrifid, four-cleft.
quadrige (kooa-), *n.m.*, (antiq.) quadriga.
quadrijumeaux (kooa-), *adj.m.pl.*, (anat.) quadrigemina. *Tubercules* — ; corpora quadrigemina.
quadrilatéral, *adj.*, quadrilateral.
quadrilatère (kooa-), *n.m.*, (geom.) quadrilateral.
****quadrillage**, *n.m.*, pavement of square stones, flags.
****quadrille**, *n.f.*, troop of horse (in a tournament).
quadrille, *n.m.*, (card game, mus., dancing) quadrille ; check, square, lozenge.
quadrillé, *adj.*, (of cloths) checkered, plaid ; (of paper) ruled both ways, in squares.
quadrillion (kooa-), *n.m.*, a thousand billions.
quadrilobé, **-e** (kooa-), *adj.*, (bot.) quadrilobate.
quadriloculaire (kooa-), *adj.*, (bot.) quadrilocular.
quadrinôme (kooa-), *n.m.*, (alg.) quadrinomial.
quadriparti, **-e** (kooa-), *adj.*, (bot.) quadripartite.
quadripartition (kooa-), *n.f.*, (l.u.) quadripartition.
quadriphylle (kooa-), *adj.*, (bot.) quadriphyllous.
quadrirème (kooa-), *n.m.*, quadrireme.
quadrisyllabe (kooa-dri-sil-lab), *n.m.*, quadrisyllable.
quadrivalve (kooa-), *adj.*, (bot.) quadrivalve, quadrivalvular.
quadrumane (kooa-), *n.m.* and *adj.*, (mam.) quadruman ; quadrumanous.
quadrupède (kooa-), *n.m.* and *adj.*, quadruped ; four-footed ; quadruped.
quadruple (kooa-), *n.m.* and *adj.*, quadruple, fourfold ; (Spanish coin) doubloon.
quadruple, *n.f.*, Spanish gold coin worth 85 francs, about $16.50.
quadrupler (kooa-), *v.a.*, to quadruple, to quadruplicate ; to increase fourfold.
quadrupler, *v.n.*, to be quadrupled ; to increase fourfold.
quai, *n.m.*, quay, wharf. *Droit de* — ; wharfage.
quaiage, *n.m.* *V.* **quayage**.
quaiche, *n.f.*, (nav.) ketch.
quaker *or* **quacre** (kooa-kr), *n.m.*, quaker.
quakeresse (kooa-kres), *n.f.*, quakeress.
quakérisme (kooa-), *n.m.*, quakerism.
qualifiable, *adj.*, that can be called, named, styled, described, termed.
qualificateur, *n.m.*, (c.rel.) qualificator.
qualificati-f, -ve, *adj.*, (gram.) qualifying.
qualificatif, *n.m.*, (gram.) qualificative.
qualification, *n.f.*, title, name ; character, nature, qualification.

qualifié, -e, *part.*, qualified, called, named. *Vol* — ; robbery with aggravated circumstances.

qualifier, *v.a.*, to qualify, to call; to entitle, to style, to name. — *quelqu'un de fourbe ;* to call any one a knave.

se **qualifier,** *v.r.*, to call one's self, to style one's self.

qualité, *n.f.*, quality; property; qualification, accomplishment; title, rank. *Il n'a pas les —s requises pour ce poste ;* he is not qualified to fill that position. *En — de ;* in the capacity of, in the character of, as. *Avoir — pour ;* to be qualified to. *Avoir de la — ;* to be of good quality.

quand, *adv.*, when, whenever, what time, what period; while, whilst. *Depuis —?* since when ? *Depuis — est-il arrivé ?* since when has he arrived, or how long has he been here ? *Jusqu'à—?* or *jusques à—?* how long? till when?

quand, *conj.*, though, although. — *même ;* though, although, even if. — *même elle voudrait ;* even if she were willing. — *même ;* in spite of everything; through thick and thin; at any price. — *bien même ;* even though. — *je le disais !* did n't I tell you so ! what did I say ! *Je le ferai — même ;* I shall do it just the same, *or* in spite of you, etc.

quant à, *adv.*, with regard to, as to, as for, concerning, respecting. — *à cela ;* as for that. *Se mettre sur son —à-soi, sur son —-à-moi ;* to stand on one's dignity. *Tenir,* or *se tenir sur, son —-à-soi,* or *son —-à-moi ;* to assume a proud and reserved air.

quantes, *adj.f.pl.*, only employed in the two phrases : *Toutes fois et — toutes et — fois que ;* whenever, as often as, (com.) on demand.

quantième, *n.m.*, day (of the month). *Quel est le — du mois ?* what day of the month is it ?

quantitati-f, -ve, *adj.*, quantitative.

quantité, *n.f.*, quantity; variety; deal, number, multitude, abundance, plenty, lot.

quantum (koo-an-tom), *n.m.*, (—s) quantum.

quarantaine, *n.f.*, about forty; age of forty; quarantine. *Faire la — ;* to perform quarantine. *Lever la — ;* to admit to pratique. *Purger sa — ;* to clear one's quarantine. *Mettre en — ;* to put into coventry.

quarante, *n.m.* and *adj.*, forty. *Les — ;* the members of the French Academy, the forty immortals. *Remettre à l'an — ;* to put off till doomsday. *Je m'en moque comme de l'an — ;* I don't care two straws about it.

quarantie (-tí), *n.f.*, tribunal of the forty (at Venice).

quarantième (-tièm), *n.m.f.* and *adj.*, fortieth.

quarderonner, *v.a.*, (arch.) to round off.

quarre, quarré, quarreau, quarrément, quarrer, quarrure. *V.* **carre, carré,** etc.

quart (kar), *n.m.*, quarter, fourth; point (of the compass); quart (measure); (nav.) watch. *Un — d'heure ;* a quarter of an hour. *Médire du tiers et du — ;* to speak ill of everybody. — *de cercle ;* quadrant. *Officier de — ;* (nav.) officer of the watch. *Faire son — ;* to do one's watch. — *de nuit ;* night-watch. *Faire bon — ;* to keep a good lookout. *Le premier — ;* the starboard-watch. *Bon — !* (nav.) all 's well ! — *de vent ;* point of the compass. *Le — d'heure de Rabelais ;* the moment of payment; the crucial moment. *Les trois —s du temps ;* generally, most frequently.

quart, -e, *adj.*, fourth; (med.) quartan. *Fièvre —e ;* quartan ague, quartan.

quartaine, *adj.f.*, (pop.) quartan. *Fièvre — ;* quartan ague.

quartan, *n.m.*, (hunt.) fourth year (of wild boars).

quartanier, *n.m.*, wild boar four years old.

quartation, *n.f.*, (metal.) quartation.

quartaut, *n.m.*, octave (cask).

quarte, *n.f.*, (mus.) fourth; (fenc.) quarte; (piquet) quart; ⊙half gallon.

quartenier, *n.m.*, local police officer.

quarteron, *n.m.*, **-ne,** *n.f.*, quadroon, quateron.

quarteron, *n.m.*, the fourth part of ꝗ pound, *or* of a hundred. *Demi—* ; the eighth part of a pound, *or* of a hundred.

quartidi (koo-ar-), *n.m.*, Quartidi (fourth day of the decade in the calendar of the first French republic).

quartier (-tié), *n.m.*, quarter, fourth part; piece, part; block; quarter (of a town, of the moon); ward; district; neighborhood ; flap (of a saddle) ; gammon (of bacon) ; block (of stone); (arch., her., milit., vet.) quarter ; descent ; study, form (in schools). *pl.*, quarters. *Un — de lard ;* half a flitch of bacon. — *de soulier ;* quarter of a shoe. — *général ;* (milit.) headquarters. *Elève du troisième — ;* pupil of the third form. *De — ;* (milit.) on duty. *Demander — ;* to beg for quarter, for mercy. *Il ne donne point de — à ses débiteurs ;* he is eternally dunning his debtors. *On n'y fait — à personne ;* they spare nobody there.

quartier-maître, *n.m.*, (—s- —s) (milit., nav.) quartermaster, second-class petty officer.

quarto. *V.* **in-quarto.**

quarto (kooar-to), *adv.*, fourthly, in the fourth place.

quartz (kooar-tz), *n.m.*, (min.) quartz.

quartzeu-x, -se (kooa-), *adj.*, (min.) quartzose, quartzy.

quasi, *n.m.*, (cook.) thick end of a loin of veal ; chump, chump end.

quasi, *adv.*, (fam.) almost, nearly ; quasi.

quasi-contrat, *n.m.*, (—-—s) (jur.) quasi contract, implied contract.

quasi-délit, *n.m.*, (—-—s) (jur.) injury caused involuntarily. [say.

quasiment, *adv.*, almost, nearly, as you would

quasimodo, *n.f.*, (c.rel.) Quasimodo, hunchback (in V. Hugo's *Notre Dame*). *Dimanche de la — ;* Low Sunday.

quassia (kooa-), *n.f.*, (pharm.) quassia.

quassier (kooa-sié), *n.m.*, (bot.) stavewood, quassia.

quater, *n.m.*, C (numeration of houses). *See* **ter.**

quaternaire (kooa-), *adj.*, quaternary.

quaterne, *n.m.*, quaternary ; four winning numbers (*V.* **quine).**

quaterné, -e, *adj.*, (bot.) quaternate.

quatorze, *n.m.* and *adj.*, fourteen, fourteenth.

quatorzième, *n.m.f.* and *adj.*, fourteenth, fourteenth day.

quatorzièmement, *adv.*, fourteenthly.

quatrain, *n.m.*, quatrain.

quatre, *adj.*, four, fourth. *Un de ces — matins ;* one of these fine days. *Marcher à — pattes ;* to go upon all fours. *Être tiré à — épingles ;* to look as if one had just come out of a bandbox. — *à — ;* four to four, four abreast ; four steps at a time, in great haste, at a furious rate; (in games) four all.

quatre, *n.m.*, four ; fourth. *Se mettre en — pour quelqu'un ;* to go through fire for any one. *Crier comme — ;* to cry out lustily. *Faire le diable à — ;* to kick up a terrible shindy ; to exert one's self to the utmost. *On le tenait à — ;* it needed four men to hold him. *Je me tenais à — pour ne pas . . . ;* it was as much as I could do not to . . . *Travailler comme — ;* to work like a nigger.

quatre-temps, *n.m.pl.*, Ember-days.

quatre-vingtième, *n.m.f.* and *adj.*, eightieth.

quatre-vingts, *adj.*, eighty. — *millions ;* eighty millions. *Ils étaient — ;* there were eighty of them. *Quatre-vingt-un ;* eighty-one. *Quatre-vingt-dix ;* ninety. *Quatre-vingt-dix-neuf ;* ninety-nine. [*Quatre-vingts* takes no *s* when it precedes another number. It likewise takes no *s* when used in dates of the Christian era : *L'an mil sept cent quatre-vingt ;* the year 1780.]

quatrième, *n.m.* and *adj.*, fourth; fourth floor; pupil of the fourth class.

quatrième, *n.f.* and *adj.*, fourth; fourth class (in schools); (piquet) quart.

quatrièmement, *adv.*, fourthly.

quatriennal, -e (-è-n-nal), *adj.*, quadrennial.

quatrillion (kooa-), *n.m.* *V.* **quadrillion.**

quatuor (kooa-), *n.m.*, (—) (mus.) quartet, quartette.

quayage, *n.m.*, wharfage, keyage.

que, *relative pron.*, whom, that, which, what. *Qu'est-ce — c'est ?* what is it? — *dites-vous ?* what do you say? — *dit-on de nouveau ?* what news have you to tell us? *Il ne sait — faire;* he does not know what to do. *L'homme — vous voyez;* the man whom you see.

que, *conj.*, that; how; how much, how many; if; as, when; unless, without; till, until; yet; lest, for fear that; in order that, for; before; since; so; than; let; because; why; only, nothing but. *J'avoue — cela est surprenant;* I confess that this is very surprising. *Afin —;* that, in order that. *De sorte —;* so that. *S'il le souhaite, et — vous le vouliez;* if he desires it, and you also wish it. *Je ne serai point content — je ne le sache;* I shall never rest content until I know it. *Attendez qu'il vienne;* wait till he comes. *Il me verrait périr, qu'il n'en serait pas touché;* even if he were to see me perish, he would not be in the least concerned. *Approchez, — je vous embrasse;* draw near, (in order) that I may kiss you. *N'approchez pas de ce chien, de peur qu'il ne vous morde;* do not go near that dog, lest he should bite you. *Il n'y a qu'une heure qu'il est parti;* he left but an hour ago. *On le régala — rien n'y manquait;* they treated him in such a way that nothing was wanting. *A peine eut-il achevé de parler qu'il expira;* he had hardly done speaking, when he expired. *Le mari est plus raisonnable — la femme;* the husband is more reasonable than the wife. *Plutôt — de le faire;* rather than do it. *Tout savant qu'il est, il a bien peu de jugement;* learned as he is, he has very little judgment. *C'est à la cour qu'on apprend à flatter;* it is at court one learns to flatter. *Qu'il parle;* let him speak. *Je vous assure — cela est ainsi;* I assure you that it is so. *Je doute — cela soit ainsi;* I doubt whether it is so. *C'est une passion dangereuse — le jeu;* gambling is a dangerous passion. *C'est être sage — de vivre ainsi;* it is acting like a wise man to live so. *C'est en vain — je me fatigue;* it is in vain that I toil and moil. *C'est — je ne savais pas — vous y étiez;* the fact is I did not know that you were there. *Il y a dix ans — je l'aime;* I have loved her these last ten years. *Je ne suis pas si fou — de le croire;* I am not such a fool as to believe it. *Il est tout autre — vous ne disiez;* he is quite different from what you said. — *Dieu vous bénisse;* God bless you. — *j'agisse contre ma conscience!* ask me to act against my conscience! — *vous aimez à parler!* how fond you are of talking! *Qu'elle est grande!* how tall she is! *Qu'il y a de sots dans le monde!* what a lot of fools there are in the world! *Le malheureux qu'il est!* wretch that he is! — *ne parlez-vous?* why do you not speak? — *ne fait-il pas pour s'enrichir?* what does he not do to grow rich? — *ne puis-je vous rendre service!* would to God that I could serve you! — *n'ai-je le temps!* oh, that I had the time! *Je ne sors point — je ne m'enrhume;* I never go out without catching cold. *Je n'ai — faire de;* I have no business with, I have nothing to do with; I have no need of. *Je n'ai — faire de vous dire;* I need not tell you. *Il ne fait — boire et manger;* he does nothing but eat and drink. *Nous ne faisons — de commencer;* we are only just beginning. *Je dis — oui;* I say yes. *Il croit —*

non; he thinks not. *Je gage — si;* I bet you it is so. *Allez, sot — vous êtes;* go, blockhead that you are. *Le moyen — je souffre cela?* how can I bear that? *Ce n'est pas trop — cela;* that 's not too much. *Ce — c'est que la vie!* what a strange thing life is! *La belle chose — d'être riche!* how nice it is to be rich!

quel, -le, *adj.* — *homme est-ce?* what sort of a man is he? — *le heure est-il?* what o'clock is it? — *le pitié?* what a pity! — *le taille!* what a figure! — *le que soit votre intention;* whatever your intention may be. — *qu'il soit;* whatever he be, whoever he be, whatever it is. *Tel —;* indifferent, so so.

quelconque, *adj.*, whatever, any; any whatsoever. *D'une manière —;* in any way whatever, anyhow. *Une raison —;* any reason whatever.

Ⓞ**quellement** (kèl-màn), *adv.* *Tellement —;* indifferently, so so.

quelque, *adj.*, some, any, a few, odd; whatever, whatsoever. *Adressez-vous à — autre;* apply to somebody else. — *jour;* some day or other. *Il y a — s années;* some years ago. *J'ai — s amis dans cette ville;* I have a few friends in this town. — *part;* somewhere. — *peu d'argent;* some little money. — *s efforts que vous fassiez;* whatever efforts you make. *En — lieu qu'il soit;* wherever he is. *En — temps que ce soit;* at any time.

quelque, *adv.*, however, howsoever; some, about. — *riches qu'ils soient;* however rich they may be. — *centaines de livres;* a few hundred pounds. — *cent francs;* about a hundred francs.

quelquefois, *adv.*, sometimes.

quelques-uns, *n.m.pl.*, **-unes**, *n.f.pl.*, some, some people; any; a few.

quelqu'un, *n.m.*, **-e**, *n.f.*, somebody, some one; anybody, any one.

quémander, *v.n.*, to beg, to beg for, to go a-begging, to solicit.

quémanderie, *n.f.*, begging, solicitation.

quémandeu-r, *n.m.*, **-se**, *n.f.*, importunate beggar.

qu'en-dira-t-on, *n.m.*, (n.p.) public talk, tittle-tattle. *Se moquer du —;* to ignore what people say.

quenelle, *n.f.*, (cook.) forcemeat ball.

quenotte, *n.f.*, (fam.) tooth (of young children).

*****quenouille**, *n.f.*, distaff; bed-post; tree cut in the form of a distaff. — *de lit;* bedpost. *A — s;* four-post. *En —;* like a distaff. *Tomber en —;* to fall to the female line. *Coiffer une —;* to cover a distaff.

*****quenouillée**, *n.f.*, distaffful.

*****quenouillette**, *n.f.*, a small distaff; (bot.) distaff-thistle. — *s de la poupe;* (nav.) stern-timbers.

quérable, *adj.*, (jur.) demandable (of a debt).

quercitron, *n.m.*, (bot.) quercitron.

querelle, *n.f.*, quarrel, quarreling, row, brawl, broil, wrangling. — *d'Allemand;* groundless quarrel. *Faire une — à;* to quarrel with. *Chercher — à;* to pick a quarrel with. *Vider une —;* to settle a quarrel. *Susciter une — à;* to raise a quarrel. *Ne pas épouser une —;* not to take up any one's quarrel.

quereller, *v.a.*, to quarrel with, to pick a quarrel with, to scold.

se **quereller**, *v.r.*, to quarrel, to wrangle, to have words.

quereller, *v.n.*, to quarrel, to wrangle.

querelleu-r, **-se**, *adj.* and *n.*, quarrelsome; quarreler, wrangler.

Ⓞ**quérir**, *v.a.*, to fetch. [Only employed in the infinitive with *aller, envoyer, venir.*] *Aller —;* to go and fetch. *Envoyer —;* to send for.

questeur (kuès-), *n.m.*, questor.

question (kès-tion), *n.f.*, question, interrogation; query, rack, torture; point, issue; (jur.) issue; question (torture). *Faire une* —; to ask a question. *De quoi est-il* —? what's the matter? *Résoudre une* —; to solve a question. *Sortir de la* —; to wander from the question. *Si c'est une* — *à faire;* if it is a fair question. *Il est* — *de;* it is in contemplation to (*i. e.* intended to). *Après cela il fut* — *de moi;* then my affair came up. *Mettre en* —; to question; to call in question, to doubt. *Mettre à la* —; to put to the rack, to torture.

questionnaire (kes-tio-nèr), *n.m.*, examination questions; book of questions; torturer, tormentor.

questionner (kès-tio-né), *v.a.*, to question, to interrogate; to ask questions.

questionneu-r, *n.m.*, **-se**, *n.f.*, questioner, querist. *adj.*, inquisitive.

questure (kuès-), *n.f.*, questorship; questors' office.

quête, *n.f.*, quest, search; collection, offertory, gathering; (hunt.) beating about; (nav.) rake. *Se mettre en* — *de;* to go in quest of.

quêter, *v.a.* and *n.*, to go in quest, *or* search, of; to gather *or* collect; to beg, *or* ask, for; to make a collection; to canvass; (hunt.) to search.

quêteu-r, *n.m.*, **-se**, *n.f.*, collector, gatherer, mendicant (friar).

queue (keû), *n.f.*, tail; stalk, stem; (l.u.) hone; hogshead; end, extremity; rear; (of documents) label; billiard-cue; handle (of a frying-pan, of mills); train (of robes, gowns); file, string (of persons). —*d'aronde*, (—*s*—) (carp.) dovetail. —*de-chat cirrus;* curl-cloud; mare's tail. — *écourtée;* bobtail. —*de-cheval,* (—*s*—) (bot.) horse-tail. —*de lion,* (—*s*—) (bot.) lion's-tail; motherwort. —*de-pourceau;* (bot.) hog's-fennel. *Demi*—, (—*s*—) half a hogshead. *La* — *d'un paon;* a peacock's train. *La* —*d'une robe;* the train of a gown. —*de moulin;* mill-handle. — *de poêle;* handle of a frying-pan. *La* — *de l'armée;* the rear of the army. *Avoir les ennemis en* —; to have the enemy at one's heels. *Il est à la* —; he is behind, at the bottom of the class. *Faire* —; to stand in a line. *Faire la* — *à;* to take in, to deceive. *On fait* — *au théâtre;* there is a crowd at the doors. *A* —*d'aronde;* (carp.) dovetailed. *A la* — *leu leu,* V. **leu.** *Faire fausse* —; to miscue (billiards).

queussi-queumi, *adv.*, neither more nor less, neither better nor worse, just the same.

queuter, *v.n.*, to strike two balls at once, *or* together; to make a foul stroke.

queux *or* **queue** (keû), *n.f.*, hone, whetstone. ☉**queux**, *n.m.*, cook. *Grand* —, *maître* —; head cook; restaurateur.

qui, *relative pron.*, who, whoever, whom, whomsoever, which, that; what; some. *L'homme* — *pense;* the man who thinks. *Les chevaux* — *tirent;* the horses that draw. *De* — *parle-t-il?* whom is he speaking of? *A* — *est ce livre?* whose book is this? *Dites-moi* —; tell me who. *Je ne sais pas* —; I don't know who. *C'est à* — *l'aura;* it is to who will have it. *C'était à* —; they vied with one another as to who. — *pis est;* what is worse. — *plus est;* what is more. *Je sais* — *vous voulez dire;* I know whom you mean. — *est là?* who's there? — *d'entre vous oserait?* which of you would dare? *Ils étaient dispersés* — *çà,* — *là;* they were dispersed some one way, some another. — *que ce soit,* — *que ce puisse être;* whoever, whosoever it be. *Je n'ai vu* — *que ce soit;* I saw nobody, not a soul. *Il ne se défiait de* — *que ce fût;* he mistrusted nobody. — *que ce soit, il s'en repentira;* let him be who he will, he shall rue it. *A* — *est-ce à?* whose turn is it to? *A* — *est?* whose is? *or* to whom is? *A* — *le tour?* whose turn is it?

Pour — *connaît;* to any one who knows. — *s'excuse, s'accuse;* a guilty conscience needs no accuser.

quia (kui-a), *adv.*, (l.u.) naught. *Etre à* —; to be at a loss, to be at a stand, to be nonplused. *Mettre à* —; to nonplus, to silence.

quibus (kui-bus), *n.m.*, (pop.) property, wealth, needful cash, tin. *Avoir du* —; to be flush of money.

quiconque (ki-kōnk), *pron.*, whoever, whosoever; whomsoever, whichever.

quida-m (ki-dān), *n.m.*, **-ne** (ki-da-n), *n.f.*, (jur.) quidam; a certain individual; a certain person, one, some fellow.

quiddité (kuid-di-té), *n.f.*, quiddity.

quiescence, *n.f.*, quiescence.

quiescent, **-e** (kui-), *adj.*, quiescent.

quiétisme, *n.m.*, quietism (the doctrine of).

quiétiste, *n.m.f.* and *adj.*, quietist.

quiétude, *n.f.*, quietude.

****quignon**, *n.m.*, (fam.) hunch (large piece).

☉****quillage**, *n.m.*, keelage. V. **ancrage.**

****quille**, *n.f.*, skittle, nine-pin; (nav.) keel. *Jeu de* —*s;* game of skittles, set of skittles; skittle-ground *or* alley. *Donner à quelqu'un son sac et ses* —*s;* to send any one packing. *Recevoir quelqu'un comme un chien dans un jeu de* —*s;* to receive any one like a dog. *Trousser ses* —*s;* to cut one's sticks.

****quiller**, *v.n.*, to throw for partners, *or* for first play (at skittles).

****quillette**, *n.f.*, osier cutting.

****quillier**, *n.m.*, skittle-ground.

****quilloir**, *n.m.*, (nav.) reel-stick.

****quillon**, *n.m.*, cross-bar (of a sword).

quina, *n.m.* V. **quinquina.**

quinaire, *n.m.*, (antiq.) quinarius.

quinaire (kui-), *adj.*, (math.) quinary.

☉**quinaud**, **-e**, *adj.* V. **penaud.**

****quincaille**, *n.f.*, ironmongery, hardware; (fig.) trash, gimcrack.

****quincaillerie**, *n.f.*, ironmongery, hardware.

****quincaillier**, *n.m.*, ironmonger, hardwareman.

quinconce, *n.m.*, quincunx.

quindécagone (kuin-), *n.m.*, (geom.) quindecagon.

quindécemvir (kuin-dé-sèm-vir), *n.m.*, quindecemvir.

quindécemvirat, *n.m.*, quindecemvirate.

quine, *n.m.*, (l.u.) two fives (trictrac); five winning numbers (in a lottery). *Avoir la* —; to be in for (anything). *Gagner la* —; to win the big prize.

quinine, *n.f.*, quinine.

quinola, *n.m.*, knave of hearts (reversi).

quinquagénaire (kuin-koua-), *n.m.f.* and *adj.*, person fifty years old; fifty years old.

quinquagésime (kuin-koua-), *n.f.*, Quinquagesima.

☉**quinque** (kuin-kué), *n.m.*, (mus.) quintet.

quinquédenté, **-e** (kuin-kué-), *adj.*, (bot.) quinquedentate.

quinquennal, **-e** (kuin-kuèn-nal), *adj.*, quinquennial.

☉**quinquennium**, *n.m.*, (n.p.) a five years' course of philosophy and theology.

quinquenove, *n.m.*, a game at dice.

quinquerce (kuin-kuèrs), *n.m.*, (antiq.) quinquertium.

quinquérème (kuin-kué-), *n.f.*, (nav.) quinquereme.

quinquet, *n.m.*, Argand lamp; lamp, common oil lamp.

quinquina, *n.m.*, quinquina; Peruvian bark; (bot.) cinchona; tonic wine, appetizer.

quint, *n.m.* and *adj.*, (l.u.) fifth. *Charles*—; Charles the Fifth. *Sixte*—; Sixtus the Fifth.

quintaine, *n.f.*, (man.) quintain.

quintal, *n.m.*, quintal, hundred-weight.

quintan, *n.m.*, (man.) quintain (to tilt at).

quintane, *adj.*, quintan, of five days (of fevers).

quinte, *n.f.*, (mus.) fifth ; quint (piquet) ; fit (of coughing) ; freak, whim; (fenc.) quinte; tenor violin ; (man.) dead stop.

quinte, *adj.f.*, of five days (of fevers). *Fièvre —;* a five-day fever. *V.* **quintane**.

***quintefeuille**, *n.f.*, (bot.) cinque-foil.

quintessence, *n.f.*, quintessence ; marrow ; (fig.) pith ; essential part.

quintessencier, *v.a.*, to draw the quintessence out of ; to refine, to be critical; to subtilize.

quintette (kuin-tèt), *n.m.*, (mus.) quintet, quintette.

quinteu-x, -se, *adj.*, fanciful, whimsical ; crotchety ; making dead stops, jibbing (of a horse).

quintidi (kuin-), *n.m.*, Quintidi (fifth day of the decade in the calendar of the first French republic).

quintillion, *n.m.*, trillion.

quintuple (kuin-), *n.m.* and *adj.*, quintuple, fivefold.

quintupler (kuin-), *v.a.*, to quintuple, to increase fivefold.

quinzain, *n.m.*, fifteen each (at tennis).

quinzaine, *n.f.*, about fifteen; fortnight.

quinze, *n.m.* and *adj.*, fifteen; fifteenth. — *jours;* fortnight. *D'aujourd'hui en —;* this day fortnight. *Il y a eu hier — jours;* yesterday fortnight. *Il y a eu Dimanche — jours;* last Sunday fortnight. *De Lundi en —;* next Monday fortnight. *Les —vingts;* Quinze-Vingts, hospital in Paris (for three hundred blind men). *Un —vingts;* an inmate of Quinze-Vingts.

quinzième, *n.m.* and *adj.*, fifteenth; fifteenth day; (mus.) fifteenth.

quinzièmement, *adv.*, fifteenthly, in the fifteenth place.

quiproquo, *n.m.*, (—*s*) quid pro quo, mistake, blunder.

quittance, *n.f.*, receipt, discharge. — *pour solde de compte;* receipt in full.

quittancer, *v.a.*, to receipt.

quitte, *adj.*, discharged (from debt) ; quit, quits, clear ; free, rid. *Jouer à — ou double;* to play double or quits. *Tenir —;* to release, to disengage. *Je suis — d'un grand embarras;* I am rid of a great deal of trouble. *Je vous tiens — de votre parole;* I release you from your word. *Vous n'en serez pas — à si bon marché;* you shall not come off so cheaply. *Il en fut — pour la peur;* he got off with a good fright. *J'irai — à être grondé;* I shall go, even if I get scolded. *Etre — envers quelqu'un;* to owe no one anything ; to be even with any one.

quittement, *adv.*, (jur.) entirely, without debt or incumbrance.

quitter, *v.a.*, to quit, to leave, to part with; to leave off, to take off ; to lay aside, to desist from; to give up, to give over ; to depart (life). *Je vous quitte pour un instant;* I leave you for a moment. *— père et mère;* to leave father and mother. — *ses habits;* to take off one's clothes. — *une charge;* to give up a post. *J'aime mieux — que disputer;* I would rather give up than wrangle (over it). *Il a quitté le service;* he has left the service. — *le commerce;* to give up business. — *la chasse;* to give up hunting. — *la partie;* to give up the game. *Qui quitte la partie la perd;* who leaves off the game, loses. *Ne pas — des yeux;* not to take one's eyes off.

quitus (kui-tus), *n.m.*, (—) (fin.) discharge.

qui va là? *or* **qui-va-là**, *n.m.*, who goes there ? *Avoir réponse à —;* to be stopped by no difficulty ; to have an answer always ready.

qui vive? *or* **qui-vive**, *n.m.*, (milit.) challenge-word; who goes there ? *Etre sur le —;* to keep a good look-out; to be on the qui vive, *or* on the alert.

***quoailler**, *v.n.*, (of a horse) to swish its tail.

quoi, *pron.*, which, what. — *que vous disiez;* whatever you may say, in short, to speak plainly; of course, to be sure. *Dites-moi en — je puis vous servir;* tell me in what way I can serve you. *C'est en — vous vous trompez;* you are mistaken in that. *A — passez-vous le temps?* how do you spend your time ? *A — bon tant de façons?* why so much ceremony ? *A propos de —?* on what occasion ? with respect to what ? *Avoir de —;* (pop.) to be rich. *Il n'y a pas de —;* it is not worth mentioning ; don't mention it ! — *qu'il en soit;* be that as it may. *Nous avons de — le faire;* we have the means to do it. *Avoir de —;* to have sufficient. *Il n'y a pas de — pleurer;* it is not worth crying about. *Il n'y a pas de — rire;* it is no laughing matter. *Le je ne sais —;* the "indescribable" something.

quoi! *int.*, what ! how ! —, *vous avez fait cela?* what ! have you done that ? — *donc, vous osez me résister en face!* how then ! dare you resist me openly ?

quoi-que, *conj.*, whatever.

quoique, *conj.*, although, though. *Quoiqu'il soit pauvre;* although he is poor.

quolibet, *n.m.*, quibble, pun, sorry joke.

quote-part, *n.f.*, (—*s*—*s*) quota, portion, share, contribution.

quotidien, -ne (-in, -è-n), *adj.*, daily, quotidian. *Notre pain —;* our daily bread ; (fig.) our daily custom, our daily round.

quotidiennement, *adv.*, daily.

quotient, *n.m.*, (arith.) quotient.

quotité, *n.f.*, quota, portion, share.

R

r (èr), *n.f.*, (re), *n.m.*, the eighteenth letter of the alphabet, r.

rabâchage, *n.m.*, tautology ; tiresome repetition; rigmarole.

rabâcher, *v.n.* and *a.*, (fam.) to make tiresome repetitions, to repeat the same thing over and over again.

rabâcherie (-bâ-shrî), *n.f.*, eternal repetition.

rabâcheu-r, *n.m.*, **-se**, *n.f.*, eternal repeater ; twaddler.

rabais, *n.m.*, abatement, reduction, diminution ; reduced price, allowance, fall; lowest tender. *Vendre, donner, au —;* to sell at reduced prices. *Etre au —;* to have fallen in price. *Il les a pris au —;* he has taken them by contract. *Vente au —;* selling off, sale.

rabaissement (-bès-mān), *n.m.*, fall, depreciation, diminution in value; (fig.) humiliation, contempt.

rabaisser, *v.a.*, to lower ; to abate, to diminish, to lessen ; to depreciate, to humble ; to disparage; to bring down, to put down. — *sa voix;* to lower one's voice. — *les monnaies;* to depreciate the coin. — *les taxes;* to lower the taxes. — *l'orgueil de quelqu'un;* to humble any one's pride.

raban, *n.m.*, (nav.) rope-band, gasket, knittle.

rabanner, *v.a.*, (nav.) to fit a sail with rope-bands and earings.

rabat, *n.m.*, band (for the neck), bands ; end of the roof (of a tennis-court) ; beating about (for game).

rabat-joie, *n.m.*, (—) damper, wet blanket, mar-joy, spoil-sport. *C'est un —;* he is a regular wet blanket, *or* spoil-sport.

rabattage, *n.m.*, cutting down, pressing down.

rabattre, *v.a.*, to bring down, to lower, to beat down, to pull *or* cut down, to turn *or* press down, to lay; to abate, to diminish, to deduct; to humble; to revoke. *Le vent rabat la fumée;* the wind beats down the smoke. — *un coup;* to ward off a blow. *Il n'en veut rien —;* he won't

abate an inch of it, he won't come down a peg.
— *l'orgueil de quelqu'un ;* to bring down or lower
any one's pride. — *le gibier ;* to beat up the
game. *En* —; to take off ; (fig.) to come down
a peg or two. — *le caquet à quelqu'un ;* to take
any one down a peg.

se **rabattre,** *v.r.,* to beat down ; to turn off, to
change one's road ; to fall back upon, to come
down, to lower one's pretensions ; to limit one's
self.

rabattre, *v.n.,* to turn under ; to turn off ; to
change (one's) direction or route.

rabattue, *n.f.,* (nav.) drift-rail.

rabbaniste, *n.m.* *V.* **rabbiniste.**

rabbi or **rabbin,** *n.m.,* rabbi, rabbin. *Grand*
—; chief rabbi.

rabbinage, *n.m.,* rabbinism.

rabbinique, *adj.,* rabbinical.

rabbinisme, *n.m.,* rabbinism.

rabbiniste or **rabbaniste,** *n.m.,* rabbinist.

rabdologie, *n.f.,* rhabdology.

rabdomancie or ⊙**rabdomance,** *n.f.,* rhab-
domancy.

rabes, *n.f.pl.,* hard roe (of cod).

rabêtir, *v.a.* and *n.,* to stupefy ; to make dull,
or stupid ; to grow dull, or stupid.

rabette, *n.f.,* rape ; rape-seed.

rabiole, *n.f.* *V.* **rave.**

rabique or **rabeique,** *adj.,* (med.) hydropho-
bic ; of rabies, rabid.

râble, *n.m.,* back of a hare, or rabbit ; (tech.)
rake, poker, stirrer ; (b.s.) back (of a person).

râbler, *v.a.,* to rake, to poke, to scrape.

râblu, -e, *adj.,* thick-backed (of a hare, or
rabbit) ; (pers.) broad-backed, strong-backed ;
(fig.) hardy, vigorous.

râblure, *n.f.,* (nav.) rabbet, channel. — *de
la quille ;* rabbet of the keel.

se **rabonnir,** *v.a.,* to improve.

rabot, *n.m.,* plane ; beater (to move lime) ;
road-scraper. *Passer le — sur ;* to plane, to
polish.

rabotage, *n.m.,* (carp.) planing.

raboter, *v.a.* and *n.,* to plane, to smooth with
a plane ; to polish.

raboteur, *n.m.,* planer, molding-worker.

raboteu-x, -se, *adj.,* knotty, rough ; rugged,
cragged, craggy ; uneven, (fig.) harsh, jagged (of
style). *Un chemin* —; an uneven road.

rabougri, -e, *part.,* stunted. *Un petit homme*
—; a small, stunted fellow or man.

rabougrir, *v.a.,* to stunt.

se **rabougrir,** *v.r.,* to become, or grow, stunted.

***rabouillère,** *n.f.,* rabbit's nest, or hole ; (fig.)
corner, spot (in Rabelais).

raboutir, *v.a.,* to piece, to join end to end, to
join on.

rabrouer, *v.a.,* to snub, to pull up short ; to
chide, to rebuke.

rabroueu-r, *n.m.,* **-se,** *n.f.,* snappish person,
scold.

racage, *n.m.,* (nav.) parrel. *Pommes de* —;
trucks of a parrel. *Bigots de* —; ribs of a parrel. *Bâtard de* —; parrel-rope. *Drosse de* —;
parrel-truss.

racahout, *n.m.,* (*n.p.*) racahout (a nutritious
fecula).

*****racaille,** *n.f.,* rabble, riffraff ; rubbish, trash.

racambeau, *n.m.,* (nav.) traveler, jib-iron.

racastillage, *n.m.,* (nav.) repair of the upper
works.

racastiller, *v.a.,* to repair the upper works (of
a vessel).

raccommodage, *n.m.,* mending, repairing,
darning.

raccommodement (-mod-mān), *n.m.,* reconciliation, reconcilement.

raccommoder, *v.a.,* to mend, to repair ; to
piece, to patch, to botch ; to adjust, to set right ;
to improve, to correct ; to reconcile, to make

friends again ; to darn. *Faire — quelque chose ;*
to have anything mended. *On les a raccommodés ;* they have been reconciled.

se **raccommoder,** *v.r.,* to be mended ; (of persons) to be reconciled ; to make it up again. *Le
mari et la femme se sont raccommodés ;* the husband and wife are friends again, or have made it
up again.

raccommodeu-r, *n.m.,* **-se,** *n.f.,* mender,
patcher.

raccord, *n.m.,* joining, fitting, junction ; union ;
piece, patch.

raccordement, *n.m.,* (arch.) leveling ; union,
junction ; mending, patching.

raccorder, *v.a.,* to join, to unite, to adjust, to
connect, to level ; to piece, to patch ; (of instruments) to tune again.

raccourci, -e, *part.,* shortened, abbreviated ;
too short. *A bras —s ;* with might and main.

raccourci, *n.m.,* epitome, abridgment, short
cut ; (paint.) foreshortening. *En* —; abridged,
briefly ; (persp.) foreshortened ; (fig.) in miniature. *Prendre au* —; to take a short cut.

raccourcir, *v.a.,* to shorten, to make shorter ;
to contract, to bend ; to curtail ; to abbreviate,
to abridge ; (persp.) to foreshorten.

se **raccourcir,** *v.r.,* to shorten ; to grow, or become, shorter ; to contract one's self ; to shrink.

raccourcir, *v.n.,* to shorten ; to become
shorter ; to shrink, to contract.

raccourcissement (-sis-mān), *n.m.,* shortening, contraction, curtailment, abridgment ;
shrinking ; foreshortening.

raccours, *n.m.,* shrinking.

raccoutrement, *n.m.,* mending (of clothes).

raccoutrer, *v.a.,* to mend, to sew up.

se **raccoutumer,** *v.r.,* to reaccustom one's self
(to), to get used (to) again.

raccroc (ra-kro), *n.m.,* chance, lucky hit ; (at
billiards) fluke. *Coup de* —; lucky stroke, fluke.

raccrocher, *v.a.,* to hook again ; to hang up
again ; to recover, to get again, to get hold of,
to pick up. *Raccrochez ce tableau ;* hang up this
picture again. — *son argent ;* to recover one's
money. *Si je pouvais — cela !* if I could only
bring that off! *Raccroché à Londres ;* (of persons)
picked up in London.

se **raccrocher,** *v.r.,* to cling ; to adhere ; to
retrieve one's losses, to recover one's self ; to
catch, or snatch, at. *Se — à une chose ;* to cling
to anything.

raccrocher, *v.n.,* to fluke. *Il ne fait que* —;
he does nothing but fluke.

raccrocheuse, *n.f.,* (pop.) street-walker.

race, *n.f.,* race ; stock, breed ; family, line,
ancestry ; (agri.) variety. *Un cheval de* —; a
thorough-bred horse. *Ce chien est de bonne* —;
this dog is of a good breed, is pure-bred. *Croiser
les —s ;* to cross the breeds. — *de vipères ;*
generation of vipers. *La — future ;* future ages.
Les bons chiens chassent de —; it runs in the
blood. *Cette fille chasse de* —; that girl is a
flirt like her mother. *Faire* —; to breed.

rachat, *n.m.,* repurchase, redemption, recovery, ransom. *Vendre à faculté de* —; to sell
with power of redemption. — *de bans ;* (marriage) license.

rachetable (rash-tabl), *adj.,* redeemable.

racheter (rash-té), *v.a.,* to buy back, to buy
again, to repurchase ; to ransom, to buy off, to
redeem ; to compensate, to make up for ; to
atone, to atone for. — *une rente ;* to redeem an
annuity. — *les prisonniers ;* to ransom the prisoners. — *ses vices par ses vertus ;* to atone for
one's vices by one's virtues.

se **racheter,** *v.r.,* to redeem one's self ; to be
compensated, to be made up for.

racheu-x, -se, *adj.,* knotty (of wood).

rachever (rash-vé), *v.a.,* (pop.) to finish (anything begun).

rachidien, -ne (-in, -èn), *adj.*, (anat.) spinal, vertebral.

rachis (ra-shis), *n.m.*. (anat.) spinal, vertebral column, spine; (bot.) stalk.

rachitique, *adj.*, (med.) rickety; (bot.) blighted, stunted, knotty.

rachitique, *n.m.f.*, rickety person, person suffering from rickets.

rachitis (-tis), *n.m.*, rachitis; rickets.

rachitisme, *n.m.*, rachitis; rickets; (agri.) white blight.

racinage, *n.m.*, esculent roots, root-crops; (dy.) walnut dye (of walnut peel).

racinal, *n.m.*, (carp.) beam, sleeper; sole; sill.

racine, *n.f.*, root; (fig.) beginning, principle, origin. *Fruits pendants par les —s;* standing crops. — *carrée;* (arith.) square root. — *cubique;* cube root. *Prendre —;* to take root.

raciner, *v.n.*, to strike root.

raciner, *v.a.*, to dye with roots, to root-figure.

racinien, -ne, *adj.*, Racinian, of *or* after Racine.

rack, *n.m.*, arrack, rack (liquor). *V.* **arack**.

râclage, *n.m.*, scraping, thinning.

râcle, *n.f.*, (nav.) scraper (used to clean a ship's side, deck, etc.).

râcle-boyau, *n.m.*, (—) catgut-scraper, fiddler.

râclée, *n.f.*, scraping; (pop.) beating, drubbing, whacking, thrashing, hiding.

râcler, *v.a.*, to scrape, to scrape off; to strike (a measure); to strum, to thrum. — *le boyau;* to scrape the fiddle.

râcleur, *n.m.*, catgut-scraper; strummer (on the piano, etc.).

râcloir, *n.m.*, scraper, road-scraper.

râcloire, *n.f.*, strike (of measures).

râclon, *n.m.*, scraped-mud (for manure).

râclure, *n.f.*, scrapings.

racolage, *n.m.*, recruiting, enlisting, crimping, impressing.

racoler, *v.a.*, to entice men to enlist, to crimp, to enlist; (fig.) to pick up.

racoleur, *n.m.*, crimp; recruiting sergeant.

racontable, *adj.*, relatable.

racontage *or* **racontar**, *n.m.*, gossip, tittle-tattle, idle tales.

raconter, *v.a.*, to relate, to tell, to narrate, to recount.

raconteu-r, *n.m.*, **-se**, *n.f.*, relater, story-teller, narrator.

racornir, *v.a.*, to make as hard as horn; to make hard, to harden; to dry up, to shrivel, to shrivel up.

se **racornir**, *v.r.*, to grow hard, to harden; to shrivel, to shrivel up, to dry up.

racornissement (-nis-màn), *n.m.*, hardening, shriveling, drying up.

racquit, *n.m.*, winning back.

racquitter, *v.a.*, to win back again; to indemnify, to recoup.

se **racquitter**, *v.r.*, to win back again; to retrieve one's losses, to recoup one's self.

rade, *n.f.*, (nav.) roads, roadstead. — *foraine;* open roadstead. *Grande —;* outer roads. *Petite —;* inner roads. *Vaisseau en —;* roadster. *Aller en —;* to go into the roads.

radeau, *n.m.*, raft.

rader, *v.a.*, (nav.) to anchor in a roadstead; to strike (a measure). — *un vaisseau;* to anchor a ship in a roadstead.

radeur, *n.m.*, salt-measurer.

radiaire, *n.m.* and *adj.*, (zool.) radiary; radiated. —*s;* radiata.

radial, -e, *adj.*, (anat., geom.) radial.

radiance, *n.f.*, radiance, radiancy; luster.

radiant, -e, *adj.*, radiant.

radiation, *n.f.*, radiation, irradiation; obliteration, erasure, crossing out, striking out.

radical, -e, *adj.*, radical.

radical, *n.m.*, radical; root.

radicalement (-kal-màn), *adv.*, radically.

radicalisme, *n.m.*, radicalism.

radicant, -e, *adj.*, (bot.) radicant.

radication, *n.f.*, radication.

radicelle, *n.f.*, (bot.) radicle.

radicule, *n.f.*, (bot.) radicle.

radié, -e, *adj.*, (bot.) radiant, radiated, stellated; (her.) radiant.

radier, *n.m.*, (arch.) inverted arch; floor (of a lock on a canal); apron (of docks, of basins); radish-plate.

radier, *v.a.*, to strike out, to cross out.

radieu-x, -se, *adj.*, radiant, beaming, shining, blazing.

radiomètre, *n.m.*, (astron.) radiometer.

radis, *n.m.*, radish.

radius (-us), *n.m.*, (anat.) radius.

radoire, *n.f.*, strike (of measures).

radotage, *n.m.*, nonsense, idle talk, drivel; dotage.

radoter, *v.n.*, to rave, to dote, to talk idly, to wander, to talk drivel.

radoterie (ra-do-trî), *n.f. V.* **radotage**.

radoteu-r, *n.m.*, **-se**, *n.f.*, dotard, driveler. *Vieille —se;* trifling old woman.

radoub (-doob), *n.m.*, (nav.) repair, refitting of a ship, graving. *Cale de —;* graving slip. *Forme de —;* graving dock. *Vaisseau en —;* ship undergoing repairs. *Mettre au —;* to lay up (a vessel).

radouber, *v.a.*, (nav.) to refit, to repair, to recalk.

se **radouber**, *v.r.*, (nav.) to be repaired.

radoubeur, *n.m.*, (nav.) calker.

radouci, *part.adj.*, softened, subdued.

radoucir, *v.a.*, to soften, to make milder, to appease, to pacify, to mitigate, to allay.

se **radoucir**, *v.r.*, to soften, to grow milder, to become milder; to get milder; to grow soft, to become soft, to get soft; to subside, to be appeased, to be pacified; to relent, to relax, to soften down. *Le temps se radoucit;* it is getting milder *or* better weather.

radoucissement (-sis-màn), *n.m.*, softening, getting milder (of the weather); mitigation, allaying, appeasement, improvement.

rafale, *n.f.*, (nav.) squall.

rafalé, *adj.*, caught in a squall; (pop. & fig.) hard up, up a tree.

raffe, *n.f. V.* **rafle**.

raffermir, *v.a.*, to harden, to make firm; to fasten; to establish, to confirm, to settle, to secure, to fortify, to strengthen. *Cet événement raffermit son autorité;* that event strengthened his authority. — *le courage de quelqu'un;* to give heart to any one.

se **raffermir**, *v.r.*, to grow stronger, to gather strength; to be established, to become established, to consolidate; to be confirmed, to become confirmed; to improve. *Sa santé se raffermit;* his health is improving.

raffermissement (-mis-màn), *n.m.*, hardening, strengthening; confirmation, establishment, fastening, securing, consolidation, improvement.

raffinade, *n.f.*, best refined sugar.

raffinage, *n.m.*, refining.

raffiné, -e, *adj.*, fashionable rake.

raffiné, -e, *adj.*, refined, delicate; keen, sharp, subtle, clever, consummate.

raffinement (ra-fi-n-màn), *n.m.*, refinement, affected nicety.

raffiner, *v.a.*, to refine.

se **raffiner**, *v.r.*, to refine, to be refined, to become refined.

raffiner, *v.n.*, to refine. — *sur le point d'honneur;* to be over-nice upon the point of honor.

raffinerie (ra-fi-n-rî), *n.f.*, refinery; sugar-refinery, refining.

raffineur, *n.m.*, refiner. — *de sucre;* sugar-refiner, sugar-baker.

raffoler, *v.n.*, to dote (upon), to be passionately fond (of), to be distractedly in love (with). *Il raffole de cette femme;* he is madly in love, or infatuated, with that woman.

raffolir, *v.n.*, (l.u.) to become mad, to go mad. *V.* **affoler**.

rafistolage, *n.m.*, patching up, mending.

rafistoler, *v.a.*, (fam.) to mend clothes, to patch up, to make new.

rafle, raffe, *or* **râpe**, *n.f.*, grape-stalk stripped of all its fruit; (dice) pair-royal. *Faire* —; (fam.) to sweep off the stakes; to sweep off everything, to make a clean sweep.

rafler, *v.a.*, (fam.) to sweep away, to sweep off, to carry off.

⊙**raflouer**, *v.a.*, (nav.). *V.* **renflouer**.

rafraîchir, *v.a.*, to cool; to refresh, to restore, to invigorate, to repair, to recruit, to renew, to freshen, to freshen up, to renovate, to rub up, to crop, to cut, to trim (cut the ends of) ; (milit.) to relieve ; to rest. — *du vin;* to cool wine. — *le sang;* to refresh the blood. — *un tableau;* to clean up, *or* freshen up, a picture. — *une tapisserie;* to restore a piece of tapestry. — *les cheveux;* to clip the hair. — *la mémoire;* to refresh one's memory. — *une muraille;* to repair a wall. — *une place;* to supply a garrison with fresh men and provisions. *Ces troupes sont fatiguées, il faut les metire dans de bons quartiers pour les* —; these troops are worn out, they must be sent into good quarters to rest. — *la mémoire à quelqu'un;* to remind any one of a thing.

se **rafraîchir**, *v.r.*, to cool, to grow cool, to become cool ; to take refreshment, to refresh one's self ; to be refreshed ; to recruit one's self ; to recruit one's strength, to rest one's self. *Venez vous rafraîchir;* come and take some refreshment. *Le vent se rafraîchit;* the wind is freshening.

rafraîchir, *v.n.*, to cool, to become cool; to be refreshing.

rafraîchissant, -e, *adj.*, cooling, refreshing, refrigerative.

rafraîchissant, *n.m.*, (med.) cooling medicine.

rafraîchissement (-shis-mân), *n.m.*, cooling ; cooling effect. *pl.*, refreshments ; provisions, supplies. *Faire les* —*s;* (nav.) to take in fresh provisions.

rafraîchisseur, *adj.*, cooling, refrigerative.

rafraîchissoir, *n.m.*, cooler, refrigerator.

*****ragaillardir**, *v.a.*, to make merry, to render merry, to render cheerful, to enliven, to cheer, to cheer up, to give a fillip to.

rage, *n.f.*, (med.) rage, fury, incensement ; mania ; rabies, hydrophobia, canine madness, mania, inveterate habit. *Ecumer de* —; to foam with rage. *Avoir la* —; to be mad (of animals). — *de dents;* violent tooth-ache; (pop.) ravenous hunger. *Il a la* — *d'écrire;* he has a mania for writing, he will write at any price. *Il l'aime à la* —; he loves her to distraction. *Il a la* — *du jeu;* he has a passion for gambling. *Faire* —; to be quite *or* all the rage; to cause great disorder, great havoc; to do one's utmost. *Dire* — *de quelqu'un;* to say all imaginable harm of any one. *Quand on veut noyer son chien, on dit qu'il a la* —; (prov.) give a dog a bad name and hang him.

rager, *v.n.*, (fam.) to be in a passion; to sulk, to be angry, to fume.

rageu-r, *n.m.*, -**se**, *n.f.*, ill-tempered person; spitfire.

ragot, *n.m.*, (hunt.) solitary wild boar; (fig.) silly talk, twaddle.

ragot, -e, *adj.*, dumpy, thick and short; thick set; squat (animal).

ragoût, *n.m.*, (cook.) ragout; stew; hash. *Faire un* —; to make a stew. *En* —; stewed.

ragoûtant, -e, *adj.*, relishing, savory; inviting, tempting. *Morceau* —; tit-bit. *Ce mets-là n'est guère* —; that dish is not very tempting.

ragoûter, *v.a.*, to restore the appetite; to quicken, to stimulate, to stir up.

se **ragoûter**, *v.r.*, to recover one's appetite.

ragrafer, *v.a.*, to clasp again, to re-clasp, to hook again.

ragrandir, *v.a.*, to enlarge again; to enlarge.

se **ragrandir**, *v.r.*, to be enlarged again; to become larger.

ragréage, *n.m.* (nav.) refitting.

ragréer, *v.a.*, (arch.) to finish, to finish off, to give the finishing touch to; to restore, to renovate, to do up; to repair; to pare again (trees), to prune; (nav.) to rig anew, to refit. — *un ouvrage de menuiserie;* to finish a piece of joiner's work. — *une branche d'arbre;* to prune a branch of a tree.

se **ragréer**, *v.r.*, (nav.) to be repaired; to obtain fresh rigging.

ragrément, *n.m.*, finishing, finishing off; restoration, renovation, doing up; pruning, reparing (of trees); (nav.) refitting.

ragué (ra-ghé), *adj.*, (nav.) chafed, rubbed, galled.

se **raguer**, *v.a.*, (nav.) to chafe, to gall.

raguet, *n.m.*, (pisc.) codling.

raia, *n.m.*, rajah, raja.

raide, *adj.*, stiff, rigid; tight; inflexible, stern; tough; steep; swift, rapid; (nav.) taught. — *de froid;* stiff with cold. *Peau* —; tough skin. *Montagne* —; steep mountain. — *comme une barre de fer;* as stiff as a poker. *Se tenir* —; to stand stiff. *Vol* —; rapid flight. *Le cours de la rivière est* —; the current of the river is very swift. — *comme balle;* in no time, in a jiffy.

raide, *adv.*, quickly, swiftly; vigorously; tightly; toughly.

raideur, *n.f.*, stiffness, rigidity; inflexibility; tightness; toughness; steepness; swiftness, velocity.

*****raidillon**, *n.m.*, ascent; hillock.

raidir, *v.a.*, to stiffen, to render inflexible, to render rigid; to tighten; to toughen; (nav.) to haul taught.

se **raidir**, *v.r.*, to stiffen; to become, to grow, to get stiff; to become inflexible, to get inflexible; to bear up against (fig.), to resist; to harden one's self (against); to withstand; to bristle up; to toughen.

raidir, *v.n.*, to stiffen; to become, to grow, to get, stiff; to tighten; to toughen.

raie, *n.f.*, line, stroke; streak, stripe; (of hair) parting; (agri.) furrow; (ich.) ray, skate. *A* —*s;* striped. *Faire sa* —; to part one's hair. *Etoffe à* —*s;* striped material. — *bouclée;* (ich.) thornback. — *mobular;* angel-fish.

raifort, *n.m.*, (bot.) radish, horse-radish.

rail, *n.m.*, (railways) rail. — *mobile;* switch-rail, point. — *ondulé;* fish-bellied rail. — *à ornière;* tram-rail. *Distance des* —*s dans œuvre;* gauge of way.

*****railler**, *v.a.*, to banter, to jeer, to rally, to joke, to jest.

se **railler**, *v.r.*, to jest, to joke, to mock, to make game of.

*****railler**, *v.n.*, to jeer, to scoff; to joke, to jest, to laugh at. — *de tout;* to jeer at everything. *Ne raillez pas davantage;* no more of your jeering, jesting. *Je ne raille pas;* I am not joking.

*****raillerie**, *n.f.*, raillery, bantering, jesting, jest, joke, banter, jeer, mockery. *Tourner une chose en* —; to turn anything into a jest. *Entendre la* —; to joke well, to be a good hand at a joke. *Entendre* —; to take a joke, to take a jest. *C'est une* — *de croire que;* it is ridiculous to think that. — *à part, sans* —; seriously, in good earnest, without joking. *La* — *en est-elle?* (fam.) is it a matter for jest, *or* joking?

*railleu-r, -se, n. and adj., banterer, jeerer, joker, scoffer, jester; bantering, jeering, joking, jesting, scoffing, fond of raillery. *D'un air —;* sneeringly.

railway, n.m., railway.

rain, n.m., skirt (of a wood). V. **lisière.**

rainceau, n.m. V. **rinceau.**

raine, n.f., (local expr.) frog.

rainette, n.f., (erp.) tree-frog; (bot.) V. **reinette.**

rainure, n.f., groove; rabbet; furrow, slot-hole, quirk.

raiponce, n.f., (bot.) rampion, rampion bell-flower.

raire or **réer,** v.n., (hunt.) to bell, to croon.

rais, n.m., spoke (of a wheel); ☉beam, ray (of light); (her.) beam. *— de cœur;* (arch.) ogee.

raisin, n.m., grape, grapes. *Une grappe de —;* bunch of grapes. *Un grain de —;* a grape. *Un pépin de —;* a grapestone. *— de Corinthe;* (grocer's) currants. *Des —s secs;* raisins. *— d'Amérique;* (bot.) poke-weed. *—d'ours;* bear's whortleberry. *— de renard;* (bot.) herb-Paris, true-love. *Grand —;* royal (paper).

raisiné, n.m., pear, quince, and grape preserve.

raisinier, n.m., (bot.) grape-tree.

raison, n.f., reason, sense, judgment, rationality; satisfaction; proof, ground, matter, argument; motive; rate; consideration; justice, right, excuse, answer; (com.) firm; share; ratio; (jur.) claim. *— sociale;* firm; name of a firm, style. *Sans —;* groundless, groundlessly. *—s d'état;* state reasons. *—s de famille;* family reasons. *Il n'a point de —;* he lacks sense, he is deficient in sense. *Mariage de —;* prudent marriage, marriage for money. *Parler —;* to talk sense, to talk sensibly. *Avoir —;* to be right. *Vous avez —;* you are right. *Donner — à quelqu'un;* to decide in favor of any one, to side with any one. *Plus que de —;* more than is reasonable, more than one ought to. *Entendre —;* to listen to reason. *Mettre quelqu'un à la —;* to bring any one to reason, to settle any one. *Comme de —;* as it is fit, of course, naturally. *Etre de —;* imaginary being, creation of the brain. *Où force domine — n'a point lieu;* where force holds sway, there's no room for reason. *Tirer — d'une injure;* to obtain satisfaction for an injury. *Se faire — soi-même;* to do one's self justice, to take the law into one's own hands. *Faire — à;* to pledge. *Faire — de;* to give satisfaction for. *Se faire une —;* to be guided by reason. *Se rendre à la —;* to yield to reason. *Rendre — de sa conduite;* to give an account of one's conduct. *Ce n'est pas une —;* that does not follow. *Ne pas entendre —;* not to listen to reason. *Puissante —;* powerful argument. *— probable;* probable proof. *Point tant de —s;* don't argue so much! *Grande —;* great cause. *Bonne —;* good grounds. *A plus forte —;* with greater reason or force; a fortiori. *— de plus;* all the more reason. *Pour — de quoi;* for which cause, wherefore. *Pour — à moi connue;* for reasons best known to myself. *A — de, en — de;* in proportion to; according to; at the rate of. *En — de;* by reason of; in consideration of. *A telle fin que de —;* in case of need; according to circumstances; at all events; in any case. *Sous la — de;* (com.) under the style of. *Sa — est d'un tiers;* his interest (in the concern) stands at one third. *Livre àe —;* ledger.

raisonnable, adj., rational, reasonable, thinking, sensible; conscionable, just, wise; proper, right; adequate; moderate; fair; tolerable. *Pension —;* adequate pension. *Prix —;* moderate price. *Il est d'une taille —;* he is moderately tall, or very fairly tall.

raisonnablement, adv., reasonably, sensibly,

agreeably to reason, wisely, fairly, justly, rationally; moderately, pretty well; tolerably.

raisonné, -e, adj., rational, intelligent, supported by proof; analytical, studied, methodical, classified.

raisonnement (rè-zo-n-mān), n.m., reasoning; argument, ratiocination, answer. *Faire des —s à perte de vue;* to reason vaguely, to wander from the point. *Point de —s;* no answers; none of your answers.

raisonner, v.n., to reason, to argue, to discourse; to answer; to murmur; (nav.) to lie to, (in order to be searched). *— faux* or *— à faux;* to reason falsely. *Faire — un vaisseau;* (nav.) to compel a ship to speak another. V. **arraisonner.**

raisonner, v.a., to reason, to apply one's reason to; to examine, to study, to consider; (nav.) to bring to and search.

se **raisonner,** v.r., to reason with one's self; (of things) to be discussed, to be considered.

raisonneu-r, -se, n. and adj., reasoner, arguer; logician; impertinent answerer; impertinent, insolent; answering when reprimanded. *Faire le —;* to argue, to answer, to grumble.

rajah or **raja,** n.m., raja, rajah.

rajeunir, v.a., to make young; to make look younger, to give a young look; to restore to youth; to revive, to renew, to modernize, to prune, to lop (trees). *— des meubles;* to renew furniture.

se **rajeunir,** v.r., to make one's self look younger.

rajeunir, v.n., to grow young again, to be restored to youth; to look young again.

rajeunissant, -e, adj., giving a youthful appearance to.

rajeunissement (-nis-mān), n.m., growing young again, making young again; rejuvenescence, restoration to youth; renewal, renovation.

rajouter, v.a., to add again or more.

rajustement, n.m., readjustment; putting or setting in order, repairing; (fig.) reconciliation.

rajuster, v.a., to readjust, to put to rights, to put or set in order again; to settle; to reconcile. *— un habit;* to arrange a coat. *On les a rajustés;* they have been reconciled.

se **rajuster,** v.r., to readjust one's self, or one's dress; to become reconciled.

râlant, -e, adj., in death's throes; dying.

râle, n.m., (orni.) rail. *— de genêts;* land-rail.

râle, n.m., rattling in the throat. *— de la mort;* death-rattle.

râlement (râl-mān), n.m., rattling in the throat, death-rattle.

ralentir, v.a., to abate, to slacken; to lessen, to diminish, to moderate, to mitigate. *— sa course;* to slacken one's pace.

se **ralentir,** v.r., to slacken; to abate, to relax, to diminish; to grow remiss, to flag, to cool.

ralentissement (-tis-mān), n.m., slackening, relenting, abatement, flagging, cooling.

râler, v.n., to have the death-rattle; to be in the throes of death.

ralingue (-lin-g), n.f., (nav.) bolt-rope (of a sail). *— de fond;* foot-rope. *— de chute;* leech-rope. *— de têtière;* head-rope. *Mettre une voile en —;* to let fly the sheets of a sail. *Mets en —!* let the sails shiver in the wind!

ralinguer (-ghé), v.a., (nav.) to sew the bolt-ropes to. *— une voile;* to sew the bolt-ropes to a sail.

ralinguer, v.n., (nav.) to let fly the sheets of a sail (loose to the wind); to fly loose to the wind (of sails); to shiver.

ralliement (-li-mān), n.m., rallying, rally. *Mot de —;* rallying-word or cry; countersign. *Signe de —;* rallying sign. *Point de —;* rallying-place.

rallier, v.a., to rally, to join, to get near. *— le navire au vent;* (nav.) to haul to the wind again; to bring the ship into the wind.

se **rallier**, *v.r.*, to rally, to join forces.

rallonge, *n.f.*, lengthening piece. — *d'une table ;* leaf of a table.

rallongement (ra-lonj-män), *n.m.*, lengthening.

rallonger, *v.a.*, to make longer, to lengthen.

rallumer, *v.a.*, to relight, to light again ; to rekindle, to kindle again, to light up anew, to revive.

se **rallumer**, *v.r.*, to light again ; to burst, to break out again ; to rekindle.

ramadan *or* **ramazan**, *n.m.*, (Mahometan religion) Ramadan (feast of).

ramadouer, *v.a. V.* **amadouer**.

ramage, *n.m.*, flowers (on stuffs) ; flowering ; singing, chirping, warbling (of birds) ; prattle, prattling ; (of peas) sticking.

ramagé, -e, *adj.*, flowered (of stuffs).

ramager, *v.n.*, (l.u.) to warble (of birds).

ramaigrir, *v.a* and *n.*, to make lean, *or* thin, again ; to grow thin again.

ramaigrissement, *n.m.*, emaciation, leanness.

***ramaillage**, *n.m.*, scraping off the hair (of skins).

***ramailler**, *v.a.*, to scrape off the hair of skins (before they are shamoyed).

ramaire, *adj.*, (bot.) rameous.

ramas, *n.m.*, collection, heap ; set, troop, lot, omnium-gatherum, scrapings, rakings, sweepings. *Un — de bandits ;* (fam.) a set of robbers.

ramasse, *n.f.*, sledge (used on mountains).

ramassé, -e, *adj.*, thick-set ; squat ; huddled up, gathered up ; compact ; (bot.) clustered. *Corps —;* thick-set body. *Taille —e;* squat figure.

ramasser, *n.m.*, (l.u.) picking up. *Cela ne vaut pas le —;* (prov., fam.) that is not worth picking up, *or* (fig.) not worth troubling about.

ramasser, *v.a.*, to collect, to gather, to get together, to rake together ; to assemble ; to pick up, to take up ; (pop.) to belabor ; to draw in (a mountain sledge). — *toutes ses forces;* to muster all one's troops.

se **ramasser**, *v.r.*, to assemble, to gather together ; to be assembled ; to roll itself up (animal) ; to pick one's self up, to get up again, to be huddled up ; to gather up one's limbs.

ramasseur, *n.m.*, gatherer, collector ; mountain sledge-driver.

ramassis, *n.m. V.* **ramas**.

ramazan, *n.m. V.* **ramadan**.

rambour, *n.m.*, a kind of apple.

rame, *n.f.*, oar ; ream (of paper) ; (hort.) stick, prop ; stick (for peas) ; (manu.) tenter-frame. *Etre*, *or tirer, à la —;* to tug at the oar ; to work hard. *Mettre un livre à la —;* to sell a book for waste-paper. *A la —;* rowing. *Aller à la —;* to row.

ramé, -e, *adj.*, branched (of peas), propped (of plants) ; bar, double-head (of shot) ; (hunt.) (of a young stag) horned. *Balles —es;* double shot. *Boulets —s;* bar-shot.

rameau, *n.m.*, bough, branch (of a tree) ; branch, subdivision ; (anat.) branch. *Le dimanche, le jour, des —x;* Palm-Sunday.

ramée, *n.f.*, green boughs, green arbor, branches with their leaves, bower, cover.

ramenable, *adj.*, reclaimable.

ramendable, *adj.*, (tech.) mendable.

ramendage, *n.m.*, (tech.) mending (gilt).

ramender, *v.a.*, to lower the price of provisions (pop.) ; (agri.) to manure again ; to mend (gilding) ; to dye again.

ramender, *v.n.*, (pop.) to fall in price (of provisions).

ramener, *v.a.*, to bring again ; to bring back ; to throw again (dice) ; to retrieve ; to restore to health ; to reclaim ; (man.) to lower its head ; to recall ; to pacify, to bring over. — *une vieille mode;* to revive an old fashion. — *quelqu'un* *à son devoir ;* to bring any one back to his duty. — *à la maison ;* to bring home.

se **ramener**, *v.r.*, (man.) to carry its head. *Se — bien ;* to carry its head well.

ramequin (ram-kin), *n.m.*, (cook.) ramekin, cheese-cake.

ramer, *v.n.*, to row, to pull ; (tech.) to tenter ; to tug at the oar ; to work hard.

ramer, *v.a.*, to stick peas ; to prop plants.

se **ramer**, *v.r.*, to be propped.

ramereau (ra-mrô), *n.m.*, young ringdove.

ramette, *n.f.*, (print.) job-case, packet (of note paper).

rameur, *n.m.*, rower, oarsman.

rameu-x, -se, *adj.*, branching, branchy, ramous. *Tige —se;* branchy stalk.

ramier, *n.m.*, ringdove, wood-pigeon.

ramière, *n.f.*, row, *or* bower, of trees *or* shrubs.

ramification, *n.f.*, ramification, branch.

se **ramifier**, *v.r.*, to ramify, to separate into branches, to branch out, to extend.

***ramilles**, *n.f.pl.*, twigs ; chatwood.

raminagrotis, *n.m.*, grimalkin.

ramingue (ra-min-gh), *adj.*, (man.) restive ; jibbing.

ramoitir, *v.a.*, to moisten, to make damp.

se **ramoitir**, *v.r.*, to become damp.

ramollir, *v.a.*, to soften, to make soft ; (fig.) to enervate. — *les cuirs*, to soak the hides.

se **ramollir**, *v.r.*, to soften, to grow soft ; (fig.) to relent.

ramollissant, -e, *adj.*, (med.) softening, emollient.

ramollissant, *n.m.*, (med.) emollient.

ramollissement (-lis-män), *n.m.*, softening. — *du cerveau ;* softening of the brain.

ramon, *n.m.*, garden-broom, besom ; sweep's apparatus.

ramonage, *n.m.*, sweeping (of a chimney).

ramoner, *v.a.*, to sweep (a chimney).

ramoneur, *n.m.*, chimney-sweeper, sweep.

rampant, -e, *adj.*, creeping, crawling ; (fig.) cringing, crouching, servile ; (her.) rampant. *Lierre —;* creeping-ivy.

rampant, *n.m.*, (arch.) coping.

rampe, *n.f.*, flight of stairs ; stairs ; handrail, baluster ; slope, incline, gradient ; (fig.) stage ; (thea.) foot-lamps, foot-lights ; (engineering) inclined plane.

rampement (ränp-män), *n.m.*, creeping, crawling (reptiles).

ramper, *v.n.*, to creep, to crawl ; (fig.) to crouch, to cringe, to truckle, to grovel. *Son style rampe ;* his style is low, flat, prosy.

rampin, *adj.m. V.* **pinçard**.

rampiste, *n.m.*, baluster-maker.

ramure, *n.f.*, branches, boughs, antlers (of a stag).

rancart, *n.m.*, (fam.) refuse, waste. *Mettre au —;* to throw aside, to cast off, to lay aside, to do away with ; (fig.) to put on the shelf.

rance, *adj.*, rancid, rank, rusty.

rance, *n.m.*, rancidness. *Sentir le —;* to smell rancid.

rancette, *n.f.*, sheet-iron (for stove pipes).

ranche, *n.f.*, round of a rack-ladder ; rack (of a crane) ; peg.

rancher, *n.m.*, rack-ladder ; roost-ladder.

ranci, -e, *adj.*, grown rancid ; rank.

rancidité *or* **rancissure**, *n.f.*, rancidness, rancidity.

se **rancir**, *v.n.*, to grow rancid.

rancissure, *n.f. V.* **rancidité**.

rançon, *n.f.*, ransom. *Mettre à —;* to demand, *or* exact, ransom of.

rançonnement (-so-n-män), *n.m.*, ransoming, exaction, extortion.

rançonner, *v.a.*, to ransom; to set a ransom upon ; to levy contributions, to tax ; (fig.) to impose upon ; to fleece.

rançonneu-r, *n.m.*, **-se**, *n.f.*, (fam. l.u.) extortioner.

rancune, *n. f.*, rancor, spite, grudge, ill-feeling, malice. *Vieille* —; old grudge. *Il lui garde* —; he owes him a grudge. *Sans* —; without ill-feeling.

rancuni-er, **-ère**, *adj.*, rancorous, spiteful.

randonnée, *n.f.*, (hunt.) round, circuit, doubling (of game); ⊙ (fig.) long walk.

rang (ran), *n.m.*, row, line, range; rank (degree, station); order ; class ; rate (of ships); (print.) frame; (nav.) tier (of cables); tier (of boxes in theaters). *Dernier* —; lowest rank. *Au même* —; in the same row. *A son* —; in one's turn. *De premier* —; first rate. *Occuper un — élevé ;* to rank high. *Tenir un* —; to hold a rank, to make a figure. *Se mettre sur les —s ;* to enter the lists, to come forward (as a candidate); to put up (for); to stand (for). *Etre sur les —s ;* to be a candidate (for). *Il aspire au premier* —; he aspires to the first place. *Mettre au — de ses amis ;* to reckon amongst one's friends. *Tel qui brille au second — s'éclipse au premier ;* a good subordinate often makes a bad leader. *En — d'oignon ;* (prov.) in a row. *V.* **oignon**.

rangé, -e, *part.*, steady; pitched (of battles). *Bataille — e ;* pitched battle. *En bataille — e ;* in a pitched battle. *Un homme* —; a steady man.

rangée, *n.f.*, row, range, file, line, tier, set.

rangement, *n.m.*, arranging, putting in order, binning (wine).

ranger, *v.a.*, to range, to put in ranks, to arrange; to put, to set, in order; to set to rights; to subdue, to subject; to rank; to reckon; to keep back; to put out of the way; to bin (wine); (nav.) to sail close to; (milit.) to draw up (soldiers). *— des gens deux à deux ;* to place people in double file. *— des livres ;* to set books in order. *— une armée en bataille ;* to draw up an army in battle array. *Les gardes firent — le peuple ;* the guards kept the people back. *Rangez cette table ;* put that table back, out of the way. *— la terre, la côte ;* (nav.) to hug the shore. *— le vent ;* (nav.) to haul close to the wind.

se ranger, *v.r.*, to make room, to make way (for); to draw back, to step aside, to stand aside, to clear the way, to get out of the way ; to reform, to take to regular habits; to draw up (of carriages, of troops); to fall in (of soldiers) ; to veer (of the wind). *Il se rangea dans un coin ;* he drew aside into a corner. *Rangez-vous donc !* make room, will you ! *Les troupes se rangèrent en bataille ;* the troops drew up in order of battle. *Se — à l'avis de quelqu'un ;* to come over (to), or fall in (with), another's opinion. *Se — du parti de quelqu'un ;* to go over to a person's side. *Il s'est rangé ;* he has settled down (after sowing his wild oats). *Le vent se range à l'arrière ;* (nav.) the wind is veering aft.

rangette, *n.f.*, sheet-iron.

rangeur, *n.m.*, binner (of wine).

ranimer, *v.a.*, to restore, to revive, to animate; to reanimate; to stir up; to enliven ; to cheer up. *— les couleurs d'un tableau ;* to revive the colors of a picture. *Le printemps ranime toute la nature ;* the spring revives all nature.

se ranimer, *v.r.*, to revive, to recover, to be restored to health ; to brighten up, to be enlivened ; to cheer up. *La nature se ranime ;* nature revives.

ranule or **grenouillette**, *n.f.*, (med.) ranula.

ranz, *n.m.*, ranz, air, tune. *— des vaches ;* song of the Swiss neatherds.

raout, *n.m.*, rout, party.

rapace, *adj.*, rapacious; (metal.) wasting.

rapace, *n.m.*, rapacious person ; rapacious bird. *pl.*, (orni.) birds of prey.

rapacement, *adv.*, rapaciously.

rapacité, *n.f.*, rapacity, rapaciousness.

râpage, *n.m.*, rasping, grating.

rapaisement, *n.m.*, reappeasement.

rapaiser, *v.a.*, to pacify, to appease again.

rapatelle, *n.f.*, horsehair cloth (for sieves).

rapatriage, *n.m.*, reconciliation, reconcilement.

rapatriement (-trî-mān), *n.m.*, repatriation, the sending back of shipwrecked sailors, etc., to their country (by consuls); return of troops from distant countries; recalling ; (l.u.) reconciliation, reconcilement.

rapatrier, *v.a.*, to repatriate, to send back, to recall ; to reconcile, to set to rights, to make friends again. *On les a rapatriés ;* they have been reconciled.

se rapatrier, *v.r.*, to return to one's native country, to return home; to be reconciled ; to be friends again, to make it up.

râpe, *n.f.*, grater ; rasp ; stalk ; stem of grapes, *V.* **rafle**. *pl.*, (vet.) malanders, *V.* **malandre**.

râpé, *n.m.*, rape-wine (fresh grapes put into a vessel of spoiled wine to improve it) ; rappee. *— de copeaux ;* chips to clarify wine.

râpé, -e, *part.*, (of clothes) shabby, threadbare, seedy, worn out. *Du tabac* —; rappee. *Un habit* —; a threadbare coat.

râper, *v.a.*, to grate, to rasp. *Se* —; to be rasped ; (fig.) to become threadbare, to be worn out.

rapetassage, *n.m.*, patching, mending, cobbling.

rapetasser (rap-ta-sé), *v.a.*, to patch, to patch up, to piece, to botch, to mend, to cobble.

rapetasseu-r, *n.m.*, **-se**, *n.f.*, botcher, piecer, cobbler; (fig.) compiler, adapter.

rapetissement, *n.m.*, shortening ; (fig.) belittling.

rapetisser (rap-ti-sé), *v.a.*, to belittle, to dwarf, to shorten, to make less, shorter, smaller. *se rapetisser*, *v.r.*, to become little, to lessen, to shrink ; to humble, or lower, one's self.

rapetisser, *v.n.*, to become little, to lessen, to grow short, to shrink.

râpette, *n.f.*, (bot.) goose-grass.

rapide, *adj.*, rapid, swift, quick, fleet, fast; hasty, sudden. *A l'aile* — ; swift-winged.

rapide, *n.m.*, rapid. *Le* — ; the fast, or express, train.

rapidement (-pid-mān), *adv.*, rapidly, swiftly, fleetly, lightly, fast ; suddenly.

rapidité, *n.f.*, rapidity, swiftness, fleetness ; speed ; suddenness ; steepness.

rapiéçage, *n.m.*, patching, piecing.

rapiécement (-piès-man), *n.m.*, piecing, patching, botching.

rapiécer, *v.a.*, to piece, to botch, to patch, to mend.

rapiécetage (-piés-taj), *n.m.*, piecing, patching ; patchwork.

rapiéceter (-piés-té), *v.a.*, to patch, to piece, to botch ; to piece all over. *— des meubles ;* to botch up furniture.

rapiéceur, *n.m.*, patcher, mender.

rapière, *n.f.*, (jest.) rapier.

rapin, *n.m.*, (fam.) painter's pupil ; (b.s.) dauber.

rapinade, *n.f.*, daub.

rapine, *n.f.*, rapine, plunder, pillage, robbery, plundering, pillaging, spoil.

rapiner, *v.n.* and *a.*, to pillage, to rob, to pilfer, to peculate.

rapineu-r, *n.m.*, **-se**, *n.f.*, plunderer, pilferer, pillager.

*rappareiller, *v.a.*, to match.

rapparier, *v.a.*, to match.

rappel, *n.m.*, recall, recalling, revocation, call (to order); (milit.) drums beating to arms or quarters; unpaid part (of a salary). *— à l'ordre ;* call to order. *— de lumière ;* (paint.) distribution of light. *Battre le —;* (milit.) to beat to arms, or to quarters.

rappeler (ra-plé), *v.a.,* to call again, to call back ; to recall, to call home, to summon up, to muster ; to restore ; to recall to mind. *Je m'en allais, et il m'a rappelé ;* I was going, and he called me back. *— quelqu'un à la vie ;* to restore any one to life. *— un homme à son devoir ;* to recall a man to his duty. *— quelqu'un à l'ordre ;* to call any one to order. *— ses esprits ;* to recover one's self. *— le temps passé ;* to recall the past. *Rappelez-moi à son bon souvenir ;* remember me kindly to him. *— la lumière ;* (paint.) to distribute the light.

se **rappeler,** *v.r.,* to recollect, to remember, to recall to mind. *Se — quelque chose ;* to remember anything. *Vous rappelez-vous ?* do you remember ? *Je me le rappelle parfaitement ;* I recollect it very well. *Je me rappelle que vous me l'avez dit ;* I recollect your telling me so. *Je me rappelle d'avoir fait cela ;* I recollect having done that.

rappeler, *v.n.,* (milit.) to beat to arms, *or* to quarters.

rapport, *n.m.,* bearing ; revenue ; produce ; report, account, information, relation, testimony, evidence ; tale, story ; return ; statement; affinity, analogy, resemblance, similitude ; harmony, correspondence, uniformity ; connection, reference ; communication, intercourse, concern; tendency ; ratio, proportion ; reimbursement, refunding ; rising (in the stomach). *Etre en —;* to be productive, to be in bearing (of land). *Etre en plein —;* to be in full bearing ; to be very productive. *Belle montre et peu de —;* a fine show and a small crop. *Faire un —;* to draw up a report, to make a return. *Aimer à faire des —s ;* to love to tell tales. *Il en a fait son —;* he has sent in his report. *Le style n'est pas en — avec le sujet ;* the style is not in harmony, or in keeping, with the subject. *Avoir — à;* to relate to, to refer to ; to have relation to. *Il n'y a aucun — entre ces choses ;* there is no connection between these things. *Mettre une personne en — avec une autre ;* to bring a person into contact with another; to bring any two persons together. *Par — à;* with reference to. *Il a fait cela par — à vous ;* he did that on your account. *Sous le — de,* with respect to. *Terres de —;* artificial soil, made soil. *Pièces de —;* patch-work, inlaid work. *Sous tous les —s ;* in all respects, in every respect.

rapportable, *adj.,* (jur.) that must be refunded, restorable.

rapporté, -e, *part.,* brought back ; (com.) brought over *or* forward. *Ouvrage de pièces —es ;* inlaid work. *Terres —es;* artificial soil, made soil.

rapporter, *v.a.,* to bring again, to bring back, to carry back ; to bring away, to bring home ; to bring home again; to carry home ; to account for ; to revoke, to recall ; to report, to tell, to relate, to give an account of ; to cite, to quote ; to direct, to refer to ; to ascribe, to attribute ; to yield, to bear ; to bring in ; to reimburse ; (book-keeping) to carry forward; to trace ; to set down ; (com.) to post (in ledgers). *Il m'en a rapporté que des coups ;* he only got blows by it. *— un fait comme il s'est passé ;* to relate a fact as it happened. *Il rapporte tout ;* he tells everything. *— tout à soi ;* to think of nothing but self. *— l'effet à sa cause ;* to refer the effect to its cause. *Une terre qui rapporte beaucoup ;* an estate that yields a good income. *Des arbres qui rapportent beaucoup ;* trees that bear a great deal of fruit. *Son argent lui rapporte six pour cent ;* his money brings him in six per cent. *Cette mauvaise action ne lui rapportera rien ;* this bad action will avail him nothing (com.). *— du journal au grand livre ;* to post from the journal to the ledger.

se **rapporter,** *v.r.,* to agree, to correspond, to tally, to coincide, to blend ; to relate, to refer, to have reference to, to allude to, to be allied, related to. *Ces deux couleurs se rapportent bien;* these two colors blend well together. *S'en rapporter à;* to leave it to (any one). *Je m'en rapporte à vous;* I leave it to you; I trust to you. *Je m'en rapporte à votre témoignage ;* I abide by what you say. *S'il faut s'en rapporter aux anciennes traditions ;* if we are to believe ancient traditions. *Je m'en rapporterai à qui que ce soit;* I will refer the thing to anybody. *Je m'en rapporte à votre serment;* I abide (by) your oath *or* I refer you (to) your oath.

rapporter, *v.n.,* to fetch and bring (of the dog); to bring in, to produce ; to tell tales ; to pay well, to be profitable.

rapporteur, *n.m.,* reporter, stenographer ; (geom.) protractor. *— d'un comité ;* committee reporter.

rapporteu-r, *n.m.,* **-se,** *n.f.,* tell-tale, tale-bearer.

rapprendre, *v.a.,* to learn again, to learn anew.

rapprivoiser, *v.a.,* to tame again.

rapprochement (-prosh-mān), *n.m.,* drawing, placing near, bringing together ; junction; reconcilement, reconciliation ; putting together, comparing; comparison.

rapprocher, *v.a.,* to draw near again, to approach again ; to bring together ; to set in opposition, to compare; to bring nearer. *— deux personnes ;* to bring two persons together, to reconcile two persons. *Rapprochez ces deux planches ;* bring these two planks closer. *— un cerf;* to put hounds on the track of a stag.

se **rapprocher,** *v.r.,* to come near again ; to come, to draw, nearer; to be brought together ; to approach, to approximate, to resemble, to begin to be friends again, to become reconciled.

rapsode, *n.m.,* (Grec. antiq.) rhapsodist.

rapsodie, *n.f.,* rhapsody ; rambling composition.

rapsodiste, *n.m.,* rhapsodist.

rapt, *n.m.,* abduction, rape.

râpure, *n.f.,* raspings.

raquetier, *n.m.,* racket-maker ; battledore-maker.

raqueton, *n.m.,* large racket.

raquette, *n.f.,* racket, battledore ; snow-shoe ; (bot.) Indian fig, opuntia.

rare, *adj.,* rare, uncommon, extraordinary ; unusual, singular; scarce ; thin, scanty, sparse ; (med.) slow (of the pulse). *Devenir — comme les beaux jours ;* to become quite a stranger. *Se rendre —;* to make one's self scarce. *Vous devenez bien —;* you are quite a stranger.

raréfacti-f, -ve, *adj.,* rarefying.

raréfaction, *n.f.,* (phys.) rarefaction.

raréfiable, *adj.,* (phys.) that can be rarefied.

raréfiant, -e, *adj.,* rarefying.

se **raréfier,** *v.n.,* to rarefy, to become rarefied.

rarement (rar-mān), *adv.,* rarely, seldom, unfrequently, not often.

rareté (rar-té), *n.f.,* rarity, rareness, scarcity, singularity.

rarissime, *adj.,* very rare, most rare.

ras, -e, *adj.,* close-shaved, short-haired ; shorn, shaved, close, bare ; smooth, open, flat ; short-naped ; (nav.) low-built, flat-bottomed, undecked. *Un chien à poil —;* a short-haired dog. *Il a la tête —e ;* his head is shorn. *Il a le menton —;* he has a bare, smooth, chin. *Il porte la barbe —e ;* he shaves close. *Du velours —;* shorn velvet. *Etoffe —e ;* smooth stuff. *Serge —e ;* napless serge. *—e campagne ;* open country. *Vaisseau —, or vaisseau à —à l'eau;* straight-sheered ship. *Faire table —e ;* to clear the board of. *A —e terre ;* level with the ground.

ras, *n.m.,* short-nap cloth. *— de carène ;*

(nav.) shipwright's floating stage. *Au — de, à
—;* nearly level with. *— de marée;* (nav.) tide-
wav, race. *A — de terre;* almost touching the
ground; skimming the ground. *V.* raz.

rasade, *n.f.*, bumper, brimmer. *Boire une
—;* to drink a bumper.

rasant, -e, *adj.*, shaving, grazing; sweeping;
(fort.) rasant; (milit.) flank. *Vue —e;* view of
a flat, open country.

rasement (raz-mān), *n.m.*, shaving; (milit.)
razing *or* leveling to the ground.

raser, *v.a.*, to shave; to shave off, to demolish, to pull down, to raze to the ground; to
graze, to touch; to skim over; to lay flat; to
glance over, to touch lightly, to suppress; to cut
down, to disable (a ship). *Se faire —;* to get
(one's self) shaved. *—une maison;* to pull down
a house. *— un vaisseau;* to cut down a ship.
Une balle lui rasa le visage; a ball grazed his
face. *— la côte;* (nav.) to hug the coast. *—
l'air;* to hover.

se **raser**, *v.r.*, to shave, to shave one's self, to
be shaved. *Cette perdrix se rase;* this partridge
keeps close to the ground.

raser, *v.n.*, to shave; to pass very close to;
(vet.) to raze, to be aged. *Ce cheval rase;* this
horse is aged.

rase-tapis, *n.m.*, (of horses) daisy-cutter.

rasibus (-bus), *prep.*, (pop.) quite close.
Couper —; to cut off quite close.

rasoir, *n.m.*, razor; (fig. and pop.) a bore.
Pierre à —; hone. *Cuir à —;* razor-strop. *Repasser un —;* to set a razor.

rason, *n.m.*, (ich.) razor-fish.

rassade, *n.f.*, glass-bead, bugle.

rassasiant, -e, *adj.*, satiating, filling, cloying.

rassasiement (-zi-mān), *n. m.*, satiety; surfeit.

rassasier, *v.a.*, to sate, to satiate; to satisfy,
to fill; to cloy, to glut, to surfeit. *Etre rassasié
d'une chose;* to be tired of a thing. *Il n'est
jamais rassasié d'argent;* he can never have
enough money.

se **rassasier**, *v.r.*, to be satiated; to sate one's
self with; to be cloyed with; to take one's fill
of.

rassemblement, *n.m.*, assembling; muster,
mustering, collecting; riotous meeting, mob;
assemblage. *Disperser un —;* to disperse a mob.

rassembler, *v.a.*, to collect, to assemble, to
reassemble, to gather together, to bring together
again; to put together again; to get together,
to muster. *— des troupes;* to muster troops.
— des matériaux pour un ouvrage; to collect
materials for a work.

se **rassembler**, *v.r.*, to assemble, to gather
together, to congregate, to meet, to unite, to
muster. *Se — en foule;* to flock, to crowd.

rasseoir (ra-soâr), *v.a.*, to seat again, to
reseat; to replace, to put in its place again; to
settle, to calm, to compose, to appease. *— une
statue sur sa base;* to replace a statue on its base.
— une pierre; to replace a stone. *Donnez-lui
le temps de — ses esprits;* give him time to compose himself.

se **rasseoir**, *v.r.*, to sit down again, to be seated
again; to settle (of liquids); to be composed.

rasseoir, *v.n.*, to settle (of liquids). *Laissez
— ce café;* let that coffee settle.

rasséréner, *v.a.*, to make serene, to clear up;
to restore serenity to. *Le soleil parut et ras-
séréna le temps;* the sun shone out and cleared
up the weather.

se **rasséréner**, *v.r.*, to clear up, to recover one's
serenity; to brighten up.

rassiéger, *v.a.*, to besiege again; to beset
again.

rassis, -e, *part.*, set down again; settled.

rassis, *adj.*, cool, staid, sedate, sober-minded.
Du pain —· stale bread. *De sang —;* in cool

blood. *De sens —;* with sound judgment, dispassionate, unmoved. *Esprit —;* sober mind.

rassis, *n.m.*, old horse-shoe reset; (fig.) soberness (in Montaigne).

rassortiment, *n.m.*, rematching (of colors,
materials); re-sorting; taking in a stock of goods
for a season, etc., restocking.

rassortir, *v.a.*, to sort, *or* match, again.

rassurance, *n.f.*, reassurance.

rassurant, -e, *adj.*, tranquillizing; encouraging, comforting, reassuring.

rassurer, *v.a.*, to strengthen; to remove any
one's fears; to consolidate; to make firm; to
tranquillize, to reassure, to comfort, to satisfy,
to cheer.

se **rassurer**, *v.r.*, to tranquillize one's self; to
recover one's self, to be reassured; to set one's
mind at rest; (of the weather) to settle, to clear
up. *Rassurez-vous;* set your mind at rest.

rat, *n.m.*, rat; whim, crotchet, fad; niggard;
taper. *— d'eau;* water-rat. *— de Pharaon;* ichneumon. *Mort aux—s;* rat's-bane. *Un nid à —s;*
a sorry lodging. *Gueux comme un — d'église;*
as poor as a church mouse. *A bon chat bon —;*
set a thief to catch a thief. *— de cave;* small
wax taper; exciseman. *Avoir des —s;* to be
whimsical. *— de l'opéra;* ballet-girl. *Prendre
un —;* to miss fire. *— d'église;* church-goer.

ratafia, *n.m.*, ratafia.

ratang, *n.m.*, ratan.

ratanhia, *n.m.*, (bot., med.) rhatany.

ratata, *n.m.*, drum-beating.

ratatiné, -e, *adj.*, shriveled, shriveled up;
shrunk. *Un petit vieillard —;* a little withered
old man.

se **ratatiner**, *v.r.*, to shrink, to shrivel, to shrivel
up.

*****ratatouille**, *n.f.*, (cook.) bad stew (made of
scraps of meat).

rate, *n.f.*, spleen, milt. *Avoir des vapeurs de
—;* to be troubled with the spleen. *Epanouir
la —;* to drive away the spleen, to make merry.
S'épanouir la —; to drive away one's spleen, to
be merry.

râteau, *n.m.*, (agri.) rake, bow (of a scythe);
(horl., nav.) rack.

râtelage (râ-tlaj), *n.m.*, (agri.) raking.

râtelée (râ-tlée), *n.f.*, raking; rakeful.

râteler (râ-tlé), *v.a.*, to rake.

râteleur (râ-tleur), *n.m.*, raker.

râteleu-x, -se, *adj.*, splenetic.

râtelier, *n.m.*, rack (in stables); set of teeth;
(milit.) arm-rack; (nav.) rack. *Manger à plus
d'un —;* to have more than one string to one's bow.
Mettre les armes au —; to quit the service.

ratelle, *n.f.*, disease (of pigs).

rater, *v.n.*, to miss fire; to flash in the pan,
to miscarry. *Son fusil rata;* his gun missed fire.

rater, *v.a.*, to miss; not to obtain; to fail in.
— une charge; to miss a place.

⊙**rati-er, -ère** (-tié, -tièr), *adj.*, whimsical. *n.m.*,
ratter, rat-catcher.

ratière (-tièr), *n.f.*, rat-trap.

ratification, *n.f.*, ratification.

ratifier, *v.a.*, to ratify.

*****ratillon**, *n.m.*, little rat.

ratine, *n.f.*, ratteen, patersham, frieze cloth.

ratiné, -e, *adj.*, friezed.

ratiner, *v.a.*, (manu.) to frieze.

ratiocination, *n.f.*, ratiocination, reasoning.

ratiociner, *v.a.*, to ratiocinate, to reason.

ration, *n.f.*, ration allowance. *Mettre à la
—;* to allowance. *— diminuée;* short allowance.

rational, *n.m.*, breast-plate (Jew. rel.).

rationalisme, *n.m.*, rationalism.

rationaliste, *n.m.*, rationalist.

rationalité, *n.f.*, rationality.

rationnel, -le, *adj.*, rational. *Horizon —;*
rational horizon. *Quantité —le;* rational quantity.

rationnellement (-nèl-màn), *adv.*, rationally.

rationnement, *n.m.*, short allowance.

rationner, *v.a.*, to allowance, to put on short allowance.

ratissage, *n.m.*, scraping, raking.

ratisser, *v.a.*, to rake; to scrape, to scrape off.

ratissoire, *n.f.*, scraper.

ratissure, *n.f.*, scrapings.

raton, *n.m.*, (mam.) raccoon; (fam.) little rat; (pers.) ducky, darling; (in fables) mouser.

rattacher, *v.a.*, to tie again, to tie up again; to fasten again, to fasten up again; to connect, to attach. — *par une chaîne;* to chain up again. — *une question à une autre;* to connect one question with another.

se rattacher, *v.r.*, to be tied; to fasten, to be fastened; to fasten upon; to be attached to, to be connected *or* allied (with).

ratteindre, *v.a.*, to retake, to catch again, to take again; to overtake, to come up again (with).

rattendrir, *v.a.*, to soften again, to make tender again, to move again.

rattiser, *v.a.*, to stir up the fire again; to stir up again. *V.* **attiser.**

rattraper, *v.a.*, to retake, to catch again, to overtake, to come up again (with), to recover. *On a rattrapé le prisonnier;* the prisoner has been retaken. *Bien fin qui m'y rattrapera;* once bit, twice shy.

se rattraper, *v.r.*, to catch hold of; to compensate one's self; to win back one's losses; to make up for.

rature, *n.f.*, erasure, scratch; word crossed out.

raturer, *v.a.*, to efface; to blot out; to erase, to scratch *or* cross out; to scrape (skins).

raucité, *n.f.*, raucity, hoarseness.

rauque, *adj.*, hoarse.

ravage, *n.m.*, ravage, havoc, waste. *Faire des —s;* to commit ravages.

ravager, *v.a.*, to ravage, to lay waste, to spoil.

ravageur, *n.m.*, ravager, spoiler.

ravale, *n.f.*, roller (to smooth the ground).

ravalement (-val-màn), *n.m.*, (l.u.) debasement, disparagement; (mas.) rough-casting; (arch.) finishing off. *Piano à —;* piano-forte with a double row of keys.

ravaler, *v.a.*, to swallow again; to put down, to run down, to lower; to press, to roll (land); to debase, to disparage; (mas.) to rough-cast. — *la gloire de;* to run down the glory of.

se ravaler, *v.r.*, to debase one's self; to lower one's self.

ravaudage, *n.m.*, mending (of old clothes); botching, bungling; darning stockings.

ravauder, *v.a.*, to mend (old clothes); to botch, to botch up; to revile; to plague, to tease, to bustle about (in-doors). — *des bas;* to darn stockings.

ravauderie (-vô-drî), *n.f.*, (fam.) silly stuff, nonsense, trash. *Dire des —s;* to talk nonsense.

ravaudeu-r, *n.m.*, **-se**, *n.f.*, mender (of stockings, old clothes); botcher, patcher; twaddler.

rave, *n.f.*, long radish, radish, colerape, turnip, beet.

ravelin (ra-vlin), *n.m.*, (fort.) ravelin.

ravenelle (ra-vnèl), *n.f.*, wall-flower.

ravi, -e, *part.*, carried away, transported; raptured; ravished, overjoyed, glad, delighted. *Être — de joie;* to be overjoyed. *J'en suis —;* I am delighted at it. — *d'admiration;* carried away by admiration. *Je suis — que vous la connaissiez;* I am delighted you know her.

ravière, *n.f.*, radish-bed.

ravigote, *n.f.*, (cook.) sharp sauce.

ravigoter, *v.a.*, (pop.) to revive the appetite of, to enliven, to cheer.

se ravigoter, *v.r.*, to revive, to recover one's strength, one's appetite.

ravilir, *v.a.*, to debase, to disgrace, to degrade, to lower. *V.* **avilir.**

ravin, *n.m.*, ravine, hollow road.

ravine, *n.f.*, mountain torrent; gully, ravine.

ravinement, *n.m.*, gullying.

raviner, *v.a.*, to gully (land).

ravir, *v.a.*, to carry off; to take away; to ravish, to rob of; to charm, to delight, to enrapture. — *le bien d'autrui;* to steal the property of another. — *l'honneur à une fille;* to dishonor a girl. *On lui a ravi son plus doux espoir;* he has been robbed of his dearest hope. *A —;* wonderfully well, to admiration, admirably. *Elle chante à —;* she sings admirably.

ravisement, *n.m.*, thinking better of; altering one's mind, second thought, after thought.

se raviser, *v.r.*, to alter one's mind, to bethink one's self; to think better of it.

ravissant, -e, *adj.*, rapacious, ravenous; admirable, ravishing, delightful, lovely, enchanting, charming.

ravissement (-vis-màn), *n.m.*, rape; transport, rapture, ravishment, delight. *Il était dans le —;* he was in raptures. — *de joie;* transport of joy.

ravisseur, *n.m.*, ravisher.

*ravitaillement, *n.m.*, revictualing; (fig.) recruiting.

*ravitailler, *v.a.*, to revictual. *Se —;* to recruit.

raviver, *v.a.*, to make a fire burn up; to revive; to reanimate; to brighten up, to cheer, to rouse. — *un tableau;* to revive a picture.

se raviver, *v.r.*, to revive.

ravoir, *v.a.*, to get again, to have again; to get back, to recover.

se ravoir, *v.r.*, to recover one's strength, to recruit, to pick up, to pick up one's crumbs.

rayé, -e, *part.*, striped, streaked; (artil.) rifled, grooved; scratched, scratched out, crossed out. *Vaisselle —e;* scratched plate. *Des mots —s;* words crossed out. *Canon —;* rifled cannon.

rayer, *v.a.*, to scratch (plate, dishes, etc.), to scratch out; to cross *or* strike out, to erase, to expunge, to streak, to stripe; (artil.) to rifle, to groove. — *une étoffe;* to stripe a stuff. *Rayez cela de vos papiers;* strike that out of your book; (fig.) look upon it as a bad debt. — *d'une liste;* to strike off a list. — *du papier;* to rule paper. — *le canon d'un fusil;* to rifle a gun-barrel.

rayère, *n.f.*, loop-hole (in towers).

rayeur, *n.m.*, ruler (instr.).

ray-grass, *n.m.*, (n.p.) (bot.) rye-grass.

rayon, *n.m.*, ray, beam, gleam; (geom.) radius; spoke (of a wheel); (ich.) ray; (agri.) furrow; shelf; comb (of honey). — *de lumière;* ray of light. *Faisceau de —s;* (opt.) pencil of rays. *Un — d'espérance;* a ray of hope. *A dix lieues de —, dans un — de dix lieues;* within a radius of ten leagues. *Une étoile à cinq —s;* a star with five rays. — *de miel;* honey-comb.

rayonnant, -e, *adj.*, radiant, shining, sparkling, beaming. — *de lumière;* beaming with light.

rayonné, -e, *adj.*, radiated, stellated; (of rooms) shelved.

rayonnés, *n.m.*, (zool.) radiary. *pl.*, radiata.

rayonnement (rè-io-n-màn), *n.m.*, radiance; radiancy; (phys.) radiation. *Le — des astres;* the radiation of the stars.

rayonner, *v.n.*, to radiate, to irradiate; to shine; to beam; to glisten; to trace furrows *or* lines. *Son visage rayonne de joie;* his face is radiant with joy. *v.a.*, to shelve (a room).

rayure, *n.f.*, stripe (of textile fabrics); streak; scratch, groove; rifling (fire-arms).

raz, *n.m.*, (nav.) race, bore. — *de marée;* bore, eagre (rush of water up an estuary; wave caused by the meeting of two tides).

razzia, *n.f.*, (—*s*) (milit.) raid, foray, razzia; inroad; (fig.) clean sweep.

ré, *n.m.*, (mus.) D ; (vocal mus.) re, D.

re, ré, prefix from Latin *re*, red.

réabonnement, *n.m.*, renewed subscription.

se **réabonner**, *v.r.*, to subscribe again; to renew one's subscription.

réabsorber, *v.a.*, to reabsorb.

réabsorption, *n.f.*, reabsorption.

réact-eur, -rice, *n. and adj.*, (pol., l.u.) reactionary.

réacti-f, -ve, *adj.*, reactive.

réactif, *n.m.*, (chem.) reagent, test.

réaction, *n.f.*, reaction.

réactionnaire, *n.m.f. and adj.*, reactionist; reactionary.

réactionner, *v.a.*, to sue again.

réactionner, *v.n.*, to react.

réadmettre, *v.a.*, to readmit, to admit again.

réadmission, *n.f.*, readmission, readmittance.

réadopter, *v.a.*, to readopt.

réadoption, *n.f.*, readoption.

réafficher, *v.a.*, to stick *or* post up again.

réaffirmer, *v.a.*, to reaffirm.

réaggrave, *n.f.*, (canon law) reaggravation.

réaggraver, *v.a.*, (canon law) to censure by a reaggravation.

réagir, *v.n.*, to react.

réajournement, *n.m.*, readjournment; fresh summons.

réajourner, *v.a.*, to readjourn.

réal, *n.m.* (*réaux*), *or* **réale**, *n.f.* (*réales*), real (Spanish coin = 5 cents).

réal, -e, *adj.*, royal, of the royal galley.

réale, *n.f.*, royal galley (old).

réalgar, *n.m.*, (min.) realgar.

réalisable, *adj.*, realizable.

réalisation, *n.f.*, realization; (fin.) conversion into money.

réaliser, *v.a.*, to realize; to convert into money.

se **réaliser**, *v.r.*, to be realized, to be converted into money; (fig.) to come to pass.

réalisme, *n.m.*, realism.

réaliste, *n.m.f.*, realist.

réalité, *n.f.*, reality; (theol.) real presence. *En* —; in reality; in fact, indeed.

réapparition, *n.f.*, reappearance.

réappel, *n.m.*, second call, second call over.

réappeler, *v.a.*, to call over a second time.

réapposer, *v.a.*, to reaffix, to put on again, to set on again; to reappend.

réapposition, *n.f.*, reaffixing, reappending; putting on again.

réargenter, *v.a.*, to resilver, to replate.

réargenture, *n.f.*, resilvering, replating.

réarmement, *n.m.*, arming again, re-arming.

réarmer, *v.a.*, to arm again.

réarpentage, *n.m.*, resurvey.

réarpenter, *v.a.*, to resurvey.

réassemblage, *n.m.*, reassemblage.

réassembler, *v.a.*, to reassemble, to gather together again.

réasservir, *v.a.*, to subjugate, enslave again.

*réassignation, *n.f.*, fresh summons, reassignment, new subpœna.

*réassigné, -e, *part.*, summoned again, reassigned.

*réassigner, *v.a.*, to reassign, to resummon, to summon again.

réassurance, *n.f.*, reinsurance, reassurance.

réassurer, *v.a.*, to reinsure, to reassure.

réatteler, *v.a.*, (of horses) to put to again.

rebaigner, *v.a.*, to bathe again. *Se* —; to bathe again.

*rebâiller, *v.n.*, to yawn again.

rebaiser, *v.a.*, to kiss again.

rebaisser, *v.a.*, to lower again, to let down again. *Se* —, to stoop down again.

rebander, *v.a.*, to bend again (a bow); to bind up again; to tie up again; to put another bandage (over the eyes).

rebaptisant (-ba-ti-), *n.m.*, rebaptizer.

rebaptisation (-ba-ti-), *n.f.*, baptizing again.

rebaptiser (-ba-ti-), *v.a.*, to rebaptize.

rébarbati-f, -ve, *adj.*, stern, gruff, crabbed, cross. *Visage* —; crabbed, gruff, stern countenance.

rebâter, *v.a.*, to resaddle, to saddle again.

rebâtir, *v.a.*, to rebuild, to build again.

rebattre, *v.a.*, to beat again; to repeat, to tell over and over; to shuffle again (cards).

rebattu, -e, *part.*, old, hackneyed, trite, oft-told. *Un conte* —; an old worn-out story. *J'en ai les oreilles* —*es*; I am sick of hearing it so often.

rebaudir, *v.a.*, (hunt.) to caress, to encourage (dogs).

⊙**rebec**, *n.m.*, (instr.) rebeck.

rebelle, *n.m.f. and adj.*, rebel; rebellious, disobedient, unyielding; (med.) obstinate; (metal.) refractory, impervious (to); ill-adapted; unfeeling. — *à la justice;* flying in the face of justice. — *à la raison;* impervious to reason. *Un sujet* — *à la poésie;* a subject ill-adapted to verse. *Une fièvre* — *aux remèdes;* an unyielding fever. *C'est une beauté* —; she is an unfeeling beauty. *Substances* —*s;* (metal.) refractory substances, substances hard to melt.

se **rebeller**, *v.r.*, to rebel, to rise in rebellion, to revolt.

rébellion, *n.f.*, rebellion, resistance, contumacy. *Faire* — *à la justice;* to resist justice.

rebénir, *v.a.*, to bless again; to consecrate anew.

se **rebéquer**, *v.r.*, to be saucy, to be pert, insolent.

rebercer, *v.a.*, to rock again.

se **rebercer**, *v.r.*, to rock one's self again.

rebiffer, *v.n.*, to turn up one's nose.

se **rebiffer**, *v.r.*, to resist, to refuse obedience; to refuse bluntly.

reblanchir, *v.a.*, to wash again; to blanch again, to bleach again; to whitewash again.

rèble *or* **rièble**, *n.m.*, (bot.) goose-grass; cleavers.

reboire, *v.a.*, to drink again.

reboisement, *n.m.*, retimbering, reafforestation.

reboiser, *v.a.*, to retimber, to replant, to reafforest.

rebond, *n.m.*, rebound.

rebondi, -e, *adj.*, plump, round, chubby, full. *Des joues* —*es;* chubby cheeks.

rebondir, *v.n.*, to rebound.

rebondissement (-dis-mãn), *n.m.*, rebounding.

rebord, *n.m.*, border, hem (of clothes); ledge; brim.

reborder, *v.a.*, to put a new border to; to border again, to rehem. — *une robe;* to put a new border, *or* new hem, to a gown. — *des souliers;* to bind shoes anew.

rebotter, *v.a.*, to make boots again for; to boot somebody again.

se **rebotter**, *v.r.*, to put on one's boots again.

rebouchement, *n.m.*, stopping up again.

reboucher, *v.a.*, to stop up again; to block up again; to stuff up; to cork up again. — *un trou;* to stop up a hole again. — *une bouteille;* to cork a bottle up again.

se **reboucher**, *v.r.*, to get, *or* become, stuffed up, or stopped up, again; to bend. *L'épée se reboucha contre sa cuirasse;* the sword bent against his cuirass.

rebouil, *n.m.*, pelt-wool.

*rebouillir, *v.n.*, to boil again.

rebouisage, *n.m.*, cleaning and polishing (of hats).

rebouiser, *v.a.*, to clean and polish (hats).

rebourgeonner, *v.n.*, to bud again.

rebours, *n.m.*, wrong side (of a stuff); wrong way (of the grain); contrary, reverse. *A* —, *au* —; the wrong way; against the grain, backwards. *Marcher à* —; to walk backwards. *Prendre à* —; to misconstrue. *Lire à* —; to read backwards.

rebours, -e, *adj.*, (fam.) cross, cross-grained, crabbed.

reboutage, *n.m.*, bone-setting.

rebouteu-r, *n.m.*, **-se**, *n.f.*, bone-setter.

reboutonner, *v.a.*, to button again, to re-button.

se **reboutonner**, *v.r.*, to button up one's clothes again.

rebrider, *v.a.*, to bridle again.

rebrocher, *v.a.*, to restitch books.

rebroder, *v.a.*, to re-embroider.

*** rebrouiller**, *v.a.*, to embroil again, to mix again, to confound again, to entangle again.

rebrousse, *n.f.*, napping-tool.

rebroussement (-bros-mãn), *n.m.*, turning back, turning up, inflection; (geom.) retrogression (of a curve).

à **rebrousse-poil**, *adv.*, against the hair; the wrong way; against the grain.

rebrousser, *v.a.*, to turn up (the hair). — *chemin;* to go back, to turn back, to retrace one's steps.

rebroussoir, *n.m.*, napping-tool.

rebroyer, *v.a.*, to grind again.

rebrûler, *v.a.*, to burn again.

rebrunir, *v.a.*, to burnish again.

rebuffade, *n.f.*, rebuff, repulse, rebuke.

rébus (-bus), *n.m.*, rebus; pun, conundrum.

rebut, *n.m.*, repulse, rebuff, rejection, refusal; refuse; trash; waste, rubbish, trumpery; riffraff, scum. *Marchandises de* —; waste goods. *Papier de* —; waste paper. *Mettre au* —; to throw aside. *Etre au* —; to be thrown aside. *Mettre une lettre au* —; to send a letter to the dead-letter office. *Bureau des* —; dead-letter office.

rebutant, -e, *adj.*, repulsive, forbidding, loathsome. *Travail* —; tedious work. *Air* —; forbidding look. *Homme* —; repulsive man.

rebuter, *v.a.*, to repulse, to rebuff, to thrust away, to cast aside; to reject, to refuse; to disgust, to shock. — *des excuses;* to refuse an apology. *Il a rebuté ces marchandises;* he rejected those goods.

se **rebuter**, *v.r.*, to be discouraged *or* disheartened, to be rebuffed, to lose courage. *Il se rebute aisément;* he is easily disheartened.

recacher, *v.a.*, to hide again.

recacheter (-kash-té), *v.a.*, to seal up again.

récalcitrant, -e, *adj.*, stubborn, refractory, perverse, reluctant, averse.

récalcitrer, *v.n.*, to be restive, to kick (of horses); (l.u.) to be refractory; to resist, to be reluctant.

recaler, *v.a.*, to wedge up again, to refix, to refasten. (fig.) *V.* **rembarrer**. *Il a été recalé;* (fam.) he has been plowed again.

récapitulati-f, -ve, *adj.*, recapitulatory.

récapitulation, *n.f.*, recapitulation, summing up.

récapituler, *v.a.*, to recapitulate, to sum up.

recarder, *v.a.*, to card again.

recarreler (-kar-lé), *v.a.*, to pave a floor anew.

recasser, *v.a.*, to break again; (agri.) to break up stubble-land, to give a first plowing to.

recassis, *n.m.*, (agri.) stubble-land that has been broken up.

recéder, *v.a.*, to re-cede, to yield again, to restore again, to let have back (again); to give up again.

recel, *n.m.*, (jur.) receiving of stolen goods.

recélé, *n.m.*, (jur.) concealment of goods; embezzlement.

recèlement (-sèl-mãn), *n.m.*, concealing, concealment (of malefactors); receiving (of stolen goods).

recéler, *v.a.*, to conceal (malefactors); to receive (stolen goods); to embezzle; to conceal, to hide; to contain. — *des effets;* to conceal wearing apparel.

recéler, *v.n.*, (hunt.) to be *or* remain concealed.

receleu-r, *n.m.*, **-se**, *n.f.*, (rè-cĕ-), receiver of stolen goods.

récemment (-sa-mãn), *adv.*, recently, newly, lately.

recensement (-sãns-mãn), *n.m.*, census; return, numbering; revisal, verification.

recenser, *v.a.*, to take the census; to verify, to examine.

recension, *n.f.*, (philos.) recension; book revised and edited (by a critic).

récent, -e, *adj.*, recent, new, fresh, late.

recépage, *n.m.*, (agri.) cutting down close (of vines).

recépée, *n.f.*, cut part of a wood.

recéper, *v.a.*, (agri.) to cut down.

récépissé, *n.m.*, receipt (for documents, papers); acknowledgment of receipt.

réceptacle, *n.m.*, receptacle; (bot.) torus.

récepteur, *n.m.*, recipient, receiver, reservoir; (of telegraphs) receiving instrument.

réceptibilité, *n.f.*, (l.u.) receptibility.

réception, *n.f.*, receiving, receipt, reception; admittance, admission, levee, drawing-room; party, entertainment. *Accuser* — *d'une lettre;* to acknowledge the receipt of a letter. *Bonne* —; welcome, good reception.

réceptionnaire, *adj.*, receiving. *n.m.*, receiver, receiving clerk.

réceptivité, *n.f.*, (l.u.) receptivity.

recerclage, *n.m.*, re-hooping.

recercler, *v.a.*, to hoop anew, to put new hoops to.

recette, *n.f.*, receipt, receipts, collection; receiving office; recipe; receiver's office, receivership, collectorship.

recevabilité, *n.f.*, (jur.) admissibility.

recevable, *adj.*, receivable, admissible, allowed.

receveu-r, *n.m.*, **-se**, *n.f.*, receiver, surveyor, comptroller, collector (of taxes).

recevoir, *v.a.*, to receive, to accept, to take, to take in, to let in; to welcome, to harbor; to admit; to allow of; to meet with, to submit to; to entertain. — *bien;* to receive well; to welcome. — *un mauvais accueil;* to meet with a bad reception. — *une opinion;* to admit an opinion. *Je reçois vos offres;* I accept your offers. *Son livre a été bien reçu;* his book has taken well. — *une excuse;* to accept an excuse. — *une proposition;* to accept a proposal. — *un coup mortel;* to be mortally wounded. — *la mort;* to meet with (one's) death.

recevoir, *v.n.*, to receive, to receive company; to be at home to visitors; to hold a levee, a drawing-room. *On recevra ce soir là;* there will be company that evening. *Elle reçoit beaucoup;* she sees a great deal of company. *Quand recevez-vous?* when is your reception, *or* at home, day? when are you at home to visitors?

recez (rĕ-sĕ), *n.m.*, recess; minutes (of a Congress).

réchampir *or* **échampir**, *v.a.*, to pick out with colors, to set off.

rechange, *n.m.*, change of anything; spare things; (com.) re-exchange; (nav.) spare stores. *Des habits de* —; spare clothes. *J'en ai de* —; I have some in reserve. *Mâts de hune de* —; spare topmasts. *De* —; spare.

rechanger, *v.a.*, to change again.

rechanter, *v.a.*, to sing again; to tell often.

réchapper, *v.n.,* to escape, to recover. *Un réchappé de la potence ;* (pop.) a villain, a gallows bird. — *d'une maladie ;* to recover from an illness.

recharge, *n.f.,* surcharge ; fresh charge. *En* — ; in addition.

rechargement, *n.m.,* reloading, loading again, reballasting.

recharger, *v.a.,* to load again, to reballast; to recharge; (milit.) to make a second charge ; to charge again, to enjoin over again. — *les ennemis ;* to charge the enemy again.

rechasser, *v.a.* and *n.,* to drive away again ; to drive back.

rechasser, *v.a.,* to hunt again.

réchaud, *n.m.,* chafing-dish, dish-warmer, hot-water dish, small stove ; (hort.) hot-bed, mulch.

réchauffage, *n.m.,* warming up again ; giving as new what is old, hash-up ; plagiarism ; reheating ; (metal.) balling.

réchauffé, *n.m.,* food, etc., warmed up ; something that is stale, old ; stale stuff, imitation ; (fig.) after-thought. *C'est du* — ; it is mere imitation.

réchauffé, -e, *adj.,* warmed up again.

réchauffement, *n.m.,* (hort.) lining anew (a hot-bed) ; mulching.

réchauffer, *v.a.,* to heat again, to make warm again, to make hot again, to warm again, to warm up ; to re-animate, to rekindle, to stir up. *Faire — la soupe ;* to warm up the soup. — *une couche ;* (hort.) to manure a bed anew, to mulch. *se* **réchauffer,** *v.r.,* to warm one's self, to get one's self warm, to grow warm ; to rekindle, to become warmer, to warm.

réchauffoir, *n.m.,* plate-warmer, dish-warmer.

rechausser, *v.a.,* to put on shoes *or* stockings again ; to set new cogs to a wheel ; (agri., hort.) to mold, to mold up ; (mas.) to line the foot of, to underpin. — *un arbre ;* to mold up a tree. — *un mur ;* to underpin a wall.

rêche, *adj.,* rough (to the taste, touch) ; crabbed (of persons). *Cette étoffe est* — ; that stuff is very rough.

recherche, *n.f.,* search, seeking, quest, pursuit ; research, inquiry, investigation ; examination, scrutiny; studied elegance, neatness, finish, labored refinement, studied refinement, care ; addresses, courtship, suit ; (mas.) research, mending (with tiles *or* slates). *Travailler à la* — *de la vérité ;* to labor in search of truth. — *exacte ;* strict search. *Faire la — d'une chose ;* to search for a thing. *Style naturel et sans* — ; natural and unaffected style. *Il fait la — d'une veuve ;* he is courting a widow.

recherché, -e, *adj.,* choice, exquisite; affected, far-fetched, sought after, run after, in great request, in great demand. *Parure* —*e ;* exquisite dress. *Expression* —*e ;* far-fetched expression. *Ornements* —*s ;* choice ornaments.

rechercher, *v.a.,* to seek again, to look again for, to seek, to seek for, to seek after, to look for, to search, to search for, to search after ; to investigate, to search into, to inquire into, to make an inquiry into ; to institute an inquiry into, to call to account ; to endeavor to obtain, to desire, to aspire to ; to run after, to court, to seek ; to solicit in marriage, to ask in marriage, to woo, to solicit the hand of ; (arts) to finish, to finish off, to polish ; (man.) to animate. *On rechercha sa vie;* they made inquiries into his mode of life. — *un cheval ;* to animate a horse. *se* **rechercher,** *v.r.,* to seek each other, *or* each other's society ; to be sought after.

****rechigné, -e,** *adj.,* sour-faced, glum, surly, sulky, cross, crabbed, gruff.

****rechignement,** *n.m.,* sulking, frowning, sullenness, crabbedness.

****rechigner,** *v.n.,* to look sulky, sullen, grim, gruff, sour, crabbed.

⊙**rechoir,** *v.n.,* to fall again ; to relapse, to have a relapse.

rechute, *n.f.,* relapse.

récidive, *n.f.,* recidivism, relapse into crime ; second offense, repetition of an offense. *Il y a* — ; it is not the first offense. *Etre en* — ; to be an old offender.

récidiver, *v.u.,* to repeat the same offense ; to commit the same crime again.

récidiviste, *n.m.f.,* previously convicted felon ; habitual criminal ; old offender.

récif, *n.m.,* (nav.) reef, ledge (of rocks); ridge.

récipé, *n.m.,* recipe, medical prescription ; receipt.

récipiendaire, *n.m.,* new member, member-elect.

récipient, *n.m.,* (chem.) recipient, receiver ; cistern, well.

réciprocation, *n.f.,* reciprocation.

réciprocité, *n.f.,* reciprocity, reciprocation.

réciproque, *n.m.,* like. *Rendre le* — ; to return the like ; to give like for like.

réciproque, *n.f.,* (math., log.) converse.

réciproque, *adj.,* reciprocal, mutual ; (math.) converse, reciprocal.

réciproquement (-prok-mān), *adv.,* reciprocally, mutually ; (math.) conversely.

recirer, *v.a.,* to wax, polish, *or* black, again.

récit, *n.m.,* recital, relation, account, story, tale, narration, narrative, statement ; report ; (mus.) recitative.

récitant, -e, *adj.,* (mus.) solo.

récitateu-r, *n.m.,* reciter, repeater.

récitatif, *n.m.,* (mus.) recitative.

récitation, *n.f.,* reciting, recitation ; repetition.

réciter, *v.a.,* to recite, to rehearse ; to repeat, to say ; to tell, to relate, to give an account of, to recount ; (mus.) to sing in recitative ; to play in recitative. *Récitez votre leçon ;* say your lesson.

réciter, *v.n.,* (mus.) to perform a recitative ; to recite.

réciteu-r, -se, *n.m.f.,* reciter, story-teller.

réclamable, *adj.,* claimable.

réclamant, *n.m., -e,* *n.f.,* (jur.) claimant.

réclamation, *n.f.,* claim, demand ; complaint, protestation, protest, opposition, objection. *Etre en* — ; to have raised an objection, to have formulated a complaint, a demand.

réclame, *n.m,* (hawking) bird-call.

réclame, *n.f.,* (print.) catch-word ; primer ; (of newspapers) editorial announcement, advertisement, puff, puffing, paragraph puff ; (thea.) cue, catchword (last words of couplets).

réclamer, *v.a.,* to implore, to entreat, to beseech; to reclaim, to claim back, to redemand, to demand back again ; to claim ; (hunt.) to call off ; (hawking) to bring back ; (jur.) to lay claim to. — *son droit ;* to claim one's right. — *un oiseau ;* to bring back a hawk. — *les chiens ;* to call off the dogs. *se* **réclamer,** *v.r.,* to be reclaimed, to be demanded ; to say one is known to a person ; to make use of any one's name, to invoke, to refer to. *Voyant qu'on allait le maltraiter, il se réclama d'un tel ;* seeing they were about to ill-treat him, he referred to so-and-so.

réclamer, *v.n.,* to oppose, to object, to protest (against), to complain (of), to make a complaint, to make objection (to). *Je réclame contre cela ;* I protest against that. *Personne ne réclame ?* does nobody raise any objection ?

reclouer, *v.a.,* to nail again.

⊙**reclure,** *v.a.,* to shut up, to confine, to cloister up, to sequester.

reclus, -e, *n.* and *part.,* recluse, monk, nun ; cloistered up, shut up, sequestered, secluded.

reclusion *or* **réclusion,** *n.f.,* reclusion, retirement, seclusion ; (jur.) confinement, imprisonment (with hard labor and loss of civil rights).

*recogner, *v.a.*, to hit again, to strike again ; to beat back, to drive back, to beat (an argument).

récognitif (-cog-), *adj.m.*, (jur.) recognitory. *Acte* — ; ratification of a liability (stating the consideration thereof).

récognition (-cog-), *n.f.*, recognition.

recoiffer, *v.a.*, to dress the head *or* hair again ; to re-adjust the hair ; to cap again, to re-cap (bottles).

recoin, *n.m.*, corner, nook, by-place, by-way. *pl.*, cricks and corners ; innermost recesses.

récolement (-kol-mān), *n.m.*, (jur.) examination ; verification.

récoler, *v.a.*, (jur.) to read the previous evidence to a witness ; to examine, to verify.

⊙**récollection** (-kol-lèk-), *n.f.*, (devotional style) contemplation.

recollement, *n.m.*, pasting, *or* gluing, again ; (of a wound) healing.

recoller, *v.a.*, to paste again (fig. and fam.). *Il a été recollé or recalé ;* he has been plowed again.

récollet, *n.m.*, **-te**, *n.f.*, recollet (Franciscan friar *or* nun).

récolte, *n.f.*, harvest, crop, vintage ; collection, gathering. *Temps de la* — ; harvest time. *Faire la* — ; to get in the harvest.

récolter, *v.a.*, to reap, to gather in, to get in. *se* **récolter**, *v.r.*, to be got in (of crops).

recommandable, *adj.*, commendable, recommendable, respectable.

recommandation, *n.f.*, recommendation ; esteem, reference, introduction ; (jur.) detainer. *Lettre de* — ; letter of introduction.

recommander, *v.a.*, to recommend, to charge, to enjoin, to bid, to intrust, to request ; (jur.) to lodge a detainer against. *Je vous recommande le secret ;* I enjoin secrecy.

se **recommander**, *v.r.*, to recommend one's self, itself ; to look for protection (to) ; to refer to. *Cette chose se recommande d'elle-même ;* the thing is its own recommendation. *Je me recommande à vous ;* I refer to you.

recommencement, *n.m.*, recommencement, beginning anew, repetition, renewal.

recommencer, *v.a.n.*, to recommence, to begin again. — *la guerre ;* to begin war afresh. — *de plus belle,* — *sur nouveaux frais ;* to renew the attempt, to begin again worse than ever. *C'est toujours à* — ; there's no end to it. *Ne recommencez pas, par exemple ;* don't do it again, though.

recomparaître, *v.n.*, to appear again (before).

récompense, *n.f.*, reward, recompense ; requital ; compensation, amends ; indemnity. *En* — ; in return (for) ; as a recompense (for).

récompenser, *v.a.*, to reward, to requite, to recompense, to remunerate ; to make amends (to), to compensate ; to requite ; to make up for, to repay. — *le temps perdu ;* to make up for lost time.

se **récompenser**, *v.r.*, to make up for, to make amends, to be recompensed.

recomposer, *v.a.*, to recompose.

recomposition, *n.f.*, recomposition.

recompter (-kon-té), *v.a.*, to count again.

réconciliable, *adj.*, reconcilable.

réconciliat-eur, *n.m.*, **-rice**, *n.f.*, reconciler. *adj.*, reconciling.

réconciliation, *n.f.*, reconciliation, reconcilement.

réconcilier, *v.a.*, to reconcile, to conciliate ; to make friends again. *On les a réconciliés ;* they have been reconciled. — *une église ;* to consecrate a church anew.

se **réconcilier**, *v.r.*, to be reconciled, to become friends again. *Il s'est réconcilié avec son père ;* he has made it up with his father.

réconduction (*tacite*), *n.f.*, (jur.) renewal of a lease, continued tenancy (upon the same terms).

reconduire, *v.a.*, to reconduct, to lead back, to show out ; to accompany, to see home, to accompany to the door.

reconduite, *n.f.*, accompanying out, *or* to the door ; seeing out, seeing home. *Faire la* — ; to accompany out, home.

reconfirmer, *v.a.*, to confirm again.

⊙**réconfort**, *n.m.*, comfort, relief, consolation.

⊙**réconfortation**, *n.f.*, cheering up, comforting, strengthening.

réconforter, *v.a.*, to cheer up, to strengthen, to fortify, to comfort ; to cheer.

reconfrontation, *n.f.*, confronting anew.

reconfronter, *v.a.*, to confront again.

reconnaissable, *adj.*, recognizable.

reconnaissance, *n.f.*, gratitude, thankfulness ; recognition ; examination ; acknowledgment, confession ; reward, return ; recognizance ; (milit., nav.) reconnoitering, econnoitering party. *Avoir de la* — ; to be grateful. *Témoigner sa* — ; to testify one's gratitude. *Faire une* — ; to reconoiter. — *d'enfant ;* acknowledgment of a child. — *de prêteur sur gages ;* pawn-broker's ticket.

reconnaissant, -e, *adj.*, grateful, thankful. — *de ;* thankful for.

reconnaître, *v.a.*, to recognize, to know again ; to know ; to identify ; to find out, to discover ; to acknowledge, to confess, to admit, to allow ; to be grateful ; (milit.) to reconnoiter, to explore, to observe. *Je ne le reconnais plus ;* he has grown out of my recollection. *Se faire* — ; to make one's self known. *On a reconnu sa trahison ;* his treachery was discovered. — *un enfant ;* to own a child. *Je vous reconnais bien là ;* that is just like you.

se **reconnaître**, *v.r.*, to know one's self ; to see one's self ; to know where one is ; to make out ; to come to one's self ; to collect one's self ; to give one's self breathing time ; to acknowledge one's guilt ; to plead guilty. *Il se reconnaît dans son fils ;* he sees himself in his son. *Je commence à me reconnaître ;* I begin to know where I am. *Je ne me reconnais plus ;* I don't know what I am about. *Je me reconnais bien là ;* that is just like me.

reconquérir, *v.a.*, to reconquer, to recover, to regain.

reconsidération, *n.f.*, reconsideration.

reconsidérer, *v.a.*, to reconsider.

reconstituer, *v.a.*, to reconstitute, to re-establish, to re-organize.

reconstitution, *n.f.*, reconstitution, reorganization, resettling ; (jur.) substitution.

reconstruction, *n.f.*, reconstruction, rebuilding.

reconstruire, *v.a.*, to build again, to reconstruct.

reconsulter, *v.a.*, to consult again.

reconter, *v.a.*, to tell again, to relate over again.

recontinuer, *v.a.*, to resume, to go on again.

recontracter, *v.a.*, to contract again.

reconvention, *n.f.*, (jur.) cross suit, cross action, set off.

reconventionnel, -le, *adj.*, (jur.) cross. *Demande* — ; cross action.

reconvoquer, *v.a.*, to convene again, to call together again.

recopier, *v.a.*, to copy again. *Se* — ; to be recopied.

*recoquillement, *n.m.*, curling up, turning up, shriveling ; being dog's-eared (of leaves).

*recoquiller, *v.a.*, to curl up ; to turn up, to shrivel up ; to dog's-ear (leaves).

*se recoquiller, *v.r.*, to turn up, to curl one's self up, to be dog's-eared, to shrivel.

recorder, *v.a.*, to rehearse (a lesson) ; to learn

or get by heart ; to cord again ; to twist again ; to measure firewood again.

se **recorder**, v.r., to concert with any one, to call to mind ; to be recorded.

recorriger, v.a., to correct again, to revise.

recors, n.m., bailiff's man.

recoucher, v.a., to put to bed again, to lay flat again.

se **recoucher**, v.r., to go to bed again.

recoudre, v.a., to sew again, or stitch again.

se **recoudre**, v.t., to be sewn up again.

recoupe, n.f., rubble, stone-chips ; chippings ; pollard.

recoupement (-coop-mān), n.m., (arch.) off-set ; recess.

recouper, v.a., to cut again.

recoupette, n.f., coarse meal.

recourbé, -e, adj., bent back, curved, crooked.

recourber, v.a., to bend back, to make crooked, to crook.

se **recourber**, v.r., to grow crooked, to bend.

recourbure, n.f., bending back, curveture.

recourir, v.n., to run again ; to have recourse to, to apply to, to resort (to) ; to appeal. — aux remèdes ; to have recourse to remedies.

recours, n.m., recourse ; refuge, resort, help, resource, redress, remedy, appeal. — en cassation ; petition of appeal. — en grâce ; petition for pardon or commutation.

⊙**recousse**, n.f. V. **rescousse**.

recousu, -e, part., sewed, stitched again.

recouvrable, adj., (fin.) recoverable.

⊙**recouvrance**, n.f., recovery.

recouvrement, n.m., recovery, regaining ; (fin.) payment ; (horl.) lid ; cap (of a watch) ; (arch.) overlapping. pl., debts due to one. — de la santé ; recovery of one's health. Faire un état de — ; to draw up a statement of debts due. Faire un — ; to recover an outstanding debt.

recouvrer, v.a., to recover, to regain, to get again, to get back possession (of), to get in, to collect. — ses forces ; to recover one's strength. — son bien ; to recover one's fortune.

recouvrir, v.a., to cover again ; to cover, to mask, to hide, to conceal.

se **recouvrir**, v.r., to cover one's self again ; to be covered again ; to be hidden again, to become cloudy again, to be overcast again.

recracher, v.a. and n., to spit out again ; to spit again ; (fig.) to fork out again ; to disgorge.

récréance, n.f., provisional possession. Lettres de — ; (diplomacy) letters of recall.

récréati-f, -ve, adj., recreative ; refreshing ; diverting, amusing.

récréation, n.f., recreation, amusement, diversion ; play (of children). Heure de — ; play-time. Être en — ; to be at play, out of school.

recréer, v.a., to re-create, to create again.

récréer, v.a., to recreate, to divert, to amuse.

se **récréer**, v.r., to divert, to amuse one's self, to take recreation.

récrément, n.m., (med.) recrement.

récrémenteu-x, -se, or **récrémentitiel**, -le, adj., (med.) recremental, recrementitious.

recrépir, v.a., to parget again, to roughcast ; to give a fresh coat of plaster to ; to paint (one's face) ; to patch up. — un vieux mur ; to replaster an old wall. — un vieux conte ; to dress up an old story.

recrépissage or **recrépissement**, n.m., re-plastering ; repatching.

recreuser, v.a., to dig up again, to dig deeper.

⊙**récri**, n.m., exclamation ; cry, outcry, clamor.

se **récrier**, v.r., to exclaim ; to utter an exclamation ; to cry out, to protest. Il n'y a pas de quoi se — ; there is nothing to cause astonishment, there is no need to cry out.

récrimination, n.f., recrimination.

récriminatoire, adj., recriminatory.

récriminer, v.n., to recriminate.

récrire, v.a., to write over again ; to write again ; to rewrite.

recroître, v.n., to grow again ; to spring up again.

recrotter, v.a., to dirty again.

recru, -e, adj., quite tired, worn out, knocked up, jaded, spent.

recrudescence, n.f., recrudescence.

recrudescent, -e, adj., recrudescent.

recrue, n.f., recruiting ; recruit ; recruits. Faire des —s ; to raise recruits.

recrutement (re-krut-mān), n.m., recruiting, recruitment.

recruter, v.a., to recruit.

se **recruter**, v.r., to recruit.

recruteur, n. and adj.m., recruiter ; recruiting, recruiting officer.

recta, adv., punctually, exactly.

rectangle, adj., (geom.) rectangular, right-angled.

rectangle, n.m., rectangle.

rectangulaire, adj., rectangular, right-angled.

recteur, n.m., rector (of a parish, of an academy) ; provost, warden.

rect-eur, -rice, adj., directing. ⊙Esprit — ; (chem.) aromatic. Pennes rectrices ; (zool.) tail-feathers.

rectifiable, adj., rectifiable.

rectificateur, n.m., rectifier.

rectificati-f, -ve, adj., rectifying.

rectification, n.f., rectification ; (jur.) amendment.

rectifier, v.a., to rectify.

se **rectifier**, v.r., to be rectified.

*rectiligne, adj., rectilineal, rectilinear.

rectitude, n.f., rectitude, uprightness.

recto, n.m., (—s) first page of a leaf ; odd page, right-handed page.

rectoral, -e, adj., rectorial.

rectorat, n.m., rectorship, rectorate, provost-ship, wardenship.

rectrice, n.f., (orni.) tail-feather. V. **rec-teur**, adj.

rectum (-tom), n.m., (—) (anat.) rectum.

reçu, -e, part., received ; admitted ; recognized, customary, usual.

reçu, n.m., receipt. Au — de ; on receipt of. Donnez-moi un — de ce que je vous remets ; give me a receipt for what I give you.

*recueil, n.m., collection, selection, miscellany. — choisi ; elegant extracts.

*recueillement, n.m., contemplation, meditation, self-communing ; gathering, collection ; (fig.) peaceful seclusion.

*recueilli, -e, part., gathered, collected ; meditative, wrapped in meditation, calm, still, quiet. C'est un homme très — ; he is a very contemplative man.

*recueillir, v.a., to gather, to get in ; to reap ; to get together, to collect ; to pick up ; to receive, to take in, to shelter. — une succession ; to inherit an estate. — ses esprits ; to collect one's self. — ses forces ; to collect one's strength. — les voix ; to collect the votes.

se **recueillir**, v.r., to collect one's self, to collect one's thoughts ; to wrap one's self up in pious meditation. — en soi-même ; to retire within one's self, to commune with one's self ; to reflect.

recuire, v.a., to cook, or do, again ; to boil over again ; to bake over again ; (manu.) to anneal. — des métaux ; to anneal metals.

recuit, -e, part., boiled, baked, or roasted again. Cela est cuit et — ; that is done to rags.

recuit, n.m., or **recuite**, n.f., annealing (of metals, glass) ; reheating (liquids).

recul, n.m., recoil ; kicking (of fire-arms).

reculade, n.f., falling back ; retreat ; backing (of carriages). Honteuse — ; shameful retreat. Faire une — ; to beat a retreat.

reculé, -e, part., put back ; distant, remote ;

backward, behind (in learning). *La postérité la plus —e ;* the remotest posterity.

reculée, *n.f.,* (l.u.) backing-space ; moving back. *Feu de —;* (l.u.) roasting fire.

reculement (-kul-mǎn), *n.m.,* drawing back ; backing (of carriages) ; breech (of saddles).

reculer, *v.a.,* to pull back ; to put back ; to put off, to defer ; to extend.

se **reculer,** *v.r.,* to draw back ; to go further off ; to put back ; to be extended, to sit further off.

reculer, *v.n.,* to go back, to fall back, to draw back ; to retreat, to recede, to shirk, to shrink (before), to back out (of) ; to give way ; to re-coil ; to rein back (a horse). — *pour mieux sauter ;* to wait for something better. *Il est trop avancé pour —;* he is too far involved to retreat. *Il ne recule jamais ;* he never flinches. *En reculant ;* in going backwards.

à **reculons,** *adv.,* backwards ; the wrong way ; with one's back to the engine, etc.

⊙**récupérable,** *adj.,* that may be recovered, retrievable, recoverable.

récupération, *n.f.,* recovery.

récupérer, *v.a.,* to recover, to retrieve ; to get back.

se **récupérer,** *v.r.,* to recover ; to retrieve one's losses.

récurer, *v.a.* V. **écurer.**

récurrence, *n.f.,* (med.) recurrence.

récurrent, -e (-kur-rǎn, -t), *adj.,* (med.) recurrent, returning.

récursoire, *adj.,* (jur.) which can give rise to an appeal, remedial.

récusable, *adj.,* (jur.) exceptionable, challengeable, doubtful.

récusation, *n.f.,* (jur.) challenge, exception, denial.

récuser, *v.a.,* to challenge (witnesses, jurors) ; to deny, to reject.

se **récuser,** *v.r.,* to excuse one's self, to decline ; (of judges, jurors) to decline judging *or* voting ; to declare one's self incompetent.

rédacteur, *n.m.,* writer (of a deed) ; clerk (in a public office) ; editor, editress ; writer (of periodicals). — *d'un journal ;* editor of a newspaper. — *en chef ;* chief editor. — *gérant ;* sub-editor.

rédaction, *n.f.,* drawing up (deeds, etc.) ; wording ; editing (periodicals) ; editors.

redan, *n.m.,* (fort.) redan ; (arch.) skew-back.

redanser, *v.n.,* to dance again.

reddition (rèd-di-), *n.f.,* (jur., milit.) surrender, reduction ; restitution, giving back ; giving in (of accounts). — *de compte ;* giving in of accounts.

redébattre, *v.a.,* to debate again.

redéclarer, *v.a.,* to declare again.

redédier, *v.a.,* to dedicate anew.

redéfaire, *v.a.,* to undo again.

redéjeuner, *v.a.,* to breakfast again.

redélibérer, *v.a.,* to deliberate again (upon), to consider again.

⊙**redélivrer,** *v.a.,* to set at liberty a second time.

redemander, *v.a.,* to redemand, to ask again ; to ask back again.

redemeurer, *v.n.,* to dwell *or* live again.

redémolir, *v.a.,* to demolish, *or* pull down, again.

rédempteur, *n.m.,* redeemer, savior.

rédempt-eur, -rice, *adj.,* redeeming, redemptive, redemptory.

rédemption, *n.f.,* redemption ; ransom.

rédemptoriste, *n.m.,* Redemptorist.

redépêcher, *v.a.,* to dispatch again.

redescendre, *v.n.,* to go, or come, down again.

redescendre, *v.a.,* to take down again.

redevable, *n.m.f.* and *adj.,* debtor ; indebted ; beholden. *Je suis votre —* or *je vous suis —;* I am your debtor. *Etre — à . . . de ;* to be indebted to . . . for.

redevance, *n.f.,* rent ; royalty ; due, service ; (feudalism) fine.

redevenir (rě-dě-vnir), *v.n.,* to become again.

redévider, *v.a.,* to wind again.

redevoir, *v.a.,* to remain in one's debt, to owe still.

rédhibition, *n.f.,* (jur.) action to set aside a sale.

rédhibitoire, *adj.,* (jur.) setting aside a sale · redhibitory.

rédiger, *v.a.,* to draw out ; to draw up ; to draught ; to write out ; to word ; to indite.

se **rédimer,** *v.a.,* to redeem one's self.

rediner, *v.n.,* to dine again.

redingote, *n.f.,* riding-coat, frock-coat ; (ladies') morning dress.

redire, *v.a.,* to repeat, to say again, to tell again ; to censure, to criticize, to find fault (with) ; to report. *Trouver à — à ;* to find fault with, to find amiss, to complain of. *Je n'y trouve rien à —;* I see nothing amiss in it. *Il n'y a rien à —;* no fault can be found with. *Se faire —;* to have repeated to one ; to require to be told again.

rediseu-r, *n.m.,* **-se,** *n.f.,* tautologist, repeater ; tell-tale, tale-bearer.

redistribuer, *v.a.,* to distribute again.

redistribution, *n.f.,* redistribution, re-issue.

redite, *n.f.,* (b.s.) repetition, gossiping.

redompter (-don-té), *v.a.,* to subdue again.

redondance or **rédondance,** *n.f.,* superfluity of words, redundancy.

redondant or **rédondant, -e,** *adj.,* redundant.

redonder or **rédonder,** *v.n.,* to be redundant.

redonner, *v.a.,* to give again, to give back again ; to restore ; to deal again (at cards).

se **redonner,** *v.r.,* to give one's self up again ; to give away again ; to indulge again in.

redonner, *v.n.,* to give one's self up again ; to fall again into ; to take to again ; (milit.) to charge again ; to be engaged again.

redorer, *v.a.,* to gild over again, to regild.

redormir, *v.n.,* to sleep again.

⊙**redoublant,** *n.m.,* pupil that remains a second year in the same class.

redoublé, -e, *part.,* redoubled, increased ; repeated. *Pas —;* (milit.) double-quick time. *Rimes —es ;* double rhymes.

redoublement, *n.m.,* redoubling, increase ; reduplication ; (med.) paroxysm.

redoubler, *v.a.,* to redouble, to increase, to reiterate ; to increase greatly ; to put a new lining to. — *ses soins ;* to be doubly careful.

redoubler, *v.n.,* to increase ; to redouble ; ⊙to continue two years in the same class (at school). — *de soins ;* to be doubly attentive.

redoul or **roudou,** *n.m.,* (bot.) coriaria myrtifolia, tanners' sumac.

redoutable, *adj.,* formidable, redoubtable, terrible, dreadful.

redoute, *n.f.,* (fort.) redoubt ; ridotto ; dancing-room.

redouter, *v.a.,* to dread, to fear. *Il n'est pas à —;* he is not to be feared.

redressage, *n.m.,* straightening.

redressement (-drès-mǎn), *n.m.,* straightening ; erection ; redressing ; redress ; relief (from a grievance).

redresser, *v.a.,* to make straight, to make straight again ; to straighten ; to erect ; to set up again ; to put right ; to correct, to reform, to put to rights, to set to rights ; to redress ; to over-reach. — *la tête ;* to hold up one's head. — *des griefs ;* to redress grievances.

se **redresser,** *v.r.,* to become straight again ; to get straight again ; to bridle up ; to stand erect again ; to set upright ; to be set right, to be redressed. *Redressez-vous ;* sit up.

redresseur, *n.m.,* redresser, avenger, righter.

redû, *n.m.,* balance due.

réducteur, *n.m.,* (surg.) apparatus for reducing a dislocation.

réductibilité, n.f., reducibleness.

réductible, adj., reducible.

réducti-f, -ve, adj., reductive.

réduction, n.f., reduction; subjugation; (com.) allowance, abatement; (chem., math., surg.) reduction.

réduire (réduisant, réduit), v.a., to reduce, to abate, to diminish, to curtail; to subdue, to subjugate; to compel; to oblige, to restrain; (chem., math., surg.) to reduce. — *une place;* to reduce a stronghold, to take a fortress. — *au désespoir;* to drive to despair.

se **réduire**, v.r., to be reduced; to diminish; to abate; to vanish; to reduce one's self; to be subdued; (fig.) to come to, to amount to.

réduit, n.m., retreat, small habitation; lodging; corner, recess; hole, hovel; (fort.) reduct.

réduplicati-f, -ve, adj., (gram.) reduplicative.

réduplicatif, n.m., (gram.) reduplicative.

réduplication, n.f., reduplication.

réédification, n.f., rebuilding.

réédifier, v.a., to rebuild.

rééditer, v.a., to publish anew (of books).

réel, -le, adj., real, true; actual; substantial. n.m., reality, truth.

réélection, n.f., re-election.

rééligibilité, n.f., re-eligibility.

rééligible, adj., re-eligible.

réélire, v.a., to re-elect.

réellement (-èl-mãn), adv., really; in reality, truly, indeed.

réemballage, n.m., repacking.

réemballer, v.a., to repack.

réémettre, v.a., to re-issue.

réémigrer, v.n., to re-emigrate.

réémission, n.f., re-issue.

réentement, n.m., regrafting.

réenter, v.a., to regraft. *Se* —; to be regrafted.

réenterrement, n.m., reburial.

réenterrer, v.a., to re-bury, to re-inter.

réer, v.n. V. **raire**.

réescompte, n.m., (com.) rediscount.

réescompter, v.a., (com.) to rediscount.

réexaminer, v.a., to examine anew.

réexpédier, v.a., to forward again, to send off again.

réexpédition, n.f., forwarding again, sending off again, return.

réexportation, n.f., re-exportation.

réexporter, v.a., to re-export.

refâcher, v.a., to vex again, to anger again.

se **refâcher**, v.r., to grow angry, *or* vexed, again.

refaçon, n.f., remaking, remake.

refaçonner, v.a., to form *or* make again, to re-fashion.

réfaction, n.f., remaking; repairing, repairs; (com.) rebate.

refaire, v.a., to do again, to do over again, to remake; to make anew; to begin anew; to recommence; to deal again (at cards); to take in, to deceive; to be refreshing (to); to refresh; to mend, to repair. — *de la viande;* to warm meat up again, to re-pot meat.

se **refaire**, v.r., to refresh one's self; to recover one's strength; to retrieve one's losses; to assume a new character. *Se* — *un habit;* to have a coat done up again, *or* a coat made again.

refait, n.m., drawn game (at play); (hunt.) new horns.

refait, -e, part., done again; (of timber) squared, prepared for use; (nav.) twice laid (of cordage).

refaucher, v.a., to mow again.

réfection, n.f., repairs; ⊙repairs to buildings; refection (meal); food, nourishment; recovery of strength.

réfectoire, n.m., refectory, dining-room *or* hall.

refend, n.m., splitting, sawing, dividing; (arch.) channel (in wall). *Mur de* —; (arch.) partition-wall. *Bois de* —; sawed timber.

refendre, v.a., to cleave, *or* split, again; to quarter (timber); to saw into slabs (stone); to saw, or cut, lengthwise.

référé, n.m., (jur.) application to a judge (sitting) in chambers. *En* —; in chambers.

référence, n.f., (com.) reference; relation, information.

référendaire, n.m., referendary.

référendariat, n.m., referendaryship.

référer, v.a., to refer; to ascribe. *En* — *à;* to refer to.

se **référer**, v.r., to refer, to have a reference; to refer, to leave it (to), to confide, to trust (in). *S'en référer à l'avis de quelqu'un;* to refer to the opinion of any one.

référer, v.n., to report, to make a report.

refermer, v.a., to shut up again, to close up. — *une plaie;* to close a wound.

se **refermer**, v.r., to shut again; to close again.

referrer, v.a., to shoe again (animal).

*****refeuilleter**, v.a., to turn over again, to turn over and over (leaves); to read again cursorily.

reficher, v.a., to thrust, *or* stick, in again; to drive in again.

refiger, v.n., to congeal again.

se **refiger**, v.r., to congeal again.

refixer, v.a., to fix again.

réfléchi, -e, adj., reflected; reflecting; deliberate; considerate; reflective, thoughtful, meditative; (bot.) reflex. *Action* —*e;* deliberate action. *Crime* —; premeditated crime. *Opinion peu* —*e;* hasty opinion. *Personne* —*e;* reflective, meditative, thoughtful, circumspect, person. *Homme peu* —; inconsiderate man.

réfléchir, v.a., to reflect, to reflect back; to mirror back; to throw back; to reverberate.

se **réfléchir**, v.r., to reflect, to be reflected.

réfléchir, v.n., to reflect, to reflect on, to think, to consider, to ponder. *J'y réfléchirai;* I'll think it over.

réfléchissant, -e, adj., reflecting.

réfléchissement (-shis-mãn), n.m., reflection, reverberation.

réflecteur, n. and adj. m., reflector; reflective, reflecting.

reflet, n.m., reflection, reflex, reflected light.

refléter, v.a., to reflect (light, etc.).

se **refléter**, v.r., to reflect, to be reflected, to be mirrored back.

refleurir, v.n., to blossom again, to blow again, to flower again; to flourish again. *Faire* —; to revive.

réflexe, adj., reflex.

réflexibilité, n.f., reflexibility.

réflexible, adj., reflexible, reflectible.

réflexi-f, -ve, adj., reflexive.

réflexion, n.f., reflection; thought, consideration. *Faire* —; to reflect. *Avez-vous fait vos* —*s?* have you considered the matter? have you pondered over it? *Un homme de* —; a thinking man. *Toute* — *faite;* all things considered; after due reflection; on second thought.

refluer, v.n., to reflow, to flow back, to ebb.

reflux, n.m., reflux, refluctuation; ebb, ebbing, flowing back. *Le flux et le* —; the ebb and flow; (fig.) the constant shifting.

⊙**refonder**, v.a., (jur.) to refund, to reimburse, to repay; to refound.

refondre, v.a., to refound, to melt again; to recast, to cast again, to mold anew; to improve; to remodel; (nav.) to repair, to improve, to correct. — *la monnaie;* to recoin money. — *un ouvrage;* to remodel, *or* re-cast, a work. — *un vaisseau;* to repair a ship thoroughly.

refonte, n.f., refounding, recasting (metal.); recoinage, recoining; remodeling; (nav.) thorough repair.

reforger, *v.a.*, to forge again.

réformable, *adj.*, reformable, that may be reformed ; (jur.) reversible ; (mil.) exemptible.

réformat-eur, *n.m.*, **-rice**, *n.f.*, reformer. *adj.*, reforming, reformatory.

réformation, *n.f.*, reformation, amendment. *La — des monnaies ;* the re-stamping of coin.

réforme, *n.f.*, reform, reformation, amendment ; (milit.) reduction, discharge. *Traitement de — ;* (milit.) half-pay. *Etre mis à la — ;* (milit.) to be put on half-pay. *Etre en — ;* (milit.) to be on half-pay. *Congé de — ;* (milit.) discharge. *Cheval de — ;* cast horse.

réformé, -e, *part.*, reformed. *La religion —e ;* the Protestant religion. *Un officier — ;* a half-pay officer.

réformé, *n.m.*, reformer, reformist.

réformer, *v.a.*, to reform, to mend, to improve. *— ses mœurs ;* to reform one's morals. *— sa vie ;* to amend one's life. *— les abus ;* to reform abuses. *— son train ;* to reduce the number of one's servants. *— les monnaies ;* to re-stamp coin. *— des troupes ;* to discharge troops. *— un officier ;* to put an officer on half-pay. *— un soldat ;* to discharge a soldier.

se **réformer**, *v.r.*, to reform, to amend ; to be reformed.

reformer, *v.a.*, to form again, to form anew.

se **reformer**, *v.r.*, to form again, to be formed anew.

réformiste, *n.m.*, reformer, reformist.

refortifier, *v.a.*, to fortify again.

refouetter, *v.a.*, to whip again.

refoulement (re-fool-mān), *n.m.*, driving back, suppression, compressing, forcing back ; ebbing (of the tide). *Le — des eaux ;* the flowing back of the waters. *Le — de la marée ;* the ebbing of the tide. *Le — d'une armée ;* the driving back of an army.

refouler, *v.a.*, to drive back, to repel ; to compress ; (artil.) to ram. *— la marée ;* to stem, to go against the tide.

refouler, *v.n.*, to ebb ; to flow back. *La marée refoule ;* the tide is ebbing.

refouloir, *n.m.*, cannon-rammer.

refournir, *v.a.*, to furnish again, to stock anew.

réfractaire, *adj.*, refractory, stubborn, obstinate, rebellious ; impervious (to) ; fire-proof.

réfractaire, *n.m.*, (milit.) defaulting conscript, defaulter.

réfracter, *v.a.*, (phys.) to refract.

se **réfracter**, *v.r.*, to be refracted.

réfracti-f, -ve, *adj.*, refractive.

réfraction, *n.f.*, (phys.) refraction.

refrain, *n.m.*, refrain, burden of a song ; constant theme ; (nav., l.u.) rolling back of billows (after breaking on rocks), surf. *C'est son — continuel ;* it is his constant theme ; he is always harping upon it.

refrangibilité, *n.f.*, refrangibility.

réfrangible, *adj.*, refrangible.

refrapper, *v.n.*, to strike again, to knock again. *— la monnaie ;* to restamp coin.

refréner, *v.a.*, to bridle, to restrain ; to curb, to repress.

réfrigérant, -e, *adj.*, refrigerant. *Mélange — ;* freezing mixture.

réfrigérant, *n.m.*, (med.) refrigerant.

réfrigérati-f, -ve, *adj.*, (med.) refrigerative.

réfrigératif, *n.m.*, (med.) refrigerative.

réfrigération, *n.f.*, (chem.) refrigeration.

⊙**réfrigératoire**, *adj.*, refrigerative.

réfringent, -e, *adj.*, refracting.

refrire, *v.a.*, to fry again.

refriser, *v.a.*, to curl again.

refrogné, -e, *or* **renfrogné, -e**, *part.*, frowning, scowling, gruff, surly, sullen. *Air — ;* scowling, sullen look.

*refrognement *or* **renfrognement**, *n.m.*, frown, scowl, knitting of the brows.

*se refrogner *or* *se* **renfrogner**, *v.r.*, to frown, to knit one's brows.

refroidi, -e, *part.*, chilled, cooled.

refroidir, *v.a.*, to cool, to chill.

se **refroidir**, *v.r.*, to cool, to grow cold *or* cool ; to slacken, to relax, to relent, to abate.

refroidir, *v.n.*, to cool, to become cold.

refroidissement (-dis-mān), *n.m.*, cooling, coolness ; coldness ; chill, cold. *J'ai pris un — ;* I have caught a chill.

refrotter, *v.a.*, to rub again.

refuge, *n.m.*, refuge, shelter, asylum, resting place ; resource, protection. *— assuré ;* safe refuge. *Lieu de — ;* place of safety.

réfugié, -e, *n.m.*, **-e**, *n.f.*, refugee.

se **réfugier**, *v.r.*, to take refuge, shelter ; (fig.) to have recourse (to) ; to shelter one's self (behind).

refuir, *v.n.*, (hunt.) to double.

refuite, *n.f.*, (hunt.) shift, doubling ; (l.u.) shuffling, evasion.

refus, *n.m.*, refusal, denial ; thing refused. *Essuyer un — ;* to meet with a refusal. *Un — net ;* a flat refusal. *Cela n'est pas de — ;* that is not to be refused, *or* is very acceptable. *Ce n'est pas à son — ;* it has not been offered him *or* he has not had the refusal of it. *Enfoncer un pieu jusqu'à — de mouton ;* (tech.) to ram a pile in (until driven home). *Ce pieu est au — ;* this pile is set, driven home.

refusable, *adj.*, refusable.

refuser, *v.a.*, to refuse ; to deny ; to decline, not to accept, to grudge, to demur. *— des présents ;* to refuse presents. *— la porte à quelqu'un ;* to deny any one admittance ; to shut one's door (against).

se **refuser**, *v.r.*, to deny one's self, to deprive one's self of ; not to permit ; to grudge one's self ; to shun, to avoid ; to withstand, to resist. *Il se refuse le nécessaire ;* he denies himself the necessaries of life.

refuser, *v.n.*, to refuse ; to decline ; (man.) to refuse to advance ; (nav.) to scant ; not to come to the wind.

refuseu-r, *n.m.*, **-se**, *n.f.*, refuser.

réfutable, *adj.*, refutable.

réfutateur, *n.m.*, refuter, confuter.

réfutation, *n.f.*, refutation, confutation, disproof.

réfuter, *v.a.*, to refute, to confute, to disprove.

se **réfuter**, *v.r.*, to refute each other ; to be refuted.

*regagner, *v.a.*, to regain, to get again, to win back, to recover ; to retrieve ; to rejoin, to overtake, to reach, to gain over. *— le dessus ;* to get the upper hand again. *— le vent sur l'ennemi ;* (nav.) to get the weather-gauge of the enemy. *— quelqu'un ;* to gain any one over *or* to overtake any one. *— la maison ;* to return home, to reach home.

*regaillardir, *v.a.*, to make merry, to enliven, to revive, to give a fillip to. *V.* **ragaillardir**.

regain, *n.m.*, aftermath, after-grass ; (fig.) revival, return ; (of life) new lease of. *— de jeunesse ;* a second youth. *— de vie ;* a new lease of life.

régal, *n.m.*, feast, entertainment, treat ; pleasure. *C'est un vrai — pour moi ;* it is a real treat for me.

régalade, *n.f.*, (fam.) gulping down ; blazing fire ; treating ; treat. *Boire à la — ;* to gulp down ; to pour (wine, etc.) down one's throat, without putting the glass to one's lips.

régalant, -e, *adj.*, amusing, pleasant, entertaining.

régale, *n.m.*, (mus.) regal, vox humana (stop).

régale, *n.f.*, right, regalia (F. Hist.).

régale, *adj.f.*, (l.u.) royal. *Eau — ;* aqua regia (nitro-hydrochloric acid).

régalement (-gal-măn), *n.m.*, ⊙assessment, equalization (of taxes) ; leveling (of ground) ; ⊙equalization (of shares in an inheritance).

régaler, *v.a.*, to regale, to treat, to feast, to entertain ; ⊙to assess taxes ; to level (ground). *se* **régaler**, *v.r.*, to feast, to entertain *or* treat one another ; to regale one's self ; to enjoy one's self.

régaleur, *n.m.*, entertainer, leveler.

⊙**régalien** (-in), *adj.m.*, regal, royal.

regard, *n.m.*, look ; gaze, stare ; glance ; eye, eyes ; (astrol.) aspect ; two pictures looking at one another. *pl.*, eyes ; attention, notice ; (tech.) draft-hole, man-hole. — *tendre ;* tender look. *Lancer un* — ; to dart a look. *Jeter ses* —*s de côté et d'autre ;* to cast one's eyes about. *Jeter un* — *sur ;* to cast a glance at. *Adoucir ses* —*s ;* to soften one's countenance. *Fixer les* —*s de quelqu'un ;* to catch any one's eye ; to arrest any one's attention. *Au* — *sombre ;* dull-eyed. *En* —; opposite. *Avoir* — *sur ;* to look into, to face. *Promener ses* —*s sur ;* to cast one's eyes upon, *or* round. *Abaisser les* —*s ;* to look down. *Au* — *de, V.* **à l'égard de.**

regardable, *adj.*, to be worth looking at ; to be looked at.

regardant, *n.m.*, beholder, looker-on, spectator.

regardant, -e, *adj.*, too strict, particular, nice ; economical, near, saving, niggardly.

regarder, *v.a.*, to look at ; to look on ; to behold ; to face, to be opposite, to look into ; to consider, to mind, to look up to ; to regard, to concern. — *quelqu'un ;* to look at any one. — *quelqu'un fixement ;* to stare at any one. — *par un trou ;* to look (at) through a hole. — *quelqu'un de haut en bas ;* to look down upon any one, to look any one down (with contempt). — *comme ;* to look upon as, to consider as, to repute. *Cela vous regarde ;* that concerns you. *Se faire* —; to attract notice.

se **regarder**, *v.r.*, to look at one's self ; to look at each other ; to look upon one's self as ; to consider one another as ; to be opposite to each other ; to be in front of each other.

regarder, *v.n.*, to look, to face, to be opposite, to front ; to mind, to pay heed to. *Ma chambre regarde sur le jardin ;* my room overlooks the garden. *Regardez-y bien ;* take heed. *Y* —; to be particular, to consider. *Y* — *à deux fois ;* to think twice. *Y* — *de près ;* to be particular about. *Je n'y regarde pas de si près ;* I am not so particular as all that.

regarnir, *v.a.*, to furnish again ; to retrim.

régate, *n.f.*, regatta, boat-race.

regayer, *v.a.*, to comb hemp.

regayoir, *n.m.*, hemp-comb.

regayure, *n.f.*, refuse of hemp.

regazonnement, *n.m.*, returfing.

regazonner, *v.a.*, to returf.

regel, *n.m.*, renewed frost, freezing again.

regeler, *v.n.*, to freeze again.

régence, *n.f.*, regency.

régénérat-eur, -rice, *n.* and *adj.*, regenerator ; regenerating, reproducing.

régénération, *n.f.*, regeneration.

régénérer, *v.a.*, to regenerate. *se* **régénérer**, *v.r.*, to be regenerated.

régent, -e, *adj.*, regent.

régent, *n.m.*, regent ; master (of a college) ; governor, director (of the bank of France) ; name of a large diamond of the French crown.

régenter, *v.a.* and *n.*, ⊙ to teach ; (fig.) to domineer, to lord it over, to hector.

regermer, *v.n.*, to regerminate.

régicide, *n.m.* and *adj.*, regicide ; regicidal.

régie, *n.f.*, administration ; administration of the taxes ; excise, excisemen ; excise-office. *Officier de la* —; exciseman.

regimbement, *n. m.*, kicking (of horses) ; resistance, revolt, kicking against.

regimber, *v.n.*, to kick (of horses) ; (fig.) to resist ; to revolt, to kick against.

régime, *n.m.*, regimen ; diet ; form of government ; rule ; reign ; law ; order of things ; (gram.) object, objective case. *Mettre au* —; to diet. *Etre au* —; to be on low diet. *Vivre de* —; to live by rule. *Se mettre au* —; to diet one's self.

régiment, *n.m.*, regiment.

régimentaire, *adj.*, regimental.

région, *n.f.*, region, country.

régional, *adj.*, local (district) ; industrial, agricultural.

régir, *v.a.*, to govern, to rule ; to administer, to manage.

régisseur, *n.m.*, manager, steward.

régistrateur, *n.m.*, registrar, recorder (in the Pope's chancellor's office).

registre, *n.m.*, register, book, account ; register (of an organ) ; (mus.) draw-stop ; (print.) register ; damper (of chimneys) ; vane (of a steam-engine). *Rapporter sur un* —; to enter in a register. *Il est sur mes* —*s ;* I have him on my books. *Tenir* —; to keep account (of).

registrer, *v.a.*, to register, to record.

regître, *n.m. V.* **registre**.

regitrer, *v.a. V.* **registrer**.

réglage, *n.m.*, ruling (of paper) ; regulating, settling ; setting, timing (of watches, clocks, etc.).

règle, *n.f.*, rule, ruler ; order ; pattern, model, example ; guide, regulation ; (arith.) sum. *pl.*, menses, courses. *Cela est de* —; that is the rule. *Dans les* —*s ;* according to rule, in due form. *Etre en* —, *se mettre en* —; to be in order, to have everything in order. — *à coulisse ;* sliding rule.

réglé, -e, *adj.*, ruled ; regulated, regular, steady. — *comme un papier de musique ;* as regular as clock-work. *Une vie* —*e ;* a regular life. *A des heures* — *es ;* at regular hours. *Il a le pouls* —; his pulse is regular.

règlement, *n.m.*, regulation ; laws, by-laws ; standing order ; settlement (of accounts) ; (mil.) roster. *Violer le* —; to commit a breach of order. *Vous manquez au* —; you are breaking the rules. — *de compte ;* settlement of an account.

réglément, *adv.*, regularly, exactly.

réglementaire, *adj.*, according to regulations, allowed, lawful, usual, customary.

réglementation, *n.f.*, regulating.

réglementer, *v.a.* and *n.*, to regulate.

régler, *v.a.*, to rule, to regulate, to square ; to order ; to settle ; to determine, to decide ; to time. — *sa dépense ;* to regulate one's expenses. — *ses affaires ;* to settle one's affairs. — *une pendule ;* to set a clock right. — *un différend ;* to settle a difference.

se **régler**, *v.r.*, to regulate one's self by ; to imitate, to follow the example of, to be guided (by) ; to be regulated, to time one's self (upon). *Se* — *sur la vertu ;* to be guided by virtue. *Je ne me règle pas sur cela ;* I don't go by that. *Je me réglerai sur vous ;* I shall time myself by you.

réglet, *n.m.*, (print.) rule ; (arch.) girth.

réglette, *n.f.*, (print.) reglet.

régleu-r, *n.m.*, -se, *n.f.*, ruler, paper-ruler.

réglisse, *n.f.*, licorice. *Du jus de* —; Spanish liquorice. — *en bâton ;* stick licorice.

réglure, *n.f.*, ruling (of paper).

***régnant, -e**, *adj.*, reigning, prevailing, present ; prevalent ; predominating, predominant, chief.

***règne**, *n.m.*, reign ; prevalence ; vogue, fashion ; crown (over the high altar in churches) ; kingdom ; tiara (of the pope). — *animal ;* animal kingdom.

***régner**, *v.n.*, to reign, to govern, to rule, to bear sway, to prevail ; to be in fashion ; (arch.) to reach. *La maladie qui règne ;* the prevailing disease.

régnicole, *n.m.f.* and *adj.* (rĕg-ni-), (jur.) native, citizen ; naturalized subject.

regonflement, *n.m.*, re-inflation, swelling anew.

regonfler, *v.n.*, to swell, to overflow.

regonfler, *v.a.*, to swell again ; to inflate, to fill again.

regorgement, *n.m.*, overflowing (of fluids) ; overflow, superabundance.

regorger, *v.n.*, to overflow, to run over, to abound with, to teem with ; to be glutted, to be crowded *or* crammed (with). *La salle regorgeait de monde ;* the hall was crowded with spectators. *Cette province regorge de blé ;* that province abounds in corn. — *de santé ;* to be in rude health. *Faire* — ; to compel to disgorge.

regouler, *v.a.*, (pop.) to snub ; to surfeit.

regoûter, *v.a.*, to taste again.

regracier, *v.a.*, to pardon again, a second time.

regrat, *n.m.*, (l.u.) huckstering ; huckster's shop ; ⊙ retail salt-shop.

regrattage, *n.m.*, (mas.) regrating, rescraping.

regratter, *v.a.*, to scratch again ; to scrape again ; (mas.) to regrate.

regratter, *v.n.*, to huckster ; (l.u.) to haggle ; to make illegitimate petty profits.

regratterie (-gra-trî), *n.f.*, huckster's trade ; huckstery, huckster's wares.

regratti-er, *n.m.*, **-ère**, *n.f.*, huckster, huck-stress ; dealer in second-hand goods ; (fig.) scribbler, compiler, hack ; haggler.

regreffer, *v.a.*, to graft again.

régressi-f, **-ve**, *adj.*, regressive, retrogressive.

régression, *n.f.*, regression, retrogression.

regret, *n.m.*, regret. *Avoir du* — ; to feel regret, to be sorry. *J'ai* — *que vous n'ayez pas vu cette pièce ;* I regret that you have not seen that play. *A* — ; with regret, with reluctance, grudgingly.

regrettable, *adj.*, lamentable, regrettable, deplorable.

regrettablement, *adv.*, lamentably.

regretter, *v.a.*, to regret, to lament, to grieve (at) ; to be sorry (for) ; to repent, to miss. *Tout le monde le regrette ;* he is regretted by every-body. *Je regrette qu'il ne soit pas ici ;* I regret that he is not here. *Je vous regrette ;* I miss you. *Le regretté . . . ;* the late lamented . . .

regrossir, *v.a.*, (engr.) to make thicker.

reguinder (-ghin-), *v.a.n.*, to hoist again ; to soar again.

se **reguinder**, *v.r.*, to soar again (of a hawk).

régularisation, *n.f.*, putting in order ; settle-ment.

régulariser, *v.a.*, to put in order, to settle.

régularité, *n.f.*, regularity, strict observance (of rules) ; strictness ; ecclesiastical state.

régulateur, *n.m.*, regulator ; standard. *Le* — *d'une horloge ;* the regulator of a clock. — *de tirage ;* damper.

régulat-eur, **-rice**, *adj.*, regulating.

régule, *n.m.*, (chem.) pure metal ; (orni.) regulus, kinglet ; (disparagingly, of persons) king-ling, kinglet.

réguli-er, **-ère**, *adj.*, regular, steady ; punctual, exact.

régulier, *n.m.*, regular (of monks, soldiers).

régulièrement (-lier-mān), *adv.*, regularly, punctually, steadily.

régurgitation, *n.f.*, reabsorption.

régurgiter, *v.a.*, to throw, *or* pour, back.

réhabilitation, *n.f.*, rehabilitation, vindica-tion ; (of bankrupts) discharge.

réhabiliter, *v.a.*, to rehabilitate, to reinstate ; to restore to ; to vindicate.

se **réhabiliter**, *v.r.*, to rehabilitate one's self, to reinstate, to re-establish one's self, to pay twenty shillings in the pound.

réhabituer, *v.a.*, to use, to reaccustom.

se **réhabituer**, *v.r.*, to reaccustom one's self.

rehacher, *v.a.*, to mince again.

rehanter, *v.a.*, to frequent again.

rehasarder, *v.a.*, to venture again.

rehaussé, **-e**, *adj.*, heightened, enhanced ; set off, enriched.

rehaussement (-hôs-mān), *n.m.*, raising, heightening ; enhancing ; increase of value (of coin).

rehausser, *v.a.*, to raise, to heighten, to set off, to enrich ; to set forth, to extol, to cry up, to enhance, to raise the value of. — *le mérite d'une action ;* to enhance the merit of an action. — *d'or et d'argent ;* to enrich with gold and silver.

rehauts (rě-hô), *n.m.pl.*, (paint.) lightest parts of a picture.

reheurter, *v.a.*, to knock, *or* to hit, again.

réimportation, *n.f.*, (com.) re-importation.

réimporter, *v.a.*, to import again.

réimposer, *v.a.*, to reassess ; to lay on again ; (print.) to reimpose.

réimposition, *n.f.*, further assessment ; (print.) reimposing.

réimpression, *n.f.*, reprinting ; reprint, reissue.

réimprimer, *v.a.*, to print again, to reissue.

rein, *n.m.*, kidney ; rein (of an arch), skirt (of a wood). *pl.*, loins, reins, back. *Douleur dans les* —*s ;* pain in the loins. *Poursuivre quelqu'un l'épée dans les* —*s ;* to pursue any one very close. *Il a les* —*s forts ;* he is strong-backed ; (fig.) he has a long purse. *Douleur des* —*s ;* pains in the back. *Se donner un tour de* —*s ;* to sprain one's back. *Chute des* —*s ;* small of the back. *Les* —*s d'une voûte ;* the haunches, or shoulder, of a vault.

reinaire, *adj.*, (bot.) having the shape of a kidney ; reniform.

réincorporer, *v.a.*, to reincorporate.

reine, *n.f.*, queen. — *régnante ;* reigning queen, queen regnant. — *mère ;* queen mother. — *douairière ;* queen dowager. *Faire la* — ; to act the queen. —*des-prés*, (—*s*—) (bot.) meadow-sweet.

reine-claude, *n.f.*, (—*s*—) (bot.) greengage.

reine-marguerite, *n.f.*, (—*s*—*s*) (bot.) China-aster, Chinese starwort, starwort. *V.* **marguerite**.

reinette, *n.f.*, russet ; rennet ; pippin. — *d'Angleterre ;* golden pippin.

réinfecter, *v.a.*, to reinfect, to taint again.

réinstallation, *n.f.*, reinstallment.

réinstaller, *v.a.*, to reinstall.

reinté, **-e**, *adj.*, broad-loined, strong-backed.

réintégrande, *n.f.*, (jur.) restoration.

réintégration, *n.f.*, reinstatement ; (com.) re-warehousing.

réintégrer, *v.a.*, to reinstate ; to re-ware-house.

réinventer, *v.a.*, to invent anew.

réinviter, *v.a.*, to invite again.

reis, *n.m.*, (—) chief. —*effendi ;* Turkish Secretary of state for Foreign Affairs.

réitérati-f, **-ve**, *adj.*, repeated, reiterative.

réitération, *n.f.*, reiteration, repetition.

réitérer, *v.a.*, to reiterate, to repeat.

reitre, *n.m.*, reiter (German horse soldier of the 14th and 15th centuries). *C'est un vieux* — ; he is an old fox.

****rejaillir**, *v.n.*, to gush, to gush out, to spurt out, to fly out, to stream, to spring out, to spout, to spout out ; to reflect, to be reflected, to flash ; to fly back ; to rebound, to cast a reflection (upon) ; to be hurled back.

****rejaillissement** (-is-mān), *n.m.*, gushing, gushing out, spouting, spouting forth, springing out, spurting, spurting out ; springing, rebound-ing ; reflection, flashing (of light) ; rebound, fly-ing back (of a solid body).

rejaunir, *v.n.*, to grow yellow again.

réjection, *n.f.*, rejection.

rejet, *n.m.*, rejection ; throwing out ; young

shoot, sprig, sprout; (geol.) out-throw; (fin.) carrying; transfer; cast, swarm (of bees); springe (for woodcock).

rejetable, *adj.*, that may be rejected, rejectable.

rejeteau, *n.m.*, weather-board *or* bead (of a door *or* window).

rejeter (rĕj-té), *v.a.*, to throw again; to drive back, to throw back; to cast *or* throw up *or* out; to throw, to throw away; to put forth (of plants); to refuse to accept, to reject; to set aside; to deny; (fin.) to carry; to transfer. — *le blâme sur;* to throw the blame on. — *un compte sur;* to carry or transfer an account (to).

se **rejeter**, *v.r.*, to have recourse to, to fall back (upon); to throw back to each other; to be rejected.

rejeter, *v.n.*, to shoot (of plants).

rejetoir, *n.m.*, springe, gin, noose.

rejeton (rĕj-ton), *n.m.*, (bot.) shoot, sprout; (hort.) offset; (fig.) scion, offspring.

rejettement, *n.m.*, rejection.

rejoindre, *v.a.*, to rejoin, to join again, to join; to reunite; to meet again; to overtake; to catch up.

se **rejoindre**, *v.r.*, to join again, to catch each other up again, to be joined together again; to reunite, to meet again.

rejointoiement (-toa-mãn), *n.m.*, (mas.) rejointing; repointing.

rejointoyer, *v.a.*, (mas.) to rejoint, to repoint.

rejouer, *v.a.*, to play again; to act again. *Se* — ; to be played *or* acted, again.

rejouer, *v.n.*, to play again; to recall a move.

réjoui, *-e*, *n.* and *adj.*, jovial, joyous, merry person; jovial, joyous, merry. *Un gros* — ; a jovial man; jolly fellow. *Grosse* —*e;* buxom woman, *or* lass.

réjouir, *v.a.*, to rejoice, to gladden, to delight, to divert, to entertain, to make merry; to cheer, to exhilarate. *Cette couleur réjouit la vue;* that color pleases the eye. *Le vin réjouit le cœur;* wine makes the heart glad.

se **réjouir**, *v.r.*, to be *or* to make merry, to enjoy one's self; to rejoice (at); to be delighted (at), to enjoy one's self, to be glad (of *or* at).

réjouissance, *n.f.*, rejoicing; coarse meat; make-weight. *pl.*, rejoicings, merry-making. *En signe de* — ; as a sign of rejoicing.

réjouissant, *-e*, *adj.*, jovial, joyous, cheerful; gladsome, rejoicing, cheering, diverting, amusing.

relâchant, *-e*, *adj.*, loosening, opening, laxative, relaxing.

relâchant, *n.m.*, opening medicine, laxative.

relâche, *n.m.*, intermission, remission; discontinuance; rest, respite; relaxation; (thea.) no performance. *Il y a* — *au théâtre ce soir;* there is no performance at the theater this evening. — *!* closed (of theaters). *Sans* — ; without intermission.

relâche, *n.f.*, (nav.) any place fit to put into; putting into port; calling at a port.

relâché, *-e*, *adj.*, loose, remiss, lax, relaxed. *Morale* —*e;* loose doctrine.

relâchement (-lâsh-mãn), *n.m.*, slackness, looseness, laxness; slackening, loosening, relaxing; diminution; intermission; abatement; relaxation, rest; remissness; laxity (of morals). — *des nerfs;* relaxing of the nerves.

relâcher, *v.a.*, to slacken, to loose, to loosen, to unbend, to relax; to let go, to release, to set at liberty; to yield, to give up, to abate.

se **relâcher**, *v.r.*, to grow slack *or* loose; to slacken, to abate; to give way, to relax, to unbend; to fall off; to flag; to get milder (of the weather). *Se* — *l'esprit;* to unbend one's mind, to take relaxation.

relâcher, *v.n.*, to abate, to remit, to relax, to flag; (nav.) to put into port, to touch at.

relais, *n.m.*, relay (fresh horses); stage; post-

ing-house (where fresh horses are taken). *Chevaux de* — ; fresh horses; (hunt.) relay; opening (in carpet-making); (fort.) V. **berme**. *Etre de* — ; to be unemployed, to have nothing to do, to be disengaged, at leisure.

relaissé, *adj.m.* (hunt.), resting (of hares).

relaisser, *v.n.*, (hunt.) to rest (of hares).

relancer, *v.a.*, (hunt.) to start again; to turn out again; to urge, to rouse, to answer sharply, to put down, to take up short (by an answer). — *quelqu'un;* to put any one down; to take any one up short.

relaps, *-e* (rĕ-laps), *n.* and *adj.*, relapser; relapsed; relapsed into heresy.

rélargir, *v.a.*, to widen, to let out (clothes).

rélargissement (-jis-mãn), *n.m.*, widening; letting out (clothes).

relater, *v.a.*, (jur.) to relate, to state.

relateur, *n.m.*, (l.u.) relater, narrator.

relati-f, *-ve*, *adj.*, relative, relating.

relatif, *n.m.*, (gram.) relative.

relation, *n.f.*, relation, reference; respect, account, recital; statement; connection. *pl.*, relations, connections, intercourse; communication, correspondence. *Etre en* —*s avec quelqu'un;* to be connected with any one, to be in correspondence with any one. — *exacte;* exact account.

relationnaire, *n.m.*, narrator, relater.

relativement (-tiv-mãn), *adv.*, relatively, comparatively.

relativité, *n.f.*, relativeness.

relatter, *v.a.*, to lath anew.

relaver, *v.a.*, to wash again.

relaxation, *n.f.*, (jur., med.) laxness; enlargement; relaxation, abatement, remission. — *d'un prisonnier;* release of a prisoner.

relaxé, *adj.*, relaxed, slackened, released.

relaxer, *v.a.*, to relax; to enlarge; to release.

relayer, *v.a.*, to take the place of, *or* to relieve, any one.

se **relayer**, *v.r.*, to relieve one another; to take it in turns.

relayer, *v.n.*, to take fresh horses, to change horses.

relayeur, *n.m.*, job post-master.

relécher, *v.a.*, to lick again.

relégation, *n.f.*, (jur.) banishment; exile; relegation.

reléguer (-ghé), *v.a.*, to banish; to send off; to shut up; to consign; to relegate; to seclude.

se **reléguer**, *v.r.*, to shut one's self up, to seclude one's self.

relent, *n.m.*, mustiness, moldiness. *Sentir le* — ; to smell moldy.

relevage, *n.m.*, raising; collection (of letters); clearing (letter boxes).

***relevailles** (rĕl-vâ-ye), *n.f.pl.*, churching of a woman. *Faire ses* — ; to be churched.

relevant, *-e* (rĕl-vãn, -t), *adj.*, held, being holden; depending.

relevé (rĕl-vé), *n.m.*, abstract, extract, statement, return; shifting (of a horse's shoe). *Faire un* — *de compte;* to make an abstract of an account.

relevé, *-e* (rĕl-vé), *adj.*, raised; erect; high, exalted, lofty, refined. *Une condition* —*e;* a high rank. *Pensée* —*e;* noble thought. *D'un ton* — ; in a refined tone. *De la viande d'un goût* — ; high-seasoned meat.

relevée (rĕl-vé), *n.f.*, (jur.) afternoon. *De* — ; in the afternoon.

relèvement (rĕ-lèv-mãn), *n.m.*, raising again; statement, account; (nav.) rising, bearing.

relever (rĕl-vé), *v.a.*, to raise again, to lift up again; to tuck up; to restore; to raise; to curl up, to twirl up; to heighten, to relieve, to set off; to cry up, to extol; to notice, to remark; to take up; to give a relish to; to liberate, to free; to retort; to criticize; (nav.) to take the bearings of. — *des fortifications;* to restore fortifications. — *un fossé;* to raise up the banks of a ditch. — *le courage de quelqu'un;* to raise any one's courage. *Relevez votre robe;* tuck up your gown. — *les bords d'un chapeau;* to turn up the rim of a hat. — *un mot;* to criticize a word. — *la tête;* to raise one's head again. *La parure relève la bonne mine;* dress sets off a handsome face. — *une action;* to extol an action. — *quelqu'un;* to raise any one. *Se faire — de ses vœux;* to get one's vows annulled. — *la garde;* to relieve guard. — *une sentinelle;* to relieve a sentry. — *un vaisseau;* to get a ship afloat again. — *l'ancre;* to shift the position of the anchor. — *une côte;* to take the bearings of a coast; to survey a coast. — *le quart;* (nav.) to set the watch.

se **relever**, *v.r.*, to rise again; to get up again, to rise; to rise up, to get up; to recover, to retrieve one's losses; to relieve each other; to take turns; to be raised; (nav.) to right itself (of a ship).

relever, *v.r.*, to recover; to get better; to turn up; to depend; to be dependent upon; to be amenable (to) (jur.). — *de maladie;* to recover from illness. — *de coucher;* to be about again (after confinement); to be churched.

releveur, *n.m.* and *adj.*, (anat.) levator; elevator.

reliage, *n.m.*, hooping (of casks).

relief, *n.m.*, relief, relievo, embossment; embossing; set-off. *Bas—,* (——*s*) bas-relief, bass-relief, basso-relievo, low-relief. *Haut, plein* —, — *entier;* high-relief, alto-relievo. *Demi-*, (——) demi-relievo. *Ouvrage de* —; work in relief. *Donner du* —; to set off; to give relief; to make conspicuous; to give importance to.

⊙**reliefs**, *n.m.pl.*, remains, leavings, broken scraps (from the table).

reliement, *n.m.*, union, joining, junction; connecting, connection.

relier, *v.a.*, to hoop (casks); to bind (books).

relieur, *n.m.*, binder, bookbinder.

religieuse, *n.f.*, nun.

religieusement (-efiz-mān), *adv.*, religiously, strictly, scrupulously, faithfully.

religieu-x, **-se**, *adj.*, religious, spiritual; exact, strict, punctual.

religieux, *n.m.*, friar, monk, brother.

religion, *n.f.*, religion, creed; religious worship; piety, godliness, faith; (fig.) scruple, conscientiousness, conscience. *Se faire une — d'une chose;* to make a thing a matter of conscience or of duty. — *réformée;* protestant religion. *Entrer en* —; to become a monk, a nun. *Mourir en* —; to die in the Lord, or to die a Christian.

religionnaire, *n.m.*, Protestant.

religiosité, *n.f.*, ⊙excessive scrupulousness in religious matters; religiousness.

relimage, *n.m.*, filing again.

relimer, *v.a.*, to file again; to polish; to work up.

reliquaire, *n.m.*, reliquary; shrine.

reliquat, *n.m.*, balance, remainder of an account; remains (of a disease); ⊙remains of a feast.

reliquataire, *n.m.*, debtor owing a balance; debtor.

relique, *n.f.*, relic. *Les —s d'un saint;* the shrine of a saint. *Je n'ai pas grand'foi à ses* —*s;* I have not much confidence in him.

relire, *v.a.*, to read over again.

reliure, *n.f.*, binding (of books).

relocation, *n.f.*, (jur.) letting anew; reletting, fresh lease.

reloger, *v.a.* and *n.*, to lodge again, to dwell again.

relouer, *v.a.*, to let again; to underlet; to rent again.

reluire, *v.n.*, to shine, to glitter, to glisten. *Tout ce qui reluit n'est pas or;* all is not gold that glitters.

reluisant, **-e**, *adj.*, bright, shining, glittering.

reluquer, *v.a.*, to cast sheep's eyes on; to ogle; to leer at; to have an eye upon, to long for (fig.). — *une terre;* to covet a certain property. — *un héritage;* to covet an inheritance.

reluqueu-r, *n.m.*, **-se**, *n.f.*, ogler; coveter.

remâcher, *v.a.*, to chew again, to ruminate; to revolve in one's mind.

remaçonner, *v.a.*, to repair (mas.). *Se —;* to be repaired.

*****rémailler**, *v.a.*, to enamel again.

remailler, *v.a.*, to mend, to repair the meshes of (in stockings, knitting, fishing nets, etc.).

remander, *v.a.*, to send word again.

remaniement *or* **remaniment**, *n.m.*, handling again; touching again; (print.) overrunning; doing over again, repairing, altering, changing.

remanier, *v.a.*, to handle again; to touch again; to repair; to retouch, to do over again; (print.) to overrun. — *le papier;* (print.) to turn the paper.

remarchander, *v.a.*, to haggle again.

remarcher, *v.n.*, to walk *or* go again; to march again.

remarier, *v.a.*, to marry again.

se **remarier**, *v.r.*, to marry a second time; to be married again.

remarquable, *adj.*, remarkable, conspicuous.

remarquablement, *adv.*, remarkably, conspicuously.

remarque, *n.f.*, remark, observation, notice. *Digne de* —; worthy of notice, noteworthy.

remarquer, *v.a.*, to mark again, to make another mark; to note, to observe, to notice, to take notice; to remark, to distinguish. *Se faire* —; to attract notice, to distinguish one's self. *Faire* —; to observe, to point out; to call attention to.

se **remarquer**, *v.r.*, to be remarked, noticed.

remasquer, *v.a.*, to mask again.

se **remasquer**, *v.r.*, to put on one's mask again.

remballage, *n.m.*, re-packing.

remballer, *v.a.*, to pack up again.

rembarquement, *n.m.*, re-embarkation; re-embarkment, re-shipping, re-shipment.

rembarquer, *v.a.*, to re-embark; to ship again.

se **rembarquer**, *v.r.*, to re-embark; to go on board again; to engage again (in anything).

rembarrer, *v.a.*, to repel, to repulse; to retort on, to set down, to take up short, to stop at once.

remblai, *n.m.*, filling up; embanking; rubbish.

remblayer, *v.a.*, to embank, to fill up (with rubbish); to resow (with corn).

remboîtement (-boat-mān), *n.m.*, setting (of a bone); fitting in again, clamping.

remboîter, *v.a.*, to set (a bone); to fit in again, to clamp (pieces of joinery).

rembourrage *or* **rembourrement** (ran-boor-), *n.m.*, stuffing, padding.

rembourrer, *v.a.*, to stuff (with flock *or* hair); to stuff out, to pad.

se **rembourrer**, *v.r.*, (pop.) to stuff up (to eat gluttonously).

remboursable, *adj.*, repayable, reimbursable; (fin.) redeemable.

remboursement, *n.m.*, reimbursement, repayment. *Contre* —; on payment, on cash remittance. *Faire suivre en* —; to require payment on delivery, to charge forward.

rembourser, *v.a.*, to reimburse, to repay, to refund.

se **rembourser**, *v.r.*, to reimburse one's self, to repay one's self.

rembraser, *v.a.*, to kindle again.

rembrasser, *v.a.*, to embrace again.

rembruni, **-e**, *adj.*, brown, dark, gloomy,

dull, cloudy. *Un air* — ; a gloomy look. *Teint* — ; dark complexion.

rembrunir, *v.a.*, to make dark or darker, to darken ; to cloud ; to sadden.

se **rembrunir**, *v.r.*, to get, or grow, darker ; to become cloudy, gloomy ; to become sad, melancholy. *Son front se rembrunit ;* his brow grew darker.

rembrunissement (-nis-măn), *n.m.*, darkening, becoming darker.

rembuchement (-bŭsh-măn), *n.m.*, (hunt.) return to covert.

se **rembucher**, *v.r.*, (hunt.) to return to covert.

remède, *n.m.*, remedy ; medicine, cure ; (med.) clyster. *Sans* — ; without remedy, past recovery. *Susceptible de* — ; remediable, not by any means hopeless. *Etre dans les* — *s ;* to take remedies. *Se mettre dans les* — *s ;* to take remedies, physic. *Apporter du* — *à ;* to remedy, to stop. *Un* — *à tous maux ;* a plaster for all sores. *Le grand* — ; the grand remedy, mercury. *A chose faite point de* — ; what is done cannot be undone. *C'est un vrai* — *d'amour que cette femme !* that woman is a horrid old fright.

remédiable, *adj.*, remediable.

remédier, *v.n.*, to remedy, to cure, to stop. — *à un mal ;* to remedy an evil. *On ne saurait y* — ; that can't be helped.

remêler, *v.a.*, to mix again ; to shuffle again.

remémora-teur, -trice, *adj.*, reminding.

remémorati-f, -ve, *adj.*, commemorative ; reminding.

⊙**remémorer**, *v.a.*, to put in mind of, to remind of.

⊙*se* **remémorer**, *v.r.*, to recollect.

remener, *v.a.*, to take back, to lead back ; to carry back, to bring back (a person).

remerciement *or* **remercîment**, *n.m.*, thanks. *Faire des* — *s ;* to return thanks.

remercier, *v.a.*, to thank, to give *or* return thanks ; to decline ; not to accept ; to discharge. *Je vous remercie ;* I thank you.

réméré, *n.m.*, (jur.) redemption, repurchase. *Faculté de* — ; power of redemption. *Vente à* —; sale with power of redemption.

remesurer, *v.a.*, to measure again.

remetteu-r, -se, *n.m.f.*, remitter, remittor.

remettre, *v.a.*, to put again, to put on again, to wear again ; to put back, to put back again, to set again ; to lay again ; to set (a bone) ; to restore, to reinstate ; to recover, to make well ; to reassure ; to remove ; to deliver, to give up ; to return, to deliver up, to hand over ; to put off, to delay ; to remit, to forgive, to pardon ; to leave the one care of ; to intrust ; to remember, to recognize. — *à la voile ;* to set sail again. — *l'épée dans le fourreau ;* to put up one's sword. — *une armée sur pied ;* to raise new forces. — *dans l'esprit ;* to remind. — *quelqu'un ;* to recollect any one, to know any one again. *Je vous remets ;* I recollect your face. — *en bon ordre ;* to restore to order. — *en bonne intelligence ;* to reconcile, to reunite. *Le voilà tout à fait remis ;* he is quite recovered. — *l'esprit ;* to soothe the mind (of). — *une lettre à son adresse ;* to deliver a letter (to its address). *Faire* — ; to have something, *or* to cause something to be, delivered, conveyed, *or* handed over ; to send, to forward. — *de l'argent ;* to remit money. — *d'un jour à l'autre ;* to put off from day to day. — *une chose à la décision de quelqu'un ;* to refer a matter to any one. — *en question ;* to unsettle, to call in question again.

se **remettre**, *v.r.*, to apply one's self again ; to resume ; to set one's self again ; to call to mind ; to recover from, to grow well again ; to recover, *or* to compose, one's self ; (hunt.) to light (of birds) ; to resign one's self ; to refer, to rely. *Se* — *à table ;* to sit down again to table. *Remettez-vous ;* compose yourself. *Se* — *une chose ;* to recollect a

thing. *S'en* — *à ;* to refer to ; to trust to. *S'en* — *à quelqu'un ;* to refer a thing to any one, to leave, to intrust (to). *Se* — *au beau ;* (of the weather) to mend, to become fine again. *Se* — *en route ;* to resume one's journey.

remeubler, *v.a.*, to refurnish.

réminiscence, *n.f.*, reminiscence.

rémipède, *n.m.*, (zool.) remiped.

remis, -e, *part.*, put back, put off ; drawn (of a game) ; (of weather) settled, fine again. *Partie* — *e ;* drawn game. *Ce n'est que partie* — *e ;* it is only a pleasure deferred.

remisage, *n.m.*, housing ; coach-house, shed.

remise, *n.f.*, giving up ; delivery ; delay ; deferring ; remittance ; reduction, abatement ; commission, allowance ; coach-house, mews ; (hunt.) cover (for game) ; place of lighting (of partridges). *Il use toujours de* — ; he is always putting off. *La* — *d'une audience ;* the putting off of a hearing. *Faire une* — ; to make a remittance, to remit. *Faire* — *de ;* to forgive, to remit. *Il est sous la* — ; he is on the shelf. *Sous la* — ; in the coach-house.

remise, *n.m.*, coach let on hire ; hired brougham. *Voiture de* — ; livery carriage (as hired from the stables, in opposition to *voiture de place,* taken from the stand).

remiser, *v.a.*, to put in the coach-house ; to house ; to put by.

rémissible, *adj.*, remissible, pardonable, excusable.

rémission, *n.f.*, remission, mercy, forgiveness, pardon.

rémissionnaire, *n.m.*, pardoned criminal.

rémittent, -e, *adj.*, (med.) remitting.

remmaillage, *n.m.*, re-stitching, mending.

remmailler, *v.a.*, to re-stitch, to mend, to re-make the meshes of. *V.* **remailler**.

***remmailloter** (răn-ma-), *v.a.*, to rewrap (in swaddling-clothes).

remmancher (răn-măn-), *v.a.*, to put a new haft or handle to, to haft again.

remmener (răn-mné), *v.a.*, to take back, to carry back, to lead back ; to take away again (a person).

remodeler (-mo-dlé), *v.a.*, to model anew.

rémolade *or* **remolade**, *n.f. V.* **rémoulade**.

remole, *n.f. V.* **remous**.

remontage, *n.m.*, new fronting, vamping (of boots) ; (tech.) remounting, putting together again, fitting up again.

remonte, *n.f.*, (milit.) remount ; (of studs) new leap ; going up stream.

remonter, *v.n.*, to reascend ; to go up again ; to go back, to trace back ; to date (from) (with reference to time) ; to rise, to rise again ; to remount. — *à cheval ;* to get on horseback again. — *sur sa bête ;* to recover one's losses. — *à la source, à l'origine d'une chose ;* to trace a thing back to its origin.

remonter, *v.a.*, to reascend ; to go up again ; to put together again ; to remount (cavalry) ; to rise (of public securities) ; to fit up ; to stock ; to go up ; to wind up (a watch, a clock) ; to new-string (of instruments). — *une rivière, un fleuve ;* to ascend a river. — *une montre ;* to wind up a watch. — *des bottes ;* to new-front, or to vamp, boots. — *un fusil ;* to new-stock a gun. — *le moral à quelqu'un ;* to revive the spirits of any one. — *un magasin ;* to stock a warehouse anew.

se **remonter**, *v.r.*, to stock one's self again ; to wind up (watches) ; (fig.) to recover one's strength, health, *or* spirits.

remontoir, *n.m.*, key (for winding up clocks) ; keyless action (in watches).

remontrance, *n.f.*, remonstrance.

remontrant, *n.m.*, remonstrant.

remontrer, *v.a.*, to demonstrate, to represent, to lay before, to point out, to show, to show again ; to remonstrate ; (hunt.) to show where the game has passed. *En — à quelqu'un ;* to be more than a match for, to outdo any one ; to put up to a thing or two. *C'est gros Jean qui remontre à son curé ;* it is teaching one's grandmother how to suck eggs.

se remontrer, *v.r.,* to show one's self again.

rémora, *n.m.,* (—*s*) (ich.) remora ; suck-fish ; (fig.) hindrance, impediment, obstacle.

remordre, *v.a.* and *n.,* to bite again anything *or* anybody ; to attack again ; to try again ; (fig., of conscience) to torment, to rack.

remords (re-mor), *n.m.,* remorse, compunction. *Avoir des —s ;* to feel remorse. *Sans —;* remorseless. *Etouffer ses —;* to stifle remorse.

rémore, *n.f.* V. **rémora.**

remorquage, *n.m.,* (nav.) towing.

remorque, *n.f.,* towing (a ship). *Prendre à la —;* to take in tow. *Se mettre à la —;* to get into tow. *Câble de —;* tow-line. *A la — de ;* in tow of ; (fig.) under the influence, *or* leadership, of ; in the train, *or* wake, of.

remorquer, *v.a.,* (nav.) to tow, to tug, to drag.

remorqueur, *n.m.,* tug, towing-vessel.

remorqueuse, *n.f.,* (railways) pilot-engine.

à rémotis (-tiss), *adv.,* (l.u.) aside, by. *Mettre à —;* to put by.

remoucher, *v.a.,* to snuff the candle again ; to wipe again the nose of.

se remoucher, *v.r.,* to blow one's nose again.

remoudre, *v.a.,* to grind again (corn, etc.).

rémoudre, *v.a.,* to sharpen, *or* to whet, again.

***remouiller,** *v.a.;* to wet again.

rémoulade, *n.f.,* (cook.) sharp mustard-sauce ; (vet.) sprain-ointment.

rémouleur, *n.m.,* grinder, knife-grinder.

remous, *n.m.,* eddy, dead-water, back-water.

***rempaillage,** *n.m.,* re-covering with straw ; restuffing, rebottoming.

***rempailler,** *v.a.,* to rebottom *or* new-bottom (a chair).

***rempailleu-r,** *n.m.,* -se, *n.f.,* chair-mender.

rempaquement (-pak-mãn), *n.m.,* barreling of herrings.

rempaqueter (-pak-té), *v.a.,* to pack up again.

remparer, *v.a.,* to fortify, to bulwark ; to intrench ; to cover.

se remparer, *v.r.,* to fortify one's self (by ramparts) ; to take possession again.

rempart, *n.m.,* rampart, bulwark.

remplaçable, *adj.,* replaceable.

remplaçant, *n.m.,* substitute.

remplacement (-plas-mãn), *n.m.,* replacing ; replacement ; fresh supply ; (fin.) reinvestment. *Bureau de —;* office for providing substitutes for the army. *Le — a été aboli en France par la loi de 1872 ;* the replacing of recruits by substitutes was abolished in France by law in 1872. *En — de ;* instead of, in place of.

remplacer, *v.a.,* to replace, to take the place of ; to serve as a substitute ; to reinvest. *Vous le remplacerez pendant son absence ;* you will fill his place during his absence. *Se faire —;* to get a substitute.

se remplacer, *v.r.,* to be replaced ; to get a fresh supply of anything.

remplage, *n.m.,* the filling up, adding (of wine-casks) ; fillings, rubble (mas.).

rempli, *n.m.,* tuck, fold, turning in.

rempli, -e, *adj.,* full, replete, fraught (with).

remplier, *v.a.,* to make a tuck, to turn in.

remplir, *v.a.,* to fill, to fill up ; to fill again ; to cram, to stuff ; to take up, to occupy ; to supply, to furnish ; to keep, to hold ; to fulfill, to discharge ; to perform ; to answer, to come up to ; to pay back. *Il remplit bien son temps ;* he employs his time well. *— un poste ;* to hold a post. *— ses engagements ;* to fulfill one's engagements. *— une tâche ;* to perform a task. *— l'attente de quelqu'un ;* to answer any one's expectation.

se remplir, *v.r.,* to fill one's self ; to cram, *or* stuff, one's self ; to fill, to become full.

remplissage, *n.m.,* filling, filling up (of casks) ; filling out ; (fig.) rubbish, trash, padding.

remplisseuse, *n.f.,* (needle-work) filler-in, point-lace mender.

remploi, *n.m.,* (jur.) re-investment, re-employment.

remployer, *v.a.,* to use again, to re-invest.

remplumer, *v.a.,* to feather again ; (mus.) to quill anew.

se remplumer, *v.r.,* to get new feathers ; to retrieve one's losses ; to get stout again ; to pick up again.

rempocher, *v.a.,* to pocket again.

rempoigner, *v.a.,* to catch hold of again, to seize again, to recapture.

rempoisonner (rãn-poa-zo-né), *v.a.* to poison again.

rempoissonnement (rãm-poa-so-n-mãn), *n.m.,* re-stocking with fish.

rempoissonner (rãn-poa-so-né), *v.a.,* to re-stock with fish.

remporter, *v.a.,* to carry, *or* take, back ; to carry away *or* off, to take away *or* off ; to get, to obtain ; to bear off ; to win. *— un prix ;* to carry off a prize. *— la victoire ;* to win the victory.

rempotage, *n.m.,* (gard.) re-potting.

rempoter, *v.a.,* (gard.) to re-pot.

remprisonnement, *n.m.,* reimprisonment.

remprisonner, *v.a.,* to reimprison.

remprunter, *v.a.,* to borrow again.

remuable, *adj.,* movable.

remuage, *n.m.,* moving, stirring.

remuant, -e, *adj.,* restless, stirring ; unquiet ; bustling, busy ; turbulent, seditious.

remue-ménage, *n.m.,* (—) stir, rummage ; disturbance, bustle, confusion.

remuement *or* **remûment,** *n.m.,* stirring ; moving, commotion, disturbance.

remue-queue, *n.m.,* (—). V. **hochequeue.**

remuer, *v.a.,* to move, to stir ; to rouse ; to turn up ; to disturb, to handle ; to affect, to shake, to wag ; to shuffle (of dominoes) ; to change the linen (of a baby). *— la tête ;* to shake one's head. *— des meubles ;* to rummage, *or* move, furniture. *— la queue ;* to wag its tail (of a dog). *— ciel et terre ;* to leave no stone unturned, to move heaven and earth.

se remuer, *v.r.,* to stir, to move ; to bestir one's self, to bustle about ; to fidget.

remuer, *v.n.,* to stir, to move ; to make a disturbance ; to fidget.

remueu-r, *n.m.,* -se, *n.f.,* mover, stirrer.

remueuse, *n.f.,* nurse-maid.

⊙**remugle,** *n.m.* V. **renfermé.**

rémunérateur, *n.m.,* rewarder, remunerator, requiter.

rémunérat-eur, -rice, *adj.,* remunerative.

⊙**rémunérati-f, -ve,** *adj.,* remunerative.

rémunération, *n.f.,* remuneration, reward.

rémunératoire, *adj.,* remuneratory.

rémunérer, *v.a.,* to remunerate, to reward.

renâcler, *v.n.,* (pop.) to snuff, to snort (in anger) ; to turn up one's nose ; to be unwilling, to be reluctant, to hang back, to demur.

renaissance, *n.f.,* regeneration, new birth, revival, renewal ; renascence, renascence. *— des lettres ;* revival of letters.

renaissant, -e, *adj.,* springing up again, growing up again, reviving, returning, renascent, recurring.

renaître, *v.n.,* to be born again ; to grow again ; to come up again ; to appear again, to spring up again, to rise again ; to revive, to reappear, to recur. *Toute la nature renaît ;* all nature revives. *Le jour renaît ;* day reappears. *— à la vie ;* to return to life. *— au bonheur ;* to be restored to happiness.

rénal, -e, *adj.*, (anat.) renal.

renard, *n.m.*, (mam.) fox; (mam.) dog-fox; fox, cunning dog, sly fellow; (astron.) Fox; (engineering) leak; (pop.) vomit, spew. — *américain;* raccoon. *Queue-de-* —, (—*s*— *)* fox's brush; (bot.) prince's-feather. — *marin;* sea-ape. *Fin* —; cunning dog, sly fox. *Se confesser au* — ; to tell one's secret to an enemy. *Le* — *prêche aux poules;* the devil rebukes sin. *Prendre marte pour* — ; to mistake one person for another. *Compère le* —, *maître* — ; Reynard the fox (Lafontaine).

renarde, *n.f.*, (mam.) she-fox; (fig.) catamaran.

renardeau, *n.m.*, fox's cub.

renarder, *v.n.*, to play the fox; (pop.) to vomit; to shoot the cat.

renardier, *n.m.*, fox-catcher.

renardière, *n.f.*, fox's burrow.

⊙**renasquer,** *v.n.* V. **renâcler.**

rencaissage or **rencaissement,** *n.m.*, (hort.) putting again into wooden boxes; (fin.) re-encashing.

rencaisser, *v.a.*, to put again into boxes; (fin.) to pay again into the bank, to re-encash; to get in money.

renchéri, -e, *adj.*, risen in price, higher-priced; over-particular, over-nice (of a person).

renchéri, *n.m.*, -**e,** *n.f.*, particular person, nice person. *Faire le* —, *faire la* —*e;* to be mighty particular, to give one's self airs.

renchérir, *v.a.* and *n.*, to raise the price of; to get dearer; to rise. — *sur;* to improve upon; to go beyond, to outstrip.

renchérissement (-ris-măn), *n.m.*, rise in price.

renclouer, *v.a.*, (milit.) to spike again.

*****rencogner,** *v.a.*, (fam.) to draw back, to drive, or to get, into a corner.

se *rencogner, *v.r.*, to hide or crouch in a corner.

rencontre, *n.f.*, meeting; encounter, accidental meeting; accident, chance; collision; accidental fight; duel; opportunity, occurrence, case; juncture; coincidence; collision. *Aller, venir, à la* — *de quelqu'un ;* to go to meet, or to come to meet, any one. *De* — ; second-hand. *Marchandise de* —; second-hand goods. *Roue de* — *d'une horloge ;* balance-wheel of a clock. *Vaisseaux de* — ; (chem.) vessels fitting into each other. *Une mauvaise* —; an unpleasant encounter.

rencontre, *n.m.*, (her.) rencounter.

rencontrer, *v.a.*, to meet, to meet with, to fall in with; to light upon; to find, to encounter; to meet, to encounter (in a hostile manner).

se rencontrer, *v.r.*, to meet, to meet each other, to meet with each other, to be met with; to be seen; to agree, to coincide; to meet, to encounter (in a duel). *Nos idées se rencontrent;* our ideas coincide, or tally. *Cela ne se rencontre pas tous les jours;* that does not happen, that is not to be met with, every day. *Les beaux esprits se rencontrent;* great wits jump together.

rencontrer, *v.n.*, to have good or ill luck, to be fortunate or unfortunate; to guess; to speak to the purpose, to make a hit. *Vous avez bien rencontré;* you have hit the right nail on the head. *Le limier rencontre;* the blood-hound is on the scent.

rencorser, *v.a.*, to put a new body (to).

rendage, *n.m.*, (tech.) product of raw materials; daily product of a lime-kiln; yield, output.

rendement (rand-măn), *n.m.*, produce, yield, output.

se rendetter, *v.r.*, to run, or get, into debt again.

rendeu-r, *n.m.*, -**se,** *n.f.*, one who renders, restorer.

rendez-vous, *n.m.*, (—) rendezvous, meeting, appointment; place of meeting, place of resort. *Donner un* — *à quelqu'un ;* to make an appoint-

ment with any one. *Prendre* —; to make an appointment. *Se donner* —; to make an appointment; to agree to meet; to resort.

rendonnée, *n.f.* V. **randonnée.**

rendormir, *v.a.*, to lull to sleep again, to send to sleep again.

se rendormir, *v.r.*, to fall, or go, to sleep again.

rendoubler, *v.a.*, to turn in, to turn down; to fold up, to double up.

rendre, *v.a.*, to render, to return, to restore, to give back, to give again; to pay back, to repay, to refund, to pay again; to deliver up, to yield, to yield up, to give up, to render up, to surrender; to carry, to convey, to transport, to take; to cast up, to cast out, to eject, to void, to throw up, to throw off one's stomach; to do, to pay, to give; to make; to produce, to bear, to bring in; to translate; to reward; to express, to convey, to represent; to issue; to exhale, to emit, to send forth, to give out; (jur.) to remit; (jur.) to surrender; (jur.) to return, to find, to bring in; to give in; to give (verdict). *Rendez-moi mon reste;* give me my change. — *de l'ouvrage;* to take work home. — *le salut;* to return a salute. — *hommage;* to render homage. *Je vous rends grâce;* I return you thanks. — *ses respects, ses devoirs à quelqu'un;* to pay one's respects, one's duty, to any one. — *compte;* to give an account. — *visite;* to pay a visit. — *à quelqu'un sa visite;* to return any one his call. — *justice à quelqu'un;* to do any one justice. — *la justice;* to administer, or to dispense, justice. — *service à quelqu'un;* to do any one a service. — *la pareille;* to return like for like. — *le bien pour le mal;* to return good for evil. — *avec usure;* to return with interest. *Dieu vous le rende!* may God reward you! — *la santé;* to restore health. — *un prisonnier à la liberté;* to set a prisoner at liberty. *L'expérience l'a rendu sage;* experience has made him wise, has taught him wisdom. — *une place;* (milit.) to surrender a town. — *les armes;* to lay down one's arms. — *une médecine;* to throw up a dose of physic. — *gorge;* to refund; to disgorge. — *raison;* to account for, to give a reason. *Rendez-moi raison de votre conduite;* explain your conduct to me. — *raison à quelqu'un;* to give any one satisfaction, to fight a duel. — *un arrêt;* to issue a decree. — *témoignage;* to bear witness. — *à quelqu'un sa parole;* to release any one from his promise. — *l'âme;* to give up the ghost. — *le pain bénit;* (c.rel.) to make the bread-offering. — *un paquet, — une lettre;* to take a parcel, a letter, to its destination. — *des marchandises en un lieu;* to take, to carry, to convey goods to a place. *Montez dans ma voiture, en deux heures je vous rendrai là;* get into my carriage, in two hours I will take you there. *Ce fermier rend tant de sa ferme;* that farmer pays so much for his farm.

se rendre, *v.r.*, to make one's self, to render one's self; to become, to turn; to go, to repair, to proceed, to resort; to wait upon any one; to flow; to yield, to surrender, to surrender one's self, to give one's self up; to be worn out, to be tired out, to be exhausted. *Se* — *partie contre quelqu'un;* to declare against any one. *Se* — *à son devoir;* to go where duty calls. *Le sang se rend au cœur;* the blood flows to the heart. *Se* — *prisonnier;* to surrender one's self prisoner, to give one's self up. *Je me rends;* I am tired out; I give up.

rendre, *v.n.*, to lead (to) (of roads); to evacuate, to void; to run (of wounds).

rendre, *n.m.*, repayment, refunding, returning.

rendu, -e, *part.*, arrived; rendered, delivered; exhausted, tired out, knocked up, spent (of a horse). *Je suis* —; I am quite exhausted, fagged out, done up. *Un cheval qui est* —; a spent horse.

rendu, *n.m.,* return, tit for tat.

renduire, *v.a.,* to plaster anew ; to daub over again ; to give a new coating (to).

rendurcir, *v.a.,* to make harder.

se **rendurcir,** *v.r.,* to become harder ; to become hardened.

rêne, *n.f.,* rein. *Prendre les —s ;* to take the reins.

renégat, *n.m.,* **-e,** *n.f.,* renegade.

reneiger, *v.n.,* to snow again.

rêner, *v.a.,* to bridle, to bridle (in) (a horse).

rénette, *n.f.,* green frog ; (vet.) paring knife ; marking tool.

rénetter, *v.a.,* (vet.) to furrow, to mark, to groove.

renettoyer, *v.a.,* to clean again.

renfaitage, *n.m.,* repairing the top of a roof, new-ridging.

renfaîter, *v.a.,* to new-ridge, to mend the top of a roof.

renfermé, *n.m.,* fustiness ; musty, *or* close, *or* confined, air. *Sentir le —;* to smell close *or* fusty.

renfermer, *v.a.,* to shut up, to confine ; to comprehend, to include, to contain ; to conceal, to hide.

se **renfermer,** *v.r.,* to shut one's self up, to confine one's self. *Se — en soi-même ;* to retire within one's self, to commune with one's self.

renfiler, *v.a.,* to thread again, to new-string.

renflammer, *v.a.,* to rekindle.

se **renflammer,** *v.r.,* to be rekindled.

renflé, -e, *adj.,* swollen, swelling ; (bot.) inflated, puffed out ; risen (of dough) ; bossed.

renflement, *n.m.,* swelling, enlargement ; (bot.) struma.

renfler, *v.n., se* **renfler,** *v.r.,* to swell, to swell out ; to rise.

renflouage, *n.m.,* (nav.) getting a ship afloat again, refloating, raising.

renflouer, *v.a.,* (nav.) to refloat, to raise.

renfoncement (-fons-mān), *n.m.,* cavity ; hollow, recess ; (of a door) doorway ; (print.) indentation ; (arch.) break ; (paint.) background.

renfoncer, *v.a.,* to drive further in, to drive deeper, to pull further on ; to pull over one's eyes ; (print.) to indent ; (of a cask) to new bottom.

renforçage, *n.m.,* strengthening.

renforcé, -e, *adj.,* strong, thick ; substantial ; wealthy ; stout ; thick-set, downright, regular. *Des vers —s de pensées ;* verses very rich in thought. *C'est un bourgeois —;* he is a substantial, purse-proud citizen. *Un bidet —;* a strong thick-set nag. *Une étoffe —e ;* a thick strong stuff. *Sottise —e ;* downright stupidity.

renforcement, *n.m.,* reënforcing, strengthening.

renforcer, *v.a.,* to reënforce ; to strengthen ; to augment, to increase. *— le son d'un instrument ;* to increase the sound of an instrument.

se **renforcer,** *v.r.,* to gather strength ; to increase, to grow stronger ; (milit.) to be reënforced.

renformir, *v.a.,* (mas.) to re-plaster, to mend (a wall, etc.).

renformis, *n.m.,* (mas.) pargeting, plastering, new coat ; repairing (of a wall).

renfort, *n.m.,* reënforcement, supply, relief, addition, increase ; strengthening piece. *A grand — de ;* with the help of, by dint of, with any amount of tugging (at) *or* plying (of). *De —;* extra, additional, fresh.

***renfrogné, renfrognement,** *se* **renfrogner.** *V.* **refrogné, refrognement,** *se* **refrogner.**

rengagement (-gaj-mān), *n.m.,* re-engagement ; (milit.) re-enlistment ; pledging, pawning again.

rengager, *v.a.,* to engage again, to re-engage ; (milit.) to re-enlist ; to pledge, to pawn again. *— un domaine ;* to mortgage a domain. *— son cœur ;* to engage one's heart again.

se **rengager,** *v.r.,* to engage again, to re-engage, to begin afresh ; (milit.) to re-enlist.

rengaîne, *n.m.,* (pop.) refusal. *Il a un furieux — ;* there is no making him accept ; there is no conciliating him.

rengaine, *n.f.,* (pop.) threadbare, commonplace story ; hackneyed expression ; harping on ; worn-out expedient. *C'est toujours la même —;* it's the same old story.

rengainer, *v.a.,* to sheath, to put up ; to suppress, to withdraw, to stop, to reserve. *— une épée ;* to put up a sword. *Rengainez votre compliment ;* pocket, *or* withhold, your compliment (*i.e.,* keep it to yourself).

rengaîner, *v.n.,* to sheath one's sword, to put up one's sword. *Rengaînez, messieurs !* put up, gentlemen.

rengorgement, *n.m.,* bridling up, carrying one's head high ; airs (of importance).

se **rengorger,** *v.r.,* to carry it with a high hand, to carry one's head high, to bridle up, to give one's self airs.

rengraisser, *v.a.,* to fatten again.

se **rengraisser,** *v.r.,* to grow fat, *or* stout, again ; to become fat again, to fatten again.

rengraisser, *v.n.,* to grow fat, to become fat, *or* stout, again.

rengrènement (-grè-n-mān), *n.m.,* (coin.) re-coinage, re-coining, re-stamping.

rengréner, *v.a.,* to grind corn again ; (coin.) to coin again, to re-coin, to re-stamp ; (mec.) to throw into gear again, to engage again.

renhardir, *v.a.,* to embolden ; to encourage again.

reniable, *adj.,* deniable.

reniement *or* **reniment,** *n.m.,* denying, disowning ; denial of St. Peter.

renier, *v.a.,* to deny, to disown ; to disavow, to abjure, to disclaim, to renounce, to forswear. *— sa religion ;* to abjure one's religion.

reniflement, *n.m.,* sniffing ; snuffing up (of horses).

renifler, *v.n.,* to sniff ; to turn up one's nose (at) ; to manifest unwillingness, to demur, to hang back. *Ce cheval renifle sur l'avoine ;* this horse is off his feed.

reniflerie, *n.f.,* sniffing.

renifleu-r, *n.m.,* **-se,** *n.f.,* sniffer.

réniforce, *adj.,* kidney-shaped.

rénitence, *n.f.,* (med.) renitency.

rénitent, -e, *adj.,* (med.) renitent.

reniveler, *v.a.,* to level again.

renivellement, *n.m.,* new-leveling.

renjamber, *v.a.,* to jump, *or* step, over again.

renne (rè-n), *n.m.,* reindeer.

renom (-non), *n.m.,* renown, fame, reputation, report, note, name. *Etre en —;* to be popular.

renommé, -e, *adj.,* renowned, famous, noted, celebrated, famed.

renommée, *n.f.,* renown, fame, name, reputation, celebrity ; report, repute ; rumor ; (myth.) Fame. *Bonne — vaut mieux que ceinture dorée ;* a good name is better than riches.

renommer, *v.a.,* to name again, to re-elect ; to render renowned, to render famous, to make renowned, to make famous. *Se faire —;* to spread one's fame ; to acquire fame ; to make one's self famous ; to have one's self re-elected.

se **renommer,** *v.r.,* to make use of the name of any one. *V. se* **réclamer** (de).

renonce, *n.f.,* renounce, revoke (at cards).

renoncement (-nōns-mān), *n.m.,* renouncing, renouncement. *— à soi-même ;* self-denial, abnegation.

renoncer, *v.n.,* to renounce, to give up, to surrender ; to forego, to relinquish, to lay down, to waive ; to revoke, to renounce (at cards). *— à la couronne ;* to renounce the crown. *— à une succession ;* to give up an inheritance. *— à sa foi ;* to renounce one's faith.

renoncer, *v.a.*, to renounce, to disclaim, to disown, to deny, to disavow.

renonciat-eur, *n.m.*, **-rice**, *n.f.*, (jur.) renouncer, relassor.

renonciation, *n.f.*, renunciation, renouncement; self-denial.

renonculacées, *n.f.pl.*, (bot.) ranunculaceæ.

renoncule, *n.f.*, (bot.) ranunculus, buttercup, crowfoot, spearwort.

ronouée, *n.f.*, (bot.) polygonum, knot-berry, knot-grass.

⊙**renouement** *or* **renoûment**, *n.m.*, renewing, renewal.

renouer, *v.a.*, to knot again, to tie again; to tie up; to put together; to resume, to renew. — *amitié;* to be friends again. — *l'amitié de parents;* to reconcile relations. — *une affaire;* to resume business. — *connaissance;* to renew acquaintance with.

renouer, *v.n.*, to resume one's relations, to resume one's connection.

renou-eur, *n.m.*, **-euse**, *n.f.* *V.* **rebouteur.**

⊙**renouveau**, *n.m.*, (fam. poet.) spring, spring-time.

renouvelable, *adj.*, renewable.

renouveler (-noo-vlé), *v.a.*, to renew, to renovate, to revive, to resuscitate; to refresh; to repeat, to do again. — *un usage;* to revive a custom.

se **renouveler**, *v.r.*, to be renewed, to be revived, to succeed each other; to happen, *or* occur, again.

renouveler, *v.n.*, to renew, to redouble, to increase. — *de jambes;* to walk briskly again with renewed strength. — *d'appétit;* to eat again with a fresh appetite. — *d'attention;* to redouble one's attention, to be doubly attentive. — *d'ardeur;* to show more eagerness.

renouvellement (-vèl-mān), *n.m.*, renewing, renewal, reviving; reiteration, repetition; recurrence; increase, redoubling.

rénovat-eur, -rice, *adj.*, renovating.

rénovation, *n.f.*, renovation, renewal.

*****renseignement**, *n.m.*, information, intelligence; account; indication, direction, inquiry. *pl.*, references, information. *Prendre des —s;* to make inquiries, to gather information. *Aller aux —s;* to make inquiries. *Bureau de —s;* intelligence-office, inquiry-office.

*****renseigner**, *v.a.*, to teach again, to instruct again; to inform, to give information, to show, to tell, to direct. *Se —;* to get information; to make inquiries; to inform one's self.

rensemencement, *n.m.*, (agri.) re-sowing.

rensemencer, *v.a.*, (agri.) to sow again, to re-sow.

rentamer, *v.a.*, to cut again, to begin again; to resume. — *un discours;* to resume a speech.

rentassé, -e, *adj.*, thick-set.

rentasser, *v.a.*, to heap up again.

rente, *n.f.*, yearly income, revenue; rent, annuity; stock, funds; pension. — *foncière;* ground-rent. — *viagère* or *à fonds perdu;* life-annuity. *Le taux de la —;* the price of stocks. —*s sur l'Etat;* government-stock. *La — hausse;* the stocks are rising. *Acheter des —s;* to buy stock, to invest in the funds. *Faire une — à;* to allow a pension to, to make an allowance to. *Vivre de ses —s;* to do nothing; to be independent; to live on one's income, to be a gentleman at large. *Racheter une —;* to redeem an annuity. *Avoir des —s;* to have an independent income; to have money invested. *Il lui fait une —;* he allows him, *or* her, a pension.

renté, -e, *adj.*, who has an income; endowed (of public establishments). *Bien —;* rich, wealthy.

renter, *v.a.*, to allow a yearly income to; to endow (public establishments).

renti-er, *n.m.*, **-ère**, *n.f.*, stockholder, fund-holder, annuitant; independent gentleman; independent lady; gentleman at large.

rentoilage, *n.m.*, new-lining, re-lining, re-canvassing. — *d'un tableau;* stretching a picture upon new cloth.

rentoiler, *v.a.*, to put new cloth (to a thing); to reline. — *un tableau;* to stretch, to paste, an old painting on new canvas.

rentrage, *n.m.*, bringing in, taking in, housing.

rentraîner, *v.a.*, to carry away again, to lead away again, to draw on, in, again.

rentraire (rentrayant, rentrait), *v.a.*, to fine-draw, to darn, to renter.

rentraiture, *n.f.*, fine-drawing, rentering, darn, darning; joining on.

rentrant, *adj.*, re-entering, returning; (geom., fort.) re-entering.

rentrant, *n.m.*, new player. *On demande un —;* a new player is wanted.

rentrayeu-r, *n.m.*, **-se**, *n.f.*, fine-drawer.

rentré, -e, *part.*, returned, re-entered; (med.) suppressed, driven in. *Sueur —e;* checked perspiration.

rentrée, *n.f.*, re-entrance; re-opening; re-appearance; taking in, housing, ingathering (of crops); (com.) incoming, receipt, payment, collection, getting-in of taxes; returns; (hunt.) return. *A la — des classes;* at the beginning of term. *Cet acteur a fait sa —;* (thea.) that actor has made his re-appearance. — *des impôts;* getting in of the taxes. *Ce revenu est d'une — difficile;* this revenue is slow in coming in. *Frais de —;* collection expenses.

rentrer, *v.n.*, to enter again, to return, to come in again, to go in again, to get in again; to re-enter, to join again; to become again, to get again; to recover; to re-open (of courts of law, schools, colleges); to make one's reappearance, to reappear (of an actor); to return to, to resume; (med.) to be suppressed, to be driven in; (engr.) to retouch; to be got in, to come in (of money); to buy in (at cards). — *en possession;* to regain possession. — *en son bien;* to recover one's property. — *en grâce;* to come into favor again. — *en soi-même;* to examine one's self, to commune with one's self. — *en son bon sens;* to come to one's senses again. — *en charge;* to return to one's post. — *en condition;* to go in service again. — *en fonctions;* to resume one's duties. — *en fureur;* to fly into a passion again, to get into a passion again. *Faire —;* to drive in. *Il m'est rentré beau jeu;* I have secured good cards. — *dans la ville;* to return to town. *Cet acteur rentre ce soir;* that actor makes his reappearance this evening.

rentrer, *v.a.*, to take in, to bring in, to put in, to get in, to house; to suppress, to check, to stifle; (med.) to drive in; (nav.) to bowse in; to house guns; (print.) to indent. *Voici le moment de — les foins;* now is the season for getting in the hay. — *une ligne;* (print.) to indent a line.

renvahir, *v.a.*, to invade again.

renvelopper (ran-vlo-pé), *v.a.*, to wrap up again.

renverger, *v.a.*, to edge (baskets).

renverguer, *v.a.*, (nav.) to bend a sail again (to the yards).

renversable, *adj.*, reversible, liable to be overthrown.

renversant, -e, *adj.*, (fam.) astounding, stupendous, amazing, extraordinary; stunning. *Un coup —;* a stunning, knock-down blow.

à la **renverse**, *adv.*, backwards, upon one's back. *Tomber à la —;* to fall backwards.

renversé, -e, *part.*, thrown down, thrown back, pliant; (her.) inverted. *Il a l'esprit —;* his brain is turning. *C'est le monde —;* it is the world turned upside down (*i. e.* it is preposterous).

renversement, *n.m.*, reversing, overturning, throwing down, throwing over, overthrowing; turning upside down; confusion, disorder; turning, alienation (of the brain); subversion, destruction; (surg.) retroversion, prolapse; (mus.) inversion, revert, reversing; (arith.) inversion; (nav.) ⊙ transshipment, *V.* **transbordement.** — *d'un état;* overthrow of a state. — *des lois;* subversion of the laws. — *de la paupière;* (med.) eversion of the eyelid.

renverser, *v.a.*, to reverse, to turn upside-down, to turn topsy-turvy; to throw down, to upset, to tumble down, to overthrow, to overturn; to spill; to turn (the brain); to disorder, to confuse; to destroy, to ruin; to astound, to stupefy, to overwhelm; to transpose; (milit.) to put to flight, to rout, to put to the rout; to invert; (surg.) to retrovert; (nav.) ⊙ to transship, *V.* **transborder.** — *à coups de canon;* to batter down. — *la table;* to upset the table. — *un bataillon;* to break, to overthrow, to battalion. — *un état;* to overthrow a state. *Ceci lui renversera l'esprit;* this will turn his brain. — *l'encre;* to spill the ink, to knock the ink over. — *la vapeur;* (rail.) to reverse the engine. — *une voiture;* to upset a carriage.

se **renverser**, *v.r.*, to fall down, to turn upside down, to upset, to be upset, to be thrown down, to overset, to be overset, to capsize; to be capsized, to be spilt; to throw one's self back, to fall back, to lie on one's back; (milit.) to be thrown into disorder, to be thrown back; (surg.) to be retroverted.

renverseur, *n.m.*, overthrower; subverter; inverter, destroyer; transposer.

renvi, *n.m.*, revy, additional stake.

renvidage, *n.m.*, winding up, winding (in spinning).

renvier, *v.n.*, to revy, to lay above the stakes, (at cards).

renvoi, *n.m.*, sending back, returning, return, sending away, dismissal, discharge; referring, sending; (jur.) adjournment; caret, reference (in books, writings); reflection, reverberation; (jur.) reference to another judge. *pl.*, (med.) rising of the stomach. *De —;* returnable. — *du son;* reverberation of sound. *Chevaux de —;* return horses. — *de troupes;* dismissal of troops. — *de la cause à huitaine;* adjournment of the case for a week.

renvoyer, *v.a.*, to send again; to send back again, to return; to send away, to dismiss; to discharge; to refer; to put off, to postpone, to adjourn, to delay; to drive back; to throw back; to reflect (light or heat); to repeat, to reverberate (sound). — *un ministre;* to dismiss a minister. — *un domestique;* to discharge a servant. — *une femme;* to repudiate a wife. *On a renvoyé l'affaire à huitaine;* the case has been adjourned for a week. — *la balle à quelqu'un;* to give one as good as he sends, to return the compliment. — *un accusé;* to acquit a prisoner. — *un plaideur de sa demande;* to nonsuit a plaintiff. — *le lecteur à une note;* to refer the reader to a note.

se **renvoyer**, *v.r.*, to be sent back *or* returned; to send from one to another. *Se — la balle;* to bandy compliments, to retort.

réoccupation, *n.f.*, reoccupation.

réoccuper, *v.a.*, to occupy again, to reoccupy.

réopiner, *v.n.*, to deliver one's opinion again.

réorchestration, *n.f.*, new-scoring.

réorchestrer, *v.a.*, (mus.) to compose a new score.

réordination, *n.f.*, re-ordination.

réordonner, *v.a.*, to ordain again, to re-ordain, to re-order.

réorganisation, *n.f.*, re-organization.

réorganiser, *v.a.*, to re-organize.

se **réorganiser**, *v.r.*, to be re-organized.

réouverture, *n.f.*, re-opening. *La — d'un théâtre;* the re-opening of a theater. *La — d'un magasin;* the re-opening of a shop.

repaire, *n.m.*, haunt, den, lair, hole; (hunt.) dung of hares, wolves, etc.; (tech.) *V.* **repère.** — *de voleurs;* den of thieves, haunt of thieves.

répaissir, *v.a.* and *n.*, to thicken again. *Se —;* to become, *or* get, thick again.

repaître, *v.n.*, (l.u.) to feed, to take refreshment; to bait.

repaître, *v.a.*, (l.u.) to feed, to nourish. *Il faut — ces animaux;* these animals must be fed. — *quelqu'un d'espérances;* to feed any one with hopes.

se **repaître**, *v.r.*, to feed on; to feast on; to delight in, to indulge in, to gloat over. *Il se repaît d'espérances vaines;* he feeds on vain hopes.

répandre, *v.a.* and *n.*, to spill, to shed, to diffuse, to scatter, to distribute, to bestow, to give out, to pour out, to exhale, to spread abroad, to propagate, to circulate. — *des larmes;* to shed tears. — *des bienfaits;* to bestow benefits. — *un bruit;* to spread a report. — *son sang;* to shed one's blood. — *des aumônes;* to distribute alms. — *l'alarme;* to spread alarm. — *son cœur;* to open one's heart.

se **répandre**, *v.r.*, to be spilt, to be shed, to be diffused, to be spread, to be scattered, to be distributed, to be bestowed, to be given out, to be poured out, to be exhaled, to be spread abroad, to be propagated, to be circulated; to be current; to flow, to spread, to go abroad, to get abroad; to burst out, to break out, to launch out, to indulge in, to fly out; to frequent society, to go into society. *La lumière se répand beaucoup plus vite que le son;* light travels much more quickly than sound. *La nouvelle de la victoire se répandit en un instant;* the news of the victory was spread abroad in an instant. *Se — en compliments;* to break out, to launch out, into compliments. *Se — en invectives;* to launch out into abuse. *Se — dans le monde;* to go out into society.

répandu, -e, *part.*, spilt, shed. *Etre fort — dans le monde;* to go out into society, to go out a great deal; to be in great request. *Etre fort —;* to be very well known.

réparable, *adj.*, reparable, mendable.

reparaître, *v.n.*, to reappear, to appear again, to appear anew, to make one's reappearance, to enter again, to come back.

réparat-eur, -rice, *n.* and *adj.*, restorer, repairer; restorative, reparative, refreshing.

réparation, *n.f.*, repairing, mending; reparation, amends, satisfaction, apology, excuse. *pl.*, repair, repairs; (jur.) damages, indemnity, relief. *Faire — à quelqu'un;* to make amends to any one. *En —;* under repair.

réparatoire, *adj.*, reparative.

réparer, *v.a.*, to repair, to mend; to make amends for, to atone for, to redeem; to indemnify; to make up for; to re-establish, to recover, to recruit. — *ses forces;* to recruit one's strength. — *son honneur;* to retrieve one's honor. — *sa faute;* to make amends for one's faults. — *ses pertes;* to retrieve one's losses. — *des torts;* to redress grievances. — *le temps perdu;* to make up for lost time.

répareur, *n.m.*, (tech.) repairer.

réparition, *n.f.*, (astron.) reappearance (of a star after an eclipse). *V.* **réapparition.**

reparler, *v.n.*, to speak again.

repartie (-tî), *n.f.*, repartee, retort, rejoinder, reply. *Avoir la — prompte, être prompt à la —;* to be quick at repartee. *Faire une —;* to make a repartee.

repartir, *v.n.*, to set out again, to set off again.

repartir, *v.a.* and *n.*, to reply, to answer, to retort.

répartir, *v.a.*, to divide, to distribute ; to portion out ; to assess. — *les contributions ;* to assess taxes.

répartiteur, *n.* and *adj.m.*, assessor ; assessing (of taxes).

répartition, *n.f.*, division, distribution ; assessment.

repas, *n.m.*, meal, repast. — *de noces ;* wedding breakfast. — *en gras ;* meat dinner ; meat breakfast. — *en maigre ;* fish dinner ; fish breakfast. *Faire un* —; to make a meal. *Faire ses* —, *prendre ses* — ; to take one's meals.

repassage, *n.m.*, ironing (of linen) ; dressing, doing up (of a hat) ; grinding, setting, honing, whetting, grinding (of cutlery) ; (agri.) raking.

repasser, *v.n.*, to pass again ; to pass by again ; to call again, to look in again. — *chez quelqu'un ;* to call again on any one, to look in again.

repasser, *v.a.*, to pass again, to repass ; to cross again, to carry over again ; to iron, to iron out ; to grind, to set, to hone, to whet ; to turn over, to think over, to revolve ; to go over, to look over ; to repeat ; (dy.) to dye again ; to curry a second time (leather) ; (fig., pop.) to beat ; to find fault with, to abuse, to scold. — *une leçon ;* to look over a lesson. — *du linge ;* to iron linen. — *la lime sur ;* to repolish. — *quelque chose dans son esprit ;* to revolve anything in one's mind. — *quelqu'un ;* to beat, to abuse, any one. — *sur un cuir ;* to strop. — *sur la pierre ;* to set,to whet. — *sur la meule ;* to grind.

se **repasser**, *v.r.*, to be ironed ; to be ground, sharpened, whetted.

repasseur, *n.m.*, pointer (of pins) ; grinder. — *de couteaux ;* knife-grinder.

repasseuse, *n.f.*, ironer.

repassoir, *n.m.*, grinding-stone. — *à crayon ;* pencil-pointer.

repavage, *n.m.*, repaving.

repaver, *v.a.*, to pave anew, to repave.

repayer, *v.a.*, to pay again.

repêcher, *v.a.*, to fish up again ; to take out of the water ; to take out again, to take up again, to recover, to catch again.

repeindre, *v.a.*, to paint again ; to retouch, to touch up.

repeint, *n.m.*, (paint.) re-painted, *or* restored, part of a picture.

repenser, *v.n.*, to think of again, to reconsider, to revolve.

repentance, *n.f.*, repentance, contrition.

repentant, -e, *adj.*, repentant, penitent.

repentie (-tĭ), *adj.* and *n.f.*, penitent. *Les filles* —*s ;* female penitentiary.

se **repentir** (se repentant, se repenti), *v.r.*, to repent, to rue. *Se — de ses fautes ;* to repent one's faults. *Il s'en repentira ;* he will rue it.

repentir, *n.m.*, repentance, contrition, compunction, penitence, regret ; ringlet. *Elle porte des* —*s ;* she wears curls ; (paint.) pentamento, correction.

repercer, *v.a.*, to pierce again, to bore again ; to tap again; to punch.

répercussi-f, -ve, *adj.*, (med.) repellent.

répercussif, *n.m.*, (med.) repellent, repercussive.

répercussion, *n.f.*, repercussion ; reverberation.

répercuter, *v.a.*, to repercuss, to drive back ; to reverberate, to echo ; to reflect ; (med.) to repel, to drive in.

reperdre, *v.a.*, to lose again.

repère, *n.m.*, mark, land-mark ; (arts) bench-mark ; joining-mark ; (mec.) datum. *Point de* —; land-mark, indication, direction.

répertoire, *n.m.*, table, list, catalogue ; repertory ; (com.) alphabet, alphabetical index. *Pièce qui fait partie du* —, *pièce restée au* —; (thea.) stock-piece. *Être un* —; (pers.) to be a living chronicle. *Pièce de* —; stock-piece.

*****répétailler**, *v.a.*, to repeat over and over again, to keep on repeating.

répéter, *v.a.*, to repeat ; to say again, to tell again ; to recite ; to reflect ; (jur.) to claim again, to demand again ; to give private lessons to, to be private tutor to ; (thea.) to rehearse. *Faire — à quelqu'un sa leçon ;* to hear any one say his lesson. *Il répète ces deux élèves ;* (at school) he is private tutor to these two boys. — *une comédie ;* to rehearse a comedy. — *une chose contre quelqu'un ;* (jur.) to claim (a thing) from any one, to redemand.

se **répéter**, *v.r.*, to be repeated ; to copy one's self ; to be renewed ; to occur again ; always to say the same thing.

répétiteur, *n.m.*, tutor, private master ; assistant professor (of certain schools) ; (nav.) repeater, repeating-ship ; call-boy.

répétition, *n.f.*, repetition ; action for ; (jur.) renewal, reproduction ; replica, duplicate ; recovery of money ; private tuition ; (thea.) rehearsal. *Pièce en* —; play in rehearsal. *Montre à* —; repeating-watch, repeater. *Donner des* —*s ;* to give private tuition, to give private lessons.

repétrir, *v.a.*, to knead again ; to form again.

repeuplement, *n.m.*, repeopling, re-stocking. — *d'un étang ;* re-stocking of a pond.

repeupler, *v.a.*, to repeople ; to re-stock. — *un étang ;* to re-stock a pond.

se **repeupler**, *v.r.*, to be repeopled ; to be re-stocked.

repic, *n.m.*, repique (piquet). *Faire quelqu'un — et capot ;* (fig., fam.) to nonplus any one.

repiquage, *n.m.*, (agri., gard.) transplantation, pricking again ; picking up.

repiquer, *v.a.*, to prick again ; (hort.) to prick ; (agri.) to transplant ; (engineering) to pick up.

repiquer, *v.n.*, to pick up ; to recover ; to pluck up courage. — *à la vie ;* to pick up one's crumbs. — *sur le rôti ;* to cut and come again.

répit, *n.m.*, respite, reprieve, delay ; rest, breathing-time.

replacement (-plas-mān), *n.m.*, replacing, putting again, setting again ; placing (servants) in a situation again ; reinvestment (of funds).

replacer, *v.a.*, to replace, to put in place again ; to reinvest (funds).

replaider, *v.a.*, (jur.) to replead, to plead again.

replanchéier, *v.a.*, to new-floor.

replanir, *v.a.*, to plane down.

replant, *n.m.*, young plant.

replantation, *n.f.*, replantation.

replanter, *v.a.*, to replant.

replâtrage, *n.m.*, re-plastering ; plastering, plastering up ; botching up, patching up ; patched up quarrel.

replâtrer, *v.a.*, to replaster ; to plaster, to plaster up, to botch, to botch up, to patch up, to bolster up.

repl-et, -ète, *adj.*, obese, bulky, corpulent, stout, lusty, portly.

réplétion, *n.f.*, repletion, stoutness, fatness, surfeit.

repleuvoir, *v.i.*, to rain again.

repli, *n.m.*, fold ; plait ; crease ; recess ; winding, sinuosity ; turning ; coil. *Les* —*s du serpent ;* the coils of the serpent. *Les plis et les* —*s du cœur humain ;* the inmost, *or* innermost, recesses of the human heart.

repliement *or* **reploiement**, *n.m.*, (milit.) falling back.

replier, *v.a.*, to fold again, to fold up again ; to wind, to twist, to writhe, to coil ; (milit.) to force back ; to draw back.

se **replier**, *v.r.*, to twist one's self, to wind one's self, to fold one's self, to writhe ; to turn, to turn up ; to bend up ; to wind, to coil ; (milit.) to fall back, to retreat. *Se — sur soi-même ;* to turn one's thoughts inwardly, to retire within one's self; to meditate, to commune with one's self; (man.) to turn suddenly round.

réplique, *n.f.,* reply, answer; rejoinder; (mus.) repeat; (thea.) cue. *Donner la* —; to give a person his cue. *Avoir la* —; to have the last say.

répliquer, *v.a.* and *n.,* to reply, to answer; to rejoin, to return, to retort; (jur.) to reply, to rejoin, to put in a rejoinder.

reploiement, *n.m.* V. **repliement.**

replonger, *v.a.,* to plunge again, to dip again, to duck again, to re-immerse, to immerse again.

se replonger, *v.r.,* to plunge anew, to plunge one's self again, to dive into again.

replonger, *v.n.,* to dive again, to dive anew.

reployer, *v.a., se* **reployer,** *v.r.* V. **replier, se replier.**

repolir, *v.a.,* to repolish, to polish again, to polish anew.

repolissage, *n.m.,* re-polishing.

répondant, *n.m.,* bail, surety, security; reference; (in schools) respondent; lay-clerk.

repondre, *v.a.n.,* to lay (eggs) again.

répondre, *v.a.,* to answer, to reply, to write back; to make the responses (to).

répondre, *v.n.,* to answer, to reply; to write back; to lead (to) (of roads); to reach, to be heard (of sound); to make a suitable return; to correspond, to respond, to agree, to come up, to satisfy, to answer; to be answerable (for), to be accountable (to *or* for); to be responsible (for); to be security (for); (man.) to obey, to answer; to maintain a thesis. — *à ceux qui appellent;* to answer those who call. — *ad rem;* to give a direct answer, to answer to the point. — *en Normand;* to answer equivocally, to give a shuffling answer. *Pour* — *à;* in answer to, in reply to. *Ces allées répondent au canal;* these walks lead to the canal. — *à l'attente publique;* to answer, to come up to public expectation. *Ne pas* — *à l'attente publique;* not to come up to, to fall short of public expectation. *Tout répond à nos vœux;* everything falls in with our wishes. *Qui pourrait* — *de l'événement?* who could answer for the event? *Je ne vous réponds que de moi;* I only answer for myself. *Je vous en réponds;* I'll be bound it is so!; I'll warrant you; I should think so, indeed!; I can tell you! *En* — *de;* to answer for (with).

se répondre, *v.r.,* to answer one's self; to answer each other; to correspond, to suit, to agree; to sympathize. *Nos cœurs se répondent;* our hearts are in sympathy.

répons, *n.m.,* response (church and print.).

réponse, *n.f.,* answer, reply; response; (jur.) rejoinder. — *à une réplique;* (jur.) rejoinder. *A sotte demande point de* —; a foolish question deserves no answer. — *de Normand;* equivocal, or shuffling answer. *Faire* —; to answer, to make answer. *Faire une* —; to give an answer. — *s'il vous plaît;* an answer will oblige.

report, *n.m.,* (book-keeping) carrying over, carrying forward, bringing forward; sum carried over, amount brought forward; continuation, prolongation. *Faire un* —; to bring forward; (exchange) to carry over.

reportage, *n.m.,* reporting.

reporter (-teur), *n.m.,* (—*s*) (in newspapers) reporter.

reporter, *v.a.,* to carry back again, to carry back, to take back; to trace back, to trace; (book-keeping) to carry forward, to carry over.

se reporter, *v.r.,* to go back (to); to return; to be carried back; to look back (upon).

reporter, *v.n.,* to carry over.

repos, *n.m.,* rest; stillness; repose, ease, quiet, peace, tranquillity; pause; resting-place; (carp.) quarter-pace. *En* —; at rest. *Se tenir en* —; to keep quiet. *Être en* —; to be at ease.

Laissez-moi en —; let me alone. *Lit de* —; couch. *Mettre un fusil dans son* —, *au* —; to half-cock a gun. *Echappement de* —; (horl.) stop; dead beat. — *!* (milit.) stand at ease!

reposé, -e, *part. adj.,* rested, refreshed; quiet, calm, cool, fresh. *A tête —e;* coolly, deliberately, at leisure. *Vin* —; wine that has settled.

reposée, *n.f.,* (hunt.) lair. *A —s;* with intervals of rest.

repose-pied, *n.m.,* foot-rest.

reposer, *v.a.,* to place again, to lay again, to set again; to rest (on anything); to lay; to repose, to settle; to refresh; (milit.) to ground arms. *Cela repose la vue;* that is restful to the eye. — *la tête;* to refresh the head.

se reposer, *v.r.,* to rest one's self, to rest, to repose, to lay one's self down, to lie down; to rely on, to confide in; to settle, to settle down; to pause; to light (of birds). *Se* — *après le travail;* to rest after labor. *Il faut que l'esprit se repose;* the mind has need of rest. *Se* — *sur;* to depend upon, to rely on. *Se* — *sur quelqu'un;* to rely on, to depend upon, any one.

reposer, *v.n.,* to rest, to lie; to repose; to lay one's self down, to lie down, to lie fallow, to settle. *Laisser* — ; (agri.) to let lie fallow.

reposoir, *n.m.,* street altar (procession of the *Fête-Dieu*); resting-place; pause.

repoussant, -e, *adj.,* repulsive, forbidding, repelling, loathsome, shocking.

repoussement (-poos-mān), *n.m.,* repulsion; recoil (of fire-arms). V. **recul,** which is more frequently used. *J'éprouve un certain* — *pour cet homme;* I feel a sort of aversion to this man.

repousser, *v.a.,* to repel; to drive back; to beat back, to force back, to push back; to thrust back, to thrust away; to reflect, to spurn; to repulse, to repel (an argument); to resent; to rebuff; to shoot out again (of plants); (print.) to prick in. — *l'ennemi;* to repulse the enemy. — *la force par la force;* to repel force by force. — *la tentation;* to repel temptation. — *une demande;* to reject a demand.

repousser, *v.n.,* to be repulsive; to recoil; to kick (of fire-arms); to spring up, to come up again, to shoot up (of plants); to grow again (of the hair).

repoussoir, *n.m.,* driving-bolt; starting-bolt; punch (of a dentist); (paint.) set-off, contrast.

répréhensible, *adj.,* reprehensible, reprovable.

répréhensiblement, *adv.,* reprehensibly.

répréhensi-f, -ve, *adj.,* reprehensive.

répréhension, *n.f.,* reprehension, reproof.

reprendre, *v.a.,* to take again; to take back; to take up again; to take to again; to catch again; (of diseases) to return; to recover; to resume, to begin again; to rebuke; to take up, to reprove; to find fault with; (arch.) to underpin. — *connaissance;* to recover consciousness. — *une ville;* to re-take a town. — *ses habits d'hiver;* to take to one's winter clothing again. *On ne m'y reprendra plus;* I will not be caught napping again. — *ses forces;* to recover one's strength. — *courage;* to take courage again. — *ses esprits;* to recover one's senses. — *haleine;* to recover one's breath, to breathe again; to take breath. — *le dessus;* to get the upper hand again. — *un mur sous œuvre, en sous-œuvre,* par-dessous œuvre; to underpin a wall. — *aigrement;* to reprove, or to take up, sharply.

se reprendre, *v.r.,* to correct one's self, to take one's self up; to be caught again; (of wounds) to close up again, to heal.

reprendre, *v.n.,* to take root again; (of wounds) to close up again; to begin to recover; to begin again; to reply, to answer; to return; (man.) to change its pace; to freeze again (of rivers); to return (of diseases). *Cet arbre a bien repris;* this tree has taken root very well. *Le* *froid a repris;* the cold has set in again. *Cette mode a repris;* this fashion has come in again.

repreneu-r, *n.m.,* **-se,** *n.f.,* carper, fault-finder, snarling critic. *adj.,* censuring.

*représaille, *n.f.,* reprisal, retaliation. *User de —s;* to make reprisals, to retaliate; (fig.) to retaliate, to return like for like; to give tit for tat. *Lettres de —s;* letters of marque and reprisal.

représentant, *n.m.,* representative.

représentati-f, -ve, *adj.,* representative.

représentation, *n.f.,* representation, exhibition, production, performance; display, show; appearance, mien; air; (empty) catafalque; remonstrance; (jur.) succession. *Il a une belle —;* he has a stately appearance, a noble deportment. *Faire des —s à;* to remonstrate (with).

représenter, *v.a.,* to represent, to present again; to show; to show again; to exhibit; to lay before; to produce; to reflect; to depict; to describe; to look like, to resemble; to perform, to act (a play); to be the representative of; to stand in the place of. *Il se fit — les registres;* he had the registers laid before him. *Cela est représenté au naturel;* that is depicted to the life.

se **représenter,** *v.r.,* to present one's self again; to appear again; to make one's appearance again; to fancy, to imagine, to picture to one's self; to occur; to present itself again (of a thing).

représenter, *v.n.,* to represent, to set forth; to maintain, to keep, one's dignity; to have an imposing appearance.

répressible, *adj.,* repressible.

répressi-f, -ve, *adj.,* repressive.

répression, *n.f.,* repression.

reprêter, *v.a.,* to lend again.

reprier, *v.a.,* to pray, *or* beg, again; to re-invite.

réprimable, *adj.,* repressible.

réprimande, *n.f.,* reprimand, reproof, rebuke. *Faire une — à quelqu'un;* to reprimand any one.

réprimander, *v.a.,* to reprimand, to reprove, to rebuke, to upbraid; to lecture.

réprimant, -e, *adj.,* repressive.

réprimer, *v.a.,* to repress, to restrain, to curb, to quell, to keep down, to check. *— le vice;* to put down vice. *— l'orgueil;* to check pride. *— ses désirs;* to check one's desires. *— les abus;* to repress abuses. *— ses passions;* to curb one's passions.

repris, -e, *part.,* retaken, resumed, taken up again; reset (of a bone).

repris de justice, *n.* and *adj.m.,* liberated convict, old offender.

reprise, *n.f.,* resumption; retaking; taking back; recovery; reconquest; revival; renewal; darn; (mus.) repetition, mark of repetition; (arch.) underpropping, underpinning; (man.) lesson; recapture (of a ship). *A plusieurs —s, à différentes —, à diverses —s;* several times, repeatedly. *A deux —s;* twice. *La — d'un procès;* the renewal of a lawsuit. *Faire des —s;* to darn. *Faire des —s perdues;* to fine-draw.

repriser, *v.a.,* to darn.

réprobat-eur, -rice, *adj.,* reproving, censuring.

réprobation, *n.f.,* reprobation.

reprochable, *adj.,* reproachable.

reproche, *n.m.,* reproach; expostulation. *pl.,* (jur.) exception, objection. *Un homme sans —;* a man free from reproach. *Faire un — à quelqu'un de quelque chose;* to reproach any one with anything. *Faire des —s amers à;* to reproach bitterly. *S'attirer des —s;* to incur reproach.

reprocher, *v.a.,* to reproach, to expostulate, to upbraid, to rebuke, to taunt, to twit, to cast in the teeth of. *— à une personne quelque chose;* to reproach a person with anything. *Il lui a reproché ses défauts;* he reproached him with his faults. *Il me l'a reproché;* he cast it in my teeth; he twitted me with it. *— les morceaux à quelqu'un;* to grudge any one the very food he eats. *— des témoins;* (jur.) to object (to), *or* to challenge, witnesses.

se **reprocher,** *v.r.,* to reproach, to upbraid one's self; to grudge one's self; to be reproached.

reproduct-eur, -rice, *adj.,* reproductive.

reproductibilité, *n.f.,* reproducibility.

reproductible, *adj.,* reproducible.

reproducti-f, -ve, *adj.,* reproductive.

reproduction, *n.f.,* reproduction; reprinting, republication; recurrence.

reproduire, *v.a.,* to produce again, to reproduce; to reprint, to republish.

se **reproduire,** *v.r.,* to come again; to be reproduced; to show one's self again; to occur, to happen again, to recur.

repromettre, *v.a.,* to promise again.

réprouvable, *adj.,* censurable, reprehensible, blamable.

réprouvé, *n.m.,* (theol.) reprobate. *Il a un visage de —;* he has a sinister-looking face.

reprouver, *v.a.,* to prove again.

réprouver, *v.a.,* to disapprove of, to disapprove, to reprobate, to condemn, to reject.

reps (rèps), *n.m.,* rep (silk *or* woolen fabric).

reptation, *n.f.,* reptation, creeping.

reptile, *n.m.* and *adj.,* reptile; creeping, crawling. *C'est un —;* he is a crawling wretch, a reptile.

républicain, -e, *n.* and *adj.,* republican.

républicaniser, *v.a.,* to republicanize.

républicanisme, *n.m.,* republicanism.

républication, *n.f.,* republication, re-issue.

républier, *v.a.,* to republish, to re-issue.

république, *n.f.,* republic; commonwealth. *La — des lettres;* the republic of letters.

répudiation, *n.f.,* repudiation, renunciation; rejection.

répudier, *v.a.,* to repudiate, to put away; to renounce, to reject.

*répugnance, *n.f.,* repugnance, dislike; reluctance, unwillingness. *J'ai de la — à le faire;* I am reluctant, *or* loath, to do it. *Avec —;* with reluctance, reluctantly, repugnantly.

*répugnant, -e, *adj.,* repugnant.

*répugner, *v.n.,* to be repugnant, to be contrary, to clash with; to feel repugnance at; to feel reluctant; to feel loath. *Cela répugne au sens commun;* that is contrary to common sense. *Cet homme me répugne;* that man is my aversion. *Cela me répugne;* I am loath to do it. *Il me répugne de vous entretenir d'un pareil sujet;* it is repugnant to me to talk to you on such a subject.

répulluler, *v.n.,* to repullulate; to abound, to swarm; to increase fast.

répulsi-f, -ve, *adj.,* (phys.) repulsive, repelling.

répulsion, *n.f.,* (phys.) repulsion; (fig.) aversion, disgust.

repurger, *v.a.,* to purge again.

réputation, *n.f.,* reputation, character, repute, fame. *Avoir la — de;* to have the reputation of, to pass for. *Je ne vous connaissais que de —;* I only knew you by report. *En —;* in repute, in request. *Se faire une —;* to get one's self a reputation. *Se mettre en —;* to get into repute. *Avoir de la —;* to have reputation, to have a name. *Perdre quelqu'un de —;* to ruin any one's reputation, character.

réputer, *v.a.,* to repute, to account, to reckon, to deem; to hold.

requérable, *adj.,* (jur.) demandable.

requérant, -e, *n.* and *adj.,* (jur.) plaintiff, applicant; petitioner.

requérir (requérant, requis), *v.a.,* to request,

to beg ; to require, to demand ; to claim, to summon. *C'est lui qui m'en a requis ;* it was he who requested me to do it.

requête, *n.f.,* request, petition, demand, application ; (hunt.) new cast, new search. *Faire une —;* to make a request, a demand. *On accorda sa —;* his demand was granted.

requêter, *v.a.,* (hunt.) to search again (for).

requiem (-kui-èm), *n.m.,* requiem.

requin, *n.m.,* (ich.) shark.

requinqué, -e, *adj.,* (fam., iron.) spruce, dressed out.

se **requinquer,** *v.r.,* (fam., iron.) to deck one's self out.

requis, -e, *part.,* requested, required, requisite, proper ; due. *Il a l'âge —;* he has the proper, the required age.

réquisition, *n.f.,* requisition, application ; motion ; call, summons, order, levy. *A la — de ;* on the application of.

réquisitionnement, *n.m.,* requisitioning.

réquisitionner, *v.a.,* to requisition ; to impound.

réquisitoire, *n.m.,* (jur.) speech for the crown.

resaluer, *v.a.,* to salute, to bow to, again.

rescellement, *n.m.,* resealing, refastening.

resceller, *v.a.,* to seal again.

rescif (rè-cif), *n.m.* V. **récif.**

rescindant, *n.m.,* (jur., ant.) motion to annul, or set aside.

rescinder, *v.a.,* (jur.) to annul, to rescind.

rescision (rès-si-zi-on), *n.f.,* (jur.) annulment, rescission.

rescisoire (rès-si-zoar), *n.m.,* (jur.) ground for annulment. *adj.,* rescissory.

⊙**rescontre,** *n.m.,* (com.) bill-book.

rescousse, *n.f.,* recapture ; help, rescue. *A la — ;* help ! help !

rescription, *n.f.,* money order ; check ; scrip, bond, debenture.

rescrit, *n.m.,* rescript ; bull.

réseau, *n.m.,* net, net-work ; (rail.) system, section ; (anat.) plexus ; (arch.) tracery ; (geom.) chain (of triangles).

résection (ré-cèk-si-on), *n.f.,* (surg.) resection [amputation].

réséda, *n.m.,* (bot.) reseda, mignonette.

réséquer (ré-cé-), *v.a.,* (surg.) to resect.

réservation, *n.f.,* reserve, reservation.

réserve, *n.f.,* reserve, reservation, caution ; modesty ; stock, stores ; preserve (for game). *Se tenir sur la — ;* to be reserved, to act with circumspection. *A la — de ;* with the reservation of. *En — ;* in reserve, in store. *Mettre en —;* to reserve, to lay by. *Sans —;* without reserve, unreservedly.

réservé, -e, *adj.,* reserved, cautious, wary, circumspect, shy ; guarded, coy.

réserver, *v.a.,* to reserve, to save, to set apart, to lay by, to lay up.

se **réserver,** *v.r.,* to reserve, to reserve to one's self ; to mean, to intend, to purpose ; to wait for an opportunity ; to be kept ; to reserve to one's self the right. *Se — la réplique ;* to reserve the right of replying. *Je me réserve de faire cela ;* I am waiting for an opportunity to do that.

réserviste, *n.m.,* (milit.) reserve-man, reservist.

réservoir, *n.m.,* reservoir, tank ; fish-pond, cistern, well ; (anat.) receptacle.

résidant, -e, *adj.,* resident, residing.

résidence, *n.f.,* residence, place of abode, dwelling, living. *Etablir sa — à ;* to take up one's abode (at).

résident, *n.m.,* resident, minister at a foreign court.

résider, *v.n.,* to reside, to dwell, to live ; to lie (in), to rest.

résidu, *n.m.,* settlement (of liquids) ; residue ; (arith.) remainder ; (chem.) residuum.

***résignant,** *n.m.,* resigner.

***résignataire,** *n.m.,* resignee.

***résignation,** *n.f.,* resignation.

resigner, *v.a.,* to sign again.

***résigner,** *v.a.,* to resign, to give up.

*se **résigner,** *v.r.,* to resign one's self (to), to submit ; to be reconciled (to) ; to put up (with).

résiliation, *n.f.,* canceling, annulling.

résiliement or **résiliment,** *n.m.* V. **résiliation.**

résilier, *v.a.,* to cancel, to annul.

résille, *n.f.,* hair-net.

résine, *n.f.,* resin, rosin ; colophony. *Un pain de — ;* a cake of resin.

résineu-x, -se, *adj.,* resinous.

résinifère, *adj.,* yielding resin, resiniferous.

résipiscence (-zi-), *n.f.,* resipiscence, repentance. *Venir à — ;* to repent ; to amend.

résistance, *n.f.,* resistance, opposition, obstacle ; (med.) obstinacy. *Pièce de — ;* (cook.) solid joint. *Sans — ;* unresistingly. *Faire de la — ;* to offer resistance, to resist.

résistant, *adj.,* tough, firm, unyielding.

résister, *v.n.,* to resist, to oppose, to withstand ; to endure, to last. *— à l'ennemi ;* to resist the enemy. *— à la tentation ;* to withstand temptation. *Je n'y saurais plus — ;* I can endure it no longer.

résistible, *adj.,* resistible.

résolu, -e, *part.,* resolved on, decided, determined on, settled, fixed.

résolu, -e, *adj.,* resolute, bold, determined, stout-hearted, undaunted.

résolubilité, *n.f.,* resolvability.

résoluble, *adj.,* solvable, resolvable.

résolument, *adv.,* resolutely, boldly, stoutly.

résoluti-f, -ve, *adj.,* (med.) resolutive ; resolvent ; discutient.

résolutif, *n.m.,* (med.) resolutive, resolvent.

résolution, *n.f.,* resolution, solution, decision, determination ; resolve ; (jur.) canceling, annulment. *Avec — ;* resolutely, stoutly. *Changer de — ;* to alter one's mind. *— d'un contrat ;* (jur.) canceling of a contract.

résolutoire, *adj.,* (jur.) resolutive, canceling.

résolvant, -e, *adj., n.m.,* (med.) resolvent.

résonance, *n.f.,* resonance.

résonnant, -e, *adj.,* resonant ; sounding, sonorous. *Voix claire et — e ;* clear and sonorous voice. *Un violon bien — ;* a well-sounding violin.

résonnement (-zo-n-mãn), *n.m.,* resounding, clanking, echoing, rattling, rattle.

résonner, *v.n.,* to resound ; to clank, to echo, to reverberate.

résorber (-zor-), *v.a.,* (med.) to reabsorb.

se **résorber** (-zor-), *v.r.,* (med.) to be reabsorbed.

résorption (-zor-), *n.f.,* reabsorption.

résoudre (résolvant, résolu *and* résous), *v.a.,* to resolve ; to dissolve, to melt ; to solve ; to decide, to settle ; (jur.) to cancel, to make void ; to resolve on, to determine on, to decide upon (a thing) ; to determine ; to decide on ; to persuade. *— une tumeur ;* (med.) to resolve a tumor. *— un problème ;* to solve a problem. *— une question ;* to settle a question. *— un bail ;* to cancel a lease. *A-t-on résolu la paix ou la guerre ?* has peace or war been decided upon ? or is it to be peace or war ?

se **résoudre,** *v.r.,* to resolve, to be resolved, to be solved ; to dissolve, to be dissolved ; to determine ; to be prevailed upon ; to make up one's mind. *L'eau se résout en vapeur ;* water is resolved into vapor. *Se — à ;* to resolve upon ; to bring one's self to. *A quoi vous résolvez-vous ?* what resolution have you come to ? *Je ne saurais m'y résoudre ;* I cannot make up my mind to do it.

résous, *part.,* resolved, dissolved, melted ; changed into. [*Résous* has no feminine.]

respect (rès-pè), *n.m.,* respect, regard, reverence, awe, deference, dutifulness. *Porter – à quelqu'un;* to show respect to any one. *Manquer de – envers quelqu'un;* to be wanting in respect towards any one. *Présenter ses –s à quelqu'un;* to pay one's respects to any one, to give one's kind regards to. *Se faire porter – ;* to make one's self respected. *Imprimer,* or *imposer, le – à;* to impress any one with respect, to awe any one. *Tenir en – ;* to keep in awe or in respect. *Sauf votre – ;* saving your presence. *Sauf le – que je vous dois;* with due deference to you.

respectabilité, *n.f.,* respectability.

respectable (rès-pèk-), *adj.,* respectable, venerable.

respectablement, *adv.,* respectably.

respecter (rès-pèk-), *v.a.,* to respect, to reverence, to revere; to spare. *— la vieillesse;* to respect old age. *Respectez ses sentiments;* spare his feelings. *Le temps n'a pas respecté ces monuments;* time has not spared those monuments. *Se faire — ;* to command respect. *se* **respecter** (rès-pèk-té), *v.r.,* to respect one's self; to respect each other.

respecti-f, -ve (rès-pèk-), *adj.,* respective.

respectivement (rès-pèk-tiv-mān), *adv.,* respectively.

respectueusement (rès-pèk-tu-euz-mān), *adv.,* respectfully, reverentially, dutifully, deferentially.

respectueu-x, -se (rès-pèk-), *adj.,* respectful, reverential, dutiful, deferential.

respirable (rès-), *adj.,* respirable, breathable.

respirateur, *adj.,* respiratory. *n.m.,* respirator.

respiration (rès-), *n.f.,* respiration, breathing. *Difficulté de — ;* shortness of breath. *Avoir la — coupée;* to be unable to get one's breath.

respiratoire (rès-pi-ra-toar), *adj.,* respiratory.

respirer (rès-pi-ré), *v.n.,* to breathe, to respire; to take breath, to draw breath, to rest; to long for. *Il a de la peine à — ;* he can scarcely breathe. *— après quelque chose;* to long for anything, to desire anything ardently.

respirer (rès-), *v.a.,* to breathe, to inhale; to thirst after, to long for; to bespeak, to betoken, to express. *Son visage respire la douceur;* his face betokens gentleness. *Il ne respire que la vengeance;* he thirsts after vengeance.

resplendir (rès-plān-), *v.n.,* to shine brightly; to be resplendent, to glitter.

resplendissant, -e (rès-plān-), *adj.,* resplendent, bright, glittering.

resplendissement (rès-plān-dis-mān), *n.m.,* resplendence.

responsabilité (rès-), *n.f.,* responsibility, liability.

responsable (rès-), *adj.,* responsible, answerable, liable, accountable.

responsi-f, -ve (rès-), *adj.,* (jur.) responsory.

ressac (rè-sak), *n.m.,* (nav.) surf.

***ressaigner** (rè-sè-), *v.a.* and *n.,* to bleed again.

ressaisir (rè-sè-zir), *v.a.,* to seize again, to take again, to recover possession of.

se **ressaisir** (rè-sè-zir), *v.r.,* to seize again, to recover possession of.

ressaler, *v.a.,* to salt again.

ressasser (rè-sa-sé), *v.a.,* to sift again; to examine minutely; to scrutinize.

ressasseu-r, -se, *n.m.f.,* tiresome repeater.

ressaut (rè-sô), *n.m.,* (arch.) ressault, projection; abrupt fall, dip.

ressauter (rè-sô-té), *v.a.n.,* to leap again; (arch.) to project.

ressécher (rè-sé-), *v.a.,* to dry again.

resseller (rè-sè-lé), *v.a.,* to saddle again.

ressemblance (rè-sān-), *n.f.,* resemblance, likeness, similarity. *Se tromper à la — ;* to be deceived by the likeness.

ressemblant, -e (rè-sān-), *adj.,* resembling, like, similar. *C'est très — ;* it is a striking likeness.

ressembler (rè-sān-), *v.n.,* to resemble, to be like, to take after. *Le fils ressemble à son père;* the son resembles his father. *Ce portrait vous ressemble peu;* this portrait is not much like you.

se **ressembler** (rè-sān-), *v.r.,* to resemble one another, to be like each other, to be alike; to be uniform. *Ils se ressemblent comme deux gouttes d'eau;* they are as like as two peas. *Qui se ressemble, s'assemble;* birds of a feather flock together.

ressemelage (rè-sè-mlaj), *n.m.,* resoling (of boots); new footing (of stockings).

ressemeler (rè-sè-mlé), *v.a.,* to sole anew (boots or shoes); to foot anew (stockings).

ressemer (rè-sè-mé), *v.a.,* to sow again.

ressenti, -e (rè-sān-), *part.,* felt; (paint.) strongly expressed, or marked; full of expression.

ressentiment (rè-sān-), *n.m.,* slight return, attack, touch (of disease, pain); desire of vengeance, resentment. *Avec — ;* resentingly. *Plein de — ;* resentful.

ressentir (rè-sān-), *v.a.,* to feel, to experience; to manifest, to show; to have a sense of. *— du malaise;* to feel uncomfortable. *Elle ressent vivement cette injure;* she feels that insult keenly.

se **ressentir** (rè-sān-), *v.r.,* to feel the effects of, to perceive, to resent; to feel (disease, pain) to feel the effects of. *Il se ressent encore de ses pertes;* he still feels the effects of his losses. *— d'une injure;* to resent an injury.

resserrement (rè-sèr-mān), *n.m.,* contraction, closing, tightening; restriction, oppression; (med.) stricture, contraction, costiveness.

resserrer (rè-sè-ré), *v.a.,* to tie again; to tie tighter, to draw closer, to bind tighter, to confine, to compress, to contract, to straighten; to rivet; to put by, away again; to keep more closely; to restrain, to confine; (print.) to lock up again; (nav.) to take in sails again; (milit.) to close again. *— une rivière dans son lit;* to confine a river to its bed. *Le froid resserre les pores;* cold contracts the pores. *— les liens de l'amitié;* to draw closer the bonds of friendship.

se **resserrer** (rè-sè-ré), *v.r.,* to contract, to be contracted; to be narrower, closer; to confine one's self, to be compressed; to become tighter; to become colder (of the weather); to retrench one's expenses; to be restricted in circulation (of money). *Le temps se resserre;* the weather is getting colder.

ressif (rè-sif), *n.m.* *V.* **récif**.

ressort (rè-sor), *n.m.,* spring; elasticity; energy; activity, force, strength; means. *À — ;* with a spring. *Faire — ;* to fly back. *Il n'agit que par — ;* he acts only at the instigation of others. *Faire jouer tous ses —s;* to use every effort.

ressort (rè-sor), *n.m.,* extent of jurisdiction; department, province, line; (jur.) resort. *En dernier — ;* (jur.) in the last resort; without appeal. *Cela n'est pas de mon — ;* that is not within my province, or not in my line.

ressortir (rè-sor-), *v.n.,* (pres. part. ressortant) to go out again; to be set off, to stand out (of a thing); to arise (from), to proceed (from), to result (from); to follow. *Faire — ;* to bring forward, to show off, to set forth, to bring out in relief.

ressortir (rè-sor-), *v.n.,* (pres. part. ressortissant), (jur.) to be under the jurisdiction of, to depend (on); to be dependent (on); to refer (to).

ressortissant, -e (rè-sor-), *adj.,* (jur.) appealable (to), amenable (to), under the jurisdiction (of), dependent (on).

ressouder (rè-sou-), *v.a.,* to solder again.

ressoudure, n.f., re-soldering.

ressource (rĕ-soors), n.f., resource, expedient, shift. pl., resources. Faire —; to procure resources; to raise the wind; to finance. C'est ma dernière —; that is my last shift. — désespérée; desperate expedient, shift. Un malheur sans —; an irreparable misfortune. Je suis perdu, ruiné, sans —; I am irretrievably ruined. Il n'y a point de —; there 's no help for it. C'est un homme de —; he is a man fertile in expedients, a man of resource.

⊙**ressouvenance** (rĕ-soo-vnans), n.f., remembrance.

ressouvenir (rĕ-soo-vnir), n.m., remembrance, recollection; reminiscence, memento; twinge, return (of pain).

se **ressouvenir** (rĕ-soo-vnir), v.r., to recollect, to remember. Faire ressouvenir; to put in mind. Vous en ressouvient-il? do you remember it?

ressuage (rĕ-), n.m., (tech.) sweating; (metal.) eliquation.

ressuer (rĕ-), v.n., (metal.) to eliquate; (tech.) to sweat.

ressui (rè-), n.m., lair (where animals dry themselves).

ressuiement, n.m., drying.

ressuscitation, n.f., or **ressuscitement,** n.m., resuscitation, revival, renewal.

ressuscitatoire, adj., reviving.

ressusciter (rè-), v.a., to resuscitate, to raise from the dead, to bring to life again, to revive.

ressusciter (rè-), v.n., to rise from the dead, to come to life again, to be resuscitated.

ressuyer (rè-), v.n., to wipe, to dry, again.

se **ressuyer** (rè-), v.r., to dry; to air (of linen).

restant, -e (rès-), adj., remaining, left. Poste —e; till called for.

restant (rès-), n.m., remainder, rest.

⊙**restaur** (rès-), n.m., (com.). V. **ristourne.**

restaurant, -e (rès-), adj., restorative.

restaurant (rès-), n.m., restorative; eatinghouse, dining-rooms, luncheon-rooms.

restaurat-eur, n.m., **-rice** (rès-), n.f., restorer.

restaurateur(rès-),n.m., eating-house keeper.

restaurati-f, -ve (rès-), adj., (med.) restorative.

restauration (rès-), n.f., restoration, repairing, re-establishment.

restaurer (rès-), v.a., to restore; to re-establish, to repair; to put in thorough repair; to revive, to refresh. — ses forces; to restore one's strength.

se **restaurer** (rès-), v.r., to take refreshment, to refresh one's self; to recover one's strength.

reste, n.m., rest, remainder, remnant. Remains, residue, scrap, relic, leavings. pl., mortal remains. Avoir de —; to have something left and to spare, to have remaining. De —; left, remaining, enough and more than enough. Et le —; and the rest of it, and so forth, et cætera. Faire son —; to stake all the money one has left. Jouer de son —; to play one's last stake. Donner son — à quelqu'un; to give it to, to abuse, to beat any one. Il ne demanda pas son —; he did not wait for anything more, he sneaked off. Etre en —; to be behindhand, to be in arrears. Il n'y a rien de —; there is nothing left. J'en ai de —; I have more than enough. Du —; however, moreover, nevertheless. Au —; besides. N'être pas de — avec; not to be beholden to.

rester, v.n., to remain, to be left; to stay, to stop, to continue, to keep; (mus.) to hold; (nav.) to bear. C'est tout ce qui me reste; that is all I have left. Il reste quelque argent; there is some money left. Que me reste-t-il à faire? what am I to do now? Il me reste à vous dire; I have still to tell you. Il resta à Rome après

notre départ; he stayed at Rome after our departure. Il est resté stupéfait; he remained thunderstruck. Restez tranquille; keep quiet, keep still. — chez soi; to stay at home. Où en sommes-nous restés? where did we leave off? En — à; to leave off, to stop. Restons-en là; let us stop there; let us say no more about it.

restituable (rès-), adj., repayable, returnable, to be refunded.

restituer (rès-), v.a., to restore, to return, to give back again, to refund. — un passage d'un livre; to restore a passage in a book.

restituteur (rès-), n.m., restorer (of the texts of authors).

restitution (rès-), n.f., restitution, restoration; (jur.) relief, release.

restreindre (rès-), (restreignant, restreint), v.a., to restrict, to restrain, to limit, to confine, to stint.

se **restreindre** (rès-), v.r., to restrain one's self, to limit one's self (to), to be restricted.

restricti-f, -ve (rès-), adj., restrictive.

restriction (rès-), n.f., restriction, restraint; reserve. — mentale; mental reservation.

restringent, -e (rès-), adj., (med.) (l.u.) astringent.

restringent, n.m., (med.) (l.u.) astringent.

résultant, -e (rès-), adj., resulting, arising; resultant.

résultante, n.f., (med.) resultant.

résultat, n.m., result. En —; finally, ultimately, eventually.

résulter, v.n., to result, to follow (from); to be the consequence (of). Que résulte-t-il de là? what follows from that? Qu'en peut-il —? what can be the consequences?

résumé, n.m., recapitulation, summary; abridgment; epitome; short account; (jur.) summing up of a judge. Au —, en —; upon the whole, after all, to sum up.

résumer, v.a., to recapitulate, to sum up, to give a summary. — un discours; to give a summary of a speech.

se **résumer,** v.r., to recapitulate, to sum up; to embody, to be comprised; to be summed up.

résurrecti-f, -ve, adj., life-giving, life-restoring.

résurrection, n.f., resurrection, rising.

résurrectionniste, n.m., resurrectionist.

rétable, n.m., (arch.) altar screen, reredos.

rétablir, v.a., to re-establish, to restore, to repair; to recover; to re-install; to set up again; to retrieve; to revive. — son honneur; to retrieve one's honor. — sa santé; to recover one's health. — quelqu'un; to set any one up again.

se **rétablir,** v.r., to recover one's health; to get well again; to be re-established, restored, repaired. Le crédit commence à se —; credit is gradually being restored.

rétablissement (-blis-mān), n.m., re-establishment, restoration, repairing, recovery, re-instatement, revival, recovery of health. Sans espoir de —; past recovery. — dans les bonnes grâces de quelqu'un; restoration to any one's good graces. — du commerce; revival of commerce.

*****retaille,** n.f., (manu.) piece cut off; shred, paring.

*****retailler,** v.a., to cut, to mend again (pens, pencils); to prune again.

rétamage, n.m., tinning over again; re-silvering.

rétamer, v.a., to tin over again; to re-silver.

rétameur, n.m., tinker.

retapé, -e, adj., done up (of hats); (pop.) spruce, natty, smart.

retaper, v.a., ⊙to cock (a hat); to do up (a hat); to curl and powder (a wig). — les cheveux; to turn up the hair.

se **retaper**, *v.r.*, to be done up (of hats) ; (pop.) to dress one's self out.

retard, *n.m.*, delay ; (mus.) retardation ; slowness (of a clock). *Apporter du —* ; to cause delay. *Eprouver du —* ; to suffer delay. *Etre en —* ; to be late ; to be in arrears ; to be backward, to be behind time. *Votre montre est en — de deux minutes ;* your watch is two minutes slow. *Nous avons dix minutes de —* ; (of railways) the train is ten minutes late. *Avoir une patte de —* ; to walk lame.

retardataire, *n.m.* and *adj.*, in arrears ; defaulter, loiterer, lagger ; in arrears ; late, behindhand.

retardat-eur, -rice, *adj.*, (phys.) retarding.

retardation, *n.f.*, (phys.) retardation.

retardement, *n.m.*, delay, retardment, putting off ; (com., nav.) over-time, demurrage.

retarder, *v.a.*, to retard, to delay, to defer, to put off ; to hinder ; to put back (clocks and watches). *— une horloge ;* to put a clock back.

retarder, *v.n.*, to lose, to go too slow (of clocks and watches) ; to come later. *Ma montre retarde ;* my watch loses. *Sa fièvre retarde tous les jours d'environ une heure ;* his fit of ague comes on one hour later every day.

retâter, *v.a.*, to touch and feel again ; to taste again ; to grope about again ; to try, to begin again, to alter, to mend, to correct.

reteindre, *v.a.*, to dye again.

retendre, *v.a.*, to bend again ; to pull again, to stretch again, to spread again.

retenir (rě-tnir), *v.a.*, to get again ; to get hold of again ; to retain, to keep, to withhold, to keep back ; to reserve ; to curb ; to bespeak, to hire ; to secure, to engage ; to detain, to keep, to confine ; to hold back, to hinder ; to restrain, to keep from ; to remember ; (arith.) to carry. *Posez sept et retenez deux ;* (arith.) put down seven and carry two. *— une chambre ;* to secure a room. *— une place à la diligence ;* to bespeak a place in the coach. *— une place ;* to keep, or secure, a place. *— un domestique ;* to engage a servant. *Il ne saurait — sa langue ;* he cannot restrain his tongue. *— sa colère ;* to restrain one's anger. *Qu'est-ce qui vous retient ?* what hinders you ? *Je ne sais ce qui me retient ;* I don't know what hinders me. *— une poutre ;* (carp.) to secure a beam. *— quelqu'un ;* to detain any one. *Je ne vous retiendrai pas ;* I won't keep you a minute.

se **retenir**, *v.r.*, to keep back, to forbear ; to control one's self ; to stop ; to seize hold, to catch hold of, to clutch, to cling to ; (man.) to hold back.

retenir, *v.n.*, to hold back (of horses) ; to breed (of mares).

retenter, *v.a.*, to re-attempt.

rétenti-f, -ve, *adj.*, retentive.

rétention, *n.f.*, reservation, reserve, retention ; (jur.) retaining.

rétentionnaire, *n.m.f.*, (jur.) detainer. *adj.*, detaining.

retentir, *v.n.*, to resound, to ring, to re-echo, to clank, to rattle.

retentissant, -e, *adj.*, resounding, ringing, echoing, sonorous, loud ; famous. *Voûte —e ;* echoing vault.

retentissement (-tis-mān), *n.m.*, resounding, echo, re-echoing, clanking, rattling, ringing ; fame, celebrity. *Avoir du —* ; to make a great noise ; to be spread abroad.

retentum (ré-tin-tom), *n.m.*, mental reserve ; (jur.) ⊙tacit clause, proviso.

retenu, -e (rě-tnu), *adj.*, circumspect, reserved, cautious, timid, discreet, wary ; prudent, coy, shy.

retenue, *n.f.*, reserve, discretion, circumspection, caution, prudence ; keeping in, detention ; (fin.) stoppage. *Il faut avoir de la —* ; one must

keep within bounds. *Etre en —* ; to be in detention ; (school) to be kept in. *Sans —* ; unreservedly. *Palan de —* ; relieving tackle.

reterçage *or* **retersage**, *n.m.*, second dressing (of vines).

retercer *or* **reterser**, *v.a.*, to dress vines again.

rétiaire (-ci-èr), *n.m.*, (antiq.) net-fighter.

réticence, *n.f.*, reserve, concealment ; (rhet.) reticence.

réticulaire, *adj.*, (anat.) reticular.

réticule, *n.f.*, reticule, reticle (of a telescope) ; bag ; hair-net.

réticulé, -e, *adj.*, (arch., bot.) reticulated.

réti-f, -ve, *n.* and *adj.*, restive ; stubborn, mulish.

rétiforme, *adj.*, retiform.

rétine, *n.f.*, (anat.) retina (of the eye).

retirable, *adj.*, withdrawable.

⊙**retirade**, *n.f.*, (fort.) retirade.

retiration, *n.f.*, (print.) working off the outer form.

retiré, -e, *adj.*, retired, lonely, solitary, secluded ; shrunk, contracted.

retirement (-tir-mān), *n.m.*, (surg.) contraction, shrinking of the nerves and muscles.

retirer, *v.a.*, to draw again ; to draw back ; to withdraw ; to draw out ; to take away ; to redeem, to recover ; to retract, to claim, to withdraw ; to reap, to get, to derive ; to receive ; to lodge, to shelter, to harbor ; to fire off again, to let off again (fireworks) ; to remove (from school, prison) ; to derive (profit). *— sa parole ;* to call back one's word. *— quelqu'un de prison ;* to remove any one from prison. *— des choses qui étaient en gage ;* to take things out of pawn. *— son enjeu ;* to withdraw one's stakes. *— du danger ;* to rescue from danger.

se **retirer**, *v.r.*, to retire, to withdraw, to go away ; (of water) to subside, to recede, to ebb ; to retire from, to leave ; to quit ; to shrink, to contract, to recoup or retrieve one's self, to be drawn back or withdrawn. *Retirez-vous ;* leave the room ; be off ; (jur.) stand down (to witnesses). *Il s'est retiré du service ;* he has quitted the service. *Se — du commerce ;* to retire from business. *Se — en lieu de sûreté ;* to retire to a place of safety. *Il se retire de bonne heure ;* he keeps good hours. *Ils se retirèrent chacun chez eux ;* they retired to their respective homes.

retirer, *v.n.*, to withdraw, to ebb, to go down (of the tide).

retisser, *v.a.*, to weave again.

retombée, *n.f.*, (arch.) springing (of an arch).

retomber, *v.n.*, to fall again ; to relapse, to fall down again ; to fall. *— malade ;* to fall ill again. *— dans la même faute ;* to relapse into the same fault.

retondre, *v.a.*, to shear again ; (arch.) to clean off, to cut away useless ornaments.

retoquer, *v.a.*, to pluck, to plow again (at exam.).

retordage, *n.m.*, (manu.) twisting.

retordement, *n.m.*, (manu.) twisting.

retordeur, *n.m.*, twister, throwster.

retordre, *v.a.*, to wring again, to twist again ; to twist (silk, thread). *Donner du fil à — à quelqu'un ;* to cut out work for any one, to give any one a great deal of trouble. *Se —* ; to be twisted.

rétorquer, *v.a.*, to retort.

retors, -e, *adj.*, twisted ; artful, deep, cunning, shrewd, crafty. *Un homme —* ; a cunning, crafty man.

rétorsion, *n.f.*, act of retorting, retortion.

retorte, *n.f.*, (chem.) retort. *V.* **cornue.**

* **retortiller**, *v.a.*, to twist again.

retouche, *n.f.*, (paint.) retouching.

retoucher, *v.n.*, to touch again, to retouch ; to touch up, to improve.

retoucher, *v.a.*, to retouch, to touch up, to

improve; to correct, to alter. *Se —;* to be retouched.

retour, *n.m.,* return, coming back; turning; winding; recurrence, conversion; (jur.) reversion; (arch.) return; thing given in to boot, into the bargain; acknowledgment; decline of life; wane; artifice, trick; change, reciprocity, caprice, whim; vicissitude; (nav.) homeward voyage. *Le — du printemps;* the return of spring. *A mon —;* on my return. *Sans —;* forever, irreparably, irrecoverably, irretrievably. *Etre de —;* to have returned. *Par — du courier;* by return of post. *Etre sur son —;* to be upon the point of returning. *Etre sur le —;* to be upon the decline of life, to be going downhill, to be on the wane; to be past middle age. *Avoir de fâcheux —s;* to be odd, whimsical. *Il n'y a point de — avec lui;* there is no peace to be made with him; there is no end to his resentment. *Amour qui n'est pas payé de —;* unrequited love. *A beau jeu, beau —;* one good turn deserves another. *La fortune a ses —s;* fortune has its vicissitudes. *Etre perdu sans —;* to be past all hope. *— de chasse;* luncheon (after shooting). *Quel — me donnerez-vous?* what will you give me to boot? *Faire un — sur soi-même;* to examine one's self. *En — de;* in return for. *Je serai de — à midi;* I shall be back at twelve. *Billet de —;* return ticket. *Sans esprit de —;* without thinking of returning. *Payer de —;* to requite (hate, love, etc.). *Faire — à;* to return to, to revert. *— d'âge;* change of life.

retourne, *n.f.,* turn-up card, trump-card, trumps.

retourner, *v.n.,* to return, to go again, to go back, to go back again; to turn up (at cards). *— sur ses pas;* to retrace one's steps. *— en arrière;* to turn back. *— à son travail;* to return to one's work. *N'y retournez pas;* don't do it again. *Il retourne cœur;* hearts are trumps. *Voyons de quoi il retourne;* (pop.) let us see what's going on, *or* how matters stand.

retourner, *v.a.,* to turn, to turn up; to revolve, to turn over, round, about, up, back; to turn (clothes); to mix (a salad). *— un habit;* to turn a coat. *— du foin;* to turn hay. *— une carte;* to turn up a card. *— une salade;* to mix a salad.

se **retourner,** *v.r.,* to turn, to turn round; to turn one's self, to be turned. *S'en retourner;* to return home, to go back again, to turn back.

retracement, *n.m.,* retracing; description, relation.

retracer, *v.a.,* to trace again; to retrace, to trace; to recount, to relate.

se **retracer,** *v.r.,* to retrace, to recall to mind, to remember; to return, to recur, to be traced again.

rétractation, *n.f.,* retractation, recantation.

rétracter, *v.a.,* to retract, to recall, to revoke.

se **rétracter,** *v.r.,* to retract; to make a retraction; to recant.

rétractile, *adj.,* retractile.

rétractilité, *n.f.,* retractility.   [tion.

rétraction, *n.f.,* (med.) retraction; contrac-

retraduire, *v.a.,* to translate again.

retraire, *v.a.,* (jur.) to redeem an estate; to milk again.

retrait, -e, *adj.,* lean, shrunk (grain); shrunk (of wood); (jur.) withdrawn, redeemed.

retrait, *n.m.,* closet, private room; (jur.) redemption, regaining possession; withdrawal (of a bill in parliament, of money from a bank); (arch.) off-set; shrinking, contraction (of clay, metals). *— conventionnel;* (jur.) re-emption. *Le — d'un projet de loi;* the withdrawal of a bill in parliament. *— d'emploi;* (milit.) being unattached (of officers).

retraite, *n.f.,* retreat; retiring; retirement;

refuge, hiding-place, haunt, lurking-place; retiring pension, pension; shrinking, contraction (of clay, of metals); (arch.) offset; nail (in the foot of a horse); (milit.) tattoo; (com.) redraft. *Battre en —;* to retreat, to draw off, to beat a retreat. *Sonner la —;* (hunt.) to call off the hounds; (milit.) to sound a retreat. *Donner — à quelqu'un;* to shelter any one, to harbour any one. *— de voleurs;* resort, den, of thieves. *Mettre à la —;* to pension off, to superannuate. *Prendre sa —;* to retire on a pension, to retire from the service. *Battre la —;* (milit.) to beat the tattoo. *Officier en —;* retired, *or* half-pay, officer.

retraité, -e, *n.* and *adj.,* one who is pensioned off, superannuated; on the retired list. *Officier —;* officer on the retired list. *Un —;* one who is pensioned off, a pensioner.

retranchement (-trănsh-măn), *n.m.,* retrenchment, abridging, suppression; curtailment; (milit.) retrenchment, intrenchment. *Forcer quelqu'un dans ses —s;* to storm any one in his stronghold.

retrancher, *v.a.,* to retrench, to curtail, to cut short; to cut off, to strike off, to erase; (arith.) to subtract; to take away, to abridge; to suppress; to deduct; to take away (from); (milit.) to intrench. *— un camp;* to intrench a camp.

se **retrancher,** *v.r.,* to restrain one's self; to confine one's self; to retrench, to curtail one's expenses; (milit.) to intrench one's self; to fall back upon, to urge, to plead, to put forward.

retranscrire, *v.a.,* to copy out again.

*retravailler, *v.a.,* to work again, to do over again.

retraverser, *v.a.,* to cross, to traverse again.

retrayant, *n.m.,* **-e,** *n.f.,* (jur.) repurchaser; re-emptor.

rêtre, *n.m.* V. **reître.**

rétréci, -e, *adj.,* narrow, cramped, contracted, confined.

rétrécir, *v.a.,* to take in, to straiten, to make narrower, to contract; to narrow, to cramp; to shrink; to limit.

se **rétrécir,** *v.r.,* to become narrow, to grow strait; to shrink, to contract; to be cramped, contracted, straitened.

rétrécir, *v.n.,* to narrow, to shrink up.

rétrécissement (-sis-măn), *n.m.,* narrowing, shrinking, cramping; contracting; narrowness, contraction; (med.) stricture.

rétreindre, *v.a.,* to hammer out (metal).

rétreinte, *n.f.,* hammering out.

retremper, *v.a.,* to temper again (metal); to give renewed force to, to strengthen.

se **retremper,** *v.r.,* to acquire renewed strength; to recruit one's strength, to be strengthened, invigorated.

rétribué, -e, *adj.,* remunerated, rewarded.

rétribuer, *v.a.,* to remunerate, to requite, to reward; to give a salary, a fee, to.

rétribution, *n.f.,* retribution, reward.

rétroacti-f, -ve, *adj.,* retroactive.

rétroaction, *n.f.,* retroaction.

rétroactivement (-tiv-măn), *adv.,* retroactively.

rétroactivité, *n.f.,* retroactive effect.

rétroagir, *v.n.,* to have a retroactive effect.

rétrocéder, *v.a.,* to give back again, to cede back; (jur.) to reconvey; to reassign.

rétrocessi-f, -ve, *adj.,* retroceding, retrocedent.

rétrocession, *n.f.,* (jur.) retrocession, redemise, reconveyance.

rétrogradation, *n.f.,* (astron.) retrogradation, retrogression, retrocession.

rétrograde, *adj.,* retrograde.

rétrograder, *v.n.,* to retrograde, to go backward; to go back.

rétrogressi-f, -ve, *adj.*, retrogressive.

rétrogression, *n.f.*, retrogression.

rétrospecti-f, -ve, *adj.*, retrospective.

retroussé, -e, *part.*, turned up, tucked up, cocked up. *Nez* —; snub nose, turned-up nose. *Avoir le bras* —; to have one's sleeves tucked up.

retroussement (-troos-mān), *n.m.*, turning up, tucking up, cocking up, curling up.

retrousser, *v.a.*, to turn up, to tuck up, to cock; to tie up; (nav.) to truss up sails. — *sa robe;* to tuck up one's gown. — *sa moustache;* to turn up one's moustache.

se **retrousser**, *v.r.*, to turn up, to cock up; to tie up; to tuck up one's gown.

retroussis, *n.m.*, cock, flap (of a hat); boot-top, top (of a boot); facing (of a uniform, livery).

retrouver, *v.a.*, to find again, to recover; to recognize; to meet again. *Je le retrouverai bien;* he will not escape me.

se **retrouver**, *v.r.*, to find one another again; to find one's self again; to be found again; to be met with again; to find one's way.

rets (ré), *n.m.*, net, netting, snare, toils.

réunion, *n.f.*, reunion, union, junction; meeting, assembly; company; concourse, gathering; party, soirée, reception. *Salle de* —; assembly-room. *Maison de* —; meeting-house.

réunir, *v.a.*, to reunite, to join again, to bring together again, to reannex; to unite, to join, to bring together, to annex; to collect, to assemble, to muster; to call together, to combine; to reconcile, to unite. — *des faits;* to collect facts.

se **réunir**, *v.r.*, to reunite, to unite, to join, to join again, to unite again; to be united, to be joined, to be collected; to meet (at an appointed place); to gather, to collect, to come together, to assemble, to muster, to club together, to combine, to blend, to be blended.

réussi, -e, *adj.*, successful, brilliant, well executed *or* carried out. *Bien* —; well done; a success, well-performed. *Mal* —; badly done; spoilt, badly performed; not a success.

réussir, *v.n.*, to succeed, to prosper, to thrive, to be successful, to have success. — *à faire quelque chose;* to succeed in doing anything. *Il a mal réussi;* he was unsuccessful. *Ce projet n'a pas réussi;* the plan did not succeed. *Tout ce qu'il entreprend lui réussit;* everything he undertakes succeeds. *Les pommiers réussissent dans ce terrain;* apple-trees thrive in this soil. *Cela m'a bien réussi;* that answered my purpose admirably.

réussir, *v.a.*, to carry out well, to execute well, to accomplish, to perform.

réussite, *n.f.*, success; issue, event, result.

revacciner, *v.a.*, to revaccinate.

revalidation, *n.f.*, (jur.) rendering valid again.

revaloir, *v.a.*, to return like for like; to be even with, to pay back. *Il me le revaudra;* he shall pay for it, I will be even with him (for it).

revanche, *n.f.*, revenge, retaliation; return; return-match (at play). *Avoir sa* —; to have one's revenge; to have one's turn. *Prendre sa* —; to take one's revenge; to return like for like; to play the return-match. *En* —; by way of retaliation; in return.

revancher, *v.a.*, (fam.) to defend; to revenge; to return like for like.

se **revancher**, *v.r.*, (fam.) to defend one's self; to be revenged, to revenge; to return like for like; to have one's turn. *Se — d'un bienfait;* to return a benefit.

revancheur, *n.m.*, (l.u.) defender.

rêvasser, *v.n.*, to have troubled dreams, to dream, to keep dreaming; to muse. — *à une affaire;* to muse over, or ponder over, any matter.

rêvasserie (-va-srī), *n.f.*, unconnected, broken dreams; musing, dreaming.

rêvasseur, *n.m.*, dreamer, muser.

rêve, *n.m.*, dream; idle fancy, day-dream, vision, illusion.

revêche, *adj.*, sharp, harsh, rough; stubborn, unruly, cross, untractable, ill-natured, dogged, cross-grained, crabbed, cantankerous. *Diamant* —; diamond not polishable in all its parts.

rêve-creux, *n.m.*, (—) dreamer.

***réveil, *n.m.*, waking, awaking; waking-time; (horl.) alarum, alarm; alarm-watch, alarm-clock; (milit.) reveille. *A mon* —; on my awaking.

***réveille-matin, *n.m.*, (—) alarm-clock, alarum; chanticleer, cock; (bot.) wartwort, spurge.

***réveiller, *v.a.*, to awake, to wake, to rouse, to rouse up, to call up; to stir up, to quicken, to revive, to recall; to evoke, to rake up. — *des souvenirs fâcheux;* to recall disagreeable recollections.

*se réveiller, *v.r.*, to wake, to awake, to wake up, to awaken; to revive; to be aroused, to be renewed, to be awakened. *Sa haine se réveilla;* his hatred was aroused. *Se — de son assoupissement;* to awake from one's lethargy. *Se — en sursaut;* to start up out of one's sleep.

réveilleu-r, -se, *n.m.f.*, waker, awakener, caller.

***réveillon, *n.m.*, midnight repast; Christmas-eve revel; (paint.) strong touch of light.

révélat-eur, -rice, *n.f.*, informer, revealer, discoverer, detector. *adj.*, revealing, tell-tale. — *d'un complot;* revealer of a plot. *Être le — de ses complices;* to inform against one's accomplices; (jur.) to turn king's, queen's, evidence.

révélation, *n.f.*, revelation; discovery, disclosure; (jur.) information.

révéler, *v.a.*, to reveal, to discover, to lay open, to disclose, to detect; to betray; to inform against; (fam., pop.) to blab.

revenant, -e, *adj.*, pleasing, prepossessing. *Physionomie —e;* pleasing physiognomy.

revenant (rĕ-vnän), *n.m.*, ghost, spirit. *Il y a des —s dans cette maison;* that house is haunted.

revenant-bon, *n.m.*, (—s—s) perquisite; bonus; emolument; windfall, godsend.

revendage, *n.m.*, huckstering.

revendeu-r, -se, *n.f.*, retail dealer, retailer; dealer in old clothes; regrater. —*se à la toilette;* wardrobe dealer, dealer in cast clothes.

revendicable, *adj.*, claimable.

revendication, *n.f.*, (jur.) claim; claiming, demand. *Action en* —; (jur.) action in pursuit of a claim.

revendiquer, *v.a.*, to claim, to demand.

revendre, *v.a.*, to sell again; to re-sell. *Il en a à* —; he has enough of it, and to spare. *En* — *à quelqu'un;* to be deeper than any one, to be more than a match for any one; to outdo.

revenir (rĕ-vnir), *v.n.*, to come again, to come back, to come back again, to return, to recover, to recover one's self; to get over, to come to one's self, to come to; to be restored; to occur, to recur, to present one's self; to resume, to reconsider; to alter one's mind, to change one's opinion, to recant, to retract; to be undeceived; to come over to, to adopt, to embrace; to retrieve; to be reconciled, to be appeased, to be pacified; to cost, to stand in; to amount, to come to; to be tantamount to; to please, to suit, to match; to arise, to accrue, to result, to proceed; to appear, to haunt, to walk; (jur.) to claim on a guarantee; (of food) to rise (in the stomach). *Faire — quelqu'un;* to call any one back. *Son nom ne me revient pas;* I do not recollect his name. *Revenons à notre propos;* let us resume, let us return to our business. *J'en reviens toujours là que;* I still persist in thinking that. *En*

— *toujours là ;* to be always harping on the same string. — *à la charge ;* to return to the charge. — *à ses moutons ;* to return to one's subject. — *sur une matière ;* to return to a subject. — *d'une maladie ;* to recover from an attack of illness. *Il revient à vue d'œil ;* he is recovering visibly. — *à soi ;* to recover one's senses, to come to one's self again, to come to, to revive ; to resume one's serenity ; to reform, to be reformed, to be reclaimed, to return to the right path. — *d'une frayeur ;* to recover from a fright. — *en santé ;* to recover one's health. — *de loin ;* to escape great danger, to have a narrow escape ; to recover from a dangerous illness. — *sur l'eau ;* to get afloat again, to recover one's losses. *N'en pas —;* to wonder at, to be lost in astonishment. *En — d'une belle ;* to have had a narrow escape. *Revenir à l'avis de ;* to come over to the opinion of, to fall in with any one's views. *Je n'en reviens pas ;* I cannot recover from my astonishment, I cannot get over it ; I cannot make it out ; (fam.) it caps me. — *de ses préjugés ;* to shake off one's prejudices. — *de ses folies ;* to leave off one's old pranks. *Je suis revenu de ces amusements-là ;* I do not care for those amusements any more *or* these amusements pall upon me now. — *sur le compte de quelqu'un ;* to have a better (*or* a worse) opinion of any one (as the case may be). *Quand on m'a fait de ces tours, je ne reviens pas ;* when people play me such tricks as those I never forgive them. *Son humeur ne me revient pas ;* his humor does not please me. *Les deux choses reviennent au même ;* the two things amount to the same, come to the same, are tantamount to the same. *Cet habit revient à tant ;* that coat costs so much. *Il me revient que ;* I hear, I am told, *or* I understand that. *Il ne m'en revient rien ;* I get nothing by it. *De la viande qui revient ;* meat that rises in one's stomach. *Le vin fait — le cœur ;* wine cheers the heart. *Faire — de la viande ;* (cook.) to parboil, to half-cook meat.

revente, *n.f.,* resale ; selling again, reselling ; regrating. *De —;* second-hand. *Lit de —;* second-hand bed.

reventer, *v.a.,* (nav.) to fill a sail again.

revenu (rĕ-vnu), *n.m.,* revenue, income, rent, profit. *État des —s ;* rental. *—s casuels ;* perquisites.

revenue, *n.f.,* young wood (of a coppice).

rêver, *v.n.,* to dream, to be in a dream ; to rave, to be light-headed ; to talk idly ; to have a wandering mind, to muse ; to think, to reflect, to consider. *Il rêve tout éveillé ;* he indulges in day-dreams. *J'ai rêvé longtemps sur cette affaire ;* I have pondered long over that affair. *Je regagnai mon hôtellerie en rêvant ;* I trudged back to my inn in a thoughtful mood.

rêver, *v.a.,* to dream, to long for, to desire ardently, to dream of. *Il ne rêve que fortune ;* he thinks of nothing but riches.

réverbérant, -e, *adj.,* reverberating.

réverbération, *n.f.,* reverberation ; reverberation, repercussion (of sound). *La — des rayons du soleil ;* the reverberation of the solar rays.

réverbère, *n.m.,* reflector, street lamp. *Feu de —;* (chem.) reverberated fire.

réverbérer, *v.a.* and *n.,* to reverberate.

reverdie, *n.m.,* (nav.) return of the high tide.

reverdir, *v.a.* and *n.,* to paint green again ; to become green again ; to grow young again ; to reblossom ; (fig.) to grow influential, powerful again. *Planter là quelqu'un pour —;* to leave any one in the lurch ; to give any one the slip. *Il faut — ces barreaux ;* these iron bars must be painted green again. *Faire —;* to make green ; to revive.

reverdissement (-dis-mãn), *n.m.,* growing green again.

révéremment (-ra-mãn), *adv.,* reverently.

révérence, *n.f.,* reverence, veneration ; bow, curtsey. *Avec —;* reverently. *Faire une profonde —;* to make a low bow, a low curtsey. *Tirer sa — à quelqu'un ;* (jest.) to bow to any one.

révérencielle, *adj.,* reverential.

révérencieusement (-euz-man), *adv.,* reverentially.

révérencieu-x, -se, *adj.,* reverential ; bowing and scraping, obsequious.

révérend, -e, *adj.,* reverend. *Très —;* right reverend. [Sometimes used as a noun in the masculine.]

révérendissime, *adj.,* most reverend.

révérer, *v.a.,* to revere, to reverence, to venerate, to hold in veneration.

rêverie (rê-vrî), *n.f.,* reverie, musing ; dream ; raving, delirium. *Tomber en —;* to fall to musing.

revernir, *v.a.,* to glaze again, to varnish over again.

⊙**reverquier,** *n.m.* V. **revertier.**

revers (-vèr), *n.m.,* back, reverse ; facing (of clothes) ; lapel (of a coat) ; back stroke ; top (of boots) ; reverse, change for the worse. *Coup de —;* back-handed stroke. *Donner un —;* to hit a back stroke. *Le — de la médaille ;* the reverse side of the medal ; (fig.) the dark side of the picture. *Le — de la tranchée ;* (fort.) the reverse of the trench. *A or de —;* (mil.) in the rear, on the flank.

réversal, -e, *adj.,* (jur.) confirmatory.

reverseau, *n.m.,* flashing-board (for doors, etc.).

reversement, *n.m.,* (nav.) trans-shipment. *V.* **transbordement.**

reverser, *v.a.,* to pour out again ; to pour off ; (nav.) to trans-ship (*V.* **transborder**) ; (com.) to transfer, to carry (forward *or* over).

reversi *or* **reversis,** *n.m.,* reversis (card game).

réversibilité, *n.f.,* (jur.) revertibility.

réversible, *adj.,* reversible ; (jur.) revertible.

réversion, *n.f.,* (jur.) reversion.

réversoir, *n.m.,* dam, weir.

revertier (-tié), *n.m.,* sort of backgammon.

revêtement (-vê-tmãn), *n.m.,* (arch., mas.) covering, lining, coating, casing, facing ; (fort.) revetement ; (joinery) veneering.

revêtir, *v.a.,* to clothe ; to give clothes to, to invest ; to dress ; to put on, to assume ; to endow a person with ; to bestow on a person ; (mas.) to line, to cover. — *les pauvres ;* to clothe the poor. — *un habit ;* to put on a coat. — *ses pensées d'un style brillant ;* to clothe one's thoughts in brilliant language. — *la figure de quelqu'un ;* to put on the air of some one else. *Les formes que revêt la pensée ;* the forms that thought assumes. — *un personnage ;* to assume a character. *Je me suis dépouillé de cet emploi pour l'en —;* I threw up this employment in his favor, to bestow it on him. — *une terrasse de gazon ;* to cover a terrace with turf.

se revêtir, *v.r.,* to clothe one's self, to array one's self, to invest one's self, to dress, to put on, to assume, to take ; to be invested.

rêveu-r, -se, *n.* and *adj.,* dreamer, muser ; thoughtful, pensive, dreamy, musing.

revidage, *n.m.,* (at auction) knock-out.

revider, *v.a.,* to empty again ; to knock out.

revient (rĕvi-in), *n.m.,* (com.) only used in : *prix de —;* net cost.

revirade, *n.f.,* (backgammon) back-game.

revirement (re-vir-mãn), *n.m.,* sudden change ; (nav.) tacking ; (com. and fin.) transfer. — *de parties ;* (com.) transfer.

revirer, *v.n.,* (nav.) to tack about, to tack, to put about ; to turn round, to change sides, to be a turn-coat, to rat. *Il a reviré de bord ;* he has ratted.

revisable, *adj.*, revisable.

reviser, *v.a.*, to revise, to review, to examine.

reviseur, *n.m.*, reviser, examiner.

revision, *n.f.*, revisal, revision, re-examination, review. *Sujet à* — *;* questionable. *— de procès ;* rehearing. *Faire la — d'une feuille ;* (print.) to revise a sheet. *Conseil de —* ; (milit.) examining-board (as to health of recruits).

revivification, *n.f.*, (chem.) revivification.

revivifier, *v.a.*, to revive, to revivify, to regenerate.

revivre, *v.n.*, to come to life again ; to live again ; to revive. *Faire —* ; to bring to life again, to revive, to restore. *Les pères revivent dans leurs enfants ;* fathers live again in their children.

révocabilité, *n.f.*, revocability.

révocable, *adj.*, revocable, reversible, repealable.

⊙**révocati-f, -ve**, *adj.*, repealing.

révocation, *n.f.*, revocation, repeal, revoking, recall.

révocatoire, *adj.*, revocatory.

revoici, *prep.*, (fam., jest) once more, here . . . again. *Me —* ; here am I again.

revoilà, *prep.*, (fam., jest) once more, there . . . again. *Les revoilà !* there they are again !

revoir, *v.a.*, to see again ; to meet again ; to revise, to review, to re-examine.

se **revoir**, *v.r.*, to see, to meet, each other again ; to be seen again. *Nous nous reverrons ;* we shall meet again.

revoir, *n.m.*, seeing, *or* meeting, again. *Au —* ; good-bye for the present, *or* till we meet again. *A* — ; to be revised.

revoler, *v.n.*, to fly again, to fly back ; to steal, *or* rob, again.

revolin, *n.m.*, (nav.) eddy-wind.

révoltant, -e, *adj.*, revolting.

révolte, *n.f.*, revolt, rebellion.

révolté, *n.m.*, rebel.

révolter, *v.a.*, to cause to revolt *or* rebel, to stir up ; to rouse, to excite ; to shock, to disgust, to horrify.

se **révolter**, *v.r.*, to revolt, to rebel, to be indignant, to be shocked.

révolter, *n.m.*, to revolt, to rebel.

révolu, -e, *adj.*, revolved, accomplished, completed, finished, ended.

révoluti-f, -ve, *adj.*, (bot.) revolute.

révolution, *n.f.*, revolution.

révolutionnaire, *n.m.* and *adj.*, revolutionist ; revolutionary.

révolutionnairement (-sio-nèr-mǎn), *adv.*, in a revolutionary manner.

révolutionner, *v.a.*, to revolutionize.

revolver (ré-vol-vèr), *n.m.*, revolver.

revomir, *v.a.*, to vomit, to throw up again ; to vomit again ; to bring up.

révoquer, *v.a.*, to recall (an ambassador) ; to dismiss (a clerk, an officer, an official, etc.) ; to revoke, to repeal. *— en doute ;* to call in question.

revouloir, *v.a.*, to wish again, to wish again for.

revoyager, *v.n.*, to travel again.

revue, *n.f.*, review ; magazine ; survey, examination, revision. *Faire la — de ;* to examine, to survey. *Faire une — de ses papiers ;* to examine one's papers. *Passer en —* ; (milit.) to review. *Etre gens de —* ; to meet often.

révulsi-f, -ve, *adj.*, (med.) revulsive.

révulsif, *n.m.*, (med.) revulsive.

révulsion, *n.f.*, revulsion.

rez, *prep.*, (l.u.) level with, even with. *— pied, — terre ;* even, *or* level, with the ground.

rez-de-chaussée, *n.m.*, (—) ground-floor ; level with the ground. *Au —* ; on the ground-floor. *A* — ; level with the ground.

rhabdologie, *n.f.* *V.* **rabdologie**.

rhabdomancie, *n.f.* *V.* **rabdomancie**.

***rhabilage**, *n.m.*, repairing, mending, botching, patching.

***rhabillement**, *n.m.* *V.* **rhabillage**.

***rhabiller**, *v.a.*, to dress again, to clothe anew ; to mend, to patch up.

***rhabilleu-r**, *n.m.*, **-se**, *n.f.* *V.* **rebouteur**.

rhagade, *n.f.*, (med.) rhagade, crack, chap, fissure.

rhapontic, *n.m.*, (bot.) bastard monk's-rhubarb, rheum rhaponticum.

rhapsode, *n.m.*, **rhapsodie**, *n.f.*, **rhapsodiste**, *n.m.* *V.* **rapsode, rapsodie, rapsodiste**.

rhénan, -e, *adj.*, (geog.) Rhenish.

rhésus (-zus), *n.m.*, pig-tailed baboon.

rhéteur, *n.m.*, rhetorician, rhetor.

rhétien, -ne (ti-in,-tiè-n), *adj.*, (geog.) Rhetian.

rhétoricien (-si-in), *n.m.*, rhetorician.

rhétorique, *n.f.*, rhetoric. *Figure de —* ; rhetorical figure. *Faire sa —* ; to be in the class of rhetoric (in the highest form but one ; the *Remove*).

rhin, *n.m.*, (geog.) Rhine. *Vin du —* ; Rhenish wine, Rhine-wine.

rhinanthe, *n.f.*, (bot.) cock's-comb.

rhingrave, *n.m.*, rhingrave (German governor).

rhingrave, *n.f.*, (formerly) a sort of knee-breeches, knickerbockers.

rhinocéros (-ros), *n.m.*, rhinoceros.

rhinoplastie, *n.f.*, (surg.) rhinoplasty.

rhodium (-om), *n.m.*, (min.) rhodium.

rhododendron, *n.m.*, (bot.) rhododendron ; rose-bay.

rhombe, *n.m.*, (geom.) rhomb, rhombus ; (ich.) rhombus.

rhomboèdre, *n.m.*, (geom.) rhombohedron.

rhomboïdal, -e, *adj.*, rhomboïdal.

rhomboïde, *n.m.*, (anat., geom.) rhomboid.

rhubarbe, *n.f.*, rhubarb. *— blanche ;* white jalap. *— des moines ;* monk's-rhubarb, herb-patience.

rhum (rom), *n.m.*, rum.

rhumatique, *adj.*, rheumatic.

rhumatisant, -e, *n.* and *adj.*, rheumatic.

rhumatismal, -e, *adj.*, rheumatic.

rhumatisme, *n.m.*, rheumatism.

rhumb, *n.m.* *V.* **rumb**.

rhume, *n.m.*, cold. *— de cerveau ;* cold in the head. *Un gros —* ; a violent cold. *— de poitrine ;* cold on the chest. *Attraper un —* ; to catch a cold.

rhus (rus), *n.m.* *V.* **sumac**.

rhythme, *n.m.* *V.* **rythme**.

rhythmique, *adj.* *V.* **rythmique**.

riant, -e, *adj.*, laughing, smiling, lively, cheerful ; pleasant, pleasing.

ribambelle, *n.f.*, swarm, string ; host, lot (of people).

ribaud, -e, *n.* and *adj.*, (l.ex.) ribald.

ribauderie (-bô-drî), *n.f.*, ribaldry.

ribaudure, *n.f.*, crease, fold (in cloth).

riblette, *n.f.*, (cook.) collop ; rasher.

riblons, *n.m.pl.*, scrap-iron.

ribord, *n.m.*, (nav.) garboard strake.

ribordage, *n.m.*, (nav.) damage by fouling.

ribote, *n.f.*, (pop.) debauch, drunken bout. *Etre en —* ; to be boozy, drunk, tight ; to be on the spree. *Faire —* ; to have a drunken bout.

riboter, *v.n.*, (pop.) to get boozy, drunk ; to be on the spree.

riboteu-r, *n.m.*, **-se**, *n.f.*, (pop.) drunkard ; boozer.

ricanement (-ka-n-mǎn), *n.m.*, chuckling, chuckle, sneering, sneer ; giggling, giggle.

ricaner, *v.n.*, to chuckle, to sneer, to snigger, to giggle.

ricanerie (-ka-n-rî), *n.f.* *V.* **ricanement**.

ricaneu-r, **-se**, *n.* and *adj.*, sneerer, sneering ; giggler, giggling.

ric-à-ric, *adv.*, in driblets; (fam.) rigorously, strictly.

richard, *n.m.*, moneyed man; rich fellow; capitalist, nabob.

riche, *n.m.* and *adj.*, rich man; rich, wealthy, opulent; sumptuous; copious; valuable, precious. *Un — parti;* a good match (marriage). *— moisson;* abundant harvest. *Langue —;* copious language. *Le mauvais —;* the rich man of the Gospel.

richement (rish-màn), *adv.*, richly, opulently, copiously, splendidly; preciously.

richesse, *n.f.*, riches, wealth, wealthiness, opulence; copiousness; richness. *La — d'une langue;* the copiousness of a language. *Contentement passe —;* enough is as good as a feast.

richissime, *adj.*, (fam.) inordinately rich.

ricin, *n.m.*, (bot.) palma Christi, castor-oil plant. *Huile de —;* castor-oil.

ricocher, *v.n.*, (artil.) to ricochet, to rebound.

ricochet, *n.m.*, duck and drake (rebound on the water); series; chain, succession; (artil.) ricochet. *Faire des —s;* (artil.) to ricochet; to make ducks and drakes on the water. *Feu à —;* (artil.) ricochet-firing *or* fire. *C'est la chanson du —;* it is the same thing over and over again. *Par —;* indirectly.

rictus, *n.m.*, grin, grinning.

ride, *n.f.*, wrinkle (on the face); (bot.) wrinkle (on the water); (nav.) laniard. *—s des haubans;* shroud laniards.

ridé, -e, *adj.*, wrinkled; (bot.) rugose. *Une pomme —e;* a shrivelled apple.

rideau, *n.m.*, curtain; screen (of trees); (fort.) rideau. *Tirer le —;* to draw the curtain. *Baisser le —;* (thea.) to drop the curtain. *Lever de —;* (thea.) curtain-raiser. *— d'entr'acte;* drop-scene.

ridée, *n.f.*, clap-net.

ridelle, *n.f.*, staff-side, standard-side (of a cart).

rider, *v.a.*, to wrinkle (the skin); to shrivel; to crumple; to ripple, to ruffle (water); to corrugate, to contract.

se **rider**, *v.r.*, to wrinkle, to shrivel, to shrivel up; to ripple, to ruffle (of water).

ridicule, *adj.*, ridiculous. *Se rendre —;* to make one's self ridiculous.

ridicule, *n.m.*, ridicule, ridiculousness; ridiculous person, ridiculous thing. *Tomber dans le —*, or *tourner au —;* to become ridiculous. *Tourner quelqu'un en —;* to ridicule any one.

ridiculement (-kul-màn), *adv.*, ridiculously.

ridiculiser, *v.a.*, to ridicule, to make ridiculous, to make fun (of).

ridiculité, *n.f.*, (l.u.) ridiculousness, ridiculous thing. *C'est une — de parler ainsi;* it is absurd to speak in this manner.

rièble, *n.m.* V. **grateron**.

rien (ri-in), *n.m.*, nothing, nought, not anything; anything; mere nothing, trifle, mere trifle. *Pour —;* for nothing, for next to nothing, for a mere trifle, for a' song. *— de plus beau;* nothing finer. *— autre chose;* nothing else. *On ne fait — de —;* nothing can be made out of nothing. *Je n'en ferai —;* I shall do nothing of the sort. *Cette montre ne vous sert à —;* that watch is of no use to you. *Il ne sert à — de;* it is of no use to. *Cet homme ne m'est —;* that man is nothing to me. *Cela ne fait —;* that does not matter. *Tout comme si de — n'était;* as if nothing at all was the matter. *Ne faites semblant de —;* pretend not to mind it, not to see it, say nothing at all. *Je ne pense à — moins qu'à cela;* nothing is further from my thoughts. *Ce n'est — moins que cela;* it is quite another thing, it is anything but that. *En moins de —;* in the twinkling of an eye, in a trice. *De —;* don't mention it! of nothing; insignificant. *— au monde ne me fera oublier cela;*

nothing in the world will make me forget that. *— de —;* absolutely nothing. *Moins que —;* very little. *S'il y a — qui me plaise;* if anything pleases me. *Y a-t-il — de nouveau?* is there any news? *N'aboutir à —;* to come to nothing.

rieu-r, *n.m.*, -se, *n.f.*, laugher, giggler, sneerer. *Il a les —s de son côté;* he has the laughers on his side.

rieu-r, -se, *adj.*, laughing, joking, sneering, mocking, jeering.

riflard, *n.m.*, old umbrella; gamp; (carp.) horse-plane; (for stones) paring-chisel; (for metal) rough file.

rigaudon, *n.m.* V. **rigodon**.

rigide, *adj.*, rigid, strict, harsh, severe, stiff.

rigidement (-jid-màn), *adv.*, rigidly, strictly, harshly, stiffly.

rigidité, *n.f.*, rigidness, rigidity, stiffness, strictness, severity, harshness.

rigodon, *n.m.*, rigadoon (dance).

rigole, *n.f.*, trench, little ditch *or* furrow, little gutter; culvert (of roads).

rigorisme, *n.m.*, rigorism, austerity; hypercriticism.

rigoriste, *n.m.f.* and *adj.*, rigorist; hypercritic; over-rigid, over-severe; hypercritical.

rigoureusement (-reûz-màn), *adv.*, rigorously, severely, strictly, harshly.

rigoureu-x, -se, *adj.*, rigorous, stern, harsh; strict; severe, sharp; close.

rigueur (-gheur), *n.f.*, rigor, severity; harshness; sternness, sharpness, closeness, precision. *La — du sort;* the sternness of fate. *Traiter quelqu'un avec —;* to be severe with any one. *Cette règle est de —;* this rule is indispensable. *Jouer de —;* to play the strict rule of the game. *La — de l'hiver;* the inclemency of the winter. *A la —;* strictly speaking; in a strict sense; for once in a way; if absolutely necessary.

*rillettes, *n.f.pl.*, minced pork.

*rimaille, *n.f.*, (b.s.) rhyming doggerel.

*rimailler, *v.n.*, to write bad verses.

*rimailleur, *n.m.*, sorry rhymer, poetaster.

rime, *n.f.*, rhyme. *pl.* verse. *—s croisées;* alternate rhymes. *—s plates;* following rhymes (line by line). *Il n'y a ni — ni raison dans ce qu'il dit;* there is neither rhyme nor reason in what he says.

rimer, *v.n.* and *a.*, to rhyme. *Cela ne rime à rien;* there's no sense in it; it is all nonsense; that means nothing at all. *De la prose rimée;* mere doggerel.

rimeur, *n.m.*, rhymer; poetaster.

rinçage, *n.m.*, rinsing.

rinceau, *n.m.*, (arch.) foliage; (her.) bough.

rincer, *v.a.*, to rinse, to wash, to cleanse. *Il a été bien rincé;* (pop.) he has been well drenched; he has been well thrashed; well paid out.

se **rincer**, *v.r.*, to rinse. *Se — la bouche;* to rinse one's mouth.

rinceu-r, -se, *n.m.f.*, rinser, washer.

rinçoir, *n.m.*, rinsing tub.

rinçure, *n.f.*, rinsings; slops; (of wine) poor watery stuff.

ringard, *n.m.*, (tech.) fire-iron, poker, iron-rake.

ringrave, *n.m.f.* V. **rhingrave**.

⊙**riolé, -e**, *adj.*, streaked.

rioter, *v.n.*, to giggle, to titter.

rioteu-r, *n.m.*, -se, *n.f.*, giggler, titterer.

riotte, *n.f.*, tiff.

ripage, *n.m.*, (tech.) scraping.

*ripaille, *n.f.*, feasting, junketing. *Faire —;* to feast, to junket.

ripe, *n.f.*, (sculpt.) scraper.

riper, *v.a.*, (sculpt.) to scrape.

ripopée, *n.f.*, slops, medley; slipslop, mishmash; bad wine.

riposte, *n.f.*, smart reply, repartee ; (fenc.) parry and thrust, return.

riposter, *v.n.*, to repartee, to make a smart reply ; to make a return ; to reply, to answer, to return it ; (fenc.) to parry and thrust. *Il riposta d'un soufflet ;* he replied with a slap in the face.

ripuaire, *adj.*, riparian, riverine.

rire (riant, ri), *v.n.*, to laugh ; to be merry ; to look pleasant, to smile ; to be in jest, to joke, to make game of ; to trifle ; to be favorable, to be propitious ; to scoff at. *Éclater de —;* to break out into laughter, to burst out laughing. *Étouffer de —;* to be suffocating with laughter. *Se tenir les côtes de —;* to split one's sides with laughing. *Se pâmer de —;* to die with laughing. *Avoir le mot pour —;* to be facetious, to be ever ready with a joke. *— à gorge déployée ;* to roar with laughter. *— du bout des dents, — jaune ;* to laugh on the wrong side of one's mouth, to force a laugh. *— dans sa barbe, — sous cape ;* to laugh in one's sleeve. *— de ;* to laugh at, not to mind, not to care for. *— de quelqu'un ;* to laugh at any one. *— au nez de quelqu'un ;* to laugh in any one's face. *Apprêter à —;* to make one's self a laughing-stock. *Rira bien qui rira le dernier* or *marchand qui perd ne peut —;* let them laugh that win. *Cela fait —;* that makes one laugh. *Il n'y a pas là de quoi —;* there 's nothing to laugh at in that. *Il n'y a pas de quoi —;* it is no laughing matter. *Et la foule de —;* up went a great shout of laughter from the crowd ! *— aux anges ;* to laugh beyond measure ; to laugh alone, or to one's self. *— aux dépens d'autrui ;* to laugh at another's expense. *Nous rirons bien ;* we shall have great fun. *La fortune lui rit ;* fortune smiles upon him. *Est-ce que vous riez ?* are you jesting ? *Vous voulez —;* you are jesting. *Je le disais pour —;* I said it in jest. *— de bon cœur ;* to laugh heartily. *Pour —;* in play, for fun. *En riant, or pour —;* jokingly, in jest, for fun. *Histoire de —;* for fun, for a lark. *Un roi pour —;* a sham king. *Un conte pour —;* a laughable story. *Pincer sans —;* to jest bitingly. *Tel qui rit vendredi, dimanche pleurera ;* laughter is akin to tears, or laugh to-day and cry to-morrow.

se **rire**, *v.r.*, to laugh ; to make sport, to jest, to trifle, to scoff. *On se rit de lui ;* he is laughed at.

rire, *n.m.*, laugh ; laughter, laughing ; giggle ; grin. *De grands éclats de —;* great shouts of laughter. *Un — moqueur ;* a sneer. *Un — niais ;* a silly laugh. *Un gros —;* loud laughter ; a horse-laugh. *— étouffé ;* suppressed laugh ; giggle. *Accès de —;* fit of laughter. *Partir d'un éclat de —;* to burst out laughing.

ris, *n.m.*, (poet.) laugh, smile, laughter ; (nav.) reef (of sails); (cook.) sweet-bread. *— forcé ;* a forced laugh. *Un — moqueur ;* a sneer. *Prendre un —;* (nav.) to take in a reef. *— de veau ;* (cook.) sweet-bread.

risban, *n.m.*, (fort.) risband.

risdale, *n.f. V.* **rixdale**.

risée, *n.f.*, laugh, laughter, mockery, derision ; butt, laughing-stock ; (nav.) gust, squall, flaw. *Être, or faire, la — de tout le monde ;* to be the laughing-stock of every one. *Objet de —;* laughing-stock.

riser, *v.a.*, (nav.) to strike a sail, to reef.

risette, *n.f.*, pretty laugh, smile.

risibilité, *n.f.*, risibility.

risible, *adj.*, risible ; comical, laughable.

risiblement, *adv.*, laughably.

risquable, *adj.*, adventurous, hazardous ; that may be ventured.

risque, *n.m.*, risk, hazard, peril. *J'en courrai le —;* I will run the risk of it. *A tout —;* at all hazards or costs. *A ses —s et périls ;* at one's own risk. *Au — de ;* at the risk of.

risqué, -e, *adj.*, risky, hazardous, hazarded ; bold ; improper, broad, free.

risquer, *v.a.*, to risk, to hazard, to venture, to run the risk of, to have to fear. *Qui ne risque rien n'a rien ;* nothing venture, nothing have. *— le paquet ;* to risk all or to brave the storm.

se **risquer**, *v.r.*, to risk, to venture, to take one's chance of.

risque-tout, *n.m.*, desperado, dare-devil.

risse, *n.f.*, (nav.) lashing-rope.

risser, *v.a.*, to lash, to frap.

rissole, *n.f.*, (cook.) minced meat fritter, rissole.

rissolé, -e, *part.*, (cook.) brown, browned ; crackling. *Il a le visage —;* his face is sunburnt.

rissoler, *v.a.*, (cook.) to roast brown.

se **rissoler**, *v.r.*, (cook.) to roast brown.

ristorne or **ristourne**, *n.f.*, (com.) canceling an insurance.

ristorner or **ristourner**, *v.a.*, (com.) to cancel an insurance ; to carry to another account.

rit or **rite**, *n.m.*, rite.

ritournelle, *n.f.*, (mus.) ritornello, flourish.

ritualiste, *n.m.f.*, ritualist.

rituel, *n.m.*, ritual, prayer-book.

rivage, *n.m.*, shore, sea-shore, strand, beach ; bank-side (of rivers) ; water-side. *Être jeté sur le —;* to be cast ashore. *Quitter le —;* to put off.

rival, -e, *n.* and *adj.*, rival. *Ils sont rivaux de gloire ;* they are rivals in glory.

rivaliser, *v.n.*, to rival, to vie, to compete, to strive, to strive with, to emulate. *Ils ont rivalisé d'efforts ;* they vied with each other in efforts.

rivalité, *n.f.*, rivalry, rivalship, competition, emulation.

rive, *n.f.*, shore, bank (of rivers) ; border, skirt (of woods). *On n'y voit ni fond ni —;* (prov.) it is beyond any man's comprehension.

rivement, *n.m.*, riveting.

river, *v.a.*, to rivet, to clinch. *— son clou à quelqu'un ;* to give any one a clincher, to silence any one.

riverain, *n.m.*, river-side resident ; borderer ; owner of riverside property.

riverain, -e, *adj.*, riparian, bordering (on rivers or woods) ; riverine ; possessing property situated along a forest, road, or street.

rivet, *n.m.*, rivet.

rivetage, *n.m.*, riveting.

rivière, *n.f.*, river, stream. *Bras d'une —;* branch of a river. *Gens de —;* watermen. *La — est marchande ;* the river is navigable. *Les petits ruisseaux font les grandes —s ;* many a little makes a mickle. *Mettre des peaux en —;* to soak skins. *— de diamants ;* diamond necklace, stream of diamonds.

rivoir, *n.m.*, riveting-hammer.

rivure, *n.f.*, hinge-pin.

rixdale, *n.f.*, rix-dollar.

rixe, *n.f.*, combat, conflict, fight, scuffle ; brawl, dispute, affray ; quarrel.

riz (ri), *n.m.*, (bot.) rice. *— au lait ;* rice-milk. *Gâteau de —;* rice-pudding, rice-cake.

rize, *n.m.*, rize (Turkish coin).

rizière, *n.f.*, rice-field, rice-plantation.

rob, *n.m.*, (pharm.) rob.

robe, *n.f.*, gown, robe, dress, frock ; coat (of certain animals); husk, peel (of certain vegetables, fruit); cloth (clergymen) ; long robe (lawyers). *— de femme ;* dress, gown. *— d'enfant ;* frock. *— de chambre ;* morning-gown, dressing-gown. *— décolletée ;* low dress. *— montante ;* dress high to the neck. *Gens de —;* gentlemen of the long robe ; barristers. *En — de chambre ;* (of potatoes) in their skins, in their jackets.

rober, *v.a.*, to bark (madder). *— un chapeau ;* to rub a hat ; (of cigars) to wrap.

robin, n.m., (b.s.) limb of the law, lawyer.

robin, proper name used in the following familiar and proverbial expressions : *Toujours souvient à — de ses flûtes;* one always remembers one's old ways. *C'est un plaisant —;* he is a contemptible fellow, *or* an easy fool.

robinet, n.m., cock ; tap, plug. *— à deux eaux, à deux faces, à deux fins;* double-valve cock. *Fermer le —;* to turn off the cock. *Ouvrir le —;* to turn on the cock.

robinier, n.m., (bot.) robinia, common acacia, locust-tree.

roborati-f, -ve, adj., (med.) (l.u.) roborant.

robre, n.m., rubber (whist).

robuste, adj., robust, hardy, strong, vigorous, sturdy.

robustement, adv., robustly, hardily, lustily, stoutly.

robustesse, n.f., robustness, strength, vigor.

roc, n.m., rock (isolated mass of stony matter) ; ⊙rook, castle (at chess). *— vif;* solid rock.

*****rocaille,** n.f., rock-work, grotto work.

*****rocailleur,** n.m., grotto-maker, rock-work-maker.

*****rocailleu-x, -se,** adj., pebbly, stony, flinty ; rugged, rough. *Style —;* harsh style.

rocambeau, n.m., (nav.) iron ring (holding the sails round the mast).

rocambole, n.f., (hort.) rocambole, seasoning ; a trite, sorry joke ; ⊙piquancy, point, zest ; cream (of anything). *Et la —;* (pop.) and the rest of it.

roccelle, n.f., (bot.) archil, orchil.

roche, n.f., rock, boulder ; quartz, stony mass (inland) ; rock (insensibility), flint, steel. *Cœur de —;* heart of flint. *Homme de la vieille —;* man of the old stamp or school. *Il y a quelque anguille sous —;* there is a snake in the grass ; I can smell a rat. *— crayeuse;* chalk rock. *Eau de —;* spring water.

rocher, n.m., rock, boulder, crag (sea-girt usually) ; (conch.) murex ; (artificial) rockery. *Plein de —s;* rocky. *Cœur de —;* heart of flint. *— escarpé;* steep rock.

rocheraie (ro-shré), n.f., (orni.) stock-dove.

rochet, n.m., rocket (surplice) ; (horl.) rack, ratch ; (of machinery) clink ; (locksmith's work) ratchet.

rocheu-x, -se, adj., (geol.) rocky, stony.

rock *or* **rouc,** n.m., roc (fabulous bird).

rococo, n.m. and adj., antiquated style, rococo style, bad taste (in arts) ; antiquated, trumpery, old, old-fashioned.

rocou, rocouer, rocouyer. *V.* **roucou, roucouer, roucouyer.**

rôder, v.n., to roam, to rove, to ramble ; to prowl.

rôdeur, n.m., roamer, rover, rambler ; vagrant ; prowler.

rodomont, n.m., rodomont, blusterer, ranter, braggadocio, bully.

rodomontade, n.f., rodomontade, boasting, bluster, bravado, swaggering.

rogations, n.f.pl., (c.rel.) rogation. *Jours des —;* rogation-days. *Semaine des —;* rogation week.

rogatoire, adj., (jur.) of inquiry. *Commission —;* judicial commission (to examine witnesses).

rogatons, n.m.pl., scraps, odds and ends, broken meat ; waste paper.

roger-bontemps, n.m., (—s —) (fam.) a jolly fellow, merry andrew.

*****rogne,** n.f., itch ; mange ; (vet.) scab.

*****rognement,** n.m., cutting, paring, clipping.

*****rogne-pieds,** n.m.pl., (vet.) farrier's knife.

*****rogner,** v.a., to clip, to cut (at the extremities) ; to pare, to crop, to prune, to lop ; to cut off, to cut short, to pare off. *— la vigne;* to prune the vine. *— un livre;* to cut a book. *— la monnaie;* to clip coin. *— les ongles à quelqu'un;* to clip any one's wings.

*****rogneu-r,** n.m., **-se,** n.f., clipper (of coin).

*****rogneu-x, -se,** adj., itchy, mangy, scabbed, scurvy.

*****rognoir,** n.m., (book-bind.) plow ; cutting-press.

*****rognon,** n.m., kidney ; (pop.) loins ; hip ; testicle (of some animals). *Blessure aux —s d'un cheval;* navel-gall. *Mine en —s;* (metal.) kidney-shaped ore.

*****rognonner,** v.n., to growl, to grumble.

*****rognure,** n.f., paring, clipping, cutting. pl., refuse, leavings.

rogomme, n.m., dram, spirits, grog. *Voix de —;* croaking voice, hoarse voice, drunkard's voice.

rogue (rog), adj., (fam.) proud, haughty, disdainful.

roi, n.m., king. *De par le —;* in the king's name. *Vive le —;* long live the king. *Le jour des —s;* Twelfth-day. *Gâteau des —s;* Twelfth-cake. *Fêter,* or *tirer, les —s;* to celebrate Twelfth-night. *Vivre en —;* to live like a king, like a prince. *C'est la cour du — Pétaud;* it is Bedlam broke loose. *— d'armes;* king at arms.

roide, adj. *V.* **raide.**

roitelet (roa-tlè), n.m., petty king, kinglet ; (orni.) wren. *— huppé;* golden-crested wren. *— triple bandeau;* fire-crested wren.

rôlage, n.m., rolling (of tobaccos).

rôle, n.m., roll, scroll ; list, rota, roster, catalogue ; (thea.) part, character, impersonation ; (jur.) cause-list. *A tour de —;* in turn, by turn, by rotation. *Jouer bien son —;* to play one's part well. *— de combat;* (nav.) quarter-bill. *— de quart;* watch-bill. *— d'équipage;* (nav.) muster-roll. *Sortir de son —;* to be out of character, to exceed one's attributes. *Saisir son —;* to catch the spirit of one's part. *Manquer son —;* (fig.) to mistake one's vocation. *Outrer son —;* to overdo one's part.

rôler, v.n., (b.s.) to spin out legal documents (to increase the costs).

rôlet, n.m., (l.u.) character, little part. *Jouer bien son —;* to play one's part well. *Être au bout de son —;* to be at one's wits' end, at the end of one's tether.

rollier, n.m., (orni.) roller.

romain, -e, adj., Roman ; Romish ; (print.) Roman. *A la —e;* Roman-like. *L'Eglise catholique —e;* the church of Rome. *Calendrier —;* Romish calendar. *Laitue —e;* cos lettuce.

romain, n.m., **-e,** n.f., Roman.

romain, n.m., (print.) Roman, primer. *Gros —;* great primer. *Petit —;* long primer.

romaine, n.f., steelyard ; (bot.) cos lettuce.

romaïque, n.m. and adj., Romaic, modern Greek language ; Greek, Grecian.

romaïque, n.f., the Greek national dance.

roman, n.m., novel, romance, fiction, romancing tale ; Romance (language). *Cela tient du —;* it is like a romance. *C'est une aventure de —;* it is a romantic adventure. *De —;* of novels, romantic, imaginary.

roman, -e, *or* **romance,** adj., Romanic, Romance.

romance, n.f., (mus.) ballad, song.

romancer *or* **romanciser,** v.n., to romance.

romancero, n.m., (—s) romancero, collection of short Spanish epic poems.

romancier, n.m., romance-writer ; novelist, novel-writer.

romane, adj., (arch.) romanesque.

romanesque, adj., fanciful, romantic ; romanesque.

romanesquement, adv., romantically, in a romantic manner.

romaniser, v.a. and n., to romanize.

romanticisme, *n.m.*, romanticism.

romantique, *n.m.* and *adj.*, romanticist, romanticism ; romantic, romantical.

romantiquement (-tik-mān), *adv.*, romantically.

romantisme, *n.m.*, romanticism.

romarin, *n.m.*, (bot.) rosemary.

rompement (ronp-mān), *n.m.*, only used in : — *de tête ;* mental fatigue, head-splitting.

rompre, *v.a.*, to break, to break asunder, to snap ; to break off, to dissolve ; to train, to break in, to train up, to use ; to divert, to turn off ; (phys.) to refract ; (med.) to rupture ; (paint.) to blend. — *un criminel ;* to break a criminal upon the wheel. — *la tête à quelqu'un ;* to break any one's head. — *les chemins ;* to spoil the roads, to break up the roads. — *la glace ;* to break the ice. — *le cou à quelqu'un ;* to break any one's neck, to ruin any one. — *les couleurs ;* to blend the colors. — *la mesure* or *la semelle ;* (fenc.) to retire in parrying, to draw back. — *le grain germé ;* to turn the barley. — *les bordages ;* (nav.) to rip off planks. — *le sommeil de quelqu'un ;* to interrupt the sleep of any one. — *un coup ;* to deaden a blow. — *le silence ;* to break silence. — *les chiens ;* (hunt.) to call off the dogs. — *l'eau à un cheval ;* to interrupt a horse in drinking. — *un traité ;* to break off a treaty. — *son ménage ;* to give up housekeeping. — *le carré ;* (milit.) to break the square. — *une armée ;* to disband an army. — *la paille ;* to break off (an agreement, a bargain, etc.) ; to break off, to fall out with, to become the enemy of any one. — *son serment ;* to break one's oath. — *son jeûne ;* to break one's fast. — *sa prison ;* to break out of prison. — *son ban ;* to break one's ban. — *la tête à quelqu'un ;* to turn any one's brain ; to worry any one. — *un homme aux affaires ;* to train a man up to business. — *un cheval ;* to break in a horse. *A tout* — ; furiously, frantically. *Cet acteur a été applaudi à tout* — ; that actor received frantic applause.

se **rompre**, *v. r.*, to break, to break off, to snap, to break up, to break asunder ; to discontinue ; (phys.) to be refracted ; (med.) to rupture. *Se* — *la tête ;* to puzzle, or rack, one's brains.

rompre, *v.n.*, to break, to break asunder, to break off, to snap, to break up ; to discontinue, to have done. — *court ;* to break off short. — *en visière avec quelqu'un ;* to tell any one the truth to his face ; to quarrel openly with any one, to break off with any one.

rompu, -**e**, *part.*, broken, snapped ; broken in ; (nav.) hogged (of a ship). *Etre — aux affaires ;* to be used, *or* accustomed, to business. *Tout — de fatigue ;* quite worn out with fatigue. *Travailler à bâtons —s ;* to work by fits and starts. *Nombre* — ; (l.u.) fraction.

ronce, *n.f.*, (bot.) bramble, brier ; blackberry-bush ; blackberry-tree ; (fig.) thorn, obstacle.

ronceraie, *n.f.*, brake, briery.

rond, -**e**, *adj.*, round ; rotund ; frank, easy, plain-dealing ; even (of money, accounts). *Un peu* — ; roundish. *Du fil* — ; coarse thread. *Pain* — ; coarse bread. *Voix —e ;* full voice. *Compte* — ; even account. *C'est un homme tout* — ; he is a plain-dealing man, *or* honesty itself. *Etre — en affaires ;* to be straightforward in business matters. *Figure de —e bosse ;* (sculpt.) figure in alto-relievo. *Période —e ;* full and rounded period.

rond, *n.m.*, round, orb, ring, circle, disk. *Danser en* — ; to dance in a ring. — *d'eau ;* circular basin of water. — *de serviette ;* napkin ring.

rondache, *n.f.*, round buckler, round shield.

ronde, *n.f.*, round ; patrol ; table song, roundelay ; (mus.) semibreve ; round hand (writing). *Faire la* — ; to go the rounds. *A la* — ; round

about. *Boire à la* — ; to drink all round. *Passer à la* — ; to hand round, to pass round. *Chemin des* —s ; round-way.

rondeau, *n.m.*, rondeau, roundelay (French poet.) ; (mus.) rondo.

rondelet, -**te** (rŏn-dlè, -t), *adj.*, roundish, plump, plumpish.

rondelette, *n.f.*, ground-ivy.

rondelettes, *n.f.pl.*, sail-cloth made in Brittany.

rondelle, *n.f.*, round shield ; rundle, ring ; washer (of a wheel) ; sculptor's rounded chisel.

rondement (rŏn-dmān), *adv.*, roundly ; quickly ; briskly, vigorously ; plainly, frankly ; with a high hand. *Mener une affaire* — ; not to dilly-dally. *Y aller* — ; to act frankly and quickly. *Il va — en besogne ;* he goes briskly to work.

rondeur, *n.f.*, roundness, smoothness, undulating expanse, rotundity ; fullness, flow ; openness, plain dealing ; curve, compass (of a piece of timber used in shipbuilding).

rondin, *n.m.*, billet, round log ; cudgel.

rondiner, *v.a.*, to cudgel. — *d'importance ;* to beat soundly.

rondon, *n.m.*, (hawking) swoop, impetuosity. *En* — ; impetuously.

rond-point, *n.m.* — (—*s*—*s*) (arch.) apsis ; circus (place where several roads, *or* walks, meet).

ronflant, -**e**, *adj.*, snoring ; sonorous, high-sounding ; loud.

ronflement, *n.m.*, snoring, snore ; roaring, peal, rumbling ; humming ; snorting (of horses). — *des vents ;* roaring of the wind. — *d'une toupie ;* humming of a top.

ronfler, *v.n.*, to snore ; (of horses) to snort ; (of cannon, thunder) to roar ; (of organs) to peal ; (of spinning-tops) to hum.

ronfleu-r, *n.m.*, -**se**, *n.f.*, snorer.

ronge, *n.m.*, (hunt.) ruminating. *Le cerf fait le* — ; the stag is ruminating.

rongeant, -**e**, *adj.*, gnawing, devouring, corroding ; (med.) corrosive.

*****ronge-maille**, *n.m.*, (—) nibble (rat). *Maître* — ; squire nibble.

ronge-ver, *n.m.*, gnawing worm.

ronger, *v.a.*, to gnaw, to nibble, to pick ; to waste, to consume, to eat up, to corrode ; to fret, to torment, to prey upon (the mind). — *un os ;* to pick, *or* gnaw, a bone. — *son frein ;* to champ the bit ; to fret inwardly, to chafe. — *ses ongles ;* to bite one's nails. *La rouille ronge le fer ;* rust corrodes iron. *Donner un os à* — *à quelqu'un ;* (fig.) to bestow upon, to grant any one, a favor ; to cut out work for any one, to give any one trouble.

rongeur, *n.* and *adj. m.*, (mam.) rodent ; gnawing, biting ; corroding ; consuming. *Ver* — ; never-dying worm.

ronron, *n.m.*, purr, purring. *Faire* — ; to purr.

roquefort, *n.m.*, Roquefort cheese.

⊙**roquelaure**, *n.f.*, roquelaure (sort of cloak).

roquentin, *n.m.*, dotard, gray-beard, old buck.

roquer, *v.n.*, to castle, to rook (at chess).

roquet, *n.m.*, pug-dog ; (fam.) dog, puppy, cur (person).

roquette, *n.f.*, (bot.) rocket. — *sauvage ;* wild rocket.

⊙***roquille**, *n.f.*, gill, quartern.

rorage, *n.m.*, dew-bleaching.

rosace, *n.f.*, (arch.) rose ; rose-work ; (Gothic arch.) rose-window.

rosacé, -**e**, *adj.*, (bot.) rosaceous.

rosacées, *n.f.pl.*, (bot.) rose-tribe, rosaceæ.

rosage, *n.m.*, (bot.) oleander, rose-bay ; rosing (dyeing).

rosagine, *n.f.*, (bot.) rose-bay.

rosaire, *n.m.*, rosary.

rosat, *adj.*, (pharm.) of roses. *Miel* — ; honey of roses.

rosbif, *n.m.*, (—*s*) roast-beef.

rose, *n.f.*, rose ; (arch.) rose-window ; rose-diamond. *Couleur de* —; rose-colored. *De* —; rosy. —*d'Inde ;* African marigold. *Laurier*—, (—*s*—*s*) rose-laurel. — *gueldre ;* Guelder-rose. — *des quatre saisons ;* monthly rose. — *de diamants ;* cluster of diamonds in the form of a rose. *Diamant en* —; rose-cut diamond. — *des vents ;* (nav.) compass-card. *Découvrir le pot aux* —*s ;* to find out the secret. *Il n'est point de* — *sans épines ;* there is no rose without a thorn.

rose, *adj.*, rosy, pink ; rose-colored.

rose, *n.m.*, rose-color.

rosé, **-e**, *adj.*, roseate, rosy.

roseau, *n.m.*, reed, reed-cane ; reed-grass. — *de marais ;* common marsh-reed. — *cultivé ;* evergreen reed. — *odorant ;* sweet-flag. — *des Indes ;* bamboo. *Lieu planté de* —*x ;* reed-bank. *Plein*, or *couvert, de* —*x ;* reedy. *C'est un* — *peint en fer ;* his looks belie his firmness.

rose-croix, *n.m.*, (—*s*—) Rosicrucian.

rosée, *n.f.*, dew ; (vet.) oozing blood. — *du soleil ;* (bot.) sun-dew. — *du matin ;* morning-dew. *Goutte de* —; dew-drop.

roselet (rô-zlè), *n.m.*, (mam.) stoat.

roselière, *n.f.*, reed-bank, reed-field.

roselle, *n.f.*, (orni.) redwing.

roséole, *n.f.*, (med.) roseola, scarlet rash.

roser, *v.a.*, to rose. *Se* —; to become rosy ; to assume a roseate hue.

roseraie (rôz-rè), *n.f.*, rosery, rose garden.

rosette, *n.f.*, rosette ; small rose ; rose-diamond ; red ink ; red chalk ; (ich.) gray gurnard ; (metal.) cake ; (orni.) redwing, swine-pipe ; (hat-making) tip ; (paint.) rosette, roset. *Diamant à* —; rose-diamond.

rosier, *n.m.*, rose-tree, rose-bush.

rosière, *n.f.*, rose-queen ; (ich.) minnow, pink.

roson, *n.m.* V. **rosace**.

rosse, *n.f.*, jade, screw ; (ich.) roach.

rosser, *v.a.*, to belabor, to lick, to thrash, to maul, to drub, to give a drubbing to.

*****rossignol**, *n.m.*, (orni.) nightingale ; pipe, flute (made of bark) ; stop (of organ) ; picklock ; skeleton key ; (carp.) wedge ; shopkeeper (old article). —*d'Arcadie ;* jackass. — *de muraille ;* (orni.) red-start.

*****rossignoler**, *v.n.*, (fam.) to imitate the nightingale's song.

rossinante, *n.f.*, Rosinante (sorry horse).

rossinante, *n.m.*, Rosinante (Don Quixote's horse).

rossolis, *n.m.*, rossolis (liquor) ; (bot.) sun-dew.

roster, *v.a.* V. **rouster**.

rostral, **-e**, *adj.*, rostral.

rostre, *n.m.*, (zoöl.) rostrum.

rostré, **-e**, *adj.*, rostrate, rostrated.

rosture, *n.f.* V. **rousture**.

rot, *n.m.*, (l.ex.) belch, eructation. *Faire un* —; to belch.

rôt, *n.m.*, roast, roast meat ; first course. *Gros* —; joint of meat. *Petit* —; roast of game.

rotacé, **-e**, *adj.*, (bot.) rotate, rotated.

rotang, *n.m.* V. **rotin**.

rotateur, *n.* and *adj. m.*, (anat.) rotator ; rotatory.

rotateurs, *n.m.pl.*, (zoöl.) rotatories.

rotation, *n.f.*, rotation.

rotatoire, *adj.*, rotatory.

rotatoires, *n.m.pl.* (ent.) rotifers, rotatories, wheel-animals, wheel-insects, wheel-animalcules.

rote, *n.f.*, rota (court of Rome).

roter, *v.n.*, (l.ex.) to belch.

rôti, *n.m.*, roast, roast meat (prov.) *Il ne faut pas s'endormir sur le* —; we must have our wits about us, or not neglect our work.

rôtie (-tî), *n.f.*, toast. *Une* —; a round of

toast. — *au beurre ;* buttered toast. — *au vin ;* toast in wine.

rotifère, *n.m.*, (ent.) rotifer, wheel-animal.

rotiforme, *adj.*, (zoöl.) wheel-shaped.

rotin, *n.m.*, (bot.) rotang ; rattan, rattan-cane.

rôtir, *v.a.*, to roast ; to broil ; to toast (bread) ; to burn, to parch. — *au four ;* to bake. *N'être bon ni à* — *ni à bouillir ;* to be fit for nothing. *se* **rôtir**, *v.r.*, to parch, to burn, to roast one's self.

rôtir, *v.n.*, to roast, to broil, to toast.

rôtissage, *n.m.*, roasting.

rôtisserie (-ti-srî), *n.f.*, cook-shop.

rôtisseu-r, *n.m.*, **-se**, *n.f.*, cook-shop keeper. — *en blanc ;* poulterer.

rôtissoire, *n.f.*, roasting screen, roaster, Dutch oven.

rotonde, *n.f.*, rotunda, back part of a diligence. *En* —; circular.

rotondité, *n.f.*, rotundity, roundness ; plumpness, fatness.

rotule, *n.f.*, (anat.) patella, knee-cap.

roture, *n.f.*, commonalty, plebeian state. *Il est né dans la* —; he is of ignoble birth.

roturi-er, **-ère**, *n.* and *adj.*, commoner ; plebeian, of mean birth ; vulgar, mean. ⊙*Air* —; vulgar air.

roturièrement (-rièr-mān), *adv.*, in a plebeian manner ; vulgarly.

rouage, *n.m.*, wheelwork, wheels ; machinery ; (horl.) movement.

rouan, **-ne**, *adj.*, (of horses) roan.

rouan, *n.m.*, roan horse.

rouanne, *n.f.*, brand-iron, marking-iron.

rouanner, *v.a.*, to brand, to mark.

rouannette, *n.f.*, (carp.). V. **rainette**.

rouble, *n.m.*, rouble, ruble (Russian coin).

rouc, *n.m.* V. **rock**.

rouche, *n.f.*, (nav.) a ship's hull.

roucou, *n.m.*, (bot.) and (dy.) arnotto.

roucouer, *v.a.*, to paint with arnotto.

se **roucouer**, *v.r.*, to paint one's self with arnotto.

roucoulement (-kool-mān), *n.m.*, cooing.

roucouler, *v.n.* and *a.*, to coo (pigeons) ; to warble (out) *or* (forth).

roucouyer, *n.m.*, (bot.) arnotto-tree.

roudou, *n.m.* V. **redoul**.

roue, *n.f.*, wheel ; paddle ; (torture) wheel ; (artil.) truck. — *d'affût de canon ;* truck of a gun-carriage. —*d'une horloge ;* clock-wheel. — *à aubes or à palees ;* paddle-wheel. — *hydraulique ;* water-wheel. *Pousser à la* —; to put one's shoulder to the wheel, to help on. *Mettre des bâtons dans les* —*s ;* to thwart, to put spokes into the wheels (of). *Un paon fait la* —; a peacock spreads his tail. *Faire la* —; to strut, to stalk, to show off, to wheel about ; to tumble over and over, to do the windmill. — *de compte ;* (horl.) notch-wheel. — *dentée ;* toothed-wheel. — *de rencontre ;* (horl.) balance-wheel. — *de câble ;* (nav.) coil. — *de gouvernail ;* steering-wheel. *Mettre à la* —; to rack, to put to the rack.

roué, *n.m.*, roué ; rake, profligate ; trickster.

roué, **-e**, *adj.*, crafty, sharp, artful ; very deep ; knocked up, broken down. — *de coups ;* soundly thrashed.

rouelle, *n.f.*, round slice, collop ; (vet.) rowel. — *de citron ;* slice of lemon. — *de veau ;* fillet of veal.

rouennerie (rooa-n-rî), *n.f.*, printed cotton goods ; Rouen goods.

rouer, *v.a.*, to break upon the wheel ; to crush ; to jade. — *quelqu'un de coups ;* to beat any one unmercifully. *Être roué de fatigue ;* to be jaded with fatigue. — *un câble ;* to coil a cable.

rouerie (roo-rî), *n.f.*, piece of knavery, sharp practice, cheat ; trickery.

rouet, *n.m.*, small wheel ; spinning-wheel ; purr (of a cat) ; (nav.) sheave. — *de moulin ;*

cog-wheel of a mill. — *de tisserand;* weaver's cloth-beam. — *d'arquebuse;* lock of an arquebuse. *Faire le* —; to purr.

rouette, *n.f.,* (tech.) osier-twig.

roue-vis, *n.f.,* (—s— —) screw-wheel.

rouge, *adj.,* red; blood-red; blood-shot; red-hot. *Fer* —; red-hot iron; (of partridges) red-legged. *Boulets* —*s;* red-hot balls. *Cuivre* —; copper. — *trogne* (fam.) red face.

rouge, *n.m.,* red; red paint, rouge; redness, blush; (orni.) shoveler. — *vif;* deep red, bright red. — *brun;* brownish red. — *d'écarlate;* scarlet. — *sanguin;* blood red. — *de garance;* madder.

rouge, *adv.,* only used in: *Se fâcher tout* —; to get downright angry.

rougeâtre (-jâtr), *adj.,* reddish.

rougeaud, -e (-jô, -d), *n.* and *adj.,* red-faced person; ruddy-faced, red-faced, ruddy.

rouge-bord, *n.m.,* (—s— —s) bumper (of red wine).

rouge-gorge, *n.m.,* (—s— —s) (orni.) redbreast, robin redbreast.

rougeole (-jol), *n.f.,* (med.) measles, (bot.) cow-wheat.

rouge-queue, *n.m.,* (—s— —s) red-start, red-tail.

rouget, *n.m.,* (ich.) gurnet, red gurnet; red surmullet; (ent.) wheal-worm. *adj.,* reddish.

rougette, *n.f.,* (mam.) pteropus.

rougeur, *n.f.,* redness, blush, glow, color. *pl.,* (med.) rosy-drop, red-spot. *La* — *lui est montée au visage;* the color came into her cheeks.

rougir, *v.n.,* to redden, to grow red; to color, to color up, to blush, to be ashamed. — *de honte;* to blush with shame. — *de colère;* to grow red with anger. — *jusqu'au blanc des yeux;* to blush up to the eyes, to color up to the eyes. *Faire* — *quelqu'un;* to put any one to the blush.

rougir, *v.a.,* to redden; to tinge with red or blood; to mix red wine with water.

roui, *n.m.,* steeping, soaking, maceration; retting; fustiness, rancidness. *Sentir le* —; to have a rancid taste.

***rouille,** *n.f.,* rust, rustiness (of metals); flaw (of mirrors); (bot.) mildew, blight, blast. *La* — *mange le fer;* rust corrodes iron. *Ces froments sont chargés de* —; this wheat is mildewed.

***rouillé, -e,** *adj.,* rusty; blighted (of corn).

***rouiller,** *v.a.,* to rust, to make rusty; to blight; to impair.

se **rouiller,** *v.r.,* to rust, to grow rusty; to get rusty, to become rusty; to rust, to be impaired.

***rouilleux, -se,** *adj.,* ferruginated.

***rouillure,** *n.f.,* rustiness, rust.

rouir, *v.a.,* to steep, to soak, to macerate (hemp, flax), to ret.

rouir, *v.n.,* to be retted.

rouissage, *n.m.,* soaking, steeping, retting.

rouissoir, *n.m.,* rettery.

roulade, *n.f.,* roll, rolling; (mus.) roulade, trill, shake; (cook.) collar. *Faire une* — *;* (cook.) to collar.

roulage, *n.m.,* rolling; carriage (of goods); wagon-office; wagoning. — *accéléré;* fly-wagon. *Voiture de* —; goods wagon.

roulant, -e, *adj.,* rolling; easy (of roads); (surg.) moving (of veins). *Chemin* —; easy way. *Feu* —; (milit.) running fire. *Presse* —*e;* (print.) press at work.

rouleau, *n.m.,* roll; roller; rolling-pin; roll, twist (of tobacco); coil (of a rope); (med.) roller; (print.) roller; (tech.) sheave. — *de papier;* roll of paper. *Plier en* —; to roll up. *Être au bout de son* —; to be at one's wits' end, *or* at the end of one's tether. — *d'imprimeur;* printer's roller.

roulée, *n.f.,* (pop.) thrashing, drubbing.

roulement (rool-mān), *n.m.,* rolling, roll, rumbling; (mus.) roll; roll (of a drum); rotation; volutation. — *d'yeux;* rolling of the eyes. — *de fonds;* (com.) circulation of capital. *Fonds de* —; floating capital.

rouler, *v.a.,* to roll, to roll up; to wind, to wind up; to revolve, to turn over; to pass, to pass away; (of meat) to collar; (fig.) to do for a person. — *une chose dans sa tête;* to turn a thing over in one's mind. — *sa vie;* to pass one's life. — *carrosse;* to keep a carriage. *Je l'ai roulé;* I did for him *or* I bowled him over.

se **rouler,** *v.r.,* to roll one's self, to roll, to tumble; to wallow; to wind; to fight, to have a set to.

rouler, *v.n.,* to roll, to revolve; to tumble; to toss; to ramble, to wander; to stroll; to keep going; to succeed by rotation; to be plentiful, to turn upon (of a thing). *Faire* — *la presse;* (print.) to set the press going. — *sur l'or et sur l'argent;* to roll in riches. *Tout roule là-dessus;* all turns upon that. *Ils roulent ensemble;* they take their turns. *Faire* —; to keep going. *Pierre qui roule n'amasse pas de mousse;* a rolling stone gathers no moss. *La conversation roula sur ce sujet;* the conversation turned upon this subject.

roulet, *n.m.,* hatter's roller.

roulette, *n.f.,* roller, truckle, little wheel; truckle-bed; ⊙hand-chaise, Bath-chair; caster; roulette (game); (geom.) cycloid. *Cela marche comme sur des* —*s;* that is getting on swimmingly. *Lit à* —*s;* bedstead on casters. — *de relieur;* book-binder's fillet.

rouleur, *n.m.,* (ent.) vine-fretter, vine-grub, (nav.) rolling vessel.

rouleuse, *n.f.,* caterpillar.

roulier, *n.m.,* wagoner, carter, carrier.

roulière, *n.f.,* wagoner's smock.

roulis, *n.m.,* (nav.) rolling, laboring; roll (of the waves). [roller, cylinder.

rouloir, *n.m.,* rolling-board (for candles);

roulotte, *n.f.,* wagon.

roupie, *n.f.,* rupee; (l.ex.) snivel. *Avoir la* —; to snivel.

roupieu-x, -se, *adj.,* (l.u.) snively, sniveling.

***roupiller,** *v.n.* (pop.) to doze, to snooze.

***roupilleu-r,** *n.m.,* -se, *n.f.,* (pop.) dozer, snoozer.

roure, *n.m.,* (bot.) English oak.

roussâtre, *adj.,* reddish, russet.

rousseau, *n.* and *adj.m.,* (fam.) red-haired fellow; red-haired.

rousselet (roo-slè), *n.m.,* (bot.) russet pear.

rousserolle (roo-srol), *n.f.,* (orni.) great sedge-warbler.

roussette, *n.f.,* (orni.) bog-rush, hedge-sparrow; (ich.) dog-fish, bounce; (mam.) pteropus.

rousseur, *n.f.,* redness; freckle. *Avoir des* —*s, avoir des taches de* —; to be freckled.

roussi, *n.m.,* burnt smell; burning, smell of burning; ⊙Russia leather.

roussin, *n.m.,* thick-set stallion. — *d'Arcadie;* ass, jackass, moke.

roussir, *v.a.* and *n.* to redden; to singe, to scorch; to dye of a rusty color, *or* of a fawn-color; to grow red, to turn red; to singe, to scorch. *Faire* —; to brown (meat, etc.).

roussissage, *n.m.,* dyeing red.

rousster *or* **rusturer,** *v.a.,* (nav.) to woold, to wind (ropes).

rousture *or* **rosture,** *n.f.,* (nav.) woolding.

rout (raoot), *n.m.,* (—) rout (assembly). *V.* **raout.**

***routailler,** *v.a.,* (hunt.) to track.

route, *n.f.,* road, way; journey, route, direction, path, course; (nav.) track, course, way, run; riding (in a forest); track, path (of planets, comets). *Grand'*—, (— — —) highway. — *ordinaire ;* common road. — *de traverse ;* cross road. *Il est resté en* — ; he remained behind. *Il est en* — ; he is on his way. *Prendre la* — *de ;* to take the way to, to go in the direction of, to make for. *Faire* — ; to make for. *Faire* —; (nav.) to sail. *A la* — *!* (nav.) steer the course ! *Porter à* — ; to go, or take, a straight course. *Faire fausse* — ; to take the wrong road ; (nav.) to alter the course ; (fig.) to take a wrong step ; to make a mistake. — *estimée ;* (nav.) dead reckoning. *Feuille de* — ; (milit.) route ; way-bill (of public conveyances). *On lui a tracé sa* — ; his course is marked out for him. *La* — *de la vertu ;* the path of virtue.

routier (-tié), *n.m.*, (geog.) tract chart, road book; (nav.) sailing orders, guide, pilot. *Vieux* — ; old stager.

routi-er, -ère, *adj.*, of roads. *Carte* —*ère ;* road-map. *Locomotive* —; traction engine, road engine.

routine, *n.f.*, routine, habit; rote (frequent repetition of sounds). *Par* — ; by routine, by habit, by rote.

routiner, *v.a.*, (l.u.) to teach by routine.

routini-er, -ère, *n.* and *adj.*, person acting by routine, red-tapist ; of routine, routine-like.

routoir, *n.m.*, retting-pond ; retting-pit.

rouverin (roo-vrin), *adj.m.*, (metal.) blistered, brittle, hot, short.

rouvieux *or* **roux-vieux,** *n.* and *adj.m.* (n.p.), (vet.) mange ; mangy.

rouvre, *n.m.*, (bot.) English oak. *V.* **roure.**

rouvrir, *v.a.*, to open again. — *une plaie ;* to reopen a wound. *Se* — ; to open again.

rou-x, -sse, *adj.*, reddish, red-haired, russet ; sandy, carroty. *Vents* — ; cold dry winds. *Lune* —*sse ;* April moon.

roux, *n.m.*, reddish color ; russet ; (mam.) field-mouse; (cook.) brown butter sauce. — *ardent ;* fiery red.

roux-vieux, *n.m.* *V.* **rouvieux.**

royal, -e (roa-yal), *adj.*, royal, regal, kingly, kinglike.

royale (roa-yal), *n.f.*, tuft of beard just below the underlip, chin-tuft.

royalement (roa-yal-mān), *adv.*, royally, regally, in a kingly manner.

royalisme (roa-ya-), *n.m.*, royalism.

royaliste (roa-ya-), *n.m.f.*, and *adj.*, royalist.

royaume (roa-yôm), *n.m.*, kingdom, realm.

royauté (roa-yô-), *n.f.*, royalty. *Abdiquer la* —; to abdicate the throne. *Les marques de la* —; the regalia.

r.p., initial letters of *Révérend Père ;* reverend father.

rr., abbreviation of *Royales,* royal.

ru, *n.m.*, channel *or* bed (of a small stream).

ruade, *n.f.*, kick (of horses, etc.). *pl.*, kicking. *Détacher,* or *lancer, une* — ; to give a kick.

rubabelle *or* **rubace,** *n.f.*, rubicel, rubicelle.

ruban, *n.m.*, ribbon ; band ; (arch.) beading. *Garniture de* —*s ;* set of ribbons. — *de fil ;* tape. —*-d'eau,* (—*s*—) blue burr-reed, reed-grass. *Canon à* — ; twisted gun-barrel. —*s de la glotte,* —*s vocaux ;* (anat.) vocal cords. — *de soie ;* silk ribbon. — *de velours ;* velvet ribbon.

rubané, -e, *part.*, (zoöl.) striped ; flattened, ribbon-like. *Canon* — ; twisted gun-barrel.

rubaner, *v.a.*, to trim with ribbons ; to arrange flax and hemp fibers ; to divide wax into bandelets; to twist a band of iron to turn it into gun-barrels.

rubanerie (-ba-n-rî), *n.f.*, ribbon-weaving ; ribbon-trade.

rubani-er, -ère, *adj.*, ribbon. *Industrie* —*ère ;* ribbon-manufacture, ribbon trade.

rubanier, *n.m.*, ribbon-weaver ; (bot.) bur-weed.

rubanière, *n.f.*, ribbon-weaver.

rubarbe, *n.f.* *V.* **rhubarbe.**

rubasse, *n.f.*, (min.) colored quartz.

rubéfaction, *n.f.*, (med.) rubefaction.

rubéfiant, -e, *adj.*, (med.) rubefacient.

rubéfiant, *n.m.*, (med.) rubefacient.

rubéfier, *v.a.*, or *se* —, *v.r.*, (med.) to rubify.

⊙**rubeline,** *n.f.* *V.* **rouge-gorge.**

rubéole, *n.f.*, (bot.) cross-wort.

rubescent, -e, *adj.*, rubescent.

rubicé, -e, *adj.*, red-colored.

rubiacées, *n.f.pl.*, plants of the madder family.

rubican, *n. m.* and *adj.*, rubican color ; rubican.

rubicon, *n.m.*, Rubicon. *Passer le* —; to take a desperate step.

rubicond, -e, *adj.*, rubicund ; bloated; blowzy.

rubification, *n.f.*, rubification.

rubigineu-x, -se, *adj.*, rubiginous.

⊙**rubine,** *n.f.*, (chem.) ruby. — *d'argent ;* red-silver, ruby-silver. — *d'arsenic ;* realgar.

rubis, *n.m.*, ruby ; red pimple, grog-blossom. *Faire* — *sur l'ongle ;* to drink to the last drop. *Payer* — *sur l'ongle ;* to pay to the last farthing. *Monté sur* — ; jeweled.

rubricaire, *n.m.*, rubrician, rubricist.

rubricateur, *n.m.*, artist who illuminated manuscripts in the Middle Ages.

rubrique, *n.f.*, method, rule, practice ; head; title ; trick ; ruddle, red chalk. *pl.*, (canon law) rubric. *Sous la* — *de ;* under the head of.

ruche, *n.f.*, hive ; swarm ; (needle-work) quilling, frilling, ruche. — *d'abeilles ;* bee-hive. *Châtrer une* — ; to cut away the wax and honey from a hive.

ruché, -e, *adj.*, quilted. *n.m.*, frilling.

ruchée, *n.f.*, hive-full.

rucher, *n.m.*, stand for bees ; apiary.

rucher, *v.a.*, (needlework) to quilt, to frill.

rudâni-er, -ère, *adj.*, (l.u.) surly, churlish, uncouth.

rude, *adj.*, harsh, rough, rugged, steep, uneven ; sharp, rude, hard ; disagreeable ; grating, violent, fierce ; severe, bitter ; rigid, strict ; formidable ; uncouth, unpolished ; impetuous, boisterous ; troublesome, difficult. *Avoir la peau* —; to have a rough skin. *Une* — *épreuve ;* a severe trial. *Chemin* — ; rugged road. *Avoir la voix* — ; to have a harsh voice. *Des manières* —*s ;* rough, coarse, uncouth manners. *Un* — *assaut ;* a fierce assault. *Les temps sont* —*s ;* times are hard. *Des paroles* —*s ;* harsh words.

rudement (ru-dmān), *adv.*, roughly, ruggedly, harshly, sharply, severely, strictly ; tumultuously, violently, impetuously, rudely. *Traiter* —; to treat roughly. *Aller* — *en besogne ;* to work with a vengeance.

rudenté, -e, *adj.*, (arch.) cabled (of columns).

rudenture, *n.f.*, (arch.) cabling, rudenture.

rudesse, *n.f.*, harshness ; roughness ; ruggedness ; severity ; tumultuousness ; fierceness, violence ; austerity, strictness ; troublesomeness ; rude thing, coarse thing ; rudeness.

rudiment, *n.m.*, rudiment.

rudimentaire, *adj.*, rudimental, elementary, rudimentary.

rudoyer, *v.a.*, to use roughly, harshly ; to speak harshly to ; to bully ; to ill-treat (a horse).

rue, *n.f.*, street ; (bot.) rue. — *passante ;* much frequented street. *Courir les* —*s ;* to run about the streets ; (fig.) to be in everybody's mouth (of news) ; to be common (of a thing). — *de traverse ;* cross-street. — *écartée ;* back street. *Il est fou à courir les* — *s ;* he is stark, staring mad. *Les* —*s en sont pavées ;* (prov.) it is as common as dust. *Etre vieux comme les* —*s ;* to be as old as the hills. — *de chèvre ;* goat's-rue.

ruelle, *n.f.*, lane, alley, by-street ; bed-side, wall-side ; (fig.) lady's alcove ; private circle ;

literary coterie. *Les belles —s de Paris;* the best drawing-rooms in the town.

rueller, *v.a.*, to mold (vines).

ruer, *v.a.*, (l.u.) to fling, to hurl, to **cast**; to throw. *— de grands coups;* to deal heavy blows.

se **ruer**, *v.r.*, to throw one's self; to rush upon.

ruer, *v.n.*, to kick (of horses, etc.).

rueu-r, -se, *n. and adj.*, (man.) kicker; given to kicking.

rugine, *n.f.*, (surg.) rugine, scalp; (dentist's) tooth-scaler.

ruginer, *v.a.*, (surg.) to scalp.

rugir, *v.n.*, to roar, to yell.

rugissant, -e, *adj.*, roaring.

rugissement (-jis-mān), *n.m.*, roaring, roar.

rugosité, *n.f.*, rugosity, roughness, unevenness; wrinkle.

rugueu-x, -se (-gheû, -z), *adj.*, rugose, rough, uneven; wrinkled.

ruilée, *n.f.*, (arch.) verge.

ruine, *n.f.*, ruin, decay; overthrow, destruction, downfall; desolation. *Tomber en —s;* to fall to, to crumble to, ruins. *Tomber en —;* to run to ruin. *Courir à sa —;* to go to one's ruin; to go to wrack and ruin. *Cet édifice menace —;* this building is falling to ruins. *Sortir de ses —s;* to rise from its ruins (of towns, etc.). *Battre en —;* (milit.) to batter down.

ruiné, -e, *adj.*, ruined. *Son crédit est —;* his credit is gone. *Un tempérament —;* a worn-out constitution.

ruiner, *v.a.*, to ruin, to lay waste; to spoil; to undo, to overthrow, to destroy. *— un cheval;* to spoil a horse.

se **ruiner**, *v.r.*, to decay; to fall into decay; to ruin one's self; to be ruined, spoilt.

ruineu-x, -se, *adj.*, falling to ruin; ruinous.

ruinure, *n.f.*, (carp.) bearing.

ruisseau, *n.m.*, brook, stream, rivulet; gutter, street kennel. *Petit —;* rivulet, brook, streamlet, rill.

ruisselant, -e (rui-slān, -t), *adj.*, streaming, running down, dripping.

ruisseler (rui-slé), *v.n.*, to gush, to stream; to trickle, to trickle down, to run down.

ⓟ**ruisselet** (rui-slè), *n.m.*, rivulet, brooklet.

rum, *n.m.* V. **rhum**.

rumb (romb), *n.m.*, (nav.) rhumb, rhomb.

rumen (-mè-n), *n.m.*, rumen, paunch.

rumeur, *n.f.*, rumor, report; clamor, uproar, noise.

ruminant, -e, *adj.*, ruminant, ruminating.

ruminant, *n.m.*, (mam.) ruminant.

rumination, *n.f.*, rumination, chewing the cud.

ruminer, *v.n.*, to ruminate; to chew the cud; (fig.) to muse on, to ponder over, to think over.

ruminer, *v.a.*, to ruminate; to think over, to muse over. *Que ruminez-vous là?* what are you thinking about or turning over in your mind?

runes, *n.f.pl.*, runes, runic characters.

runique, *adj.*, runic.

rupture, *n.f.*, breaking, rupture, breaking off; (fig.) complete separation (between two persons); bursting; (med.) rupture, hernia; fracture; (paint.) mixing of colors. *La — d'un os;* the fracture of a bone. *La — d'un tendon;* the rupture of a sinew. *La — d'un mariage;* the breaking off of a match. *En — de ban;* escaped from banishment. *Ils en sont venus à une —;* all is at end between them.

rural, -e, *adj.*, rural.

ruse, *n.f.*, artifice, wile, deceit, craft, ruse, cunning, trick; (hunt.) double. *User de —s;* to practice deceit. *— de guerre;* stratagem of war.

rusé, -e, *adj.*, artful, deceitful, cunning, crafty, sly, subtle, designing. *Un — matois;* a knowing card. *Avoir l'air —;* to look cunning.

ruser, *v.n.*, to use deceit, craft, guile, artifice, cunning; (hunt.) to double.

russe, *n.m.f.* and *adj.*, Russian.

rustaud, -e, *adj.*, (fam.) boorish, rustic, coarse, uncouth.

rustaud, *n.m.*, (fam.) rustic; clod-hopper.

rustaudement (-tô-dmān), *adv.*, (fam.). V. **rustiquement**.

rustauderie (-tô-drî), *n.f.* (fam.). V. **rusticité**.

rusticité, *n.f.*, rusticity, clownishness, churlishness, uncouthness.

rustique, *adj.*, rural, rustic, country; artless, boorish. *Vie —;* country life. *Manières —s;* rustic manners. *Langage —;* boorish language.

rustique, *n.m.*, (arch.) rustic order.

rustiquement (-tik-mān), *adv.*, rustically, rudely, clownishly, boorishly, uncouthly.

rustiquer, *v.a.*, (arch.) to rough-cast, to jag out.

rustre, *n.m.* and *adj.*, boor, clown, churl, clodhopper; boorish, clownish, rude.

rusturer, *v.a.* V. **rouster**.

rut (rut), *n.m.*, rut (of deer). *Etre en —;* to rut.

rutabaga, *n.m.*, (agri.) Swedish turnip, rutabaga.

rutilant, -e, *adj.*, rutilant, shining, brilliant.

rutiler, *v.n.*, to shine, to rutilate.

rutoir, *n.m.*, (manu.) retting-pit; retting-pond.

ryott, *n.m.*, ryot (in India).

rythme, *n.m.*, rhythm.

rythmique, *adj.*, rhythmical.

S

s (èss), *n.f.*, (se), *n.m.*, the nineteenth letter of the alphabet, s. [S is added for the sake of euphony to the second pers. sing. of the imperative of verbs of the first conjugation before *y*, as : *vas-y;* go there; and also before *en*, as : *donnes-en;* give some.] *Faire des S;* to reel about, to stagger (like a drunken man).

s', contraction of *se*.

sa, *adj.f.*, his, her, one's, its. V. **son**.

sabbat, *n.m.*, Sabbath, seventh day of the week among the Jews; Sabbath (sabbatic year); nocturnal meeting or nightly revels (of witches); racket, uproar, tumult, scolding. *— de chats;* caterwauling. *Faire un —;* to kick up a shindy. *Faire un beau — à quelqu'un;* to scold any one well.

sabbataire, *n.m.*, Sabbatarian; Seventh-day Baptist.

sabbatique, *adj.*, sabbatical (of years).

sabbatisme, *n.m.*, sabbatism.

sabéen (-in), *adj.*, sabian.

sabéisme or **sabaïsme**, *n.m.*, Sabaism.

sabin, -e, *n.m.f.*, Sabine man or woman.

sabine, *n.f.*, (bot.) savin.

sabisme, *n.m.*, Sabaism.

sable, *n.m.*, sand; gravel, ballast; (l.u.) hour-glass; (her.) sable.

sablé, -e, *adj.*, laid with sand, sanded. *Allée —e;* gravel-walk or path.

sabler, *v.a.*, to gravel, to sand, to cover with sand or gravel; to drink off. *— un verre de vin;* to toss off a glass of wine.

sableu-x, -se, *adj.*, sandy.

sablier, *n.m.*, sand-glass; hour-glass; sand-man, dealer in sand; (nav.) glass; sand-box; (bot.) sand-box.

sablière, *n.f.*, sand-pit, gravel-pit; (carp.) raising-piece; (arch.) wall-plate; torsel.

sablon, *n.m.*, fine sand, scouring sand.

sablonner, *v.a.*, to sand, to scour with sand.

sablonneu-x, -se, *adj.*, sandy, graveled; gritty.

sablonnier, *n.m.*, dealer in sand.

sablonnière, *n.f.*, sand-pit, gravel-**pit**.

sabord, *n.m.*, (nav.) port, port-hole, gun-port.

sabordement, *n.m.*, (nav.) scuttling.

saborder, *v.a.*, (nav.) to scuttle.

sabot, *n.m.*, sabot, wooden shoe, horse's hoof, clog ; shoe (of carriages) ; (conch.) turban, turban-shell ; socket (of furniture) ; top (plaything) ; sorry fiddle ; (of ships) old tub. *Dormir comme un* —; to sleep like a top.

saboter, *v.n.*, to whip a top ; to clatter with one's shoes. *v.a.*, to arm the end of a stake with an iron socket ; (pop.) to bungle, to botch.

saboteur, *n.m.*, bungler.

sabotier (-tié), *n.m.*, clog maker, wearer or maker of wooden shoes, wooden shoe-maker.

sabotière, *n.f.*, wooden-shoe shop ; dance of people (in wooden shoes).

sabouler, *v.a.*, (pop.) to push about, to jostle, to hustle ; to scold, to rate, to bully.

sabre, *n.m.*, saber ; broadsword. — *baïonnette;* rifle-sword, sword-bayonet. — *poignard;* dirk, saber-poniard.

⊙**sabrenas**, *n.m.*, cobbler ; bungler.

⊙**sabrenasser**, *v.a. V.* **sabrenauder**.

⊙**sabrenauder**, *v.a.*, to cobble, to botch, to bungle.

sabrer, *v.a.*, to strike or cut with a saber, to saber ; to hurry over, to botch, to bungle. — *une affaire;* to hurry over any business.

sabretache, *n.f.*, (milit.) sabretache.

sabreur, *n.m.*, (fam.) brave soldier, hard fighter, swash-buckler ; (fig.) bungler, botcher. *Beau* —; dashing soldier (cavalry).

⊙**sabuleu-x, -se**, *adj.*, gritty.

saburral, -e, *adj.*, (med.) saburral.

saburre, *n.f.*, (med.) indigestion, foulness of the stomach.

sac, *n.m.*, sack, bag ; knapsack ; sackcloth ; poke-net ; (surg.) sac ; bag, pouch (of certain animals) ; plunder, sack, sacking, pillage, ransacking. — *de nuit;* carpet-bag. — *à ouvrage;* work-bag. *Homme de* — *et de corde;* Newgate-bird. — *à vin;* drunkard. — *à papier!* zounds ! hang it ! bless me ! *Cul-de*—, (—*s*—) blind alley. *Mettre quelqu'un au* —; to nonplus any one. *Tirer d'un* — *deux moutures;* to take double fees. *Voir le fond du* —; to sift an affair to the bottom. *Prendre quelqu'un la main dans le* —; to catch any one in the very act, or red-handed. — *de blé;* sack of wheat. — *de procès;* lawyer's bag. *Donner communication de son* —; (jur.) to communicate papers. *Etre dans le* —; to be in a fair way (to succeed). *Remplir son* —; (fam., pop.) to fill one's belly. *Donner à quelqu'un son* —; to send any one about his business, to give any one the sack. *Dans les petites* —*s sont les fines épices;* small parcels hold fine wares. *Vider son* —; to exhaust one's budget, to have one's say out. *Prendre son* — *et ses quilles;* to pack off, bag and baggage. *Mettre une ville à* —; to plunder, to sack a town. *Juger sur l'étiquette du* —; to judge by appearances.

saccade, *n.f.*, (man.) saccade, jerk (with a bridle) ; check, rebuke, reproof, reprimand ; scolding, rating ; (fig.) sudden, brusque movement ; fit, start. *Par* —*s;* by fits and starts.

saccadé, -e, *part.*, jerked, by jerks ; broken, irregular. *Style* —; abrupt style. *Phrases* —*es;* short, pithy sentences.

saccader, *v.a.*, (man.) to jerk, to check.

saccage, *n.m.*, havoc, confusion, jumble, confused heap.

saccagement (sa-kaj-măn), *n.m.*, sack, sackage, sacking, pillaging, ransacking, plunder.

saccager, *v.a.*, to sack, to ransack, to pillage, to plunder ; to throw into confusion.

saccageur, *n.m.*, plunderer ; sacker, ravager.

saccatier, *n.m.*, coal-heaver.

saccellaire, *n.m.*, (Fr. Hist.) treasurer, keeper of the privy purse.

saccharate (sak-ka-), *n.m.*, (chem.) saccharate. — *de chaux;* saccharated solution of lime.

sacchareu-x, -se (sak-ka-), *adj.*, saccharine.

saccharifère (sak-ka-), *adj.*, sacchariferous.

saccharimètre (sak-ka-), *n.m.*, saccharimeter, saccharometer.

saccharin, -e (sak-ka-), *adj.*, saccharine.

saccharique (sak-ka-), *adj.*, saccharic.

saccharure (sak-ka-), *n.m.*, (pharm.) sugar of (certain chemicals). — *d'aconit;* sugar of aconite.

sacciforme (sak-si-), *adj.*, (bot.) bagged.

sacerdoce, *n.m.*, priesthood.

sacerdotal, -e, *adj.*, sacerdotal, priestly.

sacerdotalisme, *n.m.*, sacerdotalism.

sachée, *n.f.*, sackful, bagful.

sachem (sa-shèm), *n.m.*, sachem (Indian chief).

sachet, *n.m.*, satchel, little bag or sack ; scent-bag.

sacoche, *n.f.*, saddle-bag ; money-bag.

sacramentaire, *n.m.*, sacramentarian.

sacramental, -e, or **sacramentel, -le**, *adj.*, sacramental. *Mots sacramentaux;* decisive words.

sacramentalement (-tal-măn) or **sacramentellement**, *adv.*, sacramentally.

sacre, *n.m.*, anointing, coronation of a king ; (orni.) saker ; (fig.) blackguard. — *d'un évêque;* consecration of a bishop.

sacré, -e, *adj.*, sacred, inviolable ; holy, consecrated, anointed, crowned ; (l.ex.) damned, cursed, confounded, blasted ; (anat.) sacral.

sacrebleu, *int.*, by Jove ! confound it ! dash it !

sacrement, *n.m.*, sacrament ; matrimony, marriage. *Saint* —; Holy Sacrament ; (c.rel.) Host ; (c.rel.) monstrance. *Administrer les derniers* —*s à quelqu'un;* to administer the last sacrament to any one. *Recevoir le* —; to receive the sacrament, to take the sacrament. *Office du saint* —; communion-service.

sacrer, *v.a.*, to anoint, to crown, a king ; to consecrate a bishop.

sacrer, *v.n.*, to curse, to swear.

sacret, *n.m.*, (hawking) sakeret.

sacrificateur, *n.m.*, sacrificer. *Souverain* —; high-priest.

sacrificatoire, *adj.*, sacrificial.

sacrificature, *n.f.*, office of sacrificer.

sacrifice, *n.m.*, sacrifice, offering, peace-offering. — *d'actions de grâces,* — *de louange;* (Bibl.) thanksgiving.

sacrifier, *v.a.*, to sacrifice, to make offerings ; to immolate ; to devote (time to a thing). — *des victimes;* to sacrifice victims. — *tout à ses intérêts;* to sacrifice everything to one's interest.

sacrifier, *v.n.*, to sacrifice.

sacrilège, *n.m.*, sacrilege.

sacrilège, *n.m.f.* and *adj.*, sacrilegist, sacrilegious person ; sacrilegious.

sacrilègement (-lèj-măn), *adv.*, sacrilegiously.

sacripant, *n.m.*, hector, bully, swaggerer ; scoundrel, blackguard.

sacristain, *n.m.*, sexton ; sacristan, vestry-keeper.

sacristie, *n.f.*, sacristy, vestry, vestry-room ; audit-house (of cathedrals) ; church-plate, sacred vases, etc. ; church fees.

sacristine, *n.f.*, vestry-nun.

sacro, *adj., invariable,* (rel.) holy. —*saint;* very, doubly holy ; (anat.) sacro.

sacrum, *n.m.*, (anat.) sacrum. *Os* —; sacrum, sacral bone.

saducéen (-cé-in), **-ne** (-cé-è-n), *n.* and *adj.*, Sadducee ; Sadducean.

saducéisme, *n.m.*, Sadducism.

⊙**saette**, *n.f. V.* **sagette**.

safran, *n.m.* (bot.) saffron; crocus. — *bâtard;* meadow-saffron, mock-saffron, bastard-saffron, safflower. — *de gouvernail;* (nav.) after-piece of a rudder.

safrané, -e, *adj.*, saffron, saffroned; yellow.

safraner, *v.a.*, to saffron.

safranière, *n.f.*, saffron-plantation.

safranum (-nom), *n.m.*, (chem.) safflower.

⊙**safre**, *adj.*, (pop.) greedy, gluttonous.

safre, *n.m.*, (chem.) zaffre, zaffer.

saga, *n.f.*, saga (legend of the northern nations of Europe).

sagace, *adj.*, sagacious, acute, shrewd.

sagacité, *n.f.*, sagacity, sagaciousness, quickness, acuteness, shrewdness.

sagamore, *n.m.*, sagamore (Indian chief).

sage, *adj.*, sage, wise, sensible, wary, rational, discreet, judicious, prudent; cool, sober, staid, well-behaved, steady, virtuous, modest; quiet, gentle. *Des lois —s;* wise laws. *Conduite —;* steady, prudent conduct. — *politique;* wise policy. *Etre —;* (of children) to be good, to be well-behaved. *Femme —;* virtuous woman.

sage, *n.m.*, wise man, sage.

sage-femme, *n.f.*, (—*s—s*), midwife.

sagement (saj-mãn), *adv.*, sagely, wisely, prudently, discreetly, judiciously, warily, soberly, steadily.

sagesse, *n.f.*, wisdom; moderation, discretion, prudence; steadiness, sobriety, chastity; goodness; good behavior (of children); gentleness (of animals).

⊙**sagette** or **saette**, *n.f.*, arrow; (bot.) arrow-head; adder's-tongue.

sagination, *n.f.*, fattening.

sagine, *n.f.*, (bot.) pearl-grass, pearl-wort.

sagittaire, *n.m.*, (astron.) Sagittarius.

sagittaire, *n.f.*, (bot.) arrow-head, adder's tongue.

sagittale, *adj.f.*, (anat.) sagittal.

sagitté, -e, *adj.*, (bot.) sagittate, arrow-headed, arrow-shaped.

sagou, *n.m.*, sago.

sagouier or **sagoutier**, *n.m.*, (bot.) sago-tree.

sagouin, *n.m.*, **-e**, *n.f.*, (mam.) sagoin, squirrel-monkey; slovenly fellow, slovenly woman.

s a i, initial letters of *Son Altesse Impériale*, His *or* Her Imperial Highness.

saie, *n.f.*, (antiq.) sagum (tunic, cloak); brush (used by goldsmiths); a light kind of serge.

saietter, *v.a.*, to brush.

*****saignant, -e**, *adj.*, bleeding, bloody; nearly raw, underdone (of meat).

*****saignée**, *n.f.*, (surg.) phlebotomy, bleeding, blood-letting; small of the arm; trench (for draining); (fig.) heavy payment, expense; drain.

*****saignement** (-mãn), *n.m.*, bleeding. — *de nez;* bleeding at the nose.

*****saigner**, *v.a.*, to bleed, to draw out blood; (cook.) to kill, to stick; to drain; to get money out of, to bleed any one.

*se***saigner**, *v.r.*, to bleed one's self, to drain one's self; to make a sacrifice.

*****saigner**, *v.n.*, to bleed. *Je saigne du nez;* I am bleeding at the nose. — *du nez;* (fig.) to show the white feather, to lack courage. *Le cœur m'en saigne;* it cuts me to the heart.

*****saigneur**, *n.m.*, (fam., l.u.) bleeder, blood-letter.

*****saigneu-x, -se**, *adj.*, bloody. *Bout —;* scrag end, neck (of lamb, mutton, veal).

*****saillant, -e**, *adj.*, jutting out, projecting; striking, forcible, remarkable; (her.) salient.

*****saillant**, *n.m.*, (fort.) the salient angle of any out-work.

*****saille!** *archaic 2d pers. sing. of the imperative of the verb saillir*, (nav.) haul! (word of command).

*****saillie**, *n.f.*, jutting out, projecture; promi-

nence, protuberance; start, sudden gush, spurt; sudden fit, sally; flash of wit, witticism; (arch.) rabbet, ledge; (of a steam-engine) spindle.

*****saillir**, *v.n.*, (*irregular*) (arch.) to project, to jut, to jut out, to stand out, to protrude, to rabbet; (paint.) to stand out. *Faire —;* to bring out; to bring into prominence; to show up. *Qui saille;* prominent. *Cette corniche saille trop;* that cornice projects too much.

*****saillir**, *v.a.*, (*regular*) (of animals) to leap, to cover, to serve.

*****saillir**, *v.n.*, (*regular*) to gush, to spout out (of liquids). V. **jaillir**, which is much more generally used.

sain, -e, *adj.*, sound, hale, healthy, sane, wholesome; (nav.) clear. — *de corps et d'esprit;* sound in body and mind. *Revenir — et sauf;* to return safe and sound. *Jugement —;* sound judgment. *Nourriture —e;* wholesome food.

sainbois, *n.m.*, (bot.) spurge-flax. V. **garou**.

saindoux, *n.m.*, lard.

sainement (sè-n-mãn), *adv.*, soundly, rationally, judiciously, healthily, wholesomely.

sainfoin, *n.m.*, (bot.) sainfoin.

saint, -e, *adj.*, holy, sacred, godly, sainted; sanctified; consecrated, saintly. — *homme;* godly man. *L'Ecriture —e;* Holy-Writ. *La semaine —e;* holy-week. *Le vendredi —;* Good-Friday. *La — Jean;* Midsummer. *La — Martin;* Martinmas-day. *Le —siège;* the holy see. *—-père;* holy father, the Pope. *Le —-Esprit, l'Esprit—;* the Holy Ghost, the Holy Spirit. *Le —-empire romain, le —-empire;* (formerly) the German empire. *—-office;* the holy-office (a name for the Inquisition). *Mal —;* falling sickness. *Rendre —;* to sanctify. *Lieu —;* sanctuary. *Terre —e;* consecrated ground; Holy Land. *Feu —-Antoine;* Saint Anthony's fire, erysipelas. *La —e journée;* the blessed, *or* the whole, day. *Tout le — Frusquin;* (pop.) the whole bally lot (of clothes). [Saint is written with a capital letter and joined to the following name by a hyphen, when such name does not designate a saint: *la Saint-Jean;* Midsummer.]

saint, *n.m.*, **-e**, *n.f.*, saint, patron saint, patron. — *d'une ville;* patron saint of a town. *Mettre au nombre des —s;* to canonize. *Il ne sait à quel — se vouer;* he does not know which way to turn. *Le — des —s;* the holy of holies.

saint-augustin, *n.m.*, (n.p.) Saint Augustine; (print.) English.

sainte-barbe, *n.f.*, (—) (nav.) powder-magazine, gun-room. *Collège —;* (in Paris).

saintement (sint-mãn), *adv.*, holily, sacredly; righteously, piously, religiously.

sainte nitouche, *n.f.*, (n.p.) a sanctimonious-looking person. *Faire la —;* to sham Abraham.

sainte-pélagie, *n.f.*, (formerly) debtor's prison; the French "Marshalsea"; (now) a political prison.

sainteté (sint-té), *n.f.*, holiness, sanctity, sacredness, saintliness; godliness, righteousness; Holiness (the Pope); (b.s.) saintship.

saint-germain, *n.m.*, (—) (hort.) Saint Germain (a kind of pear).

saint-simonien, *n.m.*, **-ne**, *n.f.*, (—*—s*) Saint-Simonian.

saint-simoniser, *v.a.*, to convert (to the doctrines of) (used by de Balzac).

saint-simonisme, *n.m.*, (n.p.) Saint-Simonianism (system of the Count of Saint-Simon).

saïque, *n.f.*, (nav.) saic.

saisi, -e, *adj.*, seized, possessed, struck, impressed. *Etre — d'une affaire;* to be made cognizant with; to be called upon to look into, to examine; (jur.) distrained.

saisi, *n.m.*, (jur.) person distrained.

saisie, *n.f.*, seizure, distress, distraint, execu-

tion. — *immobilière;* distress on real property.
— *mobilière;* distress on movable goods, distress on personal property.

saisie-arrêt, *n.f.,* (—*s*——) (jur.) attachment; garnishment (in London).

saisie-brandon, *n.f.,* (—*s*——) (jur.) execution on growing crops.

saisie-exécution, *n.f.,* (—*s*——) (jur.) execution; distress.

saisie-gagerie, *n.f.,* (—*s*——) (jur.) execution by way of security (for house-rent).

saisie-revendication, *n.f.,* (—*s*——) (jur.) attachment of goods claimed (pending litigation).

saisine, *n.f.,* (jur.) seizin; (nav.) gripe, lashing.

saisir, *v.a.,* to seize, to seize upon, to catch, to lay hold of, to catch hold of, to get hold of, to take, to take hold of; to strike, to come upon, to impress, to shock, to startle; to embrace, to avail one's self of; to understand, to perceive, to discern, to comprehend; to attack; to make cognizant of, to lay before; (jur.) to distrain; (jur.) to vest; (jur.) to attach. — *quelqu'un au collet;* to collar any one. — *l'occasion;* to seize the opportunity. — *un prétexte;* to avail one's self of an excuse. *La peur les a saisis;* they were struck with fear. — *un tribunal d'une affaire;* to lay (an affair) before a court, to bring before a court of justice.

se **saisir,** *v.r.,* to seize, to catch hold (of), to lay hold (of), to grasp; to take possession, to take cognizance (of); to arrest, to apprehend. *Saisi du vol;* (of a thief) with the stolen goods upon him.

saisir-arrêter, *v.a.,* (jur.) to attach; (in London) to garnish.

saisir-exécuter, *v.a.,* (jur.) to distrain.

saisissable, *adj.,* distrainable, seizable; attachable.

saisissant, -e, *adj.,* (of cold) keen, sharp, piercing; striking, thrilling, startling, impressive.

saisissant, -e, *n.* and *adj.,* (jur.) distrainer.

saisissement (-zis-mān), *n.m.,* shock, chill, violent impression, pang; (of criminals) pinioning.

saison, *n.f.,* season, weather; proper time, moment. *Arrière*—, (—*s*——*s*) latter end of autumn; (fig.) aftermath. *La* — *est avancée;* the season is forward. *Morte*—, (—*s*——*s*) (com.) dull, dead season. *Morte* —; winter. *En temps et en* — ; in due season. *Etre en pleine* —; to be in their prime (of flowers and fruits). *Ces mets ne sont plus de* —; those dishes are out of season. *De* —; in season. *Marchand des quatre* —*s;* costermonger, hawker.

salace, *adj.,* salacious.

salacité, *n.f.,* salaciousness, salacity.

salade, *n.f.,* salad, salading; mess (for horses); sallet (kind of helmet). *Retourner, fatiguer, la* —; to mix the salad.

saladier, *n.m.,* salad-dish, salad-bowl.

salage, *n.m.,* salting.

salaire, *n.m.,* wages, pay, hire; recompense, reward, retribution, punishment. *Toute peine mérite* —; the laborer is worthy of his hire.

salaison, *n.f.,* salting; salt-provision.

salamalec, *n.m.,* (jest.) low bow, salaam.

salamandre, *n.f.,* salamander, fire-eater.

salangane, *n.f.,* (orni.) esculent swallow.

salant, *adj.,* salt; saline. *Marais* —; salt-marsh.

salarié, -e, *n.* and *part.,* salaried person; hireling; placeman; paid.

salarier, *v.a.,* to pay; to give wages, *or* a salary, *or* a stipend, to.

salaud, -e, *n.* and *adj.,* sloven, dirty fellow; dirty woman, slut; slovenly, sluttish.

sale, *adj.* and *n.m.f.,* dirty, nasty, foul; soiled; filthy, low, coarse, dirty person; sloven. *Vaisseau* —; (nav.) foul ship; (of colors) dull.

---

salé, *n.m.,* salt-pork. *Du petit* —; pork newly-salted; pickled pork.

salé, -e, *adj.,* salted, salt, briny; keen, pungent, biting; loose, coarse, broad. *Un peu* —; saltish. *Sources* —*es;* salt-springs. *Raillerie* —*e;* biting raillery. *Un propos* —; a coarse remark.

salement (sal-mān), *adv.,* dirtily, nastily, filthily; (fig.) in a slovenly manner.

salep (sa-lèp), *n.m.,* salep.

saler, *v.a.,* to salt, to salt down; to corn (beef); to overcharge, to lay it on stiff for (goods); to fleece (customers).

se **saler,** *v.r.,* to be salted (of anything).

saleron (sal-ron), *n.m.,* bowl of a salt-cellar.

saleté (sal-té), *n.f.,* dirt, soil, dirtiness, nastiness, filthiness; filth, dirty rubbish; dirty thing; dirty trick; coarseness, ribaldry, obscenity.

saleur, *n.m.,* salter, curer.

salicaire, *n.f.,* salicaria; purple willow.

salicole, *adj.,* salicultural.

salicoque, *n.f.,* prawn.

salicor, *n.m., or* **salicorne,** *n.f.,* (bot.) glasswort, saltwort.

⊙**salicot,** *n.m.* V. **salicoque.**

salicotte, *n.f.,* (bot.) saltwort.

saliculture, *n.f.,* saliculture.

salière, *n.f.,* salt-cellar; salt-box; eye-pit (of horses); hollow behind the collar-bone (of persons).

salifère, *adj.,* saliferous.

salifiable, *adj.,* (chem.) salifiable.

salification, *n.f.,* (chem.) salification.

salifier, *v.a.,* to salify.

saligaud, *n.m.,* **-e,** *n.f.,* (pop.) dirty person; dirty thing; sloven; slut.

*****salignon,** *n.m.,* salt-cat.

saligot, *n.m.,* (bot.) water-caltrop.

salin, -e, *adj.,* saline, briny.

salin, *n.m.,* salt-marsh; raw salt; brine-pan; salt-works.

saline, *n.f.,* salt provisions, salt fish; salt-mine, salt-works, salt-pit, brine-pit.

salinier, *n.m.,* the owner and worker of salt-works.

salique, *adj.,* salic. *Loi* —; salic law.

salir, *v.a.,* to dirt, to dirty, to soil, to stain, to foul, to taint, to sully, to tarnish, to disgrace.

se **salir,** *v.r.,* to dirty one's self; to get dirty; to soil; to sully one's reputation, to disgrace one's self.

salissant, -e, *adj.,* soiling, that soils, that gets dirty.

salisson, *n.f.,* (pop.) young slut.

salissure, *n.f.,* spot of dirt; soil, stain.

salivaire, *adj.,* (anat.) salivary.

salivation, *n.f.,* (med.) salivation.

salive, *n.f.,* saliva; spittle.

saliver, *v.n.,* to spit; to salivate.

salle, *n.f.,* hall, room; ward (in hospitals); (thea.) house; arbor (of gardens). — *à manger;* dining-room. *La* — *du commun;* the servants' hall. — *d'audience;* audience-chamber. — *de spectacle;* play-house. — *de billard;* billiard-room. — *d'armes;* fencing-school, school of arms. armory. — *de danse;* dancing-room, dancing-school. — *de verdure;* green arbor. — *d'asile;* infant-school. — *des festins;* banqueting-hall. — *d'étude;* study, school-room. — *de police;* (mil.) guard-room. — *du rapport;* orderly-room. — *de récréation;* play-room. — *de réunion;* assembly-room. — *du conseil;* council-chamber. — *pleine,* or *comble;* crowded house; house-full, full house.

salmigondis, *n.m.,* (cook.) hotch-potch, resurrection pie; medley, farrago.

salmis, *n.m.,* ragout of game (previously roasted).

saloir, *n.m.,* salt-box; salting-tub.

salon, *n.m.,* drawing-room; saloon, parlor;

exhibition (of paintings, of works of art). *pl.*, fashionable world; fashionable circles. *Petit —*; small drawing-room. *Fréquenter les —s;* to be a man of fashion.

salope, *n.* and *adj.f.*, slut; disorderly woman; slovenly, sluttish. *C'est une vraie —*; she is a perfect slut. *Marie —*; *(—s —s)* mud-boat.

salopement (-lop-mān), *adv.*, (pop.) sluttishly, dirtily.

saloperie (-lo-prī), *n.f.*, slovenliness, sluttishness; coarse language, ribaldry; beastliness, filth.

salorge, *n.m.*, loaf of salt.   [making.

salpêtrage, *n.m.*, nitrification; saltpeter-

salpêtre, *n.m.*, saltpeter. *Ce n'est que du —*; he fires up, *or* he takes fire, at the least thing; (fig.) hastiness; fire, vivacity.

salpêtrer, *v.a.*, to throw saltpeter (over a space of ground); to nitrify (a wall); to throw out, to produce, saltpeter.

se **salpêtrer**, *v.r.*, to nitrify, to be covered with saltpeter (of walls).

salpêtrerie, *n.f.*, saltpeter-works.

salpêtreu-x, -se, *adj.*, saltpetrous.

salpêtrier, *n.m.*, saltpeter-maker.

salpêtrière, *n.f.*, saltpeter-works. *La Salpêtrière;* asylum for women.

*** salseparelle**, *n.f.*, sarsaparilla.

salsifis (-fī), *n.m.*, (bot.) salsify. *— sauvage, — des prés;* goat's-beard. *— noir, — d'Espagne;* viper's-grass.

saltarelle, *n.f.*, saltarella, Italian dance.

saltation, *n.f.*, saltation.

saltimbanque, *n.m.*, mountebank, clown, buffoon; humbug, quack.

salubre, *adj.*, salubrious, wholesome, healthful, healthy.

salubrité, *n.f.*, salubrity, salubriousness, healthfulness, wholesomeness. *Conseil de —*; board of health. *Inspecteur de —*; sanitary inspector.

saluer, *v.a.*, to salute, to bow to; to hail, to greet; to cheer; to proclaim. *— la compagnie;* to bow to the company. *Je vous salue, j'ai l'honneur de vous —*; (in letters) your servant, your humble servant. *— le soleil;* to hail the sun. *Saluez-le de ma part;* remember me to him. *— empereur, or roi;* to proclaim emperor, *or* king. *— de onze coups de canon;* to fire a salute of eleven guns (in honor of).

se **saluer**, *v.r.*, to bow to, to salute, each other.

salure, *n.f.*, saltness, brine.

salut, *n.m.*, safety; (rel.) salvation; salute, bow; welfare, preservation, escape, hope *or* chance of success; salutation; hail; (c.rel.) benediction (after even song). *Il a cherché un — dans la fuite;* he sought safety in flight. *Un profond —*; a low bow. *Léger —*; nod; (nav., milit.) salute. *int., —!* hail! greeting! *A bon entendeur —!* a word to the wise is enough.

salutaire, *adj.*, salutary, wholesome, advantageous, beneficial.

salutairement (-tèr-mān), *adv.*, salutarily, beneficially.

salutation, *n.f.*, salutation. *pl.*, compliments; salute; bow. *Recevez mes —s empressées;* yours very truly (in letters).

⊙**salvage**, *n.m.* V. **sauvetage**.

salvanos (-nōs), *n.m.*, (—) (nav.) life-buoy.

⊙**salvations**, *n.f.*, (jur.) rejoinder.

salve, *n.f.*, (artil.) salute, volley. *Une — d'applaudissements;* a round of applause.

salvé, *n.m.*, (—) (c.rel.) Salve Regina.

samaritain (-tin), -**e** (-tè-n), *n.* and *adj.*, Samaritan.

samedi (sa-m-dī), *n.m.*, Saturday. *— saint;* Easter-eve.

samscrit, -**e**, *adj.* V. **sanscrit**.

san-benito, *n.m.*, (—) san benito.

sancir, *v.n.*, (nav.) to founder, to sink (by the bows).

sanctifiant, -**e**, *adj.*, sanctifying.

sanctificateur, *n.m.*, sanctifier. *adj.* sanctifying.

sanctification, *n.f.*, sanetification, holy-keeping.

sanctifier, *v.a.*, to sanctify, to make holy, to keep holy, to hallow.

sanction, *n.f.*, sanction; approbation; assent (of parliament).

sanctionner, *v.a.*, to sanction.

sanctuaire, *n.m.*, sanctuary; (of the temple at Jerusalem) holy of holies; (of churches) chancel, altar; (fig.) church.

sandal *or* **santal**, *n.m.*, sandal-wood, sandal.

sandale, *n.f.*, sandal; fencing-shoe.

sandalier, *n.m.*, sandal-maker.

sandaraque, *n.f.*, (bot.) sandarac, pounce.

sandjak, sandjiak, *or* **sandjiakat**, *n.m.* V. sangiac.

sandwich (-ooitch), *n.m.*, sandwich.

sang, *n.m.*, blood; race, parentage, relationship, kindred, race. *Un homme de —*; a blood-thirsty man. *Coup de —*; stroke, apoplectic fit. *Pur —*; thoroughbred. *Demi —*; halfbred. *Mettre à feu et à —*; to put to fire and sword. *Suer — et eau;* to toil and moil *or* to strain every nerve. *Se battre au premier —*; to fight till the first blood is drawn. *Cela glace le —*; that curdles one's blood. *Cela est dans le —*; that runs in the blood. *Se faire du bon —*; (fam.) to amuse one's self, to have a jolly time (of it). *Se faire du mauvais —*; to fret, to worry. *Bon — ne peut mentir;* good breeding will assert itself. *Son — n'a fait qu'un tour;* he was struck all of a heap.

sang-de-dragon, *n.m.* (—) (bot.) dragon's-blood.

sang-froid, *n.m.*, (n.p.) coolness, composure, sang-froid, presence of mind. *De —*; in cold blood; with composure; soberminded. *Perdre son —*; to lose one's presence of mind.

sangiac *or* **sangiacat**, *n.m.*, sangiac; district, province; governor (in Turkey).

sanglade, *n.f.*, lash, cut (with a whip).

sanglant, -**e**, *adj.*, bloody, covered with blood; outrageous, gross; keen, biting, cutting. *Affront —*; outrageous affront.

sangle, *n.f.*, strap, band, belt; girth (of saddles). *Lit de —*; cross, *or* folding, bedstead.

sanglé, -**e**, *adj.*, strapped; (fig.) ill-treated, cut up; tight, tight-fitting.

sangler, *v.a.*, to bind with a girth, to girth, to strap, to gird; to tighten, to lash, to beat. *— un coup de poing;* to deal a blow. *Avoir été sanglé;* to have been beaten, ill-used; (fig.) cut up.

se **sangler**, *v.r.*, to lace one's self tightly; (fig.) to stint, *or* pinch, one's self.

sanglier, *n.m.*, wild boar. *— de mer;* seahog, boar-fish.

sanglot, *n.m.*, sob. *pl.*, sobbing, moaning (of the sea: V. Hugo). *—s entre-coupés;* broken sobs.

sangloter, *v.n.*, to sob.

sangsue (san-sū), *n.f.*, leech; (fig.) blood-sucker, extortioner.

sanguification (-gu-i-), *n.f.*, sanguification.

sanguifier (-gu-i-), *v.a.*, to sanguify.

se **sanguifier**, *v.r.*, to sanguify.

sanguin, -**e** (-ghīn, -ghi-n), *adj.*, of blood, full-blooded; sanguineous, blood-colored, blood-red. *Vaisseau —*; blood-vessel.

sanguinaire (-ghi-), *adj.*, sanguinary, bloody, murderous, bloodthirsty.

sanguinaire, *n.f.*, (bot.) bloodwort.

sanguine (-ghi-n), *n.f.*, red chalk, blood-stone.

sanguinelle (-ghi-), *n.f.*, (bot.) gatter-tree.

sanguinolent, -**e** (-ghi-), *adj.*, (med.) tinged with blood.

sanhédrin, *n.m.*, sanhedrim.

sanicle, *n.f.*, (bot.) sanicle.

sanie, *n.f.*, (med.) sanies.

sanieu-x, -se, *adj.*, sanious.

sanitaire, *adj.*, sanitary.

sans, *prep.*, without; free from; but for, had it not been for, were it not for. — *amis;* friendless. — *doute;* without doubt. — *cela;* were it not for that or else. — *quoi;* otherwise or else, without that. — *y penser;* unawares, unthinkingly. —*peur;* fearless. — *le sou;* penniless. *Cela va*—*dire;* of course, as a matter of course.

sans-cœur, *adj.* and *n.m.f.*, (pop.) heartless; unfeeling person or wretch.

sanscrit, *n.m.*, Sanscrit (language).

sanscrit, -e, *adj.*, Sanscrit.

sans-culotte, *n.m.*, (——*s*) ragged fellow; sans-culotte; ultra-violent republican.

sans-culottides, *n.f.pl.*, the five supernumerary days to complete the year in the calendar of the first French republic; *also,* the festivals held during those days.

sans-dents, *n.f.*, (———*s*) toothless old woman.

sans-façon, *n.m.*, bluntness, off-handedness, familiarity.

sans-fleur, *n.f.*, (——*s*) a sort of apple.

sans-gêne, *n.m.*, unceremoniousness; impudence, coolness; off-handedness.

sansonnet, *n.m.*, (orni.) starling.

sans-peau, *n.f.*, (—) summer-pear.

sans que, *conj.*, without. *Il a passé* — *que je l'aie aperçu;* he passed without my seeing him.

sans-soin, *adj.*, careless. *n.m.f.*, careless creature.

sans-souci, *n.m.*, (—) careless, indifferent man, jolly fellow.

sans-terre, *adj.*, Lackland. *Les* —*s;* the Lacklanders.

santal, *n.m.* V. **sandal**.

santaline, *n.f.*, (chem.) santaline.

santé, *n.f.*, health, healthiness; soundness; toast. *Comment va la* —? how is your health? how are you? *Maison de* —; private asylum. *Bureau de* —; board of health. *Billet de* —; certificate of health. *Boire à la* —*de quelqu'un;* to drink any one's health. *Corps de* —; medical staff. *Officier de* —; medical practitioner.

santoline, *n.f.*, (bot.) santolina. [Sometimes, but improperly, used for *santonine,* which see.]

santon, *n.m.*, santon; a santon's tomb (in Algeria).

santonine, *n.f.*, (bot.) artemisia santonica; (chem.) santonin.

sanve, *n.f.*, (bot.) charlock.

saoul, *adj.* V. **soûl**.

saouler, *v.a.* V. **soûler**.

sapa, *n.m.*, (pharm.) grape-jelly, juice.

sapajou, *n.m.*, (mam.) sapajou; (fig. pers.) monkey.

sapan, *n.m.*, sapan-wood.

sape, *n.f.*, (milit.) sap, sapping, mine, trench. *Aller à la* —; (milit.) to sap.

saper, *v.a.*, to sap, to undermine, to cut away, to shake.

sapeur, *n.m.*, (milit.) sapper.

saphène, *n.f.*, (anat.) saphena.

saphique, *n.m.* and *adj.*, (Grec. poet.) sapphic.

saphir, *n.m.*, sapphire.

saphirine, *n.f.*, (min.) blue chalcedony.

sapide, *adj.*, sapid, palatable.

sapidité, *n.f.*, sapidity, sapidness, flavor.

sapience, *n.f.*, ⊙ sapience, wisdom (theol.).

sapientiaux, *adj.m.pl.*, (Bibl.) sapiential.

sapin, *n.m.*, fir, fir-tree; spruce, deal; (pop.) hackney-coach. *Sentir le* —; to have a foot in the grave. *Sa toux sent le* —; he has a church-yard cough.

sapine, *n.f.*, fir-plank, deal-board; scaffold-pole.

sapinière, *n.f.*, fir-plantation, fir-grove.

saponacé, -e, *adj.*, saponaceous.

saponaire, *n.f.*, (bot.) soapwort.

saponification, *n.f.*, saponification.

saponifier, *v.a.*, to saponify.

se **saponifier**, *v.r.*, to saponify.

saponine, *n.f.*, saponine.

saporifique, *adj.*, saporific.

sapote or **sapotille, n.f.*, sapota (fruit).

sapotier or **sapotillier, n.m.*, sapota (tree).

sar, *n.m.* V. **sart**.

sarabande, *n.f.*, saraband (dance).

sarbacane, *n.f.*, air-cane; pea-shooter; speaking tube; puff and dart. *Par* —; by proxy.

sarbotière, *n.f.* V. **sorbétière**.

sarcasme, *n.m.*, sarcasm.

sarcastique, *adj.*, sarcastic; sarcastical.

sarcelle, *n.f.*, (orni.) teal.

sarcite, *n.f.*, flesh-stone.

sarclage, *n.m.*, (gard.) weeding.

sarcler, *v.a.*, (gard.) to weed; (fig.) to extirpate.

sarcleur, *n.m.*, weeder.

sarcloir, *n.m.*, weeding-hook or fork, hoe.

sarclure, *n.f.*, weedings.

sarcocèle, *n.f.*, (surg.) sarcocele.

sarcocolle, *n.f.*, sarcocolla.

sarcocollier, *n.m.*, (bot.) sarcocol-tree, pænea mucronata.

sarcologie, *n.f.*, sarcology.

sarcomateu-x, -se, *adj.*, (surg.) sarcomatous.

sarcome, *n.m.*, (surg.) sarcoma.

sarcophage, *n.m.*, sarcophagus; coffin, representation of a coffin (at a funeral).

sarcophage, *n.m.* and *adj.*, (med.) caustic, corrosive, escharotic.

⊙**sarcotique**, *n.m.* and *adj.*, (med.) sarcotic.

sardanapale, *n.m.*, effeminate man.

sarde, *n.m.f.* and *adj.*, Sardinian.

sarde, *n.f.*, (ich.) scomber; a kind of sardine or pilchard (of Brazil).

sardine, *n.f.*, pilchard, sardine.

sardoine, *n.f.*, (min.) sardonyx.

sardonien, -ne (-ni-in, -ni-è-n), *adj.*, sardonian, sardonic.

sardonique, *adj.*, sardonic.

sargasse, *n.f.*, sargassum, gulf-weed.

sarge or **sargue**, *n.m.*, (ich.) sheep's head, sargus.

sarigue, *n.m.f.*, opossum.

sarisse, *n.f.*, (antiq.) sarissa, the phalanx's long pike.

sarmate, *adj.*, sarmatian.

sarment, *n.m.*, vine-shoot, vine-twig.

sarmenteu-x, -se, *adj.*, (bot.) sarmentous, branchy, climbing.

sarracénique, *adj.*, Saracenic.

sarrasin, *n.m.* and *adj.*, Saracen; (arch.) Saracenic.

sarrasin, *n.m.*, buckwheat.

sarrasine, *n.f.*, (fort.) sarasin, sarrasine, portcullis, herse.

sarrau, *n.m.*, smock-frock, smock; (children) pinafore.

sarrette, *n.f.*, (bot.) saw-wort.

sarriette, *n.f.*, (bot.) savory; common marum.

sarrot, *n.m.* V. **sarrau**.

sart or **sar**, *n.m.*, sea-wrack.

sas, *n.m.*, bolting-sieve; sieve; screen; chamber (of locks). *Passer au* —; to sift (fig.). *Passer au gros* —; to examine superficially.

sassafras, *n.m.*, (bot.) sassafras.

sasse, *n.f.*, (nav.) scoop.

sassement (sâs-mān), *n.m.*, sifting, winnowing.

sassenage (sâs-naj), *n.m.*, Sassenage cheese.

sasser, *v.a.*, to sift, to bolt; to winnow; to scan, to scrutinize.

sasset, *n.m.*, little sieve.

sasseur, *n.m.*, sifter, bolter; winnower.

satan, *n.m.*, Satan.

satanas, *n.m.*, (fam.) Satan.

satané, *adj.*, (fam.) roguish, wanton, mischievous; devilish, confounded.

satanique, *adj.*, satanic, satanical.

satellite (-tèl-lit), *n.m.*, satellite.

satellite, *adj.*, (anat.) companion. [Only used in : *veines —s ; venæ comites ;* companion veins.]

satiété, *n.f.*, satiety, surfeit, fullness.

satin, *n.m.*, satin.

satinade, *n.f.*, satinet.

satinage, *n.m.*, satining ; glazing (of paper).

satiné, -e, *adj.*, satin-like, satiny, hot *or* cold pressed ; glazed (of paper). *Peau —e ;* skin as soft as velvet.

satiner, *v.a.*, to satin ; to glaze (paper). — *à chaud ;* to hot press. — *à froid ;* to cold press.

satiner, *v.n.*, to become as soft as satin.

satire, *n.f.*, satire ; lampoon. — *piquante ;* cutting satire. — *personnelle ;* lampoon.

satirique, *n.m.* and *adj.*, satirist ; satirical.

satiriquement (-rik-mån), *adv.*, satirically.

satiriser, *v.a.*, to satirize.

satirist, *n.m.f.*, satirist.

satisfaction, *n.f.*, satisfaction, gratification, pleasure ; atonement.

satisfactoire, *adj.*, (theol.) satisfactory.

satisfaire, *v.a.*, to satisfy, to please, to gratify ; to supply (wants) ; to answer ; to meet, to discharge ; to give satisfaction (to) (to make amends) ; to perform, to execute, to fulfill ; to comply (with), to obey. — *sa passion ;* to gratify one's passion. — *l'attente de quelqu'un ;* to answer any one's expectation.

se **satisfaire**, *v.r.*, to satisfy one's self, to indulge one's self.

satisfaire, *v.n.*, to satisfy ; to discharge ; to perform, to execute ; to gratify, to indulge. — *à ses engagements ;* to meet one's engagements.

satisfaisant, -e, *adj.*, satisfactory.

satisfait, -e, *adj.*, satisfied, contented, pleased.

satisfecit, *n.m.*, (—) certificate of good conduct.

satrape, *n.m.*, satrap.

satrapie, *n.f.*, satrapy.

saturable, *adj.*, saturable.

saturant, -e, *adj.*, saturant.

saturation, *n.f.*, saturation.

saturer, *v.a.*, to saturate ; to surfeit.

se **saturer**, *v.r.*, to become saturated, surfeited.

saturnales, *n.f.pl.*, Saturnalia.

saturne, *n.m.*, (astron., chem.) Saturn.

saturnin, -e, *adj.*, (med.) lead. *Colique —e ;* lead colic.

satyre, *n.m.*, satyr.

satyre, *n.f.*, (Grec. antiq.) satyric play ; satire.

satyriasis (-zis), *n.m.*, (med.) satyriasis.

satyrion, *n.m.*, (bot.) satyrion, satyrium, standard-grass, stander-grass.

satyrique, *adj.*, pertaining to satyrs, satyric.

sauce, *n.f.*, (cook.) sauce. — *relevée ;* rich, highly-seasoned sauce. — *douce ;* sweet sauce. — *piquante ;* sharp sauce. *A toute —;* in all manner of ways, for any sort of work. *Il n'est —* (or *chère*) *que d'appétit ;* a good appetite is the best sauce. *On ne sait à quelle — le mettre ;* there is no knowing what to do with him. *Faire la — à quelqu'un ;* to give any one a smart rebuke, to pull any one up sharply. *Etre dans la —;* to be in a pickle.

saucé, -e, *part.*, drenched, soused, wet through. *Médailles —es ;* plated medals.

saucer, *v.a.*, to dip in sauce ; to sop, to souse, to wet through ; to scold ; to blow up.

saucier, *n.m.*, (nav.) saucer (of a capstan) ; sauce-maker, sauce-contriver.

saucière, *n.f.*, sauce-boat, sauce-tureen.

saucisse, *n.f.* sausage.

saucisson, *n.m.*, large sausage ; (artil.) saucisson, saucisse ; (fort.) bundle of fagots *or* fascines.

sau-f, -ve, *adj.*, safe, unhurt, unscathed, spared. *Il en est revenu sain et —;* he returned safe and sound. *La vie —ve ;* with one's life.

sauf, *prep.*, saving, save, except, but ; reserving ; subject to ; under. — *erreur ou omission ;* errors excepted. — *correction ;* under correction. — *votre respect ;* saving your presence.

sauf-conduit, *n.m.*, (——*s*) safe-conduct.

sauge, *n.f.*, (bot.) sage.

saugrenu, -e, *adj.*, absurd, ridiculous.

saulaie, *n.f.*, willow-plantation *or* grove.

saule, *n.m.*, willow. — *pleureur ;* weeping willow.

saulée, *n.f.*, row *or* avenue of willows.

saumâtre, *adj.*, brackish, briny.

saumon, *n.m.*, (ich.) salmon ; (metal.) pig, brock ; (nav.) kentledge. — *mariné ;* pickled salmon. — *de fonte ;* pig-iron.

saumoné, -e, *adj.*, salmon. *Truite —e ;* salmon-trout.

saumoneau, *n.m.*, (ich.) young salmon, grilse.

saumure, *n.f.*, brine, pickle.

saumurer, *v.a.*, to brine, to pickle, to souse.

saumurois, *adj.*, native of Saumur.

saunage, *n.m.*, salt-trade ; salt-making. *Faux- —; (n.p.)* illicit salt-trade.

sauner, *v.n.*, to make salt.

saunerie (sô-n-rî), *n.f.*, salt-house ; salt-works.

saunier *or* **saulnier**, *n.m.*, salt-maker. *Faux- —,* (——*s*) dealer in contraband salt.

saunière, *n.f.*, salt-box.

saupiquet, *n.m.*, (cook.) sharp sauce.

saupoudrage, *n.m.*, salting, besprinkling.

saupoudrer, *v.a.*, to powder ; to sprinkle with salt, pepper, etc. ; to strew ; to sprinkle ; (fig.) to intersperse, to interlard, to strew.

saur, *adj.* red (of herrings). [This word is an abbreviation of *saure*, which see below.]

saure, *adj.* yellowish brown ; sorrel (of horses) ; red, smoked (of herrings). *Un hareng —;* a red herring. *Un cheval —;* a sorrel horse.

saurer, *v.a.*, to smoke (herrings).

sauret, *adj.*, (l.u.) red (of herrings).

sauriens (-in), *n.m.pl.*, saurians ; lizards.

saurin, *n.m.*, herring (just) smoked.

saussaie, *n.f. V.* **saulaie**.

saut, *n.m.*, leap, jump, skip, bound ; spring ; waterfall ; (man.) vault, leap. *Faire un —;* to take a leap. — *de carpe* or *périlleux ;* somerset, somersault. — *de Breton ;* tripping up any one. — *de loup ;* ha-ha; ditch. *Il s'élança tout d'un —;* he sprang forward at a bound. *Au — du lit ;* on getting up, on getting out of bed. *De plein —;* at once ; point blank. *Par —s et par bonds ;* by fits and starts. — *de mouton ;* (man.) goat-leap; (game) leap-frog.

sautage, *n.m.*, exploding, blasting (mines).

saute, *n.f.*, (nav.) sudden veering of the wind, chopping.

sauté, *n.m.*, (cook.) stew.

sauté, -e, *adj.*, (cook.) stewed.

saute-en-barque, *n.m.*, boating-jacket.

sautelle, *n.f.*, vine-shoot.

sauter, *v.n.*, to leap, to leap off, to jump, to skip, to pass over, to overlook ; to spring ; (nav.) to veer, to shift, to chop round (of the wind) ; to blow up (to explode) ; to kick the bucket ; to be discharged (of a person). — *en avant ;* to leap forward. — *par-dessus une muraille ;* to leap over a wall. — *de joie ;* to jump, or leap, for joy. *Faire — un bastion ;* to blow up a bastion. *Faire — la banque ;* to break the bank. — *au collet de quelqu'un ;* to collar any one. *Cela saute aux* *yeux ;* that is obvious, self-evident. — *aux nues ;* to jump up to the ceiling. *Le vent saute ;* (nav.) the wind is shifting, *or* chopping, round. — *en l'air ;* to bounce, *or* jump, up. — *à bas du lit ;* to jump out of bed. *Reculer pour mieux — ;* to await a better opportunity. — *en selle ;* to leap into the saddle.

sauter, *v.a.*, to leap, to leap over ; to overlook, to pass over ; to leave out, to skip. — *un fossé ;* to clear a ditch. *Il a sauté une phrase ;* he has skipped a sentence. — *à pieds joints ;* to jump close-feet *or* close-legged.

sautereau (sô-trô), *n.m.*, jack (of harpsichords).

sauterelle, *n.f.*, grasshopper, locust, gutter-skipper ; (carp.) level (instrument).

saute-ruisseau, *n.m.*, (— - —*x*) (game) hopscotch ; errand-boy. — *de mer ;* squilla (sort of shrimp).

sauteu-r, *n.m.*, **-se**, *n.f.*, leaper, jumper, tumbler, mountebank ; (man.) vaulter ; leaping-horse.

sauteuse, *n.f.*, a kind of dance.

***sautillant**, **-e**, *adj.*, hopping, skipping ; (fig.) jerky (of style).

***sautillement**, *n.m.*, hopping, skipping.

***sautiller**, *v.n.*, to hop, to skip, to jump about.

sautoir (sô-toar), *n.m.*, Saint Andrew's cross ; scarf, watch-guard ; (her.) saltier ; (cook.) stewpan ; (horl.) jumper. *En —* ; cross-wise, slung over the shoulder (of muskets) ; crossways ; (her.) saltier-wise. *Porter son bagage en —* ; to have one's baggage slung over one's shoulder.

sauvage, *n.m.f.* and *adj.*, savage ; savage, wild, untamed ; shy, timid ; unsociable ; uncivilized ; rude, brutal, barbarous.

sauvagement, *adv.*, wildly ; savagely ; fiercely.

sauvageon (-jon), *n.m.*, (agri.) wild stock.

sauvagerie (sô-va-jrî), *n.f.*, unsociableness ; shyness, wildness.

sauvagesse, *n.f.*, uncivilized woman ; (fam.) a woman destitute of education and manners, a scold, a shrew.

sauvagin, *n.m.*, taste, *or* smell, of water-fowl.

sauvagin, **-e**, *adj.*, fishy (in taste). *Sentir le* — ; to taste fishy, to smell fishy.

sauvagine, *n.f.*, wild water-fowl ; odour of water-fowl ; (com.) common unprepared skins *or* furs.

sauvegarde (sôv-gard), *n.f.*, safe-keeping, safeguard ; shield, buckler, protection. —*s de beaupré ;* (nav.) man-ropes of the bowsprit ; rudder pendant.

sauvegarder (sôv-gardé), *v.a.*, to protect, to safeguard.

sauve-qui-peut, *n.m.*, (—) headlong flight, rout ; stampede ; panic.

sauver, *v.a.*, to save, to deliver, to rescue ; to keep, to be the salvation of ; to economize ; to ward off, to palliate ; to conceal ; to excuse, to vindicate. *Sauve qui peut ;* save himself who can, every one for himself. — *les apparences ;* to save appearances. — *les défauts d'un ouvrage ;* to conceal the imperfections of a work. — *la vie à quelqu'un ;* to save any one's life.

se **sauver**, *v.r.*, to escape, to make good one's escape, to run away ; to abscond ; to make off ; to take refuge ; to retrieve one's self ; to indemnify one's self ; to work out one's salvation.

sauvetage (sôv-taj), *n.m.*, (nav.) salvage, saving, rescue. *Canot de —* ; life-boat. *Ceinture de —* ; life-belt. *Bouée de —* ; life-buoy. *Société de —* ; life-boat institution. *Appareil,* or *sac, de —* ; fire-escape.

sauveteur (sôv-teur), *n.m.*, rescuer ; life-preserver ; fire-escape ; salvor.

sauvette, *n.f.* duck-stone (game).

sauveur, *n.m.* and *adj.*, saver, deliverer ; Saviour, Redeemer ; (Bib.) all-saving.

sauve-vie, *n.f.*, (—) (bot.) wall-rue.

savamment (-va-mān), *adv.*, learnedly, cleverly ; knowingly, wittingly.

savane, *n.f.*, savannah.

savant, **-e**, *adj.*, learned, clever ; masterly, able, skillful. *Une main —e ;* a skillful hand. *Femme —e ;* blue-stocking.

savant, *n.m.*, **-e**, *n.f.*, scholar, learned person. *Les —s ;* the literati, the learned.

savantasse, *n.m.*, pedant. [Sometimes spelt *savantas* in poetry.]

savanterie, *n.f.*, pedantry.

savantissime, *adj.*, most learned.

savarin, *n.m.*, tipsy cake.

savate, *n.f.*, old shoe ; awkward, clumsy person ; (nav.) shoes ; slip-shoe ; shoe down at the heel ; (game) hunt the slipper ; bungler. *Traîner la —* ; to be as poor as Job ; to shuffle along. *Tirer la —* ; to fight with the feet.

savaterie, *n.f.*, old-shoe trade *or* market ; old-shoe shop.

saveter (sav-té), *v.a.*, to cobble ; to bungle, to botch.

savetier (sav-tié), *n.m.*, cobbler ; bungler, botcher, duffer.

saveur, *n.f.*, savor, flavor, relish ; taste, zest.

savoir (sachant, su), *v.a.*, to know, to have a knowledge of, to be aware of ; to understand ; to be sensible of ; to be acquainted with. *Il n'en sait rien ;* he knows nothing about it. *Puisque vous en savez tant ;* since you know so much (about it) *or* since you are so well posted up (in the matter). *Faire —* ; to notify, to acquaint, to let know, to inform. *Je ne sais ;* I don't know. *Je ne sais que faire ;* I don't know what to do. *Je suis tout je ne sais comment ;* I am all out of sorts. *Pas que je sache ;* not that I know, not to my knowledge. *Il sait son pain manger ;* he knows what he is about. — *vivre ;* to know how to behave, to be well-bred, to have breeding. *Il ne sait pas vivre ;* he has no manners. *Il ne sait ni A ni B ;* he is a regular dunce *or* duffer. *En — plus d'une ;* to know a trick or two. *En — gré à quelqu'un ;* to be grateful, *or* thankful, to any one (for). *En — trop long ;* to know too much. *Je ne sais qu'en croire ;* I know not what to think of it. *Je le sais de bonne part ;* I have it from a good source. *Si l'on vient à — cela ;* if that comes to be known. *Je ne saurais qu'y faire ;* I cannot help it. *Je ne sais où j'en suis ;* I do not know which way to turn, or what I am about. *Autant que je sache ;* to the best of my belief. *Que nous sachions ;* as far as we know ; as far as we recollect ; as far as we can judge ; as far as we are aware. *Un je ne sais quoi ;* an indescribable something. [*Je ne sais quoi* is the "indescribable" in French.] *Qui sait plus se tait ;* (prov.) a still tongue shows a wise head.

savoir, *v.n.*, to know, to be learned, to be a scholar, to be a person of learning. —, *à —* ; viz., namely, that is to say, to wit ; that remains to be known ; perhaps.

se **savoir**, *v.r.*, to get *or* become known, to know one's self to be. *Tout se sait avec le temps ;* everything becomes known in time.

savoir, *n.m.*, knowledge, learning, scholarship, talents, skill.

savoir-faire, *n.m.*, (*n.p.*) management ; tact, ability, skill ; wits. *Il vit de son —* ; he lives by his wits.

savoir-vivre, *n.m.*, (*n.p.*) good manners, good breeding.

savoisien, **-ne**, *adj.* and *n.*, Savoyard ; of, from, Savoy.

savon, *n.m.*, soap ; rebuke, scolding, blowing up, wigging ; soaping. *Donner un — à quelqu'un ;* to blow any one up, to give a wigging to. — *marbré ;* mottled soap. — *parfumé ;* scented soap. — *noir ;* soft soap. *Eau de —* ; soapsuds.

savonnage, *n.m.*, soaping ; washing with soap, soap-suds.

savonner, *v.a.*, to soap ; to wash with soap, to lather ; (pop.) to rebuke, to scold, to blow up. *se* **savonner**, *v.r.*, to bear washing, to wash (of fabrics). *Cette étoffe se savonne ;* this material will wash, will bear washing.

savonnerie (-vo-n-rî), *n.f.*, soap-house, soap-trade ; soap-works.

savonnette, *n.f.*, wash-ball ; soap-ball.

savonneu-x, -se, *adj.*, soapy.

savonnier, *n.m.*, soap-boiler, soap-manufacturer ; (bot.) soapberry-tree.

savourement (-voor-mān), *n.m.*, savoring, tasting ; (fig.) enjoyment.

savourer, *v.a.*, to savor ; to relish, to taste ; (fig.) to enjoy, to delight in.

savouret, *n.m.*, marrow-bone.

savoureusement (-reuz-mān), *adv.*, with relish.

savoureu-x, -se, *adj.*, savory, delicious.

savoyard, *n.m.*, -**e**, *n.f.*, Savoyard ; native of Savoy ; (fig.) ill-mannered, rude, unmannerly person. *V.* **savoisien**.

saxatile, *adj.*, saxatile.

saxifrage, *adj.*, saxifragous.

saxifrage, *n.f.*, (bot.) saxifrage.

saxon, -ne, *n.* and *adj.*, Saxon.

saynète, *n.f.*, sainette (Spanish farce).

sayon, *n.m.*, sayon, tunic.

sbire, *n.m.*, sbirro, myrmidon.

scabellon, *n.m.*, (arch.) socle, small pedestal.

scabieuse, *n.f.*, (bot.) scabious.

scabieu-x, -se, *adj.*, (med.) scabious, scabby.

scabreu-x, -se, *adj.*, scabrous, rugged, rough ; dangerous, difficult, slippery ; delicate ; ticklish.

scabrosité, *n.f.*, (of plants) roughness ; ruggedness.

scalaire, *n.f.*, (moll.) wentletrap.

scalde, *n.m.*, (antiq.) Scandinavian poet.

scalène, *adj.*, (geom.) scalene, scalenous.

scalpel, *n.m.*, scalpel.

scalper, *v.a.*, to scalp. *S'entre* —; to scalp one another.

scalpeur, *n.m.*, scalper.

scammonée, *n.f.*, scammony.

scandale, *n.m.*, scandal ; offense ; exposure ; shame ; dismay, horror. *Au grand* — *de tout le monde ;* to every one's horror. *Faire du* — ; to make a scene.

scandaleusement (-leuz-mān), *adv.*, scandalously.

scandaleu-x, -se, *adj.*, scandalous.

scandaliser, *v.a.*, to scandalize, to shock. *se* **scandaliser**, *v.r.*, to be scandalized, to be shocked, to take offense. *Il se scandalise de tout ;* he takes offense at everything.

scander, *v.a.*, to scan. *se* **scander**, *v.r.*, to be scanned.

scandinave, *n.m.f.*, and *adj.*, scandinavian.

scansion, *n.f.*, scansion.

scape, *n.m.*, (bot.) flower-supporting stem, scape.

scaphandre, *n.m.*, cork-jacket (for swimming); diving apparatus.

scaphandrier, *n.m.*, diver.

scaphoïde, *adj.*, scaphoid.

scapin, *n.m.*, knave, rogue, scamp. [The " knave " of Molière's comedies.]

scapolite, *n.m.*, (min.) scapolite.

scapulaire, *n.m.*, scapular scapulary; (surg.) shoulder-band.

scapulaire, *adj.f.*, (anat., orni.) scapular.

scarabée, *n.m.*, (ent.) scarabæus, beetle.

scaramouche, *n.m.*, scaramouch.

scare, *n.m.*, (ich.) scarus, parrot-fish.

scarieu-x, -se, *adj.*, (bot.) scarious.

scarificateur, *n.m.*, (surg.) scarificator ; scarifier (instrument).

scarification, *n.f.*, scarification.

scarifier, *v.a.*, to scarify.

scariole, *n.f.* *V.* **escarole**.

scarlatine, *n.* and *adj.f.*, (med.) scarlatina ; scarlet. *Fièvre* —; scarlet fever.

sceau, *n.m.*, seal ; impression of a seal ; act of confirmation ; sanction. —*x de l'État ;* Seals of the State. *Petit* —; privy seal. *Garde des* —*x :* Keeper of the Seals. — *de Notre Dame ;* (bot.) black briony. *Apposer son* —; to affix one's seal. *Mettre le* — *à ;* to seal ; to complete, to put the finishing touch to. *Etre marqué d'un* —; to be branded with. *Marqué au* — *du génie ;* pregnant with genius (V. Hugo).

⊙**scel**, *n.m.* *V.* **sceau**.

scélérat, -e, *adj.*, flagitious, nefarious, villainous, infamous, vile.

scélérat, *n.m.*, scoundrel, villain ; wretch.

scélératesse, *n.f.*, villainy, infamy, atrociousness, wickedness.

scellé, *n.m.*, waxen stamp placed officially on locks, closets, etc. ; seals. *Apposer les* —*s ;* to affix the seals. *Lever les* —*s ;* to take off the seals. *Bris de* —; unlawful breaking of the seals.

scellement (sèl-mān), *n.m.*, sealing; fastening.

sceller, *v.a.*, to put an official seal to, to seal, to seal up ; to fix, to bind ; to ratify, to confirm ; to cement ; to make fast ; (mas.) to bed.

scelleur, *n.m.*, sealer.

scène, *n.f.*, scene ; uproar, quarrel, row, scene ; (thea.) stage, scenery. *La mise en* — *d'une pièce ;* (thea.) the getting up or staging of a piece. *Faire une* — *à quelqu'un ;* to have a row with any one, to blow any one up. *Etre en* —; (thea.) to be upon the stage.

scénique, *adj.*, scenical, scenic.

scénite, *adj.*, dwelling in tents.

scénographie, *n.f.*, scenography.

scénographique, *adj.*, scenographical.

scénopégie, *n.f.*, the feast of tabernacles.

scepticisme, *n.m.*, scepticism.

sceptique, *n.m.* and *adj.*, sceptic, sceptical.

sceptre (sèp-tr), *n.m.*, sceptre ; sway, empire, dominion.

schabraque or **chabraque** (sha-), *n.f.*, shabrack.

schah (shâ), *n.m.*, Shah (of Persia).

schako (sha-), *n.m.* *V.* **shako**.

schall (shâl), *n.m.* *V.* **châle**.

scheik (shèk), *n.m.* *V.* **cheik**.

schelling (shè-lin), *n.m.*, (—*s*) shilling.

schenante (shè-), *n.m.*, (bot.) lemon-grass.

schène (skè-n), *n.m.*, (antiq.) scheme (Egyptian measure of length ; about six miles and a half).

schérif (shé-), *n.m.* (—*s*). *V.* **chérif** and **shérif**.

scherzo (skèr-), *n.m.*, (*scherzi*) (mus.) scherzo, (sportive piece in a symphony).

schiite (shi-it), *n.m.*, shiite, schismatic Mahometan.

schismatique (shis-), *n.m.* and *adj.*, schismatic ; schismatical.

schisme (shism), *n.m.*, schism.

schiste (shist), *n.m.*, (min.) schist, slate.

schisteu-x, -se (shis-), *adj.*, schistous.

schlague (shlag), *n.f.*, (milit.) flogging.

schlich (shlik), *n.m.*, (min.) slick.

schlittage, *n.m.*, sledge (for felled trees).

schlitte, *n.f.*, sledge (for felled trees) (in Erckmann-Chatrian).

schlitteur, *n.m.*, sledger (of felled trees).

schnapan (shna-), *n.m.* *V.* **chenapan**.

scholastique (sko-). *V.* **scolastique**.

scholie (sko-). *V.* **scolie**.

schooner (shoo-nèr, skoonèr), *n.m.*, (nav.) schooner.

schorl (shorl), *n.m.*, (min.) schorl.

sciage, *n.m.*, sawing.

sciagraphie, *n.f.* *V.* **sciographie**.

sciant, -e, *adj.,* boring, annoying, bothering, tiresome, tedious.

sciatérique, *adj.,* sciatheric.

sciatique, *n.f.* and *adj.,* (anat., med.) sciatica, hip gout ; sciatical.

scie, *n.f.,* saw ; (ich.) saw-fish ; (pop.) trouble, bore (tiresome thing). — *à main ;* handsaw. — *à découper ;* fret-saw. *Quelle — !* (fig.) what a bore ! — *de scieur de long ;* pit-saw.

sciemment (si-a-mãn), *adv.,* wittingly, knowingly.

science, *n.f.,* knowledge, science, learning. *Posséder une — à fond ;* to be thoroughly master of a science. *S'adonner aux —s ;* to devote one's self to the study of sciences. *La — infuse ;* intuition. *De — certaine ;* for a positive fact.

scientifique, *adj.,* scientific.

scientifiquement (-fik-mãn), *adv.,* scientifically.

scier, *v.a.,* to saw ; to reap, to cut down. — *le dos à quelqu'un ;* (pop.) to bore any one.

se **scier,** *v.r.,* to saw, to be cut with a saw.

scier, *v.n.,* to saw ; (nav.) to back water. — *à culer ;* (nav.) to put astern, to back water.

scierie (sî-rî), *n.f.,* saw-mill.

scieur, *n.m.,* sawyer ; reaper. *Fosse de — de long ;* saw-pit.

scille, *n.f.,* (bot.) squill.

scillitique, *adj.,* (pharm.) of squill.

scindé, -e, *adj.,* divided ; (of books) in parts.

scinder, *v.a.,* to divide. *Se — ;* to be divided.

scinque, *n.m.,* (erpelotogy) skink.

scintillant, -e (-til-lãn, -t), *adj.,* scintillant.

scintillation (-til-la-), *n.f.,* scintillation.

scintillement (sin-til-mãn), *n.m.,* scintillation, sparkling, twinkling.

scintiller (-til-lé), *v.n.,* to scintillate, to sparkle, to twinkle.

sciographie, *n.f.,* (arch.) sciagraphy, sciography.

sciographique, *adj.,* (arch.) sciagraphical, sciographical.

scion, *n.m.,* (bot.) scion, shoot.

scioptique, *adj.,* (opt.) scioptic.

scirpe, *n.m.,* (bot.) club-rush.

scissile, *adj.,* scissible.

scission, *n.f.,* scission, split, secession ; division (of opinions) ; defection, separation. *Faire — ;* to secede.

scissionnaire, *n.m.* and *adj.,* seceder ; seceding.

scissure, *n.f.,* (anat.) fissure ; crack, cleft.

sciure, *n.f.,* saw-dust, saw-powder.

sclarée, *n.f.,* (bot.) clary.

sclérophtalmie, *n.f.,* (med.) ophthalmy (inflammation of the conjunctiva).

sclérotique, *n.f.,* (anat.) sclerotic.

scolaire, *adj.,* scholar, academic ; (of schools). *Année — ;* academic year (October to August in France).

scolarité, *n.f.,* course of study ; curriculum.

scolastique, *adj.,* scholastical ; academic ; of schools.

scolastique, *n.m.,* scholastic, school-man.

scolastique, *n.f.,* scholasticism.

scolastiquement (-tik-mãn), *adv.,* scholastically.

scoliaste, *n.m.,* scholiast.

scolie, *n.f.,* scholium ; (Grec. antiq.) tablesong.

scolie, *n.f.,* (geom.) scholium.

scolopendre, *n.f.,* (bot.) hart's-tongue ; (ent.) scolopendra, centiped.

scombre, *n.m.,* (ich.) scomber.

scorbut, *n.m.,* scurvy.

scorbutique, *n.m.* and *adj.,* scorbutic.

scordium (-diom), *n.m.,* (bot.) water-germander.

scorie, *n.f.,* (metal.) scoria, dross.

scorification, *n.f.,* (metal.) scorification.

scorificatoire, *n.m.,* scorifier.

scorifier, *v.a.,* to scorify.

scorpioïde, *n.f.,* (bot.) scorpion's-tail.

scorpiojelle, *n.f.,* scorpion oil.

scorpion, *n.m.,* (astron.) Scorpion ; (ent.) scorpion.

scorpione, *n.f.,* (bot.) scorpion-grass, scorpion's-tail.

scorpiure, *n.f.,* (bot.) caterpillar.

scorsonère, *n.f.,* (bot.) viper's-grass.

scotie (-tî), *n.f.,* (arch.) scotia ; casement.

scribe, *n.m.,* scribe, writer.

scripteur, *n.m.,* writer of the pope's bulls.

scrofulaire, *n.f.,* (bot.) figwort.

scrofules, *n.f.pl.,* scrofula, king's evil.

scrofuleu-x, -se, *n.* and *adj.,* scrofulous person ; scrofulous.

scrotocèle, *n.f.,* (surg.) scrotocele.

scrotum (-tom), *n.m.,* (—) (anat.) scrotum.

scrupule, *n.m.,* scruple ; qualm ; scrupulousness ; scruple (weight). *Avoir des —s ;* to be scrupulous. *Lever des —s ;* to remove scruples. *Je m'en ferais — ;* I would hesitate to do it.

scrupuleusement (-lesz-mãn), *adv.,* scrupulously, strictly, exactly.

scrupuleu-x, -se, *n.* and *adj.,* over-nice, over-scrupulous person ; scrupulous, strict, nice, rigorous, precise.

scrutat-eur, -rice, *n.* and *adj.,* investigator, explorer, searcher, scrutinizer ; (of a ballot) scrutineer ; teller ; investigating, searching, scrutinizing.

scruter, *v.a.,* to scrutinize, to search closely, to investigate, to fathom ; to look carefully into.

scrutin, *n.m.,* ballot, balloting. — *de liste ;* vote by ticket. *Dépouiller le — ;* to count the votes. *Au —,* or *au — secret ;* by ballot.

soubac, *n.m.* V. **usquebac.**

sculptable (skul-tabl), *adj.,* to be sculptured ; to be carved.

sculpter (skul-té), *v.a.,* to sculpture, to carve.

sculpteur (skul-teur), *n.m.,* sculptor, carver.

sculptural (skul-tu-), *adj.,* sculptural.

sculpture (skul-tur), *n.f.,* sculpture, carving ; carved work.

scutiforme, *adj.,* scutiform, shield-shaped.

scylla, *n.m.,* Scylla. V. **charybde.**

scytale, *n.m.,* a species of snake.

scythe, *n.m.f.* and *adj.,* Scythian.

se, s', *pron.,* one's self, himself, herself, itself, themselves ; one another, each other. *Il — ruine ;* he is ruining himself. *Ils s'aiment ;* they love one another. *Cela — peut ;* that may be. *Ils — connaissent ;* they know each other. *Ils — parlent ;* they speak to each other.

séance, *n.f.,* seat (right of sitting) ; sitting (time of meeting of deliberative assemblies) ; meeting ; sitting (for one's portrait) ; recital ; lecture. *Avoir — ;* to have a seat. *Lever la — ;* to close the meeting. *Faire une — ;* to sit (at table, at play, etc.). *En — ;* sitting ; — *tenante ;* there and then, forthwith.

séant, *part.,* (jur.) sitting.

séant, *n.m.,* sitting upright. *Etre sur son —, se mettre sur son — ;* to sit up in bed.

séant, -e, *adj.,* fitting, seemly, becoming.

seau, *n.m.,* pail, bucket. *Il pleut à —x ;* it is raining in torrents.

sébacé, -e, *adj.,* sebaceous.

sébeste, *n.m.,* sebesten-plum.

sébestier (-tié), *n.m.,* (bot.) sebesten-plum-tree.

sébifère, *adj.,* (bot.) sebiferous (yielding tallow).

sébile, *n.f.,* small wooden bowl (a receptacle for the powder used to dry ink).

sec, sèche, *adj.,* dry ; lean, spare ; barren ; plain ; unadorned ; cold, unfeeling, sharp ; dissatisfied (of looks) ; (paint.) hard ; dried (of fruit, flowers, leaves, fish, &c.) ; severe (of reprimands). *Des mains sèches ;* lean hands. *Un homme* —; a spare, thin man. *Coup* —; sharp stroke. *Avoir le gosier* —; to be very dry. *Il a le pouls* —; his pulse is sharp. *Etre à* —; to have no money. *Cœur* —; unfeeling heart. *Mine sèche ;* dissatisfied look. *Perte sèche ;* dead loss. *— comme un pendu ;* as thin as a lath.

sec, *n.m.,* dryness; fodder; dry weather. *A* —; dried up; (nav.) under bare poles; empty, low; drained, exhausted; (fig.) hard up. *A* — *sur le rivage ;* (nav.) high and dry (of ships). *Mettre un étang à* —; to drain a pond; (fig.) to exhaust. *Vaisseau à* —; ship under bare poles.

sec, *adv.,* dryly, sharply. *Boire* —; to drink hard. *Répondre* —; to answer sharply.

sécable, *adj.,* divisible.

sécant, -e *adj.,* (geom.) secant.

sécante, *n.f.,* (geom.) secant.

sécateur, *n.m.,* (gard.) pruning-shears.

sécéder, *v.n.,* to secede.

sécession, *n.f.,* secession.

sécessioniste, *adj.* and *n.m.f.,* secessionist.

séchage, *n.m.,* drying.

sèche *or* **seiche,** *n.f.,* cuttle-fish.

séchée, *n.f.,* drying.

sèchement (sèah-mān), *adv.,* dryly; sharply; barrenly, without ornament, plainly.

sécher, *v.a.,* to dry, to dry up, to cure.

se sécher, *v.r.,* to dry one's self; to dry (of a thing).

sécher, *v.n.,* to dry, to wither, to pine away. *Faire* — *du linge ;* to spread out linen to dry. — *sur pied ;* to pine away, to be extremely dejected.

sécheresse (sè-shrès), *n.f.,* dryness; drought; sharpness, barrenness.

sécherie (sé-shrî), *n.f.,* (manu.) drying-house.

séchoir, *n.m.,* (manu.) drying-room; (tech.) dryer.

second, -e (sĕ-gon, -d) *adj.,* second; junior; inferior. *Eau* —; (chem.) lye-water. *De* — *main ;* second-hand. *Sans —e ;* matchless, peerless.

second (sĕ-gŏn), *n.m.,* second, assistant; second story, second floor, second class; fore cabin (in ships). *Il demeure au* —; he lives on the second floor. *En* —; second, second in command; in the second place; in a subordinate capacity; (nav.) mate. *En —e ;* in the second class (rail.).

secondaire (se-gon-dèr) *adj.,* secondary, accessory. *Enseignement* —; secondary *or* higher education.

secondairement (se-gon-dèr-mān), *adv.,* secondarily, accessorily.

seconde (se-gond), *n.f.,* second (of time); second class (in schools); (mus.) second; (print.) revise, second proof.

secondement (se-gon-dmān), *adv.,* secondly, in the second place.

seconder (se-gon-dé), *v.a.,* to second, to assist; to favor, to back, to support; to promote, to forward.

secondine (se-gon-di-n), *n.f.,* (bot.) secundine. *pl.,* secundines, after-birth.

sécot, *adj.,* lean, lanky, bony.

secouement, *n.m.* V. **secoûment.**

secouer, *v.a.,* to shake, to shake off; to jolt, to toss; to discard, to rouse; to rate, to handle roughly. — *le tête ;* to shake one's head. — *les oreilles ;* to demur, to say nay. — *le joug ;* to shake off the yoke.

se secouer, *v.r.,* to shake one's self; to take exercise; to move about; to exert one's self.

secoûment *or* **secouement,** *n.m.,* shaking, jogging, jolting.

secourable, *adj.,* helpful, helping, willing to help; relievable.

secourir, *v. a.,* to succor, to assist, to relieve, to help, to aid; to rescue.

secours, *n.m.,* help, relief, succor, assistance; aid; rescue. *Donner du* —; to render assistance. *Crier au* —; to cry out for help. *Au* —*! help ! help !* — *à domicile ;* outdoor relief. *Société de* — *mutuels ;* benefit society.

secousse, *n.f.,* shake, shock; blow, concussion, toss, tossing, jerk; (fig.) agitation; check.

secr-et, -ète, *adj.,* secret, private, hidden, undiscovered, reserved, silent. *Tenir* —; to keep secret. *Escalier* — *or dérobé ;* back-stairs, private staircase.

secret, *n.m.,* secrecy, privacy, mystery; secret; solitary confinement; secret drawer, secret spring. *C'est mon* —; that is not a fair question. *Mettre un prisonnier au* —; to put a prisoner in solitary confinement. *En* —; secretly, privately, in private. *Sous le* —; in secrecy, under the seal of secrecy. *Le* — *de Polichinelle ;* an open secret; no secret at all. — *de deux* — *de Dieu,* — *de trois* — *de tous ;* no secret but between two.

secrétaire, *n.m.,* secretary; escritoire; writing-table; (orni.) secretary-bird. — *d'ambassade ;* secretary to an embassy. — *d'état ;* secretary of state. *Sous* — *général ;* under secretary (of state).

secrétairerie (-tèr-rî), *n.f.,* secretary's office.

secrétariat, *n.m.,* secretaryship; secretary's office.

secrète, *n.f.,* (c.rel.) secret prayer.

secrètement (-krèt-mān), *adv.,* secretly, privately, in secret, in private; inwardly.

sécréter, *v.a.,* (physiology) to secrete.

sécréteur, *adj.,* secretory.

sécrétion, *n.f.,* (physiology) secretion.

sécrétoire, *adj.,* secretory, secreting.

sectaire, *n.m.f.,* sectarian.

sectateur, *n.m.,* follower, votary.

secte, *n.f.,* sect. *Faire* —; to form a sect. *Faire* — *à part ;* to differ from most people, to form a separate body.

secteur, *n.m.,* (geom.) sector.

sectile, *adj.,* sectile.

section, *n.f.,* section, division. — *de vote ;* polling-station.

sectionnement, *n.m.,* dividing into parts; division.

sectionner, *v.a.,* to divide into parts; to divide.

séculaire, *adj.,* secular, coming once in a century; centenarian; venerable; time-honored, ancient. *Un chêne* —; a venerable oak.

sécularisation, *n.f.,* secularization.

séculariser, *v.a.,* to secularize.

sécularité, *n.f.,* secularity, secular jurisdiction.

séculi-er, -ère, *adj.,* secular, worldly. *Le bras* —; the secular power.

séculier, *n.m.,* laic, layman.

séculièrement (-lièr-mān), *adv.,* secularly.

secundo (se-gon-), *adv.,* secondly.

sécurité, *n.f.,* security, safety; confidence.

sedan, *n.m.,* Sedan-cloth.

sédanoise *or* **parisienne,** *n.f.,* (print.) pearl.

sédati-f, -ve, *adj.,* (med.) sedative.

sédatif, *n.m.,* sedative.

sédentaire, *adj.,* sedentary, settled, stationary.

sédiment, *n.m.,* sediment, grounds, dregs, lees.

sédimentaire, *adj.,* sedimentary.

séditieusement (-si-euz-mān), *adv.,* seditiously.

séditieu-x, -se, *adj.,* seditious, mutinous, rebellious, riotous.

séditieux, *n.m.,* rebel, mutineer.

sédition, *n.f.,* sedition, mutiny, riot. *Faire une* —; to promote a sedition. *Éteindre une* —; to quash a sedition.

séduct-eur, -rice, *n.* and *adj.*, seducer, enticer ; seductive, enticing, fascinating ; deluding.

séduction, *n.f.*, seduction, enticement ; allurement ; bribing, subornation. — *de témoins ;* bribing of witnesses. *La — des richesses ;* the allurements of wealth.

séduire (séduisant, séduit), *v.a.*, to seduce ; to charm, to win over ; to fascinate, to captivate ; to delude, to beguile ; to suborn, to bribe ; to bewitch. — *des témoins ;* to bribe witnesses.

séduisant, -e, *adj.*, seductive, seducing ; delusive, bewitching, fascinating, tempting. *Offres —es ;* tempting offers.

ségétal, -e, *adj.*, growing in cornfields.

segment, *n.m.*, (geom.) segment.

segmentaire, *adj.*, segmental.

ségrairie, *n.f.*, woods held in common.

ségrais, *n.m.*, detached wood.

ségrégation, *n.f.*, segregation.

ségrégativement (-tiv-mān), *adv.*, separately, segregatively.

seiche, *n.f.* V. **sèche**.

séide, *n.m.*, fanatical partisan ; assassin ; blind supporter.

seigle, *n.m.*, (bot.) rye. — *ergoté ;* spurred rye. *Faux — ;* rye-grass.

*****seigneur**, *n.m.*, lord ; the Lord, squire. *Petit — ;* lordling. — *suzerain ;* lord paramount. *Notre— ;* our Lord. *A tout —tout honneur ;* honor to whom honor is due. *En grand — ;* in grand style.

*****seigneuriage**, *n.m.*, seigniorage (duty on coinage).

*****seigneurial, -e**, *adj.*, seigniorial, manorial, lordly.

*****seigneurie**, *n.f.*, seigniory, lordship ; manor. *Votre — ;* your lordship.

seime, *n.f.*, (vet.) wire-heel.

sein, *n.m.*, breast, bosom ; heart (midst) ; middle ; womb. *Au— de l'église ;* in the bosom of the church. *Donner le — à un enfant ;* to give a child the breast, to suckle.

seine, *n.f.*, fish-net, seine. *Pêche à la — ;* seine-fishing.

seing (sin), *n.m.*, sign manual, signature. *Blanc — ;* signature in blank. — *privé ;* private seal.

seize, *n.m.* and *adj.*, sixteen, sixteenth.

seizième, *n.m.f.* and *adj.*, sixteenth.

seizièmement, *adv.*, sixteenthly.

séjour, *n.m.*, stay, abode, residence, sojourn ; place, regions ; continuance ; dwelling, habitation ; delay. *Permis de — ;* permission to reside.

séjourner, *v.n.*, to stay, to sojourn, to dwell, to make a stay, to tarry ; to remain, to continue.

sel, *n.m.*, salt ; wit ; point, humor. — *gris ;* bay salt. *De bon — ;* properly salted. *A la croque au— ;* with salt only. — *gemme ;* rock-salt. — *marin ;* sea-salt. *Un miton de — ;* a peck of salt. *Au gros — ;* (fig.) coarse. *Beurre demi— ;* salt-butter. — *Anglais ;* Epsom salts. — *blanc ;* table-salt. *Gros — ;* coarse salt. *Couche de — ;* bed of salt. — *attique ;* Attic wit. *Ils ne mangeront pas un miton de — ensemble ;* (prov.) they will soon be at sixes and sevens, or will soon fall out.

sélaciens, *n.m.pl.*, (ich.) cartilaginous fishes.

sélam *or* **sélan**, *n.m.*, (—*s*) emblematic nosegay (in the East).

sélection, *n.f.*, selection.

sélénieux, *adj.*, (chem.) selenious.

sélénite, *n.f.*, (chem.) selenite.

sélénitou-x, -se, *adj.*, selenitic.

sélénium (-om), *n.m.*, (chem.) selenium.

sélénographie, *n.f.*, selenography.

sélénographique, *adj.*, selenographical.

sélin, *n.m.*, milk-parsley (bot.).

sellage, *n.m.*, saddling.

selle, *n.f.*, saddle ; stool, motion of the bowels ; water-closet ; washing board. — *de femme ;* side-saddle, lady's saddle. *Cheval de — ;* saddle-horse. *Aller à la — ;* to go to the stool. *Etre toujours en — ;* never to be out of the saddle. — *à tous chevaux ;* common saddle ; commonplace discourse. *La première — ;* the best horse in the stable. — *de calfat ;* (nav.) calking-box.

seller, *v.a.*, to saddle.

se **seller**, *v.r.*, (agri.) to harden (as land).

sellerie (sèl-rī), *n.f.*, saddlery, saddle-room.

sellette, *n.f.*, culprits' seat ; (fig.) stool of repentance ; bed (of a carriage) ; shoe-black's box ; collar (of a plow) ; cradle (of painters) ; (nav.) calking-box. *Etre sur la — ;* to be at the bar (of criminals). *Mettre sur la — ;* to haul over the coals. *Tenir sur la — ;* to cross-question, to heckle, to pump (a person).

sellier, *n.m.*, saddler.

selon, *prep.*, according to, agreeably to, conformably to, pursuant to. *On l'a traité — son mérite ;* he was treated according to his deserts. —*moi ;* in my opinion. *C'est — ;* that depends.

selon que, *conj.*, as, according as.

*****semailles**, *n.f.pl.*, sowing ; seed ; sowing-time.

semaine, *n.f.*, week ; week's work ; week's wages ; week's money ; week's pocket-money ; week's allowance. *A la — ;* by the week. *Prêter à la petite — ;* to lend money (for a short time) at high interest. — *sainte ;* Holy Week. — *grasse ;* shrove-tide. *Par — ;* a week. *La — prochaine ;* next week. *La — des quatre jeudis ;* when two Sundays come together (i.e. never). *Etre de — ;* to be on duty (for the week).

semainier, *n.m.*, officer, monk, or actor, on duty (for the week) ; case of seven razors ; letter-rack ; bangle.

semainière, *n.f.*, nun, *or* actress, on duty (for the week).

sémaphore, *n.m.*, semaphore, signal-post.

semaque, *n.f.*, fishing-boat, fishing-smack.

semblable, *adj.*, like, alike, not unlike, similar, such. — *à un torrent ;* like a torrent.

semblable, *n.m.*, like ; fellow, match, equal ; fellow-creature, fellow-man.

semblablement, *adv.*, likewise, too, also, in like manner.

⊙**semblance**, *n.f.*, resemblance, semblance, look, likeness.

semblant, *n.m.*, appearance, semblance, seeming, air, look ; pretense, show, sham. *Faux — ;* false pretense. *Faire — ;* to feign, to pretend, to dissemble, to seem, to appear as if. *Il fait — de ne pas le voir ;* he pretends not to see it. *Ne faire — de rien ;* to appear to take no notice (of) ; to feign ignorance (of). *Sans faire — de rien ;* looking as if nothing was the matter.

sembler, *v.n.*, to seem, to appear. *Cela me semble ainsi ;* it appears so to me. *Il semble ;* it seems, it appears, it would appear. *Il me semble que je le vois ;* I think, or I fancy, I see him. *Il lui semble que ;* he fancies that. *Que vous en semble ?* what do you think of it ? *Il lui semble que cela n'est rien ;* he thinks it is nothing. *Si bon lui semble ;* if he thinks fit. *C'est ce qui me semble ;* precisely as I thought. *Il semble que ce soit ;* it seems that it is. *Il me semble que c'est ;* it seems to me that it is.

semé, -e, *part.*, sowed, sown ; strewn (with) ; interspersed (with) ; (her.) aspersed. —*d'étoiles ;* bespangled with stars. — *de fleurs ;* strewn with flowers.

séméiologie, *n.f.*, semeiology.

séméiotique, *n.f.*, semeiotics.

semelle, *n.f.*, sole (of boots, shoes) ; foot (of stockings) ; length of a foot ; (carp.) sleeper ; dormant-tree ; shoe (of an anchor). — *simple ;*

single sole. *Battre la* —; to pad the hoof, to tramp ; to warm one's feet, *or* trudge about. *Reculer d'une* —; to give way a foot. *Ne pas rompre d'une* —; not to draw back a step; not to give way an inch. *Rompre la* —; (fencing) to retire in parrying. — *de dérive ;* (nav.) leeboard.

semence, *n.f.*, seed ; seeds ; saving ; fine sprigs (small nails, tin tacks) ; (fig.) cause. — *de perles ;* seed-pearl. — *d'un procès ;* cause of a lawsuit. — *de diamant ;* diamond-sparks.

semencine, *n.f.*, (pharm.) one of the three kinds of wormwood.

semen-contra (sé-mè-n-), *n.m.*, (*n.p.*) (pharm.) semen-contra, worm-seed.

semé, -e, *part., adj.*, sown, strewn, interspersed.

semer, *v.a.*, to sow, to scatter ; to spread ; to strew, to sprinkle, to disseminate. — *du blé ;* to sow wheat. — *de l'argent ;* to scatter money. — *la discorde ;* to sow discord. — *la terreur ;* to spread terror. — *des fleurs ;* to strew flowers. *Il faut — pour recueillir ;* one must sow first to reap afterwards. *Se* —; to be sowed.

semestre (-mès-), *n.m.*, half-year ; six months; half-year's duty ; half-year's income ; (milit.) six months' furlough. *Entrer en* —; to enter upon a six months' duty. *Congé de* —; six months' furlough. *Par* —; half-yearly.

semestriel, -le (-mès-), *adj.*, half-yearly.

semestrier (-mès-), *n.m.*, (milit.) soldier absent on a six months' furlough.

semeur, *n.m.*, seedsman, sower ; disseminator, spreader.

semi, *adj. invariable*, semi, demi, half.

semi-arien, -ne, *adj. and n.*, (—-—*s*) Semi-Arian.

semi-circulaire, *adj.* semicircular.

semi-double, *adj.*, semi-double.

semi-flosculeu-x, -se, *adj.*, (bot.) semiflosculous.

semi-hebdomadaire, *adj.*, semi-weekly.

semillance, *n.f.*, sprightliness, liveliness.

*****sémillant, -e**, *adj.*, brisk, lively, frisky, sprightly.

sémiller, *v.n.*, to be sprightly *or* lively ; to be brisk.

semi-lunaire, *adj.*, semi-lunar.

semi-mensuel, -le, *adj.*, fortnightly.

séminaire, *n.m.*, seminary, clerical college ; school.

séminal, -e, *adj.*, seminal.

séminariste, *n.m.*, seminarist.

sémination, *n.f.*, semination.

semi-périodique, *adj.*, semi-periodic.

semi-preuve, *n.f.*, (—-—*s*) imperfect proof, beginning of a proof.

semis, *n.m.*, seed-plot, seedling.

sémitique, *adj.*, Semitic.

semi-ton, *n.m.*, (—-—*s*) (mus.) semitone.

semoir, *n.m.*, (agri.) seed-lip ; drill-machine, corn-drill.

semonce, *n.f.*, rebuke, reprimand, lecture ; call, summons.

semoncer, *v.a.*, to reprimand, to lecture, to summon, to call.

semoule, *n.f.*, semolina.

semper-virens (sin-pèr-vi-rīns), *n.m.adj.*, (—) (bot.) coral honeysuckle ; evergreen.

sempiternel, -le (sin-), *adj.*, sempiternal, everlasting.

sénat, *n.m.*, senate ; senate-house.

sénateur, *n.m.*, senator.

sénatorerie, *n.f.*, senatorship.

sénatorial, -e, *adj.*, senatorial.

sénatorien, -ne (-in, -è-n), *adj.*, senatorial, senatorian.

sénatrice, *n.f.*, senator's lady.

sénatus-consulte (-tus-), *n.m.*, (—-—*s*) senatus-consultum ; decree (of a senator).

senau, *n.m.*, (nav.) snow (sort of vessel). *Voile de* —; try-sail.

séné, *n.m.*, senna.

sénéchal, *n.m.*, seneschal. *Grand* —; high seneschal.

sénéchale, *n.f.*, seneschal's wife.

sénéchaussée, *n.f.*, seneschal's jurisdiction ; seneschal's court.

seneçon (sè-n-son), *n.m.*, (bot.) groundsel.

senegrain, senègre, *or* **senegré**, *n.m.*, (bot.) fenugreek.

senelle, *n.f.* V. **cenelle**.

sénestre, *adj.*, ⊙left ; (her.) sinister.

sénevé (sé-n-vé), *n.m.*, (bot.) charlock, black mustard.

⊙**sénieur**, *n.m.*, senior.

sénile, *adj.*, senile, old.

sénilité, *n.f.*, senility, old age.

senne, *n.f.* V. **seine**.

sens (sänss), *n.m.*, sense, senses, feelings, passions ; understanding, judgment ; intellect ; reason, intelligence ; opinion, sentiment ; wits, reason, judgment ; meaning, import ; way, direction. *Reprendre ses* —; to come to one's senses, to come to. *Bon* —; good sense. — *commun ;* common-sense. — *propre ;* proper meaning. — *figuré ;* figurative sense. — *intime ;* consciousness. *A double* —; with double meaning. *A mon* —; in my opinion. *Dans tous les* —; in all directions, to and fro. *En tous* —; in every direction. *N'avoir pas le* — *commun ;* to be preposterous, absurd. *Tomber sous le* —; to be obvious, self-evident. *A contre* —; wrong way, in a wrong sense. — *devant derrière ;* hind part foremost ; wrong side first. *Ce mot a deux* —; that word has two meanings. *Il abonde en son* —; he is wedded to his opinion. *J'abonde dans votre* —; I am of your opinion. — *dessus dessous ;* upside down, topsy-turvy. *Etre dans son bon* —; to be in one's right senses. *Mettre quelqu'un hors de son* —; to drive any one out of his senses. *En* — *inverse ;* in a contrary direction.

sensation, *n.f.*, sensation, feeling. *Faire* —; to cause a sensation. *A* —; sensational.

sensé, -e, *adj.*, sensible, intelligent, reasonable.

sensément, *adv.*, sensibly, judiciously.

sensibilité, *n.f.*, sensibility, sensitiveness, feeling, delicacy ; tenderness, soreness ; tenderheartedness.

sensible, *adj.*, sensible ; perceptible, obvious, palpable, evident ; feeling, sensitive ; visible (horizon) ; tender, sore (of flesh). *Il se montra* — *à ma douleur;* he seemed moved by my sorrow. *C'est son endroit* —; that's his sensitive part. *Note* —; (mus.) leading note.

sensible, *n.f.*, (mus.) leading note.

sensiblement, *adv.*, sensibly, feelingly, keenly ; vividly, deeply, obviously, perceptibly, greatly, visibly, considerably, much.

sensiblerie, *n.f.*, sentimentality.

sensiti-f, -ve, *adj.*, sensitive.

sensitive, *n.f.*, (bot.) sensitive plant.

sensorial, *adj.*, (physiol.) sensorial.

sensorium (-om), *n.m.*, sensorium.

sensualisme, *n.m.*, sensualism.

sensualiste, *n.m.f. and adj.*, sensualist ; sensual.

sensualité, *n.f.*, sensuality.

sensuel, -le, *n. and adj.*, sensualist ; sensual, voluptuous.

sensuellement (-èl-män), *adv.*, sensually.

⊙**sente**, *n.f.* V. **sentier**.

senîence, *n.f.*, sentence ; maxim ; judgment ; decree, decision, verdict.

⊙**sentencié, -e**, *n.m., -e, n.f.*, convict.

⊙**sentencier**, *v.a.*, (criminal law) to condemn, to pass sentence, to sentence.

sentencieusement (-euz-män), *adv.*, sententiously.

sentencieu-x, -se, *adj.,* sententious.

sentène, *n.f.,* thread of a skein. *V.* **centaine.**

senteur, *n.f.,* scent, fragrance, perfume, odor, smell. *Pois de* —; sweet pea.

senti, -e, *part.* and *adj.,* felt, experienced, perceived. *Bien* —, *vivement* —; heartfelt, deeply felt; (fig.) expressive, impressive, well expressed.

sentier (-tié), *n.m.,* path, foot-path, pathway, by-way; lane, track; balk (in a plowed field). — *battu ;* beaten track.

sentiment, *n.m.,* feeling, sensation; sentiment; perception; sense, consciousness, sensibility; opinion. *Avoir le — de ;* to be conscious of. *Juger par* —; to judge from feeling. — *d'amour ;* feeling of love. *Selon mon* —; in my opinion. *Faire des* —; to be sentimental.

sentimental, -e, *adj.,* sentimental.

sentimentalement, *adv.,* sentimentally.

sentimentalité, *n.f.,* sentimentality.

sentine, *n.f.,* (nav.) well-room (of a ship); (fig.) sink of vice.

sentinelle, *n.f.,* sentinel, sentry. — *perdue ;* forlorn sentinel. *Faire* —; to keep sentry, to mount guard, to be on the watch.

sentir (sentant, senti), *v.a.,* to feel, to be sensible of, to have a sense of ; to smell, to scent; to taste, to have a taste of, to savor; to look like, to perceive, to experience, to foresee, to guess, to know. *Cette carpe sent la bourbe ;* this carp tastes of the mud. *Faire — quelque chose à quelqu'un ;* to impress any one with a sense of any thing, to bring home to. *Il sent les choses de loin ;* he foresees things from afar. *Se faire* —; to make itself felt.

se **sentir,** *v.r.,* to feel one's self, to know one's self, to be sensible ; to be conscious, to feel the effects of ; to be visible or perceived; to feel within one's self. *Il se sentait mourir ;* he felt himself dying. *Il ne se sent pas de froid ;* he is quite benumbed with cold. *Ne pas se — de joie ;* to be beside one's self with joy; to be in raptures. *Il se sent bien ;* he knows himself very well.

sentir, *v.n.,* to feel; to smell, to have an odor ; to have a bad smell. — *bon ;* to smell nice. — *mauvais ;* to smell bad. *Cette viande commence à* —; this meat is beginning to be tainted. *Cela ne sent pas bon ;* (fig.) I don't like the look of it.

seoir (soàr), *v.n.,* to suit, to become, to fit. *Il vous sied mal,* or *il ne vous sied pas,* (de) ; it ill becomes you to.

seoir (soàr), *v.n.,* (l.u.) to sit, to be sitting.

séparable, *adj.,* separable.

séparation, *n.f.,* separation, severing; parting ; partition. — *de biens ;* separate estate, separate maintenance. — *de corps et de biens ;* divorce *a mensâ et thoro,* or judicial separation. *Mur de* —; partition wall.

séparatiste, *n.m.,* separatist, secessionist. *adj.,* seceding.

séparément, *adv.,* separately ; disjunctively; apart, asunder.

séparer, *v.a.,* to separate, to sever, to disunite, to divide, to part, to set apart, to drive asunder, to disjoin, to divorce ; to disconnect, to cut off. — *le bon grain d'avec le mauvais ;* to separate the good seed from the bad. — *les cheveux sur le front ;* to part the hair on the forehead. — *deux hommes qui se battent ;* to part two men fighting.

se **séparer,** *v.r.,* to separate, to sever, to part, to part company (with) ; to secede, to divide ; to break up (of assemblies) ; to come off. *Il n'y a si bonne compagnie qui ne se sépare ;* the best friends must part at last.

sépia, *n.f.,* sepia. *A la* —; in sepia.

seps (sèps), *n.m.,* (erpetology) seps.

sept (sèt), *n.m.* and *adj.,* seven, seventh.

septain, *n.m.,* seven-lined stanza.

⊙**septante** (sèp-), *adj.,* seventy. *Version des* —*s ;* septuagint.

septembre (sèp-), *n.m.,* September.

septembriseur (sèp-), *n.m.,* (French hist.) septembrist, agent of the massacres of September, 1792.

septénaire (sèp-), *n.m.* and *adj.,* septenary.

septennal, -e (sèp-tè-n-nal), *adj.,* septennial.

septennalité (sèp-tè-n-na-), *n.f.,* seven years' duration.

septentrion (sèp-), *n.m.,* North ; (astron.) Lesser Bear.

septentrional, -e (sèp-), *adj.,* North, Northern.

septidi (sèp-), *n.m.,* septidi, the seventh day of the decade of the calendar of the first French republic.

septième (sè-tièm), *n.m.f.* and *adj.,* seventh : seventh day. *Elève de* —; seventh form boy (in France); lowest-class boy (in America).

septième (sè-tièm), *n.f.,* sequence of seven cards ; (mus.) seventh ; (piquet) septieme.

septièmement (sè-tièm-mān), *adv.,* seventhly.

septier (se-tié), *n.m.* *V.* **setier.**

septillion (sèp-), *n.m.,* (arith.) one quadrillion.

septimo (sèp-), *adv.,* seventhly, in the seventh place.

septique (sèp-), *adj.,* (med.) septical, septic.

septuagénaire (sèp-), *n.m.f.* and *adj.,* septuagenarian.

septuagésime (sèp-), *n.f.,* septuagesima.

septuor (sèp-), *n.m.* (—), (mus.) a piece for seven voices, or seven instruments.

septuple (sèp-), *n.m.* and *adj.,* septuple, sevenfold.

septupler (sèp-), *v.a.,* to increase sevenfold.

sépulcral, -e, *adj.,* sepulchral, cadaverous.

sépulcre, *n.m.,* sepulchre, tomb, grave.

sépulture, *n.f.,* burial, sepulture, interment, vault (tomb). *La — ecclésiastique ;* Christian burial. *Privé de* —; left unburied. *Donner la* —; to bury, to inter.

séquelle, *n.f.,* (fam.) gang, crew (of persons); set, host (of things).

séquence, *n.f.,* sequence (at cards) ; (c. rel.) sequence.

séquestration, *n.f.,* sequestration.

séquestre, *n.m.,* sequestration; sequestrator ; deposit, depository. *Mettre en* —; to sequester.

séquestré, -e, *adj.,* sequestered, solitary, lonely, retired.

séquestrer, *v.a.,* to sequester ; to put away. *se* **séquestrer,** *v.r.,* to sequester one's self.

séquin, *n.m.,* sequin (gold coin).

*****sérail,** *n.m.,* seraglio.

séran, *n.m.,* hatchel, flax comb.

sérançage, *n.m.,* hatcheling.

sérancer, *v.a.,* to hatchel, to dress (flax).

séranceur, *n.m.,* hatcheler, flax or hempdresser.

sérançoir, *n.m.,* hatchel, flax-comb.

sérancolin, *n.m.,* Serancolin marble.

séraphin, *n.m.,* seraph.

séraphique, *adj.,* seraphic.

sérasquier, *n.m.,* seraskier, pacha (commanding the troops of a province).

serbocal, *n.m.,* small glass cylinder.

serein, *n.m.,* night-dew, evening-damp.

serein (sè-rin), **-e,** (sè-rè-n), *adj.,* serene, placid, calm; happy.

sérénade, *n.f.,* serenade. *Donner une* — *à ;* to serenade.

sérénissime, *adj.,* most serene (title).

sérénité, *n.f.,* serenity, calmness ; placidness ; equanimity. *Avec* —; serenely, calmly.

séreu-x, -se, *adj.,* (med.) serous, watery.

ser-f (sèrf), **-ve** (sèrv), *n.* and *adj.,* serf ; in bondage, of serfs.

serfouette (sèr-), *n.f.*, hoe.

serfouir (sèr-), *v.a.*, to hoe.

serfouissage (sèr-), *n.m.*, (gard.) hoeing.

serge (sèrj), *n.f.*, serge.

sergent (sèr-), *n.m.*, sergeant ; (joiner's tool) cramp. — *d'armes ;* sergeant-at-arms. — *de ville ;* policeman, constable.

⊙**sergenter** (sèr-), *v.a.*, to dun ; to plague, to bore.

⊙**sergenterie** (sèr-jan-trï), *n.f.*, sergeantship.

serger *or* **sergier** (sèr-), *n.m.*, serge-weaver.

sergerie (sèr-), *n.f.*, serge-manufactory, serge-trade.

séricicole, *adj.*, silk-producing.

sériciculteur, *n.m.*, silk-grower.

sériciculture, *n.f.*, silk culture, silk husbandry.

série, *n.f.*, series.

sérieusement (-euz-mãn), *adv.*, seriously, gravely, in earnest ; for good ; coolly, coldly.

sérieu-x, -se, *adj.*, serious, grave, staid ; earnest, real, true, solid, substantial ; said, *or* meant, in earnest. *Mine—se ;* serious look.

sérieux, *n.m.*, seriousness, importance, gravity, earnestness ; (thea.) serious business, serious side, serious part. *Garder son — ;* to preserve one's gravity, to keep one's countenance. *Prendre son — ;* to grow serious, to begin to look grave. *Au — ;* in earnest, seriously. *Reprendre son — ;* to recover one's gravity.

serin (sè-rïn), *n.m.*, -e (sè-ri-n), *n.f.*, canary, canary-bird ; (fig.) muff, flat, fool.

serinage, *n.m.*, cramming, grinding (of pupils).

seriner (sè-), *v.a.*, to teach with the bird-organ. — *un oiseau ;* to teach a bird with the bird-organ ; (fig.) to coach, to cram.

serinette (sè-), *n.f.*, bird-organ ; singer of no power.

seringa (sè-), *n.m.*, (bot.) syringa.

seringue (sè-rïngh), *n.f.*, syringe, squirt.

seringuer (sè-rin-ghé), *v.a.*, to syringe, to squirt, to inject, to flash. — *un vaisseau ;* (nav.) to rake a ship.

serment (sèr-), *n.m.*, oath, promise, solemn declaration. *pl.,* swearing. *Faux — ;* false oath. *Prêter — ;* to take an oath, to be sworn. *Rompre son —, manquer à son — ;* to break one's oath. *Sous la foi du — ;* upon oath. *Faire prêter — à ;* to swear in any one, to put any one on his oath.

⊙**serment-é, -e** (sèr-), *adj. V.* **assermenté.**

sermon (sèr-), *n.m.*, sermon ; lecture, admonition.

sermonnaire (sèr-), *n.m.* and *adj.*, collection of sermons ; author of sermons ; adapted to sermons.

sermonner (sèr-), *v.a.*, (b.s.) to sermonize, to preach, to lecture.

sermonneur (sèr-), *n.m.*, (b.s.) sermonizer, preacher, lecturer.

sérosité, *n.f.*, serosity, wateriness.

serpe (sèrp), *n.f.*, bill, bill-hook, hedge-bill, pruning-bill. *C'est fait à la — ;* it is done in a bungling way.

serpent (sèr-), *n.m.*, serpent, snake, adder ; (mus.) serpent, serpent player. — *à sonnettes ;* rattlesnake. *Œil-de—,* (*—s—*) (jewel) serpent's-eye. *Langue-de—,* (*—s—*) (bot.) serpent's-tongue.

serpentaire (sèr-), *n.f.*, (bot.) serpentaria, snake-root ; dragon's-wort.

serpentaire (sèr-), *n.m.*, (astron.) Serpentarius ; (orni.) serpent-eater.

serpente (sèr-), *n.f.*, silver-paper, tissue-paper.

serpenteau (sèr-), *n.m.*, young serpent ; (firework) serpent, squib.

serpenter (sèr-), *v.n.*, to meander, to wind, to twine.

serpentin, -e (sèr-), *adj.*, serpentine (of marble ; of a horse's tongue).

serpentin (sèr-), *n.m.*, winding-pipe, worm (of a still).

serpentine (sèr-), *n.f.*, serpentine-stone ; serpentine-marble ; (bot.) ophioxylon, snake-wood.

serpette (sèr-), *n.f.*, pruning-knife, garden-knife.

serpigineu-x, -se (sèr-), *adj.*, (med.) serpiginous.

*****serpillière** (sèr-), *n.f.*, packing-cloth ; (coarse) apron, canvas.

serpolet (sèr-), *n.m.*, (bot.) wild thyme.

serrage (sèr-), *n.m.*, tightening, pressing.

serraté, -e, *adj.*, serrate, serrated.

serratiforme, *adj.*, saw-shaped.

serratule (sèr-ra-), *n.f.*, (bot.) serratula, saw-wort.

serre (sèr-), *n.f.*, greenhouse ; conservatory ; talon, claw (of birds) ; pressure, squeeze (of fruit) ; grasp, grip, clutch, hand. — *chaude ;* hot-house. — *à raisin ;* vinery. — *à ananas ;* pinery. *Avoir la — bonne ;* to have a strong grasp, grip, *or* hand.

serré, -e (sè-ré), *part.*, close, serried, compact, tight, fast ; crowded ; close-fisted, covetous ; (bot.) serrate, serrated ; small (of writing) ; concise, terse (of style). *Un nœud — ;* a tight knot. *Drap bien — ;* close-woven cloth. *Avoir le cœur — ;* to be oppressed with grief.

serré (sè-ré), *adv.*, very much ; hard (of freezing) ; impudently (of lying). *Jouer — ;* to play prudently.

serre-bosse (sèr-), *n.f.*, (—) (nav.) shank-painter.

serre-étoupe (sèr-), *n.m.*, (—) stuffing-box.

serre-file (sèr-), *n.m.*, (—-—s) (milit.) bringer up, last man ; (nav.) sternmost vessel.

serre-frein (sèr-), *n.m.*, (—-—s) (rail.) brake-man.

serrement (sèr-mãn), *n.m.*, pressing, clasping ; squeeze, squeezing. — *de cœur ;* anguish of heart ; pang. — *de main ;* hand-squeeze.

serrément (sè-ré-), *adv.*, niggardly, closely.

serre-nez (sèr-), *n.m.*, (—) (man.) twitch.

serre-nœud (sèr-), *n.m.*, (—-—s) (surg.) ligature-tightener.

serre-papiers (sèr-), *n.m.*, (—) paper-holder, set of pigeon-holes for papers.

serrer (sè-ré), *v.a.*, to press, to press closely ; to tighten, to squeeze, to grasp, to grip, to wring ; to crowd, to condense, to put close together ; to press, to push hard ; to tie (a knot) ; (print.) to lock, to lock up ; to oppress (the heart) ; (milit.) to close (the ranks) ; to clinch (one's fist, one's teeth) ; to put away ; to clasp, to draw close, to hug (the coast). — *la main à quelqu'un ;* to shake any one by the hand, to shake hands with any one. — *un nœud ;* to tighten a knot. — *le bouton à quelqu'un ;* to urge any one on. — *les pouces à quelqu'un ;* to force any one to do a thing ; to bring pressure to bear upon. *Cela serre le cœur ;* it is a heart-rending sight. — *les rangs ;* (milit.) to close the ranks. *Serrez les rangs !* close up ! — *son écriture ;* to write close. — *les dents ;* to clench one's teeth. — *le poing ;* to clench one's fist. — *la forme ;* (print.) to lock up the form. — *la muraille ;* to pass close to, *or* to skirt, the wall. — *de près ;* to press hard. — *les voiles ;* to take in the sails. — *le vent ;* to haul close to the wind ; to keep to windward. *Serrez vos livres ;* put your books away. — *les blés ;* to house the corn. — *des vêtements ;* to put away clothes. — *la bride ;* to pull in the bridle ; to pull up.

se **serrer** (sè-ré), *v.r.*, to press each other close ; to sit close, to lie close ; to stand close ; to crowd ; to tighten one's self ; to pinch, *or* stint, one's self.

serre-tête (sèr-), *n.m.*, (—) head-band ; night-cap ; bathing-cap.

serrette (sè-rèt) *or* **sarrette**, *n.f.*, (bot.) serra-tula, saw-wort.

serron (sè-), *n.m.*, seroon.

serrure (sè-rur), *n.f.*, lock. — *de sûreté ;* safety lock. *Crocheter une* — ; to pick a lock.

serrurerie (sè-rur-rî), *n.f.*, locksmith's trade, locksmith's work.

serrurier (sè-), *n.m.*, locksmith.

sertir (sèr-), *v.a.*, to set a stone (in a bezel).

sertissure (sèr-), *n.f.*, setting (in a bezel).

sérum (-rom), *n.m.*, serum.

servage (sèr-), *n.m.*, servitude, bondage, serf-dom.

serval (sèr-), *n.m.* (mam.) tiger-cat.

servant (sèr-), *adj.*, serving, in waiting ; lay (brother).

servant (sèr-), *n.m.*, (artil.) gunner, artillery-man.

servante (sèr-), *n.f.*, servant-maid, maid-ser-vant ; servant-girl ; dumb-waiter, dinner-wagon ; (print.) frisket-stand.

serve, *n.f.*, female serf.

serveur, *n.m.*, bowler (at cricket).

serviable (sèr-), *adj.*, serviceable, willing to do a service, obliging.

service (sèr-), *n.m.*, service ; duty, attend-ance ; office, function ; divine service ; set (col-lection) ; course (of dishes at meals). *Se mettre en* — ; (of servants) to go into service. *Etre au* — *de ;* to be in the service of. *Au* — ; in the army, in the service. *Qu'y a-t-il pour votre* — ? what can I do for you ? *Il a trente ans de* — ; he has served thirty years. *Etre de* — ; to be on duty. *Hors de* — ; out of use, unfit for use. *Faire le* — ; to perform the duty, or work, of ; to do duty, or officiate, at ; (of coaches) to ply be-tween. *Se mettre en* — ; to go into service.

serviette (sèr-), *n.f.*, napkin, towel. *Rond de* — ; napkin ring. — *de dessert ;* doily. — *de toilette ;* bedroom towel.

servile (sèr-), *adj.*, servile, menial ; slavish, cringing ; mean.

servilement (sèr-vil-mān), *adv.*, servilely, slavishly, meanly.

servilité (sèr-), *n.f.*, servility, servileness, slavishness, meanness, cringing.

servir (sèr-), (servant, servi), *v.a.*, to serve, to wait on, to attend ; to serve up ; to help to, to be serviceable, to be of service ; to assist ; to be of use ; to help ; (fin.) to pay (interest) ; to supply (with goods) ; (c.rel.) to assist the priest (at mass). — *à table ;* to wait at table. *Madame est servie ;* dinner is served *or* is ready. *Pour vous* — ; at your service ; with your leave.

se **servir** (sèr-), *v.r.*, to serve one's self, to be served, to be served up (of dishes). *Se* — *de ;* to use, to employ, to make use of ; to avail one's self of. *Servez-vous ;* help yourself.

servir (sèr-), *v.n.*, to serve, to be of use, to serve up, to bring in dinner *or* supper ; to be employed, to be conducive. *On a servi ;* dinner is on the table. — *sur mer, sur terre ;* to serve in the navy, in the army. — *de ;* to serve as, to do the office of. *Cela ne sert à rien ;* that is of no use. *Cela sert à plusieurs choses ;* that is used for several purposes. *A quoi sert-il de ?* of what use is it to ? *Il ne sert à rien de ;* it is of no use to. *Il ne sert à rien de s'emporter ;* it is of no use flying into a passion. *Cela sert de pain ;* that does instead of bread. *Il m'a servi de père ;* he has been as a father to me. *Cela ne sert de rien ;* that is of no avail. *Se faire* — ; to be waited upon.

serviteur (sèr-), *n.m.*, servant, man-servant. — *de l'Etat ;* servant of the State. *Votre* — *!* your servant ; I beg to be excused ; excuse me.

servitude (sèr-), *n.f.*, servitude, slavery.

ses (sè), *adj.pl.*, his, her, its, one's. *V.* **son**.

sésame, *n.m.*, (bot.) sesame, sesamum. — *ouvre-toi !* open, sesame !

sésamoïde, *adj.m.*, (anat.) sesamoid.

séséli, *n.m.*, (bot.) seseli.

sesquialtère (sès-kui-), *adj.*, (math.) sesqui-alteral.

sessile (sès-sil), *adj.*, sessile.

session (sè-), *n.f.*, session, sitting ; term (of law courts *or* universities).

sesterce (sès-), *n.m.*, (Rom. antiq.) sesterce.

sétacé, -e, *adj.*, setaceous, bristle-shaped.

séthim (-tim), *n.m.*, (bot.) shittim.

⊙**setier** (sè-tié), *n.m.*, an obsolete measure, pint.

sétifère, *adj.*, bristle-bearing, setiferous.

sétiforme, *adj.*, bristle-shaped.

sétigère, *adj.*, (bot.) setigerous, bristly.

séton, *n.m.*, seton.

*** seuil**, *n.m.*, threshold (of a door) ; sill.

seul, -e, *n.* and *adj.*, one ; alone, by one's self ; single ; mere, only, sole. *Tout* — ; all alone. *Un* — *homme ;* one man, a single man, one man only. *Un homme* — ; a lonely man, a man by himself.

seulement (seul-mān), *adv.*, only, but, solely, merely. *Un mot* — ; but one word.

seulet, -te, *adj.*, (l.u.) alone, by one's self, all alone.

sève, *n.f.*, sap ; pith ; vigor, strength. *Cet arbre est en* — ; the sap of that tree is rising.

sévère, *adj.*, severe, stern, harsh, hard, rigid, strict ; austere ; noble and regular, correct, pure. *Un juge* — ; a stern judge.

sévèrement (-vèr-mān), *adv.*, severely, harshly ; sternly ; strictly ; purely, correctly.

sévérité, *n.f.*, severity, rigidness, strictness, sternness ; austerity ; purity, correctness. *User de* — *envers quelqu'un ;* to use any one unkindly.

séveu-x, -se, *adj.*, (bot.) sappy ; (fig.) pithy, vigorous, strong.

sévices, *n.m.pl.*, (jur.) cruelty, assault.

sévir, *v.n.*, (**contre**) to use with rigor, to be severe ; to deal rigorously with ; to rage (of war, etc.).

sevrage (sĕ-), *n.m.*, weaning.

sevrer (sĕ-), *v.a.*, to wean, to deprive (of).

sèvres, *n.m.*, Sèvres porcelain.

sevreuse (sĕ-), *n.f.*, dry nurse.

sexagénaire (sèg-za-), *n.m.f.*, and *adj.*, sexa-genarian.

sexagésimal (sèg-za-), *adj.*, (math.) sexagesi-mal.

sexagésime (sèg-za-), *n.f.*, Sexagesima.

sexangulaire (sèk-sān-), *adj.*, sexangular.

sex-digitaire (sèks-), *n.m.f.* and *adj.*, (— — *s*) six-fingered person ; six-fingered.

sex-digital, -e (sèks-), *adj.*, six-fingered ; six-toed.

sexe (sèks), *n.m.*, sex ; fair sex ; womankind. *Le beau* — ; the fair sex.

sexennal, -e (sèk-sè-n-nal), *adj.*, sexennial.

sextant (sèks-), *n.m.*, sextant.

sexte (sèkst), *n.f.*, (c.rel.) sixth canonical hour ; sixth ; the sixth book of Pope Boniface VIII.'s Decretals.

sextidi (sèks-), *n.m.*, sextidi, sixth day of the decade of the calendar of the first French republic.

sextil, -e (sèks-), *adj. Aspect* — ; (astrol.) sextile.

sextillion (sèks-), *n.m.*, (arith.) one thousand trillions.

sexto, *adv.*, sixthly, in the sixth place.

sextule (sèks-), *n.m.*, apothecaries' weight, about 65 grains.

sextuor (sèks-), *n.m.*, (—) (mus.) sextet.

sextuple (sèks-), *n.m.* and *adj.*, sextuple, sixfold.

sextupler (sèks-), *v.a.*, to increase sixfold.

sexualité (sèk-sua-), *n.f.*, sexuality.

sexuel, -le (sèk-su-èl), *adj.*, sexual.

sgraffite, *n.m.* V. **graffite.**

shako (sha-), *n.m.*, (milit.) shako.

shall, *n.m.* V. **châle.**

sheling, *n.m.* V. **schelling.**

shérif (shérif), *n.m.*, sheriff.

si, *conj.*, if ; whether ; ⊙nevertheless. — *vous le faites ;* if you do it. — *je l'avais vu ;* had I seen it. *S'il vient ;* if he comes. *S'ils veulent ;* if they like. — *bien que ;* so that. — *ce n'est que ;* unless, except. — *. . . que*, however.

si, *adv.*, so, so much ; however ; yes. *N'allez pas — vite ;* do not go so fast. — *petit qu'il soit ;* however small he is, small as he is. *Je dis que —* ; I say yes. *Je gage que —* ; I bet that it is so. — *fait vraiment ;* yes indeed, oh yes ; excuse me. *Vous ne l'avez pas vu.* —, *je l'ai vu ;* you have not seen it. Yes, I have. *Il n'y a pas de — qui fasse ;* there is no excuse for it. *Avec un — on mettrait Paris dans une bouteille ;* if wishes were horses, beggars would ride, *or* such suppositions are idle. *Oh ! que —* ; oh ! yes, I would ; is n't he, though !

si, *n.m.*, (mus.) B, si.

sialagogue, *n.m.*, (med.) sialogogue.

sialisme, *n.m.*, (med.) ptyalism.

siamois, -e, *n.* and *adj.*, Siamese.

siamoise, *n.f.*, Siam cotton.

sibarite, *n.m.* V. **sybarite.**

sibilant, -e, *adj.*, hissing, sibilant.

sibylle, *n.f.*, sibyl.

sibyllin, *adj.*, sibylline.

sic, *adv.*, (Lat.) sic, thus.

sicaire, *n.m.*, hired assassin.

siccati-f, -ve, *adj.*, siccative.

siccatif, *n.m.*, siccative, dessicative, drying.

siccité (sik-si-), *n.f.*, siccity, dryness.

sicilien, -ne (-in, -èn), *n.* and *adj.*, Sicilian.

sicilique, *n.m.*, apothecaries' weight, about 97½ grains.

sicle, *n.m.*, shekel.

sicomore, *n.f.* V. **sycomore.**

sidéral, -e, *adj.* sideral, sidereal.

sidéritis, *n.m.* V. **crapaudine.**

sidéroxylon, *n.m.*, iron wood.

siècle, *n.m.*, century, hundred years ; age, time ; world ; period. *Les mœurs de notre —* ; the manners of our age. *Il y a un — qu'on ne vous a vu ;* we have not seen you for an age. *A tous les —s, aux —s des —s, dans tous les —s des —s ;* for ever and ever, in all times, in all ages.

siège, *n.m.*, seat, coach-box ; bench (of a court of justice); bishopric, see ; dickey (of a carriage); (milit.) siege ; offices. *En état de —* ; in a state of siege ; under martial law. *Equipage de —* ; siege-train. *Pièce de —* ; siege gun. *Mettre le — devant ;* to lay siege to. *Le — d'un cocher ;* a coachman's box. *Le saint —* ; the holy see. *Le — d'une société ;* the office of any society. *Lever le —* ; to raise the siege.

siéger, *v.n.*, to hold one's see (of bishops) ; to sit (of assemblies or courts) ; to be seated (fig.) ; to lie, to reside (of a thing).

sien, -ne (si-in, si-è-n), *pron.*, his, hers, its ; one's own. *Mon père et le sien ;* my father and his, hers. *Ma sœur et la sienne ;* my sister and his, hers.

sien, *n.m.*, **-ne**, *n.f.*, one's own property ; his own, her own, one's own. *Chacun le — n'est pas trop ;* let each have his own and all is fair. *Faire des —nes ;* to play pranks. *Les —s ;* one's people, relations and friends. *A chacun le —* ; to each his own.

sienne (terre de), *n.f.*, sienna earth, sienna.

sieste, *n.f.*, siesta, afternoon nap. *Faire la —* ; to take one's afternoon's nap.

sieur, *n.m.*, (jur.) mister, Mr., the said.

sifflable, *adj.*, that deserves to be hissed.

sifflage, *n.m.*, wheezing (of lungs).

sifflant, -e, *adj.*, hissing, whistling ; sibilant ; wheezing.

sifflement, *n.m.*, whistling, whistle ; hissing, hiss ; whiz, whizzing (of the wind, an arrow, etc.); wheezing.

siffler, *v.n.*, to whistle, to hiss, to whiz ; to wheeze.

siffler, *v.a.*, to whistle ; to hiss at ; to sing (of birds); to prompt. — *quelqu'un ;* to prompt any one. — *une pièce ;* to hiss a piece. — *un acteur ;* to hiss an actor.

sifflerie, *n.m.*, hissing.

sifflet, *n.m.*, whistle, catcall ; windpipe ; (nav.) boatswain's call. *Un coup de —* ; a whistle, a signal. *Couper le — à quelqu'un ;* (triv.) to cut any one's throat ; to shut up, or silence, any one.

siffleu-r, *n.m.*, **-se**, *n.f.*, whistler, hisser, singer.

siffleur, *n.m.*, (orni.) wood-wren ; piping bull-finch.

siffleu-r, -se, *adj.*, whistling, piping (of birds) that wheezes (of horses). *n.m. ; un —*, (of horses) a roarer.

sigillé, -e (-jil-lé), *adj.*, sigillated. *Terre —e ;* bole.

sigisbée, *n.m.*, cicisbeo, lover.

sigisbéisme, *n.m.*, cicisbeism.

sigmoïde, *adj.*, (anat.) sigmoid, sigmoidal.

***signal**, *n.m.*, signal ; word.

***signalé, -e**, *adj.*, signalized ; signal ; remarkable, conspicuous.

***signalement**, *n.m.*, description (of a man).

***signaler**, *v.a.*, to give the description of ; to point out, to mention, to notice ; to mark out ; to give a signal, to signalize.

se **signaler**, *v.r.*, to signalize, *or* distinguish, one's self.

signaliste, *n.m.*, signalman.

***signataire**, *n.m.f.*, signer, subscriber. *adj.* signatory.

***signature**, *n.f.*, signature, sign, sign-manual ; signing.

***signe**, *n.m.*, sign, mark ; beck, nod ; indication, token, badge ; omen ; mark (on the skin). *Faire —* ; to make signs, to beckon. *Faire — de la main ;* to beckon with the hand. — *de la tête ;* nod. *Faire le — de la croix ;* to cross one's self.

***signer**, *v.a.*, to sign, to subscribe.

***se* signer**, *v.r.*, to cross one's self ; to make the sign of the cross.

signer, *v.n.*, to sign, to subscribe one's self.

signet (si-nè), *n.m.*, small sign ; tassel, mark (for books).

⊙***signifiance**, *n.f.*, significance, token, testimony, sign, mark.

***signifiant, -e**, *adj.*, (theol.) significant, significative, expressive.

***significati-f, -ve**, *adj.*, significative, significant.

***signification**, *n.f.*, signification ; meaning, sense, acceptation ; (jur.) legal notice.

***significativement**, *adv.*, with force, significantly.

***signifier**, *v.a.*, to signify, to mean, to notify, to declare, to announce, to intimate ; (jur.) to serve. *Que signifie ce mot ?* what is the meaning of this word ? *Faire —* ; to give notice of. *Je lui ai signifié d'avoir à s'y trouver ;* I gave him notice to be sure and be there.

***se* signifier**, *v.r.*, (jur.) to be served.

sikh, *n.m.*, *adj.*, Sikh (East Indian).

sil, *n.m.*, yellow ocher (of the ancients).

silence, *n.m.*, silence, stillness ; secrecy, omission, pause ; (mus.) rest. *Faire —* ; to keep silence, to be silent. *Rompre le —* ; to break the silence. *Imposer —* ; to silence. *Passer sous —* ; to pass over in silence, not to mention. *Réduire au —* ; to silence. *Garder, or observer, le —* ; to keep silence, *or* remain silent. *En —* ; silently, without noise, gently. *Dans le —* ; in secret, secretly.

silencieusement (-euz-mān), *adv.*, silently.

silencieu-x, -se, *adj.*, silent, still.

silène, *n.m.*, (myth.) Silenus; Satyr.

silène, *n.f.*, (bot.) catch-fly.

silex (-lèks), *n.m.*, silex, flint.

silhouette *or* **silouette,** *n.f.*, silhouette, outline; profile.

silicate, *n.m.*, (chem.) silicate.

silice, *n.f.*, (chem.) silica, flint.

siliceu-x, -se, *adj.*, silicious.

silicique, *adj.*, (chem.) silicic.

silicium, *n.m.*, (chem.) silicon, silicium.

silicule, *n.f.*, (bot.) silicle, silicula, seed-pouch.

siliculeu-x, -se, *adj.*, (bot.) siliculous, siliculose.

silique, *n.f.*, (bot.) siliqua, silique, two-valved pod.

siliqueu-x, -se, *adj.*, (bot.) siliquous, siliquose.

***sillage,** *n.m.*, (nav.) track, wake; steerage-way, sea-way.

sillée, *n.f.*, (agri.) trench.

***siller,** *v.n.*, (l.u.) (nav.) to run ahead, to make headway.

***siller,** *v.a.*, to close the eyes (of a hawk).

***sillet,** *n.m.*, nut (of stringed instruments).

***sillomètre,** *n.m.*, (nav.) sillometer, log.

***sillon,** *n.m.*, (agri.) furrow, ridge; trench, drill; track, trail (of light); wake (of ships); (anat.) groove; wrinkle; (poet.) *pl.*, fields, plains.

***sillonner,** *v.a.*, to furrow, to plow, to ridge, to cut; to streak, to flash through, to glint; (anat.) to groove.

silo, *n.m.*, pit (for preserving grain).

silouette, *n.f. V.* **silhouette.**

silphium (-fiom), *n.m.*, (n.p.) silphium, laser.

silure, *n.m.*, (ich.) silurus, silure.

silurien, -ne (ri-ĭn, -è-n), *adj.*, (geol.) silurian.

silves, *n.f.pl. V.* **sylves.**

simagrée, *n.f.*, grimace, pretense, show, affected way. *pl.*, affectation, grimaces, fuss.

simaise, *n.f. V.* **cimaise.**

simarouba, *n.m.*, (bot.) simaruba.

simarre, *n.f.*, (of priests) cassock; woman's long gown; justice's robe.

simbleau, *n.m.*, (carp.) radius-line.

similaire, *adj.*, similar.

similarité, *n.f.*, similarity, likeness.

similitude, *n.f.*, similitude, similarity; comparison; (rhet.) simile.

similivoire, *n.m.*, imitation ivory.

similor, *n.m.*, pinchbeck.

simoniaque, *n.m.* and *adj.*, simoniac; simoniacal.

simonie, *n.f.*, simony.

simoun (-moon), *n.m.*, simoom.

simple, *adj.*, simple, single; only, only one, but one, bare, mere; common, private (of soldiers); plain, unadorned, simple-minded; silly. *Des souliers à — semelle;* single-soled shoes. *Un — soldat;* a common soldier, a private. *Un homme —;* an unpretending man. *C'est tout —;* (fam.) it is quite natural; it 's a matter of course; why, of course; why not.

simple, *n.m.*, simple, medicinal plant; (mus.) simple air.

simplement, *adv.*, simply, only, solely, merely, singly; plainly, without any ornament; artlessly; silily. *Tout —;* merely, that's all.

⊙**simplesse,** *n.f.*, simplicity, simpleness.

simplicité, *n.f.*, simplicity, simpleness, artlessness, plainness; silliness.

simplification, *n.f.*, simplification.

simplifier, *v.a.*, to simplify.

simulacre, *n.m.*, image, idol; phantom; shadow; appearance, feint, sham. *Un — de combat;* a sham fight.

simulation, *n.f.*, (jur.) feigning, feint, simulation.

simulé, -e, *adj.*, fictitious, feigned, false, pretended, counterfeit, sham.

simuler, *v.a.*, to feign, to sham. — *une attaque;* to make a false attack.

simultané, -e, *adj.*, simultaneous.

simultanéité, *n.f.*, simultaneousness.

simultanément, *adv.*, simultaneously.

sinapisé, -e, *adj.*, (med.) infused with mustard.

sinapisme, *n.m.*, sinapism, mustard-plaster.

sincère, *adj.*, sincere, true, open-hearted, honest.

sincèrement (-sèr-mān), *adv.*, sincerely, truly, plainly, ingenuously, honestly.

sincérité, *n.f.*, sincerity, sincereness, open-heartedness, honesty.

sincipital, -e, *adj.*, sincipital.

sinciput (-put), *n.m.*, sinciput.

sindon, *n.m.*, Christ's shroud; (surg.) pledget.

sinécure, *n.f.*, sinecure.

sinécuriste, *n.m.*, sinecurist.

sine quâ non, *adj.inv.*, sine quâ non, indispensable.

singe, *n.m.*, ape, monkey, baboon; monkey (of pile-drivers); windlass; pantograph (copying-machine). *Payer en monnaie de —;* to jeer at a man instead of paying him, *or* to pay with promises.

singe, *adj.*, (l.u.) apish.

singer, *v.a.*, to ape, to mimic.

singerie (sin-jrĭ), *n.f.*, apish trick, antic, grimace, trick; mimicry.

singe-u°, -resse, *adj.*, that apes, apish.

singeur, *n.m.*, ape (imitator).

singulariser, *v.a.*, to singularize, to render singular, odd.

se **singulariser,** *v.r.*, to render one's self singular, odd; to affect singularity.

singularité, *n.f.*, singularity; peculiarity; oddness.

singuli-er, -ère, *adj.*, singular; peculiar; odd; single (combat). *Combat —;* single combat.

singulier, *n.m.*, (gram.) singular.

singulièrement (-lièr-mān), *adv.*, singularly, peculiarly, in a singular manner, oddly.

sinistre, *adj.*, sinister, inauspicious; lurid, forbidding; dismal. *Présage —;* sinister foreboding. *Augure —;* unlucky omen.

sinistre, *n.m.*, accident, disaster; casualty, loss, damage.

sinistrement, *adv.*, sinisterly, inauspiciously, dismally.

sinologue (-log), *n.m.*, sinologist, Chinese scholar.

sinombre, *adj.*, (of a lamp) shadowless.

sinon, *conj.*, otherwise, else, or else; except, save, if not, unless.

sinon que, *conj.*, save that; except.

sinople, *n.m.*, (her.) sinople, vert; (min.) a variety of quartz.

sinué, -e, *adj.*, (bot.) sinuate.

sinueu-x, -se, *adj.*, sinuous, winding, meandering.

sinuosité, *n.f.*, sinuosity, winding, meandering.

sinus (-nus), *n.m.*, (math.) sine; (anat.) sinus.

siphilis, *n.f. V.* **syphilis.**

siphilitique, *adj. V.* **syphilitique.**

siphon, *n.m.*, siphon; water-spout (at sea).

sire, *n.m.*, sire (title of kings and emperors); ⊙sir (lord); (in fables) squire. *Un pauvre —;* a poor wretch, wight.

sirène, *n.f.*, siren, mermaid, sea-maid.

sirius (-us), *n.m.*, (astron.) Sirius.

siroco *or* ⊙**siroc,** *n.m.*, Sirocco.

sirop, *n.m.*, syrup.

siroter, *v.a.*, to sip. *V.* **déguster.**

siroter, *v.n.*, to tipple.

siroteur, *n.m.*, tippler.

sirsacas, *n.m.*, Indian cotton-cloth.

sirtes, n.f.pl. V. **syrtes.**

sirupeu-x, -se, adj., syrupy.

sirvente, n.m., sirvente (war song).

sis, -e, adj., (jur.) seated, situate, situated.

sison, n.m., honeywort.

sistelle, n.f., (orni.) nut-hatch.

sistre, n.m., (antiq.) sistrum (Egyptian timbrel).

sisymbre, n.m., (bot.) sisymbrium.

sisyphe, n.m., Sisyphus. Le rocher de —; (fig.) long, profitless, and hard work.

site, n.m., site, landscape, scenery.

sitôt, adv., so soon, as soon. De —; for some time to come.

sitôt que, conj., as soon as.

situation, n.f., situation, site; state of affairs; position; predicament; (nav.) bearing of coasts; (com.) statement (of accounts). En —; in a conspicuous situation; in one's proper place or character.

situé, -e, adj., situate, situated, lying.

situer, v.a., to place, to seat.

six, n.m. and adj., six, sixth; sixth day. [For the pronunciation of this word, V. **dix.**]

⊙**sixain,** n.m. V. **sizain.**

sixième (si-zièm), n.m. and adj., sixth; sixth day (of a period); sixth form boy (in England); second form boy (in France); sixth class (at school).

sixième (si-zièm), n.f., six cards of the same suit (cards; piquet); sixth form (in England); second form (in France); highest class (in America).

sixièmement (si-zièm-mãn), adv., sixthly.

sixte (sikst), n.f., (mus.) sixth. Le Pape — Quint; Pope Sixtus the fifth.

sizain, n.m., stanza of six lines; six packs of cards.

sizette, n.f., sizette (card game).

slave, n.m.f. and adj., Slav; Sclavonian, Sclavonic.

sloop or sloupe (sloop), n.m., (nav.) sloop.

smalah, n.f. (n.p.), smala (Arab chief's camp).

smalt, n.m., smalt, blue glass.

smérinthe, n.m., (ent.) hawk-moth.

*****smille,** n.f., (mas.) scapple-ax.

*****smiller,** v.a., (mas.) to scapple.

sobre, adj., sober, sparing, temperate, abstemious.

sobrement, adv., soberly, moderately, temperately, sparingly, abstemiously.

sobriété, n.f., sobriety, soberness, temperance, moderation, abstemiousness.

sobriquet, n.m., nickname. Donner un — à; to nickname.

soc, n.m., plowshare.

sociabilité, n.f., sociability, sociableness, good fellowship, intercourse.

sociable, adj., sociable, social.

sociablement, adv., sociably, socially.

social, -e, adj., social; (com.) (name of) firm. Sous la raison — e; under the style, name (of).

socialement (-sial-mãn), adv., socially, in a social manner.

socialisme, n.m., socialism.

socialiste, n.m.f., socialist.

sociétaire, n.m.f. and adj., associate, partner, shareholder; member of a society, of a company; foundation member.

société, n.f., society, community; company, partnership, club, class; social life. — de commerce; trading company. — anonyme; joint-stock company. — en commandite; limited liability company. Faire une — avec quelqu'un; to enter into partnership with any one. Être en —; (at cards) to be partners. Talents de —; accomplishments. Règle de —; (arith.) fellowship, rule of fellowship.

socinianisme, n.m., Socinianism.

socinien, -ne (ni-in, -è-n), n. and adj., Socinian.

socle, n.m., (arch.) socle, pedestal, stand, base, plinth, socket. — continu; basement.

socque, n.m., clog, galoche, patten, overshoe.

socratique, adj., socratic.

sodium (-om), n.m., (chem.) sodium.

sodomie, n.f., sodomy.

sodomite, n.m., sodomite.

sœur (seur), n.f., sister; nun. —s germaines; sister of the whole blood. —s consanguines; sisters on the father's side. —s utérines; sisters on the mother's side. —s jumelles; twin sisters. — de lait; foster-sister. Demi—; step-sister. Belle—; sister in law. Les neuf —s; the Muses, the sacred Nine. — laie, — converse; lay-sister. Communauté de —s; sisterhood.

sœurette, n.f., little sister, dear little sister.

sofa, n.m., sofa, ottoman.

soffite, n.m., (arch.) soffit.

sofi or soufi, n.m., (—s) sofi, dervis, dervise.

sofi or sophi, n.m., Sofi, Sophi (a title of the King of Persia).

soi, pron., one's self, self, itself. Penser à —; to think of one's self. Etre à —; to be one's own master.

soi-disant, adj., self-styled, would-be, pretended, so-called, supposed.

soie, n.f., silk; hair (of a few species of dogs); bristle (of hogs); tongue (of knives, swords); (vet.) V. **seime.** — de bourre; floss-silk. — crue, — grège; raw silk. — plate; floss-silk. Des jours filés d'or et de —; halcyon days. Peau de —; Japanese silk.

soierie (soa-rî), n.f., silk, silk-trade; silk-manufactory. pl., silks, silk goods. Marchand de —; silk-mercer. Maison de —; silk-house.

soif, n.f., thirst. Avoir —; to be thirsty, to thirst after. Avoir grand' —; to be very thirsty. Mourir de —; to be almost dying with thirst. Etancher sa —; to quench one's thirst. — des richesses; thirst for riches, greed. Garder une poire pour la —; to lay up something for a rainy day.

soigné, -e, adj., carefully done; highly finished, elaborate; nicely got up; sound, sharp.

*****soigner,** v.a., to take care of, to look after, to attend, to attend to, to mind, to nurse. — un malade; to nurse a sick person.

*****se soigner,** v.r., to take care of one's self, to nurse one's self.

*****soigneusement** (-eûz-mãn), adv., carefully.

*****soigneu-x, -se,** adj., careful, regardful, solicitous; mindful.

soi-même, pron., one's self; itself.

soi-mouvant, adj., (philos.) self-moving.

soin, n.m., care, attendance on. pl., attentions, solicitude; pains, trouble. Avoir — de quelque chose; to take care of anything. Je vous en laisse le —; I leave it to your care. Rendre des —s à quelqu'un; to be attentive to any one. Petits —s; little, or minute, attentions. Etre aux petits —s avec quelqu'un; to be all attention to any one. Manque de —; carelessness. Avec —; carefully.

soir, n.m., evening, night. Du matin au —; from morning till, or to, night. Bon —; good evening. Hier —, hier au —; last evening, last night. Ce —; this evening, to-night. Sur le —; towards evening; at night-fall. Le — de la vie; the declining years.

soirée, n.f., evening (duration of the evening); evening party. Aller en —; to go out to a party, to go to an evening party. Passer la —; to spend the evening. Dans la —; during the evening.

soit, adv., be it so, let it be so, well and good, I grant it. Hé bien, —; well, be it so. Ainsi —-il; so be it. — dit; be it said.

soit, conj., either, whether, or. — l'un, — l'autre; either one or the other. — que; (with a verb) whether.

soixantaine (soa-săn-tĕ-n), *n.f.*, about, or some, sixty; some sixty years of age.

soixante (soa-sănt), *n.m.* and *adj.*, sixty. —*dix;* seventy. —*douze;* seventy-two.

soixanter (soa-săn-té), *v.n.*, to reckon sixty (piquet). [sixtieth.

soixantième (soa-săn-tièm), *n.m.* and *adj.*,

sol, *n.m.*, soil; ground; ground-plot; (mus.) G, sol; coin. ⊙*V.* **sou.**

solaire, *adj.*, solar. *Cadran* —; sun-dial.

solandre, *n.f.*, (vet.) solanders, sallenders.

solanées, *n.f.pl.*, (bot.) solanaceæ.

solanum (-nom), *n.m.*, (bot.) solanum.

solbatu, -e, *adj.*, (of horses) surbated.

solbature, *n.f.*, (vet.) quitter, quitter-bone.

soldanelle, *n.f.*, (bot.) soldanel; convolvulus soldanella.

soldat, *n.m.*, soldier. *pl.*, soldiery, rank and file. — *de la milice;* militiaman. *Simple* —; private soldier. — *du train;* army service corps man. *Se faire* —; to enlist.

soldatesque, *n.f.* and *adj.*, soldier-like, soldierly, soldiery.

solde, *n.f.*, (milit.) pay. *Demi-* —; half-pay.

solde, *n.m.*, (com.) settlement; clearance sale, clearance, balance. *Pour — de tout compte;* in full of all demands.

solder, *v.a.*, to pay, to settle, to discharge; to keep in pay; to liquidate; to sell off, to clear off. — *un compte;* to settle an account. — *des troupes;* to pay troops.

sole, *n.f.*, sole (of animals); (agri.) brake; (ich.) sole; (arch.) sleeper. — *battue;* (vet.) quitter, quitter-bone.

soléaire, *adj.*, (anat.) solear.

solécisme, *n.m.*, solecism.

***soleil**, *n.m.*, sun; sunshine; star; sunflower; (c. rel.) monstrance; sun-fish; (print.) squabble; (fireworks) catherine wheel. — *couchant;* sunset. *Se chauffer au* —; to bask in the sun. *Le — luit pour tout le monde;* the sun shines upon all alike. *Il fait du* —; the sun is shining. *Coup de* —; sunstroke. *Le — se couche;* the sun is setting, is going down. *Il fait un beau* —; it is beautiful sunshine. *Au* —; in the sun. *Au grand* —; at midday; in bright sunshine.

soleillé, -e, *adj. V.* **ensoleillé.**

solen (-lè-n), *n.m.*, (conch., surg.) solen.

solénite, *n.f.*, (fos.) solenite.

solennel, -le (so-la-nèl), *adj.*, solemn, awful.

solennellement (-la-nèl-măn), *adv.*, solemnly.

solennisation (-la-ni-) *n.f.*, solemnization.

solenniser (-la-ni), *v.a.*, to solemnize.

solennité (-la-ni-), *n.f.*, solemnity, solemnness, solemn occasion.

solfatare, *n.f.*, (geol.) solfatara.

solfège, *n.m.*, (mus.) solfeggio.

solfier, *v.a.*, (mus.) to sol-fa.

solidaire, *adj.*, conjointly liable; jointly and separately liable; solidary; conjointly answerable.

solidairement (-dèr-măn), *adv.*, conjointly; jointly and severally.

solidarité, *n.f.*, solidarity, joint liability; joint and separate liability, joint interest, fellowship, brotherhood.

solide, *adj.*, solid, strong, firm; steadfast, stable, fast, substantial, sound, real; solvent. *Un jugement* —; a sound judgment.

solide, *n.m.*, solid; solid body; solid figure; reality. *Viser au* —; to have an eye to the main chance.

solidement (-lid-măn), *adv.*, solidly, substantially; firmly; soundly.

solidification, *n.f.*, solidification.

se **solidifier**, *v.r.*, to solidify, to become solid; to acquire solidity.

solidité, *n.f.*, solidity, strength; steadfastness, stability, firmness, soundness.

soliloque, *n.m.*, soliloquy.

soliloquer, *v.n.*, to soliloquize.

solin, *n.m.*, (arch.) space between two joists or rafters.

solipède, *n.m.* and *adj.*, soliped; solipedous.

soliste, *n.m.*, solo singer, solo player, soloist.

solitaire, *adj.*, solitary, lonely, desert, single.

solitaire, *n.m.*, hermit, recluse, solitary individual; brilliant (diamond).

solitairement (-tèr-măn), *adv.*, solitarily.

solitude, *n.f.*, solitude, loneliness, wilderness, desert.

solive, *n.f.*, joist, rafter.

soliveau, *n.m.*, small joist.

⊙**sollicitable**, *adj.*, that may be solicited.

sollicitation (sol-li-), *n.f.*, solicitation; entreaty; application; instigation; canvassing.

solliciter (sol-li-), *v.a.*, to solicit; to apply for; to incite, to urge; to entreat, to incite; to induce; to canvass.

solliciter, *v.a.*, to solicit, to petition.

solliciteu-r, *n.m.*, -**se** (sol-li-), *n.f.*, solicitor, solicitress, petitioner, canvasser.

sollicitude (sol-li-), *n.f.*, solicitude, care, anxiety. *Avoir de la — pour;* to be solicitous (for), anxious (about).

solo, *n.m.*, (—) (mus.) solo.

solstice, *n.m.*, solstice. — *d'été;* summer solstice.

solsticial, -e, *adj.*, solstitial.

solubilité, *n.f.*, solubility.

soluble, *adj.*, solvable; soluble, dissolvable.

solution, *n.f.*, solution; break; dissolution; (math.) solution; resolution; (jur.) discharge.

solvabilité, *n.f.*, solvency.

solvable, *adj.*, solvent.

somatologie, *n.f.*, somatology.

sombrage, *n.m.*, (agri.) first dressing.

sombre, *adj.*, dark, somber, dull, dim, dingy, lurid; gloomy; overcast; melancholy, sad, sullen. *Temps* —; gloomy weather. *Lumière* —; dull, or dim, light. *Couleurs* —*s;* somber colors.

sombrer, *v.n.*, (nav.) to founder, to go down; (agri.) to give a first dressing to.

sombrero, *n.m.*, sombrero, broad-brimmed hat.

sommaire, *n.m.* and *adj.*, summary, compendium, abridgment, abstract; summary, compendious.

sommairement (-mèr-măn), *adv.*, summarily, briefly, succinctly.

sommation, *n.f.*, summons, notice; (jur.) process, summons; (math.) summation. *Signifier une — à quelqu'un;* to serve a summons on any one. *Faire les trois* —*s;* to read the Riot Act.

somme, *n.f.*, burden; sum (quantity); amount; (math.) sum; (lit.) summary, compendium. *Bête de* —; beast of burden. — *totale;* sum-total. — *toute, en* —; finally, in short. *Une — de;* a stated sum.

somme, *n.m.*, nap (sleep). *Faire un* —; to have a nap, to have forty winks. *Ne faire qu'un* —; never to wake all night, to sleep the night through.

***sommeil**, *n.m.*, sleep. *Avoir* —; to be sleepy. *J'ai bien* —; I am very sleepy. *Profond* —; deep sleep. *Cela porte au* —; that induces sleep. — *agité;* restless sleep. *Dormir d'un profond* —; to sleep soundly. *Accablé de* —; dreadfully sleepy. *Tomber de* —; *n'en pouvoir plus de* —; to be overcome with sleep. *Il n'en peut plus de* —; he is quite worn out for want of sleep. *Le — me gagne;* I am getting sleepy. *Avoir le — léger;* to be a light sleeper.

***sommeiller**, *v.n.*, to slumber, to doze.

sommeli-er, *n.m.*, -**ère**, *n.f.*, butler, cellarman.

sommellerie (so-mèl-rî), *n.f.*, butler's place; pantry, buttery.

sommer, *v.a.*, to summon, to call upon, to charge, to challenge ; (math.) to sum up, to cast up. — *quelqu'un de sa parole ;* to call upon any one to fulfil his promise. — *une place de se rendre ;* (milit.) to summon a fortress to surrender.

sommet, *n.m.*, top, apex, summit ; pinnacle ; acme, zenith ; crown, top (of the head) ; (bot.) vertex ; (arch.) crown ; (geom.) apex, vertex.

sommier, *n.m.*, pack-horse ; hair-mattress ; wind-chest (of an organ) ; wrest plank, sound-board (of pianos) ; (arch.) breastsummer ; summer ; register-book ; (print.) winter. — *élastique ;* spring mattress.

sommité (som-mi-), *n.f.*, summit, top, apex ; head, eminent man ; principal, *or* chief, point. *Une des —s ;* (fig.) one of the distinguished men.

somnambule (som-nãn-), *n.m.f.* and *adj.*, somnambulist.

somnambulisme, *n.m.*, somnambulism.

somnifère (som-ni-), *n.m.* and *adj.*, (med.) narcotic ; somniferous.

somnolence (som-no-), *n.f.*, somnolence, somnolency.

somnolent, -e, *adj.*, (med.) somnolent, sleepy, drowsy.

somptuaire, *adj.*, sumptuary.

somptueusement (-euz-mãn), *adv.*, sumptuously, splendidly.

somptueu-x, -se, *adj.*, sumptuous, gorgeous, splendid.

somptuosité, *n.f.*, sumptuousness, splendor.

son, *n.m.*, bran ; (phys.) sound ; freckle. *Tache de —;* freckle. — *aigu ;* shrill sound. — *de cloches ;* ringing of bells. — *du tambour ;* beat of the drum, sound of the drum.

son, **sa**, **ses**, *adj.*, his, her, its, one's. *Son frère, sa sœur et ses enfants ;* his brother, sister, and children. *Son âme ;* his, her, soul. [*Son* is used for the *fem.* instead of *sa* when the word following begins with a vowel or a silent *h.*]

sonate, *n.f.*, (mus.) sonata.

sondage, *n.m.*, sounding ; (mining) boring.

sonde, *n.f.*, plummet, fathom-line ; (nav.) sounding-line, sounding-lead ; (surg.) probe ; (manu.) proof-stick ; (mining) bore. *pl.*, (nav.) soundings. *Jeter la —;* (nav.) to heave the lead, to sound. *Plomb de —;* sounding lead.

sonder, *v.a.*, to sound, to fathom ; to ullage, to taste ; to scrutinize, to examine thoroughly, to investigate, to explore ; to probe, to search. — *le terrain ;* (mining) to bore ; (fig.) to see how matters stand. — *le gué ;* to sound the ford ; (fig.) to reconnoiter ; to see how matters stand. — *la côte ;* to ascertain the depth, *or* to take soundings (along the coast). — *une plaie ;* to probe a wound. — *un fromage ;* to pierce a cheese. — *quelqu'un ;* to sound, to pump, any one.

sonder, *v.n.*, (nav.) to heave the lead, to sound, to take soundings.

sondeur, *n.m.*, (nav.) leadsman ; (min.) borer.

songe, *n.m.*, dream, dreaming. *Faire un —;* to have a dream. *Voir en —;* to see in a dream, to dream. *Mal d'autres n'est que —;* other people's woes do not affect us much.

songe-creux, *n.m.*, (—) dreamer, visionary.

⊙**songe-malice**, *n.m.*, (—, *or* — - —s) mischief-maker.

songer, *v.n.*, to dream, to muse ; to think, to reflect, to mean ; to intend, to devise, to purpose, to propose, to consider, to cast about (for) ; to aim (at). — *profondément ;* to think deeply. — *à quelque chose ;* to think of anything (suddenly). *Songez à ce que vous faites ;* mind what you are about. *Sans y —;* unawares, unthinkingly. *Il songe à se marier ;* he is thinking of marrying, *or* he contemplates marriage. *Songez-y, songez-y bien ;* mind what you are about ; beware. *Maintenant que j'y songe ;* now that I think of it ; now that I remember.

songer, *v.a.*, to dream (in one's sleep) ; to dream, to imagine, to think of. — *une comédie ;* to think of a comedy, to imagine a comedy. *Ne — que bals, que fêtes ;* to think of nothing but balls, parties.

songerie, *n.f.*, dreaming, musing, idle dream.

songeur, *n.* and *adj.m.*, (l.u.) dreamer ; thoughtful, dreamy.

⊙**sonica**, *adv.*, in the nick of time, just in time. *On allait partir sans lui, il est arrivé —;* they were going to set out without him, when he arrived just in the nick of time. *Il a gagné —;* (basset) he has won just in the nick of time.

***sonnaille**, *n.f.*, bell (attached to the neck of cattle).

***sonnailler**, *v.n.*, (fam.) to ring often ; to keep ringing.

***sonnailler**, *n.m.*, bell-wether (of sheep).

sonnant, -e, *adj.*, sounding, that has a clear sound ; sonorous. *Espèces —es ;* hard cash, money down, ready money. *A sept heures —es ;* just as the clock was striking seven.

sonner, *v.n.*, to sound, to emit a sound ; to chink, to ring ; to strike (of clocks) ; to toll ; to ring the bell. *Faites — cet écu ;* ring that crown-piece. — *de la trompette ;* to sound the trumpet. — *du cor ;* to blow the French horn. *Voilà midi qui sonne ;* the clock is striking twelve, it is striking twelve. *On sonne ;* there is a ring at the door, *or* the bell is ringing.

sonner, *v.a.*, to sound, to ring ; to toll ; to strike (of watches, clocks) ; to wind (of instruments) ; (milit.) to sound. — *les cloches ;* to ring the bells. — *le dîner ;* to ring for dinner. — *ses gens ;* to ring for the servants. — *le boute-selle ;* (milit.) to sound to horse. *Ne — mot ;* not to say a word, not to let the least hint drop. — *la messe ;* to ring the bells for mass. *Il a vingt ans bien sonnés ;* he is well over twenty. *Il est trois heures sonnées ;* the clock has struck three, *or* it is past three o'clock.

sonnerie (so-n-rî), *n.f.*, ring of bells ; bells ; (horl.) striking part, clock-work ; airs, flourishes ; (milit.) sound of the trumpet. *Pendule à —;* striking clock.

sonnet, *n.m.*, sonnet.

sonnette, *n.f.*, little bell ; house-bell, hand-bell, rattle ; (tech.) pile-driver ; engraver's mallet. *Cordon de —;* bell-pull. *Agiter la —, tirer la —;* to ring, to ring the bell, to pull the bell.

sonneur, *n.m.*, bell-ringer, blower.

sonnez (-né), *n.m.*, two sixes (backgammon).

sonomètre, *n.m.*, sonometer.

sonore, *adj.*, sonorous, clear, deep-toned. *Voix —;* sonorous voice.

sonorité, *n.f.*, sonorousness.

sopeur, *n.f.*, sopor, *n.m.*, (med.) deep, comatose sleep.

sopha, *n.m.* V. **sofa**.

sophi, *n.m.* V. **sofi**.

sophisme, *n.m.*, sophism, fallacy. *pl.*, sophistry.

sophiste, *n.m.*, sophist.

sophistication, *n.f.*, sophistication ; adulteration.

sophistique, *adj.*, sophistic, sophistical. *n.f.*, sophistry.

sophistiquer, *v.a.*, to sophisticate, to adulterate.

sophistiquer, *v.n.*, to subtilize.

sophistiquerie (-ti-krî), *n.f.*, sophistry, sophistication, adulteration.

sophistiqueur, *n.m.*, subtilizer, sophisticator, adulterator.

sophore, *n.m.*, (bot.) sophora.

soporati-f, -ve, *adj.*, soporiferous, soporific.

soporeu-x, -se, *adj.*, (med.) soporous.

soporifère *or* **soporifique**, *n.m.* and *adj.*, soporific ; soporiferous.

soprano, *n.m.*, (mus.) soprano, treble (voice).

sor. *V.* **saure.**

sorbe, *n.f.*, (bot.) sorb.

sorbet, *n.m.*, sherbet.

sorbétière, *n.f.*, ice-pail.

sorbier, *n.m.*, (bot.) sorb. — *domestique ;* service, service-tree. — *sauvage,* — *des oiseaux ;* quick-beam, quick-beam tree, roan-tree, mountain ash, quicken, quicken-tree.

sorboniste, *n.m.*, Sorbonist.

sorbonne, *n.f.*, Sorbonne (seat of the university of Paris).

sorcellerie (-sèl-rî), *n.f.*, sorcery, witchcraft, witchery, enchantment.

sorcier, *n.m.*, sorcerer, wizard ; conjuror, magician, enchanter. *Il n'est pas grand* —; he is no conjuror.

sorcière, *n.f.*, sorceress, witch, enchantress. *Vieille* —; old hag. *Sabbat des* —*s ;* witches' Sabbath.

sordide, *adj.*, sordid, dirty, filthy, mean, covetous, niggardly. — *avarice ;* base avarice.

sordidement (-did-măn), *adv.*, sordidly, meanly, niggardly, stingily.

sordidité, *n.f.*, sordidness, meanness.

soret. *V.* **sauret.**

sorgho, *n.m.*, (bot.) sorghum, sorgo.

sorite, *n.m.*, (log.) sorites.

sorne, *n.f.*, scum, slag, dross.

sornette, *n.f.*, idle talk, idle story, small talk, stuff. *Conter des* —*s ;* to talk nonsense, *or* to say sweet nothings to.

sororal, -e, *or* **sororial, -e**, *adj.*, of a sister, sisterly, of sisters.

sort, *n.m.*, fate, destiny, lot ; fortune ; position, condition ; existence ; spell, charm. *Le* — *des armes ;* the fate of arms, the chances of war. *Au* —; by lot. *Tirage au* —; drawing by lots. *Tirer au* —; to cast lots, to draw lots. *Tomber au* —; to draw a bad number (at conscriptions). *Le* — *en est jeté ;* the die is cast. *Jeter un* — *à quelqu'un ;* to throw a spell over any one. *Jeter un* — *sur quelque chose ;* to throw a spell over anything. *Etre son* —; to be one's lot, to fall to one's lot. *Faire un* — *à quelqu'un ;* to procure any one an existence ; to provide for any one.

sortable, *adj.*, suitable.

sortablement, *adv.*, suitably.

sortant, *n.m.*, person going out ; person leaving office, a dignity, a place. *Les entrants et les* —*s ;* the incomers and outgoers.

sortant, -e, *adj.*, outgoing, leaving office ; drawn, coming out (of numbers in lotteries).

sorte, *n.f.*, sort, kind, species ; manner, way. *Parler de la bonne* — *à quelqu'un ;* to rate any one soundly ; (fam.) to give it him. *En aucune* —; in no wise. *De telle* —; to such a degree, in such a way. *De quelque* — *que ce soit ;* in any way whatever. *De la* —; thus, so, in that manner, in that way. *De* — *que, en* — *que ;* so that. *De toute* —, *de toutes* —*s ;* of every kind, of all kinds. *Faire en* — *que ;* to manage so that ; to see that ; to contrive that.

sorteu-r, -se, *n.m.f.*, much out, fond of going out. *C'est un grand* —; he is always out, always gadding about.

sortie (-tî), *n.f.*, going out, coming out, departure, leaving ; egress, outlet, issue, exit, way out, escape ; holiday ; outburst, attack, abuse ; tirade ; (customs) exportation ; (thea.) exit ; (milit.) sally, sortie ; low cards (at cards). *A la* — *du dîner ;* on leaving the dinner-table, *or* at the end of the dinner. *Droit de* —; export duty. — *de bal ;* opera cloak. *Faire une* — *à quelqu'un ;* to blow any one up. *Faire une* —; (milit.) to make a sally. *Faire une* — *contre ;* to launch out against. *Jour de* —; holiday. *Fausse* —; (thea.) wrong exit.

sortilège, *n.m.*, sorcery, witchcraft, spell.

sortir (sortant, sorti), *v.n.* (*irregular*), to go

out, to go forth, to come, to come out, to come forth, to emerge, to proceed, to issue ; to get out, to come off ; to rise ; to depart, to swerve, to deviate ; to proceed ; to result ; to ensue ; to wander (from a subject) ; to start (of the eyes) ; to spring up, to come up ; to peep out, to shoot out (milit.) ; to sally forth, to sally out ; to steam out (of ships) ; (thea.) to exit, to make one's exit ; to spring, to be born ; to run off (locomotives) ; (paint.) to project, to stand out ; to be in relief. — *de la chambre ;* to go out of the room. *Il est sorti ;* he has gone out. *Il vient de* —; *il ne fait que de* —; he has just gone out. *Il est sorti ce matin ;* he went out this morning. *Il ne fait qu'entrer et* —; he does nothing but go in and out. *La rivière est sortie de son lit ;* the river has overflowed its banks. *Faire* — *un homme de prison ;* to get a man out of prison. — *du port ;* to leave, to steam out of, the harbor. — *de maladie ;* to (just) recover from illness. — *de table ;* to rise from table. — *de son devoir ;* to deviate from one's duty. — *des bornes de la bienséance ;* to overstep the rules of decency. — *de l'enfance ;* to be no longer a child. — *de cadence ;* (mus.) to be out of time. *Les yeux lui sortent de la tête ;* his eyes are starting out of his head. *Faire* —; to make go out ; to drive out ; to call forth ; to elicit, to bring to light.

sortir, *v.a.* (*irregular*), to get out, to bring out, to take out, to carry out ; to extricate. *Sortez ce cheval ;* bring out that horse. — *des fleurs ;* to put flowers out in the open air. — *un enfant ;* to take a child out.

sortir, *v.a.* (*regular*), (jur.) to obtain, to have.

sortir, *n.m.*, going out, leaving, quitting, coming out, rising. *Au* — *du lit ;* on getting out of bed. *Au* — *de sa lecture ;* (Ste. Beuve) when we close his book.

sosie, *n.m.*, second self, counterpart, twin, like.

sot, -te, *n.* and *adj.*, fool, blockhead ; stupid, silly, foolish, senseless, sheepish. — *animal ;* (triv.) foolish creature. *Le voilà bien* —; he looks rather sheepish now. *Il est resté* —; he looked somewhat foolish. *A* —*te demande point de réponse ;* a silly question needs no answer *or* answer a fool according to his folly. *C'est un* — *en trois lettres ;* he is a downright fool. *Quelque* — *le ferait ;* one would be a fool to do that.

sotie, *n.f.*, sotie (kind of 14th century play in which political satire predominated).

sot-l'y-laisse, *n.m.*, (—) pope's nose (of poultry).

sotnia, *n.f.*, sotnia (company of Russian horse).

sottement (sot-măn), *adv.*, sillily, foolishly, senselessly.

sottise, *n.f.*, silliness, folly ; silly thing, foolish trick, nonsense, foolishness ; indecency ; insult. *pl.*, abuse, abusive language. *Dire des* —*s à quelqu'un ;* to abuse any one, to call any one names.

sottisier, *n.m.*, (fam.) collection of indecent tales *or* songs ; ribald person.

sou, *n.m.*, sou, copper ; cent. *Gros* —; penny-piece, copper. *Petit* —; cent, small copper. *N'avoir pas le* —, *n'avoir pas un* —; to be penniless, not to be worth a farthing, not to be worth a groat. *Sans le* —; penniless. *Une affaire de deux* —*s ;* a two-cent business, *or* trumpery affair. *Comme quatre* —*s ;* (fam.) wretchedly, shabbily, paltrily.

soubarbe, *n.f.* *V.* **sous-barbe.**

soubassement (-bâs-măn), *n.m.*, dado, bed-valance ; (arch.) basement, sub-basement. — *d'une colonne ;* (arch.) pattern of a column.

soubise, *n.f.*, onion-sauce.

soubresaut, *n.m.*, sudden leap *or* start ; jolt ; plunge (of a horse) ; (med.) subsultus.

soubresauter, *v.n.*, to start, to jump, to jolt, to plunge.

soubrette, *n.f.*, (thea.) waiting-woman, abigail, lady's maid.

soubreveste, *n.f.*, sleeveless upper coat.

soubuse, *n.f.*, (orni.) hen harrier.

souche, *n.f.*, stump, stock, stub, stem (of trees); block; blockhead; head, founder (genealogy); chimney-neck, chimney-shaft, chimney-stalk; (bot.) subterranean stock; counterfoil (of passports, etc.); voucher, counterfoil (of checks, receipts, etc.); tally. *C'est une vraie —;* he is a regular blockhead. *Faire —;* to be the first of a branch, to found a family. *— de cheminée;* chimney-stock. *— d'enclume;* anvil-block.

souchet, *n.m.*, (bot.) galingale; (mas.) ragstone; (orni.) shoveler, shoveler-duck.

souchetage (soosh-taj), *n.m.*, counting stumps (of felled timber).

soucheteur (soosh-teur), *n.m.*, surveyor of stocks, stubs, in a forest.

souci, *n.m.*, anxious care, anxiety; (bot.) marigold; (orni.) golden-crested wren. *Sans —;* free from care. *Avoir —;* to take care. *Avoir des —s;* to have cares. *Etre dévoré de —;* to be careworn. *C'est le moindre*, or *le cadet, de mes —s;* I don't care a rap about it, or it does n't trouble me in the least. *— d'eau, — des marais;* (bot.) marsh-marigold. *— des champs;* (bot.) wild marigold; cow-marigold. *— figue;* (bot.) fig-marigold.

se **soucier**, *v.r.*, to care, to mind, to be concerned, to concern one's self, to be anxious, to be uneasy; to like, to want. *Il ne s'en soucie guère;* he cares little for, or about, it. *Il ne se soucie de rien;* he cares for nothing. *Je ne m'en soucie plus;* I have no further wish for it. *S'en — comme de l'an quarante;* not to care a rush, or a rap.

soucieu-x, -se, *adj.*, anxious, full of care, careworn, pensive, thoughtful.

soucoupe, *n.f.*, saucer; salver.

soudable, *adj.*, that can be soldered.

soudage, *n.m.*, soldering, welding.

soudain, -e, *adj.*, sudden, unexpected, unlooked-for.

soudain, *adv.*, suddenly, on a sudden, all of a sudden.

soudainement (-dè-n-mān), *adv.*, suddenly, on a sudden, all of a sudden.

soudaineté (-dè-n-té), *n.f.*, suddenness, unexpectedness.

soudan, *n.m.*, (—s) sultan.

soudard or **soudart**, *n.m.*, (fam.) trooper, veteran soldier.

soude, *n.f.*, (min.) soda; (bot.) glasswort.

souder, *v.a.*, to solder, to weld; (fig.) to unite, to join.

se **souder**, *v.r.*, to be soldered or welded; to unite, to consolidate.

soudiviser, *v.a.* V. **subdiviser**.

soudoir, *n.m.*, soldering-iron.

soudoyer, *v.a.*, to hire, to pay troops; to keep in pay.

soudrille, *n.m.*, (fam.) lewd, thievish soldier.

soudure, *n.f.*, solder; soldering, welding.

soufflage, *n.m.*, glass-blowing; blowing; (nav.) sheathing.

soufflant, -e, *adj.*, blowing.

souffle, *n.m.*, breath, breathing; puff (of wind); (fig.) inspiration, influence, breath.

soufflement, *n.m.*, blowing.

souffler, *v.n.*, to blow; to breathe, to pant, to puff; to swell; to complain; to seek the philosopher's stone. *— aux oreilles de quelqu'un;* to whisper in any one's ear. *— dans ses doigts;* to blow upon one's fingers. *Il n'oserait —;* he dares not complain.

souffler, *v.a.*, to blow, to blow out; to breathe, to breathe out; to inflate; to whisper; to huff (at draughts); (nav.) to sheathe; to prompt. *— le feu;* to blow the fire. *— le*

chaud et le froid; to blow hot and cold. *— un comédien;* to prompt a player. *- - l'orgue;* to blow an organ. *— à quelqu'un un emploi;* to rob any one of a situation (by forestalling him). *— un vaisseau;* to sheath a ship. *— les canons;* (artil.) to scale the guns. *Ne pas — mot;* not to say a word, or not to open one's mouth. *se* **souffler**, *v.r.*, to be blown.

soufflerie, *n.f.*, bellows (of an organ); blast-apparatus; ⊙alchemy.

soufflet, *n.m.*, bellows, pair of bellows; head or hood (of a carriage); box on the ear, slap in the face; affront, mortification; humiliation. *Donner un — à Vaugelas;* to murder the Queen's English.

souffletade, *n.f.*, (l.u.) slapping (in the face).

souffleter, *v.a.*, to slap in the face, to box the ears of; (fig.) to strike, to insult, to buffet.

⊙**souffleteur**, *n.m.*, striker, slapper.

souffletier, *n.m.*, bellows-maker.

souffleur, *n.m.*, (zoöl.) a species of dolphin. *Les —s;* cetaceans.

souffleu-r, -se, *n.* and *adj.*, blower, organ-blower; panter; (thea.) prompter; glass-blower; alchemist; panting (of horses). *— d'orgue;* organ-blower. *Cheval —;* panting horse; roarer.

soufflure, *n.f.*, (metal.) flaw; seedy glass.

souffrable, *adj.*, (l.u.) sufferable, tolerable.

souffrance, *n.f.*, suffering, pain, suspense, sufferance; endurance; (jur.) sufferance, toleration. *En —;* suspended; (com.) standing over; (of bills) dishonored. *Jour de —;* borrowed light.

souffrant, -e, *adj.*, suffering, in pain; patient; enduring; unwell, poorly, ailing.

souffre-douleur, *n.m.*, (—) drudge; fag; butt, laughing-stock.

souffreteu-x, -se, *adj.*, miserable, unwell, poorly, sickly, weakly, puny.

souffrir (souffrant, souffert), *v.a.*, to suffer, to bear, to endure, to abide; to undergo, to sustain, to stand; to tolerate; to permit, to let, to allow, to put up with; to admit of. *— la douleur;* to endure pain. *— la fatigue;* to bear fatigue. *— un assaut;* to stand an assault. *— un affront;* to put up with an affront. *Je ne saurais — cet homme-là;* I cannot endure that man. *Il souffre tout à ses enfants;* he is too indulgent to his children. *Pourquoi souffrez-vous cela ?* why do you put up with that? *Cela ne souffre point de retardement;* that admits of no delay. *Faire —;* to pain, to grieve, to torture.

souffrir, *v.n.*, to suffer, to suffer pain, to be in pain; to be pained; to be a sufferer; to be injured. *— de la tête;* to feel a pain in one's head. *Se —;* to endure each other; to be tolerated; to be suffered (of things).

soufi, *n.m.* V. **sofi**.

soufrage, *n.m.*, sulphuring; smoking with brimstone.

soufre, *n.m.*, sulphur, brimstone. *Fleur de —;* flour of brimstone.

soufrer, *v.a.*, to dip in brimstone, to sulphur.

soufrière, *n.f.*, sulphur-mine.

soufroir, *n.m.*, sulphuring-stove.

sougarde, *n.f.* V. **sous-garde**.

sougorge, *n.f.* V. **sous-gorge**.

souhait, *n.m.*, wish, desire. *A —;* to one's heart's content, according to one's desire, as one would have it. *Avoir tout à —;* to have everything to one's liking. *A vos —s;* (fam.) God bless you ! (after sneezing).

souhaitable, *adj.*, desirable, to be wished for.

souhaiter, *v.a.*, to wish, to wish for, to long for. *Je vous souhaite le bonjour;* I wish you good morning. *Il serait à — que, etc.;* it is desirable that, etc. *Que souhaitez-vous ?* what do you wish for? *Je vous en souhaite, je t'en souhaite;* I wish you may get it. *— la bonne année à quelqu'un;* to wish any one a happy New Year.

se **souhaiter**, *v.r.*, to wish one's self, *or* each other.

souï, *n.m.*, soy (sauce).

***souille**, *n.f.*, (hunt.) wallowing place (of wild boars); bed (impression made by the bottom of a ship on the mud).

***souiller**, *v.a.*, to soil, to dirty, to stain, to blemish, to sully, to defile, to pollute, to contaminate.

se **souiller**, *v.r.*, to soil, to get dirty; to sully, to tarnish.

***souillon**, *n.m.f.*, scullion; sloven, slut, slattern, trollop.

***souillure**, *n.f.*, dirt, spot of dirt; spot, stain; blot, impurity; contamination, pollution, defilement.

soûl, -e (soo, -l), *adj.*, glutted; surfeited, drunk, tipsy; cloyed, satiated, heartily sick of. — *comme une grive;* as drunk as a lord. *Il est* — *de musique;* he is surfeited with music. *A merle* — *cerises sont amères;* plenty makes dainty. *Tout son* —; to one's heart's content.

soûl (soo), *n.m.*, one's fill, one's bellyful. *Boire et manger son* —; to eat and drink one's fill.

soulageant, -e (-jän, -t), *adj.*, easing; comforting; relieving.

soulagement (-la-jmän), *n.m.*, relief, ease, comfort, alleviation, assuagement; solace, help. *Cela me donne du* —; that relieves me. *C'est un* — *à ses peines;* it is an alleviation of his troubles.

soulager, *v.a.*, to relieve, to ease, to lighten; to alleviate, to allay, to assist, to comfort; to assist, to help.

se **soulager**, *v.r.*, to relieve one's self, *or* each other.

soûlaison, *n.m.*, (fam.) drunkenness; drinking bout, boozing.

soûlard, -e, n.f., (pop.) drunkard.

⊙**soûlaud**, *n.m.*, **-e**, *n.f.*, (pop.) drunkard.

soûler, *v.a.*, to fill, to glut, to satiate, to surfeit; to intoxicate, to make drunk.

se **soûler**, *v.r.*, to glut one's self, to satiate one's self; to get intoxicated; to riot, to get drunk.

souleur, *n.f.*, (fam.) fright, shock.

soulèvement (-lèv-män), *n.m.*, heaving, rising (of the stomach); swelling, upheaving (of the waves); insurrection, revolt; indignation.

soulever (sool-vé), *v.a.*, to raise; to lift, to heave up, to take up; to lift up; to excite, to stir up; to urge to insurrection; to excite to action; to raise the indignation of; to make indignant; to moot, *or* raise (question).

se **soulever** (sool-), *v.r.*, to raise one's self, to rise; to swell; to be urged to action; to be urged to indignation, to be indignant; to rise to revolt, to rise in insurrection, in arms.

soulever (sool-), *v.n.*, to rise, turn (of the stomach). *Le cœur me soulève à la pensée de;* my stomach rises at the thought of.

soulier, *n.m.*, shoe. —*s ferrés;* hobnailed shoes. *Être dans ses petits* —*s;* to be in an awkward situation, to be uneasy in one's mind; to be on pins and needles.

soulier-botte, *n.m.*, (—*s*—*s*) Blucher boot.

***soulignement**, *n.m.*, underlining.

***souligner**, *v.a.*, to underline.

⊙**souloir**, *v.n.*, to be wont, to use.

soulte *or* **soute**, *n.f.*, (jur. com.) balance; premium, settlement.

soumettre, *v.a.*, to subdue, to submit, to bring under subjection, to subject; to overcome; to subjugate; to subordinate, to refer. — *un pays;* to subdue a country.

se **soumettre**, *v.r.*, to submit, to yield, to be submissive, to give way; to succumb, to assent (to); to comply (with). *Il faut se* — *ou se démettre;* one must knuckle under or clear out, *or* submit *or* resign.

soumission, *n.f.*, submission, submissiveness; subjection, compliance, obedience, mark of respect; tender for a contract; contract; deed of contract; (jur.) bond; subscription. —*s cachetées;* sealed tenders.

soumissionnaire, *n.m.f.*, tendering party.

soumissionner, *v.a.*, to make a tender for *or* to tender for.

soupape, *n.f.*, plug, valve. — *dormante;* fixed valve. — *à clapet;* clack-valve. — *à gorge;* throttle valve. — *de sûreté;* safety-valve. *A* —; with a valve.

soupatoire, *adj.*, (fam.) of supper, serving as a supper. *Dîner* —; dinner-supper.

soupçon, *n.m.*, suspicion; surmise, conjecture, taste, smack, dash, jot, bit, trifle; touch. *Un* — *d'ail;* just a taste of garlic. *Un* —, *s'il vous plaît;* the smallest of pieces, please!

soupçonnable, *adj.*, suspectable, liable to be suspected.

soupçonner, *v.a.*, to suspect, to surmise.

se **soupçonner**, *v.r.*, to suspect one another; to be suspected.

soupçonneu-r, -se, *n.m.f.*, suspecter.

soupçonneu-x, -se, *adj.*, suspicious.

soupe, *n.f.*, soup, slice of bread for soup, sippet, sop; (fam.) dinner. — *à perroquet;* bread steeped in wine. — *au lait;* milk-porridge. *Ivre comme une* —; as drunk as a lord, *or* as tight as a drum. *Trempé comme une* —; drenched *or* wet to the skin. *Tremper la* —; to soak the bread in the soup. *Tailler la* —; to cut bread for the soup. — *grasse;* meat soup. — *maigre;* vegetable soup. *S'emporter comme une* — *au lait;* to be of a very hasty temper; to fly into a passion (without any warning). *Manger la* — *avec quelqu'un;* (fam.) to come and dine with any one *or* to come and have pot-luck with any one.

soupente, *n.f.*, loft, garret; brace (of a coach); strap (of a horse).

souper, *v.n.*, to sup, to take supper. *A* —; to sup; one's supper.

souper *or* **soupé**, *n.m.*, supper.

soupeser, *v.a.*, to weigh, to lift, to try the weight of.

soupette, *n.f.*, thin slice of bread, sippet.

soupeu-r, *n.m.*, **-se**, *n.f.*, supper, eater; gay man *or* woman.

soupied, *n.m.* *V.* **sous-pied**.

soupière, *n.f.*, tureen, soup-tureen.

soupir, *n.m.*, sigh, breath; breathing; gasp; (fig.) wish, longing; (mus.) crotchet-rest. *pl.*, sighing. *Pousser des* —*s;* to heave sighs. *Rendre le dernier* —; to breathe one's last.

***soupirail**, *n.m.*, air-hole, vent-hole.

soupirant, *n.m.*, wooer, lover.

soupirer, *v.n.*, to sigh; to gasp; to long. — *de douleur;* to sigh for grief. — *après une chose;* to long for a thing.

soupirer, *v.a.*, to breathe, to breathe forth, to sigh.

soupireur, *n.m.*, (fam.) sigher.

souple, *adj.*, supple, pliant, flexible, yielding, tractable, docile, compliant. *Un esprit* —; a compliant temper.

souplement, *adv.*, pliantly, flexibly, compliantly.

souplesse, *n.f.*, suppleness, pliancy, flexibility, facility, compliance, versatility. *La* — *de l'osier;* the flexibility of the osier. *Tours de* —; cunning tricks. *Sa voix a de la* —; there is a marked flexibility in his voice.

***souquenille**, *n.f.*, smock-frock; gabardine.

source, *n.f.*, source, spring, fountain, fountain-head; well-spring, rise. — *d'eau;* spring. *Eau de* —; spring water. *Prendre sa* —; to take its rise (of a river). *Avoir sa* — *dans;* (fig.) to have its rise in, to proceed from. *Couler de* —; to flow naturally; to come from the heart.

sourcier, *n.m.*, bletonist, spring-finder.

sourcil, (-ci), *n.m.*, eye-brow, brow. *Froncer le —* ; to knit one's brow.

sourcili-er, -ère, *adj.*, (anat.) superciliary.

***sourciller**, *v.n.*, to knit one's brows ; to frown ; to wince, to flinch ; (of water) to spring, to gush out. *Sans —* ; without moving a muscle or without wincing.

***sourcilleu-x, -se**, *adj.*, haughty, proud ; supercilious, cloud-topped, towering, steep ; uneasy ; melancholy. *Montagnes —ses ;* lofty mountains.

sourd, -e, *adj.*, deaf ; dull, hollow, muffled (of sound) ; insensible, dead ; (math.) ☉surd ; secret, underhand ; rumbling. *Voix —e ;* hollow voice. *— comme un pot ;* as deaf as a post. *Il court un bruit —* ; it is whispered about. *Lanterne —e ;* dark lantern. *Lime —e ;* dead file. *Douleur —e ;* dull pain. *Menées —es ;* underhand dealings. *Faire la —e oreille ;* to turn a deaf ear.

sourd, *n.m.*, **-e**, *n.f.*, deaf person ; (zoöl.) salamander (local ex.). *Frapper comme un —* ; to strike hard. *Faire le —* ; to sham deafness. *Il n'est pire — que celui qui ne veut pas entendre ;* none so deaf as those who won't hear. *— et muet ;* deaf and dumb.

sourdaud, *n.m.*, person hard of hearing.

sourdeline, *n.f.*, Italian bag-pipe.

sourdement, *adv.*, indistinctly ; with a hollow voice ; dully, rumblingly ; (of sound) with a dull rumbling noise ; secretly ; in an underhand manner. *Brûler —* ; to smoulder.

sourdine, *n.f.*, sordet, sordine (of a trumpet) ; damper (piano). *A la —* ; secretly, on the sly.

sourd-muet, *n.m.*, (— *-s*), **sourde-muette**, *n.f.*, (— *-s-s*) deaf and dumb person.

sourdon, *n.m.*, (conch.) cockle.

sourdre, *v.n.*, to spring, to issue, to gush out, to arise, to well ; (nav.) (of a cloud) to rise.

souriant, *adj.*, smiling.

souriceau, *n.m.*, little mouse.

souricier, *n.m.*, mouser.

souricière, *n.f.*, mouse-trap.

souriquois, -e, *adj.*, (jest.) of mice. *La gent —c ;* the mouse tribe, the murine race.

sourire, *v.n.*, to smile ; to countenance ; to be agreeable, to delight, to please (of a thing) ; to favor ; to tempt, to suit. *— à quelqu'un ;* to smile upon any one.

sourire or **souris**, *n.m.*, smile. *— moqueur ;* a sneer, scornful smile.

souris, *n.f.*, mouse ; mouse-color ; venison-bit, knuckle (of a leg of mutton) ; (milit.) saucisse, saucisson (to fire a mine) ; (vet.) nasal cartilage (of the horse). *Pas de —* ; (fort.) flight of steps leading to the moat. *Chauve-—*, (— *-s-—*) bat. *— qui n'a qu'un trou est bientôt prise ;* it is well to have more than one string to one's bow ; *on entendrait trotter une —* ; you could hear a pin drop.

souris, *adj. invariable*, mouse-colored. *Cheval —* ; mouse-colored horse.

sournois, -e, *n.* and *adj.*, dissembler, artful person, sly fox, sly boots ; dissembled, artful, cunning, sly, deep, crafty.

sournoisement, *adv.*, slyly, cunningly, on the sly.

sournoiserie, *n.f.*, slyness, artfulness, cunning, sly trick.

sous, *prep.*, under, beneath ; upon ; with ; in ; by ; sub ; deputy. *— le lit ;* under the bed. *— terre ;* underground. *Affirmer — serment ;* to swear upon oath. *— silence ;* in silence. *— la main ;* close at hand. *— presse ;* in the press. *— peu de jours ;* in a few days. *— peu de temps ;* in a short time. *Regarder quelqu'un — le nez ;* to stare any one in the face. *—gouverneur,* (— *-s*) deputy-governor. *— secrétaire ;* under-secretary. *—voile ;* (nav.) under sail. *— le vent ;* to leeward.

sous-affermer, *v.a.*, to underlet ; to take an under-lease.

sous-agent, *n.m.f.*, (— *-s*) under-agent.

sous-aide, *n.m.f.*, (— *-s*) under-assistant ; assistant surgeon.

sous-amendement, *n.m.*, (— *-s*) additional amendment ; amendment to an amendment.

sous-amender, *v.a.*, to make an additional amendment.

sous-arbrisseau, *n.m.*, (— *-x*) (bot.) suffrutex ; undershrub.

sous-aumônier, *n.m.*, sub-almoner ; assistant chaplain.

sous-axillaire, *adj.*, (bot.) sub-axillary.

***sous-bail**, *n.m.*, (— *-baux*) under-lease.

sous-baill-eur, -eresse, *n.m.f.*, under-lessor.

sous-barbe, *n.f.*, (— *-s*) under jaw (of horses). *— de beaupré ;* (nav.) bob-stay.

sous-bibliothécaire, *n.m.*, (— *-s*) sublibrarian.

sous-bois, *n.m.*, underwood, undergrowth.

sous-bras, *n.m.*, dress preserver.

sous-brigadier, *n.m.*, lance-corporal.

sous-carbonate, *n.m.*, sub-carbonate.

sous-chantre, *n.m.*, (— *-s*) sub-chanter, succentor.

sous-chef, *n.m.*, (— *-s*) chief-assistant, second head-clerk. [rafter.

sous-chevron, *n.m.*, (— *-s*) (carp.) under-

sous-clavi-er, -ère, *adj.*, (anat.) sub-clavian.

sous-clerc, *n.m.*, (— *-s*) under-clerk.

sous-comité, *n.m.*, (— *-s*) sub-committee.

sous-commis, *n.m.*, under-clerk, junior-clerk.

sous-commissaire, *n.m.*, (— *-s*) (nav.) under-commissary.

sous-contrefort, *n.m.*, (— *-s*) stiffener (of boots, shoes).

sous-costal, -e, *adj.*, (anat.) sub-costal.

sous-couche, *n.f.*, underlayer, substratum.

souscripteur, *n.m.*, subscriber ; (com.) underwriter.

souscription, *n.f.*, subscription ; signature ; contribution.

souscrire, *v.a.n.*, to subscribe, to sign ; (fig.) to consent, to agree to ; to approve, to indorse. *— un contrat ;* to subscribe a contract.

souscrivant, *n.m.*, underwriter.

sous-cutané, -e, *adj.*, subcutaneous.

sous-délégué, *n.m.*, (— *-s*) sub-delegate.

sous-déléguer, *v.a.*, to subdelegate.

sous-diaconat, *n.m.*, (— *-s*) subdeaconry.

sous-diacre, *n.m.*, (— *-s*) subdeacon.

sous-direct-eur, -rice, *n.m.f.*, sub-manager, sub-manageress.

sous-diviser, *v.a.* V. **subdiviser.**

sous-division, *n.f.*, (— *-s*) subdivision.

sous-dominante, *n.f.*, (— *-s*) (mus.) subdominant.

sous-double, *adj.*, (math.) subduple.

sous-doublé, -e, *adj.*, (math.) sub-duplicate.

sous-doyen, *n.m.*, (— *-s*) sub-dean.

sous-doyenné, *n.m.*, (— *-s*) sub-deanery, sub-deanship.

sous-économe, *n.m.*, sub-treasurer.

sous-entendre, *v.a.*, not to express fully, to understand, to hint, to imply. *se* **sous-entendre**, *v.r.*, to be understood. *Cela se sous-entend ;* that is understood.

sous-entendu, *n.m.*, (— *-s*) thing understood. *adj.*, understood.

sous-entente, *n.f.*, (— *-s*) mental reservation.

sous-entrepreneur, *n.m.*, (— *-s*) sub-contractor (of public works).

sous-espèce, *n.f.*, (— *-s*) sub-species.

sous-faîte, *n.m.*, (— *-s*) (carp.) under-ridge-board.

sous-ferme, *n.f.*, (— *-s*) (jur.) under-lease.

sous-fermer, *v.a.*, to underlet ; to take an under-lease.

sous-fermi-er, *n.m.*, **-ère**, *n.f.*, (——*s*) (jur.) under-lessee.

sous-fondation, *n.f.*, (——*s*) subpavement.

sous-fréter, *v.a.*, to underlet, to under-freight (ships).

sous-garantie, *n.f.*, (——*s*) (jur.) counter-bond.

sous-garde, *n.f.*, ,(—) trigger-guard.

sous-genre, *n.m.*, (——*s*) subgenus.

sous-gorge, *n.f.*, (—) throat-band (of a bridle).

sous-gouverneur, *n.m.*, (——*s*) deputy-governor.

sous-greffier, *n.m.*, (——*s*) deputy-registrar.

sous-instructeur, *n.m.*, (mil.) fugleman.

sous-intendance, *n.f.*, (——*s*) (milit.) deputy-commissaryship; under commissary's office.

sous-intendant, *n.m.*, (——*s*) (milit.) deputy-commissary, sub-commissary.

sous-jacent, *adj.*, subjacent.

sous-jupe, *n.f.*, underskirt.

sous-lieutenance, *n.f.*, (——*s*) (artil.) sub-lieutenancy; (milit.) ensigncy; (nav.) second-lieutenancy.

sous-lieutenant, *n.m.*, (——*s*) (artil.) sub-lieutenant; (milit.) ensign; (nav.) second-lieutenant.

sous-locataire, *n.m.f.*, (——*s*) under-tenant.

sous-location, *n.f.*, (——*s*) under-letting, under-tenancy.

sous-louer, *v.a.*, to underlet; to under-hire.

sous-maître, *n.m.*, (——*s*) usher, under-master, assistant (at a school).

sous-maîtresse, *n.f.*, (——*s*) assistant-teacher; governess.

sous-marin, -e, *adj.*, submarine; submersed; underset (of currents).

sous-maxillaire, *adj.*, (anat.) sub-maxillary.

sous-multiple, *n.m.*, (——*s*) (arith.) sub-multiple.

sous-noix, *n.f.*, round (of beef).

sous-normale, *n.f.*, (——*s*) (geom.) sub-normal; sub-perpendicular.

sous-occipital, -e, *adj.*, sub-occipital.

en sous-œuvre, *adv.*, (arch.) underpinning. *Reprendre un mur en—;* to underpin a wall.

sous-officier, *n.m.*, (——*s*) non-commissioned officer.

sous-orbiculaire, *adj.*, suborbicular.

sous-ordre, *n.m.*, (——*s*) subordinate. *En —;* subordinately.

sous-perpendiculaire, *n.f.* *V.* **sous-normale.**

sous-pied, *n.m.*, (——*s*) strap (of trousers).

sous-précepteur, *n.m.*, (——*s*) assistant tutor.

sous-préfecture, *n.f.*, (——*s*) sub-prefecture.

sous-préfet, *n.m.*, (——*s*) sub-prefect, under-sheriff.

sous-prieur, *n.m.*, (——*s*) sub-prior.

sous-prieure, *n.f.*, (——*s*) sub-prioress.

sous-principal, *n.m.*, (——*s*) vice-principal.

sous-sacristain, *n.m.*, (——*s*) under-sexton, under-sacristan.

sous-secrétaire, *n.m.*, (——*s*) under-secretary.

sous-secrétariat, *n.m.*, (——*s*) under-secretaryship.

sous-seing, *n.m.*, (——*s*) private deed.

sous-sel, *n.m.*, (——*s*) (chem.) sub-salt.

*****soussigné**, -e, *part.*, undersigned, underwritten. *Nous —s certifions;* we, the undersigned, certify.

sous-sol, *n.m.*, (——*s*) (agri.) sub-soil, sub-stratum; basement.

sous-tangente, *n.f.*, (——*s*) (geom.) subtangent.

sous-tendante, *n.f.*, (——*s*) (geom.) sub-tense chord.

sous-tendre, *v.a.*, (geom.) to subtend.

sous-titre, *n.m.*, (——*s*) (print.) sub-heading, second title.

soustraction, *n.f.*, (arith., jur.) subtraction; taking away.

soustraire (soustrayant, soustrait), *v.a.*, to take away, to remove; to withdraw; to shelter, to screen; (arith.) to subtract.

se **soustraire**, *v.r.*, to escape, to avoid; to flee; to exempt one's self; to withdraw; to be subtracted. *Se — au châtiment;* to avoid punishment. *Se — à la tyrannie;* to flee from tyranny. *Se — à la justice;* to fly from justice, to abscond.

sous-traitant, *n.m.*, (——*s*) sub-contractor.

sous-traité, *n.m.*, (——*s*) sub-contract.

sous-traiter, *v.a.*, to sub-contract.

sous-triple, *adj.*, (math.) sub-triple.

sous-triplé, -e, *adj.*, (math.) sub-triplicate. *En raison —e;* in a sub-triplicate ratio.

soustylaire, *n.f.*, substyle (of a dial).

sous-variété, *n.f.*, (——*s*) sub-variety.

sous-ventrière, *n.f.*, (——*s*) belly-band.

soutache, *n.f.*, braid (of a hussar's shako).

soutacher, *v.a.*, to braid (needle-work).

soutane, *n.f.*, cassock; (fig.) cloth; priests.

soutanelle, *n.f.*, short cassock.

soute, *n.f.*, (nav.) store-room. — *aux poudres;* (nav.) powder-magazine, powder-room. *V.* **soulte.** — *à charbon;* coal-bunker; coal-chute. — *au pain;* bread-room; bread-pan.

soutenable (soo-tnabl), *adj.*, sustainable, maintainable; supportable, tenable.

soutenance, *n.f.*, the sustaining of a thesis.

soutenant (soo-tnãn), *n.m.*, sustainer, mooter (student); respondent.

soutènement (soo-tèn-mãn), *n.m.*, (arch.) support, prop; (jur.) written explanation. *Mur de —;* breast-wall.

soutèneur (soo-tneur), *n.m.*, bully; pimp.

soutenir (soo-tnir), *v.a.*, to support, to sustain, to bear, to bear up; to hold, to hold up; to keep up, to uphold; to assert, to maintain; to uphold, to affirm, to back, to stand by; to countenance, to favor; to prop, to prop up; to strengthen; to afford (an expense); to endure, to bear up against. — *une famille;* to support a family. — *la conversation;* to keep up the conversation. — *son rang;* to uphold, or keep up, one's rank. — *le combat;* to maintain the fight. — *la lumière;* to bear the light. *Il ne peut — la raillerie;* he cannot stand joking. *Le vin vous soutient;* wine strengthens one. — *une thèse;* to sustain a thesis. — *un siège;* to sustain a siege. *se* **soutenir**, *v.r.*, to support one's self; to sustain one's self; to stand up, to keep one's self up; to bear up; to hold out; to succeed; to continue, to get on, not to flag. *Elle se soutient bien;* she holds out very well. *Son style ne se soutient pas;* his style is not sustained. *Se — contre;* to resist, to withstand.

soutenu, -e, *adj.*, supported, sustained; continued; unremitting, unceasing, constant; high, lofty, elevated. *Discours bien —;* well-sustained discourse. *Style —;* lofty style.

souterrain, -e, *adj.*, subterraneous, subterranean. *Voies —es;* underhand practices.

souterrain, *n.m.*, cavern, vault; tunnel; underground.

souterrainement, *adv.*, underground; (fig.) in an underhanded manner, secretly.

soutien (-ti-in), *n.m.*, stay, prop, support, staff; maintenance; sustenance; stiffening; supporter, upholder, vindicator, sustainer.

soutirage, *n.m.*, racking, drawing off (of wine).

soutirer, *v.a.*, to rack, to draw off (liquors); to get out of, to worm out of, to screw out of (to obtain).

soutre, *n.m.*, writing pad.

⊙**souvenance** (soo-vnans), *n.f.*, remembrance, recollection. *Avoir—;* to remember.

souvenez-vous-de-moi, *n.m.*, (—) (bot.) marsh scorpion-grass ; forget-me-not.

souvenir (soo-vnir), *n.m.*, remembrance, recollection, memory, reminder ; keepsake ; memorandum-book ; letter-rack. *Rappeler une chose au — de quelqu'un ;* to remind any one of a thing. *Rappelez-moi à son —* ; remember me to him. *se* **souvenir**, *v.r.*, to remember ; to call to mind, to recollect ; to bear in mind. *Se — du temps passé ;* to remember past times. *Je m'en souviendrai ;* I shall remember it. *Il me souvient ;* I remember. *Il m'en souvient ;* I remember it. *T'en souvient-il ?* do you remember ? *Autant que je puis m'en —* ; to the best of my recollection. *S'il m'en souvient bien ;* if I recollect rightly.

souvent, *adv.*, often, oftentimes, frequently, many times. *Peu —* ; rarely.

⊙**souventefois** (-vant-foa), *adv.*, oftentimes.

souverain, -e (soo-vrin, -vrè-n), *n.* and *adj.*, sovereign ; supreme, superlative, highest, extreme, most excellent, infallible ; final, without appeal. *Au — degré ;* to a sovereign degree.

souverain, *n.m.*, sovereign (coin).

souverainement (soo-vrè-n-mān), *adv.*, extremely, in the extreme; finally; sovereignly, supremely, superlatively.

souveraineté (souv-rè-n-té), *n.f.*, sovereignty, supremacy, dominion; dominions.

soy, *n.m.* V. **soui**.

soyeu-x, -se, *adj.*, silky, silken.

spacieusement (-eûz-mān), *adv.*, spaciously.

spacieu-x, -se, *adj.*, spacious, wide, roomy, large.

spadassin, *n.m.*, (b.s.) fighter, bully, hired assassin.

*****spadille**, *n.m.*, spadilla (at ombre).

spahi, *n.m.*, spahi (Algerian horse soldier).

spalme, *n.m.*, (nav.) paying-stuff. V. **courée** *or* **courai.**

spalmer, *v.a.*, to grave, to pitch, to pay (a ship). V. **espalmer.**

spalt, *n.m.*, (min.) spalt.

sparadrap (-dra-p), *n.m.*, (pharm.) cerecloth.

spare, *n.*, (ich.) gilt-head.

spargoule *or* **spargoute**, *n.f.* V. **spergule.**

spartan *or* **sparton**, *n.m.*, (nav.) rope made of esparto.

sparte, *n.f.*, (bot.) esparto ; mat-weed.

sparterie, manufacture of esparto ; esparto articles.

spartiate, *n.m.f.* and *adj.*, Spartan.

sparton, *n.m.* V. **spartan.**

spasme, *n.m.*, spasm.

spasmodique, *adj.*, spasmodic.

spasmologie, *n.f.*, spasmology.

spath (spat), *n.m.*, (min.) spar. *— perlé ;* pearl spar. *— fluor ;* fluor-spar.

spathacé, -e, *adj.*, (bot.) spathaceous.

spathe, *n.f.*, (bot.) spatha, spathe.

spathique, *adj.*, (min.) sparry, spathic.

spatule, *n.f.*, spatula ; (orni.) spoon-bill.

spécial, -e, *adj.*, special, especial, peculiar, particular; professional (of a person). *Les hommes spéciaux ;* professional men.

spécialement (-al-mān), *adv.*, especially, peculiarly, particularly.

spécialisation, *n.f.*, specialization.

spécialiser, *v.n.*, to specialize.

spécialiste, *n.m.*, (med.) specialist. *Médecin —* ; specialist.

spécialité, *n.f.*, peculiarity, specialty; line, *or* department, of business ; special study.

spécieusement (-euz-mān), *adv.*, speciously, plausibly.

spécieu-x, -se, *adj.* specious, plausible.

spécificati-f, -ve, *adj.*, specificative.

spécification, *n.f.*, specification.

spécifier, *v.a.*, to specify.

spécifique, *n.m.* and *adj.*, specific.

spécifiquement (-fik-mān), *adv.*, specifically.

spécimen (-mè-n), *n.m.*, (—*s*) specimen.

spéciosité, *n.f.*, speciousness.

spectacle, *n.m.*, play, spectacle, scene, sight, public view, show ; play-house, performance ; theater. *Salle de —* ; play-house, theater. *Etre en —* ; to be exposed to public view. *Se donner en —* ; to attract attention ; to make one's self conspicuous. *Programme*, or *affiche, de —* ; play-bill. *Servir de —* ; to be a butt for public laughter. *Jour de —* ; play-night. *Aller au —* ; to go to the play, *or* theater.

spectat-eur, -rice, *n.* and *adj.*, spectator, looker-on, by-stander. *pl.*, (thea.) spectators, audience. *adj.*, looking on.

spectral, *adj.*, (opt.) spectral ; pertaining to the spectrum.

spectre, *n.m.*, specter, phantom, ghost ; (phys.) spectrum.

spéculaire, *adj.*, (min.) specular, transparent. ⊙*Science —* ; the science of mirror-making.

spéculat-eur, *n.m.*, **-rice**, *n.f.*, speculator, investor.

spéculati-f, -ve, *adj.*, speculative.

spéculatif, *n.m.*, speculative man, speculative mind.

spéculation, *n.f.*, speculation.

spéculativement, *adv.*, in a speculative manner.

spéculer, *v.n.*, to speculate.

speculum (spé-cu-lom), *n.m.*, (—) (surg.) speculum.

⊙**spée**, *n.f.* V. **cépée.**

spencer (spin-sèr), *n.m.*, (—*s*) spencer (garment).

spergule, *n.f.*, (bot.) spurrey.

spermaceti (-céti), *n.m.*, (*n.p.*) spermaceti, sperm.

spermatique, *adj.*, spermatic.

spermatocèle, *n.f.*, (med.) spermatocele.

spermatologie, *n.f.*, (med.) spermatology.

sperme, *n.m.*, sperm, seed. *— de baleine, blanc de baleine ;* spermaceti.

spermophile, *n.m.*, ground squirrel.

sphacèle, *n.m.*, (med.) sphacelus.

sphacélé, -e, *adj.*, sphacelated.

sphénoïdal, -e, *adj.*, sphenoidal.

sphénoïde, *n.m.* and *adj.*, (anat.) sphenoid, sphenoidal.

sphère, *n.f.*, (geom.) sphere, globe ; circle, orb, orbit. *Sortir de sa —* ; to go out of one's sphere. *Etude de la —* ; use of the globes.

sphéricité, *n.f.*, sphericity.

sphérique, *adj.*, spherical, globose. *Triangle —* ; curvilinear triangle.

sphériquement, *adv.*, spherically.

sphériste, *n.m.*, (antiq.) one who taught ball playing.

sphéristère, *n.m.*, (antiq.) ball playing ground.

sphéristique, *n.f.*, (antiq.) the art of ball playing.

sphéroïdal, -e, *adj.*, spheroidal.

sphéroïde, *n.m.*, (geom.) spheroid.

sphéromètre, *n.m.*, spherometer.

sphincter (-tèr), *n.m.*, (anat.) sphincter.

sphinx (sfinks), *n.m.*, sphinx ; (ent.) sphinx, hawk-moth.

sphragistique, *n.f.*, sphragistics.

spic, *n.m.*, (bot.) spike, lavender.

spica, *n.m.*, (surg.) spica-bandage, spica.

spicanard, *n.m.*, (bot.) spikenard.

spiccato, *adv.*, (mus.) spiccato.

spiciforme, *adj.*, spike-shaped.

spicule, *n.m.*, (bot.) spicule, spikelet.

spigélie, *n.f.*, (bot.) worm-grass.

spina-bifida, *n.f.*, (*n.p.*) (med.) rickets.

spinal, -e, *adj.*, spinal.

spina-ventosa, *n.m.*, (*n.p.*) (med.) spina-ventosa.

spinelle, *n.m.*, spinel, spinelle.

spinifère, *n.m.*, spiniferous.
spiniforme, *adj.*, spiniform.
spinosisme, *n.m.*, Spinozism.
spinosiste, *n.m.*, Spinozist.
spiral, -e, *adj.*, spiral.
spiral, *n.m.*, (horl.) spiral spring ; hair-spring, balance spring.
spirale, *n.f.*, (geom.) spiral ; spire ; (conch.) turban. *En* — ; spirally, winding round. *Aller en* — ; to wind (up *or* round).
⊙**spiralement** (-ral-mãn), *adv.*, in a spiral form, spirally.
spiration, *n.f.*, (theol.) spiration.
spire, *n.f.*, (ancient arch.) spire ; (geom.) helix, revolution of the helix.
spirée, *n.f.*, (bot.) spiræa (genus). — *ulmaire*, *or reine-des-prés ;* meadow-sweet, queen of the meadow. — *filipendule ;* dropwort.
spirite, *n.m.f.*, spirit-rapper, spiritist.
spiritisme, *n.m.*, spiritism, spiritualism.
spiritualisation, *n.f.*, (chem.) spiritualization.
spiritualiser, *v.a.*, to spiritualize.
spiritualisme, *n.m.*, spiritualism.
spiritualiste, *n.m.f.* and *adj.*, spiritualist.
spiritualité, *n.f.*, spirituality.
spirituel, *n.m.*, spirituality (not temporality) ; (rel.) spiritual man.
spirituel, -le, *adj.*, spiritual (incorporeal) ; mental, intellectual ; witty, shrewd, ingenious ; sprightly, lively, intelligent. *Un homme fort* — ; a very witty man. *Une réponse —le ; a witty answer.
spirituellement (-èl-mãn), *adv.*, spiritually, in spirit, ingeniously, wittily, cleverly, shrewdly.
spiritueu-x, -se, *adj.*, spirituous.
spiritueux, *n.m.*, spirit, spirits. *pl.*, spirituous liquors.
splanchnique, *adj.*, (anat.) splanchnic.
splanchnologie (splãn-kno-), *n.f.*, (anat.) splanchnology.
spleen (spli-n), *n.m.*, spleen, melancholy.
splénalgie, *n.f.*, spleenalgy.
splendeur, *n.f.*, splendor, brightness, luster ; brilliancy, magnificence, pomp.
splendide, *adj.*, splendid, sumptuous, magnificent.
splendidement (-did-mãn), *adv.*, splendidly, sumptuously, magnificently.
splénétique, *adj.*, *n.m.f.*, splenetic.
splénique, *adj.*, (anat.) splenic.
spoliat-eur, *n.m.*, **-rice**, *n.f.*, spoiler, despoiler, spoliator. *adv.*, despoiling of spoliation.
spoliation, *n.f.*, spoliation.
spolier, *v.a.*, to spoliate, to despoil, to plunder, to rob.
spondaïque, *n.m.* and *adj.*, spondaic.
spondée, *n.m.*, spondee.
spondyle, *n.m.*, (anat.) spondyl, spondyle ; (conch.) spondylus.
spondylite, *n.f.*, (med.) inflammation of the vertebræ.
spongieu-x, -se, *adj.*, spongy.
spongiosité, *n.f.*, sponginess.
spongite, *n.f.*, (min.) spongite.
spontané, -e, *adj.*, spontaneous ; voluntary.
spontanéité, *n.f.*, spontaneity, spontaneousness.
spontanément, *adv.*, spontaneously, of one's own accord, voluntarily.
sponton, *n.m.* V. **esponton**.
sporadique, *adj.*, (med.) sporadic.
spore, *n.f.*, (bot.) spore, sporule.
sport, *n.m.*, (—*s*) sport.
sportsman, *n.m.*, sportsman.
sportule, *n.f.*, dole, bribe, alms.
sporule, *n.f.*, (bot.) sporule, spore.
spouliner, *v.a.*, to spool (thread).
spumeu-x, -se, *adj.*, spumous, foamy, frothy.
spumosité, *n.f.*, frothiness.

sputation, *n.f.*, (med.) sputation, expectoration.
squale (skooal), *n.m.*, (ich.) dog-fish, shark.
squammeu-x, -se (skooa-), *adj.*, squamous, scaly, squamose.
square (skooêr), *n.m.*, (—*s*) square (public place).
squelette, *n.m.*, skeleton ; carcass, frame (of a ship). *C'est un* —, *c'est un vrai* — ; (pers.) he, she, is a living skeleton.
****squille**, *n.f.*, squill (crustaceous animal).
squinancie. V. **esquinancie**.
squine, *n.f.*, (bot.) China-root.
squirre *or* **squirrhe** (skir), *n.m.*, (med.) scirrhus, glandular tumor.
squirreu-x, -se, *or* **squirrheu-x, -se**, *adj.*, scirrhous.
s.s., initial letters of *Sa Sainteté*, His Holiness, title of the Pope.
s.s., p.p., abbreviations of *Saints Pères ;* Holy Fathers.
st ! *int.*, here, come here ! hi ! hoy ! I say !
stabat mater, *n.m.*, (—) (c. rel.) Stabat Mater.
stabilité, *n.f.*, stability, consistence, firmness, solidity ; durability, steadfastness. *Manquer de* — ; to lack stability.
stable, *adj.*, stable, solid, firm, durable, lasting, permanent ; steadfast.
stade, *n.m.*, (antiq.) stadium (185 m.) ; furlong (Eng. measure) ; stade ; (med.) stage, period.
stage, *n.m.*, term of probation, residence ; (rail.) luggage-van. *Faire son* — ; to keep one's terms (as a probationer).
stagiaire, *n.* and *adj.m.*, licentiate in law going through his *stage. Avocat* — ; licentiate in law (not admitted to the bar) *or* probationer. *adj.*, attending terms, going through his course.
stagirite, *n.m.*, stagyrite.
stagnant, -e, *adj.*, stagnant, standing still.
stagnation, *n.f.*, stagnation, stagnancy.
****stagnon**, *n.m.* V. **estagnon**.
stalactite, *n.f.*, (min.) stalactite.
stalagmite, *n.f.*, (min.) stalagmite.
stalle, *n.f.*, stall (for horses).
stamenais, *n.m.pl.*, (nav.) lower futtocks.
staminé, -e, *adj.*, (bot.) staminate, stamened.
staminifère, *adj.*, (bot.) staminiferous.
staminiforme, *adj.*, staminiform.
stance, *n.f.*, stanza.
stangue (stãn-g), *n.f.*, (her.) shank of an anchor.
stannifère, *adj.*, stanniferous, tinny. *Terrain* — ; tin-ground. *Veine* — ; tin-floor.
staphisaigre, *n.f.*, (bot.) stavesacre, licebane, lousewort.
staphylin, *n.m.*, (ent.) staphylinus.
staphylôme, *n.m.*, (med.) staphyloma, staphylosis.
staroste, *n.m.*, starost (Polish noble).
starostie (-tî), *n.f.*, starosty (fief).
stase, *n.f.*, (med.) arrest, stagnation (of the blood).
stathouder (-dèr), *n.m.*, stadtholder.
stathoudérat, *n.m.*, stadtholdership, stadtholderate.
statice, *n.f.*, (bot.) sea-lavender.
station, *n.f.*, action of standing ; manner of standing ; stay ; station (short stay) ; stoppage ; stand (of public coaches) ; (railway) station ; halt ; stoppage. *Il n'y a point de voitures à la* — ; there are no cabs on the stand. *Chef de* — ; (rail.) station-master.
stationnaire, *adj.*, stationary.
stationnaire, *n.m.*, (nav.) guard-ship, police-ship.
stationnal, *adj.*, stational (of churches).
stationnement (-sio-n-mãn), *n.m.*, stationing, stoppage ; standing (of cabs).
stationner, *v.n.*, to stop, to stand (of cabs).

statique, *n.f.*, statics.
statisticien (-si-in), *n.m.*, statistician.
statistique, *n.f.*, statistics, returns.
statuaire, *n.m.*, (pers.) statuary.
statuaire, *adj.*, statuary.
statuaire, *n.f.*, statuary (art).
statue, *n.f.*, statue, figure; (Bibl.) pillar.
statuer, *v.a.*, to decree, to resolve, to ordain, to enact. *v.n.*, to make laws.
statuette, *n.f.*, small statue, statuette.
statu quo, *n.m.*, (*n.p.*) statu quo. *In* — ; in statu quo.
stature, *n.f.*, stature, height.
statut, *n.m.*, statute, decree; by-law, written law; article (of association).
statutaire, *adj.*, statutory, conformable to statute.
steamer (sti-meur), *n.m.*, (—*s*) steamer.
stéarine, *n.f.*, (chem.) stearine.
stéarique, *adj.*, (chem.) stearic.
stéatite, *n.f.*, (min.) steatite.
stéatocèle, *n.f.*, (med.) steatocele.
stéatôme, *n.m.*, (med.) steatoma.
steeple-chase, *n.m.*, (— — —*s*) steeple-chase.
stèle, *n.f.*, (arch.) stela;(of a sun-dial) pedestal.
stellaire, *n.f.*, (bot.) stitchwort.
stellaire, *adj.*,(astron.) stellar, stellary, starry.
stelliforme, *adj.*, stelliform, in the shape of a star.
stellion, *n.m.*, star-lizard.
stellionat, *n.m.*, (jur.) stellionate.
stellionataire, *n.m.*, (jur.) person guilty of stellionate.
sténographe, *n.m.*, stenographer, short-hand writer; reporter. — *des chambres;* parliamentary reporter.
sténographie, *n.f.*, stenography, shorthand.
sténographier, *v.a.*, to write in short-hand, to take down in short-hand, to report.
sténographique, *adj.*, stenographical.
sténographiquement, *adv.*, stenographically.
stentor, *n.m.*, Stentor. *D'une voix de* — ; in a stentorian voice.
steppe, *n.m.* or *f.*, steppe.
stercoraire, *adj.*, stercoraceous, stercorary.
stère, *n.m.*, (French measure) stere, cubic meter (35.3174 cubic feet).
stéréobate, *n.m.*, (arch.) stereobate.
stéréographie, *n.f.*, stereography.
stéréographique, *adj.*, stereographic, stereographical.
stéréométrie, *n.f.*, (geom.) stereometry.
stéréoscope, *n.m.*, stereoscope.
stéréotomie, *n.f.*, (geom.) stereotomy.
stéréotypage, *n.m.*, stereotyping.
stéréotype, *adj.*, stereotype.
stéréotyper, *v.a.*, to stereotype.
stéréotypeur, *n.m.*, stereotyper.
stéréotypie, *n.f.*, stereotypy; stereotype printing; stereotype printing-office.
stérile, *adj.*, sterile, barren, unfruitful; (fig.) fruitless, vain; farrow (of cows). *Année* — ; year of dearth. *Ouvrage* — ; dry work. *Gloire* — ; empty glory. *Vache* —; farrow cow.
stérilement, *adv.*, barrenly, unfruitfully.
stériliser, *v.a.*, to make, to render, sterile; to sterilize.
stérilité, *n.f.*, sterility, barrenness, unfruitfulness; (fig.) dearth, scarcity. — *de nouvelles;* scarcity, *or* dearth, of news.
sterling, *n.* and *adj.m.*, *invariable*, sterling. *Monnaie* —; sterling. *Livre* —; pound sterling.
sterne, *n.m.*, (orni.) tern, black tern.
sternum (-nom), *n.m.*, (—) (anat.) sternum, breast-bone.
sternutatoire, *n.m.* and *adj.*, sternutatory.
stertoreu-x, -se, *adj.*, (med.) stertorous.
stéthoscope, *n.m.*, (med.) stethoscope.
stibié, -e, *adj.*, (pharm.) stibial, antimonial.

stigmate, *n.m.*, scar, stigma, brand, mark of infamy; mark, spot, trace, stain; (ent.) spiracle; (bot.) stigma. *pl.* (theol.) stigmata. — *flétrissant;* mark of infamy, stigma of infamy. *Porter les* —*s de la petite vérole;* to be pock-marked.
stigmatiser, *v.a.*, to brand (with a hot iron); to stigmatize, to brand.
stil de grain, *n.m.*, (paint.) yellow lake.
stillation, *n.f.*, (phys.) dripping, dropping.
stimulant, -e, *adj.*, stimulating, stimulant.
stimulant, *n.m.*, stimulant, stimulus.
stimulat-eur, -rice, *adj.*, stimulating.
stimulation, *n.f.*, stimulation.
stimuler, *v.a.*, to stimulate, to excite, to rouse, to spur on, to urge forward.
stimulus, *n.m.*, (med.) stimulus.
stipe, *n.f.*, (bot.) feather-grass, stipa; ⊙ a tax on leases.
stipe, *n.m.*, (bot.) stipe; caudex.
stipelle, *n.f.*, (bot.) stipel.
stipendiaire, *adj.*, stipendiary, hired.
stipendié, *n.m.*, stipendiary, hireling.
stipendier, *v.a.*, to hire, to keep in pay.
stipulacé, -e, *adj.*, (bot.) stipulaceous.
stipulant, -e, *adj.*, (jur.) stipulating.
stipulation, *n.f.*, stipulation.
stipule, *n.f.*, (bot.) stipula, stipule.
stipuler, *v.a.*, to stipulate; (jur.) to covenant, to contract.
stock, *n.m.*, (—) (com.) stock.
stockfisch, *n.m.*, (n.p.) stockfish.
stoff, *n.m.*, stuff (cotton *or* woolen).
stoïcien, -ne, (-in, -è-n), *n.* and *adj.*, stoic; stoical.
stoïcisme, *n.m.*, stoicism, stoicalness.
stoïcité, *n.f.*, stoicism.
stoïque, *n.m.f.* and *adj.*, stoic; stoical.
stoïquement (-ik-mān), *adv.*, stoically.
stokfiche, *n.m.* *V.* **stockfisch**.
stole, *n.f.*, (antiq.) stola.
stomacal, -e, *adj.*, stomachic.
stomachique, *n.m.* and *adj.*, (med.) stomachic; (anat.) of the stomach.
stomate, *n.m.*, (bot.) stomatum.
stopper, *v.a.* and *n.*, to stop (a railway train, a steamboat, an engine).
stoppeur, *n.m.*, (nav.) stopper.
storax (-aks), *n.m.*, (bot., pharm.) storax.
store, *n.m.*, spring-roller blind, roller-blind; blind. *Lever les* —*s;* to pull up the blinds. *Baisser les* —*s;* to let the blinds down, *or* pull down the blinds.
storthing, *n.m.*, Storthing (Norway legislative body).
strabisme, *n.m.*, (med.) strabism; squinting.
strabite, *n.m.f.* and *adj.*, squint-eyed; squinting.
stramonium, *n.m.*, (bot.) stramony, thorn-apple.
strangulation, *n.f.*, strangulation.
⊙stranguler, *v.a.* *V.* **étrangler**.
strangurie, *n.f.*, (med.) strangury.
strapasser, *v.a.*, ⊙ to drub, to bang, to thrash; (paint.) (l.u.) to rough-sketch, to paint carelessly, to daub.
strapasson, *n.m.*, dauber, rough-sketcher.
strapassonner, *v.a.*, (paint.) *V.* **strapasser**.
strapontin, *n.m.*, bracket seat (of carriages).
stras (strâs), *n.m.*, strass, paste (of jewels).
strasse, *n.f.*, floss-silk.
stratagème, *n.m.*, stratagem.
strate, *n.f.*, (geol.) stratum.
stratégie, *n.f.*, strategy.
stratégique, *adj.*, strategic, strategical.
stratégiste, *n.m.*, strategist.
stratification, *n.f.*, stratification.
stratifier, *v.a.*, to stratify.
stratocratie (-ci), *n.f.*, stratocracy.
stratographie, *n.f.*, stratography.
strélitz, *n.m.*, strelitz.

strette, *n.f.*, (mus.) stretto (part of a fugue).

stribord, *n.m.* (nav.). *V.* **tribord**.

strict (strikt), -e, *adj.*, strict, precise, rigid, severe, rigorous.

strictement, *adv.*, strictly, precisely, rigidly, severely, rigorously.

stricture, *n.f.*, (med.) (l.u.) stricture.

strident, -e, *adj.*, strident, harsh, jarring, screeching, shrill. *Voix —e ;* shrill voice.

strideur, *n.f.*, harshness, creaking (of sound).

strié, -e, *adj.*, (min., arch., natural hist.) striate, striated, channeled, streaked.

strie, *n.f.*, (natural hist.) striæ ; (arch.,) fillet, fluting, streak.

strier, *v.n.*, to streak.

strige, *n.f.*, or **stryge**, *n.m.*, vampire, ghost.

strigile, *n.m.*, (antiq.) strigil.

strigueu-x, -se (-gheû, -z), *adj.*, (bot.) strigous, strigose.

striures, *n.f.pl. V.* **strie**.

strobile, *n.m.*, (bot.). *V.* **cône** (bot.).

strophe, *n.f.*, strophe.

structure, *n.f.*, structure, construction, form, make; (fig.) arrangement, disposition.

strumeu-x, -se, *adj.*, strumous, scrofulous.

strychnine (strik-), *n.f.*, (med.) strychnine, strychnia.

strychnos (stri-knôs), *n.m.*, (bot.) strychnos.

stryge, *n.m. V.* **strige**. [to stucco.

stuc, *n.m.*, stucco, stucco-work. *Enduire de —;*

stucateur, *n.m.*, stucco plasterer.

studieusement (-eûz-mān), *adv.*, studiously.

studieu-x, -se, *adj.*, studious.

stupéfacti-f, -ve, *adj.*, (med.) stupefactive.

stupéfaction, *n.f.*, (med.) stupefaction; stupefaction, great astonishment.

stupéfait, -e, *adj.*, stupefied, astonished ; astounded, dumfounded, thunderstruck.

stupéfiant, -e, *adj.*, (med.) stupefactive, stupefying, dumfounding, stunning.

stupéfiant, *n.m.*, (med.) narcotic.

stupéfier, *v.a.*, (med.) to stupefy ; to stupefy, to astonish, to astound, to amaze, to dumfound.

stupeur, *n.f.*, (med.) stupor ; stupor, astonishment, amazement.

stupide, *n.m.f.* and *adj.*, stupid person *or* fellow, blockhead; stupid, senseless, dull.

stupidement (-pid-mān), *adv.*, stupidly, senselessly.

stupidité, *n.f.*, stupidity, stupidness, dullness; stupid thing, piece of stupidity.

stupre, *n.m.*, stupration.

stygmate, *n.m. V.* **stigmate**.

style, *n.m.*, style, tone, manner, strain ; (fine arts) style ; (chronology) style ; (bot.) style. *— décousu ;* unconnected style. *— badin ;* jocular style. *— fleuri ;* florid style. *— coulant ;* fluent style. *— soutenu ;* elevated, lofty, style. *— de pratique ;* law terms. *— de cadran ;* style, *or* gnomon (of a dial). *Vieux —;* old style ; old-fashioned. *Voilà bien son —;* that is just his way, that's just like him.

stylé, -e, *adj.*, trained, taught ; clever ; stylish, dashing.

styler, *v.a.*, to train, to bring up, to use, to accustom, to form.

stylet, *n.m.*, stiletto ; (surg.) probe, stylet.

styliforme, *adj.*, (bot.) styliform.

stylite, *n.m.* and *adj.*, (rel. hist.) stylite.

stylobate, *n.m.*, (arch.) stylobate.

styloïde, *adj.*, (anat.) styloid.

styptique, *n.m.* and *adj.*, (med.) styptic.

styrax, *n.m.*, (bot. pharm.) storax.

su, *n.m.*, knowledge. *Au — de ;* to the knowledge of. *Au vu et au — de tout le monde ;* as everybody knows.

su, *part.* (of *savoir*), known.

suage, *n.m.*, dampness, oozing ; (nav.) paving-stuff.

suaire, *n.m.*, winding-sheet, shroud.

suant, -e, *adj.*, sweating, in a sweat ; perspiring, dripping with sweat.

suave, *adj.*, sweet ; agreeable, pleasant ; fragrant, odoriferous ; soft.

suavement (-av-mān), *adj.*, sweetly, agreeably, pleasantly.

suavité, *n.f.*, suavity ; sweetness, fragrance, pleasantness, agreeableness.

subalterne, *n.m.* and *adj.*, subaltern, subordinate, inferior.

subalternité, *n.f.*, subordination ; inferior position.

subdélégation, *n.f.*, subdelegation.

subdélégué (-ghé), *n.m.*, subdelegate.

subdéléguer (-ghé), *v.a.*, to subdelegate.

subdiviser, *v.a.*, to subdivide.

*se***subdiviser**, *v.r.*, to subdivide, to be subdivided.

subdivision, *n.f.*, subdivision.

subéreu-x, -se, *adj.*, (bot.) suberous, corky.

subérique, *adj.*, suberic.

subfossile, *adj.*, subfossil.

subintrant, -e, *adj.*, (med.) subintrans, quotidian (beginning before the other is over) (of attacks of fever).

subir, *v.a.*, to undergo, to suffer, to submit, to sustain, to support, to go through, to pass ; to put up with. *— son sort ;* to submit to one's fate. *— la question ;* to undergo torture. *— un examen ;* to pass an examination, to undergo an examination. *— un interrogatoire ;* to be cross-examined. *Se — ;* to put up with one another; to be suffered.

subit, -e, *adj.*, sudden, unexpected.

subitement (-bit-man), *adv.*, suddenly, on a sudden, all of a sudden, unexpectedly.

subito, *adv.*, suddenly, on a sudden, all of a sudden.

subjecti-f, -ve, *adj.*, subjective.

subjectivement (-tiv-mān), *adv.*, subjectively.

subjectivité, *n.f.*, (philos.) subjectivity.

subjonctif, *n.m.*, (gram.) subjunctive.

subjugation, *n.f.*, subjugation.

subjuguer (-ghé), *v.a.*, to subjugate, to subdue, to subject, to bring under the dominion of, to bring under subjection, to master, to get the better of, to overcome ; to captivate.

subjugueur, *n.m.*, subduer, subjugator.

sublimable, *adj.*, (chem.) sublimable.

sublimation, *n.f.*, (chem.) sublimation, subliming.

sublimatoire, *n.m.*, (chem.) subliming pot.

sublime, *n.m.* and *adj.*, sublime, sublimity.

sublimé, *n.m.*, (chem.) sublimate.

sublimement, *adv.*, sublimely.

sublimer, *v.a.*, (chem.) to sublimate.

sublimité, *n.f.*, sublimity.

sublingual, -e (-gooal), *adj.*, (anat.) sublingual.

sublunaire, *adj.*, sublunar, sublunary.

submerger, *v.a.*, to submerge, to swamp, to sink, to drown ; to overwhelm.

submersible, *adj.*, submergible; (bot.) submerse.

submersion, *n.f.*, submersion.

subodorer, *v.a.*, to scent at a distance.

subordination, *n.f.*, subordination.

subordonné, -e, *n.m.f.* and *adj.*, subordinate, inferior, dependent.

subordonnément, *adv.*, subordinately.

subordonner, *v.a.*, to subordinate.

⊙**subornateur**, *n.m. V.* **suborneur**.

subornation, *n.f.*, subornation, bribery, bribing ; (jur.) embracery (of juries).

suborner, *v.a.*, to suborn, to bribe, to tamper with ; (jur.) to embrace, to attempt to corrupt (a jury).

suborneu-r, *n.m.*, -se, *n.f.*, suborner, briber; (jur.) embracer (of juries).

suborneu-r, -se, *adj.,* suborning, bribing.

subrécargue (-kar-g), *n.m.,* (com., nav.) supercargo.

subrécot, *n.m.,* after-reckoning, fresh demand.

subreptice, *adj.,* surreptitious.

subrepticement (-tis-măn), *adv.,* surreptitiously.

subreption, *n.f.,* subreption.

subrogation, *n.f.,* (jur.) subrogation.

subrogatoire, *adj.,* subrogatory.

subrogé, -e, *adj.,* surrogated. — *tuteur;* deputy - guardian (to watch over trustees). *Evêque —;* suffragan bishop, surrogate.

subroger, *v.a.,* (jur.) to surrogate. *Se —;* to be surrogated.

subséquemment (-ka-măn), *adv.,* subsequently.

subséquent, -e, *adj.,* subsequent.

subside, *n.m.,* subsidy, aid. *pl.,* supplies, supply (of the state).

subsidiaire, *adj.,* subsidiary, auxiliary, collateral, additional.

subsidiairement (-dièr-măn), *adv.,* further, also, likewise; in a subsidiary manner, collaterally, additionally.

subsistance, *n.f.,* subsistence, sustenance, maintenance, support, allowance. *Tirer sa — de;* to get one's living by.

subsistant, -e, *adj.,* subsisting, subsistent, existing, extant, being, living.

subsister, *v.n.,* to subsist, to stand, to continue, to be extant, to have existence; to be in force; to hold good; to exist, to live. *J'ai de la peine à —;* I can hardly get a livelihood.

substance, *n.f.,* substance. *En —;* summarily, in substance.

substantiel, -le, *adj.,* substantial.

substantiellement (-sièl-măn), *adv.,* (theol.) substantially.

substantif, *n.m.* and *adj.,* (gram.) substantive.

substantive, *adj.f.,* (dy.) substantive, substantial. *Couleur —;* substantive color.

substantivement (-tiv-măn), *adv.,* substantively.

substituer, *v.a.,* to substitute, to change, to replace; (jur.) to entail; (jur.) to appoint. *Propriété substituée;* entailed estate.

se **substituer,** *v.r.,* to substitute one's self; to supersede, to replace.

substitut, *n.m.,* substitute, deputy, delegate, surrogate.

substitution, *n.f.,* substitution; (jur.) entail; (jur.) estate in tail.

substratum (-tom), *n.m.,* (*n.p.*) (philos.) substratum.

substruction, *n.f.,* (arch.) substructure.

substructure, *n.f.,* substructure.

subterfuge, *n.m.,* subterfuge, evasion, shift.

subtil, -e, *adj.,* subtile, thin, fine; acute, keen, sharp, quick, sagacious; ready, dexterous; cunning, smart, shrewd, artful, crafty.

subtilement (-til-măn), *adv.,* subtly, artfully, slyly; finely, cunningly, dexterously; acutely, sharply, smartly.

subtilisation, *n.f.,* (chem.) subtilization.

subtiliser, *v.a.,* to subtilize, to refine; (fam.) to cheat, to take in, to deceive.

subtiliser, *v.n.,* to subtilize.

subtiliseur, -se, *n.m.f.,* subtilizer; abstracter.

subtilité, *n.f.,* subtlety; fineness, penetration, refinement, acuteness; subtleness, expertness, adroitness, shrewdness, nicety of discrimination; cunning, artfulness, craftiness. *La — des sens;* the acuteness of the senses. — *d'esprit;* refinement of mind.

subulé, -e, *adj.,* (bot.) subulate, awl-shaped.

suburbain, -e (-bĭn, bè-n), *adj.,* suburban.

suburbicaire, *adj.,* (Roman antiq.) suburbicarian; (c.rel.) within the diocese of Rome.

subvenir, *v.n.,* to relieve, to help, to assist; to supply, to provide, to afford. — *aux besoins de quelqu'un;* to provide for any one's wants. *Si je puis y —;* if I can afford it, *or* find the ways and means.

subvention, *n.f.,* supply, subsidy, grant; aid, help, subvention.

subventionnel, -le, *adj.,* subventional.

subventionner, *v.a.,* to grant a relief (in public money), to subsidize, to subvention; to endow, to assist, to aid.

subversi-f, -ve (-vèr-), *adj.,* subversive.

subversion (-vèr-), *n.f.,* subversion, ruin, overthrow, destruction.

subvertir (-vèr-), *v.a.,* to subvert, to destroy, to overthrow, to ruin.

suc, *n.m.,* juice, essence, quintessence. — *gastrique;* gastric juice.

succédané, *n.m.,* (med.) succedaneum, substitute.

succédané, -e, *adj.,* (med.) succedaneous.

succéder, *v.n.,* to succeed, to follow; to inherit. *La nuit succède au jour;* night follows day. — *à quelqu'un;* to succeed any one. — *à un royaume;* to succeed to a kingdom. *Tout lui succède;* he, she, is successful in everything. *se* **succéder,** *v.r.,* to succeed one another, to follow one another.

succès, *n.m.,* success. — *de circonstance;* accidental success. — *d'estime;* indifferent success.

successeur (suk-sè-), *n.m.,* successor.

successibilité (suk-sè-), *n.f.,* (jur.) right of succession.

successible (suk-sè-), *adj.,* (jur.) heritable, capable of inheriting.

successi-f, -ve (suk-sè-), *adj.,* successive, (jur.) in succession.

succession (suk-sè-), *n.f.,* succession, inheritance, heritage, heirs, estate; series. *Renoncer à une —;* to give up one's right to a succession. *Par — de temps;* in process of time. *Droit d'administrer la —;* (jur.) letters of administration. *Recueillir une —;* to acquire an inheritance, to have an estate left one, to come into property. *Acte de —;* act of settlement. *Droit de —;* right of succession; legacy-duty, probate-duty.

sucessivement (suk-sè-siv-măn), *adv.,* successively, in succession.

succin (suk-sĭn), *n.m.,* yellow amber.

succinct, -e (suk-sĭn, -t), *adj.,* succinct, concise, brief, short.

succinctement (suk-sĭnt-măn), *adv.,* succinctly, briefly, concisely.

succion (suk-si-), *n.f.,* suction, sucking.

succomber, *v.n.,* to sink under *or* beneath, to fall; to yield, to succumb, to be overcome, to fail, to be worsted, to get the worst of it; to die, to perish. — *à la douleur;* to be overcome with grief. — *à la tentation;* to yield to temptation. — *sous le faix;* to sink under the burden.

succube, *n.m.,* succubus.

succulemment, *adv.,* succulently.

succulence, *n.f.,* succulence, succulency.

succulent, -e, *adj.,* succulent, juicy; nutritious, rich.

succursale, *n.* and *adj.f.,* (eccl.) chapel of ease, branch establishment, auxiliary branch; branch-bank.

succursaliste, *n.m.,* curate of a chapel of ease.

sucement (sus-măn), *n.m.,* sucking, suck.

sucer, *v.a.,* to suck, to suck in, to imbibe; to suck out; to suck up; to draw, to drain. *Se —;* to be sucked.

sucet, *n.m.,* (ich.) sucking-fish, sucker, remora; (orni.) common wren.

suceur, *n.m.* and *adj.,* sucker; sucking; (zoöl.) suctorian.

suçoir, *n.m.*, sucker; (ent.) proboscis.

suçon, *n.m.*, spot made by sucking; sucking-mark; stick of barley-sugar.

suçoter, *v.a.*, to keep sucking, to suck gradually, to suck at. — *un sucre d'orge;* to suck a stick of barley-sugar.

sucre, *n.m.*, sugar. — *brut;* raw sugar, moist sugar, brown sugar. — *pilé* or *en poudre;* powdered sugar, ground sugar; sifted, *or* castor, sugar. — *raffiné;* refined sugar, lump sugar, loaf sugar. — *d'orge;* barley-sugar. *Pain de —;* sugar-loaf. — *en pain;* loaf sugar. *Etre tout — et tout miel;* to be all honey.

sucré, *-e*, *part.*, sugared, sweet, sugary, luscious; (fig.) demure, prim, honeyed, bland. *Air* —; prim air. *Eau — e;* sugar and water.

sucrer, *v.a.*, to sugar, to sweeten, to put sugar in. *Se —;* to put sugar in (one's tea or coffee). *Sucrez-vous;* take some sugar.

sucrerie, *n.f.*, sugar-house, sugar-works, sugar-refinery; sweetmeat; confectionery; sweets.

sucrier, *n.m.*, sugar-bowl, sugar-basin; sugar-maker.

sucr-ier, -ière, *adj.*, sugar, of sugar. *Industrie — ère;* sugar-trade.

sucrin, *adj.*, sugary (melons).

sud (sud), *n.m.*, South; south wind. *Du —;* southern. *Vers le —;* southward. *— est;* south-east. *Au —;* southward. *Courir au —;* to steer a southerly course.

sud, *adj.*, south, southerly (of the wind).

sudation, *n.f.*, (med.) sudation, sweating.

sudatoire, *adj.*, sudatory.

sudiste, *n.m.f.* and *adj.*, Southerner (American politics).

sudorifère, *adj.*, (med.) sudoriferous.

sudorifique, *n.m.*, and *adj.*, (med.) sudorific.

sudoripare, *adj.*, sudoriparous.

sud-ouest (sud-ooèst), *n.m.*, south-west.

suédois, *-e*, *n.* and *adj.*, Swede; Swedish. *A la — e;* Swedish fashion.

suée, *n.f.*, sweating; (fam., pop.) sudden fright, sudden fear.

suer, *v.n.*, to sweat, to be in a sweat, to perspire; to toil, to drudge, to ooze, to ooze out; to sputter; to become damp (of walls). — *à grosses gouttes;* to perspire profusely. *Faire — le tabac;* to heat tobacco. *Faire —;* (fig.) to try any one's patience; to sicken any one.

suer, *v.a.*, to sweat. — *sang et eau;* to toil and moil, to strain every nerve.

suerie (sû-rî), *n.f.*, drying-place (for tobacco).

suette, *n.f.*, sweating sickness. — *miliaire;* miliary fever.

sueur, *n.f.*, sweat, perspiration; sweating. *pl.*, labor, toil, pains. — *rentrée;* (med.) suppressed perspiration. *A la — de;* by the sweat of.

suffire (suffisant, suffi), *v.n.*, to suffice, to be sufficient, to be enough; to be adequate, to be equal to. *Le peu que j'ai me suffit;* the little I have is sufficient for, *or* suffices, me. *Qu'il vous suffise que;* let it suffice you that. *Il suffit que vous le disiez pour que je le croie;* your saying so is sufficient for me to believe it. *On ne peut pas — à tout;* it is impossible to provide for everything, to attend to everything, to guard against everything. *Suffit, cela suffit;* enough, that's enough, no more! *A chaque jour suffit sa peine;* sufficient for the day is the evil thereof.

se suffire, *v.r.*, to support one's self, to keep one's self, to provide for one's self; to find resources in one's self.

suffisamment (-za-mān), *adv.*, sufficiently, enough.

suffisance, *n.f.*, sufficiency, competency; adequacy; ⊙ability; conceit, pride, presumption; self-sufficiency, bumptiousness. *Avoir — de vivres;* to have provisions enough. *A —, en* —; sufficiently, enough. *Un air de —;* a self-conceited air.

suffisant, *-e*, *adj.*, sufficient, enough; consequential, conceited, self-sufficient, stuck up.

suffisant, *n.m.*, *-e*, *n.f.*, self-conceited person, bumptious, stuck-up person.

suffixe, *n.m.*, (gram.) suffix.

suffocant, *-e*, *adj.*, suffocating, choking, stifling.

suffocation, *n.f.*, suffocation, choking, stifling.

suffoquer, *v.a.*, to suffocate, to stifle, to choke.

suffoquer, *v.n.*, to suffocate, to stifle, to choke. — *de rage, de colère;* to be choking with rage, with anger.

suffragant, *n.* and *adj.m.* suffragan.

suffrage, *n.m.*, suffrage, vote; approbation, commendation, support. — *universel;* manhood suffrage.

suffumigation, *n.f.*, (med.) suffumigation.

suffusion, *n.f.*, (med.) suffusion.

suggérer (sug-jé-), *v.a.*, to suggest, to hint, to intimate. *Se —;* to be suggested.

suggestion (sug-jès-ti-on), *n.f.*, (b.s.) suggestion, hint, instigation, intimation; inspiration.

suicide, *n.m.*, suicide, self-murder; self-destruction; (pers.) suicide, self-murderer; (jur.) (pers.) felo de se.

suicidé, *n.m.*, *-e*, *n.f.*, self-murderer, suicide.

se suicider, *v.r.*, to commit suicide, to make away with one's self.

suie, *n.f.*, soot.

suif, *n.m.*, tallow; candle-grease; (nav.) coat, stuff. *Donner un — à quelqu'un;* (pop.) to blow up any one, to give a good blowing up to. *Donner un — à un vaisseau;* (nav.) to pay a ship. *Pain de —;* crackling.

suifer, *v.a.*, to tallow; (nav.) to pay a ship.

suifeux, *-se*, *adj.*, tallowy, greasy.

sui generis, *adj.*, sui generis, of its own particular kind.

suint, *n.m.*, grease; yolk (of wool).

suintement (suint-mān), *n.m.*, oozing, ooze, sweating, leaking.

suinter, *v.n.*, to ooze, to leak, to run.

suisse, *n.m.*, Swiss; head porter (of a mansion); beadle (of a church); (mam.) ground squirrel.

suissesse, *n.f.*, Swiss woman.

suite, *n.f.*, rest; retinue, train, attendance, attendants; sequel; continuation; series, succession; connection, order; set; consequence, result, progress, course; consistency, coherence. *A la —;* after, behind; (mil.) on half-pay, honorary. *Dans la —;* eventually, afterwards. — *de médailles;* set of medals. *Cela peut avoir de fâcheuses — s;* that may be attended with disagreeable consequences. *Sans —;* unconnected; unattended. *N'avoir pas de — s;* to have no bad consequences; to have no coherence; to have no relatives; not to be followed up. *N'avoir pas d'esprit de —;* not to be consistent; to keep at nothing long. *Donner — à;* to follow up, to carry out, to proceed with. *Propos sans —;* desultory talk. *Faire — à;* to be a continuation of, to follow. *De —;* one after another, consecutively, following. *Tout de —;* immediately, at once. *Et ainsi de —;* and so forth, and so on. *La — au prochain numéro;* to be continued (of stories).

suivant, *prep.*, according to, agreeably to; in the opinion of, in pursuance of, conformably to.

suivant que, *conj.*, as, according as.

suivant, *-e*, *adj.*, next, following, succeeding, subsequent, ensuing.

suivant, *n.m.*, *-e*, *n.f.*, follower, attendant; near relation. — *e;* waiting-maid; lady's maid; (thea.) chambermaid.

suiver, *v.a.*, to tallow. *V.* **suifer.**

suivi, *-e*, *part.*, followed; connected; consistent, coherent, regular; constant, sought after, popular. *Discours bien* —, coherent discourse.

suivre (suivant, suivi), *v.a.*, to follow, to go after, to come after, to go next, to be next, to come next ; to pursue ; to attend, to go with, to accompany ; to attend ; to follow ; to observe ; (nav.) to hug (the coast) ; to give way to, to indulge. — *de près*, — *de loin ;* to follow close, to follow at a distance. — *son chemin ;* to go one's way. — *le barreau ;* to follow the profession of the law. — *la mode ;* to follow the fashion. — *sa pointe ;* to pursue one's end. *Faire* —; to have (a person) followed ; to send on, to be forwarded (of letters, etc.) ; (com.) to charge forward.

se **suivre**, *v.r.*, to follow each other, to succeed each other ; to be connected, to be continuous.

suivre, *v.n.*, to follow, to go after, to come after ; to pay attention ; to attend, to result, to ensue. *Faites* —; (print.) run on. *A* —; (of articles or stories) to be continued.

sujet, -te, *n.* and *adj.*, subject (to); subjected, amenable (to), liable (to), exposed (to); apt (to), addicted (to), inclined (to). — *aux lois ;* amenable to the laws. — *à caution ;* not to be trusted, not trustworthy, suspicious, not to be relied upon. *Etre* — *à l'heure ;* to be tied to time.

sujet, -te, *n.m.f.*, subject ; person, individual ; cause, reason ; matter, motive, occasion, ground, account; theme, argument, topic; (hort.) stock. *J'ai* — *de me plaindre ;* I have reason to complain. *S'éloigner de son* — ; to wander from one's subject. *Mauvais* —; worthless fellow, scamp, bad lot. *Petit mauvais* —; little rascal (of children).

sujétion, *n.f.*, subjection, dependence, constraint.

sulfate, *n.m.*, (chem.) sulphate.

sulfaté, -e, *adj.*, (chem.) sulphatic, sulphated.

sulfhydrate, *n.m.*, (chem.) hydrosulphate.

sulfhydrique, *adj.*, (chem.) hydrosulphuric.

sulfite, *n.m.*, (chem.) sulphite.

sulfuration, *n.f.*, (chem.) sulphuration.

sulfure, *n.m.*, (chem.) sulphuret.

sulfuré, -e, *adj.*, (chem.) sulphureted.

sulfureu-x, -se, *adj.*, sulphurous, sulphureous, sulphury.

sulfurique, *adj.*, (chem.) sulphuric.

sultan, *n.m.*, sultan ; scent-satchel, scent-basket.

sultanat, *n.m.*, sultanate.

sultane, *n.f.*, sultana, sultaness ; Turkish man-of-war.

sultanin, *n.m.*, sultanin (Turkish coin).

sumac, *n.m.*, sumac-tree ; sumac.

sund (le), *n.m.*, The Sound (between Denmark and Sweden).

sunnite, *n.m.* V. **schiite**.

super (su-pé), *v.n.*, (nav.) to be stopped up.

superbe (-pèrb), *n.m.* and *adj.*, (Bibl.) proud, haughty man ; proud, arrogant ; superb, splendid ; gorgeous, stately ; lofty ; supercilious, vainglorious. *Dieu résiste au* — ; God resisteth the proud. *Un* — *tableau ;* a splendid painting. *Un dîner* — ; a splendid dinner. *Meubles* —*s ;* gorgeous furniture.

superbe (-pèrb), *n.f.*, arrogance, haughtiness, vainglory.

superbement (-pèr-), *adv.*, proudly, arrogantly ; sumptuously, splendidly ; loftily.

supercherie (-pèr-), *n.f.*, deceit, fraud, trickery.

superfétation (-pèr-), *n.f.*, superfetation ; superfluity.

superficie (-pèr-), *n.f.*, superficies, surface ; area.

superficiel, -le (-pèr-), *adj.*, superficial, shallow.

superficiellement (su-pèr-fi-si-èl-mān), *adv.*, superficially.

superfin, -e (-pèr-), *adj.*, superfine.

superfin (-pèr-), *n.m.*, superfine quality, superfluity, excess.

superflu, -e (-pèr-), *adj.*, superfluous, exuberant, needless, unnecessary.

superflu (-pèr-), *n.m.*, superfluity, excess.

superfluité (-pèr-), *n.f.*, superfluity.

supérieur, -e, *n.* and *adj.*, superior, upper, higher. *Les classes* —*es ;* the higher classes. *Etre* — *aux événements ;* to rise superior to events.

supérieurement (-eur-mān), *adv.*, in a superior manner, in a superior degree, superlatively well, uncommonly well, capitally.

supériorité, *n.f.*, superiority.

superlati-f, -ve (-pèr-), *adj.*, (gram.) superlative.

superlatif (-pèr-), *n.m.*, superlative. *Au* —, superlatively ; (gram.) in the superlative, superlatively. *Cet homme est bête au* — ; that man is stupid to a degree.

superlativement (su-pèr-la-tiv-mān), *adv.*, superlatively.

superposer (-pèr-), *v.a.*, to superpose, to add. *Se* —; to add itself.

superposition (-pèr-), *n.f.*, superposition.

superpurgation (-pèr-), *n.f.*, superpurgation.

superséder (-pèr-), *v.n.*, (jur.) to postpone, to put off.

superstitieusement (su-pèrs-ti-si-euz-mān), *adv.*, superstitiously.

superstitieu-x, -se (-pèrs-ti-si-), *adj.*, superstitious ; overnice.

superstition (-pèrs-ti-si-), *n.f.*, superstition ; overnicety.

superstructure (-pèr-), *n.f.*, superstructure.

supersubstantiel, -le (-pèr-), *adj.*, supersubstantial.

supin, *n.m.*, (gram.) supine.

supinateur, *n.m.*, (anat.) supinator.

supination, *n.f.*, supination.

supplantation, *n.f.*, supplantation.

supplanter, *v.a.*, to supplant ; to oust.

suppléance, *n.f.*, substitution, assistantship.

suppléant, -e, *n.m.*, -e, *n.f.*, substitute, assistant, deputy. *Juge* —; assistant judge.

suppléer, *v.a.*, to supply, to fill up, to make up (what is deficient) ; to take the place of.

suppléer, *v.n.*, to make up the deficiency ; to supply the place. *La valeur suppléée au nombre ;* valor makes up for deficiency of numbers.

supplément, *n.m.*, supplement, addition ; additional price, extra.

supplémentaire, *adj.*, supplementary, supplemental, additional, extra.

suppléti-f, -ve, *adj.*, suppletory, completing.

suppliant, -e, *n.* and *adj.*, suppliant, supplicant ; beseecher, implorer ; supplicating, beseeching, entreating.

supplication, *n.f.*, supplication, entreaty, humble petition.

supplice, *n.m.*, corporal punishment ; torment, pain, anguish. *Etre au* — ; to be upon the rack, to be on thorns ; to be in great pain. *Dernier* — ; capital punishment.

supplicié, *n.m.*, criminal executed.

supplicier, *v.a.*, to put to death, to execute.

supplier, *v.a.*, to beseech, to entreat, to supplicate.

supplique, *n.f.*, petition, request, supplication, prayer, entreaty.

support, *n.m.*, support, prop ; assistance ; rest, stand, bracket ; fulcrum ; (carp.) strut ; (her.) supporter ; (arch.) pillar.

supportable, *adj.*, supportable, bearable, tolerable.

supportablement, *adv.*, tolerably, bearably.

supporter, *v.a.*, to support, to sustain, to

uphold ; to endure ; to suffer, to tolerate, to bear with, to put up with, to stand.

se supporter, *v.r.,* to be supported ; to be borne ; to be suffered ; to bear with one another.

supposable, *adj.,* supposable.

supposé, -e, *part.,* supposed ; supposititious, pretended, counterfeit, putative ; reputed. — *qu'il y consente;* suppose, *or* supposing, he consents to it.

supposer, *v.a.,* to suppose, to grant, to infer, to imply, to forge, to feign; to conjecture. — *un testament;* to forge a will. — *un enfant;* to substitute a child, to palm off a child (upon).

suppositi-f, -ve, *adj.,* suppositive.

supposition, *n.f.,* supposition, forgery ; substitution. — *d'enfant;* palming off of a child.

suppositoire, *n.m.,* (med.) suppository.

suppôt, *n.m.,* agent, instrument, tool ; (b.s.) abettor; imp (of the devil).

suppressi-f, -ve, *adj.,* suppressive.

suppression, *n.f.,* suppression, concealment.

supprimer, *v.a.,* to suppress, to pass over in silence ; to put down, to abolish, to take off, to omit, to cut off *or* down, to cancel. — *des impôts;* to take off taxes. — *une loi;* to abolish a law. *Se* —; to be suppressed.

suppurati-f, -ve, *adj.,* (med.) suppurative.

suppuratif, *n.m.,* (med.) suppurative.

suppuration, *n.f.,* suppuration.

suppurer, *v.n.,* to suppurate.

supputation, *n.f.,* computation, calculation, supputation, reckoning.

supputer, *v.a.,* to calculate, to compute, to reckon, to suppute.

suprématie (-ci), *n.f.,* supremacy.

suprême, *adj.,* supreme, highest, last. *A l'heure* —; at the last hour (death).

suprêmement, *adv.,* supremely.

sur, *prep.,* upon, on, over ; by ; in ; about ; towards ; above ; on account of, respecting, concerning ; out of. *Compter* —; to rely on, to make sure of. — *un vaisseau;* on board a ship. *Il l'a mis* — *son testament;* he has put him in his will. *N'avoir pas d'argent* — *soi;* to have no money about one. — *le soir;* towards evening. — *la brune;* about dusk. — *la fin de la semaine;* towards the end of the week. — *ma parole;* upon my word. *Il s'excusa* — *son âge;* he excused himself on account of his age. *Il prend trop* — *lui;* he undertakes too much *or* he presumes too much. — *le-champ;* immediately. — *ces entrefaites;* in the meantime. *Dix* — *quinze;* ten out of fifteen. — *toute chose,* — *toutes choses;* above all, above all things. — *le tout;* upon the whole; (her.) over all. *Donner* — to look out upon. *Six pieds* — *deux;* six feet by two.

sur, -e, *adj.,* sour.

sûr, -e, *adj.,* sure, certain ; safe, secure; firm, steady, unerring, trustworthy. *Je suis — de vous;* I can depend on you. *Il est — de son fait;* he is sure of success, *or* his doom is sealed. *Les chemins sont —s;* the roads are safe. *Le temps n'est pas* —; the weather is uncertain. *Il est en lieu* —; he is in a place of safety, he is out of harm's way. *C'est un ami* —; he is a trusty friend. *Ce port est* —; this port is safe. *A coup* —, *pour* —; surely, for certain, positively, for sure. — *comme père et mère;* as sure as a gun. — *et certain;* positive. *Peu* —; unsafe. *Pour le plus* —; to be on the safe side.

sûr, *adv.,* surely, certainly, assuredly.

surabondamment (-da-mān), *adv.,* superabundantly.

surabondance, *n.f.,* superabundance.

surabondant, -e, *adj.,* superabundant.

surabonder, *v.n.,* to superabound.

surachat, *n.m.,* overpaying.

suracheter (-ash-té), *v.a.,* to overpay.

suraigu, -ë, *adj.,* (mus.) very high, very shrill.

surajoutement (-joot-mān), *n.m.,* superaddition.

surajouter, *v.a.,* to superadd.

sural, -e, *adj.,* (anat.) sural.

sur-aller, *v.n.,* (hunt.) to go over a track (without pointing) (of a dog).

*sur-andouiller, *n.m.,* (— -—s) (hunt.) surantler.

surannation (-an-na-), *n.f.,* expiration.

suranné, -e (-ra-né), *part.,* expired ; superannuated, grown out of date ; antiquated.

se suranner (-ra-né), *v.n.,* to be past one year's date, to expire. [Little used. *V.* **périmer.**]

sur-arbitre, *n.m.,* (— -—s) umpire.

surard, *adj.,* of elder-flower. *Vinaigre* —; elder-flower vinegar.

surate, *n.f.,* surah (of the Koran).

surbaissé, -e, *adj.,* (arch.) surbased, elliptical, overhanging. *Un cintre* —; a low overhanging arch.

surbaissement (-bès-mān), *n.m.,* (arch.) surbasement.

surbaisser, *v.a.,* (arch.) to make elliptic.

surbaisser, *v.n.,* to overhang.

surbande, *n.f.,* (surg.) bandage.

surcens (-sans), *n.m.,* (feudalism) lord's rent.

surcharge, *n.f.,* additional burden ; overloading, overcharge ; extra weight, overplus ; word written over another.

surcharger, *v.a.,* to overload, to overburden, to overcharge, to surcharge; to overtax, to overstock ; (fig.) to overwhelm, to weigh down (with) ; to oppress; to write over words. — *de travail;* to overwhelm with work. — *d'impôts;* to overtax.

surchauffer, *v.a.,* to overheat.

surchauffure, *n.f.,* (metal.) overheating.

surchoix, *n.m.,* first, *or* prime, quality.

surcomposé, -e, *adj.* and *n.m.,* (gram.) double compound.

surcoupe, *n.f.,* trumping over.

surcouper, *v.a.,* to trump over (at cards).

surcroissance, *n.f.,* outgrowth, overgrowth, excrescence.

surcroît, *n.m.,* superaddition, increase, aggravation, excess. *Pour — de malheur;* to make it worse *or* as a crowning misfortune. *De* —; to boot, in addition.

surcroître, *v.n.,* to grow out (of) ; to outgrow.

Ⓢ**surcroître,** *v.a.,* to increase beyond measure.

surcuire, *v.a.,* to overbake.

surcuisson, *n.f.,* overbaking.

surdemande, *n.f.,* immoderate demand.

surdent, *n.f.,* irregular tooth ; wolf's tooth (of horses).

surdité, *n.f.,* deafness.

surdoré, -e, *part.,* double-gilt.

surdorer, *v.a.,* to double-gild.

surdos, *n.m.,* loin-strap (of a horse); porter's pad.

sureau, *n.m.,* elder, elder-tree.

surélever, *v.a.,* to increase the height of ; to make higher.

surelle, *n.f.,* (bot.) wood-sorrel.

sûrement (sur-mān), *adv.,* surely, certainly ; safely, securely ; to be sure.

suréminent, -e, *adj.,* supereminent.

surémission, *n.f.,* (fin.) over-issue.

surenchère, *n.f.,* outbidding, higher bid.

surenchérir, *v.n.,* to outbid, to bid higher.

surenchérisseur, *n.m.,* outbidder.

surérogation, *n.f.,* supererogation.

surérogatoire, *adj.,* supererogatory.

surestarie (-rès-), *n.f.,* (nav., com.) demurrage.

surestimation, *n.f.,* overestimate, overvaluation.

surestimer, *v.a.,* to overestimate, to overvalue.

suret, -te, *adj.,* sourish.

sûreté (sur-té), *n.f.,* safety, surety, security; sureness, warranty. *Etre en lieu de* —; to be out of harm's way, to be in safe keeping. *Mettre en* —; to put in safe keeping. *Coffre de* —; iron chest. *Service de* —; detective police. *Ronde de* —; police-round.

surévaluation, *n.f.,* overvaluation, over-estimate.

surévaluer, *v.a.,* to overvalue, to over-estimate.

surexcitation, *n.f.,* excitement, overexcite-ment.

surexciter, *v.a.,* to excite, overexcite.

surface, *n.f.,* surface; outside; appearances.

surfaire, *v.a.,* to overcharge, to ask too much for, to overrate, to overpraise; to exaggerate.

surfaix, *n.m.,* surcingle.

surfin, -e, *adj.,* superfine. *n.m.,* superfine quality.

surfleurir, *v.n.,* (bot.) to blow again.

surge, *adj. Laine* —; raw, unwashed wool; wool in the yolk.

surgeon (-jon), *n.m.,* (hort.) sucker, off-shoot; ⊙descendant. ⊙ — *d'eau ;* natural water-jet.

surgir, *v.n.,* to come to land, to land; to reach (port); to arise, to spring up; to rise into notice. — *au port ;* to come into port. *Faire* —; to give rise to, to bring about, to cause.

surgissement, *n.m.,* arising, springing up; arriving, landing.

surglacer, *v.a.,* to cover, *or* coat, with sugar (pastry).

surhaussement (-hôs-mān), *n.m.,* raising; forcing up (prices).

surhausser, *v.a.,* (arch.) to raise; to force up the price of.

surhumain, -e (-mīn, -mè-n), *adj.,* super-human.

surier, *n.m.,* cork-tree.

surintendance, *n.f.,* superintendence.

surintendant, *n.m.,* superintendent, comp-troller, overseer.

surintendante, *n.f.,* superintendent's wife; lady superintendent.

surjalé, *part.,* (nav.) foul (of anchors).

surjaler *or* **surjauler,** *v.n.,* (nav.) to foul (of anchors).

surjaler *or* **surjauler,** *v.a.,* (nav.) to raise the anchor to clear its stock.

surjet, *n.m.,* (of seams) whip-stitch, overcast-ing.

surjeter, *v.a.,* to whip-stitch, to overcast.

surlendemain (-land-min), *n.m.,* next day but one; second day (after); the day after the morrow. *Le* — *de son départ ;* the second day after his departure.

surlonge, *n.f.,* chuck (of beef).

surlouer, *v.a.,* to let (at an exorbitant rent); to let above value.

surlunaire, *adj.,* superlunar, superlunary.

surmener, *v.a.,* to overdrive, to override; to overwork; (fig.) to treat badly, to deal severely with (pers.).

surmesure, *n.f.,* over-measure.

surmeule, *n.f.,* runner-stone (of a mill).

surmontable, *adj.,* surmountable, superable.

surmonter, *v.a.,* to surmount; to overcome; to conquer, to subdue; to outdo, to surpass; to rise above (of fluids). — *sa colère ;* to subdue one's anger.

surmonter, *v.n.,* to rise above (of fluids).

surmoule, *n.m.,* cast taken on one of plaster.

surmouler, *v.a.,* to make a cast on a figure *or* ornament.

surmoût, *n.m.,* new wort (of wine).

surmulet, *n.m.,* (ich.) surmullet, grey mullet.

surmulot, *n.m.,* surmulot, Norway rat.

surnager, *v.n.,* to float on the surface; to survive, to remain; to hold one's ground.

surnaturalité, *n.f.,* (theol.) supernaturalness.

surnaturel, -le, *adj.,* supernatural, preter-natural.

surnaturel, *n.m.,* supernatural.

surnaturellement (-rèl-mān), *adv.,* super-naturally, preternaturally.

surnom (-non), *n.m.,* surname, cognomen.

surnommer, *v.a.,* to surname.

surnuméraire, *n.m.* and *adj.,* supernume-rary.

surnumérariat, *n.m.,* supernumerary time.

suron, *n.m.,* seroon; (bot.) earth-nut.

suros (-rô), *n.m.,* (vet.) splint.

suroxydation, *n.f.,* (chem.) peroxidizing, su-peroxidation.

suroxyde, *n.m.,* (chem.) peroxide.

suroxyder, *v.a.,* (chem.) to peroxidize.

suroxygéné, -e, *adj.,* (chem.) overcharged with oxygen.

suroxygéner, *v.a.,* to overcharge with oxy-gen; to superoxygenate.

surpasser, *v.a.,* to surpass, to exceed, to go beyond, to excel, to surmount, to outdo; to astonish, to be taller than. *Il me surpasse de trois pouces ;* he is taller than I am by three inches.

surpaye, *n.f.,* extra pay, additional pay; (mil.) batta.

surpayer, *v.a.,* to overpay.

surpeau, *n.f.,* (l.u.) epidermis. *V.* **épiderme.**

surplis, *n.m.,* surplice.

surplomb (-plon), *n.m.,* overhanging (of buildings). *Etre en* —; to overhang. *En* —; overhanging.

surplomber, *v.n.,* to hang over, to overhang.

surplus, *n.m.,* surplus, surplusage, overplus, remainder, rest, difference. *Au* —; besides, moreover, in addition to which.

surpoids, *n.m.,* overweight.

surprenant, -e, *adj.,* surprising, astonishing.

surprendre, *v.a.,* to surprise, to take by sur-prise, to overtake; to deceive, to catch, to over-hear; to entrap, to overreach, to intercept; to astonish, to amaze. — *une ville ;* to take a town by surprise. *La nuit nous surprit ;* night over-took us. *La pluie me surprit ;* I was caught in the rain.

se **surprendre,** *v.r.,* to surprise one's self; to catch one's self.

surprise, *n.f.,* surprise; amazement; deceit, deception; surprise-box. *Ménager une* — *à quelqu'un ;* to prepare a surprise for any one. *Revenir de sa* —; to recover from one's sur-prise.

surproduction, *n.f.,* overproduction.

surrénal, -e, *adj.,* (anat.) suprarenal, surre-nal.

sursaturation, *n.f.,* supersaturation.

sursaturer, *v.a.,* to supersaturate.

sursaut, *n.m.,* start. *S'éveiller en* —; to start up out of one's sleep, to start up. *Eveiller,* or *réveiller, en* —; to startle any one out of his sleep, to awake any one suddenly.

surséance, *n.f.,* suspension.

sursel, *n.m.,* (chem.) supersalt.

sursemer, *v.a.,* to sow over again.

surseoir (sursoyant, sursis), *v.a.* and *n.,* to sus-pend, to defer, to delay, to postpone, to put off, to respite.

sursis, *n.m.,* delay, respite, reprieve.

sursolide, *n.m.* and *adj.,* (alg.) sursolid.

surtare, *n.f.,* (com.) supertare, extra tare.

surtaux, *n.m.,* excessive taxation, overassess-ment.

surtaxe, *n.f.,* surtax, surcharge, additional tax; extra postage.

surtaxer, *v.a.,* to overtax, to overassess.

surtiré, *n.m.,* (com.) acceptor of a bill; drawee.

surtout, *adv.,* above all, especially, chiefly.

surtout, n.m., light cart; épergne; centre-piece; overcoat.

surusage, n.m. (com.) clough, cloff (allowance).

*****surveillance,** n.f., superintendence, inspection, supervision.

*****surveillant, -e,** n. and adj., inspector, over-seer, superintendent; vigilant, watchful.

*****surveille,** n.f. V. **avant-veille.**

*****surveiller,** v.a., to superintend, to inspect, to look after, to watch, to have an eye upon.

survenance, n.f., (jur.) unexpected birth; unforeseen arrival.

survenant, -e, n., (jur.) unexpected heir; new-comer, chance guest, chance comer.

survendre, v.a. and n., to overcharge.

survenir, v.n., to supervene, to come on, to take place, to happen unexpectedly, to befall, to arise, to come unexpectedly; to drop in.

survente, n.f., overcharge.

surventer, v.n., (nav.) to blow hard, to blow a gale.

survider, v.a., to partly empty, to lighten (anything).

survie, n.f., survivorship, survival.

survivance, n.f., reversion (of offices); survivorship. De —; reversionary.

survivancier, n.m., reversioner (of offices).

survivant, -e, n. and adj., survivor; surviving.

survivre, v.n., to survive, to outlive, to out-last. — à son père; to outlive one's father. v.a., to get over an illness, to outlive (a wife, children, etc.).

se **survivre,** v.r., to live again. Se — à soi-même; to lose one's faculties, to fall into one's dotage. Se — dans ses enfants, dans ses ouvrages; to live again in one's children, in one's works.

sus, prep., (l.u.) upon, above, afore, fore. Courir — à quelqu'un; to run at, to fall upon, to attack, any one. En —; over and above, in addition, extra, to boot.

sus, int., on! on them! at them!

susceptibilité, n.f., susceptibility, irritability, touchiness, irascibility.

susceptible, adj., susceptible, capable; irascible, easily offended, oversensitive, touchy. Elle est trop —; she takes offense too easily or she is too touchy.

susception, n.f., taking of holy orders; (c.rel.) reception (of the crown, of the cross).

⊙**suscitation,** n.f., instigation, (ant.) suscitation.

susciter, v.a., to raise, to raise up, to start, to set up, to create, to give rise to, to give birth to, to raise against, to stir up, to rouse.

suscription, n.f., superscription, address.

susdénommé, -e, adj., above-mentioned.

susdit, -e, adj., aforesaid.

susénoncé, -e, adj., above-mentioned.

susmentionné, -e, adj., (jur.) above-mentioned.

susnommé, -e, adj., (jur.) above-named.

suspect, -e (-pèk, -t), adj., suspected, suspicious. Cela m'est —; I don't like the look of it. Vous me seriez — pour cent raisons; there are a hundred reasons for my suspecting you.

suspecter, v.a., to suspect.

se **suspecter,** v.r., to suspect one another.

suspendre, v.a., to suspend, to hang, to hang up; to stop, to delay. — son travail; to lay aside one's work, to stay, to postpone, to defer.

se **suspendre,** v.r., to suspend one's self.

suspendu, -e, adj., part., suspended, hung up. Pont —; suspension bridge; (of carriages) on springs. Jardins —s; hanging gardens. Jetée —e; chain-pier.

suspens, adj., (eccl.) suspended. Prêtre —; inhibited priest. En —; in suspense; in abeyance; outstanding (of debts).

suspense, n.f., (eccl.) inhibition.

suspenseur, adj., (anat.) suspensory.

suspensi-f, -ve, adj., (gram.) of suspension; (jur.) being a bar to subsequent proceedings.

suspension, n.f., suspension, interruption, discontinuance, cessation.

suspensoir or **suspensoire,** n.m., (surg.) suspensory bandage, suspensor.

suspente, n.f., (nav.) sling (of a yard).

suspicion, n.f., (jur.) suspicion.

sus-pied, n.m., upper strap (of a spur).

sus-relaté, -e, adj., above mentioned.

susseyer, v.n., to lisp.

sustentation, n.f., sustentation, sustenance.

sustenter, v.a., to sustain, to support, to maintain.

se **sustenter,** v.n., to maintain one's self, to support one's self.

susurration (su-sur-ra-), n.f., susurration, whispering, chirping, buzzing soft murmur; soughing (of the wind).

⊙**susurrer** (su-sur-ré), v.n., to murmur softly, to whisper. V. **chuchoter.**

suttee or **suttie,** n.f., (—) suttee.

suture, n.f., (anat.) suture; (bet.) seam; joint.

suturer, v.n., to suture, to join.

suzerain, -e (suz-rin, -rè-n), n. and adj., suzerain, lord paramount; paramount, sovereign.

suzeraineté (suz-rè-n-té), n.f., suzerainty.

svelte, adj., light, slender, slim; elegant.

sybarite, n.m.f. and adj., Sybarite; Sybaritic (very particular, fond of good living).

sycomore, n.m., (bot.) sycamore.

sycophante, n.m., sycophant, knave; rogue, impostor.

syllabaire (-sil-la-), n.m., spelling-book.

syllabe (sil-lab), n.f., syllable.

syllabique (sil-la-), adj., syllabic, syllabical.

syllabiquement (sil-la-), adv., syllabically.

syllabisation (sil-la-), n.f., syllabication.

syllabus (sil-la-), n.m., (—) (c.rel.) syllabus.

syllepse (sil-lèps), n.f., (gram.) syllepsis; substitution.

syllogisme (sil-lo-), n.m., syllogism.

syllogistique (sil-lo-), adj., syllogistic, syllogistical.

sylph-e, n.m., **-ide,** n.f., sylph.

sylvain, n.m., sylvan.

sylvane, n.f., sylvanite.

sylvatique, adj., sylvatic.

sylves, n.f.pl., sylvæ, collection of poetical works.

sylvestre, adj., wild, sylvan, growing in woods.

sylvicole, adj., living in woods.

sylviculture, n.f., sylviculture, forestry.

sylvie, n.f., (orni.) sylvia, warbler.

symbole, n.m., symbol, sign, emblem; creed. — des Apôtres; Apostles' creed.

symbolique, adj., symbolic, symbolical, typical.

symboliser, v.n., to symbolize.

symbolisme, n.m., (philos.) symbolism.

symétrie, n.f., symmetry.

symétrique, adj., symmetrical.

symétriquement (-trik-mān), adv., symmetrically.

symétriser, v.n., to symmetrize, to harmonize.

sympathie, n.f., sympathy, fellow-feeling, harmony (in colors).

sympathique, adj., sympathetic, congenial.

sympathiser, v.n., to sympathize.

symphonie, n.f., symphony.

symphoniste, n.m., symphonist.

symphyse, n.f., (anat.) symphysis.

symposiaque, n.m., symposiac.

symptomatique, adj., symptomatic.

symptomatologie, n.f., symptomatology.

symptôme, n.m., symptom, indication, sign, token.

synagogue (-gog), *n.f.*, synagogue.
synalèphe, *n.f.*, (gram.) synalepha.
synallagmatique, *adj.*, (jur.) (of a contract) synallagmatic, reciprocal.
synanthéré, -e, *adj.*, (bot.) synantherous.
synanthérées, *n.f.pl.*, (bot.) compositæ.
synanthérie, *n.f.* V. **syngénésie**.
synarthrose, *n.f.*, (anat.) synarthrosis.
synchondrose (-kon-), *n.f.*, (anat.) synchondrosis.
synchrone (-krô-n), *adj.*, (phys.) synchronical.
synchronique, *adj.*, (hist.) synchronical.
synchroniser, *v.a.*, to synchronize.
synchronisme, *n.m.*, synchronism.
synchyse (-kiz), *n.f.*, (gram.) synchysis.
syncope, *n.f.*, (med.) syncope, swoon, fainting fit; (mus.) syncopation, syncope; (gram.) syncope.
syncopé, -e, *adj.*, syncopated.
syncoper, *v.n.*, (gram., mus.) to syncopate.
syncrétisme, *n.m.*, syncretism.
syndérèse, *n.f.*, (rel.) remorse, sting of conscience.
syndic, *n.m.*, syndic, trustee, assignee. — *d'office;* official assignee.
syndical, *adj.*, pertaining to a syndic. *Chambre —e;* syndics, council, committee.
syndicat, *n.m.*, syndicate. — *de faillite;* commission in bankruptcy.
se **syndiquer**, *v.r.*, to form a syndicate.
synecdoche *or* **synecdoque**, *n.f.*, (rhet.) synecdoche.
synérèse, *n.f.*, (gram.) synæresis.
synévrose, *n.f.*, (anat.) synneurosis.
syngénésie, *n.f.*, (bot.) syngenesia.
syngnathe, *n.m.*, (ich.) syngnathus, horn-fish, sea-needle.
synodal, -e, *adj.*, synodic, synodal.
synodalement (-dal-mān), *adv.*, synodically.
synode, *n.m.*, synod.
synodique, *adj.*, synodic, synodical.
synonyme, *n.m.* and *adj.*, synonym; synonymous.
synonymie, *n.f.*, synonymy.
synonymique, *adj.*, pertaining, relating to synonymy, synonymous.
synopse, *n.f.*, synopsis of the Gospel.
synoptique, *adj.*, synoptic, synoptical.
synoque, *n.f.*, synocha.
synovial, -e, *adj.*, (anat.) synovial.
synovie, *n.f.*, (anat.) synovia.
syntaxe, *n.f.*, syntax.
syntaxique, *adj.*, syntactic, syntactical.
synthèse, *n.f.*, synthesis, composition.
synthétique, *adj.*, synthetic, synthetical.
synthétiquement, *adv.*, synthetically.
syphilis (-liss), *n.f.*, syphilis.
syphilitique, *adj.*, syphilitic.
syphon, *n.m.* V. **siphon**.
syriaque, *n.m.* and *adj.*, Syriac.
syrien, -ne (-ri-ĭn, -è-n), *n.* and *adj.*, Syrian.
syringa, *n.m.*, (bot.) syringa, lilac.
syringotome, *n.m.*, (surg.) instrument to perform syringotomy.
syringotomie, *n.f.*, (surg.) syringotomy.
syrop, *n.f.* V. **sirop**.
syrtes, *n.f.pl.*, quicksands.
systaltique, *adj.*, (physiology) systaltic.
systématique, *adj.*, systematic, systematical.
systématiquement (-tik-mān), *adv.*, systematically.
systématiser, *v.a.*, to systematize.
systématiseur, *n.m.*, systematizer.
système, *n.m.*, system, plan, policy. *Par —;* systematically.
systole, *n.f.*, (anat., gram.) systole.
systolique, *adj.*, systolic.
systyle, *n.m.* and *adj.*, (arch.) systyle.
syzygie, *n.f.*, (astron.) syzygy.

T

t, *n.m.*, the twentieth letter of the alphabet, t. [T is put for the sake of euphony between a verb ending with a vowel and the pronouns *il, elle, on;* ex.: *Aime-t-il?* does he love?]
t', contraction of *te*.
ta, *possessive adj.f.*, thy. V. **ton**.
tabac (-ba), *n.m.*, tobacco, snuff. *Carotte de —;* roll of tobacco. — *en carotte;* pig-tail tobacco. *Débitant de —;* dealer in snuff and tobacco. *Marchand de —;* tobacconist. — *à chiquer;* chewing tobacco. — *à fumer;* tobacco. — *à priser;* snuff. *Prendre du —;* to take snuff.
tabagie, *n.f.*, divan, smoking-room; ⊙tobacco box.
tabarin, *n.m.*, merry-andrew, buffoon.
tabarinage, *n.m.*, buffoonery.
tabatière (-tièr), *n.f.*, snuff-box. *Fenêtre en —;* sky-light.
⊙**tabellion**, *n.m.*, notary, scrivener.
⊙**tabellionage**, *n.m.*, scrivener's office.
tabernacle, *n.m.*, tent, tabernacle.
tabide, *adj.*, tabid, tabetic.
tabifique, *adj.*, consumptive.
tabis, *n.m.*, tabby (watered silk).
tabiser, *v.a.*, to tabby, to water.
tablature, *n.f.*, (mus.) tablature. *Donner de la — à quelqu'un;* to get any one into trouble, to cause serious inconvenience to.
table, *n.f.*, table; board (food, fare); table, index (of a book); (nav.) mess (of officers); slab (of stone); belly (violin); face (anvil); (anat.) table; (of jewelry) table. *pl.*, men (at backgammon). — *à jouer;* card-table. — *à manger;* dining-table. — *de nuit;* night, *or* bedside, table. — *à coulisses;* or *à rallonges;* telescope table. — *à ouvrage;* work-table. — *de cuisine;* kitchen-dresser. — *à écrire;* writing-table. *Se mettre à —;* to sit at table. *Tenir —;* to keep a table, to sit long at table. *Tenir bonne —;* to keep a good table. *Tenir — ouverte;* to keep open house. *Donner la — à quelqu'un;* to board any one. *La — du commun;* the servants' table. *Courir les —s;* to sponge for a dinner. — *s astronomiques;* astronomical tables. — *pythagorique,* — *de Pythagore;* multiplication-table. — *d'harmonie;* sounding-board. *Jouer cartes sur —;* to act openly, above board. *Faire — rase;* to make a clean sweep. *Aimer la —;* to like good living. *Mettre la —;* to lay the table. *Servir à —;* to wait at table. *Lever la —;* to remove the cloth. *Se lever de —, sortir de —,* or *quitter la —;* to rise from table; to get up from table. *Vivre à la même —;* to mess together. *Avoir —;* to have the right of sitting down in the royal presence.
tableau, *n.m.*, painting, picture, piece, scene, view, sight, description; (nav.) breastwork; list, roll, table; panel (of juries); (paint.) painting, piece; (at races) telegraph-board. — *de chevalet;* easel-piece. — *x vivants;* tableaux vivants; living pictures. *Encadrer un —;* to frame a picture. *Former un —;* (jur.) to empanel (a jury). — *annonces;* advertising board.
tablée, *n.f.*, tableful, table-length.
tabler, *v.n.*, to dress the board (backgammon). *Vous pouvez—là-dessus;* you may depend upon it.
tableti-er (-blĕ-tié), *n.m.*, — **ère** (-blĕ-tiè-r), *n.f.*, dealer in fancy turnery *or* toys.
tablette (-blèt), *n.f.*, shelf; tablet; (nav.) rising-staff; (arch.) table; cake (of chocolate); (pharm.) lozenge. *pl.*, note-book. — *de cheminée;* mantel-piece. — *de chocolat;* cake of chocolate. *Rayez cela de vos —s;* don't depend upon that. *Vous êtes sur mes —s;* I have you in my books, *or* I'll not forget you.
tabletterie (-blè-trĭ), *n.f.*, fancy-turnery trade, fancy stationery; toy-trade.

tablier, *n.m.*, apron, pinafore; (of carriages) of docks, of basins) apron; floor, platform (of a bridge); (fort.) platform; chess-board.

tabloin, *n.m.*, (artil.) wooden platform.

tabou, *n.m.*, taboo.

tabouer, *v.a.*, to taboo.

tabouret, *n.m.*, stool; foot-stool; stool of repentance; (bot.) shepherd's pouch. — *de piano;* music-stool.

tabourin, *n.m.*, chimney cowl, *or* cawl.

tabulaire, *adj.*, tabular.

tac, *n.m.*, (vet.) rot (in sheep).

tacaud, *n.m.*, (ich.) whiting-pout.

tacet (-sèt), *n.m.*, (mus.) pause, tacet; (fig.) silence. *Il a gardé le* —; he kept silent.

tachant, -e, *adj.*, soiling.

tache, *n.f.*, spot, stain, blot, speck; speckle, blemish. — *de rousseur;* freckle. *Avoir des —s de rousseur;* to be freckled. — *de feu;* tan spot. — *de naissance;* birth-mark.

tâche, *n.f.*, task; task-work; job. *A la* —; by the task, by the job, by the piece. *Travailler à la* —, *être à la* —; to work by the task, by the piece. *Prendre à — de faire une chose;* to make it one's business to do a thing. *Ouvrier à la* —; jobber, jobbing-workman.

tacher, *v.a.*, to stain; to spot; to taint; to tarnish; to blemish.
se **tacher**, *v.r.*, to soil one's self; to soil one's clothes.

tâcher, *v.n.*, to try, to endeavor, to strive, to seek. *Pardonnez-lui, il n'y tâchait pas;* (iron.) pardon him, he did not mean it.

tâcheron, *n.m.*, (tech.) jobber.

tacheté, -e, *part.*, spotted, speckled, tabby (of cats).

tacheter (tash-té), *v.a.*, to speckle, to mark with spots, to fleck.

tachygraphe, *n.m.*, tachygrapher, shorthand writer.

tachygraphie, *n.f.*, tachygraphy, shorthand writing.

tachygraphique, *adj.*, tachygraphic.

tacite, *adj.*, tacit, implied.

tacitement (-sit-man), *adv.*, tacitly, impliedly, by implication.

taciturne, *adj.*, taciturn, silent.

taciturnité, *n.f.*, taciturnity.

tact (takt), *n.m.*, feeling, touch; tact.

tac tac, *onomatopœia*, tick tack (of clocks); rap-tap (of knockers).

tacticien (-si-in), *n.m.*, tactician.

tactile, *adj.*, tactile.

tactilité, *n.f.*, tactility, tangibility.

taction, *n.f.*, taction, touch.

tactique, *n.f.* and *adj.*, tactics, generalship; manœuvre, stratagem; plan, way, move; tactical.

tadorne, *n.m.*, (orni.) sheldrake, bergander.

tael, *n.m.*, tael (China money, about 70 cents American).

tænia, *n.m. V.* **ténia**.

taffetas (taf-tâ), *n.m.*, taffeta, lustring; plain silk. — *d'Angleterre;* court-plaster. — *gomme;* oil-silk.

tafia, *n.m.*, tafia (rum).

taïaut *or* **tayaut**, *n.m.*, (hunt.) tally-ho.

taïcoun, *n.m.*, (—*s*) Tycoon.

taie, *n.f.*, pillow-case; (med.) film, speck. — *d'oreiller;* pillow-case.

⊙*****taillable**, *adj.*, taxable (feud.).

*****taillade**, *n.f.*, slash, gash, cut.

*****taillader**, *v.a.*, to slash to cut, to gash. *Des manches tailladées;* slashed sleeves.

*****taillanderie**, *n.f.*, edge-tool trade; edge-tools.

*****taillandier**, *n.m.*, edge-tool maker.

*****taillant**, *n.m.*, edge (of a knife).

*****taille**, *n.f.*, cutting, cut; edge of a sword; size, height, stature; shape, waist, figure; tally-stick; (hort.) pruning; (surg.) cystotomy; (mus.) tenor part; (feudalism) poll-tax; subsidy; deal

(at cards); (mus.) tenor; (fig.) level. *Frapper d'estoc et de* —; to cut and thrust, *or* to hit right and left. *La — des arbres;* the pruning of trees. *La — d'un habit;* the cut of a coat. *La — des pierres;* the cutting of stones. *Pierre de* —; free-stone. *Il est de ma* —; he is my height. *—-douce*, (—*s*—*s*) (engr.) copper-plate. *Haute-* —; (mus.) upper-tenor. *Basse-* —; (mus.) bass. *Faire des coches sur une* —; to tally. *De — à;* big enough to, quite capable of. *Ils nous ont fait une France à leur* —; (fig.) they have brought France *down* to their level (Béranger). *Ma colère va haut et me monte à sa* —; my anger knows no bounds and *raises* me to his level (V. Hugo).

*****taillé, -e**, *part.*, cut, carved, trimmed. *Etre bien* —; to be well-knit.

*****taille-crayons**, *n.m.*, (—*—*—*s*) pencil-pointer.

*****taille-légumes**, *n.m.*, vegetable cutter.

*****taille-mèche**, *n.m.* (— *- —s*) wick-cutter.

*****taille-mer**, *n.m.*, (—) (nav.) cutwater.

*****taille-plume**, *n.m.*, (— *- —s*) pen-cutter.

*****tailler**, *v.a.*, to cut, to cut out; to carve; to hew; to trim, to prune; to make, to mend (pens); to frame, to tally, to deal (cards). — *un diamant;* to cut a diamond. — *des arbres;* to prune trees. — *un habit;* to cut out a coat. — *des plumes;* to make pens. — *une armée en pièces;* to cut an army to pieces. — *de la besogne à;* to cut out work for; to give a great deal of trouble to. — *des bavettes;* (fam.) to gossip, to chatter, to spin yarns.

*****tailler**, *v.n.*, to cut (shape). *Il peut — en plein drap;* he has everything at his command. — *de l'avant;* (nav.) to go very fast, to make good headway.
se **tailler**, *v.r.*, to be cut, etc.

*****tailleur**, *n.m.*, tailor; cutter; hewer; banker (at faro). — *de pierre;* stone-cutter *or* mason. — *d'habits;* tailor. *Garçon* —; journeyman tailor. — *à façon;* jobbing tailor.

*****tailleuse**, *n.f.*, tailoress, cutter out (dress-making).

*****taille-vent**, *n.m.*, sea-gull; (nav.) lug-sail.

*****taillis**, *n.m.* and *adj.*, copse, coppice, thicket, underwood; cut. *Bois* —; copse.

*****tailloir**, *n.m.*, trencher, platter; (arch.) abacus.

*****taillon**, *n.m.*, nib (of a pen).

tain, *n.m.*, foil, tin-foil, leaf-tin.

taire (taisant, tu), *v.a.*, to say nothing of; to pass over in silence; to conceal, to suppress. *Faire* —; to silence, to reduce to silence, to hush; to gag (the press); to suppress, to lay aside.
se **taire**, *v.r.*, to hold one's tongue, *or* one's peace, to be silent, to remain silent. *Taisez-vous;* hold your tongue, *or* tongues.

taisson, *n.m.*, (mam.) badger.

taissonnière, *n.f.*, badger's hole.

talapoin, *n.m.*, talapoin (Buddhist priest); (mam.) talapoin (monkey).

talc, *n.m.*, talc, isinglass-stone.

talcique, *adj.*, (min.) talcky.

taled (-lèd), *n.m.*, taled (Jew. rel.).

talent, *n.m.*, talent, power, ability, faculty, art, skill, attainments; talented person ▪ (coin) talent. *De* —; talented.

⊙**taler**, *n.m. V.* **thaler**.

talève, *n.f.*, (orni.) sultana-bird.

talion, *n.m.*, retaliation, talio. *Loi du —; law of retaliation (lex talionis).

talisman, *n.m.*, talisman.

talismanique, *adj.*, talismanic.

talitre, *n.m.*, sand-hopper.

talle, *n.f.*, (hort.) sucker. *V.* **drageon**.

taller, *v.n.*, (hort.) to shoot, to throw out suckers. *V.* **drageonner**.

tallevane, *n.f.*, butter jar.

tallipot, *n.m.*, (bot.) tallipot, *or* fan palm.

talmouse, *n.f.*, cheese-cake; (pop.) whack, slap.

talmud (-mud), *n.m.*, Talmud.

talmudique, *adj.*, Talmudical.

talmudiste, *n.m.adj.*, Talmudist, Talmudistic.

taloche, *n.f.* cuff, punch, thump.

talon, *n.m.*, heel; stock (at cards); heel (of shoes, razors); (nav.) sole (of a rudder); shoulder (of a sword); (arch.) ogee; voucher (of receipts, checks); rest (of a saddle); remnant (of bread). *Mettre des —s à ;* to heel. *Marcher sur les —s de quelqu'un ;* to tread upon any one's heels. *Jouer des,* or *montrer les, —s ;* to take to one's heels, to scuttle. *Tourner les —s ;* to go away. *Donner un coup de—;* (nav.) to ground, to strike, to bump. *Avoir l'esprit aux —;* to shine at the wrong end, to be anything but witty. *— rouge ;* aristocrat, nobleman.

talonner, *v.a.*, to be close at the heels of ; to pursue close ; to press hard, to urge, to dun.

talonner, *v.n.*, (nav.) to ground.

talonnier, *n.m.*, heel-maker.

talonnières, *n.f.*, heel-piece ; (nav.) heel (of a rudder) ; (*pl.*, myth.) talaria, Mercury's heel wings.

talpack, *n.m.*, (mil.) busby.

talqueu-x, -se, *adj.*, (min.) talcous, talcose.

talus, *n.m.*, slope, declivity, bank, embankment ; mound ; (arch., fort.) talus. *En — ;* slopingly, shelving. *Aller en — ;* to slope down ; to shelve.

talutage, *n.m.*, sloping ; embanking.

taluter, *v.a.*, (arch.) to slope, to shelve.

tamandua, *n.m.*, (mam.) a species of ant-eaters.

tamanoir, *n.m.*, (mam.) the great ant-eater.

tamarin, *n.m.*, tamarind ; tamarind-tree ; (mam.) tamarin.

tamarinier, *n.m.*, tamarind, tamarind-tree, Indian acacia.

tamaris, tamarisc, or **tamarix**, *n.m.*, (bot.) tamarisk.

tambour, *n.m.*, drum ; drummer ; (horl.) barrel; (mec.) drum, barrel, tympan ; (arch.) drum; embroidery-frame ; (anat.) tympanum ; paddle-box (of steamboats). *—-major,* (*—s——s*), *—-maître,* (*—s——s*) drum-major, drum-master. *Broderie au — ;* tambour work. *Mener — battant ;* to carry it with a high hand, to beat out and out. *— de basque ;* tambourine. *— voilé ;* muffled drum. *Sortir — battant ;* to leave with the honors of war.

tambourin, *n.m.*, tambourine, tabor ; timbrel ; player on the tambourine.

tambourinage, *n.m.*, drumming.

tambouriner, *v.n.*, to drum, to beat the drum, to tattoo.

tambouriner, *v.a.*, to advertise, to puff ; to cry by the town drummer.

tambourineur, *n.m.*, (b.s.) drummer.

taminier, *n.m.*, (bot.) Indian acacia, black briony.

tamis, *n.m.*, sieve, strainer, sifter. *Passer au —;* to sift, to strain ; (fig.) to examine thoroughly.

tamisage, *n.m.*, sifting, straining.

*****tamisaille** or **tamise**, *n.f.*, (nav.) sweep of the tiller.

tamiser, *v.a.*, to sift, to strain.

tamiser, *v.n.*, (nav.) to shake.

tamiserie, *n.f.*, sieve-making ; sieves.

tamiseur, *n.m.*, sifter (glass factory).

tamisier, *n.m.*, sieve-maker.

tampe, *n.f.*, wedge (cloth manufacture).

tamper, *v.a.*, to fix the wedge on the friezing-table.

tampon, *n.m.*, plug ; stopper ; pad ; bung ; (artil.) tampion ; (tech.) buffer.

tamponnement, *n.m.*, plugging, stopping.

tamponner, *v.a.*, to plug, to stop up ; to tent (a wound). *Se —,* (rails) to run into each other ; (fig. and pop.) to have a set-to.

tam-tam, *n.m.*, (*—-—s*) tam-tam, tom-tom.

tan, *n.m.*, tan ; tanner's bark. *Gros —;* coarse bark.

tanaisie, *n.f.*, (bot.) tansy.

tancement, *n.m.*, rebuking, lecturing, scolding.

tancer, *v.a.*, to rebuke, to lecture, to scold.

tanche, *n.f.*, (ich.) tench.

tandis que (-di-), *conj.*, whilst ; while (implying contrast) ; whereas.

tangage, *n.m.*, (nav.) pitching (of ships).

tangara, *n.m.*, (orni.) tanager.

tangence, *n.f.*, (geom.) tangency, contact.

tangent, -e, *adj.*, (geom.) tangential, tangent.

tangente, *n.f.*, (geom.) tangent.

tanger, *v.n.*, (nav.) to hug the coast.

tangibilité, *n.f.*, tangibility, tangibleness.

tangible, *adj.*, tangible.

tangon, *n.m.*, (nav.) fore-sail boom.

tangue, *n.f.*, sea-sand (used as manure).

tanguer (-ghé), *v.n.*, (nav.) to pitch, to heave.

tanière, *n.f.*, den, hole, lair (of beasts).

tanin, *n.m.*, (chem.) tannin.

tannage, *n.m.*, tanning.

tannant, -e, *adj.*, tanning ; (pop.) tiresome, irksome. *Une substance —e ;* a tanning substance. *Un homme — ;* a bore. *Une occupation —e ;* an irksome task; irksome work.

tanne, *n.f.*, (med.) comedo, grub.

tanné, *n.m.*, tan-color.

tanné, -e, *adj.*, tanned, tawny, tan-colored.

tannée, *n.f.*, waste tan ; tanner's bark.

tanner, *v.a.*, to tan ; (pop.) to vex, to plague, to tease, to annoy, to beat, to hide.

tannerie (ta-n-rî), *n.f.*, tan-yard.

tanneur, *n.m.*, tanner.

⊙**tannin**, *n.m.* *V.* **tanin**.

tant, *adv.*, so much ; so many ; as much ; as many ; both ; to such a degree ; so ; so far ; so long ; as far ; as long. *— soit peu ;* ever so little. *Tous — que nous sommes ;* every one of us, or the whole lot of us. *Nous sommes — à —;* we are even (at play). *— petits que grands ;* both small and great. *— pour vous que pour lui ;* as much for you as for him. *— il était abusé ;* so much was he deceived. *— il est vrai ;* so true is it. *— le monde est crédule ;* so credulous is, or such is the credulity of, the world. *— que ;* as long as. *— que je vivrai ;* as long as I live. *—mieux ;* so much the better. *—pis ;* so much the worse. *—s'en faut ;* far from it. *—s'en faut que ;* so far from. *— y a que ;* (fam.) at all events, however, but the fact remains that. *Si — est que je le puisse ;* if, or supposing, I can. *— de monde ;* so many people. *Vous m'en direz — !* that alters the case; now ! I understand ; that's quite another thing ! *Comme il y en a —;* (in speaking of beauty) nothing out of the common. *— bien que mal ;* indifferently, so so ; as well as one can.

tantale, *n.m.*, Tantalus. *Supplice de —;* tantalism.

tantaliser, *v.a.*, to tantalize.

tantalisme, *n.m.*, tantalism.

tante, *n.f.*, aunt ; (pawnbroker) uncle. *Grand—;* great aunt. *— à la mode de Bretagne ;* cousin german.

tantet or **tantinet**, *n.m.*, the least bit, the least little drop, dash.

tantôt, *adv.*, presently, by and by, soon, anon ; a little while ago ; just now ; sometimes. *Je finirai cela — ;* I shall finish that by and by, or in the afternoon. *Il est — nuit ;* it will soon be night. *Il se porte — bien, — mal ;* sometimes he is well, sometimes ill. *A —!* good-bye for the present.

taon (tän), *n.m.*, (ent.) ox-fly, breeze, gad-fly.

tapage, *n.m.*, noise, uproar, row, racket, piece of work ; show, display.

tapageur, *n.m.*, noisy fellow, blusterer.

tapageu-r, -se, *adj.*, rackety, roystering, noisy, loud, blustering ; gaudy, flashy.

tape, *n.f.*, rap, slap, tap, thump ; (nav.) tampion.

tapecu *or* **tape-cul** (tap-ku), *n.m.*, swing-gate ; see-saw ; (nav.) ring-tail, ring-sail ; jolting carriage.

tapée, *n.f.*, (pop.) a lot, a whole host of.

tapement, *n.m.*, striking.

taper, *v.a.*, to strike, to hit, to slap ; to frizzle (the hair) ; (paint.) to sketch freely ; to paint in a free, bold style ; (nav.) to put a tampion in (a gun).

taper, *v.n.*, to strike, to hit ; to stamp ; to strum (musical instruments) ; to be heady (of wine). — *du pied ;* to stamp with one's foot. *Ce vin tape fort,* or *tape à la tête ;* this wine is heady.

en **tapinois,** *adv.*, stealthily, clandestinely, slyly.

tapioca *or* **tapioka,** *n.m.*, tapioca.

se **tapir,** *v.r.*, to squat, to crouch, to cower, to lie hid.

tapir, *n.m.*, (mam.) tapir.

tapis, *n.m.*, carpet, rug ; tapis, cover, cloth (for tables) ; ground. *Mettre sur le* — ; to bring on the tapis ; to bring forward ; to bring under discussion. — *vert ;* grass-plot ; green cloth ; gaming-table. — *de cheminée ;* hearth-rug. — *de lit ;* bedside carpet. *Amuser le* — ; to beat about the bush ; to talk the time away. *Etre sur le* — ; to be talked about, to be much discussed. *Faire* — *net* or *nettoyer le* — ; to sweep the stakes. *Eclairer le* — ; to put down one's stakes.

tapisser, *v.a.*, to upholster, to carpet ; to paper, to cover ; to hang with tapestry ; to deck, to adorn.

tapisserie (-pi-srî), *n.f.*, tapestry, hangings ; upholstery; fancy needle-work ; carpeting. *Faire* — ; to be a wall-flower (at a ball). *Faire de la* — ; to do fancy work.

tapissier, *n.m.*, upholsterer, tapestry-worker.

tapissière, *n.f.*, upholsteress, tapestry-worker ; tilted cart, spring van.

tapon, *n.m.*, (fam.) bundle (of clothes) ; (nav.) plug, stopper.

tapoter, *v.a.*, to pat, to tap, to strum.

tapure, *n.f.*, frizzling (of hair).

taque, *n.f.*, cast-iron plate.

taquer, *v.a.*, (print.) to plane, to plane down.

taquet, *n.m.*, (nav.) whelp, pin (of the capstan) ; (nav.) kevel, cleat ; (joiner's work) angle-block.

taquin, -e, *n.* and *adj.*, tease, torment (pers.) ; teasing, of a teasing disposition.

taquinement (-ki-n-mān), *adv.*, (l.u.) teasingly.

taquiner, *v.n.*, to tease, to plague, to torment.

taquinerie (-ki-n-rî), *n.f.*, teasing.

taquoir, *n.m.*, (print.) planer.

tarabuster, *v.a.*, to pester, to plague, to tease, to bother ; to handle roughly.

tarare, *n.m.*, (agri.) winnowing-machine.

tarare ! *int.*, pshaw ! fiddlestick ! — *ponpon !* (l.u.) brag !

taraud, *n.m.*, (tech.) tap-borer, screw-tap.

taraudage, *n.m.*, tapping (screws, nuts).

tarauder, *v.a.*, (tech.) to tap (screws, nuts).

tard, *n.m.*, *adj.*, and *adv.*, late ; late hour. *Trop* — ; too late. *Plus* — ; later ; afterwards ; at some other time ; later on ; years, *or* centuries, after ; at a later period ; in after life, in after years. *Au plus* — ; at the latest. *Tôt ou* — ; sooner or later. *Il est* — ; it is late. *Il se fait* — ; it is getting late. *Mieux vaut* — *que jamais ;* better late than never.

tarder, *v.n.*, to delay, to put off, to stay, to tarry ; to loiter, to dally ; to be long ; (imper.) to long (to). *Il me tarde de le faire ;* I long to do it. *Il ne tardera pas à venir ;* it will soon be here. *Il me tarde de parler ;* I am most anxious to speak.

tardi-f, -ve, *adj.*, tardy, late, slow ; backward. *Fruits* —*s ;* late fruits.

tardiflore, *adj.*, late blooming.

tardigrade, *adj.*, tardigrade.

tardivement (-div-mān), *adv.*, tardily, slowly.

tardiveté (-div-té), *n.f.*, (hort.) lateness, backwardness.

tare, *n.f.*, (com.) tare, waste ; blemish, defect, fault, imperfection.

taré, -e, *adj.*, injured, damaged, spoiled ; of bad character ; ill-famed, disreputable.

tarentelle, *n.f.*, tarantella (an Italian dance).

tarentule, *n.f.*, (ent.) tarantula.

tarer, *v.a.*, to injure, to damage, to hurt ; (com.) to tare.

se **tarer,** *v.r.*, to spoil, to deteriorate.

taret, *n.m.*, teredo-worm, ship-worm.

targe, *n.f.*, targe, target (shield).

targette, *n.f.*, flat bolt, slide-bolt.

se **targuer** (-ghé), *v.r.*, to be proud of, to boast of, to brag of, to pride, to plume one's self on.

targum (-gom), *n.m.*, (—) targum.

tari, *n.m.*, (—) tari (oriental drink).

tarier, *n.m.*, (orni.) white bustard, whin-chat.

tarière, *n.f.*, wimble, auger ; borer ; (ent.) terebra.

tarif, *n.m.*, tariff, rate, scale of prices, price-list, list of charges.

tarifer, *v.a.*, to tariff, to price, to rate.

tarin, *n.m.*, (orni.) tarin.

tarir, *v.a.*, to drain, to dry up, to exhaust.

se **tarir,** *v.r.*, to dry up, to be exhausted, to be drained ; to cease, to stop, to end. *Ne pas se* — ; (fig.) to talk incessantly, never to have done.

tarir, *v.n.*, to be drained ; to dry up.

tarissable, *adj.*, drainable ; exhaustible.

tarissement (-ris-mān), *n.m.*, draining, exhausting, drying up.

tarlatane, *n.f.*, tarlatan (muslin).

taroté, -e, *adj.*, checkered, spotted (of cards).

tarots (-rô), *n.m.pl.*, spotted cards.

taroupe, *n.f.*, hair growing between the eyebrows.

tarpéienne, *adj.f.*, Tarpeian, only used in *Roche* —; Tarpeian rock.

tarse, *n.m.*, tarse, tarsus.

tarsien, -ne (-si-in, -si-è-n), *adj.*, tarsal.

tarsier, *n.m.*, (mam.) tarsier.

tartan, *n.m.*, tartan, plaid.

tartane, *n.f.*, (nav.) tartan (ship).

tartare, *n.m.*, Tartar ; (myth.) hell. *A la* —; (cook.) with cold mustard sauce.

tartareu-x, -se, *adj.*, tartareous.

tartarin, *n.m.*, Barbary ape.

tartarique, *adj.*, tartaric. *V.* **tartrique.**

tartariser, *v.a.*, to tartarize.

tarte, *n.f.*, (cook.) tart. *C'est sa* — *à la crème ;* (fig.) it is his one and constant objection.

tartelette, *n.f.*, tartlet.

tartine, *n.f.*, slice of bread (with butter, preserves, etc.) ; (fig.) long, tedious speech *or* newspaper article. — *de confitures ;* slice of bread and jam.

tartrate, *n.m.*, (chem.) tartrate.

tartre, *n.m.*, (chem.) tartar.

tartrique, *adj.*, (chem.) tartaric.

tartufe, *n.m.*, hypocrite.

tartuferie (-tu-frî), *n.f.*, hypocrisy.

tartufier, *v.n.*, to play the hypocrite.

tas, *n.m.*, heap, pile ; lot, set (of persons) ; hand-anvil ; (agri.) shock. *Mettre en* — ; to put into a heap *or* heaps. — *de pierres ;* heap of stones. *Un* — *de filous ;* a set of sharpers. *Prendre au* — ; to help one's self to.

tasse, *n.f.*, cup. — *à café ;* coffee-cup. — *à thé ;* tea-cup. — *de thé ;* cup of tea. *Demi* —; small cup (of coffee).

tasseau, *n.m.*, (arch.) hammer-beam, tassel.

tassée, *n.f.*, cupful.

tassement (tâs-mān), *n.m.*, (arch.) settling, sinking, subsiding, subsidence.

tasser, *v.a.*, to heap up, to pile up ; to cram, to beat down ; to compress.

se **tasser**, *v.r.*, (arch.) to sink, to settle, to subside; (of plants) to grow thick ; (of persons) to draw *or* press closer, to crowd together.

tasser, *v.n.*, (arch.) to settle; to sink; (hort.) to grow thick.

tassette, *n.m.*, tasses, tassets (of armor).

tâte-poule, *n.m.*, (—) (pop.) molly-coddle, molly.

tâter, *v.a.* and *n.*, to feel ; to try, to-taste ; to sound. — *le pouls ;* to feel the pulse. — *le courage de quelqu'un ;* to put any one's courage to the test *or* proof. — *quelqu'un sur une affaire ;* to sound any one respecting anything. — *de quelque chose;* to taste anything.

se **tâter**, *v.r.*, to examine one's self, to feel one's self.

tâteu-r, *n.m.*, **-se**, *n.f.*, feeler, taster, irresolute person.

tâte-vin, *n.m.*, (—) wine taster (instrument).

***tatillon**, *n.m.*, **-ne**, *n.f.*, meddler, busy-body.

***tatillonnage**, *n.m.*, meddling, intermeddling.

***tatillonner**, *v.n.*, to meddle, to intermeddle.

tâtonnement (-to-n-mãn), *n.m.*, feeling one's way, groping. *Méthode de* —; tentative method.

tâtonner, *v.n.*, to feel one's way, to grope.

tâtonneu-r, *n.m.*, **-se**, *n.f.*, groper, fumbler ; waverer ; irresolute person.

à **tâtons**, *adv.*, feeling one's way, groping ; gropingly. *Marcher*, or *aller, à* — ; to grope about, to feel one's way. *Chercher à* —, or *chercher en tâtonnant ;* to grope for.

tatou, *n.m.*, (mam.) armadillo, dasypus.

tatouage, *n.m.*, tattooing.

tatouer, *v.a.*, to tattoo.

tattersall, *n.m.*, (*n.p.*) tattersall.

taude, *n.f.*, (nav.) awning.

taudion, *n.m.*, (pop.). *V.* **taudis**.

taudis, *n.m.*, hole, hovel.

taupe, *n.f.*, (mam.) mole; (vet.) ⊙ poll-evil ; (med.) ⊙ wen, *V.* **loupe** (pers.) cunning fox, intriguing person.

***taupe-grillon**, *n.m.*, (—*s*-—*s*) (ent.) mole-cricket.

taupier, *n.m.*, mole-catcher.

taupière, *n.m.*, mole-trap.

taupin, *n.m.*, click-beetle. *Franc* — ; (obȝol.) militiaman.

taupinière, *n.f.*, mole-hill ; hillock, knoll.

taure, *n.f.*, yearling, heifer.

tauréador, *n.m.*, (—*s*). *V.* **toréador**.

taureau, *n.m.*, bull ; (astron.) Taurus. — *sauvage ;* wild bull. *Un combat de* —*x ;* a bull-fight.

tauricorne, *adj.*, tauricornous.

tautochrone (-krô-n), *adj.*, tautochronous.

tautochronisme (-kro-), *n.m.*, tautochronism.

tautogramme, *n.m.*, tautogram (a poem every word of which begins with the same letter).

tautologie, *n.f.*, tautology.

tautologique, *adj.*, tautological.

taux, *n.m.*, price, rate, rate of interest ; assessment.

tavaïolle, *n.f.*, chrisom-cloth ; antimacassar.

taveler (ta-vlé), *v.a.*, to spot, to speckle.

tavelle, *n.f.*, crown-lace.

tavelure (ta-vlur), *n.f.*, spots, speckles.

taverne, *n.f.*, tavern, pot-house, public-house; beer-shop.

taverni-er, *n.m.*, **-ère**, *n.f.*, tavern-keeper, publican.

taxateur, *n.m.*, (jur.) taxer, assessor ; taxing-master.

taxation, *n.f.*, taxation; fixing of prices.

taxe, *n.f.*, assize, price, price fixed ; tax, assessment, impost, toll.

taxer, *v.a.*, to rate, to fix the price of ; to assess; to tax, to lay a tax upon ; to charge (with), to accuse (of) ; to term. *On le taxa d'avarice ;* they taxed him with, *or* accused him of, avarice.

se **taxer**, *v.r.*, to tax one's self.

taxiarque, *n.m.*, (antiq.) taxiarch.

taxidermie, *n.f.*, taxidermy.

taxis, *n.f.*, (surg.) taxis.

tayaut, *n.m.*, (hunt.). *V.* **taïaut**.

tchèque, *n.m.*, (phil.) Czech (language).

té, *n.m.*, (fort.) mines having the shape of a ⊤, to blow up an enemy's fortification; anything in the shape of a ⊤.

te, *pron.*, thee, to thee, you, to you.

technique (tèk-nik), *adj.*, technical.

technique (tèk-nik), *n.f.*, technics.

technique (tèk-nik), *n.m.*, (arts) execution, make, style, technique.

techniquement (tèk-nik-mãn), *adv.*, technically.

technologie (tèk-no-), *n.f.*, technology.

technologique (tèk-no-), *adj.*, technological.

teck *or* **tek**, *n.m.*, (bot.) teak, teak-wood.

tectrices, *n.f.pl.*, coverts (of feathers of birds).

te deum (té-dé-om), *n.m.*, (—) Te Deum.

tégument, *n.m.*, tegument ; (anat.) integument.

***teignasse**, *n.f. V.* **tignasse**.

***teigne**, *n.f.*, (med.) ringworm of the scalp, trichonosis tonsurans, tinea capitis ; (ent.) corn-moth (in wheat) ; (vet.) thrush.

***teigneu-x**, **-se**, *n.* and *adj.*, scurvy ; scurvy, dirty person.

***teillage**, *n.m. V.* **tillage**.

***teille**, *n.f. V.* **tille**.

***teiller**, *v.a. V.* **tiller**.

***teilleur**, *n.m.*, **-se**, *n.f.*, (agri.). *V.* **tilleur**.

teindre (*teignant, teint), *v.a.*, to dye, to tinge, to stain, to color.

teint, *n.m.*, (dy.) dye, color ; tincture ; complexion. *Grand* —, — *solide ;* fast dye ; fast color.

teinte, *n.f.*, (paint.) tint, tinge ; tincture ; shade, hue; dye (fig.) smack, touch. *Demi-* —; (—*s*-—*s*) mezzotinto.

teinter, *v.a.*, (paint.) to tint, to tinge, to tone.

teinture, *n.f.*, dye, dyeing ; (pharm.) tincture; (fig.) superficial knowledge, smattering.

teinturerie (-tur-rî), *n.f.*, dye-shop ; dye-works.

teinturi-er, *n.m.*, **-ère**, *n.f.*, dyer.

tel, **-le**, *adj.*, such, like ; similar ; such an one. — *maître,* — *valet ;* like master, like man. *Telle vie, telle fin ;* men die as they live. *M. un* — ; Mr. so and so. *J'irai dans* —*le ville à* —*le époque;* I shall go to such a town at such a time. — *quel ;* such as it is, just as it was, indifferent, so so. *Ce sont des gens* —*s quels ;* they are no great shakes. — *est pris qui croyait prendre ;* it is a case of the biter bit.

télamons, *n.m.pl.*, (arch.) telamones.

télégramme, *n.m.*, telegram.

télégraphe, *n.m.*, telegraph. *Faire jouer le* — ; to telegraph.

télégraphie, *n.f.*, telegraphy.

télégraphier, *v.a.*, to telegraph.

télégraphique, *adj.*, telegraphic.

télescope, *n.m.*, telescope.

télescopique, *adj.*, telescopic.

tellement (tèl-mãn), *adv.*, so, in such a manner ; so much ; so far, in such sort. — *que ;* so that, so much so that. — *quellement ;* indifferently, so-so.

tellière, *n.f.*, foolscap paper.

tellure, *n.m.*, (chem.) tellurium.

tellurique, *adj.*, (chem.) telluric.

téméraire, *n.m.f.* and *adj.*, rash, reckless person ; rash, foolhardy, reckless. *Un coup* —; a rash enterprise.

témérairement (-rèr-mãn), *adv.*, rashly, foolhardily, recklessly.

témérité, *n.f.*, temerity, rashness, foolhardiness, recklessness.

***témoignage**, *n.m.*, testimony, evidence ; testimonial ; witness ; (fig.) token, mark, proof. *Rendre — à la vérité de ;* to bear witness, *or to* testify, to the truth of. *Appeler en — ;* to call to witness. *Faux — ;* false swearing, perjury. *En — de quoi ;* in witness whereof.

*témoigner, *v.a.,* to testify ; to show, to prove, to express, to convey ; to indicate, to mark. — *du chagrin ;* to show sorrow.

*témoigner, *v.n.,* to testify ; to witness, to bear witness, to give evidence.

témoin, *n.m.,* witness, evidence ; testimony ; proof ; mark ; second (in duels). — *auriculaire ;* ear-witness. — *à charge ;* witness for the prosecution. — *à décharge ;* witness for the defense. — *oculaire ;* eye-witness. *Prendre à — ;* to call to witness.

tempe, *n.f.,* (anat.) temple.

tempérament, *n.m.,* constitution, temperament ; temper ; medium, middle-course, compromise ; (com.) tally-trade. *Un — ruiné ;* a broken constitution.

tempérance, *n.f.,* temperance, sobriety.

tempérant, -e, *adj.,* temperate, sober ; (med.) sedative.

tempérant, *n.m.,* temperate man ; (med.) sedative.

température, *n.f.,* temperature.

tempéré, *n.m.,* temperate ; (rhet.) unadorned style.

tempéré, -e, *adj.,* temperate, mild ; mixed, limited (governments) ; (rhet.) tempered, unadorned.

tempérer, *v.a.,* to temper, to allay, to mollify, to soothe, to assuage, to moderate, to regulate ; to contain, to check.

se tempérer, *v.r.,* to become tempered ; to become temperate *or* mild (of the weather).

tempête, *n.f.,* tempest, storm, gale.

tempêter, *v.n.,* to storm, to bluster, to fume.

tempétueu-x, -se, *adj.,* tempestuous, boisterous, stormy.

temple, *n.m.,* temple.

templier, *n.m.,* templar, knight-templar.

temporaire, *adj.,* temporary.

temporairement, *adv.,* temporarily, for the time being.

temporal, -e, *adj.,* (anat.) temporal.

⊙temporalité, *n.f.,* temporality.

temporel, -le, *adj.,* temporal.

temporel, *n.m.,* (ecc.) temporalities ; (pol.) temporal power.

temporellement (-rèl-màn), *adv.,* temporally.

temporisat-eur, -rice, *n.* and *adj.,* procrastinator, temporizer ; procrastinating, temporizing.

temporisation, *n.f.,* temporizing, procrastination.

temporiser, *v.n.,* to temporize, to delay, to procrastinate.

temporiseur, *n.m.,* (l.u.) *V.* temporisateur.

temps (tàn), *n.m.,* time, while, period, term ; leisure ; season ; weather ; (gram.) tense ; (mus.) time-stroke. *Passer son — à étudier ;* to spend one's time in study. *Il a fait son — ;* he has had his day, he has served his time. *Du — d'Auguste ;* in the time of Augustus. — *moyen ;* mean time. *Dans le — ;* formerly, of yore. *Avec le — ;* in time, in course of time. *Grand — ;* high time. *En un rien de — or en deux — et trois mouvements ;* in a trice, in a jiffy. *En même — ;* at the same time. *A — ;* in time. *De — en — ;* from time to time, now and then. *De tout — ;* at all times. *A quelque — de là ;* some time after. *S'accommoder au — ;* to comply with the times. *Le — perdu ne se retrouve point ;* lost time is never found again. *Réparer le — perdu ;* to make up for lost time. *Se donner du bon — ;* to take it easy ; to enjoy one's self. *Prendre le — comme il vient ;* to take things easily. *Du — que Berthe filait ;* when Adam delved and Eve spun *or* when the world

was young. *Par le — qui court ;* nowadays, as times go. *Autres — autres mœurs ;* manners change with the times. *En — et lieu ;* in proper time and place. *Prendre bien son — ;* to choose one's time well. *Quel — fait-il ?* what sort of weather is it ? *Il fait beau — ;* it is fine weather. *Gros — ;* (nav.) stormy weather. *Mauvais — ;* bad weather. — *fait ;* settled weather. *Par le — qu'il fait ;* in such weather (i. e. as we are having).

tenable, *adj.,* tenable ; habitable.

tenace, *adj.,* tenacious, adhesive, sticky ; niggardly, stingy ; retentive (of the memory).

ténacité, *n.f.,* tenacity, tenaciousness, adhesiveness ; retentiveness (of the memory) ; stinginess.

*tenaille, *n.f.,* (fort.) tenaille. *pl.,* pincers, nippers, pinchers, tongs.

*tenailler, *v.a.,* to tear off, to hold tight, to squeeze ; (fig.) to torture, to torment.

*tenaillon, *n.m.,* (fort.) tenaillon.

tenance, *n.f.,* (feudalism) tenancy.

tenanci-er, *n.m.,* -ère, *n.f.,* (feudalism) holder, occupier. *Franc — ;* freeholder.

tenant, *n.m.,* (at a tournament) challenger, champion ; supporter ; defender. *Les —s et aboutissants ;* the adjacent lands, houses, etc. ; (fig.) details, particulars, circumstances.

tenant, -e, *adj.,* holding, having something of, seldom used but in the expression, *Séance —e ;* before the meeting separates, during the sitting ; there and then.

ténare, *n.m.,* (poet.) Tænarus, hell.

tendance, *n.f.,* tendency, leaning, inclination.

tendant, -e, *adj.,* tending, aiming at.

tendelet (tan-dlè), *n.m.,* (nav.) awning, canopy ; (arch.) tilt.

tender (tin-dèr), *n.m.,* (rail.) tender.

tendeu-r, -se, *n.m.f.,* stretcher, hanger (of tapestry) ; spreader, layer, setter (of snares) ; coupling-iron.

tendineu-x, -se, *adj.,* tendinous.

tendon, *n.m.,* (anat.) tendon, sinew.

tendre, *adj.,* tender, soft ; delicate, sensitive, affecting, moving, new (of bread). *Du pain — ;* new bread. *Avoir le cœur — ;* to be tender-hearted. *Un métal — ;* a soft metal. *Couleur — ;* delicate color.

tendre, *n.m.,* (fam.) tenderness, affection, liking, inclination ; love. *Le pays de — ;* Love.

tendre, *v.a.,* to bend, to stretch, to spread, to lay ; to strain ; to set ; to hold out ; to pitch (tents) ; to hang (tapestry). — *un arc ;* to bend a bow. — *une souricière ;* to set a mouse-trap. — *un lit ;* to put up a bed. *Il me tendit la main ;* he stretched out his hand to me. — *la joue ;* to hold out the cheek. — *les bras à quelqu'un ;* to hold out one's arms to any one. — *une tente ;* to pitch a tent. — *la perche à ;* to help, to lend a helping hand to. *Il vaut mieux — la main que le cou ;* it is better to beg than to steal. *L'arc toujours tendu se gâte ;* all work and no play makes Jack a dull boy.

tendre, *v.n.,* to lead to ; to tend ; to conduce ; to hang tapestry, etc. *Où tend ce chemin ?* where does that road lead to ?

tendrement, *adv.,* tenderly, dearly, affectionately.

tendresse, *n.f.,* tenderness, love, fondness. *pl.,* tender caresses.

tendret, -te, *adj.,* rather tender.

tendreté, *n.f.,* (l.u.) tenderness (of fruit, etc.).

tendron, *n.m.,* shoot, tendril (of plants) ; gristle ; (fam.) young lass.

tendu, -e, *part.* and *adj.,* bent ; tight, stiff ; strained. *Style — ;* stiff, affected, far-fetched, unnatural style. *Situation — ;* a strained *or* delicate situation.

ténèbres, *n.f.pl.,* darkness, night, gloom. *Les — de l'ignorance ;* the night of ignorance.

ténébreusement (-eûz-mān), *adv.*, darkly, gloomily ; secretly.

ténébreu-x, -se, *adj.*, dark, gloomy, obscure, overcast, melancholy ; underhand.

tènement (tè-n-mān), *n.m.*, (feudalism) tenement; block of houses.

ténesme, *n.m.*, (med.) tenesmus.

tenettes, *n.f.pl.*, (surg.) lithotomy forceps, extractor.

teneur, *n.f.*, tenor, terms, text ; purport; contents. *Je n'en comprends pas la* — ; I don't understand the purport of it.

teneur de livres, *n.m.*, book-keeper.

tenez! *int. V.* **tiens.**

ténia, *n.m.*, tænia, tape-worm.

tenir (tenant, tenu), *v.a.*, to hold, to have hold of, to have; to contain ; to possess ; to believe, to regard, to maintain, to be possessed of, to occupy; to take up, to keep; to perform ; to account, to look upon, to consider, to think, to detain. *Vous tenez trop de place ;* you take up too much room. — *maison ;* to keep house. — *boutique ;* to keep a shop. — *le lit ;* to keep one's bed. — *le large ;* (nav.) to go out into the open. — *la mer ;* (nav.) to be seaworthy. — *la campagne ;* (milit.) to have taken, *or* to hold, the field. — *la tête droite ;* to hold up one's head. — *les yeux baissés ;* to keep one's eyes down. *Cela m'a tenu plus que je ne pensais ;* that detained me longer than I thought. *Je tiens cela de bonne source ;* I have it on the best authority. *Je le tiens pour honnête homme ;* I look upon him as an honest man. *Voilà la conduite qu'il tient ;* such is the way in which he behaves. — *sa parole ;* to keep one's word. *Cessez de — ce langage ;* cease to hold this language, cease to speak in such a manner. — *table ouverte ;* to keep open house (com.). — *les livres en partie double ;* to keep books by double entry. — *la caisse ;* to be a cashier, to have charge of the cash. — *registre de quelque chose ;* to keep an account of anything. *Je tiendrai compte de cela ;* I shall take that into consideration. — *quelqu'un à distance ;* to hold any one at a distance. — *quelque chose dans la main ;* to hold anything in the hollow of one's hand. *Faire — des lettres à quelqu'un ;* to forward, or send, letters to any one. — *lieu de ;* to be instead of, to stand in the place of. *Il m'a tenu lieu de père ;* he has been like a father to me. — *le loup par les oreilles ;* to be in a critical situation. — *son homme ;* to have one's man. — *quelqu'un à quatre;* to hold any one down by force. *se* **tenir**, *v.r.*, to hold, to hold on, to hold fast, to hold each other ; to abide by; to cling, to adhere, to stick ; to keep, to stay; to keep one's self ; to be; to stand, to lie ; to remain ; to be held ; to sit ; to think one's self, to consider one's self ; to contain one's self, to refrain. *Je m'y tiens ;* I stand (at cards). *S'en tenir à ;* to rely on, to adhere to, to rest content, to stick to. *Je m'en tiens à votre avis ;* I stick to your advice. *Se — mal à cheval ;* not to sit well on horseback. *Tenez-vous en là ;* go no further in the matter ; remain content. *Se — en embuscade ;* to lie in ambush. *Se — sur ses gardes ;* to stand upon one's guard. *Se le — pour dit ;* to take it for granted ; not to forget it. *Tenez-vous en repos ;* be, or keep, quiet. *Se — à ne rien faire ;* to stand doing nothing. *Se — les bras croisés ;* to sit with one's arms crossed. *Se — à genoux ;* to be, to remain, upon one's knees. *Se — debout ;* to stand up. *Se — droit ;* to stand upright. *Je me suis tenu à quatre pour ne pas rire ;* it was almost more than I could do not to laugh. *Ne pas savoir à quoi s'en tenir ;* not to know what to believe. *Savoir à quoi s'en* — ; to know how it is, how matters stand, *or* what to do.

tenir, *v.n.*, to hold, to hold fast ; to be contiguous ; to hang; to adhere, to stick ; to be held (of fairs, markets, assemblies); to take after; to be of the nature; to keep together; to remain; to withstand, to resist; (milit.) to hold out ; to subsist ; to be connected with ; to be desirous; to proceed, to result. — *bon ;* to hold out, to stick fast. *Il tient à le faire ;* he is anxious to do it. *Il ne tient pas à moi qu'elle ne vienne pas ;* it is not my fault that she does not come. *Qu'à cela ne tienne ;* never mind, let not that be an objection. *Il n'y a pas d'amitié qui tienne ;* friendship has nothing to do with the question. *La vie ne tient qu'à un fil ;* life only hangs on a thread. *S'il ne tient qu'à cela ;* if that is all. *A quoi tient-il que ?* how is it that ? *A quoi cela tient-il ?* what is it owing to? *Il tient de son père ;* he takes after his father. *Ce clou ne tient pas ;* this nail does not hold. *Je n'y tiens plus ;* I cannot stand it any longer. *Je n'y tiens pas ;* I am not particular about it. *En — ;* to be smitten. *Il ne tient qu'à vous de ;* it only depends on you to, *or* only rests with you to. *Tiens! c'est vous ;* hullo! well, I never ! is that you ? *Tiens! tiens!* indeed, you don't say so. *Il vaut mieux — que courir or un tiens vaut mieux que deux tu l'auras ;* (prov.) a bird in the hand is worth two in the bush. *Cela lui tient au cœur ;* he thinks of nothing else. — *comme teigne ;* (pop.) to stick like wax.

tenon, *n.m.*, tenon; bolt (of fire-arms); nut (of an anchor).

ténor, *n.m.*, (—s) (mus.) tenor.

ténotomie, *n.f.*, (surg.) tenotomy.

tensi-f, -ve, *adj.*, tense.

tension, *n.f.*, tension, intenseness. — *d'esprit ;* intense application of mind.   [plaint).

tenson, *n.f.*, (ancient poet.) tenson (love-

tentacule, *n.m.*, (ent.) tentacle, feeler.

tentant, -e, *adj.*, tempting.

tentat-eur, *n.m.adj.*, **-rice**, *n.f.*, tempter, temptress, tempting.

tentati-f, -ve, *adj.*, tentative.

tentation, *n.f.*, temptation.

tentative, *n.f.*, attempt, trial, endeavor.

tente, *n.f.*, tent, pavilion, (nav.) awning. *Dresser une* — ; to pitch a tent.

tenté, *adj.*, tempted, disposed, inclined.

tenter, *v.a.*, to attempt, to try, to tempt.

se **tenter**, *v.r.*, to be attempted *or* tried.

tenture, *n.f.*, tapestry, hangings.

tenu, -e, *part.*, held, kept ; bound, obliged ; reputed, considered. *Je ne suis pas — à cela ;* I am not bound to that. *A l'impossible nul n'est* — ; there's no flying without wings.

ténu, -e, *adj.*, tenuous, thin, spare.

tenue, *n.f.*, holding (of assemblies) ; session; attitude (of a person); dress; deportment, carriage, bearing, address; appearance ; steadiness (of troops); keeping (of books); (mus.) holding-note; (nav.) anchor-hold; holding (of the pen); steadiness (of a thing). *Tout d'une* — ; contiguous (of lands). *Grande* — ; (milit.) full dress. *Petite* — ; (milit.) undress. — *des livres ;* book-keeping.

ténuirostres, *n.m.pl.*, (orni.) tenuirostres.

ténuité, *n.f.*, tenuity, thinness, spareness.

tenure, *n.f.*, tenure.

téorbe, *n.m.*, (mus.) theorbo, archlute.

tépide, *adj.*, (l.u.). *V.* **tiède.**

tépidité, *n.f.*, (l.u.). *V.* **tiédeur.**

ter (tèr), *adv.*, third ; (mus.) three times ; (of houses) B.

tératologie, *n.f.*, (physiology) teratology.

tercer *or* **terser** (tèr-), *v.a.*, to give a third dressing to.

tercet (tèr-sè), *n.m.*, tiercet (poet.).

térébenthine, *n.f.*, turpentine.

térébinthe, *n.m.*, (bot.) turpentine-tree.

térébrant, *adj.*, (med.) keen, lancinating pain ; (mol.) terebrating.

térébrants, *n.m.pl.*, (ent.) terebrantia.

térébration, *n.f.*, terebration, boring.

tergiversation, *n.f.*, tergiversation, shift, evasion, shuffling.

tergiverser, *v.n.*, to tergiversate, to shift, to practise evasion, to shuffle.

terme (tèrm), *n.m.*, term ; termination ; bound, end, limit, post ; time ; quarter's-rent, quarter-day ; boundary ; word, expression. *pl.*, state, condition, terms. *Toucher au —* ; to draw near the term, the close. *Payer son —* ; to pay one's rent. *Qui a — ne doit rien* ; no one is obliged to pay before a debt is due. *Le — vaut l'argent* ; time is money. *Ménager ses —s* ; to modify one's expressions. *A long —* ; (com.) of bills long-dated. *A court —* ; short-dated. *Avant —* ; prematurely, before one's time.

termès, *n.m. V.* termite.

terminaison, *n.f.*, termination, end, ending.

terminal, -e, *adj.*, (bot.) terminal.

terminati-f, -ve, *adj.*, (gram.) terminational.

terminer (tèr-), *v.a.*, to terminate, to end, to bound, to limit, to put an end to, to conclude, to bring to a close, to settle.

se **terminer**, *v.r.*, to end, to come to an end, to terminate, to be bounded ; to conclude, to be brought to a conclusion, to be settled.

terminologie, *n.f.*, terminology.

termite *or* **termès**, *n.m.*, (ent.) white ant ; termes. *pl.*, termites.

ternaire (tèr-nèr), *adj.*, tenary.

terne (tèr-n), *adj.*, tarnished, dull, dim ; wan, tame, spiritless.

terne (tèr-n), *n.m.*, two threes (at dice) ; trey (in a lottery).

terné, -e (tèr-), *adj.*, (bot.) ternate.

ternir, *v.a.*, to tarnish, to dull ; to deaden ; to sully; to stain. *— des couleurs* ; to deaden the colors. *— sa gloire* ; to tarnish one's glory.

se **ternir**, *v.r.*, to tarnish, to grow dull, to be sullied; to fade (of colors).

ternissure, *n.f.*, tarnishing, dullness, fading, blemish, stain.

terrage, *n.m.*, claying (of sugar).

terrain, *n.m.*, ground ; soil, earth, land ; ground-plot ; piece of ground, field, course. *Gagner du —* ; to gain ground. *Tâter le —* ; (fig.) to feel one's way. *Être sur son —* ; to be in one's element. *Sur le —* ; on the field. *Aller sur le —* ; to fight a duel. *Céder le —* ; to yield, to give way. *Disputer le —* ; to stand one's ground, to dispute every inch of the ground. *Le — des courses* ; the race course, the course. *Ménager le —* ; (fig.) to act cautiously.

terral, *n.m.*, (nav.) wind coming from land.

terraqué, -e (-ké), *adj.*, terraqueous.

terrasse, *n.f.*, terrace ; flat roof, balcony, earthwork ; (paint.) foreground.

terrassement (-ras-mān), *n.m.*, earthwork, embankment, ballasting, banking.

terrasser, *v.a.*, to fill in with earth-work ; to embank ; to throw on the ground ; to fell, to throw down ; to knock down ; to confound, to dismay, to throw into consternation, to nonplus, to beat.

terrasseu-x, -se, *adj.*, earthy (of marble).

terrassier, *n.m.*, digger, excavator, navvy.

terre, *n.f.*, earth, land, ground, soil, mold ; dominion, territory, grounds, estate, property, homestead; world; land, shore. *Cultiver la —* ; to till the ground. *— ferme* ; dry-land, terra firma, main land, continent. *Se coucher à —* ; to lie flat on the ground. *Jeter un homme à —* ; to throw a man on the ground. *Hautes —s* ; highlands. *Basses —s* ; lowlands. *— à foulon* or *— à dégraisser* ; fuller's earth. *— à potier* ; potter's earth. *Vaisselle de —* ; earthenware. *Mettre pied à —* ; to alight. *Mettre à —* ; to put down ; (nav.) to land. *Perdre —* ; to lose sight of land ; to get out of one's depth (in swimming). *Aller à —* ; to be prosy, to grovel ; (man.) to

passage low ; (nav.) to sail along the coast. *— franche* ; vegetable mold. *— sainte* ; consecrated ground ; holy land. *Pipe de*, or *en*, *—* ; clay pipe. *— à porcelaine* ; china clay. *— glaise* ; clay. *Par —* ; on the ground, on the floor ; by land. *A —* ; on the ground, on the floor. *Tomber par —*, *tomber à —* ; to fall down. *Aller par —* ; to go by land. *Qui — a, guerre a* ; much coin, much care. *Mettre en —* ; to bury. *Ventre à —* ; at full gallop. *Vivre sur ses —s* ; to live on one's property. *Vivre de ses —s* ; to live on the income of one's property. *— à —*, *adj.*, commonplace ; vulgar, low, prosy.

terreau, *n.m.*, (gard.) vegetable mold ; mold, compost.

terre d'ombre, *n.f. V.* ombre.

terre-mérite, *n.f.*, (*n.p.*) turmeric (in powder).

terre-neuve, *n.m.*, (—) Newfoundland dog.

terre-neuvier, *n.m.*, (— - —s) (nav.) banker ; Newfoundland fisherman, *or* (of a ship) trader ; Newfoundland dog.

terre-noix, *n.f.* (—), (bot.), pig-nut, earth-nut, ground-nut.

terre-plein, *n.m.*, (— - —s) (fort.) terre-plein; platform.

terrer, *v.a.*, (gard.) to renew the mold of ; to spread mold over ; to burrow ; to clay (sugar), to fuller's earth (cloth, etc.).

se **terrer**, *v.r.*, to earth one's self, to burrow.

terrer, *v.n.*, to burrow.

terrestre, *adj.*, terrestrial, earthly.

terrette, *n.f.*, ground-ivy.

terreur (tèr-reur), *n.f.*, terror, trepidation, awe, dread. *Temps de la —* ; (French hist.) Reign of Terror.

terreu-x, -se, *adj.*, terreous, earthy ; dirty ; dull (of colors) ; cadaverous (of the countenance).

terrible (tèr-ribl), *adj.*, terrible, dreadful, awful; unmanageable (of children).

terriblement (tèr-ri-) *adv.*, terribly, dreadfully, awfully ; with a vengeance.

terrien (tè-ri-in), *n.m.*, *-ne* (tè-ri-èn-), *n.f.*, landholder.

terrier (tè-riè), *n.m.*, terrier (hole) ; burrow, hole ; terrier (dog). *— griffin* ; Scotch terrier.

terrier (tè-rié), *adj.m.*, only used in the expression, *Papier —* ; court-roll, terrier.

terrifier (tèr-ri-), *v.a.*, to terrify, to dismay.

terrine (tè-ri-n), *n.f.*, earthen pan ; dish. *En —* ; potted.

terrinée (tè-ri-), *n.f.*, panful.

terrir (tè-rir), *v.n.*, to lay eggs in earth or sand (of the tortoise) ; (nav.) to approach land.

territoire (tè-ri-toar), *n.m.*, territory ; jurisdiction.

territorial, -e (tè-ri-), *adj.*, territorial.

terroir (tè-roar), *n.m.*, soil, ground. *Goût de —* ; raciness (of style).

terroriser (tèr-ro-), *v.a.*, to govern by terror, to terrorize.

terrorisme (tèr-ro-), *n.m.*, terrorism.

terroriste (tèr-ro-), *n.m.*, terrorist.

terser (tèr-), *v.a. V.* tercer.

tertiaire (tèr-siè-), *adj.*, (geol., med.) tertiary.

tertio (tèr-siô), *adv.*, thirdly.

tertre (tèr-), *n.m.*, hillock, rising ground, knoll, ridge, mound. *— funéraire* ; grave ; moldering heap (Gray).

tes (tè), *possessive adj.pl.*, thy. *V.* ton.

tesson (tè-) *or* **têt** (tè), *n.m.*, potsherd, fragment of broken glass.

test (tèst), *n.m.*, (English hist.) test.

têt (tè), *or* **têt** (tè), *n.m.*, (zöol.) shell.

testacé (tès-), *n.m.*, shelled animal, testacean.

testacé, -e (tès-), *adj.*, testaceous.

testament (tès-), *n.m.*, Testament ; testament, will, last will and testament. *Ancien —* ; Old Testament. *Nouveau —* ; New Testament.

testamentaire (tès-), *adj.*, testamentary.

⊙**testat** (tès-tat), *adj.*, testate.

testat-eur, *n.m.*, **-rice**, *n.f.*, (tès-), testator, testatrix.

tester (tès-), *v.n.*, to make one's will. *Mourir sans —*; to die intestate.

testicule (-tès), *n.m.*, testicle.

testif (tès-), *n.m.*, camel's hair.

testimonial, -e (tès-), *adj.*, testifying, of testimony, by witness.

⊙**teston** (tès-), *n.m.*, (old coin) testoon.

⊙**testonner** (tès-), *v.a.*, to dress the hair.

⊙**têt** (tè) *or* **test** (tèst), *n.m.*, (chem., metal.) test, cupel, potsherd, broken glass, etc.

tétanique, *adj.*, (med.) tetanic.

tétanos (-nos), *n.m.*, (med.) tetanus; lockjaw.

têtard, *n.m.*, tadpole; pole-socket (of carriages); (ich.) bull-head, miller's thumb.

tétasses (tè-), *n.f.pl.*, (triv.) flabby hanging-down breasts.

tête, *n.f.*, head, head-piece; brains, sense, judgment; presence of mind, self-possession; hair, head of hair; horns (of stags); front, head (of a bridge); top (of things); (milit.) van, vanguard; court-card (of playing cards); (bot.) capitulum; header (swimming). *— à perruque;* wig-block, barber's block; (fig.) blockhead, old fogy. *— de Méduse;* Medusa's head; (fig.) anything producing terror, anything horrible. *Mal de —;* headache. *Signe de —;* nod. *La — en avant;* head foremost. *— ou pile;* head or tails. *— de colonne;* foremost body. *— de ligne;* starting point, terminus, port of departure. *Payer tant par —;* to pay so much a head, a piece. *Aller la — levée;* to carry one's head high. *Donner — baissée contre;* to run full butt at. *Donner de la — contre un mur;* to hit one's head against a stone wall. *Se monter la —;* to get excited over anything. *Avoir mauvaise — mais bon cœur;* to be quick-tempered, but kind-hearted. *Avoir la — fêlée;* to be crack-brained. *Avoir des affaires par-dessus la —;* to be over head and ears in business, in work. *Avoir de la —;* to have presence of mind, to be resolute. *Ce sont deux —s dans un bonnet;* they are hand and glove together. *Crier à tue —;* to bawl out loud, to shout at the top of one's voice. *— baissée;* headlong. *— pelée, — chauve;* bald head. *Cela lui met martel en —;* that worries him to death. *La — me fend;* my head is ready to split. *La — me tourne;* I feel giddy. *En avoir par-dessus la —;* to be sick and tired of anything, to be over head and ears in. *Avoir la — près du bonnet;* to be passionate, hot-headed. *La — lui a tourné;* he has lost his senses. *Il ne sait où donner de la —;* he does not know which way to turn. *Autant de —s, autant d'opinions;* so many men, so many minds. *Il y va de votre —;* your life is at stake. *Vous en répondrez sur votre —;* your head will answer for it. *Il est homme de —;* he has a good head, he is a man of resource. *Il a la — dure;* he is dull of understanding. *C'est une mauvaise —;* he is an obstinate fellow. *Avoir une chose en —;* to have a thing in one's head, to be bent upon a thing. *Perdre la —;* to lose one's head, to lose one's self-possession; to lose one's wits. *Agir de —;* to act with prudence. *Faire à sa —;* to have one's own way, to follow one's own bent. *Avoir la — chaude;* to be hot-headed. *Tenir — à quelqu'un;* to cope with any one. *Tourner la — à quelqu'un;* to turn any one's head, brain. *De la — aux pieds;* from head to foot; from top to toe. *Faire un signe de —;* to nod. *— de mort;* death's head. *En —;* in one's head; in front, ahead. *— d'âne;* (ich.) miller's thumb, bull-head.

tête-à-tête, *n.m.*, (—) tête-à-tête, private interview *or* conversation. *En —;* face to face,

in private, by ourselves, etc.; (furniture) settee, ottoman.

têteau, *n.m.*, end of a branch.

tête-bêche, *adj.*, top against bottom.

tête-bleu! *int.*, zounds!

tête-dieu, *int.*, zounds!

teter (té-) *or* **téter**, *v.a.*, to suck (milk).

teter (té-) *or* **téter**, *v.n.*, to suck. *Donner à — à;* to give suck to, to suckle.

tétière (-ti-è-r), *n.f.*, infant's cap; antimacassar; head-stall (of a bridle).

tétin (té-), *n.m.*, nipple, teat.

tétine (té-), *n.f.*, (cook.) udder; dent (on a cuirass).

téton (té-), *n.m.*, teat, breast (of a woman). *Bouton du —;* nipple.

tétonnière (té-), *n.f.*, breast-band; (l.ex.) full-breasted woman.

tétra, a prefix from Gr. τετρα.

tétracorde, *n.m.*, tetrachord.

tétradrachme, *n.m.* and *f.*, (antiq.) tetradrachm.

tétradynamie, *n.f.*, (bot.) tetradynamia.

tétraèdre, *n.m.*, (geom.) tetrahedron.

tétragone, *n.m.* and *adj.*, (geom.) tetragon; tetragonal.

tétralogie, *n.f.*, (antiq.) tetralogy.

tétramètre, *n.m.*, tetrameter.

tétrandrie, *n.f.*, (bot.) tetrandria.

tétrapétalé, -e, *adj.*, (bot.) tetrapetalous.

tétraphylle, *adj.*, (bot.) tetraphyllous.

tétrarcat *or* **tétrarchat**, *n.m.*, tetrarchate.

tétrarchie, *n.f.*, tetrarchy.

tétrarque, *n.m.*, tetrarch.

tétras (-trâs), *n.m.*, (orni.) grouse, capercailzie.

tétrastyle, *n.m.*, (arch.) tetrastyle.

tétrasyllabe, *n.m.*, (gram.) tetrasyllable.

tette (tèt), *n.f.*, teat, dug (of animals).

tette-chèvre (tèt-), *n.m.*, (— — —*s*) (orni.) goat-sucker, fern-owl.

têtu, -e, *adj.*, headstrong, willful, stubborn, obstinate.

têtu, *n.m.*, (tech.) granite hammer.

teutonique, *adj.*, Teutonic.

texte (tèkst), *n.m.*, text, theme, matter, subject, point; (jur.) purview; passage (of Scripture). *Petit —;* (print.) brevier. *Gros—;* (print.) two-line brevier. *Revenir à son —;* to return to the point. *Restituer un —;* to restore a text. *Livre de —;* text-book.

textile (tèks-til), *n.m.* and *adj.*, textile material; textile.

textuaire (tèks-tu-è-r), *n.m.*, text. *adj.*, textuary.

textuel, -le (tèks-tu-èl), *adj.*, textual, word for word.

textuellement (tèks-tu-èl-mãn), *adv.*, textually, word for word, verbatim.

texture (tèks-tur), *n.f.*, weaving, texture; connection.

thalame, *n.m.*, (bot.) thalamus.

thaler (-lèr), *n.m.*, dollar (German coin).

thallium, *n.m.*, (n.p.) (chem.) thallium.

thalweg, *n.m.*, (—*s*) (geog.) thalweg; middle line of a river.

thane, *n.m.*, thane (Saxon or Danish baron).

thapsie, *n.f.*, (bot.) deadly carrot.

thaumaturge, *n.m.* and *adj.*, thaumaturge; thaumaturgical.

thaumaturgie, *n.f.*, thaumaturgy.

thé, *n.m.*, tea; tea-party; (bot.) tea-tree. *Boîte à —;* tea-caddy, tea-canister. *Cabaret à —, service à —;* set of tea-things, tea-service.

théatin, *n.m.*, theatine (monk *or* nun).

théâtral, -e, *adj.*, theatrical.

théâtralement, *adv.*, theatrically.

théâtre, *n.m.*, theater, playhouse; stage; plays (collection); theater (scene, place of action); scene, field, seat. *Monter sur le —;* to appear upon the stage, to act, to tread the boards.

Changement de —; change of scenery. *Coup de* —; unexpected event, striking event; (fam.) claptrap. — *de la guerre;* seat of war. — *de Corneille;* Corneille's plays. *Roi de* —; mere shadow of a king. *Accommoder un sujet au* —; to adapt anything for the stage.

thébaïde, *n.f.,* Egyptian desert; (fig.) a desert, lonely solitude.

thébain, *n.m.* and *adj.,* Theban.

thélère, *n.f.,* tea-pot.

théiforme, *adj.,* theiform (infusions).

théisme, *n.m.,* theism.

théiste, *n.m.,* theist.

thelfuse, *n.f.,* river-crab.

thème, *n.m.,* topic, subject, theme; (mus.) theme; (astrol.) scheme; composition, exercise (in schools).

thémis, *n.f.,* Themis, (poet. st. e.) justice.

théocratie (-ci), *n.f.,* theocracy.

théocratique, *adj.,* theocratic, theocratical.

théocratiquement (-tik-màn), *adv.,* theocratically.

théodicée, *n.f.,* theodicy.

théodolite, *n.m.,* (math.) theodolite.

théodosien, *adj.,* Theodosian.

théogonie, *n.f.,* theogony.

théogonique, *adj.,* relating to theogony.

théologal, *n.m.,* lecturer on divinity.

théologal, -e, *adj.,* theological, divine.

théologale, *n.f.,* lectureship on divinity.

théologie, *n.f.,* theology, divinity. *Docteur en* —; doctor of divinity.

théologien (-ji-in), *n.m.,* theologian, divine.

théologique, *adj.,* theological.

théologiquement (-jik-màn), *adv.,* theologically.

théorbe, *n.m.* *V.* **téorbe.**

théorème, *n.m.,* theorem.

théoricien (-si-in), *n.m.,* theorist.

théorie, *n.f.,* theory; speculation. *Faire des —s;* to speculate; to theorize.

théorique, *adj.,* theoretical.

théoriquement (-rik-màn), *adv.,* theoretically.

théoriser, *v.a.,* to theorize.

théoriste, *n.m.,* theorist.

théosophe, *n.m.,* theosophist.

théosophie, *n.f.,* theosophy.

thérapeutes, *n.m.pl.,* (religious order) Therapeutics.

thérapeutique, *adj.,* therapeutical.

thérapeutique, *n.f.,* (med.) therapeutics.

thériacal, -e, *adj.,* (pharm.) theriac, theriacal.

thériaque, *n.f.,* (pharm.) theriac.

thermal, -e (tèr-), *adj.,* thermal. *Eaux —es;* hot mineral waters, hot springs.

thermes (tèrm), *n.m.pl.,* thermal baths; (antiq.) thermæ.

thermidor (tèr-), *n.m.,* Thermidor, eleventh month of the calendar of the first French republic, from July 19th to August 17th.

thermidorien, -ne (tèr-), *n.* and *adj.,* Thermidorian.

thermo-manomètre (tèr-), *n.m.,* (of steam-engines) thermometer-gauge.

thermomètre (tèr-), *n.m.,* thermometer.

thermométrique (tèr-), *adj.,* thermometric.

thermoscope (tèr-), *n.m.,* (phys.) thermoscope.

thermostat (tèr-), *n.m.,* (phys.) thermostat.

thésauriser (tèr-), *v.n.,* to treasure up, to hoard up, to heap up treasure.

thésauriseu-r, *n.m.,* **-se,** *n.f.,* hoarder.

thèse, *n.f.,* thesis, theme; disputation, argument, discussion; the printed sheet containing the thesis. *Vous sortez de la* —; you are wandering from the question. *Soutenir — pour quelqu'un;* to side with any one, to stand up for any one. *Il voulut soutenir sa* —; he resolved to

maintain his point. *Cela change la* —; that alters the matter. *En — générale;* as a rule.

thessalonicien, *n.m.* and *adj.,* Thessalonian.

théurgie, *n.f.,* theurgy.

théurgique, *adj.,* theurgic, theurgical.

thibaude, *n.f.,* hair-cloth, cow-hair cloth, coarse drugget.

thlaspi, *n.m.,* (bot.) thlaspi.

thon, *n.m.,* (ich.) tunny, tunny-fish.

thoracique or ⊙**thorachique,** *n.m.* and *adj.,* (med.) pectoral; thoracic. *Canal* —; thoracic duct.

thorax (-raks), *n.m.,* (anat.) thorax, chest.

thridace, *n.f.,* (pharm.) lactucarium, lettuce-opium.

thrombus (-bus), *n.m.,* (surg.) thrombus.

thuia, *n.m.,* (bot.) thuja, arbor vitæ.

thuriféraire, *n.m.,* (c. rel.) censer-bearer.

thurifère, *n.m.,* (bot.) thuriferous.

thuya, *n.m.,* *V.* **thuia.**

thyade, *n.f.,* (antiq.) Bacchante.

thym (tin), *n.m.,* (bot.) thyme.

thymus, *n.m.,* (—) (anat.) thymus.

thyroïde, *adj.,* (anat.) thyroid.

thyrse, *n.m.,* (antiq.) thyrsus; (bot.) thyrsus.

tiare (tiar), *n.f.,* tiara.

tibia, *n.m.,* (anat.) tibia, shin, shin-bone.

tibial, -e, *adj.,* (anat.) tibial.

tibio-tarsien, -ne (-si-in, -è-n), *adj.,* (anat.) tibio-tarsal.

tic, *n.m.,* knack, ugly knack, bad habit; (vet.) crib-biting; bad habits of cattle; (med.) tic. — *douloureux;* tic douloureux, facial neuralgia.

tic tac, *n.m.,* ticktack; tick, ticking, click.

tiède, *adj.,* lukewarm, tepid; mild, soft, cool; (fig.) indifferent.

tièdement (tièd-màn), *adv.,* coldly, with indifference; lukewarmly.

tiédeur, *n.f.,* lukewarmness, tepidity, tepidness; (fig.) coldness, indifference.

tiédir, *v.n.,* to cool, to grow lukewarm, to become lukewarm; to grow cool, to become cool.

tien, -ne (ti-in, -è-n), *pron.,* thine, yours.

tien, *n.m.,* thine, thy own, yours, your own. *Les —s;* thy people, thy relations and friends.

tiens, *n.m.,* only used in the expression *Un — vaut mieux que deux tu l'auras;* (prov.) a bird in the hand is worth two in the bush.

tiens! or **tenez!** *int.,* expressing astonishment, or to call the attention of the hearer; look! look here! look there! hold! now then! there!

tierce (tièrs), *n.f.,* third (of time); (mus.) third, tierce; tierce (at cards); (fenc.) tiers; (print.) press-revise. — *majeure;* (mus.) major third; tierce major (at cards). — *mineure;* (mus.) minor third.

tiercelet (tièr-slè), *n.m.,* (hawking) tercel, tiercel, tiercelet, tarsel.

tiercement (tièrs-màn), *n.m.,* (thea.) increase of a third (in prices); ⊙(jur.) outbidding by one third a price offered.

tiercer (tièrsé), *v.a.* and *n.,* (thea.) to raise prices one third; ⊙(jur.) to outbid by one third a price offered; (agri.) to plow a third time. *V.* **tercer.**

tierceron (tièr-), *n.m.,* (arch.) tierceron.

tierçon (tièr-), *n.m.,* a measure, tierce (of a cask).

tier-s, -ce (tièr, tièrs), *adj.,* third, of a third person, third party. *Le — état;* the people, the commons. *Fièvre —ce;* tertian ague. — *porteur,* — *détenteur;* third party or hand. — *parti;* third party.

tiers, *n.m.,* third, third person; third part. *Le — et le quart;* everybody, all the world.

tiers-point, *n.m.,* (— — -s) (arch.) tierce-point; (tech.) saw-file.

tige, *n.f.,* trunk, stem, body; stalk, leg (of a boot); shank (of a candlestick); stock, head (of a family); shank (of an anchor); straw (of corn); tail (of a valve); (tech.) rod. — *de communication;* connecting rod. — *graduée;* index rod. *Arbres à haute —;* tall trees. *Arbres à basse —;* dwarf trees.

tigette, *n.f.,* (arch.) honeysuckle ornament (at the springing of a volute).

***tignasse,** *n.f.,* (fam., pop.) mop, shock (of hair); old wig.

***tignon,** *n.m.* V. **chignon.**

***tignonner,** *v.a.,* to curl the hair behind the head (of women).

***se tignonner,** *v.r.,* to seize each other by the hair (behind), to pull caps, to have a set-to.

tigre, *n.m.,* (mam.) tiger; (ich.) square fish; (conch.) tiger-shell; groom; (ent.) tiger-beetle.

tigre, *adj.,* spotted (like a tiger).

tigré, -e, *adj.,* spotted, speckled.

tigrer, *v.a.,* to spot, to speckle.

tigresse, *n.f.,* (mam.) tigress.

tilbury, *n.m.,* tilbury, gig, two-wheeled cart.

tiliacées, *n.f.pl.,* (bot.) tiliaceæ.

***tillac,** *n.m.,* (nav.) deck, poop. *Franc —;* main deck. *Faux —;* orlop deck.

***tillage** *or* **teillage,** *n.m.,* (agri.) stripping, scutching (hemp).

***tille** *or* **teille,** *n.f.,* bast of the lime-tree; cabin, cuddy (of an undecked vessel); ax-hammer; hemp-harl.

***tiller** *or* **teiller,** *v.a.,* (agri.) to peel, to strip, to scutch (hemp).

***tilleul,** *n.m.,* (bot.) linden-tree, lime-tree.

***tilleu-r,** *-se,* or *n.f.,* or **teilleu-r, -se,** (agri.) stripper, scutcher (of hemp).

timbale, *n.f.,* kettle-drum; (mus.) timbal; cup (of metal); battledore; (cook.) mold.

timbalier, *n.m.,* kettle-drummer.

timbrage, *n.m.,* stamping (of government paper).

timbre, *n.m.,* bell, clock-bell; office-bell, call-bell; ring, sound (of a bell); thrill, tone, voice; stamp (on paper); (her.) helmet; (horl.) bell; (post-office) post-mark; head, brains. — *de la voix;* tone of the voice. — *acquit, quittance;* receipt-stamp. *Droit de —;* stamp duty. *Sa voix a un — argentin;* he has a silver-toned voice. *Il a le — fêlé;* he is crack-brained, cracked.

timbré, -e, *part. adj.,* sta ped. *Papier —;* stamped paper, summons, writ. *Esprit, cerveau —;* crack-brained person. *Il est —;* he is cracked.

timbre-poste, *n.m.,* (—*s*—) postage-stamp.

timbrer, *v.a.,* to stamp (paper, parchment); (her.) to crest.

timbreur, *n.m.,* stamper.

timide, *adj.,* timid, bashful, timorous, shy.

timidement (-mid-mǎn), *adv.,* timidly, bashfully; timorously; shyly.

timidité, *n.f.,* timidity, timorousness, nervousness, shyness, bashfulness.

timon, *n.m.,* pole (of a coach); beam (of a plow); (nav.) helm, tiller (of a rudder); (fig.) helm, direction, government; (tech.) draughtbar. *Tenir le —;* to be at the helm.

timonerie (-mo-n-rî), *n.f.,* (nav.) steerage.

timonier, *n.m.,* wheeler, wheel-horse; (nav.) steersman, helmsman.

timoré, -e, *adj.,* timorous, fearful, scrupulous.

tin, *n.m.,* (nav.) block of wood; (tech.) caskstand.

tincal, *n.m.,* (chem.) tincal.

tinctorial, -e, *adj.,* tinctorial.

tine, *n.f.,* tub, water-cask, firkin.

tinet, *n.m.,* gambrel (of horses); bent stick (for suspending carcases).

tinette, *n.f.,* half tub, kit, firkin (of butter).

tintamarre, *n.m.,* hubbub, uproar, clatter, hurly-burly, din, racket.

tintement (tǐnt-mǎn), *n.m.,* ringing sound, tinkling; tingling; toll, tolling, jingling, jingle. — *funèbre;* funeral toll, knell. — *d'oreilles;* tingling, *or* ringing, in the ears.

tintenague (tǐnt-nag), *n.f.* V. **toutenague.**

tinter, *v.a.,* to toll, to ring, to ring for; (nav.) to put upon the stocks, to set on blocks, to prop, to support.

tinter, *v.n.,* to toll, to ring; to tinkle, to jingle; to tingle. *Les oreilles me tintent;* my ears tingle.

tintin, *n.m.,* jingling, tinkling (of bells, glasses).

tintouin, *n.m.,* tingling (in one's ear); noise, hubbub; anxiety, uneasiness, trouble. *Avoir du —;* to be upon thorns, to be in trouble.

tique, *n.f.,* (ent.) tick. — *ricin;* wood-tick, dog-tick.

tiquer, *v.n.,* (of horses) to be vicious.

tiqueté, -e (tik-té), *adj.,* variegated, speckled, spotted.

tiqueture, *n.f.,* spottedness, spots, speckles; variegation.

tiqueu-r, -se, *adj.,* crib-biting (of horses). *n.m.,* crib-biter.

tir, *n.m.,* shooting, firing, fire; shooting-gallery, shooting-ground. — *en écharpe;* flank-fire, rifle-range, range. — *à la cible;* target-firing. *Chasse au —;* (hunt.) shooting. *Justesse du —;* trueness of the aim. *Avoir un — infaillible;* to have an unerring aim, to be a deadly shot.

tirade, *n.f.,* tirade; (mus., thea.) tirade; passage (of prose *or* verse). *Tout d'une —;* all in one speech *or* breath, *or* at one stretch.

tirage, *n.m.,* draught; towing (of boats); towing-path; drawing (of a lottery); (print.) working, working off, pulling, printing; winding-off (of silk); (fig.) difficulty, obstacle. — *au sort;* drawing lots, balloting. *Le — d'une cheminée;* the draught of a chimney.

***tiraillement,** *n.m.,* plucking, pulling, hauling about; twitching, twinge, pain; (fig.) anxiety; jarring, jar, disagreement. — *d'estomac;* pain in the stomach, griping.

***tirailler,** *v.a.,* to pull, to haul about, to tug, to twitch; to tease, to plague, to bother, to pester.

***se tirailler,** *v.r.,* to pull one another about.

***tirailler,** *v.n.,* to shoot wildly; to bang away; (milit.) to skirmish.

***tiraillerie,** *n.f.,* (milit.) desultory, wild, aimless firing.

***tirailleur,** *n.m.,* (milit.) sharpshooter; skirmisher.

tirant, *n.m.,* string (of purses); boot-strap; cramp, cramp-iron; (carp.) collar; iron bar, bolt, holdfast; (cook.) white leather; string of parchment; brace (of a drum); ship's gauge, ship's draught. — *d'eau;* (nav.) gauge, sea-gauge, ship's draught.

tirasse, *n.f.,* (hunt.) draw-net.

tirasser, *v.a.* and *n.,* (hunt.) to catch with a draw-net; to set a draw-net.

tire, *n.f.,* tug, pull; quick jerk of the wing. *Tout d'une —;* at a stretch. *Voleur à la —;* pickpocket. *Vol à la —;* pocket-picking.

tiré, -e, *adj.,* drawn.

tiré, *n.m.,* (hunt.) shooting; (com.) drawee (of bills).

tire-balle, *n.m.,* (———*s*) (surg.) bullet-forceps; (milit.) ramrod-screw.

tire-botte, *n.m.,* (———*s*) boot-hook; boot-jack.

tire-bouchon, *n.m.,* (———*s*) cork-screw; ringlet (of hair).

tire-bouchonné, -e, *adj.,* (of hair) in ringlets.

tire-bourre, *n.m.,* (———*s*) worm-screw (to unload a gun).

tire-bouton, *n.m.,* (———*s*) button-hook.

tire-clou, *n.m.,* (— *- -s*) nail-drawer ; (tech.) claw-hammer ; slater's hammer.

à tire-d'aile, *adv.,* with a quick jerk of the wings ; at a single flight ; with outstretched wings, darting through the air. *Voler à* — ; to fly as fast as its wings can carry it ; at full speed.

tire-étoupe, *n.m.,* (—) (tech.) worm.

tire-feu. *n.m.,* (artil.) lanyard.

tire-fond, *n.m.,* (—) turrel elevator.

à tire-larigot, *adv.,* only used in *Boire à* — ; to drink hard, to drink like a fish.

***tire-ligne,** *n.m.,* (— *- -s*) drawing-pen.

tirelire, *n.f.,* money-box.

⊙**tirelire,** *n.m.,* song, carol (of the lark).

⊙**tirelirer,** *v.n.,* to sing like a lark.

tire-moelle, *n.m.,* (—) marrow-spoon.

tire-pied, *n.m.,* (— *- -s*) shoemaker's stirrup.

tire-plomb, *n.m.,* (—) glazier's vice.

tire-point or **tire-pointe,** *n.m.,* (—) pricker (used in stitching).

tirer, *v.a.,* to draw, to pull, to give a pull ; to take, to take out, to pull out ; to get, to extract, to collect ; to fire, to shoot, to fire at, to shoot at ; to trace, to delineate ; to receive, to reap, to recover ; to extricate, to free from ; to relieve ; to conclude, to infer, to deduce ; to draw on, to put on, to draw up ; to draw down ; (print.) to work, to work off, to pull, to print, to pull off ; to approach, to border, to verge (on) ; (nav.) to draw ; to tighten (a rope) ; to tap (liquors) ; to stretch (linen) ; to cast (a nativity) ; to draw (a bill) ; to take out (a tooth) ; to let (blood). — *en arrière* ; to pull back. — *de l'eau* ; to draw water. — *dedans* ; to pull in. — *en haut* ; to pull up. — *en bas* ; to pull down. — *les oreilles à quelqu'un* ; to pull any one's ears. — *la langue* ; to put out one's tongue. *Faire* — *l'épée à quelqu'un* ; to make any one draw his sword. *Se faire* — *l'oreille* ; to require (much) pressing. — *ses bottes* ; to pull off one's boots. — *de l'argent de sa poche* ; to pull money out of one's pocket. — *pied ou aile d'une chose* ; to reap some benefit (from a thing) by hook or by crook. *Il tire beaucoup de la cour* ; he gets a great deal by the court. — *parti de* ; to make the best of, to turn to account. — *satisfaction d'une injure* ; to obtain satisfaction for an injury. — *vengeance* ; to be revenged. — *vanité, or gloire, d'une chose* ; to glory in, to be proud of, to boast of, to take a pride in. — *avantage d'une chose* ; to derive advantage from anything. — *la racine carrée, la racine cubique d'un nombre* ; to extract the square, the cubic root of a number. — *le suc des herbes* ; to extract the juice of herbs. — *une conséquence* ; to draw an inference. — *une corde* ; to tighten a cord. — *quelqu'un à quatre chevaux* ; to draw and quarter any one, to tear any one to pieces. — *ses chausses,* — *ses guêtres* ; (fam., pop.) to cut one's sticks, to scamper off. — *une vache* ; to milk a cow. — *les rideaux* ; to open the curtains ; to close, to pull the curtains to. — *l'or* ; to wire-draw gold. — *les cartes* ; to tell fortunes. — *d'erreur* ; to undeceive. — *une affaire en longueur* ; to protract, to delay, to put off anything. — *une allée au cordeau* ; to make a walk in a straight line. — *en cire* ; to reproduce in wax. — *des estampes* ; to pull prints. — *un fusil* ; to shoot a gun. — *un coup de canon* ; to fire a gun. — *des fusées* ; to let off rockets. — *un oiseau* ; to shoot at a bird. — *une estocade* ; (fenc.) to make a pass. — *le diable par la queue* ; to lead a struggling existence. — *les vers du nez à quelqu'un* ; to pump any one. *Tirez le rideau, la farce est jouée* ; ring down the curtain, the play is over (Rabelais).

se tirer, *v.r.,* to extricate one's self ; to get out to, to get through ; to recover (from illness). *Se* — *d'affaire sain et sauf* ; to escape safe and sound, to get off scot free. *Se* — *d'un puits* ; to get out

of any difficulty. *Je me ferais* — *à quatre avant de parler* ; wild horses would not make me speak. *Se* — *d'affaire* ; to get out of (a scrape, a difficulty). *S'en* — ; to pull through, to manage it.

tirer, *v.n.,* to draw ; to go, to make for ; to shoot ; to tend, to border, to verge ; to fire. — *sur* ; to incline to, to border, to verge on. *Cette pierre tire sur le vert* ; that stone is greenish. — *à sa fin* ; to be closing in (of day) ; (fig.) to be on one's last legs. *Bon à* — ; order for press ; ready for press, passed for press.

tire-racine, *n.m.,* (—) stump-forceps (of a dentist).

tiret, *n.m.,* slip of parchment ; hyphen.

tiretaine (tir-tè-n), *n.f.,* linsey-woolsey. *V.* **breluche.**

tire-tête, *n.m.,* (— *- -s*) craniotomy forceps.

tireu-r, *n.m.,-se,* *n.f.,* one who draws, drawer ; marksman, shot (pers.) ; rifleman, sharpshooter ; drawer (of a bill of exchange). — *d'or* ; gold wire-drawer. ⊙ — *d'armes* ; fencing-master. — *se de cartes* ; fortune-teller. *C'est un bon* — ; he is a good shot.

***tire-veille,** *n.f.,* (—) (nav.) ladder-rope ; manrope. — *de l'échelle hors le bord* ; manropes of the sides. — *de cabestan* ; swifter.

tiroir, *n.m.,* drawer (of a table, etc.) ; (milit.) middle rank ; (tech.) slide, slide-box. *Pièce à* — ; (thea.) comedy of episodes.

tironien, -ne (-in, -è-n), *adj.,* (antiq.) Tironian. *Abréviation* — *ne* ; Tironian note.

tisane, *n.f.,* (med.) diet-drink, infusion, decoction (of herbs). — *de champagne* ; light champagne (for invalids).

tisard, *n.m.,* door (of an oven).

tiser, *v.a.,* to stoke.

tison, *n.m.,* brand, fire-brand.

tisonné, *adj.m.,* only used in *Gris* — ; (of horses) marked with black spots.

tisonner, *v.n.,* to stir, or to poke, the fire.

tisonneu-r, *n.m.,* *-se,* *n.f.,* person fond of poking the fire.

tisonnier, *n.m.,* poker ; blacksmith's poker.

tissage, *n.m.,* weaving, plaiting ; texture.

tisser, *v.a.,* to weave, to plait ; to contrive.

tisserand (tis-rãn), *n.m.,* weaver.

tisseranderie (tis-ran-drî), *n.f.,* weaver's business.

tissu, -e, *past part.* (of ⊙*tistre*), woven, spun, made up. *Des jours* — *s d'or et de soie* ; happy, halcyon days.

tissu, *n.m.,* texture, textile fabric, texture ; tissue. — *de mensonges* ; tissue of lies. — *d'argent* ; silver tissue. — *d'or* ; golden tissue. — *métallique* ; gauze wire, gauze wirework. — *réticulaire* ; (anat.) reticular body.

tissure, *n.f.,* tissue, texture, web, weaving, contexture.

tissuterie, *n.f.,* ribbon-weaving.

tissutier (-tié), *n.m.,* weaver (of silk textures).

⊙**tistre,** *v.a.,* to weave.

titan, *n.m.,* (myth.) Titan.

titane, *n.m.,* or **titanium** (-om), *n.m.,* (chem.) titanium.

titanique, titanesque, *adj.,* titanic.

tithymale, *n.m.,* (bot.) tithymal.

titi, *n.m.,* gay apprentice, roystering blade ; mummer (at carnivals).

titillant, -e (til-lãn, -t), *adj.,* titillating ; tickling.

titillation (-til-la-), *n.f.,* titillation, tickling ; slight agitation.

titiller (-til-lé), *v.n.* and *a.,* to titillate, to tickle.

titre, *n.m.,* title, style, title-page ; capacity, claim, reason, cause ; respect, way, right ; standard (of coin) ; (jur.) title, title-deed, deed, indenture. *Faux* — ; false title ; falsehood, sham ; (print.) half-title. *Donner un* — *à* ; to entitle to. *A — de ;* by right of, in virtue of. *A bon* —, *à juste — deservedly, justly. A — gratuit ;* gratuitously. *En —;* at the head of, on the title *or* title page ; chief, titular, acknowledged. *A plus d'un —;* for more reasons than one, on more grounds than one. *Se donner le — de ;* to style one's self.

titré, -e, *adj.,* titled ; conferring a title (of estates).

titrer, *v.a.,* to give a title to.

titrier, *n.m.,* forger of titles *or* deeds (l.u.) ; curator of deeds (in monasteries).

titubant, -e, *adj.,* staggering.

titubation, *n.f.,* titubation, reeling, staggering.

tituber, *v.n.,* to stagger, to reel.

titulaire, *n.m.f.* and *adj.,* titular, titulary, incumbent, head, chief.

toast *or* **toste** (tost), *n.m.,* toast, health. *Porter, donner, un —;* to toast, to give *or* propose a toast.

toaster (tos-té), *v.a. V.* **toster.**

toc! *int.* and *n.m.,* rap, knock (at a door) ; sham, *or* imitation, jewelry ; paste ; brummagem goods.

tocane, *n.f.,* unpressed wine.

tocante, *n.f.,* (pop.) ticker, watch.

tocsin, *n.m.,* tocsin, alarm-bell ; (fig.) hue and cry.

todier, *n.m.,* (orni.) tody.

toge, *n.f.,* (Rom. antiq.) toga, robe, gown.

tohu-bohu, *n.m.,* (—) (from Hebrew) chaos ; jumble, medley ; (fig.) confusion, uproar, disorder, hurly-burly, hubbub.

toi, *pron.,* thee, thyself, thou, you, yourself.

toile, *n.f.,* cloth, linen cloth ; (thea.) curtain ; canvas (for painting) ; canvas, sail ; (paint.) painting, picture, piece ; web (of a spider). *pl.* (hunt.) toils. *— à sac ;* sack-cloth. *— écrue ;* brown holland. *— ouvrée ;* huckaback. *— d'emballage ;* pack-cloth. *— grasse ;* tarpaulin. *— vernie ;* oil-skin. *— peinte ;* printed calico, print. *— pour chemises ;* shirting. *— pour draps de lit ;* sheeting. *—s de sabords ;* port-sails. *— de dunette ;* canvas-covering for the poop. *— d'or ;* gold cloth. *— cirée ;* oil-cloth. *— d'araignée ;* cobweb. *Blanchisseur de —s ;* bleacher. *Marchand de —s ;* linendraper. *— de Pénélope ;* Penelope's web. *La — est levée ;* (thea.) the curtain is up. *La — tombe ;* (thea.) the curtain falls. *Derrière la — ;* (thea.) behind the curtain.

toilerie (toal-rî), *n.f.,* linen-cloth trade, linen drapery.

toilette, *n.f.,* toilet ; attire, dress ; dressing-table, toilet-table, wash-stand ; trimming (of horses). *Revendeuse à la —;* wardrobe purchaser (of left-off wearing apparel). *Grande —;* full dress. *Cabinet de —;* dressing-closet, dressing-room. *Il, or elle, fait sa —;* or *il, or elle, est à sa —;* he, *or* she, is dressing.

toili-er, *n.m.,* **-ère,** *n.f.,* dealer in linen ; linen-cloth maker, cotton-cloth maker.

toise, *n.f.,* toise (6·39459 feet) ; fathom. *On ne mesure pas les hommes à la —;* men ought not to be judged by their size. *Mesurer les autres à sa —;* to measure others by one's own standard.

toisé, *n.m.,* measuring ; (math.) mensuration.

toiser, *v.a.,* to measure ; to survey, to examine ; to eye from head to foot, to look down upon ; to settle, to conclude. *— un soldat ;* to take the height of a soldier. *— quelqu'un ;* to look any one up and down, *or* to look down on any one. *Cela est toisé ;* (pop.) that is done for.

toiseur, *n.m.,* measurer, surveyor.

toison, *n.f.,* fleece ; (pop.) thick head of hair. *— d'or ;* golden fleece. *L'ordre de la — d'or ;* the Order of the Golden Fleece.

toit, *n.m.,* roof, house-top ; top (of a mine) ; dwelling, home. *— à cochons ;* pig-sty. *— à*

deux croupes ; (arch.) compass roof, span roof. *Dire, or crier, quelque chose sur les —s ;* to proclaim anything from the housetop. *Habiter sous les —s ;* to live in a garret, *or* an attic. *Commencer une maison par le — ;* (fig.) to begin at the wrong end.

toiture, *n.f.,* roofing, roof.

tokai *or* **tokay,** *n.m.,* Tokay wine.

tôle, *n.f.,* sheet-iron ; (metal.) plate-iron. *— ondulée ;* corrugated iron.

tolérable, *adj.,* tolerable, bearable, supportable ; middling, passable.

tolérablement, *adv.,* tolerably, supportably ; passably, middlingly.

tolérance, *n.f.,* tolerance, toleration, endurance, forbearance, indulgence ; (jur.) sufferance ; (coin.) deduction, allowance. *Maison de —;* house of ill-fame.

tolérant, -e, *adj.,* tolerant.

tolérantisme, *n.m.,* (theol.) system of toleration.

tolérer, *v.a.,* to tolerate, to suffer, to allow, to endure, to bear, to allow of ; to wink at. *Je ne puis — cet homme ;* I cannot bear, endure, that man. *Se —,* to tolerate one's self, to be tolerated.

tôlerie (tôl-rî), *n.f.,* sheet-iron manufactory ; (metal.) flatting-mills ; sheet-iron goods.

tolet, *n.m.,* (nav.) thole.

toletière (tol-tièr), *n.f.,* (nav.) rowlock.

tôlier, *n.m.,* work in sheet-iron ; manufacturer of sheet-iron.

tollé, *n.m.,* hue and cry. *Crier — sur quelqu'un ;* to raise a hue and cry against any one.

tomahawk, *n.m.,* tomahawk.

tomaison, *n.f.,* numbering (into volumes) ; number (of a volume).

tomate, *n.f.,* (bot.) tomato, love-apple.

tombac, *n.m.,* (metal.) tombac.

tombal, -e, *adj.,* (archæology) only used in *Pierre —e ;* tomb-stone.

tombant, -e, *adj.,* falling down, drooping, flowing.

tombe, *n.f.,* tomb, grave, tombstone, headstone, gravestone. *Descendre dans la —,* to die, to sink into the grave. *Être sur le bord de la — ;* to be on the brink of the grave.

tombeau, *n.m.,* tomb, grave ; tombstone ; sepulcher, death. *Mettre au — ;* to bring down to the grave or to bury.

tombée, *n.f.,* fall (of day). *A la — de la nuit ;* at nightfall. *A la — du jour ;* at close of day.

tombelier, *n.m.,* carter.

tomber, *v.n.,* to fall, to fall down ; to tumble, to tumble down ; to drop, to drop down ; to sink, to sink down ; to break in, to come, to light, to hit on, to come across ; to come down, to sink, to decay, to fall away, to dwindle, to droop, to come out ; to abate, to die away ; (nav.) to sag ; to hang, to incline. *— bien or mal ;* to be lucky or unlucky ; to come seasonably *or* unseasonably ; to come to the wrong or right person. *Il est tombé de cheval ;* he fell off his horse. *— à terre, — par terre ;* to fall down. *Le brouillard tombe ;* the fog is falling. *— malade ;* to fall ill. *— de faiblesse ;* to drop down from weakness. *— d'inanition ;* to be ready to faint for want of food. *— du haut mal ;* to have the falling sickness. *— raide mort ;* to fall down dead. *Se laisser — ;* to get a fall. *— en enfance ;* to become childish. *— dans les bras de quelqu'un ;* to fall into any one's arms. *— sur une maison ;* to come across a house. *— d'accord ;* to agree, to be at one with. *— de son haut, — des nues ;* to be amazed, to be astounded. *Les bras m'en tombèrent ;* I was struck dumb with surprise. *Le sort est tombé sur lui ;* the lot has fallen upon him. *Cela m'est tombé entre les mains ;* that fell into my hands. *Le jour tombe ;* the day is closing in. *Faire — ;* to throw, push, *or* knock, down ; to trip up. *Laisser* — ; to drop, to let fall. — *dans l'eau ;* (fig.) to fall through, to come to nothing, to fall to the ground. — *sous le vent ;* (nav.) to fall to leeward. — *de fièvre en chaud mal, — de la poêle dans la braise ;* to jump out of the frying pan into the fire.

tombereau (ton-brô), *n.m.,* (for the condemned) tumbril-cart ; dust-cart ; ballast-truck ; sledge.

tombola, *n.f.,* tombola, lottery, raffle.

tome, *n.m.,* volume, tome.

tomenteu-x, **-se**, *adj.,* (bot., zoöl., anat.) tomentous, tomentose, downy.

ton, *m.,* **ta,** *f.,* **tes,** *pl.m.f., possessive adj.,* thy, your. — *frère, ta sœur et tes cousins ;* thy brother, sister, and cousins. — *âme ;* thy soul. [*Ton* is used for the *f.* before a vowel or silent *h.*]

ton, *n.m.,* tone ; tune ; voice, accent ; manner, strain, style, taste ; manners, breeding ; color, tint, tinge. — *aigre ;* shrill tone. — *doux ;* soft, sweet tone. *Mauvais* — ; ill-breeding, ill-manners, vulgarity. *De mauvais* — ; ill-bred, unmannerly, ungentlemanly, low, vulgar, improper. *Donner le* — ; to give the tone, to lead the fashion ; (mus.) to pitch, to tone. *Parler d'un* — *fier ;* to speak haughtily. *Parler d'un* — *de maître ;* to speak in a magisterial manner, to be very masterful. *Le prendre sur un* — ; to assume airs. *Le prendre sur un haut* — ; to speak with arrogance ; to carry it high. *Changer de* — ; to sing to another tune, to change one's tone. *Il donne le* — *à la conversation ;* he takes the lead in conversation. *Donner le* — *à l'orchestre ;* to lead the orchestra. *C'est le* — *qui fait la musique ;* it is the manner which shows the intention.

tonalité, *n.f.,* (mus.) tonality.

tondaison, *n.f.* V. **tonte.**

tondeu-r, *n.m.,* **-se,** *n.f.,* shearer, clipper. — *de draps ;* shearman, clothworker.

tondeuse, *n.f.,* shearing-machine. — *de gazon ;* lawn-mower.

tondre, *v.a. and n.,* to shear, to clip, to crop ; to shave, to trim, to pare. — *des brebis ;* to shear sheep. — *du drap ;* to shear cloth. — *une haie ;* to clip a hedge. — *sur un œuf ;* to skin a flint.

tondu, -e, *part.,* shorn. *Il n'y avait que trois* —*s et un pelé ;* there was nothing but the ragtag and bobtail.

tonicité, *n.f.,* (med.) tonicity.

tonique, *adj.,* (med., mus., gram.) tonic.

tonique, *n.m.,* (med.) tonic.

tonique, *n.f.,* (mus.) tonic, key-note, key.

⊙**tonisme,** *n.m.* V. **tonicité.**

tonlieu, *n.m.,* market-toll (feudalism).

tonnage, *n.m.,* tonnage. *Droit de* — ; tonnage dues.

tonnant, -e, *adj.,* thundering. *Jupiter* — ; (myth.) Jupiter the thunderer, Jupiter tonans, thundering Jove.

tonne, *n.f.,* tun (wooden vessel) ; (conch.) spotted tun ; (nav.) can-buoy ; ton (20 cwts. = 1000 kil.).

tonneau, *n.m.,* tun (wooden ship) ; cask ; tun (measure) ; (nav.) ton (1000 kil. ; 1 mètre cube). *Enfoncer un* — ; to stave in a cask. *Mettre un* — *en perce ;* to broach a cask. — *percé ;* leaky cask ; (fig.) spendthrift.

tonneler (to-n-lé), *v.a.,* (hunt.) to tunnel.

tonnelet (to-n-lè), *n.m.,* small cask, keg.

tonneleur (to-n-leur), *n.m.,* (hunt.) tunneler (one who takes partridges with a tunnel-net).

tonnelier, *n.m.,* cooper.

tonnelle, *n.f.,* (hunt.) tunnel-net ; arbor, green arbor, bower, alcove ; (arch.) semicircular vault.

tonnellerie (to-nèl-rî), *n.f.,* cooperage ; cooper's trade ; (nav.) cooper's shed.

tonner, *v.n.,* to thunder ; to inveigh (against) ; to exclaim. *Il tonne ;* it thunders.

tonnerre, *n.m.,* thunder, thunderbolt ; thun-

dering noise. *Coup de* — , *éclat de* — ; clap of thunder, peal of thunder. — *! int.,* by jingo ! bedad ! by Jove !

tonsille, *n.f.,* (l.u.) (anat.) tonsil. V. **amygdale.**

tonsure, *n.f.,* tonsure ; orders, clergy.

tonsuré, *adj.n.m.,* tonsured, shaven ; priest.

tonsurer, *v.a.,* to tonsure.

tonte, *n.f.,* shearing, sheepshearing, fleecing, clipping ; clippings, clip ; shearing-time.

tontine, *n.f.,* tontine.

tontini-er, *n.m.,* **-ère,** *n.f.,* sharer in, *or* annuitant of, a tontine.

tontisse, *adj.,* of shearings of woolen cloth.

tontisse, *n.f.,* hangings coated with the shearings of cloth. *Papier*— ; flock-paper.

tonton, *n.m.,* (child) nuncle.

tonture, *n.f.,* shearing (of leaves, grass) ; shearings, clippings, flock (of cloth) ; (nav.) sheer. — *de drap ;* flock. — *des ponts ;* sheer (of a ship's decks).

topaze, *n.f.,* topaz.

toper, *v.n.,* to cover one's adversary's stake ; to agree. *Je tope à cela ;* I agree to that. *Tope là !* done ! agreed ! your hand upon it ! *Je tope et tingue ;* (at dice) I cover and I hold.

tophacé, -e, *adj.,* (med.) gouty.

tophus (-fus), *n.m.,* (med.) tophus.

topinambour, *n.m.,* Jerusalem-artichoke.

topique, *adj.,* (med.) topic, topical.

topique, *n.m.,* (rhet., med.) topic.

topographe, *n.m.,* topographer.

topographie, *n.f.,* topography.

topographique, *adj.,* topographical.

toquade, *n.f.,* (fam., pop.) infatuation, mad fancy, fad.

toque, *n.f.,* flat cap, bonnet ; toque (plaited all round).

toqué, -e, *adj.,* cracked, crazy, touched ; infatuated, in love (with).

toquer, *v.a.,* (l.u.) to offend ; to hit, to strike, to knock ; (pop.) to craze, to turn the brain of ; to infatuate.

toquet, *n.m.,* toquet, cap.

torche, *n.f.,* torch, link ; twist, pad ; (paint.) rubber.

torche-cul, *n.m.,* (—-—*s*) (fig.) worthless writing, trash.

torche-nez, *n.m.,* (—) (man.) twitch.

torche-pinceau, *n.m.,* rubber.

torche-pot, *n.m.,* (—) (orni.) nut-hatch.

torcher, *v.a.,* to wipe ; to knock off, to botch ; to beat, to drub.

se **torcher,** *v.r.,* to be wiped ; to wipe one's self ; (triv.) to fight.

torchère, *n.f.,* torch, cresset, tall candelabrum.

torchis, *n.m.,* mud, loam. *Mur de* — ; mud-wall.

torchon, *n.m.,* dish-cloth, dish-clout ; house-cloth, duster.

torcol, torcou, *n.m.,* (orni.) wry-neck.

tordage, *n.m.,* twisting, twist.

tord-boyaux, *n.m.,* rotgut, fiery brandy ; rat's bane.

tordeu-r, *n.m.,* **-se,** *n.f.,* twister ; throwster (of silk). *f.,* wringing-machine.

tord-nez, *n.f.,* (—) (man.) twitch (for horses).

tordre, *v.a.,* to twist, to wring, to wring out ; to contort, to disfigure ; to throw (silk) ; to buckle (a wheel). — *la bouche ;* to twist one's mouth. *Il ne fait que* — *et avaler ;* he gives but one twist, and down it goes.

se **tordre,** *v.r.,* to twist ; to writhe. *Se* — *de rire ;* to be convulsed, to split one's sides with laughter.

tore, *n.m.,* (arch., bot.) torus, tore.

toréador, *n.m.,* (—*s*) matador, toreador, bull-fighter.

torisme, *n.m.* V. **torysme.**

*tormentille, *n.f.,* (bot.) tormentil, septfoil.

torminal, -e, *adj.,* (med.) griping, torminal.

toron, *n.m.,* (nav.) strand (of a rope); (arch.) torus.

torpeur, *n.f.,* torpor, torpidity, torpidness.

***torpille,** *n.f.,* (ich.) torpedo, cramp-fish; (explosive) torpedo.

torpilleur, *n.m.,* torpedo-boat.

torquer, *v.a.,* to twist (tobacco).

⊙**torquet,** *n.m.,* (pop.) snare. *Donner un —, donner le — à quelqu'un;* to humbug any one, to take any one in. *Donner dans le —;* to fall into the snare, to be taken in.

torquette, *n.f.,* wicker-basket (for fish); game-basket.

torréfaction (tor-ré-), *n.f.,* torrefaction.

torréfier (tor-ré-), *v.a.,* to torrefy.

torrent (tor-rān), *n.m.,* torrent, stream; flood (of tears); flow (of words).

torrentueu-x, -se (tor-ran-), *adj.,* torrent-like; impetuous.

torride (tor-rid), *adj.,* torrid.

tors, -e, *adj.,* twisted, wry, crooked; wreathed, contorted. *Jambes —es;* crooked legs. *Bouche —e;* wry mouth.

torsade, *n.f.,* twisted fringe *or* cord; bullion (of epaulets).

torse, *n.m.,* trunk, chest (of a person); (sculpt., paint.) torso, trunk, bust.

torser, *v.a.,* to twist (to wreathe (the shaft of a column).

torsil, -e, *adj.,* (bot.) twisted, contorted.

torsion, *n.f.,* torsion; twisting.

tort, *n.m.,* wrong, harm, injury, hurt; mischief, offense; prejudice, detriment. *Faire — à quelqu'un;* to wrong any one. *Réparer le — qu'on a fait;* to repair the wrong one has done. *Se faire —;* to injure one's self. *Avoir —;* to be wrong, to be in the wrong. *Donner — à quelqu'un;* to decide against any one. *Mettre quelqu'un dans son —;* to leave (a person) no loophole, no excuse. *A —;* wrong, wrongly, wrongfully, injuriously. *Il parle à — et à travers;* he speaks at random, thoughtlessly. *A — et à droit;* at random. *A — ou à droit, à — ou à raison;* rightly or wrongly. *Etre dans son —;* to be in the wrong. *Se mettre dans son —;* to put one's self in the wrong.

tortelle, *n.f.,* hedge-mustard. *V.* **vélar.**

torticolis, *n.m.,* wry-neck, stiff neck; crick (in the neck); (fig.) hypocrite, canter.

tortil, *n.m.,* (her.) a baron's wreath.

***tortillage,** *n.m.,* rigmarole, embarrassed language, shuffling.

***tortille** *or* **tortillère,** *n.f.,* serpentine *or* winding walk.

***tortillé, -e,** *adj.,* twisted, wreathed.

***tortillement,** *n.m.,* twisting, twist; wrench; (fig.) shifting, shuffling, shift, evasion.

***tortiller,** *v.n.,* to twist, to wriggle, to waddle. *Il n'y a pas à —;* (fig.) it must be done; there is no shuffling out of it. *— bien de la fourchette;* to tuck in, to lay to. *Il tortille en marchant;* he waddles along.

***se tortiller,** *v.r.,* to wriggle, to writhe.

***tortiller,** *v.n.,* to wriggle, to shuffle.

***tortillère,** *n.f.* *V.* **tortille.**

⊙***tortillon,** *n.m.,* coarse cap; pad (for the head); country servant-girl, little slavey.

tortionnaire (tor-sio-), *n.m.* and *adj.,* ⊙executioner; (jur.) wrongful, unjust.

tortionnairement (tor-sio-nèr-mān), *adv.,* (jur.) wrongfully.

⊙**tortionner** (tor-sio-), *v.a.,* to strain a text, to twist a passage of an author. *V.* **torturer.**

tortis, *n.m.,* twist (of threads); ⊙wreath, garland; (her.) circle of pearls round a baron's coronet.

tortu, -e, *adj.,* crooked, tortuous, bandy. *Jambes —es;* crooked legs.

tortue, *n.f.,* tortoise, turtle; transport-ship; (Rom. antiq.) testudo. *A pas de —;* at a snail's pace. *Potage —;* turtle-soup. *Fausse —;* mock-turtle.

torturer, *v.a.,* to make crooked, to crook, to bend.

se torturer, *v.r.,* to grow crooked, to crook, to bend.

tortueusement (-eûz-mān), *adv.,* crookedly, tortuously.

tortueu-x, -se, *adj.,* tortuous, winding, bending in and out; (fig.) artful, crafty; unfair, disingenuous.

tortuosité, *n.f.,* (l.u.) tortuosity, crookedness; winding.

torture, *n.f.,* torture, rack, pain. *Mettre à la —;* to put to the rack.

torturer, *v.a.,* to torture, to put to the rack. *— un texte, un passage;* to strain *or* twist (the meaning of) a text, a part of a book, a writing.

tory, *n.m.* and *adj.,* Tory.

toryisme, *n.m.,* Toryism.

toscan, -e, *n.* and *adj.,* Tuscan.

toste, *n.m.* *V.* **toast.**

toster, *v.a.* and *n.,* to toast; to give, *or* to propose, a toast; to drink the health of.

tôt, *adv.,* soon, shortly. *Trop —;* too soon. *— ou tard;* sooner or later. *Au plus —,* *or* *le plus —, possible;* as soon as possible, at soonest, as early as possible; at once. *Aussi — que;* as soon as, as early as. *Plus — que;* sooner than. *Le plus —;* the soonest, the earliest. *Le plus — que;* as early as.

total, -e, *adj.,* total, whole, entire, utter, universal, complete.

total, *n.m.,* whole, whole sum, total, sum total. *Au —, en —;* upon the whole, taken all in all, after all.

totalement (-tal-mān), *adv.,* totally, wholly, entirely, utterly, completely.

totaliser, *v.a.,* to form a total of, to foot up *or* total up.

totalité, *n.f.,* totality, whole. *En —;* the whole.

toton *or* **touton,** *n.m.,* teetotum; (child) nuncle.

touage, *n.m.,* (nav.) towage, towing; warping.

***touaille,** *n.f.,* roller-towel, jack-towel.

toucan, *n.m.,* (orni., astron.) toucan.

touchable, *adj.,* touchable.

touchant, -e, *adj.,* touching, moving, affecting.

touchant, *n.m.,* the moving, affecting, impressive, touching part (of).

touchant, *prep.,* concerning, respecting, touching, about, with respect to.

⊙**touchante,** *n.f.,* (geom.) *V.* **tangente.**

touchau *or* **touchand,** *n.m.,* touch-needle.

touche, *n.f.,* touch, assay; trial; pointer: (paint.) stroke, touch; fret (of violins, guitars); key (of a piano, organ, harpsichord); (print.) inking (the form); drove (of oxen); hit, touch (fenc.). *Pierre de —;* touch-stone.

touché, -e, *part., adj.,* touched, affected. *Pièce —e, pièce jouée* (chess), *dame —e, dame jouée* (draughts, backgammon); if you touch your man *or* piece you must play it. *Bien —;* (fig.) well-written, well-said, well-done, well-hit.

touche-à-tout, *n.m.f.,* meddler; Jack of all trades.

toucher, *v.a.,* to touch, to handle, to feel, to finger; to assay, to try (precious metals); to receive (money); to beat, to whip, to strike (animals); (mus.) to play; to express, to convey; to describe; (print.) to ink; to paint, to draw, to depict; to touch on, to allude to; to move, to affect; to concern, to regard; to interest, to inspire interest in. *— le, ou du, piano;* to play the piano. *— un ulcère;* (surg.) to touch an ulcer with caustic. *— ses appointements;* to receive one's salary. *Cela ne me touche point;* that does not concern me. — *la grosse corde;* to come to, *or* to speak upon, the main point (of an affair). *Se laisser* — *par les larmes de quelqu'un;* to be affected, to be moved, by any one's tears. — *un mot;* to let drop a hint, to send word. *Je vous toucherai un mot;* I 'll drop you a line. — *le fond de la douleur possible;* (V. Hugo) to drain to the dregs the cup of human sorrow. — *un cheval;* to drive on.

se **toucher**, *v.r.*, to touch, to touch one another, each other, to join, to be adjoining, to meet.

toucher, *v.n.*, to touch; to reach; to take away; to play a musical instrument; to draw near, to approach; to change, to alter; to concern, to regard, to interest; to be affected, to be moved; to drive, to drive on; (man.) to whip; to be related, to be akin; to be like; (nav.) to touch; (nav.) to ground; (nav.) to strike. *Sa maison touche à la mienne;* his house is next to mine. — *à une île;* (nav.) to touch at an island. *Touchez, cocher, allons plus vite;* drive on, coachman, faster, please ! *J'y touche de la main;* I reach it with my hand. — *dans la main;* to strike hands (in concluding a bargain). — *à un certain temps;* to be very near a particular time. *Il n'osa* — *à la religion;* he dared not meddle with religion. *Il y a touché;* he had a hand in it. — *de près à quelqu'un;* to be nearly related to any one. *N'avoir pas l'air d'y* —; to look as if butter would not melt in one's mouth. *Ne touchez pas à la reine !* hands off the queen !

toucher, *n.m.*, touch, feeling; touch (manner of playing an instrument).

toucheur, *n.m.*, cattle drover; (print.) inking-roller.

tou-col, *int.*, (hunt.) lie down ! down !

toue, *n.f.*, ferry-boat, barge.

touée, *n.f.*, (nav.) towage, towing, warping; towline. *Amarre de* —; towline. *Câble de* —; stream-cable. *Ancre de* —; kedge-anchor.

touer, *v.a.*, (nav.) to tow, to warp.

se **touer**, *v.r.*, (nav.) to haul herself ahead.

toueur, *n.m.*, towing-boat, tow-boat (on rivers).

touffe, *n.f.*, tuft, bunch, cluster, clump; wisp (of straw, hay). — *de cheveux;* tuft of hair. — *d'arbres;* cluster of trees.

touffer, *v.a.*, to tuft.

se **touffer**, *v.r.*, to bunch, to cluster.

touffeur, *n.f.*, (fam.) stifling heat.

touffu, -e, *adj.*, tufted, bushy, branchy, leafy; full, thick.

toug, *n.m. V.* **touc.**

toujours, *adv.*, always, for ever, ever, evermore; still; nevertheless, at least. *Est-il* — *à Paris ?* is he still in Paris ? *Se dire adieu pour* —; to bid each other adieu for ever. — *plus;* more and more. — *est-il que;* still; the fact remains that; as it is. *C'est* — *ça* or *cela !* that 's always as much, or something !

toupet, *n.m.*, tuft of hair; forelock; front, foretop; (fig.) presumption, brass, effrontery; cheek, impudence. *Avoir du* —; to have any amount of brass *or* cheek. *Se prendre au* —; to take each other by the hair. *Quel* — *!* what impudence ! what effrontery ! what cheek !

toupie, *n.f.*, spinning-top, peg-top; humming-top; top; (fig.) (pers., pop.) trollop, drab. — *d'Allemagne;* humming-top. *Faire aller une* —; to spin a top.

*****toupiller**, *v.n.*, to spin, to whirl about; (fam.) to do nothing but run up and down, *or* about, the house.

*****toupillon**, *n.m.*, little tuft of hair; waste branch (of an orange-tree).

tour, *n.f.*, tower; rook, castle (at chess).

tour, *n.m.*, turn, going round, winding; revolution; turn; circumference, circuit; trick;

feat; order; manner; twist, strain; lathe; turning-box; tour, trip; valance (of bed); turn (act); tour, front, foretop (of hair). *Faire le* — *de;* to go round. *En un* — *de main;* in the twinkling of an eye; in a trice. *Faire un* — *de jardin;* to take a turn round, *or* in, the garden. *Faire un* —; to take a stroll. — *de promenade;* turn, walk, stroll. *Cet arbre a dix pieds de* —; that tree is ten feet in circumference. — *s de gobelets;* juggler's tricks, legerdemain. *Vous aurez votre* —; you will have your turn. *Faire, jouer, un mauvais* — *à quelqu'un;* to serve, *or* play, any one a nasty trick. — *de reins;* twist, *or* strain, in the back. *A chacun son* —; every dog has his day. *Chacun à son* —; every one in his turn. — *de cou;* necktie *or* band. — *à* —; by turns. — *en l'air;* mandrel-lathe. *Fait au* —; made with a lathe, turned; extremely well made. *A* — *de rôle;* in turn, in succession. *Mon sang n'a fait qu'un* —; I turned deathly pale ; I nearly fainted ; I was thoroughly upset. *Faire ses quinze* — *s;* to do a hundred useless things. *Fermer à double* —; to double-lock. *Elle est faite au* —; she has a splendid figure.

*****touraille**, *n.f.*, malt kiln.

tourang-eau, -elle, *n.adj.*, of Touraine ; native of Touraine.

tourbe, *n.f.*, turf, peat ; mob, vulgar herd.

tourbeu-x, -se, *adj.*, turfy, peaty.

tourbière, *n.f.*, peat-bog, peat-moss.

*****tourbillon**, *n.m.*, whirlwind, vortex, tornado; whirlpool ; eddy ; hurly-burly, bustle ; tour-billon (fireworks).

*****tourbillonnement**, *n.m.*, whirling, eddying.

*****tourbillonner**, *v.n.*, to eddy, to whirl, to wind, to curl.

tourd, *n.m.*, **tourdelle**, *n.f.*, (orni.) fieldfare, thrush ; (ich.) sea fish (of the genus Labrax).

*****tourdille**, *adj.*, spotty gray ; dirty gray.

tourelle, *n.f.*, turret.

touret, *n.m.*, wheel (of a lathe) ; reel, drill.

tourie, *n.f.*, carboy ; (wicker) jar.

tourière, *n.f.*, nun attendant, *or* in attendance (at the turning-box in a nunnery).

*****tourillon**, *n.m.*, trunnion ; spindle, pivot (of a gate) ; axle, axle-tree, arbor.

touriste, *n.m.*, tourist.

tourlourou, *n.m.*, (pop.) foot-soldier.

tourmaline, *n.f.*, tourmalin, turmalin.

tourment, *n.m.*, torment, torture ; anguish, pain ; plague, scourge, vexation.

tourmentant, -e, *adj.*, tormenting, troublesome.

tourmente, *n.f.*, tempest, storm, hurricane, foul weather ; (fig.) disturbance, turmoil.

tourmenter, *v.a.* and *n.*, to torment, to torture, to rack ; to grieve, to distress, to vex, to trouble, to plague; to harass, to annoy, to pester ; to jolt; to strain (a ship) ; to labor hard (of a ship). *Son procès le tourmente;* his lawsuit worries him. *Que cela ne vous tourmente point;* don't let that worry, *or* trouble, you.

se **tourmenter**, *v.r.*, to toss, to tumble ; to torment one's self, to labor very hard ; to be uneasy, to fret; (of wood) to warp; to be restless, agitated (of horses).

tourmenteur, *adj.m.*, torturing, tormenting.

tourmenteu-x, -se, *adj.*, (nav., l.u.) stormy (of regions).

tourmentin, *n.m.*, (nav.) storm-jib, fore-stay sail.

tournage, *n.m.*, (man.) turning.

*****tournailler**, *v.n.*, (fam.) to turn, to go round and round a place ; to prowl, *or* hover, round a place.

tournant, *n.m.*, turn, turning, bend ; turning-space (for a carriage) ; whirlpool, vortex ; (fig.) indirect means. *Au* — *de la rue;* at the corner of the street. *A un* — *de la route;* at a turn of, *or* in, the road.

tournant, -e, *adj.,* turning. *Pont* —; revolving, swing-bridge. *Mouvement* —; (milit.) turning, outflanking movement, outflanking of an enemy's position.

tourné, -e, *part.,* turned; awry; sour, spoilt, nearly ripe. *Avoir l'esprit mal* —; to be cross-grained.

tourne-à-gauche, *n.m.,* (—) (tech.) tap wrench.

⊙**tournebride,** *n.m.,* tavern, roadside inn.

tournebroche, *n.m.,* jack, kitchen-jack, roasting-jack; turnspit.

tournée, *n.f.,* circuit; progress, visit; round, turn, walk; journey. *Faire sa* —; to go one's rounds. *Il est en* —; he is on his rounds; he is on circuit (of judges, barristers).

tourne-feuillet, *n.m.,* book-marker.

tourne-gants, *n.m.,* (—) glove-stick, glove-stretchers.

⊙**tournelle,** *n.f.,* small tower; Tournelle (criminal chamber of the Parliament of Paris); prison.

⊙**tournemain,** *n.m.,* trice, twinkling, instant. *En un* —; in a trice, in a twinkling. *V. tour de main* under **tour.**

tournement, *n.m.,* turning, whirling. *— de tête;* swimming in the head, giddiness.

***tourne-oreille,** *n.m.,* (—) (agri.) turning moldboard. *Charrue* —; turnwrist plow.

tourne-pierre, *n.m.,* (—-*s*) (orni.) turnstone.

tourner, *v.a.,* to turn, to turn round, to wind round, to revolve, to move round, to twirl, to twirl round; to do, to translate; to construe, to interpret; to turn off; to turn up *or* over. *— une broche;* to turn a spit. *— le dos à quelqu'un;* to turn one's back on any one. *— ses souliers;* to wear one's shoes on one side. *— une personne à son gré;* to manage any one as one likes, to wind any one round one's little finger. *— tout en bien;* to put a good construction upon everything. *— tout en mal;* to put a wrong construction upon everything. *— casaque;* (fig.) to change sides, to rat. *— la conversation;* to change the subject of conversation. *— le sang à quelqu'un;* to upset any one. *Faire* —; to turn, to spin, to curdle. *— une chose en raillerie;* to make a jest of anything, to turn anything into ridicule. *— du latin en français;* to turn Latin into French. *Il tourne bien un vers;* he is a good hand at turning a verse.

se **tourner,** *v.r.,* to turn; to turn round, to turn about; to turn, to change, to become changed. *Le temps se tourne au beau;* the weather is changing to fair.

tourner, *v.n.,* to turn, to turn round, to wheel, to revolve, to tack about; to turn out; to change; to color, to ripen; to turn up (of cards); to spoil, to curdle (of liquids); (of the tongue) to trip, to slip. *— vers;* to turn towards. *Le vent a tourné;* the wind has shifted. *Il tourne comme une girouette;* he turns like a weather-cock. *La tête me tourne;* I feel quite giddy. *La tête lui a tourné;* he lost his head. *— autour du pot;* to beat about the bush. *— du côté de quelqu'un;* to go over to any one. *Il ne sait plus de quel côté* —; he does not know which way to turn. *Cela tournera mal;* that will come to no good. *La chance a tourné;* the luck has changed; (fig.) the tables are turned. *— court;* to cut short, to make an end.

tournerie, *n.f.,* turner's shop.

tournesol, *n.m.,* (bot.) turnsol, girasole, sunflower; dyer's croton.

tournette, *n.f.,* squirrel's cage; cotton winder (of candle-makers); (l.u.) skein-holder

tourneur, *n.m.,* turner.

tourneuse, *n.f.,* reeler, winder.

tourne-vent, *n.m.,* (—) cowl (on chimneys).

tournevire, *n.f.,* (nav.) voyol, viol (for weigh-

ing an anchor). *Garcettes de* —; nippers. *Œillets de* —; eyes of the voyol.

tournevis (-viss), *n.m.,* turn-screw, screw-driver.

tourniole, *n.f.,* whitlow.

tourniquet, *n.m.,* turnstile, turnpike; roundabout; (carp.) screw-jack; sash-pulley; (nav.) roller; (surg.) tourniquet; swivel.

tournis, *n.m.,* (vet.) sturdy, turnsick, staggers.

tournoi, *n.m.,* tournament.

tournoiement *or* **tournoiment** (-noa-măn), *n.m.,* turning round, wheeling round; (vet.) sturdy, turnsick, staggers. *Un — de tête;* a swimming in the head, giddiness.

tournois, *adj.,* of Tours. *Livre* —; livre, Tours currency, worth about 10 pence.

tournoyer, *v.n.,* to turn round and round, to wheel round, to wind, to eddy; (fig.) to beat about the bush, to shuffle.

tournure, *n.f.,* figure, shape; tournure, bustle (part of dress); turn, direction, course; cast; appearance; turn (of mind, style). *Avoir bonne* —; to be a good figure, to have a good figure; (fig.) to look well. *Avoir mauvaise* —; to be a bad figure, to have a bad figure; (fig.) to look bad. *Les choses commencent à prendre une mauvaise* —; things are beginning to look bad.

tourte, *n.f.,* tart, fruit-pie; pie.

tourteau, *n.m.,* (agri.) oil-cake; ⊙a cake; (ich.) hermit-crab.

tourtereau, *n.m.,* young turtle-dove.

tourterelle, *n.f.,* turtle-dove.

tourtière (-ti-èr), *n.f.,* tart-dish.

tous, *adj.m.pl.,* **toutes,** *adj.f.pl.* V. **tout.**

touselle, *n.f.,* (agri.) lammas wheat.

La **toussaint,** *n.f.,* All Saints' day.

tousser, *v.n.,* to cough; to hem.

tousserie, *n.f.,* (fam.) habitual coughing.

tousseu-r, *n.m.,* -**se,** *n.f.,* cougher.

tout, -e, *adj.,* all, whole, the whole of, each, any; every; full, long; only, sole. *— le monde;* all the world, everybody. *—e la famille;* all the, or the whole, family. *Tous mes livres;* all my books. *—es les fois que;* as often as, every time that. *Courir à —es jambes;* to run full speed, *or* at the top of one's speed. *C'est — un;* it is all the same. *— homme qui;* any man who. *Tous les jours;* every day. *Tous les deux jours;* every other day. *— le jour;* the whole day. *Tous les huit jours;* every week. *Tous les quinze jours;* every fortnight.

tout, *n.m.,* (touts), whole, all, the whole; every one, every thing, chief point; only thing. *Il veut — avoir;* he wants to have all. *Est-ce là — ?* is that all? *Avez-vous — dit?* have you said everything; have you had your say? *— bien considéré;* all things considered. *A — prendre;* on the whole; all things considered. *Il est propre à* —; he is fit for anything. *Du* —; not at all. *Comme* —; exceedingly, extremely, awfully, dreadfully, furiously, like anything. *Il n'aura rien du* —; he shall have nothing at all. *En* —; in all, upon the whole. *Voilà* —; that is all. *C'est* —; that is all. *Par-dessus* —; above all. *Point du* —; not at all. *Plusieurs —s distincts;* several distinct wholes.

tout, *adv.,* wholly, entirely, quite, completely, thoroughly; all, for all; although, though, however. [*Tout, adv.,* coming before an adjective or past participle beginning with a consonant, or *h* aspirate, and qualifying a feminine noun or pronoun, is changed into *toute;* and into *toutes,* if the noun or pronoun is in the plural.] *Je suis — à vous;* I am quite at your service. *— à vous;* sincerely yours. *— à fait;* quite, wholly, entirely. *— malades qu'ils sont;* ill as they are. *—es malades qu'elles sont;* ill as they are. *Des femmes — éplorées;* women all in tears. *— nu;* stark naked. *Ces fleurs sont —es fraîches;* these flowers are quite fresh. —*e femme qu'elle est ;* although she is a woman, or woman though she is. —*es bonnes qu'elles sont ;* however good they may be. — *prêt ;* quite ready. *Parler — haut ;* to speak aloud. — *comme vous voudrez ;* just as you please. — *le long de la rivière ;* all along the river. — *beau,* — *doux ;* softly, gently, stop a bit, hold ! not so fast. — *de go ;* bluntly. *de bon ;* in earnest. — *à coup ;* suddenly. — *d'un coup ;* all on a sudden, all at once. — *au moins ;* at least. — *au plus ;* at the most. — *de suite ;* directly. — *au long ;* in detail, at full length. — *à l'heure ;* just now.

tout à fait, *adv.,* quite, wholly, entirely.

toute-bonne, *n.f.,* (—*s*—*s*) (bot.) clary, all good ; (a sort of pear).

toute-bonté, *n.f.,* supreme goodness.

toute-épice, *n.f.,* (—*s*—*s*) allspice.

toutefois (toot-foa), *adv.,* yet, nevertheless, however, still.

toutenague (toot-nag), *or* **tintenague,** *n.f.,* (metal.) tutenag.

tout-ensemble, *n.m.,* (—) (arts) whole, tout ensemble, viewed as a whole.

toute-présence, *n.f.,* (*n.p.*) omnipresence, ubiquity.

toute-puissance, *n.f.,* (*n.p.*) omnipotence, almighty power.

toute-saine, *n.f.,* (—*s*—*s*) (bot.) tutsan.

toute-science, *n.f.,* (*n.p.*) omniscience.

toute-table *or* **toutes-tables,** *n.m.,* tables (backgammon).

tou-tou, *n.m.,* (—*—*—*s*) bow-wow, doggy.

tout-ou-rien, *n.m.,* (—) (horl.) all or nothing.

tout-puissant, *adj.m.,* **toute-puissante,** *adj.f.,* Almighty, Omnipotent, all-powerful.

tout-puissant, *n.m.,* (*n.p.*) Omnipotent, Almighty.

toux, *n.f.,* cough, coughing. — *opiniâtre ;* obstinate cough. — *qui sent le sapin* or — *de renard ;* church-yard cough. *Quinte de —* or *accès de —;* fit of coughing.

toxicodendron, *n.m.,* (bot.) toxicodendron.

toxicologie, *n.f.,* toxicology.

toxique, *n.m.,* and *adj.,* (med.) poison ; poisonous.

traban, *n.m.,* traban (soldier).

trabée, *n.f.,* (Roman antiq.) trabea (toga).

⊙**trac,** *n.m.,* track, trace (of animals) ; pace of horses, mules. *Avoir le —;* (fam.) to be funky.

traçant, -e, *adj.,* (bot.) running (of roots).

tracas, *n.m.,* bustle, confusion, turmoil, disorder ; worry, annoyance, bother ; splutter. — *des affaires ;* turmoil of business. — *du monde ;* turmoil of the world.

tracasser, *v.n.,* to bustle, to be busy, to be full of bustle, to stir ; to meddle, to fidget.

tracasser, *v.a.,* to plague, to trouble, to vex, to pester, to annoy.

tracasserie (-ka-srî), *n.f.,* cavil, chicane ; quarrel ; bickering, broil ; pester, bother, annoyance, vexation.

tracassi-er, -ère, *n.* and *adj.,* caviler ; troublesome person, mischief-maker ; pesterer ; busybody ; shuffling, caviling ; mischief-making ; pestering, bothering, annoying.

trace, *n.f.,* trace, track, step, footstep, print (of the foot) ; sign, mark, impression, vestige ; remains ; outline, sketch ; (hunt.) trail ; slot (of deer).

tracé, *n.m.,* laying out (of ground) ; outline, sketch, drawing ; direction ; (rail) line ; draught. *Faire le — de ;* to lay out.

tracelet, *n.m.,* tracer, tracing-point.

tracement (tras-mãn), *n.m.,* laying out (of grounds, roads).

tracer, *v.a.,* to draw, to trace, to draw out, to trace out, to make out, to sketch ; to lay out (grounds, roads) ; (fig.) to lay down, to set forth, to mark out,

tracer, *v.n.,* (of trees) to spread their roots ; to run out. *Se —;* to be traced.

traceret, *n.m.,* tracing-point.

traceu-r, -se, *n.m.f.,* tracer.

trachée, *n.f.,* (ent.) (bot.) air-vessel, trachea.

trachée-artère, *n.f.,* (—*s*—*s*) (anat.) trachea, windpipe.

trachéite, *n.f.,* (med.) trachitis.

trachéotomie, *n.f.,* (surg.) tracheotomy.

trachyte, *n.m.,* (min.) trachyte.

traçoir, *n.m.,* tracer.

traction, *n.f.,* traction ; draught ; thrust (of suspension-bridges).

traditeur, *n.m.,* (ecc. hist.) traditor.

tradition, *n.f.,* tradition ; (jur.) delivery. — *de la chose vendue ;* delivery of the thing sold. *De —;* traditional.

traditionnaire, *n.m.,* traditionary.

traditionnel, -le, *adj.,* traditional, traditionary, traditive.

traditionnellement (-nèl-mãn), *adv.,* traditionally.

traducteur, *n.m.,* translator.

traduction, *n.f.,* translation.

traduire (traduisant, traduit), *v.a.,* to translate, to interpret, to construe, to render ; to convey, to express ; to show, to betray, to indicate, to denote ; (jur.) to remove, to arraign, to indict. — *facilement, à livre ouvert ;* to translate easily, at sight.

se **traduire,** *v.r.,* to be translated ; to be depicted, denoted ; to be construed, to be interpreted, to be expressed.

traduisible, *adj.,* translatable.

trafic, *n.m.,* traffic, trading, trade. *Faire — de ;* to deal in. *Il fait — de toute sorte de marchandises ;* he traffics, or trades, in all sorts of goods.

trafiquant, *n.m.,* trafficker.

trafiquer, *v.n.,* to traffic, to trade, to deal (in), to sell.

tragacanthe, *n.f.,* (bot.) tragacanth.

tragédie, *n.f.,* tragedy.

tragédien, *n.m.,* **-ne,** *n.f.* (-in, -è-n), tragedian.

tragi-comédie, *n.f.,* tragi-comedy.

tragi-comique, *adj.,* tragi-comic, tragicomical.

tragique, *adj.,* tragic, tragical.

tragique, *n.m.,* tragedy, tragic art ; tragedian ; tragic writer ; tragicalness ; tragic part *or* side. *Prendre une chose au —;* to take a thing too seriously. *Tourner au —;* to assume a tragical appearance, to take a tragical turn, to become a tragedy.

tragiquement (-jik-mãn), *adv.,* tragically.

trahir, *v.a.,* to betray ; to disclose, to denote ; to reveal, to discover ; to be false to, to deceive ; to disappoint. — *sa patrie ;* to betray one's country. — *le secret de quelqu'un ;* to divulge, to betray any one's secret.

se **trahir,** *v.r.,* to betray one's self ; to betray one another ; to be denoted, to be depicted (on).

trahison, *n.f.,* treachery, treacherousness ; treason, perfidy, foul play ; breach of faith, breach of trust.

***traille,** *n.f.,* ferry-boat (of a large size).

train, *n.m.,* pace, rate ; train, suite, attendants ; way, manner ; noise, dust ; carriage, skeleton (of carriages) ; quarters (of a horse) ; train (of boats) ; (print.) carriage ; raft ; (railways) train ; (railways) truck. — *d'artillerie ;* train of artillery. — *de presse ;* (print.) carriage. — *de bois ;* raft of wood. — *direct ;* through train. — *omnibus ;* slow train. — *mixte ;* mixed train. — *express ;* — *rapide ;* express train. —*-poste ;* (—*s*—) mail-train. — *d'aller ;* down train. — *de marchandises ;* goods train. — *de plaisir ;* excursion train. — *de retour ;* up train. — *de grande vitesse ;* fast train. — *de petite vitesse ;* goods train. — *de voyageurs;* passenger-train. *Mise en* —; (print.) making ready. — *de maison;* establishment. *Aller grand* —; to go at a great rate, to go very fast. *Le cocher nous a menés bon* —; the coachman drove us very fast. *Faire du* —; to make a noise, a fuss, to kick up a shindy. *L'affaire est en bon* —; the business is in a fair way. *Mettre quelqu'un en — de faire une chose;* to put any one in the way of doing a thing. *Mettre en* —; to set going, to start, to put in hand. *Tel était notre — de vie;* such was our way of living. *Il va toujours son* —; he goes on in his old way or as usual. *Aller son* — (of a thing) to have its course. *Être en* —; to be in good spirits, to be in the mood (for). *N'être pas en* —; not to be up to the mark. *Au — dont il y va;* at the rate he goes on. *Fort en* —; in high spirits, in high fettle. *Se mettre en — de faire une chose;* to prepare to do, to set about doing, a thing. *Tout d'un* —; all together. *Pas dans le* —; not up to date, of an older school. *Mener bon* —; to drive hard. *Mener grand* —; to drive at a great pace; (fig.) to live in great style. *A fond de* —; at full speed, at full gallop.

traînage, *n.m.,* sledging, sleighing; (racing) training.

traînant, -e, *adj.,* dragging, trailing, tiresome, languid. *Drapeaux —s;* trailing colors. *Style* —; heavy style. *Voix —;* drawling voice.

traînard, *n.m.,* loiterer, straggler, laggard.

traînasse, *n.f.,* (bot.) florin; knot-grass; drag-net.

traînasser, *v.a.* and *n.,* (fam.) to draw out, to spin out, to drag about, to delay, to protract; to be dilatory, to linger.

traîne, *n.f.,* dragging, being dragged or drawn. *Bateau à la* —; boat in tow at the stern of a ship. *Perdreaux en* —; young partridges that cannot fly; unfledged partridges.

traîneau, *n.m.,* sledge, sleigh; trammel, drag-net, draw-net.

traîne-buissons, *n.m.,* (orni.) hedge-sparrow.

traînée, *n.f.,* train (of gunpowder); trail, long line (of anything spilt); (hunt.) track; (pers.) street-walker, trollop.

traîne-malheur, *n.m.f.,* (—) wretch.

traîne-potence, *n.m.,* (—) hang-gallows-fellow, Newgate-bird, gaol-bird, gallows-bird.

traîner, *v.a.,* to draw, to drag, to drag along, to trail; to put off, to spin out, to draw out, to protract, to lengthen; to drawl. — *un homme en prison;* to drag a man off to prison. *Il traîne la jambe;* he drags his leg. *Cet oiseau traîne l'aile;* that bird hangs its wing. — *ses paroles;* to draw out one's words. — *les choses en longueur;* to protract, or to delay, things. — *dans la boue;* to draggle, to defame. *Laisser* —; to leave littered about.

se **traîner,** *v.r.,* to crawl, to creep along; to lag, to lag behind, to drag one's self along.

traîner, *v.n.,* to trail, to drag, to lag; to droop; to lie about; to languish, to linger, to be in abeyance or in suspense; to be spun out, to be protracted, to be drawn out, to be lengthened; to be found. *Votre robe traîne;* your gown sweeps the ground, drags along the ground. *L'affaire traîne;* the matter hangs fire. *Il y a longtemps qu'il traîne;* he has been in a lingering state for a long time. *Cela traîne dans tous les livres;* that is found in every book.

traînerie, *n.f.,* dragging, drawling; string (of words); series, long speech.

traîneur, *n.m.,* straggler, lagger; poacher (with a trammel); (nav.) ship lagging behind. — *d'épée,* — *de sabre;* trooper, sword dangler, swashbuckler.

train-train, *n.m.,* routine, habits, regular course.

traire (trayant, trait), *v.a.,* to milk, to draw.

trait, -e, *part.,* milked; (of precious metals) wire-drawn.

trait, *n.m.,* arrow, dart, bolt, shaft, thunderbolt; stroke, hit, trait; trace (of harness); leash (for dogs); turn (of the scale); draught, gulp; dash (of the pen); (paint.) touch; kerf (of a saw); feature, lineament; act; prime move (at chess, draughts); (c.rel.) tract; gold or silver wire. *Au* —; (of a drawing) in outline. — *d'union;* hyphen, connecting link. *Décocher, lancer un* —; to shoot, to let fly an arrow. *Il partit comme un* —; he darted off (like an arrow from the bow). — *s de l'Amour;* Love's shafts. — *piquant;* smart hit. — *de satire;* satirical stroke. *Chacun me lança son* —; every one had a fling at me. — *s de l'envie;* shafts of envy. *Avaler tout d'un* —; to swallow at one draught. *Boire à longs —s;* to quaff. *Avoir — à;* to have reference to. *A longs —s;* deep, in long draughts. *Copier — pour* —; to copy stroke for stroke. — *d'esprit;* witticism, flash of wit. *Cheval de* —; draught-horse. *D'un seul* —; at a stretch. *Boutons de* —; gold or silver wire buttons. *Ce sont là de ses —s;* that's just like him, or some of his tricks.

traitable, *adj.,* tractable, manageable; (metal.) ductile, pliant, soft, malleable.

traitant, *n.m.,* farmer (of the revenue); contractor.

traite, *n.f.,* stage, journey, stretch; trade, trading (on the African coast); milking; (com.) draft, bill; banking; exportation; ⊙customs duty. *Je m'y rendis tout d'une* —; I made but one stage of it. — *des nègres,* — *des noirs;* slave-trade. *Tout d'une* —; at a stretch. *Bâtiment de* —; slaver, slave-ship. *Faire la* —; to carry on the slave-trade; to trade with the coast of Africa.

traité, *n.m.,* treatise, tract, dissertation; treaty; agreement. — *de paix;* treaty of peace. — *de commerce;* commercial treaty.

traitement (trèt-mān), *n.m.,* treatment; reception, honors; usage; entertainment (to ambassadors or envoys); salary, stipend, emoluments (of a place); (med., chem.) treatment; (nav.) full pay. *Mauvais —s;* ill-usage, ill-treatment.

traiter, *v.a.,* to treat; to discuss, to handle, to discourse upon; to use, to behave to; to call, to style; to negotiate, to treat for, to be in treaty for; to treat of; to entertain, to board; to execute, to do; (med., chem.) to treat. *Il m'a traité en frère;* he treated me like a brother. — *quelqu'un avec honneur;* to show any one great honor. — *de haut en bas;* to treat with contempt. *Il l'a traité de fat;* he called him a fop. — *quelqu'un de Turc à More;* to treat any one like a Turk, to use any one shamefully.

se **traiter,** *v.r.,* to be treated; to treat one's self; to treat one another; to live (well or badly); to be one's own doctor.

traiter, *v.n.,* to treat, to discuss; to negotiate, to be in negotiation for; to come to terms; to entertain, to treat; to keep an ordinary; to keep a boarding-house. — *d'une matière;* to treat of a matter. — *à tant par tête;* to keep an ordinary at so much a head; to board people at so much a head.

traiteur, *n.m.,* eating-house keeper; Louisi ana trader.

traître, -sse, *n.* and *adj.,* traitor, treacherous man; traitress, treacherous woman; treacherous, false, perfidious; traitorous. *Les chats sont —s;* cats are treacherous. *En* —; treacherously, perfidiously. *Prendre en* —; to fall upon, or attack, in a treacherous manner. *Pas un — mot;* not a single word.

traîtreusement (-eûz-mān), *adv.,* traitorously, treacherously.

traîtrise, *n.f.,* treachery, perfidy.

trajectoire, *n.f.*, (ballistics) trajectory.

trajet, *n.m.*, passage, voyage, journey; (surg.) course, direction. — *d'une plaie;* direction of a wound. *Faire le* —; to perform the journey, to make the passage, etc.

*tramail *or* **trémail**, *n.m.*, trammel, drag-net.

trame, *n.f.*, weft, woof, web; plot, conspiracy; course, progress, thread. *La* — *de sa vie;* the course of his life. *Ourdir une* —; to lay, or to hatch, a plot.

tramer, *v.a.*, to weave; to plot, to brew, to contrive, to hatch. — *une étoffe de soie;* to weave a stuff with a silk woof. — *une conspiration;* to hatch a plot. *V.* **ourdir**.

se **tramer**, *v.r.*, to be woven; to be hatched, plotted; to be in course of being hatched, plotted.

⊙**tramontain**, -e (-tin, -tè-n), *adj.*, tramontane (lying beyond the mountains).

tramontane, *n.f.*, tramontane, North wind; North; North star (in the Mediterranean). *Perdre la* —; to be at a loss what to do, to be at one's wits' end.

tramway, *n.m.*, (—*s*) tramway, tramroad.

tranchant, -e, *adj.*, sharp, cutting; trenchant, salient, prominent; peremptory, decisive. *Epée* —*e;* sharp sword. *Ecuyer* —; gentleman-carver. *Couleurs* —*es;* strong, glaring colors.

tranchant, *n.m.*, edge (of cutting instruments); web (of colters). *Epée à deux* —*s;* two-edged, or double-edged, sword.

tranche, *n.f.*, slice, chop, collop, steak; (of beef) aitchbone; (of a book) edge; (arith.) period, set. *Doré sur* —*s;* with gilt edges, gilt-edged. — *de lard;* rasher of bacon.

tranchée, *n.f.*, trench, drain. *pl.*, throes, pains (of a woman in labor); cut, cutting, excavation. *pl.*, gripes, griping, colic. *Avoir des* —*s;* to be griped. —*s rouges;* (vet.) gripes (of horses).

tranchefile (transh-fil), *n.f.*, (book-bind.) headband; bar (in a shoe); cross-chain (of a bridle).

tranche-gazon, *n.m.*, turfing-iron.

tranchelard (transh-lâr), *n.m.*, larding-knife.

*tranche-montagne, *n.m.*, (——*s*) hector, bully, swaggerer, blusterer, braggart.

trancher, *v.a.*, to cut, to cut off; to decide, to determine, to settle. — *la tête à quelqu'un;* to cut off any one's head. *Ceci tranche la difficulté;* this removes the obstacle. — *le mot;* to say the word, to speak out. — *la question;* to settle, *or* clinch, the matter; to cut the Gordian knot; to solve the difficulty.

trancher, *v.n.*, to decide, to determine, to resolve, to set up for, to affect; to cut; (of colors) to glare, to show. — *court;* to cut short. — *net;* to speak one's mind plainly. — *du grand seigneur;* to give one's self the airs of a lord, to lord it (over). — *du philosophe;* to set up for a philosopher. — *du petit-maître;* to affect the beau, the dandy. *Ce couteau tranche comme un rasoir;* this knife cuts like a razor. — *dans le vif;* to cut to the quick; (fig.) to set to work in good earnest.

tranchet, *n.m.*, shoemaker's knife; paring-knife; shank (of chisels).

tranchoir, *n.m.*, trencher, plate.

tranquille, *adj.*, quiet, calm, still, tranquil, peaceful; easy (in mind). *Tenez-vous* —; be quiet. *Soyez* —; never fear; don't trouble about that; set your mind at ease (about it). *Laissez-moi* —; leave me alone; stuff! nonsense! *Séjour* —; tranquil, peaceful abode.

tranquillement (-kil-mān), *adv.*, tranquilly, quietly, peaceably, calmly, sedately.

tranquillisant, -e, *adj.*, tranquillizing.

tranquilliser, *v.a.*, to tranquillize, to make easy, to still, to quiet, to set at ease, at rest.

se **tranquilliser**, *v.r.*, to grow tranquil, easy; to become tranquil, to be tranquillized, to make one's self easy (about anything).

tranquillité, *n.f.*, tranquillity, calmness, quiet, stillness, peace.

trans, a prefix from Lat. *trans*.

transaction (-zak-ci-), *n.f.*, transaction, compromise, arrangement.

transalpin, -e (-zal-pĭn, -pi-n), *adj.*, beyond the Alps, transalpine.

transatlantique, *adj.*, transatlantic.

transbordement, *n.m.*, transshipment.

transborder, *v.a.*, to transship.

transcendance, *n.f.*, transcendency.

transcendant, -e, *adj.*, transcendent.

transcendantal, -e, *adj.*, (philos.) transcendental.

transcripteur, *n.m.*, transcriber.

transcription, *n.f.*, transcription, transcript, copy.

transcrire, *v.a.*, to transcribe, to copy.

transe, *n.f.*, affright, fright, fear, apprehension. *Etre dans des* —*s;* to be in mortal terror.

transept, *n.m.*, (arch.) transept.

transférable, *adj.*, transferable; (com.) endorsable.

transfèrement, *n.m.*, removal, transference, conveying (of convicts).

transférer, *v.a.*, to transfer, to transport, to convey; to translate (bishops); to remove; to put off; to make over; to postpone. — *son droit;* to make over one's right. — *une fête;* to postpone a fête. *Se* —; to be transferred.

transfert, *n.m.*, transfer; (jur.) conveyance.

transfiguration, *n.f.*, transfiguration.

transfigurer, *v.a.*, to transfigure.

se **transfigurer**, *v.r.*, to be transfigured.

transfilage, *n.m.*, (nav.) marling.

transfiler, *v.a.*, (nav.) to marl.

transformation, *n.f.*, transformation, transmutation.

transformer, *v.a.*, to transform, to transmute; to change, to convert, to turn.

se **transformer**, *v.r.*, to transform, to be transformed, to be transmuted.

transfuge, *n.m.*, (milit.) deserter; fugitive, turncoat.

transfuser, *v.a.*, to transfuse.

transfuseur, *n.m.*, transfuser.

transfusion, *n.f.*, transfusion.

transgresser, *v.a.*, to transgress, to trespass against, to violate.

transgresseur, *n.m.*, transgressor.

transgression, *n.f.*, transgression, violation.

transi, -e, *part.*, chilled, benumbed. — *de froid;* chilled with cold. *Un amoureux* —; a bashful lover.

transiger (-zi-jé), *v.n.*, to compound, to compromise, to come to terms; to treat (with).

transiger, *v.a.*, to transact.

transir, *v.a.*, to chill, to benumb; to overcome with fear or affliction, to paralyze.

transir, *v.n.*, to be chilled (with cold); to be overcome or paralyzed with fear or affliction.

transissement (-sis-mān), *n.m.*, (l.u.) chill, numbness, shivering, trembling.

transit (tran-zit), *n.m.*, (com.) transit.

transiti-f, -ve (tran-zi-), *adj.*, transitive. *Verbe* —; transitive verb.

transition (tran-zi-), *n.f.*, transition.

transitoire (tran-zi-), *adj.*, transitory, transient.

⊙**translater**, *v.a.*, to translate.

⊙**translateur**, *n.m.*, translator.

translati-f, -ve, *adj.*, (jur.) transferring.

translation, *n.f.*, translation (of bishops); removal; postponement (of a ceremony); (jur.) transfer.

translucide, *adj.*, translucid.

translucidité, *n.f.*, translucency, translucidity.

transmarin, -e (-rĭn, -ri-n), *adj.*, transmarine.

transmetteur, *n.m.*, (in telegraphy) transmitting-key.

transmettre, *v.a.*, to transmit, to convey ; to forward ; to send on ; to transfer, to make over, to hand down. — *son nom à la postérité ;* to hand down one's name to posterity.

transmigrant, -e, *adj.*, (zoöl.) migratory.

transmigration, *n.f.*, transmigration.

transmissibilité, *n.f.*, transmissibility.

transmissible, *adj.*, transmissible, transferable.

transmission, *n.f.*, transmission ; (com.) transfer.

transmuable, *adj.*, transmutable.

transmuer, *v.a.*, to transmute.

transmutabilité, *n.f.*, transmutability.

transmutation, *n.f.*, transmutation.

transparence, *n.f.*, transparency.

transparent, -e, *adj.*, transparent.

transparent, *n.m.*, (paint.) transparency ; black lines (for writing straight).

transpercer, *v.a.*, to transpierce, to pierce through and through, to run through.

transpirable, *adj.*, (l.u.) perspirable.

transpiration, *n.f.*, perspiration, transpiration.

transpirer, *v.n.*, to perspire ; to exhale, to ooze out ; (fig.) to transpire.

transplantable, *adj.*, (gard.) transplantable.

transplantation, *n.f.*, transplantation.

⊙**transplantement**, *n.m.*   *V.* **transplantation.**

transplanter, *v.a.*, to transplant.   *Se —;* to be transplanted.

transplanteur, *n.m.*, (hort.) (pers.) transplanter.

transplantoir, *n.m.*, transplanter (instrument).

transport, *n.m.*, carriage ; conveyance ; transfer, assignment ; (fig.) rapture, transport, ecstasy, delirium ; (nav.) transport-ship, transport. *Vaisseau de —;* transport-ship. — *de joie ;* transport of joy. — *au cerveau ;* delirium, deliriousness. *Commerce de —;* carrying-trade. *Frais de —;* (com.) carriage.

transportable, *adj.*, that may be conveyed, transportable.

transportation, *n.f.*, transportation, banishment.

transporté, -e, *n.* and *adj.*, convict ; transported, rapt.

transporter, *v.a.*, to convey, to transport ; to transfer ; to make over ; to banish ; to enrapture, to transport. — *une créance ;* to transfer a debt. *La joie l'a tout transporté ;* he is quite overcome with joy.

se **transporter**, *v.r.*, to transport one's self, to go, to repair (to). *Se — sur les lieux ;* to go, to repair, to the place.

⊙**transposable**, *adj.*, transposable.

transposer, *v.a.*, to transpose. *Se —;* to be transposed.

transpositeur, *adj.m.*, only used in *Piano, instrument —;* transposing piano, instrument.

transpositi-f, -ve, *adj.*, transpositive.

transposition, *n.f.*, transposition.

transrhénan, -e, *adj.*, from beyond the Rhine, transrhenish.

transsubstantiation (-stăn-ci-a-cion), *n.f.*, transubstantiation.

transsubstantier (-stăn-cié), *v.a.*, to transubstantiate.

transsudation, *n.f.*, transudation.

transsuder, *v.n.*, to transude.

transvasation, *n.f.*, decanting, transfusion.

transvasement, *n.m.*, decantation, transfusion.

transvaser, *v.a.*, to decant, to transfuse.

transvaseur, *n.m.*, decanter.

transversal, -e, *adj.*, transversal, transverse.

transversalement (-sal-măn), *adv.*, transversely.

transverse, *adj.*, transversal, transverse.

trantran, *n.m.*, (fam.) routine, habits, regular course ; knack (in treating certain things). *Savoir le —;* to be an old stager. *Savoir le — du palais ;* (fam.) to know the ins and outs of the law courts. *V.* **train-train.**

trapèze, *n.m.*, (geom.) trapezium ; (anat.) trapezium (bone) ; trapezius (muscle) ; (gymnastics) trapeze. [In the language of anatomy this word is also used adjectively : *os —;* trapezium ; *muscle —;* trapezius.]

trapéziforme, *adj.*, trapeziform.

trapézoïde, *n.m.* and *adj.*, (geom.) trapezoid ; (anat.) trapezoidal.

trapp, *n.m.*, (geol., min.) trap.

trappe, *n.f.*, trap-door ; trap, pitfall ; (of the gallows) drop. *Tendre une —;* to lay a trap.

trappeur, *n.m.*, trapper.

trappiste, *n.m.* and *adj.*, Trappist.

trapu, -e, *adj.*, squat, dumpy, thick-set, stubby.

traque, *n.f.*, (hunt.) inclosing, beating (for game).

traquenard (trak-nar), *n.m.*, racking-pace (of a horse) ; trap (for noxious animals).

traquer, *v.a.*, (hunt.) to beat a wood for game ; to inclose ; to encircle ; to ferret out ; to surround, to hem in. — *un bois ;* to inclose a wood. — *des voleurs ;* to surround thieves.

traquet, *n.m.*, trap (for fetid animals) ; (orni.) stone chatter ; mill-clapper. *Donner dans le —;* to be entrapped.

traqueur, *n.m.*, (hunt.) beater up.

trass, *n.m.*, (min.) trass.

traumaticine, *n.f.*, (med.) pigment (of guttapercha).

traumatique, *adj.*, traumatic.

****travail**, *n.m.*, (*travaux*), labor, work, toil ; piece of work ; employment ; study ; travail. *pl.*, works ; workmanship. *Vivre de son —;* to live by one's labor. *A force de —;* by dint of labor. *Se mettre au —;* to set to work. — *d'enfant ;* child-birth, labor, travail. *Travaux forcés ;* penal servitude. *Cabinet de —;* study.

****travail**, *n.m.*, (*travails*) trave, brake (for the shoeing of refractory horses) ; reports (of Ministers to the Head of the State, of heads of departments to Ministers).

travaillé, -e, *part. adj.*, worked, wrought, labored ; elaborate, (fig.) laboring (under), a prey (to). — *à jour ;* open-worked.

****travailler**, *v.n.*, to labor, to work ; (of wine) to ferment ; to study ; to make it one's study ; to endeavor ; to digest with difficulty ; (of a ship) to be strained ; (of wood) to warp ; (of a wall) to chink. — *à l'aiguille ;* to do needlework. — *à la terre ;* to till the ground.

****travailler**, *v.a.*, to work, to work at, to labor ; to do with care ; to fashion ; to work up ; to cultivate, to improve (ground) ; to exercise, to overwork (a horse) ; to torment. *Un cheval trop travaillé ;* a horse overworked. — *les esprits ;* to rouse, to excite, the minds (of the populace). — *son style ;* to overdo, to elaborate one's style.

*se **travailler**, *v.r.*, to torment one's self ; to make one's self uneasy ; to torment each other ; to work up ; to endeavor, to study.

****travailleu-r, -se**, *n.* and *adj.*, workman ; laborer, artisan ; industrious, hard-workingman ; industrious, laborious woman ; laborious, industrious, hard-working.

travée, *n.f.*, (arch.) bay ; triforium (of a church) ; truss (of bridges). — *de balustres ;* balustrade.

travers. *n.m.*, breadth, side (of a ship) ; whim, caprice, fancy, oddity, eccentricity. *A —;* athwart, through, across. *Au — de ;* through. *Au — du corps ;* through the body. *A — les bois ;* across the woods. *A — champs ;* across country. *Parler à tort et à —;* to talk at random. *De* —; awry, crooked; askew, cross, wrong. *Marcher de* —; to walk crooked. *Regarder quelqu'un de* —; to look black, to look daggers, at any one. *Il prend tout de* —; he takes everything in a wrong sense; he puts a wrong construction upon everything. *Avoir l'esprit de* —; to be of a cross-grained temper; to be wrong-headed. *En* —; across, cross-wise.

traverse, *n.f.*, cross-bar, cross-piece; (carp.) cross - beam girder; cross - road; (railways) sleeper; (fort.) traverse; (fig.) misfortune. *A la* —; (obstacle) in the way. *Se jeter, venir, à la* —; to place one's self in the way. *Chemin de* —; cross-road. *Rue de* —; cross-street, side-street.

traversée, *n.f.*, (nav.) passage, voyage, crossing.

traversement, *n.m.*, crossing.

traverser, *v.a.*, to cross, to go *or* pass over, to travel over, to travel through; to lie across; to traverse, to get over; to go across; to run through (with a sword); to penetrate, to go, to run through; to thwart, to disturb, to vex. — *une rivière à la nage;* to swim over a river. — *l'ancre;* (nav.) to stow the anchor. — *les voiles;* (nav.) to flat in the sails. — *un projet;* to thwart a project. *Faire* —; to get, *or* send, through; to get, *or* bring, over.

se **traverser,** *v.r.*, to be crossed; to cross each other; to thwart each other; (man.) to traverse.

traversi-er, -ère, *adj.*, cross, that plies across. *Barque —ère;* ferry-boat. *Flûte —ère;* German flute.

traversin, *n.m.*, bolster; (carp., nav.) cross beam; transom; (of 'oats) stretcher.

traversine, *n.f.*, (arch.) sleeper, transom.

travertin, *n.m.*, (min.) travertin.

travesti, -e, *adj.*, disguised, travestied, parodied, burlesqued. — *en paysan;* disguised as a peasant.

travestir, *v.a.*, to disguise, to travesty; (fig.) to misinterpret, to misrepresent.

se **travestir,** *v.r.*, to disguise one's self.

travestissement (-tis-mān), *n.m.*, disguise, travesty.

travestisseur, *n.m.*, parodist, travestier.

trayon, *n.m.*, dug, teat (of cows, etc.).

trébuchage, *n.m.*, (coin) weighing and sorting.

trébuchant, -e, *adj.*, stumbling; (coin.) of weight, of full weight.

trébuchant, *n.m.*, (coin.) full weight.

trébuchement (-bush-man), *n.m.*, (l.u.) stumbling, fall; blunder.

trébucher, *v.n.*, to stumble, to slip, to trip, to err; to weigh down.

trébuchet, *n.m.*, assay-balance *or* scales; bird-trap. *Prendre quelqu'un au* —; to entrap any one.

tréfiler, *v.a.*, to wire-draw.

tréfilerie (-fil-rî), *n.f.*, wire-drawing mill.

tréfileur, *n.m.*, wire-drawer.

trèfle, *n.m.*, (bot.) trefoil, clover, shamrock; clubs (at cards); (arch.) trefoil.

tréfoncier, *n.m.*, land-owner; mine-owner.

tréfonds *or* **très-fonds** (-fon), *n.m.*, subsoil; (fig.) bottom. *Savoir le fond et le — d'une affaire;* to know the ins and outs of, to know all about, an affair.

***treillage,** *n.m.*, trellis-work; lattice-work (of gardens); fence.

***treillageur,** *n.m.*, lattice-maker, trellis-maker.

***treille,** *n.f.*, vine-arbor; shrimp-net. *Le jus de la* —; the juice of the grape.

***treillis,** *n.m.*, trellis, lattice; lattice-work; glazed calico; sackcloth.

***treillissé, -e,** *adj.*, trellised, latticed.

***treillisser,** *v.a.*, to trellis, to lattice.

treizaine, *n.f.*, baker's dozen.

treize, *n.m.* and *adj.*, thirteen, thirteenth.

treizième, *n.m.f.* and *adj.*, thirteenth.

treizièmement (trè-zièm-mān), *adv.*, thirteenthly.

tréma, *n.m.*, diæresis.

trémail, *n.m.* V. **tramail.**

tremblaie, *n.f.*, aspen-grove.

tremblant, -e, *adj.*, trembling, quaking, tremulous, shivering, quivering; twinkling, flickering (of light).

tremble, *n.m.*, (bot.) aspen.

tremblé, *n.m.*, (print.) waved rule.

tremblé, -e, *adj.*, waved (of lines); shaking (of writing). *Ecriture —e;* shaking, trembling handwriting.

tremblée, *n.f.*, (vet.) thwarter (disease in sheep).

tremblement, *n.m.*, trembling, quaking, trepidation, shaking, shivering, tremor; fluttering (of wings); flickering (of light); (mus.) shake, trill. — *de nerfs;* nervous shivering, trembling. — *de terre;* earthquake. *Et tout le —!* (fam.) and the whole blessed lot; and all the rest of it.

trembler, *v.n.*, to tremble, to shake, to shiver; to quake, to fear, to flutter (of wings), to quiver (of light). — *de froid;* to shiver with cold. *La main lui tremble;* his hand shakes. *A faire* —; enough to make one shiver; thundering (of noise).

trembleu-r, *n.m.*, **-se,** *n.f.*, trembler, quaker.

tremblotant, -e, *adj.*, trembling (of the voice); tremulous (of sound); shivering, quivering, fluttering.

trembloter, *v.n.*, to tremble (of sound); to quiver, to shiver, to flutter (of wings); to flicker (of light).

trémie, *n.f.*, hopper, mill-hopper.

trémière, *adj.f.*, only used in *Rose* —; hollyhock, rose-mallow.

tremolo (tré-), *n.m.*, (—) (mus.) tremolo.

trémoussement (-moos-mān), *n.m.*, fluttering, joggling; frisking; flutter. *Se donner du* —; to bestir one's self; to frisk about.

trémousser, *v.a.*, to stir, to bestir, to shake (any one).

se **trémousser,** *v.r.*, to flutter about, to frisk, to joggle; to bestir one's self, to bustle about.

trémoussoir, *n.m.*, swinging-chair, revolving-chair.

trempage, *n.m.*, steeping; soaking; (print.) wetting.

trempe, *n.m.*, temper (of steel); constitution; character, stamp, quality; (print.) wetting. *Donner la — au fer;* to temper iron. *Ce sont des gens de la même* —; they are people of the same stamp.

trempé, -e, *part.*, soaked, wet; tempered (of iron and steel). *Il est tout* —; he is wet to the skin. *Du vin* —; diluted wine.

trempée, *n.f.*, steeping, soaking, drenching; (fig. and pop.) whacking, drubbing.

tremper, *v.a.*, to dip, to soak, to steep, to drench, to wet, to temper (iron and steel); to dilute (wine); (print.) to wet (paper); to imbrue. — *la soupe;* to pour the soup on the bread. — *de larmes;* to wet with tears. — *ses mains dans le sang;* to imbrue one's hands in blood.

tremper, *v.n.*, to soak, to be steeped; to be implicated (in); to be a party (to); to be concerned (in); to participate (in). — *dans un crime;* to be implicated in a crime.

tremperie (tran-prî), *n.f.*, (print.) wetting-room, sink.

tremplin, *n.m.*, spring-board, leaping-board.

trentain, *n.m.*, thirty all (at tennis).

trentaine, *n.f.*, about thirty, some thirty; age of thirty. *Il a passé la* —; he is over thirty.

trente, *n.m.* and *adj.*, thirty, thirtieth.

trentenaire, *adj.*, of thirty years' duration.

trentième (-tièm), *n.m.f.* and *adj.*, thirtieth.

tréou, *n.m.*, (nav.) lug-sail.

trépan, *n.m.*, (surg.) trepan (instrument); trepanning.

trépanation, *n.f.*, (surg.) trepanning.

trépaner, *v.a.*, (surg.) to trepan.

trépang, *n.m.*, (zoöl.) trepang.

trépas, *n.m.*, (poet.) decease, death.

trépassé, *n.m.*, dead person. *Les —s;* the dead.

trépassement (-pâs-mãn), *n.m.*, death, decease.

trépasser, *v.n.*, to die, to depart this life.

trépidation, *n.f.*, trepidation, trembling, tremor; (ancient astron.) libration; slight shock of earthquake.

trépied, *n.m.*, trivet; tripod.

*****trépignement,** *n.m.*, stamping.

*****trépigner,** *v.n.*, to stamp, to stamp one's foot. *— de colère;* to stamp with rage.

trépointe, *n.f.*, welt (of a shoe).

très, *adv.*, very; most; very much; quite, widely; deeply; greatly. *Le — Haut;* the Almighty.

tré-sept (-sèt), *n.m.*, (*n.p.*) a card game.

très-fonds, *n.m.* (—). *V.* **tréfonds.**

trésor, *n.m.*, treasure; treasury; exchequer; record-office; (c. rel.) relics and ornaments. *Amasser des —s;* to heap up riches.

trésorerie (-zor-rî), *n.f.*, treasury.

trésorier, *n.m.*, treasurer; (milit.) paymaster.

trésorière, *n.f.*, treasurer.

tressage, *n.m.*, weaving.

*****tressaillement,** *n.m.*, start, starting; tremor, thrill; flutter, trepidation.

*****tressaillir** (tressaillant, tressailli), *v.n.*, to start, to leap, to tremble, to shudder, to give a start; to thrill; to quake, to start into life. *— de peur;* to start with fear. *— de joie;* to leap for joy.

tressaillure, *n.f.*, cracking, chipping (in pottery).

tresse, *n.f.*, tress, plait, plat, braid.

tresser, *v.a.*, to weave, to interweave, to plait, to braid; to wreathe; to form into tresses. *— des cheveux;* to braid hair.

tresseu-r, *n.m.*, **-se,** *n.f.*, plaiter, braider.

trest, *n.m.*, sail-cloth (for fishing boats).

tréteau, *n.m.*, trestle, trestles. *pl.,* stage, boards (of a mountebank). *— de meule;* (agri.) stack-stand. *Monter sur les —x;* to make a mountebank of one's self; to tread the boards, to go on the stage.

*****treuil,** *n.m.*, windlass; hand-winch; (mec.) wheel and axle.

trêve, *n.f.*, truce. *— de compliments;* a truce to compliments. *— à ces niaiseries!* no more of these fooleries!

trévire, *n.f.*, (nav.) parbuckle.

trévirer, *v.a.*, (nav.) to parbuckle.

tri, a prefix from Lat. *tri,* and Gr. τρι.

tri, *n.m.*, "tri" (card game); sorting; trick (whist).

triable, *adj.*, sortable.

triade, *n.f.*, triad.

triage, *n.m.*, choosing, picking, sorting; choice, selection.

triandre, *adj.*, (bot.) triandrous.

triandrie, *n.f.*, (bot.) triandria.

triangle, *n.m.*, (geom., astron., mus.) triangle; (nav.) triangular hanging stage (for calking).

triangulaire, *adj.*, triangular.

triangulairement, *adv.*, triangularly.

triangulation, *n.f.*, triangulation; trigonometrical survey.

triangulé, -e, *adj.*, triangled.

trianon, *n.m.*, pavilion. *Le petit —, le grand —;* royal summer palaces in the park at Versailles.

trias, *n.m.*, (geol.) trias.

triasique, *adj.*, (geol.) triassic.

tribade, *n.f.*, (l.ex.) shameless, unnatural woman.

tribal, -e, *adj.*, tribal.

tribart, *n.m.*, clog; yoke.

tribord, *n.m.*, (nav.) starboard. *— tout!* (nav.) hard a starboard!

tribordais, *n.m.*, (nav.) starboard-watch.

triboulet, *n.m.*, (gold.) triblet; (fig.) fool, jester.

tribraque, *n.m.*, tribrach.

tribu, *n.f.*, tribe.

tribulation, *n.f.*, tribulation.

tribun, *n.m.*, tribune; demagogue.

tribunal, *n.m.*, tribunal, bench, judgment-seat; court of justice.

tribunat, *n.m.*, tribuneship; tribunate.

tribune, *n.f.*, tribune (rostrum); gallery; grand-stand (at races); platform, hustings. *Monter à la —;* to mount the rostrum; to speak (in parliament). *— aux enchères;* auctioneer's rostrum. *— d'orgues;* organ-loft.

tribunitien, -ne (-ci-in, -ci-è-n), *adj.*, tribunitial.

tribut, *n.m.*, tribute; grant, contribution; duty, debt. *Payer le — à la nature;* to pay the debt of nature. *Payer le — à Neptune;* to be sea-sick.

tributaire, *n.m.* and *adj.*, tributary.

triceps (-sèps), *n.m.* and *adj.*, (anat.) triceps.

tricher, *v.a.* and *n.*, (fam.) to cheat; to bilk; to trick.

tricherie (tri-shrî), *n.f.*, cheat, cheating, trick, trickery. *— revient à son maître;* curses, like chickens, come home to roost.

tricheu-r, *n.m.*, **-se,** *n.f.*, cheat, trickster.

trichine (-ki-n), *n.f.*, thread worm, trichina spiralis (of the pig).

tricoises, *n.f.pl.*, farrier's pincers.

tricolor, *n.m.*, (bot.) tricolored amaranth.

tricolore, *adj.*, tricolored.

tricorde, *n.m. adj.*, trichord.

tricorne, *n.m.*, three-cornered hat; shovel-hat. *adj.*, three-cornered, three-horned.

tricot, *n.m.*, cudgel; knitting; knitted vest.

tricotage, *n.m.*, knitting.

tricoter, *v.a.* and *n.*, to knit; to make lace. *Se —;* to knit for one's self; to be knitted.

tricoteu-r, *n.m.*, **-se,** *n.f.*, knitter. *f.,* knitting-frame.

trictrac, *n.m.*, trick-track, backgammon; trick-track-board, backgammon-board.

tricycle, *n.m.*, a three-wheeled carriage, three-wheeler, tricycle.

tricycliste. *n.m.f.*, tricyclist.

tride, *adj.*, (riding) swift, quick, fleet. *Mouvement —;* quick and strong movement (of a horse).

trident, *n.m.*, trident; fish-gig.

tridenté, -e, *adj.*, (bot.) tridented; trident-pointed.

tridi, *n.m.*, tridi, third day of the decade in the calendar of the first French republic.

triduo, *n.m.*, (—*s*) (c.rel.) religious exercises which last three days.

trièdre, *adj.*, (geom.) trihedral.

triennal, -e (-è-n-nal), *adj.*, triennial.

triennalité (-è-n-na-), *n.f.*, term of three years; triennial duration.

triennat (-è-n-na), *n.m.*, space of three years; trienniate, triennial period.

trier, *v.a.*, to pick, to pick out, to cull, to sort, to choose, to select. *Des hommes triés;* picked men.

se **trier,** *v.r.*, to be sorted.

triérarchie, *n.f.*, (antiq.) trierarchy.

triérarque, *n.m.*, (antiq.) trierarch.

trieu-r, *n.m.*, **-se,** *n.f.*, sorter, picker.

trifide, *adj.*, (bot.) trifid.

triflore, *adj.*, (bot.) three-flowered, triflorous.

triforium (-om), *n.m.*, (arch.) triforium, blind story.

trigame, *n.adj.*, trigamous; trigamist.

trigamie, *n.f.*, trigamy.

trigaud, -e, *adj.*, (fam.) shuffling, cunning, crafty. *n.* shuffler.

trigauder, *v.n.*, (fam.) to shuffle.

trigauderie (-gô-drî), *n.f.*, (fam.) shuffling trick; artful trick.

trigle, *n.f.*, (ich.) gurnard, gurnet.

triglyphe, *n.m.*, (arch.) triglyph.

trigone, *n.m.*, trigon.

trigonométrie, *n.f.*, trigonometry.

trigonométrique, *adj.*, trigonometrical.

trigonométriquement, *adv.*, trigonometrically.

tril, *n.m.*, (mus.). *V.* **trille**.

trilatéral, -e, *adj.*, trilateral.

trilatère, *n.m.*, (l.u.). *V.* **triangle**.

*****trille**, *or* **tril**, *n.m.*, (mus.) quaver, trill, shake.

*****triller**, *v.a.*, (mus.) to shake, to trill, to quaver.

trillion, *n.m.*, one billion.

trilobé, -e, *adj.*, (bot.) trilobate, thrice-lobed; (arch.) three-cusped.

triloculaire, *adj.*, (bot.) trilocular.

trilogie, *n.f.*, trilogy.   [about.

trimbaler, *v.a.*, to trail; (pers.) to drag, *or* lug, *se* **trimbaler**, *v.r.*, to go about, *or* to and fro; to knock about (the streets).

trimer, *v.n.*, to run up and down; to trudge.

trimestre, *n.m.*, quarter of a year; quarter's money; three months', quarter's salary. *Toucher son* —; to receive one's (quarter's) salary. *Par* —; quarterly.

trimestriel, -le, *adj.*, quarterly.

trimestriellement, *adv.*, every quarter.

trimètre, *n.m.*, trimeter.

trin *or* **trine**, *adj.m.*, trine. — *aspect* ; (astron.) trine aspect.

tringa, *n.m.*, (orni.) tringa.

tringle, *n.f.*, curtain-rod; rod, rail, bar; (arch.) tringle; rod; (carp.) mark; connecting-rod.

tringler, *v.a.*, (carp.) to mark out, to chalk.

trinitaire, *n.m.*, Trinitarian.

trinité, *n.f.*, trinity. *La* — ; Trinity Sunday.

trinôme, *n.m.*, and *adj.*, (alg.) trinomial.

trinquart, *n.m.*, small fishing-boat, herring-boat.

trinquer, *v.n.*, to touch, or clink, glasses in drinking; (fig.) to hobnob (with).

trinquet, *n.m.*, (nav.) fore-mast (in a lateen vessel).

trinquette, *n.f.*, (nav.) storm-jib, fore-stay sail.

trio, *n.m.*, (—*s*) trio ; triplet.

triolet, *n.m.*, (poet.) triolet ; (mus.) triplet.

triomphal, -e, *adj.*, triumphal.

triomphalement (-fal-mãn), *adv.*, triumphantly.

triomphant, -e, *adj.*, triumphant.

triomphateur, *n.m.*, triumpher.

triomphe, *n.m.*, triumph.

triomphe, *n.f.*, (card game) triumph.

triompher, *v.n.*, to triumph (over); to overcome; to be triumphant; to exult, to be exultant, to glory (in); to excel. — *de ses passions;* to overcome one's passions.

trioste, *n.m.*, (bot.) feverwort.

*****tripaille**, *n.f.*, garbage, offal.

tripan, *n.m. V.* **trépang**.

tripartite, *adj.*, tripartite.

tripe, *n.f.*, tripe; imitation velvet, velveteen.

tripe-madame, *n.f.*, (—). *V.* **trique-madame**.

tripée, *n.f.*, garbage, offal.

triperie (tri-prî), *n.f.*, tripe-house, tripe-shop.

tripette, *n.f.*, small tripe. *Il ne vaut pas* —; he is not worth a straw.

triphtongue (-tong), *n.f.*, (gram.) triphthong.

triphylle, *adj.*, (bot.) triphyllous.

tripi-er, *n.m.*, -**ère**, *n.f.*, dealer in tripe.

tripier, *adj.*, (hawking) untamable.

triple, *n.m.* and *adj.*, treble; triple, threefold, treble, three times as much *or* as many; three times the number *or* quantity.

triplement, *adv.*, trebly, triply.

triplement, *n.m.*, trebling, tripling.

tripler, *v.a.* and *n.*, to treble, to triple.

triplicata, *n.m.*, triplicate. *Faire un acte en* —; to draw up a deed (in three copies).

triplicité, *n.f.*, triplicity.

tripoli, *n.m.*, tripoli ; rotten-stone.

tripolir, *v.a.*, to polish with rotten-stone.

tripot, *n.m.*, gaming-house; pot-house; hell; house of ill-fame, brothel.

tripotage, *n.m.*, medley, jumble ; mish-mash; jobbing ; underhand dealing ; scandal ; gossiping story.

tripotée, *n.f.*, (pop.) a beating, a drubbing.

tripoter, *v.a.* and *n.*, (fam.) to plot; to hatch, to brew mischief ; to slander, to job ; to make a mess of ; to act in an underhand manner ; (pers.) to pull about, to handle (roughly).

tripoti-er, *n.m.*, -**ère**, *n.f.*, (-tié, -tièr), low intriguer, slanderer ; gambling-house keeper, brothel-keeper.

tripsac, *n.m.*, (bot.) gama grass.

triptère, *adj.*, three-winged.

triptote, *n.m.*, (gram.) triptote.

triptyque, *n.m.*, (paint.) triptych.

trique, *n.f.*, cudgel ; stick, bludgeon.

triqueballe, *n.m.* or *f.*, (artil.) truck.

trique-madame, *n.f.*, (—) (bot.) white stone-crop.

triquer, *v.a.*, (pop.) to cudgel, to beat; (tech.) to sort, to range (timber) ; to mix.

triquet, *n.m.*, tennis-bat ; (tech.) trestle.

triquetrac, *n.m.*, clatter.

*****trirègne**, *n.m.*, tiara ; pope's triple crown.

trirème, *n.f.*, trireme.

trisaïeul, *n.m.*, great-great-grandfather.

trisaïeule, *n.f.*, great-great-grandmother.

trisection, *n.f.*, trisection.

trismégiste, *n.m.*, (print.) two-line pica, double pica.

trismus, *n.m.*, (med.) trismus, lock-jaw.

trissement (tris-mãn), *n.m.*, cry (of swallows).

trissyllabe, *n.m.* and *adj.*, trisyllable; trisyllabic.

triste, *adj.*, sorrowful, mournful, sad; melancholy; dull ; dark, gloomy, dreary, dismal; (pers.) poor, sorry; mean, wretched, paltry. *Une — nouvelle ;* a sad piece of news. *Un — spectacle ;* a sad, or sorry, spectacle. *Faire un — repas ;* to make a sorry meal. *Le temps est* — ; the weather is dull. — *comme un bonnet de nuit* or *comme un enterrement ;* (pers.) as dull as ditch-water.

tristement, *adv.*, in a melancholy manner, sadly, sorrowfully, mournfully, drearily, dismally ; sorrily, poorly ; dully.

Les **tristes**, *n.m.pl.*, Ovid's Tristia.

tristesse, *n.f.*, sadness, melancholy, dreariness, dullness, gloom, gloominess.

triton, *n.m.*, Triton, sea-god ; (mus.) tritone.

tritoxyde, *n.m.*, (chem.) tritoxide.

triturable, *adj.*, triturable.

trituration, *n.f.*, trituration.

triturer, *v.a.*, to triturate.

triumvir (-om-vir), *n.m.*, (—*s*) triumvir.

triumviral, -e, *adj.*, triumviral.

triumvirat, *n.m.*, triumvirate.

trivalve, *adj.*, (bot.) trivalvular.

trivelin, *n.m.*, (l.u.) buffoon, merry-andrew ; (tech.) dentist's forceps.

trivelinade, *n.f.*, (l.u.) buffoonery.

triviaire, *adj.*, only used in *Carrefour* — ; a place where three roads end; junction of three roads.

trivial, -e, adj. and n., trivial, trite, vulgar, slangy; trifling, light; triviality, vulgarity.

trivialement (-mān), adv., trivially, vulgarly.

trivialité, n.f., triviality, vulgarity, commonness; triteness.

trivium (-vio-m), n.m., (n.p.) trivium.

trivoie, n.f., junction of three roads.

troc (trok), n.m., swop, barter, exchange.

trocart or **trois-quarts,** n.m., (surg.) trocar.

trochaïque (-ka-ik), n.m. and adj., trochaic.

trochanter (-kan-tèr), n.m., (anat.) trochanter.

trochée (-shé), n.f., (agri.) brushwood, branches (of a seedling).

trochée (-shé), n.m., (poet.) trochee.

trochereau, n.m., long-leaved pine.

troches (trosh), n.m.pl., (hunt.) fumet, fewmet (the dung of deer).

trochet (-shè), n.m., cluster (of fruit or flowers); (tech.) block.

trochile (-kil), n.m., (arch.) trochilus; (orni.) trochil.

trochisque (-shisk), n.m., (pharm.) troche, cake (of colors).

trochure (-shur), n.f., (hunt.) cluster of horns, trochings, surantler.

troène, n.m.; (bot.) privet.

troglodyte, n.m., troglodyte; (mam.) chimpanzee; (orni.) wren.

*trogne, n.f., face, phiz. — enluminée; large red face. — d'ivrogne; drunkard's face.

*trognon, n.m., core (of a pear or apple); stump (of a cabbage). Un petit —; (pop.) a dear little girl; (pop.) head.

trois, n.m. and adj., three; third. Règle de —; rule of three.

troisième, n.m.f. and adj., third.

troisième, n.m., pupil of the 3d form (in a public school); third story, third floor (of houses).

troisième, n.f., third class of a college.

troisièmement (troa-zièm-mān), adv., thirdly.

trois-mâts, n.m., (—) (nav.) three-master.

trois-ponts, n.m., (nav.) three-decker.

trois-quarts, n.m., (—). V. **trocart.**

trois-six, n.m., (—) (com.) brandy or alcohol (36 deg.); raw spirits; common brandy.

trôle, n.f., used only in Ouvrier à la —; furniture hawker. Filet à la —; drag-net.

trôlée, n.f., company, set.

trôler, v.a. and n., to lead, or drag, somebody about; to stroll about, to ramble, to rove, to tramp about.

trolle, n.m., (bot.) globe-flower, trollius.

trombe, n.f., (phys.) water-spout.

tromblon, n.m., blunderbuss (fire-arm).

trombone, n.m., (mus.) trombone.

tromboniste, n.m., trombonist, tromboneplayer.

trompe, n.f., horn, trumpet, trump; proboscis, trunk (of elephants, of insects); (tech.) blast-engine; Jew's-harp. —s de fallope; (anat.) Fallopian tubes.

trompe-la-mort, n.f., death's match (person desperately ill who recovers, etc).

trompe-l'œil, n.m., (—) (paint.) still-life deception; (fig.) illusion, sham.

tromper, v.a., to deceive, to impose upon; to cheat, to baffle, to put out; to delude, to beguile; to take in; to impose on; to elude. — la loi; to elude the law. — la confiance de quelqu'un; to abuse any one's confidence. — son ennui; to beguile one's weariness. C'est ce qui vous trompe; there you are mistaken.

se tromper, v.r., to be mistaken, to mistake, to make a mistake; to deceive one's self, to be deceived. Vous vous trompez; you are mistaken. A s'y —; enough to be mistaken, so as to take one for the other. Se — de chemin; to take the wrong road. Se — de livre; to take the wrong book. Se — de travail; to do the wrong work.

tromperie (trõn-prî), n.f., deception, cheating, fraud, deceit, imposition, illusion, delusion.

trompeter, v.n., to publish by sound of trumpet; to trumpet forth; to blab out, to publish; (of the eagle) to scream.

trompeteur, n.m., (anat.) buccinator.

trompette, n.f., (mus.) trumpet; (fig.) trumpeter, gossip, tell-tale; (conch.) trumpet-shell. — parlante; (l.u.) speaking-trumpet. V. **porte-voix.** — marine; one-stringed violoncello. — à clef; key-bugle. Sonner de la —; to blow the trumpet. En —; (of the nose) turned up. Sans —, sans tambour ni —; silently, quietly, without noise; privately. Déloger sans —; to decamp silently, without noise.

trompette, n.m., trumpeter.

trompeu-r, -se, n. and adj., deceiver, cheat; deluder, betrayer; deceitful, delusive, fallacious, beguiling, designing, cheating, false.

trompeusement, adv., deceitfully, deceptively.

*trompillon, n.m., (arch.) small pendentive.

tronc (tron), n.m., trunk, stem, stump; stock; poor box, box; (arch.) broken shaft (of a column, pillar); (geom.) frustum.

troncature, n.f., truncation.

tronce, n.f., stump (of a tree); Yule-log.

tronchet, n.m., cooper's block.

tronçon, n.m., broken piece, fragment, stump; portion, section (of a line of railway).

tronçonnement, n.m., cutting up.

tronçonner, v.a., to truncate, to lop, to cut into long pieces, to cut up.

trône, n.m., throne.

trôner, v.n., to sit on a throne; (fig.) to lord it over.

tronquer, v.a., to mutilate, to truncate, to detruncate; (fig.) to garble, to mangle (book).

trop, adv., too much, too many, too, over. Par —; too much. Je ne sais (pas) —; I hardly know, I am not quite sure. Qui dit — ne dit rien; (prov.) who would prove too much, proves nothing. Pas — bon; not very good. Pas — bien; not very well. — peu; too little. De —; too much, too many, over. Etre de —; to be one too many, not to be wanted. — de peine; too much trouble. — cuit; over-done. — plein; too full. Tuyau de — plein; wastepipe.

trop, n.m., excess, exuberance, superfluity.

trope, n.m., (rhet.) trope.

trophée, n.m., trophy. Faire — d'une chose; to glory in a thing.

tropical, -e, adj., tropic, tropical. Plante —e; tropical plant.

tropique, n.m. and adj., tropic; tropical; (bot.) ⊙diurnal. Année —; tropical year. Plante —; ⊙diurnal plant.

tropologique, adj., tropological.

trop-plein, n.m., (— — —s) overflow, waste; overplus, surplus, excess.

troquer, v.a., to truck, to barter, to exchange, to chop and change, to swap. — son cheval borgne contre un aveugle; to change for the worse.

troqueu-r, n.m., -se, n.f., barterer, trucker.

trot, n.m., trot.

trotte, n.f., trot, run, way, walk.

trotte-chemin, n.m., (—) (orni.). V. **traquet.**

trotte-menu, adj., slow-trotting.

trotter, v.n., to trot; to trot about, to run about, to go about; (of children) to toddle. Cette idée me trotte dans la tête; this idea keeps running into my head.

trotter, v.a., (man.) to cause to trot. — un cheval; to trot out a horse. Faire —; to put into a trot.

trotterie (tro-trî), *n.f.*, excursion, jaunt, trip.

trotteur, *n.m.*, trotter. *adj.*, trotting.

⊙**trotti-er, -ère,** *adj.*, fond of walking.

trottin, *n.m.*, errand-boy ; ⊙page. *Aller chercher les pardons de Saint —* ; to take a walk instead of going to church.

trottiner, *v.n.*, to go a jog trot ; (pers.) to toddle along.

trottoir, *n.m.*, foot-path, footway, sidewalk, foot-pavement (of streets). *Faire le —* ; to walk the streets.

trou, *n.m.*, hole, gap, orifice, mouth ; (anat.) foramen, orifice ; hazard (at tennis). *— de la serrure ;* key-hole. *— du chat ;* (nav.) lubber's hole. *— d'homme ;* man-hole. *Boucher un — ;* to stop a hole, to fill a gap ; to pay a debt or portion of a debt. *Boire comme un — ;* to drink like a fish. *N'avoir rien vu que par le — d'une bouteille ;* to have seen nothing of the world. *Faire un — à la lune ;* to shoot the moon ; to fly from one's creditors.

troubadour, *n.m.*, troubadour, bard.

troublant, -e, *adj.*, disturbing, troubling, disquieting.

trouble, *adj.*, thick, muddy, troubled, turbid, foul ; dull, cloudy, overcast, dim. *Avoir la vue —;* to be dim-sighted. *Pêcher en eau — ;* to fish in troubled waters ; to take advantage of confusion *or* disorder.

trouble, *adv.*, dimly, confusedly.

trouble, *n.m.*, confusion, disorder, disturbance, agitation, turmoil ; dispute, quarrel. *pl.*, troubles, broils, commotions, disturbances, dissensions. *—s civils ;* civil broils. *Exciter des —s dans un Etat ;* to raise dissensions in a state.

troublé, -e, *adj. part.*, disturbed ; confused, put out, abashed, bashful.

trouble *er* **truble,** *n.f.*, hoop-net.

troubleau, *n.m.*, small hoop-net.

trouble-fête, *n.m.*, (—) mar-joy, troublesome guest.

troublement, *n.m.*, confusion, disturbance.

troubler, *v.a.*, to trouble, to make thick, to make muddy ; to muddle, to turn ; to disturb, to disorder, to distract, to confound, to agitate, to perplex, to disconcert, to unsettle ; to unhinge ; to put to trouble ; to interrupt ; to destroy the harmony of ; to ruffle, to annoy, to discompose, to confuse ; to dim, to dull. *La peur lui trouble la raison ;* fear unhinges his mind. *— quelqu'un ;* to put anyone out.

se **troubler,** *v.r.*, to grow thick, to become thick, to grow muddy, to become muddy, to grow turbid, to become turbid ; to turn, to become sour, to turn sour ; to be confused, to be disconcerted, to become agitated ; to become foggy, to be foggy, to become overcast, to get overcast, cloudy ; to become confused, dim.

trouée, *n.f.*, opening, gap, pass ; large hole.

trouer, *v.a.*, to bore, to perforate, to make a hole in ; (tech.) to hole.

se **trouer,** *v.r.*, to have a hole.

trou-madame, *n.m.*, (—s——) bagatelle, nine-holes (game).

troupe, *n.f.*, troop, band, company, crew, gang, set ; soldiery, soldiers ; crowd (of children) ; flock. *pl.*, troops, forces. *Aller en — ;* to flock together. *—s de terre ;* land-forces. *—s de mer ;* sea-forces.

troupeau, *n.m.*, flock, herd, drove. *— de moutons ;* flock of sheep. *— de gros bétail ;* drove of cattle.

troupier, *n.m.*, soldier, trooper. *Vieux — ;* old campaigner, veteran.

⊙**trousse,** *n.f.*, bundle, truss ; (surg.) case of instruments ; case (of a barber) ; ⊙quiver. *Etre aux —s de l'ennemi ;* to be upon the enemy's heels. *Je suis à ses —s ;* I am after him.

troussé, -e, *adj.*, tucked up. *Bien — ;* well set up, neat, nice, well got up, well turned ;

dapper. *Compliment bien — ;* well turned compliment.

trousseau, *n.m.*, bunch (of keys) ; ⊙small sheaf of arrows ; trousseau (of a lady about to be married) ; outfit (of nuns, school-boarders, etc.) ; (anat.) fasciculus.

trousse-col, *n.m.*, (— -—s). *V.* **torcol.**

trousse-étriers, *n.m.*, (—) stirrup-leather.

trousse-galant, *n.m.*, (n.p.) (fam.) cholera.

trousse-pète, *n.f.*, (—) (pop.) hussy, jade.

trousse-queue, *n.m.*, (—) (man.) tail-case.

troussequin, *n.m.*, cantel, cantle (of a saddle).

trousser, *v.a.*, to tie up, to tuck up, to turn up, to pin up ; to truss ; to dispatch (business) ; to hasten. *— ses jupes ;* to tuck up one's petticoats. *— un poulet ;* to truss a chicken. *— baggage or ses guenilles ;* to make off, to cut one's sticks, to be off, to hook it, to cut it. *— de la besogne ;* to get through a lot of work (quickly).

se **trousser,** *v.r.*, to tuck up one's clothes ; to be tucked up.

troussis, *n.m.*, tucking up, tuck.

trouvable, *adj.*, that can be found, discoverable.

***trouvaille,** *n.f.*, thing found (by chance) ; godsend, windfall ; discovery, hit, lucky hit. *Faire une — ;* to make a discovery, to discover something.

trouvé, -e, *part.*, found. *Bien — ;* felicitous, happy, new, original (of words). *Enfant — ;* foundling. *Croire avoir trouvé la pie au nid ;* to have found a mare's nest. *Mot bien — ;* happy word, felicitous expression.

trouver, *v.a.*, to find, to find out, to discover, to detect ; to meet with, to meet, to light on, to hit upon, to come across ; to like ; to think, to deem, to deem it, to dream, to judge. *Comment le trouvez-vous ?* how do you like it ? *Aller —or venir — ;* to go to, to go and see, to call *or* wait upon, to visit. *Je lui trouve bon visage ;* I think he looks well. *— à dire, or — à redire ;* to find fault with. *— bon ;* to approve, to think fit. *— mauvais ;* to blame, to dislike, to disapprove, to be displeased with. *— beau, belle ;* to admire, to think handsome. *Où avez-vous trouvé cela ?* what made you think of that ? what put that in your head ? *Vous trouvez !* that's your opinion, is it !

se **trouver,** *v.r.*, to find one's self ; to be present, to be, to be by ; to feel, to feel one's self, to prove, to turn out ; to happen, to chance, to chance to be. *Il s'est trouvé à cette action ;* he was in that action. *Se — mal ;* to faint, to feel unwell, to be taken ill ; to fare ill. *Se — bien ;* to be well, to feel comfortable, to derive benefit from. *Cela se trouve bien ;* that is lucky. *Il se trouve ;* there is *or* there are ; we find ; it happens, *or* turns out.

trouvère *or* ⊙**trouveur,** *n.m.*, Trouvère, northern bard (name of old poets of the North of France).

truand, *n.m.*, **-e,** *n.f.*, *adj.*, (pop.) (l.u.) vagrant, beggar, vagabond.

***truandaille,** *n.f.*, (pop.) (l.u.) vagrants, beggars, vagabonds.

truander, *v.n.*, (pop.) (l.u.) to beg, to mump, to rove, to loaf.

truanderie (-an-drî), *n.m.*, (pop.) (l.u.) mumping, begging ; vagrancy, loafing.

truble, *n.f.* *V.* **trouble.**

truc, *n.m.*, (thea.) machinery ; (pop.) knack, dodge, trick. *Il a le — ;* he has the knack of doing it, he is up to it. *V.* **truck.**

trucage, *n.m.*, Jewing.

trucheman (trush-mãn) *or* **truchement,** *n.m.*, interpreter ; dragoman, drogman.

⊙**trucher,** *v.n.*, (pop.) to beg from laziness.

⊙**trucheu-r,** *n.m.*, **-se,** *n.f.*, (pop.) beggar.

***truck** *or* **truc,** *n.m.*, (railways) truck, trolley.

truculent, -e, *adj.* truculent.

truelle, *n.f.,* trowel ; fish-slice, fish-carver.

truellée, *n.f.,* trowelful.

truffe, *n.f.,* (bot.) truffle.

truffer, *v.a.,* to stuff with truffles.

truffière, *n.f.,* truffle-ground.

truflier, *n.m.,* (bot.) privet.

truie, *n.f.,* (mam.) sow.

truisme, *n.m.,* truism.

truite, *n.f.,* (ich.) trout. — *saumonée ;* salmon trout. *Vivier à —s ;* trout stream.

truité, -e, *adj.,* spotted (porcelain) ; speckled ; trout-colored (of dogs and horses). *Fonte —e ;* (metal.) pig-iron spotted white and gray.

trullisation, *n.f.,* (arch.) troweling.

trumeau, *n.m.,* (arch.) pier ; pier-glass ; leg, *or* shin, of beef.

trusquin, *n.m. V.* **troussequin.**

tsar, *n.m. V.* **czar.**

tsarien, tsarine, tsarowitz. *V.* **czarien, czarine, czarowitz.**

tu, *pron.,* thou, you. — *es ;* thou art, you are. *Etre à — et à toi avec quelqu'un ;* to be on very familiar terms, *or* very intimate, with any one.

tuable, *adj.,* fit for killing.

tuage, *n.m.,* killing, slaughter (of an animal).

tuant, -e, *adj.,* killing, toilsome, tiresome, laborious, tedious. *C'est un homme —;* he is a regular bore. *V.* **assommant.**

tu-autem (-ô-tèm), *n.m.,* (*n.p.*) main thing, difficulty, rub.

tube, *n.m.,* tube, pipe ; (anat.) duct ; (bot.) tube ; (zoöl.) duct, tube.

tuber, *v.a.,* to tube.

tubercule, *n.m.,* (bot., med.) tubercle.

tuberculé, -e, *adj.,* (med.) tuberculate, tubercled.

tuberculeu-x, -se, *adj.,* tubercular, tuberculous ; (bot.) tubercular, tuberculous, grained ; (med.) tubercled, tubercular, tuberculous.

tuberculisation, *n.f.,* (med.) formation and growth of tubercles.

tubéreuse, *n.f.,* (bot.) tuberose.

tubéreu-x, -se, *adj.,* (bot.) tuberous.

tubérifère, *adj.,* tuberiferous.

tubérosité, *n.f.,* (anat.) tuberosity.

tubiforme, *adj.,* tubiform.

tubulaire, *adj.,* tubular.

tubule, *n.m.,* small tube, tubule.

tubulé, -e, *adj.,* tubular, tubulated, tubulous.

tubuleu-x, -se, *adj.,* tubulated, tubulous.

tubulure, *n.f.,* (chem.) tubulature ; (bot.) tubes, tubing.

tudesque, *n.m.* and *adj.,* Teutonic, Germanic (language) ; inelegant, rough, coarse.

tudieu, *int.,* zounds !

tue-chien, *n.m.,* (— — —s) (bot.) meadow saffron, dog's bane, colchicum.

tuer, *v.a.,* to kill, to slay, to slaughter, to butcher ; to kill, to tire to death, to be the death of ; to while away. — *des bœufs ;* to slaughter oxen. — *le temps ;* to kill time. *Se faire —;* to get killed, to expose one's life.

se **tuer,** *v.r.,* to kill one's self, to make away with one's self, to commit suicide ; (fig.) to wear one's self out. *Se — de peine ;* to work one's self to death.

tuer, *v.n.,* to kill, to be baneful (to) ; to tire, to be irksome.

tuerie (tû-rî), *n.f.,* slaughter, massacre, butchery, carnage ; slaughter-house.

à **tue-tête,** *adv.,* (of shouting and quarreling) with all one's might, as loud as one can, at the top of one's voice.

tueur, *n.m.,* killer, slayer. — *de gens ;* bully, braggart.

tuf, *n.m.,* (min.) tuff, tufa.

tufacé, -e, *adj.,* (min.) tufaceous.

tuffeau, *n.m.,* (min.) tuff, tufa.

tufi-er, -ère, *adj.,* tufaceous.

?uile, *n.f.,* tile. — *faîtière ;* crest-tile ; ridge-tile. — *en S ;* pantile. — *de Guienne ;* gutter-tile. — *vernissée ;* glazed tile ; (fig.) blow ; hard luck, mishap.

tuileau, *n.m.,* broken tile, shard.

tuilerie (tuil-rî), *n.f.,* tile-works, **tile-fields.** *Les —s ;* Tuileries, a palace in Paris.

tuilier, *n.m.,* tile-maker.

tulipe, *n.f.,* (bot.) tulip.

tulipier, *n.m.,* (bot.) tulip-tree.

tulle, *n.m.,* tulle, net.

tulliste, *n.m.f.,* tulle-maker.

tuméfaction, *n.f.,* (med.) tumefaction.

tuméfier, *v.a.,* (med., surg.) to tumefy.

se **tuméfier,** *v.r.,* (med., surg.) to tumefy.

tumeur, *n.f.,* tumor. *pl.,* (vet.) warbles.

tumulaire, *adj.,* of the grave, sepulchral. *Pierre —;* tombstone.

tumulte, *n.m.,* tumult, uproar, riot, hubbub, confusion.

tumultuaire, *adj.* tumultuary ; against the law.

tumultuairement (-èr-mān), *adv.,* in a tumultuary manner.

tumultueusement (-euz-mān), *adv.,* tumultuously.

tumultueu-x, -se, *adj.,* tumultuous, riotous.

tumulus (-lus), *n.m.,* tumulus, barrow ; cairn ; mound (burial-place).

tungstène, *n.m.* (*n.p.*), (chem.) tungsten.

tunique, *n.f.,* tunic ; (bot.) tunic ; (anat.) tunic, coat, film ; wall, coat (of the stomach) ; tunic (of the eye).

tuniqué, -e, *adj.,* (bot.) tunicated.

tunnel, *n.m.,* tunnel.

tuorbe, *n.m. V.* **téorbe.**

turban, *n.m.,* turban. *Prendre le —;* to turn Mahometan.

turbine, *n.f.,* (mec.) turbine.

turbiné, -e, *adj.,* turbinate, turbinated.

turbinite, *n.f.,* (conch.) turbinite, turbite.

turbith, *n.m.,* (pharm.) turbith, turpeth. — *minéral ;* turpeth mineral, subsulphate of mercury.

turbot, *n.m.,* (ich.) turbot.

turbotière (ti-è-r), *n.f.,* turbot-kettle.

turbotin, *n.m.,* (ich.) young turbot.

turbulemment (-la-mān), *adv.,* turbulently.

turbulence, *n.f.,* turbulence, wildness.

turbulent, -e, *adj.,* turbulent, noisy ; rude, wild (of children).

turc, *n.m.,* Turk ; wood-worm. *Se faire —;* to turn Turk.

tur-c, -que, *adj.,* Turkish.

turcie, *n.f.,* (l.u.) dike, embankment.

turcisme, *n.m.,* Turcism.

turco, *n.m.,* (—s), turco (Algerian soldier).

turcoin, *n.m.,* mohair.

turelure (tur-lur), *n.f.,* tol de rol, fol de rol, words (burden of a song). *C'est toujours la même —;* it is always the same thing over and over again.

turf, *n.m.,* (*n.p.*) turf.

turfiste, *n.m.,* turfite.

turgescence, *n.f.,* turgescence, turgidness.

turgescent, -e, *adj.,* turgid, turgescent.

turlupin, *n.m.,* punster ; sorry jester.

turlupinade, *n.f.,* sorry jesting ; bad joke.

turlupiner, *v.n.,* to pun (badly).

turlupiner, *v.a.,* to laugh at, to turn into ridicule, to jeer (at), to banter, to provoke.

turlurette, *n.f.,* kind of guitar (in use in the 14th century).

turlut, *n.m.,* (orni.) titlark.

turlututu, *n.m.,* (bot.) reed-pipe.

turnep (-nèp), *n.m.,* field-turnip.

turpitude, *n.f.,* turpitude, baseness, vileness, filthy language. *Dire des —s ;* to tell filthy stories.

turque, *n.f.*, Turkish woman.

turquette, *n.f.*, (bot.) rupture-wort.

turquin, *adj.*, dark (of blue); deep blue.

turquoise, *n.f.*, turquoise.

tussilage, *n.m.*, (bot.) colt's-foot, horse-foot.

tutélaire, *adj.*, tutelary, protecting, guardian.

tutelle, *n.f.*, (jur.) tutelage, guardianship, protectorship; committeeship (of lunatics). *Enfants en* —; children under the care of a guardian, minors.

tut-eur, *n.m.*, **-rice**, *n.f.*, (jur.) guardian, trustee; protector; (hort.) prop.

tutie (-tî), *n.f.*, (chem.) tutty.

tutoiement or **tutoîment** (-toa-mān), *n.m.*, theeing and thouing, saying thou and thee.

tutoyer, *v.a.*, to thee and thou. *se tutoyer*, *v.r.*, to thee and thou each other; to be on familiar terms.

tutrice, *n.f.* *V.* tuteur.

tuyau, *n.m.*, pipe, tube, tunnel, funnel; barrel (of a quill); stalk (of corn); stalk, stem (of feathers); nozzle (of bellows, of candlesticks); shank, stem (of tobacco-pipes); goffering (of frills, etc.). — *aspirant*; suction pipe. — *atmospherique*; vacuum-pipe. — *de conduite*; delivery-pipe. — *de dégagement de la vapeur*; waste steam-pipe. — *d'embranchement*; branch-pipe. — *de trop-plein*; waste-pipe. — *de descente*; stack-pipe. — *de la cheminée*; flue of the chimney. — *de cheminée*; chimney flue.

tuyautage, *n.m.*, goffering, quilling, fluting.

tuyauter, *v.a.*, to goffer, to frill, to plate (frills, linen, etc.).

tuyauterie (tui-io-trî), *n.f.*, system of pipes; pipe-store; pipe-trade.

tuyère (tu-ie-r), *n.f.*, tue-iron; tewel; blast-pipe.

tympan, *n.m.*, (anat.) tympanum; drum of the ear; (print., arch., mec.) tympan; spandrel (of bridges).

tympaniser, *v.a.*, (fam.) to run down, to inveigh against, to decry, to lampoon, to traduce.

tympanite, *n.f.*, tympanite, tympany; wind (in horses).

tympanon, *n.m.*, (mus.) dulcimer.

type, *n.m.*, type, model; symbol; emblem; standard, character; (astron.) plan drawing; (print.) type. *C'est un véritable* —; (fig.) he is quite a character. *Quel* — *d'homme!* what a character!

typha, *n.m.*, (bot.) reed-mace, Indian grass.

typhoïde, *adj.*, (med.) typhoid, typhus.

typhon, *n.m.*, (phys.) water-spout; typhoon.

typhus (-fus), *n.m.*, (med.) typhus, typhus fever, camp-fever, gaol-fever. — *du gros bétail*; cattle-plague.

typique, *adj.*, typic, typical, emblematic, emblematical, symbolical.

typographe, *n.m.*, typographer, printer.

typographie, *n.f.*, typography; printing; printing-office.

typographique, *adj.*, typographical. *Caractères* —*s*; printing-type.

typographiquement (-fik-mān), *adv.*, typographically.

tyran, *n.m.*, tyrant, despot, oppressor. *Cette femme est un vrai* —; that woman is a regular shrew.

tyranneau (-ra-nô), *n.m.*, petty tyrant.

tyrannicide (-ra-ni-), *n.m.*, tyrannicide.

tyrannie (-ra-nî), *n.f.*, tyranny, oppression. *S'affranchir de la* —; to free one's self from tyranny; to throw off the yoke of tyranny.

tyrannique, *adj.*, tyrannical.

tyranniquement (-ra-nîk-mān), *adv.*, tyrannically.

tyranniser (-ra-ni-), *v.a.*, to tyrannize (over), to oppress.

tyrolienne, *n.f.*, mountain song (dance or waltz popular in the Tyrol).

tzar, *n.m.* *V.* czar.

tzigane, *n.m.f.*, gypsy (Hungarian).

U

u, *n.m.* the twenty-first letter of the alphabet, u.

ubiquiste (-kuist), *n.m.*, (ecc. hist.) Ubiquist.

ubiquitaire (-kui-), *n.m.*, (ecc. hist.) Ubiquitarian, Ubiquitary. *adj.*, ubiquitous, omnipresent.

ubiquité (-kui-), *n.f.*, ubiquity.

udomètre, *n.m.*, (phys.) udometer, pluvio-meter, rain-gauge.

uhlan, *n.m.*, (—*s*) uhlan (German lancer).

ukase, *n.m.*, ukase (edict of the Emperor of Russia).

ulcération, *n.f.*, (med.) ulceration.

ulcère, *n.m.*, ulcer.

ulcéré, -e, *part.*, (med.) ulcerated, gangrened; (fig.) embittered, full of deep resentment, cankered.

ulcérer, *v.a.*, to ulcerate; (fig.) to exasperate, to embitter, to provoke, to incense. *s'ulcérer*, *v.r.*, (med.) to ulcerate, to exulcerate.

ulcéreu-x, -se, *adj.*, (med.) ulcerous.

uléma, *n.m.*, (—*s*) ulema (in Turkey a doctor of law).

ulex, *n.m.*, (bot.) ulex, whin, gorse.

uligineu-x, -se, *adj.*, (bot.) uliginous.

ulmaire, *n.f.*, (bot.) common meadow-sweet.

ulmine, *n.f.*, (chem.) ulmine.

ulmique, *adj.*, (chem.) ulmic. *Acide* —; ulmic acid.

ultérieur, -e, *adj.*, ulterior, subsequent; further.

ultérieurement (-eur-mān), *adv.*, subsequently, later, beyond, further, besides.

ultimatum (-to-m), *n.m.*, (—*s*) ultimatum.

ultra, *n.m.*, (—*s*) ultra (person of violent opinions).

ultraïsme, *n.m.*, ultraism.

ultra-mondain, -e (-dĭn, -dè-n), *adj.*, ultra-mundane.

ultramontain, -e (-tĭn, -tè-n), *n.* and *adj.*, ultramontane; tramontane.

ultramontanisme, *n.m.*, ultramontanism.

ultrazodiacal, *adj.*, (astron.) ultrazodiacal (applied to those planets, the orbit of which is not limited to the width of the zodiac).

ululation, *n.f.*, ululation; howling, hooting.

ululer, *v.n.*, to ululate, to hoot, to howl.

umble, *n.m.*, (ich.) umber, char or charr, grayling.

un, *n.m.*, one; unit.

un, -e, *pron.*, one. — *pour cent*; one per cent. *L'* — *vaut l'autre*; one is as good as the other. *L'* — *après l'autre*; one after another. — *à* —; one by one. *Les* —*s disent oui, les autres disent non*; some say yes, the others say no. *L'* — *ou l'autre*; either, the one or the other. *L'* — *et l'autre*; both. *Les* —*s et les autres*; all, all together. *Ni l'* — *ni l'autre*; neither the one nor the other, neither. *L'* — *portant l'autre*; (taking) one with another, on an average. *En donner d'* —*e à quelqu'un*; to take any one in. *N'en faire ni* —*e ni deux*; to make no bones about; not to hesitate, to decide there and then. *C'est tout* —; it matters not, it is all one.

un, -e, *art.*, a, an, any.

un, -e, *adj.*, one. *Sur les* —*e heure*; about one o'clock.

unanime, *adj.*, unanimous.

unanimement (-nim-mān), *adv.*, unanimously.

unanimité, *n.f.*, unanimity.

unau, *n.m.*, (mam.) sloth.

unciale (ōn-), *adj.f.* *V.* onciale.

undécennal, -e, *adj.,* undecennial.

unguis (on-gu-iss), *n.m.,* (anat.) unguis.

unguiculé, -e, *adj.,* unguiculate, unguiculated.

uni, -e, *adj.,* united ; smooth, even, level ; plain, simple, unaffected ; uniform. *Chemin —;* level road. *Du linge —;* plain linen. ⊙ *A l'—, adv.,* level. *Etoffe —e;* plain material. *Les Etats —s;* The United States.

unicorne, *n.m.,* unicorn ; sea-unicorn, narwhal, narwal.

unième, *adj.,* first. [Only used in *vingt et —, trente et —,* etc. ; 21st, 31st, etc.]

unièmement (-èm-mān), *adv.,* firstly. [Only used when preceded by 20, 30, 40, etc.]

unification, *n.f.,* unification, amalgamation.

unifier, *v.a.,* to amalgamate, to unite.

uniflore, *adj.,* (bot.) uniflorous.

uniforme, *adj.,* uniform. *D'—;* regimental.

uniforme, *n.m.,* uniform ; uniform, regimentals. *Quitter l'—;* to quit the service. *Grand —;* full-dress uniform.

uniformément, *adv.,* uniformly.

uniformité, *n.f.,* uniformity.

unilatéral, *adj.,* (bot.) unilateral ; (of contracts) binding on one party only.

uniloculaire, *adj.,* (bot.) unilocular.

uniment, *adv.,* evenly, even, smoothly ; plainly, simply. *Tout —;* simply, plainly, and no more.

uninominal, -e, *adj.,* of one name.

union, *n.f.,* union, conjunction ; concord, agreement, harmony, blending, mixture ; (jur.) deed of agreement ; (jur.) concurrence.

unionisme, *n.m.,* unionism.

unipare, *adj.,* uniparous.

unipersonnel, -le, *adj.,* (gram.) unipersonal, impersonal.

unique, *adj.,* only, sole ; single, unique ; matchless, unrivaled ; unparalleled, unprecedented ; odd, singular. *Fils —;* only son.

uniquement (u-nik-mān), *adv.,* only, solely ; above the rest; above all things.

unir, *v.a.,* to unite, to join, to combine ; to smooth, to level, to plane, to make smooth ; to pair.

s'unir, *v.r.,* to unite, to be united, to join together, to coalesce.

unisexué, -e (-ni-cèksué), *or* **unisexuel, -le** (-ni-cèksu-èl), *adj.,* (bot.) unisexual.

unisson, *n.m.,* (mus.) unison, keeping, harmony, concert. *Deux cordes à l'—;* two strings in unison. *A l'—;* in unison, in concert.

unitaire, *n.m.f.* and *adj.,* Unitarian.

unitarisme, *n.m.,* unitarianism.

unité, *n.f.,* unity, unit ; unity, concord, agreement.

unitif, -ve, *adj.,* (theol.) of pure love.

univalve, *adj.,* (bot., conch.) univalve, unival-vular.

univers, *n.m.,* universe.

universaliser, *v.a.,* to make universal.

universalité, *n.f.,* universality, generality.

universaux, *n.m.pl.* of **universel,** *n.,* q. v.

universel, -le, *adj.,* universal ; residuary sole (of legatees).

universel, *n.m.,* (*universaux*) (log.) predicable, universal.

universellement (-sèl-mān), *adv.,* universally, generally.

universitaire, *adj.,* of, *or* belonging to, the university ; academic.

université, *n.f.,* university.

univocation, *n.f.,* univocation.

univoque, *adj.,* univocal.

upas (u-pâs), *n.m.,* (bot.) poison-tree, bohun upas.

urane *or* **uranium** (-nio-m), *n.f.,* (min.) uranite, uranium.

uranie (astron.) Urania ; (bot.) traveler's tree.

uranographie, *n.f.,* uranography.

uranographique, *adj.,* uranographic, uranographical.

uranoscope, *n.m.,* (ich.) uranoscopus.

uranus (-nus), *n.m.,* (astron.) Uranus, (Georgium Sidus).

urate, *n.m.,* (chem.) urate.

urbain, -e (-bin, -bè-n), *adj.,* urban.

urbaine, *n.f.,* hackney carriage (sort of).

urbains, *n.m.pl.,* townspeople.

urbanité, *n.f.,* urbanity.

urcéolé, -e, *adj.,* (bot.) urceolate.

ure, aurochs, *or* **urus,** *n.m.,* (mam.) ure, ure-ox, urus.

urédo, *n.m.,* (bot.) uredo.

urée, *n.f.,* (chem.) urea.

uretère, *n.m.,* (anat.) ureter.

urètre *or* **urèthre,** *n.m.,* (anat.) urethra.

urgence, *n.f.,* urgency. *D'—;* urgent, immediate ; in case of urgency.

urgent, -e, *adj.,* urgent, cogent, pressing.

urinaire, *adj.,* urinary.

urinal, *n.m.,* urinal.

urine, *n.f.,* urine, chamber-lye ; stale (of animals).

uriner, *v.n.,* to urine, to make water ; to stale (of animals).

urineu-x, -se, *adj.,* urinous.

urinoir, *n.m.,* urinary, urinal.

urique, *adj.,* (chem.) uric.

urne, *n.f.,* urn ; ballot-box. *— de scrutin* or *— électorale;* ballot-box.

ursuline, *n.f.,* Ursuline nun, Ursuline.

urticaire, *n.f.,* (med.) urticaria, nettle-rash.

urtication, *n.f.,* (surg.) urtication.

urticées, *n.f.pl.,* (bot.) nettle tribe, urticaceæ.

urus, *n.m.* V. **ure.**

us, *n.m.,* (n.p.) used only in ; *un savant en —;* a man learned in Latin ; Latin scholar.

us (us), *n.m.pl.,* (n.s.) usage, use, way. *Les — et coutumes;* the ways and customs.

usage, *n.m.,* custom, practice, use, usage; wear (of clothes). *pl.,* church-books. *L'— le veut ainsi;* custom will have it so. *Cela est hors d'—;* that 's out of use. *Mettre une chose en —;* to use a thing. *Hors d'—;* obsolete. *Peu en —;* little used. *Mettre tout en —;* to spare no pains, to use every endeavor. *L'— du monde;* knowledge of the world ; ways of the world. *Avoir de l'—;* to have manners, a certain breeding.

usager, *n.m.,* (jur.) commoner.

usance, *n.f.,* (com.) usance. *A l'—;* at usance.

usante, *adj.f.,* (jur.) (of spinsters) making use of, using.

usé, -e, *adj.,* worn out, threadbare ; stale, common, trite, hackneyed. *Conte —;* stale story.

user, *v.n.,* to use, to make use of. *— de violence;* to use violence. *— de douceur;* to use gentle means. *En — bien avec quelqu'un;* to use, or treat, any one well. *En — mal avec quelqu'un;* to use, or treat, any one ill. *En — bien, en — mal;* to make a good, or bad, use of.

user, *v.a.,* to use, to consume ; to wear out, to wear off ; to use up, to spend, to waste ; to wear away ; to wear down ; (surg.) to eat off, to consume. *— des souliers;* to wear out shoes. *— ses yeux;* to impair one's sight (by reading, etc.).

s'user, *v.r.,* to wear out ; to be worn out, to be used, to be consumed ; to waste, to decay ; to be spent.

user, *n.m.,* wear, service. *Ce drap est d'un bon —;* this cloth wears well. *On ne connaît les gens qu'à l'—;* (fig.) it takes time to know people. *Etre bon à l'—;* to improve on acquaintance.

usine, *n.f.,* works, mills, manufactory, factory.

usinier, *n.m.*, manufacturer, mill-owner.

usité, -e, *adj.*, usual; customary; used, in use. *Ce mot n'est guère —;* that word is seldom used.

usquebac (us-kĕ-bak), *n.m.*, usquebaugh (spirits).

ustensile, *n.m.*, utensil; tool, implement. *—s de cuisine;* kitchen utensils.

ustion (u-sti-on), *n.f.*, ustion, combustion.

usuel, -le, *adj.*, usual, customary, ordinary, common.

usuellement (-èl-mān), *adv.*, usually, customarily.

usufructuaire, *adj.*, (jur.) usufructuary.

usufruit, *n.m.*, (jur.) usufruct, use.

usufruiti-er, *n.m.*, **-ère**, *n.f.* (-tié, -tiè-r), usufructuary, tenant for life.

usufruit-ier, **-ière**, *adj.*, (jur.) usufructuary.

usuraire, *adj.*, usurious.

usurairement (-rèr-mān), *adv.*, usuriously.

usure, *n.f.*, usury, unlawful interest; wearing, wear, wear and tear. *Prêter à —;* to lend upon usury. *Rendre avec —;* to return with interest.

usuri-er (-rié), *n.m.*, **-ère** (-riè-r), *n.f.*, usurer.

usurpat-eur, *n.m.*, **-rice**, *n.f.*, usurper.

usurpation, *n.f.*, usurpation, encroachment.

usurper, *v.a.* and *n.*, to usurp; to encroach.

ut (ut), *n.m.*, (mus.) ut, do, c.

utérin, -e, *adj.*, (med.) uterine; (jur.) uterine, on the mother's side.

utérins, *n.m.pl.*, (jur.) brothers of the half blood, by the same venter; brothers and sisters of the half blood, by the same venter.

utérus (-rus), *n.m.*, womb, matrix, uterus.

utile, *adj.*, useful, of use, advantageous; expedient, proper, due, beneficial; profitable, serviceable; subservient. *En temps —;* in proper, or due, or good, time.

utile, *n.m.*, utility, usefulness. *Joindre l'— à l'agréable;* to combine utility and pleasure.

utilement (u-til-mān), *adv.*, usefully, profitably, beneficially, advantageously.

utiliser, *v.a.*, to find use for, to turn to account, to make use of, to avail one's self of. *S'—*, to be utilized.

utilitaire, *n.m.* and *adj.*, utilitarian.

utilité, *n.f.*, utility, use, usefulness, benefit, profit, service, avail, advantage, purpose ; (thea.) utility (actor). *But d'—;* purpose, useful end.

utopie, *n.f.*, utopia.

utopique, *adj.*, utopian.

utopiste, *n.m.f.* and *adj.*, utopist; utopian.

utricule, *n.m.*, utricle.

utriculé, -e, *adj.*, utricular.

uvée, *n.f.*, (anat.) uvea.

uvelte, *n.f.*, (bot.) sea-grape.

uviforme, *adj.*, uviform, grape-shaped.

uvulaire, *adj.*, (anat.) uvular.

V

v, *n.m.*, the twenty-second letter of the alphabet, **v**.

v. (initial letter of *voir*, to see), V., vide.

va, imperative of *aller*, to go. *— pour cela;* I consent to it; done, agreed.

va, *n.m.*, va (at basset, faro).

vacance, *n.f.*, vacancy. *pl.* vacation, holidays; recess (of parliament). *Entrer en —s;* to break up (of schools).

vacant, -e, *adj.*, vacant, unfilled, unoccupied, empty; (jur.) in abeyance, unclaimed.

vacarme, *n.m.*, hubbub, tumult, uproar. *Faire du —;* to kick up a shindy; to create a disturbance.

vacation, *n.f.*, attendance, sitting (of public officers); day's sale (of auctions); vacation (of courts); ⊙ trade, profession. *— avenante;* in case of a vacancy.

vaccin, *n.m.*, (med.) vaccine matter, vaccine; lymph.

vaccinal, -e, *adj.*, vaccinal, vaccine.

vaccinateur, *n.m.*, vaccinator.

vaccination, *n.f.*, vaccination.

vaccine, *n.f.*, vaccinia, cow-pox; vaccination.

vacciner, *v.a.*, to vaccinate.

vache, *n.f.*, (mam.) cow; cow-hide (prepared for use). *Etable à —s;* cow-house, cow-stable or shed. *— à lait;* milk cow, milch cow, dairy cow. *Manger de la — enragée;* to endure great hardships, to rough it. *Le grand chemin des —s;* the beaten track. *Le plancher des —s;* dry land, terra firma. *Parler français comme une — enragée;* to murder the French language.

vach-er, *n.m.*, **-ère**, *n.f.*, cowherd, cow-keeper, neat-herd.

vacherie (va-shrî), *n.f.*, cow-house.

vaciet, *n.m.*, (bot.) grape-hyacinth.

vacillant, -e (-sil-lān, -t), *adj.*, vacillating; reeling, staggering, tottering; wavering, uncertain, undecided; (bot.) versatile; (fig.) flickering (of light).

vacillation (-sil-la-), *n.f.*, vacillation; wavering, flickering (of light).

vaciller (-sil-lé), *v.n.*, to vacillate; to waver; to reel, to stagger; (fig.) to flicker (of light).

vacuité, *n.f.*, vacuity, emptiness.

vade, *n.f.*, vade, stake (at play).

vademanque, *n.f.*, (banking) decrease of money in reserve.

vade-mecum (va-dé-mé-ko-m), *n.m.* (—), vade-mecum, manual.

va-et-vient, *n.m.* (—), (mec.) reciprocating motion, swing, sweep, see-saw motion; (fig.) oscillation; (nav.) small ferry-boat; pass-rope, traversing gear.

vagabond, -e, *n.* and *adj.*, vagabond, vagrant; wandering.

vagabondage, *n.m.*, vagrancy; roguery.

vagabonder or ⊙**vagabonner**, *v.n.*, to be a vagabond, to wander, to roam, to tramp about.

vagant, *n.m.*, wrecker.

vagin, *n.m.*, (anat.) vagina.

vaginal, -e, *adj.*, (anat.) vaginal.

vagir, *v.n.*, (of infants) to wail, to mewl, to pule.

vagissant, *adj.*, mewling, wailing, puling.

vagissement, *n.m.*, crying, wailing, mewling (of infants).

vague (vag), *n.f.*, wave, billow, surge.

vague, *adj.*, vague, indeterminate, loose, uncertain; faint, indistinct, hazy; empty. *Terres —s;* waste-land.

vague, *n.m.*, vagueness, looseness; uncertainty; space, empty space, emptiness; void, vacuum.

vaguement (vag-mān), *adv.*, vaguely.

vaguemestre (vag-mès-tr), *n.m.*, (milit.) wagon-master, baggage-master, paymaster, orderly, post-sergeant (nav.) postman.

vaguer (va-ghé), *v.n.*, to ramble, to rove, to range about, to wander, to stray, to straggle. *v.a.*, to mash (in brewing).

vaguesse, *n.f.*, (paint.) lightness, airiness.

vaigrage, *n.m.*, (nav.) outer-planking, ceiling, wale.

vaigre, *n.f.*, (nav.) plank (for ceiling).

*****vaillamment** (va-ia-mān), *adv.*, valiantly, valorously, courageously, stoutly.

*****vaillance**, *n.f.*, valiance, valor, courage, bravery.

*****vaillant, -e**, *adj.*, valiant, valorous, brave, courageous, gallant.

*****vaillant**, *n.m.*, all a man is worth, one's substance. *Tout son —;* one's all.

*****vaillant**, *adv.*, worth, value. *N'avoir pas un sou —;* not to be worth a penny (of a person). *Il n'a rien —;* he is penniless. *Il a dix mille écus —;* he is worth 30,000 francs.

⊙*vaillantise, *n.f.*, (fam.) prowess, valorous deed.

vain, -e (vin, vè-n), *adj.*, vain, fruitless, in-effectual, unprofitable; empty, shadowy, foolish, trifling, frivolous; vainglorious, presumptuous, self-conceited. *En* —; vainly, in vain, to no purpose. *Homme* —; vain, conceited man.

vaincre (vainquant, vaincu), *v.a.*, to van-quish, to conquer, to overcome, to master, to defeat, to get the better of; to outdo, to surpass, to excel. *Se laisser* —; to give way to, to yield. *Se laisser — à la pitié*; to be moved to pity. *se* vaincre, *v.r.*, to conquer one's self; to con-quer one's passions.

vaincre, *v.n.*, to win; to be victorious.

vaincu, *n.m.*, conquered, vanquished (enemy).

vainement (vè-n-màn), *adv.*, vainly, in vain, fruitlessly; to no purpose.

vainqueur, *n.m.* and *adj.*, vanquisher, con-queror, subduer, victor, overcomer; prize-win-ner, prize-man, prize-boy, prize-holder; conquer-ing, victorious, triumphant.

vair, *n.m.*, (her.) vair.

vairé, -e, *adj.*, (her.) vairy.

vairon, *adj.*, silver-eyed (of horses); (pers.) wall-eyed, odd-eyed. *Œil* —; wall-eye.

vairon, *n.m.*, (ich.) minnow.

vaisseau, *n.m.*, ship, vessel; structure, fab-ric; pile (inside of a building); (anat.) vessel, tube; (bot.) duct. *pl.*, (nav.) shipping. — *d'approvisionnement;* victualing-ship. — *mar-chand;* merchantman. — *de guerre;* man-of-war. — *à deux ponts;* two-decker. — *de la marine royale;* His, Her, Majesty's ship. — *frégate;* frigate-built ship. — *de compagnie;* (nav.) good company keeper. — *école;* training-ship. — *armé en guerre;* armed ship.

vaisselle, *n.f.*, plates and dishes; plate (of gold *or* silver). — *de terre;* earthenware. — *d'or;* gold plate. — *d'argent;* silver plate. — *ciselée;* carved plate. — *plate;* (of gold *or* sil-ver) plate.

vaissellerie, *n.f.*, pots and pans.

val, *n.m.*, valley, vale, dale. *Par monts et par vaux;* up hill and down dale.

valable, *adj.*, valid, good for.

valablement, *adv.*, validly.

valenciennes, *n.f.*, valenciennes (lace).

valériane, *n.f.*, (bot.) valerian.

valet, *n.m.*, footman, valet; knave (at cards); door weight; hold-fast (of a joiner); support (of a looking-glass). — *de pied;* footman. — *de chambre;* valet. — *de bourreau;* assistant-exe-cutioner, aid. *Faire le bon* —; to be officious. *Maître* —; (agri.) headman. — *de ferme;* farm-servant. — *de chiens;* whipper-in. *Tel maître, tel* —; like master, like man. *C'est un — de cartes;* (fig.) he is a nobody, a contemptible fel-low. *Il n'y a pas de grand homme pour son — de chambre;* no man is a hero to his valet. *On ne prend pas de — pour se servir soi-même;* what! keep a dog and bark thyself!

valetage (val-taj), *n.m.*, duty of a valet, drudgery.

*valetaille (val-tâ-i), *n.f.*, pack of men-ser-vants, footmen, flunkies, lackeys, menials.

valet-à-patin, *n.m.*, (—*s* —) (surg.) forceps (for ligatures).

valeter (val-té), *v.n.*, to cringe, to dance attendance, to fawn upon.

valétudinaire, *n.m.f.* and *adj.*, valetudinary, valetudinarian, invalid.

valeur, *n.f.*, value, worth, consideration; import, meaning. *pl.*, (com.) bills, paper, stocks, shares, securities; valor, bravery, courage, gal-lantry. *Etre en* —; to bear a good price. *Etre de nulle* —; to be of no value, to be valueless. *Abaisser la* —; to depreciate. — *en espèces;* value in cash. —*s mobilières;* transferable securities. *Mettre en* —; to improve (land).

valeureusement (-reûz-màn), *adv.*, valiantly, valorously, bravely, courageously.

valeureu-x, -se, *adj.*, valiant, valorous, brave, courageous, gallant.

validation, *n.f.*, (jur.) validation, rendering valid.

validé, *n.f.*, (n.p.) the title of the Sultan's mother.

valide, *n.m.* and *adj.*, person in health; healthy; in health, valid, good.

validement (-lid-màn), *adv.*, (jur.) validly.

valider, *v.a.*, to validate, to confirm, to ratify, to make valid.

validité, *n.f.*, validity, validness.

valise, *n.f.*, valise, portmanteau.

valisnère *or* valisnérie, *n.f.*, (bot.) frogbit.

valkyrie, *n.f.*, (—*s*) Scandinavian myth, valkyrie, goddess, wish-maiden.

vallaire, *adj.*, (antiq.) vallary, vallar. *Cou-ronne* —; vallary crown.

vallée, *n.f.*, valley, vale.

vallon, *n.m.*, dale, vale, small valley.

valoir (valant, valu), *v.n.*, to be worth, to be as good as, *to* be equal to; to yield, to bring, to win for, to procure. — *mieux;* to be better, to be preferable. *Il vaut mieux ne pas y aller;* it is better not to go there. *Cela ne vaut rien;* that is good for nothing. *Cet habit ne vaut plus rien;* this coat is quite worn out. *Cela ne vaut pas la peine d'y penser;* that is not worth a moment's thought. *Il ne vaut pas la peine qu'on lui réponde;* he is not worth answering. *Vous ne faites rien qui vaille;* nothing you do is worth anything; you do nothing to speak of. *Chaque chose vaut son prix;* everything has its price. *Cela vaut son pesant d'or;* that is worth its weight in gold. *Faire — une terre;* to improve, to cultivate, an estate. *Faire — son argent;* to turn one's money to account, to put it out at interest. *Faire — son talent;* to turn one's tal-ent to account. *Faire — sa marchandise;* to set off one's goods. *Il fait bien — ce qu'il sait;* he makes the best of his knowledge. *Faire — son droit;* to assert, *or* maintain, one's right. *Se faire* —; to push one's self forward, to brag too much. *Cela vaut fait;* that's as good as done. *Vaille que vaille;* at all events, for better or worse. *Que lui a valu son ambition?* what has his ambition brought him, *or* won for him?

valonnement, *n.m.*, disposing in vales.

ad valorem, *adj.*, (com.) ad valorem.

valse, *n.f.*, waltz.

valser, *v.n.*, to waltz.

valseu-r, *n.m.*, -se, *n.f.*, waltzer, dancer, partner (in a dance).

value, *n.f.*, value. *Plus* —; superior value. *Moins* —; inferior value.

valvaire, *adj.*, (bot.) valvate.

valve, *n.f.*, valve; (tech.) clack, *or* trap, door.

valvé, -e, *adj.*, (bot.) valved, valvate.

valvule, *n.f.*, (anat.) valvule.

vampire, *n.m.*, vampire.

van, *n.m.*, (agri.) fan, van; winnowing-baskets.

vandale, *n.m.* and *adj.*, Vandal; vandalic.

vandalisme, *n.m.*, vandalism.

vandoise, *n.f.*, (ich.) dart; dace.

*vanille, *n.f.*, (bot.) vanilla, vanilla-tree; (bot.) vanilla (fruit).

*vanillier, *n.m.*, (bot.) vanilla-tree, vanilla.

vanité, *n.f.*, vanity, self-conceit. *Que vous avez de* —! how full of vanity you are! *Faire — d'une chose;* to be proud of a thing. *Sans* —; vanity apart.

vaniteu-x, -se, *adj.*, vainglorious, absurdly vain.

vannage, *n.m.*, (agri.) winnowing; (hydraul.) system of water-gates in a dam, etc.

vanne, *n.f.*, water-gate, sluice, sluice-gate; paddle-door. *adj.* *Eaux* —*s;* waste waters (from factories, etc.).

vanneau, *n.m.*, (orni.) lapwing, peewit, plover.

vanner, *v.a.*, to winnow, to fan, to sift, to hull; (hydraul.) to make, *or* to place, water-gates in dams, etc.

vannerie (va-n-rî), *n.f.*, basket-trade; basket-work.

vannet, *n.m.*, scallop, scollop (shell-fish).

vannette, *n.f.*, server, flat basket (to give horses their corn). — *crible;* oat-sieve.

vanneur, *n.m.*, winnower.

vannier, *n.m.*, basket-maker.

******vantail,** *n.m.*, leaf of a folding-door; window-shutter; lock-gate. *Fermer les vantaux;* to shut the folding-doors.

vantard, -e, *n.* and *adj.*, boaster, bragger; braggart; boasting, boastful; bragging.

vantardise, *n.f.*, (fam.) habitual boasting, bragging.

vanter, *v.a.*, to vaunt, to cry up, to praise up, to extol.

se **vanter,** *v.r.*, to boast, to vaunt, to brag; to praise one's self; to plume one's self upon. *Il n'y a pas de quoi se* —; there is nothing to brag of.

vanterie (văn-trî), *n.f.*, boasting, bragging, vaunting; brag, boast.

⊙**vanteur,** *n.m.* *V.* **vantard.**

va-nu-pieds, *n.m.* and *f.*, (—) tatterdemalion, ragged rascal, ragamuffin, waif and stray; vagabond, beggar.

vapeur, *n.f.*, vapor, fume, steam, damp, exhalation. *pl.*, vapors, hysterics. *A la* —; by steam. *Bateau à* —; steam-boat, steamer. *Remorqueur à* —; steam-tug. *Chaudière à* —; steam-boiler. *Machine à* —; steam-engine. *Registre de* —; throttle-valve (of a steam-engine). *En* —; with the steam on. *A toute* —; at full speed. *Mettre en* —; to put the steam on, to get up steam. *On est en pleine* —; steam is up.

vapeur, *n.m.*, steamer. — *poste;* mail-steamer.

vaporeu-x, -se, *adj.*, vaporous, vaporish; (paint.) aerial.

vaporisation, *n.f.*, vaporization.

vaporiser, *v.a.*, to vaporize.

se **vaporiser,** *v.r.*, to vaporize, to be vaporized.

vaquer (va-ké), *v.n.*, to be vacant, void, empty; to be in vacation-time, not to sit; to attend, to devote one's self to. *Il vaque à ses affaires;* he is attending to his business.

******varaigne,** *n.f.*, tide-sluice (of salt marshes).

varaire, *n.f.*, (bot.) white hellebore.

varangue (-răng), *n.f.*, (nav.) floor-timbers of a ship. — *plate* or — *de fond;* flat floor-timber. — *fort acculée;* rising floor-timber (amidships).

vare, *n.f.*, Spanish measure of length, about a yard.

varec or **varech,** *n.m.*, (bot.) varec, wrack, sea-wrack, sea-weed; (jur.) wreck (things washed upon the shore by the sea); sunken ship.

varenne, *n.f.*, waste-land; (hunt.) ⊙ chase, royal preserve.

vareuse, *n.f.*, oil-skin (jacket); pilot-jacket; jersey, blazer.

variabilité, *n.f.*, variableness, variability, changeableness; (alg.) variability.

variable, *adj.*, variable, changeable, fickle, unsettled, unsteady. *La fortune est* —; fortune is fickle. *Pouls* —; changeable pulse.

variable, *n.m.*, variable, change. *Le baromètre est au* —; the barometer is at change.

variant, -e, *adj.*, (l.u.) variable, fickle.

variante, *n.f.*, different reading, *or* interpretation; various, *or* different, spelling; alteration, difference (in different editions of a book), etc.

variation, *n.f.*, variation, variety, change, changeableness; alteration.

varice, *n.f.*, (med.) varix, varicose vein.

varicelle, *n.f.*, (med.) varicella, swine-pox.

varicocèle, *n.f.*, (med.) varicocela.

varier, *v.a.*, to vary, to variegate, to diversify. — *la phrase;* to say the same thing in other words.

varier, *v.n.*, to vary, to change, to be changeable; to disagree, to be at variance; to be fickle.

variété, *n.f.*, variety, diversity, change. *pl.*, miscellanea; varieties; medley; extracts.

ne **varietur** (né varié-tur), (jur.) in order that no change may be made; "final edition" of an author's works.

variole, *n.f.*, small-pox, variola.

varioleu-x, -se, *adj.* and *n.*, (a person) suffering from small-pox.

variolique, *adj.*, (med.), variolous, variolar, variolic.

variolite, *n.f.*, (min.) variolite.

varioloïde, *n.f.*, (med.) varioloid, chicken-pox.

variorum, *n.m.* and *adj.*, (—) variorum. *Edition* —; variorum edition.

variqueu-x, -se, *adj.*, varicose, varicous.

⊙**varlet,** *n.m.*, varlet, page.

varlope, *n.f.*, jointer, jointing-plane.

vasculaire or (l.u.) **vasculeu-x, -se,** *adj.*, (anat.) vascular.

vase, *n.m.*, vase, vessel, urn. —*s antiques;* antique vases. —*s étrusques;* Etruscan vases. —*s cinéraires;* funeral urns. — *de nuit;* chamber utensil.

vase, *n.f.*, slime, mud, mire, ooze, silt.

vaseu-x, -se, *adj.*, slimy, muddy, miry, silty, oozy.

vasi-er, -ère, *n.* and *adj.*, mud, of mud.

vasière, *n.f.*, salt-pan, brine-pan; mussel-bed.

vasistas (-tâs), *n.m.*, casement-window, casement; hatch-door; shutter; blind (of a carriage).

vasque, *n.f.*, basin (of a fountain).

vassal, *n.m.*, vassal.

vassalité, *n.f.*, vassalage; land held by vassals.

vasselage (vas-laj), *n.m.*, vassalage.

vaste, *adj.*, vast, wide, great, spacious, extensive. — *pays;* vast country. *De* —*s desseins;* great designs. *Un lieu* —; a vast place. *int.* (nav.) avast!

vastement, *adv.*, vastly, extensively, hugely, widely, greatly.

vatican, *n.m.*, Vatican, the Palace of the Pope.

va-tout, *n.m.*, (—) staking all one has, one's all (at cards).

à **vau-de-route,** *adv.* *V.* **à vau-l'eau.**

vaudeville (vôd-vil), *n.m.*, (thea.) vaudeville; ballad; (thea.) ballad-opera, ballad-farce (corruption of *Vaux de Vire*, by Olivier Basselin).

vaudevilliste, *n.m.*, vaudeville-writer; ballad-writer.

vaudois, *n.m.*, Vaudois, native of Vaud.

à **vau-l'eau,** *adv.*, with the current, down stream; (fig.) to wrack and ruin; at sixes and sevens.

vaurien (-in), *n.m.*, good-for-nothing wretch, worthless fellow, scamp, scape-grace; rogue, vagabond.

vautour, *n.m.*, (orni.) vulture.

vautrait, *n.m.*, (hunt.) boar-hunting equipage.

vautre, *n.m.*, boar-hound.

vautré, -e, *adj.*, wallowing, weltering; sprawling.

se **vautrer,** *v.r.*, to wallow, to welter, to roll; to spread one's self out, to sprawl.

vavasseur, *n.m.*, vavasor (vassal of a vassal).

vayvodat, *n.m.*, waywodate, waywodeship.

vayvode, *n.m.*, (—*s*) waiwode, waywode.

vayvodie, *n.f.*, waywodeship.

veau, *n.m.*, calf; bull-calf; calf's leather;

veal; lazy fellow. — *marin;* seal, sea-calf; sealskin. *Chair de* —; veal. *Longe de* —; loin of veal. *Rouelle de* —; fillet of veal. *Des pieds de* —; calves' feet. *Eau de* —; veal broth. *Faire le pied de* —; (fig.) to cringe, to bow and scrape, to truckle (to). *Faire le* —; to sprawl; to indulge one's self, to idle one's time away.

vecteur, *adj.,* (astron.) vector. *Rayon* —; radius vector.

Véda, *n.m.,* Veda (sacred books of the Hindoos).

védasse, *n.f.,* (dy.) weed-ashes.

vedette, *n.f.,* scout, vedette, mounted sentinel; watch-box, watch-tower. *Ecrire quelque chose en* —; to write anything in a line by itself. *Mettre en* —; to place on vedette.

védique, *adj.,* Vedic.

végétable, *adj.,* capable of vegetation.

végétal, *n.m.,* vegetable; plant.

végétal, -e, *adj.,* vegetable.

végétalité, *n.f.,* vegetability.

végétant, -e, *adj.,* vegetating.

végétarien, -ne, *n.m.f.,* vegetarian.

végétati-f, -ve, *adj.,* vegetative.

végétation, *n.f.,* vegetation.

végéter, *v.n.,* to vegetate. *Il ne fait plus que* —; he merely vegetates.

véhémence, *n.f.,* vehemence, vehemency, impetuosity; force, violence.

véhément, -e, *adj.,* vehement, impetuous, hot, passionate. *Naturel* —; hot temper. *Orateur* —; vehement orator, impassioned orator.

véhémentement, *adv.,* ⊙ (jur.) strongly; (fam., fig.) vehemently.

véhicule, *n.m.,* vehicle.

vehme, *n.f.,* (n.p.) Vehmic Court.

vehmique, *adj.,* Vehmic.

*veille, *n.f.,* watch, watching, sitting up; eve, vigil, day before; point, verge. *Etre à la — de;* to be on the point of, on the verge of. *Entre la — et le sommeil;* between sleeping and waking.

*veillée, *n.f.,* sitting up to work in company; evening (in company); night attendance (upon a sick person). *Les —s d'hiver;* the winter evenings.

*veiller, *v.n.,* to watch, to sit up, to wake, to be awake, to lie awake; to be on the watch; to attend, to take care, to see, to have an eye upon. — *au salut de l'état;* to watch over the safety of the state. — *sur soi même;* to be upon one's guard. *Faire — quelqu'un;* to keep any one up. *Veillez-y;* see to it.

*veiller, *v.a.,* to watch over, to look after, to sit up with. — *un malade;* to sit up with, *or* to watch by the bedside of, a sick person.

*veilles, *n.f.pl.,* labors; night-studies, nightwatches, vigils.

*veilleur, *n.m.,* watcher; night watchman.

*veilleuse, *n.f.,* night-lamp; float-light, watchlight.

*veillote *or* **veillotte,** *n.f.,* hay-cock; (bot.) meadow-saffron.

veinage, *n.m.,* (paint.) veining.

veinard, *n.m.* and *adj.,* (pop.) lucky fellow, in luck's way.

veine, *n.f.,* (anat., geol., min.) vein; (of marble *or* wood) vein; (geol.) seam; underground spring of water; (fig.) vein. *Je suis en* —; my hand is in; I am in luck's way. *En — de;* in the vein for, in the humor for. *Bonne* —; good run of luck (at play). *Avoir de la* —; to be in luck. *Je ne suis plus en* —; my luck has turned.

veiné, -e, *adj.,* veiny, veined.

veiner, *v.a.,* (paint.) to vein.

veineu-x, -se, *adj.,* veined, veining; (anat.) venous, venal.

veinule, *n.f.,* (anat.) small vein.

vêlage, *n.m.,* calving (of cows).

vélar, *n.m.,* hedge-mustard, hedge-garlic.

vélarium (-rio-m), *n.m.,* (—*s*) (Rom. antiq.)

velarium (awning stretched above the theater to keep off the sun).

vélaut! *int.,* (hunt.) tally-ho.

velche, *n.m.,* Goth, ignoramus.

velcherie, *n.f.,* ignorance, stupidity.

vêle, *n.f.,* cow-calf.

vêler, *v.a.,* (of cows) to calve.

vélin, *n.m.,* vellum; fine Alençon lace.

vélite, *n.m.,* (Rom. antiq.) light-armed soldier, skirmisher.

velléité (vél-lé-), *n.f.,* velleity, slight desire, fancy, mind.

⊙**véloce,** *adj.,* (astron.) swift, rapid.

vélocipède, *n.m.,* velocipede, cycle.

vélocité, *n.f.,* velocity, swiftness, rapidity, speed.

velours, *n.m.,* velvet. — *ras;* short-nap velvet. — *façonné;* figured velvet. — *de soie;* silk velvet. — *de coton;* cotton velvet. — *à côtes;* corduroy. — *de coton croisé;* velveteen. — *glacé;* shot velvet. *Faire patte de* —; to speak smoothly; to draw in one's claws. *Habits de — ventre de son;* (prov.) silks and satins put out the kitchen fire. *Passe* —; (bot.) prince's feathers.

velouté, *n.m.,* velveting, flock surface; velvetpile; softness; (bot.) velvet; (med.) ⊙mucous membrane.

velouté, -e, *adj.,* velvet, velvety; cut in imitation of velvet; velvet-like; with the softness of velvet; soft and smooth to the palate (of wines).

velouter, *v.a.,* to give (to some material) the appearance of velvet; to make velvet-like.

veloutier (-tié), *n.m.,* velvet-worker.

veltage, *n.m.,* measuring liquids by the *velte.*

velte, *n.f.,* an (obsolete) measure of capacity, about 7 quarts English; a sort of gauge to measure the capacity of casks.

velter, *v.a.,* to measure liquids by the *velte.*

velteur, *n.m.,* gauger; one who measures by the *velte.*

velu, -e, *adj.,* hairy (not applied to the head or beard); shaggy, rough. *n.m.,* shagginess; hairy part.

velverette, *n.f.,* corduroy.

velvet, *n.m.,* **velvetine,** *n.f.,* velveteen.

velvote, *n.f.,* (bot.) (spurious) toad-flax.

venaison, *n.f.,* venison.

vénal, -e, *adj.,* venal, mercenary.

vénalement (-nal-mān), *adv.,* in a venal, mercenary manner.

vénalité, *n.f.,* venality.

venant, *n.m.* and *adj.,* comer; coming. *A tout* —; to the first comer; to any one, *or* as the fancy takes one.

vendable, *adj.,* salable, vendible.

vendange, *n.f.,* vintage; grape-gathering. *Faire* —; to gather the grapes; (fig.) to make a good thing of, to profit by.

vendanger, *v.a.* and *n.,* to gather grapes; to vintage; (fig.) to make illicit profits; to ravage, to spoil, to devastate, to sweep away.

vendangeu-r, *n.m.,* **-se,** *n.f.,* vintager, grapegatherer.

vendéen, -ne, *n.,* *adj.,* Vendean.

vendémiaire, *n.m.,* Vendémiaire, the first month of the calendar of the first French republic, from September 22d *or* 23d to October 21st *or* 22d.

venderesse (vān-drès), *n.f.,* (jur.) vendor.

vendetta, *n.f.,* (—*s*) vendetta, vengeance.

vendeu-r, *n.m.,* **-se,** *n.f.,* seller, vendor, dealer. — *d'orviétan;* quack.

vendication, *n.f.* V. **revendication.**

vendiquer, *v.a.* V. **revendiquer.**

⊙**vendition,** *n.f.,* (jur.) sale.

vendre, *v.a.* and *n.,* to sell, to vend, to sell out; (fig.) to betray. — *cher;* to sell dear. — *à bon marché;* to sell cheap. — *argent comptant;* to sell for ready money. *A* —; to be sold, for sale. *Chose qui plaît est à moitié vendue;* good wares make quick sales.

se **vendre,** *v.r.,* to sell one's self; to sell, to go off (of a thing).

vendredi, *n.m.,* Friday. *Le — saint;* Good-Friday.

vené, -e, *adj.,* high (of meat).

⊙**vénéfice,** *n.m.,* (jur.) poisoning by malefice.

⊙**venelle,** *n.f.,* small street, alley, lane. [Only used in the popular expression *Enfiler la* —; to run away, to take to one's heels.]

vénéneu-x, -se, *adj.,* venomous, poisonous (of plants only).

vener, *v.a.,* to run (cattle) to make their flesh tender. *Faire — de la viande;* to keep meat until it gets high.

vénérable, *adj.,* venerable, reverend.

vénérablement, *adv.,* venerably, reverently.

vénération, *n.f.,* veneration. *Sa mémoire est en* —; his memory is held in veneration.

vénérer, *v.a.,* to venerate, to reverence.

vénerie (vé-n-rî) *n.f.,* venery, hunting; hunting-train; kennel.

vénérien, -ne (-in, -è-n), *adj.,* venereal, syphilitic.

venette, *n.f.,* (pop.) fright, funk. *Avoir la* —; to be in a funk. *Donner la* —; to frighten, to put into a funk.

veneur, *n.m.,* huntsman. *Grand* —; master of the hounds.

venez-y-voir, *n.m.,* (—) (fam., iron.) sight, show, raree-show; trifle, catch, cheat.

vengeance (-jans), *n.f.,* vengeance, revenge. *Tirer — d'un affront;* to be revenged for an affront. *Demander,* or *crier,* —; to call, or cry, for vengeance. *Esprit de* —; revengefulness. *Par* —; out of revenge.

venger, *v.a.,* to revenge, to avenge, to take revenge for, to resent. *— une injure;* to avenge an injury.

se **venger,** *v.r.,* to revenge one's self, to avenge one's self; to be revenged. *Se — de quelqu'un;* to be revenged on any one.

venge-ur, -resse, *n.* and *adj.,* avenger, revenger; revengeful, avenging.

véniel, -le, *adj.,* venial.

véniellement (-nièl-mān), *adv.,* venially.

veni-mecum (vé-ni-mé-co-m), *n.m.,* (—). V. **vade-mecum.**

venimeu-x, -se, *adj.,* communicating poison, venomous (of animals); poisonous, malignant.

venin, *n.m.,* venom, poison, spite, rancor, malice. *Morte la bête, mort le* —; dead dogs can't bite *or* dead men tell no tales. *Il a jeté tout son* —; he has vented all his spite.

venir (venant, venu), *v.n.,* to come, to be coming; to come along, to arrive; to chance, to fall out, to occur, to happen; to be descended; to grow, to grow up, to thrive (of plants); to issue, to run, to flow; to emanate, to proceed, to arise, to derive; to reach. *Je le vois* —; I see him coming; (fig.) I see what he is driving at. *Le voilà qui vient;* here he comes. *Venez ici;* come here. *Voulez-vous — avec nous à Londres?* will you go with us to London? *Faire* —; to send for. *Faire — le médecin;* to send for the doctor. *Il va et vient;* he goes in and out. *Il s'en est allé comme il est venu;* he has had his labor for his pains. *Je ne ferai qu'aller et* —; I will not stay, I shall be back again directly. *En — aux extrémités;* to come to extremities. *S'en* —; to come away. *Il en vint jusqu'à le menacer;* he went so far as to threaten him. *En — aux mains;* to come to blows. *Il en faut — là;* we must come to that at last. *Si ma lettre venait à se perdre;* if my letter should happen to be lost, *or* to miscarry. *Tout lui vient à souhait;* everything succeeds according to his wishes. *Cette nouvelle est venue jusqu'à moi;* that news reached even me.

Il me vint une pensée; a thought came into my head. *D'où vient-il que?* how is it that? *D'où vient cela?* what is the cause of that? *D'où vient que?* how is it that? *Quand il vint à parler de;* when he came to speak of. *— au monde;* to come into the world. *— de;* to come from; (followed by an infinitive) to have just. *Je viens de le quitter;* I have just left him. *Se faire bien — de;* to ingratiate one's self (with), to curry favor (with). *Il vient de partir;* he has only just gone, *or* started. *Il vient d'arriver;* he has just arrived. *Je viens le voir;* I come to see him. *Je viens de le voir;* I have just seen him. *Cet arbre vient bien;* that tree thrives well. *Viens donc, venez donc;* come away, come along. *Où voulez-vous en —?* what are you aiming, driving, at? *D'où venez-vous?* where do you come from? where were you brought up? *Il faut le voir —;* we must first see what he is driving at. *Vouloir en — à;* to aim at, to be driving at, to mean, to be up to. *Temps à —;* future time. *— à bout de;* to succeed, to master, to get through (anything). *Tout vient à point à qui sait attendre;* everything comes to him who waits. *C'est un beau — y voir;* a pretty sight, indeed!

venir, *n.m.,* coming.

vent, *n.m.,* wind, gale; flatulence; breath; (hunt.) scent; vanity, emptiness; (artil.) windage. *Un souffle de* —; a puff of wind. *Un — coulis;* a slight draught. *Il fait du* —; it is windy. *Etre à l'abri du* —; to be sheltered from the wind. *Jeter la plume au* —; to allow chance to decide. *Autant en emporte le* —; all that is idle talk. *Aller comme le* —; to go swiftly, like the wind. *Aller selon le* —; to sail with the wind; (fig.) to go with the times; to be a time-server. *— fait;* settled wind. *Au* —; to the wind; (nav.) to windward. *Sous le* —; (nav.) to leeward. *— de terre;* land breeze. *— de mer;* sea breeze. *Avoir — et marée;* to have both wind and tide (in one's favor). *Avoir le dessus du* —; (nav.) to have the weather-gauge; (fig.) to have the upper hand of any one. *Avoir des —s;* to be troubled with wind, flatulence (fig.). *Lâcher un* —; to break a wind. *Tout cela n'est que du* —; all that means nothing. *Si le — le permet;* weather permitting. *Filer — arrière;* (nav.) to sail before the wind. *Gagner le — sur;* to get to windward of; to weather. *Prendre le* —; to scent; (nav.) to sail near the wind. *frais;* fresh gale. *Gros coup de* —; strong gale. *Etre logé aux quatre —s;* to be exposed to every wind that blows. *Avoir le — contraire;* to have the wind against one. *Flotter au gré du* —; to float in the wind. *Iles du* —; (geog.) Windward Islands. *— au visage rend un homme sage;* (prov.) adversity makes a man wise, not rich.

*****ventail,** *n.m.,* (her.) ventail, visor (of a helmet).

vente, *n.f.,* sale; selling, auction; felling, cutting out (of timber). *En* —; for sale, now ready (of a book). *Mettre en* —; to offer for sale; to put up for sale, to publish (a book). *— aux enchères;* auction. *— judiciaire;* sale under warrant, *or* before the sheriff. *Marchandise de bonne* —; goods that go off well. *Asseoir les —s;* to mark the trees that are to be felled. *Lods et —s;* tax on the sale of heritages.

ventelle, *n.f.* paddle-valve (of lock-gates).

venter, *v.n.imp.,* to blow, to be windy. *Il vente;* the wind is blowing, it is windy.

venteu-x, -se, *adj.,* windy, flatulent.

ventier, *n.m.,* wood-salesman.

ventilateur, *n.m.,* ventilator, fan; (phys.) air-exhauster.

ventilation, *n.f.,* ventilation, airing; (jur.) valuation.

ventiler, *v.a.,* to ventilate, to air; (jur.) to value; (fig.) to discuss, to moot.

ventis, *n.m.,* wind-fallen timber.

ventolier, *n.m.*, (hawking) bird that flies well against the wind.

ventôse, *n.m.*, Ventose, the sixth month of the calendar of the first French republic, from February 19th or 20th to March 20th.

ventosité, *n.f.*, flatulence, ventosity.

ventouse, *n.f.*, cupping-glass, sucker ; the devil-fish ; ventilator, vent-hole, air-hole ; (arch.) ventiduct. *pl.*, cupping-glasses. *Appliquer les —s ;* to cup. *—s-sèches ;* dry-cupping.

ventouser, *v.a.*, to cup.

ventouseur, *n.m.*, cupper.

ventral, -e *adj.*, ventral.

ventre, *n.m.*, belly, stomach; (of bottles) belly; womb; chest, body, inside. *— à terre ;* at full speed. *Passer sur le — à ;* to bear down upon, to rout, to put to rout. *Prendre du — ;* to get a corporation. *Le bas— ;* (anat.) the abdomen. *J'ai mal au — ;* I have a stomach-ache. *Remettre le cœur au — à quelqu'un ;* to give any one fresh courage. *A plat — ;* flat on the face. *Faire — ;* to bulge, to swell out. *Manger à — déboutonné ;* to eat like a glutton. *— affamé n'a point d'oreilles ;* a hungry man will not listen to reason *or* a hungry man is an angry man. *Savoir ce que quelqu'un a dans le — ;* (fam.) to know what a person is worth, *or* is thinking of. *N'avoir pas à trois mois dans le — ;* (fam.) not to have three months to live. *— affamé prend tout à gré ;* any food is good food when you are starving.

ventrebleu ! *int.* zounds !

ventrée, *n.f.*, litter (of animals).

ventricule, *n.m.*, ventricle.

ventrière, *n.f.*, girth (of a horse), belly-band, abdominal belt; sling ; (carp.) purlin ; (machinery) brace.

ventriloque, *n.m.* and *adj.*, ventriloquist ; ventriloquous, ventriloquial.

ventriloquie, *n.f.*, ventriloquy, ventriloquism.

*se **ventrouiller**, *v.r.*, to wallow in the mire, *or* in the mud.

ventru, -e, *adj.*, big-bellied, corpulent; bulging (out).

venu, -e, *part.*, come. *Bien — ;* welcome, well-grown (of trees, etc.). *Mal — ;* ill-received ; not welcome ; ill-grown, stunted (of trees, etc.) ; not justified, wrong. *Le premier —, la première —e ;* the first-comer, the first that comes, the first person one meets, any one, no matter which *or* who. *Le dernier — ;* the last comer. *Nouveau — ;* new-comer (*m.s.*). *Des nouveaux —s ;* new-comers (*m.pl.*). *Une nouvelle —e ;* a new-comer (*f.s.*). *Des nouvelles —es ;* new-comers (*f.pl.*).

venue, *n.f.*, coming, arrival, advent, growth. *Allées et —s ;* goings and comings. *Tout d'une —* ; at a stretch, all at once. *A la bonne — ;* come what may, at all hazards.

☉**vénule**. *n.f.* V. **veinule**.

vénus (-nus), *n.f.*, (astron., myth.) Venus ; ☉ (chem.) copper.

vénusté, *n.f.*, (l.u.) handsomeness, gracefulness, elegance.

vêpres, *n.f.pl.*, vespers.

ver (vèr), *n.m.*, worm, maggot ; moth ; mite. *— luisant ;* glowworm. *— de fumier ;* muckworm. *— à soie ;* silk-worm. *— rongeur ;* neverdying worm. *— de fromage ;* cheese-mite. *— solitaire ;* tape-worm. *—de terre ;* earth-worm. *Mangé, or rongé, des —s ;* worm-eaten. *Nu comme — ;* stark naked. *Tuer son — ;* (pop.) to have a morning nip.

véracité, *n.f.*, veracity.

véraison, *n.f.*, turning, ripening (of grapes).

véranda, *n.f.*, verandah.

vératre, *n.m.*, (bot.) veratrum.

vératrine, *n.f.*, (chem.) veratria, veratrine.

verbal, -e, *adj.*, verbal. *Promesse —e ;* promise by word of mouth.

verbalement (-bal-mān), *adv.*, verbally, by word of mouth.

verbaliser, *v.n.*, to draw up a written statement ; to state facts, to be long-winded.

verbe, *n.m.*, (gram.) verb ; voice ; (theol.) the Word.

verbénacées, *n.f.pl.*, (bot.) verbenaceæ.

verbération, *n.f.*, verberation.

verbeusement, *adv.*, verbosely, with many words.

verbeu-x, -se, *adj.*, verbose, prolix.

verbiage, *n.m.*, verbiage.

verbiager, *v.n.*, to be verbose.

verbiageu-r, *n.m.*, **-se**, *n.f.*, verbose, *or* wordy, talker ; twaddler.

verbosité, *n.f.*, verbosity.

ver-coquin, *n.m.*, (—s—s) (ent.) vine-grub; (vet.) staggers ; caprice, whim.

verd, *adj.* V. **vert**.

verdal, *n.m.*, basement-light, cellar-light.

verdâtre, *adj.*, greenish.

verdée, *n.f.*, white wine of Tuscany.

verdelet, -te, *adj.*, tart (of wine) ; vigorous, strong, hale (of old people).

verderie, *n.f.*, verderer's range ; verderer's jurisdiction.

verdet, *n.m.*, verdigris.

verdeur, *n.f.*, greenness, viridity, sap ; tartness, harshness (of wine) ; acrimony ; (of old people) vigor, freshness.

verdict (-dikt), *n.m.*, (jur.) verdict, finding. *Rendre un — ;* to deliver a verdict.

verdier, *n.m.*, verderer, verderor ; (orni.) greenfinch, green-linnet.

verdir, *v.a.* and *n.*, to paint green; to grow green, to become green ; to get covered with verdigris (of copper).

verdoyant, -e, *adj.*, verdant, green.

verdoyer, *v.n.*, to be verdant, to become green.

verdure, *n.f.*, verdure, greenness, green ; potherbs.

verdurier, *n.m.*, greengrocer.

véreu-x, -se, *adj.*, worm-eaten, maggoty, full of maggots, rotten ; suspicious, suspected of a concealed vice *or* defect ; (com.) (of bills) insecure, unsafe, doubtful.

verge, *n.f.*, rod, wand ; shank (of an anchor) ; handle (of a whip) ; penis. *pl.*, rod, birch (old) ; yard (measure). *— de bedeau ;* verger's wand. *Cet enfant craint les —s ;* that child fears the rod. *Donner des —s pour se faire fouetter ;* to give a rod to beat one's self. *Passer (quelqu'un) par les —s ;* (mil.) to flog. *Etre passé par les —s or passer par les —s ;* to run the gauntlet. *Faire passer (un soldat) par les—s ;* (mil.) to flog through the lines.

vergé, -e, *adj.*, (of paper) laid; (of textile fabrics) streaky.

vergée, *n.f.*, about a rood.

verger, *v.a.*, to measure by the rod.

verger, *n.m.*, fruit-garden, orchard.

vergeté, -e, *part.*, beaten (cleaned with a cane) ; streaked (of skin).

vergeter, *v.a.*, to beat, to whisk, to brush (with a cane).

vergetier (-tié), *n.m.*, brushmaker, rodmaker.

vergette, *n.f.*, brush, clothes-brush, bundle of rods, switch (generally used in the plural) ; hoops (of a drum). *Donner un coup de —s (à) ;* to give a brushing, to brush.

vergeure (-jur), *n.f.*, wire-mark (of paper).

verglacé, -e, *part. adj.*, covered with rime, coated over with frost, frozen over.

verglacer, *v.imp.* (old). *Il verglace ;* the rain freezes as it falls. V. **verglas**.

verglas, *n.m.*, glazed frost, frozen rain, rime. *Il fait — or il tombe du — ;* the rain freezes as it falls.

***vergne**, *n.m.*, alder-tree.

***vergogne**, *n.f.*, shame. *Sans— ;* shameless.

vergogneu-x, -se, *adj.*, shy, reserved, modest, bashful.

vergue (vèrg), *n.f.*, (nav.) yard (of a sail). *Grande* —; main-yard.

véricle, *n.f.*, paste, imitation (jewelry).

véridicité, *n.f.*, veracity, credibility.

véridique, *adj.*, veracious, credible.

véridiquement, *adv.*, veraciously, truthfully.

vérificateur, *n.m.*, verifier, examiner (of work); auditor (of accounts).

vérification, *n.f.*, verification, examining, auditing; (of wills) probate.

vérifier, *v.a.*, to inspect, to examine, to verify; to try (weights, measures); to audit, to prove (a will).

vérin, *n.m.*, screw-jack.

vérine, *n.f.*, verinas (tobacco); (nav.) binnacle-lamp.

vérissime, *adj.*, most true, most faithful.

véritable, *adj.*, true, genuine, pure, real, staunch. *Un — ami ;* a true friend.

véritablement, *adv.*, truly, really, in reality, indeed, in truth.

véritas, *n.m.*, Lloyd's register (French). *Bureau —;* (French) Lloyd's rooms.

vérité, *n.f.*, truth, verity, truthfulness. *Dire la —;* to speak the truth. *En —;* indeed, truly. *A la —;* indeed ; it is true ; I confess. *Toute — n'est pas bonne à dire ;* all truths are not to be spoken at all times. *On dit souvent la — en riant ;* there 's many a true word spoken in jest. *Dire ses —s à quelqu'un ;* (not to be afraid) to tell any one his faults ; to be outspoken with any one.

verjus, *n.m.*, verjuice ; sour grapes. *C'est jus vert et —;* it is six of one and half a dozen of the other.

verjuté, -e, *adj.*, sharp, tart, acid.

verjuter, *v.a.*, to flavor with verjuice.

***vermeil, -le**, *adj.*, vermilion, ruby, ruddy, rosy, coral. *Teint —;* rosy complexion.

***vermeil**, *n.m.*, silver-gilt.

vermicel or **vermicelle**, *n.m.*, vermicelli.

vermicelier, *n.m.*, vermicelli manufacturer.

vermiculaire, *adj.*, vermicular, worm-shaped; (anat.) vermiform.

vermiculaire, *n.f.*, (bot.) stone-crop.

vermiculé, -e, *adj.*, (arch.) vermicular, vermiculated.

vermiculures, *n.f.pl.*, (arch.) vermiculated work.

vermiforme, *adj.*, worm-shaped ; (anat.) vermiform.

vermifuge, *n.m.*, (med.) vermifuge.

***vermiller**, *v.n.*, (hunt.) (of boars) to scratch for worms, etc.

***vermillon**, *n.m.*, vermilion.

***vermillonner**, *v.a.*, to vermilion ; to paint in red.

vermine, *n.f.*, vermin, (fig.) rabble.

vermineu-x, -se, *adj.*, (med.) caused by worms.

vermisseau, *n.m.*, vermicule, grub, earth-worm, little worm.

*se***vermouler**, *v.r.*, to be worm-eaten.

vermoulu, -e, *adj.*, worm-eaten, decayed, crumbling to pieces.

vermoulure, *n.f.*, worm-hole, rottenness in wood, dry-rot.

vermout or **vermouth**, *n.m.*, bitters.

vernaille, *n.f.*, (min.) telesia.

vernal, -e, *adj.*, vernal, spring-like.

vernation, *n.f.*, (bot.) vernation, foliation.

verne, *n.m.*, (bot.). *V.* **vergne**.

vernier, *n.m.*, vernier, sliding-rule.

vernir, *v.a.*, to varnish ; to glaze; to japan, to lacquer, to polish.

vernis, *n.m.*, varnish, polish, glaze, glazing. *— gras ;* oil-varnish. *Donner un — à ;* to polish, to set off.

vernissage, *n.m.*, varnishing ; glazing.

vernisser, *v.a.*, to varnish, to glaze, to japan.

vernisseur, *n.m.*, varnisher.

vernissure, *n.f.*, the application of varnish, or glazing, on anything.

vérole, *n.f.*, pox. *La petite —;* the small-pox. *Grain de petite —;* pock-mark. *Petite — volante ;* chicken pox.

vérolé, -e, *n.* and *adj.*, (l.ex.) (med.) poxed, syphilitic.

vérolique, *adj.*, (med.) syphilitic.

véron, *n.m.* *V.* **vairon**.

véronique, *n.f.*, (bot.) veronica, speedwell.

***verraille**, *n.f.*, small glass wares ; old glass.

verrat, *n.m.*, boar.

verre, *n.m.*, glass. *— à boire ;* drinking glass. *Choquer les —s ;* to touch glasses. *— grossissant ;* magnifying-glass. *— ardent ;* burning-glass. *Grand —;* tumbler. *— à pied ;* rummer. *— à vin ;* wine-glass. *— de vin ;* glass of wine. *— de couleur ;* stained glass, colored glass.

verrée, *n.f.*, glassful.

verrerie (vér-rî), *n.f.*, glass-works ; glass-making ; glass-wares.

verrier, *n.m.*, glass-maker, glassman, glass-blower; dealer in glassware ; glass-basket.

verrière, *n.f.*, glass-stand, monteith ; (in churches) stained window.

verrine or **verrière**, *n.f.*, glazed box ; glass picture frame.

verroterie (vè-ro-trî), *n.f.*, glass-ware ; glass trinket ; glass beads.

verrou, *n.m.*, bolt. *Fermer une porte au —;* to bolt a door. *S'enfermer au —;* to bolt one's self in. *Au —;* under lock and key, locked up.

verrouiller, *v.a.*, to bolt, to bar.

***se* verrouiller**, *v.r.*, to bolt one's self in.

verrucaire, *n.f.*, (bot.) wartwort.

verrue, *n.f.*, wart.

verruqueu-x, -se, *adj.*, warty ; wart-like; verrucose ; (med.) tubercled.

vers (vèr), *n.m.*, verse, line (of poetry). *Faire des —;* to write verses. *Grand —;* Alexandrine (twelve-syllabled verse).

vers, *prep.*, towards, about, to. *Tournez-vous — moi ;* turn towards me. *— les quatre heures ;* about four o'clock.

versable, *adj.*, apt to overturn, liable to upset.

versade, *n.f.*, upsetting, overturning.

versage, *n.m.*, (agri.) first dressing (of land).

versant, -e, *adj.*, liable to be overturned.

versant, *n.m.*, declivity, side, slope (of mountains) ; watershed.

versatile, *adj.*, versatile, variable, changeable.

versatilité, *n.f.*, versatility variableness.

verse, *adj.*, (geom.) versed. *Sinus —;* versed sine.

à **verse**, *adv.*, (of rain) very fast, in torrents. *Il pleut à —;* it is raining in torrents, *or* cats and dogs.

versé, -e, *part.adj.*, poured, overturned; (fig.) versed, skilled, conversant.

verseau, *n.m.*, (astron.) Aquarius.

versement, *n.m.*, payment ; deposit. *— partiel ;* installment.

verser, *v.a.*, to pour, to pour out ; to shoot, to discharge, to empty ; to shed, to spill ; to lodge, to deposit (money) ; to overturn, to upset, to cast, to throw.

verser, *v.n.*, to overturn, to upset, to be over-turned, to overset (of vehicles); to be laid, to be beaten down (of standing corn).

verset, *n.m.*, (Bibl.) verse.

versicules or **versiculets**, *n.m.pl.*, (fam., jest.) little verses, versicles.

versificateur, *n.m.*, versifier, poetaster.

versification, *n.f.*, versification.

versifier, *v.n.*, to versify, to make verses.

versifier, v.a., to turn into verses.

se **versifier**, v.r., to be versified, to be put into verse.

version, n.f., version, translation.

verso, n.m., (—s) back (of a leaf); (print.) reverse, even, left-hand page.

versoir, n.m., mold-board (of a plow).

verste, n.f., verst (Russian measure of length, about 1166 yards).

vert, -e, adj., green; sharp, harsh (of things); tart (of wine); raw (of hides); vigorous, robust (of old age); resolute. *Bois* —; green wood. *Morue —e ;* salt fish (that has not been yet dried). *Cuir* —; raw leather. *Fruit* —; green fruit. *Du vin* —; tart wine. *Pomme —e;* unripe apple. *Pierres —es;* stones just cut out of the quarry. *Une —e vieillesse ;* a vigorous, or hale, old age. *Une —e réponse ;* a sharp answer. *Ils sont trop —s ;* the grapes are sour. *Il a la tête —e;* he is a hare-brained fellow, *or* a greenhorn.

vert, n.m., green, green color; grass; green meat; green food; tartness (of wine). *— de mer ;* sea-green. *Employer le — et le sec ;* to leave no stone unturned. *Mettre des chevaux au — ;* to turn horses out to grass. *Vous ne le prendrez pas sans —;* you will not catch him napping. *Manger son blé en — ;* (prov.) to anticipate one's income.

vert d'eau *or* **vert de mer**, n.m., sea-green.

vert-de-gris, n.m., (n.p.) verdigris.

vert de vessie, n.m., sap-green.

vert-pomme, n.m., apple-green.

vertébral, -e, adj., vertebral.

vertèbre, n.f., vertebra.

vertébré, -e, adj., vertebral, vertebrate.

vertébré, n.m., (zoöl.) vertebral, vertebrate. *Les —s ;* the vertebrates.

vertement, adv., vigorously, briskly, sharply; harshly, severely. *Je l'ai tancé — ;* I reprimanded him most severely; I gave him a good talking to.

vertical, -e, adj., vertical.

verticalement (-kal-män), adv., vertically.

verticalité, n.f., verticalness.

*verticille, n.m., (bot.) verticil; whorl.

*verticillé, -e, adj., (bot.) verticillate.

verticité, n.f., verticity (of the sea compass).

vertige, n.m., dizziness, giddiness, vertigo, swimming in the head; (vet.) staggers; (fig.) folly, madness, intoxication.

vertigineu-x, -se, adj., giddy, dizzy (of heights, etc.), subject to giddiness.

vertigo, n.m., (—s) vertigo; whim, crotchet; (vet.) staggers.

vertu, n.f., virtue, chastity; property, faculty, quality; power, force. *Faire de nécessité — ;* to make a virtue of necessity. *En — de ;* by virtue of, in pursuance of. *— de ma vie !* why, bless my heart !

⊙**vertubleu ! vertuchou !** int., bless my heart ! zounds !

vertueusement (-efiz-män), adv., virtuously.

vertueu-x, -se, adj., virtuous.

⊙**vertugadin**, n.m., farthingale.

verve, n.f., warmth, fancy, inspiration; animation, liveliness; spirit; fervor; rapture; raciness, humor; (l.u.) fancy, whim, crotchet. *Avoir de la — ;* to be sprightly, spirited.

verveine, n.f., (bot.) vervain, verbena.

vervelle, n.f., (falconry) varvel.

verveux *or* **vervier**, n.m. and adj., hoop-net (for fishing).

vésanie, n.f., (med.) madness, insanity.

vesce, n.f., (bot.) vetch, tare.

vésical, -e, adj., vesical.

vésicant, -e, adj., causing blisters, vesicatory.

vésication, n.f., (med.) vesication.

vésicatoire, n.m. and adj., blister; vesicatory; blistering. *Un emplâtre — ;* a blistering plaster. *Un — ;* a blister. *Mouche à — ;* blister-fly.

vésiculaire, adj., vesicular.

vésicule, n.f., vesicle, bladder.

vésiculeu-x, -se, adj., vesiculate, bladdery.

vesou, n.m., sugar-cane juice.

vespasienne (-zi-èn), n.f., urinal (public).

vesper (vès-pèr), n.m., (astron.) Vesper, Venus.

⊙**vespériser**, v.a., to scold, to reprimand.

vespétro, n.m., ratafia (a cordial).

vesse, n.f., (1.) fizzling (school-slang). *Vesse !* cave! *Avoir la — ;* (fig.) to be in a funk.

vesse-de-loup, n.f., (—s —) (bot.) puff-ball.

vesser, v.n., (l. ex.) to fizzle; (fig.) to funk.

vesseu-r, n.m., **-se**, n.f., (l. ex.) one who fizzles; coward, funk.

vessie, n.f., bladder; blister; (ich.) bladder; (fig.) trifle, nonsense. *— natatoire ;* swimming bladder. *Faire croire que des —s sont des lanternes ;* (prov.) to make any one believe that the moon is made of green cheese. *Il vaut nous faire prendre des —s pour des lanternes;* he would make us believe . . ., etc. *Faire venir des —s ;* to blister.

vessigon, n.m., (vet.) vessicnon, wind-gall.

vesta, n.f., (astron.) Vesta.

vestale, n.f., vestal.

veste, n.f., round jacket.

vestiaire (-ti-èr), n.m., vestiary; robing-room; wardrobe; dressing-room; cloak-room; charity clothing-club; clothes-money (in convents).

vestibule, n.m., vestibule, lobby, hall, porch, gateway; passage.

vestige, n.m., footstep, track; vestige, sign, mark, foot-print; trace, remains.

veston, n.m., lounge-jacket, dress-jacket.

vésuvien, -ne, adj., Vesuvian.

vêtement (vêt-män), n.m., garment; garb. *pl.*, dress, clothes, raiment, wearing apparel. *— manqué ;* misfit.

vétéran, n.m., veteran; unpromoted pupil.

vétérance, n.f., quality of a veteran, veteranship.

vétérinaire, n.m. and adj., veterinary surgeon; veterinary.

*vétillard, -e. V. **vétilleur**.

*vétille, n.f., trifle.

*vétiller, v.n., to trifle, to stand upon trifles.

vétillerie, n.f., hair-splitting.

*vétilleu-r, n.m., -se, n.f., one who stands upon trifles, trifler, hair-splitter.

*vétilleu-x, -se, adj., overnice, fastidious, captious, hair-splitting (of a person); ticklish, minute, tedious, trifling (of a thing).

vêtir (vêtant, vêtu), v.a., to clothe, to vest, to array, to dress.

se **vêtir**, v.r., to put on one's clothes, to dress one's self.

vétiver (-vèr), n.m., (bot.) whorl-flowered bent-grass.

veto (vé-tô), n.m., (n.p.) veto.

vêtu, -e, part., dressed, clothed, clad, arrayed. *Mal — ;* ill-dressed. *— de blanc, de noir ;* dressed in white, in black.

vêture, n.f., taking the habit *or* the veil (of friars and nuns). [*Prise d'habit* is more frequently used.]

vétusté, n.f., antiquity, oldness, decay.

vétyver (-vèr), n.m. V. **vétiver**.

veu-f, -ve, n. and adj., widower; widow; widowed. *Cette église est —ve de son évêque;* this church is deprived of its bishop. *Eglise —ve ;* a church no longer, a cathedral. *Epouser la — ;* (pop.) to be guillotined.

veule, adj., (gard.) too light (of earth); long, small and weak (branches); (pers.) weak, powerless.

veuvage, n.m., widowhood.

veuve, n.f., widow; (bot.) tulip streaked white and violet; (orni.) widow-bird, whidah-finch, vidua.

veuvier, *adj.*, widower.

vexant, -e, *adj.*, vexing, provoking, annoying.

vexat-eur, -rice, *adj.*, vexatious.

vexation, *n.f.*, vexation, molestation, annoyance.

vexatoire, *adj.*, vexatious, annoying.

vexer, *v.a.*, to vex, to plague, to molest, to torment, to annoy.

vexillaire, *n.m.*, (Rom. antiq.) vexillary, standard-bearer.

vexillaire, *adj.*, (nav.) vexillary (of signals made by means of flags); (bot.) having the shape of a flag.

viâ, *prep.*, via, by way of.

viabilité, *n.f.*, (med., jur.) viability (of infants); condition of the roads of a country; good repair.

viable, *adj.*, viable, likely to live.

viaduc, *n.m.*, viaduct.

viag-er, -ère, *adj.*, for life, during life. *Rente —ère;* life-annuity. *Placer en —;* to sink (money); to invest in a life-annuity.

viager, *n.m.*, (fin.) life-interest.

viande, *n.f.*, meat, viand. *— de boucherie or grosse —;* butcher's meat. *Menue —;* fowl and game. *— blanche;* white meat (poultry, veal, etc.). *— noire;* brown meat (game). *Basse —;* inferior, coarse meat. *Un mangeur de —s apprêtées;* a lazy fellow, a sponger.

viander, *v.n.*, (hunt.) to graze (of deer).

viandis, *n.m.*, pasture, grazing (of deer).

viatique, *n.m.*, Viaticum; last sacrament; provisions for a journey; traveling money.

vibord, *n.m.*, (nav.) waist (of a ship).

vibrant, -e, *adj.*, vibrating; vibrant; jarring.

vibration, *n.f.*, vibration.

vibratoire, *adj.*, vibratory.

vibrer, *v.n.*, to vibrate.

vibrion, *n.m.*, (zoöl.) vibrio, microscopic eel.

vicaire, *n.m.*, vicar (delegate); curate of a parish. *Le — de Jésus-Christ;* the Pope. *Grand —;* grand vicar.

vicairie, *n.f.*, or **vicariat**, *n.m.*, curacy, curateship, vicarage, living.

vicarial, -e, *adj.*, vicarial.

vicarier, *v.n.*, to officiate as a curate.

vice, *n.m.*, vice, fault; blemish, defect, flaw, imperfection, error. *Pauvreté n'est pas —;* poverty is no crime. *— de forme;* informality.

vice, *Latin particle*, vice, instead of. [Only used in French in composition with nouns.]

vice-amiral, *n.m.*, (*—-amiraux*), vice-admiral; second ship of a fleet.

vice-amirauté, *n.f.*, (*—-—-s*) vice-admiralty.

*****vice-bailli**, *n.m.*, (*—-—-s*) vice-bailiff.

vice-chancelier, *n.m.*, (*—-—-s*) vice-chancellor.

vice-consul, *n.m.*, (*—-—-s*) vice-consul.

vice-consulat, *n.m.*, (*—-—-s*) vice-consulship.

vice-gérant, *n.m.*, (*—-—-s*) vicegerent, deputy manager.

vice-gérent, *n.m.*, (*—-—-s*) vicegerent.

vice-légat, *n.m.*, (*—-—-s*) vice-legate.

vice-légation, *n.f.*, (*—-—-s*) vice-legateship.

vicennal, -e, *adj.*, vicennial (of twenty years).

vice-préfet, *n.m.*, vice-prefect.

vice-présidence, *n.f.*, (*—-—-s*) vice-presidency.

vice-président, *n.m.*, (*—-—-s*) vice-president.

vice-reine, *n.f.*, (*—-—-s*) vice-queen.

vice-roi, *n.m.*, (*—-—-s*) viceroy.

vice-royauté, *n.f.*, (*—-—-s*) viceroyalty, viceroyship.

vice-sénéchal, *n.m.*, (*—-sénéchaux*) deputy-seneschal.

vice versa, *adv.*, vice versa.

vicié, -e, *adj.*, vitiated, depraved, corrupted; foul (air).

vicier, *v.a.*, to vitiate, to taint, to corrupt, to make or render foul.

se **vicier**, *v.r.*, to become vitiated or corrupt; to become, or get, tainted or foul.

vicieusement (-euz-mān), *adv.*, viciously.

vicieu-x, -se, *adj.*, vicious, faulty, defective.

vicinal, -e, *adj.*, (of roads) parish, parochial, connecting.

vicinalité, *n.f.*, condition of the roads of a parish, connection, communication (of roads).

vicissitude, *n.f.*, vicissitude; revolution, change.

vicomtal, -e, *adj.*, of a viscount or viscountess.

vicomte, *n.m.*, viscount.

vicomté, *n.f.*, viscountship; viscounty.

vicomtesse, *n.f.*, viscountess.

victimaire, *n.m.*, (antiq.) victimarius. *adj.*, of a victim, or victims.

victime, *n.f.*, victim, sufferer. *Etre — de;* to be a sufferer by. *Mourir — de;* to die a victim to.

victimer, *v.a.*, to victimize; to sacrifice; to immolate; to ridicule; to quiz; to make a laughing-stock of.

victoire, *n.f.*, victory, conquest. *Remporter la —;* to gain the victory. *proper noun,* Victoria.

victoria, *n.f.*, victoria, park-phaeton.

victorieuse, *n.f.*, (bot.) a variety of anemone.

victorieusement (-euz-mān), *adv.*, victoriously, triumphantly.

victorieu-x, -se, *adj.*, victorious, triumphant.

victorieux, *n.m.*, (bot.) a variety of carnation.

*****victuaille**, *n.f.*, (l.u.) provisions. *pl.*, (nav.) ⊙stores, victuals, eatables. *V.* **vivres**.

⊙*****victuailleur**, *n.m.*, (nav.) victualer, victualing-agent.

vidage, *n.m.*, emptying.

vidame, *n.m.*, (feudalism) vidame.

vidamé, *n.m.*, or **vidamie**, *n.f.*, dignity of a vidame.

vidange, *n.f.*, clearing, emptying, removing; (of cess-pools) night-work; ullage (of liquor); *pl.*, night-soil; (med.) lochia. *En —;* (of corks) ullaged.

vidangeur, *n.m.*, night-man, scavenger.

vide, *adj.*, empty, void, blank, devoid, destitute, vacant, vacuous; (mus.) open. *Corde à —;* open string.

vide, *n.m.*, void, gap, chasm, hole; vacuum, emptiness, vanity; blank, empty space. *A —;* empty, upon nothing. *Mâcher à —;* (fig.) to feed on false hopes.

vidé, -e, *part.*, emptied, empty. *Jarrets bien —s;* (of a horse) clean hocks.

*****vide-bouteille**, *n.m.*, (*—-—-s*) small country house, country-box (house).

vide-poches, *n.m.*, (*—*) lady's work-table, carriage-basket.

vider, *v.a.*, to empty; to vacate; to decide, to end; to settle; to draw (poultry); to gut (fish); to drain. *— un étang;* to drain a pond. *— une clef;* to bore a key. *— du drap;* to pink cloth. *— un procès;* to adjust, or to settle, a lawsuit. *— un différend;* to settle a dispute. *—ses comptes;* to make up one's accounts. *— les lieux, une province, etc.;* to leave, to be driven from, a place, a province, etc. (by force).

se **vider**, *v.r.*, to be emptied; to empty itself (of a thing); to be settled, to be adjusted.

vidimer, *v.a.*, (jur.) to collate, to compare (the copy of a document with the original).

⊙**vidimus**, *n.m.*, the certifying the copy of a document as conforming to the original.

vidrecome, *n.m.*, (l.u.) tumbler, large drinking-glass.

viduité, *n.f.*, widowhood.

vidure, *n.f.*, emptying, drawing; pinking.

vie, *n.f.*, life, existence, days; morals, character; lifetime; livelihood, living; food, subsistence; way of living, course of life; vitality; spirit, animation. *Rendre la — à quelqu'un;* to restore life to any one. *Rendre la — dure à quelqu'un;* to make any one miserable; to make life a burden to any one. *Etre en —;* to be alive. *Il y va de la —;* it is a case of life and death. *Demander la —;* to beg for life. *Je n'ai rien vu de pareil de ma —;* I never saw anything like it in all my life. *Gagner sa —;* to get one's livelihood. *Mendier sa —;* to beg one's bread. *Faire bonne —;* to lead a merry life. *Faire la —;* to live fast; to racket. *Faire — qui dure;* to lead a sober life; (fig.) to husband one's resources. *Mener une — heureuse;* to lead a happy life. *Avoir la — dure;* to have a hard time; to have nine lives. *Train de —;* way of living. *Tourmenter sa —;* to bestir one's self. *Faire — de garçon;* to live like a bachelor. *Mener une — réglée;* to lead a regular life. *C'est ma —;* it is my very life. *Telle —, telle fin;* people die as they live. *Il a écrit lui-même sa —;* he has written his own life. *A la — et à la mort;* in life and death. *Une pension à —;* a pension for life. *Sa — durant;* during his life. *Prodiguer sa —;* to throw away one's life, to expose one's self to danger. *S'ôter la —;* to make way with one's self.

viédase, *n.m.,* (l.ex.) (pers.) puppy, jackanapes.

*vieil, *adj.* V. **vieux.**

*vieillard, *n.m.,* old man.

*vieille, *adj.* V. **vieux.**

*vieille, *n.f.,* old woman.

*vieillement, *adv.,* in an old way, *or* manner.

*vieillerie, *n.f.,* old things; old clothes, old goods, old stuff, old lumber, rubbish.

*vieillesse, *n.f.,* old age; oldness. *Elle est morte de —;* she died of old age.

*vieillir, *v.n.,* to grow old; to get old; to look old; to become obsolete (of words).

*vieillir, *v.a.,* to make old; to make look old.

*se vieillir, *v.r.,* to make one's self look old; to give one's self out as older than one actually is.

*vieillissant, -e, *adj.,* growing old.

*vieillissement (-is-mān), *n.m.,* growing old.

*vieillot, -te, *adj.,* oldish.

vielle, *n.f.,* hurdy-gurdy. *Il est du bois dont on fait les —s ;* he is of a pliant temperament.

vieller, *v.n.,* to play upon the hurdy-gurdy; (pop.) ⊙to stand trifling.

vielleu-r, *n.m.,* **-se,** *n.f.,* hurdy-gurdy player.

vierge, *n.f.,* virgin, maid; (astron.) Virgo.

vierge, *adj.,* virgin, virginal, maiden; pure, untrodden, unwrought; free from. *Métaux —s;* native, *or* virgin, metals. *Forêt —;* primeval, untrodden, virgin forest. *Epée —;* unfleshed, maiden sword.

vieux, vieil, *adj.m.,* **vieille,** *f.,* old; aged, advanced in years; ancient, venerable. *Un vieux soldat;* an old soldier. *Un vieil arbre;* an old tree. *Un vieil harpagon;* an old miser. *Une vieille femme;* an old woman. [*Vieil* may be used instead of *vieux* before a vowel or a silent *h.*]

vieux, *n.m.,* old man, old boy, old fellow; *un — de la vieille;* a veteran of the Old Guard.

vieux, *n.m.,* anything that is old (especially clothes, shoes, etc.).

vi-f, -ve, *adj.,* alive, live, living; quick; lively, brisk, sprightly, smart, animated, fiery, mettlesome, ardent, eager, hasty, keen, alert, nimble; sharp, violent (of pain); vivid, bright (of colors). *Cheval —;* mettlesome horse. *Des yeux —s;* sparkling eyes. *Couleur —ve;* bright color. *Un froid —;* a piercing cold. *Une —ve douleur;* a violent pain. *Eau —ve;* spring-water. *Chaux —ve;* quicklime. *Haie —ve;* quickset hedge. *De —ve voix;* by word of mouth; vivâ voce; verbally, orally. *Il est — comme la poudre;* he is quick-tempered, as hot as a pepper-corn; he is quick at work. *Mort ou —;* dead or alive.

vif, *n.m.,* quick; (jur.) person living; shaft (of a column). *Etre touché au —;* to be touched to the quick. *Trancher,* or *couper, dans le —;* to cut to the quick; (fig.) to set to work in earnest. *Piquer au —;* to sting to the quick. *Etre pris sur le —;* (of pictures, descriptions) to be very life-like.

vif-argent, *n.m.,* (*n.p.*) quicksilver.

vigie, *n.f.,* (nav.) look-out; look-out man; lurking rock; rock above water; (railways) seat (on the top of cars). *Etre en —;* (nav.) to be on the look-out, on the watch.

vigilamment (-la-mān), *adv.,* vigilantly, watchfully.

vigilance, *n.f.,* vigilance, watchfulness.

vigilant, -e, *adj.,* vigilant, watchful.

vigile, *n.f.,* vigil, eve.

*vigne, *n.f.,* vine; vineyard. *— sauvage;* wild vine. *— vierge;* wild-grape, wild-briony. *— noire;* black briony *or* bryony. *— blanche;* white briony, traveler's joy. *— de Judée;* woody nightshade, bitter-sweet. *Etre dans les —s du Seigneur;* to be in one's cups, to be half-seas-over.

*vigneau, *n.m.* V. **vignot.**

*vigneron, *n.m.,* **-ne,** *n.f.,* vine-dresser, wine-grower.

*vignette, *n.f.,* (engr.) vignette; (bot.) meadow-sweet.

vignettiste, *n.m.,* vignettist, vignette-maker.

*vignoble, *n.m.,* vineyard. *Propriétaire de —s;* wine-grower.

*vignoble, *adj.,* wine-growing.

*vignot *or* **vigneau,** *n.m.,* periwinkle.

*vigogne, *n.m.,* vicuna-felt hat.

*vigogne, *n.f.,* vicugna, vicuña, vicuna; vicuna-wool, swan's down.

vigoureusement (-reŭz-mān), *adv.,* vigorously, stoutly, forcibly, energetically.

vigoureu-x, -se, *adj.,* vigorous, stout, hardy, lusty, forcible, energetic.

viguerie, *n.f.,* provostship (in Languedoc, Provence).

vigueur, *n.f.,* vigor, strength, force; power, sturdiness; energy, spirit. *Mettre en —;* to put in force, to enforce. *— d'esprit;* strength of mind. *Entrer en —;* to come into force.

viguier, *n.m.,* provost (Languedoc, Provence).

vil, -e, *adj.,* vile, base, mean, despicable, low, wretched. *A — prix;* very cheap, dirt-cheap.

vilain, *n.m.,* (feudalism) villain, villein; niggard; blackguard, cad, nasty fellow; miser. *Oignez — il vous poindra, poignez — il vous oindra;* a bad man will return evil for good.

vilain, -e (-lïn, -lè-n), *adj.,* ugly, vile, villainous, pitiful, miserable, unhandsome; shabby, worthless, nasty, filthy, slovenly, wicked; sordid, wretched, infamous, scandalous. *Il m'a joué un — tour;* he has played me a nasty trick. *— temps;* bad weather. *Il fait — ;* it is nasty weather. *C'est un — monsieur;* he is a nasty fellow, an ugly customer.

vilain (-lïn), *n.m.,* **-e** (-lè-n), *n.f.,* (fam.) naughty boy, naughty girl.

vilainement (-lè-n-mān), *adv.,* uglily; basely, nastily, shamefully, scandalously, unworthily, villainously, wretchedly, naughtily, sordidly, improperly, deplorably.

vilayet, *n.m.,* vilayet, large Turkish province.

vilebrequin (vil-brĕ-kïn), *n.m.,* center-bit, wimble.

vilement (vil-mān), *adv.,* vilely, basely, meanly, abjectly, contemptibly.

vilenie (vil-nï), *n.f.,* filth, nastiness, foulness, dirt; sordid avarice, niggardliness; trash, unwholesome food; mean, base, vile action. *pl.,* offensive words; filthiness, obscenity.

vileté (vil-té) *or* **vilité,** *n.f.,* cheapness, low price; unimportance, baseness, meanness.

vilipendement, *n.m.,* vilification.

vilipender, *v.a.*, to vilify, to despise, to cry down; to undervalue.

vilité, *n.f.* V. **vileté**.

villa, *n.f.*, villa.

villace, *n.f.*, (fam., l.u.) large, straggling, thinly-peopled city.

village, *n.m.*, village. *Des gens de* — ; country-folk. *Il est bien de son* — ; he knows nothing of what is going on in the world.

villageois (-joâ), *n.m.*, **-e** (-joaz), *n.f.*, villager, rustic, cottager. *adj.* rustic, country.

villanelle, *n.f.*, pastoral poetry; a dancing tune.

ville, *n.f.*, town, city. — *de commerce ;* commercial town. — *maritime ;* sea-port town. — *de bains* or *d'eaux ;* watering-place. — *de guerre ;* fortress. *Robe,* or *toilette, de* — ; walking-dress. *Habit de* — ; (of officers) plain clothes, mufti. *Costume de* — ; morning-coat, frock coat. *Corps de* — ; corporation, town-council. *Etre en* — ; to be out (not at home). *Il est allé dîner en* — ; he has gone out to dinner, he is dining out. *Etre à la* — ; to be in town.

villégiature, *n.f.*, sojourn in the country. *En* — ; staying in the country.

villette, *n.f.*, (fam.) small town, townlet.

villeu-x, **-se**, *adj.*, (bot.) villous, villose.

villifère, *adj.*, villiferous.

villiforme, *adj.*, villiform.

villosité, *n.f.*, (bot.) villosity.

vimaire, *n.f.*, damage caused (to forests) by storms.

vin, *n.m.*, wine, vinosity, strength. — *mousseux ;* sparkling wine. — *non mousseux ;* still wine. *Du* — *éventé ;* dead wine. — *de Bordeaux ;* claret. *Du* — *paillet ;* pale wine. — *du Rhin ;* Rhenish wine. — *de deux feuilles ;* wine two years old. — *qui a beaucoup de corps ;* full-bodied wine. — *ordinaire ;* dinner wine. — *pur ;* neat wine (without water). — *coupé ;* diluted wine. — *de la comète ;* vintage wine. — *brûlé ;* — *chaud ;* mulled wine, negus. *Marchand de* —, or *négociant en* —*s ;* wine-merchant. *Un doigt de* — ; a drop of wine. *Tremper son* — ; to dilute one's wine. *Il est en pointe de* — ; he has had a drop too much. *Etre pris de* — ; to be the worse for liquor. *Etre entre deux* —*s ;* to be half-seas over. *Cuver son* — ; to sleep one's self sober. *Un sac à* — ; a drunken sot. *Il a le* — *mauvais ;* he is quarrelsome in his cups. *Il a le* — *bon ;* he is merry on his cups. *A bon* — *point d'enseigne ;* good wine needs no bush. *Du* — *à faire danser les chèvres ;* wine not fit to drink. *Le* — *entré, la raison sort ;* (prov.) when ale is in, wit is out. *Mouiller trop son* — ; to drown the miller.

vinage, *n.m.*, putting alcohol into wine.

vinaigre, *n.m.*, vinegar.

vinaigré, **-e**, *adj.*, seasoned with vinegar.

vinaigrer, *v.a.*, to season with vinegar.

vinaigrerie, *n.f.*, vinegar manufactory.

vinaigrette, *n.f.*, vinegar sauce; meat seasoned with vinegar; Bath chair, hand-chair.

vinaigrier, *n.m.*, vinegar merchant; vinegar cruet; (bot.) sumac tree.

vinaire, *adj.*, for wine. *Vaisseaux* —*s ;* wine-vessels, wine-casks.

vinasse, *n.f.*, very weak wine.

vindas (-dâs), *n.m.*, (tech.) windlass.

vindicati-f, **-ve**, *adj.*, vindictive, revengeful.

vindicte, *n.f.*, (jur.) prosecution (of crime). *La* — *publique ;* prosecution (by the public prosecutor). *A la* — *publique ;* held up to public reprobation.

vinée, *n.f.*, crop of wine, vintage.

viner, *v.a.*, to put alcohol into wine.

vinetier (vi-n-tié) or **vinettier** (-nè-tié), *n.m.*, barberry-tree.

vineu-x, **-se**, *adj.*, vinous; winy, wine-colored.

vingt (vîn), *n.m.* and *adj.*, twenty, score;

twentieth. *Quatre-vingts hommes ;* eighty men. *Quatre-vingt-six bœufs ;* eighty-six oxen. [*Vingt* takes an *s* when preceded and multiplied by another number, but remains invariable when it is followed by another number.]

vingtaine (vin-tè-n), *n.f.*, a score, about twenty. [game.

vingt et un, *n.m.*, (*n.p.*) vingt-et-un (card

vingtième (vin-ti-èm), *n.m.* and *adj.*, twentieth.

vinicole, *adj.*, wine-growing, wine-producing.

vinification, *n.f.*, wine-making.

viol, *n.m.*, rape, violation; indecent assault.

violacé, -e, *adj.*, violaceous; (med.) purple.

violacées or **violariées**, *n.f.pl.*, (bot.) violaceæ.

violat, *adj.*, of violets.

violat-eur, *n.m.*, **-rice**, *n.f.*, violator, infringer, breaker, transgressor. *adj.*, violating, transgressing, infringing.

violation, *n.f.*, violation, transgression, breach, infringement.

violâtre, *adj.*, inclining to a violet color, purplish.

viole, *n.f.*, (mus.) tenor-violin ; viol.

violement (viol-mān), *n.m.*, (l.u.) violation ; (old) infringement, infraction; rape.

violemment (-la-mān), *adv.*, violently, with violence.

violence, *n.f.*, violence; (jur.) force, stress. *Faire* — *à quelqu'un ;* to offer violence to any one.

violent, -e, *adj.*, violent; strong (of suspicion); (fig.) too bad. *C'est par trop* — ; it is really too bad. *Douleur* —*e ;* violent pain. *Mort* —*e ;* violent death.

violenter, *v.a.*, to force, to offer violence to ; to compel, to constrain; to ill-use.

violer, *v.a.*, to violate, to ravish; to break, to infringe, to transgress. — *sa foi ;* to break one's faith. — *le droit des gens ;* to break the law of nations.

violet, *n.m.*, violet-color.

violet, -e, *adj.*, violet-colored.

violette, *n.f.*, (bot.) violet. — *tricolore ;* heart's-ease, pansy. — *de la chandeleur ;* snow-drop. — *marine ;* Canterbury-bell.

violeur, *n.m.*, violator, ravisher.

violier, *n.m.*, wall-flower, gilly-flower. — *des jardins ;* stock.

violiste, *n.m.*, violist.

violon, *n.m.*, violin, fiddle ; violinist, violin-player, fiddler ; cell, round-house, lock-up (prison). *Mettre quelqu'un au* — ; to put any one in quod. *Il a payé les* —*s ;* he paid the piper. *Jouer du* — ; to play on the violin.

violoncelle, *n.m.*, violoncello.

violoncelliste, *n.m.*, violoncellist.

violoniste, *n.m.f.*, violinist.

viorne, *n.f.*, (bot.) viburnum.

vipère, *n.f.*, viper, adder.

vipereau, *n.m.*, young viper.

vipérin, -e (-rîn, -ri-n), *adj.*, viperine.

vipérine (-ri-n), *n.f.*, (bot.) viper's-bugloss.

virago, *n.f.*, virago, catamaran.

virée, *n.f.*, veering.

virelai, *n.m.*, virelay (ancient French poem on two rhymes).

virement (vir-mān), *n.m.*, turning ; (nav.) veering, tacking about; (fin.) clearing. — *d'eau ;* (nav.) turn of the tide.

virer, *v.n.* and *a.*, to turn, to turn about ; (nav.) to tack; to heave. — *de bord ;* (nav.) to tack about, to put about ; (fig.) to change sides, to turn round, to rat. *Vire !* 'bout ship !

vireur, *n.m.*, turning-gear; (phot.) toning.

vireu-x, **-se**, *adj.*, poisonous, noxious, fetid, nauseous.

virevau or **vireveau** (vir-vô), *n.m.*, (nav.) winch.

virevaude, n.f. V. **vire-vire**.

virevent (vir-vän), n.m., (orni.) kingfisher.

vire vire, n.f., (—) (nav.) whirlpool.

virevolte, n.f., (man.) volt right and left, quick turning.

⊙**virevousse** or **virevouste**, n.f., bustle; (fig.) prevarication, shuffling, shifting.

virginal, -e, adj., virginal, maidenly.

virginalement, adv., maidenly, in a maiden-like manner.

virginité, n.f., virginity, maidenhead.

virgouleuse, n.f., a sort of winter pear.

virgule, n.f., (gram.) comma; (horl.) hook escapement. Point et —; semicolon.

viril, -e, adj., male, virile, manly. Age —; manhood, man's estate.

virilement (-ril-män), adv., manfully, manly, like a man.

virilité, n.f., virility, manhood, man's estate, vigor, force.

virole, n.f., ferrule.

virolé, -e, adj., (her.) virole.

viroler, v.a., to ferrule, to hoop.

virtualité, n.f., virtuality, potentiality.

virtuel, -le, adj., virtual, potential.

virtuellement (-èl-män), adv., virtually, potentially.

virtuose, n.m.f., virtuoso.

virulence, n.f., virulence, virulency.

virulent, -e, adj., virulent.

virus (-rus), n.m., virus.

vis (vis), n.f., screw. Escalier à —; winding, corkscrew staircase.

visa, n.m., (—) visa, signature, indorsement (on passports).

visage, n.m., face, visage; countenance, aspect, look, air. — pâle; pale face. A deux —s; double-faced. A — découvert; openly, barefacedly. Avoir bon —; to look well. Faire bon, or mauvais, — à quelqu'un; to look pleasantly, or unpleasantly, at any one; to give any one a good, or bad, reception. Se composer le —; to compose one's countenance. Changer de —; to change countenance; to turn pale; to have one's face at command. Trouver — de bois; to find the door shut, to find nobody there.

vis-à-vis, adv., opposite, in juxtaposition.

vis-à-vis (vi-za-vī), n.m., (—) vis-a-vis (in dancing); vis-a-vis (carriage); opposite neighbor (at table).

vis-à-vis, prep., opposite, over against, over the way; towards, relatively. — de l'église; opposite the church.

viscéral, -e (vis-sé-), adj., visceral.

viscère (vis-sèr), n.f., (anat.) viscus. pl., viscera, vital organs.

viscosité, n.f., viscosity, viscidity, viscousness; clamminess.

visée, n.f., aim; end; design, plan, scheme.

viser, v.n., to aim, to take aim; to aspire (to), to endeavor. Il visait à ce but; that was his goal.

viser, v.a., to aim, to aim (at), to take aim (at); to drive (at); to countersign, to indorse (passports). Faire — un passeport; to get a passport countersigned, or indorsed.

viseur (n.m., aimer.

vishnou (vis-noo), n.m., Vishnu (name of one of the Hindoo deities).

visibilité, n.f., visibility, visibleness, obviousness.

visible, adj., visible, evident, manifest, obvious.

visiblement, adv., visibly, evidently, manifestly, obviously.

visière, n.f., visor (of a helmet); foresight (of fire-arms); shade (for the eyes); peak (of caps, etc.); (fam.) eyesight. Rompre en — à quelqu'un; to break one's lance in the visor of one's adversary; (fig.) to attack any one to his face; to break

off with, to fall out with. Elle lui a donné dans la —; he was smitten with her.

visigoth (-gô), n.m., Visigoth; barbarian, Goth.

vision, n.f., vision, sight, phantom, chimera, fancy.

visionnaire, n.m.f. and adj., a visionary, a dreamer; visionary, fanciful.

visir, n.m. V. **vizir**.

visirat, n.m. V. **vizirat**.

visitandine, n.f., Visitandine (nun).

visitation, n.f., visitation. L'ordre de la —; the Order of the Visitation.

visite, n.f., visit; call; visiting; visitation; examination, inspection, search. Aller en —; to go visiting. En —; visiting, on a visit; as a visitor. Faire —, rendre —, à quelqu'un; to make a call upon any one, to pay any one a visit. Rendre sa — à quelqu'un; to return any one his, or her, call. Faire la — des caves; to search the cellars. Droit de —; right of search. Faire la — des bagages; to examine baggage.

visiter, v.a. and n., to visit; to make a visit, a visitation; to search, to examine, to inspect, to look. — un vaisseau; to search a ship.

visiteu-r, n.m., **-se**, n.f., visitor; searcher.

vison, n.m., American marten.

vison-visu, adv., opposite one another.

visorium (-om), n.m., (print.) copy-holder, catch, jigger.

visqueu-x, -se, adj., viscous, slimy, clammy, sticky.

vissage, n.m., screwing.

visser, v.a., to screw; to screw on; to screw up; to screw down.

se**visser**, v.r., to screw; to screw on; to screw up; to screw down; to be screwed.

visserie, n.f., screws.

visu (de), adv., with one's own eyes.

visuel, -le, adj., visual.

vital, -e, adj., vital, essential.

vitalement (-tal-män), adv., vitally; essentially.

vitalisme, n.m., doctrine of the vitalists.

vitaliste, n.m., vitalist.

vitalité, n.f., vitality.

vitchoura, n.m., (—s) fur greatcoat.

vite, adj., swift, quick, fleet, speedy, rapid. Pouls —; quick pulse. — comme le vent; as fleet as the wind.

vite, adv., quick, quickly, fast, speedily; rapidly; expeditiously. Allez —; go quickly. Aller — en besogne; to go fast at work; (fig.) not to mince matters. — ! quick! —! — ! quick! make haste! look sharp. Au plus —; as fast as possible; that instant, that very moment. Faire —; to be quick, to make haste, to expedite matters. Allons! plus — que ça; come! hurry up! look sharp about it!

vitelotte (vi-tlot), n.f., kidney potato.

vitement (vit-män), adv., quickly, speedily.

vitesse, n.f., swiftness, speed, celerity, quickness, rapidity. A la — de; at a speed of, at the rate of. Gagner quelqu'un de —; to outstrip, to outrun, any one. A grande —; at full speed. A toute —; at full speed. Train de grande —; (railways) express, express train. Train de petite —; goods train, slow train.

vitex, n.m., (bot.) vitex, chaste-tree.

viticole, adj., relating, pertaining to vine culture, wine-growing.

viticulture, n.f., vine-culture; viticulture.

vitonnière, n.f., (nav.) timber-hole.

vitrage, n.m., glazing; glass windows; glass partition.

vitrail, n.m., stained glass window, church-window.

vitre, n.f., window-glass or pane; pane of glass; window. Carreau de —; pane of glass. Casser les —s; to break the windows; (fig.) to speak boldly, to speak out one's mind, not to mince matters.

vitré, -e, *adj.*, glazed ; (of doors) glass ; (anat.) vitreous. *Porte —e ;* glass door.

vitrer, *v.a.*, to furnish with glass windows, to glaze.

vitrerie, *n.f.*, glaziery, glazier's work.

vitrescibilité, *n.f.*, vitrescence.

vitrescible, *adj.*, vitrescible.

vitreu-x, -se, *adj.*, vitreous, glassy.

vitri-er, *n.m.*, **-ère**, *n.f.*, glazier ; glazier's wife.

vitrifiable, *adj.*, vitrifiable.

vitrification, *n.f.*, vitrification.

vitrifier, *v.a.*, to vitrify.

se **vitrifier**, *v.r.*, to vitrify.

vitrine, *n.f.*, shop-window ; show-case ; glass case (in museums, etc.).

vitriol, *n.m.*, vitriol.

vitriolé, -e, *adj.*, vitriolated.

vitriolique, *adj.*, vitriolic.

vitriolisation, *n.f.*, vitriolisation.

vitupérer, *v.a.*, to vituperate, to reprimand.

vivable, *adj.*, (fam.) sociable, pleasant to live with.

vivace, *adj.*, long-lived, perennial ; inveterate, deep-rooted. *Plantes —s ;* perennial plants, perennials.

vivacité, *n.f.*, vivacity, vivaciousness, liveliness, sprightliness, briskness ; spirit, life, animation ; ardor, vividness, brightness.

vivandi-er, *n.m.*, **-ère**, *n.f.*, sutler, canteenman *or* woman.

vivant, -e, *adj.*, living, alive ; quick, animate, animated. *Langue —e ;* living language. *Rue —e ;* lively street.

vivant, *n.m.*, person living, person alive ; determined character ; life, lifetime. *De son —;* in his lifetime. *Du — de son frère ;* when his brother was alive. *Un bon —;* a jolly, or boon, companion ; a high liver.

vivat (-vat), *int.*, hurrah! huzza! *Pousser des —;* to cheer to the echo.

vivat (-vat), *n.m.*, (—s) hurra, huzza. *Crier —;* to cheer, to hurra.

vive, *n.f.*, (ich.) viver, weever.

⊙**vive-la-joie**, *n.m.*, (—) jolly, boon companion.

vivelle, *n.f.*, darn, darning ; gusset.

vivement (viv-mān), *adv.*, quickly, briskly, sharply, smartly, vigorously, eagerly, keenly, deeply ; angrily ; poignantly ; acutely ; spiritedly ; with animation.

viveur, *n.m.*, high liver, free liver, fast man, man about town.

vivier, *n.m.*, fish-pond.

vivifiant, -e, *adj.*, vivifying, quickening, strengthening, recuperating, refreshing ; invigorating, life-giving.

vivification, *n.f.*, vivification, vivifying ; revival.

vivifier, *v.a.*, to vivify, to quicken ; to give life to, to enliven, to animate, to refresh, to revive.

vivifique, *adj.*, (l.u.) vivifying, life-giving. *V.* **vivifiant**.

vivipare, *adj.*, viviparous.

vivisecter, *v.a.*, to vivisect.

vivisecteur, *n.m.*, vivisector.

vivisection, *n.f.*, vivisection.

vivoter, *v.n.*, to live poorly ; to live from hand to mouth, to make shift to live, to rub along ; to keep body and soul together.

vivre (vivant, vécu), *v.n.*, to live, to be living, to be alive ; to exist, to subsist, to be maintained, to board, to take one's meals at ; to behave. *Il vit mal ;* he lives badly. *Il vit mal avec son frère ;* he is on bad terms with his brother. *Il vit aux dépens d'autrui ;* he lives at other people's expense. *Bien —;* to live a good life. — *bien ;* to live well (to have abundance of every-

thing). *Il fait cher — à Londres ;* living is dear in London. *Faire —;* to feed, to keep alive, to maintain. — *de son travail ;* to live by one's labor. — *d'industrie,* — *d'invention ;* (b.s.) to live by one's wits. — *d'espérance ;* to live in hopes. *Il faut que tout le monde vive ;* everybody must live. — *dans les sapes ;* (Saint-Simon) to be mixed up in underhand intrigues. — *en prince ;* to live like a prince. *Savoir —;* to be a person of good manners, of good breeding. *Il ne sait pas —;* he has no manners. *Apprendre à —;* to learn, *or* to teach, manners. *Vive le roi !* long live the king ! *Vive !* hurrah for ! *Ne pas trouver âme qui vive ;* not to find a soul at home. *Qui vivra verra ;* he who lives longest will see most. *Il fait bon — ici ;* this is a good place to live in. *Vivent les ministres !* long live the ministers !

vivre, *n.m.*, living, board, food. *pl.*, provisions, victuals. *Couper les —s à quelqu'un ;* to cut off any one's supplies. *Agents des —s ;* (nav.) agent-victualer. *Bureau des —s ;* victualing-office.

vivres-pain, *n.m.pl.*, (n.s.) (milit.- nav.) bread-store.

vivres-viande, *n.m.pl.*, (n.s.) (milit.- nav.) meat-store.

vivrier, *n.m.*, victualer.

vizir, *n.m.*, vizier.

vizirat *or* **viziriat**, *n.m.*, vizierate, viziership.

vocable, *n.m.*, vocable, word, term, name.

vocabulaire, *n.m.*, vocabulary.

vocabuliste, *n.m.*, (l.u.) author of a vocabulary.

vocal, *n.m.*, **-e**, *n.f.*, (ecc.) vocal (voter).

vocal, -e, *adj.*, vocal.

vocalement (-kal-mān), *adv.*, (l.u.) vocally, orally.

vocalisation, *n.f.*, vocalization.

vocalise, *n.f.*, piece of music for exercising the voice.

vocaliser, *v.n.*, (mus.) to vocalize.

vocatif, *n.m.*, (gram.) vocative, vocative case.

vocation, *n.f.*, vocation, calling, call ; inclination ; destination, talent. *Suivre sa —;* to follow one's vocation, one's bent.

vociférat-eur, *n.m.*, **-rice**, *n.f.*, clamorer, brawler. *adj.*, clamoring, brawling, roaring.

vociférations, *n.f.pl.*, vociferations.

vociférer, *v.a.* and *n.*, to vociferate, to cry out, to roar.

vœu, *n.m.*, vow ; votive offering ; vote, suffrage ; prayer, wish, will, desire. *pl.*, vows (religious ceremony). *Faire — de jeûner ;* to make a vow of abstinence. *Faire des —x pour quelqu'un ;* to offer up prayers for any one, to wish any one success. *Etre au comble de ses —x ;* to have reached the summit of one's happiness.

vogue (vog), *n.f.*, (nav.) rowing, sailing, going ; (fig.) vogue, fashion, credit, repute, reputation. *Avoir de la —;* to be in vogue, in fashion. *Mettre en —;* to bring into vogue, into fashion. *Succès de —;* temporary success.

vogue-avant, *n.m.*, bow-oarsman, bow.

voguer (-ghé), *v.n.*, (nav.) to impel a boat (by rowing) ; to ride, to sail ; to row (l.u.). *V.* **ramer, nager**. *Vogue la galère !* come what may !

⊙**vogueur** (-gheur), *n.m.*, rower ; cork-bladder.

voici, *prep.*, see here, behold, here is, here are, here come, this is, these are. — *mon livre, voilà le vôtre ;* here is my book, there is yours. *En — d'une autre ;* this is still more singular. *Me —, le voilà ;* here I am, there he is, here he comes. *Monsieur que —;* this gentleman. *Le — qui vient ;* here he comes. *Nous y —;* here we are. — *venir votre frère ;* here comes your brother. — *venir le printemps ;* spring is coming, is at hand, is near.

voie, *n.f.*, way, road, track; path, organ, medium, channel; course, breadth (between the wheels of carriages); (hunt.) track (of deer, boars); conveyance, means of conveyance; load (of wood, stone, sand); means; (nav.) leak; (railways) gauge, permanent way, four-foot way; (chem.) process. *Il est toujours par — et par chemin;* he is always rambling about, always on the move. *La — lactée;* the Milky Way. — *d'eau;* two pailfuls of water; (nav.) leak. *Faire une — d'eau;* (nav) to spring a leak. *Boucher une — d'eau;* to stop a leak. —*s de fait;* (jur.) assault, blows. *En venir aux —s de fait;* to come to blows. — *ferrée;* railway, railroad. *Les affaires sont en — de hausse;* things are looking up. *Etre sur la —;* to be on the track, on the scent. *Etre en — de;* to be in a fair way (of). — *de garage, d'évitement;* (railways) siding, shunting-line.

voilà, *prep.*, see there, behold, that is, those are, there is, there are. — *l'homme;* that is the man. *Le —;* there he is. *Ah! vous —;* oh! there you are. — *qui va bien;* that is getting on well now, that's all right now, that's capital. *Le — qui arrive;* there he comes. — *qu'on m'appelle;* I am called, some one is calling me. *Comme la — triste!* how sad she is! *Comme vous — fait!* what a strange figure you cut! what a plight you are in! — *ce que c'est;* that is what it is. — *tout;* that is all. *En — assez;* that is enough. *En — t-il!* what a lot there is! *En — pour!* that will do for. — *comme vous êtes;* that is just like you. — *comme je suis;* you must take me as I am, I'm that sort of man. *Ne — t-il pas que . . .;* why, I declare it is . . . or lo! and behold! it is. . . . *Comme le — sale!* see how dirty he is. — *près d'un an;* it is now nearly a year. — *une heure qu'il parle;* he has been speaking for an hour. *Ne — t-il pas qu'il pleut;* well! I declare, it is raining.

voile, *n.m.*, vail; cover, mask, disguise; cloak, color, show, pretense. *Avoir un — devant les yeux;* to have a mist before one's eyes.

voile, *n.f.*, (nav.) sail; (fig.) sail, ship. *La — de misaine;* the foresail. *La — d'artimon;* the mizzen. — *de fortune;* lug sail. *Faire force de —s;* to crowd all sail. *Aller à —s et à rames;* to go with sails and oars. *Déployer les —s;* to unfurl the sails. *A pleines —s or à toutes —s;* (nav.) with full sail, all sails set; at full speed; (fig.) willingly, heartily. *Faire —;* to sail. *Caler la —;* to strike sail. *Mettre à la —;* to set sail. *A la —;* under sail, sailing.

voilé, -e, *adj.*, (nav.) provided with sails, rigged; (fig.) veiled, dull, dim, soft, gentle. *Peu —;* broad (of hints or language).

voiler, *v.a.*, to veil, to cover; to cloak, to color, to blind, to disguise; to conceal, to muffle. *se* **voiler**, *v.r.*, to wear a veil; to be veiled, concealed, covered, muffled.

voilerie (voal-rî), *n.f.*, (nav.) sail-loft; sail-making.

voilier, *n.m.*, sail-maker; sailer (ship). *Un bon —;* a fast sailer (ship).

voilure, *n.f.*, set of sails; trim of the sails.

voir (voyant, vu), *v.a.*, to see; to look at, to behold, to observe, to view; to witness; to inspect, to superintend; to overlook; to keep company with; to be on visiting terms with, to frequent the society of. *Je l'ai vu de mes propres yeux;* I have seen it with my own eyes. *Il veut tout — par lui-même;* he insists on seeing everything with his own eyes, or for himself. *Que vois-je?* what do I see? — *quelque chose en songe;* to see anything in a dream. — *le jour;* to be born, to see the light of day. *Faire —;* to show, to let see. *On n'a jamais rien vu de pareil;* the like was never seen before. *Vit-on jamais rien d'égal!* was anything like it ever seen? *Voyez ce tableau;* look at that picture.

Faire — du pays à quelqu'un; to lead any one a dance. — *tout en beau;* to see the bright side of anything. *Il ne voit personne;* he sees no company. *Se faire —;* to appear, to show one's self. *Je vous vois venir;* I see what you are driving at.

se **voir**, *v.r.*, to see one's self; to see one another; to visit one another; to be, or to find, one's self. *Ils ne se voient point;* they do not visit one another, they are not on visiting terms.

voir, *v.n.*, to see; to have one's sight; to superintend; to inspect, to look, to look out. *Je vois bien quelle est son intention;* I see plainly what he is driving at. *Je ne vois point à quoi cela peut servir;* I don't see what purpose that can serve. *Je lui ferai bien — à qui il s'adresse;* I'll show him what sort of a person he has to deal with. — *clair;* to see clearly. *Y — trouble;* to see dimly. *Au vu et au su de tout le monde;* openly, before every one. *Ceci est à —;* it remains to be seen. — *de loin;* to be far-sighted. *N'y — goutte;* not to see a bit, not to see a wink, not to see in the least. *Voyons! let us see! come! now then! Ma maison voit sur un jardin;* my house looks out into a garden.

voire, *adv.*, even; ⊙indeed, truly. — *même;* nay even.

voirie, *n.f.*, commission of public ways or highways; common sewer, carrion, offal.

voisin, -e, *adj.*, neighboring, bordering, adjacent, next; next door. *La maison —e;* the next house. *Etre — de sa ruine;* (fig.) to be on the verge of ruin.

voisin, *n.m.*, -e, *n.f.*, neighbor. *Etre —s;* to be next-door neighbors.

voisinage, *n.m.*, neighborhood; vicinity; proximity, nearness; neighbors; (jur.) venue, visne.

voisiner, *v.n.*, to visit one's neighbors; to go a neighboring.

voiturage, *n.m.*, conveying, transporting, carriage of goods (in cars, carts, vans, etc.).

voiture, *n.f.*, carriage; coach; conveyance, vehicle; fare; load. — *publique;* stage-coach. — *à deux chevaux;* coach, or carriage, and pair. — *de maître;* private carriage. — *d'arrosement;* watering cart. — *à bagages;* luggage van. *Station de —;* cab-rank. — *de louage;* hired carriage. — *de place;* cab, hackney-carriage. — *de remise;* fly, hired carriage. *Bureau de la —;* coach-office. *Place de —s;* cab-stand. *Descendre de —;* to alight from a carriage. *Se promener en —, aller en —;* to ride in a carriage, to drive.

voiturer, *v.a.*, to carry, to convey, to transport, to cart.

voiturier, *n.m.*, carrier; wagoner; driver. *V.* **roulier.**

voiturin, *n.m.*, driver (owner of a carriage usually lent on hire); the carriage so hired.

voix, *n.f.*, voice, tone, sound; vote, suffrage; opinion, judgment; singer. — *grêle;* faint voice. — *de tête;* falsetto, head-note. *Faire la petite —;* to speak small. — *aiguë;* shrill voice. *De vive —;* by word of mouth, orally. *A — basse;* in a low voice, in an undertone, in a whisper. *A haute —;* in a loud voice, loudly, audibly. *Aller aux —;* to put to the vote, to divide. *Donner sa —;* to give one's vote. *Mettre aux —;* to put to the vote. *Aux —!* vote! divide! *A l'unanimité des —;* without a dissentient voice. *D'une seule, or d'une commune, —;* with one voice, unanimously.

vol, *n.m.*, robbery, theft, robbing, extortion, fleecing; larceny; stolen goods. — *de nuit avec effraction;* burglary. — *de grand chemin;* highway robbery. *On l'a trouvé saisi du —;* they found the stolen goods upon him.

vol, *n.m.*, flying; flight, soaring; flock; cast (of hawks). *Prendre un — trop haut;* to soar too high. *Prendre son* —; to soar, to take one's flight, *or* its flight. *A* — *d'oiseau ;* as the crow flies. *Au* —; flying, on the wing.

volable, *adj.*, liable to be stolen.

volage, *adj.*, fickle, volatile, inconstant, unsteady, flighty. *La jeunesse est* —; youth is inconstant, flighty.

*****volaille**, *n.f.*, poultry, fowl. *Marchand de* —; poulterer.

*****volailler**, *n.m.*, poulterer ; poultry-yard.

volant, -e *adj.*, flying, loose, floating, volatile; movable, portable (of paper), loose ; (nav.) traveling; (paint.) floating (of drapery). *Assiettes* —*es ;* extras, extra dishes.

volant, *n.m.*, shuttle-cock ; flounce (of a dress); fly-wheel (of machinery); sail (of a windmill). *Jouer au* —; to play at battle-door and shuttle-cock.

volatil, -e, *adj.*, volatile ; airy, light.

volatile, *n.m.f.*, and *adj.*, winged animal ; winged.

volatilisation, *n.f.*, volatilization.

volatiliser, *v.a.*, to volatilize.

se **volatiliser**, *v.r.*, to volatilize, to become volatilized.

volatilité, *n.f.*, volatility, volatileness.

*****volatille**, *n.f.*, (fam.) small birds for the table.

vol-au-vent, *n.m.*, (—) (cook.) vol-au-vent, puff-paste.

volcan, *n.m.*, volcano.

volcanique, *adj.*, volcanic.

volcanisé, -e, *adj.*, vulcanized.

volcanite, *n.m.*, vulcanite.

vole, *n.f.*, vole (at cards).

volée, *n.f.*, flight (of birds); flock; covey, bevy, brood ; rank ; discharge (of one gun); volley (of guns); shower (of blows) ; peal (of bells); swing-tree, splinter-bar *or* bar (of a coach); drubbing, thrashing. *Il a pris sa* —; he has taken wings. *Tirer à toute* —; to fire a random shot. *Sonner à toute* —; to ring a full peal. *A toute* —; (of bells) in full and furious swing. *Une* — *de coups de bâton ;* a shower of blows. *Etre de la première* —; to be of the first water, of high rank ; tip-top, crack, swell. *Haute* —; high rank, high class, society, aristocracy. *Donner une* — *à quelqu'un ;* to give any one a drubbing. *A la* —; flying, in the air ; (fig.) at random, rashly, unthinkingly. *Entre bond et* —; at a lucky moment.

voler, *v.n.*, to fly, to fly about, to take wings, to soar, to be upon the wing. *Le temps vole ;* time flies. — *en éclats ;* to fly into pieces. *Entendre* — *une mouche ;* to hear a pin drop.

voler, *v.a.*, (hawking) to chase ; to fly at, to fly.

voler, *v.a.*, to steal, to rob, to fleece ; to plunder ; to take away, to usurp. — *la bourse de quelqu'un ;* to steal any one's purse. — *de l'argent ;* to steal money. *Ne l'avoir pas volé ;* to have richly deserved it, to have well earned it; to have got one's deserts.

voler, *v.n.*, to steal, to rob. — *sur le grand chemin ;* to rob on the highway.

⊙**volereau** (vol-rô), *n.m.*, petty thief, pilferer.

volerie (vol-rî), *n.f.*, robbery ; robbing, pilfering; (falconry) flying.

volet, *n.m.*, shutter, window-shutter; pigeonhouse ; dove-cot ; ledge (of a pigeon-house), sorting-board (for seeds); (bot.) water-lily; (nav.) boat-compass.

voleter (vol-té), *v.n.*, to flutter, to hover, to flicker.

volette, *n.f.*, small hurdle, fly-net (for a horse).

voleu-r, *n.m.*, **-se**, *n.f.*, thief, robber, stealer, extortioner, fleecer. — *de grand chemin ;* highwayman, foot-pad. *Au* —*! stop thief ! Crier au* —; to cry out, stop thief ! *Quand les* —*s se battent, les larcins se découvrent ;* when thieves

fall out, honest men get their own. *Etre fait comme un* —; to be in tatters.

volière, *n.f.*, aviary, pigeon-house, large bird-cage.

volige, *n.f.*, (carp.) scantling, batten.

volition, *n.f.*, volition.

volontaire, *n.m.f.* and *adj.*, obstinate, headstrong person ; voluntary ; intended, intentional ; spontaneous ; obstinate, willful, heady, headstrong.

volontaire, *n.m.*, volunteer.

volontairement (-tèr-mān), *adv.*, voluntarily, willingly, willfully, intentionally, spontaneously.

volontariat, *n.m.*, (milit.) condition of the volunteer ; volunteering.

volonté, *n.f.*, will, mind, pleasure, intention, way. *pl.*, whims, fancies, caprices. *La bonne* — *est réputée pour le fait ;* the will is as good as the deed. *Tout plie sous sa* —; everything yields to his will. *Il aime à faire ses* —*s ;* he likes to have his own way. *Dernières* —*s ;* last will and testament. *Bonne* — ; good-will, readiness, willingness. *Avoir de la bonne* —; to be willing. *Mauvaise* —; ill-will, unwillingness. *A* —; at pleasure, at will.

volontiers (-tié), *adv.*, willingly, readily, gladly, with pleasure.

volsque, *n.m.f.* and *adj.*, Volscian.

voltaïque, *adj.*, voltaic. *Pile* —; voltaic pile.

voltairien, *n.m.*, **-ne**, *n.f.*, voltairian (a follower of Voltaire).

voltaïsme, *n.m.*, voltaism.

volte, *n.f.*, (fenc.) (man.) volt.

volte-face, *n.f.*, (—) turning of the head, turning round. — *! face about ! Faire* —; (milit.) to face about ; (fig.) to turn completely round, to rat.

volter, *v.n.*, (fenc.) to make a volt.

voltige, *n.f.*, slack-rope ; dancing on the slack-rope ; tumbling ; (man.) vaulting.

voltigeant, -e (-jan, -t), *adj.*, fluttering, hovering.

voltigement (-tij-mān), *n.m.*, tumbling; hovering, flying, fluttering, flutter ; vaulting on a slack-rope.

voltiger, *v.n.*, to flutter, to fly about, to hover; to vault on a slack rope, *or* on a horse; to tumble.

voltigeur, *n.m.*, vaulter, voltigeur, tumbler, leaper ; (milit.) footsoldier. *pl.*, riflemen, light infantry.

volubile, *adj.*, (bot.) volubile, volubilate, voluble.

volubilis, *n.m.*, (bot.) convolvulus.

volubilité, *n.f.*, volubility, rapidity, fluency. — *de langue ;* volubility.

voluble, *adj.*, (bot.) volubile, volubilate ; voluble, fluent, quick (of speech).

volume, *n.m.*, volume ; bulk, size, mass; compass (of the voice).

volumineu-x, -se, *adj.*, voluminous, bulky, large, considerable.

volupté, *n.f.*, voluptuousness ; pleasure, delight, luxury. *Il y a de la* — *à boire quand on a soif ;* it is a luxury to drink when one is thirsty.

voluptuaire, *n.m.adj.*, voluptuary ; luxurious; (jur.) of expenses on ornamental repairs.

voluptueusement (-eûz-mān), *adv.*, voluptuously.

voluptueu-x, -se, *n.* and *adj.*, voluptuary, epicure; voluptuous, sensual.

volute, *n.f.*, (arch.) volute, scroll ; (conch.) voluta.

voluté, -e, *adj.*, voluted, scrolled.

voluter, *v.a.*, to wind silk thread ; (arch.) to make volutes, to scroll.

volva *or* **volve**, *n.f.*, (bot.) volva, wrapper.

volvé, -e, *adj.*, (bot.) having a volva.

⊙**volvulus** (-lus), *n.m.*, (med.) ileus, (bot.) convolvulus.

vomer (vomèr), *n.m.*, (anat.) os vomer.

vomique, *n.f.*, (med.) vomica.

vomique, *adj.*, vomic. *Noix* —; vomic-nut ; nux vomica.

vomiquier, *n.m.*, (bot.) strychnos nux vomica, nux vomica tree.

vomir, *v.a.* and *n.*, to vomit, to bring up, to throw up ; to belch out, to cast up, to vomit forth. *Avoir envie de* —; to feel sick. *Faire des efforts pour* —; to retch. *— de la flamme ;* to belch out flame.

vomissement (-mis-mān), *n.m.*, vomiting, sickness.

vomiti-f, -ve, *adj.*, vomitive.

vomitif, *n.m.*, vomit, emetic.

vomitoire, *n.m.*, (med.) ⊙emetic ; (arch.) vomitory (large doors).

vorace, *adj.*, voracious, ravenous.

voracement (-ras-mān), *adv.*, voraciously, ravenously.

voracité, *n.f.*, voracity, ravenousness.

vos, *possessive adj.pl.*, your. *V.* **votre.**

votant, *n.m.*, voter.

votant, -e, *adj.*, voting, having a vote.

votation, *n.f.*, voting.

vote, *n.m.*, vote, voice, suffrage, poll, polling. *— à main levée ;* show of hands. *— au scrutin ;* ballot. *Adopté par un* —; carried. *Rejeté par un* —; lost, defeated.

voter, *v.n.*, to vote.

voter, *v.a.*, to vote. *— des remercîments à quelqu'un ;* to pass a vote of thanks to any one.

voti-f, -ve, *adj.*, votive, votary.

votre, *possessive adj.m.f.,* **vos,** *pl.*, your. *— serviteur ;* your servant. *Vos parents ;* your relations.

le **vôtre,** *possessive pron. m.,* **la vôtre,** *f.,* **les vôtres,** *pl.m.f.,* yours. *Il a pris ses livres et les —s ;* he has taken his books and yours.

le **vôtre,** *n.m.,* your own, yours. *pl.*, your relations, friends, etc. ; your pranks, tricks. *Je suis des —s ;* I am one of your party. *Etre des —s ;* to be one of you, to belong to your body ; to form one of your party. *Vous avez fait des —s ;* you have played one of your pranks.

vouer, *v.a.*, to vow, to devote, to dedicate, to consecrate, to doom.

se **vouer,** *v.r.*, to dedicate one's self, to apply one's self (to), to devote one's self (to). *Ne pas savoir à quel saint se* —; not to know which way to turn.

vouge, *n.m.*, boar-spear, bill-hook.

vouloir (voulant, voulu), *v.a.*, to will, to be willing, to be inclined, to have a fancy, to be pleased, to intend, to wish, to require ; t̃ consent ; to resolve, to determine ; to want; to try, to attempt, to endeavor ; to admit, to grant. *Je le veux ainsi ;* I will have it so. *Il veut que vous obéissiez ;* he will have you obey. *Je ne veux pas ;* I wont, I don't mean to. *Que voulez-vous ?* what do you want? what can I do for you? what can you expect? what was to be done? *Il ne sait ce qu'il veut ;* he does not know his own mind. *Dieu le veut ;* God wills it. *Dieu le veuille !* God grant it ! *Ce que femme veut, Dieu le veut ;* a woman must have her way. *— c'est pouvoir ;* where there 's a will, there 's a way. *Il veut que cela soit ;* he will have it so. *— du bien à quelqu'un ;* to wish any one well. *Je vous veux du bien ;* I am your well-wisher. *Se faire bien, mal, — de ;* to win any one's regard, to get disliked by. *S'en — de ;* to be angry with one's self for having. *— du mal à quelqu'un ;* to wish any one harm. *Vous l'avez voulu !* it is your own fault; you would have it. *En — à quelqu'un ;* to bear any one ill-will, to owe any one a grudge. *Elle m'en veut du mal ;* she bears me a grudge for it. *Il en voulait à l'argent ;* he was after the money. *Il nous demanda ce que nous lui voulions ;* he asked us what we

wanted of him. *A qui en veut-il ?* of whom, of what, does he complain? *En veux-tu, en voilà ;* as much as ever you like, heaps and heaps of. *Il y en avait à bouche en veux-tu ;* there was enough and to spare ; heaps of it. *Savoir ce que parler veut dire ;* to take the hint; to understand the (hidden) meaning. *Que veut dire cet homme ?* what does that man mean ? *Que veut dire cela ?* what does that mean ? *or* what is the meaning of this ? *Que veut dire ce mot ?* what is the meaning of this word ? *Si vous le voulez, il le voudra aussi ;* if you consent to it, he will do so too. *Oui, je le veux bien ;* yes, I consent to it, I am willing. *Je veux que vous sachiez ;* I wish you to know. *Veuillez me dire ;* please, or kindly, tell me. *Je le veux bien ;* with pleasure ! I have no objection. *Veuillez agréer ;* be pleased to accept.

vouloir, *n.m.*, will. *Bon* —; good-will. *Mauvais* —; ill-will.

voulu, -e, *adj., part.,* wished, wanted, desired ; requisite, required ; due, casual, received, accepted.

vous, *personal pron.*, you, ye. *— dites ;* you say. *De — à moi ;* between you and me.

vousseau *or* **voussoir,** *n.m.,* (arch.) wedge, archstone, vault-stone.

voussure, *n.f.*, (arch.) curve, elevation of an arch, coving.

voûte, *n.f.*, vault, arch, canopy. *pl.*, (of a horse-shoe) hollow, vaulting. *— surbaissée ;* surbased vault. *La clef de —;* the keystone. *— imparfaite ;* diminished arch. *— oblique ;* skew arch. *— d'arête ;* groined vault. *— de décharge ;* relieving vault. *— acoustique ;* whispering dome *or* gallery. *La — du ciel ;* the canopy of heaven.

voûter, *v.a.*, to vault, to arch. *— un fer à cheval ;* to hollow a horseshoe.

se **voûter,** *v.r.*, to arch, to vault ; (pers.) to be bent, to stoop, to grow round-shouldered.

voyage, *n.m.*, voyage, journey, travel, trip. *pl.*, travels. *— de long cours ;* (nav.) long voyage, voyage in foreign parts. *— d'aller ;* (nav.) outward voyage. *— de retour ;* (nav.) return voyage. *Faire un —;* to travel, to take a journey. *Faire un petit —;* to go a short trip. *Bon — !* pleasant journey to you ! *Etre en —;* to be traveling, to be abroad. *De —;* traveling. *En —;* traveling, journeying abroad.

voyager, *v.n.*, to travel, to voyage, to journey. *— à pied ;* to travel on foot. *— à cheval ;* to travel on horseback.

voyageu-r, *n.m.*, **-se,** *n.f.*, traveler ; passenger. *Commis —;* (com.) commercial traveler, traveler. *Oiseau —;* migratory bird. *Pigeon* —; carrier pigeon.

voyant, -e, *adj.*, gaudy, showy (of colors) ; person who can see, who is not blind.

voyant, *n.m.*, (Bibl.) seer, prophet.

voyelle, *n.f.*, (gram.) vowel.

voyer, *n.* and *adj. m.*, surveyor of roads, inspector of highways ; relating, pertaining, to roads.

voyou, *n.m.*, (pop.) young blackguard, cad.

vrac, vrague, *or* **vraque,** *n.m.*, (nav.) disorder. *En —;* pell-mell, unpacked, loose, in bulk. *Charger en —;* (nav.) to load with a loose cargo, or cargo in bulk.

vrai, -e, *adj.*, true, real, right, genuine ; proper ; fit; regular, arrant; very. *Il est — que je l'ai dit ;* it is true I said so. *Est-il — que vous l'ayez dit ?* is it true you said it ? *Toujours est-il —;* it is nevertheless true. *Un — savant ;* a thorough scholar. *Un — coquin ;* an arrant knave. *Pas — !* (fam.) is n't it true ! is n't it a fact !

vrai, *n.m.*, truth. *A dire —, à — dire ;* to speak the truth. *Cela sort du —;* that is going from the truth, that is out of character. *Au —;*

in truth, truly. *Le — n'est pas toujours vraisemblable ;* truth is stranger than fiction.

vrai, *adj.*, in truth, truly.

vraiment, *adv.*, truly, indeed ; verily, in truth, forsooth ! *Oui, — ;* yes, indeed.

vraisemblable (-san-), *n.m.* and *adj.*, probability, likelihood ; likely, probable.

vraisemblablement (-san-), *adv.*, likely, probably.

vraisemblance (-san-), *n.f.*, probability, likelihood.

vraque, *n.m. V.* **vrac.**

*****vrille**, *n.f.*, gimlet ; wimble, borer, piercer ; (bot.) clasper, tendril.

vrillé, -e, *adj.*, *part.*, bored ; spiral ; curled ; (bot.) claspered.

*****vriller**, *v.a.* and *n.*, to bore, to make holes with a gimlet ; (fig.) to ascend spirally (of fireworks).

*****vrillerie**, *n.f.*, gimlet-making.

*****vrillier**, *n.m.*, gimlet-maker.

*****vrillon**, *n.m.*, small wimble.

vu, *prep.*, seeing, considering. *— son âge ;* considering his age.

vu, *n.m.*, sight, examination, inspection; (jur.) introductory part. *Au — et au su de tout le monde ;* in the sight of the whole world, with the knowledge of everybody ; openly.

vu que, *conj.*, seeing that, since.

vue, *n.f.*, sight, eyesight ; eyes ; view, survey, inspection ; prospect ; light, window; design. *Il a perdu la — ;* he has lost his sight. *Avoir la — bonne ;* to have good eyes. *Avoir la — courte ;* to be short-sighted. *Avoir la — basse ;* to be near-sighted. *Jeter la — sur un objet ;* to cast one's eye upon an object. *Baisser la — ;* to look down. *Donner dans la — ;* to strike upon the eyes, to catch one's eye. *A perte de — ;* farther than the eye can reach ; out of sight ; at random ; far-fetched. *Des compliments à perte de — ;* long-winded compliments. *Perdre de — une chose ;* to lose sight of a thing. *A — ;* at sight. *A — de pays ;* by guess. *Garder un prisonnier à — ;* not to let a prisoner out of sight. *A — d'œil ;* by the eye, visibly. *Avoir la — sur quelqu'un ;* to keep a watch over any one. *Avoir des —s sur ;* to have designs upon. *Connaître de — ;* to know by sight. *A dix jours de — ;* ten days after sight. *Une — de côté ;* a side view. *Un plan à — d'oiseau ;* a bird's-eye view. *Cette maison a une belle — ;* that house has a fine view. *Son appartement a — sur la rivière ;* his apartment looks out upon the river. *Dans la — de ;* with a view of. *Il a de grandes —s ;* he aims at great things, he aims high. *Je l'ai fait dans cette — ;* I did it with that end in view. *Avoir une chose en — ;* to have a thing in one's eye, in view.

vulcain, *n.m.*, (myth.) Vulcan ; (fig.) smith, blacksmith; (butterfly) red-admiral.

vulcanien, -ne (-ni-in, -ni-è-n), *adj.*, (geol.) plutonian, vulcanian.

vulcanisation, *n.f.*, vulcanization.

vulcanisé, -e, *adj.*, vulcanized.

vulcaniser, *v.a.*, to vulcanize.

vulgaire, *n.m.* and *adj.*, vulgar, common people ; vulgar, common. *Le — ;* the vulgar herd, the common run of people.

vulgairement (-ghèr-mān), *adv.*, vulgarly, commonly, generally.

vulgarisateur, *n.m.*, *adj.*, vulgarizer (of knowledge); vulgarizing, popularizing.

vulgarisation, *n.f.*, vulgarization, diffusing (of knowledge).

vulgariser, *v.a.*, to vulgarize, to popularize ; *se* **vulgariser**, *v.r.*, to be, to become vulgarized, popularized.

vulgarité, *n.f.*, vulgarity, commonness, triviality.

vulgate, *n.f.*, vulgate (Latin Bible).

vulgivague, *adj.*, prostituted. *Femme — ;* prostitute.

vulnérabilité, *n.f.*, vulnerableness.

vulnérable, *adj.*, vulnerable.

vulnérablement, *adv.*, vulnerably.

vulnéraire, *n.m.* and *adj.*, (pharm.) vulnerary.

vulnéraire, *n.f.*, (bot.) kidney-vetch, woundwort.

vulnérant, -e, *adj.*, wounding.

vulnération, *n.f.*, wounding, wounds.

vulpin, *n.m.*, (bot.) foxtail (grass).

vulpin, -e, *adj.*, vulpine, fox-like. [face.]

vultueu-x, -se, *adj.*, (med.) flushed (of the

vulve, *n.f.*, (anat.) vulva.

W

w (double vé), *n.m.*, (this letter does not belong to the French alphabet, and is used in foreign words only), w.

wacke, *n.m.*, (min.) wacke.

wagon (va-gon), *n.m.*, wagon, truck, van, railway carriage. *— écurie ;* (rail.) horse-box. *— étable ;* cattle-truck. *— frein ;* brake-van. *— lit ;* sleeping-car. *— poste ;* mail carriage. *En — !* take your seats ! *— restaurant ;* dining car. *— salon ;* Pullman car.

walhalla, *n.m.*, (n.p.) Odin's paradise.

walkyrie, *n.f.* (—s). *V.* **valkyrie.**

wallon, *n.m.*, **-ne**, *n.f.*, Walloon.

wallon, *n.m.*, Walloon (language).

warrant, *n.m.*, warrant.

warranter, *v.a.*, (com.) to warrant, to certify.

watergang or **watregan**, *n.m.*, small canal ; ditch (in Flanders).

wesleyen, -ne, *adj.*, Wesleyan.

whig (ooig), *n.m.*, Whig.

whiggisme, *n.m.*, Whiggism.

whiskey (ooiski), *n.m.*, whisky (spirit).

whist, *n.m.*, whist.

wicléfisme, *n.m.*, Wicliffism.

wicléfiste, *n.m.*, Wicliffite.

wigwam, *n.m.*, wigwam.

wisk, *n.m. V.* **whist.**

wiskey, *n.m. V.* **whiskey.**

wolfram (vol-fram), *n.m.*, (min.) wolfram.

wombat, *n.m.*, (mam.) wombat.

X

x (iks), *n.m.*, the twenty-third letter of the alphabet, x.

xanthe, *n.m.*, (bot.) burweed.

xbre (ab. of *décembre*), Dec.

xérasie (ksé-), *n.f.*, (med.) xerasia, alopecia.

xerès, *n.m.*, sherry-wine.

xérophagie (ksé-), *n.f.*, xerophagy.

xérophtalmie (ksé-), *n.f.*, xerophthalmy.

xiphias (ksi-fias), *n.m.*, (ich., astron.) xiphias.

xiphoïde (ksi-), *adj.*, (anat.) xiphoid, ensiform.

xylocope, *n.m.*, (zoöl.) xylocope, carpenter bee.

xylographe (ksi-), *n.m.*, xylographer, wood-engraver.

xylographie (ksi-), *n.f.*, xylography, wood-engraving.

xylographique (ksi-), *adj.*, xylographic, of wood-engraving.

xyloïdine, *n.f.*, (chem.) xyloidine.

xylophage (ksi-), *n.m.* and *adj.*, (ent.) xylophagan ; wood-fretter, bark-chafer ; xylophagous.

xylophagie, *n.f.*, xylophagy.

xylophone, *n.m.*, (mus.) xylophone.

xyste (ksist), *n.m.*, (antiq.) xyst, xystos.

Y

y (i-grèk), *n.m.*, the twenty-fourth letter of the alphabet, y.

y, *adv.*, there, thither ; within, at home. *Je l'y ai vu;* I saw him there. *Allez-y;* go there. *Voulez-vous y aller?* will you go there ? *Monsieur A., y est-il?* is Mr. A. in, or at home ? *Oui, il y est;* yes, he is at home.

y, *personal pron.*, by it, by them ; for it, for them ; in it, in them, therein ; at it, at them ; to him, to her, to it, to them. *Il n'y est pas propre;* he is not fit for it. *Il n'y gagnera rien;* he will get nothing by it. *Ne vous y fiez pas;* don't trust him. *Sans y penser;* without thinking of it. *Il — a;* there is or there are.

yac, *n.m.*, Union Jack.

yacht (iak), *n.m.*, yacht.

yacou, *n.m.*, (orni.) yacou.

yankee (-ki), *n.m.*, Yankee.

yard (iard), *n.m.*, yard (measure).

yatagan, *n.m.*, yataghan.

yèble, *n.m.* V. **hièble.**

yénite, *n.f.*, (min.) yenite.

yeuse, *n.f.*, ilex, holm, evergreen oak, holly oak.

yeux, *n.m.pl.*, eyes (*plur.* of œil, q.v.).

yole, *n.f.*, (nav.) yawl. *— gig;* gig.

youyou, *n.m.*, dingey, small boat (China).

ypréau, *n.m.*, Ypres-elm, wych-elm.

ysard, *n.m.* V. **isard.**

yucca, *n.m.*, (bot.) yucca, Adam's needle.

Z

z (zèd), *n.m.*, the twenty-fifth letter of the alphabet, z.

zabre, *n.m.*, corn-ground beetle.

zagaie, *n.f.*, assegai (African javelin).

zaïm, *n.m.*, zaïm (Turkish soldier).

zain, *adj.*, whole-colored (of horses, etc.).

zamie, *n.f.*, (bot.) zamia.

zani, *n.m.*, zany.

zèbre, *n.m.*, zebra.

zébré, -e, *adj.*, striped like the zebra.

zébrure, *n.f.*, stripes (like the zebra's).

zébu, *n.m.*, (mam.) zebu.

zédoaire, *n.f.*, (bot.) zedoary.

zée, *n.m.*, (ich.) zeus.

zélat-eur, *n.m.*, **-rice,** *n.f.*, zealot, zealous person.

zèle, *n.m.*, zeal, warmth, ardor. *Avoir du — pour,* or *à;* to be zealous in. *Avoir peu de —;* not to be zealous, to be lukewarm. *Avec —;* zealously. *S'enflammer de — pour;* to be fired with zeal (for).

zélé, -e, *adj.*, zealous.

zélote, *n.f.*, zealot.

zélotisme, *n.m.*, zealotry.

zend (zïnd), *n.m.*, (n.p.) Zend; religious doctrine of Zoroaster.

zend, -e (zïnd), *adj.*, relating to Zend.

zend-avesta (zïnd-), *n.m.*, (n.p.) Zendavesta (sacred book of the Guebers or Parsees).

zénith (-nit), *n.m.*, (astron.) zenith.

zénonique, *adj.*, Zenonic.

zénonisme, *n.m.*, Zenonism.

zéolithe, *n.m.*, zeolite.

zéphire or **zéphyr,** *n.m.*, zephyr, gentle breeze.

zéro, *n.m.*, nought; cipher; zero (of the thermometer). *A —;* at zero. *Au-dessous de —;* below zero. *C'est un — or un — en chiffre;* he is a mere cipher.

zest (zèst), *n.m.*, only used in the proverbial and familiar expression *Entre le zist et le —;* pretty well, so-so ; middling; undecided, wavering (of persons).

zest (zèst), *int.*, pshaw ! nonsense ! presto !

zeste (zèst), *n.m.*, zest (of a lemon, orange, walnut) ; straw, fig, nothing. *Cela ne vaut pas un —;* it is not worth a straw.

zététique, *n.f.* and *adj.*, zetetics ; zetetic.

zeugme, *n.m.*, (rhet.) zeugma.

zézaiement, *n.m.*, lisping, lisp (bad pronunciation which consists in giving to g or j the soft sound of z).

zézayer, *v.n.*, to lisp.

zibeline, *n.f.*, sable. *Martre —;* sable fur.

zigzag (zig-zag), *n.m.*, zigzag ; crankle ; (of lightning) fork. *Faire des —s;* to reel about, to stagger. *Aller en —;* to zigzag. *Eclair en —;* forked lightning.

zigzaguer, *v.n.*, to zigzag ; to reel about.

zinc, *n.m.*, zinc.

zincage or **zingage,** *n.m.*, zinking, covering with zinc.

zincographe, *n.m.*, zincographer.

zincographie, *n.f.*, zincography.

zincographique, *adj.*, zincographic, zincographical.

zingari, *n.m.*, (—s) Gypsy.

zinguer (-ghé), *v.a.*, to cover with zinc; to lay with zinc.

zinguerie, *n.f.*, zinc-works.

zingueur (-gheur), *n.m.*, zinc-worker.

zinzolin, *n.m.*, red violet.

zircon, *n.m.*, (min.) zircon.

zirconium, *n.m.*, (chem.) zirconium.

zist (zist), *n.m.* V. **zest.**

zizanie, *n.f.*, (bot.) ☉tare, darnel-grass ; Canada rice ; (fig.) division, dissension, discord, variance. *Semer la —;* to sow dissension, discord.

zizi, *n.m.*, (orni.) cirl-bunting.

zodiacal, -e, *adj.*, zodiacal.

zodiaque, *n.m.*, zodiac.

zoïle, *n.m.*, (—s) Zoïlus ; (fig.) a snarling critic.

zona or **zoster** (-tè-r), *n.m.*, (med.) shingles.

zone, *n.f.*, zone, belt. *— glaciale;* frigid zone. *— tempérée;* temperate zone. *— torride;* torrid zone.

zoné, -e, *adj.*, zoned.

zoographe, *n.m.*, zoögrapher.

zoographie, *n.f.*, zoögraphy.

zoolâtre, *n.m.*, zoölater.

zoolâtrie, *n.f.*, zoölatry.

zoolithe, *n.m.*, zoölite.

zoologie, *n.f.*, zoölogy.

zoologique, *adj.*, zoölogic, zoölogical.

zoologiste, *n.m.*, zoölogist.

zoologue, *n.m.* V. **zoologiste.**

zoonomie, *n.f.*, zoönomy.

zoophage, *n.m.* and *adj.*, zoöphagan (carnivorous quadruped); zoöphagous.

zoophore, *n.m.*, (arch.) zoöphorous.

zoophyte, *n.m.*, zoöphyte.

zootigue, *adj.*, zoötic.

zootomie, *n.f.*, zoötomy.

zootomiste, *n.m.*, zoötomist.

zopolite, *n.m.*, vulture (Mexican).

zopissa, *n.m.*, (nav.) zopessa (pitch scraped off ships).

zostère, *n.f.*, sea-weed, wrack-grass.

zouave, *n.m.*, zouave (soldier).

zoulou, *n.m.*, zulu.

zut, *int.* be blowed ! hang it ! not if I know it ! no use ! no go !

zygène, *n.m.*, (ich.) hammer-fish.

zygoma, *n.m.*, zygoma.

zygomatique, *adj.*, zygomatic. *Arcade —;* zygomatic arch.

zymosimètre, *n.m.*, zymosimeter (instrument).

zymotique, *adj.*, zymotic.

VOCABULARY OF PROPER NAMES,

INCLUDING THOSE OF

HISTORY AND MYTHOLOGY.

A

Aaron (aarōn), *m.*, Aaron.
Abdias (abdiäs), *m.*, Obadiah.
Abel, *m.*, Abel.
Abigail, *f.*, Abigail.
Abner (abnèr), *m.*, Abner.
Abraham, *m.*, Abraham.
Absalon, *m.*, Absalom.
Acaste, *m.*, Acastus.
Aceste, *m.*, Acestes.
Achab (akab), *m.*, Ahab.
Achate (akat), *m.*, Achates.
Achille (ashïl), *m.*, Achilles.
Achmet (akmèt), *m.*, Achmet.
Actéon, *m.*, Actæon.
Ada, *f.*, Adah.
Adam (adān), *m.*, Adam.
Adélaïde (adé-la-ï-d), *f.*, Adelaide.
Adèle, *f.*, Adela.
Admète, *m.*, Admetus.
Adolphe, *m.*, Adolphus.
Adonis (-nîs), *m.*, Adonis.
Adraste, *m.*, Adrastus.
Adrastée, *f.*, Adrastia.
Adrien (adriin), *m.*, Adrian.
Agamemnon, *m.*, Agamemnon.
Agar, *f.*, Hagar.
Agathe, *f.*, Agatha.
Agathocle, *m.*, Agathocles.
Agésilas (-lâs), *m.*, Agesilaus.
Aggée, *m.*, Haggai.
Agis (ajis), *m.*, Agis.
Aglaé, *f.*, Aglaia.
*Agnès (-ès), *f.*, Agnes.
Agricola, *m.*, Agricola.
Agrippine, *f.*, Agrippina.
Aimée, *f.*, Amy.
Aladin, *m.*, Aladdin.
Alain, *m.*, Allen.
Alaric, *m.*, Alaric.
l'Albane, *m.*, Albano.
Albert, *m.*, Albert.
Albertine, *f.*, Albertina, Alberta.
Alcée, *m.*, Alcæus.
Alceste, *f.*, (myth) Alcestis.
Alcibiade, *m.*, Alcibiades.
Alcide, *m.*, Alcides.
Alcinoüs, *m.*, Alcinous.
Alcmène, *f.*, Alcmena.
Alecton, *f.*, Alecto.
Alexandre (alèksändr), *m.*, Alexander.
Alfred (-frèd), *m.*, Alfred.
Aliboron, *m.*, Grizzle.
Alice, *f.*, Alice.
Alphée, *m.*, Alpheus.
Alphonse, *m.*, Alphonso.
Althée, *f.*, Althæa.
Aluin, *m.*, Alwin.
Amalec, *m.*, Amalek.

Amalthée, *f.*, Amalthæa.
Aman, *m.*, Haman.
Ambroise, *m.*, Ambrose.
Amédée, *m.*, Amedeus.
Amélie, *f.*, Amelia.
Améric Vespuce, *m.*, Americus Vesputius, Amerigo Vespucci.
Amilcar, *m.*, Hamilcar.
Amphitryon, *m.*, Amphitryon.
Amurat, *m.*, Amurath.
Anacharsis (-karsis), *m.*, Anacharsis.
Anacréon, *m.*, Anacreon.
Anastase, *m.*, Anastasius.
Anaxagore, *m.*, Anaxagoras.
Anaxarque, *m.*, Anaxarchus.
Anaximandre, *m.*, Anaximander.
Anchise, *m.*, Anchises.
André, *m.*, Andrew.
Androclès, *m.*, Androcles.
Andromaque, *f.*, Andromache.
Andromède, *f.*, Andromeda.
Ange, *m.*, Angelus.
Angélique, *f.*, Angelica.
Anna, *f.*, Hannah.
Anne, *f.*, Anne, Ann, Anna.
Annette, *f.*, Annie, Nancy.
Annibal, *m.*, Hannibal.
Anselme, *m.*, Anselmo.
Antée, *m.*, Antæus.
Antigone, *m.*, Antigonus.
Antigone, *f.*, Antigone.
Antiloque, *m.*, Antilochus.
Antipater (-tèr), *m.*, Antipater.
Antoine, *m.*, Anthony, Antony. Marc —; *Marc Antony*.
Antoinette, *f.*, Antoinette.
Antonin, *m.*, Antoninus.
Antonine, *f.*, Antonina.
Aod *or* Ahod, *m.*, Ehud.
Apelle (apèl), *m.*, Apelles.
Apollodore, *m.*, Apollodorus.
Apollon, *m.*, Apollo.
Appien (apiïn), *m.*, Appian.
Apulée, *m.*, Apuleius.
Aquin, *m.*, Aquinas. Saint Thomas d'—; *Thomas Aquinas.*
Arabelle, *f.*, Arabella.
Arbace, *m.*, Arbaces.
Arcade, *m.*, Arcadius.
Arcésilas (-lâs), *m.*, Arcesilaus.
Archambaud (-bô), *m.*, Archibald.
Archélaüs (-kéla-ûs), *m.*, Archelaus.
Archiloque, *m.*, Archilochus.
Archimède, *m.*, Archimedes.
Aréthuse, *f.*, Arethusa.
l'Arétin, *m.*, Aretino.
Ariane, *f.*, Ariadne.
Aricie, *f.*, Aricia.

Aridée, *m.*, Arridæus.
l'Arioste, *m.*, Ariosto.
Arioviste, *m.*, Ariovistus.
Aristarque, *m.*, Aristarchus.
Aristée, *m.*, Aristeus.
Aristide, *m.*, Aristides.
Aristophane, *m.*, Aristophanes.
Aristote, *m.*, Aristotle.
Arlequin, *m.*, Harlequin.
Armide, *f.*, Armida.
Arnaud, *m.*, Arnold.
Arrien (ariïn), *m.*, Arrian.
Arsène, *m.*, Arsenius.
Artaban, *m.*, Artabanus.
Artaxerce (-gzer-s), *m.*, Artaxerxes. — Longue-Main; *Artaxerxes Longimanus.*
Artémise, *f.*, Artemisia.
Arthur, *m.*, Arthur.
*Ascagne, *m.*, Ascanius.
Asclépiade, *m.*, Asclepiades.
Asmodée, *m.*, Asmodeus.
Aspasie, *f.*, Aspasia.
Asser (a-cè-r), *m.*, Asher.
Assuérus (-rûs), *m.*, Ahasuerus.
Astrée, *f.*, Astræa.
Astyage, *m.*, Astyages.
Atalante, *f.*, Atalanta.
Athalie, *f.*, Athaliah.
Athanase, *m.*, Athanasius.
Athelstan, *m.*, Athelstane.
Atlas, *m.*, Atlas.
Atrée, *m.*, Atreus.
Atride, *m.*, Atrides.
Attale, *m.*, Attalus.
Atticus (-kûs), *m.*, Atticus.
Augias (ôjiäs), *m.*, Augeas.
Auguste, *m.*, Augustus.
Augustin, *m.*, Austin, Augustine. Saint —; *Saint-Augustin.*
Augustule, *m.*, Augustulus.
Aulu-Gelle, *m.*, Aulus-Gellius.
Aurèle, *m.*, Aurelius. Marc —; *Marcus Aurelius.*
Aurélie, *f.*, Aurelia.
Aurélien (-liin), *m.*, Aurelian.
Aurore, *f.*, Aurora.
Ausone, *m.*, Ausonius.
Aventin, *m.*, Aventine.
Avicenne, *m.*, Avicenna.
Azarias, *m.*, Azariah.

B

Babet, *f.*, Betsy, Bess.
*Bailleul, *m.*, Baliol.
Bajazet, *m.*, Bajazeth.
Bajala, *f.*, Bilhah.
Balthazar, *m.*, Balthazar, Belshazzar.
Baptiste (batist), *m.*, Baptist.

Barabbas (-bâs), *m.*, Barabbas.
Barbe, *n.f.*, Barbara.
Barbe Bleue, *f.*, Bluebeard.
Barberousse, *m.*, Barbarossa.
Bardesane, *m.*, Bardesanes.
Barnabé, *m.*, Barnaby, Barnabas.
Barthélemi (-télmi) *m.*, Bartholomew.
Barthole, *m.*, Bartolo.
Basile, *m.*, Basil.
Basilide, *m.*, Basilides.
Bathuel, *m.*, Bethuel.
Baudouin, *m.*, Baldwin.
Béatrice, *f.*, Beatrice.
Béatrix, *f.*, Beatrix.
Bède, *m.*, Beda.
Bélisaire, *m.*, Belisarius.
Bellone, *f.*, Bellona.
Belzébuth, *m.*, Beelzebub.
Bénédict (-dict), Benoît, *m.*, Benedict.
Bénédicte, *f.*, Benedicta.
Benjamin (bin-), *m.*, Benjamin.
Benoît, *m.*, Benedict.
Benoite, *f.*, Benedicta.
Benserade (binsrad), *m.*, Benserade.
Bérénice, *f.*, Berenice, Beronice.
Bernard, *m.*, Bernard.
Bernardin, *m.*, Bernardine.
Berthe, *f.*, Bertha.
Bertrand, *m.*, Bertram.
Bethsabée, *f.*, Bathsheba.
Bèze, *m.*, Beza.
Blaise, *m.*, Blase.
Blanche, *f.*, Blanch, Blanche.
Boccace, *m.*, Boccaccio.
Boèce, *m.*, Boethius.
Boleslas (-lâs), *m.*, Boleslaus.
le Bolognèse, *m.*, Bolognese.
Bonaventure, *m.*, Bonadventure.
Boniface, *m.*, Boniface.
Bonne, *f.*, Bona.
Booz (booz), *m.*, Boaz.
Borée, *m.*, Boreas.
Bouddha, *m.*, Buddha.
Briarée, *m.*, Briareus.
Brigitte, *f.*, Bridget.
Britannicus (-kûs), *m.*, Britannicus.
Bucéphale, *m.*, Bucephalus.

C

Caïn, *m.*, Cain.
Caïnan, *m.*, Cainan.
Caïphe, *m.*, Caiaphas.
Caïus (ka-iûs), *m.*, Caius.
Caligula, *m.*, Caligula.
Caliste, *m.*, Calistus.
Callicrate (kal-li-), *m.*, Callicrates.
Callimaque, *m.*, Callimachus.
Calliope, *f.*, Calliope.
Callisthène, *m.*, Callisthenes.
Calpurnie, *f.*, Calpurnia.
Calvin, *m.*, Calvin.
Calypso, *f.*, Calypso.
Cambyse, *m.*, Cambyses.
*Camille, *m.*, Camillus.
*Camille, *f.*, Camilla.
le Camoens, *m.*, Camoens.
Canut, *m.*, Canute. — le Hardi ; Hardicanute.
Capitolin, *m.*, Capitolinus.
Carbon, *m.*, Carbo.

Caroline, *f.*, Caroline.
Caron, *m.*, Charon.
Casimir, *m.*, Casimir.
Cassandre, *m.*, Cassander.
Cassandre, *f.*, Cassandra.
Catherine (ka-tri-n), *f.*, Catharine, Catherine.
Catilina, *m.*, Catilina, Catiline.
Catin, *f.*, Kate, Kitty.
Caton, *m.*, Cato.
Catulle, *m.*, Catullus.
Cécile, *f.*, Cecilia.
Célestin, *m.*, Celestine.
Célie, *f.*, Celia.
Celse, *m.*, Celsus.
Cendrillon, *f.*, Cinderella.
Céphale, *m.*, Cephalus.
Cerbère, *m.*, Cerberus.
Cérès (-rès), *f.*, Ceres.
Cérinthe, *m.*, Cerinthus.
Césaire, *m.*, Cæsarius.
César, *m.*, Cæsar.
Chabrias (-âs), *m.*, Chabrias.
Cham (kam), *m.*, Ham.
*Charlemagne, *m.*, Charlemagne.
Charles, *m.*, Charles. — Quint ; Charles the Fifth (of Spain). — le Téméraire ; Charles the Bold.
Charlot, *m.*, Charly.
Charlotte, *f.*, Charlotte.
Charon (kâron), *m.*, Charon.
Chloé, *f.*, Chloe.
Chrétien (krétiin), *m.*, Christian.
Christienne, *f.*, Christiana.
le Christ (krist), *m.*, Christ.
Christine (kris-), *f.*, Christina.
Christophe (kris-), *m.*, Christopher.
Chryséis (krizéis), *f.*, Chryseïs.
Chrysès (krizès), *m.*, Chryses.
Chrysippe (krizip), *m.*, Chrysippus.
Chrysostôme (kri-), *m.*, Chrysostom.
Cicéron, *m.*, Cicero.
les Cimbres, *m.pl.*, the Cimbri.
Cincinnatus (-ci-n-na-tûs), *m.*, Cincinnatus.
Circé, *f.*, Circe.
Clara or Claire, *f.*, Clara.
Clarisse, *f.*, Clarissa.
Claude, *m.*, Claudius. — le Lorrain; Claude Lorraine.
Claude, *f.*, Claudia.
Claudie, *f.*, Claudia.
Claudien (-diin), *m.*, Claudian.
Cléanthe, *m.*, Cleanthes.
Cléarque, *m.*, Clearchus.
Clélie, *f.*, Clœlia.
Clémence, *f.*, Mercy.
Clément, *m.*, Clement.
Clémentine, *f.*, Clementina.
Cléomène, *m.*, Cleomenes.
Cléopâtre, *f.*, Cleopatra.
Clio, *f.*, Clio.
Cloanthe, *m.*, Cloanthus.
Clotaire, *m.*, Clotharius, Clothaire.
Clotilde, *f.*, Clotilda.
Clytemnestre (klitèmnèstr), *f.*, Clytemnestra.
Collatin, *m.*, Collatinus.
Colomb (kolon), *m.*, Columbus.
Colombine, *f.*, Columbine.
Commode, *m.*, Commodus.
Comnène (komnè-n), *m.*, Comnenus.

Confucius (-ûs), *m.*, Confucius.
Conrad (-rad), *m.*, Conrad.
Constance, *m.*, Constantius.
Constance, *f.*, Constance.
Constantin, *m.*, Constantinus.
Copernic, *m.*, Copernicus.
Coré, *m.*, Korah.
Corinne, *f.*, Corinna.
Coriolan, *m.*, Coriolanus.
Cornélie, *f.*, Cornelia.
Cornélius (-ûs), *m.*, Cornelius.
le Corrège, *m.*, Correggio.
Cosme (kô-m), *m.*, Cosmus, Cosmo.
Créon, *m.*, Creon.
Crépin, *m.*, Crispin.
Crésus (-zus), *m.*, Crœsus.
Créuse, *f.*, Creusa.
Cupidon, *m.*, Cupid.
les Curiaces, *m.pl.*, the Curiatii.
Curion, *m.*, Curio.
Cyaxare, *m.*, Cyaxares.
Cybèle, *f.*, Cybela.
les Cyclopes, *m.pl.*, Cyclopes.
Cynégire, *m.*, Cynegirus.
Cyprien (sipriin), *m.*, Cyprianus.
*Cyrille, *m.*, Cyril.
Cythérée, *f.*, Cytheræa.

D

Dalila, *f.*, Delilah.
Damoclès (-clès), *m.*, Damocles.
Danaüs (-us), *m.*, Danaus.
le Dante, *m.*, Dante.
Daphné, *f.*, Daphne.
Daphnis (-nîs), *m.*, Daphnis.
Darius (-ûs), *m.*, Darius. — Codoman; Darius Codomanus.
Débora, *f.*, Deborah.
Dèce, *m.*, Decius.
Dédale, *m.*, Dædalus.
Déidamie, *f.*, Deïdamia.
Déjanire, *f.*, Dejanira.
Délie, *f.*, Delia.
Démade, *m.*, Demades.
Démocède, *m.*, Democedes.
Démocrate, *m.*, Democrates.
Démocrite, *m.*, Democritus.
Démosthène, *m.*, Demosthenes.
Denis, *m.*, Dionysius ; Denis. — l'Ancien ; Dionysius the elder. — le Jeune ; Dionysius the younger.
Denise, *f.*, Dionysia.
Descartes (dèkart), *m.*, Descartes.
Diane, *f.*, Diana.
Didon, *f.*, Dido.
Dieudonné, *m.*, Deodatus.
Dioclétien (-siin), *m.*, Diocletian.
Diodore, *m.*, Diodorus. — de Sicile; Diodorus Siculus.
Diogène, *m.*, Diogenes. — Laerce ; Diogenes Laertius.
Diomède, *m.*, Diomedes.
Dominique, *m.*, Dominic.
le Dominiquin, *m.*, Dominichino.
Domitien (-siin), *m.*, Domitian.
Donat, *m.*, Donatus.
Dorothée, *f.*, Dorothea, Dorrit, Dorothy.

Dracon, *m.,* Draco.
*Drusille, *f.,* Drusilla.
Dulcinée, *f.,* Dulcinea.

E

Éaque, *m.,* Æacus.
Edmond, *m.,* Edmund. —
Côte-de-fer ; *Edmund Iron-side.*
Édouard, *m.,* Edward.
Égée, *m.,* Ægeus.
Égéon, *m.,* Ægæon.
Égérie, *f.,* Egeria.
Égisthe, *m.,* Ægisthus.
Églé, *f.,* Ægle.
Électre, *f.,* Electra.
Éléonore, *f.,* Eleanor.
Éliacin, *m.,* Eliakim.
Élie, *m.,* Elias, Elijah.
Élien (élin), *m.,* Ælianus.
Élisabeth, *f.,* Elizabeth.
Élise, *f.,* Eliza ; Ailsa.
Élisée, *m.,* Elisha.
Éloi, *m.,* Eloy.
Elvire, *f.,* Elvira.
Émeri, *m.,* Emery.
Émile, *m.,* Æmilius. Paul— ;
Paulus Æmilius.
Émilie, *f.,* Emily, Amelia.
Émilien (-liin), *m.,* Æmilian.
Emmanuel (è-m-manuèl), *m.,*
Emmanuel.
Empédocle, *m.,* Empedocles.
Encelade, *m.,* Enceladus.
Endymion, *m.,* Endymion.
Énée, *m.,* Æneas.
Énoch, *m.,* Enoch.
Éole, *m.,* Æolus.
Épaminondas (-dâs), *m.,* Epaminondas.
Épictète, *m.,* Epictetus.
Épicure, *m.,* Epicurus.
les **Épigones,** *m.pl.,* the Epigoni.
Épiménide, *m.,* Epimenides.
Épiphane, *m.,* Epiphanius.
Érasme, *m.,* Erasmus.
Érato, *f.,* Erato.
Éraste, *m.,* Erastus.
Ératosthène, *m.,* Eratosthenes.
Érèbe, *m.,* Erebus.
Ernest, *m.,* Ernest.
Érostrate, *m.,* Erostratus.
Ésaü, *m.,* Esau.
Eschine (ès-ghi-n), *m.,* Æschines.
Eschyle (ès-shil), *m.,* Æschylus.
Esculape, *m.,* Æsculapius.
Esdras (-drâs), *m.,* Esdras,
Ezra.
Éson, *m.,* Æson.
Ésope, *m.,* Æsop.
Esron, *m.,* Esrom.
Esther (éstèr), *f.,* Esther.
Étéocle, *m.,* Eteocles.
Étienne (étiè-n), *m.,* Stephen.
Euclide, *m.,* Euclid.
Eudoxie, *f.,* Eudoxia.
Eugène, *m.,* Eugenius, Eugene.
Eugénie, *f.,* Eugenia.
Eulalie, *f.,* Eulalia.
Eumée, *m.,* Eumæus.
Eumène, *m.,* Eumenes.

Euripide, *m.,* Euripides.
Europe, *f.,* Europa.
Euryale, *m.,* Euryalus.
Eurybate, *m.,* Eurybates.
Eurydice, *f.,* Eurydice.
Eurysthée, *m.,* Eurystheus.
Eusèbe, *m.,* Eusebius.
Eustache, *m.,* Eustace.
Eustathe, *m.,* Eustathius.
Eutrope, *m.,* Eutropius.
Évandre, *m.,* Evander.
Ève, *f.,* Eve.
Éveline, *f.,* Evelyn, Evelina.
Ézéchias (-kiâs), *m.,* Hezekiah, Ezechias.
Ézéchiel (-kièl), *m.,* Ezekiel.

F

Fabien (-biin), *m.,* Fabian.
Fabrice, Fabricius (-ûs), *m.,*
Fabricius.
Fallope, *m.,* Fallopio.
Fanchette,Fanchon,*f.,*Fanny,
Fanchon.
Fatima, *f.,* Fatima.
Faust (fôst), *m.,* Faustus,
Faust.
Faustine, *f.,* Faustina.
Félicie, *f.,* Felicia.
Félicien, *m.,* Felician.
Félicité, *f.,* Felicity.
Félix (-liks), *m.,* Felix.
Fernand, *m.,* Fernando.
Fiesque, *m.,* Fiesco.
Flavien (-viin), *m.,* Flavian.
Flore, *f.,* Flora.
Florence, *f.,* Florence.
Fortune, *f.,* Fortuna.
Fortuné, *m.,* Fortunatus.
Foulque, *m.,* Fulk.
François, *m.,* Francis.
Françoise, *f.,* Frances.
Frédégonde, *f.,* Fredegond.
Frédéric, *m.,* Frederick, Frederic.
Fulvie, *f.,* Fulvia.

G

Gabrielle, *f.,* Gabriella.
Galatée, *f.,* Galatea.
Galère, *m.,* Galerius.
Galien (-liin), *m.,* Galen.
Galilée, *m.,* Galileo.
Gallien (-liin), *m.,* Gallienus.
Ganymède, *m.,* Ganymede.
Gaspard, *m.,* Jasper.
Gauthier, *m.,* Walter, Wat.
Gédéon, *m.,* Gideon.
Gédouin, *m.,* Goodwin.
Gélon, *m.,* Gelo, Gelon.
Genséric, *m.,* Genseric.
Geoffroy (jofroa), *m.,* Geoffrey, Jeffrey.
Georges (jorj), *m.,* George.
Georgette (jorjèt), *f.,* Georgetta.
Georgine (jorji-n),*f.,* Georgina.
les **Gépides,** *m.pl.,* Gepidæ.
Géralde, *m.,* Gerald.
Géraldine, *f.,* Geraldine.
Gérard, *m.,* Gerard.
Germain, *m.,* German.
Gertrude, *f.,* Gertrude.
Gervais, *m.,* Gervase.
Gilles (jil), *m.,* Giles.

Glycère, *f.,* Glycera.
Godefroi, Godefroy (godfroa),
m., Godfrey.
Gordien (-diin), *m.,* Gordian.
Gorgias (-âs), *m.,* Gorgias.
Gracchus (grakûs), *m.,* Gracchus.
les **Gracques** (grak), *m.pl.,* the
Gracchi.
Gratien (-siin), *m.,* Gratian.
Grégoire, *m.,* Gregory.
Grippeminaud, *m.,* Grimalkin.
le **Guerchin,** *m.,* Guercino.
le **Guide,** *m.,* Guido.
*Guillaume (ghi-iô-m), *m.,*
William. — le conquérant :
William the Conqueror. — le
Roux ; *William Rufus.*
*Guillot (ghi-io), *m.,* Bill, Billy.
Gustave, *m.,* Gustavus.
Guy (ghi), *m.,* Guy.
Gylippe, *m.,* Gylippus.

H

Habacuc, *m.,* Habakkuk.
Haggée, *m.,* Haggai.
Hannon, *m.,* Hanno.
†Hardi Canut, *m.,* Hardicanute.
†Harold, *m.,* Harold.
Harpale, *m.,* Harpalus.
Harpocrate, *m.,* Harpocrates.
Hébé, *f.,* Hebe.
Hécate, *f.,* Hecate.
Hector, *m.,* Hector.
Hécube, *f.,* Hecuba.
Hégésippe, *m.,* Hegesippus.
Helcias (-âs), *m.,* Helkiah.
Hélène, *f.,* Helen, Helena.
Héliodore, *m.,* Heliodorus.
Héliogabale, *m.,* Heliogabalus.
Héloïse, *f.,* Eloisa, Heloisa.
Hénoch (ènok), *m. V.* **Énoch.**
†Henri, *m.,* Henry. [Henri in
familiar style has the *h* mute.]
Henriette, *f.,* Henrietta, Harriet.
Héraclide, *m.,* Heraclide.
Héraclite, *m.,* Heraclitus.
Hercule, *m.,* Hercules.
Hermione, *f.,* Hermione.
Hermocrate, *m.,* Hermocrates.
Héro, *f.,* Hero.
Hérode, *m.,* Herod.
Hérodien (-diin), *m.,* Herodian.
Hérodote, *m.,* Herodotus.
Hérophile, *m.,* Herophilus.
Hersilie, *f.,* Hersilia.
Hésiode, *m.,* Hesiod.
Hiéron, *m.,* Hiero.
Hiéronyme, *m.,* Hieronymus.
Hilaire, *m.,* Hilary.
Himilcon, *m.,* Himilco.
Hipparque, *m.,* Hipparchus.
Hippocrate, *m.,* Hippocrates.
Hippolyte, *f.,* Hippolyta.
Hippolyte, *m.,* Hippolytus.
Hippomène, *m.,* Hippomenes.
Hircan, *m.,* Hyrcanus.
Holopherne, *m.,* Holophernes,
Holofernes.
Homère, *m.,* Homer.
†Homfroi, *m.,* Humphrey.
Honoré, *m.,* Honoratus, Honorius.
Honorée, *f.,* Honoria.
Horace, *m.,* Horatio, Horatius;
Horace.

les **Horaces**, *m.pl.* the Horatii.
Hortense, *f.*, Hortensia.
†**Hugues** (hug), *m.*, Hugh.
Hunyade, *m.*, Huniades.
Hyacinthe, *m.*, Hyacinthus.
Hygie, *f.*, Hygeia.
Hymen, Hyménée, *m.*, Hymen, Hymenæus.
Hypéride, *m.*, Hyperides.
Hypérion, *m.*, Hyperion.
Hypermnestre, *f.*, Hypermnestra.
Hystaspe, *m.*, Hystaspes.

I

Icare, *m.*, Icarus.
Idoménée, *m.*, Idomeneus.
Ignace, *m.*, Ignatius.
Iphicrate, *m.*, Iphicrates.
Iphigénie, *f.*, Iphigenia.
Irène, *f.*, Irene.
Irénée, *m.*, Irenæus.
Isaac (izàak), *m.*, Isaac.
Isabelle, *f.*, Isabella.
Isaïe, *m.*, Isaiah.
Isidore, *m.*, Isidore, Isidorus.
Isis (izís), *f.*, Isis.
Ismaël, *m.*, Ishmael.
Isocrate, *m.*, Isocrates.
Israël (izraèl), *m.*, Israel.
Iule, *m.*, Iulus.

J

Jacob, *m.*, Jacob.
Jacques (jâk), *m.*, James.
— Bonhomme ; *Hodge.*
Jacquet, *m.*, Jem, Jim.
Jacquot, *m.*, Jack, Jim ; Poll, Pug.
James, *m.*, James. La Cour St.
— ; *the court of St. James.*
Jansénius (-ûs), *m.*, Jansenius.
Janvier, *m.*, Januarius.
Japhet, *m.*, Japheth.
Jean (jan), *m.*, John, Jack.
— sans terre ; *John Lackland.*
Jean-Jacques, *m.*, J. J. Rousseau.
Jeanne (jâ-n), *f.*, Jane, Joan.
— Darc ; *Joan of Arc.*
Jeannette (ja-nèt), **Jeanneton**, *f.*, Jenny.
Jeannot, *m.*, Johnny, Jacky.
Jenny, *f.*, Jenny.
Jephté, *m.*, Jephthah.
Jérémie, *m.*, Jeremy, Jeremiah.
Jérôme, *m.*, Jerome, Hieronymus.
Jessé, *m.*, Jesse.
Jésus (jézu), *m.*, Jesus.
Jésus-Christ (jézu-kri), *m.*, Jesus Christ.
Jézabel, *f.*, Jezebel.
Joachim (-ki-m), *m.*, Joachim.
Joad *or* **Joiada**, *m.*, Jehoiada.
Joas, *m.*, Joash.
Jocaste, *f.*, Jocasta.
Jocrisse, *m.*, Jack-Pudding.
Jonas (-nâs), *m.*, Jonah.
Jonathan *or* **Jonathas** (-tâs), *m.*, Jonathan.
Joram, *m.*, Jehoram.
Josaphat, *m.*, Jehoshaphat.
Josèphe (Flavien), *m.*, Josephus (Flavius).
Josias (-âs), *m.*, Josiah, Josias.

Josué, *m.*, Joshua.
Juda, *m.*, Judah.
Judas, *m.* — Iscariote ; *Judas Iscariot.*
Jude, *m.*, Judas (the apostle).
Jules, *m.*, Julius. — Romain ; *Giulio Romano.*
Julie, *f.*, Julia.
Julien (-liin), *m.*, Julian.
Julienne, *f.*, Juliana.
Juliette, *f.*, Juliet.
Junie, *f.*, Junia.
Junius (-ûs), *m.*, Junius.
Junon, *f.*, Juno.
Jupiter (-tèr), *m.*, Jupiter, Jove.
— Férétrien ; *Jupiter Feretrius.* — Olympien ; *Jupiter Olympius.* — Tonnant ; *Jupiter the Thunderer.*
Juste, *m.*, Justus.
Justine, *f.*, Justina.
Justinien (-niin), *m.*, Justinian.

L

Lactance, *m.*, Lactantius.
Ladislas (-lâs), *m.*, Ladislaus.
Laerce, *m.*, Laertius. *V.* **Diogène**.
Laërte, *m.*, Laertes.
Lancelot (lanslô), *m.*, Launcelot.
Laodamie, *f.*, Laodamia.
les **Lapithes**, *m.pl.*, Lapithæ.
Latone, *f.*, Latona.
Laure, *f.*, Laura.
Laurent, *m.*, Laurence, Lawrence.
Lavinie, *f.*, Lavinia.
Lazare, *m.*, Lazarus.
Léandre, *m.*, Leander.
Léon, *m.*, Leon, Leo.
Léonard, *m.*, Leonard. — de Vinci ; *Leonardo da Vinci.*
Léonat, *m.*, Leonatus.
Léonce, *m.*, Leontius.
Léonidas (-dâs), *m.*, Leonidas.
Léonie, *f.*, Leonia.
Léonore, *f.*, Leonora.
Lépide, *m.*, Lepidus.
Leucippe, *m.*, Leucippus.
Leucothoé, *f.*, Leucothoe.
Lévi, *m.*, Levy.
Lia, *f.*, Leah.
Libère, *m.*, Liberius.
Libitine, *f.*, Libitina.
Linné, *m.*, Linnæus.
Lise, Lisette, *f.*, Lizzie, Lizzy.
Livie, *f.*, Livia.
Longin, *m.*, Longinus.
Lothaire, *m.*, Lothaire, Lothario.
Louis, *m.*, Lewis, Louis.
Louise, Louison, *f.*, Louisa, Louise.
Luc, *m.*, Luke.
Lucain, *m.*, Lucan.
Lucie, *f.*, Lucy.
Lucien (-siin), *m.*, Lucian.
Lucile, *f.*, Lucilla.
Lucinde, *f.*, Lucinda.
Lucine, *f.*, Lucina.
Lucius (-ûs), *m.*, Lucius.
Lucrèce, *m.*, Lucretius.
Lucrèce, *f.*, Lucretia.
Lycurgue (-kurg), *m.*, Lycurgus.
Lydie, *f.*, Lydia.
Lyncée, *m.*, Lynceus.
Lysandre, *m.*, Lysander.

Lysimaque, *m.*, Lysimachus.
Lysippe, *m.*, Lysippus.

M

Macaire, *m.*, Macarius.
Machabée (makabé), *m.*, Maccabeus.
les **Machabées**, *m.pl.*, the Maccabees.
Machiavel, *m.*, Machiavelli, Machiavel.
Macrin, *m.*, Macrinus.
Macrobe, *m.*, Macrobius.
Madeleine (mad-lè-n), *f.*, Magdalen, Magdalene ; Madeline.
Madelon (madlon), *f.*, Maud.
Magnence, *m.*, Magnentius.
Magon, *m.*, Mago.
Mahomet, *m.*, Mahomet, Mahommed.
Mainfroi, *m.*, Manfred.
Malachie, *m.*, Malachi.
Mammée (mam-mé), *f.*, Mammea.
Manassé, *m.*, Manasseh, Manasses.
Mannasès, *m.*, (King) Manasseh.
Manon, *f.*, Molly.
Marc, *m.*, Mark. — Antoine ; *Mark Antony.*
Marc-Aurèle, *m.*, Marcus Aurelius.
Marcellin (-cèl-lin), *m.*, Marcellinus.
Marcelline, *f.*, Marcellina.
Marcien (-siin), *m.*, Marcian.
Mardochée, *m.*, Mordecai.
Margot, *f.*, Marget, Mag, Meg.
Marguerite (-grit), *f.*, Margaret.
Maria, *f.*, Maria, Mary.
Marianne, *f.*, Marian.
Marie, *f.*, Mary.
Mariette, Marion, *f.*, Molly, Marion.
Marthe, *f.*, Martha.
Martin, *m.*, Martin ; (bear) Bruin.
Mathan, *m.*, Matthan.
Mathieu, *m.*, Matthew.
Mathilde, *f.*, Matilda.
Mathusalem (-lè-m), *m.*, Methuselah.
Matthias, *m.*, Matthias.
Matthieu, *m.*, Matthew.
Maurice, *m.*, Maurice, Morice.
Mausole, *m.*, Mausolus.
Maviaël, *m.*, Mehujael.
Maxence, *m.*, Maxentius.
Maxime, *m.*, Maximus.
Maximien (-miin), *m.*, Maximianus, Maximian.
Maximilien (-liin), *m.*, Maximilian.
Maximin, *m.*, Maximinus.
Mécène, *m.*, Mecænas.
Médée, *f.*, Medea.
Médicis, *m.*, Medici.
Méduse, *f.*, Medusa.
Mégère, *f.*, Megæra.
Mélampe, *m.*, Melampus.
Mélanie, *f.*, Melania.
Melcha (mèlka), *f.*, Milcah.
Melchisédech (mèlkizédèk), *m.*, Melchizedek, Melchizedec.
Méléagre, *m.*, Meleager.

Mélicerte, *m.*, Melicerta.
Mélisse, *f.*, Melissa.
Melpomène, *f.*, Melpomene.
Mélusine, *f.*, Melusina.
Ménandre, *m.*, Menander.
Ménèce, *m.*, Menœtius.
Ménélas (-lâs), *m.*, Menelaus.
Ménippe, *m.*, Menippus.
Mercure, *m.*, Mercury.
Messaline, *f.*, Messalina.
Métastase, *m.*, Metastasio.
Michaud, *m.*, Mike.
Michée, *m.*, Micah.
Michel, *m.*, Michael.
Michel-Ange (mikèl-ānj), *m.*, Michael-Angelo.
Milon, *m.*, Milo.
Miltiade, *m.*, Miltiades.
Minerve, *f.*, Minerva.
Minos (minôs), *m.*, Minos.
Mithridate, *m.*, Mithridates.
Mohammed, *m.*, Mohammed, Mahomet.
Moïse, *m.*, Moses.
Monime, *f.*, Monima.
Morphée, *m.*, Morpheus.
Mucien, *m.*, Mucianus.
Myrtée, *f.*, Myrtea.
Myrtile, *m.*, Myrtilus.

N

Nabuchodonosor (-ko-), *m.*, Nebuchadnezzar.
Nannette, *f.*, Nancy.
Napoléon, *m.*, Napoleon.
Narcisse, *m.*, Narcissus.
Néarque, *m.*, Nearchus.
Néhémie, *m.*, Nehemiah.
Némésis (-zîs), *f.*, Nemesis.
Nemrod, *m.*, Nimrod.
Néoptolème, *m.*, Neoptolemus.
Nérée, *m.*, Nereus.
Néron, *m.*, Nero.
Nicaise, *m.*, Nicasius.
Nicéphore, *m.*, Nicephorus.
Nicodème, *m.*, Nicodemus.
Nicolas, *m.*, Nicholas, Nick.
Nicomède, *m.*, Nicomedes.
Ninon, *f.*, Nino, Nina.
Noé, *m.*, Noah.
Noël, *m.*, Noel. Le petit —; *Santa Claus.*
Noémi, *f.*, Naomi.

O

Océan, *m.*, (myth.) Oceanus.
Ochozias (okozîâs),*m.*, Ahaziah.
Octave, *m.*, Octavius.
Octavie, *f.*, Octavia.
Octavien (-viin), *m.*, Octavian.
Odin, *m.*, Odin, Woden.
Odoacre, *m.*, Odoacer.
Œdipe (edip), *m.*, Œdipus.
Olivie, *f.*, Olivia.
Olivier, *m.*, Oliver.
Olympe, *f.*, Olympia.
Olympiodore, *m.*, Olympiodorus.
Onésime, *m.*, Onesimus.
Onomacrite, *m.*, Onomacritus.
Onomarque, *m.*, Onomarchus.
Ophélie, *f.*, Ophelia.
Oppien (opin), *m.*, Oppian.
Oreste, *m.*, Orestes.
Origène, *m.*, Origen.
Oronte, *m.*, Orontes.

Orphée, *m.*, Orpheus.
Osée, *m.*, Hosea.
Osmond, *m.*, Osmund.
Othon, *m.*, Otho.
Ouen, *m.*, Owen. Saint —; *Saint Owen.*
Ovide, *n.m.*, Ovid.

P

Palamède, *m.*, Palamedes.
Palémon, *m.*, Palœmon.
Paléologue (-log), *m.*, Palæologus.
Palinure, *m.*, Palinurus.
Pandore, *f.*, Pandora.
Panthée, *m.*, Pantheus.
Paolo (Fra), *m.*, Paul of Venice; Paolo.
Papinien (-niin), *m.*, Papinian.
Paracelse, *m.*, Paracelsus.
Pâris (-rîs), *m.*, Paris.
Paris (Monsieur de), *m.*, Jack Ketch.
Parménide, *m.*, Parmenides.
Parménion, *m.*, Parmenio.
les Parques, *f.pl.*, the Parcæ, the Fates.
Patrice, *m.*, Patrick, Patricius.
Patrocle, *m.*, Patroclus.
Paul (pol), *m.*, Paul, Paulus.
Pauline, *f.*, Paulina, Pauline.
Pégase, *m.*, Pegasus.
Pélage, *m.*, Pelagius.
Pélée, *m.*, Peleus.
Pénélope, *f.*, Penelope.
Penthée, *m.*, Pentheus.
Penthésilée, *f.*, Penthesilea.
Pepin, *m.*, Pepin. — le Bref; *Pepin the Short.*
Périandre, *m.*, Periander.
Périclès (-klès), *m.*, Pericles.
Pérosès (-zès), *or* Firouz, *m.*, Perozes, Firouz.
Perse, *m.*, Persius.
Persée, *m.*, Perseus.
Pétrarque, *m.*, Petrarch.
Pétrone, *m.*, Petronius.
Phaéton, *m.*, Phaeton, Phaethon.
Pharaon, *m.*, Pharaoh.
Pharnabaze, *m.*, Pharnabazus.
Pharnace, *m.*, Pharnaces.
Phébé, *f.*, Phœbe.
Phébus (-bûs), *m.*, Phœbus.
Phédon, *m.*, Phædon.
Phèdre, *m.*, Phædrus.
Phèdre, *f.*, Phædra.
Phidias (-dîâs), *m.*, Phidias.
Philadelphe, *m.*, Philadelphus.
Philarète, *m.*, Philaretus.
Philippe, *m.*, Philip. — le Bel ; *Philip the Fair (of France).* — le Beau ; *Philip the Handsome (of Spain).*
Philippe, *f.*, Philippa.
Philippine, *f.*, Philippina.
Philocrate, *m.*, Philocrates.
Philoctète, *m.*, Philoctetes.
Philologue (-log), *m.*, Philologus.
Philomèle, *f.*, Philomela.
Philomèle, *m.*, Philomelus.
Phinée, Phinéas, *m.*, Phineas.
Phryné, *f.*, Phryne.
Phylée, *m.*, Phyleus.
Pie, *m.*, Pius.
Pierre, *m.*, Peter.

Pilate, *m.*, Pilate. Ponce —; *Pontius Pilate.*
Pindare, *m.*, Pindar.
Pisandre, *m.*, Pisander.
Pisistrate, *m.*, Pisistratus.
Pison, *m.*, Piso.
Pitthée, *m.*, Pittheus.
Placide, *f.*, Placidia.
Plancine, *f.*, Plancina.
Planude, *m.*, Planudes.
Platon, *m.*, Plato.
Plaute, *m.*, Plautus.
Plautien (-siin), *m.*, Plautian.
Pline, *m.*, Pliny. — l'Ancien ; *Pliny the Elder.* — le Jeune ; *Pliny the Younger.*
Plutarque, *m.*, Plutarch.
Pluton, *m.*, Pluto.
Polichinelle, *m.*, Punch.
Politien (-siin), *m.*, Politiano.
Pollion, *m.*, Pollio.
Polybe, *m.*, Polybius.
Polycarpe, *m.*, Polycarp.
Polyclète, *m.*, Polycletus.
Polycrate, *m.*, Polycrates.
Polydore, *m.*, Polydorus.
Polymnie (-lim-nî), *f.*, Polymnia.
Polynice, *m.*, Polynices.
Polyphème, *m.*, Polyphemus.
Polyxène, *f.*, Polyxena.
Pomone, *f.*, Pomona.
Pompée, *m.*, Pompey.
Pompéius, *m.*, Pompeius.
Pompilius (-ûs), *m.*, Pompilius.
Ponce, *m.*, Pontius.
Poppée, *f.*, Poppæa.
Porcie, *f.*, Porcia, Portia.
Porphyre, *m.*, Porphyry.
Poucet (le Petit), *m.*, Hop o' my Thumb.
Praxitèle, *m.*, Praxiteles.
Priape, *m.*, Priapus.
Priscien (pri-siin), *m.*, Priscian.
Priscille, *f.*, Priscilla.
Priscillien (-liin), *m.*, Priscillian.
Procope, *m.*, Procopius.
Procuste *or* Procruste, *m.*, Procrustes.
Prométhée, *m.*, Prometheus.
Properce, *m.*, Propertius.
Proserpine, *f.*, Proserpina.
Protée, *m.*, Proteus.
Protésilas (-lâs), *m.*, Protesilaus.
Protogène, *m.*, Protogenes.
Prudence, *m.*, Prudentius.
Prudence, *f.*, Prudence.
Psamménit, *m.*, Psammenitus.
Psammétique, *m.*, Psammetichus.
Psyché, *f.*, Psyche.
Ptolémée, *m.*, Ptolemy.
Pulchérie (-kérî), *f.*, Pulcheria.
Putiphar, *m.*, Potiphar.
Pylade, *m.*, Pylades.
Pyrame, *m.*, Pyramus.
Pyrrhon (pir-ron), *m.*, Pyrrho.
Pythagore, *m.*, Pythagoras.
Pythée, *m.*, Pytheas.

Q

Quichotte (Don) (ki-shot), *m.*, Don Quixote.
Quinte-Curce (kuint-kurs), *m.*, Quintus Curtius.

Quintilien (kuintiliin), *m.*, Quintilian.

R

Radegonde (radgond), *f.*, Radegund.
Rahab, *f.*, Rahab.
Raminagrobis, *m.*, Grimalkin.
Ramsès, *m.*, Rameses.
Randolphe, *m.*, Randolph, Randal.
Raoul, *m.*, Ralph.
Raphaël, *m.*, Raphael.
Raymond, *m.*, Raymond, Raymund.
Rémi, *m.*, Remy.
Renaud, *m.*, Reynold, Reginald.
Rhadamanthe, *m.*, Rhadamanthus.
Rhadamiste, *m.*, Rhadamistus.
Rhée, *f.*, Rhea.
Rhésus, *m.*, Rhesus.
Richard, *m.*, Richard.
Robert, *m.*, Robert.
Roboam (-am), *m.*, Rehoboam.
Rodolphe, *m.*, Rodolph.
Rodrigue, *m.*, Roderick, Roderic.
Roland, *m.*, Rowland, Rolando.
Romain, *m.*, Romanus. Jules —; *Giulio Romano.*
Roméo, *m.*, Romeo.
Rosalie, *f.*, Rosaline.
Rose, *f.*, Rose, Rosa.
Rosemonde (rôz-mond), *f.*, Rosamund, Rosamond.
Rosine, *f.*, Rosine, Rosina.
Roxane, *f.*, Roxana.
Ruben (-bin), *m.*, Reuben.
Rufin, *m.*, Rufinus.
Ruisdael, *m.*, Ruysdael.

S

Sabine, *f.*, Sabina.
Salluste, *m.*, Sallust.
Salmonée, *m.*, Salmoneus.
Salomon, *m.*, Solomon.
Salvien (-viin), *m.*, Salvian.
Samson (sanson), *m.*, Samson, Sampson.
Sancho Pança, *m.*, Sancho Panza.
Sapho, *f.*, Sappho.
Sara, *f.*, Sarah.
Sardanapale, *m.*, Sardanapalus.
Saturne, *m.*, Saturn.
Saturnin, *m.*, Saturninus.
Saül, *m.*, Saul.
Saumaise, *m.*, Salmasius.
Savinien, *m.*, Savinian.
Savonarole, *m.*, Savonarola.
Scipion, *m.*, Scipio. — l'Africain; *Scipio Africanus.* — l'Asiatique; *Scipio Asiaticus.*
Sébastien (-tiin), *m.*, Sebastian.
Sédécias (-âs), *m.*, Zedekiah.
Séjan, *m.*, Sejanus.
Sélène, *f.*, Diana ; Selene.
Sem (sè-m), *f.*, Shem.
Sémélé, *f.*, Semele.
Sénèque, *m.*, Seneca.
Sennachérib, *m.*, Sennacherib.
Séphora, *f.*, Zipporah.
Septime, *m.*, Septimius, Septimus.

Sergeste, *m.*, Sergestus.
Sévère, *m.*, Severus.
Sforce, *m.*, Sforza.
Sichée, *m.*, Sichæus.
Sidoine Apollinaire, *m.*, Sidonius Apollinaris.
Sigismond, *m.*, Sigismund.
Silène, *m.*, Silenus.
Silvain, *m.* *V.* **Sylvain**.
Silvestre, *m.*, Silvester.
Siméon, *m.*, Simeon.
Simonide, *m.*, Simonides.
Sisyphe, *m.*, Sisyphus.
Sixte, *m.*, Sextus. — Quint; *Sixtus the Fifth.*
Sminthée, *m.*, Smintheus.
Socin, *m.*, Socinus.
Socrate, *m.*, Socrates.
Sophie, *f.*, Sophia, Sophy.
Sophocle, *m.*, Sophocles.
Sophonie, *m.*, Zephaniah.
Sophonisbe, *f.*, Sophonisba.
Sosie, *m.*, Sosia.
Sosthène, *m.*, Sosthenes.
Stace, *m.*, Statius.
Stanislas (-lâs), *m.*, Stanislaus.
Stéphanie, *f.*, Stephania.
Stésichore (-kor), *m.*, Stesichorus.
Stilicon, *m.*, Stilicho.
Strabon, *m.*, Strabo.
Suénon, *m.*, Sweyn.
Suétone, *m.*, Suetonius.
Sulpice, *m.*, Sulpicius.
Susanne, *f.*, Susan, Susannah.
Susette, Suzon, *f.*, Susey, Susy.
Sylvain, *m.*, Sylvan, Sylvanus.
Sylvestre, *m.*, Sylvester.
Sylvie, *f.*, Sylvia.
Symmaque (sim-mak), *m.*, Symmachus.

T

Tacite, *m.*, Tacitus.
Tamerlan, *m.*, Tamerlane.
Tancrède, *m.*, Tancred.
Tantale, *m.*, Tantalus.
Tarquin, *m.*, Tarquinius.
Tarquinie, *f.*, Tarquinia.
le **Tasse**, *m.*, Tasso.
Tatius (ta-sius), *m.*, Tatius.
Taxile, *m.*, Taxilus.
Télégone, *m.*, Telegonus.
Télémaque, *m.*, Telemachus.
Télèphe, *m.*, Telephus.
Térée, *m.*, Tereus.
Térence, *m.*, Terence.
Terpandre, *m.*, Terpander.
Terpsichore (-kor), *f.*, Terpsichore.
Tertullien (-liin), *m.*, Tertullian.
Thaïs (ta-îs), *f.*, Thais.
Thalès (-lès), *m.*, Thales.
Thalie, *f.*, Thalia.
Thamar, *f.*, Tamar.
Thémis (-mîs), *f.*, Themis.
Thémistocle (-cle), *m.*, Themistocles.
Théocrite, *m.*, Theocritus.
Théodat, *m.*, Theodatus.
Théodora, *f.*, Theodora.
Théodore, *m.*, Theodorus, Theodore.
Théodose, *m.*, Theodosius.
Théodose, *f.*, Theodosia.
Théophane, *m.*, Theophanes.
Théophile, *m.*, Theophilus.

Théophraste, *m.*, Theophrastus.
Théopompe, *m.*, Theopompus.
Théramène, *m.*, Theramenes.
Thérèse, *f.*, Theresa.
Thersite, *m.*, Thersites.
Thésée, *m.*, Theseus.
Thibaut, *m.*, Theobald.
Thomassine, *f.*, Thomasin.
Thrasybule, *m.*, Thrasybulus.
Thrasymède, *m.*, Thrasymedes.
Thucydide, *m.*, Thucydides.
Thyeste, *m.*, Thyestes.
Tibère, *m.*, Tiberius.
Tibulle, *m.*, Tibullus.
Tigrane, *m.*, Tigranes.
Timagène, *m.*, Timagenes.
Timarque, *m.*, Timarchus.
Timée, *m.*, Timæus.
Timocrate, *m.*, Timocrates.
Timoléon, *m.*, Timoleon.
Timophane, *m.*, Timophanes.
Timothée, *m.*, Timothy, Timotheus.
le **Tintoret**, *m.*, Tintoretto.
Tiridate, *m.*, Tiridates.
Tite, *m.*, Titus.
Tite-Live, *m.*, Livy.
Tithon, *m.*, Tithonus.
le **Titien** (-siin), *m.*, Titian.
Titus (-tûs), *m.*, Titus.
Tobie, *m.*, Tobias.
Toinette, Toinon, *f.*, Antonia.
Tribonien (-niin), *m.*, Tribonian.
Triptolème, *m.*, Triptolemus.
le **Trissin**, *m.*, Trissino.
Trogue-Pompée (trog-), *m.*, Trogus Pompeius.
Troïle, *m.*, Troïlus.
Tubalcaïn, *m.*, Tubal-Cain.
Tullie (tul-lî), *f.*, Tullia.
Tullius (tul-liûs), *m.*, Tully, Tullius.
Tydée, *m.*, Tydeus.
Tyndare, *m.*, Tyndareus.
Typhée, *m.*, Typhœus.
Typhon, *m.*, Typhon.
Tyrtée, *m.*, Tyrtæus.

U

Ugolin, *m.*, Ugolino.
Ulpien (-piin), *m.*, Ulpian.
Ulrique, *f.*, Ulrica.
Ulysse, *m.*, Ulysses.
Uranie, *f.*, Urania.
Urbain, *m.*, Urban.
Urie, *m.*, Uriah.
Ursule, *f.*, Ursula.

V

Valentin, *m.*, Valentine.
Valentine, *f.*, Valentine.
Valentinien (-niin), *m.*, Valentinian.
Valère, *m.*, Valerius.
Valérie, *f.*, Valeria.
Valérien (-riin), *m.*, Valerian.
Varron, *m.*, Varro.
Vatace, *m.*, Vataces.
Venceslas, *m.*, Wenceslas.
Vénus (-nûs), *f.*, Venus.
Véronèse, *m.*, Veronese.
Véronique, *f.*, Veronica.
Vertumne (-tum-n), *m.*, Vertumnus.

Vespasien(-ziin), m., Vespasian.
Vespuce, Améric, m., Amerigo Vespucci.
Véturie, f., Veturia.
Vichnou, m., Vishnu.
Victoire, f., Victoria.
Victoria, f., Victoria.
Victorien, m., Victorian.
Victorin, m., Victorinus.
Virgile, m., Virgil.
Virginie, f., Virginia.
Viriathe, m., Viriathus.
Vitruve, m., Vitruvius.
Vivien (-viin), m., Vivian.
Vulcain, m., Vulcan.

W

Wiclef, m., Wicliffe, Wycliffe.
Wilhelmine, m., Wilhelmina.

X

Xanthippe, m., Xantippus.
Xanthippe, f., Xantippe.
Xénocrate, m., Xenocrates.
Xénophane, m., Xenophanes.
Xerxès (gzèrcès), m., Xerxes.
Ximénès (gzim-nès), m., Ximenes.

Z

Zacharie (zakari), m., Zachariah, Zachary.
Zachée, m., Zaccheus.
Zébédée, m., Zebedee, Zebediah.
Zénobie, f., Zenobia.
Zénon, m., Zeno.
Zéphire, m., Zephyr, Zephyrus.
Zoïle, m., Zoilus.
Zopyre, m., Zopyrus.
Zoroastre, m., Zoroaster.
Zorobabel, m., Zerubbabel.
Zosime, m., Zosimus.

VOCABULARY

OF

ANCIENT AND MODERN GEOGRAPHICAL NAMES.

A

Abdère, f., Abdera.

Abruzze, L', f., Abruzzo.

Abruzzes, Les, f.pl., the Abruzzi.

Abyssinie, f., Abyssinia.

Acadie, f., Acadia.

Acarnanie, f., Acarnania.

Achaïe (aka-ï), f., Achaia.

Achantis, L', m., Ashantee.

Achéron, L', m., the Acheron.

Açores, Les, f.pl., the Azores.

Acre, or **St. Jean d'Acre,** m., Acre.

Adriatique, f., the Adriatic.

Afrique, f., Africa.

Agrigente, m., Agrigentum.

Aigle, Cap de l', m., Eagle-Point.

Aix-la-Chapelle, n.f., Aix-la-Chapelle, Aachen.

Albanie, f., Albania.

Albe, f., Alba, Alva.

Albion, L', f., Albion.

Aléoutiennes (îles), f.pl., the Aleutian Islands.

Alep, m., Aleppo.

Alexandrette, f., Alexandretta.

Alexandrie, f., Alexandria.

Algarve, f., Algarva.

Alger, m., Algiers.

Algérie, f., Algeria.

Alicante, f., Alicant.

Allegany, Les Monts, m., the Alleghany Mountains.

*Allemagne, f., Germany. La mer d'— ; the German Ocean.

Alpes, f.pl., Alps. Basses—; the Lower Alps. Hautes—; the Upper Alps.

Alphée, m., Alpheus.

Alsace (alza-s), L', f., Alsace.

Amarapoura or **Umerapoura,** m., Amarapoora.

Amazones (fleuve des), m., the Amazon river, Maranon.

Ambracie, f., Ambracia.

Amérique, f., America. Etats Unis d'—; United States of America.

Amirauté, îles de l', f., Admiralty Islands.

Amis, îles des, f., Friendly Islands.

Anatolie, f., Anatolia.

Ancône, f., Ancona.

Andalousie, f., Andalusia.

Andes, Les, f., the Andes.

Andorre, La République d', m., Andorra.

Andrinople, f., Adrianople.

Angleterre, f., England.

*Anguille, L', f., Snake's Island.

Annam, L', m., Annam.

Anse, f. V. **Hanse.**

Anséatiques, Villes, f. V. **Hanséatiques.**

Antigoa, f., Antigua.

*Antilles, Les, f.pl., the West Indies. Grandes —; the Greater Antilles. Petites —; the Lesser Antilles. La mer des —; the Caribbean Sea.

Antioche, f., Antioch.

Anvers (anvèrs), m., Antwerp.

Aorne, m., Aornus.

Aoude, m., Oude.

Apennins, Les, m.pl., Apennines.

Apulie, f., Apulia.

Aquilée, f., Aquilea.

Aquitaine, f., Aquitaine, Aquitania.

Arabie, f., Arabia. — Heureuse; Arabia Felix. — Déserte; Arabia Deserta. — Pétrée; Arabia Petræa.

Aragon, m., Aragon.

Arbèles, f., Arbela.

Arcadie, f., Arcadia.

Archipel, L', m., the Archipelago.

Arcole, f., Arcola.

Ardennes (ardè-n), **Les,** f., Ardennes.

Argentine, La République, the Argentine Republic, Argentina.

Argolide, f., Argolis.

Argovie, f., Aargau.

Arménie, f., Armenia.

Armorique, f., Armorica.

Asie, m., Asia. — Mineure; Asia Minor.

Assise, f., Assisi.

Assyrie, f., Assyria.

Astrakan, m., Astrakhan.

Asturies, Les, f.pl., the Asturias.

Athènes, f., Athens.

Atlantique, L', m., the Atlantic.

Atlas (-lâs), m., Atlas.

Attique, f., Attica.

Augsbourg, m., Augsburg.

Aulide, f., Aulis.

*Aurigny, m., Alderney.

Ausonie, L', f., Ausonia (poet. for Italy).

Australasie, L', f., Australasia.

Australie, L', f., Australia.

Autriche, f., Austria.

Auxerre (ô-sèr), m., Auxerre; x sounded as ss.

Auxonne (ô-so-n), m., Auxonne.

Aventin, L', m., the Aventine.

Averne, L', m., Averno.

Azincourt, m., Agincourt.

Azof, Azov. La mer d'—; the Sea of Azov.

B

Babylone, f., Babylon.

Babylonie, f., Babylonia.

Bactriane, f., Bactriana.

Bade, f., Baden.

Baffin, Baie de, f., Baffin's Bay.

Bahama, Les îles, f., the Bahama Islands or the Bahamas.

Bahia, m., Bahia.

Bâle, f., Basle, Basel.

Baléares, Les îles, f.pl., the Balearic Isles.

Baltique, La, f., the Baltic.

Barbade, f., Barbadoes.

Barbaresques, États, m., the Barbary States.

Barbarie, La, f., Barbary.

Barboude, f., Barbuda.

Barcelone, f., Barcelona.

Barcelonnette, f., Barcelonnette.

Basan, m., Bashan.

Batavia, f., Batavia (capital of Java).

Batavie, La, f., Batavia (Holland).

Bavière, f., Bavaria.

Belgique, La, f., Belgium.

Béloutchistan, m., Beloochistan.

Bénarès (-rès), m., Benares.

Bénévent, m., Benevento.

Bengale (bingal), m., Bengal. Le Golfe du —; the Bay of Bengal.

Béotie, f., Beotia.

Bergame, f., Bergamo.

Berg-op-zoom, m., Bergen-op-zoom.

Berks, (Comté de), Berkshire.

Berlin, m., Berlin.

Bermudes, Les, f.pl., the Bermudas.

Berne, f., Bern.

Bersabée, f., Beersheba.

Bessarabie, f., Bessarabia.

Béthanie, f., Bethany.

Bethléem (bètlé-èm), f., Bethlehem.

Bétique, f., Bætica.

Beydjapour, *m.*, Bejapoor.

Birman Empire, Le, *m.*, Burmah.

Biscaye, *f.*, Biscay. La Mer or le Golfe de —; *the Bay of Biscay.* V. Gascogne.

Bithynie, *f.*, Bithynia.

Blanc, Le Cap, *m.*, Cape Blanco.

Bohème, La, *f.*, Bohemia.

*Bologne, *f.*, Bologna.

Bolonais, *m.*, Bolognese.

Bone, *f.*, Bona.

Borysthène, *m.*, Borysthenes.

Bosnie, *f.*, Bosnia.

Bosphore, Le, *m.*, Bosphorus.

Bothnie, *f.*, Bothnia.

Boukarest, Bucharest (-rèst), *m.*, Bucharest.

Boukharie, *f.*, Bukaria, Bucharia.

*Boulogne, Boulogne.

*Bourgogne, *f.*, Burgundy.

Bragance, *f.*, Braganza.

Brahmapoutre, *m.*, Brahmapootra.

Brandebourg (brandbour), *m.* *m.*, Brandenburg.

Brème, *m.*, Bremen.

Brésil, Le, *m.*, Brazil.

*Bretagne, *f.*, Brittany (France). La Grande —; *Great Britain.* La Nouvelle —; *New Britain.*

Brindes, *m.*, Brindisi.

Britanniques, Les Îles, *f.*, British Isles.

Brousse, *m.*, Broussa.

Brunswick (bronsvick), *m.*, Brunswick.

Bruxelles (brussèl; *x* sounded as *ss*), *f.*, Brussels.

Bucharie (bukarf), *f.* V. Boukharie.

Bude, *n.*, Buda.

Buénos-Ayres (buénozèr), *m.*, Buenos Ayres.

Bulgarie, *f.*, Bulgaria.

Byzance, *f.*, Byzantium.

C

Caboul, *m.* V. Kaboul.

Cachemire, Le, *m.*, (kashmir), Cashmere, (town) Cashmere.

Cadix, *f.*, Cadiz.

Cadmée, La, *f.*, Cadmea.

Cafrerie, La, *f.*, Kaffraria.

Caire, Le, *m.*, Cairo.

Calabre, *f.*, Calabria.

Calais (kalè), *m.*, Calais. Le Pas-de-—; *the Straits of Dover.*

Calédonie, *f.*, Caledonia.

Calicut (-kut), *m.*, Calicut.

Californie, *f.*, California. Basse-—, Vieille-—; *Lower,* or *Old, California.* Haute-—, Nouvelle-—; *Upper California.*

Calvados (-dos), *m.*, Calvados.

Calvaire, *m.*, Calvary. Le Mont-—; *Mount Calvary.*

Cambaye (kambè), *m.*, Cambay.

Cambodge, *f.*, Cambodia.

*Campagne de Rome, *f.*, Campagna Romana.

Campanie, *f.*, Campania.

Campêche, *f.*, Campeachy.

Canada, *m.*, Canada. Bas-—;

Lower Canada. Haut-—; *Upper Canada.*

Canarie, la Grande, *f.*, Grand Canary. Les Îles —s; *the Canary Isles.*

Candie, Île de, *f.*, Candia.

Canée, *f.*, Canea.

Cannes, *f.*, Cannæ (in Italy), Cannes (France).

Cantorbéry, *m.*, Canterbury.

Cap, *m.*, Cape. Le —de Bonne Espérance; *Cape of Good Hope.* Le —; *Cape Town.* La Colonie du —; *Cape Colony.*

Capharnaüm (-na-om), *m.*, Capernaum.

Capoue, *f.*, Capua.

Cappadoce, *f.*, Cappadocia.

Caraïbes, Îles, *f.*, Leeward and Windward Islands.

Carinthie, *f.*, Carinthia.

Carniole, *f.*, Carniola.

Caroline, *f.*, Carolina.

Carpathes, Les Monts, *m.* Carpathian Mountains.

Carrare, *f.*, Carrara.

Carthagène, *f.*, Carthagena.

Caspienne, La Mer, *f.*, Caspian Sea.

Castalie, *f.*, Castalia.

*Castille, *f.*, Castile.

*Catalogne, *f.*, Catalonia.

Catane, *f.*, Catana.

Caucase, Le, *m.*, Caucasus.

Céphalonie, *f.*, Cephalonia.

Césarée, *f.*, Cæsarea.

Cervin, Le Mont, *m.*, the Matterhorn.

Cévennes (sé-vè-n), *f.*, Cevennes.

Ceylan, *m.*, Ceylon.

Chalcédoine (kal-), *f.*, Chalcedon, Chalcedonia.

Chaldée (kal-), *f.*, Chaldea.

Chambéry, *m.*, Chambery.

Chanaan (kana-an), *m.*, Canaan.

Charybde (karibe), *m.*, Charybdis.

Chéronée (ké-), *f.*, Chæronea.

Chersonèse (kèr-), *f.*, Chersonese.

Chili, Le, *m.*, Chili.

Chine, La, *f.*, China.

Chypre, *f.*, Cyprus.

Cilicie, *f.*, Cilicia.

Circassie, *f.*, Circassia.

Cithéron, *m.*, Cithæron.

Cobourg, *m.*, Coburg.

Cochinchine, *f.*, Cochin China.

Cocyte, *m.*, Cocytus.

Coïmbre, *f.*, Coimbra.

Colchide (-kid), *f.*, Colchis.

*Cologne, *f.*, Cologne.

Colombie, *f.*, Columbia.

Colone, *f.*, Colonus.

Colonnes d'Hercule, Les, *f.pl.*, Hercules' Pillars.

Compostelle, *f.*, Compostella.

Congo, *m.*, Congo.

Constantine, *f.*, Constantine, Constantina.

Copenhague (kopè-nag), *f.*, Copenhagen.

Corcyre, *f.*, Corcyra.

*Cordillères, Les, *f.pl.*, Cordilleras.

Cordoue, *f.*, Cordova.

Corée, La, *f.*, Corea.

Corfou, *f.*, Corfu.

Corinthe, *f.*, Corinth.

*Cornouailles, Le, *m.*, Cornwall. La pointe de —; *Land's End.*

*Corogne, La, *f.*, Corunna.

Corse, *f.*, Corsica.

Cortone, *f.*, Cortona.

Côte des Esclaves, *f.*, Slave Coast.

Côte d'Ivoire, *f.*, Ivory Coast.

Côte d'Or, *f.*, Gold Coast (in Africa).

Courlande, *f.*, Courland.

Cracovie, *f.*, Cracow.

Crémone, *f.*, Cremona.

Crète, *f.*, Crete.

Crimée, *f.*, Crimea.

Croatie, *f.*, Croatia.

Cume, *f.*, Cuma.

Cumes, *f.*, Cumæ.

Curaçao, *m.*, Curaçoa.

Cynthe, *m.*, Cynthus.

Cynurie, *f.*, Cynuria.

Cythère, *f.*, Cythera.

D

Dacie, *f.*, Dacia.

Dalécarlie, *f.*, Dalecarlia.

Dalmatie, *f.*, Dalmatia.

Damas (-mâs), *f.*, Damascus.

Damiette, *f.*, Damietta.

Danemark (da-n-mark), Le, *m.*, Denmark.

Dantzick, *m.*, Danzig.

Danube, Le, *m.*, the Danube.

Dardanelles, Les, *f.pl.*, the Dardanelles.

Dauphiné, Le, *m.*, Dauphiny.

Davis, Le Détroit, or Canal, de, *m.*, Davis' Strait.

Deccan, Le, *m.*, Deccan.

Dekhan, *m.* V. Deccan

Delphes, *f.*, Delphi.

Dents, Côte des, *f.*, Ivory Coast.

Devon, Le Comté de, *m.*, Devonshire.

Diémen (diéme-n), Terre de Van, *f.*, Van Diemen's Land.

Djaguernat, *m.*, Juggernauth.

Djihoun, *m.*, Jihoon, Oxus, Amoo.

Dniéper, *n.m.*, Dnieper.

Dniester, *m.*, Dniester.

Dominique, La, *f.*, Dominica.

*Dordogne, La, *f.*, Dordogne.

Doride, *f.*, Doris.

Dorylée, *f.*, Dorylæum.

Doubs (doo), Le, *m.*, Doubs.

Douvres, *m.*, Dover.

Dresde, *f.*, Dresden.

Dunkerque, *n.m.*, Dunkirk.

E

Ebre, *m.*, Ebro.

Ecbatane, *f.*, Ecbatana.

Écluse, L', *f.*, Sluys.

Écosse, *f.*, Scotland. La Nouvelle—; *Nova Scotia.*

Édimbourg, *m.* or *f.*, Edinburgh.

Égée, La Mer, *f.*, the Ægean Sea.

Égine, *f.*, Ægina.

Égypte, *f.*, Egypt. Basse-—; *Lower Egypt.* Haute-—; *Upper Egypt.* Moyenne —; *Middle Egypt.*

Élatée, *f.*, Elatea.
Elbe, Île d', *f.*, the island of Elba, Elba.
Elbe, (river) *m.*, Elbe.
Élide, *f.*, Elis (country).
Élis (élîs), *f.*, Elis (capital).
Elseneur, *f.*, Elsinore.
Emmatis (èm-ma-ûs), *m.*, Emmaus.
Engadine, L', *f.*, the Engadine.
Éolie, Éolide, *f.*, Eolia.
Éphèse, *f.*, Ephesus.
Épices, Îles aux, *f.*, the Spice Islands
Épidamne (-dam-n), *m.*, Epidamnus. Dyrrachium.
Épidaure, *f.*, Epidaurus.
Épire, *f.*, Epirus.
Équateur, République de l', *f.*, Ecuador.
Érétrie, *f.*, Eretria.
Érié, Le Lac, *m.*, Lake Erie.
Escaut, *m.*, Scheldt.
Esclave, Lac de l', *m.*, Slave Lake.
Esclaves, Côte des, *f.*, Slave Coast.
Esclavonie, *f.*, Sclavonia.
*Espagne, *f.*, Spain.
Estramadure, L', *f.*, Estramadura.
États-Unis, Les, *m.pl.*, the United States.
Éthiopie, *f.*, Ethiopia.
Etna, *m.*, Etna.
Étolie, *f.*, Etolia.
Étrurie, *f.*, Etruria.
Eubée, *f.*, Euboea.
Euphrate, L', *m.*, Euphrates.
Europe, L', *f.*, Europe.

F

Falkland, Les Îles, *f.pl.*, the Falkland Islands.
Feroë (fèr), **Les Îles**, *f.pl.*, the Faroe Islands.
Fernambouc, *m.* *V.* **Pernambouc.**
Ferrare, *f.*, Ferrara.
Figuères (fighièr), *f.*, Figueras.
Finistère, Cap, *m.*, Land's End (in England) ; Cape Finisterra (in Spain).
Finistère (Département du), *m.*, Department of Finistère (France).
Finlande, *f.*, Finland.
Fionie, *f.*, Fuhnen, Funen, Fyen.
Flandre, *f.*, Flanders.
Flessingue (flè-sing), *m.*, Flushing.
Floride, *f.*, Florida.
Fontarabie, *f.*, Fontarabia.
Forêt-Noire, *f.*, Black Forest.
Formose, *f.*, Formosa.
Forth, Golfe du, *m.*, the Frith or Firth of Forth.
France, *f.*, France.
Francfort, *m.*, Frankfort.
Franconie, *f.*, Franconia.
Fribourg, *m.*, Fribourg (Switz.).
Fribourg, *m.*, Freiburg (Ger.).
Frioul, *m.*, Friuli.
Frise, La, *f.*, Friesland.

G

Gabaon, *m.*, Gibeon.
Gabon, Le, *m.*, the Gaboon.
Gadès, *m.*, Gades (Cadiz).
Gaète, *f.*, Gaeta.
Galaad, *m.*, Gilead.
Galatie, *f.*, Galatia.
Galgala, *m.*, Gilgal.
Galice, *f.*, Galicia (in Spain).
Galicie, *f.*, Galicia (in Austria).
Galilée, *f.*, Galilæa, Galilee.
Galles, Le Pays de, *m.*, Wales. La Nouvelle-Galles du Sud ; *New South Wales.*
Gambie, *f.*, Gambia.
Gand, *m.*, Ghent.
Gange, *m.*, Ganges.
*Gascogne, *f.*, Gascony. Le Golfe de — ; *the Bay of Biscay.*
Gaule, La, *f.*, Gaul.
Géants, Chaussée des, *f.*, Giant's Causeway.
Gédrosie, *f.*, Mekran.
Gènes, *f.*, Genoa.
Genève, *f.*, Geneva.
Géorgie, *f.*, Georgia.
Germanie, *f.*, Germany.
Gessen (jèce-n), *m.*, Goshen.
Ghattes, Les, *f.pl.*, the Ghauts.
Girone, *f.*, Gerona.
Glasgow, *m.*, Glasgow.
Gnesne, *f.*, Gnesen.
Gœttingue (gheutïn-g), *m.*, Göttingen.
Golconde, *f.*, Golconda.
Gothembourg (gotanbour), *m.*, Gottenburg.
Gothie, *f.*, Gothland.
Gottingue, *m.* *V.* **Gœttingue.**
Goudelour (goodloor), *m.* *V.* **Kaddalor.**
Goudjerate, *m.* *V.* **Guzzerat.**
Graines, Côtes des, *f.*, Grain Coast.
Grampians, Monts, *m. pl.*, Grampian Mountains.
Granique, Le, *m.*, the Granicus.
Grèce, *f.*, Greece.
Grenade, *f.* (province and island), Granada. La Nouvelle — ; *New Granada.*
Groënland (gro-inlan), *m.*, Greenland.
Groningue (-nïng), **Groningen**, *m.*, Groningen.
Guadalquivir (gooadalkivir), *m.*, Guadalquivir.
Guadeloupe (gooadloop), *f.*, Guadeloupe.
Guatémala (gooa-), *m.*, Guatemala.
Gueldre (ghèldr), *f.*, Guelders, Guelderland.
Guernesey, *f.*, Guernsey.
Guyane, Guiane (ghia-n), **La**, *f.*, Guiana.
Guinée, *f.*, Guinea.
Guyenne, *f.*, Guienne.
Guzzerat, *m.*, Guzerat.

H

†**Haarlem**, *m.* *V.* **Harlem.**
†**Hainaut**, *m.*, Hainault.
Haïti, *f.*, Hayti.
Halicarnasse, *f.*, Halicarnassus.

†**Hambourg**, *m.*, Hamburg.
†**Hanovre, Le**, *m.*, Hanover.
†**Hanse**, *f.*, Hanse-Towns.
†**Hanséatiques, Villes**, *f.*, Hanse-Towns.
Hapsbourg, *m.*, Hapsburg.
†**Harlem** (-lè-m), *m.*, Harlem, Haarlem.
†**Havane, La**, *f.*, Havana.
†**Havre, Le**, *m.*, Havre.
Hawaii, *m.*, Hawaii, Owhyhee.
†**Haye** (hê), **La**, *f.*, the Hague.
Hèbre, L', (river), *m.*, Hebreus.
Hébrides, Les, *f.*, Hebrides.
Hélicon, *m.*, Helicon.
Hellespont, *m.*, Hellespont.
Helvétie, *f.*, Helvetia.
Héraclée, *f.*, Heraclea.
Herculanum (-nom), *m.*, Herculaneum.
Herzégovine, *f.*, Herzegovina.
Hespérie, *f.*, Hesperia.
Hesse, La, *f.*, Hesse.
Hibernie, *f.*, Hibernia.
Hindoustan, *m.*, Hindoostan, Hindustan.
†**Hollande**, *f.*, Holland.
†**Hombourg**, *m.*, Homburg.
Honduras, Le, *m.*, Honduras.
Hongrie, *f.*, Hungary.
Hudson, La Baie de, *f.*, Hudson's Bay.
Huningue (unin-g), *m.*, Huningen.
Hydaspe, *m.*, Hydaspes (Jeloum).
Hydraote, *m.*, Hydraotes (Ravee).
Hymette, L' (mountain), *m.*, Hymettus, *or* Mount Hymettus.
Hyphase, *m.*, Hyphasis (Beyas, Sutlej ?).
Hyrcanie, *f.*, Hyrcania.

I

Ibérie, *f.*, Iberia.
Icarie, *f.*, Icaria.
Icarienne, Mer, *f.*, Icarian Sea.
Idalie, *f.*, Idalia.
Idumée, *f.*, Idumea.
Iéna, *m.*, Jena.
Île, *f.*, island. —s du Vent ; *the Windward Islands.* —s sous le Vent ; *the Leeward Islands.*
Île - de - France, *f.*, Isle of France, Mauritius.
Illyrie (il-lirf), *f.*, Illyria.
Ilion, *m.*, Ilium (Troy).
Inde, *f.*, India. Les —s ; *the Indies, India.* —s Occidentales ; *West Indies.* —s Orientales ; *East Indies.* La mer des —s ; *the Indian Ocean.*
Indo-Chine, *f.*, Indo-China.
Indostan, *m.* *V.* **Hindoustan.**
Ingrie, *f.*, Ingria.
Ionie, *f.*, Ionia.
Ioniennes, Îles, *f.pl.*, the Ionian Isles.
Irlande, *f.*, Ireland. La mer d'— ; *the Irish Sea.*
Isaurie, *f.*, Isauria.
Islande, *f.*, Iceland.
Istrie, *f.*, Istria.
Italie, *f.*, Italy.
Ithaque, *f.*, Ithaca.
Ivoire, La Côte d', *f.*, the Ivory Coast.

J

Jagernaut, *m.* *V.* **Djaguernat.**
Jamaïque, La, *f.*, Jamaica.
Japon, Le, *m.*, Japan.
Jéricho (jériko), *f.*, Jericho.
Jersey (jerzè), *f.*, Jersey.
Jérusalem (-lè-m), *f.*, Jerusalem.
Jourdain, Le, *m.*, Jordan.
Judée, *f.*, Judæa.
Jutland, Le, *m.*, Jutland.

K

Kaboul, *m.*, Cabool, Kabul, Cabul.
Kachgar, *m.*, Cashgar.
Kaddalor, *m.*, Cuddalore.
Kamtchatka, Le (k mtchatka), *m.*, Kamtschatka.
Karnatic, Le, *m.*, the Carnatic.
Kécho, Kachao.
Kouriles, *f.pl.*, Kuriles.
Krapacks (Monts), *m.*, the Carpathian Mountains.

L

Lacédémone, *f.*, Lacedæmon.
Lacknau, *m.* *V.* **Luknow.**
Laconie, *f.*, Laconia.
Lancastre, *m.*, Lancaster.
Laodicée, *f.*, Laodicea.
Laponie, La, *f.*, Lapland.
Laquedives (lakdive), **Les** (îles), *f.*, Laccadives, Laccadive Islands.
Larisse, *f.*, Larissa.
Larrons, îles des, *or* **Mariannes, îles**, *f.*, the Ladrone Islands, Mariana Islands.
Leipsick (lèpsik), *m.*, Leipsic, Leipzig.
Lemnos, *f.*, Lemnos.
Lépante, *f.*, Lepanto.
Lerme, *f.*, Lerma.
Lerne, *m.*, Lerna.
Léthé, Le, *m.*, Lethe.
Leuctres, *f.*, Leuctra.
Levant, Le, *m.*, the Levant.
Leyde, *f.*, Leyden.
Liban, *m.*, Lebanon.
Liburnie, *f.*, Liburnia.
Libye, *f.*, Libya.
Liège, *m.*, Liège.
Ligurie, *f.*, Liguria.
Limbourg, *m.*, Limburg (Holl.); Limbourg (Belg.).
Limousin, Le, *m.*, Limousin.
Lisbonne, *f.*, Lisbon.
Lithuanie, *f.*, Lithuania.
Livadie, *f.*, Livadia.
Livonie, *f.*, Livonia.
Livourne, *m.*, Leghorn.
Loire, La (river), Loire.
Lombardie, *f.*, Lombardy.
Londres, *m.*, London.
Lorette, *f.*, Loretto.
Lorraine, *f.*, Lorraine.
Louisbourg, *m.*, Louisburg.
Louisiane, La, *f.*, Louisiana.
Lucanie, *f.*, Lucania.
Lucayes (lukê), **Les**, *f.pl.*, the Bahama Islands.
Luçon, *f.*, Luzon.
Lucques, *f.*, Lucca.
Luknow, *m.*, Lucknow.

Lunebourg, *m.*, Luneburg.
Lusace, *f.*, Lusatia.
Lusitanie, *f.*, Lusitania.
Lutèce, *f.*, (ancient Paris) Lutetia.
Lutzen (-zè-n), *m.*, Lutzen.
Luxembourg, *m.*, Luxemburg.
Lycaonie, *f.*, Lycaonia.
Lycie, *f.*, Lycia.
Lydia, La, *f.*, Lydia.
Lyon, *m.*, Lyons.
Lysimachie, *f.*, Lysimachia.

M

Macédoine, *f.*, Macedonia.
Madère, *f.*, Madeira.
Maëstricht (maèstrik), *m.*, Maastricht.
Magdebourg, *m.*, Magdeburg.
Magellan, Le Détroit de, *m.*, the Straits of Magellan.
Mahrattes (Indian tribe), *m.*, Mahrattas.
Maine, Le, *m.*, Maine.
Maïssour, *m.*, Mysore.
Majorque, *f.*, Majorca.
Malaisie, La, *f.*, Malaysia.
Maldives, Les îles, *f.pl.*, the Maldive Islands.
Malines, *f.*, Mechlin.
Malouines, îles, *f.*, the Falkland Islands.
Malte, *f.*, Malta.
Man, L'île de, *f.*, the Isle of Man.
Manche, La, *f.*, the British *or* English Channel ; (in Spain) La Manche. Les îles de la — *the Channel Islands.*
Mandchourie, La, *f.*, Manchuria.
*Manille, *f.*, Manila.
Mantinée, *f.*, Mantinea.
Mantoue, *f.*, Mantua.
Maragnon, *m.*, Maranon, Amazon.
Marguerite (-ghèrit), **La**, *f.*, Margarita.
Mariannes, îles, *f.*, Mariana Islands. *V.* **Larrons.**
Marienbourg (mariinboor), *f.*, Marienburg.
Marmara, La Mer de, *f.*, the Sea of Marmora.
Maroc, *m.*, Morocco.
Marquises, Les (îles), *f.pl.*, the Marquesas.
*Marseille, *f.*, Marseilles.
Martinique, La, *f.*, Martinique.
Maurice, L'île, *f.*, Mauritius. *V.* **France.**
Mauritanie, *f.*, Mauritania.
Mayence (ma-ian-s), *f.*, Mentz, Mainz.
Mayenne (ma-iè-n), **La**, *f.*, the Mayenne.
Mecklembourg (mèklinboor), *m.*, Mecklenburg.
Mecque, La, *f.*, Mecca.
Médine, *f.*, Medina.
Méditerranée, La Mer, *f.*, the Mediterranean.
Mégare, *f.*, Megara.
Mein, Le, *m.*, the Main.
Mélinde, *f.*, Melinda.
Menton, *m.*, Mentone.
Méonie, *f.*, Mæonia.
Mésie, *f.*, Mœsia.

Mésopotamie, La, *f.*, Mesopotamia.
Messénie, *f.*, Messenia.
Messine, *f.*, Messina. Le Phare de — ; *the Straits of Messina.*
Meuse, *f.*, the Meuse, Maas.
Mexico, *m.*, Mexico (town).
Mexique, Le, *m.*, Mexico (country).
Michigan, Lac, *m.*, Lake Michigan.
Middelbourg, *m.*, Middleburg.
Milanais, Le, *m.*, the Milanese.
Milet, *m.*, Miletus.
Mingrélie, *f.*, Mingrelia.
Minorque, *f.*, Minorca.
Minturnes, *f.*, Minturnæ.
Mississippi, Le, *m.*, the Mississippi.
Missouri, Le, *m.*, the Missouri.
Modène, *f.*, Modena.
Mœsie (mézî), *f.* *V.* **Mésie.**
Moka, *f.*, Mocha, Mokha.
Moldavie, La, *f.*, Moldavia.
Moluques, Les, *f.pl.*, the Moluccas.
Mongolie, *f.*, Mongolia.
Moravie, *f.*, Moravia.
Morée, *f.*, Morea.
Moscou, *m.*, Moscow.
Moscovie, *f.*, Muscovy (Russia).
Moskova, *or* **Moskva**, *f.*, Moscow.
Mossoul, *f.*, Mosul.
Mozambique, Le, *m.*, Mosambique.
Murcie, *f.*, Murcia.
Mycènes, *f.*, Mycenæ.
Mysie, *f.*, Mysia.

N

Nancy, *f.*, Nancy.
Nankin, *m.*, Nankin, *or* Nanking.
Nauplie, *f.*, Nauplia.
Navarin, *m.*, Navarino.
Navigateurs, Archipel des, *m.*, the Navigators' Islands.
Néerlande, La, *f.*, the Netherlands.
Négrepont, *f.*, Negropont.
Népal, *or* **Nepaul**, *m.*, Nepaul.
Neustrie, La, *f.*, Neustria.
Nice, *f.*, (in France) Nice.
Nicée, *f.*, Nicæa, Nice.
Nicomédie, *f.*, Nicomedia.
Nicosie, *f.*, Nicosia.
Niger (nijèr), **Le**, *m.*, the Niger.
Nigritie, La, *n.f.*, Nigritia, Central Africa, Negroland.
Nil, Le, *m.*, Nile.
Nimègue (nimè-g), *m.*, Nimeguen.
Ninive, *f.*, Nineveh.
*Noailles, *m.*, Noailles.
Norique, La, *f.*, Noricum.
Normandie, La, *f.*, Normandy.
Norvège, *or* **Norwège, La**, *f.*, Norway.
Nouvelle-Écosse, La, *f.*, Nova Scotia.
Nouvelle-Zemble, La, *f.*, Nova Zembla.
Novara, *f.*, Novare.
Nubie, *f.*, Nubia.
Numance, *f.*, Numantia.
Numidie, La, *f.*, Numidia.

O

Océanie, f., Oceania.
Oder (odèr), L', m., the Oder.
Ohio, L', m., the Ohio.
Oldenbourg (oldinboor), m., Oldenburg.
Olympe, m., Olympus.
Olympie, f., Olympia.
Olynthe, f., Olynthus.
Orange, La Colonie du Fleuve, the Orange River Colony.
Orcades, Les, f.pl., the Orkneys, or the Orkney Islands.
Orchomène (-ko-), m., Orchomenus.
Orégon, L', m., Oregon.
Orenbourg (orinbour), m., Orenburg.
Orénoque, L', m., the Orinoco.
Orléans, m. or f., Orleans.
Osnabruck, m., Osnabruck.
Ostende, m., Ostend.
Otahiti, f., Otaheite. V. Taïti.
Otrante, m., Otranto.
Ouessant, m., Ushant.
Oural, m., Ural. Les Monts —s; the Ural Mountains.

P

Pactole, Le, m., Pactolus.
Padoue, f., Padua.
Palatinat, m., Palatinate.
Palerme, f., Palermo.
Palestine, f., Palestina.
Palmyre, f., Palmyra.
Pampelune (panplu-n), f., Pampeluna.
Pamphylie, La, f., Pamphylia.
Panama, f., Panama.
Pannonie, f., Pannonia.
Papouasie, f., Papua.
Paraguay (-ghè), Le, m., Paraguay.
Paris (pari), m., Paris.
Parme, f., Parma.
Parnasse, Le, m., Parnassus.
Parthie, n.f., Parthia.
Patagonie, f., Patagonia.
Pathmos (-môs), f., Patmos.
Patras (patrâs), f., Patras.
Pausilippe, m., Pausilippo.
Pavie, f., Pavia.
Pays-bas, Les, m.pl., the Netherlands.
Pégou, m., Pegu.
Pékin, m., Pekin, Peking.
Péloponnèse, Le, m., Peloponnesus.
Pensylvanie (pin-), f., Pennsylvania.
Péonie, f., Pæonia.
Pergame, f., Pergamos.
Périnthe, f., Perinthus.
Permesse, Le, m., the Permessus.
Pernambouc, m., Pernambuco.
Pérou, m., Peru.
Pérouse, f., Perugia.
Perse, f., Persia.
Perside, f., Persis, Fars, Farsistan.
Persique, Le Golfe, m., the Persian Gulf.
Pétersbourg, St., m., St. Petersburg.
Phalsbourg, m., Phalsburg.
Pharsale, f., Pharsalia.

Phénicie, f., Phœnicia.
Philadelphie, f., Philadelphia.
Philippes, f., Philippi.
Philippines, Les Îles or Les, f., the Philippine Islands, or the Philippines.
Philipsbourg, m., Philipsburg.
Phocée, f., Phocæa.
Phocide, La, f., Phocis.
Phrygie, f., Phrygia.
Picardie, La, f., Picardy.
Piémont, Le, m., Piedmont.
Pinde, Le, m., Pindus.
Pirée, Le, m., the Piræus.
Pise, f., Pisa.
Plaisance, f., Placentia.
Platée, f., Platæa.
Podolie, f., Podolia.
Polésie, f., Polesia.
Pologne, La, f., Poland.
Polynésie, La, f., Polynesia.
Poméranie, La, f., Pomerania.
Pomérellie, f., Minor Pomerania.
Pompéi, Pompéies (ponpèis), f., Pompeii.
Pondichéry, m., Pondicherry.
Pont, Le, m., Pontus.
Pont-Euxin, Le, m., the Euxine Sea.
Pontins, Marais, m., Pontine Marshes.
Porto, m., Porto, Oporto.
Pouille, f., Apulia.
Presbourg, f., Presburg.
Propontide, La, f., Propontis.
Prusse, La, f., Prussia.
Ptolémaïs (-ma-îs), f., Ptolemais.
Pultava, m., Pultava, Poltava.
Pyrénées, Les, f.pl., the Pyrenees. Basses— ; the Lower Pyrenees. Hautes— ; the Upper Pyrenees.

Q

Quebec (kébèk), m., Quebec.
Queensland, Le, m., Queensland.
Quiberon (kibron), m., Quiberon.
Quimper (kinpèr), m., Quimper.
Quirinal, Le, m., the Quirinal.

R

Raguse, f., Ragusa.
Rangoun (-goon), m., Rangoon.
Ratisbonne, f., Ratisbon.
Ravenne, f., Ravenna.
Reims, or Rheims (-rins), m., Rheims.
Rhétie, La, f., Rhætia.
Rhin, Le, m., the Rhine.
Rhodes (rod), f., Rhodes.
Rhône, Le, m., the Rhone.
Riviéra, La, f., the Riviera.
Rochelle, La, f., Rochelle.
Rocheux, Monts, m.pl., the Rocky Mountains.
*Romagne, f., Romagna.
Rome, f., Rome.
Rosette, f., Rosetta.
Rotterdam (rotèrdam), m., Rotterdam.
Roumanie, f., Roumania.
Roumélie, f., Roumelie.
Rubicon, Le, m., the Rubicon.

Russie, f., Russia. La—d'Asie; *Russia in Asia.* La — d'Europe ; *Russia in Europe.*

S

Saba, f., Saba ; Sheba.
Sabine, f., Sabina.
Sagonte, f., Saguntum.
Sahara, m., Sahara.
Saigon, m., Saigon.
Saint-Ange, m., Saint Angelo.
Saint-Domingue (Île de), f., San Domingo.
Salamanque, f., Salamanca.
Salamine, f., Salamis.
Salerne, f., Salerno.
Salonique, n.f., Salonica.
Salzbourg, m., Salzburg.
Samarcande, f., Samarcand.
Samarie, f., Samaria.
Samothrace, f., Samothracia.
Santander (-dèr), m., Santander.
Saragosse, La, f., Saragossa.
*Sardaigne, La, f., Sardinia.
Sardes, f., Sardis.
Sarmatie, f., Sarmatia.
Savoie, f., Savoy.
Saxe, La, f., Saxony.
Scamandre, Le, m., Scamander.
Scandinavie, La, f., Scandinavia.
Schaffhouse (shafoo-z), f., Schaffhausen.
Schwarzbourg (shvarzboor), m., Schwarzburg.
Sclavonie or Slavonie, f., Sclavonia.
Scythie, f., Scythia.
Sébastopol or Sévastopol, m., Sebastopol.
Ségovie, f., Segovia.
Séleucide, f., Seleucis.
Séleucie, f., Seleucia.
Sénégal, Le, m., Senegal.
Sénégambie, La, f., Senegambia.
Servie, or Serbie, f., Servia.
Seychelles, Les Îles, f.pl., the Seychelles Islands, the Seychelles.
Shetland, Les Îles, f.pl., the Shetland Islands, the Shetlands.
Sibérie, f., Siberia.
Sichem (sishè-m), f., Shechem.
Sicile, La, f., Sicily.
Sienne (siè-n), f., Sienna.
Silésie, La, f., Silesia.
Silistrie, f., Silistria.
Siloé, f., Siloah, Siloam.
Siloh, m., Shiloh.
Sinaï, m., Sinai.
Sind, Le, m., Sind or Indus.
Sindhy, Le, m., Sind (province).
Singapour, m., Singapore.
Sion, f., Zion.
Slavonie, La, f., Slavonia.
Smyrne, f., Smyrna.
Société, Îles de la, f., Society Islands.
Sodome, f., Sodom.
Sogdiane, f., Sogdiana.
Soleure, (canton, m.; town, f.), Soleure.
Solfatare, La, f., the Solfatara.
Solway, Le Golfe de, m., the Solway Firth or Frith.

Sonde, Archipel de la, *m.,* Sunda Isles. Le Détroit de la —; *the Sunda Straits.*

Sorlingues (-lin-g), **Îles,** *f.,* the Scilly Isles.

Souabe, *f.,* Suabia.

Sparte, *f.,* Sparta.

Spire, *m.,* Speyer, Spires.

Spitzberg, *m.,* Spitzbergen.

Stagire, *f.,* Stagira.

Steinkerque or **Steenkerke,** *m.,* Steenkerque.

Strasbourg, *m.,* Strasburg, Strasbourg.

Stuttgard, *m.,* Stuttgart.

Styrie, *f.,* Styria.

Suède, *f.,* Sweden.

Suisse, Le, *f.,* Switzerland.

Sund (Le Sond), *m.,* The Sound.

Supérieur, Le Lac, *m.,* Lake Superior.

Surate, *f.,* Surat.

Suse, *f.,* Susa.

Syrie, La, *f.,* Syria.

T

Tabago, *f.,* Tobago.

Table, *n.f.* La Baie de la —; *Table Bay.* Le Mont de la —; *Table Mountain.*

Tage, Le, *m.,* the Tagus.

Taïti, *f.,* Otaheite, Tahiti.

Tamise, *f.,* Thames.

Tananarive, *f.,* Antananarivo.

Tanger, *m.,* Tangier.

Tarente, *f.,* Taranto.

Tarragone, *f.,* Tarragona.

Tarse, *f.,* Tarsus.

Tartarie, *f.,* Tartary.

Tasmanie, La, *f.,* Tasmania.

Tauride, *f.,* Taurida.

Ténare, *m.,* Tænarus.

Ténériffe, *f.,* Teneriffe.

Terceiro, *f.,* Terceira.

Terracine, *f.,* Terracina.

Terre de Feu, *f.,* Tierra del Fuego.

Terre de Van Diémen, *f.,* Van Diemen's Land, Tasmania.

Terre-Ferme, *f.,* Terra-Firma.

Terre-Neuve, *f.,* Newfoundland.

Terre-Sainte, *f.,* Holy Land.

Tessin, Tésin, Le, *m.,* Tessin; Ticino.

Thébaïde, La, *f.,* Thebaid.

Thèbes, *f.,* Thebes.

Thermopyles, *f.pl.,* Thermopylæ.

Thessalie, *f.,* Thessaly.

Thessalonique, *f.,* Thessalonica.

Thurgovie, *f.,* Thurgau.

Thuringe, *f.,* Thuringia.

Tibre, Le, *m.,* the Tiber.

Tigre, Le, *m.,* the Tigris.

Tilsitt (tilsit), *m.,* Tilsit.

Tolède, *f.,* Toledo.

Tonkin, Tonquin, Le, *m.,* Tonquin.

Tortone, *f.,* Tortona.

Tortose, *f.,* Tortosa.

Toscane, *n.f.,* Tuscany.

Transvaal, Le, *m.,* the Transvaal.

Transcaucasie, La, *f.,* Transcaucasia.

Transylvanie, La, *f.,* Transylvania.

Trasimène, Le Lac, *m.,* Lake Trasimene.

Travnik, *m.,* Travinik.

Trébie, *f.,* Trebia.

Trébizonde, *f.,* Trebizond.

Trente, *f.,* Trent.

Trèves, *m.,* Treves, Trier.

Trévise, *f.,* Treviso.

Trieste, *f.,* or *m.,* Trieste.

Trinité, *f.,* La Trinité, Trinidad.

Trinquemale, or **Trincomaly,** *m.,* Trincomalee.

Triphylie, *f.,* Triphylia.

Troade, *f.,* Troas, Troad.

Troie, *f.,* Troja, Troia.

Tubingue, *f.,* Tubingen.

Tunisie, La, *f.,* Tunisia.

Turcomanie, *f.,* Turkomania.

Turquie, *f.,* Turkey.

Tyr, *f.,* Tyre.

U

Ukraine, *f.,* Ukraine, Ukraina.

Umerapoura, *m. V. Amarapoura.*

Upsal, *m.,* Upsala.

Urbin, *m.,* Urbino.

Utique, *f.,* Utica.

Utrecht (utrèk), *m.,* Utrecht.

V

Valachie (-kî), *f.,* Wallachia.

Valence, *f.,* Valencia.

Valette, La, *f.,* Valetta.

Valteline, *f.,* Valtellina.

Vancouver, L'Île de, *f.,* Vancouver Island.

Van Diémen, Terre de, *f.,* Van Diemen's Land, Tasmania.

Varsovie, *f.,* Warsaw.

Vénétie, *f.,* Venetia.

Venise, *f.,* Venice.

Venosa, *f.,* Venosa.

*Vermeille, Mer, *f.,* the Gulf of California.

Vérone, *f.,* Verona.

*Versailles (vèr-), *m.,* Versailles.

Vert, Le Cap, Cape Verd.

Vésuve, *m.,* Vesuvius.

Vicence, *f.,* Vicenza.

Vienne (viè-n), *f.,* Vienna (in Austria) ; Vienne (France).

Virginia, La, *f.,* Virginia.

Vistule, *f.,* Vistula.

Viterbe, *f.,* Viterbo.

Vitoria, *f.,* Vittoria.

Volhynie, La, *f.,* Volhynia.

W

Westphalie (vès-fa-lî), *f.,* Westphalia.

Wight (waïte), **Île de,** *f.,* Isle of Wight.

Wurtzbourg, *m.,* Wurzburg.

X

Xanthe, Le, *m.,* the Xanthus.

Xérès, or **Xérez** (gzérès), *m.,* Xeres.

Y

Yémen (iémè-n), **Le,** *m.,* the Yemen.

Yucatan, Le, *m.,* Yucatan.

Z

Zélande, *f.,* Zealand. La Nouvelle —; *New Zealand.*

Zoulouland, Le, *m.,* Zululand.

Zurich (zurik), *m.,* Zurich.

Zuyderzée, Le, *m.,* the Zuider Zee or Zuyder Zee.

Zollverein, Le, *m.,* the Zollverein.

TABLE OF FRENCH COINS, MEASURES, AND WEIGHTS,

REDUCED TO AMERICAN MONEY, MEASURES, AND WEIGHTS.

Francs. Centimes.	Dollars. Cents.	Francs. Centimes.	Dollars. Cents.	Francs. Centimes.	Dollars. Cents.
Fr. c.	$ cts.	Fr. c.	$ cts.	Fr. c.	$ cts.
0 05	0 01·0	5 00	0 96·5	13 00	2 50·9
0 10	0 01·9	6 00	1 15·8	14 00	2 70·2
0 25	0 04·8	7 00	1 35·1	15 00	2 89·5
0 50	0 09·6	8 00	1 54·4	16 00	3 08·8
1 00	0 19·3	9 00	1 73·7	17 00	3 28·1
2 00	0 38·6	10 00	1 93·0	18 00	3 47·4
3 00	0 57·9	11 00	2 12·3	19 00	3 66·7
4 00	0 77·2	12 00	2 21·6	20 00	3 86·0

SUPERFICIAL MEASURE.

Are (100 square mètres)..0·098845 rood.
Hectare (10,000 square mètres)..2·471143 acres.
Centiare (1 square mètre)..1·196033 sq. yd.

SOLID MEASURE.

Stère (1 cubic mètre).... { 1·31 cubic yard *or* 35 cubic feet, 547 cubic inches.
Décastère (10 stères).... 13·1 cubic yards.
Décistère (10th of a stère) { 3 cubic feet, 918·7 cubic inches.

WEIGHTS.

Gramme (weight of 1 cubic centimètre of water in its state of maximum density, or 39¼° Fahr., or 4 degrees centigrade)..... } 15·4325 grains troy.
Décagramme (10 grammes) 6·43 dwt.
Hectogram. (100 grammes) { 3·527 oz. avoir. *or* 3·216 oz. troy.
Kilogram. (1,000 grammes) { 2·2055 lb. avoir. *or* 2·6803 lb. troy.
Quintal métrique (100 kilogs.) 220·548 lb.
Millier, tonneau de mer (1,000 kilogrammes)............ 19 cwt. 12 oz. 5 dwt.
Décigram. (10th of 1 gram.) 1·5432 grain.
Centigramme (100th do.).. 0·15432 grain.
Milligramme (1,000th do.).. 0·015432 grain.

ITINERARY MEASURE.

Mètre (ten-millionth part of the arc of a meridian between the pole and the equator) .... } 3·2808992 feet.
Décamètre (10 mètres)........ 32·808992 feet.
Kilomètre (1,000 mètres)......1093·633 yards.
Myriamètre (10,000 mètres)... 6·2138 miles.

LONG MEASURE.

Décimètre (10th of a mètre)..3·937079 inches.
Centimètre (100th of a mètre)..0·393708 inch.
Millimètre (1,000th of a mètre)..0·03937 inch.

MEASURE OF CAPACITY.

Litre (1 cubic décimètre). 1·760773 pint.
Décalitre (10 litres)....... 2·2009668 gallons.
Hectolitre (100 litres).... { 22·009668 gallons *or* 2·7512 bushels.
Kilolitre, mètre cube (1,000 litres)................. 3·426 quarters.
Décilitre (10th of a litre).. 0·1760773 pint.
Centilitre (100th of a litre) 0·01760773 pint.

THERMOMETER.

0° Centigrade Melting ice....	32°	Fahrenheit.
100° do. Boiling water..	212°	do.
0° Réaumur Melting ice....	32°	do.
80° do. Boiling water..	212°	do.

TABLE OF AMERICAN COINS, MEASURES, AND WEIGHTS,

REDUCED TO FRENCH MONEY, MEASURES, AND WEIGHTS.

	$	Cts.		Feet.	Inches.
	f. c.	f. c.		Mètres.	Centimèt.
1	5·18	0·05	1	0·30479449	2·539954
2	10·26	0·10	2	0·60953898	5·079908
3	15·54	0·16	3	0·91438348	7·619862
4	20·73	0·21	4	1·21917796	10·159816
5	25·91	0·26	5	1·52397245	12·699770
6	32·09	0·31	6	1·82876694	15·239724
7	36·27	0·36	7	2·13356143	17·779678
8	41·45	0·41	8	2·43835592	20·319632
9	46·63	0·47	9	2·74315041	22·859586
10	51·81	0·52	10	3·0479449	25·399540
11	56·99	0·57	11	3·3527394	27·939494
12	62·18	0·62	12	3·6575338	30·479448
13	67·36	0·67	13	3·9623284	33·019402
14	72·54	0·73	14	4·2671229	35·559356
15	77·72	0·78	15	4·5719173	38·09931
20	103·63	1·04	20	6·0953898	50·79908
25	129·53	1·30	25	7·6198622	63·49885
50	259·07	2·59	50	15·2397245	126·99770
75	388·60	3·89	75	22·8595867	190·49655
100	518·13	5·18	100	30·4794490	252·99540

TROY WEIGHT.

Grain = 0·064798 grammes.
Pennyweight = 1·55517 "
Ounce = 31·1035 "
Pound = 0·373242 kilogrammes.

LONG MEASURE.

3 feet	(1	yard)	=	0·914383 mètres.
Fathom	(2	yards)	=	1·828766 "
Pole, Rod	(5½	")	=	5·02911 "
Furlong	(220	")	=	201·16437 "
Mile	(1760	")	=	1609·3149 "

AVOIRDUPOIS WEIGHT.

Dram .... = 1·17718 grammes.
Ounce......... = 28·3495 "
Pound .... = 0·4535926 kilogrammes.
Quarter .... = 12·6956 "
Hundredweight = 50·802 "
Ton .... = 1016·048 "

SUPERFICIAL MEASURE.

Square inch = 6·451366 centimètres carrés.
" foot = 0·0929 mètres carrés.
" yard = 0·836097 " "
Rod = 25·291939 " "
Rood (1,210 square yards) = 10·116775 ares.
Acre (4,840 " ") = 40·4671 "
Square mile = 2·588881 kilomètres carrés.

SOLID MEASURE.

Cubic inch = 16·386176 centimètres cubes.
" foot = 0·028214 mètre cube.
" yard = 0·764502 " "

MEASURE OF CAPACITY.

Pint............ = 0·5679 litres.
Quart.......... = 1·1359 "
Gallon......... = 4·543458 "
Peck........... = 9·086916 "
Bushel........ = 36·34766 "
Sack .... = 1·0904 hectolitres.
Quarter .... = 2·90781 "
Chaldron........ = 13·08516 "

ENGLISH–FRENCH DIVISION.

For the explanation of the Abbreviations used in the English-French Division, see pages xxiv., xxv.

— indicates the repetition of the English word.

Words in parentheses serve to complete the sense of those words that precede or follow them.

When two or more French nouns of the same gender follow, their gender is indicated after the last noun only.

The pronunciation of English words is indicated, in the English-French Division, in the same manner as that of French words in the French-English division, and represented in *all* cases by means of the French spelling, with the exception of :

        1st, *th* hard, which is expressed by (th);
        2d, *th* soft,   "   "   *(th)*;
        3d, *g*, when hard before *e*, *i*, or *y*, by (gh).

⊙ Indicates obsolete French words.

(ant.) Indicates obsolete English words.

A

GENERAL ENGLISH-FRENCH DICTIONARY.

a, première lettre de l'alphabet, a; (mus.) la *m*. A Number 1; *A Numéro 1 bis*. A 1; *de première classe*; (fig.) *de première qualité*. Not to know A from B; *ne savoir ni A ni B*.

a (é), *indefinite art.*, un, *m*., une, *f*. Three — day; *trois par jour*. — shilling — pound; *un schelling la livre*.

aback' (a-bak), *adv*., en arrière, à l'improviste, au dépourvu; (nav.) sur le mât; coiffé. To lay a sail —; (nav.) *coiffer une voile*. To take —; *déconcerter, interdire*.

ab'acus (-keuss), *n*., (arch. math.) abaque, *m*.

abaft', *adv*., (nav.) à l'arrière, en arrière.

abaft', *prep*., (nav.) en arrière **de**; arrière.

abai'sance, *n. V.* **obeisance**.

aban'don (a-ba'n'do'n), *v.a.*, abandonner, délaisser, quitter, renoncer à, se désister de.

aban'doned, *adj*., abandonné; perdu de débauches, dissolu. — wretch; *misérable*, *n.m*.

aban'doning (-don'igne), *n*., abandon, *m*.

aban'donment (-don'mè-nte), *n*., abandon, délaissement; laisser aller, *m*.

abase' (-béss), *v.a.*, abaisser, avilir, ravaler.

abase'ment (-béss-mè-nte), *n*., abaissement, avilissement, ravalement, *m*.

abash' (abashe), *v.a.*, déconcerter, intimider, interdire, confondre, décontenancer.

abate', *v.a.*, rabattre; diminuer; amoindrir; remettre; abolir; (to lower *or* weaken) affaiblir, atténuer; calmer, apaiser; (com.) faire remise **de**.

abate' (-béte), *v.n.*, diminuer, s'affaiblir, s'arrêter; (of the weather) se calmer, s'apaiser; (of the wind *or* temperature, etc.) tomber, baisser, s'abattre; perdre de sa force.

abate'ment (-mè-nte), *n*., diminution, *f*.; rabais, *m*., réduction; remise, *f*., affaiblissement, *m*.

abat'ing (-bét'igne), *n*., diminution, remise, *f*.; rabais, *m*.

ab'ature (-tiour), *n*., (hunt.) abattures, *f.pl*.

abb, *n*., chaîne de tisserand, *f*.

ab'bacy, *n*., dignité d'abbé, *f*.; droits abbatiaux, *m.pl*.

abbat'ical *or* **abba'tial** (-shial), *adj*., abbatial.

ab'bé (-bé), *n*., abbé, *m*.

ab'bess, *n*., abbesse, *f*.

ab'bey, *n*., abbaye, *f*.

ab'bot, *n*., abbé, supérieur d'abbaye, *m*.

ab'botship, *n*., dignité d'abbé, fonctions d'abbé, *f*.

abbre'viate (ab-bri-vié-te), *v.a.*, abréger; raccourcir.

abbrevia'tion, *n*., abréviation, *f*.

abbre'viator (-teur), *n*., abréviateur, *m*.

abbre'viatory (-via-tori) *adj*., qui abrège, abréviatif.

abbre'viature (-via-tioure), *n*., abrégé, *m*.

a b c, *n*., a b c, a b c d (alphabet), *m*.

ab'dicate (-kéte), *v.a.* and *n*., abdiquer.

abdica'tion (-ké-), *n*., abdication, *f*.

abdic'ative, *adj*., qui fait abdiquer.

abdo'men, *n*., (anat.) abdomen. Lower part of the —; *bas-ventre, m*.

abdom'inal *or* **abdom'inous** (-neusse), *adj*., abdominal.

abdu'cent (-diou-cè-nte), *adj*., (anat.) abducteur.

abduct' (-deucte), *v.a.*, détourner, enlever (clandestinement et par force).

abduc'tion (-deuk-), *n*., abduction, *f*.; détournement (de mineur), *m*.; (jur.) enlèvement, *m*.

abduc'tor (-deuk-teur), *n*., (anat.) abducteur, muscle abducteur, *m*.

abeceda'rian (é-bi-ci-da-ri-a-n), *n*., abécédaire, *m*.

abece'dary (é-bi-ci-dé-ri), *adj*., abécédaire.

abed' (-bède), *adv*., au lit, couché.

aber'rance *or* **aber'rancy** (-bèr-ra-nse, -ci), *n*., égarement, *m*., aberration, erreur, *f*.

aber'rant, *adj*., égaré.

aberra'tion (-bèr-ré-), *n*., aberration, *f*.; éloignement, écart, égarement, *m*.; erreur, *f*.

abet' (-bète), *v.a.*, soutenir, encourager, appuyer; exciter, soutenir, favoriser; provoquer.

abet'ment (-bèt'mè-nte), *n*., appui, encouragement, *m*., provocation, *f*.

abet'ter *or* **abet'tor** (-teur), *n*., fauteur, instigateur, *m*.

abey'ance, *n*., (jur.) vacance; attente, suspension, *f*. In —; *en suspens*; *périmé*. To fall into —; *tomber en désuétude*; *périmer*; *cesser d'être en vigueur*.

abhor', *v.a.*, abhorrer, avoir en horreur, détester.

abhor'rence (-rè-nce), *n*., horreur, *f*.

abhor'rent (-rè-nte), *adj*., odieux, en horreur; incompatible, contraire.

abhor'rently, *adv*., avec horreur.

abhor'rer (-reur), *n*., ennemi juré *or* déclaré, *m*.

abide' (-baïde), *v.a.*, attendre; supporter, subir, souffrir.

abide', *v.n.*, demeurer; rester, souffrir. To — by (a decision); *s'en tenir à*; *rester fidèle à*. To — by (the laws); *respecter, se conformer à, ne pas enfreindre*.

abid'er (-baïdeur), *n*., personne qui demeure, *f*., habitant, *m*.

abid'ing (-baïdigne), *n*., séjour, *m*., demeure, *f*.

abid'ing, *adj*., constant, permanent.

ab'igail, *n*., suivante, soubrette, *f*.

abil'ity, *n*., capacité, portée, *f*., pouvoir, talent, *m*., habileté, faculté, *f*., moyens, *m.pl*.; pouvoir, *m*.

abintes'tate (-bi-n-tès-téte), *adv*., (jur.) ab intestat.

ab'ject, *adj*., abject, bas, vil.

ab'ject, *n*., (ant.) un homme abject, un misérable, *m*.

abject'edness, *n*., abjection, *f*., avilissement, *m*.

abjec'tion (-sheune), *n*., abjection, *f*., abaissement, *m*., bassesse, *f*.

ab'jectly, *adv*., d'une manière abjecte.

ab'jectness, *n*., abjection, *f*.

abjura'tion (-jiou-ré-), *n*., abjuration, *f*.

abjure' (-jiour), *v.a.*, abjurer, renoncer.

abjur'er (-jiour'eur), *n*., (personne) qui abjure, *f*.

ablac'tate (-téte), *v.a.*, sevrer.

ablaquea'tion (-koui-é-), *n*., (hort.) déchaussement, *m*.

abla'tion (-blé-), *n*., enlèvement, *m*.; soustraction, *f*., retranchement, *m*.

ab'lative, *n*., (gram.) ablatif, *m*. In the —; *à l'ablatif*.

a'ble (ê-b'l), *adj*., capable; habile; robuste. To

be — to; *pouvoir; être à même* de; *être en état*
de; *être en mesure* de. He is — to do it; *il peut*
le faire. As one is —; *selon ses moyens.*

a′ble-bodied (ê-b′l-bodie), *adj.*, fort, robuste,
vigoureux ; (nav.) habile, valide ; bon pour le
service.

ab′len (a-blène) *or* **ab′let** (-blète), *n.*, (ich.)
able, *m.*, ablette, *f.*

a′bleness (ê-b′l-nèsse), *n.*, pouvoir, *m. ;* habileté, force ; capacité, *f.*

ab′luent (a-bliou-), *adj.*, qui nettoie, détersif.

ablu′tion (-bliou-), *n.*, ablution, *f.*

a′bly (ê-bli), *adv.*, habilement, adroitement.

abnega′tion (-ni-ghé-), *n.*, abnégation, renonciation, *f.*

ab′negator (-ni-ghé-teur), *n.*, personne qui
nie, *f.*

abnoda′tion (-dé-), *n.*, (hort.) enlèvement des
nœuds, *m.*

abnorm′al, *adj.*, anormal, irrégulier, difforme.

abnorm′ally, *adv.*, anormalement, irrégulièrement.

aboard′ (a-bôrde), *adv.*, (nav.) à bord. To fall
— a ship ; *aborder un navire.*

abode′ (a-bôde), *n.*, séjour, *m.*, demeure, résidence, habitation, *f.*

abol′ish, *v.a.*, abolir ; détruire ; anéantir ; annuler.

abol′ishable, *adj.*, abolissable.

abol′isher, *n.*, (personne) qui abolit, *f.*

abol′ishment, *n.*, abolissement, *m.*

aboli′tion (abolish′eunn), *n.*, abolition, destruction ; suppression, extinction, *f.*

aboli′tionist, *n.*, abolitionniste, *m.*

abom′inable, *adj.*, abominable, infâme, détestable.

abom′inableness, *n.*, abomination, *f.*

abom′inably, *adv.*, abominablement.

abom′inate (-mi-néte), *v.a.*, avoir en abomination, détester.

abomina′tion, *n.*, abomination, horreur, *f.*

aborig′inal (-bô-rid′ji-), *adj.*, aborigène, primitif.

aborig′ines (-nize), *n.pl.*, aborigènes, *m.pl.*

abor′tion, *n.*, avorton ; avortement, *m.*

abor′tive, *adj.*, abortif ; avorté.

abor′tively, *adv.*, en avortant ; avant terme ;
(fig.) prématurément; sans résultat, sans succès.

abor′tiveness, *n.*, état d'avorton ; avortement ; (fig.) insuccès, *m.*

abound′ (-baou-n-de), *v.n.*, abonder en, regorger de. To — with ; *avoir en abondance,*
avoir abondance de.

abound′ing (-digne), *adj.*, abondant. — in;
abondant en.

about′ (a-baoute), *adv.*, autour, tout autour, à
l'entour ; à la ronde ; çà et là ; environ : sur le
point de. To be — to ; *être sur le point* de. All
—; *partout.* Round —; *tout autour* de. Somewhere — here ; *près d'ici, de ce côté, dans les*
environs. Left —; *demi-tour à gauche.* Right —;
demi-tour à droite.

about′, *prep.*, autour de ; auprès de ; touchant,
au sujet de ; sur ; vers ; dans ; par. — that; *là-*
dessus, à ce sujet, à cet égard. To talk —; *parler*
de. To set — anything ; *se mettre à quelque*
chose. — the streets ; *par les rues.* — two
o'clock ; *vers les deux heures.* I have no money
— me ; *je n'ai pas d'argent sur moi.* To be —
anything ; *être occupé à quelque chose ; s'occuper*
de. To go —; (nav.) *virer de bord.* What is it
all — ? *de quoi s'agit-il ? qu'est-ce que c'est ?* To
bring —; *accomplir, faire réussir, venir à bout* de.

above′, *prep.*, au-dessus de ; au-delà de ; plus
de; (nav.) en amont de. To be — (a thing) ; *être*
trop fier pour.

above′, *adv.*, en haut ; là-haut ; au-dessus ;
ci-dessus. — all ; *surtout, pardessus tout.* —
board ; *ouvertement, franchement ; à jeu décou-*
vert. To play fair and — board ; *jouer cartes sur*

table. — ground ; *sur terre ; de ce monde, en vie.*
— named ; *susdit ; précité.* —named; *surnommé.*

abrade′ (-bréde), *v.a.*, user par le frottement ;
produire (abrasion) ; faire une écorchure,
écorcher ; miner, rouger.

a′braham *or* **a′bram**, *n.*, fourbe fieffé, *m.*
To sham —; *jouer l'innocence patriarcale ; faire*
le bon apôtre.

abra′sion (a-b′ré-jeune), *n.*, action d'enlever
par le frottement, *f.*; (med.) abrasion, écorchure, *f.* ; (coin) frai, *m.*

abreast′ (-brèste), *adv.*, de front ; à côté l'un
de l'autre ; vis-à-vis; (nav.) par le travers.

abridge′, *v.a.*, abréger ; retrancher, réduire ;
restreindre ; priver de.

abridg′er (-djeur), *n.*, abréviateur, *m.*

abridg′ment (-brid-je-), *n.*, abrégé, *m.*, réduction, diminution, *f. ;* précis, *m.*

abroach′ (-brôt-she), *adv.*, en perce ; (fig.) en
avant, en train.

abroad′ (a-brôde), *adv.*, dehors ; à la promenade ; à l'étranger ; au large, au loin, au dehors ;
partout. To, get *or* be, —; (fig.) (of news) *courir,*
se répandre ; transpirer. To be all —; *être tout*
désorienté, tout ahuri. To be blazed —; *être*
éventé, proclamé, publié, colporté. The schoolmaster is —; *l'éducation est partout.*

ab′rogate (a-brô-ghéte), *v.a.*, abroger.

abroga′tion, *n.* abrogation ; révocation, *f.*

abrupt′, *adj.*, brusque ; brisé ; saccadé ; abrupt ;
rocailleux, escarpé ; précipité, à pic.

abrup′tion, *n.*, rupture, *f.*

abrupt′ly, *adv.*, brusquement, avec précipitation ; subitement.

abrupt′ness, *n.*, brusquerie, rudesse, précipitation, aspérité, *f. ;* (of rocks, etc.) escarpement, *m.*

ab′scess, *n.*, abcès, *m.*

abscind′, *v.a.*, retrancher.

ab′sciss *or* **abscis′sa**, *n.*, (geom.) abscisse, *f.*

abscis′sion (-j'eune), *n.*, amputation, *f.*

abscond′ (-ko'nde), *v.n.*, se cacher ; disparaître ; fuir la justice ; se soustraire aux poursuites
de la justice.

abscond′edly, *adv.*, en cachette.

abscond′er (-deur), *n.*, fugitif, contumax, *m.*

abscond′ing, *n.*, action de se cacher ; fuite, *f.*

ab′sence (-sè-nse), *n.*, absence, *f.;* éloignement, *m. ;* absence d'esprit, distraction, *f.*, manque, *m.*

ab′sent, *adj.*, absent ; distrait.

absent′, *v.a.*, éloigner. To — one's self; *s'ab-*
senter.

absentee′ (-ti), *n.*, absent, *m.* — landlord ;
propriétaire forain.

absentee′ism (-ti-izme), *n.*, absentéisme, *m.*

absent′er (-deur), *n.*, absent, déserteur (de son poste),
m.

absinthe′, *n.*, absinthe, *f.*

absin′thiated (-thié-), *adj.*, absinthé.

ab′sis, *n.* V. **apsis.**

ab′solute (-liou-te), *adj.*, absolu ; vrai ; parfait ; pur et simple, positif ; (arrant) vrai, franc,
véritable. He is an — knave ; *c'est un franc*
coquin.

ab′solutely, *adv.*, absolument, positivement.

ab′soluteness, *n.*, pouvoir absolu ; arbitraire,
m.

absolu′tion, *n.*, absolution ; (rel.) absoute, *f.*

ab′solutism, *n.*, absolutisme, *m.*

ab′solutist, *n.*, absolutiste, *m.*

absol′utory, *adj.*, absolutoire.

absolve′ (-zolve), *v.a.*, absoudre de, délier, décharger, dégager, affranchir, exempter de.

ab′sonant, *adj.*, en contradiction, absurde,
contraire à la raison ; discordant.

absorb′, *v.a.*, absorber ; engloutir.

absorbabil′ity, *n.*, faculté d'absorber, *f.*

absorb′able, *adj.*, (chem.) qui peut être
absorbé, absorbable.

absorb′ent, *n.*, absorbant, *m.*

absorb'ent, *adj.*, absorbant.

absorp'tion, *n.*, absorption; extinction, *f.*

absorp'tive, *adj.*, qui a la faculté d'absorber; (chem.) absorbant.

abstain' (-tè-ne), *v.n.*, s'abstenir **de**, se priver **de** ; se réfuser.

abstain'er, *n.*, abstenant. Total —; *abstème, qui ne boit pas d'alcool.*

abstain'ing, *n.*, abstinence, *f.*

abste'mious (-mieusse), *adj.*, abstème, sobre, modéré.

abste'miously, *adv.*, sobrement; avec abstinence, avec modération.

abste'miousness, *n.*, abstinence, modération ; sobriété, *f.*

absten'tion (-tè'n-), *n.*, abstinence, privation, abstention, *f.*

absterge' (-teurd'je), *v.a.*, (surg.) absterger ; nettoyer.

abster'gent, *n.*, abstergent, *m.*

abster'gent, *adj.*, abstergent, abstersif.

abster'sion (-teur-), *n.*, (med.) abstersion, *f.*

abster'sive, *adj.*, abstersif, abstergent.

ab'stinence *ou* **ab'stinency**, *n.*, abstinence, abstention, *f.*

ab'stinent, *adj.*, abstinent, sobre.

ab'stinently, *adv.*, avec abstinence.

abstract', *v.a.*, abstraire, extraire, soustraire à, dérober à, (to sum up) résumer; séparer **de** ; (to exclude) faire abstraction **de**.

abstract', *adj.*, abstrait.

ab'stract, *n.*, résumé, *m.* ; analyse, *f.* ; extrait, relevé, précis, *m.* ; état sommaire, *m.* In the —; *par abstraction, en théorie.*

abstract'ed, *adj.*, séparé ; soustrait, dérobé; purifié, abstrait ; distrait.

abstract'edly, *adv.*, d'une manière abstraite ; par abstraction.

abstract'edness, *n.*, caractère abstrait, *m.*

abstract'er (-teur-), *n.*, abréviateur, *m.*

abstrac'tion, *n.*, abstraction ; distraction, préoccupation ; soustraction, *f.*

abstract'ive, *adj.*, abstractif; extrait.

ab'stractly, *adv.*, abstractivement, abstraitement, d'une manière abstraite.

ab'stractness, *n.*, abstraction; nature abstraite, *f.*

abstruse' (-strouss), *adj.*, caché ; abstrus, abstrait, obscur.

abstruse'ly, *adv.*, d'une manière abstruse, abstraitement, obscurément.

abstruse'ness, *n.*, qualité abstruse, obscurité, *f.*

absurd' (-seurde), *adj.*, absurde.

absurd'ity, *n.*, absurdité, *f.*

absurd'ly, *adv.*, absurdement.

absurd'ness, *n.*, absurdité, *f.*

abun'dance (-beune-), *n.*, abondance ; prospérité ; quantité, *f.* ; grand nombre, *m.*

abun'dant, *adj.*, abondant, riche. — in; *abondant* en.

abun'dantly, *adv.*, abondamment; largement ; en abondance.

abuse' (-biouze), *v.a.*, abuser **de** ; médire **de** ; dire des sottises à, injurier, dire des injures à, maltraiter; tromper.

abuse' (-biousse), *n.*, abus, *m.* ; sottises, insultes, injures, *f. pl.*

abus'er (-biou-zeur), *n.*, abuseur, insulteur ; grossier personnage, *m.*

abus'ive (-biouss'-), *adj.*, injurieux ; abusif.

abus'ively, *adj.*, injurieusement, abusivement.

abus'iveness, *n.*, langage injurieux *ou* outrageant ; grossièreté, *f.*

abut' (-beute), *v.n.*, aboutir à ; s'embrancher; confiner à.

abut'ment, *n.*, but, *m.* ; borne ; contre-fiche ; (of a bridge) culée, *f.* ; arc-boutant, *m.*

abut'ment - pier (-pieurre), *n.*, pile - culée, butée, *f.*

abut'ting, *n.*, embranchement (of a road), *m.*

abyss', *n.*, abîme, gouffre, *m.*

aca'cia (-shia), *n.*, acacia, *m.* Indian —; *tamarinier, m.* Common —; *acacia vulgaire.* Bastard —; *robinier, m.*

academ'ic (-dé-), *n.*, académicien, *m.*

academ'ic *ou* **academ'ical**, *adj.*, académique, universitaire, classique, scolaire.

academ'ically, *adv.*, académiquement.

academi'cian (-di-), *n.*, académicien, *m.* ; de l'académie.

acad'emism, *n.*, système académique, *m.*

acad'emist, *n.*, académicien ; académiste, *m.*

acad'emy (-di-), *n.*, académie ; école, pension, institution, *f.*, pensionnat, *m.* — figure ; *académie, étude, f.*

acan'tha (-tha), *n.*, (bot.) acanthe, branche-ursine, *f.*

acan'thine (-thine), *adj.*, fait d'épine.

acan'thus (-theusse), *n.*, (bot., arch.) acanthe, *f.*

accede' (-cîde), *v.n.*, accéder à, consentir à, monter **sur** le trône.

accel'erate (-leu-rête), *v.a.*, accélérer, hâter, activer, précipiter, presser.

accelera'tion (-ré-), *n.*, accélération, *f.*

accel'erative (-leu-), *adj.*, accélérateur.

accel'eratory (-leu-ra-tori), *adj.*, accélérant.

accendibil'ity, *n.*, (chem.) inflammabilité, *f.*

accend'ible, *adj.*, (chem.) inflammable.

accen'sion, *n.*, (chem.) inflammation, *f.*

ac'cent, *n.*, accent ; ton ; parler, *m.*

accent', *v.a.*, accentuer ; articuler.

accent'ing, *n.*, accentuation, *f.*

accent'uate (-tiou-éte), *v.a.*, accentuer.

accentua'tion, *n.*, accentuation, *f.*

accept', *v.a.*, accepter, agréer, accueillir, recevoir ; comprendre, entendre (l.u.).

accept'able, *adj.*, acceptable, agréable.

accept'ableness, *n.*, acceptabilité, *f.* ; mérite, bon accueil, droit au bon accueil, *m.*

accept'ably, *adv.*, agréablement.

accept'ance, *n.*, acceptation, *f.* ; accueil, *m.* Worth —; *qui vaut la peine d'être accepté ; digne d'être offert.* To beg any one's — of anything ; *prier quelqu'un d'accepter, de vouloir bien accepter quelque chose.* To cancel an —; (com.) *annuler une acceptation.* To furnish with an —; *revêtir d'une acceptation.* To leave for —; *laisser à l'acceptation.* To refuse —; *refuser à l'acceptation.* To present for —; *présenter à l'acceptation.* To send out for —; *envoyer à l'acceptation.*

accepta'tion (-té-), *n.*, accueil, *m.* ; réception, faveur ; (gram.) acception, *f.* ; sens, *m.*

accept'er (-teur), *n.*, (com.) accepteur, *m.*

accep'tion, *n.*, (gram.) acception, *f.* ; sens, *m.*

ac'cess, *n.*, accès, abord, *m.* Difficult of —; *d'un accès, ou abord, difficile.*

ac'cessary. *V.* **accessory**.

acces'sible, *adj.*, accessible, abordable.

acces'sion, *n.*, accession, acquisition ; addition, *f.* ; accroissement ; (to a throne) avènement, *m.*

acces'sional, *adj.*, additionnel.

accesso'rial, *adj.*, de complicité.

acces'sorily, *adv.*, accessoirement.

acces'soriness, *n.*, état accessoire, *m.*, complicité, *f.*

acces'sory, *adj.*, accessoire.

acces'sory, *n.*, complice, *m.*

ac'cidence, *n.*, rudiments de grammaire, *m. pl.*

ac'cident, *n.*, accident ; incident ; (of fire) sinistre ; hasard, *m.*

accident'al, *adj.*, accidentel, fortuit, casuel. — light, *accident de lumière.*

accident'al, *n.*, accident.

accident'ally, *adv.*, accidentellement, fortuitement, par accident, casuellement, par hasard.

accident'alness, *n.*, nature accidentelle *or* accessoire, *f.* ; cas imprévu, *m.*

acclaim', n., acclamation, f.

acclaim', v.a., acclamer à, applaudir à.

acclama'tion (-mé-), n., acclamation, f.

acclam'atory, adj., d'acclamation, d'applaudissement.

accli'mated, adj., acclimaté.

acclima'tion (-mé-), n., acclimatement, m. ;
acclimatation, f.

acclimatiza'tion (-mâ-taï-zè-sheunn), n., acclimatation, f.

acclivity, n., montée, pente, élévation,
rampe, f.

accli'vous (-veusse), adj., en rampe, montant.

accolade' (-caou-n-te), n., accolade, f. ; embrassement, m.

accom'modable, adj., accommodable.

accom'modate (-déte), v.a., accommoder,
ajuster ; disposer ; loger ; obliger, servir ;
fournir, procurer. To — with a seat; donner un
siège à une place à. To — one's self to ; s'accommoder à ; se prêter à.

accom'modated, adj., accommodé.

accom'modately, adv., convenablement.

accom'modating, adj., accommodant ; flexible.

accommoda'tion, n., adaptation, f. ; accommodement, m. ; convenance, f. ; logement, m. ;
(com.) facilités, f.pl. — bill ; billet de complaisance. The accommodations are very good in this
hotel; on est très bien dans cet hôtel. — ladder ;
(nav.) échelle de commandement.

accom'modator (-teur), n., personne qui
accommode, f.

accom'paniment (n., accompagnement, m.

accom'panist, n., (mus.) accompagnateur, m.,
accompagnatrice, f.

accom'pany, v.a., accompagner. — with ;
accompagner de.

accom'plice, n., complice, m.f. — with ;
complice de.

accom'plish, v.a., accomplir ; former ; effectuer ; remplir ; achever ; opérer.

accom'plished (-plish'te), adj., accompli,
parfait, achevé ; émérite.

accom'plisher (-sheur), n., exécuteur, m.

accom'plishment, n., accomplissement ; talent, mérite, art d'agrément, m., connaissances,
f.pl., qualité, f.

accompt'. V. account.

accord', n., accord, consentement, accommodement, m. Of one's own — ; de son propre
mouvement. With one — ; d'un commun accord.
In — ; d'accord avec, conformément à.

accord', v.a., accorder ; ajuster.

accord', v.n., s'accorder, être d'accord.

accord'ance, n., accord, m. ; conformité,
union, f.

accord'ant, adj., d'accord avec, conforme à.

accord'ing, adj., conforme à.

accord'ing as, conj., selon que, suivant que.

accord'ing to, prep., selon, suivant, conformément à, d'après.

accord'ingly, adv., en conséquence, donc,
aussi.

accord'ion, n., accordéon, m.

accost', v.a., accoster, aborder.

accost'able, adj., abordable.

accoucheur', n., accoucheur, m.

account' (-caou-n-te), n., compte ; récit, exposé, compte rendu, m., relation ; importance,
considération ; raison ; histoire ; description, f. ;
motif, sujet ; poids, m. ; (com.) facture, f. Old
—; ancien compte. Current —; compte courant.
Outstanding —; compte non soldé. — agreed
upon ; arrêté de compte. Overdrawn —; compte
découvert. Bank —; compte de banque. Cash
—; compte de caisse. Stock —; compte de capital. Statement of an —; état de compte. Abstract of an —; relevé de compte. In — with ;
en compte avec. As per — rendered ; suivant
compte remis. On — of ; pour le compte de. On

— and risk of ; aux risques et pour le compte de.
On no —, pour rien au monde. To call to —;
demander des explications, or compte, à. To take
an — of ; prendre note de. To take into —;
tenir compte de, (com.) mettre en ligne de compte.
To turn to — ; tirer parti de. On joint —; de
compte en participation. Per —; suivant compte.
To appear in any one's —; figurer sur le compte
de quelqu'un. To audit an —; vérifier un compte.
To balance an — ; balancer un compte. To carry
to —; porter en compte. To close an —; clore un
compte. To compare —s; confronter un compte.
To deliver an —; remettre un compte. To have a
current — with ; être en compte courant avec.
To keep —s; tenir des livres. To make out any
one's —; établir le compte de quelqu'un. To
make up an —; balancer un compte. To note an
—; pointer un compte. To open an —; ouvrir un
compte. To pass to —; passer en compte. On
joint or mutual —; de compte à demi. Short —s
make long friends ; les bons comptes font les bons
amis. On — of ; à cause de. On your —; par
égard pour vous. By all —s ; au dire de tout le
monde or de l'aveu de tous. To turn anything to
—; mettre quelque chose à profit or tirer profit de
quelque chose. To make — of ; faire cas de.
To make no — of ; ne faire aucun cas de. The
—s from China ; les nouvelles de la Chine.

account' (-caou-n-te), v.a., compter ; estimer,
regarder comme, réputer.

account', v.n., rendre compte de ; expliquer ;
répondre de, rendre raison de. — for; expliquer,
justifier son action.

accountabil'ity, n., responsabilité, f.

account'able, adj., responsable, comptable ;
explicable.

account'ableness, n., responsabilité, f.

account'ant, n., comptable ; teneur de livres,
m. — general; chef de comptabilité.

account'-book (-bouke), n., livre de comptes, m.

accou'ple (-ac-keu-p'l), v.a., accoupler.

accou'ter (-teur), v.a., équiper ; accoutrer ;
parer ; (pop.) affubler, fagoter.

accou'terment, n., accoutrement, équipement,
m.

accred'it, v.a., accréditer.

accredita'tion (-té-). V. credence.

accred'ited, adj., accrédité.

accre'tion, n., accroissement ; (of earth) atterrissement, m.

accre'tive, adj., croissant.

accrue' (-crou), v.n., s'accroître ; provenir
de, résulter de, s'ensuivre, revenir à.

accum'bent, adj., à demi couché.

accu'mulate (ac-kiou-miou-léte), v.a., accumuler, entasser, amonceler.

accu'mulate, v.n., s'accumuler, s'amonceler,
s'entasser.

accu'mulate, adj., accumulé.

accu'mulating, adj., toujours croissant.

accumula'tion, n., accumulation, f. ; amoncellement, amas ; entassement ; (jur.) cumul, m.

accu'mulative, adj., qui accumule, accumulateur.

accu'mulatively, adv., par accumulation.

accu'mulator (-lé-teur), n., accumulateur, f.,
accumulatrice, f.

ac'curacy (-kiou-), n., exactitude, justesse,
attention, f., soin, m. ; correction, précision, f.

ac'curate (-kiou-réte), adj., exact ; juste ; correct, fidèle, précis.

ac'curately, adv., exactement, soigneusement.

ac'curateness, n., précision, justesse, f.

accurse' (-keurse), v.a., maudire, excommunier.

accursed' (-keurste or -keur'sède), adj., maudit, détestable, exécrable.

accu'sable (-kiou-za-b'l), adj., accusable.

accusa'tion (-zé-), n., accusation, f.

accu'sative, n., (gram.) accusatif, m.

accu'sative, adj., (gram.) de l'accusatif.

accu'satively, adv., (gram.) comme accusatif.

accu'satory (-teuri), adj., accusatoire.

accuse' (-kiouze), v.a., accuser.

accus'er, n., accusateur, m., accusatrice, f.

accus'tom (-keus-teume), v.a., accoutumer à ; habituer à. To — one's self to ; s'accoutumer à ; s'habituer à, se faire à.

accus'tomable, adj., (l.u.) habituel.

accus'tomably, adv., (l.u.) habituellement.

accus'tomarily, adv., (l.u.) ordinairement.

accus'tomary, adj., (l.u.) ordinaire.

ace (éce), n., (cards) as ; (fig.) point, iota, m. Within an — of ; à deux doigts de. I was within an — of ; j'ai failli, or il s'en est fallu de peu que.

aceph'alous (-céf-al-eusse), adj., (zoöl.) acéphale, sans tête.

acerb'ate (-seur-béte), v.a., rendre acerbe, aigrir.

acerb'ity, n., acerbité, aigreur ; dureté, âpreté, sévérité, rigueur, f.

ac'erous (-seu-reusse), adj., acéré.

aces'cency, n., acescence, f.

aces'cent, adj., acescent (qui tourne à l'aigre).

ac'etate (-ci-té-te), n., (chem.) acétate, m.

acet'ic, adj., (chem.) acétique.

ac'etite, n., (chem. ant.) acétate, m.

ace'tous, adj., (chem.) acéteux.

ache (éke), n., mal, m., douleur, f. Head—; mal de tête, mal à la tête. Tooth—; mal de dents, mal aux dents. To have a head—; avoir mal à la tête, avoir un mal de tête.

ache (éke), v.n., faire mal ; souffrir. My head aches ; j'ai mal à la tête. My feet —; les pieds me font mal.

achiev'able, adj., exécutable, faisable.

achieve' (a-tshîve), v.a., exécuter, accomplir, gagner, (a victory) remporter. To — a reputation ; se faire une réputation.

achieve'ment, n., exploit, fait d'armes, accomplissement, haut-fait, succès, m. ; œuvre, production, découverte, victoire, f. ; (her.) écusson, m., armoiries, f.pl.

achiev'er, n., auteur, or exécuteur, d'un exploit, m.

ach'ing (é-kigne), n., douleur, souffrance, f.

ach'ing, adj., endolori, douloureux.

a'chor (é-kor),n., (med.) croûte de lait, teigne, f.

achromat'ic (-krô-), adj., (opt.) achromatique.

ac'id, adj., acide.

ac'id, n., acide, m.

acid'ity, n., acidité, f.

acid'ulate (-diou-léte), v.a., aciduler.

acid'ulous (-leusse), adj., acidule.

ac'inose (-nôss) ou ac'inous (-neusse), adj., granulaire, granulé.

acknowl'edge (ak-no-lèdje), v.a., reconnaître ; répondre à ; avouer, confesser, convenir de ; (of letters) accuser réception de.

acknowl'edgment (-lèdj'), n., reconnaissance, f., aveu, m., excuse, f. ; tribut ; accusé de réception, reçu, certificat, m. ; attestation, f. ; remerciments or remerciements, m.pl. ; récompense, f.

ac'me (-mi), n., (med.) acmé ; (fig.) apogée ; comble, m., faîte, m. ; sommet, m.

ac'olyte (-laïte), n., acolyte, m.

ac'onite (-naïte), n., aconit, m.

a'corn (-), n., gland, m. ; (nav.) pomme de girouette, f. ; (conch.) barnacle, gland de mer, m.

a'corned (-côrn'de), adj., chargé de glands.

acotyle'don (-ti-lé-done), n., (bot.) acotylédone, f.

acotyle'donous, adj., (bot.) acotylédone.

acous'tic (-caous-), adj., acoustique.

acous'tics, n., acoustique, f.

acquaint' (ac-coué-nte), v.a., informer ; avertir ; faire savoir à, familiariser avec. To make any one —ed with anything ; faire con-

naître, or faire savoir, quelque chose à quelqu'un. To get —ed with any one ; faire la connaissance de quelqu'un. To be —ed with ; connaître, se mettre au courant de or au fait de, prendre connaissance de. To be intimately —ed with any one ; être très lié avec quelqu'un.

acquaint'ance, n., connaissance, liaison, accointance, f. To have a great many —s ; avoir beaucoup de connaissances. To make — with any one ; faire connaissance avec quelqu'un. To make his, or her, —; faire sa connaissance.

acquaint'ed, adj., connu ; instruit de ; familier avec.

acquest' (ac-couèste), n., acquisition ; conquête, f. ; (law) acquêt, m.

acquiesce' (ac-koui-èsse), v.n., acquiescer à ; adhérer à ; accéder à ; consentir à ; se soumettre à.

acquies'cence ou acquies'cency, n., acquiescement, m. ; soumission, f.

acquies'cent, adj., résigné, soumis, facile, accommodant.

acquir'able, adj., acquérable.

acquire' (ac-kouaïeur), v.a., acquérir ; obtenir ; gagner ; apprendre.

acquire'ment, n., acquis, m. ; acquisition ; instruction, connaissance, f., talent, m.

acquir'er, n., acquéreur, m., acquéreuse, f.

acquisi'tion (ac-koui-zi-), n., acquisition ; connaissance, f.

acquis'itive, adj., qui est acquis ; porté à acquérer.

acquit' (ac-kouite), v.a., acquitter, absoudre de, décharger de. To — one's self of ; s'acquitter de ; faire son devoir. To — one's self well ; se bien tirer de.

acquit'tal, n., acquittement, m.

acquit'tance, n., acquittement, m., décharge ; quittance, f. ; (com.) acquit, m.

a'cre (é-keur), n., arpent, demi-hectare, m.

ac'rid, adj., âcre.

acrid'ity ou ac'ridness, n., âcreté, f.

acrimo'nious, adj., acrimonieux, âcre.

acrimo'niously, adv., avec aigreur, avec acrimonie.

ac'rimony, n., acrimonie, âcreté, aigreur, f.

ac'ritude (-tioude), n., âcreté, f.

ac'rospire (-païeur), n., germe, m., plumule, f.

across', prep., à travers ; au travers de ; par. adv., de travers, en travers ; de l'autre côté. To come —; rencontrer, trouver sur son passage, tomber sur.

acros'tic, n., acrostiche, m.

act, n., action, f., fait, acte, trait, coup, m. In the —; sur le fait. In the very —; sur le fait même, en flagrant délit. In the — of ; en train de. — of indemnity ; bill d'indemnité. It is not the — of an honest man ; ce n'est pas le fait d'un honnête homme.

act, v.a., représenter, jouer ; feindre, contrefaire.

act, v.n., agir sur ; se conduire ; se comporter ; opérer ; influer sur.

act'ing, n., action, f. ; (thea.) jeu, m. ; (fig.) feinte, f. His affection is not sincere, it is mere —; son affection est jouée, ce n'est qu'une feinte.

act'ing, adj., qui agit ; (tech.) à effet ; (taking the place of) suppléant, faisant fonctions de. — manager ; directeur gérant. — corporal ; élève-caporal or caporal postiche.

ac'tion, n., action, f. ; fait, événement ; (jur.) procès ; combat, m., affaire, bataille, f. ; (tech.) effet, m. To call into —; mettre en action, mettre en jeu, faire jouer, employer. Naval —; combat naval. To bring an — against a person ; intenter un procès à quelqu'un or poursuivre quelqu'un en justice. Civil —; action au civil. To clear (decks) for —; (nav.) faire branle-bas de combat.

ac'tionable, adj., actionnable, sujet à procès, punissable.

act'ive, adj., actif ; agile, ingambe.

act'ively, adv., activement, agilement, avec activité.

activ'ity, n., activité, agilité, f.

act'or, n., acteur, comédien, (fam.) cabotin, m.

act'ress, n., actrice, comédienne, f.

act'ual (act-iou-al), adj., réel, effectif, véritable, actuel, positif.

actual'ity, n., réalité, actualité, f.

actualiza'tion, n., actualisation.

ac'tualize, v.a., actualiser.

act'ually, adv., réellement, positivement, véritablement, actuellement, effectivement.

act'ualness, n., réalité, f.

act'uary (act-iou-), n., secrétaire, expert-comptable, m.

act'uate (-tiou-ête), v.a., mettre en action, influencer, pousser, animer, guider, inciter à.

acu'leate (-kiou-li-éte) ou **acu'leated** (-kiou-li-étède), adj., (bot.) aiguillonné, pointu, piquant.

acu'men (-kiou-mène), n., finesse, pénétration, f.

acu'minate, v.n., s'élever en cône ; se terminer en pointe.

acu'minate (-kiou-mi-néte) adj., aigu, pointu ; (bot.) acuminé.

acu'minated, adj., (bot.) acuminé ; terminé en pointe.

acumina'tion, n., pointe aiguë ; finesse, f.

acupunc'ture (-kiou-peu-nkt-iour), n., (surg.) acuponcture, f.

acute' (-kioute), adj., aigu, violent, perçant ; fin ; poignant ; pénétrant.

acute'ly, adv., finement, subtilement ; vivement.

acute'ness (-kiout'nèsse), n., état aigu, m. ; force, intensité, finesse, perspicacité, f.

A. D., l'an de grâce.

ad'age (-dèdje), n., adage, m.

adag'ial, adj., (ant.) passé en adage, proverbial.

ada'gio (-dadjiô), n., (mus.) adagio, m.

ad'amant, n., diamant, m.

adamant'ine, adj., de diamant ; (min.) adamantin.

adapt', v.a., adapter, approprier, ajuster ; appliquer.

adapt'able, adj., adaptable, qui peut s'adapter.

adapta'tion (-dap-té-), n., adaptation, f. ; arrangement, m.

adapt'ed, part., propre à ; adapté à.

adapt'er, n., adaptateur, qui adapte.

adaptibil'ity, n., faculté d'être adapté, f.

adays', adv., aujourd'hui. Now—; de nos jours ; actuellement.

add, v.a., ajouter, joindre ; adjoindre ; additionner. — to this; ajoutez à cela.

ad'dable. V. **ad'dible**.

ad'der, n., vipère, f.

ad'derlike (ad-deur-laïke), adj., en serpent.

ad'der's-tongue, n., (bot.) langue de serpent, f.

ad'der's-wort, n., (bot.) vipérine, f.

addibil'ity, n., qualité de ce qui peut être ajouté, f.

ad'dible ou **ad'dable**, adj., qui peut être ajouté.

addict', v.r. To — one's self to; s'adonner à, se consacrer à, se livrer à. To be —ed to; s'adonner à ; être adonné à.

addict'edness ou **addic'tion**, n., attachement, goût, penchant, m., disposition, f.

addi'tion (ad-di-), n., addition, f., surcroît, supplément ; accroissement, m. In — to; outre, en sus de. Revised with —s; (of books) édition revue et augmentée.

addi'tional, adj., additionnel, supplémentaire, de plus.

addi'tionally, adv., par addition, en outre, en sus.

ad'dle, n., tartre (from wine).

ad'dle, adj., couvi (of eggs) ; trouble ; (fig.) stérile.

ad'dle, v.a., rendre couvi ; troubler.

ad'dled, part., couvi, gâté, trouble ; (fig.) stérile, pourri.

ad'dle-headed (-hè-dède) **ad'dle-pated** (-pé-tède), adj., à cerveau vide, écervelé.

address', v.a., adresser ; s'adresser à ; parler à, adresser la parole à, apostropher ; aborder ; (of letters) adresser, mettre l'adresse à.

address', n., adresse, allocution, f., discours, plaidoyer ; port, m., tenue, f. To pay one's —es to ; faire la cour à, rechercher en mariage. Of good —; comme il faut, de bonne tournure, à l'air distingué. Style of —; titre, m.

addressee', n., destinataire.

address'er (ad-drèss-seur), n., pétitionnaire, m.

adduce' (-diouce), v.a., présenter, alléguer ; apporter, fournir, avancer, produire ; citer.

addu'cible, adj., allégable ou qui peut être allégué.

adduc'tion (-deuk-), n., citation, f.

adduc'tive, adj., **adduc'tor**, n., adducteur.

ademp'tion, n. (jur.) ademption, révocation (d'un legs), f.

adept', adj., adepte, habile, versé dans.

adept', n., adepte, m.f.

ad'equacy (-di-koua-), **ad'equateness**, n., juste proportion ; suffisance, f.

ad'equate (-di-kouéte), adj., proportionné, égal ; suffisant ; équivalent, compétent.

ad'equately, adv., en juste proportion, justement, suffisamment.

adhere' (ad-fre), v.n., adhérer à, s'attacher à ; (fig.) se fier à, s'en tenir à.

adher'ence, n., adhérence, adhésion, f., attachement, m.

adher'ent, n. adhérent, partisan, dépendant, disciple, m.

adher'er, n., partisan, adhérent, m.

adhe'sion (-dî-jeune), n., adhésion, adhérence, f.

adhe'sive (-dî-cive), adj., qui adhère ; tenace ; (med.) adhésif.

adhe'sively, adv., avec adhérence.

adhe'siveness, n., adhérence, adhésion, (fig.) ténacité, f.

adhor'tatory, adj., exhortatoire, f.

adiaph'orous (-di-a-fo-reusse), adj., indifférent, neutre.

adieu', adv., adieu.

adieu' (-diou), n., adieu, m. To bid any one —; faire ses adieux à quelqu'un.

ad infini'tum (-teume), adv., à l'infini.

ad in'terim, adv., par intérim.

ad'ipocere (-cîre), n., adipocire, f.

ad'ipose (-pôss) ou **ad'ipous** (-peusse), adj., adipeux.

ad'it, n., (mines) entrée ; galerie d'écoulement, f.

adja'cency, n., contiguïté, f., voisinage, m., proximité, f.

adja'cent, adj., adjacent à, contigu à, voisin de ; (of countries) limitrophe de.

ad'jective, n., adjectif, m.

ad'jective, adj., (dy.) adjective.

ad'jectively, adv., adjectivement.

adjoin' (-joïne), v.a., joindre à, adjoindre à, ajouter à, toucher.

adjoin', v.n., être attenant, or contigu, à ; se joindre à.

adjourn' (-djeurn), v.a., ajourner, différer, remettre. Let us —; remettons la partie.

adjourn', v.n., s'ajourner.

adjourn'ment, n., ajournement, m.

adjudge' (-djeudje), v.a., adjuger ; décerner ; juger, condamner ; décréter ; arrêter.

adjudg'ment, n., jugement, m., décision, f.

adju'dicate, v.a., juger.

adju'dicate (-jiou-di-kéte), *v.a.*, adjuger.
adjudica'tion, *n.*, jugement, *m.*; décision, *f.*; arrêt, *m.*, déclaration de faillite, *f.*
adju'dicator (-teur), *n.*, juge, *m.*
ad'junct, *adj.*, joint, adjoint, secondaire, accessoire.
ad'junct (ad-jeu'n'kte), *n.*, accessoire; adjoint, *m.*
adjunc'tion, *n.*, adjonction, addition, *f.*
adjunc'tive, *adj.*, qui joint.
adjunc'tive, *n.*, chose jointe, *f.*
adjunc'tively, *adj.*, par addition.
adjura'tion (-jiou-ré-), *n.*, appel sacré, *m.*, invocation, adjuration, *f.*
adjure' (-jioure), *v.a.*, adjurer.
adjur'er, *n.*, personne qui adjure, *f.*
adjust' (-jeuste), *v.a.*, ajuster, régler, arranger, fixer, déterminer.
adjust'er, *n.*, ajusteur, *m.*, personne qui ajuste, *f.*
adjust'ment, *n.*, ajustement, accord, arrangement, *m.* Amicable —; *arrangement à l'amiable.*
ad'jutancy, *n.*, (milit.) grade d'adjudant; ordre, *m.*, classification, *f.*
ad'jutant (-jiou-), *n.*, (milit.) adjudant; (fig.) second, *m.* — general; *chef d'état-major, m.*
ad'juvant, *n.*, aide, *f.*; (pharm.) adjuvant, *m.*
ad lib'itum, *adv.*, à volonté.
admeas'urement, *n.*, mesurage, *m.*; dimension, *f.*; règlement, *m.*
ad'measurer, *n.*, mesureur, *m.*
admensura'tion, *n.* V. **admeasurement**.
admin'ister, *v.a.*, administrer; gérer; régir; donner; fournir; faire prêter (an oath).
admin'ister (-teur), *v.n.*, subvenir à; pourvoir à.
admin'istrate (-tréte), *v.a.*, administrer; régir; donner.
administra'tion, *n.*, administration, *f.*; gouvernement, *m.*; (law) gestion, gérance, *f.*
admin'istrative, *adj.*, administratif.
admin'istratively, *adv.*, administrativement.
administra'tor, *n.*, administrateur, régent, *m.*
administra'torship, *n.*, fonctions d'administrateur, *f.pl.*, administration, *f.*
administra'trix, *n.*, administratrice, *f.*
ad'mirable, *adj.*, admirable.
ad'mirableness, *n.*, excellence, beauté, *f.*
ad'mirably, *adv.*, admirablement, à ravir, à merveille.
ad'miral, *n.*, amiral; (flag-ship) vaisseau amiral, *m.* Rear——; *contre-amiral.* Vice——; *vice-amiral.*
ad'miralship, *n.*, amiralat, *m.*
ad'miralty, *n.*, amirauté, *f.* Board of ——; *conseil d'amirauté, m.* First lord of the ——; *ministre de la marine, m.*
admira'tion (-ré-), *n.*, admiration, *f.*; étonnement, *m.* To ——; *à ravir.*
admire', *v.a.*, admirer, trouver beau, aimer; être épris de.
admire' (-maïeur), *v.n.*, s'étonner.
admir'er, *n.*, admirateur, *m.*, admiratrice, *f.*
admir'ingly, *adv.*, avec admiration.
admissibil'ity, *n.*, admissibilité, *f.*
admis'sible, *adj.*, admissible.
admis'sibly, *adv.*, d'une manière admissible.
admis'sion, *n.*, réception, admission, entrée, *f.*; accès; aveu, *m.*, concession, *f.* Free ——; *entrée libre.* Free — ticket; *billet de faveur, m.* — money; *prix d'entrée, prix des places, m.*
admit', *v.a.*, admettre; laisser entrer; recevoir; faire entrer; (admit of) comporter; (to confess) avouer, reconnaître; donner entrée à; souffrir, tolérer.
admit'table, *adj.*, admissible.
admit'tance, *n.*, accès, *m.*; admission, entrée, *f.* No — except on business; *le public n'entre pas ici; défense d'entrer.*
admix', *v.a.*, mêler, mélanger.

admix'tion, *n.*, mélange, *m.*
admix'ture, *n.*, mélange, *m.*
admon'ish, *v.a.*, avertir; exhorter; reprendre, réprimander, admonester.
admon'isher, *n.*, moniteur, *m.*, monitrice, *f.*
admon'ishment, *n.*, admonition, *f.*; avertissement, *m.*; (as a reproof) admonestation, remontrance, réprimande, *f.*
admoni'tion, *n.*, avertissement, avis, conseil, *m.*; admonition, *f.*
admon'itive, *adj.*, d'avertissement, avertissant.
admon'itor (-teur), *n.*, moniteur, conseiller, *m.*
admon'itory, *adj.*, d'avertissement, monitorial.
ado' (-dou), *n.*, fracas, tintamarre, *m.*; peine; difficulté, affaire, *f.*; façons, cérémonies, *f.pl.*; embarras, *m.* To make no more ——; *n'en faire ni une ni deux* or *n'en pas faire à deux fois.* Much — about nothing; *beaucoup de bruit pour rien.* Without any more ——; *sans plus de façons, d'embarras, de cérémonie.*
adoles'cence *ou* **adoles'cency**, *n.*, adolescence, *f.*
adoles'cent, *n.*, adolescent, jeune homme, *m.*
adoles'cent, *adj.*, adolescent.
adopt'able, adoptable.
adopt', *v.a.*, adopter.
adopt'ed, *adj.*, adoptif, adopté, d'adoption.
adopt'edly, *adv.*, par adoption.
adopt'er, *n.*, personne qui adopte, *f.*, adoptant, *m.*
adop'tion, *n.*, adoption, *f.*, choix, *m.*
adop'tive, *adj.*, adoptif, adopté, d'adoption.
ador'able, *adj.*, adorable, charmant.
ador'ableness, *n.*, qualité, nature adorable, *f.*
ador'ably, *adv.*, d'une manière adorable, adorablement.
adora'tion (-ré-), *n.*, adoration, *f.*, culte, *m.*
adore', *v.a.*, adorer.
ador'er, *n.*, adorateur, *m.*, adoratrice, *f.*
adorn', *v.a.*, orner; parer, embellir; (fig.) faire l'ornement **de**. To — one's self; *se parer.*
adorn'ment, *n.*, ornement, *m.*, parure, *f.*, embellissement, *m.*
adown' (-daoune), *adv.*, en bas, à terre, par terre.
adown', *prep.*, en bas **de**, le long **de**. — the stream; *en aval.*
adrift', *adv.*, (nav.) en dérive, à l'abandon; (fig.) abandonné, sans ressources. To run ——; *dériver.* To turn ——; *mettre dehors, abandonner, déserter.* To go ——; (nav.) *aller à la dérive*; (fig.) *se laisser aller; ne plus connaître de bornes.*
adroit' (-droïte), *adj.*, adroit, habile.
adroit'ly, *adv.*, adroitement.
adroit'ness, *n.*, adresse, dextérité, *f.*
adsciti'tious (-sheusse), *adj.*, étranger, emprunté.
adstrin'gent. V. **astringent**.
ad'ulate (-diou-léte), *v.a.*, aduler.
adula'tion, *n.*, adulation, *f.*
ad'ulator, *n.*, adulateur, *m.*, adulatrice, *f.*
ad'ulatory, *adj.*, adulateur.
adult', *adj.*, adulte.
adult' (-deulte), *n.*, adulte, *m.f.*
adul'terate (-deul-teur-éte), *v.a.*, frelater, falsifier, adultérer, sophistiquer; (fig.) altérer, corrompre.
adul'terate, *adj.*, adultère; frelaté, falsifié, faux.
adultera'tion, *n.*, falsification, frelaterie, sophistication, *f.*; frelatage, *m.*
adul'terator, *n.*, frelateur, falsificateur, *m.*
adul'terer (-deul-teur-eur), *n.*, adultère, *m.*
adul'teress (-deul-teur-èsse), *n.*, adultère, femme adultère, *f.*
adul'terine, *adj.*, adultérin; falsifié.
adul'terous (-deul-teur-eusse), *adj.*, adultère; (fig.) impur, faux, corrompu.

adul'terously, adv., par l'adultère.

adul'tery (adeul-teuri), n., adultère, m.

adum'brant, adj., ébauché, esquissé.

adum'brate (-deu'm'bréte), v.a., ébaucher ; esquisser.

adumbra'tion, n., ébauche, esquisse, f.

adun'city (-deu'n'), n., courbure, f.

adun'cous (-keusse), adj., crochu.

adust' (-deuste), adj., brûlé ; (med.) aduste.

adus'tion, n., (surg.) adustion ; cautérisation, f.

advance', v.a., avancer, hâter, faire avancer, élever ; (com.) hausser, augmenter, élever.

advance', v.n., s'avancer, avancer, se porter en avant, faire des progrès. To — ; (in the service) arriver.

advance', n., avancement, progrès, mouvement, (step) pas, m., marche ; (com.) hausse, augmentation ; avance, f. ; (com.) avances, f.pl. On the — ; (com.) en hausse. In — ; en avant ; d'avance. To make —s ; faire des avances, faire le premier pas. To pay in — ; payer d'avance.

advance'-guard (-gârde), n., (milit.) garde avancée, avant-garde, f.

advance'-money, n., avance, f.

advanced', part., avancé.

advance'ment, n., avancement, progrès, m. ; promotion ; (com.) avance, f.

advan'cer (-seur), n., personne qui avance, f. ; prêteur ; promoteur, m.

advan'cive, adj., tendant, or qui tend, à avancer.

advan'tage (-tèdge), n., avantage, m., supériorité, f. ; profit, intérêt, m. To take — of ; profiter de, tirer profit de, se prévaloir de. To take — of any one's kindness ; abuser de la bonté de quelqu'un or exploiter quelqu'un. To the best —; au plus grand avantage. To any one's best —; au mieux des intérêts de quelqu'un. To his or her —; à son avantage. To turn to —; mettre à profit, tirer parti de.

advan'tage, v.a., avantager, favoriser ; avancer les intérêts de.

advan'taged (-tèdj'de), part., avantagé.

advan'tage-ground (-graounde), n. V. vantage-ground.

advanta'geous (-té-djeusse), adj., avantageux.

advanta'geously, adv., avantageusement.

advanta'geousness, n., avantage, m., utilité, f.

advene' (-vîne), v.n., (ant.) survenir, advenir.

ad'vent (-vè'n'te), n., venue, arrivée, f. ; Avent, m.

adventi'tious (-vè-n-ti-sheusse), adj., adventice, accidentel, fortuit, accessoire.

adventi'tiously, adv., accidentellement.

advent'ive, adj., adventice.

advent'ive, n., immigrant, étranger, m.

advent'ual (-tioual), adj., de l'Avent.

adven'ture, n., aventure, f., incident, hasard, risque, m. ; chance, spéculation, f. At all —s ; à tout hasard. To stand upon one's — ; tenter l'aventure, courir la chance des armes.

adven'ture (-tioure), v.a., aventurer, risquer, hasarder.

adven'ture, v.n., s'aventurer, se hasarder, se risquer.

adven'turer (-tiour-eur), n., aventurier, spéculateur, m.

adven'turesome, adj., aventurier, aventureux. V. venturesome.

adven'turess, n., aventurière.

adven'turine, n., (min.) aventurine, f.

adven'turous, adj., aventureux.

adven'turously, adv., aventureusement.

adven'turousness, n., esprit aventureux, caractère aventureux, m.

ad'verb (-veurbe), n., adverbe, m.

adverb'ial, adj., adverbial.

adverb'ially, adv., adverbialement.

ad'versary, n., adversaire, m. f.

advers'ative, adj., adversatif.

ad'verse (-veurse), adj., adverse, défavorable, malheureux, contraire à, opposé à, hostile à, ennemi de.

ad'versely, adv., d'une manière hostile, défavorablement.

ad'verseness, n., opposition ; hostilité, f.

advers'ity, n., adversité, f.

advert' (-veurte), v.n., faire allusion à ; considérer, mentionner ; parler de, appeler l'attention sur.

advert'ence ou advert'ency, n., attention, f.

advertise' (-veur-taïze), v.a., annoncer, faire annoncer, afficher, publier.

adver'tisement (-veur-tize-), n., avis, avertissement, m. ; annonce ; réclame, f.

adverti'ser (-veur-taïzeur), n., personne qui fait des annonces, f. ; journal d'annonces, m.

adverti'sing, n., annonces, f.pl. ; publicité, f.

adverti'sing-agent, n., agent de publicité, m.

adverti'sing-frame, n., porte-affiches, m.

adverti'sing-office, n., bureau des annonces, m. ; agence de publicité, f.

adverti'sing-sheet, n., feuille d'annonces, f.

advice' (-vaïce), n., avis, conseil, m., consultation, f. To take — ; prendre conseil de ; consulter. To give — of ; donner avis de. To take a person's — ; suivre le conseil de quelqu'un. If you take my — ; si vous m'en croyez. Letter of — ; (com.) lettre d'avis, f.

advice'-boat (-bôte), n., aviso, m.

advis'able, adj., judicieux, convenable, utile, bon de.

advis'ableness, n., utilité, convenance, prudence, sagesse, f.

advise' (-vaïze), v.a., conseiller ; donner avis de ; prévenir de ; (com.) aviser de. To keep any one constantly advised of ; tenir quelqu'un au courant de.

advise', v.n., aviser, délibérer, considérer, prendre conseil ; se consulter.

advised' (-vaïz'de), adj., avisé ; mûri ; prudent. Ill— ; mal avisé. Well— ; bien avisé. Be — by me ; croyez m'en.

advis'edly (-vaï-zèd'li), adv., avec réflexion ; de propos délibéré ; exprès, judicieusement, prudemment, à dessein ; sciemment.

advis'edness (-vaï-zèd'nèsse), n., sagesse, prudence, circonspection, f.

advis'er, n., conseiller, m.

ad'vocacy, n., défense, intercession, f. ; appui, soutien, m.

ad'vocate (-vô-kéte), n., avocat, défenseur, intercesseur, m.

ad'vocate, v.a., soutenir, défendre, plaider, appuyer.

advoca'tion, n., défense, intervention, f. ; soutien, m.

advowee' (-vaou-î), n., patron, collateur, f.

advow'son, n., patronage, m., collation, f.

adynam'ic, adj., (med.) adynamique.

adyn'amy, n., (med.) adynamie, f.

adz ou adze, n., erminette ; doloire, f.

æ'gis (idjisse), n., égide, f.

æ'glogue (igl'oghe), n., églogue, f.

ægo'phony (igo-), n., (med.) égophonie, voix chevrotante, f.

ænig'ma. V. enigma.

a'erate (-euréte), v.a., (chem.) aérer.

ae'rial (é-i-ri-al), adj., aérien, d'air.

ae'rie or ae'ry (iri), n., aire, f.

a'eriform (é-eur-i-), adj., aériforme.

a'erify (é-eur-i-faïe), v.a., remplir d'air.

aerog'raphy, n., aérographie, f.

a'erolite ou a'erolith, n., aérolithe, m.

aerolog'ical, adj., aérologique.

aerol'ogist, n., savant dans l'aérologie, m.

aerol'ogy, n., (med.) aérologie, f.

aerom'eter (é-eur-o-miteur), n., aéromètre, m.

aerom'etry, *n.*, aérométrie, *f.*

a'eronaut (é-eur-ô-), *n.*, aéronaute, *m.f.*

aeronaut'ic, *adj.*, aérostatique, aéronautique.

aeronaut'ics, *n.pl.*, science de l'aéronaute, *f.*

aer'ostat, *n.*, aérostat, *m.*

aerostat'ic, *adj.*, aérostatique.

aerostat'ics, *n.pl.*, art aérostatique, *m.*

aerosta'tion, *n.*, aérostation, *f.*

aeru'ginous (i-rioud'jineusse), *adj.*, érugineux.

aesthet'ic *ou* aesthet'ical, *adj.*, esthétique.

aesthet'ics (is-thè-), *n.pl.*, esthétique, *f.*

aetiol'ogy *ou* etiol'ogy (i-tio-lod'ji), *n.*, (med.) étiologie, *f.*

aeti'tes (î-taï-tize), *n.*, aétite, pierre d'aigle, *f.*

afar', *adv.*, de loin, loin, au loin. — off; *au loin.*

affabil'ity, *n.*, affabilité, *f.*

af'fable, *adj.*, affable, doux, gracieux.

af'fableness, *n.*, affabilité, *f.*

af'fably, *adv.*, affablement, avec affabilité.

affair', *n.*, affaire, *f.* Mercantile —s ; *les affaires, f.pl.; le commerce.* As —s stand; *au point où en sont les affaires.* To liquidate, to wind up, one's —s ; *liquider ses affaires.*

affect' (af-fècte), *v.a.*, affecter ; intéresser ; toucher à ; aimer ; viser à, aspirer à ; influer **sur**.

affecta'tion (-fec-té-), *n.*, affectation, *f.*

affect'ed, *adj.*, disposé ; affecté ; précieux ; touché, ému, attendri ; (of style) maniéré, prétentieux.

affect'edly, *adv.*, d'une manière affectée, avec affectation.

affect'edness, *n.*, affectation, *f.*

affect'ing, *adj.*, touchant ; affectant, concernant, ayant trait à.

affect'ingly (-tigne-), *adv.*, d'une manière touchante.

affec'tion, *n.*, affection ; inclination, *f.* ; attachement, penchant, *m.* ; maladie, *f.* ; (fig.) sentiment, *m.*, émotion, *f.*

affec'tionate (-sheunéte), *adj.*, affectueux, affectionné.

affec'tionately, *adv.*, affectueusement, avec affection, affectionnément.

affec'tionateness, *n.*, affection, tendresse, *f.*

affec'tioned (-sheu-n-de), *adj.*, disposé ; affectionné ; (ant.) affecté.

affi'ance (af-faïa-n-se), *n.*, fiançailles, *f.pl.*

affi'ance, *v.a.*, fiancer.

affi'anced (af-faïa'nste), *part.*, fiancé.

affida'vit, *n.*, déclaration, attestation (écrite et affirmée) sous serment, *m.*

affil'iate (af-fil-i-éte), *v.a.*, affilier ; adopter (comme fils) ; attribuer, rattacher à.

affilia'tion, *n.*, affiliation ; adoption (comme fils), *f.* ; recherche de la paternité, *f.*

af'finage (-néd'je), *n.*, (metal.) affinage, *m.*

affin'ity, *n.*, affinité, alliance, *f.*

affirm' (af-feurme), *v.a.*, affirmer ; confirmer ; assurer à.

affirm', *v.n.*, affirmer ; déclarer.

affirm'able, *adj.*, qu'on peut affirmer.

affirma'tion (-mé-), *n.*, affirmation ; confirmation ; déclaration, *f.*

affirm'ative (-ma-), *adj.*, affirmatif.

affirm'ative, *n.*, affirmative, *f.* To reply in the — ; *répondre affirmativement.*

affirm'atively, *adv.*, affirmativement.

affirm'er, *n.*, personne qui affirme, *f.*

affix', *v.a.*, apposer à ; ajouter ; fixer, attacher à.

af'fix, *n.*, affixe, *m.*

affla'tion (-flé-), *n.*, action de souffler, *f.*

affla'tus (-flé-teusse), *n.*, souffle, *m.*, haleine, inspiration, *f.*

afflict', *v.a.*, affliger ; tourmenter.

afflict'edness (-tèd-nèsse), *n.*, douleur, affliction, *f.*

afflict'ing, *adj.*, affligeant, chagrinant.

afflic'tion, *n.*, affliction, calamité, misère, *f.* ; malheur, *m.*

afflict'ive, *adj.*, affligeant, (jur.) afflictif.

afflict'ively, *adv.*, d'une manière affligeante.

af'fluence (af-flou-è-nse), *n.*, abondance, opulence, affluence, *f.* ; richesses, *f.pl.*

af'fluent, *adj.*, abondant ; opulent, riche. *n.*, (geog.) affluent, *m.*

af'fluent, *n.pl.*, les affluents, les riches, *m.pl.*

af'flux (af-fleuxe), *n.*, (med.) afflux, *m.*

afflux'ion, *n.*, (med.) afflux, *m.*

afford', *v.a.*, donner ; fournir ; offrir ; procurer ; avoir le moyen, les moyens ; pouvoir ; être en position, en état **de**. I cannot — the time; *je ne puis pas trouver le temps.* I cannot — it ; *mes moyens ne me le permettent pas, je n'en ai pas les moyens ; je ne puis me le permettre.* He could not — me a minute's interview ; *il n'a pu me donner un moment d'entretien.*

affor'est, *v.a.*, convertir en forêt, boiser.

afforesta'tion, *n.*, conversion en forêt, *f.* ; boisement, *m.*

affran'chise (af-fra-n-tchaïze), *v.a.*, affranchir.

affran'chisement, *n.*, affranchissement, *m.*

affray', *n.*, querelle, échauffourée, rixe, batterie, *f.*, tumulte, trouble, *m.*, émeute, *f.*

affright' (af-fraïte), *v.a.*, effrayer.

affright', *n.*, effroi, *m.*, épouvante, *f.*

affright'edly, *adv.*, avec effroi, avec épouvante.

affront' (af-freu'nte), *v.a.*, (ant.) (to meet) rencontrer ; affronter ; offenser, insulter, outrager ; faire un affront à.

affront', *n.*, affront, *m.*, insulte, injure, *f.*, outrage, *m.* ; (ant.) rencontre, *f.* To put an — on any one ; *faire un affront à quelqu'un.* To brook an — ; *digérer un affront.* To pocket an — ; *boire, avaler un affront.*

affront'er, *n.*, offenseur, *m.*

affront'ing, *adj.*, offensant, choquant, insultant, outrageant.

affuse' (af-fiouze), *v.a.*, verser **sur**.

affu'sion (af-fiou-jeune), *n.*, action de verser ; (pharm.) affusion, *f.*

afield' (-fîlde), *adv.*, aux champs, à la campagne. To go far — ; *aller très loin.*

afire' (-faïeu-), *adv.*, en feu.

aflat', *adv.*, à plat.

afloat' (-flôte), *adv.*, (nav.) à flot ; sur l'eau ; en train; (fig.) en circulation ; sur pied, en train. To set a ship — ; *mettre un vaisseau à flot.*

afoot' (-foute), *adv.*, à pied ; sur pied ; en train, en chemin, en route.

afore', *prep.*, devant, avant.

afore', *adv.*, auparavant ; en avant ; sur le devant ; (nav.) avant.

afore'going (-goïgne), *adj.*, précédent.

afore'hand, *adv.*, par avance.

afore'mentioned (-mèn-sheun'de), *adj.*, mentionné plus haut, susdit, précité.

afore'named (-né-m'de), *adj.*, susnommé.

afore'said, *adj.*, susdit, le dit, ledit.

afore'thought (-thôte), *adj.*, prémédité.

afore'time (-taïme), *adv.*, autrefois, jadis.

a forti'ori (-ti-ô-), *adv.*, à plus forte raison, à fortiori.

afraid' (-fréde), *adj.*, effrayé, craintif, qui a peur. To be — of anything ; *avoir peur de quelque chose.* To make — ; *faire peur à ; faire craindre à.*

afresh' (-frè-she), *adv.*, de nouveau, encore ; de plus belle.

Af'ric *ou* Af'rican, *adj.*, africain, d'Afrique.

Af'rican (-ca-n), *n.*, Africain, *m.*, Africaine, *f.*

afront' (a-freu'nte), *adv.*, en face.

aft, *adj.*, (nav.) arrière, de l'arrière. Fore and — ; (nav.) *avant et arrière.*

aft'er, *adv.*, après ; suivant, d'après.

aft'er, *prep.*, après ; après que ; selon ; sur ; d'après ; (in the train of) à la suite **de**.

aft'er, *adj.*, ultérieur, futur ; arrière ; (nav.) d'arrière.

aft′er-ages (-éd′jèze), *n.pl.*, siècles futurs, *m.pl.*; postérité, *f.*

aft′er-all (-ôl), *adv.*, après tout; enfin; au fond.

aft′er-birth (-beurth), *n.*, arrière-faix; (med.) placenta, délivre, *m.*, secondines, *f.pl.*

aft′er-clap, *n.*, coup inattendu, contre-coup, second coup, *m.*

aft′er-cost, *n.*, frais ultérieurs, *m.pl.*

aft′er-crop, *n.*, seconde récolte, *f.*; regain, *m.*

aft′er-days, *n.pl.*, jours à venir, *m.pl.*

aft′er-dinner, *n.*, après-dîner, après-dîné, *m.*

aft′er-dream (-drîme), *n.*, rêverie, *f.*

aft′er-for′tune (-tioune), *n.*, destinée ultérieure, *f.*

aft′er-game (-ghéme), *n.*, revanche, dernière ressource, *f.*

aft′er-grass, *n.*, regain, *m.*

aft′er-growth (-grôth), *n.*, regain, *m.*

aft′er-guard (-gârde), *n.*, (nav.) surveillant de l'arrière, *m.*

aft′er-hope (-hôpe), *n.*, espérance future, *f.*

aft′er-hours (-aourze), *n.pl.*, heures en sus, *f.pl.* V. **overtime.**

aft′er-life (-laïfe), *n.*, vie ultérieure, *f.*; avenir, *m.*

aft′er-love, *n.*, second amour, *m.*

aft′ermath (-math), *n.*, regain, *m.*

aft′ernoon (-noune), *n.*, après-midi, *m.f.*; après-dîner, *m.*

aft′er-pains (-pè′nze), *n.pl.*, douleurs qui suivent l'accouchement; (med.) tranchées, *f.pl.*

aft′er-part (-pârte), *n.*, dernière partie, *f.*

aft′er-piece (-pîce), *n.*, (thea.) petite pièce, *f.*

aft′er-proof (-prouf), *n.*, preuve ultérieure, *f.*

aft′er-reckoning, *n.*, révision de compte, *f.*

aft′er-repentance, *n.*, repentir tardif, *m.*

aft′er-sail (-séle), *n.*, (nav.) voile de l'arrière, *f.*

aft′er-state (-stéte), *n.*, état futur, *m.*

aft′er-sting (-stigne), *n.*, nouvelle piqûre, *f.*

aft′er-storm, *n.*, tempête nouvelle, *f.*

af′ter-supper (-seup-peur), *n.*, après-souper, après-soupé, *m.*, après-soupée, *f.*

aft′er-swarm (-swôrme), *n.*, arrière-essaim, *m.*

aft′er-taste (-téste), *n.*, arrière-goût, déboire, *m.*

aft′er-thought (-thôte), *n.*, pensée ultérieure, réflexion tardive, *f.*

aft′er-times (-taïm′ze), *n.pl.*, temps à venir, *m.pl.*

aft′er-tossing (to-cigne), *n.*, (nav.) agitation de la mer après une tempête, houle, *f.*

aft′er-touch (-teut′she), *n.*, (paint.) retouche, *f.*

aft′erward (-weurd) *ou* **aft′erwards** (-weurdze), *adv.*, ensuite, puis, plus tard.

aft′er-wise (-waïze), *adj.*, sage après coup.

aft′er-wit (-wite), *n.*, esprit tardif, *m.*; sagesse après coup, *f.*

aft′er-years (-yirs), *n.*, années à venir, *f.pl.*

a′ga, *n.*, aga, *m.*

again′ (-ghéne), *adv.*, encore; encore une fois, de nouveau. As much —; *encore autant.* — and —, *à plusieurs reprises, sans cesse, à coups redoublés.* As large —, *deux fois aussi grand.* Never —; *ne . . . plus jamais.*

against′ (-ghé′nste), *prep.*, contre; vis-à-vis; sur; vers, près de. — my coming back; *pour le moment de mon retour.* Over —; *vis à vis, en face.*

ag′ami, *n.*, (orni.) agami, *m.*

ag′amous (-meusse), *adj.*, (bot.) agame.

agape′ (-ghépe), *adv.*, la bouche béante.

ag′ape (-pi), *n.* (*agapæ*), (theol.) agape, *f.*

ag′aric, *n.*, (bot.) agaric, *m.*

ag′ate (-ghéte), *n.*, agate, *f.*

ag′aty (-ghé-ti), *adj.*, d'agate.

aga′ve (-gé-vi), *n.*, (bot.) agavé, *m.*

age′ (édje), *n.*, âge ; siècle, *m.* Brazen —; *âge d'airain.* Golden —; *âge d'or.* Silver —; *âge d'argent.* Middle —s ; *moyen âge.* Dark —s; *siècles de ténèbres, m.pl.* — of discretion ; *âge de*

raison. To be of —; *être majeur.* Under —; *mineur.* To come of —; *atteindre sa majorité.* To be of an — to ; *être d'âge* **à**. To look one's —; *paraître son âge.* To bear one's — well ; *porter bien son âge.*

age, *v.n.*, vieillir.

a′ged (é-djède *ou* édj′de), *adj.*, vieux, âgé ; (of horses) hors d'âge. Middle —; *entre deux âges.* The —; *les vieillards, m.pl.*

a′gedly, *adv.*, en vieillard.

a′gency, *n.*, agence ; régie ; maison de commission; (fig.) action, entremise, influence, *f.*

agen′da, *n.*, agenda, *m.*

a′gent (édjè-n-te), *n.*, agent; homme d'affaires, commissionnaire, représentant, *m.*

agglom′erate, *v.a.*, agglomérer.

agglom′erate (-meur-éte), *v.n.*, s'agglomérer.

agglom′erated, *adj.*, (bot.) aggloméré.

agglomera′tion (-meur-é-), *n.*, agglomération, *f.*

agglu′tinant, *n.*, agglutinant, *m.*

agglu′tinant (-gliou-), *adj.*, agglutinant.

agglu′tinate (-gliou-ti-néte), *v.a.*, agglutiner.

agglutina′tion (-gliou-ti-né-), *n.*, agglutination, *f.*

agglu′tinative (-gliou-ti-né-), *adj.*, agglutinatif.

ag′grandize (-daïze), *v.a.*, agrandir.

aggrand′izement, *n.*, agrandissement, *m.*

ag′gravate (-véte), *v.a.*, aggraver, exagérer ; (to vex) taquiner, provoquer; agacer, pousser à bout, faire endêver.

aggrava′tion, *n.*, aggravation ; circonstance aggravante ; exagération; (vexation) provocation, *f.*; agacement, *m.*; taquinerie, agacerie, *f.*

ag′gregate, *v.a.*, réunir, rassembler, recueillir.

ag′gregate, *adj.*, rassemblé, réuni ; agrégé.

ag′gregate (-gri-ghéte), *n.*, agrégation, masse, *f.*; total, *m.*; somme totale, *f.*; agrégat, *m.* In the —; *en somme, tout ensemble, à tout prendre.*

ag′gregately, *adv.*, en masse, collectivement.

aggrega′tion, *n.*, agrégation, réunion, *f.*; assemblage, *m.*

ag′gregative, *adj.*, agrégatif.

aggres′sion, *n.*, agression, attaque, *f.*

aggress′ive, *adj.*, offensif, hostile ; agressif.

aggress′iveness, *n.*, caractère agressif, *m.*; agressivité, *f.*

aggress′or, *n.*, agresseur, *m.*

aggriev′ance. V. **grievance.**

aggrieve′ (ag-grîve), *v.a.*, affliger ; peiner ; blesser, molester, léser, offenser.

aggroup′, *v.a.*, (paint.) grouper, agrouper.

aghast′, *adj.*, frappé *ou* saisi d'effroi ; épouvanté, consterné, ébahi, ahuri.

ag′ile (adjile), *adj.*, agile, leste, dispos.

ag′ileness, *n.*, agilité, légèreté, *f.*

agil′ity, *n.*, agilité, légèreté, *f.*

a′gio (édji-ô), *n.*, change; agio, *m.*

ag′itate (adj-i-téte), *v.a.*, agiter, exciter, remuer, troubler ; (a question) discuter, soulever.

agita′tion, *n.*, agitation, *f.*; trouble, *m.*; discussion, *f.*, examen, *m.* To be in —; (of things) *être en question, être sur le tapis.*

ag′itator (-teur), *n.*, agitateur ; meneur, *m.*

ag′let *ou* **aig′let**, *n.*, aiguillette, *f.*; (bot.) onglet, *m.*

ag′nail (ag-néle), *n.*, envie, *f.*; panaris, *m.*

ag′nate (ag-néte), *n.*, agnat, *m.*

ag′nate, *adj.*, d'agnat, agnatique.

agnat′ic (ag-nat-), *adj.*, agnatique.

agna′tion (ag-né-), *n.*, agnation, *f.*

agno′men (ag-nô-mè-n), *n.*, surnom, *m.*

agnomina′tion (ag-no-mi-né-), *n.*, surnom, *m.*

ago′, *adv.*, passé, il y a, il y a eu. Long —; *il y a longtemps.* A long while —; *il y a bien longtemps.* Two days —; *il y a deux jours.* Not long —; *il n'y a pas longtemps.* How long

ago is it? *combien de temps y a-t-il?* It was ten years —; *il y a de cela dix ans.*

agog', *adv.*, enflammé, excité; avec feu, en émoi; en l'air. To be all —; *avoir la tête montée, être dans l'agitation; griller* **de**. To set —; *monter la tête à quelqu'un, mettre en train, donner envie* **de**; *faire griller* **de**. They are all — about it; *ils en grillent tous.*

ago'ing (-gŏïgne), *adv.*, en train, en branle, en mouvement, en action.

ag'onize, *v.n.*, souffrir l'agonie, être au supplice.

ag'onize (ag-ŏ-naïze), *v.a.*, torturer, faire souffrir, martyriser; mettre au supplice.

ag'onized (ag-ŏ-naïz'de), *adj.*, (of persons) qui souffre l'agonie; (of things) poignant, déchirant.

ag'onizing (ag-ŏ-naïz-igne), *adj.*, qui fait souffrir; qui torture; le plus cruel; déchirant.

ag'onizingly, *adv.*, avec angoisse.

ag'ony, *n.*, agonie; douleur, angoisse, *f.* To suffer —ies; *souffrir le martyre; être au supplice.*

agou'ti, *n.*, (mam.) agouti, *m.*

agra'rian, *adj.*, agraire, agricole, d'agriculture.

agree', *v.n.*, s'accorder; tomber d'accord; être d'accord; (of the health) convenir **à**; se convenir; consentir **à**; donner son assentiment à. I — with you there; *je suis de votre avis là-dessus* ou *je partage votre avis là-dessus.* My dinner agreed with me; *mon dîner ne m'a pas fait de mal,* ou *a bien passé.* That is agreed on by all; *tout le monde en convient; on est tous d'accord là-dessus.*

agree', *v.a.*, (l.u.) accorder, mettre d'accord, réconcilier.

agree'able, *adj.*, agréable; conforme **à**. I am —; *je veux bien.*

agree'ableness, *n.*, agrément, *m.*; conformité; harmonie, *f.*; rapport, *m.*

agree'ably, *adv.*, agréablement; conformément à.

agreed', *adj.*, convenu, d'accord. *int.*, c'est entendu, c'est une affaire entendue; c'est convenu!; va, pour!

agree'ment, *n.*, accord; rapport, *m.*; convention; bonne intelligence; conformité, *f.*; contrat, *m.* To come to an —; *en venir,* ou *arriver, à un accommodement.*

agricul'tural, *adj.*, agricole, d'agriculture; aratoire. — implement maker; *fabricant de machines d'agriculture, m.*

ag'riculture (-keult-iour), *n.*, agriculture, *f.*

agricul'turist, *n.*, agriculteur, agronome, *m.*

ag'rimony, *n.*, (bot.) aigremoine, *f.*

a'griot, *n.*, griotte, *f.*

aground' (-graou-n'de), *adj.*, (nav.) échoué; à terre. To run —; *échouer; faire échouer; mettre,* ou *jeter, à la côte.*

a'gue (é-ghiou), *n.*, fièvre, fièvre intermittente, *f.*

a'gue-fit, *n.*, accès de fièvre intermittente, *m.*

a'gue-powder, *n.*, poudre fébrifuge, *f.*

a'gue-proof, *adj.*, à l'épreuve de la fièvre intermittente.

a'gue-spell, *n.*, charme fébrifuge, *m.*

a'gue-struck (-streuke), *adj.*, atteint de fièvre intermittente.

a'gue-tree (-trî), *n.*, (bot.) sassafras, *m.*

a'guish (é-ghiou-ishe), *adj.*, fièvreux; fébricitant.

a'guishness, *n.*, état fébrile, *m.*

ah! *int.*, ah! hélas!

aha! *int.*, aha!

ahead' (-hède), *adv.*, (nav.) en avant, devant; (fig.) à la tête. To get —; *(nav.) gagner l'avant* **de**; *(fig.) devancer.* To go on —; *prendre les devants.* To have the wind —; *avoir vent debout.* Go —! *allez-y! en avant!* Right —; *tout droit.*

ahoy'! (a-hôi), *int.*, (nav.) ho! Ship —; *ôhé du navire.*

ahull' (-heul), *adv.*, (nav.) à mâts et à cordes; à sec.

ahun'gry (-heugn'gri), *adj.*, (ant.) tourmenté par la faim.

a'i (é-i), *n.*, (mam.) aï, *m.*

aid, *v.a.*, aider; secourir, assister. To — each other; *s'entr'aider.*

aid, *n.*, aide, assistance, *f.*; secours, concours; subside, *m.* With the — of; *à l'aide* **de**, *avec le concours* **de**. To come to any one's —; *venir à l'aide* **de** *quelqu'un, venir en aide* **à** *quelqu'un.* In — of; *au profit* **de**, *au bénéfice* **de**.

aide'-de-camp, *n.*, aide de camp, *m.*

aid'er, *n.*, aide, complice, *m.f.*

aid'less, *adj.*, sans secours; délaissé.

ai'glet, *n.*, (her.) aiglon, *m.*

ai'gret *ou* **ai'grette'**, *n.*, aigrette, *f.*

ai'gulet (é-ghiou-lette), *n.*, aiguillette, *f.*

ail (éle), *v.a.*, avoir, ou faire, mal **à**; chagriner. What —s you? *qu'avez-vous? qu'est-ce qui vous fait mal?* Nothing —s me; *je n'ai rien.* Something —s him; *il a quelque chose.*

ail'ing (él-igne), *adj.*, souffrant, maladif.

ail'ment, *n.*, mal, malaise, *m.*; incommodité, indisposition, *f.*

aim, *v.a.*, viser; ajuster, diriger; (a blow) lancer, porter.

aim, *v.n.*, viser **à**, aspirer **à**, tendre **à**; avoir pour but **de**.

aim (éme), *n.*, intention, visée, *f.*; but; point de mire, dessein; (sight of a gun) guidon, *m.* To take —; at; *viser; coucher en joue.* To miss one's —; *manquer son coup.*

air, *n.*, air, *m.*, mine, apparence, *f.*; vent, *m.* To build castles in the —; *faire des châteaux en Espagne.* To give one's self — *se donner des airs.* To give one's self an — of; *se donner un air* **de**. To vanish into thin —; *s'en aller à vau l'eau.* To let the — into a room; *donner de l'air à une chambre, aérer une chambre.* To take the —; *prendre l'air.* To enjoy the evening —; *prendre le frais.* To go out in the open —; *prendre l'air.* In the open —; *en plein air, au grand air.* In the —; *en l'air.* Foul —; *air vicié.* Confined —; *air renfermé.* Downcast —; *air abattu.* Breath of —; *souffle de vent, m.*

air, *v.a.*, aérer; mettre à l'air; ressuyer, chauffer. This linen must be —ed; *il faut mettre ce linge à l'air* or *il faut chauffer ce linge.* To — one's self; *prendre l'air.*

air'-ball (-bôl), *n.*, petit ballon, *m.*

air'-balloon (bal-loune), *n.*, ballon aérostatique, *m.*

air'-blad'der (-blad-deur), *n.*, vessie pleine d'air; (ich.) vessie aérienne, vessie natatoire, *f.*

air'-brav'ing (-brév-igne), *adj.*, qui brave les vents.

air'-bubble (-beub-b'l), *n.*, bulle d'air, *f.*

air'-built (-bilte), *adj.*, bâti en l'air, chimérique.

air'-cell, *n.*, (bot.) cellule aérienne, *f.*

air'-current, *n.*, courant d'air, *m.*

air'-cushion (-coush-eune), *n.*, coussin à air, *m.*

air'-drawn (-drône), *adj.*, imaginaire.

air'-exhauster, *n.*, (phys.) ventilateur, *m.*

air'-gun (-gheune), *n.*, fusil à vent, *m.*

air'-holder, *n.*, tube à air, *m.*

air'-hole, *n.*, soupirail; évent (of a furnace), *m.*

air'ily, *adv.*, légèrement, gaîment.

air'iness, *n.*, exposition à l'air; (fig.) légèreté, gaieté, *f.*

air'ing (air-igne), *n.*, aérage (of linen); éventage (of skins), *m.*; promenade, *f.* To take an —; *prendre l'air, prendre le frais, faire une promenade.* To give an — **to**; *faire prendre l'air* **à** or *mener promener.*

air'-jacket (-djak-ète), *n.*, ceinture de natation, ceinture à air, *f.*

air'-lamp, *n.*, lampe à courant d'air, *f.*

air'less, *adj.*, privé d'air.

air'-mattress, *n.*, matelas à air, *m.*

air'-passages (-pass'èdjize), *n.*, voies aériennes, *f.pl.*

air'-poise (-poïze), *n.*, aéromètre, *m.*

air'-pump (-peu'mpe), *n.*, machine pneumatique, pompe à air, *f.*

air'-shaft, *n.*, (tech.) puits d'aérage, *m.*

air'-stirring (-steu'rigne), *adj.*, qui bat l'air.

air'-stove (-stôve), *n.*, calorifère, *m.*

air'-thread (-thrède), *n.*, fil de la Vierge, *m.*

air'-tight (-taïte), *adj.*, imperméable à l'air.

air'-tightness, *n.*, imperméabilité à l'air, *f.*

air'-trap, *n.*, machine à ventiler, *f.*, ventilateur, *m.*

air'-tubes (-tioub'ze), *n.*, conduits aériens, *m.pl.*

air'-valve. *n.*, soupape à air, *f.*

air'-vessel (-vès's'l), *n.*, (bot.) vaisseau aérien ; (tech.) réservoir d'air, récipient, *m.*

air'y, *adj.*, aérien ; ouvert à l'air, aéré ; léger, délicat ; dégagé, gai, enjoué, sémillant. —*words*; *paroles en l'air*, *f.pl.* — *nothings* ; *des riens, de petits riens*, *m.pl.*

air'y-light (-laïte), *adj.*, léger comme l'air.

aisle (aïle), *n.*, (of a church) aile, nef latérale, *f.*, bas côté, *m.*

aisled, *adj.*, à bas côtés ; à nefs latérales.

ait (a-ït), *n.*, îlot, *m.*

aitch'bone, *n.*, tranche (du cimier de bœuf), *f.*

ajar' (adjàr), *adj.*, entr'ouvert, entre-bâillé.

akim'bo (-ki-m'bô), *adv.*, appuyé sur la hanche. With one's arms — ; *les poings sur les hanches.*

akin' (-kine), *adj.*, allié à ; parent ; voisin de ; qui ressemble à, semblable à ; qui a rapport avec. Laughter is — to tears ; (prov.) *tel qui rit vendredi, dimanche pleurera.*

al'abaster (-teur), *n.*, albâtre, *m.*

al'abaster, *adj.*, d'albâtre.

alack' ! *int.*, hélas !

alack'aday ! *int.* hélas !

alac'rity, *n.*, vivacité, ardeur, *f.*, empressement, *m.*

alamode' (-môde), *adv.*, à la mode.

alarm', *n.*, alarme, *f.* ; (horl.) réveille-matin, *m.* To beat the — ; *battre la générale.*

alarm', *v.a.*, alarmer, donner d'alarme à, effrayer, faire peur à. Don't be alarmed ; *soyez sans inquiétude* or *ne craignez rien, n'ayez pas peur.*

alarm'-bell, *n.*, cloche d'alarme, *f.*, tocsin, *m.*

alarm'-clock, *n.*, réveille-matin, *m.*

alarm'-gun (-gheune), *n.*, canon d'alarme, *m.*

alarm'ing, *adj.*, alarmant.

alarm'ingly, *adv.*, d'une manière alarmante.

alarm'ist, *n.*, alarmiste, *m.*

alarm-post, *n.*, point de ralliement, *m.*

alar'um (-la-reume, -lê-), *n.* V. **alarm**.

alas' ! *int.*, hélas !

alb, *n.*, aube (priest's vestment), *f.*

al'batross, *n.*, (orni.) albatros, *m.*

albe'it (ôl-bi-ite), *adv.*, quoique, bien que; malgré que (used only with *avoir*) ; néanmoins, toutefois.

albes'cent (al-bès-sè-nte), *adj.*, blanchissant.

albi'no, *n.*, albinos ; ⊙nègre-blanc, *m.*

albugin'eous (-bioud'ji-n'i-eusse), *adj.*, albuginé, albugineux.

albu'go (-biou-gô), *n.*, (med.) albugo, *m.*, taie, *f.*

al'bum, *n.*, album, *m.*

albu'men (-biou-), *n.*, albumine, *f.*

albu'minous (-neusse), *adj.*, albumineux.

albur'num (-beur-neume), *n.*, (bot.) aubier, *m.*

alca'ic (-ké-ike), *adj.*, alcaïque.

alca'ic, *n.*, alcaïque, *m.*

alcaid' (-kéde), *n.*, alcade, *m.*

alchem'ic *ou* **alchem'ical** (-ké-), *adj.*, alchimique.

alchem'ically, *adv.*, par un procédé alchimique.

al'chemist (-ké-), *n.*, alchimiste, *m.*

alchemist'ic *ou* **alchemist'ical**, *adj.*, d'alchimiste, alchimique.

al'chemy (-ké-), *n.*, alchimie, *f.*

al'cohol (-cô-), *n.*, alcool, *m.*

.alcohol'ic, *adj.*, alcoolique.

alcoholiza'tion (-zé-), *n.*, alcoolisation, *f.*

al'coholize (-lïze), *v.a.*, alcooliser.

alcohol'meter *ou* **alcoho'meter** (-miteur), *n.*, alcoolmètre, alcoomètre, *m.*

al'coran, *n.* V. **alkoran**, **koran**.

al'cove, *n.*, renfoncement, *m.*, alcôve ; niche ; (gard.) loge, tonnelle, *f.*, berceau, pavillon, *m.*

al'der (ôl-deur), *n.*, (bot.) aune, vergne, *m.* — grove; *aunaie, f.*

al'derman (ôl-deur-mane), *n.*, conseiller municipal, alderman, *m.*

al'der-plot (-plote), *n.*, aunaie, *f.*

ale (éle), *n.*, ale, bière, *f.*

ale'-bench (-bè-nshe), *n.*, banc de cabaret, *m.*

ale'-brewer (-brou-eur), *n.*, brasseur, *m.*

ale'-conner (-con-neur), *n.*, inspecteur de mesures pour les liquides, *m.*

ale'cost (éle-), *n.* V. **tansy**.

alee' (alî), *adv.*, (nav.) sous le vent.

ale'-hoof (-houfe), *n.*, (bot.) lierre terrestre, *m.*

ale'-house (-haouce), *n.* cabaret, *m.*

ale'-knight (-naïte), *n.*, (ant.) pilier de cabaret, *m.*

alem'bic, *n.*, alambic, *m.*

alert' (-leurte), *n.*, alerte, *f.* On the — ; *sur le qui-vive.*

alert', *adj.*, alerte, vigilant, vif, éveillé.

alert'ness, *n.*, activité, vigilance, promptitude, vivacité, *f.*

ale'-shot, *n.*, écot de cabaret, *m.*

ale'-stake (él-stéke), *n.*, bouchon de cabaret, *m.*

ale'-taster (-tésteur), *n.*, dégustateur, *m.*

ale'-wife (-waïfe), *n.*, cabaretière, *f.*

Alexan'drian, *adj.*, alexandrien, d'Alexandrie.

Alexan'drian *ou* **Alexan'drine**, *n.*, alexandrin, *m.*

al'ga (algha), *n.*, (*algæ*) (bot.) algue, *f.*

algazel', *n.*, gazelle, *f.*

al'gebra (al-dji-), *n.*, algèbre, *f.*

algebra'ic (-bré-ik) *ou* **algebra'ical** (-bré-i-), *adj.*, algébrique.

algebra'ically, *adv.*, algébriquement.

algebra'ist (-bré-iste), *n.*, algébriste, *m.*

al'gor, *n.*, (med.) (ant.) froid extrême *or* glacial, *m.*

al'gorithm (-gô-rith'm), *n.*, (math.) algorithme, *m.*

al'gous (-gheusse), *adj.*, qui a rapport aux algues.

alguazil', *n.*, alguazil, *m.*

a'lias (é-li-), *n.*, faux nom, pseudonyme, nom de guerre, *m.*

a'lias, *adv.*, dit, autrement dit.

al'ibi, *n.*, (jur.) alibi, *m.*

al'ible, *adj.*, (ant.) (med.) alibile.

al'ien (éliène), *adj.*, étranger à ; éloigné de.

al'ien, *n.*, étranger, *m.*, étrangère, *f.* — *act* ; *loi sur les étrangers, f.*

al'ienability (éliè-), *n.*, aliénabilité, *f.*

al'ienable, *adj.*, aliénable.

al'ienage, *n.*, pérégrinité.

al'ienate, *v.a.* aliéner, éloigner.

al'ienate, *adj.* V. **alien**.

aliena'tion (-né-), *n.*, aliénation, *f.* ; éloignement, *m.* Mental — ; *aliénation mentale.*

al'ienator, *n.*, aliénateur, *m.*, aliénatrice, *f.*

alienee', *n.*, aliénataire, *m.f.*, acheteur, *m.*

al'ienism, *n.*, pérégrinité, *f.*

al'iform, *adj.*, ayant la forme d'une aile.

alight' (-laïte), *adj.*, allumé. To be — ; *être allumé*. The house is — ; *le feu est à la maison.*

alight', *v.n.*, descendre ; mettre pied à terre ; (of birds) s'abattre, tomber.

align', *v.a.*, aligner.

align'ment, *n.*, alignement, *m.*

alike' (-laïke), *adv.*, également ; de même ; à la fois ; aussi ; tout autant.

alike', *adj.*, semblable, pareil ; ressemblant.

al'iment, *n.*, aliment, *m.*

aliment'al, *adj.*, alimentaire, nutritif.

aliment'ally, *adv.*, d'une manière nutritive.

aliment'ary, *adj.*, alimentaire.

alimenta'tion (-té-), *n.*, alimentation, *f.*

al'imony, *n.*, pension alimentaire, *f.*

al'iquant (-kwa-n-te), *adj.*, aliquante, *adj f.*

al'iquot (-kwote), *adj.*, aliquote, *adj f.*

alive' (-laïve), *adj.*, en vie, vivant ; vif, gai ; éveillé ; attentif **à**, animé ; sensible **à**. While — ; *de son vivant.* Dead or — ; *mort ou vif.* More dead than — ; *plus mort que vif.* Look — ! *remuez-vous un peu.* To keep — ; (fig.) *entretenir, aviver.* To burn, bury, flay — ; *brûler, enterrer, écorcher vif.* To be — with ; *regorger de, fourmiller de.* To be — to one's interests ; *avoir ses intérêts à cœur.* The best man — ; *le meilleur homme du monde.* No man — ; *personne au monde.* To be quite — to the gravity of the situation ; *sentir, ou comprendre, toute la gravité de la situation.*

alkales'cency, *n.*, (chem.) alcalescence, *f.*

alkales'cent, *adj.*, alcalescent.

al'kali, *n.*, alcali, *m.*

al'kalify (-faïe), *v.a.*, alcaliser.

al'kalify, *v.n.*, s'alcaliser.

alkalim'etor (-miteur), *n.*, (chem.) alcalimètre, *m.*

al'kaline, *adj.*, alcalin.

al'kaline (-laïne), *n.*, substance alcaline, *f.*

alkaliza'tion (-laï-zé-), *n.*, (ant.) alcalisation, *f.*

al'kalize (-laïze), *v.a.*, alcaliser.

al'kanet (-nète), *n.*, (bot.) orcanète, *f.*

al'koran (-kôra-n), *n.*, alcoran, coran, *m.*

all (ôl), *adj.*, tout, tous. — of you ; *vous tous.* That is — ; *voilà tout, c'est tout.* — the better ; *tant mieux.* With — speed ; *au plus vite.* For — that ; *malgré cela.* It is — the same ; *c'est tout de même ou la même chose.* One and — ; *tous sans exception.* Above — ; *surtout, par-dessus tout.* — in — ; *entièrement, tel quel.* — at one price ; *au choix.* It is — the same to me ; *cela m'est égal ou je m'en bats l'œil.* If that be — ; *s'il ne tient qu'à cela ou si ce n'est que cela.* It is — nonsense ; *c'est absurde ; tout cela n'a pas le sens commun ; allons donc ! que me dites vous là !* Four, five — ; *quatre à quatre, cinq à cinq.*

all, *adv.*, tout, entièrement, souverainement. Not at — ; *point du tout.* — at once ; *tout d'un coup.* Nothing at — ; *rien du tout.* At — ; *tant soit peu, tant que de.* — in the wind ; *incertain, irrésolu, inconstant.*

all, *n.*, tout, *m.* My — ; *tout mon avoir.* If that's — ; *s'il ne tient qu'à cela.* To stake one's — ; *jouer son tout.*

all-aban'doned, *adj.*, abandonné de tous.

all-abhorred' (-ab-hord), *adj.*, abhorré de tous.

all-absorb'ing, *adj.*, qui absorbe l'esprit, du plus haut intérêt.

all-admir'ing (-maïeur-), *adj.*, tout dans l'admiration.

allay', *v.a.*, apaiser, soulager, adoucir, calmer.

allay', *n.*, affaiblissement, *m.*

allay'er (al-lé-eur), *n.*, qui soulage, qui calme ; calmant, soulagement, *m.*

allay'ment, *n.*, (ant.) adoucissement, *m.*

all-beau'teous (-biouti-eusse), *adj.*, souverainement beau.

all-boun'tiful (-baoun-tifoul), *adj.*, infiniment bon.

all-cheer'ing (-tshîrîne), *adj.*, qui réjouit tout.

all-comply'ing (-ko-m-plaïgne), *adj.*, qui se prête à tout.

all-dread'ed (-drè-dède), *adj.*, redouté de tous.

all-effi'cient (-shi-è-nte), *adj.*, tout efficace.

allega'tion (al-li-ghé-), *n.*, allégation, *f.*

allege' (al-lèdje), *v.a.*, alléguer, prétendre.

allege'able, *adj.*, qu'on peut alléguer.

alleg'er (al-lè-), *n.*, allégateur, -trice, *f.*, celui, celle qui allègue.

alle'giance (al-lîd-jia-nce), *n.*, fidélité ; obéissance, *f.* Oath of — ; *serment de fidélité, m.*

allegor'ic *ou* **allegor'ical**, *adj.*, allégorique.

allegor'ically, *adv.*, allégoriquement.

allegor'icalness (al-li-), *n.*, nature allégorique, *f.*

al'legorist, *n.*, allégoriste, *m.*

al'legorize (-raïze), *v.a.*, allégoriser.

al'legorize, *v.n.*, faire des allégories.

al'legory (al-li-), *n.*, allégorie, *f.*

alle'gro (al-lé-), *adv.*, (mus.) allegro.

all-el'oquent (-èl-ô-kouè-n-te), *adj.*, tout éloquent.

allelu'jah (al-li-liou-ya), *n.*, alléluia, *m.*

all-endur'ing (è-n-diourîgne), *adj.*, résigné à tout, qui endure tout.

alle'viate (al-li-vié-te), *v.a.*, alléger, soulager, adoucir.

allevia'tion, *n.*, allégement, adoucissement, soulagement, *m.*

al'ley (al-li), *n.*, (of a town) ruelle, allée, *f.* Blind — ; *impasse, f. ; cul de sac, m.*

all-fours' (ôl-fôrze), *n.*, (cards) impériale, *f.* To go on — ; *marcher*, or *aller, à quatre pattes.*

all-giv'er (-ghiveur), *n.*, dispensateur de tous les biens, *m.*

all-good' (ôl-goude), *adj.*, souverainement bon.

all-good', *n.*, (bot.) chenopode, épinard sauvage, *m.*

all-hail' ! (-hèle), *int.*, salut !

all-hal'lows (ôl-hal-lôze), *n.*, La Toussaint, *f.*

all-hap'py, *adj.*, bienheureux.

all'-heal (-hîle), *n.*, (bot.) berce, branche-ursine bâtarde, *f.*

allia'ceous (al-lié-shi-eusse), *adj.*, (bot.) alliacé.

alli'ance (al-lai-a-nce), *n.*, alliance ; (kindred) parenté, *f.*

al'lied, *adj.*, allié, parent.

alliga'tion, *n.*, (arith.) règle d'alliage, *f.*

al'ligator (al-li-ghé-teur), *n.*, alligator, caïman, *m.*

allitera'tion (al-li-teuré-), *n.*, (rhet.) allitération, *f.*

allit'erative (al-li-teura-), *adj.*, allitératif.

all-judg'ing (-djeud'jigne), *adj.*, juge suprême.

all-just' (-djeuste), *adj.*, qui est la justice même.

all-kind' (-kaï-n-de), *adj.*, de toute bonté ; extrêmement bon.

all-know'ing (-nôîgne), *adj.*, de science infinie, omniscient ; qui sait tout.

all-lov'ing, *adj.*, dont l'amour est infini ; qui est tout amour.

al'locate (al-lôkéte), *v.a.*, allouer ; assigner.

alloca'tion, *n.*, allocation ; disposition, *f.*, arrangement, *m.*

allocu'tion (al-lô-kiou-), *n.*, allocution, *f.*

allo'dial (al-lô-), *adj.*, allodial.

allo'dium (al-lô-dieume), *n.*, franc-alleu, *m.*

allonge' (al-leu'n-je), *n.*, (fenc.) botte, *f.*

allonge', *v.a.*, (fenc.) allonger, porter.

alloo'. *V.* **halloo.**

allopath'ic, *adj.*, allopathique.

allop'athist, *n.*, allopathe, *m.*

allop'athy, *n.*, allopathie, *f.*

allot' (al-lote), *v.a.*, assigner en partage, donner, départir, répartir, accorder ; (appointment) désigner, destiner, affecter.

allot'ment, n., partage, lot; décret, m.; distribution, répartition; (agri.) sole, f.

allot'tery, n., (ant.) V. **allotment**.

allow' (al-laou), v.a., permettre, autoriser; donner; allouer, approuver, avouer, admettre, reconnaître; souffrir, sanctionner. To — any one to do anything; *permettre à quelqu'un de* (ou *autoriser quelqu'un à*) *faire quelque chose*. To — for; *deduire*; *faire la part de*; *tenir compte de*; (fig.) *avoir égard à*. To — of; *comporter, admettre de*. I will not — it; *je ne le souff.irai*, or *permettrai, pas*. — me; *permettez-moi*. I am allowed to; *il m'est permis de, je suis autorisé à, on me laisse*. I am allowed wine; *le vin m'est permis ou on me permet le vin*. To allow one's self to be; *se laisser* (followed by infinitive). — me! *permettez!*

allow'able, adj., légitime, juste, permis, admissible; convenable.

allow'ableness, n., légitimité, légalité, f.

allow'ance, n., allocation, pension; gratification; ration; (com.) remise, réduction, sanction, permission, indulgence; (mil.) indemnité, f. Short —; *ration réduite, ration diminuée*. Trade —; (com.) remise, réduction. Mess —; *indemnité de table*. To be on short —; *être rationné*. To make — for; *avoir de l'indulgence pour*; *avoir égard à, tenir compte de*. To put on short —; *rationner*. Mcuthly —; *mois*, m. Weekly —; *semaine, f.*

allow'ance, v.a., mettre à la ration, rationner

alloy' (al-lo-i), n., alliage, mélange, m. There is no joy without —; *il n'y a pas de bonheur sans mélange*.

alloy', v.a., (metal.) allier; altérer, diminuer, flétrir.

alloy'age (al-lo-yèdge), n., (metal.) alliage, m.

all-pow'erful (-paoueurfoul), adj., tout-puissant.

all-saints'-day (-sé-ntse-), n., jour de la Toussaint, m.

all-souls'-day (-sôlze-), n., jour des morts, m.

all'-spice (-spaïce), n., (bot.) piment, m.

all-suffi'cient (-seuf-fi-shiè-n-te), adj., suffisant.

allude' (al-lioude), v.a., faire allusion à; avoir trait à; vouloir parler de; vouloir dire.

allure' (al-lioure), v.a., amorcer, attirer, séduire, engager, inviter à.

allure'ment, n., amorce, séduction, f.; appât, charme, attrait, m.

allur'er, n., séducteur, flatteur, tentateur, m.

allur'ing, adj., entraînant, attrayant, séduisant.

allur'ingly, adv., d'une manière séduisante, attrayante, entraînante.

allur'ingness, n., entraînement, m.; séduction, f.

allu'sion (al-liou-jeune), n., allusion; comparaison; figure, f. In — to; *par allusion à* or *en faisant allusion à*.

allu'sive, adj., faisant allusion; figuré.

allu'sively, adv., par allusion.

allu'via (al-liou-), n.pl., terres d'alluvion, f.pl., alluvion, f.

allu'vial, adj., d'alluvion, alluvial.

allu'vious (al-liou-vi-eusse), adj., (ant.). V. **alluvial**.

allu'vium (al-liou-vieume), n., alluvion, f., atterrissement, m.

all-wise' (-waïze), adj., d'une sagesse infinie.

all-wor'shiped (-shipte), adj., adoré de tous.

all-wor'thy (-weur*th*i), adj., infiniment digne.

ally' (al-laï), v.a., allier à, unir à, joindre à. To — one's self to; *s'allier à* ou *avec*.

ally', n., allié, parent, ami, confédéré, m.

al'magist (-djiste), n., almageste, m.

al'manac (ôl-ma-nak), n., almanach, m.

almigh'tiness (ôl-maï-ti-nèsse), n., toute-puissance, omnipotence, f.

almight'y (ôl-maï-ti), adj., tout-puissant, omnipotent.

almight'y, n., Tout-Puissant, m.

a'lmond (â-meu-n-de), n., amande, f. Burnt —; *praline, amande pralinée, f.* Sugared —, *dragée, f.* — rock; *nougat, m.* Milk of —s; *lait d'amandes, m.* Bitter —; *amande amère.* Sweet —; *amande douce.* African —; *amande d'Afrique.* Italian —; *amande d'Italie.* Shelled —s; *amandes cassées.* Oil of —s; *huile d'amandes, f.* — paste; *pâte d'amande, f.* — soap; *savon d'amande, m.* — of the ear, *parotide, f.*

a'lmond-flower (-flaoueur), n., fleur d'amande, f.

a'lmond-tree (-tri), n., amandier, m.

al'moner, n., aumônier, m.

al'monry (-meun'ri), n., aumônerie, f.

al'most (ôl-môste), adv., presque, (before a numeral) près **de**.

alms (â'mze), n., aumône, f. To give —, *faire* or *donner l'aumône.*

alms'-box, n., tronc des pauvres, m.

alms'-deed (-dîde), n., œuvre de charité, f.

alms'-giving (-ghi-), n., aumônes, f.pl.

alms'-house (-haouce), n., maison de charité, f.; hospice pour les pauvres, m.

alms'-man, n., qui vit d'aumônes, m.

al'muce, n., aumusse, f.

al'nage (al-nèdje), n., aunage, m.

al'night (al-naïte), n., (ant.) veilleuse, f.

al'oe (-lô), n., (bot.) aloès, m.

al'oes (-lôze), n., (med.) aloès, m.

al'oes-wood (-woude), n., bois d'aloès, m.

aloet'ic (-ètic) ou **aloet'ical** (-ètical), adj., aloétique.

aloet'ic, n., médicament aloétique, m.

aloft', adv., en haut, haut, en l'air; (nav.) dans les hunes. To go —; *monter au haut du mât ou dans les hunes.* —! (int.) *à la hune!*

alone' (-lône), adj., seul; unique. To let —; *laisser, laisser de côté, laisser là.* Let me —; *laissez-moi tranquille.*

along', adv., le long, au long, le long **de**. — with; *avec*; *en même temps que, ainsi que.* Come —; *venez donc.* All —; *tout le temps*; *tout le long* **de**; *tout le long du chemin.* Go —; *allez-vous promener.* — side; (nav.) *contre à contre, bord à bord.*

aloof' (-loufe), adv., loin; au loin, au large; éloigné, à distance, à l'écart; (nav.) au lof. To keep —; *se tenir à l'écart.* To hold —; *tenir à distance.*

alo'sa (-lô-ça), n., (ich.) alose, f.

aloud' (-laoude), adv., haut; à haute voix; à grand bruit.

alpa'ca, n., (al-pa-ca) (fabric) alpaga, alpaca; (zoöl.) alpaca, m.

al'pha, n., alpha (of the Greek alphabet); alpha, commencement, principe, m.

al'phabet, n., alphabet; (com.) répertoire alphabétique, m.

al'phabet, v.a., classer par ordre alphabétique.

alphabet'ic ou **alphabet'ical**, adj., alphabétique. In — order; *par ordre alphabétique.*

alphabet'ically, adv., alphabétiquement.

al'pine (-païn), adj., alpin; des Alpes, alpestre.

alread'y (ôl-rè-), adv., déjà.

alsa'tia, n., cour des miracles, f.

al'so (ôl-sô), adv., aussi, également.

al'tar (-teur), n., autel, m. High —; *maître-autel, m.*

al'tar-cloth (-clô*th*), n., nappe, f., or parement, m., d'autel.

al'tar-piece (-pîce), n., tableau d'autel, m.

al'tar-screen (-), n., retable, m.

al'tarwise (-waïze), adj., en forme d'autel.

al'ter, v.a., changer; modifier; retoucher, retoucher à; corriger.

al'ter (ôl-teur), v.n., changer, se changer.

al'terable, adj., changeant, variable.

altera′tion (-teuré-), *n.*, changement, *m.*, correction, modification, *f.* To require —; *demander, or exiger, du changement.*

al′terative (-teura-), *adj.*, (med.) altérant.

al′terative, *n.*, (med.) altérant, *m.*

altercate, *v.n.*, se disputer, se quereller.

alterca′tion (ŏl-teur-ké-), *n.*, altercation, dispute, *f.*

altern′ate (ŏl-teur-néte), *adj.*, alterne, alternant; (of rhymes) croisé.

altern′ate, *n.*, alternative (succession), *f.*

al′ternate, *v.a.*, alterner, faire alterner, exercer alternativement.

al′ternate, *v.n.*, alterner.

altern′ately, *adv.*, alternativement, tour à tour.

altern′ateness, *n.*, alternat, *m.*

alterna′tion, *n.*, alternative, choix ; (geol.) alternance, *f.*

altern′ative (ŏl-teur-né-), *adj.*, alternatif, alternant.

altern′ative, *n.*, alternative, *f. ;* choix, *m.*

altern′atively, *adv.*, alternativement.

although′ (ŏl-*lhô*), *conj.*, bien que, quoique.

altil′oquence (-lo-kwè-n-se), *n.*, (ant.) discours pompeux, *m.*

altim′etry, *n.*, altimétrie, *f.*

al′titude (-tioude), *n.*, élévation, hauteur, altitude, *f.*

altogeth′er (ŏl-tou-ghè-*theur*), *adv.*, tout à fait, entièrement, tout à la fois, (in all) en tout.

al′to-relie′vo (-tô-ri-lî-vo), *n.*, plein, haut relief, *m.*

al′udel (-liou-) *n.*, (chem.) aludel, *m.*

al′um (-leume), *n.* alun, *m.* Rock —; *alun de roche.*

al′um, *v.a.*, aluner.

al′umed (-leum′de), *adj.*, aluné.

alu′mina *ou* **alu′mine** (-liou-), *n.*, (min.) alumine, *f.*

al′uming (-leumigne), *n.*, (dy.) alunage, *f.*

alu′minous (-liou-mi-neusse), *adj.*, alumineux.

alu′minum, *n.*, aluminium, *m.*

al′umish (-leu-mishe), *adj.*, alumineux.

al′um-ma′king (-mé-kigne), *n.*, alunation, *f.*

al′um-pit, *n.*, alunière, *f.*

al′um-wa′ter (-wŏ-teur), *n.*, eau alumineuse,*f.*

al′um-works (-weurkse), *n.pl.*, fabrique d'alun, *f.*

al′veole (-vi-ole) *ou* **al′veolus** (-vi-oleusse), **n.**, (*alveoli*) (anat.) alvéole, *m.*

al′ways (ŏlwéze), *adv.*, toujours. [ès-arts, *m.*

A.M., *adv.*, du matin ; l'an du monde ; maître-**amabil′ity**, *n.*, amabilité, *f.*

amain′ (-méne), *adv.*, vigoureusement, avec force, de toutes ses forces ; (nav.) tout de suite ; (nav.) amène !

amal′gam (-game), *n.*, amalgame, *m.*

amal′gamable, *adj.*, qui peut s'amalgamer.

amal′gamate (-méte),*v.a.*, amalgamer, fusionner.

amal′gamate, *v.n.*, s'amalgamer, se fusionner; (fig.) se combiner.

amalgama′tion (-ga-mé-), *n.*, amalgamation, *f. ;* (fig.) amalgame, fusionnement, *m.*

amanuen′sis (-niou-è-n), *n.* (*amanuenses*) secrétaire, copiste, *m.*

am′aranth (-ra-nth) *ou* **amaran′thus** (-rantheusse), *n.*, amarante, *f.*

amaranth′ine (-ra-n-thine), *adj.*, d'amarante.

amaryl′lis, *n.*, (bot.) amaryllis, *f.*

amass′, *v.a.*, amasser, entasser.

amateur′ (-teur), *n.*, amateur, *m.*

amato′rial (-tô-), *adj.*, d'amour; amoureux.

amato′rially, *adv.*, amoureusement.

am′atory (-to-), *adj.*, d'amour ; amoureux.

amauro′sis, *n.*, (med.) goutte sereine, amaurose,*f.*

amaze′ (-méze), *v.a.*, surprendre, étonner,

frapper d'étonnement, confondre, interdire; (dazzle) éblouir, émerveiller.

amazed′ (-méz′de), *part.*, étonné ; **surpris** ; ébahi ; confondu, interdit.

amaz′edly (-mézèdli), *adv.*, avec étonnement.

amaz′edness (-mézèd′nèsse), *n.*, étonnement, *m.*

amaze′ment, *n.*, étonnement, stupeur, *f.; ;* ébahissement, effroi, *m.*

amaz′ing, *adj.*, étonnant, épatant, extraordinaire.

amaz′ingly, *adv.*, étonnamment, furieusement, au possible.

am′azon, *n.*, amazone, *f.*

Amazo′nia (myth., lit.) pays des amazones, *m.*

Amazo′nian (-zŏ-), *adj.*, d'amazone, hardi.

amba′ges (a-m-bé-d'jize), *n.pl.*, ambages, *f.pl.*, détours, *m.pl.*

ambas′sador (-deur), *n.*, ambassadeur, *m.*

ambas′sadress (-drèsse), *n.*, ambassadrice, *f.*

am′ber (-beur), *n.*, ambre, *m.*

am′ber, *adj.*, d'ambre.

am′ber, *v.a.*, ambrer.

am′ber-colored (-keu-leurde), *adj.*, ambré.

am′ber-drink, *n.*, boisson de couleur ambrée,*f.*

am′bergris (-grîsse), *n.*, ambre gris, *m.*

am′ber-seed (-sîde), *n.*, graine musquée, ambrette,*f.*

ambidex′ter (-teur), *n.*, ambidextre, *m.f.*

ambidexter′ity, *n.*, ambidextérité, (fig.) duplicité, fourberie, *f.*

ambidex′trous (-treusse), *adj.*, ambidextre.

am′bient, *adj.*, ambiant.

ambigu′ity, *n.*, ambiguïté ; équivoque, *f.*

ambig′uous (-ghiou-eusse), *adj.*, ambigu, équivoque, douteux.

ambig′uously, *adv.*, ambigument, d'une manière équivoque.

ambig′uousness, *n.*, ambiguïté, *f.*

am′bit, *n.*, contour, *m.*, circonférence, *f.*

ambi′tion, *n.*, ambition, *f.*

ambi′tious (-sheusse), *adj.*, ambitieux.

ambi′tiously, *adv.*, ambitieusement.

am′ble, *v.n.*, aller l'amble, trottiner, aller son chemin, son train. To make a horse —; *mettre un cheval à l'amble.*

am′ble, *v.a.*, faire aller l'amble **à**.

am′ble, *n.*, amble, *m.*

am′bler (-bleur), *n.*, haquenée, *f. ;* cheval qui va l'amble, *m.*

am′bling, *adj.*, à l'amble. — pace, *n.*, amble, *m.*

am′blingly, *adv.*, à l'amble.

ambro′sia (-brô-jia), *n.*, ambroisie, *f.*

ambro′sial, *adj.*, d'ambroisie, délicieux, doux.

ambro′sian (-brô-ji-), *adj.*, d'ambroisie.

ambs′-ace (é'mz′éce), *n.*, beset, bezet, ambesas, *m.*

am′bulance, *n.* (-biou-), hôpital militaire, *m.;* ambulance, *f.* — cart; *fourgon d'ambulance, m.*

am′bulant (-biou-), *adj.*, ambulant.

am′bulatory, *adj.*, ambulatoire.

am′bury (-biou-), *n.*, (vet.) furoncle, *m.*

ambuscade′ (-beus-kéde), *n.*, embuscade, *f.* To lay an — for; *dresser une embuscade* **à**. To fall into an —; *tomber dans une embuscade.*

ambuscade′, *v.a.*, embusquer, mettre en embuscade.

am′bush (-boushe), *n.*, (b.s.) embûche ; (milit.) embuscade, *f.*, guet-apens, *m.*

am′bush, *v.a.*, embusquer.

am′bush, *v.n.*, s'embusquer.

am′bushment (-n-), *n.* (ant.) embûche,*f.*

ameer′ (-mieur) *or* **amir′**, *n.*, Emir, *m.*

amel′iorate (-mi-lieu-réte), *v.a.*, améliorer, perfectionner.

amel′iorate, *v.n.*, s'améliorer, se perfectionner.

ameliora′tion, *n.*, amélioration, *f. ;* perfectionnement, *m.*

amen' (é-mè-ne), *adv.*, amen ; ainsi soit-il.

ame'nable (-mi-), *adj.*, responsable, comptable ; (jur.) justiciable **de**, soumis **à**, sujet **à**. He is — to reason ; *on peut lui faire entendre raison*. To make any one — to reason ; *faire entendre raison à quelqu'un*.

ame'nableness, *n.*, responsabilité ; soumission.

amend', *v.a.*, amender, corriger ; réparer ; réformer, modifier.

amend', *v.n.*, s'amender, s'améliorer, se corriger.

amend'able (-dab'l), *adj.*, amendable.

amend'er, *n.*, personne qui amende, chose qui amende, *f.* ; correctif, *m.*

amend'ment, *n.*, amendement, changement, *m.* ; amélioration, rectification, réforme, *f.*

amends' (-mè-n-dze), *n.pl.*, dédommagement, *m.* ; compensation ; réparation, *f.* To make — for ; *dédommager de, compenser ; réparer.*

amen'ity (-mè-), *n.*, aménité, *f.*

Amenta'ceæ, *n.pl.*, (bot.) amentacées, *f.pl.*

amerce' (-meurse), *v.a.*, mettre, *or* condamner, à l'amende.

amerce'ment, *n.*, amende, peine, *f.*

Amer'ican, *adj.*, américain.

Amer'ican, *n.*, Américain, *m.*, Américaine, *f.*

Amer'ican, *n.*, (print.) américaine, *f.*

Amer'icanism, *n.*, idiotisme américain, *m.*

Amer'icanize (-naïze), *v.a.*, naturaliser Américain.

am'ethyst (-mé-thiste), *n.*, améthyste, *f.*

amethyst'ine (-taïne), *adj.*, de la nature de l'améthyste ; fait d'améthyste.

amiabil'ity (é-mia-), *n.*, amabilité, *f.*

a'miable, *adj.*, aimable ; attrayant, gracieux.

a'miableness, *n.*, amabilité, bonne grâce, *f.*

a'miably, *adv.*, avec amabilité, gracieusement.

am'ianth (-a-nth) *ou* **amian'thus** (-theusse), *n.*, (min.) amiante, *m.*

am'icable, *adj.*, amical ; (of a settlement) à l'amiable.

am'icableness, *n.*, état amical, *m.*, cordialité, *f.*

am'icably, *adv.*, amicalement ; amiablement, (of a settlement) à l'amiable, de gré **à** gré.

am'ice (-misse) *or* **am'ict** (-mikte), *n.*, amict, *m.*

amid' *ou* **amidst'**, *prep.*, au milieu **de**.

amid'ships, *adv.*, (nav.) par le travers. Helm —! *droite la barre !*

amiss', *adj.*, mauvais, hors de propos.

amiss', *adv.*, mal, en mal, en mauvaise part ; (unseasonably) mal à propos. To do — ; *mal faire.* Do not take — what I am going to tell you ; *ne prenez pas en mauvaise part ce que je vais vous dire.* Nothing comes — to him ; *il s'arrange de tout ; tout lui va.*

am'ity, *n.*, amitié, *f.* ; entente cordiale, *f.*

am'mi, *n.*, (bot.) ammi, sison, *m.*

ammo'nia (am-mô-), *n.*, ammoniaque, *f.*

ammo'niac *ou* **ammoni'acum** (-keume), *n.*, gomme ammoniaque, *f.*

ammo'niac *ou* **ammoni'acal**, *adj.*, ammoniac, ammoniacal.

ammuni'tion (am-miou-), *n.*, munitions de guerre, *f.pl.* — bread ; *pain de munition*, *m.*

am'nesty, *n.*, amnistie, *f.* *v.a.*, amnistier.

amo'mum (-mô-meume), *n.*, (bot.) amome, *m.*

among' (-meu'gne), **amongst'** (-meu'gnst), *prep.*, entre, parmi ; avec, au milieu de, chez. From —; *d'entre.* — others ; *entre autres.* One — a thousand ; *un sur mille.*

am'orous (-reusse), *adj.*, amoureux.

am'orously, *adv.*, amoureusement.

am'orousness, *n.*, galanterie, passion, tendance à l'amour, *f.*

amor'phous (-feusse), *adj.*, amorphe.

amort' (-morte), *adj.*, abattu, mélancolique, triste à la mort.

amortiza'tion (-taïzé-), *n.*, amortissement, *m.*

amort'ize (-taïze), *v.a.*, amortir ; (ant.) annuler, détruire.

amort'izement, *n.*, amortissement, *m.*

amount' (-maou-n'te), *v.n.*, se monter à, monter à, revenir à, s'élever à, se réduire à. That amounts to the same thing ; *cela revient au même.* His argument amounts to this ; *son argument se reduit à ceci.*

amount', *n.*, montant, total, *m.* ; quantité, somme, *f.* ; (fig.) valeur, *f.*, résultat, *m.* To the — of ; *jusqu'à concurrence de.*

amour', *n.*, amours (intrigue amoureuse), *f.pl.*, galanterie, amourette, *f.*

Amphib'ia, *n.pl.*, amphibies, *m.pl.*

amphib'ian, *n.*, amphibie, *m.*

amphib'ious (-bieusse), *adj.*, amphibie.

amphib'iousness, *n.*, nature amphibie, *f.*

amphibolog'ical (-lod'ji-), *adj.*, amphibologique.

amphibolog'ically, *adv.*, amphibologiquement.

amphibol'ogy, *n.*, amphibologie, *f.*

amphicty'on'ic (-ti-o-), *adj.*, amphictyonique.

amphic'tyons (-ti-o-n-ze), *n.pl.*, amphictyons, *m.pl.*

amphis'cians (-fis-si-a-n-ze) *ou* **amphis'cii** (-fis-si-aïe), *m.pl.*, (geog.) amphisciens, *m.pl.*

amphithe'atral (-thi-), *adj.*, en amphithéâtre.

amphithe'ater (-thi-a-teur), *n.*, amphithéâtre, *m.*

amphitheat'rical, *adj.*, amphithéâtral, d'amphithéâtre.

am'ple, *adj.*, ample, large ; vaste, grand, suffisant, très suffisant.

am'pleness, *n.*, ampleur, grandeur, étendue, *f.*

amplia'tion (-pli-é-), *n.*, (Rom. antiq.) ajournement d'un jugement criminel, *m.* ; (l.u.) amplification, prolixité, *f.*

amplifica'tion (-ké-), *n.*, amplification, *f.*

am'plifier (faï-eur), *n.*, amplificateur, *m.*

am'plify (-faïe), *v.a.*, agrandir, amplifier, augmenter, étendre, grossir, développer.

am'plitude (-tioude), *n.*, amplitude, étendue, largeur, *f.*

am'ply, *adv.*, amplement.

ampul'la (-peul-la), *n.*, (bot.) ampoule, *f.*

am'putate (-piou-téte), *v.a.*, amputer.

amputa'tion, *n.*, amputation, *f.* To perform an —; *faire une amputation.*

amuck', *adv.* To run — at ; *attaquer en fou furieux ; parcourir les rues comme un forcené.*

am'ulet (-mioulète), *n.*, amulette, *f.*

amuse' (-miouze), *v.a.*, amuser, divertir, récréer, distraire. To be —d at ; *s'amuser, se divertir, rire de.*

amuse'ment, *n.*, amusement, divertissement, plaisir, *m.* ; distraction, *f.*

amus'er, *n.*, amuseur, *m.*

amus'ing, *adj.*, amusant, agréable, divertissant.

amus'ingly, *adv.*, d'une manière amusante.

amus'ively, *adv.*, agréablement, de manière à amuser.

amyg'dalate (-da-léte), *adj.*, fait d'amandes.

amyg'dalate, *n.*, amandé, lait d'amande, *m.*

amyg'daloid (-loïde), *n.*, (min.) amygdaloïde, *f.*

amyla'ceous (-lé-shi-eusse), *adj.*, amylacé.

an, *art.*, un, m., une, *f.*

an, *conj.*, (ant.) si. Catch me — thou canst, *attrape-moi, si tu peux.*

Anabap'tism (-bap-tiz'me), *n.*, anabaptisme, *m.*

Anabap'tist, *n.*, anabaptiste, *m.f.*

Anabaptis'tic *ou* **Anabaptis'tical**, *adj.*, des anabaptistes.

Anabaptis'tically, *adv.*, en anabaptiste.

Anabap'tistry, *n.*, (l.u.) anabaptisme, *m.*

anacar'dium (-câr-dieume), *n.*, (bot.) anacarde, *m.*

anach'oret (-kô-rète) *ou* **anach'orite** (-kô-raïte), *n.* *V.* **anchoret.**

anach'ronism, n., anachronisme, m.

anachronis'tic, adj., qui contient un anachronisme.

anacolu'thon (-liou-tho-n), n., (gram.) anacoluthe, f.

Anacreon'tic (-cri-o-n-), adj., anacréontique.

Anacreon'tic, n., poème anacréontique, m.

anagog'ical (-god'ji-), adj., (theol.) anagogique.

an'agram, n., anagramme, f.

anagrammat'ic ou anagrammat'ical, adj., d'anagramme.

anagrammat'ically, adv., par anagramme.

anagram'matist, n., faiseur d'anagrammes, m.

anagram'matize, v.n., faire des anagrammes.

analec'ta ou an'alects (-lèkta, -lèktse), n. pl., analectes, m.pl.

analem'ma, n., (astron.) analemme, m.

analep'tic, adj., analeptique.

analep'tic, n., analeptique, m.

analog'ical (-lod'ji-), adj., analogique.

analog'ically, adv., analogiquement.

anal'ogism (-lod'jiz'me), n., (phil.) analogisme, m.

anal'ogist, n., personne qui fait des analogies, f.

anal'ogize (-lod'jaïze), v.a., expliquer analogiquement.

anal'ogous (-logheusse), adj., analogue.

anal'ogously, adv., d'une manière analogue.

anal'ogy (-lod'ji), n., analogie, f. By —; par analogie.

anal'ysis, n., analyse, f.

an'alyst, n., analyste, m.

analyt'ic or analyt'ical, adj., analytique, raisonné.

analyt'ically, adv., analytiquement.

analyt'ics, n., art de l'analyse, m. ; algèbre, f.

an'alyze (-laïze), v.a., analyser, faire l'analyse de.

an'alyzer, n., analyste ; analyseur, m.

anamor'phosis (-cisse), n., anamorphose, f.

ana'nas ou ananas'sa, n., ananas, m.

an'apæst ou an'apest, n., anapeste, m.

anapest'ic, adj., anapestique.

anapest'ic, n., mesure anapestique, f.

anaph'ora, n., (rhet.) anaphore, f.

anarch'ic ou anarch'ical (-kik, -ki-kal), adj., anarchique.

an'archist, n., anarchiste, m.f.

an'archy (-ki-), n., anarchie, f.

anasar'ca (-çâr-), n., (med.) anasarque, f.

anasar'cous (-çâr-keusse), adj., hydropique.

anath'ema (-nath-i-), n., anathème, m.

anathemat'ical, adj., d'anathème.

anathemat'ically, adv., en forme d'anathème.

anathematiza'tion (-nath-i-matizé-), n., action d'anathématiser.

anath'ematize (-nath-i-ma-taïze), v.a., anathématiser, frapper d'anathème, excommunier.

anath'ematized (-nath-i-ma-taïz'de), adj., anathème, excommunié.

anatom'ical, adj., anatomique.

anatom'ically, adv., anatomiquement.

anat'omist (-to-), n., anatomiste, m.

anat'omize (-to-maïze), v.a., anatomiser.

anat'omy (-to-), n., anatomie, f.

an'cestor (-cès-teur), n., ancêtre, aïeul, m.

an'cestors (-cès-teurze), n.pl., ancêtres, pères, aïeux, m.pl.

ances'tral, adj., d'ancêtres ; de mes, de tes, de ses, etc., ancêtres ; héréditaire.

an'cestry, n., ancêtres, m.pl. ; race, origine, naissance, haute extraction, f.

an'chor (aign-keur), n., ancre, f. Best bower —; seconde ancre. Bower —; ancre de poste. Ebb —; ancre de jusant. Flood —; ancre de flot. Foul —; ancre surjalée. Kedge —; ancre à empenneler, ancre de toue. Sea —; ancre du large. Sheet--; maîtresse ancre, ancre de

miséricorde; (fig.) ancre de salut, planche de salut, f. Shore —; ancre de terre. Small bower —; ancre d'affourche. Spare —; ancre de rechange. Stream —; ancre de touée. To lie or ride at —; être à l'ancre. To let go the —; mouiller l'ancre. To weigh —; lever l'ancre. To drag the —s; chasser sur les ancres. —stock; jas, jouail, jouet, m.

an'chor, v.n., mouiller, ancrer, s'ancrer ; (fig.) se fixer, s'arrêter, s'ancrer.

an'chor, v.a., mouiller, ancrer.

an'chorage (-keur-édje), n., mouillage, ancrage ; droit d'ancrage, m. ; ancres, f.pl.

an'chored (-keur'de), adj., mouillé, ancré.

an'choret (-keu-rète) ou an'chorite (-keuraïte), n., anachorète, ermite, m.

an'chor-ground (-graounde), n., (nav.) mouillage, m.

an'chor-hold, n., (nav.) tenue, f.

an'choring, n., (nav.) mouillage, ancrage, m.

an'choring-ground, n., mouillage, m.

an'choring-place (-keurigne-plèce), n., mouillage, m.

an'chor-smith, n., forgeur d'ancres.

an'chor-stock, n., (nav.) jas d'ancre, m.

ancho'vy (a-n-tshô-), n., anchois, m.

anchylo'sis (-ki-lô-cisse), n., (med.) ankylose, f.

an'cient (é'n'shi-è-nte), n., ancien, vieux ; (milit.) drapeau ; (nav.) pavillon, m. The — of days ; Dieu, le Tout-Puissant, m.

an'cient, adj., ancien, antique ; (old) vieux.

an'ciently, adv., anciennement.

an'cientness, n., ancienneté, f.

an'cientry, n., ancienneté (of a family), f.

and, conj., et. Better — better ; de mieux en mieux. Carriage — pair ; voiture à deux chevaux, f. Carriage — four; voiture à quatre chevaux, f.

andan'te, n., (mus.) andante, andanté, m.

An'dean (-di-), adj., des Andes.

and'iron (a-n-daï-eurn), n., chenet, m.

andro'gynal (-drod'ji-) ou andro'gynous (-drod'ji-neusse), adj., (bot.) androgyne ; (zoöl.) hermaphrodite.

an'drogyne (-drod'jaïne), n., androgyne, hermaphrodite, m.

an'ecdote (-dôte), n., anecdote, f.

anecdot'ical (-do-), adj., anecdotique.

anem'ometer (-ni-mo-mi-teur), n., anémomètre, m.

anem'one ou anem'ony (-mô-ni), n., anémone, f.

anem'one-root, n., patte, griffe d'anémone, f.

anem'oscope (-né-mo-scôpe), n., anémoscope, m., girouette, f.

an-end', adj., (nav.) debout, guindé.

anent', prep., concernant, touchant, sur, au sujet de, à propos de.

a'net, n., (bot.) fenouil puant, aneth, m.

an'eurism (-iou-), n., anévrisme, m.

aneuris'mal, adj., anévrismal.

anew' (-niou), adv., de nouveau.

anfractuos'ity (-tiou-), n., (ant.) anfractuosité, f.

anfrac'tuous (-tiou-eusse), adj., anfractueux.

an'gel (é-n-d'jèle), n., ange, m. —-winged ; aux ailes d'ange.

an'gel-fish, n., angelot, ange de mer, m.

angel'ic ou angel'ical, adj., angélique.

angel'ica, n., angélique, f.

angel'ically, adv., angéliquement.

angel'icalness, n., nature angélique, f.

an'gelot (a-n-d'jèlote), n., angelot, m.

an'gel-shot, n., (nav.) boulet ramé, ange, m.

an'gelus, n., angélus, m.

an'gel-water, n., eau de Portugal, f.

an'gel-worship (-weur-), n., culte des anges, m.

an'ger (aign'gheur), *n.*, colère, *f.*; courroux, *m.* To provoke any one to —; *exciter la colère de quelqu'un.*

an'ger, *v.a.*, fâcher, irriter, provoquer, mettre en colère.

angi'na (a-nd'jaïna), *n.*, (med.) angine, *f.*

angiog'raphy (a-nd'jio-), *n.*, (anat.) angiographie, *f.*

angiol'ogy, *n.*, angiologie, *f.*

angiosperm'ous (a-nd'jïo-speurmeusse), *adj.*, (bot.) angiosperme.

an'gle (aign-g'l), *n.*, angle; coin, *m.*

an'gle, *v.n.*, pêcher à la ligne. To — after; (fig.) *essayer de savoir.*

an'gled (aign-gl'de), *adj.*, à angles. Acute— ; *acutangle.* Eight— ; *octogone.* Five- — ; *pentagone.* Four— ; *quadrangulaire.* Many— ; *polygone.* Nine- — ; *ennéagone.* Obtuse — ; *obtusangle.* Right- — ; *rectangle, rectangulaire.* Seven- — ; *heptagone.* Six— ; *hexagone.* Ten- — ; *décagone.* Twelve- — ; *dodécagone.*

an'gler, *n.*, pêcheur à la ligne, *m.*; (ich.) baudroie, *f.*

An'glican, *adj.*, anglican.

An'glican, *n.*, anglican, *m.*, anglicane, *f.*

An'glicism, *n.*, anglicisme, *m.*

An'glicize (-çaïze), *v.a.*, rendre anglais, angliciser.

an'gling, *n.*, pêche à la ligne, *f.*

Angloma'nia, *n.*, anglomanie, *f.*

An'glo-Sax'on, *adj.*, anglo-saxon.

An'glo-Sax'on, *n.*, Anglo-saxon; (lang.) anglosaxon, *m.*

an'grily, *adv.*, avec colère.

an'gry, *adj.*, fâché, en colère, irrité, furieux, courroucé. To be — with any one; *être en colère* **contre** *quelqu'un; en vouloir* **à.** To get — ; *se fâcher; se mettre en colère.* To make — ; *mettre en colère.* An — word ; *un mot plus haut que l'autre ; une parole vive.*

an'guish (-gouishe), *n.*, angoisse, *f.*

an'guish, *v.a.*, navrer de douleur.

an'guished, *adj.*, navré *(de douleur).*

an'gular (-ghiou-leur), *adj.*, angulaire.

an'gularity, *n.*, forme angulaire, angularité, *f.*

an'gularly, *adv.*, angulairement.

an'gulated (-ghiou-lé-tède), *adj.*, (ant.) angulé.

an'gulous (-ghiou-leusse), *adj.*, (ant.) anguleux.

anight' (-naïte) *ou* **anights** (-naïtse), (ant.) *adv.*, de nuit, la nuit.

an'il, *n.*, (bot.) anil, *m.*

an'ile (-naïle), *adj.*, de vieille femme.

an'ileness (-naïl-) *ou* **anil'ity** (-ni-li-), *n.*, radotage, *m.*

animadver'sion (-veur-), *n.*, animadversion, *f.*, blâme, *m.*

animadvert' (-veurte), *v.n.*, **s'attaquer à ;** critiquer, censurer, blâmer.

animadvert'er (-veur-), *n.*, censeur, frondeur, *m.*

an'imal, *n.* and *adj.*, animal, *m.*

animal'cular (-kiou-leur) *ou* **animal'culine** (-kiouline), *adj.*, animalculaire.

animal'cule (-kioule), *n.*, (*animalcula*) animalcule, *m.*

an'imalish, *adj.*, d'animal.

animal'ity, *n.*, animalité, *f.*

animaliza'tion (-li-zé-), *n.*, animalisation, *f.*

an'imalize (-laïze), *v.a.*, animaliser. *v.n.*, s'animaliser.

an'imate (-méte), *v.a.*, animer; ranimer, purifier. To — with ; *animer* **de.**

an'imate, *adj.*, animé.

an'imated, *adj.*, animé, vif.

an'imating, *adj.*, qui anime, qui ranime.

an'imatingly, *adv.*, vivement.

anima'tion, *n.*, animation, vivacité, chaleur, vie, *f.*; feu, *m.* Suspended —; *asphyxie, léthargie, f.*

an'imative, *adj.*, animateur.

an'imator (-méteur), *n.*, personne qui anime, chose qui anime, *f.*

animet'ta, *n.*, (c.rel.) voile du calice, *m.*

animos'ity, *n.*, animosité, *f.*; acharnement, *m.*

an'imus, *n.*, animosité, *f.*; but, *m.*, intention, *f.*; esprit, esprit **de**, *m.*; hostilité, *f.*

an'ise (-nice), *n.*, anis, *m.*

an'ise-seed (-nis-sîde), *n.*, (bot.) graine d'anis, *f.*; anis, *m.*

an'ise-seed-tree (-trî), *n.*, badiane, *f.*

an'kle (aign-k'l), *n.*, cheville du pied, *f.* — deep; *jusqu'aux chevilles.*

an'kle-bone (-bône), *n.*, astragale, *m.*

an'kled (aign-k'lde), *adj.*, pourvu de chevilles.

an'kle-joint (-djoï'n'te), *n.*, cou-de-pied, *m.*

an'nalist, *n.*, annaliste, *m.*

an'nals, *n.pl.*, annales, *f.pl.*, fastes, *m.pl.*, histoire, *f.*

an'nats, *n.pl.*, annate, *f.*

anneal' (-nîle), *v.a.*, recuire, tempérer.

anneal'ing, *n.*, recuite, *f.*

annel'ides (-nè-li-dize), *n.pl.*, annélides, *m.pl.*

annex', *v.a.*, annexer **à**, joindre **à**, attacher **à.**

annex', *v.n.*, se joindre **à**, s'attacher **à.**

an'nex, *n.*, annexe, *f.*

annexa'tion (-nèk-sé-), *n.*, annexion, annexation, jonction, *f.*

annexed' (-nèkste), *adj.*, ci-joint; annexé.

anni'hilable (an-naï-hi-la'-b'l), *adj.*, qui peut être anéanti, qui peut être annihilé.

anni'hilate (-naï-hi-léte), *v.a.*, anéantir, détruire, annihiler, mettre à néant.

anni'hilating, *v.a.*, **annihila'tion**, anéantissement, *m.*; annihilation, *f.*

anniver'sarily (-veur-), *adv.*, annuellement, tous les ans.

anniver'sary (-veur-), *n.*, anniversaire, *m.*

anniver'sary, *adj.*, anniversaire.

An'no Dom'ini, *latin ex.*, l'an du Seigneur, l'an de grâce.

annomina'tion (-mi-né-), *n.*, allitération, *f.*

an'notate (-no-téte), *v.a.*, annoter.

annota'tion, *n.*, annotation, *f.*

annota'tionist, *n.*, (l.u.) annotateur.

an'notator (-no-té-teur), *n.*, annotateur, *m.*

announce' (-naou-nse), *v.a.*, annoncer, proclamer.

announce'ment, *n.*, annonce, nouvelle, *f.*, avis, *m.*

announ'cer, *n.*, personne qui annonce une nouvelle, *f.*, messager, -ère, *m. f.*

annoy' (-a-n-no-ye), *v.a.*, incommoder, ennuyer, molester, contrarier, agacer; être désagréable **à.**

annoy'ance, *n.*, tracasserie, contrariété, *f.*; ennui, tourment, désagrément, déplaisir, *m.*

annoy'er, *n.*, taquin, *m.*, taquine, *f.*, tourment, *m.*

annoy'ing, *adj.*, ennuyant, contrariant, vexant, agaçant, désagréable. — person ; *être fatigant, m.*

an'nual (-niou-), *adj.*, annuel.

an'nual, *n.*, annuaire, *m.*; (bot.) plante annuelle, *f.*

an'nually, *adv.*, annuellement, tous les ans.

annu'itant (-niou-i-), *n.*, rentier; détenteur d'annuité, rentier viager, *m.*

annu'ity (-niou-i-), *n.*, rente annuelle, pension, *f.* Life —; *rente viagère.* Contingent —; *rente viagère.* Consolidated annuities; *rentes consolidées, f.pl.* Perpetual —; *rente perpétuelle.* Long —; *annuité à long terme, f.* Reduced —; *rente réduite.* Terminable —; *annuité rachetable* ou *remboursable* (à date fixe). Government —; *rente sur l'Etat, f.* Writ of —; *bref d'annuité, m.* To buy up an —; *amortir une rente.* To redeem an —; *racheter une rente.* To settle an — on; *constituer une rente* **à.**

annul' (an-neul), *v.a.*, annuler.

an'nular (-niou-leur) *ou* **an'nulary** (-niou-), *adj.*, annulaire.

an'nulate (an-niou-léte), *adj.*, annelé.

an'nulated (an-niou-lé-tède), *adj.*, annelé.

an'nulet (an-niou-lète), *n.*, annelet, *m. ;* (arch.) armilles, *f. pl.*

annul'ment (an-neul-), *n.*, annulation, *f.*

an'num (an-neume), *n.*, an, *m.* Per —; *par an.*

annuncia'tion (an-neu-n-ci-é-), *n.*, annonce, promulgation, *f. ;* avis, *m. ;* Annonciation, *f.*

an'odyne (-no-daïne), *adj.*, anodin.

an'odyne, *n.*, remède anodin ; calmant, *m.*

anoint' (-noï-n'te), *v.a.*, oindre.

anoint'ed, *adj.*, oint.

anoint'ed, *n.*, oint, *m.* The Lord's —; *l'oint du Seigneur.*

anoint'er, *n.*, personne qui oint, qui sacre, *f.*

anoint'ing, *n.*, **anoint'ment**, onction, *f.*

anomalist'ic *ou* **anomalist'ical**, *adj.*, (astron.) anomalistique; hétéroclite.

anom'alous (-leusse), *adj.*, anomal, irrégulier, hétéroclite.

anom'alously, *adv.*, irrégulièrement.

anom'aly, *n.*, irrégularité, anomalie, *f.*

ano'mia, *n.*, (conch.) anomie, *f.*

anon' (-none), *adv.*, tout à l'heure ; tantôt ; à l'instant, aussitôt. Ever and —; *de temps en temps, de temps à autre, à tout moment, à tout bout de champ.*

anon'ymous (-meusse), *adj.*, anonyme.

anon'ymously, *adv.*, anonymement; sous l'anonyme.

an'orexy, *n.*, (med.) anorexie, *f.*

anorm'al, *adj.*, anormal.

anoth'er (a-n'euther), *adj.*, un autre, encore un. One —; *l'un l'autre ; les uns les autres.* One with —; *l'un dans l'autre, l'un portant l'autre.* One after —; *l'un après l'autre.* That is — thing; *c'est autre chose, c'est différent.* That is quite — thing; *c'est une autre paire de manches.*

an'sated (-sé-tède), *adj.*, (ant.) à anses, ansé.

an'serine (-seuraïne), *adj.*, d'oie.

an'swer (-seur), *v.a.*, répondre; répondre à ; satisfaire, suffire à ; remplir ; résoudre ; (a door) ouvrir. This —s my purpose ; *cela remplit mon but.* To — several purposes ; *servir à plusieurs fins.*

answer, *v.n.*, répondre **de** *ou* **pour** ; (b.s.) raisonner, faire le raisonneur; réussir. That did not —; *cela n'a pas réussi.*

answer, *n.*, réponse, *f. ;* (b.s.) raisonnement, *m.*, réplique, *f.* In — to your letter; *en réponse à votre lettre.* Awaiting an —; *en attendant le plaisir de vous lire.* No —s! *point de raisonnements !*

an'swerable, *adj.*, susceptible de réponse ; conforme à ; responsable **de.**

an'swerableness, *n.*, convenance ; conformité, *f.*, rapport, *m.*

an'swerably, *adv.*, convenablement.

an'swerer, *n.*, personne qui répond, *f. ;* répondant, *m.*

an'swering, *adj.*, qui répond **à** ; correspondant **à.**

ant (an-n'te), *n.*, fourmi, *f.*

ant'-eater (-îteur), *n.*, (mam.) fourmilier, *m.*

ant'-hill, *n.*, fourmilière, *f.*

ant'-lion, *n.*, fourmi-lion.

antag'onism (-go-niz'me), *n.*, contestation, lutte, opposition, *f.*, antagonisme, *m.*

antag'onist, *n.*, antagoniste, *m.*

antag'onist, *adj.*, (anat.) antagoniste.

antarc'tic (-târk-), *adj.*, antarctique.

an'te-act (-ti-), *n.*, acte antérieur, *m.*

anteced'ence (-ti-ci-), *n.*, antécédence, antériorité, *f.*

anteced'ent, *adj.*, antécédent, antérieur.

anteced'ent, *n.*, antécédent, *m.*

anteced'ently, *adv.*, antécédemment, antérieurement.

an'te-chamber (-ti-tshé'm'beur), *n.*, antichambre, *f.*

an'te-chapel (-ti-tshap'l), *n.*, avant-corps de chapelle, *m.*

an'te-court, *n.*, avant-cour, *f.*

antecur'sor (-ti-keur-seur), *n.*, (antiq.) éclaireur; avant-coureur, *m.*

an'tedate (-ti-déte), *n.*, antidate, *f.*

an'tedate, *v.a.*, antidater; anticiper.

antedilu'vial *ou* **antedilu'vian** (-ti-di-liou-), *adj.* and *n.*, antédiluvien.

an'telope (-ti-lô-), *n.*, antilope, *f.*

antemerid'ian (-ti-mé-), *adj.*, avant midi.

antemun'dane (-ti-meu-n'déne), *adj.*, antérieur à la création.

anten'na (-tèn-na), *n.*, (*antennæ*) antenne, *f.*

an'tenumber (-ti-neu-m'beur), *n.*, nombre antécédent, *m.*

antenup'tial (-ti-neup-shial), *adj.*, d'avant le mariage.

antepas'chal (-ti-pâs-kal), *adj.*, d'avant Pâques.

antepenult' (-ti-pi-neulte) *ou* **antepenult'ima** (-ti-pi-neul-), *n.*, antépénultième, *f.*

antepenult'imate (-méte), *n.* and *adj.*, antépénultième, *f.*

ante-posi'tion (a'n-ti-), *n.*, (gram.) inversion, *f.*

ante'rior (-ti-rieur), *adj.*, antérieur.

anterior'ity, *n.*, antériorité, *f.*

an'te-room (-ti-roume), *n.*, antichambre, *f. ;* vestibule, *m.*

an'te-saloon (-ti-sa-loune), *n.*, antichambre de salon, *f.*

an'them (-thème), *n.*, antienne, hymne, *f. ;* chant, *m.*

an'ther (-theur), *n.*, (bot.) anthère, *f.*

antholog'ical (-tho-lod'ji-), *adj.*, d'anthologie.

anthol'ogy (-tho-lod'ji), *n.*, anthologie, chrestomathie, *f.*

An'thony's fire (-thôniz' faïeur), *n.*, (med.) feu Saint Antoine (l.u.), érésipèle, *m.*

an'thracite (-thra-), *n.*, (min.) anthracite, *m.*

an'thrax (-thrakse), *n.*, (med.) anthrax, charbon, *m.*

anthropolog'ical (-thro-po-lod'ji-), *adj.*, anthropologique.

anthropol'ogist, *n.*, anthropologiste, *m.*

anthropol'ogy, *n.*, anthropologie, *f.*

anthropomor'phism (-thrô-pô-), *n.*, anthropomorphisme, *m.*

anthropomor'phous (-feusse), *adj.*, anthropomorphe.

anthropoph'agous (-gheusse), *adj.*, anthropophage.

anthropoph'agus (-gheusse), *n.*, (*anthropophagi*) anthropophage, *m.f.*

anthropoph'agy, *n.*, anthropophagie, *f.*

an'tic, *n.*, bouffon, *m. ;* bouffonnerie, *f. ;* mouvement grotesque, *m. ;* farce, cabriole, *f.*

an'tic, *adj.*, grotesque, étrange, drôle.

an'tichrist, *n.*, antéchrist, *m.*

antichris'tian, *adj.* and *n.*, antichrétien.

antichristian'ity, *n.*, antichristianisme, *m.*

antic'ipate (-péte), *v.a.*, anticiper, prévenir; s'attendre à ; devancer; se proposer **de**, jouir d'avance **de** ; compter **sur** ; se promettre.

antic'ipated, *adj.*, prématuré, anticipé.

anticipa'tion, *n.*, anticipation, attente, espérance, *f. ;* avant-goût, *m.* By —; *d'avance, par anticipation.*

antic'ipatory, *adj.*, par anticipation.

anti-cli'max (-claï-), *n.*, (rhet.) gradation renversée, *f.*

anti-constitu'tional (-sti-tiou-), *adj.*, anti-constitutionnel.

anti-convuls'ive (-veul-), *adj.*, anticonvulsif.

anti-corro'sive, *n.* and *adj.*, anticorrosif.

anti-democrat'ic *ou* **anti-democrat'ical** (-mô-), *adj.*, contraire à la démocratie.

an'tidotal (-dô-), *adj.*, qui sert d'antidote,

an'tidote (-dôte), n., antidote, contre-poison, m.

an'tidote, v.a., (ant.) fournir des antidotes.

antidot'ically, adv., comme antidote.

anti-epis'copal, adj., opposé à l'épiscopat, contre l'épiscopat.

anti-evangel'ical (-i-va-n'd'jè-), adj., anti-évangélique.

anti-feb'rile, adj., antifébrile, fébrifuge.

anti-feb'rile, n., fébrifuge, m.

antil'ogy (-lod'ji), n., (ant.) antilogie, f.

antimacas'sar, n., têtière, f.; dessus de fauteuil, m.

anti-ministe'rial (-nis-tî-), adj., opposé au ministère.

anti-ministe'rialist, n., antiministériel, m.

anti-monarch'ic ou anti-monarch'ical (-kik, -kikal), adj., antimonarchique.

antimo'nial (-mô-), adj., antimonial. — wine; vin émétique, m.

an'timony, n., antimoine, m.

antin'omy, n., antinomie, f.

anti-pa'pal (-pé-), adj., opposé au papisme.

anti-pathet'ic ou anti-pathet'ical (-thè-), adj., antipathique.

anti-pathet'ically, adv., par antipathie.

antip'athy (-thi), n., antipathie, f.

anti-patriot'ic (-pé-), adj., anti-patriotique.

anti-pestilen'tial, adj., antipestilentiel.

anti-philosoph'ical, adj., antiphilosophique.

antiph'ony (-fo-), n., contre-chant, m.

antiph'rasis (-cisse), n., antiphrase, f.

antip'odal (-po-), adj., des antipodes.

an'tipode (-pôde), n., antipode, m.

an'ti-pope (-pôpe), n., antipape, m.

antiqua'rian (-kwé-), adj., d'antiquaire, antique.

antiqua'rian (-kwé-) ou an'tiquary (-kwa-), n., antiquaire, m.

an'tiquate (-kwéte), v.a., faire tomber en désuétude; (jur.) abroger.

an'tiquated, adj., vieilli, antique; suranné; (out of fashion) démodé.

antique', n., antique, m.; antiquité; (print.) normande, f.

antique', adj., ancien, antique.

antique'ness, n., ancienneté, antiquité, f.

antiq'uity (-kwi-), n., antiquité, f.

anti-revolu'tionary (-vo-liou-), adj., anti-révolutionnaire.

anti-revolu'tionist, n., antirévolutionnaire, m.

anti-rheumat'ic, adj., anti-rhumatismal.

antiscorbu'tic ou antiscorbu'tical (-biou-), adj., antiscorbutique.

antiscorbu'tic, n., (med.) antiscorbutique, m.

antisep'tic, adj., (med.) antiseptique.

antisep'tic, n., antiseptique, m.

anti-so'cial (-sô-shial), adj., antisocial.

antispasmod'ic, adj., antispasmodique.

antispasmod'ic, n., antispasmodique, m.

antis'trophe (-fî), n., antistrophe, f.

antisyphilit'ic, adj., antisyphilitique.

antith'esis (-thè-cisse), n., antithèse, f.

antithet'ic ou antithet'ical (-thè-), adj., antithétique.

an'titype (-taïpe), n., antitype, m.

anti-vene'real (-vè-ni-ri-), adj., antivénérien.

ant'ler, n., andouiller, m.

ant'lered (-leurde), adj., à andouillers.

antonoma'sia (-mé-jia), n., (rhet.) antonomase, f.

an'tonym, n., (gram.) antonyme, contraire, m.

anton'ymous, adj., antonyme.

anton'ymy, n., antonymie, f.

an'tre (-teur), n., (ant.) antre, m.; caverne, f.

a'nus (é-neusse), n., (anat.) anus, m.

an'vil, n., enclume, f.; (fig.) métier, m. Upon the —; sur le métier, en préparation.

an'vil-block, n., billot d'enclume, m.

anxi'ety (aign'-zaï-èti), n., anxiété, inquiétude, sollicitude, f.; empressement, m.

anx'ious (aignk-shi-eusse), adj., inquiet; désireux, curieux. To be — to; désirer vivement de, tenir à.

anx'iously, adv., avec inquiétude; avec sollicitude, avec impatience, avec anxiété.

anx'iousness, n., anxiété; inquiétude, sollicitude, f.; empressement, vif désir, m.

a'ny (è-ni), adj., quelque; tout; du, de la, de l', des; de; en, quelqu'un, aucun, n'importe lequel, le premier venu, qui que ce soit, (aff.) quelque part, (neg.) nulle-part. In — wise; de quelque manière que ce soit. — thing; quoi que ce soit. — one; qui que ce soit, quelqu'un. — man; tout homme. Have you — wine? avez-vous du vin? Have you —? en avez-vous? I do not know — of your judges; je ne connais aucun de vos juges. Scarcely —; presque pas. — further; plus loin. — where; dans quelque endroit que ce soit, n'importe où. — better; mieux. — more; plus, encore, davantage. I doubt that — of them; je doute qu'aucun d'entre eux (subj.). — body can do it; tout homme peut le faire ou n'importe qui peut le faire. — of them; aucun d'eux (neg.); quelqu'un d'entr'eux (aff.).

a'nyhow (-haou), adv., n'importe comment, de quelque manière que ce soit, de toute façon.

a'orist (ê-oriste), n., (gram.) aoriste, m.

aor'ta (é-or-), n., (anat.) aorte, f.

aor'tal ou aor'tic, adj., aortique.

apace' (-péce), adv., vite; à grands pas.

apart' (-pârte), adv., à part, de côté, en dehors.

apart'ment (-pârt'), n., chambre; pièce (d'un appartement), f.; logement, m. A suite of —s; un appartement, m.

apathet'ic (-thè-), adj., apathique.

ap'athy (-thi), n., apathie, f.

ape (épe), n., singe, m.

ape, v.a., singer.

apeak' (-pîke), adv., (nav.) à pic, en pantenne.

ap'ennine (-pèn-naïne), adj., des Apennins.

ape'rient (-pi-), n. and adj., laxatif, m.

aper'itive (-pé-), adj., laxatif.

ap'erture (-pœr-tioure), n., ouverture, f.; orifice, m.

a'pery, n., singerie, f.

apet'alous (-pè-ta-leusse), adj., (bot.) apétale.

a'pex (é-peks), n., (apices, apexes) sommet; cimier (of a helmet), m.

aphæ'resis ou aphe'resis (-fî-ri-cisse), n., (gram.) aphérèse, f.

aphe'lion (-fî-), n., aphélie, m.

apho'nia or aph'ony (-fô-), n., aphonie, f.

aph'orism, n., aphorisme, m.

aphoris'tic ou aphoris'tical, adj., aphoristique.

aphoris'tically, adv., par aphorisme.

aphrodis'iac ou aphrodis'iacal, adj., aphrodisiaque.

aphrodis'iac, n., aphrodisiaque, m.

aphrodi'ta ou aphrodi'te (-daï-ta, -daï-tî), n., magnésite, (pop.) écume de mer, f.

aph'yllous (-fil-leusse), adj., aphylle.

a'piary (é-pi-), n., rucher, m.

apiece' (-péce), adv., la pièce; chacun, (pers.) par tête, par personne.

a'pish (é-), adj., badin, bouffon; de singe. — trick; singerie, f.

a'pishly, adv., en singe, en badin.

a'pishness, n., bouffonnerie, singerie, sottise, f.

apit'pat, adv. V. pitapat.

apoc'alypse, n., apocalypse, f.

apocalyp'tic ou apocalyp'tical, adj., apocalyptique.

apocalyp'tically, adv., d'une manière apocalyptique.

apoc'ope (-pi), n., (gram.) apocope, f.

apoc'rypha, n., les apocryphes, les livres apocryphes, m.pl.

apoc'ryphal, adj., apocryphe.

apoc'ynum (-neume), *n.*, (bot.) apocyn, *m.*

ap'odal, *adj.*, (ich.) apode.

ap'ode (-pôde), *n.* (*apodes, apoda*), (zoöl.) apode, *m.*

ap'ogee (-pod'ji), *n.*, apogée, *m.*

apologet'ic *ou* apologet'ical (-lod'jè-), *adj.*, apologétique.

apologet'ically, *adv.*, en forme d'apologie.

apol'ogist (-lod'jiste), *n.*, apologiste, *m.*

apol'ogize (-lod'jaïze), *v.n.*, faire une apologie ; s'excuser auprès de, faire des excuses à, demander pardon. To — for any one ; *faire des excuses pour quelqu'un ; excuser une personne auprès d'une autre.*

ap'ologue, *n.*, apologue, *m.*

apol'ogy (-lod'ji), *n.*, apologie ; excuse, *f.* To make an — for ; *faire des excuses, s'excuser de.*

aponeuro'sis (-niou-rô-cisse), *n.*, (anat.) aponévrose, *f.*

ap'ophthegm (-po-thème), *n.* *V.* apothegm.

apoplec'tic *ou* apoplec'tical (-pô-plèk-), *adj.*, apoplectique.

ap'oplexy (-pô-), *n.*, apoplexie, *f.* To fall down in a fit of —; *tomber en apoplexie.* To be seized with —; *être frappé d'apoplexie.*

aport' (a-porte), *adv.*, (nav.) à bâbord.

apos'tasy (-ci), *n.*, apostasie, *f.*

apos'tate (-téte), *n.*, apostat, *m.*

apos'tate, *adj.*, apostat, d'apostat.

apostat'ical, *adj.*, apostat.

apos'tatize (-taïze), *v.n.*, apostasier, renier, abjurer.

ap'ostema *ou* ap'osteme (-sti-ma, -stîme), *n.*, abcès, ⊙apostème, ⊙apostume, *m.*

apostema'tion (-ti-mé-), *n.*, (med.) formation d'un ⊙apostème, d'un abcès, *f.*

apostem'atous (-tèm-ateusse), *adj.*, d'apostème, de la nature de ⊙l'apostème, de l'abcès.

a posterio'ri (-pôs-ti-riô-), *adv.*, à posteriori.

apos'tle (a-pos-s'l), *n.*, apôtre, *m.* The acts of the —s ; *les actes des apôtres, m.pl.*

apos'tleship, *n.*, apostolat, *m.*

apostol'ic *ou* apostol'ical, *adj.*, apostolique. — creed ; *symbole des apôtres, m.*

apostol'ically, *adv.*, apostoliquement.

apostol'icalness, *n.*, caractère apostolique, *m.*

apos'trophe (-fi), *n.*, apostrophe, *f.*

apos'trophize (-faïze), *v.a.*, apostropher ; mettre une apostrophe.

apoth'ecary (-po-thi-), *n.*, (ant.) apothicaire ; médecin, *m.*

ap'othegm *ou* ap'othem (-thème), *n.*, apophtegme, *m.*

apothegmat'ical, *adj.*, en forme d'apophtegme.

apotheg'matize (-thèg-ma-taïze), *v.n.*, parler par apophtegmes.

apotheo'sis (-thî-o-cisse), *n.*, apothéose, *f.*

ap'ozem (-zème), *n.*, apozème, *m.*

apozem'ical, *adj.*, d'apozème.

appall', *v.a.*, épouvanter, terrifier, consterner.

appal'ling, *adj.*, effrayant, épouvantable, terrifiant.

appall'ment, *n.*, (ant.) frayeur, épouvante, terreur, *f.*

ap'panage (-nèd'je), *n.*, apanage, *m.*

appara'tus (-ré-teusse), *n.*, appareil, attirail, *m.*

appar'el, *v.a.*, vêtir, parer ; (nav.) équiper.

appar'el, *n.*, habit, vêtement ; habillement, appareil ; (nav.) équipement, *m.* Wearing —; *habits, m.pl., hardes, f.pl.*

appa'rent (-pé-), *adj.*, apparent, évident, clair, manifeste. Heir —; *héritier présomptif, m.*

appa'rently, *adv.*, évidemment, en apparence, apparemment.

appari'tion, *n.*, apparition, *f.*

appar'itor (-teur), *n.*, apparitour, *m.*

appeach', *v.a.*, (ant.) *V.* impeach.

appeal' (-pîle), *v.a.*, porter à un tribunal supérieur.

appeal', *v.n.*, (jur.) appeler, en appeler à ; (fig.) s'adresser à ; supplier ; (jur.) se pourvoir en cassation, (for a reprieve) se pourvoir en grâce.

appeal', *n.*, appel, *m.* Court of —; *cour d'appel, cour de cassation, f.* To lodge an —; *interjeter appel.* Without —; *en dernier ressort.*

appeal'able, *adj.*, sujet à appel.

appeal'ant, *n.*, (ant.) (jur.) appelant, *m.*

appear' (ap-pîre), *v.n.*, paraître ; apparaître à ; se montrer à, comparaître devant, se présenter à. It would —; *il paraîtrait.* To — against any one ; (jur.) *se présenter contre quelqu'un ; se porter partie contre quelqu'un.* To — for ; *représenter, répondre pour.* To make —; *faire paraître, prouver, démontrer.*

appear'ance, *n.*, apparition, apparence, figure, *f.* ; air, aspect, extérieur, *m.* ; (persp.) perspective ; (jur.) comparution, *f.* At first —; *au premier abord, au premier coup d'œil.* To save —s ; *sauver les apparences.* For the sake of —; *pour sauver les apparences.* There is every —; *il y a toute apparence.* To all —s ; *selon toute apparence.* To judge by —s ; *à en juger d'après les apparences ; juger sur la mine.* To make one's —; *faire son apparition ; faire son entrée, arriver, venir ;* (jur.) *comparaître.* To make one's first —; (thea.) *faire son début, débuter.* To make one's last —; *paraître pour la dernière fois.* To put in an —; *faire acte de présence ;* (jur.) *faire acte de comparution.*

appear'er, *n.*, (jur.) comparant.

appeas'able (ap-pîzab'l), *adj.*, apaisable, qu'on peut apaiser.

appease' (ap-pîze), *v.a.*, apaiser, calmer ; pacifier.

appease'ment, *n.*, apaisement, *m.*

appeas'er, *n.*, pacificateur, *m.*

appeas'ing, *adj.*, qui apaise.

appel'lant (ap-pèl-la'nte), *n.*, (jur.) appelant ; (dueling) provocateur, *m.*

appel'lant, *adj.*, appelant ; en appel.

appel'late (ap-pèl-léte), *adj.*, d'appel.

appel'late, *n.*, (ant.) intimé ; accusé, *m.*

appella'tion (ap-pèl-lé-) *n.*, nom, *m.* ; qualification, appellation, dénomination, *f.*

appel'lative, *adj.*, appellatif.

appel'latory, *adj.*, d'appel.

appellee' (ap-pèl-li), *n.*, (jur.) intimé, *m.*, intimée, *f.*

appellor' (ap-pèl-lor), *n.*, (jur.) appelant, *m.*, appelante, *f.*

append' (ap-pè-n-d), *v.a.*, apposer, annexer, attacher.

append'age (ap-pé-n-dèd'je), *n.*, accessoire, appendice, apanage, *m.*

append'ant, *adj.*, dépendant de, accessoire à, attaché à, annexé à.

appendic'ular, *adj.*, appendiculaire.

append'ix (*appendices, appendixes*), *n.*, appendice, *m.*

appercep'tion (ap-peur-cèp-), *n.*, (philos.) perception, *f.*

appertain' (ap-peur-téne), *v.n.*, appartenir à.

apper'tenance (ap-peur-te-), *n.*, appartenance, *f.*

ap'petence (ap-pi-tè-n-se) *ou* ap'petency (ap-pi-tè-n-ci), *n.*, appétence, envie, *f.*, désir, *m.*

ap'petent (ap-pi-tè-n-te), *adj.*, avide de.

appetibil'ity (ap-pi-), *n.*, (ant.) appétibilité, *f.*

appet'ible, *adj.*, (ant.) désirable, appétible.

ap'petite (ap-pi-taïte), *n.*, appétit ; (fig.) penchant, *m.*, soif, *f.* A good — to you ; *bon appétit.* Ravenous —; *appétit de cheval.* To get an —; *gagner de l'appétit.* To have an —; *avoir de l'appétit.* To have a good —; *avoir bon appétit.* To give an —; *donner de l'appétit.*

ap'petize, *v.a.*, mettre en appétit.

ap'petizer (ap-pi-taïzeur), *n.*, apéritif, *m.*

ap'petizing, *adj.*, appétissant.

Ap'pian, *adj.* The — Way ; *la voie appienne.*

applaud' (ap-plō-de), *v.a.*, applaudir (quelqu'un), applaudir **à** (quelque chose).

applaud'er, *n.*, applaudisseur, *m.*

applause', *n.*, applaudissement, *m.*, applaudissements, *m.pl.*

ap'ple (ap-p'l), *n.*, pomme, *f.* Apple of the eye ; *pupille, prunelle, f.* Crab— ; *pomme sauvage.* Pine— ; *ananas, m.* Oak— ; *noix de galle, f.* — of love, love— ; *pomme d'amour, tomate, f.* Fir— ; *pomme de pin.* Baking — ; *pomme à cuire.* Adam's — ; *pomme d'Adam, f.; citron, m.*

ap'ple-core, *n.*, trognon de pomme, *m.*

ap'ple-fritter, *n.*, beignet de pommes, *m.*

ap'ple-green, *n.adj.*, vert pomme, *m.*

ap'ple-grove (-grōve), *n.*, pommeraie, *f.*

ap'ple-harvest, *n.*, cueillette de pommes, *f.*

ap'ple-jelly, *n.*, gelée de pommes, *f.*

ap'ple-loft, *n.*, fruiterie, *f.*

ap'ple-peel (-pîle), *n.*, pelure de pomme, *f.*

ap'ple-puff (-peuf), *n.*, (cook.) chausson, beignet de pommes, *m.*

ap'ple-sauce (-sô-ce), *n.*, compote de pommes, *f.*

ap'ple-shaped, *adj.*, en forme de pomme.

ap'ple-tree (-trî), *n.*, pommier, *m.*

ap'ple-woman (-wou-ma-ne), *n.*, marchande de pommes, *f.*

appli'ance (ap-pla'ya-n-ce), *n.*, action, condition, *f.;* moyen ; remède, ustensile, instrument, appareil, *m. ;* machine, *f. ;* agencement, *m.*

applicabil'ity (ap-pli-), *n.*, applicabilité, *f.*

ap'plicable (ap-pli-ca-b'l), *adj.*, applicable **à**.

ap'plicableness, *n.* *V.* **applicability**.

ap'plicably, *adv.*, de manière à pouvoir être appliqué.

ap'plicant, *n.*, postulant ; candidat, pétitionnaire ; (jur.) demandeur, *m. ;* postulante ; (jur.) demanderesse, *f.*

ap'plicate (ap-pli-kéte), *adj.*, (math.) concret, nombré.

applica'tion (ap-pli-ké-), *n.*, application, *f. ;* usage, emploi, *m. ;* sollicitation, demande, *f.* To make — to ; *s'adresser* **à**, *faire une demande* **à**.

applique'-lace, *n.*, application.

apply' (ap-pla'ye), *v.a.*, appliquer **à** ; adresser **à** ; porter ; (arith.) diviser. To — the brake ; *serrer le frein.* To — for a situation ; *solliciter un poste.*

apply', *v.n.*, s'appliquer **à**, s'adresser **à**, s'attacher **à** ; se mettre **à**. — to ; (imperative mood) *s'adresser* **à** ou **chez**.

appoint' (ap-poï-nte), *v.a.*, nommer ; établir ; arrêter, désigner, fixer, indiquer ; ordonner **à**, meubler, garnir, équiper.

appoint', *v.n.*, arrêter, décréter.

appoint', *n.*, (com.) appoint.

appoint'able, *adj.*, qui peut être nommé.

appoint'ed (-tède), *part.*, nommé, établi, arrêté, désigné, fixé, indiqué ; fourni (of troops).

appointee' (-tî), *n.*, fonctionnaire nommé, *m.*

appoint'er (-teur), *n.*, nominateur, -trice.

appoint'ment, *n.*, rendez-vous ; ordre, équipement ; traitement, *m.*, appointments, *m.pl. ;* décret, arrêt ; établissement ; emploi, *m.*, charge ; nomination, *f.* To make an — with any one ; *donner un rendez-vous à quelqu'un ; prendre rendez-vous* **avec**. To — by ; (*fournisseur*) breveté.

appor'tion (ap-pôr-), *v.a.*, proportionner, partager, répartir, assigner.

appor'tioner (-eur), *n.*, répartiteur, *m.*

appor'tionment, *n.*, répartition, distribution, *f.*, partage, *m.*

appose', *v.a.*, apposer.

ap'posite, *adj.*, à propos ; applicable **à** ; convenable **à**, bien placé ; approprié **à**.

ap'positely, *adv.*, convenablement, justement, à propos.

ap'positeness, *n.*, convenance ; justesse, applicabilité, *f.*, à-propos, *m.*

apposi'tion, *n.*, apposition, *f.*

apprais'able, *adj.*, évaluable.

appraise' (ap-préze), *v.a.*, priser, évaluer, estimer, expertiser.

apprise'ment, *n.*, prisée (at auctions); évaluation, estimation, expertise, *f.*

apprais'er (-zeur), *n.*, estimateur, commissaire-priseur, expert, *m.*

appre'ciable (ap-prî-shiab'l), *adj.*, appréciable.

appre'ciate (ap-pri-shiéte), *v.n.*, apprécier, estimer.

apprecia'tion (ap-pri-shié-), *n.*, appréciation, *f.*

appre'ciative, *adj.*, appréciatif.

apprehend' (ap-pri-hè-nde), *v.a.*, prendre, saisir, arrêter, appréhender au corps; embrasser; comprendre ; présumer ; croire.

apprehend'er, *n.*, personne qui arrête, *f.*

apprehen'sible, *adj.*, appréhensible ; concevable.

apprehen'sion (ap-pri-hè-n-), *n.*, appréhension ; conception ; arrestation, prise de corps ; crainte, inquiétude, *f.* To be dull of — ; *avoir l'esprit lourd.*

apprehen'sive, *adj.*, intelligent, prompt à saisir ; appréhensif, inquiet, alarmé. To be — of ; *appréhender.*

apprehen'sively, *adv.*, avec intelligence; avec crainte.

appren'tice (ap-prè-n-), *n.*, apprenti ; (of lawyers) clerc ; (of medical men) élève ; (nav.) novice, *m.* To place as — to ; *mettre en apprentissage* **chez**.

appren'tice, *v.a.*, mettre en apprentissage.

appren'ticeship, *n.*, apprentissage, *m.*

apprise' (ap-praîze), *v.a.*, apprendre, informer, instruire, donner avis **à** ; prévenir.

approach' (ap-prôt-she), *n.*, approche, *f.;* abord, accès ; pas ; rapprochement, *m. ;* (math.) approximation, *f.* On his —, on her — ; *à son approche.* An — towards ; *un pas* **vers** ; *un rapprochement* **vers**. To be easy of — ; *être d'un accès*, ou *d'un abord*, *facile.* To make —es; *faire des avances* **à**.

approach', *v.a.*, approcher **de**, s'approcher **de** aborder.

approach', *v.n.*, approcher, s'approcher.

approach'able, *adj.*, abordable, accessible.

approach'ing, *adj.*, dont on s'approche; approchant ; prochain.

approach'ing, *n.*, (hort.) greffe par approche, *f.*

approach'ment, *n.*, (ant.) approche, *f.*

approba'tion (ap-prô-bé-), *n.*, approbation, *f.* On — ; *à condition.*

ap'probatory, *adj.*, approbateur.

appro'priate (ap-prô-pri-éte), *adj.*, approprié **à**, propre **à**, convenable **à** ; affecté **à** ; à propos ; juste.

appro'priate, *v.a.*, approprier **à** ; s'approprier ; destiner **à**, réserver **à**, affecter **à**.

appro'priately, *adv.*, à juste titre ; proprement ; convenablement ; à l'avenant **de**.

appro'priateness, *n.*, convenance, *f.*, à-propos, *m. ;* justesse, *f.*

appropria'tion (ap-prô-prié-), *n.*, application, destination ; appropriation ; (jur.) propriété, *f. ;* emploi, *m.*

appro'priator (ap-prô-pri-é-teur), *n.*, bénéficier, *m. ;* qui approprie.

appro'vable (ap-prou-vab'l), *adj.*, digne d'approbation ; estimable, approuvable.

appro'val, *n.*, approbation, *f.* On — ; *à condition.*

approve' (ap-prouve), *v.a.*, approuver, confirmer, recommander. To — of ; *approuver*: *être content* **de**. To — one's self ; *se montrer.*

approved' (ap-prouv'de), *adj.*, approuvé, recommandé, confirmé.

appro'ver (ap-prou-veur), *n.*, approbateur, *m.*, approbatrice, *f. ;* (jur.) (ant.) révélateur de complices, *m.*

appro'ving (ap-prou-vigne), *adj.*, approbateur, approbatif.

appro'vingly, *adv.*, avec approbation.

approx'imate (ap-prok-si-méte), *v.a.*, rapprocher **de**.

approx'imate, *v.n.*, se rapprocher **de**; approcher **de**.

approx'imate, *adj.*, approximatif.

approxima'tion (ap-prok-si-mé-), *n.*, approximation, *f. ;* rapprochement, *m.*

approx'imative, *adj.*, approximatif.

approx'imatively, *adv.*, approximativement.

appulse' (ap-peulse), *n.*, choc, *m. ;* (astron.) rencontre, approche, *f.*

appur'tenance (ap-peur-te-), *n.*, appartenance, dépendance, *f.*

appur'tenant, *adj.*, appartenant **à**, dépendant **de**.

ap'ricot (-cote), *n.*, abricot, *m.* — tree ; *abricotier, m.*

A'pril (é-pril), *n.*, Avril, *m.* — shower ; *giboulée de mars, f.*

A'pril-fool (-foule), *n.*, qui a reçu un poisson d'avril, *f.* To be made an —; *recevoir un poisson d'avril.* To make an —; *donner un poisson d'avril* **à**.

a'pron (é-preune *ou* -peurne), *n.*, tablier ; (artil.) couvre-lumière ; (nav.) éperon, *m. ;* contre-étrave, *f.* An — full; *plein son tablier.* Tied to the — strings of; *sous la domination* **de**.

a'proned, *adj.*, portant tablier.

apse *or* **apsis,** *n.*, (arch., rel.) abside, *f. ;* chevet, *m.;* (astron.) apside, *f.*

apt, *adj.*, sujet **à** ; enclin **à** ; porté **à** ; propre **à**, convenable **à**. To be — to; *être porté* **à**, *être disposé* **à**.

Ap'tera (-teu-) *ou* **ap'terans** (-teura'n'ze), *n.pl.*, (ent.) aptères, *m.pl.*

ap'terous (ap-teureusse), *adj.*, aptère.

apt'itude (-tioude), *n.*, aptitude, disposition, *f.;* penchant, *m.*

apt'ly, *adv.*, à propos ; justement, convenablement.

apt'ness (-nèsse), *n.*, disposition, convenance, aptitude ; propriété, tendance, *f.*

ap'yrous (a-païreusse), *adj.*, apyre, infusible.

a'qua (é-kwa), *n.*, eau, *f.*

a'qua-for'tis (é-kwa-), *n.*, eau-forte, *f.*

a'qua-mari'na (é-kwa-), *n.*, aigue-marine, *f.*

a'qua-re'gia (é-kwa-rid'jia), *n.*, eau régale, *f.*

aquarelle', *n.*, aquarelle, *f.*

aqua'rium (-rieume), *n.*, aquarium, *m.*

Aqua'rius (-rieusse), *n.*, (astron.) Verseau.

aquat'ic *ou* **aquat'ical,** *adj.*, aquatique.

aquat'ic, *n.*, plante aquatique, *f.*

a'qua-tint (é-kwa-ti-n-te) *ou* **a'qua-tint'a** (é-kwa-ti-n-ta), *n.*, (engr.) aquatinte, *f.*

a'qua-vi'tæ (é-kwa-vaïti), *n.*, eau de vie, *f.*

aq'ueduct (a-kwi-deuct), *n.*, aqueduc, *m.*

a'queous (é-kwi-eusse), *adj.*, aqueux.

a'queousness, *n.*, aquosité, *f.*

aq'uiline (a-kwi-laïne), *adj.*, aquilin, d'aigle.

Aq'uilon (a-kwi-lone), *n.*, aquilon, *m.*

aquos'ity (a-kwociti), *n.*, aquosité, *f.*

Ar'ab, *n.*, Arabe, *m.f.* *adj.*, arabe.

ar'abesque, *adj.*, arabesque.

ar'abesque, *n.*, arabesque, *f.*

Ara'bian (a-ré-bia-n), *n.*, Arabe, *m.f.*

Ara'bian, *adj.*, arabe ; (geog.) arabique. — bedstead; *lit à baldaquin.*

ar'abic, *adj.*, arabe, arabique. Gum —; *gomme arabique.*

Ar'abic, *n.*, arabe (language), *m.*

ar'able, *adj.*, arable, labourable.

arach'noid (-rak-noïde), *n.*, arachnoïde, *f.*

ara'neous (-ré-ni-eusse) *ou* **ara'neose** (-ré-ni-ôss), *adj.*, d'araignée.

ar'balist (âr-), *n.*, arbalète, *f.*

ar'biter (âr-), *n.*, arbitre, *m.*

arbit'rament (âr-), *n.*, arbitrage, jugement, compromis, *m. ;* décision, *f.*

ar'bitrarily, *adv.*, arbitrairement.

ar'bitrariness (-nèsse), *n.*, arbitraire, *m.*

ar'bitrary, *adj.*, arbitraire.

ar'bitrate (âr-bi-tréte), *v.a.*, arbitrer, décider.

ar'bitrate, *v.n.*, arbitrer, décider, prononcer.

arbitra'tion (âr-bi-tré-), *n.*, arbitrage, *m. ;* décision, *f.* By —; *par arbitrage; arbitralement.*

arbitra'tion-bond (-bo-n'd), *n.*, (jur.) compromis, *m.*

ar'bitrator (âr-bi-tré-teur), *n.*, arbitre, *m.*

arbit'rement (âr-bi-tri-), *n.*, (ant.) décision, *f. ;* jugement, compromis; (philos.) arbitre, *m.*

ar'bitress (âr-bi-trèsse), *n.*, arbitre, *f.*

ar'bor, *n.*, (bot., tech.) arbre, *m.* — vitæ; *thuia ou thuya, m.*

arbo'reous (âr-bô-ri-eusse) *ou* **ar'borous** (âr-bo-reusse), *adj.*, d'arbre ; (bot.) arborescent.

arbores'cence, *n.*, arborescence, *f.*

arbores'cent (âr-bo-rès-sè-nte), *adj.*, arborescent.

arboricul'ture (âr-bo-ri-keul-tioure), *n.*, arboriculture, culture des arbres, *f.*

ar'boriform, *adj.*, arboriforme.

ar'borist, *n.*, arboriste, *m.*

ar'borize (âr-bo-raïze), *v.a.*, arboriser (l.u.).

ar'bor (âr-beur), *n.*, berceau, *m. ;* tonnelle, *f.*

ar'bute (âr-bioute) *ou* **arbu'tus** (âr-biou-teusse), *n.*, (bot.) arbousier, *m.*

arbu'tean (âr-biou-ti-a'n), *adj.*, (bot.) d'arbousier.

ar'bute-berry, *n.*, (bot.) arbouse, *f.*

arc, *n.*, arc, *m.*

arcade' (âr-kéde), *n.*, arcade, galerie, *f. ;* passage, *m.*

arca'dian (âr-ké-di-a'n), *adj.*, arcadien.

arca'num (âr-ké-neume), *n.*, arcane, secret, mystère, *m.*

arc-boutant', *n.*, arc-boutant, *m.*

arch (ârt'she), *n.*, arche, *f. ;* arc, cintre, *m. ;* voûte, *f.* Triumphal —; *arc de triomphe.*

arch, *v.a.*, voûter ; cintrer ; arquer, courber.

arch, *adj.*, fin ; malin ; grand, insigne, fieffé.

archæolog'ic (âr-ki-olod'jik), *adj.*, archéologique.

archæol'ogy (âr-ki-olod'ji) *ou* **archaiol'ogy** (âr-ké-), *n.*, archéologie, *f.*

arch'aism (âr-ké-izme), *n.*, archaïsme, *m.*

archan'gel (âr-ké-nd'jèle), *n.*, archange, *m.*

archangel'ic, *adj.*, archangélique, de l'archange.

archbish'op (ârt'sh-bi-sheupe), *n.*, archevêque, *m.*

archbish'opric, *n.*, archevêché, *m.*

arch-but'tress, *n.*, arc-boutant, *m.*

archdea'con (ârt'sh-dîk'n), *n.*, archidiacre, *m.*

archdea'conry, *n.*, archidiaconat, *m.*

archduch'ess (ârt'sh-deut'shèsse), *n.*, archiduchesse, *f.*

archduch'y (-deutshi), *n.*, archiduché, *m.*

archduke' (-diouke), *n.*, archiduc, *m.*

archduke'dom, *n.*, archiduché, *m.*

arched (ârt'shte), *adj.*, voûté, cintré ; arqué.

arch'er (ârt'sh'eur), *n.*, archer ; (astron.) Sagittaire, *m.*

arch'ery, *n.*, tir à l'arc, *m.*

arch'es-court (ârt'shèze-côrte), *n.*, cour des arches, *f.*

arch'etypal (âr-ki-taï-pal), *adj.*, archétype.

arch'etype (âr-ki-taïpe), *n.*, archétype ; (coin) étalon, *m.*

arch-fiend' (ârt'sh-ffn'de), *n.*, démon, *m.*

arch-foe' (-fô), *n.*, grand ennemi, ennemi juré, *m.*

arch-head' (art'sh-hède), *n.*, (arch.) tête de voûte, *f.*

arch-her'esy (ârt'sh-hè-ri-ci), *n.*, hérésie principale, *f.*

arch-her'etic (-hè-ri-), *n.*, grand hérétique, *m.*

arch-hyp'ocrite (-po-), *n.*, grand hypocrite, *m.*

arch'ical (âr-ki-), *adj.*, principal.

archidiac'onal (âr-ki-di-ako-), *adj.*, d'archidiacre.

archiepis'copacy (âr-ki-i-pis-ko-), *n.*, archiépiscopacy.

archiepis'copal, *adj.*, archiépiscopal.

arch'ing (ârt'shigne), *n.*, arche, voûte, *f.*

archipel'ago (âr-ki-), *n.*, archipel, *m.*

arch'itect (âr-ki-), *n.*, architecte; (fig.) artisan, *m.*

architecton'ic, *adj.*, architectonique.

architect'ural (-tiou-), *adj.*, architectural.

arch'itecture (âr-ki-tèk-tioure), *n.*, architecture, *f.*

arch'itrave (âr-ki-tréve), *n.*, architrave, *f.*

arch'ival (-kaï-), *adj.*, d'archives, des archives.

arch'ivault (-ki-vôlte) *ou* **archivolt** (-ki-volte), *n.*, (arch.) archivolte, *f.*

ar'chives (-kaïv'ze), *n.pl.*, archives, *f.pl.*

ar'chivist (-kiviste), *n.*, archiviste, *m.*

arch'like (ârt'sh-laïke), *adj.*, en forme d'arche, en voûte; voûté.

arch'lute (ârt'sh-lioute), *n.*, téorbe, théorbe, tuorbe, *m.*

arch'ly (ârt'shli), *adv.*, avec malice, malicieusement, d'un air malin, avec espièglerie.

arch'ness (art'shnèsse), *n.*, malice, espièglerie, *f.*

arch'on (âr-ko'n), *n.*, archonte, *m.*

arch-priest' (ârt'sh-prïste), *n.*, archiprêtre, *m.*

arch-pri'mate (-praï-méte), *n.*, grand primat, *m.*

arch-pro'phet, *n.*, grand prophète, *m.*

arch'-stone (-stône), *n.*, (arch.) voussoir, *m.*; clé de voûte, *f.*

arch-trai'tor (-teur), *n.*, traître insigne, *m.*

arch-vil'lain (-vil-la-n), *n.*, grand misérable, *m.*

arch-vil'lainy, *n.*, profonde scélératesse, *f.*

arch'way, *n.*, passage (sous une voûte); portail; arceau, *m.*; voûte, *f.*

arch'wise (ârt'shwaïze), *adv.*, en forme de voûte, en forme d'arche.

arch'-work, *n.*, arcature, *f.*

arc'tic (ârk-tike), *adj.*, arctique.

arc'uate (âr-kiou-éte), *adj.*, en forme d'arc.

ar'dency, *n.*, ardeur, *f.*

ar'dent, *adj.*, ardent, brûlant. — spirits; *spiritueux, m.pl.*

ar'dently, *adv.*, ardemment, avec ardeur.

ar'dor (-deur), *n.*, ardeur, *f.*

ard'uous (-diou-eusse), *adj.*, ardu, rude, pénible, difficile.

ard'uously, *adv.*, difficilement, péniblement.

ard'uousness, *n.*, difficulté, *f.*

a'rea (é-ri-a), *n.*, aire, étendue, enceinte, *f.*; (of halls) pourtour; surface, superficie, arène; (of a house) avant-cour; sous-sol; (of churches) parvis, *m.* — steps; *escalier de service, m.*

a'real (é-ri-al), *adj.*, de superficie.

are'ca, *n.*, arec, *m.* — nut; *noix d'arec, f.*

arefac'tion (ar-i-), *n.*, aréfaction, *f.*

ar'efy (-ri-faïe), *v.a.*, dessécher.

are'na (-rî-), *n.*, arène; (med.) gravelle, *f.*

arena'ceous (-ri-né-shi-eusse), *adj.*, arénacé.

arena'tion (-ri-né-), *n.*, arénation, *f.*

arenose' (-ri-nôss), *adj.*, aréneux, sabionneux.

are'ola (-ri-ô-), **ar'eole** (-ri-ôle), *n.*, (anat. med.) aréole, *f.*

are'olar, *adj.*, aréolaire.

areom'eter (-ri-o'mi-teur), *n.*, aréomètre, *m.*

areom'etry, *n.*, art de mesurer la gravité spécifique des fluides, *m.*; aréométrie, *f.*

Areop'agite (-ri-op-a'jaïte), *n.*, aréopagite, *m.*

Areop'agus (-ri-o-pa-gheusse), *n.*, aréopage, *m.*

a'reostyle (-ri-ostaïle), *n.*, aréostyle, *m.*

ar'gal, *n.*, tartre brut, *m.*

ar'gemone (ard'ji-mô-ni), *n.*, (bot.) argémone, *f.*, pavot épineux, *m.*

ar'gent (ard'j'è-n'te), *adj.*, d'argent, argenté.

ar'gent, *n.*, (her.) argent, *m.*

argent'al, *adj.*, d'argent.

ar'gentate (-téte), *n.*, (chem.) fulminate d'argent, *m.*

argenta'tion (-té-), *n.*, argenture, *f.*

argentif'erous (-ti-feureusse), *adj.*, argentifère.

ar'gentine (-taïne), *n.*, (bot., ich.) argentine, *f.*

ar'gentine, *adj.*, argentin.

ar'gil (ârd'jile), *n.*, argile, *f.*

ar'gil (ârd'jile), *n.*, (orni.) cigogne à sac, *f.*; marabout, *m.*

argilla'ceous (ârdjil-lé-shieusse), *adj.*, argilacé.

argillif'erous (ârd-jil-li-feu-reusse), *adj.*, argilifère.

ar'gonaut (-go-), *n.*, argonaute, *m.*

ar'gosy (-go-ci), *n.*, (nav.) vaisseau marchand, navire, *m.*; caraque, *f.*

ar'gue (-ghiou), *v.n.*, argumenter; raisonner **de**, arguer **de**, soutenir, prétendre; (jur.) plaider.

ar'gue, *v.a.*, discuter; annoncer; (fig.) dénoter; indiquer, accuser.

ar'guer (-ghiou-eur), *n.*, argumentateur, logicien, disputant, controversiste, raisonneur, *m.*

ar'guing, *n.*, argumentation, discussion, *f.*; raisonnement, *m.* *adj.*, raisonneur.

ar'gument (-ghiou-), *n.*, argument, raisonnement, sujet, *m.*; thèse, discussion, preuve, *f.*

argument'al, *adj.*, d'argument.

argumenta'tion (-té-), *n.*, argumentation, *f.*

argument'ative, *adj.*, de raisonnement, d'argumentation; disposé à argumenter. — declamation; *argumentation oratoire, f.*

argument'atively, *adv.*, par argument.

Ar'gus (-gheusse), *n.*, argus, *m.*

argute' (-ghioute), *adj.*, (ant.) fin, subtil.

A'rian, *adj.*, arien.

A'rian (a-ria-n), *n.*, arien, arienne, *f.*

A'rianism (-a-), *n.*, arianisme, *m.*

ar'id, *adj.*, aride.

arid'ity, *n.*, aridité, *f.*

ar'idness (-nèsse), *n.* *V.* **aridity.**

A'ries (éri-îze), *n.*, (astron.) Bélier, *m.*

ariet'ta (arièt-ta), *n.*, ariette, *f.*

aright' (araïte), *adv.*, droitement; bien.

arise' (araïze), *v.n.*, se lever; s'élever, survenir; se soulever, surgir, se présenter; provenir **de**; naître **de**.

ar'istarch, *n.*, aristarque, *m.*

aristoc'racy (-a-), *n.*, aristocratie, *f.*

aris'tocrat, *n.*, aristocrate, *m.f.*

aristocrat'ic *ou* **aristocrat'ical**, *adj.*, aristocratique.

aristocrat'ically, *adv.*, aristocratiquement.

Aristote'lian (-tî-), *adj.*, aristotélicien.

Aristote'lian, *n.*, aristotélicien, *m.*, aristotélicienne, *f.*

Aristote'lianism, *n.*, aristotélisme, *m.*

arith'metic (-rith-mi-), *n.*, arithmétique, *f.*; calcul, *m.*

arithmet'ical, *adj.*, arithmétique.

arithmet'ically, *adv.*, arithmétiquement.

arithmeti'cian (arith-mi-ti-sha'n), *n.*, arithméticien, *m.*

ark, *n.*, arche, *f.*; coffret, *m.* Noah's —; *l'arche de Noé, f.* The — of the covenant, the — of the Lord; *l'arche d'alliance, l'arche du Seigneur, f.*

arm, *n.*, bras; (horl.) levier, *m.* With —s folded; *les bras croisés.* With open —s; *à bras ouverts.* — in —; *bras dessus, bras dessous.* In —s; *en armes; les armes à la main;* (of children) *au maillot.* Under —; *sous les armes.* At —'s length; *à distance.* Within —'s reach; *à portée du bras.*

arm, *v.a.*, armer; donner des armes à.

arm, *v.n.*, s'armer, armer; prendre les armes.

arma'da (-mé-), *n.*, flotte, armada, *f.*

armadil′la, *n.*, armadille, *f.*

armadil′lo, *n.*, (mam.) tatou, *m.*

ar′mament, *n.*, armement, *m.*

arm′-chair (ârm-tshère), *n.*, fauteuil, *m.*

armed (ârm′de), *adj.*, armé.

arm′ful (-foule), *n.*, brassée, *f.*

arm′-guard, *n.*, garde-bras, brassard, *m.*

arm′hole (-hôle), *n.*, aisselle; emmanchure, entournure, *f.*

arm′illary, *adj.*, armillaire.

arm′istice, *n.*, armistice, *m.*

arm′less (-lèsse), *adj.*, sans bras; sans armes.

arm′let (-lète), *n.*, brassard, bracelet; petit bras (de mer), *m.*

armo′rial (-mô-), *adj.*, armorial. — bearings; *armoiries, f.pl.*

arm′orist (ârmeuriste), *n.*, (ant.) armoriste, *m.*

arm′or (-meur), *n.*, armure, *f.; armement, m.* — cased, plated; *cuirassé, blindé.* — casing *ou* plating; *blindage, m.* — plate; *plaque de blindage, f.*

arm′ored, *adj.*, cuirassé, blindé. — train; *train blindé, m.*

arm′orer (âr-meureur), *n.*, armurier, *m.*

arm′ory (-meuri), *n.*, arsenal, *m.; salle d'armes; armure, f.*

arm′pit (-pite), *n.*, aisselle, *f.*

arms (ârm′ze), *n.pl.*, armes; (her.) armes, armoiries, *f.pl.* Man at —; *homme d'armes, m.* Passage of —; *pas d'armes, m.* Small —; *armes portatives.* Side —; *armes blanches.* Irregular —; (her.) *armes fausses, armes à enquerre.* By force of —; *par la force des armes.* To beat to —; (milit.) *battre le rappel, battre la générale.* To take up —; *prendre les armes.* Ground — ! (milit.) *reposez vos armes, descendez armes!* Slope — ! (milit.) *armes à volonté!* Support —; (milit.) *arme au bras!* Unpile — ! (milit.) *rompez les faisceaux!* Shoulder — ! (milit.) *portez armes!* Lodge — ! (milit.) *haut les armes!* To have long — ; *avoir les bras longs.* In — ; *les armes à la main.* To give up one's —; *rendre les armes.*

arms′-manufactory, *n.*, armurerie, manufacture d'armes, *f.*

ar′my, *n.*, armée; (fig.) foule, multitude, *f.* To enter the —; *entrer dans l'armée.* To be in the —; *être militaire, être au service.* — corps; *corps d'armée, m.*

ar′nica, *n.*, arnique, *f.; arnica, m.*

arnot′to, *n.*, (bot.) rocou, rocouyer; (dy.) rocou, *m.*

ar′nuts (-neutse), *n.*, avoine cultivée, *f.*

aro′ma, *n.*, arome, *m.; (of wine) bouquet, m.*

aromat′ic *ou* **aromat′ical** (-ro-), *adj.*, aromatique.

aromatiza′tion (-ro-matizé-), *n.*, aromatisation, *f.*

aro′matize (-rô-mataïze), *v.a.*, aromatiser.

around′ (-raou′nde), *prep.*, autour **de**, à l'entour **de**.

around′, *adv.*, autour, à l'entour, à la ronde, aux environs; aux alentours.

arouse′ (-raouze), *v.a.*, soulever, réveiller, éveiller, exciter, animer.

arow′ (arô), *adv.*, en rang, l'un après l'autre.

aroynt′ (arô-ï-n′te), *adv.*, (ant.) va-t-en; loin d'ici; arrière!

arpeg′gio (-pèd′ji-ô), *n.*, (mus.) arpège, *m.*

arquebusade′ (-kwi-beu-céde), *n.*, arquebusade; (pharm.) eau d'arquebusade, *f.*

ar′quebuse (-kwi-beusse), *n.*, arquebuse, *f.*

arquebusier′ (ârkwi-beu-cir), *n.*, arquebusier, *m.*

ar′rack, *n.*, arack, rack, *m.*

arraign′ (ar-réne), *v.a.*, traduire en justice, accuser; mettre en accusation; poursuivre (en justice).

arraign′er, *n.*, accusateur.

arraign′ment (-ré-n′-), *n.*, mise en accusation; accusation, *f.*

arrange′ (-ré-n′je), *v.a.*, arranger, ranger, agencer; disposer, distribuer, aménager, organiser. *v.n.*, s'arranger, faire des arrangements. — to meet me; *arrangez-vous pour me rencontrer.*

arrange′ment, *n.*, arrangement; agencement, accommodement, aménagement, *m.; disposition, organisation, f.*

arran′ger (-ré-n′jeur), *n.*, arrangeur; meneur, *m.*

ar′rant, *adj.*, vrai, insigne, grand, fieffé, déterminé.

ar′rantly, *adv.*, notoirement; impudemment, ouvertement.

array′, *n.*, ordre, *m.; revue; suite, troupe, f.; cortège; nombre, m.; foule, f.; appareil, m.; pompe, f.; atours, m.pl.; (jur.) liste des jurés, f.* In battle —; *en ordre de bataille.*

array′, *v.a.*, déployer, ranger; revêtir **de**; parer **de**, orner **de**; (jur.) dresser.

arrear′ (ar-rire), **arrears′**, *n.*, arriéré, *m. pl.*, arrérages, *m.pl.* In —; *en arrière, arriéré, en retard.* To pay up one's —s; *payer son arriéré.*

arrest′ (ar-rèste), *n.*, empêchement; arrêt, *m.; arrestation, prise de corps, f.* — for debt; *contrainte par corps, f.* Under —; *en état d'arrestation;* (mil.) *aux arrêts.*

arrest′, *v.a.*, arrêter, saisir; fixer, suspendre; surseoir (à).

arresta′tion (-rès-té-), **arrest′ment**, *n.*, arrestation, opposition, *f.*

arri′val (ar-raï-), *n.*, arrivée, *f.; arrivage, m.* — platform; *quai d'arrivée, débarcadère, m.*

arrive′ (ar-raïve), *v.n.*, arriver; parvenir **à**.

ar′rogance *ou* **ar′rogancy** (-ro-), *n.*, arrogance, *f.*

ar′rogant (-ro-), *adj.*, arrogant.

ar′rogantly, *adv.*, arrogamment.

ar′rogate (-ro-ghéte), *v.a.*, s'arroger. *v.n.*, (to one's self) s'arroger.

arroga′tion (-ro-ghé-), *n.*, prétention, *ou* demande, arrogante, *f.*

ar′row (ar-rô), *n.*, flèche, *f.; (fig.) trait, m.* Shower of —s; *grêle de flèches, f.*

ar′row-grass, *n.*, troscart, *m.; herbe des pampas, f.*

ar′row-head (-hède), *n.*, tête de flèche; (bot.) sagittaire, fléchière, *f.*

ar′row-ma′ker (-mék-eur), *n.*, fléchier, *m.*

ar′row-root (-route), *n.*, arrow-root, *m.; herbe à la flèche, f.*

ar′row-shaped (-ro-shépte), *adj.*, sagitté.

ar′rowy (ar-ro-i), *adj.*, de flèche, en flèche.

arse, *n.*, (l.ex.) derrière, *m.*, fesse, *f.; (of meat) cimier, gîte, m.*

ar′senal (-si-), *n.*, arsenal, *m.*

arse′niate (-sï-niéte), *n.*, arséniate, *m.*

ar′senic (-sè-nike), *n.*, arsenic, *m.*

arsen′ical (-sè-), *adj.*, arsenical.

arsen′icate (-sè-ni-kéte), *v.a.*, combiner avec l'arsenic.

arse′nious (-sï-), *adj.*, arsénieux.

ar′senite (-sè-naïte), *n.*, arsénite, *m.*

ar′son (-so′n), *n.*, incendie prémédité, *m.*

art (ârte), *n.*, art; artifice, *m.; adresse, f.; beaux-arts, m.pl.* Black —; *magie noire, f.* The fine —s; *les beaux-arts, m.pl.* School of —; *école des beaux-arts, f.* — club; *cercle des beaux-arts.* — sale; *vente d'objets d'art, f.*

arte′rial (-tï-), *adj.*, (anat.) artériel.

arteriol′ogy (âr-tï-riolod′ji), *n.*, artériologie, *f.*

ar′tery (âr-teuri), *n.*, artère, *f.*

arte′sian (ar-tïzia′n), *adj.*, artésien.

art′ful (ârt′foul), *adj.*, rusé, fin; fait avec art; adroit, habile; (b.s.) (crafty) artificieux, astucieux.

art′fully (-foul-li), *adv.*, avec artifice, artificieusement, avec finesse ; artistement; (craft) astucieusement, insidieusement.

art'fulness (ârt'foulnèsse), n., ruse, finesse, f. ; art, m. ; habileté, astuce, f., artifice, m.

arthrit'ic ou **arthrit'ical** (ar-thri-), adj., arthritique.

arthro'sis (âr-thrô-cisse), n., (anat.) articulation, f.

ar'tichoke (âr-tit'shôke), n., artichaut, m. Jerusalem —; topinambour, m.

ar'ticle (âr-tik'l), n., article; objet, colis, m. ; marchandise, f. pl., (of a society) statuts, m. pl., (jur.) contrat d'apprentissage, m. Definite (gram.) article défini, m.

ar'ticle, v.a., engager par contrat ; mettre (chez un avoué), comme clerc (chez un médecin), comme élève.

ar'ticled (ar-tik'lde), adj., rédigé en articles ; lié, obligé, engagé par contrat écrit ; apprenti. — pupil ; (in schools) élève maître, m., élève-maîtresse, f.

artic'ular (ar-ti-kiou-leur), adj., articulaire.

artic'ulate (ar-ti-kiou-léte), adj., articulé.

artic'ulate, v.a., articuler ; traiter.

artic'ulate, v.n., articuler, parler distinctement.

artic'ulately, adv., distinctement; article par article.

articula'tion (ar-ti-kiou-lé-), **artic'ulateness**, n., articulation, f.

ar'tifice (âr'-), n., artifice, art, m.

artif'icer (-seur), n., artisan, ouvrier, artiste, m.

artifi'cial (-shial), adj., artificiel.

artificial'ity, n., état artificiel, m. ; nature artificielle, f.

artifi'cially, adv., artificiellement ; artistement.

artil'lerist (-til-leurist), n., artilleur, m.

artil'lery, n., artillerie, f. Horse—; artillerie à cheval. Field—; artillerie de campagne. — ground ; polygone, m. — practice ; tir du canon, m. — train ; équipage d'artillerie, m.

artil'lery-man, n., artilleur, m.

art'isan (-za-n), n., artisan, ouvrier, m.

art'ist, n., artiste, m.

artist'ic ou **artist'ical**, adj., artistique.

artist'ically, adv., artistement ; avec art.

art'less, adj., ingénu, simple, naïf ; sans art, naturel.

art'lessly, adv., ingénument, simplement, naïvement, sans art.

art'lessness, n., naturel, m. ; naïveté, simplicité, f.

a'rum (é-reume), n., arum, m.

arundin'eous (-reu'n-di-ni-eusse), adj., couvert de roseaux.

arus'pex (-reus-pèkse) ou **arus'pice** (-reus-), n., (aruspices) aruspice, m.

as (âce), n., (Rom. antiq.) as, m. ; (arith.) entier, nombre entier, m.

as (aze), conj., comme, ainsi que, selon que, suivant que ; à mesure que ; en. — it were ; pour ainsi dire. — yet ; jusqu'à présent, encore. — though ; comme si. — much — ; autant que. — . . . — ; aussi . . . que. — great — ; aussi grand que. — it is ; comme il est ; dans le cas présent ; vu l'état de choses. Be it — it may; quoi qu'il en soit. — it is ; toujours est-il que. Rich — she is ; toute riche qu'elle est. — for; quant à. — he advanced; à mesure qu'il avançait. She was dressed — a page ; elle était habillée en page.

asafœt'ida ou **asafet'ida** (a-ça-), n., assa fœtida, f. V. assafoetida.

asbes'tos (-bès-tosse) ou **asbestus** (-bès-teusse), n., asbeste, m.

ascend', v.n., monter à or sur, remonter, s'élever; (of mountains) faire l'ascension de.

ascend', v.a., monter, gravir ; remonter (a river).

ascend'able (as-cè-n'dab'l), adj., où l'on peut monter.

ascend'ant, n., ascendant, m. ; influence, supériorité, f., dessus, m. To be in the — ; prédominer, aller croissant.

ascend'ant (-da'nte), adj., ascendant, supérieur.

ascend'ency (-dè-nsi), n., ascendant, m. ; supériorité, influence, f.

ascend'ing (-digne), adj., ascendant.

ascen'sion (as-cè-n-sheune), n., ascension, f.

ascen'sional, adj., ascensionnel.

Ascen'sion-day, n., jour de l'Ascension, m.

ascent' (as-cè-n'te), n., ascension ; hauteur, élévation, montée, pente, inclinaison, f. ; coteau, m.

ascertain' (as-ceur-téne), v.a., assurer ; s'assurer ; s'assurer de ; constater ; vérifier, prouver ; fixer, déterminer.

ascertain'ment, n., fixation, vérification, règle établie, f.

ascet'ic, adj., ascétique.

ascet'ic (as-sè-tike), n., ascète, ascétique, m.

ascet'icism, n., ascétisme, m.

asci'tes (as-saï-tîze), n., (med.) ascite, f.

ascit'ic ou **ascit'ical** (as-si-), adj., ascitique, ascite.

asciti'tious (as-si-ti-shieusse), adj., additionnel.

ascle'piad (-klî-), n., (poet.) asclépiade, m.

ascri'bable (-craï-), adj., que l'on peut attribuer ; imputable à.

ascribe' (-craïbe), v.a., attribuer à; imputer à, accorder à.

ascrip'tion, n., imputation, attribution, f.

ash, n., (bot.) frêne, m. ; cendre, f.

ash, adj., de frêne, cendré.

ashamed' (-shê-m'de), adj., honteux, confus. To be — of ; avoir honte de. I am — of you ; vous me faites honte.

ash'-colored (ashe-keuleurde), adj., cendré.

ash'en (a-shène), adj., de frêne, cendré.

ash'es (ashèze), n.pl., cendre, f. ; cendres, f.pl.

ash'-fire (-faïeur), n., feu couvert, m.

ash'-gray, gris cendré.

ash'-grove, frênaie, f.

ash'lar, n., moellon, libage, m.

ashore' (-shore), adv., à terre ; (of a ship) échoué, à la côte.

ash'-pit, n., ash'-pan, ash'-tub, cendrier, m.

Ash-Wednes'day (-wè-n'z'dè), n., mercredi des cendres, m.

ash'y, adj., cendré ; terreux, pâle.

ash'y-pale (-péle), adj., pâle comme la mort.

Asiat'ic (ê-shia-tike), adj., asiatique.

Asiat'icism, n., orientalisme, m.

aside' (-çaïde), adv., de côté ; à part ; à l'écart, en aparté. Putting, setting —; sans compter; abstraction faite de. Putting, setting that — ; à part cela.

asine'go (a-ci-ni-gô), n., (pers.) âne, sot, aliboron, m.

as'inine (a-ci-naïne), adj., d'âne; (zoöl.) asine, adj.f.

ask (âske), v.a., demander; inviter à ; prier de ; s'informer de. To — in ; prier d'entrer, faire entrer. To — up ; prier de monter, faire monter. To — to do ; demander à faire. To — to see ; demander à voir. To — after any one's health ; demander des nouvelles de la santé de quelqu'un. To — a question ; faire une question.

askance' ou **askant'**, adv., de travers ; de côté, obliquement, du coin de l'œil.

ask'er (âsk-eur), n., demandeur, questionneur, solliciteur, m. ; demandeuse, questionneuse, solliciteuse, f.

askew' (a-skiou), adv., de travers, de côté ; de biais, en biais.

aslant', adv., obliquement, de biais, de côté, f.

asleep' (a-slîpe), adv., endormi.

aslope' (a-slôpe), *adv.*, en pente.

asp *ou* **asp'ic**, *n.*, aspic, *m.*

aspar'agus (-gheusse), *n.*, asperge, *f.* Bundle of —; *botte d'asperges, f.* — bed; *aspergerie, f.* — dish; *berceau à asperges, m.* — tongs; *pinces à asperges, f.pl.*

as'pect (-pèkte), *n.*, aspect, regard, point de vue, *m.*; exposition, *f.* To have a south —; *être exposé au midi.*

asp'en (-pène), *n.*, (bot.) tremble, *m.*

asp'en-grove (-grôve), *n.*, tremblaie, *f.*

asp'en-tree (-tri), *n.*, tremble, *m.*

asper'ity (-pè-), *n.*, aspérité, âpreté, rudesse, sévérité, *f.*

asperse' (as-peurse), *v.a.*, diffamer, noircir; vilipender, calomnier.

asper'ser (-seur), *n.*, calomniateur, diffamateur, *m.*

asper'sion (-peur-), *n.*, aspersion; diffamation, calomnie, *f.*

asphalt', **asphalte'**, *ou* **asphalt'um** (-teume), asphalte, *m.*

asphalt'ic (-taïte), *adj.*, d'asphalte.

asphalt'ite (-taïte), *adj.*, d'asphalte; Asphaltite (of the Dead Sea).

asphyx'ia *ou* **asphyx'y**, *n.*, (med.) asphyxie, *f.*

asp'ic, *n.*, (erpetol.: bot,.) aspic, *m.*; (artil.) ⊙couleuvrine, *f.*

aspi'rant *ou* **as'pirant** (-païeur- *ou* -pi-), *n.*, aspirant, *m.*, aspirante, *f.*; candidat, postulant, *m.*

as'pirate, *adj.*, aspiré.

as'pirate (-réte), *v.a.*, aspirer.

as'pirate, *v.n.*, s'aspirer.

as'pirate, *n.*, (gram.) aspirée, *f.*; esprit rude, *m.*

aspira'tion (-ré-), *n.*, aspiration, *f.*; élan, désir, *m.*

aspire' (as-païeur), *v.n.*, aspirer, s'aspirer à; aspirer à, prétendre à; viser à; ambitionner.

aspir'er (as-païeur-eur), *n.*, aspirant, postulant, candidat, *m.*

aspir'ing, *n.*, aspiration, *f.*; vif désir, *m.*

aspir'ing (as-païeur-igne), *adj.*, ambitieux, qui désire faire son chemin.

asquint', *adv.*, de travers; en louchant.

ass, *n.*, âne, *m.* She- —; *ânesse, f.* Young —; *ânon, m.* —es' bridge; *pont aux ânes, m.*

assafœt'ida, *n.*, assa fœtida, *f.*

as'sagai, *n.*, zagaïe, *f.*

assail' (as-sèle), *v.a.*, assaillir, attaquer.

assail'able (-lab'l), *adj.*, attaquable.

assail'ant (-la-n'te), assaillant, *m.*

assail'er (-leur), *n.*, assaillant, *m.*

assail'ment (-mè-n'te), *n.*, attaque, *f.*

assart' (as-sarte), *n.*, (ant.) essartement; arbre essarté, *m.*

assart', *v.a.*, essarter.

assas'sin (-cine), *n.*, assassin, *m.*

assas'sinate (-néte), *v.a.*, assassiner.

assas'sinating (-nétigne), *adj.*, d'assassinat, assassinant.

assassina'tion (-né-), *n.*, assassinat, *m.*

assas'sinator (-né-teur), *n.*, assassin, *m.*

assas'sin-like (-laïke), *adj.*, d'assassin.

assault' (as-sôlte), *n.*, assaut, *m.*; attaque, agression, *f.*; jeu; épreuve, vérification, *f.*; contrôle, *m.* — office; *bureau de garantie, m.* — scales, trébuchet, *m.*; *balance d'analyse ou d'essayeur, f.*

assay'-balance (-la-n'ce), *n.*, trébuchet, *m.*; balance d'essayeur, *f.*

assay'er (as-sé-eur), *n.*, essayeur, *m.*

assay'-master, *n.*, maître-essayeur, *m.*

assem'blage (-sè-m'bléd'je), *n.*, assemblage, *m.*; assemblée, *f.*

assem'ble (-sè-m'b'l), *v.a.*, assembler, réunir, rassembler.

assem'ble, *v.n.*, s'assembler, se réunir, se rassembler.

assem'bler (-bleur), *n.*, personne qui rassemble, *f.*; chef, meneur, *m.*

assem'bly, *n.*, assemblée, réunion, *f.* To meet in —; *se réunir en assemblée publique.*

assem'bly-room (-roume), *n.*, salle d'assemblée, de réunion, *f.*

assent' (as-sè-n'te), *n.*, assentiment, consentement, *m.*; sanction, *f.*

assent', *v.n.*, donner son assentiment à; approuver; assentir à, consentir à.

assent'er (-teur), *n.*, approbateur, *m.*, approbatrice, *f.*

assent'ingly (-tigneli), *adv.*, avec approbation.

assent'ment, *n.*, (ant.) assentiment, *m.*

assert' (-seurte), *v.a.*, avancer; soutenir; prononcer, proclamer, constater, affirmer, prétendre; revendiquer, faire valoir (rights).

asser'tion, *n.*, assertion, revendication, *f.*

assert'ive, *adj.*, (ant.) assertif, affirmatif.

assert'or (-teur), *n.*, défenseur, soutien, *m.*

assert'ory, *adj.*, affirmatif.

assess', *v.a.*, taxer, imposer, coter, répartir, fixer, évaluer.

assess'able, *adj.*, imposable.

assessed' (as-sès-ste), *part.*, taxé, imposé, fixé, déterminé. *adj.*, direct.

asses'sionary (-sheunari), *adj.*, assessorial.

assess'ment, *n.*, cote, imposition, répartition, assiette, fixation, *f.*; cadastre, *m.*

assess'or (-seur), *n.*, fonctionnaire chargé d'asseoir les impôts, assesseur, répartiteur, estimateur, expert, *m.*

as'sets, *n.pl.*, actif, *m.* — and liabilities; *actif et passif, m.*

assev'er (as-sèv-eur) *or* **assev'erate** (as-sèv-euréte), *v.a.*, affirmer solennellement.

assevera'tion (-ré-), *n.*, affirmation solennelle, *f.*

assidu'ity (-diou-i-), *n.*, assiduité, *f.*

assid'uous (-diou-eusse), *adj.*, assidu.

assid'uously, *adv.*, assidûment.

assign' (as-saïne), *n.*, (jur.) ayant droit, ayant cause, *m.*

assign', *v.a.*, assigner à; determiner, fixer; transférer à, appliquer à.

assign'able (-nab'l), *adj.*, assignable; (jur.) transférable; déterminable.

assigna'tion (as-sig-né-), *n.*, assignation, désignation; (jur.) cession, *f.*; rendez-vous, *m.*

assignee' (as-saï-nî), *n.*, syndic; cessionnaire; mandataire, *m.* Official —; *syndic provisoire.*

assign'er (-neur), *n.*, personne qui assigne, *f.*; (jur.) cédant, *m.*

assign'ment (as-saï-n-mè-n'te), *n.*, transfert, *m.*; cession de biens; allocation, *f.*

assign'or (-neur), *n.*, (jur.) cédant, *m.*

assim'ilable, *adj.*, assimilable.

assim'ilate (-léte), *v.a.*, assimiler, s'assimiler.

assimila'tion (-lé-), *n.*, assimilation, *f.*

assim'ilative, *adj.*, assimilatif, assimilateur.

assist', *v.a.*, assister; secourir, aider.

assist'ance, *n.*, assistance, aide, *f.*; secours, concours, *m.*

assist'ant, *n.*, aide; assistant; appui; adjoint, suppléant, second, *m.*; (in a shop) garçon de comptoir, chef de rayon; (pop.) calicot, *m.*; demoiselle de comptoir, *f.* — examiner; *examinateur adjoint.*

assist'ant, *adj.*, qui aide; auxiliaire.

assist'er (-teur), *n.*, aide, *m.f.*; personne qui assiste, qui aide, *f.*

assize' (as-saïze) *ou* **assiz'es** (-saïize), *n.*,

assises, *f.pl.;* tarif, *m.,* taxe, *f.* Court of —s ; *cour d'assises, f.* — of bread; *taxe du pain.* The case is down for hearing at the —s ; *c'est porté aux assises* (V. Hugo).

assize', *v.a.,* taxer, imposer; fixer le prix des denrées.

assiz'er (-zeur), *n.,* vérificateur des poids et mesures, *m.*

associabil'ity (as-sô-shia-), *n.,* sociabilité, *f.*

asso'ciable (-shiab'l), *adj.,* sociable.

asso'ciate (-shi-éte), *n.,* associé, *m.;* (in crime) complice, *m.;* collègue ; compagnon, *m.*

asso'ciate, *v.a.,* associer **avec** *ou* **à** ; servir **avec,** joindre **à.**

asso'ciate, *v.n.,* s'associer **avec** *ou* **à.** To — with ; *fréquenter.*

associa'tion (-cié-), *n.,* association, corporation, idée, notion, union,*f.;* rapport, souvenir, *m.*

as'sonance (as-so-na'nce), *n.,* (rhet.) assonance, *f.*

as'sonant, *adj.,* assonant.

assort' (as-sorte), *v.a.,* assortir.

assort'ed, *part.,* assorti.

assort'ment, *n.,* assortiment; assemblage, *m.*

assuage' (as-swéd'je), *v.a.,* adoucir, apaiser, calmer, *v.n.,* s'apaiser, se calmer.

assuage'ment, *n.,* adoucissement, soulagement, apaisement, *m.*

assua'sive (as-swé-cive), *adj.,* soulageant, adoucissant, apaisant.

assume' (as-sioume), *v.a.,* prendre, s'arroger, s'attribuer, prendre sur soi ; assumer, prendre *(une responsabilité)* ; supposer ; prétendre ; se permettre, se donner.

assume', *v.n.,* être arrogant, faire l'important; s'en faire accroire, afficher des prétentions.

assu'mer (-meur), *n.,* arrogant, présomptueux, prétentieux, *m.*

assu'ming (-migne), *adj.,* arrogant, prétentieux; ambitieux, tranchant.

assump'sit (as-seu-m-site), *n.,* (jur.) promesse verbale, *f.*

assump'tion (as-seu-m-sheune), *n.,* (rel.) Assomption (la fête de l') ; (fig.) présomption ; prétention; supposition, *f.*

assump'tive (as-seu-m-tive), *adj.,* qu'on peut prendre; (log.) assomptif.

assu'rance (a-shiou-ra'nce), *n.,* assurance, certitude, promesse, *f.* V. **insurance.**

assure' (a-shiour), *v.a.,* assurer.

assured' (-shiour'de), *part. adj.,* assuré; sûr.

assur'edly (-shiour-ède-), *adv.,* assurément, certainement. Most — ; *certes, bien assurément, bien certainement.*

assur'edness, *n.,* certitude, *f.*

assur'er (-reur), *n.,* assureur, *m.*

as'teism (asti-iz'me), *n.,* (rhet.) ironie raffinée, *f.*

as'ter (-teur), *n.,* (bot.) aster, *m.*

aste'rias (-tî-), *n.,* astérie, *f.*

aste'riated (as-tî-ri-étède), *adj.,* étoilé.

aste'riatite (as-tî-rié-taïte), *n.,* astérie pétrifiée, *f.*

as'terisk (as-teuriske), *n.,* astérisque, *m.*

as'terism (as-teu-riz'me), *n.,* astérisme, *m.*

astern' (as-teurne), *adv.,* (nav.) à l'arrière, de l'arrière, en poupe, arrière. To leave —; *laisser à l'arrière.*

asth'ma (as-ma), *n.,* asthme, *m.*

asthmat'ic, *adj.,* asthmatique.

astir', *adj.,* agité, en l'air, en rumeur, en émoi, debout ; agissant, actif. We were — betimes ; *nous fûmes debout, ou sur pied, de bonne heure.*

aston'ish, *v.a.,* étonner, surprendre.

aston'ished, *adj., part.,* étonné **de,** surpris **de.**

aston'ishing (-shigne), *adj.,* étonnant, surprenant.

aston'ishingly (-shigne-li), *adv.,* étonnamment.

aston'ishment, *n.,* étonnement, *m.* To strike with —; *frapper d'étonnement.* To recover from one's —; *revenir de son étonnement.* To the — of all; *au grand étonnement de tous.*

astound' (as-ta-ou'nde), *v.a.,* étonner ; abasourdir, étourdir.

astound'ingly, *adv.,* étonnamment.

astrad'dle, *adv.,* à califourchon. V. **astride.**

Astræ'a *ou* **Astre'a** (astri-a), *n.,* astrée, *f.*

as'tragal, *n.,* (arch.) astragale, *m.*

As'trakhan, *n.,* astracan, *m.*

as'tral, *adj.,* astral.

astray', *adv.,* de travers ; égaré. To go —; *s'égarer.* To lead —; *égarer.*

Astre'a, *n.* V. **Astræa.**

astrict' (-trikte), *v.a.,* (l.u.) resserrer, comprimer.

astric'tion (as-trik-sheune), *n.,* contrainte, (med.) constriction; (surg.) compression,*f.*

astride' (astraïde), *adv.,* à califourchon (avec) les jambes écartées. — upon; *à cheval* **sur.**

astringe' (-tri-nd'je), *v.a.,* resserrer.

astrin'gency (-tri-n-), *n.,* astringence,*f.*

astrin'gent, *adj.,* astringent.

astrin'gent (-tri-n-), *n.,* astringent, *m.*

astrog'raphy, *n.,* description des astres, *f.*

as'trolabe (-tro-lébe), *n.,* astrolabe, *m.*

astrol'oger (-lod'jeur), *n.,* astrologue, *m.*

astrolog'ic *ou* **astrolog'ical** (-lod'jik, -lod-jical), *adj.,* astrologique.

astrolog'ically, *adv.,* par l'astrologie.

astrol'ogize (-lod'jaïze), *v.n.,* pratiquer l'astrologie.

astrol'ogy (-lod'ji), *n.,* astrologie, *f.*

astron'omer (-no-meur), *n.,* astronome, *m.*

astronom'ic *ou* **astronom'ical** (as-tro-no-), *adj.,* astronomique.

astronom'ically (as-tro-no-), *adv.,* astronomiquement.

astron'omy (as-tro-nô-), *n.,* astronomie, *f.*

astrut' (a-streute), *adv.,* en se rengorgeant; bouffi **de.**

astute' (as-tioute), *adj.,* fin, pénétrant, rusé.

asun'der (a-ceu-n'deur), *adv.,* séparé, séparément, éloigné l'un de l'autre ; en deux.

asy'lum (a-çaï-leume), *n.,* asile, refuge ; hospice, asile, *m.* Lunatic —; *maison d'aliénés, petite-maison, maison de santé,f.*

as'ymptote (a-ci-m'tôte), *n.,* (geom.) asymptote,*f.*

asymptot'ical, *adj.,* asymptotique.

at, *prep.,* à, dans ; en; après. — peace; *en paix.* — war ; *en guerre.* They are all — me; *ils sont tous après moi.* To be hard — it; *travailler ferme.* — home; *chez soi, à la maison.* — . . .'s ; *chez. . .* — my brother's; *chez mon frère.* — London ; *à Londres.* — a bound ; *d'un bond, d'un trait.* — his request; *sur sa demande.* To be — anything ; *être occupé à quelque chose.* What are you — ? *que diable faites vous?*

at'aghan (-ga'n), *n.,* yatagan, *m.*

at'araxy, *n.,* (ant.) ataraxie,*f.*

atax'ia *ou* **at'axy,** *n.,* (ant.) ataxie,*f.*

atax'ic, *adj.,* ataxique.

Athana'sian (ath-a-né-shia'n), *adj.,* de Saint Athanase. — creed; *symbole de Saint Athanase, m.*

a'theism (é-thi-iz'me), *n.,* athéisme, *m.*

a'theist (é-thi-iste), *n.,* athée, *m.*

a'theist, atheist'ic, *ou* **atheist'ical,** *adj.,* athée, d'athée.

atheist'ically, *adv.,* en athée.

Athenæ'um *ou* **Athene'um** (ath-i-nî-eume), *n.* (*Athenæa, -nea*) Athénée, *m.*

Athe'nian (a-thî-ni-a'n), *adj.,* Athénien.

Athe'nian, *n.,* Athénien, *m.,* Athénienne, *f.*

athirst' (atheurste), *adj.,* altéré, qui a soif. — for glory ; *altéré de gloire.*

ath'lete (ath-lîte), *n.,* athlète, *m.*

athlet'ic (ath-lè-tike), *adj.*, athlétique, robuste, fort.

athwart' (a-thwŏrte), *adv.*, de travers; à la traverse, en travers **de**.

athwart', *prep.*, à travers; à l'encontre; (nav.) en travers **de**, par le travers.

atilt', *adv.*, en jouteur, en champ clos; (of casks) debout. To run — against; *rompre une lance* **avec**.

Atlante'an *ou* **Atlan'tian** (at-la-n-tia-n), *adj.*, de l'Atlantide; d'Atlas.

Atlan'tes (at-la-n-tize), *n.pl.*, (arch.) atlante, *m.*

Atlan'tic, *adj.*, atlantique.

Atlan'tic (at-la-n-), *n.*, Atlantique, *f.*

Atlan'tis, *n.*, Atlantide, *f.*

at'las, *n.*, (geog., anat.) atlas, *m.*

at'mosphere (-ffre), *n.*, atmosphère, *f.*

atmospher'ic *ou* **atmospher'ical** (-fè-), *adj.*, atmosphérique.

at'om (a-teume), *n.*, atome, *m.*

atom'ic *ou* **atom'ical**, *adj.*, atomique.

at'om-like (-laïke), *adj.*, comme un atome.

atone', *v.a.*, expier; racheter.

atone' (-tône), *v.n.*, expier, apaiser.

atone'ment, *n.*, expiation, *f.* In — for his crimes; *en expiation de ses crimes.*

aton'er (-neur), *n.*, personne qui expie, expiateur, *f.*

aton'ic (-to-nike), *adj.*, atonique, (gram.) atone.

at'ony (-to-ni), *n.*, (med.) faiblesse, atonie, *f.*

atop' (atope), *adv.*, en haut, au sommet.

atrabila'rian (-lé-ria-n) *ou* **atrabil'ious** (-bili-eusse), *adj.*, atrabilaire.

at'rabile, *f.*, (med.) atrabile, *f.*

atrament'al (-mè-n-) *ou* **atrament'ous** (mèn'-teusse), *adj.*, noir comme de l'encre.

atrip' (atripe), *adv.*, (nav.) (of anchor) dérapé; (of top-sails) guindé.

atro'cious (-trô-shieusse), *adj.*, atroce.

atro'ciously, *adv.*, atrocement.

atro'ciousness, *n.*, atrocité, *f.*

atroc'ity (atro-ci-), *n.*, atrocité, *f.*

at'rophy (-tro-), *n.*, (med.) atrophie, consomption, *f.*

attach' (at-tat'she), *v.a.*, attacher à, lier à; arrêter; (jur.) mettre opposition à, contraindre par corps, saisir.

attach'able (at-tat'shab'l), *adj.*, (jur.) saisissable, contraignable par corps.

attaché', *n.*, attaché, *m.*

attach'ment, *n.*, attachement, *m.;* (jur.) opposition, contrainte, saisie, *f.*

attack', *n.*, attaque, *f.;* accès, *m.*

attack', *v.a.*, attaquer.

attack'er (-keur), *n.*, attaquant, agresseur, *m.*

attain' (at-té-n), *v.a.*, atteindre, parvenir à, arriver à.

attain'able (-nab'l), *adj.*, qu'on peut atteindre, accessible.

attain'ableness, *n.*, possibilité d'atteindre, *f.*

attain'der (-té-n-deur), *n.*, atteinte, tache, souillure, (jur.) flétrissure; dégradation, mort civile, *f.*

attain'ment (-té-n-), *n.*, acquisition; portée; possession, connaissances, *f.;* talent, *m.*

attaint' (-té-nte), *n.*, tache, flétrissure; (man.) atteinte; (jur.) inscription en faux, *f.*

attaint', *v.a.*, atteindre, entacher; vicier, flétrir; frapper de mort civile; dégrader, déshonorer, accuser **de**, convaincre **de**; (ant.) déclarer faux (le verdict d'un jury).

attaint'ure (-t-én-tioure), *n.*, note d'infamie, flétrissure, *f.*

attempt' (at-tè-m'te), *n.*, essai, effort, *m.;* entreprise, *f.;* (jur.) attentat, *m.*, tentative, *f.* An — on any one's life; *un attentat contre la vie de quelqu'un.* First —; *coup d'essai, m.*

attempt', *v.a.*, entreprendre **de**; essayer **de**, chercher à, tâcher **de**, vouloir; attenter à; (jur.) faire une tentative **de**.

attempt'able (-tab'l), *adj.*, attaquable; qui peut être essayé, tenté.

attempt'er (-teur), *n.*, personne qui essaye, *f.;* (b.s.) agresseur, *m.*

attend' (at-tè-n'de), *v.a.*, faire attention à; s'occuper **de**; soigner (un malade); suivre (des leçons); écouter, accompagner; servir; attendre. To — the lectures on chemistry; *suivre le cours de chimie.*

attend', *v.n.*, faire attention, écouter, prêter l'oreille; assister, être présent; servir; accompagner; observer; avoir égard à; veiller, vaquer à, avoir soin **de**; s'appliquer à. I shall —; *j'y serai ou je m'y trouverai.*

attend'ance (at-tè-n'da-nce), *n.*, attention, *f.;* service, *m.;* assiduité; présence, *f.;* soins (pour un malade), *m.pl.* To dance —; *faire antichambre, le pied de grue; croquer le marmot.*

attend'ant (-da-n'te), *adj.*, qui suit, qui accompagne; qui dépend **de**.

attend'ant, *n.*, assistant; compagnon, *m.*, compagne, *f.;* serviteur, domestique, *m.;* personne de suite, *f.* *pl.*, escorte, suite, *f.*, cortège, *m.*

atten'tion (at-tè-n-), *n.*, attention, *f.* To pay —; *faire attention.* To turn one's — to; *s'occuper de.* To call any one's — to; *appeler l'attention de quelqu'un sur; faire remarquer à.* — ! garde à vous! To be all —s to; *être aux petits soins* **avec** *ou* **pour**.

atten'tive, *adj.*, attentif à, soigneux **de**.

atten'tively, *adv.*, attentivement.

atten'tiveness, *n.*, attention, *f.*

atten'uant (at-tè-niou-a-nte), *adj. and n.*, atténuant.

atten'uate, *v.a.*, atténuer, amoindrir, diminuer, affaiblir; amincir, amaigrir.

atten'uated (-tède), *adj.*, atténué; diminué, amoindri, affaibli.

attenua'tion (-niou-é-), *n.*, atténuation, diminution, *f.;* amoindrissement, *m.*

attest' (at-tèste), *v.a.*, attester; (to denote) témoigner **de**.

attesta'tion (-tès-té-), *n.*, attestation, *f.;* témoignage, *m.*

attest'or (-teur), *n.*, personne qui atteste, *f.*

At'tic, *adj.*, attique. *n.*, (dialect) attique, *m.*

at'tic, *n.*, (arch.) attique, *m.*, mansarde, *f.*, grenier, *m.* — window; *fenêtre en mansarde, f.*

At'ticism, *n.*, atticisme, *m.*

At'ticize (at-ti-çaïze), *v.a.*, donner une forme attique à.

At'ticize, *v.n.*, affecter l'atticisme.

attire' (at-taïeur), *n.*, vêtement, costume, *m.;* parure, *f.*, atours, *m.pl.*

attire', *v.a.*, vêtir **de**, parer **de**, orner **de**.

atti'rer (at-taïeureur), *n.*, personne qui habille, qui pare, *f.*

at'titude (at-ti-tioude), *n.*, attitude, pose, *f.*, air, *m.*

attitu'dinize, *v.n.*, poser; se donner des airs.

attor'ney (at-teur-ni), *n.*, procureur, avoué, fondé de pouvoir, *m.* Power of —; *procuration, f.; pouvoir, m.* — general; *procureur général.* — at law; *avoué, notaire, m.*

attor'neyship, *n.*, charge d'avoué, de procureur, *f.*

attract' (at-trakte), *v.a.*, attirer.

attractabil'ity, *n.*, propriété d'être attiré, *f.*

attract'able, *adj.*, attirable.

attract'ile, *adj.*, attractif.

attract'ingly (at-trac-tigne-li), *adv.*, par attraction.

attrac'tion (-trak-sheune), *n.*, attraction, *f.;* attrait, *m.*

attract'ive, *adj.*, attrayant; (drawing to) attractif.

attract'ively, *adv.*, d'une manière attrayante.

attract'iveness, *n.*, vertu attractive, *f.;* attrait, charme, *m.*

attrib'utable (-biou-t-ab'l), *adj.*, attribuable, imputable.

at'tribute, *n.*, attribut, *m.*; qualité, *f.*

attrib'ute (-bioute),*v.a.*, attribuer à, imputer à.

attribu'tion (-biou-sheune), *n.*, attribution, *f.*; attribut, éloge, *m.*

attrib'utive, *adj.*, qui attribue; attributif.

attrib'utive, *n.*, (gram.) attributif, *m.*

attrite (at-traïte), *adj.*, frotté; (theol.) attrit, pénétré d'attrition.

attrite'ness, *n.*, état de ce qui est usé par le frottement, *m.*

attri'tion (at-tri-sheune), *n.*, attrition, trituration, *f.*; (theol.) attrition, *f.*

attune' (at-tiou-ne), *v.a.*, accorder, mettre à l'unison, au diapason.

au'burn (ŏ-beurne), *adj.*, châtain-clair.

auc'tion (ŏk-sheune), *n.*, encan, *m.*; enchère, criée, adjudication, *f.*; enchères, *f.pl.*; vente à l'encan, *f.* Sale by —; *vente aux enchères, à l'encan.* To sell by —; *vendre aux enchères, vendre à l'encan, vendre à la criée.* — mart; *hôtel, m.,* ou *salles de ventes, f.*

auctioneer' (ŏk-sheunîre), *n.*, commissaire-priseur, encanteur; (markets) crieur, *m.*

auctioneer'ing, *adj.*, qui vend aux enchères.

auda'cious (ŏ-dé-shieusse), *adj.*, audacieux.

auda'ciously, *adv.*, audacieusement.

auda'ciousness, *n.*, audace, *f.*

audac'ity (ŏ-da-ci-), *n.*, audace, *f.*

au'dible (ŏ-dib'l), *adj.*, qu'on peut entendre; perceptible; intelligible. He, *or* it, was scarcely —; *on l'entendait à peine.*

au'dibleness, *n.*, faculté de produire un son, de se faire entendre, *f.*

au'dibly, *adv.*, de manière à être entendu; à haute et intelligible voix.

au'dience (ŏ-di-è-nce), *n.*, audience, assistance, assemblée, *f.*; auditoire, *m.*; les assistants, *m.pl.*

au'dience-cham'ber (-tshé-m'beur), *n.*, salle d'audience, *f.*

au'dit (ŏ-dite), *n.*, audition, vérification de comptes, *f.* — office; *cour des comptes, f.*

au'dit, *v.a.*, apurer, vérifier des comptes.

au'dit-house (-haouce), *n.*, sacristie.

au'ditor, *n.*, auditeur; vérificateur, *m.*

au'ditory, *n.*, auditoire, tribunal, *m.*; assemblée, *f.*

au'ditory, *adj.*, auditif.

au'ditress, *n.*, femme qui écoute, *f.* She was the sole —; *elle seule composait l'auditoire.*

Auge'an (ŏdji-a-n), *adj.*, d'Augias. The — stable; *l'écurie d'Augias, f.*

au'ger (ŏ-gheur), *n.*, (tech.) tarière, *f.* — bit; *mèche de tarière, f.*

aught (ŏte), *n.*, quelque chose; quoi que ce soit; rien, tout. For — I know; *autant que je sache; à ma connaissance.* For — I care; *pour ce qui m'importe.*

augment' (ŏg-mè-n-te), **n.**, accroissement; (gram.) augment, *m.*

augment',*v.a.*, augmenter, accroître.

augment', *v.n.*, augmenter, s'augmenter, s'accroître.

augmenta'tion (ŏg-mè-n-té-sheune), *n.*, augmentation, *f.*

augment'ative (ŏg-mè-n-ta-), *adj.*, augmentatif.

au'gur (ŏgheur), *n.*, augure, devin, *m.*

au'gur, *v.n.*, augurer, présager.

au'gural (-ghiou-), *adj.*, augural.

augura'tion (ghiou-ré-sheune), *n.*, (ant.) divination par les augures, *f.*

augu'rial (-ghiou-), *adj.*, des augures.

au'gurship (-gheur-), *n.*, charge d'augure, *f.*

au'gury (-ghiou-), *n.*, divination par les augures, *f.*; augure, présage, *m.* Of good —; *de bon augure.* Of ill —; *de mauvais augure.*

au'gust, *adj.*, auguste.

Au'gust (-gheuste), (month of) *n.*, août, *m.*

Augus'tan (-gheusta-n), *adj.*, d'Auguste. — confession; *confession d'Augsbourg, f.*

Augus'tin (-gheusti-ne), *n.*, augustin, *m.*

august'ness, *n.*, caractère auguste, *m.*; majesté, *f.*

auk, *n.*, alque, pingouin, *m.*

au'lic, *adj.*, aulique.

aunt (ān-n-t), *n.*, tante, *f.* Great —; *grand'-tante.*

au'ra, *n.*, exhalaison, *f.*

au'ral, *adj.*, de l'air; de l'oreille. — surgeon; *auriste, m.*

au'rated (-ré-tède), **au'riate**, *adj.*, qui ressemble à l'or; d'or, doré.

aure'lia (-ré-), *n.*, chrysalide, nymphe, *f.*

au'ricle (-rik'l), *n.*, auricule, *f.*; pavillon de l'oreille, *m.*; (of the heart) oreillette, *f.*

auric'ular, *adj.*, auriculaire.

auric'ularly, *adv.*, à l'oreille; secrètement.

aurif'erous (-fé-reuss), *adj.*, aurifère.

au'rist, *n.*, auriste, *m.*

Auro'ra, *n.*, aurore, *f.* — Borealis; *aurore boréale.*

auro'ral, *adj.*, d'aurore.

auscul'tate (-keul-téte), *v.a.*, (med.) ausculter.

ausculta'tion (-keul-té-sheune), *n.*, auscultation, *f.*

au'spice, *n.*, auspice, *m.* Under the —s of; *sous les auspices* **de.**

auspi'cious (-shieusse), *adj.*, de bon augure, propice, favorable, heureux.

auspi'ciously, *adv.*, sous d'heureux auspices, favorablement.

auspi'ciousness, *n.*, aspect favorable, *m.*, heureux auspices, *m.pl.*

aus'ter (-teur), *n.*, vent du midi, autan, *m.*

austere' (-tîre), *adj.*, austère, âpre, rigide.

austere'ly, *adv.*, austèrement.

austere'ness, **auster'ity**, *n.*, austérité; âpreté (of taste), *f.*

Aus'tin (-ti'ne), *adj.*, (friar) augustin.

aus'tral, *adj.*, austral.

Austra'lian (-li-a'n), *adj.*, australien.

Aus'trian, *adj.*, autrichien.

Aus'trian, *n.*, Autrichien, *m.*, Autrichienne, *f.*

authen'tic *ou* **authen'tical** (-thè'n'), *adj.*, authentique.

authen'tically, *adv.*, authentiquement.

authen'ticate, *v.a.*, constater; légaliser; établir l'authenticité **de.**

authentica'tion,*n.*, authenticité; (jur.) légalisation, *f.*

authentic'ity, *n.*, authenticité, *f.*

au'thor (-thor), *n.*, auteur, *m.*; (fig.) cause, *f.*

au'thoress, *n.*, auteur, *m.*; femme auteur, *f.*

author'itative (-tho-), *adj.*, d'autorité; revêtu d'autorité, impérieux.

author'itatively, *adv.*, avec autorité.

author'itativeness, *n.*, autorité, *f.*; air *ou* ton d'autorité, *m.*

author'ity, *n.*, autorité, *f.*; pouvoir, *m.* To have from good —; *tenir de bonne source.*

authoriza'tion (-zé-), *n.*, autorisation, *f.*

au'thorize (-raï-ze), *v.a.*, autoriser.

au'thorship, *n.*, profession d'auteur, qualité d'auteur; (fam.) paternité, *f.* The — is unknown; *l'auteur est inconnu.* To own the — of; *avouer qu'on est l'auteur* **de.**

autobiog'rapher, *n.*, autobiographe.

autobiograph'ical, *adj.*, autobiographique.

autobiog'raphy, *n.*, autobiographie, *f.*

autoc'racy, *n.*, autocratie, *f.*

au'tocrat, *n.*, autocrate, *m.*

autocrat'ic *ou* **autocrat'ical**, *adj.*, autocratique.

au'to-da-fe', *n.*, autodafé, *m.*

au'tograph, *n.*, autographe, *m.*

au'tograph, *v.a.*, autographier.

autograph'ic *ou* **autograph'ical**, *adj.*, autographe, autographique.

autog'raphy, *n.*, autographie, *f.*

automat'ic *ou* **automat'ical**, *adj.*, automatique.

autom'aton (-to'n), *n.*, (*automata, automatons*) automate, *m.*

autom'atous (-teusse), *adj.*, (ant.) automatique.

au'topsy, *n.*, autopsie, *f.*

au'tumn (-teume), *n.*, automne, *m.f.*

autum'nal (-teum-nal), *adj.*, automnal, d'automne.

autum'nal, *n.*, plante automnale, *f.*

auxil'iary, *adj.n.*, auxiliaire, *m.*

avail', *n.*, avantage, service, *m. ;* utilité, *f.* To be of no —; *ne servir de rien, ne servir à rien.* Of what — is it? *à quoi sert de ? que sert de ?* **avail'**, *v.n.*, servir. That —s nothing; *cela ne sert à rien.*

avail', *v.a.*, profiter à, servir à. To — one's self of ; *profiter de, se prévaloir de.*

avail'able (-lab'l), *adj.*, utile, profitable ; disponible.

avail'ableness, *n.*, utilité; efficacité, validité,*f.*

avail'ably, *adv.*, utilement, avec profit.

av'alanche *ou* **av'alange**, *n.*, avalanche, *f.*

av'arice, *n.*, avarice, *f.*

avari'cious (-shieusse), *adj.*, avare, avaricieux.

avari'ciously, *adv.*, avec avarice, avaricieusement.

avari'ciousness, *n.*, avarice, *f.*

avast', *int.*, (nav.) tiens bon ; baste !

avaunt', *int.*, loin d'ici ! arrière ! loin de moi !

a've, *n.*, avé, *m.* — Maria; *avé Maria, m.*

avena'ceous, *adj.*, avénacé.

av'enage (-nédje), *n.*, avénage, *m.*

avenge' (-vè'n'dje), *v.a.*, venger. To — one's self; *se venger de.*

aven'ger (-vè'n'djeur), *n.*, vengeur, *m. ;* vengeresse, *f.*

aven'geress, *n.*, vengeresse, *f.*

aven'ging, *adj.*, vengeur.

av'ens, *n.*, (bot.) benoîte, *f.*

av'enue (-vi-niou), *n.*, avenue, *f.*

aver' (-veur), *v.a.*, affirmer, avérer; assurer, certifier.

av'erage (-édje), *n.*, moyenne, *f.*, prix moyen; terme moyen, *m.;* mercuriale (des grains); (com., nav.) avarie, *f.* Petty —s; *menues avaries.* General —s; *avaries communes.* Weekly —s; (of corn) *mercuriale hebdomadaire.* Statement of —s ; *règlement d'avaries.* Free of —; *franc d'avarie.* On an —; *en moyenne, l'un dans l'autre.* To make good an —; *indemniser d'une avarie.* To state the —s; *régler les avaries.* Above the —; *au-dessus du commun.*

av'erage, *adj.*, commun; moyen. — prices of corn; *mercuriale, f.*

av'erage, *v.a.*, calculer, prendre le terme moyen de, prendre la moyenne de.

av'erage, *v.n.*, revenir en moyenne à, donner une moyenne de.

aver'ment (-veur-mè-nte), *n.*, affirmation, déclaration formelle, *f.*

averse' (-veurse), *adj.*, opposé à, défavorable à, éloigné de, qui a de l'éloignement pour, en-nemi de. To be — to ; *avoir de l'éloignement pour, avoir de l'aversion pour, être peu disposé à.*

averse'ly, *adv.*, à regret, à contre-cœur.

averse'ness, *n.*, répugnance, aversion, *f. ;* éloignement, *m.*

aver'sion, *n.*, aversion, *f.;* éloignement, *m.* To take an — to; *prendre en aversion.* That man is my pet —; *cet homme est ma bête noire.*

avert', *v.a.*, détourner de, éloigner de, écarter de ; préserver de.

avert' (-veurte), *v.n.*, se détourner.

a'viary, *n.*, volière, *f.*

avid'ity, *n.*, avidité, *f*

avoca'tion (-vo-ké-sheune), *n.*, métier, *m. ;* occupation; distraction,*f.*

avoid' (-voïde), *v.a.*, éviter, fuir; (ant.) annuler.

avoid', *v.n.*, se retirer, s'esquiver.

avoid'able, *adj.*, qu'on peut éviter, évitable; (jur.) résoluble.

avoid'ance, *n.*, action d'éviter ; vacance, annulation, *f. ;* écoulement, *m.*

avoid'less (-voïd'), *adj.*, inévitable, inéluctable.

avoirdupois', *n.*, (com.) avoir du poids, *m.*

avouch' (-va-outshe), *v.a.*, affirmer, déclarer.

avouch'ment, *n.*, (ant.) déclaration, *f.*

avow' (-va-ou), *v.a.*, avouer, confesser, déclarer, maintenir.

avow'able, *adj.*, avouable.

avow'al, *n.*, aveu, *m.*

avow'edly, *adv.*, de son propre aveu; ouvertement.

avow'er, *n.*, personne qui avoue, *f.*

avow'ry, *n.*, (jur.) aveu, *m.*

avul'sion (-veul-sheune), *n.*, avulsion, *f.,* arrachement, *m.*

awaft', *adv.*, (nav.) en berne.

await', *v.a.*, attendre.

awake' (-wéke), *v.a.*, éveiller, réveiller.

awake', *v.n.*, s'éveiller, se réveiller ; (fig.) revenir de.

awake', *adj.*, éveillé, vigilant.

awa'ken, *v.a.*, éveiller, réveiller.

awa'kened, *adj.*, éveillé.

awa'kener, *n.*, réveilleur, -euse, *m.f.*

awa'kening (-wékenigne), *n.*, réveil, *m.*

awa'king, *n.*, réveil, *m.*

award', *v.a.*, décerner, adjuger.

award', *v.n.*, décréter, décider.

award', *n.*, arrêt, décret, jugement, jugement arbitral, *m.*, sentence,*f.*

aware' (-wére), *adj.*, qui sait ; instruit. To be — of ; *savoir, connaître; être instruit de, s'apercevoir de.* Not to be —; *ignorer.* Not that I am — of ; *pas que je sache.*

away' (-wé), *adv.*, absent; loin, au loin, à distance. To go —; *s'en aller.* To fly —; *s'envoler.* To send —; *renvoyer.* To talk —; *parler toujours.* To take —; *enlever.* He is —; *il est absent.*

away'! *int.*, en avant ! arrière ! loin de moi ! loin d'ici ! — with you ! *allez-vous-en !* — with; *laissons là !* Right —; *sans arrêt, sans interruption.* Right —; (rail.) *partez ! en route !*

awe (ô), *n.*, terreur, crainte, *f.;* effroi; respect, *m.* To fill with —; *remplir de terreur.* To strike with —; *frapper de terreur.* To stand in — of; *craindre, redouter.* To keep in —; *tenir en, ou dans, le respect ; tenir en haleine.*

awe, *v.a.*, inspirer du respect à ; tenir en respect; imprimer la terreur à; imposer à.

aweath'er (-wétheur), *adv.*, (nav.) au vent.

aweigh' (a-wé), *adv.*, (nav.) (of anchor) pendant.

awe'-struck (ô-streuke), *adj.*, frappé de terreur; saisi de respect.

aw'ful, *adj.*, terrible; solennel, redoutable ; imposant.

aw'fully, *adv.*, horriblement; terriblement ; avec respect; (triv.) excessivement.

aw'fulness, *n.*, crainte, terreur, horreur, *f. ;* caractère terrible, *m.*, solennité, *f.*

awhile' (-waïle), *adv.*, pendant quelque temps; un instant, un peu. Wait —; *attendez un peu, un instant.*

awk'ward (ôk-weurde), *adj.*, maladroit, gauche, embarrassant, malencontreux, fâcheux.

awk'wardly, *adv.*, gauchement, maladroitement, d'une manière embarrassante.

awk'wardness, *n.*, gaucherie, maladresse, *f. ;* embarras, *m.*

awl (ôl), *n.*, alène, *f. ;* poinçon, *m.* — maker; *alénier.*

aw'less, adj., sans crainte; courageux, intrépide; impudent, effronté.

awl'-shaped (-shépte), adj., en alêne; subulé.

awn, n., (bot.) barbe, arête, f.

awned', adj., épié, monté en épi, barbu, à barbes.

aw'ning, n., tente, banne, bâche, f.

awry', adv., de travers, de côté.

ax ou **axe,** n., hache, cognée, f. — case; porte-hache, m.

ax'il ou **axil'la,** n., (anat., bot.) aisselle, f.

ax'illary, adj., axillaire.

ax'iom, n., axiome, m.

axiomat'ic ou **axiomat'ical,** adj., d'axiome.

ax'is, n., (axes) axe, m.

ax'le ou **ax'le-tree** (ax'l-trî), n., essieu, m. — box; boîte d'essieu, f. — grease; vieux oing, m. — guard; garde-essieu, f.

ay ou **aye,** adv., oui; bien plus; et qui plus est; (nav.) bon quart !

aye, adv. For —; à jamais, pour toujours.

aye, n., (ayes) affirmation, f., oui; (ayes) voix pour, f.

az'arole, n., (bot.) azerole, f.

az'imuth, n., (astron.) azimut, m.

azote', n., (chem.) azote, m.

azot'ic, adj., azotique.

a'zure (a-jiour or é-), adj., d'azur.

a'zure, n., azur, m.

a'zure, v.a., azurer.

a'zured (a-jiour'de or é-), adj., azuré.

a'zure-stone (-stône), n., pierre d'azur, f.; lapis lazuli, m.

a'zurite (a-jiouraïte or é-), n., (min.) lazulite, f.

az'yme, n., (ant.) pain azyme, m.

az'ymites (-maït'se), n.pl., azymites, m.

az'ymous (-meusse), adj., azyme.

B

b, n., seconde lettre de l'alphabet, b, m.; (mus.) si, m. — natural; si bécarre. — flat; si bémol.

B. A., bachelier-ès-lettres, ès-arts.

baa (bâ), v.n., bêler.

baa, n., bêlement, m.

Baal, n., Baal, m.

bab'ble, v.n., babiller; gazouiller, jaser; (fig.) (of a stream) murmurer, babiller.

bab'ble, n., babil, caquet; (fig.) murmure, m.; jaserie, f.

bab'bler, n., babillard, m., babillarde, f.; bavard.

bab'bling, n., babil, babillage, bavardage, caquetage, m.

bab'bling, adj., babillard.

babe (bébe), n., enfant nouveau-né, petit enfant, poupon, m., pouponne, f.

Ba'bel (bé-), n., Babel, f.

bab'ery (bé-biri), n., babiole, f., joujou, m.

ba'bishly, adv., (ant.) en enfant.

baboon' (ba-boune), n., babouin, m.

ba'by (bé-bi), n., enfant nouveau-né, petit enfant, poupon, bébé, m., pouponne, poupée, f. — linen; layette, f.

ba'byhood (bé-bi-houde), n., bas âge, m., enfance, f.

ba'byish (bé-bi-ish), adj., enfantin, de petit enfant.

Babylo'nian ou **Babylo'nish,** adj., babylonien; de Babel.

Babylo'nian, n., Babylonien, m., Babylonienne, f.; (ant.) astrologue, m.

baccalau'reate, n., baccalauréat, m.

bac'carat, n., baccarat, m.

bac'chanal (bak-ka-), ou **bacchana'lian** (bakka-na-lia'n), n., ivrogne, débauché, m., ivrognesse, f.

bacchana'lia ou **bac'chanals,** n.pl., bacchanales, f.pl.

bacchana'lian, adj., bachique.

bac'chanals, n.pl. V. **bacchana'lia.**

bacchant', n., prêtre de Bacchus, m.

bacchan'te, n., bacchante, f.

bac'chic (bak-kik) ou **bac'chical** (-kikal), adj., bachique.

baccif'erous (bak-si-feuresse), adj., baccifère.

bach'elor (bat'sheu-leur), n., célibataire, garçon; (of arts) bachelier, m. — of arts, of science; bachelier ès arts, ès sciences, m. — of medicine, of laws, of divinity; bachelier en médecine, en droit, en théologie. —'s degree; grade de bachelier, m.

bach'elorship, n., célibat ; (of arts) baccalauréat, m.

back, adv., en arrière; de retour, rentre. To call —; rappeler. To come —; revenir. To give —; rendre. To send —; renvoyer. To go —; retourner. To come —; revenir. To ask —; redemander. To be —; être de retour. A few years —; il y a de cela quelques années.

back, n., dos; derrière, m.; reins, m.pl.; (of a hill, embankment) revers, m.; (of hares, etc.) râble, m. — of a chair; dos, dossier de chaise, m. — of the head; derrière de la tête. — of the stage ; fond du théâtre, m. — of a chimney; fond de cheminée, m. — of a house; derrière d'une maison. — to —; dos à dos. Behind one's —; derrière le dos. To break any one's —; casser les reins à quelqu'un. To turn one's — on any one; tourner le dos à quelqu'un. At the — of; au dos de; derrière. To fall on one's —; tomber à la renverse. When his — is turned; quand il a le dos tourné.

back, v.a., faire reculer; soutenir, appuyer; (bet) parier pour ; (nav.) coiffer; (anchors) empenneler ; viser (a warrant) ; (com. bills) endosser.

back, v.n., reculer ; (nav.) nager à culer. To — out of; se dédire ; reculer devant ; se tirer de; tirer son épingle du jeu.

back'bite (-baïte), v.a., médire de ; calomnier.

back'biter (-baïteur), n., médisant, détracteur, calomniateur, m.

back'biting (-baïtigne), n., médisance, calomnie, détraction, f.

back'bitingly, adv., avec médisance.

back'board (-bôrde), n., (nav.) dossier, m.

back'bone (-bône), n., épine du dos, f. To the —; jusqu'à la moelle des os. To have no —; n'avoir pas de force de caractère; manquer de décision. [m.

back'-building, n., arrière corps de batiment,

back'-door (-dore), n., porte de derrière, f.

backed' (bak'te), adj., à dos ; à dossier (com.); (of bills) endossé.

back'er, n., partisan, second; parieur pour, m.

back'gammon (-gam-meune), n., trictrac, m.

back'-garden, n., jardin de derrière, m.

back'ground (-gra-ou'n'de), n., terrain de derrière ; fond ; (paint.) arrière-plan, fond, m.

back'-handed (-ha-ndède), adj., donné avec le revers de la main.

back'-handed, adv., avec le revers de la main.

back'-kitchen, n., arrière-cuisine, f.

back'-parlor, n., petit salon de derrière, m., arrière-salle, f. (V. Hugo).

back'-pedal, v.n., contrepédaler.

back'room (-roume), n., chambre de derrière, f.

back'-shop, n., arrière-boutique, f.

back'side (-saïde), n., derrière, m.

back'sight (-saïte), n., (of firearms) hausse, f.

backslide (-slaïde), v.n., apostasier, retomber.

backsli'der (-deur), n., apostat; renégat; transgresseur ; relaps, m.

backsli'ding (-digne), n., infidélité, tergiversation, faute, rechute, f.

back′-slums, *n.pl.*, bas quartiers, *m.pl.*

back′stair, *adj.* — influence ; *intrigue de cour*, *f.*

back′stairs (-stèrze), *n.*, escalier dérobé, *m.*

back′-stroke, *n.*, coup de revers, *m. ;* (at games) bricole ; (fig.) coup de patte, *f. ;* contre-coup, *m.*

back′sword (-sôrde), *n.*, sabre, *m.*

back′-train, *n.*, train de retour, *m.*

back′ward (-worde) *ou* **back′wards**, *adj.*, arriéré, en retard, en arrière; lent, tardif, peu empressé. To be —; (of studies) *être fort peu avancé ; ne pas savoir grand′chose.*

back′ward, *adv.*, à reculons; à la renverse; à rebours ; en arrière. To fall —; *tomber à la renverse.* To walk — and forward ; *se promener de long en large.* — and forward motion; *mouvement de va et vient.*

backwarda′tion, *n.*, déport, *m.*

back′wardly, *adv.*, en arrière, à contre-cœur.

back′wardness (-nèsse), *n.*, état arriéré, manque de progrès, *m. ;* répugnance, lenteur, *f.*

back′wards (-wordze), *adv.* *V.* **backward**.

back′wood (-woude), *n.*, arrière-bois, *m.*

back′woods, *n.*, terres incultes, *f.pl.* In the —; *dans le fin fond des bois.*

back′woodsman, *n.*, habitant des bois, *m.*

back′-yard, *n.*, arrière-cour, cour de derrière, *f.*

ba′con (bé-k′n), *n.*, lard, *m.* Rasher of —; *tranche de lard ; barde, f.* Flitch of —; *flèche de lard, f.* To save one′s —; *sauver sa peau ; se tirer d′affaire.*

Baco′nian, *adj.*, baconien, de Bacon.

Bac′trian, *adj.*, bactrien, -ne.

bac′ule (bakioule), *n.*, (fort.) herse, *f.*

bad (bade), *adj.*, méchant; mauvais; (of health) malade. That is too —; *c′est trop fort or c′est par trop fort.* — money; *fausse monnaie, f.* — cold; *gros rhume, m.* — is the best; *le meilleur n′en vaut rien.* It is very — of you ; *c′est très mal à vous.* To have a — finger, hand, etc.; *avoir mal au doigt, etc.*

badge, *n.*, plaque, marque, *f. ;* signe, symbole ; (on the arm) brassard ; insigne, *m.*

badge, *v.a.*, marquer d′une plaque.

badge′less (-lèsse), *adj.*, sans plaque ; sans marque.

bad′ger (-jeur), *n.*, blaireau, *m.*

bad′ger-legged (-lèg′de), *adj.*, à jambes de blaireau.

bad′ly, *adv.*, mal; grandement, fort, beaucoup, bien. — dressed; *mal mis.* To want —; *avoir grandement besoin, ou bien besoin, de.* To be — off ; *être dans le besoin.*

bad′ness (-nèsse), *n.*, méchanceté; mauvaise qualité, *f. ;* mauvais état, *m.*

baf′fle (baf-f′l), *v.a.*, confondre, déjouer; bafouer; dérouter, dépister, rendre inutile.

baf′fler (-fl′eur), *n.*, qui déjoue.

bag, *n.*, sac, cabas, *m. ;* bourse (for the hair); (of animals) outre, poche, *f. ;* (letters) courier, *m.* Carpet—; *sac de nuit, m.* To pack up — and baggage; *plier bagage.* With — and baggage; *avec armes et bagage.* —man; *commis-voyageur, m.* — wig; *perruque à bourse, f.*

bag, *v.a.*, ensacher, mettre en sac; gonfler comme un sac; (at billiards) blouser; (of game) tuer; (to steal) voler, chiper.

bag, *v.n.*, faire le sac ; être gonflé; bouffer.

bagatelle′, *n.*, bagatelle, *f. ;* joujou ; billard de dame, *m.* — board; *billard-bagatelle, m.*

bag′ful (-foule), *n.*, sachée, *f.*, sac plein, *m.*

bag′gage (baghé′dje), *n.*, bagage, *m. ;* (jest.) coquine, prostituée, *f.* Saucy —; *impertinente, péronnelle, f.*

bag′ging (baghigne), *n.*, toile à sac, *f.*

bagn′io (ba-niô), *n.*, maison de bains; maison de débauche ; prison, *f. ;* quartier des esclaves, *m.*

bag′pipe (-païpe), *n.*, cornemuse, musette, *f.*

bag′pipe, *v.a.*, (nav.) masquer, coiffer.

bag′piper (-païpeur), *n.*, joueur de corne-muse, *m.*

baguette′ (baghète), *n.*, (arch.) baguette, *f.*

bah, *int.*, bah.

bail (béle), *n.*, caution, *f. ;* cautionnement, *m.* On —; *sous caution.* To put in — for ; *fournir caution pour.*

bail, *v.a.*, cautionner.

bail′able (bélab′l), *adj.*, recevable à caution, qui admet le cautionnement.

bail-bond (-bo′nde), *n.*, cautionnement, *m.*

bailee′ (bél-i), *n.*, dépositaire, *m.f.*

bail′er *ou* **bail′or** (bél-eur), *n.*, déposant, *m. ;* caution, *f.*

bail′iff (bé-life), *n.*, huissier ; (Chan. Isl.) chef-magistrat, *m.* Farm —; *régisseur, m.* —′s man ; *recors, m.*

bail′ing, *n.*, cautionnement, *m.*

bail′iwick (bél′i-wike), *n.*, bailliage, *m.*

bail′ment, *n.*, dépôt, nantissement, gage, *m.*

bait, *v.a.*, (of horses) rafraîchir ; (hook) amorcer ; (of bulls, etc.) faire combattre ; (of persons) harceler, tourmenter.

bait (béte), *v.n.*, (on a journey) se rafraîchir.

bait, *n.*, amorce, *f. ;* appât, *m.* White-—; *able, m., ablette, clupée blanche, blanchaille, f.* To take, *ou* swallow, the —; *mordre à l′hameçon.*

bait′ing (-tigne), *n.*, amorçage, rafraîchissement, combat, *m.* Bull—; *combat de taureaux, m.*

baize (béze), *n.*, drap de billard, *m.*, serge espagnolette, *f.*

bake (béke), *v.a., v.n.*, cuire au four, faire du pain; boulanger ; se dessécher.

bake′house (-haouce), *n.*, fournil, *m.*, boulangerie, *f.*

ba′ker (bék-eur), *n.*, boulanger, *m.*, -ère, *f.* —′s shop, —′s trade; *boulangerie, f.* —′s man; *mitron, m.*

ba′ker-legged (-lèg′de), *adj.*, bancal.

ba′kery (bék-euri), *n.*, boulangerie, *f.*

ba′king (bék′igne), *n.*, cuisson ; (batch) fournée, cuite, *f.*

bal′ance (-la′nce), *n.*, balance, *f. ;* équilibre, contrepoids ; (horl.) balancier, *m.* — of an account; *reliquat de compte, m.* — of power ; *balance politique.* To turn the —; *faire pencher la balance.* To lose one′s —; *perdre l′équilibre.* To strike a —; (com.) *établir une balance.*

bal′ance, *v.a.*, balancer ; tenir, maintenir en équilibre, équilibrer, pondérer ; arrêter, balancer.

bal′ance, *v.n.*, se balancer ; (fig.) balancer, hésiter.

bal′ance-beam (-bîme), *n.*, (tech.) balancier, *m.*

bal′ance-maker (-mék-eur), *n.*, fabricant de balances, *m.*

bal′ancer (-ceur), *n.*, personne qui balance, *f. ;* peseur, *m.*

bal′ance-sheet (-shîte), *n.*, (com.) balance, *f. ;* bilan, *m.*

bal′ance-weight (-wéte), *n.*, poids de balance; contrepoids, *m.*

bal′ancing (-cigne), *n.*, balancement, *m.*

bal′cony (-kô-), *n.*, balcon, *m.*

bald (bôld), *adj.*, chauve ; (fig.) (of style) plat, sec, nu, découvert.

bal′dachin (bôld′akine), *n.*, baldaquin, *m.*

bal′derdash (bôldeurdashe), *n.*, galimatias ; fatras, *m.*

bald′-head (-hède), *n.*, tête chauve, *f.*

bald′ly, *adv.*, nûment, platement, sèchement.

bald′ness (-nèsse), *n.*, calvitie ; (fig.) platitude, nudité, sécheresse, *f.*

bald′pate (-péte), *n.*, tête chauve, *f.*

bald′pated (-pétède), *adj.*, à tête chauve.

bald′rick *ou* **bald′ric** (bôld′rike), *n.*, baudrier, ceinturon, *m. ;* ceinture, *f.*

bale (béle), *n.*, (com.) balle, *f.*, ballot, colis, *m.*

bale, *v.a.*, emballer; (nav.) vider l'eau avec l'écope, écoper.

Balea'ric (-li-), *adj.*, des îles Baléares.

bale'ful (bélefoule), *adj.*, malheureux, sinistre, funeste, triste.

bale'fully, *adv.*, funestement, nuisiblement.

bale'fulness, *n.*, nature funeste, nuisible, pernicieuse, *f.*

balk (bōke), *n.*, désappointement, contretemps, mécompte, (of land) entre-deux, *m.;* (of timber) bille, poutre, *f.*

balk, *v.a.*, frustrer; entraver, contrarier, désappointer; déjouer.

ball (bōl), *n.*, boule; (of snow) boule, pelote; (of a musket) balle, *f.;* (of cannon) boulet, *m.;* (at billiards) bille; (cook.) boulette, *f.;* (for playing) balle, *f.* — of the eye; *globe*, *m.; prunelle, pupille, f.* — lightning; *foudre globulaire, f.* — of thread; *peloton de fil, m.* — cartridge; *cartouche à balle, f.* — cock; *robinet-flotteur, m.* — practice; *tir à balle, m.* — proof; *à l'épreuve des balles.*

ball, *v.n.*, (of snow) se peloter.

ball, *n.*, bal, *m.* — dress; *costume de bal, m.* — room; *salle, f.*, (ou *salon, m.*) de bal. Fancy —; *bal costumé.*

bal'lad (bal-lade), *n.*, ballade; romance, *f.* — opera, *vaudeville, m.*

bal'lad, *v.n.*, chanter des ballades; faire des ballades.

bal'lad-maker (-mék-eur), *n.*, faiseur de ballades, *m.*

bal'lad-monger (-meugn'gheur), *n.*, marchand de ballades, *m.*

bal'lad-singer, *n.*, chanteur des rues, *m.*

bal'lad-writer (-raïteur), *n.*, auteur de ballades, chansonnier, *m.*

bal'last (bal-laste), *n.*, (nav.) lest, *m.;* (railways) ballast, *m.* — pit; *ballastière, f.* In —; *sur lest.*

bal'last, *v.a.*, (nav.) lester; empierrer, ensabler.

bal'laster, *n.*, terrassier, *m.*

bal'lasting (-tigne), *n.*, (engineering) ensablement, empierrement; (nav.) lestage, *m.*

bal'last-heaver, *u.*, délesteur, *m.*

bal'last-lighter (-laï-teur), *n.*, bateau lesteur, *m.*

bal'last-train, *n.*, train de ballast, *m.*

bal'let (bal-lè), *n.*, ballet, *m.* — girl; *danseuse, f.*

bal'let-master (-mâs-teur), *n.*, directeur des ballets, *m.*

ball'ing (bōl-ligne), *n.*, (metal.) ballage, réchauffage, *m.*

ballis'ta, balis'ta (bal-lis-), *n.*, baliste, *f.*

ballis'tics (bal-lis-tikse), *n.pl.*, balistique, *f. sing.*

balloon' (ba-loune), *n.*, ballon, aérostat, *m.*

bal'lot (bal-lote), *n.*, boule, *f.;* bulletin, *m.* By —; *au scrutin secret.* First —; *premier tour de scrutin, m.* Second —; *second tour de scrutin, m.*

bal'lot, *v.n.*, voter au scrutin.

bal'lot-box, *n.*, urne du scrutin, *f.*

bal'loting (-tigne), *n.*, scrutin; vote au scrutin, *m.*

bal'lot-paper, *n.*, bulletin de scrutin, *m.*

balm (bâme), *n.*, baume, *m.;* (bot.) mélisse, *f.*

balm, *v.a.*, parfumer; servir de baume à.

balm'-mint (-mi-n'te), *n.*, mélisse, citronnelle, *f.*

balm'y (bâm'i), *adj.*, balsamique; embaumé, parfumé, doux; (pop. and jest.) ivre, pris de vin.

bal'neary (-ni-), *n.*, (ant.) salle de bain, *f.*

balnea'tion (-ni-é), *n.*, (ant.) action de baigner, *f.*

bal'neatory (-ni-a-to-), *adj.*, de bain.

bal'sam (bōl-çame), *n.*, baume, *m.;* balsamine, *f.*

balsam'ic (bal-), *n.*, balsamique, *m.*

balsam'ic *ou* **balsam'ical**, *adj.*, balsamique.

bal'samine (bōl-ça-), *n.*, balsamine, *f.*

bal'sam-tree (-trî), *n.*, balsamier, baumier, *m.*

bal'uster (ba-leus-teur), *n.*, rampe (of a staircase), *f. ;* (arch.) balustre, *m.*

bal'ustered (-teurde), *adj.*, à balustres.

balustrade' (-tréde), *n.*, balustrade, *f.*

bamboo' (ba-m'bou), *n.*, bambou, *m.*

bamboo'zle (-bou'z'l), *v.a.*, embrouiller, tromper, mettre dedans, refaire, enjôler.

bamboo'zler (-z'leur), *n.*, embrouilleur, trompeur, enjôleur, *m.*

bamboo'zling, *n.*, enjôlement, *m.;* duperie, *f.*

ban (ba-n), *n.*, ban, *m.;* interdiction; malédiction. Under the —; *au ban.*

ban, *v.a.*, anathématiser, maudire.

ban, *v.n.*, proférer des malédictions.

bana'na (ba-nâ-na), *n.*, (bot.) banane, *f.*

bana'na-tree (-trî), *n.*, bananier, *m.*

ban'co (bâgn-kō), *adj.*, (com.) banco, de banque.

band (ba-n'de), *n.*, bande; musique, troupe, *f. ;* lien; ruban, *m.;* (for the waist) ceinture; (of guns, etc.) capucine, *f.;* (of priests) rabat, *m.* — master; *chef de musique, m.* — stand; *tribune de musiciens, f.*

band, *v.a.*, bander; liguer, réunir en troupe.

band, *v.n.*, se liguer.

band'age (ba-n'dédje), *n.*, bandeau; (surg.) bandage, *m.*, bande, *f.*

band'age-maker (-mék-eur), *n.*, bandagiste, *m.*

bandan'a *ou* **bandan'na** (ba'n-),*n.*, indienne,*f.*

band'box (ba'nd'-), *n.*, carton, *m.*

band'elet *ou* **band'let** (ba'nd'lète), *n.*, bandelette, *f.*

ban'dit (bân'dite), *n.*, (*banditti*) bandit, *m.*

bandit'ti, *n.*, bandits, *m.pl.*

ban'dog (ban'doghe), *n.*, chien d'attache, *m.*

bandoleer' (ban'do-lîre), *n.*, bandoulière, *f.*

band'rol (ban'drôle), *n.*, banderole, *f.*

band'ster, *n.*, (agri.) botteleur, *m.*

band'y, *v.a.*, renvoyer (a ball); ballotter, échanger; se renvoyer. To — words; *faire assaut de paroles ; se renvoyer des paroles.*

band'y, *v.n.*, se mesurer, rivaliser; se disputer.

band'y, *adj.*, tortu. — leg; *jambe tortue, f.*

band'ying, *n.*, dispute, rivalité, *f.*

band'y-legged (-lèg'de), *adj.*, bancal; (fam.) bancroche.

bane (béne), *n.*, poison; (fig.) fléau, *m.;* ruine, *f.*

bane, *v.a.*, (l.u.) empoisonner.

bane'berry (-bé-), *n.*, (bot.) herbe de saint Christophe, *f.*

bane'ful (-foule), *adj.*, empoisonné, vénéneux, funeste, mortel, nuisible.

bane'fully, *adv.*, nuisiblement, funestement, mortellement.

bane'fulness (-nèsse), *n.*, chose fatale, (fig.) action destructive, nature funeste, *f.*

bang (bagne), *n.*, coup, grand bruit, *m.*

bang, *v.a.*, rosser, étriller; pousser violemment. To — a door; *claquer une porte ; pousser violemment une porte.* He went out —ing the door after him; *il sortit en claquant la porte* (Daudet).

bang! *int.*, pan! paf!

bang'ing (-ghigne), *n.*, roulée, volée, *f.*

ban'gle (-n), *n.*, porte-bonheur, *m.*

ban'ian (ban'i-a-n), *n.*, banian, *m.* — day; *jour maigre, m.*

ban'ian-tree (-trî), *n.*, figuier d'Adam, *m.*

ban'ish (ban'ishe), *v.a.*, bannir, exiler; proscrire; (fig.) (*to dismiss*) écarter.

ban'isher (-sheur), *n.*, proscripteur, *m.*

ban'ishment, *n.*, bannissement, exil, *m.*, proscription, *f.*

ban'ister (-teur), *n.* V. **baluster**.

bank (bâgn'ke), *n.*, terrasse, *f.*, remblai, talus, *m.;* berge; rive, *f. ;* rivage, bord; banc de sable, de gazon, *m.*

bank (baign'ke), *v.a.*, terrasser; encaisser.

bank, *n.*, (com.) banque, *f.* Branch — ; *successale de banque, f.* Savings- — ; *caisse d'épargne, f.* Joint-stock — ; *banque par actions,* ou *en commandite.*

bank, *v.a.*, déposer dans une banque; **encaisser** (*de l'argent*).

bank (with), *v.n.*, avoir pour banquier.

bank'-account (-ak-kaou'nte), *n.*, compte de banque, *m.*

bank'-book (-bouke), *n.*, carnet de banque, *m.*

bank'-clerk (-clàrke), *n.*, commis de banque, *m.*

bank'er (-keur), *n.*, banquier, *m.*

bank'-holiday, *n.*, fête légale, *f.*

bank'ing (baign'k'igne), *n.*, banque, *f.* — *establishment; établissement de banque, m.*

bank'-note (-nôte), *n.*, billet de banque, *m.*

bank'-porter (-por-teur), *n.*, garçon de banque, *m.*

bank'-post bill (-pôste-), *n.*, mandat de banque, *m.*

bank'rupt (baign'k'reupte), *n.*, banqueroutier, *m.*, banqueroutière, *f.:* failli, *m.*, faillie, *f.* Fraudulent —; *banqueroutier frauduleux.* To be, to become, a —; *faire banqueroute.* To be adjudicated *ou* adjudged a — ; *être déclaré en faillite.* —'s certificate ; *concordat, m.*

bank'rupt, *adj.*, en faillite, en banqueroute; (fig.) ruiné.

bank'rupt, *v.a.*, mettre en faillite, ruiner.

bank'ruptcy (baign'k'reup'ci), *n.*, banqueroute, faillite, *f.* Fraudulent — ; *banqueroute frauduleuse, f.* Court of — ; *cour des faillites, f.*

bank'-stock, *n.*, actions de banque, *f.pl.*, consolidés, *m.pl.*

ban'ner (ba'n'neur), *n.*, bannière, *f.;* étendard, *m.*

ban'nered (ba'n'neurde), *adj.*, portant des bannières, garni de bannières; pavoisé.

ban'neret (ba'n'neurète), *n.*, banneret, *m.*

ban'nerol (ba'n'neurôle), *n.* V. **bandrol.**

ban'nock, *n.*, gâteau d'avoine, *m.*

banns (ba'n'ze), *n.pl.*, bans de mariage, *m.*, publication de bans, *f.*

ban'quet (baign'kwète), *n.*, banquet, festin, *m.;* (fort.) V. **banquette.**

ban'quet, *v.a.*, donner un banquet **à.**

ban'quet, *v.n.*, banqueter, festiner, faire festin.

ban'queter (baign'kwèteur), *n.*, amateur de banquets, *m.*

ban'queting (-tigne), *n.*, banquet, festin, *m.*

ban'queting-house (-haouce), *n.*, salle de banquet, *f.*

ban'queting-room (-roume), *n.*, salle de banquet, de festin, *f.*

banquette' (bai'gn'kète), *n.*, (fort.) banquette, *f.*

ban'ter (ban'teur), *n.*, plaisanterie, raillerie, *f.*

ban'ter, *v.a.*, plaisanter, railler.

ban'terer (ban'teureur), *n.*, railleur, *m.*, railleuse, *f.*

ban'tering (ba'n'teurigne), *n.*, raillerie, *f.*

ban'tering, *adj.*, railleur.

ban'tling (ba'n'tligne), *n.*, poupon, bambin, marmot, *m.*

ban'yan, *n.* V. **banian.**

bap'tism (bap'tiz'm), *n.*, baptême, *m.* Certificate of —; *extrait de baptême, m.*

baptis'mal (bap'tiz-), *adj.*, baptismal, de baptême.

bap'tist (bap'tiste), *n.*, anabaptiste, *m.*

bap'tistery (bap-tis-teuri), *n.*, baptistère, *m.*

baptist'ic *ou* **baptist'ical** (bap'tis-), *adj.*, du baptême.

baptize' (bap'taïze), *v.a.*, baptiser.

baptiz'er (bap-taïzeur), *n.*, baptiseur, *m.*, personne qui baptise, *f.*

bar, *n.*, barre, *f.;* barreau, parquet; obstacle; (of public houses) comptoir; (jur.) banc des ac-

cusés, *m.;* (rod) tringle, *f.;* (swingbar) palonnier, *m.;* (of lace) bride ; (of a bit) barre; (of medals) barrette; (mus.) mesure, *f.;* (jur.) empêchement, *m.* Prisoner at the — ; *accusé, m.* Stirrup — ; *porte-étrivières, m.* — iron ; *fer en barres, m.* To be called to the — ; *être reçu avocat.*

bar, *v.a.*, barrer ; exclure, empêcher **de** ; (jur.) interrompre, exclure; interdire **à** ; ôter; priver **de.**

barb, *n.*, barbe, *f.;* pointe, dent (of a fish-hook, of an arrow), *f.*

barb, *n.*, cheval de Barbarie; barbe, *m.*

barb, *v.a.*, barder (a horse); garnir de pointes (an arrow); faire des dents à un hameçon, à une flèche.

bar'bacan (bar-ba-ca'n), *n.*, barbacane, *f.*

barba'rian (bar-bé-ri-a'n), *adj.*, barbare.

barba'rian, *n.*, barbare, *m.f.*

barbar'ic, *adj.*, barbare, des barbares.

bar'barism (bàr-ba-), *n.*, barbarie, *f.;* (gram.) barbarisme, *m.*

barbar'ity, *n.*, barbarie, cruauté, *f.*

bar'barize (bàr-ba-raïze), *v.a.*, rendre barbare; barbariser.

bar'barous (bàr-bareusse), *adj.*, barbare.

bar'barousness (-nèsse), *n.*, barbarie, *f.*

bar'bary, *n.*, cheval barbe, *m.*

bar'bate (bàr-béte) *ou* **bar'bated** (bàr-bétède), *adj.*, barbelé; (bot.) barbé, barbu.

bar'becue (bàr-bí-kiou), *v.a.*, faire cuire, *ou* rôtir (un animal tout entier).

bar'becue, *n.*, animal rôti entier, *m.*

barbed (bàrb'de), *adj.*, barbelé ; bardé. — wire ; *grillage à pointes de fer, fil de fer barbelé, m.*

barb'el (bàr-b'l), *n.*, (ich.) barbeau, *m.* ; (vet.) barbillons, *m.pl.*

barb'er (bàr-beur), *n.*, barbier, coiffeur, *m.* —'s block; *tête à perruque, f.*

barb'er-mon'ger (-meugn'gheur), *n.*, petit-maître, dandy, *m.*

bar'berry, *n.*, épine-vinette, *f.*

barb'er-sur'geon (-seur'd'jeune), *n.*, chirurgien-barbier, *m.*

bar'bican (bàr-bi-ca-n), *n.* V. **barbacan.**

bar'bles (bàr-b'lze), *n.pl.*, (vet.) barbillons, *m.pl.*

bar'carolle, *n.*, barcarolle, *f.*

bard, *n.*, barde, troubadour, trouvère, *m.*

bard'ic, *adj.*, de barde.

bard'ish, *adj.*, de barde.

bard'ism, *n.*, science des bardes, *f.*

bare (bére), *adj.*, nu, découvert; tout juste; seul; simple; (fig.) dépourvu **de.** The — necessaries; *le strict nécessaire, m.*

bare, *v.a.*, découvrir; dépouiller **de** ; mettre à nu; exposer ; (of swords) tirer du fourreau.

bare'back, *adv.*, à dos nu ; à nu ; à poil.

bare'-bone, *n.*, corps décharné, squelette, *m.*

bare'boned (-bôned), *adj.*, décharné.

bare'boned, *n.*, cagot, cafard, *m.*

bare'faced (-fés'te), *adj.*, à visage découvert ; effronté, éhonté, sans déguisement.

bare'facedly (-fés'tli), *adv.*, ouvertement; sans déguisement; effrontément.

bare'facedness (-fés't'nèsse), *n.*, effronterie, *f.*

bare'foot (-foute), *adj.*, nu-pieds ; pieds nus.

bare'gnawn (-nône), *adj.*, rongé au vif.

bare'headed (-hè-dède), *adj.*, nu-tête, tête nue.

bare'legged (-lég'de), *adj.*, nu-jambes.

bare'ly (bér'li), *adv.*, à peine ; simplement ; seulement; pauvrement, chétivement, tout juste.

bare'-necked, *adj.*, le cou nu ; (of a woman) décolletée, la gorge nue.

bare'ness (bér'nèsse), *n.*, nudité; pauvreté, misère, *f.*, dénûment, *m.*

bar'gain (bàr-ghi-n), *n.*, marché ; accord, contrat, *m.*, bonne affaire, occasion, *f.* To make a good — ; *faire un bon marché* ; *acheter quelque chose à bon marché.* Great — ; *marché d'or, excellent marché.* To have a thing a great — ; *avoir quelque chose pour rien, pour presque rien, à excellent compte.* It is a — ; *tope là! ; j'y* *consens; voilà qui est fait; c'est convenu.* It is no —; *marché nul.* To strike a —; *faire un marché.* Into the —; *par-dessus le marché.* To get the best of the —; *avoir la meilleure part.* To drive hard —s; *être serré en affaires.* To make the best of a bad —; *se tirer d'affaire le mieux possible.*

bar'gain, *v.n.,* marchander; faire marché, convenir **de**; faire affaire. I did not — for that; (fig.) *je ne comptais pas là-dessus; je ne m'attendais pas à cela.* You are always bargaining; *vous ne faites que marchander.*

bargainee' (-ni), *n.,* (jur.) acquéreur, *m.*

bar'gainer (-neur), *n.,* vendeur, *m.,* personne qui marchande, *f.*

barge (bârdje), *n.,* barque, *f.;* bateau, chaland, *m.;* (nav.) canot de parade, *m.*

barge'man (-mane), *n.,* batelier, canotier, *m.*

barge'master (-mâsteur), *n.,* patron de barque, *m.*

barge'-owner, *n.,* propriétaire de chalands, *m.f.*

baril'la (ba-ril'la), *n.,* (bot., chem.) barille, soude, *f.*

bar'itone, *n.,* baryton, *m.*

bark (bârke), *n.,* écorce, *f.;* (of tanners) tan; (pharm.) quinquina; (of a dog) aboiement, *m.*

bark, *v.a.,* écorcer, enlever l'écorce à un arbre; décortiquer.

bark, *v.n.,* (of dogs) aboyer.

bark *ou* **barque,** *n.,* barque, *f.;* trois-mâts, *m.*

bark'bared (-bér'de), *adj.,* écorcé.

barked (bârk'te), *adj.,* écorcé; (of limbs) écorché.

bark'er (-keur), *n.,* aboyeur; écorceur, *m.*

bark'ing (bark'igne), *n.,*(of dogs) aboiement, *m.*

bark'ing, *n.,*(hort.) écorcement, *m.;* décortication, *f.* — iron; *écorçoir, m.*

bark'less (-lèsse), *adj.,* sans écorce.

bark'-mill, *n.,* moulin à tan, *m.*

bark'y, *adj.,* d'écorce.

bar'ley (bâr-li), *n.,* orge, *f.* Peeled, hulled —; *orge mondé, m.* Pearl —; *orge perlé, m.* Malted —; (tech.) *orge maltée, f.* —water; *eau d'orge, f.* —sugar; *sucre d'orge, m.*

barm (bârme), *n.,* levure, *f.*

bar'maid (-méde), *n.,* fille, *ou* demoiselle, de comptoir, *f.*

bar'man (-mane), *n.,* garçon de comptoir, *m.*

barm'y, *adj.,* qui contient de la levure.

barn (bârne), *n.,* grange, *f.* — door fowls; *oiseaux de basse-cour, m.pl.;* volaille, *f.* — floor; *aire de grange, f.*

barn, *v.a.,* (ant.) engranger, mettre en grange.

bar'nacle (bâr-na'k'l), *n.,* (orni.) barnache, barnacle, *f.;* (mol.) cirripède, *m.;* (mol.) anatife, pousse-pieds, *m.* pl., (vet.) morailles, *f.pl.*

barom'eter (-mi-teur), *n.,* baromètre, *m.*

baromet'ric *ou* **baromet'rical** (-ro-mè-), *adj.,* barométrique.

bar'on (bar'eu'n), *n.,* baron; (jur.) mari, *m.;* (her.) armes mi-parties, *f.pl.* — of beef; (cook.) *aloyau-double, m.*

bar'onage (bar'eu'n'adje), *n.,* baronnage, *m.;* baronnie; contribution prélevée sur les barons, *f.*

bar'oness (bar'eun'èsse), *n.,* baronne, *f.*

bar'onet (bar'o'n'ète), *n.,* baronnet, *m.*

bar'onetage (bar'o-n'ètadje), *n.,* corps des baronnets, *m.*

bar'onetcy (bar'o-nèt'ci), *n.,* dignité de baronnet, *f.*

baro'nial (-rô-), *adj.,* baronnial; de baron.

bar'ony, *n.,* baronnie, *f.*

barouche', *n.,* barouche, calèche, *f.*

bar'racan (bar-ra-ka-n), *n.,* bouracan, *f.*

bar'rack (bar-rake) *ou* **bar'racks,** *n.,* caserne, *f.;* quartier, *m.* — master; *intendant de caserne, quartier-maître, m.* — porter; *casernier, m.* — room; *chambrée, f.* — sergeant; *garde-magasin, m.*

bar'rator (bar-ra-teur), *n.,* (jur.) personne qui incite aux procès, *f.;* (nav.) marin coupable de baraterie, *m.*

bar'ratrous (-treusse) *adj.,* (nav.) entaché de baraterie.

bar'ratrously, *adv.,* avec, de, par, baraterie.

bar'ratry, *n.,* excitation aux procès; (nav.) baraterie, *f.*

barred, *adj., part.,* barré; (striped) à raies; (jur.) nul, périmé, caduc.

bar'rel (bar-rèle), *n.,* baril; (of machines) cylindre, tambour; canon de fusil; fût; barillet, *m.;* fusée, *f.* — of the capstan; (nav.) *mèche du cabestan, f.* — of a gun; *canon de fusil, m.* — of a drum; *fût de tambour, m.* Watch —; *barillet de montre, m.* — of a pump; *corps de pompe, m.* — of tar; *gonne, f.* — organ; *orgue de barbarie, m.*

bar'rel, *v.a.,* embariller, entonner, mettre en baril, encaquer; (of roads) arrondir en dos d'âne, bomber.

bar'rel-bellied (-bèl'lide), *adj.,* à gros ventre, pansu, ventru.

barreled, *adj.,* (of machines) à cylindre; (of fire-arms) à canon; (of roads) bombé.

bar'ren (bar-rène), *adj.,* stérile, improductif.

bar'renly, *adv.,* stérilement.

bar'renness (bar-rè-n-nèsse), *n.,* stérilité, *f.*

barricade' (-kéde), *n.,* barricade; (nav.) batayole, *f.*

barricade', *v.a.,* barricader; (nav.) bastinguer.

barrica'ding (-digne), *n.,* action de barricader, *f.;* (nav.) bastingage, *m.*

bar'rier (bar-ri-eur), *n.,* barrière; limite, *f.*

bar'ring, *prep.,* excepté, hormis, sauf, à part. — a few; *hormis quelques-uns, à quelques-uns près.* — mistakes; *sauf erreur.*

bar'row (bar-rô), *n.,* brouette, *f.;* (ant.) pourceau, porc (châtré); (mines) amas de décombres; bois, bosquet; (antiq.) tumulus; (salt-works) égouttoir, *m.;* trémie, *f.* — grease; *saindoux, m.* Hand— —; *brancard, m.;* civière, *f.*

bar'rowman (-mane), *n.,* brouettier, brouetteur, *m.*

barse (bârse), *n.,* (ich.) perche commune, *f.*

bar'shot, *n.,* boulet ramé, *m.*

bar'ter (-teur), *n.,* échange, troc, trafic, *m.*

bar'ter, *v.a. and n.,* troquer, échanger, trafiquer.

bar'terer (-teureur), *n.,* trafiquant, troqueur, brocanteur, *m.*

bar'tizan (bâr-ti-za-n), *n.,* (arch.) galerie en saillie, *f.*

bary'ta (ba-raï-ta) *ou* **baryte'** (bar'aïte), *n.,* (min.) baryte, *f.*

bar'ytone (-tône), *n.,* baryton, *m.*

bar'ytone, *adj.,* (mus.) de baryton. — voice; *voix de baryton, f.*

basalt', *n.,* basalte, *m.*

basalt'ic (-ik), *adj.,* basaltique.

bas'cule-bridge (-kioule-), *n.,* pont-levis; pont à bascule, *m.*

base (béce), *adj.,* vil, bas, infâme, indigne, méprisable; illégitime; de mauvais aloi; (of all metals, except gold and silver) non précieux, de peu de valeur; (coin) faux. —born; *bâtard; de basse naissance, de basse extraction.* —minded; *qui a l'âme basse.* — mindedness; *bassesse d'âme.*

base (béce), *n.,* base, *f.;* fondement; (arch.) soubassement, *m.;* (mus.) basse, *f.;* (game) barres, *f.pl.;* (of roads) encaissement, *f.* (tech.) fond, *m.* — of a pedestal; *socle, m.* — of a bed; *soubassement de lit.* Double —; *contre-basse, f.* — voice; *voix de basse-taille, f.*

base, *v.a.,* baser, asseoir.

base'less (-lèsse) *adj.,* sans base, sans fondement.

base'ly, *adv.,* bassement, lâchement, honteusement, vilement.

base'ment (-mè-nte), n., fondation, f. ; fondement ; (arch.) soubassement ; sous-sol, m.

base'ness (-nèsse), n., bassesse, lâcheté ; illégitimité ; altération, mauvaise qualité (of metals) ; gravité (of sound), f.

bashaw' (-shô), n., bacha, pacha, m.

bash'ful, adj., timide, modeste, honteux.

bash'fully, adv., timidement, modestement.

bash'fulness (-nèsse), n., timidité, pudeur, modestie, mauvaise honte, f.

ba'sic (bé-cike), n., adj., (chem.) basique.

bas'il (baz'il), n., biseau ; (bot.) basilic, m.

bas'il (baz'l) ou **bas'an** (baz'a'n), n., basane, f.

bas'il, v.a., tailler en biseau.

bas'ilar (béss'i-lâr) ou **bas'ilary** (béss'i-lari), adj., basilaire.

basil'ic ou **basil'ica**, n., (arch., anat.) basilique, f.

basil'ic ou **basil'ical**, adj., (anat.) basilique ; (arch.) d'une basilique.

basil'icon (-ko-n), n., (pharm.) basilicon, basilicum, m.

bas'ilisk (-ske), n., basilic, m.

ba'sin (béss'n), n., bassin ; réservoir ; bol, m. ; cuvette, (nav.) darse, darce (in the Mediterranean), f. Holy-water —; bénitier, m. Wash- —; cuvette, f.

ba'sis (bé-cisse), n., (bases) base, f. ; fondement, m.

bask (baske), v.a., chauffer au soleil.

bask, v.n., se chauffer, (fig.) prospérer, s'endormir. To — in the sun ; se chauffer au soleil.

bask'et (bas-kète), n., corbeille, f. ; panier, m. ; (of apple women) éventaire ; (of carriages) vide-poches, m. ; (fish ou game) bourriche, f. Fruit- — ; corbeille à fruits, f. Table- — ; (hamper) manne, f. Back- —; hotte, f. Hand- —; panier à bras, m. Little —; corbillon, m. — full ; panier plein, m. ; panerée (fruits), f. — handle ; anse de panier, f. —hilt ; garde en coquille, f. —hilted ; en coquille. —maker ; vannier, m. —rod ; osier, m. —woman ; porteuse, f. — work ; vannerie, f.

ba'son (bèss'n), n. V. **basin**.

bas-relief', **bass-relief'** (bass'rèlîfe), or **basso-relie'vo** (basso-rèlî-vo), n., bas-relief, m.

bass (bésse), n., (mus.) basse, clef de fa, f. ; (musical instrument) basse, f., violoncelle, m. ; (mus.) basse-taille, f. — viol ; (mus.) basse de viole, f. Thorough- — ; basse continue, f. Double- — ; (mus.) contre-basse, f. — of an organ ; jeu de bourdon, m.

bass (basse), n., natte, f. ; (bot.) tilleul d'Amérique ; (pisc.) bar, bars, m.

bas'set (bas'sète), n., bassette (card game), f. — hound ; basset, m.

bas'sinet, n., barcelonnette, f. ; petit berceau, m.

bas'sock, n., natte, f. ; paillasson, m.

bassoon' (bas'soune), n., basson, m.

bassoon'ist, n., qui joue du basson (pers.), m.

bas'so-relie'vo, **bass-relief'**, n. V. **bas-relief**.

bast, n., (of limes) teille, tille ; filasse, f. ; agenouilloir, m.

bas'tard (bas'teurde), n., bâtard ; faux.

bas'tard, n., bâtard, m., bâtarde, f. ; (jur.) enfant naturel, m.

bas'tardize (-daïze), v.a., déclarer bâtard.

bas'tardy, n., bâtardise, f.

baste (béste), v.a., bâtonner ; arroser la viande qui rôtit ; (needle-work), faufiler, bâtir.

bastinade' ou **bastina'do** (-néde, -nédô), n., bastonnade, f.

bastinade' ou **bastina'do**, v.a., bâtonner, donner la bastonnade à.

ba'sting (bés'tigne), n., bastonnade, f. ; arrosement (de viande), m., (needle-work) faufilure, couture à points espacés, f.

bas'tion (bas'ti-o-n), n., bastion, m.

bas'to, n., baste, as de trèfle (hombre, quadrille), m.

bat (bate), n., bâton, battoir, m. ; (cricket) crosse ; (mam.) chauve-souris, f. Off his own —; par ses propres efforts.

bat, v.n., jouer du bâton ; (game) jouer du battoir, de la crosse, manier la crosse.

bata'tas (baté-tass), n., (bot.) patate, f.

Bata'vian (-té-vi-a-n), adj., batave.

Bata'vian, n., Batave, m. f.

batch (bat'she), n., fournée ; (fig.) troupe, bande, f. ; tas, ramassis, m.

bate (béte), v.a., (ant.) rabattre, rabaisser, diminuer ; ôter, retrancher ; excepter ; faire remise de. He will not —an inch of it ; il n'en veut point démordre.

bath (bâth), n., bain, m. ; baignoire, f. — -keeper ; baigneur, m. Hot, or warm, —; bain chaud, m. Medicated —; bain médicinal, m. Tepid — ; bain tempéré, m. Hip- —; bain de siège, m. Slipper- — ; sabot, m. ; baignoire en forme de sabot, f. Hot air —; bain d'air chaud, m. Shower- —; douche, douche en arrosoir, f. —room ; salle de bain, f. Vapor — ; bain de vapeur, m. — drawers ; caleçon de bain, m. — chair ; vinaigrette, roulette, f. — towel ; serviette de bain, f. The Order of the Bath ; l'Ordre du Bain, m. Go to Bath ! allez-vous promener.

bathe (béthe), v.a., baigner, arroser, tremper, mouiller ; bassiner, étuver. To — a wound ; bassiner une plaie.

bathe, v.n., se baigner. n., baignade, f. To go for a — ; aller se baigner. To — one's eyes ; se bassiner les yeux.

ba'ther (bétheur), n., baigneur, m., baigneuse, f.

ba'thing (béthigne), n., action de baigner, de se baigner, f. ; bain, m. Sea- — ; bains de mer, m.pl. River- — ; bains de rivière, m.pl. — dress, — gown ; peignoir, m. — -establishment ; établissement de bains, m. — tub ; baignoire, f. — room ; salle de bain, f. — machine ; voiture de bain ou voiture-baignoire, f.

ba'thos (béthoss), n., pathos, galimatias, m.

ba'ting (bétigne), prep., sauf. V. **barring**.

bat'let (bat'lète), n., battoir, m.

bat'man, m., (mil.) brosseur, m.

bat'on, bat'oon (bat'on), n., bâton, tricot, m., trique, f., gourdin, m. ; baguette, f.

batra'chia ou **batra'chians** (-tré-kia, -kia-nze), n., batraciens, m.

batra'chian (-tré-kia-n), adj., des batraciens.

bats'man, n., qui manie la crosse, m.

bat'ta, n., supplément de solde, m.

battal'ion (bat-ta-lieune), n., bataillon, m.

bat'ten (bat't'n), v.a., (ant.) engraisser, fertiliser ; (carp.) voliger.

bat'ten, v.n., (ant.) s'engraisser de ; se bourrer de ; se gorger de ; (carp.) construire en volige. V. **fatten**.

bat'ten, n., (ant.) (carp.) volige, f. ; battant, m. ; chasse de tisserand, f. ; chevron, m. ; latte ; (nav.) latte, f. —s of the hatches ; lattes des écoutilles, f.pl. To — down ; enfermer dans la cabine, défendre le pont aux passagers (pendant une grosse tempête).

bat'ter (bat'teur), n., pâte de farine, f.

bat'ter, v.a., battre en brèche ; battre ; délabrer ; ébranler ; écraser ; démolir. To — with ordnance ; battre à coups de canon, canonner. To — in ; battre en brèche. To — down ; abattre, renverser, battre en ruine.

bat'tered (bat'teurde), adj., battu en brèche ; (of metals) bossué, bosselé, battu ; délabré ; (print.) mauvais.

bat'terer, n., abatteur ; batteur, m.

bat'tering (bat'teurigne), n., (milit.) action de battre en brèche, f. —-piece ; pièce de siège, f. —ram ; bélier, m. —train ; artillerie de siège, f.

bat'tery (bat'teuri), n., batterie ; action de bat-

tre en brèche, f. ; (jur.) voies de fait, f. pl. ; (phys.)
batterie, f. Galvanic —; pile galvanique, f.

bat'ting (bat'tigne), n., jeu de crosse, m.

bat'tish (bat'ishe), adj., de chauve-souris.

bat'tle (bat't'l), n., bataille, f. ; combat, m.
—array; ordre de bataille, m. To do —; combattre **pour**. — piece; (paint.) bataille, f. To give
—; livrer bataille. To die in —; mourir au champ
d'honneur.

bat'tle, v.n., se battre ; combattre ; batailler.

bat'tle-ax (-axe), n., hache d'armes, f.

bat'tledore (bat't'l-dore), n., battoir, m. ;
raquette, f.

bat'tlement (bat't'l-mè-nte), n., créneau ;
(fig.) rempart, m.

bat'ton (bat't'n), n., (ant.). V. **batten.**

bat'ty, adj. V. **battish.**

bau'ble (bô-b'l), n. V. **bawble.**

bav'in (-vi-n), n., bourrée, fascine, f. ; cotret,
m. ; javelle (of vine branches), f.

baw'ble ou **bau'ble** (bô-b'l), n., babiole, bagatelle, f. ; colifichet, hochet, m. ; fanfreluche ;
breloque, f. Fool's —; marotte de fou, f.

baw'bling (bô-bligne), adj., (ant.) mesquin,
de nulle valeur, qui n'est qu'une babiole.

baw'cock (bô-koke), n., (ant.) godelureau, m.

baw'diness, n., obscénité, impudicité, f.

bawd'rick (bô-drike), n. V. **baldric.**

baw'dy, adj., obscène, paillard. — house;
lieu de débauche, bordel, m.

bawl (bôl), v.n., crier, brailler.

bawl, v.a., crier.

bawl'er (bôl-eur), n., crieur, m., crieuse, f. ;
brailleur, m., brailleuse, f. ; criailleur, m., criailleuse, f. ; braillard, m., braillarde, f.

bawl'ing (bôl-igne), n., cri, m. ; cris, m. pl. ;
braillement, m. ; crierie, criaillerie, clabauderie, f.

bawn (bô-n), n., (ant.) enclos, m.

bay (béie), n., baie ; écluse ; (arch.) travée,
f. ; abois, m. pl. ; (bot.) laurier, laurier femelle,
m. — of joists ; travée, f. —window ; fenêtre
en saillie, f. The stag stands at —; le cerf est
aux abois. To keep any one at —; mettre quelqu'un aux abois, le tenir en échec, en respect.
Small —; anse, f. —berry ; baie de laurier, f.
—-cherry ; laurier-cerise, m. —tree ; laurier,
m. — salt ; sel gris, sel marin brut, m.

bay, adj., bai. Light —; bai clair. Dark —;
bai brun. Chestnut —; bai châtain. Gilded —;
bai fauve.

bay, v.n., aboyer. To — the moon; aboyer à
la lune.

bay'adere, n., bayadère, f., (Hindoo dancing
girl).

bay'ard (bé-arde), n., bai, cheval bai. adj.,
(fig.) aveuglé par l'amour-propre.

bay'ardly (bé-ardly), adj., aveugle; stupide.
adv., stupidement, aveuglément.

bayed (bé-de), adj., (mas.) à ouvertures, à
intervalles, à baies.

bay'onet, n., baïonnette, f.

bay'onet, v.a., tuer à coups de, ou d'un coup
de, baïonnette. — charge; charge à la baïonnette. — belt; porte-baïonnette, m.

bazaar' ou **bazar'** (bazâre), n., bazar.

B.C., avant J. Christ.

B.D., bachelier en théologie.

bdel'lium (dèl'lieume), n., bdellium, m.

be (bi), v.n., (preterit, Was ; past part., Been)
être, exister ; devoir, falloir. The title is to
descend to his heir ; le titre doit passer à son
héritier. To — very well; se porter très bien.
What is the matter? qu'est-ce qu'il y a? qu'y
a-t-il ? To — out ; (to be mistaken) se tromper.
To — right; avoir raison. To — wrong; avoir
tort. I am to ; je dois. I was to ; je devais. I
ought to ; je devrais. I ought to have ; j'aurais
dû. I must have; j'ai dû, j'avais dû. Why is it
that . . . ? pourquoi faut-il que . . . ? How is it
that . . . ? comment se fait-il que . . . ? That is

nothing to me ; cela ne me regarde pas; cela
ne me fait rien. If that is the same to you ; si
cela vous est égal. To — a witness; servir de
témoin. To — better ; valoir mieux ; se porter
mieux. It is no matter ; il n'importe, n'importe.
Nobody is to know it ; personne ne doit le savoir ;
il faut que personne ne le sache. Is it to be won-
dered at if . . . ; faut-il s'étonner si . . . Union
is strength ; l'union fait la force. Were I to ;
quand je devrais ou dussé-je. To — cold, warm,
thirsty, hungry ; avoir froid, chaud, soif, faim.
It is warm, cold, fine ; il fait chaud, froid, beau.
How cold your hands are ! que, ou comme, vous
avez les mains froides ! My hands are cold ;
j'ai froid aux mains. It begins to — cold ; il
commence à faire froid. To — twenty, thirty
years old ; avoir vingt ans, trente ans. It is
ten; il est dix heures. There to —; y avoir ; être.
There is ; il y a ; il est. There are; il y a ; il
est. If it were not for; sans ; ne fût-ce. Had it
not been for; n'eût été. — that as it may ; quoi
qu'il en soit. As it were ; pour ainsi dire. It
being ; comme il était. It being cold ; comme
il faisait froid. It were to be wished that ; il
serait à désirer que. It is to be hoped that ; il
est à espérer que. That is not to be seen ; cela
ne se voit pas. I took you to —; je vous prenais
pour. You would take him to — forty ; vous
lui donneriez quarante ans.

beach (bîtshe), n., rivage, m., plage, f. ; (of a
lake) bord, m., rive, f.

bea'con (bî'k'n), n., balise, f. ; fanal, phare, m.

bea'con, v.a., allumer, éclairer, baliser.

bea'conage (-édje), n., droit de balise, m.

bea'coned (bî'k'n'de), adj., surmonté d'un
fanal, d'un phare ; à fanal, à phare ; balisé.

bead (bîde), n., grain de chapelet, de bracelet, de collier ; chapelet, rosaire, m. ; perle ;
bulle, f. ; globule, m. String of —s ; collier,
chapelet, m. To thread —s ; enfiler des perles.
To tell one's —s ; dire son chapelet. Steel —s ;
grains d'acier, m. pl.

bead, v.n., perler ; former des globules.

bea'dle (bîd'l), n., bedeau, suisse ; huissier ;
huissier audiencier, m.

bead'-maker (-mék'eur), n., fabricant de
perles, de grains de perle ; patenôtrier, m.

bead'roll (-rôl), n., liste de ceux pour qui les
prêtres doivent prier, f.

bead'tree (-trî), n., (bot.) mélie, f., azédarac, m.

bea'gle (bi'g'l), n., chien basset, m.

beak (bîke), n., bec ; (nav.) éperon, m. ; bigorne, f. ; (pop.) magistrat. — full ; becquée, f.

beak'er, n., gobelet, m. ; coupe, f.

beak'-iron (-aï'eur'ne), n., bigorne, f.

beam (bîme), n., (of timber) poutre, f. ; (of
light) rayon ; (of a plow, a carriage) timon :
(of scales) fléau ; (nav.) bau, m. Cross —; traverse, f.

beam, v.n., rayonner.

beam, v.a., lancer, darder des rayons.

beam'-ends (-è'nd'ze), n.pl., (nav.) côté, m.
To be on her —; (of a ship) donner à la bande ;
(fig., of pers.) être à la dernière extrémité.

beam'ing, n., rayonnement, m.

beam'ing, adj., rayonnant, radieux.

beam'less, adj., sans rayon, sans éclat, terne.

beam'-tree (-trî), n., alisier blanc, m.

beam'y, adj., rayonnant, brillant ; massif ;
cornu.

bean (bîne), n., fève, f. French —; haricot
vert, m. Horse —; féverole, f. Kidney —;
haricot blanc, m.

bear (bère), n., ours, m., ourse, f. ; (astron.) Ourse, f. ; (at
the Exchange) joueur à la baisse, baissier, m.

bear, v.a., (preterit, Bore ; past part., Borne,
Born) porter ; soutenir ; supporter, souffrir,
subir ; essuyer ; avoir ; enfanter ; tenir ; faire ;
garder. To — away; emporter, remporter. To —
down ; entraîner ; renverser ; (nav.) courir. To —

out; *maintenir; justifier; avancer.* To — the bell; *l'emporter.* To — company; *tenir compagnie à.* To — off; *emporter, enlever; remporter.* To — off the land; (nav.) *courir au large.* You will — me out when I say that he is . . . ; *vous direz avec moi que . . .* To — sway; *dominer, régner,* To — upon; *porter* sur. To — the charges; *payer les frais.* To — fruit; *porter fruit.* To — interest; (com.) *porter intérêt.* To — with; *supporter, endurer.* To be born; *naître.* To be borne; *être porté, supporté, soutenu.* To bring to — upon; *agir* sur, *mettre en jeu.*

bear, *v.n.,* souffrir; rapporter, être fertile; porter; se porter; peser. — towards; *se diriger* sur *ou* vers. Beyond —ing; *d'une manière insupportable.* — with me a little; *un peu de patience.* To — one's self ; *se comporter, se conduire.* To — upon (a question); *avoir trait à.* To — up; *ne pas perdre courage, ne pas se laisser abattre.*

bear'able, *adj.,* supportable.
bear'-baiting (-bêt'-), *n.,* combat d'ours, *m.*
bear'-berry, *n.,* (bot.) raisin d'ours, *m.*
bear'-bind (-baï'n'de), *n.,* (bot.) liseron des haies, *m.*
beard (bîrde), *n.,* barbe ; (of an arrow) dent, pointe, *f.* To do, to say anything to any one's —; *dire, faire quelque chose à la barbe de quelqu'un.*
beard, *v.a.,* braver, défier, faire quelque chose à la barbe de (quelqu'un), narguer; (an arrow) barbeler.
beard'ed, *adj.,* barbu; barbelé.
beard'less, *adj.,* sans barbe; imberbe. — boy; *blanc-bec, m.*
beard'lessness, *n.,* défaut, *ou* manque, de barbe, *m.*
bear'er, *n.,* porteur, *m.,* porteuse, *f.,* arbre de rapport ; (arch.) support, *m.* —s of a tree ; *crochets d'arbre, m.pl.* Stretcher —; (mil.) *brancardier, m.* To —; *au porteur.*
bear'-garden (-gârd'n), *n.,* arène, fosse aux ours, *f.;* scène de désordre, *m.; pétaudière, f.; la cour du roi Pétaud, f.*
bear'herd (-heurde), *n.,* meneur d'ours, *m.*
bear'ing, *n.,* rapport ; maintien, port, *m.;* conduite, contenance, attitude; portée; face, *f.;* air, aspect; (nav.) gisement, *m.;* hauteur, situation, *f.;* (her.) armes, armoiries, *f.pl.* — out; (arch.) *saillie, avance, f.*
bear'ing-block, *n.,* (tech.) support, *m.*
bear'ing-cloth (-clôth), *n.,* robe baptismale, *f.*
bear'ing-neck (-nèke), *n.,* tourillon, *m.*
bear'ing-rein (-rêne), *n.,* rêne, *f.*
bear'ing-surface (-seur-féce), *n.,* point d'appui, *m.*
bear'ing-up, *n.,* étayement (d'un mur).
bear'ing-wall (-wôl), *n.,* mur de refend, *m.*
bear'ish, *adj.,* d'ours; brutal.
bear'like (-laïke), *adj.,* qui tient de l'ours, semblable à un ours.
bear's-ear, *n.,* (bot.) oreille d'ours, *f.*
bear's-whortleberry, *n.,* (bot.) raisin d'ours, *m.*
beast (bîste), *n.,* bête; (card game) bête, *f.;* (of a person) animal, cochon, *m.,* bête, bête brute, salope, *f.* Wild —; *bête sauvage, f.* — of burden; *bête de somme, f.* — of the chase; *bête de chasse, f.*
beast'liness, *n.,* brutalité; saleté, saloperie, obscénité, *f.*
beast'ly, *adj.,* bestial; sale, vilain, malpropre, dégoûtant.
beat (bîte), *n.,* battement; son, *m.;* station; ronde (of policemen), *f.;* (of postmen), parcours; (hunt.) lieu où se fait une battue, *m.* — of the drum ; *batterie de tambour, f.* That is out of his own proper —; *cela ne rentre pas dans sa spécialité.*
beat, *v.a.* (preterit, Beat ; past part., Beaten),

battre ; frapper ; piler, broyer; l'emporter sur ; (of rain, snow) battre, fouetter. To — the alarm; *battre la générale.* To — down ; *abattre; diminuer.* To — back; *repousser.* To — in ; *faire entrer de force.* To — time ; *battre la mesure.* That beats all; *cela l'emporte sur tout ou cela passe les bornes.* To — any one hollow, to — any one all to nothing; *battre quelqu'un à plate couture.* That beats me ; *cela me passe.* To — about ; *aller à droite et à gauche, chercher de tous côtés;* (fig.) *se casser la tête, se torturer l'esprit.* To — a wood; *battre un bois.* To — about the bush; *tourner autour du pot.* To — away; *éloigner, écarter.* To — black and blue; *meurtrir.* — to death; *assommer.* — up; (eggs) *fouetter.* To — the country; *battre le pays.*
beat, *v.n.,* battre; être agité. To — up for soldiers ; *recruter des soldats.* To — about ; (nav.) *louvoyer.* To — up to windward; *courir des bordées.* — against; *battre, se briser.*
beat'en, *adj.,* battu, (trite) (fig.) frayé, rebattu.
beat'er, *n.,* batteur, *m.;* (instrument) batte ; (print.) balle, *f.;* (tech.) fouloir, *m.*
beatif'ic *ou* **beatif'ical** (bi-a-), *adj.,* béatifique.
beatif'ically, *adv.,* d'une manière béatifique.
beatifica'tion (-fi-ké-), *n.,* béatification, *f.*
beat'ify (-faïe), *v.a.,* béatifier.
beat'ing (bît'igne), *n.,* batterie ; bourrade ; volée, rossée, *f.;* coups, *m.pl.;* battement, battage, *m.*
beat'itude (biati-tioude), *n.,* béatitude, félicité, *f.*
beau, *n.,* damoiseau; ⊙plumet (military beau); petit-maître ; prétendant ; futur, *m.* To set up for a —; *faire le petit maître.*
beau'ish (beau-ishe), *adj.,* pimpant, élégant, recherché, fat.
beau'teous (biou-ti-euse), *adj.,* beau.
beau'teously, *adv.,* avec beauté.
beau'teousness, *n.,* beauté; bonne grâce, *f.*
beau'tifier (-fa'i'eur), *n.,* personne, chose qui embellit, *f.*
beau'tiful (-foul), *adj.,* beau, superbe.
beau'tifully, *adv.,* admirablement, d'une belle manière ; parfaitement bien.
beau'tifulness, *n.,* beauté, *f.*
beau'tify (-faïe), *v.a.,* embellir, orner.
beau'tify, *v.n.,* s'embellir.
beau'ty (biouti), *n.,* beauté, *f.;* charme, *m.*
beau'ty-spot, *n.,* mouche, *f.;* grain de beauté, *m.*
beau'ty-wash (-woshe) *ou* **beau'ty-water** (-wôteur), *n.,* eau de beauté, *f.*
bea'ver (bi'veur), *n.,* castor; chapeau de castor, *m.,* visière (of a helmet), *f.*
becalm' (bi-câme), *v.a.,* apaiser, calmer; (nav.) abriter. To be becalmed; (nav.) *être abrié ou abrié, être pris de calme.*
because' (bicôze), *conj.,* parce que. — of ; à cause de.
beccafi'co (béc-a-fi-cô), *n.,* (orni.) becfigue, *m.*
bechance' (bi-tshâ'nse), *v.n.,* arriver à, advenir à.
bechance', *adv.,* par accident.
becharm' (bi-tshârme), *v.a.,* charmer, ensorceler.
bechic (bi'kike), *n.,* (med.) béchique.
beck, *n.,* signe (of the hand, of the head), *m.*
beck (bèke) *ou* **beck'on** (bèk'k'n), *v.n.,* faire signe à (of the hand, of the head); faire signe, inviter à.
beck'on, *v.a.,* faire signe à ; appeler.
becloud' (bi-claoude), *v.a.,* couvrir de nuages, voiler.
become' (bi-keume), *v.n.,* (preterit, Became ; past part., Become) devenir, commencer à être. To — accustomed to ; *s'accoutumer à.* What will — of me ? *que deviendrai-je ?* To — interested in some one; *s'intéresser à quelqu'un.* To —

known; *se faire connaître*. To — detached ; *se détacher de*.

become', *v.a.*, aller bien à, seoir à, convenir à, être propre à. To ill — ; *convenir mal, peu*.

becom'ing, *adj.*, séant, bienséant, convenable, qui sied bien, qui va bien.

becom'ingly (bi-), *adv.*, avec bienséance, convenablement, avec grâce.

becom'ingness, *n.*, convenance ; bienséance, grâce, *f.*

bed (bède), *v.a.*, coucher, mettre au lit ; coucher **avec** ; loger ; fixer, enfoncer ; semer, planter ; parquer (of oysters, mussels).

bed, *v.n.*, coucher, se coucher, cohabiter.

bed, *n.*, lit, *m.* ; couche, *f.*, (of oysters) parc ; (gard.) massif, carré, *m.* ; (of mines) couche, *f.*, gisement ; (of roads) encaissement, *m.* ; planche, plate-bande, *f.* — of a river ; *lit de rivière*. Feather— ; *lit de plume*. Field — ; *lit de camp*. State— ; *lit de parade*. Folding— ; *lit brisé, lit de sangle*. Tent— ; *lit à tombeau*. Press— ; *lit en forme d'armoire*. Four-post — ; *lit à quenouilles*. Double-bedded ; *à deux lits*. — of a ship ; (nav.) *souille, f.* — of a gun ; *coussin de mire, m.* To turn down the — ; *faire la couverture*. From — and board ; (jur.) *séparation de corps et de biens, f.* To be in — ; *être au lit, être alité*. To be brought to — ; *accoucher*. To confine to — ; *retenir au lit*. To keep one's — ; *garder le lit*. To lie in — ; *rester au lit, se tenir au lit*. To take to one's — ; *s'aliter*. To sleep in separate —s ; *faire lit à part*. As you make your — so you must lie ; *comme on fait son lit on se couche*.

bedab'ble (bi-dab'b'l), *v.a.*, éclabousser, asperger.

bedag'gle (bi-dag-g'l). V. **bedrag'gle**.

bedark'en (bi-där-k'n), *v.a.*, assombrir, obscurcir.

bedash' (bi-), *v.a.*, éclabousser **de**, arroser **de**, mouiller **de**.

bedaub' (bi-), *v.a.*, souiller, salir ; barbouiller.

bedaz'zle (bi-daz'z'l), *v.a.*, éblouir.

bed'-bolt (-bôlte), *n.*, boulon (qui traverse l'affût d'un canon), *m.*

bed'chamber (-tshé-m-beur), *n.*, chambre à coucher, *f.*

bed'clothes, *n.*, couvertures, *f.pl.* ; draps, *m.pl.*

bed'cover, *n.*, couvre-lit, *m.*

bed'ding (bèd'digne), *n.*, literie, *f.*, coucher, *m.*

bedeck' (bi-dèke), *v.a.*, orner **de**, parer **de**, décorer **de**.

be'del (bî-dèle), *n.*, appariteur, *m.*

be'delry, *n.*, fonctions d'appariteur, de massier, *f.pl.*

bedev'il (bi-dev'v'l), *v.a.*, faire endiabler ; lutiner ; ensorceler.

bedew' (bi-diou), *v.a.*, arroser **de**, humecter de rosée.

bed'fellow (-fèl-lô), *n.*, camarade de lit, coucheur, *m.* ; compagne de lit, coucheuse, *f.* Troublesome — ; (fig.) (ill-tempered person) *mauvais coucheur, m.*

bed'frame (-fréme), *n.*, bois de lit, *m.*

bed'hangings (-haign-ign'ze), *n.pl.*, tour de lit, *m.* ; tenture de lit, *f.*

bedight' (bi-daïte), *v.a.*, (ant.) décorer **de**, parer **de**, orner **de**.

bedim' (bi-dime), *v.a.*, obscurcir, rembrunir.

bediz'en (bidaï-z'n *ou* bidiz'n), *v.a.*, parer, orner, attirer ; chamarrer.

Bed'lam, *n.*, Bedlam (hôpital des fous), *m.* ; petites maisons, *f.pl.* ; (l.u.) fou, *m.*, folle, *f.*

bed'lamite (-lam'aïte), *n.*, fou, *m.*, folle, *f.*

bed'lamlike (-laïke), *adv.*, en fou, en insensé.

bed'maker (-mék'-), *n.*, chambrière, *f.*

bed'molding (-môld-igne), *n.*, (arch.) filet, *m.*

bed'post (-pôste), *n.*, colonne de lit, quenouille de lit, *f.*

bed'presser (-prèss'-), *n.*, (ant.) dormeur, *m.* dormeuse, *f.*, (fig.) paresseux, *m.*, paresseuse, *f.*

bedrag'gle (bi-drag'g'l), *v.a.*, crotter, salir ; (fig.) traîner dans la boue.

bedrench' (bi-drè'nshe), *v.a.*, tremper.

bed'rid (bèd'ride) *ou* **bed'ridden** (-rid'd'n), *adj.*, grabataire, alité.

bed'room (bèd'roume), *n.*, chambre à coucher, *f.*

bed'screw (bèd'scrou), *n.*, écrou de lit, *m.*, vis de lit, *f.*

bed'side (bèd'saïde), *n.*, ruelle, *f.* ; bord du lit, *m.* — carpet ; *descente de lit, f.*

bed'stead (-stède), *n.*, bois de lit, lit, châlit, *m.*

bed'straw (-strô), *n.*, paillasse, *f.* ; (bot.) caille-lait ; gaillet, *m.*

bed'time (-taïme), *n.*, heure du coucher, *f.* ; temps de se coucher, *m.*

bedung' (bi-dugn'e), *v.a.*, (engraisser avec du fumier), fumer.

bed'ward (bèd'worde), *adv.*, vers le lit.

bedwarf' (bi-dwôrfe), *v.a.*, rapetisser.

bedye' (bi-daïe), *v.a.*, teindre.

bee (bî), *n.*, abeille ; mouche à miel, *f.* Hive— ; *abeille domestique, abeille ouvrière, de ruche, f.* Bumble— ; *bourdon, m.* Queen— ; *reine abeille, mère abeille, f.* To ring —s ; *carillonner les abeilles.* Swarm of —s ; *essaim d'abeilles, m.* To have a — in one's bonnet ; *avoir une araignée dans le plafond, ou au plafond.*

bee'-board (-bôrde), *n.*, tablette à ruches, *f.*

bee'-bread (-brède), *n.*, pain d'abeilles, *m.*

beech, beech-tree (bîtshe-trî), *n.*, (bot.) hêtre, fouteau, fayard, *m.* Plantation of —s ; *foutelaie, f.*

beech'-martin (-tine), *n.*, (mam.) fouine, *f.*

beech'mast *ou* **beech'nut** (-maste, -neute), *n.*, (bot.) faîne, *f.*

beech'oil (-oïle), *n.*, huile de faîne, *f.*

bee'-eater (bî-ît'eur), *n.*, (orni.) guêpier, *m.*

beef (bîf), *n.*, (beeves) bœuf, *m.*

beef'-eater (-ît'eur), *n.*, mangeur de bœuf ; gros-bœuf (stout man) ; (orni.) pique-bœuf ; (yeoman) cent-gardes, *m.*

bee'-flower (-flaou-eur), *n.*, (bot.) orchis, *m.*

beef'steak (bîfe-stèke), *n.*, bifteck, *m.*

beef'witted (-wit'téde), *adj.*, (ant.) lourd comme un bœuf.

bee'-garden (-gärd'n), *n.*, rucher, *f.*

bee'hive (-haïve), *n.*, ruche, *f.*

bee'-house (-haouce), *n.*, rucher, *m.*

bee'like (-laïke), *adj.*, d'abeille, comme les abeilles.

bee'master (-mâs'teur), *n.*, éleveur d'abeilles, apiculteur, *m.*

beer (bîre), *n.*, bière, *f.*

beer'-engine (-èn-djine), *n.*, pompe à bière, *f.*

beer'house (-haouce), *n.*, taverne, brasserie, *f.*, cabaret, *m.* — keeper ; *cabaretier, m.*

beer'shop (-shope), *n.*, débit de bière, *m.*

beet (bîte), *n.*, (bot.) bette, betterave, *f.*

beet'-chard (-tshärde), *n.*, (bot.) carde poirée, *f.*

bee'tle (bî't'l), *n.*, maillot, *m.* ; mailloche ; batte, *f.* ; battoir (laundress's), *m.* ; hie, demoiselle (pavior's), *f.* ; mouton (of a pile-driver), *m.* ; (ent.) scarabée, escarbot, *m.* Horn— , stag— ; *cerf-volant, m.*

bee'tle, *v.n.*, surplomber, avancer, faire saillie. Beetling crags ; *rochers surplombants.*

bee'tle-browed (-braoude), *adj.*, à sourcils épais.

bee'tle-head (-hède), *n.*, souche, bûche, ganache, *f.*

bee'tle-stock, *n.*, (tech.) manche de mail, de mailloche, *m.*

beet'radish (bîte-rad'ishe), **beet'rave** (-réve), *ou* **beet'root** (-route), *n.*, (bot.) betterave, *f.*

befall' (bi-fôl), *v.a.* and *n.*, (preterit, Befell ; past part., Befallen) arriver à, survenir à ; échoir à.

befeath'ered (bi-fè-*theur*'de), adj., emplumé, couvert de plumes.

befit' (bi-fite), v.a., convenir à.

befoam' (bi-fôme), (l.u.) v.a., couvrir d'écume.

befool' (bi-foule), v.a., duper, tromper, infatuer.

before' (bi-), prep., (of time) avant; (of place) devant; par devant; (jur.) par-devant.

before', adv., (of time) auparavant, avant; (of place) en avant; (above) plus haut; (till then) jusqu'alors, jusque là; (till now) jusqu'ici, jusqu'à présent.

before', conj., avant que (*subj.*); (*rather*) plutôt que, avant de.

before'hand (-han'n'de), adv., par avance, à l'avance, d'avance. To be — with somebody ; *devancer, prévenir quelqu'un.*

before'time (-taïme), adv., (ant.) autrefois, jadis, anciennement. *V.* **aforetime.**

befoul' (bi-faoule), v.a., salir, souiller.

befriend' (bi-frè'nde), v.a., favoriser, seconder, aider; appuyer, protéger ; être l'ami de, faire du bien à ; traiter en ami.

befringe' (bi-fri'n'je), v.a., franger, garnir d'une frange.

beg (bèghe), v.a., mendier; demander à (of), de (to), prier de; supposer. I — to inform you; *j'ai l'honneur de vous informer.* To — the question; *tourner dans un cercle vicieux* ou *faire une pétition de principe.* To go —ging ; (of things) *chercher un possesseur.*

beg, v.n., mendier. To — of; *prier de.*

beget' (bi-ghète), v.a., (*preterit,* Begot'; *past part.,* Begot'ten), engendrer; produire; causer; amener; entraîner, faire naître.

beget'ter, n., auteur, père, m.

beg'gar (bèg-gheur), n., mendiant, m., mendiante, *f. ;* gueux, m. To be a —; (fig.) *être dans la misère.*

beg'gar, v.a., réduire à la mendicité; appauvrir, ruiner, épuiser. — my neighbor; (game) *bataille, f.* Poor —; *pauvre diable, m.* Set a — on horseback and he will ride to the devil; *il n'est orgueil que de sot enrichi.* —cannot be choosers ; *ne choisit pas qui emprunte.*

beg'gar-girl (-gheur'l) ou **beg'gar-maid** (-méde), n., jeune mendiante, *f.*

beg'garliness, n., gueuserie, pauvreté, misère, *f.*

beg'garly, adj., chétif, pauvre, misérable.

beg'garly, adv., misérablement, chétivement.

beg'gar-man (-ma'n), n., mendiant, m.

beg'gar-woman (-woum'a'n), n., mendiante, *f.*

beg'gary, n., mendicité, misère, *f.* To be in —; *être au berniquet, à la besace.*

beg'ging, n., mendicité, *f.* — the question; *cercle vicieux, m., pétition de principe, f.*

begin' (bi-ghi'n), v.a., (*preterit,* Began'; *past part.,* Begun'), commencer, entamer, débuter, entonner ; se mettre à. To — the discussion; *entamer la discussion.*

begin', v.n., commencer (by, with) par. — afresh; *recommencer, se renouveler.* To — with; *pour commencer ; et d'abord, tout d'abord.*

begin'ner, n., commençant ; débutant, m.

begin'ning (bi-ghin'), n., commencement, début, principe, m., origine, *f.* The first —s; *les éléments, m.pl.*

begird' (bi-gheurde) ou **begirt'** (ant.), v.a., ceindre de, enceindre de ; entourer de ; cerner.

begone' ! (bi-), int., va-t'en ! allez-vous-en ! retire-toi ! retirez-vous ! loin d'ici !

begot'ten (bi-got't'n). *V.* **beget.**

begrease' (bi-grize), v.a., graisser, enduire de graisse.

begrime' (bi-graïme), v.a., barbouiller, souiller, salir, noircir.

begrudge' (bi-greud'je), v.a., regretter; envier à ; refuser à ; marchander à ; donner à contre cœur à.

beguile' (bi-gaïle), v.a., décevoir; abuser; surprendre ; tromper ; séduire, charmer ; faire oublier à.

begui'ler, n., trompeur, séducteur, m. ; trompeuse, séductrice, *f.*

Beguin' (bi-ghine), n., béguin, m.

Beguine' (bi-ghîne), n., béguine; dévote, *f.*

behalf' (bi-hâfe), n., faveur; part, *f. ;* (com.) profit, m. On — of ; *de la part de ; au nom de.* In — of ; *en faveur de* ; (com.) *au profit de.*

behave', v.n., se comporter, se conduire.

behaved', adj. Ill —; *qui se conduit mal ; mal-appris, grossier.* Well —; *qui se conduit bien ; sage, poli.*

beha'vior (bi-hév'ieur), n., conduite, tenue, *f. ;* procédé, m. ; procédés, m.pl. ; manière d'être, *f.,* manières, *f.pl.*

behead' (bi-hède), v.a., décapiter, guillotiner.

behead'ing, n., décapitation; (of St. John the Baptist) décollation, *f.*

be'hemoth (bî-hi-moth), n., béhémoth, m.

behest' (bi-hèste), n., commandement, ordre, précepte, m. ; injonction, *f.*

behind', prep., derrière; après; en retard de, en arrière de.

behind' (bi-haï'n'de), adv., derrière, par derrière, en arrière, en retard; (riding) en croupe.

behind'hand, adj., en arrière, en retard; en reste.

behold' (bi-hôl'de), v.a., (*preterit* and *past part.,* Beheld'), voir, regarder; contempler, considérer.

behold' ! int., vois ! voyez ! voici ! voilà ! tenez ! voilà que !

behold'en (-dène), adj., redevable à ; obligé à.

behold'er, n., spectateur, témoin, assistant, m.

behoof' (bi-houfe), n., avantage, profit, intérêt, m. ; faveur, *f.*

behoofed' (-houf'te), adj., (of horses) à sabot.

behove' (bi-houve), v.n.imp., convenir à (ant.). It behoves — ; *il faut, il importe, il convient, il sied.* It behoves you to ; *il est séant que . . .* (with subj.) ou *il vous sied de . . .* (with inf.).

be'ing (bi-igne), n., être, m. ; existence, *f.*

be'ing, pres. part. (of To be), étant. The time —; *le temps présent, le moment, m.*

Bei'ram, n., (Mahom. rel.) beiram, bairam, m.

bejade' (bi-d'jéde), v.a., (ant.) harasser; surmener.

bela'bor (bi-lé'beur), v.a., rosser, battre.

bela'ted (bi-lét'ède), adj., attardé, anuité, surpris par la nuit.

belay' (bi-), v.a., attendre au passage, arrêter, entraver ; (nav.) amarrer. —ing-pin ; (nav.) *cabillot, m.* —ing cleat; (nav.) *taquet, m.*

belch (bèlshe), n., rot (l.ex.); rot, m. ; éructation, *f.*

belch, v.a., vomir. To — out flames; *vomir des flammes.*

belch, v.n., roter (l.ex.); vomir.

belch'er, n., roteur, m. (l.ex.).

bel'dam, bel'dame, n., sorcière; vieille, *f.*

belea'guer (bi-lî-gheur), v.a., assiéger, cerner, investir.

belea'guerer, n., assiégeant, m.

belee' (bi-lî), v.a., (nav.) faire dériver; dérober le vent à.

bel'fry (-n), n., clocher; beffroi; (nav.) montant de cloche, m.

Bel'gian (-d'ji-a'n), adj., belge.

Bel'gian, n., Belge, m.f.

belie' (bi-laïe), v.a., contrefaire ; calomnier ; démentir, donner le démenti à.

belief' (bi-lîfe), n., foi, créance, croyance, opinion, *f. ;* credo, m. Light of —; *crédule.* Hard of —; *incrédule.* Past —; *incroyable.* To the best of one's —; *autant qu'on le sache.*

believ'able, adj., croyable, probable.

believe' (bi-lîve), v.n., croire en ou à. To —

in God; *croire en Dieu.* I — so; *je crois que oui; je le crois.* I — not; *je crois que non; je ne le crois pas.*

believe', *v.a.*, croire. I — you; *je vous crois; je crois bien.* If you are to be believed; *à vous en croire.* To make any one —; *faire croire à quelqu'un.* To make a person —; (to deceive) *en faire accroire à quelqu'un.* To make —; *faire semblant de, prétendre.* It is a mere make- —; *c'est une pure prétention ou c'est un simple subterfuge.*

believ'er, *n.*, croyant, *m.*, croyante, *f.*; fidèle, *m.f.*

believ'ingly, *adv.*, avec foi.

belike' (bi-laïke), *adv.*, apparemment, peut-être, probablement.

belime' (bi-laïme), *v.a.*, engluer.

bell, *n.*, cloche, clochette, *f.*; (on horses) grelot, *m.*; (house) sonnette, *f.*; (arch.) vase, *m.*, corbeille, *f.*; (horl.) timbre, *m.* Chime of —s; *carillon, m.* Dumb—; *haltère, m.* — of a trumpet; *pavillon de trompette, m.* — of a flower; (bot.) *calice d'une fleur, m.* To ring, pull, ou touch the —; *sonner, tirer, la sonnette.* To bear the —; *être le meneur, le boute-en-train; remporter la palme, l'emporter (sur les autres).* To ring the —s; *donner l'alarme.* Electric —; *sonnette électrique.*

bell, *v.a.* To — the cat; *attacher le grelot.*

bell, *v.n.*, fleurir en forme de grelot, de cloche; (hunt.) réer, raire, bramer.

belladon'na, *n.*, (bot.) belladone, *f.*

belle, *n.*, belle, belle dame, *f.*

belled (bèl'de), *adj.*, à clochette, à grelot.

belles-let'tres, *n.*, belles-lettres, *f.pl.*

bell'-crowned, *adj.*, (of hats) évasé.

bell'-fashioned (-fasheu'n'de), *adj.*, en cloche, en forme de cloche.

bell'flower (-flaou'eur), *n.*, (bot.) campanule, clochette, *f.* [clochea, *m.*

bell'founder (-faoun'deur), *n.*, fondeur de —

bell'-foundry, *n.*, fonderie de cloches, *f.*

bell'-gable (-ghé'b'l), *n.*, (arch.) clocheton (en forme de pignon), *m.*

bell'-glass (-glâce), *n.*, cloche (de jardin), *f.*

bell'hanger (-haign'eur), *n.*, poseur de son- nettes, *m.*

bell'lied (bèl'lide), *adj.*, à ventre. Big —; *à gros ventre; ventru.*

bellig'erent (bèl-li'd'jère'n'te), *adj.*, belli- gérant.

bellig'erent, *n.*, belligérant, *m.*

bell'ing, *n.*, (hunt.) bramement, *m.*

bell'ing, *adj.*, (of hops) croissant en forme de cloche.

bell'man, *n.*, homme à la cloche; crieur public, *m.*

bell'metal, *n.*, métal de cloche, *m.*

bell'-mouth (-maouth), *n.*, (tech.) évasement, *m.*

bell'-mouthed (-maouth'de), *adj.*, (tech.) évasé.

bel'low (bèl-lô), *v.n.*, crier, beugler; (of the sea) mugir; (of thunder) gronder.

bel'lows (bèl-loze), *n.pl.*, soufflet, *m.sing.*

bell'pull (-poule), *n.*, cordon de sonnette, *m.*

bell'ringer (-rigu'eur), *n.*, sonneur de cloches, *m.*

bell'rope (-rôpe), *n.*, corde de cloche, *f.*; cor- don de sonnette, *m.*

bell'-shaped (-shép'te), *adj.*, en cloche, évasé en cloche.

bell'-tower (-taoueur), *n.*, beffroi, clocher, *m.*

bell'-turret (-teur'rète), *n.*, (arch.) clocheton, *m.*

bell'-wether (-wètheur), *n.*, sonnailler, *m.*

bel'ly, *n.*, ventre, estomac, *m.*; panse, *f.* — of a lute; *table de luth, f.*

bel'ly, *v.n.*, bomber, faire ventre, pousser en dehors; se gonfler.

bel'ly-ache (-éke), *n.*, mal au ventre, mal à l'estomac, *m.*

bel'ly-band, *n.*, sous-ventrière, sangle, *f.*

bel'ly-bound (-baou'n'de), *adj.*, constipé.

bel'ly-cheer (-tahîre), *n.*, (ant.) bonne chère, *f.*

bel'ly-ful (-foule), *n.*, (pop.), soûl, *m.* I had my — of it; *j'en ai eu tout mon soûl or j'en ai eu assez.*

bel'ly-god, *n.*, (ant.) glouton, *m.*

bel'ly-pinched (-pi'n'shte), *adj.*, (ant.) af- famé.

bel'ly-slave (-sléve), *n.*, (ant.) esclave de son ventre, *m.*

bel'ly-timber, *n.*, (pop.) nourriture, *f.*; vivres, *m.pl.*

belong' (bi-lòn'ghe), *v.n.*, appartenir à, être à; (to come from) être de.

beloved' (bi-leuv'de *ou* -leuvède), *adj.*, chéri de, bien-aimé de; favori.

below', *prep.*, sous, en dessous de; après, depuis; (nav.) en aval de; au-dessous de; in- digne de. To be — par; (com.) (of shares) *perdre au change*; (fig.) *n'être pas dans son état normal.* To be far —; *être bien inférieur à.*

below' (bi-lô), *adv.*, au-dessous, en bas; à la cuisine, à l'office; ici-bas, dessous; ci-dessous. See —; *voir ci-dessous.* To be —; (dead) *être sous terre.*

belt, *n.*, ceinturon, baudrier; ceinture, cour- roie, *f.*; (surg.) bandage, *m.*; (of land) bande, *f.*

belt, *v.a.*, ceindre, entourer; attacher en sau- toir.

belt'ing, *n.*, ceinture, *f.*

belt'ing-course (-côrse), *n.*, (arch.) chaîne, *f.*

belt'-maker (-mék-eur), *n.*, ceinturier, *m.*

belt'-strap, *n.*, allonge de ceinturon; bélière, *f.*

bel'vedere (-vè-dîre), *n.*, belvédère, *m.*

bemire' (bi-maïeur), *v.a.*, embourber, crotter; couvrir de boue.

bemoan' (bi-mône), *v.a.*, plaindre, lamenter, pleurer, déplorer; gémir sur.

bemoan'er, *n.*, faiseur de lamentations, *m.*

bemoan'ing, *n.*, lamentation, *f.*

bemock' (bi-moke), *v.n.* and *a.*, (l.u.) se moquer; se moquer de; railler; tourner en ridi- cule.

bemol' (bi-), *n.*, (mus.) bémol, *m.*

bemourn', *v.a.*, pleurer, déplorer.

ben, *n.*, ben; (montagne en Ecosse) pic, *m.* — nut; *noix de ben, f.* — oil; *huile de ben, f.*

bench (bè'n'she), *n.*, banc, (in tiers) gradin, *m.*; banquette, *f.*; (tech.) établi; banc, siège, tribunal, *m.*, cour de justice, magistrature, *f.* Court of King's —, of Queen's —; *cour du Banc du roi, de la reine.* — of a canal; berme, *f.* Treasury —; *banc ministériel.* To play to empty —es; (thea.) *jouer devant les banquettes.*

bench, *v.a.*, garnir de bancs.

bench'er, *n.*, juge; conseiller; avocat du pre- mier rang, *m.*

bend (bè'n'de), *v.a.*, (*preterit and past part.*, Bent) plier, fausser; courber, faire plier; incliner, tendre, bander; fléchir; appliquer, diriger; (nav.) nouer. To — one's brows; *froncer le sourcil, rider le front.* To — all one's endeavors; *ap- pliquer tous ses efforts à.* To — down; *courber; abaisser.* To — round; *recourber.* To — up; *cambrer.* To — one's knee; *fléchir le genou.* To — a sail; (nav.) *enverguer une voile.* To — a cable; *étalinguer un câble.* On bended knees; *à genoux.*

bend, *v.n.*, plier, ployer; se courber, être courbé; se pencher, (bow) s'incliner; s'appli- quer à; tourner; fléchir; (to overhang) avancer, surplomber, faire saillie. To — forward; *se pencher en avant.*

bend, bend'ing, *n.*, courbure; inclinaison, *f.*; (of ground) pli, détour; coude, *m.*; (nav.) pré- ceinte, lisse; (of the back) chute des reins, *f.*

bend'er, *n.*, (spring) ressort, *m.*

bend'ing, *adj.*, courbé, incliné, penchant, penché, sinueux.

beneath' (bi-nîth), *prep.*, sous; au-dessous **de**.

beneath', *adv.*, dessous, au-dessous, en bas.

ben'edict, *n.*, homme marié; nouveau marié, *m.* To turn —; *se marier; faire une fin.*

benedic'tine (bè'n'îdictine), *n.*, bénédictin, *m.*, (liqueur) bénédictine, *f.*

Benedic'tine, *adj.*, de l'ordre de saint Benoît; bénédictin.

benedic'tion (bè'n'i-), *n.*, bénédiction, *f.*; (thanks) actions de grâces, *f.pl.*; investiture d'un abbé, *f.*

benefac'tion (bè'n'i-), *n.*, don, bienfait, *m.*, œuvre de bienfaisance; grâce, faveur, donation, *f.*

benefac'tor (bè'n'i-), *n.*, bienfaiteur, *m.*

benefac'tress (bè'n'i-), *n.*, bienfaitrice, *f.*

ben'efice (bè'n'i-), *n.*, bénéfice, *m.*

ben'eficed (bè'n'i-fiste), *adj.*, qui a un bénéfice.

benef'icence (bi-nèf'i-), *n.*, bienfaisance, *f.*

benef'icent, *adj.*, bienfaisant.

benef'icently, *adv.*, avec bienfaisance.

benefi'cial (bè'n'i-fish'al), *adj.*, bienfaisant, salutaire; avantageux, utile, profitable.

benefi'cially, *adv.*, salutairement, avantageusement, utilement.

benefi'cialness, *n.*, avantage, profit, *m.*; utilité, *f.*

benefi'ciary (bè'n'i-fish'iari), *n.*, bénéficier; (feudalism) feudataire, bénéficiaire, *m.*

benefi'ciary, *adj.*, (feud.) bénéficiaire.

benefi'cient (bèn'i-fish'è'n'te), *adj.*, bienfaisant, avantageux, profitable.

ben'efit (bè'n'i-fite), *n.*, bienfait; service; bénéfice; profit, avantage, *m.*; (thea.) représentation à bénéfice, *f.* For the — of; *au profit de*; *pour le bien de*; *dans l'intérêt de.* To give any one the — of a bargain; *faire profiter quelqu'un d'un bon marché.*

ben'efit, *v.a.*, avoir du bénéfice, tirer du profit **de**, profiter **de**; faire du bien à.

ben'efit, *v.n.*, profiter, se trouver bien **de**, gagner à.

ben'efit-night (-naïte), *n.*, (thea.) représentation à bénéfice, *f.*

ben'efit-soci'ety (-so-çaï'yiti), *n.*, société de secours mutuels, *f.*

benev'olence (bi-nèv'o-), *n.*, bienveillance, bonté, bienfaisance, *f.*; don gratuit, *m.*

benev'olent, *adj.*, bienveillant, bienfaisant, de bienfaisance.

benev'olently, *adv.*, avec bienveillance, avec bienfaisance, bénévolement.

Bengalee' (bè'n'galî), *n.*, bengali; dialecte du Bengale, *m.*

Bengalese' (-lîze), *n.*, Bengalais, natif du Bengale, *m.*

benight' (bi-naïte), *v.a.*, obscurcir.

benight'ed (-tède), *adj.*, anuité; surpris par la nuit; couvert de ténèbres; ignorant. To be —; *être plongé dans les ténèbres, dans l'ignorance.*

benign' (bi-naïne), *adj.*, bénin, bienfaisant, généreux, bon, affable.

benig'nant (bi-nig-na'nte), *adj.*, bon, gracieux, bienveillant.

benig'nity (bi-nig'niti), *n.*, bénignité, douceur, *f.*

benign'ly (bi-naï'n'li), *adv.*, bénignement.

ben'ison (bè'n'i-ceune), *n.*, (ant.) bénédiction, *f.*

ben'jamin (bè'n'djamine), *n.*, benjoin, *m.*, assa dulcis, *f.*

ben'net (herb) (bè'n'nète), *n.*, (bot.) benoîte, *f.*

bent, *n.*, pli; penchant, *m.*; pente; courbure, tension, disposition, tendance, *f.*

bent (bè'n'te), *past part.* (of to bend), courbé, plié. — on; *déterminé à, décidé à; porté à, appliqué à.*

bent'grass, *n.*, (bot.) agrostide, *f.*

benumb' (bi-neume), *v.a.*, engourdir; glacer.

benumb'edness (bi-neum'ednèss) *ou* **benumb'ing**, *n.*, engourdissement, *m.*

benzo'ic (bè'n'zoïke), *adj.*, (chem.) benzoïque.

benzoin' (-zôïne), *n.* *V.* **benjamin**.

bepaint' (bi-pé'n'te), *v.a.*, (l.u.) peindre; barbouiller, peinturer.

bepep'per (bi-pèp'peur), *v.a.*, poivrer.

bepinch' (bi-pi'n'she), *v.a.*, pincer.

beplas'ter (bi-plâsteur), *v.a.*, (fam.) plâtrer.

beplume' (bi-plioume), *v.a.*, (fam.) emplumer.

bepow'der (bi-paoudeur), *v.a.*, (fam.) poudrer.

bepraise' (bi-préze), *v.a.*, louanger.

bequeath' (bi-kwîthe), *v.a.*, léguer.

bequeath'er, *n.*, testateur, *m.*, testatrice, *f.*

bequeath'ment, *n.*, (ant.) legs, *m.*; action de léguer, *f.*

bequest' (bi-kwèste), *n.*, legs, héritage, *m.*

berate' (bi-réte), *v.a.*, insulter; vilipender.

berat'tle (bi-rat'tl), *v.a.*, remplir de bruit.

ber'berry (beur-), *n.*, (bot.) épine-vinette, *f.*

bereave' (bi-rîve), *v.a.*, dépouiller **de**, priver de, enlever à, ravir à.

bereave'ment, *n.*, privation, perte, *f.*; vide; abandon, *m.*; solitude, *f.*

ber'gamot (beur-ga-mote), *n.*, (pear) bergamote; (tapestry) bergame, *f.*

berhyme' (bi-raïme), *v.a.*, rimailler.

ber'lin (beur-line *ou* bèr-), *n.*, berline (carriage), *f.* — wool; *laine à broder*, *f.* — work; *broderie*, *f.* — repository; *magasin de laine à broder*, *m.*

berme (beurme), *n.*, berme, *f.*

Ber'nardin (beur-), *adj.*, bernardin.

ber'ry, *n.*, grain, *m.*; baie; fève, *f.* Coffee in the —; *café au grain*, *m.*

ber'ry, *v.n.*, (bot.) porter des baies.

ber'ry-bear'ing (-bèr'igne), *adj.*, (bot.) baccifère, qui porte des baies.

berth (beurth), *n.*, (nav.) cabine, *f.*; (nav.) (ship's station) évitage, *m.*; case, *f.*; lit, *m.*; couchette; (place) place, *f.*, emploi, *m.*

ber'yl (bèr'ile), *n.*, (min.) béryl, *m.*

ber'ylline (-laïne), *adj.*, de béryl.

bescrawl' (bi-scrôl), *v.a.* (ant.) griffonner.

bescrib'ble (bi-), *v.a.*, (ant.) barbouiller.

beseech' (bi-cîtshe), *v.a.*, (*preterit and past part.*, Besought) supplier, conjurer, implorer.

beseech'er, *n.*, suppliant, *m.*, suppliante, *f.*

beseech'ing, *n.*, supplication, *f.*; instances, *f.pl.*

beseem' (bi-cîme), *v.n.*, convenir **à**, seoir **à**.

beseem'ly, **beseem'ing**, *adj.*, convenable, bienséant.

beseem'ingness, *n.*, convenance, bienséance, *f.*

beset' (bi-cète), *v.a.*, (*preterit and past part.*, Beset) assiéger, obséder; entourer, embarrasser, serrer de près.

beset'ting, *adj.*, habituel; obsesseur. — sin; *péché mignon ou d'habitude*, *m.*

beshrew' (bi-shrou), *v.a.*, maudire.

beside' (bi-çaïde) *ou* **besides'** (-çaïd'ze), *prep.*, à côté **de**, auprès **de**; outre; hors, hors **de**; hormis, excepté, en dehors **de**. To be — one's self; *être hors de soi.*

beside' *ou* **besides'**, *adv.*, d'ailleurs, du reste, en outre, encore, de plus; hors de là; au delà.

beside' that (-*thate*), *conj.*, outre que.

besiege' (bi-cî'dje), *v.a.*, assiéger.

besieged' (bi-cî'dj'd), *n.*, assiégé, *m.*

besie'ger, *n.*, assiégeant, *m.*

besie'ging, *n.*, action d'assiéger, *f.*; siège, *m.*

besie'ging, *adj.*, assiégeant, e.

besmear' (bi-smîre), *v.a.*, barbouiller, salir; enduire; souiller.

besmirch' (bi-smeurt'she), *v.a.*, souiller, salir, tacher. To — any one's reputation; *perdre quelqu'un de réputation ou noircir quelqu'un.*

besmoke' (bi-smôke), *v.a.*, enfumer, noircir.

besmut' (bi-smeute), *v.a.*, noircir de suie.

be'som (bi-zeume), *n.*, balai, *m.*

be'som, *v.n.*, balayer.

besot' (bi-çote), *v.a.*, assoter ; abrutir, hébéter.

besot'ted (bi-çot'tède), *past part.*, infatué ; stupéfié ; abruti, hébété.

besot'tedly (bi-çot'tèd-), *adv.*, sottement, stupidement.

besot'tedness, *n.*, abrutissement, *m.*

besought' (bè-çôte), *V.* **beseech.**

bespan'gle (bi-spa'gn'g'l), *v.a.*, orner de paillettes ; (dot) passementer **de** ; parsemer **de.**

bespat'ter (bi-), *v.a.*, éclabousser, couvrir de boue ; asperger ; noircir, diffamer, flétrir.

bespeak' (bi-spîke), *v.a.*, (*preterit,* Bespoke ; *past part.,* Bespoken) commander, faire faire ; retenir ; annoncer, dénoter, montrer ; discourir ; parler à, s'adresser à, demander d'avance à. To — a place : *retenir une place.* To — a coat : *commander un habit.*

bespeck'le (bi-spèc'k'l), *v.a.*, tacheter, marqueter, moucheter.

bespice' (bi-spaïce), *v.a.*, épicer ; assaisonner.

bespot' (bi-spote), *v.a.*, tacher, salir, souiller, crotter.

bespread' (bi-sprède), *v.a.*, tendre, étendre ; semer ; couvrir **de.**

besprent' (bi-sprè'n'te), *adj.*, (ant.) arrosé ; semé ; couvert.

besprink'le (bi-spri'gn'k'l), *v.a.*, arroser **de,** parsemer **de.**

besprink'ler, *n.*, arroseur, *m.*

bespurt' (bi-speurte), *v.a.*, asperger.

best (bèste), *adj.*, meilleur, le meilleur, le mieux. The — man on earth ; *le meilleur homme du monde.* — man (at weddings) : *garçon d'honneur,* m. To do one's — ; *faire tout son possible ; faire de son mieux.* To act for the — ; *faire, agir pour le mieux.* To the — of my recollection ; *autant que je puis m'en souvenir.* To the — of my belief ; *à ce que je crois, autant que je sache.* To the — of one's ability ; *de son mieux.* The — of it is that ; *le meilleur est que.* At — ; *au mieux, tout au mieux ; au plus, tout au plus, à tout prendre.* For the — ; *pour le mieux, au mieux.* To have the — of it ; *avoir le dessus.* To make the — of ; *tirer tout ce qu'on peut* **de** ; *tirer le meilleur parti* **de.** To make the — of one's way ; *se rendre tout droit ; aller droit, en toute hâte.* The — of the way ; *la plus grande partie du chemin.* To have the — of it ; *avoir l'avantage.* To do one's — to ; *faire tout ce qui dépend de soi* **pour.** The — of everything ; *ce qu'il y a de meilleur.* To make the — of circumstances ; *s'adapter aux circonstances.* To put the — construction on anything ; *voir les choses du bon côté.*

best, *adv.*, mieux, le mieux. To strive as to who shall do their — to ; *faire à qui mieux mieux* **pour.** One had — ; *mieux vaudrait, mieux vaut ; ce qu'il y a mieux à faire c'est* **de.**

bestain' (bi-sténe), *v.a.*, tacher.

bes'tial (bèst'ial), *adj.*, bestial, brutal, de bête.

bestial'ity, *n.*, bestialité, *f.*

bes'tialize (bèst'ial'aïze), *v.a.*, abrutir.

bes'tially, *adv.*, bestialement.

bestir' (bi-steur), *v.a.*, remuer, agiter, mettre en mouvement. To — one's self ; *se remuer ; se donner du mouvement ; s'agiter ; se trémousser.*

bestow' (bi-stô), *v.a.*, donner ; appliquer ; dispenser ; accorder **à** ; conférer **à** ; employer **à,** consacrer **à.** To — a kindness on any one ; *faire une faveur, rendre un service* **à** *quelqu'un.*

bestow'al, *n.*, dispensation, *f.*

bestow'er, *n.*, dispensateur, *m.*, dispensatrice, *f.*

bestow'ing, *n.*, donation, *f.* ; don, *m.*

bestrad'dle (bi-), *v.a.*, enfourcher.

bestraught' (bi-strôte), *adj.* *V.* **distraught.**

bestrew' (bi-strou), *v.a.*, joncher, parsemer **de.**

bestride' (bi-straïde), *v.a.*, monter (a horse) ; enjamber, enfourcher.

bestud' (bi-steude), *v.a.* *V.* **stud.**

bet (bète), *n.*, pari, *m.* ; gageure, *f.* To lay a — ; *parier.*

bet, *v.a.*, parier, gager, faire un pari, faire une gageure.

betake' (bi-téke), *v.a.* (*preterit,* Betook ; *past part.,* Betaken). To — one's self to ; *se livrer* **à,** *se mettre* **à,** *s'adonner* **à,** *se retirer* **dans,** *recourir* **à,** *avoir recours* **à** ; *se porter* **vers.** To — one's self to one's study ; *se retirer dans son cabinet.* To — one's self to one's heels ; *se sauver, s'enfuir.* To — one's self to one's studies ; *se livrer à ses études.*

bethink' (bi-thign'k), *v.n.*, (*preterit* and *past part.,* Bethought) ruminer ; s'aviser **de,** réfléchir **à.**

bethink', *v.a.*, se rappeler, se ressouvenir **de.** To — one's self ; *imaginer ; avoir l'idée, songer* **à** ; (twice) *se raviser.*

Beth'lehem (bèth-li'ème), *n.*, hospice pour les aliénés, *m.* *V.* **Bedlam.**

Beth'lemite (bèth-lè'm'aïte), *n.*, (geog.) Bethléhémite, *m.f.* ; habitant de Bedlam, *m.*, habitante de Bedlam, *f.* *V.* **Bedlam.**

bethump' (bi-theu'm'pe), *v.a.*, rosser, étriller, assommer.

betide' (bi-taïde), *v.a.*, arriver **à,** advenir **à** ; prédire, annoncer. Woe — you ; *malheur à vous.*

betide', *v.n.*, arriver, advenir.

betime' (bi-taïme) *ou* **betimes'** (bi-taï'mze), *adv.*, de bonne heure.

beto'ken (bi-tô'k'n), *v.a.*, indiquer ; annoncer, dénoter, présager, désigner.

bet'on (bèt'eune), *n.*, béton, *m.*

bet'ony (bèt'o'ni), *n.*, (bot.) bétoine, *f.*

betray' (bi-tré), *v.a.*, trahir ; livrer ; tromper ; révéler ; faire tomber, entraîner. To — (lead) into error ; *entraîner dans l'erreur.*

betray'al, *n.*, trahison, perfidie, *f.*

betray'er, *n.*, traître, *m.*, traîtresse, *f.*

betrim' (bi-trime), *v.a.*, parer, orner, décorer.

betroth' (bi-troth), *v.a.*, fiancer, accorder **à.**

betrothed' (bi-trothte), *n.*, fiancé, accordé, *m.* ; fiancée, accordée, *f.*

betrothed', *adj.*, fiancé, accordé, **à.**

betroth'ing *ou* **betroth'al**, *n.*, fiançailles, (pop.) accordailles, *f.pl.*

bet'ter (bèt'teur), *adj.*, meilleur. — and — ; *de mieux en mieux.* For the — ; *en mieux.* To be — ; *se trouver mieux, se rétablir ; valoir mieux.* To grow — ; *devenir meilleur ; se porter mieux, se rétablir.* — late than never ; *mieux vaut tard que jamais.* The — day, the — the deed ; *bon jour, bonne œuvre.* To get the — of ; *prendre le dessus* **sur** ; *avoir le dessus* **de** ; *l'emporter sur* ; *venir à bout* **de** ; *se rétablir* **de.** To have the — ; *avoir l'avantage, la supériorité* **sur,** *l'emporter* **sur.** To be the — for ; *se trouver bien* **de.** To be none the — for (a thing) ; *n'en être pas plus avancé.*

bet'ter, *adv.*, mieux. To be — off ; *être dans une meilleure position.* For — for worse ; *vaille que vaille.* So much the — ! *tant mieux !* — and — ; *de mieux en mieux.* To be — ; *valoir mieux, se porter mieux, être mieux.* To get — ; *aller mieux, se porter mieux.* I had — ; *je ferais mieux.* To think the — of ; (reflect) *se raviser.* I like her the — for it ; *je l'en aime davantage.* To think the — of ; (pers.) *avoir meilleure opinion* **de,** *estimer d'avantage.* The more I know you, the — I like you ; *plus je vous connais, plus je vous aime.*

bet'ter, *n.*, supérieur, *m.* One's elders and —s ; *gens qui valent mieux que soi,* m.pl.

bet'ter, *v.a.*, améliorer, avancer. To — one's self ; *améliorer sa position.*

bet'terment, **bet'tering**, *n.*, amélioration, *f.* ; perfectionnement, embellissement, *m.*

bet'ting (bèt-tigne), n., pari (action), m., paris, m.pl. — man ; parieur. — woman ; parieuse.

bet'tor (bèt-tor), n., parieur; joueur, m.

bet'ty (bèt'ti), n., monseigneur (instrument), m., (slang) pince, f.

betum'bled (bi-teu'm'b'lde), adj., en désordre; chiffonné.

between' (bi-twine), prep., entre. — us ; entre nous. — us two, three, etc.; à nous deux, à nous trois, etc. — wind and water; à fleur d'eau. — this and then; d'ici là. — this and to-morrow; d'ici à demain. — whiles ; dans l'intervalle. — this and Monday ; d'ici à lundi. — decks ; (nav.) entrepont, m.

between', n., intervalle, m.

betwixt' (bi-), prep., entre. — and between ; entre les deux.

bev'el (bè-vèl), n., (tech.) fausse équerre, f.

bev'el, adj., de biais; en biseau.

bev'el, v.a., équarrir, tailler en biseau.

bev'el, v.n., aller en biais, biaiser ; (mines) diriger.

bev'eling, n., coupe en biais, f. ; biseau, m.

bev'eling, adj., de biais.

bev'erage (bèv'eur'èdge), n., breuvage, m. ; boisson, f.

bev'il. V. **bevel**.

bev'y (bè-vi), n., volée; troupe, bande, f. — of partridges; compagnie de perdrix, f. — of quails; volée de cailles, f. — of animals; troupe d'animaux, f. — of roebucks ; troupe de chevreuils, f. — of women; assemblée de femmes, f. — of young girls ; troupe de jeunes filles.

bewail' (bi-wéle), v.a., regretter, pleurer.

bewail', v.n., se lamenter de.

bewail'ing, n., plainte, lamentation, f.

beware' (bi-wère), v.n., se garder de, prendre garde à ; se défier de, se méfier de.

bewet' (bi-wète), v.a., humecter.

bewhis'kered (bi-), adj., paré de favoris.

bewil'der (bi-), v.a., égarer, embrouiller, embarrasser, dérouter; transporter, ravir; ahurir, effarer.

bewitch' (bi-wit'she), v.a., ensorceler ; enchanter ; fasciner.

bewitch'er, n., ensorceleur, m., ensorceleuse, f.

bewitch'ery, bewitch'ment, n., ensorcellement, m.

bewitch'ing, adj., enchanteur, séduisant, ravissant.

bewitch'ingly, adv., d'une manière séduisante; à ravir.

bewray' (bi-ré), v.a., déceler ; tromper ; trahir.

bewray'er (bi-rê'y'eur), n., (ant.) traître, m.

bey, n., bey, m.

beyond' (bi-yon'de), prep., delà, par delà, au-delà de; au dessus de; outre ; hors de. — measure ; outre mesure, démesurément. To be — reach of ; être hors de la portée de. To go —; (any one) surpasser, aller plus loin que. This is — me ; cela me passe.

beyond', adv., là-bas. V. **yonder**.

bez'el (bè-zèl) ou **bez'il**, n., chaton (of a ring), m.

bez'oar (bèz-ôre), n., bézoard, m.

bi'a, n., cauris, coris, m.

bian'gulate (baï-aï'gn-ghiou-léte), **bian'gulated** (-létède), ou **bian'gulous** (-leusse), adj., à deux angles.

bi'as (baï'ass), n., (biasses) biais, m. ; pente, f., penchant, parti pris, m. ; tendance, direction, f. ; but; préjugé, m. ; prévention, f. On the —; en travers, en croix, en sautoir.

bi'as, v.a., incliner, faire pencher; prévenir ; influencer ; porter à ; diriger.

bi'as, adj., de biais, de travers.

bi'as, adv., de biais, de travers.

bi'ased, adj., prévenu.

bib, n., bavette, f. ; (pisc.) tacaud, m.

bib, v.a., buvoter.

biba'cious (baï-bé-sheusse), adj., buveur.

bib'ber (bib'-), n., buveur, biberon, m., biberonne, f.

Bi'ble (baï'b'l), n., bible, f. — Society ; société biblique, f.

bib'lical (bi-), adj., biblique.

bibliog'rapher, n., bibliographe, m.

bibliograph'ic ou **bibliograph'ical**, adj., bibliographique.

bibliog'raphy, n., bibliographie, f.

biblioma'nia (-mé-), n., bibliomanie, f.

biblioma'niac (-mé-), n., bibliomane, m.

biblioph'ilist (-fi-), n., bibliophile, m.

bib'liopole (-pôle), **bibliop'olist**, n., libraire, m.

bib'ulous (-biou-leusse), adj., spongieux, absorbant, qui boit.

bice ou **bise** (baïce), n., (paint.) bleu pâle ; vert pâle, m.

bi'ceps (baï-), n., (anat.) biceps, m.

bick'er (bik'-), v.n., se quereller, disputer, contester, se picoter, se chamailler.

bick'erer, n., querelleur, chamailleur, m.

bick'ering, n., picoterie ; querelle, bisbille, f.

bick'ern (bik'èrne), n., bec, m. ; bigorne, f.

bicorn'ous (baï-cor'neusse), adj., à deux cornes, bicorne.

bi'colored, adj., bicolore.

bicor'poral (baï-), adj., à deux corps.

bi'cycle (baï-), n., bicyclette, f. ; velocipède, (pop.) vélo, m.; (pop.) bécane, f. — handle bars; guidon, m. — pneumatic tire ; pneumatique, m. tire-cover ; enveloppe, f. — inner tube ; chambre à air, f.

bid, v.a., offrir ; ordonner de ; enchérir ; dire de ; convier à ; commander de ; inviter à (at auctions). To — fair to ; être en passe de ; promettre de. To — good-by to ; dire adieu à ou faire ses adieux à.

bid, n., enchère, f.

bid'der, n., enchérisseur, acheteur, m. Highest —; plus offrant, m.

bid'ding, n., commandement, ordre, m. ; invitation, prière, demande, f.; (at auctions) enchère, f.

bide (baïde), v.a., endurer, souffrir ; attendre. To — one's time ; attendre le bon moment.

bide, v.n., demeurer, rester, habiter.

bident'al, bident'ate, ou **bident'ated** (baïde'n-, -téte, -tétéde), adj., bidenté. [ture), m.

bid'et (bi-dète), n., bidet (horse); bidet (furni-

bid'ing (baïd'-), n., (fig.) demeure, f. ; séjour, m. — one's time ; attendant l'occasion.

bid'on (bid'eune), n., bidon, m.

bien'nial (baï'è'n-ni-), adj., biennal, de deux ans; (bot.) bisannuel.

bien'nially, adv., tous les deux ans, de deux ans, en deux ans.

bier (bieur), n., bière, f., cercueil, m. ; civière, f. ; brancard, m.

bif'erous (bif'eureusse), adj., bifère.

bif'fin, n., pomme tapée, f.

bi'fid (baï-fide), adj., bifide.

bi'fold (baï-fôlde), adj., double.

bifur'cate (baï-feur-kéte) ou **bifur'cated** (-tède), adj., bifurqué. — s, se bifurquer.

bifurca'tion, n., bifurcation, f.

big, adj., gros; superbe, fier ; grand, vaste ; plein; (of women) enceinte, grosse; (of animals) pleine. To look —; faire le gros dos ; faire l'important. To talk —; parler haut ; trancher du grand ; faire l'important ; (to threaten) parler des grosses dents. — with ; gros de.

big'amist, n., bigame, m.f.

big'amy, n., bigamie, f.

big'ly, adv., fièrement, superbement.

big'ness (big'nèsse), n., grosseur, grandeur, f.

big'ot (big'ote), n., bigot, cagot, m.; bigote, cagote, f., fanatique, m. and f.

big'ot, adj., (ant.). V. **bigoted**.

big'oted (big'ot'ède), adj., bigot, cagot.

big'otedly, adv., avec bigoterie; en bigot.

big'otry, n., bigoterie, cagoterie, f.

bil'ander, n., (nav.) bélandre, f.

bilat'eral (baï-), adj., bilatéral.

bil'berry, n., (bot.) airelle; myrtille, f.

bil'bo, n., (bilboes) rapière, f.; pl., (nav.) fers, m.pl.

bile (baïle), n., bile, f.

bile'-duct (-deucte), n., canal, conduit, biliaire, m.

bilge (bild'je), n., (nav.) sentine (of a ship), f. — -water; eau de cale, f. — ways; coittes, anguilles, f.pl.

bilge, v.n., (nav.) faire une voie d'eau (à fond de cale); crever, se défoncer.

bil'iary (bil'iari), adj., biliaire.

bil'ious, adj., bilieux.

bilk, v.a., flouer, tromper, frustrer.

bill, n., bec d'oiseau, m.; hache, f.

bill, v.n., se becqueter.

bill, v.a., afficher.

bill, n., note, f.; mémoire, compte, m., facture, f.; billet, effet; compte, m., (at dining-rooms) carte à payer, addition, f.; (of parliament) bill, projet de loi, m. Hand—; affiche, f., placard, m. Stick no — ! défense d'afficher! Exchequer— ; bon du trésor, m. To discount a — ; escompter un billet, un effet. Tradesman's — ; mémoire de fournisseur, m., facture, f. — of parcels; facture. To make a — payable to: passer un effet à l'ordre de; faire un billet à l'ordre de. To honor a — ; faire honneur à, payer, un billet. To dishonor a — ; ne pas faire honneur à, ne pas payer, un billet. — payable to bearer; billet au porteur. — at sight; billet à vue. — on demand; billet à présentation. To take up a —; acquitter un billet, payer un billet. The expiration of a —; l'échéance d'un effet, f. To provide for the payment of a —; faire les fonds d'un effet. — of exchange; lettre de change, f. — of fare; menu, m., carte, f. — of lading; connaissement, m. — of health; patente de santé, f. — of rights; (jur.) déclaration des droits, f. True —; arrêt d'accusation or arrêt de mise en accusation. To find a true —; prononcer la mise en accusation de.

bill'-broker (-brô-), n., courtier de change, m.

bill'-brokerage (-édje), n., courtage de change, m.

bill'et (bil'lète), n., bûche; (her.) billette, f.; billet; billet de logement, m.

bill'et, v.a., délivrer des billets de logement à, loger.

bill'et-doux (bil'lè-), n., (billets-doux) billet doux, m.

bill'-file, n., pique-notes, m.

bill'-frame, n., porte-affiches, m.

bill'-head, n., tête de facture, f.

bill'-hook, n., serpe, f.

bil'liard (bil'ieurde), adj., de billard. — ball; bille, f. — cloth; tapis, m. — cushion; bande, f. — marker; garçon de billard, m. — playing; le jeu de billard.

bil'liard-room (-roume), n., salle de billard, f.

bil'liards (bil'ieurdze), n.pl., billard, m.sing. To play a game at —; faire une partie de billard.

bil'liard-table (-tè'b'l), n., billard, m.; table de billard, f.

bil'lingsgate (bil'ligne'z'ghête), n., langage de la halle, m.

bil'lion (bil'ien'ne), n., trillion, m.

bil'low (bil'lô), n., flot, m.; vague, houle, lame, f.

bil'low, v.n., s'élever en vagues, ondoyer.

bil'lowy (bil-lô-i), adj., houleux.

bill'sticker, n., afficheur, colleur d'affiches, m.

bill'-sticking, n., affichage, m.

bil'lycock-hat', n., feutre; chapeau rond, m.

bima'nous (-neusse), adj., bimane.

bin (bine), n., huche, caisse, f., coffre, m. Wine —; porte-bouteilles, m.; cave, f.

bin, v.a., ranger; empiler (bottles).

bi'nary (baï-), adj., binaire.

bi'nary, n., (arith.) nombre binaire, m.

bind (baï'n'de), v.a., lier; obliger; resserrer; constiper; ceindre, border, garotter, serrer; (with hoops) cercler de. To — a book; relier un livre. To — down; lier, astreindre à. To — a wound; bander une blessure. To be bound to; être tenu de. To — over; contraindre de comparaître. To be bound over; (jur.) être tenu de comparaître. That is bound to happen; cela ne peut manquer d'arriver. I'll be bound; j'en réponds.

bind, v.n., se lier, durcir.

bind'er, n., lieur; relieur; bandeau, m., bande, attache, f.

bind'ery (baï'n'deuri), n., atelier de reliure, m.

bind'ing, n., reliure, f.; bandeau, galon, m., bordure, f.

bind'ing, adj., obligatoire, astringent; (jur.) commissoire.

bind'weed (baï'n'd'wîde), n., (bot.) liseron, m.

bin'nacle, n., (nav.) habitacle, m.

bin'ocle, n., binocle, m.

binoc'ular (baï-), adj., binoculaire.

bino'mial (baï-nô-), adj., (alg.) binôme.

biog'rapher (baï'og'graf'-), n., biographe, m.

biograph'ic ou **biograph'ical** (baï'o-), adj., biographique.

biog'raphy (baï'o-), n., biographie, f.

bip'artite (bip'ar-taïte), adj., biparti.

bi'ped (baï-pède), n., bipède, m.

bip'edal (bi-pi-), adj., bipède.

biquadrat'ic (baï-kwo-), adj., (alg.) bi-carré.

birch (beurtshe), n., bouleau, m.; verge, f.; verges, f.pl. v.a., battre à coups de verges, fouetter; donner le fouet à.

birch'-broom, n., balai de bouleau, m.

birch'en (beurtsh'n), adj., de bouleau.

birch'-grove, n., boulaie, bouleraie, f.

birch'ing, n., coups de verges, m.pl.; le fouet, m.

birch'-tree (-trî), n., bouleau, m.

bird (beurde), n., oiseau, m. A — in hand is worth two in the bush; un Tiens vaut mieux que deux Tu l'auras. A little — told me; mon petit doigt me l'a dit. To kill two —s with one stone; faire d'une pierre deux coups.

bird, v.n., oiseler. V. **fowl**.

bird'-cage, n., cage d'oiseau, f.

bird'-call (-côl), n., appeau, pipeau, m.

bird'-catcher, n., oiseleur, m.

bird'-eyed (-aïe'de), adj., à œil d'oiseau.

bird'-fancier, n., amateur d'oiseaux, m.

bird'like (-laïke), adj., comme un oiseau.

bird'lime (-laïme), n., glu, f.

bird'man, n., oiseleur, m.

bird'-organ, n., serinette, f.

bird'seller, n., oiselier, m.

birds'eye (beurd'z'aïe), adj., à vue d'oiseau. — view; vue à vol d'oiseau, f.

birds'foot (-foute), n., (bot.) ornithope; pied d'oiseau, m.

bird'show, n., exposition d'oiseaux, f.

bird'snarer, n., oiseleur, m.

birds'nest, n., nid d'oiseau, m.; (bot.) carotte sauvage, f.

birds'nest, v.a. To go birdsnesting; aller dénicher des oiseaux.

birds'nester, n., dénicheur d'oiseaux, m.

bird'stuffer, n., empailleur (d'oiseaux), m.

bird'-trap, n., trébuchet, m.

bird'witted (-tède), adj., à tête de linotte.

birth (beurth), n., naissance; origine, source; couche, f., enfantement, m.; (nav.) évitée, f., évitage, *m.* By — ; *de naissance.* To give — to; *donner le jour à,* (fig.) *donner lieu à, occasionner.*

birth'day, *n.,* jour de naissance, *m.,* fête, *f.* — card ; *billet de faire part.*

birth'place (-pléce), *n.,* lieu natal, *m.*

birth'right (-raïte), *n.,* droit de naissance, (primogeniture) droit d'aînesse, *m.*

bis, *adv.,* bis.

bis'cuit (bis'kite), *n.,* biscuit, *m.* — dust ; *poudre de biscuit, m.* — root ; *camassie, f.* Bread and — baker ; *boulanger, pâtissier, f.*

bise, *n. V.* **bice.**

bisect' (baï-cèkte), *v.a.,* diviser en deux.

bisec'tion (baï-), *n.,* bissection, *f.*

bisex'ual (baï-), *adj.,* bissexuel.

bish'op (bish'eupe), *n.,* évêque ; (at chess) fou, *m.,* (of a fowl) mitre, *f.,* bonnet d'évêque, *m.* —'s palace ; *évêché, m.*

bish'oping, *n.,* maquignonnage, *m.*

bish'op-like (-laïke), *adj.,* d'évêque.

bish'opric, *n.,* évêché, *m.*

bish'ops-wort (-weurte), *n.,* ammi, *m.*

bisk, *n.,* bisque, *f. ;* coulis, *m.*

bis'muth (biz'meuth), *n.,* bismuth, *m.*

bissex'tile, *n.,* année bissextile, *f.*

bissex'tile, *adj.,* bissextil.

bis'tort (-teurte), *n.,* bistorte, *f.*

bis'toury (bis-teuri), *n.,* bistouri, *m.*

bis'ter *ou* **bis'tre** (bisteur), *n.,* bistre, *f.*

bit, *n.,* morceau, *m. ;* pièce, *f. ;* brin, bout; peu, bout de chemin, *m.,* distance ; (nav.) bitte, *f. ;* (man.) mors, frein, *m.* Not a — of it ! *pas un brin, pas le moins du monde, pas du tout.* — by — ; *pièce à pièce.* I don't care a — ; *je m'en bats l'œil.* Every —, *ou* every — of it ; *en entier, entièrement, tout à fait.*

bit, *v.a.,* emboucher ; (nav.) bitter.

bitch, *n.,* chienne, *f. ;* (in compounds) femelle, *f.*

bite (baïte), *n.,* morsure ; piqûre ; bouchée; (fig.) attrape; (fig.) attrapoire, *f. ;* (print.) larron ; coup de dent, *m.* I have not had a single — ; (fishing) *il ne m'est pas venu un seul poisson.*

bite, *v.a.,* (*preterit,* Bit ; *past part.,* Bit, Bitten) mordre ; ronger ; (of the wind) couper ; attraper, duper, mettre dedans. — off ; *déchirer avec les dents.* To — one's lips ; *se mordre les lèvres.* To — one's thumb (at a person) ; *faire la nique à quelqu'un.* To — the bit; (of horses) *ronger le frein.* To — one's nails ; *se ronger les ongles.*

bite, *v.n.,* mordre. To — ; (to take the bait) *mordre à l'hameçon.* Do the fish — ? *faites vous bonne pêche?* ou *le poisson mord-il ?*

bi'ter, *n.,* personne qui mord, *f. ;* (fig.) trompeur, *m.* It is a case of the — bit ; *c'est fin contre fin ou tel est pris qui croyait prendre.* *f coupant.*

bi'ting, *adj.,* mordant, piquant ; (of the wind)

bi'ting, *n.,* morsure, *f.*

bi'tingly, *adv.,* d'une manière mordante, d'une manière piquante.

bit'less (bit'lèsse), *adj.,* sans mors.

bit'tacle, *n. V.* **binnacle.**

bit'ter, *adj.,* amer, aigre; acharné, mordant, cruel, piquant, rigoureux, vif.

bit'ter, *n.,* amer, *m. ;* amertume, *f.*

bit'terish, *adj.,* un peu amer.

bit'terishness, *n.,* légère amertume, *f.*

bit'terly, *adv.,* avec amertume; amèrement.

bit'tern (bit'teurne), *n.,* (orni.) butor, *m. ;* (chem.) eau mère, *f.*

bit'terness, *n.,* amertume, aigreur, *f.,* fiel; acharnement, *m.*

bit'umen (bi-tiou-mène), *n.,* bitume, *m*

bitu'minate (-néte), *v.a.,* bituminer.

bitu'minous (-neusse), *adj.,* bitumineux.

bi'valve, bivalv'ular, *ou* **bivalv'ous** (baï-, -leur, -veusse), *adj.,* bivalve.

biv'ouac, *n.,* bivouac, *m.*

biv'ouac, *v.n.,* bivouaquer.

blab, *n.,* bavard, jaseur, *m. ;* bavarde, jaseuse, *f. ;* rapporteur, *m.,* rapporteuse, *f.*

blab, *v.a.,* jaser **de,** bavarder **de.**

blab, *v.n.,* jaser, bavarder.

black, *v.a.,* noircir, cirer (of boots).

black, *n.,* noir, *m. pl.,* (smuts) noirs, *m.pl.,* particules de suie, *f.pl.* Ivory — ; *noir d'ivoire.* Lamp — ; *noir de fumée.* Dressed in — ; *habillé de noir.* The —s ; *les noirs, les nègres, m.pl.* In — and white ; *en toutes lettres, par écrit.*

black, *adj.,* noir ; (print.) imprimé; obscur, sombre, triste. To look — at any one ; *regarder quelqu'un de travers, de mauvais œil.* He is hardly ever seen without a — eye ; *on ne le voit guère sans un œil poché.* To beat — and blue ; *rouer de coups.* To be — and blue; *être tout meurtri.* To make — ; (fig.) *noircir.*

black'amoor (-mour), *n.,* More, nègre; (fam.) moricaud, *m.,* moricaude, *f.* You cannot wash a — white ; *à laver la tête d'un More on perd sa lessive.*

black'ball (-bôle), *n.,* cirage en boule, *m. ;* boule noire, *f. ;* rejet, *m.,* diffamation, *f.*

black'ball, *v.a.,* rejeter au scrutin.

black'berry, *n.,* mûre sauvage, mûre de ronce, *f.*

black'berry-bush, *n.,* mûrier sauvage, *m.,* ronce, *f.*

black'bird (-beurde) *n.,* merle, *m.*

black'board, *n.,* tableau noir, *m.*

black'-book, *n.,* registre des punitions ; (sorcery) grimoire, *m.*

black'-cap, *n.,* bonnet noir, *m.,* toque noire, *f.*

black'-cock, *n.,* coq de bruyère, *m.*

black'-cur'rant, *n.,* cassis, *m.*

black'death, *n.,* peste, *f.*

black'-earth, *n.,* terreau, *m.*

black'en (blak'n), *v.a.* and *n.,* noircir; obscurcir.

black'guard (blag'gârde), *n.,* polisson, gredin, galopin, vaurien ; (fam.) goujat, voyou, *m.*

black'guard, *adj.,* de polisson ; de galopin; ignoble, sale, canaille.

black'guardism, *n.,* polissonnerie, *f.*

black'hole, *n.,* cachot, trou noir, cabanon, *m.*

black'ing, *n.,* cirage, *m.*

black'ish, *adj.,* noirâtre.

black'-lead, *n.,* mine de plomb, plombagine, *f.*

black'leg (-lèghe), *n.,* escroc, grec, *m.*

black'-letter, *n.,* lettre gothique, *f.*

black'ly, *adv.,* avec noirceur.

black'-mail (-méle), *n.,* redevance en blé, *ou* en bœufs, *f. ;* tribut payé à des bandes de voleurs, *m. ;* (fig.) fraude, extorsion, exaction, *f.,* chantage, *m. v.a.,* faire chanter.

black'ness, *n.,* noirceur, *f.*

black'-sheep, *n.,* (fig.) brebis galeuse, *f.*

black'-smith (-smith), *n.,* forgeron, *m.* —'s shop ; *forge, f.*

black'y-top, *n.,* (orni.) traquet, *m.*

blad'der, *n.,* vessie, vésicule, ampoule, *f. ;* (fig.) bulle. — wort ; (bot.) utriculaire, *f.*

blad'dered (-deurde), *adj.,* gonflé, enflé.

blad'dery, *adj.,* vésiculaire; vésiculeux.

blade (bléde), *n.,* lame (of cutting instruments), *f. ;* brin (of grass) ; plat (of an oar) gaillard, compagnon, compère, *m.* Old — ; *vieux routier.* Young — ; *jeune luron.* Jolly — ; *joyeux compagnon.*

blade, *v.a.,* garnir d'une lame, mettre une lame à.

blade'bone (-bône), *n.,* omoplate, *f.*

bla'ded (-'ède), *adj.,* à feuilles, lamelleux ; (min.) lamellé. Double — ; *à deux lames.*

blain (bléne), *n.,* tumeur, pustule, *f.*

bla'mable (blêm'-), *adj.,* blâmable.

blame (bléme), *n.,* blâme, *m. ;* faute, *f.*

blame, *v.a.,* blâmer, reprendre, s'en prendre **à** ; censurer, accuser **de.** To lay the — on; *rejeter le blâme sur.*

blame'ful (-foule), *adj.*, coupable, blâmable.

blame'less, *n.*, irrépréhensible, irréprochable, innocent, sans tache.

blame'lessly, *adv.*, irréprochablement.

blame'lessness, *n.*, innocence, *f.*

bla'mer, *n.*, désapprobateur, *m.*

blame'worthy (-weur*thi*), *adj.*, cigne de blâme.

blanch, *v.a.*, blanchir ; (to peel) peler ; (fig.) pâlir ; faire pâlir.

blanch, *v.n.*, pâlir ; faiblir ; tergiverser.

blanch'ing, *n.*, blanchiment, *m.*

blanc-mange', *n.*, blanc-manger, *m.*

bland (bla'n'de), *adj.*, doux, aimable ; (in a bad sense) doucereux, mielleux.

blandil'oquence (-kwè'n'ce), *n.*, doux parler, langage caressant, *m.*

bland'ish, *v.a.*, caresser, flatter, cajoler.

bland'ishing *ou* **bland'ishment**, *n.*, caresse, *f.* ; attrait, charme, *m.*

bland'ness, *n.*, douceur, affabilité, *f.*

blank (blai'gnke), *adj.*, blanc, en blanc ; (fig.) pâle ; confus, déconcerté ; (arch.) faux ; (of cartridges) à blanc, sans balle. To fire with — cartridge ; *tirer à blanc.*

blank, *n.*, blanc ; (of lotteries) billet blanc, billet perdant ; (fig.) vide, *m.*, lacune, *f.* In — ; *en blanc.* My mind is a perfect — ; *mon esprit est, pour ainsi dire, un grand feuillet blanc.*

blank, *v.a.*, laisser vide, laisser en blanc ; faire pâlir, pâlir ; confondre ; annuler.

blank'et (blai'gnk'ète), *n.*, couverture, *f.* ; (print.) blanchet, *m.*

blank'et, *v.a.*, envelopper avec une couverture.

blanketeer' (-f'eur), *n.*, berneur, *m.*

blank'ly, *adv.*, avec confusion.

blank'ness, *n.*, blancheur, pâleur, *f.*

blare (blère), *v.n.*, (l.u.) rugir, beugler.

blar'ney, *v.a.*, encenser, enjôler, flagorner ; payer en monnaie de singe.

blar'ney, *n.*, eau bénite de cour, flagornerie, monnaie de singe, *f.*

blaspheme' (-fîme), *v.a.* and *n.*, blasphémer.

blasphe'mer, *n.*, blasphémateur, *m.*

blas'phemous (-fi-meusse), *adj.*, blasphématoire.

blas'phemously, *adv.*, avec blasphème.

blas'phemy (-fi-), *n.*, blasphème, *m.*

blast, *n.*, souffle ; vent, coup de vent ; vent pestilentiel ; son d'un instrument à vent, *m.* ; explosion, *f.* ; (fig.) souffle destructeur.

blast, *v.a.*, flétrir ; brûler ; détruire, ruiner ; (mines) faire sauter.

blast'-engine, *n.*, machine soufflante, *f.*

blast'er, *n.*, destructeur, détracteur, *m.*

blast'-furnace (-feur-nèce), *n.*, haut fourneau, *m.*

blast'ing, *adj.*, destructeur.

blast'ing, *n.*, (mines) sautage, *m.* ; explosion, *f.*

blast'pipe (-païpe), *n.*, tuyau d'échappement, *m.* ; tuyère, *f.*

bla'tant, *adj.*, bruyant, beuglant ; (fig.) pompeux, ronflant.

blay, *n.*, (ich.) able, *m.*, ablette, *f.*

blaze (bléze), *n.*, flamme ; lumière, *f.* ; feu ; éclat, bruit, tumulte, *m.* ; (man.) étoile, *f.* To be a— ; *s'enflammer.*

blaze, *v.n.*, être en flammes ; flamber, brûler, briller.

blaze, *v.a.*, répandre ; (abroad) crier par dessus les toits ; faire connaître, publier.

bla'zing, *adj.*, flamboyant ; brillant ; enflammé, embrasé. *n.*, flamboiement.

bla'zon (blé-z'n), *n.*, blason, *m.* ; révélation, divulgation, *f.*

bla'zon, *v.a.*, blasonner ; faire briller ; proclamer, publier. To — abroad ; *crier par-dessus les toits.*

bleaoh (blîtshe), *v.a.*, rendre blanc, blanchir ; pâlir.

bleach, *v.n.*, blanchir.

bleach'er, *n.*, blanchisseur (of linen cloth), *m.*

bleach'ing, *n.*, blanchiment, *m.*

bleach'ing-liq'uid (-lik'wide), *n.*, eau de javelle, *f.*

bleach'-works (-weurkse), *n.*, blanchisserie, *f.*

bleak (blîke), *adj.*, froid ; glacial ; désert, triste ; ouvert, sans abri.

bleak'ish, *adj.*, assez froid, assez triste.

bleak'ly, *adv.*, froidement.

bleak'ness, *n.*, froidure, *f.* ; froid glacial, *m.* tristesse, nudité, *f.*

bleak'y, *adj.* (ant.). *V.* **bleak**.

blear (blîre), *adj.*, chassieux. —-eyed ; *chassieux.*

blear, *v.a.*, rendre chassieux ; (fig.) troubler.

blear'edness (blîr'èd'-), *n.*, chassie, lippitude, *f.*

bleat (blîte), *v.n.*, bêler.

bleat, *n.*, bêlement, *m.*

bleat'ing, *adj.*, bêlant.

bleat'ing, *m.*, bêlement, *m.*

bleb (blèbe), *n.*, ampoule, vésicule, *f.*

bleb'by, *adj.*, vésiculaire.

bleed (blîde), *v.n.*, (preterit and past part., Bled) saigner ; périr ; couler ; pleurer (of vines).

bleed, *v.a.* and *n.*, saigner ; (pop.) faire débourser, faire rendre gorge à ; (pop.) débourser. To — at the nose ; *saigner du nez.*

bleed'ing, *n.*, saignement, *m.* ; (surg.) saignée, *f.*

bleed'ing, *adj.*, ensanglanté, couvert de sang.

blem'ish (blè'-), *v.a.*, flétrir, ternir.

blem'ish, *n.*, flétrissure, tache, *f.* ; défaut, *m.*

blend (blè'n'de), *v.a.*, fondre, mêler, mélanger ; marier, allier à *ou* avec.

blend, *v.n.*, se fondre, se marier à *ou* avec ; (engraving) grener. To — with ; *se confondre* avec, *se mêler* avec.

blende, *n.*, (min.) blende, *f.*

blend'ing, *n.*, fusion, *f.* ; mélange, *m.* ; (engr.) grenure, *f.*

blennorrhœ'a, *n.*, (med.) blennorrhée, *f.*

bless, *v.a.*, bénir ; rendre heureux, faire le bonheur de ; charmer ; réjouir. God — you ! *Dieu vous bénisse !* — my heart, my soul ; *mon dieu ! sapristi !* To — with ; *douer* de.

blessed' (blèste *ou* blèss'ède), *adj.*, béni, saint ; bienheureux ; heureux. To be — with ; *avoir le bonheur d'avoir* ; être doué de ; *jouir de.* The — Virgin ; *la sainte Vierge.* The whole — day|; *toute la sainte*, ou *la bénite, journée.*

bless'edly (blèss'èd'li), *adv.*, heureusement.

bless'edness (blèss'èd'-), *n.*, béatitude, félicité, grâce, *f.* ; bonheur, *m.* Single — ; *célibat, m.*

bless'er, *n.*, personne qui bénit, *f.*

bless'ing, *n.*, bénédiction, *f.* ; bonheur, bénédicité ; bienfait ; bien, *m.* ; grâce, *f.*

blest, *adj. V.* **blessed**.

blight (blaïte), *v.a.*, (of the wind) flétrir ; (of the sun) brouir ; (of fungi) nieller ; (fig.) frustrer, détruire, ruiner, briser, anéantir.

blight, *n.*, (of flowers and fruit) brouissure ; (of corn) nielle, rouille ; (fig.) flétrissure, tache, *f.*

blind (blaï'n'de), *adj.*, aveugle ; obscur ; (of doors) faux. — one eye ; *borgne.* Stone- — ; *complètement aveugle.* — alley ; *cul-de-sac, m.*, impasse, *f.*

blind, *n.*, (fort.) blinde, *f.* ; store, abat-jour, *m.* ; jalousie, persienne, *f.* ; (fig.) voile, masque, *m.* Venetian — ; *jalousie.*

blind, *v.a.*, aveugler ; bander les yeux à, obscurir, voiler, embrouiller.

blind'fold (-fôlde), *v.a.*, bander les yeux à, empêcher de voir.

blind'fold, *adj.*, les yeux bandés ; (fig.) aveugle.

blind'ly, *adv.*, aveuglément.

blind'-maker, *n.*, fabricant de persiennes, etc.

blind'man's-buff (blaï'n'd'ma'n'z'beufe), *n.*, colin-maillard, *m.*

blind'ness, n., cécité, f.; aveuglement, m.; ignorance, f.

blind'side (-saïde), n., côté faible, m.

blink (blign'ke), v.n., cligner **de**; clignoter **de**.

blink, v.a., offusquer, fermer les yeux **sur**, se refuser **à**, refuser de voir; éluder.

blink, n., clignement; clignotement.

blink'er, n., personne qui cligne des yeux; visière, f.; bandeau, m.; (horses) œillère, f.

bliss, n., félicité, béatitude, f.; bonheur, m.

bliss'ful (-foule), adj., bienheureux.

bliss'fully, adv., dans la félicité; heureusement.

bliss'fulness, n., félicité, béatitude, f.

blis'ter, n., ampoule, cloche, bulle, vessie, f.; (med.) vésicatoire, m.

blis'ter, v.a., appliquer un vésicatoire; faire venir des ampoules.

blis'ter, v.n., s'élever en forme de vessie; se couvrir d'ampoules.

blis'ter-fly (-flaïe), n., mouche à vésicatoire, cantharide, f.

blite (blaïte), n., (bot.) blette, blète, f.

blithe (blaïthe), adj., gai, joyeux.

blithe'ly, adv., joyeusement, gaîment ou gaiement.

blithe'some (blaïth'ceume), adj., gai, joyeux.

blithe'someness, n., gaîté, joie, f.

bloat (blôte), v.a., gonfler, bouffir, boursoufler, enfler, rendre vain; fumer, saurer (of herrings).

bloat, v.n., bouffir, s'enfler.

bloat'ed (blôt'ède), adj., bouffi **de**, gonflé **de**. — aristocrat; (fam.) aristo, m.

bloat'edness, n., bouffissure, enflure, f.

bloat'er, n., hareng saur, m.

blob'ber, n., bulle, f.

blob'ber-lip, n., grosse lèvre, f.

blob'ber-lipped (-lipte), adj., lippu.

block, n., bloc, billot, m.; (hair-dressing) tête à perruque, f.; (of wood-cuts) planche, f.; (for ribbons) rouleau, m.; forme (of a hat); (nav.) poulie, f.; (print.) encrier; (of coopers) charpi, m.; (of a pulley) chape; (nav.) poulie, f.; (of stereoplates) cliché, m.; (fig.) bûche, f. — of houses; pâté de maisons, m. Stumbling —; pierre d'achoppement, f.

block, v.a., bloquer. — up; fermer, boucher; condamner, murer.

blockade' (blok'éde), n., blocus, m. — runner; forceur de blocus, m. — running; forcement de blocus, m.

blockade', v.a., bloquer, faire le blocus **de**.

block'head (-hède), n., ganache, bûche, f.; imbécile, m.f.; sot, m., sotte, f.

block'headed, adj., sot, stupide.

block'ishly, adv., stupidement.

block'ishness, n., stupidité, f.

block'like (-laïke), adj., comme un imbécile.

block'tin, n., étain en saumon, m.

blood (bleude), n., sang, m.; (fig.) parenté, f.; tempérament, m; (man.) race, f. That makes one's — run cold; cela glace le sang. One cannot draw — out of a stone; on ne saurait tirer de l'huile d'un mur. In cold —; de sang froid.

blood, v.a., saigner; ensanglanter, mettre en curée (of dogs); (fig.) exaspérer, échauffer.

blood'-colored (-keul'leur'de), adj., couleur de sang.

blood'-guiltiness (-ghil-), n., crime de meurtre, m.

blood'-heat (-hîte), n., chaleur du sang, chaleur animale, f.

blood'-horse, n., cheval de race, cheval pur sang; cheval de course, m.

blood'hound (-haou'n'de), n., limier, m.

blood'ily, adv., d'une manière sanglante; d'une manière sanguinaire.

blood'iness, n., disposition sanguinaire, f.; état sanglant, m.

blood'less, adj., qui n'a point de sang; pâle, inanimé. — victory; victoire non sanglante, ou sans effusion de sang, f.

blood'let (-lète), v.a., phlébotomiser, saigner.

blood'letter, n., phlébotomiste, m.

blood'letting, n., phlébotomie, saignée, f.

blood'shed (-shède), n., effusion de sang, f.; sang répandu, m.

blood'shedder, n., meurtrier, m.

blood'shedding, n., effusion de sang, f.

blood'shot (-shote), adj., rouge; (of the eyes) éraillé, injecté de sang.

blood'-stone (-stône), n., sanguine, f.; jaspe sanguin, m.

blood'sucker (-seuk'-), n., suceur de sang; buveur de sang, m.

blood'thirstiness (-theurs'-), n., soif de sang, f.

blood'thirsty, adj., sanguinaire, altéré de sang.

blood'vessel, n., vaisseau sanguin, m.

blood'-wood (-woude), n., bois de campêche, m.

blood'wort (-weurte), n., (bot.) sanguinaire, f.

blood'y, adj., de sang, sanglant, sanguinaire.

bloom (bloume), n., fleur; fraîcheur; (of fruit) fleur, f.; velouté, m.; (metal.) loupe, f. In —; en fleur.

bloom, v.n., fleurir, briller; être éclatant; (of varnish) chancir.

bloom'ingly, adv., d'une manière florissante, avec éclat.

bloom'y, adj., fleuri, fleurissant.

blos'som (blos'seume), n., fleur, f.

blos'som, v.n., fleurir, être en fleur. To — into; avoir comme floraison; s'épanouir **en**.

blos'somy, adj., couvert de fleurs.

blot (blote), n., tache; effaçure, rature, f.; (of ink) pâté, m., tache, f.

blot, v.a., tacher, noircir; (of ink) faire un pâté **sur**; effacer; souiller. To — out; rayer, effacer.

blot, v.n., (of paper) boire.

blotch, n., pustule, f.

blotch, v.a., couvrir de pustules, tacher, noircir.

blotched, adj., couperosé; bourgeonné.

blote (blôte), v.a., (of herrings) fumer, saurer.

blot'ting (blot'-), adj., qui fait des taches; (of paper) qui boit, buvard.

blot'ting-case (-kéce), n., buvard, m.

blot'ting-paper (-pé-peur), n., papier brouillard, buvard, m.

blouse, n., blouse; chemisette, f.

blow, n., coup; (nav.) grain, m., brise, f. A — with a stick; un coup de bâton. To deal any one a —; porter un coup **à** quelqu'un. Without striking a —; sans coup férir. At a single —; d'un seul coup. To come to —s; en venir aux mains, en venir aux voies de fait. A fly —; chiure de mouche, f.

blow, v.n., (preterit, Blew; past part., Blown) souffler; faire, y avoir, du vent; (of wind-instruments) sonner; (of flowers) s'épanouir. To — over; passer, se dissiper. To — up; (by gunpowder) sauter; éclater. It is blowing; il fait du vent. It is blowing great guns; il fait une tempête à tout casser.

blow, v.a., chasser; souffler; (of wind-instruments) sonner; (of flies) couvrir de piqûres, couvrir d'œufs. To — one's nose; se moucher. To — away; chasser; dissiper. To — down; renverser, abattre (par le vent), casser, briser, enfoncer. To — out; souffler, éteindre (une lumière); faire sauter (la cervelle). To — out one's brains; se faire sauter, se brûler, la cervelle. To — hot and cold; souffler le froid et le chaud. To — up; souffler en l'air; faire sauter (**par**

la poudre). To — any one up; *faire une scène à quelqu'un ; donner un savon à quelqu'un.* You be blowed ! *allez au diable ! allez-vous promener !*

blow'er, n., souffleur, m., souffleuse, f. ; rideau de cheminée, m.

blow'fly (-flaïe), n., mouche à viande, f.

blow'ing, n., action de souffler, f. ; souffle ; (of glass) soufflage; (of wind-instruments) son, m.

blowing-up, n., savon, m. To give a good — to ; *lancer vertement.*

blow'-out, n., bombance, ripaille, f.

blow'pipe (-païpe), n., chalumeau, m.

blowze (blaouze), n., grosse joufflue, f.

blow'zy, adj., haut en couleur, hâlé, joufflu, rubicond.

blub'ber (bleub'beur), n., lard de baleine, m., graisse de baleine; ortie de mer, f.

blub'ber, v.n., pleurer comme un veau.

blub'berer, n., **blub'bering,** adj., pleurard, -e, m.f.

bludg'eon (bleud'jeune), n., assommoir, casse-tête, m. ; trique, f. [*grimace.*

blue, adj., bleu, azur. To look — ; *faire la* blue (blou), n., bleu, azur, m. Prussian — ; *bleu de Prusse.* Sky — ; *bleu de ciel.*

blue, v.a., bleuir ; (dy.) mettre, *ou* teindre, en bleu ; (washing) passer au bleu.

blue'bell, n., jacinthe des prés, clochette, f.

blue'bottle (-bot-t'l), n., (bot.) bluet, m. ; (ent.) mouche bleue, f.

blue'-book, n., livre jaune, m.

blue'-devils (-dèv'lze), n.pl., maladie noire,f.; papillons noirs, m.pl.

blue'ness (-nèsse), n., couleur bleue, f.

blue'-pill, n., pilule mercurielle, f.

blue'stocking, n., bas bleu, m., femme savante, f.

blue'-throat, n., gorge-bleue, m.

bluff (bleufe), adj., gros ; rude ; criard, colère, violent, brusque ; (steep) escarpé, accore.

bluff, n., (nav.) accore, m., falaise, berge, f., escarpement, m.

bluff'ness (-nèsse), n., rudesse, rondeur, brusquerie, f.

blu'ish (blou-ishe), adj., bleuâtre.

blu'ishness (-nèsse), n., couleur bleuâtre, teinte bleuâtre, f.

blun'der (bleun'-), n., bévue, grosse faute, étourderie, balourdise ; (pop.) gaffe, f.

blun'der, v.n., faire une bévue. — about ; *agir en étourdi.*

blun'der, v.a., embrouiller. — a thing out ; *lâcher quelque chose, dire sans y penser, laisser échapper.*

blun'derbuss (-beusse), n., espingole, f.; tromblon, m.

blun'derer, n., faiseur de bévues, m., faiseuse de bévues, f. ; maladroit, m., maladroite, f., étourdi, m., étourdie, f.

blun'der-head (-hède), n., brouillon, m., brouillonne, f.

blun'dering, adj., qui fait des bévues; étourdi.

blun'deringly, adv., étourdiment, en étourdi.

blunt (bleun'te), adj., émoussé, épointé; (fig., pers.) brusque, grossier, obtus; bourru.

blunt, v.a., émousser, épointer ; (fig.) adoucir, amortir.

blunt'ly, adv., brusquement, crûment ; de but en blanc.

blunt'ness (-nèsse), n., épointement, m. ; (fig.) brusquerie, rudesse, f.

blunt'-witted, adj., stupide, lourd, borné.

blur (bleur), n., tache, f.

blur, v.a., tacher, barbouiller; souiller, ternir.

blurt out' (bleurte), v.a., jeter, dire à l'étourdie, laisser échapper, lâcher.

blush (bleushe), v.n., rougir de *ou* pour, avoir honte de.

blush, n., rougeur, f. Her color rose ; *la rougeur lui monta au visage.* At the first — ;

au premier aspect, au premier abord. To put to the — ; *faire rougir.*

blush'ing, adj., rougissant; qui rougit.

blush'less (-lèsse), adj., impudent; effronté.

blus'ter (bleus'teur), v.n., faire du fracas ; tempêter, crier **contre.**

blus'ter, n., fracas, bruit, tapage, m. ; fanfaronnade, (of storms) fureur, f.; (of anger) emportement, m. Why all this — ? *pourquoi tout cet emportement ?*

blus'terer, n.,fanfaron, rodomont, tapageur, m.

blus'tering, adj., (of weather) orageux ; (of noise) bruyant; fanfaron. — fellow; *fanfaron,* m.

blus'teringly, adv., en tempêtant, en criant.

boa, n., (zoöl.) boa ; (fur) boa, m.

bo'a-constrict'or (-con'stric-teur), n., boa, boa constricteur; devin, m.

boar (bôre), n., verrat, m. Wild —; *sanglier,* m. Young wild —; *marcassin,* m. —hound ; *chien de sanglier,* m. — hunt ; *chasse au sanglier,* f.

board (bôrde), n., planche, f.; ais, écriteau, m. ; (aliments) table, pension, nourriture, f.; (print.) carton; (of tailors) établi; (council) conseil; (book-bind.) plat; (nav.) bord, m. — of Trade; *ministère du commerce,* m. — of works; *ministère des travaux publics,* m. To bind in —s ; *cartonner.* To put out to — ; *mettre en pension.* — of examiners; *jury d'examen,* m. — of directors; *conseil d'administration,* m. On —; *à bord.* On — a ship ; *à bord d'un vaisseau.* To go on — ; *aller à bord, s'embarquer.* On — one's ship; *à son bord.*

board, v.a., planchéier ; (nav.) aborder; nourrir, mettre en pension.

board, v.n., être, se mettre en pension.

board'able, adj., abordable.

board'er, n., pensionnaire ; interne, pensionnaire (at school), m.f.

board'ing, n., planchéiage ; table, nourriture; pension, f. ; (nav.) abordage, m.

board'ing-house (-haouce), n., pension bourgeoise, pension de famille, f.

board'ing-pike (-païke), n., (nav.) pique d'abordage, f.

board'ing-school (-skoule), n., pension, institution, f. ; pensionnat, m.

board'-wages (-wé'djize), n.pl., gages pour frais de nourriture, m.pl. To be on —; *avoir tant pour frais de nourriture.*

boar'ish (bôr'ishe), adj., de sanglier ; brutal, grossier.

boar'-spear (-spîre), n., (hunt.) épieu, m.

boast (bôste), v.a., vanter ; (mas., sculpt.) ébaucher.

boast, v.n., se vanter **de,** se glorifier **de** ; se faire fort **de.**

boast, n., vanterie, jactance, f. To make a — of ; *se vanter* **de,** *se faire gloire* **de,** *tirer vanité* **de.**

boast'er, n., vantard ; (mas., sculpt.) ébauchoir, m.

boast'ful (-foule), adj., vantard ; arrogant, orgueilleux; vain.

boast'ing, n., vanterie, jactance, fanfaronnade, gloriole, f.

boast'ingly, adv., avec vanterie, avec jactance.

boast'ing-tool (-toule), n., (mas., sculpt.) ébauchoir, m.

boat (bôte), n., bateau, canot, m. ; barque, f. Long—; *chaloupe,* f. She is a fine — ; *c'est un superbe bâtiment.* By—; *par eau* (fig.). To be in the same — with ; *être dans le même pétrin, être dans la même galère ; être du même côté que.*

boat, v.a., transporter par bateau. To — the oars ; *rentrer les avirons.*

boat'builder (-bild'eur), n., constructeur de bateaux, m.

boat'-hook (-houke), n., gaffe, f.

boat'-house (-haouce), n., hangar à bateaux, m.

boat'ing, n., batelage, m. ; promenade en bateau, f. ; canotage, m.

boat'-keeper, n., canotier, m.

boat'-load (-lôde), n., batelée, f.

boat'man ou **boats'man** (bôt'ma'n, bôt's'-ma'n), n., batelier, m.

boat'-oar (-ôre), n., rame, f. ; aviron, m.

boat'-rope (-rôpe), n., câbleau, câblot, m.

boats'man, n. V. **boatman**.

boat'swain (-swéne, bôs'n), n., (nav.) maître d'équipage, m. —'s mate; contre-maître, m.

boat' up, v.a., remonter en bateau.

bob, n., (end) bout ; (tassel) gland; pendant, m. ; (wig) perruque à nœuds ; lentille (of a pendulum), f. ; (blow) coup, m., tape, f. ; (of a stanza) refrain ; (pop.) schelling, m.

bob, v.a., écourter (the tail) ; (to drub) houspiller, rosser ; (to cheat) attraper, mettre dedans ; secouer, ballotter, balancer ; bafouer ; (to strike) taper; escamoter.

bob, v.n., heurter; pendiller, osciller, s'agiter. To — down ; se baisser rapidement. To — up; reparaître, revenir à la surface.

bob'bin (bob'bine), n., bobine, f. ; fuseau à dentelle, m. ; ganse, f.

bob'bin-work (-weurke) n., ouvrage fait à la bobine, m.

bob'by, n., (pop.) gardien de la paix; (pop.) cogne, m.

bob'tail (-téle), n., queue écourtée : canaille, f.

bob'tailed (-tél'de), adj., à queue écourtée.

bob'wig, n., perruque à nœuds ou perruque ronde, f.

boc'asine (boc'a-cine), n., (com.) boucassin, m.

bode (bôde), v.a., présager.

bode well', ill', v.n., être de bon augure, de mauvais augure.

bod'ice (bod'ice), n., cache-corset ; corsage, m.

bod'ied (bod'ide), adj., à corps. Full — wine ; vin corsé, m.

bod'iless (-lèsse), adj., sans corps ; incorporel.

bod'ily, adj., corporel, matériel, réel.

bod'ily, adv., corporellement ; entièrement ; en masse.

bod'ing, n., présage, pronostic, m.

bod'kin (bod'kine), n., poinçon ; passe-lacet, m. ; (print.) pointe, f.

bod'y, n., corps ; (geom.) solide ; (principal thing) fond ; (center) cœur, center ; (main body of an army) gros, m. ; (of a church) nef ; (of a carriage) caisse, f. ; (of a dress) corsage, m. ; (jur.) personne, f. Dead — ; corps mort ; cadavre, m. To have — ; (of wine) être corsé. Public — ; corporation, f. Some— ; quelqu'un. Any— ; quelqu'un, tout le monde. No— ; ne personne. Every— ; tout le monde. In a — ; en corps, en masse. Any— ; personne. — snatcher ; déterreur de cadavres, m. — linen ; linge de corps, m. — snatching ; déterrement (de cadavres).

bod'y, v.a. V. **embody**.

bod'y-clothes (-cloze), n.pl., (for a horse) housse, couverture, f.

bod'y-guard, n., garde du corps, escorte, f.

bog, n., marais, marécage, m., fondrière, f.

bog, v.a., embourber.

bog'bean (-bîne), n., (bot.) ménianthe trifolié, trèfle d'eau, m.

bog'gle (bog'g'l), v.n., hésiter à ; dissimuler ; reculer **devant** ; (to haggle) marchander, barguigner ; (to dissemble) feindre, dissimuler.

bog'gler, n., couard, peureux, m., peureuse, f. ; barguigneur, m., barguigneuse, f.

bog'gling, n., hésitation, irrésolution, f. ; (fam.) barguinage, m.

bog'gy (bog'ghi), adj., marécageux.

bog'-trotter, n., habitant des marais, m.

bohea' (bô-hî), n., thé bohé, m.

boil (bo-île), v.a., faire bouillir.

boil, v.n., bouillir ; (to bubble) bouillonner ; pétiller. To — away ; ébouillir. To — fast ;

bouillir, ou faire bouillir, à gros bouillons. To — slowly ; bouillir, ou faire bouillir, à petits bouillons, doucement. To —over; déborder, bouillonner. To — up ; monter. To — to rags; pourrir à force de cuire.

boil, n., (med.) furoncle ; clou, m.

boil'er, n., (pers.) bouilleur, m. ; (thing) bouilloire ; chaudière, f., bouilleur (of a steam-engine), m.

boil'er-ma'ker, n., chaudronnier, m.

boil'er-manufac'tory, n., chaudronnerie, f.

boil'er-tube (-tioube), n., (mec.) tube de bouilleur, m.

boil'ery, n., bouillerie, f. (salt-works).

boil'ing, n., bouillonnement, m. ; ébullition, f.

boil'ing, adj., bouillant ; en ébullition. — hot ; tout bouillant.

bois'terous (bo-is'teur'eusse), adj., orageux ; violent, impétueux, furieux ; vif ; bruyant ; turbulent.

bois'terously, adv., impétueusement, violemment, bruyamment.

bois'terousness, n., impétuosité ; turbulence, violence, f.

bo'lary, adj., (min.) bolaire, sigillé, argileux.

bold (bôlde), adj., hardi ; audacieux, téméraire ; impudent, effronté; assuré ; (clear) saillant, net ; escarpé ; (steep) accore. To make — to ; prendre la liberté **de** ; se permettre **de**. To make — with; prendre des libertés **avec** ; agir cavalièrement **avec**. As — as brass ; hardi comme un page.

bold'face, n., impudence, effronterie, f. ; (pers.) impudent, effronté, m.

bold'faced, adj., impudent, effronté.

bold'ly, adv., hardiment, courageusement, intrépidement, impudemment; (clearly) nettement.

bold'ness, n., hardiesse, audace, assurance; impudence; netteté, f.

bole (bôle), n., bol ; (of a tree) tronc, m.

bo'lis (bô-lisse), n., bolide, m., (nav.) sonde, f.

boll (bôl), n., (bot.) balle, f.

boll, v.n., monter en graine.

bol'ster (bôl-), n., traversin ; coussin ; (arch.) couchis ; (nav.) coussin de ferrure, m.

bol'ster, v.a., mettre un traversin **sous**; (fig.) appuyer, soutenir.

bol'sterer, n., défenseur, appui, soutien, m.

bol'stering, n., appui, soutien, m.

bolt (bôlte), n., verrou; pène; bluteau, blutoir, sas, m. ; cheville, f. ; (fig.) trait ; (leap) saut, bond, m. To draw a — ; tirer un verrou. — upright, adj. ; tout droit, droit comme un I.

bolt, v.a., verrouiller ; fermer au verrou; (to sift) bluter; sasser; (to swallow) gober; avaler sans mastiquer. To — in; enfermer au verrou. To — one's self in; s'enfermer au verrou. To — any one out; mettre le verrou contre quelqu'un.

bolt, v.n., se lancer; décamper, filer; prendre la clef des champs; (of a horse) s'emporter. To — in; entrer brusquement. To — out; sortir brusquement.

bolt'er, n., bluteau, sas, m.

bolt'ing, n., (with a pin) chevillage; verrouillement (of doors); (sifting) blutage, m.

bolt'ing-cloth (-clôth), n., étamine, f.

bolt'ing-house (-haouce), n., bluterie, f.

bolt'ing-hutch (-heutshe), n., huche à bluter, f.

bolt'ing-mill, n., bluteau mécanique; blutoir, m.

bolt'ing-pin, n., cheville, f.

bolt'-rope (-rôpe), n., (nav.) ralingue, f.

bo'lus (bô-leusse), n., (pharm.) bolus, bol, m.

bomb (beume), n., bombe, f. ; bruit éclatant, m. —shell; bombe, f. ; obus, m.

bombard', v.a., bombarder.

bombardier' (-bardieur), n., bombardier, m.

bombard'ment (-bârd'-), n., bombardement, m.

bombar'do (beu'm'bârdo), n., (mus.) bombarde, f.

bom'bast (beu'm'bàste *ou* bo'm'-), *n.*, pathos, boursouflage, *m.;* enflure, *f.;* (pers.) vantard, *m.*

bombas'ter, *n.*, le capitaine Fracasse, *m.*

bombas'tic, *adj.*, enflé, ampoulé.

bom'bastry, *n.*, enflure, *f.;* boursouflage, *f.*

bombazine' (beu'm'ba-zine), *n.*, alépine, *f.*

bomb'ketch (-kètshe) *ou* bomb'-vessel (-vès's'l), *n.*, galiote à bombes, bombarde, *f.*

bomb'-proof (-proufe), *adj.*, à l'épreuve de la bombe.

bo'na-fi'de (bô'na-faï-di), *adj.*, sérieux et de bonne foi.

bo'na-fi'de, *adv.*, sérieusement et de bonne foi.

bond (bo'n'de), *n.*, lien; engagement; (carp.) assemblage, *m.;* (jur., fin.) obligation, *f.;* (fin.) bon, billet, *m.;* signature, *f.;* (of the customs) entrepôt, *m.* Matrimonial—; *lien conjugal.* To enter into a —; (jur.) *passer une obligation.* In —; *à l'entrepôt.* In —s; *dans les fers.*

bond, *v.a.*, entreposer. —ed goods; *marchandise entreposée, f. sing.*

bond'age (bo'n'd'édje), *n.*, esclavage, servage, *m.;* servitude, *f.*

bond'er, *n.*, entrepositaire, *m.f.*

bond'-holder (-hôld'-), *n.*, porteur de bon, détenteur de bon, d'obligation, *m.*

bond'ing, *n.*, entreposage, *m.*

bond'man (-ma'n), *n.*, (*bondmen*) serf, esclave, ⊙bonhomme, *m.*

bond'servant (-seur-), *n.*, esclave, *m.f.*

bond'service (-seur-), *n.*, esclavage, *m.*

bond'slave (-slève), *n.*, esclave, *m.f.*

bonds'man (bo'n'dz'ma'n), *n.*, (*bondsmen*) (jur.) caution, *f.*, (ant.) esclave, *m.*

bond'-stone (-stône), *n.*, (mas.) boutisse, *f.*

bonds'woman (-wou'm'a'n), *n.*, esclave, *f.*

bone (bône), *n.*, os, *m.;* (of fish) arête; (of whale) baleine; (of teeth) ivoire, *f. pl.*, ossements; restes mortels, *m.pl.* — of contention; *pomme de discorde, f.* To the back—; *jusqu'à la moelle des os.* He makes no —s about that; *il ne se fait pas scrupule de le faire; il n'en fait ni une ni deux.* To have a — to pick with any one; *avoir maille à partir, quelque chose à démêler,* avec *quelqu'un.* What is bred in the — will never come out of the flesh; *la caque sent toujours le hareng.* To make no —s; *ne pas se faire scrupule* de. To make —s about; *faire des façons* pour. To make old —s; *vivre vieux.* Not to make old—s; *mourir jeune.*

bone, *v.a.*, désosser; (pop.) chiper.

bone'-ache (-éke), *n.*, douleurs ostéocopes, *f.pl.*

bone'black, *n.*, charbon, noir animal, *m.*

boned (bô'n'de), *past part.*, désossé; à os; pourvu d'os. High—; *à os saillants.* Large—; *ossu.* Strong—; *qui a les os solides.*

bone'-earth, *n.*, phosphate de chaux, *m.*

bone'less, *adj.*, sans os.

bone'-man (rag and), *n.*, chiffonnier, *m.*

bone'-setter, *n.*, rebouteur, renoueur, *m.*

bon'fire (bo'n'faïeur), *n.*, feu de joie, *m.*

bon-mot', *n.*, bon mot, *m.*

bon'net (bo'n'nète), *n.*, chapeau (woman's); (Scotchman's) bonnet, béret, *m.;* (fort., nav.) bonnette, *f.*

bon'net, *v.a.*, enfoncer le chapeau sur la tête à; (fig.) houspiller.

bon'net-box, *n.*, carton à chapeau, *m.*

bon'neted (-nèt'ède), *adj.*, coiffé d'un chapeau.

bon'neting, *n.*, houspillement, *m.*

bon'nilass, bon'ny lass, *n.*, belle fille, *f.*

bon'nily, *adv.*, gentiment; gaiement *ou* gaîment.

bon'niness, *n.*, gentillesse, gaieté, *f.*

bon'ny, *adj.*, gentil, joli, joyeux, gai; (plump) grassouillet, potelé.

bo'num mag'num, *n.*, (bot.) prune royale, *f.*

bo'nus (bo-neusse), *n.*, boni; pot de vin, *m.;* prime, *f.*

bo'ny (bô-ni), *adj.*, osseux; fort; (of fish) plein d'arêtes.

bonze, *n.*, bonze, bonzesse, *m.f.*

boo'by (bou-bi), *n.*, nigaud, benêt, dadais, *m.;* (orni.) fou, *m.*, boubie, *f.*

boo'byish, *adj.*, nigaud.

book (bouke), *v.a.*, enregistrer, inscrire. To — a seat; *retenir une place.* To — through to; *prendre un billet direct* pour.

book, *n.*, livre, livret; cahier, *m.* Note —; carnet, *m.* Depositor's — (at a savings-bank); *livret, m.* Day-—; (com.) *journal, m.* To keep —s; *tenir des livres.* To be in any one's good —s; *être bien dans les papiers de quelqu'un;* *être bien* avec; (com.) *avoir un compte ouvert* avec. To turn over the leaves of a —; *feuilleter un livre.* Old —; *vieux livre, bouquin, m.* To bring to —; *forcer à s'expliquer.*

book'binder (bouk'baï'n'd'-), *n.*, relieur, *m.*

book'binding, *n.*, reliure, *f.*

book'case (-kéce), *n.*, bibliothèque, *f.;* corps de bibliothèque, *m.*

book'debt (-dète), *n.*, dette active, créance, *f.*

book'ful (-foule), *adj.*, érudit, pédant.

book'ing, *n.*, enregistrement (parcels, etc.), *m.*

book'ing-office, *n.*, bureau d'enregistrement, de factage; bureau de messagerie; bureau des billets, *m.*

book'ish, *adj.*, studieux, attaché aux livres, passionné pour la lecture.

book'keeper (bouk'kîp'eur), *n.*, teneur de livres, *m.*

book'keeping, *n.*, comptabilité, tenue des livres, *f.*

book'learned (-leur'n'ède), *adj.*, savant, lettré.

book'learning, *n.*, savoir, *m.;* érudition, *f.*

book'maker (-mék'eur), *n.*, faiseur de livres; parieur de profession, *m.*

book'making, *n.*, fabrication de livres, *f.*

book'man (-ma'n), *n.*, savant, *m.*

book'marker, *n.*, signet, *m.*

book'mate (-méte), *n.*, camarade d'études, *m.*

book' muslin, *n.*, organdi, *m.*

book'-post, *n.* By —; *en imprimés; sous bande.*

book'seller (-sèll'-), *n.*, libraire, *m.* Second-hand —; *marchand de livres d'occasion, bouquiniste, m.* — and publisher; *libraire-éditeur, m.*

book'selling, *n.*, profession de libraire, *f.*

book'shelf, *n.*, rayon (de bibliothèque), *m.*

book'-shop *ou* store, *n.*, librairie, *f.*

book'-slide *ou* rest, *n.*, porte-livres, *m.*

book'-stall (-stôl), *n.*, étalage de livres, *m.*

book'-trade, *n.*, commerce de la librairie, *m.*

book'-worm (-weurme), *n.*, dévoreur de livres; (ent.) lépisme, ciron, *m.*

book'writer, *n.*, auteur, *m.f.*

book'writing, *n.*, composition des livres, *f.*

boom (boume), *n.*, (nav.) boute-hors, *m.;* (of harbors) chaîne, estacade; (of piles) estacade en pilotis, *f.;* arc-boutant, *m.*

boom, *v.a.*, (com.) faire valoir. *v.n.*, gronder (of cannon).

boom'ing (boum'-), *n.*, bruit retentissant, grondement, *m.*

boon (boune), *n.*, bienfait, don, *m.;* faveur, *f.;* bien, avantage, *m.* It will be a great —; *ce sera un grand bien, ou un grand avantage.*

boon, *adj.*, bon, gai, joyeux. — companion; *compagnon de débauché; joyeux compère, m.*

boor (bour), *n.*, paysan, rustre, *m.*

boor'ish, *adj.*, rustre, grossier.

boor'ishly, *adv.*, grossièrement.

boor'ishness, *n.*, rusticité, grossièreté, *f.*

booze *ou* booze (bouze), *v.n.*, boire à l'excès, riboter.

boos'y *ou* booz'y, *adj.*, gris, en ribote.

boot (boute), *v.a.*, servir à; profiter à; botter. What boots it? *à quoi sert? que sert?*

boot, n., profit, avantage ; butin, m. To —; en sus, de plus, par-dessus le marché.

boot, n., (of men) bottine ; (of women) bottine, f.; (of women and children) brodequin ; (instr. of torture) brodequin ; (of a carriage) coffre, m., cave, f. Half- —s ; bottines. Blucher —s ; souliers-bottes, m.pl. Top—s ; bottes à revers. Hessian, Wellington, —s ; bottes à l'écuyère. Spring-side —s, Congress —s ; bottines à élastiques. Dress- —s ; bottes fines. —maker ; bottier, m. — cleaner ; décrotteur, cireur de bottes, m. Patent leather —s ; bottes vernies, souliers vernis.

boot'ed (bout'ède), part., botté.

booth (bouth), n., baraque, tente, f.; pavillon, m.

boot'hooks (-houkse), n., tirants, m.

boot'-hose (-hôze), n., houseaux, m.pl.

boot'jack, n., tire-botte, m.

boot'-last (-lâste), n. V. **boot-tree**.

boot'leg (-lèghe), n., tige de botte, f.

boot'less (-lèsse), adj., sans botter, sans chaussures ; (fig.) inutile, vain.

boot'lessly, adv., inutilement ; vainement.

boot'lessness, n., inutilité, f.

boot'trade, n., botterie, cordonnerie, f.

boot'-tree (-trî), n., embauchoir, m., forme, f.

boot'y, n., butin, m.

bo-peep' (-pîpe), n. cligne-musette, f., cache-cache, m.

bor'age (bor'adge), n., (bot.) bourrache, f.

bo'rax, n., borax, m.

bor'der, n., bord, m.; (edging) bordure ; (of a country) frontière, marche, f.; (of forests) bord, m.; lisière, f.; (of flowers), parterre, m., plate-bande ; (of a forest) lisière, f. — land ; pays limitrophe, m. — town ; ville frontière, f.

bor'der, v.a., border, confiner.

bor'der, v.n., confiner à ou avec ; toucher à ; être contigu à ; être limitrophe de, avoisiner ; (fig.) approcher de, friser. To — on sixty ; approcher de la soixantaine. That borders upon license ; cela frise la licence.

bor'derer, n., habitant de la frontière, m.

bor'dering, adj., contigu à ; voisin de ; approchant de, limitrophe de.

bore, v.a., percer, forer ; sonder, creuser ; (fig.) ennuyer, importuner, assommer ; scier le dos à.

bore, v.n., percer ; (man.) porter le nez au vent.

bore, n., trou ; calibre ; (of a musket) âme, f.; foret ; (fig.) (per.) ennuyeux, cauchemar ; (of things) ennui, m., corvée, scie, f.; (nav.) ras de marée, mascaret, m.

bo'real (bô-ri-al), adj., boréal.

Bo'reas (bô-ri-asse), n., Borée, m.

bore'dom, n., état d'ennui, m.

bor'er, n., foreur ; perceur ; (instrument) perçoir, foret, m., vrille, f.; (ent.) perce-bois, m.

bor'ing, n., sondage, forage, m.

bor'ing, adj., ennuyeux, assommant.

born, past part., né ; de naissance. Still — ou — dead ; mort-né. Low —; de basse naissance ; V. **bear**. — to ; né pour, destiné à. I was — in ; je suis né en. He was — in ; (if dead) il était né en. Wellington was —; Wellington naquit.

borne, past part. V. **bear**. — down ; écrasé.

bo'ron (bô-ro'n), n., (chem.) bore, m.

bor'ough (beur'ô), n., bourg, m. Rotten —; bourg pourri.

bor'row (bor'rô), v.a., emprunter à ou de (of or from persons) ; (of things) emprunter de.

bor'rowed, adj., (factitious) d'emprunt.

bor'rower, n., emprunteur, m., -euse, f.

bor'rowing, n., emprunt, m.

bos'cage (bos'kédje), n., bocage, m.

bosh, n., esquisse, ébauche ; (pop.) absurdité, bêtise, niaiserie, sottise, galimatias, m.; fadaises, f.pl.

bosk'y, adj., boisé.

bos'om (bouz'eume, bôu'zeume), n., sein ;

(fig.) cœur, m., intimité, f. — friend ; ami de cœur, ami intime, m. In the — of ; au sein de.

bos'om, v.a., renfermer dans son sein.

boss, n., bosse ; bossette, f.; (United States) contremaître, directeur, m.

boss'age (bos'sèdje), n., bossage, m.

botan'ic ou **botan'ical**, adj., botanique.

botan'ically, adv., conformément à la botanique.

bot'anist, n., botaniste, m.f.

bot'anize (-naïze), v.n., botaniser, herboriser.

bot'any, n., botanique, f.

botch, n., pustule, f.; (fig.) ravaudage, replâtrage, bousillage, m.

botch, v.a., rapetasser, ravauder ; replâtrer.

botch'er, n., ravaudeur, m., ravaudeuse, f.

botch'ing, n., ravaudage, m.

botch'y, adj., de pièces et de morceaux ; tacheté.

both (bôth), adj., l'un et l'autre ; les deux ; tous les deux ; tous deux. — of us ; nous deux. — sides ; les deux côtés, m.pl.

both, adv., tant. — . . . et . . . ; et . . . et . . . ; tant . . . que . . . ; à la fois, aussi bien que, comme. — you and I ; et vous et moi. — for you and him ; tant pour vous que pour lui. — by sea and land ; tant par mer que par terre ; et par mer et par terre. — dishonoring and dishonorable ; à la fois déshonorant et déshonorable.

both'er (both'eur), v.a., ennuyer ; tracasser, tourmenter, (triv.) embêter.

both'er ou **bothera'tion** (-ré-), n., ennui, tracas, tourment, m.

bot'tle (bot't'l), n., bouteille, carafe, f.; flacon, m.; (of hay) botte, f.

bot'tle, v.a., mettre en bouteille. To — up ; (fig.) contenir, étouffer, rengaîner.

bot'tle-companion (-co'm'pa'n'ieune), n., camarade de bouteille, m.

bot'tled (bot't'lde), part., en bouteille ; (fig.) ventru.

bot'tle-flower (-flaou-eur), n., bluet, m.

bot'tle-friend (-frè'nd), n., ami de bouteille, m.

bot'tle-gourd, n., gourde, f.

bot'tle-jack, n., tournebroche mécanique, m.

bot'tle-making, n., bouteillerie, f.

bot'tle-nose, n., gros nez, m.

bot'tle-nosed (-noz'de), adj., à gros nez.

bot'tler, n., metteur en bouteilles, m.; (of hay) botteleur, m.

bot'tle-rack, n., planche à bouteilles, f.

bot'tle-tit, n., (orni.) mésange à longue queue, f.

bot'tle-trade, n., bouteillerie, f.

bot'tling, n., mise en bouteilles, f., (of hay) bottelage, f.

bot'tom (bot'teume), n., fond ; bas ; bout, m.; base ; (dale) vallée ; (nav.) carène, f.; (nav.) navire, bâtiment, m.; (fig.) borne, limite ; lie, f.; sédiment, m. From top to —; de haut en bas ; de fond en comble. At —; au fond. To probe to the —; examiner à fond. To sink to the —; couler à fond. To be at the — of ; être l'âme de (quelque intrigue), être le principal instigateur.

bot'tom, v.a., mettre un fond à ; asseoir, baser.

bot'tom, v.n., se fonder ; être assis.

bot'tomed (bot'teu'm'de), adj., à fond. Flat- —; à fond plat. Copper —; doublé de cuivre. Double ou false —; à double fond.

bot'tomless (-lèsse), adj., sans fond.

bot'tomry, n., (nav.) contrat à la grosse aventure ; prêt à la grosse aventure, m.

bou'doir, n., boudoir, m.

bough (baou), n., branche, f., rameau, m.

bought, preterit and past part. V. **buy**. — book ; (com.) livre d'achats, m.

bou'gie, n., (surg.) bougie, f.

boul'der, n., fragment de roc ; quartier de roc,

brisant à pic, *m.* ; grosse pierre, roche, *f.* — wall ; *mur en galet, m.*

bounce (baou'n'ce), *v.n.*, éclater ; sauter avec grand bruit ; faire le tapageur ; faire le matamore ; se vanter.

bounce, *n.*, éclat, coup sec, *m.* ; hâblerie, vanterie, fracas, *f.*

boun'cer, *n.*, fanfaron ; hâbleur, **menteur**, *m.* ; menterie, blague, bourde, colle, *f.*

boun'cingly, *adv.*, en fanfaron ; avec jactance.

bound (ba'ou'n'de), *preterit* et *past part.* V. **bind**.

bound, *adj.*, tenu **de** ; lié à ; redevable à ; (nav.) destiné **pour** ; allant à, en destination **de**. Where are you — to ? *où allez-vous ; où va le navire ?* Homeward- —; *en retour.*

bound, *n.*, borne ; limite, *f.* ; (jump) bond, saut, *m.* At a — ; *d'un saut, d'un bond.*

bound, *v.a.*, borner, limiter, (fig.) retenir.

bound, *v.n.*, bondir **de**, sauter **de**.

bound'ary, *n.*, limite, borne, frontière, *f.*

bound'en (-dène), *adj.*, obligatoire, impérieux, indispensable, rigoureux ; sacré. It is your — duty ; *c'est votre devoir sacré.*

bound'ing, *n.*, bondissement, *adj.*, bondissant.

bound'less (-lèsse), *adj.*, sans bornes ; illimité ; infini.

bound'lessness (-nèsse), *n.*, étendue infinie, infinité, immensité, *f.*

boun'teous (baou'n'ti'eusse), *adj.*, libéral, généreux ; bienfaisant.

boun'teously, *adv.*, libéralement, généreusement.

boun'teousness, **boun'tifulness** (-nèsse), *n.*, libéralité, munificence, générosité, abondance, *f.*

boun'tiful (-foule), *adj.*, généreux, libéral.

boun'tifully, *adv.*, généreusement ; avec bienfaisance.

boun'ty, *n.*, bienfaisance, largesse, douceur ; libéralité, gratification, *f.* ; don, *m.* ; (com.) prime, *f.*

bouquet', *n.*, bouquet, *m.* — **holder** ; *portebouquet, m.*

bourgeois' (beur-djoïce), *n.*, (print.) gaillarde, *f.*

bourn, **bourne** (bourne), *n.*, borne, limite, *f.* ; (end in view) terme, but, *m.* ; (ant.) ruisseau, torrent, *m.*

bout (baoute), *n.*, coup, *m.*, fois ; partie de plaisir ; (fight) peignée ; (of a game) manche, *f.* ; (of pain) accès, *m.* Second — ; *reprise, f.* To have a — of it ; *s'en donner.* At one — ; *d'un seul coup.*

bo'vine (bô'vaïne), *adj.*, bovine, *adj.f.*

bow (baou), *v.a.*, courber ; plier, fléchir, incliner. To — out ; *éconduire, congédier.*

bow, *v.n.*, plier ; se courber ; s'incliner ; saluer ; (to comply) se plier à, se soumettre à, se rendre à. To — down ; *v.n.*, *se prosterner, s'humilier ; v.a.*, *courber, baisser ; accabler.* I — to your decision ; *je me rends à votre décision* ou *je respecte votre décision.* One must — to circumstances ; *où la chèvre est attachée il faut qu'elle broute.*

bow, *n.*, salut, *m.* ; (b.s.) courbette, *f.* ; (nav.) avant (of a ship), *m.*

bow (bô), *n.*, arc ; (of a violin) archet ; (math.) demi-cercle ; (of a saddle) arçon ; (of ribbons) nœud, *m.* — **window** ; *fenêtre cintrée, fenêtre en saillie, en rotonde, f.* To draw the long — ; *en dire à, en conter à, exagérer, blaguer.*

bow'el (baou-èl), *v.a.*, éventrer ; enlever les entrailles à.

bow'els (-èlze), *n.*, entrailles, *f.pl.* ; intestins, boyaux, *m.pl.* ; sein, *m.* ; compassion, pitié, *f.* ; entrailles, *f.pl.*

bow'er (baou'eur), *n.*, berceau de verdure, bosquet, *m.* ; tonnelle, retraite, *f.* — **anchor** ; (nav.) *ancre de poste, de bossoir, f.*

bow'er, *v.a.*, enfermer dans un berceau de verdure ; entourer, loger.

bow'ery, *adj.*, en charmille, en berceau ; touffu, ombragé.

bowl (bôle), *n.*, bol, bassin ; vase, *m.* ; jatte, *f.* ; (of a spoon) cuilleron ; (of a pipe) fourneau, *m.* ; (spherical body) boule ; (milit., nav.) gamelle, *f.*

bowl, *v.a.*, faire rouler (a bowl, a ball) ; servir la balle (at cricket). *v.n.*, jouer à la boule, jouer à la balle.

bow'legged (bô-lèg'bé), *adj.*, à jambes en manches de veste, à jambes arquées.

bowl'er (bôl'eur, baoul'eur), *n.*, joueur de boule ; (at cricket) serveur, *m.*

bow'line (bô-laïne), *n.*, (nav.) bouline, *f.*

bowl'ing, *n.*, jeu de boule, *m.*

bowl'ing-green (-grîne), *n.*, jeu de boule, boulingrin, *m.*

bow'man (-ma'n), *n.*, (bô-) archer ; (nav.) (baou-) brigadier, *m.*

bow'net (bô-nète), *n.*, nasse de pêcheur, *f.*

bowse (baouce), *v.a.*, (nav.) haler, palanquer.

bow'shot (bô-shote), *n.*, portée de trait, *f.*

bow'sprit (bô'sprite), *n.*, (nav.) beaupré, *m.*

bow'string (bô-strigne), *n.*, corde d'arc, *f.* ; cordon (to strangle with), *m.*

box, *n.*, (for the poor) tronc, *m.* ; boîte, malle, caisse ; (thea.) loge, *f.* ; (of wheels) écrou ; (of a shoeblack) sellette, *f.* ; (of houses) pied-à-terre ; (bot.) buis ; (print.) cassetin, *m.* Coach- — ; *siège de cocher, m.* Horse — , wagon — ; *écurie, f.* — on the ear ; *soufflet, m.* Christmas- — ; *étrennes, f.pl.* Strong- — ; *coffre-fort, m.* Hunting- — ; *pied à terre, m.* Sentry- — ; *guérite, f.* Snuff- — ; *tabatière, f.* In the wrong — ; *fourvoyé, égaré, loin de compte.* To be in the wrong — ; *se tromper, se fourvoyer, le prendre à gauche.*

box, *v.n.*, boxer, se boxer.

box, *v.a.*, enfermer dans une boîte ; encaisser ; souffleter. To — the compass ; *savoir la rose des vents.*

box'en (bok's'n), *adj.*, de buis.

box'er, *n.*, boxeur, pugiliste, *m.*

box'ing, *n.*, boxe, *f.*, pugilat, *m.*

box'keeper (-kîp'eur), *n.*, (thea.) ouvreur de loges, *m.*, ouvreuse de loges, *f.*

box'maker (-mék'eur), *n.*, layetier, *m.*

box'-office, *n.*, bureau de location, *m.*

box'-order, *n.*, coupon de loge, *m.*

box' plantation *ou* **grove**, *n.*, buissaie, buissière, *f.*

box'-thorn, *n.*, lyciet, *m.*

box'-tree (-trî), *n.*, buis, *m.*

boy (boï), *n.*, garçon, petit garçon, enfant, (at school) élève, (nav.) mousse, *m.* Bad — ; *mauvais sujet, m.* Mere — ; *gamin, m.* Old — ! *mon vieux, m.*

boy'ar (bo-yâr), *n.*, boyard, boïard, *m.*

boy'cott, *v.a.*, mettre à l'index.

boy'cotting, mise à l'index, *f.*

boy'hood (-houde), *n.*, enfance, adolescence, *f.*

boy'ish (boï-ishe), **boy'like**, *adj.*, puéril ; d'enfant, enfantin, en enfant.

boy'ishly, *adv.*, puérilement ; en enfant.

boy'ishness, *n.*, enfantillage, *m.* ; puérilité, *f.*

brace (bréce), *v.a.*, lier, serrer, attacher, tendre, bander, fortifier ; donner du ton à ; (nav.) brasser.

brace, *n.*, couple (of game) ; paire (of pistols), *f.* ; (arch.) tirant, *m.* ; (of a drum) tirant, *m.* ; (for a child) brassière, *f.* ; (of arms) brassard, *m.* ; (carp.) ancre, *f.* ; (mec.) vilebrequin, *m.* ; (mus., print.) accolade, *f.* ; (nav.) bras (of a yard), *m.* ; (of a coach) soupente, *f.* ; (of greyhounds) laisse, *f.* *pl.*, bretelles, *f.pl.*

brace'let (bréss'lète), *n.*, bracelet, *m.*

bra'cer, *n.*, bandage, brassard ; tonique, *m.*

brach (brake), *n.*, chien de chasse, braque, *m.*

brach'ial (brak'ial, bré-ki-al), *adj.*, brachial.

bra'cing (brécigne), *adj.*, fortifiant, tonique, vivifiant, vif.

brack'et (brakète), *n.*, (print.) crochet; (arch.) tasseau, *m.* ; console, étagère; accolade, *f.* ; (for lights) bras de lumière, *m.*

brack'ish (brak'ishe), *adj.*, saumâtre.

brack'ishness (-nèsse), *n.*, goût saumâtre, *m.*

brad (brade), *n.*, clou sans tête, *m.*

brad'awl (brad'ŏl), *n.*, poinçon effilé, *m.*

brad'shaw, *n.*, tableau des heures; indicateur (rail.), *m.*

brag, *v.n.*, se vanter de.

brag, *n.*, fanfaronnade, vanterie, *f.*

braggado'cio (brag'ga-dô-shi-ô), *n.*, bravache; fanfaron, *m.*

brag'gart (brag'garte), *adj.*, fanfaron, vantard.

brag'gart *ou* **brag'ger** (brag'gheur), *n.*, vantard, fanfaron, *m.*

brag'ging (brag'ghigne), *n.*, vanterie, forfanterie, *f.*

brag'gingly, *adv.*, en fanfaron.

Brah'man (brâ'mi'n), *n.*, brame; brahmane, *m.*

Brahman'ical, *adj.*, brahmanique.

Brah'manism, *n.*, brahmanisme, *m.*

braid (bréde), *n.*, tresse ; soutache, ganse, *f.* ; lacet ; cordonnet, galon, liséré, *m.* Braiding machine ; *machine à lacets, f.*

braid, *v.a.*, tresser, soutacher.

brails (brél'z), *n.pl.*, (nav.) cargue, *f.*

brail-up' (-eupe), *v.a.*, (nav.) carguer.

brain (bréne), *n.*, cerveau, *m.* ; cervelle, *f.* ; jugement, esprit, *m.* ; tête, *f.* To puzzle one's —s ; *se creuser la cervelle, se casser la tête à.* To blow one's —s out; *se faire sauter, se brûler la cervelle.*

brain, *v.a.*, faire sauter, brûler la cervelle à.

brain'ish (brén'ishe), *adj.*, insensé ; à tête chaude.

brain'less (-lèsse), *adj.*, sans cervelle ; à cerveau vide.

brain'lessness, *n.*, absence, *f.*, manque de cervelle, *m.* ; étourderie, *f.*

brain'sick, *adj.*, à cerveau malade.

brain'sickly, *adv.*, en cerveau malade.

brain'sickness (-nèsse), *n.*, folie, *f.* ; état d'un écervelé, *m.*, étourderie, indiscrétion, *f.*

brain'-work, *n.*, travail de tête, *m.*

brake (bréke), *n.*, fougère ; fougeraie, ronceraie, *f.* ; (waste land) lande, *f.* ; (thicket) fourré, *m.* ; (agri.) casse-motte, *m.* ; (hydr.) brimbale, *f.* ; (man.) bridon; (tech.) frein, *m.* ; (for kneading) huche au pain, *f.* ; pétrin ; (for curriers) brisoir, *m.*

brake'man, *n.*, garde-frein, *m.*

bra'ky, *adj.*, épineux.

bram'ble (bra'm'b'l), *n.*, ronce, *f.* — bush ; *buisson de ronces, m.*

Bra'min, etc. *V.* **Brahman**, etc.

bran (bra'n), *n.*, son, *m.*

branch (bra'n'she), *v.n.*, pousser des branches. To — off; *se ramifier* ; (of roads) *s'embrancher, se bifurquer* ; (of pers.) (into) *se jeter, se lancer dans.*

branch, *v.a.*, diviser en branches.

branch, *n.*, branche; (of public establishments) succursale, *f.* ; (railways) embranchement, *m.*

branch'iness (-nèsse), *n.*, état branchu, *m.*

branch'less (-lèsse), *adj.*, sans branches ; ébranché.

branch'y, *adj.*, branchu.

brand (bra'n'de), *n.*, brandon, tison ; (of infamy) stigmate, *m.* ; flétrissure; (com.) marque; (kind) sorte, qualité, *f.* — new; *tout neuf ; flambant neuf.*

brand, *v.a.*, flétrir, stigmatiser; marquer.

bran'died, *adj.*, mêlé d'eau de vie; à l'eau de vie.

brand'ing, *n.*, action de marquer, flétrissure, *f.*

brand'ing-iron, *n.*, fer à marquer, fer chaud (of criminals), *m.*

brand'-iron (-aïeurne), *n.*, fer à marquer ; trépied, *m.*

bran'dish (-dishe), *v.a.*, brandir.

bran'disher, *n.*, personne qui brandit, *f.*

bran'dy, *n.*, eau-de-vie, *f.*

bran'gle (bragn'g'l). *V.* **wrangle**.

brank'-ursine (-eur'saïne), *n.*, branche-ursine, branc-ursine, berce, acanthe, *f.*

bran'ny, *adj.*, de son.

bra'sier (bré-jeur), *n.*, dinandier; ouvrier en cuivre jaune; braisier (coal-pan), *m.*

brass (brâce), *n.*, airain, cuivre jaune, laiton; toupet, *m.* ; effronterie, *f.* As bold as —; *avec un front d'airain.* — band ; *musique d'instruments de cuivre, f.*

brass, *v.a.*, couvrir de laiton.

brass'-button, *n.*, bouton de cuivre, *m.*

brass'-cannon, *n.*, canon de fonte, *m.*

brass'-finisher, *n.*, polisseur de cuivre, *m.*

brass'-foil (-fo-il), *n.*, cuivre battu, *m.*

brass'-founder (-faou'n'deur), *n.*, fondeur en cuivre, *m.*

brass'-foundry, *n.*, fonderie de cuivre, *f.*

brass'iness (-nèsse), *n.*, ressemblance avec le cuivre, *f.*

brass'-instrument, *n.*, instrument de cuivre, *m.*

brass'-visaged (-viz'èdj'de), *adj.*, à front d'airain, effronté.

brass'-wares (-wèr'ze), *n.pl.*, dinanderie, *f.*

brass'-wire (-waïeur), *n.*, fil de laiton, *m.*

brass'-work, *n.*, objet, ouvrage en cuivre, *m.*

brass'-works (-weurkse), *n.pl.*, usine à cuivre, *f.*

brass'y, *adj.*, d'airain.

brat (brate), *n.*, marmot, *m.*, marmotte, *f.*

brava'do (-vâdô), *n.*, bravade, *f.* Out of —; *par bravade.*

brave (bréve), *adj.*, brave, vaillant, noble, grand; excellent.

brave, *v.a.*, braver, défier.

brave'ly, *adv.*, courageusement, bravement.

bra'very (-veur-), *n.*, bravoure, *f.*

bra'vo (brâ-vô, bré-vô), *n.*, bravo, assassin, *m.*

bra'vo ! *int.*, bravo !

bravu'ra (bra-viou-ra), *n.*, (mus.) air de bravoure, *m.*

brawl (brôl), *n.*, clabauderie, dispute, querelle, *f.* ; tapage, *m.*

brawl, *v.n.*, brailler, clabauder, disputer.

brawl'er, *n.*, clabaudeur ; braillard, *m.*, braillarde, *f.* ; brailleur, *m.*, brailleuse, *f.* ; querelleur, *m.*, querelleuse, *f.*

brawl'ing, *n.*, clabauderie, criaillerie, *f.*

brawl'ingly, *adv.*, en clabaudant, en braillant.

brawn (brô'n), *n.*, chair de sanglier, *f.* ; (of the body) partie charnue, *f.* ; muscles, *m.pl.* ; fromage de cochon, *m.* ; (fig.) force musculaire, *f.*

brawn'iness (-nèsse), *n.*, force musculaire, *f.*

brawn'y, *adj.*, charnu, musculeux, robuste.

bray (bré), *v.a.*, broyer, piler; faire résonner, faire retentir.

bray, *v.n.*, braire ; (fig.) résonner, retentir.

bray *ou* **bray'ing** (bré-igne), *n.*, braiment, braire, *m.*

bray'er (bré-eur), *n.*, braillard; (tech.) pilon, *m.*

braze (bréze), *v.a.*, travailler en airain; souder; braser ; endurcir.

bra'zen (bré-z'n), *adj.*, d'airain ; (fig.) effronté, impudent.

bra'zen, *v.n.*, montrer un front d'airain. To — it out; *payer d'effronterie ou d'audace.* To — out; *traiter de haut, v.a.*

bra'zen-face (-féce), *n.*, front d'airain; (pers.) effronté, *m.*, effrontée, *f.* To put on a — ; *s'armer d'effronterie.*

bra'zen-faced (-féss'te), *adj.*, à front d'airain.

bra'zenness (bré-z'n'nèsse), *n.*, qualité propre à l'airain ; impudence, effronterie, *f.*

brazil′ ou **Brazil′-wood** (bra-zîl-woude), *n.*, brésillet ; bois de Brésil, *m.*

Brazil′ian, *adj.*, brésilien.

Brazil′-nut (-neute), *n.*, noix du Brésil, *f.*

breach (brîtshe), *n.*, fracture, *f.*, bris, *m. ;* (fig.) brèche ; rupture ; violation, infraction, atteinte, *f.* — of trust ; *abus de confiance, m.* — of the peace ; *délit contre l'ordre public, m.*

breach, *v.a.*, battre en brèche.

bread (brède), *n.*, pain, *m.* Daily —; *pain quotidien.* New —; *pain frais.* Stale —; *pain rassis.* Brown — ; *pain bis.* —stuffs ; *farines, céréales, f. pl.* To take the — out of one's mouth; *ôter à quelqu'un le pain de la main.* To be in want of —; *manquer de pain.* On — and water; *au pain et à l'eau.* To get one's —; *gagner sa vie.*

bread′less, *adj.*, sans pain.

bread′-room (-roume), *n.*, (nav.) soute au pain, *f. ;* soute à biscuit, *f.*

breadth (brèd'th), *n.*, largeur, *f. ;* (of stuffs) lé, *m.*

bread′-tree (-trî), *n.*, jaquier ; arbre à pain, *m.*

break (bréke), *v.a.* (*preterit,* Broke ; *past part.,* Broken), rompre ; casser ; briser ; violer, enfreindre ; faire faire faillite à ; ruiner. To — open a door ; *enfoncer une porte.* To — asunder ; *briser, rompre ; séparer, désunir.* To — open a letter ; *décacheter une lettre.* To — off ; *rompre, interrompre.* To — up ; *démolir ; dissoudre, licencier.* To — through ; *se frayer, ou s'ouvrir, un passage à travers ; se faire jour à travers.* To — in a horse ; *rompre un cheval.* To — any one of a bad habit ; *faire perdre à quelqu'un une mauvaise habitude, corriger d'une mauvaise habitude.* To — one's arm, one's neck; *se casser un bras, le cou.* To — any one's heart ; *briser le cœur à quelqu'un.* To — one's oath ; *violer, fausser son serment.* To — an engagement (matrimonial) ; *rompre un projet de mariage.* To — the news to somebody ; *préparer quelqu'un à entendre la nouvelle.* To — one's word ; *manquer à sa parole.* To — the square ; *rompre le carré.* To — the bank (at play) ; *faire sauter la banque.* To — one's journey ; *s'arrêter en route.* To — upon the wheel ; *rouer.*

break, *v.n.*, rompre, se rompre, casser, se casser, briser, se briser ; éclater ; (com.) faire faillite ; (of daybreak) poindre ; (of an abscess) percer ; (of age) décliner, baisser, changer, se casser. To — in ; *envahir, pénétrer, s'introduire.* To — up ; (of an assembly) *se séparer ; (of schools, etc.) entrer en vacances ; (of cold) s'adoucir ; (of weather) se gâter.* To — asunder ; (of clouds) *se déchirer.* To — out ; *éclater ; (of diseases) se déclarer.* To — off ; *cesser.* To — down ; (of carriages) *verser ; (of horses) s'abattre ; (of orators) rester court, s'arrêter tout court ; (of a bridge) s'effondrer ; s'écrouler.* To — away ; *s'arracher ; (fig.) se dissoudre ; (of clouds) se dissiper.* To — from ; *échapper à, s'échapper de.* To — with ; *rompre avec, se brouiller avec.*

break, break′ing, *n.*, cassure, rupture ; percée, trouée, clairière ; (fig.) interruption, *f. ;* (of the weather) changement ; (print.) alinéa, *m. ;* (man.) voiture de dressage, *f. ;* (of the voice) mue, *f.* — of day ; *point du jour, m. ; pointe du jour, f.* — down ; (railw.) accident, *m. ; débâcle, déconfiture, détérioration, f. ;* (failure) *insuccès, m.*

break′able, *adj.*, cassable.

break′age (-èdje), *n.*, (com.) casse, *f. ;* cassage, *m. ;* cassure, *f.*

break′er, *n.*, infracteur ; briseur, *m.*, briseuse, *f. ;* violateur, *m.*, violatrice, *f.*, transgresseur ; (tamer) dompteur ; (of the sea) brisant ; écueil, *m.* — in ; *dresseur.* Ice — ; *brise-glace, m.*

break′fast (brèk′feuste), *n.*, déjeuner, *m.* — cup ; *grande tasse, f.* — room ; *petite salle à manger, f.* — time ; *heure du déjeuner, f.*

break′fast, *v.n.*, déjeuner. — on ou off; *déjeuner de.*

break′-iron (-aï′eurne), *n.*, enclume, *f.*

break′man, *n. V.* **brakeman.**

break′neck (-nèke), *n.*, casse-cou, *m.* — place ; *endroit à se casser le cou, f.*

break′-stone (-stône), *n.*, (bot.) saxifrage, *f.*

break′water (-wôteur), *n.*, (of bridges) avant-bec ; arrière-bec ; éperon ; (of harbors) brise-lames, *m. ;* digue, *f. ;* rempart, *m.*

bream (brîme), *n.*, (ich.) brème, *f.*

bream, *v.a.*, (nav.) chauffer (a ship).

breast (brèste), *n.*, poitrine, mamelle, *f.; sein ;* (fig.) cœur, *m.*, âme, conscience, *f. ;* (nav.) flanc; (of a horse) poitrail ; (of a goose) filet; (of a fowl) blanc, *m. ;* (of a coat) revers, *m.pl. ;* (of a plow) versoir, *m.* — to — ; (of duels) *à bout portant.* At the — ; (of a child) *à la mamelle.* To make a clean — of ; *tout avouer ; faire un aveu complet.*

breast, *v.a.*, attaquer de front ; affronter, braver ; lutter **contre.**

breast′-bone, *n.*, sternum, *m.*

breast′-collar, *n.*, bricole, *f.*

breast′-deep, *adj.*, *adv.*, jusqu'à la poitrine.

breast′-high (-haïe), *adj.*, à hauteur d'appui.

breast′-pad ou **piece,** *n.*, plastron, *m.*

breast′-pin, *n.*, épingle de cravate, *f.*

breast′plate (-pléte), *n.*, cuirasse, *f.*

breast′wall, *n.*, mur de soutènement.

breast′work (-weurke), *n.*, parapet; (nav.) fronteau, *m.*

breath (brèth), *n.*, haleine, *f.;* souffle, *m.; (*fig.*) vie, existence, *f.* To be out of — ; *être hors d'haleine, être essoufflé.* To get out of — ; *se mettre hors d'haleine ; perdre haleine.* Last — ; *dernier soupir, m.* To draw — ; *respirer.* To take —; *reprendre haleine.* To hold one's — ; *retenir son haleine.* To take one's — away ; *couper la respiration à ; (fig.) interdire, déconcerter.* There is not a — of wind ; *il n'y a pas une haleine, un souffle de vent.* There is not a — of air stirring ; *il ne fait pas un souffle de vent.* Shortness of — ; *courte haleine, f.*

breathe (brîthe), *v.n.*, respirer. To — after; *souhaiter ; soupirer après.*

breathe, *v.a.*, respirer, souffler. To — one's last ; *rendre le dernier soupir.* To — out ; *exhaler, pousser.*

breath′er, *n.*, personne qui respire, *f.*

breath′ing, *adj.*, qui respire, vivant ; pour respirer.

breath′ing, *n.*, respiration, *f. ;* (gram.) esprit, *m.* — hole ; *soupirail, m.*

breath′ing-place, *n.*, place pour respirer, *f.*

breath′ing-time (-taïme), *n.*, temps de respirer, relâche, répit, *m.*

breath′less (brèth′lèsse), *adj.*, essoufflé ; haletant ; inanimé. —ness, *f.*, essoufflement, *m.*

bred (brède), *past part.* (of To breed), élevé. Ill— ; *mal élevé.* Well— ; *bien élevé.*

breech (brît′she), *n.*, derrière, *m. ;* (of fire-arms) culasse, *f.* —band ; (of saddles) *reculement, m.* —loader ; *fusil se chargeant par la culasse, m.*

breech, *v.a.*, mettre en culotte ; (to whip) fesser ; mettre une culasse **à.**

breech′es (brît′shize), *n.pl.*, culotte, *f.sing.* To wear the — ; (fig.) *porter la culotte.*

breed (brîde), *v.a.*, (*preterit* and *past part.*, Bred) enfanter, engendrer ; élever ; produire, occasionner, faire naître ; (to bring up) élever.

breed, *v.n.*, s'engendrer ; multiplier.

breed, *n.*, race ; (of birds) couvée, *f.*

breed′er, *n.*, mère ; (of horses) poulinière, *f. ;* éleveur, *m. ;* (fig.) cause, source, *f.*

breed′ing, *n.*, génération, production, éducation, *f. ;* (of cattle) élevage, *m.* Good— ; *politesse, bonne éducation, f. ; savoir-vivre, m.*

breeze (brîze), *n.*, brise, *f. ;* vent, *m. ;* (fig.) altercation, dispute, affaire, *f.*

breez'y, *adj.*, rafraîchi par la brise, frais ; (fig.) orageux.

breth'ren (brèth'rène), *n.pl.*, frères, *m.pl.*

breve (brĭve), *n.*, (mus.) brève, maxime, *f.*

brevet' (bri'vète, brèvèt'e), *adj.*, (milit.) à brevet.

brevet', *n.*, brevet, *m. v.a.*, breveter.

brev'iary (brĭv'ia-rĭ), *n.*, bréviaire ; abrégé, *m.*

brevier' (bri-vieur), *n.*, (print.) petit texte, *m.*

brev'ity (brèv'iti), *n.*, brièveté ; concision, *f.*

brew (brou), *v.a.*, brasser ; mêler ; (fig.) tramer ; (to plot) machiner.

brew, *v.n.*, faire de la bière ; (fig.) (of a storm) se préparer ; s'amasser, se dessiner, couver.

brew'er, *n.*, brasseur, *m.*

brew'ery, *n.*, brasserie, *f.*

brew'house (-haouce), *n.*, brasserie, *f.*

brew'ing, *n.*, brassage ; (quantity brewed) brassin, *m.*

bri'ar (braï'ar), *n.* *V.* **brier.**

bribe (braïbe), *n.*, présent (*dans le but de corrompre*) ; prix ; appât, pot-de-vin, *m. ;* largesse ; tentation, *f.*

bribe, *v.a.*, gagner, corrompre ; suborner.

bri'ber, *n.*, suborneur, corrupteur, *m.*, corruptrice, *f.*

bri'bery, *n.*, corruption, subornation, (fig.) séduction, *f.*

brick (brike), *n.*, brique, *f.; (*fig.) brave garçon, bon enfant. *adj.*, de briques, en *ou* à briques.

brick, *v.a.*, bâtir de briques, briqueter.

brick'bat (-bate), *n.*, morceau, *ou* éclat, de brique, *m. ;* briquaillons, *m.pl.*

brick'dust (-deuste), *n.*, poussière de briques, *f.*

brick'field *ou* **brick'kiln**, briqueterie, *f.;* four à briques, *m.*

brick'laye (-lé-eur) *n.*, maçon en briques, maçon ; (for chimneys) fumiste, *m.*

brick'maker (-mék'eur), *n.*, briquetier, *m.*

brick'work (-weurk), *n.*, briquetage, *m.*

bri'dal (braï-), *n.*, fête nuptiale, noce, *f.*

bri'dal, *adj.*, nuptial, de noce.

bride (braïde), *n.*, nouvelle mariée ; épousée ; fiancée, future, prétendue, *f.*

bride'bed (-bède), *n.*, lit nuptial, *m.*

bride'cake (-kéke), *n.*, gâteau de noce, *m.*

bride'groom (-groume), *n.*, marié, fiancé, *m.*

bride'maid *ou* **brides'maid** (-méde), *n.*, demoiselle d'honneur, *f.*

bride'man *ou* **brides'man**, *n.*, garçon d'honneur, *m.*

bride'well (braïd'wèle), *n.*, maison de correction, *f.*

bridge, *n.*, pont, *m.; (*of a boat) passerelle, *f.;* (of stringed instruments) chevalet ; (of the nose) dos ; (of a comb) champ, *m. ;* (of a gun-carriage) hausse, *f.* — head ; tête de pont, *f.* Wire — ; *pont de fil de fer, m.*

bridge, *v.a.*, construire, *ou* jeter, un pont **sur.**

bri'dle (braï'd'l), *n.*, bride, *f. ;* (fig.) frein, *m. ;* (nav.) branche, *f.* — path ; *route cavalière, f.* — hand ; *main gauche, f.*

bri'dle, *v.a.*, brider ; (fig.) mettre un frein **à** ; tenir en frein, contenir.

bri'dle, *v.n.*, redresser la tête. To — up ; *se redresser, se rengorger.*

bridoon' (braï-doune), *n.*, (man.) filet, bridon, *m.*

brief (brĭfe), *adj.*, bref, court, de courte durée, passager ; (fig.) concis. — spoken ; *laconique.*

brief, *n.*, bref ; abrégé, *m.;* (of barristers) cause, *f.*, dossier, *m.*

brief'less, *adj.*, sans causes.

brief'ly, *adv.*, brièvement ; en peu de mots.

brief'ness, *n.*, brièveté, concision, *f.*

bri'er (braï'eur), *n.*, ronce, *f.* Wild — ; *églantier, m.* Sweet — ; *églantier odorant, m.*

bri'ery, *adj.*, plein de ronces.

brig, *n.*, (nav.) brig, brick, *m.*

brigade' (-ghéde), *n.*, brigade, *f. ;* (of firemen) corps de pompiers, *m.*

brigade', *v.a.*, former en brigades.

brigadier' (brig-a-dîre), *n.*, général de brigade, *m.*

brigad'ing, *n.*, embrigadement, *m.*

brig'and (brig'a'n'de), *n.*, brigand, *m.*

brig'andage (-'d'édje), *n.*, brigandage, *m.*

brig'antine (brig-a'n'-tĭne), *n.*, (nav.) brigantin, *m.*, brigantine, *f.*

bright (braïte), *adj.*, brillant, clair, éclatant, lumineux, beau, intelligent. To see the — side of things ; *voir tout en beau, voir tout couleur de rose.* —er days ; *jours plus heureux, m.pl.*

brigh'ten (braït'n), *v.a.*, faire briller ; polir ; (fig.) répandre de l'éclat **sur**, illustrer, embellir ; (to cheer) égayer ; dégourdir. To — up ; *éclaircir ;* (fig.) *égayer.*

brigh'ten, *v.n.*, s'éclaircir, briller, étinceler, devenir plus gai. To — up ; (of the face) *rayonner ; s'épanouir ;* (of the weather) *s'éclaircir.*

bright'ly, *adv.*, d'une manière brillante ; brillamment, avec éclat.

bright'ness, *n.*, brillant, lustre, éclat, *m. ;* (fig.) joie, vivacité, *f.*

brill'iance *ou* **brill'iancy**, *n.*, brillant, lustre, éclat, *m.*

brill'iant, *adj.*, brillant, éclatant.

brill'iant, *n.*, brillant (diamond), *m.*

brill'iantly, *adv.*, brillamment, avec éclat.

brills (brilze), *n.*, cils (of the horse), *m.pl.*

brim (brime), *n.*, bord, *m.*

brim, *v.a.* and *n.*, remplir jusqu'au bord ; être plein jusqu'au bord.

brim'ful (-foule), *adj.*, plein jusqu'au bord ; tout plein. — of tears ; *gros de larmes.*

brim'less, *adj.*, sans bords.

brimmed, *adj.*, à bords, à rebords.

brim'mer, *n.*, rasade, *f. ;* rouge bord, *m.*

brim'stone (bri'm'stône), *n.*, soufre, *m.*

brim'stony, *adj.*, sulfureux.

brin'ded (bri'n'dède), *adj.*, tavelé, tacheté.

brin'dle (bri'n'd'l), *n.*, taveture, *f.*

brin'dled (-d'lde), *adj.*, tavelé, tacheté.

brine (braïne), *n.*, saumure, *f.*

brine, *v.a.*, mettre dans la saumure, saler.

bring (brigne), *v.a.*, (preterit **and** past part., Brought), apporter ; (to lead in) amener ; conduire ; (to carry) porter ; transporter ; (to reduce) réduire. To — about ; *amener, ramener, venir à bout de.* To — away ; *emporter ;* (of persons) *emmener.* To — back ; *rapporter, ramener.* To — down ; *descendre, amener en bas ; abattre ; humilier ; faire baisser ; faire descendre ; diminuer ;* (an audience) *enlever.* To — forth ; *produire ; mettre au monde ; mettre bas.* To — forward ; *faire avancer ;* (com.) *reporter.* To — nearer ; *rapprocher.* To — in ; *faire entrer, introduire.* To — on ; *amener, occasionner.* To — out ; *sortir, faire sortir, tirer ; faire paraître, publier ; représenter sur la scène.* To — over ; *transporter ; faire passer ; convertir, attirer.* To — under ; *soumettre à ; assujettir à.* To — up ; *nourrir ; élever ; monter ; vomir.* To — upon ; *attirer* **sur**, *faire tomber* **sur.** To — to ; *faire reprendre connaissance* **à** ; (nav.) *amener.* To — close to ; *approcher.* To — into fashion ; *mettre à la mode.* To — into question ; *mettre en question.* To — actions ; *intenter des actions.* To — into trouble ; *engager dans de mauvaises affaires.* To — to bed ; *accoucher.* To — to pass ; *exécuter, effectuer.* To — to perfection ; *perfectionner.* To — together ; *assembler ; réconcilier, raccommoder.* To — word of ; *apporter des nouvelles* **de.**

bring'er, *n.*, porteur, *m.* — up ; (milit.) *serre-file.*

bri'nish (braïnishe), *adj.* *V.* **briny.**

brink (brign'ke), *n.*, bord, *m.* The — of a precipice ; *le bord d'un précipice.* On the — of ruin ; *sur le penchant de la ruine ; à deux doigts de sa perte.*

bri'ny (braï-), *adj.*, saumâtre, **salé** ; **amer.**

brisk, *adj.*, vif ; piquant ; animé, actif, éveillé ; frais, dispos.

brisk′et (-kè′e), *n.*, poitrine (butcher′s meat), *f.*

brisk′ly, *adv.*, vivement.

brisk′ness, *n.*, vivacité, activité, *f.*

brisk up′, *v.a.*, animer. *v.n.*, s′animer ; se tenir droit ; prendre une attitude hardie.

bris′tle (bris′s′l), *n.*, (of pigs, etc.) soie, *f.* ; poil raide, *m.*

bris′tle, *v.a.* and *n.*, hérisser ; se hérisser ; se hérisser **de** (with) ; se raidir **contre**.

bris′tly, bris′tling, *adj.*, hérissé **de** ; poilu.

Britan′nic, *adj.*, britannique.

Brit′ish, *adj.*, britannique ; anglais. — India; *l′Inde anglaise, f.* — Guiana ; *La Guyane anglaise, f.*

brit′tle (brit′t′l), *adj.*, fragile ; cassant.

brit′tleness, *n.*, fragilité, *f.*

broach (brŏt′she), *n.*, broche, *f.*

broach, *v.a.*, embrocher ; (a cask) mettre en perce ; émettre, communiquer ; (a subject) introduire, entamer ; effleurer. To — to ; (nav.) *se coiffer ; faire chapelle.*

broach′er, *n.*, broche (for roasting), *f.* ; (fig.) auteur, *m.*

broad (brŏde), *adj.*, large, grand, gros, vaste ; (fig.) grossier, hardi ; (of hints) assez clair, peu voilé ; (accent) bien prononcé. — awake ; *bien éveillé.* — daylight ; *grand jour, m.* — footed ; *aux larges pieds.* As — as it is long ; *tout un ; la même chose.*

broad′-breasted, *adj.*, à large poitrine, à la poitrine large.

broad′-brimmed (-bri′m′de), *adj.*, à larges bords.

broad′cast, *adj.*, (agri.) à la volée ; (fig.) jeté au hasard.

broad′cast, *n.*, (agri.) semis, *m.*, *ou* semailles, *f.pl.* ; à la volée.

Broad-Church, *n.*, Eglise libérale, *f.*

broad′cloth, *n.*, drap fin, *m.*

broad′en (brŏ′d′n), *v.n.*, s′élargir, s′agrandir, s′étendre.

broad′ humor, *n.*, grosse gaieté, *f.*

broad′ish, *adj.*, un peu large, assez large.

broad′ laugh, *n.*, gros rire, *m.*

broad′-leaved, *adj.*, à larges feuilles.

broad′ly, *adj.*, largement.

broad′ness, *n.*, largeur, *f.* ; (fig.) grossièreté, *f.*

broad′-shouldered, *adj.*, aux larges épaules, qui a les épaules larges.

broad′side (-saïde), *n.*, (nav.) bordée, *f.* ; (nav.) côté, bord ; (print.) in-plano, *m.* To fire a — ; *tirer une bordée.*

broad′ stone, *n.*, pierre de taille, *f.*

broad′sword (-sŏrde), *n.*, sabre, *m.*

broad′wise (-waïze), *adv.*, en largeur, en large.

brocade′ (-kéde), *n.*, brocart, *m.*

broca′ded (-dède), *adj.*, de brocart ; (pers.) vêtu de brocart.

bro′cage *ou* **bro′kage**. *V.* **brokerage**.

bro′catel, *n.*, brocatelle, *f.* ; brocard, *m.*

broc′coli, *n.*, brocoli, chou fleur, *m.*

brock′et (brok′ète), *n.*, jeune cerf, daguet, *m.*

bro′gan, *n.*, (shoe) brogan, *f.*

brogue (brŏghe), *n.*, accent très prononcé, patois, *m.* ; (shoe) brogue, *f.*

broil (broïle), *n.*, discussion, dispute ; querelle, *f.* ; tumulte, *m.*

broil, *v.a.*, griller, faire griller.

broil, *v.n.*, griller ; se griller.

broil′er, *n.*, gril ; (fig.) boute-feu, *m.*

bro′ken (brŏ′k′n), *adj.*, cassé, brisé, rompu ; navré ; (of meetings) dissous ; dispersé ; (of language) décousu ; baragouiné, écorché, sans suite ; (of country) accidenté ; (of time) perdu. — voice; *voix entrecoupée, f.* — sleep ; *sommeil interrompu, m.*

bro′ken-backed (-bak′te), *adj.*, qui a le dos rompu ; qui a les reins cassés ; (nav.) cassé.

bro′ken-hearted (-hârt′ède), *adj.*, qui a le cœur brisé, qui a le cœur navré. To die — ; *mourir de chagrin.*

bro′ken-kneed, *adj.*, (of horses) couronné.

bro′kenly, *adv.*, par morceaux ; sans suite.

bro′ken meat, *n.*, restes de viande, rogatons, graillons, *m.pl.*

bro′ken-wind′ed (-wi′n′dède), *adj.*, (vet.) poussif.

bro′ker (brŏ-), *n.*, courtier ; fripier, brocanteur, *m.* Stock —; *agent de change, m.* Ship —; *courtier maritime, m.* Outside — ; *coulissier, m.*

bro′kerage (-édje), *n.*, courtage, *m.*

brome *ou* **bro′mine** (brôme, -maïne), *n.*, (chem.) brome, *m.*

bron′chi, bron′chia, *ou* **bron′chiæ** (-ki, -ki-a, -ki-i), *n.pl.*, bronches, *f.pl.*

bron′chial *ou* **bron′chic** (-kial, -kike), *adj.*, bronchique.

bronchi′tis (-kaï-tisse), *n.*, bronchite, *f.* ; catarrhe pulmonaire, *m.*

bronchot′omy (-ko-), *n.*, bronchotomie, *f.*

bronze, *n.*, bronze, *m.* — powder ; *bronze jaune, ou en coquille.*

bronze, *v.a.*, bronzer ; durcir comme l′airain.

bronz′er, *n.*, bronzeur.

bronz′ing, *n.*, bronzage, *m.*

brooch (brŏ′tshe), *n.*, (jewel) broche, *f.* ; (paint.) camaïeu, *m.*

brood (broude), *v.a.*, couver ; (fig.) nourrir, chérir, soigner.

brood, *v.n.*, couver ; se couver ; se préparer. To — over ; *méditer* **sur** ; *rêver* **à.**

brood, *n.*, couvée ; engeance, race, *f.*

brook (brouke), *n.*, ruisseau, *m.*

brook, *v.a.*, souffrir ; endurer, avaler, digérer, boire.

brook′let (-lète), *n.*, petit ruisseau, *m.*

broom (broume), *n.*, balai ; (bot.) genêt, *m.* A new — always sweeps clean ; *rien ne vaut balai neuf ; il n′est rien tel que balai neuf.*

broom′rape (-répe), *n.*, (bot.) orobanche ; clandestine, *f.*

broom′staff (-stâfe) *ou* **broom′stick**, *n.*, manche à balai, *m.*

broom′y, *adj.*, rempli de genêts.

broth (brôth), *n.*, bouillon, *m.* Black —; *brouet noir, m.*

broth′el, *n.*, bordel, *m.*

broth′er (breuth*er*), *n.*, frère, *m.* —-in-law; *beau-frère.* Foster— ; *frère de lait.* Elder —; *frère aîné.* Younger —; *frère cadet.* — officer, — in arms ; *frère, ou compagnon, d′armes, m.*

broth′erhood (-houde), *n.*, fraternité ; confrérie ; confraternité, *f.*

broth′erless, *adj.*, sans frère.

broth′erlike (-laïke), *adj.*, en frère ; fraternel.

broth′erly, *adj.*, fraternel.

broth′erly, *adv.*, fraternellement.

brought (brŏte), *preterit* and *past part.* *V.* **bring.**

brow (braow), *n.*, sourcil ; front; (fig.) sommet, *m.* ; croupe, *f.* —-ague ; *migraine, f.* To knit the — ; *froncer le sourcil.* To smooth one′s — ; *se dérider.*

brow′beat (-bîte), *v.a.*, mater, déconcerter, intimider, traiter avec hauteur.

brow′beaten, *past part.*, maté, déconcerté, intimidé.

brow′beating, *n.*, langage arrogant, *m.* ; arrogance, *f.* ; ton impérieux, *m.*

brow′bound (-baou′n′de), *adj.*, couronné **de** ; à l′extrême bord **de.**

brown (braoune), *adj.*, brun ; sombre, rembruni ; (of the hair) châtain. — bread ; *pain bis, m.* — paper ; *papier gris, m.* — sugar ; *cassonade, f.* — bill ; (milit.) *fusil de munition, m.* — holland ; *toile écrue, f.* — study ; *sombre rêverie,* *humeur noire, f. ; songe creux, m.* To be in a — study ; *songer creux.*

brown, *n.*, brun ; (cook.) rissolé, *m.*

brown, *v.a.*, brunir ; (cook.) rissoler ; faire roussir.

brown, *v.n.*, brunir, se brunir.

brown'ish, *adj.*, brunâtre.

brown'ness, *n.*, couleur brune, *f.*

browse (braouze), *v.a.* and *n.*, brouter.

browse'wood (-woude), *n.*, brout, *m.*

bruise (brouze), *v.a.*, meurtrir, contusionner ; écraser, piler ; concasser.

bruise, *n.*, meurtrissure, contusion, *f.*

bruis'er, *n.*, écraseur, concasseur ; boxeur.

bruis'ing, *n.*, meurtrissure, contusion, *f. ;* écrasement, broiement, *m.;* (pop.) roulée, volée, *f.*

bruit (broute), *v.a.*, ébruiter, faire courir le bruit (que).

bru'mal (brou-), *adj.*, d'hiver, brumal.

brunette' (brou-), *n.*, brune, brunette, *f.*

brunt (brun'n'te), *n.*, choc, *m. ;* force ; violence, fureur, *f.* — of battle ; *fort de la bataille, m.* The — of fortune ; (fig.) *les coups du sort, m. pl.* To bear the — of anything ; *faire les frais de.* I shall have to bear the — of it ; *c'est moi qu'on rendra responsable* ou *c'est moi qui devrai en faire les frais.*

brush (breushe), *n.*, brosse, *f. ;* balai ; pinceau ; (fig.) coups, *m.pl.*, batterie ; (mil.) escarmouche, querelle ; queue (of a fox) ; (of electric light) traînée lumineuse, *f.*

brush, *v.a.*, brosser ; effleurer, raser. To — past ; *frôler ; passer rapidement* **auprès de.** To — away ; *enlever (avec la brosse), secouer ;* (tears) *essuyer.* To — up ; *donner un coup de brosse à ;* (a subject, language) *repasser ; se remettre à.*

brush'er, *n.*, brosseur, *m.*, -se, *f.*

brush'ing, *n.*, brossée ; action de brosser, *f. ;* brossage, *m.*

brush'maker (-mék'-), *n.*, brossier, fabricant de brosses, *m.*

brush'wood (-woude), *n.*, broussailles, *f.pl.*

brush'y, *adj.*, comme une brosse ; rude, hérissé.

bru'tal (brou-), *adj.*, brutal, cruel, inhumain.

brutal'ity, *n.*, brutalité, cruauté, *f.*

bru'talize (-aïze), *v.a.*, abrutir.

bru'talize, *v.n.*, s'abrutir.

bru'tally, *adv.*, brutalement.

brute (broute), *n.*, brute, bête, *f. ;* brutal, *m.*

brute, *adj.*, insensible ; (of animals) sauvage ; brutal ; privé de raison ; grossier ; farouche ; (of matter) brut. The — creation ; *l'espèce animale, f.*

bru'tify (-faïe), *v.a.*, abrutir.

bru'tish (brout'-), *adj.*, abruti, de brute, brutal, grossier.

bru'tishly, *adv.*, brutalement, comme une brute, en brute.

bru'tishness, *n.*, brutalité, *f.*

bru'tism, *n.*, (ant.) caractère de la brute ; abrutissement, *m.*

bry'ony (braï'o-), *n.*, (bot.) bryone, couleuvrée, *f.*

bub'ble (beub'b'l), *n.*, bulle d'air ; (fig.) chimère, utopie; dupe, *f. ;* jouet, *m. ;* duperie, flouerie, *f.* — company ; *flouerie.*

bub'ble, *v.a.*, duper.

bub'ble, *v.n.*, bouillonner ; (of streams) murmurer. To — up ; *bouillonner ;* (of wine) *pétiller.*

bub'bler, *n.*, trompeur, *m.*

bub'bling, *n.*, bouillonnement ; pétillement ; (fig.) murmure, *m.*

bu'bo (biou-), *n.*, (med.) bubon, *m.*

buccaneer' (beuk-ka-nîre), *n.*, boucanier, *m.*

buck (beuke), *n.*, (of linen) lessive, *f. ;* daim ; chevreuil ; mâle (of the hare, of the rabbit) ; (fig.) gaillard ; beau, élégant, *m.* — hound ; *limier, m.* — shot ; *chevrotine, f.* — skin ; *peau de daim, f.*

buck, *v.a.*, lessiver, laver.

buck, *v.n.*, (man.) faire le saut de mouton. To — up ; (fam.) *se hâter, se trémousser.*

buck'basket (-kète), *n.*, panier au linge sale, *m.*

buck'bean (-bîne), *n.* V. **bogbean.**

buck'et (-kète), *n.*, seau, baquet, *m.* To kick the —; (pop.) *sauter le pas ; passer l'arme à gauche ; claquer.*

buck'ing, *n.*, lessive, *f.*

buck'ing-cloth (-clôth), *n.*, charrier, *m.*

buck'ing-tub (-teube), *n.*, cuvier, *m.*

buck'le (beuk'k'l), *n.*, boucle, *f.*

buck'le, *v.a.*, boucler, attacher, agrafer. To — on ; *revêtir.*

buck'le, *v.n.*, plier, se plier, se courber ; se boucler ; s'attacher avec une boucle. To — to; *s'appliquer* **à.** To — with ; *être aux prises* **avec.** To — a wheel ; tordre.

buck'ler (beuk'-), *n.*, bouclier, *m.*

buck'ram (beuk'-), *n.*, bougran, *m.* Man in —; *homme de carton, soldat pour rire, m.*

buck'wheat (beuk'hwîte), *n.*, sarrasin, blé noir, *m.*

bucol'ic (biou-), *adj.*, bucolique. [noir,

bucol'ic, *n.*, poème bucolique; poète bucolique, *m.*

bud (beude), *n.*, bourgeon, bouton ; (fig.) germe, *m.*, racine, *f.*

bud, *v.n.*, bourgeonner ; s'épanouir ; fleurir ; germer, boutonner.

bud, *v.a.*, écussonner, greffer. A budding poet ; *un poète en herbe, m.*

Bud'dhism (boud'-), *n.*, bouddhisme, *m.*

Bud'dhist (-), *n.*, bouddhiste, *m.f.*

bud'ding, *n.*, bourgeonnement ; germe, *m. ;* greffe en écusson, *f.*

bud'dle (beud'd'l), *n.*, (metal.) caisse à laver, *f.*

bud'dle, *v.a.*, (metal.) laver.

budge (beudje), *v.n.*, bouger, bouger **de;** se remuer.

budge, *n.*, peau d'agneau, *f.*

bud'get (beud'jète), *n.*, budget; sac, *m.*

buff (beufe), *n.*, buffle (skin), *m.;* couleur chamois ; (med.) couenne, *f.* To stand —; *tenir ferme ; tenir tête* **à.**

buff, *adj.*, de peau de buffle ; de couleur chamois.

buf'falo (beuf'fa-lô), *n.*, buffle, *m.*

buf'falo-snake (-snéke), *n.*, boa, boa constricteur ; devin, *m.*

buf'fer (beuf'-), *n.*, tampon (de choc), *m.* — stop ; (rail.) *butoir, m.* Old — ; (pers.) *vieux bonhomme.*

buf'fet (beuf'fète), *n.*, buffet ; soufflet, coup de poing, *m.*

buf'fet, *v.n.*, se battre à coups de poing ; boxer.

buf'fet, *v.a.*, frapper à coups de poing, battre, souffleter ; assaillir ; étouffer la son (of bells). Buffeted by the waves ; *battu des vagues.*

buf'feting, *n.*, bourrade, *f. ;* (fig.) attaque, *f.*, assaut, *m.*

buf'fle-headed (-hèdède), *adj.*, stupide ; à grosse tête.

buffoon' (beuf'foune), *n.*, bouffon, *m.*

buffoon', *v.a.*, bafouer, ridiculiser. *v.n.*, faire le bouffon, bouffonner.

buffoon'ery, *n.*, bouffonnerie, *f.*

buf'fy, *adj.*, (med.) de couenne ; couenneux.

bug (beughe), *n.*, punaise, *f.*

bug'bear (-bère), *n.*, épouvantail ; loup-garou, *m.*

bug'-bite, *n.*, morsure de punaise, *f.*

bug'gy (beug'ghi), *adj.*, plein de punaises.

bug'gy, *n.*, américaine (*phaeton*), *f.*

bu'gle (biou'g'l), *n.*, perle de Venise ; (bot.) bugle, *f.*

bu'gle ou **bu'gle-horn**, *n.*, cor de chasse, (mil.) clairon, *m.*

bu'gler, *n.*, clairon, *m.*

bu'gle-weed (-wîde), *n.*, (bot.) marrube, *m.*

bu'gloss (biou-), *n.*, buglosse, *f.*

bug'-wort, cimicaire, *f.*

buhl (bioule), *n.*, Boule, *m.*   *adj.*, **de boule.** — work; *marqueterie de boule,f.*

build (bilde), *v.a.n.* (*preterit* and *past part.*, Built), bâtir ; construire ; édifier ; (fig.) fonder, baser. — on ; *compter* **sur,** *se fonder* **sur.**

build, *n.*, construction, forme, *f. ;* (nav.) gabari *ou* gabarit, *m.* Of English —; *de construction anglaise.*

build'er, *n.*, constructeur, entrepreneur de bâtiments; (of organs) facteur; (fig.) fondateur, créateur, architecte, *m.*

build'ing, *n.*, construction, structure, bâtisse, *f.;* édifice, monument; bâtiment, *m.* — **materials;** *matériaux de construction, m.pl.* — society; *société immobilière, f.*   [construction.

built, *part. adj.*, construit ; construit **en** ; de

bulb (beulbe), *n.*, (anat.) bulbe, *m. ;* (bot.) bulbe, *f.*, ognon, *m. ;* (of thermometers) boule, *f.*

bulb'ous, *adj.*, bulbeux.

Bulgarian, *adj.*, bulgare.

bulge (beul'dje), *n.*, ventre; (nav.) fond de cale, *m.*, sentine, *f.*

bulge (out), *v.n.*, faire ventre, bomber.

bu'limy (biou-), *n.*, boulimie, *f.*

bulk (beulke), *n.*, volume, *m. ;* grosseur, masse ; grandeur, capacité, charge, *f.* To break —; (nav.) *entamer ; commencer le déchargement ; rompre charge.* Laden in —; *chargé en grenier.*

bulk'head (beulk'hède), *n.*, (nav.) cloison étanche, *f.*

bulk'iness, *n.*, grosseur, taille, *f.;* volume, *m.*

bulk'y, *adj.*, gros, volumineux, grand, massif.

bull (boule), *n.*, taureau, *m.;* (of the pope) bulle ; (blunder) bêtise, boulette, bévue, gaffe, *f.;* (at the exchange) joueur à la hausse, haussier, *m.*   *v.a.* To —; *jouer à la hausse.*

bul'lace (boul'léce), *n.*, (bot.) prunelle, *f.*

bul'lace-tree (-trî), *n.*, prunellier, *m.*

bull'-baiting (-bét'-), *n.*, combat de taureaux contre des chiens, *m.*

bull'-beggar (-bèg-gheur), *n.*, croquemitaine, *m.*

bull'-calf, *n.*, veau mâle, taurillon, *m.*

bull'-dog, *n.*, dogue, bouledogue, *m.*

bul'len (beul'lène), *n.*, chènevotte, *f.*

bul'len-nail (-néle), *n.*, clou de tapissier, *m.*

bul'let (boul'lète), *n.*, balle, *f.* — proof ; *à l'épreuve des balles.* — mold; *moule à balles, m.*

bul'letin (boul'li-tîne), *n.*, bulletin, *m.*

bull'fighter, *n.*, toréador, *m.*

bull'-fight (-faîte), *n.*, combat de taureaux (avec des hommes), *m.*

bull'-finch (-fi'n'she), *n.*, bouvreuil, *m.*

bull'-fly *ou* **bull'-bee** (-flaïe, -bî), *n.*,taon, *m.*

bull'-head (-hède), *n.*, grosse bête, *f. ;* (ich.) cotte, chabot, cabot, *m. ;* têtard, *m.*

bul'lion (boul'ieune), *n.*, lingot, *m. ;* matières d'or et d'argent, *f.pl. ;* numéraire, *m.* Stock of —; *encaisse métallique, f.* — dealer ; *changeur, m.*

bul'lion-office, *n.*, (com.) bureau pour l'achat des matières d'or et d'argent, *m.*

bull'ish (boull'-), *adj.*, ridicule, saugrenu.

bull'ock (boul'-), *n.*, bœuf, *m.* Young —; *bouvillon, m.*

bull's-eye, *n.*, œil-de-bœuf, *m. ;* lanterne sourde, *f. ;* (nav.) (skylight) lentille, *f. ;* (mil.) point de mire, *m.*

bull'-terrier, *n.*, boule-terrier, *m.*

bul'ly (boul'-), *n.*, fier-à-bras, matamore, fendant, bravache, *m.*

bul'ly, *v.a.*, rudoyer, maltraiter, malmener ; intimider.

bul'ly, *v.n.*, faire le fendant, le fier-à-bras, le matamore.

bul'lying, *adj.*, grossier, brutal. *n.*, crânerie, brutalité, *f.*

bul'rush (boul'reushe), *n.*, jonc, *m.* To look for knots in a —; *chercher midi à quatorze heures.*

bul'wark (boul'weurke), *n.*, boulevard, rempart, *m.*

bum (beume), *n.*, derrière, *m.*

bum-bail'iff (-bé-), *n.*, huissier (pop.), garde de commerce ; recors, *m.*

bum'ble-bee (beu'm'b'l-bî), *n.*, bourdon, *m.*

bum'boat (-bôte), *n.*, bateau de provisions, *m.*

bum'kin (beu'm'-), *n.*, (nav.) arc-boutant, porte-lof, *m.*

bump (beu'm'pe), *n.*, bosse, *f.;* coup, choc, *m.;* secousse, chute d'un corps lourd, *f.*

bump, *v.a.*, frapper. *v.n.*, cogner, heurter ; rebondir.

bump'er, *n.*, rasade, *f. ;* rouge bord, *m.*

bump'kin (beu'm'p-), *n.*, rustre, rustaud, *m.*, rustaude, *f.*

bunch (beu'n'she), *n.*, (of keys) trousseau, *m. ;* (things tied together) botte, grappe, *f.*, bouquet, *m.;* (on the back) bosse ; (agri.) javelle, *f.* — of onions ; *botte d'oignons, f.* — of grapes; *grappe de raisin, f.*

bunch, *v.n.*, faire bosse. To — out ; *bomber.*

bunch, *v.a.*, lier en botte, en bouquet.

bunch'backed (-bak'te), *adj.*, bossu.

bunch'y, *adj.*, touffu, en grappe.

bun'dle (beu'n'd'l), *n.*, paquet ; faisceau, tas, *m. ;* botte ; (agri.) javelle, *f.* — of asparagus ; *botte d'asperges, f.* — of papers; *liasse de papiers, f.*

bun'dle, *v.a.*, empaqueter. To — out ; *mettre, ou jeter, ou flanquer, à la porte.* To — one's self off ; *plier bagage ; décamper, filer. v.n.* To — in and out; *entrer, sortir à la hâte, en masse.*

bung (beugn'ghe), *n.*, bondon ; (artil.) tampon, *m.* —borer; *bondonnière, f.*

bung, *v.a.*, bondonner, boucher.

bung'hole (-hôle), *n.*, bonde, *f.*

bun'gle (beugn'g'l), *n.*, bousillage, *m. ;* gâchis, *m. ;* bévue, *f.*

bun'gle, *v.a.*, saveter, gâcher, massacrer.

bun'gle, *v.n.*, s'y prendre de travers, s'y prendre mal, faire de mauvaise besogne.

bun'gler, *n.*, maladroit, savetier, gâcheur, bousilleur, *m.*

bun'gling, *n.*, gâchage, *m.*

bun'gling, *adj.*, maladroit; (of things) saveté, saboté.

bun'glingly, *adv.*, en savetier, maladroitement, absurdement, inhabilement.

bun'ion (beu'n'io'n), *n.*, oignon (on the foot), *m.*

bun'ker, *n.*, (nav.) soute à charbon, *f.*

bunt (beu'n'te), *n.*, (nav.), fond de voile, *m.*

bunt, *v.n.*, (nav.) s'enfler.

bunt'ing, *n.*, étamine, *f.;* (orni.) bruant ; pavillon, *m. ;* (flags) drapeaux, *m.pl.*

buoy (b'oï), *n.*, (nav.) bouée, *f.* Life —; *bouée de sauvetage, f.*

buoy, *v.a.*, soutenir sur l'eau, baliser. To — up ; *soutenir sur l'eau ;* (fig.) *soutenir, appuyer, ranimer, relever. v.n.*, flotter, surnager. To — up with false hopes ; *bercer (quelqu'un) de fausses espérances.*

buoy'ance *ou* **buoy'ancy** (bo'y'a'n'ce, -ci), *n.*, faculté de surnager ; légèreté, *f. ;* élan, *m. ;* fermeté, vivacité; énergie, activité, *f.*

buoy'ant, *adj.*, léger, flottant, élastique, ferme, énergique ; animé.

bur (beur), *n.*, (of a spear) arrêt ; (bot.) bardane, *f.*, glouteron, *m.*

bur'bot (beur'bote), *n.*, (ich.) lotte commune, *f.*

bur'den (beur'd'n), *n.*, fardeau, *m.;* charge, *f.;* poids ; (nav.) port, *m.* The — of years; *le poids des années.* Beast of —; *bête de somme, f.* — of a song ; *refrain, m.* To be a — ; *être à charge à.* The —of proof lies with him ; *c'est à lui à prouver que.*

bur'den, *v.a.*, imposer un fardeau **à** ; charger, opprimer ; surcharger. To be —ed with years ; *être chargé d'années.*

bur'densome (-seume), *adj.*, onéreux; lourd; ennuyeux, à charge.

bur'dock (beur-), *n.*, (bot.) bardane, *f.* ; glouteron, *m.*

bu'reau (biou-), *n.*, bureau, *m.*

bureau'cracy, *n.*, bureaucratie, *f.*

bu'reaucrat, *n.*, bureaucrate, *m.*

bureaucrat'ic, *adj.*, bureaucratique.

bur'gess (beur'djèce), *n.*, bourgeois, citoyen, habitant, *m.*

burgh (beurghe), *n.*, bourg, *m.*

burgh'er (beurgh'-), *n.*, bourgeois; citoyen, *m.*

burgh'ership, *n.*, droit de bourgeoisie, *m.*

bur'glar (beurg'leur), *n.*, voleur; auteur de vol de nuit avec effraction, cambrioleur, *m.*

burgla'rious, *adj.*, de vol de nuit avec effraction.

burgla'riously, *adv.*, la nuit avec effraction.

bur'glary (beurg'leuri), *n.*, vol de nuit avec effraction, cambriolage, *m.*

bur'gomaster (beur'go-mas-teur), *n.*, bourgmestre, *m.*

bur'ial (bè-), *n.*, enterrement; ensevelissement, *m.*; sépulture, inhumation, *f.* Christian —; *sépulture ecclésiastique, sépulture en terre sainte, f.* — service; *office des morts, m.* — place; *lieu de sépulture, m.* — board; *administration des pompes funèbres, f.*

bur'ial-ground (-graou'n'de), *n.*, cimetière, *m.*

bur'ier (bè-ri-eur), *n.*, fossoyeur, *m.*

bu'rin (biou-ri'n), *n.*, burin, *m.*

burke, *v.a.*, étouffer; étrangler.

burk'er, *n.*, étouffeur.

burl (beurl), *v.a.*, épinceter, noper (woollen cloth).

burlesque' (beur-), *adj.* and *n.*, burlesque, bouffon.

burlesque', *v.a.*, parodier, travestir.

burlesq'uer, *n.*, qui fait du burlesque, qui tourne en ridicule.

bur'letta (beur-), *n.*, vaudeville, *m.*, farce, bluette, *f.*

bur'liness (beur-), *n.*, grosseur; corpulence; emphase, *f.*

bur'ly (beur-), *adj.*, gros et grand; solidement bâti; bruyant; emphatique.

burn (beurne), *n.*, brûlure; cuite (of bricks), *f.*

burn, *v.a.*, (*preterit* and *past part.*, Burnt, Burned) brûler; (tech.) cuire; (to long) brûler **de.** To — down; *brûler.* To — down to the ground ; *brûler de fond en comble.* To — up; *brûler entièrement.* To — to ashes; *réduire en cendres.*

burn, *v.n.*, brûler. To — out; *se consumer.*

burn'er, *n.*, brûleur; (of a lamp) bec, *m.*

burn'ing, *n.*, brûlure, *f.*; incendie, *m.*; combustion; cautérisation, *f.*

burn'ing, *adj.*, en feu; brûlant. — mirror; *miroir ardent, m.* To smell anything —; *sentir quelque chose qui brûle.*

burn'ing-glass (-glâce), *n.*, verre ardent, *m.*, lentille, *f.*

burn'ish (beur-), *v.a.*, brunir, polir.

burn'ish, *v.n.*, prendre du brillant.

burn'isher, *n.*, (pers.) brunisseur, *m.*, brunisseuse, *f.*; (tool) brunissoir, *m.*

burn'ishing, *n.*, brunissage, *m.*

burnt. *V.* burn.

burnt'-offering (beurn't'of-feur'-), *n.*, holocauste, *m.*

burr (beure), *n.*, lobe (of the ear); ris de veau; ciseau triangulaire; (language) roulement, grasseyement, *m.*

bur'rel-shot (beur'rèl-shote), *n.*, mitraille, *f.*

burr'ing, *n.*, grasseyement, *m.*

bur'row (beur'rô), *n.*, terrier, clapier, *m.*

bur'row, *v.n.*, terrer, se terrer.

bur'sar (beur-), *n.*, économe; boursier, *m.*

bur'sarship, *n.*, économat, *m.* ; bourse, *f.*

burst (beurste), *n.*, fracas, éclat, *m.*, explosion; rupture, hernie, *f.* ; (fig.) transport, mouvement ;

déchaînement, débordement, *m.* ; explosion, *f.* — of laughter; *éclat de rire, m.* — of applause ; *tonnerre d'applaudissements, m.* — of tears; *torrent de larmes, m.* — of eloquence ; *mouvement d'éloquence, m.* — of passion; *transport de colère, m.*

burst, *v.a.*, (*preterit* and *past part.*, Burst) crever ; faire éclater ; fendre ; rompre, briser. To — open a door; *enfoncer une porte.*

burst, *v.n.*, crever, éclater ; se fendre ; faire explosion, jaillir, s'élancer. To — into tears; *fondre en larmes.* To — out into; *éclater* **en.**

burt (beurte), *n.*, turbot, *m.*, limande, *f.*

bur'then (beur'*th*'n), *n.* *V.* **burden.**

bur'y (bèr'ré), *v.a.*, enterrer; ensevelir, cacher; (fig.) (to plunge) enfoncer, plonger. To — the hatchet ; *faire la paix; passer l'éponge* **sur.**

'bus (beuce), *abréviation de* omnibus.

bush (boushe), *n.*, buisson, fourré, taillis; (signboard) bouchon, *m.* ; (hunt.) queue de renard; terre inculte, *f.* Good wine needs no —; *à bon vin point d'enseigne.* To beat about the —; *tourner autour du pot.*

bush, *v.n.*, devenir touffu.

bush'-beater, *n.*, batteur de buissons, *m.*

bush'el (boush'èl), *n.*, boisseau, *m.*

bush'iness (boush'-), *n.*, état touffu, *m.* ; épaisseur, *f.*

bush'y (boushi), *adj.*, buissonneux ; touffu. — whiskered ; *aux épais favoris.*

bus'ily, *adv.*, activement ; avec empressement; d'un air officieux, important, affairé.

bus'iness (biz'nès), *n.*, affaire, occupation, besogne, *f.*, état, métier, *m.* ; affaires, *f.pl.* ; commerce ; fonds, fonds de commerce, *m.* ; (of a banker) clientèle, *f.* Extensive —; *affaires considérables.* Line of —; *genre de commerce, m.* Run of —; *courant d'affaires, m.* In —; *dans les affaires ; dans le commerce.* Old established —; *ancienne maison, f.* On —; *pour affaire.* To attend to one's —; *soigner ses affaires;* être à ses affaires. To be in — for one's self ; *être établi pour son compte.* To buy a —; *acheter un fonds de commerce.* To do —; *faire des affaires.* To do a great deal of —; *faire de bonnes affaires.* To do — with; *être en relations commerciales* **avec.** To give up —; *se retirer des affaires.* To give up one's —; *céder son fonds de commerce.* To put to —; *mettre dans les affaires.* To have a good —; *faire de bonnes affaires.* To make it one's —; *en faire son affaire.* Mind your own —! *mêlez-vous de ce qui vous regarde !* You have no — here; *vous n'avez que faire ici.* To settle a —; *arranger une affaire.* To send any one about his —; *envoyer promener quelqu'un.* Go about your —; *allez vous promener.* What — is that of yours? *est-ce que cela vous regarde?* You have done a fine piece of — indeed! *vous avez fait là une belle équipée!* What — have you to? *qu'avez-vous besoin de?* What — had you there? *qu'alliez-vous faire là ?* *qu'alliez-vous faire dans cette galère ?*

bus'iness-like (-laïke), *adj.*, d'affaires, propre aux affaires; pratique, régulier ; franc, droit, sérieux, rond en affaires.

busk (beuske), *n.*, busc, *m.* — case ; *busquière, f.*

bus'kin (beus'-), *n.f.*, cothurne, brodequin, *m.*, (fig.) tragédie, *f.*; style élevé, *m.*

bus'kined (beus'ki'n'de), *adj.*, en brodequins ; en cothurnes; (fig.) tragique.

buss (beuce), *n.*, (triv.) baiser, *m.*

buss, *v.a.*, (triv.) embrasser, baiser, baisoter.

bust (beuste), *n.*, buste, *m.* ; bosse, *f.* From the —; *d'après la bosse.*

bust'ard (beus'-), *n.*, outarde, *f.*

bust'er, *n.*, affaire, *f.* A regular —; *une vraie bombance, f.*

bus'tle (beus's'l), *n.*, mouvement ; tumulte,

bruit, *m.*, confusion ; activité, agitation ; (part of a lady's dress) tournure, *f.*

bus'tle, *v.a.*, tracasser, mettre en mouvement.

bus'tle, *v.n.*, se donner du mouvement ; se hâter ; se trémousser, se remuer.

bus'tler, *n.*, homme remuant, intrigant.

bus'tling, *adj.*, actif, affairé ; empressé ; remuant, bruyant. — old woman ; *vieille alerte, f.* (V. Hugo) ; *vieux lutin, m.*

bus'y (biz'zi), *adj.*, affairé, occupé ; actif ; en mouvement ; agité.

bus'y, *v.a.*, occuper. To — one's self about ; *s'occuper de ; se mêler de ; s'agiter.*

bus'y-body, *n.*, officieux, *m.*, officieuse, *f.* ; tatillon, *m.*, tatillonne, *f.* ; brouillon, *m.*

but (beute), *conj.*, mais, qui ne ; (without) sans que. There is not one of them — knows it ; *il n'y en a pas un qui ne le sache.* — that ; *sans que.* Not — that ; *non que.* That cannot — be ; *cela doit être.* He never heard of a quarrel — his fingers itched ; *il n'entendait jamais parler d'une querelle, sans que les doigts lui démangeassent.* It cannot — be accounted natural ; *on ne peut que le considérer comme naturel.* — few executions take place ; *il ne se fait que peu d'exécutions.* — yesterday ; *hier seulement, pas plus tard qu'hier, hier encore.* To do nothing — ; *ne faire que.* I cannot — see ; *je ne peux m'empêcher de voir,* ou *il m'est impossible de ne pas voir.*

but, *adv.*, excepté ; ne . . . que ; moins ; seulement ; si ce n'est que ; ne fût-ce que. — for ; *sans ; si ce n'était que.* I should have died, — for him ; *sans lui, je serais mort.* The last — one ; *l'avant-dernier.* There is — you who ; *il n'y a que vous qui.* All — ; *presque.*

but, *n.* V. **butt.**

but, *prep.*, sans. — for his entreaties ; *sans ses supplications ; n'eussent été ses instances.*

butch'er (bout'sh'eur), *n.*, boucher, *m.*, bouchère, *f.* — 's boy ; *garçon boucher, m.* Journeyman — ; *étalier, m.* — 's shop ; *boucherie, f.* — stall ; *étal de boucher, m.* — 's meat ; *viande de boucherie, grosse viande, f.*

butch'er, *v.a.*, égorger, massacrer.

butch'erliness, *n.*, cruauté, *f.*

butch'erly, *adj.*, cruel, barbare.

butch'ery, *n.*, boucherie, *f.*, massacre, carnage, *m.*

but'ler (beut'-), *n.*, sommelier, maître d'hôtel, *m.* — 's tray ; *plateau à découper, m.*

but'ment (beut'-), *n.*, contrefort, contre-boutant, *m.* V. **abutment.**

butt (beute), *n.*, bout ; gros bout ; (of animals) coup de tête, *m.* ; (of muskets) crosse ; (of cues) masse, *f.* ; (fig.) but, point de mire, *m.*, cible ; (nav.) butte, tête de bordage ; (cask) pipe ; pièce (anglaise) ; (fencing) botte, *f.* ; (for water) tonneau ; (pers.) plastron, *m.*

butt, *v.n.*, cosser (of rams).

butt'-end (beut-è'n'de), *n.*, gros bout, *m.* ; crosse, *f.*

but'ter (beut'-), *n.*, beurre, *m.* She looks as if — would not melt in her mouth ; *elle fait la sainte Nitouche.*

but'ter, *v.a.*, beurrer ; (at play) doubler les enjeux ; (fig.) flagorner, encenser. Fair words — no parsnips ; (prov.) *je vis de bonne soupe et non de beau langage* (Molière).

but'ter-boat (-bôte), *n.*, beurrier, *m.*, petite saucière, *f.*

but'tercup (-keupe), *n.*, (bot.) bouton d'or, *m.*

but'ter-dairy, *n.*, beurrerie, *f.*

but'ter-dish, *n.* V. **butter-boat.**

but'ter-fingers, *n.pl.*, mains de beurre, *f.pl.*

but'terfly (-flaïe), *n.*, papillon, *m.*

but'ter-knife, *n.*, couteau à beurre, *m.*

but'ter-man (-ma'n), *n.*, beurrier, marchand de beurre, *m.*

but'termilk, *n.*, lait de beurre, petit-lait, *m.*

but'ter-pear (-père), *n.*, (bot.) beurré, *m.*

but'ter-sauce, *n.*, sauce blanche, *f.*

but'ter-scotch, *n.*, caramel au beurre, *m.*

but'ter-stamp, *n.*, moule à beurre, *m.*

but'ter-tub, *n.*, tinette, *f.*

but'ter-wife ou **but'ter-woman** (-waïfe, -wouma'n), *n.*, beurrière, marchande de beurre, *f.*

but'terwort (-weurte), *n.*, (bot.) grassette, *f.*

but'tery (beut'teur'i), *adj.*, de beurre ; butyreux. *n.*, dépense, *f.*

but'tock (beut'-), *n.*, fesse, *f.* ; (of an ox) cimier, *m.*, culotte de bœuf, *f.*

but'ton (beut't'n), *n.*, bouton, *m.*

but'ton, *v.a.*, boutonner.

but'ton, *v.n.*, se boutonner.

but'ton-hole (-hôle), *n.*, boutonnière, *f.* To — any one ; *accoster quelqu'un (à l'imprévu).*

but'ton-hook, *n.*, tire ou tourne-bouton, *m.*

but'toning, *n.*, boutonnement, *m.*

but'ton-maker (-mék'eur), *n.*, boutonnier, *m.*

but'ton-mold, *n.*, moule à bouton, *m.*

but'ton-shank, *n.*, queue de bouton, *f.*

but'tress (beut'trèce), *n.*, arc-boutant, éperon, *m.*

but'tress, *v.a.*, arc-bouter.

bux'om (beuk'seume), *adj.*, beau ; enjoué, gai, folâtre, gaillard, réjoui. — woman ; *grosse réjouie* ou *gaillarde, f.*

bux'omly, *adv.*, gaiement, joyeusement, gaillardement.

bux'omness, *n.*, gaillardise, *f.*

buy (ba'ye), *v.a.*, (*preterit* and *past part.*, Bought), acheter ; (to bribe) corrompre, gagner. To — off ; *racheter.* To — out ; *racheter, libérer du service,* (com.) *acheter la part de.* To — up ; *accaparer.* To — of ; *acheter à.*

buy'er, *n.*, acheteur, acquéreur, *m.*

buy'ing, *n.*, achat, *m.* — out, off, in ; *rachat, m.*

buzz (beuze), *v.a.*, chuchoter, dire tout bas, murmurer.

buzz, *n.*, bourdonnement, chuchotement, murmure, *m.*

buzz, *v.n.*, bourdonner.

buz'zard (beuz'zarde), *n.*, buse, *f.*

by (baïe), *prep.*, près de ; auprès de ; à côté de ; par ; de ; à ; d'après ; en. — far ; *de beaucoup.* — day ; *durant la journée.* — the day ; *pour la journée, à la journée.* He will lose none — me ; *il n'en perdra aucune par ma faute, de mon fait.* — no means ; *nullement.* — the way ; *chemin faisant ;* (fig.) *à propos.* — this time ; *à ce temps, alors, en ce moment, à l'heure qu'il est.* — way of ; *pour ; en guise de, par manière de.* He was — me ; *il était près de moi, à côté de moi.* — that means ; *par ce moyen.* Loved — all ; *aimé de tous.* One — one ; *un à un.* — what you say ; *d'après ce que vous dites.* — doing that ; *en faisant cela.* — that time ; *d'ici là.* Money — one ; *de l'argent par devers soi.* — one's self ; *tout seul.* — my watch ; *à ma montre.* — sight ; *de vue.* I know him — his walk ; *je le connais à sa marche.* — measure, weight ; *à la mesure, au poids.* — seven o'clock ; *avant sept heures.* — the end of the day ; *à la fin du jour.* — to-morrow ; *d'ici à demain.* Two feet — six ; *deux pieds sur six.* Longer — two feet ; *plus long de deux pieds.*

by, *adv.*, près ; là, par là ; passé. To be standing — ; *être là.* Close — ; *tout près.*

by ou **bye**, *n.*, (ce qui n'occupe l'attention qu'indirectement). By the — ; *en passant ; à propos.*

by and by, *adv.*, tout à l'heure.

by-by, *n.*, dodo, *m.*

bye (baïe), *n.*, demeure, *f.*, village, *m.* ; ville, *f.*

by'gone, *adj.*, passé ; qui n'est plus. Let — s be — s ; *ne revenons pas sur le passé ; oublions le passé, passons l'éponge là-dessus.*

by'-lane (-léne), *n.*, ruelle écartée, *f.* ; sentier, chemin détourné ; chemin de traverse, *m.*

by'-law (-lō), *n.*, loi réglementaire, loi locale, *f.* ; règlement, statut, arrêté, *m.*

by'-name (-néme), *n.*, sobriquet, surnom, *m.* To be a — ; *être l'objet du mépris général.*

by-name, *v.a.*, surnommer.

by-play, *n.*, jeu de scène, jeu muet, jeu accessoire, *m.* [détourné, *m.*]

by-road, *n.*, chemin de traverse, *m.* ; chemin

Byron'ian, *adj.*, byronien.

By'ronism, *n.*, byronisme, *m.*

by'-stander, *n.*, assistant ; spectateur, *m.* ; spectatrice, *f.* [tournée, *f.*]

by'street, *n.*, rue de traverse, *f.*, rue dé-

by'way (-wé), *n.*, chemin détourné, obscur, écarté, *m.*

by'word (-weurde), *n.*, dicton, proverbe, *m.* ; (fig.) risée, *f.* To have become a — ; *être passé en proverbe* ; (fig.) *être devenu la risée* **de.**

Byzan'tian (biz'a'n'shi'a'n) *ou* **Byzan'tine** (-taïne), *adj.*, byzantin.

C

c, troisième lettre de l'alphabet, c, *m.* ; (mus.) ut, do, *m* ; (mus.) clef d'ut, *f.*

cab, *n.*, cabriolet ; fiacre, *m.*, voiture de place, *f.* To — it ; *venir*, ou *aller*, *en voiture.* — driver ; *cocher de fiacre, m.* — fare ; *prix de la course, tarif, m.* — horse ; *cheval de fiacre, m.* — stand ; *station de voitures de place, f.*

cabal', *n.*, cabale, *f.* *v.n.*, cabaler.

cab'ala, *n.*, cabale, *f.*

cab'alism, *n.*, science de cabale, *f.*

cab'alist, *n.*, cabaliste, *m.*

cabalist'ic *ou* **cabalist'ical**, *adj.*, cabalistique.

cabal'ler, *n.*, cabaleur, *m.*

cab'bage (-bédje), *n.*, chou, *m.* ; (material) gratte, *f.* Turnip— ; *chou-navet.* Savoy — ; *chou frisé.* — lettuce ; *laitue pommée, f.*

cab'bage, *v.a.*, gratter (to preserve material) ; chiper, rogner du drap.

cab'bage, *v.n.*, (hort.) pommer.

cab'bage-head (-hède), *n.*, pomme de chou, *f.*

cab'bage-rose, *n.*, rose à cent feuilles, *f.*

cab'bage-sprout (-spraoute), *n.*, chou cavalier, *m.*

cab'bage-stalk (-stōke), *n.*, tige de chou, *f.*

cab'bage-stump (-steu'm'pe), *n.*, trognon de chou, *m.*

cab'bage-tree (-trî), *n.*, chou palmiste, *m.*

cab'by, *n.*, cocher, *m.*

cab'in (-bine), *n.*, cabane ; (nav.) chambre, cabine, *f.* — passenger ; *passager de première classe, m.* Chief — ; *grande chambre.* Fore— ; *chambre d'avant.*

cab'in, *v.n.*, vivre dans une cabane; loger à l'étroit.

cab'in, *v.a.*, enfermer dans une cabane; emprisonner.

cab'in-boy (-boï), *n.*, (nav.) mousse, *m.*

cab'ined, *adj.*, emprisonné, enfermé ; cagé, à l'étroit.

cab'inet (-nète), *n.*, cabinet, *m.*

cab'inet-coun'cil (-caou'n'-), *n.*, conseil des ministres, *m.*

cab'inet-maker (-mék'-), *n.*, ébéniste, *m.*

cab'inet-piano, *n.*, grand piano droit, *m.*

cab'inet-size, *n.*, (photog.) carte-album, *f.*

cab'inet-wood, *n.*, bois d'ébénisterie, *m.*

cab'inet-work, *n.*, ébénisterie, *f.*

ca'ble (ké'b'l), *n.*, câble, *m.* — length ; *en-câblure, f.* —gram ; *télégramme sous-marin, m.*

ca'ble, *v.a.*, (arch.) orner ; endenter ; (nav.) amarrer; télégraphier.

ca'bled, *adj.*, (nav.) amarré ; télégraphié.

ca'blet (ké-blète), *n.*, (nav.) câbleau, câblot, *m.*

caboose' (ca-bouce), *n.*, (nav.) fourneaux, *m.pl.*, cuisine, *f.*

cabriolet' (-lé), *n.*, cabriole, *f.*, cabriolet, *m.*

caca'o, *n.*, (bot.) cacao ; (tree) cacaoyer, cacaotier, *m.*

caca'o-pod (-pode), *n.*, (bot.) cabosse, *f.*

cachec'tic *ou* **cachec'tical** (-kèk-), *adj.*, (med.) cachectique.

cachex'y (-kèk-si), *n.*, (med.) cachexie, *f.*

cachinna'tion (cak'i'n'né-), *n.*, (ant.) fou rire; éclat de rire, *m.*

cack'le (cak'k'l), *n.*, caquet, *m.*

cack'le, *v.n.*, caqueter (of hens) ; criailler, cacarder (of geese) ; (fig.) ricaner.

cack'ler, *n.*, poule qui caquette ; oie qui criaille, qui cacarde, *f.* ; caqueteur, *m.*, caqueteuse, *f.*

cack'ling, *n.*, caquetage, *m.*

cacochym'ical (-ki'm'-), *adj.*, (med.) cacochyme.

cac'ochymy (kak'o-ki'm-i), *n.*, (med.) cacochymie, *f.*

cacoph'ony, *n.*, cacophonie, *f.*

cac'tus (-teusse), *n.*, cactus, *m.*

cad, *n.*, (triv.) conducteur d'omnibus ; voyou; gamin, goujat, *m.*

cadas'tral, *adj.*, cadastral. — survey, *cadastre, m.*

cadav'erous (-èr-), *adj.*, cadavéreux.

cad'dis (cad'dice), *n.*, cadis, *m.* ; charrée, *f.*

cad'dy, *n.*, boîte à thé, *f.*

cade (kéde), *adj.*, doux ; apprivoisé.

cade (kéde), *n.*, caque, *f.*, baril, *m.*

cade (kéde), *v.a.*, élever à la main ; apprivoiser.

ca'dence *ou* **ca'dency** (ké-dè'n'ce, -ci), *n.*, cadence ; (mus.) chute, *f.*

ca'dence, *v.a.*, cadencer.

cadet' (-dète), *n.*, cadet, *m.* ; élève d'une école militaire, d'une école navale, *m.* Naval — ; *aspirant de marine, m.*

cad'ger, *n.*, (triv.) regrattier, mendiant, *m.*

cadme'an (-mi-) *ou* **cad'mian**, *adj.*, cadméen.

cadu'ceus (-diou-sheusse), *n.*, caducée, *m.*

cadu'city (-diou-), *n.*, caducité, *f.*

caesu'ra (si-ziou'-), *n.*, césure, *f.*

caesu'ral, *adj.*, de césure.

cag, *n.* V. **keg.**

cage (kédje), *n.*, cage, *f.* ; (prison) violon, *m.* — bird ; *oiseau de cage, m.* —ful ; *cagée, f.* — maker ; *cagier, m., cagière, f.*

cage, *v.a.*, mettre en cage, encager ; mettre au violon, coffrer.

cais'son (ké'çô'n), *n.*, (arch., milit.) caisson, *m.*

cai'tiff (ké-), *n.*, misérable, pendard, gueux, *m.*

cajole' (ca'djôle), *v.a.*, cajoler.

cajol'er, *n.*, cajoleur, *m.*, cajoleuse, *f.*

cajol'ery, *n.*, cajolerie, *f.*

cake (kéke), *n.*, gâteau ; (agri.) tourteau ; (of wax) pain, *m.* ; (metal.) rosette ; (concreted matter) masse, croûte, *f.* Twelfth — ; *gâteau des rois.* — of chocolate ; *tablette de chocolat, f.* — of soap ; *pain de savon.* — mold ; *moule à gâteaux, m.* — shop ; *boutique de pâtissier, f.*

cake, *v.n.*, se cailler, se prendre, se lier, se coller, se durcir.

cal'abash, *n.*, (bot.) calebasse, *f.* — tree ; *calebassier, m.*

cal'amine (-maïne), *n.*, calamine, *f.*

calam'itous, *adj.*, calamiteux, désastreux, affreux, funeste.

calam'itously, *adv.*, désastreusement.

calam'ity, *n.*, calamité, *f.* ; désastre, malheur, *m.*

cal'amus, *n.*, roseau, *m.*

calash', *n.*, calèche ; galoche, *f.*

calc'arate (-réte), *adj.*, (bot.) éperonné.

calca'reous (-ké-ri-), *adj.*, calcaire.

cal'ceated (-si-étéde), *adj.*, chaussé.

cal'ciform, *adj.*, semblable à la chaux.

cal'cinate (-néte), *v.a.* V. **calcine.**

calcina'tion (-né-), *n.*, calcination, *f.*

calcine' (-saïne), *v.a.*, calciner.

calcine', *v.n.*, se calciner.

calc'-spar (-spâr), *n.*, spath calcaire, *m.*

cal'culable (-kiou-), *adj.*, calculable.

cal'culate (-léte), *v.a.*, calculer ; adapter, ajuster.

cal'culate, *v.n.*, calculer, compter **sur**.

calcula'tion (-lé-), *n.*, calcul, *m.*

cal'culative (-lé-), *adj.*, de calcul.

cal'culator (-lé-teur), *n.*, calculateur, *m.*

cal'culatory, *adj.*, qui a rapport au calcul.

cal'culose *ou* **cal'culous** (-kiou-lôss, -leusse), *adj.*, calculeux.

cal'culus (-leusse), *n.*, (math. med.) calcul, *m.*

cal'dron (côl'dreu'ne), *n.*, chaudron, *m. ;* chaudière, *f.*

Caledo'nian (-li-dô-), *adj.*, calédonien.

Caledo'nian, *n.*, Calédonien, *m.*, Calédonienne, *f.*

calefa'cient (-lifé-shè'n'te), *adj.*, chauffant.

calefac'tion (-l'i-fac-), *n.*, caléfaction, *f.*

calefac'tive *ou* **calefac'tory** (cal-i-, -teuri), *adj.*, qui chauffe.

cal'efy (cal-i-faïe), *v.n.*, (l.u.) s'échauffer.

cal'efy, *v.a.*, (l.u.) chauffer ; échauffer.

cal'endar (cal-è'n'-), *n.*, calendrier, tableau, almanach, *m. ;* (jur.) liste d'accusés, *f.* — month ; *mois solaire, m.*

cal'ender, *n.*, cylindre, *m. ;* calandre, *f. ;* (Eastern dervish) calender, *m.*

cal'ender, *v.a.*, cylindrer, calandrer.

cal'endering, *n.*, calandrage, *m.*

cal'ends (cal-è'n'd'ze), *n.pl.*, calendes, *f.pl.*

calf (kâfe), *n.*, (*calves*) veau ; (of tne deer) faon ; (of the leg) mollet, gras, *m. ;* (fig.) buse, *f.*, nigaud, niais, veau, *m.* Fatted — ; *veau gras.* With — ; (of cows) pleine. — binding ; (book bind.) *reliure en veau, f.* — bound ; *relié en veau.* —'s foot ; *pied de veau, m.* —'s head ; *tête de veau, f.* —'s liver ; *foie de veau, m.* —'s sweet-bread ; *ris de veau, m.*

cal'iber *ou* **calibre** (cal'i-beur), *n.*, calibre ; (tech.) compas d'épaisseur, *m.*

cal'ice (cal'ice), *n.* V. **chalice**.

cal'ico (cal'ice), *n.*, calicot, *m.* Printed — ; *indienne, toile peinte, f.*

cal'ico-printer, *n.*, imprimeur d'indiennes, imprimeur de toiles peintes, *m.*

cal'ico-printing, *n.*, impression d'indiennes, *f.*

ca'lif, *n.* V. **caliph**.

cal'ifate, *n.* V. **caliphate**.

caliga'tion (-ghé-), *n.*, (l.u.) obscuscissement de la vue, *m.*

calig'inous (-dji-), *adj.*, (l.u.) obscur, sombre.

caligraph'ic, *adj.* V. **calligraphic**.

calig'raphy, *n.* V. **calligraphy**.

cal'ipash, *n.*, carapace, *f.*

ca'liph (ké'life), *n.*, calife, *m.*

cal'iphate (-'éte), *n.*, califat, *m.*

calk, caulk (kôke), *v.a.*, calfater ; (of horses) ferrer à glace.

calk'er, caulker, *n.*, calfat, *m.*

calk'in, *n.*, crampon, *m.*

calk'ing, caulk'ing, *n.*, calfatage, *m.*

calk'ing-iron, caulk'-(-aï'eurne), *n.*, (tech.) calfait, *m.*

call (kôl), *n.*, appel, *m. ;* ordres, *m.pl. ;* demande, *f. ;* (nav.) sifflet, *m. ;* (of a trumpet) sonnerie ; visite, *f. ;* (money) appel de fonds, *m.* Bird— ; *appeau, pipeau, m.* To give any one a — ; *faire une visite à quelqu'un ; passer chez quelqu'un.* At any one's — ; *aux ordres de tout le monde.* At — ; (com.) *à commandement.* Within — ; *à portée de la voix.* He is at his beck and — ; *il lui obéit au doigt et à l'œil.* — to order ; *rappel à l'ordre, m.*

call, *v.n.*, appeler, crier ; venir **chez**, faire visite **à**. To — on any one, at any one's house ; *passer chez quelqu'un.* To — at (of trains, etc.) ; passer **par** ; s'arrêter **à** ; (nav.) toucher **à**. To — on ; *solliciter une faveur ; prier, conjurer* **de**. To — out ; *crier, parler à haute voix.* To —

upon ; *implorer.* To — again (to come) ; *repasser* **chez**, *revenir.* To — one's self ; *s'intituler.* To be called ; *s'appeler.*

call, *v.a.*, appeler, invoquer, nommer. To — a cab ; *faire venir, ou faire avancer, une voiture.* To — the roll ; *faire l'appel.* To — again, to — back ; *rappeler, révoquer, rétracter.* To — aside ; *prendre à part.* To — down ; *appeler, faire descendre ;* (fig.) *faire tomber, attirer.* To — for ; *appeler, demander, exiger ; réclamer ; aller prendre.* To — to order ; *rappeler à l'ordre.* To — forth ; (fig.) *provoquer, produire, inspirer, faire naître.* To — into action ; *mettre en action.* To — into play ; *mettre en jeu.* To — to mind ; *se rappeler.* To — in ; *faire rentrer.* To — in a doctor ; *faire venir un médecin.* To — in money ; *retirer de la monnaie de la circulation.* To — out ; *appeler ; provoquer ; appeler en duel ;* (mil.) *appeler sous les drapeaux.* To — up ; *faire monter ; réveiller, faire lever ;* (fig.) *évoquer ;* (jur.) *appeler, citer.* To — off ; *appeler, rappeler.* To — to ; *crier* **à** ; *appeler ; invoquer, appeler à son secours.* To — up ; (fig.) *évoquer.* To — together ; *assembler, réunir.*

call'-bell, *n.*, timbre de table, *m.*

call'-bird, *n.*, chanterelle, *f.*, (*oiseau*).

call'-boy (bo-i), *n.*, (thea.) avertisseur ; (nav.) répétiteur, *m.*

calligraph'ic *ou* **calligraph'ical**, *adj.*, calligraphique.

callig'raphy, *n.*, calligraphie, *f.*

call'ing, *n.*, appellation ; profession, vocation, *f. ;* métier, état, *m.* — in (of coin) ; *retrait, m. ;* démonétisation, *f.* — out, — over ; *appel, m.*

callisthen'ic, *adj.*, callisthénique.

callisthen'ics, *n.pl.*, callisthénie, *f.*

callos'ity (cal-loss'iti), *n.*, callosité, *f.*, cal, calus, *m.*

cal'lous, *adj.*, calleux ; endurci, insensible.

cal'lously, *adv.*, d'une manière calleuse ; avec insensibilité.

cal'lousness, *n.*, callosité ; insensibilité, *f. ;* endurcissement, *m.*

cal'low (-lô), *adj.*, sans plume ; (fig.) jeune, novice.

cal'lus, *n.*, cal, calus, *m. ;* callosité, *f.*

calm (kâme), *n.*, calme, *m.*

calm, *adj.*, calme. To get, *ou* become, — ; *se calmer.*

calm, *v.a.* and *n.*, calmer, apaiser.

calm'er, *n.*, adoucissant ; calmant ; (pers.) consolateur, *m. ;* -trice, *f.*

calm'ly, *adv.*, avec calme ; tranquillement.

calm'ness, *n.*, calme, *m. ;* tranquillité, *f.*

cal'omel, *n.*, calomel, *m.*

calor'ic, *n.*, calorique, *m.*

calor'ic, *adj.*, de calorique.

calorif'ic, *adj.*, calorifique.

cal'trop, *n.*, (bot.) herse, croix de Malte ; (milit.) chausse-trape, *f.*

calum'ba (-leu'm'-), *n.*, (bot.) colombo, *m.*

cal'umet (cal'iou-mète), *n.*, calumet, *m.*

calum'niate (-leu'm'niéte), *v.a.* and *n.*, calomnier.

calumnia'tion (-ni-é-), *n.*, calomnie, *f.*

calum'niator (-teur), *n.*, calomniateur, *m.*

calum'niatory *ou* **calum'nious**, *adj.*, calomnieux.

calum'niously, *adv.*, calomnieusement.

calum'niousness, *n.*, caractère calomnieux, *m.*

cal'umny (cal'eu'm'ni), *n.*, calomnie, *f.*

cal'vary, *n.*, calvaire, *m.*

calve (kâve), *v.n.*, vêler.

Cal'vinism, *n.*, calvinisme, *m.*

Cal'vinist, *n.*, calviniste, *m.f.*

Calvinist'ic *ou* **Calvinist'ical**, *adj.*, calviniste.

calv'ish (kâv'ishe), *adj.*, de veau ; comme un veau.

cal'yx, *n.*, calice, *m.*

cama'ieu (ka-mé-yô), *n.* V. **cameo**.

camaril'la, n., camarilla, f.
cam'ber, v.a., cambrer. v.n., se cambrer.
cam'ber, n., cambre, cambrure, f.
cam'bering, adj., cambré. [f.
Cam'berwell-beau'ty, n., (butterfly) vanesse,
cam'bist, n., agent de change, ⊙cambiste, m.
cam'bric (ké'm'-), n., batiste, f. — muslin —
percale, f.
came (kéme), v.n. V. come.
came (kéme), n., plomb de vitrier, m.
cam'el (cam'èl), n., chameau, m., chamelle, f.
cam'el-backed (-bak'te), adj., à dos de chameau.
cam'el-driver (-draïv'-), n., chamelier, m.
came'leon ou came'leon-mineral (-mî-li-),
n., (chem.) caméléon minéral, permanganate de
potasse, m.
came'lia, n., camélia, m.
camel'opard (-pârde), n., girafe, f., ⊙camé-
lopard, caméléopard, m.
cam'el's hair (-el'z'hère), n., poil de chameau,
m. — brush ; pinceau, m.
cam'eo (ca'm'i-ô), n., camaïeu, camée, m.
cam'era-lu'cida (-'i-ra-liou-), n., chambre
claire, f.
cam'era-obscu'ra (-'i-ra-ob-skiou-), n., chambre obscure, f.
cam'erate, v.a., voûter, arquer.
cam'erated (ca'm'i-ré-tède), adj., voûté.
camera'tion (ca'm'i-ré-), n., courbure, voûte,
f.
camisade' ('-i-céde), n., attaque de nuit, f.
cam'let, n., camelot, m.
cam'leted, adj., cameloté ; moiré.
cam'omile (-maïle), n. V. chamomile.
camp (ca'm'pe), n., camp, m. To pitch a — ;
asseoir un camp. To break up a — ; lever un
camp. — equipage ; articles de campement, m.
— kettle ; bidon, m. — follower ; goujat, mer-
canti, m. — stool ; pliant, m.
camp, v.a. and n., camper.
campaign' (ca'm'péne), n., campagne, f.
campaign', v.n., (milit.) faire campagne.
campaign'er, n., vieux soldat, vétéran, m.
campa'na, n., (bot.) pulsatille, f.
campani'le (-nî-lé), n., campanile, m., cam-
panille, f.
campan'ula (-niou-), n., campanule, f.
campan'ulate, adj., (bot.) campanulé, en
cloche.
campeach'y wood (-pi-tshi woude), n. V.
logwood.
cam'phire ou cam'phor (-feur), n., camphre,
m.
cam'phorate ou cam'phorated (-feur'éte,
-étède), adj., camphré.
can (cane), n., pot, broc, bidon, m.; burette, f.
can, v.a., mettre en boîte.
can (cane), v.n. (preterit and conditional,
Could), (to be able) pouvoir, (to know how to)
savoir. I — do it ; je peux, ou je sais, le faire.
— I? puis-je? That — not be ; cela ne peut pas
être ; cela ne se peut pas. He — read ; il sait
lire. — it be true? serait-ce vrai? As true as
— be ; aussi vrai que possible.
canal', n., canal, m.
canalic'ulate ou canalic'ulated (-kiou-léte,
-létède), adj., cannelé.
canal'izable, adj., canalisable.
canaliza'tion, n., canalisation.
cana'ry (-né-), n., vin des Canaries ; (orni.)
serin, m.
cana'ry-bird (-beurde), n., serin, m. Cock-
— ; serin, m. Hen— ; serine, f.
cana'ry-grass (-grâce), n., alpiste ; blé des
Canaries, m.
cana'ry-seed (-sîde), n., graine des Canaries, f.
can'cel, v.a., annuler ; résilier ; effacer, biffer,
rayer ; (com.) résilier ; (jur.) ⊙canceller ; (print.)
refaire.

can'cel, n., (print.) feuillet refait, m.
can'cellated (-létède), adj., rayé ; cellulaire.
cancella'tion (-lé-), n., (jur.) cancellation, f.
can'cer, n., cancer, m.
can'cerate (-ceur'éte), v.n., devenir cancéreux ;
s'ulcérer.
cancera'tion (-ceur'é-), n., ulcération can-
céreuse, f.
can'cerous, adj., cancéreux.
can'cerousness, n., état cancéreux, m.
can'criform, adj., cancriforme.
can'crine (-craïne), adj., de cancre ; cancéreux.
candela'brum (-lé-breu'me), n., (candelabra),
candélabre, m.
can'dent (-dè'n'te), adj., chauffé à blanc.
can'did, adj., candide, franc, sincère, ingénu ;
loyal, impartial.
can'didate (-déte), n., candidat, aspirant, m.
can'didly, adv., candidement, franchement,
ingénument, loyalement, en bonne foi, en conscience.
can'didness, n., candeur, franchise, sincérité ;
bonne foi, f.
can'died (ca'n'dide), adj., candi.
can'dle (ca'n'd'l), v.a., (eggs) mirer.
can'dle, n., chandelle ; lumière, bougie, (church)
cierge, f. Wax — ; bougie. Mold — ; chandelle
moulée. Dipped — ; chandelle plongée. A —
studied, labored speech ; un discours qui sent la
chandelle.
can'dle-end (-è'n'de), n., bout de chandelle,
m. ; débris, brins, fragments, m.pl.
can'dle-grease (-grîce), n., suif, m.
can'dle-light (-laïte), n., lumière de la chandelle, f. By — ; à la lumière ; à la lumière de la
chandelle, ou des chandelles ; aux chandelles.
can'dle-maker, n., fabricant de chandelles,
m.
can'dlemas (-meusse), n., la Chandeleur, f.
can'dle-mold, n., moule à chandelles, m.
can'dle-power, n., pouvoir éclairant de la
chandelle, m.
can'dlestick, n., chandelier, m. Bedroom
— ; bougeoir, m.
can'dle-stuff (-steufe), n., suif, m.; cire,
stéarine, f.
can'dle-wick, n., mèche de chandelle, f.
can'dor (-deur), n., candeur, franchise, sincérité, bonne foi, f.
can'dy, v.a., faire candir.
can'dy, v.n., se candir, se cristalliser.
can'dy, n., candi, m.
cane (kéne), n., canne, f. ; (of an umbrella)
jonc, m., tige, f. ; (agri.) plant, cep, m. — chair ;
chaise de canne, f. — basket ; panier de jonc,
m. — knob ; pomme de canne, f. — sugar ;
sucre de canne, m.
cane-juice, n., suc de canne, m.
cane, v.a., donner des coups de canne à.
cane'-mill, n., moulin à sucre, m. ; sucrerie, f.
canes'cent (-nès-cè'n'te), adj., blanchissant,
blanchâtre, tirant sur le blanc.
cane'trash (-trashe), n., bagasse, f.
cane'-work (-weurke), n., objet, ouvrage de
canne, m.
canic'ula ou can'icule (-nik'iou-), n., (astron.)
canicule, f.
canic'ular, adj., caniculaire.
canine' (-naïne), adj., canin, de chien.
ca'ning (ké-), n., coups de canne, m.pl., râclée,
f.
ca'ning, n., (of chairs) cannage, m.
can'ister, n., boîte de fer blanc, f.
can'ister-shot (-shote), n., mitraille ; boîte à
balles, f. V. case-shot.
can'ker (kagn'keur), n., (fig.) ver rongeur,
fléau, m.; gangrène, f. ; (med.) chancre ; (bot.)
gratte-cul, m.
can'ker, v.a., ronger ; corrompre, envenimer,
empoisonner.

can′ker, *v.n.*, se ronger ; se gangrener, se corrompre.

can′ker-bit (-bite), *adj.*, gangrené.

can′kered (-keurde), *adj.*, rongé, gangrené ; hargneux (fig.).

can′ker-fly (-flaïe), *n.*, ver rongeur des fruits, *m.*

can′kerous, *adj.*, chancreux ; rongeant.

can′ker-worm (-weurme), *n.*, ver rongeur, *m.* ; chenille, *f.* ; (pop.) argent comptant, *m.*

can′nibal (ca′n′ni-bal), *n.*, cannibale, anthropophage, *m.f.*

can′nibalism, *n.*, cannibalisme, *m.* ; anthropophagie, *f.*

can′nibally, *adv.*, en cannibale.

can′non (ca′n′no′n), *n.*, (artil.) print.) canon ; (billiards) carambolage, *m.*, bouche à feu, *f.*

can′non, *v.n.*, caramboler.

cannonade′ (-′éde), *n.*, canonnade, *f.*

cannonade′, *v.a.*, canonner.

cannonade′, *v.n.*, se canonner.

can′non-ball (-bôl), *n.*, boulet de canon, *m.*

cannoneer′ *ou* **cannonier′** (-îre), *n.*, canonnier, *m.*

can′noning, *n.*, (at billiards) carambolage, *m.* — game ; *jeu de carambolage, m.*

can′non-proof (-proufe), *adj.*, à l'épreuve du canon.

can′non-shot (-shote), *n.*, boulet de canon, coup de canon, *m.* ; portée de canon, *f.* Within — ; *à portée de canon.*

can′nular (-′niou-), *adj.*, tubuleux, tubulaire.

canoe′ (-nou), *n.*, canot, *m.* ; pirogue, périssoire, *f.*

can′on (ca′n′-o′n), *n.*, (ecc.) canon ; chanoine, *m.* ; (print.) canon, gros çanon.

ca′ñon *ou* **can′yon**, *n.*, gorge, *f.*, défilé, *m.*

can′oness, *n.*, chanoinesse, *f.*

canon′ical, *adj.*, canonique.

canon′ically, *adv.*, canoniquemenɬ.

canon′icalness, *n.*, canonicité, *f.*

canon′icals (-calze), *n.pl.*, (ecc.) vêtements sacerdotaux, *m.*

canon′icate (-kéte), *n.*, canonicat, *m.*

can′onist, *n.*, canoniste, *m.*

canonist′ic, *adj.*, de canoniste.

canoniza′tion (-′aïzé-), *n.*, canonisation, *f.*

can′onize (-naïze), *v.a.*, canoniser.

can′on-law (-lô), *n.*, droit canon, *m.*

can′onry *ou* **can′onship**, *n.*, canonicat, *m.*

can′opy, *n.*, dais ; pavillon ; (arch.) baldaquin, *m.* ; (of heaven) voûte, *f.* — bed ; *lit à baldaquin, m.*

can′opy, *v.a.*, couvrir d'un dais.

cant (ka′n′te), *n.*, jargon, argot, *m.* ; afféterie ; hypocrisie, cafarderie, *f.* ; langage hypocrite, *m.*, (tech.) chanfrein, pan coupé, *m.*

cant, *v.n.*, parler avec afféterie, avec cafarderie, avec affectation ; enjôler.

cant, *v.a.*, pousser, jeter ; (arch.) chanfreiner ; (nav.) rouler, capoter ; incliner. To — over ; *renverser ;* (timber) *débiller* der *;* (stones) *épanneler.*

Can′tab, *n.*, étudiant de l'université de Cambridge.

can′talever *ou* **can′tilever**, *n.*, modillon, *m.*

can′taloupe (-loupe), *n.*, (hort.) cantaloup, *m.*

cantan′kerous, *adj.*, acariâtre, revêche.

canta′ta (-tâ-), *n.*, cantate, *f.*

canteen′ (-tîne), *n.*, (milit.) cantine, *f.* ; bidon, *m.*

cant′er, *n.*, hypocrite, *m.f.* ; cafard, tartufe, *m.* ; cafarde, *f.* ; galop de chasse ; petit galop, *m.*

cant′er, *v.n.*, aller au petit galop.

can′terbury, *n.*, casier à musique, *m.* ; (geog.) Cantorbéry, *m.*

Can′terbury-bell, *n.*, (bot.) violette marine, *f.* ; campanule, *f.*

can′tharis (-tha-), *n.*, (*cantharides*) cantharide, *f.*

can′ticle (-ti′k′l), *n.*, cantique, *m.*

can′tillate (-léte), *v.a.*, chantonner.

cant′ing, *adj.*, affété, cafard ; hypocrite, tartufe ; (her.) parlant.

cant′ingly, *adv.*, avec afféterie, avec cafarderie, avec affectation.

can′tle (ka′n′t′l), *v.a.*, (ant.) diviser, morceler.

can′to (-tô), *n.*, chant, *m.*

can′ton, *n.*, canton, *m.*

can′ton, *v.a.*, diviser en cantons ; (milit.) cantonner.

can′tonal, *adj.*, cantonal.

can′tonize (-aïze), *v.a.*, diviser en cantons.

can′tonment, *n.*, cantonnement, *m.*

can′ula (-′iou-), *n.*, (surg.) canule, *f.*

can′vas (-′vace), *n.*, canevas, (fig.) tableau, *m.*, peinture ; toile, voile, (sail-cloth) toile à voiles, *f.* Mellowing — ; *peinture qui s'agatise* (Th. Gautier). Under — ; (mil.) *sous tentes ;* (nav.) *sous voiles.* — shoe ; *soulier en toile, m.*

can′vass (-′vace), *n.*, débat, *m.*, discussion, brigue ; sollicitation de suffrages, *f.* ; (com.) sollicitation de commandes, *f.*

can′vass, *v.a.*, agiter, débattre, discuter, solliciter.

can′vass, *v.n.*, briguer ; solliciter des suffrages, (com.) solliciter des commandes, faire la place.

can′vasser, *n.*, brigueur ; solliciteur de suffrages, courtier électoral, (com.) placier, *m.*

ca′ny (ké-ni), *adj.*, de canne, de jonc.

canzonet′ (-nète), *n.*, chansonnette, *f.*

caoutchouc′ (-′tshouke), *n.*, caoutchouc, *m.*

cap, *n.*, (woman's) bonnet, *m.* ; (man's) casquette ; (of a cardinal) barrette ; (universities) toque ; (smoking) calotte, *f.* ; (of fire-arms) capsule, amorce ; (of foils) mouche, *f.* ; (of a bell) chapeau ; (nav.) chouquet ; (horl.) recouvrement, *m.*, cuvette, *f.* Skull — ; *calotte, f.* Knee — ; *boîte, noix, f.* — and bells ; *marotte, f.* If the — fits wear it ; *qui se sent morveux, qu'il se mouche.* To set one's — at ; *vouloir captiver, chercher à plaire à.*

cap, *v.n.*, coiffer, couronner ; (of foils) moucheter ; (tech.) bonneter, capsuler ; (fig.) surpasser ; dépasser **de** ; mettre le comble **à**. To — a statement ; *renchérir* **sur.** That caps me ; *cela me passe.*

capabil′ity (ké-), *n.*, capacité, *f.*

ca′pable (ké-pa′b′l), *adj.*, capable, susceptible **de.**

ca′pableness, *n.*, capacité, *f.*

capa′cious (-pé-sheusse), *adj.*, ample, vaste, étendu ; grand, spacieux.

capa′ciousness, *n.*, capacité ; étendue, *f.*

capac′itate (-téte), *v.a.*, rendre capable **de,** *ou* propre **à** ; mettre en état **de.**

capac′ity, *n.*, capacité ; (employment) qualité, *f.*, titre, *m.* In the — of ; *en qualité* **de.** In that — ; *à ce titre.*

cap-a-pie′ (-pî), *adv.*, de pied en cap.

capar′ison (-ceune), *n.*, caparaçon, *m.*

capar′ison, *v.a.*, caparaçonner.

cape (képe), *n.*, collet, carrick, *m.* ; pèlerine, rotonde, berthe, *f.* ; (geog.) cap, *m.*

cap′elin, *n.*, (ich.) capelan, caplan, *m.*

Capel′la, *n.*, (astr.) la Chèvre.

capell′-master, *n.*, maître de chapelle, *m.*

ca′per (ké-), *n.*, cabriole, *f.* ; (dancing) bond, entrechat, *m.* ; (bot.) câpre, *f.* — sauce ; *sauce aux câpres, f.*

ca′per, *v.n.*, cabrioler ; (dancing) faire des entrechats ; bondir, sauter, faire des cabrioles.

ca′per-bush (-boushe), *n.*, câprier, *m.*

ca′perer, *n.*, cabrioleur, *m.*

ca′pias (ké-), *n.*, (jur.) prise de corps, *f.* ; mandat d'arrêt, mandat d'amener, *m.*

capilla′ceous (-lé-sheusse), *adj.*, capillaire.

capillaire′, *n.*, sirop de capillaire, *m.*

cap′illariness *ou* **capillar′ity**, *n.*, capillarité, *f.*

cap'illary, _adj._, capillaire.

cap'ital, _n._, (com., fin.) capital, _m._, capitaux, _m.pl._; (arch.) chapiteau, _m._; (town) capitale, _f._; (com.) fonds social, _m._; (print., writing) majuscule, capitale, _f._ To make — out of ; _exploiter._

cap'ital, _adj._, capital; excellent, parfait ; essentiel ; majuscule. That 's —; _c'est parfait._ — ! _parfait !_ — fellow ; _excellent garçon._

cap'italist, _n._, capitaliste, _m._

cap'itally, _adv._, parfaitement; principalement; admirablement, à merveille.

capita'tion (-té-), _n._, dénombrement, _m._; capitation, _f._ — fee ; _rétribution par tête, f._

cap'itol (-tôle), _n._, capitole, _m._

capito'lian _ou_ cap'itoline (-tô-li-a'n, -laïne), _adj._, capitolin.

capit'ular _ou_ capit'ulary (-pit'iou-), _n._, capitulaire, membre d'un chapitre, _m._

capit'ularly, _adv._, capitulairement.

capit'ulate (-pit'iou-léte), _v.n._, capituler.

capitula'tion (-pit'iou-lé-), _n._, capitulation, _f._

ca'pon (ké'p'n), _n._, chapon, _m._

ca'pon, _v.a._, chaponner.

caponniere' (-nîre), _n._, caponnière, _f._

capot', _adj._, (at cards, etc.), capot. _v.a._, faire capot.

capote', _n._, capote, _f._

capped (cap'te), _adj._, coiffé ; couronné ; (horl.) à recouvrement.

cap'ping, _n._, (of fire-arms) amorçage ; (tech.) bonnetage, _m._ _pl._, armature, _f._

caprice' (-prîce), _n._, caprice, _m._

capri'cious (-prish'eusse), _adj._, capricieux.

capri'ciously, _adv._, capricieusement.

capri'ciousness, _n._, caractère capricieux, _m._; humeur capricieuse, _f._

Cap'ricorn (-côrne), _n._, capricorne, _m._

cap'riform _ou_ cap'rine (cap'raïne), _adj._, en chèvre ; lascif.

cap'rizant, _adj._, capricant (of the pulse).

cap'sicum, _n._, piment, _m._

capsize' (-saïze), _v.a._, chavirer ; faire chavirer.

capsize', _v.n._, (nav.) chavirer, verser.

cap'stan, _n._, cabestan, _m._

cap'sular _ou_ cap'sulary (-siou-), _adj._, capsulaire.

cap'sulate (-siou-léte) _ou_ cap'sulated (-siou-létède), _adj._, enfermé dans une capsule.

cap'sule, _n._, capsule, _f._

cap'tain (kap'ti'n), _n._, capitaine, _m._ Post —; (nav.) _capitaine de vaisseau._ — of a gun ; _chef de pièce ;_ (merc. navy) _capitaine de navire._

cap'taincy, cap'tainship, _n._, grade de capitaine, _m._; capitainerie, _f._

capta'tion (-té-), _n._, (ant.) capture ; (jur.) captation, _f._; (courtship) cour, _f._

cap'tion, _n._, prise de corps, arrestation, _f._; (of things) saisie, _f._; (of articles, chapters) entête, _m._

cap'tious (-sheusse) _adj._, captieux ; pointilleux, chicaneur ; susceptible.

cap'tiously, _adv._, captieusement.

cap'tiousness, _n._, disposition à la critique, pointillerie, chicanerie ; susceptibilité, _f._

cap'tivate (-véte), _v.a._, captiver ; charmer, séduire ; capter ; assujettir.

cap'tivating, _adj._, enchanteur, séduisant ; qui captive.

captiva'tion (-vé-), _n._, assujettissement, _m._; séduction, _f._

cap'tive, _n._, captif, _m._, captive, _f._; prisonnier, _m.f._; prisonnière, _f._

cap'tive, _adj._, captif ; de captif.

captiv'ity, _n._, captivité, _f._

cap'tor (-teur), _n._, (nav.) capteur ; preneur, _m._

cap'ture (capt'ioure), _n._, capture ; prise, arrestation, _f._

cap'ture, _v.a._, capturer, prendre, arrêter.

capuchin' (cap'iou-shîne), _n._, capucin, _m._, capucine ; mante à capuchon (woman's), _f._

car (câre), _n._, char, chariot, _m._; (gig) carriole, _f._; (of a balloon) nacelle, _f._

car'abine (-baïne) _ou_ car'bine (câr-baïne), _n._, carabine, _f._; mousqueton, _m._

carabineer' (-nîre), _n._, carabinier, _m._

car'ack _ou_ car'rack, _n._, caraque, _f._, (a galleon).

car'acole (-côle), _n._, caracole, _f._

car'acole, _v.n._, (man.) caracoler.

car'amel, _n._, caramel, _m._

caran'na, _n._, caragne, gomme caragne, _f._

car'apace, _n._, carapace, _f._

car'at (-ate), _n._, carat, _m._

caravan' (-va'n), _n._, caravane, _f._

caravan'sary (-va'n'sa-) _ou_ caravan'serai (-va'n'sé-), _n._, caravansérail, _m._

car'avel _ou_ car'vel (câr-), _n._, caravelle, _f._

car'away (-wé), _n._, carvi, cumin des prés, _m._ — seed ; _graine de carvi, f._

car'bon (câr-bo'n), _n._, (chem.) carbone, _m._

car'bonate (-'éte), _n._, carbonate, _m._

carbon'ic, _adj._, carbonique.

carbonif'erous, _adj._, carbonifère.

carboniza'tion (-aïzé-), _n._, carbonisation, _f._

car'bonize (-'aïze), _v.a._, carboniser.

car'boy, _n._, tourie, dame-jeanne, _f._; bocal, _m._

car'buncle (câr-bugn'k'l), _n._, escarboucle, _f._; (med.) charbon, _m._

car'buncled (-k'lde), _adj._, garni d'escarboucles ; (of the nose) bourgeonne.

carbunc'ular (-kiou-), _adj._, d'escarboucle ; rouge ; (med.) charbonneux.

car'buret (câr-biou-rète), _n._, (chem.) carbure, _m._

car'bureted, _adj._, carburé.

car'cajou, _n._, carcajou, _m._

car'canet (câr-ca-nète), _n._, carcan; collier de pierreries, _m._

car'case _ou_ car'cass (câr-), _n._, carcasse, _f._; cadavre, corps mort, _m._

carcino'ma (câr-ci-nô-), _n._, carcinome, cancer, _m._

card (cârde), _n._, carte ; (manu.) carde ; (of the winds) rose des vents ; (of address) carte d'adresse, _f._

card, _v.a._, carder.

card'amine (câr-da-maïne), _n._, (bot.) cardamine, _f._

card'amom (câr-da-meume), _n._, (bot.) cardamome, _m._

card'-basket, _n._, corbeille à cartes, _f._

card'board, _n._, carton, _m._

card'-case (-kéce), _n._, étui à cartes, _f._

card'er (cârd'-), _n._, cardeur, _m._, cardeuse, _f._

car'diac, _adj._, cardiaque.

car'diac, _n._, (med.) cardiaque, _m._

cardi'acal (câr-), _n._, fortifiant.

car'dialgy (câr-di-al-dji), _n._, cardialgie, _f._

car'dinal (câr-), _n._, cardinal, _m._

car'dinal, _adj._, cardinal. — points ; _points cardinaux, m.pl._ — virtues ; _vertus cardinales, f.pl._

car'dinalate (-éte) _ou_ car'dinalship, _n._, cardinalat, _m._

card'ing, cardage, _m._ — house ; _carderie, f._ — machine ; _machine à carder, cardeuse, f._

card'maker (-mék'-), _n._, cartier, _m._

card'-paper (-pé-peur), _n._, carton fin, _m._

card'-player (cârd'-), _n._, joueur, _m._, ou joueuse, _f._, de cartes.

card'-playing, _n._, jeu de cartes, _m._, (les) cartes, _f.pl._

card'-rack (-rack), _n._, porte-cartes, _m._

card'-room (-roume), _n._, salon de jeu, _m._

card'-sharper, _n._, grec, fileur de cartes, bonneteur, _m._

card'-table (-téb'l), _n._, table de jeu, _f._

card'-tray, _n._, plateau à cartes, _m._

care (kère), _n._, soin ; souci, _m._; précaution, sollicitude ; attention, _f._ To the — of; _aux soins_

de. To take — of ; *prendre soin* **de**. To take — to ; *prendre garde* à ; *se garder* **de** ; *avoir soin* **de**. — of ; *aux bons soins* **de**. With — ; *avec soin ;* (of packages) *fragile ;* (of souls) *à charge d'âmes*. Take — he does not touch you ; *prenez garde qu'il ne vous touche* (subj.). Take great — NOT to do it ; *gardez-vous bien de le faire.* Take — of yourself ; *soignez-vous bien ;* (beware of harm) *prenez garde à vous*. They are old enough to take — of themselves ; *ils sont d'âge à se conduire*. To place under the — of ; *confier* à ; *confier aux soins* **de**.

care, *v.n.*, se soucier **de**, s'inquiéter **de**. To — for ; *tenir* à, *se mettre en peine* **de**. I don't — for it ; *je n'y tiens pas ; je ne m'en soucie pas.* I don't — ! *je m'en moque!* What do I — ? *que m'importe?* ou *qu'est-ce que cela me fait ?*

care'-crazed (-créz'de), *adj.*, accablé de soucis.

careen' (-rîne), *n.*, (nav.) carène, *f.*

careen', *v.a.*, (nav.) mettre en carène, caréner, abattre.

careen', *v.n.*, (nav.) donner de la bande, se coucher ; être à la bande.

careen'ing, *n.*, carénage, *m.*

career' (-rieur), *n.*, carrière, course, *f.*

career', *v.n.*, courir rapidement ; courir sur ; s'élancer, voler.

care'ful (kér'foule), *adj.*, soigneux, attentif ; prudent ; plein de soucis, soucieux.

care'fully, *adv.*, soigneusement, attentivement.

care'fulness, *n.*, attention, *f. ;* soin ; souci, *m.*

care'less, *adj.*, sans souci ; insouciant, nonchalant ; négligent **de** ; indifférent à ; sans souci **de** ; oublieux **de**.

care'lessly, *adv.*, sans souci, avec insouciance, nonchalamment, négligemment.

care'lessness, *n.*, insouciance, nonchalance, négligence, *f.*, incurie, indifférence, *f.*

caress' (-rèce), *n.*, caresse, *f.*

caress', *v.a.*, caresser.

ca'ret (ké'rète), *n.*, renvoi, *m.*

care'worn (-wôrne), *adj.*, usé par les soucis.

car'go (cârgô), *n.*, cargaison, *f. ;* chargement, *m.*

car'ibou, *n.*, caribou, *m.*

car'icature (-tioure), *n.*, caricature, charge, *f.*

car'icature, *v.a.*, caricaturer.

car'icaturist (-tiouriste), *n.*, caricaturiste, *m.*

ca'ries (ké-ri-ize), *n.*, carie, *f.*

car'illon (ca-ril-leune), *n.*, petite cloche, *f. ;* (mus.) carillon, *m.*

ca'rious (ké-), *adj.*, carié. To become — ; *se carier.*

cark'ing, *adj.*, cuisant ; fatigant ; douloureux, cruel.

car'man (câr-ma'n), *n.*, (*carmen*) charretier, *m.*

car'line (câr-line), *n.*, (nav.) carlingue, *f.*

carmagnole', *n.*, carmagnole, *f.*

Car'melite (câr-mèl-aïte), *adj.*, de carme, de carmélite.

Car'melite, *n.*, carme, *m.* — nun; *carmélite, f.*

car'minate, *v.a.*, carminer.

carmin'ative, *adj.*, carminatif.

carmin'ative, *n.*, carminatif, *m.*

car'mine (câr-maïne), *n.*, carmin, *m.*

car'nage (câr-nédje), *n.*, carnage, *m.*

car'nal (câr-), *adj.*, charnel. —-minded, *adj. ;* sensuel, charnel ; mondain. —-mindedness, *n. ; sensualité, f.*

car'nally, *adv.*, charnellement ; par la chair.

carna'tion (-né-), *n.*, carnation, *f. ;* (bot.) œillet giroflée, œillet des fleuristes, *m.*

carna'tion-color (-keul'leur), *n.*, incarnat, *m.*

car'neous (câr-ni-eusse), *adj.*, charnu.

carnifica'tion (câr-ni-fi-ké-), *n.*, carnification, *f.*

car'nify (câr-ni-faïe), *v.n.*, se carnifier.

car'nival (câr-), *n.*, carnaval, *m.*

carniv'orous, *adj.*, carnivore.

carnos'ity (-noss'i-), *n.*, carnosité, *f.*

car'nous, *adj.*, charnu.

car'ny (câr-), *v.n.*, pateliner.

car'nying, *adj.*, patelin. *n.*, patelinage, *m.*

car'ob, *n.*, (bot.) (tree) caroubier, *m. ;* (fruit) caroube, carouge, *f.*

car'ol, *n.*, chanson, *f. ;* chant, (of larks) grisollement, *m.* Christmas — ; *chant de Noël*, *m.*

car'ol, *v.a.n.*, chanter, (of larks) grisoller.

carot'id, *n.*, (anat.) carotide, *f.*

carot'id, *adj.*, (anat.) carotide, carotidien.

carous'al (-zal), *n.*, carrousel, *m. ;* orgie, ripaille, *f.*

carouse' (ca-raou-ze), *v.n.*, boire, riboter.

carou'ser, *n.*, grand buveur, riboteur, ripailleur, *m.*

carp (cârpe), *n.*, (ich.) carpe, *f.* — pond ; *étang à carpes, carpier, m.*

carp (cârpe), *v.a.* and *n.*, blâmer ; censurer, épiloguer sur ; trouver à redire à ; gloser sur. To — at ; *gloser* sur.

car'penter (câr-pè'n'-), *n.*, charpentier, menuisier, *m.*

car'pentry, *n.*, charpenterie, menuiserie, *f.*

carp'er, *n.*, gloseur, épilogueur, *m.*

car'pet (câr-pète), *n.*, tapis, *m.* — bag; *sac de nuit, m.* — broom; *balai de jonc, m.* — knight ; *chevalier de salon, m.* — walk ; *tapis vert, m.*

car'pet, *v.a.*, garnir de tapis ; (fig.) tapisser.

carp'ing (cârp'-), *adj.*, pointilleux, caustique.

carp'ing, *n.*, glose, censure, critique, *f.*

carp'ingly, *adv.*, en glosant, en critique ; malignement.

car'riage (car'ridje), *n.*, voiture, *f. ;* équipage ; (rail.) wagon, *m.*, voiture, *f. ;* (of parcels) port, factage, camionnage ; (of the body) port, maintien, *m. ;* tenue, démarche, conduite, *f. ;* (of cannon) affût, *m. ;* (com.) frais de transport, *m.pl.* To keep one's — ; *avoir équipage*, ou *voiture ; tenir équipage*. Gentleman's — ; *voiture de maître*. — and pair, and four ; *voiture à deux chevaux, à quatre chevaux*. — paid ; *port payé*. — not paid ; *port dû.* — free ; *franc de port*. — basket ; *vide-poches, m.* — clock ; *pendule de voyage, f.* — window; *glace, f.* — horse ; *cheval d'attelage, m.* — entrance ; *porte-cochère, f.* — rug ; *couverture de voyage, f.* — way; *route carrossable ;* (of streets) *chaussée, f. ;* *pavé, m.*

car'rier (car'rieur), *n.*, porteur ; voiturier, camionneur, roulier, *m.* — pigeon ; *pigeon voyageur, pigeon messager, m.*

car'rion (-r'i-o'n), *n.*, charogne, *f.*

car'rion, *adj.*, de charogne.

car'ronade, *n.*, (large bore cannon) caronade, *f.*

car'rot (car'rote), *n.*, carotte, *f.* — soup ; *soupe aux carottes, f. ;* *potage à la crécy, m.*

car'rotiness, *n.*, couleur rousse, *f.*

car'roty, *adj.*, couleur de carotte ; roux.

car'ry, *v.a.*, porter ; mener ; entraîner ; emporter ; (of dogs) rapporter ; (arith.) retenir. To — it high ; *le prendre* sur *un haut ton*. To — about ; *porter à droite et à gauche ; porter partout ; mener à droite et à gauche ; mener partout*. To — away ; *emporter ; enlever ; emmener ; entraîner par persuasion ; ravir en extase*. To — back ; *reporter, se reporter à*. To — down ; *descendre*. To — forward ; (com.) *reporter*. To — forth; *sortir*. To — in ; *rentrer*. To — off ; *emporter ; remporter ; enlever ; tuer*. To — on ; *pousser ; poursuivre ; continuer ; gérer, exercer*. To — out ; *porter dehors ; développer ; exécuter ; mettre à exécution, effectuer*. To — over to ; *faire passer à*. To — through ; *accomplir, mener à bonne fin*. To — it off ; *s'en tirer, réussir*. To — up ; *porter en haut ; monter*. To — it over any one ; *l'emporter sur quelqu'un*. — the day ; *remporter la victoire, l'emporter*. — to and fro ; *porter çà et là*. To — over ; *transporter, faire* *passer;* (com.) *reporter.* To — through; *faire surmonter, faire triompher.* To — one's self; *se comporter, se conduire.* To — coals to New-castle; *porter de l'eau à la rivière.*

car'ry, *v.n.,* (artil.) porter. — wind; (man.) (of a horse) *porter, porter la tête.*

car'rying, *n.,* transport, port, *m.* — of arms; *port d'armes, m.*

cart (cârte), *n.,* charrette, *f.;* camion; tombereau; chariot; (milit.) fourgon, *m.* To put the — before the horse; *mettre la charrue devant les bœufs.*

cart (cârte), *v.a.,* charrier, charroyer, voiturer. *v.n.,* faire des charrois. To — away; *enlever, emporter.*

cart'age (cârt'èdje), *n.,* charriage, charroi, transport, *m.*

carte (cârte), *n.,* carte, *f.;* menu, *m.*

carte-blanche' (cârte-), *n.,* carte blanche, *f.*

cartel', *n.,* cartel, *m.*

cartel'-ship (-shipe), *n.,* cartel, bâtiment parlementaire, *m.*

cart'er, *n.,* charretier, roulier, voiturier, *m.*

Carte'sian (-tî-), *adj.,* cartésien.

Carte'sian, *n.,* cartésien, *m.*

Carte'sianism, *n.,* cartésianisme, *m.*

cart'grease, *n.,* oing, cambouis, *m.*

Carthagin'ian (câr-tha-dji-),*adj.,* carthaginois.

Carthagin'ian, *n.,* Carthaginois, *m.,* Carthaginoise, *f.*

car'thamus (câr-tha-), *n.,* (bot.) carthame, *m.*

cart'-horse (-hôrse), *n.,* cheval de trait, *m.*

Carthu'sian (-thiou'ja'n), *n.,* chartreux.

car'tilage (câr-ti-lèdje), *n.,* cartilage, *m.*

cartilag'inous (câr-ti-ladj'i-), *adj.,* cartilagineux.

cart'-load (-lôde), *n.,* charretée, voie, *f.*

cartoon' (-toune), *n.,* carton, *m.*

cartouch', *n.,* (artil.) boîte à mitraille, *f.;* (arch.) cartouche, *m.;* (milit.) giberne, *f.*

car'tridge (câr-), *n.,* cartouche; (of cannon) gargousse, *f.* Blank —; *cartouche à blanc, f.* — case; *étui de cartouche, m.* — pouch; *cartouchière, f.*

car'tridge-box, *n.,* giberne, (sport) cartouchière, *f.*

car'tridge-factory, *n.,* cartoucherie, *f.*

cart'rut (-reute), *n.,* ornière, *f.*

cart'-shed (-shède), *n.,* hangar, *m.*

cart'way, *n.,* chemin de charroi, *m.;* route charretière, *f.*

cart'wheel, *n.,* roue de charette, *f.*

cart'wright (-raïte), *n.* V. **wheelwright.**

car'uncle (-'ugn'k'l), *n.,* caroncule, *f.*

carve (cârve), *v.a.* and *n.,* sculpter; tailler; graver; couper; ciseler; (meat) découper; dépecer.

carv'er, *n.,* découpeur, *m.;* écuyer tranchant; (sculpt.) sculpteur; graveur, ciseleur, *m.*

carv'ing, *n.,* découpage, *m.;* (sculpt.) sculpture, gravure, ciselure, *f.* — knife, fork; *couteau, m.; fourchette à découper, f.*

caryat'ides, *n.pl.,* cariatide, caryatide, *f.*

cascade' (-kéde), *n.,* cascade, *f.*

case (kéce), *n.,* étui, fourreau, *m.;* gaîne; trousse, *f.;* (for jewels) écrin; (of an organ) buffet, *m.;* (wrapper) enveloppe; (for packing) caisse; (print.) casse; (of a watch) boîte; (showcase) vitrine, montre; (of a pillow) taie, *f.;* cas, état, question; (gram., math., med.) cas, *m.;* (jur.) cause, *f.* —-ful; (print.) cassetée, *f.* In that —; *dans ce cas, en ce cas, cela étant.* In —; *au cas que; en cas que; dans le cas où.* That alters the —; *c'est une autre paire de manches; c'est une autre affaire.* Should the — occur; *le cas échéant.* As the — may be; *selon les circonstances.* Such being the —; *cela étant.* If that is the —; *s'il en est ainsi.* In any —; *en tout cas.* In such a —; *en pareil cas.* It is a very hard —; *cela est rude; c'est dur.*

case, *v.a.,* mettre dans un étui; enfermer; envelopper, encaisser; (of mines) cuveler; (to iron) ferrer.

cased, *part. adj.,* mis dans un étui, encaissé; (nav.) cuirassé. Double —; (of watches) *à double boîte.*

case'maker, *n.,* gainier, *m.*

case'mate (késs'méte), *n.,* casemate, *f. v.a.,* casemater.

case'ment (késs'-), *n.,* fenêtre; croisée, *f.* — window; *fenêtre croisée, f.*

case'mented, *adj.,* à vasistas.

ca'seous, *adv.,* caséeux.

cash (cashe), *n.,* argent, numéraire, *m.;* espèces, *f.pl.* — down; *argent comptant, m.* To sell for —; *vendre au comptant.* To be in —; *être en fonds.*

cash, *v.a.,* (com.) convertir en espèces; changer; escompter; recevoir, toucher. To get cashed; *faire changer.*

cash'-account (-ac-cou'n'te), *n.,* compte de caisse, *m.* — balance; *encaisse, f.*

cash'-book (-bouke), *n.,* livre de caisse, *m.*

cash'-box, *n.,* cassette; (com.) caisse, *f.*

cashew'-nut (ca-shou-neute), *n.,* noix d'acajou, *f.*

cashew'-tree (-trî), *n.,* (bot.) anacardier, *m.*

cashier' (-shîre), *n.,* caissier, *m.*

cashier', *v.a.,* destituer, (milit.) casser, dégrader.

cash'-keeper (-kîp'-), *n.,* caissier, *m.*

cash'mere (-mîre), *n.,* cachemire, *m.*

cash' note, *n.,* mandat à payer, bon de caisse, *m.*

cashoo' (-shou), *n.,* cachou, *m.*

ca'sing (-késs'-), *n.,* (carp.) revêtement; chambranle; entourage, *m.;* enveloppe, couverture, *f.*

cask (câske), *n.,* baril, *m.;* barrique, *f.;* tonneau, *m.* — stand; *chantier, m.*

cask, *v.a.,* (ant.) mettre en baril, en tonneau, en barrique.

cask'et (câskète), *n.,* cassette, *f.;* écrin, *m.*

casque *ou* **cask** (câske), *n.,* casque, *m.*

cassa'tion (-sé'-), *n.,* cassation, *f.*

cas'sava (-sé-, *ou* -sa-), *n.,* cassave, *f.*

cas'sia (cash'shi-a), *n.,* casse, *f.*

cas'sock, *n.,* soutane, (ant.) casaque, *f.*

cas'socked, *adj.,* en soutane.

cast (câste), *v.a.,* (*preterit* and *past part.,* Cast) jeter; lancer; condamner; (metal.) couler; (of trees and animals) dépouiller; (reptiles) changer (skin); (thea.) distribuer les rôles; (print.) clicher; (mold) mouler. To — about; *jeter de tous côtés.* To — about for; *songer à; chercher.* To — aside; *jeter à l'écart.* To — away; *jeter; renoncer à, bannir.* To — down; *affliger; abattre; décourager;* (of the eyes) *baisser.* To — forth; *exhaler; rejeter.* To — headlong; *précipiter.* To — off; *rejeter, repousser, abandonner.* To — lots; *tirer au sort.* To — out; *chasser.* To — up; *additionner, faire l'addition de;* (of food) *vomir.* To be —; (jur.) *être débouté* (**de**). To — anchor; *jeter l'ancre.* To — by; *rejeter.* — cannon; *canon de fonte, m.* — off clothes; *vêtements de rebut, m.pl.; défroque, f.* — glass; *verre coulé, m.* — iron; *fonte, f.* — net; *épervier, m.*

cast, *v.n.,* se jeter; (of wood) se déjeter; se couler; (nav.) abattre. To be — away; *être jeté à la côte; faire naufrage.*

cast, *n.,* (throw) jet; coup; moule, *m.;* (metal.) fonte; (thea.) distribution des rôles, *f.;* rôles, acteurs, *m.pl.;* (fig.) nuance, trempe, expression, *f.;* air, caractère, *m.;* (sculpt.) statuette, *f.;* buste, bronze, plâtre, modèle, *m.;* (agri.) volée, *f.* To have a — in the eye; *loucher.* To take a — of; *mouler.* — clothes; *vêtements de rebut;* défroque, *f.*

cas'tanet, *n.,* castagnette, *f.*

cas'tellan, *n.*, châtelain, *m.*

cas'tellany, *n.*, châtellenie, *f.*

cast'er (câst'eur), *n.*, personne qui jette, *f.;* calculateur; saupoudroir, *m.;* roulette (of furniture), *f.*

cas'tigate (-ghéte), *v.a.*, châtier, punir.

castiga'tion (-ghé-), *n.*, châtiment, *m.*, correction, punition, *f.*

cas'tigator (-ghéteur), *n.*, personne qui punit, qui châtie, *f.*

cas'tigatory, *adj.*, qui punit, qui châtie.

cast'ing (câst'-), *n.*, fonte, *f.;* moulage; (print.) clichage; calcul, *m.;* (nav.) abatée, *f.*

cast'ing-vote, *n.*, voix prépondérante, *f.*

cas'tle (câs's'l), *n.*, château, *m.;* (at chess) tour, *f.* —s in the air; châteaux en Espagne.

cas'tle, *v.a.*, (at chess) roquer.

cas'tled (câs's'lde), *adj.*, chargé de châteaux, couronné de tours.

cas'tor, *n.*, (mam., astron.) castor; chapeau de castor, *m.*

cas'torine (-raïne), *n.*, castorine, *f.*

cas'tor-oil (câs'tor-oïle), *n.*, huile de ricin, *f.*

cas'tor-sugar, *n.*, sucre en poudre, *m.*

castrameta'tion (-mi-té-), *n.*, (antiq.) castramétation, *f.*

cas'trate (-tréte), *v.a.*, châtrer.

castra'tion (-tré-), *n.*, castration, *f.*

castra'to (-trâ-tô), *n.*, castrat, *m.*

cas'ual (caj'iou-), *adj.*, fortuit, accidentel, casuel, de passage.

cas'ually, *adv.*, fortuitement, accidentellement, par hasard, en passant.

cas'ualty (caj'iou-), *n.*, hasard, cas fortuit, accident, sinistre, *m.;* (mil., nav.) perte, *f.* Return of casualties; *liste des morts, des blessés et des prisonniers, f.*

cas'uist (ca-jiou-), *n.*, casuiste, *m.*

casuist'ic *ou* casuist'ical, *adj.*, de casuiste.

casuist'ically, *adv.*, en casuiste.

cas'uistry, *n.*, science du casuiste, *f.*

cat (cate), *n.*, chat, *m.*, chatte, *f.;* (milit., nav.) fouet; (nav.) capon (of a ship); (game) bâtonnet, *m.* Tom- —; *matou, m.* When the —'s away the mice will play; *le chat parti, les souris dansent.* To live a — and dog life; *s'accorder comme chien et chat.* To let the — out of the bag; *éventer la mèche ou la mine.* When candles are away all —s are gray; *la nuit tous les chats sont gris.* A muffled — catches no mice; *chat botté n'attrape pas de souris.* Like a — on hot bricks; *comme chat sur braise.*

cat, *v.a.*, (nav.) caponner (of anchors).

catachre'sis (-krî-cisse), *n.*, (rhet.) catachrèse, *f.*

catachres'tical (-krèss-), *adj.*, de catachrèse.

catachres'tically, *adv.*, par catachrèse.

cat'aclysm, *n.*, cataclysme, *m.*

cat'acombs (-counes), *n.pl.*, catacombes, *f.pl.*

catacous'tics, *n.pl.*, catacoustique, *f.sing.*

catadiop'tric *ou* catadiop'trical, *adj.*, catadioptrique.

catafal'co, *n.*, catafalque, *m.*

cat'alepsy, *n.*, catalepsie, *f.*

catalep'tic, *adj.*, cataleptique.

cat'alogue, *n.*, catalogue, *m.*

catame'nia (-mî-), *n.*, flux menstruel, *m.*, règles, *f.pl.*

cat'apult (-peulte), *n.*, catapulte, *f.*

cat'aract, *n.*, cataracte, *f.*

catarrh' (ka-târ), *n.*, catarrhe, *m.*

catarrh'al, *adj.*, catarrhal.

catas'trophe (-fi), *n.*, catastrophe, *f.;* (thea.) dénoûment, *m.*

cat'call (-kôl), *n.*, (thea.) sifflet, *m.*

catch, *n.*, prise; (fig.) belle affaire, attrape, *f.*, jeu de mot, attrape-nigaud, *m.;* (of a door) crampon; anneau; (of a latch) mentonnet; (mus.) air à reprises; (print.) visorium, *m.;* (of fish) pêche, *f.;* (tech.; of locks) cliquet, loquet,

crochet d'arrêt, *m.* She is a good —; *elle a de la fortune.* She's no great —in the way of money; *ce n'est pas une fortune qu'il épouse.*

catch, *v.a.*, (*preterit* and *past part.*, Caught) attraper; prendre; saisir; (pop.) pincer; surprendre. —at; *s'empresser de saisir.* —cold; *s'enrhumer.* To — on; *avoir du succès.* —up; *saisir; relever; rattraper, atteindre.* To — any one crying; *surprendre quelqu'un à pleurer.* I shall —him up; *je le rattraperai.* If I —you at it; *si je vous y prends.* Her eye caught mine; *nos yeux se rencontrèrent.* To — the train; *arriver à temps pour le train, ne pas manquer le train.*

catch, *v.n.*, s'accrocher à, s'engager dans; s'attraper à; se prendre à. To — it; (scold) *en avoir, en recevoir.*

catch'er, *n.*, attrapeur, *m.*, attrapeuse, *f.*

catch'fly (-flaïe), *n.*, (bot.) silène, *f.*, attrape-mouche, gobe-mouches, *m.*

catch'ing, *adj.*, qui saisit; contagieux; séduisant. To be —; *être contagieux, se communiquer, se gagner.*

catch'penny (-pèn'ni), *n.*, attrape-nigauds, *adj.*, d'attrape, de réclame, de boutique.

catch'word (-weurde), *n.*, (print.) réclame, *f.*

cat'echism (cat'i-kiz'm), *n.*, catéchisme, *m.*

cat'echist (-kiste), *n.*, catéchiste, *m.*

catechis'tical (-kis'-), *adj.*, de catéchiste; de catéchisme.

cat'echize (cat'i-kaïze), *v.a.*, catéchiser; interroger.

cat'echizer (-kaïz'-), *n.*, catéchiste, *m.*

catechu'men (-kiou-mène), *n.*, catéchumène, *m.f.*

categor'ical (cat'i-), *adj.*, catégorique.

categor'ically, *adv.*, catégoriquement, *m.*

cat'egory (cat'i-), *n.*, catégorie, *f.*

cat'enarian (cat'i-né-), *adj.*, en chaîne, comme une chaîne.

cat'enate (cat'i-néte), *v.a.*, (l.u.) enchaîner, lier.

catena'tion (-né-), *n.*, enchaînement, *m.*

ca'ter (for), (cât-), *v.n.*, pourvoir à.

ca'ter, *n.*, (at cards) quatre, *m.*

ca'terer, *n.*, pourvoyeur, *m.*, pourvoyeuse, *f.;* approvisionneur, *m.*, approvisionneuse, *f.*

cat'erpillar, *n.*, chenille, *f.*

cat'erwaul, *n.*, (of the cat) appeler; miauler; crier, faire du tintamarre.

cat'erwauling, *n.*, sabbat des chats, tintamarre, *m.*

cat'fall, *n.*, (nav.) garant de capon, *m.*

cat'fish (-fishe), *n.*, (ich.) loup de mer, loup *ou* chat marin, *m.*

cat'gut (-gheute), *n.*, corde à boyau, *f.* —scraper; *râcleur, m.*

cathar'tic (-thâr-), *adj.*, cathartique.

cathar'tic, *n.*, cathartique, *m.*

cathar'ticalness, *n.*, qualité cathartique, *f.*

cat'head (cat'hède), *n.*, (nav.) bossoir, *m.*

cathe'dral (-thi-), *n.*, cathédrale, *f.* — town; *ville épiscopale, f.*, évêché, *m.*

cath'eter (cath-), *n.*, cathéter, *m.*

cat'-hole (-hôle), *n.*, chatière, *f.*

cath'olic (cath-), *adj.*, catholique.

cath'olic, *n.*, catholique, *m.f.*

cathol'icism, *n.*, catholicisme, *m.*

catholic'ity, *n.*, catholicité, *f.*

cath'olicly, *adv.*, catholiquement; universellement.

cath'olicness, *n.*, universalité, *f.*

cathol'icon (ca-tho-), *n.*, électuaire purgatif, catholicon, *m.*

cat'kin (cat'kine), *n.*, (bot.) chaton, *m.*

cat'like, *adj.*, comme un chat, de chat.

cat'ling, *n.*, corde à violon, *f.*

cat'mint (cat'mi'n'te), *n.*, (bot.) cataire, *f.*

cat-o'-nine'-tails (-naïne't'élze), *n.*, fouet à neuf lanières, martinet, *m.;* garcette, *f.*

catop'tric *ou* catop'trical, *adj.*, catoptrique.

catop'trics (-trikse), *n.pl.*, catoptrique, *f.sing.*

cat's'-eye (-aïe), *n.*, (min.) œil-de-chat, *m.*

cat's'-foot (-foute), *n.*, (bot.) pied-de-chat, lierre terrestre, *m.*

cat's' litter, *n.*, chattée, *f.*

cat's'-paw (-pō), *n.*, patte de chat, *f. ;* (nav.) (of wind) vent léger, souffle de vent, *m.* To be any one's —; *tirer les marrons du feu pour quelqu'un*, ou *être la dupe de quelqu'un.*

cat's'-purr (-peur), *n.*, (med.) frémissement cataire, *m.*

cat's'-skin, *n.*, peau de chat, *f.*

cat's'-tail (-téle), *n.*, (bot.) massette, *f.*

cat'sup (cat'seupe), *n.*, sauce piquante, *f.*

cat'-thyme (-taïme), *n.*, marum, *m.*

cat'tle, *n.*, bétail, *m. ;* bestiaux, *m.pl.* Black —; *gros bétail*, *m.* — shed; *étable*, *f.* — market; *marché aux bestiaux*, *m.* — pen ; *parc à bestiaux*, *m.* — plague ; *peste bovine*, *f.* — train ; *convoi de bestiaux*, *m.* — truck ; *wagon-étable*, *m.*

cat'tle show (-shō), *n.*, exposition de bétail, *f.*

cat'-tribe (cat'traïbe), *n.sing.*, (zoöl.) félins, *m.pl.*

cau'dal, *adj.*, caudal.

cau'dex, *n.*, (*caudices*) caudex, *m.*

cau'dine, *adj.*, caudine. — forks ; *fourches caudines*, *f.pl.*

cau'dle, *n.*, brouet, chaudeau, *m.*

caught (côte). *V.* **catch**.

caul, *n.*, réseau, filet, *m. ;* coiffe de réseau ; coiffe d'enfant, *f.*

cau'liflower (col'li-flaou'eur), *n.*, chou-fleur, *m.*

cau'line (cō-laïne), *adj.*, (bot.) caulinaire.

caus'al, *adj.*, causal, causatif.

causal'ity, *n.*, causalité, *f.*

caus'ally, *adv.*, suivant l'ordre des causes.

caus'ative, *adj.*, causatif.

cause (cō-ze), *n.*, cause, raison, *f.*, motif, sujet, *m.* There is — to believe ; *il y a lieu de croire.* To show —; *exposer ses raisons.*

cause, *v.a.*, causer, être cause de ; occasionner, faire naître. To — sorrow ; *donner du chagrin.* To — to be punished ; *faire punir.* To — a thing to be done ; *faire faire.*

cause'less, *adj.*, sans cause, sans motif, sans sujet, non-motivé.

cause'lessly, *adv.*, sans cause.

cause'lessness, *n.*, absence de motifs, *f.*

cause'-list, *n.*, (jur.) rôle, *m.*

caus'er, *n.*, cause, *f.*, auteur, *m.*

cause'way (-wé), *n.*, chaussée ; digue, jetée, *f.*

caus'tic, *adj.*, caustique.

caus'tic, *n.*, caustique, *m.* Lunar —; *pierre infernale*, *f.*

cauteriza'tion (-teur'aï-zé-), *n.*, cautérisation, *f.*

cau'terize (-teur'aïze), *v.a.*, cautériser.

cau'terizing, *n.*, cautérisation, *f.*

cau'tery (-teur'i), *n.*, cautère, *m.*

cau'tion (cō'sheune), *n.*, avis, *m. ;* précaution, prévoyance, prudence, circonspection ; garantie, *f.*

cau'tion, *v.a.*, précautionner ; avertir **de**, aviser **de** ; mettre en garde **contre** ; prémunir **contre**.

cau'tionary, *adj.*, d'avertissement, de prévoyance, de précaution ; pour avertir.

cau'tious (cō'sheusse), *adj.*, précautionné, circonspect, prudent ; en garde **contre**.

cau'tiously, *adv.*, avec précaution, prudemment, avec circonspection.

cau'tiousness, *n.*, prévoyance, circonspection, prudence, *f.*

cavalcade' (-kéde), *n.*, cavalcade, *f.*

cavalier' (-lîre), *n.*, cavalier, *m.*

cavalier', *adj.*, vaillant, courageux ; cavalier.

cavalier'ly, *adv.*, cavalièrement.

cav'alry, *n.*, cavalerie, *f.*

cavati'na (-tî-), *n.*, cavatine, *f.*

cava'tion (-vé-), *n.*, (ant.) (arch.) excavation, *f.*

cave (kéve), *n.*, caverne, *f. ;* antre, souterrain, *m.*

cave, *v.a.*, caver, creuser.

cave, *v.n.*, habiter une caverne. To — in ; (fig.) céder, *se soumettre, mettre les pouces ;* (of buildings) *s'affaisser, s'effondrer.*

ca'vern (cav'eurne), *n.*, caverne.

cav'ernous, *adj.*, caverneux.

cav'esson (cav'ès'seune), *n.*, (man.) caveçon, *m.*

caviare' (-âre), *n.*, caviar, *m.*

cav'il, *n.*, pointillerie ; chicane, *f.*

cav'il, *v.n.*, pointiller ; chicaner ; ergoter **sur** (at).

cav'iler, *n.*, chicanier, chicaneur, ergoteur, *m.*

cav'ilingly, *adv.*, par esprit de chicane.

cav'ilous, *adj.*, chicanier.

cav'ilously, *adv.*, par pointillerie, en chicaneur.

cav'ing-in, *n.*, soumission, *f.*

cav'ity, *n.*, cavité, *f.*

caw (cō), *v.n.*, croasser.

caw'ing, *n.*, croassement, *m.*

cay'man, *n.*, (zoöl.) caïman, *m.*

cease (cîce), *v.n.*, cesser, discontinuer.

cease, *v.a.*, cesser, faire cesser. — firing ! *cessez le feu !*

cease'less, *adj.*, incessant, continuel.

cease'lessly, *adv.*, sans cesse, continuellement.

ceas'ing, *n.*, cessation, *f.* Without —; *sans discontinuer.*

ce'city (cè-ci- ou cî-ci-), *n.*, cécité, *f.*

ce'dar (cî-), *n.*, cèdre, *m.* — bird ; *jaseur d'Amérique*, *m.* — wood ; *bois de cèdre*, *m.*

cede (cîde), *v.a.* and *n.*, céder.

cedil'la (ci-), *n.*, (gram.) cédille, *f.*

ce'drate (cî-dréte), *n.*, cédrat, *m.*

ce'drine (cî-), *adj.*, de cèdre.

ce'dry (cî-), *adj.*, de la couleur du cèdre.

ceil (cîle), *v.a.*, plafonner.

ceil'ing, *n.*, plafond ; plafonnage, *m.*

cel'ebrate (cèl'i-bréte), *v.a.*, célébrer.

cel'ebrated (-tède), *past part.*, célébré ; célèbre, renommé, fameux, *adj.*

celebra'tion (-bré-), *n.*, célébration ; louange, *f. ;* éloge, *m.*

cel'ebrator (-teur), *n.*, panégyriste, *m.*

celeb'rity (ci-lèb'-), *n.*, célébrité, *f.*

celer'ity (ci-lèr'-), *n.*, célérité, vitesse, *f.*

cel'ery (cèl'eur-), *n.*, céleri, *m.* Bundle of —; *botte de céleri*, *f.*

celes'tial (ci-lès-), *adj.*, céleste.

celes'tial, *n.*, habitant du ciel, esprit céleste, *m.* The —s ; *les Chinois*, *m.pl.*

celes'tially, *adv.*, d'une manière céleste.

ce'liac (cî-), *adj.*, (anat.) céliaque.

cel'ibacy (cèl'-), *n.*, célibat, *f.*

cell (cèle), *n.*, cellule, case, loge ; (of bees) alvéole, *f. ;* compartiment ; (mil.) cachot ; (lockup) violon, *m.*

cel'lar (cèl'lar), *n.*, cave, *f. ;* cellier, caveau, *m.*

cel'larage (-èdje), *n.*, caves, *f.pl. ;* (dues) cavage, droit de cave, *m.*

cellaret' (-rète), *n.*, cave à liqueurs, *f.*

celled (cèl'de), *adj.*; à cellules.

cel'lular (cèl'liou-), *adj.*, cellulaire.

Celt (kelte), *n.*, Celte, *m.f.*

Celt'ic, *adj.*, celtique.

cem'ent (cèm'-), *n.*, ciment, mastic ; cément, *m.*

cement', *v.a.*, cimenter ; cémenter ; (of jewels) mastiquer ; (fig.) consolider, fortifier.

cementa'tion (-té-), *n.*, cémentation, *f.*

cem'etery (cèm'i-tèr'i), *n.*, cimetière, *m.*

cen'atory (cèn'a-teuri), *adj.*, du, ou de, souper ; soupatoire.

cen'obite (cèn'o-baïte), *n.*, cénobite, *m.*

cenobit'ic ou **cenobit'ical**, *adj.*, (ant.) cénobitique.

cen'otaph (cèn'-), *n.*, cénotaphe, *m.*

cense (cèn'se), *n.*, (ant.) impôt, *m. ;* taxe, *f.*

cense, *v.a.*, (ant.) encenser.

cen'ser (cèn'n'-), *n.*, encensoir, *m.*

cen'sor (cè'n'-seur), *n.*, censeur, *m.*

censo'rial *ou* **censo'rian** (-sô-), *adj.*, censorial, sévère.

censo'rious (-sô-), *adj.*, de censeur ; critique, disposé à blâmer et à condamner, hargneux.

censo'riously, *adv.*, en censeur, en critique ; sévèrement.

censo'riousness, *n.*, disposition à la censure, *f. ;* manie de critiquer, *f.*

cen'sorship (-seur-), *n.*, fonctions de censeur, *f.pl. ;* censure, *f.*

cen'surable (cè'n'shiou-), *adj.*, censurable, blâmable.

cen'surably, *adv.*, d'une manière censurable.

cen'sure (cè'n'shioure), *n.*, censure, critique, *f.*, blâme, *m.*

cen'sure, *v.a.*, censurer, critiquer, blâmer.

cen'surer, *n.*, censeur ; critique, *m.*

cen'sus (cè'n'-), *n.*, recensement, dénombrement, *m.*

cent (cè'n'te), *n.*, cent, *m.* Ten per —; *dix pour cent.*

cen'taur (cè'n'-), *n.*, centaure, *m.*

cen'taury (cè'n'-), *n.*, (bot.) centaurée, érythrée, *f.*

cen'tenary (cè'n'ti-né-), *adj.*, centenaire. *n.*, centième anniversaire, centenaire, *m.*

centen'nial (cè'n'tè'n'-), *adj.*, séculaire, centennal.

centes'imal (cè'n'tèss'-), *adj.*, centésimal.

centes'imal, *n.*, centième, *m.*

cen'tigrade (cè'n'ti-grède), *adj.*, centigrade.

cen'tigramme (cè'n'ti-), *n.*, centigramme, *m.*

cen'time (cè'n'tîme), *n.*, centime, *m.*

centim'eter *ou* **cen'timetre** (cè'n'tim'i-teur), *n.*, centimètre, *m.*

centip'edal, *adj.*, centipède.

cen'tipede (cè'n'ti-pide), **cen'tiped** (-pède), *n.*, (ent.) scolopendre, *f. ;* mille-pieds, *m.*

cen'to (cè'n'tô), *n.*, centon, *m.*

cen'tral (cè'n'-), *adj.*, central.

central'ity, *n.*, état central, *m. ;* position centrale, *f.*

centraliza'tion (-tral'aïzé-), *n.*, centralisation, *f.*

cen'tralize (-'aïze), *v.a.*, centraliser.

cen'trally, *adv.*, d'une manière centrale.

center *ou* **cen'tre** (cè'n'teur), *n.*, centre, milieu, *m.* — bit; mèche anglaise, tarière, *f. ;* (in Anjou) vilebrequin, *m.* — piece ; épergne, *f.* — ottoman ; pouf, *m.* — table ; table de milieu, *f. ;* guéridon, *m.*

cen'ter, *v.a.*, placer au centre ; concentrer.

cen'ter, *v.n.*, faire centre ; se concentrer, être placé au centre ; (to rest) reposer **sur.**

cen'tric *ou* **cen'trical** (cè'n'-), *adj.*, central, placé au milieu.

cen'trically, *adv.*, dans une position centrale.

centri'city, *n.*, position centrale, *f. ;* état central, *m.*

centrif'ugal (-trif'iou-), *adj.*, centrifuge.

centrip'etal (-trip'i-), *adj.*, centripète.

centum'vir (cè'n'-teu'm'veur), *n.*, centumvir, *m.*

centum'virate (-éte), *n.*, centumvirat, *m.*

cen'tuple (-tiou-p'l), *adj.*, centuple.

cen'tuple, *v.a.*, centupler.

centu'rion (cè'n'tiou-ri-eune), *n.*, centurion, *m.*

cen'tury (cè'n'tiou-), *n.*, siècle, *m. ;* centurie, *f.*

ceph'alalgy (cèf'alal'dji), *n.*, céphalalgie, *f. ;* mal de tête, *m.*

cephal'ic (ci-), *adj.*, céphalique.

ce'rate (cî-réte), *n.*, cérat, *m.*

cere (cîre), *v.a.*, cirer ; enduire de cire.

ce'real (cî'ri-), *adj.*, céréale, *f.*

cerebel'lum (cèr'i-bèl'leume), *n.*, (anat.) cervelet, *m.*

cer'ebral (cèr'i-), *adj.*, cérébral.

cere'cloth (cîr'clôth), *n.*, toile d'embaumement, *f.*

cere'ment (cîre-), *n.*, suaire d'embaumement, *m.*

ceremo'nial (cèr'i-mô-), *adj.*, de cérémonie.

ceremo'nial, *n.*, cérémonie, étiquette, *f. ;* cérémonial, *m.*

ceremo'nially, *adv.*, suivant les cérémonies.

ceremo'nious, *adj.*, de cérémonie, cérémonieux.

ceremo'niously, *adv.*, avec cérémonie.

ceremo'niousness, *n.*, manières cérémonieuses, *f.pl.*

cer'emony (cèr'i-mo-), *n.*, cérémonie ; façon, *f. ;* cérémonial, *m.* Without —; sans façon ; sans cérémonie. To stand on, *ou* upon, —; faire des façons, des cérémonies.

cer'tain (ceur'ti'n), *adj.*, certain. A — thing; (something) une certaine chose, (a positive thing) une chose certaine. For —; pour certain ; à coup sûr. One thing is —, that ; ce qu'il y a de certain, c'est que.

cer'tainly, *adv.*, certainement.

cer'tainty, *n.*, certitude ; chose certaine, *f.* To a —; à coup sûr ; pour sûr et certain.

certif'icate (cer-tif'i-kète), *n.*, certificat ; (of a bankrupt) concordat ; (of birth, marriage, death), acte ; (copy of) extrait, *m.*

cer'tifier, *n.*, certificateur, *m.*

cer'tify (ceur-tî-faïe), *v.a.*, certifier, déclarer, notifier, donner avis à.

cer'titude (ceur-ti-tioude), *n.*, certitude, *f.*

ceru'lean (ci-rou-li-), *adj.*, bleu, azuré.

ceru'leous, *adj.*, (ant.) *V.* **ceru'lean.**

ceru'men (ci-rou-mè'ne), *n.*, cérumen, *m.*

ceru'minous, *adj.*, cérumineux.

ce'ruse (ci-rouce), *n.*, céruse, *f. ;* blanc de céruse, *m.*

cer'vical (ceur-), *adj.*, (anat.) cervical.

cesa'rean (ci-za-ri-), *adj.*, (surg.) césarienne, *adj., f.*

ces'pitous (cèss'pi-), *adj.*, de gazon.

cessa'tion (cès'sé-), *n.*, cessation, suspension, *f.*

ces'sion (cèsh'eune), *n.*, cession, *f.*

ces'sionary, *adj.*, cessionnaire.

cess'pool (cèss'poule), **cess'pit**, *n.*, puisard, *m. ;* fosse d'aisances, *f.*

ces'tus (cès-), *n.*, ceste, *m.*

ce'sure (cî-jeur), *n.* *V.* **cæsura.**

ceta'cean (ci-té-sheune), *n.*, (zoöl.) cétacé, *m.*

ceta'ceous (-sheusse), *adj.*, cétacé.

chad (shade), *n.*, alose, *f.*

chafe (tshéfe), *n.*, irritation, *f. ;* courroux, *m.*

chafe, *v.a.*, chauffer ; courroucer, irriter ; (a cable) érailler.

chafe, *v.n.*, s'écorcher, frotter ; (of cables) s'érailler, se raguer ; s'irriter ; s'enflammer.

cha'fer, *n.*, (ent.) hanneton, scarabée ; (tech.) réchaud, *m.*

cha'fery, *n.*, chaufferie, *f.*

chaff (tshafe), *n.*, menue paille ; paille hachée, (pop.) plaisanterie, raillerie, blague, *f.* — cutter; hache-paille, *m.*

chaff, *v.a.*, blaguer, berner, taquiner, gausser. You are only chaffing me ; vous ne faites que me blaguer, ou me berner ; ou ce n'est qu'une blague ce que vous me dites là.

chaf'fer, *v.n.*, barguiner, marchander.

chaf'ferer, *n.*, barguigneur, *m.*

chaf'finch (tshaf'fi'n'she), *n.*, (orni.) pinson, *m.*

chaff'ing, *adj.*, (fam.) gausseur, gouailleur.

chaff'ing, *n.*, gausserie, gouaillerie, *f.*

chaff'y, *adj.*, de paille ; plein de paille ; (fig. pers.) frivole, léger.

cha'fing (tshéf'-), *n.*, action d'échauffer, *f. ;* échauffement, *m. ;* irritation, *f.*

cha'fing-dish (-dishe), n., réchaud, m.

cha'fing-pan (-pane), n., chaufferette, f.

chagreen' (sha-grîne), n., chagrin; m., peau de chagrin, f.

chagrin' (sha-grîne), n., chagrin; dépit, m.

chagrin', v.a., chagriner, vexer.

chain (tshéne), n., chaîne, f. Gunter's —; (surveying) chaîne d'arpenteur, f. — armor; cotte de mailles, f. Albert —; chaîne de gilet, f. — cable; câble-chaîne, m. — bridge; pont suspendu, m. — gang; cadène, f. — pier; jetée suspendue, f.

chain, v.a., enchaîner, attacher avec une chaîne ou avec des chaînes, fermer par une chaîne.

chain'shot (-shote), n., boulets ramés, m.pl.; ange, m.

chair (tshère), n., chaise, f.; siège, m.; (of a professor) chaire, f.; (of the chairman or president of an assembly) fauteuil, m.; (rail) coussinet, m. Arm—; fauteuil. Bath—; vinaigrette, f. Sedan-—; chaise à porteurs, f. Easy —; bergère, f. Rocking-—; chaise berceuse, f. Deck —; chaise longue, f.; pliant, m. To be in the —; occuper le fauteuil. —! —! à l'ordre! à l'ordre! To fill the —; présider. To leave the —; lever la séance. With . . . in the —; sous la présidence de . . .

chair'-bottomer, n., rempailleur, m., rempailleuse, f.

chair'-cover, n., housse, f.; garniture de fauteuil, f.

chair'-maker (-mék'-), n., fabricant de chaises, m.

chair'man (-ma'n), n., porteur de chaise; traîneur de vinaigrette, (of an assembly) président, m.

chaise (shéze), n., chaise, f.

chalcog'rapher (kal-), n., chalcographe, m.

chalcog'raphy, n., chalcographie, f.

chal'dron (tshôl-), n., mesure de trente-six boisseaux, f.; (for coal) poids de 2,500 livres, m.

chal'ice (tshal'-), n., calice, m., coupe, f.

chal'iced (tshal'iste), adj., à calice.

chalk (tshôke), n., craie, f.; (for drawing) pastel, crayon, m. — drawing; pastel, m.

chalk, v.a., blanchir avec de la craie; marquer avec de la craie; tracer; (agri.) marner.

chalk'iness, n., nature crayeuse, f.

chalk'-pit (-pite), n., carrière de craie, f.

chalk'-stone (-stône), n., pierre à chaux, f.; petit morceau de craie; (med.) calcul arthritique, m.

chalk'y, adj., de craie, crayeux.

chal'lenge (tshal'lè'n'dje), n., cartel; défi, m.; provocation; prétention, demande; (jur.) récusation, f.; (milit.) qui-vive, m. To send a — to; envoyer ses témoins à.

chal'lenge, v.a., défier; provoquer en duel; réclamer; (jur.) récuser; sommer; (milit.) reconnaître; crier qui vive à.

chal'lenger, n., auteur d'un cartel; provocateur, aggresseur, m.; personne qui jette un défi; (jur.) personne qui récuse un juré, un jury, f.

chalyb'eate (ka-lib'i-éte), adj., ferrugineux.

chalyb'eate, n., eau ferrugineuse, f.

chamade' (sha-méde), n., (milit.) chamade, f.

cham'ber (tshé'm'-), n., chambre; (of the nose) fosse, f.; (of a mine) fourneau, m.; (artil.) chambre, âme, f.; (of pistols) barillet, m.; bureaux, m.pl., étude, f.; —ful; chambrée, chambre pleine, f. In ou at —s; (of judges) en référé. — counsel; avocat consultant, m.

cham'ber, v.a., enfermer dans une chambre.

cham'ber, v.n., libertiner; résider.

cham'bered, part. adj., chambré, à coups. Six-— revolver; révolver à six coups, m.

cham'berer, n., (l.u.) homme à intrigues, libertin, m.

cham'berlain (tshé'm'beur-line), n., chambellan; trésorier; (of the pope) camérier, m.

cham'berlainship, n., charge de chambellan, f.

cham'ber-maid (-méde), n., femme de chambre; fille de chambre, fille de service, f.

cham'ber-pot (-pote), n., pot de chambre, m.

cham'ber-practice, n., consultations, clientèle (d'avocat consultant).

chame'leon (ka-mî-li-), n., (zoöl.) caméléon, m.

chame'leonize (-'aïze), v.a., changer de couleurs comme le caméléon.

cham'fer ou **cham'fret** (tsha'm-, -frète), n., (arch.) chanfrein, m.

cham'fer, v.a., (arch.) tailler en chanfrein, chanfreiner.

cha'mois (sham'mé ou sha-moi), n., chamois, m.

cha'mois leather (-lètheur), n., chamois, m., peau de chamois, f.

cham'omile (ca-mô-maïle), n., (bot.) camomille, f.

champ (tsha'm'pe), v.a., ronger, mâcher. To — the bit; ronger le frein.

champ, v.n., ronger son frein.

champagne' (sha'm'péne), n., vin de Champagne, m. — brandy; fine champagne, m., eau-de-vie de champagne, f.

champaign' (sha'm'péne), n., campagne, f. — country; pays ouvert, m., rase campagne, f.

champaign', adj., de campagne.

champi'gnon (-pi'n'ieune), n., champignon, m.

cham'pion (tsha'm'pi'eune), n., champion, m.

cham'pion, v.a., défier au combat, provoquer; (fig.) soutenir, défendre. To — any one's cause; prendre fait et cause pour; prendre la défense de; prendre les armes pour.

cham'pionship, n., championnat, m.

chance (tshâ'n'ce), n., chance, fortune, f.; hasard, sort; (jur.) cas fortuit, m. To take one's —; courir la chance. — contest; lutte amenée par le hasard. The main —; le solide, m.

chance, v.n., arriver par hasard, venir à. To — to meet; rencontrer par hasard. To — it; risquer le paquet.

chance, adj., du hasard, par hasard, de hasard.

chance'able (-'sab'l), adj., accidentel.

chan'cel (tshâ'n'cèle), n., sanctuaire, m.

chan'cellor (tshâ'n'cèl'leur), n., chancelier, m. Lord-—; grand chancelier, m. — of the exchequer; Ministre des Finances, m.

chan'cellorship, n., charge de chancelier, f.

chan'cery (tshâ'n'ceur-), n., cour de la chancellerie, f. Master in —; maître des requêtes à la cour, m.

chan'cre (sha'gn'k'eur), n., chancre, m.

chan'crous (sha'gn'k'reusse), adj., chancreux.

chandelier (sha'n'di-lîre), n., lustre, m.

chan'dler (tsha'n'dleur), n., marchand, ou fabricant, de chandelles; petit épicier, m.

chan'dlery, n., petite épicerie, f.; regrat, m.

change (tshé'n'dje), n., changement, m.; (of moon) phase, f.; (abbreviation of exchange) bourse; (money) monnaie, f., appoint, m. To give — for; faire la monnaie de. I have no —; je n'ai pas de monnaie. For a —; pour changer. A — of linen; du linge blanc; du linge de rechange, m. On —; à la Bourse. To be a gainer ou loser by the —; gagner ou perdre au change. To ring the —s; (fig.) revenir sur, rabâcher. To — carriages; (rail.) changer de voiture. All — here! tout le monde descend! ou tout le monde change de voiture. — of life; retour d'âge, m.

change, v.a., changer; (a sentence) commuer.

change, v.n., changer de; (of the moon) se renouveler.

change'able (-'djab'l), adj., changeant, variable, inconstant.

change'ableness, n., caractère variable, m.; inconstance; mobilité, f.

change′ably, *adv.*, inconstamment, variablement ; d′une manière variable.

change′ful (-foule), *adj.*, inconstant, changeant.

change′less, *adj.*, immuable ; constant ; invariable.

change′ling, *n.*, esprit changeant ; enfant substitué, *m.*

chan′ger, *n.*, changeur, *m.*

chan′nel (tsha′n′nèle), *n.*, canal, *m. ;* rigole (of streets), *f. ;* lit (of rivers), *m. ;* passe (of harbors) ; (fig.) voie, *f. ;* moyen, *m. ;* entremise, *f.* The British — ; *la Manche, f.* The — Islands ; *les Iles de la Manche, les Iles Anglo-Normandes, f.pl.* St. George′s — ; *le canal St. Georges, m.*

chan′nel, *v.a.*, creuser ; sillonner ; (arch.) canneler.

chant (tshâ′n′te), *n.*, chant ; plain-chant, *m.*

chant, *v.a.*, chanter.

chant, *v.n.*, chanter ; chanter le plain-chant.

chant′er, *n.*, chanteur ; chantre, *m.*

chant′icleer (-ti-clîre), *n.*, réveille-matin (le coq) ; chantre du jour, ⊙chanteclair, *m.*

chant′ing, *n.*, chant ; plain-chant, *m.*

chant′ress (-trèce), *n.*, chanteuse, *f.*

cha′os (ké-oss), *n.*, chaos, *m.*

chaot′ic (ké-), *adj.*, chaotique, de chaos.

chap (tshape *ou* tshope), *n.*, homme, garçon, gaillard, compère, gars, (pop.) gosse, *m. ;* (on the hands, etc.) gerçure, crevasse, *f.* Bad — ; *mauvais garnement, m.*

chap, *v.a.*, gercer. *v.n.*, gercer, se gercer.

chape (tshépe), *n.*, chape, bouterolle, *f.*

chap′el (tshap′l), *n.*, chapelle, *f. ;* (print.) atelier, *m.* — of ease ; (*église*) *succursale, f.*

chape′less (tshép′lèsse), *adj.*, sans bouterolle.

chap′eron (chap′èr′ône), *n.*, chaperon, *m.*

chap′eron, *v.a.*, chaperonner.

chap′fallen (tshop′fôl′n), *adj.*, à mâchoire tombante ; l′oreille basse ; penaud, abattu.

chap′lain (tshap′line), *n.*, chapelain ; aumônier, *m.*

chap′laincy *ou* **chap′lainship,** *n.*, chapellenie, *f. ;* fonctions d′aumônier, *f.pl.*

chap′let (tshap′lète), *n.*, chapelet, *m. ;* guirlande ; (of a peacock) aigrette, *f.*

chap′py (tshap′- *ou* tshop′-), *adj.*, plein de gerçures.

chaps (tshopse), *n.*, gueule, *f. ;* mâchoires, *f.pl. ;* (of a vice) mâchoires d′étau, *f.pl.*

chap′ter (tshap′-), *n.*, chapitre, *m. ;* lettre capitulaire, *f.*

chap′ter, *v.a.*, chapitrer.

chap′ter-house (-haouce), *n.*, chapitre, *m.*

char (tshâr), *v.a.*, réduire en charbon, carboniser ; purifier (by heat).

char *ou* **chare** (tshar), *v.n.*, aller en journée.

char *ou* **charing** (tshar), *n.*, ouvrage à la journée, *m.*

char (tshar), *n.*, (ich.) ombre, *m.*

char′acter (kar′ak-teur), *n.*, caractère ; (state) rang ; (thea.) rôle ; personnage ; genre, *m. ;* nature, couleur, renommée, réputation, moralité, *f. ;* certificat de moralité ; (capacity) qualité ; (pers.) personnage, type ; (kind) genre, *m. ;* nature, *f.* He is quite a —; *c′est un vrai original.* Bad —; *mauvais sujet ou homme perdu de réputation, m.* A man of bad — ; *un homme de mauvaise réputation, m.* I do not like books of that —; *je n′aime pas les livres de ce genre.* What —? does he play ? *quels rôles joue-t-il ?* To go for a —; (of servants) *aller aux renseignements.* In —; *dans son rôle ; à sa place.* In the — of ; *déguisé* **en,** *dans son rôle* **de.** Out of —; *déplacé, sorti de son rôle.*

characteris′tic *ou* **characteris′tical,** *adj.*, caractéristique.

characteris′tic, *n.*, trait caractéristique, *m. ;* (gram., math.) caractéristique, *f.*

characteris′tically, *adv.*, d′une manière caractéristique.

char′acterize (-′aïze), *v.a.*, caractériser.

characteriza′tion, *n.*, action de caractériser, *f.*

char′acterless, *adj.*, sans caractère.

charade′ (sha-réde), *n.*, charade, *f.*

char′coal (tshâr′côle), *n.*, charbon de bois ; (chem.) carbone, *m.* Animal —; *noir animal, m.* — burner ; *charbonnier, m.* — dust ;*fraisil, poussier, m.* — pit ; *charbonnière, f.*

chard (tshârde), *n.*, carde, *f.*

charge (tshârdje), *n.*, charge, *f. ;* fardeau, soin ; (of a judge) résumé ; (jur.) chef d′accusation, *m.*, accusation ; (milit., vet.) charge, *f. ;* (of a bishop) mandement, *m. ;* (protection) garde, direction, *f. ;* dépôt, objet confié aux soins **de** ; (price) prix, *m. pl.*, frais, dépens, *m.pl.* To give any one in — ; *faire arrêter quelqu′un.* To take — of ; *se charger* **de.** To bring a — against ; *porter une accusation* **contre** ; *accuser.* — sheet ; *livre de police, écrou, m.*

charge, *v.a.*, charger **de** ; accuser **de** ; faire payer ; prendre, demander ; (fig.) adjurer ; ordonner **à** ; enjoindre **de** ; sommer **de** ; (of taxes) grever.

charge, *v.n.*, (milit.) charger.

charge′able, *adj.*, à charge **à** ; accusable **de** ; imputable **à** ; imposable, taxable.

char′ger, *n.*, grand plat, plateau ; cheval de bataille, *m.*

cha′rily (tshé′rili), *adv.*, avec précaution, avec circonspection ; frugalement ; chichement.

cha′riness (tshé-), *n.*, précaution, prudence, circonspection, sobriété, *f.*

char′iot (tshar′i-ote), *n.*, coupé, (antiq.) char, chariot, *m.* — race ; *course de chars, f.*

charioteer′ (-′îre), *n.*, conducteur de chariot ; (astron.) cocher, charretier, *m.*

char′itable (tshar′i-ta′b′l), *adj.*, charitable.

char′itably, *adv.*, charitablement.

char′ity, *n.*, charité, bienveillance ; (alms) aumône, bienfaisance ; œuvre de bienfaisance, *f.* — begins at home ; *charité bien ordonnée commence par soi-même.* — school ; *école gratuite, f.* To ask for —; *demander l′aumône.* Out of —; *par charité.*

char′latan (tshâr-), *n.*, charlatan, *m.*

charlatan′ic *ou* **charlatan′ical,** *adj.*, charlatanesque, de charlatan.

char′latanism *ou* **char′latanry,** *n.*, charlatanerie, *f. ;* charlatanisme, *m.*

Charles′s Wain (tshârlz′iz′wéne), *n.*, (astron.) chariot, *m.*, grande ourse, *f.*

charm (tshârme), *n.*, charme, *m.*, (trinket) breloque, *f.*

charm, *v.a.*, charmer, enchanter.

charm′er, *n.*, enchanteur, *m.*, enchanteresse, *f. ;* charmeur, *m.*, charmeuse, *f.*

charm′ing, *adj.*, enchanteur ; charmant ; joli, délicieux, ravissant.

charm′ingly, *adv.*, d′une manière charmante ; à ravir.

charm′less, *adj.*, sans charme, *m.*

char′nel (tshâr′nèle), *adj.*, de charnier.

char′nel-house (-haouce), *n.*, charnier, *m.*

chart (tshârte), *n.*, carte de géographie ; carte marine, *f.*

char′ter (tshar′-), *n.*, ⊙chartre ; charte, *f.*, acte, *m.*

char′ter, *v.a.*, instituer par une charte ; établir par un acte ; (com., nav.) fréter, affréter, noliser.

char′terer, *n.*, affréteur, *m.*

char′ter-party (-pâr′-), *n.*, charte partie, *f.*

char′-woman (tshar-woum′a′n), *n.*, femme de journée, femme de ménage, *f.*

char′-work, *n.*, ouvrage à la journée, *m.*

cha′ry (tshér′-), *adj.*, prudent ; économe ; circonspect ; soigneux ; sobre. — of words ; *sobre de paroles.*

chase (tshéce), *n.*, chasse ; poursuite ; (of cannon) volée, *f. ;* (print.) châssis, *m.*

chase, v.a., chasser ; poursuivre ; donner la chasse à ; (metal.) ciseler. — away; *faire prendre la fuite* à.

cha'ser, n., chasseur ; (metal.) ciseleur; (nav.) vaisseau chasseur, m.

chasm (kaz'm), n., brèche. f. ; vide, abîme, m.

chaste (tshéste), adj., chaste, pudique ; (of language) pur ; (of taste) de bon goût, m.

chaste'ly, adv., chastement, pudiquement.

chas'ten (tshés's'n), v.a., châtier ; réprimer; purifier.

chas'tener (tshés's'-neur), n., celui qui châtie, m.

chaste'ness (tshést'-), n., pureté de langage, f.

chas'tening, n., châtiment, m., correction, f.

chastise' (tshas'taïze), v.a., châtier.

chas'tisement, n., châtiment, m.

chasti'ser, n., personne qui châtie, f. ; châtieur, m.

chas'tity (tshas'-), n., chasteté, pureté, f.

chas'uble (tshaz'iou-b'l), n., chasuble, f.

chat (tshate), n., causerie, (pop.) causette, f., entretien ; (orni.) traquet, m. — wood; *menu bois*, m., *bourrée*, f. To have a —; *faire la causette*. To have a little — ; *faire un bout de causette*.

chat, v.n., causer ; jaser, (pop.) faire la causette.

chat'ellany (shâ'tèl'-), n., châtellenie, f.

chatoy'ant (sha-toïa'nte), adj., chatoyant.

chatoy'ment (sha-toï-), n., chatoiement, chatoîment, m.

chat'tel (tshat't'l), n., mobilier. pl., biens, effets, m.pl.

chat'ter (tshat'-); v.n., jaser, babiller ; (of the teeth) claquer.

chat'terbox (-bokse), n., babillard, m., babillarde, f. ; moulin à paroles, m.

chat'terer, n., jaseur, babillard, m.

chat'tering (tshat'-), n., jaserie, f. ; babil, caquetage ; (of the teeth) claquement, m.

chat'ty (tshat'-), adj., causeur, causant ; bavard.

chaw (tsho), v.a., mâcher. n., chique, f. V. chew.

cheap (tshîpe), adj., à bon marché ; à bon compte ; peu coûteux ; économique. Dirt —; *pour rien ; à vil prix.* To hold — ; *faire bon marché* de. To make one's self —; *se prodiguer ; se déprécier.* —-jack wares; *camelote*, f.

cheap'en, v.a., marchander; diminuer la valeur de, faire baisser le prix de.

cheap'ener, n., marchandeur, -euse, m.f.

cheap'er, adj., à meilleur marché ; à meilleur compte ; moins ; moins coûteux. — and —; *de moins en moins cher.*

cheap'ly, adv., à bon marché, à vil prix, à bon compte ; économiquement ; (expense) à peu de frais.

cheap'ness, n., bon marché, bas prix, m.

cheat (tshîte), n., (thing) fourberie, tromperie, f. ; (pers.) fourbe, trompeur, m., trompeuse, f. ; (at cards) tricheur, m., tricheuse, f.

cheat, v.a., tromper, attraper, duper ; (at cards) tricher.

cheat'ing, n., fourberie ; tromperie, filouterie, (at cards) tricherie, f.

check (tshèke), v.a., faire éprouver un échec à ; contenir, arrêter, mater, maîtriser ; réprimer; reprendre ; vérifier ; contrôler ; pointer ; (of stuffs) quadriller ; (at chess) faire échec à.

check (tshèke), n., échec, obstacle, m. ; réprimande ; (thea.) contremarque, f. ; (com.) mandat, bon, chèque, m. ; étoffe quadrillée ; toile de coton rayée, f. ; (at chess) échec, m. With —s ; à *carreaux*. To hold, or keep, in — ; *tenir en échec.*

check'-book (-bouke), n., livre de mandats, de chèques, m. ; carnet de chèques, m.

check'er, v.a., marqueter ; diaprer ; tacheter. — board ; *échiquier, damier*, m. A —ed career; *une carrière pleine de vicissitudes.*

check'er-work (-weurke), n., marqueterie, f.

check'mate (-méte), n., échec et mat, m.

check'mate, v.a., faire échec et mat à ; mater, entraver.

check'-rail, n., contre-rail.

check'-roll, n., état de maison ; (mil.) contre-appel, m.

check'string (-strigne), n., cordon de communication, m.

check'-taker (-té-), n., receveur de contremarques, m.

cheek (tshîke), n., joue ; (of a press) jumelle ; (of scales) chasse ; (of pigs) bajoue ; (of a door) feuillure ; (fig. and fam.) impudence, f. ; front, toupet, m. — by jowl; *côte à côte* ; *tête à tête* ; *dans une étroite intimité.*

cheek'-bone (-bône), n., pommette, f. To have high —s; *avoir les pommettes saillantes.* With high —s ; *aux pommettes saillantes.*

cheek'y, adj., impudent ; peu gêné.

cheer (tshîre), n., (food) chère ; acclamation, f. ; applaudissement, m. ; gaieté ; consolation, f. ; vivat, m. To be of good — ; *avoir bon courage.*

cheer, v.a., égayer, réjouir ; animer ; applaudir, acclamer.

cheer, v.n., se réjouir ; applaudir ; crier vivat. To — up ; *se ranimer ; s'égayer ; prendre courage.*

cheer'er, n., applaudisseur, acclamateur, m.

cheer'ful (-foule), adj., joyeux, gai; (prospect) riant.

cheer'fully, adv., gaiement, gaîment, joyeusement ; de bon cœur.

cheer'fulness, n., gaieté, gaîté, bonne humeur, f.

cheer'ily, adj., gaiement, gaîment.

cheer'ing, n., consolation, f. ; applaudissements, m.pl., acclamations, f.pl., vivats, hourras, m.pl.

cheer'ing, adj., consolant, réjouissant, encourageant, égayant.

cheer'less, adj., triste, sombre, morne.

cheer'y, adj., gai, joyeux, réjoui.

cheese' (tshîze), n., fromage, m. — cake; *talmouse*, f. — mold ; *moule à fromage*, m. — stand ; *porte-fromage*, m. — taster ; *sonde à fromage*, f. — knife ; *couteau à fromage.*

cheese'-curds, n.pl., caillebotte, f.

cheese'-monger (-meu'gn'gh'eur), n., marchand de fromage.

cheese'-paring (-pèr'-), n., pelure de fromage, f. — economy ; (fig.) *économie de bouts de chandelle*, f.

cheese'-rennet (-rè'n'nète), n., (bot.) gaillet, caille-lait, m.

cheese'-trade (-), n., commerce des fromages, m.

cheese'-vat (-vate), n., éclisse à fromage, f.

chees'y (tshîzi), adj., fromageux, caséeux.

chem'ical (kè'm'-), adj., chimique.

chem'ically, adv., chimiquement.

chemise' (shi-mîze), n., chemise, f.

chem'ist (kè'm'-), n., chimiste; pharmacien, m.

chem'istry (kè'm'- ou ki'm'-) n., chimie, f.

cheque (tshèke), n., (com.) bon, mandat, chèque, m. ; bulletin, m. ; contremarque, f.

chequ'er (tshèk'-), n., mosaïque ; trésorerie, f. ; trésor, m. ; *abréviation de* exchequer.

cher'ish (tshèr'-), v.a., chérir ; (of hopes) nourrir, entretenir.

cher'ry (tshèr'-), n., cerise, f. — pit; (game) *fossette*, f. — pie ; *tourte aux cerises*, f.

cher'ry, adj., de cerise, de cerisier. — -red ; *rouge cerise.*

cher'ry-brandy, n., ratafia de cerises, m.

cher'ry-cheeked (-tshîk'te), adj., aux joues vermeilles.

cher'ry-garden, **orchard**, n., cerisaie, f.

cher'ry-laurel (-lō-), *n.*, laurier-cerise, *m.*

cher'ry-stone (-stōne), *n.*, noyau de cerise, *m.*

cher'ry-tree (-trî), *n.*, cerisier, *m.*

cher'ub (tshèr'eube), *n.*, (*cherubs, cherubim*) chérubin, *m.*

cheru'bic (tshè-roub'-), *adj.*, de chérubin, angélique.

cher'ubin, *n.*, (*cherubim*). *V.* **cherub.**

cher'vil (tsheur-), *n.*, cerfeuil, *m.*

chess (tshèsse), *n.*, échecs, *m.pl.*

chess'-board (-bōrde), *n.*, échiquier, *m.*

chess'man (-ma'n), *n.*, pièce, *f.*, pion, *m.* A set of chessmen ; *un jeu d'échecs.*

ches'som (tshè's'-), *n.*, terre franche, terre végétale, terre meuble, *f.*

chess'-player (-plé-eur), *n.*, joueur d'échecs, *m.*

chest (tshèste), *n.*, caisse, *f.*, coffre, *m.; (of the body) poitrine, *f.; (of a horse) poitrail ; (milit.) caisson, *m.* — of drawers ; *commode, f.;* — protector ; *plastron hygiénique, m.*

chest, *v.a.*, encoffrer, encaisser.

chest'ed, *adj.*, à poitrine ; (of horses) à poitrail. Broad, deep — ; *à large poitrine ; au poitrail large* (of horses). Narrow — ; *à poitrine étroite.*

chest'-foundering (-faou'n'd'-), *n.*, (vet.) courbature, *f.*

chest'-foundered (-faou'n'd'eurde), *adj.*, (vet.) courbatu.

chest'nut (-neute), *n.*, châtaigne, *f.; marron, m.* That's a — ; (fig.) *c'est connu ! vieille histoire ! f., vieux conte ! m.*

chest'nut, *adj.*, (of color) châtain ; (of horses) alezan.

chest'nut-tree (-trî), *n.*, châtaignier, marronnier, *m.* — grove ; *châtaigneraie, f.*

cheval'-glass (shèv'al-glâce), *n.*, psyché, *f.*

chevalier' (-lîre), *n.*, chevalier, cavalier, *m.*

chevaux'-de-frise' (shèv-ô-de-frîze), *n.pl.,* (fort.) chevaux de frise, *m.pl.*

chev'en, *n.*, chabot, *m.*

chev'eril, *n.*, chevreau (leather). — conscience ; (fig.) *conscience élastique, f.*

chev'ron, *n.*, chevron. —-work ; *chevronnage, m.*

chew (tshiou), *v.a.*, mâcher ; ruminer. To — tobacco ; *chiquer.* To — the cud ; *ruminer.*

chew'er, *n.*, mâcheur, *m.*

chew'ing, *n.*, mastication, *f.*

chicane' (tshi-kéne), *n.*, chicane, *f.*

chicane', *v.n.*, chicaner.

chica'ner, *n.*, chicaneur, *m.*, chicaneuse, *f.*

chica'nery, *n.*, chicanerie, chicane, *f.*

chick (tshike), *n.*, poussin, poulet, *m.*, poulette, *f.* — pea ; *pois chiche, m.* — weed ; *morgeline, f.* He's no — ; *ce n'est plus un enfant, tant s'en faut.*

chick'en (tshick'ène), *n.*, poulet, *m.* Don't count your —s before they are hatched ; (fig.) *il ne faut pas vendre la peau de l'ours avant de l'avoir mis par terre, ou tué.* She's no — ; (fam.) *elle est bien sur le retour.*

chick'en-bone, *n.*, os de poulet, *m.*

chick'en-broth, *n.*, bouillon de poulet, *m.*

chick'en-coop, *n.*, poussinière, *f.*

chick'en-heart'ed (-hûrtède), *adj.*, au cœur de poule ; timide, peureux, poltron.

chick'en-pox (-pokse), *n.*, petite vérole volante, *f.*

chick'ling, *n.*, poussin, *m.*

chic'ory (tshik'-), *n.*, chicorée, *f.*

chide (tshaïde), *v.a.*, gronder, blâmer, réprimander, censurer.

chide, *v.n.*, gronder ; murmurer **contre.**

chi'der, *n.*, grondeur, *m.*, grondeuse, *f.*

chi'ding, *n.*, gronderie, *f.*

chi'dingly, *adv.*, en grondant.

chief (tshîfe), *n.*, chef, *m.; partie principale, f.; (com.) associé principal, m.*

chief, *adj.*, principal, premier ; suprême. In — ; *en chef.*

chief'dom, *n.*, souveraineté, suprématie, *f.*

chief'less, *adj.*, sans chef.

chief'ly, *adv.*, surtout, principalement.

chief'tain (-tène), *n.*, chef de clan, *m.*

chiff'chaff, *n.*, (orni.) grand pouillot, *m.*

chiffonnier' (shif-fo'n'fre), *n.*, chiffonnier, *m.*, chiffonnière, *f.*

chil'blain (tshil'bléne), *n.*, engelure, *f.*

child (tshaïlde), *n.*, (*children*) enfant, *m.f.* Good, *ou* naughty, — ; *enfant sage, méchant.* To be a good, *ou* naughty — ; *être sage, être méchant.* From a — ; *dès l'enfance.* A burnt — dreads the fire ; *chat échaudé craint l'eau froide.* To be with — ; *être enceinte, être grosse.* To get with — ; *faire un enfant à ;* (l.ex.) *engrosser.*

child'-bearing (-bèr'-), *n.*, travail d'enfant, *m.*

child'bed (-bède), *n.*, couches, *f.pl.* In — ; *en couches.*

child'birth (-beurth), *n.*, enfantement, *m.;* couches, *f.pl.*

childe (tshaïlde), *n.*, chevalier, *m.*

child'hood (-houde), *n.*, enfance, *f.*

child'ish, *adj.*, enfant, puéril, enfantin. To get, *ou* grow, — ; *tomber en enfance.*

child'ishly, *adv.*, puérilement, comme un enfant.

child'ishness, *n.*, puérilité, *f. ;* enfantillage, *m.;* seconde enfance, *f.*

child'less, *adj.*, sans enfant.

child'like (-laïke), *adj.*, comme un enfant, enfantin, puéril.

child' murder, murderer, *n.*, infanticide, *m.*

child's' play, *n.*, jeu d'enfant, *m.*, amusette, *f.*, enfantillage, *m.* It is mere — ; *ce n'est pas difficile à faire, c'est facile comme tout.*

chil'dren, *n.pl.* *V.* **child.**

chil'i (tshili), *n.*, poivre de Guinée, de Cayenne, *m.*

chill (tshile), *n.*, froid, *m.; glace, f.*, refroidissement, frisson, *m.* To take the — off ; *faire dégourdir.* Cold —s ; *frissons, n.pl.* To catch a — ; *attraper un refroidissement.*

chill, *adj.*, froid ; glacé.

chill, *v.a.*, refroidir ; glacer ; décourager.

chill'iness *ou* **chill'ness**, *n.*, froid, frisson ; (med.) frissonnement, *m.*

chil'ly, *adj.*, (pers.) frileux ; (of things) un peu froid.

Chil'tern Hund'reds (tshilteurne hun'n'-dredze), *n.*, communes de Chiltern, *f.* To accept the — — ; *donner sa démission de membre de la Chambre des Communes.*

chime (tshaïme), *n.*, carillon; accord de sons; son harmonieux, *m. ;* harmonie, *f.*

chime, *v.a.*, carillonner, mettre en mouvement.

chime, *v.n.*, s'accorder **avec** ; faire chorus.

chi'mer, *n.*, carillonneur, *m.*

chime'ra (kaï-mî-), *n.*, chimère, *f.*

chimer'ical (-mèr'i-), *adj.*, chimérique.

chimer'ically, *adv.*, chimériquement.

chim'ney (tshim'ni), *n.*, cheminée, *f.; (of a lamp) verre, m.*

chim'ney-board, *n.*, devant de cheminée, *m.*

chim'ney-corner (-cor-neur), *n.*, coin du feu, *m.*

chim'ney-cowl, *n.*, tabourin, *m.*

chim'ney-draught (-drâfte), *n.*, tirage de cheminée, *m.*

chim'ney-flue (-fliou), *n.*, tuyau de cheminée, *f.*

chim'ney-glass, *n.*, glace de cheminée, *f.*

chim'ney-piece (-pîce), *n.*, cheminée, *f.;* chambranle de cheminée, *m.*

chim'ney-pot (-pote), *n.*, mitre de cheminée, *f.*

chim'ney-stack, *n.*, corps de cheminée, *m.;*

chim′ney - sweep *ou* chim′ney - sweeper (-swîpe, -′eur), *m.*, ramoneur, *m.*

chim′ney-sweeping, *n.*, ramonage, *m.*

chim′ney-sweeping machine, *n.*, hérisson, ramon, *m.*

chin (tshi′n), *n.*, menton, *m.* —strap ; *mentonnière* ; (mil.) *jugulaire, f.*

chi′na (tshaī-), *n.*, porcelaine, *f.* —ware, stone ; *porcelaine, f.* —aster ; *reine marguerite, f.* —man ; *Chinois ; marchand de porcelaine, m.; vaisseau faisant le commerce avec la Chine.* — shop ; *magasin de porcelaine, m.* — clay ; *argile à porcelaine, f.* — ink ; *encre de Chine, f.* — painter ; *peintre sur porcelaine, m.* — painting ; *peinture sur porcelaine, f.*

chin′cough (-kôf), *n.*, coqueluche, *f.*

chine (tshaïne), *n.*, (anat.) échine ; (of pork) échinée, *f.*

Chinese′ (tshaï-nize), *adj.*, chinois. —bells ; *chapeau chinois, m.* — figure ; *chinoiserie, f.*

Chinese′, *n.*, Chinois, (language) chinois, *m.*

chink (tshign′ke), *n.*, crevasse, fente, lézarde, *f.;* (pop.) argent, *m.*, pécune, *f. ;* son, tintement, *m.*

chink, *v.a.*, crevasser, faire crevasser ; faire sonner.

chink, *v.n.*, se fendiller, se crevasser; s′ouvrir; (of metals) sonner.

chinned, *adj.*, à menton.

chink′y, *adj.*, fendu, crevassé.

chintz (tshi′n′tse), *n.*, indienne ; perse, *f.*

chip (tshipe), *n.*, copeau, fragment, éclat, *m.* — ax ; *doloire, f.* — hat, *ou* bonnet ; *chapeau latanier, m.* To be a — of the old block ; *chasser de race ou être bien le fils de son père.* It is like — in porridge ; *c′est comme un coup d′épée dans l′eau.*

chip, *v.a.*, couper, tailler, écorner ; chapeler (bread).

chip, *v.n.*, s′écorner, s′ébrécher, éclater ; s′éclater, (of china, etc.) s′écailler. To — from the shell ; *sortir de la coquille en la faisant éclater.* To — off ; *s′écailler.*

chip′ping, *n.*, fragment, éclat, *m. ;* (of bread) chapelure, *f.*

chira′gra (kaï-ré-), *n.*, (med.) chiragre, *f.*

chirol′ogy (ki-rol-o-dji), *n.*, chirologie, *f.*

chi′romancy (ki-), *n.*, chiromancie, *f.*

chi′roplast (ki-), *n.*, (piano) guide-main, *m.*

chirop′odist, *n.*, pédicure, *m.*

chirp (tsheurpe), *n.*, gazouillement, ramage; chant ; (of insects) cri, *m.*

chirp, *v.n.*, gazouiller ; (of larks) grisoller ; (of insects) crier.

chirp′er, *n.*, oiseau qui gazouille, *m.*

chirp′ing, *n.*, gazouillement, ramage ; (of insects) cri, *m.*

chis′el (tshiz′èl), *n.*, ciseau, *m.* Cold —; *ciseau à froid.*

chis′el, *v.a.*, ciseler ; (pop.) filouter, carotter, enfoncer.

chis′eling, *n.*, ciselure ; (fig.) filouterie, *f.*

chit (tshite), *n.*, germe ; (fig.) marmot, bambin, mioche, *m.* — of a girl ; *gamine, f.*

chit, *v.n.*, germer.

chit′chat (tshit′shate), *n.*, babil, caquet, *m.*, causerie, *f.*

chit′terlings (tshit′teur-lign′ze), *n.pl.*, tripes, andouilles, *f.pl.*

chiv′alrous (shiv′-), *adj.*, chevaleresque.

chiv′alry, *n.*, chevalerie, *f.*

chives, *n.pl.*, ciboulette, *f.*

chlam′ys, *n.*, chlamyde, *f.*

chlo′rate (klô-réte), *n.*, (chem.) chlorate, *m.*

chlo′ride (-ride), *n.*, (chem.) chlorure, *m.*

chlo′rine (-rine), *n.*, (chem.) chlore, *m.*

chloro′sis (klo-rô-cice), *n.*, (med.) chlorose, *f. ;* pâles couleurs, *f.pl.*

choak (tshôke), *v.a.* V. choke.

choc′olate (tshok′o-léte), *n.*, chocolat, *m.* — —

pot ; *chocolatière, f.* —-cracker; *diablotin, m.* — cake ; *tablette de chocolat, f.* — drop ; *pastille de chocolat, f.* — stick ; *bâton de chocolat, m.* — color; *couleur chocolat.* — maker ; *chocolatier, m.*

choice (tshoïce), *n.*, choix, *m. ;* élite, *f. ;* assortiment, *m.* To have Hobson′s —; *n′avoir pas de choix, avoir la main forcée.*

choice, *adj.*, rare, choisi; de choix ; d′élite; recherché; (of wines) fin.

choice′less, *adj.*, qui n′a pas de choix.

choice′ly, *adv.*, avec choix ; avec grand soin.

choice′ness, *n.*, valeur ; qualité recherchée, excellence, supériorité, *f.*

choir (kwaïeur), *n.*, chœur, *m.* — master ; *maître de chant ou de chapelle, m.*

choke (tshôke), *n.*, foin d′artichaut, *m.* —full; *tout plein ; plein comme un œuf.*

choke, *v.a.*, étouffer, suffoquer, étrangler ; engorger, boucher, — *v.n.*, s′engorger, se boucher.

choke′-damp (-da′m′pe), *n.*, air vicié, *m. ;* mofette, moufette, *f.*

choke′-pear (-père), *n.*, poire d′angoisse, *f.*

chok′ing, *n.*, étouffement, *m. ;* suffocation, *f.*, (of things) engorgement, *m.*

chok′y, *adj.*, étouffant, suffoquant.

chol′er (kol′eure), *n.*, bile ; colère, *f.*

chol′era (kol′eur′a), *n.*, (med.) choléra, *m.* —-morbus ; *choléra-morbus, m.*

chol′eric (kol′eur′-), *adj.*, cholérique, bilieux ; de colère; colérique, irascible.

chol′erine (kol′eur′-), *n.*, cholérine, *f. ;* faux choléra, *m.*

choose (tshouze), *v.a.n.*, (preterit, Chose ; past part., Chosen) choisir; élire ; préférer ; vouloir ; se décider à. I — to do it ; *il me plaît de le faire.*

choos′er, *n.*, personne qui choisit, *m.*

choos′ing, *n.*, choix, *m.*

chop (tshope), *n.*, tranche, *f. ;* (tech.) mâchoires, *f. pl.*, (of an animal) gueule, *f.* The —s of the Channel ; *l′embouchure (f.)*, ou *les approches (f. pl.)*, de la Manche. To lick one′s —s ; *se lécher les babines.* Mutton —; *côtelette de mouton, f.*

chop, *v.a.*, couper ; hacher ; trafiquer, troquer, échanger. To — off ; *trancher, couper.* To — up; *hacher menu.* To — logic ; *ergoter, disputailler.* Let not the counsel — with the judge ; *que l′avocat ne se chamaille pas, ne dispute pas, avec le juge.*

chop, *v.n.*, trafiquer, troquer ; (nav.) (of the wind) tourner, sauter, changer ; (of the sea) clapoter.

chop′-fallen (-fôl′n), *adj.*, à mâchoire tombante ; l′oreille basse; démonté, abattu, penaud. *V.* chap-fallen.

chop′-house (-haouce), *n.*, café restaurant, *m.*

chopped, *part.*, coupé à l′emporte-pièce.

chop′per, *n.*, couperet, *m.*, hachette, *f.*

chop′ping, *n.*, coupe, action de couper, *f. ;* (nav.) clapotage, *m.* — board ; *hachoir, ais, m.* — block ; *billot, m.*

chop′ping-knife (-naïfe), *n.*, couperet, *m.*, hachette, *f.*

chop′py, *adj.*, crevassé; (of the sea) houleux, clapoteux.

chop′stick, *n.*, baguette, aiguille, *f.*, bâtonnets, *m.pl.*

cho′ral (kô-), *adj.*, en chœur, de chœur.

chord (corde), *n.*, corde, *f. ;* (mus.) accord, *m.*

chord, *v.a.*, mettre des cordes à.

chor′ister (kor′-), *n.*, chantre, choriste, *m.*

chorog′raphy (ko-), *n.*, chorographie, *f.*

cho′rus (kô-reusse), *n.*, chœur, concert ; refrain, *m.*

chose, cho′sen (tshôze, -z′n). *V.* choose.

chrism (kriz′m), *n.*, chrême, *m.*

Christ (kraïste), *n.*, le Christ, *m.*

christ′en (kris′s′n), *v.a.*, baptiser.

Christ′endom (kris′s′n′deume), *n.*, chrétienté, *f.*

christ'ening, n., baptême, m.
Christ'ian (krist'-), adj., chrétien.
Christ'ian, n., chrétien, m., chrétienne. —
brethren ; *frères de la doctrine chrétienne*, m.pl.
— brother, sister ; *frère, sœur en Jésus Christ.*
— name ; *nom de baptême*, m.
Christian'ity, n., christianisme, m.
Chris'tianize (-'aïze), v.a., christianiser.
Chris'tianly, adj., chrétien.
Chris'tianly, adv., chrétiennement, en chrétien.
Christ'mas (kris'meusse), n., Noël, m., la fête de Noël ; la Noël, f. — carol ; *chant*, ou *cantique, de Noël*, m. — eve; *la veille de Noël*, f.
Christ'mas-box (-bokse), n., étrennes,f.pl.
Christ'mas-card, n., carte du jour de l'an, f.
Christ'mas-gift, n., cadeau du jour de l'an, m.
Christ'mas-holidays, n., fêtes de Noël ; vacances de Noël, f.pl.
Christ'mas-log, n., bûche de Noël, f.
Christ'mas-party, n., réunion de Noël, f.
chromat'ic (kro-), adj., chromatique.
chron'ic ou **chron'ical** (kro-), adj., chronique.
chron'icle (kro'n'-), n., chronique, f.
chron'icle, v.a., faire la chronique de, enregistrer, raconer, consigner.
chron'icler, n., chroniqueur, m.
chronol'oger ou **chronol'ogist** (-djeur, -djiste), n., chronologiste, m.
chronolog'ic ou **chronolog'ical** (kro'n'olodjik, -cal), adj., chronologique.
chronolog'ically, adv., chronologiquement.
chronol'ogy, n., chronologie, f.
chronom'eter (kro-no'm'i-), n., chronomètre, m. ; montre marine, f.
chrys'alis (kriss'-), n., (*chrysalides*) chrysalide, f.
chrys'olite (kriss'o-laïte), n., chrysolithe, f.
chub (tsheube), n., (ich.) chabot ; meunier, m.
chubbed (tsheub'de), adj., à grosse tête.
chub'by (tsheub'bi), adj., joufflu ; dodu ; (of the hands) potelé.
chuck (tsheuke), n., gloussement ; (term of endearment) poulet, m., poulette ; petite tape sous le menton, f.
chuck (tsheuke), v.n., (of the cock) appeler ; (of the hen) glousser.
chuck, v.a., donner des petits coups sous le menton à ; caresser; jeter.
chuck'-farthing (-fâr-*thi*gne), n., fossette, f.
chuc'kle (tsheuk'k'l), v.n., rire ; rire tout bas de ; rire sous cape de; ricaner. To — over ; *faire des gorges chaudes de.*
chuc'kle, v.a., (of the hen) appeler, glousser ; caresser.
chuc'kle, n., rire étouffé, ricanement, m.
chuff (tsheufe), n., butor, gros rustre, m.
chuf'fily, adv., en butor, grossièrement.
chuf'finess, n., grossièreté, rusticité,.f.
chuff'y, adj., grossier, rustique.
chum (tsheume), m., camarade de chambre, intime, inséparable, copain, m.
chum, v.n., être camarades de chambre. To — with; *être bien* avec ; *s'accorder* avec ; *s'entendre* avec.
chump (tsheu'm'pe), n., tronçon de bois, m. — end ; *bas de gigot*, m. — chop ; *côtelette de gigot*, f.
church (tsheurtshe), n., église, f., office ; (protestants) temple, m. — clerk ; *chantre*, m.
church, v.a., célébrer l'office des relevailles.
church-goer, n., qui va à l'église, qui fréquente les églises. Regular —; *pilier d'église*, m.
church'ing, n., relevailles, f.pl.
church' law, n., droit canon, m.
church'man (-ma'n), n., homme d'église ; anglican, m.
church'-music, n., plain-chant, m.
church'-rate (-réte) ou **church'-tax** (-takse), n., taxe pour l'entretien de l'église, f.

church'-service, n., (time) office, service divin, (book) paroissien, m.
church'-warden (-wŏr-d'n), n., marguillier, m. —'s pew ; *banc de l'œuvre, banc d'œuvre*, m.
church'yard (-yârde), n., cimetière, m. — cough ; *toux qui sent le sapin, toux de renard*, f.
churl (tsheurle), n., paysan, rustre, manant ; ladre, avare, m.
churl'ish, adj., grossier, rude ; dur, ladre, avare.
churl'ishly, adv., grossièrement ; rudement, durement.
churl'ishness, n., grossièreté, dureté, f.
churn (tsheurne), n., baratte, f.
churn, v.a., baratter, battre.
chyle (kaïle), n., chyle, m.
chylifac'tion (kaïl'i-fak-), n., chylification, f.
chyme (kaïme), n., chyme, m.
chym'ist (kim'-). V. **chemist**.
cibo'rium, n., ciboire, m.
cic'atrice ou **cic'atrix**, n., (*cicatrices*) cicatrice, f.
cic'atrize (-traïze), v.a. and n., cicatriser ; se cicatriser.
cicero'ne (tshī-tsheur'ô-nè), n., cicérone, m.
ci'der (çaï-), n., cidre, n. Strong — ; *gros cidre.* New — ; *cidre doux.* — mill ; *pressoir à pommes*, m.
ci'der-maker, n., fabricant de cidre, m.
ci'der-kin (-kine), n., petit cidre, m.
cigar', n., cigare, m. — ash ; *cendre de cigares*, f. — box ; *boîte à cigares*, f. — case ; *porte-cigares*, m. — cutter ; *coupe-cigares*, m. — holder ; *brûle* ou *fume-cigare*, m. — stand ; *porte-cigares*, m. — end; *bout de cigare*, m. — shop ; *bureau* ou *débit de tabac*, m.
cigarette', cigarette, f. — holder ; *fume* ou *brûle-cigarette*, m. — paper ; *papier à cigarettes*, m.
cil'iated ('-ède), adj., (bot.) cilié.
cim'eter (sim'i-teur), n., cimeterre, m.
cinc'ture (ci'nkt'ieur), n., ceinture, f.
cin'der, n., cendre ; (of coal) escarbille, f., fraisil, m. — pail ; *étouffoir*, m.
cin'erary (-'eur'é-), adj., cinéraire.
cinera'tion (-'eur'é-), n., cinération, f.
cin'nabar, n., cinabre, m.
cin'namon, n., cannelle, f.
cinque (cign'ke), n., (at cards) cinq, m.
cinque'-foil (-foïl), n., (bot.) quintefeuille ; potentille, f.
cinque'-ports (-pôrtse), n.pl., cinq ports, m.pl. Warden of the —; *gouverneur des cinq ports*, m.
cinque'-spotted (-tède), adj., à cinq taches.
ci'pher (saï-), n., chiffre ; zéro; (fig.) homme nul, m. ; nullité, f. — key ; *clé de chiffre*, m. In —; *en chiffre.* He is a mere — ; *c'est tout simplement une nullité que cet homme là.*
ci'pher, v.a., chiffrer ; écrire en chiffre.
ci'pher, v.n., (pop.) chiffrer ; calculer.
ci'phering, n., calcul, m. ; arithmétique, f.
ci'phering-book (-bouke), n., cahier d'arithmétique, m.
circe'an (seur-cî-), adj., de Circée.
cir'cinate (-néte), v.a., (l.u.) faire un cercle.
cir'cle (ceur'k'l), n., cercle ; (log.) cercle vicieux, m. Dress —; (theat.) *premières*, f.pl.
cir'cle, v.a., entourer de ; environner de ; ceindre de.
cir'cle, v.n., former un cercle ; faire le tour ; se mouvoir autour de ; tournoyer.
cir'cled (-k'lde), adj., circulaire, en cercle ; en forme de cercle.
cir'clet (-clète), n., petit cercle, anneau, m.
cir'cling, adj., circulaire, tournoyant ; environnant.
cir'cuit (ceur-kite), n., circuit ; tour, m. ; circonférence; (of the judges) tournée, f. On —; *en tournée.*

circu'itous (ceur-kiou-i-), *adj.*, détourné, sinueux.

circu'itously, *adv.*, d'une manière détournée, par des détours.

circu'ity (ceur-kiou-i-), *n.*, circuit, *m.* ; (of words) circonlocution, *f.*, détours, *m.pl.*

cir'cular (ceur-kiou-), *adj.*, circulaire ; de ceinture ; (of bills of exchange) indirect.

cir'cular, *n.*, circulaire, *f.*, bulletin, *m.* — note *ou* ticket ; *billet circulaire, m.* — railway; *chemin de fer de ceinture, m.*

circular'ity, *n.*, forme circulaire, *f.*

cir'cularly, *adv.*, circulairement ; par circulation.

cir'culate, *v.a.*, mettre en circulation, faire circuler, répandre.

cir'culate, *v.n.*, circuler.

cir'culating, *adj.* — decimal ; *fraction périodique, f.* — medium ; *monnaie légale d'un pays, f.* — library ; *cabinet de lecture, m.*

circula'tion (-lé-), *n.*, circulation, *f.*

cir'culatory (-teu-ri), *adj.*, circulaire ; circulatoire.

circumam'bient, *adj.*, environnant ; ambiant.

cir'cumcise (-saïze), *v.a.*, circoncire.

circumci'sion (-keu'm'si-jeune), *n.*, circoncision, *f.*

circum'ference(ceur-keu'm'feur'-), *n.*, circonférence, *f.*

circumferen'tor (-teur), *n.*, boussole d'arpenteur, *f.*

cir'cumflex (-flèkse), *adj.*, circonflexe.

cir'cumflex, *n.*, (gram.) circonflexe, accent circonflexe, *m.*

circum'fluent *ou* **circum'fluous** (-fliou-), *adj.*, qui coule autour ; environnant.

circumfuse' (-fiouze), *v.a.*, répandre autour ; disperser.

circumfu'sion (-fiou-jeune), *n.*, action de répandre ; expansion, *f.*

circumja'cent (-keu'm'djé-), *adj.*, circonvoisin, circonjacent.

circumlocu'tion (-kiou-), *n.*, circonlocution, *f.*

circumnav'igable, *adj.*, dont on peut faire le tour en naviguant.

circumnav'igate, *v.a.*, naviguer autour de, faire le tour de ; contourner.

circumnaviga'tion (-ghé-), *n.*, circumnavigation, *f.*

circumscribe' (-scraïbe), *v.a.*, circonscrire.

circumscrip'tion, *n.*, circonscription, *f.*

circumscrip'tive, *adj.*, circonscrit.

circumscrip'tively, *adv.*, d'une manière circonscrite.

cir'cumspect, *adj.*, circonspect, mesuré.

circumspec'tion, *n.*, circonspection, *f.*

circumspec'tive, *adj.*, circonspect.

cir'cumspectly, *adv.*, avec circonspection.

cir'cumstance, *n.*, circonstance, *f.* ; détail, état, *m.* *pl.*, moyens, *m.pl.* ; position, *f.* In straitened —s ; *gêné dans ses affaires, dans la gêne. Under any* —s ; *dans tous les cas. Under no* —s ; *en aucun cas, sous aucun prétexte.* To be in good, *ou* bad, —s ; *être bien, ou mal, dans ses affaires.* To be in easy —s ; *être dans l'aisance.*

circumstance, *v.a.*, placer. As I was —d ; *dans la position où je me trouvais.* They are so —d that . . . ; *il sont dans une position telle que . . .*

circumstan'tial (-sta'n'shal), *adj.*, des circonstances ; circonstancié, minutieux; (evidence) indirect, par induction.

circumstan'tially, *adv.*, suivant les circonstances.

circumstan'tiate (-shi-éte), *v.a.*, circonstancier.

circumvalla'tion (-val'lé-), *n.*, circonvallation, *f.*

circumvent' (-vè'n'te), *v.a.*, circonvenir.

circumven'tion, *n.*, circonvention, *f.*

circumvest' (-vèste), *v.a.*, envelopper.

circumvolu'tion (-liou-), *n.*, circonvolution, *f.*

cir'cus (ceur-keusse), *n.*, cirque; (of streets) rond-point, *m.* — girl ; *écuyère, f.*

cir'rus, *n.*, (bot.) cirre (a tendril); (of clouds) cirrus, *m.*

cisal'pine (ciss'al-païne), *adj.*, cisalpin.

cist, *n.*, ciste ; boîte, caisse, *f.* ; sac, *m.*

cist'ed, *adj.*, enkysté.

cis'tern (-teurne), *n.*, citerne ; fontaine ; (of barometers) cuvette, *f.* ; (of pumps and steam engines) réservoir, *m.*

cis'tus, *n.*, (bot.) ciste, *m.*

cit, *n.*, bon bourgeois, badaud, *m.*

cit'adel, *n.*, citadelle, *f.*

cita'tion (-té-), *n.*, citation, *f.*

cite (caïte), *v.a.*, citer; astreindre à; sommer de.

ci'ter, *n.*, citateur, *m.*

cith'ara, *n.*, cithare, *f.*

cit'icism, *n.*, manières bourgeoises, *f.pl.*

cit'izen (cit'i-z'n), *n.*, citoyen, bourgeois; habitant, *m.*, habitante, *f.* Fellow —; *concitoyen, m.* —like, *adj.*, bourgeois.

cit'izenship, *n.*, droit de cité, droit de bourgeoisie, *m.*

cit'rine (-'raïne), *adj.*, citrin.

cit'ron (-'reune), *n.*, citron, *m.* — tree; *citronnier, m.*

cit'rul (-'reule), *n.*, (l.u.) citrouille, *f.*, potiron, *m.*

cit'y, *n.*, ville; cité; (commercial part) la cité, *f.* — article (newspapers), *bulletin financier, m.* — intelligence ; *compte rendu de la Bourse, m.* ; *revue de la Bourse, f.*

civ'et (-'ète), *n.*, civette, *f.*

civ'ic, *adj.*, civique.

civ'il, *adj.*, civil, municipal ; honnête, poli. —service examination ; *concours d'admission aux emplois civils, m.*

civil'ian, *n.*, légiste en droit civil ; étudiant en droit civil ; bourgeois, civil, *m.*

civil'ity, *n.*, civilité, honnêteté, politesse, *f.*

civiliza'tion (-aïzé-), *n.*, civilisation, *f.*

civ'ilize (-aïze), *v.a.*, civiliser.

civ'ilizer, *n.*, civilisateur, *m.*, civilisatrice, *f.*

civ'illy, *adv.*, civilement, honnêtement, poliment.

clack, *n.*, caquet ; (of a mill) claquet, *m.*

clack, *v.a.*, caqueter ; (of a mill) cliqueter.

clack'ing, *n.*, caquetage, *m.*

clad. *V.* **clothe.** Iron — ; *navire cuirassé, m.*

claim (cléme), *n.*, demande, prétention, *f.* ; titre, droit, *m.* ; (jur.) réclamation, *f.* To lay — to ; *prétendre à* ; *faire valoir ses droits à, revendiquer.*

claim, *v.a.*, demander ; réclamer ; prétendre à, avoir la prétention de.

claim'able, *adj.*, qu'on peut réclamer ; réclamable.

claim'ant (clém'-), *n.*, réclamateur, prétendant ; ayant droit, *m.*

claim'er, *n.* *V.* **claim'ant.**

clam, *n.*, (mollusque) peigne, *m.* ; clovisse, *f.* *v.a.*, engluer, poisser. *v.n.*, s'attacher **sur**, adhérer à.

clam'ber (cla'm'-beur), *v.n.*, grimper **sur** *ou* **à.**

clam'miness, *n.*, viscosité, (of the hands) moiteur, *f.*

clam'my, *adj.*, visqueux, gluant ; pâteux ; (of the hands) humide, moite.

clam'orous, *adj.*, bruyant, tumultueux; criard.

clam'orously, *adv.*, bruyamment, à grands cris.

clam'or (clam'eur), *n.*, clameur, *f.* ; bruit, *m.*

clam'or, *v.n.*, crier, vociférer. To — against; *crier* **contre**, *se récrier* **contre.** To — for ; *demander à grands cris.*

clamp, *n.*, crampon, *m.* ; (carp.) emboîture, *f.*, tas de briques ; (fig.) pas lourd, *m.*

clamp, *v.a.*, (carp.) emboîter, (nav.) acclamper.

clan (cla'n), *n.*, clan, *m.* ; troupe, clique, coterie, *f.*

clandes'tine, *adj.*, clandestin.

clandes'tinely, *adv.*, clandestinement.

clandes'tineness, *n.*, clandestinité, *f.*

clang, *n.*, cliquetis, *m.*

clang, *v.a. and n.*, faire résonner ; résonner. To — out ; *faire résonner.*

clang'orous, *adj.*, aigu, perçant, résonnant.

clank, *n.*, cliquetis, son aigu, cri perçant, *m.*

clank, *v.a.*, faire résonner.

clan'nish, *adj.*, de clan ; étroitement uni.

clan'nishness, *n.*, union étroite, *f.*

clan'ship, *n.*, esprit de famille, *m.* ; union étroite; autorité sous un clan, *f.* To claim — with ; *se dire du même clan que.*

clans'man (cla'n'z'ma'n), *n.*, membre d'un clan, *m.*

clap, *n.*, coup, *m.* ; claque ; (med.) blennorrhée, *f.* ; battement de mains ; (of thunder) coup, *m.* — trap; *coup de théâtre, m.; chose à effet,réclame, f. adj.*, à effet, à sensation.

clap, *v.a.*, frapper, battre, fermer (the hands, the wings) applaudir; claquer; flanquer, fourrer, mettre. To — one's sides ; *se battre les flancs.* To — up; *enfermer, claquemurer ;* (fig.) *bâcler.* To — down; (windows) *fermer avec bruit.* To — together ; *mettre ensemble.* To — the handcuffs on ; *appliquer, ou mettre, les menottes à.*

clap, *v.n.*, faire résonner ; claquer des mains, battre des mains ; (of birds) battre des ailes.

clap'per, *n.*, claqueur ; (of a bell) battant ; (of a mill) claquet, *m.*

clap'per-claw (-clô), *v.a.*, se battre du bec et des ongles ; (fig.) gronder; injurier, vilipender.

clap'per-clawing, *n.*, bataille à coups de langue, *f.*

clare'-obscure' (clèr'obs-kioure), *n.*, (paint.) clair-obscur, *m.*

claret (-'ète), *n.*, bordeaux, vin de Bordeaux, *m.* — jug ; *carafe à bordeaux, f.*

clarifica'tion (-ké-), *n.*, clarification, *f.*

clar'ify (-faïe), *v.n.*, se clarifier.

clar'ify, *v.a.*, clarifier.

clar'ion, *n.*, clairon, *m.*

clar'y (clè-), *n.*, (bot.) orvale, toute-bonne, *f.*

clash, *n.*, fracas, coup, choc, cliquetis (of arms); conflit, *m.* ; opposition, *f.*

clash, *v.n.*, résonner, se heurter, s'entre-choquer ; être aux prises ; être en opposition, en conflit **avec** ; être en désaccord **avec.** To — with ; *aller à l'encontre de ; s'opposer à.*

clash, *v.a.*, faire résonner (en frappant); (glasses) choquer ; heurter.

clasp, *n.*, fermoir, *m.* ; agrafe, *f.* ; cadenas ; embrassement, *m.* ; étreinte, *f.*

clasp, *v.a.*, fermer avec un fermoir ; agrafer; cadenasser; serrer; presser; enlacer. To — any one round the neck ; *sauter ou se jeter au cou de quelqu'un.* To — one's hands; *joindre les mains.* With clasped hands; *les mains jointes.*

clasp'er, *n.*, (bot.) vrille, main, *f.*

class, *n.*, classe, catégorie, *f.* ; cours; genre, *m.* —room ; *classe, f.* — book; *livre de classe, m.* —mate ; *camarade de classe, m.*

class, *v.a.*, classer.

clas'sic, *n.*, classique, *m.*

clas'sic *ou* **clas'sical**, *adj.*, classique.

clas'sically *adv.*, d'une manière classique.

classif'ic, *adj.*, par classes.

classifica'tion (-ké-), *n.*, classification, *f.*

clas'sify (-faïe), *v.a.*, classifier.

class'ing, *n.*, classement, *m.*

clat'ter, *n.*, bruit, tapage, fracas, tintamarre; claquetage, babillage, *m.*

clat'ter, *v.n.*, faire du bruit ; claquer ; re-tentir ; résonner ; (talk) caqueter.

clat'terer, *n.*, tapageur ; babillard, *m.*

clat'tering, *n.*, bruit, fracas, *m.*

clause (clôze), *n.*, clause, *f.* ; (gram.) membre de phrase, *m.*, proposition, *f.*

claus'tral, *adj.*, claustral.

cla'vate (clé-véte), *adj.*, (bot.) claviforme.

clava'tion (-vé-), *n.*, (anat.) gomphose, *f.*

clav'icle (-'k'l), *n.*, (anat.) clavicule, *f.*

cla'vus, *n.*, (bot.) ergot (disease of rye, etc.). (med.) cor (on the feet), *m.*

claw (clô), *n.*, griffe, *f.* ; (bot., zoöl.) ongle, *m.* ; (of crabs) pince, *f.* ; (of a bench) valet ; (of a hammer) pied de biche, *m.* — foot; *pied de griffon, m.* — hammer; *marteau à dent, m.*

claw, *v.a.*, tirer, égratigner, déchirer avec les griffes; mettre en pièces, déchirer ; railler, gronder ; (fig., ant.) flatter ; gratter, chatouiller ; (nav.) faire, courir des bordées à, louvoyer. To — off ; *déchirer.*

clawed (clô'd), *adj.*, armé de griffes.

claw'less, *adj.*, sans griffe.

clay (clè), *n.*, argile; boue, terre glaise, glaise, *f.* ; limon, *m.* Baked — ; *terre cuite, f.* — pipe; *pipe en terre ;* (pop.) *bouffarde, f.*

clay, *v.a.*, glaiser, (agri.) glaiser, marner; (sugar) terrer.

clay'-cold (-côlde), *adj.*, glacé, froid comme l'argile ; sans vie ; mort.

clay'ey (clé-i), *adj.*, argileux.

clay'ing, *n.*, (sugar-making) terrage; (mas.) corroi, *m.*

clay'ing-house (-haouce), *n.*, étuve à sucre, *f.*

clay'-land, *m.*, terre argileuse, *f.*

clay'-marl, *n.*, marne argileuse, *f.*

clay'more, *n.*, claymore, *f.*

clay'-pit, *n.*, argilière, marnière, *f.*

clay'-slate (-sléte), *n.*, schiste argileux, *m.*

clay'-soil, *n.*, sol argileux, *m.*

clean (clîne), *adj.*, propre ; (of shoes) ciré; (of linen) blanc ; (print.) (of proofs) peu chargé ; (fig.) adroit ; net ; droit, raide. — bill of health; *patente nette, f.* — hands; *mains propres ;* (fig.) *mains nettes, f.pl.*

clean, *adv.*, heureusement, adroitement, entièrement, tout à fait ; droit, raide.

clean, *v.a.*, nettoyer ; (sewers, canals, etc.) curer ; (of shoes) décrotter, cirer ; (chem.) décaper ; (manu.) dégraisser.

clean'able, *adj.*, nettoyable.

clean'er, *n.*, nettoyeur, -euse ; (of boots) décrotteur ; dégraisseur ; (of sewers) écureur, *m.*

clean'ing, *n.*, nettoyage, *m.* ; (of sewers, canals) curage; (manu.)dégraissage;(chem.)décapage,*m.*

clean'liness, *n.*, propreté ; netteté,*f.*

clean'ly, *adj.*, propre ; pur.

clean'ly, *adv.*, proprement, nettement.

clean'ness, *n.*, propreté, pureté, innocence ; (fig.) netteté, justesse, pureté, *f.*

cleans'able, *adj.*, nettoyable.

cleanse (clè'n'ze), *v.a.*, nettoyer ; laver; (sewers, canals) curer ; (fig.) purifier. To — the blood ; *purifier le sang.*

cleans'er, *n.*, chose qui nettoie, *f.* ; détersif, (of sewers, canals, etc.) cureur ; (med.) abstergent, *m.*

cleans'ing, *n.*, nettoyage, *m.* ; (fig.) purification, *f.* ; (of sewers, canals) curement, *m.*

clear, *adj.*, clair ; net, évident ; sûr; innocent; sans tache ; (arch.) dans l'œuvre. — of ; *exempt* **de.** To keep — of ; *ne pas se heurter* **contre**, *ne pas s'approcher* **de** ; *se tenir à distance* **de**, *éloigné* **de** ; *éviter.* To get — of; *se tirer d'affaire.* To get — of; *se débarrasser* **de**, *sortir* **de**, *se justifier* **de.** To make — ; *rendre clair.* To steer — of ; *éviter.* To keep — ; (streets) *faire la police des rues.*

clear, *adv.*, clair; net.

clear, *v.a.*, éclaircir ; clarifier ; faire évacuer ; gagner ; (agri.) défricher ; (nav.) parer, dégager. To — a hedge ; *franchir une haie.* To — the

customs; *acquitter les droits de douane.* To —
from ; *dégager* de; *débarrasser* de. To — of ;
purger de; *acquitter* de. To — a good deal of
money ; *gagner beaucoup d'argent.* To — the
table ; *desservir.* To — one's brow ; *se dérider
le front.* To —; (letter boxes) *faire la levée* de.
To — for action ; (nav.) *faire branle-bas de combat.* To — away ; (of obstructions) *déblayer,
ouvrir un chemin.* To — a cape ; *doubler un
cap.* The streets were —ed by the musketry
fire ; *les rues furent balayées par la fusillade.*
To — out ; *se retirer.* To — off ; *s'en aller.* To —
up accounts; (com.) *liquider.* To — the customs;
passer (quelque chose) en douane. To — goods ;
acquitter les droits de. To — one's self ; *se réhabiliter ; faire reconnaître son innocence.*

clear, *v.n.,* s'éclaircir, se rasséréner ; se dissiper. To — up; (of the weather) *s'éclaircir ; se
rasséréner, se remettre ;* (fig.) *s'éclaircir, se débrouiller.* To — away; *desservir.* To — off *ou*
out ; *filer, décamper.* It is —ing up ; *le temps
s'éclaircit ou se remet.*

clear'ance, *n.,* dégagement ; (of rubbish, etc.)
déblaiement ; (nav.) congé ; (com.) solde, *m.;* liquidation, *f.* — sale ; *solde,* m.; *liquidation,f.*

clear'-headed (-hèdède), *adj.,* qui a l'esprit
clair ; à l'esprit clair; qui a la tête libre.

clear'ing, *n.,* éclaircissement, débrouillement,
acquittement (of land), défrichement, déblaiement, *m.;* (of letter boxes) levée ; (in woods)
éclaircie, *f. ;* (of rubbish) déblaiement; (of profits) clair et net, *m.* — out ; *enlèvement, m. ;
rafle, f.* — up; *éclaircissement, m.*

clear'ing-house, *n.,* (rail.) bureau central ;
(of banks) comptoir de règlement, *m.*

clear'ly, *adv.,* avec clarté, bien ; nettement ;
clairement ; évidemment.

clear'ness, *n.,* clarté; netteté; pureté, *f.*

clear'-sighted (-saït'ède), *adj.,* clairvoyant.

clear-sight'edness, *n.,* clairvoyance, *f.*

clear'-starch (-stärtshe), *v.a.,* blanchir à
neuf ; empeser.

clear'-starcher, *n.,* blanchisseur de fin, *m.,*
blanchisseuse de fin, *f.*

clear'-starching, blanchissage de fin *ou* à
neuf.

cleat (clîte), *n.,* (nav.) taquet, *m.*

cleav'able, *adj.,* clivable, qui peut se fendre.

cleav'age (clî'vêdje), *n.,* fendage, *m. ;* (min.)
fente, *f. ;* clivage, *m.*

cleave, *v.a.* and *n.,* (*preterit,* Clove, Cleft;
past part., Cloven, Cleft) fendre, diviser ; se
fendre ; se coller à; (fig.) s'attacher à, s'unir à.

cleav'er, *n.,* (pers.) fendeur ; (thing) couperet,
fendoir, merlin, *m.*

cleav'ers (clî-veurze), *n.,* (bot.) gaillet, caille-
lait, grateron, *m.*

cleav'ing, *n.,* fendage, (fig.) attachement, *m.*

clef (clèfe), *n.,* (mus.) clef, clé, *f.*

cleft (clèfte), *n.,* fente; ouverture, crevasse,*f.*

clem'ency (clè'm'è'n'-), *n.,* clémence; (of the
weather) douceur, *f.*

clem'ent (clè'm'èn'te), *adj.,* doux, clément.

clep'sydra (clèp'-), *n.,* clepsydre, *f.*

cler'gy (cleur'djî), *n.,* clergé, *m.*

cler'gyman, *n.,* ecclésiastique ; (c.rel.) prêtre, abbé; (protestant) ministre, pasteur, *m.*

cler'ical (clèr'-), *adj.,* clérical.

cler'ically, *adv.,* cléricalement.

clerk (clärke *ou* cleurke), *n.,* (of lawyers and
churches) clerc ; (com.) commis ; (in public
offices) employé, comptable ; (of law courts)
greffier, *m.* Managing —; *premier commis.*
Senior, chief —; *chef de bureau, m.* Lawyers'
—; *clerc d'avoué.*

clerk'ship, *n.,* secrétariat, *m. ;* place de clerc,
place de commis, *f.*

clev'er (clèv'-), *adj.,* adroit, habile, ingénieux ;
savant, spirituel ; bien écrit, bien exécuté. To
be — at ; *être fort en.*

clev'erly, *adv.,* habilement, adroitement.

clev'erness, *n.,* habileté, adresse, *f.,* savoir,
m.; intelligence, *f.;* moyens, *m.pl.*

clew (cliou), *n.,* peloton de fil; peloton; fil,
guide; (nav.) point de voile, *m.*

clew (cliou), *v.a.,* (nav.) carguer.

click, *v.n.,* faire tic-tac ; (print.) mettre en
pages.

click'er, *n.,* (print.) metteur en pages ; (man.)
cheval qui forge; (shoes) coupeur, cordonnier, *m.*

click'ing, *n.,* (print.) mise en pages, *f. ;* tic-
tac, *m.*

cli'ent (claïe'n'te), *n.,* client, *m. ;* cliente, *f.*
pl., clientèle, *f.*

cliff, *n.,* falaise, *f. ;* rocher, *m. ;* (hill) colline, *f.*

cliff'y, *adj.,* à falaises ; rocailleux.

climacter'ic *ou* **-al** (-tèr'-), *adj.,* climatérique.

cli'mate (claï-), *n.,* climat, *m.*

cli'max (claï-), *n.,* gradation, *f. ;* comble,
climax, *m. ;* fin de tout, *f.*

climb (claïme), *n.,* ascension, *f.* Stiff —;
ascension raide.

climb, *v.n.,* grimper **sur;** monter **sur;** gravir; (fig.) s'élever. To — down; *en rabattre,
rabattre ses prétentions.*

climb, *v.a.,* escalader, gravir, monter **sur.**

climb'er, *n.,* grimpeur, *m. ;* (bot.) plante
grimpante, *f. ;* (orni.) grimpeur, *m.*

clime (claïme), *n.,* climat; pays, *m.*

clinch (cli'n'she), *n.,* crampon, *m. ;* (nav.)
étalingure, *f.*

clinch, *v.a.,* tenir à main fermée ; fermer le
poing; serrer; (of nails) river ; (nav.) étalinguer.
To — an argument; *confirmer un argument.*

clinch'er, *n.,* crampon; (fig.) mot sans réplique, *m.* To give any one a —; *river son clou à
quelqu'un.*

clinch'er-built, *adj.,* (of boats) bordé à clin.

cling (cligne), *v.n.,* (*preterit* and *past part.,*
Clung), se cramponner à, s'attacher à, se tenir à,
s'accrocher à; (of dresses) se coller à. To —
together ; *se tenir ensemble, se tenir embrassés.*
A drowning man clings to anything ; *un homme
qui se noie se raccroche à tout.*

cling'-stone (-stône), *n.,* (fruit) pavie, *m.*

cling'y, *adj.,* qui s'attache, qui s'accroche.

clin'ical, *adj.,* (med.) clinique, de clinique.

clin'ically, *adv.,* d'une manière clinique.

clink (cli'gnk), *n.,* tintement, cliquetis, *m.*

clink, *v.n.,* tinter; résonner.

clink, *v.a.,* faire tinter ; faire résonner.

clink'er, *n.,* mâchefer, *m.*

clink'ing, *n.,* cliquetis, tintement, *m.*

clip, *v.a.,* couper ; (with scissors) rogner;
(dogs and horses) tondre; (to abridge) écourter ;
(of words) manger, estropier ; (of tickets) contrôler.

clip, *n.,* tonte, *f. ;* pince-notes, *m.*

clip'per, *n.,* rogneur, *m.,* rogneuse, *f. ;* (nav.)
fin voilier, *m.*

clip'ping, *n.,* rognure, *f. ;* (of tickets) con-
trôlement, *m.*

cloak (clôke), *n.,* manteau ; (with a hood)
caban; (fig.) masque, prétexte, *m. ;* (mil.) capote,
f. — room ; (railways) *vestiaire, dépôt, m. ;
consigne, f.* In the — room ; *au dépôt.*

cloak, *v.a.,* couvrir d'un manteau ; (fig.) masquer, voiler, cacher.

cloak'edly, *adv.,* sous le manteau, en cachette.

clock, *n.,* horloge; pendule, *f. ;* (of stockings)
coin, *m.* Eight-day —; *pendule, ou horloge, qui
marche huit jours.* What o'— is it ? *quelle heure
est-il ?* It is one o'—; *il est une heure.* Ornamental --; *pendule, f.* — dial ; *cadran d'horloge,
m.* — case ; *cage, ou boîte, d'horloge, f.*

clock'-maker (-mèk'-), *n.,* horloger, *m.*

clock'-making, *n.,* horlogerie, *f.*

clock'-tower, *n.,* tour d'horloge, *f.*

clock'-work (-weurke), *n.,* (horl.) mouvement, *m.,* rouages, *m.pl. ;* (fig.) travail régulier,

bien ajusté, *m. ;* régularité, *f.* As regular as ; *réglé comme un papier de musique.*

clod, *n.*, motte de terre, *f. ;* morceau, *m.*, masse, *f. ;* grumeau, caillot, *m.*

clod, *v.n.*, se cailler, se coaguler, se grumeler.

clod, *v.n.*, lancer des mottes de terre **contre.**

clod'dy, *adj.*, plein de mottes ; grumeleux.

clod'hopper, *n.*, rustre, rustaud, manant, lourdaud, *m.*

clod'pate, *n.*, claude, lourdaud, sot, imbécile, *m.*

clod'pated (-pét'ède), *adj.*, claude ; lourd, hébété.

clod'poll (clod'pol), *n.*, claude, lourdaud, sot, imbécile, *m.*

clog, *n.*, (for an animal) entraves, *f.pl. ;* (for the foot) socque ; galoche, *f. ;* sabot ; (fig.) empêchement, embarras, *m.*, entrave, *f. ;* entraves, *f.pl.*

clog, *v.a.*, (animal) entraver ; (fig.) entraver, embarrasser ; obstruer, encombrer.

clog, *v.n.*, s'embarrasser ; s'attacher à ; se boucher, s'obstruer.

clog'gy (-ghi), *adj.*, embarrassant ; pesant.

clois'ter (clois'-), *n.*, cloître, *m.*

clois'ter, *v.a.*, cloîtrer.

close (clôce), *n.*, clos, enclos ; (of a cathedral) cloître, *m.*

close (clôce), *adj.*, clos, bien fermé ; compact, étroit ; (avaricious, tight) serré ; (of the weather) lourd ; (of the air) renfermé ; (fig.) mystérieux ; discret ; attentif, appliqué. — to ; *près de.* In — confinement ; *au secret.* — to the ground ; *à fleur de terre, à ras de terre.*

close (clôce), *adv.*, serré, de près. — by ; *tout près.* — to one another ; *tout près les uns des autres.* To be — upon ; *serrer de près.*

close (clôze), *v.a.*, clore, fermer ; terminer ; conclure ; serrer. To — in ; *clore ;* (the ranks) *serrer.* To — up ; *fermer.*

close (clôze), *v.n.*, se fermer ; clore, terminer, conclure ; finir ; (milit.) en venir aux mains ; (of a wound) se fermer, se cicatriser. To — with ; *convenir de, s'entendre* **avec** ; (to grapple with) *prendre corps à corps ;* (to come to an arrangement) *s'arranger* **avec.** To — upon ; *s'arrêter* à, *se déterminer* à. I —d by saying that ; *je finis en disant que.*

close (clôze), *n.*, fin ; clôture ; prise (in wrestling), *f.* To bring to a — ; *terminer.* To draw to a — ; *tirer, ou toucher,* à *sa fin.*

close'ly (clôss'li), *adv.*, serré ; de près ; étroitement ; secrètement ; strictement ; intimement ; attentivement. To observe — ; *veiller de près, ne pas perdre de vue.*

close'ness (clôss'-), *n.*, fidélité ; concision, logique serrée, *f. ;* état serré, *m. ;* compacité, étroitesse, *f. ;* (of the weather) état lourd ; air renfermé, *m. ;* (fig.) connexion ; avarice ; discrétion, réserve ; (of pursuit) vigueur, *f.*

clos'er (cloz'-), *n.*, finisseur, *m. ;* (of boots) joigneur, *m. ;* joigneuse, *f.*

close'stool (clôss'stoule), *n.*, chaise percée, *f.*

clos'et (kloz'ète), *n.*, cabinet, placard ; boudoir, *m. ;* grande armoire, *f.* Dark — ; *cabinet noir, m.*

clos'et (kloz'ète), *v.a.*, enfermer dans un cabinet, prendre en particulier. To be —ed with ; *être enfermé* **avec** ; *être en tête-à-tête* **avec.**

clos'eting, *n.*, conférence particulière, *f. ;* tête-à-tête, *m.*

clos'ing (clôz'-), *n.*, clôture ; fin, conclusion ; (of shops) fermeture, *f. adj.*, de clôture ; (last) dernier, final.

clo'sure (clô'jeur), *n.*, clôture, fermeture, *f. ;* enclos, *m. ;* enceinte, *f.*

clot, *n.*, grumeau ; caillot, *m.*

clot, *v.n.*, se cailler ; se grumeler.

cloth (clôth), *n.*, (woolen, gold *ou* silver tissue) drap, *m. ;* (linen tissue) toile, *f. ;* (cotton tissue) calicot, coton ; (cover for a table)

tapis, *m. ;* (binding) toile, percaline, *f.* Table — ; *nappe, f.* To lay the — ; *mettre le couvert.* To remove the — ; *desservir.* Long — ; *percale, cretonne, f.* — merchant ; *marchand de draps, drapier, m.* — presser ; *presse-étoffes, m.* — trade ; *commerce des draps, m., draperie, f.* — weaver ; *tisserand en draps, m.* — worker ; *ouvrier en draps, m.*

clothe (clôthe), *v.a.* (*preterit* and *past part.*, Clad, Clothed), vêtir, revêtir **de**, couvrir **de,** habiller.

clothes (clôthze), *n.*, hardes, *f.pl. ;* habits, vêtements, *m.pl.* Bed — ; *couvertures, f.pl.* Long — ; *maillot, m.* Old — ; *vieux habits, m.pl.* Old — man ; *fripier, m.* In plain — ; *en civil, en bourgeois, en paysan.*

cloth'ier (clôth'hieur), *n.*, drapier, tailleur, marchand de confection, d'habits tout faits, *m.*

cloth'ing (clôth'-), *n.*, vêtement, habillement, *m. ;* couvertures, *f.pl.*

cloth'-shearer, *n.*, tondeur de drap, *m.*

clot'ty, *adj.*, grumeleux.

cloud (claoude), *n.*, nuage, *m. ;* nue ; (fig.) nuée ; (in stones) veine, tache, *f.* To be under a — ; *être discrédité, être mal vu du monde ; avoir quelque chose contre soi.* To fall from the —s ; *tomber des nues.*

cloud, *v.a.*, couvrir de nuages ; obscurcir ; voiler ; (of sorrow) assombrir, répandre un nuage **sur.**

cloud, *v.n.*, se couvrir de nuages ; se couvrir, s'obscurcir ; (of the brow) se rembrunir.

cloud'capt, *adj.*, couvert de nuages ; s'élevant jusqu'aux nues ; qui se perd dans les nues.

cloud'-compelling, *adj.*, qui amasse des nuages.

cloud'ily, *adv.*, avec des nuages ; (fig.) obscurément.

cloud'iness, *n.*, état nuageux, *m. ;* obscurité, couleur terne ; (fig.) tristesse, *f.*

cloud'less, *adj.*, sans nuage.

cloud'y, *adj.*, nuageux, couvert ; nébuleux ; (fig.) ténébreux, sombre ; (of liquids) trouble. — weather ; *temps couvert, m.* It is getting — ; *le temps se couvre.*

clout (claoute), *n.*, torchon ; chiffon, *m. ;* (thump) tape, claque, taloche, *f. ;* (nail) clou à tête plate, *m. ;* (of axle-tree) rondelle, *f. ;* pièce pour raccommoder, *f.* — for children ; *lange, m.*, couche, ⊙braie, *f.*

clout, *v.a.*, rapetasser ; taper ; garnir de clous ; (fig.) donner une claque à ; talocher.

clove (clôve), *n.*, clou de girofle, *m.* — of garlic ; *gousse d'ail, f.*

clove'bark (-bârke), *n.*, cannelle giroflée, *f.*

clo'ven (clô'v'n), *adj.*, fendu ; fourchu. To show the — foot ; *laisser voir le bout de l'oreille.*

clo'ven-footed *ou* **clo'ven-hoofed** (-foutède, -houf'te), *adj.*, qui a le pied fendu, fourchu.

clo'ver (clô-), *n.*, trèfle, *m.* — field ; *champ de trèfle, m.*, tréflière, *f.* In — ; *dans l'abondance ;* à *gogo.* To be in — ; *avoir du foin dans ses bottes.*

clo'vered (clô-veurde), *adj.*, couvert de trèfle.

clove'-oil, *n.*, huile de girofle, *f.*

clove'-stalk (-stôke), *n.*, griffe de girofle, *f.*

clove'tree, *n.*, giroflier, *m.*

clown (claoune), *n.*, bouffon, paillasse ; clown ; pitre ; (with Columbine) Gille ; (b.s.) rustre, manant, *m.*

clown'ish, *adj.*, de paysan ; rustre, grossier.

clown'ishly, *adv.*, en manant, grossièrement.

clown'ishness, *n.*, rusticité ; gaucherie, grossièreté, rudesse, *f.*

cloy (cloïe), *v.a.*, (glut) rassasier ; affadir.

cloy'ing, *n.*, affadissement, *m.*, satiété, *f.*

cloy'less, *adj.*, qui ne rassasie pas.

club (cleube), *n.*, massue ; (assembly) réunion, *f.*, cercle, club, *m. ;* cotisation, *f. ;* (at cards) trèfle, *m. ;* (of the hair) catogan, *m.*

club, *v.a.*, cotiser, réunir ; renverser ; (the hair) relever en catogan.

club, *v.n.*, se réunir pour, se cotiser pour ; s'associer avec ; contribuer à.

club'-foot (-foute), *n.*, pied bot, *m.*

club'-headed (-hèdède), *adj.*, à grosse tête ; stupide, bête.

club'-law (-lō), *n.*, loi du plus fort, anarchie, *f.*

club'-room, *n.*, salle de cercle, *f.*

club'-shaped, *adj.*, en forme de massue ; claviforme.

cluck (cleuke), *v.n.*, glousser.

cluck (cleuke), *v.a.*, appeler.

cluck'ing, *n.*, gloussement, *m.*

clue (cliou), *n.* V. **clew**. (fig.) fil, indice, signe, *n.*, idée. To give a — to ; *mettre sur la voie ; mettre sur la piste ; donner un indice* de.

clue, *v.a.* V. **clew**.

clump (cleu'm'pe), *n.*, gros bloc ; (fig.) groupe, *m.* — of trees ; *massif* ou *groupe d'arbres, bouquet d'arbres, m. ; touffe d'arbres, f.*

clum'sily (cleu'm'-), *adv.*, gauchement, maladroitement ; grossièrement.

clum'siness, *n.*, gaucherie, maladresse, *f.*

clum'sy, *adj.*, gauche ; maladroit, disgracieux, laid, mal fait, rude.

clus'ter (cleus'-), *n.*, grappe, *f. ;* (of nuts) paquet, *m. ;* (of trees) bouquet, groupe, massif ; (of bees) peloton, essaim ; groupe ; amas, *m. ;* (of diamonds) attache, *f.*

clus'ter, *v.n.*, croître en grappes ; s'amasser ; se grouper autour de ; s'attrouper, se rassembler ; (of bees) se pelotonner.

clus'ter, *v.a.*, réunir en grappe ; amasser, rassembler.

clus'tery, *adj.*, en grappe.

clutch (cleutshe), *v.a.*, saisir, empoigner, serrer. To — the hand, the fist ; *serrer, ou fermer, le poing.* To — at anything ; *s'accrocher à tout.*

clutch, *n.*, griffe, prise, étreinte, *f.* To fall into any one's —es ; *passer sous la patte de quelqu'un.*

clut'ter (cleut'-), *n.*, amas confus, vacarme, *m.*

clut'ter, *v.n.*, faire du bruit.

coach (côtshe), *n.*, voiture, *f. ;* carrosse, *m. ;* (nav.) chambre de conseil, *f. ;* (universities) préparateur, répétiteur, instructeur, *m.* Slow —; *lambin, m.* A — and six ; *une voiture à six chevaux.* Mail —; *malle-poste, f.* Stage —; *diligence, f.* — step ; *marchepied, m.* — window ; *glace (de voiture), f.*

coach, *v.a.*, voiturer. To — up ; (fig.) *préparer aux examens.*

coach, *v.n.*, aller en voiture.

coach'-box (-bokse), *n.*, siège du cocher, *m.*

coach'-door, *n.*, portière, *f.*

coach'-full, *n.*, carrossée ; voiture pleine, *f.*

coach'-hire (-haïeur), *n.*, prix de louage, *m.*

coach'-house, *n.*, remise, *f.*

coach'ing, *n.*, voyage en voiture, *m. ;* (fig.) préparation aux examens, instruction, *f.*

coach'-maker (-mék'-), *n.*, carrossier, *m.*

coach'man (-ma'n), *n.*, cocher, *m.*

coach'-office, *n.*, bureau des voitures, des diligences, *m.* To be left at the — ; *bureau restant, m.*

coach'-stand (-sta'n'de), *n.*, place, *ou* station, de fiacres, *f.*

coac'tion, *n.*, coaction, *f.*

coact'ive, *adj.*, coactif.

coact'ively (-), *adv.*, par coercition.

coadju'tor (cô-ad-jou-teur), *n.*, coadjuteur, adjoint, collègue, collaborateur, *m.*

coadven'tur-er, **-ess** (cô-ad-vè'n'tiour-), *n.*, compagnon, *m.*, compagne, *f.*, d'aventure.

coa'gent (-é'djè'n'te), *n.*, aide, coopérateur, *m.*

coag'ulable (-agh'iou-), *adj.*, coagulable.

coag'ulate, *v.a.* and *n.*, coaguler ; se coaguler.

coagula'tion, *n.*, coagulation, *f.*

coag'ulative, *adj.*, coagulant.

coal (côl), *n.*, charbon de terre, *m. ;* (tech.) houille, *f.* To carry —s to Newcastle ; *porter de l'eau à la rivière.* To call over the —s ; *mettre sur la sellette.* To haul over the —s ; *blâmer ; trouver à redire à.*

coal, *v.a.*, charbonner. *v.n.*, (of steamers) faire sa provision de charbon.

coal'-bed (-bède), *n.*, couche de houille, *f.*

coal'-black, *adj.*, noir comme du charbon.

coal'-box (-bokse), *n.*, boîte à charbon, *f.*

coal'-bunker, *n.*, soute à charbon.

coal'-cellar, *n.*, charbonnier, *m.*

coal'-cinders (-ci'n'deurze), *n.pl.*, escarbilles, *f.pl.*

coal'-drawing (-drô-), *n.*, extraction de la houille, *f.*

coal'-dust, *n.*, poussier de charbon, fraisil, *m.*

coal'ery (-eur'-), *n.*, (l.u.) houillère, *f.*

coalesce' (-lèce), *v.n.*, s'unir, se confondre, se fondre, s'allier ; se fusionner.

coales'cence (-lès'cè'n'ce), *n.*, union, coalescence, adhésion, *f.*

coales'cent, *adj.*, coalescent.

coal'-field (-fîlde), *n.*, terrain houiller, *m.*

coal'-heaver (-hîv'-), *n.*, porteur de charbon de terre, *m.*

coal'-hole (-hôl), *n.*, (nav.) charbonnier, *m. ;* soute au charbon, *f.*

coal'-hood (-houde), *n.*, (orni.) bouvreuil, *m.*

coali'tion (cô-a-lish'eune), *n.*, coalition, *f.*

coal'-master (-mâs'-), *n.*, exploitant de houillère, *m.*

coal'-measure (-mèj'eur), *n.*, (min.) gisement houiller, *m. ;* formation houillère, *f.*

coal'-merchant (-meur'tsha'n'te), *n.*, marchand de charbon de terre, *m.*

coal'-mine (-maïne), *n.*, mine de houille, *f.*

coal'-miner, *n.*, charbonnier, *m.*

coal'-scuttle (-skeut't'l), *n.*, seau, panier, *m.*, boîte à charbon, *f.*

coal'-stone (-stône), *n.*, anthracite, *m.*

coal'-wharf (-hwôrfe), *n.*, dépôt de houille, *m.*

coal'-whipper (-hwip'-), *n.*, déchargeur de houille, *m.*

coal'-work (-weurke), *n.*, houillère, *f.*

coal'y, *adj.*, houilleux.

coapta'tion (cô-ap-té-), *n.*, adaptation, *f. ;* arrangement, *m. ;* (surg.) coaptation, *f.*

coarct' *ou* **coarct'ate** (cô-ârcte, -téte), *v.a.*, (ant.) resserrer, rétrécir.

coarcta'tion (-té-), *n.*, (ant.) pression, contraction, contrainte, *f.*

coarse (côrse), *adj.*, gros, grossier. — grained ; (of tissues, etc.) à *gros grain ;* (of fabrics) à *gros poil ;* (of wood) à *gros fil.*

coarse'ly, *adv.*, grossièrement.

coarse'ness, *n.*, grossièreté, *f.*

coast (côste), *n.*, côte, plage, *f. ;* rivage, littoral, *m.* The — is clear ; *vous pouvez passer ; il n'y a plus personne.*

coast, *v.n.*, suivre la côte ; caboter, ranger *ou* suivre la côte, côtoyer.

coast, *v.a.*, côtoyer. To — along ; *côtoyer.*

coast'er, *n.*, cabotier, *m.*

coast'-guard (-gârde), *n.*, garde-côtes, *m.*

coast'ing, *n.*, cabotage, *m.*

coat (côte), *n.*, habit, *m. ;* (mas., paint.) couche ; (of serpents) peau ; (of some animals) robe ; fourrure, *f. ;* poil, *m. ;* (her.) écusson, *m.*, cotte ; (anat.) paroi, tunique ; (nav.) braie, *f.*, suif, *m.* Frock — ; *redingote, f.* Tail —, dress — ; *habit, m.* Great — ; *pardessus, paletot, m. ;* (mil.) capote, *f.* — tail ; *basque, f.* — of mail ; *cotte de mailles, f.* Cut your — *according to your cloth ; selon ta bourse gouverne ta bouche.* To turn one's — , to be a turn — ; *tourner casaque.*

coat, *v.a.*, habiller ; revêtir ; enduire.

coat'ing, n., étoffe pour habits, f. ; enduit, m. ; couche, f. Rough —; crépi, m.

coax (côkse), v.a., amadouer, cajoler, enjôler.

coax'er, n., cajoleur, enjôleur, amadoueur, m.

coax'ing, n., cajolerie, f., enjôlement, m.

cob, n., pince-maille, m. ; balle (of maize) ; (for feeding fowls) boulette ; (orni.) mouette, f. ; (man.) petit cheval entier, m.

co'bail (-béle), n., cofidéjusseur, m.

co'balt (cô-bâlte), n., cobalt, m.

cob'ble (cob'b'l), v.a., saveter, rapetasser. n., (boat) bateau pêcheur ; (of stones) galet, m. pl., (of coals) gaillette, f. ; gailletin, m.

cob'bler, n., savetier, m. —'s wax ; poix de cordonnier, f.

cob'bling, n., raccommodage de souliers, m.

cob'nut, n., aveline, f.

cob'web (-wèbe), n., toile d'araignée, f.

co'calon (cô-), n., gros cocon, m.

coc'cyx (cok'sikse), n., coccyx, m.

coch'ineal (cotsh'i-nîle), n., cochenille, f.

coch'lea (cok'li-a), n., (anat.) limaçon, m.

cochlear'iform ou **coch'leary** (cok'li-ér'-, cok'li-a-), adj., en forme de vis ; en spirale.

cochlea'ria (-a), n., cochléaria, m.

cock, n., coq ; (of small birds) mâle ; (tap) robinet ; (of fire-arms) chien ; (of hats) retroussis ; (of dials) style, m. ; (of a balance) aiguille ; (of hay) tas, m. ; meule, f. Black —; coq de bruyère, m. Weather—; girouette, f. — and bull story ; coq-à-l'âne, conte à dormir debout, m. — of the walk ; coq du village, m. At full —; (of weapons) armé. At half —; au repos.

cock, v.a., redresser, retrousser ; relever ; (fire-arms) armer ; (hay) mettre en meule.

cockade' (-éde), n., cocarde, f. ; signe, emblème, m.

cock-a-doo'dle-doo' (cok-a-dou'd'l'dou), n., coquerico, m., cocorico, m.

cock'-a-hoop, adj., triomphant.

cockatoo' (-a-tou), n., kakatoès ; cacatois, m.

cock'atrice (-trice), n., basilic, m.

cock'boat (-bôte), n., petit bateau, coquet, m.

cock'brained (-bré'n'de), adj., étourdi, écer-cock' canary, n., serin, m. [velé.

cock'chafer (-tshéf'-), n., hanneton, m.

cock'-crow (-crô), n., chant du coq, m. From —; dès patron-minette.

cocked (cok'te), adj., (of hats) à cornes ; (of fire-arms) armé.

cock'er, v.a., (ant.) choyer, dorloter.

cock'et (-ète), n., acquit, sceau de douane, m.

cock'fight ou **cock'fighting** (-faïte, -faït'-), n., combat de coqs, m. ; joute de coqs, f.

cock'-horse, n., dada, m.

coc'kle (cok'k'l), n., (conch.) bucarde, coque ; (bot.) agrostide ; (of corn) nielle, f.

coc'kle, v.a. and n., recoquiller ; se recoquiller ; (of the sea) moutonner.

coc'kled (cok'k'lde), adj., à coquille.

coc'kle-stairs (-stèrze), n., escalier à vis, m.

cock'loft, n., grenier, galetas, m.

cock'match, n., joute de coqs, f.

cock'ney (-ni), n., badaud de Londres, m.

cock'pit, n., arène des combats de coqs, f. ; (nav.) poste des malades, m.

cock'roach (-rôtshe), n., blatte, f.

cocks'-comb (coks'kôme), n., crête de coq ; (bot.) célosie à crête ; crête-de-coq, amarante des jardiniers, f. ; (pers.) fat, freluquet, m.

cocks'head (coks'hède), n., (bot.) sainfoin, m.

cock'-spur, n., éperon de coq, ergot, m.

cock'-spur thorn, n., alisier, m.

cock'sure (kok'shioure), adj., sûr et certain.

cock'swain. V. **coxswain**.

cock's weed, n., passerage, f.

cock'y, adj., suffisant, vaniteux ; qui fait l'important.

co'coa (cô'cô), n., coco ; cocotier ; cacao en poudre, cacao, m.

co'coa-nut (cô-cô-neute), n., coco, m. ; noix de coco, f., cocotier, m.

cocoon' (co-coune), n., cocon, m.

coc'tion (cok'-), n., coction, f.

cod (code), n., (ich.) morue ; (pod) cosse ; (anat.) scrotum, m., bourses, f.pl. —-fish ; morue, f. —-liver oil ; huile de foie de morue, f.

cod'dle, v.a., mitonner ; câliner ; dorloter, choyer.

code (côde), n., code, m.

cod'ger, n., bonhomme, original ; butor, rustre ; pingre, m.

cod'icil, n., codicille, m.

codifica'tion, n., codification.

cod'ify, v.a., codifier.

cod'lin ou **cod'ling**, n., pomme à cuire, f.

cod'ling, n., (ich.) petite morue, f.

coef'ficacy (cô-èf'-), n., efficacité égale, f.

coeffi'ciency (cô-èf-fish'è'n-), n., coopération, f. ; concours, m.

coeffi'cient, n., coefficient, m.

coemp'tion, n., coemption, f.

coengage' (-è'n-ghédje), v.a., engager conjointement.

coenjoy' (-è'n'djoï), v.a., jouir conjointement de.

coe'qual (-î-kwôl), adj., égal, (theol.) coégal.

coequal'ity (-î-kwôl'-), n., égalité, (theol.) coégalité, f.

coerce' (cô-eurce), v.a., forcer, contraindre, réprimer.

coer'cible, adj., qui peut être contraint.

coer'cion (cô-eur-), n., coercition, f.

coer'cive, adj., coercitif.

coer'cively, adv., par coercition.

coessen'tial (cô-ès'sè'n-shal), adj., (theol.) de même essence.

coessential'ity, n., (theol.) communauté d'essence, f.

coeter'nal (cô-î-teur-), adj., (theol.) coéternel.

coeter'nally, adv., de toute éternité.

coeter'nity, n., (theol.) coéternité, f.

coe'val (cô-î-), adj., contemporain, du même âge.

coexist', v.n., coexister.

coexist'ence, n., coexistence, f.

coexist'ent ou **coexist'ing**, adj., coexistant.

cof'fee (cof-fi), n., café, m. — cup ; tasse à café, f. — roaster ; brûloir à café, m. — mill ; moulin à café, m.

cof'fee-berry (-bèr'-), n., grain, m., ou fève, f., de café.

cof'fee-broker, n., courtier en cafés, m.

cof'fee-grounds, n.pl., marc de café, m.

cof'fee-house, n., café, m., crêmerie, f. — keeper ; cafetier, limonadier, m.

cof'fee-plantation (-pla'n'té-), n., caféière, f.

cof'fee-pot (-pote), n., cafetière, f.

cof'fee-room (-roume), n., salon d'hôtel, café, m.

cof'fee-service, service à café, m.

cof'fee-tree (-trî), n., caféier, cafier, m.

cof'fer, n., coffre, coffret, m. ; caisse, cassette, f.

cof'fer, v.a., encoffrer, encaisser.

cof'fer-dam, n., batardeau, m.

cof'fin, n., cercueil, m. ; bière, f.

cof'fin, v.a., enfermer dans un cercueil.

cog, n., dent, f. ; cran, m. — -wheel ; roue dentée, f. — boat ; bateau pêcheur, m.

cog, v.a., cajoler ; enjôler ; (dice) piper ; (tech.) garnir de dents, denter.

cog, v.n., faire des cajoleries.

co'gency (cô-djè'n-), n., force, puissance, f.

co'gent, adj., puissant, fort.

co'gently, adv., avec force.

cogged, adj., denté, à dents ; (of dice) pipé.

cog'ger (cog-gheur), n., (l.u.) cajoleur, m., cajoleuse, f.

cog'itate (codj'i-téte), v.a., penser à, ruminer sur. v.n., méditer.

cogita'tion, n., réflexion, pensée, méditation, f.

cog'itative, adj., pensif, réfléchi.

cog'nate (cog-néte), adj., de la même famille; analogue, (jur.) cognat.

cogna'tion, n., analogie; parenté; (jur.) cognation, f.

cogni'tion (cog-nish'eune), n., connaissance, f.

cog'nitive, adj., capable de savoir, de comprendre, de la compétence **de**.

cog'nizable (cog-), adj., (jur.) du ressort **de**; de la compétence **de**.

cog'nizance (cog-), n., marque, f.; insigne, m.; connaissance; (jur.) juridiction, compétence, f.

cog'nizant (cog-), adj., instruit; (jur.) compétent.

cogno'men (cog-nô-mène), n., surnom, nom de guerre, m.

cognom'inal, adj., de surnom, homonyme.

cohab'it (cô-), v.n., cohabiter.

cohabita'tion (-té-), n., cohabitation, f.

co'heir (cô-ère), n., cohéritier, m.

coheir'ess, n., cohéritière, f.

cohere' (cô-hîre), v.n., adhérer **à**; convenir **à**, concorder **avec**; être attaché **à**.

coher'ence ou **coher'ency**, n., cohésion, cohérence, f.

coher'ent, adj., conséquent; cohérent, adhérent.

coher'ently, adv., d'une manière cohérente.

cohesibil'ity (cô-hi-), n., tendance à la cohésion, f.

cohe'sible, adj., susceptible de cohésion.

cohe'sion (cô-hi-jeune), n., cohésion, f.

cohe'sive (-cive), adj., qui peut adhérer; gluant.

cohe'siveness, n., cohésion, f.

co'hobate (cô-), v.n., cohober.

cohoba'tion, n., cohobation, f.

co'hort (cô-), n., cohorte, f.

coif (coïfe), v.a., coiffe, calotte, f.

coif, n., coiffer.

coil (coïl), n., (of hair) rouleau; (of serpents) repli, m.; (nav.) glène, f.

coil, v.a., replier, rouler, enrouler; (nav.) gléner, lever, rouer.

coil, v.n., se replier, s'enrouler.

coin, n., (money) monnaie; pièce de monnaie, f.; coin, m. Base ou counterfeit —; fausse monnaie. To pay any one back in his own —; rendre à quelqu'un la monnaie de sa pièce.

coin, v.a., monnayer; (b.s.) forger, fabriquer, inventer. To — words; faire, forger des mots. To — money; battre monnaie; (fig.) amasser de l'or, s'enrichir. To — (into) money; monnayer. —ed money; argent monnayé, m.

coin'age (coï'n'èdje), n., monnayage, m., monnaie; invention, fabrication, f.

coincide' (cô-i'n-çaïde), v.n., s'accorder **avec**, coïncider **avec**, se rencontrer.

coin'cidence (cô-i'n-ci-), n., coïncidence; rencontre, f.; accord, hasard, m.

coin'cident, adj., coïncident; d'accord.

coin'er (coï'n-), n., monnayeur; (b.s.) faux monnayeur, m.

coin'ing-press (-prèce), n., balancier monétaire, m. — tool; outil de monnayeur, m.

coit, n. V. quoit.

coi'tion (co-ish'eune), n., coït, m.; conjonction, copulation, f.

coke (côke), n., coke, m. — dust; fraisil, m.

col'ander (-l'n), n., passoire, f.

col'chicum (-tshi-keume), n., colchique, m.

col'cothar (-thar), n., colcotar, m.

cold (côlde), adj., froid. To be —; avoir froid. To be — to (any one); battre froid à. To grow —; se refroidir.

cold, n., froid; (illness) rhume; refroidissement; frisson; catarrhe, m., froidure, f. To have a — in the head; être enrhumé du cerveau. To

have a —; être enrhumé. To take —; attraper un rhume; s'enrhumer. In — blood; de sang froid; prémédité, délibéré. — bloodedness; sang froid, m. — chisel; ciseau à froid, m. — drawn; étiré à froid. — hearted; froid, insensible. — heartedness; froideur, insensibilité, f. — press, v.a.; satiner à froid. — pressing; satinage à froid, m. — short (of metals); cassant. — water cure; traitement médical par l'eau froide, m.

cold'ish, adj., un peu froid, frais.

cold'ly, adv., froidement. To look — on any one; battre froid à quelqu'un.

cold'ness, n., froid, m.; froideur, f.

cole ou **cole'wort** (côl, -weurte), n., chou, m.

coleop'ter, n., coléoptère, m.

colessee' (cô-lès'sî), n., (jur.) copreneur, m.

col'ic, n., colique, f.

colise'um (-si-eume), n. V. colosse'um.

collapse' (col'lapse), v.n., s'affaisser; tomber ensemble; s'écrouler; s'ébouler, s'effondrer; (of balloons) se désenfler.

collapse', n., rapprochement; (med.) prostration, f.; affaissement, écroulement, m., débâcle, f.

col'lar (col'leur), n., collier; (of a shirt) col; (of a coat, a dress) collet, m.; (for ladies) collerette; (arch.) ceinture, f. — of brawn; (butch.) rouleau de sanglier. Against the —; à perte, à contre-cœur. To slip the —; s'échapper; devenir libre. To take up the — again; reprendre le collier. To seize by the —; saisir ou prendre au collet.

col'lar, v.a., colleter, saisir, prendre au collet; (cook.) rouler; mettre un collier à (fig.).

col'lar-bone (-bône), n., (anat.) clavicule, f.

col'lar-pin (-pine), n., bouton à clavette, m.

collate' (col'léte), v.a., collationner; comparer; (of livings) conférer.

collate', v.n., présenter à un bénéfice; user du droit de collation.

collat'eral (-lat'eur-), n., (jur.) collatéral, m.

collat'eral, adj., collatéral; côte à côte; indirect, parallèle, additionnel.

collat'erally, adv., en ligne collatérale; indirectement, côte à côte.

colla'tion (-lé-), n., collation; comparaison, f., don, présent, m.; (repast) collation, f.

colla'tor (-lé-teur), n., celui qui compare, collateur, m.

col'league (-l'îghe), n., collègue, m.

col'league, v.a., adjoindre; unir **à**.

collect' (col'lècte), v.a., collecte; quête, f.

collect', v.a., recueillir; ramasser, rassembler, collectionner; (taxes) percevoir; (debts) recouvrer; (charity) quêter; faire la levée (des lettres); inférer, déduire. To — one's self; se recueillir, se remettre, se calmer.

collect', v.n., s'amasser, s'entasser.

collecta'neous (col'lèc'té-ni-), adj., recueilli, amassé.

collect'ed (-'ède), adj., rassemblé, réuni; calme, tranquille; recueilli.

collect'edly, adv., ensemble; avec calme, avec recueillement.

collect'edness, n., recueillement, calme; sang-froid, m.

collec'tion, n., assemblage, rassemblement, m.; collection; collecte, quête, f.; reception; (postal) levée, f.; recouvrement, m.

collec'tive, adj., collectif.

collec'tively, adv., collectivement.

collec'tor (-teur), n., collecteur, receveur; (of curios) collectionneur; (of taxes) percepteur; compilateur; (for charity) quêteur, m.

collec'torship, n., charge de percepteur, de receveur; perception, recette, f.

col'lege (col'lèdje), n., collège, lycée, m., société, f. — of physicians; faculté de médecine, f. — of priests; séminaire, m.

colle'gial (col-lî'djial), adj., collégial.

colle'gian (-djia'n), n., collégien, m.

colle′giate (-djiéte), *adj.*, de collège ; collégial. — *school* ; *institution, f.*

col′let (col′lète), *n.*, (tech.) collet, *m.*

collide′, *v.n.*, heurter **contre** ; se heurter ; s'entrechoquer ; se rencontrer ; (nav.) s'aborder.

collid′ing, *n.*, collision, *f.*, choc, *m.*

col′lier (col′lieur), *n.*, houilleur ; (nav.) charbonnier ; (ship) vaisseau charbonnier, *m.*

col′liery, *n.*, houillère, *f.*

col′ligate (col′li-ghéte), *v.a.*, (ant.) lier *ou* attacher ensemble.

colli′sion (-lijeune), *n.*, collision, *f.*, choc, *m.*, (nav.) abordage, *m.* To come into — with ; *heurter* **contre**, *rencontrer* ; (nav.) *aborder.*

col′locate (col′lo-kéte), *v.a.*, placer ; (jur.) colloquer.

colloca′tion (-ké-), *n.*, placement, *m.* ; place, *f.*

col′lop (col′lope), *n.*, tranche de viande ; escalope ; grillade, *f.*

collo′quial (-′lô′kwi-al), *adj.*, dialogué, de conversation, familier.

col′loquy (col-lô-kwi), *n.*, colloque, entretien, *m.*

collude′ (col-lioude), *v.n.*, (jur.) colluder, être d'intelligence.

collud′er, *n.*, complice, *m.*

collu′sion (col′liou′jeune), *n.*, collusion, connivence, entente secrète, *f.*

collu′sive (col′liou′cive), *adj.*, collusoire.

collu′sively, *adv.*, collusoirement.

col′ly, *n.*, suie, *f.*

col′ly, *v.a.*, noircir, barbouiller avec de la suie.

colly′rium (-eume), *n.*, collyre, *m.*

col′ocynth (-ci′n'th), *n.*, (bot.) coloquinte, *f.*

co′lon (cô-), *n.*, (anat.) colon, *m.* ; (gram.) deux points, *m.pl.*

colo′nel (keur′n'l), *n.*, colonel, *m.*

colo′nelcy *ou* **colo′nelship** (keur-), *n.*, grade de colonel, *m.*

colo′nial, *adj.*, colonial.

col′onist, *n.*, colon, *m.*

coloniza′tion (-naï-zé-), *n.*, colonisation, *f.*

col′onize (-naïze), *v.a.*, coloniser. To become —d ; *se coloniser.*

colonnade′ (-néde), *n.*, colonnade, *f.*

col′ony, *n.*, colonie, *f.*

col′ophony, *n.*, colophane, *f.*

coloquint′ida (-kwi′n'-), *n.*, coloquinte, *f.*

Colora′do-bee′tle, *n.*, doryphore, *f.*

col′orate, *adj.*, (ant.) coloré ; teint.

colos′sal, *adj.*, colossal.

colosse′um (-′sî-eume), *n.*, Colisée, *m.*

colos′sus (-ceusse), *n.*, (*colossi*) colosse, *m.*

col′or (keul′leur), *n.*, couleur, *f.* (fig.) ombre, apparence, *f.*, (painting) coloris, prétexte ; (housepainting) badigeon, *m. pl.*, (milit.) drapeau ; (nav.) pavillon, *m.* Man of — ; *nègre, m.* Off — ; *qui a perdu son brillant* (of gems). To fear no —s ; *ne pas craindre d'ennemi.* With flying —s ; *à enseignes déployées.* To lend — to ; (of anything) *sembler justifier.*

col′or-blind, *adj.*, affecté de daltonisme.

col′or-blindness, *n.*, daltonisme, *m.*

col′or, *v.a.*, colorer ; colorier ; enluminer ; badigeonner ; nuancer ; culotter (une pipe).

col′or, *v.n.*, (of persons) rougir ; (of things) se colorer ; (of pipes) se culotter.

col′orable, *adj.*, plausible, spécieux.

col′ored (keul′leurde), *adj.*, coloré, colorié, enluminé ; nuancé.

col′oring, *n.*, coloris, *m.* ; couleur, *f.* ; badigeonnage, (fig.) prétexte, *m.*

col′orist, *n.*, coloriste, *m.*

col′orless, *adj.*, sans couleur, incolore ; (of style) terne, pâle.

col′or-sergeant, *n.*, porte-drapeau, *m.*

colt (côlte), *n.*, poulain, novice, *m.* —**′s-foot** ; *pas-d'âne, m.* —**′s-tooth** ; *dent de lait, f.*

col′umbine (col′eu′m′baïne), *adj.*, de pigeon ; gorge-de-pigeon.

col′umbine, *n.*, (thea.) Colombine ; (bot.) aquilégie, herbe de lion, ancolie, *f.* ; gant de Notre-Dame, *m.*

colum′bo, *n.* *V.* **calumba.**

col′umn (col′leume), *n.*, colonne, *f.*

colum′nar (kol′leu′m′-neur), *adj.*, en colonne.

col′umned, *adj.*, à colonnes.

colure′ (-lioure), *n.*, colure, *m.*

col′za, *n.*, colza, *m.*

co′ma (cô-), *n.*, (med.) coma, assoupissement, *m.* ; (astron.) chevelure, *f.*

co′-mate (cô-méte), *n.*, compagnon, camarade, compère, *m.*

co′matose *ou* **co′matous** (-tôss, -teusse), *adj.*, comateux.

comb (côme), *n.*, peigne, *m.* ; (of horses) étrille, *f.* ; (of a cock) crête, *f.* ; (of honey) rayon, *m.* Large tooth — ; *démêloir, m.* Small — ; *peigne fin, m.* — bag ; *porte-peigne, m.*

comb, *v.a.*, peigner ; (a horse) étriller.

com′bat (keu′m′- *ou* co′m′-), *n.*, combat, *m.*

com′bat, *v.a.* and *n.*, combattre.

com′batant, *n.*, combattant, *m.*

comb′er (cô′m′eur), *n.*, peigneur, *m.*

combina′tion (-bi-né-), *n.*, combinaison ; union, association, cabale, ligue, coalition, *f.* ; concours de circonstances, *m.*

combine′ (-baïne), *v.a.*, combiner ; réunir ; coaliser ; allier, liguer.

combine′, *v.n.*, se combiner **à**, se coaliser **avec**, se liguer, s'allier **à**, s'unir **à**. —d movement ; *mouvement d'ensemble, m.*

comb′ing, *n.*, action de peigner, *f.*, (tech.) peignage, *m.*

comb′less (cô′m′lèce), *adj.*, sans crête.

comb′-maker (-mék′-), *n.*, peignier, fabricant de peignes, *m.*

combust′ible (-beus′-), *adj.*, combustible.

combustibil′ity, *n.*, combustibilité, *f.*

combus′tion (-beust′ieune), *n.*, combustion ; conflagration, *f.* ; embrasement, *m.*

come (keume), *v.n.*, (*preterit*, Came ; *past part.*, Come) venir. To — about ; *arriver, survenir.* To — after ; *venir après ; suivre ; venir chercher.* To — again ; *venir de nouveau ; revenir.* To — against ; *heurter, frapper.* To — asunder ; *se détacher.* To — at ; *arriver* **jusqu'à** ; *s'aboucher* **avec.** To — away ; *partir ; venir.* To — back ; *revenir.* To — between ; *intervenir, s'interposer.* To — by ; *venir* **par** ; *passer* **par** ; *entrer en possession* **de.** To — down ; *descendre.* To — down to ; *arriver* **jusqu'à** ; *être transmis, descendre* **à.** To — down upon ; *tomber* **dessus.** To — home ; *rentrer.* To — for ; *venir* **pour,** *venir chercher.* To — forward ; *s'avancer ; se présenter.* To — in ; *entrer ; arriver* ; (of the tide) *monter.* To — in again ; *rentrer.* To — in for ; (property) *hériter* **de** ; *entrer pour, entrer pour chercher.* To — in and out ; *entrer et sortir.* To — next ; *suivre immédiatement.* To — of ; *résulter* **de** ; *provenir* **de** ; *venir* **de.** To — off ; (fig.) *se détacher, s'enlever ; réussir ; se dégager* **de.** To — off with ; *en être quitte* **pour.** To — off victorious ; *remporter la victoire, gagner la journée.* To — on ; *s'avancer ; arriver ; avoir lieu.* To — out ; *sortir ; se déclarer ;* (of the hair) *tomber ;* (of the stars) *se montrer, paraître ;* (of stains) *s'effacer, disparaître ;* (of difficulty) *se tirer d'affaire, s'en tirer ;* (of society, etc.) *débuter, se lancer ;* (of books) *paraître, être publié.* Just — out ; *vient de paraître.* To — out again ; *ressortir.* To — out with ; *lâcher ; dire, laisser échapper.* To — round ; *venir ; arriver ;* (of health) *se remettre, se rétablir, revenir à soi.* To — to ; *se remettre, recouvrer ses sens, reprendre connaissance.* To — to the same ; *revenir au même.* To — to terms ; *en venir à un arrangement.* — what may ; *advienne que pourra.* To — together ; *venir ensemble ; se réunir.* To — under ; *être compris* **sous** ; *être soumis* **à.** To —

undone, unsewed; *se défaire, se découdre*. How —s it that; *comment se fait-il que*. To — up; *monter; s'élever*. To — upon; *se précipiter* **sur.** To — up with; *atteindre, attraper*.

come'dian (-mî-), *n.*, comédien, *m.*, comédienne, *f.*; comique, acteur, *m.*

com'edy, *n.*, comédie, *f.*

come'liness (keu'm'-), *n.*, beauté, grâce, *f.*; agréments, *m.pl.*

come'ly, *adj.*, avenant; beau; bienséant, convenable, digne.

come'ly, *adv.*, avec convenance.

come' off (keum'ôfe), *n.*, défaite, évasion, échappatoire, *f.*; faux-fuyant, *m.*

com'er (keum'eur), *n.*, venant; venu, *m.*, venue, *f.* New —; *nouveau venu*. First —; *premier venu*.

com'et (com'ète), *n.*, comète, *f.*

com'etary *ou* **comet'ic,** *adj.*, cométaire.

com'fit (keu'm'-), *n.*, dragée, *f.*

com'fort (keum'feurte), *n.*, aisance, aise, *f.*; bien-être; agrément; soulagement, *m.*; consolation, *f.* To be of good —, to take —; *prendre courage; se consoler.* To like one's —s; *aimer ses aises; aimer le confortable.*

com'fort, *v.a.*, conforter, soulager; consoler; encourager.

com'fortable, *adj.*, (pers.) à son aise; rassis, posé, qui jouit de son bien-être; (of things) agréable, bon, confortable, commode, consolant. To make —; *cajoler, gâter, mettre bien.* To make one's self —; *se mettre à son aise, prendre ses aises; se donner du bien-être.*

com'fortably, *adv.*, à son aise, agréablement, avec aisance, confortablement, commodément.

com'forter (keum'feurt'eur), *n.*, consolateur (Holy Ghost), *m.*; consolatrice, *f.*; (kerchief) cache-nez de laine, *m.*

com'fortless, *adj.*, sans agrément; sans consolation; désolé, triste; inconsolable.

com'fortlessly, *adv.*, incommodément, mal, mal à son aise; (fig.) inconsolablement, tristement.

com'fortlessness, *n.*, incommodité; gêne, *f.*, malaise, *m.*

com'frey (keum'fri), *n.*, (bot.) consoude, *f.*

com'ic *ou* **com'ical,** *adj.*, comique, drôle.

com'ically, *adv.*, comiquement.

com'icalness, *n.*, caractère comique, *m.*

com'ing (keum'-), *n.*, venue; arrivée, approche, *f.* — in; *entrée, f.*

com'ing, *adj.*, qui arrive, qui vient; arrivant; à venir; prochain. I am —; *je viens; on y va l; voilà! voilà!*

comi'tia, *n.pl.*, comices, *m.pl.*

comi'tial, *adj.*, de comices.

com'ity, *n.*, politesse, courtoisie, urbanité, *f.* The — of nations; *l'accord entre les nations* (as regards the laws, conventions, etc.).

com'ma (com'ma), *n.*, virgule, *f.*; (mus.) comma, *m.* Inverted —; *guillemet, m.*

command' (com'mâ'n'de), *n.*, commandement; pouvoir, empire, *m.*; autorité; connaissance, facilité, *f.* To have the — of words; *avoir une grande facilité d'expression.* To — a view; *dominer le paysage.* Word of —; (mil.) *commandement.* To give the word of —; *commander.* At —; *à sa disposition.* Yours to —; *à vos ordres ou votre obéissant serviteur.* To be at any one's —; *être aux ordres de quelqu'un.*

command', *v.a.*, commander; avoir à sa disposition; posséder; (of respect) commander, inspirer; (to impose) imposer; (a view) dominer.

command'ant, *n.*, commandant, *m.*

command'er, *n.*, commandant; (of knighthood) commandeur; (nav.) capitaine de frégate, *m.* — in chief; *généralissime, général en chef, m.*; (tech.) (for paving) demoiselle, *f.*

command'ing, *adj.*, commandant; imposant; (overlooking) dominant: (authoritative) impérieux, d'autorité.

command'ingly, *adv.*, d'une manière imposante; avec autorité.

command'ment, *n.*, commandement, ordre, précepte, *m.*

commeas'urable, *adj.*, ayant une commune mesure; égal; proportionnel; commensurable.

commem'orable (-mèm'-), *adj.*, notable, mémorable.

commem'orate, *v.a.*, célébrer, solenniser; commémorer.

commemora'tion (-ré-), *n.*, souvenir, *m.*; mémoire; commémoration; solennisation, *f.*

commem'orative *ou* **commem'oratory** (-tori), *adj.*, commémoratif.

commence' (com'mè'n'ce), *v.a.*, commencer. To — one's duties; *entrer en fonctions.*

commence',*v.n.*, commencer, débuter comme.

commence'ment, *n.*, commencement, début, *m.*, origine, *f.*

commend' (com'mè'n'de), *v.a.*, approuver, louer; recommander; recommander au souvenir de; commettre **à,** confier **à.**

commend'able, *adj.*, louable; recommandable.

commend'ableness, *n.*, qualité d'être louable, *f.*; mérite, *m.*

commend'ably, *adv.*, d'une manière louable.

commend'am, *n.*, (ecc.) commende, *f.*; bénéfice par intérim, *m.*

commend'atary, *n.*, ecclésiastique commendataire, *m.*

commenda'tion (-dé-sheune), *n.*, éloge, *m.*; louange, recommandation, *f.* Worthy of the highest —; *digne des plus grands éloges.*

commend'atory (-tori), *adj.*, de recommandation; d'éloges; commendataire.

commend'er, *n.*, panégyriste, *m.*

commen'sal, *n.*, commensal, *m.*

commensurabil'ity (-mè'n'siou-), *n.*, commensurabilité, *f.*

commen'surable, *adj.*, commensurable.

commen'surate, *adj.*, réductible à une mesure commune; proportionnel, égal; proportionné **à,** en rapport **avec;** (of measure, of space) commensurable.

commen'surate. *v.a.*, réduire à une mesure commune; proportionner; mesurer.

commen'surately, *adv.*, proportionnellement, proportionnément, dans d'égales proportions.

commensura'tion, *n.*, commensurabilité, *f.*

com'ment, *n.*, commentaire, *m.*

comment' *ou* **com'mentate,** *v.n.*, commenter.

com'mentary, *n.*, commentaire, *m.*

com'mentator (-té-teur), *n.*, commentateur, *m.*

comment'er, *n.*, annotateur, *m.*

commenti'tious (-tish'eusse), *adj.*, inventé, imaginaire.

com'merce (com'meurce), *n.*, commerce, échange, *m.*

commer'cial (-'meur'shal), *adj.*, commercial, commerçant. — treaty; *traité de commerce, m.* — navigation; *commerce maritime, m.* — house; *maison, f.* — law; *droit commercial, m.* — traveler; *commis voyageur, m.* — broker; *courtier de commerce, m.* — dictionary; *dictionnaire de commerce, m.* — harbor; *port marchand, port de commerce, m.*

commer'cially, *adv.*, commercialement.

commina'tion (-né-), *n.*, menace; (rhet.) commination, *f.*

commin'atory (-teuri), *adj.*, comminatoire, menaçant.

commin'gle (-mign'g'l), *v.a.*, mêler ensemble; mêler, confondre.

commin'gle, *v.n.*, se mêler ensemble, *ou* avec; se confondre; se fondre dans, *ou* en.

com'minute (-nioute), *v.a.*, réduire en petits fragments.

comminu'tion (-niou-), *n.*, pulvérisation, *f.*

commis'erable (-miz'eur'-), *adj.*, (l.u.) digne de commisération.

commis'erate (-miz'eur-), *v.a.*, avoir de la commisération **pour** ; plaindre, avoir compassion **de** ; avoir pitié **de**.

commisera'tion (-miz'eur'é-), *n.*, commisération, *f.*

commis'erator (-teur), *n.*, personne qui a de la commisération, *f.*

commissa'riat (-cé-ri-ate), *n.*, commissariat, *m.* ; commissaires des vivres, *m.pl.* ; intendance, *f.*

com'missary, *n.*, commissaire, intendant, *m.*

com'missaryship, *n.*, commissariat, *m.*

commis'sion (-mish'eune), *n.*, commission, *f.* ; (com.) courtage ; (milit.) brevet ; (jur.) mandat, *m.* ; (of faults) commission, *f.* — of a crime ; *perpétration d'un crime, f.* — agent ; *commissionnaire en marchandises, m.* On —; *à commission.* Sin of —; *péché de commission, m.* To throw up one's —; *donner sa démission.*

commis'sion, *v.a.*, charger **de**, commissionner ; autoriser à, déléguer ; donner pouvoir à.

commis'sioner (-mish'eu'n'eur), *n.*, commissaire, commissionnaire, *m.* — in bankruptcy ; *juge-commissaire de faillite, m.* Chief — of police ; *préfet de police, m.*

commis'sionership, *n.*, commissariat, *m.*

com'missure (-mish'ioure), *n.*, (anat.) commissure, *f.*

commit', *v.a.*, commettre ; confier **à** ; livrer, entraîner ; engager, lier ; mettre ; envoyer en prison. To —; (a bill) *renvoyer à une commission.* To — to memory ; *apprendre par cœur, graver dans sa mémoire.* To — for trial ; *délivrer un mandat de dépôt* **contre**. To — one's self ; *se commettre ; se compromettre.*

commit'ment, *n.*, perpétration, *f.* ; emprisonnement ; mandat de dépôt ; (parl.) renvoi à une commission, *m.*

commit'tee (-mit'tî), *n.*, comité, *m.* ; (in parliament) commission, *f.* — room ; *salle de commission, f.* Select — ; *commission d'enquête. f.* To go into — ; (of the House of Commons) *se former en comité.* To call a — of the whole House ; *demander le comité secret.*

commit'teeship, *n.*, curatelle, tutelle, *f.*

commit'ter, *n.*, auteur de, *m.*

commode' (com'môde), *n.*, ancienne coiffure de femme ; baigneuse, commode, *f.* ; buffet à étagère, *m.* Night — ; *chaise percée, f.*

commo'dious (-mô-), *adj.*, commode ; utile ; confortable.

commo'diously (-mô-), *adv.*, commodément ; utilement, confortablement.

commo'diousness (-mô-), *n.*, commodité, *f.* ; avantage, *m.*

commod'ity, *n.*, commodité ; marchandise, denrée, *f.* ; profit, avantage ; produit, *m.*

com'modore (-dôre), *n.*, commodore ; chef de division ; bâtiment convoyeur, *m.*

com'mon, *adj.*, commun ; ordinaire ; vulgaire ; trivial ; simple. — people ; *menu peuple, m.* — soldier ; *simple soldat, m.* — law ; *droit coutumier, droit commun, m.* — prayer (book of) ; *liturgie anglicane, f.* — sense ; *sens commun, m.*

com'mon, *n.*, commune, *f.* ; communal, *m.*, (jur.) vaine pâture, *f.* ; terrain vague, *m.* ; lande, *f.* In —; *en commun.* To have nothing in — with ; *n'avoir rien de commun* **avec**. To live in —; *faire maison commune.* To be on short —s ; *être à la ration.* To put on short —s ; *mettre à la ration, rationner.*

com'mon, *v.n.*, vivre en commun.

com'monable, *adj.*, du domaine public ; pour lequel le droit de vaine pâture est admis.

com'monage (-édje), *n.*, droit de vaine pâture ; droit d'usage, *m.*

com'monalty, *n.*, bourgeoisie, *f.*

com'mon-council, *n.*, conseil municipal, *m.*

com'mon-councilor, *n.*, conseiller municipal, *m.*

com'moner, *n.*, membre de la Chambre des Communes ; bourgeois ; (b.s.) roturier, *m.* ; personne qui jouit du droit d'usage, du droit de vaine pâture, *f.* ; (at the university) étudiant sans bourse.

common'tion, *n.*, (ant.) avertissement, *m.*

com'monly, *adv.*, ordinairement, communément.

com'monness, *n.*, participation (l.u.) ; généralité, fréquence ; jouissance en commun, *f.*

com'monplace (-plèce), *adj.*, banal, commun, trivial, terre à terre. — pedant ; *pédant vulgaire, m.*

com'monplace, *n.*, lieu commun ; resumé, *m.* ; note, *f.*, banalité, *f.*

com'monplace, *v.a.*, résumer, rendre en peu de mots.

com'mons (-meu'n'ze), *n.*, ordinaire, *m.* ; table, nourriture en commun ; Chambre des Communes ; bourgeoisie, *f.*

com'mon-sailor, *n.*, simple matelot, *m.*

com'mon-sewer, *n.*, égout public, *m.*

commonweal' (-wîle), *n.*, bien public, *m.*

commonwealth' (-wélth), *n.*, chose publique, république, *f.* ; état, gouvernement, *m.*

commo'tion (-mô-), *n.*, commotion, *f.*

com'mune, *n.*, commune, *f.*

commune' (-mioune), *v.n.*, conférer, parler ; converser, s'entretenir. To — with one's self ; *se recueillir.*

commu'nicable (-miou-), *adj.*, communicable ; qu'on peut communiquer.

commu'nicant (-miou-), *n.*, communiant, *m.*, communiante, *f.*

commu'nicate (-miou-), *v.a.*, communiquer, faire connaître, faire part **de**.

commu'nicate, *v.n.*, communiquer ; se communiquer ; correspondre ; (ecc.) communier.

communica'tion (-miou-ni-ké-), *n.*, communication, *f.*

commu'nicative, *adj.*, communicatif.

commu'nicativeness, *n.*, caractère communicatif, *m.*

commun'ion (-miou'n'ieune), *n.*, communion, *f.* ; commerce, *m.* ; relations, *f.pl.* — cup ; calice, *m.* — table ; *sainte table, f.*

commun'ion-service (-seur-), *n.*, office du saint sacrement, *m.*

commu'nity (-miou-), *n.*, communauté, société, *f.*, public ; état, *m.* ; classe, *f.*

commutabil'ity (-miou-), *n.*, permutabilité, *f.* ; (jur.) commuabilité, *f.*

commut'able (-miou-), *adj.*, permutable, échangeable ; (jur.) commuable.

commuta'tion (-miou-té-), *n.*, commutation, permutation, *f.* ; échange, *m.* ; (jur.) commuation, *f.*

commu'tative (-miou-té-), *adj.*, commutatif.

commute' (-mioute), *v.a.*, échanger ; changer ; (jur.) commuer, racheter.

commute', *v.n.*, tenir lieu **de**.

com'pact, *n.*, pacte ; contrat, *m.* ; convention, *f.*

com'pact, *adj.*, compact ; serré ; lié ; uni, concis.

compact', *v.a.*, rendre compact ; unir, condenser.

compact'ly, *adv.*, d'une manière serrée ; brièvement ; (of style) avec concision.

compact'ness, *n.*, caractère compact, *m.* ; (phys.) compacité, densité, *f.*

compan'ion (-ieune), *n.*, compagnon, *m.*, compagne, *f.* ; camarade, *m.f.* ; (to a lady) dame de compagnie, demoiselle de compagnie. *f.* ; (furniture) pendant, *m.* ; (nav.) capot ; échelle, *m.* — ladder ; (nav.) *échelle de dunette, f.*

compan'ionable, *adj.*, sociable ; d'un commerce facile.

compan'ionableness, *n.*, sociabilité, *f.*
compan'ionably, *adj.*, sociablement.
compan'ionship, *n.*, camaraderie ; compagnie, société, *f.*
com'pany, *n.*, compagnie ; société, corporation, *f.* ; monde, entourage, *m.* ; (of actors) troupe, *f.* ; (nav.) équipage, *m.* Joint-stock —; *société par actions, société anonyme.* We have — to-day ; *nous avons du monde aujourd'hui.* To bear —; *accompagner ; tenir compagnie* à. To keep — with ; *fréquenter ;* (to court) *faire la cour* à. To keep —; *voir du monde.* To sail in —; (nav.) *aller ou naviguer de conserve.* To keep good *ou* bad —; *fréquenter la bonne ou la mauvaise compagnie.* To part —; *se séparer.* To request the — of, at dinner, etc. ; *inviter à (venir) dîner,* etc.
com'parable, *adj.*, comparable.
compar'ative, *adj.*, comparatif, relatif ; du comparatif.
compar'ative, *n.*, comparatif, *m.*
compar'atively, *adv.*, comparativement, relativement.
compare' (-père), *v.a.*, comparer ; (of accounts) confronter. *v.n.*, rivaliser **avec** ; le disputer à. Compared with ; *en comparaison* **de**, *auprès* **de**.
compar'ison (-ceune), *n.*, comparaison, *f.* In — with ; *auprès* **de** ; *en comparaison* **de**. Beyond —; *sans comparaison, sans contredit.* —s are odious ; *toute comparaison cloche* (ou *pèche*).
compart'ment, *n.*, compartiment, *m.* ; subdivision d'un bâtiment ; partie d'un terrain, d'un dessin, *f.*
com'pass (keu'm'-), *n.*, enceinte, *f.* ; cercle, *m.* ; (fig.) sphère, étendue, *f.;* (nav.) compas de route, *m.*, boussole ; (reach) portée, *f.* ; (of the voice) étendue, *f.* Within —; *avec modération, sans exagération.* To keep within —; *retenir dans de justes bornes.* *v.n.*, *observer les convenances, se tenir dans de justes limites.* — card ; *rose des vents, f.* —needle ; *aiguille de boussole, f.*
com'pass (keu'm'-), *v.a.*, faire le tour **de** ; environner ; assiéger ; venir à bout **de**, embrasser ; méditer, imaginer, accomplir. To — any one's ruin ; *comploter la ruine de quelqu'un.*
com'passes (keu'm'pass'ize), *n.pl.*, compas, *m.sing.*
compas'sion (ko'm'pash'eune), *n.*, compassion, pitié, *f.*
compas'sionate, *adj.*, compatissant.
compas'sionate, *v.a.*, compatir à ; avoir pitié **de**.
compas'sionately, *adv.*, avec pitié.
compater'nity, *n.*, compérage, *m.*
compatibil'ity, *n.*, compatibilité, *f.*
compat'ible, *adj.*, compatible **avec**.
compat'ibleness, *n.*, compatibilité.
compat'ibly, *adv.*, d'une manière compatible.
compa'triot (-pé-), *n.*, compatriote, *m.f.*
compeer' (-pîre), *n.*, égal, pair, compagnon, *m.*, compagne, *f.* ; confrère, compère, *m.*
compel' (-pèle), *v.a.*, contraindre **de** ; forcer **de** ; obliger à or **de**.
compel'lable (-pèl'lab'l), *adj.*, (jur.) contraignable ; qu'on peut forcer.
compel'lably, *adv.*, par force.
compel'ler, *n.*, personne qui contraint, *f.*
compend'ious, *adj.*, raccourci, abrégé, concis, compact.
compend'iously, *adv.*, brièvement, en abrégé, en raccourci, compendieusement.
compend'iousness, *n.*, brièveté, concision, *f.*
compend'ium (-pè'n'di-eume), *n.*, compendium, abrégé, précis, épitomé, *m.*
compen'sable, *adj.*, (ant.) compensable.
com'pensate (-séte), *v.a.*, compenser **de** ; dédommager **de**.
com'pensate, *v.n.*, se compenser.

compensa'tion (-sé-), *n.*, compensation, *f.* — balance ; (horl.) *balancier compensateur, m.*
compen'sative *ou* **compen'satory** (-tori), *adj.*, compensatoire, compensateur.
compete' (-pîte), *v.n.*, concourir ; rivaliser **avec** ; disputer à ; faire concurrence à ; être en concurrence **avec**. To — for ; *concourir* **pour**, *disputer* à.
com'petence *ou* **com'petency** (-pi-), *n.*, capacité, aptitude ; (jur.) compétence ; (fortune) aisance, *f.* To have a —; *avoir de quoi vivre.*
com'petent (-pi-), *adj.*, compétent ; raisonnable ; suffisant ; convenable. To be — to fill ; *être à la hauteur* **de** ; *être capable de remplir.*
com'petently, *adv.*, convenablement ; suffisamment ; raisonnablement.
competi'tion (-pi-tish'-), *n.*, (of commerce) concurrence, *f.* ; (for a prize, a place) concours, *m.* To offer for —; *mettre au concours.*
compet'itor (-teur), *n.*, compétiteur ; concurrent, rival, *m.*
compila'tion (-paï-lé-), *n.*, compilation, *f.*, recueil, *m.*
compile' (-païle), *v.a.*, compiler, composer.
compi'ler, *n.*, compilateur, *m.*
compla'cence *ou* **compla'cency** (-plé-), *n.*, plaisir, *m.* ; satisfaction ; complaisance, *f.*
compla'cent (-plé-), *adj.*, de complaisance.
compla'cently, *adv.*, avec complaisance.
complain' (-plé'ne), *v.n.*, se plaindre.
complain'ant, *n.*, plaignant, *m.*, plaignante, *f.;* demandeur, *m.*, demanderesse, *f.*
complain'er, *n.*, personne qui se plaint, *f.*
complaint' (-plé'n'te), *n.*, plainte ; (illness) maladie, *f.* ; grief, *m.* ; (admin.) réclamation, *f.* Cause of —; *sujet de plainte, m.*
com'plaisance (-za'n'ce), *n.*, complaisance, *f.*
com'plaisant, *adj.*, complaisant.
com'plaisantly, *adv.*, complaisamment.
com'plement (-pli-), *n.*, complément ; (fig.) ornement, *m.* Full —; (nav., mil.) *grand complet, m.* To have one's full —; *être au grand complet.*
complement'al, *adj.* complémentaire.
complete' (-plîte), *adj.*, complet, achevé ; accompli, parfait.
complete', *v.a.*, compléter, achever ; accomplir ; réaliser, mettre le comble à.
complete'ly, *adv.*, complètement.
complete'ness (-plît'-), *n.*, caractère complet, *m.* ; perfection, *f.*
comple'tion (-plî-), *n.*, achèvement, accomplissement, *m.*, perfection, *f.*
com'pletories, *n.pl.*, (rel.) complies, *f.pl.*
com'pletory (-plî-), *adj.*, qui accomplit.
com'plex (-plèkse), *adj.*, complexe, compliqué ; (arith.) composé.
complex'edness, *n.*, complication, *f.*
complex'ion (-plèk'sheune), *n.*, teint, *m.* ; couleur, *f.* ; (med.) tempérament, *m.;* complexion, *f.;* (fig.) caractère, *m.* To put a different — upon ; *voir sous un autre jour.*
complex'ional, *adj.*, de tempérament.
complex'ionally, *adv.*, par le tempérament.
complex'ity *ou* **com'plexness** (-plèks'-), *n.*, complexité, complication, *f.*
com'plexly, *adv.*, d'une manière complexe.
compli'ance (-plaï'-), consentement, acquiescement, *m.* ; complaisance ; condescendance, *f.* In — with ; *conformément à, suivant.*
compli'ant, *adj.*, soumis ; souple, flexible ; complaisant, accommodant.
compli'antly, *adv.*, avec complaisance, avec soumission.
com'plicate, *v.a.*, compliquer ; embrouiller ; composer. To — matters ; *pour compliquer l'affaire.*
com'plicated (-pli-), *adj.*, compliqué. To become —; *se compliquer.*
complica'tion (-pli-ké-), *n.*, complication, *f.*

compli'er (-plaï'eur), n., complaisant, m. ; qui se plie facilement.

com'pliment, n., compliment ; présent, cadeau, m. ; gracieuseté, galanterie, f. pl., salutations, f.pl. With the author's —s ; respectueux hommages de l'auteur, m.pl. —s of the season ; souhaits de bonne année, m.pl. Best —s ; salutations empressées, f.pl.

com'pliment, v.a., complimenter, féliciter ; faire son compliment à ; faire cadeau à.

compliment'ary, adj., complimenteur ; flatteur.

com'plimenter, n., complimenteur, m., complimenteuse, f.

com'plin (-pline) ou **com'pline** (-pline), n., (ecc.) complies, f.pl.

comply' (-plaï), v.n., acquiescer à ; se soumettre à ; se conformer à ; s'accommoder à ; se plier à ; se rendre à ; adhérer à ; obéir à ; accéder à ; (fulfil) remplir, observer ; satisfaire à.

compo'nent (-pô-), adj., constituant ; composant.

compo'nent, n., (mech.) composante ; partie constituante, f., composant, m.

comport', v.n., s'accorder avec ; convenir à ; comporter. To — with ; supporter.

comport', v.a., souffrir, endurer. To — one's self ; se comporter.

comport'ment, n., conduite, f.

com'pos men'tis (-mè'n'-), adj., (jur.) sain d'esprit.

compose' (-pôze), v.a., composer ; écrire ; rédiger, arranger ; calmer ; apaiser ; tranquilliser. To — one's self ; se calmer ; se remettre, s'arranger. To — one's looks ; se composer le visage.

composed' (-pôz'de), adj., calme, tranquille, apaisé.

compos'edly (-pôz'èdli), adv., tranquillement, avec calme.

compos'edness (-poz'èd'-), n., calme, m. ; tranquillité, f.

compos'er (-pôz'-), n., personne qui règle un différend, f. ; auteur ; (music) compositeur, m.

compos'ing (-pôz'-), adj., (pharm.) calmant ; (print.) à composer. — draught ; potion calmante, f. — room ; (print.) atelier de composition, m.

compos'ing-stick, n., (print.) composteur, m.

compos'ite (-poz'aïte), adj., composite ; composé. — candle ; bougie composée, f.

composi'tion (-zish'-), n., composition, (fig.) nature, f. ; (com.) atermoiement, atermoîment, arrangement, m. ; (jur.) transaction, f., concordat, m.

compos'itor (-poz'i-teur), n., (print.) compositeur, m.

com'post (-pôste), n., compost ; engrais, m.

compo'sure (-pô-jeur), n., calme, sang-froid, m. ; tranquillité, (l.u.) composition, f. — of carriage ; maintien calme, m.

compota'tion (-té-), n., libation, f.

com'pound (-paou'n'de), n., composé, m. ; composition, f.

com'pound, adj., composé, complexe. — interest ; (com.) intérêt composé, intérêt des intérêts, m.

compound', v.a., composer ; (com.) entrer en composition pour, venir à composition pour ; atermoyer ; mêler, combiner ; arranger. To — a felony ; entrer en composition avec le voleur (en vue de restitution). To — with one's creditors ; s'arranger, faire un concordat avec ses créanciers.

compound', v.n., s'arranger ; entrer en arrangement ; transiger.

compound'able, adj., qui peut être composé.

compound'er, n., personne qui mélange, f. ; auteur de transactions ; arbitre, entremetteur, (jur.) compositeur à l'amiable, m.

comprehend' (-pri-hè'n'de), v.a., comprendre ; renfermer.

comprehen'sible (-pri-), adj., compréhensible ; saisissable ; intelligible.

comprehen'sibly (-pri-), adv., intelligiblement.

comprehen'sion (-pri-), n., action de comprendre ; compréhension, f.

comprehen'sive (-pri-), adj., étendu, vaste ; compréhensif.

comprehen'sively, adv., avec étendue, largement.

comprehen'siveness, n., étendue, portée, f. ; richesse (of ideas), f.

com'press (-prèce), n., compresse, f.

compress' (-prèce), v.a., resserrer, comprimer.

compressibil'ity, n., compressibilité, f.

compress'ible, adj., compressible.

compres'sion (-prèsh'-), n., compression ; concision, f. ; refoulement, m.

compress'ive, adj., compressif.

comprise' (-praïze), v.a., contenir, renfermer, comprendre.

com'promise (-maïze), n., compromis ; arrangement, accommodement, m. ; transaction, f.

com'promise, v.a., compromettre ; arranger.

com'promise, v.n., transiger.

com'promiser, n., personne qui fait un compromis, f.

compul'sion (-peul-), n., contrainte, f.

compul'sive (-peul-), adj., par contrainte, forcé, obligatoire, coercitif.

compul'sively, adv., par force, par contrainte ; forcément.

compul'sorily (-peul-), adv., par force, de force, forcément.

compul'sory (-peul-), adj., obligatoire.

compunc'tion (-peugnk'sheune), n., componction, f. ; vif remords, m.

comput'able (-piout'-), adj., qui peut être compté, computé, supputé ; calculable.

computa'tion (-piou-té-), n., supputation, f. ; compte, calcul, m.

compute' (-pioute), v.a., calculer ; supputer ; compter, estimer, évaluer ; (of the calendar) computer.

comput'er, n., calculateur, m. ; (of the calendar) computiste, m.

com'rade (-rède), n., camarade, copain, m.

com'radeship, n., camaraderie, f.

con, n., contre, m.

con (over), v.a., savoir ; répéter ; étudier, repasser, relire.

concat'enate (-cat'i-), v.a., enchaîner, lier.

concatena'tion (-né-), n., enchaînement, m.

con'cave (cogn'kéve), adj., concave ; creux.

con'caveness (-kév'-) ou **concav'ity** (-cav'i-), n., concavité, f.

conca'vo-con'cave (-ké'vo-, -kéve), adj., concavo-concave.

conca'vo-con'vex (-ké'vo-), adj., concavo-convexe.

conceal' (-cîle), v.a., cacher ; (fig.) dissimuler ; céler (from, à) ; dérober à ; taire ; (jur.) receler, ne pas divulguer.

conceal'able, adj., déguisable.

conceal'er, n., (jur.) receleur ; non-révélateur, m.

conceal'ment, n., action de cacher, dissimulation, f. ; secret, mystère ; abri, m. ; retraite, cachette, f. ; (jur.) recèlement, secret, m. — of birth ; suppression de part, f. In — ; en secret, en cachette. To keep in — ; v.a., tenir caché ; v.n., se tenir caché.

concede' (-cîde), v.a., concéder, accorder, admettre. To — the point ; tomber d'accord sur le point, être d'accord.

concede', v.n., faire des concessions.

conceit' (-cîte), n., imagination, opinion, pensée ; idée plaisante ; suffisance, vanité, pointe, f. To be out of — with ; être dégoûté de. To put out of — ; dégoûter de. Full of — ; enflé de vanité.

conceit'ed, *adj.*, suffisant ; vain, maniéré, prétentieux, enflé de vanité.

conceit'edly, *adv.*, avec suffisance ; avec vanité, avec prétention.

conceit'edness, *n.*, vanité, suffisance, *f.*

conceiv'able (-cîv'-), *adj.*, concevable.

conceiv'ably, *adv.*, d'une manière concevable.

conceive' (-cîve), *v.a.*, concevoir ; imaginer ; croire, penser.

conceive', *v.n.*, concevoir.

conceiv'er, *n.*, qui conçoit, qui pénètre (le sens d'une chose). Wise —s ; *esprits pénétrants, m.pl.*

concen'ter (-cè'n'teur), *v.a.*, concentrer ; réunir en un centre.

concen'ter, *v.n.*, se concentrer.

con'centrate, *v.a.*, concentrer.

con'centrate, *v.n.*, se concentrer.

concentra'tion (-tré-), *n.*, concentration, *f.*

concen'tric *ou* **concen'trical,** *adj.*, concentrique.

concep'tible, *adj.*, (ant.) concevable.

concep'tion (-cèp'-), *n.*, conception ; idée, notion, *f.;* projet, dessein, *m.*

concern' (-ceurne), *n.*, affaire, *f.;* intérêt ; soin, souci, chagrin, *m.;* préoccupation ; (com.) entreprise, *f.;* établissement, *m.*

concern', *v.a.*, concerner ; regarder ; intéresser (with, à) ; inquiéter. To — one's self about ; *s'intéresser* à ; *s'occuper* de ; *s'inquiéter* de ; *se mettre en peine de*. To be —ed ; *être inquiet* de ; (in) *prendre part* à. To all whom it may —; *à tous ceux à qui il appartiendra*. It concerns me to know ; *il m'importe de savoir*.

concerned', *adj.*, inquiet ; (as counsel in a suit) occupant.

concern'edly (-ceurn'èd-), *adv.*, avec intérêt, avec affection, avec peine, avec inquiétude.

concern'ing, *prep.*, touchant, concernant, sur ; à l'égard de.

concern'ment, *n.*, intérêt, *m.;* affaire ; interposition ; sollicitude, inquiétude, *f.*

concert' (-ceurte), *v.a.* and *n.*, concerter ; ajuster ; composer ; se concerter.

con'cert, *n.*, concert ; (fig.) unisson, *m.* In —; *de concert, à l'unisson.* — room ; *salle de concert, f.*

concert'ed, *adj.*, concerté ; (mus.) d'ensemble.

concer'to (-ceur-), *n.*, (mus.) concerto, *m.*

conces'sion (-cèsh'-), *n.*, concession, *f.;* aveu, *m.*

conces'sionary, *adj.*, par concession.

conces'sive (-cès'sive), *adj.*, qui implique concession.

conces'sively, *adv.*, par concession.

conch (cogn'ke), *n.*, conque ; coquille, *f.*

conch'a (-ka), *n.*, (anat.) conque, *f.*

conchif'erous (-kif'eur'-), *adj.*, conchifère.

conch'ite (-kaïte), *n.*, conchite, *f.*

conch'oid (-koïde), *n.*, (geom.) conchoïde, *f.*

conchol'ogist (-kol'-), *n.*, conchyliologiste, *m.*

conchol'ogy (-kol'-), *n.*, conchyliologie, *f.*

conchyl'ious (-kil'-), *adj.*, de coquillage.

concil'iable, *adj.*, (ant.) réconciliable.

concil'iate, *v.a.*, concilier.

concilia'tion (-cil-i-é-), *n.*, conciliation, *f.*

concil'iator (-é-teur), *n.*, conciliateur, *m.*, conciliatrice, *f.*

concil'iatory (-tori), *adj.*, conciliant, conciliatoire.

concise' (-çaïce), *adj.*, concis.

concise'ly, *adv.*, avec concision, succinctement, laconiquement.

concise'ness, *n.*, concision, *f.*

conci'sion (-cij'eune), *n.*, coupure ; excision, *f.*

con'clave (con'cléve), *n.*, conclave, *m.*, assemblée, *f.*

conclude' (-clioude), *v.a.*, conclure ; terminer, finir ; considérer comme ; juger, estimer.

conclude', *v.n.*, conclure ; se terminer à, par *ou* en ; finir par.

conclud'ing, *adj.*, final, dernier.

conclu'sion (-cliou'jeune), *n.*, conclusion ; décision ; fin, *f.* To try —s with ; *se mesurer* avec.

conclu'sive (-cliou-cive), *adj.*, concluant, final, décisif, conclusif.

conclu'sively, *adv.*, d'une manière concluante, décisive.

conclu'siveness, *n.*, caractère concluant, *m.*

concoct', *v.a.*, digérer ; élaborer, préparer ; mûrir ; concevoir, dresser (un plan).

concoc'tion, *n.*, coction, concoction ; élaboration ; (plotting) machination, *f.*

concoct'ive, *adj.*, (med.) concocteur.

concom'itance *ou* **concom'itancy,** *n.*, concomitance, *f.*, concours, *m.*

concom'itant, *adj.*, concomitant, qui accompagne.

concom'itantly, *adv.*, par concomitance, en compagnie avec d'autres.

con'cord, *n.*, concorde ; harmonie, *f.;* accord, *m.;* (mus.) consonance ; (gram.) concordance, *f.*

concord', *v.n.*, (ant.) s'unir, concorder, s'accorder.

concord'ance, *n.*, concordance, *f.;* index de l'Ecriture sainte, *m.*

concord'ancy, *n.*, concordance, *f.*, accord, *m.*

concord'ant, *adj.*, d'accord ; concordant.

concord'at, *n.*, concordat, *m.*

con'course (cogn'côrse), *n.*, concours, *m.;* affluence ; foule ; réunion, *f.*

concres'cence (-crès'-), *n.*, concrétion, *f.*

con'crete (-crîte), *n.*, concret, corps concret ; (mas.) béton, *m.* — work ; *bétonnage, m.*

con'crete, *adj.*, concret ; figé.

concrete', *v.n.*, devenir concret ; se coaguler ; se solidifier.

concrete', *v.a.*, rendre concret ; solidifier.

concrete'ly, *adv.*, d'une manière concrète.

concrete'ness, *n.*, état concret, *m.*

concre'tion (-crî-), *n.*, concrétion, *f.*

concre'tive, *adj.*, coagulant.

concu'binage (congn'kiou-bi-nédje), *n.*, concubinage, *m.*

con'cubine (-kiou-baïne), *n.*, concubine, *f.*

concu'piscence (-kiou-), *n.*, concupiscence, *f.*

concu'piscent, *adj.*, lascif, libidineux.

concu'piscible, *adj.*, concupiscible.

concur' (-keur), *v.n.*, concorder ; s'accorder ; concourir ; (in) être d'accord **avec** ; partager.

concur'rence (-keur-), *n.*, concours ; assentiment, *m.*

concur'rent, *adj.*, qui concourt, qui s'accorde ; concourant.

concur'rently, *adv.*, concurremment.

concus'sion (-keush'-), *n.*, secousse, *f.;* ébranlement, choc, *m.;* (ant.) concussion, exaction, extorsion, *f.*

concus'sive (-keus'-), *adj.*, qui ébranle.

condemn' (-dème), *v.a.*, (as unfit for use) réformer, condamner, blâmer ; (to blame for) condamner de, blâmer **de**.

condem'nable (-dèm-na-), *adj.*, condamnable.

condemna'tion (-dèm-né-),*n.*,condamnation,*f.*

condem'natory (-dèm'na-tori), *adj.*, condamnatoire.

condem'ner (-dèm-neur), *n.*, personne qui condamne, *f.;* condamnateur, -trice, *m.f.*

condens'able, *adj.*, condensable.

condensa'tion (-sé-), *n.*, condensation, *f.*

condense', *v.a.*, condenser, (food) concentrer, (fig.) resserrer, abréger.

condense', *v.n.*, se condenser, (fig.) se resserrer.

condens'er, *n.*, (phys.) condensateur ; (mec.) condenseur, *m.*

condens'ing, *n.*, condensation, *f.*

condens'ing-engine (-è'n'djine), *n.*, machine à condenser ; condenseuse, *f.*

condens'ing-jet (-djète),*n.*, jet d'eau froide,*m.*

condens'ity, n., condensation; densité, f.

condescend', v.n., condescendre à; s'abaisser à ou jusqu'à, daigner; se soumettre à; céder.

condescend'ence, **condescend'ency**, n., condescendance, f.

condescend'ingly, adv., par condescendance.

condescen'sion (-di-), n., condescendance, f. ; acte de condescendance, m.

condign' (-daïne), adj., proportionné; mérité, juste.

condign'ly, adv., justement.

con'diment, n., assaisonnement, condiment, m.

condisci'ple (-dis-çaï-), n., condisciple, m.

condi'tion (-dish'-), n., condition, f. ; état, m. Out of —; en mauvais état. In good ou bad —; en bon, en mauvais état. On — that; à condi- tion que. In a — to; en état de.

condi'tional (-dish'eu'n'-), adj., conditionnel.

condi'tional, n., (ant.) restriction, f. ; (gram.) conditionnel, m.

condi'tionally, adv., conditionnellement.

condi'tioned (-dish'eu'n'de), adj., condi- tionné; de condition, de rang. Good ou well —; bien conditionné; en bon état ; (fig.) d'un bon naturel.

condole' (-dôle), v.n. and a., partager la dou- leur de; prendre part à la douleur de. To — with ; faire ses compliments de condoléance à.

condo'lence, n., condoléance, f.

condona'tion, n., pardon, m.

condone', v.a., (things) pardonner.

con'dor, n., condor, m.

conduce' (-diouce), v.n., contribuer à; servir à ; conduire à; tendre à.

condu'cible, adj., utile; avantageux; qui contribue.

condu'cibleness, n., utilité, f.

condu'cive (-diou-cive), adj., utile à; avanta- geux à; propre à; qui contribue à. To be — to; contribuer à, tendre à.

condu'civeness, n., utilité; propriété de conduire, de contribuer, f.

con'duct (-deucte), n., conduite; direction, f. ; procédé; guide, m., démarches, f.pl.

conduct', v.a., conduire; diriger, mener, guider, introduire dans. To — one's self; se conduire, se comporter.

conduct'or (-deuct'eur), n., (mus.) chef d'or- chestre; directeur; guide; (of an omnibus) conducteur, m. ; (mil.) vaguemestre. Lightning —; paratonnerre, m.

conduct'ress, n., conductrice, f.

con'duit (-dite), n., conduit; couloir, passage, m.

con'dyle (-dil), n., (anat.) condyle, m.

cone (côn), n., (math.) cône; (bot.) cône, strobile, m. ; pomme de pin, f.

co'ney (cô-), n. V. co'ny.

co'ney-wool, n. V. co'ny-wool.

confab'ulate (-fab'iou-), v.n., confabuler ; s'entretenir familièrement avec.

confabula'tion (-fab'iou-lé-), n., confabula- tion, f. ; entretien familier, m.

con'fect ou **confec'tion** (-fèk-), n., confection, confiture, sucrerie, f.

confec'tioner (-eur), n., confiseur, patissier, m.

confec'tionery (-euri), n., confiserie, f. ; magasin, m., fabrique, f., de bonbons, de sucre- ries; bonbons, m.pl., sucreries, f.pl.

confed'eracy (-fèd'eur'-), n., confédération, f. ; ligue; (jur.) association illégale, f. ; compérage, m.

confed'erate (-fèd'eur'-), v.a., confédérer.

confed'erate, v.n., se confédérer avec.

confed'erate, adj., confédéré; de confédéré, ligué à ou avec.

confed'erate, n., allié; complice, compère, m.

confedera'tion (-fèd'eur'é-), n., fédération, confédération, f.

confer' (-feur), v.a., conférer; accorder. To — upon; conférer à. To — an honor upon; faire un grand honneur à.

confer', v.n., conférer de.

con'ference (-feur-), n., conférence, f.

confer'va (-feur-), n., (bot.) conferve, f.

confess' (-fèce), v.a., confesser; avouer; re- connaître, admettre.

confess', v.n., se confesser; (jur.) faire des aveux.

confessed', adj., reconnu, confessé, avoué.

confess'edly (-fèss'èd-), adv., de son aveu ; de l'aveu de tout le monde; ouvertement.

confes'sion (-fèsh'-), n., confession, f. ; aveu, m., (jur.) aveux, m.pl. To go to —; aller à con- fesse. A frank — is good for the soul; rien ne soulage comme un aveu sincère.

confes'sional, n., confessionnal, m.

confes'sor (-ceur), n., confesseur, m.

con'fidant (-fi-), n., confident, m.

con'fidante, n., confidente, f.

confide' (-faïde), v.n., se confier à; se fier à, avoir confiance en; s'en remettre à.

confide', v.a., confier à, charger de.

con'fidence (-fi-), n., confiance; confidence ; hardiesse, assurance, f. To put — in; avoir confiance en.

con'fident, n., confident, m., confidente, f.

con'fident, adj., confiant; certain; sûr; assuré, hardi.

confiden'tial, adj., de confiance; confidentiel.

confiden'tially, adv., de confiance; confiden- tiellement.

con'fidently, adv., avec confiance, positive- ment.

configura'tion (-figh'iou-ré-), n., configura- tion, f.

confi'nable (-faï'n'-), adj., que l'on peut limiter.

con'fine (-faïne), n., confins, m.pl.; bord, m. ; limite, borne, f.

confine', v.n., confiner à.

confine', v.a., confiner, enfermer, reléguer ; retenir, limiter, borner. To be —d ; faire ses couches, accoucher. To be —d to one's room, one's bed; garder la chambre, le lit. To — one's self to; se limiter, se borner à. To —; (to barracks) consigner. —d air; air renfermé, m.

confine'less (-faï'n'-), adj., illimité.

confine'ment (-faï'n'-), n., confinement; em- prisonnement, m. ; (milit.) arrêts, m.pl.; con- signe, f. ; (of women) couches, f.pl. In close —; au secret. Solitary —; emprisonnement cellulaire.

confin'ity, n., proximité; contiguïté, f.

confirm' (-feurme), v.a., confirmer; fortifier, affermir ; (to harden) endurcir.

confirm'able, adj., confirmable.

confirma'tion, n., confirmation, f. ; affer- missement, m.

confirm'atory, adj., confirmatif ; qui con- firme ; en confirmation de, à l'appui de.

confirmed' (-feurm'de), adj., positif, certain ; invétéré, fieffé, incorrigible, endurci.

confirm'edness (-feurm'èd'-), n., caractère invétéré, m.

confirm'er, n., confirmateur, m.

confis'cable, adj., confiscable.

confis'cate, v.a., confisquer.

confisca'tion (-ké-), n., confiscation, f.

con'fiscator (-ké-teur), n., auteur de confisca- tion, m.

confis'catory, adj., de confiscation.

confit'eor, n., confiteor, m.

conflagra'tion (-gré-), n., conflagration, f. ; embrasement ; incendie, m.

con'flict, n., conflit, entrechoquement, m. ; lutte, contradiction, f.

conflict', v.n., s'entrechoquer; lutter ; être en contradiction avec ; être en conflit avec.

conflict'ing, adj., en conflit, contradictoire ; en contradiction avec ; opposé, contraire.

con'fluence (-fliou-), n., confluent, m. ; afflu- ence, f. ; concours, m., (med.) confluence, f.

con'fluent, adj., confluent, qui conflue. To be —; confluer.

conform', v.a., conformer.

conform', v.n., se conformer.

conform'able, adj., conforme à; d'accord avec.

conform'ably, adv., conformément à.

conforma'tion (-mé-), n., conformation; conformité, f.

conform'ist, n., conformiste, m.

conform'ity, n., conformité, f. In — with; conformément à.

confound' (-faou'n'de), v.a., confondre; renverser; embarrasser; rendre confus; troubler. — him! que le diable l'emporte! — it! diable!

confound'ed (-faou'n'd'ède), part., adj., confondu; maudit, vilain, sacré.

confound'edly, adv., terriblement, furieusement, diablement.

confound'edness, n., confusion, f.; embarras, m.

confrater'nity (-teur-), n., confrérie; confraternité, f.

confront' (-freu'n'te), v.a., confronter; affronter; se présenter de front à; attaquer de front; faire face à; tenir tête à; se trouver en face de.

confronta'tion (-freu'n'té-), n., confrontation, f.

confuse' (-fiouze), v.a., mettre la confusion dans; rendre confus, déconcerter; embrouiller; confondre, troubler; mettre en désordre.

confus'edly (-fiouz'èdli), adv., confusément.

confus'edness (-fiouz'kèd-), n., confusion, f.

confu'sion (-fiou-jeune), n., confusion; ruine, f.; embarras, désordre, trouble, m.

confu'table (-fiou-), adj., réfutable.

confuta'tion, n., réfutation, f.

confute', v.a., réfuter.

confut'er, n., réfutateur, m.

congeal' (-djîle), v.a., congeler, glacer, geler.

congeal', v.n., se congeler, se geler; (of rivers) prendre.

congeal'able, adj., congelable.

congeal'ment, n., congélation, f.

con'gener (-djî-neur), n., congénère.

congener'ic, adj., congénère.

conge'nial (-djî-), adj., de la même nature; naturel; sympathique à, conforme à. A — task; une tâche agréable. — to the language; dans le génie de la langue.

congenial'ity ou conge'nialness, n., affinité, analogie, conformité, sympathie, f.

congen'ital (-djè'n'-), adj., (med.) congénital.

con'ger-eel (cogn'gh'eur), n., congre, m.; anguille de mer, f.

conge'ries (co'n'djî-ri-îze), n.s. and pl., masse informe, f.; amas, m.

congest' (-djeste), v.a., amasser, entasser, amonceler; engorger. To become —ed; se congestionner; s'engorger.

conges'tion (-djèst'ieune), n., amas, m.; (med.) congestion, f.

congest'ive, adj., congeste ou qui provoque la congestion.

conglo'bate (-glô-), v.a., former en globe, englober.

conglo'bate, adj., conglobé; en forme de globe.

conglobe' (-glôbe), v.a. and n., (ant.) conglober; se conglober.

conglob'ulate (-glob'iou-), v.n., (of animals) se pelotonner; (of fluids) se réunir en globules.

conglom'erate (-glom'eur'-), v.a., conglomérer. v.n., se conglomérer.

conglom'erate, adj., congloméré.

conglom'erate, n. (geol.) conglomérat, m.

conglomera'tion (-eur'é-), n., conglomération, f.

conglu'tinate (-gliou-), v.a., conglutiner.

conglu'tinate, v.n., s'unir par conglutination, se conglutiner.

conglutina'tion, n., conglutination; fusion, union, f.

conglu'tinative, adj., conglutinatif, conglutinant.

congrat'ulate (-grat'iou-), v.a., féliciter de, complimenter de; faire son compliment à. To — one's self; se féliciter de.

congratula'tion (-lé-), n., félicitation, f.; compliment, m.

congrat'ulator (-lé-teur), n., personne qui félicite, f.; congratulateur, m.

congrat'ulatory, adj., de félicitation; congratulatoire.

con'gregate (cogn'gri-), v.a., rassembler.

con'gregate, v.n., se rassembler, s'assembler chez; se rendre à ou dans.

congrega'tion (-gri-ghé-), n., congrégation; (in a church) assemblée, f.; auditoire, m.; assistance; (of things) agrégation, f.; amas; assemblage, m.; de l'assemblée.

congrega'tional, adj., de la congrégation;

congrega'tionalist, n., congréganiste, m.f.

con'gress (cogn'grèce), n., congrès, m.; rencontre, f. —man; Membre du Congrès, m.

congres'sional, adj., congressional.

con'gruence ou **con'gruency** (-grou-), n., convenance, f.

con'gruent, adj., convenable, congru; conforme, correspondant; (geom.) superposable.

congru'ity (-grou-), n., convenance, conformité, (theol.) congruité, f.

con'gruous, adj., convenable à, conforme à; congruent, (geom.) homogène.

con'gruously, adv., convenablement, correctement, pertinemment, régulièrement; ⊙congrûment.

con'ic ou **con'ical**, adj., conique.

con'ically, adv., en forme de cône.

con'icalness, n., forme conique, f.

con'ics, n.pl., (geom.) sections coniques, f.pl.

conif'erous (-'eur'-), adj., conifère.

conject'ural (-djèkt'iou-), adj., conjectural, de conjecture.

conject'urally, adv., conjecturalement.

conject'ure (-djèkt'ioure), v.a. and n., conjecturer.

conject'ure, n., conjecture, f.

conject'urer, n., faiseur de conjectures, m.

conjoin' (-djoïne), v.a., joindre, conjoindre, unir; adjoindre.

conjoin', v.n., se joindre à; s'unir à.

conjoint' (-djoï'n'te), adj., lié; (mus.) uni, conjoint.

conjoint'ly, adv., conjointement, d'accord; de concert.

con'jugal (-djiou-), adj., conjugal, matrimonial.

con'jugally, adv., conjugalement.

con'jugate (-djiou-), v.a., conjuguer. To be —d; se conjuguer.

conjuga'tion, n., conjugaison, f.

conjunct' (-djeugn'kte), adj., réuni.

conjunc'tion (-djeugn'k'sheune), n., union, liaison, conjonction, f. In — with; conjointement avec.

conjunc'tive, adj., uni; conjonctif. — mood; subjonctif, m.

conjunc'tively, adj., conjointement.

conjunc'tiveness, n., propriété de joindre, f.

conjunct'ly, adv., conjointement.

conjunct'ure (-djeugn'kt'ioure-), n., conjoncture; occasion, rencontre, f.; concours de circonstances, m.

conjura'tion (keu'n'djiou-ré-), n., conjuration; adjuration; évocation; sorcellerie, f.

conjure' (co'n'-djioure), v.a., conjurer, adjurer, lier par un serment.

con'jure (keu'n'djeur), *v.a.*, **ensorceler**, escamoter. To — up; *évoquer.* To — away ; *exorciser.*

con'jure (keun'djeur), *v.n.*, faire de la sorcellerie ; escamoter.

con'jurer (keu'n'djeur-eur), *n.*, conjurateur,
sorcier, *m.*, sorcière, *f. ;* escamoteur, prestidigitateur, physicien, (jest.) habile homme, *m.* He
is no — ; *il n'a pas inventé la poudre.*

con'juring, *n.*, magie, *f.*, sorcellerie, prestidigitation, *f. ;* escamotage, *m.* — book ;
grimoire, m. — trick; *tour de prestidigitation, m.*

con'nate (co'n-néte), *adj.*, né en même temps;
(bot.) conné.

connat'ural (-nat'iou-), *adj.*, qui naît en
même temps; de même nature; en rapport
naturel.

connat'urally, *adv.*, naturellement, originairement.

connect' (co'n-nèkte), *v.a.*, lier à, attacher à,
allier à, joindre à, unir à ; (tech.) accoupler,
mettre en communication.

connect', *v.n.*, se lier.

connect'ed, *adj.*, joint, uni, lié ; continu ; en
rapport. To be — with; *être joint* **à** ; *se lier* **à** ;
se rattacher **à** ; *se rapporter* **à**.

connec'tion, *n.* *V.* **connexion.**

connect'ive, *n.*, (gram.) liaison, conjonction,
f. ; (bot.) connectif, *m.*

connect'ive, *adj.*, de liaison.

connect'ively, *adv.*, ensemble.

con'ner, *n.*, vérificateur de mesures, (fig.)
bouquineur, liseur enragé, *m.*

connex'ion *ou* **connec'tion**, *n.*, liaison; suite;
connexion, *f. ;* rapport, *m. ;* relations, *f.pl. ;*
(com.) clientèle, *f. ;* (family) parent, *m. ;* parenté ; famille, *f. ;* parents, *m.pl.* In this — ;
sous ce rapport, sur l'affaire en question. To
run in — ; (of trains) *être en correspondance*
avec *ou* **correspondre avec.**

conniv'ance *ou* **conniv'ency** (-naï-), *n.*, connivence, *f.*

connive' (-naïve), *v.n.*, conniver à ; être de
connivence **pour** ; tolérer, fermer les yeux **sur.**

conniv'ency, *n.* *V.* **connivance.**

connoisseur' (ko'n-nès'ceure), *n.*, connaisseur, amateur, *m.*

connu'bial (-niou-), *adj.*, du mariage ; conjugal.

co'noid (cô-noïde), *n.*, conoïde, *m.*

conoid'al, conoid'ic *ou* **conoid'ical** (-noïd'-),
adj., conoïde.

con'quer (cogn'keur *ou* -'kweur), *v.a.*, vaincre, dompter; (a country, or, fig., to gain, to
win) conquérir.

con'quer, *v.n.*, vaincre, remporter la victoire.

con'querable, *adj.*, à vaincre ; domptable.

con'queress, *n.*, conquérante, *f.*

con'queror (-keur'eur), *n.*, vainqueur, conquérant, *m.*

con'quest (cogn'kwèste), *n.*, conquête ; victoire, *f.*

consanguin'eal *ou* **consanguin'eous** (con-
sa'n'gwi'n'i-), *adj.*, de même sang.

consanguin'ity, *n.*, consanguinité, parenté, *f.*

con'science (co'n'shè'n'se), *n.*, conscience, *f.*
In all — ; *en bonne conscience.*

conscien'tious (-shi'è'n'sheusse), *adj.*, consciencieux; de conscience.

conscien'tiously, *adv.*, consciencieusement.

conscien'tiousness, *n.*, conscience, *f. ;* sentiment de justice, *m. ;* droiture, *f.*

con'scionable (-sheu'n'-), *adj.*, raisonnable ;
juste, équitable.

con'scionableness, *n.*, équité, justice, *f.*

con'scionably, *adv.*, raisonnablement, justement, équitablement.

con'scious (co'n'sheusse), *adj.*, conscient, qui
a conscience **de** ; qui a sa connaissance, sa tête; (of
things), dont on a une conscience. To be — ; *avoir
sa connaissance, sa tête.* To be — of ; *avoir la*

conscience **de** ; *avoir le sentiment* **de** ; *savoir ; être
instruit* **de.**

con'sciously, *adv.*, sciemment, avec conscience de soi-même, en parfaite connaissance.

con'sciousness, *n.*, sentiment intérieur, *m. ;*
conscience, perception; (med.) connaissance, *f.*
To regain — ; *reprendre connaissance.*

con'script (-scripte), *adj.*, conscrit.

con'script, *n.*, conscrit, *m.*

conscrip'tion, *n.*, conscription, *f.*

con'secrate (-si-), *v.a.*, consacrer; (a church-
yard) bénir ; (a bishop, a king) **sacrer** ; (of
saints) canoniser. —d ground ; *terre sainte, f.* —
bread ; *pain bénit, m.*

consecra'tion (-cré-), *n.*, consécration; canonisation, *f.*, (of a king, a bishop) sacre, *m.*

con'secrator (-si-cré-teur), *n.*, consécrateur,
consacrant, *m.*

con'secratory, *adj.*, de consécration ; sacramental, sacramentel.

con'sectary, *adj.*, résultant.

con'sectary, *n.*, conséquence, déduction, *f.*,
corollaire, *m.*

consecu'tion (-si-kiou-), *n.*, conséquence, succession, *f. ;* enchaînement de conséquences, *m.*

consec'utive (-sèk'iou-), *adj.*, consécutif, qui
suit.

consec'utively, *adv.*, consécutivement.

consent', *n.*, consentement ; accord ; rapport,
m., (physiology) sympathie, *f.* With one — ;
d'un commun accord, d'une commune voix.

consent', *v.n.*, consentir à.

consenta'neous (-té-ni-), *adj.*, conforme **à** ;
d'accord **avec.**

consenta'neously, *adv.*, conformément **à,**
d'accord **avec.**

consenta'neousness, *n.*, accord, *m. ;* conformité, *f.*

consent'er, *n.*, personne qui consent, *f.*

consen'tient (-sè'n'shè'n'te), *adj.*, du même
sentiment ; unanime ; (jur.) consentant.

con'sequence (-sè-kwè'n'se), *n.*, conséquence,
suite, effet ; importance, *f.* In — ; *en conséquence.* In — of ; *par suite* **de.** Of no — ; *de
nulle importance.* The — is ; *il s'ensuit que ; il
en résulte que.*

con'sequent (-si-), *n.*, suite, *f. ;* (log., math.)
conséquent, *m.*

con'sequent, *adj.*, conséquent. — upon ; *qui
est la conséquence* **de** ; *qui suit; en conséquence* **de.**

consequen'tial (-kwè'n'shal), *adj.*, conséquent ; logique ; (b.s.) (fig. and pers.) suffisant,
important.

consequen'tially, *adv.*, conséquemment ; avec
suite ; (b.s.) avec suffisance, d'un air important.

consequen'tialness, *n.*, justesse do raisonnement, logique ; (b.s.) (fig.) suffisance, *f. ;*
air d'importance, *m.*

con'sequently, *adv.*, conséquemment ; par
conséquent, en conséquence.

conserv'able (-seur-), *adj.*, conservable *ou* qui
peut être conservé.

conserva'tion (-seur-vé-), *n.*, conservation, *f.*

conserv'atism, *n.*, conservatisme, toryisme, *m.*

conserv'ative (-seur-), *adj.*, conservateur.

con'servator (-seur-vé-teur), *n.*, conservateur, *m. ;* conservatrice, *f.*

conserv'atory (-seur-va-tori), *n.*, (for arts
and music) conservatoire ; magasin ; dépôt, *m. ;*
(hort.) serre, *f.*

conserv'atory, *adj.*, conservateur.

conserve' (-seurve), *n.*, conserve, *f.*

conserve', *v.a.*, conserver ; (fruit, etc.) confire.

conserv'er, *n.*, conservateur, *m.*, conservatrice, *f. ;* personne qui fait des conserves, *f.*

consid'er, *v.a.*, considérer ; estimer ; envisager ; tenir **pour,** regarder comme ; examiner ;
avoir égard **à.**

consid'er, *v.n.*, considérer, penser à, songer **à,**
réfléchir **à.**

consid′erable (-sid′eur′-), *adj.*, considérable ; grand, important.

consid′erableness, *n.*, importance ; grandeur, valeur, *f.*

consid′erably, *adv.*, considérablement.

consid′erate (-sid′eur′-), *adj.*, réfléchi, modéré ; indulgent ; attentif, plein d'égards, attentionné ; attentif à ; prévenant **pour.** It is very — of you to ; *c′est très aimable à vous* **de.**

consid′erately, *adv.*, d'une manière réfléchie ; avec modération, avec indulgence ; avec attention, avec égards, avec prévenance.

consid′erateness, *n.*, caractère réfléchi, *m. ;* attention, prudence, discrétion, délicatesse, *f.*

considera′tion, *n.*, considération, *f. ;* examen, *m.*, égards, *m.pl. ;* compensation, récompense, *f.;* dédommagement, équivalent, *m.* On, upon, on further — ; *tout bien considéré, réflexion faite.* Out of — for ; *par égard* **pour** *ou vu.* In — of ; *en considération* **de.** Under no — ; *sous aucun compte.* To be under — ; *être à l'examen, être en délibération.* To take into — ; *prendre en considération ; tenir compte* **de.**

consid′erer, *n.*, penseur, *m.*

consid′ering, *prep.*, considérant ; en égard **à ;** vu, attendu.

consign′ (-saïne), *v.a.*, (com.) consigner **à ;** livrer **à,** confier **à,** remettre **à.** To — to the grave ; *déposer* ou *coucher dans le tombeau.*

consignee′ (-si-nî), *n.*, (com.) consignataire, destinataire, *m.f.*

consign′er(-saï′n′eur) *ou* **consign′or** (-si-nor), *n.*, consignateur, expéditeur, *m.*

consign′ment (-saï′n′-), *n.*, consignation, *f.*, envoi, *m. ;* lettre de consignation, *f.*

consist′, *v.n.*, consister, exister. To — in ; *consister* **en,** *consister* **à.** To — of ; *consister* **en,** *consister* **dans,** *se composer* **de.** To — with ; *se maintenir, exister, s'accorder* **avec ;** *être compatible* **avec.** [*Consister* requires the preposition **à** before a verb ; the preposition **dans** before a noun taken in a limited sense ; and the preposition **en** in any other case.]

consis′tence *ou* **consis′tency,** *n.*, consistance, suite, *f. ;* esprit de suite ; accord, *m.*, harmonie ; liaison ; stabilité, solidité, *f.*

consis′tent, *adj.*, solide ; conséquent ; compatible **avec,** toujours égal ; conforme **à.**

consis′tently, *adv.*, d'une manière conséquente, conséquemment ; conformément **à ;** d'une manière compatible **avec.**

consisto′rial *ou* **consisto′rian** (-tô-), *adj.*, consistorial.

consis′tory (-to-ri), *n.*, consistoire, *m.*

consol′able (-sô-la′b′l), *adj.*, consolable.

consola′tion (so-lé-), *n.*, consolation, *f.*

consol′atory (-sol′a-tori), *adj.*, consolant ; de consolation, consolatoire.

con′sole (-sôle), *n.*, console, *f.*

console′ (-sôle), *v.a.*, consoler (for) **de.**

consol′er (-sôl′-), *n.*, consolateur, *m.*, consolatrice, *f.*

consol′idate, *v.a.*, consolider ; (jur.) réunir.

consol′idate, *v.n.*, se consolider.

consolida′tion (-dé-), *n.*, consolidation, *f.*

con′sols (-solze), *n.pl.*, consolidés ; fonds publics, *m.pl. ;* rentes consolidées, *f.pl.*

con′sonance *ou* **con′sonancy,** *n.*, consonance, *f. ;* accord, *m.*, union, harmonie, conformité, *f.* In — with ; *en conformité* **avec.**

con′sonant, *adj.*, consonant ; conforme **à ;** d'accord **avec.**

con′sonant, *n.*, (gram.) consonne, *f.*

con′sonantly, *adv.*, d'accord **avec.**

con′sonous, *adj.*, à l'unisson.

con′sort, *n.*, compagnon, *m.*, compagne, *f. ;* époux, *m.*, épouse ; (nav.) conserve, *f. ;* vaisseau de conserve, *m.* *pl.*, conjoints ; (jur.) consorts, *m.pl.* Prince— ; *prince-époux, mari de la reine, m.* Queen— ; *reine, f.*

consort′, *v.a.*, unir ; marier.

consort′ (with), *v.n.*, s'associer **à ;** s'unir **à ;** fréquenter. To — with ; *être le compagnon* **de.**

con′sound (-saou′n′de), *n.*, (bot.) consoude, *f.*

conspic′uous (-spik′iou-), *adj.*, en vue ; en évidence ; bien visible ; remarquable, éminent, marquant, distingué.

conspic′uously, *adv.*, évidemment, en évidence ; visiblement, éminemment ; d'une manière apparente.

conspic′uousness, *n.*, visibilité, évidence ; renommée, *f. ;* caractère remarquable, *m. ;* position, distinction, *f. ;* éclat, *m.*

conspir′acy, *n.*, conspiration, conjuration, *f.*

conspira′tion (-spi-ré-), *n.*, conspiration, *f.*

conspir′ator (-spir-a-teur), *n.*, conspirateur ; conjuré, *m.*

conspire′ (-spaïeur), *v.n.*, conspirer, comploter.

conspi′rer, *n.*, conjuré, *m.*

conspi′ringly, *adv.*, par conspiration.

con′stable (keu′n′-), *n.*, connétable ; constable, officier de police ; gouverneur ; gardien, *m.* Chief — ; *commissaire de police, m.* High — ; *grand connétable, m.* To outrun the — ; *faire des extravagances ; s'endetter.*

con′stableship, *n.*, dignité de connétable, *f. ;* fonctions de connétable, *f.pl.*

con′stancy, *n.*, stabilité ; constance ; fermeté ; persévérance, *f.*

con′stant, *adj.*, stable ; constant ; fidèle ; continuel.

con′stant, *n.*, (math., phys.) constante, *f.*

con′stantly, *adv.*, constamment ; invariablement ; continuellement.

constel′late, *v.a.*, consteller.

constella′tion (-stèl-lé-), *n.*, constellation, *f.*

consterna′tion (-steur-né-), *n.*, consternation, *f.*

con′stipate, *v.a.*, serrer, constiper.

constipa′tion, *n.*, resserrement, *m. ;* constipation, *f.*

constit′uency (-stit′iou-), *n.*, collège électoral, *m. ;* circonscription électorale, *f.* My — ; *mes commettants, m.pl.*

constit′uent, *n.*, constituant, *m. ;* partie constituante, *f.;* auteur, créateur ; élément commettant, (politics) commettant, *m.*

constit′uent, *adj.*, constituant ; nécessaire, essentiel, élémentaire.

con′stitute (-tioute), *v.a.*, constituer.

con′stituter, *n.*, constituteur, *m.*

constitu′tion (-tiou-), *n.*, constitution ; complexion, *f. ;* tempérament, *m.*

constitu′tional, *adj.*, constitutionnel. *n.*, promenade de santé, *f.* To take one's — ; *faire sa petite promenade, prendre l'air.*

constitu′tionalist, *n.*, constitutionnel, *m.*

constitutional′ity, *n.*, constitutionnalité, *f.*

constitu′tionally, *adv.*, par tempérament ; constitutionnellement.

constitu′tionist, *n.*, constitutionnel zélé, *m.*

con′stitutive (-tiou-), *adj.*, constitutif.

constrain′ (-stréne), *v.a.*, contraindre ; forcer ; (check) retenir, comprimer ; enfermer, astreindre ; (hinder) gêner.

constrain′able, *adj.*, (jur.) contraignable.

constrain′edly, *adv.*, par contrainte.

constrain′er, *n.*, personne qui contraint, *f.*

constraint′, *n.*, contrainte ; gêne, *f.*

constrict′, *v.a.*, resserrer, contracter.

constric′tion, *n.*, constriction, *f.;* (med.) rétrécissement, *m.*

constric′tor (-teur), *n.*, (anat.) constricteur ; (zoöl.) boa, boa constricteur, *m.*

constrin′gent (-stri′n′djè′n′te), *adj.*, (med.) constringent, qui resserre.

construct′ (-streukte), *v.a.*, construire, **bâtir ;** dresser ; composer, interpréter.

construct′er, *n.*, constructeur, *m.*

constru'tion, *n.*, construction; interprétation, *f.*, sens, *m.* To put the best — on; *donner la meilleure interprétation* à. To put a wrong — on everything; *interpréter tout en mal.* What — do you put upon his conduct ? *comment expliquez-vous sa conduite?*

construc'tive, *adj.*, constructif; interprétatif; implicite; supposé; censé.

construc'tively, *adv.*, par interprétation, par induction.

con'strue (-strou), *v.a.*, traduire ; expliquer ; interpréter; construire.

consubsist' (-seub'-), *v.n.*, subsister ensemble.

consubstan'tial (-seub-sta'n'shal), *adj.*, consubstantiel.

consubstan'tialist. *n.*, consubstantiateur, *m.*

consubstantial'ity, *n.*, consubstantialité, *f.*

consubstan'tially, *adv.*, consubstantiellement.

consubstan'tiate (-shi-éte), *v.a.*, unir en une seule et même substance.

consubstantia'tion (-shi-é-), *n.*, consubstantiation ; impanation, *f.*

con'suetudinary (-swi-tioude), *adj.*, coutumier.

con'sul (-seul), *n.*, consul, *m.*

con'sular, *adj.*, consulaire.

con'sulate *ou* **con'sulship**, *n.*, consulat, *m.*

consult' (-seulte), *v.a.*, consulter.

consult', *v.n.*, délibérer, se consulter.

consulta'tion (-té-), *n.*, consultation ; délibération, *f.*

consult'er, *n.*, consultant, *m.*

consult'ing, *adj.*, consultant. — room ; *cabinet de consultation*, *m.*

consu'mable (-sioum'-), *adj.*, consumable ; (eatable, drinkable) consommable.

consume' (-sioume), *v.a.*, consumer, dévorer ; dissiper, gaspiller, perdre ; (to use) consommer.

consume', *v.n.*, se consumer.

consu'mer, *n.*, personne, chose, qui consume, *f.* ; consommateur, *m.*

con'summate (-seu'm'-), *v.a.*, consommer, achever, accomplir, parachever.

con'summate, *adj.*, consommé ; parfait, complet, achevé, fini.

con'summately, *adj.*, parfaitement, complètement.

consumma'tion (-seu'm'-mé-), *n.*, consommation ; fin, *f.* ; accomplissement ; comble, *m.* It is the — of my hopes; *c'est le comble de mes désirs.*

consump'tion (-seu'm'-sheune), *n.*, consomption, action de consumer ; consommation ; (med.) consomption, maladie de poitrine, phtisie, *f.* To be in a — ; *être poitrinaire; être atteint de la poitrine.* To die of — ; *mourir de la poitrine, ou de phthisie.*

consump'tive (-seu'm'-tive), *adj.*, qui consume ; (med.) de consomption, poitrinaire, phtisique, pulmonaire. To become — ; *tomber en consomption.*

consump'tiveness, *n.*, prédisposition à la phtisie, *f.*

con'tact, *n.*, contact ; rapport, *m.* To bring into — ; *mettre en rapport, rapprocher.* To come into — ; *se rencontrer avec, se mettre en rapport avec.*

conta'gion (-té-djeune), *n.*, contagion, *f.*

conta'gious (-té-djeusse), *adj.*, contagieux.

conta'giousness, *n.*, nature contagieuse, *f.*

contain' (-téne), *v.a.*, contenir ; réprimer, retenir, renfermer.

contain'able, *adj.*, qui peut être contenu.

contain'er, *n.*, contenant, *m.*

contam'inate, *v.a.*, souiller ; contaminer.

contamina'tion (-né-), *n.*, souillure ; contamination, *f.*

contemn' (-tème), *v.a.*, mépriser, dédaigner.

contem'ner (-tè'm'neur), *n.*, contempteur, *m.*

con'template, *v.a.*, contempler ; méditer, projeter.

con'template, *v.n.*, contempler, projeter, avoir en vue ; prévoir, espérer; s'attendre à ; songer à ; envisager.

contempla'tion (-plé-), *n.*, contemplation ; pensée, méditation, *f.* ; projet, *m.* To have in — ; *avoir en vue* de ; *se proposer* de. It was in — to ; *il était question* de.

con'templative (-plé-), *adj.*, contemplatif.

con'templatively, *adv.*, contemplativement.

con'templator (-plé-teur), *n.*, contemplateur, *m.*, contemplatrice, *f.*

contemporane'ity (-nî-iti), *n.*, contemporanéité, *f.*

contempora'neous (-ré-ni-), *adj.*, contemporain.

contem'porary, *adj.*, contemporain.

contem'porary, *n.*, contemporain, *m.*, contemporaine, *f.* ; (of newspapers) confrère, *m.*

contempt' (-tè'm'te), *n.*, mépris, dédain, *m.* — of court ; *refus de comparaître, m. ; contumace, désobéissance aux ordres de la cour, f.* To feel — for ; *avoir du mépris* pour. To fall into — ; *tomber dans le mépris.* In — ; *par mépris.* In — of ; *au mépris* de. To purge one's — ; *purger sa contumace.*

contemp'tible (-tè'm'ti-b'l), *adj.*, méprisable ; chétif ; à dédaigner.

contemp'tibleness, *n.*, caractère méprisable, *m.*

contemp'tibly, *adv.*, d'une manière méprisable ; avec mépris.

contemp'tuous (-tè'm't'iou-eusse), *adj.*, méprisant, dédaigneux.

contemp'tuously, *adv.*, avec mépris, dédaigneusement.

contemp'tuousness, *n.*, caractère méprisant ; mépris, *m.* ; humeur dédaigneuse, *f.*

contend', *v.n.*, lutter, combattre ; contester ; soutenir, affirmer, prétendre. To — for ; *combattre pour; se battre ;* (prizes, places) *concourir* pour ; *se disputer.*

contend'er, *n.*, contendant, compétiteur, concurrent, combattant, belligérant; champion, *m.*

contend'ing, *adj.*, contendant ; en lutte ; opposé, rival, contraire. *n.pl.* disputes, contestations, *f.pl.* The — parties ; *les belligérants, les contestants, m.pl.*

content', *n.*, contentement, *m.* ; satisfaction, *f. pl.*, (things) contenu, *m.s.* Table of —s ; *table des matières, f. ; index, m.*

content', *adj.*, content, satisfait. To be — (with); *être content* de ; *se contenter* de. I am —; *je consens ; je veux bien.*

content', *v.a.*, contenter, satisfaire.

content'ed (-tè'n'tède), *adj.*, satisfait de, content de, résigné à.

content'edly, *adv.*, avec contentement ; patiemment, sans se plaindre.

content'edness, *n.*, contentement, *m.*

conten'tion, *n.*, contention ; dispute, lutte, discorde, *f.*, débat, *m.*

conten'tious (-tè'n'sheusse), *adj.*, (jur.) contentieux, litigieux, disputeur, querelleur.

conten'tiously, *adv.*, en disputant ; (jur.) contentieusement.

conten'tiousness, *n.*, disposition contentieuse; humeur querelleuse, *f.* ; (jur.) esprit litigieux.

content'less, *adj.*, mécontent.

content'ment, *n.*, contentement, *m.*, résignation, soumission, *f.* — is beyond riches ; (prov.) *contentement passe richesses.*

contents', *n.pl.*, contenu, *m. sing.* Table of — ; *table des matières, f.*

conter'minous (-teur-), *adj.*, contigu à, limitrophe de, voisin de.

con'test, *n.*, contestation, lutte, *f.* ; débat, combat, *m.*

contest', *v.a.*, contester, disputer.
contest', *v.n.*, contester, disputer, lutter; (to vie) rivaliser de.
contes'table, *adj.*, contestable.
contesta'tion, *n.*, contestation, *f.*; témoignage, *m.*
con'text, *n.*, contexte, sens, *m.*
context'ural, *adj.*, de contexture.
context'ure (-tèkst'ioure), *n.*, contexture; suite, série, *f.*; tissu; (fig.) enchaînement, *m.*
contigu'ity (-ghiou-i-), *n.f.*, contiguïté, proximité, *f.*
contig'uous (-tigh'iou-eusse), *adj.*, contigu à, attenant à.
contig'uously, *adv.*, d'une manière contiguë; en contiguïté.
contig'uousness, *n.*, contiguïté, *f.*
con'tinence *ou* **con'tinency**, *n.*, continence; chasteté; (fig.) retenue, modération, *f.*
con'tinent, *adj.*, continent; modéré; retenu; chaste.
con'tinent, *n.*, (geog.) continent, *m.*
continen'tal, *adj.*, continental.
con'tinently, *adv.*, avec continence, chastement; avec retenue, avec modération.
contin'gence *ou* **contin'gency** (-ti'n'djè'n'ce, -'djè'n'-), *n.*, contingence, éventualité, *f.*; cas imprévu, cas fortuit, *m.*
contin'gent (-ti'n'djè'n'te), *n.*, contingent; événement fortuit, *m.*
contin'gent, *adj.*, contingent, éventuel; casuel, fortuit, accidentel, aléatoire.
contin'gently, *adv.*, fortuitement, par accident, casuellement.
contin'ual (-ti'n'iou-al), *adj.*, continuel; (jur.) continu.
contin'ually, *adv.*, continuellement; (jur.) continûment.
contin'uance (-ti'n'iou-), *n.*, continuation; continuité; durée, *f.*; séjour; (jur.) ajournement, *m.*; remise, *f.*
contin'uate (-ti'n'iou-), *adj.*, (l.u.) continu; étroitement uni; interrompu; (jur.) continuel.
continua'tion (-ti'n'iou-é-), *n.*, continuation; continuité, persévérance; durée, *f.*
contin'uator (-ti'n'iou-é-teur), *n.*, continuateur, *m.*
contin'ue (-ti'n'iou), *v.a.*, continuer; prolonger; conserver, perpétuer, maintenir. To — one's way; *reprendre son chemin; se remettre en route.*
contin'ue, *v.n.*, continuer; demeurer, rester; continuer de vivre, être toujours, persévérer; persister.
contin'ued, *adj.*, continu, prolongé; soutenu, suivi; (of articles) à suivre. To be — in our next; *la suite au prochain numéro.*
contin'uedly (-ti'n'iou'-dli), *adv.*, continûment, sans interruption.
contin'uer, *n.*, personne qui persévère, *f.*; continuateur, *m.*
continu'ity (-niou-i-ti), *n.*, continuité, *f.*
contin'uous (-ti'n'iou-eusse), *adj.*, continu.
contin'uously, *adv.*, continûment; sans interruption.
contort', *v.a.*, tordre, contourner, défigurer.
contort'ed (-tort'ède), *adj.*, tordu; tors, contourné; défiguré; (bot.) tortile.
contor'tion (-sheune), *n.*, contorsion; (med.) luxation, *f.*
contour', *n.*, contour, *m.*
con'tra, *prep.*, contre; (com.) d'autre part. Per —; *par contre.*
con'traband, *adj.*, de contrebande.
con'traband, *n.*, contrebande, *f.*
contract', *v.a.*, contracter; abréger, resserrer; rétrécir; rider; (a habit) prendre, contracter; (admin.) adjuger.
contract', *v.n.*, se contracter, se resserrer, se rétrécir, se rider; (com.) traiter, contracter,

s'engager à; entreprendre. To — for; *traiter pour.*
con'tract, *n.*, contrat; pacte, convention, *m.f.*; (for public works) adjudication, soumission, entreprise à forfait, *f.*; (marriage) contrat, *m.*; fiançailles, *f.pl.* Conditions of —; *cahier des charges, m.* By private —; *de gré à gré, à l'amiable.* To put up to —; *mettre en adjudication.*
contrac'table, *adj.*, contractable.
contrac'tedness (-tract'èd-), *n.*, caractère borné, *m.*; brièveté, *f.*; rétrécissement, resserrement, *m.*
contractibil'ity, *n.*, contractilité, faculté de se contracter; force contractive, *f.*
contrac'tible, *adj.*, contractile, susceptible de contraction.
contrac'tibleness, *n.* *V.* **contractibility**.
contrac'tile, *adj.*, contractile.
contractil'ity, *n.*, force contractive, contractilité, *f.*
contrac'tion, *n.*, contraction, *f.*; rétrécissement; raccourcissement, *m.*
contrac'tor (-teur), *n.*, contractant, *m.*, contractante, *f.*; entrepreneur; (for the army, navy) fournisseur; (tech.) adjudicataire, *m.*
contradict', *v.a.*, contredire, démentir.
contradic'ter, *n.*, contradicteur, *m.*
contradic'tion, *n.*, contradiction, *f.*; (denial) démenti, *m.*
contradic'tious (-dik'sheusse), *adj.*, contradictoire; plein de contradictions; opposé, contraire à.
contradic'tiousness, *n.*, contradiction, *f.*; esprit de contradiction, *m.*
contradic'torily, *adv.*, contradictoirement.
contradic'toriness, *n.*, nature contradictoire, *m.*
contradic'tory, *adj.*, contradictoire.
contradistinc'tion, *n.*, opposition, *f.*; contraste, *m.* In — to; *par opposition* à.
contradistinc'tive, *adj.*, (ant.) qui marque une distinction tranchée.
contradistin'guish (-tign'gwish), *v.a.*, distinguer.
contra-fis'sure (-fish'ioure), *n.*, contre-fissure; contrefente, contre-fracture, *f.*
contra-in'dicate, *v.a.*, (med.) contre-indiquer.
contra-in'dicant *ou* **contra-indica'tion** (-ké-), *n.*, (med.) contre-indication, *f.*
contral'to, *n.*, (mus.) contralto, *m.*
con'tramure (-mioure), *n.*, (fort.) contremur, *m.* *v.n.*, contre-murer.
contraposi'tion (-po-zi-), *n.*, contre-position, *f.*
con'traries (-rize), *n.pl.*, contraires, *m.pl.*
contrari'ety (-tra-raï'-è-), *n.*, opposition; contradiction; contrariété, *f.*
con'trarily, *adv.*, contrairement; en sens contraire.
con'trariness, *n.*, contrariété, opposition, *f.*
contra'riously, *adv.*, contrairement.
con'trariwise (-waïze), *adv.*, au contraire; en sens opposé.
con'trary, *n.*, contraire, *m.* On the —; *au contraire.* To the —; *contre; en sens contraire.* Quite the —; *tout le contraire; bien au contraire.*
con'trary, *adj.*, contraire, opposé.
con'trast (-trâste), *n.*, contraste, *m.* To stand in —; *être en contraste; faire contraste.*
contrast', *v.a.*, contraster; mettre en contraste. *v.n.*, contraster, être en contraste, faire contraste.
con'trate-wheel (-hwîle), *n.*, (horl.) roue de rencontre, *f.*
contravalla'tion (-val-lé-), *n.*, (fort.) contrevallation, *f.*
contravene' (-vîne), *v.a.*, contrevenir à, enfreindre.
contrave'ner, *n.*, contrevenant, *m.*
contraven'tion, *n.*, contravention, infraction, *f.*

contrib'utary (-trib'iou-), *adj.*, tributaire.

contrib'ute (-trib'ioute), *v.a.*, contribuer à, payer sa part **de.**

contrib'ute, *v.n.*, contribuer à ; concourir à ; aider à, collaborer à.

contribu'tion (-biou-), *n.*, contribution ; (com.) assurance mutuelle, *f.*, article (de journal, etc.), *m.*

contrib'utive (-trib'iou-), *adj.*, qui contribue, contributif. To be — to ; *contribuer* à.

contrib'utor (-trib'iou-teur), *n.*, contribuant, garant, *m. ;* collaborateur, rédacteur, correspondant, *m.* To be a — to ; *écrire* **pour,** ou **dans.**

con'trite (-traïte), *adj.*, contrit, pénitent.

con'tritely, *adv.*, avec contrition.

con'triteness, *n.*, contrition, *f.*

contri'tion (-trish'-), *n.*, contrition, *f.*

contri'vable (-traïv'-), *adj.*, possible à faire, à arranger, à combiner.

contri'vance (-traïv'-), *n.*, invention ; combinaison, idée, *f. ;* artifice, moyen, *m.,* machine, *f. ;* projet, *m.*

contrive' (-traïve), *v.a.*, inventer ; trouver, combiner ; imaginer, pratiquer ; se pratiquer.

contrive', *v.n.*, s'arranger de manière à ; s'arranger **pour ;** trouver moyen **de ;** parvenir à ; venir à bout **de ;** s'y prendre **pour.**

contri'ver, *n.*, inventeur, *m.,* inventrice, *f. ;* (l.u.) combinateur, *m.,* combinatrice, *f. ;* auteur, *m.*

contri'ving, *adj.*, ingénieux ; artificieux.

control' (-trôl), *n.*, contrôle, empire, *m. ;* influence, autorité, *f.,* frein, *m.* To keep under —; *être maître* **de.**

control', *v.a.*, contrôler ; exercer de l'empire **sur,** gouverner, régler, diriger ; réprimer.

control'lable (-trôl'la-b'l), *adj.*, sujet à contrôle ; soumis à l'autorité ; gouvernable, docile.

control'ler, *n.*, contrôleur, *m.*

control'lership, *n.*, charge de contrôleur, *f. ;* contrôle, *m.*

control'ment, *n. V.* **control.**

controver'sial (-veur-shal), *adj.*, de controverse ; polémique.

controver'sialist, *n.*, controversiste, *m.*

con'troversy (-veur-), *n.*, controverse ; polémique, dispute, *f. ;* différend, *m.*

con'trovert (-veurte), *v.a.*, controverser, mettre en controverse, disputer, débattre, agiter.

controver'tible, *adj.*, sujet à controverse.

controver'tist, *n.*, controversiste, *m.*

contuma'cious (-tiou-mé-sheusse), *adj.*, obstiné, récalcitrant ; opiniâtre ; pervers ; (jur.) contumace.

contuma'ciously, *adv.*, avec obstination ; opiniâtrément ; (jur.) par contumace.

contuma'ciousness, *n.*, opiniâtreté, obstination ; perversité, *f.*

con'tumacy (-tiou-), *n.*, obstination ; opiniâtreté ; (jur.) contumace ; désobéissance, *f.*

contume'lious (-tiou-mi-), *adj.*, injurieux, outrageant, méprisant.

contume'liously, *adv.*, injurieusement, outrageusement.

con'tumely (-tiou-mè-), *n.*, injure, *f. ;* outrage, mépris, dédain, *m.,* insulte, *f.*

contuse' (-tiouze), *v.a.*, contusionner, meurtrir.

contu'sion (-tiou-jeune), *n.*, contusion, meurtrissure, *f.*

conun'drum (-neu'n'-dreume), *n.*, énigme ; turlupinade, *f. ;* jeu de mots, quolibet, *m.*

convales'cence ou **convales'cency** (-lès'-), *n.*, convalescence, *f.*

convales'cent, *adj.*, convalescent. — home ; *asile de convalescence, m.*

convales'cent, *n.*, convalescent, *m.,* convalescente, *f.*

convalla'ria (-val-lé-), *n.*, (bot.) convallaire, *f. ;* muguet, *m.*

conve'nable (-vî'n'-), *adj.*, qui peut être convoqué.

convene' (-vîne), *v.a.*, convoquer ; réunir, assembler ; citer **devant.**

convene', *v.n.*, s'assembler, se réunir.

conve'ner (-vî'n'-), *n.*, personne qui convoque, *f.*

con'venience ou **conve'niency** (-vî'n'-), *n.,* commodité, convenance, aise, *f. ;* objet de commodité, *m. pl.,* commodités ; (nav.) emménagements. At your earliest — ; *aussitôt que vous le pourrez, à la première occasion.* At your — ; *à votre commodité ; sans vous déranger.* To meet the — of ; *arranger, accommoder.*

conve'nient (-vî'n'-), *adj.*, commode, convenable. If you could make it — to; *si vous pouvez vous arranger de manière à ce que* (with subj.) ou *de manière à* (with infinitive). If it is — to you ; *si cela ne vous dérange pas ; si cela vous arrange.*

conve'niently, *adv.*, commodément, convenablement, à son aise ; sans se gêner.

con'vent, *n.*, couvent, *m.*

conven'ticle (-tik'l), *n.*, conciliabule, conventicule, *m.*

conven'tion, *n.*, convention ; assemblée, *f.*

conven'tional, *adj.*, conventionnel, de convention.

conven'tionalism, *n.,* ce qui est conventionnel, *m.,* phrase de convention, *f. ;* usage de convention, *m.*

conventional'ity, *n.*, nature conventionnelle, *f.*

conven'tionally, *adj.*, par convention.

conven'tionary, *adj.*, réglé par convention.

conven'tioner, *n.*, membre d'une convention, *m.*

conven'tual (-vè'n't'iou-), *n.*, conventuel ; religieux, *m.,* religieuse, *f.*

conven'tual, *adj.*, conventuel.

conven'tually, *adv.*, conventuellement.

converge' (-veurdje), *v.n.*, converger à ou vers.

conver'gence ou **conver'gency** (-veur-djè-n'ce, -ci), *n.*, convergence, *f.*

conver'gent ou **conver'ging** (-veurdj'-), *adj.*, convergent.

conver'sable (-veur'sa-b'l), *adj.*, de bonne conversation ; causeur ; sociable.

conver'sableness, *n.*, amabilité ; sociabilité, *f.*

conver'sably, *adv.*, d'une manière sociable.

con'versant (-veur-), *adj.*, familier ; familiarisé **avec.** — with ; *versé* **dans** ; *au fait* **de,** *au courant* **de.**

conversa'tion (-sé-), *n.*, conversation, *f. ;* entretien ; commerce, *m.* To carry on a — ; *soutenir une conversation.* Private — ; *entretien particulier.* Earnest — ; *entretien sérieux.* To change the — ; *changer de conversation* ou *changer de sujet.*

conversa'tional, *adj.*, de, ou de la, conversation. A man of great — powers ; *un homme qui a une grande facilité de conversation ; un excellent causeur, m.*

conversazio'ne (-vèr-sât'zi-ô'né), *n.*, assemblée littéraire, réunion, *f. ;* cercle, *m.*

converse' (-veurse), *v.n.*, causer, converser, s'entretenir **avec** ; fréquenter.

con'verse, *n.*, commerce, *m. ;* relations, *f.pl. ;* entretien, *m. ;* conversation ; (log.) converse ; (math.) réciproque, *f.*

con'verse, *adj.*, (math.) réciproque, inverse.

con'versely, *adv.*, (log.) réciproquement.

conver'sion (-veur-), *n.*, conversion, *f. ;* (of firearms) transformation ; (jur.) appropriation, *f. ;* changement, *m.*

con'vert (-veurte), *n.*, converti, *m.,* convertie, *f.* To become a — ; *se convertir.*

convert' (-veurte), *v.a.*, convertir ; (of firearms) transformer ; faire servir, appliquer à, approprier.

convert', v.n., se convertir ; se transformer, se changer.

conver'ter (-veurt'-), n., convertisseur, m.

convertibil'ity ou **conver'tibleness** (-veurt'-), n., convertibilité, f.

conver'tible, adj., (of things) convertible (of persons) convertissable, (fin.) convertible.

conver'tibly, adv., réciproquement.

con'vex, adj., convexe, bombé.

con'vex, n., corps convexe, m.

con'vexed (-vèkste), adj., convexe.

convex'edly (-vèks'èd'-), adv., de forme convexe.

convex'ity, n., convexité, f. ; (of roads) bombement, m.

con'vexly, adv., de forme convexe.

convex'o-con'cave (-kéve), adj., convexoconcave.

convex'o-con'vex, adj., convexo-convexe.

convey' (-vé), v.a., transporter ; transmettre, porter, conduire, amener ; présenter ; rendre, exprimer, donner ; communiquer ; (jur.) faire transport **de**. To — away ; *emporter ;* (to lead) *emmener.* To —; (meanings) *donner l'idée* **de**. To — to posterity ; *transmettre à la postérité.*

convey'able (-vè-a'b'l), adj., transportable ; portable, charriable ; communicable, exprimable, transférable.

convey'ance (-vé-a'n'ce), n., transport ; passage, m. ; voie ; voiture, transmission, f. ; envoi, moyen de transport, m. ; (jur.) translation de propriété, f. ; (jur.) acte translatif de propriété, transfert, m. Deed of —; *acte de vente, m.*

convey'ancer, n., notaire qui dresse les actes translatifs de propriété ; notaire, m.

convey'ancing, n., rédaction des actes translatifs de propriété, f. ; notariat, m., transferts, m.pl.

convey'er (-vé-eur), n., personne qui transporte, qui transmet, f. ; porteur, voiturier, m.

convict', v.a., condamner ; déclarer coupable ; convaincre.

con'vict (-vik'te), n., condamné, m., condamnée, f. ; criminel ; forçat, déporté, m. ; (on ticket of leave) forçat libéré, m. — prison ; *bagne, m.*

con'vict-keep'er (-kîp'-peur), n., gardechiourme, m.

convic'tion, n., conviction, persuasion ; (jur.) condamnation, f.

convic'tive, adj., convaincant ; (jur.) convictionnel.

convince', v.a., convaincre, persuader ; mettre en évidence.

convin'cing, adj., convaincant. part., convainquant.

convin'cingly, adv., d'une manière convaincante.

convin'cingness (-cign'nèce), n., caractère convaincant, m., évidence, force, f.

conviv'ial, adj., de fête ; (of persons) sociable ; joyeux, jovial.

convivial'ity, n., sociabilité, gaieté, f.

convoca'tion (-ko-), n., convocation ; assemblée, f.

convoke' (-vôke), v.a., convoquer, assembler.

con'volute ou **con'voluted** (-lioute, -ède), adj., (bot.) convoluté.

convolu'tion (-liou-), n., enroulement, m., circonvolution, f.

convolve', v.a., rouler, enrouler.

convol'vulus (-vol-viou-), n., (convolvuli), belle-de-jour, f. ; liseron ; volubilis, m.

con'voy (-voï), v.a., convoyer, escorter.

con'voy, n., convoi, m. ; escorte, f. —-ship ; *bâtiment convoyeur, bâtiment d'escorte, m., escorte, f.*

convulse' (-veulse), v.a., convulser, convul-

sionner, jeter dans des convulsions ; crisper, agiter ; (fig.) ébranler ; bouleverser.

convulsed', adj., crispé, agité ; ébranlé, convulsé, bouleversé. To be — with laughter ; *se pâmer de rire.*

convul'sion (-veul-sheune), n., convulsion, f. ; mouvement convulsif, m., commotion, f. To be seized with —s ; *tomber en convulsions.* Fit of —s ; *accès de convulsion, m.*

convul'sive, adj., convulsif.

convul'sively, adv., convulsivement.

co'ny (keu- ou cô-), n., lapin, (fig.) niais, m.

co'ny-wool (-woule), n., poil de lapin, m.

coo (coû), v.n., roucouler.

coo'ing (coû-igne), n., roucoulement, m.

cook, n., cuisinier, m., cuisinière, f. ; (nav.) coq, m. Man- —; *cuisinier, m.* Woman —; *cuisinière, f.* —-shop ; *restaurant, m. ; rôtisserie, f.* —-shop keeper ; *restaurateur, traiteur, m.*

cook (couke), v.n., cuire ; faire la cuisine, cuisiner ; (fig.) arranger, préparer ; (accounts) falsifier.

cook, v.a., faire cuire ; apprêter.

cook'ery (-'eur'i), n., cuisine (art), f.

cook'ery-book (-bouke), n., livre de cuisine, m.

cool (coûl), adj., froid ; frais ; (pers.) calme, tranquille, froid ; impudent, peu gêné. How — that man is ; *comme cet homme est sans gêne, a de l'aplomb.* To grow —; *se refroidir.*

cool, n., frais, m., fraîcheur, f. In the —; *au frais.*

cool, v.a., rafraîchir ; refroidir ; calmer, modérer.

cool, v.n., se refroidir ; refroidir. To — down ; *se calmer, s'apaiser, se modérer.*

cool'er, n., rafraîchissoir, réfrigérant ; (med.) rafraîchissant, m.

cool'headed, adj., froid, de sang froid.

coo'lie (coû-li), coolie, couli, m.

cool'ing, adj., rafraîchissant, calmant.

cool'ish, adj., un peu frais.

cool'ly, adv., fraîchement, froidement ; de sang-froid, tranquillement, avec calme.

cool'ness, n., fraîcheur, f., frais, m. ; (fig.) froideur, indifférence, f. ; refroidissement ; sangfroid, calme, m. ; impudence, f., sans gêne.

coom (coume), n., suie, f. ; cambouis, m.

coop (coupe), n., (hen) poulailler, m., mue, f. ; (of sheep) parc, m.

coop, v.a., enfermer dans une mue ; enfermer étroitement, claquemurer ; parquer. To be —ed up ; *être enfermé comme dans une cage ; être parqué comme des moutons.*

coo'per (coup'-), n., tonnelier, boisselier, m.

coo'perage (-'édje), n., tonnellerie, boissellerie, f.

coöp'erate (-cô-), v.n., coopérer à, concourir à.

coöpera'tion (cô-op'eur-é-), n., coopération, f., concours, m.

coöp'erative, adj., coopérant, coopératif.

coöp'erator (-teur), n., coopérateur, m.

coör'dinate (-cô-), adj., du même rang ; égal ; (math.) coordonné.

coör'dinately, adv., également ; au même degré.

coör'dinateness, n., égalité de rang, coordination, f.

coör'dinates (cô-or-di-nétse), n.pl., (math.) coordonnées, f.pl.

coördina'tion (-né-), n., égalité de rang ; coordination, f.

coör'dinator, n., coordonnateur, -trice, m.f.

coot (coute), n., poule d'eau, foulque, f. ; (fig.) nigaud, m.

cop, n., cime, crête, f., sommet, m. ; (of birds) huppe, aigrette, f.

copai'ba (-pê-) ou **copi'vi**, n., copahu, baume de copahu, m.

co'pal (cô-), n., copal, m.

copar'cenary ou **copar'ceny** (côpâr-cè-), n., (jur.) indivis, m.; succession par indivis, f.

copar'cener (cô-pâr-cè-), n., (jur.) propriétaire indivis, m., propriétaire indivise, f.

copart'ner (cô-pârt'-), n., associé, coassocié, m.

copart'nership ou **copart'nery** (cô-pârt'-), n., égalité de part; société en nom collectif, f.

copay'va (-pê-), n. V. **copaïba**.

cope (côpe), n., coiffe; (sacerdotal vestment) chape; (arch.) chape; voûte, f. — maker; chapier, m.

cope, v.a., couvrir, chaperonner.

cope, v.n., opposer; résister; lutter. To — with; tenir tête à; lutter contre; rivaliser avec.

Coper'nican, adj., copernicien.

cop'ier ou **cop'yist** (cop'i-, cop'i-iste), n., copiste, m.

co'ping (cô'-), n., (of a building) faîte; (of a wall) couronnement, chevron, m.

co'pious (cô'-), adj., abondant; copieux; riche.

co'piously, adv., copieusement, abondamment; richement.

co'piousness, n., abondance, richesse, f.

copped (copte), adj., qui s'élève en pointe; conique; (ant.) (of birds) huppé.

cop'pel (cop-), n. V. **cupel**.

cop'per (cop-), adj., de cuivre.

cop'per, n., cuivre, m.; (boiler) chaudière, f.; (small boiler) chaudron, m. pl., sous, m.pl., petite monnaie, f. —hued; cuivré. — nose; nez couperosé, m.

cop'per, v.a., cuivrer; (vessels) doubler en cuivre.

cop'peras (cop'peur-ace), n., couperose, f.

cop'per-bottomed (-bot'teu'm'de), adj., doublé en cuivre, à fond de cuivre.

cop'per-colored (-keul'leurde), adj., cuivré.

cop'per-plate, n., planche de cuivre; taille-douce, f.

cop'per-plate engraver, n., graveur en taille douce, m.

cop'per-plate engraving, n., gravure en taille douce, f.

cop'per-sheathing, n., doublage en cuivre, m.

cop'per-smith (-smith), n., chaudronnier, m.

cop'per-wares, n., cuivrerie, f.

cop'per-wire (-waïeur), n., fil de cuivre, fil de laiton, m.

cop'per-works (-weurkse), n., usine à cuivre, f.

cop'pery (cop'peur'i), adj., cuivreux.

cop'pice ou **copse**, n., taillis, m.

cop'pled (cop'p'lde), adj., qui s'élève en pointe; conique.

copse, v.a., conserver en taillis.

copse, n. V. **coppice**.

Copt, n., Cophte, Copte, m.

Cop'tic, n., (language) cophte, copte, m.

Cop'tic, adj., cophte, copte.

cop'ula (cop'iou-), n., (log.) copule, f.

cop'ulate (cop'iou-léte), v.n., s'accoupler.

copula'tion (-lé-), n., copulation, f.

cop'ulative, adj., (gram.) copulatif.

cop'ulative, n., (gram.) copulative, f.

cop'y, n., copie, f.; (model for writing) exemple; (of printed books) exemplaire, m.; (jur.) expédition, grosse, f.; (for drawing) modèle; (of newspapers) numéro, m. Rough —; brouillon, m. To make a fair —; mettre au net. A true —; pour copie conforme, pour ampliation.

cop'y, v.a., copier, transcrire.

cop'y-book (-bouke), n., cahier, m.

cop'yhold (-hôlde), n., tenure en vertu de copie du rôle de la cour seigneuriale, f.

cop'yholder, n., tenancier par copyhold, m.

cop'ying-clerk, n., expéditionnaire, m.

cop'ying-press (copi'ign'-prèce), n., presse à copier, f.

cop'yist, n. V. **copier**.

cop'yright (-raïte), n., droit d'auteur, droit de reproduction, m.; propriété littéraire, f. This is —; reproduction interdite.

coquet' (co-kète), v.a., faire des coquetteries à; dire des douceurs à; faire les doux yeux à; faire la coquette avec.

coquet', v.n., faire le coquet; faire la coquette; (l.u.) coqueter.

coquet' ou **coquette'**, n., coquette, f.

co'quetry (co-kèt'ri), n., coquetterie, f.

coquet'tish, adj., coquet, en coquette.

coquet'tishly, adv., coquettement.

cor'acle, n., nacelle, f., bateau pêcheur, m.

cor'al, n., corail; (rattle) hochet de corail, m. —reef; banc de corail, m. —diver, —fisher; corailleur, m. —fishing, —fishery; pêche du corail, f. —wort; (bot.) clandestine, dentaire, f.

cor'al, adj., de corail.

cor'alline (cor-al-laïne), n., (natur. hist.) coralline, f.

cor'beil (-bèle), n., (fort.) corbeille, f.

cor'bel, n., (arch.) corbeau, m.; niche, f.

cord, n., corde, ganse, f.; lien; cordon, cordage; (velvet) velours à cordes, m.

cord, v.a., corder; (needlework) ganser.

cor'dage (-édje), n., cordes, f.pl.; (nav.) cordage, m. — of a cannon; comblan, comblau, combleau, m.

cor'date ou **cor'dated** (-dé'-), adj., cordé, cordiforme.

cor'ded ('-ède), adj., de corde; cordé, à côtes.

cor'delier (-dè-lîre), n., cordelier, m.

cor'dial, adj., cordial.

cor'dial, n., cordial, m.; liqueur, f.

cordial'ity (-), n., cordialité, f.

cor'dially, adv., cordialement.

cord'-maker (-mék'-), n., cordier, m.

cor'don (-deune), n., (arch., fort., milit.) cordon, m.

cor'duroy (-diou-roï), n., velours (de coton) à côtes, m.

cord'-wood (-woude), n., bois de stère, m.

core (côre), n., cœur, m.; (of fruit) trognon, cœur, m.; (fig.) cœur, milieu, centre, m.; âme, f.; (of an abscess) bourbillon, fond, m.

cored (cô'rd), adj., (herrings) salé.

co-re'gency (-), n., corégence, f.

co-re'gent, n., (ant.) corégent, m.

co-reli'gionist, n., coreligionnaire, m.f.

co-respon'dent, n., complice, m.; codéfendeur, m.

corian'der (cô-), n., (bot.) coriandre, f.

Corin'thian (-thi-), adj., corinthien; de Corinthe.

co-ri'val (cô-raï-), n., rival; compétiteur, m.

co-ri'valry (cô-raï-), n., rivalité, f.

cork, n., liège; bouchon, m.; (float for swimming) nageoire, f. — cutter; bouchonnier, m. — tree; chêne liège, m.

cork, v.a., boucher.

cork'ing, n., bouchage, m.

cork'screw (-scrou), n., tire-bouchon, m. — staircase; escalier en limaçon ou à vis, m.

cork'y, adj., de liège, subéreux.

cor'morant, n., (orni.) cormoran; glouton, m.

corn (côr'n), n., blé; grain, froment, m.; grains, m.pl.; céréales, f.pl.; (on the foot) cor, m. Soft —; œil de perdrix, m. Indian —; maïs, blé de Turquie, m. Ear of —; épi de blé, m. — brandy; eau de vie de grains, f.

corn, v.a., saler; grener.

corn'chandler (-tsha'n'd'-), n., blatier; marchand de blé; grainetier, m.

corn'-cockle, n., nielle, f.

corn'-crops, n., céréales, f.pl.

corn'cutter (-keut'-), n., pédicure, m.

corn'dealer (-dîl'-), n., marchand de blé, m.

corn'-drill, n., (agri.) semoir, m.

cor'nea (-ni-), n., (anat.) cornée, f.

corned'-beef (cor'n'de-bîfe), *n.*, bœuf salé, *m.*

corne'lian (-nî-), *n.*, (min.) cornaline, *f.*

corne'lian-tree (-trî), *n.*, cornouiller, *m.*

cor'nel-tree (-trî), *n.*, cornouiller, *m.*

cor'neous (-ni-), *adj.*, corné.

cor'ner, *n.*, coin, angle, *m. ;* encoignure, encognure ; extrémité ; (tech.) cornière, *f.* — stone ; *pierre angulaire*, *f.* — tooth ; *incisive externe*, *f.* — house ; *maison du coin* ou *qui fait le coin*, *f.* — dish ; *plat d'entrée ;* (com.) *accaparement*, *m.*

cor'ner, *v.a.*, (wheat, salt, etc.) (com.) accaparer ; pousser dans un coin ; acculer ; (fig.) mettre au pied du mur.

cor'nerwise (-waïze), *adv.*, diagonalement.

cor'net (-nète), *n.*, (mus., conch.) cornet ; (milit.) porte-étendard, sous-lieutenant, cornette, *m. ;* (vet.) couronne, *f. ;* (of paper) cornet, *n.*

cor'netcy, *n.*, sous-lieutenance, *f.*

corn'-exchange, *n.*, halle au blé, *f.*

corn'-factor (-teur), *n.*, facteur en blé, ou aux grains ; blatier, *m.*

corn'field (-fîlde), *n.*, champ de blé, *m.*

corn'flag, *n.*, (bot.) glaïeul, *m.*

corn'-flower, *n.*, bluet, *m.*

cor'nice, *n.*, corniche, *f.*

cor'nicle (-ni'k'l), *n.*, (little horn) cornichon, *m. ;* cornicule, *f.*

cornif'ic, *adj.*, qui produit des cornes.

Corn'ish, *adj.*, de Cornouailles.

corn'ist, *n.*, corniste, *m.*

corn'-laws (-lôze), *n.pl.*, lois sur les céréales, *f.pl.*

corn'-market, *n.*, halle au blé, *f.*

corn'-merchant (-tsha'n'te), *n.*, négociant en blé, *m.*

corn'-pipe (-païpe), *n.*, chalumeau de paille, *m.*

corn'-poppy, *n.*, coquelicot, *m.*

corn'-salad, *n.*, mâche, doucette, *f.*

corn'-sheaf (-shîfe), *n.*, gerbe de blé, *f.*

corn'-stack, *n.*, meule de blé, *f.*

corn'-stalk (-stôke), *n.*, épi de blé, *m.*

corn'-trade, *n.*, commerce des grains, *m.*

cornuco'pia (-niou-cô-), *n.*, corne d'abondance, *f.*

cor'ny, *adj.*, de corne ; de grains.

corol'la, *n.*, (bot.) corolle, *f.*

cor'ollary, *n.*, corollaire, *f.*

coro'na (-rô-), *n.*, couronne, *f. ;* (arch.) larmier, *m. ;* (anat., astron., bot.) couronne, *f.*

cor'onal, *n.*, couronne, guirlande ; (anat.) suture coronale, *f.*

cor'onal, *adj.*, (anat.) coronal.

cor'onary, *adj.*, de couronne ; (med.) coronaire.

corona'tion (-né-), *n.*, couronnement, sacre, *m.*

cor'oner, *n.*, coroner, *m.*

cor'onet (-nète), *n.*, couronne ; (head-dress) ferronnière, *f.*

cor'poral, *n.*, (nav.) caporal ; (of infantry) caporal ; (of cavalry, of artillery) brigadier, *m.*

cor'poral, *adj.*, corporel.

corporale' (-rél), *n.*, (c.rel.) corporal, *m.*

corporal'ity, *n.*, (theol.) corporalité, matérialité, *f.*

cor'porally, *adv.*, corporellement ; de corps.

cor'porate, *adj.*, érigé en corporation ; de corporation, collectif, corporatif.

corpora'tion (-ré-), *n.*, corporation, communauté, société, *f. ;* (of a town) conseil municipal, *m.*, municipalité ; (jest.) bedaine, *f.*

corpo'real (-pô-ri-), *adj.*, corporel, matériel.

corpo'really, *adv.*, corporellement, matériellement.

corpore'ity (-pô-rî-î-), *n.*, matérialité, *f.*

corpo'reous (-pô-ri-), *adj.*, (ant.). *V.* **corporeal**.

corpo'rify (-faïe), *v.a.*, corporifier, corporiser.

cor'posant (-za'n'te), *n.*, (nav.) feu Saint-Elme, *m.*

corps (côr ; *pl.* côrze), *n.*, corps, *m.*, troupe, *f.* Army — ; *corps d'armée*, *m.*

corpse (corpse), *n.*, cadavre ; corps mort, *m.*

cor'pulence ou **cor'pulency** (-piou-), *n.*, corpulence, *f. ;* embonpoint, *m.*

cor'pulent (-piou-), *adj.*, corpulent ; replet, gras.

Cor'pus - Chris'ti (cor'peusse-kris-taïe), *n.*, (c.rel.) la Fête-Dieu, *f.*

cor'puscle (-peus's'l), *n.*, corpuscule, *m.*

corpus'cular (-peus'kiou-) ou **corpuscula'rian** (-peus'kiou-lé-), *adj.*, corpusculaire.

corpuscula'rian (-peus'kiou-lé-), *n.*, corpusculiste, *m.*

correct', *adj.*, correct, convenable, régulier, en règle, exact ; juste ; (of style) pur, bon.

correct', *v.a.*, corriger, rectifier ; réparer, régler, reprendre. To stand — ed ; *reconnaître son erreur ; avouer qu'on a tort.* — ed copy ; *corrigé*, *m.*, *copie corrigée*, *f.*

correc'tion, *n.*, correction, *f.* Under — ; *sauf correction.*

correctional, *adj.*, correctionnel, -le.

correc'tive, *adj.*, de correction ; correctif.

correc'tive, *n.*, correctif, *m.*

correct'ly, *adv.*, correctement, exactement, justement, juste ; convenablement ; purement, regulièrement.

correct'ness, *n.*, exactitude, justesse, convenance, (of style) pureté ; (of a copy) fidélité, *f.*

correc'tor (-teur), *n.*, correcteur, *m.*

cor'relate (-ri-léte), *v.n.*, être corrélatif, correspondre.

correla'tion (-ri-lé-), *n.*, corrélation, *f.*

correl'ative (-rèl-è-), *adj.*, corrélatif.

correl'ative, *n.*, corrélatif, *m.*

correl'atively, *adv.*, par corrélation, d'une manière corrélative.

correl'ativeness, *n.*, caractère corrélatif, *m.*

correspond', *v.n.*, correspondre à ou avec ; se correspondre ; se rapporter à ; répondre à ; s'accorder avec ; être en rapport avec ; être conforme à.

correspon'dence, *n.*, correspondance, *f. ;* rapport, *m.*, relations, *f.pl. ;* intelligence, *f.*

correspon'dent, *adj.*, correspondant à, conforme à ; qui se rapporte à.

correspon'dent, *n.*, correspondant, *m.*

correspon'dently, *adv.*, d'une manière correspondante, conformément à.

correspon'ding, *adj.*, correspondant à.

correspon'sive, *adj.*, correspondant à, conforme à.

cor'ridor (-dôr), *n.*, corridor ; (fort.) chemin couvert, *m.*

cor'rigible (-ri-dji-b'l), *adj.*, corrigible ; punissable.

cor'rigibleness, *n.*, caractère corrigible, *m.*

corrob'orant, *adj.*, (pharm.) corroborant.

corrob'orant, *n.*, (pharm.) corroborant, *m.*

corrob'orate, *v.a.*, corroborer, fortifier, confirmer.

corrobora'tion (-ré-), *n.*, corroboration ; confirmation, *f.* In — of ; *à l'appui de.*

corrob'orative, *adj.*, corroboratif.

corrob'orative, *n.*, (pharm.) corroborant, *m.*

corrode' (-rôde), *v.a.*, corroder, ronger ; (fig.) miner, détruire.

corro'dent, *adj.*, corrodant.

corrodibil'ity ou **corro'sibility** (-ci-), *n.*, qualité de ce qui peut être corrodé, *f.*

corro'dible ou **corro'sible** (-ci-), *adj.*, qui peut être corrodé, susceptible de corrosion.

corro'sion (-rô-jeune), *n.*, corrosion ; (fig.) destruction, *f.*

corro'sive (-rô-cive), *adj.*, corrosif ; (fig.) rongeur. — care ; (fig.) *souci rongeur*, *m.*

corro'sive, *n.*, corrosif, *m.*

corro'sively, *adv.*, comme un corrosif.

corro'siveness, *n.*, nature corrosive, *f.*

cor'rugant (-riou-), *adj.*, qui ride, qui plisse.

cor'rugate, *v.a.*, rider, plisser, froncer ; onduler. —d iron ; *fer cannelé, m. ; tôle ondulée, f.*

cor'rugate, *v.n.*, se plisser, se froncer, se rider.

corruga'tion (-riou-ghé-), *n.*, cannelure, *f. ;* (fig.) plissement, froncement, *m.*

corrupt' (cor-reupte), *v.a.*, corrompre, altérer.

corrupt', *v.n.*, se corrompre, se gâter, s'altérer. To become — ; *se corrompre, se dépraver.*

corrupt', *adj.*, corrompu, dépravé, gâté, vicié.

corrupt'er, *n.*, corrupteur, *m.*, corruptrice, *f.*

corruptibil'ity, *n.*, corruptibilité, *f.*

corrupt'ible, *adj.*, corruptible.

corrupt'ibly, *adv.*, d'une manière corruptible.

corrupt'ing, *adj.*, corrupteur.

corrup'tion, *n.*, corruption, dégradation, *f. ;* (matter) pus, *m.*

corrup'tive (cor-reup'-), *adj.*, (l.u.) corruptif.

corrupt'less, *adj.*, incorruptible.

corrupt'ly, *adv.*, par la corruption ; par corruption, d'une manière corrompue.

corrupt'ness, *n.*, corruption, *f.*

corrupt-prac'tices, *n.*, (in elections) subornation (directe *ou* indirecte), *f.*

corrupt'ress, *n.*, corruptrice, *f.*

cor'sair, *n.*, corsaire, *m.*

corse, *n.*, (poet.) cadavre, *m.*

corse'let (cors'lète), *n.*, corselet, *m.*

corse'let, *v.a.*, revêtir d'un corselet.

cor'set (-sète), *n.*, corset, *m.*

cor'set-maker (-mék'-), *n.*, fabricant de corsets, *m. ;* corsetière, *f.*

Cor'sican, *adj.*, corse ; de Corse.

Cor'tes (-tîze), *n.pl.*, cortès, *f.pl.*

cor'tical, *adj.*, cortical.

corun'dum (co-reun'deume), *n.*, corindon, *m.*

corus'cant (-reus'-), *adj.*, scintillant, brillant.

corus'cate, *v.n.*, scintiller, briller.

corusca'tion (-eus'ké-), *n.*, coruscation ; (fig.) éclat, *m.*, éclair, *f.*

corvette', *n.*, corvette, *f.*

co'rymb, *n.*, (bot.) corymbe, *m.*

coryphe'us, *n.*, coryphée, *m.*

co-se'cant (cô-cî-), *n.*, (geom.) cosécante, *f.*

co'sey, co'sy, *ou* **co'zy** (cô-zi), *adj.*, (of apartments) commode et petit ; chaud, confortable. *n.*, (tea) coussinet de théière, *m.*

co'sily (cô-zi-), *adv.*, à l'aise ; agréablement.

co'sine (co-caïne), *n.*, (geom.) cosinus, *m.*

cos-let'tuce (-lét'tiss), *n.*, laitue romaine, *f.*

cosmet'ic (coz'-), *adj.*, cosmétique.

cosmet'ic, *n.*, cosmétique, *m.*

cos'mic *ou* **cos'mical** (coz'-), *adj.*, cosmique.

cos'mically, *adv.*, avec le soleil (*à son lever ou à son coucher*).

cosmog'ony (coz'-), *n.*, cosmogonie, *f.*

cosmog'rapher (coz'-), *n.*, cosmographe, *m.*

cosmograph'ic *ou* **cosmograph'ical**, *adj.*, cosmographique.

cosmograph'ically, *adv.*, d'une manière cosmographique.

cosmog'raphy (coz'-), *n.*, cosmographie, *f.*

cosmolog'ical (coz'-), *adj.*, cosmologique.

cosmol'ogist, *n.*, personne versée dans la cosmologie, *f.*

cosmol'ogy (coz'-), *n.*, cosmologie, *f.*

cosmopol'itan (coz'-) *ou* **cosmop'olite** (coz'-mop-o-laïte), *n.*, cosmopolite, *m.*

cosmora'ma (coz'mo-râ-), *n.*, (opt.) cosmorama, *m.*

Cos'sack, *m.*, cosaque, *m.*

cos'set (cos'sète), *n.*, agneau favori ; agneau privé ; favori, *m.*, favorite, *f. v.a.*, dorloter, caresser.

cost, *n.*, prix ; frais, *m. ;* dépense, *f. ;* (com.) coût, *m. ;* dépens, *m.pl. pl.*, (jur.) dépens, *m. pl. — price ; prix coûtant*, ou *prix de revient, m.* To one's — ; *à ses dépens.* To carry —s ; (jur.) *entraîner les dépens.* At your own —; *à vos risques et périls.* At any —; *à tout prix, à tous hasards.*

cost, *v.n.*, (*preterit* and *past part.*, Cost), coûter. — what it may ; *coûte que coûte.* It costs me (pain) to find fault with you ; *il m'en coûte de vous blâmer.*

cos'tal, *adj.*, (anat.) costal.

cos'termonger *ou* **cos'ter** (cos'-'teur-meugn'-gh'eur), *n.*, marchand ambulant de (pommes et d'autres fruits), marchand des quatre saisons, *m.*

cos'tive, *adj.*, constipé.

cos'tiveness, *n.*, constipation, *f.*

cost'less, *adj.*, qui ne coûte rien, sans frais.

cost'liness, *n.*, haut prix, prix élevé, *m. ;* dépense ; somptuosité ; richesse, *f.*

cost'ly, *adj.*, coûteux, de prix ; somptueux ; de luxe.

cost'mary, *n.*, (bot.) balsamite, balsamite odorante, *f.*

cos'tume (-tioume), *n.*, costume, *m.*

cos'tumer *ou* **-ier**, *n.*, costumier, *m.*

co-suf'ferer, *n.*, compagnon d'infortune, *m.*

co-sure'ty (cô-chour'-), *n.*, (jur.) cofidéjusseur, *m.*

cos'y (cô-zi), *adj.*, petit et commode, etc. *V.* **co'sey.**

cot, *n.*, cabane ; chaumière, *f. ;* (for sheep) parc ; (bed) petit lit, lit d'enfant ; lit volant ; (nav.) lit de bord, cadre, hamac à l'anglaise, *m.*

cotan'gent (cô-ta'n'-dje'n'te),*n.*, cotangente, *f.*

cotem'porary (cô-). *V.* **contem'porary.**

coten'ant (cô-tè'n'-), *n.*, (jur.) co-tenancier, *m. ;* colocataire, *m.f.*

co'terie (cô-teu-rî), *n.*, coterie, clique, *f.*

coter'minous, *adj.*, limitrophe **de**, voisin **de**, contigu à.

cothurn' (-theurne), *n.*, cothurne, *m.*

cothur'nate *ou* **cothur'nated** (-theur'-), *adj.*, qui a chaussé le cothurne ; (fig., ant.) tragique.

cot'quean (cot'kwîne), *n.*, jocrisse ; fouille au pot, *m.*

co-trustee', *n.*, cotuteur, curateur, *m.*, -trice, *f.*

cots'wold (cots'wôlde), *n.*, parc, en pleine campagne, *m.*, (of sheep).

cot'tage (cot'tédje), *n.*, chaumière, cabane, petite maison, villa, *f.* Swiss — ; *châlet, m. —* piano ; *piano droit, m. —* farming ; *petite culture, f.*

cot'tager, *n.*, paysan, *m.*, paysanne, *f.*, villageois, *m.*

cot'ter (cot'-) *ou* **cot'tier** (cot'tieur), *n.*, paysan, *m.*, paysanne, *f. ;* villageois, *m. ;* (tech.) clavette, *f.*

cot'ton (cot't'n), *n.*, coton ; calicot ; fil d'Ecosse, *m.* Darning-— ; *coton plat.* Sewing-—; *fil d'Ecosse, coton à coudre.* Knitting-—; *coton à tricoter.* Ball of —; *pelote de coton, f.* Reel of —; *bobine de coton, f.*

cot'ton, *v.n.*, cotonner ; se cotonner, être intimement lié **avec**. To— to ; *prendre en amitié ;* (with) *corder* **avec**.

cot'ton-check (-tshèke), *n.*, cotonnade, *f.*

cot'ton-cloth (-clôth), *n.*, toile de coton, *f.*, calicot, *m. ;* cotonnade, *f.*

cot'ton-cord, *n.*, ganse de coton, *f.*

cot'ton-fabric, *n.*, tissu de coton, calicot, *m.*

cot'ton-factory (-teu'ri), *n.*, filature de coton, *f.*

cot'ton-gin (-djine), *n.*, (tech.) machine à égrener le coton, égreneuse à coton, *f.*

cot'ton-goods, *n.pl.*, cotonnade, *f.*

cot'ton-jen'ny (-djè'n'ni), *n.*, métier à filer le coton, *m.*

cot'ton-mill, *n.*, moulin à coton, *m. ;* filature de coton, *f.*

cot'ton-plant, cot'ton-shrub (-shreube), *ou* **cot'ton-tree** (-trî), *n.*, cotonnier, *m.*

cot'ton-spinner, *n.*, filateur de coton, *m.*

cot'ton-spinning, *n.*, filage du coton, *m.*

cot'ton-trade, *n.*, commerce des cotons, *m.*

cot'ton-velvet, *n.*, velours de coton, *m.*

cot'ton-waste, *n.*, bourre de coton, *f.*

cot'ton-wool (-woule), *n.*, ouate, *f.*

cot'ton-yarn (-yârne), *n.*, fil de coton, *m.*

cotyle'don (-lĭ-deune), *n.*, (bot., anat.) cotylédon, *m.*

cotyle'donous, *adj.*, cotylédoné.

couch (caoutshe), *n.*, couche, chaise longue, *f.* ; lit de repos ; canapé, *m.*

couch, *v.n.*, coucher ; se coucher ; se baisser ; se tapir.

couch, *v.a.*, coucher ; étendre ; (of writing) rédiger ; exprimer, mettre, *ou* coucher, par écrit ; cacher ; (surg.) abaisser la cataracte ; (mil.) tenir (la lance) en arrêt.

couch'ant, *adj.*, couché, accroupi, tapi ; (her.) couché.

couch'er, *n.*, oculiste, *m.*

couch'grass (-grâce), *n.*, chiendent, *m.*

cough (cofe), *n.*, toux, *f.* Hooping- —; *coqueluche, f.* — drop ; *pastille* (pour la toux), *f.* To have a —; *avoir la toux.* To have a bad —; *avoir une mauvaise toux.*

cough, *v.n.*, tousser.

cough (**up**), *v.a.*, expectorer.

cough'er, *n.*, tousseur, *m.*, tousseuse, *f.*

cough'ing, *n.*, toux. Fit of —; *accès*, *m.*, *quinte de toux, f.*

could (coude). *V.* **can** (verb).

coul'ter (côl'-), *n.*, coutre, *m.*

coun'cil (caou'n-), *n.*, conseil ; (eccl.) concile, *m.* Cabinet ; *réunion du Cabinet, f.*

coun'cil-board (-bôrde), *n.*, table du conseil, *m.*

coun'cil-chamber, *n.*, salle du conseil, *f.*

coun'cilor (-'leur), **coun'cilman**, *n.*, conseiller, conseiller municipal, *m.*

coun'sel (-sèle), *n.*, conseil, avis, *m.*, discrétion, *f.*; défenseurs, avocats d'une partie, *m.pl.*, avocat, défenseur, *m.* To hold —; *tenir conseil.* To keep one's —; (loc.) *n'en parlez à personne.* —keeper ; *personne discrète, f.* ; *confident, m.* To take —'s opinion ; *consulter un avocat.*

coun'sel, *v.a.*, conseiller.

coun'selable, *adj.*, conseillable.

coun'selor (-sèl'leur), *n.*, conseil, avocat, *m.*

coun'selorship, *n.*, fonctions de conseil, *f.pl.*, charge d'avocat, *f.*

count (caou'n'te), *n.*, calcul ; compte, *m.* ; (jur.) charge, *f.* ; chef d'accusation ; (title) comte, *m.*

count, *v.a.*, compter ; (to esteem, consider) regarder, considérer, compter ; (to place to account) imputer à. To — out ; *ajourner* (une réunion). *v.n.*, to — upon ; *compter sur.* The House was counted out at 8 o'clock ; *on a ajourné la Chambre à huit heures.* That was —ed to him for righteousness ; *cela lui fut imputé à justice.*

coun'tenance (caou'n'tĕ'n-), *n.*, figure, mine, expression, physionomie ; contenance, *f.* ; air, *m.* ; (fig.) faveur, protection ; approbation, *f.* ; appui, *m.* How looks her —? *quelle mine a-t-elle ?* The knight of the rueful —; *le chevalier à la triste figure.* To be out of —; *perdre contenance, être décontenancé.* To keep one's —; *garder son sérieux, faire bonne contenance.* The light of his —; (biblically) *la lumière de son visage.* To look any one out of —; *faire baisser les yeux à quelqu'un.* To put in —; *mettre à son aise,* ou *donner de l'assurance à.* To give — to ; *favoriser, encourager.* To change —; *changer de visage.* To put out of —; *décontenancer.* To stare out of —; *dévisager quelqu'un.*

coun'tenance, *v.a.*, appuyer, encourager, favoriser, autoriser ; soutenir, défendre ; approuver ; être en faveur **de**.

coun'ter, *n.*, calculateur, compteur ; (at cards) jeton ; (of a shop) comptoir, *m.* ; (mus.) haute-contre, *f.*, (instrument) compteur, *m.* —jumper ; (pop.) *calicot, m.*

coun'ter, *adv.*, contre ; contrairement à ; à l'encontre **de**. To run — to a thing ; *aller à*

l'encontre de quelque chose. To go *ou* run — to a person ; *heurter, contrarier quelqu'un, aller à l'encontre* **de**.

counteract' (caou'n'teur'acte), *v.a.*, compenser ; détruire ; faire obstacle à ; contrecarrer ; balancer ; déjouer ; neutraliser.

counterac'tion, *n.*, action contraire, *f.*, mouvement opposé, *m.* ; opposition, résistance, *f.*, empêchement, obstacle, *m.*

coun'ter-alley, *n.*, contre-allée, *f.*

coun'ter-attraction, *n.*, attraction opposée, *f.*

coun'ter-balance, *n.*, contrepoids, *m.*

counterbal'ance, *v.a.*, contre-balancer.

coun'ter-bass (-béce), *n.*, (mus.) contre-basse, *f.*

coun'terbond, *n.*, (jur.) sous-garantie (donnée au garant), *f.*

coun'terbuff (-beufe), *v.a.*, rendre un coup ; arrêter, faire reculer par un coup.

coun'terbuff, *n.*, coup rendu, *m.*

coun'terchange (-tshè'n'dje), *n.*, contre-échange, *m.*

counterchange', *v.a.*, échanger.

coun'tercharge, *n.*, contre-accusation, contre-plainte, *f.*

coun'tercharm (-tshârme), *n.*, contre-charme, *m.*

coun'tercheck (-tshèke), *n.*, frein, obstacle, *m.*, censure, réprimande, *f.*

counter-check', *v.a.*, opposer, réprimer, blâmer, contrecarrer.

coun'ter-current, *n.*, contre-courant, *m.*

coun'ter-deed, *n.*, contre-lettre, *f.*

coun'ter-drain (-drone), *n.*, contre-fossé, *m.*

counterdraw' (-drô), *v.a.*, calquer.

coun'terdrawing (-drô-igne), *n.*, calque, *m.*

coun'ter-evidence, *n.*, déposition contradictoire, *f.*, témoignage contraire, *m.*

coun'terfeit (-fîte), *n.*, contrefaçon ; imitation, *f.* ; (pers.) imposteur, *m.*

coun'terfeit, *adj.*, contrefait, feint, simulé, faux.

coun'terfeit, *v.a.*, contrefaire ; imiter ; feindre.

coun'terfeit, *v.n.*, feindre.

coun'terfeiter, *n.*, contrefacteur ; imitateur, faussaire, faux-monnayeur, *m.*

coun'terfeiting, *n.*, contrefaçon, *m.*

coun'ter-ferment (-feur-), *n.*, ferment agissant en sens contraire, *m.*

coun'ter-fissure. *V.* **contra-fissure**.

coun'terfoil, *n.*, contre-taille, talon de souche, *m.*

coun'terfort (-fôrte), *n.*, contre-boutant, contrefort, *m.*

coun'ter-fugue (-fioughe), *n.*, (mus.) contre-fugue, *f.*

coun'terguard (-gârde), *n.*, (fort.) contre-garde, *f.*

coun'ter-indication (-ké-), *n.*, contre-indication, *f.*

coun'ter-lath (-lâth), *n.*, (carp.) contre-latte, *f.*

counter-lath', *v.a.*, (carp.) contre-latter.

coun'terlight (-laïte), *n.*, (paint.) contre jour, *m.*

coun'termand, *n.*, contre-ordre, contremandement, *m.*

countermand', *v.a.*, contremander, décommander.

counter-march' (-mârtshe), *n.*, (milit.) contremarche, *f.*

coun'ter-march, *v.n.*, (milit.) exécuter, *ou* faire, une contremarche.

coun'termark (-mârke), *n.*, contremarque, *f.*

countermark', *v.a.*, contremarquer.

coun'termine (-maïne), *n.*, contre-mine, *f.*

countermine', *v.a.*, contre-miner ; (fig.) opposer, détruire, déjouer, combattre.

coun'ter-motion (-mô-), *n.*, contre-projet, *m.* ; contre-proposition, *f.*

coun'termovement (-mouv'-), *n.*, (milit.) contremarche, *f.;* mouvement opposé, *m.*

coun'termure (-mioure), *n.*, contre-mur, *m.*

countermure', *v.a.*, contre-murer.

coun'ter-natural (-nat'iou-), *adj.*, contre nature.

coun'ter-negociation, *n.*, négociation contraire, *f.*

coun'terpace (-péce), *n.*, contre-pas, *m.*

coun'terpane (-péne), *n.*, courtepointe, *f.;* couvre-pied, *m.*

coun'terpart (-pârte), *n.*, contre-partie, *f.;* pendant; (jur.) (of deeds) double, duplicata, *m.;* (mus.) contre-partie, *f.*

coun'ter-petition (-pi-), *n.*, pétition opposée, *ou* contre pétition.

coun'terplea (-plî), *n.*, (jur.) réplique, *f.*

coun'terplot, *n.*, contre-ruse, (l.u.) *f.*

counterplot', *v.a.*, combattre par une contre-ruse.

coun'terpoint (-poï'n'te), *n.*, (mus.) contre-point, *m.*

coun'terpoise (-poïze), *n.*, contrepoids, *m.*

coun'terpoise, *v.a.*, contre-balancer.

coun'terpoison (-poï-z'n), *n.*, contrepoison, *m.*

coun'terpressure (-prèsh'eur), *n.*, pression contraire, *f.*

coun'terproject (-prodj'ècte), *n.*, contre-projet, *m.*

coun'terproof (-proufe), *n.*, contre-épreuve, *f.*

counterprove' (-prouve), *v.a.*, contre-tirer, tirer une contre-épreuve.

coun'ter-revolution (-liou-), *n.*, contre-révolution, *f.*

coun'ter-revolutionary, *adj.*, contre-révolutionnaire.

coun'ter-revolutionist, *n.*, contre-révolutionnaire, *m.f.*

coun'terroll (-rôle), *n.*, (jur.) contrôle, duplicata, *m.*

coun'terscarp (-scârpe), *n.*, (fort.) contre-scarpe, *f.*

coun'terseal (-sîl), *v.a.*, contre-sceller.

coun'ter-security (-sèkiou-), *n.*, (jur.) sous-garantie, *f.*

countersign' (-saïne), *v.a.*, contresigner.

coun'tersign, *n.*, (milit.) mot de ralliement, *m.*

coun'ter-signature (-sig-na-tioure), *n.*, contreseing, *m.*

coun'ter-statement (-stéte'-), *n.*, assertion, exposition, contraire d'un fait, *f.*

coun'ter-statute (-stat'ioute), *n.*, statut contraire, *m.*

coun'ter-struggle (-streug'g'l), *n.*, lutte en sens contraire, *f.*

coun'tersway (-swé), *n.*, influence opposée, *f.*

coun'tertally, *n.*, (com.) contre-taille, *f.*

coun'tertaste (-téste), *n.*, faux goût, *m.*

coun'tertenor (-tè'n'-), *n.*, (mus.) haute-contre, *f.*

coun'tertide (-taïde), *n.*, retour de marée, *m.*, *ou* contre-marée, *f.*

coun'tertime (-taïme), *n.*, résistance, opposition, *f.;* défense, résistance (d'un cheval).

coun'tervail (-véle), *n.*, équivalence, compensation, *f.*

countervail', *v.a.*, contre-balancer; compenser, balancer.

coun'terview (-viou), *n.*, contraste; point de vue opposé, *m.*

counterwheel' (-hwîl), *v.a.*, (milit.) commander, exécuter une conversion en arrière.

counterwork' (-weurke), *v.a.*, contreminer; confondre, déjouer, contrecarrer.

coun'terworks, *n.pl.*, (fort.) contre-attaque, *f.*

count'ess (caou'n't'-), *n.*, comtesse, *f.*

count'ing-house (-haouce), *n.*, bureau, comptoir, *m.;* caisse, *f.*

count'less, *adj.*, innombrable, sans nombre.

coun'trified (keu'n'trie-faïde), *adj.*, provincial; campagnard; agreste, champêtre; rustique.

coun'try (keu'n'trie), *n.*, patrie; contrée, *f.;* pays, *m.;* région; campagne, *f.* To live in the —; *demeurer à la campagne*. — town; *ville de province*, *f.* — gentleman; *gentilhomme campagnard, gentilhomme de province*, *m.* — girl; *petite villageoise, payse, paysanne, f.* — life; *vie champêtre; vie de province*, *f.*

coun'try-box, *n.*, pied-à-terre, *m.*

coun'try-house (-haouce), *n.*, maison de campagne, *f.*

coun'try-man (-ma'n), *n.*, habitant d'un pays; compatriote; paysan, campagnard, homme de la campagne, *m.* What — are you? *de quel pays êtes-vous?* Fellow-—; *compatriote*, *m.*

coun'try-parson, *n.*, curé de village *ou* de campagne, *m.*

coun'try-people, *n.pl.*, campagnards, provinciaux, gens de la campagne, *m.pl.*

coun'try-seat (-sîte), *n.*, campagne; maison de campagne, *f.;* château, *m.*

coun'ty (caou'n'-), *n.*, comté, *m.* — court; *tribunal de première instance*, *m.* — town; *chef-lieu*, *m.* — rate; *impôt départemental*, *m.*

cou'pée (-pé), *n.*, (dance) coupé, *m.*

couple (keup'p'l), *n.*, couple, *f.;* (a male and female) couple, *m.;* (carp.) moise, *f.;* (mec.) couple, *m.*

couple, *v.n.*, s'accoupler.

couple, *v.a.*, coupler, accoupler, attacher, atteler; joindre.

couplet (keup'lète), *n.*, couplet, distique, *m.*, strophe, *f.*

coupling, *n.*, accouplement, assemblage, *m.* *pl.*, (rail.) attelage, *m.* — chain; *chaîne de sûreté, chaîne d'attelage, f.* — iron; *tendeur*, *m.*

cou'rage (keur'édje), *n.*, courage, *m.*

coura'geous (keur'ré'djeusse), *adj.*, courageux.

coura'geously, *adv.*, courageusement.

coura'geousness, *n.*, courage, *m.*

cou'rier (cou'rieur), *n.*, courrier, *m.*

course (côrse), *n.*, cours, *m.;* course, carrière, voie, suite, succession, *f.;* (of life) genre; (at a meal) service; (duration) courant, *m.;* (for races) arène, *f.*, terrain de course; (for horse-races) hippodrome, *m.;* (mas.) assise, *f.;* (geol.) filon, *m.;* (nav.) route, *f.* *pl.*, (med.) règles, *f.pl.* In due —; *en ordre, en son temps, en temps utile, en temps et lieu.* In the — of; *dans le cours de;* (of time) *dans le courant de.* In — of time; *avec le temps.* Of —; *naturellement; bien entendu, cela va sans dire;* (jur.) *de droit.* That is a matter of —; *cela va sans dire.* To take its —; *prendre son cours.* Water-—; *lit de rivière; cours d'eau*, *m.* In — of formation; *en train de se constituer; en voie de formation.*

course, *v.a.*, courir; faire courir, parcourir; chasser, poursuivre.

course, *v.n.*, courir, circuler (of the blood).

cours'er, *n.*, coureur, coursier, chasseur (à courre), *m.*

court (côrte), *n.*, cour, *f.;* tribunal, *m.;* (small street) impasse, *f.;* passage, *m.* Criminal —; *cour de justice criminelle.* To go to —; *aller à la cour.* To pay one's — to; *faire sa cour à.* In open —; *en plein tribunal.* — yard; *cour*, *f.* — day; *jour d'audience*, *m.*

court, *v.a.*, faire la cour à; courtiser; fêter; solliciter; rechercher, briguer; prier, inviter. To — inquiries; *inviter les renseignements ou être prêt à donner tous les renseignements.*

court'-baron, *n.*, cour seigneuriale, *f.*

court'-bred (-brède), *adj.*, élevé à la cour.

court'-card, *n.*, figure, *f.*

court'-chaplain, *n.*, aumônier de la cour, *m.*

court′-day, *n.*, jour d'audience, *m.* ; jour de palais, *m.*

court′-dress, *n.*, habit de cour, *m.*

court′eous (keur-tè- *ou* kôrtieusse), *adj.*, courtois ; poli.

court′eously, *adv.*, courtoisement ; poliment.

court′eousness, *n.*, courtoisie ; politesse, *f.*

court′er, *n.*, amant, soupirant, prétendant, *m.*

court′esy (keur-tè-ci), *n.*, courtoisie ; politesse ; (keur't'ci) (*V.* curtsey) révérence, *f.*

courte′sy, *v.n.* (*V.* curtsey).

cour′tezan (keur-tè-z'ne), *n.*, courtisane, *f.*

court′-hand, *n.*, écriture de palais, *f.*

court′-house, *n.*, salle des réunions, *f.* ; palais de justice, *m.*

court′ier (côrt′ieur), *n.*, courtisan, *m.*

court′like (côrt′laïke), *adj.*, de cour ; poli ; élégant.

court′liness (côrt′-), *n.*, élégance, politesse, *f.* ; poli, élégant ; courtois, gracieux.

court′ly, *adj.*, de cour ; poli, élégant ; courtois, gracieux.

court′ly, *adv.*, dans le ton de la cour ; poliment, avec grâce.

court-mar′tial (-mâr′sh'al), *n.*, conseil de guerre, *m.*

court′-plaster (-plâs′-), *n.*, taffetas d'Angleterre, *m.*

court′-roll, *n.*, ⊙terrier, *m.*

court′ship, *n.*, cour, *f.*

court′yard, *n.*, cour, *f.*

cous′in (keuz'z'n), *n.*, cousin, *m.*, cousine, *f.* First —; *cousin germain, cousine germaine.* Second —; *cousin issu, ou cousine issue, de germain.*

cove (côve), *n.*, (geog.) anse, crique, *f.* ; (pers.) gaillard, individu, *m.*

cove, *v.a.*, voûter, cintrer.

cov′enant (keuv'è-), *n.*, convention, *f.* ; pacte, contrat ; (Eng. hist.) covenant, *m.* To enter into a —; *s'engager par contrat* à.

cov′enant, *v.n.*, convenir **de** ; s'engager à.

cov′enant, *v.a.*, accorder, promettre, stipuler par contrat.

covenantee′, *n.*, obligataire, *m.f.*

cov′enanter, *n.*, partie contractante, *f.* ; (jur.) débiteur, *m.*, débitrice, *f.* ; (English hist.) covenantaire, religionnaire, *m.*

Cov′entry, *n.* To send to —; *mettre en quarantaine.* To be sent to —; *être mis en quarantaine.* To be in —; *être en quarantaine.*

cov′er (keuv′-), *v.a.*, couvrir **de** *ou* **en**, recouvrir **de** *ou* **en**, déguiser ; cacher ; (of birds) couver ; (of animals) couvrir, saillir. To — distances ; *parcourir du pays.*

cov′er, *n.*, couverture ; (of a dish, a plate) cloche ; (of a letter, a parcel) enveloppe ; (of a chair) housse, *f.* ; (of a saucepan) couvercle ; (bot.) involucre ; (fig.) voile, masque ; abri, (of a table) tapis ; couvert, *m.* Under —; *à couvert, à l'abri de.* Under registered —; *sous enveloppe chargée.* Under —; *sous enveloppe ; sous la protection ; à la faveur de ; sous le masque de ; à l'abri de* ; (fig.) *sous l'apparence de ; sous de faux semblants de.*

cov′ering, *n.*, couverture, enveloppe ; (of chairs) housse, *f.* ; (of clothing) habits, vêtements, *m.pl.*

cov′erlet (keuv′eur′lète), *n.*, couvre-pied, couvre-lit, *m.*

cov′ert (keuv′eurte), *n.*, couvert, abri ; gîte, fort, *m.* ; tanière, *f.*

cov′ert, *adj.*, couvert ; caché, secret ; insidieux ; (jur.) en puissance de mari.

cov′ertly, *adv.*, secrètement, en cachette.

cov′erture (keuv′eurt′ioure), *n.*, abri ; (jur.) état de la femme en puissance de mari, *m.*

cov′ert-way (-wè), *n.*, (fort.) chemin couvert, *m.*

cov′et (keuv′ète), *v.a.*, convoiter ; ambitionner ; désirer ardemment.

cov′etable, *adj.*, convoitable.

cov′etous, *adj.*, avide, avare, cupide, convoiteux.

cov′etously, *adv.*, avec convoitise ; avidement.

cov′etousness, *n.*, convoitise, avarice ; cupidité, avidité, *f.*

cov′ey (keuv′è), *n.*, (of birds of the same nest) couvée ; (of birds) volée ; bande, compagnie, *f.*

cov′ing (côv′-), *n.*, voussure, *f.*

cow (cao), *n.*, vache, *f.* Milch —; *vache laitière, vache à lait.* — hair ; *bourre de vache, f.* — house, — shed ; *vacherie, étable à vaches, f.*

cow, *v.a.*, intimider ; dompter ; accabler ; atterrer.

cow′ard (caou′eurde), *n.*, lâche, couard, poltron, *m.*, poltronne, *f.*

cow′ardice, *n.*, couardise, poltronnerie, lâcheté, *f.*

cow′ardliness, *n.*, couardise, lâcheté, *f.*

cow′ardly, *adj.*, couard, lâche, poltron.

cow′ardly, *adv.*, couardement, lâchement, en poltron ; en lâche.

cow′-bane, *n.*, (bot.) cicutaire aquatique, ciguë vireuse, *f.*

cow′-berry (-bèr′-), *n.*, (bot.) airelle, canneberge, *f.* ; comaret, *m.*

cow′-boy (-boï), *n.*, jeune vacher, *m.*

cow′-catcher (-catsh′-), *m.*, (rail.) chasse-pierres, *m.*

cow′-dung (-deu′gne), *n.*, bouse de vache, *f.*

cow′er, *v.n.*, s'accroupir, se blottir ; s'affaisser, se tapir.

cow′-grass (-grâce), *n.*, (bot.) trèfle des prés, *m.*

cow′-herd, *n.*, vacher, *m.*, vachère, *f.*

cow′-keeper (-kîp′-), *n.*, vacher, *m.*, vachère, *f.* ; nourrisseur, *m.*

cowl (caoul), *n.*, capuce ; capuchon, *m.* ; tabourin (of chimneys), *m.*

cow′-leech (-lîtshe), *n.*, vétérinaire, *m.*

cow′-parsnip (-pârs′-), *n.*, (bot.) berce ; branche-ursine bâtarde, *f.*

cow′-pen (-pène), *n.*, parc aux vaches, *m.*

cow′-pox, *n.*, (med.) vaccine, *f.*

cow′slip, *n.*, (bot.) primevère, *f.*

cows′-lungwort (caoz′leu′gn′weurte), *n.*, (bot.) bouillon-blanc, *m.*

cow′-tree (-trî), *n.*, arbre à la vache, brosimon, *m.*

cow′-weed (-wîde), *n.*, cerfeuil sauvage, *m.*

cow′-wheat (-hwîte), *n.*, (bot.) mélampyre, blé de vache, *m.* ; queue-de-renard, *f.*

cox′comb (-côme), *n.*, fat, petit-maître, freluquet, *m.* ; (bot.) célosie, *f.*, passe-velours, *m.*, amarante, *f.*

cox′combry (-côm′ri), *n.*, fatuité, *f.*

coxcomb′ical, *adj.*, fat, plein de fatuité ; de fat.

cox′swain, *n.*, patron de chaloupe, *m.*

coy (coï), *adj.*, modeste ; timide ; réservé.

coy, *v.n.*, être réservé ; se comporter avec timidité, faire des difficultés.

coy′ly, *adv.*, modestement, timidement ; avec réserve.

coy′ness, *n.*, modestie, timidité, réserve, *f.*

coz (keuze), *abréviation de* cousin, *m.*, cousine, *f.*

coz′en (keuz′z'n), *v.a.*, duper, tromper.

coz′enage (-édje), *n.*, fourberie, fourbe, tromperie, *f.*

coz′ener, *n.*, fourbe, trompeur, *m.*

co′zy, *adj.* V. cosey.

crab, *n.*, crabe, cancre, *m.* ; écrevisse de mer ; (bot.) pomme sauvage, *f.* ; (astron.) cancer, *m.*, écrevisse, *f.* ; (nav.) cabestan volant ; (of men) loup-garou, mauvais coucheur, *m.* ; (of women) pie-grièche, *f.* To catch a —; (nav.) *manquer son coup de rame.*

crab′-apple (-ap′p'l), *n.*, pomme sauvage, *f.*

crab'bed (crab'ède), *adj.*, acariâtre, revêche ; dur, rude ; bourru, chagrin. — look ; *mine rechignée, f.*

crab'bedly (-'èd'-), *adv.*, d'une manière bourrue, durement, rudement.

crab'bedness (-'èd'-), *n.*, humeur acariâtre ; âcreté, rudesse ; difficulté, *f.*

crab'-fish, *n.*, crabe, *m. ;* écrevisse de mer, *f.*

crab'-tree (-trî), *n.*, pommier sauvage, *m.*

crack, *n.*, (noise) craquement, *m. ;* fente ; crevasse ; (in glass) fêlure, *f. ;* (boaster) hâbleur, *m.*, hâbleuse, *f. ;* craqueur, *m.*, craqueuse, *f. ;* (tech.) fissure, *f. ;* (of a whip) claquement, *m. ;* (of firearms) détonation ; lézarde ; (of voice) hue de la voix ; (boast) hâblerie, *f.* In a —; *en un clin d'œil.* — of doom; *le jugement dernier.* To be a — shot ; *être un excellent tireur ; avoir un tir infaillible.*

crack, *v.a.*, fêler, gercer ; fendre ; (nuts) casser ; (a whip) faire claquer ; claquer ; (a bottle of wine) faire sauter ; décoiffer ; (a joke) dire, faire, lâcher ; (fig.) rompre, briser. To — a crib ; (pop.) *s'introduire à l'aide d'effraction dans une maison.* To — up ; (pop.) *faire mousser ;* (fig.) *vanter, exalter, prôner.*

crack, *v.n.*, craquer, se fendre, se lézarder ; (of the ground, the skin) se gercer ; craqueter ; (of a whip) claquer ; (of glass, pottery-ware, etc.) se fêler ; (pers.) se vanter ; (of the voice) muer ; (of boots) se crever, se percer.

crack'-brained (-bré'n'de), *adj.*, timbré, fou. — fellow ; *cerveau fêlé, m.*

cracked (crak'te), *adj.*, fendu, fêlé ; (fig.) timbré ; détraqué. To be a little —; *avoir un grain de folie.*

crack'er, *n.*, vantard, craqueur ; (firework) pétard ; (bonbon) diablotin ; biscuit, *m.*

crac'kle (crak'k'l), *v.a.*, pétiller, craqueter, crépiter.

crack'nel (-nèle), *n.*, craquelin, *m.*

cra'dle (kré'd'l), *n.*, berceau, *m. ;* (of house painters) sellette, *f. ;* (of a ship) ber, *m. ;* (of a mower) ramassette, *f.* From the —; *dès le berceau.* In the —; *au berceau.*

cra'dle, *v.a.*, coucher dans un berceau, bercer ; (to lull) endormir.

craft (crâfte), *n.*, (trade) métier, art, *m. ;* (cunning) ruse, astuce ; (nav.) embarcation, *f.* The —; *la franc-maçonnerie, f.* Small — ; (nav.) *petits bâtiments de tous genres, m.pl.*

craft'ily, *adv.*, artificieusement, avec ruse.

craft'iness, *n.*, artifice, *m. ;* ruse, astuce, *f.*

crafts'man (crâfts'ma'n), *n.*, artisan habile, artiste, *m.*

crafts'master (-mâs-), *n.*, maître en son art, expert, *m.*

craft'y, *adj.*, artificieux ; rusé, astucieux.

crag, *n.*, rocher escarpé ; roc à pic, *m. ;* pointe de rocher, *f. ;* (geol.) falun *ou* sable coquillier du terrain pliocène, *m.*

crag'ged (crag'ghède), *adj.*, rocailleux ; escarpé, abrupt.

crag'gedness *ou* **crag'giness** (crag'ghèd'-, -'ghi-), *n.*, état rocailleux, *m. ;* anfractuosité, *f.*

crag'gy (crag'ghi), *adj.*, rocailleux, escarpé, abrupt.

crake, *n.*, (orni.) râle, *m.*

cram, *n.*, (fib) colle, bourde, *f.* What a —! *quelle colle !*

cram (crame), *v.a.*, fourrer, remplir ; bourrer ; gorger ; farcir ; seriner, élever en serre chaude (of students). To — poultry ; *gaver, empâter de la volaille.*

cram (crame), *v.n.*, se bourrer, se gaver ; s'empiffrer ; (fig.) en conter là.

cram'bo (cra'm'bô), *n.*, bout rimé ; jeu des bouts rimés, *m.*

cram'mer, *n.*, répétiteur, préparateur ; (pop.) bachotier ; (colleges) colleur ; (fibber) bourdeur, *m.*

cram'ming, *n.*, études surmenées, indigestes, *f.pl.* — establishment ; *four à bachot, m. ;* (a lie) *bourde, colle, f.*

cramp (cra'm'pe), *n.*, crampe, *f.*, (tech.) crampon, *m. ;* (fig.) gêne, entrave, *f.*

cramp, *v.a.*, courbaturer, engourdir, serrer ; resserrer ; donner la crampe ; (fig.) gêner ; entraver, restreindre ; (tech.) cramponner. To — in ; *sceller, cramponner.* To — out ; *arracher, tirer de force.*

cramped, *adj.*, gêné, -e. A — style ; *un style dur, serré.* — writing ; *pattes de mouche, f.pl.*

cramp'-fish, *n.*, (ich.) torpille, *f.*

cramp'-iron (-aï'eur'n), *n.*, crampon, *m.*

cramp'it (cra'm'pite), *n.*, bouterolle, *f.*

cran'age (cré-nédje), *n.*, droit de grue, *m.*

cran'berry (cra'n'bèr'-), *n.*, (bot.) airelle, canneberge, *f.*

cranch (cra'n'she), *v.a.* *V.* **crunch.**

crane, *n.*, (orni., tech.) grue, *f. ;* (hydr.) siphon, *m.* Steam — ; *grue à vapeur.* — neck ; (of a carriage) *cou de cygne, m.* *v.a.* To — up ; *hausser, lever (au moyen d'une grue).*

crane's'bill (cré'n'z'-), *n.*, (bot.) bec-de-grue, géranium, *m.*

craniolog'ical (cré-ni-o-lodj'-), *adj.*, craniologique.

craniol'ogist (-djiste), *n.*, craniologiste, craniologue, *m.*

craniol'ogy (-dji), *n.*, craniologie, cranologie, *f.*

craniom'etry (-ét'-), *n.*, craniométrie, *f.*

cranios'copy (-), *n.*, cranioscopie, *f.*

cra'nium (cré-ni-eume), *n.*, (anat.) crâne, *m.*

crank (cra'gn'ke), *n.*, coude ; détour ; sens forcé, jeu de mots ; (tech.) cran, *m. ;* bielle ; manivelle, *f.*

crank, *adj.*, vif, gaillard, dispos, éveillé ; volage ; (nav.) qui a le côté faible.

crank, *v.a.*, couder. *V.* **crankle.**

cran'kle (cra'gn'k'l), *v.n.*, sortir et rentrer ; aller en zigzag.

cran'kle, *v.a.*, couper en zigzag.

cran'kle, *n.*, détour ; zigzag, *m.*

crank'y, *adj.*, irritable, capricieux, fantasque, inquiet, impatient.

cran'nied (cra'n'ide), *adj.*, crevassé, lézardé, gercé.

cran'ny, *n.*, crevasse, fente, lézarde, fissure, *f. ;* trou, *m.*

crape, *n.*, crêpe, *m.* Smooth —; *crêpe lisse.*

crape, *v.a.*, crêper.

crap'ulous (crap'iou-), *adj.*, crapuleux ; soûl, ivre.

crash, *n.*, fracas ; grand bruit, *m. ;* débâcle ; ruine ; (fig.) faillite, banqueroute, *f.*

crash, *v.n.*, faire un grand fracas. *v.a.*, fracasser, briser. To — down ; *tomber avec fracas.*

cra'sis (cré-ciss), *n.*, (gram.) crase, *f.*

crass, *adj.*, épais, grossier, stupide, obtus ; crasse, *adj.f.*

cras'situde (cras'si-tioude), *n.*, épaisseur, *f.*

crate (créte), *n.*, caisse à claire-voie, *f. ;* panier à verrerie, *m. ;* manne, *f.*

cra'ter (cré-), *n.*, cratère, *m.*

craunch (cra'n'she) *ou* **crunch** (creu'n'she), *v.a.*, croquer.

cravat', *n.*, cravate, *f.*

crave, *v.a.*, solliciter ; implorer ; demander avec instance ; soupirer après.

cra'ven (cré'v'n), *adj.*, de lâche ; poltron, lâche.

cra'ven, *n.*, lâche, poltron, *m.*

cra'ven, *v.a.*, rendre lâche, intimider.

crav'er (crév'-), *n.*, (ant.) demandeur, solliciteur, *m.*

crav'ing, *n.*, désir ardent, besoin impérieux, désir insatiable, *m.*

craw (crô), *n.*, jabot (of a bird), *m.*

craw'fish (crô-) *ou* **cray'fish** (cré-), *n.*, écrevisse, *f.* Sea-—; *langouste, f.*

crawl (crôl), *v.n.*, ramper ; se traîner ; se glisser **dans**, s'insinuer **dans** ; avoir la chair de poule. My flesh —s ; *j'ai la chair de poule*. To — down ; *se traîner en bas*. To — up ; *grimper*, ou *monter, à quatre pattes*. To —; (of cabmen) *faire la maraude*.

crawl, *n.*, (a pen for fish on the sea-coast) parc à poisson, bouchot, *m.*

crawl'er, *n.*, reptile, *m.* ; (pop.) voiture de place, hirondelle, *f.* ; (cabman) maraudeur, *m.*

crawl'ing, *adj.*, rampant. *n.*, rampement, *m.* ; (of cabmen) maraude, *f.*

cray'on (cré-eune), *n.*, crayon de pastel ; pastel, *m.*

cray'on, *v.a.*, dessiner au pastel ; crayonner ; dessiner ; esquisser.

craze, *v.a.*, briser ; broyer ; frapper de folie ; déranger, affaiblir le cerveau **de** ; rendre fou.

craze, *n.*, folie ; passion folle, *f.*

crazed, *adj.*, fou, démenté.

cra'zedness (cré-), *n.*, caducité ; démence ; folie, *f.*

cra'zily, *adv.*, follement.

cra'ziness, *n.*, caducité ; démence, folie, *f.*

cra'zy (cré-zi), *adj.*, caduc ; infirme ; fou ; (fig.) délabré, en mauvais état, hors de service.

creak (crîke), *v.n.*, craquer ; crier ; (of the crane) glapir, trompeter.

creak'ing (crîk-), *n.*, cri, craquement, *m.* *adj.*, qui crie, qui craque.

cream (crîme), *n.*, crème, *f.* — -cheese ; *fromage à la crème*, *m.* Whipped —; *crème fouettée*. — laid ; *vergé blanc*, *m.* — sauce ; *béchamel*, *f.* — jug ; *pot à crème*, *m.*

cream, *v.a.*, écrémer.

cream, *v.n.*, crémer, mousser.

cream'-colored (-keul'leurde), *adj.*, couleur café au lait ; (of horses) isabelle.

cream'y, *adj.*, crémeux ; de crème.

crease (crî-ce), *n.*, pli ; faux pli, *m.*, raie, *f.*

crease, *v.a.*, faire des plis à ; faire des faux plis à ; chiffonner.

cre'asote (crî-a-côte), *n.* V. **creosote**.

cre'at (crî-ate), *n.*, (man.) créat, *m.*

create' (crî-éte), *v.a.*, créer ; faire naître ; produire ; engendrer ; occasionner, susciter, causer ; constituer, faire.

crea'tion, *n.*, création ; nature, *f.*, univers, *m.*

crea'tive, *adj.*, créateur.

crea'tiveness, *n.*, (ant.) faculté de créer, *f.*, pouvoir créateur, *m.* ; puissance créatrice, *f.*

crea'tor (-teur), *n.*, créateur, *m.*

crea'ture (crît'ioure), *n.*, créature, personne, *f.* ; être, *m.* ; bête, *f.*, animal, *m.* — comforts ; *mangeaille, bonne chère*, *f.* ; *vivres*, *m.pl.*

cre'dence (crî-), *n.*, créance ; croyance, foi ; (ecc.) crédence, *f.* To give — to ; *ajouter foi à*. — table ; *crédence*, *f.*

creden'da (crî-dèn'-), *n.pl.*, articles de foi, *m.pl.*

creden'tials (crî-dèn'shalze), *n.*, lettres de créance, *f.pl.*

credibil'ity (crèd'-), *n.*, véridicité ; crédibilité, *f.*

cred'ible (crèd'i-b'l), *adj.*, croyable ; digne de foi.

cred'ibleness, *n.*, crédibilité, *f.*

cred'ibly, *adv.*, d'une manière digne de foi. To be — informed ; *tenir de source certaine*.

cred'it (crèd'ite), *n.*, croyance, foi, *f.* ; honneur ; crédit, *m.*, influence, *f.* ; (com.) crédit, *m.* To give —; (com.) *faire crédit*. To give — to ; *ajouter foi à*. To do — to ; *faire honneur à*. Worthy of —; *digne de foi*. On —; *à crédit*. I gave you — for more sense ; *je vous croyais plus de jugement*. To give — to a person for ; *rendre justice à, tenir compte de . . . à*.

cred'it, *v.a.*, ajouter foi à ; croire à ; faire honneur à ; (com.) donner crédit à, faire crédit **de** ; (book-keeping) créditer ; porter au crédit **de**.

cred'itable, *adj.*, honorable ; estimable, digne d'éloge.

cred'itableness, *n.*, estime, *f.*, crédit, honneur, *m.*

cred'itably, *adv.*, honorablement.

cred'itor (-teur), *n.*, créancier, *m.*, créancière, *f.* ; (book-keeping) crédit, avoir, *m.*

credu'lity (crè-diou-), *n.*, crédulité, *f.*

cred'ulous, *adj.*, crédule.

cred'ulousness, *n.*, crédulité, *f.*

creed (crîde), *n.*, credo, *m.* ; croyance, foi, *f.* ; symbole, *m.*, profession de foi, *f.* The Apostles' —; *le symbole des Apôtres*.

creek (crîke), *n.*, (geog.) crique, anse, *f.*

creek'y, *adj.*, plein de criques ; sinueux.

creep (crîpe), *v.n.*, (*preterit* and *past part.*, Crept) se traîner, ramper ; se glisser. To — in ; *se glisser dans* ; *s'insinuer dans* ; *se faufiler dans*. To — on ; *s'avancer peu à peu* ; *s'avancer en rampant*. To — out ; *sortir en rampant* ; *sortir à l'improviste* ; *s'esquiver*. To — up ; *grimper à quatre pattes*, ou *lentement*. To — over ; *ramper par-dessus*.

creep'er, *n.*, reptile, *m.* ; (orni.) grimpereau, *m.* ; (bot.) plante grimpante, *f.* ; (fig.) traînard, *m.*

creep'hole (crîp'hôl), *n.*, trou, *m.* ; (fig.) échappatoire, *f.*, faux-fuyant, *m.*

creep'ingly, *adv.*, en rampant ; lentement.

cre'mate, *v.a.*, incinérer.

crema'tion (cri-mé-), *n.*, crémation, incinération, *f.*

cre'nate *ou* **cre'nated** (crî-néte, -'ède), *adj.*, entaillé ; échancré, crénelé.

cre'nature (crî'n'a-tioure), *n.*, crénelure, *f.*

cre'nellated (crî- *ou* crè'n'èl'lé-tède), *adj.*, crénelé.

cre'nelled (crî- *ou* crè'n'èlde), *adj.*, entaillé, échancré.

cre'ole (crî-ôl), *n.*, créole, *m.f.*

cre'osote (crî-o-çote), *n.*, créosote, *f.*

crep'itate (crèp'-), *v.n.*, crépiter, décrépiter.

crepita'tion (crèp'i-té-), *n.*, décrépitation, crépitation, *f.*

crepus'cle (cri-peus's'l) *ou* **crepus'cule** (cri-peus'kioul), *n.*, (ant.) crépuscule, *m.*

crescen'do (crès'cè'n'dô), *adv.*, (mus.) crescendo.

cres'cent (crès'-), *n.*, croissant, *m.* ; demi-lune, *f.*

cres'cent *ou* **cres'cive**, *adj.*, croissant. The — moon ; *le croissant de la lune* ou *la lune à son croissant*.

cress (crèce), *n.*, cresson, *m.* Water- —; *cresson de fontaine*. — bed ; *cressonnière*, *f.*

cres'set (crès'sète), *n.*, feu de fanal ; flambeau, *m.* ; torche, *f.*

crest (crèste), *n.*, (of a cock) crête ; (orni.) huppe ; (of a peacock) aigrette, *f.* ; (of a helmet) her.) cimier ; écusson, *m.* ; (anat., fig.) crête, *f.*, (fig.) orgueil, courage, *m.*, (of a wave) crête houppée, *f.*

crest, *v.a.*, orner d'un cimier.

crest'ed (-ède), *adj.*, orné d'un cimier ; à crête ; huppé ; à aigrette, crêté.

crest'fallen (-fôln), *adj.*, abattu, penaud, l'oreille basse.

crest'less, *adj.*, sans crête ; sans cimier ; (ast.) de basse naissance.

creta'ceous (cri-té-sheusse), *adj.*, (geol.) crétacé.

cre'tin (crî-), *n.*, crétin, *m.*

cre'tinism, *n.*, crétinisme, *m.*

crev'ice (crèv'iss), *n.*, crevasse, lézarde, fente, *f.* *v.a.*, crevasser, lézarder.

crew (crou), *n.*, bande, clique, troupe, *f.* ; (nav.) équipage, *m.*

crew'el (crou'èl), *n.*, laine à border, *f.*

crib, *n.*, berceau, lit d'enfant, *m.* ; (in a cow-house) crèche, mangeoire, *f.*, (cottage) chaumière, *f.* ; (grain) coffre, *m.*, huche ; (salt) salière, _f._ ; (fig.) plagiat, _m._ ; traduction littérale d'un auteur, clef ; (pop.) place, _f._; emploi, _m._

crib, _v.a._, piller, chiper.

crick, _n._, douleur spasmodique des muscles du cou, du dos ; crampe, _f._

crick'et (crik'ète), _n._, (ent.) grillon, criquet, _m._ ; (game) jeu de crosse, _m._ — bat ; _battoir_, _m._ — field ; _champ de cricket, m._

crick'eter, _n._, joueur de cricket, _m._

cri'er (craï'eur), _n._, crieur ; (of a court) huissier, _m._

crime (craïme), _n._, crime, _m._ Heinous —; _forfait, crime énorme, m._ To charge with a —; _accuser d'un crime._

crime'less, _adj._, (ant.) exempt de crime, innocent.

crim'inal (crim'-), _adj._, criminel.
crim'inal (crim'-), _n._, criminel, _m._

criminal'ity, _n._, (ant.) culpabilité, criminalité, _f._

crim'inally, _adv._, criminellement.

crim'inate, _v.a._, incriminer.

crimina'tion (-né-), _n._, incrimination, accusation, _f._

crim'inative (-né-) _ou_ **crim'inatory** (-néto'ri), _adj._, (ant.) accusatoire.

crimp (cri'm'pe), _adj._, friable ; fragile.

crimp, _n._, commissionnaire pour la vente de la houille ; (for the army, etc.) racoleur, _m._; (harbors) propriétaire de cabaret borgne, _m.f._

crimp, _v.a._, gaufrer ; friser, boucler ; (milit.) racoler ; attirer (**dans**) ; (cook.) taillader.

crimp'er, _n._, gaufreur, friseur, _m._

crimp'ing, _n._, frisure, _f._ ; crêpage ; gaufrage ; racolage, _m._ — iron ; _fer à friser, à gaufrer, m._

crim'ple (cri'm'p'l), _v.a._, plisser, froncer, rider.

crim'son (cri'm'z'n), _adj._, cramoisi ; rouge, incarnat.

crim'son, _n._, cramoisi ; rouge, incarnat, _m._

crim'son, _v.a._, teindre en cramoisi.

crim'son, _v.n._, devenir tout cramoisi ; rougir.

cringe (cri'n'dje), _n._, courbette ; bassesse, _f._

cringe, _v.a._, contracter, froncer, tordre.

cringe, _v.n._, faire des courbettes ; ramper. To — to ; _faire le chien couchant_ **auprès de.**

crin'gle (cri'gn'g'l), _n._, erseau, _m._ ; patte, _f._ (pour porte) ; (nav.) branche de bouline, _f._

crin'kle (cri'gn'k'l), _v.n._, serpenter ; aller en zigzag.

crin'kle, _v.a._, former en zigzag.

crip'ple (crip'p'l), _n._, boiteux, _m._, boiteuse, _f._ ; estropié, _m._

crip'ple, _adj._, boiteux, estropié, perclus.

crip'ple, _v.a._, estropier ; mettre hors de combat, (fig.) paralyser ; (nav.) causer des avaries à.

cri'sis (craï-ciss), _n._, (_crises_) crise, _f._

crisp, _adj._, fragile, friable, cassant ; croquant ; (bot.) crépu, crispé ; (of hair) frisé, bouclé.

crisp, _v.a._, friser, boucler ; (stuffs) crêper ; (fig.) faire serpenter. _v.n._, se rider, onduler, serpenter.

crisp'ing, _n._, action de friser, de boucler, _f._

crisp'ing-i'ron (-aï'eur'n) _ou_ **crisp'ing-pin** (-pine) _n._, fer à friser, _m._

crisp'ness, _n._, fragilité ; qualité de ce qui est croquant, sec, cassant, _f._ ; état de ce qui est frisé, _m._ ; frisure ; friabilité, _f._

crisp'y, _adj._, frisé ; (of pastry) croquant ; sec, cassant.

crite'rion (craï-tî-ri-eune), _n._, épreuve, _f._ ; critérium, _m._

crit'ic, _n._, critique, _m._

crit'ical, _adj._, de la critique ; critique ; difficile, délicat, judicieux. — affair; _affaire délicate, f._

crit'ically, _adv._, d'une manière critique ; de crise ; en critique, avec soin.

crit'icalness, _n._, (ant.) caractère critique, _m._ ; délicatesse d'appréciation, _f._

crit'icism (-ciz'm), _n._, critique, censure, _f._

crit'icizable, _adj._, critiquable.

crit'icize (-çaïze), _v.a._, critiquer ; faire la critique **de.**

crit'icize, _v.n._, faire de la critique.

critique' (-tîke), _n._, observation critique ; critique, _f._

croak (crôke), _n._, (of frogs) coassement ; (of rooks) croassement ; (fig.) grognement, _m._

croak, _v.n._, (of frogs) coasser ; (of rooks) croasser ; (fig.) gronder, grogner, (pop.) (to die) crever, claquer.

croak'er (crôk'-), _n._, grognon ; faiseur de jérémiades, _m._, pessimiste, _m._

croak'ing, _n._ V. **croak** (noun).

cro'ceous (crô-sheusse), _adj._, safrané, de safran.

crock (croke), _n._, pot de terre, _m._ ; cruche, suie, _f._ ; noir de fumée, _m._

crock'ery (crok'eur'i) _ou_ **crock'ery-ware** (-wère), _n._, faïence, vaisselle, _f._

croc'odile (-daïl _ou_ -dil), _n._, crocodile, _m._ _adj._, de crocodile.

cro'cus (crô-), _n._, safran, crocus, _m._

croft, _n._, petit clos, _m._ ; petite ferme, _f._ ; pré, courtil, _m._

croft'er, _n._, petit fermier, paysan, closier, _m._

croisade', _n._ V. **crusade.**

crone (crône), _n._, vieille brebis ; vieille femme ; vieille, _f._

cro'net (crô-nète), _n._, (vet.) couronne, _f._

cro'ny (crô-), _n._, vieux ami ; vieux camarade ; compère, _m._ ; vieille connaissance, _f._

crook (crouke), _n._, courbure ; (of a shepherd) houlette, _f._, (of bishops) crosse, _f._ ; (fig.) détour, _m._ By hook or by — ; _de quelque façon que ce soit ; de manière ou d'autre ; par un moyen ou par un autre._

crook, _v.a._, courber, tortuer ; pervertir, appliquer mal à propos.

crook'-back, _n._, bossu, _m._, bossue, _f._

crook'-backed (-bak'te), _adj._, à dos voûté ; voûté ; bossu.

crook'ed (crouk'ède), _adj._, courbe ; courbé ; tortueux ; crochu ; (fig.) pervers ; tortu, de travers.

crook'edly, _adv._, tortueusement, de travers.

crook'edness (-), _n._, courbure, _f._ ; état tortu ; (fig.) travers, _m._, perversité, _f._

crook'-kneed (-nîde), _adj._, bancal, cagneux.

crook'-legged (-lègd'e), _adj._, bancal, qui a les jambes cagneuses, tortues. To be — ; _avoir les jambes cagneuses, tortues ; être bancal._

crook'-neck (-nèke), _n._, (bot.) gourde ; calebasse, _f._

crook'-shouldered (-shôl'deur'de), _adj._, qui a une épaule plus haute que l'autre.

croon, _v.n._, gémir, geindre ; (to sing in a low voice) chanter à voix basse. _v.a._, (fig.) murmurer doucement, susurrer.

crop, _n._, (of a bird) jabot, _m._ ; (agri., hort.) récolte, moisson ; cueillette ; tonte, _f._ Neck and — ; _entièrement, complètement._ Second — ; _regain, m._

crop, _v.a._, cueillir (of fruit) ; récolter ; moissonner, faucher ; couper le bout ; (horses) écourter ; (of animals) brouter ; tondre.

crop, _v.n._, donner une récolte. To — out ; (geol.) _affleurer._

crop'-eared (-îr'de), _n._, cheval essorillé, cheval bretaudé, _m._

crop'per, _n._, pigeon à gros jabot, _m._ To come a — ; _tomber de son haut ;_ (fig.) _faire fiasco ; aller à vau l'eau._

crop'ping, _n._, action de couper ; mutilation ; (of animals) action de brouter ; (agri.) exploitation d'un champ, _f._

cro'sier (crô-jeur), _n._, crosse (of a bishop), _f._

cros'let (cros'lète), *n.*, (her.) croisette, *f.*

cross, *n.*, croix, *f.*; (of roads, streets) carrefour, *m.*, croisée, *f.*; (fig.) revers, malheur, *m.*; traverse, contrariété, *f.*; (of breeds) croisement, *m.* On the —; *de travers, en biais.* Sign of the —; *signe de croix, signe de la croix, m.* Criss-cross; *croisé, en croix.* To take up the —; (fig.) *se sacrifier à quelque pieux objet.*

cross, *adj.*, oblique ; en travers ; de travers ; fâcheux, contraire ; bourru, maussade ; méchant, de mauvaise humeur. — woman ; *femme de mauvaise humeur, f.* — answer ; *réponse de travers, f.*

cross, *v.a.*, croiser ; faire le signe de la croix **sur** ; faire une croix **sur** ; (zoöl.) croiser ; (of letters) se croiser ; (fig.) franchir ; contrarier, contrecarrer. To — again ; *repasser.* To — out ; *effacer, rayer, biffer.* To — over ; *traverser.* To — a threshold ; *franchir un seuil.* To — one's self ; *faire le signe de la croix ; se signer ; se croiser.* To — one's mind ; *se présenter à l'esprit.*

cross, *v.n.*, être en travers ; traverser.

cross, *prep.*, à travers. — country ; *à travers champs.*

cross'-action, *n.*, procès en reconvention, *m.*

cross'-armed (-ârm'de), *adj.*, qui a les bras croisés ; (bot.) à paires croisées ; opposé, croisé.

cross'-arrow, *n.*, flèche d'arbalète, *f.*, carreau, *m.*

cross'bar (-bâr), *n.*, (carp.) traverse, *f.*

cross'bar-shot, *n.*, (artil.) boulet ramé, ange, *m.*

cross'-beam (-bîme), *n.*, (carp.) traverse, *f.*, traversin, *m.*, solive croisée, *f.*; (nav.) traversin, *m.*

cross'-bearer (-bèr'-), *n.*, porte-croix, *m.*

cross'bow (-bô), *n.*, arbalète, *f.*

cross'bow-man (-ma'n), *n.*, arbalétrier, archer, *m.*

cross'-bred, *adj.*, métis.

cross'-breed (-brîde), *n.*, race croisée, *f.*

cross'-breeding, *n.*, croisement, *m.*

cross'bun (-beune), *n.*, baba marqué, *m.*, *ou* brioche marquée, *f.*, d'une croix.

cross'-cut (-keute), *v.a.*, couper en travers, *n.*, traverse, *f.*, raccourci, *m.*

cross'cut-saw (-sô), *n.*, scie à deux mains, *f.*

cross'-examination (-né-), *n.*, (jur.) interrogatoire contradictoire, *m.*

cross'-examine (-ègz'am'ine), *v.a.*, (jur.) interroger contradictoirement.

cross'-eye, *n.*, strabisme, *m.*

cross'-eyed, *adj.*, affecté de strabisme, louche.

cross'-fire, *n.*, feu croisé, *m.*

cross'-framing (-fré'm'-), *n.*, (carp.) traverse, *f.*

cross'-grained (gré'n'de), *adj.*, (of wood) dont la veine est à rebours ; dont le fil est irrégulier ; (pers.) rebours, revêche, acariâtre. To be —; *avoir l'esprit mal tourné ; être acariâtre.*

cross'-hands (-ha'n'dze), *n.*, (dancing) chaîne anglaise, *f.*

cross'-hatch (-hat'she), *v.a.*, (engr.) contrehacher.

cross'-hatching, *n.*, (engr.) contre-hachure, *f.*

cross'ing, *n.*, passage à niveau, *m.*; (of streets) passage d'un trottoir à l'autre, *m.*; (on the sea) traversée, *f.*; (of animals) croisement ; (fig.) travers, *m.*, contrariété, *f.*; (ant.) signe de croix, *m.* — point ; (railways) croisière, *f.*

cross'jack (-djak), *n.*, (nav.) voile carrée, *f.*

cross'-keys, *n.*, clefs en sautoir, *f.pl.*

cross'-legged (-lég'de), *adj.*, qui a les jambes croisées.

cross'-like (-laïke), *adj.*, (bot.) cruciforme ; en croix ; (surg.) crucial.

cross'ly, *adv.*, en travers ; (fig.) malheureusement ; mal ; de travers ; avec mauvaise humeur ; contrairement.

cross'ness, *n.*, travers, *m.*; mauvaise humeur, méchanceté, *f.*

cross'-patch, *n.*, mauvais coucheur (of a man) *m.*; pie-grièche (of a woman), *f.*

cross'-path, *n.*, chemin de traverse, *m.*

cross'-pawl (-pôl), *n.*, (nav.) lisse, *f.*

cross'piece (-pîce), *n.*, (carp.) entretoise ; traverse, *f.*

cross'-post (-pôste), *n.*, service de correspondance des postes, *m.*

cross'-purpose (-peur'poss), *n.*, système contraire, but contraire, *m.*, opposition, contradiction, *f.*; contresens ; malentendu ; quiproquo, *m.*; énigme, *f.*; (game) propos interrompu, *m.* To be at —s ; *se contrecarrer.*

cross-ques'tion (-kwèst'ieune), *v.a.*, interroger contradictoirement. *n.*, question captieuse, *f.*

cross'-road (-rôde), *n.*, chemin de traverse, *m.*

cross'-sea, *n.*, mer clapoteuse, *f.*

cross'-shaped (-shé'p'te), *adj.*, en forme de croix ; cruciforme.

cross'-street, *n.*, rue transversale, *f.*

cross'-summons, *n.*, reconvention, *f.*

cross'-wind (-wi'n'de), *n.*, vent contraire, *m.*

cross'-wise (-waïze), *adv.*, en croix ; en forme de croix ; en travers ; en sautoir.

crotch'et (crotsh'ète), *n.*, (mas.) étai, *m.*; (mus.) noire, *f.*; (surg.) crochet, *m.*; (idea) lubie, marotte, *f.*; (knitting) crochet, *m.*

crotch'eted (-èt'ède), *adj.*, (mus.) mesuré.

crotch'ety (-èt'i), *adj.*, sujet aux lubies, capricieux.

crouch (craoutche), *v.n.*, se tapir ; se blottir ; (fig.) ramper, s'abaisser **devant**, faire le chien couchant **auprès de**.

croup, *n.*, (of animals) croupe, *f.*; (of birds) croupion ; (med.) croup, *m.*

croupade', *n.*, (man.) croupade, *f.*

crow (crô), *n.*, (orni.) corbeau, *m.*; corneille, *f.*; levier de fer ; chant du coq, *m.* As the — flies ; *à vol d'oiseau ; en ligne directe.* To have a — to pluck with any one ; *avoir maille à partir avec quelqu'un.* To pluck *ou* pull a —; *disputer pour des riens.*

crow, *v.n.*, (preterit Crew, Crowed ; *past part.*, Crowed) (of cocks) chanter. To — over ; *chanter victoire* **sur**.

crow'-bar (-bâr), *n.*, pince, *f.*, levier, monseigneur, *m.*

crow'berry, *n.*, (bot.) camarine, *f.*

crowd (craoude), *n.*, foule, cohue, *f.*, rassemblement, *m.*

crowd, *v.a.*, presser ; serrer, encombrer. To — with ; *remplir* **de**. To — sail ; (nav.) *forcer de voiles ; faire force de voiles.*

crowd, *v.n.*, affluer ; se presser ; se présenter en foule. To — in ; *arriver en foule.* To — out ; *sortir en foule.* To — round ; *entourer en foule.*

crow'foot (-foute), *n.*, (milit.) chausse-trape ; (bot.) renoncule ; (nav.) araignée, *f.*

crow's'foot, *n.*, patte d'oie, *f.*, éperon, *m.*

crow'-keeper (-kîp'-), *n.*, épouvantail, *m.*

crown (craoune), *n.*, couronne, *f.*; sommet ; (piece of money) écu, *m.*, couronne, *f.*; (nav.) collet ; (of a hat) fond, *m.*; forme ; (of a stag) couronne, meule, *f.*; sommet (of the head) ; accomplissement, *m.*; (jur.) partie publique ; (arch.) clef, *f.* — prince ; *prince royal ; prince héréditaire ; prince impérial, m.* The —; *l'État.* To come to the —; *monter sur le trône.* On his coming to the —; *à son avènement au trône.*

crown, *v.a.*, couronner ; (at draughts) damer. To — all ; *pour comble de malheur.*

crown'ing, *n.*, couronnement, comble, accomplissement, *m.* *adj.*, dernier, final, suprême. As a — misfortune ; *pour comble de malheur.*

crown'land (-la'n'de), *n.*, domaine de la couronne, *m.*

crown'-side (-saïde), *n.*, (jur.) cour criminelle, partie publique, *f.*

crown'-wheel (-hwîl), n., (horl.) roue de champ, roue de rencontre, f.

crown'-witness (-witn's), n., témoin à charge, m.

crown'-work (-weurke), n., (fort.) ouvrage à couronne, m. ; couronne, f.

croyn (croïne), v.n., (hunt.) réer, raire.

cruch'et (creutsh'ète), n., (orni.) ramier, m.

cru'cial (crou-shi-), adj., crucial, en croix ; (fig.) définitif, décisif. — test ; épreuve décisive, f.

cru'cible (crou-ci-b'l), n., creuset, m.

crucif'erous (crou-cif-eur-), adj., crucifère.

cru'cifier (crou-ci-faï'eur), n., celui qui crucifie, m.

cru'cifix (crou-ci-fikse), n., crucifix, christ, m.

crucifix'ion (-fik'sheune), n., crucifiement, m. ; crucifixion, f.

cru'ciform, adj., cruciforme.

cru'cify (-faïe), v.a., crucifier.

crude (croude), adj., cru; informe; indigeste; brut, grossier; imparfait.

crude'ly, adv., crûment.

crude'ness, n., crudité, f.

cru'dity, n., crudité, nature informe, f.

cru'el (crou'èl), adj., cruel.

cru'elly, adv., cruellement.

cru'elty, n., cruauté, f., acte barbare, inhumain, m. ; (jur.) mauvais traitements, m.pl. ; voies de fait, f.pl.

cru'et (crou'ète), n., burette, f. ; huilier, m.

cru'et-stand (-sta'n'd), n., huilier, m. ; ménagère, f.

cruise (crouze), n., croisière, course, f. On a —; en croisière. Cruising squadron ; croisière, f.

cruise, v.n., croiser; faire la course.

cruis'er, n., croiseur, m.

crum ou **crumb** (creume), n., mie; miette, f. v.a., émietter, paner. —brush ; brosse à miettes, f. —cloth ; dessus de table, m.

crum'ble (creu'm'b'l), v.a., émietter; pulvériser; broyer; réduire en poussière.

crum'ble, v.n., s'émier ; s'émietter ; tomber en poussière. — down ; tomber en ruine, s'écrouler ; (of earth) s'ébouler.

crum'my, adj., plein de mie; tendre.

crump (creu'm'pe), adj., courbé, crochu.

crum'pet (creu'm'pète), n., madeleine, f.

crum'ple (creu'm'p'l), v.a., rider; chiffonner; froisser.

crum'ple, v.n., se rider, se chiffonner, se ratatiner.

crum'pling, n., (ant.) pomme ratatinée, f.

crunch (creu'n'she), v.a. V. craunch.

cru'or (crou-eur), n., sang; grumeau, m.

crup'per (creup'-), n., croupe; croupière, f.

cru'ral (crou'-), adj., crural.

crusade' (crou-céde), n., croisade, f.

crusad'er, n., croisé, m.

cru'set (crou-cète), n., creuset, m.

crush (creushe), n., écrasement, choc, m. ; foule, cohue, bagarre, f.

crush, v.a., écraser; détruire, accabler; opprimer; étouffer, anéantir. To — in; enfoncer. To — out; tirer de, faire sortir de; exprimer. To — out a rebellion; étouffer une rébellion.

crush, v.n., se serrer ; se presser.

crush'er, n., écraseur, concasseur ; pilon, m.

crush'-hat, n., (theat.) claque, m.

crush'ing, n., écrasement, broiement, écrasement, m.

crush'ing-machine (-ma-shîne), n., machine à broyer, f. ; (metal.) bocard, (agr.) concasseur ; pilon, m.

crush'-room, n., (theat.) foyer, m.

crust (creuste), n., croûte, f.

crust, v.a., incruster, couvrir d'une croûte.

crust, v.n., s'incruster, former une croûte, s'encroûter.

crusta'cea (creus-té-shi-a), n.pl., crustacés, m.pl.

crusta'ceous (-té-sheusse), adj., crustacé.

crus'tily, adv., d'une manière morose, d'une manière hargneuse, d'un air bourru.

crus'tiness, n., qualité de ce qui a de la croûte ; (fig.) humeur hargneuse, mauvaise humeur, dureté, f.

crus'ty, adj., qui a beaucoup de croûte, couvert d'une croûte ; (fig.) hargneux, morose, maussade.

crutch (creutshe), n., béquille, f. On —es ; avec des béquilles.

crutch, v.a., soutenir avec des béquilles.

cry (craïe), n., cri, m. ; (ant.) (pack of hounds) meute, f. Much — and little wool ; plus de bruit que de besogne. In full — ; (of hounds) donnant de la voix.

cry, v.n., crier; (to weep) pleurer. To — aloud; élever la voix. To — off; quitter la partie, refuser de procéder. To — out ; s'écrier ; crier ; se récrier. To — to ; réclamer, invoquer. To — out against ; se récrier contre.

cry, v.a., crier. To — down ; décrier, censurer, blâmer. To — out ; crier très fort. To — up ; exalter, prôner ; vanter.

cry'ing, n., cri, m., cris, m.pl., (weeping) pleurs, m.pl., larmes, f.

cry'ing, adj., criant; qui pleure. A —shame; une vraie honte.

crypt (cripte), n., (ecc.) crypte, f. ; (anat.) crypte, m. and f.

cryp'tic ou **cryp'tical**, adj., secret, occulte.

cryp'tically, adv., secrètement.

cryp'togam, n., (bot.) cryptogame, f.

cryptog'amous, adj., (bot.) cryptogame.

cryptog'raphy, n., cryptographie, stéganographie, f.

crys'tal, n., cristal, m.

crys'tal, adj., de cristal.

crys'talline (-laïne ou -line), adj., cristallin. — lens ; cristallin (of the eye), m.

crystalliza'tion (-laï-zé-), n., cristallisation, f.

crys'tallize (-laïze), v.a., cristalliser.

crys'tallize, v.n., se cristalliser.

crys'tal-oil, n., naphte pur, m.

cub (keube), n., petit ; (of a bear) ourson ; (of a lion) lionceau ; (of a wolf) louveteau ; (of a fox) renardeau ; (pop.) gamin, m. An unlicked —; un ours mal léché.

cub, v.n., mettre bas.

cu'bature (kiou-ba-tioure), n., cubature, f., cubage, m.

cube (kioube), n., cube, m. — root ; racine cubique, f.

cube, v.a., cuber.

cu'beb (kiou-bèbe), n., cubèbe, m.

cu'bic ou **cu'bical** (kiou-), adj., cubique, cube.

cu'biform, adj., cubique, en cube.

cu'bit (kiou-), n., (anat.) cubitus, m. ; (measure) coudée, f.

cu'bital, adj., cubital.

cuck'ing-stool (keuk'ign'stoul), n., (jur.) sellette de correction, f.

cuck'old (keuk'-), n., cocu, cornard, m.

cuck'old, v.a., faire cocu.

cuck'oldom (-deume), n., cocuage, m.

cuc'koo (couk'ou), n., coucou, m.

cu'cullate ou **cucullated** (kiou-keul-léte, -ède), adj., encapuchonné.

cu'cumber (kiou-keu'm'-), n., concombre, m.

cucurbita'ceous (kiou-keur-bi-té-sheusse), adj., cucurbitacé.

cu'curbite (kiou-keur-), n., cucurbite, f.

cud (keude), n., aliments, m.pl. ; (of ruminants) panse, f. ; chique de tabac, f. To chew the —; ruminer.

cud'bear (-bère), n., couleur pourpre, f.

cud'dle (keud'd'l), v.a., embrasser étroitement, serrer, caresser.

cud'dle, v.n., se blottir ; se ramasser, se pelotonner ; s'embrasser étroitement, s'étreindre.

cud'dy (keud'-), *n.*, (nav.) petite cabine, cuisine, *f.* ; (ich.) charbonnier, *m.*

cudg'el (keud'djèl), *n.*, gourdin ; bâton, *m.*, trique, *f.*

cudg'el, *v.a.*, bâtonner. To be —ed ; *recevoir des coups de bâton.*

cud'geling, *n.*, coups de bâton, *m.pl.* ; volée de coups, *f.* ; bastonnade, *f.*

cudg'el-proof (-proufe), *adj.*, à l'épreuve du gourdin.

cue (kiou), *n.*, queue de billard ; (thea.) réplique, *f.* ; (fig.) avis, mot, *m.*, instruction ; (fig.) veine, *f.* To give the — ; (thea.) *donner la réplique* ; (fig.) *donner le mot* à ; *faire la leçon* à. To miss — ; *faire fausse queue.* — rack ; *porte-queues,* m. — tip ; *procédé,* m.

cue, *v.a.*, tresser en queue.

cuff (keuf), *v.a.*, souffleter ; donner des coups de patte à ; gourmer.

cuff, *n.*, coup de poing ; coup de patte, *m.* ; taloche, *f.* ; (of a coat) parement ; (of a gown) poignet, *m.* ; manchette, *f.*

cuirass' (kwî-), *n.*, cuirasse, *f.*

cuirassier' (kwî-ras'sîre), *n.*, cuirassier, *m.*

cuish *ou* **cuisse** (kwice), *n.*, cuissard, *m.*

cu'linary (kiou-), *adj.*, de cuisine ; culinaire.

cull (keul), *v.a.*, recueillir, cueillir, choisir, trier.

cul'lender, *n.*, couloire, passoire, *f.*

cul'ler (keul'-), *n.*, trieur, *m.*, trieuse, *f.*

cul'let, *n.*, (broken glass) grésil, *m.*

cul'lis, *n.*, (broth) coulis, *m.*

culm (keulme), *n.*, (bot.) chaume, *m.* ; (min.) houille sèche, anthracite, *f.*

cul'minate (keul-), *v.n.*, (astron.) culminer ; (fig.) se terminer **en** ; finir **par.**

culmina'tion (-né-), *n.*, (astron.) culmination, *f.*

culpabil'ity (keul-), *n.*, culpabilité, *f.*

cul'pable, *adj.*, coupable.

cul'pableness, *n.*, culpabilité, *f.*

cul'pably, *adv.*, d'une manière coupable, coupablement.

cul'prit (keul'-), *n.*, accusé, *m.*, accusée, *f.* ; criminel, *m.*, criminelle, *f.* ; coupable, prévenu, inculpé, *m.*, inculpée, *f.*

cult, *n.*, hommage, culte, *m.*

cul'ter (keul'-), *n.*, soc ; coutre, *m.* *V.* **coulter.**

cul'tivable, *adj.*, cultivable.

cul'tivate (keul'-), *v.a.*, cultiver.

cultiva'tion (-vé-), *n.*, culture, *f.* Under — ; *en culture.*

cul'tivator (-vé-teur), *n.*, cultivateur, *m.*

cul'ture (keult'ioure), *n.*, culture, *f.* ; (fig.) instruction, éducation, culture, *f.*

cul'ture, *v.a.*, cultiver.

cul'tureless, *adj.*, sans culture ; inculte.

cul'verin (keul-veur'ine), *n.*, coulevrine, *f.*

cul'vert (keul-veurt), *n.*, rigole, *f.* ; ponceau, petit aqueduc, *m.*

cum'ber (keu'm'-), *n.*, embarras, obstacle, *m.* —field ; *traînasse, renouée des oiseaux, f.*

cum'ber, *v.a.*, embarrasser **de** ; encombrer **de.**

cum'bersome (-seume), **cum'brous**, *adj.*, embarrassant, gênant, incommode, lourd ; à charge.

cum'bersomely, *adv.*, d'une manière embarrassante.

cum'bersomeness, *n.*, embarras, fardeau, *m.*

cum'brance, *n.*, embarras, fardeau, *m.*, gêne, *f.*

cum'in (keu'm'ine), *n.*, (bot.) cumin, *m.*

cu'mulate (kiou-miou-), *v.a.*, accumuler ; cumuler.

cumula'tion (-lé-), *n.*, accumulation ; (jur.) cumulation, *f.*

cu'neal (kiou-ni-), *adj.*, en forme de coin ; cunéaire.

cu'neate *ou* **cu'neated** (-ède), *adj.*, en coin, cunéaire.

cune'iform (kiou-nî-i-) *ou* **cu'niform** (kiou-ni-), *adj.*, cunéiforme, en forme de coin.

cun'ning (keu'n'-), *n.*, finesse ; adresse ; ruse, astuce, *f.*

cun'ning, *adj.*, fin, rusé, adroit, astucieux.

cun'ningly, *adv.*, avec finesse ; avec artifice ; adroitement ; par ruse.

cun'ningness, *n.*, ruse, finesse, *f.*

cup (keupe), *n.*, tasse, coupe, *f.* ; gobelet ; (bot.) calice, *m.* ; (med.) ventouse, *f.* In one's —s ; *dans les vignes du Seigneur* ; *ivre* ; *pris de vin.* — and ball ; *bilboquet,* m. —ful ; *tassée* ; *plein une tasse.* The parting — ; *le coup de l'étrier, m.*

cup, *v.a.*, ventouser.

cup'bearer (-bèr'-), *n.*, échanson, *m.*

cup'board (keub'eurde), *n.*, armoire, *f.* ; buffet, placard, *m.*

cu'pel (kiou-), *n.*, (chem.) coupelle, *f.*

cupella'tion (kiou-pèl-lé-), *n.*, coupellation, *f.*

cu'pola (kiou-), *n.*, coupole, *f.*

cup'ping, *n.*, application de ventouses, *f.*

cup'ping-glass (-glâce), *n.*, ventouse, *f.*

cu'preous (kiou-pri-), *adj.*, cuivreux.

cu'pulate (kiou-piou-), *adj.*, (bot.) muni d'une cupule, cupulé.

cu'pule (kiou-pioul), *n.*, (bot.) cupule, *f.*

cur (keur), *n.*, chien de rue, mauvais chien, chien hargneux, *m.* ; (pers.) vilain chien, vilain animal, *m.*

cur'able (kiou-ra-b'l), *adj.*, guérissable, curable.

cur'ableness, *n.*, curabilité, *f.*

cur'açoa (kiou-ra-çô), *n.*, curaçao (liqueur), *m.*

cur'acy (kiou-), *n.*, vicariat, *m.* ; cure, *f.*

cur'ate (kiou-), *n.*, vicaire, desservant, *m.*

cur'ative (kiou-ré-), *adj.*, curatif.

cura'tor (kiou-ré-teur), *n.*, administrateur, (museum) conservateur ; (jur.) curateur, *m.*

curb (keurbe), *n.*, (man.) gourmette, *f.* ; (fig.) frein, *m.* ; (of a well) margelle ; (of a foot pavement) bordure ; (vet.) tare, *f.* — chain ; *gourmette, f.*

curb, *v.a.*, (man.) gourmer ; (fig.) réprimer, contenir, brider ; mettre un frein **à.**

curb'less, *adj.*, effréné, sans frein.

curb'-stone (-'stône), *n.*, bordure, *f.*

curcu'lio (keur-kiou-), *n.*, (ent.) charançon, *m.*

cur'cuma (keur-kiou-), *n.*, (bot.) curcuma, *m.*

curd (keurde), *n.*, caillé, lait caillé, *m.* ; caillebotte, *f.* ; grumeau, *m.*

curd, *v.a.*, cailler, figer.

cur'dle (keur'd'l), *v.a.*, cailler ; figer.

cur'dle, *v.n.*, se cailler, se figer.

curd'y, *adj.*, caillé, figé.

cure (kioure), *n.*, guérison ; cure, *f.* ; remède, *m.* ; (ecc.) cure, *f.* — of souls ; *charge d'âmes, f.*

cure, *v.a.*, guérir ; (of hay) sécher ; (meat) mariner, saler ; (fig.) remédier **à**, corriger.

cure'less, *adj.*, incurable.

cur'er, *n.*, guérisseur, médecin ; (of meat, fish) saleur, *m.*

cur'few (keur-fiou), *n.*, couvre-feu, *m.*

cur'few-bell, *n.*, couvre-feu, *m.*

curios'ity (kiou-ri-oss'-), *n.*, curiosité, *f.* Old — ; *bric à brac, m.* Dealer in curiosities ; *marchand de bric à brac* ; *antiquaire, m.*

cu'rious (kiou-), *adj.*, curieux ; exact ; délicat ; difficile. — of *ou* after ; *curieux* **de**, *à la recherche* **de.**

cu'riously (kiou-), *adv.*, curieusement. — enough ; *par une singulière coïncidence.*

curl (keurl), *n.*, boucle ; ondulation, *f.*

curl, *v.a.*, boucler ; friser ; (fig.) faire onduler. To — up ; *retrousser, faire tourbillonner.*

curl, *v.n.*, friser, boucler ; (of the serpent) se replier, s'entortiller ; (of the vine) s'entrelacer ;

(of smoke, waves) tourbillonner, onduler, ondoyer. To — up; *se pelotonner* (of cats); *se blottir*; *se recoquiller*; *se retrousser*.

curl'-cloud, *n.*, cirrus, *m.*

curled (keur'l'de), *adj.*, (bot.) crispé, crépu; frisé, bouclé.

cur'lew (keur-liou), *n.*, (orni.) courlieu, courlis, *m.*

curl'iness (keurl'-), *n.*, frisure, *f.*, frisé, *m.*

curl'ing, *n.*, frisure; (of waves) ondulation, *f.*

curl'ing-irons (-ai'eurn'z) *ou* **curl'ing-tongs** (-to'ngze), *n.pl.*, fer à friser, *m.sing.*

curl'-paper, *n.*, papillote, *f.*

curl'y, *adj.*, frisé; bouclé; (fig.) qui ondule. — headed; *qui a la tête frisée, qui a les cheveux bouclés.*

curmud'geon (keur-meud'jeune), *n.*, ladre, pingre; grippe-sou, *m.*, pingresse, *f.*

curmud'geonly, *adv.*, en ladre, de ladre.

cur'rant (keur'ra'n'te), *n.*, groseille à grappes, *f.* Dried —s; *raisin de Corinthe*, *m.* Black —; *cassis*, *m.* Red —; *groseille rouge*, *f.* White —; *groseille blanche*, *f.*

cur'rant-bush (-boushe), *n.*, groseiller à grappes; gadellier, *m.*

cur'rency (keur-rè'n'-), *n.*, (of money) cours, *m.*, circulation, *f.*; (fig.) cours, crédit, *m.*, vogue, *f.* Legal —; *monnaie légale*, *f.* Paper —; *circulation de papier-monnaie*, *f.* To give — to; *donner cours à.*

cur'rent, *adj.*, courant; (fig.) admis, reçu, qui a cours. — account; (com.) *compte courant*, *m.* — price; *prix courant*, *m.* To pass —; *avoir cours; être admis.*

cur'rent, *n.*, courant d'eau; courant; cours, *m.*

cur'rently, *adv.*, continuellement; couramment; généralement. It is — reported that; *on prétend que ou le bruit court que.*

cur'ricle (keur'ri-k'l), *n.*, cabriolet à deux roues, *m.*; chaise de poste, *f.*

curric'ulum, *n.*, cours; cours d'études, *m.*

cur'rier (keur-ri-eur), *n.*, corroyeur, *m.*

cur'rish (keur-rishe), *adj.*, hargneux, brutal.

cur'rishly, *adv.*, d'une manière hargneuse.

cur'ry (keur-ri), *v.a.*, corroyer; (a horse) étriller; (pers.) rosser, étriller; (cook.) accommoder au cari. To — favor with; *s'insinuer dans les bonnes grâces de ou se faire bien venir de.*

cur'ry, **cur'ry-powder**, *n.*, cari, *m.*

cur'ry-comb (-côme), *n.*, étrille, *f.*

curse (keurse), *n.*, malédiction, *f.*, blasphème; fléau, malheur, *m.*

curse, *v.a.*, maudire, affliger.

curse, *v.n.*, proférer des malédictions; jurer, (pop.) sacrer. To be —d with; *être affligé de; avoir pour son malheur.* He is —d with; *il a le malheur d'avoir.*

curs'ed (keurs'ède), *adj.*, maudit, exécrable.

curs'edly, *adv.*, abominablement; terriblement.

curs'edness, *n.*, (ant.) noirceur, méchanceté, *f.*

curs'er, *n.*, qui maudit, blasphémateur, *m.*

cur'sitor (keur-si-teur), *n.*, (ant.) greffier de la Cour de Chancellerie, *m.*

cur'sorily (keur-), *adv.*, rapidement; à la hâte, superficiellement.

cur'soriness (keur-), *n.*, examen rapide, *m.*

cur'sory (keur-) *adj.*, rapide, léger, superficiel; précipité.

curst (keurste), *adj.*, (ant.) odieux, détestable, vexatoire, méchant, malfaisant.

curt (keurte), *adj.*, court, bref; sec; concis.

curtail' (keur-téle), *v.a.*, retrancher; réduire; raccourcir; abréger, rogner, tronquer; amoindrir, diminuer; écourter. To — of; *priver de.*

curtail'ment, *n.*, réduction, *f.*; retranchement, raccourcissement, abrégé, *m.*

cur'tain (keur-tine), *n.*, rideau, *m.*; (fort.) courtine, *f.*; (thea.) rideau, *m.*, toile, *f.* —rod; tringle, *f.* — lecture; *semonce conjugale*, *m.f.* — hook, pin, rest; *patère*, *f.* — pole; *porte-rideaux*, *m.f.*

cur'tain, *v.a.*, garnir de rideaux; (fig.) envelopper, voiler.

cur'tain-arm (-arme) *ou* **cur'tain-band** (-ba'n'd), *n.*, embrasse, *f.*

curt'sy (keurt'-), *n.*, révérence. *v.n.*, faire la révérence.

cur'vated (keur-vé-tède), *adj.*, courbé.

curva'tion (keur-vé-), *n.*, courbure, *f.*

cur'vature (keur-va-tioure), *n.*, courbure, *f.*

curve (keurve), *adj.*, courbe.

curve, *n.*, (geom.) courbe, *f.*

curve, *v.a.*, courber; cintrer. *v.n.*, se courber, devenir courbe, décrire une courbe.

curvet' (keur-vète), *v.n.*, (man.) faire des courbettes; sauter, gambader.

curvet', *n.*, (man.) courbette, *f.*; tour, *m.*; (fig.) fredaine, *f.*

curvilin'eal *ou* **curvilin'ear** (keur-), *adj.*, curviligne.

cush'ion (coush'eune), *n.*, coussin; (of a steam engine) matelas; (of a pump) coussinet, *m.*; (billiards) bande, *f.*

cush'ion, *v.a.*, asseoir sur un coussin; garnir de coussins; (fig.) mettre de côté; étouffer; (at billiards) acculer à la bande.

cush'ioned (coush'eu'n'de), *adj.*, garni de coussins; (billiards) acculé à la bande.

cusp (keuspe), *n.*, corne du croissant, pointe; (anat.) cuspide, *f.*; (arch.) lobe, *m.*

cus'pated (keus-pét'ède) *ou* **cus'pidal** (keus'-) *adj.*, (ant.) terminé en pointe.

cus'pidated (keus'pi-dét'ède), *adj.*, terminé en pointe.

cuss, *n.*, vaurien, chenapan, *m.*

cuss'edness, *n.*, perversité, méchanceté, *f.*

cus'tard (keus-), *n.*, crème cuite au four, *f.*; flan, *m.* — apple; (bot.) anone, *f.*; cœur de bœuf, *m.*

cus'tody (keus'-) *n.*, garde; arrestation, prison, détention, *f.* To give any one into —; *faire arrêter quelqu'un.* To commit to any one's —; *confier à la garde de quelqu'un.* In —; *en état d'arrestation.* In close —; *au secret.*

cus'tom (keus'-), *n.*, coutume, habitude, *f.*; usage, *m.*; pratique; douane; (of a shop) pratique, *f.*, chalands, *m.pl.*, achalandage, *m.* To clear the —s; *passer* (quelque chose) *en douane.*

cus'tomable (keus'to'm'a-b'l), *adj.*, (l.u.) habituel; accoutumé; sujet aux droits de douane.

cus'tomably, *adv.*, de coutume; par habitude, habituellement.

cus'tomarily (keus'-), *adv.*, ordinairement; communément, habituellement, d'habitude.

cus'tomariness, *n.*, habitude, fréquence, *f.*

cus'tomary (keus'-), *adj.*, ordinaire; (jur.) coutumier; d'usage; reçu.

cus'tomer (keus'-), *n.*, chaland, client; habitué, *m.*; pratique, *f.*; (pop.) individu, particulier, *m.* To know one's —; *connaître son monde.* Ugly —; *mauvais coucheur*, *m.* Queer —; *drôle d'individu*, *m.*

cus'tom-house (-haouce), *n.*, douane, *f.* — officer; *employé de la douane; douanier*, *m.*

cus'toms-duty (-diou-), *n.*, droit de douane, *m.*

cut (keute), *n.*, (with a sharp instrument) coup, *m.*; balafre, estafilade, *f.*; (piece cut off) morceau, *m.*; (place cut open) coupure; (of clothes) coupe; (engr.) gravure, vignette, estampe; (at cards) coupe; (channel) coupure, *f.*; chenal, *m.*; (words) ironie incisive, *f.*, reproche vif, mot piquant, trait; coup de patte, *m.*; (figure) tournure; (short way) traverse, *f.*; le plus court, au plus court. To draw —s; *tirer à la courte paille.* To take a short —; *prendre un* *raccourci*. To take the shortest —; *prendre le chemin le plus court*.

cut, *v.a.,* (preterit and *past part.*, Cut) couper. tailler, fendre ; trancher. To — one's teeth ; *faire ses dents.* To — a figure; *faire figure.* To — capers ; *faire des siennes.* To — some one; *rompre* **avec,** *planter là, laisser là; passer quelqu'un dans la rue.* To — a loaf; *entamer un pain.* To — down ; *abattre;* (mil.) *tailler en pièces, écraser;* (to clip) *rogner, abréger, réduire.* To — off; *supprimer; retrancher; extirper; élider; séparer; couper, trancher, tailler; intercepter; priver; empêcher.* To — small ; *hacher; rapetisser.* To — short; *interrompre; abréger.* To — to the heart; *fendre le cœur à; affliger.* To — up; *ouvrir; couper; écharper; disséquer; découper.* To — asunder; *déchirer; trancher; exclure; couper; briser;* (mil.) *écharper; tailler en pièces.* To — out; *tailler; couper; ôter, retrancher;* (fig.) *surpasser, éclipser.* To — out work for any one; *tailler de la besogne à.* To — one's way; *se frayer un chemin.* To — one's sticks, to — it; *filer, déguerpir.* To — across; *couper en travers.* To — along; *filer, jouer des jambes.* To — off with a shilling; *ne rien laisser à; déshériter.* To — to pieces; (mil.) *écharper, tailler en pièces;* (criticism) *abîmer.*

cut, *v.n.,* couper, se couper, percer, tailler. To — and come again; *revenir au plat.*

cut and dried, *adj.,* tout prêt, tout fait.

cuta′neous (kiou-té-ni-), *adj.,* cutané.

cu′ticle (kiou-ti-k'l), *n.,* cuticule, pellicule, *f. ;* épiderme, *m.*

cutic′ular (kiou-tik′iou-), *adj.,* épidermique.

cut′lass (keut′-), *n.,* coutelas, *m.*

cut′ler (keut′-), *n.,* coutelier, *m.*

cut′lery, *n.,* coutellerie, *f.*

cut′let (keut′-), *n.,* côtelette, *f.*

cut′purse (-peurse), *n.,* coupeur de bourse, *m.*

cut′ter (keut′-), *n.,* coupeur, coupoir ; (nav.) canot, cotre, cutter ; (tech.) burin, *m.*

cut′throat (-thrôte), *n.,* coupe-jarret, *m.* — place; *coupe-gorge, m.*

cut′ting (keut′-), *n.,* incision ; (of wood, of cards, of hair) coupe; (hort.) bouture, *f.*

cut′ting, *adj.,* incisif ; piquant; poignant, caustique ; tranchant, mordant.

cut′ting-en′gine (-è′n′djine), *n.,* machine à diviser, *f.*

cut′ting-knife (-naïfe), *n.,* (print.) coupoir, *m.*

cut′ting-out-machine (-aoute-ma-shîne), *n.,* (coin.) emporte-pièce, m.

cut′ting-press (-prèce), *n.,* (bookbind.) rognoir, *m.*

cut′tle *ou* **cut′tle-fish** (keut't'l, -fishe), *n.,* (mol.) sèche, seiche ; pieuvre, *f.*

cut′tle-bone (-bône), *n.,* (conch.) os de sèche, *m.*

cut′tle-fish, *n.,* seiche, *f.*

cut′ty-pipe (-wôteur), *n.,* brûle-gueule, *m.*

cut′water (-wôteur), *n.,* (engineering) avant-bec ; arrière-bec ; (orni.) coupeur d'eau, bec-en-ciseaux ; (nav.) taille-mer, *m.*

cy′cle (çaï′k'l), *n.,* cycle, *m.* — of the sun; *cycle solaire.* — of the moon; *cycle lunaire.*

cy′cloïd (çaï-cloïde), *n.,* cycloïde, *f.*

cy′clop (çaï-), *n.,* cyclope, *m.*

cyclopæ′dia (çaï-klo-pî-), *n.,* encyclopédie, *f.*

cyclope′an (çaï-clo-pî-), *adj.,* cyclopéen.

cyclop′ic (çaï-), *adj.,* de cyclope ; cyclopéen.

cyg′net, *n.,* jeune cygne, *m.*

cyl′inder (ci-), *n.,* cylindre ; (of a pump) corps de pompe, *m.*

cylindra′ceous (ci-li′n′dré-sheusse), *adj.,* (l.u.) cylindrique.

cylin′dric *ou* **cylin′drical** (ci-li′n′-), *adj.,* cylindrique.

cyma′tium (si-mé-shi-eume), *n.,* (arch.) cymaise, *f.*

cym′bal (si′m′-), *n.,* cymbale, *f.*

cym′bal-player (-plé′-), *n.,* cymbalier, *m.*

cynan′che (si-na′gn′ki), *n.,* (med.) esquinancie, *f.*

cyn′ic, *n.,* cynique, *m.*

cyn′ic *ou* **cyn′ical,** *adj.,* cynique.

cyn′ically, *adj.,* cyniquement, d'une manière cynique.

cyn′icism (-ciz′m), *n.,* cynisme, *m.*

cyn′osure (çaï-no-shioure *ou* ci-), *n.,* cynosure, *f.,* point d'attraition, point de mire, *m.* The — of all eyes ; *l'objet de tous les regards, m.*

cy′press *ou* **cy′press-tree** (çaï-prèce, -trî), *n.,* cyprès, *m.*

cy′press-wood (-woude), *n.,* cyprès, bois de cyprès, *m.*

cyst *ou* **cys′tis** (ciste *ou* -tiss), *n.,* (surg.) kyste, *m.*

cysti′tis (cis-taï-tiss), *n.,* (med.) cystite, *f.*

cystot′omy (cis′to-), *n.,* cystotomie, *f.*

cyt′isus (-ceuss), *n.,* (bot.) cytise ; faux ébénier, *m.*

czar (zâr), *n.,* tsar, czar, *m.*

czari′na (-rî-), *n.,* tsarine, czarine, *f.*

czar′ish, *adj.,* tsarien, czarien.

czar′owitz (zar′o-vitse) *n.,* tsarowitz, czarowitz, *m.*

D

d, quatrième lettre de l'alphabet, d, *m. ;* (mus.) ré, *m.*

dab, *n.,* coup léger, *m. ;* éclaboussure, tache ; (pers., pop.) expert, adepte, *f. ;* (a bit) petit morceau, *m. ;* (ich.) limande, *f.* To be a — at ; *exceller* à ou **en** ; *s'entendre à ;* *être au fait de.*

dab, *v.a.,* toucher légèrement ; éponger à petits coups ; étuver.

dab′ble (dab′b′l), *v.a.,* barbouiller, souiller, éclabousser.

dab′ble, *v.n.,* barboter, patauger. To — in ; *se mêler de, s'ingérer dans ; toucher à.*

dab′bler, *n.,* barboteur ; bousilleur ; barbouilleur, *m.*

dab′chick (-tshik), *n.,* (orni.) le petit grèbe, grèbe castagneux, *m.*

dab′ster, *n.,* malin ; passé maître, *m.*

dace, *n.,* (ich.) vandoise, *f. ;* dard, *m.*

dachs′hund (-), *n.,* basset allemand, *m.*

dac′tyle, *n.,* dactyle, *m.*

dac′tylic, *n.,* dactylique.

dad *ou* **dad′dy,** *n.,* papa, *m.* —-long-legs ; (ent.) faucheur, faucheux, *m.*

da′do (dé-dô), *n.,* (arch.) dé ; fût vertical, (of rooms) lambris, *m.*

daf′fodil, *n.,* asphodèle, narcisse des prés, *m.*

daft, *adj.,* stupide, sot ; à moitié fou.

dag, *n.,* (ant.) dague, *f.*

dag′ger (dag′gheur), *n.,* poignard, *m. ;* dague ; (print.) croix, *f.* At — s drawn ; *à couteaux tirés.* — knife ; *couteau-poignard, m.* To look — s at; *lancer des regards foudroyants* à.

dag′gers-drawing (-′gheurz′drô′-), *n.,* action de tirer les poignards du fourreau ; mettre l'épée à la main ; mettre flamberge au vent ; violente querelle, *f.* To be at — ; *être à couteaux tirés* **avec,** *être toujours à se quereller.*

dag′gle (dag′g′l), *v.n.,* se crotter ; se traîner dans la boue.

dag′gle, *v.a.,* crotter ; traîner dans la boue.

dag′gle-tail (-téle), *adj. V.* **draggle-tailed.**

Da′gon (flé-), *n.,* Dagon, *m.*

daguerre′otype (-taïpe), *n.,* daguerréotype, *m.*

dah′lia (dâ-), *n.,* (bot.) dahlia, *m.*

dai′ly (dé-li), *adj.,* journalier, quotidien ; (astron.) diurne.

dai′ly, *adv.,* journellement, tous les jours.

dain′tily (dé′n′-), *adv.,* délicatement, élégamment; avec délicatesse ; avec friandise.

dain′tiness, *n.,* délicatesse, *f.,* goût difficile, *m,*

dain'ty, _n._, friandise, _f._

dain'ty (dé'n'-), _adj._, friand, délicat ; difficile.

dai'ry (dé-ri), _n._, laiterie ; (shop) crémerie, _f._

dai'ry-farm (-fârme), _n._, laiterie en gros, _f._

dai'ryist (-ri-iste), _n._, (l.u.) laitier, crémier, _m._

dai'ry-maid (-méde), _n._, fille de laiterie, laitière, _f._

dai'ry-man (-ma'n), _n._, garçon de laiterie ; laitier, crémier, _m._

dai'ry-room (-roume), _n._, laiterie (lieu où l'on tient le lait), _f._

dai'ry-wom'an (-woum'a'n), _n._, laitière, crémière, _f._

dais, _n._, estrade, _f._ ; (ant.) dais, _m._

dai'sy (dé-zi), _n._, marguerite, pâquerette, _f._

dai'sy-cutter (-cut'-), _n._, (man.) cheval qui rase le tapis, _m._

dai'sy-rake (-réke), _n._, râteau à gazon, _m._

dale, _n._, vallon, _m._ ; vallée, _f._ Up hill and down — ; _par monts et par vaux._

dales'man, _n._, habitant des vallées, _m._

dal'liance (dal'li-), _n._, folâtrerie, _f._ ; badinage, _m._ ; caresses, _f.pl._ ; (ant.) délai, _m._

dal'lier (dal'li-), _n._, folâtre, _m._ ; personne légère, _f._

dal'ly (dal'li), _v.n._, tarder, différer ; s'amuser ; badiner ; folâtrer ; perdre son temps.

dam (dame), _n._, (of animals) mère ; (at draughts) dame damée, dame ; (of a canal) dame, _f._ ; (of a river) barrage, bâtardeau, _m._ ; digue, _f._

dam, _v.n._, diguer, barrer, endiguer, contenir ; (fig.) arrêter.

dam'age (dam'édje), _n._, dommage ; tort, dégât ; (fig.) préjudice, détriment, _m._ ; (nav.) avarie, _f._ _pl._, (jur.) dommages-intérêts, dommages et intérêts, _m.pl._

dam'age, _v.a._, endommager ; avarier ; (fig.) faire tort à ; nuire à, compromettre.

dam'age, _v.n._, s'endommager.

dam'ageable (-'édj'a-b'l), _adj._, susceptible de s'endommager, avariable.

damascene' (-'cîne), _n._, prune de Damas, _f._

dam'ask, _n._, damas, _m._ adj., damassé. rose ; _rose incarnate, f._

dam'ask, _v.a._, damasser.

damaskeen' (-'kîne), _v.a._, damasquiner.

damaskeen'ing, _n._, (art.) damasquinerie ; (ornament) damasquinure, _f._

dam'asking, _n._, damassure, _f._

dam'ask-worker, _n._, damasseur, _m._

dam'assin, _n._, damassin, _m._ ; damesquette, _f._

dame (déme), _n._, dame ; mère ; maîtresse d'école, _f._ —'s violet ; (bot.) _julienne des jardins, f._

damn (da'm'), _v.a._, damner ; condamner ; désapprouver ; siffler (as a mark of disapprobation) ; jurer après ; envoyer au diable. —! _sacrebleu ! maudit, odieux, pernicieux._

dam'nable (da'm'na-b'l), _adj._, damnable, maudit, odieux, pernicieux.

dam'nably, _adv._, odieusement, abominablement, diablement.

damna'tion (da'm'né-), _n._, damnation, _f._

dam'natory (da'm'na-tori), _adj._, condamnatoire.

damned (da'm'de _ou_ da'm'nède), _adj._, damné ; (l.ex.) maudit, odieux, détestable, exécrable.

damp (da'm'pe), _n._, humidité, vapeur, _f._ ; froid, _m._ ; (fig.) tristesse, _f._, abattement, _m._ Choke — ; _mofette, f._ ; _acide carbonique, m._

damp, _adj._, humide ; moite ; (fig.) triste, abattu.

damp, _v.a._, rendre humide ; humecter ; (fig.) décourager, abattre, ralentir, refroidir. To — the spirits of ; _décourager._

damp'er, _n._, éteignoir ; (piano) étouffoir, _m._ ; pédale douce, sourdine, _f._ ; (of a chimney) registre ; (nav.) éteignoir ; rabat-joie, _m._ To put a — on ; _jeter un voile de tristesse sur._

damp'ish, _adj._, un peu humide, moite.

damp'ness, _n._, humidité, moiteur, _f._

dam'sel (da'm'zèl), _n._, jeune fille, suivante, demoiselle, _f._

dam'son (da'm'z'n), _n._, prune de Damas, _f._

dam'son-tree (-trî), _n._, prunier de Damas, _m._

dance (da'n'se), _n._, danse, _f._, bal, _m._ To lead the — ; _mener la danse._ — music ; _air de danse, air dansant, m._ The — of death; _danse macabre._ To lead any one a — ; _houspiller, ou malmener, quelqu'un._

dance, _v.n._, danser ; agiter. — attendance ; _faire le pied de grue ; faire antichambre ;_ (fam.) _croquer le marmot._

dance, _v.a._, danser ; faire danser.

dan'cer, _n._, danseur, _m._, danseuse, _f._

dan'cing, _n._, danse, _f._

dan'cing, _adj._, de danse. —master ; _maître de danse, m._ —room ; _salle de danse, f._ — party ; _soirée dansante, f._, bal, m._

dan'delion (da'n'dé-lai'one), _n._, (bot.) dent-de-lion, _f._ ; pissenlit, _m._

dan'dle (da'n'd'l), _v.a._, dorloter ; bercer, dodiner.

dan'druff (da'n'dreufe), _n._, dartre farineuse, crasse (de la tête), _f._ ; pellicules, _f.pl._

dan'dy, _n._, dandy, élégant, petit-maître, gandin, _m._

dan'dy, _adj._, de dandy ; élégant.

dan'dyism, _n._, dandysme, _m._

Dane, _n._, Danois, _m._, Danoise, _f._

dane'wort (-weurte), _n._, hièble, yèble, _f._

dan'ger (dé'n'djeur), _n._, danger, péril, _m._

dan'gerless, _adj._, sans danger.

dan'gerous, _adj._, dangereux.

dan'gerously, _adv._, dangereusement.

dan'gle (da'ng'g'l), _v.n._, pendiller. _v.a._, laisser pendre, balancer, agiter. To — after ; _être aux trousses de ; être pendu à la ceinture de._

dan'gler, _n._, godelureau, parasite, _m._

Dan'ish (dé'n'-), _adj._, danois.

Dan'ish, _n._, danois (language), _m._

dank, _adj._, moite, humide.

dank, _n._, humidité, _f._

dank'ishness, _n._, humidité, _f._

dap'per, _adj._, éveillé ; leste ; vif, fringant, pimpant. — couplets ; _couplets sémillants, m.pl._

dap'perling, _n._, nain, petit bonhomme, _m._

dap'ple (dap'p'l), _adj._, pommelé, truité, miroité. —gray ; _gris pommelé, m._

dap'ple, _v.a._, tacheter, pommeler, barioler. _v.n._, se pommeler, se tacheter.

dare, _v.n._ (_preterit_, Durst), oser, risquer.

dare, _v.a._, défier ; braver ; affronter, provoquer. I — say ; _j'ose dire que ; il est probable que ; je crois bien que ; sans doute que ; je parie que._ I — say ! _eh bien, oui ! ; par exemple !_ To — to do ; _oser faire._ If you — me to do it ; _si vous me défiez de le faire._

dare'-devil, _n._ and _adj._, audacieux, désespéré ; un risque-tout.

dar'ing, _adj._, audacieux, hardi, vaillant.

dar'ing, _n._, hardiesse, audace, _f._

dar'ingly, _adv._, audacieusement, hardiment.

dark (dârke), _n._, ténèbres, _f.pl._ ; obscurité, ignorance, nuit, _f._

dark, _adj._, obscur, sombre ; noir ; (fig.) caché, mystérieux. — lantern ; _lanterne sourde, f._ To be — ; _faire sombre ; faire nuit._ The — ages ; _l'âge des ténèbres, le moyen-âge, m._ To see only the — side (of anything) ; _voir tout en noir._ — working ; _mystérieux._

dark'en (dâr'k'n), _v.a._, obscurcir, assombrir ; (the complexion) brunir ; (colors in painting) assourdir ; (fig.) troubler, embarrasser.

dark'en, _v.n._, s'obscurcir ; se rembrunir, s'assombrir.

dark'ening, _n._, obscurcissement, assombrissement ; rembrunissement ; (of colors) assourdissement, _m._

dark'ish, _adj._, un peu sombre ; noirâtre, un peu brun.

dark′ling, adj., (ant.) dans l'obscurité, dans les ténèbres.

dark′ly, adv., obscurément; sourdement; dans les ténèbres.

dark′ness, n., obscurité, f.; ténèbres, f.pl., (of colors) teinte sombre, f.; (of the skin), teint brun, m.

dark′some (-seume), adj., sombre.

dar′ky, n., (fam.) moricaud, m.

dar′ling (dâr-), n.f., favori, m.; favorite, f.; chéri, m., chérie, f.; mignon, m., mignonne, f.; bien-aimé, m., bien-aimée, f.; ange; chou, m.

dar′ling, adj., chéri, favori, bien-aimé.

darn (dârne), n., reprise, f.

darn, v.a., repriser; faire des reprises à.

dar′nel (dâr-), n., ivraie, f.

darn′ing, n., reprise, f. — cotton; coton à repriser, m. — needle; aiguille à repriser, f.

dart (dârte), n., dard; trait, m.

dart, v.a., darder; lancer **contre**.

dart, v.n., se lancer, s'élancer **sur**; fondre **sur**; partir comme un trait.

dash, n., choc; coup, élan; (with a pen) trait, m.; (small quantity) teinte, f., (fig.) grain, m., pointe, f.; soupçon, m. To cut a —; mener grand train, trancher du grand. A — of vinegar; un filet de vinaigre.

dash, v.a., frapper; écraser, heurter, briser; barrer, biffer; (fig.) détruire; (writing) souligner. To — against; heurter **contre**. To — away; jeter, repousser. To — up; faire sauter, faire jaillir. To — in pieces; briser en morceaux. To — down; précipiter, renverser. To — out; effacer; faire sauter. To — off; ébaucher, esquisser; (fam.) brocher.

dash, v.n., se heurter, se briser; se précipiter, jaillir. To — through; se précipiter, s'élancer à travers. To — in; interrompre vivement. To — up (to a carriage); s'élancer **jusqu'à**.

dash′ing, adj., fougueux; brillant, superbe; pimpant, élégant.

das′tard, n., lâche, m.f.; poltron, m., poltronne, f.

das′tard, adj., lâche; poltron.

das′tardize (-'aïze), v.a., (ant.) effrayer, faire peur à.

das′tardliness, n., poltronnerie, lâcheté, f.

das′tardly, adj., lâche; poltron.

das′tardy, n., (ant.) lâcheté, poltronnerie, f.

da′ta (dé-), n.pl., données, f.pl.

date, n., date, échéance, f.; (of money) millésime, m.; (bot.) datte, f. — rack; semainier, m. Out of —; suranné, vieilli; passé de mode, démodé; (com.) (i.e. overdue) périmé. To pass out of —; passer, vieillir; (com.) périmer. Dated, under — of; en date **de**. To bring up to —; mettre à jour.

date, v.a. and n., dater; (from) dater **de**.

date′less, adj., sans date.

date′-tree (-trî), n., dattier, m.

da′tive (dé-), adj., datif.

da′tive (dé-), n., datif, m.

da′tum (dé-teume), n., (data) donnée, f.; (mec.) repère, m. — line; ligne de repère, f.

daub (dôbe), v.a., barbouiller; enduire; (fig.) surcharger, déguiser; flatter grossièrement, flagorner.

daub, n., barbouillage, m.; (paint.) croûte, f.

daub′er, n., barbouilleur, crouton m., (fig.) flagorneur.

daub′y, adj., gluant, visqueux.

daugh′ter (dô′teur), n., fille, f. — -in-law; belle-fille, bru, f. Step- —; belle-fille, f. Grand- —; petite-fille, f.

daugh′terly, adj., filial. adv., en fille, filialement.

daunt (dâ′n'te ou dô′n'te), v.a., dompter; effrayer, intimider, abattre.

daunt′less, adj., indomptable, intrépide.

daunt′lessness, n., intrépidité, f.

dau′phin (dô-fine), n., Dauphin, m.

dau′phiness, n., Dauphine, f.

dav′enport, n., bureau, secrétaire, m.

da′vit (dé-vite), n., (nav.) davier, bossoir, m.

daw′dle (dô′d'l), v.n., lambiner, muser, baguenauder, flâner.

daw′dler, n., flâneur, lambin, musard, m.

dawn (dô′ne), n., aube, aurore, f.; point du jour, m.

dawn, v.n., poindre, paraître, se lever, luire, (fig.) briller; naître, percer.

day (dé), n., jour, m.; journée, f.; (fig.) bataille, victoire, f. To —; aujourd'hui. — before yesterday; avant-hier. — after to-morrow; après-demain. Better —s; des jours meilleurs. — by —; de jour en jour. Every —; tous les jours. All —; tout le jour; toute la journée. The — after; le lendemain. This —; aujourd'hui; ce jour-ci. From this —; dès aujourd'hui. Two —s after; le surlendemain, m. Two —s before; l'avant veille, f. The — of the month; le quantième du mois. Broad —; plein jour. Every two —s, every other —; tous les deux jours. In our —s; de nos jours. Good —; bonjour. Any —; d'un jour à l'autre; n'importe quel jour. By the —; à la journée. At the present —; de nos jours. In the —s of old; au temps jadis. In the —s of; au temps des; du temps de. In former —s; autrefois, jadis. The — before; la veille. The — before that on which; la veille du jour où. This — last year; l'an dernier à pareil jour. This — week; d'aujourd'hui en huit. This — fortnight; d'aujourd'hui en quinze. The better the — the better the deed; bon jour, bonne œuvre. Sufficient for the — is the evil thereof; à chaque jour suffit sa peine. To carry, ou win, the —; remporter la victoire. To have one's —s; avoir ses jours; être journalier. To have had its —; (of a thing) avoir servi son temps.

day′boarder, n., demi-pensionnaire, m.

day′book (-bouke), n., (com.) journal; livre journal, m.

day′break (-brèke), n., point du jour, m.; pointe du jour, aube, aurore, f.

day′light (-laïte), n., jour, m., lumière du jour, f. Broad —; grand jour. By —; de jour. In broad —; au grand jour, en plein jour.

day′ly. V. daily.

day′pupil, n., externe, m.

day′spring, n., jour naissant, m.; aurore, aube, f.

day′-star, n., étoile du matin, f.; soleil, m.

day′s'-work (dé′z'weurke), n., ouvrage d'un jour, m.; journée, f.; travail du jour, m.

day′time (-taïme), n., (from sunrise to sunset) jour, m.; journée, f. In the —; pendant le jour, pendant la journée.

day′-wearied (-wî-ride), adj., fatigué de sa journée.

daze, n., pierre brillante, f.

daz′zle ou **daze** (daz'z'l), v.a., éblouir, étourdir, stupéfier.

daz′zle, v.n., (l. u.) être ébloui, s'éblouir.

daz′zling, n., éblouissement, m.

daz′zling, adj., éblouissant.

daz′zlingly, adv., d'une manière éblouissante.

dea′con (dî′k'n), n., diacre, m.

dea′coness (dî′kn'èce), n., diaconesse, f.

dea′conry (dî′k'n-ri) ou **dea′conship** (dî′-k'n-), n., diaconat, m.

dead (dède), adj., mort; inanimé; inerte, insensible; lourd, pesant; (of liquor) éventé; (of fire) sans flamme; (of sound) sourd; (of colors) terne, mat. — body; cadavre, corps mort, m. — coal; charbon éteint, m. — sleep; profond sommeil, m. — of the night; silence de la nuit, m. — time of the year; morte-saison, f. — wall; muraille isolée ou sans baies, f.; mur blanc, m. — calm; calme plat, m. Money lying —; *de l'argent qui dort, m.* To drop down —; *tomber mort.* — drunk; *ivre-mort.* — beat; *éreinté.* — house; *morgue, f.* — letter; (inoperative) *lettre morte, f.; lettre tombée au rebut.* — letter office; *bureau des rebuts, m.* — lift; *dernière extrémité, f.; état désespéré, m.* — march; *marche funèbre, f.* — season; *morte-saison, f.* — lock; (fig.) *impasse, f.; arrêt forcé, m.* — level; *niveau, m.* — reckoning; (nav.) *route estimée, f.* — set; *vive attaque; tentative désespérée, f.* — shot; *qui a un tir infaillible.* — stop; *halte subite, f.* — weight; *poids inerte; fardeau pesant, m.* — water; *remous, m.* — wood; *bois mort, m.*

dead, *n.*, (of the winter) cœur, fort; (of the night) milieu, *m.* The —; *les morts, m.pl.*

dead'en (dèd'd'n), *v.a.*, amortir; (to blunt) émousser; (liquor) éventer; (gold and silver) matir, amatir; (of sounds) assourdir.

dead'liness, *n.*, caractère mortel, *m.*, nature mortelle, *f.*

dead'ly, *adj.*, mortel, à mort; (fig.) extrême-ment, profondément. — dull; *profondément triste.* — nightshade; *belladonne, f.*

dead'ly, *adv.*, mortellement.

dead'ness, *n.*, mort, *f.;* (fig.) engourdisse-ment, *m.*, stagnation, froideur, (of sound) ma-tité, *f.*

deaf (dèfe), *adj.*, sourd; (fig.) insensible. — as a post; *sourd comme un pot.*

deaf'en (dèf'f'n), *v.a.*, rendre sourd; assour-dir; étourdir.

deaf'ening, *adj.*, assourdissant.

deaf'ly (dèf'li), *adv.*, (of hearing) mal, impar-faitement.

deaf'ness (dèf'-), *n.*, surdité, *f.*

deal (dîl), *n.*, quantité; (at cards) donne, *f.;* (wood) bois blanc, sapin, bois de sapin, *m.* A great —, a good —; *beaucoup de.* By a good —; *à beaucoup près.* A good — to do; *beaucoup, ou fort, à faire.*

deal, *v.a.*, distribuer; répartir; (at cards) donner; (blows) porter. To — blows; *frapper.*

deal, *v.n.*, agir, traiter, en user **avec**; mener; conduire, (to throw) lancer; diriger, gouverner (of commerce). To — by any one; *traiter quel-qu'un; en user à l'égard de quelqu'un.* To — with any one; *en user* **avec** *quelqu'un;* (com.) *donner sa pratique, se faire servir chez quelqu'un.* To have to — with; *avoir affaire à.*

deal'er, *n.*, marchand, *m.;* (at cards) per-sonne qui donne, *f.*, donneur, *m.*

deal'ing, *n.*, conduite, manière d'agir, *f.;* procédé, *m.;* affaire, occupation, *f.;* relations, *f.pl.*, rapports, *m.pl.* Double —; *duplicité, f.*

dean, *n.*, doyen, *m.*

dean'ery (dî'n'euri) *ou* **dean'ship** (dî'n'-), *n.*, doyenné, décanat, *m.*

dear (dîre), *n.*, cher; cher ami, *m.;* chère; chère amie, bonne, *f.*

dear ! *int.*, mon Dieu ! Oh — me ! *Ah, mon Dieu !*

dear, *adj.*, cher; chéri; précieux, joli, gentil, charmant.

dear, *adv.*, cher; beaucoup.

dear'ly, *adv.*, chèrement; tendrement.

dear'ly-bought, dear'bought (-bôte), *adj.*, acheté cher, payé cher.

dear'ness, *n.*, cherté; (fig.) tendresse, *f.*

dearth (deurth), *n.*, disette, *f.*

death (dèth), *n.*, mort, *f.;* (hunt.) hallali; (poet.) trépas; (jur.) décès, *m.* It will be the — of me ; *j'en mourrai.* To be frozen to —; *mourir de froid.* To beat to —; *assommer de coups.* To catch one's —; *attraper la mort.* To bleed to —; *saigner à blanc; perdre tout son sang.* That child will be the — of me ; *cet enfant me tuera.* To drink one's self to —; *se tuer à force de boire.* To die a natural —; *mourir de sa belle mort.* To be sick unto —; *être malade à en*

mourir. To pine to —; *mourir de chagrin.* To put to —; *mettre à mort.* To frighten to —; *faire mourir de frayeur.* To sound the —; (hunt.) *sonner l'hallali.*

death'-bed (-bède), *n.*, lit de mort, *m.* On one's —; *à son lit de mort; au lit de la mort.*

death'-bell, *n.*, cloche funèbre, *f.;* glas funèbre, *m.*

death'-blow (-blô), *n.*, coup de la mort; coup mortel, *m.;* (fig.) ruine complète; destruction, *f.;* coup de grâce, *m.*

death'-boding (-bod'-), *adj.*, qui présage la mort.

death'-darting (-dârt'-), *adj.*, qui lance la mort; meurtrier.

death'-dealing, *adj.*, qui donne la mort.

death'-hunter (-heu'nt'-), *n.*, croque mort, *m.*

death'less, *adj.*, immortel, impérissable.

death'like (-laïke), *adj.*, semblable à la mort; de mort; cadavéreux.

death'-note (-nôte), *n.*, son de mort, *m.*

death'-psalm (-sâme), *n.*, psaume des morts, de Profundis, *m.*

death'-rate, *n.*, mortalité, proportion des décès, *f.*

death'-rattle (-rat't'l), *n.*, râle de la mort, râle de l'agonie, râle, *m.*

death's'-door (dèths'dôre), *n.*, porte du tom-beau, *f.* At —; *à deux doigts de la mort, à l'article de la mort.*

death's-head (dèths'hède), *n.*, tête de mort, *f.*

death's-shot (-shote), *n.*, coup mortel, *m.*

death'-struggle (-strug'g'l), *n.*, agonie, *f.*

death'-throes (-thrôze), *n.*, agonie, *f.* To be in one's —; *agoniser.*

death'-warrant (-wor'ra'n'te), *n.*, ordre d'exé-cution; arrêt de mort, *m.*

death'-watch (-wôtshe), *n.*, (ent.) horloge de la mort, *f.*

death'-wound, *n.*, blessure mortelle, *f.*

debar' (di-bâr), *v.a.*, exclure de; priver **de**; empêcher **de**; frustrer **de**, défendre, interdire.

debark' (di-bârke), *v.n.*, débarquer.

debarka'tion, *n.*, débarquement, *m.*

debase' (di-béce), *v.a.*, avilir; abaisser; abâtardir, ravaler; (chem.) adultérer, falsifier, frelater; dénaturer; (coin.) altérer, falsifier.

debase'ment (-béce-), *n.*, abaissement, avilisse-ment, *m.;* (chem.) falsification, (coin.) altéra-tion, sophistication, *f.;* frelatage, *m.*

debas'er (-béce-), *n.*, personne qui abaisse, qui avilit, *f.*

debas'ing (-béce-), *adj.*, avilissant.

debat'able (di-bét'a-b'l), *adj.*, contestable, sujet à contestation.

debate' (di-béte), *n.*, débat, *m.;* débats, *m.pl.;* discussion, contestation, dispute, *f.*

debate', *v.a.*, débattre, discuter, disputer.

debate', *v.n.*, discuter **sur**; délibérer **sur**.

deba'ter, *n.*, personne qui discute, *f.;* orateur parlementaire ; argumentateur, *m.*

debauch' (di-bôtsh), *n.*, débauche, *f.*

debauch', *v.a.*, débaucher, corrompre, per-vertir.

debauch'edly (di-bôtsh'èd-), *adv.*, dans la débauche, en débauché.

debauchee' (dèb-ô-shî), *n.*, libertin, débauché, *m.*

debauch'er (di-bôtsh'-), *n.*, débaucheur, *m.*, débaucheuse, *f.;* corrupteur, *m.*, corruptrice, *f.*

debauch'ery (di-bôtsheur'i), *n.*, débauche, *f.*

debauch'ment, *n.*, (ant.) débauche, *f.*

deben'ture (di-bè'n't'ioure), *n.*, reconnais-sance d'une dette, obligation, *f.;* (at the cus-toms) certificat de prime, *m.* — holder ; *porteur d'obligations, m.*

debil'itate (di-), *v.a.*, débiliter, affaiblir.

debilita'tion (-li-té-), *n.*, debilitation, *f.;* af-faiblissement, *m.*

debil'ity, *n.*, débilité ; faiblesse, *f.*

deb'it (dèb'ite), *n.*, débet, débit, doit, *m.* To carry to any one's —; *porter au débit de quelqu'un.* — balance ; *solde débiteur, m.* — side ; *débit, doit.*

deb'it, *v.a.*, débiter de, passer au débit de.

debonair' (dèb'o-nére), *adj.*, débonnaire, doux, poli, complaisant.

debonair'ly, *adv.*, (ant.) débonnairement.

debonair'ness, *n.*, (ant.) débonnaireté, bonhomie, *f.*

debouch' (dè-boushe), *v.n.*, déboucher.

debou'ching, *n.*, débouchement.

debt (dète), *n.*, dette ; obligation ; créance, *f. pl.*, dettes, *f.pl.* ; passif, *m.sing.* Bad —; *mauvaise créance.* Floating —; *dette courante,* (fin.) *dette flottante.* Large —; *grosse dette.* National —; *dette publique.* Outstanding —; *créance courante, créance à recouvrer.* Passive —; *dette passive.* Privileged —; *créance privilégiée.* — due ; *créance exigible.* To admit a —; *reconnaître une dette.* To be in — to any one ; *devoir à quelqu'un, être le débiteur de.* To contract a —; *contracter une dette.* To discharge a —; *acquitter une dette.* To prove a —; *produire ses titres de créance.* To run, *ou* get, into —; *faire des dettes, s'endetter.* To recover a —; *recouvrer une créance.* Deeply in —; *accablé de dettes.* I am in your —; *je suis votre débiteur.* To pay the — of nature ; *payer le tribut de la nature.* Out of — out of danger ; *qui ne doit rien n'a rien à craindre.* To get out of some one's —; *s'acquitter* **envers.**

debtee' (dèt'î), *n.*, (jur.) créancier, *m.*

deb'tor (dèt'teur), *n.*, débiteur, *m.*, débitrice, *f.* — and creditor ; *débiteur et créancier, m.* — side ; *débit, doit, m.* —s' prison ; *prison pour dettes, f.*

dec'ade (dèk-éde), *n.*, dizaine ; décade, *f.*

deca'dence *ou* **deca'dency** (di-ké-), *n.*, décadence, *f.*

dec'agon (dèk'-), *n.*, (geom.) décagone, *m.*

dec'agram (dèk'-), *n.*, décagramme, *m.*

decahe'dron (dèk'a-hî-), *n.*, décaèdre, *m.*

dec'alitre (-lî-teur), *n.*, décalitre, *m.*

dec'alogue (dèk'a-loghe), *n.*, décalogue, *m.*

Decam'eron, *n.*, décaméron, *m.*

decamp' (di-ca'm'pe), *v.n.*, (milit.) lever le camp ; (fig.) décamper ; déguerpir.

decamp'ment, *n.*, décampement, *m.*

decan'gular (dèk'a'gn-ghiou-), *adj.*, décagone.

decant' (di-), *v.a.*, décanter, transvaser.

decant'er, *n.*, carafe, *f.* Small —; *carafon, m.*

decap'itate (di-), *v.a.*, décapiter.

decapita'tion (-'î-té-), *n.*, décapitation, *f.*

dec'astich (dèk'a-stike), *n.*, dizain, *m.*

dec'astyle (dèk'a-staïle), *n.*, décastyle, *m.*

decay' (di-ké), *n.*, décadence ; ruine, *f.* ; déclin, délabrement, dépérissement, *m.* To fall into —; *tomber en ruine, en décadence, se délabrer.* — of bones, teeth ; *carie des os, des dents, f.*

decay', *v.n.*, tomber en décadence, se délabrer, se perdre ; dépérir ; se gâter ; se carier.

decease' (di-cîce), *n.*, décès, *m.* ; mort, *f.*

decease', *v.n.*, décéder ; mourir.

deceased' (di-cîste), *adj.*, décédé ; mort.

deceased', *n.*, défunt, *m.*, défunte, *f.*

deceit' (di-cîte), *n.*, déception ; supercherie, fourberie, tromperie, ruse ; (jur.) fraude, *f.* ; artifice, *m.*

deceit'ful (-foule), *adj.*, trompeur ; (of things) décevant.

deceit'fully, *adv.*, frauduleusement.

deceit'fulness, *n.*, caractère trompeur, *m.* ; fausseté, tromperie, *f.*

deceit'less, *adj.*, sincère.

deceiv'able (di-cîv'a-b'l), *adj.*, facile à tromper ; trompeur ; illusoire ; décevant.

deceive' (di-cîve), *v.a.*, décevoir ; tromper.

deceiv'er, *n.*, imposteur, trompeur, *m.*, trompeuse, *f.*

Decem'ber (di-cè'm'beur), *n.*, décembre, *m.*

decem'vir (di-cè'm'veur), *n.*, décemvir, *m.*

decem'virate, *n.*, décemvirat, *m.*

de'cency (dî-cè'n'-), *n.*, bienséance ; décence, *f.* ; convenances, *f. pl.*

decen'nial (di-), *adj.*, décennal.

de'cent (dî-), *adj.*, bienséant, décent, honnête, propre, présentable, passable.

de'cently, *adv.*, décemment ; convenablement, modérément.

decentraliza'tion, *n.*, décentralisation.

decen'tralize, *v.a.*, décentraliser.

decep'tible (di-), *adj.*, décevable.

decep'tion (di-), *n.*, tromperie, fraude, déception, illusion, *f.*

decep'tive (di-cèp'-), *adj.*, décevant, trompeur, mensonger, déceptif.

decharm' (di-tshârme), *v.a.*, désenchanter ; rompre un charme.

decide' (di-çaïde), *v.a.*, décider ; décider de.

decide', *v.n.*, décider ; se décider ; se prononcer pour.

deci'ded (-'ède), *adj.*, décidé, prononcé ; positif, bien arrêté ; ferme, résolu.

deci'dedly, *adv.*, décidément ; positivement, certainement, résolument.

deci'der (di-caïd'eur), *n.*, arbitre, juge, *m.*

decid'uous (di-cid'iou-), *adj.*, (bot.) caduque (of leaves), *f.*

dec'igram, *n.*, décigramme, *m.*

dec'ilitre (dè-ci-lî-teur), *n.*, décilitre, *m.*

dec'imal, *adj.*, décimal.

dec'imal, *n.*, décimale, fraction décimale, *f.*

dec'imate, *v.a.*, décimer.

decima'tion (-mé-), *n.*, décimation, *f.*

deci'pher (di-çaï'-), *v.a.*, déchiffrer.

deci'pherable, *adj.*, déchiffrable.

deci'pherer, *n.*, déchiffreur, *m.*

deci'sion (di-ci-jeune), *n.*, décision ; résolution ; fermeté ; (end) issue, *f.* To come to a —; *prendre un parti.*

deci'sive (di-çaï-cive), *adj.*, décisif ; tranchant, prononcé. To be — of ; *décider de.*

deci'sively, *adv.*, décisivement, d'une manière décisive.

deci'siveness, *n.*, caractère décisif, *m.*

deck (dèke), *n.*, (nav.) pont ; (of merchant ships) tillac, *m.* Lower —; *franc tillac.* Quarter-—; *gaillard d'arrière, m.* Fore-—; *gaillard d'avant, m.*

deck (dèke), *v.a.*, parer de ; orner ; embellir de ; (nav.) ponter, couvrir d'un pont.

deck'er, *n.*, personne qui pare, *f.* ; vaisseau ponté, *m.* Three-—; *vaisseau à trois ponts, m.*

deck'ing, *n.*, ornement, *m.*

declaim' (di-cléme), *v.a.* and *n.*, déclamer, haranguer.

declai'mer, *n.*, déclamateur, *m.*

declama'tion (dèk-la-mé-), *n.*, déclamation, *f.* ; discours public, *m.*

declam'atory (-ma-), *adj.*, déclamatoire.

declar'able (di-clèr-a-b'l), *adj.*, déclarable.

declara'tion (dèk-la-ré-), *n.*, déclaration ; proclamation ; manifestation, *f.*

declar'ative (di-clèr-a-), *adj.*, explicatif ; (jur.) déclaratif.

declar'atorily (di-clèr-a-), *adv.*, par déclaration.

declar'atory (di-clèr-a-), *adj.*, énonciatif ; (jur.) déclaratoire ; déclaratif.

declare' (di-clère), *v.a.*, déclarer ; annoncer ; constater, assurer, affirmer, proclamer. To — one's self guilty ; *s'avouer coupable.*

declare', *v.n.*, se déclarer, se prononcer **pour.** I —! *par exemple ! ma parole !* To — off ; *quitter la partie, refuser de procéder ; tirer son épingle du jeu.*

declar'edly (di-clèr'èd-), *adv.*, formellement, ouvertement.

declar'er, *n.*, personne qui annonce, *f.*

declen'sion (di-clè'n'-), *n.*, (gram.) déclinaison ; (fig.) décadence, *f. ;* déclin, *m. ;* pente, inclinaison, *f.*

decli'nable (di-claï'n'a-b'l), *adj.,* déclinable.

declina'tion (dèk-li-né-), *n.,* déclin, *m. ;* descente ; décadence ; (gram., ant.) déclinaison, (astr., phys.) déclinaison, *f.*

declin'atory (di-cli'n'a-tori), *adj.,* (jur.) déclinatoire.

decline' (di-claïne), *n.,* déclin, *m. ;* décadence; (med.) maladie de langueur, *f. ;* marasme, *m.* To be in a —; *être atteint de marasme.*

decline', *v.a.,* pencher, incliner ; refuser ; éviter ; (gram.) décliner.

decline', *v.n.,* pencher ; décliner ; (of price) baisser. To — from ; *dévier de.*

decliv'ity, *n.,* déclivité, pente, *f. ;* penchant, *m.*

decliv'ous (di-claï'-), *adj.,* en pente ; déclive.

decoct', *v.a.,* faire bouillir.

decoc'tible (-i-b'l), *adj.,* (ant.) qui peut être bouilli.

decoc'tion, *n.,* décoction, *f.*

decol'late, *v.a.,* décoller, décapiter.

decolla'tion (-lé-), *n.,* décollation, *f.*

decolora'tion (di-keul-eur'é-), *n.,* décoloration.

decol'or (di-keul-eur) *ou* **decol'orate** (di-keul'eur'éte), *v.a.,* décolorer.

decom'plex (dî-co'm'-), *adj.,* composé d'idées complexes.

decompos'able, *adj.,* décomposable.

decompose' (dî-co'm'poze), *v.a.,* décomposer. *v.n.,* se décomposer.

decompos'ite, *adj.,* surcomposé.

decomposi'tion (dî-co'm'po-zish'eune), *n.,* décomposition, *f.*

decompound' (dî-co'm'paou'n'de), *v.a.,* (l.u.) décomposer par moyens mécaniques.

dec'orate (dèk'-), *v.a.,* décorer, orner, embellir.

decora'tion (-ré-), *n.,* décoration, *f. ;* ornement, embellissement, *m.*

dec'orative (-ré-), *adj.,* de décoration, décoratif.

dec'orator (-ré-teur), *n.,* décorateur, *m.*

deco'rous (di-cô- *ou* dèk'o-), *adj.,* bienséant, convenable, décent.

deco'rously, *adv.,* convenablement ; avec bienséance, décemment.

decor'ticate, *v.a.,* décortiquer.

decortica'tion (-ké-), *n.,* décortication, *f.*

deco'rum (-cô-reume), *n.,* bienséance, *f. ;* décorum, *m. ;* convenances, *f.pl.*

decoy' (di-coïe), *v.a.,* leurrer, attirer dans un piège, amorcer.

decoy', *n.,* leurre, piège, (pers.) mouchard, mouton, *m.* — bird ; *appeau, appeleur, m.* — duck ; *appelant, canard privé ;* leurre, *m.*

decrease' (di-crîce), *n.,* décroissement, *m. ;* décroissance, diminution, *f. ;* déclin, *m. ;* (of water) décrue, *f. ;* (of the moon) décours ; (com.) déchet, *m.*

decrease', *v.n.,* diminuer ; décroître.

decrease', *v.a.,* faire décroître, diminuer, amoindrir.

decree' (di-crî), *n.,* décret, arrêt, jugement, *m. ;* ordonnance, *f.*

decree', *v.a.,* décréter ; ordonner ; arrêter, décerner.

dec'rement (dèc'ri-), *n.,* décroissement ; décours, *m.*

decrep'it (di-crèp'ite), *adj.,* décrépit, cassé, affaibli par l'âge, caduc.

decrep'itate (di-crèp'-), *v.a.,* calciner une substance qui décrépite ; faire décrépiter.

decrep'itate (di-crèp'-), *v.n.,* décrépiter, crépiter.

decrepita'tion (-té-), *n.,* décrépitation, crépitation, *f.*

decrep'itness (di-crèp'-) *ou* **decrep'itude** (dè-crèp'i-tioude), *n.,* décrépitude, vieillesse, *f.*

decres'cent (di-crès'-), *adj.,* décroissant.

decre'tal (-crî-), *adj.,* décrétal.

decre'tal, *n.,* décrétale, *f. ;* recueil de décrétales, *m.*

dec'retory (dèc'ri-tori), *adj.,* décrété ; décisif, définitif, péremptoire.

decri'al (di-craï-), *n.,* décri, dénigrement, *m.*

decry' (di-craïe), *v.a.,* décrier.

decum'bent (di-keu'm'-), *adj.,* (bot.) couché, décombant.

dec'uple (dèk'iou-p'l), *adj.,* décuple.

decu'rion (di-kiou-), *n.,* décurion, *m.*

decus'sate (di-keus'-) *ou* **decus'sated** (-tède), *adj.,* (bot.) décussé ; (conch.) strié en croix.

decussa'tion (-sé-), *n.,* décussation, *f.*

ded'icate (dèd-), *v.a.,* dédier à ; dévouer à ; consacrer à.

ded'icated, *adj.,* dédié à, consacré à.

dedica'tion (-ké-), *n.,* dédicace, *f.*

ded'icator (-ké-teur), *n.,* personne qui fait une dédicace, *f.*

ded'icatory (-ké-tori), *adj.,* dédicatoire.

deduce' (di-diouce), *v.a.,* déduire de, inférer de, conclure de, tirer de.

deduce'ment, *n.,* déduction, *f.*

dedu'cible (-ci-b'l), *adj.,* qu'on peut déduire.

deduct' (di-deukte), *v.a.,* déduire, rabattre ; retrancher, défalquer.

deduc'tion, *n.,* déduction ; conséquence ; (com.) remise, *f.*

deduc'tive, *adj.,* conséquent, déductif. — reasoning ; *raisonnement par déduction, m.*

deduc'tively, *adv.,* par déduction.

deed (dîde), *n.,* action, *f. ;* acte ; fait ; exploit; (com.) titre, contrat, *m.* Private — ; *acte sous seing privé, m.*

deed'less, *adj.,* inactif ; obscur.

deem (dîme), *v.a.,* juger ; penser, croire, estimer ; prendre pour ; considérer ou regarder comme. To — it a favour ; *l'estimer une faveur.* To — it right ; *juger convenable de ; croire devoir.* To — it prudent ; *penser qu'il est prudent de.* To be —ed ; *être réputé, passer* pour.

deep (dîpe), *n.,* mer, *f. ;* océan ; abîme, *m. ;* profondeur, *f.* — sea lead ; (nav.) *grande sonde, f.*

deep (dîpe), *adj.,* profond ; (fig.) grand, extrême ; (of color) foncé ; (at play) gros ; (of sound) grave ; (of mourning) grand ; (b.s.) rusé, fin. This well is thirty feet — ; *ce puits a trente pieds de profondeur,* ou *est profond de trente pieds,* ou *a une profondeur de trente pieds.* — mourning ; *grand deuil, m.* Two, three — ; (mil.) *sur deux, sur trois rangs.* To go — into ; *traiter* à *fond.* — in debt ; *accablé de dettes.* To be eight feet — ; *avoir huit pieds de profondeur.*

deep'en (dîp'p'n), *v.a.,* approfondir ; assombrir ; (color) rendre plus foncé ; (sound) rendre plus grave.

deep'en, *v.n.,* devenir plus profond, plus foncé.

deep'drawn, *adj.,* long, profond.

deep'-fetched (-fètsh'te), *adj.,* profond, tiré par les cheveux.

deep'-laid, *adj.,* infernal ; ténébreux, secret.

deep'ly, *adv.,* profondément ; vivement ; extrêmement ; (of color) fortement ; (of sound) gravement ; (b.s.) avec ruse.

deep'ness, *n.,* profondeur ; (b.s.) ruse, *f.* V. **depth.**

deep'-read, *adj.,* érudit.

deep'-rooted, *adj.,* enraciné, invétéré.

deep'-sea line, *n.,* grande sonde, *f.*

deep'-seated, *adj.,* profond, enraciné.

deep'toned, *adj.,* aux tons graves, *m.pl.*

deep'waisted, *adj.,* (of a ship) haut-encastillé.

deer (dîre), *n.,* daim, *m.,* daine, *f. ;* bête fauve, *f. ;* cerf, *m.* Fallow — ; *daim.* Red — ; *cerf commun.* — hound ; *limier, m.*

deer'-stalker (-stôk'-), *n.,* chasseur à l'affût (de bêtes fauves).

deer'-stalking, n., chasse à l'affût.

deface' (di-), v.a., défigurer ; effacer ; dégrader, détériorer.

deface'ment, n., dégradation ; détérioration ; action d'effacer, f.

defa'cer, n., destructeur, -trice, m.f.

defal'cate (di-), v.a., défalquer ; retrancher, détourner.

defalca'tion (di-fal-ké-), n., défalcation, diminution, déduction, f. ; (com.) détournement de fonds, déficit, m.

defama'tion (dèf-a-mé-), n., diffamation, f.

defama'tory (-tori), adj., diffamatoire, diffamant.

defame' (di-), v.a., diffamer.

defa'mer, n., diffamateur, m.

default' (di-fôlte), n., défaut, manque, m. ; (jur.) contumace, f. In — of ; à défaut de. To suffer —; (jur.) faire défaut. By —; par contumace, par défaut.

default', v.n., (jur.) faire défaut, ne pas comparaître.

default'er (-fôlt'-), n., délinquant, m., délinquante, f. ; (jur.) défaillant, m., défaillante, f. ; contumace, m.f. ; personne qui ne remplit pas ses engagements, f. ; (of recruits) conscrit réfractaire ; (private money) auteur d'un détournement de fonds ; (of public moneys) concussionnaire, m.

defea'sance (di-fî-za'n'ce), n., (jur.) abrogation ; contre-lettre, f.

defea'sible (di-fîz'i-b'l), adj., annulable.

defeat' (di-fîte), n., défaite ; déroute, f., échec, insuccès, m.

defeat', v.a., défaire, mettre en déroute, vaincre ; faire échouer ; (fig.) annuler, repousser, déjouer, frustrer ; (evade) échapper à, éluder.

def'ecate (dèf'i-kéte), v.a., déféquer.

defeca'tion, n., défécation, f.

defect' (di-fècte), n., défaut, m. ; défectuosité, imperfection, f., (jur.) vice, m.

defec'tion (di-fèk-), n., défection ; apostasie ; révolte, f.

defec'tive (di-fèc-), adj., défectueux, défectif ; en défaut, fautif ; (jur.) vicieux ; (gram.) défectif.

defec'tively, adv., défectueusement.

defec'tiveness, n., (jur.) état vicieux, m. ; défectuosité, f.

defend' (di-), v.a., défendre, protéger, préserver.

defend'able (-a-b'l), adj., qui peut se justifier ; tenable.

defend'ant, n., défendeur, m., défenderesse, f. ; intimé, intimée, f.

defend'er, n., défenseur, m.

defense' (di-), v.a., défense, protection, f.

defense'less, adj., sans défense.

defen'sible (-si-b'l), adj., défendable ; soutenable ; justifiable ; excusable.

defen'sive, adj., défensif.

defen'sive, n., défensive, f. On the —; sur la défensive.

defen'sively, adv., pour la défense.

defer' (di-feur), v.a., différer, remettre, renvoyer ; ajourner.

defer' (di-feur), v.n., différer ; (submit) déférer à. To — to any one ; déférer à quelqu'un ; s'en rapporter à quelqu'un.

def'erence (dèf'eur-), n., déférence, f. Out of — to ; par déférence pour.

def'erent (dèf'eur-), adj., qui transporte ; conducteur.

def'erent, n., véhicule ; moyen de transport ; (anat.) canal, m.

deferen'tial (dèf'i-rè'n'shal), adj., de déférence, déférentiel ; respectueux.

deferen'tially, adv., avec déférence, avec respect.

defi'ance (di-faï'-), n., défi, m. To set at —;

---

défier, braver. In — of ; au mépris de, en dépit de.

defi'cience ou **defi'ciency** (dè-fish'-), n., manque, défaut, m. ; insuffisance, imperfection, faiblesse, f. ; déficit, m.

defi'cient (di-fish'-), adj., défectueux ; insuffisant, faible, peu avancé, imparfait. To be — in ; être faible en ; manquer de ; ne pas avoir ; être dépourvu de. He is — in those qualities ; ces qualités lui manquent.

def'icit (dèf-), n., déficit, m.

defi'er (di-faï'-), n., qui défie, qui brave, provocateur.

defile' (di-faïl), n., défilé, m.

defile' (di-faïl), v.a., souiller ; déshonorer, corrompre, débaucher ; violer.

defile', v.n., (mil.) défiler.

defile'ment (di-faïl-), n., action de souiller ; souillure, f. ; (fort.) défilement, m.

defi'ler, n., corrupteur, m., corruptrice, f. ; ravisseur, m.

defi'nable (di-faï'n'-), adj., définissable.

define' (di-faïne), v.a., définir ; déterminer ; limiter ; accentuer, marquer.

defi'ner, n., qui définit, f.

def'inite (dèf'i-nite), adj., défini ; déterminé.

def'inite, n., défini, m.

def'initely, adv., d'une manière déterminée.

def'initeness, n., caractère déterminé, m.

defini'tion (dèf'i-nish'eune), n., définition, f.

defin'itive (di-fi'n'i-tive), adj., définitif.

defin'itive, n., (gram.) déterminatif, m.

defin'itively, adv., définitivement, en définitive.

defin'itiveness, n., caractère définitif, m.

deflagrabil'ity (di-flé-gra-), combustibilité, f.

defla'grable ou **def'la** (di-flé-gra-b'l ou dèf'la-), adj., combustible.

def'lagrate (dèf-la-), v.a., (chem.) faire brûler avec flamme. v.n., brûler avec flamme.

deflagra'tion (-gré-), n., déflagration, f.

deflect' (di-flècte), v.a., faire dévier. v.n., dévier ; (of the needle) décliner.

deflec'tion, n., déviation, déclinaison, f.

deflora'tion (dèf'lo-ré-), n., défloration.

deflour' ou **deflower'** (di-flaoueur), v.a., déflorer ; déshonorer ; (fig.) flétrir.

deflour'er ou **deflower'er**, n., celui qui déflore, ravisseur, m.

defluxion'ion (di-fleuk'sheune), n., (med.) écoulement, m.

deforce' (di-fôrce), v.a., (jur.) détenir, déposséder.

deforce'ment, n., (jur.) détention, usurpation, f.

defor'ciant (di-fôr-shi-), n., (jur.) détenteur, m.

deform', v.a., déformer, défigurer, enlaidir.

deforma'tion (di-form'é-), n., déformation, f. ; défigurement, m.

deformed', adj., difforme, contrefait.

deform'edly (di-form'èd'-), adv., d'une manière difforme.

deform'ity, n., difformité, laideur, f.

defraud' (di-frôde), v.a., frauder, frustrer, tromper ; priver de, dépouiller de.

defraud'er, n., fraudeur, m., fraudeuse, f.

defray' (di-fré), v.a., défrayer ; payer ; (to make up for) couvrir.

defray'er (di-fré-eur), n., qui défraye, amphitryon, m.

defray'ment ou **defray'ing**, n., défrayement, m.

deft (dèf'te), adj., adroit, habile ; leste, accort, convenable.

deft'ly, adv., adroitement, lestement.

deft'ness, n., gentillesse, adresse, habileté, f.

defunct' (di-feu'gn'cte), adj., défunt, trépassé, décédé.

defunct', n., défunt, m., défunte, f.

defy' (di-faïe), *v.a.*, défier, braver ; narguer.

defy'er, *n.* *V.* **defier.**

degen'eracy (di-djè'n'èr'-), *n.*, dégénération, *f.* ; abâtardissement, *m.*

degen'erate (di-djè'n'èr'-), *adj.*, dégénéré, abâtardi.

degen'erate, *v.n.*, dégénérer, s'abâtardir.

degen'erately, *adv.*, avec dégénération.

degen'erateness *ou* **degenera'tion**, *n.*, dégénération, *f.* ; abâtardissement, *m.*

degen'erous, *adj.*, dégénéré ; bas, vil, misérable ; indigne.

deglu'tinate (di-gliou'-), *v.a.*, décoller, dégluer.

degluti'tion (dèg-liou-tish'eune), *n.*, déglutition, *f.*

degrada'tion (dèg-ra-dé-), *n.*, dégradation, *f.* ; avilissement, *m.*

degrade' (di-), *v.a.*, dégrader ; avilir.

degra'ded (-éde), *adj.*, dégradé.

degra'ding, *adj.*, dégradant.

degra'dingly, *adv.*, d'une manière dégradante, *ou* avilissante.

degree' (di-grî), *n.*, degré ; rang, ordre, *m.* ; qualité, condition, *f.* University —; *grade universitaire*, *m.* To a certain —; *jusqu'à un certain point.* By —s, *peu à peu, graduellement.* To a — ; *à l'extrême, au possible.*

degusta'tion (di-gheus-té-), *n.*, (ant.) dégustation, *f.*

dehisce' (di-hice), *v.n.*, (bot.) s'ouvrir ; être déhiscent.

dehis'cence, *n.*, (bot.) déhiscence, *f.*

dehis'cent, *adj.*, (bot.) déhiscent.

de'icide (dî-i-caïde), *n.*, déicide, *m.*

deifica'tion (dî-i-fi-ké-), *n.*, déification, *f.*

de'iform (dî-i-), *adj.*, divin.

de'ify (dî-i-faïe), *v.a.*, déifier, diviniser.

deign (déne), *v.a.*, daigner. *v.a.*, accorder, daigner accorder.

de'ism (dî-iz'm), *n.*, déisme, *m.*

de'ist (dî-iste), *n.*, déiste, *m.*

de'ity (dî-i-), *n.*, divinité ; (myth.) déité, *f.*

deject', *v.a.*, abaisser ; abattre ; affliger.

deject'ed, *adj.*, abattu, triste.

deject'edly, *adv.*, dans l'abattement ; tristement, d'un air triste.

deject'edness, *n.*, abattement, *m.*

dejec'tion, *n.*, abattement, *m.* ; (med.) défécation, déjection, *f.*

dejec'ture (-'ioure), *n. sing.*, (med.) évacuations alvines, *f.pl.*

delay' (di-lé), *n.*, délai, retardement, retard, *m.*

delay', *v.a.*, différer, remettre, retarder, arrêter. *v.n.*, tarder, s'arrêter. All is not lost that is —ed ; *ce qui est différé n'est pas perdu.*

delay'er (di-lé-eur), *n.*, temporiseur, *m.*

de'le (dî-li), *v.a.*, (print.) deleatur, *m.*

delect'able (di-lèc-ta-b'l), *adj.*, délectable.

delect'ableness, *n.*, délectation, *f.*, caractère délectable, *m.*

delect'ably, *adv.*, délectablement, d'une manière délectable.

delecta'tion (-té-), *n.*, délectation, *f.*

del'egacy, *n.*, délégation, *f.*

del'egate (dèl'î-), *adj.*, délégué.

del'egate (dèl'î-), *n.*, délégué, *m.*

del'egate (dèl'î-), *v.a.*, déléguer.

delega'tion (dèl-i-ghé-), *n.*, délégation, *f.*

del'egator, *n.*, (jur.) délégant, délégateur, *m.*, délégatrice, *f.*

delete', *v.a.*, effacer, rayer, biffer.

delete'rious (dèl-i-tî-), *adj.*, délétère, nuisible.

dele'tion (di-lî-), *n.*, rature, *f.* ; grattage, *m.*

del'etory (dèl-i-tori), *n.*, chose qui efface, *f.*

delf, delft, *ou* **delft'-ware** (-wère), *n.*, faïence de Delft, *f.*

delib'erate (di-lib'eur'-) *adj.*, délibéré ; mûri, réfléchi, avisé.

delib'erate, *v.n.*, délibérer. To — upon ; *délibérer* **sur.**

delib'erately, *adv.*, mûrement ; de propos délibéré ; à dessein.

delib'erateness, *n.*, délibération, réflexion ; circonspection, prudence, *f.*

delibera'tion (-eur'é-), *n.*, délibération, *f.*

delib'erative (-eur-a-), *adj.*, délibérant ; délibératif.

delib'eratively, *adv.*, par délibération.

del'icacy (dèl-i-), *n.*, délicatesse, *f.*, (dainty) friandise, *f.*

del'icate (dèl-i-), *adj.*, délicat.

del'icately, *adv.*, délicatement.

del'icateness, *n.*, délicatesse, *f.*

deli'cious (di-lish'eusse), *adj.*, délicieux.

deli'ciously, *adv.*, délicieusement.

deli'ciousness, *n.*, délices, *f.pl.*, excellence, volupté, *f.* ; charme, *m.*

delight' (di-laïte), *n.*, délices, *f.pl.*, délice ; plaisir, *m.*

delight', *v.a.*, plaire à ; faire les délices **de**, enchanter ; ravir, charmer.

delight', *v.n.* To — in ; *faire ses délices de ; se plaire à ; prendre plaisir à ; goûter ; se faire un plaisir de ; trouver son bonheur à ou dans.* To be —ed to ; *être enchanté* **de.**

delight'ful (-foule), *adj.*, délicieux, charmant, ravissant.

delight'fully, *adv.*, délicieusement, à ravir.

delight'fulness, *n.*, charme, *m.* ; délices, *f.pl.*

delight'less, *adj.*, sans charme.

delight'some (-seume) *adj.*, agréable, délicieux.

delight'somely, *adv.*, agréablement.

delight'someness, *n.*, agrément, *m.*

delin'eament (di-li'n'i-), *n.*, délinéation, *f.*

delin'eate (di-li'n'i-), *v.a.*, faire la délinéation **de** ; esquisser, de'siner, tracer ; (fig.) décrire ; peindre.

delinea'tion (di-li'n'i-é-), *n.*, délinéation ; esquisse ; (fig.) peinture, description, *f.*

delin'eator (di-li'n'i-é-teur), *n.*, dessinateur ; peintre, *m.*

delin'quency (di-li'gn'kwè'n'-), *n.*, délit, *m.* ; faute, *f.*

delin'quent (di-li'gn'kwè'n'te), *n.*, délinquant, *m.* ; délinquante, *f.*

del'iquate (dèl-i-kwéte) *ou* **deliq'uiate** (di-lik-kwi-éte), *v.a.* and *n.*, liquéfier ; se liquéfier.

deliqua'tion (dèl-i-kwé-), *n.*, (ant.) déliquescence, *f.*

deliquesce' (dè-li-kwèce), *v.n.*, tomber en déliquescence.

deliques'cence, *n.*, déliquescence, *f.*

deliques'cent, *adj.*, déliquescent.

deliq'uium (di-lik'wi-eume), *n.*, (chem.) deliquium, *m.* ; (med.) syncope, *f.*

delir'ious (di-li-), *adj.*, délirant, en délire ; dans le délire ; de délire. To be — ; *avoir le délire, délirer.* To become — ; *tomber dans le délire.*

delir'iousness, *n.*, délire, *m.*

delir'ium (di-lir-i-eume), *n.*, délire, transport de joie, *m.* — tremens ; *delirium tremens, m.*

deliv'er (di-), *v.a.*, délivrer ; sauver ; (letters) distribuer ; (a letter, a parcel) remettre ; (goods, a place) livrer ; (a speech) prononcer ; (a woman) délivrer, accoucher. To — from ; *délivrer* **de** ; *sauver* **de.** To — in ; *délivrer* ; *donner.* To — up ; *livrer* ; *remettre* ; *rendre.* To — one's self up to ; *se livrer* à. To — a message to ; *remettre un message* à. To — one's self over to ; *se rendre, s'abandonner* à.

deliv'erable, *adj.*, (com.) livrable.

deli'verance, *n.*, délivrance, *f.* ; acquittement par un jury ; (of a woman) accouchement, *m.*, délivrance, *f.*

deliv'erer, *n.*, libérateur, *m.*, libératrice, *f.* ; sauveur, *m.*, (of circulars) distributeur, *m.* ; (com.) livrancier, livreur, *m.*

deliv'ery, _n._, délivrance, remise, _f._ ; (of speech) débit, _m._, diction; (com.) livraison; (of letters) distribution, _f._; (of a woman) accouchement, _m._, délivrance, _f._ Payment on — ; (com.) _payement contre livraison_, _m._

dell, _n._, creux; vallon, _m._

del'phine, _adj._, du Dauphin (de France).

delu'dable (di-lioud'a-b'l), _adj._, facile à tromper.

delude' (di-lioude), _v.a._, tromper, abuser. To — one's self; _se faire illusion_, _s'abuser._

delu'der, _n._, trompeur, séducteur, imposteur, _m._

del'uge (dèl'lioudje), _n._, déluge, _m._

del'uge, _v.a._, inonder de.

delu'sion (di-liou-jeune) _n._, illusion, déception, _f._

delu'sive (di-liou-cive) _ou_ delu'sory (-ço-), _adj._, illusoire, trompeur.

delu'siveness, _n._, caractère illusoire, _m._, nature trompeuse, _f._

delve (dèlve), _v.a._, creuser; fouir, bêcher; (fig.) sonder, pénétrer.

dem'agogue, _n._, démagogue, _m._

demain' (di-méne) _ou_ demesne' (di-mîne), _n._, domaine, _m._; propriété, _f._; bien-fonds, _m._

demand' (di-mâ'n'de), _n._, demande, réclamation, requête, _f._; appel, (outlet) débouché, débit, _m._; (fig.) recherche, _f._ In great —; _très demandé_, _très recherché._ In little —; _peu demandé._ On — ; (com.) _à présentation._ In full of all —s; _pour solde de tout compte._

demand', _v.a._, demander; réclamer; exiger, requérir.

demand'able (-'a-b'l), _adj._, exigible.

demand'ant, _n._, (jur.) demandeur, _m._, demanderesse, _f._

demand'er, _n._, demandeur, personne qui demande, _f._

demarca'tion (dî-mar-ké-), _n._, démarcation, _f._

demean' (di-mîne), _v.a._, abaisser, avilir, dégrader; conduire; traiter. To — one's self; _s'abaisser_ jusqu'à, _s'avilir_, _se dégrader_, _se ravaler_; _se comporter_, _se conduire._

demea'nor (di-mî'n'eur), _n._, conduite, _f._; maintien, _m._; tenue, allure, _f._

demen'tate, _adj._, fou, en démence.

demen'tate, _v.a._, rendre fou, aliéner.

demen'ted, _adj._, fou, insensé.

demer'it, _n._, démérite, _m._

demer'it, _v.a._, (ant.) démériter.

demerito'rious (-), _adj._, déméritoire.

dem'i (dèm'i), _adj._, demi, à demi.

dem'i-deify (-dî-i-faïe), _v.a._, déifier à demi.

dem'i-devil (-dèv'l), _n._, demi-démon, _m._

dem'i-ditone (-daï-tône), _n._, (mus.) tierce mineure; petite tierce, _f._

dem'i-god, _n._, demi-dieu, _m._

dem'i-john (-djone), _n._, dame-jeanne, _f._

dem'i-lance, _n._, demi-pique, _f._

dem'i-lune (-lioune), _n._, (fort.) demi-lune, _f._

dem'i-quaver (-kwé-), _n._, (mus.) double croche, _f._

dem'i-rep (-rèpe), _n._, (ant.) demi-vertu, _f._

demi'sable (di-maïz'a-b'l), _adj._, (jur.) qui peut être affermé; affermable.

demise' (dî-maïze), _n._, décès, _m._; mort; (jur.) translation, _ou_ transmission, de propriété, _f._

demise', _v.a._, affermer, donner à ferme _ou_ à bail, louer; léguer; (jur.) faire transport de.

dem'i-semi'-quaver, _n._, triple croche, _f._

demis'ing, _n._, affermage, _m._

demis'sion (dî-mish'eune), _n._, relâchement, _m._; dégradation, démission, _f._

dem'i-tone (-tone), _n._, demi-ton, _m._

dem'i-wolf (-woulfe), _n._, chien métis _ou_ chien-loup, _m._

demobiliza'tion, _n._, démobilisation, _f._

demob'ilize, _v.a._, démobiliser.

democ'racy, _n._, démocratie, _f._

dem'ocrat, _n._, démocrate, _m._

democrat'ic _ou_ democrat'ical, _adj._, démocratique.

democrat'ically, _adv._, démocratiquement.

demol'ish (di-), _v.a._, démolir.

demol'isher, _n._, démolisseur.

demoli'tion (-lish'eune), _n._, démolition, _f._

de'mon (dî-), _n._, démon, diable, _m._

demo'niac, _n._, démoniaque, _m._ _f._

demo'niac (-mô-) _ou_ demoniacal (dèm'o-naï'a-), _adj._, démoniaque.

demo'nian (-mô-), _adj._, démoniaque.

demonol'ogy (-dji), _n._, démonographie, _f._

demon'strable (di-mo'n'stra-b'l), _adj._, démontrable.

demon'strably, _adv._, par la démonstration; démonstrativement.

dem'onstrate, _v.a._, démontrer.

demonstra'tion (-stré-), _n._, démonstration, _f._

demon'strative (-stra-), _adj._, démonstratif; qui montre clairement.

demon'stratively, _adv._, démonstrativement.

dem'onstrator (-stra-teur _ou_ -stré-), _n._, démonstrateur, _m._

demon'stratory, _adj._, qui tend à démontrer.

demoraliza'tion (di-mor-al-i-zé-), _n._, démoralisation, _f._

demor'alize (-aïze), _v.a._, démoraliser.

demul'cent (di-meul-), _adj._, adoucissant, émollient.

demur' (di-meur), _n._, hésitation, objection, incertitude; difficulté, _f._; doute, _m._

demur', _v.n._, hésiter; balancer; temporiser; (jur.) opposer une exception péremptoire. To — to; _objecter_, _faire objection_ à, _s'opposer_ à; _se refuser_ à; _ne pas admettre._

demure' (di-mioure), _adj._, réservé, posé, grave, modeste; (b.s.) prude, d'une modestie affectée.

demure'ly, _adv._, gravement, modestement; (b.s.) avec une modestie affectée.

demure'ness, _n._, gravité, modestie; (b.s.) pruderie, modestie affectée, _f._

demur'rage (di-meur'rédge), _n._, (com. nav.) indemnité pour détention de marchandises, pour surestarie, _f._

demur'rer (di-meur-'), _n._, personne qui hésite, qui balance, _f._; temporiseur, _m._; (jur.) exception péremptoire, _f._

demy' (di-maïe), _n._, (of paper) coquille, _f._, papier carré, _m._; (of a book) petit format; (at Oxford) boursier, _m._

demy'ship, _n._, bourse, _f._

den (dène), _n._, antre, repaire, _m._; tanière (menageries); loge, _f._; bouge, taudis, _m._

den'ary (dè'n'-), _adj._, décimal; (l.u.) dénaire.

dena'tionalize (di-nash'eu'n'al-aïze), _v.a._, dénationaliser.

den'droid (dè'n'droïd), _adj._, (bot.) dendroïde, arborescent.

deni'able (di-naï-a-'l), _adj._, niable.

deni'al (di-naï-al), refus, déni, _m._, _f._; dénégation, _f._; (of St. Peter) reniement, reniment, _m._ Flat —; _démenti_; _refus net_, _m._; _dénégation formelle_, _f._

deni'er (di-naï'eur), _n._, personne qui nie, _f._

den'igrate (dè'n'i-), _v.a._, noircir; calomnier; dénigrer.

denigra'tion (-'gré-), _n._, dénigrement, _m._; calomnie, médisance, _f._

deniza'tion (dè'n'i-zé-), _n._, petite naturalisation, _f._; droit de cité, _m._

den'izen (dè'n'i-z'n) _ou_ den'ison (dé'n'i-z'n), _n._, (English jur.) étranger qui a obtenu les petites lettres de naturalisation en Angleterre; citoyen, habitant, _m._

den'izen, _v.a._, donner droit de cité à.

denom'inate (di-), _v.a._, nommer, appeler; désigner sous le nom de.

denomina'tion (-né-), n., dénomination, f.; nom, m.

denom'inative, adj., dénominatif.

denom'inator (-né-teur), n., dénominateur, m.

denota'tion (dî'n'o-té-), n., dénotation, f.

denote' (di-nôte), v.a., dénoter, marquer, moutrer, indiquer, démontrer.

denounce' (di-naou'n'ce), v.a., dénoncer ; déclarer.

denounce'ment, n., dénonciation, déclaration, f.

denoun'cer, n., dénonciateur, m., dénonciatrice, f.

dense (dè'n'se), adj., dense ; épais, compact.

densely, adv., en masse ; à l'excès, par une foule compacte.

den'sity, n., densité, épaisseur, f.

dent (dè'n'te), n., creux, m., coche, bosse, entaille, f.

dent, v.a., denteler, bossuer ; faire une coche, des coches, une entaille ; marquer.

dent'al (dè'n-), adj., dentaire, dental, des dents ; (gram.) dental.

dent'al, n., (gram.) dentale, f.; (conch.) dentale, m. — surgeon ; chirurgien dentiste, m.

den'tate (dè'n'-) ou **den'tated** (-'ède), adj., (bot.) denté, dentelé.

den'ticle (dè'n'-ti-k'l), n., (arch.) denticules, m.pl.

denticu'ulate (dè'n'tik'iou-) ou **dentic'ulated** (-ède), adj., (arch.) dentelé ; (bot.) denticulé.

denticula'tion, n., dentelure, f.

den'tifrice, n., dentifrice, m.

den'til (dè'n'-) ou **den'tel** (dè'n'-), n., (arch.) modillon, m.

den'tist, n., dentiste, m.

den'tistry, n., art du dentiste, m.; dentisterie, f.

denti'tion, n., dentition, f.

denu'date (di-niou-) ou **denude'** (di-nioude), v.a., dénuder, dénuer, dépouiller, dégarnir.

denuda'tion (-dé-), n., dénudation, f.

denuncia'tion (di-neu'n'shi-), n., dénonciation, f.

denun'ciator (-é-teur), n., dénonciateur, m., dénonciatrice, f.

deny' (di-naïe), v.a., nier, démentir, (jur.) dénier ; renier ; refuser ; rejeter ; renoncer à. — one's self ; faire abnégation de soi-même ; faire dire qu'on n'est pas chez soi, faire défendre sa porte à; se refuser quelque chose. To — anything to any one ; refuser quelque chose à quelqu'un. Not to be denied ; incontestable. He is not to be denied ; il le veut à tout prix ; rien ne peut le retenir, le repousser, l'arrêter.

deobstruct' (dî-ob-streucte), v.a., dégager, débarrasser, nettoyer ; désobstruer.

deob'struent (di-ob-strou'-), adj., désobstruant, désobstructif.

deodoriza'tion, n., désinfection, f.

deo'dorize, v.a., désinfecter.

deo'dorizer, n., désinfectant, désinfecteur.

deo'dorizing, adj., désinfectant, désinfecteur. n., désinfection.

deop'pilate (di-), v.a., désopiler, désobstruer.

deox'idate (di-), v.a., désoxyder.

deoxidiza'tion (-'aïzé-), n., désoxydation, f.

deox'idize (-daïze), v.a., désoxyder.

deox'ygenate (di-oks'i-djè'n'-), v.a., désoxygéner.

deoxygena'tion, n., désoxygénation, f.

depart', v.n., partir ; sortir ; s'éloigner ; (fig.) se départir de, se désister de, renoncer à ; s'évanouir ; mourir. To — from ; s'écarter de.

depart', v.a., quitter. To — this life ; mourir ; quitter ce monde.

depart'ment, n., département, service, m. ; partie, f.; rayon, m. Manager of a —; (com.) chef de service ; chef de rayon, m. Intelligence —; service des renseignements, m.

depart'ure (-ioure), n., départ ; éloignement ; désistement, écart, m. ; déviation, séparation, mort, f.; trépas, m.

depend' (di-), v.n., pendre ; dépendre de; reposer sur ; demeurer dans la dépendance de. To — on ; dépendre de, se fier à, compter sur, se reposer sur. — upon it; soyez en sûr, comptez y bien, comptez là-dessus, croyez le bien.

depend'able (-'a-b'l), adj., sur lequel on peut compter.

depend'ance, n. V. **dependence**.

depend'ant ou **depend'ent**, adj., dépendant ; pendant, qui pend.

depend'ant ou **depend'ent**, n., personne dépendante, f.; subordonné, m. To be — on ; dépendre de.

depend'antly ou **depend'ently**, adv., dépendamment.

depend'ence ou **depend'ency**, n., dépendance ; confiance, f. Foreign —; possession à l'étranger, colonie, f. No — can be placed on what he says ; il est impossible de se fier à ce qu'il dit ; on ne saurait compter sur lui.

depend'er, n., personne dépendante, f.

dephlegm' (di-flème), v.a., (ant.) déflegmer.

dephlegma'tion (di-flè'm'é-), n., déflegmation, f.

depict' (di-), v.a., peindre, dépeindre, décrire.

dep'ilate (dèp'-), v.a., (med.) épiler.

depila'tion (-lé-), (med.) n., épilation, dépilation, f.

depil'atory (-tori), adj., dépilatif ; dépilatoire, épilatoire.

depil'atory, n., dépilatoire, m.

deplor'able (di-plô-ra-b'l), adj., déplorable, pitoyable.

deplor'ableness, n., état déplorable, m.

deplor'ably, adv., déplorablement ; pitoyablement.

deplore' (di-plôre), v.a., déplorer, lamenter.

deplor'er, n., personne qui déplore, f.

deploy' (di-ploïe), v.a., (milit.) déployer. v.n., (milit.) se déployer. In —ing distance ; à intervalle de déploiement.

deploy'ing ou **deploy'ment**, n., déploiement, f.

depluma'tion (di-plou-mé-), n., action de plumer, f.

deplume' (di-ploume), v.a., plumer, déplumer.

depon'ent (di-pô-), n., (jur.) déposant ; (gram.) déponent, m.

depop'ulate (di-pop'iou-), v.a., dépeupler.

depop'ulate, v.n., (ant.) se dépeupler.

depopula'tion (-lé-), n., dépeuplement, m. ; dépopulation, f.

depop'ulator (-teur), n., personne qui dépeuple, destructeur, m.

deport', v.a., déporter. To — one's self ; se comporter ; se conduire.

deporta'tion (dî-por-té-), n., déportation, f.

deport'ment (di-pôrt'-), n., maintien, air, m. ; tenue ; conduite, f., manières, f.pl.

depos'al (di-pô-zal), n., déposition, destitution, f.

depose' (di-pôze), v.a. and n., déposer (from) de. To — to a fact ; déposer sur ou de.

depos'er, n., qui dépose, qui prive d'une dignité, f.

depos'it (di-poz'ite), n., dépôt, versement, m. ; arrhes, f.pl. To leave a —; déposer des arrhes. — account ; compte de dépôt, m.

depos'it, v.a., déposer, mettre bas.

depos'itary (di-poz'-), n., dépositaire, m.

deposi'tion (dèp'o-zish'eune), n., déposition, f. ; dépôt, m.

depos'itor (-'eur), n., (at a bank) déposant, m., déposante, f. ; (com.) dépositeur, m., dépositrice, f.

depos'itory (-tori), n., dépôt, (pers.) dépositaire ; (book) répertoire, m.

de'pot (dé-pô), *n.*, dépôt, *m.*

deprava'tion (dèp-ré-vé-), *n.*, dépravation, *f.*

deprave' (di-), *v.a.*, dépraver, corrompre.

depraved' (di-prév'dé), *adj.*, dépravé, corrompu. To become —; *se dépraver, se corrompre.*

deprav'edly (-'èd'-), *adv.*, d'une manière dépravée.

deprav'edness (-'èd'-), *n.*, corruption, dépravation, *f.*

deprave'ment, *n.*, (ant.) dépravation, *f.*

depra'ver, *n.*, corrupteur, *m.*; corruptrice, *f.*

deprav'ity (di-prav'-), *n.*, dépravation, *f.*

dep'recate (dèp'ri-kéte), *v.a.*, détourner par la prière; conjurer; repousser; désapprouver; regretter; s'opposer à. I strongly — his interfering; *je m'oppose fortement à ce qu'il intervienne.*

dep'recatingly, *adv.*, en suppliant, en s'excusant.

depreca'tion, *n.*, déprécation, supplication, excuse, *f.*

dep'recative *ou* **dep'recatory** (-tori), *adj.*, de déprécation, de supplication, suppliant, d'excuse.

depre'ciate (di-prî-shi-), *v.a.*, déprécier.

depre'ciate, *v.n.*, se déprécier, tomber, perdre sa valeur.

deprecia'tion, *n.*, dépréciation, *f.*

depre'ciator (-teur), *n.*, dépréciateur, *m.*

dep'redate (dèp'ri-), *v.a.*, piller, saccager, ravager, détruire.

dep'redate, *v.n.*, commettre des déprédations.

depreda'tion (-dé-), *n.*, déprédation, destruction, *f.*; ravage, *m.*

dep'redator (-teur), *n.*, pillard, déprédateur, *m.*

depress' (di-prèce), *v.a.*, baisser; abaisser; abattre, accabler, ruiner; déprimer; décourager; (to sink) incliner; (to flatten) aplatir; humilier; faire languir; (of prices) faire baisser.

depressed', abattu, (low) bas; (flat) aplati; (hollow) creux.

depres'sion (-prèsh'eune), *n.*, abaissement; affaissement, aplatissement; (fig.) abattement, *m.*; (surg.) dépression, *f.*

depres'sor (dè-prèss'eur), *n.*, oppresseur; (anat.) abaisseur, *m.*

depriva'tion (dèp'raïv'é-), *n.*, privation; perte, *f.*

deprive' (dè-praïve), *v.a.*, priver **de**; dépouiller **de**; (fig.) révoquer, interdire à.

depth (dèp'th), *n.*, profondeur; hauteur, *f.*; (recess) enfoncement; (of the seasons) fort, cœur; (of the night) milieu; (print.) (of the letters) corps, *m.*; (math.) hauteur, épaisseur, *f.*; (nav.) (of the hold) creux, *m.*; (of a sail) chute, *f.* — of winter; *cœur de l'hiver, m.* To go beyond one's —; *perdre pied;* (fig.) *parler sans connaissance de cause, ou de ce qu'on ignore.* To be in one's —; *avoir pied.* To get in one's —; *prendre fond.*

depth'less, *adj.*, sans profondeur.

dep'urate (dèp'iou-), *v.a.*, (ant.) dépurer.

dep'urate, *adj.*, dépuré.

depura'tion (-ré-), *n.*, (med.) dépuration, *f.*

dep'uratory (-tori), *adj.*, (med.) dépuratoire.

deputa'tion (dèp'iou-té-), *n.*, députation, délégation, *f.*

depute' (di-pioute), *v.a.*, députer; déléguer.

dep'uty, *n.*, député, délégué, adjoint, *m.* — governor; *lieutenant-gouverneur, m.* —chairman; *vice-président, m.* —mayor; *adjoint au maire, adjoint, m.* —manager; *sous-directeur, m.* — judge; *juge suppléant, m.*

derac'inate, *v.a.*, (l.u.) déraciner.

derange' (di-ré'n'dje), *v.a.*, déranger; désorganiser; troubler l'esprit **de**. To be —d; *avoir le cerveau dérangé; être fou.*

derange'ment, *n.*, dérangement; trouble, *m.*; aliénation mentale, folie, *f.*

der'elict (dèr'i-), *adj.*, délaissé, abandonné. — ship; *vaisseau abandonné, m.*

der'elict, *n.*, (jur.) objet abandonné, *m.*; épave, *f.*

derelic'tion, *n.*, abandon, *m.*

deride' (di-raïde), *v.a.*, tourner en dérision; railler; se moquer **de**, se rire **de**.

deri'der, *n.*, moqueur, *m.*; moqueuse, *f.*; railleur, *m.*, railleuse, *f.*

deri'dingly, *adv.*, par dérision.

deri'sion (di-rij'eune), *n.*, dérision, moquerie, *f.*; objet de dérision, *m.*

deri'sive (di-raï-cive), *adj.*, dérisoire.

deri'sively, *adv.*, par dérision.

deri'sory (di-rai-sori), *adj.*, dérisoire.

deri'vable (di-raïv'a-b'l), *adj.*, dérivable; qui dérive, qui peut dériver; à puiser; qu'on peut tenir **de**.

deriva'tion (dèr-i-vé-), *n.*, dérivation; origine, *f.*

deriv'ative (di-riv'-), *adj.*, dérivé; (med.) dérivatif.

deriv'ative, *n.*, (gram.) dérivé; (mus.) accord dérivé; (med.) dérivatif, *m.*

deriv'atively, *adv.*, par dérivation.

derive' (di-raïve), *v.a.*, (water) faire dériver; dériver **de**; (gram.) faire dériver; (fig.) recueillir, retirer, tirer **de**.

derive', *v.n.*, venir **de**, provenir **de**.

derm, **der'ma**, *ou* **der'mis** (deurm'-), *n.*, (anat.) derme, *m.*

dern'ier (deur-ni-eur), *adj.*, (jur.) dernier.

der'ogate (dèr-o-ghéte), *v.a.*, dénigrer, déprécier; (jur.) déroger à.

der'ogate, *v.n.*, dégénérer; se dégrader. To — from; *déroger à; porter atteinte à.*

der'ogated (-ède), *part.*, diminué de valeur; dégradé, endommagé.

deroga'tion (-ghé-), *n.*, dérogation, *f.*; détriment, *m.*; atteinte, *f.*

derog'atory, *adj.*, dérogatoire, qui porte atteinte à, dérogeant à.

derog'ative, *adj.*, dérogatoire, indigne.

der'rick, *n.*, (nav.) martinet, *m.* — boom; mât de charge, *m.* To rig a —; *pousser une vergue en bataille.*

der'vis (deur-) *ou* **der'vise** (-vaïze), *n.*, dervis, derviche, *m.*

des'cant (dès'-), *n.*, chant, air, morceau d'ensemble; discours, *m.*; dissertation, *f.*

des'cant, *v.n.*, discourir de ou sur; s'étendre sur. To — on; *commenter sur; s'appesantir sur.*

descend' (di-), *v.a.* and *n.*, descendre, tomber. To — upon; *tomber sur;* (of inheritance) passer à; (to lower one's self) s'abaisser jusqu'à ou à. To be — ed from; *descendre de, tirer son origine de.*

descend'ant, *n.*, descendant, *m.*, descendante, *f.*

descend'ent, *adj.*, descendant, issu **de**; qui descend, provenant **de**.

descen'sion (di-cè'n'sheune), *n.*, descente, *f.*, (fig.) abaissement, *m.*; chute, *f.*

descent' (di'-), *n.*, descente; chute; descendance, postérité, *f.*; (of lineage) naissance, origine, souche; (of pistons) descente, *f.*

descri'bable, *adj.*, descriptible.

describe' (di-scraïbe), *v.a.*, décrire, dépeindre, peindre.

descri'ber, *n.*, auteur d'une description, (st. e.) peintre, descripteur, *m.*

descri'er (di-scraï-), *n.*, personne qui découvre, *f.*

descrip'tion (di-scrip'-), *n.*, description, *f.*; (of a person) signalement, *m.*; qualité, sorte, espèce, *f.*; genre, *m.*

descry', *v.a.*, découvrir, apercevoir; explorer, reconnaître.

des'ecrate (dèss'i-), *v.a.*, profaner.

desecra'tion (-cré-), *n.*, profanation, *f.*

desert' (di-zeurte), *n.*, mérite, *m. ;* mérites, *m.pl. ; désert, m. ; solitude, f.*

des'ert (dèz'eurte), *adj.*, désert, solitaire.

desert' (di-zeurte), *v.a.*, abandonner ; déserter, quitter.

desert' (di-zeurte), *v.n.*, (mil.) déserter.

desert'er (di-zeurt'-), *n.*, déserteur ; transfuge, *m.*

deser'tion (di-zeur-), *n.*, désertion, *f.*, abandon, *m.*

deserve' (di-zeurve), *v.a.* and *v.n.*, mériter.

deserv'edly (-ède-), *adv.*, à bon droit, justement, à juste titre.

deser'ver, *n.*, personne méritante, *f.*

deserv'ing, *adj.*, de mérite ; méritant.

deshabille' (dèss'a-bile), *n.*, déshabillé, *m.*

desic'cant (di-cik'-), *adj.*, dessiccatif, siccatif.

desic'cant, *n.*, dessiccatif, siccatif, *m.*

des'iccate (di-cik'-), *v.a.*, sécher, dessécher.

des'iccate, *v.n.*, sécher, se dessécher.

desicca'tion ('ké-), *n.*, dessiccation, *f.*

desic'cative (di-cik'-), *adj.*, dessiccatif, siccatif.

desic'cative, *n.*, dessiccatif, siccatif, *m.*

desidera'tum (di-cid'eur'é-teume), *n.*, chose à désirer, lacune, *f. ;* desideratum, *m.*

design' (di-çaïne *ou* -zaïne), *n.*, dessein, projet ; (drawing) dessin, *m.*, (manu.) modèle, *m.* By — ; *à dessein.* To have —s upon ; (of things) *convoiter, rechercher, aspirer à posséder ;* (of persons) *avoir des desseins* **sur**.

design', *v.a.*, dessiner ; destiner à ; désigner ; avoir le dessein **de**, projeter, concevoir ; se proposer **de**.

design'able (di-çaï'n'ab'l), *adj.*, que l'on peut désigner.

des'ignate (dèss'ig-néte), *v.a.*, désigner ; nommer. *adj.*, désigné, nommé.

designa'tion (dèss'ig-né-), *n.*, désignation, (Scotch jur.) destination, *f.*

design'edly (di-çaï'n'èd-), *adv.*, à dessein, avec intention, de propos délibéré.

design'er (di-çaï'n'eur), *n.*, dessinateur ; inventeur ; (b.s.) machinateur, intrigant, *m.*

design'ing (di-çaï'n'-), *adj.*, artificieux, intrigant.

design'less (di-çaï'n-), *adj.*, sans dessein.

design'lessly, *adv.*, par inadvertance, sans dessein.

desir'able (di-zaïeur'a-b'l), *adj.*, désirable, à désirer, à souhaiter, agréable.

desir'ableness, *n.*, caractère désirable, avantage, *m.*

desir'ably, *adv.*, désirablement, avantageusement.

desire' (di-zaïeur), *n.*, désir, *m.*, envie, prière, demande, *f.* By — ; *sur demande ; à la demande* **de**.

desire' (di-zaïeur), *v.a.*, désirer ; souhaiter ; prier ; ordonner à, charger **de**.

desire'less, *adj.*, exempt de désirs.

desir'er, *n.*, personne qui désire, *f.*

desir'ous (di-zaïeur'-), *adj.*, qui désire ; désireux **de**, empressé **de**. To be — of ; *avoir le désir* **de** ; *avoir envie* **de** ; *être empressé* **de**.

desist' (di-ciste), *v.n.*, se désister **de** ; cesser **de** ; renoncer **à**, abandonner.

desist'ance (di-ci'st'-), *n.*, désistement, abandon, refus, *m.*

desk (dèske), *n.*, pupitre, bureau, *m. ;* (in a church or school) chaire, *f. ;* (for music or lectern) lutrin, *m.*

des'olate (dèss'o-), *adj.*, désolé, isolé, inhabité, solitaire, dévasté.

des'olate, *v.a.*, désoler ; dévaster, ravager ; dépeupler.

des'olately, *adv.*, d'une manière désolée.

desola'tion (-lé-), *n.*, désolation, *f.* Abomination of — ; (script.) *l'abomination de la désolation, f.*

des'olator, *n.*, désolateur, *m.*, -trice, *f.*

despair' (di-spère), *n.*, désespoir, *m.* In — ; *au désespoir.*

despair', *v.n.*, désespérer **de**, se désespérer. His life is despaired of ; *on désespère de le sauver.*

despair'er, *n.*, désespéré, personne au désespoir, *f.*

despair'ingly, *adv.*, d'une manière désespérante ; sans espoir, avec désespoir.

despatch' (di-) *ou* **dispatch'**, *n.*, dépêche, *f. ;* envoi, *m. ;* promptitude, expédition, diligence, *f.* — boat ; *aviso, m.* To use all — ; *user de diligence.*

despatch' *ou* **dispatch'**, *v.a.*, dépêcher, envoyer ; expédier, exécuter.

despatch'ful *ou* **dis-**, *adj.*, expéditif, prompt.

despera'do (dès-peu-ré-dô), *n.*, énergumène ; homme dangereux, enragé, forcené, *m.*

des'perate (dès-peur-), *adj.*, désespéré, désespérant ; dont on désespère ; furieux, forcené ; à outrance, acharné, terrible. — fight ; *combat acharné, m.*

des'perately, *adv.*, en désespéré ; (l.u.) désespérément ; d'une manière désespérée ; terriblement, excessivement, éperdument.

des'perateness, *n.*, fureur, furie, *f.*, acharnement, *m.*

despera'tion (-ré-), *n.*, désespoir, *m. ;* fureur, exaspération, *f.*, acharnement, *m.*

des'picable (dès-pi-ca-b'l), *adj.*, méprisable.

des'picableness, *n.*, caractère méprisable, *m. ;* bassesse, *f.*

des'picably, *adv.*, bassement, d'une manière méprisable.

despi'sable (di-spaïz'a-b'l), *adj.*, méprisable.

despise' (di-spaïze), *v.a.*, mépriser, dédaigner.

despi'sedness (di-spaïz'èd-), *n.*, avilissement, *m.*

despi'ser (di-spaïz'-), *n.*, contempteur, *m.*

despi'sing, *n.*, mépris, dédain, *m.*

despi'singly, *adv.*, avec mépris.

despite' (di-spaïte), *n.*, dépit, *m. ;* haine, *f.*

despite', *v.a.*, dépiter.

despite', *prep.*, en dépit **de**, malgré.

despite'ful (-foule), *adj.*, qui a du dépit.

despite'fully, *adv.*, avec dépit.

despite'fulness, *n.*, dépit, *m.*

despoil' (di-spoïl), *v.a.*, dépouiller.

despoil'er, *n.*, spoliateur, *m.*, spoliatrice, *f.*

despolia'tion (di-spo-li-é-), *n.*, spoliation, *f.*

despond' (di-spo'n'de), *v.n.*, se décourager ; être abattu, se laisser abattre ; désespérer **de**.

despon'dency, *n.*, abattement, *m.*, désespoir, découragement, *m.*

despon'dent, *adj.*, découragé, abattu, désespéré.

despon'dently, *adv.*, dans l'abattement ; avec désespoir.

des'pot, *n.*, despote, tyran, *m.*

despot'ic *ou* **despot'ical** (dès'-), *adj.*, despotique.

despot'ically, *adv.*, despotiquement ; en despote.

des'potism (-'iz'm), *n.*, despotisme, *m.*

desquama'tion (dès'kwa-mé-), *n.*, desquamation, *f.*

dessert' (dèz'zeurte), *n.*, dessert, *m.* At — ; *au dessert. adj.*, de dessert. — apple, pear ; *pomme, poire, à couteau,* ou *à dessert, f.* — knife, plate ; *couteau, m.*, assiette, *f.*, à dessert. — wine ; *vin de dessert, m.* — spoon and fork ; *couvert à dessert, m.*

destina'tion (-né-), *n.*, destination, *f.*

des'tine (dès-tine), *v.a.*, destiner à, désigner, marquer, fixer, indiquer.

des'tiny, *n.*, destin, *m. ;* destinée, *f.*

des'titute (dès-ti-tioute), *adj.*, dépourvu **de**, destitué **de** ; privé **de** ; dénué **de** ; dans le dénûment, dans la misère, abandonné, délaissé.

destitu'tion (-ti-tiou-), *n.*, dénuement, dénûment, délaissement, abandon, *m. ;* privation, *f.*

destroy' (di-stroïe), *v.a.*, détruire, exterminer, ruiner, perdre ; gâter, abîmer.

destroy'er, *n.*, destructeur, *m.*

destroy'ing, *adj.*, destructeur, destructif, *n.*, destruction, *f.*

destructibil'ity (di-streuct'-), *n.*, destructibilité, *f.*

destruc'tible (di-streuct'i-b'l), *adj.*, destructible.

destruc'tion, *n.*, destruction, *f. ;* meurtre, massacre, carnage, *m. ;* (fig.) perte, ruine, perdition, *f.*

destruc'tive, *adj.*, destructeur, destructif, funeste, mortel, fatal. — distillation ; (chem.) *distillation sèche, f.*

destruc'tively, *adv.*, d'une manière destructive.

destruc'tiveness, *n.*, caractère, *ou* pouvoir, destructeur, *m.*, nature destructive, *f.*

des'uetude (déss'-wi-tioude), *n.*, désuétude, *f.*

des'ultorily (dèss'-eul-tori-), *adv.*, par sauts et par bonds ; à bâtons rompus, sans suite, d'une manière décousue.

des'ultoriness, *n.*, défaut de liaison ; défaut de méthode ; manque d'esprit de suite, *m.*

des'ultory (dèss-eul-tori), *adj.*, (of work) par sauts et par bonds ; à bâtons rompus ; décousu ; sans suite ; changeant, irrégulier. In a — manner ; *sans méthode, sans suite.*

detach' (di-tatshe), *v.a.*, détacher, isoler, séparer. To become —ed ; *se détacher.*

detached', *adj.*, détaché, isolé ; (of houses) entre cour et jardin.

detach'ment, *n.*, action de détacher, *f. ;* détachement, *m.*

detail' (di-téle), *n.*, détail, *m.* In —; *minutieusement, en détail.*

detail', *v.a.*, détailler.

detail'er, *n.*, narrateur de détails, (liter.) détailliste, *m.*

detain' (di-téne), *v.a.*, retenir ; tenir ; détenir, arrêter, empêcher.

detain'er, *n.*, personne qui retient ; détenteur, *m. ;* détention, *f.* Writ of — ; (jur.) *mandat d'arrestation provisoire, m.* Forcible — ; (jur.) *usurpation ou prise de possession par violence, f.*

detect' (di-tècte), *v.a.*, découvrir ; surprendre.

detect'er, *n.*, personne qui découvre, *f. ;* dénonciateur, révélateur, *m.*

detec'tion, *n.*, découverte, *f.*

detec'tive, *n.*, agent, espion de la police criminelle, la police secrète, *m. ;* agent de sûreté, mouchard, flic, argousin, *m.*

detent' (di-), *n.*, (horl.) détente, *f.*

deten'tion (di-), *n.*, action de retenir, *f. ;* retard, *m. ;* (jur.) détention, *f. ;* (delay) retard, *m.*

deter' (di-teur), *v.a.*, détourner de ; empêcher de ; retenir ; arrêter ; effrayer, décourager.

deterge' (di-teurdje), *v.a.*, déterger.

deter'gent, *adj.*, détergent, détersif.

deter'gent, *n.*, détersif, *m.*

dete'riorate (di-tî-), *v.a.*, détériorer ; faire dégénérer.

dete'riorate, *v.n.*, (of things) se détériorer ; (pers.) dégénérer.

deteriora'tion (-rio-ré-), *n.*, (of things) détérioration ; (pers.) dégénération, *f.*

deter'minable (di-teur-mi-na-b'l), *adj.*, déterminable.

deter'minate (di-teur-), *adj.*, déterminé, établi, réglé, arrêté, décidé ; définitif, décisif, fixé ; (pers.) résolu.

deter'minately, *adv.*, déterminément, résolument.

determina'tion (-né-), *n.*, détermination ; décision ; résolution ; direction, (jur.) fin, expiration, *f.*

deter'minative, *adj.*, déterminatif ; déterminant.

deter'mine (di-teur-mine), *v.a.*, déterminer, décider, régler.

deter'mine, *v.n.*, se déterminer ; se décider ; résoudre ; finir, expirer, se terminer.

deter'mined (-mi'n'de), *adj.*, déterminé.

deter'minedly (-mi'n'dli), *adv.*, déterminément.

deter'sion (di-teur-), *n.*, détersion, *f.*

deter'sive (di-teur-), *adj.*, détersif.

deter'sive, *n.*, détersif, *m.*

detest' (di-tèste), *v.a.*, détester, abhorrer.

detest'able, *adj.*, détestable ; abominable, odieux, atroce.

detest'ably, *adv.*, détestablement, abominablement.

detesta'tion (-ès-té-), *n.*, détestation, exécration, *f.* To hold in — ; *avoir en horreur, exécrer.*

detest'er, *n.*, personne qui déteste, ennemi juré, *f.*

dethrone' (di-thrône), *v.a.*, détrôner.

dethrone'ment, *n.*, détrônement, *m.*

dethro'ner, *n.*, personne qui détrône, *f. ;* détrôneur (Voltaire).

det'onate (dèt-o-), *v.n.*, détoner, fulminer.

det'onate, *v.a.*, faire détoner.

det'onating, *n.*, détonation, *f. adj.*, à détonation, fulminant. Detonating powder ; *poudre fulminante, f.*

detona'tion (dèto-né-), *n.*, détonation, fulmination, *f.*

detour' (dé-tour), *n.*, détour, *m. ;*

detract' (di-tracte), *v.a.* and *n.*, enlever à ; diminuer de, ôter à ; dénigrer, rabattre.

detract'er, *n.*, détracteur, *m.*

detract'ingly, *adv.*, par détraction, par dénigrement.

detrac'tion (di-trac-), *n.*, action d'enlever ; détraction, *f. ;* dénigrement, *m.*

detrac'tive, *adj.*, détracteur.

detrac'tory (-'eur-), *adj.*, dérogatoire ; détracteur.

detrac'tress, *n.*, médisante, *f.*

det'riment, *n.*, détriment ; préjudice ; dommage, *m.*

detrimen'tal, *adj.*, préjudiciable à, nuisible à, *n.*, (fig.) valet de cœur, *m.*

detrimen'tally, *adv.*, d'une manière préjudiciable.

detri'tus (di-traï-), *n.*, (geol.) détritus, débris, *m.*

detrude' (di-troude), *v.a.*, précipiter, repousser ; refouler ; chasser, reléguer.

detrun'cate (di-treu'gn-), *v.a.*, tronquer, écourter, couper.

detrunca'tion, *n.*, coupe ; mutilation, *f.*

deuce (diouce), *n.*, deux, *m.*

deuce *ou* **deuse** (diouce), *n.*, (l. ex.) diable ; diantre, *m.* The —! *diantre! diable!* The — is in it ; *le diable s'en mêle ;* (at play) deux. Double — ; *double deux.*

Deuteron'omy (diou-teur'-), *n.*, Deutéronome, *m.*

dev'astate (dèv'as-), *v.a.*, dévaster.

dev'astating, *adj.*, dévastateur.

devasta'tion, *n.*, dévastation, *f.*

devel'op (di-vèl'-), *v.a.*, développer.

devel'opment, *n.*, développement, *m. ;* exposition, *f.* — theory ; *théorie de l'évolution, du transformisme, f.* — of doctrine ; (theol.) *évolution du dogme, f.*

devest' (di-vèste), *v.a.*, (jur.) désinvestir de.

devex'ity (di-vèks'-), *n.*, courbure, inclinaison, *f.*

de'viate (di-vî-), *v.n.*, dévier de, se dévier ; s'égarer, s'écarter de.

devia'tion, *n.*, déviation, *f. ;* égarement, écart, *m.*

device' (di-vaïce), *n.*, devise, *f. ;* dessein,

plan, projet ; artifice, moyen, stratagème, *m.* ; invention, *f.*

dev'il (dèv'l), *n.,* diable, démon, *m.* She—; *diablesse, f.* The —! *ah diable !* How, *ou* what, the —; *que diable.* The — take ; *(que) le diable emporte.* The — is in him ; *il a le diable au corps.* The — on two sticks ; *le diable boiteux.* There is the — to pay ; *c'est le diable à confesser.* Dare—; *téméraire, audacieux.* — may care ; *imprudent, téméraire, insouciant.* To give the — his due ; *rendre justice au diable.* To play the very —; *faire le diable à quatre.* Talk of the — and you 're sure to see his horns ; *quand on parle du loup, on en voit la queue.* —*fish ; poulpe, m., pieuvre* (V. Hugo), *f.*

dev'ilet *ou* **dev'iling,** *n.* V. **dev'ilkin.**

dev'ilish (dèv'l-ishe), *adj.,* maudit, diabolique, satané.

dev'ilishly, *adv.,* diaboliquement, diablement, en diable.

dev'ilishness, *n.,* caractère diabolique, *m.*

dev'ilkin (dèv'l-), **dev'ilet** (dèv'lète) *ou* **dev'iling** (dèv'l-), *n.,* diablotin, *m.*

de'vious (di-vi-), *adj.,* détourné, écarté ; (fig.) errant, vagabond, faux. — course ; *fausse direction.*

de'viously, *adv.,* en déviant ; d'une manière détournée ; (fig.) à tort.

devi'sable (di-vaïz'-a-b'l), *adj.,* imaginable ; (jur.) (of property) disponible.

devise' (di-vaize), *n.,* disposition testamentaire, *f.,* legs, *m.*

devise', *v.a.,* projeter ; imaginer, inventer ; chercher, songer à ; tramer ; machiner ; (jur.) disposer par testament **de** ; léguer **à.**

devise', *v.n.,* projeter.

devisee' (dèv-i-zî), *n.,* (jur.) héritier institué, légataire universel, *m.*

devi'ser (di-vaïz'-), *n.,* inventeur, *m.*

devi'sor (di-vaï-zeur *ou* -zor), *n.,* (jur.) testateur, *m.,* testatrice, *f.,* légateur, *m.,* -trice, *f.*

devoid' (di-voïde), *adj.,* privé **de** ; exempt **de** ; dénué **de** ; dépourvu **de.**

devolu'tion (dèv'o-liou-), *n.,* dévolution, *f.*

devolve' (di-), *v.a.,* rouler ; transférer, transmettre.

devolve', *v.n.,* échoir **à** ; tomber ; être dévolu **à** ; incomber **à.** It —s upon me ; *c'est à moi qu'il appartient de* ; ou *c'est à moi qu'il incombe de.*

devolved', *adj.,* dévolu, échu.

devote' (di-vôte), *v.a.,* dévouer **à,** vouer **à,** consacrer **à.**

devote', *n.,* dévot, *m.,* dévote, *f.*

devo'ted, *adj.,* dévoué, consacré, voué ; (accursed) maudit, -e.

devo'tedly, *adv.,* avec dévouement.

devo'tedness, *n.,* dévouement, *m.*

devotee' (dèv'o-tî), *n.,* dévot, *m.,* dévote, *f.* ; (b.s.) faux dévot, *m.,* fausse dévote, *f.* ; bigot, *m.,* bigote, *f.,* cagot, *m.,* cagote, *f.*

devo'tion (di-vô-), *n.,* dévotion ; offrande ; prières, *f.pl.* ; empressement ; dévouement, *m.* — chair ; *prie-dieu, m.*

devo'tional, *adj.,* (of things) de dévotion ; (pers.) religieux ; porté à la dévotion.

devo'tionalist *ou* **devo'tionist,** *n.,* dévot, *m.,* dévote, *f.* ; (b.s.) faux dévot, *m.,* fausse dévote, *f.* ; bigot, *m.,* bigote, *f.*

devour' (di-vaour), *v.a.,* dévorer.

devour'er, *n.,* monstre dévorant ; dévoreur, vorace, *m.,* dévoreuse, *f.,* (of things) destructeur, *m.* To be a — of books ; *dévorer les livres.*

devour'ingly, *adv.,* en dévorant, avec voracité.

devout' (di-vaoute), *adj.,* dévot, pieux, fervent, sincère.

devout'less, *adj.,* indévot.

devout'lessness, *n.,* indévotion (l.u.), *f.*

devout'ly, *adv.,* dévotement.

devout'ness, *n.,* dévotion, piété, *f.*

dew (diou), *n.,* rosée, *f.*

dew, *v.a.,* (ant.) couvrir de rosée ; mouiller, arroser, tremper.

dew'-bent (-bè'n'te), *adj.,* qui plie sous la rosée ; chargé de rosée.

dew'-bespan'gled (-bè-spa'gn'g'l'de), *adj.,* parsemé de rosée.

dew'-besprent', *adj.,* couvert de rosée.

dew'-drop, *n.,* goutte de rosée, *f.*

dew'-dropping, *adj.,* qui dégoutte de rosée.

dew'-lap, *n.,* fanon, *m.*

dew'-lapt, *adj.,* qui a un fanon ; à fanon.

dew'-sprinkled (-spri'gn'k'l'de), *adj.,* couvert de rosée.

dew'-worm (-weurme), *n.,* (ent.) lombric terrestre ; ver de terre, *m.*

dew'y (diou-i), *adj.,* de rosée ; couvert, *ou* humide, de rosée.

dex'ter (dèks'teur), *adj.,* droit ; (her.) dextre.

dexter'ity (-tèr'-), *n.,* dextérité, adresse, *f.*

dex'terous (-teur'-), *adj.,* adroit ; habile.

dex'terously, *adv.,* adroitement, habilement.

dex'terousness, *n.,* dextérité, adresse, *f.*

dex'tral, *adj.,* (l.u.) droit.

dextral'ity, *n.,* (l.u.) situation à droite, *f.*

dex'trine, *n.,* (chem.) dextrine, *f.*

dey, *n.,* dey, *m.*

diabe'tes (daï'a-bî-tize), *n. sing.* and *pl.,* (med.) diabète, *m.sing.*

diabet'ic *ou* **diabet'ical** (daï-a-bèt'-), *adj.,* diabétique.

diabol'ic *ou* **diabol'ical** (daï-a-), *adj.,* diabolique.

diabol'ically, *adv.,* diaboliquement.

diabol'icalness, *n.,* caractère diabolique, *m.*

diach'ylum (daï'ak'i-leume), *ou* **diach'ylon** (-lone), *n.,* diachylum, diachylon, *m.*

diaco'dium (daï-a-cô-di-eume), *n.,* diacode, *m.*

diac'onal (daï-ac'o-), *adj.,* diaconal.

diacous'tics (daï-a-caous-tikse), *n.pl.,* diacoustique, *f.sing.*

diadel'phia (daï-a-), *n.,* (bot.) diadelphie, *f.*

di'adem (daï-a-), *n.,* diadème, *m.*

di'ademed (-dè'm'de), *adj.,* ceint d'un diadème.

di'adrom (daï-a-), *n.,* (l.u.) vibration du pendule ; durée de cette vibration, *f.*

diær'esis (daï-èr-i-ciss), *n.* (diæreses) tréma, *m.* ; (surg.) diérèse, *f.*

diagnos'tic (daï-ag-), *adj.,* diagnostique.

diagnos'tic, *n.,* diagnostique, *m.*

diag'onal (daï-ag-), *adj.,* diagonal.

diag'onal, *n.,* diagonale, *f.*

diag'onally, *adv.,* diagonalement.

di'agram (daï-a-), *n.,* diagramme, *m.* ; figure, *f.*

di'al (daï'al), *n.,* cadran, *m.* Sun-— ; *cadran solaire, m.*

di'alect (daï-a-), *n.,* dialecte ; langage, *m.*

dialec'tic *ou* **dialec'tical,** *adj.,* dialectique.

dialec'tically, *adv.,* dialectiquement.

dialecti'cian (daï-a-lèc-tish'a'n), *n.,* dialecticien, logicien, *m.*

dialec'tics (daï-a-lèc-tikse), *n.pl.,* dialectique, *f.sing.*

di'aling (daï-al'-), *n.,* gnomonique, *f.*

di'alist (daï-al'-), *n.,* faiseur de cadrans, *m.*

dial'ogist (daï-al'o-djiste), *n.,* interlocuteur ; auteur de dialogues ; (l.u.) dialogiste, *m.*

dialogis'tic *ou* **dialogis'tical,** *adj.,* dialogique.

dialogis'tically, *adv.,* en forme de dialogue.

di'alogue (daï-a-loghe), *n.,* dialogue ; entretien, *m.*

di'alogue-writer (-raït'-), *n.,* auteur de dialogues, (l.u.) dialogiste, *m.*

di'al-plate (daï-al-pléte), *n.,* cadran, *m.*

di'al-work (-weurke), *n.,* (horl.) cadrature, *f.*

diam'eter (daï-am'i-), *n.,* diamètre, *m.*

diam'etral, diamet'ric, *ou* **diamet'rical** (daï-a-), *adj.,* diamétral.

diam'etrally *ou* **diamet'rically**, *adv.*, diamétralement.

di'amond (daï'a-meu'n'de), *n.*, diamant ; (at cards) carreau ; (geom.) rhombe, *m.* Set of —s ; *garniture de diamants, f.* Cut —; *diamant taillé.* False —; *faux diamant ; diamant faux.* Polished —; *diamant poli.* Rough —; *diamant brut.* True —; *vrai diamant.* Wrought —; *diamant travaillé.* Glazier's —; *diamant de vitrier.* Rose —; *diamant en rose, m. ; rose, f.* — of the first water; *diamant de première eau.* To set a —; *monter un diamant.* — setter; *sertisseur de diamants.* —cutter ; *diamantaire ; lapidaire, m.* —cutting ; *taille du diamant, f.* — shaped ; *rhomboïdal, en carreau, en losange.* — cut ; *taillé en diamant.* —dust ; *égrisé, m. ; égrisée, f.* — cut —; *fin contre fin.* — beetle ; *entîme, m.*

dian'dria (daï-), *n.*, (bot.) diandrie, *f.*

diapa'son (daï'a-pé-z'n), *n.*, diapason, *m.*

di'aper (daï'a-), *n.*, toile ouvrée, *f.*, linge ouvré, *m. ;* (arch.) panneau à arabesques, *m.*

di'aper, *v.a.*, varier de plusieurs couleurs, diaprer ; ouvrer, damasser.

diaphane'ity (daï-a-fa-nî-i-), *n.*, diaphanéité, *f.*

diaphan'ic *ou* **diaph'anous**, *adj.*, diaphane.

diaphore'sis (daï-a-fo-rî-cice), *n.*, diaphorèse, *f.*

di'aphragm (daï-a-frame), *n.*, diaphragme, *m.*

di'arist (daï-a-), *n.*, personne qui tient un journal, *f.*

diarrhœ'a (daï-a-rî-a), *n.*, diarrhée, *f.*

diarthro'sis (daï-ar-thrô-cice), *n.*, diarthrose, *f.*

di'ary (daï-a-), *n.*, journal, agenda, *m.* Weekly —; *semainier, m.*

di'astase (daï-as-téce), *n.*, (chem.) diastase, *f.*

dias'tasis (daï-as-ta-cice), *n.*, (surg.) diastase, *f.*

dias'tole (daï-as-to-lî), *n.*, (physiol.) diastole, *f.*

di'astyle (daï-a-staïle), *n.*, (arch.) diastyle, *m.*

diath'esis (daï-ath-i-cice), *n.*, diathèse, *f.*

diaton'ic (daï-a-), *adj.*, (mus.) diatonique.

di'atribe (daï-a-traïbe), *n.*, diatribe, *f.*

dib'ble (dib'b'l), *n.*, plantoir, *m.*

dib'ble, *v.a.*, (agri.) planter au plantoir.

dib'stone (-stône), *n.*, palet, *m.*

dice (daïce), *n.pl.* *V.* **die**, *in.*

dice'-box (-bokse), *n.*, cornet à dés, *m.*

di'cer, *n.*, joueur aux dés, *m.*

dichot'omy (daï-cot'-), *n.*, (bot.) dichotomie, *f.*

the **dick'ens !** (dik'è'n'ze), *int.*, (l.ex.) diantre !

dick'y, *n.*, siège de derrière, *m. ;* (shirt-front) chemisette, *f.* Come — bird ! *venez petit !*

dicotyle'don (daï-cot'i-li-), *n.*, (bot.) dicotylédone, *f.*

dicotyle'donous, *adj.*, dicotylédone.

dic'tate (daï-), *n.*, précepte ; ordre, *m. ;* règle, inspiration, voix, impulsion, *f.*

dic'tate, *v.a.*, dicter. *v.n.*, faire la loi à ; commander à.

dicta'tion (dic-té-), *n.*, dictée ; (fig.) injonction, prescription, *f.*

dicta'tor (-té-teur), *n.*, dictateur, *m.*

dictato'rial (-tô-), *adj.*, dictatorial, de dictateur ; impérieux ; dogmatique ; (fig.) arrogant, autoritaire ; magistral.

dicta'torship (-té-teur'-), *n.*, dictature, *f.*

dic'tatory (-té-tori), *adj.*, arrogant; dogmatique ; tranchant; magistral.

dicta'ture (-té-tioure), *n.*, dictature, *f.*

dic'tion (dik'sheune), *n.*, diction, *f.;* débit, *m.*

dic'tionary (dik'sheu'n'a-), *n.*, dictionnaire, *f.*

did, *v.* *V.* **do**.

didac'tic *ou* **didac'tical**, *adj.*, didactique.

didac'tically, *adv.*, didactiquement.

did'apper (did'ap'eur), *n.*, (orni.) plongeon, *m.*

did'dle (did'd'l), *v.n.*, chanceler en marchant ; vétiller ; perdre son temps.

did'dle, *v.a.*, duper, (pop.) enfoncer, mettre dedans, flouer, filouter.

didel'phys (daï-), *n.*, (mam.) didelphe, *m.*

did'ymous, *adj.*, (bot.) didyme.

didyna'mia (-né), *n.*, (bot.) didynamie, *f.*

die (daïe), *n.*, (*dice*) dé à jouer, *m. ;* (fig.) chance, *f.*, hasard, *m.* The — is cast ; *le sort, ou le dé, en est jeté.* A cast of the —; *un coup de dé.*

die (daïe), *n.*, (*dies*) (for stamping) coin, *m.* — sinking ; *gravure en creux, f.*

die (daïe), *v.n.*, mourir ; s'éteindre. To — away; *s'éteindre, se mourir ;* (fig.) *s'évanouir, se dissiper ; disparaître, cesser.* To — off, *ou* out; *s'éteindre ; disparaître, s'oublier.* To be dying; *se mourir.* To be dying with; *mourir* **de.** To — broken-hearted ; *mourir de chagrin.* To — the death of ; *mourir de la mort* **de.** To — a natural death ; *mourir de sa belle mort.* To — hard; *avoir la vie dure; lutter contre la mort.* I am dying to see you ; *je meurs d'envie de vous voir.*

die'sis (daï'î-cice), *n.*, (mus.) dièse, *m. ;* (print.) croix double (‡), *f.*

di'et (daï'ète), *n.*, (assembly) diète ; (food) nourriture ; (med.) diète, *f.*, régime, *m.*

di'et, *v.a.*, (med.) mettre à la diète, mettre au régime ; nourrir.

di'et, *v.n.*, faire diète, être au régime ; se nourrir.

di'etary, *n.*, diète, *f. ;* régime alimentaire, régime diététique, *m. ;* nourriture, *f.*

di'etary, *adj.*, de diète.

di'eter (daï-èt'-), *n.*, diététiste, *m.*

dietet'ic *ou* **dietet'ical** (daï'-), *adj.*, diététique.

dietet'ics (daï-), *n.pl.*, diététique, *f.*

di'etine (daï'-è-), *n.*, diétine, *f.*

dif'fer (dif'feur), *v.n.*, différer **de** ; n'être pas de l'avis **de** ; différer d'opinion **avec** ; se quereller **avec** ; être brouillé **avec** ; être en désaccord **avec.**

dif'ference, *n.*, différence ; (quarrel) dispute, *f. ;* différend, *m.* To pay the —; *faire l'appoint.* It makes no —; *cela ne fait rien ; cela est égal.* To split the —; *partager le différend.*

dif'ference, *v.a.*, différencier.

dif'ferent, *adj.*, différent.

differen'tial (-shal), *adj.*, différentiel.

differen'tiate, *v.a.*, (math.) différentier.

differentia'tion, *n.*, (math.) différentiation, *f.*

dif'ferently, *adv.*, différemment.

dif'ficult (-keulte), *adj.*, difficile ; malaisé. It was — for him to ; *il avait de la difficulté* **à.**

dif'ficulty (-keul-), *n.*, difficulté ; peine, *f. ;* embarras, *m. ;* (pl.) embarras pécuniaires, *m.* Without —; *sans peine, aisément.* With —; *avec peine.* To be in —ies ; *être dans la gêne, être gêné.*

dif'fidence, *n.*, défiance, diffidence, *f.;* manque de confiance en soi-même, *m. ;* hesitation, modestie, réserve ; timidité, *f.*

dif'fident, *adj.*, défiant ; timide ; hésitant ; modeste. To be — of ; *se défier* **de** ; *n'avoir pas de confiance* **en** ; *douter* **de.**

dif'fidently, *adv.*, avec défiance ; avec hésitation ; timidement.

dif'fluent (dif'flou'-), *adj.*, (ant.) coulant, fluide.

difform', *adj.*, difforme, irrégulier.

difform'ity, *n.*, difformité, *f.*

diffrac'tion, *n.*, (phys.) diffraction, *f.*

diffuse' (dif'fiouce), *adj.*, diffus, verbeux ; répandu, étendu.

diffuse' (-fiouze), *v.a.*, répandre.

diffused' (dif'fiouz'de), *past part.*, répandu; irrégulier, (opt.) diffus.

diffus'edly (-fiouz'èd-), *adv.*, diffusément, d'une manière étendue.

diffuse'ly (-fiouss'-), *adv.*, diffusément.

diffu'sion (dif'fiou-jeune), *n.*, diffusion, dispersion ; propagation, *f.*

diffu'sive (-flou-cive), *adj.*, qui se répand, qui peut se répandre ; qui s'étend au loin ; (of style) diffus, étendu.

diffu'sively, *adv.*, au loin, dans toutes les directions.

diffu'siveness, *n.*, abondance ; extension ; verbosité, diffusion, *f.*

dig, *v.a.*, (*preterit* and *past past.*, Dug *ou* Digged) creuser ; bêcher ; piocher ; fouiller. To — out ; *retirer, extraire, déterrer.* To — up ; *défoncer, déterrer ; arracher.* To — open ; *ouvrir.* To — through ; *percer, transpercer.*

dig, *v.n.*, bêcher, piocher ; creuser la terre ; faire des fouilles. *n.*, coup de coude, *m.*

di'gest (daï-djèste), *n.*, digeste, sommaire, *m.*

digest' (di-djèste), *v.a.*, classer, rédiger, arranger, élaborer, étudier, méditer, digérer ; (food) digérer ; (chem.) faire digérer.

digest', *v.n.*, digérer.

digest'er (di-), *n.*, (chem.) digesteur, *m. ;* marmite de Papin, *f.*

diges'tible (di-), *adj.*, digestible ; qui se digère.

diges'tion (di-djèst'ieune), *n.*, digestion, *f. ;* (fig.) examen approfondi, *m.*

diges'tive (di-), *adj.*, digestif.

diges'tive, *n.*, digestif, *m.*

dig'ger (dig'gheur), *n.*, personne qui bêche, *f. ;* terrassier ; (for gold) chercheur d'or, mineur, *m.*

dig'ging (-ghigne), *n.*, fouille, *f. ;* déblai ; terrassement, *m.* *pl.*, mines d'or, *f.*, placers, *m.pl.*

dight (daïte), *adj.*, (ant.) orné, paré.

dig'it (didj'ite), *n.*, mesure de 20 millimètres, *f. ;* doigt ; (arith.) chiffre, *m.*

dig'ital (didj'i-), *adj.*, (anat.) digital.

dig'itate (didj'i-) *ou* **dig'itated** (-ède), *adj.*, (bot., anat.) digité.

dig'nified (dig-ni-faïde), *adj.*, revêtu d'une dignité ; plein de dignité, digne, noble, fier ; solennel.

dig'nify (dig-ni-faïe), *v.a.*, dignifier (V. Hugo) ; élever à une dignité ; donner de la dignité à ; élever, illustrer ; revêtir d'un titre ; honorer, exalter, ennoblir ; décorer **de.**

dig'nitary (dig-ni-), *n.*, dignitaire, *m.*

dig'nity (dig-ni-), *n.*, dignité, *f.*

di'graph (daï-), *n.*, digramme, *m.*

digress' (di-), *v.n.*, faire une digression ; s'écarter **de** ; s'égarer **dans.**

digres'sion (di-grèsh'eune), *n.*, digression ; faute, *f. ;* écart, *m.*

digres'sional (-grèsh'eu'n'-), *adj.*, de digression.

digres'sive (di-), *adj.*, de digression.

digres'sively, *adv.*, par digression.

dike (daïke), *n.*, digue, *f. ;* fossé, *m.*

dike, *v.a.*, endiguer ; entourer d'un fossé.

dilac'erate (di-lass'eur'-), *v.a.*, dilacérer.

dilacera'tion (-'eur'é-), *n.*, dilacération, *f.*

dilania'tion (di-lé-ni-é-), *n.*, (ant.) action de déchirer, action de mettre en pièces, *f.*

dilap'idate, *v.a.*, délabrer, dilapider. —d ; *en mauvais état, tombant en ruine.*

dilap'idate, *v.n.*, se délabrer, se dilapider, tomber en ruine.

dilapida'tion (di-lap-i-dé-), *n.*, délabrement, *m. ;* dilapidation, *f.*

dilap'idator (-dé-teur), *n.*, dilapidateur, *m. ;* dilapidatrice, *f.*

dilatabil'ity (di-lét'-), *n.*, dilatabilité, *f.*

dila'table (di-lét'-a-b'l), *adj.*, dilatable.

dilata'tion (dil-a-té-), *n.*, dilatation, *f.*

dilate' (daï-), *v.a.*, dilater, élargir, étendre.

dilate', *v.n.*, se dilater ; (to descant) s'appesantir, s'étendre **sur.**

dila'tor (daï-lé-teur), *n.*, (med.) dilatateur, *m.*

dil'atoriness (dil-a-tori-), *n.*, lenteur, négligence, *f. ;* retard, *m.*

dil'atory (dila-tori), *adj.*, négligent, lent, (jur.) dilatoire.

dilem'ma (di-), *n.*, dilemme ; embarras, *m.*

dilettan'te (dil-èt-ta'n'ti), *n.*, (*dilettanti*) amateur des beaux arts ; (mus.) dilettante, *m.*

dil'igence (dil-i-djè'n'ce), *n.*, diligence, assiduité, *f. ;* soin, *m. ;* (coach) diligence, *f.*

dil'igent (dil-i-djè'n'te), *adj.*, diligent, appliqué.

dil'igently (-), *adv.*, diligemment, avec application.

dill, *n.*, (bot.) anet, *m.*

dil'ly-dally, *v.n.*, lanterner, barguigner.

dil'ly-dallying, *n.*, lanternerie, *f. ;* (fam.) barguignage, *m.*

dil'uent (dil'iou-), *adj.*, délayant, qui délaye.

dilute' (di-lioute), *v.a.*, détremper ; délayer ; diluer ; étendre d'eau ; (wine) couper ; (fig.) affaiblir.

dilu'ter, *n.*, (med.) délayant, *m.*

dilu'tion, **dilu'ting** (di-liou-), *n.*, (of liquids) dilution, *f. ;* délayement ; (fig.) affaiblissement, *m.*

dilu'vial *ou* **dilu'vian** (di-liou-), *adj.*, diluvien.

dim, *adj.*, obscur, obscurci, trouble, blafard ; (of light) terne, pâle, faible ; sombre. To be — sighted ; *avoir la vue trouble.*

dim, *v.a.*, obscurcir ; offusquer ; (to sully) ternir ; (to surpass) éclipser.

dimen'sion, *n.*, dimension, proportion, étendue, *f.*

dimidia'tion (-mi-di-é-), *n.*, division en deux parties égales, *f.*

dimin'ish, *v.a.*, diminuer, abaisser, amoindrir ; (to take away) ôter, retrancher **de.**

dimin'ish, *v.n.*, diminuer.

dimin'ishingly, *adv.*, désavantageusement.

diminu'tion (-niou-), *n.*, diminution, *f.*

dimin'utive, *adj.*, petit, diminutif.

dimin'utive, *n.*, diminutif, *m.*

dimin'utively, *adv.*, dans de petites proportions ; désavantageusement ; en petit.

dimin'utiveness, *n.*, petitesse ; exiguïté, *f.*

dim'issory (-'is'sori), *adj.*, dimissorial.

dim'ity, *n.*, basin, *m.*

dim'ly, *adv.*, obscurément, indistinctement, faiblement, confusément ; sans éclat.

dim'mish, *adj.*, un peu obscur ; terne.

dim'ness, *n.*, état obscurci ; obscurcissement, *m. ;* obscurité ; faiblesse ; couleur terne, *f.*

dim'ple (-di'm'p'l), *n.*, fossette, *f.*

dim'ple, *v.a.*, former en fossette.

dim'ple, *v.n.*, former des fossettes ; (fig.) se plisser, se rider.

dim'ply, *adv.*, plein de fossettes.

din, *n.*, bruit étourdissant, fracas, tumulte ; (of arms) cliquetis, *m.*

din, *v.a.*, étourdir, assourdir ; (to repeat) corner.

dine (daïne), *v.n.*, dîner (**de**). To — out ; *dîner en ville, dîner dehors.* To — out in the country ; *dîner à la campagne.* To — with Duke Humphrey ; *dîner par cœur.*

dine, *v.a.*, donner à dîner **à** ; nourrir.

di'ner, *n.*, dîneur, (b.s.) pique-assiette, *m.*

ding'-dong (dign'dogne), *n.*, tintement des cloches, dine-dindon, carillon, *m.*

din'giness (di'n'-dji-), *n.*, couleur sombre ; air sombre, *m. ;* pauvreté, *f. ;* aspect sale, *m.*

din'gle (di'gn'g'l), *n.*, vallon, *m.*

din'gle-dan'gle (di'gn'g'l-da'gn'g'l), *adv.*, en pendillant.

din'gy (di'n'-dji), *adj.*, sombre ; sale ; petit, mesquin.

di'ning (daï'n'-), *n.*, action de dîner, *f.* — hall ; *réfectoire, m.*

di'ning-room (-roume), *n.*, salle à manger, *f.*

di'ning-rooms (-roum'ze), *n.pl.*, restaurant, *m.sing.*

di'ning-table (-té-b'l), *n.*, table à manger, table, *f.*

din'ner (di'n'eur), _n._, dîner, dîné, _m._ — time ; _heure du dîner, f._ — service ; _service de table, m._ — lift ; _monte-plats, m._ — wagon ; _servante, étagère de service, f._ —napkin; _serviette de table, f._

dint (di'n'te), _n._, coup, _m._; coche, dent, marque d'un coup ; (fig.) force, puissance, _f._ By — of ; _à force de._

dint, _v.a._, bossuer, bosseler.

dinumera'tion (daï-niou-meur'é-), _n._, énumération, _f._; dénombrement, _m._

dioc'esan (daï-o-cî-ça'n), _adj._, diocésain.

dioc'esan, _n._, évêque diocésain, _m._

di'ocese (daï-ô-cice), _n._, diocèse, _m._

diœ'cia (daï-î-shi-a), _n._, (bot.) diœcie, _f._

diop'tric _ou_ **diop'trical** (daï-), _adj._, dioptrique.

diop'trics (daï-op-trikse), _n.pl._, dioptrique, _f.sing._

dio'rama (daï-o-râ-), _n._, diorama, _m._

dip, _v.a._, plonger ; tremper ; mouiller.

dip, _v.n._, plonger ; (of the needle) incliner ; (mines) s'incliner. To — into ; _s'engager_ **dans** ; (of books) _feuilleter, parcourir, effleurer._

dip, _n._, plongeon, (geol.) plongement, _m._; (of the needle) inclinaison ; (candle) chandelle à la baguette, _f._ To have a — ; _prendre un bain (de mer)_

diph'thong (dip'tho'gne), _n._, diphtongue, _f._

dip'loe (dip-lo-i), _n._, (anat.) diploé, _m._

diplo'ma (di-plô-), _n._, diplôme, _m._

diplo'macy (di-plô-), _n._, diplomatie, _f._

dip'lomat, _n._, diplomate, _m._

diplomat'ic, _adj._, diplomatique.

diplomat'ics (-'ikse), _n.pl._, diplomatique, _f.sing._

diplo'matist (-plô-), _n._, diplomate, _m._

dip'per, _n._, plongeur, _m._

dip'ping, _n._, plongement, (fall) abaissement, _m._; (mines) inclinaison ; (into books) lecture rapide, _f._; effleurement, _m._

dip'tera (dip-tira) _ou_ **dip'terans** (dip-tî-ra'n'ze), _n.pl._, (ent.) diptères, _m.pl._

dip'teral _ou_ **dip'terous** (-teur-), _adj._, (ent.) diptère.

dire (daïeur), _adj._, terrible, affreux ; cruel.

direct', _adj._, direct, droit, exprès, formel, positif, clair. — taxes ; _contributions directes, f.pl._

direct', _adv._, directement.

direct', _v.a._, diriger ; rapporter, conduire ; commander ; ordonner ; conseiller, prescrire ; enseigner, renseigner, indiquer, donner des renseignements, des instructions, à. To — a letter; _adresser une lettre._ To — attention ; _appeler l'attention_ de ... à _ou_ sur.

direc'tion, _n._, direction, conduite, _f._; ordre, _m.,_ instruction, _f._; sens, côté, _m._; (of a letter) adresse, suscription, _f._; (of the wind) lit, _m._ In all —s ; _de tous côtés._

direc'tive, _adj._, directeur, qui dirige, qui guide ; indicatif.

direct'ly, _adv._, directement, immédiatement ; (of time) tout de suite, immédiatement ; (as soon as) aussitôt que.

direct'ness, _n._, mouvement direct, _m._; direction en droite ligne ; (fig.) droiture, _f._ — of purpose ; _à propos, m._; _justesse, précision, f._; _droiture, m._

direct'or (-teur), _n._, directeur, administrateur, guide, chef ; (of the Bank of France) régent, _m._

direct'orate, _n._, conseil d'administration, _m._

directo'rial, _adj._, directorial, de directeur.

direc'tory, _n._, directoire, _m._; direction, _f._; conseil d'administration ; (for addresses) almanach des adresses, _m._

direc'tress, _n._, directrice, _f._

dire'ful (daïeur'foule), _adj._, terrible, affreux ; cruel.

dire'fully, _adv._, terriblement, affreusement, cruellement.

dire'fulness, _n._, horreur, calamité, _f._

dirge (deurdje), _n._, chant funèbre, chant de mort, _m._

dirk (deurke), _n._, dague, _f._; poignard, _m._

dirt (deurte), _n._, boue ; saleté ; fange ; ordure ; crotte, crasse, _f._

dirt, _v.a._, salir, souiller, crotter.

dirt'ily, _adv._, salement ; vilainement, bassement.

dirt'iness, _n._, saleté, malpropreté ; (fig.) bassesse, vilenie, _f._

dirt'y, _adj._, sale, crasseux ; crotté ; malpropre ; (fig.) bas, sale, vilain. — action ; _action sale, f._ — fellow ; _saligaud, m._ — work ; _saleté, f._ To be — ; (of roads) _faire sale._

dirt'y, _v.a._, salir, crotter ; (fig.) souiller.

disabil'ity (diss'-), _n._, incapacité ; impuissance ; (jur.) inhabilité, _f._

disa'ble (diz'é-b'l), _v.a._, rendre incapable ; mettre hors d'état de ; mettre hors de service ; renverser ; détruire ; (jur.) rendre inhabile à ; (mil.) mettre hors de combat ; (of a battery) démonter ; (nav.) désemparer.

disa'bled, _adj._, hors d'état **de** ; hors de service ; rendu incapable **de** ; (mil.) hors de combat ; estropié ; (nav.) désemparé. — soldier ; _invalide, m._

disa'bling, _adj._, qui rend incapable ; (jur.) qui frappe d'incapacité légale, qui rend inhabile.

disabuse' (diss'a-biouze), _v.a._, désabuser.

disabus'ing, _n._, désabusement, _m._

disaccus'tom (diss'ac'keus'teume), _v.a._, désaccoutumer, déshabituer.

disacknowl'edge, _v.a._, renier, désavouer.

disacquain'tance (diss'ac'kwé'n't'-), _n._,(ant.) cessation de connaissance, _f._

disadvan'tage (diss'ad-vâ'n'tédje), _n._, désavantage, inconvénient, _m._; (loss) perte, _f._ At a —, to — ; _avec désavantage; à son désavantage ; à perte._

disadvan'tage, _v.a._, désavantager.

disadvanta'geous (-té'djeusse), _adj._, désavantageux.

disadvanta'geously, _adv._, désavantageusement.

disadvanta'geousness, _n._, désavantage, _m._

disaffect' (diss'-), _v.a._, aliéner les esprits; indisposer, mécontenter ; (disorder) déranger.

disaffect'ed (-ède), _adj._, mal disposé ; indisposé ; mécontent.

disaffect'edly, _adv._, avec désaffection, avec mécontentement.

disaffect'edness _ou_ **disaffec'tion,** _n._, désaffection, _f._

disaffirm' (diss'af'feurme), _v.a._, nier, désavouer ; (jur.) infirmer.

disaffirm'ance, _n._, réfutation ; (jur.) infirmation, _f._; rejet, _m._

disaffor'est (diss'af'for'èste), _v.a._, déclarer ne plus être forêt ; (fig.) cultiver ; (to denude) déboiser.

disag'gregate (diss'ag'grî-), _v.a._, désagréger.

disaggrega'tion (diss'ag'grî-ghé-), _n._, désagrégation, _f._

disagree' (diss'a-grî), _v.n._, différer ; ne pas s'accorder ; ne pas convenir **à.** To — with ; _faire mal à ; incommoder._ To — with any one ; _ne pas s'accorder_ **avec,** _être brouillé_ **avec** _quelqu'un ; ne pas être de l'avis_ **de.** To — to ; ne pas accéder **à** ; _refuser d'accéder_ **à.** My dinner disagreed with me ; _mon dîner m'a fait mal,_ ou _n'a pas bien passé._

disagree'able (diss'a-grî-a-b'l), _adj._, désagréable ; fâcheux.

disagree'ableness, _n._, désagrément, _m.,_ nature désagréable, _f._

disagree'ably, _adv._, désagréablement.

disagree'ment (diss'a-grî-), _n._, différence, dissemblance, diversité, _f._; différend, désaccord, _m._; différence d'opinion ; brouillerie, _f._

disallow' (diss'al'laou), _v.a._, désapprouver,

rejeter, désavouer ; ne **pas** admettre, refuser, défendre, interdire.

disallow', *v.n.*, ne pas permettre.

disallow'able (-a-b'l), *adj.*, défendu, interdit ; qui n'est pas permis ; inadmissible.

disallow'ance, *n.*, défense, désapprobation ; prohibition, *f. ;* refus d'admettre, *m.*

disappear' (diss'ap'pîre), *v.a.*, disparaître.

disappear'ance (diss'-), *n.*, disparition, *f.*

disappoint' (diss'ap-pôï'n'te), *v.a.*, contrarier ; désappointer, désillusionner ; frustrer ; manquer de parole **à** ; tromper ; (to defeat) déconcerter, déjouer. He was —ed in love ; *il a eu des chagrins d'amour.*

disappoint'ment (diss'ap-pôï'n't'-), *n.*, contrariété, *f. ;* désappointement, *m. ;* espérance déçue, *f. ;* contretemps, mécompte, *m.*

disapproba'tion (diss'ap-pro-bé-), *n.*, désapprobation, *f.*

disap'probatory (diss'ap-pro-ba-tori), *adj.*, désapprobateur.

disapprove' (diss'ap-prouve), *v.a.*, désapprouver, blâmer.

disarm' (diz'ârme), *v.a.*, désarmer.

disarm'ing, **disarm'ament**, *n.*, désarmement, *m.*

disarrange', *v.a.*, déranger, désajuster.

disarrange'ment (diss'ar-ré'n'dje-), *n.*, dérangement ; désordre ; désajustement, *m.*

disarray' (diss'ar-ré), *v.a.*, déshabiller ; mettre en désarroi, en désordre ; déranger.

disarray', *n.*, désarroi, désordre, *m. ;* déroute, confusion, *f.*

disas'ter (diz'-), *n.*, désastre, malheur, sinistre, *m.*

disas'trous, *adj.*, désastreux.

disas'trously, *adv.*, désastreusement.

disas'trousness, *n.*, nature désastreuse, *f.*

disavow' (diss'a-vaou), *v.a.*, désavouer.

disavow'al (-), *n.*, désaveu, *m.*

disband', *v.a.*, licencier ; congédier ; disperser.

disband', *v.n.*, se séparer, se disperser, se débander, (milit.) être licencié.

disband'ing, *n.*, licenciement, *m. ;* (fig.) débandement, *m. ;* dispersion, *f.*

disbar', *v.a.*, rayer du tableau des avocats.

disbelief' (-bi-lîfe), *n.*, incrédulité, *f. ;* manque de foi, *m.*

disbelieve' (-bi-lîve), *v.a.*, ne pas croire, refuser de croire. To — every word of ; *ne pas croire un seul mot* **de.**

disbeliev'er, *n.*, incrédule, *m.f.*

disbench' (diz'bè'n'she), *v.a.*, chasser de son siège, chasser de son banc (ant.) ; (jur.) rayer du tableau des avocats.

disbranch' (diz'brâ'n'she), *v.a.*, ébrancher.

disbud' (diz'beude), *v.a.*, ébourgeonner.

disbud'ding, *n.*, ébourgeonnement, *m.*

disbur'den (diz'beur-d'n), *v.a.*, décharger **de** ; débarrasser **de** ; alléger **de** ; (fig.) ouvrir, soulager. To — one's heart to ; *ouvrir son cœur* **à.**

disburse' (diz'beurse), *v.a.*, débourser, dépenser.

disburse'ment, *n.*, déboursement, *m. ;* déboursés, *m.pl. ;* mise de fonds, *f. ;* paiement, *m. ;* dépense, *f.*

disbur'ser, *n.*, personne qui débourse, *f.*

disc (diske), *n.*, disque, *m.*

discard' (dis'cârde), *v.a.*, congédier ; écarter ; mettre de côté ; exclure, éliminer, supprimer ; renvoyer ; (to reject) rejeter, repousser. To — ; (at cards) *faire son écart, écarter.*

discern' (diz'zeurne), *v.a.*, discerner, distinguer ; (fig.) juger.

discern'er, *n.*, juge, observateur, *m.*

discern'ible (diz'zeurn'i-b'l), *adj.*, perceptible, visible, qui peut être discerné.

discern'ibleness, *n.*, visibilité, *f.*

discern'ibly, *adv.*, visiblement.

discern'ing, *adj.*, judicieux, éclairé, attentif.

discern'ingly, *adv.*, avec discernement.

discern'ment, *n.*, discernement ; jugement, *m.*

discharge' (dis-tshârdje), *n.*, déchargement, *m. ;* émission, *f. ;* écoulement, *m. ;* (of fire-arms, etc.) décharge, volée, *f. ;* (of arrows) décochement, *m. ;* (from prison) mise en liberté, libération, *f. ;* élargissement ; (of a duty) accomplissement, *m.*, exécution, *f. ;* exercice ; (of a servant) congé, *m.*, (exemption) exemption de service, libération, *f. ;* (milit.) congé définitif, *m. ;* (payment) quittance, (med.) suppuration ; (of bankrupts) réhabilitation, *f.* — pipe ; *tuyau de décharge, m.*

discharge' (dis-tshârdje), *v.a.*, décharger ; (a servant) congédier, renvoyer ; (from confinement) (to let out) lâcher, laisser échapper ; libérer, élargir ; (a debt) acquitter, payer, liquider ; (arrows) décocher, lancer ; (fire-arms) décharger ; (a duty) s'acquitter **de**, accomplir ; (milit., nav.) congédier, (as unfit for service) réformer ; (jur.) acquitter ; (to emit) lancer, jeter ; (from an oath, etc.) délier, exempter **de**, dispenser **de.**

dischar'ger, *n.*, qui décharge, qui congédie, *f. ;* (phys.) excitateur, *m.*

dischar'ging, *n.*, (nav.) désarmement, *m.* — pipe ; *tuyau de décharge* ; (nav.) *tuyau de vidange, m.* — rod ; (electricity) *excitateur, m.*

disci'ple (dis'çaï'p'l), *n.*, disciple, *m.*

disci'ple, *v.a.*, enseigner, endoctriner, instruire.

disci'pleship, *n.*, état de disciple, *m.*

dis'ciplinable (-a-b'l), *adj.*, disciplinable ; soumis à la discipline.

disciplina'rian (-né-), *adj.*, disciplinaire.

disciplina'rian, *n.*, personne rigide pour la discipline, *f. ;* (milit.) instructeur, *m.* To be a good —; *savoir tenir une classe ; entendre bien la discipline.*

dis'ciplinary, *adj.*, disciplinaire.

dis'cipline, *n.*, discipline, *f.*

dis'cipline, *v.a.*, discipliner, former, instruire, accoutumer à l'ordre ; (fig.) contenir, restreindre, tenir en laisse.

disclaim' (dis-cléme), *v.a.*, désavouer, renier, nier, répudier ; se défendre **de.**

disclaim'er, *n.*, personne qui désavoue, qui renie, *f. ;* désaveu public, *m.*

disclose' (-clôze), *v.a.*, découvrir, révéler ; divulguer ; (fig.) mettre au jour, faire voir.

disclo'ser, *n.*, révélateur, *m.*, révélatrice, *f.*

disclo'sure (-clô'jeur), *n.*, déclaration, révélation ; découverte, divulgation, *f.*

discol'or (dis'keul'leur), *v.a.*, décolorer.

discolora'tion (dis'keul'leur-é-), *n.*, décoloration, *f.*

discom'fit (dis-keu'm'fite), *n.*, défaite, déroute ; dispersion, *f. ;* renversement, *m.*

discom'fit, *v.a.*, défaire ; mettre en déroute ; mettre en fuite ; disperser ; vaincre ; (fig.) dérouter, déconfire.

discom'fiture (-'ioure), *n.*, défaite, déroute, (fig.) déconfiture, *f.*

discom'fort (-keu'm'feurte), *n.*, désolation, affliction, gêne, douleur ; privation, incommodité, *f. ;* désagrément, malaise, *m.*

discom'fort, *v.a.*, affliger ; chagriner, incommoder, gêner, inquiéter ; attrister.

discommend', *v.a.*, blâmer, censurer.

discommend'able (-'a-b'l), *adj.*, blâmable, censurable.

discommend'ableness, *n.*, caractère blâmable, *m.*

discommenda'tion, *n.*, blâme, *m.*

discommend'er, *n.*, désapprobateur, censeur, *m.*

discommode' (-môde), *v.a.* V. **incommode.**

discommo'dious, *adj.*, (ant.) incommode.

discom'mon, *v.a.*, priver du droit de vaine pâture.

discompose' (-pôze), *v.a.*, déranger, troubler; mettre hors de soi, agiter; irriter, chagriner; (of the features) défaire.

discompo'sure (-pô'jeur), *n.*, dérangement; trouble, désordre, *m.*, agitation, *f.*

disconcert' (-ceurte), *v.a.*, déconcerter, troubler.

disconform'ity, *n.*, dissemblance, contradiction, *f.*

discongru'ity (-grou-), *n.*, disconvenance, *f.*

disconnect', *v.a.*, désunir, séparer, diviser; (machinery) désembrayer.

disconnec'tion, *n.*, désunion, séparation, division, *f.*

discon'solate, *adj.*, inconsolable, désolé.

discon'solately, *adv.*, inconsolablement.

discon'solateness, *n.*, désolation, *f.*

discontent', *adj.*, mécontent.

discontent', *n.*, mécontentement, *m.*

discontent', *v.a.*, mécontenter.

discontent'ed, *adj.*, mécontent de (with).

discontent'edly, *adv.*, avec mécontentement; à contre-cœur.

discontent'edness, *n.*, (ant.) mécontentement, *m.*

discontent'ing, *adj.*, peu satisfaisant.

discontent'ment, *n.*, mécontentement, *m.*

discontin'uance (-'iou-) *ou* **discontinua'tion** (-'iou-é-), *n.*, cessation; discontinuation; (separation) discontinuité, *f.*

discontin'ue (-ti'n'iou), *v.a.* and *n.*, discontinuer.

discontinu'ity (-niou-), *n.*, discontinuité, *f.*

discontin'uous, *adj.*, (ant.) discontinu.

dis'cord, **discor'dance**, *ou* **discor'dancy**, *n.*, discorde; (mus.) dissonance, *f.*; discordance, *f.*

discor'dant, *adj.*, discordant, en désaccord.

discor'dantly, *adv.*, sans accord; d'une manière discordante.

dis'count (dis-caou'n'te), *n.*, escompte, *m.*; (abatement) remise, diminution de prix, *f.*; rabais, *m.*; (arith.) règle d'escompte, *f.* At a —; *déprécié*; *au rabais*; *en baisse*; *à perte*; (fig.) *en défaveur*, *décrédité*, *tombé*. To be at a —; *ne pas valoir cher.* — bank; *comptoir d'escompte*, *m.*

dis'count, *v.a.*, déduire; décompter; retrancher; (allow) faire une remise de; (com.) escompter. To — one's losses; *faire la part du feu.*

dis'count, *v.n.*, (com.) faire l'escompte.

dis'count'able (-a-b'l), *adj.*, escomptable.

discoun'tenance (-tè-), *n.*, défaveur, *f.*; mauvais accueil, *m.*; froideur, *f.*

discoun'tenance, *v.a.*, décontenancer, désapprouver, décourager, recevoir froidement; (fig.) s'opposer à; combattre.

dis'counter, *n.*, (com.) escompteur, *m.*

dis'counting, *n.*, escompte, *m.*

discour'age (-keur'édje), *v.a.*, décourager, rebuter; détourner, dissuader.

discour'agement, *n.*, découragement, *m.*

discour'ager, *n.*, personne qui décourage, *f.*

discourse' (-côrse), *n.*, discours; traité; entretien, langage, propos, *m.*; conversation, *f.*

discourse', *v.n.*, discourir de *ou* sur; parler de *ou* sur; s'entretenir de; raisonner de; traiter de. To — in public; *parler en public.*

discour'ser, *n.*, discoureur, *m.*

discour'sive, *adj.*, discursif; dialogué.

discour'teous (-kôrt'ieusse), *adj.*, impoli, incivil; discourtois.

discour'teously, *adv.*, discourtoisement, impoliment, incivilement.

discour'tesy (-keur-té-ci), *n.*, impolitesse; discourtoisie, *f.*

discov'er (-keuv'-), *v.a.*, découvrir; révéler; montrer; constater; faire voir; voir, apercevoir; laisser percer; s'apercevoir de.

discov'erable (-a-b'l), *adj.*, qui peut être découvert; facile à découvrir; visible; apparent.

discov'erer, *n.*, auteur d'une découverte; révélateur, *m.*, révélatrice, *f.*

discov'ery, *n.*, découverte, révélation, *f.*, scandale, éclat, *m.*

discred'it (dis-crèd'ite), *n.*, discrédit; déconsidération; déshonneur, *m.*, honte, *f.*

discred'it, *v.a.*, ne pas croire; décréditer; déshonorer; discréditer, déconsidérer.

discred'itable (-a-b'l), *adj.*, peu honorable; compromettant; déshonorant; honteux.

discreet' (dis'crîte), *adj.*, discret, prudent, circonspect, sage.

discreet'ly, *adv.*, discrètement, sagement; prudemment.

discreet'ness, *n.*, discrétion, *f.*

discrep'ance *ou* **discrep'ancy** (-crèp'-), *n.*, différence, contradiction, *f.*

discrep'ant, *adj.*, different; opposé; en contradiction avec.

discrete' (dis'crîte), *adj.*, séparé, discret; (arith.) simple.

discre'tion (-krèsh'eune), *n.*, discrétion, prudence, sagesse, *f.*; jugement, discernement, *m.* Years of —; *âge de discrétion, de raison, m.* To surrender at —; *se rendre à discrétion.* To use one's own —; *faire ce que l'on juge à propos, faire à sa guise.*

discre'tional. *V.* **discretionary.**

discre'tionary (-krèsh'-), *adj.*, discrétionnaire, facultatif. — power; (jur.) *pouvoir discrétionnaire; pouvoir illimité, m.*

discre'tionally *ou* **discre'tionarily**, *adv.*, à discrétion, à la discrétion, au jugement de quelqu'un.

discre'tive (-crî-), *adj.*, disjonctif; séparé, distinct, (med.) discret.

discre'tively, *adv.*, d'une manière disjonctive.

discrim'inable (-na-b'l), *adj.*, qui peut être distingué.

discrim'inate, *v.a.* and *n.*, distinguer, séparer; reconnaître, discerner.

discrim'inately, *adv.*, distinctement, avec discernement.

discrim'inateness, *n.*, distinction, *f.*

discrim'inating, *adj.*, distinctif, caractéristique.

discrimina'tion (-na-), *n.*, distinction, marque distinctive, *f.*; discernement, *m.* Without —; *indistinctement, sans discernement.*

discrim'inative (-né-), *adj.*, distinctif, qui distingue, caractéristique; judicieux, bien entendu.

discrown' (-craoune), *v.a.*, découronner; priver de la couronne.

discul'pate (-keul-), *v.a.*, disculper, exculper, justifier, excuser.

discum'ber (-keu'm'-), *v.a.*, (l.u.) débarrasser, dégager, désencombrer.

discur'sive (-keur-), *adj.*, errant; décousu, vague, étendu; discursif.

discur'sively, *adv.*, d'une manière discursive, vaguement.

discur'sory, *adj.*, raisonnable, rationnel; d'argument.

dis'cus (-keusse), *n.*, disque, *m.*

discuss' (-keusse), *v.a.*, discuter, débattre.

discus'sion, *n.*, discussion; analyse, *f.*; débat, *m.*

discu'tient (-kiou-shè'n'te), (med.) résolutif, résolutive.

disdain' (diz'déne), *n.*, dédain, mépris, *m.*

disdain', *v.a.*, dédaigner, mépriser.

disdain'ful (-foule), *adj.*, dédaigneux, méprisant.

disdain'fully, *adv.*, dédaigneusement.

disdain'fulness, *n.*, dédain, *m.*

disease' (diz'ize), *n.*, maladie, *f.*; mal; (fig.) vice, affaissement, *m.*

diseased' (diz'iz'de), *adj.*, malade, indisposé; (fig.) dérangé, troublé.

disedge', v.a., émousser, épointer.

disedged' (diz'édj'de), adj., émoussé, épointé.

disembark' (diss'è'm'bârke), v.a., désembarquer ; débarquer.

disembark', v.n., débarquer.

disembarka'tion (-bârk'-é-) ou **disembark'ment**, n., débarquement ; désembarquement, m.

disembar'rass (diss'-), v.a., débarrasser.

disembel'lish, v.a., désembellir.

disembel'lishment, n., désembellissement, m.

disembit'ter (diss'-), v.a., adoucir.

disembod'ied (diss'è'm'bod'ide), adj., dépouillé de son corps ; (mil.) désincorporé, licencié.

disembod'y, v.a., dépouiller du corps ; (mil.) désincorporer, licencier.

disembod'ying, n., (mil.) licenciement, m.

disembogue' (diss'è'm'bôghe), v.n., se décharger **dans** ; déboucher ; tomber **dans, se jeter dans** (of rivers) ; (nav.) débouquer.

disembogue', v.a., jeter, décharger.

disembogue'ment (-boghe'-), n., débouchement, m. ; décharge, f. ; (nav.) débouquement, m.

disembow'el (diss'è'm'baouèl), v.a., éventrer, éviscérer ; arracher les entrailles **à**.

disembroil' (diss'è'm'broïl), v.a., débrouiller.

disembroil'ing, n., débrouillement, m.

disena'ble (diss'è'n'-é-b'l), v.a., rendre incapable **de**, rendre inhabile **à**.

disenam'ored (diss'è'n'am'eurde), adj., (ant.) qui n'est plus amoureux.

disenchant' (diss'è'n'tshâ'n'te), v.a., désenchanter.

disenchant'ment, n., désenchantement, m.

disencum'ber (diss'è'n'keu'm'-), v.a., débarrasser **de**, dégager **de**, désencombrer.

disencum'brance, n., débarras, désencombrement, m. ; délivrance, f.

disengage' (diss'è'n'ghédje), v.a., dégager, débarrasser ; délivrer ; affranchir ; libérer ; détacher.

disengaged' (-ghédj'de), adj., dégagé ; libre ; de loisir.

disengage'ment (-ghédj'-), n., dégagement, affranchissement, loisir, m. ; libération, f.

disenno'ble (diss'è'n'nô-b'l), v.a., faire perdre la noblesse **à** ; avilir, dégrader.

disenroll' (diss'è'n'rôl), v.a., effacer d'un registre, d'une liste.

disentan'gle (diss'è'n'ta'gn'g'l), v.a., démêler ; débarrasser **de** ; débrouiller ; dégager **de** ; (the feet) dépêtrer **de**.

disentan'glement, n., débrouillement ; dégagement ; démêlement, dépêtrement, m.

disenthrall' (diss'è'n'throl), v.a., affranchir ; libérer ; tirer d'esclavage.

disenthrall'ment, n., affranchissement, m. ; mise en liberté, f.

disenthrone' (diss'è'n'thrône), v.a., (ant.) détrôner.

disenti'tle (diss'è'n'taï't'l), v.a., dépouiller ; priver du droit **à**, ôter le droit **à**.

disentomb', v.a., exhumer.

disentrance' (diss'è'n'-), v.a., réveiller d'un sommeil léthargique.

disentwine' (diss'è'n'twaïne), v.a., détordre, détortiller, séparer.

disespouse' (diss'ès'paouze), v.a., (ant.) démarier ; divorcer.

disestab'lish, v.a., priver du caractère d'un établissement public.

disestab'lishment, n., séparation de l'Eglise et de l'Etat, f.

disesteem' (diss'ès'tîme), n., déconsidération, mésestime, f.

disesteem', v.a., mésestimer, mépriser.

disfa'vor (-fé-veur), n., défaveur, disgrâce, f. To be in great —with ; être très mal vu **de**.

disfa'vor, v.a., jeter la défaveur **sur** ; voir avec défaveur ; désapprouver ; recevoir froidement.

disfigura'tion (-figh'iou-ré-), n., action de défigurer ; difformité, f.

disfig'ure (-figh'ioure), v.a., défigurer ; déformer.

disfig'urement, n., état de ce qui est défiguré ; enlaidissement ; défaut, m. ; tache, f.

disfran'chise (-'tshaïze), v.a., priver de ses privilèges électoraux ; priver du droit électoral.

disfran'chisement, n., privation de ses privilèges électoraux ; privation du droit électoral, f.

disfur'nish (-feur-), v.a., dépouiller, dégarnir ; démeubler.

disgar'nish (diz'gâr'-), v.a., dégarnir ; (milit.) dégarnir.

disglo'rify (diz'glô-ri-faïe), v.a., ne plus glorifier ; priver de gloire ; humilier, dégrader.

disgorge' (diz'gordje), v.a. and n., vomir ; rendre ; se dégorger **de** ; (fig.) dégorger ; rendre gorge.

disgorge'ment, n., vomissement, dégorgement, m.

disgrace' (diz'-), n., disgrâce, honte, f. ; déshonneur, m. To be the — of ; à la honte **de**. To be the — of ; être la honte **de** ; faire la honte **de**, être l'opprobre **de**. To be in — ; être en disgrâce ; (of a child) être en pénitence.

disgrace', v.a., disgracier ; déshonorer ; avilir, décréditer.

disgrace'ful (-foule), adj., infâme ; honteux ; déshonorant, ignoble.

disgrace'fully, adv., honteusement ; avec déshonneur ; avec disgrâce.

disgrace'fulness, n., infamie, honte, ignominie, f., déshonneur, m.

disgra'cer, n., personne qui fait honte ; personne qui déshonore, f.

disgra'cious (diz'gré-sheusse), adj., disgracieux, déplaisant.

disguis'able, adj., déguisable.

disguise' (diz'gaïze), n., déguisement ; travestissement ; (fig.) masque, voile, m. In — ; déguisé.

disguise', v.a., déguiser, cacher, voiler ; masquer, contrefaire.

disguise'ment, n. V. disguise.

disgui'ser, n., qui se déguise ; qui déguise.

disgui'sing, n., déguisement, m. ; mascarade, f.

disgust' (diz'gheuste), n., dégoût, m., aversion, f. ; ennui, m.

disgust', v.a., dégoûter **de** ; ennuyer **de**.

disgust'ful (-foule), adj., dégoûtant.

disgust'ing, adj., dégoûtant.

disgust'ingly, adv., d'une manière dégoûtante.

dish, n., (dishes) (utensil) plat ; (food) mets, plat ; (of a pair of scales) plat, plateau, bassin, m. pl., plats, m.pl. ; vaisselle, f.sing. Made up — ; plat apprêté. To wash the —es ; laver la vaisselle.

dish, v.a., mettre dans le plat ; dresser, servir ; apprêter ; (fig.) attraper, enfoncer ; mettre dedans. To — up ; mettre dans le plat ; servir.

dishabille' (diss'a-bil), n., déshabillé, m.

dish'cloth (-cloth) ou **dish'clout** (-claoute), n., torchon de cuisine, m. ; lavette, f.sing.

dish'-cover (-keuv'-), n., couvercle, couvre-plat, m. ; cloche de plat, f.

dishear'ten (diss'hârt't'n), v.a., décourager ; désespérer, désoler.

disher'ison (diss'hè-ri-z'n), n., (jur.) exhérédation, f.

dishev'el (di-shè-vèl), v.a., mettre en désordre ; décheveler, écheveler.

dishev'eled (-vèlde), adj., en désordre ; déchevelé, échevelé, épars.

dish'-mat, n., dessous de plat, m.

dishon'est (diz'o'n'èste), adj., qui n'a pas de

probité ; qui n'est pas probe, déloyal ; malhonnête ; déshonnête.

dishon'estly, *adv.*, sans probité ; déloyalement ; malhonnêtement ; déshonnêtement.

dishon'esty, *n.*, improbité ; déloyauté ; malhonnêteté, *f.*

dishon'or (diz'o'n'eur), *n.*, déshonneur ; (com.) non-paiement, *m.*

dishon'or, *v.a.*, déshonorer ; avilir ; (com.) ne pas faire honneur à ; ne pas faire bon accueil à ; laisser protester (un effet).

dishon'orable (-a-b'l), *adj.*, (pers.) sans honneur ; (of things) déshonorant, honteux.

dishon'orer, *n.*, personne qui déshonore, *f.* ; débaucheur, *m.*

dishorn' (diss'-), *v.a.*, décorner, écorner.

dish'-warmer, *n.*, réchaud, *m.*

dish'-washer (-wŏsh'-), *n.*, (orni.) lavandière, bergeronnette, *f.* ; hoche-queue, *m.*

dish'water (-wŏ-), *n.*, eau de vaisselle ; lavure de vaisselle, *f.*

disimprove'ment (diss'i'm'prouve-), *n.*, progrès en arrière, mouvement rétrograde, *m.*

disinclina'tion (diss'i'n'cli-né-), *n.*, éloignement, *m.* ; aversion, répugnance, *f.*

disincline' (-claïne), *v.a.*, indisposer, éloigner.

disincor'porate (diss'i'n'-), *v.a.*, désincorporer ; priver des priviléges d'une corporation.

disincorpora'tion, *n.*, désincorporation, *f.*

disinfect' (diss'i'n'-), *v.a.*, désinfecter.

disinfec'tion, *n.*, désinfection, *f.*

disingenu'ity (diss'i-n'dji-niou-), *n.*, mauvaise foi, *f.*

disingen'uous (-djè'n'iou-eusse), *adj.*, sans candeur, de mauvaise foi ; dissimulé, faux ; déloyal.

disingen'uously, *adv.*, sans candeur ; avec dissimulation ; de mauvaise foi, déloyalement.

disingen'uousness, *n.*, dissimulation ; mauvaise foi, fausseté ; déloyauté, *f.*

disinher'it (diss'i'n'hèr'-), *v.a.*, déshériter, (jur.) exhéréder.

disinher'itance, *n.*, (jur.) exhérédation, *f.*, déshéritement, *m.*

disinhume' (diss'i'n'hioume), *v.a.*, exhumer.

disin'tegrable (diz'i'n'tè-gra-b'l), *adj.*, susceptible de se désagréger.

disin'tegrate (-gréte), *v.a.*, désagréger, séparer, diviser.

disintegra'tion (-gré-), *n.*, désagrégation, séparation, *f.*

disinter' (diss'i'n'teur), *v.a.*, déterrer ; exhumer.

disin'terested (diz'i'n'teur-èst'ède), *adj.*, désintéressé.

disin'terestedly, *adv.*, avec désintéressement.

disin'terestedness, *n.*, désintéressement, *m.*

disinter'ment (diss'i'n'teur-), *n.*, exhumation, *f.*

disinvite' (diss'in'vaïte), *v.a.*, déprier.

disjoin' (diz'djoï'ne), *v.a.*, déjoindre, disjoindre, désunir.

disjoint' (diz'djoï'n'te), *v.a.*, démettre, désarticuler ; disloquer ; démonter ; désunir ; démembrer.

disjoint'ed (-ède), *adj.*, désarticulé, disloqué, démis ; démembré, démonté ; (fig. of style, etc.) décousu, sans suite.

disjoint'edly, *adv.*, d'une manière décousue, incohérente.

disjunct' (diz'djeu'gn'k'te), *adj.*, disjoint, séparé.

disjunc'tion (diz'-), *n.*, disjonction, séparation, *f.*

disjunc'tive (diz'djeu'gn'k'-), *adj.*, disjonctif, incapable d'union.

disjunc'tive, *n.*, (gram.) disjonctive, *f.*

disjunc'tively, *adv.*, séparément.

disk *ou* **disc**, *n.*, disque, *m.*

dislike' (diz'laïke), *n.*, éloignement, *m.* ; aversion, *f.* ; dégoût, *m.* To take a — to any one ; *prendre quelqu'un en aversion, en grippe* ; *se dégoûter* **de**. To have a — for ; *avoir de l'éloignement* **pour**. Likes and —s ; *goûts et antipathies, m.pl.*

dislike', *v.a.*, ne pas aimer ; avoir de l'éloignement **pour** ; avoir du dégoût **pour**. To be —d ; *n'être pas aimé* **de** ; *être mal vu* **de**. Not to — ; *ne pas trouver mauvais* ; *aimer assez.*

dislike'ness (-laïk'nése), *n.*, dissemblance, *f.*

disli'ker, *n.*, désapprobateur, *m.*

dislimb' (diz'lime), *v.a.*, démembrer, découper un corps par membres, arracher les membres à *ou* **de**.

dis'locate, *v.a.*, disloquer, démettre.

disloca'tion (-ké-), *n.*, dislocation ; luxation, *f.*

dislodge' (diz'-), *v.a.*, déloger ; déplacer ; chasser de sa position ; (hunt.) débucher.

dislodge', *v.n.*, déloger.

disloy'al (diz-lo'i-), *adj.*, peu attaché au souverain ; perfide, déloyal ; infidèle.

disloy'ally, *adv.*, perfidement, déloyalement, infidèlement.

disloy'alty, *n.*, manque de fidélité au souverain, *m.* ; défection, déloyauté, perfidie, *f.*

dis'mal (diz'-), *adj.*, lugubre, sombre, horrible, triste, sinistre.

dis'mally, *adv.*, lugubrement, horriblement, tristement, d'une manière sombre.

dis'malness, *n.*, état lugubre, état sombre, *m.* ; horreur ; tristesse, *f.*

disman'tle (diz'ma'n't'l), *v.a.*, dévêtir ; dépouiller ; (milit.) démanteler ; (nav.) désarmer, dégréer, démanteler.

dismast' (diz'mâste), *v.a.*, démâter.

dismast'ing, *n.*, démâtage, *m.*

dismay' (diz'mé), *n.*, effroi, découragement, abattement, *m.* ; terreur, épouvante, consternation, *f.*

dismay', *v.a.*, effrayer, terrifier, épouvanter, consterner.

dismem'ber (diz'-), *v.a.*, démembrer.

dismem'bering, *n.*, démembrement, *m.*, mutilation, *f.*

dismem'berment, *n.*, démembrement, *m.*, mutilation, *f.*

dismiss' (diz'-), *v.a.*, renvoyer ; congédier ; destituer **de** ; (a subject) abandonner, quitter ; (of thoughts, etc.) bannir, chasser. To — from one's mind ; *écarter, bannir, de son esprit*. Let us — the subject ; *n'en parlons plus.*

dismis'sal, *n.*, renvoi, congé, *m.* ; destitution, *f.*

dismis'sible, *adj.*, amovible ; renvoyable.

dismis'sion (diz'mish'eune), *n.*, renvoi, congé, *m.* ; destitution, *f.*

dismort'gage (diz'mor-ghédje), *v.a.*, dégrever un immeuble ; purger d'hypothèques.

dismount' (diz'maou'n'te), *v.a.*, démonter, désarçonner ; faire descendre de cheval.

dismount', *v.n.*, descendre de cheval ; descendre **de**, mettre pied à terre.

disobe'dience (diss-o-bi-), *n.*, désobéissance, *f.*

disobe'dient, *adj.*, désobéissant.

disobey' (diss'o-bé), *v.a.*, désobéir à.

disoblige' (diss-o-blaïdje), *v.a.*, désobliger.

disobli'ging, *adj.*, désobligeant.

disobli'gingly, *adv.*, désobligeamment, d'une manière désobligeante.

disobli'gingness, *n.*, désobligeance, *f.*

disor'der (diz'-), *n.*, désordre, déréglement, *m.* ; (illness) indisposition, maladie, *f.* ; dérangement, *m.*

disor'der, *v.a.*, mettre en désordre ; déranger ; troubler ; (to make ill) rendre malade, incommoder, indisposer.

disor'dered (diz'or'deurde), *adj.*, en désordre ; dérangé ; déréglé, désordonné ; malade.

disor'derly, *adj.*, en désordre ; tumultueux, désordonné, turbulent, indocile, déréglé ; immoral ; vicieux ; de débauche.

disor'derly, *adv.*, déréglément, en désordre, d'une manière désordonnée.

disorganiza'tion (diz'or-ga'n'i-zé-), *n.*, désorganisation, *f.*

disor'ganize (diz'or-ga'n'aïze), *v.a.*, désorganiser. *v.n.*, se désorganiser.

disown' (diz'ône), *v.a.*, désavouer, nier, renier.

disox'idate, disoxida'tion (diss'oks'idé-), **disox'ygenate, disoxygena'tion** (diss-oks'i-djè'n'é-). *V.* **deox'idate,** etc.

dispair' (dis'-), *v.a.*, (l.u.) dépareiller, séparer.

dispar'adised (-daïste), *adj.*, (l.u.) chassé du paradis.

dispar'age (dis'par'édje), *v.a.*, dépriser, déprécier, ravaler ; dénigrer ; déshonorer ; faire injure, *ou* tort, **à** ; (by marriage) mésallier.

dispar'agement, *n.*, avilissement ; dénigrement ; déshonneur, reproche, *m.;* honte, *f.;* tort, *m. ;* (by marriage) mésalliance, *f.* Without — to you ; *sans vouloir vous faire tort ; sans rien ôter de votre mérite ; sans déshonneur pour vous.*

dispar'ager, *n.*, dénigreur, -euse, *m.* and *f.*

dispar'aging, *adj.*, dépréciateur, désavantageux, injurieux, déshonorant, de mépris.

dispar'agingly, *adv.*, avec dénigrement ; par dénigrement ; avec mépris ; avec déshonneur.

dis'parate, *adj.*, disparate.

dis'parates (-rétse), *n.pl.*, disparates ; choses disparates, *f.pl.*

dispar'ity, *n.*, disparité, inégalité, *f.*

dispark' (dis'pârke), *v.a.*, déclore un parc ; déparquer.

dispart' (dis'pârte), *v.a.*, diviser ; séparer ; (artil.) marquer la mire sur un canon.

dispart', *v.n.*, être divisé, séparé ; se diviser, se séparer.

dispas'sion (dis'pash'eune), *n.*, apathie, absence de passion, *f. ;* calme, *m.*

dispas'sionate, *adj.*, sans passion ; calme ; impartial.

dispas'sionately, *adv.*, sans passion ; avec calme ; avec impartialité.

dispel', *v.a.*, dissiper, chasser, écarter. *v.n.*, se dissiper, disparaître.

dispens'able (-sa-b'l), *adj.*, dont on peut se dispenser, *ou* se passer ; distribuable.

dispen'sary, *n.*, dispensaire, *m. ;* (of hospitals) pharmacie, *f.*

dispensa'tion (-sé-), *n.*, dispensation ; dispense ; distribution, *f.;* (fig.) bienfait, don ; arrêt, *m.*, épreuve (de la providence), *f.*

dispensa'tor (-sé-teur), *n.*, dispensateur, *m.*

dispen'satory, *adj.*, qui peut accorder des dispenses.

dispen'satory, *n.*, (pharm.) codex ; dispensaire, *m.*

dispense', *v.a.*, distribuer, administrer, dispenser ; départir ; (pharm.) dispenser, préparer (des médicaments). To — with ; *se dispenser* de ; *se passer* **de.** To — any one from ; *dispenser quelqu'un* **de,** *excuser quelqu'un* **de.**

dispen'ser, *n.*, dispensateur, *m.*, dispensatrice, *f. ;* distributeur, *m.*, distributrice, *f. ;* pharmacien, *m.*

dispeo'ple (dis'pî-p'l), *v.a.*, dépeupler.

disperse' (dis'peurse), *v.a.*, disperser ; dissiper ; répandre, disséminer ; (med.) résoudre.

disperse', *v.n.*, se disperser ; s'enfuir ; se dissiper.

dispers'edly (-'èdli), *adv.*, çà et là ; séparément.

disper'ser, *n.*, qui disperse, qui dissipe.

disper'sion, *n.*, dispersion ; (opt.) dispersion, *f.*

dispir'it, *v.a.*, décourager, abattre, démoraliser ; ôter le moral **à.**

dispir'itedness (-'èd'-), *n.*, abattement, découragement, *m. ;* démoralisation, *f.*

displace', *v.a.*, déplacer, déranger ; ôter ; (from a post) destituer.

displace'ment, *n.*, déplacement, *m. ;* révocation, destitution, *f.*

displant', *v.a.*, déplanter.

displanta'tion (-té-), *n.*, déplantation, *f.*, déplantage, *m.*

display', *n.*, exposition, parade, *f. ;* étalage ; faste ; (of troops) déploiement, *m.* To make a — of ; *faire parade* **de,** *faire étalage* **de.**

display', *v.a.*, déployer ; étendre ; exposer ; développer ; étaler ; faire parade **de** ; manifester, montrer.

displease' (dis'plîze), *v.a.*, déplaire **à** ; mécontenter ; contrarier, fâcher, vexer.

displeased', *adj.*, mécontent **de,** offensé **de.**

displea'sing, *adj.*, déplaisant, désagréable.

displeas'ure (dis'plèj'eur), *n.*, déplaisir ; courroux, *m. ;* disgrâce, défaveur, *f.* To incur any one's — ; *s'attirer la colère, le mécontentement* **de** (*quelqu'un*).

displume' (-ploume), *v.a.*, déplumer.

disport' (-pôrte), *n.*, divertissement, passetemps, *m.*, récréation, *f.*, ébats, *m.pl.*

disport', *v.n.*, se divertir, se jouer, s'amuser, s'ébattre ; prendre ses ébats ; folâtrer.

disport', *v.a.*, divertir, amuser. To — one's self ; *s'amuser ; se divertir ; prendre ses ébats ; s'ébattre.*

dispo'sable, *adj.*, disponible.

dispo'sal (-pôz'-), *n.*, disposition, vente, cession, *f.* To have at one's —; *avoir à sa disposition.*

dispose', *v.a.*, disposer ; préparer ; arranger ; disposer **de.** To — (the mind to) ; *disposer* **à,** *porter* **à.** To — of ; *transférer, aliéner, céder, vendre ; disposer* **de,** *se défaire* **de.** To be —d of ; (house) *à vendre.* To be —d of by private contract ; *à vendre à l'amiable.* To — of any one ; *se défaire de quelqu'un.* To — of one's time ; *employer son temps.* Evil—d ; *mal intentionné.* Well—d ; *bien intentionné.* —d to ; *porté* **à,** *disposé* **à.**

dispo'ser, *n.*, personne qui dispose, *f. ;* distributeur ; donateur, dispensateur, *m.*

disposi'tion (-zish'-), *n.*, disposition, *f. ;* (pers.) caractère, naturel, *m.*

dispossess' (-poz'zèss), *v.a.*, déposséder **de,** dépouiller **de** ; priver **de** ; (jur.) exproprier.

disposses'sion (poz'zèsh'eune), *n.*, dépossession ; (jur.) expropriation, *f.*

disposses'sor (-poz'zèss'-), *n.*, personne qui dépossède, *f. ;* spoliateur, *m.*, spoliatrice, *f.*

dispraise' (-prèze), *n.* *V.* **blame.**

dispraise', *v.a.* *V.* **blame.**

disprai'singly, *adv.*, avec blâme ; avec reproche.

disproof' (-proufe), *n.*, réfutation, *f.*

dispropor'tion (-pôr-), *n.*, disproportion, *f.*

dispropor'tion, *v.a.*, mal proportionner, disproportionner.

dispropor'tional, *adj.*, disproportionné, disproportionnel.

dispropor'tionally, *adv.*, d'une manière disproportionnée ; inégalement, sans symétrie.

dispropor'tionate, *adj.*, disproportionné.

dispropor'tionately, *adv.*, d'une manière disproportionnée.

dispropor'tionateness, *n.*, disproportion, *f. ;* caractère disproportionné, *m.*

disprove' (-prouve), *v.a.*, réfuter, prouver le contraire **de.**

disprov'er, *n.*, réfutateur, *m.*

dis'putable (-piou-ta-b'l), *adj.*, disputable, contestable.

dis'putant, *n.*, disputant, *m.*

disputa'tion (-té-), *n.*, dispute ; discussion, contestation, *f.*, débat, *m.*

disputa'tious (-piou-té-sheusse) *ou* **dis'putative** (-piou-), *adj.*, disputeur ; (fam.) disputailleur, chicaneur.

dispute' (-pioute), *n.*, dispute, *f.* ; débat, *m.* ; discussion, *f.* Beyond —; *sans contredit ; incontestable, incontestablement.*

dispute', *v.a.*, disputer ; discuter ; débattre, contester.

dispute', *v.n.*, disputer ; discuter ; être en débat.

dispu'ter, *n.*, disputant, disputeur, controversiste, *m.*

disqualifica'tion (dis-kwol-i-fi-ké-), *n.*, incapacité, *f.* ; (jur.) défaut de qualité, *m.*, incapacité légale, inhabilité, *f.*

disqual'ify (-faïe), *v.a.*, rendre incapable **de** ; rendre inhabile **à** ; frapper d'incapacité.

disqui'et (-kwaïète), *n.*, inquiétude, *f.* ; trouble, *m.*

disqui'et, *v.a.*, inquiéter.

disqui'eter, *n.*, perturbateur, *m.*

disqui'etude (-tioude) *ou* **disqui'etness**, *n.*, inquiétude, agitation, *f.*

disquisi'tion (-kwi-zish'-), *n.*, disquisition ; recherche ; investigation, *f.* ; examen, *m.*

disregard' (-ri-gârde), *n.*, mépris, dédain, *m.* ; insouciance, indifférence, *f.* In — of ; *au mépris de.*

disregard', *v.a.*, ne pas considérer ; mépriser ; négliger ; (to reject) écarter ; éloigner ; regarder avec indifférence ; dédaigner ; ne faire aucun cas **de**, ne tenir aucun compte **de** ; repousser.

disregard'ful (-foule), *adj.*, dédaigneux ; insouciant **de**, négligent.

disregard'fully, *adv.*, négligemment ; dédaigneusement.

disrel'ish (diz'rèl'-), *n.*, dégoût, *m.* ; aversion, répugnance, *f.*

disrel'ish, *v.a.*, avoir du dégoût **pour** ; avoir de l'aversion **pour** ; donner de l'aversion **pour**, trouver mauvais.

disrep'utable (-rèp'iou-ta-b'l), *adj.*, (pers.) de mauvaise réputation, mal famé, taré ; (of things) compromettant, déshonorant.

disrep'utably, *adv.*, avec déshonneur ; honteusement.

disrepute' (-rè-pioute), *n.*, discrédit, déshonneur, *m.* ; mauvaise renommée ; mauvaise réputation, *f.* To bring into —; *déconsidérer, faire tomber en discrédit.* To fall into —; *perdre sa réputation, tomber en discrédit.*

disrespect' (-ri-spèkte), *n.*, irrévérence, *f.* ; manque d'égards ; manque de respect, *m.*

disrespect'ful, *adj.*, irrespectueux, irrévérencieux. To be — to ; *manquer de respect* **à**.

disrespect'fully, *adv.*, irrespectueusement ; avec irrévérence ; sans respect.

disrobe' (diz'rôbe), *v.a.*, déshabiller ; dépouiller **de**.

disrobe', *v.n.*, se déshabiller, se dépouiller **de**.

disrup'tion (diz'reup'-), *n.*, rupture ; disruption, *f.*

dissatisfac'tion, *n.*, mécontentement, déplaisir, *m.*

dissatisfac'tory (-tori) *adj.* V. **unsatisfactory.**

dissat'isfied, *adj.*, mécontent **de**.

dissat'isfy (-faïe), *v.a.*, mécontenter.

dissect', *v.a.*, découper, disséquer.

dissec'tion, *n.*, dissection, *f.*

dissec'tor (-teur), *n.*, disséqueur, dissecteur, *m.*

disseize' (dis-size), *v.a.*, (jur.) déposséder illégalement.

disseizee' (-zî), *n.*, (jur.) partie dépossédée illégalement, *f.*

dissei'zin (dis-si-zine), *n.*, (jur.) dépossession illégale, *f.*

dissei'zor, *n.*, (jur.) partie qui dépossède illégalement, *f.*

dissem'ble, *v.n.*, dissimuler, feindre ; user de feinte, faire l'hypocrite.

dissem'ble, *v.a.*, dissimuler, simuler, déguiser, cacher.

dissem'bler, *n.*, dissimulé, *m.*, dissimulée, *f.* ; hypocrite, *m.f.*

dissem'bling, *n.*, dissimulation, feinte, hypocrisie, *f.*

dissem'blingly, *adv.*, en dissimulant, avec dissimulation.

dissem'inate, *v.a.*, disséminer, répandre, propager, circuler, faire circuler (news).

dissemina'tion (-né-), *n.*, dissémination, propagation, *f.*

dissem'inator (-né-teur), *n.*, propagateur, *m.*

dissen'sion, *n.*, dissension ; zizanie, *f.*

dissent', *n.*, dissentiment, *m.* ; dissidence, *f.* ; (rel.) schisme, *m.*

dissent', *v.n.*, différer **avec**, opposer ; différer de sentiment **avec** ; être d'une opinion contraire à ; différer de l'Eglise établie.

dissent'er, *n.*, dissident, *m.*, dissidente, *f.* ; non-conformiste, *m.f.*

dissen'tient (-shè'n'te), *adj.*, différent, opposé, contraire. Without a — voice ; *à l'unanimité ; nemine contradicente.*

dissep'iment (-sèp-), *n.*, (bot.) cloison, *f.*

dissert' (dis'seurte), *v.n.*, (ant.) disserter ; discuter, disputer.

disserta'tion (-seur-té-), *n.*, dissertation, *f.*

dis'sertator (-té-teur), *n.*, auteur d'une dissertation ; dissertateur, *m.*

disser'vice (-seur-), *n.*, mauvais service ; mauvais office ; tort, *m.*

disser'viceable, *adj.*, nuisible **à** ; préjudiciable **à**.

disser'viceableness, *n.*, caractère préjudiciable, *m.*

disser'viceably, *adv.*, d'une manière préjudiciable.

dissev'er (dis-sèv'-), *v.a.*, séparer **de** ; enlever ; arracher **de** ; diviser ; désunir.

dissev'erance, *n.*, séparation ; division ; désunion, *f.*

dis'sidence, *n.*, dissidence, discorde, *f.* ; désaccord, *m.*

dissim'ilar, *adj.*, dissemblable ; dissimilaire, différent.

dissimilar'ity, *n.*, dissemblance, *f.*

dissimula'tion (-'iou-lé-), *n.*, dissimulation, *f.*

dis'sipable (-pa-b'l), *adj.*, qui peut être dissipé, sujet à se dissiper.

dis'sipate, *v.a.*, dissiper. *v.n.*, se dissiper.

dissipa'tion (-pé-), *n.*, dissipation ; évaporation ; distraction, *f.*

disso'ciate (-sô-shi'-), *v.a.*, séparer, désunir, désassocier.

dissocia'tion, *n.*, séparation, désunion, (chem.) dissociation.

dissolubil'ity, *n.*, solubilité, *f.*

dis'soluble (-sô-liou-b'l), *adj.*, dissoluble ; soluble.

dis'solute (-lioute), *adj.*, dissolu.

dis'solutely, *adv.*, dissolument, dans la dissolution.

dis'soluteness, *n.*, dissolution, débauche, *f.*

dissolu'tion (-liou-), *n.*, dissolution ; mort, *f.*

dissolv'able (diz'zolv'a-b'l), *adj.*, soluble ; dissoluble.

dissolve' (diz'zolve), *v.a.*, dissoudre ; désunir ; détruire, annuler ; (fig.) résoudre. The partnership is —d ; *l'association est dissoute.*

dissolve', *v.n.*, se dissoudre ; se séparer ; (fig.) mourir. To — into tears ; *fondre en larmes.*

dissol'vent, *n.*, dissolvant, *m.*

dissol'vent, *adj.*, dissolvant.

dissol'ver, *n.*, dissolvant, *m.*

dis'sonance *ou* **dis'sonancy**, *n.*, dissonance, discordance, *f.*

dis'sonant, *adj.*, dissonant, discordant.

dissuade' (-swéde), *v.a.*, dissuader **de**, détourner **de**.

dissua'der, n., (personne) qui dissuade, f.

dissua'sion (-swé-jeune), n., dissuasion, f.

dissua'sive (-swé-cive), adj., qui dissuade.

dissyllab'ic, adj., dissyllabe.

dissyl'lable (-sil'la-b'l), n., dissyllabe, m.

dis'taff (-tâfe), n., quenouille, f.

dis'tance, n., distance, f.; éloignement ; lointain, (journey) trajet, m.; (fig.) réserve, f.; (mus.) intervalle, m. In the —; au loin; dans le lointain; dans l'éloignement. Point of —; (persp.) point de vue, m. To keep one's —; se tenir à distance; garder sa distance; se tenir à sa place. At a —; à distance, à quelque distance; loin; au loin. To keep at a —; tenir à distance. To keep one's self at a —; se tenir à distance.

dis'tance, v.a., éloigner ; dépasser, devancer ; distancer ; laisser en arrière.

dis'tant, adj., distant de; éloigné de, lointain; (fig.) réservé, froid; faible. A — likeness; une faible ressemblance. He is very —; il est très réservé.

dis'tantly, adv., de loin; à quelque distance ; d'une manière éloignée ; (fig.) avec réserve ; froidement, faiblement, avec froideur.

distaste' (dis-téste), n., dégoût; déplaisir ; m.; aversion, répugnance, f.

distaste'ful (-foule), adj., dégoûtant ; odieux à; désagréable à ou de; offensant.

distaste'fulness, n., goût désagréable, m.; aversion, répugnance, f.

distem'per, n., mal, dérangement, (in dogs) catarrhe, m.; maladie, indisposition; (paint.) détrempe, f.

distem'per, v.a., déranger, incommoder ; troubler ; (paint.) peindre en détrempe.

distem'perature (-tioure), n., (ant.) perturbation ; confusion, f.; tumulte, m.; indisposition, intempérance, f.

distem'pered (-peurde), adj., incommodé, malade; (fig.) troublé; froissé, chiffonné.

distem'pering, n., art de peindre en détrempe, m.

distend', v.a., étendre ; dilater ; (med.) distendre ; enfler, gonfler.

distend', v.n., se détendre, se distendre, se gonfler.

disten'sible, adj., dilatable.

disten'sion ou **disten'tion**, n., (med.) distension, dilatation, f.; écartement, (med.) ballonnement, m.

dis'tich (-tike), n., distique, m.

distill', v.a., distiller ; faire tomber goutte à goutte ; extraire de.

distill', v.n., distiller; tomber goutte à goutte.

distil'lable (-la-b'l), adj., distillable.

distilla'tion (-lé-), n., distillation, f.

distil'latory (-la-tori), adj., distillatoire.

distil'ler, n., distillateur, m.

distil'lery, n., distillerie, f.

distil'ling, n., distillation, f.

distinct' (-tign'kte), adj., distinct, distingué, séparé, spécifié, exprès, catégorique, clair.

distinc'tion, n., distinction, f.

distinc'tive, adj., distinctif.

distinc'tively, adv., d'une manière distinctive.

distinc'tiveness, n., caractère distinctif, m.

distinct'ly, adv., distinctement, clairement ; (fig.) expressément, catégoriquement.

distinct'ness, n., caractère distinct, m.; clarté, netteté, f.

distin'guish (-tign'gwishe), v.a., distinguer.

distin'guish, v.n., distinguer ; établir une distinction.

distin'guishable, adj., que l'on peut distinguer ; qui mérite d'être distingué, remarquable.

distin'guished (-tign'gwish'te), adj., distingué. A — foreigner ; un étranger de distinction. A — man ; un homme éminent.

distin'guisher, n., observateur judicieux, m.

distin'guishing, adj., distinctif.

distin'guishingly, adv., avec distinction; avec discernement ; spécialement.

distort', v.a., tordre, déformer ; contourner ; dénaturer, (one's features) décomposer ; (fig.) torturer ; défigurer, fausser.

distort'ed (-ède), adj., tordu ; contourné ; décomposé ; (fig.) torturé, faussé.

distor'tion, n., distorsion, contorsion, altération; (of writing) sens forcé, f.

distract', v.a., distraire de, détourner de ; jeter dans la confusion ; tourmenter, troubler ; bouleverser ; mettre hors de soi ; rendre fou.

distract'ed (-ède), adj., bouleversé, éperdu ; fou, insensé, hors de soi.

distract'edly, adv., follement ; éperdument.

distract'edness, n., folie, démence, f.

distract'ing, adj., cruel, atroce, déchirant, dévorant. — cares ; soucis dévorants, m.pl.

distrac'tion, n., déchirement, trouble, m.; confusion, f.; désespoir, m.; angoisse, démence, folie, (diversion) distraction, f. To drive to —; mettre hors de soi ; faire devenir fou. To love to —; aimer éperdument, ou à la folie.

distrain' (-tréne), v.a. and n., saisir. v.n., faire, ou opérer, une saisie.

distrain'able, adj., saisissable. Not —; insaisissable.

distrain'er, n., saisissant, m., saisissante, f.

distraint', n., saisie, f.

distress', n., détresse, affliction, peine, f., chagrin, m.; (poverty) gêne, misère; (jur.) saisie, f.; (ant.) malheur, m., calamité, f.

distress', v.a., affliger, désoler, désespérer ; inquiéter ; (jur.) saisir.

distress'ful (-foule), adj., affligeant ; misérable ; de détresse ; malheureux, cruel.

distress'fully, adv., cruellement.

distress'ing, adj., affligeant, désolant, désespérant ; douloureux, pénible, cruel.

distrib'utable, adj., distribuable.

distrib'ute (-'ioute), v.a., distribuer, (allot) répartir ; (justice) administrer.

distribu'tion, n., distribution, répartition ; (justice) administration, f.

distrib'utive, adj., distributif.

distrib'utive, n., mot distributif, m.

distrib'utively, adv., distributivement ; dans un sens distributif ; par distribution.

dis'trict (-trik'te), n., district, arrondissement, m.; contrée, région ; (electoral) circonscription, f.; (of a town) quartier, m.

distrin'gas (dis-tri'gn'gace), n., (jur.) mandat de comparution, ordre de saisir, m.

distrust' (-treuste), n., méfiance, défiance, f.

distrust', v.a., se méfier de ; se défier de.

distrust'ful (-foule), adj., défiant ; méfiant ; réservé ; timide ; modeste.

distrust'fully, adv., avec méfiance ; avec défiance.

distrust'fulness, n., caractère méfiant, m.

disturb' (-teurbe), v.a., troubler, déranger, changer.

disturb'ance, n., trouble ; tumulte, désordre, dérangement, m.; confusion ; émeute, f.; bruit, tapage, m.

disturb'er, n., perturbateur, m., perturbatrice, f.; (jur.) auteur de troubles, m.

disu'nion (diss'iou'n'ieune), n., désunion, f.

disunite' (diss'iou-naïte), v.a., désunir, séparer.

disunite', v.n., se désunir, se séparer.

disu'sage (diss'iou-zédge) (ant.) ou **disuse'** (diss-iouce), n., cessation d'usage, désuétude, f.; (jur.) non-usage, m. To fall into —; tomber en désuétude, cesser d'être en vigueur.

disuse' (diss'iouze), v.a., cesser de faire usage de ; (ant.) déshabituer de, désaccoutumer de.

disused', adj., dont on ne se sert plus ; (of words) inusité, vieilli.

ditch, n., fossé, m. By the — side; *au bord du fossé.* To die in the last —; *résister jusqu'à la dernière extrémité.* — water; *eau croupie, f.* As dull as — water; (pers.) *triste comme un bonnet de nuit.*

ditch, v.a., fossoyer, entourer d'un fossé.

ditch, v.n., faire, ou creuser, un fossé.

ditch'er, n., ouvrier qui creuse des fossés, m.

ditch'ing, n., fossoyage.

dith'yramb, dithyram'bic, ou **dithyram'bus** (dith-), n., dithyrambe, m.

dithyram'bic, adj., dithyrambique, exagéré.

di'tone (daï-tône), n., (mus.) diton, m.

dittan'der, n., (bot.) passerage, f.

dit'tany, n., (bot.) dictame, m.; fraxinelle, f.

dit'tied (dit'tide), adj., (ant.) cadencé.

dit'to (dit'tô), adv., (com. fin.) idem, dito.

dit'ty, n., chansonnette, chanson, f. — bag; *ménagère, f.* (of sailors).

diuret'ic (daï-ou-rèt'-), n., diurétique, m.

diuret'ic, adj., diurétique.

diur'nal, adj., journalier, du jour, de jour; (med.) quotidien ; (astron.) diurne.

diur'nally, adv., journellement, chaque jour.

divan' (di-va'ne), n., divan, sofa, fumoir, salon-fumoir, m.

divaga'tion, n., divagation, f.

divar'icate (daï-var'i-), v.n., se séparer ; se partager en deux; faire la fourche, fourcher, se bifurquer. adj., (bot.) divariqué.

divarica'tion, n., séparation, division en deux branches ; intersection, bifurcation, f.; croisement, m.

dive (daïve), v.n., plonger ; faire le plongeon. To — into ; *sonder, approfondir; examiner à fond.*

di'ver (daïv'-), n., plongeur; (orni.) plongeon, m.

diverge' (di-veurdje), v.n., diverger.

diver'gence ou **diver'gency** (-veur'djè'n-), n., divergence, f.

diver'gent (-veur'djè'n'te), adj., divergent.

di'vers (daï-vèrze), adj., divers ; plusieurs, quelques-uns. — colored ; *de diverses couleurs; de diverses nuances.*

di'verse (daï-vèrse), adj., divers ; différent de, varié.

di'versely (-veurs'-), adv., diversement.

diversifica'tion (di-veur-si-fi-ké-), n., changement, m. ; variation, variété, diversité, f.

diver'sify (di-veur-si-faïe), v.a., diversifier; (of colors) varier, nuancer.

diver'sion (-veur-), n., diversion, distraction, récréation, f. ; divertissement, amusement, m. ; détournement, m. ; (mil.) diversion, f.

diver'sity (-veur-), n., diversité, variété, f.

divert' (di-veurte), v.a., divertir, réjouir, récréer ; distraire, détourner de ; (milit.) faire diversion.

divert'er, n., personne qui distrait, qui divertit ; chose qui distrait, f.

divert'ing, adj., divertissant, amusant.

divert'isement, n., divertissement, m.

diver'tive, adj., (l.u.) divertissant, amusant.

divest' (di-véste), v.a., dépouiller de ; (jur.) se dévêtir, se dessaisir de.

dives'titure (-tioure), n., (jur.) dessaisissement, dévêtissement, m.

divid'able, adj., divisible, répartissable.

divide' (di-vaïde), v.a., diviser ; partager, distribuer ; (in parliament) mettre aux voix. — ! aux voix!

divide', v.n., se diviser, se partager ; (in parliament) aller aux voix. They were —d ; *ils différaient d'opinion.* The opinions were —d ; *les avis étaient partagés.*

div'idend (di-vi-), n., dividende, m.

divi'der (di-vaïd'-), n., personne qui divise ; chose qui divise, f. ; distributeur ; diviseur, m. pl., compas (de dessin), m.

divina'tion (di-vi-né-), n., divination ; prédiction, f.

divin'atory (-tori), adj., divinatoire.

divine' (di-vaïne), adj., divin.

divine' (di-vaïne), n., ecclésiastique, prêtre ; théologien, m.

divine' (di-vaïne), v.a., deviner ; prédire, pressentir ; conjecturer.

divine'ly (di-vaïn'-), adv., divinement.

divine'ness (di-vaï'n'-), n., divinité ; excellence, perfection, f.

divi'ner (di-vaï'n'-), n., devin ; devineur, m., devineuse, f.

divi'neress, n., devineresse, f.

di'ving (daïv'-), n., plongement, m. ; action de plonger, f.; plongeon, m. — dress; *scaphandre, m.*

di'ving-bell (daïv'-), n., cloche à plongeur, cloche à plonger, f.

divi'ning-rod, n., baguette divinatoire, f.

divin'ity (di-vi'n'-i-), n., divinité ; théologie, f. ; (fig.) être céleste, m. Student in —; *étudiant en théologie, m.*

divisibil'ity (-viz'-), n., divisibilité, f.

divis'ible (-viz'i-b'l), adj., divisible.

divi'sion (-vij'eune), n., division, f. ; partage, m. ; (fig.) scission, discorde ; (mus.) roulade, f. Compound —; (arith.) *division des nombres complexes, f.* Simple —; *division des nombres entiers.* On a —; (parl.) *en allant aux voix.* Without a —; *sans aller aux voix.*

divi'sionary (-vij'-), adj., de division, divisionnaire.

divi'sor (-vaï'zeur), n., (arith., alg.) diviseur, m.

divorce' (-vôrce), n., (jur.) divorce, m. ; séparation, désunion, f. To sue for a —; *faire une demande en divorce.*

divorce', v.a., (jur.) prononcer le divorce ; séparer. v.n.; divorcer ; divorcer **avec.**

divorce'ment, n., divorce, m.

divor'cer, n., personne qui divorce ; cause de divorce, f.

divor'cive, adj., de divorce ; qui entraîne le divorce.

divulge' (di-veul'dje), v.a., divulguer ; publier, révéler.

divul'gence, n., divulgation, f.

divul'ger, n., divulgateur, m., divulgatrice, f.

divul'sion, n., arrachement, m.

diz'ziness, n., vertige, éblouissement, étourdissement, m.

diz'zy, adj., étourdissant, étourdi, ébloui ; (of a height) vertigineux, étourdissant. To make —; *étourdir ; donner le vertige à.*

do (dou), v.a., (preterit Did ; past part., Done) faire ; accomplir, commettre ; (service, justice) rendre ; (to finish) finir ; (to cook) cuire, faire cuire ; (to cheat) enfoncer ; mettre dedans, duper, flouer. To — good ; *faire le bien.* To — evil ; *faire le mal.* To — again, to — over again ; *refaire.* To — it again ; *recommencer.* To — up ; *remettre en état ; arranger ; empaqueter ; emballer.* To have nothing to — with ; *n'avoir que faire de, n'avoir rien à y voir.* To have something to — with ; *y être pour quelque chose.* To — nothing ; *ne faire rien ; ne rien faire.* It is as good as done ; *cela vaut fait.* To — up ; *refaire, réparer ; remettre à neuf.* To — over ; *enduire de, recouvrir de.* To — for ; *tuer ; ⊙occire.* Such things are not done ; *ces choses ne se font pas.* He is done for ; *c'en est fait de lui.* It is done, but badly ; *ce n'est ni fait, ni à faire.* What is done, cannot be undone ; *à chose faite, point de remède.* What is to be done ? *comment faire ?* What would you have me — ? *que voulez-vous que je fasse ?* To — nothing of the sort ; *n'en faire rien.* To — no work on Monday ; *faire le lundi.* What am I, ou are we, to — ? *que faire ?* To be done up ; *n'en pouvoir plus ; être éreinté.*

do, v.n., se porter ; se conduire ; (to suit) aller, faire ; (to finish) finir. How do you — ? *comment vous portez-vous ?; comment allez-vous ?* To

— by; *agir* **envers**; *en agir* **avec**. To have to
— with; *avoir affaire* **à**; *avoir affaire* **de**; *avoir
à démêler* **avec**. To have done with; *n'avoir
plus besoin* **de**; *en finir* **avec**; *en avoir assez
de*; *avoir rompu* **avec**. To — without; *se passer
de*. — ! *je t'en prie* ! *je vous en prie* ! Have
done ! *finissez* ! *assez* ! *cessez* ! Will that — ?
cela va-t-il ?; *est-ce bien comme cela* ? That will
—; *c'est bien comme cela*; *cela suffit*; *cela va*;
c'est cela. That will never — ; *cela n'ira jamais*;
cela ne se passera pas ainsi; *ce n'est pas tolérable*; *ce n'est pas permis*. To — away with;
faire cesser; *abolir*; *supprimer*; *se défaire de*;
ôter, enlever, faire disparaître. A shake won't
— ; *ce n'est pas une secousse qu'il faut*.

do, *n.,* fait, acte, *m.; action, f.; (cheat)* duperie, flouerie, *f.* —nothing; *fainéant, m.* Ne'er-
—well; *vaurien, m.*

do'cile, *adj.,* docile.

docil'ity, *n.,* docilité, *f.*

doc'imacy, *n.,* (metal.) docimasie, *f.*

dock, *v.a.,* (horses) courtauder; (dogs) écourter; (fig.) (of accounts) rogner; supprimer;
(nav.) mettre dans le bassin; (com., nav.) faire
entrer aux docks; (on rivers) garer.

dock, *n.,* (stump of a horse's tail) tronçon;
(bot.) rumex, *m.; patience, f.;* (nav.) bassin;
(com., nav.) dock; (courts) banc des accusés,
des prévenus, *m.* Dry —; *bassin d'échouage, m.*
Floating —, wet —; *bassin à flot, m.* — keeper;
gardien de bassin, m.

dock'-due (-diou), *n.,* droit de bassin, droit de
dock, *m.*

dock'et (-'ète), *n.,* bordereau, *m.; cote, étiquette; ouverture ou déclaration d'une faillite, f.;*
(jur.) extrait, *m.* To strike a —; *faire déclarer
en faillite.*

dock'et, *v.a.,* étiqueter; (jur.) faire un extrait
de, faire un bordereau **de.**

dock'-gate (-ghéte), *n.,* vanne de bassin, *f.*

dock'-house (-haouce), *n.,* hôtel de la compagnie des docks, *m.*

dock'ing, *n.,* (vet.) écourtage. — iron; (vet.)
brûle-queue, m. — knife; (vet.) *coupe-queue, m.*

dock'-master (-mâs-), *n.,* surintendant des
docks, *m.*

dock'-yard (-yârde), *n.,* arsenal de port, arsenal de marine; chantier de construction, *m.*

doc'tor (-teur), *n.,* docteur; médecin, *m.* —
of divinity; *docteur en théologie.* — of laws;
docteur en droit. — of medicine; *docteur en médecine, docteur-médecin.* — of science; *docteur-
ès-sciences.* —s Commons; *Collège des docteurs
en droit, m.*

doc'tor (-teur), *v.a.,* (triv.) médicamenter,
(fam.) médeciner, droguer; (fig.) altérer, changer,
fausser; (of wine) frelater.

doc'toral (-teur-), *adj.,* doctoral.

doc'torally, *adv.,* en docteur.

doc'torate (-tor-), *n.,* doctorat, *m.*

doc'toress, doc'tress, *n.,* doctoresse, *f.*

doc'torship (-teur-), *n.,* doctorat, *m.*

doc'trinal, *adj.,* de doctrine; dogmatique;
doctrinal.

doc'trine, *n.,* doctrine, *f.*

doc'ument (dok'iou-), *n.,* document, titre, *m.;*
pièce, *f.*

doc'ument, *v.a.,* munir de documents; munir
de titres.

documen'tal ou documen'tary, *adj.,* de documents; justificatif, authentique. — evidence;
preuve authentique, f.

dod'der, *n.,* (bot.) cuscute, *f.*

dodec'agon (dô-dè-), *n.,* (geom.) dodécagone,
m.

dodecan'dria (dô-dè-), *n.,* (bot.) dodécandrie,
f.

dodge, *v.n.,* changer rapidement de place;
s'esquiver; ruser, biaiser, (fig.) faire des détours.

dodge, *v.a.,* esquiver; éviter; suivre la piste

de; tenir (quelqu'un) le bec dans l'eau; amuser
de fausses espérances.

dodge, *n.,* tour, biais, détour, *m.; ruse, ficelle,
f.*

dodg'er, *n.,* biaiseur, *m.,* biaiseuse, *f.,* finaud,
m., -e, *f.,* intrigant, *m.,* -e, *f.* An artful —; *un fin
matois, un rusé compère;* (pop.) *un roublard.*

doe (dô), *n.,* daine; chevrette, *f.* — hare;
hase, f. — rabbit; *lapine, f.*

do'er (dou'eur), *n.,* faiseur; auteur, *m.*

doff, *v.a.,* ôter, tirer.

dog, *n.,* chien; (andiron) chenet; (jest.) coquin, gaillard, *m.* Cunning —; *rusé coquin.* Old
ou wild —; *vieux routier, vieux farceur, m.* Sad
— ; *triste sujet, m.* Alpine —; *chien du grand
Saint-Bernard.* Bull— ; *bouledogue, m.* House-
—; *chien de garde, chien de basse-cour.* Lap—;
chien de dame, bichon, m. Watch— ; *chien de
garde.* Sporting—; *chien de chasse.* —iron;
chenet, landier, m. To go to the —s; *prendre le
chemin de l'hôpital.* To send to the —s; *envoyer
promener, envoyer au diable.* To set a — at any
one; *haler un chien après quelqu'un.* Give a —
a bad name and hang him; *qui veut noyer son
chien l'accuse de la rage.* The — in the manger;
le chien du jardinier.

dog, *v.a.,* suivre à la piste; espionner; harceler, guetter, épier, pourchasser. To — any one's
footsteps; *être toujours aux trousses de quelqu'un.*

dog'ate, *n.,* dogat, *m.*

dog'bane, *n.,* V. **dog's-bane.**

dog'berry (-bèr'-), *n.,* cornouille, *f.*

dog'-brier, *n.,* églantier, *m.*

dog'-cart, *n.,* voiture à deux roues, *f.,* tilbury, *m.*

dog'cheap (-tshîpe), *adj.,* à vil prix.

dog'days (-dèze), *n.pl.,* jours caniculaires, *m.
pl.; canicule, f.sing.* To be in the —; *être dans
la canicule.*

doge (dôdje), *n.,* doge, *m.*

dog'-faced (-féste), *adj.,* à face de chien.

dog'-fight (-faîte), *n.,* combat de chiens, *m.*

dog'fish, *n.,* (ich.) roussette, *f.,* chien de mer,
squale, aiguillat, *m.*

dog'ged (-ghède), *adj.,* bourru, hargneux;
revêche; rébarbatif; acariâtre, acharné, opiniâtre, entêté.

dog'gedly, *adv.,* comme un chien; d'une manière hargneuse; opiniâtrément, avec acharnement; avec entêtement; obstinément; mordicus.

dog'gedness, *n.,* caractère hargneux, *m.;* opiniâtreté, *f.,* acharnement, entêtement, *m.*

dog'ger (-gheur), *n.,* (nav.) dogre, dogre-bot,
m.

dog'gerel (dog-gheu'-), *adj.,* sans mesure;
sans rime ni raison; burlesque; rimaillé.

dog'gerel, *n.,* vers sans mesure, vers burles-
ques, *m.pl.; rimaille, f.; mauvais vers, m.pl.*

dog'gish (-ghishe), *adj.,* de chien.

dog'-hole (-hôl), *n.,* niche à chien, *f.;* (fig.)
trou à chien, taudis, chenil, *m.*

dog'-house (-haouce), *n.,* niche à chien, *f.,*
chenil, *m.*

dog'-keeper (-kîp'-), *n.,* piqueur, *m.*

dog'-kennel (-), *n.,* chenil, *m.*

dog'-leech (-lîtshe), *n.,* médecin pour les
chiens, vétérinaire, *m.*

dog'-legged (-lèg'de), *adj.,* à patte de chien.

dog'ma, *n.,* dogme, *m.*

dogmat'ic ou dogmat'ical, *adj.,* dogmatique.

dogmat'ically, *adv.,* dogmatiquement.

dogmat'icalness, *n.,* caractère dogmatique,
m., manière tranchante, *f.*

dog'matism, *n.,* dogmatisme, *m.*

dog'matist, *n.,* dogmatiste, *m.*

dog'matize (-taïse), *v.n.,* dogmatiser.

dog'matizer (-taïz'-), *n.,* dogmatiseur, *m.*
(b. s.)

dog's'-bane (dog'z'-), *n.,* (bot.) colchique, tue-
chien, *m.,* noix vomique, *f.*

dog's'-ear (dog'z'îre), n., corne, oreille, f., pli au coin d'une page de livre, m.

dog's'-ear, v.a., faire des cornes aux pages d'un livre.

dog's-grass (dog'z'grâce), n., (bot.) chiendent, m.

dog'sick, adj., qui a envie de vomir.

dog'show, n., exposition de chiens, f.

dog'-star (-stăr), n., (astron.) Canicule, f., Sirius, m.

dog'wood (-woude), n., (bot.) cornouiller, m.

doi'ley ou **doi'ly**, serviette de dessert; nappe de toilette, f.; dessous de lampe, m.

do'ing (dou'-), n., (doings) faits, m.pl.; actions, f.pl.; exploits, actes, m.pl.; œuvre, f., ouvrage; (jobbing) tripotage; événement, m., chose, affaire, f. **—s** and sayings; faits et dires, faits et gestes, actes et paroles, m.pl. That requires some **—**; ce n'est pas fait en un tour de main, ou sans y mettre du sien.

dole (dôle), n., part; aumône, pitance, gratification, f.; don gratuit, m.; coups, m.pl.; chagrin, m., tristesse, lamentation, f.

dole, v.a., distribuer avec parcimonie. To **—** out; distribuer chichement; faire l'aumône **de**.

dole'ful (-foule), adj., malheureux; plaintif; douloureux, triste, lugubre.

dole'fully, adj., douloureusement, plaintivement, tristement.

dole'fulness, n., tristesse, mélancolie, douleur, f.

doll, n., poupée, f.

dol'lar, n., dollar, m.

dol'man, n., dolman (cloak), m.

dol'men, n., dolmen (druidical stone), m.

do'lor (dô-leur), n., douleur, f.; chagrin, m.

dol'orous, adj., douloureux, triste.

dol'orously, adv., douloureusement.

dol'phin, n., (ich.) dauphin, m.; (nav.) baderne, f.

dolt (dôlte), n., balourd, m., balourde, f.; benêt; sot, m.; bûche, f.

dolt'ish, adj., sot; stupide; lourd, lourdaud.

dolt'ishly, adv., avec balourdise; sottement, en lourdaud.

domain' (do-méne), n., domaine, m., propriété, f.

dome, n., dôme, m., dôme, m.

domes'day-book (dou'm'z'dé-bouke), n. V. **dooms'day-book**.

domes'tic, n., domestique, m.f., servante, f.

domes'tic, adj., domestique, de famille; du foyer domestique, casanier, -ère.

domes'tically, adv., dans son intérieur; par rapport aux affaires domestiques.

domes'ticate, v.a., rendre casanier; accoutumer à la vie domestique; domestiquer, apprivoiser.

domes'ticated, adj., (persons) qui entend le ménage; casanier, f.; (of animals) domestique, apprivoisé.

domestica'tion (-ti-ké-), n., vie casanière, retraite, f.; (of animals) apprivoisement, m.

domestic'ity, n., domesticité, f.

dom'icile (-çaïl), n., domicile, m.

dom'icile (-çaïl) ou **domicil'iate** (-cil'i-), v.a., domicilier.

dom'iciled, adj., domicilié.

domicil'iary (-cil'-), adj., domiciliaire. **—** visit; (jur.) visite domiciliaire, f.

dom'inant, adj., dominant, dominateur.

dom'inant, n., (mus.) dominante, f.

dom'inate, v.n., dominer; prévaloir, prédominer.

domina'tion (-né-), n., domination, f.

dom'inator (-né-teur), n., dominateur, m.

domineer' (-nîre), v.n., tempêter; régenter; commander en despote. To **—** over; dominer **sur**; maîtriser; tyranniser **sur**.

domineer'ing, adj., impérieux, arrogant, dic-

tatorial, insolent. n., arrogance, humeur impérieuse. To like **—** over people; aimer à régenter son monde.

domin'ical, adj., dominical. n., dominicale, f.

domin'ioan, n., dominicain, m.

dom'inie, n., magister, pédagogue, maître d'école, m.

domin'ion (-'ieune), n., domination, autorité, f.; empire, pouvoir, m. pl., états, m.pl., possessions, f. pl., empire, m.

dom'ino, n., camail; domino, m. In a **—**; en domino. To play at **—es**; jouer aux dominos.

don, n., don (title); (jest.) grand seigneur: professeur à l'université, m.

don, v.a., mettre; revêtir, endosser.

dona'tion (-né-), n., donation, f.; don, m.

don'ative, n., don, présent, m.; largesse, f.

done (deune). V. **do**. I have **—**; j'ai fini. **—** for; flambé, perdu, fichu, enfoncé. **—**! tope là!; ça y est! Well **—**! à la bonne heure!; bravo!; à merveille!; très bien! (of meat) bien cuit. **—** brown; (fig.) refait; éreinté. Over **—**; (of meat) trop cuit. Under **—**; saignant.

donee' (dô-nî), n., donataire, m.f.

don'key (do'gn'ké), n., âne, baudet, m., bourrique, f. To ride a **—**; aller à âne. Riding (on) a **—**; monté sur un âne. **—** ride; promenade à âne, f. **—** boy; ânier, m. **—** chaise; voiture à âne, f.

don'key-engine, n., pompe alimentaire, f.

don'key-race, n., course d'ânes, f.

don'nism, n., fatuité, suffisance, f.; (univ.) morgue doctorale, f.

do'nor (dô-), n., donateur, m., donatrice, f.

doo'dle (dou'd'l), n., niais, nigaud, m.

doom (doume), v.a., condamner à; destiner à; vouer à; ordonner, commander, juger.

doom, n., arrêt, jugement; sort, destin, m.; condamnation, sentence, f. Crack of **—**; le jugement dernier.

dooms'day (dou'm'z'dé), n., jour du jugement dernier, m. To put off till **—**; remettre à l'an quarante.

dooms'day-book, n., grand cadastre d'Angleterre, m.

door (dôr), n., porte, f.; (of a steam-engine) registre, m. Folding **—s**; porte à deux battants. House **—**; porte de maison. In **—s**; à la maison, chez soi. Out of **—s**; hors de la maison, dehors. At death's **—**; aux portes du tombeau. Next **—** to; voisin, à côté **de**. To close one's **—** against; fermer sa porte **à**. To turn out of **—**; mettre à la porte. To lie at the **—** of; être imputable **à**. With closed **—s**; à huis clos. To lay it at any one's **—**; s'en prendre à quelqu'un **de**. The fault lies at his **—**; la faute en est à lui. He lives next **—**; il loge à ma porte; ou nous demeurons porte à porte. It is next **—** to a lie; si ce n'est pas un mensonge, c'est bien près d'en être un.

door'-bell, n., sonnette, f.

door'-case (-kéce), n., châssis de porte, m.

door'-frame, n., chambranle, châssis, m.

door'-handle (-ha'n'd'l), n., poignée de porte, f., bouton, m.

door'-hangings, n.pl., portière, f.

door'ing, n., (ant.) châssis de porte, m.

door'-jamb (-dja'm), n., jambage de porte, m.

door'-keeper (-kîp'-), n., (of a house) concierge, portier; (of public places) gardien, m.

door'-knob (-nobe), n., bouton de porte, m.

door'-mat, n., paillasson, m.

door'-nail (-néle), n., clou de marteau de porte, m. Dead as a **—**; bien mort, archi-mort.

door'-plate, n., plaque, f.

door'-post (-pôste), n., montant de porte, m.

door'-scraper, n., décrottoir, m.

door'-sill, n., seuil, pas, m.

door'-spring, n., bascule, f., ferme-porte, m.

door'-stead (-stède), n., baie de porte, f.

door'-step, n., pas de porte, seuil, m.

door'-stone, n., seuil, pas de porte, m.

door'way (-wè), n., entrée, f., renfoncement de porte, m. In a — ; *dans le renfoncement d'une porte, ou sous une porte.*

dor *ou* **dorr**, n., (ent.) bousier ; hanneton, m.

dora'do (-ré-dô), n., (ich.) dorade, (astron.) Dorade, f., Xiphias, m.

doree', do'ry (do'rî), n., (ich.) dorée, f., zée, zée forgeron, m. John — ; (ich.) *dorée, f.*

Do'rian, adj., dorien.

Do'ric, adj., dorique.

dor'mancy, n., repos, m.

dor'mant, adj., endormi, assoupi ; (her.) dormant ; (capital) qui dort, mort ; (of partners) commanditaire ; (fig.) latent, caché. To be, *ou* to lie, — ; *sommeiller* ; (capital) *dormir.*

dor'mer-window (-wi'n'dô), n., lucarne, f.

dor'mitive, adj., (med.) dormitif ; qui provoque le sommeil.

dor'mitive, n., (med.) dormitif, m.

dor'mitory (-tori), n., dortoir, m.

dor'mouse (-maouce), n., (mam.) loir, m.

dor'noc, n., toile d'Ecosse, f.

dor'sal, adj., dorsal.

dose (dôce), n., dose, f.

dose, v.a., médicamenter, doser ; proportionner ; donner quelque chose d'un goût désagréable.

dos'sil, n., (surg.) bourdonnet, m.

dot, n., point, m.

dot, v.a., ponctuer, marquer d'un point ; (of arts) pointiller, marquer avec des points ; (fig.) parsemer de.

do'tage (dô-tédje), n., seconde enfance, f. ; radotage, m. ; tendresse extrême, f.

do'tal (dô-), adj., dotal.

do'tard (dô-), n., radoteur, m.

dota'tion (dô-té-), n., dotation, f.

dote (dôte), v.n., radoter, extravaguer. To — on ; *aimer éperdument ; aimer à la folie ; raffoler de.*

do'ter (dôt'-), n., radoteur, m., radoteuse, personne folle de, f.

do'tingly (dôt'-), adv., à la folie, avec extravagance.

dot'tard (dot'-), n., arbre étêté *ou* rabougri, m.

doub'le (deub'b'l), n., double ; pendant ; détour ; (mil.) pas redoublé ; artifice, m. ; ruse, f. ; (print.) doublon, m. ; (mus.) variation, f. My — ; *mon pendant.* At the — ; *au pas redoublé.* To fold — ; *plier en deux.* — that ; *le double de cela.* To grow — ; (pers.) *se voûter.*

doub'le, adv., double ; au double. — jointed ; *membré comme deux.*

doub'le, v.a., doubler ; faire un pli à ; (of fists) serrer, fermer.

doub'le, v.n., doubler ; s'esquiver ; (fig.) user de ruse, biaiser. To — back ; *revenir sur ses pas.*

doub'le, adj., double. Bent — ; (pers.) *voûté.* — Dutch ; *baragouin,* m. In — quick time ; *en moins de rien ; sans faire ni une ni deux.*

doub'le-bar'reled, adj., à deux coups, à double canon.

doub'le-bass, n., contre-basse, f.

doub'le-biting (baït'-), adj., à deux tranchants.

doub'le-buttoned (-beut'n'de), adj., à deux rangs de boutons.

doub'le-chin, n., menton à double étage, m.

doub'le-chinned, adj., à double menton.

doub'le-dealer (-dîl'-), n., trompeur, fourbe, m.

doub'le-dealing, n., dissimulation, hypocrisie, duplicité, fausseté, f.

doub'le-dye (-daïe), v.a., teindre deux fois. —d ; *noté d'infamie ; doublement infâme.*

doub'le-entendre (dou'b'l-â'n-tâ'n'd'r), n., mot à double entente, m.

doub'le-entry, n., tenue des livres en partie double, f.

doub'le-faced, adj., trompeur, fourbe.

doub'le-lock, v.a., fermer à double tour. n., serrure à double tour, f.

doub'le-minded (-maï'n'd'ède), adj., faux, trompeur.

doub'leness, n., état double, m. ; duplicité, f.

doub'ler, n., personne qui double, f. ; (manuf.) doubleur, m., doubleuse, f.

doub'let (deub'lète), n., pourpoint ; (at games) doublet, m.

doub'le-tongued (-teu'gn'g'd), adj., fourbe, dissimulé.

doubloon' (doub'loune), n., doublon, m.

doub'ly, adv., doublement.

doubt (daoute), n., doute, m. ; hésitation, appréhension, f. Beyond a — ; *sans aucun doute.* Beyond all — ; *hors de doute, indubitable.* No — ; *sans doute.* No — that ; *nul doute que* (subj.).

doubt, v.a., douter de.

doubt, v.n., douter, soupçonner ; craindre, hésiter.

doubt'er, n., personne qui doute, f.

doubt'ful (-foule), adj., douteux ; indécis ; incertain. To be — of ; *douter de, avoir des doutes sur.*

doubt'fully, adv., d'une manière douteuse ; avec indécision, d'une manière ambiguë, avec ambiguïté.

doubt'fulness, n., doute, m. ; incertitude, ambiguïté, f.

doubt'ingly, adv., d'une manière douteuse.

doubt'less, adv., sans doute, indubitablement, assurément.

doubt'lessly, adv., incontestablement, sans contredit.

douceur' (dou-ceur), n., douceur, gratification, f. ; pot-de-vin, présent, m.

doucine' (dou-cîne), n., (arch.) doucine, f.

dough (dô), n., pâte, f.

dough'nut (-neûte), n., pet de nonne, beignet, m.

dough'ty (daou'ti), adj., vaillant, brave, preux.

dough'y (dô-i), adj., pâteux ; mou ; maladif.

douse (daouce), v.a., plonger, jeter dans l'eau, arroser d'eau ; éteindre. v.n., tomber dans l'eau.

dove (deuve), n., colombe, f. ; pigeon, m.

dove'-color (-keul'leur), n., gorge-de-pigeon, m.

dove'-colored (-keul'leur'de), adj., gorge-de-pigeon.

dove'-cot *ou* **dove'-house** (-haouce), n., colombier, m.

dove'tail (-téle), n., (carp.) queue d'aronde, f.

dove'tail, v.a., assembler à queue d'aronde ; réunir, joindre ; arranger.

dow'ager (daou'é-djeur), n., douairière, femme âgée, f.

dow'cets (daou-cètse), n.pl., (vet.) daintiers ; rognons, m.pl.

dow'dy (daou-di), n., femme gauche, (mal) fagotée, f. ; gros paquet, m.

dow'dy, adj., gauche ; mal mise ; vulgaire.

dow'er *ou* **dow'ry** (daou'-), n., douaire, m. ; dot, f. ; présent, don, m. v.a., doter de.

dow'ered (daou'eurde), adj., doté ; (fig.) favorisé de la nature.

dow'erless, adj., sans dot.

dow'las, n., toile de Doulens, f.

down (daoune), n., duvet ; (bot.) duvet, coton ; (plain) plateau bas, m., plaine, f. The Downs ; *les dunes, f.pl.* — bed ; *lit de plume ;* duvet, m.

down, prep. au bas de ; en bas de ; le long de ; jusqu'en bas de. — dale ; *en aval.* — the stream ; *en aval.* — to here ; *jusqu'ici.*

down, adv., en bas ; à bas ; bas ; à terre ; (of the wind) tombé, apaisé ; (of the sun) couché ; (of clocks, watches) pas remonté, arrêté ; (of prices) en baisse ; (of the tide) bas, basse ; (fig.) sur le déclin, en défaveur. — with ! *à bas !* ; (to dogs) *à bas les pattes !* ; *couchez !* — with it ! *avalez !* Up and —; *çà et là ; de long en large.* — in the mouth ; *découragé, abattu, penaud.* — upon one's luck ; (fam.) *n'avoir pas de chance.* — stream ; *en aval, avec le courant.* To go —; *aller en aval ; avaler.*

down'cast (-câste), *adj.*, abattu.

down'fall (-fôl), *n.*, chute ; décadence, *f.*

down'fallen (-fôl'n), *adj.*, tombé ; déchu, ruiné.

down'hearted (-hârt'ède), *adj.*, abattu, découragé.

down'hill, *n.*, pente, descente, *f.*

down'hill, *adj.*, incliné ; en pente. — *adv.*, en descendant, dans les descentes (V. Hugo).

down'-line, *n.*, (rail.) voie descendante, *f.*

down'-pour, *n.*, (of rain) averse, pluie torrentielle, *f.*

down'right (-raïte), *adj.*, direct ; franc ; véritable ; vrai ; (b.s) fieffé.

down'right, *adv.*, net, tout net ; tout à fait, complètement.

down'sitting, *n.*, repos, *m.* ; action de s'asseoir, *f.*

down'-stairs, *adv.*, en bas de l'escalier.

down'trodden, *adj.*, foulé aux pieds, opprimé.

down'ward (-wôrde) *ou* **down'wards** (-wôrdze), *adj.*, penché ; qui descend ; descendant ; incliné. — *course ; chute, f.*

down'ward *ou* **down'wards**, *adv.*, en bas ; en descendant, en aval.

down'y, *adj.*, de duvet ; (fruit) couvert de duvet ; (of birds) duveté.

dow'ry, *n. V.* **dower**.

doxol'ogy (-dji), *n.*, Gloria Patri ; Gloria, *m.*

doze (dôze), *v.n.*, être assoupi, s'assoupir, s'endormir, sommeiller ; être à moitié endormi.

doze, *n.*, somme, *m.* To — away the time ; *passer ou perdre son temps à dormir.* To have a —; *faire un somme.* To — over one's work ; *s'endormir sur son ouvrage.*

doz'en (deuz'z'n), *n.*, douzaine, *f.*

do'ziness (dô-), *n.*, assoupissement, *m.*

do'zy (dô-), *adj.*, assoupi, engourdi.

drab, *n.*, gris brun ; drap gris brun, drap noisette, *m.* ; (woman) coureuse, salope, *f.*

drab, *adj.*, gris brun.

drab'ble (drab'b'l), *v.n.*, pêcher des barbeaux (à la ligne).

drab'ble, *v.a. V.* **draggle**.

drab'bling, *n.*, pêche de barbeaux à la ligne, *f.*

drab'bling, *adj.*, qui pêche des barbeaux à la ligne.

drachm (drame), *n.*, drachme, *f.*

dra'co (dré-cô), *n.*, feu follet ; (astron.) Dragon ; (zoöl.) dragon, *m.*

draco'nian *ou* **dracon'ic**, *adj.*, draconien, -ne.

draff (drâfe), *n.*, lavure, rinçure, lie, *f.*, balayures, ordures, *f.pl.* ; rebut, *m.*

draft (drâfte), *n.*, tirage ; trait ; (sketch) dessin, plan, (document) brouillon, *m.* ; minute, (com.) traite, *f.* ; mandat, effet, *m.*; (milit., nav.) détachement ; (depth of water) tirant ; tirant d'eau, *m.*

draft, *v.a.*, dessiner, rédiger ; (milit.) détacher. To —into ; *incorporer* **dans**, **à**, *ou* **avec**; *enrôler* **dans** ou **à.**

drag, *n.*, croc ; harpon ; train, radeau, *m.* ; (nav.) drague, gaffe, *f.* ; (coach) diable ; (of a coach) sabot, *m.*, enrayure, *f.* ; (of machinery) frein, sabot, *m.* ; (agr.) herse, *f.* To be a — upon ; être à charge à. To put on the —, *mettre le sabot* ; (fig.) *s'arrêter.*

drag, *v.a.*, traîner, tirer ; (nav.) draguer. To —away from ; *entraîner ; arracher de.* To —in ; *faire entrer de force.* To —about ; *traîner, trimbaler.* To —out ; *faire sortir de force; entraîner.*

— for oysters ; *draguer ou pêcher des huîtres.* To — the anchor ; *chasser sur son ancre.*

drag, *v.n.*, se traîner ; traîner ; (nav.) (of the anchor) chasser. To — on, *ou* out ; traîner, languir ; traîner en longueur.

drag'-chain (-t'shéne), *n.*, chaîne de drague, *f.*

drag'gle (drag'g'l), *v.a.* and *n.*, traîner dans la crotte, traîner dans la boue ; traîner par terre.

drag'gle-tailed (-tél'de), *adj.*, traîné dans la crotte, *ou* dans la boue.

drag'-hook (-houke), *n.*, croc, *m.*

drag'-man (-ma'ne), *n.*, pêcheur à la seine ; pêcheur à la drague, *m.*

drag'-net (-nète), *n.*, seine, *f.* ; chalon, *m.*

drag'oman (drag'o-ma'ne), *n.*, dragoman ; drogman ; trucheman ; truchement, *m.*

drag'on (dragh'eune), *n.*, dragon ; (astron.) Dragon ; (bot.) bistorte ; langue de serpent, *f.* ; pied-de-veau, *m.*

drag'on-beam (-bîme), *n.*, (carp.) contre-fiche, *f.*

drag'onet (-eun'ète), *n.*, petit dragon, *m.*

drag'on-fly, *n.*, (ent.) demoiselle, libellule, *f.*

drag'onish, *adj.*, en forme de dragon ; de dragon.

drag'on-like (-laïke), *adj.*, en dragon ; comme un dragon.

drag'onnade, *n.*, dragonnade, *f.*

drag'on's-blood (-eu'n'z'bleude), *n.*, sang-de-dragon ; sang-dragon, *m.*

drag'on's-head (-eu'n'z'hède), *n.*, (astron.) tête du Dragon, *f.* ; (bot.) dracocéphale, *m.*

drag'on-tree (-trî), *n.*, (bot.) dragonnier, *m.*

dragoon' (dra-goune), *n.*, (milit.) dragon, *m.*

dragoon', *v.a.*, livrer à la fureur des soldats ; opprimer ; harasser ; persécuter ; forcer par des mesures violentes ; soumettre, assujettir, asservir par les armes.

drain (dréne), *n.*, tranchée, *f.*;égouttoir ;drain ; égoût ; fossé d'écoulement, épuisement, *m.*

drain, *v.a.*, faire écouler ; (a marsh, a river) saigner, dessécher, drainer ; (fig.) épuiser, saigner.

drain, *v.n.*, s'égoutter, s'écouler.

drain'age (-édje), *n.*, écoulement, égouttage ; drainage ; dessèchement ; épuisement, *m.*

drain'ing, *n.*, écoulement ; égouttage, drainage, *m.* — well ; *puisard, m.*

drake, *n.*, canard, *m.* To play ducks and —s ; *faire des ricochets.* To play ducks and —s with one's money ; *jeter l'argent par les fenêtres.*

dram, *n.*, drachme ; (drink) goutte, *f.* — drinker ; buveur, godailleur, *m.* — drinking ; *abus des liqueurs fortes, m.* ; *godaille, f.*

dra'ma (dra-ma), *n.*, drame, *m.*

dramat'ic *ou* **dramat'ical**, *adj.*, dramatique.

dram'atist, *n.*, auteur dramatique ; dramaturge, *m.*

dram'atize (-taïze), *v.a.*, dramatiser.

dra'per (drép'-), *n.*, drapier ; marchand de drap ; marchand de nouveautés, *m.* Linen —; *linger, m., lingère, f., marchand de nouveautés, m., marchande de nouveautés, f.*

dra'pery, *n.*, draperie, *f.* ; nouveautés, *f.pl.*

dras'tic, *n.*, (med.) drastique, *m.*

dras'tic, *adj.*, drastique.

draught (drâfte), *n.*, tirage ; trait ; (of air) courant d'air ; (from a chink) vent coulis ; (of drink) coup ; (drawing) dessin, *m.*, esquisse, ébauche, *f.* ; (of fish) coup de filet, *m.* ; quantité prise ; (com.) traite, *f.*, mandat, effet ; (depth of water) tirant ; (milit.) détachement, *m.* ; (pharm.) potion, *f.* ; (game) dames, *f.pl.* Rough —; *brouillon, m.* At a, *ou* one, —; *d'un trait, d'un seul coup.* A deep —; *un grand coup.* In long —s ; *à grands traits.*

draught'-beer, *m.*, bière à la mesure, *f.*

draught'-board (-bôrde), *n.*, damier, *m.*

draught'-compasses (-pass'ize), *n.*, compas à pointes changeantes, *m.*

draught'-hole (-hôl), n., (tech.) regard, m.

draught'-horse, n., cheval de trait, m.

draughts'man, n., dessinateur, m.

draw (drŏ), v.a. (preterit, Drew ; past part., Drawn), tirer ; retirer ; traîner ; prendre, retirer ; (a picture) dessiner, tracer, représenter, peindre ; (salary) toucher ; (teeth) arracher ; (poultry) vider ; (tech.) étirer ; (water) puiser ; (fig.) (consolation, information) puiser . . . (from) **dans**. To — and quarter ; écarteler. To — up contracts ; rédiger des contrats. To — a sigh ; pousser un soupir. To — water ; puiser de l'eau. To — information; puiser des renseignemens. To — a bow ; tendre un arc. To — in one's horns ; rabattre ses prétentions. To — the long bow; dire des gasconnades. To — again ; tirer de nouveau. To — along ; traîner. To — aside ; tirer à l'écart ; (fig.) détourner. To — asunder ; séparer, diviser. To — away ; entraîner ; retirer, ôter. To—back ; tirer en arrière ; retirer. To — down ; tirer en bas ; faire descendre. To — forth ; tirer en avant ; faire avancer ; faire sortir ; (fig.) faire paraître, faire ressortir. To—in ; enjôler, attirer ; séduire ; tirer dedans ; faire entrer de force ; rentrer. To — nearer ; approcher. To — off ; tirer ; ôter. To — on ; tirer ; (fig.) attirer ; amener. To — out ; tirer dehors ; faire avancer ; prolonger ; ranger en bataille. To — over ; faire passer ; entraîner, gagner. To — up ; tirer en haut ; relever ; (milit.) ranger ; (deeds, etc.) rédiger ; (jur.) dresser ; (nav.) aligner.

draw, v.n., tirer ; se resserrer ; se rétrécir ; se contracter ; (of swords) tirer l'épée ; (of a play) prendre ; (with a pencil) dessiner ; (of tea) s'infuser, se faire ; (at dominoes) pêcher ; (of sails) porter, être tendu. To — in ; se raccourcir ; se resserrer, décroître, diminuer ; (of the day) baisser. To — near ; approcher, s'approcher. To — off ; se retirer. To — out ; s'étendre. To — together ; se rassembler ; se réunir. To — up ; s'arrêter ; se ranger. To — back ; se retirer ; reculer. To — together ; aller bien ensemble ; marcher d'accord.

draw'back, n., (com.) drawback, m. ; remise, f. ; (fig.) décompte, mécompte ; désavantage, défaut, inconvénient, obstacle, m. ; entrave, résistance, reculade, f. It is a great — ; c'est un grand désavantage, ou inconvénient, ou c'est très fâcheux.

draw'-bench (-bè'n'she), n., (tech.) banc à étirer, m.

draw'bridge, n., pont-levis, m.

drawee' (drŏ-i), n., (com.) tiré, m., tirée, f.

draw'er (drŏ'eur), n., tireur, m., tireuse, f. ; (of water) puiseur ; dessinateur ; (of teeth) arracheur; corps attirant ; (sliding box) tiroir ; (com.) tireur, m. Chest of —s, commode, f.

draw'ers (drŏ'eurze), n.pl., caleçon, m.sing. Pair of — ; caleçon, pantalon de femme, m. sing.

draw'-gear (-ghîre), n., attelage, harnais, m.

draw'ing, n., tirage, m. ; action d'attirer, f. ; (sketch) dessin, m. Freehand — ; dessin à main levée. [m.

draw'ing-book (-bouke), n., cahier de dessin, m.

draw'ing-frame (-fréme), n., (tech.) filière, f.

draw'ing-knife (-naïfe), n., plane, f.

draw'ing-pen (-pène), n., tire-ligne, m.

draw'ing-pencil, n., crayon à dessiner, m.

draw'ing-pin, n., punaise (pour le dessin), f.

draw'ing-room (-roume), n., salon, m. ; réception, f. To hold a — ; recevoir. — suite ; ameublement de salon, m. There was a — to-day; il y a eu réception à la cour aujourd'hui.

drawl (drŏl), v.a., passer en lambinant ; (one's words) traîner ses paroles.

drawl, v.n., avoir un débit traînant.

drawl, n., débit traînant ; son traînant, m. ; voix traînante, f. [paroles.

drawl'ing, adj., traînant ; qui traîne ses paroles.

drawn (drŏ'ne), adj., (combats) égal ; (of

games) nul, (of swords) nu. A — battle ; bataille indécise, f. A — game ; partie nulle, partie remise, f. A — sword ; épée nue, f.

draw'-net, n., pantière, tirasse, f. V. **drag-net**.

draw'-plate, n., (tech.) filière, f.

draw'-sheet, n., alèze, f.

draw'-stop, n., (mus.) registre, m.

draw'-well, n., puits à poulie, m.

dray (dré), n., camion, haquet, m.

dray'-horse, n., cheval de haquet, m.

dray'-man, n., camionneur ; haquetier, m.

dread (drède), n., terreur, crainte, f. ; effroi, m. In — of ; de crainte **de**. To be in — of ; redouter **de**, craindre **de** ; redouter, craindre.

dread, adj., redoutable, terrible ; révéré, auguste, imposant.

dread, v.a., craindre, redouter.

dread'ful (-foule), adj., affreux, terrible, épouvantable.

dread'fully, adv., terriblement, affreusement, horriblement.

dread'fulness, n., effroi, m. ; horreur, f.

dread'less, adj., sans peur ; intrépide.

dread'lessness, n., intrépidité, f.

dread'naught (-nŏ'te), n., intrépide ; audacieux ; (of a garment) imperméable, vêtement imperméable, caban, m.

dream (drî'me), n., songe, rêve, m.

dream, v.n. (preterit and past part., Dreamed ou Dreamt), rêver, songer ; s'imaginer. To — of ; rêver **de**.

dream, v.a., songer, rêver. To — away one's time ; consumer le temps dans de vaines pensées ou passer le temps à rêver.

dream'er, n., rêveur, m., rêveuse, f. ; songeur, visionnaire, (l.u.) mage, m.

dream'less, adj., qui ne rêve pas ; sans rêve.

dream'lessly, adv., sans rêver.

dream'y, adj., chimérique, vain, visionnaire ; (pers.) adonné aux rêves.

drea'rily (drî'r-), adv., tristement, lugubrement.

drea'riness, n., tristesse, solitude, f.

drea'ry (drî'r'i), drear, adj., triste, lugubre, solitaire, affreux, horrible.

dredge (drèdje), n., drèche, f., mélange d'avoine et d'orge, m. ; (net) drague, f.

dredge, v.a., saupoudrer de farine ; (pisc.) draguer.

dred'ger, n., pêcheur à la drague, dragueur, m. ; boîte à farine, f. ; (nav.) bateau dragueur, m.

dreg'giness (drèg'ghi-), n., féculence, lie, bourbe, f.

dreg'gy (drèg'ghi), adj., féculent ; fangeux ; plein de lie.

dregs (drèg'ze), n., lie, f. ; effondrilles, f.pl. ; sédiment, m. To the — ; jusqu'à la lie.

drench (drè'n'she), n., breuvage, m.

drench, v.a., tremper **de**, submerger **de**, mouiller **de**, inonder **de**, noyer **de** ; (vet.) donner un breuvage à, abreuver.

drench'er, n., personne qui trempe ; (of rain) averse ; personne qui donne des breuvages à, f.

dress (drèce), n., habillement, vêtement, habit, m. ; mise ; toilette, f. ; ornement, m. ; parure, f. ; uniforme, m. ; (of a woman) robe ; (milit.) tenue, f. — goods ; vêtements pour femmes et enfants, m. Full — ; grande toilette ; (milit.) grande tenue, f. — clothes ; habit de soirée, m. — circle ; (theat.) premières, f. pl. — rehearsal; répétition générale, f. — preserver, sous bras, m.

dress, v.a., habiller, vêtir ; parer, orner ; (a wound) panser ; (agri.) donner une façon à ; labourer, fumer ; (food) accommoder, apprêter ; assaisonner ; (cloth) lustrer ; (nav.) (of a ship) pavoiser ; (manu.) apprêter ; (milit.) aligner. To — one's self ; s'habiller ; faire sa toilette. To — out, ou up ; parer, orner ; harnacher, affubler, attifer ; (fig.) donner une fausse apparence à.

To — hair ; *coiffer.* To — one's hair ; *se coiffer.*
To — to death ; *se parer avec excès.*

dress, *v.n.,* s'habiller ; faire sa toilette ;
(milit.) s'aligner. —! (mil.) *alignement !*

dressed', part. adj., habillé, vêtu. Well — ;
bien mis, bien mise. Badly — ; *mal mis, mal
mise.*

dress'er, n., personne qui habille ; personne
qui panse, *f. ;* (manu.) apprêteur, *m.,* apprê-
teuse ; (in a kitchen) table de cuisine, *f. ;* (med.)
externe d'hôpital, *m.* To be a good —; *se mettre
bien, s'habiller bien.*

dress'ing, n., toilette, *f.,* habillement, ajustement ; (of a wound) appareil, pansement ; (agri.)
labour, *m.,* fumure, *f. ;* (manu.) apprêtage,
apprêt, *m. ;* (chastisement) coups, *m.pl.,* râclée,*f.*

dress'ing-case (-kéce), n., nécessaire de
toilette, *m.*

dress'ing-gown, n., robe de chambre, *f. ;*
peignoir, *m.*

dress'ing-room (-roume), n., cabinet de toilette, *m.*

dress'ing-table, n., toilette, *f.*

dress'-maker (-mék'-), n., couturière, *f.*

dres'sy (drèss'i), adj., qui aime la toilette ;
recherché dans sa mise *ou* tiré à quatre épingles ;
fastueux, paré, habillé ; (of clothes) qui habille
bien.

drib'ble, *v.a.,* laisser dégoutter, faire dégoutter ; verser, répandre goutte à goutte.

drib'ble (drib'b'l), *v.n.,* dégoutter ; baver.

drib'blet, n., chiquet, *m.;* petite somme, *f.* In
—s ; *par bagatelles ; petites sommes, f.pl.*

dri'er (draï'-), n. *V.* **dryer.**

drift, *v.a.,* chasser, pousser, amonceler, entasser.

drift, *v.n.,* dériver, aller à la dérive, flotter à
la dérive ; s'entasser, s'amonceler, s'amasser ;
(fig.) être emporté **par.**

drift, n., objet qui flotte au gré du vent, de
l'eau ; tourbillon ; amas, *m. ;* (fig.) tendance, *f.,*
but, objet, *m.,* portée ; (nav.) dérive, *f. ;* (geol.)
diluvium, *m.;* terrains de transport, *m.pl. ;* (of
ice) glaces flottantes, *f.pl.* — of a current ; *vélocité d'un courant, f.* — ice ; *glace flottanté, f.*
— net ; *manet, m.* — sand ; *sable mouvant, m.*
—wood ; *bois flottant, m.*

drill, n., (agri.) semoir ; (furrow) sillon ;
(manu.) coutil de fil ; (milit.) exercice, m.; manœuvre, *f. ;* (tech.) foret ; (zoöl.) mandrill, m.

drill, *v.a.,* forer, percer ; (agri.) semer par
sillons ; (milit.) exercer ; faire faire l'exercice **à.**

drill, *v.n.,* (agri.) semer par sillons ; (milit.)
faire l'exercice.

drill-hus'bandry (-heuz'ba'n'd'-), n., (agri.)
semaille au semoir, *f.*

drill'ing, n., forage ; (agri.) semis au semoir ;
(milit.) exercice, m.

drill'-machine (-ma-shîne), n., (metal.) machine à forer, *f.*

drill'-officer, n., (milit.) officier instructeur, m.

drill'-sergeant, n., sergent-instructeur, m.

drink (dri'gn'ke), n., boisson, *f. ;* (fig.) ivresse, *f.*

drink, *v.n.* (preterit, Drank ; past part.,
Drunk), boire. To — in ; *imbiber, absorber.* To
— off ; *boire d'un coup, d'un trait.* To — to ;
boire à la santé **de.** To — like a fish ; *boire
comme une éponge, ou comme un trou, comme un
chantre.*

drink'able (-'a-b'l), adj., buvable, potable.

drink'ableness, n., état potable, m.

drink'er, n., buveur, m., buveuse, f. ; ivrogne,
m., ivrognesse, f.

drink'ing, adj., adonné à la boisson ; qui
boit. — song ; *chanson bachique, f.*

drink'ing, n., action de boire ; boisson, ivrognerie, f., boire, m.

drink'ing-booth, n., buvette, f.

drink'ing-bout, n., orgie, f.

drink'ing-fountain, n., fontaine publique, f.

drink'ing-house (-haouce), n., cabaret, m.,
taverne, f.

drink'-money (-meu'n'-nè), n., pourboire, m.

drink'-offering, n., offrande de vin, f.

drip, n., goutte, f. ; égout ; (arch.) larmier, m.
To be dripping wet ; *être tout trempé.*

drip, *v.a.,* faire dégoutter.

drip'ping, n., graisse de rôti, f. ; gouttes, f.pl.

drip'ping-pan (-pa'ne), n., lèchefrite, f.

drip'stone (-stône), n., filtre en pierre ; (arch.)
larmier, m.

drive (draïve), *v.a.,* (preterit, Drove ; past
part., Driven), forcer, pousser, réduire ; porter ;
(carriages, horses) conduire, mener ; chasser,
pousser. To — away ; *chasser, renvoyer.* To
— back ; *repousser, refouler.* To — in ; *planter,
faire entrer ; enfoncer.* To — off ; *renvoyer,
chasser ; différer.* To — on ; *pousser à ; entraîner* **à,** *exciter* **à.** To — out ; *faire sortir, chasser.*

drive, *v.n.,* mener, conduire ; courir ; se
diriger ; aller en voiture. To — by ; *passer en
voiture.* To — against ; *pousser* **vers** ; *s'élancer*
contre. To — at ; *tendre* **à** ; *vouloir en venir*
à. To — off ; *partir.* To — about ; *se promener
en voiture.* To — down ; (in a carriage) *se rendre
en voiture.* To — off ; *partir en voiture.* To —
on ; *pousser en avant.* — on ! *fouette, cocher ! en
avant !* To — out ; *sortir en voiture.* To — up ;
arriver en voiture.

drive, n., promenade en voiture ; (place) promenade pour les voitures, f. ; (up to a house)
avenue, allée, f.

driv'el (driv'v'l), n., bave, f. This is mere —;
(fig.) *c'est tout simplement du bavardage.*

driv'el, *v.n.,* baver ; radoter.

driv'eler (driv'l'-), n., radoteur, m., radoteuse, f.

dri'ver (draïv'-), n., personne qui pousse, qui
chasse, f. ; cocher, conducteur, voiturier, m. ;
(mil.) (artil.) canonnier conducteur ; (rail.) mécanicien, m.

driv'ing, adj., qui pousse, qui conduit ; moteur.
— box ; *siège de cocher, m.* — shaft ; *arbre moteur, m.* — wheel ; *roue motrice, f.*

driz'zle (driz'z'l), *v.n.,* bruiner, tomber en
petites gouttes.

driz'zle, n., bruine, pluie fine, f.

driz'zling, adj. ; — rain ; *pluie fine, f.*

driz'zly, adj., de bruine.

droll (drôl), n., plaisant, farceur, m.

droll, adj., plaisant, drôle. — thing ; *drôlerie,
drôle de chose, f.* — fellow ; *drôle de corps, m.*

droll'ery, n., plaisanterie ; drôlerie, farce, f.

droll'ish, adj., assez drôle, un peu drôle.

drom'edary (dreu'm'e-), n., dromadaire, m.

drone (drône), n., faux bourdon, frelon ; (pers.)
fainéant, m. ; (sound) bourdonnement, m. —
bee ; *faux bourdon.* — fly ; *mouche-abeille, f.*
— pipe ; (of an organ) *bourdon, m.*

drone, *v.n.,* bourdonner ; (fig.) vivre dans la
fainéantise ; lambiner. To — out ; *bourdonner,
chantonner, psalmodier.*

dro'ning, adj., fainéant ; bourdonnant.

dro'ning, n., débit monotone, m.

dro'nish, adj., fainéant.

droop (droupe), *v.n.,* tomber ; faiblir, languir ;
se flétrir ; pencher.

droop, *v.a.,* laisser tomber, laisser pendre.

droop'ing, adj., languissant, abattu, découragé ; baissé, penché.

droop'ing, n., accablement, abattement, m. ;
langueur, tristesse, f.

droop'ingly, adv., languissamment.

drop, n., goutte, larme ; (of a gibbet) bascule,
f. ; (for the ear) pendant, m. ; (thea.) chute ;
(nav.) chute of the principal square sails), f. —
scene ; *rideau d'entr'acte, m.*

drop, *v.a.,* laisser tomber ; (the anchor) (nav.)
jeter ; (of letters) mettre, jeter (à la poste) ; (a

courtesy) tirer ; (let down) faire descendre de voiture (en chemin) ; (utter) laisser échapper ; (to desist) laisser là, cesser de voir, planter là, quitter, abandonner. To — anchor ; *jeter l'ancre.* To — a letter into the post ; *jeter une lettre à la poste.* To — an acquaintance ; *cesser de voir quelqu'un, planter là quelqu'un.* To let — ; (of words) *laisser échapper.*

drop, *v.n.*, tomber en gouttes, dégoutter ; échapper ; tomber ; (of animals) s'abattre. To — astern ; (nav.) *culer.* To — away ; *tomber l'un après l'autre.* To — down ; *tomber.* To — in ; *arriver à l'improviste ; faire une visite en passant.* To — into ; *arriver inopinément.* To — off ; *s'en aller, mourir, tomber, se détacher.* To — out ; *se dérober, s'esquiver.* To — with fatigue ; *tomber de fatigue.*

drop'let (-lète), *n.*, gouttelette, *f.*

drop'per, *n.*, (fishing) bout de ligne, *m.*

drop'sical, *adj.*, hydropique, d'hydropisie.

drop'sy, *n.*, hydropisie, *f.*

drop'wort (-weurte), *n.*, (bot.) spirée, filipendule, senanthe fistuleuse, *f.*

dross, *n.*, écume ; (fig.) rouille, *f.* ; rebut, *m.* ; (metal.) scorie, *f.*

dros'siness, *n.*, écume, rouille ; (fig.) impureté, *f.*

dros'sy, *adj.*, écumeux, plein d'écume ; impur, sans valeur.

drought (draoute), *n.*, sécheresse ; soif, *f.*

drought'iness, *n.*, sécheresse, *f.*

drough'ty, *adj.*, sec ; aride ; (pers.) altéré.

drove (drôve), *n.*, troupeau, *m.* ; (fig.) foule, troupe, *f.*, (agri.) drain, *m.* ; rigole d'irrigation, *f.*

dro'ver, *n.*, conducteur de bestiaux, *m.*

drown (draoune), *v.a.*, noyer ; inonder, submerger, absorber ; (noise) dominer, couvrir, étouffer. To be —ed ; *être noyé.* To — care ; *mettre fin aux soucis.* To be —ed in ; *être plongé* **dans.**

drown, *v.n.*, se noyer. To be —ing ; *se noyer.*

drow'sily, *adv.*, dans un état de torpeur ; d'un air endormi ; (fig.) nonchalamment ; avec indolence ; sans énergie.

drow'siness, *n.*, somnolence, *f.* ; assoupissement, *m.* ; indolence, *f.* ; manque d'énergie, *m.*

drow'sy, *adj.*, assoupi, endormi ; léthargique, lourd, stupide ; indolent ; assoupissant.

drub (dreube), *v.a.*, rosser, étriller, battre, frotter.

drub, *n.*, coup de bâton, *m.* ; taloche, volée, *f.*

drub'bing, *n.*, roulée, volée, râclée ; grêle de coups, *f.*

drudge (dreudje), *n.*, homme de peine ; souffre-douleur, esclave, *m.*

drudge, *v.n.*, travailler sans relâche ; s'échiner, piocher.

drud'ger, *n.*, homme de peine, *m.*

drud'gery, *n.*, travail fatigant, travail pénible, *m.* ; peine, corvée, vile besogne, *f.*

drud'gingly, *adv.*, péniblement ; laborieusement.

drug (dreughe), *n.*, drogue, *f.*

drug, *v.a.*, mettre des drogues **dans** ; empoisonner ; droguer.

drug, *v.n.*, ordonner, administrer, préparer, dispenser, des drogues, *ou* des médecines, **à.**

drug'get (dreug'ghète), *n.*, bure, *f.* ; ⊙droguet, *m.*

drug'gist (dreug'ghiste), *n.*, droguiste, pharmacien, *m.f.*

druid, *n.*, druide, *m.*

drum (dreume), *n.*, tambour, *m.* ; caisse, *f.* — of the ear ; *tympan, m.* Big — ; *grosse caisse.* Muffled — ; *tambour voilé.*

drum, *v.n.*, battre le tambour ; tambouriner ; faire le tambour ; (fig.) tinter. To — into the ears ; *répétailler, corner aux oreilles.* To — into the head ; *finir par faire entrer dans la tête* **à.**

drum, *v.a.*, (milit.) chasser au son du tambour ;

(fig.) seriner. To — out of ; *chasser ignominieusement, dégrader.*

drum'-barrel, *n.*, (tech.) tambour, *m.*

drum'-head (-hède), *n.*, dessus du tambour, *m.* — court-martial ; *conseil de guerre assemblé sur le champ, m.*

drum'-hole (-hôle), *n.*, trou de la caisse du tambour, *m.*

drum'-major (-mé-djeur), *n.*, tambour-major, *m.*

drum'-maker (-mék'-), *n.*, faiseur de tambours, *m.*

drum'mer, *n.*, tambour, *m.*

drum'-stick, *n.*, baguette de tambour ; (of big drum) mailloche, batte, *f.* ; (cook.) pilon, *m.*

drunk (dreu'gn'ke), *adj.*, ivre, gris. Dead — ; *ivre-mort.*

drunk'ard, *n.*, ivrogne, *m.*, ivrognesse, *f.*

drunk'en (dreu'gn'k'n), *adj.*, ivre ; ivrogne ; d'ivresse, d'ivrognie.

drunk'enly, *adv.*, en ivrogne.

drunk'enness, *n.*, ivrognerie ; ivresse, *f.*

dry (draïe), *adj.*, sec, desséché ; tari ; à sec ; aride ; altéré ; (fig.) mordant, piquant, froid, décourageant, caustique, sévère. To be — ; (pers.) *avoir soif ; être altéré* ; (of the weather) *faire sec.* — nurse ; *bonne d'enfant, sevreuse, f.* To — nurse ; *élever au biberon, sevrer.* — goods ; *étoffes, f.pl., tissus, m.pl., mercerie, f.* — harbor ; *port d'échouage, m.*

dry, *v.a.*, sécher ; mettre à sec ; dessécher. To — up ; *sécher ; dessécher.* To — one's tears ; *sécher, essuyer ses larmes.* To — one's eyes ; *s'essuyer les yeux.*

dry, *v.n.*, sécher. To — up ; *tarir.*

dry'-beat (-bîte), *v.a.*, battre à tour de bras, rosser.

dry'-dock, *n.*, bassin de radoub, *m.*, cale sèche, *f.*

dry'er, *n.*, siccatif, dessiccatif, *m.*

dry'-eyed (-aïe'-de), *adj.*, à l'œil sec ; les yeux secs ; sans larmes.

dry'-foot (-foute), *adv.*, (hunt.) à la piste ; à la trace.

dry'ing, *adj.*, qui sèche, siccatif.

dry'ing-house (-haouce), *n.*, essui, séchoir, *m.* ; étuve ; sécherie, *f.*

dry'ness, *n.*, sécheresse ; aridité, *f.*

dry'-rot, *n.*, pourriture sèche, *f.*

dry'-rub (-reube), *v.a.*, frotter à sec.

dry'-salter (-sôlt'-), *n.*, marchand de salaisons, droguiste, *m.*

dry'-shod (-shode), *adj.*, à pied sec.

dry'-stove (-stôve), *n.*, serre chaude, *f.*

du'al (diou'-), *n.*, double ; (gram.) duel, *m.* — number ; *duel, m.*

dual'ity, *n.*, dualité, *f.*

dub, *v.a.*, créer, faire, *ou* armer, chevalier ; qualifier **de**, baptiser ; (tech.) passer (les peaux) en huile ; (mas.) renformir.

dub'bing, *pres. part.* V. **dub.**

dub'bing, *n.*, mélange de dégras et de suif ; (mas.) renformis, *m.*

du'bious (diou'-), *adj.*, douteux, incertain, indécis. — light ; *jour douteux, m.* ; *lumière douteuse, f.*

du'biously, *adv.*, douteusement.

du'biousness, *n.*, doute, *m.* ; incertitude ; indécision, *f.*

du'cal (diou-), *adj.*, ducal.

duc'at (deuc'ate), *n.*, ducat, *m.*

duch'ess, *n.*, duchesse, *f.*

duch'y, *n.*, duché, *m.*

duck (deuke), *n.*, (orni.) cane, *f.*, canard, *m.* ; (nav.) toile à voile, *f.* ; (plunging) plongeon ; (term of endearment) chou, chat, poulet, *m.*, poulette, *f.* Russian — ; *toile de Russie, f.* —s and drakes ; (game) ricochets, *m.pl.* To play —s and drakes with one's money ; *jeter l'argent par les fenêtres.*

duck, *v.a.*, plonger dans l'eau ; plonger ; (head) baisser ; (nav.) donner la cale **à**.

duck, *v.n.*, plonger ; faire le plongeon, courber la tête.

duck'-bill *ou* **duck'-mole**, *n.*, (zool.) ornithorynque, *m.*

duck'-gun (-gheune), *n.*, canardière, *f.*

duck'hawk, *n.*, harpaye, *m.*

duck'ing, *n.*, action de plonger, *f.* ; plongeon ; (nav.) baptême du tropique, de la ligne, *m.*

duck'-legged (-lèg'de), *adj.*, à jambes courtes, dandinantes.

duck'ling, *n.*, caneton, *m.* ; canette, *f.*

duck'-meat (-mîte), *n.*, (bot.) lenticule, lentille d'eau, lentille de marais, *f.*

duck'-moor, *n.*, (ornith.) busard des marais,*m.*

duck's'-foot (deuks'foute), *n.*, (bot.) alchimille, *f.* ; podophyllum, *m.*

duck'-shooting (-shout'-), *n.*, chasse aux canards, *f.*

duck'-stone (-stône), *n.*, (boy's game) sauvette, *f.*

duck'weed, *n.*, lenticule, *f.*

duck'y, *n.*, petit chat ; petit chou, *m.*

duct (deucte), *n.*, conduit ; tube, (anat.) vaisseau, canal, (bot.) vaisseau, *m.* Alimentary —; *tube digestif, canal alimentaire, m.*

duc'tile (deuc'tile), *adj.*, ductile, souple.

duc'tileness *ou* **ductil'ity**, *n.*, ductilité, flexibilité, souplesse, *f.*

dud'geon (deud'jeune), *n.*, brouille, brouillerie ; mauvaise part ; colère, *f.* ; ressentiment, *m.* ; (dagger) (ant.) petite dague, *f.* To take in —; *prendre en mauvaise part ; prendre de travers, s'offenser* **de**. In high —; *fort en colère.*

due (diou), *adj.*, dû ; convenable ; juste, (com.) échu, arrivé à l'échéance, (fig.) requis, voulu ; suffisant. The train is — at eight o'clock ; *le train doit arriver à huit heures.* In — form ; *dans les formes voulues ; en règle, dans les règles.* In — time; *en temps utile ; au moment voulu ; à temps.* In — time and place ; *en temps et lieu.*

due, *n.*, dû ; droit, impôt, *m.*, redevance, *f.* To give the devil his — ; *rendre justice au diable, ne pas peindre le diable plus noir qu'il n'est.* To give any one his — ; *prendre à quelqu'un ce que lui est dû ; rendre justice à quelqu'un.*

due, *adv.*, droit, directement. — west ; *en plein ouest.*

du'el (diou'-), *n.*, duel ; combat, *m.*, (fig.) lutte, contestation, *f.* To fight a —; *se battre en duel.*

du'eling, *n.*, (le) duel, *m.*

du'elist, *n.*, duelliste, *m.*

duen'na (diou'è'n'-), *n.*, duègne, *f.*

duet' (deu'ète), *n.*, (mus.) duo, *m.*

dug (deughe), *n.*, bout de sein, *m.* ; (of animals that are milked) trayon, *m.*

duke (diouke), *n.*, duc, *m.*

duke'dom (-deume), *n.*, duché, *m.* ; dignité de duc, *f.* ; titre de duc, *m.*

dul'cet (deul'cète), *adj.*, (ant.) doux, harmonieux.

dul'cify (deul-ci-faïe), *v.a.*, (ant. pharm.) dulcifier.

dul'cimer (deul'-), *n.*, tympanon, dulcimer, *m.*

dull (deul), *adj.*, (of persons) lourd, borné, stupide ; (of the weather) lourd, gris, sombre, couvert, triste ; (of sound) sourd ; (melancholy) triste, sombre ; (blunt) émoussé ; (com.) plat, calme ; (color) sombre, terne, blafard ; (of surface) mat. — of hearing ; *qui entend dur ; sourdaud ; un peu sourd.* A — fire ; *un triste feu.* To be —; (melancholy) *s'ennuyer.* To be —; (tiresome) *être ennuyeux, assommant, sciant.* To feel —; *s'ennuyer.*

dull (deul), *v.a.*, rendre lourd ; lasser ; hébéter ; (to blunt) émousser ; ternir ; affaiblir ; stupéfier ; (to numb) engourdir.

dull, *v.n.*, devenir lourd ; s'hébéter, s'engourdir, s'émousser.

dul'lard (deul'-), *n.*, lourdaud, imbécile, *m.* ; cruche, *f.*

dull'ish, *adj.*, un peu lourd, un peu triste.

dull'-brained (-bré'n'de), *adj.*, à l'esprit lourd ; qui a l'esprit lourd, stupide ; lourd.

dull'-browed (-braou'de), *adj.*, au front sombre ; qui a le front sombre, triste, mélancolique.

dull'-eyed (-aïe'de), *adj.*, au regard sombre ; mélancolique, au regard terne.

dull'-head (-hède), *n.*, esprit lourd ; lourdaud, benêt, *m.*

dull'ness, *n.*, stupidité ; lenteur, *f.* ; ennui ; état émoussé ; manque d'éclat, *m.*, matité, ternissure, *f.*

dull'-season, *n.*, morte-saison, *f.*

dull'-sighted (-saït'ède), *adj.*, qui a la vue faible ; à la vue faible, myope.

dull'-witted (-wit'tède), *adj.*, lourd, stupide.

dul'ly, *adv.*, lourdement, lentement, sottement, sans énergie.

du'ly (diou-li), *adv.*, dûment, en temps utile ; justement ; convenablement ; régulièrement, bien. I have — received ; *j'ai bien reçu.*

dumb (deume), *adj.*, muet, réduit au silence. — -waiter ; *servante, f.*

dumb'-ague *ou* **dumb'-chill**, *n.*, fièvre intermittente, *f.*

dumb'-bells, *n.pl.*, haltères, *m.pl.*

dumb'-crea'ture, *n.*, bête, *f.*, animal, *m.*

dumb'ly (deu'm'li), *adv.*, sans rien dire, sans paroles, en silence.

dumb'ness (deu'm'nèce), *n.*, silence ; mutisme, *m.*

dumb'-show, *n.*, pantomime, *f.*, jeu muet, *m.*

dum'found *ou* **dumfoun'der** (deu'm'faou'n'd, -'eur), *v.a.*, confondre ; abasourdir, interdire, étonner, troubler, (pop.) épater.

dum'my (deu'm'-), *n.*, muet, *m.*, muette, *f.* ; mannequin, personnage muet, (fig.) homme de paille, (whist) mort, *m.*

dump (deu'm'pe), *n.*, tristesse ; mélancolie ; humeur noire, *f.* To be in the —s ; *être triste comme un bonnet de nuit.*

dump'ish, *adj.*, chagrin, mélancolique.

dump'ishness, *n.*, tristesse, mélancolie, *f.*

dump'ling (deu'm'p'-), *n.*,(cook.) chausson, *m.*

dum'py, *adj.*, trapu ; gros et court.

dun (deune), *adj.*, brun foncé, noisette ; (of horses) bai brun, alezan foncé, isabelle.

dun, *n.*, créancier importun, *m.*

dun *ou* **don**, *n.*, (ant.), éminence, *f.*, fort, *m.*

dun, *v.a.*, importuner, poursuivre.

dunce (deu'n'ce), *n.*, ignorant, crétin, cancre, *m.*, ignorante ; ganache, cruche, *f.*

dun'-colored (-keul'leurde), *adj.*, brun foncé ; (of horses) isabelle.

dun'-fish, *n.*, morue salée, *f.*

dun'-fly, *n.*, taon, *m.*

dung (deu'gne), *n.*, fiente, *f.* ; (agri.) fumier, *m.* ; (of mice, sheep, rabbits) crotte, *f.* ; (of horses) crottin, *m.* ; (of oxen, cows) fiente, bouse, *f.* ; (of stags) fumées, *f.p.*

dung, *v.a.*, fumer.

dung, *v.n.*, fienter.

dung'-cart (-cârte), *n.*, tombereau à fumier, *m.*

dun'geon (deu'n'djeu'ne), *n.*, cachot, *m.*, basse-fosse, *f.*

dung'-fork (-forke), *n.*, fourche à fumier, *f.*

dung'hill, *n.*, fumier, (fig.) taudis, *m.*, baraque, *f.*

dung'hill, *adj.*, de fumier ; sale, ignoble.

dung'ing (deu'gn'-), *n.*, (agri.) fumure, *f.* ; (manu.) bousage, *m.*

dung'y (deu'gn'i), *adj.*, de fumier ; (fig.) vil, bas, sale.

dun'lin, *n.*, (orni.) cocorli, *m.*

dun'nage (deu'n'nèdje), *n.*, (nav.) fardage, *m.*

dun'ning (deu'n'-), *n.*, importunité ; (curing) salaison, *f.*

dun'nish, *adj.*, qui tire sur le gris foncé ; brunâtre.

du'o (diou-ô), *n.*, duo, *m.*

duodec'imal (diou-o-dèc'i-), *adj.*, duodécimal.

duodec'imals (-malze), *n. ;* (arith.) multiplication des nombres complexes, *f.*

duodec'imo, *n.*, (print.) in-douze, *m.*

duode'nal (diou-o-dî'-nal), *adj.*, (anat.) duodénal.

duoden'ary, *adj.*, duodénaire.

dupe (dioupe), *n.*, dupe, *f.*

dupe, *v.a.*, duper, tromper, (fam.) flouer.

du'pion (diou-), *n.*, cocon double, *m.*

du'ple (diou-p'l), *adj.*, double.

du'plicate (diou-pli-kéte) *adj.*, double.

du'plicate, *n.*, double, duplicata, *m. ;* (of a pawnbroker) reconnaissance, *f.* In — ; *en duplicata, en double.*

du'plicate, *v.a.*, doubler ; copier ; (ant.) plier en double.

duplica'tion (diou-pli-ké-), *n.*, duplication, *f.*

duplic'ity (diou-), *n.*, duplicité, mauvaise foi, dissimulation, *f.*

durabil'ity (diou-), *n.*, durabilité, *f.*

du'rable (diou-ra-b'l), *adj.*, durable.

du'rableness, *n.*, durabilité, *f.*

du'rably, *adv.*, d'une manière durable.

du'rance (diou-), *n.*, emprisonnement, *m. ;* prison, *f.* To be in — ; *être en prison, ou en cage.*

dura'tion (diou-ré-), *n.*, durée, *f.*

duress' (diou-), *n.*, emprisonnement, *m. ;* contrainte, pression, *f.*

du'ring (diour'-), *prep.*, pendant, durant.

dur'ra, *n.*, (bot.) doura, sorgho, *m.*

dusk (deuske), *n.*, brune, *f. ;* crépuscule, *m.*, (color) teinte sombre, *f.* In the — of the evening ; *à la brune, à la nuit tombante, à la tombée de la nuit, entre chien et loup.*

dusk, *adj.*, obscur, sombre.

dusk'ily, *adv.*, obscurément.

dusk'iness, *n.*, obscurité, teinte sombre, .

dusk'y, *adj.*, obscur, sombre, foncé, noirâtre, brunâtre.

dust (deuste), *n.*, poussière ; poudre ; confusion, commotion, *f. ;* cendres des morts, *f.pl. ;* tombe ; condition basse et misérable, poussière, *f.* Saw— ; *sciure, f.* Coal— ; *poussier de charbon, m.* To raise a — ; *produire une commotion.* To throw — in any one's eyes ; *jeter de la poudre aux yeux de quelqu'un.* To trample in the — ; *fouler aux pieds.* To trample into — ; *réduire en poussière ; réduire au néant.*

dust, *v.a.*, épousseter ; couvrir de poussière ; pulvériser, battre. To — any one's jacket ; *étriller quelqu'un.*

dust'-brush (-breushe), *n.*, plumeau, *m.*

dust'er, *n.*, torchon, *m. ;* vergette, *f.*, plumeau, *m.*, (for horses) époussette, *f.*

dust'-heap, *n.*, tas d'ordures, *m.*

dust'-hole (-hôle), *n.*, trou aux ordures, *m.*

dust'iness, *n.*, état poudreux, *m.*

dust'man (-mane), *n.*, boueur, *m.*

dust'-pan, *n.*, pelle à ordures, *f.*

dust'y, *adj.*, poudreux, couvert de poussière ; de poussière.

Dutch (deutshe), *adj.*, hollandais.

Dutch, *n.*, hollandais (language), *m.*

Dutch'man, *n.*, Hollandais, *m.*

Dutch'woman (-woum'ane),*n.*, Hollandaise, *f.*

du'teous (diou-ti-), *adj.*, soumis, obéissant, respectueux.

du'tiable (diou-ti-a-b'l), *adj.*, imposable, assujetti aux droits et impositions.

du'tiful (diou-ti-foule), *adj.*, obéissant, soumis, respectueux, humble.

du'tifully, *adv.*, avec soumission, respectueusement.

du'tifulness, *n.*, soumission ; déférence, *f.*

du'ty (diou-ti), *n.*, devoir ; respect ; (at the customs) droit ; (milit.) service, *m.* On — ; *de service, de garde ;* (of sentinels) *en faction ;* (fam.) *de corvée.* To do — for ; *servir de ; prendre la place de.* To do one's — ; *faire son devoir.* To enter upon one's duties ; *entrer en fonctions.*

duum'vir (diou-eu'm'veur), *n.*, duumvir, *m.*

duum'virate (-éte), *n.*, duumvirat, *m.*

dwale (dwéle), *n.*, (her.) couleur noire ; (bot.) belladone ; douce-amère, *f.*

dwarf (dworfe), *n.*, nain, *m.*, naine, *f.*

dwarf, *adj.*, nain.

dwarf, *v.a.*, rapetisser ; (hort.) rabougrir, naniser.

dwarf, *v.n.*, se rapetisser, se rabougrir.

dwarf'ing, *n.*, (hort.) nanisation, *f.*

dwarf'ish, *adj.*, de nain, insignifiant, petit, minime.

dwarf'ishly, *adv.*, en nain.

dwarf'ishness (dwarf-), *n.*, taille de nain ; petitesse, *f.*

dwell (dwèle), *v.n.*, demeurer, habiter ; rester. To — on ; *s'étendre* **sur**, *appuyer* **sur** ; *s'arrêter* **à**, *s'appesantir* **sur**, *insister* **sur**.

dwell'er, *n.*, habitant, *m.*, habitante, *f.*

dwell'ing, *n.*, demeure, habitation, résidence, *f. ;* domicile, *m.*

dwell'ing-house (-haouce), *n.*, maison d'habitation, demeure, résidence, *f. ;* domicile, *m.*

dwin'dle (dwi'n'd'l), *v.n.*, diminuer ; dépérir ; dégénérer ; disparaître ; se réduire **à**.

dwin'dle, *v.a.*, diminuer, réduire ; briser ; disperser.

dye (daïe), *v.a.*, teindre, colorer ; tacher.

dye, *v.n.*, teindre, se teindre. To — black, red ; *teindre en noir, en rouge.*

dye, *n.*, teinture, teinte ; couleur ; matière tinctoriale, *f.*, (fig.) caractère, *m. ;* qualité, noirceur, *f.* A crime of a deeper — ; *un crime plus atroce.* A villain of the deepest — ; *un coquin fieffé.*

dye'-drug (-dreughe), *n.*, drogue de teinture ; drogue tinctoriale, matière tinctoriale, *f.*

dye'-house (-haouce), *n.*, teinturerie, *f.*

dye'ing, *n.*, teinture, *f.*

dye'-mill, *n.*, teinturerie, *f. ;* atelier de teinture, *m.*

dy'er (daïeur), *n.*, teinturier, *m.*, teinturière, *f.*

dy'er's-broom (-'z'broume), *n.*, (bot.) herbe des teinturiers ; genestrole, genétrelle, *f.*

dy'er's-weed (-'z'wîde), *n.*, (bot.) réséda des teinturiers, *m. ;* gaude, *f. ;* pastel, *m.*, guède, *f.* *V.* **dyer's broom**.

dye'stuff (-steufe), *n.*, couleur pour teindre ; matière tinctoriale, *f.*

dye'-wood (-woude), *n.*, bois de teinture ; bois tinctorial, *m.*

dye'-works (-weurkse), *n.pl.*, teinturerie, *f.sing.*

dy'ing (daï'i'gne), *adj.*, mourant, moribond ; (of things) de la mort ; suprême, dernier, fait au lit de la mort. — man ; *mourant, moribond, au lit de la mort.* — woman ; *mourante, moribonde, f.* To be — ; *se mourir, être mourant* (only used in Present and Imperfect tenses).

dyke (daïke), *n.*, digue, *f. ;* fossé ; (mines) filon stérile, *m. ;* (geol.) faille ; veine de basalte, *f.*

dynam'ic *ou* **dynam'ical** (di-), *adj.*, dynamique. [*f.sing.*

dynam'ics (di-na'm'ikse), *n.pl.*, dynamique, *f.*

dy'namo, *n.*, dynamo, *m.*

dynamom'eter (din'a-mo-m'i-), *n.*, (mec.) dynamomètre, *m.*

dynas'tic (di-), *adj.*, dynastique.

dyn'asty, *n.*, dynastie, famille, *f.*

dyne, *n.*, (phys.) dyne, *f.*

dys'enteric *ou* **dysenter'ical** (diss'è-n'tèr'-), *adj.*, (med.) dysentérique.

dys'entery (diss'è'n'tèr'i), n., dysenterie, f.
dyspep'sia ou **dyspep'sy** (dis-pèp'-), n., dyspepsie, f.
dys'pnœa (disp'nî-a), n., dyspnée, f.
dys'ury (diss'iou-ri), n., dysurie, f.

E

e, cinquième lettre de l'alphabet, e, m.; (mus.) mi, m.

each (îtshe), pron. and adj., chaque; chacun, m., chacune, f. — one; chacun, m., chacune, f.; — other; l'un l'autre; les uns les autres. For — other; l'un pour l'autre, les uns pour les autres. Of — other; l'un de l'autre, les uns des autres. To — other; l'un à l'autre, les uns aux autres.

ea'ger, (î-gheur), adj., vif, ardent; impatient, curieux, avide, désireux, empressé.

ea'gerly, adv., ardemment, impatiemment, avec empressement.

ea'gerness, n., ardeur, impatience, vivacité; avidité, f.; empressement, m.

ea'gle (î-g'l), n., (orni., astron.) aigle, m.; (her., Rom. hist.) aigle, f., (ecc.) lutrin, m.

ea'gle-eyed (-aïe'de), adj., aux yeux d'aigle.

ea'gle-owl, n., grand-duc, m.

ea'gle-sighted (-saït'ède), adj. V. **eagle-eyed**.

ea'gle-stone (-stône), n., (min.) aétite, pierre d'aigle, f.

ea'glet (î-glète), n., aiglon, m.

ea'gle-winged (-wign'de), adj., aux ailes d'aigle.

ea'gre (î-gheur), n., raz; raz de marée, m.

ear (îr), n., oreille, f.; (of corn) épi, m.; (of a vessel) anse, f. All —s; tout attention, très attentif. Up to the —s; jusqu'aux oreilles; complètement; très avant; profondément. Over head and —s; par-dessus les oreilles. To be by the —s; être en guerre, être aux prises. To set by the —s; mettre aux prises, brouiller. At first —; immédiatement. To turn a deaf —; faire la sourde oreille. To listen with both —; écouter de toutes ses oreilles.

ear, v.n., monter en épi.

ear'ache (îr-éke), n., mal d'oreille; mal à l'oreille, m.

ear'-bored (îr-bôrde), adj., aux oreilles percées; qui a les oreilles percées.

ear'-cap, n., oreillette, f.

ear'-deafening (-dèf'fn'-), adj., étourdissant.

ear'-drop, n., pendant d'oreille, m.

ear'-drum (-dreume), n., (anat.) tympan; tambour de l'oreille, m.

eared (îr-de), adj., qui a des oreilles; garni d'épis; (bot.) auriculé. Long— ; aux longues oreilles. Full —; (of corn) à épis pleins.

earl (eur'l), n., comte, m. — marshal; comte maréchal, m.

ear'-lap (îr'lape), n., lobe, bout inférieur de l'oreille, m.

earl'dom (eur'l'deume), n., comté, titre de comte, m.

ear'less (îr'lèce), adj., sans oreilles.

ear'liness (eur'li'-), n., heure peu avancée; précocité; arrivée prématurée, f.; (of fruits) précocité, hâtiveté, f.

ear'ly (eur'li) adv., de bonne heure; tôt; dès le matin, de bon matin, de grand matin; matinalement; (fig.) au commencement de; dans les premiers jours ou mois de.

ear'ly, adj., matinal, (pers.) matineux; prématuré, précoce; (hort.) hâtif. — age; âge tendre; bas âge, m. — ages; premiers âges, premiers temps, m.pl. — old age; vieillesse prématurée, f. — church; Eglise primitive, f. To be an — riser; avoir l'habitude de se lever de bonne heure; être matineux,

earn (eurne), v.a., gagner, obtenir; acquérir; mériter.

ear'nest (eur'nèste), adj., ardent, vif, sérieux, empressé, zélé, sincère.

ear'nest, n., sérieux, gage, m.; arrhes, f.pl.; denier à Dieu, m. In good —; sérieux; au sérieux; de bonne foi; tout de bon; pour tout de bon. Are you in —? parlez-vous sérieusement? To be in —; être sérieux, parler sérieusement.

ear'nestly, adv., ardemment; sérieusement; instamment, avec empressement.

ear'nest-money (-meu'n'ni), n., arrhes, f.pl.

ear'nestness, n., ardeur, f.; empressement; sérieux, zèle, m.

earn'ings (eurn'ign'ze), n.pl., gain; fruit du travail, m., gages, m.pl.

ear'-pick (îr-pike), n., cure-oreille, m.

ear'piercing (îr-pîrs'-), adj., qui perce l'oreille; au son perçant.

ear'-ring (îr-rigne), n., boucle d'oreille, f.

ear'-shaped (îr-shép'te), adj., en forme d'oreille.

ear'shot (îr-shote), n., à portée de l'oreille, de l'ouïe, de la voix, m.

earth (eurth), n., terre, f.

earth, v.a., enterrer, enfouir, couvrir de terre. To — up; (agri.) butter. To — one's self; se terrer. Made —; terre rapportée, f. Mother —; mère commune, f.

earth'bag, n., sac de, ou à, terre, m.

earth'bank, n., jetée de terre, f.

earth'board (-bôrde), n., (agri.) versoir, m.

earth'born, adj., né de la terre, terrestre; de basse naissance.

earth'bound (-baou'n'de), adj., attaché à la terre; (fig.) attaché aux biens terrestres.

earth'bred (-brède), adj., (ant.) de basse naissance; vil, abject.

earthed, adj., enterré; (of animals) terré, dans son terrier.

earth'en (eurth'n), adj., de terre.

earth'enware (-wére), n., poterie; vaisselle de terre; faïence, f.

earth'fed (-fède), adj., (ant.) nourri de substances terrestres, bas, rampant, charnel.

earth'flax, n., (min.) amiante, asbeste, m.

earth'iness, n., nature terreuse; féculence, (ant., fig.) bassesse, grossièreté, f.

earth'liness, n., (ant.) mondanité, f.; attachement aux biens terrestres; (l.u.) caractère terrestre, m.

earth'ling, n., (ant.) mortel, m.

earth'ly, adj., terrestre.

earth'ly-minded (-maï'n'd'ède), adj., mondain.

earth'ly-mindedness, n., caractère mondain, m., mondanité, f.

earth'-nut (-neute), n., (bot.) terre-noix; châtaigne, ou pistache, de terre, f.

earth'quake (-kwéke), n., tremblement de terre, m.

earth'shaking (-shék'-), adj., qui fait trembler la terre.

earth'ward (-weurde), adv., vers la terre.

earth'work (-weurke), n., terrassement, m., travaux de terrasse, m.pl.; (fort.) ouvrage en terre, m.

earth'worm (-weurme), n., ver de terre, m.

earth'y, adj., de terre; terrestre; terreux.

ear'-trumpet (îr-treu'm'pète), n., cornet acoustique, m.

ear'-wax (îr-wakse), n., cérumen, m., cire, f.

ear'wig (îr'wighe), n., (ent.) perce-oreille, m.; forficule auriculaire, f.

ease (îze), n., aisance, aise, tranquillité, facilité, f., repos, m.; (fig.) abandon, m.; (of pain) soulagement, m. At —; tranquille; à l'aise; (mil.) à volonté. At one's —; à l'aise; dans l'aisance. To take one's —; se mettre à l'aise; prendre ses aises. Stand at —! (mil.) en place! repos!

ease, v.a., tranquilliser, calmer ; soulager, alléger, adoucir, calmer, mettre à l'aise. To — off ; (nav.) *larguer* (a ship), *amener au vent.* — her ! *doucement !*

ease'ful (-foule), adj., tranquille, paisible.

ea'sel (î'z'l), n., (paint.) chevalet, m.

ease'ment, n., soulagement, m. ; (jur.) servitude, f.

ea'sily, adv., facilement, aisément, à l'aise.

ea'siness, n., facilité ; douceur, aisance, f.

east (îste), n., est, orient, levant, m. — Indiaman ; *navire des Indes orientales,* m. — wind ; *vent d'est.*

east, adj., d'orient, oriental, d'est.

Eas'ter (îst'eur), n., (Christian rel.) Pâque ou Pâques, m. (f. ou m. in the plur.) ; (Jewish rel.) Pâque, f. — Monday ; *lundi de Pâques,* m. Monday in — week ou Monday before — ; *lundi saint.* On — eve ; *veille de Pâques,* f., *samedi saint,* m. — day ; *jour de Pâques,* m.

east'erly, adj., d'orient ; d'est.

east'erly, adv., vers l'orient, vers l'est ; à l'est, à l'orient.

east'ern, adj., oriental, d'orient, d'est. Great — railway ; *chemin de fer de l'est,* m.

east'ward (îst'worde), adv., vers l'orient ; vers l'est.

ea'sy (î-zi) adj., aisé, facile ; tranquille ; (of style) doux, coulant ; à l'aise ; dans l'aisance. — chair ; *fauteuil,* m. — of belief ; *crédule.* I am — in my mind ; *j'ai l'esprit tranquille ;* je *suis sans inquiétude.* To take it — ; *ne pas se faire de bile ; ne pas se tourmenter ;* (fam.) *ne pas se fouler la rate.* To make one's self — about ; *se tranquilliser* sur. I am quite — on that score ou I have no misgivings ; *je suis tranquille là-dessus.* It is as — as possible ; *c'est facile comme bonjour.* In — stages ; *en grand seigneur.* — going ; *accommodant, complaisant, qui ne se fait pas de bile.*

eat (île), v.a., (preterit, Eat, Ate ; *past part.,* Eaten) manger ; gruger ; (to corrode) ronger. To — a good dinner ; *faire un bon dîner.* To — away ; *consumer ; ronger.* To — up ; *manger entièrement ; dévorer ; achever de manger.* To — one's words ; *se rétracter ;* (fam.) *en être au repentir.* To — one's terms ; *étudier le droit.* To — out ; *consommer, gruger ; ronger, dévorer, consumer.*

eat, v.n., manger. To — into ; *ronger ; faire des ravages* dans ; *miner.* Rust —s into iron ; *la rouille ronge le fer.*

eat'able (ît'a-b'l), adj., mangeable, comestible, bon à manger.

eat'able, n., comestible, m.

eat'age, n., (for horses, etc.) regain, m.

eat'er, n., mangeur, m., mangeuse, f. ; (ant.) valet, laquais, m.

eat'ing, n., action de manger, f. ; manger ; (fig.) dévorant, rongeur, m. — and drinking ; le *boire et le manger,* m. To be fond of good — ; *aimer la bonne chère.*

eat'ing-house (-haouce), n., restaurant, m. ; — keeper ; *restaurateur ; traiteur,* m.

eaves (îv'ze), n., bord du toit, égout ; (arch.) larmier, m.

eaves'drop, v.n., écouter aux portes.

eaves'dropper, n., écouteur aux portes, m.

ebb (èbe), v.n., (fig.) baisser, décliner ; refluer, s'écouler, se retirer. To — and flow; *monter et baiser.*

ebb, n., reflux, m. ; (nav.) jusant; (fig.) déclin, m. ; décadence, f. At a low — ; *très bas.* The — and flow ; *le flux et le reflux,* m. — tide ; *marée descendante,* f.

ebb'ing, n., qui reflue ; sur le déclin.

ebb'-tide (-taïde), n., reflux ; (nav.) jusant, m.

eb'on, adj., (ant.) d'ébène, noir.

eb'onize (-'aïze), v.a., ébéner.

eb'ony (èb'-), n., ébène, f. ; bois d'ébène,

(bot.) plaqueminier, ébénier, m. Dealer in — ; *négrier,* m. — work ; ébène, m.

eb'ony-tree (-trî), n., (bot.) ébénier, m.

ebul'lience ou **ebul'liency** (è-beull'-), n., (ant.) ébullition ; effervescence, f.

ebul'lient, adj., en ébullition, bouillonnant.

ebulli'tion (èb'eul'-), n., ébullition ; effervescence, f. ; transport, accès, m.

ec'ce-ho'mo (èk-sè-hô-mô), n., ecce homo (behold the man !), m.

eccen'tric, adj., excentrique ; bizarre ; original, singulier. — gear ; (mec.) *appareil à transformer les mouvements ; excentrique,* m.

eccen'tric (èk'cè'n'-), n., (geom.) cercle excentrique, m.

eccentric'ity, n., (geom.) excentricité ; (fig.) originalité, f.

ecchymo'sis (èk-ki-mô-cice), n., ecchymose, f.

Ecclesias'tes (èk-cli-zi-as-tize), n., Ecclésiaste, m.

ecclesias'tic (-cli-), n., ecclésiastique, m.

ecclesias'tic ou **ecclesias'tical** (-cli-), adj., ecclésiastique.

ecclesias'tically (-cli-), adv., ecclésiastiquement.

Ecclesias'ticus (-cli-), n., Ecclésiastique, m.

echi'nus (i-ki-), n., (conch.) oursin, hérisson de mer, m. ; (arch.) échine, f.

ech'o (èk'ô), n., (phys.) écho, m.

ech'o, v.a., (fig.) répéter ; (phys.) renvoyer, répercuter.

ech'o, v.n., faire écho ; retentir, résonner.

ech'oless, adj., sans écho.

eclat' (écla), n., éclat, m.

eclec'tic, adj., éclectique.

eclec'tic, n., éclectique, m.

eclec'ticism, n., éclectisme, m.

eclipse', n., éclipse, f.

eclipse', v.a., éclipser ; (fig.) surpasser, exceller.

eclipse', v.n., s'éclipser.

eclip'tic, n., écliptique, f.

eclip'tic, adj., écliptique ; de l'écliptique.

ec'logue (èk'loghe), n. V. **æg'logue.**

ecod', int., ma foi ! parbleu !

econom'ic ou **econom'ical,** adj., (of things) économique ; (pers.) économe, ménager.

econom'ically, adv., économiquement.

econom'ics, n.pl., économie, f.sing. Political — ; *économie.*

econ'omist, n., économe ; économiste, m.

econ'omize (-maïze), v.a., économiser.

econ'omize, v.n., économiser ; user d'économie.

econ'omy, n., économie, f. ; système, m.

ecs'tasied, adj., ravi en extase, extasié.

ecs'tasy (èk-sta-ci), n., extase, f. ; transport, m.

ecstat'ic ou **ecstat'ical,** adj., extatique ; d'extase.

ectro'pium (èk-trô-), n., (med.) ectropion, m.

ec'type, n., ectype, f.

ecumen'ical, adj., œcuménique, écuménique.

ec'zema, n., (med.) eczéma, m.

eczem'atous, adj., (med.) eczémateux, -euse.

eda'cious (è-dé-sheusse), adj., vorace, gourmand.

Ed'da, n., Edda, f.

edac'ity (è-dass'-), n., voracité, gourmandise, f.

ed'dy (èd-), n., (of water) contrecourant, remous ; (of wind) tourbillon, m.

ed'dy, adj., tourbillonnant.

ed'dy, v.n., tourbillonner, tournoyer.

ed'dy-water (-wô-), n., remous, m.

ed'dy-wind (-wi'n'de), n., revolin, m.

edem'atose (è-dè'm'a-tôss) ou **edem'atous,** adj., œdémateux.

E'den (î-dène), n., Eden, m.

eden'talous ou **eden'tated** (è-dè'n'ta-, -tétède), adj., (zool.) édenté.

edge (èdje), *n.*, bord ; (of sharp instruments) fil, tranchant, *m.* ; (of a wood, forest) lisière, *f.* ; (coin) cordon, *m.* ; (of a prism) angle, *m.* ; arête saillante ; (of a book) tranche, *f.* To give an — to ; *donner le fil à.* To take off the — ; *ôter le fil à, émousser.* To set one's teeth on — ; *agacer les dents.* To put to the — of the sword ; *passer au fil de l'épée.* With gilt —s ; *doré sur tranche.* To take the — off one's appetite ; *étourdir la grosse faim.*

edge, *v.a.,* affiler ; aiguiser ; (to border) border ; (carp.) abattre les angles ; (fig.) exaspérer, aiguillonner ; inciter, pousser, exciter ; provoquer. To — in ; *faire entrer difficilement* ; (fig.) *glisser, couler.* [Au figuré, on trouve quelquefois *egg,* qui n'est qu'une orthographe erronée du mot *edge.*]

edge, *v.n.,* s'avancer de côté. To — away ; (nav.) *s'éloigner graduellement.* To — upon ; (of the wind) *aller contre.*

edged (èdj'de), *adj.,* affilé, aigu, tranchant ; bordé. Two— ; *à deux tranchants.* Gilt— ; *doré sur tranche.* To play with — tools ; *jouer avec le feu.*

edge'less, *adj.,* sans tranchant ; émoussé.

edge'-tool (-toule), *n.,* instrument tranchant, *m.* — maker ; *taillandier, m.* — trade ; *taillanderie, f.*

edge'wise (-waïze), *adv.,* de côté, sur le bord, de champ.

edg'ing, *n.,* bord, *m.* ; bordure ; garniture, *f.*

ed'ible (èd'i-b'l), *adj.,* mangeable, comestible, bon à manger.

e'dict (î-dicte), *n.,* édit, *m.*

edifica'tion (èd'i-fi-ké-), *n.,* édification, *f.*

ed'ifice, *n.,* édifice, *m.*

ed'ifier (èd'i-faï'-), *n.,* (l.u.) qui édifie ; (l.u.) édificateur, *m.*

ed'ify (èd'i-faïe), *v.a.,* édifier.

ed'ifying, *adj.,* édifiant.

ed'ifyingly, *adv.,* d'une manière édifiante.

e'dile (î-daïl), *n.,* édile, *m.*

e'dileship, *n.,* édilité, *f.*

ed'it (èd'ite), *v.a.,* publier ; être éditeur de ; éditer, annoter ; rédiger, diriger.

edi'tion (è-dish'eune), *n.,* édition, *f.*

ed'itor (èd'i-teur), *n.,* éditeur, annotateur ; (of newspapers) rédacteur, gérant, directeur, *m.*

ed'itorship, *n.,* fonctions d'éditeur, *f.pl.* ; direction d'un journal, rédaction, *f.*

ed'ucate (èd'iou-kéte), *v.a.,* élever ; faire l'éducation de, instruire.

educa'tion (èd-iou-ké-), *n.,* éducation, *f.*

educa'tional, *adj.,* d'éducation.

ed'ucator (-két'eur), *n.,* instituteur, *m.,* institutrice, *f.* ; éducateur, *m.* ; éducatrice, *f.*

educe' (è-diouce), *v.a.,* tirer, faire sortir, extraire.

educ'tion (è-deuk'-), *n.,* émission ; extraction ; décharge, *f.* ; dégagement, *m.*

edul'corate (è-deul-co-réte), *v.a.,* (pharm.) édulcorer.

edulcora'tion, *n.,* (pharm.) édulcoration, *f.*

eel (îl), *n.,* anguille, *f.* —spear ; *trident, m.* —buck ; *nasse, f.* —fare ; *montée d'anguillettes, f.* —fishing ; *pêche à l'anguille, f.* —fork ; *trident, m.* —pout ; (ich.) *lotte, barbote, f.*

ef'fable (èf'fa-b'l), *adj.,* (ant.) qui peut s'exprimer.

efface' (-féce), *v.a.,* effacer.

efface'able (-féss'a-b'l), *adj.,* effaçable.

effect' (èf'fèkte), *n.,* effet, *m.* ; action, *f.* ; objet, *m.* ; (jur.) biens, *m.pl.* In — ; *en réalité* ; *de fait* ; *en effet.* To the same — ; *à la même intention.* Without — ; *invalide* ; *sans résultat.* For — ; *pour faire de l'effet.* To give — to ; *valider* ; *rendre valide* ; *mettre à exécution.* To feel the —s of ; *se ressentir de.* Of no — ; *nul et invalide.* To no — ; *en vain* ; *sans résultat* ; *inutile.* To take — ; *faire effet* ; *agir* ; *produire son*

effet ; *porter coup* ; *opérer.* To produce — ; *faire de l'effet.* To carry into — ; *accomplir, exécuter, mettre à exécution, mettre à effet.*

effect', *v.a.,* effectuer, exécuter, accomplir, opérer.

effect'ible (-i-b'l), *adj.,* (ant.) praticable, possible.

effect'ive, *adj.,* effectif, efficace.

effect'ively, *adv.,* effectivement ; efficacement.

effect'less, *adj.,* inefficace, sans effet ; inutile.

effect'or (-teur), *n.,* créateur, auteur, producteur, *m.*

effect'ual (-'iou-), *adj.,* efficace.

effect'ually, *adv.,* efficacement.

effem'inacy, *n.,* mollesse ; délicatesse efféminée, *f.*

effem'inate, *adj.,* efféminé, lâche, mou.

effem'inate, *v.a.,* efféminer, amollir.

effem'inately, *adv.,* d'une manière efféminée ; avec mollesse.

effem'inateness, *n.,* mollesse ; nature efféminée.

effervesce', *v.n.,* être en effervescence ; faire effervescence ; (of beverages) mousser, être en effervescence.

efferves'cence, *n.,* effervescence, *f.*

efferves'cent *ou* **efferves'cing,** *adj.,* effervescent ; mousseux ; (of aerated waters) gazeux.

effete' (èf'fîte), *adj.,* frappé de stérilité ; usé ; stérile, émoussé ; épuisé, éventé.

effica'cious (èf'fi-ké-sheusse), *adj.,* efficace.

effica'ciously, *adv.,* efficacement ; avec efficacité.

ef'ficacy (èf'fi-ca-), *n.,* efficacité, *f.* ; (pers.) capacité.

effi'cience *ou* **effi'ciency** (èf'fish'-), *n.,* efficacité ; action productrice ; (of armies) bonne condition ; capacité, *f.* ; (mec.) rendement, *m.*

effi'cient, *n.,* cause efficiente, *f.* ; (philos., theol.) premier moteur, *m.* ; (mil.) volontaire qui a passé à l'école de bataillon ; (math.) facteur, *m.*

effi'cient, *adj.,* efficient ; efficace ; capable.

effi'ciently, *adv.,* efficacement, d'une manière compétente.

ef'figy (-dji), *n.,* effigie, *f.* ; portrait, *m.* ; image, représentation, *f.* To burn, *ou* hang, in — ; *brûler,* ou *pendre, en effigie.*

effloresce', *v.n.,* (chem.) effleurir, s'effleurir, tomber en efflorescence.

efflores'cence *ou* **efflores'cency,** *n.,* (chem.) efflorescence ; (bot.) fleuraison, floraison, *f.*

efflores'cent, *adj.,* efflorescent ; (bot.) fleurissant.

ef'fluence *ou* **ef'fluency** (èf'fiou'-), *n.,* effluence, émanation, *f.*

ef'fluent, *adj.,* effluent ; qui émane.

efflu'vium (èf'fiou-vi-eume), *n.,* (*effluvia*) exhalaison, *f.,* effluve, *m.*

efflux' (èf'fleukse), *n.,* (ant.) écoulement, *m.* ; émanation, effusion ; (of population) émigration, *f.* — of time ; *l'expiration du temps, f.*

ef'fort (èf'fôrte), *n.,* effort, *m.* To use every — ; *faire tous ses efforts pour.* It is an —, a great — for me ; *il m'en coûte beaucoup de.*

ef'fortless, *adj.,* sans effort.

effront'ery (èf'freu'n'ti-ri), *n.,* effronterie, audace, *f.*

efful'gence, *n.,* éclat, resplendissement, *m.* ; splendeur, *f.*

efful'gent, *adj.,* resplendissant, éclatant.

effuse' (èf'fiouze), *v.a.,* répandre, verser ; (med.) épancher.

effuse', *v.n.,* émaner, se répandre ; (med.) s'épancher.

effu'sion (èf-fiou-jeune), *n.,* effusion, *f.* ; épanchement, *m.* ; (b.s.) harangue ; (med.) effusion, *f.*

effu'sive (èf'fiou-cive), *adj.,* qui répand ; (fig.) excessif, extravagant.

eft (èfte), n., (zoöl.) salamandre, f., triton, m.

egad'! (è-gade), int., ma foi !

egg (èghe), n., œuf ; (arch.) ove, m. Addled —; œuf couvi. New-laid —; œuf frais. Boiled —s ; œufs à la coque. Fried —s ; œufs sur le plat. Scrambled —s ; œufs brouillés. Yolk of —; jaune d'œuf, m. Poached —s ; œufs pochés. To lay —s ; pondre.

egg, v.a., V. **edge,** v., (fig.) exciter, pousser à.

egg'-boiler, n., (cook.) œufrier, vase à bouillir des œufs, m.

egg'-cup (-keupe), n., coquetier, m.

egg'-flip, n., lait de poule, m.

egg'-glass (-glâce), n., sablier, m.

egg'like, adj. oviforme.

egg'-merchant (-meur-tsha'n'te), n., coquetier, marchand d'œufs, m.

egg'-nog (èghe-noghe), n., lait de poule à l'eau-de-vie, au rhum, m.

egg'-plant, n., (bot.) mélongène, aubergine, f.

egg'-sauce, n., sauce aux œufs, f.

egg'-shaped (-shép'te), adj., en œuf ; (bot.) ovale.

egg'-shell, n., coque, coquille d'œuf, f.

egg'-slice, n., écumoire, f.

egg'-spoon, n., cuiller à œufs, f.

egg'-stand, n., porte-coquetiers, m.

egg'-trade, n., commerce des œufs, m.

egg'-whisk, n., fouet à blanc d'œufs, m.

e'gilops (î'dji-), n., (med.) égilops, m.

eg'lantine (-taïne, ou '-tine), n., églantier, m. ; (flower) églantine, f.

eg'logue (èg-loghe), n. V. **æg'logue.**

e'goism (î-go-iz'me), n., (philos.) égoïsme, m.

e'goist (î-go-iste), n., (philos.) égoïste, m.

e'gotism (î-go-tiz'me ou èg-o-), n., habitude de parler de soi, f. ; égoïsme ; amour-propre, m. ; vanité, f.

e'gotist, n., personne qui a l'habitude de parler de soi, f. ; vaniteux ; égoïste, m., f.

egotis'tic ou **egotis'tical,** adj., qui a l'habitude de parler trop de soi ; vaniteux ; égoïste.

e'gotize (î-go-taïze), v.n., parler trop de soi.

egre'gious (i-grî-djeusse), adj., insigne, énorme ; fameux ; (pop.) pommé.

egre'giously, adv., d'une manière insigne ; grandement ; énormément ; fameusement.

egre'giousness, n., caractère insigne, m. ; énormité, f.

e'gress ou **egres'sion** (i-gress, i-grèsh'-), n., sortie, issue, f.

e'gret (î-grète), n., (orni.) aigrette, f.

e'griot (î-gri-ote), n., (hort.) griotte, f. — tree ; griottier, m.

Egyp'tian (î-djip-'sheu'ne), adj., égyptien.

Egyp'tian, n., Egyptien, m., Egyptienne, f.

ei'der (aï-) ou **ei'der-duck** (-deuke), n., (orni.) eider, m.

ei'der-down (-daoune), n., édredon, m. — quilt ; édredon, m.

eight (ê-te), adj., huit.

eigh'teen (ê-tîne), adj., dix-huit.

eigh'teenth (-tî'n'th), adj., dix-huitième, dix-huit.

eight'fold (-fôlde), adj., octuple ; huit fois plus grand.

eighth' (êt'th), adj., huitième ; huit.

eighth', n., (mus.) octave, f.

eighth'ly (êt'th'lî), adv., huitièmement, en huitième lieu.

eigh'tieth (ê-ti-èth), adj., quatre-vingtième, quatre-vingt.

eight'-score (-scôre), adj., huit vingtaines, f.pl. ; cent soixante.

eigh'ty (ê-ti), adj., quatre-vingt.

ei'ther (î-theur), pron., l'un ou l'autre, m.sing. ; l'une ou l'autre, f.sing. ; les uns ou les autres, m.pl. ; les unes ou les autres, f.pl. ; chacun, m., chacune, f. ; l'un d'eux, m. ; l'une d'elles, f. ; (used negatively) aucun, m., aucune,

f., ni l'un ni l'autre, m.sing., ni les uns ni les autres, m.pl., ni l'une ni l'autre, f.sing., ni les unes ni les autres, f.pl. On — side ; des deux parts, de l'un et de l'autre côté. I do not expect — of them ; je n'attends ni l'un ni l'autre.

ei'ther, conj., ou, soit. — he or his friend ; soit lui, soit son ami. — he knows it or you do ; ou bien il le sait, ou vous le savez.

ei'ther, adv., non plus. Nor I — ; ni moi non plus.

ejac'ulate (î-djak'iou-léte), v.a., prononcer avec ferveur ; (ant.) lancer, éjaculer.

ejac'ulate, v.n., s'écrier.

ejacula'tion, n., prière fervente ; éjaculation, f. ; élan, m. ; (ant.) action de lancer ; émission ; éjaculation, f.

ejac'ulatory, adj., (anat.) éjaculateur. — prayers ; éjaculations, f.pl.

eject' (è-djècte), v.a., jeter, rejeter ; chasser, expulser, (jur.) évincer, (med.) évacuer.

ejec'tion, n., expulsion, f. ; rejet, m. ; (med.) évacuation ; (jur.) éviction, évincement, m.

eject'ment, n., expulsion, f.

eject'or, n., auteur d'une expulsion, m.

eke (îke), v.a., allonger ; suppléer à, augmenter, agrandir. To — out ; suppléer à ; allonger. To — out a living ; se faire une maigre pitance.

ek'ing, n., augmentation, addition ; allonge, f.

elab'orate (è-lab'o-réte), adj., élaboré, soigné, fini.

elab'orate, v.a., élaborer.

elab'orately, adv., d'une manière élaborée, laborieusement, soigneusement.

elab'orateness, n., élaboration, f. ; travail fini, m.

elabora'tion, n., élaboration, f.

elapse' (î-), v.n., s'écouler, passer, se passer.

elas'tic ou **elas'tical** (î-), adj., élastique. — band ; bande élastique, f. With — sides (of boots) ; à élastiques.

elas'tically, adv., d'une manière élastique.

elastic'ity, n., élasticité, f.

elate' (î-léte), adj., fier, enflé, enorgueilli.

elate', v.a., élever ; enfler ; exalter ; enorgueillir.

ela'tedly, adv., orgueilleusement.

ela'tion (î-lé-), n., enflure (of mind) ; fierté, vanité, f. ; orgueil, m.

el'bow (èl-bô), n., coude, angle ; (of an armchair) bras, m. — chair ; fauteuil, m.   — grease ; huile de bras, f.   — room ; coudées franches, f.pl.   — rest ; accoudoir, m. At one's — ; près de, à côté de soi. Out at — s ; mal vêtu ; (pop.) dans la panne. To push with the — ; toucher, ou pousser, du coude. To lift the — ; hausser le coude. Up to the — s ; des mains, ou du bras, jusqu'au coude.

el'bow, v.a., coudoyer ; presser. To — out ; repousser à coups de coude ; (fig.) écarter, mettre de côté ; prendre la place **de.** To — one's way out ; se frayer un chemin à coups de coude.

el'bow, v.n., faire coude ; faire angle.

el'der (èl-), n., aîné ; doyen, ancien, (among the Jews, the Presbyterians) ancien ; (bot.) sureau, m. —flower ; fleur de sureau, f. — berry ; baie de sureau, f. — bush ; sureau, m. — wine ; vin de sureau, m.

el'der, adj., aîné, plus âgé.

el'derly, adj., qui tire sur l'âge, d'un certain âge.

el'dership, n., aînesse ; qualité d'ancien, f. ; (of the Presbyterians) conseil des anciens, m.

el'dest (èl-dèste), adj., le plus âgé, l'aîné.

elecam'pane (èl-i-ca'm'pêne), n., aunée, f.

elect' (î-lècte), adj., élu, choisi, nommé.

elect', n., élu, m.

elect', v.a., élire, nommer, choisir ; (fig.) aimer mieux, préférer ; se décider à.

elec'tion, n., élection, f. ; choix, m. General — ; élections générales, élections, f.pl.

electioneer' (-îre), v.n., briguer les suffrages (à une élection) ; solliciter des votes, travailler les électeurs.

electioneer'ing, n., manœuvres électorales, f.pl. — agent ; agent, ou courtier, électoral.

elec'tive, adj., électif, électoral.

elec'tively, adv., par choix ; par élection.

elec'tor (-teur), n., électeur, m.

elec'toral, adj., électoral, d'électeur.

elec'torate, n., électorat, m.

elec'tress, n., (hist.) électrice, f.

elec'tric ou **elec'trical** (î-lèc-), adj., électrique. — bell ; sonnette électrique. [teur, m.

elec'tric, n., corps électrique, non conducteur.

elec'trically, adv., au moyen de l'électricité.

electri'cian (-trish'a'ne), n., électricien, m.

electric'ity, n., électricité, f.

elec'trifiable (-faï-a-b'l), adj., électrisable.

electrifica'tion (-fi-ké-), n., électrisation, f.

elec'trify (-faïe), v.a., électriser.

elec'trify, v.n., s'électriser.

electrom'eter (î-lèc-trom'i-), n., (phys.) électromètre, m.

elec'tro-plate, n., plaqué, m.

elec'tro-plate, v.a., plaquer, argenter.

electroph'orus, n., (phys.) électrophore, m.

elec'troscope (-tro-scôpe), n., (phys.) électroscope, m.

elec'trotype, n., (tech.) électrotype, m. v.a., électrotyper.

elec'trotyping, n., galvanoplastie, f.

elec'tuary (-lèct'iou-), n., (pharm.) électuaire, m.

eleemos'ynary (èl-î-môz'-), adj., de charité ; d'aumône, qui vit d'aumônes ou de charité.

eleemos'ynary, n., qui vit d'aumône.

el'egance ou **el'egancy** (èl-i-), n., élégance, f.

el'egant, adj., élégant. n., élégant, beau, m.

el'egantly, adv., élégamment.

ele'giac (è-lî-dji-) ou **elegi'acal** (èl-i-djaï a-), adj., élégiaque.

ele'giac (è-lî-dji-ake ou èl-i-djaï-), n., vers élégiaque, m.

el'egist, n., élégiaque ; poète élégiaque, m.

el'egy (èl'i-dji), n., élégie, f.

el'ement (è-li-), n., élément, m. pl., connaissances premières ou rudimentaires, f.pl.

elemen'tal, adj., (ant.) élémentaire ; naturel, inné.

elemen'tally, adv., littéralement.

elemen'tarity, n., (ant.) état élémentaire, m.

elemen'tary, adj., élémentaire. — school ; école primaire, f. —substance ; (chem.) élément, m.

el'ephant (èl'i-), n., éléphant, m.

el'ephant-driver (-draïv'-), n., cornac, m.

elephanti'asis (-taï-a-cice), n., éléphantiasis, f.

elephan'tine, adj., éléphantin, d'éléphant, d'ivoire.

elevate (èl-i-véte), v.a., élever, exalter ; enorgueillir ; exciter, animer.

el'evate ou **el'evated**, adj., élevé, excité ; (with wine) lancé, en train.

eleva'tion (èl-i-vé-), n., élévation, f.

el'evator (-vé-teur), n., personne qui élève, f. ; (anat., mec.) élévateur, m.

el'evatory (-vé-tori), adj., qui peut élever.

el'evatory, n., (surg.) élévatoire, m.

elev'en (i-lèv'n), adj., onze. The — ; les apôtres, m.pl.

elev'enth (i-lèv'n'th), adj., onzième.

elf (èlfe), n., (elves) esprit follet, m. ; fée, f. ; lutin ; nabot, m., nabote, f. ; nain, (folklore) elfe, m. —child — ; (folklore) enfant substitué, m.

elf, v.a., entortiller.

el'fin, adj., des lutins, des elfes.

el'fin, n., nabot, m., nabote, f. ; gamin, marmot, bambin.

elf'ish, adj. V. elfin, adj.

elf'-lock, n., cheveux tordus en boucles (comme par les lutins), m.pl.

elic'it (î-), v.a., faire jaillir ; faire sortir ; mettre en lumière ; déduire, découvrir ; faire avouer à, faire dire à.

elide' (î-laïde), v.a., (gram.) élider. v.n., s'élider.

eligibil'ity (èl-i-dji-), n., éligibilité, f. ; avantage, m.

el'igible (-dji-b'l), adj., éligible ; désirable, convenable pour ; avantageux à ou pour. — match ; un parti avantageux.

el'igibly, adv., convenablement, avantageusement.

Eli'jah, n., Elie, m.

elim'inate (è-li'm-), v.a., éliminer ; (fig.) chasser, expulser.

elim'inating, adj., éliminateur.

elimina'tion (-né-), n., élimination ; expulsion, f.

Eli'sha, n., Elisée, m.

eli'sion (i-lij'eune), n., élision ; division, f.

elite' (é-lite), n., élite, f.

elix'ir (i-liks-eur), n., élixir, m. ; quintessence, f.

Elizabeth'an (-bèth'-), adj., du temps d'Elisabeth ; gothique.

elk (èlke), n., (mam.) élan, m.

elk (èlke), n., (orni.) cygne sauvage, m.

ell, n., aune, f.

ellipse', n., (geom.) ellipse, f.

ellip'sis, n., (ellipses) (gram., print.) ellipse, f.

ellip'soid (-soïde), n., (geom.) ellipsoïde, m.

ellip'tic ou **ellip'tical**, adj., elliptique.

ellip'tically, adv., elliptiquement, (gram.) par ellipse ; (geom.) en forme d'ellipse.

elliptic'ity, n., différence entre le grand axe et le petit axe d'une ellipse, f.

elm (èlme), n., (bot.) orme, m. Young — ; ormeau, m. Witch — ; ormille, f.

elm'-grove (-grôve), n., ormaie, f.

elocu'tion (èl-o-kiou-), n., élocution, déclamation, f. ; débit, m. Teacher of — ; professeur de déclamation, m.

elocu'tionist, n., déclamateur, professeur de déclamation, m.

elo'gium ou **el'ogy** (èl'o-djieume, -dji), n. V. eulo'gium.

elon'gate, v.a., allonger ; prolonger ; étendre.

elon'gate ou **elon'gated**, adj., allongé.

elonga'tion (-ghé-), n., prolongement ; (ant.) éloignement, m. ; (med.) élongation ; (astron.) distance apparente d'une planète du soleil, f.

elope' (î-lope), v.n., quitter clandestinement la maison conjugale, la maison paternelle ; s'enfuir de. To — with ; se faire enlever par.

elope'ment, n., enlèvement, m. ; fuite, f.

e'lops (i-lopse), n., (ich.) stelet ; esturgeon, m.

el'oquence (èl-o-kwè'n'-), n., éloquence, f.

el'oquent, adj., éloquent.

el'oquently, adv., éloquemment.

else (èlse), adj., autre. Nothing — ; pas autre chose. What —? vous faut-il autre chose? quoi encore? quoi de plus? Who —? qui encore? Something — ; autre chose, quelque chose de plus, m. Everything — ; toute autre chose ; tout le reste. Everybody — ; tout autre. Nobody — ; aucun autre, personne autre. Everywhere — ; partout ailleurs. Nowhere — ; nulle autre part ; nulle part ailleurs ; en aucun autre lieu, ou pays. Where —? où encore?

else, adv., autrement ; sans quoi, ou bien.

else'where (èls'hwère), adv., ailleurs, autre part.

elu'cidate (è-liou-ci-), v.a., rendre lucide, expliquer, éclaircir, élucider.

elucida'tion, n., éclaircissement, m. ; élucidation, explication, f.

elu'cidator (è-liou-ci-dé-teur), n., commentateur, m.

elude' (è-lioude), v.a., éluder ; éviter ; échapper à ; esquiver.

elu′dible (′i-b′l), *adj.*, (ant.) qui peut être éludé, éludable.

elu′sion, *n.*, subterfuge, faux-fuyant, réponse évasive, *f.*

elu′sive, *adj.*, trompeur.

Elys′ian (i-lij′i-a′ne), *adj.*, élyséen, (ant.) élysien. — **fields** ; *champs élysées, m.pl.*

Elys′ium (i-lij′i-eume), *n.*, Elysée, *m.*

el′ytron (èl′i-), *n.*, (*elytra*) élytre, *m.* and *f.*

ema′ciate (i-mé-shi-éte), *v.n.*, maigrir ; se décharner ; s'étioler.

ema′ciate, *v.a.*, amaigrir.

ema′ciated, *adj.*, maigre, décharné, étiolé.

emacia′tion (-shi-é-), *n.*, maigreur, *f.* ; état décharné ; amaigrissement ; étiolement, *m.*

em′anate, *v.n.*, émaner.

emana′tion (-né-), *n.*, émanation, *f.*

eman′cipate, *v.a.*, émanciper ; affranchir **de**.

eman′cipate *ou* **eman′cipated** (-pét′ède), *adj.*, émancipé ; (fig.) affranchi **de**.

emancipa′tion (-pé-), *n.*, émancipation, *f.* ; affranchissement, *m.*

emar′ginate (-mâr-dji-), *v.a.*, ôter la marge (**de**), émarger.

emar′ginate *ou* **emar′ginated**, *adj.*, émargé ; (bot.) tronqué.

emargina′tion, *n.*, émargement, *m.*

emas′culate (-kiou-), *v.a.*, châtrer ; (fig.) affaiblir, énerver, efféminer.

emas′culate, *adj.*, châtré ; efféminé, énervé.

emascula′tion (-kiou-lé-), *n.*, castration ; émasculation ; mollesse ; (fig.) mollesse, *f.*

embalm′ (è′m′bâ-me), *v.a.*, embaumer.

embalm′er, *n.*, embaumeur, *m.*

embalm′ing, *n.*, embaumement, *m.*

embank′, *v.a.*, faire une digue, une levée **à** ; endiguer, remblayer ; encaisser ; terrasser.

embank′ment, *n.*, levée, digue, *f.* ; remblai ; terrassement, talus, quai, *m.*, quais, *m.pl.* ; encaissement, *m.* ; construction de quais, *f.*

embarca′tion, *n.*, embarquement, *m.*

embar′go (-bâr-), *n.*, embargo, *m.*

embar′go, *v.a.*, mettre un embargo **sur**.

embark′ (-bârke), *v.a.*, embarquer ; (fig.) engager.

embark′, *v.n.*, s'embarquer **sur** ; (fig.) s'engager **dans**.

embarka′tion (-ké-), *n.*, embarquement, *m.*

embar′rass (-ra), *v.a.*, embarrasser ; gêner ; déranger.

embar′rassing, *adj.*, embarrassant.

embar′rassingly, *adv.*, d'une manière embarrassante.

embar′rassment, *n.*, embarras, *m.* ; (fig.) perplexité, *f.* ; (in one's business) dérangement, *m.*, gêne, *f.*

embas′sador (-deur), *n.* *V.* **ambas′sador**.

em′bassy, *n.*, ambassade, *f.*

embat′tle (-bat′t′l), *v.a.*, ranger en bataille ; (arch.) créneler ; (mil.) mettre en état de défense, armer ; créneler.

embat′tle, *v.a.*, former, *ou* ranger, en bataille.

embat′tled (-bat′t′l′de), *adj.*, crénelé.

embat′tlement, *n.*, crénelure, *f.* ; créneau.

embay′ (-bé), *v.a.*, (ant.) renfermer dans une baie ; affaler sur la côte ; encaper.

embed′ (-bède), *v.a.*, enfouir ; enfoncer ; coucher ; fixer, incruster.

embel′lish, *v.a.*, embellir, orner.

embel′lisher, *n.*, embellisseur.

embel′lishment, *n.*, embellissement, *m.*

Em′ber-days (-dèze), *n.pl.*, Quatre-Temps, *m.pl.*

em′ber-goose, *n.*, (orni.) grand plongeon.

em′bers (-beurze), *n.pl.*, braise ; cendre, *f.sing.*

Em′ber-week (-wîke), *n.*, semaine des Quatre-Temps, *f.*

embez′zle (-bèz′z′l), *v.a.*, détourner ; soustraire frauduleusement.

embez′zlement, *n.*, détournement de fonds, *m.*

embez′zler, *n.*, auteur d'un détournement, *m.*

embit′ter, *v.a.*, rendre amer ; (fig.) abreuver d'amertume, empoisonner ; irriter, aigrir.

emblaze′ *ou* **embla′zon** (-blé-z′n), *v.a.*, blasonner ; (fig.) embellir ; publier, proclamer ; exalter.

embla′zoner, *n.*, écrivain héraldique ; graveur héraldique, *m.*

embla′zonry, *n.*, blason, *m.* ; armes, armoiries, *f.pl.*

em′blem, *n.*, emblème, *m.*

emblemat′ic *ou* **emblemat′ical**, *adj.*, emblématique.

emblemat′ically, *adv.*, d'une manière emblématique.

emblem′atize (è′m-blè′m-a-taïze), *v.a.*, figurer, représenter par emblèmes ; symboliser.

em′blements, *n.pl.*, (agri.) fruits pendants par racines, *m.pl.* ; récoltes pendantes, *f.pl.*

embod′iment, *n.*, corporisation ; (fig.) incarnation, personnification ; (mil.) incorporation.

embod′y, *v.n.*, (ant.) s'incorporer ; (fig.) s'unir.

embod′y, *v.a.*, revêtir d'un corps ; (theol.) corporifier ; (mil.) incorporer ; rassembler ; (fig.) personnifier, réunir ; renfermer. To — a clause in a bill ; *incorporer une clause*, ou *un article, dans un projet de loi.*

embol′den, *v.a.*, enhardir.

em′bolism, *n.*, (calendar) embolisme ; temps intercalé ; (med.) embolisme, *m.* ; pyémie, *f.*

embo′som (-bou-zeume), *v.a.*, serrer contre son sein ; renfermer dans son sein ; entourer ; caresser ; (fig.) ensevelir.

emboss′, *v.a.*, bosseler, relever en bosse ; (gold.) bosseler ; (linen) brocher ; (cutlery) damasquiner ; (sculpt.) travailler en bosse ; graver en relief.

emboss′ing, *n.*, relief ; (arch.) bossage, (gold.) bosselage, *m.* ; (of cutlery) damasquinerie, *f.*

emboss′ment, *n.*, relief, *m.* ; (sculpt.) bosse ; protubérance, *f.*

embot′tle (-bot′t′l), *v.a.*, mettre en bouteilles. *V.* **bottle**.

embow′el (-baou′èl), *v.a.* *V.* **disembowel**.

embrace′, *n.*, embrassement, *m.* ; étreinte, *f.*

embrace′, *v.a.*, embrasser ; saisir ; adopter ; accepter ; comprendre, renfermer. To — the opportunity ; *saisir*, ou *profiter **de**, l'occasion.*

embrace′ment, *n.*, embrassement, *m.* ; étreinte, *f.*

embra′cer, *n.*, personne qui embrasse, *f.* ; (follower) partisan, *m.*

embra′sure (bréj′eur), *n.*, embrasure *f.*

em′brocate, *v.a.*, fomenter ; bassiner.

embroca′tion (-ké-), *n.*, embrocation, *f.*

embroi′der (-brôïd′-), *v.a.*, broder.

embroi′derer, *n.*, brodeur, *m.* ; brodeuse, *f.*

embroi′dery, *n.*, broderie, *f.*

embroil′ (-brôïle), *v.a.*, brouiller, embrouiller ; bouleverser, jeter, précipiter, engager.

embroil′ment, *n.*, embrouillement ; désordre, *m.*, confusion, brouille, brouillerie, *f.*

em′bryo (è′m-bri-ô) *ou* **em′bryon** (-one), *n.*, embryon, *m.* In —; *à l'état rudimentaire ; en embryon.*

em′bryo *ou* **em′bryon**, *adj.*, d'embryon ; à l'état d'embryon.

embryol′ogy (-dji), *n.*, embryologie, *f.*

emend′, *v.a.*, corriger, améliorer, (jur.) émender.

emend′able (-′a-b′l), *adj.*, (ant.) corrigible, susceptible de correction.

emenda′tion (-dé-), *n.*, correction, émendation, réforme, *f.* ; changement, *m.*

em′endator (-dé-teur), *n.*, correcteur, *m.*

em′erald (èm-eur-), *n.*, émeraude, *f.* — **isle** ; *l'Irlande, f.*

emerge' (è-meurdge), *v.n.*, surgir ; sortir **de**, (geol., opt.) émerger ; paraître, se dégager **de**.

emer'gence, *n.*, action de surgir ; (geol.) émergement, *m.* ; (opt.) émergence, *f.*

emer'gency, *m.*, circonstance imprévue; occurrence ; conjoncture ; crise, *f.* ; cas urgent, besoin, *m.* — man; (in Ireland) *gardien de la saisie, m.*

emer'gent (è-meur-djè'n'te), *adj.*, qui surgit ; naissant ; imprévu ; critique, difficile ; (phys., geol.) émergent. — year ; *ère, f.* Upon — occasions ; *dans les circonstances critiques.*

em'eroids (èm'eur-oïdze), *n.pl.*, hémorroïdes, *f.pl.*

emer'sion (i-meur-sheune), *n.*, (astron.) émersion ; sortie, *f.*

em'ery (èm-eur-i), *n.*, émeri, *m.* — cloth ; *toile émerisée, f.* — dust ; *poudre d'émeri, f.* — stone ; *pierre à polir, f.*

emet'ic (-î-mèt'ike), *n.*, émétique, *m.*

emet'ic *ou* **emet'ical**, *adj.*, émétique.

emet'ically, *adv.*, comme un émétique.

em'igrant (èm'i-), *n.*, émigrant, *m.*, émigrante, *f.* ; (political) émigré, *m.*, émigrée, *f.*

em'igrant, *adj.*, émigrant.

em'igrate, *v.n.*, émigrer.

emigra'tion (-gré-), *n.*, émigration, *f.*

em'inence *ou* **em'inency** (èm-i-), *n.*, éminence, élévation ; (fig.) grandeur, distinction, célébrité, *f.* ; réputation. His —; *son Eminence, f.* To have the — of ; *l'emporter sur.*

em'inent, *adj.*, éminent, élevé; distingué, illustre.

em'inently, *adv.*, éminemment, au suprême degré.

e'mir (î-mir), *n.*, émir.

em'issary (èm'-), *n.*, émissaire, *m.*, (anat.) émissaire, émonctoire ; (hydr.) émissaire, *m.*

em'issary, *adj.*, d'émissaire ; (anat.) excrétoire, excréteur.

emis'sion (i-mish'eune), *n.*, émission, *f.*

emis'sive, *adj.*, émissif.

emit' (è-mite), *v.a.*, jeter, lancer, exhaler, dégager, (fin.) émettre ; (fig.) émettre.

em'met (èm'mète), *n.*, (ent.) fourmi, *f.*

emol'lient (î-), *n.*, émollient, *m.*

emol'lient, *adj.*, émollient.

emol'ument (î-mol'iou-), *n.*, émolument, profit, gain, avantage, *m.* ; rémunération, *f.*

emo'tion (î-mô-), *n.*, émotion, *f.*

e'motional, *adj.*, émotionnel, porté à l'émotion, susceptible d'émotion.

empale' (èm'péle), *v.a.*, (ant.) (to fortify) palissader ; (a man) empaler ; transpercer, percer, (fig., ant.) environner.

empale'ment, *n.*, empalement, supplice du pal, (fort.) palissadement, *m.* ; (her.) pal, *m.*

empan'el (è'm'pa'n'èl), *v.a.*, (jur.) dresser la liste du jury ; inscrire sur la liste du jury.

empark', *v.a.*, parquer ; (to inclose) ceindre, entourer **de**.

empas'sion (è'm'pash'-), *v.a.*, affecter, émouvoir, passionner.

em'peror (è'm'peur'eur), *n.*, empereur, *m.* ; (ent.) mars, *m.* — paper ; *papier grand aigle, m.*

em'phasis (è'm'pha-cice), *n.*, (emphases) force ; énergie ; emphase, *f.* ; accent, *m.*, accentuation ; (b.s.) emphase, *f.* To lay — upon ; *appuyer sur.*

em'phasize (-çaïze), *v.a.*, appuyer **sur** ; enchérir, renchérir **sur** ; prononcer avec force, accentuer.

emphat'ic *ou* **emphat'ical**, *adj.*, énergique ; expressif ; accentué ; emphatique ; (fig.) positif, décidé.

emphat'ically, *adv.*, énergiquement, expressivement ; avec force ; formellement, expressément ; d'une manière accentuée, emphatiquement.

emphyse'ma (è'm'fi-cî-), *n.*, (med.) emphysème, *m.*

emphyteu'sis (è'm'fi-tiou-cice), *n.*, (jur.) emphytéose, *f.*

em'pire (è'm'païeur), *n.*, empire, *m.*

empir'ic (è'm'-), *n.*, empirique ; charlatan, *m.*

empir'ic *ou* **empir'ical**, *adj.*, versé dans les expériences ; empirique, guidé par l'expérience.

empir'ically, *adv.*, expérimentalement, empiriquement, en empirique.

empir'icism, *n.*, empirisme, *m.*

employ' (è'm'plôïe), *n.*, emploi, service, *m.*, charge, occupation, *f.*

employ', *v.a.*, employer ; se servir **de**, mettre en usage ; (to occupy) occuper **à**, employer **à**. To — oneself in ; *s'employer* **à** ; *s'occuper* **à** ou **de**.

employ'able (-a-b'l), *adj.*, qui peut servir ; que l'on peut employer ; employable.

employee' (-), *n.*, employé, *m.*

employ'er, *n.*, personne qui emploie, *f.* ; maître, *m.*, maîtresse, *f.* ; patron, *m.*, patronne, *f.* ; chef ; (com.) commettant, *m.*

employ'ment, *n.*, emploi, *m.* ; occupation, *f.* Out of —; *sans emploi.* To be in search of —; *chercher un emploi.*

empo'rium (è'm'pô-ri'-), *n.*, grand marché ; entrepôt, *m.*

empov'erish (è'm'pov'èr-), *v.n.* V. **impoverish**.

empow'er (è'm'paoueur), *v.a.*, autoriser **à**, charger **de**, (jur.) donner plein pouvoir **à**, donner procuration **à**, rendre capable **de**, mettre à même **de** ; permettre **à**.

em'press (è'm'-), *n.*, impératrice, *f.*

emp'tier (è'm'ti-), *n.*, videur, *m.*, videuse, *f.*

emp'tiness (è'm'ti-), *n.*, vide, *m.* ; (fig.) vanité, inanité ; nullité, *f.* ; néant, *m.*

emp'ty (è'm'ti), *v.a.*, vider, décharger. To — itself ; *se vider, se décharger, se jeter* **dans**.

emp'ty, *adj.*, vide ; à vide ; (of streets) désert ; (fig.) vain, stérile. — -hearted ; *sans cœur.* — words ; *mots vides de sens, m.pl.* — -headed ; *sot, ignorant, à tête vide.* — -handed ; *les mains vides.*

emp'ty, *n.*, caisse vide, *f.* Returned —; (fig.) *fruit sec, m.*

emp'tysis, *n.*, (med.) crachement de sang, *m.*

empur'ple (è'm'peur'p'l), *v.a.*, (ant.) empourprer.

empye'ma (è'm'pi-î-), *n.*, (med.) empyème, *m.*

empyr'eal *ou* **empyr'ean** (è'm'pir'i-), *adj.*, empyrée.

Empyr'ean, *n.*, Empyrée, *m.*

empyreu'ma (è'm'pi-rou-), *n.*, empyreume, *m.*

e'mu, *n.*, (orni.) casoar, *m.*

em'ulate (èm'iou-), *v.a.*, s'efforcer d'égaler, d'imiter ; rivaliser **avec** ; (ant.) imiter. To — any one's example ; *suivre, ou imiter, quelqu'un.*

emula'tion (-lé-), *n.*, émulation ; rivalité, *f.* In — of each other ; *à l'envi l'un de l'autre.*

em'ulative (-lé-), *adj.*, plein d'émulation.

em'ulator (-lé-teur), *n.*, émule, *m.f.* ; émulateur, rival, *m.*

emul'gent (è-meul-djè'n'te), *adj.*, (anat.) émulgent.

em'ulous, *adj.*, qui rivalise **avec**, qui s'efforce d'égaler ; (ant.) jaloux, envieux, factieux.

em'ulously, *adv.*, avec émulation ; à l'envi.

emul'sion (è-meul-), *n.*, émulsion, *f.*

emul'sive, *adj.*, émulsif.

emunc'tory (è-meugn'k'to-), *n.*, (anat.) émonctoire, *m.*

ena'ble (è'n'é-b'l), *v.a.*, rendre capable **de** ; mettre à même **de** ; donner le moyen **a** ; mettre en état **de**; permettre **de**. To be —d to ; *être en état de* ; *être à même* **de** ; *avoir le moyen* **de**.

enact' (èn'-), *v.a.*, ordonner, arrêter ; (a law) passer, rendre, établir, faire, décréter, édicter ; (a part) représenter, remplir, jouer, faire ; (fig.) se dérouler. A terrible tragedy was —d ; *un drame horrible s'est déroulé.*

enac'tive, *adj.*, ayant force de loi.

enact'ment, *n.*, établissement d'une loi, *m.;* ordonnance, *f.;* décret ; acte législatif, *m.*

enac'tor (-'eur), *n.*, auteur, *m.*

enal'lage (èn'al'ladje), *n.*, (gram.) énallage, *m.*

enam'el (èn'am'èle), *n.*, émail, *m.*

enam'el, *v.a.*, émailler **de** ; (leather) glacer ; (faces) maquiller. *v.n.*, peindre en émail.

enam'eler *ou* **enam'elist**, *n.*, émailleur, peintre en émail, *m.;* maquilleuse, *f.*

enam'eling, *n.*, émaillure, *f.*, émaillage, *m.;* peinture en émail, *f.;* (of faces) maquillage, *m.*

enam'el-painting, *n.*, peinture sur émail, *f.*

enam'el-work (-weurke), *n.*, émaillure, *f.*

enam'or (èn'am'eur), *v.a.*, (used now only in past participle) rendre amoureux ; rendre épris ; amouracher. To be —ed with; *être épris* **de**, *être amoureux* **de**.

enarthro'sis (èn'ar-thrô-cice), *n.*, (anat.) énarthrose, *f.*

encage' (è'n'-kédje), *v.a.*, encager ; enfermer dans une cage, mettre en cage.

encamp' (è'n'-), *v.a.* and *n.*, camper.

encamp'ment, *n.*, campement, *m.*

encase', *v.a.*, encaisser, enfermer ; (to en-shrine) enchâsser.

encaus'tic (è'n'-), *adj.*, (paint.) encaustique.

encaus'tic, *n.*, peinture encaustique, *f.*

enceinte' (a'gn'sé'n'te), *adj.*, enceinte.

enceinte', *n.*, (fort.) enceinte, *f.*

enceph'alon (è'n'cèf'a-lone), *n.*, (anat.) encéphale, *m.*

enchain' (è'n'théne), *v.a.*, enchaîner.

enchant' (è'n'tshâ'n'te), *v.a.*, enchanter, ravir (with **de**).

enchant'er, *n.*, enchanteur, *m.* —'s-night-shade ; *herbe aux magiciennes, f.*

enchant'ing, *adj.*, enchanteur.

enchant'ingly, *adv.*, par enchantement ; à ravir ; d'une manière ravissante.

enchant'ment, *n.*, enchantement, *m.*, fascination, *f.*

enchan'tress, *n.*, enchanteresse, *f.*

enchase' (è'n'théce), *v.a.*, (ant.) enchâsser ; ciseler ; enrichir de diamants ; graver.

enchymo'sis, *n.*, (med.) enchymose, *f.*

encir'cle (è'n'ceur'k'l), *v.a.*, environner ; ceindre, entourer ; embrasser.

enclit'ic (è'n'-), *n.*, (gram.) enclitique, *f.*

enclose' (è'n'clôze), *v.a.*, enclore, clore ; en-tourer, environner ; (parcels, letters) renfermer ; envoyer ci-inclus ; mettre sous enveloppe ; en-voyer **avec** ; joindre **à** ; envoyer sous le même pli.

enclosed' (-klôz'de), *adj.*, entouré, environné ; (of parcels, letters) inclus, ci-inclus, sous ce pli.

enclo'sure (-klôjeur), *n.*, action de clore ; clôture, *f.;* (space inclosed) enclos, *m.*, enceinte ; (thing inclosed) chose incluse, *f.*, contenu, *m.*

enco'miast (è'n'cô-), *n.*, panégyriste, louan-geur, *m.*

encomias'tic. *V.* eulogistic.

enco'mium (è'n'cô-mi-), *n.*, éloge, panégy-rique, *m.*, louange, *f.*

encom'pass (è'n'keu'm'-), *v.a.*, entourer ; enfermer, embrasser, comprendre, renfermer.

encore' (a'gn'kôre), *adv.*, bis.

encore', *v.a.*, crier bis **à**, bisser, redemander. *n.* bis, *m. int.* bis.

encoun'ter (è'n'caou'n'-), *n.*, rencontre ; attaque, *f.;* combat, *m.;* escarmouche, (fig.) lutte, dispute, *f.*

encoun'ter, *v.a.*, rencontrer, affronter ; aborder ; aller au-devant **de** ; attaquer ; s'op-poser **à** ; (fig.) éprouver, essuyer.

encoun'ter, *v.n.*, se rencontrer hostilement ; engager le combat ; s'affronter ; se rencontrer.

encour'age (è'n'keur-édje), *v.a.*, encourager.

encour'agement, *n.*, encouragement, *m.*

encour'ager, *n.*, protecteur, *m.*

encour'aging, *adj.*, encourageant.

encour'agingly, *adv.*, d'une manière encou-rageante.

en'crinite, *n.*, (geol.) encrinite, *m.*

encroach' (è'n'crôtshe), *v.n.a.*, empiéter **sur** ; usurper ; abuser de.

encroach'er, *n.*, personne qui empiète, *f.;* usurpateur, *m.*, usurpatrice, *f.*

encroach'ing, *adj.*, qui empiète, empiétant.

encroach'ingly, *adv.*, par empiètement, en empiétant.

encroach'ment, *n.*, empiètement, *m.;* usur-pation, *f.*

encum'ber (è'n'keu'm'-), *v.a.*, encombrer **de**, accabler **de**, embarrasser **de** ; (an estate) grever, hypothéquer. An —ed estate ; *un domaine grevé d'hypothèques.*

encum'brance, *n.*, encombrement, embarras, obstacle, *m.;* charge, hypothèque, *f. pl.*, famille, *f.*, enfants, *m.pl.*

ency'clical (è'n'-), *n.adj.*, encyclique, *f.*

encyclope'dia *ou* **encyclopæ'dia** (è'n'çaï-clo-pî-), *n.*, encyclopédie, *f.*

encyclope'dian (è'n'caï-clô-pî-), **encyclo-ped'ic**, *ou* **encycloped'ical** (è'n'çaï-clô-pèd'-), *adj.*, encyclopédique.

encyclope'dist (è'n'çaï-clo-pî-), *n.*, encyclo-pédiste, *m.*

encyst'ed (è'n'cist-ède), *adj.*, (med.) en-kysté. To become —; *s'enkyster, s'ankyloser* (V. Hugo).

end (è'n'de), *n.*, bout, *m.;* extrémité ; fin, *f.;* but, objet, *m.;* fin, conclusion, issue, *f.;* ré-sultat, (of time) bout, *m.* The —s of the earth ; *le bout de l'univers ou du monde.* No — of; *force ; une infinité* **de**. At an —; *fini, terminé, passé ; guéri, apaisé, calmé.* At the — of two months; *au bout de deux mois.* Approaching —; *fin prochaine.* Odd —; *reste, m.* By the — of ; *avant la fin* **de**. To no —; *sans effet ; en vain.* To the—that ; *afin que.* From — to —; *d'un bout à l'autre.* In the —; *à la fin, à la longue, au bout du compte.* To be at an —; *être arrivé à sa fin.* To attain one's —s ; *parvenir à son but.* To come to a bad —; *finir mal ; faire une mauvaise fin.* To make an — of ; *en finir* **avec**. To put an — to ; *tuer ; mettre fin* **à** ; *mettre un terme* **à**. The — crowns all ; (prov.) *la fin couronne l'œuvre.* The — justifies the means ; (prov.) *la fin justifie les moyens* ou *le bois tortu fait le feu droit.* There's an — to everything ; (prov.) *au bout de l'aune faut* (ou *manque*) *le drap ; ou il y a un terme à tout.* On —; *debout.* At one's wit's —; *au bout de son rouleau, ou de son latin, ou de sa gamme.* To make both —s meet ; *joindre les deux bouts.* To draw to an —; *tirer, ou toucher, à sa fin.* To make one's hair stand on —; *faire dresser les cheveux sur la tête.* There's an — of it ; *c'est fini ; tout est dit.* There's an — of it all ; *tout est bien fini.* There's no — to them ; *cela n'en finit pas, ou plus.*

end, *v.a.*, finir ; terminer **en** ; achever ; tuer ; decider. All's well that —s well ; *la fin cou-ronne l'œuvre.*

end, *v.n.*, finir ; se terminer **en** ; cesser (de par-ler) ; aboutir **à** ; se réduire **à**. Never —ing ; *qui n'en finit pas ; éternel, perpétuel, incessant.*

endan'ger (è'n'da'n'djeur), *v.a.*, exposer au danger, mettre en danger, compromettre, risquer, hasarder.

endan'gering, *adj.*, qui met en danger, qui compromet.

endear' (è'n'dîre), *v.a.*, faire aimer **de**, rendre cher **à**, faire chérir **de**.

endear'ment, *n.*, caresse, tendresse, *f.;* attrait, charme, attachement, *m.*

endeav'or (è'n'dèv'eur), *n.*, effort, essai, *m.;* tentative, *f.* To use every —; *faire tous ses efforts* **pour**.

endeav'or, *v.n.*, tâcher **de**, s'efforcer **de**, essayer **de**, tenter **de**, chercher **à**, viser **à**.

endem'ic (è'n'dèm'-) *ou* **ende'mial** (è'n'dî-), *adj.*, endémique. — **disease** ; *endémie, f.*

end'ing (è'n'd'-), *n.*, fin, conclusion ; (gram.) terminaison, désinence, *f.*

en'dive (è'n'-), *n.*, chicorée, endive, escarole, *f.*

end'less, *adj.*, infini, sans fin ; éternel ; perpétuel, interminable ; sans but, sans résultat. — **screw** ; *vis sans fin, f.*

end'lessly, *adv.*, à l'infini ; éternellement, sans cesse.

end'lessness, *n.*, perpétuité, infinité, *f.*

endorse' (è'n'-), *v.n.*, (com.) endosser ; (passports) viser ; (fig.) sanctionner, appuyer, approuver.

endorsee' (è'n'dorsî), *n.*, (com.) porteur, *m.*

endorse'ment, *n.*, suscription, *f.* ; (com.) endossement, endos, (of passports) visa, *m.* ; (fig.) sanction, *f.* ; appui, *m.* ; approbation, *f.*

endor'ser, *n.*, (com.) endosseur, *m.*

en'dosmose, endosmo'sis, *n.*, (phys.) endosmose, *f.*

endow' (è'n'daou), *v.a.*, douer **de**, doter **de**.

endow'ment, *n.*, dotation, *f.* ; (fig.) don, *m.*, qualité, *f.*, avantage naturel, *m.*

end'-piece (-pîce), *n.*, (tech.), bout, *m.*

endur'able (è'n'diour'a-b'l), *adj.*, supportable, endurable, tolérable.

endur'ance (è'n'diour'-), *n.*, patience, *f.* ; pouvoir d'endurer, *m.* ; souffrance, *f.* Beyond — ; *insupportable.*

endure' (è'n'dioure), *v.n.*, (to last) durer ; continuer ; endurer la souffrance ; souffrir ; souffrir patiemment.

endure', *v.a.*, endurer, souffrir, supporter.

endur'er, *n.*, qui endure, qui souffre.

endur'ing, *adj.*, endurant, patient ; (lasting) durable.

endur'ingly, *adv.*, patiemment.

end'ways (è'n'd'wèze) *ou* **end'wise** (-waïze), *adv.*, bout à bout ; debout, perpendiculaire ; de champ.

Ene'id (è-nî-ide), *n.*, Enéide, *f.*

ene'ma, *n.*, lavement, *m.*

en'emy (è-ni-mi), *n.*, ennemi, *m.*, ennemie, *f.* The — ; (theol.) *l'ennemi, le démon.* — **of** (*ou* to); *ennemi* **de.**

energet'ic *ou* **energet'ical** (è-nèr-djèt'-), *adj.*, énergique, actif.

energet'ically, *adv.*, énergiquement.

energu'men (è'n'eur'ghiou-mène), *n.*, énergumène ; démoniaque, *m.f.*

en'ergy (è'n'èr-dji), *n.*, énergie, force, vigueur, *f.*

ener'vate (è-neur-), *v.a.*, énerver.

enerva'tion (-vé-), *n.*, état énervé, affaiblissement, *m.* ; (vet.) énervation, *f.* ; (state) énervement, *m.*

enfee'ble (èn'fî-b'l), *v.a.*, affaiblir, débiliter, priver de force, énerver.

enfee'blement, *n.*, affaiblissement, énervement, *m.* ; débilitation, *f.*

enfeoff' (è'n'fife), *v.a.*, inféoder.

enfeoff'ment, *n.*, inféodation, *f.*

enfilade' (è'n'fi-léde), *n.*, enfilade, *f.* — **fire**; *tir d'enfilade, m.*

enfilade', *v.a.*, (milit.) enfiler ; tirer en enfilade **sur.**

enforce' (è'n'fôr'-), *v.a.*, donner de la force à ; faire respecter ; faire, *ou* contraindre à, observer ; faire exécuter ; appliquer avec rigueur ; (fig.) fortifier, appuyer ; faire triompher, faire prévaloir.

enforce'able (-'a-b'l), *adj.*, (jur.) exécutoire.

enfor'cedly (-'èd'li), *adv.*, forcément ; de force.

enforce'ment, *n.*, contrainte ; force ; sanction ; mise à exécution, mise en vigueur ; exécution par la force, *f.*

enfor'cer, *n.*, personne qui emploie la force, qui met à exécution, *f.* ; agent, *m.*

enfran'chise (è'n'fra'n'shize), *v.a.*, affranchir ; conférer droit de bourgeoisie **à** ; naturaliser.

enfran'chisement, *n.*, affranchissement, *m.* ; admission au droit de bourgeoisie ; naturalisation, *f.*

enfran'chiser, *n.*, affranchisseur, *m.*

engage' (è'n'ghédje), *v.a.*, engager ; (secure, take) retenir, prendre ; (hire) louer ; arrêter ; (to pawn) mettre en gage, mettre au mont-de-piété, (servant, workman) embaucher ; occuper ; (for dancing) inviter ; (fig.) attaquer, combattre. To — **attention** ; *attirer l'attention* **avec**, *avoir l'attention* **de.**

engage', *v.n.*, s'engager ; engager le combat ; livrer combat, en venir aux mains. To — **in** ; (an enterprise) *s'embarquer* **dans.**

engaged', *part.*, engagé ; (wed.) promis, fiancé ; (not at leisure) occupé ; (fighting) aux prises, aux mains ; (of newspapers) en main, en lecture. The regiment is — ; *le régiment donne.* To be — **in** conversation (with) ; *avoir un entretien* **avec.**

engage'ment, *n.*, engagement, *m.* ; occupation, *f.*, fiançailles, *f.pl.* ; (milit.) combat, *m.* To be under an — **to** ; *être lié par un engagement* **de.** To make —**s** (with) ; *prendre des engagements* **avec.** To make an — ; *prendre un rendez-vous* **avec.** Not to keep an — ; *manquer à un engagement.*

enga'ging, *adj.*, engageant, prévenant, attrayant.

enga'gingly, *adv.*, d'une manière engageante.

engar'rison (è'n'gar-ri-s'n), *v.a.*, mettre en garnison, mettre une garnison **dans** (une place).

engen'der (è'n'djè'n'-), *v.a.*, engendrer, faire naître, causer, produire ; donner lieu **à.**

engen'der, *v.n.*, s'engendrer ; être engendré ; naître ; être causé **par** ; être produit **par.**

en'gine (è'n'djine), *n.*, machine, locomotive, *f.* ; instrument ; (fig.) levier, moyen, agent, *m.* **Fire**— ; *pompe à incendie, f.* **Steam**— ; *machine à vapeur.* **Single-acting** — ; *machine à simple effet.* **Double-acting** — ; *machine à double effet.* **Ten-horse power** — ; *machine de la force de dix chevaux.* **High-pressure** — ; *machine à haute pression.*

en'gine-driver (-draïv'-), *n.*, mécanicien, conducteur de machines ; (rail.) conducteur de locomotive, *m.*

engineer' (è'n'dji-nîre), *n.*, mécanicien ; cannonier ; ouvrier mécanicien, machiniste ; constructeur mécanicien ; (milit.) soldat du génie, officier du génie, *m.* **Civil** — ; *ingénieur civil, ou des ponts et chaussées.* **Mining** — ; *ingénieur des mines.*

engineer'ing, *n.*, art de l'ingénieur ; (milit.) génie, *m.* **Civil** — ; *génie civil, m.* ; *les ponts et chaussées, m.pl.* (under Government).

engineer'ing, *adj.*, de l'art de l'ingénieur ; du génie.

en'gine-house (-haouce), *n.*, bâtiment pour la machine ; dépôt de pompes à incendie, *m.*

en'gine-ma'ker (-mék'-), *n.*, constructeur de machines ; mécanicien, *m.*

en'gine-ma'king, *n.*, construction de machines, *f.*

en'gine-man, *n.*, machiniste ; (of steam-engines) mécanicien ; ouvrier mécanicien, *m.*

en'gine-room (-roume), *n.*, chambre de la machine (*ou* des machines), *f.*

en'gine-shaft (-shâfte), *n.*, puits de machine, *m.*

en'gine-tender (-tè'n'd'-), *n.*, tender de machine, *m.*

engird' (è'n'gheurde), *v.a.* V. **gird.**

En'glish (ign'glishe), *adj.*, anglais. — **girl** ; jeune Anglaise, *f.*

En'glish, *n.*, Anglais ; (language) anglais ;

(print.) saint-augustin, *m.* Two line —; *petit canon*, *m.* Old — ; (writing) *gothique*, *f.*

En'glish, *v.a.*, rendre en anglais.

En'glish-built, *adj.*, de construction anglaise.

En'glish-engined, *adj.*, pourvu de machines anglaises.

En'glishman, *n.*, Anglais, *m.*

En'glishwoman (-woum'-), *n.*, Anglaise *or* dame anglaise, *f.*

engorge' (é'n'gordje), *v.a.*, (ant.) dévorer, avaler, engloutir.

engorge', *v.n.*, (ant.) se gorger de.

engorge'ment, *n.*, engorgement, *m.*

engraft', *v.a.* *V.* graft.

engrail' (è'n'gréle), *v.a.*, (her.) engrêler.

engrain' (è'n'gréne), *v.a.*, teindre foncé, peindre en décor.

engrave' (è'n'-), *v.a.*, graver.

engra'ver (-'grév'-), *n.*, graveur, *m.*

engra'ving (è-), *n.*, gravure, *f.* Dealer in —s; *marchand d'estampes*, *m.* Copper-plate —; *gravure en taille-douce.* Wood— —; *gravure sur bois.* Steel—; *gravure sur acier.* Stone— —; *gravure sur pierre.* Line— —; *gravure au trait.* Letter— —; *gravure en caractères d'imprimerie.* Seal— —; *gravure en pierres fines.*

engross' (è'n'grôce), *v.a.*, (to copy) grossoyer; (to forestall) accaparer, monopoliser ; s'emparer de ; (to occupy) absorber, occuper. —ed by ; *préoccupé de.*

engross'er, *n.*, accapareur, *m.*

engross'ment, *n.*, action de grossoyer, *f.*; (forestalling) accaparement, *m.*

enhance' (è-nhã'n'ce), *v.a.*, enchérir, renchérir, augmenter, aggraver ; (fig.) rehausser, relever, augmenter.

enhance'ment, *n.*, (price) enchérissement, renchérissement, *m.*; augmentation, *f.*; (fig.) rehaussement, *m.*, hausse, *f.*

enig'ma (è-nig-), *n.*, énigme, *f.*

enigmat'ical, *adj.*, énigmatique ; obscur.

enigmat'ically, *adv.*, énigmatiquement ; obscurément.

enig'matist, *n.*, faiseur d'énigmes, *m.*

enjoin' (é'n'djoï'ne), *v.a.*, enjoindre à, prescrire à, faire une injonction à ; prohiber ; imposer à, commander à.

enjoin'ment, *n.*, injonction, *f.*

enjoy' (è'n'djo'i), *v.a.*, jouir de, trouver bon ; posséder ; goûter ; aimer à. To — one's self ; *s'en donner ; s'amuser, se divertir, se donner du bon temps.* Did you — yourself ? *vous êtes-vous bien amusé?* I —ed that very much ; *j'ai trouvé cela très bon.* I shall — my dinner ; *je dînerai avec plaisir.*

enjoy'able, *adj.*, agréable, dont on peut jouir.

enjoy'ment, *n.*, jouissance, *f.*, plaisir, *m.*, satisfaction, *f.*

enkin'dle (è'n'ki'n'd'l), *v.a.*, enflammer ; exciter, allumer.

enlarge' (è'n'lârdje), *v.a.*, agrandir, augmenter, étendre, dilater ; (to set free) élargir.

enlarge', *v.n.*, grandir, s'agrandir, s'accroître, se développer ; s'étendre sur.

enlarge'ment, *n.*, agrandissement, accroissement, *m.*; augmentation, *f.*; (from prison) élargissement, *m.*; extension, *f.*; développement, *m.*; mise en liberté ; (med.) dilatation ; (of the heart) hypertrophie, *f.*, anévrisme, *m.*

enlight'en (-laï-t'n), *v.a.*, éclairer.

enlight'ener, *n.*, qui éclaire ; instructeur, *m.*

enlight'enment, *n.*, éclaircissement, *m.* ; instruction, *f.*, lumières, *f.pl.*

enlist', *v.a.*, enrôler, inscrire ; engager.

enlist', *v.n.*, s'enrôler, s'engager.

enlist'ment, *n.*, enrôlement, engagement, *m.*

enli'ven (è'n'laï'v'n), *v.a.*, vivifier ; égayer ; animer, aiguillonner, exciter.

enli'vener, *n.*, qui vivifie, qui égaye, qui anime; (pers.) boute-en-train, *m.*

enli'vening, *adj.*, qui anime ; qui égaye.

en'mity (è'n'-), *n.*, inimitié, animosité, haine, *f.* At — with ; *en hostilité* avec, ennemi de.

en'neagon (è'n'ni-), *n.*, ennéagone, *m.*

ennean'dria (è'n'ni-), *n.*, (bot.) ennéandrie, *f.*

enno'ble (è'n'nô-b'l), *v.a.*, (to confer a title) anoblir ; (fig.) (to dignify) ennoblir ; illustrer.

enno'blement, *n.*, anoblissement; (fig.) ennoblissement, *m.* ; élévation, *f.*

enorm'ity (è-), *n.*, énormité ; atrocité, *f.*; crime énorme, *m.*

enor'mous, *adj.*, énorme ; atroce ; monstrueux ; anormal.

enor'mously, *adv.*, énormément.

enor'mousness, *n.*, énormité, *f.*, excès de grandeur, *m.*

enough' (i-neufe), *adj.*, assez. More than —; *plus qu'il n'en faut.* That is —; *c'en est assez;* assez ; en voilà assez ; cela suffit. To be —; *suffire, être suffisant.*

enrage' (è'n'rédje), *v.a.*, faire enrager ; irriter, exaspérer, rendre furieux.

enrapt'ure (è'n'rapt'ioure), *v.a.*, transporter, ravir. *n.*, ravissement, transport, *m.*

enrich' (è'n'ritshe), *v.a.*, enrichir. *v.n.*, s'enrichir.

enrich'ment, *n.*, enrichissement, *m.*

enring' (è'n'-), *v.a.*, (ant.) entourer.

enrobe' (è'n'rôbe), *v.a.*, vêtir, revêtir.

enroll' (è'n'rôl), *v.a.*, enrôler, enregistrer, inscrire.

enroll'er, *n.*, personne qui enregistre, qui enrôle, *f.*

enroll'ment, *n.*, enrôlement ; enregistrement, *m.*

ensconce' (è'n'-), *v.a.*, couvrir, mettre à couvert, cacher. To — oneself ; *se cacher* dans.

enshrine' (è'n'shraïne), *v.a.*, enchâsser ; enfermer; mettre sous verre.

enshroud' (è'n'shraoude), *v.a.*, couvrir, abriter, cacher.

en'siform, *adj.*, ensiforme.

en'sign (è'n'saïne), *n.*, enseigne, *f.* ; signal ; drapeau ; (nav.) pavillon de poupe ; (milit.) drapeau ; (pers.) porte-drapeau, enseigne ; sous-lieutenant ; (sign) signe, insigne, *m.*

en'sign-bea'rer (-bèr'-), *n.*, porte-drapeau, *m.*

en'signcy (-'saï'n'ci), *n.*, grade d'enseigne, *m.*

enslave' (è'n'-), *v.a.*, réduire à l'esclavage ; asservir ; rendre esclave, assujettir.

enslave'ment, *n.*, esclavage, asservissement, *m.*

ensla'ver, *n.*, qui réduit à l'esclavage ; asservisseur, despote, tyran, *m.*

ensnare', *v.a.*, prendre au piège, faire tomber dans le panneau, dans un piège ; (fig.) attraper, abuser, tromper.

ensue' (e'n'siou), *v.n.*, s'ensuivre, suivre ; résulter.

ensu'ing, *adj.*, suivant ; ultérieur ; prochain.

ensure' (è'n'shioure), *v.a.* *V.* insure.

entab'lature (è'n'tab-la-tioure) *ou* **enta'blement** (-té-b'l-), *n.*, (arch.) entablement, *m.*

entail' (è'n'téle), *n.*, (jur.) bien substitué, majorat, *m.* ; substitution, *f.*

entail', *v.a.*, imposer à ; (fig.) nécessiter, entraîner, occasionner ; léguer ; (jur.) substituer. —ed estate; *bien substitué*, *m.*

entail'ment, *n.*, (jur.) substitution, *f.*

entan'gle (è'n'ta'gn'g'l), *v.a.*, emmêler ; empêtrer ; enchevêtrer ; engager ; (fig.) embrouiller, embarrasser.

entan'glement, *n.*, (fig.) embrouillement, embarras, *m.* ; confusion, *f.*

entan'gler, *n.*, brouillon, *m.*

en'tasis (è'n'ta-cice), *n.*, (arch.) galbe, renflement, *m.* ; (med. ant.) maladie spasmodique, *f.*

en'ter (è'n'-), *v.a.*, entrer dans ; (to register) inscrire, enregistrer ; (jur.) (an action) intenter;

(book-keeping) porter, inscrire ; (a claim) avancer, mettre en avant, revendiquer. To — the army ; *entrer au service ; devenir militaire ; se faire soldat.* To — the navy ; *entrer au service de la marine ; se faire marin.* To — the church ; *entrer dans les ordres ; se faire ecclésiastique.* To — the law ; *entrer au barreau.* To — a profession ; *embrasser une carrière.*

en'ter, *v.n.,* entrer. To — into ; *entrer dans, prendre part à.* To — upon ; *commencer ; entrer dans; entrer en possession de, débuter dans.* To — upon an office ; *entrer en fonctions.* To — on; *s'embarquer dans ; s'engager dans.*

en'terer, *n.,* entrant, *m.*

enter'ic, *adj.,* entérique.

en'tering, *n.,* entrée, *f.* On —; *à son entrée.*

enteri'tis, *n.,* (med.) entérite, *f.*

en'terprise (è'n'teur-praïze), *n.,* entreprise, hardiesse, *f. ;* caractère entreprenant, esprit d'entreprise, *m.*

en'terpriser, *n.,* (ant.) homme entreprenant, *m.*

entertain' (è'n'teur-téne), *v.a.,* (to receive) accueillir, recevoir ; (to amuse) divertir ; (to feast) régaler de, fêter, amuser ; (an idea, etc.) entretenir ; concevoir ; (with vain hopes) nourrir ; amuser de ; (a proposal) accepter, accueillir. To — at dinner ; *donner à dîner à.* Do you — a great deal ? *voyez-vous beaucoup de monde ?* ou *recevez-vous beaucoup de monde ?*

entertain'er, *n.,* qui accueille, qui divertit, qui conçoit, qui régale, *f. ;* amuseur ; amphitryon, hôte, *m. ;* hôtesse, *f.*

entertain'ingly, *adv.,* agréablement ; d'une manière agréable.

entertain'ment, *n.,* accueil, *m. ;* hospitalité, *f. ;* (feast) repas, banquet ; (amusement) divertissement, amusement, *m. ;* réception, *f.*

enthrall' (è'n'thrôl), *v.a.,* asservir ; assujettir, tenir en servitude ; (fig.) captiver, ravir, transporter.

enthrone' (è'n'thrône), *v.a.,* placer sur le trône ; (a bishop) introniser.

enthrone'ment, *n.,* intronisation.

enthu'siasm (è'n'thiou'zi-az'me), *n.,* enthousiasme, *m.*

enthu'siast, *n.,* enthousiaste, *m.* and *f.*

enthusias'tic ou **enthusias'tical,** *adj.,* enthousiaste.

enthusias'tically, *adv.,* avec enthousiasme, en enthousiaste.

en'thymeme (è'n'thi-mème), *n.,* (log.) enthymème, *m.*

entice' (è'n'taïce), *v.a.,* attirer, inciter ; exciter ; pousser ; entraîner ; tenter, séduire. To — into ; *entraîner à ; engager à ; exciter à, pousser à.* To — away ; *enlever.*

entice'ment, *n.,* attrait, appât, charme, *m. ;* tentation, attraction, séduction, *f.*

enti'cer, *n.,* séducteur, *m.,* séductrice, *f. ;* instigateur, *m.,* instigatrice, *f. ;* (thing) appât, *m.*

enti'cing, *adj.,* séduisant, attrayant, tentant.

enti'cingly, *adv.,* d'une manière séduisante ou attrayante.

entire' (-'taïeur), *adj.,* entier, complet, parfait, intact. — horse ; *cheval entier; cheval pur sang, m.*

entire'ly, *adv.,* entièrement, en entier.

entire'ty, *n.,* entier, ensemble, *m. ;* totalité, intégrité, *f. ;* tout, *m.*

en'title (è'n'taï-t'l), *v.a.,* intituler, appeler; donner droit à. To be —d to ; *avoir droit à ; avoir le droit de ; être en droit de. v.r.,* s'intituler, s'appeler.

en'tity (è'n'-), *n.,* être, *m. ;* entité, essence, existence, *f.*

entoil' (è'n'toïl), *v.a.,* prendre dans des filets ; prendre au piège ; (fig.) enlacer, prendre dans un lacs.

entomb' (è'n'toume), *v.a.,* ensevelir.

entomb'ment (è'n'toum'mè'n'te), *n.,* sépulture, *f.*

entomolog'ical (è'n'to-mol'-o-dji-), *adj.,* entomologique.

entomol'ogist, *n.,* entomologiste, *m.*

entomol'ogy (è'n'to-mol-o-dji), *n.,* entomologie, *f.*

entozo'on (è'n'to-zô-), *n.,* (entozoa) (ent.) entozoaire, *m.*

en'trails (è'n'trél'ze), *n.pl.,* entrailles, *f.pl.*

en'trance (è'n'trân'ce), *n.,* entrée, *f. ;* (beginning) commencement ; (nav.) avant, *m. ;* initiation, *f. ;* début, *m.* — door, ou gate ; *porte d'entrée, porte-cochère, f.* — hall ; *vestibule, m.* — money ; *prix d'entrée ou droit d'entrée, m.*

en'trance (è'n-trâ'n'ce), *v.a.,* faire tomber en léthargie, rendre insensible ; (fig.) extasier, ravir, fasciner.

entrap', *v.a.,* prendre au piège ; attraper.

entreat' (è'n'trîte), *v.a.,* supplier de ; conjurer de ; adjurer de ; prier avec instance de, prier en grâce de, prier instamment de.

entrea'ty, *n.,* supplication ; prière ; sollicitation, *f.,* instances, *f.pl.*

entrepot' (a'gn't'r'pô), *n.,* entrepôt, *m.*

entresol' (a'gn't'r'-), *n.,* entresol, *m.*

entrust', *v.a. V.* intrust.

en'try (è'n'-), *n.,* entrée, *f. ;* (at the customs) droit d'inscription, *m.,* déclaration d'entrée ; (jur.) prise de possession, *f. ;* (of the mass) introït, *m. ;* (registration) inscription, *f. ;* (book-keeping) article, *m. ;* inscription, *f.* By double —; *en partie double.* By single —; *en partie simple.* To make an — against ; (com.) *débiter.*

entwine' (è'n'twaïne), *v.a.,* enlacer, entrelacer ; tresser, entortiller.

entwine', *v.n.,* s'enlacer, s'entrelacer, s'entortiller.

enu'merate (i-niou-meur'-), *v.a.,* énumérer.

enumera'tion (i-niou-meur-é-), *n.,* énumération, *f.*

enun'ciate (i-neu'n'shi-), *v.a.,* énoncer, prononcer, proférer.

enuncia'tion (-shi-é-), *n.,* énonciation, diction, *f. ;* débit, *m. ;* (geom.) énoncé, *m.*

enun'ciative ou **enun'ciatory** (-teuri), *adj.,* (log. ant.) énonciatif.

enun'ciatively, *adv.,* (ant.) d'une manière énonciative.

envel'op (è'n'vèl'-), *v.a.,* envelopper de, ou dans; entourer de.

en'velop, *n.,* enveloppe ; (astron.) chevelure (of comets), *f.* In an —; *sous enveloppe.*

envel'opment, *n.,* enveloppement, *m.*

enven'om (è'n'vè'n'eume), *v.a.,* envenimer ; empoisonner ; rendre odieux à ; (to embitter) exaspérer.

en'viable (è'n'vi-a-b'l), *adj.,* digne d'envie ; enviable.

en'vier, *n.,* envieux, *m.,* envieuse, *f.*

en'vious, *adj.,* envieux. With — eyes ; *d'un œil d'envie.*

en'viously, *adv.,* avec envie, par envie.

envi'ron (è'n'vaï-), *v.a.,* environner de (with).

envi'ronment, *n.,* environnement, *m.*

envi'rons (è'n'vaï-ro'n'ze ou -vi-), *n.pl.,* environs, *m.pl.*

en'voy (è'n'voïe), *n.,* envoyé ; (poet.) envoi, *m.* — extraordinary ; *ministre plénipotentiaire, m.*

en'vy (è'n'-), *n.,* envie, haine, *f.*

en'vy, *v.a.,* envier ; porter envie à.

eol'ic (è-), *adj.,* éolique, éolien.

e'pact (i-), *n.,* épacte, *f.*

epaule' (é-), *n.,* (fort.) épaule, *f.*

epaule'ment, *n.,* (fort.) épaulement, *m.*

ep'aulet (è'-), *n.,* épaulette, *f.*

epen'thesis (è-pè'n'thi-cice), *n.,* (epentheses) épenthèse, *f.*

epergne' (é-peurne), *n.,* surtout, ou dormant, de table, *m.*

eph'elis (èf'i-lice), *n.,* (med.) éphélide ; tache de rousseur, *f.*

ephem'era (è-fèm'i-), *n.*, (ent.) éphémère, *m.*

ephem'eral, **ephemer'ic**, *ou* **ephem'erous** (-eur'al, -èr'ik, -eur'eusse), *adj.*, éphémère.

ephem'eris (è-fèm'eur'ice), *n.*, (*ephemerides*) éphémérides, *f.pl.*

ephem'erist, *n.*, auteur d'éphémérides, astrologue, *m.*

Ephe'sian (è-fî-zia'ne), *adj.*, éphésien.

Ephe'sian, *n.*, Ephésien, *m.*, Ephésienne, *f.*

eph'od (èf'-), *n.*, éphod, *m.*

ep'ic (èp'-), *adj.*, épique.

ep'ic, *n.*, poème épique, *m.*

ep'icene (èp'i-cîne), *adj.*, (gram.) épicène.

epicra'nium (èp'i-cré-ni-), *n.*, (anat.) épicrâne, *m.*

ep'icure (èp'i-kioure), *n.*, épicurien, *m.*, épicurienne, *f.*; gastronome, gourmet, gourmand; épicure, *m.*

Epicure'an (èp'i-kiou-ri-), *adj.*, d'Epicure; épicurien; de gastronome.

Epicure'an, *n.*, épicurien, sectateur d'Epicure, *m.*

Epicure'anism, *n.*, épicurisme (doctrine), *m.*

ep'icurism, *n.*, épicurisme, *m.*

epidem'ic *ou* **epidem'ical** (èp'i-dèm'-), *adj.*, épidémique.

epidem'ic *ou* **ep'idemy** (èp'i-dè'm'-), *n.*, épidémie, *f.*

epider'mis (èp'i-deur'mice), *n.*, épiderme, *m.*

epigas'trium (èp'i-), *n.*, (anat.) épigastre, *m.*

epiglot'tis (èp'-) *n.*, (anat.) épiglotte, *f.*

ep'igram (èp'-), *n.*, épigramme, *f.*

epigrammat'ic *ou* **epigrammat'ical**, *adj.*, épigrammatique.

epigram'matist, *n.*, épigrammatiste, *m.*

ep'igraph (èp-), *n.*, épigraphe, *f.*

ep'ilepsy (èp'i-lèp-), *n.*, (med.) épilepsie, *f.*

epilep'tic, *adj.*, épileptique. — fit; *attaque d'épilepsie, f.*

epilogis'tic (i-pil'o-djis-), *adj.*, en forme d'épilogue.

ep'ilogue (èp'i-), *n.*, epilogue, *m.*

Epiph'any (i-pif-), *n.*, Epiphanie, *f.*

epip'loce (i-pip-lo-ci), *n.*, (rhet.) gradation, *f.*

epip'loon (i-pip-lo-one), *n.*, (anat.) épiploon, *m.*

epis'copacy (i-pis-cô-), *n.*, épiscopat, *m.*

episcopa'lian, *adj.*, épiscopal.

episcopa'lian, *n.*, épiscopal, *m.*

epis'copally, *adv.*, épiscopalement.

epis'copal, *adj.*, épiscopal. — see; *évêché, m.* — palace; *palais épiscopal, évêché; palais de l'évêque, m.*

epis'copate, *n.*, épiscopat, *m.*

ep'isode (èp'i-çôde), *n.*, épisode, *m.*

episod'ic *ou* **episod'ical**, *adj.*, épisodique.

episod'ically, *adv.*, en forme d'épisode.

epispas'tic (èp-), *adj.*, (med.) épispastique.

epispas'tic, *n.*, épispastique, *m.*

epis'tle (è-pis's'l), *n.*, épître, *f.*

epis'tolary (è-), *adj.*, épistolaire.

epis'tolize, *v.n.*, écrire des lettres.

epis'tolizer, *n.*, épistolier, -ère, *m.f.*

ep'itaph (èp'-), *n.*, épitaphe, *f.*

epit'asis (i-pit'a-cice), *n.*, (ancient drama) épitase, *f.*; (log.) conséquent; (med.) paroxysme, *m.*; (rhet.) péroraison, *f.*

epithala'mium (èp'i-tha-lé-mi-), *n.*, (ant.) épithalame, *m.*

ep'ithet (èp-i-thète), *n.*, épithète, *f.*

epithet'ic, *adj.*, d'épithète.

epit'ome (i-pit'o-mi), *n.*, épitomé, abrégé, précis, *m.*

epit'omist, *n.*, auteur d'un épitomé, abréviation, *m.*

epit'omize (-maîze), *v.a.*, faire un épitome de, un abrégé de, un précis de; abréger, raccourcir.

epit'omizer, *n.*, auteur d'un épitomé; abréviateur, *m.*

epizoot'ic (èp'-), *adj.*, épizootique.

epizo'oty, *n.*, épizootie, *f.*

ep'och (èp-oke *ou* î-poke), *n.*, époque, *f.* — making; *qui fait époque; mémorable.*

ep'ode (èp'ôde), *n.*, épode, *f.*

ep'opee (èp-o-pî) *ou* **ep'opœia** (-pi-ia), *n.*, épopée, *f.*

equabil'ity (î-kwa-), *n.*, uniformité, égalité, *f.*

e'quable (î-kwa-b'l), *adj.*, uniforme, égal.

e'quably, *adv.*, avec égalité, avec uniformité, uniformément.

e'qual (î-kwol), *adj.*, égal, uniforme; (fig.) impartial, juste. — to; *de force à, en état de; à la hauteur de*; (of things) *égal à*. — with; *à l'égal de*. To be — to a journey; *être de force à faire*, ou *à entreprendre, un voyage.* To be — to (anything); *en avoir la force, en avoir les moyens.* Other things being —; *toutes choses égales d'ailleurs.*

e'qual, *n.*, égal, *m.*, égale, *f.* *pl.*, pareils, égaux, *m.pl.*; pareilles, égales, *f.pl.*

e'qual, *v.a.*, égaler; être égal à.

equal'ity, *n.*, égalité, *f.*

equaliza'tion (-aîzé-), *n.*, égalisation, *f.*

e'qualize (-aïze), *v.a.*, égaliser; égaler.

e'qually, *adv.*, également, pareillement; uniformément; impartialement.

equanim'ity (î-kwa-), *n.*, égalité d'âme, *f.*; calme d'esprit, *m.*; sérénité, *f.*

equan'imous, *adj.*, qui à l'âme égale, d'un caractère égal.

equa'tion (i-kwé-), *n.*, équation, *f.*

equa'tor (i-kwé-), *n.*, équateur, *m.*

equato'rial (i-kwa-tô-), *adj.*, équatorial, de l'équateur.

e'querry (èk-wi-ri *ou* i-kwèr-i), *n.*, écuyer, *m.*

eques'trian (i-kwès-), *adj.*, équestre.

eques'trian, *n.*, cavalier, *m.*; (circus) écuyère, *f.*

equian'gled (î-kwi-à'gn'g'l'de) *ou* **equian'gular** (-a'gn'ghiou-), *adj.*, équiangle.

equibal'ance, *v.a.*, équilibrer, contrebalancer.

equidis'tance (î-kwi-), *n.*, équidistance, *f.* (l.u.)

equidis'tant, *adj.*, équidistant.

equidis'tantly, *adv.*, à égale distance.

equilat'eral (î-kwi-lat'eur-), *adj.*, équilatéral; équilatère (l.u.)

equilat'eral, *n.*, figure équilatérale, *f.*

equili'brate (î-kwi-laî-), *v.a.*, (ant.) équilibrer.

equilibra'tion (-laî-bré-), *n.*, équilibre, *m.*; action d'équilibrer, *f.*

equilib'rious (î-kwi-li-), *adj.*, (ant.) en équilibre.

equilib'riously, *adv.*, (ant.) en équilibre.

equil'ibrist (i-kwil'i-), *n.*, bateleur, équilibriste; danseur de corde, *m.*

equilib'rity (i-kwi-), *n.*, équilibre, *m.*

equilib'rium (î-kwi-), *n.*, équilibre, *m.* To keep one's —; *garder l'équilibre.* To remain in —; *se tenir en équilibre.*

e'quine (è-kwaî-), *adj.*, de cheval, chevaline, hippique.

equinoc'tial (î-kwi-nok-shal), *adj.*, équinoxial, d'équinoxe; de l'équinoxe, des équinoxes.

equinoc'tial, *n.*, ligne équinoxiale, *f.*; équateur céleste, *m.*

equinoc'tially, *adv.*, dans la direction de la ligne équinoxiale.

e'quinox (î-kwi-), *n.*, équinoxe, *m.*

equip' (i-kwipe), (ant.) *v.a.*, équiper.

eq'uipage (èk'wi-pèdje), *n.*, équipage; (nav.) équipement, *m.*

equip'ment (i-kwip'-), *n.*, équipement, *m.*

e'quipoise (i-kwi-poïce), *n.*, équilibre, *m.*; pondération, *f.*

equipol'lence *ou* **equipol'lency.** *V.* **equivalence.**

equipon'derance *ou* **equipon'derancy** (î-kwi-po'n'deur'-) *n.*, égalité de poids, *f.*; équilibre, *m.*

equipon'derant, *adj.*, de même poids; se faisant équilibre.

eq'uitable (èk'wi-ta-b'l), *adj.*, équitable, juste.

eq'uitableness, *n.*, équité, impartialité, nature équitable, *f.*

eq'uitably, *adv.*, équitablement.

equita'tion (èk'wi-té-), *n.*, équitation, *f.*

eq'uity (èk'wi-), *n.*, équité, justice, *f.*

equiv'alence (i-kwiv'-), *n.*, équivalence, égalité de valeur ; égalité de force, *f.*

equiv'alent, *adj.*, équivalent à. To be —; *être équivalent à* ou *équivaloir à; revenir à.*

equiv'alent à ou, équivalent, *m.*

equiv'alently, *adv.*, d'une manière équivalente.

equiv'ocal (ĭ-kwiv'-), *adj.*, équivoque, ambigu.

equiv'ocal, *n.*, terme équivoque, *m.*

equiv'ocally, *adv.*, d'une manière équivoque.

equiv'ocalness, *n.*, équivoque ; nature équivoque ; ambiguïté, *f.*

equiv'ocate, *v.n.*, user d'équivoque, équivoquer ; tergiverser ; chercher des faux-fuyants.

equivoca'tion (-'o-ké-), *n.*, équivoque, *f.;* faux-fuyant, *m.*

equiv'ocator (-ké-teur), *n.*, qui use d'équivoque, *f.;* tergiversateur ; prévaricateur, *m.*

e'ra (ĭ-ra), *n.*, ère ; époque, *f.* Christian —; *ère chrétienne.* To mark an —; *faire époque; V.* **epoch.**

era'diate (i-ré-di-), *v.n.*, rayonner.

eradia'tion (-di-é-), *n.*, radiation, émanation, *f.;* rayonnement, *m.*

erad'icable, *adj.*, déracinable, extirpable.

erad'icate (è-rad'i-), *v.a.*, déraciner ; (fig.) déraciner, extirper, détruire, exterminer.

eradica'tion (-'i-ké-), *n.*, déracinement, *m.;* éradication, extirpation, *f.*

erad'icative (-'i-ké-), *adj.*, (ant.) éradicatif, qui tend à extirper.

erad'icator, *n.*, extirpateur, *m.*

eras'able, *adj.*, effaçable.

erase' (è-réze), *v.a.*, raturer, effacer, rayer.

erase'ment, *n.*, rature, *f.;* effacement, *m.*

era'sure (i-ré-jeur), *n.*, effaçure, rature, *f.;* effacement, *m.*

ere (ère), *adv., conj.,* and *prep.,* avant, avant que, (rather than) plutôt que. —long ; *avant peu.* — while ; *naguère.* — yet ; *avant que.* — now ; *avant, avant ce temps.*

erect' (i-rèkte), *adj.,* debout, droit ; haut ; élevé ; levé ; dressé.

erect', *v.a.,* ériger, dresser, élever ; construire ; (fig.) établir, fonder.

erec'table (i-rèk-ta-b'l), (ant.) ou **erec'tile** (i-rèk'-), *adj.,* que l'on peut dresser ; (anat.) érectile.

erect'er, *n.,* constructeur ; fondateur, *m.*

erec'tile, *adj.,* susceptible d'érection, érectile.

erec'tion, *n.,* action de dresser ; érection, construction, élévation ; (fig.) fondation, *f.;* établissement, *m.*

erect'ness, *n.,* (ant.) posture droite, *f.;* aplomb, *m.*

erec'tor, *n.,* constructeur ; (fig.) fondateur ; (anat.) muscle érecteur, *m.*

er'emite (èr'i-maïte), *n.,* ermite. *V.* **hermit.**

erep'tion (i-rèp'-), *n.,* (ant.) enlèvement par violence, *m.*

er'ethism (èr-i-thiz'me), *n.,* éréthisme, *m.*

er'go (eur-gô), *adv.,* ergo, par conséquent.

er'got (eur-gote), *n.,* ergot, *m.*

er'gotine, *n.,* ergotine, *f.*

er'mine (êur-), *n.,* hermine, *f.;* roselet, *m.* In —; *vêtu d'hermine.*

er'mined (-mi'n'de), *adj.,* fourré d'hermine ; revêtu d'hermine.

ern ou **erne** (eurne), *n.,* (orni.) orfraie, *f.*

erne ou **æerne** (eurne), *n.,* chaumière, *f.* ; lieu de retraite, *m.*

erode' (i-rôde), *v.a.,* corroder, ronger.

ero'dent (i-rôd'-), *n.,* (pharm.) caustique, corrosif, érosif, *m.*

ero'sion (i-rô-jeune), *n.,* érosion, *f.*

erot'ic (i-), *n.,* composition érotique, *f.;* poème érotique, *m.*

erot'ic ou **erot'ical**, *adj.,* érotique.

erotoma'nia (-mé-), *n.,* érotomanie, *f.*

erpetol'ogy (eur-pi-tol-o-dji), *n.,* erpétologie, herpétologie, *f.*

err (eure), *v.n.,* faillir, errer, se tromper ; s'égarer **de,** s'écarter **de.**

er'rand (èr'-), *n.,* message, *m.* ; commission ; course, *f.* On an —; *en course.* To go an —; *aller faire une commission ; aller en commission.*

er'rand-boy (-boï), *n.,* garçon qui fait des courses ; petit messager, commissionnaire ; (of a lawyer) saute-ruisseau, *m.*

er'rant (èr'-), *adj.,* errant ; ambulant.

er'rantry, *n.,* (ant.) vie errante, *f.* Knight —; *chevalerie errante.*

errat'ic, *n.,* (ant.) vagabond, original, *m.;* planète, *f.;* bloc erratique, *m.*

errat'ic ou **errat'ical**, *adj.,* errant, vagabond, variable ; excentrique ; (astron., geol., med.) erratique.

errat'ically, *adv.,* sans règle, sans ordre.

erra'tum (èr-ré-), *n.,(errata)* erratum, errata, *m.*

erro'neous (èr-rô-ni-), *adj.,* erroné, faux, inexact.

erro'neously, *adv.,* incorrectement, faussement, à faux, à tort.

erro'neousness, *n.,* caractère erroné, *m.* faussété, *f.*

er'ror (èr-reur), *n.,* erreur, faute, *f.;* (theol.) péché, *m.* —s excepted ; *sauf erreur ou omission.* In —; *dans l'erreur.* To labor under —; *être dans l'erreur, se tromper grandement.* To induce into —; *induire en erreur.*

erst (eurste), *adv.,* autrefois, jadis, auparavant ; d'abord, jusqu'à présent, jusqu'ici.

erubes'cence ou **erubes'cency** (è-riou-), *n.,* rougeur ; (med.) érubescence, *f.*

erubes'cent, *adj.,* rougeâtre, (med.) érubescent.

eruc'tate (i-reuk'-), *v.a.,* (ant.) avoir des éructations, roter ; (med.) éructer ; vomir.

eructa'tion (-té-), *n.,* éructation, *f.;* rot, *m.*

er'udite (èr-iou-daïte ou -dite), *adj.,* érudit, savant, *n.,* érudit, *m.*

erudi'tion, *n.,* érudition, *f.,* savoir, *m.*

eru'ginous (i-riou-dji-), *adj.,* érugineux.

erup'tion (i-reup-), *n.,* éruption ; irruption, invasion ; sortie (of bands of troops), *f.*

erup'tive, *adj.,* éruptif.

erysip'elas (èr-i-cip'i-lace), *n.,* (med.) érysipèle, érésipèle, *m.*

erysipel'atous (-cip'èl-), *adj.,* érysipélateux.

escalade' (ès-ca-léde), *n.,* escalade, *f. v.a.,* escalader.

escapade' (ès-ca-péde), *n.,* escapade ; (man.) allure irrégulière, *f.*

escape' (ès-), *n.,* évasion, fuite ; (fig.) délivrance, *f.* Fire —; *appareil de sauvetage, m.* — of steam ; *échappement de la vapeur, m.* — of gas ; *fuite de gaz.* There is no — from it ; *il n'y a pas moyen d'y échapper ; il faut y passer à tout prix.* To make good one's —; *s'échapper ; s'enfuir ;* (from prison) *s'évader.* To have a narrow —; *l'échapper belle.*

escape', *v.a.,* échapper à ; éviter. To — one's memory ; *échapper à ; sortir de la mémoire.*

escape', *v.n.,* s'échapper, s'enfuir, se sauver ; (from prison) s'évader ; (fig.) se soustraire à.

escape'ment, *n.,* (horl.) échappement, *m.*

escarp' (ès-cârpe), *v.a.,* (fort.) escarper. *V.* **scarp.**

escarp'ment, *n.,* (fort.) escarpement, *m.*

eschalot' (èsh-a-), *n.,* (bot.) échalote, *f.*

es'char (ès-kar), *n.,* (surg.) eschare, *f.*

escheat' (ès-tshîte), *n.,* déshérence, aubaine, *f.;* bien en déshérence, *m.*

escheat', *v.n.,* tomber en déshérence ; échoir à.

escheat'able, *adj.*, sujet à déshérence.

escheat'age, *n.*, droit de déshérence, droit d'aubaine, *m.*

eschew' (ès-tshou), *v.a.*, éviter, fuir; renoncer à.

escort', *v.a.*, escorter.

escort', *n.*, escorte, *f.*

escort'er, *n.*, cavalier, *m.*

escritoire' (ès-cri-toire), *n.*, écritoire, *f.*; secrétaire, bureau, *m.*

es'culent (ès-kiou-), *adj.*, comestible.

escutch'eon (ès-keut'sheune), *n.*, écusson; (of a key-hole) cache-entrée, *m.*

escutch'eoned, *adj.*, écussonné.

esoter'ic *ou* **esoter'ical** (ess'o-tèr'-), *adj.*, ésotérique.

espal'ier (ès-pal'ieur), *n.*, espalier, *m.*

espal'ier, *v.a.*, mettre en espalier.

espar'cet (ès-pâr-cète), *n.*, (bot.) esparcette, *f.*, esparcet, *m.*

espar'to (ès-pâr-tô), *n.*, (bot.) sparte, *m.*

espe'cial (ès-pèsh'al), *adj.*, spécial, particulier, singulier.

espe'cially, *adv.*, spécialement, surtout, particulièrement.

es'pionage (ès'pi-o-nédje *ou* -naje), *n.*, espionnage, *m.*

esplanade' (ès-pla-), *n.*, esplanade, *f.*

espou'sal (ès-paou-zal), *adj.*, nuptial, de mariage.

espou'sal, *n.*, adoption, adhésion, *f. pl.*, épousailles, fiançailles, accordailles, *f.pl.*

espouse' (ès-paouze), *v.a.*, épouser, fiancer; (fig.) adopter, embrasser, défendre.

espou'ser, *n.*, protecteur, défenseur, *m.*

espy' (ès-païe), *v.a.*, voir, découvrir, apercevoir, reconnaître, remarquer; (to watch) épier, observer, surveiller.

esquire' (ès-kwaïeur), *n.*, écuyer, *m.* (The "esquire" given in England, by courtesy, to "gentlemen" has no equivalent in French.)

es'say (ès-sè), *n.*, essai, *m.*; épreuve, composition, *f.*

essay', *v.a.*, essayer de, éprouver de, tenter de.

es'sayist, *n.*, auteur d'essais, *m.*; qui écrit des essais.

es'sence (ès'-), *n.*, essence, *f.*; parfum, *m.*; odeur, *f.*

essen'tial (ès-sè'n'shal), *adj.*, essentiel.

essen'tial, *n.*, essentiel, *m. C'est l'—*; that's the chief thing, the important point.

essential'ity, *n.*, caractère essentiel, *m.*

essen'tially, *adv.*, essentiellement.

essen'tialness, *n.*, extrême importance, *f.*

essoin' (ès'-), *v.a.*, (jur.) accorder un délai de grâce à; excuser l'absence de.

estab'lish (ès-), *v.a.*, établir, ériger, fonder; instituer, affermir; (fig.) confirmer.

estab'lished, *part.adj.*, établi, institué; (agreed) convenu, reçu; (of churches) établi, dominant. — in 1760; *maison fondée en 1760.*

estab'lishment, *n.*, établissement, *m.*, institution, maison, *f.*; état de maison, *m.*; Eglise dominante, *f.*; (fig.) affermissement, *m.*, confirmation, *f.* To be on the —; (print.) *travailler à la conscience.* Branch —; *succursale, f.*

estafette', *n.*, estafette, *f.*

estate' (ès-), *n.*, (property) bien, *m.*, propriété, terre, fortune, *f.*; (condition) état, rang, *m.*; (jur.) propriété, masse des biens; (of a deceased person) succession, *f.*; (political body) Etat, *m.* The third —; *le tiers état, le tiers, m.* Real —; (jur.) *masse des biens immeubles, f.* Personal —; (jur.) *masse des biens meubles, f.* Man's —; *l'âge viril, m.* — *office*; *bureau de gérance de propriétés, m.*

esteem' (ès-tîme), *n.*, estime, considération, *f.*

esteem', *v.a.*, estimer; considérer comme.

esteem'er, *n.*, personne qui estime, *f.*; appréciateur, *m.*

es'timable (ès-ti-ma-b'l), *adj.*, dont on peut estimer la valeur; estimable.

es'timate (ès-), *n.*, estimation, évaluation; appréciation, opinion, *f.*; jugement; (com.) devis, *m.* Rough —; *devis approximatif.*

es'timate, *v.a.*, estimer, apprécier, évaluer; juger; calculer.

estima'tion (-mé-), *n.*, estimation, appréciation, opinion, estime, *f.*, jugement, *m.*

es'timative, *adj.*, (ant.) appréciateur d'opinion; imaginatif.

es'timator (-méteur), *n.*, estimateur, appréciateur, *m.*

es'tival (ès-), *adj.*, estival, d'été.

estiva'tion (-vé-), *n.*, (bot. and zoöl.) estivation, *f.*

estop' (ès-tré), *v.a.*, empêcher, barrer, exclure; (jur.) opposer une exception, opposer une fin de non-recevoir.

estop'pel, *n.*, (jur.) exception, fin de non-recevoir, *f.*

esto'vers (ès-tô-veurze), *n.pl.*, (jur.) pension alimentaire, *f.sing.*; aliments, *m.pl.*

estrange' (ès-tré'n'dje), *v.a.*, aliéner; éloigner de, indisposer contre.

estrange'ment, *n.*, aliénation, *f.*; éloignement, *m.*

estrapade' (ès-tra-péde), *n.*, estrapade, *f.*; (man.) efforts que fait un cheval rétif pour se débarrasser de son cavalier, *m.pl.*

estray' (ès-tré), *n.*, (jur.) bête épave, *f.*

estreat' (ès-trîte), *n.*, (jur.) expédition, grosse, *f.*; extrait authentique, *m.*

estreat', *v.n.*, faire une grosse, faire un extrait.

estreat', *v.a.*, (jur.) enregistrer comme amende à payer.

es'tuary (ès-tiou-a-), *n.*, estuaire, bras de mer; (bath) bain de vapeur, *m.*

etc. (è't'cè-teura), (ab. of *et cætera*), &c., etc., et cætera.

etch (ètshe), *v.a.*, graver à l'eau-forte; (fig.) esquisser, tracer, dessiner.

etch'er, *n.*, graveur à l'eau-forte, *m.*

etch'ing, *n.*, gravure à l'eau-forte, *f.*

etch'ing-needle (-nî'd'l), *n.*, pointe à graver, *f.*

Eter'nal (i-teur-), *n.*, Eternel, *m.*

eter'nal, *adj.*, éternel.

eter'nalize (-'aïze), *v.a.*, (ant.) éterniser, rendre éternel.

eter'nally, *adv.*, éternellement.

eter'nity, *n.*, éternité, *f.*

e'ther (î-theur), *n.*, éther, *m.*

ethe'real *ou* **ethe'reous** (î-thî-ri-), *adj.*, éthéré; céleste, aérien.

eth'ic *ou* **eth'ical** (èth'-), *adj.*, éthique, moral.

eth'ically, *adv.*, suivant les principes de l'éthique.

eth'ics, *n.pl.*, morale, éthique, *f.sing.*

E'thiop (î-thi-) (ant.) *ou* **Ethio'pian** (î-thi-ô-), *n.*, Ethiopien, *m.*, Ethiopienne, *f.*

eth'moid (èth'moïde), *n.*, (anat.) ethmoïde, os ethmoïde, *m.*

eth'moid *ou* **ethmoi'dal**, *adj.*, ethmoïde, ethmoïdal.

ethnolog'ical (èth-no-lo-dj'ical), *adj.*, ethnologique, *m.*

ethnol'ogist, *n.*, ethnologue, ethnologiste; ethnographe, *m.*

ethnol'ogy (eth-nol-o-dji), *n.*, ethnologie; ethnographie, *f.*

ethol'ogy (i-thol-o-dji), *n.*, éthologie, *f.*

e'tiolate (î-ti-), *v.n.*, s'étioler.

e'tiolate, *v.a.*, étioler.

e'tiolated, *adj.*, (bot.) étiolé.

etiola'tion (-lé-), *n.*, étiolement, *m.*

etiol'ogy (î-ti-ol-o-dji), *n.*, étiologie, *f.*

etiquette' (èt'i-), *n.*, étiquette, *f.*, convenances, *f.pl.*, cérémonial de cour, *m.*

Etrus'can (i-treuss'-), *adj.*, étrusque.
etymolog'ical (èt'i-mo-lodj'i-), *adj.*, étymologique.
etymol'ogist, *n.*, étymologiste, *m.*
etymol'ogy (èt'i-mol-o-dji), *n.*, étymologie, *f.*
eu'charist (you-ka-), *n.*, eucharistie, *f.*
eacharis'tical, *adj.*, eucharistique.
euchol'ogy (you-kol'o-dji), *n.*, eucologe, *m.*
eu'crasy (you-cra-ci), *n.*, (med.) eucraisie, eucrasie, *f.*
eudiom'eter (you-di-om'i-), *n.*, eudiomètre, *m.*
eudiomet'ric *ou* **eudiomet'rical**, *adj.*, eudiométrique.
eudiom'etry, *n.*, eudiométrie, *f.*
eulog'ic *ou* **eulog'ical** (you-lodj'-), *adj.*, d'éloge, laudatif, louangeur, élogieux.
eulog'ically, *adv.*, avec éloge.
eu'logist, *n.*, panégyriste, élogiste, *m.*
eulo'gium (you-lô-dji-) *ou* **eu'logy** (-lodji), *n.*, éloge, panégyrique, *m.*
eu'logize (-lo-djaïze), *v.a.*, louer, élogier ; faire l'éloge **de.**
eu'nuch (you-neuke), *n.*, eunuque, *m.*
eu'nuchate, *v.a.*, châtrer.
eu'patory (you-pa-tori), *n.*, (bot.) eupatoire, *f.*
eu'phemism (you-fèm'iz'me), *n.*, (rhet.) euphémisme, *m.*
euphon'ic, euphon'ical (you-fo'n'-), *ou* **eupho'nious** (-fô-), *adj.*, euphonique ; (fig.) mélodieux, harmonieux, agréable à l'oreille.
eupho'niously, *adv.*, agréablement, mélodieusement, harmonieusement.
eu'phony (-fo-), *n.*, euphonie, *f.* For the sake of — ; *par euphonie.*
eu'phuism, *n.*, style précieux, *m.;* préciosité, *f.*
eu'phuist, *n.*, précieux, -euse, *m.f.*
euphuis'tic, *adj.*, précieux, affecté (of style).
Europe'an, (you-ro-pî-), *adj.*, européen.
Europe'an, *n.*, Européen, *m.*, Européenne, *f.*
euryth'my (you-rith'-), *n.*, (med.) régularité du pouls ; (arch., mus., paint.) eurythmie, *f.*
evac'uant (i-vak'iou-), *n.*, (ant.) évacuant, *m.*
evac'uant, *adj.*, (ant.) évacuant.
evac'uate (è-vak'iou-), *v.a.*, évacuer, vider.
evac'uating, *adj.*, évacuateur.
evacua'tion (è-vak'iou-é-), *n.*, évacuation ; sortie.
evac'uative, *adj.*, qui évacue, évacuatif.
evac'uator (-ét'eur), *n.*, personne qui annule, *f.*
evade' (i-véde), *v.n.*, s'échapper, s'esquiver, s'évader.
evade', *v.a.*, échapper **à**, se soustraire **à**, éluder, éviter, déjouer ; (fig.) user de subterfuges, biaiser.
evanes'cence (èv'a-), *n.*, disparition, évanescence ; (fig.) instabilité, *f.;* état éphémère, *m.*
evanes'cent, *adj.*, passager ; disparaissant, graduellement ; (fig.) passager, fugitif, éphémère.
evangel'ic *ou* **evangel'ical** (è-va'n'djèl'-), *adj.*, évangélique.
evangel'ically, *adv.*, évangéliquement.
evan'gelism, *n.*, prédication de l'Evangile, *f.*
evan'gelist, *n.*, évangéliste, *m.*
evangeliza'tion, *n.*, évangélisation, *f.*
evan'gelize (-'aïze), *v.a.*, évangéliser.
evap'orable (i-vap'o-ra-b'l), *adj.*, évaporable.
evap'orate, *v.n.*, s'évaporer.
evap'orate, *v.a.*, faire évaporer ; (fig.) donner un libre cours à, exhaler.
evap'orative, *adj.*, évaporatif.
evapora'tion (-ré-), *n.*, évaporation.
eva'sible, *adj.*, éludable.
eva'sion (i-vé-jeune), *n.*, moyen évasif ; subterfuge, *m.;* défaite, (fig.) évasion, *f.*, fauxfuyant, *m.*
eva'sive (i-vé-cive), *adj.*, évasif, qui élude.
eva'sively, *adv.*, évasivement.
eva'siveness, *n.*, caractère évasif, *m.*
eve (îve), *n.*, soir, *m.;* veille, (ecc.) vigile, *f.*
At — ; *le soir.* On the — of ; *à la veille* **de.**

e'ven (î-v'n), *n.*, soir, *m.* — song ; *antienne du soir, f.* (V. Hugo). — tide ; *soir, m.*, soirée, veillée, *f.*
e'ven, *adj.*, égal ; (smooth) uni ; (level with) de niveau ; (of number) pair. To be — with any one ; *rendre la pareille à quelqu'un ; être quitte avec quelqu'un.* — reckoning makes lasting friends ; *les bons comptes font les bons amis.* To make all doubts — ; *éclaircir les doutes.* To bet — money ; *parier à l'égalité.* To make it — money ; *faire un compte rond.*
e'ven, *adv.*, même ; aussi bien ; parfaitement. — as ; *comme.* — now ; *à l'instant ; dès à présent.* — so ; *de même, ainsi.* — though ; *quand même.*
e'ven, *v.a.*, égaler ; niveler ; égaliser ; mettre de niveau, aplanir.
even-hand'ed (-ha'n'd'ède), *adj.*, impartial, équitable.
even-hand'edness, *n.*, impartialité, équité, *f.*
e'vening (î-v'n'-), *n.*, soir, *m.;* soirée, *f.;* (fig.) déclin, *m.* In the — ; *le soir ; dans la soirée.* To-morrow — ; *demain soir ; demain au soir.* Last — ; *hier soir, hier au soir.* The — after to-morrow ; *après-demain soir.* The next — ; *le lendemain soir.* The — before ; *la veille au soir.* The — after to-morrow ; *après demain soir.*
e'vening, *adj.*, du soir. — party ; *soirée, f.*
e'vening-dew, *n.*, serein, *m.*
e'venly (i-v'n'-), *adv.*, également ; de niveau ; (fig.) impartialement.
e'venness (i-v'n'nèce), *n.*, égalité ; sérénité, *f.*, (ant.) impartialité, *f.*, calme, *m.*
e'ven-song (-so'gne), *n.*, chant du soir, *m.;* prière du soir, *f.*
e'ven-tempered, *adj.*, serein, calme, placide, égal.
event' (i-vè'n'te), *n.*, événement, *m.;* issue, *f.;* (of a poem, a play, etc.) dénouement, dénoûment, *m.* At all — s ; *à tout événement ; en tout cas ; à tout hasard ; en tous cas.*
event'erate (i-vè'n'teur'-), *v.a.*, (ant.) éventrer.
event'ful (-foule), *adj.*, plein d'événements ; mémorable.
e'ventide *ou* **e'vening-tide** (-taïde), *n.*, (ant.) déclin du jour ; soir, *m.*, soirée, *f.;* (fig.) déclin des ans, *m.* (V. Hugo).
event'ual (i-vè'n'tiou-), *adj.*, éventuel ; aléatoire ; final, définitif.
event'ually, *adv.*, éventuellement ; définitivement, finalement ; avec le temps, à la longue.
ev'er (èv'eur), *adv.*, toujours ; jamais. For — ; *pour toujours ; pour jamais ; à jamais ; à tout jamais.* For — and — ; *pour toujours ; pour jamais ; à jamais ;* (biblically) *jusqu'à la fin des siècles.* Scarcely — ; hardly — ; *presque jamais.* — and anon ; *de temps en temps ; de temps à autre.* Wine for — ; *vive le vin !* If I have — . . . ; *si j'ai jamais . . .* — after ; *pour toujours.* — since ; *depuis le temps où.* — so much ; *je ne sais combien ;* (by far) *infiniment, sans comparaison.* Be they — so many ; *quel que soit leur nombre.* — so little ; *tant soit peu.* Be it — so little ; *si peu que ce soit.* — so long ; *un temps infini.* — drunk — dry ; (prov.) *plus il boit, plus il a soif.*
ev'er-bub'bling (-beub'-), *adj.*, toujours bouillonnant.
ev'er-burn'ing (-beurn'-), *adj.*, inextinguible.
ev'er-endur'ing (-diour'-), *adj.*, éternel.
ev'ergreen (-grîne), *adj.*, toujours vert.
ev'ergreen, *n.*, arbuste toujours vert, *m.*
ev'er-hon'ored (-o'n'eurde), *adj.*, de glorieuse mémoire.
everlast'ing (-lâst'-), *adj.*, qui dure toujours ; éternel, perpétuel. — flower ; *immortelle, f.*
everlast'ing, *n.*, éternité, *f.;* Eternel ; (bot.) gnaphale, *m.*, immortelle, *f.*
everlast'ingly, *adv.*, éternellement, à jamais.

everlast'ingness, *n.*, éternité ; durée perpétuelle, *f.*

ever-liv'ing (-liv'-), *adj.*, immortel.

ever-recur'ring, *adj.*, périodique.

evermore' (-môre), *adv.*, toujours ; éternellement.

ever'sion (i-veur-), *n.*, (ant.) renversement, *m.* — of the eyelids ; *ectropion, m.*

ev'ery (èv'euri), *adj.*, chaque, tout, tous les. — body that ; *tous ceux qui.* — now and then ; *de temps à autre.* — one of them ; *tous sans exception.* — other combatant ; *un combattant sur deux.* It 's all true, — word of it ; *c'est vrai au pied de la lettre.* —body ; *tout le monde, chacun.* — day ; *tous les jours, chaque jour.* — other day ; *de deux jours l'un ; tous les deux jours.* —thing ; *tout.* —where ; *partout.* — body's business ; *les affaires de tout le monde.* — dog has his day ; (prov.) *cent ans bannière, cent ans civière ; un clou chasse l'autre.* — inch a king ; *un roi jusqu'au bout des ongles.* — Jack has his Jill ; (prov.) *il n'y a si méchant pot qui ne trouve son couvercle ; tout homme trouve chaussure à son pied.* — little helps ; *tout fait nombre.* — man for himself ; *chacun pour soi ;* (mil.) *sauve qui peut !* —thing comes to him who waits ; *tout vient à point à qui sait attendre.*

evict' (i-victe), *v.a.*, (jur.) évincer, (ant.) prouver.

evic'tion, *n.*, (jur.) éviction, *f.*, (ant.) preuve.

ev'idence (èv'-), *n.*, évidence, déposition, preuve, *f. ;* témoignage ; (pers.) témoin, *m.* — for the prosecution ; *témoin à charge.* Prisoner's —; *témoin à décharge.* King's —, Queen's —, *témoin révélateur de ses complices.* Circumstantial —; *preuves déduites des circonstances, f.pl.* To sum up the —; *résumer les débats.* To give —; *rendre témoignage ; déposer.* To give — of ; *montrer, faire voir ; faire, ou donner, preuve de.*

ev'idence, *v.a.*, montrer ; prouver, démontrer.

ev'ident, *adj.*, évident.

eviden'tial (-shal), *adj.*, d'évidence, prouvant clairement.

ev'idently, *adv.*, évidemment.

e'vil (î-v'l), *adj.*, mauvais ; (of spirits) malfaisant, malin, méchant ; cruel ; malheureux ; de malheur.

e'vil, *n.*, mal ; crime, *m. ;* maladie, *f. ;* malheur, *m. ;* calamité, *f.* King's —; *écrouelles, f.pl.* Let — be to him that — thinks ; *honni soit qui mal y pense.* Sufficient for the day is the — thereof ; *à chaque jour suffit sa peine.*

e'vil, *adv.*, mal.

e'vil-affect'ed (-af-fèkt'ède), *adj.*, mal disposé.

e'vil-do'er (-dou'eur), *n.*, malfaiteur ; méchant, *m.*, méchante, *f.*

e'vil-fa'vored (fé-veurde), *adj.*, laid, difforme.

e'vil-fa'voredness, *n.*, laideur, difformité, *f.*

e'vil-mind'ed (-maï'n'd'-), *adj.*, mal intentionné.

e'vilness, *n.*, méchanceté, *f.*

e'vil-speak'ing (-spîk'-), *n.*, médisance, *f.*

e'vil-worker (-weurk'-), *n.*, méchant, *m.*

evince' (i-vi'n'-), *v.a.*, faire voir ; montrer, manifester ; prouver, démontrer ; faire preuve de.

evin'cible (-ci-b'l), *adj.*, qui peut être prouvé ; démontrable.

evin'cibly, *adv.*, incontestablement.

evis'cerate (i-vis'ceur-), *v.a.*, éventrer, vider.

evoca'tion (èv'o-ké-), *n.*, évocation, *f.*

evoke' (i-vôke), *v.a.*, évoquer.

evola'tion (èv'o-lé-), *n.*, (ant.) action de s'envoler ; volée, *f.*

ev'olute (èv'o-lioute), *n.*, (geom.) développée, *f.*

evolu'tion (èv'o-liou-), *n.*, action de déployer ; (philos., milit.) évolution, *f. ;* (geom.) développement, *m. ;* (alg.) extraction des racines, *f. ;* (fig.) mouvement, *m.*

evolve' (i-volve), *v.a.*, dérouler ; développer ; (chem.) dégager.

evolve', *v.n.*, se dérouler ; se développer ; (chem.) se dégager.

evol'vent, *n.*, (geom.) développante, *f.*

evul'sion (i-veul-), *n.*, action d'arracher, *f.*, arrachement, *m.*

ewe (you), *n.*, brebis, *f.* — lamb ; *agnelle, f.*

ew'er (you-eur), *n.*, aiguière, *f.*

ew'ry (you-ri), *n.*, office (in the Royal Household), *m.*

exac'erbate (ègz'ass'eur-), *v.a.*, (ant.) irriter, exaspérer ; (med.) rendre plus aigu ; empirer.

exacerba'tion *ou* **exacerbes'cence** (ègzass'eur-), *n.*, irritation, exaspération ; aggravation ; (med.) exacerbation, *f.*

exact' (ègz'-), *v.a.*, exiger, demander impérieusement, extorquer.

exact', *v.n.*, commettre des exactions.

exact', *adj.*, exact, précis, strict. [torsion, *f.*

exac'tion, *n.*, action d'exiger ; exaction, ex-

exact'ly, *adv.*, exactement ; juste ; au juste.

exact'ness, *n.*, exactitude, justesse, *f.*

exact'er *ou* **exact'or** (-'eur), *n.*, exacteur, *m. ;* personne qui exige, *f. ;* extorqueur, *m.*

exag'gerate (ègz-adj'eur'-), *v.a.*, exagérer, outrer.

exaggera'tion (ègz'adj'eur'-é-), exagération, *f.*

exag'gerator, *n.*, exagérateur, trice, *m.f.*

exalt' (ègz'ôlte), *v.a.*, exalter, élever.

exalta'tion (-ôl-té-), *n.*, exaltation, élévation, *f.*

exalt'edness (-), *n.*, élévation, hauteur, position élevée, *f. ;* caractère élevé, *m.*

examina'tion (ègz'a'm'i-né-), *n.*, examen, *m. ;* vérification, *f. ;* (jur.) (of prisoners) interrogatoire, *m. ;* (of witnesses) audition, *f.* Private —; (jur.) *instruction, f.* Post mortem —; *autopsie, f.* Written —; *épreuve écrite, f.* Vivâ voce —; *épreuve orale, f.* — paper ; *questions d'examen, f.pl.* On or after —; *après examen.* — board ; *corps d'examinateurs.*

exam'ine (ègz'a'm'ine), *v.a.*, examiner ; faire l'examen de ; visiter ; vérifier ; (jur.) interroger.

exam'iner, *n.*, examinateur ; interrogateur ; (jur.) juge d'instruction, *m.* — of plays ; *censeur dramatique, m.*

exam'ple (ègz'â'm'p'l), *n.*, exemple, *m.* To set an —; *donner l'exemple.* For —; *par exemple.*

exan'imate (ègz'a'n'-), *adj.*, inanimé ; abattu.

exanthe'ma (èks'a'n'thima), *n.*, (med.) (*exanthemata*) exanthème, *m.*

exanthem'atous, *adj.*, (med.) exanthémateux, exanthématique.

exas'perate (ègz'as'peur-), *v.a.*, exaspérer ; irriter, aigrir ; énerver, agacer, provoquer ; (ant.) aggraver.

exas'perater (-'ét'eur), *n.*, personne qui irrite, qui exaspère, *f. ;* provocateur, *m.*

exaspera'tion (-peur'é-), *n.*, exaspération ; irritation, provocation, *f.*

excar'nate *ou* **excar'nificate** (èks'câr-), (ant.) *v.a.*, décharner ; dépouiller les os de la chair ; mettre en pièces ; mettre à la torture.

ex'cavate (èks'-), *v.a.*, creuser ; excaver.

excava'tion (-vé-), *n.*, excavation ; fouille ; tranchée, *f. ;* déblai, *m.*

ex'cavator (-vé-teur), *n.*, terrassier, *m.*

exceed' (èks'cîde), *v.a.*, excéder, dépasser ; outrepasser ; (fig.) surpasser.

exceed'ing, *adj.*, excessif, extrême.

exceed'ing, *adv.*, (ant.) excessivement.

exceed'ingly, *adv.*, excessivement, extrêmement.

excel' (èks'cèl), *v.a.*, surpasser ; l'emporter **sur**. To — in ; *surpasser* **en**.

excel', *v.n.*, exceller (with **à** before an infinitive, with **en** before nouns used by themselves or without the definite article ; with **dans in** other cases).

ex'cellence *ou* **ex'cellency**, *n.*, excellence, perfection, supériorité, *f.* ; mérite, *m.* His — ; *son Excellence*, *f.*

ex'cellent, *adv.*, excellent, parfait ; (b.s.) consommé, achevé.

ex'cellently, *adv.*, excellemment ; parfaitement.

except' (èks'cèpte), *v.a.*, excepter, omettre ; exclure **de**, défendre, interdire. Present company —ed ; *on excepte toujours les présents ; les sentiments exprimés ne s'appliquent en rien aux personnes présentes.*

except', *v.n.*, (jur.) fournir ses exceptions. To — against, to — to ; *s'opposer à* ; (witness) récuser. To — to a tribunal ; *décliner la compétence d'un tribunal.*

except', *prep.*, excepté ; hors ; sauf.

except', *conj.*, à moins que, à moins **de**.

except'ing, *prep.*, excepté, hormis, à l'exclusion **de**.

excep'tion, *n.*, exception ; objection, *f.* With this — ; *à cette exception près*. By way of — ; *par exception.* Without — ; *sans exception.* To take — at ; *s'offenser de ; se formaliser de, se blesser de.* To take — to ; *trouver à redire à ; trouver mauvais, ne pas admettre ;* (jur.) *s'opposer à ; récuser.*

excep'tionable (-a-b'l), *adj.*, blâmable, répréhensible, (ant.) exceptionnel ; (jur.) récusable.

excep'tional, *adj.*, exceptionnel.

excep'tionally, *adv.*, exceptionnellement.

excerpt', *n.*, extrait, *m.*

excess', *n.*, excès ; (arith., of weight) excédent, *m.* — baggage ; *excédant de bagages.*

exces'sive, *adj.*, excessif ; exagéré ; outré ; immodéré.

exces'sively, *adv.*, excessivement, à l'excès.

exces'siveness, *n.*, nature excessive, *f.*

exchange' (èks-tshé'n'dje), *n.*, échange ; (com.) change, *m.* ; (edifice) Bourse, *f.* — of prisoners ; *échange de prisonniers, m.* In — for ; *en échange de.* Average — ; *change commun.* Current — ; *cours du change ; cours, m.* Foreign — ; *change extérieur, change étranger.* Nominal — ; *change nominal.* Bill of— ; *lettre de change, f.* Foreign bill of — ; *lettre de change sur l'étranger.* First of — ; *première de change, f.* Rate of — ; *taux du change, m. ; cote du change, f.* To be a loser or gainer by the — ; *perdre ou gagner au change.*

exchange', *v.a.*, échanger **contre** ; changer **pour**.

exchange'-broker, *n.*, courtier de change, *m.*

exchange'-office, *n.*, bureau de change, *m.*

exchan'ger, *n.*, changeur, banquier qui fait le change, *m.*

excheq'uer (èks-tshèk'eur), *n.*, trésor ; trésor royal ; trésor de l'Etat ; ministère des finances ; (ant.) damier, échiquier, *m.* Court of — ; *cour de l'Echiquier, f.* Chancellor of the — ; *Ministre des finances, m.* — bill ; *bon du trésor, m.*

exci'sable (-saïz'a'b'l), *n.*, sujet à l'excise, à l'accise ; (in France) sujet aux contributions indirectes.

excise' (-saïze), *n.*, (in England) accise, excise, *f.* ; (in France) contributions indirectes, *f.pl.*, régie, *f.* — duty ; *droit de régie, m.*

excise', *v.a.*, soumettre à l'accise ; soumettre aux contributions indirectes.

excise'man (-ma'n), *n.*, préposé de l'accise, employé de l'accise ; préposé des contributions indirectes, de la régie ; employé des contributions indirectes, de la régie, *m.*

exci'sion (èx-cijeune), *n.*, destruction ; (surg.) excision, (ecc.) excommunication, *f.*

excitabil'ity (èx-saït'-), *n.*, (med.) excitabilité, *f.*

exci'table (èx-saït'a'b'l), *adj.*, excitable, irritable ; impressionnable.

exci'tant, *adj.n.*, excitant, *m.*

excita'tion (èx-saït'é-), *n.*, excitation, *f.*

excite' (èx-saïte), *v.a.*, exciter, animer, irriter ; (fig.) échauffer ; provoquer, porter **à**.

excite'ment, *n.*, surexcitation ; excitation, *f.* ; motif d'excitation, *m.* ; commotion, agitation, animation, *f.* ; stimulant, *m.*

exci'ter, *n.*, excitateur, *m.*, excitatrice, *f.* ; (fig.) mobile ; (med.) excitant, stimulant ; (phys.) corps idioélectrique, *m.*

exci'ting, *adj.*, excitant, stimulant ; entraînant ; (fig.) piquant, émouvant, violent.

exclaim' (-clême), *v.n.*, s'écrier, crier ; se récrier, s'exclamer. To — against ; *se récrier contre.*

exclaim'er, *n.*, personne qui s'écrie, qui se récrie, *f.* ; déclamateur, *m.*

exclama'tion (-mé-), *n.*, exclamation, clameur, *f.* ; cri, *m.* Note of — ; *point d'exclamation, m.*

exclam'atory (-tori), *adj.*, exclamatif, déclamatoire ; d'exclamation.

exclude' (-cloude), *v.a.*, exclure, excepter.

exclud'ing, *prep.* sans compter ; non compris.

exclu'sion (-clou'jeune), *n.*, exclusion, *f.*

exclu'sionist (-clou-jeun'iste), *n.*, personne exclusive.

exclu'sive (-clou-cive), *adj.*, exclusif ; d'exclusion. — of ; *à l'exclusion de ; non compris ; sans compter.*

exclu'sively, *adv.*, exclusivement. — of ; *à l'exclusion de, abstraction faite de.*

exclu'siveness, *n.*, caractère exclusif, *m.* ; nature exclusive, *f.*

excog'itate (-codj'i-téte), *v.a.*, inventer, créer, imaginer, trouver à force de méditation ; méditer **sur**.

excogita'tion (-codj'i-té-), *n.*, méditation ; invention, *f.*

excommu'nicable (-miou-), *adj.*, passible d'excommunication.

excommu'nicate (-miou-ni-kéte), *v.a.*, excommunier.

excommunica'tion (-ké-), *n.*, excommunication, *f.*

exco'riate (-cô-ri-éte), *v.a.*, écorcher, enlever ; gercer, faire gercer ; (surg.) excorier. The heat —s the skin ; *la chaleur gerce la peau.*

excoria'tion, *n.*, écorchure ; (surg.) excoriation, *f.*

excortica'tion (-ké-), *n.*, (ant.) décortication, *f.*

ex'crement (-cri-), *n.*, excrément, *m.*

excremen'tal *ou* **excrementi'tious** (-ti-shieusse), *adj.*, excrémenteux, excrémentiel, excrémentitiel.

excres'cence *ou* **excres'cency**, *n.*, excroissance, *f.* ; (fig.) excès, *m.* — of joy ; *un transport de joie excessif, m.*

excres'cent, *adj.*, qui forme une excroissance ; surcroissant ; (fig.) superflu ; (gram.) épenthétique.

excre'tion (-cri-), *n.*, excrétion (physiologie), *f.*

ex'cretive *ou* **ex'cretory** (-cri-, -tori), *adj.*, excrétoire, excréteur.

ex'cretory (-cri-tori), *n.*, vaisseau excrétoire, *ou* excréteur, *m.*

excru'ciable (-crou-shi-a'b'l), *adj.*, (ant.) sujet à être tourmenté.

excru'ciate (-crou-shi-éte), *v.a.*, tourmenter affreusement, torturer, mettre au supplice.

excru'ciating, *adj.*, atroce, affreux, cruel, horrible.

excrucia'tion, *n.*, tourment atroce, *m.* ; affreuse torture, *f.*

excul'pate (-keul'péte), *v.a.*, disculper, justifier, acquitter.

exculpa'tion, *n.*, excuse, justification, disculpation, *f.*

excul'patory, *adj.*, qui disculpe ; apologétique.

excur'sion (-keur-), *n.*, excursion, digression,

course; (milit.) incursion, invasion, razzia, *f.* — train ; *train de plaisir, m.* — ticket ; *billet de train de plaisir, m.* To be on an —; *être en excursion.*

excur'sive, *adj.,* errant, divagant, qui erre ; (fig.; of style) décousu, vague, errant.

excur'sively, *adv.,* (ant.) en errant.

excur'siveness, *n.,* (ant.) tendance à s'écarter de son sujet, divagation, *f.,* écart, *m.*

excu'sable (-kiouz'a'b'l), *adj.,* excusable.

excu'sableness, *n.,* caractère excusable, *m.*

excu'satory (-tori), *adj.,* d'excuse ; apologétique, justificatif.

excuse' (-kiousse), *n.,* excuse, *f.* To offer an —; *présenter une excuse.*

excuse' (-kiouze), *v.a.,* excuser, pardonner ; faire grâce **de** ; dispenser **de** ; faire remise **de.** To — one's self for ; *s'excuser* **de.** — me ! *excusez ! pardon !*

excu'ser, *n.,* (ant.) personne qui excuse, *f. ;* apologiste, *m.,f.*

ex'eat (èks'i'ate), *n.,* exéat (permission de s'absenter donnée à un étudiant des Universités anglaises); (ecc.) exeat, *m.*

ex'ecrable (èks'i-cra'b'l), *adj.,* exécrable.

ex'ecrably, *adv.,* exécrablement.

ex'ecrate (èks'i-créte), *v.a.,* exécrer, maudire, abominer, abhorrer, avoir en abomination.

execra'tion, *n.,* exécration, *f.*

ex'ecratory (-cré-tori), *n.,* formule d'exécration, (ecc.) exécratoire, *f.*

execut'able, *adj.,* exécutable, à faire.

ex'ecute (èks'i-kioute), *v.a.,* exécuter; exercer ; accomplir. To — a deed; *signer un contrat.*

execu'tion, *n.,* exécution, *f. ;* exercice ; (slaughter) massacre, carnage, *m.; (jur.)* saisie mobilière, saisie-exécution ; exécution, *f.,* supplice, *m.* In the — of one's duty ; *dans l'exercice de ses fonctions.* To carry into —, to put in —; *mettre* à *exécution.* Warrant of —; *ordre d'exécution, m.*

execu'tioner, *n.,* exécuteur ; bourreau ; (jur.) exécuteur des hautes œuvres, *m.*

exec'utive, *adj.,* exécutif.

exec'utive, *n.,* pouvoir exécutif, gouvernement, *m.*

exec'utor (-teur), *n.,* (jur.) exécuteur testamentaire, *m.*

executo'rial, *adj.,* d'exécuteur testamentaire.

exec'utorship, *n.,* fonctions d'exécuteur testamentaire, *f.pl.*

exec'utrix, *n.,* exécutrice testamentaire, *f.*

exege'sis (èks'i'dji-cisse), *n.,* exégèse, *f.*

exeget'ical (-djét'-), *adj.,* exégétique.

exeget'ically, *adv.,* par exégèse; d'une manière exégétique.

exem'plar (ègz'è'm'pleur), *n.,* modèle, *m.*

ex'emplarily, *adj.,* exemplairement.

ex'emplariness *ou* **exemplar'ity,** *n.,* qualité de ce qui est exemplaire, *f.*

ex'emplary (-plari), *adj.,* exemplaire ; (her.) à armes parlantes.

exemplifica'tion (-ké-), *n.,* démonstration, explication par des exemples ; (jur.) ampliation, *f.*

exem'plifier (-faïeur), *n.,* personne qui donne l'exemple, *f.*

exem'plify (-faïe), *v.a.,* démontrer par des exemples ; donner un exemple **de** ; (jur.) copier, faire une ampliation **de.**

exempt' (ègz'è'm'te), *v.a.,* exempter **de,** dispenser **de,** exonérer **de** ; (mil.) libérer **de.**

exempt', *adj.,* exempt **de.**

exemp'tion, *n.,* exemption, dispense ; (mil.) exonération, *f.*

exequa'tur (èks-i-koué-teur), *n.,* exequatur, *f.*

exerci'sable (èks'èr-saïz'a'b'l), *adj.,* susceptible d'être exercé.

ex'ercise (èks'èr-saïze), *n.,* exercice ; (task) thème, devoir, *m. ;* (milit.) manœuvre, *f.,* exercice, *m.* — book; *cahier de thèmes, m.*

ex'ercise, *v.a.,* exercer ; employer, user **de** ;

(animal) promener. *v.n.,* s'exercer ; (mil.) faire l'exercice.

ex'erciser, *n.,* personne qui exerce ; personne qui s'exerce, *f.*

exergue' (ègz'eurghe), *n.,* exergue, *m.*

exert' (ègz'eurte), *v.a.,* mettre en œuvre ; déployer, montrer ; employer ; accomplir ; exercer avec effort, faire un effort. To — one's self; *faire des efforts* **pour** ; *s'efforcer* **de,** *tâcher* **de** ; *se remuer, se donner de la peine.* To — one's self to the utmost ; *faire tout son possible* **pour.**

exer'tion, *n.,* effort, *m.* It is an — to make to speak ; *c'est pour lui un effort pénible de parler.*

exfo'liate (èks'fô-lié-te), *v.a.,* exfolier. *v.n.,* s'exfolier.

exfolia'tion, *n.,* exfoliation, *f.*

exha'lable (ègz'hé-la-b'l), *adj.,* qui peut s'évaporer; évaporable.

exhala'tion (-'ha-lé-), *n.,* exhalaison; exhalation, *f.*

exhale' (ègz'héle), *v.a.,* exhaler, faire exhaler. *v.n.,* s'exhaler.

exhale'ment, *n.,* exhalaison, *f.*

exhaust' (ègz'hôste), *v.a.,* épuiser ; (phys.) faire le vide dans. To — a vessel of the air contained therein; *faire le vide dans un récipient.* To — any one's patience ; *lasser quelqu'un, mettre quelqu'un à bout.*

exhaust'ed, *adj.,* épuisé ; (phys.) aspiré. I am quite —; *je suis rendu.* — receiver ; *récipient dans lequel on a fait le vide, m.*

exhaust'er, *n.,* personne qui épuise ; chose qui épuise, *f. ;* (phys.) aspirateur, *m.*

exhaust'ible, *adj.,* épuisable.

exhaust'ing, *adj.,* qui épuise ; (phys.) d'aspiration. — pipe; *tuyau d'épuisement, m.*

exhaus'tion (ègz'hôst'ieune), *n.,* épuisement, *m. ;* aspiration, *f. ;* (math.) épuisement, *m.,* méthode par épuisement, *f.*

exhaus'tive, *adj.,* qui épuise ; (fig.) complet, plein, entier.

exhaus'tively, *adv.,* à fond, complètement, entièrement.

exhaust'less, *adj.,* inépuisable.

exhib'it (ègz'hibite *ou* -'i-), *v.a.,* exhiber, montrer, produire, exposer, déployer, faire voir, offrir ; (jur.) exhiber.

exhib'it, *n.,* produit exposé, *m. ;* objet exposé, *m.; (jur.)* pièce produite, pièce à l'appui, *f.*

exhib'iter, *n.,* personne qui montre, qui produit, *f.;* (at public exhibitions) exposant, *m.*

exhibi'tion (èks'hi- *ou* -'i-), *n.,* (action) exposition; (representation) représentation, *f.,* spectacle, *m.;* (universities) bourse ; (jur.) exhibition, production, *f.* Industrial —; *exposition de l'industrie.*

exhibi'tioner, *n.,* (in universities) boursier, *m.*

exhib'itor, *n.,* exposant, *m.*

exhil'arate (ègz'hil-a-réte *ou* -'il-), *v.a.,* réjouir, divertir, récréer ; égayer.

exhil'arating, *adj.,* qui égaye ; réjouissant, divertissant, hilarant.

exhilara'tion, *n.,* réjouissance, joie, animation, *f.,* hilarité, gaieté, *f.*

exhort' (ègz'horte *ou* -'orte), *v.a.,* exhorter à. *v.n.,* faire des exhortations.

exhorta'tion (-té-), *n.,* exhortation, *f.*

exhor'tative, *adj.,* exhortatif.

exhor'tatory, *adj.,* exhortatoire.

exhort'er, *n.,* personne qui exhorte, *f. ;* exhortateur, *m.*

exhuma'tion (ègz'hiou-mé-), *n.,* exhumation, *f.*

exhume' (ègz'hioume) *ou* **exhu'mate** (-méte), *v.a.,* exhumer, déterrer.

ex'igence *ou* **ex'igency** (èks'i'djè'nse, -ci), *n.,* exigence, nécessité, *f. ;* besoin, *m. ;* situation critique, extrémité, *f.*

ex'igent, *adj.,* critique ; urgent, pressant. — of rest; *ayant besoin de repos.*

exigu'ity (èks-i-ghiou-), *n.,* exiguïté, petitesse, *f.*

exig'uous (èks-i-ghiou-eusse), *adj.*, exigu.

ex'ile (èks'aïle), *n.*, exil, exil volontaire, *m.;* (pers.) exilé, *m.*, exilée, *f.*, proscrit, *m.* To drive into —; *exiler, proscrire.*

ex'ile (èks'aïle *ou* ègz'-), *v.a.*, exiler.

ex'ilement, *n.*, (ant.) exil, bannissement, *m.*

exil'ity (ègz'i-li-ti), *n.* (ant.) petitesse; ténuité; faiblesse, légèreté, finesse, *f.*

exist', *v.n.*, exister.

exis'tence, *n.*, existence, *f.;* être, *m.* To be in —; *exister.* To call into —; *faire naître; produire; évoquer.*

exis'tent, *adj.*, existant, qui existe, actuel.

ex'it (èks'ite), *n.*, sortie, issue; (thea.) sortie, (fig.) mort, fin, *f.* To make one's —; *sortir, s'en aller;* (fig.) *mourir.*

ex'odus (èks-ô-deusse), *n.*, Exode, *m.;* sortie, *f.*

exon'erate (ègz-o'n'euréte), *v.a.*, décharger; soulager; exonérer, justifier, acquitter; exempter.

exonera'tion, *n.*, décharge, justification, exemption, exonération, *f.*, soulagement, *m.*

exon'erative, *adj.*, qui décharge; qui soulage, qui exonère.

exophthal'mia (èks'of-thal-), *n.*, (surg.) exophtalmie, *f.*

exor'bitance *ou* **exor'bitancy**, *n.*, excès, *m.;* extravagance, énormité, *f.*

exor'bitant, *adj.*, exorbitant, excessif, exagéré.

exor'bitantly, *adv.*, exorbitamment; excessivement.

ex'orcise (èks'or-saïze), *v.a.*, exorciser.

ex'orciser, *n.*, exorciste, *m.*

ex'orcism (-ciz'me), *n.*, (ant.) exorcisme, *m.*

ex'orcist, *n.*, exorciste, *m.*

exor'dial (ègz'-), *adj.*, de l'exorde; initial.

exor'dium (-dieume), *n.*, exorde, *m.*

exos'ceous, *adj.*, sans os.

exosto'sis (-tô-cisse), *n.*, (med.) exostose, *f.*

exoter'ic, *adj.*, exotérique; vulgaire; public.

exot'ic, *adj.*, exotique.

exot'ic, *n.*, plante exotique, *f.*

expand', *v.a.*, faire épanouir, étendre, répandre, déployer; dilater; (math.) développer.

expand', *v.n.*, s'épanouir; se répandre; se dilater; s'étendre; se déployer.

expanse', *n.*, étendue, *f.*

expansibil'ity, *n.*, (phys.) expansibilité, *f.*

expan'sible, *adj.*, (phys.) expansible.

expan'sion, *n.*, expansion; extension, étendue, épanouissement; (math.) développement, *m.*

expan'sive, *adj.*, expansif.

expan'siveness, *n.*, expansibilité, *f.*

ex par'te, *adj.*, d'un seul côté; d'une seule partie.

expa'tiate (èks-pé-shi-éte), *v.n.*, errer. To — on; *s'étendre* **sur**, *discourir* **sur**.

expatia'tion (-pé-shi-é-), *n.*, action de s'étendre, de discourir (**sur**).

expa'tiator (-pé-shi-é-teur), *n.*, personne qui s'étend, qui discourt, *f.;* discoureur, *m.*

expa'triate (-pé-tri-éte), *v.a.*, expatrier.

expatria'tion, *n.*, expatriation, *f.*

expect', *v.a.*, attendre; espérer, se promettre; (of things) s'attendre à, compter **sur**. He is not —ed to live; *on désespère de sa vie; les médecins l'ont condamné.* He is —ed to make a speech; *il est censé prononcer un discours* ou *on compte sur lui pour prononcer un discours.* That must be —ed; *on doit s'y attendre,* ou *il faut s'y attendre.* You are —ed; *on vous attend; on compte sur vous.* I — a great deal of pleasure; *je me promets beaucoup de plaisir.*

expec'tance *ou* **expec'tancy**, *n.*, attente, *f.;* espoir, *m.;* (jur.) expectative, *f.* Tables of expectancy; *tables de mortalité, f.pl.*

expec'tant, *adj.*, expectant. — heir; *héritier présomptif, m.*

expec'tant, *n.*, personne qui est dans l'attente; personne qui est dans l'expectative, *f.;* aspirant, *m.*

expecta'tion (-té-), *n.*, expectation, expectative, attente, espérance, *f.* He always lives in —; *il vit toujours dans l'expectative.* In — of; *dans l'attente* **de**; *dans l'espérance* **de**. To have —s; *avoir des espérances de fortune.* To answer one's —s; *répondre à ses espérances.* Beyond one's —s; *au delà de ses espérances.* — week; *semaine qui précède la Pentecôte, f.*

expect'er, *n.*, personne qui attend, qui espère, *f.*

expect'ingly, *adv.*, dans l'attente.

expec'torant, *adj.*, expectorant.

expec'torant, *n.*, expectorant, *m.*

expec'torate (-réte), *v.a.*, expectorer.

expectora'tion (-ré-), *n.*, expectoration, *f.*

expec'torative (-ra-), *adj.*, expectorant.

expe'dience *ou* **expe'diency** (-pî-), *n.*, convenance, utilité, *f.;* à-propos, avantage; (politically) opportunisme, *m.*

expe'dient, *n.*, expédient.

expe'dient, *adj.*, convenable, à propos, utile, bon, avantageux; expédient (only used with neuter pronouns *il* or *ce* with verb *être*).

expe'diently, *adv.*, convenablement; à propos.

ex'pedite, *v.a.*, expédier, hâter, dépêcher, faciliter; activer, accélérer.

expedi'tion, *n.*, expédition; promptitude, hâte, *f.* On an —; *en expédition.*

expedi'tionary, *adj.*, (milit.) expéditionnaire.

expedi'tious (-pi-dish'eusse), *adj.*, expéditif, prompt.

expedi'tiously, *adv.*, rapidement; promptement.

expedi'tiousness, *n.*, expédition, promptitude, *f.*

exped'itive, *adj.*, (ant.) expéditif.

expel', *v.a.*, expulser, chasser, faire sortir; (of schoolboys) renvoyer.

expel'ler, *n.*, personne qui chasse, qui expulse, *f.*

expel'ling, *adj.*, expulseur.

expend', *v.a.*, dépenser; employer; consacrer; consumer.

expen'diture (-di-tioure), *n.*, dépense, *f.;* dépenses, *f.pl.;* (fig.) sacrifice, *m.;* consommation, *f.*

expense', *n.*, dépense, *f.;* (fig.) dépens; frais, *m.pl.* Free of —; *sans frais; franco.* At a great —; *à grands frais.* To go to —; *se mettre en dépense* ou *en frais; faire des frais.* To put to —; *induire en dépenses.* To clear, ou cover, one's —s; *faire ses frais.* To pay its —s; (of things) *couvrir les frais.* At any —; *à tout prix.* At the — of; *aux frais* **de**; (fig.) *aux dépens* **de**.

expense'less, *adj.*, (ant.) sans frais.

expen'sive, *adj.*, (pers.) dépensier, prodigue; (of things) dispendieux, coûteux. An — victory; *une victoire coûteuse, f.*

expen'sively, *adv.*, à grands frais; dispendieusement.

expen'siveness, *n.*, dépense, *f.;* prix élevé, *m.;* prodigalité, *f.*

expe'rience (-pî-ri-), *n.*, expérience, *f.;* essai, *m.* By —, from —; *par expérience.*

expe'rience, *v.a.*, éprouver; faire l'expérience **de**, expérimenter.

expe'rienced (èks'pî-ri-è'n'ste), *adj.*, qui a de l'expérience; expérimenté.

exper'iment, *n.*, expérience, *f.*

exper'iment, *v.a. and n.*, expérimenter.

experimen'tal, *adj.*, expérimental; (pers.) qui procède par expérience.

experimen'talist, *n.*, expérimentateur, *m.*

experimen'tally, *adv.*, par expérience.

exper'imenter, *n.*, expérimentateur, *m.*

expert' (-peurte), *adj.*, expert, habile.

ex'pert, *n.*, expert, *m.*

expert'ly, *adv.*, habilement, adroitement.

expert'ness, *n.*, habileté, adresse, *f.*

ex'piable, adj., (ant.) que l'on peut expier, qui peut être expié; expiable.

ex'piate (-éte), v.a., expier, réparer.

expia'tion (-pi-é-), n., expiation, f.

ex'piatory, adj., expiatoire.

expira'tion (-pi-ré-), n., expiration; cessation; (end) fin, f., terme, m. ; (com.) échéance, f. ; (death) dernier soupir, m.

expire' (-païeur), v.n., expirer; mourir; périr.

expir'ing, adj., expirant.

ex'piry (-piri), n., expiration, f. ; terme, m. ; fin, échéance, f.

explain' (-pléne), v.a., expliquer, éclaircir.

explain', v.n., s'expliquer. To — away ; expliquer.

explain'able (-'a-b'l), adj., explicable.

explain'er, n., explicateur ; commentateur, interprète, m.

explana'tion (-né-), n., explication, f. ; éclaircissement, m.

explan'atory, adj., explicatif.

ex'pletive (-pli-), adj., explétif.

ex'pletive, n., explétif, m.

ex'plicable (-ca-b'l), adj. V. explainable.

ex'plicative, adj., explicatif.

ex'plicatory, adj., explicatif.

expli'cit, adj., explicite ; clair ; franc ; (math.) explicite. — function ; fonction explicite, f.

expli'citly, adv., explicitement.

expli'citness, n., caractère explicite, m. ; clarté ; franchise, f.

explode' (-plôde), v.a., rejeter ; repousser ; abandonner, faire éclater, (a mine) faire sauter ; (fig.) condamner, abandonner. —d theory ; théorie abandonnée, condamnée, rejetée.

explode', v.n., éclater, faire explosion.

explo'der, n., personne qui repousse, qui condamne, personne qui cause une explosion, f.

explo'ding, n., (of mines) sautage, m.

exploit' (-ploïte), n., exploit ; haut fait ; fait d'armes, m.

explor'able, adj., qui peut être exploré ; explorable.

explora'tion (-ré-), n., exploration, f. ; (fig.) examen, m. ; recherche, f.

explor'atively, adv., explorativement.

explor'atory explor'ative, adj., exploratoire ; explorateur, d'exploration.

explore' (-plôre), v.a., explorer, examiner, sonder.

explor'er, n., explorateur, m.

explo'sion (-plô-jeune), n., explosion, f.

explo'sive (-plô-cive), adj., explosif, explosible. — consonant ; (gram.) consonne explosive, f.

explo'siveness, n., explosibilité, f.

expo'nent (-pô-), n., (math.) exposant ; (fig.) représentant, interprète, m.

exponen'tial (-shial), adj., (math.) exponentiel.

ex'port, n., marchandise exportée ; qui peut être exportée, exportation, f. — trade ; commerce d'exportation, f. — duty ; droit d'exportation ; droit de sortie, m.

export' (-pôrte), v.a., exporter.

exporta'tion (-por-té-), n., exportation, f. ; transport, m.

export'er, n., exportateur, m.

expose', v.a., exposer, révéler, démasquer, faire connaître ; découvrir, compromettre. — a fraud ; démasquer une fraude. To — one's self ; s'exposer, se montrer. To — one's self to ridicule ; se donner en spectacle à ; se rendre ridicule.

expo'ser, n., personne qui expose, f.

exposi'tion (-zi-), n., exposition, f. ; commentaire, m.

expos'itor (-teur), n., interprète ; commentateur ; glossateur, m.

ex post fac'to, adj., adv., après coup ; (jur.) avec effet rétroactif.

expos'tulate (with) (-post'iou-léte), v.n., se plaindre ; faire des reproches à ; faire des remontrances à.

expostula'tion (-lé-), n., reproche, m. ; remontrance, plainte, f.

expos'tulator (-lé-teur), n., personne qui fait des reproches, des remontrances, f., remontreur, m.

expos'tulatory, adj., de reproche ; de remontrance.

expo'sure (-pô-jeur), n., exposition, f. ; danger ; péril ; scandale ; éclat, esclandre, m.

expound' (-pa-ou'n'de), v.a., expliquer, exposer, commenter, interpréter.

expound'er, n., interprète, commentateur, m.

expound'ing, n., exposition, explication, interprétation, f.

express', n., exprès, express, train express, m.

express', adj., exprès ; formel, clair, explicite ; d'une ressemblance exacte. — train ; train express ; express ; rapide, m. Lightning — ; train-éclair, m.

express', v.a., exprimer ; représenter ; désigner, manifester ; déclarer à.

expres'sible (-'si-b'l), adj., exprimable.

expres'sion, n., expression ; énonciation, f.

expres'sive, adj., expressif. To be — of ; exprimer.

expres'sively, adv., avec expression, d'une manière expressive. [gie, f.

expres'siveness, n., force d'expression, énergie, f.

express'ly, adv., expressément, distinctement, directement, formellement.

expro'priate (-prô-priéte), v.a., exproprier, se dessaisir de ; dégager ; abandonner ; renoncer à.

expropria'tion (-prié-), n., abandon, f., renonciation ; (jur.) expropriation, f.

expug'nable, adj., (ant.) expugnable.

expulse' (-peul'se), v.a., (ant.). V. expel.

expul'sion, n., expulsion, f.

expul'sive, adj., expulsif.

expunc'tion (-peu'gn'k-), n., effaçure, f.

expunge' (-peu'n'dje), v.a., effacer, rayer ; retrancher ; raturer, faire disparaître.

expur'gate (-peur-ghéte), v.a., nettoyer ; (a book) expurger.

expurga'tion, n., nettoiement, m. ; purgation ; (a book) expurgation ; purification, f.

expur'gatory, adj., expurgatoire. — index ; index expurgatoire, index, m.

ex'quisite (-kwi-zite), adj., exquis ; (of pain) atroce, affreux, vif, extrême ; (fig.) excellent, choisi ; adroit. — malice ; malice consommée, f.

ex'quisite, n., élégant, petit-maître, dandy, m.

ex'quisitely, adv., d'une manière exquise ; parfaitement, nettement, vivement, extrêmement.

ex'quisiteness, n., goût exquis, m. ; perfection ; délicatesse ; excellence ; (of grief, pain) violence, f.

exsic'cant, adj., (ant.). V. desiccant.

exsic'cate (-kéte), v.a., (ant.). V. desiccate.

exsuda'tion, n. V. exuda'tion.

exsude'. V. exude'.

ex'tant, adj., qui existe, existant, subsistant, actuel.

extempora'neous (èks-tè'm'po-ré-ni-eusse) ou extem'porary (-ra-), adj., pour le moment ; improvisé, impromptu, fait sous l'impulsion du moment.

extempora'neously, adv., d'abondance, impromptu, sans préparation.

extem'porary. V. extemporaneous.

extem'pore (-pô-ri), adv., sur-le-champ, sans préparation ; par improvisation. To speak — ; improviser (un discours).

extemporiza'tion, n., improvisation, f.

extem'porize (-raïze), v.n., improviser.

extem'porizer, n., improvisateur, m., improvisatrice, f.

extend', v.a., étendre; continuer, prolonger; (to hold out) tendre.

extend', v.n., s'étendre; (of time) se prolonger; (to spread) se propager.

extend'ible, adj., extensible; susceptible d'extension; (jur.) saisissable.

exten'sibleness ou **extensibil'ity** (-tè'n'-), n., extensibilité, f.

exten'sion, n., extension; étendue, f., prolongement; (jur.) (of time) délai; atermoiement, m., (anat., surg., gram., log.) extension, f.

exten'sive (-tè'n'-), adj., étendu, vaste; ample, grand, considérable, spacieux.

exten'sively, adv., d'une manière étendue; avec étendue; grandement, amplement, bien, très, au loin.

exten'sor (-tè'n'-), n., (anat.) extenseur, muscle extenseur, m.

extent' (-tè'n'te), n., étendue, f.; (fig.) degré, point, m.; (bearing) portée; (jur.) expertise pour estimer les biens d'un débiteur saisi; (mus.) portée, f. To a certain —; jusqu'à un certain point. To a great —; en grande partie. To the — of; jusqu'à; (com.) jusqu'à concurrence de.

exten'uate (-tè'n'iouéte), v.a., exténuer; affaiblir, diminuer, atténuer, mitiger.

extenua'tion, n., exténuation; atténuation; mitigation, f.

exte'rior (-ti-), adj., extérieur; en dehors de.

exte'rior, n., (pers., things) extérieur; (pers.) physique, m.

exte'riorly, adv., extérieurement.

exter'minate (-teur-mi-néte), v.a., exterminer; déraciner; (alg., ant.) éliminer.

extermina'tion, n., extermination; extirpation; (alg., ant.) élimination, f.

exter'minator (-né-), n., exterminateur, m.

exter'minatory, adj., d'extermination.

exter'nal (-teur-), adj., extérieur, externe.

exter'nally, adv., extérieurement, au dehors, à l'extérieur.

exter'nals (-nalze), n.pl., forme extérieure, f.sing.; dehors, m.pl.; extérieur, m.; (ecc.) cérémonies, pratiques, formes extérieures du culte, f.pl.

exterra'neous (-teur'ra-ni-eusse), adj., étranger.

extinct' (-ti'gn'k'te), adj., éteint; (ant.) aboli, tombé en désuétude.

extinc'tion, n., extinction, f.

extin'guish (-ti'gn'gwishe), v.a., éteindre; faire cesser; obscurcir; éclipser; surpasser en splendeur.

extin'guishable (-'a-b'l), adj., qu'on peut éteindre, extinguible.

extin'guisher, n., (thing) éteignoir, m.; personne qui éteint, f., éteigneur, -euse, m.f.

extin'guishing, adj., extincteur.

extin'guishment, n., extinction, abolition, f.

extir'pable, adj., (ant.) que l'on peut extirper.

extir'pate (-péte), v.a., extirper.

extirpa'tion, n., action d'extirper; extirpation, f.

ex'tirpator (-teur), n., extirpateur, m.

extol', v.a., exalter, élever, louer, vanter, célébrer.

extol'ler, n., panégyriste, m.

extol'ment, n., (ant.) panégyrique, m.; louange, action de louer, f.

extort' (-torte), v.a., extorquer, arracher. To — a promise from a person; arracher une promesse à quelqu'un. To — an answer; arracher une réponse.

extor'tion, n., extorsion; violence, f.

extor'tionate, adj., extorsionnaire.

extor'tioner, n., concussionnaire, exacteur; extorqueur, m.

ex'tra, adj., en sus; supplémentaire; (mil.) de rechange.

ex'tra, adv., en sus; de plus; au delà.

extra-charge', n., frais en sus, m.pl.; (admin.) surcharge, f., excédant, m.

extract', n., extrait, m.

extract', v.a., extraire de; tirer de; retirer de, recueillir de; (teeth) arracher à.

extrac'tion, n., extraction, f.; (pharm.) extrait, m. — of a tooth; extraction d'une dent, f.

extrac'tive, adj., que l'on peut extraire; (chem.) extractif.

extrac'tive, n., (chem.) extractif, m.

extrac'tor (-teur), n., (pers.) arracheur, -euse, m.f.; forceps, m.; appareil extracteur; curette, f.

ex'tradite, v.a., extrader.

extradi'tion, n., extradition, f.

extra'dos (-tré-dosse), n., (arch.) extrados, m.

extra-judi'cial (-djiou-di'sh'al), adj., extra-judiciaire.

extra-judi'cially, adv., extrajudiciairement.

extra-horse', n., cheval de renfort, m.

extra-lim'itary, adj., au delà des limites.

extra-mun'dane (-meu'n'dé-ne), adj., au delà du monde matériel.

extra'neous (-tré-ni-eusse), adj., étranger à, en dehors de, extérieur, non essentiel.

extraor'dinarily, adv., extraordinairement.

extraor'dinariness, n., caractère extraordinaire, m.; rareté, singularité, f.

extraor'dinary, adj., extraordinaire, rare, remarquable.

extra-paro'chial (-rô-kial), adj., qui n'est pas de la paroisse.

extra-post'age, n., surtaxe, f.

extra-provin'cial (-vi'n'-shal), adj., qui n'est pas de la même province.

extra-reg'ular (-rè-ghiou-leur), adj., hors des règles.

extra-stamp', n., timbre supplémentaire, m.

extrav'agance (-ga'n'ce), n., extravagance; bizarrerie, f.; prodigalité, f., folles dépenses, f.pl., gaspillage, m.

extrav'agant, adj., extravagant; bizarre; prodigue, dépensier; (of things) dispendieux, exorbitant.

extrav'agant (-ga'n'te), n., extravagant, m., extravagante, f., prodigue, m.

extrav'agantly, adv., d'une manière extravagante; prodigalement, follement.

extrav'asated (-cé-tède), adj., (med.) extravasé.

extravasa'tion, n., (med.) extravasation, extravasion, f.

extra-weight', n., excédent, m.

extreme' (-trîme), n., extrémité, f.; extrême, (arith., alg.) extrême, m. —s meet; les extrêmes se touchent. To an —; jusqu'à l'extrême, au dernier degré. To carry to —s; pousser à l'extrême.

extreme', adj., extrême.

extreme'ly, adv., extrêmement, au plus haut degré, au dernier degré.

extrem'ity (-trè-), n., extrémité, f.; extrême, m., calamité, f.; cas extrême, bout, m.; fin, f., comble, m. The extremities; (zoöl.) les extrémités, f.pl. To drive to extremities; pousser à bout.

ex'tricable, adj., qu'on peut dégager.

ex'tricate (-kéte), v.a., débarrasser de, dégager de; tirer d'affaire.

extrica'tion, n., dégagement, m., débarrassement; délivrance, f.

extrin'sic ou **extrin'sical** (-tri'n'-), adj., extrinsèque.

extrin'sically, adv., extrinsèquement, de dehors.

extrude' (-troude), v.a., (ant.) expulser; repousser, déposer.

extru'sion (-trou-jeune), n., (ant.) expulsion, f.

exu'berance ou **exu'berancy** (ègz'iou-beur'-), n., exubérance, surabondance, f.

exu'berant, adj., exubérant, surabondant.

exu'berantly, adv., avec exubérance.

exu'berate (-beur'éte), *v.n.*, exubérer, surabonder.

exuda'tion (èks'iou-dé-), *n.*, exsudation, *f.*

exude' (èks'ioude), *v.n.*, exsuder.

exude', *v.a.*, faire exsuder, décharger par les pores.

exul'cerate (ègz'eul-ceu-réte), *v.a.*, exulcérer, ulcérer.

exul'cerate, *v.n.*, s'ulcérer.

exulcera'tion (-ceur'é-), *n.*, ulcération ; (fig.) exaspération ; (med.) exulcération, *f.*

exult' (ègz'eulte), *v.n.*, se réjouir de ; témoigner une joie triomphante ; exulter de. To — at ; *triompher* de. To — over ; *triompher* sur. Our neighbors —ed over our defeats ; *nos voisins se réjouissaient de nos défaites.*

exul'tant, *adj.*, joyeux, triomphant.

exulta'tion (-té-), *n.*, allégresse, *f.* ; triomphe, *m.* ; joie, exultation, *f.*

exult'ingly, *adv.*, d'un air de triomphe ; avec une joie triomphante.

exus'tion (ègz'eust'-ieune), *n., f.*, (ant.) combustion, destruction par le feu.

exu'viæ (ègz'iou-vi-î), *n.pl.*, dépouilles, *f.pl.* ; (zoöl.) dépouille, *f.* ; (geol.) débris organiques, *m.pl.*

exu'viate, *v.n.*, changer de peau.

exuvia'tion, *n.*, changement de peau, *m.*

ey'as (aï'asse), *n.*, jeune faucon ; niais, *m.*

eye' (aïe), *n.*, œil, *m.* ; (fig.) vue, *f.* ; (persp.) point de vue ; (of a needle) trou ; (nav.) œillet ; (arch., and in cheeses) œil ; (bot.) œil, bouton, *m.* ; (catch for a hook) porte, *f.* pl., yeux. False —; *œil postiche.* Practised —; *œil exercé.* Black —; *œil noir, œil poché.* Sore —s ; *mal d'yeux,* *m.* Blind of one —; *borgne.* In the twinkling of an —; *en un clin d'œil.* With one's own —s ; *de ses propres yeux.* Farther than the — can reach ; *à perte de vue.* Before any one's —s ; *sous les yeux de quelqu'un.* To be before any one's —s ; *avoir sous le nez.* To cry one's —s out ; *s'épuiser en larmes.* With tears in one's —s ; *les larmes aux yeux.* To have a black —; *avoir l'œil en compote, avoir un œil poché.* To have in one's —s ; *avoir dans l'œil ; avoir en vue.* To tear out any one's —s ; *arracher les yeux à quelqu'un.* To open any one's —s ; *ouvrir les yeux à quelqu'un ; dessiller les yeux de quelqu'un.* To shut one's —s to ; *fermer les yeux* sur. To strike the —; *frapper les yeux.* To cast down one's —s ; *baisser les yeux.* To have an — to ; *avoir l'œil à ; veiller à ; avoir l'œil ouvert* sur ; *avoir en vue ; songer à.* To give an — to ; *avoir l'œil* sur ; *surveiller de près, ne pas perdre de vue.* The tears stood in his —s ; *il avait les larmes aux yeux.* There was not a dry — in the room, etc. ; *tous les yeux étaient mouillés de larmes.* To find favor in any one's —s ; *trouver grâce auprès de quelqu'un.* The sun is in my —s ; *le soleil me donne dans les yeux.* To have an — to the main chance ; *songer au solide.* That's all my —; *tout cela est bel et bon.*

eye, *v.a.*, regarder ; contempler ; suivre des yeux ; (b.s.) lorgner, toiser.

eye'ball (-bôl), *n.*, globe de l'œil, *m.* ; prunelle, pupille, *f.*

eye'-bath, *n.*, bassin oculaire, *m.*

eye'bright, *n.*, (bot.) eufraise, *f.*

eye'brow (-braou), *n.*, sourcil, *m.* To knit the —s ; *froncer les sourcils.*

eyed' (aïe'-de), *adj.*, aux yeux. Blue —; *aux yeux bleus.* One—; *borgne.* Dull—; *au regard sombre.* In the kingdom of the blind the one-— is king ; (prov.) *au royaume des aveugles les borgnes sont rois.*

eye'-dazzling (-dâ-), *adj.*, éblouissant.

eye'-drop (-drope), *n.*, (ant.) larme, *f.*

eye'-glance (-glâ'n'ce), *n.*, coup d'œil ; regard, *m.*

eye'-glass (-glâce), *n.*, lorgnon, *m.* ; lunette,

f. ; (opt.) oculaire, verre oculaire, *m.* Single —; *monocle, m.* Double —; *binocle ; lorgnon à deux branches, m. ; jumelle, f.*

eye'-hole (-hôle), *n.*, (anat.) orbite, orbite de l'œil, *f.*

eye'lash (-lashe), *n.*, cil, *m.*

eye'less (-lèsse), *adj.*, (ant.) sans yeux ; aveugle.

eye'let *ou* **eye'let-hole** (-lète, -hôle), *n.*, œillet (petit trou), *m.*

eye'lid (-lide), *n.*, paupière, *f.*

eye'-offending, *adj.*, qui blesse la vue.

eye'piece (-pîce), *n.*, (opt.) oculaire, *m.*

eye'-pleasing, *adj.*, qui plaît à l'œil.

eye'-reach, *n.*, portée de la vue, *f.*

eye'-salve (-sâve), *n.*, (med.) onguent pour les yeux, *m.*

eye'sight (-saïte), *n.*, vue, *f.*

eye'sore, *n.*, chose qui blesse *ou* qui offense l'œil, *f.* ; objet d'aversion, *m.* ; bête noire, bête d'aversion, *f.*

eye'string (-strigne), *n.*, fibre de l'œil, *f.*

eye'-tooth, *n.*, dent œillère, *f.*

eye'-water (-wô-teur), *n.*, collyre, *m.*

eye'-witness, *n.*, témoin oculaire, *m.*

ey'ot (aïote), *n.*, îlot, *m.*

eyre (ère), *n.*, (jur.) tournée (of judges), *f.* Justice in —; *juge qui va en tournée, juge ambulant, m.*

ey'ry (aïri), *n.*, aire (of birds of prey), *f.*

F

f, sixième lettre de l'alphabet, f, *m.f.* ; (mus.) fa, *m.* — sharp ; *fa dièse, m.*

faba'ceous (fa-bé-sheusse), *adj.*, de fève.

faba'go, *n.*, (bot.) fabago, *m.*, fabagelle, *f.*

Fa'bian (fé-), *adj.*, temporisateur.

fa'ble (fé-b'l), *n.*, fable, *f.* ; apologue, *m.*

fa'ble, *v.a.*, feindre ; imaginer, inventer ; supposer, prétendre ; dire faussement.

fa'bled, *adj.*, inventé ; fabuleux. — in story ; *célèbre dans la mythologie.*

fa'bler, *n.*, fabuliste ; conteur, *m.*

fab'ric, *n.*, édifice, ouvrage, *m.* ; construction, fabrique, manufacture, fabrication ; étoffe, *f.* ; tissu, *m.* ; (fig.) système, *m.*

fab'ricate (-kéte), *v.a.*, fabriquer ; construire ; (fig.) inventer.

fabrica'tion, *n.*, constructeur, fabrication ; (fig.) invention, *f.*

fab'ricator, *n.*, constructeur ; fabricateur, *m.*, fabricatrice, *f.* The Almighty — of the universe ; *le grand architecte de l'univers.*

fab'ric-lands (-la'n'dze), *n.pl.*, biens de fabrique, *m.pl.*

fab'ulist (-biou-), *n.*, fabuliste, *m.*

fab'ulous (-biou-leusse), *adj.*, fabuleux ; (fig.) vaste, immense.

fab'ulously, *adv.*, fabuleusement.

fab'ulousness, *n.*, (ant.) caractère fabuleux, *m.*, fabulosité, *f.*

face (féce), *n.*, visage, *m.* ; face, figure ; physionomie, *f.* ; (fig.) apparence ; (impudence) audace, impudence ; (grimace) grimace ; (look) mine, physionomie, *f.* ; (situation) état, aspect, *m.* ; situation ; (front) face, façade, *f.*, devant, *m.* ; (of a cannon) tranche ; (of a diamond) facette, *f.* ; (of a watch) cadran ; (of a wall) parement, *m.* ; (anat., arch., fort., geom.) face, *f.* To make —s at any one ; *faire des grimaces à quelqu'un.* To wash one's —; *se laver la figure, se débarbouiller.* To put a good — on the matter ; *faire bonne contenance à mauvais jeu ; prendre son parti en brave.* To laugh in any one's —; *rire au nez de quelqu'un.* To slap any one's —; *donner un soufflet à quelqu'un.* Before any one's —; *sous les yeux, à la barbe, au nez, de quelqu'un.* — to —; *face à face.* With a full —; *de face.*

— ache, *tic douloureux, m.* He had the — to assert ; *il eut l'audace d'affirmer.* In the very — of the court ; *en présence même de la cour.* To put a good — on a bad business ; *faire bonne mine à mauvais jeu* ou *faire contre fortune bon cœur* ou *faire bonne contenance à.* To set one's — against ; *s'opposer à ; se déclarer con-tre.* To show one's — ; *se montrer, se présenter ; paraître.* To tell (anything) to any one's — ; *dire en face.* To shut the door in any one's — ; *fermer la porte au nez de quelqu'un.*

face, *v.a.,* faire face à ; affronter ; (garments) mettre un revers là, mettre un retroussis à ; (to cover) revêtir. To — a thing out ; *soutenir une assertion ; persister dans sa conduite, dans son entreprise.* To — out ; *braver sans rougir, payer d'audace.* To — down ; *résister avec effronterie, avec audace.* To — the music ; *faire face à la musique,* ou *à l'événement ; payer les pots cassés.* —d with ; *à revers de.* —d tea ; *thé coloré frauduleusement.*

face, *v.n.,* prendre un faux dehors ; (milit.) faire front. To — about ; *faire volte-face.* — about ! *volte-face !*

faced (féss'te), *adj.,* à visage ; à figure. Double — ; *à deux visages.* Full — ; *qui a la figure pleine.* Fair — ; *beau de visage.* Bold — ; *effronté, impudent.* Ugly — ; *laid de visage.*

face'-guard, *n.,* (metal, fenc.) masque, *m.*
face'less (-lèsse), *adj.,* (ant.) sans face.
face'-painter (-pé'n't'eur), *n.* *V.* **portrait-painter.**
face'-painting, *n.,* maquillage, *m.*
fac'et (fass'ète), *n.,* facette, *f.* *v.a.,* facetter.
face'tiæ, *n.pl.,* facéties, *f.pl.*
face'tious (fa-ci-sheusse), *adj.,* facétieux.
face'tiously, *adv.,* facétieusement.
face'tiousness (-nèsse), *n.,* caractère, *ou* esprit, facétieux, *m.,* facétie, plaisanterie, *f.*
fac'eted, *adj.,* à facettes.
fac'eting, *n.,* facettage, *m.*
fa'cial, *adj.,* facial, -e.
fa'cies (fé-shi-ize), *n.,* (anat.) face, *f. ;* (geol., zoöl.) aspect de la flore, de la faune ; (bot.) aspect d'une plante, *m.* — hippocratica ; (med.) *facies hippocratique, m.*
fac'ile, *adj.,* facile, complaisant, accessible, facile à mener, à persuader.
fac'ileness (-nèsse), *n.,* (ant.) facilité, complai-sance, *f.,* manque de fermeté, *m.*
facil'itate (-téte), *v.a.,* faciliter.
facilita'tion, *n.,* action de faciliter ; facilité, *f.*
facil'ity, *n.,* facilité, *f.*
fa'cing (fé-cigne), *n.,* (of garments) parement, (mil.) parements, *m.pl. ;* revers, retroussis ; (of structures) parement, revêtement ; (milit.) front, *m. ;* (com.) falsification du thé par des matières colorantes, *f. ;* (fig.) signe extérieur, *m.* *pl.,* mouvements, *m.pl.*
fac'-similar, *adj.,* fac-similaire.
fac-sim'ile (-li), *n.,* fac-similé, *m.*
fac-sim'ile, *v.a.,* fac-similer.
fact, *n.,* fait, *m.* Matter of — ; *fait.* Matter-of-— man ; *homme positif, m.* In — ; *en effet, au fait, de fait, par le fait, effectivement.* In point of — ; *au fait.* To catch in the — ; *V.* **act.** To know for a positive — ; *savoir de source,* ou *de science, certaine.*
fac'tion, *n.,* faction ; discorde, dissension, *f.*
fac'tionist, *n.,* (ant.) factieux, *m.*
fac'tious (fak-shi-eusse), *adj.,* factieux.
fac'tiously, *adv.,* factieusement, d'une ma-nière factieuse ; en factieux.
fac'tiousness (-nèsse), *n.,* esprit factieux, *m.*
facti'tious (fak-tish'eusse), *adj.,* factice, arti-ficiel, faux.
facti'tiously, *adv.,* facticement.
facti'tiousness, *n.,* nature factice, *f.*
fac'tor (-teur), *n.,* agent ; (com., math., fig.) facteur, *m.*

fac'tory, *n.,* usine, manufacture, fabrique, *f. ;* ateliers ; (com.) comptoir, *m.,* factorerie, *f.* — hand ; *ouvrier de fabrique, m.*
facto'tum (fak-tô-teume), *n.,* factotum ; (print.) passe-partout, *m.*
fac'ulty, *n.,* (fak'eul-), *n.,* faculté, *f. ;* pouvoir, ta-lent, *m. ;* habileté, *f. ;* moyens, *m.pl. ;* puissance, *f.*
fac'und ou **facund'ious** (fak'eu'n'de, -di-eusse), *adj.,* (ant.) éloquent.
fad, *n.,* marotte, lubie, toquade, *f. ;* dada, *m.*
fad'dle, *v.n.,* baliverner, baguenauder.
fad'dy, *adj.,* à lubies.
fade (féde), *v.n.,* se faner, se flétrir ; s'éva-nouir ; s'obscurcir, disparaître, périr ; se passer, passer.
fade, *v.a.,* faner, flétrir, affaiblir.
fadge, *v.n.,* (ant.) s'accorder ; réussir.
fa'ding, *adj.,* qui se fane, qui se flétrit ; qui périt.
fa'dingly, *adv.,* en se flétrissant.
fæ'ces (fi-cèze), *n.pl.,* matière fécale, *f.sing. ;* (med.) fèces, *f.pl.*
fag, *v.a.,* forcer à travailler, à piocher ; faire aller ; battre ; fatiguer ; tyranniser.
fag, *v.n.,* travailler dur à, piocher à.
fag, *n.,* piocheur, travailleur ; (in schools) souffre-douleur ; (knot in cloth) nœud, *m.*
fag'-end (-è'n'de), *n.,* (of a tissue) lisière, queue, *f. ;* chef ; (nav.) (of a rope) bout, *m.* The — of the week ; *les derniers jours de la semaine, m.pl.* The — of a letter ; *le dernier paragraphe d'une lettre, m.*
fag'ot (fag'ote), *n.,* fagot, *m. ;* (fort.) fascine, *f. ;* (milit., nav.) ⊙passe-volant, *m.*
fag'ot, *v.a.,* lier ensemble ; fagoter.
fail (féle), *n.,* manque ; insuccès, *m.* Without — ; *sans faute, sans manque.*
fail, *v.a.,* manquer à ; faire défaut à ; (to desert) abandonner.
fail, *v.n.,* faillir ; (to miss) manquer ; (not to succeed) échouer ; faiblir ; (com.) faire faillite. I shall not — (to do it) ; *je n'y manquerai pas.* I shall not — to come ; *je ne manquerai pas de venir* ou *je viendrai sans faute, sans manque.*
fail'ing, *n.,* défaut, *m. ;* faute ; imperfection ; faiblesse ; (com.) faillite, *f.*
fail'ing, *adj.,* qui s'affaiblit, défaillant, qui manque. *prep.,* — that ; *à défaut de cela.*
fail'ure (fél'ioure), *n.,* manque, défaut ; affai-blissement, insuccès, *m. ;* affaire manquée ; chute ; (com.) faillite, *f.*
fain (féne), *adj.,* joyeux, bienheureux ; trop obligé.
fain, *adv.,* bien, volontiers. I — would come, but . . . ; *je viendrais volontiers, mais . . .* ou *je serais fort heureux de venir, mais.*
faint (fé'n'te), *adj.,* faible, défaillant ; affaibli ; languissant ; abattu ; découragé ; lâche ; (of the weather) mou. — blue ; *bleu pâle.* — heart never won fair lady ; *jamais honteux n'eut belle amie.*
faint, *v.n.,* s'évanouir, défaillir, perdre cou-rage, faiblir. To — away ; *s'évanouir ; se trouver mal, perdre connaissance.*
faint-heart'ed (-hârt'ède), *adj.,* poltron, ti-mide, abattu ; sans cœur ; sans courage, découragé.
faint-heart'edly, *adv.,* lâchement, pusillani-mement ; dans l'abattement.
faint-heart'edness (-nèsse), *n.,* manque de cœur, abattement, *m. ;* pusillanimité ; timidité ; lâcheté.
faint'ing, *n.,* évanouissement, *m. ;* défail-lance, *f.,* (med.) syncope, *f.* *adj.,* défaillant. In a — fit ; *sans connaissance, évanoui.*
faint'ishness (fé'n't'ish'nèsse), *n.,* légère faiblesse, *f.*
faint'ly, *adv.,* faiblement, mollement ; dans l'abattement.
faint'ness (-nèsse), *n.,* faiblesse, langueur, *f. ;* abattement, manque de vigueur, *m.*

fair (fère), *adj.*, beau ; clair ; pur ; net ; (of the hair) blond ; (of the complexion) blanc ; (of the weather) beau ; (of the wind) bon, favorable ; (just) juste, équitable, probe, loyal ; (com.) courant ; (fig.) direct ; (fig.) bon, compétent ; (fig.) libéral, rond en affaires. To be a — judge ; *être un bon juge.* — and square ; *honorable.* To be in a — way ; *être en bonne voie* (de) *ou être en passe* de. That is not — ; (at games) *cela n'est pas du jeu.* — words never did harm ; (prov.) *jamais beau parler n'écorcha la langue.* To make a — copy ; *mettre au net.* — words butter no parsnips ; (prov.) *je vis de bonne soupe et non de beau langage* (Molière).

fair (fère), *adv.*, bien ; agréablement ; favorablement ; avec justice ; avec équité ; de bonne foi ; loyalement. — play ; *traitement juste, traitement équitable, m.* To give — play ; *donner beau jeu* à ; *jouer franc jeu* avec ; *jouer cartes sur table* avec. To stand — with the world ; *être en bons termes avec le monde.* He charged — for the goods ; *il vendait les marchandises à un prix raisonnable.* — and square ; *honorablement ; avec droiture, rondement.* To bid — ; *promettre* de. — and softly goes far ; (prov.) *doucement va bien loin.*

fair, *n.*, belle femme, belle ; (market) foire, *f.* The — ; *le beau sexe, les belles.*

fair'-boding, *adj.*, de bon augure ; propice ; favorable.

fair'-dealing, *n.*, loyauté, bonne foi, *f. adj.*, loyal, honnête ; (com.) rond en affaires.

fair'-faced, *adj.*, bien de figure.

fair'-haired (-hèr'de), *adj.*, aux cheveux blonds.

fair'ing, *n.*, cadeau de foire, *m.*

fair'ish, *adj.*, assez bien, passable.

fair'ly, *adv.*, bien ; proprement ; complètement ; favorablement ; avec impartialité ; avec justice, honnêtement ; avec probité ; loyalement ; doucement, poliment, lisiblement.

fair'ness (-nèsse), *n.*, beauté, clarté, pureté ; netteté ; (of the hair) couleur blonde ; (of the complexion) blancheur ; (justice) équité, probité ; justice ; loyauté, impartialité, *f.*

fair'-price, *n.*, juste prix, prix raisonnable, *m.*

fair'-spoken (-spôk'n), *adj.*, à langue dorée, doux, aimable, doucereux.

fai'ry (fèr-i *ou* fé-ri), *n.*, fée, *f.*

fai'ry, *adj.*, de fée ; féerique.

fai'ry-land, *n.*, royaume *ou* empire des fées, *m.*

fai'ry-like (-laïke), *adj.*, comme une fée.

faith (féth), *n.*, foi ; fidélité, promesse, parole d'honneur, confiance, véracité, *f.* In — ! *ma foi !* Breach of — ; (jur.) *violation de foi, f.* In good — ; *de bonne foi.* To put — in ; (of things) *ajouter foi* à ; (of persons) *avoir foi* en.

faith ! *int.*, ma foi ! en vérité ! parbleu !

faith'ful (-foule), *adj.*, fidèle.

faith'ful, *n.*, fidèle ; (Mahometan) croyant, *m.*

faith'fully, *adv.*, fidèlement.

faith'fulness (-nèsse), *n.*, fidélité, *f.* [déloyal.

faith'less (-lèsse), *adj.*, sans foi ; infidèle ;

faith'lessness (-lèss'nèsse), *n.*, infidélité ; déloyauté, perfidie, mauvaise foi, *f.*

fake, *v.a.*, truquer, carotter.

fakir', *n. V.* faquir.

fal'cate *ou* **fal'cated** (-kéte, -két'ède), *adj..* courbe ; (bot.) falciforme.

fal'chion (fâl'sheune), *n.*, cimeterre, *m.*

fal'con (fô'k'n), *n.*, faucon, *m.*

fal'coner, *n.*, fauconnier, *m.*

fal'conet, *n.*, fauconneau, *m.*

fal'conry, *n.*, fauconnerie, *f.*

fald'stool (fâld'stoule), *n.*, prie-Dieu ; siège d'évêque ; siège pliant, *m.*

fall (fôl), *n.*, chute, *f.* ; (of night) tombée ; (in price) baisse ; (of rain, of snow) quantité tombée, *f.* ; (of earth) éboulement, *m.* ; (of water, of rivers) chute, cascade, cataracte ; (of waters) décrue, *f.* ; pente ; chute des feuilles, *f.*, automne, *m.*, *f.* ; (decrease) diminution, *f.* There has been a — of snow ; *il est tombé de la neige.* To speculate on a — ; (com.) *jouer à la baisse.* To have *ou* meet with a — ; *faire une chute, tomber.*

fall, *v.n.*, (*preterit*, Fell ; *past part.*, Fallen) tomber ; retomber ; (in value) baisser, diminuer ; (fig.) s'abaisser, descendre. To — away ; *maigrir, dépérir ; se révolter, apostasier.* To — back ; *tomber en arrière, reculer, se retirer, se replier.* To — back upon ; (mil.) *se replier* sur. To — down ; *tomber par terre, se prosterner.* To — away from ; *abandonner, quitter ; se départir* de. To — in ; *tomber dedans ; s'écrouler ; s'ébouler ;* (milit.) *se ranger ; s'aligner.* To — off ; *tomber.* To — on ; *tomber dessus ; rencontrer ; attaquer.* To — out ; *tomber ;* (pers.) *se quereller, se brouiller, rompre* avec ; (milit.) *quitter, ou rompre, les rangs ;* (of things) *arriver, advenir.* — out ! *rompez les rangs !* To — out with ; *se brouiller* avec. To — to ; *tomber en partage* à ; *échoir* à ; *se mettre* à ; *se livrer* à ; *se rendre* à ; *se jeter* sur ; *tomber* dessus. To — into ; *se conformer* à ; *contracter.* To — foul of ; *faire collision ; attaquer ; réprimander ; s'emporter* contre. To — short ; *manquer* de. To — through ; *n'arriver à rien, échouer, tomber dans l'eau.* To — in with ; *rencontrer, tomber* sur. To — within ; *rentrer* dans. To — under ; *être compris* dans *ou* sous. To — on ; *descendre* sur ; (fig.) *incomber* à ; *être à la charge* de. To — between two stools ; *être assis entre deux chaises.* Between two stools one falls to the ground ; (prov.) *qui deux choses chasse, ni l'une ni l'autre ne prend.* To — to blows ; *en venir aux coups.*

falla'cious (fal-lé-sheusse), *adj.*, trompeur ; fallacieux, illusoire.

falla'ciously, *adv.*, d'une manière trompeuse ; fallacieusement, illusoirement.

falla'ciousness (-nèsse), *n.*, caractère trompeur, *m.* ; fausseté, *f.*

fal'lacy, *n.*, illusion, déception, erreur ; apparence trompeuse, *f.* ; faux raisonnement ; sophisme, *m.*

fallibil'ity, *n.*, faillibilité, *f.*

fal'lible (-li-b'l), *adj.*, faillible.

fall'ing (fôl-), *n.*, chute, *f.* — away ; *amaigrissement ; dépérissement, m. ;* (fig.) *décadence, défection, f.* — in ; *enfoncement, écroulement,* (of earth) *éboulement, m.* — off ; *chute ; défection ; apostasie, f.* — out ; *brouillerie, rupture, f.*

fall'ing-sickness, *n.*, épilepsie, *f. ;* mal caduc ; haut mal, *m.*

fall'ing-star, *n.*, étoile filante *ou* tombante, *f.*

fal'low (fal'lô), *n.*, jachère, *f.*

fal'low, *v.a.*, jachérer.

fal'low, *adj.*, fauve ; (agri.) en friche, en jachère ; (fig.) inculte. To lie — ; *être en friche.* To let lie — ; *laisser en friche.* — deer ; *daim, m.*

fal'low-finch (-fi'n'she), *n.*, (orni.) motteux, cul-blanc, *m.*

fal'lowness (-nèsse), *n.*, jachère, stérilité, *f.*

false (fôlse), *adj.*, faux, menteur, trompeur, artificiel, postiche, infidèle, déloyal ; (of imprisonment) illégal.

false'-bottom, *n.*, double fond, *m.*

false'-faced (-fés'-te), *adj.*, hypocrite.

false'hair, *n.*, faux cheveux, *m.pl.*

false-heart'ed (-hâr't'ède), *adj.*, perfide, trompeur, au cœur faux.

false-heart'edness (-nèsse), *n.*, perfidie, *f.*

false'hood (-houde), *n.*, fausseté, *f. ;* faux, mensonge, *m.*

false'ly, *adj.*, faussement.

false'ness (-nèsse), *n.*, fausseté, duplicité, perfidie, infidélité, *f.* The — of a report ; *la fausseté d'une nouvelle.*

falset'to (-fâl-), *n.*, (mus.) voix de tête, de fausset, *f.* ; fausset, *m.*

fal'sifiable (fôls'i-faï'a'b'l), *adj.*, qui peut être falsifié.

falsifica'tion (-fi-ké-), *n.*, falsification, *f.*

fal'sifier (-faï'eur), *n.*, falsificateur; faussaire; (of coin) faux monnayeur, *m.*

fal'sify (-faïe), *v.a.*, falsifier; altérer; fausser; (to disprove) prouver la fausseté **de**, réfuter.

fal'sifying, *adj.*, falsificateur.

fal'sity, *n.*, fausseté, *f.*

fal'ter (fôl'-), *v.n.*, hésiter; se troubler, bégayer, balbutier; trembler; chanceler. A —ing voice; *une voix altérée, f.*

fal'tering, *n.*, hésitation, *f.*; trouble, *m.*

fal'teringly, *adv.*, avec hésitation; avec trouble; en tremblant; en balbutiant; en hésitant.

fame (féme), *n.*, gloire; renommée; réputation, *f.*; (ant.) bruit; renom, *m.* Of ill —; *mal famé.* House of ill —; *maison de débauche, maison de tolérance, maison publique, f.*

famed (fém'de), *adj.*, renommé; fameux; célèbre.

fame'less (-lesse), *adj.*, sans renommée; sans renom.

famil'iar, *n.*, ami intime; démon; esprit; (Inquisition) familier, *m.*

famil'iar, *adj.*, de la famille; familier, intime. To be — with; *être familier* **avec**; *connaître intimement.* To grow —; *se familiariser.* To make oneself — with; *se familiariser* **avec**. To make (any one) — with; *familiariser avec*.

familiar'ity, *n.*, familiarité, *f.* — breeds contempt; *la familiarité engendre le mépris ou chose accoutumée n'est pas fort prisée.*

famil'iarize (-aïze), *v.a.*, familiariser.

famil'iarly, *adv.*, familièrement.

fam'ily, *n.*, famille, *f.* To be in the — way; *être enceinte.* To come of a high —; *être d'une grande, ou illustre, famille.*

fam'ily, *adj.*, de famille, de la famille.

fam'ine, *n.*, famine, disette, *f.*

fam'ish, *v.a.*, affamer, faire mourir de faim.

fam'ish, *v.n.*, être affamé; mourir de faim.

fam'ished, *adj.*, affamé, mort de faim.

fam'ishment, *n.*, faim extrême, famine, *f.*

fa'mous (fé'meusse), *adj.*, fameux, célèbre, renommé.

fa'mously, *adv.*, avec une grande renommée; d'une manière éclatante; furieusement, prodigieusement, fameusement.

fan, *n.*, éventail, *m.*; (of a windmill) aile, *f.*; gouvernail; (of bellows) soufflet; (agri.) van mécanique, tarare ventilateur, *m.*

fan, *v.a.*, éventer; souffler; (agri.) vanner; (fig.) allumer, exciter, activer, aviver.

fanat'ic *ou* **fanat'ical**, *adj.*, fanatique.

fanat'ic, *n.*, fanatique, *m.f.*

fanat'ically, *adv.*, d'une manière fanatique; avec fanatisme.

fanat'icism, *n.*, fanatisme, *m.*

fanat'icize (-çaïze), *v.a.*, fanatiser.

fan'-carrier, *n.*, porte-éventail, *m.*

fan'-case, *n.*, étui à éventail, *m.*

fan'cied, *adj.*, imaginaire, imaginé, supposé. Much —; *très prisé, très en vogue.*

fan'ciful (-foule), *adj.*, fantastique; qui a des fantaisies; fantasque; capricieux.

fan'cifully, *adv.*, fantastiquement; capricieusement, fantasquement.

fan'cifulness, *n.*, caprice; caractère fantastique; caractère fantasque, *m.*, bizarrerie, *f.*

fan'cy, *n.*, imagination; fantaisie; idée, *f.*; goût, caprice, *m.*, envie, *f.* To take a — to any one; *prendre quelqu'un en affection.* To take a — to; *prendre du goût* **pour**. They took a — to; *il leur prit la fantaisie* **de**. To take a — to a place; *affectionner un endroit.* Where is — bred? *où naît l'amour?*

fan'cy, *adj.*, de fantaisie; (of a ball) costumé, travesti.

fan'cy, *v.a.*, s'imaginer; avoir dans l'idée; se figurer; avoir du goût **pour**.

fan'cy, *v.n.*, s'imaginer; se figurer. Just —! *figurez-vous!*

fan'cy-dress, *n.*, costume de bal paré, *m.* — ball; *bal costumé, bal paré, m.*

fan'cy-fair, *n.*, bazar au profit des pauvres, *m.*

fan'cy-framed (-fré'm'de), *adj.*, créé par l'imagination.

fan'cy-goods, *n.pl.*, articles de fantaisie, *m. pl.*

fan'cy-monger (-meu'gn'gheur), *n.*, songecreux, *m.*

fan'cy-sick, *adj.*, qui a l'imagination malade; hypocondriaque.

fan'cy-stationer, *n.*, marchand d'articles de fantaisie, *m.*

fan'cy-work, *n.*, tapisserie, broderie, *f.*

fandan'go, *n.*, fandango, *m.*

fane (féne), *n.*, temple; édifice sacré, *m.*

fan'faron (-rô'n), *n.*, fanfaron, *m.*

fanfaronade' (-éde), *n.*, fanfaronnade, *f.*

fang (fai'gne), *n.*, (of birds) griffe, serre; (of persons' teeth) racine, *f.*, chicot, (of dogs) croc, *m.*; (of boars) défense; (fig.) griffe, *f.*

fanged (fai'gn'de), *adj.*, armé de dents; armé de griffes; armé de serres; armé de crocs; armé de défenses.

fan'gle (fai'gn'g'l), *n.*, (ant.) nouvelle, mais stupide invention, *f.*

fan'gled (fai'gn'glde), *adj.*, (ant.) trop voyant; éclatant. New— —; *de nouvelle invention, d'invention nouvelle.*

fang'less, *adj.*, sans dents, sans crocs; sans serres; sans griffes; sans défenses.

fan'light (-laïte), *n.*, fenêtre en éventail, *f.*

fan'like (-laïke), *adj.*, en éventail.

fan'maker (-mék-), *n.*, éventailliste, *m.*

fan'nel (ant.) *ou* **fan'on**, *n.*, (c.rel.) fanon, (surg.) fanon, *m.*

fan'ner, *n.*, personne qui évente, *f.*; vanneur; tarare; ventilateur, *m.*

fan'-palm, *n.*, palmier-éventail, *m.*

fan'shaped (-shépte), *adj.*, en éventail.

fan'-stick, *n.*, lame d'éventail, *f.*

fan'-tail, *n.*, (orni.) pigeon paon, pigeon trembleur, *m.*; (gas-lighting) bec éventail, *m.*

fan'-tailed, *adj.*, à queue d'aronde.

fantas'tic, *n.*, personne fantasque, *f.*

fantas'tic *ou* **fantas'tical**, *adj.*, fantastique; (pers.) fantasque.

fantas'tically, *adv.*, fantastiquement; fantasquement.

fantas'ticalness, *n.*, fantaisie, bizarrerie, *f.*; caractère fantasque, *m.*

fan'tasy (-ci), *n.*, fantaisie, *f.*

fan'tom. *V.* **phan'tom**.

faquir', *n.*, faquir, fakir, *m.*

far (fâre), *adv.*, loin; au loin; bien; de beaucoup; beaucoup. As — as; *aussi loin que; jusqu'à.* By —; *de beaucoup.* How —; *jusqu'où? jusqu'à quel point? jusqu'à quelle distance?* How — is it to . . . .? *combien y a-t-il d'ici à . . . .?* So — as to; *jusqu'à.* In so — as; *en tant que.* Thus —; *jusque là; jusqu'ici.* — from; *loin* **de**. — from it; *bien loin de là; tant s'en faut.* The day was — spent; *la journée était fort avancée.* — inferior; *bien, ou fort, inférieur.* — off; *au loin.* So — so good; *jusque là c'est très bien.* — and near; *de loin et de près ou de tous côtés.* — between; *à de longs intervalles, de loin en loin.* — be it from me to; *loin de moi la pensée* **de** *ou à Dieu ne plaise que* (with subjunctive).

far, *adj.*, lointain; éloigné; reculé.

faran'dole, *n.*, farandole (a dance), *f.*

farce, *n.*, (thea.) farce, *f.*

far'cical, *adj.*, de farce; burlesque, drôle; risible.

far'cically, adv., burlesquement, drôlement.

far'cin (ant.) *ou* **far'cy** (fär-), n., (vet.) farcin, m.

fard (färde), v.a., farder.

fare (fère), v.n., aller, se porter ; se nourrir. To — ill *ou* badly ; être mal ; faire mauvaise chère. To — well ; faire bonne chère.

fare, n., course, f. ; (price) prix de la course ; prix de la place ; (pers.) voyageur, m. ; (food) chère, f., menu, m. ; plats, mets, m.pl. Bill of —; menu d'un repas, m. ; (at an eating-house) carte du jour, f. To pay full —; payer place entière. Half —; demi-place, f. Here is my —; voici le prix de ma place.

farewell' *ou* **fare'-well** (fèr'wèle), n., adieu, m. To bid any one —; dire adieu à quelqu'un.

farewell' *ou* **fare'-well**, adj., d'adieu. — -summer ; (bot.) saponaire, f.

farewell' *ou* **fare'-well**, adv., porte-toi bien ; portez-vous bien ; adieu ; bon voyage.

far'-famed, adj., célèbre au loin, partout.

far'-fetched (-fètsh'te), adj., cherché au loin ; amené, tiré de loin ; (fig. of style) recherché ; tiré par les cheveux, forcé, affecté.

far'-gone, adj., avancé.

fari'na (rī-), n., farine, f. ; (bot., ant.) pollen, m. ; (chem.) fécule, f. Fossil —; (espèce de carbonate de chaux) farine fossile, f.

farina'ceous (-né'sheusse), adj., farineux, farinacé.

farm (fârme), v.a., affermer ; exploiter ; prendre à ferme ; faire valoir. — out ; donner à ferme.

farm (fârme), n., ferme, f.

farm'able (fârm'a'b'l), adj., que l'on peut affermer.

farm'-bailiff (-bé-life), n., régisseur de ferme, m.

farm'-buildings, n.pl., bâtiments de ferme, [m.pl.

farm'er, n., fermier, m. —'s-plague ; (bot.) podagraire, f.

farm'ery, n., corps de ferme, m.

farm'-house (-haouce), n., ferme (habitation), f.

farm'ing, n., exploitation d'une ferme ; agriculture, f.

farm'-laborer, n., ouvrier de ferme, m.

far'most (fâr'môste), adj., le plus éloigné.

farm'-servant, n., garçon de ferme, m. ; fille de ferme, f.

farm'stead, n., ferme, f.

farm'-yard (-yârde), n., cour de ferme, basse-cour, f.

far'ness, n., éloignement, m. ; distance, f.

fa'ro (fé'ro), n., (game) pharaon, m.

farra'go (far-régô), n., farrago, fatras, m.

far'rier, n., maréchal ; maréchal ferrant ; vétérinaire, médecin vétérinaire, m.

far'row (-rô), n., cochonnée, f. With —; pleine, adj.f.

far'row, adj., stérile.

far'row, v.a., mettre bas (of pigs).

far'row, v.n., cochonner.

far'-seeing, adj., clairvoyant, pénétrant.

far'-sighted, adj., qui a la vue longue, presbyte.

far'-sightedness, n., presbytie, f. ; (fig.) pénétration, clairvoyance.

far'-sought (-sôte), adj., V. **far'-fetched**.

far'ther (fârtheur), adj., ultérieur, plus éloigné ; autre, encore un. — end ; extrémité, f., fond, m.

far'ther, adv., plus loin, de plus, ultérieurement ; en outre, davantage.

far'thermore, adv., de plus.

far'thest (fârthèste), n., le plus loin. At —; (of time) au plus tard ; (of quantity) au plus.

far'thing (fârthigne), n., farthing (centimes 2.42) ; liard, m. Not to be worth a —; n'avoir pas un sou vaillant.

far'thingale (fârthign'-ghéle), n., cerceau ; cerceau de jupon, vertugadin, m.

far'thingsworth (fârthign'z'weurth), n., quantité pour la valeur d'un farthing, f.

far' west', n., extrême ouest, m.

fas'ces (fas'size), n.pl., (antiq., hist.) faisceaux, m.pl.

fas'cia (fash'i'a), n., (arch.) fasce, frise, bande ; (astron.) bande ; (anat.) aponévrose, f., fascia ; (surg.) bandage, m.

fas'cial (fas'sial), adj., des faisceaux.

fas'ciated (fa-shi-ét'ède), adj., fascié.

fascia'tion (fa-shi-é-), n., (bot.) fasciation, f. ; (surg.) bandage, m.

fas'cicle (fas-si-c'l'), n., (bot.) fascicule, m.

fascic'ular (fas-sik'iou-), adj., (bot.) fasciculé.

fascic'ulate, adj., (bot.) fasciculé.

fascic'ulated (fas-sik'iou-lét'ède), adj., (bot.) fasciculé.

fas'cinate (-néte), v.a., fasciner ; enchanter, charmer, séduire.

fas'cinating, adj., fascinateur, enchanteur, séduisant. — look ; regard fascinateur, m.

fascina'tion (-né-), n., fascination, séduction, f. ; charme, m.

fascine' (-sine), n., fascine, f.

fash'ion (fash'eune), n., mode ; façon, forme, f. ; modèle ; le beau monde ; le grand monde, m. ; fashion, f. In —; à la mode. It is the —; c'est la mode. In the French —; à la française. In the English —; à l'anglaise. Out of —; passé de mode, démodé. To bring into —; mettre à la mode, mettre en vogue. To come into —; devenir à la mode. To go out of —; passer de mode. To be in —; être à la mode. To set the —; donner le ton. People of —; gens à la mode, m.pl. Woman of —; femme à la mode, f. Man of —; homme à la mode, homme du monde, m. In a —; after a —; jusqu'à un certain point ; tel quel.

fash'ion, v.a., façonner, former, accommoder, adapter.

fash'ionable (fash'eu'n'ab'l), adj., à la mode ; élégant ; fashionable, de luxe, de bon ton. — man ; élégant, homme du beau monde, m. — woman, lady ; femme à la mode, grande dame, élégante, f. — people ; gens du beau monde, gens à la mode, m.pl. — world ; le monde élégant, le grand monde, le beau monde.

fash'ionableness, n., élégance ; vogue, f.

fash'ionably, adv., à la mode, élégamment.

fash'ionist, n., (ant.) esclave de la mode, m.f.

fast (fâste), n., jeûne, m. — day ; jour de jeûne, m.

fast, v.n., jeûner.

fast, adj., (firm) ferme ; fixé à, fixe ; (quick) vite, rapide ; (faithful) fidèle ; (of sleep) profond ; (of colors) bon teint ; (nav.) amarré ; (of a door, a window) qui ne s'ouvre pas. To make —; attacher, fixer, assujétir ; (doors, windows) fermer ; (nav.) amarrer. A — man ; un homme dissipé, viveur, m. — young lady ; demoiselle qui se moque du qu'en dira-t-on, f. To be —; aimer les plaisirs, faire la vie. This clock is —; cette pendule avance. To play— and loose ; tergiverser ; agir avec duplicité. —train ; train de grande vitesse ; train rapide, m.

fast, adv., (firm) ferme, fortement ; (quick) vite, rapidement ; (of raining) fort, à verse ; (of any one asleep) profondément. To hold —; tenir ferme ; s'attacher à ; ne pas lâcher prise ; (of teeth or of doors) serrer. To live —; faire la vie. To stand —; s'arrêter, rester debout, montrer du courage, ne pas broncher.

fas'ten (fâs's'n), v.a., fixer ; attacher, lier ; (windows, doors) fermer, serrer, assujétir, assujettir. To — (anything) upon (any one) ; imputer à, mettre sur le dos à.

fas'ten, v.n., s'attacher à ; se cramponner à ; se fixer sur ; s'acharner à.

fas′tener, *n.*, personne qui attache ; qui lie ; (of windows) espagnolette, *f.*

fas′tening, *n.*, attache ; fermeture, *f.*

fast′er (fåst′eur), *n.*, jeûneur, *m.*, jeûneuse, *f.*

fast′er, *adv.*, plus vite ; plus fort.

fas′ti, *n.pl.*, fastes, *m.pl.*

fastid′ious, *adj.*, dédaigneux ; difficile ; délicat ; (over nice) exigeant.

fastid′iously, *adv.*, dédaigneusement, d'un air dégoûté.

fastid′iousness, *n.*, dédain ; goût difficile, *m.*

fasti′giate *ou* **fasti′giated** (fas-tidj′iéte, -tède), *adj.*, (bot.) fastigié.

fast′ing (fåst′-), *n.*, jeûne, *m.*

fast′ing-day, *n.*, jour de jeûne, jour maigre, *m.*

fast′ness (fåst′-), *n.*, fermeté, solidité ; (fig.) sûreté ; (stronghold) place forte, forteresse, *f.*

fas′tuous (fåst′iou-), *adj.*, (ant.) dédaigneux ; hautain ; arrogant ; orgueilleux.

fat (fate), *n.*, gras, *m.* ; graisse ; (fig.) substance, *f.* To live on the — of the land ; *faire bonne chère.* To run to — ; *prendre de l'embonpoint.* To make — ; *engraisser.*

fat, *adj.*, gras ; gros ; riche ; fertile. A — living ; *un gros bénéfice.* — as a mole ; *gras comme un moine.*

fa′tal, *adj.*, fatal, funeste, mortel.

fa′talism, *n.*, fatalisme, *m.*

fa′talist, *n.*, fataliste, *m.*

fatal′ity, *n.*, fatalité, *f.*

fa′tally, *adv.*, fatalement, funestement (l.u.), mortellement.

fate (féte), *n.*, destin, sort, *m.* The —s ; *les Parques, f.pl.*

fa′ted (fét′ède), *adj.*, destiné, réglé par le destin ; écrit, dit. It was — to be ; *c'était écrit.*

fa′ther (få-theur), *n.*, père, *m.* *pl.*, pères ; ancêtres ; aïeux, *m.pl.* Grand— ; *grand-père, m.* God— ; *parrain, m.* Step— ; *beau-père, m.* —in-law ; *beau-père, m.* Almighty — ; *Père Eternel, m.* Holy — ; *Saint-Père, m.* The early —s ; *les Pères de l'Eglise ; les Pères, m.pl.* The wish is — to the thought ; (prov.) *on croit aisément ce qu'on désire.*

fa′ther, *v.a.*, adopter. To — upon ; *attribuer à ; prêter à, imputer à ; gratifier de.*

fa′therhood (-houde), *n.*, paternité, *f.*

fa′therland (-lä′nde), *n.*, pays natal, *m.*, patrie, *f.*

fa′therless, *adj.*, orphelin, sans père.

fa′therlessness, *n.*, état d'orphelin ; orphelinage (l.u.), *m.*

fa′therliness, *adj.*, amour paternel, *m.*

fa′therly, *adj.*, paternel ; de père.

fa′therly, *adv.*, paternellement ; en père.

fath′om (fa*th*′eume), *n.*, toise ; (fig.) portée, profondeur, *f.*

fath′om (fa*th*′eume), *v.a.*, sonder, embrasser ; approfondir ; pénétrer.

fath′omable (-′a-b′l), *adj.*, pénétrable, compréhensible.

fath′omless, *adj.*, sans fond, impénétrable ; insondable, incompréhensible.

fat′igable (-ga-b′l), *adj.*, (ant.) qui se fatigue aisément, fatigable.

fatigue′ (-tighe), *n.*, fatigue, lassitude, *f.* To stand — ; *supporter, endurer la fatigue.* To be worn out with — ; *n'en pouvoir plus de fatigue ; être rendu, être excédé de fatigue.* — duty, — party ; (mil.) corvée, *f.* — dress ; *tenue de corvée, f.*

fatigue′, *v.a.*, fatiguer, lasser.

fatig′uing, *adj.*, fatigant ; *pr.part.*, fatiguant.

fat′ling, *n.*, bête grasse, *f.*

fat′ness, *n.*, graisse, *f.* ; (pers.) embonpoint, *m.* ; (fig.) fertilité, abondance, *f.*

fat′ted, *adj.*, engraissé ; gras. The — calf ; *le veau gras.*

fat′ten (fat′t'n), *v.a.*, engraisser ; nourrir, alimenter ; enrichir.

fat′ten, *v.n.*, engraisser, s'engraisser ; (fig.) s'enrichir. To — on ; *s'engraisser de, s'enrichir de.*

fat′tener, *n.*, engraisseur, *m.*, -euse, *f.*

fat′tening, *adj.*, engraissant. *n.*, engraissement, *m.*

fat′tiness, *n.*, nature graisseuse, onctuosité, *f.*

fat′tish, *adj.*, un peu gras, grasset, grassouillet.

fat′ty, *adj.*, graisseux, huileux. — acids ; (chem.) *acides gras, m.pl.*

fatu′ity (fa-tiou-i-ti), *n.*, stupidité, imbécillité, sottise, *f.*

fat′uous (fat′-iou-eusse), *adj.*, (ant.) stupide, imbécile.

fat-wit′ted, *adj.*, imbécile, stupide.

fau′ces (fô-cize), *n.pl.*, (anat.) isthme du gosier ; gosier, *m.* ; trachée artère, *f.*

fau′cet (fô-cète), *n.*, canule (in a cask), cannelle, cannette, *f.*

faul′chion (fôl-sheune), *n.* V. **falchion**.

fault (fôlte), *n.*, faute, *f.* ; défaut, vice, péché, *m.* ; (geol.) faille, *f.* To find — with ; *trouver à redire à, trouver mauvais ; s'en prendre à.* At— ; *en défaut.* To a — ; *à l'excès ; par trop.* Whose — is it? *à qui la faute?* A — confessed is half redressed ; (prov.) *péché avoué est à demi pardonné.*

fault′-finder (-faï′n′deur), *n.*, personne qui trouve toujours à redire, *f.* ; censeur, critiqueur, épilogueur, *m.*

fault′-finding, *n.*, critique, censure, *f.*

fault′-finding, *adj.*, épilogueur.

fault′ily, *adv.*, d'une manière fautive, imparfaite ; défectueusement.

fault′iness, *n.*, défauts, *m.pl.* ; imperfections, *f.pl.* ; caractère fautif, *m.* ; imperfection ; nature vicieuse, *f.*

fault′less, *adj.*, sans défaut, sans faute ; parfait, irréprochable.

fault′lessly, *adv.*, irréprochablement.

fault′lessness, *n.*, perfection, *f.*

fault′y, *adj.*, en faute, coupable ; fautif, blâmable, erroné, défectueux.

fau′na (fô-), *n.*, faune, *f.*

fa′vor (fé-veur), *n.*, faveur ; permission ; grâce, *f.* ; (ribbons) couleurs, faveurs, *f.pl.* ; (com.) honorée ; (order) commande, *f.* To wear a — ; *porter des couleurs.* To ask a — of ; *demander une faveur à.* To be in — with ; *être dans les bonnes grâces de.* By — ; *par la faveur.* By — of, under — of ; *à la faveur de ; aux soins de.* Your — of the 3d instant ; (com.) *votre honorée du trois courant.* To find — with ; *trouver grâce, ou faveur, auprès de.* To get into — with ; *se rendre agréable à ; se faire aimer de.* To curry — with ; *flatter ; chercher à plaire à ; s'insinuer dans les bonnes grâces de.*

fa′vor, *v.a.*, favoriser de ; gratifier de ; honorer de.

fa′vorable, *adj.*, favorable.

fa′vorableness, *n.*, caractère favorable, *m.* ; bienveillance, *f.*

fa′vorably, *adv.*, favorablement.

fa′vored (fé-veurde), *adj.*, favorisé. Ill- — ; *laid, de mauvaise mine.* Well— ; *de bonne mine, beau, bien fait ;* (fig.) *bien partagé de.*

fa′vorer, *n.*, personne qui favorise, *f.* ; protecteur, partisan, *m.*

favorite (fé-veur′ite), *n.*, favori, *m.*, favorite, *f.* To be a great — ; *être très aimé de ; plaire beaucoup à ; être très populaire.*

fa′vorite (fé-veur-ite), *adj.*, favori, couru.

fa′voritism, *n.*, favoritisme, *m.*

fa′vorless, *adj.*, (ant.) non favorisé. — fortune ; *fortune contraire, f.*

fawn (fô′n), *n.*, (mam.) faon, *m.* ; (fig.) (pers.) caresse servile, basse flatterie ; (fig.) (of animals) caresse, *f.*

fawn, *v.n.*, (of animals) faonner. To — upon ; (animal) *caresser ;* (pers.) *caresser servilement, flatter, flagorner, cajoler, câliner.*

fawn′er, *n.*, flatteur servile ; flagorneur, cajoleur, *m.*

fawn′ing, *n.*, (of animals) caresse ; (pers.) caresse servile ; flatterie, flagornerie, *f.*

fawn′ingly, *adv.*, en caressant ; d'une manière caressante ; servilement.

fay (fé), *n.*, (ant.) fée ; foi, *f.* By my —; *par ma foi.*

fay, *v.a.*, (carp.) joindre ; affleurer.

fe′alty (fi-), *n.*, fidélité, constance, loyauté, *f.*

fear (fîre), *n.*, crainte, peur, inquiétude, *f.* ; respect, *m.* For — of ; *de peur* **de**, *de crainte* **de**. From —, out of — ; *par peur.* Bodily —; *crainte pour sa personne, pour ses jours.* To stand in — of ; *avoir peur* **de**. There is no — ; *il n'y a rien à craindre.* No — of that ! *il n'y a pas de danger, allez !*

fear, *v.a.*, craindre, redouter ; se méfier **de**.

fear, *v.n.*, craindre ; avoir peur, être craintif. Never — ! *soyez sans crainte ! ; soyez tranquille ! ; rassurez-vous !*

fear′ful (-foule), *adj.*, qui a peur ; craintif ; timide ; terrible ; affreux ; (of things) effrayant. To be — of ; *craindre, redouter.* To be — that ; *craindre que* (with subj. and *ne*).

fear′fully, *adv.*, craintivement ; avec crainte ; avec effroi ; terriblement ; d'une manière effrayante.

fear′fulness, *n.*, crainte, terreur, horreur, *f.*, effroi, *m.*

fear′less, *adj.*, sans peur ; intrépide ; sans crainte.

fear′lessly, *adv.*, sans peur, sans crainte, avec intrépidité.

fear′lessness, *n.*, intrépidité, *f.*

feasibil′ity, *n.*, possibilité d'exécution, praticabilité, *f.*

fea′sible (fi-zi'b'l), *adj.*, faisable, exécutable, praticable.

feast (fîste), *n.*, festin, *m.* ; fête, *f.* ; régal, *m.* Enough is as good as a — ; (prov.) *assez vaut un festin ou contentement passe richesse.* Nothing like a miser's — ; *il n'est chère que de vilain.*

feast, *v.a.*, faire fête **à** ; fêter, régaler, festoyer.

feast, *v.n.*, faire festin ; se régaler ; festiner. To — on ; (fig.) *se repaître* **de**.

feast′er, *n.*, (ant.) donneur de festins ; amateur de bonne chère, *m.*

feast′ful (-foule), *adj.*, (ant.) joyeux ; de fête.

feast′ing, *n.*, festin, régal, *m.*

feat, *n.*, action, *f.* ; explo.t ; fait, haut fait, tour d'adresse, tour de force, *m.*

feath′er (fèth′eur), *n.*, plume ; (bot.) aigrette ; (of a bird's wing and tail) penne, *f.* ; (milit.) plumet, *m.* ; (of horses) petite touffe de poils, *f.* ; épi, *m.* Bunch of —s ; *bouquet de plumes, m.* Birds of a — ; *gens de même acabit, ou de même pâte.* Prancing in full — ; *en piaffant.* Birds of a — flock together ; *qui se ressemble s'assemble.* A — in the cap ; *un honneur ; une distinction.* To be in high — ; *être gai ; être de bonne humeur ; triompher.* To show the white — ; *saigner du nez ; montrer le bout de l'oreille ; faire le capon ; caponner.* To cut a — ; *se mettre en évidence ; attirer l'attention.*

feath′er, *v.a.*, mettre des plumes **à** ; orner d'une plume ; empenner ; donner des ailes **à** ; (of birds) cocher ; (to enrich) enrichir. To — one's nest ; *faire son nid ; faire fortune ; faire ses foins ; s'enrichir ; mettre du foin dans ses bottes.*

feath′er-bed (-bède), *n.*, lit de plume, *m.*

feath′er-driver (-draïv′eur), *n.*, plumassier, nettoyeur de plumes, *m.*

feath′ered (fèth′eurde), *adj.*, garni de plumes, emplumé ; (of birds) ailé, emplumé ; (of arrows) empenné ; (fig.) enrichi.

feath′er-edged (-èdj′de), *adj.*, en biseau.

feath′er-grass (-grâce), *n.*, (bot.) stipe ; stipe empennée, houque molle, houlque molle, *f.*

feath′erless, *adj.*, (ant.) sans plumes.

feath′er-seller (-sèl′eur), *n.*, plumassier, *m.*

feath′er-trade (-tréde), *n.*, plumasserie, *f.*

feath′ery, *adj.*, garni de plumes, emplumé ; (bot.) plumeux ; (fig.) léger comme une plume ; (of birds) ailé, emplumé. — spray ; (of waterfalls) panache ; *bouquet de plumes fines, m.* ; *poussière d'argent, f.*

fea′ture (fît′ioure), *n.*, trait, *m.* ; figure, *f.* ; trait caractéristique, *m.*, partie saillante, forme, particularité, *f.* ; signe, point de vue, *m.* ; marque, *f.*

fea′tured (fît′iourde), *adj.*, qui a des traits. Hard— ; *aux traits durs.* Well — ; *beau, qui a de beaux traits.* Ill — ; *laid.*

fea′tureless, *adj.*, sans traits.

febri′citant, *adj.*, (med.) fébricitant, fiévreux.

feb′rifuge (fè-bri-fioud′je), *adj.*, fébrifuge.

feb′rifuge, *n.*, fébrifuge, *m.*

feb′rile *ou* **fe′brile** (fè-braïle *ou* fi-), *adj.*, fébrile.

Feb′ruary (fèb′rou-), *n.*, février, *m.*

fe′cal (fi-), *adj.*, fécal, excrémentitiel.

fo′ces (fî-cîze), *n.* V. **fæces**.

fe′cial (fî-shi-al), *adj.*, fécial.

fec′ula (fèk′iou-), *n.*, fécule, *f.* ; amidon, *m.*

fec′ulence *ou* **fec′ulency**, *n.*, (chem.) féculence, *f.*

fec′ulent, *adj.*, (ant.) féculent.

fec′und (fèc′un'n'd), *adj.*, (chem.) fécond.

fec′undate (-déte), *v.a.*, féconder.

fecunda′tion (-dé-), *n.*, fécondation, *f.*

fecun′dity, *n.*, fécondité, *f.*

fed′eral (fèd′eur-), *adj.*, fédéral.

fed′eralism, *n.*, fédéralisme, *m.*

fed′eralist, *n.*, fédéraliste, *m.*

fed′erate (-éte), *adj.*, ligué, fédéré.

fed′erate, *v.n.*, se fédérer.

federa′tion (-ré-), *n.*, fédération, alliance, ligue, *f.*

fed′erative (-ré-), *adj.*, fédératif.

fee (fî), *n.*, (feudalism) fief, *m.* ; (jur.) propriété héréditaire, *f.* ; salaire, *m.* ; gages, *m.pl.* ; (of doctors, etc.) honoraires, *m.pl.* ; (ant.) bétail, *m.* ; biens, *m.pl.* Surplice — ; (ecc.) *casuel, m.*

fee, *v.a.*, payer ; payer des honoraires **à** ; graisser la patte **à**, gagner à prix d'argent, corrompre, suborner ; tenir à ses gages ; (Scotch) louer.

fee′ble (fî'b'l), *adj.*, faible, débile, sans vigueur. To grow — ; *s'affaiblir.*

fee′ble-minded (-maï'n'dède), *adj.*, faible d'esprit, sans résolution, sans fermeté.

fee′bleness, *n.*, faiblesse, *f.* ; manque d'énergie, *m.*

fee′bly, *adv.*, faiblement.

feed (fîde), *n.*, nourriture ; (for cattle) pâture, pâturage, *m.* — of oats ; picotin d'avoine, *m.* To be off one's — ; *perdre l'appétit.*

feed (fîde), *v.a.*, (*pret.* and *p.p.*, Fed) nourrir ; (cattle) paître, faire paître ; (animal) donner à manger **à** ; nourrir, entretenir ; alimenter. He fed him with the hope of liberty ; *il le reput de l'espérance de la liberté.*

feed, *v.n.*, se nourrir ; (of animals) paître, manger. To — upon ; *se nourrir* **de** ; *se repaître* **de** ; (fig.) *se bercer* **de**.

feed′er, *n.*, personne qui nourrit, qui donne à manger, *f.* ; mangeur, convive ; (tech.) appareil d'alimentation, *m.* ; (of mills, etc.) trémie, *f.*

feed′ing, *n.*, nourriture ; (for cattle) pâture, *f.* — bottle ; *biberon, m.*

feel (fîle), *n.*, toucher ; attouchement ; tact, *m.*

feel, *v.a.*, (*preterit* and *past part.*, Felt), sentir ; tâter ; toucher ; palper ; éprouver ; ressentir ; se ressentir **de**. To — any one's pulse ; *tâter le pouls à quelqu'un.*

feel, *v.n.*, sentir ; se sentir ; chercher ; sympathiser **avec**. To — like ; *faire l'effet* **de**. To — for ; *avoir de la sympathie* **pour**. To — cold ;

avoir froid. To — soft ; *être doux au toucher.*
To — rough ; *être âpre, ou dur au toucher.* How
do you —? *comment vous sentez-vous ?*

feel'er, n., personne qui sent, *f. ;* (mol.) tentacule, *m. ;* (of a cat) moustache ; (ent.) palpe,
antenne ; (fig.) allusion détournée, *f. ;* ballon
d'essai, *m.*

feel'ing, n., attouchement, toucher, tact ;
sentiment, *m. ;* sensibilité, *f.* — of cold, of
warmth ; *sensation du froid, de la chaleur, f.* To
hurt a person's —s ; *froisser les sentiments de
quelqu'un.* To have no — ; *n'avoir pas de sensibilité, n'avoir pas d'entrailles.* Bad, *ou* ill, — ;
rancune, f., mauvais vouloir, ressentiment, m.

feel'ing, adj., tendre, touchant ; sensible à.
He spoke in a most — manner ; *il parla de la
manière la plus touchante.*

feel'ingly, adv., d'une manière touchante ;
d'une manière sensible ; sensiblement, avec attendrissement.

fee-sim'ple (fî-si'm'p'l), n., droit de propriété
absolu, (feudal) fief simple, franc-alleu, *m.*

feet (fîte), n.pl. V. **foot.**

feet'less, adj., sans pieds.

feign (féne), v.a., feindre, inventer, imaginer,
simuler ; dissimuler.

feign (féne), v.n., feindre ; dissimuler ; faire
semblant de.

feigned (fé'n'de), adj., feint, inventé ; dissimulé ; imaginé.

feign'edly, adv., avec feinte.

feign'ing, n., feinte ; dissimulation, *f.*

feign'ingly, adv., avec feinte.

feint (fé'n'te), n., feinte, *f.*

feld'spar *ou* **feld'spath** (fèld'spâr, -spath), n.,
(min.) feldspath, *m.*

feldspath'ic *ou* **feldspath'ose** (-spath'ik,
-spath'oze), adj., feldspathique.

feli'citate (fi-li-ci-téte), v.a., féliciter ; (ant.)
rendre heureux.

felicita'tion (fi-li-ci-té-), n., félicitation, *f.*

feli'citous (fi-), adj., heureux ; bien trouvé.

feli'citously, adv., heureusement, avec bonheur.

feli'city (fi-), n., félicité, *f. ;* bonheur, *m. ;*
convenance, propriété, *f.*

fe'line (fî-laïne), adj., félin ; de chat.

fell (fèle), n., peau, fourrure, *f.*

fell, adj., barbare, cruel, féroce, diabolique.

fell, v.a., abattre ; assommer ; terrasser ; renverser.

fell'er, n., personne qui abat, *f. ;* bûcheron, *m.*

fell'monger (-meu'gn'gheur), n., marchand
de peaux, peaussier, *m.*

fel'loe (fèl'lô), n., jante, *f.* V. **felly.**

fel'low (fèl'lô), n., compagnon ; camarade ;
membre ; garçon ; gaillard ; (b.s.) individu,
drôle ; (of a university) agrégé ; (of things) pendant, pareil, *m.* Bad — ; *mauvais garnement,
méchant drôle, mauvais sujet, m.* Good — ; *bon
enfant, bon diable, brave garçon, m.* Fine — ;
beau garçon, m. Coarse — ; *grossier personnage,
m.* Poor — ; *pauvre garçon, m.* Cunning — ;
rusé compère, fin matois, m. Odd — ; *drôle
de corps, m.* Odd— ; *membre d'une certaine
société de secours mutuels, m.* Mean — ; *individu méprisable, m.* Old — ; *vieux bonhomme, m.* Bed— ; *camarade de lit, m.*
School— ; *camarade de classe, m.* A very pleasant — ; *un charmant garçon.* Merry little — ;
gentil petit drôle, m. I say, you —s ! *dites donc,
vous autres !* You — ! *vous, l'ami.* — of the
Royal Society ; *membre (agrégé) de la Société
royale de Londres, m.* These shoes are not —s ;
ces souliers ne sont pas pareils. To be hail —
well met with ; *se traiter de pair à compagnon.*
Here is the — to this picture ; *voici le pendant
de ce tableau.* The poor — ! *le pauvre homme !*

fel'low, v.a., assortir ; associer ; s'accorder
avec, s'assortir avec.

fel'low-cit'izen, n., concitoyen, *m. ;* -ne, *f.*

fel'low-cit'izenship (-), n., concitoyenneté, *f.*

fel'low-coun'selor, n., collègue au conseil, *m.*

fel'low-crea'ture (-krît-ioure), n., semblable,
m.f.

fel'low-feel'ing, n., sympathie, *f. ;* esprit de
corps ; intérêt commun, *m.* A — makes us wondrous kind ; *la sympathie* (ou *l'intérêt commun*)
rapproche les gens.

fel'low-heir (-ère), n., cohéritier, *m.*

fel'low-help'er (-hèlp'eur), n., coadjuteur,
m., aide, *m.f.*

fel'low-la'borer (-lé-beur'eur), n., collaborateur, camarade, compagnon de travail, *m.*

fel'low-like (-laïke) *ou* **fel'lowly** (ant.), adj.,
sociable, en égal.

fel'low-pris'oner, n., compagnon de captivité, codétenu, coaccusé.

fel'low-serv'ant (-seur-) n., compagnon de
service, camarade, *m.*

fel'lowship, n., société, confraternité, *f. ;* (in
universities) grade d'agrégé, *m. ;* (arith.) règle
de société, règle de compagnie, *f.*

fel'low-sol'dier (-sôl'djeu'r), n., frère
d'armes, *m.*

fel'low-stu'dent (-stiou'-), n., condisciple, *m.*

fel'low-suf'ferer, n., compagnon d'infortune,
m.

fel'low-towns'man, n., concitoyen, *m.*

fel'low-trav'eler, n., compagnon de voyage,
m.

fel'ly (fèl'li), n., jante, *f.*

fe'lo-de-se (fîlô-di-cî), n., (jur.) suicidé, suicide, *m.*

fel'on (fèl'o'n), n., auteur d'un délit, d'un
crime, d'un crime capital ; criminel ; (med.)
panaris, *m.*

fel'on, adj., félon, traître ; inhumain ; cruel.

felo'nious, adj., félon, traître perfide ; (jur.)
criminel.

felo'niously, adv., en traître ; (jur.) avec une
intention criminelle.

fel'ony, n., (jur.) délit, crime, crime capital, *m.*

felt (fèlte), n., feutre, chapeau de feutre, *m.*

felt *ou* **fel'ter,** v.a., feutrer.

felt'ing, n., feutrage, *m.*

feluc'ca (fé-leuk'ka), n., felouque, *f.*

fe'male (fî-méle), n., femme ; personne ;
jeune personne ; (of animals only) femelle, *f.*

fe'male, adj., féminin ; de femme ; (bot., and
of animals) femelle. A — friend ; *une amie.*
A — poor relative ; *une parente pauvre.* —
penitentiary ; *maison centrale pour les femmes, f.*

feme-cov'ert *ou* **femme-cov'ert** (fè'm'keuv'-
eurte), n., (jur.) femme en puissance de mari, *f.*

feme'sole *ou* **femme'-sole** (fè'm'sôle), n.,
(jur.) fille, *f.*, femme non-mariée, *f.*

fem'inacy *ou* **feminal'ity** (fè'm'i-), n., (ant.)
nature de femme, *f.*

fem'inine (fè'm-i-), adj., féminin ; efféminé.
In the — gender ; (gram.) *au féminin.*

fem'ininely, adv., (ant.) comme une femme,
en femme.

fem'oral (fè'm'o-), adj., fémoral ; crural.

fen (fè'n), n., marais, marécage, *m.* — fire ;
feu follet, m. — cricket ; (ent.) *courtilière, f.*

fence (fè'n'ce), n., clôture, enceinte, palissade,
barrière, balustrade ; (art of fencing) escrime,
(fig.) défense, *f.* To sit on the — ; (fig.) *ne pas
s'engager à une opinion de part ou d'autre ; menager la chèvre et le chou.*

fence, v.a., enclore ; mettre une clôture à ;
mettre une enceinte à ; protéger, défendre. To
— in ; *enclore.*

fence, v.n., faire des clôtures ; (with foils)
faire des armes, tirer des armes.

fence'less, adj., ouvert ; sans clôture, sans
défense.

fen'cer, n., tireur d'armes, (man.) sauteur, *m.*

fen'cible (fè'n'-ci'b'l), adj., capable de défense.

fen'cibles, *n.pl.*, miliciens, *m.pl.*, (soldats pour la défense du territoire, lesquels ne peuvent être envoyés à l'étranger).

fen'cing, *n.*, enceinte, clôture ; (with foils) escrime, *f.*

fen'cing-glove, *n.*, gant bourré, *m.*

fen'cing-mas'ter (-mâs-teur), *n.*, maître d'armes, maître d'escrime, *m.*

fen'cing-match, *n.*, assaut d'armes, *m.*

fen'cing-pad, *n.*, plastron, *m.*

fen'cing-school (-skoule), *n.*, salle d'armes, salle d'escrime, *f.*

fen'cing-shoe, *n.*, sandale d'armes, *f.*

fend (fè'n'd), *v.a.*, (ant.) se défendre de. — off ; *parer ; écarter ; détourner.*

fend'er, *n.*, garde-feu, *m. ;* (nav.) défense, *f.*

fen'nel (fè'n'nèl), *n.*, (bot.) fenouil ; aneth doux, *m.*

fen'nish (ant.) *ou* **fen'ny** (fè'n'-), *adj.*, marécageux, des marais.

fen'ugreek (fè-niou-grîke), *n.*, (bot.) fenugrec, *m. ;* trigonelle, *f.*

feoff (fèfe), *v.a.*, (ant.) investir d'un fief ; donner l'investiture à ; (fig.) douer.

feof'fee (fèf'fî), *n.*, personne investie d'un héritage foncier, *f.*

feoff'ment (fèf-), *n.*, (ant.) inféodation, *f. ;* investiture d'un héritage foncier, *f.*

fer'ial (fîr-), *adj.*, férial, férié.

fer'ment (feur-), *n.*, ferment, *m. ;* fermentation, *f.* In a — ; *en rumeur* (V. Hugo).

fer'ment, *v.n.*, fermenter.

fer'ment, *v.a.*, faire fermenter.

ferment'able (-'a-b'l), *adj.*, fermentescible.

fermenta'tion (feur-mè'n-té-), *n.*, fermentation, *f.*

fermen'tative, *adj.*, fermentatif ; de fermentation.

fermen'tativeness, *n.*, qualité de ce qui est fermentatif, *f.*

fern (feurne), *n.*, (bot.) fougère, *f.* — brake ; *fougeraie, f.* — stand ; *jardinière à fougères, f.*

fern'y, *adj.*, plein de fougères ; couvert de fougères.

fero'cious (fi-rô-sheusse), *adj.*, féroce.

fero'ciously, *adv.*, avec férocité.

fero'ciousness *ou* **feroc'ity**, *n.*, férocité, *f.*

fer'reous (fèr-ri-), *adj.*, ferrugineux.

fer'ret (fèr'rète), *n.*, (mam.) furet, *m. ;* (tape) padou, *m.*

fer'ret, *v.a.*, fureter. To — out ; *traquer, dépister, dénicher ;* (fig.) *découvrir, éventer.*

fer'ret, *v.n.*, chasser au furet, fureter.

fer'reter, *n.*, fureteur ; (fig.) fureteur, *m.*

fer'riage (fè'ri-édge), *n.*, pontonnage, prix du passage dans un bac, *m.*

ferrif'erous (fèr'rif-eur'-), *adj.*, (geol.) ferrifère.

fer'rous, *adj.*, ferreux.

fer'ru'ginated (fèr'rou'djinétède), *adj.*, ayant les propriétés *ou* la couleur de la rouille ; ferrugineux.

ferru'gineous *ou* **ferru'ginous** (fer'roudji-n'-), *adj.*, ferrugineux.

fer'rule (fèr-ril *ou* fèr'reule), *n.*, (ring) virole, *f.*

fer'ry, *v.a.*, passer dans un bac. To — over, to — across ; *passer dans un bac ;* (ant.) *porter, transporter.*

fer'ry-boat (-bôte), *n.*, bac ; barque, nacelle, *f.*

fer'ry-man (-ma'n), *n.*, passeur, *m. ;* (poet.) nocher, nautonier, *m.*

fer'tile (feur'til), *adj.*, fertile, fécond.

fer'tilely, *adv.*, abondamment ; fertilement.

fer'tileness *ou* **fertil'ity**, *n.*, fertilité, *f.*

fer'tilize (-aîze), *v.a.*, fertiliser.

fer'ula (fèr'iou-) *ou* **fer'ule** (fèr'eule), *n.*, (bot.) férule, *f. ;* (of the Eastern empire) sceptre impérial, *m. ;* (a cane) férule, *f.*

fer'vency (feur'vè'n-), *n.*, ardeur, ferveur, *f.*

fer'vent, *adj.*, vif, ardent ; fervent.

fer'vently, *adv.*, ardemment, avec ferveur.

fer'vid (feur-), *adj.*, ardent, chaud, vif, brûlant.

fer'vidly, *adv.*, avec chaleur ; ardemment.

fer'vidness, *n.*, chaleur, ardeur, *f.*

fer'vor (feur-veur), *n.*, chaleur ; ferveur, ardeur, *f.*

fes'cennine (-naïne), *adj.*, (archæol.) fescennin ; licencieux.

fes'cennine, *n.sing.*, vers fescennins, *m.pl.*

fes'cue (fès'kiou), *n.*, (ant.) touche, *f.*, (pour montrer les lettres aux enfants qui apprennent à lire).

fesse, *n.*, (her.) fasce, *f.*

fes'tal, *adj.*, de fête.

fes'ter (fès'teur), *v.n.*, s'ulcérer ; se corrompre ; s'envenimer.

fes'ter, *n.*, abcès, *m.*, tumeur, *f.*

fes'tival, *adj.*, de fête, joyeux, gai.

fes'tival, *n.*, fête, *f. ;* festival, *m.*

fes'tive *ou* **fes'tivous**, *adj.*, de fête ; joyeux.

festiv'ity, *n.*, fête ; gaîté, joie, réjouissance, *f.*

festoon' (-toune), *n.*, feston, *m.*

festoon', *v.a.*, festonner (with de).

fetch (fètshe), *n.*, ruse ; finesse, *f. ;* tour, stratagème, *m.*

fetch, *v.a.*, chercher ; aller chercher ; amener ; apporter ; (of price) rapporter, valoir ; se vendre à ; (one's breath) prendre, reprendre ; (a pump) amorcer ; (a sigh) pousser ; (a blow) porter. To — away ; *emporter, emmener.* To — down ; *faire descendre, descendre, abaisser ;* (fig.) *rabattre, humilier.* To — back ; *rapporter ; ramener.* To — in ; *faire entrer, rentrer, amener.* To — off ; *ôter, enlever, emporter, emmener.* To — out ; *faire sortir, aller chercher.* To — up ; *faire monter, monter, atteindre, rattraper, rejoindre.* These goods — a great deal ; *cette marchandise rapporte beaucoup.*

fetch, *v.n.*, se mouvoir. To — and carry for any one ; *obéir à quelqu'un au doigt et à l'œil ;* (of dogs) rapporter.

fetch'er, *n.*, chercheur, *m.*, chercheuse, *f. ;* (of dogs) rapporteur.

fe'tich, *n.*, fétiche, *m.*

fe'ticism *ou* **fe'tichism**, *n.*, fétichisme, *m.*

fet'id, *adj.*, fétide.

fet'idness, *n.*, fétidité, *f.*

fet'lock (fèt'-), *n.*, fanon (du cheval), *m.*

fet'ter (fèt'teur), *v.a.*, mettre dans les fers ; enchaîner ; (fig.) entraver. To — a horse ; *entraver un cheval.*

fet'terless, *adj.*, sans fers ; libre ; sans entraves.

fet'ters (fèt'teurze), *n.*, fers, *m.pl.*, chaînes ; (of a horse) entraves, *f.pl.*

fet'tle (fèt't'l), *v.n.*, être occupé à épousseter et à ranger. Pretend to — about the room ; *ayez l'air d'épousseter les meubles et de mettre chaque chose à sa place.*

fet'tle, *n.*, bonne condition, *f.*, bon état, *m.*

fe'tus (fî-), *n.*, (*fetuses*) fœtus, *m.*

feud (fioude), *n.*, fief, *m. ;* (quarrel) brouillerie, querelle ; inimitié, dissension, *f.*

feu'dal, *adj.*, féodal.

feu'dalism, *n.*, féodalité, *f.*

feudal'ity, *n.*, féodalité, *f.*

feu'datory, *n.*, feudataire, *m.*

feu'datory, *adj.*, feudataire, qui relève d'un seigneur.

feu'dist, *n.*, feudiste, *m.*

feuillemort', *n.*, (color) feuille-morte, *m. ;* couleur feuille-morte, *f.* (*Invariable ; not used in plural.*)

fe'ver (fî-veur), *n.*, fièvre, *f.* Fit of — ; *accès de fièvre, m.* Burning — ; *fièvre ardente.* Intermittent — ; *fièvre intermittente.* Tertian — ; *fièvre tierce.* Scarlet — ; *fièvre scarlatine.* Typhoid — ; *fièvre typhoïde.* Milk — ; *fièvre de lait.* Miliary — ; *suette miliaire, f.* To be in a

—; *avoir la fièvre ;* (fig.) *être dans une grande agitation.*

fe'ver, *v.a.,* (ant.) donner la fièvre à.

fe'verfew (-fiou), *n.,* (bot.) pyrèthre, *m. ;* matricaire, *f.*

fe'ver-hospital, *n.,* hôpital de fiévreux, *m.*

fe'verish, *adj.,* fiévreux ; fébrile ; brûlant.

fe'verishness, *n.,* indisposition fébrile ; (fig.) fièvre, *f. ;* enfièvrement, *m.*

fe'ver-stricken, *adj.,* atteint de la fièvre.

few (fiou), *adj.,* peu **de** ; peu de gens. A —; *peu de* ; *quelques ; quelques-uns,* *n., quelques-unes, f.* — people think thus ; *peu de gens pensent ainsi.* Give me a — of these pears ; *donnez-moi quelques-unes de ces poires.* One of the — good ministers ; *un des rares bons ministres.* A good —; *un nombre considérable.* Not a —; *pas mal de* ; *bon nombre* **de.**

few'er, *adj.,* moins nombreux, en plus petit nombre ; moins.

few'est, *adj.,* le plus petit nombre **de** ; le moins possible **de.**

few'ness, *n.,* petit nombre, *m. ;* petite quantité, *f.*

fi'at (faï-), *n.,* ordre, commandement, décret, *m.*

fib, *n.,* conte, mensonge, *m. ;* menterie, *f.*

fib. *v.n.,* mentir ; faire des contes.

fib'ber, *n.,* menteur, *m.,* menteuse, *f. ;* faiseur de contes, *m.,* faiseuse de contes, *f.*

fi'ber *ou* **fi'bre** (faï-beur), *n.,* fibre, *f.*

fi'bril (faï-bril), *n.,* (anat., bot.) fibrille, *f.*

fibril'lous, *adj.,* (anat., bot.) fibrilleux.

fi'brous (faï-), *adj.,* fibreux.

fib'ula (fi-biou-), *n.,* (anat.) péroné, *m. ;* (surg.) aiguille (qui sert à coudre les lèvres d'une plaie), *f. ;* (ordinary language) fermoir, *m.,* broche, *f.*

fic'kle (fik'k'l), *adj.,* volage, inconstant, changeant. A — light ; *une lumière incertaine, vacillante.*

fic'kleness, *n.,* inconstance, légèreté ; instabilité, *f.*

fic'tile (fik'til), *adj.,* fait d'argile ; plastique ; (of pottery) céramique. — earth ; *terre à potier ; argile plastique, f.*

fic'tion (fik'sheune), *n.,* fiction, fable, *f.* Works of —; *ouvrages de l'esprit, romans, m.pl.*

ficti'tious (-tish'eusse), *adj.,* fictif ; imaginaire, allégorique, faux, supposé ; (fig.) factice.

ficti'tiously, *adv.,* fictivement.

ficti'tiousness, *n.,* caractère fictif, *m.*

fid, *n.,* (nav.) épissoir, *m. ;* (of a mast) clef, *f.*

fid'dle, *n.,* violon, *m.* To play second — to ; (fig.) *jouer le second rôle* auprès **de.**

fid'dle, *v.n.,* jouer du violon ; (to trifle) baguenauder, niaiser. To be always fiddling ; *être toujours à baguenauder, à niaiser ; perdre son temps à des riens.*

fid'dle, *v.a.,* jouer un air sur le violon.

fid'dle-bow, *n.,* archet, *m.*

fid'dle-de-dee', *int.,* allons donc ; laissez donc !

fid'dle-faddle, *n.,* (pop.) fadaise ; niaiserie ; faribole ; sornette, *f.*

fid'dle-faddle, *adj.,* (pop.) qui s'occupe de fadaises, de niaiseries, de sornettes.

fid'dle-pattern, *n.,* (of spoons, etc.) couvert violon, *m.*

fid'dler, *n.,* joueur de violon ; ménétrier, *m.*

fid'dle-stick, *n.,* archet de violon, *m. ;* (nonsense) fadaise ; baliverne, *f.* —s ! *tarare ! allons donc ! quelle blague !*

fid'dle-string (-strigne), *n.,* corde de violon, *f.*

fid'dle-wood (-woude), *n.,* (bot.) bétoine aquatique, herbe-du-siège, *f.*

fid'dling, *n.,* action de jouer du violon, *f.*

fid'dling, *adj.,* frivole.

fidejus'sor (faï-di-djeuss'eur), *n.,* (jur.) fidéjusseur, *m.*

fidel'ity, *n.,* fidélité, *f.*

fidg'et (fidjète), *v.n.,* se remuer ; se tourmenter ; frétiller, gigoter, s'agiter.

fidg'et, *n.,* mouvement ; tourment, *m. ;* inquiétude, agitation, *f. ;* (of persons) mouvement perpétuel, être remuant, *m.* What a — you are ! *quel tourment vous êtes !; comme vous vous tourmentez !; quel mouvement perpétuel vous faites !* I have the —s ; *je ne puis tenir en place ; je suis sur les épines ; j'ai la puce à l'oreille.*

fidg'ety, *adj.,* remuant, inquiet ; (troublesome) tracassier, impatient, ennuyeux.

fidu'ciary (fi-diou-shi-), *adj.,* fiduciaire.

fidu'ciary, *n.,* fiduciaire, *m.*

fie ! (faïe), *int.,* fi !; fi donc ! — for shame !; *fi l'horreur !* — on ... ! *fi* **de ...** !

fief (fîfe), *n.,* fief, *m.*

field (fîlde), *n.,* champ, *m. ;* campagne, *f. ;* (fig.) champ, *m.,* carrière, *f.* — of battle ; *champ de bataille, m.* In the open —s ; *en pleins champs.* On the —; *sur le terrain* (dueling). In the —; (mil.) *en campagne.* To take the —; (milit.) *se mettre en campagne.*

field'-artillery, *n.* artillerie de campagne, *f.*

field'-bed (-bède), *n.,* lit de camp, *m.*

field'-colors (-keul'leurze), *n.pl.,* (milit.) guidon, fanion, *m.sing.*

field'-day, *n.,* (milit.) jour de revue, *m.,* revue, *f.*

field'fare (-fère), *n.,* (orni.) litorne, *f.*

field'-glass, *n.,* jumelles de campagne, *f.pl.*

field'-marshal (-mâr-), *n.,* maréchal, *m.*

field'-mouse (-maouce), *n.,* mulot, *m.*

field'-officer, *n.,* officier supérieur, *m.*

field'-piece (-pîce), *n.,* pièce de campagne, *f.*

field'-practice, *n.,* grandes manœuvres, *f.pl.*

field'-sports, *n.pl.,* sport, *m. ;* exercices en plein air, *m.pl.*

field'-staff (-stâfe), *n.,* (milit.) boutefeu, *m.*

field'-surgeon, *n.* chirurgien d'ambulance, *m.*

field'-works, *n.,* (fort.) travaux, *m.pl. ;* défenses érigées par une armée assiégeante, *f.pl.*

fiend (fî'n'de), *n.,* esprit malin ; démon, *m.* — like ; *diabolique, infernal.*

fiend'ish, *adj.,* diabolique, satanique, infernal.

fiend'ishness, *n.,* méchanceté infernale, *f.*

fierce (fîrce), *adj.,* féroce, farouche, furieux, violent.

fierce'ly, *adv.,* férocement ; furieusement.

fierce'ness, *n.,* férocité ; ardeur ; fureur ; violence ; impétuosité, *f.*

fi'eriness (faïeur'-), *n.,* fougue, ardeur, *f.,* emportement, *m.*

fi'ery, *adj.,* de feu ; ardent, fougueux, emporté ; bouillant.

fife (faïfe), *n.,* fifre, *m.*

fife, *v.n.,* jouer du fifre.

fi'fer, *n.,* fifre, joueur de fifre, *m.*

fifteen' (fif'tîne), *adj.,* quinze.

fifteenth' (fif'tî'n'th), *adj.,* quinzième.

fifteenth', *n.,* quinzième, *m. ;* (mus.) quinzième ; double octave, *f. ;* (of the days of the month) quinze.

fifteenth'ly, *adv.* quinzièmement.

fifth (fif'th), *adj.,* cinquième ; cinq. Charles the —; *Charles-Quint* (of Spain). Pope Sixtus the —; *le pape Sixte-Quint.*

fifth, *n.,* cinquième, *m. ;* (mus.) quinte, *f.*

fifth'ly, *adv.,* cinquièmement.

fif'tieth (fif-ti-èth), *adj.,* cinquantième.

fif'ty, *adj.,* cinquante. About —; *une cinquantaine.* — fold ; *cinquante fois.*

fig, *n.,* figue, *f. ;* (tree) figuier, *m.* A — for ! *foin* **de** !; *nargue* **de** !; *fi* **de** !; *au diable avec* ! Not to care a — for ; *ne pas se soucier d'un fétu* **de** ; *se moquer* **de.** In full —; *en grande toilette, f.* (milit.) *en grande tenue.*

fig'-eater (-ît'eur), *n.,* (orni.) becfigue, *m.*

fig'-garden (-gârd'n), *n.,* figuerie, *f.*

fig'-house (-haouce), *n.,* serre à figuiers, *f.*

fig'-leaf, *n.,* feuille de figuier, *f.*

fight (faïte), *v.n.*, (*preterit* and *past part.*, Fought), se battre ; combattre ; se combattre. To — shy of any one ; *se méfier de quelqu'un ; éviter quelqu'un.* To — hard ; *se battre avec acharnement.*

fight, *v.a.*, se battre **avec** ; combattre ; combattre **contre** ; défendre ; (a battle) livrer. To — a question ; *débattre une question.* To — a point ; *discuter un point de droit.* To — cocks ; *faire combattre des coqs.* To — a battle out ; *soutenir un combat.* To show — ; *montrer les dents.* To — one's way ; *se frayer un chemin à travers* (fig.) *faire son chemin (en dépit des obstacles).* To — it out ; *lutter jusqu'au bout ; vider une querelle les armes à la main.* To — a battle ; *livrer bataille.* To — the battles of one's country ; *combattre pour son pays.* The battle was obstinately fought ; *la bataille fut obstinée.* To — another man's battles ; *prendre la défense de quelqu'un.*

fight, *n.*, combat, *m. ;* bataille, lutte, *f.*

fight'er, *n.*, combattant ; (b.s.) batailleur, bretteur, ferrailleur, *m.* Prize— ; *boxeur de profession, pugiliste, m.*

fight'ing, *adj.*, qui combat ; (of things) de combat. — men ; *combattants, hommes de guerre, m.pl.* — field ; *champ de bataille, m.*

fight'ing, *n.*, combat, *m. ;* combats, *m.pl.*, lutte, *f.* Prize— ; *combat de boxeurs ; pugilat, m.*

fig'-marigold (-gôlde), *n.*, ficoïde, glaciale, *f.*

fig'ment (-mè'n'te), *n.*, (ant.) fiction, invention, fable, *f. ;* mensonge, *m.*

fig'-orchard (-tsharde), *n.*, figuerie, *f.*

fig'pecker (-pèk'eur), *n.*, (orni.) becfigue, *m.*

fig'-tree (-trî), *n.*, figuier, *m.*

figurabil'ity (figh'iou-), *n.*, (ant.) figurabilité, *f.*

fig'urable, *adj.*, (ant.) susceptible de recevoir une forme, une figure ; figurable.

fig'urant (figh'iou-), *n.*, (thea.) figurant, *m.*, figurante, *f.*

fig'urate (-réte), *adj.*, (ant.) qui a une forme, une figure ; (math., mus.) figuré. — stones ; *pierres figurées, f.pl.* — numbers ; *figurés, m. pl.*

fig'urated (-rétède), *adj.*, (ant.) formé ; figuré ; ayant une forme déterminée.

figura'tion (-ré-), *n.*, (ant.) configuration, *f. ;* type, *m.*, figure ; (mus.) figure, *f.*

fig'urative (-ré-), *adj.*, figuratif ; figuré, typique, allégorique, métaphorique. In a — sense ; *au figuré.*

fig'uratively, *adv.*, figurément ; au figuré ; figurativement.

fig'urativeness, *n.*, caractère métaphorique ; caractère symbolique, *f.*

fig'ure (figh'ioure), *n.*, figure ; forme, taille, tournure, mine, *f.;* air, *m.;* (of stuffs) dessin, *m.;* (arith.) chiffre, *m.* What a — you are ! *comme vous voilà fagoté, ou arrangé !* ; *comme vous voilà fait !* To cut a — ; *faire figure ; trancher du grand ; jeter de la poudre aux yeux.* Academical —; *académie, f.* — of speech ; *façon de parler, f.*

fig'ure, *v.a.*, figurer, façonner ; représenter, former ; imaginer. To — to one's self ; *se figurer, s'imaginer.*

fig'ured (figh'iour'de), *adj.*, à dessin ; façonné, ouvragé ; (ant.) métaphorique.

fig'ure-drawing, *n.*, dessin de figure, *m.*

fig'ure-head (-hède), *n.*, (nav.) figure, *f. ;* buste à l'avant d'un navire, (fig.) mannequin, *m.*

fig'urist (figh'iour'-), *n.*, (ant.) figuriste, *m.*

fig'wort (-weurte), *n.*, (bot.) scrofulaire ; herbe aux écrouelles, bétoine aquatique ; ficaire, *f.*

fila'ceous (-lé-sheusse), *adj.*, (ant.) filamenteux.

fil'ament (-), *n.*, filament ; (bot.) filet, filament, *m.*

filamen'tous, *adj.*, filamenteux.

fil'bert (-beurte), *n.*, aveline, noisette, *f.*

fil'bert-orchard (-tsharde), *n.*, coudraie, coudrette, *f.*

fil'bert-tree (-trî), *n.*, coudrier, avelinier, *m.*

filch (filshe), *v.a.*, escamoter, filouter, voler, chiper.

filch'er, *n.*, filou, voleur, fripon, escroc, *m.*

file (faïle), *n.*, (tool) lime, *f. ;* (of papers) liasse, *f.*, dossier, pique-notes, *m. ;* (list) liste ; (of newspapers) collection ; (milit.) file, (theat.) queue, *f.* Cunning — ; *fin matois, m.* Cunning old — ; *vieux renard, m.* On — ; *en liasse.* Left —! (mil.) *par file à gauche !* Right —! *par file à droite !* To stand in — ; *faire queue.*

file, *v.a.*, limer ; enfiler ; (newspapers) **faire** une collection **de** ; mettre en liasse ; (jur.) produire ; (a schedule) déposer. To — off ; *limer, polir.*

file, *v.n.*, (milit.) marcher sur un rang. To — off *ou* past ; *défiler.*

file'-cutter (-keut'-), *n.*, tailleur de limes, *f.*

file'cutting, *n.*, taille des limes, *f.*

file'-firing, *n.*, feu de file, *m.*

file'-leader (-lîd'-), *n.*, (milit.) chef de file, *m.*

fi'ler, *n.*, limeur, *m.*

fil'ial, *adj.*, filial.

fil'ially, *adv.*, filialement.

filia'tion (fil-i-é-), *n.*, (ant.) filiation, *f. ;* (jur.) recherche de la paternité, *f.*

fil'ibuster, *n.*, flibustier, *m.*

fil'ibuster, *v.n.*, faire le flibustier.

fil'iform, *adj.*, filiforme.

fil'igrane (fil'i-grêne) *ou* **fil'igree** (fil'i-grî), *n.*, filigrane, *m.*

fil'igraned (-gré'n'de) *ou* **fil'igreed** (-grîde), *adj.*, à filigrane.

fil'ing, *n.*, limage, *m.*, limure, *f. ;* (of papers) mise en liasse, *f. ;* classement, *m.* — off ; *défilé, m. ;* défilade, *f.*

fi'lings (faïl'ign'ze), *n.pl.*, limaille, *f.sing.*

fill, *n.*, suffisance, *f. ;* soûl, content, *m.*

fill, *v.a.*, emplir, remplir ; rassasier, combler ; (to occupy) occuper, remplir. To — up ; *remplir, combler.* To — a pipe ; *bourrer une pipe.* To — a tooth ; *plomber une dent.* The wind — s the sails ; *le vent gonfle les voiles.* To — up a vacancy in an office ; *pourvoir à un office, à un emploi.* To — up the time ; *employer le temps à.* To — in (insert) ; *insérer.*

fill, *v.n.*, se remplir, s'emplir. To — out ; *verser ; gonfler, se gonfler, s'enfler ;* (to get stout) *prendre de l'embonpoint ;* (fig.) *amplifier.*

fill'er, *n.*, personne qui remplit, *f.*, (tech.) chargeur, remplissage, cheval limonier ; limonier, *m.*

fil'let (-lète), *n.*, bandeau ; (bot.) filet ; (anat.) frein, filet ; (of coin) lame, *f. ;* (arch.) astragale, filet, *m.* — of veal ; *rouelle de veau, f.* — of beef ; *filet de bœuf, m.* — steak ; *chateaubriand, m.*

fil'let, *v.a.*, nouer, *ou* ceindre, d'un bandeau ; (arch.) orner d'un filet.

fill'ing, *n.*, action de remplir ; chose pour remplir, *f. ;* remplissage ; (of teeth) plombage, *m.* — up stuff ; *remplissage, m.*

fill'ing, *adv.*, qui remplit ; rassasiant.

fil'lip (fil'lipe), *n.*, chiquenaude, *f. ;* (fig.) coup de fouet, *m.;* ce qui sert à exciter le courage (fig.). To give a — to ; *ragaillardir* (Molière).

fil'lip, *v.a.*, donner une chiquenaude à ; chiquenauder ; (fig.) encourager.

fil'ly (fil'li), *n.*, pouliche ; (fig.) coquette, *f.*

film, *n.*, (bot.) pellicule ; (anat.) tunique ; (med.) taie, *f.;* (fig.) nuage, voile, *m.;* (photography) couche, pellicule, *f.*

film, *v.a.*, couvrir d'une tunique, d'une pellicule.

fil'my, *adj.*, membraneux.

fil'ter, *n.*, filtre, couloir, *m.*

fil'ter, *v.a.*, filtrer.

fil'tering, *adj.*, filtrant.

fil'tering-machine, *n.*, filtre, *m,*

filth (filth), *n.*, ordure, saleté ; (fig.) corruption, *f.* ; langage obscène, *m.*

filth'ily (-thi-), *adv.*, salement.

filth'iness (-thi-), *n.*, saleté, *f.* ; ordures, *f.pl.* ; (fig.) corruption, *f.*

filth'y (-thi), *adj.*, sale, dégoûtant ; (fig.) corrompu, ignoble, impur ; honteux, obscène.

fil'trate (-tréte), *v.a.*, filtrer.

filtra'tion (-tré-), *n.*, filtration, *f.*

fim'briate (-éte), *adj.*, (bot.) frangé, bordé.

fim'briate, *v.a.*, franger, border.

fim'briated (-étéde), *adj.*, (her.) bordé.

fin (fine), *n.*, (ich.) nageoire, *f.* ; (of flatfish) barbes, *f.pl.* ; (of whales) fanon, *m.* — like ; *en forme de nageoire.*

fi'nable (faï'n'a'b'l), *adj.*, passible d'amende ; (of things) punissable d'une amende.

fi'nal (faï-), *adj.*, final, dernier, définitif, décisif.

fina'le (fi-nâ-li), *n.*, (mus.) finale, *m.* ; (quadrille) finale, *f.*

fi'nally (faï-), *adv.*, enfin, finalement ; définitivement, en dernier lieu.

finance' *ou* **finan'ces**, *n.*, finance, *f.* ; finances, *f.pl.*

finan'cial (-shial), *adj.*, financier.

finan'cially, *adv.*, en matière de finances.

financier' (-cîre), *n.*, financier.

finch (fi'n'she), *n.*, (orni.) pinson, *m.*

find (faï'n'de), *v.a.*, (*preterit and past part.* Found), trouver ; (jur.) (guilty) déclarer ; (verdict) rendre, prononcer ; (to deem) juger, penser, croire, estimer. To — fault with ; *trouver mauvais ; trouver à redire à.* To — in ; *pourvoir de.* To — out ; *découvrir ; résoudre ; démasquer.* To — it necessary to ; *reconnaître ; se trouver dans la nécessité de ; se voir obligé de.*

find'er, *n.*, trouveur, *m.*, trouveuse, *f.* ; inventeur, *m.*, inventrice, *f.*

find'ing, *n.*, découverte, trouvaille, *f.* ; (jur.) jugement, *m.*, déclaration, *f.* ; verdict, *m.* —s is keepings ; (prov.) *ce qui est bon à prendre est bon à garder* (Beaumarchais).

fine (faïne), *adj.*, fin, délicat ; subtil ; (handsome) beau ; (fig.) bon, accompli, élégant. It is —; (of the weather) *il fait beau.* That is all very —, but ; *tout cela est bel et bon, mais.* — clothes do not fill stomach ; (prov.) *la belle cage ne nourrit pas l'oiseau.* — feathers make — birds; *la belle plume fait le bel oiseau.*

fine (faïne), *n.*, amende, *f.* ; pot-de-vin, *f.*

fine, *v.a.*, (to mulct) mettre à l'amende ; condamner à une amende de ; (to refine) affiner ; (wine) coller, clarifier.

fine'-arts, *n.pl.*, beaux arts, *m.pl.*

fine'-bred, *adj.*, (of horses) fin.

fine'-draw (-drô), *v.a.*, faire des reprises perdues à ; rentraire ; repriser.

fine'-drawer, *n.*, ouvrier en reprises perdues, *m.*, ouvrière en reprises perdues, *f.* ; rentrayeur, *m.*, rentrayeuse, *f.*

fine'-drawing, *n.*, reprise perdue ; rentraiture, *f.*

fine'-grained, *adj.*, (of metals) à grain fin ; (of stuffs) à poil fin ; (of wood) à fil fin.

fine'ly, *adv.*, fin ; délicatement ; finement ; subtilement ; élégamment ; (b.s.) joliment, de la belle manière.

fine'ness (faïne-), *n.*, finesse, délicatesse ; élégance ; pureté ; subtilité ; beauté, *f.*

fi'ner (faïneur), *n.*, affineur, *m.*

fi'nery (faï'n'ri), *n.*, parure, *f.* ; ornement, *m.* ; toilette, *f.* ; beaux habits, *m.pl.* ; (metal.) affinerie, *f.*, foyer d'affinerie, *m.*

fine'-spoken (-spô'k'n), *adj.*, beau parleur.

fine'-spun (-speune), *adj.*, filé fin ; (fig.) subtil, délicat, délié.

finesse' (finèce), *n.*, finesse, *f.* ; (coin.) titre; aloi, *m.*

finesse', *v.n.*, user de finesse, finasser.

finess'ing, *n.*, finasserie, *f.*

fin'-footed (fine-foutède), *adj.*, (zool.) palmipède.

fin'ger (fi'g'n'gheur), *n.*, doigt ; (mus.) doigter, *m.* ; (fig.) main, *f.* Fore— ; *doigt indicateur ; index, m.* Little — ; *petit doigt, m.* Middle— ; *doigt du milieu, médius, m.* Ring— ; *annulaire, doigt annulaire, m.* My —s were itching to ; *les doigts me démangeaient de.* To have anything at one's —s' ends ; *savoir quelque chose sur le bout du doigt.* To point with one's — ; *indiquer du doigt, montrer du doigt, au doigt.* To have a — in a thing ; *être intéressé dans une affaire ; être mêlé dans une affaire, être pour quelque chose dans.* He has a — in every pie ; *il se mêle de toutes les affaires de la paroisse, il fourre son nez partout.* To be like — and thumb ; *être unis comme les deux doigts de la main.* To blow on one's — ; *souffler dans ses doigts.*

fin'ger, *v.a.*, toucher, manier, palper ; toucher à ; exécuter **avec** les doigts ; (mus.) toucher, toucher de. To — a piece of music ; *doigter un morceau de musique.*

fin'ger, *v.n.*, (mus.) doigter.

fin'ger-board (-bôrde), *n.*, (mus.) clavier ; (of a violin) manche, *m.*

fin'gered (fi'g'n'gheurde), *adj.*, qui a des doigts; (bot.) digité ; (mam.) à doigts. Light— ; *qui a la main légère ; enclin à voler.* Light— gentry ; *les filous, m.pl. ; le gent aux doigts crochus, f.*

fin'ger-fish, *n.*, (ich.) étoile de mer, astérie, *f.*

fin'ger-glass (-glâce), *n.*, rince-doigts, *m.*

fin'ger-grass (-grâce), *n.*, (bot.) panic glabre ; panic à patte de coq, *m.*

fin'gering, *n.*, touche, *f.* ; maniement ; ouvrage délicat fait à la main ; (mus.) doigter, doigté, *m.* To have the — of ; (fig.) *avoir le maniement de.*

fin'gerling, *n.*, (ich.) saumoneau, tacon, rené, parr, *m.*

fin'ger-nail, ongle de la main, *m.*

fin'ger-part'ed (-pârtède), *adj.*, (bot.) digité.

fin'ger-plate (-pléte), *n.*, plaque de propreté, *f.*

fin'ger-post, *n.*, poteau indicateur, *m.*

fin'ger-stall (-stôl), *n.*, doigtier, *m.*

fin'gle-fangle (fi'g'n'g'l-faï'g'n'g'l), *n.*, (pop.) bagatelle, babiole, baliverne, fadaise, *f.*

fin'ical, *adj.*, précieux, affété, prétentieux.

fin'ically, *adv.*, précieusement, avec prétention.

fin'icalness, *n.*, affèterie, *f.* ; ton précieux, *m.*, préciosité, *f.* Gray's — was excessive ; *Gray poussait trop loin l'affèterie ; l'affèterie de Gray était excessive.*

fi'ning (faï'n-), *n.*, (metal.) affinage, *m.* ; (of wine) clarification, *f.* ; collage, *m.*

fi'ning-forge, *n.*, forge d'affinage, *f.*

fi'ning-pot, *n.*, creuset, *m.*

fi'nis (faï'nice), *n.*, fin, *f.*

fin'ish, *v.a.*, finir, terminer ; achever, consommer.

fin'ish, *n.*, fini, *m.* ; la dernière main, *f.* ; (mas.) la dernière couche de plâtre, *f.*

fin'ished (fin'ishte), *adj.*, fini ; (fig.) parfait, soigné.

fin'isher, *n.*, personne qui finit, qui achève, *f.*, polisseur, *m.*, polisseuse, *f.* A — ; (fig.) *le coup de grâce, m.*

fin'ishing, *adj.*, de perfectionnement ; qui complète ; dernier. —school ; *école supérieure, f.* — stroke ; *dernière touche, f. ; coup de grâce, m.*

fin'ishing, *n.*, fini ; achèvement, *m.* ; dernière touche ; dernière main, *f.*

fi'nite (faï-naïte), *adj.*, fini.

fi'nite, *n.*, fini, *m.*

fi'nitely (faï-naï't'li), *adv.*, dans de certaines limites.

fi'niteness, *n.*, caractère fini, *m.* ; **borne** ; limite, *f.*

fin′less, *adj.*, sans nageoires.

fin′like (-laïke), *adj.*, en forme de nageoire.

finned (fi'n'de), *adj.*, qui a des nageoires ; à nageoires ; (her.) loré.

fin′ny, *adj.*, qui a des nageoires ; à nageoires ; (poet.) qui habite les eaux ; qui abonde en poissons. The — tribe; *la race qui habite les eaux, f., les poissons, m.pl.* The — deep; *l'océan qui fourmille de poissons, m.*

fin′toed (fi'n'tôde), *adj.*, à doigts palmés, palmipède.

fi′orin-grass (faï'o'ri'n'grâce), *n.*, (bot.) agrostide stolonifère, *f.*

fir (feur), *n.*, (bot.) sapin ; bois de sapin, *m.*

fir′-apple (-ap'p'l), **fir′-cone**, *n.*, pomme de pin, *f.*

fire (faï'eur), *n.*, feu, incendie, *m.* Incendiary —; *incendie par malveillance.* —! *au feu!* To be on —; *être en feu.* On —; *en feu ;* (fig.) *ardent.* To catch —; *prendre feu.* To take —; *s'enflammer ; se mettre en colère.* Running —; *feu roulant, m.* To make a —; *faire du feu.* To miss, *ou* hang, —; *rater, faire long feu.* To put out a —; *éteindre un feu, un incendie.* To set on —, to set — to; *mettre le feu* à. He will never set the Thames on —; *il n'a pas inventé la poudre.* To fall from the frying-pan into the —; *tomber de fièvre en chaud mal.* To add fuel to the —; *jeter de l'huile sur le feu.* To put to — and sword ; *mettre à feu et à sang.* To go through — and water for ; *se mettre au feu pour, se mettre en quatre* **pour.** St. Anthony's —; *érésipèle, érysipèle, m.*

fire, *v.a.*, mettre le feu à ; embraser ; incendier ; enflammer ; (fire-arms) tirer ; faire le coup de feu. To — with; *enflammer de.* To — off; *tirer ; décharger.* To — up; *s'enflammer ; s'échauffer, prendre feu.*

fire, *v.n.*, prendre feu ; s'enflammer. To — at; *faire feu* **sur.** —! (milit.) *feu!* To — from the shoulder ; *tirer à bras francs.* To — away ; (fam.) *commencer ; continuer.*

fire′-alarm, *n.*, avertisseur d'incendie, *m.*

fire′-arms (-ârm'ze), *n.pl.*, armes à feu, *f.pl.*

fire′-ball (-bôl), *n.*, (milit.) grenade, *f. ;* (meteor) globe de feu, bolide, *m.*

fire′-balloon, *n.*, montgolfière, *f.*

fire′-bar (-bâre), *n.*, barre de fourneau ; barre de foyer, *f.*

fire′-blast (-blâste), *n.*, (agri.) charbon, *m. ;* rouille ; nielle, *f.*

fire′brand (-bra'n'de), *n.*, tison ardent, *m. ;* brandon ; (fig.) boutefeu de rébellion (V. Hugo); brandon de discorde, *m.*

fire′-brasses, *n.pl.*, garniture de foyer, *f.*

fire′-brick, *n.*, brique réfractaire, *f.*

fire′-brigade, *n.*, corps de sapeurs pompiers, *m.*

fire′-bucket, *n.*, seau à incendie, *m.*

fire′-chest (-tshèste), *n.*, (nav.) coffre à feu, *m.*

fire′-clay, *n.*, (tech.) argile réfractaire, *f.*

fire′-damp (-da'm'pe), *n.*, feu grisou; grisou, *m.*

fire′-dog, *n.*, chenet, landier, *m.*

fire′drake (-dréke), *n.*, (ant.) dragon volant ; feu follet; chauffeur, *m.*

fire′-eater, *n.*, pyrophage ; (fig.) matamore, sacripant, avaleur de gens, *m.*

fire′-engine (-è'n'djine), *n.*, pompe à incendie, *f.*

fire′-escape (-ès-képe), *n.*, appareil de sauvetage, échelle de sauvetage, *f.*

fire′-extinguisher, *n.*, extincteur, *m.*

fire′-fly (-flaïe), *n.*, (ent.) lampyre, *m.*, mouche à feu, *f.*

fire′-grate (-gréte), *n.*, grille de foyer, *f.*

fire′-guard, *n.*, garde-feu, *m.*

fire′-hose, *n.*, boyau, *m.*

fire′-irons (-aï'eur'n'ze), *n.*, garniture de foyer, *f. ;* (tech.) ringard ; tisonnier, *m.* Set of —s ; *garniture de foyer, f.*

fire′less, *adj.*, sans feu.

fire′lock, *n.*, arme à feu, *f. ;* fusil, mousquet, *m.*

fire′man (-ma'n), *n.*, pompier ; (in factories) chauffeur, *m.*

fire′-office, *n.*, bureau d'assurance contre l'incendie, *m.*

fire′-pan (-pa'n), *n.*, (fire-arms) bassinet, *m. ;* pelle à feu, bassinoire, *f.*

fire′place (-pléce), *n.*, cheminée, *f. ;* foyer de cheminée ; âtre, *m.*

fire′-plug, *n.*, bouche d'eau, bouche d'incendie, *f.*

fire′-policy, *n.*, police d'assurance contre l'incendie, *f.*

fire′-proof (-proufe), *adj.*, à l'épreuve du feu, incombustible.

fir′er, *n.*, incendiaire, *f.*

fire′-range, *n.*, fourneau de cuisine, *m.*

fire′-screen (-scrîne), *n.*, écran, *m.*

fire′-ship (-shipe), *n.*, brûlot, *m.*

fire′side (-saïde), *n.*, coin du feu, foyer domestique, *m.* By the —; *au coin du feu.*

fire′side, *adj.*, du coin du feu.

fire′-station, *n.* poste de pompiers, *m.*

fire′stone (-stône), *n.*, (min.) silex pyromaque, *m. ;* pierre à fusil, pierre réfractaire, *f.*

fire′-tile (-taïle), *n.*, (tech.) tuile réfractaire, *f.*

fire′-tongs, *n.pl.*, pincettes, *f.pl.*

fire′wood (-woude), *n.*, bois à brûler, bois de chauffage, *m.*

fire′work (-weurke), *n.*, feu d'artifice, *m.* To let off —s ; *tirer un feu d'artifice.* [Firework s'emploie généralement au pluriel.]

fire′-worship, *n.*, culte du feu, *m.*

fire′-worshiper, *n.*, guèbre, *m.f.*

fir′-grove, *n.*, sapinière, *f.*

fir′ing, *n.*, action d'incendier, *f. ;* chauffage, combustible ; (milit.) feu, tir, *m.*, fusillade ; (vet.) cautérisation, *f.* Independent —; (mil.) *feu à volonté, m.* — party ; *peloton d'exécution, m.*

fir′ing-iron (-aïeur'ne), *n.*, (vet.) fer à cautériser, *m.*

fir′ing-range, *n.*, tir, *m.*

fir′kin (feur-ki'n), *n.*, quartaut, barillet, *m. ;* (of butter) tinette, *f.*

firm (feurme), *adj.*, ferme, solide, fort, constant.

firm (feurme), *n.*, (com.) maison de commerce, raison sociale, *f.*

fir′mament (feur'-) *n.*, firmament ; (ant.) fondement, *m.*, base, *f.*

firmamen′tal, *adj.*, du firmament.

fir′man (feur-), *n.*, firman, *m.*

firm′ly, *adv.*, fermement ; solidement, fortement.

firm′ness, *n.*, fermeté ; solidité, force, *f.*

fir′-plank (-pla'gn'k), *n.*, planche de sapin, *f.*

first (feurste), *adj.*, premier ; unième. Twenty-—; *vingt et unième.*

first, *adv.*, le premier ; premièrement, d'abord. — or last ; *tôt ou tard.* At —; *d'abord, au commencement, à l'origine.* From the very —; *dès le début.* He was the very — to complain ; *il s'est plaint tout le premier.* The — that comes; *le premier venu, m.* — and last ; *d'un bout à l'autre.* — come — served ; *les premiers vont devant.* To be — in the field ; *prendre les devants.* — catch your hare ; *il ne faut pas vendre la peau de l'ours avant de l'avoir tué.*

first′-born, *adj.*, premier-né ; premier.

first′-class, *n.*, (ticket *ou* carriage) voiture de première classe, *f.*, billet de première classe, *m. adj.*, (of things) de premier choix ; (of pers.) éminent, de première force, de premier ordre.

first′-fruits (-froutse), *n.pl.*, prémices, *f.pl.*

first′-hand, *n.*, premier ouvrier, *m. ;* première ouvrière, *f. adj., adv.*, de la première main ; de première main.

first′ling, *n.*, premier-né, *m.*

first'ly, *adv.*, premièrement.

first'-rate, *adj.*, de première force, distingué, excellent.

firth (feurth), *n.*, estuaire, *m.*; embouchure, *f.* (of a river); détroit, *m.*

fir'-tree (-trî), *n.*, (bot.) sapin, *m.*

fis'cal (fiscal), *adj.*, fiscal.

fis'cal, *n.*, (Spain and Portugal) procureur du roi, (Scotland) procureur fiscal; (ant.) fisc, *m.*

fis'cally, *adv.*, fiscalement.

fish (fishe), *n.*, poisson, *m.*; (at play) fiche; (nav.) jumelle, *f.*; (pers.) individu, animal, pistolet, *m.* Neither — nor fowl; *ni chair, ni poisson.* To have other — to fry; *avoir d'autres chats à fouetter.* To be like a — out of water; *être comme un poisson sur la paille.* A fine kettle of —; *une jolie affaire.*

fish, *v.n.*, pêcher. To go —ing; *aller à la pêche.* To — for; *tâcher de découvrir.* To — for compliments; *quêter des compliments.* To — in troubled waters; *pêcher en eau trouble.* — for it! *allez-y; vous en serez pour vos frais!*

fish, *v.a.*, pêcher; fouiller dans; (nav.) traverser, jumeler; (fig.) chercher, attraper, surprendre. To — out a man's reasons; *tirer à quelqu'un les vers du nez.*

fish'-basket, *n.*, bourriche, manne à poisson, *f.*

fish'-bone (-bône), *n.*, arête de poisson, *f.*

fish'-cart (-cârte), *n.*, voiture à poisson, *f.*

fish'-carver, *n.* *V.* **fish-slice**.

fish'-curer (-kiour'-), *n.*, saleur, *m.*

fish'-day, *n.*, jour maigre, jour de poisson, *m.*

fish'er, *n.*, pêcheur, *m.*

fish'er-boat (-bôte), *n.*, bateau pêcheur, *m.*

fish'er-man (-ma'n), *n.*, pêcheur, *m.*

fish'ery, *n.*, pêche; pêcherie, *f.* Herring —; *pêche aux harengs, f.* The fisheries of Newfoundland; *les pêcheries de Terre-Neuve, f.pl.*

fish'-fag, *n.*, poissarde; marchande de poisson, *f.*

fish'ful (-foule), *adj.*, (ant.) poissonneux.

fish'-hook (-houke), *n.*, hameçon, *m.*

fish'iness, *n.*, goût de poisson, *m.*

fish'ing, *n.*, pêche, *f.*; (place) pêcherie, *f.* Mackerel —; *pêche du maquereau.*   [*m.*

fish'ing-boat or **smack**, *n.*, bateau pêcheur, *m.*

fish'ing-line (-laïne), *n.*, ligne, ligne à pêcher, *f.*

fish'ing-rod (-rode), *n.*, canne à pêcher, *f.*

fish'ing-tac'kle (-tak'k'l), *n.*, ustensiles (ou sngins) de pêche, *m.pl.*; attirail de pêche, *m.*

fish'-kettle (-kèt't'l), *n.*, poissonnière (ustensile), *f.*

fish'like (-laïke), *adj.*, de poisson.

fish'-market (-mâr-kète), *n.*, poissonnerie, *f.*; marché au poisson, *m.*

fish'monger (-mun'gn'gheur), *n.*, poissonnier; marchand de poisson, *m.*; poissonnière; marchande de poisson, *f.*

fish'-pond ou **fish'-pool** (-po'n'de, -poule), *n.*, étang; vivier, *m.*

fish'-slice (-slaïce), *n.*, truelle à poisson, *f.*

fish'-spear (-spîre), *n.*, harpon, *m.*

fish'-tail bur'ner, *n.*, bec en forme de queue de poisson, *m.*

fish'wife (-waïfe) ou **fish'woman** (-woum'-a'n), *n.*, poissonnière, marchande de poisson; poissarde, *f.*

fish'y, *adj.*, poissonneux; qui sent le poisson; de poisson.

fis'siped (-pède), *adj.*, fissipède.

fis'sure (fish'ioure), *n.*, fissure, fente, *f.*

fis'sure, *v.a.*, fracturer; faire des fentes à; fendre.

fist, *n.*, poing, *m.* —**ful**; *poignée, f.*

fist'ed, *adj.*, au poing. Close —; *serré, pingre, avare; dur à la détente, à la desserre.*

fis'ticuffs (-keufse), *n.pl.*, coups de poing, *m.*

fis'tula (-tiou-), *n.*, fistule, *f.*

fis'tular (-tiou-), *adj.*, fistuleux; fistulaire.

fis'tuliform, *adj.*, fistulaire.

fis'tulous, *adj.*, fistuleux.

fit, *n.*, accès, paroxysme, *m.*; attaque; convulsion, *f.* By —s and starts; *par accès; à bâtons rompus, par sauts et par bonds, par boutades.*

fit, *adj.*, propre à; juste, à propos; convenable; capable, bon (**pour** ou à); en état (**de**). — for use; *propre au service, en état de servir.* — to drink; *buvable, potable.* — to eat; *bon à manger, mangeable.* To think —; *juger convenable, juger bon* **de**.

fit, *v.a.*, convenir à; arranger; adapter à; ajuster; (tech.) encastrer; (of clothes) aller à. Let him whom the cap —s wear it; *qui se sent morveux qu'il se mouche.* To — to; accommoder à. To — with; *pourvoir* **de**. To — out; *équiper, monter; donner un trousseau à*; (a ship) armer. To — in; *encastrer.* To — up; *arranger, aménager.* That coat —s you well; *cet habit vous va bien ou vous va comme un gant.* To — any one for; *préparer quelqu'un* **pour**.

fit, *v.n.*, convenir; s'adapter à; s'ajuster; (of clothes) aller.

fitch'et (-tshète) ou **fitch'ew** (-tshiou), *n.*, (mam.) putois, *m.*

fit'ful, *adj.*, agité, vacillant; capricieux, plein de boutades; irrégulier; saccadé.

fit'fully, *adj.*, avec agitation; par accès, par boutades; irrégulièrement.

fit'ly, *adv.*, à propos, convenablement, justement.

fit'ness, *n.*, convenance, propriété, *f.*; à-propos, *m.*; capacité, *f.*

fit'ter, *n.*, personne qui adapte, *f.*; (tech.) ajusteur, *m.*

fit'ting, *adj.*, convenable; à propos; juste.

fit'ting, *n.*, adaptation, *f.*; ajustement, *m.* *pl.*, garniture, *f.* — in; emboîtement, *m.* — out; (nav.) *armement*; (milit.) *équipement*; *arrangement, aménagement, ameublement, montage, m.*

fit'tingly, *adv.*, convenablement.

five (faïve), *n.* and *adj.*, cinq.

five'fold (-fôlde), *adv.*, cinq fois; quintuple.

fives (faïv'ze), *n.*, (vet.) avives, *f.pl.*; (game) balle au mur, *f.* Bunch of —; *girofiée à cinq feuilles, f.* — court; *cour où l'on joue à la balle, f.*; *jeu de balle, m.*

fix, *v.a.*, fixer, attacher, arrêter, déterminer. To — one's self; *s'établir; se fixer.* To — bayonets; *mettre la baïonnette au canon.* With —ed bayonets; *la baïonnette au bout du fusil.* — bayonets! *baïonnette au canon!*

fix, *v.n.*, se fixer. To — upon; *se fixer sur, s'arrêter à; choisir.*

fix, *n.*, difficulté, impasse, *f.*; embarras, cas embarrassant, *m.* To be in a —; (fam.) *être dans le pétrin.*

fix'able (fiks'ab'l), *adj.*, (ant.) qui peut être fixé, qui peut s'adapter, adaptable.

fixa'tion (fiks'é'-), *n.*, fixité; place fixe; fixation, *f.*

fixed (fiks'te ou fiks'ède), *adj.*, fixe; fixé.

fix'edly (fiks'èdli), *adv.*, fermement; (pers.) à porte fixe; fixement.

fix'edness (fiks'èd-), **fix'ity**, *n.*, fixité, *f.*

fixt'ure (fiks'tioure), *n.*, stabilité, *f.*; (in a house) meuble à demeure fixe; immeuble, *m.* *pl.*, agencements, *m.pl.*

flab'biness, *n.*, flaccidité; nature flasque, *f.*

flab'by, *adj.*, flasque; mollasse.

flac'cid (flak-side), *adj.*, flasque, faible.

flaccid'ity ou **flac'cidness**, *n.*, flaccidité, *f.*

flag, *v.n.*, pendre, flotter; (fig.) s'affaisser; (fig.) se relâcher, faiblir; languir; s'user. The pleasures of the town begin to —; *les plaisirs de la ville commencent à perdre de leur intérêt, à languir, à s'user.*

flag, *v.a.*, laisser tomber; (fig.) abattre, épuiser.

flag, *v.a.*, paver, daller.

flag, v.a., (ant.) orner de drapeaux ; pavoiser.

flag, n., (milit.) drapeau : (nav.) pavillon, m. ; (bot.) glaïeul. — of truce ; *drapeau blanc ; pavillon blanc ; drapeau parlementaire.* Bearer of a — of truce ; *parlementaire*, m. Signaling — ; *fanion*, m. To strike the — ; *amener son pavillon, amener.*

flag'ellate (flådj'èl-léte), v.a., flageller.

flagella'tion (flådj'èl-lé-), n., flagellation, f.

flag'eolet (flådj'o-lète), n., flageolet, m.

flag'giness (flag'ghi-), n., état flasque, relâchement, m.

flag'ging, adj., pendant, qui pend ; flottant, qui flotte; qui se relâche; qui s'affaiblit.

flag'ging, n., dallage ; (fig.) relâchement, m.

flag'gy (flag'ghi), adj., faible ; qui flotte ; insipide ; mou ; flasque.

flagi'tious (fla-djish'eusse), adj., pervers ; infâme, atroce, abominable.

flagi'tiously, adv., (ant.) avec perversité ; d'une manière infâme.

flagi'tiousness, n., (ant.) perversité ; scélératesse; infamie, f.

flag'-officer, n., officier général de marine; chef d'escadre, m.

flag'on, n., flacon, m. ; (in churches) burette, f.

fla'grance ou **fla'grancy** (flé-), n., feu, éclat, m. ; chaleur ; notoriété ; énormité, f.

fla'grant, adj., flagrant, patent.

fla'grantly, adv., d'une manière flagrante.

flag'-ship, n., vaisseau amiral, m.

flag'-staff (-stâfe), n., lance de drapeau, f. ; (nav.) bâton, ou mât, de pavillon, m. ; hampe, f.

flag'-stone (-stône), n., dalle, f., pavé, m.

flail (fléle), n., fléau (à battre le blé), m.

flake (fléke), n., flocon, m. ; (of metals) lame ; écaille ; étincelle, f.

flake, v.a., (ant.) former en flocons, écailler ; (of metals) laminer.

flake, v.n., (ant.) s'écailler ; floconner, se floconner.

fla'ky, adj., floconneux, en flocons, par flocons; écailleux ; (of pastry) feuilleté. — paste ; *pâté feuilletée, f.*

flam, n., sornette, blague, bourde, f. ; conte, m.

flam, v.a., amuser avec des sornettes, blaguer.

flam'beau, n., flambeau, m.

flame (fléme), n., flamme, f. ; feu, m.

flame, v.n., flamber, jeter de la flamme ; s'enflammer; flamboyer. To — up ; (fig.) *s'emporter.*

flame'-colored (-keul'leurde), adj., couleur de feu, ponceau.

flame'less, adj., sans flamme.

flame'let, n., flammette, f.

fla'men (flé-mène), n., flamine, m.

fla'ming (flém'-), adj., flamboyant ; éclatant, flambant ; (fig.) véhément, violent, ardent.

fla'mingly, adv., avec éclat ; avec ardeur, avec véhémence.

flamin'go (-mi'gn'gô), n., (orni.) phénicoptère, flamant, m.

flammif'erous, adj., flammifère.

fla'my (flé-), adj., de flamme ; éclatant.

flanconade' (-con'éde), n., (fenc.) flanconade, f.

flange (fla'n'dje), n., rebord ; (railways) bandage, m. ; saillie ; bride ; collerette, f. ; (of wheels) boudin, m.

flank, n., flanc ; côté, m. — company ; *compagnie de flanc, f.*

flank, v.a., flanquer ; (milit.) prendre en flanc, attaquer en flanc.

flank, v.n., border, toucher à.

flank'er, n., (fort.) flanc ; (milit.) flanqueur, m.

flank'er, v.a., (fort.) flanquer.

flan'nel, n., flanelle, f. adj., de, ou en, flanelle.

flap, n., tape, f. ; léger coup ; (of trousers) pont ; (of a hat, a cap) bord, bord rabattu, m. ; (of a pocket) patte, f. ; (of a coat) pan ; (of a saddle) quartier ; (of the ear) bout, m. ; (of a shoe) oreille, f.

flap, v.a., frapper légèrement ; battre, agiter. To — its wings ; *battre des ailes.*

flap, v.n., battre légèrement ; battre des ailes; pendre, retomber.

flap'-eared (-îrde), adj., aux oreilles pendantes.

flap'per, n., clapet ; (orni.) halbran, m.

flap'ping, n., battement d'ailes, coup d'aile, m.

flare (flère), n., flamme, vive clarté, f. ; éclat, m. — up ; *chamaillis, tapage, vacarme* ; (fam.) *bousin, boucan, m. ; violente querelle, f.*

flare, v.n., étinceler ; flamber ; (of candles) filer ; (fig.) briller. To — up ; *se mettre en colère, s'emporter, s'enflammer.*

flash, n., éclat ; (of water, of light) jet ; éclair, m. ; (of fire-arms) lumière, f. — of lightning ; *éclair*, m. — of wit ; *trait d'esprit*, m. — of the eye ; *vif coup d'œil*, m. — in the pan; *faux feu ; coup d'épée dans l'eau; feu de paille*, m. To — in the pan ; *faire faux feu, faire fiasco.*

flash, v.a., faire jaillir ; envoyer, jeter, lancer.

flash (flashe), v.n., luire ; jaillir ; étinceler ; passer comme un éclair, éclater. To — with ; briller **de** ; *étinceler* **de.**

flash'ily, adv., superficiellement.

flash'y, adj., éclatant ; brillant ; voyant ; à effet ; superficiel ; insipide, fade.

flask, n., bouteille, f. ; flacon, m. ; poire à poudre, f.

flas'ket (flâsk'ète), n., corbeille, manne, f.

flat, adj., plat ; (of wine, beer, etc.) éventé ; (com.) calme, languissant ; (mus.) bémol ; (of sound) grave ; (fig.) net, clair, franc, formel ; (taste) fade, insipide ; (mind) simple, bête, sot. — nosed ; *camard ; qui a le nez camus.* To get — scenes ; (thea.) *coulisses du fond ; toiles de fond*, f.pl. To lay — ; *coucher à plat ; coucher ; renverser, terrasser.* To lie — ; *être couché à plat ventre ; être étendu à terre.* To fall — on the ground ; *tomber de son long.*

flat, n., surface unie, plaine, f. ; terrain plat ; (of a house) étage ; (pers.) nigaud, niais ; (mus.) bémol; (nav.) bas-fond, m.

flat, v.a. aplatir ; (fig.) amortir ; (metal.) laminer.

flat, v.n., s'aplatir ; (fig.) s'amortir.

flat'ly, **flat**, adv., de niveau, à plat ; (fig.) nettement, clairement, péremptoirement.

flat'ness, n., aplatissement, m. ; égalité ; (of wine, beer, etc.) évent, goût éventé, m. ; fadeur ; (of sound) gravité ; (fig.) insipidité, platitude, f. ; (mind) abattement, m.

flat'ten (flat't'n), v.a. aplatir ; aplanir ; (fig.) affadir ; (mus.) adoucir ; (mind) abattre ; (metal.) laminer.

flat'ten, v.n., s'aplatir ; s'aplanir ; (fig.) s'affadir ; s'éventer.

flat'tening, n., aplatissement ; aplanissement ; (of metals) laminage, m.

flat'ter, n., (pers.) lamineur ; (thing) marteau de relieur, de batteur d'or, aplatisseur, m.

flat'ter, v.a., flatter.

flat'terer, n., flatteur, m., flatteuse, f.

flat'tering, adj., flatteur.

flat'teringly, adv., d'une manière flatteuse ; avec flatterie, flatteusement.

flat'tery, n., flatterie, f.

flat'ting-mill, n., laminoir, m.

flat'tish (-tishe), adj., un peu plat.

flat'ulence ou **flat'ulency** (-tiou-), n., (med.) flatuosité ; (fig.) vide, creux, néant, m.

flat'ulent, adj., (med.) flatueux ; (fig.) ampoulé, gonflé, vain, creux.

flatuos'ity, n., (ant.) flatuosité, f.

flat'uous, adj., (ant.) flatueux.

flat'wise, adv., à plat.

flaunt (flô'n'te), n., étalage, m., vaine parure, parade, impertinence, f.

flaunt, *v.a.*, faire parade **de**; étaler, déployer, promener.

flaunt, *v.n.*, s'étendre; flotter; (fig.) se pavaner, briller, parader.

flaunt'ing, *adj.*, voyant; fier; qui se pavane.

fla'vor (flé-veur), *n.*, saveur, *f.*; (of meat) goût, fumet; (of tea, coffee, etc.) arome; (of wine) fumet, bouquet, *m.*; (of flowers) senteur, *f.*, parfum, *m.*

fla'vor, *v.a.*, donner un arome **à**; donner un parfum **à**; donner un fumet **à**; donner du bouquet **à**, assaisonner **de**.

fla'vored (flé-veurde) *adj.*, qui a un arome, un parfum; qui a un fumet, un bouquet, un goût savoureux. Full-— cigar; *cigare fort*, m. Mild-— cigar; *cigare doux*, m. — fruits; *fruits d'une bonne eau*, m.pl.

fla'voring, *n.*, assaisonnement, *m.*

fla'vorless, *adj.*, sans arome, sans senteur; sans parfum; sans goût; sans fumet; sans bouquet.

fla'vorous, **fla'vory**, *adj.*, (ant.) odorant, savoureux; qui flatte le palais.

flaw (flô), *n.*, défaut, *m.*; (of a diamond) glace; (in precious stones) paille; brèche, fente; (nav.) risée de vent; (jur.) nullité, *f.*; vice, *m.*

flaw, *v.a.*, (ant.) fendre; fêler, gercer, crevasser.

flaw'less, *adj.*, parfait, sans défaut; (of gems) sans paille, sans tache.

flaw'y, *adj.*, (ant.) qui a des défauts; défectueux; fendillé, crevassé; (of gems) paillé, pailleux.

flax, *n.*, lin, *m. adj.*, de lin.

flax'-comb (-côme), *n.*, séran, peigne, *m.*

flax'-dresser (-drès'-), *n.*, séranceur de lin, peigneur, *m.*

flax'-dressing, *n.*, peignage du lin; sérançage, *m.*

flax'en (flaks'n), *adj.*, de lin; (of the hair) blond.

flax'-field (-fîlde), *n.*, linière, *f.*

flax'-grower (-grô-), *n.*, cultivateur de lin, *m.*

flax'-growing, *n.*, culture du lin, *f.*

flax'-mill, *n.*, manufacture de lin, filature de lin, *f.*

flax'-wench (-wè'n'she), *n.*, peigneuse de lin, *f.*

flay (flé) *v.a.*, écorcher.

flay'er (flé-eur), *n.*, écorcheur, *m.*

flay'ing, *n.*, écorchement, *m.*

flea (flî), *n.*, puce, *f.* To have **a** — in one's ear; *avoir la puce à l'oreille*.

flea'-bane, *n.*, herbe aux mouches, *f.*

flea'-bite (-baïte), *n.*, piqûre, *ou* morsure, de puce; (fig.) bagatelle, *f.*, rien, petit mal, *m.*

flea'-bitten (-bit't'n), *adj.*, mordu des puces.

fleam (flîme), *n.*, (surg.) flammette, (vet.) flamme, *f.*

flea'wort (-weurte), *n.*, herbe aux puces,*f.*

fleck, *n.*, tache, moucheture, marque, *f.*

fleck, *v.a.*, moucheter, tacheter.

fledged (flèdje), *adj.*, (ant.) garni de plumes.

fledge, *v.a.*, garnir de plumes.

fledged, *adj.*, couvert de plumes. Full —; *en état de voler*.

fledge'ling, *n.*, oisillon, *m.*

flee, *v.a.*, éviter, fuir.

flee (flî), *v.n.*, (*preterit* and *past part.*, Fled), s'enfuir, fuir; prendre la fuite, se réfugier.

fleece (flîce), *n.*, toison, *f.* Golden —; *toison d'or*.

fleece, *v.a.*, abattre la toison **de**; tondre; dépouiller **de**; (fig.) écorcher, plumer, rançonner.

fleeced (flîss'te), *adj.*, couvert d'une toison; (fig.) plumé, écorché, rançonné.

flee'cer, *n.*, exacteur, voleur, écorcheur, *m.*

flee'cy, *adj.*, laineux, floconneux, moutonneux. — clouds; *nuages moutonnés*, *m.pl.*

fleer (flîre), *n.*, raillerie, grimace, *f.*

fleer, *v.a.* and *n.*, railler.

fleer'er, *n.*, (ant.) railleur, *m.*, railleuse, *f.*

fleet (flîte), *n.*, flotte, escadre, *f.*

fleet, *adj.*, vite, léger, rapide, léger à la course.

fleet, *v.a.*, (ant.) passer rapidement; (to skim over) effleurer, raser.

fleet, *v.n.*, (ant.) fuir, passer; s'envoler.

fleet'ing, *adj.*, fugitif, passager.

fleet'ingly, *adv.*, d'une manière rapide, passagère.

fleet'ly, *adv.*, vite, rapidement.

fleet'ness, *n.*, rapidité; légèreté à la course; vitesse,*f.*

flesh (flèshe), *n.*, chair; viande, *f.*; embonpoint, *m.*; (paint.) chairs, *f.pl.* Proud —; *bourgeons charnus*, *m.pl.* Hard —; *durillon*, m. To make one's — creep; *donner la chair de poule à*. To put on, *ou* pick up, —; *prendre de l'embonpoint*. In — and blood; *en chair et en os*. Neither fish — nor fowl; *ni chair, ni poisson*. In the —; *en vie*. To be one —; *ne faire qu'un corps*.

flesh, *v.a.*, repaître; assouvir; accoutumer **à**; endurcir; (hunt.) acharner; (hides) écharner.

flesh'brush (-breushe), *n.*, brosse à friction,*f.*

flesh'-color (-keul'ieur), *n.*, couleur de chair, *f.*

flesh'-colored (-keul'leurde), *adj.*, couleur de chair; incarnat.

flesh'-day (-dé), *n.*, jour gras, *m.*

flesh'hook (-houke), *n.*, croc, *m.*

flesh'iness, *n.*, état charnu, *m.*

flesh'less, *adj.*, maigre, décharné.

flesh'liness, *n.*, disposition charnelle, *f.*

flesh'ly, *adj.*, de chair, de la chair; charnel.

flesh'-meat (-mîte), *n.*, viande, *f.*

flesh'pot (-pote), *n.*, (fig.) marmite, *f.*, pot au feu, *m.* The —s of Egypt; *les bonnes choses, f.pl.*, ou *les oignons*, m.pl., *d'Egypte*.

flesh'-red (-rède), *adj.*, incarnat.

flesh'-tint, *n.*, teinte de chair, *f.*

flesh'y, *adj.*, charnu; de chair.

fleur-de-lis' (fleur-dè-lî), *n.*, (her.) fleur de lis,*f.*

flexibil'ity, *n.*, flexibilité, *f.*

flex'ible, *adj.*, qui peut se plier; flexible.

flex'ion (flèk'sheune), *n.*, courbure; flexion,*f.*

flex'or (flèk'seur), *n.*, (anat.) fléchisseur; muscle fléchisseur, *m.*

flex'uose *ou* **flex'uous** (flèk'shiou-eusse), *adj.*, sinueux; tortueux; vacillant; (bot.) flexueux.

flex'ure (flèk'sioure), *n.*, flexion, génuflexion; (geom.) courbure, *f.*

flick'er, *v.n.*, (of a light) vaciller; trembloter; ondoyer; trémousser de l'aile; battre des ailes; (fig.) vaciller, voltiger, hésiter.

flick'ering, *n.*, trémoussement, battement d'ailes, *m.*; (fig.) vacillation, fluctuation, *f.*

flick'ering, *adj.*, vacillant, tremblotant; voltigeant; incertain.

fli'er (flaï'.),*n.*,fugitif,fuyard; (mec.)volant,*m.*

flight (flaïte), *n.*, fuite, *f.*; vol, *m.*; (of birds, etc.) volée, *f.*; (fig.) élan, essor; (of time) cours, *m.*; (ant.) volée, décharge, *f.* To betake one's self to —; *prendre la fuite*. — of stairs, — of steps; *escalier*, (before a house) *perron*, *m.* At one —; *d'une volée*. At a single —; *à tire d'aile*. To put to —; *mettre en fuite*. To take —; *prendre son vol, prendre sa volée*; (fig.) *prendre son essor*.

flight'iness, *n.*, légèreté, étourderie, *f.*

flight'y, *adj.*, fugitif; étourdi, léger, volage.

flim'siness (flî'm'zi-), *n.*, légèreté; (fig.) pauvreté, mesquinerie, *f.*

flim'sy (flî'm'zi), *adj.*, mince; mesquin; mollasse; léger; faible, pauvre, frivole.

flinch (flî'n'she), *v.n.*, reculer, faiblir, céder. To — from; *se retirer de, se désister de, reculer* **devant**. Without —ing; *sans broncher, sans sourciller, de pied ferme*.

fling (fligne), *n.*, coup, *m.*; danse écossaise, *f.*; (fig.) trait, coup de patte, *m.*, moquerie, raillerie, *f.* To have one's —; *jeter sa gourme ; faire des fredaines; faire des folies; s'en donner à cœur joie.* To have a — at ; *donner un coup de patte à.*

fling, *v.a.* (preterit and past part., Flung), jeter, lancer. To — away ; *jeter, prodiguer, rejeter ; se débarrasser de, repousser.* To — about ; *lancer de tous côtés.* To — down ; *abattre, démolir, renverser.* To — open; *ouvrir brusquement.* To — off ; *jeter ; se dépouiller de.* To — out ; *jeter dehors.* To — over ; *abandonner, déserter.* To — up ; *jeter en haut, ou en l'air ; abandonner.*

fling, *v.n.*, (man.) ruer, s'élancer (l.u.); (fig.) invectiver, s'emporter, regimber. To — open ; *s'ouvrir tout à coup.*

flint (fli'n'te), *n.*, caillou, silex, *m.*, pierre à briquet, pierre à fusil; (fig.) roche ; dureté, *f.* —glass; *cristal d'Angleterre, m.* —lock ; *fusil à pierre, m.* To skin a —; *tondre sur un œuf ; faire des économies de bouts de chandelle.*

flint'y, *adj.*, de caillou ; caillouteux ; siliceux ; (fig.) dur, insensible, inexorable.

flip'pancy (flip'p'a'n'-), *n.*, ton léger ; air cavalier ; verbiage, bavardage, *m. ;* légèreté, étourderie, *f.* — of speech ; *volubilité de langage, f. ; verbiage, m.*

flip'pant (flip'pa'n'te), *adj.*, inconsidéré, léger ; bavard ; cavalier, dégagé. — tongue; *langue bien pendue, langue déliée, f.*

flip'pantly, *adv.*, légèrement ; cavalièrement ; d'un ton dégagé.

flirt (fleurte), *n.*, mouvement vif, *m. ;* (woman) coquette,*f.* One — at him, and then I'm for the voyage ; (gibe) (ant.) *je m'en vais lui donner un coup de patte, et puis me voilà parti.*

flirt, *v.n.*, voltiger ; faire la coquette, coqueter, folâtrer, papillonner ; (ant.) railler, bafouer.

flirt, *v.a.*, jeter, lancer, agiter ; (ant.) railler.

flirta'tion (fleur-té-), *n.*, coquetterie ; intrigue, *f.*

flit (flite), *v.n.*, fuir ; voltiger ; passer ; déménager, changer de demeure.

flitch (flit'she), *n.*, flèche de lard, *f.*

flit'ter-mouse (-maouce), *n.*, chauve-souris, *f.*

flit'ting, *n.*, fuite, *f.*, passage ; voltigement ; (change of residence) déménagement, *m.*

flit'ting, *adj.*, fugitif, rapide.

float (flôte), *n.*, chose qui flotte, *f. ;* radeau ; (hydr.) flotteur ; (swimming) scaphandre, *m. ;* nageoire, *f. ;* (of wood) train ; radeau ; flot, *m. ;* (of a wheel) aube ; (of a fishing-line) flotte, *f.*

float, *v.n.*, flotter; surnager ; faire la planche.

float, *v.a.*, faire flotter (fig.), former ; mettre à flot, lancer. To — a company ; *former une compagnie, une société industrielle.*

float'-board (-bôrde), *n.*, (mec.) aube, *f.*

float'er, *n.*, personne qui flotte ; flotteur ; personne qui fait la planche ; (fig.) personne qui forme une compagnie,*f.*

floatabil'ity, *n.*, flottabilité, *f.*

float'able, *adj.*, flottable.

float'ing, *adj.*, flottant. — battery · *batterie flottante, f.* — bridge; *pont flottant, m.* —capital; *capital flottant, m.* — debt; *dette flottante, f.*

float'ing, *n.*, flottement, *m.*, mise à flot; action de flotter; (agr.) irrigation ; (fig.) formation d'une compagnie, *f.*

float'-stone (-stône), *n.*, (min.) pierre spongieuse, *f.*

floc'culent (flok'kiou-), *adj.*, floconneux.

flock, *n.*, troupeau, *m. ;* bande; foule, troupe, *f. ;* (of a clergyman) ouailles, *f.pl. ;* (of wool, etc.) flocon, *m.*; bourre, *f.*

flock, *v.n.*, s'attrouper ; se rassembler ; se porter en foule ; (of birds) aller par bandes. Birds of a feather — together ; *qui se ressemble s'assemble.*

flock'-bed, *n.*, lit de bourre, *m.*

flock'-paper, *n.*, papier soufflé, papier velouté, papier tontisse, *m.*

flock'-surface (-seur-féce), *n.*, velouté, *m.*

floe, *n.*, (nav.) champ de glace, glaçon flottant, *m.*

flog, *v.a.*, fouetter ; donner le fouet à, fesser, flageller, fustiger. To — a dead horse; *chercher à ressusciter un mort.*

flog'ger (flogh'eur), *n.*, fouetteur, *m.*

flog'ging (flogh-'), *n.*, fouet, *m.*, coups de fouet, *m.pl. ;* flagellation, correction, *f.*

flood (fleude), *n.*, cours d'eau, *m. ;* (wave) onde, *f. ;* flux, déluge, *m. ;* inondation, crue, *f.* — of tears ; *torrent de larmes, m.* — tide ; *marée montante, f.; flux, flot, m.* On the top of the —; *à marée haute.*

flood, *v.a.*, inonder, submerger, noyer. To — with ; *inonder de.*

flood'gate (-ghéte), *n.*, écluse ; vanne ; (fig.) porte, *f. ;* passage, *m. ;* cataracte, *f.*

flood'ing, *n.*, inondation, (med.) hémorragie utérine ; perte de sang,*f.*

flook, *n.* V. **Fluke**.

flook'ing (flouk'-), *n.*, (mines) interruption d'un filon métallique, *f.*

floor (flôre), *n.*, plancher ; carreau, parquet ; (of a house) étage ; (of bridges) tablier, *m. ;* (nav.) varangue, *f.*, (geol.) sol, *m.* Inlaid — ; *parquet, m.* On the first — ; *au premier.* On the same —; *sur le même palier.*

floor, *v.a.*, planchéier, parqueter, carreler ; jeter par terre, terrasser ; réduire au silence, désarçonner.

floor'-cloth, *n.*, toile cirée, *f.*

floor'ing, *n.*, plancher ; parquet ; parquetage, planchéiage ; (of tiles) carrelage ; (nav.) fond, *m.*

floor'-polisher, *n.*, frotteur, *m.*

flop'-hat', *n.*, claque-oreilles, *m.*

flo'ra, *n.*, (bot.) flore, *f.*

flo'ral, *adj.*, floral. — games ; *jeux floraux, m.pl.* — beetle ; *cétoine, f.*

Flor'entine (-'è'n'-taïne), *adj.*, florentin ; de Florence.

Flor'entine, *n.*, Florentin, *m.*, Florentine, *f.*

flores'cence (-rès'cè'n'-), *n.*, (bot.) floraison, fleuraison, *f.*

flo'ret (flô'rète), *n.*, fleurette, *f.*, fleuron, *m.*

flor'iculture, *n.*, floriculture, *f.*

flor'id, *adj.*, fleuri ; florissant; coloré.

florid'ity *ou* **flor'idness**, *n.*, teint fleuri ; style fleuri, *m. ;* fraîcheur, *f.*

flor'idly, *adv.*, d'une manière fleurie.

flor'in (-'ine), *n.*, florin, *m.*

flo'rist, *n.*, fleuriste, *m.* and *f.*

flos'culous (-kiou-), *adj.*, (bot.) flosculeux.

floss, *n.*, (of silk) bourre, *f. ;* (metal.) laitier, *m.*, scorie, *f. ;* floss, *m.*

floss'-hole, *n.* (metal.) chio ; trou du chio ; laiterol, *m.*

floss'-silk, *n.*, soie plate ; filoselle, bourre de soie,*f. ;* fleuret, *m.*

flotil'la (-til'la), *n.*, flottille, *f.*

flounce (flaou'n'ce), *n.*, volant (de robe), *m.*

flounce, *v.n.*, se débattre, s'agiter, se trémousser, se démener.

flounce, *v.a.*, garnir de volants.

floun'der (flaou'n'd'-), *n.*, carrelet, *m. ;* plie franche,*f.*

floun'der, *v.n.*, se débattre, se démener, barboter.

flour (flaour), *n.*, farine ; (of potatoes, etc.) fécule, *f.* —box, —dredger; *boîte à farine, f.* — dealer ; *marchand de farines, m.* — merchant ; *négociant en farines, m.* — mill ; *moulin à farine, m.* — trade; *commerce des farines, m.*

flour, *v.a.*, convertir en farine; enfariner, saupoudrer de farine.

flour'ish (fleur'ishe), *n.*, éclat ; enjolivement, embellissement, *m. ;* (with a sword) action de brandir, *f. ;* (rhet.) fleur, *f. ;* (with a pen) trait, trait de plume, parafe ; (mus.) air rapide, prélude, *m. ;* (of a trumpet) fanfare, *f.*

flour'ish, v.a., fleurir ; embellir ; (with a pen) parafer ; (a stick, a sword) brandir.

flour'ish, v.n., fleurir ; prospérer, être florissant ; (of plants) venir bien ; (with a pen) faire des traits de plume ; (mus.) préluder, sonner une fanfare ; (fig.) s'agiter ; (in speaking) s'exprimer en style fleuri ; faire des phrases.

flour'isher, n., qui brandit ; qui fait des phrases, des traits de plume ; qui fait parade, qui fait le fanfaron.

flour'ishing, adj., florissant.

flour'ishingly, adv., d'une manière florissante.

flout (flaoute), n., (ant.) insulte, moquerie, raillerie, f.

flout, v.a., (ant.) insulter ; railler ; se moquer de ; se rire de.

flow (flô), n., écoulement, flux ; épanchement, m. ; effusion ; abondance, f.

flow, v.n., s'écouler, couler ; (of the sea) monter, fluer ; (of the tide) monter, fluer. To — in ; affluer, arriver en foule. To — from ; découler de, provenir de, venir de. To — back ; refluer. To — down ; couler, descendre. To — off ; s'écouler. To — over ; déborder, se déborder.

flow, v.a., inonder, submerger.

flow'er (flaou-eur), n., fleur, f. ; (in a crown) fleuron, m.

flow'er, v.a., orner de fleurs artificielles, de figures de fleurs.

flow'er, v.n., fleurir, être en fleur ; (of ale) fermenter ; (fig.) être en vogue.

flow'er-bed, plate-bande, f.

flow'er-bud, bouton de fleur, m.

flow'er-de-luce' (-di-liouce), n., fleur de lis, f. ; (bot.) iris de Florence, iris des marais, m. V. **fleur de lis**.

flow'er-dust (-deuste), n., (bot.) pollen, m. ; poussière fécondante, f.

flow'ered (flaoueurde), adj., figuré ; à fleurs ; fleuri. Double — ; à fleurs doubles.

flow'eret (-ète), n., petite fleur, fleurette, f. ; fleuron, m.

flow'er-fence (-fè'n'ce), n., (bot.) poincillade, poinciane, f., santal rouge, m.

flow'er-garden (-gârd'n), n., jardin fleuriste ; parterre, m.

flow'er-gentle (-djè'n't'l), n., (bot.) amarante, f.

flow'er-girl, n., bouquetière, f.

flow'eriness, n., abondance de fleurs, f. ; caractère fleuri ; style fleuri, m.

flow'er-leaf (-lîfe), n., (bot.) pétale, m.

flow'erless, adj., sans fleurs ; défleuri.

flow'er-market, n., marché aux fleurs, m.

flow'er-pot (-pote), n., pot à fleurs ; vase à fleurs, m.

flow'er-show (-shô), n., exposition de fleurs, f.

flow'er-stalk (-stôke), n., (bot.) pédoncule, m., hampe, f.

flow'er-stand (-sta'n'de), n., jardinière (meuble), f. ; porte-fleurs, m.

flow'er-work (-weurke), n., fleurs artificielles, f.pl. ; ouvrage à fleurs, m. ; fleurons, m.pl.

flow'ery, adj., orné de fleurs, plein de fleurs, fleuri ; (her.) fleuré, fleureté, fleuronné.

flow'ing (flô-), adj., coulant, débordant ; naturel ; (waving) flottant.

flow'ing, n., cours, écoulement, m. ; (fig.) épanchement, torrent, m. ; effusion, abondance, affluence, f.

flow'ingly, adv., coulamment ; couramment ; avec abondance.

flown, adj. part., envolé. High — ; (of style) gonflé, ampoulé, outré ; fier, altier.

fluc'tuant, **fluc'tuating** (fleukt'-iou-), adj., flottant ; incertain ; irrésolu, indécis, variable, changeant.

fluc'tuate (fleukt'iou-éte), v.n., balancer, flotter ; hésiter, varier.

fluctua'tion (-'iou-é-), n., balancement, doute, m. ; agitation, fluctuation, f.

flue (fliou), n., duvet, poil, m. ; tuyau de cheminée ; (of an engine) carneau, m.

flu'ency (fliou-), n., facilité, volubilité, abondance, f.

flu'ent, adj., coulant, aisé ; abondant ; éloquent ; disert.

flu'ently, adv., coulamment ; couramment, facilement.

flue'-surface (-seur-fèce), n., surface de chauffe, f.

fluff, n., bourre, f.

flu'id (fliou'-), n., fluide, liquide, gaz, m.

flu'id, adj., fluide, liquide ; gazeux, gazéiforme.

fluid'ity ou **flu'idness**, n., fluidité, f.

fluke (fliouke), n., (ich.) plie franche, f., carrelet, m. ; (nav.) patte d'ancre, f. ; (fig.) coup de hasard, m. ; (at billiards) raccroc, m. By a —; par un raccroc ; par un coup de hasard.

flum'mery (fleum'meuri), n., gelée d'avoine, bouillie, f. ; (jest.) fadaises, sornettes, blagues, f.pl.

flunk'ey, n., valet, laquais ; plat valet ; (fig.) valet de carreau, m.

flu'or (fliou-), n., (min.) fluor, spath fluor, m. — spar ; spath fluor.

flu'orin ou **flu'orine**, n., (chem.) fluor, m.

flur'ry (fleur'-), n., agitation, hâte, f., désordre ; trouble, émoi, m.

flur'ry, v.a., agiter, troubler ; ahurir.

flush (fleushe), n., rouge, m. ; rougeur, f. ; (of water) flux ; (at cards) flux ; (mus.) fredon ; (of joy) accès de joie, transport de joie, m. ; agitation ; (ant.) fraîcheur, f. ; éclat, m.

flush, v.a., colorer ; faire rougir, rougir ; (sewers, etc.,) inonder ; (pour nettoyer) laver à grande eau ; (hunt.) lever, faire lever, faire partir ; animer, exciter, enfler.

flush, v.n., rougir, (of the blood) monter au visage ; survenir ; partir tout à coup ; accourir ; briller, resplendir, rayonner.

flush, adj., frais, plein de vigueur ; élevé ; animé ; (level) à fleur ; (of doors) à saillies ; (arch.) affleuré. To be — of money ; être bien pourvu d'argent ; avoir les poches pleines.

flush'-deck (-dèke), n., (nav.) pont entier, franc-tillac, m.

flush'er, n., (orni.) lanier, m.

flush'ing, n., rougeur, f. ; rouge qui monte au visage, m. ; (of drains) nettoiement à grande eau, f. ; flaquées d'eau, f.pl. What can be more significant than this sudden —? quoi de plus expressif que cette rougeur subite ?

flush'ness, n., fraîcheur, f. ; éclat, m. ; abondance, f.

flus'ter (fleus'teur), v.a., déconcerter ; enivrer à moitié ; exciter ; échauffer, agiter, ahurir.

flus'ter, n., excitation ; confusion, f. ; emportement, trouble, m.

flute (flioute), n., flûte ; (arch.) cannelure (en creux), f. ; (baking) flûte, f. Beaked — ; flûte à bec. German — ; flûte allemande, flûte traversière, f.

flute, v.a., (arch.) canneler (en creux) ; tuyauter.

flute, v.n., jouer de la flûte, (jest.) flûter.

flu'ted, adj., flûté.

flu'ting (fliout'-), n., (arch.) striure ; cannelure, f. ; tuyautage, m.

flu'tist, n., joueur de flûte, flûtiste, m.

flut'ter ou **flut'tering** (fleut'-), n., trémoussement ; fracas, émoi ; désordre, trouble ; battement d'ailes, m. ; agitation ; vibration ; ondulation, f. To put in a — ; mettre en émoi. I'm all of a — ; je suis tout agité, tout déconcerté ; je ne sais où j'en suis.

flut'ter, v.a., mettre en désordre, faire voltiger ; agiter ; déranger, troubler, déconcerter ; ahurir, effaroucher.

flut'ter, v.n., battre des ailes ; se trémousser ; voltiger, s'agiter, palpiter, tressaillir ; (of the pulse) onduler.

flu'vial, adj., fluvial, fluviatile.

flux (fleukse), n., flux ; courant, m. ; dysenterie, f. ; (metal.) flux, m.

flux, v.a., (ant.) fondre ; (med.) faire saliver ; purger.

flux'ion (fleuk'sheune), n., fluxion, f. ; écoulement, m.

fly (flaïe), n., mouche ; voiture de place, de louage, f. ; (of wheels) volant, m. ; (of trousers) brayette, f. Spanish —; (ent.) cantharide, f. Gad—; taon, m. The — on the coach wheel ; la mouche du coche (La Fontaine).

fly, v.a., (preterit, Flew ; past part., Flown), faire voler ; fuir, éviter, quitter, abandonner. To — one's country ; quitter, abandonner son pays. To — a kite ; enlever, ou faire voler, un cerf volant.

fly, v.n. (preterit, Flew ; past part., Flown), fuir ; s'enfuir ; voler ; s'envoler, se sauver, prendre la fuite ; (wave) flotter ; (fig.) échapper à, se soustraire à. Time flies ; le temps fuit. The wind flies about ; le vent saute. To — to the head ; monter, ou porter, à la tête. To — in the face of ; insulter, défier, braver ; sauter au visage de. To — on, ou at ; se jeter sur, s'élancer sur, sauter sur. To — asunder ; se détacher, se séparer ; (to break) éclater, se briser. To — away ; s'envoler, s'enfuir. To — off ; se détacher subitement. To — back ; faire un saut en arrière, reculer ; (of things) faire ressort. To — back ; (of the horse) ruer. To — open ; s'ouvrir de soi-même, ou subitement. To — up ; monter, voler, sauter ; (of sparks) jaillir. To — out ; s'élancer, se précipiter dehors ; entrer en fureur, faire des sorties, éclater. To — into a passion ; s'emporter, se mettre en colère. To — from justice ; se soustraire à la justice. To — in a battle ; tourner le dos. To — for refuge ; se réfugier. To — the kingdom ; émigrer, s'exiler. To — in pieces ; se rompre, éclater, se briser, voler en éclats. To — abroad, about (of rumors) ; se répandre.

fly'-bane (-béne), n., (bot.) silène, herbe aux mouches, f., attrape-mouche, behen blanc, m.

fly'-bitten ('-t'n), adj., marqué de chiures de mouches, piqué des mouches.

fly'-blow (-blō), n., chiure de mouche, f. ; œuf de mouche, m.

fly'-blown, part. adj., gâté, corrompu ; sali par les mouches ; plein de vers.

fly'-boat (-bôte), n., (nav.) flûte, mouche, f. ; flibot, m.

fly'-catcher, n., attrapeur de mouches ; nigaud ; gobe-mouches, m. ; personne crédule, f. ; (orni.) gobe-mouches, m.

fly'-driver, n., cocher de cabriolet ; cocher de voiture de place, de remise, m.

fly'-fish, v.n., pêcher à la ligne avec des mouches.

fly'-fishing, n. pêche à la mouche, f.

fly'-flap, n., chasse-mouches, émouchoir, m.

fly'ing (flaï-igne), part. adj.,volant. — camp; camp volant, m. — colors ; enseignes déployées, f.pl. — squadron ; (nav.) escadre d'évolution, f. — gib; clinfoc, m. — horse; cheval ailé, m. — report ; bruit qui court, m. To come off with — colors ; s'en tirer avec honneur.

fly'-leaf, n., feuillet blanc, m., garde, f.

fly'-paper, n., mort aux mouches, f.

fly'-sheet, n., feuille volante, f.

fly'-speck, n., chiure de mouche, f.

fly'-trap, n., (bot.) dionée, f. ; attrape-mouche, m.

fly'-wheel (-hwïle), n., (mec.) volant, m.

foal (fôle), n., poulain, m. ; pouliche, f. ; petit d'une bête de somme, m. — of the ass ; ânon, m. In, ou with, —; pleine.

foal, v.n., pouliner ; mettre bas.

foal'-bit, n., (bot.) chardon aux ânes, m.

foaled, p.p. and adj., mis bas, né.

foam (fôme), n., écume, f. ; bouillon, m.

foam, v.n., écumer ; jeter de l'écume ; (nav.) moutonner ; (fig.) être en colère. To — with rage; écumer de rage, de colère.

foam'ing, part., écumant ; couvert d'écume.

foam'y, adj., écumeux, écumant.

fob, n., gousset, ⊙bourson, m. ; petite poche ; (ant.) tromperie, f.

fob (off), v.a., (ant.) duper, tromper, tricher, frauder.

fo'cal (fô-), adj., focal, du foyer ; qui appartient au foyer.

fo'cus (fô-keusse), n., (geom. and opt.) foyer, m. The — of a mirror ; le foyer d'un miroir. The — of a parabola ; le foyer d'une parabole. In —; au point, à portée.

fo'cus, v.a., (opt.) mettre au foyer ; mettre au point.

fo'cusing, n., (opt.) mise au foyer; mise au point.

fo'cusing-glass, n.,(photography) objectif, m.

fod'der, n., fourrage, m. ; pâture, f.

fod'der, v.n., fourrager ; aller au fourrage ; (nav.). V. **foth'er**.

fod'dering, n., affouragement, m.

foe (fô), n., ennemi ; adversaire, m. —man; ennemi, m.

fœtus (fï-), n., fœtus, embryon, m.

fog, n., brouillard, m. ; brouée ; (fig.) obscurité, confusion, perplexité, f. Sea—; brume, f. — signal ; signal de brume, m. — bank ; banquise,f. (V. Hugo).— bell; cloche d'avertissement, f. — horn; sirène, f.

fog, v.a., embarrasser, embrouiller, (pop.) coller.

fog'gily (-'ghi), adv., obscurément.

fog'giness (-'ghi-), n., (of the air) état brumeux, obscur ; brouillard, m., brume, f. ; (fig.) obscurité,f.

fog'gy (-'ghi), adj., épais ; brumeux ; embrumé, (fig.) sombre, obscur. It is —; il fait du brouillard.

fo'gy ou **fo'gey**, n., fossile, croûton, m. ; ganache, vieille perruque, f. Old —; vieille croûte, f.

foh ! (feu), int., fi ! pouah !

foi'ble (foï'b'l), n., faible, m. pl., faiblesses, f.pl. Wise men know their own —s (weak side); les gens d'esprit connaissent leur faible.

foil (foïl), n., défaite, f. ; échec ; (set off) ornement, relief, contraste, repoussoir ; (fenc.) fleuret, m. ; (for a stone) feuille, f. ; étain en feuilles, tain, m. To act as a — to ; donner de l'éclat, du relief à ; faire ressortir.

foil, v.a., vaincre ; déjouer, faire échouer ; désarmer, frustrer, dépister.

foil'ing, n., (hunt.) abattures, foulées, foulures, f.pl. ; (fig.) déconcertement, m.

foin (foïne), n., (fenc.) botte, f. ; coup, m.

foin, v.n., porter, ou allonger, ou pousser, une botte.

foist, v.a., fourrer, interpoler ; insérer ; intercaler ; introduire ; glisser ; couler ; (ant.) tromper, mystifier, attraper. To — anything upon any one ; passer à, glisser à ; (fam.) faire avaler à, couler à, fourrer à.

fold (fôlde), n., (fig.) l'Eglise; plissure, f.; pli, (fig.) repli, m. ; enveloppe, f. ; troupeau ; parc, bercail, m. ; (of a door) battant, m. ; (of a screen) feuille, f. — of sheep ; bergerie, f., bercail, m. Two—; double. Three—; triple. A hundred—; centuple.

fold, v.a., plisser ; plier, ployer ; envelopper ; serrer. To — a letter ; plier une lettre. To — sheep; parquer des moutons. To — one's arms; croiser les bras.

fold'age (fôld'édje), n., (ant.) droit de parcage, m.

fold'er, n., (pers.) plieur, m., plieuse, f.; (tool) plioir, m. pl., pince-nez, m.

fold'ing, n., pliage; parcage, m.

fold'ing, part. adj., pliant; brisé, (of screens) à feuilles. —-chair; fauteuil pliant, m., chaise pliante, f. —-doors; porte à deux battants, porte brisée, f. —-screen; paravent, m. —-stick; plioir, m. —-bed; lit pliant, m. —-stool; pliant, siège pliant, m. —-machine; plieuse, f. —-table; table pliante, f.

fold'less, adj., sans plis.

folia'ceous (fô-li-é-sheusse), adj., (bot.) foliacé.

fo'liage (fô-li-édje), n., feuillage, m.; (arch.) feuille, f.

fo'liage, v.a., orner de feuillage; (arch.) orner de feuilles.

fo'liaged, adj., garni de feuillage; à feuillage.

fo'liate (fô-), v.a., (ant.) battre en feuilles; étamer (un miroir).

fo'liate ou **fo'liated**, adj., (bot.) feuillé, garni de feuilles.

folia'tion (fô-lié-), n., réduction d'un métal en feuilles, f., étamage, m.; (bot.) feuillaison; foliation, f.

fo'lio (fô-liô), n., in-folio, m.; page, f.; le chiffre qui désigne le numéro des pages d'un livre, folio, m.; feuillet; feuille, f.; (com.) folio, m.

fo'lio, v.a., (print.) paginer.

fo'liomort (fô-li-o-meurte), adj., (color) feuille-morte (invariable).

folk (fôke), n., gens, personnes, f.pl.; monde, m. They are good kind of —; ce sont de bonnes gens.

folk'-lore, n., légendes, traditions, superstitions, f.pl.; croyances populaires, f.pl.

folk'mote (fôk'môte), n., assemblée du peuple, f.

fol'licle (-'k'l), n., (bot., anat.) follicule, m.

follic'ular, adj., folliculaire.

fol'low (-lô), v.a. and n., suivre; poursuivre; rechercher; observer; imiter; s'ensuivre; s'appliquer à, s'abandonner à; continuer, s'attacher à. To — a profession; exercer une profession, un état. As —s; ainsi qu'il suit, comme il suit. It does not — that; il ne s'ensuit pas que. To — that; il s'ensuit que. That does not —; ce n'est pas une conséquence nécessaire, ce n'est pas une raison.

fol'lower, n., sectateur; suivant; dépendant; partisan; imitateur; compagnon; (pop.) amoureux, m.

fol'lowing, part.adj., suivant, (consecutive) de suite. The year —; l'année suivante, f.

fol'lowing, n., suite, f., gens, m.pl.; parti, m.

fol'ly (fol'li), n., folie, sottise, imprudence, f.

foment', v.a., échauffer; animer, fomenter, encourager.

fomenta'tion (fô-mè'n'té-), n., fomentation, f.

foment'ed, part.adj., fomenté.

foment'er, n., fomentateur; fauteur, m.

fond, adj., passionné pour; (foolish) sot, peu judicieux; vain; fou de; (kind) indulgent pour, bon pour, f.; (of hopes) doux, cher, vif, ardent. — ways; manières caressantes, tendresses, f.pl. To be — of; aimer, affectionner, tenir à. To be — of a rubber; aimer à faire un robre; aimer à faire une partie de whist. To be passionately — of; aimer à la folie; être fou de; être passionné pour.

fon'dle (fo'n'd'l), v.a., dorloter, caresser; To — a child; caresser un enfant.

fon'dler, n., celui qui dorlote; qui caresse.

fon'dling, n., mignon, favori, enfant gâté, m.; caresses, f.pl.

fond'ly, adv., tendrement; passionnément; à la folie; follement, sottement.

fond'ness, n., passion; douceur; tendresse, tendresse aveugle, f.; attachement, m.; (fig.) inclination, f., penchant, goût, m.

font (fo'n'te), n., fonts baptismaux, m.pl., (ant.) source, fontaine; (print.) fonte, f.

fon'tanel (-nèle), n., (surg.) cautère; vésicatoire; séton, m.; (anat.) fontanelle, f.

fontange' (fo'n'tâ'n'dje), n., (head-dress knot) fontange, f.

food (foude), nourriture, subsistance, f.; aliment, m.; vivres, m.pl.; (animals) pâture, f. Article of —; comestible, produit, m.

fool (foule), n., sot; insensé, imbécile, niais; nigaud, m.; bête; dupe, f.; (jester) fou, bouffon, m.; (of shows) pitre, paradiste, m. To make a — of one; se jouer de quelqu'un. To play the —; faire la bête; badiner. To play the — with; se moquer de; se ficher de. To make a — of one's self; se rendre ridicule; se faire moquer de soi. To be a — for one's pains; être un jobard (V. Hugo). A fool's bolt is soon shot; (prov.) de fou juge brieve sentence. —s have the best luck; (prov.) la fortune rit aux sots; aux innocents les mains pleines. Not such a —; pas si bête.

fool, v.a., se moquer de, badiner; tromper, duper, refaire; (fam.) bafouer, berner, blaguer. To — any one out of his money; plumer quelqu'un. To — away; gaspiller; dissiper follement; (of time) baguenauder; perdre le temps à des bagatelles.

fool, v.n., faire la bête; s'amuser à des riens.

fool'-born, adj., niais, idiot de naissance.

fool'ery, n., folie, sottise; niaiserie, bouffonnerie; badinerie, f.; badinage, m.

fool'hardily, adv., témérairement.

fool'hardiness, n., folle audace; témérité, f.

fool'hardy, adj., téméraire.

fool'ing, n., badinage, m.; niaiserie, bouffonnerie, f.

fool'ish, adj., simple, sot; imbécile, vain, ridicule.

fool'ishly, adv., follement, sottement, bêtement; folâtrement.

fool'ishness, n., folie; simplicité, sottise, f.

fool's'-cap, n., papier écolier, papier tellière, f.; (fig.) bonnet d'âne, m.

fool's-par'sley, n., (bot.) petite ciguë, f

fool'-trap, n., attrape-nigaud, m.

foot (foute), n. (feet), pied, m.; patte, (of a pair of compasses) jambe; (of a pillar) base, f.; (of a sail) fond, m. —-soldiers; infanterie. — by —; pied à pied. Cat's—; (bot.) pied-de-chat, m. Dove's—; pied-de-pigeon, m. Hare—; pied-de-lièvre, m. — of a page; bas d'une page, m. At —; ci-dessous, ci-bas, ci-après. To set on —; mettre en train. To put one's — into anything; se mettre dans le pétrin; faire un gâchis; mettre les pieds dans le plat. To put one's best — foremost; se trémousser; user de toute la diligence possible; partir du bon pied. To set on —; mettre en train, mettre sur pied; (a subject, a conversation) commencer, entamer. To set on —; mettre le pied sur.

foot, v.a., fouler aux pieds; donner des coups de pied à. To — a stocking; mettre un pied à un bas.

foot, v.n., marcher, aller à pied; danser. To — it; y aller à pied.

foot'-artillery, n., artillerie à pied, f.

foot'ball (-bôl), n., ballon, m.

foot'-bath, n., bain de pieds, m.

foot'board (-bôrde), n., marchepied, m.; (of musical instruments) pédale, f.

foot'boy (-boï), n., petit laquais; valet de pied, petit groom, m.

foot'bridge, n., passerelle, f.

foot'cloth (-cloth), n., (ant.) housse, f.

foot'ed (-ède), adj., qui a des pieds. Broad—; qui a le pied large; au pied large. Four—; à quatre pattes.

foot'fall, n., pas, m.

foot'-guards (-gârdze), n.pl., les gardes à pied, m.pl.

foot'hold (-hôlde), *n.*, place pour le pied, *f.*; prise pour le pied, *f.* To get a — ; *prendre pied.* To lose one's — ; *perdre pied, perdre l'équilibre.*

foot'ing, *n.*, position, *f.*; pied, établissement, point d'appui, *m.* To pay one's — ; *payer les droits d'admission.* On a war —, *ou* peace — ; *sur un pied de guerre, ou de paix.* On the same — as; *sur le même pied que; aux mêmes conditions que.* He missed his — ; *le pied lui manqua.*

foot'-lamps *ou* **foot'-lights** (-laïtse), *n.pl.*, (thea.) rampe, *f.sing.*

foot'man (-ma'n), *n.*, laquais; valet de pied, *m.*

foot'note, *n.*, note au bas de la page, *f.*

foot'pace (-péce), *n.*, (arch.) palier, *m.*; estrade, *f.*; pas à pas; pas, *m.* At a — ; *au pas.*

foot'pad, *n.*, voleur de grand chemin, *m.*

foot'path (-pâth), *n.*, sentier; (in streets) trottoir, *m.*

foot'-pavement, *n.*, trottoir, *m.*

foot'-post, *n.*, messager à pied, *m.*

foot'-print, *n.*, empreinte du pied, *f.*

foot'-race (-réce), *n.*, course à pied, *f.*

foot'-rope (-rôpe), *n.*, (nav.) marchepied, *m.*; ralingue de voile, *f.*

foot'-rot (-rote), *n.*, (vet.) fourchet, *m.*

foot'-rule, *n.*, pied-de-roi, *m.*

foot'sore, *adj.*, les pieds meurtris.

foot'stalk (-stôke), *n.*, (bot.) pétiole, *m.*

foot'stall (-stôl), *n.*, étrier de femme, *m.*

foot'step (-stèpe), *n.*, trace, *f.*; vestige; (tech.) marchepied, pas, *m.*

foot'stool (-stoule), *n.*, marchepied; tabouret, *m.*

foot'-warmer, *n.*, chaufferette, bouillotte, *f.*

foot'way (-wé), *n.*, sentier; trottoir, *m.*

fop, *n.*, petit-maître; freluquet, damoiseau, fat, *m.*

fop'ling, *n.*, petit fat; dameret; freluquet, *m.*

fop'pery, *n.*, niaiserie; sottise; afféterie, ostentation; affectation, fatuité, *f.*

fop'pish, *adj.*, recherché; affecté; vain.

fop'pishly, *adv.*, avec affectation; avec vanité; en fat.

fop'pishness, *n.*, impertinence; fatuité; élégance affectée, prétention, ostentation, *f.*

for, *prep.*, pour, avant, par, de, à, pendant, malgré, nonobstant que, sans, n'eût été. — your sake; *pour l'amour de vous.* — pity's sake; *par pitié.* — the present; *pour le présent; pour le moment; quant à présent.* — aught we know; *autant qu'on sache, autant que nous sachions.* — one's self; *pour son compte.* It is not — you to; *ce n'est pas à vous de.* In exchange —; *en échange de.* — (since) a month; *depuis un mois.* Had it not been — him; *n'eût été, ou sans, lui.*

for, *conj.*, car. — that (because); *par la raison que.*

for'age (-'èdje), *n.*, fourrage, *m.*; (ant.) provisions, *f.pl.* — cap; (milit.) *bonnet de police, m.*

for'age, *v.n.*, fourrager; piller; ravager; désoler.

for'ager, *n.*, fourrageur, *m.*

for'aging, *n.*, fourrage; ravage, *m.*; déprédation, *f.*

forasmuch', *conj.*, vu que; d'autant que, attendu que.

fo'ray (fô'ré), *n.*, incursion, razzia, *f.*; ravage, pillage, *m.* *v.a.*, ravager, piller.

forbear' (-bère), *v.a.* and *n.*, cesser; épargner; supporter; éviter de; se dispenser de; se retenir de, s'abstenir de; s'arrêter de; traiter avec clémence; ménager; prendre patience.

forbear'ance, *n.*, clémence; patience; tolérance, indulgence, *f.*; ménagement, *m.*

forbear'ingly, *adv.*, avec patience, avec tolération, avec indulgence.

forbid', *v.a.*, défendre de, interdire de; pro-

hiber; empêcher de; s'opposer à. To — a person to (do); *défendre à quelqu'un de.* To — a thing to (any one); *défendre quelque chose à quelqu'un.* He is forbidden to; *on lui défend de ou il lui est défendu de.* God — ! *ou* Heaven — ! *à Dieu ne plaise !*

forbid'ding, *n.*, défense, interdiction, *f.*

forbid'ding, *adj.*, rebutant; repoussant, répulsif.

force (fôrce), *n.*, force; violence; contrainte; nécessité, vertu; validité, *f.* In — ; (jur.) en vigueur ; (milit.) en force.

force, *v.a.*, forcer à, réduire à, contraindre à *ou* de; violenter; violer. To — back; *repousser, refouler.* To — down; *faire descendre de force.* To — in; *enfoncer, cogner.* To — open; *forcer.* To — on; *imposer à.* To — out; *chasser de force, faire sortir, débusquer.* To — a passage; *forcer un passage.* To — one's way through; *s'ouvrir un chemin par la force.* To — one's way into; *entrer de force dans.*

forced (fôrste), *past part. adj.*, forcé; contraint; obligé; (of style) guindé.

for'cedly (fôrcèd'li), *adv.*, de force; forcément; par contrainte; nécessairement.

force'less, *adj.*, (ant.) faible; sans force.

force'meat (-mîte), *n.*, godiveau, *m.*, farce, *f.* — balls; *boulettes de viande, quenelles, f.pl.*

for'ceps (for'cèpse), *n.pl.*, (surg.) pince, *f.*; forceps, *m.sing.*

for'cer (fôr-), *n.*, personne qui force, *f.*; (mec.) piston foulant, refouleur, *m.* pl., (surg.) davier (to draw teeth), *m.*

for'cible, *adj.*, puissant; efficace; emphatique; énergique; violent; forcé; fort; (jur.) par force.

for'cibleness, *n.*, force; vigueur; violence, *f.*

for'cibly, *adv.*, puissamment; par force; fortement; emphatiquement.

for'cing, *part.*, contraignant; (gard.) l'action de forcer, d'avancer, de hâter, de mûrir les fruits, *f.*

for'cing-house, *n.*, serre chaude, *f.*

for'cing-pipe, *n.*, tuyau de refoulement, *m.*

for'cing-pump (-peu'm'pe), *n.*, pompe foulante, *f.*

ford (fôrde), *n.*, gué, *m.*; (fig. and poet.) fleuve, *m.*; onde, *f.*

ford, *v.a.*, passer à gué; guéer, traverser à gué.

ford'able (fôrd'a'b'l), *adj.*, guéable; qu'on peut passer à gué.

fore (fôre), *n.*, (nav.) avant, *m.* — and aft; *de l'avant à l'arrière.*

fore, *adj.*, antérieur; de devant. The — part; *la partie antérieure; le devant.*

fore, *adv.*, devant, auparavant, antérieurement.

fore'-arm (-ârme), *n.*, avant-bras, *m.*

fore'arm, *v.a.*, armer, munir; prémunir, fortifier par avance. Forewarned, forearmed; ⊙*qui dit averti, dit muni; un bon averti en vaut deux.*

forebode' (-bôde), *v.a.*, présager; prédire; pressentir; avoir le pressentiment de; pronostiquer.

forebo'der, *n.*, devin, prophète, *m.*; personne qui prédit, *f.*

forebo'ding, *n.*, présage, pressentiment, *m.*, prédiction, *f.*

fore'-cabin, *n.*, chambre de l'avant, *f.*; secondes, *f.pl.*

fore'-carriage, *n.*, avant-train, *m.*

fore'cast (-câste), *n.*, prévoyance, prévision, prédiction, *f.*; pressentiment; calcul, projet, plan, *m.*

forecast', *v.a.*, prédire, prévoir; (ant.) préméditer, projeter; concerter d'avance.

forecast'er, *n.*, devin, *m.*, (ant.) personne qui prémédite *ou* prévoit, *f.*

forecas'tle (foque-s'l), *n.*, (nav.) château d'avant; gaillard d'avant, *m.*

forecho'sen (-tshô'z'n), *part. adj.*, choisi d'avance ; élu d'avance.

foreci'ted (-çaït'ède), *adj.*, (ant.) précité ; cité auparavant.

foreclose' (-clôze), *v.a.*, exclure ; (jur.) forclore ; prévenir.

foreclo'sure (-jioure), *n.*, empêchement, *m. ;* (jur.) forclusion, *f.*

fore'court (-côrte), *n.*, avant-cour, *f.*

foredate', *v.a.*, (ant.) antidater. *V.* **postdate**.

fore'deck (-dèke), *n.*, (nav.) l'avant d'un navire ; gaillard d'avant, *m.*

fore'ditch, *n.*, (fort.) avant-fossé, *m.*

foredoom' (-doume), *v.a.*, (ant.) prédestiner ; déterminer par avance.

fore'-end (-è'n'de), *n.*, partie de devant ; partie antérieure, *f. ;* commencement, *m.*

fore'father (-fâ-*theur*), *n.*, aïeul, ancêtre, *m. pl.*, aïeux, ancêtres, *m.pl.*

fore'finger (-fi'gn'gheur), *n.*, index, *m.*

fore'foot (-foute), *n.*, pied de devant, *m.*

fore'front, *n.*, façade, face d'une maison, *f. ;* frontispice, *m.* In the — ; (mil.) *au premier rang.*

forego' (-gô), *v.a.*, céder ; renoncer **à**, abandonner ; résigner ; se désister **de** ; précéder ; (ant.) perdre, quitter.

forego'er (-gô-eur), *n.*, aïeul ; ancêtre ; précurseur ; prédécesseur, *m.*

forego'ing (-gô'-), *part. adj.*, précédent, antérieur. The — day ; *le jour précédent, m.*

foregone', *adj.*, passé ; déterminé, résolu, pris d'avance. — conclusion ; *parti pris, m. ; opinion toute faite ; opinion préconçue, f.*

fore'ground (-graou'n'de), *n.*, devant ; (paint.) premier plan, *m.*

fore'hand, *n.*, devant d'un cheval, *m. ;* partie principale, préférence, *f.*, avantage, *m.*

fore'handed (-dède), *adj.*, fait à temps, de bonne heure, à propos ; formé en tête, en avant, sur le devant.

fore'head (-hède), *n.*, front, *m. ;* (fig.) audace, assurance, effronterie, *f.* Low — ; *front bas.* High — ; *front haut.* Broad — ; *front large.* — of a horse ; *chanfrein, m.* — cloth ; *bandeau, frontal, m.*

for'eign (for'ine), *adj.*, étranger ; (of plants) exotique ; (com. ; of bills) sur l'étranger ; qui vient du dehors ; à l'étranger ; extérieur ; (fig.) incompatible **avec**. That is — to his nature ; *cela lui répugne, est incompatible avec son caractère.* — office ; *ministère des affaires étrangères, m.* In — parts ; *à l'étranger, dans les pays étrangers.* — built ; *de construction étrangère.* — grown ; *de provenance étrangère.*

for'eigner (for'in'eur), *n.*, étranger ; (jur.) aubain (l.u.), *m.*

for'eignness, *n.*, (ant.) éloignement ; air étranger, *m. ;* inapplicabilité, étrangeté, nouveauté, *f.*

forejudge' (-djeu'dje), *v.a.*, (jur.) rayer de la matricule ; (ant.) préjuger ; juger par avance, ou d'avance ; être prévenu **contre**.

forejudg'ment, *n.*, jugement par contumace, *m. ;* prévention, *f.*

foreknow' (-nô), *v.a.*, connaître, savoir d'avance ; prévoir.

fore-knowl'edge (-nol'èdje), *n.*, prescience, prévision, *f.*

for'el (for'èle), *n.*, parchemin (for the cover of books), *m.*

fore'land, *n.*, (geog.) promontoire, cap, *m. ;* pointe de terre, pointe, *f.*

foreleg', *n.*, jambe de devant, *f.*

fore'lock, *n.*, (nav.) goupille, *f. ;* cheveux de devant, toupet, *m.pl. ;* (on carriages) esse, *f.* To take time by the — ; *saisir, ou prendre, l'occasion aux cheveux.*

fore'man, *n.*, chef ; premier ouvrier, contremaître ; (of a shop) chef d'atelier ; (of a jury) chef du jury ; (of a printing-office) prote, *m.*

fore'mast (-mâste), *n.*, (nav.) mât d'avant ; mât de misaine, *m.*

foremen'tioned (-mè'n'sho'n'de), *adj.*, précité, dont on a fait mention auparavant, ci-dessus, mentionné ci-dessus ; (jur.) susmentionné.

fore'most (-môste), *adj.*, premier ; le plus avancé de tous ; en tête ; au premier rang. First and — ; *tout d'abord.*

fore'named (-né'm'de), *adj.*, nommé auparavant ; susnommé.

fore'noon (-noune), *n.*, matin, *m.*, matinée, *f.* In the — ; *dans la matinée.*

foren'sic *ou* **foren'sical** (fo-rè'n'-), *adj.*, (jur.) du barreau, de palais. — medicine ; *médecine légale, f.*

fore-ordain' (-fôr-or-déne), *v.a.*, préordonner ; prédestiner ; régler d'avance.

fore'part (-pârte), *n.*, devant ; (nav.) avant, *m. ;* proue ; tête, *f.*

forepast', *adj.*, passé.

fore'-rank (-ra'gn'ke), *n.*, premier rang ; front, *m. V.* **first-rank**.

forereach' (-rîtshe), *v.a.*, (nav.) dépasser ; gagner **sur**.

fore'roof (-roufe), *n.*, (arch.) avant-toit, *m.*

forerun' (fôr'reune), *v.a.*, précéder ; devancer ; présager.

forerun'ner, *n.*, avant-coureur, précurseur ; présage, pronostic ; (ant.) prédécesseur, ancêtre, *m.*

fore'sail (-s'l), *n.*, (nav.) voile de misaine, *f.*

foresee' (-sî), *v.a.*, prévoir, avoir la prescience **de**. *v.n.*, (ant.) pourvoir **à**.

foreshad'ow (-shad'ô), *v.a.*, figurer, représenter d'avance ; faire pressentir ; annoncer.

foreshad'ow, *n.*, type, symbole, *m.*

fore'ship, *n.*, (nav.) avant d'un vaisseau, *m.*

fore'shore, *n.*, plage, *f. ;* estran *ou* estrand, *m.*

foreshort'en (-shor't'n), *v.a.*, (paint.) raccourcir.

foreshort'ening, *n.*, raccourci, *m.*

foreshow' (-shô), *v.a.*, prédire ; pronostiquer ; faire voir par avance.

fore'sight (-'saïte), *n.*, prévoyance ; (theol.) prescience ; (of fire-arms) mire, *f. ;* guidon, *m.*

fore'skin, *n.*, prépuce, *m.*

fore'skirt (-skeurte), *n.*, basque, *f. ;* pan de devant ; devant, *m.*

for'est (forèste), *n.*, forêt, *f.* Woods and —s ; *eaux et forêts, f.pl.* — ranger ; *garde forestier, m.*

for'est, *adj.*, de bois, de forêt, forestier. — laws ; *lois forestières, f.pl.*

forestall' (-stôl), *v.a.*, accaparer ; anticiper ; prévenir ; devancer ; surprendre.

forestall'er, *n.*, monopoleur, accapareur, *m.*

forestall'ing, *n.*, accaparement, *m.*

fore'stay-sail, *n.*, petit foc ; foc de misaine, *m.*

for'est-born (forèste-), *adj.*, sauvage ; né dans une forêt.

for'ested (-tède), *adj.*, couvert de forêts ; garni d'arbres ; boisé.

for'ester, *n.*, forestier, habitant d'une forêt, (ant.) arbre forestier, *m.*

fore'-tackle (-tak'k'l), *n.*, (nav.) gréement de l'avant, *m. ;* cordages du mât de misaine, *m.pl.*

fore'taste (-téste), *n.*, avant-goût, *m. ;* anticipation, *f.*

foretaste', *v.a.*, goûter par avance ; avoir un avant-goût **de**.

foretell', *v.a.*, prédire, présager, prophétiser, annoncer.

foretell'er, *n.*, prophète, *m.*

forethink' (fôr'thi'gn'k), *v.a.* and *n.*, préméditer ; prévoir ; concevoir d'avance, projeter.

fore'thought (-thôte), *n.*, prévoyance ; préméditation ; prescience, *f.*

fore'token (-tô-k'n), *n.*, (ant.) présage, pronostic ; signe, *m.*

foreto'ken, *v.a.*, (ant.) présager, pronostiquer.

fore'tooth (fôr'touth), *n.*, dent de devant,

f. The **foreteeth**; *les dents de devant*; *les incisives, f.pl.*

fore'top, *n.,* (nav.) hune de misaine, (head-dress) fontange, *f.,* tour de cheveux; toupet, *m.* — gallant-mast; *petit mât de perroquet, m.* — mast; *petit mât de hune, m.* — gallant royal mast; *petit mât de cacatois, m.*

fore'vigil (-vid'jile), *n.,* avant-veille, *f.*

fore-vouched' (-vaoutshe), *adj.,* déclaré d'avance; affirmé ci-devant.

forewarn' (-wŏrne), *v.a.,* avertir par avance; précautionner, prévenir.

fore'wheel (-hwîle), *n.,* roue de devant, *f.;* train de devant, *m.*

fore'woman (-wouma'n), *n.,* première ouvrière, *f.*

fore'wrist (-riste), *n.,* avant-poignet, métacarpe, *m.*

fore'yard (-yârde), *n.,* (arch.) avant-cour; (nav.) vergue de misaine, *f.*

for'feit (-fîte), *n.,* amende; faute; (jur.) forfaiture; confiscation, *f.;* gage; (in a bargain) dédit, *m.*

for'feit, *adj.,* confisqué; perdu.

for'feit, *v.a.* and *n.,* forfaire à; manquer à; confisquer; perdre, être passible d'une amende. To — one's word; *manquer de parole, ou manquer à sa parole.*

for'feitable, *adj.,* (ant.) confiscable; sujet à confiscation.

for'feiture (-fit'ioure), *n.,* amende; confiscation; déchéance; (jur.) forfaiture, *f.*

forfend' (for-), *v.a.,* (ant.) défendre; prévenir; garder de; détourner. God — that; *Dieu me garde de.*

forge (fôrdje), *n.,* forge, *f.*

forge, *v.a.* and *n.,* forger, contrefaire; commettre un faux; falsifier (l'écriture de); inventer, controuver, fabriquer.

for'ger, *n.,* forgeur; inventeur; faussaire; faux monnayeur, *m.*

for'gery, *n.,* falsification, *f.;* faux, *m.*

forget' (-ghète), *v.a.,* oublier de; perdre le souvenir de. —-me-not; *myosotis, m.* To — one's self; *s'oublier.*

forget'ful (-foule), *adj.,* oublieux de; négligent de. To be — of; *négliger, oublier.*

forget'fulness, *n.,* oubli, manque de mémoire, *m.;* inattention; négligence, *f.*

forget'ter, *n.,* celui qui oublie, qui néglige.

forgive' (-ghive), *v.a.,* pardonner; faire grâce de, faire remise de; remettre. To — a thing; *pardonner quelque chose à, pardonner une chose à.* To — a person; *pardonner à quelqu'un de.*

forgive'ness, *n.,* pardon, *m.;* clémence; remise, grâce, (theol.) rémission, *f.*

forgiv'er, *n.,* personne qui pardonne, *f.*

forgiv'ing, *adj.,* clément, généreux, indulgent, miséricordieux.

fork, *n.,* fourchette; fourche, (roads) bifurcation; (bot., zoöl.) (of trousers) enfourchure, *f.;* (of points) pointe, *f.;* (of lightning) zigzag, *m.*

fork, *v.n.,* fourcher, se fourcher; finir en forme de fourche.

fork, *v.a.,* enlever avec la fourche; (agri.) fourcher. To — out money; *avancer de l'argent; financer;* (fam.) *jouer du pouce; rendre gorge.*

forked (fork'te), *adj.,* fourchu; (bot.) bifurqué. — lightning; *éclair en zigzag, m.*

fork'edly (fork'èd'li), *adv.,* (ant.) en forme de fourche; en fourche.

fork'edness (fork'èd'-), *n.,* (ant.) état de ce qui est fourchu, bifurqué.

fork'-head (-hède), *n.,* (ant.) pointe de flèche, *f.*

forlorn', *adj.,* abandonné; désespéré; délaissé, solitaire; perdu. — hope; (milit.) *enfants perdus, m.pl.*

forlorn'ness, *n.,* délaissement, abandon; état désespéré, *m.;* misère, *f.*

form, *n.,* forme, figure; formalité, cérémonie,

f.; banc, *m.;* (of schools, etc.) classe, *f.;* (of horses) encolure, *f.;* (of a hare) gîte, *m.;* forme, *f.;* (print.) forme, *f.* To set a —; *composer une forme.* To take off a —; *lever une forme.* To wash the —; *laver la forme.* In due —; *dans les règles.* In the fifth —; (at school) *en cinquième* (in France); *en troisième* ou *en seconde* (in England).

form, *v.a.,* former; façonner; régler; concevoir. To — part; *faire partie de.* To — an idea of; *se faire une idée de.*

form, *v.n.,* se former; (of hares) se gîter. *pro* **formâ,** pour la forme.

for'mal, *adj.,* formel, précis, méthodique, pointilleux, minutieux; affecté; étudié; grave; cérémonieux, de forme; (of style) guindé, de convention. — cause; *cause formelle, f.*

for'malist, *n.,* formaliste; façonnier; faux dévot, *m.*

formal'ity, *n.,* formalité; cérémonie; affectation; bienséance, *f.*

for'malize (-aïze), *v.a.,* (l.u.) modifier, modeler.

for'malize, *v.n.,* (l.u.) être façonnier.

for'mally, *adv.,* avec formalité; en forme, formellement, expressément; par cérémonie.

forma'tion (-mé-), *n.,* formation, *f.*

for'mative, *adj.,* formateur; plastique; qui a le pouvoir de former. — arts; *arts plastiques, m.pl.*

form'er, *n.,* formateur, créateur, *m.;* personne qui forme, qui fait, *f.;* coupeur, *m.;* forme, *f.,* moule, *m.*

for'mer, *adj.,* premier, précédent, celui-là; passé; ancien.

for'merly, *adv.,* autrefois, jadis; anciennement, auparavant.

formica'tion (-ké-), *n.,* (med.) formication, *f.;* picotement, *m.*

for'midable (-da'b'l), *adj.,* formidable, redoutable, terrible.

for'midableness, *n.,* nature formidable, *f.;* aspect formidable, *m.*

for'midably, *adv.,* d'une manière formidable; terriblement.

form'less, *adj.,* informe, irrégulier, confus.

for'mula (-miou-), *n.,* (*formulæ*), (theol., med., and math.) formule, *f.*

for'mulary, *n.,* formulaire, *m.*

for'nicate (-k'éte), *v.n.,* forniquer.

for'nicate, *adj.,* (arch.) arqué, voûté.

fornica'tion (-ké-), *n.,* fornication, *f.;* concubinage, *m.;* (theol.) idolâtrie, *f.*

for'nicator (-ké-), *n.,* fornicateur, *m.*

for'nicatress (-ké-), *n.,* fornicatrice, *f.*

forsake' (-séke), *v.a.,* délaisser, abandonner; renoncer à; se défaire de; (of duty) manquer à. To — a vice; *se corriger d'un vice.* — one's colors; *quitter les drapeaux, déserter.* — one's religion; *apostasier.*

forsa'ker, *n.,* personne qui abandonne, *f.;* déserteur, *m.;* (theol.) apostat, *m.*

forsa'king, *n.,* délaissement, abandon, *m.,* désertion; (rel.) apostasie, *f.*

forsooth' (-south), *adv.,* en vérité; ma foi; assurément.

forswear' (-swère), *v.a.* and *n.,* abjurer; répudier; se parjurer; renoncer à; répudier; renier. To — one's self; *se parjurer.*

forswear'er, *n.,* parjure, *m.*

forswear'ing, *n.,* parjure, *m.*

fort (fôrte), *n.,* fort, *m.,* forteresse, place forte, *f.*

forte, *n.,* fort, *m.;* (mus.) forté, *m.*

forth (fôrth), *adv.,* en avant; au dehors; au loin. And so —; *et ainsi de suite; et ainsi du reste; et cætera.*

forth'coming (forth'keum'-), *adj.,* prêt à paraître, approchant, prochain, tout prêt, imminent.

forthwith' (-with), adv., incontinent, aussitôt, sur-le-champ; sans délai, tout de suite, séance tenante.

for'tieth (-ti-èth), adj., quarantième.

for'tifiable (-faï'ab'l), adj., qu'on peut fortifier, fortifiable.

fortifica'tion (-ké-), n., fortification, f.

for'tifier (-faï'-), n., ingénieur, m., personne qui fortifie, f., (b.s.) suppôt, m.

for'tify (-faïe), v.a., fortifier ; munir de, armer de ; (wine) rehausser.

for'tifying, adj., réconfortant, fortifiant.

fort'ilage (fôr-ti-lédje) (ant.) ou **fort'alice** (fôr-), n., (fort.) donjon, m., forteresse, f.

a **fortiori**, adv., à plus forte raison.

for'titude (-tioude), n., bravoure ; force, force d'âme, f., courage, m.

fort'night (-naïte), n., quinze jours, m.pl., quinzaine, f. A — ago ; il y a quinze jours. To-day — ; d'aujourd'hui en quinze. A — ago yesterday ; il y a eu hier quinze jours.

fort'nightly, adv., tous les quinze jours.

for'tress, n., forteresse, place forte, f. ; (fig.) appui, soutien, m.

fortu'itous (-tiou-i-), adj., fortuit, casuel, accidentel.

fortu'itously, adv., fortuitement ; par hasard ; accidentellement.

for'tunate (-tiou-), adj., heureux, fortuné.

for'tunately, adv., heureusement ; par bonheur.

for'tune (fort'ioune), n., fortune ; destinée, bonne aventure, f. ; sort, riche parti, m., biens, m.pl., richesses, f.pl. People of — ; les gens riches, m.pl. To have one's — told ; se faire dire la bonne aventure. To make a — ; faire fortune. To seek one's — ; chercher fortune. — knocks once at every man's door ; chacun dans sa vie a un souris de la fortune.

for'tune-hunt'er (-heun'n't'-), n., intrigant ; aventurier, m. ; qui cherche de riches partis ; coureur de dot, m.

for'tune-tell'er, n., diseur de bonne aventure, m.

for'ty, adj., quarante.

fo'rum (fô-reume), n., forum, m., place publique, f.

for'ward (-wôrde), adj., vif ; entreprenant ; hardi ; avancé ; empressé, prêt, précoce ; ardent ; impatient, impertinent, présomptueux. To bring one's self — ; se mettre en évidence.

for'ward, adv., en avant ; en évidence ; (nav.) à l'avant. From this time — ; depuis ce temps-là. From this day — ; depuis ce jour ; dorénavant.

for'ward, v.a. and n., avancer, hâter ; accélérer ; envoyer, transmettre ; faire pousser ; (com.) expédier, adresser ; (of letters) faire suivre. Please — ! prière de faire suivre !

for'warder, n., promoteur, m. ; (of goods) envoyeur, expéditionnaire, m.

for'wardly, adv., (ant.) ardemment ; avec empressement ; effrontément ; hardiment.

for'wardness, n., empressement ; avancement ; progrès, m. ; ardeur ; présomption ; précocité ; assurance, hardiesse, f.

fosse (foss), n., fossé, m. ; (anat.) fosse, f.

fos'set, n. V. **fau'cet**.

fosse'-way (-wè), n., route militaire exécutée par les Romains en Angleterre, f.

fos'sil, n., fossile, m.

fos'sil, adj., fossile. — botany ; paléontologie végétale, f.

fos'silize, v.n., se fossiliser.

fos'ter, v.a., élever, nourrir ; protéger ; favoriser, encourager.

fos'ter-broth'er (-breuth'-), n., frère de lait, m.

fos'ter-child (-tshaïlde), n., nourrisson, m.

fos'terer, n., nourrice, f. ; nourricier ; (fig.) protecteur, m. ; protectrice, f.

fos'ter-father (-fâ-theur), n., père nourricier, m. ; (fig.) père adoptif.

fos'tering, n., nourriture, éducation, f. ; tendres soins, m.

fos'tering, part. adj., bienfaisant, protecteur ; maternel, paternel ; (fig.) tendre.

fos'ter-mother (-meuth'-), n., nourrice, f.

fos'ter-sister, n., sœur de lait, f.

foth'er (foth'-), v.a., (nav.) aveugler, boucher. To — a leak ; aveugler une voie d'eau.

fougade' (-gâde), n., (milit.) fougasse, f.

foul (faoul), adj., sale, infect, vilain, impur, souillé ; (of water) trouble, bourbeux. A — stomach ; un estomac chargé. — breath ; mauvaise haleine, f. — tongue ; (fig.) mauvaise langue ; (med.) langue chargée, f. — copy ; brouillon, m. — wind ; (nav.) vent contraire, m. — weather ; gros, sale temps, m. To run — of ; heurter ; aborder par accident ; tomber sur. A — action ; (fig.) une action basse, ou vile. — dealing ; conduite déshonnête, f. — air ; air vicié, impur, m. — language ; langage obscène, grossier, bas, m. — play ; mauvais tour ; mauvais jeu ; trait de perfidie, m. ; tricherie, perfidie, f. To fall — of one another ; se brouiller ; se quereller. To fall, ou run, — of ; (nav.) aborder par accident.

foul, v.a., salir, gâter, souiller, barbouiller, troubler ; (of fire-arms) crasser ; (nav.) aborder ; (of ropes) se mêler.

foul'-faced (-féss'te), adj., laid, odieux, hideux.

foul'ing, n., encrassement ; (nav.) abordage, m.

foul'ly, adv., salement ; bassement ; vilainement ; honteusement ; d'une manière dégoûtante.

foul'-mouthed (-maouth'de), adj., grossier, qui tient des discours obscènes ; insolent.

foul'ness, n., saleté, impureté ; laideur, turpitude, perfidie, déloyauté, f.

found (faou'nde), v.a., fonder, poser les fondements de ; établir ; (to cast) fondre, jeter en moule.

founda'tion (-dé-), n., base ; (endowment) fondation ; dotation, f. ; (cause, origin) fondement, commencement, m. ; source, f. To be on the — ; être boursier. To lay the —s of ; poser les fondements de.

founda'tioner, n., boursier, m.

found'ed (-dède), part. adj., fondé, bâti, établi, basé ; (metal.) fondu, jeté en moule.

found'er. n., fondateur, auteur ; (metal.) fondeur, m. ; (vet.) courbature ; fourbure, f.

foun'der, v.a., and n., surmener un cheval, le rendre fourbu, lui fouler les jambes ; (nav.) couler à fond ; sombrer, couler bas ; (fig.) se méprendre ; échouer.

foun'dered (-'eurde), adj., (of a horse) courbatu ; fourbu ; (of ships) sombré, coulé à fond. — at sea ; sombré en mer.

foun'dery ou **foun'dry** (faou'n'-), n., fonderie, f.

found'ling, n., enfant trouvé ; enfant abandonné, m.

found'ress, n., fondatrice, f.

fount ou **foun'tain** (faou'n'te, -téne), n., fontaine, source, f. ; jet d'eau, m.

fount, n., (print.) V. **font**.

foun'tain-head (-hède), n., source, origine, f.

foun'tainless, adj., sans fontaine, sans eau.

foun'tain-maker, n., fontainier, m.

four (fôre), adj., quatre. On all —s ; à quatre pattes. Carriage and — ; voiture à quatre chevaux, f.

four'-angled, adj., à quatre angles.

four'-cornered, adj., à quatre coins.

four'fold (-fôlde), adj., quatre fois autant, quadruple ; quatre fois.

four'-footed (-foutède), adj., quadrupède, à quatre pieds.

four'-foot way, n., (rail.) voie, f. ; entre-rails, m.

four'-in-hand, n., break, m.; voiture à quatre chevaux à grandes guides.

four'-in-hand, adv., à grandes guides. To drive —; conduire à grandes guides.

four'score, adj., quatre-vingts. — and ten; quatre-vingt-dix. [gulaire.

four'square (-skwère), adj., carré; quadran-

fourteen' (fôrtîne), adj., quatorze.

fourteenth' (-tî'n'th), adj., quatorzième; (of kings and dates) quatorze.

fourth (fôrth), adj., quatrième; (of kings and dates) quatre. The — part; la quatrième partie, le quart.

fourth'ly (fôrthli), adv., quatrièmement.

four'-wheeled (-hwîlde), adj., à quatre roues.

fowl (faoul), n., oiseau, m.; volaille, f.; poulet, m. Barndoor —; poule commune, f.

fowl, v.n., tirer, chasser aux oiseaux.

fowl'er, n., oiseleur; chasseur aux oiseaux, m. —'s service; (bot.) sorbier des oiseaux, m.

fowl'-house, poulailler, m.

fowl'ing, n., chasse aux oiseaux, f.

fowl'ing-piece (pîce), n., fusil de chasse, m.

fox (fokse), n., (foxes) renard; (fig.) rusé, m. Young —; renardeau, m. A sly —; un rusé compère, m. To set the — to keep the geese; (prov.) renfermer le loup dans la bergerie.

fox'-evil (-î-v'l), n., (med.) alopécie, f.

fox'glove, n., (bot.) digitale, f.

fox'-hound (-haou'n'de), n., chien de renard, m.

fox'-hunt ou **fox'-hunting,** n., chasse au renard, f.

fox'-hunter, n., chasseur au renard, m.

fox'ish ou **fox'like** (-laïke), adj., de renard; rusé. [dière, f.

fox'-kennel ou **hole** (-kè'n'nèle), n., renar-

fox'tail (-téle), n., (bot.) queue-de-renard, f.; mélampyre des champs, m.

fox'-trap, n., trappe, f.; piège à renard, traquenard, m.

fox'y, adj., (ant.) de renard, vulpin; (fig.) rusé; (red) roux.

frac'tion (frak'sheune), n., fraction, f. Vulgar —; fraction ordinaire.

frac'tional ou **frac'tionary,** adj., fractionnaire.

frac'tious (-sheusse), adj., querelleur; maussade; hargneux, méchant, chicaneur.

frac'tiously, adv., de mauvaise humeur.

frac'tiousness, n., humeur querelleuse, hargneuse, maussade; maussaderie, f.

frac'ture (frak'tioure), n., fracture, cassure; rupture, f.

frac'ture, v.a. and n., casser, rompre, briser; (surg.) fracturer, se fracturer, se rompre.

frag'ile (fradjil), adj., fragile, frêle; faible, délicat.

fragil'ity, n., fragilité; (fig.) instabilité; faiblesse, f.

frag'ment, n., fragment, éclat, reste, débris, m. Chosen —s of an author; analectes; morceaux choisis d'un auteur, m.pl.

fra'grance ou **fra'grancy** (fré-), n., odeur suave, f.; parfum, m.

fra'grant, adj., odoriférant; odorant, parfumé; qui sent bon.

fra'grantly, adv., avec un parfum agréable.

frail (fréle), n., cabas, panier, m. A — of raisins; un panier de raisins secs.

frail (fréle), adj., frêle, fragile, faible, périssable.

frail'ness ou **frail'ty,** n., faiblesse, fragilité, infirmité, f.

frame (fréme), n., forme; charpente; figure, f.; châssis, (of picture) cadre, m., bordure, f.; (of a ship) couples, m.pl.; (of artisans) métier; (of farriers) travail, m.; (of mind) disposition, f. — maker; encadreur, m.

frame, v.a., façonner, former, construire; inventer; exprimer; régler; former, encadrer.

framed (fré'm'de), part. adj., formé, fabriqué, fait; encadré.

fra'mer, n., encadreur; (fig.) auteur, artisan, m.

frame'work (-weurke), n., ouvrage fait sur le métier; (of a house) charpente, f.

fram'ing, n., (of pictures) encadrement, m.; charpente, f.

franc, n., franc, m.

fran'chise (fra'n'tshize), n., franchise, immunité, f.; privilège, droit électoral, m.

Francis'can, n., franciscain, m.

fran'gible (-dji'b'l), adj., fragile, cassant, qui se brise aisément.

frank, n., lettre affranchie.

frank, adj., franc, libéral, généreux, sincère.

frank, v.a., affranchir, envoyer franc de port.

frank'incense, n., encens, m.

Frank'ish, adj., franc, m., franque, f.

frank'ly, adv., franchement; sans contrainte; sans hésitation; sans déguisement, volontairement, de son plein gré.

frank'ness, n., franchise, sincérité, bonté, f.

fran'tic, adj., fou; frénétique; forcené; furieux. — with joy; ivre de joie.

fran'tically, adv., follement; en frénétique; en furieux.

fran'ticness, n., folie, frénésie, fureur, f.

frap, v.a., (nav.) ceintrer; brider; aiguilleter. To — a tackle; aiguilleter un palan. To — a ship; ceintrer un vaisseau.

frap'ping, n., (nav.) aiguilletage, ceintrage, m.

frater'nal (-teur-), adj., fraternel.

frater'nally, adv., fraternellement, en frère.

frater'nity, n., fraternité, confrérie, société, f.

frat'ernize, v.n., fraterniser.

frat'ernizer, n., qui fraternise.

frat'ricide (-caïde), n., fratricide, m.

frat'ricidal, adj., fratricide.

fraud, fraud'ulence ou **fraud'ulency** (frôd'iou-), n., fraude, tromperie, supercherie, circonvention, imposture, f. To commit a — upon; tromper. That man is a perfect —; impossible de se fier à cet homme.

fraud'ulent (frôd'iou-), adj., frauduleux, trompeur, de mauvaise foi.

fraud'ulently, adv., frauduleusement; en fraude.

fraught (frôte), part. adj., rempli de, chargé de, gros de, plein de; riche en, fertile en. — with misfortunes; fertile en malheurs. — with events; gros d'événements.

fray (fré), n., combat, m.; querelle; bagarre; émeute, mêlée; éraillure, f. In the thick of the —; au plus fort de la mêlée.

fray, v.a. and n., érailler; s'érailler; effiloquer, effilocher, s'effiloquer, s'effilocher.

fray'ing, n., éraillure, f.

freak (frîke), n., fantaisie; boutade, f.; caprice, m. — of nature; caprice de la nature.

freak, v.a., bigarrer de; tacheter de; barioler de.

freak'ish, adj., quinteux, bizarre, fantasque, capricieux.

freak'ishly, adv., capricieusement, par fantaisie.

freak'ishness, n., boutade; bizarrerie, humeur capricieuse, f.

frec'kle (frèk'k'l), n., rousseur, tache de rousseur, f.

frec'kled (frèk'k'lde) ou **frec'kly,** adj., tacheté; plein de taches de rousseur.

free (frî), adj., libre, exempt; sincère, franc, gratuit, volontaire, libéral; aisé, dégagé; sans contrainte, immodéré; (nav.) largue. To make — with; prendre des libertés avec, user librement de. — and easy; familier; sans cérémonie. To set —; affranchir, mettre en liberté; (of vapors, etc.) dégager. To sail —; (nav.) naviguer avec le vent largue.

free, v.a., affranchir, exempter; délivrer,

libérer ; dégager. To — one's self ; *s'affranchir.*

free'booter (frî-bout'-), *n.*, bandit, voleur, pillard, picoreur, flibustier ; maraudeur, *m.*

free'born, *adj.*, né libre.

free'cost, *adv.*, (ant.) sans frais, sans dépense ; gratis.

freed'man (frîd'ma'n), *n.*, affranchi, homme libre, *m.*

free'dom (frî-deume), *n.*, liberté ; indépendance ; immunité ; maîtrise, aisance, *f. ;* (fig.) facilité, assurance ; (of a city) bourgeoisie, *f.*, les franchises d'un bourgeois, *f.pl.*

freeheart'ed (-hârtède), *adj.*, libre, libéral, généreux, franc, de cœur.

free'hold (-hôlde), *n.*, franc-fief, franc-alleu, *m. ;* propriété foncière libre, *f.*

free'holder, *n.*, propriétaire foncier ; (hist.) franc tenancier, *m.*

free'ly, *adv.*, librement, sans contrainte, gratuitement, volontiers ; copieusement, libéralement.

free'man (-ma'n), *n.*, bourgeois, citoyen, homme libre, *m.*

freema'son (-mé-s'n), *n.*, franc-maçon, *m.*

freema'sonry (-mé-s'n-), *n.*, franc-maçonnerie, *f.*

free'minded (-maï'n'dède), *adj.*, (ant.) exempt de soucis, sans souci ; libre de soins.

free'ness, *n.*, sincérité, libéralité, candeur, *f.*

free'-school (-skoul), *n.*, école gratuite ; école publique, *m.*

free'-spoken (-spô'k'n), *adj.*, qui dit librement sa pensée, qui a son franc parler **avec.**

free'stone (-stône), *n.*, pierre de taille, pierre sableuse, *f.*

free'thinker (-thi'gn'k'-) *n.*, esprit fort, libre penseur ; incrédule, *m.*

free'-trade, *n.*, libre-échange, *m.*

free'-trader, *n.*, libre-échangiste, *m.*

free'-will, *n.*, (philos., theol.) libre arbitre, franc arbitre, *m.*

freeze (frîze), *v.a.* and *n.*, geler, se geler, glacer, se glacer, congeler, se congeler.

freez'ing, *n.*, gelée, congélation, *f.*

freez'ing, *adj.*, glacial. It is — hard ; *il gèle à pierre fendre.* — machine ; *glacière, f.* — mixture ; *mélange réfrigérant, m.* — point ; *zéro, m. ; point de congélation, f.*

freight (frète), *n.*, fret, nolis, nolisement, *m.*, cargaison, *f.*, chargement, *m.*

freight, *v.a.*, fréter, affréter ; charger, noliser.

freight'er, *n.*, fréteur, affréteur, *m.*

freight'ing, *n.*, affrétement, *m.*

French (frè'n'she), *adj.*, français. After the — fashion ; *à la française.* To take — leave ; *décamper sans mot dire* ou *filer à l'anglaise.* — wheat ; *sarrasin, blé noir, m.* — ambassador ; *ambassadeur de France, m.*

French, *n.*, (language) français, *m.*

French'-grass, *n.*, sainfoin, *m.*

French'-horn, *n.*, cor de chasse, cor d'harmonie, *m.*

French'ify (-shifaïe), *v.a.*, franciser ; donner les manières françaises. To become —ied ; *se franciser.*

French'man, *n.*, Français, *m.*

French'-roll, *n.*, petit pain, *m.*

French'-window, *n.*, croisée, *f.*

French'woman (-wouma'n), *n.*, Française, *f.*

fren'zy (frè'n'-), *n.*, frénésie, folie, *f. ;* égarement d'esprit, délire, *m.*, ivresse, *f.*

fre'quence ou **fre'quency** (frî-kwè'n-), *n.*, fréquence ; réitération, répétition fréquente, *f.*

fre'quent, *adj.*, fréquent ; ordinaire, commun.

fre'quent (fri-kwè'n'te), *v.a.*, fréquenter ; hanter.

frequent'able, *adj.*, fréquentable.

frequent'ative, *n.*, (gram.) fréquentatif, *m.*

frequent'er (fri-kwè'n't'-), *n.*, qui fréquente ; habitué, *m.*

frequent'ing (fri-), *n.*, fréquentation.

fre'quently (frî-), *adv.*, fréquemment, souvent.

fres'co (frès-cô), *n.*, fresque, *f.* To paint in — ; *peindre à fresque.* — painting ; *peinture à fresque.*

fresh (frèshe), *adj.*, frais ; récent ; vif ; nouveau ; vigoureux ; (fig.) novice, vert. — water ; (not salt) *de l'eau douce ;* (fresh-drawn) *de l'eau fraîche, f.* — horses ; *chevaux de relais, m.* — complexion ; *un teint frais, m.* — in my memory ; *j'en ai la mémoire toute fraîche.* — from ; *tout frais débarqué* **de** ; *tout frais arrivé* **de.** Is there anything — ? *y a-t-il du nouveau ?*

fresh'en (frèsh'n), *v.a.* and *n.*, rafraîchir, devenir frais, fraîchir ; se rafraîchir, dessaler. The wind —s ; (nav.) *le vent fraîchit.*

freshes (*pl.*) ou **fresh'et** (frèsh'èze, -'ète), *n.*, courant d'eau douce, *m.*, crue, *f.*

fresh'-gathered, *adj.*, frais - cueilli, *m. ;* fraîche-cueillie, *f.*

fresh'ly, *adv.*, fraîchement ; récemment, nouvellement, depuis peu.

fresh'man, *n.*, novice ; (acad.) étudiant de première année, *m.*

fresh'ness, *n.*, fraîcheur ; (fig.) nouveauté ; naïveté, *f.*

fresh'-shaved, *adj.*, rasé de frais.

fresh'water (-wô-teur), *adj.*, d'eau douce ; (fig.) maladroit, inhabile, qui n'a point d'expérience, novice. — sailors ; *marins d'eau douce, m.pl.*

fresh'-watered, *adj.*, nouvellement arrosé.

fret (frète), *n.*, (of liquor) fermentation ; (mus.) touche ; (arch.) grecque ; (of silk) éraillure, *f. ;* (borer) perçoir, *m. ;* (fig.) agitation de l'âme, *f.*

fret, *v.a.*, chagriner, fâcher ; irriter ; corroder, ronger ; écorcher ; agiter ; courroucer ; découper ; relever en bosse. To — inwardly ; *ronger son frein.*

fret, *v.n.*, se chagriner ; s'inquiéter ; se fâcher ; se vexer ; s'user ; se couper, s'érailler ; se corroder ; (fig.) s'agiter, se courroucer ; se faire du mauvais sang.

fret'ful (-foule), *adj.*, chagrin, acariâtre ; de mauvaise humeur ; agité, irritable ; inquiet, troublé.

fret'fully, *adv.*, avec chagrin ; de mauvaise humeur ; avec irritation, avec dépit.

fret'fulness, *n.*, humeur chagrine ; mauvaise humeur ; irritation, *f. ;* dépit, *m.*

fret'ting, *n.*, corrosif, *m. ;* (fig.) agitation ; commotion ; affliction, *f. ;* tracas, *m. ;* (of the skin) excoriation, *f.*

fret'ting, *adj.*, corrosif, corrodant ; (fig.) chagrinant, inquiétant.

fret'ty, *adj.*, relevé en bosse ; ciselé ; découpé ; (arch.) orné d'une grecque ; (her.) fretté, entrelacé.

fret'work (-weurke), *n.*, ouvrage relevé en bosse ; découpage, *m. ;* ciselure ; (arch.) grecque, *f. ;* (her.) entrelacs, *m.*

friabil'ity ou **fri'ableness** (fraï-a-), *n.*, friabilité, *f.*

fri'able, *adj.*, friable ; facile à réduire en poudre.

fri'ar (fraï-), *n.*, religieux, moine, *m.* Black —s ; *dominicains ; frères prêcheurs, m.pl.* Austin —s ; *augustins, m.pl.* White —s ; *carmélites, m.pl.* —'s lantern ; *feu follet, m.*

fri'ar-like (-laïke) ou **fri'arly**, *adj.*, monacal, de moine ; (fig.) simple, ingénu.

fri'ary, *n.*, confrérie, *f. ;* monastère, couvent de moines, *m.*

frib'ble, *n.*, freluquet, *m. ;* personne frivole, *f.*, moqueur, *m. v.a.* and *n.*, baguenauder. To — away ; (one's time, etc.) *perdre, gaspiller.*

frib'bler, *n.* V. **fribble.**

fricassee' (-sî), *n.*, fricassée, *f.*

fric'tion, *n.*, frottement, *n.*, friction, *f.*

fric'tion-tube, *n.*, (mil.) étoupille à friction, *f.*

Fri'day (fraï-), *n.*, vendredi, *m.* Good-—; *vendredi saint, m.*

friend (frè'n'de), *n.*, ami, *m.*, amie, *f.*; camarade; quaker, *m. pl.*, parents, *m. pl.* Short reckonings make long —s; *les bons comptes font les bons amis.* To make —s; *se réconcilier, se raccommoder.* The best of —s must part; *il n'est si bonne compagnie qui ne se sépare.* A — in need is a — indeed; *on connaît les amis au besoin.* A — at court; *un ami en voie.* For loan oft loses both itself and —; (prov.) *qui prête à l'ami perd au double* (Hamlet). Trust not a new — nor an old enemy; *les amis sont comme le melon, il faut en essayer plusieurs pour en trouver un bon* (C. Mermet).

friend'less, *adj.*, sans amis; délaissé, abandonné.

friend'liness, *n.*, bonté; bienveillance, *f.*

friend'ly, *adj.*, serviable, d'ami, amical; favorable à, propice à; bienveillant **pour**.

friend'ship, *n.*, amitié, faveur, affection mutuelle, *f.*

frieze *ou* **frize** (frize), *n.*, frise, ratine; (arch.) frise, *f.*

frig'ate (frigh'éte), *n.*, frégate, *f.* — bird; *frégate, f.*

frigatoon', *n.*, frégaton, *m.*

fright (fraïte), *n.*, peur soudaine, *f.*; effroi, *m.*, épouvante, frayeur, *f.* What a — she is! (fig.) *elle est laide à faire peur.* What a — you are! *comme vous voilà fait!*

fright (ant.) *ou* **frigh'ten** (fraït'n), *v.a.*, épouvanter; faire peur à, effrayer.

fright'ful (fraït'foule), *adj.*, épouvantable, effroyable, affreux; terrible, horrible.

fright'fully, *adv.*, effroyablement, affreusement.

fright'fulness, *n.*, horreur, frayeur, *f.*

frig'id (fri'jide), *adj.*, froid; glacial; privé de chaleur. — zone; *zone glaciale, f.*

frigid'ity *ou* **frig'idness**, *n.*, frigidité, froideur, *f.*

frig'idly, *adv.*, froidement.

frill, *n.*, jabot de chemise, *m.*; fraise, *f.*

frill, *v.a.*, orner d'un jabot, de fronces.

fringe, *n.*, frange; crépine, *f.*; effilé; bout; bord, *m.*, extrémité, *f.*

fringe, *v.a.*, franger; rucher; garnir de crépine.

fringe'maker (-mék'-), *n.*, frangier, faiseur de franges, *m.*

frin'gy, *adj.*, à frange, à crépine.

frip'pery, *n.*, friperie, *f.*, vieux habits, haillons, *m.pl.*

frisk, *n.*, (ant.) gambade, escapade, *f.*; frétillement, *m.*

frisk, *v.n.*, sautiller, gambader, frétiller, se trémousser, folâtrer.

frisk'er, *n.*, homme volage, inconstant, *m.*

frisk'iness, *n.*, frétillement; gaîté, vivacité, *f.*

frisk'y *ou* **frisk'ing**, *adj.*, fringant, gai, sémillant, vif, enjoué, frétillant, folâtre.

frit, *n.*, (glass manu.) fritte, *f.*

frith (frith), *n.*, détroit, *m.*; estuaire, *m.*, embouchure (of a river), *f.*

frit'illary, *n.*, (bot.) fritillaire, *f.*

frit'ter, *n.*, beignet; hachis frit; fragment, *m.*

frit'ter, *v.a.*, couper en morceaux, morceler, consumer. To — away (one's time or money); *gaspiller, perdre, dissiper.*

frivol'ity, *n.*, frivolité, *f.*

friv'olous, *adj.*, frivole, vain, léger, volage.

friv'olously, *adv.*, d'une manière frivole; superficiellement.

friv'olousness, *n.*, frivolité, insignifiance, *f.*

frizz *ou* **friz'zle** (-z'l), *v.a.*, friser; frisotter, taper; crêper.

friz'zle (-z'l), *n.*, boucle de cheveux frisés, *m.*; frisure, *f.*

friz'zler, *n.*, friseur, *m.*; personne qui frise, *f.*

fro (frô), *adv.*, en arrière. To go to and —;

---

aller çà et là; aller et venir. To walk to and—; *se promener de long en large; arpenter.* Coming to and —; *allées et venues, f.pl.* Motion to and —; *mouvement oscillant; (mouvement de) va et vient* (V. Hugo).

frock, *n.*, froc; habit, *m.*; **robe d'enfant**, de dame; blouse, jaquette, *f.*

frocked, *adj.*, portant le froc.

frock'coat (-côte), *n.*, redingote, *f.*

frog, *n.*, grenouille, *f.*; (of a **horse's foot**) fourchette, *f.*

frogged, *adj.*, (of coats) à brandebourgs.

frol'ic, *n.*, espièglerie, fredaine, plaisanterie, escapade, folie, *f.*; badinage, *m.*

frol'ic, *v.n.*, folâtrer, badiner, faire le fou; jouer; gambader.

frol'icsome (-ceume), *adj.*, folâtre, gaillard, badin, espiègle, joyeux; fantasque.

frol'icsomely, *adv.*, joyeusement; en badinant, gaiement.

frol'icsomeness, *n.*, gaillardise, boutade; folâtrerie, gaieté, espièglerie, *f.*

from, *prep.*, de; de devant; de par; de la part; depuis; dès, par; d'après; par suite **de**; en conséquence **de**; du haut **de**; avec; sur; dans; de la part **de**; (above) d'en haut; (afar) de loin; (amidst) du milieu **de**; (among) d'entre; (behind) de derrière; (beneath) d'en bas; (beyond) d'au delà; (high) de haut; (hence) d'ici; (thence) de là; (under) de dessous; (within) de dedans; (without) de dehors. — me; *de ma part.* To come —; *venir* **de chez**. — afar; *de loin.* — his manner; **à en juger par** *son air.* A helmet hanging — his saddle-bow; *un casque suspendu à son arçon.* — the midst of; *du sein de.* — among; *d'entre.* — without; *du dehors.* — ...to; *depuis...jusqu'à; de...à.* — age to age; *de siècle en siècle.*

frond, *n.*, (bot.) fronde, *f.*; feuillage, *m.*

fronda'tion (-dé-) *n.*, (hort.) émondage, élagage, *m.*

frondes'cence (fro'n'd'ès'-), *n.*, (bot.) feuillaison, *f.*

frondif'erous, fron'dose, *ou* **fron'dous**, *adj.*, (bot.) frondifère, feuillu, feuillé.

front (freu'n'te), *n.*, front, devant, portail, *m.*; devanture, face, façade; (box) première loge, loge de face; (of a building) façade; (room) chambre sur le devant; (bonnet) passe; (shirt) chemisette, *f.* In — of: *en face* **de**; *devant; en avant* **de**. Eyes — ! (mil.) *fixe!* To come to the —; *prendre une position élevée; faire figure; se distinguer, se faire remarquer.*

front (freu'n'te), *v.a.* and *n.*, rencontrer, faire face à, faire tête à; être vis-à-vis **de**; (ant.) attaquer de front, affronter, défier. To — a house with marble; *orner une maison d'une façade en marbre.*

fron'tage (freu'n't'-), *n.*, façade, *f.*

fron'tal (freu'n't'-), *n.*, frontal; (arch.) fronton; bandeau, *m.*

front'-box, *n.*, loge de face, *f.*

front'-court, *n.*, avant-cour, *f.*

front'-door, *n.*, porte d'entrée, *f.*

front'ed (freu'n't'ède), *adj.*, à façade; qui a un front.

fron'tier (fro'n'tîre), *n.* and *adj.*, frontière, limite, *f.*; (town) ville frontière, *f.*

front'ing (freu'n't'-), *adj.*, en face **de**; vis-à-vis; qui fait face.

fron'tispiece (freu'n'tis-pîce), *n.*, frontispice, *m.*

front'less (freu'n't-), *adj.*, (ant.) effronté, déhonté, éhonté, impudent.

front'let (freu'n't-), *n.*, fronteau, frontal, bandeau, *m.*

front'-rank, premier rang, *m.*

front'-room, *n.*, pièce sur le devant, *f.*

front'-view, *n.*, vue de face, *f.*

frost, *n.*, gelée; glace, *f.* Hoar-—; *gelée*

blanche, f. Glazed —; *verglas, m.* White, *ou* hoar, —; *givre, f.*

frost, v.a., glacer; damasquiner.

frost'-bitten (-bit'n), adj., gelé.

frost'-bound, adj., retenu par les glaces.

frost'ed, adj., glacé; damasquiné.

frost'ily, adv., (ant.) froidement; **avec une** froideur glaciale.

frost'iness, n., froid glacial; grand froid, m.

frost'nail (-néle), n., clou à glace, m.

frost'-work (-weurke), n., glacé, m.

frost'y, adj., de gelée; glacé, glacial; (weather) temps de gelée; (fig.) froid. It is a — morning; *il gèle ce matin.*

froth (froth), n., écume, mousse, f.; crème fouettée, f.; (fig.) vain étalage de paroles, m.; paroles en l'air, *f.pl.*

froth, v.n., écumer; mousser, jeter de l'écume.

froth, v.a., faire mousser.

froth'ily, adv., (ant.) avec de l'écume, légèrement; avec futilité; en bavardant.

froth'y, adj., écumeux; écumant; mousseux; plein de vent; (fig.) vain, frivole, verbeux, futile.

frounce (fraou'n'ce), v.a, (ant.) friser; froncer.

frou'zy (fraou-), adj., sale; moisi, rance, fétide.

fro'ward (frô-weurde), adj., revêche, bourru, chagrin, pervers, insolent, rude, opiniâtre, méchant, indocile.

fro'wardly, adv., méchamment; insolemment; opiniâtrément; avec perversité; de mauvaise humeur.

fro'wardness, n., humeur revêche; opiniâtreté; perversité, indocilité, désobéissance, insolence, f.

frown (fraou'ne), n., froncement de sourcils, dédain; air refrogné; (fig.) revers, m. The —s of fortune; *les revers de la fortune.*

frown, v.n., froncer les sourcils; être contraire; regarder de mauvais œil, se refrogner.

frown'ing, adj., chagrin, rechigné, refrogné; (fig.) menaçant.

frown'ingly, adv., d'un air chagrin, de mauvais œil; (fig.) d'un air menaçant.

fro'zen (frôz'n), part.adj., glacé, gelé, glacial.

frow'zy, adj. V. **frouzy.**

fructif'erous (freuk-tif'eur'-), adj., (ant.) fertile, productif, fructifère.

fructifica'tion (-ké-), n., fructification; fertilité; fécondation, f.

fruc'tify (-faïe), v.a. and n., fructifier; fertiliser, féconder, rapporter du fruit.

fru'gal (friou-), adj., frugal, économe, sobre, ménager.

frugal'ity, n., économie, frugalité; tempérance; sobriété, f.

fru'gally, adv., frugalement; avec économie sobrement.

frugiv'orous (-djiv'-), adj., frugivore.

fruit (froute), n., fruit; (fig.) avantage, profit, m. First-—s; *prémices, f.pl.*

fruit, v.n., donner, *ou* produire, du fruit.

frui'tage (frout'édje), n., fruitage, m.

fruit'-basket (-baskète), n., cueilloir, m.; corbeille à fruit, f.

fruit'-bearer (-bèr'eur), n., arbre fruitier; arbre qui porte du fruit, m.

fruit'eror, n., fruitier, m., fruitière, f.

fruit'ful (-foule), adj., fertile, abondant, chargé de fruit; (fig.) fécond **en.**

fruit'fully, adv., fertilement, abondamment; avec fruit.

fruit'fulness, n., fertilité, abondance, fécondité, f.

fruit'-grove (-grôve), n., petit verger; jardin fruitier, m.

frui'tion (friou-ish'eune), n., jouissance, possession, f.

fruit'less (frout'-), adj., stérile, infructueux, inutile, vain, sans fruit.

fruit'lessly, adv., inutilement, vainement, infructueusement, sans fruit.

fruit'-market (-mâr-), n., marché au fruit, m.

fruit'-stalk (-stôke), n., (bot.) pédoncule, m.

fruit'-time (-taïme), n., automne, f.; temps de la récolte des fruits, m.

fruit'-tree (-trî), n., arbre fruitier, m. Wall —; *arbre d'espalier, m.* Standard —; *arbre fruitier en plein vent, m.* Dwarf —; *arbre nain, m.*

fruit'-wall (-wôl), n., (hort.) espalier, m.

frumen'taceous (friou-mè'n'té-sheusse), adj., (ant.) (bot.) fromentacée.

fru'menty (friou-), n., ⊙fromentée; bouillie de farine de froment, f.

frump (freu'm'pe), v.a and n., (ant.) railler, plaisanter; se moquer de.

frump, n., femme revêche, mégère; femme désagréable; antiquaille démodée, f.

frush (freushe), n., (vet.) fourchette (du pied dé cheval), f.

frus'trate, v.a., frustrer; faire manquer; rendre inutile; déconcerter, désappointer, tromper l'espoir **de**; (jur.) annuler.

frustra'tion (-tré-), n., frustration, privation, f.; insuccès; échec, m.; nullité, déception, f.; renversement, m.

frus'trating, adj., trompeur, frustrateur.

frus'tum (freus'teume), n. (*frusta*) fragment, tronc, m. — of a cone; *tronc de cône, m.*

fry (fraïe), n.. fretin, frai, m.; (cooking) friture, fressure; (fig.) foule, f., amas, m. Small — of nobility; (fig.) *hobereau, m.* Small —; *menu peuple, menu fretin, m.*

fry, v.a., frire, faire frire; fricasser. He has other fish to —; *il a bien d'autres chats à fouetter.*

fry'ing-pan (-pane), n., poêle à frire, f. To fall from the — into the fire; *tomber de Charybde en Scylla, ou de fièvre en chaud mal.*

fu'chsia (fiou'shia), n., (bot.) fuchsia, m.

fud'dle (feud'd'l), v.a. and n., enivrer, soûler; griser; se griser, s'enivrer.

fud'dled, adj., à moitié gris; abruti.

fud'dler, n., ivrogne, débauché, m.

fudge! (feudje), int., ah! bah!

fudge, n., (triv.) conte, m.; baliverne, sottise, blague, fariboie, bêtise, absurdité, f., mensonge, m.

fu'el (fiou-), n., chauffage; combustible, m. To add — to the fire; *verser de l'huile sur le feu.* To keep in —; (of engines) *alimenter en combustible; entretenir le feu.*

fuga'cious (fiou-ghé-sheusse), adj., fugace, fugitif; passager; qui fuit; (bot.) fugace.

fuga'ciousness *ou* **fugac'ity**, n., (ant.) fugacité, volatilité, instabilité, inconstance, incertitude, f.

fugh! (fou), int., pouah!

fu'gitive (fiou-dji-), n., fugitif, transfuge, fuyard, déserteur, (mil.) réfugié, m.

fu'gitive, adj., fugitif; errant; qui s'enfuit; passager, inconstant.

fu'gitiveness, n., (ant.) fugacité, nature fugitive, inconstance, instabilité, incertitude, f.

fu'gleman, n., sergent instructeur; chef de file; guide, m.

fugue (flougñe), n., (mus.) fugue, f. To maintain a —; *faire une fugue.*

ful'crum (feul-creume), n., (bot.) soutien, support; (mec.) point d'appui, m.

fulfill' (foul'file), v.a., accomplir, remplir, achever, exécuter; combler, satisfaire.

fulfill'er, n., qui accomplit, remplit, exécute, m.

fulfill'ing, n., accomplissement, m.

fulfill'ment, n., exécution, f., accomplissement, m.

ful'gency (feul-djè'n'-), n., vif éclat, resplendissement, m.; splendeur; clarté, f.

ful'gent, *adj.*, (ant.) reluisant, éclatant, brillant, resplendissant.

ful'gurate (feul-ghiou-), *v.n.*, (ant.) émettre des éclairs, resplendir.

fulgura'tion (-ré-), *n.*, (ant.) éclair, *m.* ; fulguration; (chem.) fulguration, *f.*

fulig'inous (fiou-lidj'i-), *adj.*, fuligineux, plein de suie ; noir, sombre, triste ; couleur de suie.

full (foule), *n.*, plein ; comble, *m.* ; satiété ; mesure complète, *f.* ; soûl, comble, *m.* To give a passage in —; *citer un passage en entier.* To write in —; *écrire en toutes lettres.* To the —; *entièrement.* At its —; (of the moon) *dans son plein.* In — of all demands ; (com.) *pour solde de tout compte.*

full, *adj.*, plein, rempli, ample, entier, complet ; copieux, abondant ; rassasié **de** ; (face) visage plein. — stop ; *point, m.* — moon ; *pleine lune, f.* — meal ; *un bon repas ou un repas copieux, m.* In — light ; *en pleine lumière.* — light of day ; *plein jour, m.* — supply ; *ample provision, f.* At — speed ; *à toute vapeur* ou *à toute vitesse.*

full, *v.a.*, fouler. To — cloth ; *fouler du drap.*

full, *adv.*, plein, en plein, pleinement, tout à fait, entièrement, exactement, juste. She is — twenty ; *elle a vingt ans accomplis.* — as liable to ; *tout aussi sujet à.* — in one's face ; *en plein visage.* To know — well ; *savoir parfaitement.*

full'-blooded, *adj.*, sanguin.

full'-blown (-blône), *adj.*, épanoui, en pleine floraison ; (fig.) dans tout son éclat.

full'-bodied (-bodide), *adj.*, gros ; replet ; (of wine) corsé.

full'-bottomed (-bot'teu'm'de), *adj.*, à large fond.

full'-butt (-beute), *adv.*, en se heurtant ; nez à nez ; tête baissée.

full'-dress, *n.*, (mil.) grande tenue ; (general) grande toilette, *f.* ; (of ministers) grand uniforme, *m.*

full'-drive (-draïve), *adv.*, au grand galop, ventre à terre, à bride abattue.

full'-eared (- îr'de), *adj.*, rempli de grains.

full'er (foul'-), *n.*, foulon, *m.*

full'er's-earth (foul'leurz'eurth), *n.*, terre à foulon, terre à dégraisser, *f.*

full'ery, *n.*, foulerie, *f.* ; moulin à foulon ; atelier de foulage, *m.*

full'-eyed (-aïe'de), *adj.*, ayant de gros yeux.

full'-faced (-face'de), *adj.*, joufflu, potelé.

full'-fed (-fède), *adj.*, gras ; bien nourri ; dodu.

full'-grown (-grône), *adj.*, qui a toute sa croissance. — girl ; *grande fille, f.*

full'-growth (-grôth), *n.*, crue, *f.*, développement, accroissement, *m.*

full'ing, *n.*, foulage, *m.*

full'ing-mill, *n.*, moulin à foulon, *m.*

full-laden (-léd'n), *adj.*, tout à fait chargé.

full'-length, *adj.*, (of portraits) en pied.

full'-mouthed, *adj.*, qui a la voix pleine, sonore.

full'ness (foul-), *n.*, plénitude, abondance, *f.* ; trop plein, *m.* ; ampleur (of sound), *f.* ; volume, *m.*

full'nigh (-naïe), *adv.*, presque, tout près **de.**

full'-relief, *n.*, ronde bosse, *f.* ; plein relief, *m.*

full'-sized, *adj.*, (of paper) de grand format ; (general) de grand modèle.

full'-spread (-sprède), *adj.*, tout à fait étendu.

full'-steam, *adv.*, à toute vapeur.

full'-tilt, *adv.*, au grand galop, à toute bride. To run — against ; *courir*, ou *donner, tête baissée* **contre.**

full'-voice, *n.*, voix pleine, nourrie, *f.*

ful'ly, *adv.*, pleinement, entièrement, amplement.

ful'mar (feul'mar), *n.*, (orni.) pétrel, pinson de tempête, pinson de mer ; (zoöl.) putois, *m.*

ful'minant (feul'-), *adj.*, (chem.) fulminant.

ful'minate (feul'-), *v.a.* and *n.*, fulminer, tonner **contre**, faire un grand bruit.

fulmina'tion (-né-), *n.*, fulmination, *f.*

ful'minatory (-tori), *adj.*, fulminant.

ful'some (feul'seume), *adj.*, dégoûtant ; honteux ; infâme ; bas, vil ; nauséabond, servile, révoltant ; (of style) gonflé.

ful'somely, *adv.*, d'une manière dégoûtante ; d'une manière honteuse, bassement, vilement.

ful'someness, *n.*, dégoût, *m.* ; infamie, honte, bassesse, servilité, *f.*

fu'mage (fiou-mèdje), *n.*, (feudal) fouage, *m.*

fu'matory (fiou-ma-tori), **fu'mitory**, *n.*, (bot.) fumeterre, *f.* ; fiel de terre, *m.*

fum'ble (feu'm'b'l), *v.a.* and *n.*, faire de travers, faire maladroitement ; chiffonner ; fouiller ; tâtonner. — along ; *aller à tâtons.* — up ; *mal plier.* To — papers ; *chiffonner des papiers.*

fum'bler, *n.*, maladroit, tâtonneur, patineur, *m.*

fum'blingly, *adv.*, maladroitement, gauchement ; en tâtonnant.

fume (fioume), *n.*, fumée, vapeur, exhalaison ; (fig.) colère, vanité, *f.*

fume, *v.a.* and *n.*, fumer, jeter de la fumée ; parfumer ; exhaler ; s'exhaler, s'évaporer ; (fig.) s'échauffer, s'indigner, être en colère, rager, maugréer. To — away ; *bouillir de colère*, *rager.* To fret and — ; *se faire du mauvais sang* ; *se tourmenter.*

fu'met (fiou-mète), *n.*, (ant.) (hunt.) fumées (of the stag) ; crottes (of the hare), *f.pl.*

fumette' (fiou-), *n.*, (ant.) (cook.) fumet, *m.*

fu'migate (fiou-), *v.a.* and *n.*, fumiger ; désinfecter.

fumiga'tion, *n.*, fumigation, désinfection, *f.*

fu'migator, *n.*, (surg.) personne qui désinfecte, qui fumige, *f.*

fu'mingly (fiou-), *adv.*, en colère ; avec rage.

fu'mitory (fiou-). *V.* **fu'matory.**

fu'mous ou **fu'my** (fiou-), *adj.*, fumeux ; qui exhale des vapeurs.

fun (feune), *n.*, amusement, badinage, *m.*, plaisanterie ; gaieté, joie, gaillardise ; bourde, *f.* Full of — ; *très gai, qui aime à rire.* For — ; **pour** *badiner*, **pour** *rire.* To make — of ; *tourner en ridicule, se moquer* **de.** To have good — ; *s'en donner, se bien amuser, avoir du bon temps.*

funam'bulist (fiou-), *n.*, (ant.) funambule, voltigeur, danseur de corde, *m.*

func'tion (feu'gn'k'sheune), *n.*, fonction ; faculté, occupation, *f.* ; métier, emploi ; (acc.) service, office, *m.*

func'tional, *adj.*, fonctionnel, -le.

func'tionary, *n.*, fonctionnaire public, *ou* officiel, *m.*

fund (feunde), *n.*, fonds, capital, *m.* ; finance, caisse, *f.* The public —s ; *les fonds publics, m.pl.* Sinking — ; *caisse d'amortissement, m.* My —s are very low ; *mes fonds sont en baisse*, ou *ma bourse est fort à sec* (V. Hugo).

fund, *v.a.*, affecter des fonds ; placer, verser des fonds.

fun'dament (feu'n'-), *n.*, (fig.) fondement ; siège, (phy.) anus, *m.*

fundamen'tal, *adj.*, fondamental. *n.pl.*, principe fondamental, *m.*

fundamen'tally, *adv.*, fondamentalement, essentiellement.

fu'neral (fiou-neur'-), *n.*, enterrement, convoi funèbre, *m.* ; funérailles, obsèques, *f.pl.*

fu'neral, *adj.*, funèbre, funéraire. — oration ; *oraison funèbre, f.* — service ; *office des morts, service funèbre, m.*

fune'real (fiou-ni-ri-), *adj.*, triste, funèbre, lugubre, sépulcral.

fungos'ity (feu'gn'goss'-), *n.*, fongosité, *f.*

fun'gous (feu'gn'-), *adj.*, fongueux, spongieux, poreux.

fun'gus (feu'gn'-), *n.*, champignon, (med.) fongus, *m.* ; excroissance de chair, *f.*

fu'nicle (fiou-ni-k'l), n., (anat.) cordon ombilical, m. ; fibre nerveuse,f.; (bot.) funicule, podosperme, m.

funic'ular (fiou-nik'iou-), adj., (mec., math.) funiculaire; (bot.) fibreux, funiculé.

funk (feu'gn'ke), n., puanteur; peur, panique; (pop.) venette,f., trac, m. ; (touchwood) amadou, m. ; (anger) colère, f. ; accès de colère, m. To be in a — ; avoir la venette; avoir le trac. To put in a — ; donner la venette, le trac à.

funk'y, adj., qui a le trac, la venette.

fun'nel (feu'n'-), n., entonnoir, tuyau; (of a chimney) tuyau de cheminée, m. ; (of steamers) cheminée, f.

fun'ny (feu'n'-), adj., bouffon, facétieux, comique, drôle, risible, amusant.

fur (feur), n., fourrure, pelleterie, f. ; poil, dépôt, sédiment, m.

fur, v.a., fourrer, garnir de fourrure; (a ship) doubler un vaisseau; former un dépôt. v.n., (of the tongue) être chargé; s'encrasser.

fura'cious (fiou-ré'-sheusse), adj., (ant.) enclin à voler.

fur'below (feur-bi-lô), n., volant, falbala, m.; (ant.) pretintaille, f.

fur'below, v.a., orner, garnir de falbalas; (ant.) pretintailler.

fur'bish (feur-), v.a., fourbir, polir, brunir.

fur'bisher, n., fourbisseur, m.

fur'-cap, n., bonnet de fourrure, m.

fur'-cape, n., pèlerine, f.

furca'tion (feur-ké-), n., bifurcation, fourchure, f.

fur'chel, n., (of a coach) armon, m.

fur'fur (feur-feur), n., dartre furfuracée, f.

furfura'ceous (feur-feur-é-sheusse), adj., (med.) furfuracé.

fu'rious (fiou-), adj., furieux, acharné, frénétique, outré, insensé.

fu'riously, adv., avec fureur; avec acharnement; en insensé, en furieux, furieusement; à toute bride.

fu'riousness, n., furie, rage, frénésie, démence, f.

furl (feurle), v.n., (nav.) ferler; ployer (the sails).

fur'ling-line, n., (nav.) raban de ferlage, m. ; garcette à ferler, f.

fur'long (feur-), n., (la huitième partie d'un mille anglais) 201 mètres.

fur'lough (feur-lô), n., congé, semestre, m. ; feuille de route, f. On — ; en congé.

fur'nace (feur-), n., fournaise, f. ; fourneau ; (of engines) foyer, m.

fur'nish (feur-), v.a., fournir, pourvoir **de** ; (a house) garnir **de**, meubler; (with linen) fournir de linge ; (with arms) armer. To — (examples, etc.); donner, offrir.

fur'nisher, n., pourvoyeur, fournisseur, m.

fur'nishing, n., ameublement, m. ; garniture, f.

fur'niture (feur-ni-tioure), n., appareil, mobilier, ameublement; équipement, materiel; équipage, m. ; fourniture, f. ; (print.) garniture, f. ; (of a house) meubles, m.pl. A piece of — ; un meuble, m. — broker; brocanteur, marchand de meubles d'occasion, m. — depository, — warehouse; garde-meuble, m. — van; tapissière, f.

furred, adj., fourré; (of the tongue) chargé.

fur'rier (feur-ri-eur), n., fourreur, pelletier, m.

fur'row (feur-rô), n., ride, rainure, f. ; sillon; rayon; conduit, m.

fur'row, v.a., sillonner, rider; (tech.) rainer.

fur'ry (feur'ri), adj., fourré, couvert de fourrures. — tongue; langue chargée, f.

fur'ther (feur'theur), adj., ultérieur; autre; nouveau. — end; le fond, le bout, m. — obligation; surcroît d'obligation, m.

fur'ther (feur'theur), v.a. and n., avancer;

faciliter, aider; favoriser; pousser; appuyer; seconder.

fur'ther, adv., plus loin; de plus; ultérieurement; au delà; encore; outre cela; plus amplement.

fur'therance, n., avancement, progrès, appui, m., aide, f.

fur'therer, n., protecteur; promoteur, patron; fauteur, m.

fur'thermore, adv., de plus; en outre; outre cela.

fur'thermore, conj., qui plus est, d'ailleurs.

fur'thermost (-môste), adj., le plus éloigné, le plus reculé, le plus lointain.

fur'thest (feur'thèste), adj., le plus éloigné; le plus reculé; le plus lointain; ultérieur.

fur'thest, adv., à la distance la plus grande, le plus loin; à l'époque la plus reculée.

fur'-tippet, n., palatine, f.

fur'tive (feur-), adj., furtif; dérobé; secret.

fur'tively, adv., furtivement, à la dérobée.

fur'-trade, n., pelleterie, f.

fu'runcle (fiou-reu'gn'k'l), n., furoncle, clou, m.

fu'ry (fiou-), n., furie, fureur, frénésie, rage, violence, fougue, f., acharnement, m.

furze (feurze), n., (bot.) ajonc; genêt épineux; genêt d'Angleterre, m. — brake; genêtière, f.

fur'zy, adj., plein d'ajoncs, de genêts.

fu'sarole (fiou-ça-rôl), n., (arch.) fusarolle, f.

fusca'tion (feus-ké-), n., action d'obscurcir, obscurité, f., obscurcissement, m.

fus'cous (feus'-), adj., terne, brun foncé, sombre.

fuse, n. V. fusee.

fuse (fiouze), v.a. and n., fondre, se fondre, liquéfier.

fusee' (fiou-zî), n., fusée, f. ; (hunt.) foulées, f.pl. ; (of a watch or bomb) fusée, f.

fu'sel oil, n., huile de pomme de terre, f. ; alcool amylique, m.

fusibil'ity (fiouz'i-), n., fusibilité, f.

fu'sible (fiou-zi-), adj., fusible.

fusileer' ou **fusilier'** (fiou-zi-lîre), n., (milit.) fusilier, m.

fusillade' (-léde), n., fusillade, f.

fu'sion (fiou-jeune), n., fusion; fonte des métaux, f.

fusionist, adj., fusioniste.

fuss (feuce), n., fracas, bruit, embarras, m. ; façons, f.pl. To make a — ; faire du bruit, de l'embarras; faire des façons.

fuss'ily, adv., avec embarras.

fuss'iness, n., embarras; air, ou ton, d'importance, m.

fuss'y, adj., façonnier, qui fait des embarras.

fust (feuste), n., odeur de renfermé, f. ; (arch.) fût, m.

fus'tian (feus'-), n., futaine, f. ; (fig.) phébus, galimatias, m. adj., de futaine; (fig.) boursouflé, ampoulé.

fus'tic (feus'-), n., fustet, fustel, m.

fus'tigate (feus'-), v.a., (ant.) fustiger; battre à coups de bâton.

fus'tiness (feus'-), n., moisissure; odeur de moisi, de renfermé, f.

fus'ty (feus'-), adj., chanci, puant; (air) renfermé.

fu'tile (fiou-tile), adj., futile, vain; frivole.

futil'ity (fiou-), n., futilité, vanité, frivolité, f.; babil, caquet, bavardage, m.

fut'terill (feut'teur'ile), n., (min.) galerie d'extraction, f.

fut'tock (feut-), n.pl., (nav.) courbaton; genou, m. ; allonge, f.

fu'ture (fiout'ioure), adj., futur, à venir.

fu'ture, n., avenir; (gram.) futur, m. For the — ; à l'avenir.

futu'rity, n., avenir, m., éternité, f.

fuze (fiouze), n., (of a shell) fusée, mèche, f.

fuzz (feuze), *v.n.*, s'évaporer, s'en aller en poussière.

fuzz, *n.*, particules fines et légères, *f.pl.* ; matière volatile, *f.sing.*

fuzz'ball (-bōl), *n.*, (bot.) vesse-de-loup, *f.*

fuz'zle, *v.a.*, enivrer, griser.

fy! *ou* **fie!** (faïe), *int.*, fi! fi donc! — for shame! *fi! c'est une honte.*

G

g, septième lettre de l'alphabet, g ; (mus.) sol, *m.*

gab, *n.*, faconde, *f.* ; bavardage, *m.* To have the gift of the —; *avoir le don de la parole ; avoir la langue bien pendue.*

gab'ardine (-dîne), *n.*, souquenille, *f.*, caban, balandras, balandran, *m.*

gab'ble (gab'b'l), *n.*, babil, bourdonnement, bavardage, *m.*

gab'ble, *v.n.*, (of some birds) cacarder, crier ; bavarder, babiller, causer, caqueter.

gab'bler, *n.*, babillard, causeur, bavard, *m.*

ga'bel, *n.*, (ant.) gabelle, *f.*

ga'bion (ghé-), *n.*, (fort.) gabion, *m.*

ga'ble (ghé-b'l), *n.*, toit, pignon, *m.*

ga'ble-end (-è'n'de), *n.*, bord d'un toit, pignon, *m.*

gad, *n.*, coin d'acier, *m.* ; pointe, *f.* ; burin, poinçon, *m.*

gad, *v.n.*, battre le pavé ; rôder, flâner ; courir çà et là. To — about; *courir la pretantaine.*

gad'der, *n.*, coureur, *m.*, coureuse, *f.* ; flâneur, *m.*, flâneuse, *f.*

gad'dingly (gad'-), *adv.*, en rôdant ; en courant çà et là.

gad'fly (-flaïe), *n.*, (ent.) taon, *m.*

gaff, *n.*, gaffe, *f.*, harpon, croc, *m.*

gaf'fer, *n.*, (ant.) compère ; vieux bonhomme ; contremaître, *m.*

gaf'fle, *n.*, (ant.) éperon (pour les coqs de combat), *m.*

gag, *n.*, bâillon, *m.*

gag, *v.a.*, bâillonner.

gage (ghédje), *n.*, gage, *m.*, assurance ; jauge, *f.*, calibre, *m. V.* **gauge.**

gage, *v.a.*, jauger ; gager ; mettre en gage.

ga'ger, *n.*, jaugeur, maître jaugeur, *m.*

gag'ger, *n.*, bâillonneur, *m.*

gag'ging, *n.*, bâillonnement, *m.*

gag'gle, *v.n.*, (ant.) crier comme une oie.

gag'-tooth (-touth), *n.*, surdent, *f.*

gai'ety *ou* **gay'ety** (ghé-i-), *n.*, gaieté, gaîté, *f.* ; enjouement, *m.* ; pompe, *f.* ; faste ; (pleasure) plaisir, *m.*

gai'ly, *adv.*, gaiement, joyeusement.

gain (ghéne) *n.*, gain, profit, avantage, lucre, *m.* ; (arch.) gaîne, *f.*

gain, *v.a.* and *n.*, gagner ; acquérir ; obtenir ; l'emporter **sur** ; (a victory, a prize) remporter ; (of watches, etc.) avancer. To — ground ; *gagner du terrain.* To — over ; *convertir ; attirer à soi.* To — time ; *gagner du temps.* To — upon ; *avoir l'avantage* **sur**, *gagner* **sur**. To — the day ; *l'emporter* **sur**, *réussir.* To — friends ; *se faire des amis.*

gain'er, *n.*, gagneur, *m.* ; personne qui gagne, bénéficiaire, *f.* To be a — by ; *gagner* **à**.

gain'ful (-foule), *adj.*, (ant.) profitable, lucratif, avantageux.

gain'fully, *adv.*, (ant.) utilement ; avec profit.

gain'fulness, *n.*, (ant.) avantage, profit, gain, *m.*

gain'ings, *n.pl.*, gains ; profits, *m.pl.*

gain'less, *adj.*, (ant.) inutile ; qui n'est point profitable, sans profit.

gain'lessness, *n.*, (ant.) inutilité, *f.*

gain'ly, *adv.*, (ant.) facilement ; avec dextérité ; adroitement.

gain'say (ghé'n'séi), *v.a.*, contredire ; démentir ; nier ; contrarier.

gain'sayer (-sé-eur), *n.*, contradicteur, adversaire, *m.*

gain'saying (-sé-igne), *n.*, contradiction, opposition, dementi, *f.*

gait (ghéte), *n.*, port, air, *m.* ; démarche ; (of a horse) marche, allure, *f.*

gai'ter (ghét'-), *n.*, guêtre, *f. v.a.*, guêtrer.

ga'la (ghé-), *n.*, gala, *m.* ; réjouissance, *f.* — day ; *jour de gala, m.*

gal'axy, *n.*, (astron.) voie lactée, galaxie, *f.* ; assemblage brillant, *m.* ; réunion brillante, *f.*

gale (ghéle), *n.*, vent frais ; (nav.) grain, coup de vent, *m.* ; forte brise, tempête, *f.*

ga'lea (ghé-li-), *n.*, (bot.) coiffe, *f.* ; casque, *m.* ; (med.) céphalalgie générale, *f.*

ga'leate *ou* **ga'leated** (ghé-li-), *adj.*, casqué ; (bot.) ayant des fleurs en casque, *f.pl.*

gale'ga (-li-), *n.*, (bot.) rue de chèvre, *f.* ; galéga, *m.*

gale'na (-li-), *n.*, (min.) galène, *f.*

galeop'sis (gal-i-), *n.*, (bot.) chanvre bâtard, galéopsis, *m.* ; ortie rouge, *f.*

gal'ingale, *n.*, (bot.) souchet odorant, *m.*

gal'iot, *n.*, galiote ; petite galère, *f.*

gal'ipot, *n.*, galipot, *m.*

gall (gōl), *n.*, fiel ; amer, *m.*, bile, *f.* ; (fig.) rancune, malice, *f.*, chagrin, *m.* ; (bot.) noix de galle ; écorchure, *f.* — bladder ; *vésicule biliaire, f.* — duct ; *conduit biliaire, m.* — nut ; *noix de galle, f.* — stone ; *calcul biliaire, m.*

gall, *v.a.* and *n.*, écorcher ; se couper ; (fig.) se chagriner ; fâcher, irriter ; froisser, blesser, vexer ; harasser.

gal'lant (gal'la'n'te), *n.*, homme brave, vaillant, courageux ; galant homme, preux, *m.*

gal'lant (gal-la'n'te), *adj.*, brave, courageux, noble, vaillant, intrépide.

gallant' (gal-lâ'nte), *n.*, galant ; amant ; homme galant, *m.*

gallant' (gal-lâ'nte), *adj.*, gai ; bien mis ; galant, poli, courtois.

gal'lantly (gal'la'n'tli), *adv.*, noblement ; généreusement ; bravement, courageusement.

gallant'ly (gal'lâ'ntli), *adv.*, galamment ; poliment, courtoisement.

gal'lantry (gal'la'nt'-), *n.*, galanterie, intrigue amoureuse ; générosité, valeur, bravoure, *f.*

gal'leass (-li-), *n.*, (nav.) galéasse, galéace, *f.*

galled (gōl'de), *adj.*, écorché ; foulé ; blessé ; froissé ; piqué ; chagriné.

gal'leon (gal'li-eune), *n.*, (nav.) galion, *m.*

gal'lery (gal'leu'ri), *n.*, galerie ; (parliament) tribune, *f.* To play to the — ; *gueuser des encens.*

gal'ley (gal'li), *n.*, galère, *f.* ; (boat) caïque, *m.* ; (print.) galée, *f.* — proof ; *épreuve en placard, f.*

gal'ley-slave, *n.*, galérien, forçat, *m.*

Gal'lic, *adj.*, gaulois, gallique, gallican.

Gal'licism, *n.*, gallicisme ; idiotisme français, *m.*

galligas'kins (-ki'n'ze), *n.*, chausses larges à l'antique ; braies, grègues, *f.pl.*

gallimau'fry (-), *n.*, mélange ridicule ; salmigondis, *m.f.*

gallina'ceous (-né-sheusse), *adj.*, (orni.) gallinacé.

gall'ing (gōll'-), *n.*, inflammation, écorchure, (fig.) irritation, *f.*

gall'ing, *adj.*, irritant, piquant, mordant, vexant ; incommode. — fire ; (artil.) *feu bien nourri, feu meurtrier, m.*

gal'lingale (gal'lin'ghéle), *n.*, (bot.). *V.* **galingale.**

gal'linule (gal'li-nioule), *n.*, (orni.) poule d'eau, *f.*

gal'lipot (gal'li-), *n.*, pot de faïence, *m.*

galloma'nia, *n.*, gallomanie, *f.*

galloma'niac, *n.*, gallomane, *m.*

gal'lon (gal'lone), *n.*, gallon (quatre litres et demi), *m.*

galloon' (gal'loune), *n.*, galon, *m.* To bind with —; *galonner*, *border de galon.*

gallooned', *adj.*, galonné.

gal'lop (gal'lope), *n.*, galop, *m.* Full —; *grand galop.* Easy —; *petit galop.*

gal'lop, *v.n.*, galoper, aller au galop. To — off; *partir au galop.* To — back; *revenir au galop.* To — down; *descendre au galop.* To — up; *monter au galop.* To — past; *défiler au galop.*

gal'loper, *n.*, cheval qui galope, *m.*

gal'loping, *n.*, galop, *m.*, galopade, *f.*

gal'loping, *adj.*, (med.) galopant. — consumption ; *phtisie galopante, f.*

gal'loway (gal'lo-wè), *n.*, cheval de petite taille, bidet, *m.*

gal'lows (gal'leusse), *n.*, potence, *f.*, gibet, *m.* — bird; *gibier de potence, m.*

galoche' (ga-lôshe), *n.*, galoche, *f.*

gal'vanism (-'iz'me), *n.*, galvanisme, *m.*

gal'vanize (-'aïze), *v.a.*, galvaniser.

galvanom'eter, *n.*, galvanomètre, *m.*

gam'bet, *n.*, (orni.) gambette, *f.*

gam'bit, *n.*, (at chess) gambit, *m.*

gam'ble (ga'm'b'l), *v.n.*, jouer gros jeu. He —d away his money ; *il perdit son argent au jeu.*

gam'bler, *n.*, joueur, brelandier, *m.*

gam'bling, *n.*, jeu, *m.* ; passion du jeu, *f.* — house ; *maison de jeu, f.* — table; *table de jeu, f.*

gamboge' (-bôdje), *n.*, gomme-gutte, *f.*

gam'bol, *n.*, gambade, réjouissance, *f.*, saut de joie, bond, *m.* ; ébats, *m.pl.*

gam'bol, *v.n.*, gambader, danser de joie, folâtrer, s'ébattre, prendre ses ébats.

gam'brel, *n.*, jambe de derrière du cheval, *f.*

game, *n.*, jeu, *m.*, récréation ; partie de (one of a rubber) manche, *f.* ; gibier, *m.* ; chasse, *f.* ; (drawn game) refait, *m.*, partie nulle, *f.* Small —; *menu gibier.* To die —; *ne pas faiblir; mourir en brave ; résister jusqu'au bout.* To make — of ; *se moquer de.* To play a losing —; *jouer un jeu à perdre.*

game, *v.a.* and *n.*, jouer ; folâtrer, s'amuser, se divertir.

game'-cock, *n.*, coq de combat, *m.*

game'keeper (-kîp'-), *n.*, garde-chasse, *m.*

game'-laws, *n.pl.*, lois sur la chasse, *f.pl.*

game'-license, *n.*, permis de chasse, *m.*

game'some, *adj.*, folâtre, badin ; enjoué.

game'somely, *adv.*, en badin ; d'une manière folâtre.

game'someness, *n.*, badinage, enjouement, *m.*

game'ster (ghé'm'steur), *n.*, joueur de profession, brelandier, *m.*

ga'ming-house (-haouce), *n.*, brelan, *m.*, maison de jeu, *f.*

gam'mer (ga'm'-), *n.*, commère, bonne femme, bonne mère, *f.*

gam'mon (ga'm'-), *n.*, quartier de lard; tric-trac, *m.* ; (fig.) mauvaise plaisanterie, blague, *f.*

gam'mon, *v.a.*, saler et fumer du lard ; (fig.) embabouiner, blaguer ; (nav.) faire des liures ; (at backgammon) battre.

gamp, *n.*, (umbrella) riflard, *m.*

gam'ut (ga'm'eute), *n.*, (mus.) gamme, *f.*

gan'der, *n.*, (orni.) jars, *m.*

gang, *n.*, bande, troupe ; clique, cabale, séquelle, *f.*, (of workmen) atelier, *m.*, brigade, *f.*

gang, *v.n.*, aller, s'en aller, marcher.

gan'glion (ga'gn'gli-), *n.*, (anat.) ganglion, *m.*

gan'grene (ga'gn'grîne), *n.*, gangrène, *f.*

gan'grene, *v.a.* and *n.*, gangrener, se gangrener, être gangrené.

gan'grenous, *adj.*, gangreneux.

gang'way (ga'gn'wé), *n.*, (nav.) passage étroit ; passavant, *m.* ; passerelle, galerie du faux pont, *f.* — ladder ; *échelle hors le bord, f.*

gan'net (ga'n'nète), *n.*, (orni.) fou, *m.*

gan'ny, *n.*, (orni.) coq d'Inde, dindon, *m.*

gant'let *ou* **gant'lope** (ga'n't'lète, -'lôpe), *n.*, gantelet, *m.*, baguettes, *f.pl.* To run the —; *passer par les baguettes ;* (nav.) *courir la bouline.*

gan'za, *n.*, oie sauvage, *f.*

gaol (djél), *n.*, prison, geôle, *f.*

gaol'-bird, *n.*, gibier de galère, *m.*

gaol'-book (-bouke), *n.*, livre d'écrou, *m.*

gaol'-deliv'ery (-dè-liv'oar'i), *n.*, élargissement, *m.* ; évacuation des prisons, *f.* [prison).

gaol'er (djél'eur), *n.*, geôlier, *m.*, concierge (de

gap, *n.*, brèche ; ouverture, *f.*, vide, passage, trou, interstice, *m.* ; (in a book) lacune, *f.* ; (in a forest) trouée, *f.* To stop a —; *boucher un trou ; payer une dette.* To stand in the —; *se tenir sur la brèche.* To fill a —; *remplir une lacune.*

gape (gâpe *ou* ghêpe), *v.n.*, bâiller ; (of doors, etc.) s'ouvrir, s'entr'ouvrir ; bayer. To — after; *soupirer après.* To — at ; *regarder fixement.*

gape *ou* **ga'ping**, *n.*, bâillement, *m.*

ga'per, *n.*, bâilleur, bayeur, *m.*

ga'ping, *part.adj.*, béant, qui bâille ; entr'ouvert ; (fig.) ébahi.

ga'ping, *n.*, bâillement, *m.* ; ouverture, *f.*

gap'-toothed (-toutht't), *adj.*, brèche-dent, *f.*

garavan'ces (-cèss), *n.*, (bot.) pois chiches, *m.pl.*

garb, *n.*, façon, *f.*, costume; habit, habillement ; manteau, *m.* ; dehors, *m.pl.*

gar'bage (gâr'bèdje), *n.*, tripailles, *f.pl.* ; curée, *f.* ; restes, *m.pl.* ; (fig.) saleté, obscénité, *f.*

gar'ble (gar'b'l), *v.a.*, trier, éplucher, cribler; (fig.) mutiler, dénaturer, tronquer (a quotation).

gar'bler, *n.*, personne qui trie ; qui mutile, qui tronque (a quotation).

gar'boil (gar'boil), *n.*, (ant.) désordre, trouble, tumulte, grabuge, *m.*, confusion, *f.*

gard. *V.* **guard.**

gar'den (gâr'd'n), *n.*, jardin, *m.*

gar'den, *v.n.*, jardiner.

gar'dener, *n.*, jardinier, *m.*

garde'nia, *n.*, (bot.) gardénie, *f.*

gar'dening, *n.*, jardinage, *m.*

gar'den-mold (-môlde), *n.*, terreau, *m.*

gar'den-plot, *n.*, parterre, *m.*

gare, *n.*, écouailles (coarse wool), *f.pl.*

gar'fish (gâr-), *n.*, (ich.) brochet, *m.*, aiguille, *f.*, de mer ; orphie, *f.*

gar'ganey (gâr-ga'n'i), *n.*, (orni.) sarcelle commune, *f.*

gargan'tuan, *adj.*, immense, prodigieux.

gar'gle (gâr-), *n.*, gargarisme, *m.*

gar'gle, *v.a.*, gargariser.

gar'goyle, *n.*, gargouille, *f.*

gar'ish *ou* **ga'rish** (gâr'-), *adj.*, éclatant, trop voyant; (fig.) extravagant, outré.

gar'ishness, *n.*, excès d'éclat, *m.*, extravagance, *f.*

gar'land (gâr-), *n.*, couronne de fleurs, guirlande, *f.* *v.a.*, guirlander.

gar'lic (gâr-), *n.*, ail, *m.* Clove of —; *gousse d'ail, f.*

gar'lic-eater (-ît'-), *n.*, mangeur d'ail ; maraud, *m.*

gar'ment (gâr-), *n.*, vêtement, habit, *m.* ; parure, *f.*

gar'ner (gâr-), *n.*, grenier à grain, *m.*

gar'ner, *v.a.*, engranger ; amasser, entasser; recueillir.

gar'net (gâr-), *n.*, grenat ; (nav.) bredindin, *m.*

gar'nish (gâr-), *n.*, ornement, embellissement, *m.*, bienvenue ; parure, garniture, *f.*

gar'nish, *v.a.* and *n.*, embellir ; parer **de**, garnir **de**, orner **de**.

gar'nishment *ou* **gar'niture**, *n.*, garniture, parure, *f.* ; ornement, embellissement, *m.*

ga'rous (ghé-), *adj.*, de saumure de thon.

gar'ran *ou* **gar'ron** (gar'-), *n.*, bidet ; mauvais cheval, criquet, *m.*, rosse, *f.*

gar'ret (gar'rète), *n.*, galetas, grenier, *m.*; mansarde, *f.*

garreteer' (-îre), *n.*, habitant d'un galetas; (fig.) pauvre écrivain, *m.*

gar'rison (gar'ris'n), *n.*, garnison, *f.*

gar'rison, *v.a.*, mettre une garnison **dans**; mettre en garnison.

gar'risoned (at), *adj.*, en garnison **à**; (place) à garnison.

gar'ron, *n.*   V. **gar'ran**.

garru'lity (gar-riou-), *n.*, garrulité, loquacité, *f.*; babil, caquet, *m.*

gar'rulous, *adj.*, babillard, bavard, loquace.

gar'ter (gar-), *n.*, jarretière, *f.*

gar'ter, *v.a.*, attacher ses jarretières; lier avec une jarretière.

gas (gace), *n.*, (*gases*) (chem.) gaz, *m.*

gas'-apparatus, *n.*, appareil à gaz, *m.*

gas'-burner (-beurn'-), *n.*, bec de gaz, *m.*

gasconade', *n.*, gasconnade, hâblerie, *f.*

gaselier', *n.*, lustre à gaz, *m.*

gas'eous (gaz'i-), *adj.*, gazeux.

gas'-fitter (fit'-), *n.*, gazier, *m.*

gash, *n.*, balafre, estafilade, entaille, large blessure, *f.*

gash, *v.a.*, balafrer, taillader; faire une estafilade **à**.

gashed (gash't), *adj.*, incisé, découpé.

gas'iform, *adj.*, gazéiforme.

gas'ify (gass'i-faïe), *v.a.*, (chem.) gazéifier.

gas'ket (gas'kète), *n.*, (nav.) garcette, *f.*, raban, *m.*

gas'kins (gas'ki'n'ze), *n.pl.*, large culotte, *f.*

gas'-light, gas'-lighting (-laïte), *n.*, éclairage au gaz, *m.*

gas'-meter (-mî-), *n.*, compteur à gaz, *m.*

gasom'eter (gass'om'-), *n.*, gazomètre, *m.*

gasp, *n.*, soupir; abois, *m.*; agonie, *f.* At the last —; à la dernière extrémité; aux abois.

gasp, *v.n.*, respirer avec peine. To — after; *soupirer* **après**. To — for breath; *haleter*.

gas'-pipe, *n.*, tuyau ou conduit de gaz, *m.*

gasp'ing, *n.*, respiration, haletante.

gastral'gia (-djia), *n.*, (med.) gastralgie, *f.*

gas'tric (-), *adj.*, (anat.) gastrique.

gastri'tis (-traï-), *n.*, (med.) gastrite, *f.*

gas'tronome (-nôme), *n.*, épicurien, gastronome, *m.*

gastronom'ic, *adj.*, gastronomique.

gastron'omist, *n.*, gastronome, *m.*

gastron'omy, *n.*, gastronomie, *f.*

gas'-works, *n.pl.*, usine à gaz, *f.*

gate, *n.*, porte, *f.*; portail, *m.*; barrière, *f.*; guichet, *m.*; grille, *f.*   Flood —; *vanne*; (in ponds) *bonde*, *f.*

gate'way (-wé), *n.*, porte cochère, porte d'entrée, *f.*; guichet, passage, *m.*

gath'er (gath'-), *n.*, pli, froncis, *m.*

gath'er, *v.a.*, cueillir; amasser, ramasser; assembler, rassembler, recueillir; recevoir; froncer, plisser, récolter, rentrer. To — taxes; *percevoir les impôts*. To — breath; *prendre haleine*. To — grapes; *vendanger*. To — corn; *moissonner*. To — strength; *se rétablir*; (fig.) *prospérer, s'affermir*. To — wealth; *s'enrichir*. To — one's self up; *se ramasser, se pelotonner*.

gath'er (gath'-), *v.n.*, s'assembler, se rassembler; se condenser; s'amonceler; s'épaissir, s'approcher. To — from; *inférer de, conclure de.* To — to a head; *commencer à mûrir*; être prêt à suppurer, venir à suppuration.

gath'erer, *n.*, collecteur, quêteur, cueilleur; (of taxes) percepteur des impôts; (of grapes) vendangeur; (of corn) moissonneur, *m.*

gath'ering, *n.*, (agri.) récolte, cueillette; (for charity) quête, collecte; (of taxes) perception; (assembly) rassemblement, *m.*; assemblée, réunion, foule; (tumor) tumeur, *f.*, abcès, *m.*

gaud (gô'd), *n.*, (ant.) parure, *f.*, ornement, jouet; tour, *m.*; plaisanterie, *f.*

gau'dily, *adv.*, fastueusement, avec éclat.

gau'diness, *n.*, faste, *m.*; ostentation, *f.*, luxe, éclat, clinquant, faux brillant, *m.*

gau'dy, *adj.*   V. **showy**.

gauge (ghédje), *n.*, jauge; mesure, *f.*; (nav.) tirant d'eau, *m.*; largeur entre les rails d'un chemin de fer, *f.*, entre-rails, *m.*

gauge, *v.a.*, jauger; mesurer; (fig.) juger.

gau'ger, *n.*, jaugeur, *m.*

gau'ging, *n.*, jaugeage, *m.*   —-rod; *jauge*, *f.*

Gaul (gô'l), *n.*, Gaulois, *m.*; la Gaule, *f.*

Gaul'ish, *adj.*, gaulois.

gaunt (gâ'n'te), *adj.*, maigre, décharné.

gaunt'let (gâ'n't'-), *n.*, gantelet, *m.*   To throw down the — to; *jeter le gant* **à**.   To take up the —; *ramasser le gant*.   To run the —; (nav.) *courir la bouline*.

gaunt'ly, *adv.*, maigrement, avec maigreur, d'un air décharné.

gauze (gôze), *n.*, gaze, *f.*

gav'el, *n.*, terrain, *m.*; terre; javelle, *f.*; tribut, *m.*, extorsion; usure, *f.*

gav'el-kind (-kaï'n'de), *n.*, partage égal (des terres).

gav'ot, *n.*, (dance) gavotte, *f.*

gawk (gôke), *n.*, coucou; sot; maladroit, *m.*

gaw'ky, *adj.*, gauche, stupide, maladroit. — fellow; *grand maladroit, lourdaud, m.*

gay, *adj.*, gai, réjoui, joyeux; pimpant; dissipé; adonné au plaisir; lancé; leste.   As — as a lark; *gai comme un pinson*.   To lead a — life; *mener une vie de plaisirs*.   — with bunting; (of streets) *pavoisé*.

gay'ety *ou* **gai'ety**, *n.*, gaieté, *f.*; enjouement, éclat, plaisir, *m.*

gay'ly *ou* **gai'ly**, *adv.*, gaiement; avec éclat; élégamment.

gaze (ghéze), *n.*, regard fixe *ou* attentif, d'étonnement *ou* d'admiration, *m.*

gaze, *v.n.*, regarder fixement, contempler, regarder la bouche béante.

gazelle', *n.*, (mam.) gazelle, *f.*

ga'zer (ghéz'-), *n.*, contemplateur, spectateur, *m.*

gazette', *n.*, gazette, *f.*; journal, Journal officiel, *m.*

gazette', *v.a.*, publier **dans**, insérer **à**, annoncer **dans** le Journal officiel.   He is not yet —d; *sa nomination n'est pas encore officielle*.

gazetteer' (-tîre), *n.*, gazetier, nouvelliste; dictionnaire géographique, *m.*

ga'zing-stock (ghéz'-), *n.*, spectacle; (fig.) objet de mépris, *m.*

gazon' (-zô'n), *n.*, (fort.) gazon, *m.*

gean (djîne), *n.*, (bot.) cerise sauvage, merise, *f.*

gear (ghîre), *n.*, habit, habillement, accoutrement, *m.*; marchandise, *f.*, attirail; colifichet, *m.*; (nav.) apparaux, *m.pl.*, drisse, *f.*; (of a horse) harnais; (mec.) engrenage, jeu, *m.*; action; roue dentée, roue d'engrenage, *f.*   To be out of —; *être désengrené*; (fig.) *être dérangé*. To throw out of —; *désengrener*; (fig.) *déranger*.

gear'-case, *n.*, carter, *n.m.*

gear'ing (ghîr'-) *ou* **gear**, *n.*, disposition d'une machine, *f.*; appareil, engrenage; agencement, *m.*

gee (djî), *v.n.*, hurhau! huhau! hue!   — up! *houp-là!*

geese (ghîce), *n.*, (*pl.* of Goose) oies, *f.pl.*

Gehen'na, *n.*, géhenne, *f.*

gel'atine (djèl'-), *n.*, gélatine, *f.*

gelat'inate, gelat'inize, *v.n.*, se prendre en gelée.

gelat'inous, *adj.*, visqueux, gélatineux.

geld (ghèlde), *v.a.*, châtrer, couper, hongrer (horses).

gel'der, *n.*, châtreur, *m.*

gel'der-rose *ou* **guelder-rose**, *n.*, boule-de-neige, rose de Gueldre, *f.*; viorne, *f.* and *m.*

geld'ing, *n.*, hongre, cheval coupé, *m.*

gem (djème), *n.*, pierre précieuse, *f.* ; bijou, joyau, fleuron ; (hort.) bouton ; bourgeon, *m.*

gem, *v.a.* and *n.*, orner **de**, *ou* parer **de**, pierres précieuses ; bourgeonner ; émailler ; parsemer **de**.

Gem'ini (djèm'i'naï), *n.pl.*, (astron.) Gémeaux, *m.pl.*

gem'meous (djèm'-), *adj.*, de diamant ; de pierre précieuse ; ressemblant aux pierres précieuses.

gendarme' (jã'n'dârm), *n.*, gendarme, *m.*

gen'der (djè'n'-), *n.*, genre, *m.* ; (fig.) espèce, sorte, *f.*

genealog'ical (djèn'i-al'o-dji-), *adj.*, généalogique.

geneal'ogist, *n.*, généalogiste, *m.*

geneal'ogy (djèn'i-al-odji), *n.*, généalogie, *f.*

gen'eral (djèn'-), *n.*, général, chef, *m.* ; (drum-call) générale, *f.*

gen'eral, *adj.*, général, commun, ordinaire. Attorney- — ; *procureur général*, *m.* Vicar- — ; *vicaire général*, *m.* —shop ; *boutique où l'on vend de tout, f.* — agency ; *agence, f.* — servant ; *bonne à tout faire, f.* In — ; *en général.* The public in — ; *la masse du public.*

generalis'simo, *n.*, généralissime, *m.*

general'ity, *n.*, généralité ; la plupart ; masse ; foule, *f.*

gen'eralize (-aïze), *v.a.*, généraliser.

gen'erally, *adv.*, en général, ordinairement, généralement.

gen'eralship, *n.*, généralat, talent de général, *m.* ; stratégie ; tactique, *f.*

gen'erant (djèn'eur'-), *n.*, générateur, *m.* ; puissance productrice, *f.*

gen'erate, *v.a.* and *n.*, engendrer, produire ; propager.

genera'tion (djèn'eur'é-), *n.*, génération, race, famille ; production, *f.* ; siècle, *m.*

gen'erative, *adj.*, générateur ; producteur, fécond, fertile.

gen'erator (-'eur), *n.*, générateur, *m.*

gener'ic *ou* **gener'ical** (djèn'èr-), *adj.*, générique, distinctif.

generos'ity (djèn'eur'-), *n.*, générosité, magnanimité, libéralité, *f.*

gen'erous, *adj.*, généreux ; (fig.) abondant, riche **en** ; (of wine) plein de vinosité.

gen'erously, *adv.*, généreusement ; noblement, libéralement.

gen'esis (djèn'è-ciss), *n.*, Genèse, origine, *f.* ; (math.) génération, *f.*

gen'et (djèn'ète), *n.*, genet, *m.* ; haquenée, genette, *f.*

gene'va (djè-ni-), *n.*, genièvre, gin, *m.*

ge'nial (dji-), *adj.*, naturel ; réjouissant ; gai, joyeux, enjoué. — disposition ; *caractère sympathique, m.*

genial'ity *ou* **ge'nialness**, *n.*, gaieté, bonne humeur, nature sympathique, douceur, *f.*

ge'nially, *adv.*, naturellement, gaîment, avec bonté.

ge'nii (djî'-ni-aï), *n.pl.*, génies, *m.pl.*

gen'ital (djèn'-), *adj.*, génital. *pl.*, parties génitales, *f.pl.*

gen'itive (djèn'-), *n.*, (gram.) génitif, *m.*

ge'nius (djîn'-), *n.*, génie ; talent, *m.* ; disposition naturelle, *f.*

genteel' (djèn'-tîl), *adj.*, de bon ton, comme il faut, distingué, de bon goût, joli, élégant, galant ; poli, civil, noble.

genteel'ly, *adv.*, poliment, galamment, noblement, de bonne grâce, élégamment.

genteel'ness, *n.*, grâce, urbanité, élégance, *f.*, bon ton, *m.*

gen'tian (djè'n'sha'ne), *n.*, (bot.) gentiane, *f.*

gen'tile (djè'n'taïle), *n.*, païen, gentil, *m.*

gen'tilism (-taïl'iz'm), *n.*, paganisme, *m.* ; idolâtrie, *f.*

gentil'ity (-til'i-), *n.*, politesse, *f.* ; bon ton, *m.* ; naissance distinguée, distinction ; élégance, *f.*

gen'tle (djè'n't'l), *adj.*, doux, modéré ; aimable ; gentil. Of — birth ; *bien né.* — reader ; *ami lecteur, m.*

gen'tle-folk (-fōke) *ou* **gen'tle-folks** (-fōkse), *n.pl.*, personnes de bon ton, distinguées, comme il faut, *f.pl.* ; gens comme il faut, gens de condition, *m.pl.*

gen'tleman (-ma'n), *n.*, monsieur, homme de bon ton, comme il faut ; galant homme ; homme d'honneur ; homme bien né ; (in the service of a sovereign) gentilhomme ; (of independent means) rentier, *m.* A young — ; *un jeune homme, m.* —performer ; *amateur, m.* A perfect — ; *un parfait gentilhomme ; un homme très comme il faut.* To play the fine —; *faire le monsieur.*

gen'tleman-like (-laïke) *ou* **gen'tlemanly**, *adj.*, distingué, de bon ton, comme il faut, bien né.

gen'tlemanliness, *n.*, bon ton, urbanité, savoir-vivre, *m.*

gen'tleness, *n.*, douceur ; bonté ; bienveillance, *f.*

gen'tlewoman (-woum'a'n), *n.*, dame, femme de bon ton, de bonne famille, *f.*

gen'tly, *adv.*, doucement, lentement, avec bonté. — ! *tout beau !*

gen'try (djè'n'-), *n.*, petite noblesse ; haute bourgeoisie, *f.* ; messieurs, *m.pl.* ; (b.s., iron.) braves gens, *m.pl.* Small — ; *petite bourgeoisie, f.*, *hobereaux, m.pl.*

genuflec'tion (djè-niou-flek-sheune), *n.*, génuflexion, *f.*

gen'uine (djè'n'iou-ine), *adj.*, naturel, réel, pur, vrai, véritable, sincère ; authentique.

gen'uinely, *adv.*, purement, réellement ; naturellement, légitimement.

gen'uineness, *n.*, réalité ; authenticité ; pureté, vérité, *f.*

ge'nus (dji-), *n.*, (*genera*) genre, *m.* ; espèce, *f.*

geod'esy (-ci), *n.*, (geom.) géodésie, *f.*

geog'nosy (dji-og'-no-ci), *n.*, géognosie, *f.*

geog'rapher (dji-og'-ra-), *n.*, géographe, *m.*

geograph'ical, *adj.*, géographique.

geog'raphy (dji-og'-ra-), *n.*, géographie, *f.*

geol'ogy (dji-ol-o-dji), *n.*, géologie, *f.*

ge'omancy (djî-), *n.*, divination par la terre, géomancie, *f.*

geom'eter (dji-om'è-) *ou* **geometri'cian** (dji-o-mî-trish'è'n), *n.*, géomètre, *m.*

geomet'ric *ou* **geomet'rical**, *adj.*, géométrique, géométral.

geomet'rically, *adv.*, géométriquement, géométralement.

geom'etrize (-traïze), *v.n.*, procéder géométriquement.

geom'etry (dji-om'è-tri), *n.*, géométrie, *f.*

geora'ma (djî-o-râ-ma), *n.*, géorama, *m.*

by **George**, *int.*, sapristi ! mâtin ! sacrebleu !

Geor'gics (djor-djikse), *n.pl.*, géorgiques, *f.pl.*

Geor'gium Si'dus (djor-dji-eume-saï-), *n.*, (astron.) Herschel, Uranus, *m.*

gera'nium (dji-ré'-), *n.*, (bot.) bec-de-grue, géranium, *m.*

ger'bua (djeur-bou-a), *n.*, (mam.) gerboise, *f.*

ger'falcon (djeur-fō-k'n), *n.*, (orni.) gerfaut, *m.*

germ (djeurme), *n.*, germe, bourgeon, *m.* ; pousse, *f.* ; (bot.) embryon, *m.*

ger'man (djeur-), *adj.*, germain ; qui est parent, qui est proche ; allemand. A cousin — ; *un cousin germain, m.* — flute ; *flûte traversière, f.* — silver ; *métal blanc, m.*

Ger'man (djeur-), *n.*, Allemand, *m.*, Allemande, *f.* ; (language) allemand, *m.*

german'der (djeur-), *n.*, (bot.) germandrée, *f.*

germane', *adj.*, de la même souche ; pertinent, applicable **à** ; en rapport **avec**, qui touche **à** ; qui a rapport **à**.

German'ic (djeur-), *adj.*, germanique.

Ger'manism (djeur-), *n.*, germanisme, *m.*

ger'minal, *adj.*, germinal ; de germe.

ger'minate (djeur-), *v.a.n.*, germer, faire germer ; pousser, bourgeonner.

germina'tion, *n.*, (bot.) germination, *f.*

ger'minative, *adj.*, germinatif.

ger'und (djèr'eu'n'de), *n.*,(gram.) gérondif, *m.*

gesta'tion (djès-té-), *n.*, gestation, *f.*

gest'atory, *adj.*, gestatoire.

gestic'ulate (djès-tik-iou-), *v.n.*, gesticuler.

gesticula'tion, *n.*, gesticulation, *f.*

gestic'ulator, *n.*, gesticulateur, mime, *m.*

gestic'ulatory, *adj.*, mimique.

gest'ure (djèst'ioure), *n.*, geste ; mouvement expressif, *m.*, action, *f.*

gest'ure, *v.a.*, faire des gestes, gesticuler, accompagner de gestes.

get (ghète), *v.a.* and *n.* (*preterit*, Got; *past. part.*, Gotten *and* Got), gagner, acquérir, obtenir ; recevoir ; remporter ; avoir, tirer, faire, se faire, prendre ; (to buy, to procure) acheter, procurer, se procurer ; (to become) devenir, se faire ; (to arrive, to reach) arriver **à**, atteindre ; (to fetch) aller chercher; (to find) trouver; (to go) aller ; (to induce) engager, faire, obtenir **de**; (anything bad) attraper, s'attirer. To — about; *sortir, prendre de l'exercice*. To — about again; *reprendre ses occupations*. To — above; *surpasser*. To — abroad ; *faire sortir, publier, devenir public, s'ébruiter*. To — ahead ; *avancer, prospérer, réussir*. To — across; *traverser*. To — along ; *avancer, prospérer ; traîner, faire marcher*. To — at ; *connaître, savoir; s'informer de*. To — away ; *faire retirer ; ôter ; s'en aller ; s'évader*. To — back ; *revenir, recevoir de nouveau ; recouvrer*. To — before ; *prévenir, devancer*. To — behind ; *rester en arrière ; être en retard (de ses payements) ; pénétrer, démêler*. To — by heart ; *apprendre par cœur*. To — clear ; *se tirer de*. To — down; *descendre ; avaler*. To — forward ; *avancer, profiter*. To—free ; *s'échapper ; se dégager*. To — from ; *tirer, arracher ; se tirer, se débarrasser*. To — in ; *entrer, faire entrer, engager ; serrer ; s'insinuer*. To — off; *tirer ; débarrasser ; vendre ; échapper, se tirer, s'en tirer ; ôter ; s'ôter ; mettre pied à terre, descendre*. To — on ; *mettre ; avancer ; réussir*. To — out; *sortir ; tirer de, se tirer de ; arracher, faire sortir*. To — through, *ou* over ; *passer* **par**, *passer* à **travers** ; *surmonter, vaincre*. To — to; *arriver* à *aller* **à**, *atteindre*. To — together ; *amasser, assembler*. To — up; *lever, se lever ; organiser ; provoquer, exciter ;* (thea.) *mettre en scène, monter*. To — up again ; *relever, ramasser ; se relever*. To — upon; *monter* **sur**. To—under ; *maîtriser, dompter ; v.n., se mettre sous*. To — well again ; *se rétablir*. To — a fall; *tomber*. To — a footing ; *s'établir*. To — friends ; *se faire des amis*. To — ready ; *préparer, apprêter, se préparer*. To — the better of ; *avoir l'avantage* **sur**, *l'emporter* **sur**. To — with child ; *engrosser* (ant.). To — old ; *vieillir*. To — young again ; *rajeunir, se rajeunir*. To — married ; *se marier*. To — rich ; *s'enrichir*. To — made, *ou* done ; *faire faire*. To — mended ; *faire raccommoder*. To — to sleep ; *s'endormir*. To — loose; *lâcher, relâcher, s'échapper*. To — drunk; *s'enivrer*. To — wet ; *se mouiller*. To — tired ; *se lasser, se fatiguer*. That's all I have got to say ; *voilà tout ce que j'ai à dire*. To — the credit of ; *passer pour avoir fait*. To — hold of ; *s'emparer* **de**; *influencer*. He got him to draw up a prescription ; *il lui fit écrire une ordonnance*. To — well paid ; *être rémunéré largement ; se faire bien payer*. To — into a scrape; *mettre dans l'embarras, dans le pétrin ; se mettre dans*

le pétrin, se faire une mauvaise affaire. To — into **a** dispute ; *s'engager dans une querelle*. It was —ting late ; *il se faisait tard*. To — blood from a stone ; *tirer de l'huile d'un mur*. To — out of bed the wrong side; *mettre son bonnet de travers*.

get'ter (ghèt'-), *n.*, personne qui gagne, qui obtient, qui se procure. — up ; *promoteur*, *m.*

get'ting (ghèt'-), *n.*, acquisition, *f.* ; gain, profit, *m.* — up ; (thea.) *mise en scène*, *f.*; montage, *m.*

gew'gaw (ghiou-gô), *n.*, babiole, bagatelle, *f.* ; joujou, bijou, jouet, colifichet, *m.*

ghast'liness, *n.*, pâleur ; mine affreuse, *f.* ; air terrible, aspect horrible, *m.*

ghast'ly (gâst'-), *adj.*, de fantôme, pâle, triste, sombre, hagard, lugubre, hideux, horrible, pâle comme la mort.

gher'kin (gheur-), *n.*, (bot.) cornichon, *m.*

ghost (gôste), *n.*, esprit, *m.* ; âme ; ombre, *f.* ; revenant, fantôme, *m.* The Holy —; *le Saint-Esprit*.

ghost'like (-laïke), *adj.*, de fantôme ; flétri ; pâle, triste, sombre, hagard.

ghost'ly, *adj.*, spirituel, divin ; de spectre.

ghoul, *n.*, goule, *f.*

ghoul'ish, *adj.*, goulique.

gi'ant (djaï'-), *n.*, géant, colosse, *m.*

gi'antess, *n.*, géante, *f.*

gi'ant-like (-laïke), *adj.*, gigantesque; de géant.

gi'antship, *n.*, grandeur démesurée ; forme gigantesque, *f.*

giaour, *n.*, giaour, *m.*

gib, *n.*, vieux matou, *m.* ; (tech.) clavette, *f.*

gib'ber (ghib'-), *v.n.*, baragouiner.

gib'berish (ghib'beur-), *n.*, baragouin, jargon, patois, *m.*

gib'bet (djib'bète), *n.*, potence, *f.* ; gibet, *m.* ; croix, *f.*

gib'bet, *v.a.*, pendre à une potence ; exposer sur un gibet ; (fig.) pilorier.

gib'bon (ghib'bone), *n.*, (mam.) gibbon, *m.*

gib'bose (ghib'bôss) *ou* **gib'bous** (ghib'-), *adj.*, gibbeux, cornu, bossu.

gibbos'ity (ghib'-), *n.*, gibbosité, bosse, convexité, *f.*

gibe (djaïbe), *n.*, sarcasme, *m.* ; raillerie, moquerie, *f.*

gibe, *v.a.* and *n.*, se gausser **de** ; railler ; se moquer **de**, se rire **de**.

gi'ber, *n.*, railleur, gausseur, *m.*

gi'bingly, *adv.*, d'un air railleur, d'un air moqueur ; ironiquement.

gib'lets (djib'lètse), *n.pl.*, abattis de volaille, etc., *m.pl.*, petite-oie, *f.*

gid'dily (ghid'-), *adv.*, étourdiment ; capricieusement.

gid'diness, *n.*, vertige, étourdissement, *m.* ; étourderie, humeur folâtre, *f.*

gid'dy (ghid'di), *adj.*, étourdi, évaporé ; volage, capricieux ; (med.) vertigineux ; qui a le vertige.

gid'dy-brained (-bré'n'de) *ou* (ant.) **gid'dy-head'ed** (-hèd'ède), *adj.*, étourdi, écervelé, sot, bête, volage, léger.

gift (ghif'te), *n.*, présent, don, cadeau ; (fig.) talent, *m.* ; donation, *f.* New Year's —s ; *présents du nouvel an*, *m.pl.*, *étrennes*, *f.pl.* One must not look a — horse in the mouth ; *à cheval donné on ne regarde pas à la bride*. To have the — of the gab ; *avoir la langue bien pendue*.

gift, *v.a.*, douer **de**, inspirer ; (ant.) donner.

gift'ed (-ède), *adj.*, doué **de** ; de talent.

gig (ghig), *n.*, tilbury, cabriolet, *m.* ; (boat) chaloupe, pinasse, *f.* ; (tech.) laineuse, *f.*

gigan'tic (djaï-ga'n'-tî-), *adj.*, gigantesque ; de géant.

gig'gle (ghig'g'l), *v.n.*, ricaner, rire tout bas.

gig'gle, *n.*, ricanement, rire étouffé, *m.*

gig'gler, *n.*, ricaneur, rieur, *m.*

gi'got (dji-gote), n., gigot, m.

gild (ghilde), v.a., dorer; embellir. To — the pill; dorer la pilule.

gild'er, n., doreur, m.

gild'ing, n., dorure, f., (fig.) clinquant, oripeau; (fig.) faux dehors, m.pl.

gill (ghill), n., (of the cock) barbe, f.; (measure) roquille, f.; (bot.) gléchome, lierre terrestre; ruisseau, ravin, m.; (of fish) branchies, ouïes, f.pl.; (mam.) abajoue, f.; (bot.) feuillet, m., lame, f.

gil'ly-flower (djï'l-), n., (bot.) giroflée, f.

gilt (ghilte), n., dorure, f. adj., doré.

gilt'edged (-èdj'de), adj., doré sur tranche.

gilt'head (-hède), n., (ich.) daurade, f.

gim'crack (djïm'-), n., joujou, bibelot, m., bagatelle, babiole; patraque, f.

gim'let (ghi'm'lète), m., foret, m., vrille, f.

gimp (ghi'm'pe), n., guipure, f.; cordonnet, brandebourg, m.

gin (djine), n., trébuchet, m., trappe, f.; (liquor) genièvre, m., eau-de-vie de genièvre; (mec.) grue à trois pieds; chèvre, f.; (tech.) moulin à cylindre; moulin sciant, m. — palace; débit de vins et spiritueux, m.; buvette, f.

gin, v.a., prendre au trébuchet; égrener.

gin'ger (dji'n'djeur), n., gingembre, m.

gin'gerbread (-brède), n., pain d'épice, m.

gin'gerly, adv., tout doucement; délicatement; à pas comptés.

ging'ham (ghign'-), n., guingan (umbrella), riflard, m.

gin'gival (dji'n'dji-), adj., des gencives.

gin'gle (dji'gn'g'l), n. V. jingle.

gin'gle, v.a. V. jingle.

gin'gling, n. V. jingling.

gin'ning, n., égrenage, m.

gin'seng (dji'n'sè'gne), n., (bot.) ginseng, m.

gip'sy (djip'si), n., gipsy, bohémien, bohème, m., gipsy, égyptienne, bohémienne; fine matoise, f.

giraffe' (dji-), n., (zoöl.) girafe, f., ⊙caméléopard, m.

gird (gheurde), v.a. and n., ceindre de, entourer de; lier; vêtir de; sangler; pincer, railler. To — up one's loins; se ceindre les reins.

gird'er, n., (carp.) solive, traverse, longrine, f.

gir'dle (gheur'd'l), n., ceinture, f.; ceinturon, m.

gir'dle, v.a. V. gird.

gir'dle-belt (-bèlte), n., ceinturon, m.

gir'dle-maker, n., ceinturier, m.

girl (gheur'l), n., fille; jeune fille; jeune personne; servante, domestique, f.

girl'ish, adj., de jeune fille; enfantin.

girl'ishly, adv., en jeune fille.

girt (gheurte). V. gird.

girth, n., enceinte; ceinture, sangle, f.; contour, pourtour, m.

gist (djiste), n., fin, fin mot; fond, point principal, m.; substance, f.

give (ghive), v.a. and n. (preterit, Gave; past part., Given) donner, accorder; rendre; (an answer, credit, one's compliments, one's love) faire; (one's respects) présenter. To — a call; appeler; visiter, faire une visite. To — a description; décrire. To — a fall; faire tomber. To — a guess; deviner. To — a look; regarder. To — a portion; doter. To — a present; faire un cadeau. To — a shriek; jeter un cri de terreur. To — battle; livrer bataille. To — check; faire échec à, mettre en échec. To — content; contenter. To — ear; être attentif à, écouter; prêter l'oreille à. To — fire; tirer. To — ground; reculer; enfoncer. To — heed; prendre garde. To — in; céder. To — in charge; charger; faire arrêter. To — joy; féliciter. To — judgment; rendre, ou prononcer, jugement. To — notice; avertir. To — one leave; permettre à. To — one's mind; s'adonner, s'attacher à. To — place; céder à,

faire place à. To — suck; allaiter. To — the slip; se dérober, faire faux bond, fausser compagnie, s'échapper. To — trouble; incommoder. To — way; céder; enfoncer; s'abandonner, se relâcher, s'affaisser, s'enfoncer. To — way to; faire place à, être remplacé par; céder. To — away; donner. To — back again; rendre. To — forth; publier. To — quarter; faire quartier à. To — out; distribuer, rapporter, annoncer, déclarer publiquement, se dire; manquer. To — over; abandonner, céder; cesser, laisser, quitter. To — up; abandonner, renoncer, rendre, céder, se dessaisir de, quitter, remettre; se désister de. To — one's self up to; se constituer prisonnier. To — one's self up to; s'abandonner à; s'adonner à. To — it to (anyone); en donner à, arranger, (fam.) donner son paquet à. To — anyone the slip; fausser compagnie à. — him an inch, he will take an ell; si vous lui en donnez long comme le doigt, il en prendra long comme le bras. — the devil his due; à chacun son dû. He gives twice who gives in a trice; qui donne tôt donne deux fois.

giv'en, adj., adonné à, livré à, porté à; s'occupant de.

giv'er, n., donneur, donateur, m.

giz'zard (dji'zeurde), n., gésier, m.; (fig.) esprit, m., imagination, f.

gla'cial (glé-shi'-) ou gla'cious (glé-), adj., glacial, gelé.

gla'cier (gla-ci-eur), n., glacier, m.

gla'cis (glé-ciss ou glâ-), n., (fort.) glacis, talus, m.; pente, f.

glad, adj., content, charmé, bien aise, joyeux, réjoui, heureux de.

glad'den (glad'd'n), v.a., réjouir, récréer, rendre heureux. v.n., se réjouir, s'égayer.

glade (gléde), n., clairière; percée; avenue, f.

glad'iator (glad'i-é-), n., ♦ladiateur, m.

glad'iole (-ôl), n., (bot.) glaïeul, m.

glad'ly, adv., volontiers, avec plaisir.

glad'ness ou (ant.) glad'someness, n., joie, gaieté, allégresse, f.; contentement, plaisir, m.

glad'some, adj., (ant.) enjoué, joyeux, gai, réjouissant.

glad'stone, n., valise jumelle, f. [m.

glad'win, n., (bot.) iris fétide, glaïeul puant,

glair (glère), n., glaire, f.; blanc d'œuf, m.

glair, v.a., (bookbind.) glairer.

glance (glâ'n'-), n., regard, coup d'œil, m.; œillade, vue rapide, f.

glance, v.n., étinceler; effleurer, raser; glisser; dévier; lancer un regard sur; jeter un coup d'œil sur, des œillades à; (fig.) insinuer. To — over; parcourir.

glan'cingly, adv., en passant; légèrement.

gland (gla'n'de), n., (anat.) glande, f.; (bot.) glande, f.

glan'ders (gla'n'deurze), n.pl., (vet.) morve, f.

glandif'erous (-dif'eur'-), adj., qui porte des glands.

glan'dular ou glan'dulous (-diou-), adj., (anat.) glandulaire, glanduleux; (bot.) glanduleux.

glan'dule (-dioule), n., glandule, petite glande, f.

glare, n., vif éclat, éclat de lumière éblouissante, m.; lueur, f.; coup d'œil perçant; regard féroce; regard fixe, m.

glare, v.n., éblouir; luire, briller; regarder d'un air terrible; regarder fixement, lancer des regards terribles à.

glar'ing (glèr'-), adj., éblouissant, éclatant, tranchant; choquant; manifeste, patent, notoire.

glar'ingly, adv., (fig.) manifestement, notoirement.

glass (glâce), n., verre, m.; (window) vitre, f. pl., lunettes, f.pl. Looking—; miroir, m., glace, f. Plate —; verre poli, m. Cut —; cristal taillé, m. —, with care! fragile! Hour—;

sablier, m. Weather-—; *baromètre, m.* Eye-—; *lorgnon, m.*

glass, *adj.,* de verre.

glass, *v.a.,* (ant.) vitrer. [*terie, f.*

glass' beads (-bîdze), *n.pl.,* rassade, verroterie, *f.*

glass'-blower, *n.,* souffleur de verre, *m.*

glass'-blowing, *n.,* soufflage de verre, *m.*

glass' bottle (-bot't'l), *n.,* bouteille de verre, *f.*

glass' case (-kéce), *n.,* vitrine, *f.*

glass' door, *n.,* porte vitrée, *f.*

glass'-furnace (-feur-), *n.,* fourneau de verrerie, *m.*

glass'-gazing (-ghéz'-), *adj.,* qui se mire souvent.

glass'-grinder (-graï'n'd'-), *n.,* polisseur de glaces, *m.*

glass'house (-haouce), *n.,* verrerie, *f.*

glas'siness, *n.,* soufflage du verre, *m.;* nature vitreuse, transparence, *f.;* aspect vitreux, poli, *m.*

glass'-like, *adj.,* semblable au verre ; (fig.) transparent, fragile.

glass'-maker (-mék'-), *n.,* verrier, *m.*

glass'man, *n.,* marchand de verre, de verrerie, *m.*

glass'-metal (-mèt't'l), *n.,* verre fondu, *m.*

glass'work (-weurke) *n.,* manufacture du verre, *f.*

glass'works (-weurkse), *n.,* verrerie, manufacture de verre, *f.*

glas'sy, *adj.,* vitreux ; fragile.

glauco'ma (-cô-), *n.,* (med.) glaucome, *m.*

glau'cous, *adj.,* glauque ; verdâtre.

glaze, *v.a.* and *n.,* vitrer ; vernir ; glacer ; lustrer ; dorer.

gla'zier (glé-jeur), *n.,* vitrier, *m.*

gla'zing, *n.,* vitrage ; vernissage ; glaçage, *m.*

gleam (glîme), *n.,* rayon, *m.;* lueur, vive clarté, *f.;* trait de lumière, *m.*

gleam, *v.n.,* rayonner, briller, luire.

gleam'y ou **gleam'ing,** *adj.,* étincelant, brillant, éclatant, lumineux.

glean (glîne), *v.a.* and *n.,* glaner ; grappiller ; (fig.) recueillir, glaner.

glean'er, *n.,* glaneur, grappilleur, *m.*

glean'ing, *n.,* glanage, *m. ;* glanure, *f.*

glebe (glîbe), *n.,* glèbe ; terre, *f. ;* sol, *m.*

gle'bous ou **gle'by** (glîb'-) *adj.,* de gazon ; plein de tourbe.

glede (glîde), *n.,* (orni.) milan, *m.*

glee (glî), *n.,* gaillardise, joie, gaieté ; (mus.) chanson à reprise, *f.;* morceau d'ensemble, *m.* — maiden ; *chanteuse des rues, f.*

glee'ful (-foule), *adj.,* joyeux, gai.

glee'fully, *adv.,* gaîment, joyeusement.

gleet (glîte), *n.,* sanie ; blennorrhée, *f.;* pus, *m.*

gleet, *v.n.,* produire de la sanie ; dégoutter.

gleet'y, *adj.,* sanieux ; ichoreux.

glen (glène), *n.,* vallon, *m.,* vallée, *f.*

glib, *adj.,* coulant ; glissant, délié, voluble. A — tongue ; *une langue bien pendue.*

glib, *v.a.,* châtrer ; rendre coulant, rendre lisse.

glib'ly, *adv.,* coulamment, avec volubilité.

glib'ness, *n.,* volubilité, facilité, *f.*

glide (glaïde), *v.n.,* couler doucement ; glisser ; se glisser **dans.**

glid'ingly, *adv.,* coulamment, doucement.

glim'mer ou **glim'mering,** *n.,* lueur, *f. ;* faible rayon, *m.*

glim'mer, *v.n.,* entreluire, luire faiblement ; (of the day) poindre.

glim'mering, *n.,* lueur, faible lueur ; (fig.) légère apparence, *f.;* léger aperçu, *m. adj.,* faible.

glimpse (gli'm'pse), *n.,* sillon de lumière, trait de lumière, *m.;* lueur, *f. ;* reflet ; rayon, *m.* To catch, *ou* get, a — of ; *entrevoir.* To only catch a — of ; *ne faire qu'entrevoir.*

glis'ten (glis's'n) ou (ant.) **glis'ter** (glis'teur), *v.n.,* étinceler, briller, reluire, éclater ; rayonner.

glis'tening ou (ant.) **glis'tering,** *n.,* lueur, *f. ;* éclat, *m.*

glis'tening ou (ant.) **glis'tering,** *adj.,* luisant, brillant.

glit'ter, *n.,* éclat, lustre, *m. ;* splendeur, *f.*

glit'ter, *v.n.,* éclater, briller, reluire, étinceler. All is not gold that —s ; *tout ce qui brille* (ou *reluit) n'est pas or.*

glit'tering, *adj.,* brillant, luisant, étincelant.

glit'teringly, *adv.,* avec éclat.

gloar (glôre), *v.n.,* loucher ; regarder de travers.

gloat (glôte) (on, over, upon), *v.n.,* dévorer, couver des yeux ; (fig.) triompher **de,** se régaler **de.**

glo'bate ou **glo'bated** (glô-bé-), *adj.,* sphérique, sphéroïdal, en globe, globeux.

globe (glôbe), *n.,* globe, *m. ;* sphère, boule ; terre, *f.* The use of the —s ; (geog.) *étude de la sphère, f.*

globe, *v.a.,* (ant.) arrondir en forme de globe ; mettre en boule.

globe'holder, *n.,* porte-globe, *m.*

globe'-shaped, *adj.,* en globe, en forme de globe.

globose' (glo-bôss), **glo'bous** (glô-), ou **glob'ular** (glob'iou-), *adj.,* sphérique, globuleux, rond ; (bot.) globeux.

globos'ity (glo-bôss'-), *n.,* sphéricité, *f.*

glob'ule (glob'ioule), *n.,* globule, *m.*

gloom ou **gloom'iness** (gloum'-), *n.,* obscurité, *f.;* chagrin, *m.;* tristesse, *f.* To throw a —over ; *assombrir ; jeter un voile de tristesse* **sur.**

gloom, *v.n.,* être obscur, sombre ; s'attrister

gloom'ily, *adv.,* obscurément ; d'un air triste.

gloom'y, *adj.,* sombre, obscur ; triste ; mélancolique. — weather ; *temps sombre, m.*

glorifica'tion (glô-ri-fi-ké-), *n.,* glorification, *f.*

glo'rify (glô-ri-faïe), *v.a.,* glorifier ; exalter ; honorer.

glo'rious, *adj.,* glorieux ; illustre ; superbe ; admirable.

glo'riously, *adv.,* glorieusement, avec gloire.

glo'ry (glô-), *n.,* gloire, honneur ; (paint.) auréole, gloire, *f.,* nimbe, *m.*

glo'ry, *v.n.,* se faire gloire **de,** se glorifier **de.**

gloss, *n.,* luisant, éclat, vernis, apprêt, lustre, *m. ;* (fig.) glose, *f.;* commentaire, *m.*

gloss, *v.n.,* gloser ; interpréter ; lustrer ; donner de l'éclat à. To — over ; *masquer, colorer, déguiser, pallier.*

glos'sary, *n.,* glossaire, *m.*

gloss'er ou **gloss'arist,** *n.,* glossateur ; commentateur ; apprêteur, *m.*

gloss'iness, *n.,* poli, lustre, brillant, apprêt, *m.*

gloss'y, *adj.,* lustré, poli, éclatant, luisant.

glot'tis (glot'tiss), *n.,* (anat.) glotte, *f.*

glove (gleuve), *n.,* gant, *m.*

glove, *v.a.,* ganter.

glov'er, *n.,* gantier, *m.*

glove'-stretcher, *n.,* baguettes à gants, *f.pl. ;* ouvre-gants, *m.*

glow (glô), *n.,* chaleur ; ardeur, *f. ;* feu, éclat, *m.* To be in a —; *sentir une douce chaleur (par tout le corps).* To set in a —; *allumer, enflammer, embraser.*

glow, *v.n.,* brûler, être embrasé **de ;** brûler **de ;** briller, luire.

glow'ing, *adj.,* éclatant ; brûlant, embrasé ; ardent, animé.

glow'ingly, *adv.,* vivement, chaleureusement, avec ardeur.

glow'worm (-weurme), *n.,* ver luisant, *m.*

gloze (glôze), *v.a.* and *n.,* flatter ; cajoler ; caresser ; gloser.

glo'zer, *n.,* flatteur, cajoleur, *m.*

glo'zing, *n.,* cajolerie, flatterie, *f.*

glue (glou), *n.,* colle forte, *f.* Fish-—; *colle de poisson, f.*

glue, *v.a.,* coller ; attacher, unir.

glue'-boiler (-boïl'-), *n.,* fabricant de colle forte, *m.*

glu'er, *n.,* colleur, *m.*

glu'ey *ou* **glu'ish**, *adj.*, gluant, collant, visqueux, glutineux.

glum (gleume), *adj.*, chagrin, de mauvaise humeur.

glume (gloume), *n.*, (bot.) glume, balle, *f.*

glut (gleute), *n.*, surabondance, satiété, *f. ;* excès, *m.*

glut, *v.a.* and *n.*, avaler, gorger, soûler ; se rassasier **de** ; assouvir, s'assouvir ; repaître ; se repaître **de**. To — one's self ; *se gorger* **de**.

glu'teal (glou-ti-al), *adj.*, (anat.) fessier.

glu'ten (glou-tène), *n.*, gluten, *m.*

glu'tinous (glou-), *adj.*, glutineux, gluant, visqueux.

glu'tinousness (glou-), *n.*, viscosité, *f.*

glut'ting, *n.*, assouvissement, rassasiement ; (of streets by crowds, etc.) encombrement, *m.*

glut'ton (gleut't'n), *n.*, gourmand, glouton, *m.*

glut'tonize (gleut't'naïze), *v.n.*, manger en glouton ; manger excessivement.

glut'tonous, *adj.*, glouton, gourmand, goulu, vorace.

glut'tonously, *adv.*, en glouton, en gourmand, goulûment.

glut'tony (gleut't'ni), *n.*, gourmandise, gloutonnerie, *f.*

glyn, *n.* *V.* glen.

glyp'tics, *n.pl.*, art de graver sur les pierres précieuses, *m. ;* glyptique, *f.*

gnar (nâr) *ou* **gnarl** (nârl), *v.n.*, murmurer, gronder ; être revêche, bourru, rebours.

gnarled (nârl'de) *ou* **gnar'ly** (nâr-), *adj.*, noueux ; plein de nœuds.

gnash (nashe), *v.a.*, grincer les dents.

gnash'ing, *n.*, grincement de dents, *m.*

gnash'ingly, *adv.*, en grinçant des dents.

gnat (nate), *n.*, (ent.) cousin ; moucheron, *m.* — strainer ; *vétilleur, m.* To strain at a — ; *s'amuser*, ou *s'attacher, à des vétilles.* To strain at a — and swallow a camel ; (prov.) *rejeter le moucheron et avaler le chameau.*

gnat'snapper (nate'-), *n.*, (orni.), pivoine, *m.* and *f.*, bouvreuil ; gobe-mouche, *m.*

gnaw (nô), *v.a.*, ronger ; corroder ; mordre.

gnaw'er, *n.*, rongeur, *m.*

gnaw'ing, *n.*, rongement, *m. ;* corrosion, *f. ;* (fig.) déchirement, *m.*

gnaw'ing, *adj.*, corrosif, rongeant, (fig.) rongeur.

gneiss (naïce), *n.*, (min.) gneiss, *m.*

gnome (nôme), *n.*, gnome, *m.*, gnomide, *f. ;* esprit, *m.*

gno'mon (nô-mone), *n.*, style (de cadran solaire), *m.*

gnomon'ics (no-mo'n'ikse), *n.pl.*, gnomonique, *f.*

gnos'tic (nos-tik), *n.*, gnostique, *m.*

go (gô), *v.n.a.*, (*preterit*, Went ; *past part.*, Gone) aller, s'en aller ; passer ; partir, marcher. To — one's own way ; *aller son chemin ;* (fig.) *faire comme on l'entend.* To — into mourning ; *se mettre en deuil.* To — to sleep ; *s'endormir.* To let — ; *lâcher prise.* To — without one's dinner ; *dîner par cœur.* To — for nothing ; *ne compter pour rien ; ne pas compter.* To — in for ; *se présenter* **à** ; *se mettre sur les rangs ; concourir* **pour** ; *se décider* **pour** ; (to attempt) *tenter, essayer, entreprendre.* To — about ; *faire le tour, se détourner ; entreprendre ;* (nav.) *virer de bord.* To — ahead ; *aller en avant ; aller de l'avant.* To — on ahead ; *prendre les devants.* To — on ahead ; (nav.) *grande vitesse, f.* To — between ; *s'interposer, s'entremettre.* To — abroad ; *sortir, partir, voyager.* To — against ; *s'opposer* **à**, *avoir de la répugnance* **à**, *aller* **contre**. To — along ; *poursuivre son chemin, accompagner, passer.* To — ashore ; *débarquer, aborder ; échouer.* To — aside ; *se mettre de côté.* To — astray ; *s'égarer.* To — asunder ; *aller séparément.* To — away ; *s'en aller, se retirer, sortir.* To — back ; *reculer, s'en re-*

tourner. To — backwards ; *reculer.* To — backwards and forwards ; *aller et venir,* (fig.) *se contredire.* To — beyond ; *passer, surpasser, dépasser.* To — by ; *passer auprès, passer ; se régler* **sur** ; *passer sans être remarqué ; prendre le nom* **de** ; (of time) *s'écouler.* To — down ; *descendre, se coucher ; descendre le courant ; rétrograder ;* (nav.) *couler* **à** *fond, sombrer.* To — far ; *aller loin ;* (fig.) (to) *contribuer beaucoup* **à**. To — for ; *aller chercher, passer* **pour**. To — forth ; *sortir ; avancer.* To — forward ; *avancer, pousser, profiter, poursuivre.* To — from ; *quitter ; partir* **de**. To — from the matter ; *s'écarter du sujet.* To — halves ; *être de moitié ; être de compte à demi* **dans**. To — in ; *entrer ;* (fig.) *concourir.* To — near ; *approcher.* To — off ; *quitter ; s'en aller ; partir.* To — off ; (of goods) *se vendre, s'écouler ;* (of beauty) *passer.* To — on ; *se passer, se pratiquer ; avancer, continuer ; continuer* **de**, *aller jusqu'au bout, reprendre.* To — out ; *sortir ; s'éteindre.* To — over ; *passer, traverser.* To — through ; *passer, passer au travers, enfiler, percer, fendre ; subir, souffrir.* To — up ; *monter.* To — up a river ; *remonter un fleuve.* To — up and down ; *courir de côté et d'autre.* To — up to ; *aborder, accoster.* To — upon ; *se baser* **sur** ; *se fonder* **sur** ; *attaquer.* To — with ; *accompagner.* To — without ; *se passer* **de**. To — out of (the way) ; *se détourner* **de**. As times — ; *par le temps qui court.* To — the whole hog ; *s'en donner à cœur joie ; aller jusqu'au bout.* — it ! *allez de l'avant ! allez-y !* To — out of one's way ; *se donner bien de la peine* **pour**. I do it, but it goes against the grain ; *je le fais, mais c'est à contre-cœur.*

go, *n.*, mode, vogue, *f. ;* (fig.) entrain, brio, *m.* To be all the — ; *faire fureur.* It is no — ; *il n'y a pas mèche.* A fine — ! *une belle affaire.*

goad (gôde), *n.*, aiguillon (de bouvier), *m.*

goad (gôde), *v.a.*, aiguillonner ; piquer ; (fig.) exciter, stimuler, pousser.

go-ahead', *adj.*, entreprenant.

goal (gôle), *n.*, but, terme ; point de départ, *m.*

goat (gôte), *n.*, chèvre, *f.* He — ; *bouc, m.* She — ; *chèvre, f.* — skin ; *peau de bouc, f.*

goat'-footed, *adv.*, chèvre-pied.

goat'herd, *n.*, chevrier, *m.*

goat'ish, *adj.*, de bouc, lascif.

goat'-sucker (-seuk-), *n.*, (orni.) crapaud volant, tette-chèvre, engoulevent, *m.*

gob'ble (gob'b'l), *v.a.*, gober ; avaler ; (of turkeys) glouglouter.

gob'bler, *n.*, glouton, goulu, avaleur ; dindon, *m.*

go'between (gô-bi-twîne), *n.*, (b.s.) entremetteur, *m.*, entremetteuse, *f.*

gob'let (gob'lète), *n.*, gobelet, *m. ;* coupe, *f.*

gob'lin (gob'line), *n.*, lutin, spectre, follet, *m.* —shapes ; *formes de lutins, f.pl.*

go'-by (gô-baïe), *n.*, mauvaise raison, défaite, *f.*, détour, artifice, *m. ;* action d'éluder, d'écarter, de repousser, de changer, *f.* To give the — to ; *éluder ; passer sans saluer ; passer sans faire attention ; abandonner, repousser, planter là.*

go'-cart (gô-cârte), *n.*, chariot d'enfant, *m. ;* petite chaise à roulettes, *f.*

God, *n.*, Dieu, *m.* Would to — ! *plût à Dieu !* — forbid ! *à Dieu ne plaise !* — helps those who help themselves ; (prov.) *aide-toi, le ciel t'aidera.* — tempers the wind to the shorn lamb ; *à brebis tondue Dieu mesure le vent.*

god'child (-tshaïlde), *n.*, filleul, *m.*, filleule, *f.*

god'daughter (-dô'-), *n.*, filleule, *f.*

god'dess (-dèce), *n.*, déesse, divinité, *f.*

god'father (-fâ-theur), *n.*, parrain, *m.*

god'head (-hède), *n.*, divinité, *f.*

god'less, *adj.*, athée, impie.

god'like (-laïke), *adj.*, divin.

god'liness, *n.*, sainteté, piété, *f.*

god'ly, *adj.*, pieux, dévot, saint.

god'ly, *adv.*, religieusement, dévotement.

god'mother (-meuth'eur), *n.*, marraine, *f.*

god'send, *n.*, bonne aubaine, trouvaille, *f.*

god'ship, *n.*, divinité, *f.*

god'son (-seune), *n.*, filleul, *m.*

god'ward (-wôrde), *adv.*, (ant.) vers, envers Dieu.

god'wit (-wite), *n.*, (orni.) francolin, *m.*

go'er (gô'-), *n.*, marcheur, *m.* Comers and —s; *allants et venants*, *m.pl.* Play—; *amateur du théâtre*, *m.*

gof'fer, *v.a.*, gaufrer.

gog'gle (gog'g'l), *v.n.*, regarder de travers, rouler les yeux, loucher.

gog'gle-eyed (-aïe'de), *adj.*, louche; aux gros yeux, aux yeux à fleur de tête.

gog'gles (gog'g'lze), *n.pl.*, lunettes, *f.pl.*; (for horses) œillères, *f.pl.*

go'ing (gô'-), *n.*, marche, démarche, allure, allée, *f.*; départ, *m.* —s on; *faits et gestes*, *m.pl.* — back; *retour*, *m.*

goi'tre (goï'teur), *n.*, (med.) goître, *m.*

go'la (gô-), *n.*, (arch.) cymaise, doucine, *f.*

gold (gôlde), *n.*, or, *m.* A — ring; *un anneau d'or ou une bague en or*.

gold, *adj.*, d'or, en or.

gold'beater (-bît'-), *n.*, batteur d'or, *n.*

gold'beater's-skin (-'teur'z'skine), *n.*, baudruche, *f.*

gold'bound (-baou'n'de), *adj.*, couvert d'or, entouré d'or.

gold'-digger (-dig'gheur), *n.*, chercheur d'or, *m.*

gold'-drawer (-drô'-), *n.*, tireur d'or, *m.*

gold'-dust (-deuste), *n.*, poudre d'or, *f.*

gold'en, *adj.*, d'or.

gold'finch (-fi'n'she), *n.*, (orni.) chardonneret, *m.*

gold'-finder (-faï'n'd'-), *n.*, orpailleur; (iron.) vidangeur, *m.*

gold'-finer (-faï'n'-), *n.*, affineur d'or, *m.*

gold'fish, *n.*, (ich.) poisson rouge, *m.*; dorade, *f.*

gold'leaf, *n.*, feuille d'or, *f.*; or en feuilles, *m.*

gold'-lettered, *adj.*, en lettres d'or.

gold'-seeker, *n.*, chercheur d'or; orpailleur, *m.*

gold'smith (-smith), *n.*, orfèvre, *m.*

gold'-spink (-spi'gn'k), *n.*, (orni.) bruant, ou bréant, commun; verdier, *m.*

gold'thread, *n.*, fil d'or, *m.*

gold'-worked, *adj.*, broché d'or, tissu d'or.

gold'-working, *n.*, orfévrerie, *f.*

golosh', *n.*, galoche, *f.*

gome (gôme), *n.*, cambouis, *m.*

gompho'sis (go'm'-phô-ciss), *n.*, (anat.) gomphose, articulation immobile des os, *f.*

gon'dola, *n.*, gondole, *f.*

gondolier' (-lîre), *n.*, gondolier, *m.*

gone (gone), *past. part.* (of To go), allé, parti, disparu, passé, écoulé, (at auctions) adjugé. His money is all —; *il a dépensé tout son argent*. In days — by; *au temps jadis*. He is —; *il s'en est allé*; (dead) *il est mort*. Far —; *avancé*.

gon'falon *ou* **gon'fanon**, *n.*, (her.) gonfalon, *m.*

goniom'etry (-ô-), *n.*, goniométrie, *f.*

gonorrhœ'a (-or-rî-), *n.*, (med.) gonorrhée, *f.*

good (goûde), *adj.*, bon, d'un bon naturel, honnête; convenable; solide; favorable; avantageux; valide; sage. As — as; *presque*. To make —; *réparer*; *établir*, *prouver*; *exécuter*; *suppléer à*, *compenser*; *dédommager de*, *indemniser de*. To stand, *ou* hold, —; *être valide*. — fellowship; *bonnes relations*; *relations amicales*, *f.pl.* To be —; (of children) *être sage*. It is as — as done; *c'est une affaire faite ou c'est fait ou autant vaut*. To be as — as gold; (of children) *être sage comme une image*. — breeding always tells; *bon sang ne peut mentir*. To be in anyone's — books; *être dans les petits papiers de quelqu'un*.

good, *n.*, bien; avantage; profit, *m.*; utilité,

f. For — and all; *pour tout de bon*. What's the — of? *à quoi bon?* What — will it be to you; *à quoi cela vous avancera-t-il?* Much — may it do you! *grand bien vous fasse!* To come to no —; *n'aboutir à rien* (de bon). To do no —; *ne faire rien qui vaille*.

good, *adv.*, bien, bon. Very —; *fort bien*. As —; *aussi bien*.

good! *int.*, bon! bien! c'est très bien!

good-breed'ing (-brîd'-), *n.*, bonne éducation, politesse, *f.*; savoir-vivre, *m.*

good-bye'! *int.*, adieu! — but not farewell; *au revoir*, *mais sans adieu*.

good-condi'tioned (-dish'eu'n'de), *adj.*, bien conditionné; en bon état.

good'-for-nothing, *n.*, vaurien, *m.*

Good-Fri'day (-fraï-), *n.*, vendredi saint, *m.*

good-hu'mor (-hiou-meur), *n.*, bonne humeur, *f.*, enjouement, *m.*

good-hu'mored (-hiou-meur'de), *adj.*, de bonne humeur, enjoué.

good'liness, *n.*, beauté, grâce, bienveillance, *f.*

good'-luck (-leuke), *n.*, bonheur, *m.*; chance, prospérité, *f.*

good'ly, *adj.*, beau, bel; joli; gracieux; fort; bon; considérable.

good'man (-ma'n), *n.*, bonhomme, compère, *m.*

good-na'ture (-nét'ioure), *n.*, bonté, bonhomie, humanité, complaisance, *f.*; bon naturel, *m.*

good-na'tured (-nét'iourde), *adj.*, d'un bon naturel, bénin, bon, bienveillant.

good'ness, *n.*, bonté, *m.*; probité, *f.* — knows; *Dieu sait!* Thank —! *Dieu merci!* My —! *mon Dieu!*

good'-now! (-nao), *int.*, à la bonne heure!

goods (goûdze), *n.pl.*, meubles, effets, biens, *m.pl.*; marchandises, *f.pl.*

good'-will, *n.*, bienveillance, bonne volonté, considération, bonté; (com.) clientèle, *f.*; achalandage, *m.*

good-wom'an (-woum'a'n) *ou* **good'y**, *n.*, bonne femme, *f.*; (fam.) la mère (*une telle*).

goose (gouce), *n.*, (geese) oie, *f.*; idiot, imbécile, nigaud; (tailor's) carreau, *m.* A green —; *un oison*. A wild —; *une oie sauvage*. To go on a wild-— chase; *tenter l'impossible, chercher midi à quatorze heures*.

goose'berry (-bèr'-), *n.*, groseille à maquereau, groseille verte, *f.* — bush; *groseillier*, *m.*

goose'-cap, *n.*, imbécile, niais, sot, *m.*

goose'-flesh, *n.*, chair de poule, *f.*

goose'-grass (-grâce), *n.*, (bot.) grateron, rièble, *m.*; rapette; aspérule odorante, *f.*

goose'neck (-nèke), *n.*, (nav.) crochet, crapaud, *m.*

goose'-quill, *n.*, plume d'oie, *f.*

goose'-step, *n.*, cadence, *f.*

gor'cock, *n.*, (orni.) coq de bruyère, *m.*

gor'crow (-crô), *n.*, (orni.) corneille, *f.*

gord (gôrde), *n.*, dé pipé, *m.*

gore (gôre), *n.*, sang figé, sang, *m.*; (ant.) (of gowns) pointe; (of land) pointe de terre triangulaire, *f.*

gore, *v.a.*, piquer, percer; couper en pointe; donner un coup de corne à; forcer un passage.

gorge (gordje), *n.*, gosier, *m.*, gorge, *f.*, jabot, *m.*; (fort.) gorge, *f.*, (ravine) gorge, *f.*

gorge, *v.a.*, gorger, remplir, avaler, rassasier.

gorge, *v.n.*, se gorger; avaler.

gor'geous (gor'djeusse), *adj.*, superbe, magnifique, somptueux, éclatant, fastueux.

gor'geously, *adv.*, superbement, magnifiquement.

gor'geousness, *n.*, magnificence, pompe, splendeur, *f.*

gor'gerin (gor'djeur'ine), *n.*, (arch.) gorgerin, colarin, *m.*

gor'get (gor'djète), *n.*, gorgerin, hausse-col, *m.*

gor'hen (-hène), *n.*, poule de bruyère, *f.*

gor'ing, n., piqûre, f., coup de corne, m.

gor'mand (gor-) *ou* gour'mand (gôr-), n., gourmand ; goulu, glouton, m.

gor'mandize (-'aïze), v.n., bâfrer, goinfrer.

gor'mandizer (-'aïz'-), n., glouton, goinfre, gourmand, m.

gor'mandizing (-aïz'-), n., gourmandise, gloutonnerie, f.

gorse, n., (bot.) ajonc ; genêt, m.

gor'y (gô-), adj., sanglant, couvert de sang, ensanglanté.

gos'hawk (goss'hōke), n., (orni.) autour, m.

gos'ling (goz'-), n., (orni.) oison ; (bot.) chaton, m.

gos'pel (gos'pèl), n., évangile, m.   To take for —; *prendre pour argent comptant.*

gos'samer (gos'sa-), n., filandres, f.pl. ; fils de la Vierge, m.pl. ; gaze, f.

gos'sip, n., commère, causeuse ; babillarde, f.; causerie ; caquet, bavardage, commérage, m.; les on dit, m.pl.   To have a good —; *faire une bonne causerie.*

gos'sip, v.n., jaser, caqueter, babiller, bavarder.

gos'siping, n., commérage, bavardage, m.

Goth'ic (goth'-), adj., gothique.

Goth'icize (goth-iss'aïze), v.a., rendre gothique ; ramener à la barbarie.

go'-to! (gô-tou), int., allons! par exemple! çà! sus! courage!

gouge (gaoudje), n., gouge, f.

gouge' (out), v.a., gouger ; arracher les yeux à.

gourd (gourde), n., gourde ; calebasse, citrouille, f.   — plant ; *calebassier,* m.

gourd'iness, n., (vet.) enflure à la jambe, f.

gourd'-worm, n., entozoaire, m.

gourd'y, adj., (vet.) qui a les jambes enflées.

gour'mand. n.   V. gormand.

gout (gaoute), n., (med.) goutte, f.

gout'y, adj., goutteux.

gov'ern (gheuv'eurne), v.a. and n., gouverner, régir, diriger, tenir en bride.   To — one's self ; *se contenir, être maître de soi.*

gov'ernable (-'a-b'l), adj., qui peut être gouverné, docile, gouvernable.

gov'ernance, n., (ant.) gouvernement, m., administration, conduite ; gouverne, f.

gov'erness *ou* (ant.) gov'ernante, n., institutrice, sous-maîtresse, gouvernante, f.   — pupil; *élève-maîtresse.*

gov'ernment, n., gouvernement, m., administration, direction,f.; régime, empire, m.; (gram.) régime, m.   — official ; *employé du gouvernement,* fonctionnaire public, officiel, m.   — loan ; *emprunt public,* m.   — securities ; *fonds,* ou *effets, publics,* m.pl.

gov'ernor (gheuv'eur-neur), n., gouverneur ; gouvernant ; (of a person) directeur, régulateur ; (ant.) précepteur ; (employer) maître, patron, m.

gov'ernorship, n., direction, f.

gow'an (gaou'a'n), n., (bot.) pâquerette commune, marguerite, f.

gown (gaoune), n., robe ; toge, f.   Night-—; *chemise de nuit,* f.   Morning-—, dressing-—; *robe de chambre,* f. peignoir, m.

gowned' (gaou'n'de), adj., vêtu d'une robe, en robe.

gown'man (gaoun'ma'n) *ou* gowns'man, n., (-men) homme de robe, ou de robe longue, m.   —, pl., gens de robe, étudiants, m.pl.

grab'ble (grab'b'l), v.a. and n., (ant.) tâter, tâtonner ; aller à tâtons ; fouiller ; se traîner, se vautrer.

grace (grèce), n., grâce, bonté, faveur, f.; pardon ; agrément, ornement, bon air, m. ; (title) grandeur,f. ; (rel.) bénédicité, m. ; grâces,f.pl.

grace, v.a., orner, embellir ; illustrer, honorer.

graced (grèss'te), adj., orné, doué de, élégant.

grace'ful (-foule), adj., beau, gracieux, agréable, bien fait, enjoué.

grace'fully, adv., gracieusement, de bonne grâce.

grace'fulness, n., bonne grâce, f., agrément, charme, m., beauté, f.

grace'less, adj., sans grâces, disgracieux ; abandonné, effronté, dépravé.

grace'note (-nôte), n., (mus.) note d'agrément, f.

Gra'ces (gré-cèze), n.pl., (myth.) Grâces, f.pl.

gra'cile (grass'il) *ou* gra'cilent (grass'-), adj., (ant.) grêle, mince, menu, petit.

gracil'ity, n., (ant.) gracilité, ténuité, petitesse, f.

gra'cious (gré-sheusse), adj., gracieux, bénin, clément, bon, favorable, agréable, propice.   Good —! *bonté divine!*

gra'ciously, adv., gracieusement, obligeamment, avec clémence, favorablement.   To be — pleased to ; *daigner.*

gra'ciousness, n., bonté, bénignité ; bienfaisance, bienveillance, grâce, f.

grada'tion (gra-dé-), n., gradation, f. ; degré, m.

grad'atory (-tori), adj., gradatif, progressif, par degrés.

grade, n., grade ; degré, rang, m.

gra'dient, adj., avançant ; ambulant.

gra'dient, n., (railways) pente, rampe, inclinaison, f.

grad'ual, adj., graduel, par degrés, gradué, réglé.

gradual'ity, n., (ant.) gradation, progression régulière, f.

grad'ually, adv., graduellement, par degrés, pas à pas, peu à peu.

grad'uate (grad'iou-), n., gradué, m.

grad'uate, v.a., graduer.

grad'uate, v.n., prendre ses degrés à une université, se faire graduer.

gradua'tion (-'iou-é-), n., graduation ; gradation ; (univ.) prise de grade, f.

graft (gràft'e), n., greffe, ente, f.

graft, v.a. and n., greffer, enter.

graft'er, n., personne qui ente, greffeur.

graft'ing, n., (hort.) greffe, f.

graft'ing-knife (-naïfe), n., greffoir, m.

grain (gréne), n., grain ; pépin, m.; céréales, f.pl. ; veine, f. ; fil, m.   — of allowance ; *indulgence,* f.   — of wood ; *veine de bois.*   Against the —; (of wood) *contre le fil ; à contre fil ;* (fig.) *à contre-cœur, malgré soi ; à rebrousse-poil.*

grain, v.a., grener, greneler ; peindre en décors.

grained (gré'n'de), adj., grenu ; dur ; rude ; indélible ; peint en décors.

grain'er, n., peintre décorateur, marbrier, m.

grain'ing, n., grenure ; peinture en décors, marbrure, f.

grains (gré'n'ze), n., drèche, f., marc, m.

grain'y, adj., plein de grains, grenelé, grenu.

gral'lic, adj., (orni.) des échassiers.

gramer'cy! int., grand merci!

gramin'eous (-mi'n'i-eusse), adj., (bot.) herbeux, herbacé ; graminée (only used in feminine).

gramin'orous, adj., herbivore.

gram'mar, n., grammaire, f.   That is bad —; *c'est incorrect.*

gramma'rian (-mé-), n., grammairien, m.

gram'mar-school (-scoule), n., collège, m.

grammat'ic *ou* grammat'ical, adj., grammatical ; de grammaire.

grammat'ically, adv., grammaticalement.

grammat'icize (-çaïze), v.a. and n., (ant.) faire le grammatiste ; rendre grammatical.

gram'pus, n., (ich.) épaulard, m., orque, f.

granadil'la, n., (bot.) grenadille, fleur de la passion, f.

gran'ary, n., grenier, m. ; grange, f.

grand (gra'n'de), adj., grand, superbe, noble, illustre, sublime, grandiose.

gran'dam, *n.*, grand'mère ; vieille femme, *f.*
grand'child (-tshaïlde), *n.*, petit-fils, *m.*, petite-fille, *f.*
grand'daughter (-dô-teur), *n.*, petite-fille, *f.* A great— ; *une arrière-petite-fille.*
grandee' (gra'n'di), *n.*, grand d'Espagne, *m.*
gran'deur (-'ieur), *n.*, grandeur, *f.*, éclat, *m.*, pompe, splendeur, *f.*
grand'father (-fâ-theur) *ou* **grand'sire** (-saïeur), *n.*, grand-père, aïeul, *m.* A great— ; *un bisaïeul.*
grandil'oquence (-kwè'n'se), *n.*, langage pompeux, *m. ;* emphase, *f.*
grandil'oquent (-kwè'n'te) *ou* **grandil'o-quous** (-kweusse), *adj.*, (of speeches) sublime, pompeux ; enflé ; emphatique.
gran'dinous, *adj.*, (ant.) plein de grêle.
grand'ly, *adv.*, grandement ; fastueusement.
grand'mother (-meuth'eur), *n.*, grand'mère, aïeule, *f.* A great— ; *une bisaïeule.*
grand'-nephew, *n.*, arrière-neveu, *m.*
grand'-niece, *n.*, arrière-nièce, *f.*
grand'son (-seune), *n.*, petit-fils, *m.* A great— ; *un arrière-petit-fils.*
grand' vizier, *n.*, grand-vizir, *m.*
grange (gré'n'dje), *n.*, ferme, métairie ; grange, *f.*
gran'ger, *n.*, régisseur, intendant, *m.*
gran'ite, (*n.*, (min.) granit, *m.*
gran'itel, *n.*, (min.) marbre granitelle, *m.*
graniv'orous, *adj.*, granivore.
grant (grâ'n'te), *n.*, concession, allocation, subvention, *f.*, don, privilège, octroi, *m.*
grant, *v.a.*, donner, accorder, céder, concéder ; avouer ; (jur.) entériner ; octroyer ; supposer, admettre. To — a pardon ; *pardonner ; accorder une grâce.* God —! *Dieu veuille !*
grant'able (-'a-b'l), *adj.*, qui peut être accordé.
grant'ed (-ède), *part.adj.*, accordé, octroyé ; avoué ; reconnu ; d'accord ; soit ! — that ; *supposant que, admettant que.* To take as, *ou* for, — ; *supposer la vérité de, supposer ; tenir pour fait ; tenir pour dit.*
grantee' (-ti), *n.*, donataire, concessionnaire ; (jur.) cessionnaire, *m.f.*
grant'er *ou* **grant'or** (-tor), *n.*, donateur ; (jur.) cédant, concédant, *m.*
gran'ular *ou* **gran'ulary** (-'iou-), *adj.*, en grains, grenelé, grenu, granulé, granulaire.
gran'ulate (-'iou), *v.a.*, greneler, grener, granuler. *v.n.*, se granuler.
granula'tion (-lé), *n.*, granulation, *f.*
gran'ule (-'ioule), *n.*, petit grain, granule, *m.*
gran'ulous, *adj.*, grenu, granuleux.
grape (grépe), *n.*, raisin ; (berry) grain de raisin, *m.* A bunch of —s ; *une grappe de raisin.* Cluster of — ; *grappillon, m.* The —s are sour ; (prov.) *ils sont trop verts* (La Fontaine).
grape'-gatherer, *n.*, vendangeur, *m.*, -euse, *f.*
grape'-gathering, *n.*, vendange, *f.*
grap'ery, *n.*, serre à raisin, *f.*
grape'-shot (grépe-shote), *n.*, (milit.) mitraille, *f.*
grape'stone (grépe-stône), *n.*, pépin de raisin, *m.*
grape'-vine (-vaïne), *n.*, vigne, *f.*
grape'-wine (-vaïne), *n.*, vin de raisin, *m.*
graph'ic *ou* **graph'ical**, *adj.*, graphique, bien tracé, exact, parfait ; pittoresque.
graph'ically, *adv.*, graphiquement, exactement, pittoresquement.
graph'ite (-'aïte), *n.*, graphite, plombagine, *f.*
graphom'eter (-fo'mi²-), *n.*, (math.) graphomètre, *m.*
grap'nel, *n.*, grappin, *m.*, petite ancre, *f.*
grap'ple (grap'p'l), *n.*, grappin, croc, barpon, *m. ;* lutte, *f.*, combat de lutteurs, *K.*
grap'ple, *v.a.*, accrocher ; grappiner, harponner, arrêter ; happer ; saisir à bras le corps. To — a ship ; *accrocher, ou aborder, un navire.*

grap'ple, *v.n.*, en venir aux mains, *ou* aux prises ; se saisir de ; lutter ; (nav.) en venir à l'abordage ; (fig.) combattre. To — with ; *combattre, en venir aux prises, en venir aux mains.* To — with a subject ; *traiter, ou manier, un sujet.*
gra'py (grépi), *adj.*, (ant.) de raisin, qui a un goût de raisin.
grasp (grâsp), *n.*, poignée ; prise ; étreinte, portée ; possession, *f.*; pouvoir, *m.* Within one's — ; *à sa portée, entre les mains.* To loose one's — ; *lâcher prise.* To lose one's — ; *perdre prise.*
grasp, *v.a.*, empoigner, saisir, prendre avec la main, serrer, tenir, embrasser. — all, lose all ; (prov.) *qui trop embrasse, mal étreint.*
grasp, *v.n.*, s'emparer de ; tâcher d'attraper, se saisir. To — at ; *tâcher de saisir ; s'accrocher à ; aspirer à.*
grasp'er, *n.*, personne qui empoigne ; homme avide, ambitieux ; (ant.) grappin, *m.*
grasp'ing, *adj.*, avide, cupide, avare.
grass (grâce), *n.*, herbe, verdure, *f. ;* gazon, herbage, *m.* To turn out to — ; *mettre en pâture, mettre au vert.* Not to let the — grow under one's feet ; *prendre la balle au bond ; mettre le temps à profit.*
grass'hopper (-hop'-), *n.*, sauterelle, cigale, *f.*
grass'iness, *n.*, état herbu, *m.*
grass'-land, *n.*, prairie, *f.*
grass'-mower, *n.*, faucheuse, *f.;* (pers.) faucheur, *m.*
grass'-plot (-plote), *n.*, boulingrin, *m.*, pelouse, *f.;* tapis vert, *m.*
grass'y, *adj.*, herbu, herbeux.
grate (gréte), *n.*, grille, *f.;* grillage, *m.;* jalousie, *f.;* foyer, âtre, *m.*
grate, *v.a.* and *n.*, râper, griller ; frotter, crisser, grincer. To — the teeth ; *grincer les dents.* To — up ; *fermer avec une grille.* To — upon ; *grincer.*
grate'ful (grét'-foule), *adj.*, reconnaissant, agréable ; délicieux.
grate'fully, *adv.*, avec gratitude ; avec reconnaissance ; agréablement.
grate'fulness, *n.*, gratitude, reconnaissance, *f. ;* agrément, *m.*
gra'ter, *n.*, râpe, *f.*
gratifica'tion (-fi-ké-), *n.*, gratification ; récompense ; volupté ; satisfaction, *f. ;* plaisir, *m.*
grat'ify (-faïe), *v.a.*, gratifier, satisfaire, récompenser ; contenter.
grat'ifying (-ti-faï-igne), *adj.*, satisfaisant, agréable, flatteur.
gra'ting (grét'-), *n.*, grille, *f.*, grillage ; (nav.) égouttoir ; grincement, *m. ;* (of bread) chapelure ; irritation, contrariété, *f.*
gra'ting, *adj.*, rude, dur, discordant, choquant, blessant ; qui choque l'oreille.
gra'tingly, *adv.*, rudement, d'une manière discordante.
gra'tis (gré-tiss), *adv.*, gratuitement, gratis, pour rien.
grat'itude (-tioude), *n.*, gratitude, reconnaissance, *f.*
gratu'itous (-tiou-i-), *adj.*, gratuit, qui n'a pas de raison suffisante, pas de motif ; volontaire ; bénévole. — assumption ; *supposition gratuite, f.*
gratu'itously, *adv.*, gratuitement ; bénévolement ; sans motif, sans raison suffisante.
gratu'ity (-tiou-i-), *n.*, don, présent, *m.*, gratification, largesse, *f.;* pourboire ; pot-de-vin, *m.*
grava'men (gra-vé-) *n.*, grief, poids ; (fig.) fonds, motif, *m.*
grave (gréve), *n.*, sépulcre, tombeau, *m.*, tombe, fosse, *f. ;* (fig.) tombeau, *m.*
grave, *adj.*, grave, sérieux ; réservé, retenu, modeste ; (gram.) grave.
grave, *v.a.* and *n.*, graver, tailler, ciseler. To — a ship ; *espalmer un navire.*
grave'-clothes (-clôze), *n.pl.*, linceul, drap mortuaire, suaire, *m.*

grave'-digger (-dig'gheur), *n.*, fossoyeur, *m.*

grave'-digging, *n.*, fossoyage, *m.*

grav'el (grav'èl), *n.*, gravier, sable, *m.;* (med.) gravelle, *f.* A —pit ; *une sablonnière, f.* — walk ; *allée sablée, f.*

grav'el, *v.a.*, sabler, couvrir de gravier; embarrasser, inquiéter, vexer.

grave'less (grév'-), *adj.*, sans sépulture.

grav'elly (grav'èl-li), *adj.*, graveleux, sablonneux.

grave'ly (grév'li), *adv.*, gravement, sérieusement ; modestement.

gra'ven (gré'v'n), *past. part.* (of To grave), gravé, taillé, ciselé. A — image ; *une image taillée.*

grave'ness (grév'-), *n.* V. **gravity.**

gra'ver (grév'-), *n.*, graveur ; burin, *m.*

graves (grév'z), *n.pl.* V. **greaves.**

grave'stone (-stône), *n.*, tombeau, *m.*, tombe, *f.*

gravida'tion (-dé-) *ou* **gravid'ity**, *n.*, (ant.) grossesse, *f.*

gra'ving (grév'-), *n.*, gravure, *f. ;* (nav.) action d'espalmer. — -tool ; *burin, m.*

grav'itate, *v.n.*, graviter.

gravita'tion (-té-), *n.*, gravitation, *f.* Terrestrial — ; *pesanteur, f.*

grav'ity, *n.*, air sérieux, *m.*, gravité ; pesanteur, *f.* Specific — ; *pesanteur spécifique, f.*

gra'vy (gré-vi), *n.*, jus, suc de viande, coulis, *m.*, sauce, *f.*

gray *ou* **gray'-brock**, *n.*, (zoöl.) blaireau, taisson, *m.*

gray *ou* **grey** (gré), *adj.*, gris ; (fig.) vieux. To grow, *ou* turn, — ; *grisonner ; blanchir.* The — mare is the better horse ; *c'est elle qui porte la culotte.*

gray'beard (-bîrde), *n.*, barbe grise, *f. ;* vieillard, grison, barbon, *m.*

gray'-eyed (-a'ïe-de), *adj.*, aux yeux gris.

gray' hair, *n.*, cheveux gris, *m.pl.*

gray'-haired (-hèr'de), *adj.*, aux cheveux gris, grison, chenu.

gray'-headed (-hèd'ède), *adj.*, qui a la tête grise.

gray'hound, *n.* V. **grey'hound.**

gray'ish, *adj.*, grisâtre.

gray'ishness, *n.*, teinte grisâtre, *f.*

gray'ling, *n.*, (ich.) ombre-chevalier, *m.*

gray'ness, *n.*, couleur grise, *f. ;* gris, *m.*

gray'wacke (-wac'ki), *n.*, (min.) grès des houillères, psammite, *m.*, grauwacke, *f.*

graze, *v.a.*, effleurer, raser, friser, frôler; (the skin) érafler.

graze, *v.n.*, paître, faire paître, brouter.

graze, *n.*, écorchure, éraflure, *f.*

gra'zier (gré-jeur), *n.*, engraisseur de bétail, éleveur, herbager, *m.*

graz'ing-farm, *n.*, ferme où l'on prend le bétail en pâture.

graz'ing-ground *ou* **land**, *n.*, pâturage, *m.*

grease (grîce), *n.*, graisse, *f.*, oing, *m.*

grease (grîze *ou* grîce), *v.a.*, graisser ; frotter de graisse.

grea'siness (grîz-'), *n.*, graisse, crasse, saleté, *f.*

grea'sy (grîz'i), *adj.*, graisseux, taché de graisse; crasseux, sale.

great, *adj.*, grand, gros ; noble, illustre, important, principal ; habile ; fort. — with child; *enceinte.* — with young; *pleine.* The — ; *les grands, m.pl.* To make —er ; *agrandir.* — cry, little wool ; *grand bruit, petite besogne.* — wits jump together; *les beaux esprits se rencontrent.*

great'bellied (-bel'ïde), *adj.*, ventru.

great'-grand'daughter (-dô'-), *n.*, arrière-petite-fille, *f.*

great'-grand'father (-fâ-*theur*), *n.*, bisaïeul, *m.*

great'-grand'mother (-meu*th*-eur), *n.*, bisaïeule, *f.*

great'-grand'son (-seune), *n.*, arrière-petit-fils, *m.*

great'hearted (-hârt'ède), *adj.*, courageux, généreux ; au cœur noble.

great'ly, *adv.*, grandement, fort, beaucoup.

great'ness, *n.*, grandeur, dignité ; grosseur ; sublimité ; intensité, force, énormité, *f.*

greave (grîve), *n.*, grève ; jambière, armure pour les jambes, *f.*

greaves (grîv'ze) *ou* **graves**, *n.pl.*, cretons, pains de cretons, *m.pl.*

Gre'cian (grî'sha'n), *n.*, Grec ; (antiq.) Helléniste ; (one versed in the Greek language) helléniste, *m.*

Gre'cian, *adj.*, grec.

Gre'cism (grî'ciz'm), *n.*, hellénisme, idiotisme grec, grécisme, *m.*

greed (grîde), *n.*, cupidité, avidité ; gourmandise, gloutonnerie ; (fig.) passion, *f.*, désir ardent, *m.*

greed'ily (grîd'-), *adv.*, goulûment ; avidement, avec avidité.

greed'iness, *n.*, cupidité, avidité ; gourmandise, gloutonnerie, *f. ;* (fig.) désir ardent, *m.*, passion, *f.*

greed'y (grîd'-), *adj.*, cupide, avide ; gourmand, goulu, vorace ; passionné. — of honors; *ambitieux.* — of gain ; *avare, cupide.*

greed'y-gut (-gheute) *ou* **-guts**, *n.*, (triv.) glouton, gourmand, goinfre, *m.*

Greek (grîke), *n.*, Grec, *m.*, Grecque, *f. ;* (language) grec, *m.* — fire ; *feu grégeois.* It is all — to him; *c'est de l'algèbre pour lui.* It is all — to me ; *c'est de l'hébreu pour moi* (Molière).

Greek, *adj.*, grec.

green (grîne), *adj.*, vert; frais, récent; novice. — old age ; *verte vieillesse, f.*

green, *n.*, vert, *m.*, verdure, *f. ;* gazon, *m.*

green'broom (-broume), *n.*, (bot.) genêt épineux, *m.*

green'cloth (-clôth), *n.*, (ant.) tapis vert, *m.* The board of — ; *la cour du tapis vert, de la maison royale.*

green'-eyed (-a'ïe'-de), *adj.*, aux yeux verdâtres, ou verts.

green'finch (-fï'n'she), *n.*, (orni.) verdier, bréant, *m.*

green'gage (-ghédje), *n.*, reine-claude, *f.*

green'grocer (-grô-ceur), *n.*, fruitier, *m.*, fruitière, *f.*

green'horn, *n.*, blanc-bec, novice, *m.*

green'house (-haouce), *n.*, serre, *f.*

green'ish, *adj.*, verdâtre.

green'ly, *adv.*, (ant.) vertement ; nouvellement, prématurément ; sans expérience ; en novice.

green'ness, *n.*, verdure ; fraîcheur ; (unripeness) verdeur ; simplicité, inexpérience, *f.*

green'room (-roume), *n.*, (thea.) foyer des acteurs, *m.*

greens (grî'n'ze), *n.pl.*, (gard.) légumes, choux, *m.pl. ;* herbes potagères, *f.pl.*

green'sickness, *n.*, (med.) chlorose, *f.*, pâles couleurs, *f.pl.*

green'sward (-swôrde), *n.*, pelouse, *f.*, gazon, *m.*

green'weed, *n.*, genêtrelle, genestrolle, *f.*

green'wood (-woude), *n.*, bois vert, *m.*

greet (grî'te), *v.a.*, saluer, recevoir, accueillir.

greet'ing, *n.*, salutation, réception, *f.*, salut, accueil, *m.*, compliments, *m.pl.*

grega'rious (gri-ghé-), *adj.*, qui va en troupes, par bandes; grégaire.

Grego'rian (gri-gô-), *adj.*, grégorien.

grenade' (gri-néde), *n.*, (artil.) grenade, *f.*

grenadier' (grén'a-dîre), *n.*, grenadier, *m.*

gren'adine, *n.*, grenadine, *f.*

grey, *adj.* V. **gray.**

grey'hound *ou* **gray'hound** (gré-haou'n'de), *n.*, lévrier, *m.*, levrette, *f.*

grice (graïce), n., cochon de lait; marcassin, m.

gride (graïde), v.a., (ant.) couper, trancher, fendre.

grid'elin (grid'è-), n., gris de lin, m.

grid'iron (grid'aï'eur'ne), n., gril, m.

grief (grîfe), n., douleur, tristesse, peine, affliction, f.; chagrin, déplaisir, m. To come to —; faire fiasco; finir mal; mourir sur la paille.

griev'ance (grîv'-), n., grief; tort, abus, m.

grieve, v.a., chagriner, attrister; affliger; fouler, opprimer.

grieve, v.n., se chagriner, s'attrister; se désoler, gémir.

griev'ingly, adv., avec douleur, avec chagrin.

griev'ous (grîv'-), adj., lourd, pesant, douloureux, grave, affligeant; cruel, énorme, atroce, fâcheux.

griev'ously, adv., grièvement; gravement, cruellement, douloureusement.

griev'ousness, n., grièveté, énormité; affliction, calamité, f.; chagrin, m.

grif'fin ou **grif'fon**, n., (orni.) griffon, m.

grig, n., petite anguille, f.; grillon, m., sauterelle, f. Merry as a —; gai comme un pinson.

grill (grile), v.a., griller; mettre sur le gril; mettre à la torture.

grillade' (gril'léde), n., grillade, viande grillée, f.

grilse, n., saumonneau, m.

grim, adj., refrogné; horrible; affreux; hideux; cruel, féroce, farouche. — faced; au visage hideux, à la mine féroce.

grimace' (gri-méce), n., grimace, minauderie, f. v.n., grimacer.

grima'cing, adj., grimacier.

grimal'kin (graïme), n., vieux chat, rominagrobis, m.

grime (graïme), n., saleté, noirceur, f., barbouillage, m.; suie, f.; noir, m.

grime, v.a., salir, barbouiller, tacher, noircir.

grim'ly (gri'm'-), adv., d'un air refrogné, d'un air farouche, horriblement, hideusement.

grim'ness (gri'm'-), n., air refrogné, air féroce, m.; férocité, f.; aspect effrayant, air farouche, m.

grin (grine), n., grimace, f.; ricanement, m. Broad —; rire satanique.

grin, v.a., ricaner, grimacer; tordre la bouche.

grind (graï'n'de), v.a., (pret. and past part., Ground), moudre; mâcher; broyer; grincer; (knives, etc.) aiguiser, émoudre, repasser, (fig.) opprimer, fouler, pressurer. To — away; (at work) piocher.

grind'er, n., émouleur, gagne-petit, rémouleur; broyeur; meunier, m.; molaire; dent mâchelière, meule, f., joueur (d'orgue de Barbarie); préparateur (aux examens), m.

grind'ing, n., broiement, mouture, m., oppression, f.; (of the teeth) grincement; repassage, polissage (of stones), m.

grind'stone (-stône), n., meule; pierre à aiguiser, à repasser, f.

grin'ner (gri'n'-), n., ricaneur; grimacier, m.

grin'ning, n., ricanement, m. adj., grimacier.

grin'ningly, adv., en ricanant, en grimaçant.

grip, n., petit fossé, m., rigole, f.; griffon, serrement de main, m.; poignée, f.

gripe (graïpe), n., poignée; prise, étreinte, colique, f.; tranchées, f.pl.; serrement; (nav.) bas du taille-mer, m.

gripe, v.a., empoigner, saisir, gripper, serrer; donner la colique à, donner des tranchées à. — penny; grippe-sou, m.

gripe, v.n., avoir la colique; gripper, agripper, escroquer; (nav.) serrer le vent de trop près.

gripes (graïpe), n.pl., colique, f., tranchées; (nav.) risses de chaloupe, f.pl.

grip'ing, n., colique, f.; tranchées, f.pl. adj., de colique; (fig.) poignant, cuisant, affreux; (of a miser) avare, rapace.

gri'pingly, adv., avec des tranchées.

gris'-amber (griz'a'm'-), n., (ant.) ambre gris, m.

gris'kin (griss'-), n., épine du dos d'un porc, f.

gris'ly (griz'-), adj., hideux, affreux, horrible. — bear; V. **grizzly bear**.

grist (griste), n., blé à moudre, m., farine, mouture, f.; (fig.) gain, profit, m. To bring — to the mill; être une source de profit; faire venir l'eau au moulin. —-mill; moulin à blé, m.

gris'tle (gris's'l), n., cartilage, m.

gris'tly (gris's'li), adj., cartilagineux.

grit (grite), n., sable, gravier, m.; (groats) grosse farine, f. To have —; (fig.) avoir du courage, de la décision, du cœur. There is no — in him; le cœur lui faut; il manque de décision, de courage.

grits, n.pl. V. **groats**.

grit'-stone (-stône), n., (min.) grès dur, m.

grit'tiness, n., état graveleux, m.

grit'ty, adj., graveleux, plein de sable.

griz'elin, n. V. **grid'elin**.

griz'zle (griz'z'l), n., couleur grise, f.; grison, gris, m.; (ant.) perruque, f.

griz'zled (griz'z'l'de), adj., grison, grisâtre.

griz'zly, adj., grisâtre. — bear; ours gris d'Amérique, m.

groan (grône) ou **groan'ing** (grô'n'-), n., gémissement, soupir, m.; plainte, f.; grognement; murmure, m.

groan, v.n., gémir, geindre; soupirer; grogner.

groat (grôte), n., environ huit cents (monnaie américaine); environ 40 centimes (monnaie française). He is not worth a —; il n'a pas le sou.

groats (grôtse), n.pl., gruau d'avoine, m., farine grosse, f.

gro'cer (grô-ceur), n., épicier, m.

gro'cery (grô-ceuri), n., épicerie, f.

grog, n., grog, m. — shop; débit de liqueurs, m. — blossom; bourgeon, m.

grog'gy, adj., ivre; gris, pochard; (of a horse) aux jambes faibles.

grog'ram, n., étoffe à gros grains, filoselle, f.

groin (gro-i-ne), n., aine; (arch.) arête, f.; brise-lames, m.

groined (gro-i'n'de), adj., (arch.) à arête, d'arête.

grom'met, n., esseau, m.

grom'well ou **grom'il**, n., (bot.) lithosperme, grémil, m., herbe-aux-perles, f.

groom (groume), n., palefrenier, valet d'écurie, garçon, valet, groom, m. —'s man; garçon d'honneur.

groom, v.a., panser.

groom'ing, n., pansement, f.

groove (grouve), n., rainure, coulisse, entaille, f. Always in the same —; toujours dans la même routine.

groove, v.a., évider; creuser en gorge, creuser, canneler; faire une rainure à.

grope (grôpe), v.n., tâter, tâtonner. To —, to — along; aller à tâtons. To — in; entrer à tâtons.

grop'ingly, adv., à tâtons.

gross, n., gros, m., grosse; masse, f. In the —; en gros.

gross, adj., gros, épais; grossier, rude; (com.) brut; (fig.) flagrant. — weight; (com.) poids brut, m.

gross'ly, adv., grossièrement; d'une manière flagrante.

gross'ness, n., grossièreté, (fig.) énormité, f.

grot ou **grot'to**, n., grotte, f.

grotesque', adj., grotesque.

grotesque'ly, adv., grotesquement.

grotesque'ness, n., grotesque, m.; grotesquerie, f.

ground (graou'n'de), n., terre, f., terrain, bien-fonds, sol; fondement; (fig.) sujet, motif, m., raison, f. ; (of pictures, of flowered cloths) fond, m. The — of accusation ; (jur.) chef d'accusation, m. The —s of a gentleman's seat ; le parc, les jardins, d'une maison de campagne. To be above — ; (pers.) vivre, exister. To break — ; (mil.) ouvrir la tranchée ; (fig.) commencer. To be under — ; être sous terre ; (fig.) être enterré. To be on sure — ; être bien fondé ; être sûr de son fait. To get — ; (of news, etc.) se répandre. To gain — ; gagner du terrain ; (of news) se répandre, s'ébruiter. To lose — ; perdre du terrain, lâcher pied ; céder, faiblir ; perdre l'avantage. To stand, ou keep, one's — ; tenir ferme, tenir bon ; conserver son avantage. To fall to the — ; tomber ; se réduire à rien, ne pas aboutir. To raze with the — ; raser de fond en comble. To burn to the — ; brûler de fond en comble. To bite the — ; mordre la poussière.

ground, v.a., fonder, établir, enseigner ; appuyer, motiver ; mettre à sec ; faire le fond, mettre à terre, reposer. To — a ship ; échouer un vaisseau. — arms ! reposez vos armes !

ground (past part. of To grind) broyé, moulu ; (fig.) (down) opprimé, foulé ; (sharpened) aiguisé.

ground'age (-'èdje), n., droit d'ancrage, droit de port, droit d'amarrage, m.

ground'-ash, n., rejeton de frêne, m.

ground'ed (-'ède), part. adj., fondé, établi, enseigné ; mis à terre, échoué.

ground'edly (-'èdli), adv., sur de bons principes, solidement ; avec raison.

ground'-floor (-flôre), n., rez-de-chaussée, m.

ground'-ivy (-aïvi), n., lierre terrestre, m.

ground'less, adj., mal fondé, sans fondement, dénué de fondement.

ground'lessly, adv., sans fondement, sans raison.

ground'lessness, n., manque de fondement, m. ; futilité, f.

ground'-line, n., ligne de fond, f.

ground'ling, n., (ant.) homme de bas étage, m. ; (ich.) loche, f.

ground'-plate, n., (carp.) sablière, sole, f.

ground'-plot, n., sol, plan ; terrain ; fondement, m. ; base, f.

ground'-rent, n., rente foncière, f.

grounds (graou'n'dze), n.pl., sédiment, m., lie, f. ; marc de café, m. ; (fig.) principes, m.pl., bases, f.pl.

ground'sel, n., (bot.) seneçon, m.

ground'sill ou ground'sel, n., traverse, f. ; (ant.) seuil, m.

ground'work (-weurke), n., fond, plan, fondement, m. ; base, fondation, f.

group (groupe), n., groupe ; (hort.) massif, bouquet, m.

group, v.a., grouper, agrouper.

grouse (graousse), n., (orni.) coq de bruyère, m.

grout (graoute), n., sédiment ; son, m. ; grosse farine ; lie ; pomme sauvage, f. ; mortier, m.

grove (grôve), n., bocage, bosquet, m.

grov'el (grov'v'l), v.n., ramper, se traîner, se vautrer.

grov'eler, n., être abject, rampant, m.

grov'eling, adj., bas, rampant, abject, vil, n., bassesse, f.

grow (grô), v.n. (pret., Grew, past part., Grown), croître ; pousser ; devenir ; (of darkness, of age, of time) se faire ; s'accroître, s'augmenter. To — together ; être étroitement uni. To — again ; recroître ; reprendre racine ; redevenir. To — into fashion ; venir à la mode. To — out of fashion ; passer de mode. To — into ; devenir, passer en. To — into favor ; s'insinuer dans les bonnes grâces de. To — out of esteem ; perdre son crédit. To — out of favor ; perdre les bonnes grâces. To — out of kind ; dégénérer. To — out of use ; passer, vieillir. To — in years ; vieillir, se faire vieux. To — gray ; grisonner. To — up ; croître, lever. To — up again ; revenir. To

— old ; vieillir. To — dear ; enchérir. To — less ; diminuer. To — near, ou on ; approcher de. To — tame ; s'apprivoiser. To — weary ; se lasser, s'ennuyer. To — young again ; rajeunir. To — better ; s'améliorer, se remettre. To — big ; grossir. To — cold ; se refroidir. To — fat ; engraisser. To — handsome ; embellir. To — hot ; s'échauffer. To — poor ; s'appauvrir. To — rich ; s'enrichir. To — sleepy ; s'assoupir. To — strong ; se fortifier. To — lean ; maigrir. To — ugly ; enlaidir. To — worse ; empirer ; être plus mal. To — fainter and fainter ; devenir de plus en plus faible ; s'affaiblir de plus en plus. To — confused ; se troubler. To — hard ; se durcir, s'endurcir. He has grown out of his clothes ; ses habits sont devenus trop petits.

grow, v.a., cultiver, semer.

grow'er, n., cultivateur, planteur, m. To be a good — ; (of plants) pousser vite, ou bien.

grow'ing, adj., naissant ; croissant. n., croissance, culture, production, f.

growl (graoul), n., grognement, grondement, m.

growl, v.n., grogner, gronder, murmurer.

grown (grône), (part. of To grow), crû ; fait ; devenu. Full — ; qui a pris toute sa croissance. —, ou full—, girl ; grande fille. — people ; les grandes personnes, f., les adultes, m. English — ; de provenance anglaise.

growth (grôth), n., croissance, f., accroissement ; (produce) cru ; (fig.) progrès, développement, m. ; extension, augmentation ; récolte, f.

grub (greube), n., larve, f. ; ver ; (fig.) nain, m. ; (l.ex.) nourriture, f., aliments, m.pl.

grub, v.a., défricher, essarter, déraciner. To — up ; arracher, extirper.

grub'bing-up, n., essartement, m.

grub'by, adj., véreux ; (pers.) sale, mal peigné, mal ficelé.

grudge (greudje), n., rancune, animosité, haine, malice, f., mauvais vouloir, m. To have an old — against any one ; avoir une dent contre quelqu'un. To have a — against ; en vouloir à ; garder rancune à.

grudge, v.a. and n., regretter de ; reprocher à ; envier à ; marchander à ; plaindre, pleurer ; donner à contre cœur.

grudg'ingly, adv., à contre cœur, avec peine, à regret, de mauvaise grâce.

gru'el (grou'èl), n., gruau, m.

grue'some, adj., triste, lugubre, terrifiant.

gruff (greufe), adj., bourru, rechigné ; refrogné ; rude.

gruff'ly, adv., d'un air rechigné ; rudement.

gruff'ness, n., mauvais naturel, m. ; rudesse, brusquerie ; mine refrognée, f. ; ton bourru, m.

grum'ble (greu'm'b'l), v.n., grommeler, bougonner, murmurer, se plaindre, grogner.

grum'bler, n., grondeur, grogneur, grognon, m.

grum'bling, n., murmure, grognement, m. ; plainte, f.

grum'blingly, adv., d'un air chagrin, en grognant, en grommelant.

gru'mose (-môze) ou gru'mous (-meusse), adj., grumeleux ; épais.

grump'y, adj. V. surly.

grunt (greu'n'te), n., grognement ; gémissement, m.

grunt, v.n., grogner, grommeler.

grunt'er, n., grognard, pourceau ; cochon, m.

grunt'ling, n., grognement, m. ; plainte, f.

grunt'ling, n., petit cochon, goret, m.

gua'iacum (gouéïakeume), n., gaïac, m.

gua'no (goua-nô), n., guano, m.

guarantee' ou guar'anty (gar'a'n'ti), n., garant, m., caution, garantie, f.

guarantee', v.a., garantir ; être garant de ; se porter garant de.

guarantor', n., garant, m.

guard (gârde), n., garde, défense, f.; (man.) garde; (of trigger) pontet, m.; (of a watch) chaîne longue, f., sautoir, m.; (fig.) caution, réserve, f. —-house, — room; corps de garde, m. Railway — line. To be on — duty; être de garde. To mount, ou go, on —; monter la garde. To come off —; descendre la garde. To catch anyone off his — ; prendre sans vert. To be thrown off one's —; être pris au dépourvu. To be, ou stand, on one's — ; être, se tenir, en garde; être, se tenir, sur ses gardes. To be off one's —; être insouciant, négligent; ne pas être sur ses gardes.

guard, v.a., garder, défendre, protéger, veiller sur. To — one's self against; se donner garde de; se prémunir contre.

guard, v.n., se garder, se tenir en garde, sur ses gardes; se prémunir contre.

guard'ed, adj., prudent, circonspect; gardé, réservé.

guard'edly, adv., avec circonspection, avec réserve.

guard'edness, n., circonspection, réserve, f.

guard'-house, n., corps de garde, m.

guar'dian (gâr-di-a'n), n., gardien; (of minors) tuteur; curateur, m.

guar'dian, adj., gardien, tutélaire.

guar'dianship, n., curatelle; tutelle; protection, défense, f.

guard'-iron (-aïeur'n), n., (railways) chasse-pierres, m.

guard'less, adj., sans défense; exposé; délaissé.

guard'-room, n., corps de garde, m. ; salle de police, f.

guard'-ship, n., (nav.) vaisseau de garde; garde-côte, m.

gua'va (gouava), n., (bot.) goyave, f.

gud'geon (gheud'jeune), n., (ich.) goujon, (fig.) jobard, m., dupe, f.

guel'der-rose, n., boule de neige, f.; obier, m.

gueril'la, n., guérilla, f.

guess (ghèce), n., conjecture, estimation, f. At a —; au juger, ou jugé. At a rough —; approximativement; à peu près. To make a good —; deviner juste.

guess, v.a. and n., deviner, conjecturer.

guess'er, n., devineur, m. To be a good, ou bad, —; deviner juste ou mal.

guess'work (-weurke), n., supposition, conjecture, f. ; action de deviner, f.

guest (ghèste), n., convié, hôte, m., convive, m.f., hôtesse, f. ; invité, m.

guest'-chamber (-tshé'm'beur), n., (ant.) salle à manger, f., réfectoire, cénacle, m.

guffaw', n., gros rire, rire fou, m.; grosse gaieté, f.

gui'dance (gaïd'-), n., conduite, f.; auspices, m.pl.; direction, gouverne, f. I tell you that for your —; je vous dis cela pour votre gouverne.

guide (gaïde), n., guide, conducteur; directeur; (rail.) indicateur, livret, m.

guide, v.a., conduire, guider; diriger; régler, gouverner.

guide'less, adj., sans guide.

guide'-post, n., poteau indicateur, m.

guild (ghilde), n., corps de métier, m.; corporation, f.

guil'der (ghild'-), n., (Dutch coin) florin, m.

Guild'hall (-hôl), n., hôtel de ville, m., maison de ville, maison commune, mairie, f.

guile (gaïl), n., fraude, fourberie; astuce, f.; artifice, m.

guile'ful (-foule), adj., fourbe, trompeur; astucieux.

guile'fully, adv., astucieusement; frauduleusement; en traître.

guile'fulness, n., fourberie, f.; artifice, m.

guile'less, adj., franc, sincère, loyal; simple, ingénu.

guile'lessness, n., sincérité, franchise; simplicité, naïveté, f.

guil'lotine (ghil'lo-tîne), n., guillotine, f.

guilt (ghilte), n., crime, forfait, m.; culpabilité; criminalité; faute, f.

guilt'ily, adv., criminellement.

guilt'iness, n., crime, m., méchanceté, culpabilité, f.

guilt'less, adj., innocent. To hold —; tenir pour innocent.

guilt'lessly, adv., innocemment, sans crime.

guilt'lessness, n., innocence; pureté, f.

guilt'y, adj., coupable. The — party ; le coupable, To find —; (jur.) déclarer coupable. To plead —; se déclarer, s'avouer coupable.

guin'ea (ghi'n'è), n., guinée, f.

guin'ea-hen (-hène), n., pintade, f.

guin'ea-pep'per (-pèp'-), n., poivre d'Inde, Guinée, piment, m.

guin'ea-pig, n., cochon d'Inde, m.

guise (gaïze), n., guise, manière, façon, apparence, forme, f., masque, costume, m.; dehors, m.pl.

guitar' (ghi-târ), n., guitare, f.

gules (ghioulze), n., (her.) gueules, m.

gulf (gheulfe), n., golfe, m., baie, f.; (fig.) gouffre, abîme, m.

gulf'y, adj., plein de golfes.

gull (gheule), n., (orni.) mouette, f.; goéland, (fig.) gobe-mouches, jobard, m.; dupe, f.; (ant.) fraude, fourberie, duperie, f.

gull, v.a., tromper, duper, attraper.

gull'-catcher (-catsh'-) ou **gull'er**, n., (ant.) fourbe, floueur, imposteur, trompeur, faiseur de dupes, m.

gul'let (gheul'lète), n., gosier, m., gorge, f.

gullibil'ity, n., crédulité, f.

gul'lible (gheul'lib'l), adj., crédule, facile à duper.

gul'ly (gheul'-), n., ravin, m., ravine, f.

gul'ly-hole (-hôle), n., entrée d'égout, m.

gulp (gheulpe), n., (pop.) goulée; gorgée, f.; trait, m. At one, ou at a, —; d'un trait.

gulp, v.a., avaler, gober.

gum (gheume), n., gomme; (of the teeth) gencive, f.

gum, v.a., gommer.

gum'miness ou **gummos'ity** (ant.), n., viscosité, f.

gum'ming, n., gommage, m.

gum'mous (ant.) ou **gum'my**, adj., gommeux, gluant.

gums (gheum'ze), n.pl., gencives, f.pl.

gun (gheune), n., fusil, mousquet; canon, m., arme ou bouche à feu, f. Smooth-bore —; canon lisse, m. Rifled —; canon rayé, m. Machine —; mitrailleuse, f. Great —; canon; (fig.) personnage distingué, m. ; illustration, f. Heavy —s; grosse artillerie, f. To blow great —s; souffler à tout casser, à tout rompre, à tout détraquer.

gun'boat (-bôte), n., (nav.) chaloupe canonnière, f. [m.

gun'-carriage (-car'ridje), n., affût de canon,

gun'-cotton, n., coton poudre, fulmicoton, m.

gun'-deck (-dèke), n., (nav.) batterie, f.

gun'-drill, n., tir du canon, m.

gun'-license, n., port d'armes, m.

gun'-maker, n., armurier, m.

gun'-metal, n., fonte, f., bronze, m.

gun'nel ou **gun'wale**, n., (nav.) plat-bord, m.

gun'ner, n., canonnier, artilleur, servant, m.

gun'nery, n., artillerie, f.

gun'port (-pôrte), n., (nav.) sabord, m.

gun'powder (-paou-deur), n., poudre à canon, f. The — plot ; la conspiration des poudres, f.

gun'-rack, n., (milit.) ratelier, m.

gun'room (-roume), n., (nav.) sainte-barbe, f.

gun'shot (-shote), n., (range) portée de fusil; portée de canon, f. ; coup de feu, m.

gun′smith (-smith), *n.*, armurier, *m.*

gun′stick, *n.*, baguette (de fusil), *f.*; (artil.) refouloir, *m.*

gun′stock, *n.*, monture, *f.*, fût, bois de fusil, *m.*

Gun′ter′s-chain (gheu′n′teurz′tshéne), *n.*, chaîne d'arpentage, *f.*

gur′gle (gheur′g′l), *v.n.*, faire glouglou; (fig.) murmurer, gazouiller.

gur′nard *ou* **gur′net** (gheur-), *n.*, (ich.) rouget, rouget grondin, grondin rouge, *m.*, trigle, *f.*

gush *ou* **gush′ing** (gheush′-) *n.*, bouillonnement; jaillissement; (fig.) enthousiasme, *m.*, effusion, *f.*

gush (gheushe), *v.n.*, saillir, jaillir, ruisseler; (fig.) être sentimental à l'excès. To — out; *bouillonner, jaillir.*

gus′set (gheus′sète), *n.*, gousset, *m.*

gust (gheuste), *n.*, bouffée, rafale, *f.*, coup; transport, accès, *m.* — of wind; *bouffée de vent, f., coup de vent, m.* — of passion; *accès de colère, m.*

gust′y (gheusti), *adj.*, orageux, venteux.

gut (gheute), *n.*, boyau, intestin, *m.* *pl.*, appareil, digestif, canal alimentaire, ventre, *m.*, panse, *f.*

gut (gheute), *v.a.*, éventrer, vider; (fig.) détruire; voler, piller. The house was entirely —ted; *il ne restait plus que les quatre murs.*

gut′-scraper, *n.*, (ant.) racleur de boyau, racleur, *m.*

gut′-spinner, *n.*, boyaudier, *m.*

gut′ter (gheut′-), *n.*, gouttière, rigole, *f.*; ravin, sillon, ruisseau, *m.*; cannelure, *f.* — of lead; *chéneau, m.* — of a cross-bow; *coulisse, f.*

gut′ter, *v.a.*, canneler; sillonner.

gut′ter, *v.n.*, dégoutter; s'égoutter; couler. The candle —s; *la chandelle coule.*

gut′ter-spout (-spaoute), *n.*, gargouille, *f.*

gut′ter-tile (-taïle), *n.*, faîtière, tuile faîtière, *f.*

gut′ting, *n.*, (of fish) vidage, *m.*

gut′tle (gheut′t′l), *v.a.* and *n.*, (ant.) bâfrer, goinfrer, dévorer.

gut′tler, *n.*, (ant.) bâfreur, goinfre, *m.*

gut′tural (gheut′teur-), *adj.*, guttural.

gut′turally, *adv.*, gutturalement.

guz′zle (guz′z′l), *v.a.* and *n.*, boire avidement, lamper, ingurgiter.

guz′zler, *n.*, buveur, ivrogne, *m.*

gybe (djaïbe), *n.* V. **gibe.**

gymna′sium (dji′m′né-ji-eume), *n.*, gymnase, *m.*

gymnas′tic, *adj.*, gymnastique.

gymnas′tics, *n.pl.*, gymnastique, *f.*

gym′nic *ou* **gym′nical** (dji′m³-), *adj.*, (antiq.) gymnique.

gyn′archy (dji′n′ar-ki), *n.*, gouvernement de femmes, *m.*; gynécocratie, *f.*

gypse *ou* **gyp′sum** (djipse, -seume), *n.*, (min.) gypse, *m.*

gyp′seous (djip′si-), *adj.*, gypseux.

gy′rate, *v.n.*, tournoyer, pivoter.

gyra′tion (djaï′r′é-), *n.*, mouvement giratoire, *m.*

gyre (djaïre), *n.*, cercle, *m.*

gy′romancy (djaï-), *n.*, gyromancie, *f.*

gyve (djaïve), *v.a.*, mettre les fers (aux pieds), enchaîner.

gyves (djaïves), *n.pl.*, fers, *m.pl.*; chaînes, menottes, *f.pl.*

H

h, huitième lettre de l'alphabet, h, *m.f.*

ha! (hâ), *int.*, ha! ha!

ha′beas cor′pus (hé-bi-ass′cor-peusse), *n.*, habeas corpus, *m.*

hab′erdasher, *n.*, mercier, *m.* A —'s shop; boutique de mercier, *f.*

hab′erdashery, *n.*, mercerie, *f.*

hab′erdine (-dîne), *n.*, morue sèche, **merluche** salée, *f.*; stockfish, *m.*

haber′geon (-bèr-dji-), *n.*, haubergeon, corselet, *m.*

habil′iment, *n.*, habillement, apprêt; équipage, *m.*

hab′it, *n.*, habitude, coutume, *f.*; (dress) habit, habillement, *m.* Riding——; *habit de cheval, m.*, amazone, *f.* — of the body; *disposition habituelle, f.*, tempérament, *m.* A man of full —; *un homme replet.* To be in the — of; *avoir pour habitude de, avoir coutume de.* To get into the — of; *contracter l'habitude de*, prendre l'habitude **de.**

hab′it, *v.a.*, habiller, vêtir.

hab′itable (-a-b′l), *adj.*, habitable.

hab′itant, *n.*, (ant.) habitant, Canadien français, *m.*

hab′itat, *n.*, habitat, *m.*

habita′tion (hab′i-té-), *n.*, habitation, *f.*, domicile, *m.*; demeure, *f.*, séjour, *m.*

habit′ual (-bit′iou-), *adj.*, habituel.

habit′ually, *adv.*, habituellement, d'habitude.

habit′uate (-bit′iou-), *v.a.*, habituer, accoutumer.

hack, *v.a.*, hacher, couper, ébrécher, écharper; massacrer; tuer; écorcher. To — the English language; *écorcher l'anglais.*

hack, *n.*, cheval de louage, *m.*; (sorry horse) rosse, *f.*; fiacre, *m.*

hack′ing-knife, *n.*, hachette, *f.*

hack′le (hac′k′l), *n.*, mouche artificielle pour pêcher; filoselle; filasse; soie écrue, *f.*, séran, peigne, *m.*

hack′le, *v.a.*, sérancer; déchirer.

hack′ney (hak′ni) *ou* **hack**, *n.*, cheval de louage, *m.*

hack′ney (hak′ni), *v.a.*, avilir par l'usage; user.

hack′ney-coach (-côtshe), *n.*, fiacre, carrosse de louage, *m.*

hack′neyed (-nide), *adj.*, avili par l'usage; banal; rebattu; commun; (pers.) mercenaire, stipendié.

had′dock, *n.*, aiglefin, *m.* Dried —; *merluche, f.*

hæmatu′ria (hî-mat′iou-), *n.*, (med.) hématurie, *f.*

hæmop′tysis (hî-mop-ti-cice), *n.*, (med.) hémoptysie, *f.*

haft (hâfte), *n.*, manche, *m.*, poignée, *f.*

haft, *v.a.*, emmancher.

haft′er, *n.*, emmancheur, *m.*

hag, *n.*, vieille sorcière, furie, *f.*

hag, *v.a.*, (ant.) tourmenter; effrayer.

hag′gard, *adj.*, hagard, farouche, égaré.

hag′gardly, *adv.*, d'un air hagard.

hag′gish (hag′ghish), *adj.*, (ant.) laid, difforme, hideux.

hag′gle (hag′g′l), *v.n.*, marchander; barguigner; chipoter; couper, hacher.

hag′gler, *n.*, barguigneur, chipotier, marchandeur, *m.*; personne qui coupe maladroitement, *f.*

hagiog′rapher (hé-dji-o-), *n.*, hagiographe, auteur qui écrit sur les saints, *m.*

hagiol′ogy (hé-dji-), *n.*, traité des choses saintes, *m.*; hagiologie, *f.*

hag′-ridden (-rid′d′n), *adj.*, qui a le cauchemar.

hail (héle), *n.*, grêle, *f.*; salut, *m.*, santé, *f.*, appel, *m.* Within —; *à portée de la voix.*

hail, *int.*, salut! salut à vous!

hail, *v.a.*, saluer; (nav.) héler.

hail, *v.n.*, grêler; (nav.) venir, arriver **de.**

hail-fellow (-fèl-lô), *n.*; ami, compagnon, intime, *m.* He is — well met with him; *il est de pair à compagnon* **avec** *lui ou il le traite de pair à compagnon.*

hail'shot (-shote), n., mitraille, chevrotine, f.
hail'stone (-stōne), n., grêlon, m.
hail'-storm, n., tempête de grêle, f.
hail'y, adj., de grêle.

hair (hère), n., cheveu; poil, m.; chevelure, f.; (of a beast) poil, crin, m.; (of a boar), soies, f.pl. Head of —; cheveux, m.pl., chevelure, f.sing. Downy —; poil follet, m. Against the —; à contre-poil. To a —; exactement. Not worth a —; de nulle valeur. Both of a —; du même acabit. To split —s; ergoter; chicaner sur les mots; épiloguer; fendre, couper un cheveu en quatre; disputer sur la pointe d'une aiguille. To part one's —; faire sa raie. To dress one's —; se coiffer. To dress any one's —; coiffer quelqu'un. To tear one's —; s'arracher les cheveux.

hair'breadth (-brèd'th), n., épaisseur d'un cheveu, f. He had a — escape; il l'a échappé belle.

hair'brush (-breushe), n., brosse à cheveux, f.
hair'cloth (-cloth), n., haire, f., cilice, m.
hair'-cutting, n., coupe de cheveux, f.
hair'dresser ou **hair'cutter** (-drèss'-), n., coiffeur, m.

haired (hèr'de), adj., aux cheveux. Red—; qui a les cheveux roux, aux cheveux roux.

hair'iness, n., quantité de cheveux, nature velue, f.

hair'less, adj., chauve, sans cheveux; (of animals) sans poil.

hair'-sieve (-sive), n., tamis de crin, m.
hair'-trigger, n., double détente, f.
hair'-worker (-weurk'-), n., crinier; artiste en cheveux, m.

hair'y, adj., velu, chevelu, poilu.
hake (héke), n., (ich.) merlus, m., merluche, f., gade, m.

hal'berd (hōl'beurde), n., hallebarde, f.
halberdier' (-dîre), n., hallebardier, m.
hal'cyon (hal-ci-o'ne), n., (orni.) alcyon, m.
hal'cyon, adj., tranquille, serein. — days; des jours heureux.

hale (héle), adj., robuste, sain, vigoureux, bien portant, vert. To be — and hearty; avoir bon pied, bon œil; avoir des jambes de vingt ans; être frais et gaillard.

hale, v.a., haler, tirer, traîner avec violence. To — before a magistrate; traîner devant un magistrat; traduire en police correctionnelle.

hal'er, n. V. hauler.

half (hâfe), n., (halves) moitié, f., demi, m., demie, f. One hour and a —; une heure et demie. —and —; moitié ale et moitié porter. To divide in halves; partager en deux; diviser en deux parties égales. To go halves; être de moitié. Halves! part à deux! Better —; moitié, chère moitié, f. To do things by halves; faire les choses à demi. Too long by —; trop long de moitié. Too much by —; moitié trop, ou de trop. — as much; la moitié autant. — as much again; la moitié plus, ou de plus. — a loaf is better than no bread; (prov.) faute de grives on mange des merles ou pays ruiné vaut mieux que pays perdu. To be — seas over; être entre deux vins ou être à moitié ivre. — in jest — in earnest; moitié figue, moitié raisin.

half, adj., demi. To — an inch; à un demi-pouce près. — mast high; à mi-mât, en berne.

half, adv., à demi, à moitié.

half'-allowance, n., demi-ration, f.
half-bind'ing, n., demi-reliure, f.
half-blood'ed (-bleud'ède), adj., de sang croisé, de race croisée; (of horses) demi-sang, demi-race.
half'-bred (-brède), adj., métis; bas.
half'-breed, n., métis, m., métisse, f.
half-broth'er (-breu'th'-), n., frère consanguin ou utérin, m.
half-cry'ing, adj., à moitié pleurant; les larmes aux yeux.

half'-dead, adj., à demi-mort, à moitié mort.
half'-done, adj., à moitié fait, à moitié cuit (of meat).
half-empty, adj., à moitié vide.
half'-fare, n., demi-place, f.
half'-finished, adj., à moitié fait; imparfait; ébauché.
half'-holiday, n., demi-congé, m.
half-life'size, n., demi-nature, f.
half'-moon (-moune), n., demi-lune, f.
half'-mourning, n., demi-deuil, m.
half'-pay (-pé), n., demi-solde, f.
half'-penny (-pèn'ni), n., un sou; cinq centimes, m.
half'-pint (-païn'te), n., demi-pinte, f.
half'-sister (-sistre), n., sœur consanguine ou utérine, f.
half'-sphere (-sfire), n., (ant.) hémisphère, m.
half'-sword (-sorde), n., (ant.) combat chaud, combat corps à corps, m.
half'-way (-wé), adv., à mi-chemin, à moitié chemin. — up the hill; à mi-côte.
half'-witted (-'tède), adj., niais, sot, timbré, idiot.
half'-year, n., semestre, m.
half'-yearly, adv., par semestre, tous les six mois.

hal'ibut, n.m., (pisc.) flétan.

hall (hōl), n., salle, f.; palais; barreau; vestibule, manoir, château; (univ.) collège, m. — porter; concierge, m. — mark; n., contrôle; v.a., contrôler. — marking; contrôlage, m.

hallelu'iah ou **hallelu'jah** (hal-li-lou-ya), n., alléluia, m.

hall'iard ou **hal'yard**, n., (nav.) drisse, f.
halloo' (-'lou), n., huée, f., cri, holà, m.
halloo', v.a., crier; huer; exciter par des cris.
halloo'! int., holà! holà ho! hé là-bas!
hal'low (hal'lō), v.a., sanctifier; consacrer; dédier.

Hal'low-mas ou **-tide**, n., la Toussaint, f.
hallucina'tion (hal'liou-ci-né-), n., hallucination; méprise, bévue, déception, illusion, f.
ha'lo (hé-lō), n., halo, cercle lumineux, m.; auréole, f.

halt (hōlte), n., halte, f.; clochement, m.
halt, adj., boiteux; estropié.
halt, v.n., boiter; s'arrêter, faire halte à; (fig.) hésiter, balancer.

hal'ter, n., licou, m., corde, f.; boiteux, m.
hal'ter, v.a., enchevêtrer; mettre un licou à.
halt'ing-place, n., (mil.) étape, f.
halve (hâve), v.a., partager en deux.

ham, n., jarret, jambon, m.
ham'let, n., hameau, petit village, m.
ham'mer, n., marteau; (of fire-arms) chien, m.; enchère, f. — and tongs; avec fureur; avec violence. To bring under the —; mettre aux enchères. To — out a line; marteler un vers.
ham'mer, v.a., marteler, forger, battre, façonner à coups de marteau; enfoncer.
ham'mer, v.n., marteler; travailler; s'agiter. To — at; s'attaquer à. To — away; travailler d'arrache-pied à.
ham'mer-cloth (-cloth), n., housse de siège, f.
ham'mer-dressed (-drès'te), adj., dégrossi au marteau; (of stone) équarri.
ham'mered (-dd), adj., martelé, rebattu.
ham'merer, n., marteleur, forgeron, m.
ham'mering, n., bruit des marteaux, martelage, m.
ham'mock, n., hamac, branle, m.
ham'per, n., mannequin, m.; hotte, f., panier, m.
ham'per, v.a., embarrasser, empêtrer, entraver.
ham'-string (-strigne), n., tendon du jarret, m.
ham'string, v.a., (preterit and past part, Hamstrung), couper les jarrets à.
hand, n., main, f.; (measure) palme, m.; signa-

ture, écriture, *f.;* (at cards) jeu, *m.;* (of a watch) aiguille, *f.;* ouvrier, bras, *m.* A horse fifteen —s high ; *cheval qui a quinze palmes.* — to —; *corps à corps.* At —; *sous la main.* Bound — and foot; *pieds et poings liés.* In —; *en main ;* (com.) *en caisse.* On —; (com.) *en magasin.* By —; *à la main.* From — to —; *de main en main.* To live from — to mouth; *vivre au jour le jour.* To bring up by—; *élever au biberon.* Out of —; *fini, achevé.* To play into each other's —s; *être d'intelligence ; s'entendre comme larrons en foire.* To change —s; *changer de maître.* To have one's —s full; *avoir des affaires par dessus les bras.* To lend a — to any one; *donner un coup de main à quelqu'un.* They are — and glove together ; *ils sont à pot et à rôt; ce sont deux têtes dans un bonnet.* With both —s; *à deux mains.* On one's —s ; *sur les bras.* To be a good — at; *savoir s'y prendre.* To be an old —; *n'être pas novice ou s'y connaître.* To get one's —s in ; *se faire la main.* To get the upper —; *avoir le dessus.* To have a — in; *être pour quelque chose* **dans** ; (fig.) *tremper* **dans.** To have no — in; *n'être pour rien* **dans.** To keep in —; *tenir en bride.* To keep one's — in ; *s'entretenir la main.* To lend a —; *donner un coup d'épaule* **à.** To set one's —s ; *mettre la main* **à.** To lay violent —s on; *violenter, maltraiter.* To lay violent —s on one's self; *attenter à ses jours.* To lead with a high —; *mener tambour battant.* second —; *d'occasion.*

hand, *v.a.,* donner avec la main ; transmettre ; offrir ; conduire, mener ; passer, faire passer, remettre ; (nav.) ferler les voiles. To — down ; *transmettre; descendre ; aider à descendre.* To — over; *livrer* **à,** *remettre* **à.** To — round; *faire passer.* To — about; *passer de main en main.* To — up; *remettre, tendre, donner.* [card, *m.*

hand'-barrow (-bar'rô), *n.,* civière, *f.;* brancard. *f.*

hand'-basket, *n.,* panier à anse, *m.,* bourriche, *f.*

hand'-bell, *n.,* clochette, sonnette, *f.*

hand'-bill, *n.,* prospectus, *m.;* feuille volante, serpe, *f.*

hand'-book (-bouke), *n.,* manuel, *m.*

hand'-breadth (-bréd'th), *n.,* paume, *f.;* empan, *m.*

hand'cuff (-keufe), *n.,* menotte, *f.*

hand'cuff, *v.a.,* mettre les menottes **à.**

hand'-drawn, *adj.,* dessiné à la main.

hand'ful (-foule), *n.,* poignée, *f.;* (fig.) petit nombre, peu, *m.*

hand'-gallop (-), *n.,* petit galop, *m.*

hand'-grenade (-gri-), *n.,* grenade, *f.*

hand'-gun (-gheune), *n.,* fusil, *m.*

han'dicraft (-), *n.,* métier, *m.;* main-d'œuvre, *f.*

han'dicraftsman, *n.,* artisan, *m.*

han'dily, *adv.,* adroitement ; avec dextérité ; commodément ; à son aise.

han'diness, *n.,* adresse, dextérité, commodité, *f.*

han'diwork (-weurke), *n.,* ouvrage manuel, *m.,* main-d'œuvre (œuvre, *f.*

hand'kerchief (-tshîfe), *n.,* mouchoir, *m.*

han'dle (ha'n'd'l), *n.,* anse, *f.,* manche, *m. ;* (fig.) armes, *f.pl. ;* prise, *f.,* instrument ; (of a door) bouton, *m. ;* (of a sword) poignée ; (of a pump) brimbale ; (of a frying-pan) queue ; (of a printing-press) manivelle, *f. ;* (of a wheelbarrow) bras, *m.* — bar; (of a bicycle) guidon, *m.* To give a —; *donner prise* **à.** A — to one's name; *un titre.*

han'dle, *v.a.,* manier, toucher ; traiter.

hand'-leather (-lèth'-), *n.,* manique, *f.*

han'dling, *n.,* maniement, traitement, *m.*

hand'maid (-méde), *n.,* servante, *f.*

hand'mill, *n.,* moulin à bras, *m.*

hand'rail (-réle), *n.,* garde-fou, *m. ;* rampe, *f.*

hand'saw (-sô), *n.,* petite scie, scie à main, *f.*

hand'sel, *n.,* étrenne (première vente), *f.*

hand'sel, *v.a.,* étrenner.

hands' off! *int.,* à bas les mains ! ôtez vos mains ! — the Queen ; *ne touchez pas à la Reine !*

hand'some, *adj.,* beau, bel; élégant; gracieux; bien fait.

hand'somely, *adv.,* joliment ; galamment ; généreusement ; convenablement ; avec grâce.

hand'someness, *n.,* beauté ; élégance ; délicatesse ; grâce ; générosité, *f.*

hand'spike (-spaïke), *n.,* levier; (nav.) anspect, *m.*

hand'-vice (-vaïce), *n.,* étau à main, *m.*

hand'writing (-rait'-), *n.,* écriture, *f.*

han'dy, *adj.,* adroit, habile ; commode ; sous la main, tout près.

han'dy-dan'dy, *n.,* jeu de main, *m.*

hang (hai'gne), *v.a.* and *n.,* (*preterit* and *past part.,* Hanged *ou* Hung ; en général, *hanged* s'emploie en parlant du supplice) pendre, suspendre ; tendre ; tapisser ; baisser ; poser ; pencher ; (nav.) monter, mettre en place, être pendu ; rester, suspendre ; se pencher ; s'accrocher. To — fire ; (of fire-arms) *être lent à partir ;* (of a play) *manquer de chaleur, d'animation ;* (fig.) vaciller, hésiter. To — heavily; (of time) *durer.* To — up a question ; *ajourner la solution d'une question ; laisser une question indécise.* To — on a thread ; *ne tenir qu'à un fil.* To — in doubt ; *être en suspens.* To get the — of a thing; *acquérir le truc d'une chose.* To — a room ; *tapisser une chambre.* To — about; *s'attacher* **à** ; *traîner ; stationner.* To — back; *reculer, hésiter.* To — by; *appendre ;* (fig.) *ne tenir qu'à.* To — down; *baisser.* To — loose; *pendiller.* To — out; *arborer; demeurer.* To — over ; *pencher ; menacer.* To — together; *tenir ; s'accorder ; faire la paire.* To — the rudder ; *monter le gouvernail.* To go and be —ed ; *aller se promener, aller se faire fiche.* — it ! *fichtre !* peste ! *diable !*

hang'-dog, *n.,* pendard, *m.* — look; *mine patibulaire, f.*

hang'er, *n.,* coutelas, couteau de chasse, crochet, *m.*

hang'er-on, *n.,* écornifleur ; parasite ; importun, *m.*

hang'ing, *n.,* pendaison ; tenture ; pose, *f. adj.;* — matter ; *cas pendable, m.* — wardrobe ; *armoire à robes, à effets.*

hang'ings, *n.pl.,* tapisserie, tenture, *f.*

hang'man, *n.,* bourreau, *m.*

hang'-nail, *n.,* envie, *f.*

hank (haign'ke), *n.,* écheveau, *m.;* pantine, *f.;* (nav.) anneau de bois, *m.*

hank'er, *v.n.,* désirer ardemment ; soupirer après ; avoir bien envie **de** ; convoiter.

hank'ering, *n.,* penchant, *m.,* inclination ; grande envie, *f.,* vif désir, *m.*

hap *ou* **hap-haz'ard,** *n.,* hasard, sort ; accident, *m. ;* fortune, *f.*

hap'less, *adj.,* misérable ; infortuné ; malheureux.

hap'lessly, *adv.,* malheureusement.

hap'ly, *adv.,* par hasard ; peut-être ; par malheur.

hap'pen, *v.n.,* arriver, advenir ; se passer ; tomber ; se trouver. He —ed to hear ; *il apprit par hasard.* Not to — again ; *n'arriver plus.* — what may ! *advienne que pourra !* To — to somebody to ; *arriver à quelqu'un* **de.** If he —ed to come ; *si par hasard il arrivait.* If he —ed to see you ; *s'il vous voyait par hasard* ou *s'il venait à vous voir.* You don't — to have ; *vous n'auriez pas par hasard.* If you — to be in need of ; *s'il se trouve que vous ayez besoin.* As if nothing had —ed ; *comme si de rien n'était.* A man —ed to pass ; *un homme vint à passer.*

hap'pily, *adv.,* heureusement, par bonheur.

hap'piness, *n.,* félicité, *f.,* bonheur, *m.*

hap'py, *adj.,* heureux, fortuné. — to; *heureux* **de.**

harangue', *n.,* harangue, *f.,* discours, *m.*

harangue', v.a., haranguer, faire un discours.

haran'guer (ha-rai'gn'gh'eur), n., orateur ; (b.s.) haranguer, m.

har'ass, v.a., harasser, lasser, fatiguer ; harceler, excéder.

har'binger (hâr-bi'n'djeur), n., avant-coureur, précurseur ; fourrier, m.

har'bor (hâr-beur), n., havre, port ; refuge ; asile ; gîte, abri, m.; retraite, f. — dues; péage, m.; droits de mouillage, m.pl. — master ; officier de port, m.

har'bor, v.a. and n., loger, recéler ; héberger; se réfugier ; (fig.) entretenir, avoir, nourrir. How can you — such a thought ? comment pouvez-vous entretenir, ou avoir, une pareille idée ?

har'borer, n., receleur, hôte, m.

har'borless, adj., sans port, sans abri, sans asile.

hard (hârde), adj., dur, ferme, solide ; pénible, difficile ; rude, cruel, rigoureux ; (at disbursing money) dur à la détente, ou à la desserre. Muscles in — condition ; muscles fermes, m. — and fast rule ; règle rigoureuse, ou stricte, f. — cherries; guignes, f.pl. — drinking ; débauche, f. — frost ; forte gelée, f. — labor ; travaux forcés, m. — of belief ; incrédule. — of hearing ; dur d'oreille. — to deal with ; intraitable. — to please ; difficile à contenter ; (fig.) aguerrir ; accoutumer, habituer. — words ; duretés, f.pl. — up ; à sec ; à court d'argent. To hold — ; tenir bon, ou ferme. — a-starboard ! lof tout ! — a-port ! bord bas tout !

hard, adv., fort, fort et ferme, rudement ; difficilement ; beaucoup. He looked — at ; il regarda fixement, attentivement. — by ; tout près, auprès de.

hard'bound (-baou'n'de), adj., constipé.

hard'-drinker, n. To be a — ; boire sec.

hard'-earned, adj., amassé péniblement.

hard'en, v.a., endurcir, durcir, rendre dur.

hard'en, v.n., durcir, s'endurcir, devenir dur.

hard'ening, n., durcissement ; (pers.) endurcissement, m. ; (of steel) trempe, f.

hard'-favored (-fé-veurde), adj., laid ; disgracié de la nature.

hard'-featured, adj., aux traits durs.

hard'fought (-fôte), adj., fortement contesté ; acharné, opiniâtre.

hard'handed (-ède), adj., dont les mains sont endurcies au travail ; (fig.) dur, sévère, cruel.

hard'-hearted (-hârt'éde), adj., dur, insensible, cruel.

hard'-heartedness, n., dureté de cœur, insensibilité, inhumanité, f.

har'dihood (-houde), n., hardiesse, audace, force, vigueur ; effronterie ; bravoure, intrépidité, f.

har'dily, adv., durement, à la dure ; hardiment ; (ant.) sévèrement ; sans mollesse.

har'diness, n., force, vigueur, hardiesse, f. ; tempérament robuste, m. ; (fig.) effronterie, impudence, assurance, f.

hard-la'bored (-lé-beurde), adj., (ant.) travaillé avec soin, élaboré.

hard'ly, adv., à peine ; rudement, durement, difficilement. — so soon as ; guère avant ; (fig.) à une époque qui ne remonte guère qu'à.

hard'mouthed (-maouth'de), adj., insensible au frein ; grossier, dur en paroles.

hard'ness, n., dureté, fermeté, solidité ; rigueur, difficulté ; avarice, f. ; (of water) crudité, f. — of the heart ; endurcissement du cœur, m.

hards (hardze), n.pl., chènevottes, f. pl. ; étoupe, f.

hard'ship, n., dureté ; fatigue, peine, tribulation, injustice, oppression, misère, privation, f. ; travail, m.

hard'ware (-wère), n., quincaille, quincaillerie, f.

hard'wareman, n., quincaillier, m.

hard'-worker, n., grand travailleur.

hard'-working, adj., laborieux, travailleur ; piocheur.

har'dy, adj., hardi, courageux ; fort, robuste ; (of plants) de pleine terre.

hare (hère), n., lièvre, m. A young — ; levraut, m. Jugged — ; civet de lièvre, m. To make a — of ; rendre ridicule. To run with the — and hunt with the hounds ; ménager la chèvre et le chou.

hare'bell, n., (bot.) scille penchée, jacinthe des bois ; campanule, f.

hare'brained (-bré'n'de), adj., écervelé ; volage, léger, étourdi.

hare'foot (-foute), n., (bot.) pied-de-lièvre, m.

hare'lip, n., (surg.) bec-de-lièvre, m.

ha'rem (hé-), n., harem, m.

hare's'-ear (-z'ïre), n., (bot.) buplèvre, m., oreille-de-lièvre, f. ; vélar, m.

har'icot (-cô), n., (cook.) haricot ; (bot.) haricot, m.

hark (hârke) ou **heark'en** (hârk'-), v.n., écouter, prêter l'oreille, entendre. To — back; revenir à son sujet.

hark ! int., écoutez !

harl (hârle), n., filaments du chanvre, du lin, m.pl. ; filasse, f. ; barbes d'une plume de paon, f.pl.

har'lequin (hâr-li-kine), n., arlequin, m.

harm (hârme), n., tort, dommage, préjudice, mal, malheur, m. Out of — 's way ; en sûreté. Bodily — ; voies de fait, f.pl. There is no — in him ; il n'y entend pas malice. There is no — in that ; il n'y a pas de mal à cela.

harm, v.a., nuire à, faire du mal à, faire du tort à.

harm'ful (-foule) adj., nuisible, malfaisant; dangereux.

harm'fully, adv., dangereusement ; avec préjudice ; d'une manière nuisible.

harm'fulness, n., préjudice, dommage, m.

harm'less, adj., innocent, inoffensif. To hold (a person) — ; protéger, mettre à couvert (une personne).

harm'lessly, adv., innocemment.

harm'lessness, n., innocence, f.

harmon'ic ou **harmon'ical**, adj., harmonique; musical; harmonieux.

harmo'nious (-mô-), adj., harmonieux ; mélodieux.

harmo'niously, adv., harmonieusement ; mélodieusement.

harmo'niousness (-mô-) ou **har'mony**, n., harmonie ; mélodie ; concorde, f. ; accord, m.

har'monize (-mô-naïze), v.a., rendre harmonieux ; cadencer ; accorder ; ajuster ; harmoniser, mettre d'accord.

har'monize, v.n., s'accorder ; correspondre ; se marier **avec**. They — ; ils font bon ménage ensemble.

har'monizer, n., conciliateur ; (mus.) harmoniste, m.

har'monizing, adj., qui harmonise.

har'ness, n., harnais ; harnachement, m. To die in — ; blanchir sous le harnais ; mourir sur la brèche, mourir à la peine. To go well in — ; (of horses) être bon à la voiture.

har'ness, v.a., harnacher, enharnacher ; (to a carriage) atteler.

har'ness-ma'ker (-mék'-), n., fabricant de harnais, sellier ; bourrelier, m.

har'ness-ma'king (-mék'-), n., fabrication de harnais ; bourrellerie, f.

harp (hârpe), n., harpe, f. Jews'- — ; guimbarde, f.

harp, v.n., pincer, ou jouer de, la harpe ; répéter ; rabâcher. To — on one string ; rabâcher toujours la même chose ; chanter la même antienne.

harp'er, n., joueur de harpe, harpiste, m.

harp'ing-iron (-aï'eurne) ou **harpoon'** (-poune), n., harpon, m.

harpoon', v.t., harponner.

harpoon'er, n., harponneur, m.

harp'sichord (hârp'si-corde), n., clavecin, m.

har'py, n., harpie, f.

har'ridan, n., haridelle, mégère, souillon, vieille guenon, f.

har'rier, n., harrier ; (orni.) busard, m.

har'row (har'rô), n., herse, f.

har'row, v.a., herser ; déchirer ; agiter ; torturer ; (ant.) piller.

har'rower, n., herseur, m.

har'rowing, n., hersage, m. ; (fig.) déchirement, m. adj., déchirant, navrant.

har'ry, v.a. and n., harceler, harasser, tourmenter ; piller ; dévaster.

harsh (hârshe), adj., rude, âpre ; dur ; sévère.

harsh'ly, adv., rudement ; sévèrement ; âprement.

harsh'ness, n., rudesse, âpreté ; sévérité, f.

hars'let (hârs'-) ou **has'let** (hâs'-), n., fressure de cochon, f.

hart (hârte), n., cerf, m. — of ten ; cerf dix-cors, m.

harts'horn, n., corne de cerf ; (med.) essence de corne de cerf, f.

harts'tongue (-teu'gn'e), n., (bot.) scolopendre, langue-de-cerf, f.

hart'-wort (-weurte), n., (bot.) séséli (de Marseille), m.

ha'rum-sca'rum (hèr'eume-skèr'eume), adj., écervelé, braque, étourdi ; (of things) en l'air.

har'vest (hârveste), n., moisson ; récolte, f. — tick ; (ent.) rouget, lepte automnal, m. To get in the — ; faire la moisson.

har'vest, v.a., moissonner ; récolter.

har'vester ou **har'vestman** (-ma'n), n., moissonneur, m.

har'vest-home (-hôme), n., chanson du moissonneur ; fête des moissonneurs, fête de la moisson, f.

har'vest-time (-taïme), n., temps de la moisson, m.

hash, n., hachis, m., galimafrée, capilotade, f. To make a — of ; (fig.) gâcher, faire un joli gâchis de.

hash, v.a., hacher, couper en petits morceaux ; (fig.) gâcher, embrouiller.

hash'ish (-), n., hachisch, m.

hasp (hâspe), n., fermoir, crochet ; morailion ; loquet, m.

hasp, v.a., fermer avec des crochets, fermer avec un loquet, accrocher, verrouiller.

has'sock (-), n., paillasson, agenouilloir, m.

haste (héste), n., hâte, vitesse ; précipitation ; diligence ; colère, f. To make — ; se hâter, se dépêcher. — makes waste ; (prov.) ouvrage hâté, ouvrage gâté. In — ; à la hâte. In great — ; en grande hâte ; très pressé. More — less speed ; hâtez-vous lentement.

haste ou **hast'en** (hé's'n), v.a., hâter, dépêcher, presser.

haste ou **hast'en**, v.n., se hâter, se dépêcher, se presser, s'empresser. To — away ; se hâter de fuir, s'enfuir précipitamment. To — along ; courir le long de ; presser, allonger le pas. To — back ; revenir à la hâte.

hast'ener, n., personne qui se hâte, f.

hast'ily (hés'-), adv., à la hâte ; brusquement ; en colère ; avec vivacité.

hast'iness, n., promptitude, hâte, f. ; emportement, m. ; vivacité, f.

hast'ing-pear, n., hâtiveau, m.

hast'ings, n.pl., primeur, f., fruits, légumes précoces, hâtifs, m.pl. Green —; pois hâtifs, m.pl.

hast'y (hés'ti), adj., prompt, rapide ; pétulant, violent, emporté. — sketch ; croquis, m.

hast'y-pud'ding (-poud'digne), n., bouillie, f.

hat, n., chapeau, m. —s off ! chapeaux bas ! To hang up one's — in a house ; s'installer chez quelqu'un. To pass round the — ; faire la quête. To raise the — to any one ; ôter son chapeau à quelqu'un ou saluer quelqu'un.

hat'band, n., cordon de chapeau, bourdalou, m. Mourning — ; crêpe, m.

hat'box ou **hat'case** (-kéce), n., étui à, ou de, chapeau ; carton à chapeau, m.

hat'-brush, n., brosse à chapeau, f.

hatch, n., couvée ; éclosion ; découverte ; porte coupée ; (nav.) écoutille, f.

hatch, v.a., faire éclore ; produire ; tramer ; (drawing) hacher, faire des hachures ; (to incubate) couver. Don't count your chickens before they are —ed ; ne vendez pas la peau de l'ours avant de l'avoir pris.

hatch, v.n., couver, être prêt à éclore.

hatch'el, n., séran, peigne à chanvre, m.

hatch'el, v.a., sérancer, passer par le séran ; vexer.

hatch'eler, n., séranceur, m.

hatch'el, n., inventeur, auteur, faiseur de projets, m.

hatch'es (hatsh'èze), n.pl., (nav.) panneaux des écoutilles, m.pl. To be under —; être à fond de cale.

hatch'et (hatsh'ète), n., cognée, hachette, hache, f. To bury the — ; se réconcilier, faire la paix. To take up the — ; faire la guerre. To throw the — ; faire assaut de menterie ; ⊙gaber.

hatch'ing, n., hachure ; (of eggs) éclosion, f.

hatch'ment, n., (her.) écusson, m. ; armoiries, f.pl.

hatch'way (-wé), n., (nav.) écoutille, f.

hate (héte), n., haine, aversion, inimitié, f.

hate, v.a., haïr, détester, abhorrer, avoir en horreur.

hate'ful (-foule), adj., haïssable, odieux, détestable.

hate'fully, adv., odieusement ; avec haine.

hate'fulness, n., qualité odieuse, abomination, noirceur, f.

ha'ter (hét'eur), n., ennemi, m. To be a good —; savoir haïr.

hat'-making, n., chapellerie, f.

hat'-stand, n., porte-chapeaux, m.

hat'-trade, n., chapellerie, f.

ha'tred (hé'trède), n., haine, aversion, inimitié, f.

hat'ter (hat'teur), n., chapelier, m.

hau'berk (hô-beurke), n., haubert, m. ; cotte de mailles, cuirasse, f.

haugh'tily (hô-ti-), adv., hautainement, fièrement, d'une manière hautaine.

haugh'tiness, n., hauteur, fierté, arrogance, f.

haugh'ty (hô-ti), adj., altier, fier, hautain, arrogant.

haul (hôl), n., action de tirer, de trainer, f. ; tiraillement ; coup de filet, m. At a —; d'un coup de filet.

haul, v.a., tirer ; tirailler ; haler ; traîner. To — over the coals ; réprimander, gronder. To — in ; (nav.) haler à bord. To — up ; hisser.

haum (hôme), n., chaume, m. ; paille, f.

haunch (hâ'n'she), n., hanche, f. ; (of venison) cuisse, f. ; cuissot, m.

haunt (hâ'n'te), n., repaire ; lieu que l'on fréquente, m. ; retraite, f.

haunt, v.a., hanter, fréquenter, visiter souvent ; (fig.) obséder, tourmenter. That house is —ed ; il y a des revenants dans cette maison ou cette maison est "visionnée" (V. Hugo).

haunt'er, n., personne qui hante, f. ; habitué, visiteur habituel, m.

haunt'ing, n., fréquentation, hantise, f.

haut'boy (hô-boï), n., hautbois, m.

have (hève), v.a., (preterit and past part., Had) avoir, tenir ; faire (to avoid repetition of a verb). Had all the soldiers fought ; *si tous les soldats avaient combattu*. Had it not been for the filial respect ; *n'eût été* (ou *sans*) *le respect filial*. Had he known ; *s'il avait su*. To — to deal with ; *avoir affaire* à. What will you — ? *que prendrez-vous? que voulez-vous?* She will not — him ; *elle ne veut pas de lui*. To — nothing for it but to ; *être réduit à*. To — pain ; *avoir de la peine ; souffrir ; sentir de la douleur*. To — pleasure ; *avoir du plaisir*. To — sorrow ; *avoir du chagrin*. Let him — that book ; *donnez-lui ce livre*. I — it ; *j'y suis, j'ai trouvé*. He will — it so ; *il veut que ce soit ainsi*. He will not — me do that ; *il me défend de le faire ; il ne veut pas que je le fasse*. I — to be at the office at 4 o'clock ; *il faut que je sois, ou je dois être rendu, au bureau à quatre heures*. This may be had at . . . ; (com.) *cela est en vente chez* . . . To — (a thing) done ; *faire faire*. — after ; *suivez ; suivons*. — at ; *sus! à l'attaque!* — with! *allons! convenu!* To — a care ; *être prudent ; prendre garde* **de**. To — away ; *enlever*. To — from ; *tenir* **de**. To — in ; *contenir, comprendre, renfermer*. I had as lief ; *j'aime autant*. I had rather ; *j'aime mieux, j'aimerais mieux*. To — back ; (pers.) *faire revenir ;* (things) *faire rendre*. To — on ; (to wear) *avoir, porter*. To — about one ; *avoir sur soi*. To — in ; *faire entrer*. To — up ; *faire monter*. To — with one ; *garder, posséder*.

ha'ven (hé'v'n), *n*., havre, port ; asile, *m.*

hav'ing (hav'ĭgne), *n*., avoir, *m. ;* possession, fortune, *f. ;* biens, *m.pl.*

hav'oc, *n*., dégât, ravage, *m.*

haw (hŏ), *n*., fruit de l'aubépine, *m.*, cenelle ; (vet.) caroncule, *f.*

haw, *v.n.*, hésiter en parlant ; ânonner.

hawk (hŏke), *n*., (orni.) épervier, faucon, *m.*

hawk, *v.a.* and *n*., chasser à l'oiseau ; (fig.) colporter.

hawk'-bell, *n*., grelot ; (her.) grillet, *m.*

hawked (hŏk'te), *adj*., aquilin ; crié dans les rues. — about ; *proclamé partout.*

hawk'er, *n*., colporteur, *m.* [m.

hawk'ing, *n*., chasse au faucon, *f.*, colportage,

haw'ser (hŏss'-) *ou* **halser** (hŏss'-), *n*., (nav.) haussière, *f.*, grelin, câblot, *m.*

haw'thorn (hŏ-thorne), *n*., (bot.) aubépine, *f.*

hay (héï), *n*., foin, *m.* To make — ; *faire les foins*. To make — while the sun shines ; *battre le fer pendant qu'il est chaud ; profiter de l'occasion ; mettre le temps à profit.*

hay'bird (-beurde), *n*., (orni.) grand pouillot, *m.*

hay'cock, *n*., (agri.) tas de foin, *m.*

hay'harvest (-vèste), *n*., fenaison ; récolte des foins, *f.*

hay'loft, *n*., grenier à foin, fenil, *m.*

hay'maker (-mék'-), *n*., faneur ; faucheur, *m.*

hay'making (-mék'-), *n*., fenaison, *f.* [m.

hay'-market (-mâr-kète), *n*., marché au foin,

hay'rick *ou* **hay'stack**, *n*., meule de foin, *f.*

haz'ard, *n*., hasard, risque, *m. ;* (at cards) chance, *f.* To run the — ; *courir le risque* **de**.

haz'ard, *v.a.*, risquer, hasarder.

haz'ard, *v.n.*, se hasarder ; s'aventurer ; s'exposer à ; se risquer.

haz'ardous, *adj*., hasardeux ; dangereux.

haz'ardously, *adv*., hasardeusement, dangereusement.

haze, *n*., brouillard, *m. ;* brume, vapeur, *f. ;* (fig.) obscurité, *f.*

ha'zel (hé-z'l) *ou* **ha'zel-tree** (-trî), *n*., (bot.) noisetier, coudrier, *m.*

ha'zel, *adj*., de coudrier ; couleur de noisette. — eyed ; *aux yeux couleur de noisette.*

ha'zel-copse, *n*., coudraie, coudrette, *f.*

ha'zel-nut (-neute), *n*., noisette, *f.*

ha'zy (hé'zĭ), *adj*., brumeux. To have — notions ; *avoir des idées confuses, peu claires.*

he (hi), *pron*., il, celui, lui. [He s'emploie souvent comme **préfixe** pour désigner les ani-

maux mâles. Ex. : he-elephant, éléphant mâle; he-goat, bouc.] — that ; — who ; *celui qui*. — and I ; *lui et moi*. I am —, that unfortunate —; *je suis l'infortuné mortel en question.*

head (hède), *n*., tête, *f. ;* chef, *m. ;* (of cattle) tête, *f. ;* (nav.) avant, éperon, *m. ;* (of hair) chevelure, *f.*, cheveux, *m.pl. ;* (of game) pièce, *f. ;* (of a book) titre, *m. ;* (of a river) source ; (of an arrow) pointe ; (of a cane) pomme ; (of a wild boar) hure, *f. ;* (of a college) principal, proviseur, *m.* To be over — and ears in debt; *avoir des dettes par-dessus la tête.* He is — and shoulders taller than you ; *il est plus grand que vous de la tête et des épaules.* —s or tails ; *pile ou face.* — to wind ; *cap au vent*. To give the —; *lâcher la bride* à. To come to a —; *suppurer; mûrir*. To eat its — off ; (of horses) *ne pas travailler.* To gather —; *gagner de la force.* To make —; *résister avec succès* à ; *avancer ; faire des progrès.* To lay one's —s together ; *se donner la main* **pour** ; *s'entendre* **pour**, *se concerter.* To knock in one's — ; *renverser, détruire.* To run in one's — ; *trotter dans la tête.* To trouble one's — about ; *se mêler* **de**, *s'inquiéter* **de**. Not to be able to make — or tail of ; *n'y rien comprendre ; n'y voir que du feu ; ne pas s'y reconnaître*. From — to foot ; *de pied en cap ; des pieds à la tête.* To be hot-—ed ; *avoir la tête près du bonnet.* A — ou per — ; *par tête, par personne.* At the — of ; *en tête* **de**. To eye from — to foot ; *toiser*. To make — against ; *tenir tête* à, *résister* à. To lay one's — upon anything ; *parier sa tête à couper que.* The wine gets into his — ; *le vin lui monte à la tête.* At the — of the table ; *au haut bout de la table.* To take into one's — ; *se mettre dans la tête* **de**, *s'aviser* **de**. — foremost ; *la tête la première ; V.* **headlong**.

head, *v.a.*, conduire, commander en chef ; se mettre à la tête **de** ; diriger ; (pins, nails) façonner la tête **de**.

head, *adj*., principal, en chef.

head'ache (-éke), *n*., mal de tête, *m. ;* migraine, *f.*

head'band, *n*., bandeau, *m.*, bande ; (books) tranchefile, *f.*

head'-cheese, *n*., fromage de cochon, *m.*

head'dress, head'-gear, *n*., coiffe ; coiffure, *f.*

head'er, *n*., chef ; (of nails) ouvrier qui façonne les têtes ; (of pins) entêteur, *m.* To take a — ; (swimming) *piquer une tête.*

head'iness, *n*., emportement, *m. ;* impétuosité ; étourderie ; (of drink) qualité, nature, capiteuse, *f.*

head'ing, *n*., titre, *m.*, inscription en tête d'un article, *f. ;* (print.) lettrine, *f. ;* (of casks) fond, *m.*

head'land, *n*., cap, *m. ;* pointe, *f. ;* promontoire, *m.*

head'less, *adj*., sans tête ; sans chef.

head'long, *adv*., la tête en avant, la tête la première ; (fig.) à corps perdu, tête baissée, en étourdi, de gaieté de cœur.

head'long, *adj*., escarpé ; (fig.) irréfléchi, inconsidéré, imprudent, impétueux.

head'man (-ma'ne), *n*., chef, *m. ;* (West Indies) factotum, *m.*

head'-master, *n*., proviseur, principal, directeur, *m.*

head'-money, *n*., rétribution par tête, *f.*

head'most (-môste), *adj*., de tête, en tête, à la tête, le premier.

head'-office, *n*., bureau central, *m.*

head'piece (-pîce), *n*., armet, casque, *m. ;* tête de page, *f.*, en-tête, *m. ;* (fig.) tête, caboche, *f.*

head'quar'ters (-kwor-teurze), *n.pl.*, quartier général, *m.sing.* — staff ; *état-major du général en chef*, *m.*

head'ship, *n*., autorité suprême, primauté, *f.*

heads'man (hèdz'ma'ne), *n*., bourreau, (collieries) rouleur, *m.*

head'stall (-stōl), n., (horse) têtière, f.

head'-stick, n., (nav.) corne, f.; bois de foc, m.

head'stone (-stōne), n., pierre angulaire ; pierre tumulaire, tombe, f.

head'strong, adj., opiniâtre, têtu, obstiné, entêté.

head'way, n., (nav.) marche, f. To make — ; avancer, progresser.

head'-wind, n., vent contraire, m.

head'-work, n., travail de tête, m.

head'y, adv., (of drink) capiteux.

heal (hīl), v.a., guérir ; cicatriser ; (fig.) apaiser. —all ; panacée, f.

heal, v.n., guérir ; se guérir ; se cicatriser.

heal'er, n., guérisseur, m., guérisseuse, f.; remède, (ant.) couvreur en ardoise, m.

heal'ing, adj., propre à guérir ; salutaire. The — art ; l'art de guérir, m.

heal'ing, n., guérison, f.

health (hĕlth), n., santé, f.; toast, m.; hygiène ; (jur.) salubrité, f. To drink any one's — ; boire à la santé de quelqu'un. Out of — ; malade.

health'ful (-foule), adj., bien portant ; en bonne santé ; sain, salubre ; salutaire.

health'fully, adv., en bonne santé ; salutairement.

health'fulness, n., santé ; salubrité, f.

health'ily, adv., en bonne santé ; sainement.

health'iness, n., santé ; salubrité ; nature salutaire, f.

health'y, adj., bien portant ; en bonne santé ; sain ; salutaire.

heam (hīme), n., (of animals) arrière-faix, délivre ; placenta, m.

heap (hīpe), n., tas, monceau, amas, m.

heap, v.a., entasser, amonceler, accumuler, amasser. To — up ; entasser ; amonceler. To — the measure ; combler la mesure.

heaped (hīp'te), adj., entassé.

hear (hīre), v.a.n., (preterit and past part., Heard), entendre, entendre dire ; écouter ; (fig.) apprendre ; (jur.) exaucer. To — say : entendre dire. To — of ; entendre parler de. To — from any one ; recevoir des nouvelles de quelqu'un. To — of any one ; avoir des nouvelles de quelqu'un. Let us — from you ; donnez-nous de vos nouvelles. —, — ! très-bien ; bravo. — him ! écoutez le donc. To — any one his lesson ; faire répéter sa leçon à quelqu'un. I — a bird so sing ; mon petit doigt me l'a dit.

heard (heurde), past part. V. hear.

hear'er, n., personne qui écoute, qui entend, f.; auditeur, assistant, m.

hear'ing, n., (the sense) ouïe ; (of witnesses) audition, (jur.) audience, f. To be hard of — ; avoir l'oreille dure. He said it in my — ; il l'a dit devant moi. Within — ; à portée de la voix. Without a — ; sans l'entendre. To give a — ; donner audience à. To get a — ; se faire écouter.

hark'en (hărk'ène), v.n., écouter.

hark'ener, n., écouteur, m., écouteuse, f.

hear'say (hīr'sé), n., ouï-dire, m.

hearse (heurse), n., corbillard, char funèbre, m. —cloth ; poêle ; drap mortuaire, m.

hearse, v.a., (ant.) mettre dans le cercueil ; (fig.) ensevelir.

heart (hārte), n., cœur ; courage ; (centre) centre, m. ; (nav.) moque, f. By — ; par cœur. To take to — ; prendre à cœur. At — ; au fond. I could not for my — deny it him ; je ne pourrais la lui refuser, s'il y allait de ma vie. To set the — on ; vouloir absolument avoir, prendre en affection, avoir à cœur. To wear one's — upon one's sleeve ; agir et parler à cœur ouvert ; avoir le cœur sur la main (Daudet). To take — of grace ; prendre courage. To one's — 's content ; à cœur joie. With all my — ; de tout mon cœur. With open — ; à cœur ouvert. To find in

one's — ; avoir le courage de ; être tout disposé à, prendre sur soi de. To learn by — ; apprendre par cœur. To have one's — in one's mouth ; avoir la venette. To set the — at rest ; mettre le cœur en repos. To speak to one's — ; parler, ou aller, au cœur. To do one's — good ; réjouir le cœur. To have at — ; avoir à cœur de. To lay to — ; graver dans son cœur ou se graver (quelque chose) dans le cœur. To be out of — ; être découragé. To put in good — ; donner du cœur à ; rendre le courage à. In one's — of —s ; au fin fond du cœur. To break the — of ; briser le cœur de.

heart'-ache (-éke), n., douleur de cœur, f.; chagrin, m. ; affliction, f.

heart'-bond, n., (mas.) parpaing, m., pierre parpaigne, f.

heart'-break (-bréke), n., (ant.) crève-cœur, m.

heart'-breaking, n., déchirement de cœur, m.

heart'-breaking, adj., qui fend le cœur ; navrant.

heart'-broken (-brōk'n), adj., qui a le cœur navré, brisé.

heart'burn (-beurne), n., (med.) ardeur d'estomac, f., aigreurs, f.pl., cardialgie, gastralgie, f.

heart'burning, n., ardeur d'estomac ; (fig.) aigreur, animosité, jalousie, f.

heart'-dear (-dîre), adj., (ant.) chéri.

heart'-ease (-îze), n., paix du cœur, f.

heart'ed (hârtède), adj., doué d'un cœur. Broken- — ; qui a le cœur navré, brisé. Good- — ; qui a bon cœur. Hard- — ; au cœur dur. Light- — ; au cœur gai. Open- — ; au cœur sincère, franc. Tender- — ; tendre. Stout- — ; courageux.

heart'edness, n., (ant.) cœur, m., de cœur, du cœur. Cold- — ; froideur de cœur, insensibilité, f. Hard- — ; dureté de cœur, f.

heart'en (hâr't'n), v.n., (ant.) encourager ; animer.

hearth (harth), n., âtre ; foyer, m. — brush, — broom ; balai de cheminée, balai à main, m. — money ; fouage, m.

hearth'-rug (-reughe), n., tapis de foyer, m.

hearth'stone (-stōne), n., pierre de cheminée, f.

hear'tily (hârt'ili), adv., cordialement ; de bon cœur ; vigoureusement ; (of eating) de bon appétit.

heart'iness (hârt'-), n., sincérité ; cordialité, (of the appetite) force, f.

heart'less (hârt'-), adj., sans cœur ; cruel ; (ant.) lâche.

heart'lessly, adv., sans cœur, cruellement ; (ant.) lâchement.

heart'lessness, n., manque de courage, m.; insensibilité, cruauté, f.

heart'-oak, n., cœur de chêne, m.

heart'-rending, adj., qui fend le cœur, navrant.

heart's'-blood ou **heart'-blood** (-bleude), n., le plus pur de son sang, m.; (fig.) essence, f.

heart'-searching, adj., qui sonde le cœur.

heart's'-ease (hârt's'îze), n., (bot.) pensée sauvage, f.

heart'-sick, adj., qui a la mort dans l'âme ; navré ; soucieux ; qui a le cœur malade.

heart'-sore, n., plaie du cœur, f.; crève-cœur, m.

heart'-string (-strigne), n.pl., fibre, f., nerf, tendon, m., du cœur.

heart'-struck (-streuke), adj., touché au cœur ; frappé au cœur ; consterné ; terrifié ; atterré.

heart'whole, adj., qui a le cœur libre, libre de cœur.

heart'-wounded (-wou'n'dède), adj., blessé au cœur.

heart'y (hârti), adj., du cœur ; sincère ;

cordial ; robuste ; (of meals) abondant, bon, copieux ; (of eaters) fort.   To be hale and — ; *avoir bon pied, bon œil ; avoir des jambes de vingt ans.*

heat (hîte), *n.*, chaleur, ardeur ; (fig.) colère, animosité, fougue, passion, *f.*

heat, *v.a.*, chauffer, échauffer, enflammer.   To get into a — ; *s'animer, s'enflammer, s'emporter.* The deciding — (in a race) ; *la belle, f.*

heat, *v.n.*, chauffer ; s'échauffer, s'enflammer.

heat'ed (hît'ède), *adj.*, chauffé ; échauffé.

heat'er (hît'-), *n.*, personne qui chauffe ; chose qui chauffe, bassine, *f. ;* appareil de chauffage ; fer rouge (d'un fer à repasser), *m.*

heath (hîth), *n.*, lande, bruyère, *f.*

heath'-cock, *n.*, coq de bruyère, *m.*

hea'then (hî-*th*'n), *n.*, (*heathen* ou *heathens*), païen, *m.*, païenne, *f.*

hea'then, *adj.*, païen.

hea'thenish, *adj.*, de païen ; (fig.) barbare, cruel.

hea'thenishly, *adv.*, en païen.

hea'thenism, *n.*, paganisme, *m. ;* (fig.) barbarie, *f.*

heath'er (hèth-), *n.*, (bot.) bruyère, *f.*

heath'y (hîth'i), *adj.*, plein de bruyères.

heave (hîve), *n.*, secousse, *f. ;* soulèvement, *m. ;* élévation ; agitation, *f. ;* (ant.) vomissement ; soupir, *m. ;* (nav.) levée, *f.*

heave, *v.a.*, (*preterit*, Heaved, Hove ; *past. part.*, Heaved, Hoven), lever ; élever ; soulever ; jeter, lancer ; (a sigh) pousser ; (nav.) haler, virer.

heave, *v.n.*, haleter, soulever ; (of the heart) palpiter, battre ; (nav.) haler, virer.   To — to ; (nav.) *mettre en panne.*   To — in sight ; (nav.) *paraître ; être en vue.*

heav'en (hèv'v'n), *n.*, ciel, *m. ;* cieux, *m.pl.* — hued ; *bleu, azur.*   Good —s! *juste ciel !*   To be in the seventh — of delight ; *être aux anges.*

heav'en-born, *adj.*, divin, céleste.

heav'en-bred (-brède), *adj.*, céleste.

heav'enly, *adj.*, céleste, angélique, divin.

heav'enly, *adv.*, d'une manière céleste ; divinement.   — minded ; *plein de pensées divines.*

hea'ver (hîv'-), *n.*, chargeur, porteur, *m.* Coal — ; *porteur de charbon, m.*

heaves (hîv'ze), *n.pl.*, (vet.) pousse, *f.sing.*

heav'ily (hèv'-), *adv.*, pesamment ; lourdement, fortement, violemment ; avec acharnement ; tristement ; d'un air abattu.   To lie, — ; hang, — ; *être à charge ; peser lourdement* **sur.**

heav'iness (hèv'-), *n.*, pesanteur ; lourdeur, *f. ;* poids, *m. ;* (fig.) tristesse, *f.*, abattement, *m.*

hea'ving (hîv'-), *adj.*, qui se soulève ; soulevé.

hea'ving (hîv'-), *n.*, agitation, *f. ;* (of the sea) soulèvement, *m.*

heav'y (hèv'-), *adj.*, lourd, pesant ; (of the sea) gros ; (of the pavement) gras ; (fig.) triste ; (vet.) poussif. — cavalry ; *grosse cavalerie,f.* — road ; *mauvais chemin, m.* — task ; *tâche difficile, f.* — crop ; *récolte abondante, f.* — spar ; *barytine, f.* — armed ; *pesamment armé.* — gaited ; *qui marche à pas lourds, à pas pesants.* — handed ; *qui a la main lourde ; maladroit, gauche.* — headed ; *stupide, lourd, assommant.* — laden ; (fig.) *qui porte un lourd fardeau.* — father ; (theat.) *père noble.*

hebdom'adal ou **hebdom'adary**, *adj.*, hebdomadaire.

He'braism (hî-bra-iz'm), *n.*, hébraïsme, *m.*

He'brew (hî-brou), *n.*, Hébreu ; Israélite, *m.*, *f. ;* (language) hébreu, *m.*

He'brew, *adj.*, hébraïque ; hébreu ; israélite.

hec'atomb (hèk'a-toume), *n.*, hécatombe, *f.*

heck'le (hèk'k'l), *v.a.*, sérancer ; (at public meetings) fatiguer de questions, harasser.

heck'le, *n.*, séran, *m.*

heck'ler, *n.*, séranceur, *m.*

hec'tic ou **hec'tical**, *adj.*, hectique ; étique.

hec'togram ou **hec'togramme**, *n.*, hectogramme, *m.*

hec'tolitre, *n.*, hectolitre, *m.*

hec'tometre (-mi'tr), *n.*, hectomètre, *m.*

hec'tor (-teur), *n.*, fendant ; fier-à-bras ; matamore, *m.*

hec'tor, *v.n.*, faire le fendant.

hec'tor, *v.a.*, malmener, bousculer, maltraiter ; tourmenter, agacer.

hedge (hèdje), *n.*, haie, *f.* —-berry ; *merisier, m.* —-hyssop ; *gratiole ; herbe-au-pauvre-homme, f.* —-marriage ; *mariage clandestin, m.* — school ; *école en plein air, ⊙école buissonnière, f.*

hedge, *v.a.*, entourer d'une haie ; border.   To — a bet ; *parier pour et contre.*   To — in ; *enfermer ; renfermer ; entourer, encombrer.*

hedge, *v.n.*, se cacher ; bouder ; parier pour et contre.

hedge'bill ou **hedg'ing-bill**, *n.*, serpe, *f. ;* croissant, *m.*

hedge'hog (-hoghe), *n.*, hérisson, *m.* —-thistle ; *cactus, m.*

hedge'-knife, *n.*, serpette, *f.*

hedge'-pig, *n.*, jeune hérisson, *m.*

hedg'er, *n.*, faiseur de haies, *m.*

hedge'shears, **hedge'scissors**, *n.pl.*, sécateur, *m.*

hedge'sparrow (-rô), *n.*, fauvette d'hiver, *f. ;* traîne-buissons, *m.*

heed (hîde), *n.*, attention, *f. ;* soin, *m.*   To give — ; *faire attention à.*   To take — ; *prendre garde.*

heed, *v.a.n.*, observer, écouter ; faire attention à, prendre garde à.

heed'ful (-foule), *adj.*, attentif, vigilant, prudent, circonspect.

heed'fully, *adv.*, attentivement ; avec soin.

heed'fulness, *n.*, attention, vigilance, *f. ;* soin, *m.*

heed'less, *adj.*, étourdi, inattentif, insouciant.

heed'lessly, *adv.*, sans soin, négligemment ; inconsidérément, étourdiment, par mégarde.

heed'lessness, *n.*, inattention, négligence, étourderie, *f.*

heel (hîl), *n.*, talon ; éperon, *m.*   To be at, *ou* upon, the —s ; *être sur les talons* **de**, *être aux talons* **de** ; *être aux trousses* **de** ; *poursuivre vivement ; serrer de près.*   To be down, *ou* out, at —, *traîner la savate.*   Down at the —s ; (of shoes) *éculés.*   To cool the —s ; *faire antichambre, faire le pied de grue.*   To go —s over head ; *faire un saut périlleux, faire la culbute.*   To lay by the —s ; *enchaîner, mettre aux fers.*   To show one's —s ; *prendre la fuite.*   To take to one's —s ; *s'enfuir ; jouer des talons, prendre ses jambes à son cou.* To tread upon any one's —s ; *marcher sur les talons de quelqu'un.*

heel, *v.n.*, danser ; (nav.) avoir un faux côté.   To — over ; (nav.) *donner à la bande, être à la bande.*

heel, *v.a.*, mettre un talon à ; (a cock) armer.

heeled, *adj.*, à talons.

heel'-piece (-pîce), *n.*, bout ; talon, *m.*

heft (hèfte), *n.*, (ant.) poids, manche, *m.*

hegem'ony, *n.*, hégémonie, *f.*

heg'ira (hèdj'i-ra *ou* hi-dji-ra), *n.*, hégire, *f.*

heif'er (hèf'-), *n.*, génisse, taure, *f.*

heigh/ho ! (haï'hô), *int.*, ho ! ah !

height (haïte), *n.*, élévation, hauteur, *f. ;* (fig.) plus haut point, comble, faîte, apogée ; (centre) fort, cœur, *m.*   The — of presumption ; *le comble de la présomption.*

heigh'ten (haï't'n), *v.a.*, relever, rehausser, embellir, orner ; accroître, augmenter ; rendre plus évident.

hei'nous (hé-), *adj.*, odieux, affreux, atroce.

hei'nously, *adv.*, odieusement, affreusement, horriblement, atrocement, avec atrocité.

hei'nousness, *n.*, atrocité, énormité, *f.*

heir (ère), n., héritier; successeur, m. — apparent; héritier présomptif, m. — at law; héritier légitime, m.

heir'ess, n., héritière, f.

heir'less, adj., sans héritier.

heir'loom (-loume), n., meuble de famille, m.

heir'ship, n., hérédité, qualité d'héritier, f.

he'liac (hî-li-) ou **heli'acal** (hî-laï-), adj., héliaque.

heliocen'tric ou **heliocen'trical** (hî-), adj., héliocentrique.

he'liograph, n., héliographe, m.

heliog'raphy, n., héliographie, f.

he'lioscope (hî-li-o-scôpe), n., hélioscope, m.

he'liotrope (hî-li-o-trôpe), n., (bot. min.) héliotrope, m.

he'lix (hî-likse), n., (helices) (math.) hélice, f.; (anat.) (zoöl.) limaçon, m.; hélice, f.

hell, n., enfer, m.; (fig.) tripot, m. — born; infernal.

hell'-cat, n., furie, harpie, vieille sorcière, f.

hel'lebore (-li-bôre), n., (bot.) ellébore, m.

Hellen'ic (hèl-lè'n'-), adj., hellénique.

Hel'lenism, n., hellénisme, m.

Hel'lenist, n., helléniste, m.

hell'-hound (-haou'n'de), n., chien de l'enfer; (fig.) tison d'enfer, m.

hell'ish, adj., infernal, d'enfer.

hell'ishly, adv., infernalement.

hell'ishness, n., caractère infernal, m.

helm, n., timon, gouvernail, m.; barre, f. Man at the —; l'homme à la barre. To be at the —; être au timon; (fig.) être à la tête des affaires. To answer her —; (of a ship) gouverner.

hel'met (-mète), n., casque, m.

helms'man (hèlm'z'ma'n), n., timonier, m.

hel'ot, n., (a Spartan slave) ilote, m.

help, n., aide, assistance, f.; secours; remède, m.; ressource, f.; concours, m. — ! au secours! To cry for —; crier au secours. With the — of; au moyen de. There's no — for it; il le faut; c'est inévitable.

help (hèlpe), v.a., aider, secourir, assister, empêcher; (at table) servir. I cannot — it; je n'y puis rien; (of feelings) c'est plus fort que moi. How can it be —ed? qu'y faire? que voulez-vous? How can I — it? que voulez-vous que j'y fasse? That won't — us much; cela ne nous servira pas à grand' chose. That won't — us at all; cela ne nous avancera pas du tout. God — you! Dieu te vienne en aide! — yourself and God will — you; aide-toi et le ciel t'aidera. To — forward; avancer; pousser. To — off time; faire passer le temps. To — on; favoriser; pousser à. To — out; tirer d'affaire; aider à sortir. To — to; (table) servir; (to give) procurer. To — up; aider à monter; soutenir; relever. To — over; aider à surmonter, à passer. To — down; aider à descendre.

help, v.n., aider; se défendre, s'empêcher. I cannot — saying; je ne puis m'empêcher de dire.

help'er, n., aide; auxiliaire, m.

help'ful (-foule), adj., secourable; utile.

help'less, adj., sans secours, faible, impuissant; sans ressource, sans défense.

help'lessly, adv., sans secours; faiblement; sans ressource.

help'lessness, n., faiblesse, impuissance, f.; abandon, m., misère, f. Around this —; autour de cette misère. The — of the limbs; la misère des membres (V. Hugo).

help'mate, n., aide, compagnon, m., compagne, f.

hel'ter-skel'ter, adv., pêle-mêle, sens dessus dessous.

helve, n., manche de hache; (metal.) martinet, m. —-hammer; martinet, m. To throw the — after the hatchet; jeter le manche après la cognée.

helve, v.a., emmancher une hache.

helved, adj., à manche.

Helvet'ic, adj., helvétique.

hem (hème), n., ourlet; bord, m.

hem, v.a., ourler; border. To — in; enfermer; entourer, cerner.

hem, int., hem!

hem, v.n., faire hem.

he'matite (hî'm'a-taïte), n., (min.) hématite, f.

hemat'ocele (hè-ma-to-cîle), n., (surg.) hématocèle, f.

hemato'sis (hî-ma-to-ciss), n., (anat.) hématose, f.

hemerocal'lis (hèm'i-), n., (bot.) hémérocalle, f.

hem'i (hè-mi), prefixe grec ἡμί, demi, semi.

hem'icycle (-çaï'k'l), n., hémicycle, m.

hem'iplegy (-plèdj'i), n., (med.) hémiplégie, f.

hemip'tera (hi-mip-tira), n.pl., (ent.) hémiptères, m.pl.

hem'isphere (hèm'i-sfîre), n., hémisphère, m.

hemispher'ic ou **hemispher'ical**, adj., hémisphérique.

hem'istich (hèm'is'tike), n., hémistiche, m.

hem'lock (hèm'-), n., (bot.) ciguë, f.

hemop'tysis (hi-mop-ti-ciss), n. V. **hæmop'tysis**.

hem'orrhage (hèm'or-'radje), n., hémorragie, f.

hemorrhoi'dal (-roïd'-), adj., hémorroïdal.

hem'orrhoids (-roïd'ze), n.pl., hémorroïdes, f.pl.

hemp (hè'm'pe), n., (bot.) chanvre, m.; (fig.) corde, f. — -nettle; galéopsis, m.

hemp'-comb (-côme), n., séran, m.

hemp'-dresser (-drèss'-), n., séranceur, chanvrier, m.

hemp'en (hèm'p'n), adj., de chanvre.

hemp'-field (-fîlde), n., chènevière, f.

hemp'-seed (-sîde), n., chènevis, m.

hem'-stitch, v.a., ourler à jour.

hen (hène), n., poule; (of birds) femelle, f.

hen'-canary, n., serine, f.

hen'bane (hè'n'-), n., (bot.) jusquiame, f.

hence (hè'n'sse), adv., d'ici; (for this reason) de là; loin d'ici; dorénavant. A week —; dans huit jours.

henceforth', **hencefor'ward** (-forth), adv., désormais; dorénavant, à l'avenir.

hench'man, n., écuyer, valet; (fig.) partisan, m.

hen'-coop (-coupe), n., cage à poule, mue, f.

hendec'agon (hè'n'dèk-'), n., (geom.) endécagone, hendécagone, m.

hendecasyllab'ic (hè'n'dèk'-), adj., hendécasyllabe, hendécasyllabique.

hendecasyl'lable, n., hendécasyllabe, m.

hen-heart'ed (-hârt'ède), adj., lâche, poltron.

hen'-house (-haouce), n., poulailler, m.

hen'-parrot, n., perruche, f.

hen'-pecked (-pèk'te), adj., gouverné par sa femme, qui se laisse mener par le nez. A — husband; un jocrisse, m.

hen'-pheasant, n., faisane, f.

hen'-roost (-rouste), n., juchoir, m.

hepat'ic ou **hepat'ical** (hè-), adj., hépatique.

hep'atite (hèp'a-taïte), n., (min.) hépatite, f.

hepati'tis (-taï-tice), n., (med.) hépatite, inflammation du foie, f.

hep'tagon (hèp'ta-gone), n., (geom.) heptagone, m.

heptan'dria (hèp'-), n., (bot.) heptandrie, f.

hep'tarchy (hèp'târ-ki), n., heptarchie, f.

her (heure), pron., (person.) elle, la, lui; (possess.) son, sa, ses; (demonst.) celle, f.

her'ald (hèr'-), n., héraut; messager; avant-coureur; précurseur, m.

her'ald, v.a., proclamer, annoncer. To — into; introduire dans. To — in; (of the seasons) annoncer.

heral'dic, *adj.*, héraldique.

her'aldry, *n.*, science héraldique, *f.; blason*, *m.*

herb (heurbe), *n.*, herbe, *f.* Pot —s; *herbes potagères*, *f.pl.* Sweet —s; *herbes fines*, *f.pl.*

herba'ceous (-bé-sheusse), *adj.*, herbacé.

her'bage (-bèdje), *n.*, herbage, pâturage, *m.*

her'bal (heurbal), *n.*, herbier, *m.*

her'bal, *adj.*, des herbes.

her'balist, *n.*, herboriste, *m.*

herba'rium (heur-bé-rieume), *n.*, (*herbariums*) (bot.) herbier, *m.*

herbes'cent (heur'-), *adj.*, herbeux.

herbiv'orous, *adj.*, herbivore.

herb'orist, *n.*, (ant.) herboriste, *m.*

herboriza'tion (heur-bo-ri-zé-), *n.*, herborisation, *f.*

her'borize (heur-bo-raïze) *ou* **herbarize** (heurba-raïze), *v.n.*, herboriser.

her'bous (heurb'-) (ant.) *ou* **herb'y**, *adj.*, herbu, herbeux.

herb'-shop (-shope), *n.*, herboristerie, boutique d'herboriste, *f.*

herb'woman (heurb'woum'a'n),*n.*, herbière,*f.*

hercu'lean (hèr-kiou-li-), *adj.*, herculéen, d'Hercule.

herd (heurde), *n.*, troupeau, *m.; troupe* ; (of deer) herde, *f.* The common, *ou* vulgar, —; *le commun, le vulgaire*, *m.*

herd, *v.n.*, vivre en sociétés ; **vivre en troupes** ; s'associer.

herds'man (heurdz'-), *n.*, pâtre, *m.*

here (hïre), *adv.*, ici ; par ici. —by ; *tout près*. The little boy —; *le petit garçon que voici.* — and there ; *çà et là ; par ci par là.* — below ; *ici-bas.* — 's my point ; *voici le point où je veux venir.* — 's for you ; *voici quelque chose pour vous.* — 's to you ; *à votre santé.* It is neither — nor there ; *nous voilà loin de la question.* — he comes ; *le voici qui vient.* — they are ; *les voici ; les voilà.* —! *présent !*

here'about (-abaoute) *ou* **here'abouts** (-abaoutse), *adv.*, par ici ; près d'ici ; ici près.

hereaf'ter, *adv.*, désormais, dorénavant ; ci-après ; dans la vie future.

hereaf'ter, *n.*, vie future, *f. ;* l'autre monde, *m.*

hereat', *adv.*, à ceci, à cela ; de ceci, de cela.

here'by (-baïe), *adv.*, par ce moyen, par là ; par ceci ; par la présente ; (jur.) par les présentes ; par le présent acte.

heredit'ament (hèr'-i-), *n.*, (jur.) bien, héritage, *m.*

hered'itarily (hi-rèd'-), *adv.*, héréditairement.

hered'itary (hi-rèd'-), *adj.*, héréditaire.

hered'ity, *n.*, atavisme, *m.*

herein' (hïr'-), *adv.*, en ceci ; ici ; ci-inclus. —after ; (in a document) *désormais ; plus loin.*

hereof' (hïr'ove), *adv.*, de ceci, de cela, de là, en, d'où.

hereon' (hïr'-), *adv.*, là-dessus ; sur ceci, sur cela.

here'siarch (hè-rï-zi-ârke), *n.*, hérésiarque, *m.*

here'siarchy (-ki), *n.*, principale hérésie, *f.*

her'esy (hèr'i-ci), *n.*, hérésie, *f.*

her'etic (hèr'i-), *n.*, hérétique, *m.f.*

heret'ical, *adj.*, hérétique.

heret'ically, *adv.*, en hérétique.

hereto' (hïr-tou) *ou* **hereunto'** (hïr-eu'n'tou,), *adv.*, à ceci, à cela ; jusqu'à présent ; outre cela ; jusqu'à ce point.

heretofore' (hïr-tou-fôre), *adv.*, jusqu'à présent ; jadis, jusqu'ici.

hereupon' (hïr-eup'-), *adv.*, là-dessus, sur ces entrefaites.

herewith' (hïr-wi*th*), *adv.*, là-dessus ; avec ceci ; ci-joint ; ci-inclus.

her'itable (hèr-it-a-b'l), *adj.*, héritable, dont on peut hériter (par droit de succession).

her'itage (-tèdje), *n.*, héritage, *m.*

hermaph'rodite (-daïte),*n.*,hermaphrodite,*m.*

hermeneu'tics (heur-mi-niou-tikse), *n.*, herméneutique, *f.*

hermet'ic *ou* **hermet'ical** (heur-mèt'-), *adj.*, hermétique.

hermet'ically, *adv.*, hermétiquement.

her'mit (heur-), *n.*, ermite, reclus, *m.*

her'mitage (-'èdje), *n.*, ermitage, *m.*

hermit'ical (hèr'-), *adj.*, d'ermite.

her'nia (heur'-), *n.*, (med.) hernie, *f.*

he'ro (hï-rô), *n.*, (*heroes*) héros, *m.* —worship ; *culte des héros*, *m.*

hero'ic (hi-rô-ike), *adj.*, héroïque.

hero'ical (hï-rô-i-), *adj.*, héroïque.

hero'ically, *adv.*, héroïquement.

heroi-com'ic *ou* **heroi-com'ical** (hi-rô-i-), *adj.*, héroï-comique.

her'oine (hèr-o-ine *ou* hï-), *n.*, héroïne, *f.*

her'oism (hèr-o-iz'me *ou* hï-ro-), *n.*, héroïsme, *m.*

her'on (hèr-), *n.*, (orni.) héron, *m.*

her'pes (heur-pize), *n.*, (med.) herpès, *m. ;* dartre, *f.*

herpet'ic (heur-pè-), *adj.*, (med.) herpétique, dartreux.

herpetol'ogy (heur-pi-tol'o'dji), *n.*, (zoöl.) erpétologie, herpétologie, *f.*

her'ring (hèr-), *n.*, hareng, *m.* — boat ; *touque*, *f.* The —-pond ; *l'Océan.* Red —; *hareng saur.* —woman ; *harengère*, *f.* — fishery ; *harengaison ; pêche du hareng*, *f.*

hers (heurze), *pron.*, (person.) d'elle, à elle ; (possess.) le sien, la sienne, les siens, les siennes. I have nothing of —; *je n'ai rien à elle.* A friend of —; *un de ses amis, une de ses amies.*

herse (heurse), *n.*, (fort.) herse, *f.*

herself' (heur-), *pron.*, elle-même, se, soi, soi-même.

hes'itancy (hèz'-), *n.*, (ant.) hésitation, incertitude, *f.*

hes'itate (hèz'-), *v.n.*, hésiter, balancer. Who —s is lost ; *qui hésite est perdu.*

hes'itating (-tét'-), *adj.*, hésitant, qui hésite.

hes'itatingly, *adv.*, avec hésitation.

hesita'tion (hèz'i-té-), *n.*, hésitation, *f.*

het'eroclite (hèt'-i-ro-claïte), *n.*, mot hétéroclite, *m. ;* (ant.) chose hétéroclite, *f.*

heteroclit'ic *ou* **heteroclit'ical** (-clit'-), *adj.*, (ant.) hétéroclite.

het'erodox (hèt-eur-), *adj.*, hétérodoxe.

het'erodoxy, *n.*, hétérodoxie, *f.*

heterogene'ity (hèt-i-rô-djî'n'i-), *n.*, hétérogénéité, *f.*

heteroge'neous, **het'erogene**, *ou* **heteroge'neal**, *adj.*, hétérogène.

heteros'cian (hèt-i-rosh'a'n), *n.*, (geog.) hétérosciens, *m.pl.*

hew (hiou), *v.a.*, (*preterit*, Hewed ; *past part.*, Hewn) tailler, couper. To — down ; *abattre, renverser* ; (mil.) *tailler en pièces.*

hew'er, *n.*, (of stone) tailleur ; (of wood) fendeur de bois, bûcheron, *m.*

hew'ing, *n.*, coupe, taille, *f.*

hex'agon (hèks'-), *n.*, hexagone, *m.*

hexag'onal, *adj.*, hexagone. —prism; *prisme hexagonal*, *m.*

hexahe'dron (hèks'a-hï-), *n.*, hexaèdre, *m.*

hexam'eter (hèks'am'i-), *n.*, hexamètre, *m.*

hexamet'rical (hèks'a-), *adj.*, hexamètre.

hexan'dria (hèks'-), *n.*, hexandrie, *f.*

hey ! (hê), *int.*, hé ! hein !

hey'day, *n.*, beaux jours, *m.pl. ;* extravagance, folie, fredaine, escapade, *f.* The — of youth ; *le matin des jours* (V. Hugo).

hey'day ! *int.*, ouais ! hé !

hia'tus (haï-é-), *n.*, brèche, lacune, ouverture, *f. ;* (gram.) hiatus, *m.*

hi'bernate (haï-), *v.n.*, hiverner.

Hiber'nian (haï-beur-), *n.*, Hibernien, *m., Hibernienne, f.*

Hiber'nian, *adj.*, hibernien.

hic'cough (hik-kofe) *ou* **hic'cup** (hik-keupe), *n.*, hoquet, *m.*

hic'cough *ou* **hic'cup**, *v.n.*, avoir le hoquet.

hid'den (hid'd'n), *adj.*, caché, secret ; occulte ; mystérieux, latent.

hide (haïde), *n.*, peau, *f. ;* cuir, *m.*

hide (haïde), *v.n.*, (*preterit*, Hid ; *past part.*, Hid, Hidden) se cacher, se tenir caché.

hide, *v.a.*, cacher ; (in the ground) enfouir ; dérober à la vue ; masquer ; (to beat) rosser. — and seek ; *cache-cache*, *m.*, *cligne-musette*, *f.* To — the face from ; *passer* sur ; *excuser ; pardonner.*

hide'bound (haïde-baou'n'de), *adj.*, (vet.) dont la peau adhère aux muscles ; (fig.) intraitable.

hid'eous (hid'i-), *adj.*, hideux, horrible, affreux.

hid'eously, *adv.*, hideusement, horriblement.

hid'eousness, *n.*, caractère hideux, *m. ;* laideur ; difformité ; horreur, *f.*

hi'der (haïd'-), *n.*, personne qui cache, *f.*

hi'ding (haïd'-), *n.*, coups, *m.pl.*, roulée, raclée, *f.* To give any one a —; (triv.) *tanner le cuir à quelqu'un.*

hie (haïe), *v.n.*, se hâter ; courir ; se rendre à.

hi'erarch (haï-i-rär-ke), *n.*, (ant., ecc.) hiérarque, *m.*

hi'erarchal *ou* **hi'erarchical**, *adj.*, hiérarchique.

hi'erarchy (haï-i-rär-ki), *n.*, hiérarchie, *f.*

hieroglyph'ic (haï-i-ro-), *n.*, hiéroglyphe ; symbole, *m.*

hieroglyph'ic *ou* **hieroglyph'ical**, *adj.*, hiéroglyphique.

hieroglyph'ically, *adv.*, par hiéroglyphes.

hier'ophant (haï-èr-), *n.*, hiérophante, *m.*

hig'gle (hig'g'l), *v.n.*, vendre des denrées dans les rues ; barguigner, marchander.

hig'gledy-pig'gledy (hig-g'l-di-pig-g'l-di), *adv.*, (pop.) pêle-mêle, sens dessus dessous.

hig'gler, *n.*, marchand des rues, regrattier, revendeur, barguigneur, *m.*

high (haïe), *adj.*, haut, élevé, grand ; sublime ; fier, altier ; important ; (of cheekbones) saillant ; (of meat) faisandé. The High Church ; *la haute Église, f.* The Most High ; *le Très-Haut, m.* — price ; *prix élevé, m.* To speak of any one in — terms ; *parler de quelqu'un en termes flatteurs.* —stepping ; *au pas superbement allongé.* — mass ; *grand' messe, f.* —er and —er ; *de plus en plus.* This meat is —; *cette viande est faisandée.* — diet ; *nourriture substantielle, f. ; régime fortifiant, m.* 'T is — time ; *il est grand temps.* To mount the — horse ; *monter sur ses grands chevaux.* — and dry ; *à sec.* — and low ; *grands et petits.*

high, *n.*, haut ; ciel, *m.* From on —; *d'en haut.* On —; *au ciel ; dans les airs.*

high, *adv.*, haut, hautement ; grandement ; très, fort.

high'-born, *adj.*, de haute naissance.

high'-colored, *adj.*, haut en couleur.

high'-crowned, *adj.*, haut de forme.

high'-fed, *adj.*, bien nourri.

high'-flier (-flaï'-), *n.*, (ant.) enthousiaste, *m.*

high'-flown (-flône), *adj.*, fier ; enflé ; (of style) outré, ampoulé.

high'-flying (-flaï'lgne), *adj.*, extravagant.

high'land (-la'n'd), *n.*, pays montagneux, *m.*

high'lander, *n.*, montagnard, *m.*

high'-low (-lô), *n.*, bottine lacée, *f.*

high'ly (haïe'li), *adv.*, hautement ; d'une manière élevée ; grandement, fortement. To speak — of some one ; *parler en termes flatteurs de quelqu'un.* —blamable ; *fort blâmable.*

high'mettled (-mèt't'l'de), *adj.*, plein de feu, fougueux, ardent.

high'-minded (-maï'n'd'ède), *adj.*, ambitieux, altier, fier, magnanime.

high'mindedness, *n.*, élévation, hauteur d'âme ; magnanimité, noblesse, *f.*

high'most (-môste), *adj.*, le plus haut.

high'ness (haïe'nèce), *n.*, hauteur, élévation ; cherté ; (title) Altesse ; (title of the Sultan) Hautesse, *f.*

high'-pressure,, *n.*, haute pression, *f.*

high'-priest, *n.*, grand-prêtre, *m.*

high'-souled, *adj.*, qui a l'âme haute, grande, noble.

high'-sounding, *adj.*, (of style) pompeux ; ronflant.

high'-spirited (-'ède), *adj.*, fier, audacieux, fougueux, plein de courage, plein de cœur.

high'-street, *n.*, grand'rue, *f.*

hight (haïte), *adj.*, (ant.) nommé, appelé.

high'-water (-wô-teur), *n.*, haute marée, *f.* — mark ; *niveau des eaux au-dessus de l'étiage, m.*

high'way (-wé), *n.*, grand chemin ; *m.*

high'wayman (-ma'n), *n.*, voleur de grand chemin, *m.*

high'way robbery, *n.*, vol de grand chemin, *m.*

hilar'ity (haï-), *n.*, hilarité, *f.*

hill, *n.*, montagne, colline, *f. ;* coteau, *m.*, butte, côte, *f.* —wort ; *serpolet, thym bâtard, m.* Up—and down dale ; *par monts et par vaux.*

hill, *v.a.*, (agri.) chausser.

hill'iness, *n.*, montuosité, *f.*

hill'ock, *n.*, monticule, tertre, *m. ;* hauteur, butte, colline, *f.*

hill'y, *adj.*, montagneux, accidenté.

hilt, *n.*, poignée, garde, *f.* Up to the —; *jusqu'à la garde.*

hi'lum (haï-leume), *n.*, (bot.) hile, *m.*

him, *pron.*, (pers.) lui, le ; (demonstr.) celui.

himself', *pron.*, lui-même ; se, soi, soi-même. By —; *seul ; sans aide ; de son propre mouvement, de lui-même.* He thinks —; *il se croit.*

hind (haï'n'de), *n.*, biche, *f. ;* domestique, *m. f. ;* valet de ferme ; paysan, rustre, *m.* —calf ; *jaon, m.*

hind (haï'n'de), *adj.*, de derrière. — legs ; *jambes de derrière, f.pl.*

hind'er (haï'n'd'-), *adj.*, de derrière, postérieur, arrière.

hin'der (hi'n'-), *v.a.*, empêcher, détourner ; gêner ; retarder ; embarrasser, entraver. Frost —s the growth of plants ; *le froid (la gelée) retarde la croissance des plantes.* V. **hamper.**

hin'derance *ou* **hin'drance** (hi'n'-), *n.*, obstacle, empêchement, *m. ;* entrave, *f.*

hin'derer (hi'n'-), *n.*, personne qui empêche ; chose qui empêche, *f.*

hind'ermost (haï'n'd'eur-môste) *ou* **hind'most** (haï'n'd'-môste), *adj.*, dernier.

hinge (hi'n'dje), *n.*, gond, *m. ;* charnière, *f. ;* (fig.) ressort, pivot, *m.*, base, *f.* To be off the —s ; (fig.) *être en désordre, en confusion.* To fly off the —s ; *sortir des gonds, s'emporter.*

hinge, *v.a.*, garnir de gonds ; (fig.) plier, courber.

hinge, *v.n.*, tourner sur, rouler sur. The matter —s on this point ; *l'affaire repose sur ce point.*

hint (hi'n'te), *n.*, allusion indirecte, *f. ;* avis ; demi-mot, *m. ;* insinuation, *f.*, mots couverts, *m.pl. ;* (fig.) aperçu, *m.*, donnée, note, *f.* He understood the —; *il comprit à demi-mot.* To take the —; *comprendre ; entendre à demi-mot.* Broad —; *allusion marquée, insinuation directe, f.* —s on ; *notes sur.*

hint, *v.a.n.*, donner à entendre à, suggérer ; faire allusion à ; faire remarquer à.

hip, *n.*, hanche, *f. ;* (bot.) cynorrhodon, gratte-cul, *m.* To have on the —; *avoir l'avantage sur ; tenir.* If I can catch him once upon the —; *si jamais il tombe en mon pouvoir, si jamais il est à ma merci.* To smite — and thigh ; *défaire, détruire complètement ; anéantir.* — bath ; *bain de siège, m.*

hip (hipe), *v.a.*, déhancher, disloquer.

hip'-bone (-bône), *n.*, (anat.) ischion, *m.*

hip'-gout (-gaoute), *n.*, goutte sciatique, *f.*

hip'-joint (-djoï'n'te), *n.*, (anat.) articulation coxale, *f.*

hippocam'pus, *n.*, (ich.) hippocampe, *m.*

hippocen'taur (hip-po-cè'n'-), *n.*, hippocentaure, commun, *m.*

hip'pocras (-crace), *n.*, hypocras, *m.*

hip'podrome (-drôme), *n.*, hippodrome, *m.*

hip'pogriff, *n.*, hippogriffe, *m.*

hip'polith (-lith), *n.*, (vet.) hippolithe, *f.*

hip'pomane (-méne), *n.*, hippomane, *m.*

hippopot'amus (-meusse), *n.*, (*hippopotami*) hippopotame, *m.*

hip'-roof (-roufe), *n.*, (arch.) croupe, *f.*

hip'shot, *adj.*, déhanché.

hire (haïeur), *n.*, louage, prix de louage; prix de location; loyer; salaire, *m.*, gages, *m.pl.* To let out for —; *louer à volonté* (V. Hugo). On —; *à louage.* The labourer is worthy of his —; (prov.) *toute peine mérite salaire.*

hire, *v.a.*, louer; prendre à louage, embaucher, engager, employer; (mil.) soudoyer. To — one's self out; *se louer, se donner à louage.*

hired (haïeurde), *adj.*, loué, de louage.

hire'ling (haïeur'-), *n.*, personne salariée, *f.*; mercenaire, *m.*

hire'ling, *adj.*, salarié; mercenaire.

hi'rer, *n.*, personne qui loue, *f.*, loueur, *m.*

hi'ring, *n.*, louage, *m.*

hirsute' (hir-sioute), *adj.*, hérissé; velu.

his (hize), *pron.*, (person.) de lui; (possession) à lui; (possess.) son, sa, ses; le sien, la sienne; les siens, les siennes. Those lips of —; *ses lèvres.* — own; *le sien, la sienne, à lui.* A game of — own; *une partie où il est intéressé.*

his'pid, *adj.*, velu; (bot.) hispide.

hiss, *n.*, sifflement; coup de sifflet; sifflet, *m.*

hiss, *v.a.* and *n.*, siffler. To — at; *siffler.*

hiss'ing, *n.*, sifflement; sifflet, *m.*

hiss'ing, *adj.*, sifflant. — sound; *sifflement, bruit strident, m.*

hist! *int.*, chut! psit!

histo'rian (-tô-), *n.*, historien, *m.*

histor'ic *ou* **histor'ical**, *adj.*, historique.

histor'ically, *adv.*, historiquement.

historiog'rapher (-to-), *n.*, historiographe, *m.*

his'tory, *n.*, histoire, *f.*; (relation) historique, *m.*

his'tory-piece(-pîce),*n.*,tableau d'histoire, *m.*

his'trion, *n.*, (ant.) comédien; ⊙histrion, *m.*

histrion'ic (ant.) *ou* **histrion'ical**, *adj.*, du comédien; de la scène; de la comédie; d'histrion.

his'trionism, *n.*, représentation théâtrale, *f.*, jeu de théâtre, *m.*

histrion'ically, *adv.*, en comédien, en histrion.

hit, *n.*, succès, coup, *m.*; chance, trouvaille; (fig.) idée, invention, *f.* Lucky —; *coup heureux, m.* Happy —; *remarque à propos, f.*

hit, *v.a.* and *n.*, (*preterit* and *past part.*, Hit) donner un coup à; frapper, heurter; rencontrer; (fig.) atteindre le but; arriver; s'accorder; réussir; (not to miss) toucher. To — off; *deviner juste.* To — out; *jouer des poings; asséner* (des coups). To — off; (a likeness) *saisir, attraper; imiter parfaitement.* To — with a vengeance; *n'y pas aller de main morte.* To — against; *donner contre.* To — home; *porter coup; frapper juste.* To — upon; *trouver, rencontrer; se ressouvenir de, tomber sur.* To — the right nail on the head; *mettre le doigt dessus.* — or miss; *à tout hasard.* You have — it; *vous y êtes, vous avez mis le doigt dessus.* You have — him; *vous avez touché la corde; vous l'avez piqué au vif.*

hitch, *v.n.*, se trémousser; se démener; se nouer; s'accrocher; s'embarrasser; (man.) s'entrecrocher, se couper.

hitch, *v.a.*, accrocher; (nav.) amarrer.

hitch, *n.*, empêchement, obstacle, *m.*; entrave, *f.*; accroc, *m.*, anicroche, *f.*; (nav.) nœud,

m. Without a —; *sans entrave.* There's a — somewhere; *il y a quelque chose qui cloche.*

hith'er (hith'-), *adv.*, ici, par ici; y. — and thither; *par ci par là; çà et là.*

hith'er, *adj.*, de ce côté-ci; en deçà; le plus rapproché; citérieur.

hith'ermost (-môste), *adj.*, le plus proche.

hith'erto (-tou), *adv.*, jusqu'ici, jusqu'à présent, jusqu'alors.

hith'erward (-wôrd) *ou* **hith'erwards** (-wôrdze), *adv.*, de ce côté-ci.

hive (haïve), *n.*, ruche, *f.*; essaim, *m.*

hive, *v.a.*, mettre dans une ruche.

hive, *v.n.*, vivre dans la même ruche; vivre ensemble.

hive'-bee, *n.*, abeille de ruche, *f.*

hives (haïv'ze), *n.*, (med.) varicelle pustuleuse, *f.*

ho *ou* **hoa!** *int.*, hé! ho!

hoar (hôre), *adj.*, blanc, blanchi, chenu.

hoard (hôrde), *n.*, monceau, amas; magot, trésor, *m.*

hoard, *v.a.* and *n.*, amasser, accumuler, entasser, thésauriser.

hoard'er, *n.*, thésauriseur, accapareur, *m.*

hoard'ing, *n.*, accumulation, *f.*

hoard'ing, *adj.*, qui amasse, qui thésaurise.

hoar'-frost (hôr'froste), *n.*, gelée blanche, *f.*

hoar'iness, *n.*, blancheur, *f.*

hoarse (hôrse), *adj.*, enroué, rauque. — throat; *enrouement, m.* To get —; *s'enrouer.*

hoarse'ly, *adv.*, d'une voix enrouée, rauque.

hoarse'ness, *n.*, enrouement, *m.*; raucité, *f.*

hoar'y (hôr'i), *adj.*, blanc; blanchi; aux cheveux gris; chenu; (of frost) couvert de frimas. — headed; *aux cheveux gris.*

hoax (hôkse), *v.a.*, mystifier, attraper.

hoax, *n.*, mystification, *f.*; (false news) canard; (trick) mauvais tour, *m.*, mauvaise plaisanterie, attrape, *f.*

hob, *n.*, (of a fire-grate) plaque, *f.*; (of a wheel) moyeu, *m.*; (peasant) paysan, rustre, manant; (myth.) lutin, *m.*

hob'ble (hob'b'l), *n.*, clochement, *m.*; (fig.) difficulté, nasse, *f.*, embarras, pétrin, *m.* To get into a —; *se mettre dans le pétrin.*

hob'ble, *v.n.*, clocher, clopiner; marcher avec des béquilles; aller clopin-clopant.

hob'ble, *v.a.*, mettre dans l'embarras, entraver.

hob'by, *n.*, cheval de bois; dada, *m.*, (favorite pursuit) marotte, *f.*

hob'by-horse, *n.*, cheval de bois, dada, *m.*; (favorite pursuit) marotte, *f.*

hob'goblin (-gob'line), *n.*, lutin, spectre, fantôme, *m.*

hob'like (-laïke), *adj.*, en paysan, en rustre.

hob'nail (-néle), *n.*, clou de fer à cheval, clou à grosse tête; (fig., ant.) paysan, rustre, manant, *m.*

hob'nailed (-nél'de), *adj.*, garni de clous à grosse tête; (fig.) grossier.

hob'nob, *v.n.*, boire avec quelqu'un; trinquer. To — with; (fig.) *être de pair à compagnon avec.*

hob'nob, *adv.*, au hasard; pêle-mêle; à prendre ou à laisser.

Hob'son's-choice, *n.*, choix forcé, *m.* It is —; *c'est à prendre ou à laisser, ou à laisser ou à prendre.*

hock, *n.*, (of a horse) jarret; (wine) vin du Rhin, *m.*

hoc'kle (hoc'k'l), *v.a.*, couper le jarret à.

ho'cus, *v.a.*, (l.ex.) attraper, filouter; droguer, stupéfier.

ho'cus po'cus (hô'keusse po'keusse), *n.*, (ant.) tour de passe-passe, *m.*; jonglerie, filouterie, *f.*

hod, *n.*, (mas.) oiseau, *m.*; auge, *f.*

hodge'-podge, *n.*, salmigondis, hochepot, *m.*

hod'-man, *n.*, aide-maçon, manœuvre, *m.*

hodom'eter, *n.*, odomètre, compte-pas, *m.*

hoe (hô), *n.*, houe, (gard.) binette, *f.*

hoe, *v.a.* and *n.*, houer ; (gard.) biner, sarcler.

ho'er, *n.*, sarcleur, houeur, *m.*

hoe'ing, *n.*, sarclage, houage, *m.*

hog, *n.*, pourceau, cochon, porc, *m.* To go the whole —; (fig.) *aller jusqu'au bout ; ne pas connaître de bornes.*

hogged (hog'de), *adj.*, (nav.) cassé.

hog'gish, *adj.*, de cochon (fig.) grossier.

hog'gishly, *adv.*, en cochon ; grossièrement.

hog'gishness, *n.*, cochonnerie ; gloutonnerie ; (fig.) grossièreté, *f.*

hog'herd (hog'heurde), *n.*, porcher, *m.*

hog'mane (-méne), *n.*, crinière en brosse, *f.*

hogs'head (hog'z'hède), *n.*, demi-pièce (de litres 238), *f.*

hog'sty (hog'staïe), *n.*, porcherie, *f.*

hog'wash (-wôshe), *n.*, lavure d'écuelles ; lavure de vaisselle, *f.*

hoi, *v.n.*, dia ! hue !

hoi'den (hoï'd'n), *n.*, garçonnière, gamine, *f.*

hoi'den, *v.n.*, garçonner, gaminer.

hoi'den *ou* **hoi'denish**, *adj.*, garçonnière, *f.;* (fig.) grossier, mal-appris.

hoist (hoïste), *v.a.*, guinder ; lever, hausser, arborer, hisser.

hoist, *n.*, effort ; (nav.) guindal, (mec.) élévateur, *m.*

hoi'ty-toi'ty ! (hoï-ti-toï-ti), *int.*, bah ! allons donc ! doucement !

hoi'ty-toi'ty, *adj.*, étourdi, irréfléchi, léger.

hold (hôlde), *n.*, action de tenir ; prise, *f. ;* (support) soutien, pouvoir, *m. ;* (custody) garde, serre ; griffe ; (fortress) place forte ; (nav.) cale, *f.;* (mus.) point d'orgue, *m.* To get, to take — of ; *prendre ; saisir ; empoigner ; s'accrocher à ; se saisir de ; s'emparer de ;* (fig.) *trouver, découvrir.* To let go one's —; *lâcher prise ;* lâcher. To have a — on ; *avoir prise* sur. To have — of ; *tenir.* To put in —; (ant.) *mettre en prison.*

hold, *v.a.*, (preterit and past part., Held) tenir ; retenir ; arrêter ; soutenir ; maintenir ; contenir ; garder ; conserver ; considérer comme ; regarder comme ; avoir ; occuper ; jouir de ; célébrer ; (a review) faire passer (la revue à). — ! *tenez ! arrêtez !* To — down ; *retenir, baisser.* To — from ; *tenir* de. To — a wager ; *tenir un pari.* To — fast ; *tenir ferme.* To — together ; *tenir ensemble.* To — one's self ; *se tenir ; se regarder comme.* To — back ; *retenir, arrêter ; cacher, ne pas produire.* To — forth ; *tendre ; avancer ; proposer ; offrir ; promettre ; présenter ; mettre en avant.* To — down ; *maintenir, contenir, retenir.* To — in ; *retenir.* To — off ; *tenir éloigné ; tenir à distance.* To — on ; *continuer de tenir ; persévérer* dans, *tenir bon.* To — out ; *promettre, tendre ; présenter ; offrir ; résister ; supporter ; endurer.* To — up ; *lever ; soulever ; soutenir ; maintenir ; présenter ; exposer.* To — any one to his promise ; *astreindre quelqu'un à tenir sa promesse.* To — one's tongue ; *se taire.* To — one's peace ; *se taire.* To — a candle to the devil ; *assister à,* ou *se prêter à, une turpitude.* To — a candle to any one ; *être le complice de quelqu'un.* He cannot — a candle to him ; (fig.) *il ne le vaut pas, tant s'en faut ;* ou *il n'est rien auprès de lui.* To — one's own ; *se maintenir ; ne pas lâcher prise.* To — over ; *ajourner, détenir ; tenir en suspens.* To — water ; *être étanche ;* (fig.) *souffrir un examen rigoureux.*

hold, *v.n.*, tenir ; se soutenir ; se maintenir ; rester ; durer ; être vrai ; supporter ; endurer. To — fast ; *tenir ferme, avec force.* To — good ; *être vrai ; ne pas se démentir, être juste, être applicable ; s'appliquer* à ; *être valable.* To — together ; *tenir ensemble ; rester uni.* To — back ; *se tenir en arrière, être en retard.* To — forth ; *haranguer ; pérorer ; discourir.* To — in ; *se*

contenir ; se retenir. To — on ; *tenir toujours ; tenir bon ; aller toujours.* To — out ; *tenir bon.* To — up ; *se soutenir ;* (of the rain) *cesser ;* (of the weather) *s'éclaircir.* To — with ; *prendre parti* pour ; *prendre fait et cause* pour ; *être du parti* de.

hold'-all, *n.*, enveloppe de voyage.

hold'back, *n.*, empêchement, obstacle, *m. ;* entrave, *f.*

hold'er, *n.*, personne qui tient ; (thing) chose pour tenir, poignée, anse, *f.*, manche ; (chem.) support ; (possessor) détenteur ; locataire, tenancier ; (com.) porteur, *m.*   [valet, *m.*

hold'fast, *n.*, crampon ; croc ; (tech.)

hold'ing, *n.*, possession ; prise ; influence ; possession, jouissance, occupation, tenure, *f. ;* fermage, *m.*

hole (hôle), *n.*, trou, orifice ; antre, *m. ;* caverne ; ouverture, brèche, *f.* To be put in a —; *être dans une impasse.* To make a — in a pie ; *faire une brèche à un pâté.* A — in one's coat ; *brèche à la reputation, f.* — and corner, *adj.*, *secret, clandestin.* To drive into a —; *mettre dans une impasse ; mettre à quia.* To pick — s in a person's coat ; *critiquer* (quelqu'un) ; *chercher à redire* à *ce que fait* (quelqu'un) ; *blâmer.*

hole, *v.a.*, trouer ; (at billiards) blouser.

hol'idam (hol'i-dame), *n.*, (ant.) la sainte Vierge, *f.*

hol'iday (-dè), *n.*, jour de fête, *m. ;* fête, *f. ;* (schools) congé, campos, *m. pl.*, vacances, *f.pl.* Bank-—; *fête légale.* Home for the —s ; *en vacances.*

hol'iday, *adj.*, de jour de fête, de fête ; de jour de congé, de congé ; de vacances, en vacances.

ho'lily, *adv.*, saintement.

ho'liness, *n.*, sainteté, *f.* His Holiness ; (the Pope) *Sa Sainteté.*

hol'land, *n.*, toile de Hollande, *f.*

hol'lands, *n.*, genièvre de Hollande, *m.*

hollo' (hol'lô), *n.*, huée, *f. ;* holà, *m.*

holloa' (hol'lô), *v.n.*, huer, crier. Do not — before you are out of the wood ; (prov.) *il ne faut pas se moquer des chiens avant d'être hors du bois.*

holloa'! *ou* **hollo'!** (hol'lôa, -lô), *int.*, holà ! hé !

hol'low (-lô), *n.*, creux ; antre, *m. ;* caverne, cavité, fosse, *f.*

hol'low, *adj.*, creux, vide ; (of sound) sourd. — eyes ; *yeux creux, enfoncés dans la tête, m.pl.* —-hearted ; *faux, dissimulé, trompeur.* — square ; (milit.) *carré,* m. —-ware : *batterie de cuisine, f.* — friend ; *faux ami, m.* — defeat ; *défaite complète, f.* He was beaten — ; *il fut battu à plate couture.*

hol'low, *v.a.*, creuser, évider ; courber.

hol'lowness, *n.*, creux, vide, *m. ;* (fig.) fausseté, perfidie, *f.*

hol'ly, *n.*, (bot.) houx, *m.*

hol'ly-grove (-grôve), *n.*, houssaie, *f.*

hol'lyhock, *n.*, alcée ; rose trémière ; passerose, *f.*

hol'ly oak, holm'-oak, *n.*, (bot.) yeuse, *f.*

holm (hôlme), *n.*, îlot ; terrain d'alluvion, *m. ;* terre riveraine, *f. ;* (ant.) chêne vert, *m. ;* yeuse, *f.*

hol'ocaust, *n.*, holocauste, *m.*

hol'ograph, *n.*, (jur.) olographe, *m.*

holothu'ria (-lô-thiou-), *n.*, (zoöl.) holothurie, *f.*

hol'ster, *n.*, fonte (de pistolet), *f.*

ho'ly (hô-), *adj.*, saint, sacré ; bénit. — Ghost ; *le Saint-Esprit.* — land ; *terre sainte, f.* —-water ; *eau bénite, f.* —-week ; *la semaine sainte, f.* — alliance ; *sainte-alliance, f.* — Writ ; *Ecriture Sainte, f.*

hom'age (-èdje), *n.*, hommage, *m.*

hom'ager (-èdj'-), *n.*, hommager, *m.*

home (hôme), *n.*, chez soi ; logis ; foyer domestique ; intérieur, *m. ;* demeure, maison, *f. ; pays, m.* — rule ; *autonomie ; indépendance législative, f.* At — ; *chez soi ; à la maison.* At — day ; *jour de réception.* The long — ; *le dernier gîte.* To feel one's self at — ; *se sentir à son aise.* To be at — in, *ou* with, anything ; *être versé* **dans.** To come — to a person ; *toucher quelqu'un au vif.* To make one's self at — ; *se mettre à son aise ; faire comme si l'on était chez soi ; ne pas se gêner.* — office ; *ministère de l'Intérieur, m.* The nation at — ; *la nation elle-même, la nation chez elle.* To have a — of one's own ; *avoir pignon sur rue.* To bring — to ; *rappeler* **à.** — use ; *consommation intérieure, f.* To bring — to ; *prouver* **contre.** To come — ; *rentrer ; revenir chez soi ; retourner dans son pays.* To strike — ; *porter coup ; frapper juste.* To press — ; *presser fort ; pousser à bout.* The argument went straight — ; *l'argument est allé à son adresse,* ou *droit au fait,* ou *droit au but.* There is no place like — ; (prov.) *il n'y a pas de petit chez soi* ou *à tout oiseau son nid est beau.*

home, *adj.,* de la maison, domestique ; qui porte coup, bon.

home, *adv.,* chez soi, au logis ; à la maison ; dans son pays ; (fig.) directement, vigoureusement.

home'-bound, *adj.,* (nav.) retournant au port, de retour. [tique.

home'bred (-brède), *adj.,* naturel ; domestique.

home'felt (-fèlte), *adj.,* intime, du cœur, intérieur, profondément senti.

home'-keeping (-kîp'-), *adj.,* sédentaire, casanier.

home'-life, *n.,* vie d'intérieur, de famille, *f.*

home'liness, *n.,* caractère domestique, *m. ;* simplicité, grossièreté ; (of the face) sans beauté, *f.*

home'ly, *adj.,* de la maison ; de ménage ; simple ; ordinaire ; commun ; dépourvu de beauté.

home'made (-méde), *adj.,* de ménage ; fait à la maison ; de fabrication indigène. — bread ; *pain de ménage, m.*

home'sick, *adj.,* qui a le mal du pays.

home'-sickness, *n.,* mal du pays, *m. ;* nostalgie, *f.*

home'-speaking (-spîk'-), *n.,* discours énergique, *m.*

home'spun (-speune) *adj.,* fait à la maison, de ménage, grossier ; sans façon ; vulgaire. — cloth ; *drap épais.*

home'stall (-stôl) *ou* **home'stead** (-stède), *n.,* château et dépendances ; lieu de naissance ; domicile originaire, château, manoir, *m. ; ferme, f.*

home'ward (-wôrde), *ou* **home'wards** (-wôrdze), *ou* **home'ward-bound** (-baou'n'de), *adv.,* vers la maison ; vers son pays ; (nav.) de, *ou* au, retour.

hom'icidal (-çaï'-), *adj.,* homicide ; meurtrier.

hom'icide (-çaïde), *n.,* homicide, *m.*

hom'ily, *n.,* homélie, *f. ;* sermon, *m.*

homocen'tric (hô-), *adj.,* (astron.) homocentrique ; (math.) concentrique.

homœopath'ic ou **homœopath'ical** (hô-mi-o-path-i-), *adj.,* homéopathique.

homœop'athist, *n.,* homéopathe, *m.*

homœop'athy, *n.,* homéopathie, *f.*

homoge'neal *ou* **homoge'neous** (-dji-ni-), *adj.,* homogène, semblable.

homogene'ity *ou* **homoge'neousness** (-djini-), *n.,* homogénéité, *f.*

homol'ogous, *adj.,* (geom.) homologue.

hom'onym, *n.,* homonyme, *m.*

homon'ymous, *adj.,* homonyme.

homon'ymy, *n.,* homonymie ; ambiguïté, *f.*

homoph'ony, *n.,* homophonie, *f.*

hone (hône), *n.,* pierre à rasoir, pierre à l'huile, *f.*

hone, *v.a.,* affiler sur la pierre, repasser.

hon'est (on'èste), *adj.,* honnête ; loyal ; probe,

intègre, de bonne foi, sincère. — man ; *homme de bien, honnête homme, m.* An — man's word is as good as his bond ; (prov.) *un honnête homme n'a que sa parole.*

hon'estly, *adv.,* honnêtement ; avec probité ; de bonne foi ; sincèrement.

hon'esty, *n.,* honnêteté, probité, bonne foi, sincérité, loyauté, intégrité, franchise, *f.* — is the best policy ; (prov.) *c'est avec la bonne foi qu'on va le plus loin.*

hon'ey (heu'n'i), *n.,* miel, *m. ;* (pers.) cœur, *m.,* chérie, *f.,* ange, *m.*

hon'ey, *v.a.,* (ant.) mettre du miel **dans,** sucrer avec du miel ; cajoler, amadouer.

hon'ey-bag, *n.,* sac à miel, *m.*

hon'ey-bee, *n.,* abeille, mouche à miel, *f.*

hon'ey-comb (-côme), *n.,* rayon de miel, gâteau de miel, *m.*

hon'ey-cup (-keupe), *n.,* (bot.) nectaire, *m.*

hon'ey-dew (-diou), *n.,* miellat, *m. ;* tabac à fumer, *m.*

hon'eyed (heu'n'ède), *adj.,* emmiellé ; doux ; miellé ; mielleux.

hon'ey-flower (-flaoueur), *n.,* (bot.) grand mélianthe, *m. ;* fleur miellée, *f.*

hon'ey-guide (-gaïde), *n.,* (orni.) coucou indicateur, *m.*

hon'eymoon (-moune), *n.,* lune de miel, *f.*

hon'ey-mouthed, *adj.,* doucereux, mielleux.

hon'eysuckle (-seuc'k'l), *n.,* chèvrefeuille, *m.*

hon'eywort (-weurte), *n.,* (bot.) mélinet, sison, *m.*

hon'orary, *adj.,* honoraire.

hon'or (o'n'or), *n.,* honneur, *m. ;* dignité, estime, (at cards) figure, *f.,* honneur ; (com.) accueil, m. On, ou upon, (one's) — ; *sur l'honneur, en honneur, d'honneur, foi d'homme d'honneur.* Sense of — ; *loyauté, f.* There is — among thieves ; (prov.) *les loups ne se mangent pas entre eux.* — to whom — is due ; (prov.) *à chaque saint sa chandelle* ou *à tout seigneur tout honneur.*

hon'or, *v.a.,* honorer, faire honneur **à ;** glorifier ; (com.) accueillir, faire bon accueil **à.**

hon'orable, *adj.,* honorable, honorifique.

hon'orableness, *n.,* caractère honorable, honneur, *m. ;* honorabilité, *f.*

hon'orably, *adv.,* honorablement.

hon'orer, *n.,* personne qui honore, *f.*

hood (houde), *n.,* coiffe de femme, *f. ;* capuchon, chaperon, *m. ;* (of a carriage) capote, *f.,* soufflet, *m.*

hood, *v.a.,* encapuchonner ; couvrir ; (a hawk) chaperonner.

hood'wink (-wi'gn'ke), *v.a.,* bander les yeux **à ;** (fig.) en imposer **à,** tromper.

hoof (houfe), *n.,* sabot ; ongle, *m.* To beat, *ou* pad, the — ; *battre le pavé.*

hoof'-bound (-baou'n'de), *adj.,* (vet.) encastelé.

hoofed, *adj.,* à sabot, ongulé.

hook (houke), *n.,* crampon, crochet, croc ; (for fishing) hameçon, *m. ;* (sickle) faucille, *f.* — and eye ; *agrafe et porte, f.* By — or by crook ; *d'une manière et d'une autre ; de bric et de broc ; coûte que coûte.* On one's own — ; *pour,* ou à, *son propre compte.*

hook, *v.a.,* accrocher ; agrafer ; prendre à l'hameçon ; attraper. To — it ; (fam.) *déguerpir.*

hooked (houk'te), *adj.,* crochu, recourbé.

hook'edness (houk'èd'-), *n.,* forme crochue ; courbure, *f.*

hook'er, *n.,* (nav.) hourque, *f.*

hook'-nose (-nôze), *n.,* nez aquilin, *m.*

hook'-nosed (-nôz'de), *adj.,* qui a un nez aquilin.

hoop (houpe), *n.,* cerceau ; cercle, *m. ;* (of birds) huppe, *f. ;* (of a wheel) jante, *f. ;* (cry) cri, *m. ;* (for ladies) crinoline, *f.,* cerceau, panier, *m.* — ring ; *bague jonc, bague collier, f.*

hoop, *v.a.,* cercler ; entourer ; garnir de jantes.

hoop, *v.n.*, crier ; pousser des cris.

hoop'er, *n.*, tonnelier, *m.*

hoop'ing-cough (-kŏ'fe), *n.*, coqueluche, *f.*

hoot (houte), *v.a.*, huer.

hoot, *v.n.*, huer. To — at ; *huer.*

hoot *ou* **hoot'ing,** *n.*, huée, vocifération, *f.*, cri, (of night birds) houhou (V. Hugo), *m.*

hop (hope), *n.*, saut, sautillement ; (bot.) houblon, *m.*

hop, *v.a.* and *n.*, houblonner ; faire la cueillette du houblon.

hop, *v.n.*, sautiller ; folâtrer. To — on one leg ; *sauter à cloche-pied.*

hop'-bine, *m.*, sarment de houblon, *m.*

hop'-garden, *n.*, houblonnière, *f.*

hop'-gathering, *n.*, cueillette du houblon, *f.*

hope (hôpe), *n.*, espérance ; attente, *f.* ; espoir, *m.* It is his last — ; *c'est sa planche de salut.* Forlorn — ; (mil.) *enfants perdus, m.pl.* I am in —s that; *j'ai l'espoir que, j'ose espérer que.*

hope, *v.a.*, espérer ; s'attendre à.

hope, *v.n.*, espérer, aimer à croire. I do — to come ; *j'espère bien venir.* I — that ; *j'aime à croire que.*

hope'ful (hôp'foule), *adj.*, de grande espérance ; qui promet beaucoup ; encourageant ; qui ne désespère pas de. Young — ; *jeune viveur, jeune dépensier, m.* To be — of ; *espérer.* To be — that ; *avoir bon espoir que.*

hope'fully, *adv.*, de manière à faire espérer beaucoup ; avec espoir, avec confiance ; avec chance de succès.

hope'fulness, *n.*, bon espoir, *m.* ; apparence de succès ; confiance, *f.*

hope'less, *adj.*, sans espoir, sans chance de succès, désespéré ; inattendu.

ho'per, *n.*, personne qui espère, *f.*

ho'pingly, *adv.*, avec espoir.

hop'per (hop'peur) *n.*, sauteur, *m.*, personne qui sautille ; (of a mill) trémie, *f.* ; (agri.) semoir, *m.*

hop'ping, *n.*, action de sauter à cloche-pied ; cueillette du houblon, *f.*

hop'-pole (-pôle), *n.*, perche à houblon, *f.*, échalas, *m.*

hop'scotch (hop'scotshe), *n.*, marelle, *f.*

ho'ral *ou* **ho'rary** (hŏ-), *adj.*, horaire.

horde (hôrde), *n.*, horde, *f.*

hore'hound (hŏr'haou'n'de), *n.*, (bot.) marrube blanc, *m.*

hori'zon (ho-raï'-), *n.*, horizon, *m.* On the — ; *à l'horizon.*

horizon'tal (hor-i-), *adj.*, horizontal.

horizon'tally, *adv.*, horizontalement.

horn, *n.*, corne, *f.* ; (of stags) bois, *m.* ; (ent.) antenne, *f.* ; (mus.) cor, cornet, *m.* ; (cup) coupe, *f.* French — ; *cor d'harmonie* ; *cor, m.* — of plenty ; *corne d'abondance, f.* To draw in one's —s ; *mettre un frein* à, *ou réprimer son ardeur* ; *mettre de l'eau dans son vin* ; *en rabattre.*

horn'beam (-bîme), *n.*, (bot.) charme, *m.*

horn'-beetle *ou* **horn'-bug,** *n.*, cerf-volant, *m.*

horn'blende, *n.*, (min.) actinote, *m.*, amphibole, *f.*

horn'-blower, *n.*, sonneur de cor, *m.*

horn'book (-bouke), *n.*, abécédaire, *m.*

horned (horn'de), *adj.*, cornu, à cornes.

horned'-owl (horn'd'aoul), *n.*, (orni.) duc, *m.*

hor'net (hor-nète), *n.*, (ent.) frelon, *m.* To bring a —'s nest about one's ears ; *se mettre dans un guêpier.*

horn'fish, *n.*, (ich.) brochet de mer, *m.*, orphie, *f.*

horn'pipe (-païpe), *n.*, cornemuse ; danse au son de la cornemuse, *f.*

horn'work (-weurke), *n.*, (fort.) ouvrage à corne, *m.*

horn'wort (-weurte), *n.*, (bot.) cornifle, *m.* ; mille-feuille cornue, *f.*

horn'y, *adj.*, calleux ; de corne.

horolog'ical (hor-o-lodj'-), *adj.*, d'horloge; d'horlogerie.

horol'ogy (-dji), *n.*, horlogerie, *f.*

hor'oscope (-scŏpe), *n.*, horoscope, *m.*

hor'rible (hor'ri-b'l), *adj.*, horrible, affreux.

hor'ribleness, *n.*, caractère affreux, *m.* ; horreur, *f.*

hor'ribly, *adv.*, horriblement; affreusement.

hor'rid (hor'ride), *adj.*, affreux, horrible.

hor'ridness, *n.*, horreur, *f.* ; caractère horrible, *m.*

horripila'tion (hor-ri-pi-lé-), *n.*, (med.) horripilation, *f.*

hor'ror, *n.*, horreur, *f.* The —s ; (med.) *delirium tremens, m.*

hor'ror-strick'en (-strick'n) *ou* **horror-struck** (-streuke), *adj.*, frappé d'horreur.

horse, *n.*, cheval, *m.* ; (milit.) cavalerie, *f.* ; (tech.) chevalet, séchoir, *m.* Spare, *ou* extra, — ; *cheval haut le pied, cheval de rechange, m.* Led — ; *cheval de main, m.* Towel — ; *porte-serviettes, m.* Master of the — ; *grand écuyer, m.* To flog a dead — ; *chercher à ressusciter un mort.* To take — ; *monter à cheval.* To get on —back ; *monter en selle.* To ride on —back ; *aller à cheval.* To ride the high — ; *monter sur ses grands chevaux.* It is a good — that never stumbles ; *il n'est si bon cheval qui ne bronche.* That's a — of another color ; *c'est une autre paire de manches.* To send a — to grass ; *mettre un cheval au vert.*

horse, *v.a.*, monter un cheval ; porter ; (of horses) saillir, couvrir.

horse'-ant, *n.*, (ent.) fourmi fauve, *f.*

horse'-artillery, *n.*, artillerie à cheval, *f.*

horse'back, *n.*, dos de cheval, *m.* On — ; *à cheval.*

horse'bean (-bîne), *n.*, petite fève, féverole, *f.*

horse'block, *n.*, montoir, *m.*

horse'-box, *n.*, wagon-écurie, *m.*

horse'boy (-boï), *n.*, valet d'écurie, palefrenier, *m.*

horse'breaker (-brék'-), *n.*, personne qui dresse les chevaux, *f.* ; piqueur, écuyer, *m.*

horse'chestnut (-tshès'neute), *n.*, marron d'Inde ; (tree) marronnier d'Inde, *m.*

horse'cloth (-clôth), *n.*, housse, *f.*

horse'dealer, *n.*, maquignon, *m.*

horse'-dung, *n.*, crottin de cheval, *m.*

horse'-exercise, *n.*, équitation, *f.*

horse'-fair, *n.*, foire aux chevaux, *f.*

horse'fly (-flaïe), *n.*, taon, *m.*

horse'-gin, *n.*, (metal.) manège, *m.*

horse'guard (-gârde), *n.*, garde à cheval, *m.*

horse'guards (-gârd'ze), *n.pl.*, gardes à cheval, *m.pl.* ; (England) état-major général, *m.*

horse'hair (-hère), *n.*, crin de cheval, *m.*

horse'laugh (-lâfe), *n.*, rire outré, gros rire, rire grossier, *m.*

horse'leech (-lîtshe), *n.*, sangsue de cheval, haemopis chevaline, *f.* ; (ant.) maréchal-ferrant, vétérinaire, *m.*

horse'litter (-lit'teur), *n.*, litière, *f.*

horse'load (-lôde), *n.*, charge d'un cheval, *f.*

horse'man, *n.*, cavalier, écuyer, *m.* To be a good — ; *être bon écuyer* ; *bien monter à cheval.*

horse'manship, *n.*, manège, *m.* ; équitation, *f.*

horse'path (-pâth), *n.*, (towing) chemin de halage, *m.* ; route cavalière, *f.*

horse'pick, *n.*, cure-pied, *m.*

horse'play, *n.*, jeu de mains, *m.* ; raillerie grossière, *f.*

horse'pond (-po'n'de), *n.*, abreuvoir, *m.*

horse'-power, *n.*, force de chevaux, *f.*

horse'-race, *n.*, course de chevaux, *f.*

horse'-radish, *n.*, raifort, *m.*

horse'shoe (-shou), *n.*, fer de cheval ; fer à cheval, *m.* *adj.*, en fer à cheval.

horse'shoeing, *n.*, ferrage des chevaux, *m.*

horse′stealer (-stîl′-), *n.*, voleur de chevaux, *m.*

horse′-tail, *n.*, (bot.) queue-de-cheval, *f.*

horse′-trainer, *n.*, dresseur de chevaux, *m.*

horse′-trappings (-trap′pign′ze), *n.pl.*, harnais, *m.*

horse′whip (-hwipe), *n.*, fouet, *m.;* cravache, *f.*

horse′whip, *v.a.*, donner des coups de cravache à.

horse′woman (-woum′a′n), *n.*, cavalière, écuyère, *f.*

hor′tatory, *adj.*, (ant.) exhortatoire, d'exhortation.

horticult′ural (-keult′iour′-), *adj.*, d'horticulture.

hor′ticulture (-keult′ioure), *n.*, horticulture, *f.*

horticult′urist (-keult′iour′-), *n.*, horticulteur, *m.*

hosan′na (ho-za′n′-), *n.*, hosanna, *m.*

hose (hôze), *n.*, bas, *m.pl.;* (pipe) boyau, tuyau élastique, *m.;* (nav.) manche, *f.;* (dress) bas de chausses, caleçon, bas, *m.*

ho′sier (hô-jeur), *n.*, linger, bonnetier, *m.*

ho′siery (hô-jeur′i), *n.*, bonneterie, lingerie, *f.*

hos′pitable (-ta-b′l), *adj.*, hospitalier.

hos′pitably, *adv.*, avec hospitalité.

hos′pital, *n.*, hôpital ; hospice, *m.* Chelsea —; *Hôtel des Invalides*, *m.* — attendant ; *infirmier*, *m.*

hospital′ity, *n.*, hospitalité, *f.*

host (hôste), *n.*, hôte ; hôtelier, aubergiste, *m.;* armée, foule, multitude ; (c.rel.) hostie, *f.* He who reckons without his — must reckon twice ; *qui compte sans son hôte compte deux fois.*

hos′tage (hôst′èdje), *n.*, otage ; (fig.) gage, *m.*

hos′tel (hôs′tèle), *n.*, (ant.). *V.* **hotel.**

hos′telry (hôs′tèl-), *n.*, (l.u.) hôtel, *m.;* auberge, hôtellerie, *f.*

host′ess (hôst′-), *n.*, hôtesse, *f.*

hos′tile, *adj.*, hostile, ennemi, *f.;* (fig.) opposé à, contraire à.

hos′tilely, *adv.*, hostilement, d'une manière hostile.

hostil′ity, *n.*, hostilité, *f.*

host′ler (os′leur), *n. V.* **ostler.**

hot, *adj.*, chaud, ardent, brûlant ; piquant, épicé ; (fig.) vif, violent, échauffé. — fight ; *combat acharné*, *m.* — argument ; *discussion animée*, *f.* To be —; *avoir chaud.* To grow —; *s'échauffer.* To make —; *chauffer.* To be burning —; *brûler, être brûlant.* — baths ; *bains chauds, thermes, m.pl.* Boiling —; *tout bouillant.* To be in — water ; *être dans le pétrin.* — as a peppercorn ; *vif comme la poudre.*

hot′bed (-bède), *n.*, couche ; serre chaude, *f.* — of treason ; *foyer de trahison*, *m.*

hot′-blooded, *adj.*, excitable, irritable, passionné.

hot′brained (-bré′n′de) *ou* **hot′headed** (-hèd′ède), *adj.*, violent, fougueux, emporté.

hotch′potch, *n.*, hochepot, salmigondis, pot pourri, *m.*

hot-cock′les (-kok′k′l′ze), *n.pl.*, (game) mainchaude, *f.*

hotel′ (hô-tèl), *n.*, hôtel, *m.;* hôtellerie, auberge, *f.* — keeper ; *maître d'hôtel, hôtelier, m., maîtresse d'hôtel*, *f.*

hot′house (-haouce), *n.*, serre chaude, *f.*

hot′ly, *adv.*, avec chaleur, chaudement ; vivement.

hot′-mouthed (-maouth′de), *adj.*, entêté, obstiné, opiniâtre.

hot′ness, *n.*, chaleur ; passion, violence, fureur, *f.*

hot′press (-prèce), *v.a.*, presser à chaud ; (cloth) catir ; (paper) satiner.

hot′spur (-speur), *n.*, (ant.) homme violent, fougueux, *m.*

hough (hoke), *n.*, jarret (of animals), *m.*

hough (hoke), *v.a.*, couper les jarrets **à.**

hound (haou′n′de), *n.*, chien de chasse, chien courant, *m.* —s tongue ; *langue-de-chien, herbe-au-diable*, *f.*

hound, *v.a.*, chasser au chien courant ; (fig.) exciter, presser, pousser.

hound′fish, *n.*, aiguillat, squale, chien de mer, *m.*

hour (aou′eur), *n.*, heure, *f.* An — and a half ; *une heure et demie.* Half an —; *une demi-heure.* An — ago, an — since ; *il y a une heure.* Within an —, an — hence ; *dans une heure.* In a lucky —; *dans un moment heureux.* At the eleventh —; *au dernier moment.* To keep good —s; *rentrer, se coucher, de bonne heure.* To keep bad —s ; *rentrer, se coucher, tard, à des heures indues.*

hour′-glass (-glâce), *n.*, sablier, *m.*

hour′-hand (-ha′n′de), *n.*, aiguille des heures, petite aiguille, *f.*

hour′ly (aou′eur′li), *adj.*, fréquent, continuel, d'heure en heure ; d'un instant à l'autre, à tout moment.

hour′ly, *adv.*, à toute heure, à tout moment, d'heure en heure.

hour′-plate, *n.*, cadran, *m.*

house (haouce), *n.*, maison, *f.;* bâtiment, logis, *m.;* demeure, habitation ; (family) race, famille ; (thea.) salle, *f.* A religious — ; *une maison religieuse, un couvent, un monastère.* A nobleman's — ; *un hôtel.* The — of lords ; *la chambre des pairs.* The — of commons; *la chambre des communes.* The two —s of parliament ; *les deux chambres.* A town- — ; *une maison de ville, un hôtel.* A country- — ; *une maison de campagne.* To keep a good — ; *tenir bonne table.* To keep open — ; *tenir table ouverte.* — of call; *bourse du travail*, *f.* — of correction ; *prison*, *f., pénitencier*, *m.* To bring down the — ; *recevoir une ovation au théâtre ; exciter les applaudissements de tout l'auditoire.* From — to — ; *de maison en maison.* To keep — ; *tenir maison.* To keep the — ; *garder la maison.* — of cards ; *château de cartes*, *m.* — agent ; *agent de location*, *m.* — sparrow ; *moineau*, *m.* — steward ; *intendant ; maître d'hôtel*, *m.* — surgeon ; *interne des hôpitaux*, *m.* A man's — is his castle ; *charbonnier est maître chez soi.* To have neither — nor home ; *n'avoir ni feu ni lieu.*

house (haouze), *v.a.*, loger, recevoir chez soi ; donner le couvert à, héberger ; (things) serrer, rentrer. To — cattle ; *établer le bétail.* To — corn ; *serrer le blé, mettre le blé en grange.*

house, *v.n.*, (one's self) se loger, se mettre à couvert.

house′-bell (haouce-), *n.*, sonnette, *f.*

house′breaker (-brék′-), *n.*, voleur avec effraction, cambrioleur, *m.*

house′breaking, *n.*, vol avec effraction, cambriolage, *m.*

house′-carpenter, *n.*, menuisier en bâtiments, *m.*

house′-cricket, *n.*, grillon du foyer, *m.*

house′-dog, *n.*, chien de garde, *m.*

house′ful, *n.*, maisonnée ; (thea.) salle comble, *f. adj.*, maison pleine.

house′hold (-hôlde), *n.*, maisonnée (pop.) ; maison, famille, *f.;* domestique (used only in the sing. in this sense) ; ménage, *m.*

house′hold, *adj.*, domestique ; de ménage. — goods ; *meubles, m.pl.* — utensils ; *ustensiles de ménage, m.pl.* — gods ; *pénates, f.pl., dieux domestiques, m.pl.*

house′holder, *n.*, chef de famille, maître de maison, *m.*

house′hold-removal, *n.*, déménagement, *m.*

house′keeper (-kîp′-), *n.*, chef de maison, *m.;* femme de charge, gouvernante, *f.*

house′keeping, *n.*, ménage, *m.;* économie domestique, administration (V. Hugo), *f.*

house′leek (-lîke), *n.*, (bot.) joubarbe, *f.*

house′less, adj., qui n'a point de maison, de demeure, d'habitation ; sans asile, sans abri.

house′-maid (-méde), n., servante, fille de service, f.

house′-porter, n., portier, concierge, m.

house′-rent, n., loyer d'une maison, m.

house′-room (-roume), n., place, f. ; espace ; abri, logement, m.

house′-sparrow, n., moineau domestique, m.

house′-steward, n., maître d'hôtel, m.

house′-surgeon, n., interne, m.

house′-tax, n., impôt personnel et mobilier.

house′-top, n., faîte, toit, m. To proclaim on the —s ; crier par-dessus les toits.

house′-warming (-wŏr′m′-), n., fête donnée en prenant possession d'une nouvelle maison. To give a — ; pendre la crémaillère.

house′wife (-waïfe), n., ménagère, maîtresse de maison, f. ; (case for needles, etc.) nécessaire de femme, m., ménagère, trousse, f.

house′wifery, n., ménage, m. ; économie domestique, f.

house′-work, n., ménage, m.

hous′ing, n., logement, asile ; (storing) magasinage, m. ; (of horses) housse, f.

hov′el, n., chaumière, cabane, baraque, hutte ; ménage, m. ; bicoque, cahute, masure, f. ; taudis, trou, m.

hov′er (heuv′-), v.n., voltiger, planer, se balancer, voler par-dessus, prendre l'essor ; rôder, papillonner ; (fig.) balancer, hésiter **entre**.

how (haou), adv., comment, de quelle manière, combien, que, quel. — do you do ? comment allez-vous ? You see — I love you ; vous voyez combien je vous aime. — amiable virtue is ; que la vertu est aimable. — beautiful ! comme, ou que, c'est beau ! — old are you ? quel âge avez-vous ? — long have you been here ? combien y a-t-il que vous êtes arrivé ? depuis quand êtes-vous ici ? — long ! jusques à quand ? — far ; jusqu'où, jusqu'à quel point. — large ; de quelle grandeur. — heartily ; avec quel zèle, quelle ardeur, quelle chaleur. — very much ; combien ; à quel degré ; à quel haut degré. — kind you are ! comme, ou que, vous êtes bon, ou aimable ! — now ! qu'est-ce donc !

howbe′it (haou-bî-ite), adv., (ant.). V. **however**.

howev′er (haou-èv′-) ou **howsoev′er** (haou-ço-èv′-), adv., cependant, quoi qu'il en soit, néanmoins, pourtant ; (before an adj. or adv.) quelque . . . que. — rich he may be ; quelque riche qu'il soit ; tout riche qu'il est. Threats — frequently repeated ; les menaces quelque fréquemment qu'elles fussent répétées. — wisely ; quelque sagement que. — important ; si important que (with subj.). — he may do it ; de quelque manière qu'il le fasse.

how′itzer (haou-it-zeur), n., obusier, m.

howl (haoul), n., hurlement, cri, m. ; (of the sea, etc.) mugissement, grondement, m.

howl, v.n., hurler, crier ; (of the sea, etc.) mugir, gronder ; se lamenter. To — at ; hurler, crier **contre** ou **après**.

how′let (haou-lète), n., (orni.) hulotte, huette, f.

howl′ing (haoul′-), n., hurlement ; cri, m. ; (fig.) mugissement, grondement.

howl′ing, adj., qui hurle ; qui pousse des hurlements.

hoy (hoï), n., (nav.) vaisseau côtier, m.

hoy ! int., hé ! holà !

hub′bub (heub′beube), n., tumulte, grabuge, charivari, vacarme, tintamarre, m. ; bagarre, f.

huck′aback (heuk′a-), n., toile ouvrée, f.

huc′kle (heuk′k'l), n., (ant.) hanche ; bosse, f.

huc′kle-backed (-bak′te), adj., bossu, voûté.

huc′kle-bone (-bône), n. V. **hip-bone**.

huck′ster (heuck′steur), n., revendeur, regrattier, m.

huck′ster, v.n., (ant.) revendre en détail, vendre du regrat.

huck′stering, n., regratterie, f.

huck′stress (heuck′strèce), n., (ant.) regrattière, f.

hud′dle (heud′d'l), n., désordre, m. ; confusion ; foule, f. All in a — ; pêle-mêle, en désordre, confusément.

hud′dle, v.a., brouiller, confondre ensemble, mêler, jeter pêle-mêle ; (perform hastily) bâcler ; affubler. To — up ; (work) bâcler. To be —d up ; être entassé, être rencogné.

hud′dle, v.n., se fouler, se mêler, se coudoyer, se confondre en désordre, se presser en désordre.

hue (hiou), n., teint, m. ; couleur, teinte ; nuance ; (cry) huée, clameur, f., cri, m. Flowers of all —s ; fleurs de toutes les couleurs, f.pl. — and cry ; cri de haro, m. ; (journal) gazette de poursuites judiciaires, f. To raise a — and cry after one ; crier haro sur quelqu'un. With — and cry ; a cor et à cri.

huff (heufe), n., emportement, accès de colère, mouvement d'arrogance, m. ; bisbille, f.

huff, v.a., gonfler ; enfler ; maltraiter, traiter avec arrogance, brusquer ; (at draughts) souffler.

huff, v.n., gonfler ; s'enfler, se mettre en colère. To — at ; pester **contre**. To — and puff ; souffler comme un bœuf.

huf′finess, n., fanfaronnerie, arrogance, f.

huf′fish, adj., (ant.) fanfaron ; arrogant ; fier ; vexé, de mauvaise humeur.

huf′fishly, adv., (ant.) avec fanfaronnerie ; avec arrogance ; avec humeur.

huf′fishness, n., (ant.) pétulance ; vanterie ; arrogance, f.

hug (heughe), n., embrassade, accolade, étreinte, f.

hug, v.a., embrasser, serrer entre les bras ; chérir. To — one's self ; se féliciter **de** ; s'applaudir **de**. To — the wind ; (nav.) pincer le vent ; tenir le lit du vent. To — the land ; (nav.) serrer la côte.

huge (hioudje), adj., vaste, grand, immense, énorme.

huge′ly, adv., énormément, immensément, extrêmement, grandement.

huge′ness, n., grandeur énorme, f.

hug′ger-mug′ger (heug′gheur-meug′gheur), n., secret, m. ; saleté, négligence, f. In —; en secret. In — fashion ; salement ; négligemment.

Hu′guenot, n., huguenot, m.

hulk (heulke), n., carcasse, f. pl., pontons, m.pl. ; bagne, f. To send to the —s ; envoyer aux galères.

hulk′ing, adj., fainéant. — fellow ; gros pataud, m.

hull (heul), n., (of a ship) coque ; (of walnuts, etc.) écale, cosse, f.

hull, v.a., (a ship) percer le bordage d'un vaisseau d'un coup de canon ; (walnuts) écaler, écosser ; monder. To — ; (nav.) (of a ship) mettre à sec.

hull, v.n., flotter au gré du vent.

hum (heume), n., bourdonnement ; murmure, bruit, m. ; mystification, f. ; (fig.) bourdon, m. ; attrape, f.

hum, v.a. and n., fredonner ; chantonner ; bourdonner ; murmurer ; ronfler ; parler d'une manière confuse ; (ant.) applaudir ; tromper, mystifier. To — and ha ; faire une réponse évasive ; hésiter. To make things — ; faire aller, ou mener rondement, les choses.

hu′man (hiou-ma′n), adj., humain.

humane′ (hiou-méne), adj., bon, bénin ; humain, qui a de l'humanité ; bienfaisant.

humane′ly (hiou-mé′n′li), adv., humainement ; avec humanité.

hu′manist (hiou-), n., (ant.) personne qui connaît la nature humaine, f. ; (scholar) humaniste, m.

human'ity (hiou-), *n.*, humanité, *f.*

hu'manize (hiou-ma'n'aïze), *v.a.*, humaniser; adoucir.

hu'man-kind (-kaï'n'de), *n.*, genre humain, *m.*

hu'manly, *adv.*, humainement.

hum'ble (heu'm'b'l *ou* eu'm'-), *adj.*, humble, modeste. —-mouthed ; *modeste en parlant.*

hum'ble, *v.a.*, humilier, abaisser, mortifier.

hum'ble-bee (-bî), *n.*, bourdon, *m. ;* abeille sauvage, *f.*

hum'bleness, *n.*, humilité, modestie, *f.*

hum'ble-pie, *n.*, pâté (d'entrailles de cerf), *m.* To eat — ; *filer doux ; faire d'humbles excuses ; avaler un affront ou des couleuvres.*

hum'ble-plant, *n.*, (bot.) sensitive, *f.*

hum'bly, *adv.*, humblement.

hum'bug (heu'm'beughe), *n.*, hâblerie, blague, farce, tromperie, charlatanerie, (pop.) fumisterie, *f.;* (pers.) hâbleur, blagueur, farceur, charlatan, (pop.) fumiste, *m.*

hum'bug, *v.a.*, friponner, tromper ; faire le charlatan ; *conter des sornettes* à.

hum'drum (heu'm'dreu'me), *n.*, personne stupide ; personne assommante, *f.*

hum'drum, *adj.*, monotone endormant; (pers.) assommant, lourd, stupide, fatigant.

humec'tate (hiou-mèk't-), *v.a.*, (ant.) humecter, arroser.

humecta'tion (-mèk'té'-), *n.*, humectation, *f.;* arrosement, *m.*

hu'meral, *adj.*, huméral.

hu'merus (hiou-meur'-), *n.*, (anat.) humérus, *m.*

hu'mic, *adj.*, (chem.) humique.

hu'mid (hiou-), *adj.*, humide.

humid'ity, *n.*, humidité, *f.*

humil'iate, *v.a.*, humilier, abaisser.

humil'iating (hiou-mil'iét'-), *adj.*, humiliant.

humilia'tion (hiou-mil'ié-), *n.*, humiliation, *f.*

humil'ity (hiou-mil-), *n.*, humilité, *f.*

hum'ming, *n.*, bourdonnement ; fredonnement, *m. ;* (fig.) murmure, *m.*

hum'ming-bird (-beurde), *n.*, oiseau-mouche ; colibri, *m.*

hum'ming-top, *n.*, toupie d'Allemagne, *f.*

hu'mor (hiou-meur), *n.*, humeur ; disposition, verve comique, *f ;* caractère, goût, caprice ; esprit, *m.;* gaîté, *f. ;* enjouement, *m.* To be in a good, a bad, — ; *être de bonne, de mauvaise, humeur.* To put any one in a good — ; *mettre quelqu'un en bonne humeur.* To put out of — ; *mettre de mauvaise humeur.* In a — for ; *en veine* de ; *en train* de ; *disposé* à ; *d'humeur* à.

hu'mor, *v.a.*, complaire à ; laisser faire à ; flatter; chercher à plaire à ; se prêter à. To — anybody ; *ménager quelqu'un.*

hu'moral (hiou-meur'-), *adj.*, humoral.

hu'mored (hiou-meur'de), *part.*, satisfait, contenté ; qu'on écoute trop, pour qui l'on a un trop d'indulgence. Ill— ; *de mauvaise humeur.* Good— ; *de bonne humeur, d'un bon caractère.*

hu'morist (hiou-meur'-), *n.*, personne spirituelle, *f. ;* plaisant, original, capricieux, *m.*

hu'morless (hiou-), *adj.*, sans esprit, sans caractère.

hu'morous (hiou-), *adj.*, spirituel ; plaisant ; enjoué, badin; fantasque ; bizarre ; capricieux.

hu'morously, *adv.*, spirituellement ; plaisamment ; bizarrement ; capricieusement.

hu'morousness, *n.*, caractère spirituel ; esprit ; caractère fantasque, bizarre, capricieux, *m. ;* originalité, *f.*

hu'morsome (hiou-mor-seume), *adj.*, de mauvaise humeur ; pétulant ; spirituel ; plaisant.

hu'morsomely, *adv.*, (ant.) de mauvaise humeur ; avec méchanceté ; spirituellement.

hump (heu'm'pe), *n.*, bosse, *f.* To have the — ; *être maussade, avoir le spleen.*

hump'-backed (-'bak'te), *adj.*, bossu.

humph! *int.*, hein !

Hun, *n.*, Hun, *m.*

hunch (heu'n'she), *n.*, bosse (on the back), *f.;* gros morceau, chanteau, *m. ;* coup de coude, *m.*

hunch'back (-bake), *n.*, bossu, *m.*, bossue, *f.*

hunch'backed (-bak'te), *adj.*, voûté, bossu.

hun'dred (heu'n'drède), *adj.*, cent.

hun'dred, *n.*, cent ; centaine ; (a territorial division) canton, district, *m.* A — eggs ; *un cent d'œufs.* In — s ; *par centaines.*

hun'dred-fold (-fôlde), *adj.*, centuple.

hun'dredth (-drèd'th), *adj.*, centième.

hun'dredth, *n.*, centième, *m.*

hun'dredweight (-wê-te), *n.*, quintal, cent, *m.*

Hunga'rian (heu'gn-ghé'-), *adj.*, hongrois.

Hunga'rian, *n.*, Hongrois, *m.*, Hongroise, *f. ;* (language) hongrois, *m.*

hun'ger (heu'gn'gheur), *n.*, faim ; (fig.) soif, *f.* To feel a keen pang of — ; *sentir vivement la faim* (V. Hugo). — is the best sauce ; (prov.) *il n'est sauce que d'appétit.* — will break through stone-walls ; *la faim chasse le loup hors du bois.*

hun'ger, *v.n.*, avoir faim, être affamé. To — after ; *languir* après ; *être affamé* de ; *avoir soif* de ; *soupirer* après.

hun'ger-bit *ou* **hun'ger-bit'ten** (-bit't'n), *adj.*, (ant.) affamé ; pressé par la faim.

hun'gered (-gheurde), *adj.*, (ant.) qui a faim, affamé.

hun'gerly (-gheur-) (ant.) *ou* **hun'grily**, *adv.*, avec un appétit dévorant, avidement.

hun'gry, *adj.*, affamé ; qui a faim ; famélique. To be — ; *avoir faim.* To feed the — ; *nourrir ceux qui ont faim.* A — man is an angry man ; (prov.) *ventre affamé n'a pas d'oreilles.* To be as — as a hunter ; *avoir l'estomac dans les talons.*

hunks (heugn'kse), *n.*, ladre, avare, *m.*

hunt (heu'n'te), *n.*, chasse à courre ; (ant.) (pack of hounds) meute, *f.*

hunt (heu'n'te), *v.a.*, chasser, courre, courir ; poursuivre, chercher, rechercher. To — out ; *découvrir, dépister.* To — down ; *harceler, persécuter, mettre aux abois.* To — up ; *être à la recherche* de ; *chercher, dénicher.*

hunt, *v.n.*, chasser ; aller à la chasse.

hunt'er, *n.*, chasseur ; cheval de chasse, *m.*

hunt'ing, *n.*, chasse; (fig.) recherche, *f.* —-ground ; *terrain, ou pays, de chasse, m.* It is his happy —-ground ; (fig.) *c'est là qu'il est dans son élément.* —-box, —-seat ; *muette, f., pavillon, rendez-vous de chasse, m.* —-horn ; *cor de chasse, m.* —-watch ; *montre à savonnette, f.*

hun'tress, *n.*, chasseuse ; (poetry) chasseresse, *f.*

hunts'man, *n.*, chasseur, piqueur, veneur, *m.*

hunts'manship, *n.*, chasse, vénerie, *f.;* talent de chasseur, *m.*

hur'dle (heur'd'l), *n.*, claie, *f. ;* échalier, *m. ;* (milit.) fascine, *f.* — race ; *course de haies, f.*

hurds (heurdze), *n.pl.*, étoupe, *f.sing.*

hur'dy-gur'dy (heur'di-gheur'di), *n.*, vielle, *f.*

hur'gil (heur'ghil), *n.*, (orni.) cigogne à sac, *f.;* marabout, *m.*

hurl, *v.a.*, précipiter, lancer, jeter, rejeter dans.

hurl'er, *n.*, personne qui lance, *f.*

hur'ly-bur'ly (heur'li-beur-li), *n.*, brouhaha; tohu-bohu ; tintamarre, *m.*

hurrah' (hour'râ), *n.*, hourra, vivat, *m.*

hurrah', *v.a.*, pousser des hourras.

hur'ricane (heur-ri-), *n.*, ouragan, *m. ;* tempête, *f.*

hur'ried (heur-ride), *adj.*, précipité, pressé, rapide ; fait à la hâte.

hur'riedly, *adv.*, précipitamment, à la hâte.

hur'ry (heur-ri), *n.*, hâte, *f. ;* (fig.) tumulte, *m.*, confusion, précipitation, hâte, presse, *f.* To be in a — ; *être pressé.* Done in a — ; *fait à la hâte ; fait avec précipitation.* There is no — ; *rien ne presse ; il n'y a pas de presse.* The more — the less speed ; *grand bruit, petite besogne.*

hur'ry, v.a., presser; précipiter; faire dépêcher. To — away ; *emmener précipitamment.* To — back ; *hâter le retour* de ; *ramener en toute hâte.* To — in ; *faire entrer précipitamment.* To — on ; *entraîner, pousser, presser.* To — through, *ou* over ; (a work) *bâcler, brocher, faire à la hâte.*

hur'ry, v.n., se dépêcher ; se presser ; se hâter. To — into ; *se hâter d'entrer* dans. To — down ; *descendre à la hâte, se précipiter.* To — back ; *revenir à la hâte.* To — in ; *entrer précipitamment.* To — on ; *se hâter, se presser.*

hurt (heurte), n., mal, m. ; blessure, f. ; (fig.) tort, préjudice, dommage, m.

hurt, v.a., blesser ; faire mal à ; faire du mal, *ou* tort, à ; (fig.) nuire à, offenser, blesser, choquer. To — any one's feelings ; *blesser quelqu'un au cœur.* To — one's self ; *se faire mal* à.

hurt, v.n., faire du mal ; faire mal. It does not — ; *cela ne fait pas,* ou *point, de mal.*

hurt'ful (-foule), adj., malfaisant pour ; nuisible à, pernicieux à ; (fig.) préjudiciable à.

hurt'fully, adv., d'une manière nuisible ; pernicieusement.

hurt'fulness, n., qualité nuisible, f. ; tort, préjudice, m.

hur'tle, v.n., se choquer, se heurter; (of sound) retentir. —berry ; *airelle, f.*

hurt'less, adj., qui ne fait point de mal ; innocent ; intact.

hurt'lessly, adv., innocemment.

hurt'lessness, n., innocuité, f.

hur'tling, n., choc ; retentissement, m.

hus'band (heuz'ba'n'd), n., mari, époux, m. Ship's — ; *gérant à bord, m.* As — and wife ; *maritalement.*

hus'band, v.a., ménager, économiser.

hus'bandless, adj., (ant.) sans mari.

hus'bandman, n., laboureur, cultivateur, m.

hus'bandry, n., labourage, m. ; culture, industrie agricole ; frugalité, économie, f.

hush (heushe), adj., (ant.) silencieux, paisible.

hush ! int., chut ! paix ! motus !

hush, v.n., se taire ; faire silence.

hush, v.a., taire ; faire taire, imposer silence à ; (fig.) calmer, apaiser. To — up ; *étouffer, taire, supprimer.*

hush'-money (-meu'n'ni), n. ; prime du silence, f. Extortion of — ; (pop.) *chantage, m.*

husk (heuske), n., (of grain) balle ; (bot.) (graminaceæ) glume ; (papilionaceæ) cosse, gousse ; (of grapes) peau ; (walnuts) écale, f. ; brou, m.

husk, v.a., (fruit and vegetables) écosser ; (grain) vanner ; monder ; (walnuts) écaler.

husked (heusk'te), adj., (of fruit and vegetables) écossé ; à cosse ; (grain) vanné ; mondé; (walnuts) écalé.

husk'iness, n., sécheresse, rugosité, (of the voice) raucité, f.

husk'y (heus'-), adj., cossu ; rude, âpre ; (of the voice) rauque, éraillé, enroué.

hussar' (heuz'zâr), n., hussard, m.

hus'sif, n., (for needles, etc.) ménagère, f.

hus'sy (heuz'zi), n., coquine ; gueuse, friponne, f.

hus'tings (heus'tign'ze), n., estrade (pour haranguer les assemblées en plein air), f. ; assemblée électorale, f.

hus'tle (heus's'l), v.n., se pousser, se presser, se bousculer.

hus'tle, v.a., bousculer, presser, pousser.

hus'wife (heuz'zif), **hus'wifery** (heuz'-), n. V. **house'wife.**

hut (heute), n., hutte, cabane ; (milit.) baraque, f.

hut, v.n., (milit.) se hutter, se baraquer.

hut, v.a., loger dans des baraques.

hutch (heutshe), n., huche, f. ; (for rabbits) clapier, (kneading-trough) pétrin, m. — rabbit; *lapin de clapier, m.*

huzza' ! (heuz'zâ), int., hourra !

hy'acinth (haï-a-ci'n'th), n., hyacinthe, jacinthe, f.

hy'ades (haï'a-dize), n.pl., hyades, f.pl.

hy'brid (haï-bride), n., hybride, m.

hy'brid, adj., hybride.

hy'dra (haï-dra), n., hydre, f.

hy'dragogue (haï-.), n., (med.) hydragogue, m.

hydran'gea (haï-dra'n'dji-a), n., (bot.) hortensia, m.

hy'drant, n., bouche d'incendie, f.

hydrau'lic *ou* **hydrau'lical** (haï-), adj., hydraulique.

hydrau'lics, n.pl., hydraulique, f.*sing.*

hy'dride (-draïde), n., (chem.) hydrure, m.

hy'drocele (haï-dro-cîle), n., (med.) hydrocèle, f.

hydroceph'alus (haï-dro-cèf'a-), n., hydrocéphale, f.

hydrochlo'rate (haï-dro-klo-), n., (chem.) (ant.) hydrochlorate, m.

hydrochlo'ric (haï-dro-klô-), adj., hydrochlorique, chlorhydrique.

hydrocot'yle (haï-dr6-co-ti-li), n., (bot.) hydrocotyle, f.

hydrodynam'ic (haï-dro-daï-), adj., hydrodynamique.

hydrodynam'ics, n.pl., hydrodynamique, f.

hy'drogen (haï-dro-djène), n., (chem.) hydrogène, m.

hy'drogenize (-aïze), v.a., (chem.) hydrogéner.

hydrog'rapher (haï-), n., hydrographe, m.

hydrograph'ical, adj., hydrographique.

hydrog'raphy, n., hydrographie, f.

hydrol'ogy (haï-drol'o-dji), n., hydrologie, f.

hy'dromel, n., (pharm.) hydromel, m.

hydrom'eter (haï-dro'm'i-), n., aréomètre, pèse-liqueur, m.

hydromet'ric *ou* **hydromet'rical**, adj., aréométrique.

hydrom'etry, n., aréométrie, f.

hydropho'bia *ou* **hy'drophoby** (haï-dro-fô-), n., hydrophobie ; rage, f.

hydrophob'ic, adj., hydrophobe.

hy'drophyte (haï-dro-faïte), n., (bot.) algue, f.

hydrop'ic *ou* **hydrop'ical** (haï-), adj., hydropique.

hydropneumat'ic (hai-dro-niou-mat'ike), adj., hydropneumatique.

hydrostat'ic *ou* **hydrostat'ical** (haï-), adj., hydrostatique.

hydrostat'ically, adv., suivant l'hydrostatique.

hydrostat'ics, n.pl., hydrostatique, f.

hy'druret (haï-drou-rète), n., (chem.) (ant.) hydrure, m.

hyema'tion (haï-i-m'é-), n., (ant.) hiémation, f.

hye'na (haï-î-), n., (zoöl.) hyène, f.

hy'giene (haï-dji-îne), n., hygiène, f.

hygien'al *ou* **hygien'ic** (haï-dji-è'n'-), adj., hygiénique.

hygrom'eter (haï-gro'm'i-), n., hygromètre, m.

hygromet'ric *ou* **hygromet'rical** (-gro'm'-), adj., hygrométrique.

hygrom'etry (haï-gro'm'i-), n., hygrométrie, f.

hy'men (haï-mène), n., hymen, hyménée, m.

hymene'al *ou* **hymene'an** (haï-mi-nî-), adj., de l'hymen ; de l'hyménée ; du mariage, nuptial.

hymene'al *ou* **hymene'an**, n., chant d'hyménée, m.

hymenop'tera *ou* **hymenop'ters** (haï-mè-n'op-teur'a, -teurze), n.pl., (ent.) hyménoptères, m.pl.

hymenop'teral, adj., hyménoptère.

hymn (hime), n., (ode) hymne, m. ; (rel.) hymne, f.

hymn, v.a., célébrer par des hymnes.

hymn, v.n., chanter des hymnes.

hymn'-book (-bouke), n., livre d'hymnes, m.

hyosci'amus (haï-os-saï-a-), n., (bot.) jusquiame, f.

hypal'lage (haï-pal-la-dji), n., (rhet.) hypallage, m.

hyperba'ton (haï-peur-), n., (rhet.) hyperbate, f.

hyper'bola (haï-peur-), n., (geom.) hyperbole, f.

hyper'bole (haï-peur-bo-li), n., (rhet.) hyperbole, f.

hyperbol'ic ou **hyperbol'ical**, adj., hyperbolique.

hyperbol'ically, adv., hyperboliquement.

hyper'bolist, n., faiseur d'hyperboles, m.

hyper'bolize (-laïze), v.a., exagérer.

hyper'bolize, v.n., user de l'hyperbole, parler par hyperbole.

hyperbo'rean (haï-peur-bo-ri-), adj., hyperboréen, hyperborée.

hypercrit'ic (haï-peur-), n., hypercritique, m.

hypercrit'ical, adj., hypercritique, critique à l'excès. To be —; épiloguer.

hypercrit'icism, n., critique exagérée, f.

hy'phen (haï-fène), n., tiret ; trait d'union, m.

hypnot'ic, adj., hypnotique, narcotique, soporifique.

hypnot'ic, n., (med., pharm.) narcotique, soporifique, hypnotique, m.

hypochon'driac (haï-po-co'n'-), n., hypocondriaque, hypocondre, m.

hypochondri'acal, adj., hypocondriaque, hypocondre.

hypoc'risy (hi-pok'ri-ci), n., hypocrisie, f.

hyp'ocrite, n., hypocrite, m.f.

hypocrit'ic ou **hypocrit'ical**, adj., hypocrite.

hypocrit'ically, adv., hypocritement, en hypocrite, par hypocrisie, avec hypocrisie.

hypogas'trium (haï-), n., (anat.) hypogastre, m.

hypoglos'sal (haï-), n., hypoglosse, f.

hypo'pium (haï-pô-), n., (surg.) hypopyon, m.

hypos'tasis (haï-pos-ta-cice), n., (med.) (theol.) hypostase, f.

hypostat'ic ou **hypostat'ical** (haï-), adj., (theol.) hypostatique.

hypostat'ically, adv., (theol.) hypostatiquement.

hypoth'enuse (haï-poth'i-niouce), n., (geom.) hypoténuse, f.

hypoth'esis (haï-poth'i-cice), n., (log.) hypothèse, f.

hypothet'ic ou **hypothet'ical**, adj., (log.) hypothétique.

hypothet'ically, adv., (log.) hypothétiquement.

hy'son (haï-çone), n., thé hyson, thé vert, m.

hys'sop, n., (bot.) hysope, f.

hyster'ic ou **hyster'ical** (his'tèr-), adj., hystérique.

hyster'ics, n.pl., attaque de nerfs ; hystérie, f. sing.

hyster'ocele (his'tèr'o-cîle), n., (med.) hystérocèle, f.

hysterot'omy, n., (surg.) opération césarienne, f.

I

i, neuvième lettre de l'alphabet, i, m.

I, pron., je, moi. — speak ; je parle. Who speaks ? qui est-ce qui parle ? —; moi. It is —; c'est moi. It is — who am speaking ; c'est moi qui parle.

iam'bic (aï-), adj., iambique, iambe.

iam'bic ou **iam'bus**, n., iambe, m.

Iber'ian, adj., Ibérien, -ne.

i'bex (aï-bèkse), n., (mam.) bouquetin, m.

i'bis (aï-bice), n., (orni.) ibis, m.

ice (aïce), n., glace, f. To break the —; rompre la glace ; faire les premières démarches ou avances.

ice, v.a., glacer ; (of wine) frapper.

ice'-age, n., (geol.) période glaciaire, f.

ice'-ax, n., piolet, m.

ice'berg (aïce-beurghe), n., glace flottante, montagne de glace, f. ; banc de glace, m.

ice'-boat (-bôte), n., bateau-traîneau, m.

ice'-bound (-baou'n'de), adj., fermé, ou pris, par les glaces ; entouré de glace.

ice'-box, n., glacière, f.

ice'-breaker (-brék'-), n., brise-glace, m.

ice'-cream (-crîme), n., crème glacée, glace, f.

iced (aïste), adj., glacé ; à la glace ; (of wine, etc.) frappé.

ice'-field, n., banc de glace, m.

ice'-floe, n., banquise flottante, f.

ice'-house (-haonce), n., glacière, f.

Ice'lander, n., Islandais, m., Islandaise, f.

Icelan'dic, adj., islandais ; d'Islande.

ice'-pack, n., embâcle, m.

ice'-plant, n., ficoïde cristalline ; glaciale, f.

ice'-safe, n., glacière, f.

ichneu'mon (ik'niou-), n., ichneumon, m.

ichnograph'ic ou **ichnograph'ical** (ik'nog'-), adj., ichnographique.

ichnog'raphy (ik'nog'-), n., ichnographie, f.

i'chor (aï-kor), n., (med.) ichor, pus, m.

i'chorous, adj., ichoreux.

ich'thyolite (ik-thi-o-laïte), n., ichtyolithe, m.

ichthyolog'ical (ik'thi-ol-o-djik'-), adj., ichtyologique.

ichthyol'ogy (ik'thi-ol-o-dji), n., ichtyologie, f.

i'cicle (aï-cik'k'l), n., glaçon, m.

i'ciness (aï-), n., froid glacial, m.

i'cing, n., glaçage ; (of wine) frappage, m.

icon'oclast (aï-), n., iconoclaste, m.

iconog'raphy (aï-), n., iconographie, f.

iconol'ater (aï-co-nol'é-), n., iconolâtre, m.

iconol'ogy (aï-co-nol-o-dji), n., iconologie, f.

icosahe'dron (aï-cô-ça-hî-), n., (geom.) icosaèdre, m.

icosan'dria, n., (bot.) icosandrie, f.

icter'ical (ik'tèr'-), adj., ictérique.

ic'terus (ik'teur-), n., (med.) ictère, m., jaunisse, f.

i'cy (aï-cy), adj., de glace ; glacé, glacial.

ide'a (aï-dî-a), n., idée, f. To have an — of ; avoir, ou se faire, une idée de. To have no — that ; ne pas se douter que, ne pas savoir que. The —! par exemple ! a-t-on jamais vu ! What an — too ! aussi a-t-on idée ! (V. Hugo).

ide'al, adj., idéal ; (philos.) mental.

ide'al, n., idéal, m.

ide'alism (-'iz'me), n., idéalisme ; spiritualisme, m.

ide'alist, n., idéaliste ; spiritualiste, m.

ide'alize (-aïze), v.n., former des idées ; idéaliser.

ide'ally, adv., en idée, mentalement.

iden'tical (aï-), adj., identique.

iden'tically, adv., identiquement.

identifica'tion (-fi-ké-), n., identification, f.

iden'tify (aï-dè'n'ti-faïe), v.a., identifier, constater l'identité de ; reconnaître.

iden'tify, v.n., s'identifier.

iden'tity (aï-dè'n'ti-ti), n., identité, f.

ideolog'ical (aï-di-ol-o-dj'-), adj., idéologique.

ideol'ogist (aï-), n., idéologue, idéologiste, m.

ideol'ogy (aï-di-ol-o-dji), n., idéologie, f.

ides (aïd'ze), n.pl., ides, f.pl.

id'iocy (aï-), n., imbécillité, f. ; (med.) idiotisme, m.

id'iom, n., (dialect) idiome ; idiotisme ; génie d'une langue, m. The —s of our language ; les idiotismes de notre langue.

idiomat'ic *ou* **idiomat'ical**, adj., conforme au génie de la langue; qui renferme un idiotisme; idiomatique. — expression; *idiotisme, m.*

idiomat'ically, adv., conformément à l'idiome; d'une manière idiomatique.

idiopath'ic (-thike), adj., idiopathique.

idiopath'ically, adv., par idiopathie.

idiop'athy (id-i-op-a-thi), n., (med.) idiopathie, f.

idiosyn'crasy (id-i-o-ci'n'-cra-ci), n., idiosyncrasie, f.

id'iot (id-i-ote), n., idiot, m., idiote, f.; imbécile, m.f.

id'iotcy (-ot'ci), n., imbécillité, f.; (med.) idiotisme, m.

idiot'ic *ou* **idiot'ical**, adj., idiot, idiotique; d'imbécile; imbécile.

id'iotish, adj., idiot, idiotique; imbécile.

id'iotism (-iz'me), n., (ant.) (idiom) idiotisme, m.; (idiocy) imbécillité, f.; (med.) idiotisme, m.

i'dle (aï'd'l), adj., fainéant, oisif, paresseux, indolent, désœuvré; inutile, vain, frivole, oiseux. — fellow; *fainéant; paresseux, m.* — hours; *heures de loisir, f.pl.; moments perdus, m.pl.* — words; *paroles en l'air, f.pl.* — tale; *conte frivole, conte bleu, m.* — talk; *paroles en l'air; sornettes, f.pl.*

i'dle, v.a.n., faire le paresseux, fainéanter; flâner; gaspiller, passer dans la paresse. To — away one's time; *perdre, gaspiller, dissiper son temps.*

i'dleness, n., paresse, fainéantise; oisiveté, inutilité, f.; désœuvrement, m.

i'dler, n., fainéant, m., fainéante, f.; désœuvré, m., désœuvrée, f.; paresseux, m., paresseuse, f.; oisif, m.

i'dly, adv., dans la paresse; oisivement; en paresseux; avec indolence; nonchalamment; inutilement, vainement, follement.

i'dol (aï-), n., idole, f. — worship; *culte des idoles, m.*

idol'ater, n., idolâtre, m.

idol'atress, n., femme idolâtre, f.

idol'atrous, adj., idolâtre.

idol'atrously, adv., avec idolâtrie.

idol'atry, n., idolâtrie, f.

i'dolize (-'aïze), v.a., idolâtrer; adorer; aimer avec idolâtrie; faire une idole de.

i'dolizer, n.; **i'dolizing**, adj., idolâtre, m.f.

i'dyl (aï-), n., idylle, f.

if, conj., si. — necessary; *s'il le faut; au besoin.* — ever there was one; *s'il en fut jamais.* — anything, I am paying more than was agreed between us; *s'il y a une différence, je vous paye plus que le prix convenu entre nous.* Little — any difference; *peu, — any différence.* — not; *sinon; si ce n'est.* We will buy it — it costs us double; *nous l'achèterons, quand même il nous coûterait le double.* — possible; *s'il y a moyen; si cela est possible; s'il se peut.* — ever there was; *s'il fut jamais.* — so; *s'il en est ainsi.* To look as —; *avoir l'air de.*

ig'neous (ig-ni-), adj., igné, de feu.

ig'nis-fat'uus (ig-niss-fat'iou-), n., (*ignes-fatui*) feu follet, m.

ignite' (ig-naïte), v.a., enflammer; mettre en ignition.

ignite', v.n., s'enflammer; entrer en ignition; prendre feu; s'allumer.

igni'tible (ig-naït'i-b'l), adj., (ant.) inflammable.

igni'tion (-iz'me), n., ignition, f.

igno'ble (ig-nô-b'l), adj., ignoble; roturier.

igno'bleness, n., bassesse, f.; manque de dignité, m.

igno'bly, adv., ignoblement; d'une manière ignoble, basse. — born; *de basse naissance.*

ignomin'ious (ig-no-min'-), adj., ignominieux, indigne; (jur.) infamant.

ignomin'iously, adv., ignominieusement; indignement; (jur.) d'une manière infamante.

ig'nominy (ig-no-), n., ignominie; (jur.) infamie, f.

ignora'mus (ig-no-ré-), n., ignare, m.f.; ignorant, m.; ignorante, f.

ig'norance (ig-no-), n., ignorance, f.

ig'norant, adj., ignorant. To be — of; *ignorer; ne pas savoir; ne pas connaître.* Not to be — of; *savoir bien.*

ig'norantly, adv., ignoramment; par ignorance.

ignore', v.a., (jur.) (a bill of indictment) déclarer qu'il n'y a pas lieu à poursuivre; rendre une ordonnance de non-lieu; ignorer; écarter; mépriser; rejeter; dédaigner; ne pas vouloir reconnaître (une personne); méconnaître; ne tenir aucun compte de.

il'eum (il-î-), n., (anat.) iléon, iléum, m.

il'eus (il-i-), n., (med.) iléus, m.; colique de miséréré, f.

i'lex (aï-lèkse), n., houx, m.

il'ia, n.pl., flancs, m.pl., région lombaire, f.sing.

il'iac, adj., iliaque. — passion; *passion iliaque, f.; iléus, m.*

Il'iad, n., Iliade, f.

ill (il), n., mal, m.

ill, adj., mauvais, méchant; (of the health) malade. To fall —; *tomber malade; être pris de maladie.* To take it —; (fig.) *trouver mauvais; prendre mal.*

ill, adv., mal; peu. —able to; *peu capable de.*

ill-affect'ed, adj., mal intentionné.

illau'dable (-a-b'l), adj., peu louable.

illau'dably, adv., d'une manière peu louable.

ill-bred', adj., mal élevé.

ill-consid'ered, adj., irréfléchi, peu considéré.

ill-contrived', adj., mal imaginé; mal concerté, mal pratiqué.

ill-deserved', adj., peu mérité.

ill-design'ing (-dè-zaï'n'-), adj., mal intentionné.

ill-disposed', adj., mal intentionné.

ill-do'ing (-dou'-), n., mal, m.; mauvaise action, f.

ille'gal (il-lî-), adj., illégal; (ant.) illicite.

illegal'ity, n., illégalité, f.

ille'galize (-aïze), v.a., rendre illégal.

ille'gally, adv., illégalement.

illegibil'ity (il-lèdj'i-), n., état illisible, m.

illeg'ible (-lèdj'i-b'l), adj., illisible.

illeg'ibly, adv., illisiblement.

illegit'imacy (il-li-djit'i-), n., illégitimité, f.

illegit'imate, adj., illégitime; non autorisé.

illegit'imately, adv., illégitimement.

ill-fa'ted (-fét'ède), adj., infortuné, malheureux.

ill-fa'vored (-fé-veurde), adj., disgracié; vilain; laid.

ill-fa'voredly, adv., (ant.) laidement; disgracieusement; mal; rudement.

ill-fa'voredness, n., difformité, laideur, f.

ill-fea'tured, adj., laid.

ill-found'ed, adj., mal fondé.

ill-got'ten, adj., mal acquis.

ill-ground'ed, adj., mal fondé.

illib'eral (il-lib'eur-), adj., illibéral; peu généreux; mesquin; borné, étroit; peu relevé.

illiberal'ity, n., illibéralité; mesquinerie, f.; manque de générosité; manque de lumière, m.; petitesse; inélégance, f.

illib'erally, adv., sans libéralité; sans générosité; mesquinement; d'une manière bornée; sans élégance.

illic'it, adj., illicite.

illic'itly, adv., illicitement.

illic'itness, n., nature illicite, f.

illim'itable (-a-b'l), adj., illimitable.

illim'itably, adv., d'une manière illimitable.

illim'ited (-ède), adj. V. **unlimited**.

illim′itedness, n., (ant.) nature illimitée ; infinité, f.

illit′erate (-′eur′éte), adj., illettré.

illit′erately, adv., en homme illettré.

ill-judged′, adj., malavisé, mal compris, imprudent.

ill-man′nered, adj., grossier, malappris.

ill-mean′ing (-mîn′-), adj., malintentionné.

ill-mind′ed (-maï′n′d′-), adj., mal disposé ; enclin au mal.

ill-na′ture (-nét′ieure), n., mauvais naturel, m.

ill-na′tured (-nét′ieurde), adj., d′un mauvais naturel ; méchant.

ill-na′turedly, adv., méchamment.

ill′ness, n., maladie, f. ; mal, m. ; indisposition, f.

illog′ical (il-lodj′i-cal), adj., peu logique ; illogique.

illog′ically, adv., peu logiquement ; illogiquement.

illog′icalness, n., absence de logique, f.

ill-o′mened (-ô-mè′n′de), adj., de mauvais présage, de mauvais augure.

ill-seem′ing (-sîm′-), adj., d′un aspect peu agréable.

ill-shaped′, adj., mal bâti, mal fait.

ill-sound′ing (-saou′n′d′-), adj., sans harmonie ; maisonnant, inharmonieux.

ill-spir′ited (-spirit′ède), adj., mal disposé.

ill-starred′ (-stär′de), adj., né sous une mauvaise étoile ; de mauvais augure ; (fig.) infortuné, malheureux.

ill-suit′ing (-siout′-), adj., malséant.

ill-tem′pered, adj., mauvais, grincheux. To be —, avoir mauvais caractère.

ill-treat′, v.a., maltraiter, brutaliser, rudoyer.

ill-timed′ (-taï′m′de), adj., hors de saison ; déplacé ; importun.

illude′ (il-lioude), v.a., décevoir, tromper.

illum′inant, n., lumière, f., principe éclairant, m.

illu′minate (il-liou-), v.a., éclairer ; illuminer ; éclaircir ; (to decorate) enluminer.

illu′minate, n., illuminé, m., illuminée, f.

illu′minating, adj., qui éclaire.

illu′minating, n., enluminure, f.

illumina′tion (-mi-né-), n., illumination, f. ; (fig.) éclat, m., splendeur ; (books, etc.) enluminure, f.

illu′minative, adj., (ant.) illuminatif.

illu′minator (-né-) ou **illu′miner**, n., personne qui éclaire, chose qui éclaire, f. ; illuminateur ; (paint.) enlumineur, m., enlumineuse, f.

illu′mine, v.a., (ant.) éclairer ; (fig.) honorer.

illuminee′ (il-liou-mi′n′î), n., (illuminati) illuminé, m., illuminée, f.

illu′minism, n., illuminisme, m.

illu′sion (il-liou-jeune), n., illusion, f.

illu′sive (il-liou-cive), adj., illusoire.

illu′sively, adv., illusoirement.

illu′siveness, n., caractère illusoire, m.

illu′sory (il-liou-çô-), adj., illusoire.

illus′trate (il-leus′-), v.a., illustrer ; expliquer ; démontrer ; faire voir ; prouver ; (to adorn) orner ; embellir ; (of books) illustrer.

illustra′tion (il-leus-tré-), n., illustration, explication ; comparaison, f. ; éclaircissement, exemple, m.

illus′trative ou **illus′tratory** (-tra-), adj., qui éclaircit ; explicatif.

illus′tratively, adv., pour servir d′explication.

illus′trator (-tré-), n., illustrateur, interprète, commentateur.

illus′trious, adj., illustre, célèbre ; glorieux, noble ; beau.

illus′triously, adv., d′une manière illustre ; avec éclat ; glorieusement.

illus′triousness, n., illustration, f. ; éclat, m., gloire, éminence, f.

ill-vis′aged (-viz′èdj′de), adj., laid.

I′m (aï′m), ab. de I am ; je suis.

im′age (i′m′èdje), n., image, statuette, f. ; portrait, m. ; idole ; idée, f.

im′age, v.a.n., représenter, figurer, peindre ; (to conceive in the mind) se figurer, se représenter, s′imaginer.

im′age-break′er (-brék′eur), n., briseur d′images ; iconoclaste, m.

im′agery, n., images, f.pl. ; forme ; apparence, f. ; peinture, représentation ; chimères ; visions, f.pl. ; tableau, m. ; figures de rhétorique, f.

im′age-mak′er, n., mouleur de statuettes, m.

im′age-ven′dor (-vè′n′deur), n., marchand d′images, m.

im′age-wor′ship (-weur-), n., idolâtrie, f. ; culte des images, m.

imag′inable (i′m′adj′-i′n′-a-b′l), adj., imaginable.

imag′inary (i′m′adj′i′n′-), adj., imaginaire.

imagina′tion (i′m′adj′i-né-), n., imagination, conception, idée, pensée, f.

imag′inative, adj., imaginatif.

imag′ine (i′m′adj′ine), v.a.n., imaginer ; se faire une idée **de** ; s′imaginer, se figurer ; (jur.) préméditer.

imag′iner, n., personne qui imagine, f. ; rêveur, homme à projets, faiseur de projets, m.

imag′ining, n., création, imagination, conception, f.

ima′go, n., (zoöl.) insecte parfait, m., image, f.

im′becile (i′m′bi-cîle), adj., imbécile.

imbecil′ity, n., imbécillité ; impuissance, faiblesse, f.

imbed′ (i′m′bède), v.a., fixer ; empâter ; coucher, poser ; sceller ; encastrer.

imbibe′ (i′m′baïbe), v.a., imbiber, absorber ; (fig.) puiser, prendre ; être imbu **de**.

imbi′ber, n., chose qui imbibe, f. ; absorbant, m.

imbibi′tion (i′m′bi-bish′-), n., imbibition, f.

imbit′ter (i′m′bit′-). V. **embit′ter**.

imbod′y. V. **embod′y**.

imbol′den. V. **embol′den**.

imbo′som (-bouz′eume). V. **embo′som**.

im′bricated (-két′-ède), adj., en tuile faîtière ; en forme de tuile creuse ; (bot., zoöl.) imbriqué.

imbrica′tion (-bri-ké′-), n., imbrication, f.

imbrogl′io (i′m′brôl′yi-ô), n., imbroglio, m.

imbrown′ (-braoune), v.a.n., (ant.) rembrunir ; assombrir ; se rembrunir.

imbrue′ (-brou), v.a., tremper ; souiller.

imbrute′ (-broute), v.a., (ant.) abrutir.

imbrute′, v.n., s′abrutir.

imbue′ (-biou), v.a., imbiber, teindre ; (fig.) pénétrer ; inspirer, remplir **de**.

imbued′, adj., imbibé ; (fig.) imbu **de**, pénétré **de**.

im′itable (-a-b′l), adj., imitable.

im′itate, v.a.n., imiter ; contrefaire.

imita′tion (-i-té-), n., imitation ; contrefaçon, f. ; (paint.) pastiche, m.

im′itative (-i-té-), adj., qui imite, imitatif ; fait à l′imitation **de**, imitateur. The monkey is an — animal ; le singe est un animal imitatif.

im′itator (-i-té-), n., imitateur, m., imitatrice, f. ; contrefacteur, m.

immac′ulate (-′mak′iou-), adj., sans tache, immaculé.

immac′ulately, adv., sans tache ; purement.

immac′ulateness, n., pureté sans tache, f.

immate′rial (-ma-tî-), adj., immatériel ; indifférent, égal. It is —; peu importe, c′est égal ; cela n′a pas d′importance.

immate′rialism (-iz′me), n., (philos.) idéalisme, m.

immate′rialist, n., (philos.) idéaliste, m.

immaterial′ity, n., immatérialité, f.

immate′rialize (-aïze), v.a., rendre immatériel.

immate'rially, *adv.*, immatériellement ; sans importance.

immature' (-tioure), *adj.*, pas mûr ; pas mûri, sans être mûr ; prématuré.

immature'ly, *adv.*, prématurément ; avant la maturité.

immature'ness *ou* **immatu'rity**, *n.*, état de ce qui n'est pas mûr, *m.*, prématurité, *f.*

immeas'urable (-mèj'iou-ra-b'l) *adj.*, incommensurable ; infini ; immense.

immeas'urably, *adv.*, outre mesure ; sans mesure ; immensément, infiniment.

imme'diate (-mî-), *adj.*, immédiat ; instantané ; (fig.) pressant, urgent ; (on letters) très pressé.

imme'diately, *adv.*, immédiatement ; tout de suite ; sur-le-champ.

imme'diateness, *n.*, caractère immédiat, *m.*; grande promptitude, *f.*

immemo'rial (-mi-mô-), *adj.*, immémorial, de temps immémorial.

immemo'rially, *adv.*, de toute antiquité ; de temps immémorial.

immense', *adj.*, immense.

immense'ly, *adv.*, immensément.

immen'sity, *n.*, immensité, *f.*

immerge' (-meurdje), *v.a.*, plonger ; immerger, enfoncer.

immerse' (-meurse), *v.a.*   *V.* **immerge**.

immer'sion (-meurse), *n.*, immersion, *f.*

immesh' (-mèshe), *v.a.*, (ant.) prendre dans un filet ; envelopper, enlacer.

im'migrant, *n.*, immigrant, *m.*

im'migrate, *v.n.*, immigrer.

immigra'tion (-gré-), *n.*, immigration, *f.*

im'minence (-mi-), *n.*, imminence, *f.* ; (l.u.) péril, *m.*

im'minent, *adj.*, imminent.

im'minently, *adv.*, sur le point d'arriver.

immiscibil'ity, *n.*, (ant.) qualité de ce qui n'est pas miscible, *f.*

immis'sion, *n.*, (ant.) immission, action d'introduire, d'injecter, de faire entrer, *f.*

immobil'ity, *n.*, immobilité, *f.*

immod'erate (mod'eur'-), *adj.*, immodéré, extravagant, excessif, fou.

immod'erately, *adv.*, immodérément.

immodera'tion (-'eur'é-), *n.*, excès ; défaut de modération, *m.* ; immodération, *f.*

immod'est, *adj.*, immodeste ; peu modeste ; impudique.

immod'estly, *adv.*, immodestement ; sans modestie ; impudiquement.

immod'esty, *n.*, immodestie ; impudeur, impudicité, *f.*

im'molate (-mô-), *v.a.*, immoler.

immola'tion (-lé-), *n.*, immolation, *f.* ; sacrifice, *m.*

im'molator (-lé-), *n.*, personne qui immole, qui sacrifie, *f.*

immor'al, *adj.*, déréglé, immoral.

immoral'ity, *n.*, immoralité, *f.*

immor'ally, *adv.*, immoralement.

immor'tal, *adj.*, immortel ; perpétuel.

immortal'ity, *n.*, immortalité ; (jur.) perpétuité, *f.*

immortaliza'tion (-tal'aïzé-), *n.*, action d'immortaliser, *f.*

immor'talize (-aïze), *v.a.*, rendre immortel ; immortaliser, perpétuer.

immor'tally, *adv.*, immortellement ; éternellement.

immovabil'ity (-mouv'-), *n.*, immobilité, *f.*

immov'able (-mouv'a-b'l), *adj.*, immobile ; inébranlable ; (fig.) insensible ; (jur.) immeuble, immobilier.

immov'ableness, *n.*, immobilité, *f.*; caractère inébranlable, *m.* ; (fig.) insensibilité, *f.*

immov'ably, *adv.*, d'une manière immobile ; inébranlablement ; (fig.) insensiblement, avec insensibilité.

immu'nity (-miou-), *n.*, immunité, exemption, *f.* ; privilège, *m.*

immure' (-mioure), *v.a.*, entourer de murs ; enfermer ; claquemurer, cloîtrer, tenir captif.

immur'ing, *n.*, immuration, *f.*

immutabil'ity (-miou-ta-), *n.*, immutabilité, immuabilité, *f.*

immu'table (-miou-ta-b'l), *adj.*, invariable ; immuable ; irrévocable.

immu'tably, *adv.*, immuablement, irrévocablement.

imp (i'm'pe), *n.*, rejeton ; diablotin, démon ; (urchin) petit drôle ; (of the devil) suppôt, *m.*

im'pact, *n.*, contact ; choc, impact, *m.* ; empreinte, impression, *f.* ; (phys.) choc, *m.*, collision, *f.*

impair', *v.a.*, détériorer ; (fig.) nuire **à**, altérer, délabrer ; diminuer, affaiblir.

impair'ment, *n.*, détérioration, diminution, altération, *f.* ; délabrement, *m.*

impale'.   *V.* **empale'**.

impale'ment, *n.*, palissade, *f.* ; (of criminals) empalement, *m.*

impalpabil'ity, *n.*, (ecc. hist.) impalpabilité, *f.*

impal'pable (-pa-b'l), *adj.*, impalpable ; (fig.) subtil.

impana'tion (-né-), *n.*, (theol.) impanation, consubstantiation, *f.*

impan'el *ou* **impan'nel**, *v.a.*, dresser une liste du jury ; inscrire sur la liste du jury.

imparisyllab'ic, *adj.*, imparisyllabique.

impar'ity, *n.*, disparité, imparité, disproportion ; inégalité, *f.*

impark' (-pârke), *v.a.*   *V.* **empark**.

impart' (-pârte), *v.a.*, accorder, donner ; conférer ; communiquer ; faire savoir **à** ; instruire **de** ; faire part **à**.

impar'tial (-pâr-shal), *adj.*, impartial.

impartial'ity, *n.*, impartialité, *f.*

impar'tially, *adv.*, impartialement.

impas'sable (-pàss'a-b'l), *adj.*, impassable, impraticable ; infranchissable.

impassibil'ity (-pas'si-), *n.*, impassibilité, *f.*

impas'sible (-pas'si-b'l), *adj.*, impassible.

impas'sibleness, *n.*, impassibilité, *f.*

impas'sion (-pash'-), *v.a.*, (ant.) passionner, enflammer.

impas'sioned (-pash'eu'n'de), *adj.*, passionné, animé, excité, enflammé.

impas'sive (-pas'sive), *adj.*, impassible, insensible.

impas'sively, *adv.*, impassiblement ; avec insensibilité.

impas'siveness, *n.*, impassibilité, *f.*

impasta'tion (-pés-té-), *n.*, impastation, *f.*

impaste' (-péste), *v.a.*, pétrir ; réduire en pâte ; (paint.) empâter.

impa'tience (-pé-shè'n'se), *n.*, impatience, *f.*

impa'tient (-pé-shè'n'te), *adj.*, impatient, emporté. To get —; *s'impatienter* ; *devenir impatient.* — of, at, for, under, to ; *impatient de.*

impa'tiently, *adv.*, impatiemment.

impeach' (-pîtshe), *v.a.*, mettre en accusation ; accuser ; attaquer ; dénoncer.

impeach'able (-pîtsh'a-b'l), *adj.*, sujet à être mis en accusation ; accusable ; attaquable.

impeach'er, *n.*, dénonciateur ; accusateur, *m.*

impeach'ment, *n.*, mise en accusation ; accusation ; atteinte, *f.* ; blâme, *m.*

impeccabil'ity (-pèk'ka-), *n.*, (ant., theol.) impeccabilité, *f.*

impec'cable (-pèk'ka-b'l), *adj.*, (theol.) impeccable.

impede' (-pîde), *v.a.*, empêcher ; mettre obstacle **à** ; retarder, gêner.

imped'iment (-pèd'i-), *n.*, empêchement ; obstacle, *m.* ; entrave, difficulté, *f.* — in the speech ; embarras de la langue ; bégayement, *m.*;

difficulté à *articuler, f.* To throw —s in the way ; *mettre des bâtons dans les roues.*

impel' (-pèl), *v.a.*, pousser à ; porter à ; mettre en mouvement ; forcer à *ou* de ; exciter.

impel'ler, *n.*, force impulsive, *f. ;* moteur, *m.*

impel'ling, *adj.*, impulsif, moteur.

impend' (-pè'n'de), *v.n.*, être suspendu ; être imminent ; menacer ; être prêt à fondre **sur.**

impen'dence *ou* **impen'dency**, *n.*, imminence, *f.*

impen'dent, *adj.*, imminent, menaçant.

impenetrabil'ity (-pè'n'i-tra-), *n.*, (phys.) impénétrabilité, *f.*

impen'etrable (-pè'n'i-tra-b'l), *adj.*, impénétrable ; inaccessible ; insensible.

impen'etrableness. *V.* **impenetrabil'ity.**

impen'etrably, *adv.*, impénétrablement.

impen'itence *ou* **impen'itency** (-pè'n'i-), *n.*, impénitence, *f.*

impen'itent, *adj.*, impénitent.

impen'itently, *adv.*, dans l'impénitence.

impen'nate *ou* **impen'nous** (-pè'n'-), *adj.*, sans plumes ; sans ailes ; aptère.

imper'ative (-pèr'a-), *adj.*, impératif, obligatoire.

imper'ative, *n.*, impératif, *m.* In the — ; à *l'impératif.*

imper'atively, *adv.*, impérativement.

impercep'tible (-peur'cèp'ti-b'l), *adj.*, imperceptible.

impercep'tibleness, *n.*, imperceptibilité, *f.*

impercep'tibly, *adv.*, imperceptiblement.

imper'fect (-peur-fècte), *adj.*, imparfait ; incomplet.

imperfec'tion (-peur-fèk'-), *n.*, imperfection, *f.*

imper'fectly (-peur-), *adv.*, imparfaitement.

imper'fectness (-peur-), *n.*, état imparfait, *m.*

imper'forate (-peur-) *ou* **imper'forated** (-rét'-ède), *adj.*, (med.) imperforé.

imperfora'tion (-ré-), *n.*, (med.) imperforation, *f.*

impe'rial (-pî-), *adj.*, impérial ; royal ; souverain ; princier ; (of paper) grand jésus. — Federation ; *fédération de l'empire, f.*

impe'rial (-pî-), *n.*, (beard) impériale, royale ; (of a diligence) impériale, *f. ;* (arch.) dôme, *m.*, coupole moresque ; impériale, *f.*

impe'rialist, *n.*, impérialiste, *m. pl.*, impériaux (soldiers of the German Emperor).

impe'rially, *adv.*, (ant.) impérialement ; en empereur ; en roi.

impe'rious (-pî-), *adj.*, impérieux ; arrogant ; urgent, pressant.

impe'riously, *adv.*, impérieusement.

impe'riousness, *n.*, caractère impérieux, *m. ;* arrogance ; hauteur, *f.*

imper'ishable (-pèr'ish'a-b'l), *adj.*, impérissable.

imper'ishableness, *n.*, qualité de ce qui est impérissable, *f. ;* caractère impérissable, *m.*

imper'ishably, *adv.*, d'une manière impérissable, indestructible.

impermeabil'ity (-peur-mi-), *n.*, (phys.) imperméabilité, *f.*

imper'meable (-peur-mi-a-b'l), *adj.*, (phys.) imperméable.

imper'sonal (-peur-), *adj.*, impersonnel ; unipersonnel.

impersonal'ity, *n.*, défaut d'individualité, *m. ;* impersonnalité, *f.*

imper'sonally, *adv.*, impersonnellement ; unipersonnellement.

imper'sonate (-peur-), *v.a.*, personnifier ; représenter ; jouer le rôle **de.**

imper'sonated (-ét'ède), *adj.*, personnifié.

impersona'tion (-so'n'é-), *n.*, personnification, représentation, *f. ;* rôle, *m.*

imper'tinence *ou* **imper'tinency** (-peur-), *n.*, chose étrangère ; (rudeness) impertinence ; (trifle) futilité, *f.*

imper'tinent, *adj.*, étranger, hors de propos ; déplacé ; (rude) impertinent ; (trifling) futile.

imper'tinent, *n.*, impertinent, *m.*, impertinente, *f.*, insolent, *m.*, insolente, *f.*

imper'tinently, *adv.*, hors de propos, mal à propos ; d'une manière étrangère ; (rudely) impertinemment.

impertur'bable (-peur-teur-ba'b'l), *adj.*, imperturbable.

imper'vious (-peur-), *adj.*, impraticable ; impénétrable ; imperméable.

imper'viously, *adv.*, d'une manière impénétrable.

imper'viousness, *n.*, impénétrabilité ; imperméabilité, *f.*

impetuos'ity (-pèt'iou-o-ci-), *n.*, impétuosité, *f.*

impet'uous (-pèt'iou-), *adj.*, impétueux.

impet'uously, *adv.*, impétueusement.

impet'uousness, *n.*, impétuosité, *f.*

im'petus (-pi-), *n.*, impulsion ; force impulsive ; impétuosité, *f. ;* (fig.) essor, *m.*

impi'ety (-paï-è-), *n.*, impiété, *f.*

impinge' (-pi'n'dje), *v.n.*, heurter **contre** ; frapper.

im'pious (-pi-), *adj.*, impie.

im'piously, *adv.*, d'une manière impie ; en impie ; avec impiété.

implacabil'ity (-plé-ka-), *n.*, inflexibilité ; haine implacable, *f.*

impla'cable (-plé-ka-b'l), *adj.*, implacable, acharné.

impla'cableness, *n.*, inflexibilité, *f.*

impla'cably, *adv.*, implacablement.

implant', *v.a.*, planter ; implanter ; graver, imprimer, inculquer.

implanta'tion (-pla'n'té-), *n.*, (ant.) implantation, *f.*

im'plement (-pli-), *n.*, outil ; instrument ; ustensile ; attirail, *m.*

im'plicate, *v.a.*, impliquer ; compromettre.

implica'tion (-ké-), *n.*, implication ; induction, *f.* By — ; *implicitement.*

impli'cit, *adj.*, implicite ; aveugle. — obedience ; *obéissance passive, absolue, f.*

impli'citly, *adv.*, implicitement.

impli'citness, *n.*, caractère implicite, *m. ;* foi implicite, confiance aveugle, *f.*

implied' (-plaïde), *adj.*, implicite, tacite, qui va sans dire.

impli'edly, *adv.*, implicitement ; tacitement, aveuglément, avec une confiance aveugle.

implore' (-plôre), *v.a. and n.*, implorer, conjurer de, supplier **de.**

implor'er, *n.*, personne qui implore, *f. ;* suppliant, *m.*

implor'ingly, *adv.*, avec instance, instamment.

imply' (-plaïe), *v.a.*, impliquer ; signifier ; vouloir dire ; supposer ; contenir ; (to hint) donner à entendre.

impol'icy, *n.*, nature impolitique ; mauvaise politique ; inconvenance ; maladresse, *f.*

impolite' (-laïte), *adj.*, impoli, malhonnête.

impolite'ly, *adv.*, impoliment ; malhonnêtement.

impolite'ness, *n.*, impolitesse ; malhonnêteté, *f.*

impol'itic, *adj.*, peu politique, maladroit ; (of things) impolitique ; imprudent.

impol'iticly, *adv.*, impolitiquement, maladroitement.

imponderabil'ity (-deur'-), *n.*, (phys.) imponderabilité, *f.*

impon'derable (-deur-a-b'l) *ou* **impon'derous** (-deur'-), *adj.*, impondérable.

im'port (-pôrte), *n.*, portée, *f. ;* sens, *m. ;* importance ; (of words) valeur ; (com.) importation, *f.*

import', *v.a.*, importer ; introduire ; signifier ; impliquer ; vouloir dire ; indiquer.

impor'tance, *n.*, importance, *f.*

impor'tant, *adj.*, important.

impor'tantly, *adv.*, avec importance ; d'une manière importante.

importa'tion (-té-), *n.*, importation, *f.*

import'er (-pôrt'-), *n.*, importateur, *m.*

impor'tunate (-port'iou-), *adj.*, importun ; pressant.

impor'tunately, *adv.*, importunément, avec importunité.

importune' (-tioune), *v.a.*, importuner.

importu'nity, *n.*, importunité, *f.*

impos'able (-pôz'a-b'l), *adj.*, imposable.

impose' (-pôze), *v.a. and n.*, imposer. To — upon (to deceive) any one ; *en imposer à, tromper, quelqu'un.*

impos'er, *n.*, personne qui impose, *f.*

impos'ing, *adj.*, imposant.

impos'ing, *n.*, (print.) imposition, *f.*

impos'ing-stone (-stône), *n.*, (print.) marbre, *m.*

imposi'tion (-po-zish'-), *n.*, imposition, *f.* ; (tax) impôt, *m.* ; (deceit) imposture, *f.* ; (at school) pensum, *m.*

impossibil'ity, *n.*, impossibilité, *f.* ; impossible, *m.* There is no doing impossibilities ; *à l'impossible nul n'est tenu.*

impos'sible (-pos'si-b'l), *adj.*, impossible.

im'post (-pôste), *n.*, impôt ; droit d'entrée, *m.* ; (arch.) imposte, *f.*

impos'tor (-pos'teur), *n.*, imposteur, *m.*

impos'ture (-post'ioure), *n.*, imposture, *f.*

im'potence *ou* **im'potency**, *n.*, impuissance ; faiblesse, *f.*

im'potent, *adj.*, impuissant ; faible ; (med.) impotent, perclus.

im'potently, *adv.*, avec impuissance ; faiblement.

impound' (-paou'n'de), *v.a.*, mettre en fourrière ; (fig.) enfermer, confisquer.

impracticabil'ity. *V.* **impracticableness.**

imprac'ticable (-ca-b'l), *adj.*, impraticable ; inexécutable ; (pers.) insociable, intraitable.

imprac'ticableness, *n.*, impraticabilité, impossibilité, insociabilité, *f.*

imprac'ticably, *adv.*, d'une manière impraticable.

im'precate (-pri-), *v.a.*, faire des imprécations **contre** ; maudire.

impreca'tion (-pri-ké-), *n.*, imprécation, *f.*

im'precatory (-pri-ké-), *adj.*, (ant.) d'imprécation.

impreg'nable (-prèg-na-b'l), *adj.*, imprenable ; inexpugnable ; inébranlable.

impreg'nably, *adv.*, de manière à être imprenable ; dans une position imprenable.

impreg'nate (-prèg-), *v.a.*, imprégner ; féconder.

impreg'nated (-prèg-nét'ède), *adj.*, imprégné ; fécondé.

impregna'tion (-prèg'né-), *n.*, fécondation, *f.*

imprescriptibil'ity (-pri-scrip-), *n.*, (jur.) imprescriptibilité, *f.*

imprescrip'tible (-pri-scrip-ti-b'l), *adj.*, imprescriptible.

im'press (-prèce), *n.*, impression, empreinte ; (of sailors) presse, *f.*

impress', *v.a.*, imprimer ; empreindre ; (fig.) inculquer, graver ; (fig.) pénétrer ; impressionner ; faire sentir à ; (sailors) presser ; mettre en réquisition.

impressibil'ity, *n.*, (ant.) sensibilité, *f.*

impres'sible (-près'si-b'l), *adj.*, impressionnable ; sensible.

impres'sion (-près'h-), *n.*, impression ; empreinte ; idée, *f.* My — is that ; *j'ai dans l'idée que.*

impres'sive (-près'-), *adj.*, qui fait une profonde impression ; frappant, touchant, solennel ; émouvant.

impres'sively, *adv.*, d'une manière touchante, d'une manière pénétrante.

impres'siveness, *n.*, force, puissance, grandeur, nature touchante, nature pénétrante, *f.*

impress'ment, *n.*, réquisition, *f.* ; (mil.) racolage, *m.* ; (of sailors) presse, *f.*

imprima'tur (-mé-teur), *n.*, permis d'imprimer, *m.* ; (fig.) sanction, approbation, *f.*

imprint' (-pri'n'te), *v.a.*, imprimer ; empreindre ; graver ; inculquer.

im'print, *n.*, nom de l'éditeur sur le frontispice, *m.*

impris'on (-priz'z'n), *v.a.*, emprisonner, mettre en prison, enfermer.

impris'onment (-priz'-), *n.*, emprisonnement, *m.* ; prison ; détention, *f.* False — ; *détention illégale.* A year's — ; *un an de prison.*

improbabil'ity, *n.*, improbabilité ; invraisemblance, *f.*

improb'able (-'a-b'l), *adj.*, improbable ; invraisemblable.

improb'ably, *adv.*, invraisemblablement.

improb'ity, *n.*, improbité, *f.*

impromp'tu (-tiou), *adj.*, impromptu, improvisé.

impromp'tu, *adv.*, par improvisation, d'abondance.

impromp'tu, *n.*, impromptu, *m.*

improp'er, *adj.*, (pers.) qui convient peu ; (of things) peu convenable à, peu propre à ; (of language) impropre, inconvenant. — character ; *personne de mauvaise réputation, f.* He is an — person for that employment ; *il convient peu à cet emploi ; il est peu fait pour cet emploi.* — fraction ; *nombre fractionnaire, m.*

improp'erly, *adv.*, d'une manière peu convenable ; d'une manière inconvenante ; avec inconvenance ; à tort ; improprement ; mal à propos.

impro'priate (-prô), *v.a.*, approprier ; (canon law) séculariser.

impro'priate, *adj.*, sécularisé.

impropria'tion (-prô-pri-é-), *n.*, sécularisation, *f.* ; bénéfice sécularisé, *m.*

impro'priator (-prô-pri-é-teur), *n.*, possesseur d'un bénéfice sécularisé, *m.*

impropri'ety (-praï-é-), *n.*, (of speech) inconvenance ; (of language) impropriété, *f.*

improv'able (-prouv'a-b'l), *adj.*, susceptible d'amélioration, de perfectionnement.

improve' (-prouve), *v.a.*, améliorer, perfectionner ; utiliser ; profiter **de** ; faire faire des progrès **à** ; faire avancer ; (money) faire valoir ; (land) bonifier ; (to embellish) embellir ; (to cultivate) faire valoir, exploiter. To have —d ; *avoir fait des progrès* ; (in looks) *être embelli.*

improve', *v.n.*, s'améliorer ; se perfectionner ; (of wine) se bonifier ; faire des progrès ; avancer ; (to embellish) embellir, s'embellir ; (com.) hausser, augmenter de prix ; (to recover from illness) se rétablir peu à peu. To — on anything ; *perfectionner quelque chose.* To — on acquaintance ; *gagner à être connu.*

improve'ment, *n.*, amélioration, *f.* ; perfectionnement ; (in learning) progrès, avancement, *m.* ; instruction, *f.* ; (use) emploi, *m.* ; application pratique, *f.* ; (embellishment) embellissement, *m.* ; (of wine) bonification, *f.*

improv'er, *n.*, personne qui améliore, qui perfectionne, qui utilise, *m.* ; réformateur, *m.* ; réformatrice ; cause d'amélioration, *f.*

improv'idence (-prov'-), *n.*, imprévoyance, *f.*

improv'ident, *adj.*, imprévoyant.

improv'idently, *adv.*, avec imprévoyance ; sans prévoyance.

improvisa'tion (-vi-zé-), *n.*, improvisation, *f.*

improv'isator (-), *n.*, improvisateur, *m.*

improvisatri'ce (-ça-trî-tshé), *n.*, improvisatrice, *f.*

im'provise (-vize *ou* -vaïze), *v.a.* and *n.*, improviser.

im'proviser, *n.*, improvisateur.

impru'dence (-prou-), *n.*, imprudence, *f.*

impru'dent, *adj.*, imprudent. An — act; *une imprudence.*

impru'dently, *adv.*, imprudemment.

impu'berty (i'm-piou-beur-ti), *n.*, (jur.) impuberté; enfance, *f.*

im'pudence, *n.*, impudence, effronterie, *f.*

im'pudent, *adj.*, impudent, effronté.

im'pudently, *adv.*, impudemment, effrontément.

impugn' (-piou'ne), *v.a.*, attaquer, combattre; (fig.) mettre en doute, contester.

impugn'er, *n.*, adversaire; antagoniste, *m.*

im'pulse (-peulse) *ou* impul'sion (-peulsh'-), *n.*, impulsion, besoin, *f.*; entraînement; mouvement; motif, élan, *m.*, envie, *f.*

impul'sive, *adj.*, impulsif; qui agit sous l'impulsion du moment.

impul'sively, *adv.*, (ant.) par impulsion; par un mouvement involontaire.

impu'nity (-piou-), *n.*, impunité, *f.* With —; *impunément; sans punition.*

impure' (-pioure), *adj.*, impur; impudique; immonde, obscène.

impure'ly, *adv.*, impurement; impudiquement; d'une manière immonde; avec impureté.

impu'rity (-piou-ri-), *n.*, impureté; impudicité; immondice, obscénité, *f.*

impur'ple (-peur'p'l), *v.a.*, (ant.) empourprer.

impu'table (-piou-ta'b'l), *adj.*, imputable.

imputa'tion (-piou-té-), *n.*, (theol.) imputation; accusation, *f.*; (ant.) avis, *m.* Have you heard any — to the contrary? *avez-vous reçu avis du contraire?*

impu'tative (-piou-), *adj.*, (ant.) imputable; attribué à.

impu'tatively, *adv.*, (ant.) par imputation.

impute' (-pioute), *v.a.*, imputer à, attribuer à.

impu'ter, *n.*, personne qui attribue, qui impute, *f.*

imputres'cible (-piou-très-ci-b'l), *adj.*, imputrescible.

in, *prep.*, en, dans; à; par; pour; sur; (among) chez. — -doors; *chez lui, chez elle, chez eux.* — the air; *dans l'air.* — good health; *en bonne santé.* — the class-room; *dans la classe.* — Germany; *en Allemagne.* — Paris; *à Paris.* — the City; *dans la cité.* — black and white; *par écrit.* — for a penny, — for a pound; *autant vaut bien battu que mal battu; ou le vin est tiré, il faut le boire.* — vino veritas; *qui a bu n'a point de secrets.* To be clothed —; *être vêtu de.* — a black coat; *en habit noir.* The way — which; *la manière dont.* — as much as; *vu que; attendu que.* — blank; *en blanc.* — that; *vu que, puisque.* — the name of; *au nom de.* To know all the —s and outs of a matter; *savoir les tenants et aboutissants d'une affaire, ou savoir le fort et le faible d'une affaire, ou savoir le fonds et le tréfonds de.* — his country; *dans son pays.* — the country (out of town); *à la campagne.* — an hour; *dans, ou en, une heure.* They came — bands; *ils sont venus par bandes.* — self-defense; *pour sa propre défense.* One — ten; *un sur dix.* You must expect that — children; *il faut s'attendre à cela chez les enfants.* He will start — one hour; *il partira dans une heure.* He will do it — one hour; *il fera cela en une heure.* To hold — one's hand; *tenir à la main, tenir en main.*

in, *adv.*, (at home) chez soi, à la maison, y; (in power) au pouvoir; là dedans, en dedans, dedans. Is my brother —? *mon frère est-il à la maison, est-il chez lui, y est-il?* No, he is — *non, il n'y est pas, il n'est pas chez lui, il n'est pas à la maison.* The Whigs are — now; *les Whigs sont au pouvoir à présent.* To be — for

it; *être dedans; s'être mis dedans.* To have —; (pers.) *faire entrer;* (things) *faire provision de; acheter, se procurer.* I have had my coals —; *j'ai fait ma provision de charbon de terre.* My hand is —; *je suis en train, en veine.* —! (nav.) *amène!* Put it —; *mettez-le dedans.* The harvest is —; *la moisson est rentrée.* To take —; (harvest) *rentrer;* (to cheat) *duper; mettre dedans.* To keep — with; *être dans de bons termes avec;* (nav.) *côtoyer (le rivage).* To keep one's hand —; *s'entretenir la main.* To be — for; *en être pour.* To be — and out; *ne faire qu'aller et venir.*

inabil'ity, *n.*, manque de moyens, *m.*; impuissance; incapacité; inhabileté, *f.*

inab'stinence, *n.*, (ant.) intempérance, *f.*

inab'stinent, *adj.*, intempérant.

inaccessibil'ity *ou* (ant.) inacces'sibleness, *n.*, qualité (*f.*) ou état (*m.*) de ce qui est inaccessible, inaccessibilité, *f.*

inacces'sible (-cès'-si-b'l), *adj.*, inaccessible, inabordable.

inac'curacy (-kiou-), *n.*, inexactitude, *f.*

inac'curate (-'kiou-), *adj.*, inexact.

inac'curately, *adv.*, inexactement.

inac'tion, *n.*, inaction, *f.*; repos, *m.*

inac'tive, *adj.*, inactif; (of things) sans action, d'inaction, inerte.

inac'tively, *adv.*, inactivement; dans l'inactivité.

inactiv'ity, *n.*, inactivité, *f.*; (of things) manque d'action, *m.*; inertie, *f.*

inad'equacy (-i-kwa-), *n.*, insuffisance; disproportion, imperfection, *f.*; état incomplet, *m.*

inad'equate (-i-kwéte), *adj.*, insuffisant; imparfait; disproportionné; incomplet.

inad'equately, *adv.*, insuffisamment; imparfaitement; incomplètement; d'une manière disproportionnée.

inad'equateness. *V.* inad'equacy.

inadmissibil'ity, *n.*, inadmissibilité, *f.*

inadmis'sible (-si-b'l), *adj.*, inadmissible.

inadver'tence *ou* inadver'tency (-veur-), *n.*, inadvertance, *f.*

inadver'tent, *adj.*, négligent, étourdi.

inadver'tently (-veur-), *adv.*, par mégarde, par inadvertance.

inaffabil'ity, *n.*, (ant.) manque d'affabilité, *m.*

inaf'fable (-fa-b'l), *adj.*, (ant.) peu affable; réservé.

ina'lienable (-'él-iè'n'a-b'l), *adj.*, inaliénable; inséparable.

ina'lienableness, *n.*, inaliénabilité, *f.*

ina'lienably, *adv.*, d'une manière inaliénable.

inalterabil'ity (-teur'a-), *n.*, (ant.) inaltérabilité, *f.*

inal'terable (-teur'a-b'l), *adj.*, (ant.) inaltérable.

inane', *adj.*, vide; insensé, absurde, vain.

inan'imate, *adj.*, inanimé.

inani'tion (-nish'-), *n.*, inanition, *f.*

inan'ity, *n.*, vide, *m.*; inanité, *f.*

inap'petence *ou* (ant.) inap'petency (-ap-pi-), *n.*, (med.) inappétence, *f.*

inapplicabil'ity (-ap-pli-ca-), *n.*, caractère inapplicable, *m.*

inap'plicable (-pli-ca-b'l), *adj.*, inapplicable.

inapplica'tion (-pli-ké-), *n.*, inapplication, *f.*

inap'posite (-po-zite), *adj.*, peu approprié; déplacé; inapplicable; peu conforme, peu juste; sans rapport.

inappre'ciable (-prî-shi-a-b'l), *adj.*, inappréciable, insensible.

inapprehen'sible (-pri-hè'n'si-b'l), *adj.*, (ant.) incompréhensible, inintelligible.

inappro'priate (-prô-pri-éte), *adj.*, peu approprié.

inap'titude (-ti-tioude), *n.*, inaptitude, *f.*

inarch' (-ârtshe), *v.a.*, (hort.) enter; greffer par approche.

inartic'ulate (-tik'iou-léte), *adj.*, inarticulé.

inartic'ulately, *adv.*, d'une manière inarticulée ; confusément, indistinctement.

inartic'ulateness *ou* **inarticula'tion**, *n.*, inarticulation, *f. ;* défaut d'articulation.

inartifi'cial (-fish'al), *adj.*, (ant.) peu artificiel ; naturel, sans art.

inartifi'cially, *adv.*, naturellement ; sans art.

inatten'tion, *n.*, inattention ; distraction, *f.*

inatten'tive, *adj.*, inattentif ; distrait ; inappliqué.

inatten'tively, *adv.*, peu attentivement ; avec distraction ; sans attention.

inau'dible (-di-b'l), *adj.*, imperceptible, qui ne peut être entendu.

inau'dibly, *adv.*, à ne pouvoir être entendu.

inau'gural (-ghiou-), *adj.*, inaugural.

inau'gurate, *v.a.*, inaugurer, dédier.

inaugura'tion (-ré'-), *n.*, inauguration, *f.*

inau'guratory, *adj.*, d'inauguration.

inauspi'cious (-spish'-), *adj.*, funeste, malheureux, peu propice.

inauspi'ciously, *adv.*, sous de mauvais auspices ; d'une manière funeste.

inauspi'ciousness, *n.*, mauvais auspices, *m.pl. ;* nature funeste, *f.*

inbe'ing (-bî'-), *n.*, (ant.) inhérence, *f.*

in'board (-bôrde), *adv.*, dans la cale d'un vaisseau.

in'born, *adj.*, inné, naturel.

in'bred (-brède), *adj.*, inné, né en soi, naturel.

In'ca, *n.*, Inca, *m.*

incage' (-kédje), *v.*   *V.* **encage'**.

incal'culable (-kiou-la-b'l), *adj.*, incalculable.

incal'culably, *adv.*, d'une manière incalculable.

incandes'cent (-dès'-), *adj.*, incandescent.

incanta'tion (-té-), *n.*, incantation, *f. ;* enchantement, *m.*

incapabil'ity, *n.*, incapacité, *f.*

inca'pable (-ké-pa-b'l), *adj.*, incapable **de** ; non susceptible **de**.

incapa'cious (-pé-shi-), *adj.*, (ant.) de peu de capacité ; (fig.) étroit, borné.

incapa'ciousness, *n.*, (ant.) défaut d'espace, *m. ;* (fig.) étroitesse, *f.*

incapac'itate (-pass'i-), *v.a.*, rendre incapable **de** ; (jur.) frapper d'incapacité, rendre inhabile **à**.

incapacita'tion (-ci-té-), *n.*, défaut de capacité, *m. ;* privation de capacité légale, *f.*

incapac'ity, *n.*, incapacité ; (jur.) inhabilité, *f.*

incar'cerate (-câr-ceur'-), *v.a.*, incarcérer.

incar'cerate, *adj.*, incarcéré.

incarcera'tion (-ceur'é-), *n.*, incarcération, *f.*

incar'nate (-câr-), *adj.*, (theol.) incarné.

incar'nate, *v.a.*, revêtir de chair ; vivifier ; (theol.) incarner.

incarna'tion (-né-), *n.*, (theol., surg.) incarnation, *f.*

incase' (-kéce), *v.a.*, encaisser ; couvrir, enfermer, enchâsser.

incau'tious (-cô-shi-), *adj.*, inconsidéré, imprudent.

incau'tiously, *adv.*, imprudemment, inconsidérément ; par mégarde.

incau'tiousness, *n.*, imprudence, négligence, *f.*

incen'diarism, *n.*, incendie par malveillance, incendie prémédité *ou* volontaire, *m.*

incen'diary, *n.*, incendiaire ; (fig.) boute-feu, *m.*

incen'diary, *adj.*, incendiaire.

in'cense (i'n'cè'n's), *n.*, encens, *m.* —breathing ; *exhalant de douces odeurs.*

in'cense (i'n'cè'n's), *v.a.*, encenser.

incense' (i'n-cè'n'se), *v.a.*, courroucer ; irriter ; exaspérer ; provoquer.

incen'tive (-tive), *n.*, aiguillon ; motif, mobile, encouragement, stimulant, *m.*

incen'tive, *adj.*, excitant ; encourageant.

incep'tion (-cèp'-), *n.*, commencement, *m.*

incep'tive, *adj.*, (ant.) qui commence ; qui marque le commencement ; (gram.) inchoatif.

incer'titude (-ceur-ti-tioude), *n.*, (ant.) incertitude, *f.*

inces'sant, *adj.*, incessant ; continuel.

inces'santly, *adv.*, sans cesse, sans relâche, continuellement, incessamment.

in'cest, *n.*, inceste, *m.*

inces'tuous (-cèst'iou-), *adj.*, incestueux.

inces'tuously, *adv.*, incestueusement.

inces'tuousness, *n.*, état incestueux, *m.*

inch (i'n'tsh), *n.*, pouce (centimètres 2.539), *m.* Every — ; (fig.) *dans toute la force du terme ; jusqu'à la moelle des os ; jusqu'au bout des ongles, dans l'âme.* Within an — of ; *à deux doigts* **de**. By —es ; *peu à peu, à coups d'épingle ; à petit feu, petit à petit.* — by — ; *pouce par pouce ;* (fig.) *pied à pied, petit à petit.* Give him an — and he 'll take an ell ; (prov.) *laissez lui prendre un pied chez vous, il en aura bientôt pris quatre* (Lafontaine) ; ou *si vous lui en donnez long comme le doigt, il en prendra long comme le bras.*

inched, *adj.*, (in compounds) à . . . pouces.

in'choate (ign'co'éte), *adj.*, (ant.) commencé, incomplet, rudimentaire, à l'état d'ébauche.

in'choate, *v.a.*, (ant.) commencer.

in'choately, *adv.*, au premier degré ; à l'état rudimentaire.

inchoa'tion, *n.*, commencement, *m.*

in'choative (-cô-a-tive), *adj.*, qui commence ; inchoatif.

in'cidence, *n.*, (gram., phys., geom.) incidence, *f.*

in'cident, *n.*, incident, *m.*

in'cident, *adj.*, accidentel ; qui arrive ; particulier **à**, qui appartient **à** ; qui fait partie **de** ; (gram., opt.) incident.

inciden'tal, *adj.*, accidentel, fortuit; accessoire. — expenses ; *faux frais, m.pl.*

inciden'tally, *adv.*, incidemment ; fortuitement ; accessoirement, par hasard.

incin'erate (-ci'n'eur'éte), *v.a.*, incinérer.

incinera'tion, *n.*, incinération, *f.*

incip'iency, *n.*, commencement, *m.*

incip'ient, *adj.*, qui commence, premier, naissant.

incise' (-çaïze), *v.a.*, (ant.) couper, tailler ; inciser ; graver.

incised' (-çaïz'de), *adj.*, incisé. — wound ; *blessure par incision, f.*

inci'sion (-cij'eune), *n.*, incision, coupure, *f.*

inci'sive (-çaï-cive), *adj.*, incisif.

inci'sor (-çaï-zor), *n.*, dent incisive ; incisive, *f.*

inci'sory, *adj.*, (ant.) incisif ; tranchant.

incita'tion (-ci-té-), *n.*, (med.) incitation, *f.*

incite' (-çaïte), *v.a.*, inciter, exciter, animer, stimuler ; encourager **à** ; porter **à**.

incite'ment (-çaït'-), *n.*, encouragement, aiguillon, motif, stimulant, *m. ;* incitation, *f.*

incit'er, *n.*, instigateur, *m.*, -trice, *f.*, incitateur, *m.*

inciv'il, *adj.*, (ant.) incivil, impoli.

incivil'ity, *n.*, incivilité, malhonnêteté, impolitesse, *f.*

in'civism (-'iz'me), *n.*, incivisme, manque de patriotisme, *m.*

inclem'ency (-clè'm'-), *n.*, inclémence ; (of the weather) inclémence, intempérie ; rigueur ; (pers.) inflexibilité, dureté, sévérité, *f.*

inclem'ent (-clè'm'-), *adj.*, inclément ; (pers.) inflexible, dur, impitoyable ; (weather) rigoureux, inclément.

incli'nable (-claï'n'a-b'l), *adj.*, (ant.) enclin **à**, porté **à**, tendant **à**.

inclina'tion (-cli-né-), *n.*, inclinaison, pente ; (of the head or body) inclination, *f. ;* (liking) penchant, goût, *m.*, inclination, *f.* From — ; *par inclination, par goût.*

inclin'atory (-claï'n'a-), *adj.*, (ant.) qui incline ; incliné.

incline' (-claïne), *v.a.*, incliner; pencher; porter à, disposer à.

incline', *v.n.*, incliner, baisser, pencher; être enclin, être disposé; (math.) s'incliner; (of colors) tirer **sur**.

inclined' (-claï'n'de), *adj.*, incliné; enclin à, disposé **à**. —plane; (mec.) *plan incliné*, m. I am that way —; *je suis porté à cela.*

incli'ner, *n.*, cadran solaire incliné, m.

incli'ning, *adj.*, incliné; penché; (of colors) tirant **sur**.

inclose' (-clôze), *v. V.* **enclose.**

inclos'ure, *n. V.* **enclosure.**

include' (-cloude), *v.a.*, comprendre, renfermer. Including; *comprenant, compris, y compris.* Including the ladies; *y compris les dames; les dames y comprises.* This room —; *y compris cette chambre.*

includ'ed (-cloud'ède), *adj.*, renfermé; compris; y compris. Not —; *sans compter, non-compris.*

inclu'sion (-clou-jeune), *n.*, inclusion, action de renfermer, de comprendre, f.

inclu'sive (-clou-cive), *adj.*, inclusif, qui renferme, qui comprend. — of; *y compris.*

inclu'sively, *adv.*, inclusivement.

incoer'cible (-co-eur-ci-b'l), *adj.*, incoercible.

incog', *adv.*, incognito.

incog'nito (-cog-ni-tô), *adv.*, incognito.

incohe'rence *ou* **incohe'rency** (-hi-), *n.*, incohérence, f.

incohe'rent (-hi-), *adj.*, incohérent.

incohe'rently, *adv.*, sans cohérence; d'une manière incohérente; sans liaison.

incombustibil'ity *ou* **incombus'tibleness** (-beus'-), *n.*, (ant.) incombustibilité, f.

incombus'tible (-beus'ti-b'l), *adj.*, incombustible.

in'come (-keume), *n.*, rente, f.; revenu, m.; rentes, recettes, f.pl.; revenus, m.pl. — tax; *impôt sur le revenu*, m.

incommensurabil'ity (-'mè'n's'iou-ra-), *n.*, incommensurabilité, f.

incommen'surable (-mè'n's'iou-ra-b'l), *adj.*, incommensurable.

incommen'surate, *adj.*, disproportionné; incommensurable.

incommen'surately, *adv.*, d'une manière disproportionnée.

incommode' (-môde), *v.a.*, incommoder, gêner, embarrasser, déranger.

incommo'dious (-mô-di-), *adj.*, incommode, gênant.

incommo'diously, *adv.*, incommodément.

incommo'diousness *ou* **incommod'ity**, *n.*, incommodité, f.

incommunicabil'ity, *n.*, incommunicabilité, f.

incommu'nicable (-miou-ni-ca-b'l), *adj.*, incommunicable.

incommu'nicably, *adv.*, d'une manière incommunicable.

incommu'nicative (-két'-), *adj.*, (ant.) peu communicatif, insociable.

incommutabil'ity, *n.*, (jur.) incommutabilité, f.

incommu'table (-miout'a-b'l), *adj.*, (ant.) incommuable; (jur.) incommutable.

incompact', *adj.*, non compact.

incompact'ness, *n.*, incompacité, f.

incom'parable (-pa-ra-b'l), *adj.*, incomparable.

incom'parableness, *n.*, incomparabilité, f.

incom'parably, *adv.*, incomparablement.

incompas'sionate (-pash'eu'n'éte), *adj.*, (ant.) peu compatissant; sans compassion.

incompas'sionately, *adv.*, (ant.) sans compassion.

incompas'sionateness, *n.*, (ant.) défaut de compassion, m.

incompatibil'ity (-pat-i-), *n.*, incompatibilité, f.

incompat'ible (-pat'i-b'l), *adj.*, incompatible.

incompat'ibly, *adv.*, d'une manière incompatible.

incom'petence *ou* **incom'petency** (-pi-), *n.*, insuffisance; impuissance; (jur.) incapacité, incompétence, f.

incom'petent, *adj.*, impuissant, insuffisant; incompétent; (jur.) incompétent, incapable.

incom'petently, *adv.*, insuffisamment; (jur.) incompétemment.

incomplete' (-plîte), *adj.*, imparfait; inachevé, incomplet.

incomplete'ly, *adv.*, incomplètement; imparfaitement.

incomplete'ness, *n.*, état incomplet, inachevé, imparfait, m.; imperfection, f.

incom'plex' (-plèkse), *adj.*, (ant.) incomplexe.

incomplex'ity, *n.*, incomplexité, f.

incompli'ance (-plaï'a'n'ce), *n.*, (ant.) manque de complaisance, m.; raideur, f.

incompli'ant, *adj.*, (ant.) peu complaisant; insoumis.

incomposed' (-pôz'de), *adj.*, (ant.) dérangé, troublé.

incompos'ite (-poz'ite), *adj.*, (ant.) simple, incomplexe; (arith.) premier.

incomprehensibil'ity *ou* **incomprehen'sibleness** (-pri-hè'n'-), *n.*, incompréhensibilité, f.

incomprehen'sible (-si-b'l), *adj.*, incompréhensible.

incomprehen'sibly, *adv.*, incompréhensiblement.

incomprehen'sive (-pri-hè'n'cive), *adj.*, peu étendu; borné.

incompressibil'ity (-près'si-), *n.*, incompressibilité, f.

incompres'sible (-près'si-b'l), *adj.*, incompressible.

inconceal'able (-cîl'a-b'l), *adj.*, qu'on ne peut cacher; qui ne peut se cacher.

inconceiv'able (-cîv'a-b'l), *adj.*, inconcevable.

inconceiv'ableness, *adj.*, nature inconcevable, f.

inconceiv'ably, *adv.*, d'une manière inconcevable.

inconclu'sive (-clou-cive), *adj.*, peu concluant.

inconclu'sively, *adv.*, d'une manière peu concluante.

inconclu'siveness, *n.*, nature peu concluante, f.

inconcoct'ed (-coct'ède), *adj.*, (ant.) indigeste; peu mûr.

incondensabil'ity (-sa-), *n.*, (ant.) état de ce qui n'est pas condensable, m.

inconden'sable (-sa-b'l), *adj.*, (ant.) non condensable.

inconfor'mity, *n.*, (ant.). *V.* **non-conformity.**

incongeal'able, *adj.*, incongelable.

incongru'ity (-grou-), *n.*, incongruité; inconvenance, f.

incon'gruous (-grou-), *adj.*, incongru, inconvenant, impropre; saugrenu; (fig.) hétérogène.

incon'gruously, *adv.*, incongrûment; peu convenablement.

incon'sequence (-si-kwè'n'-), *n.*, fausse conséquence; fausse déduction, f.; manque de logique, m.

incon'sequent *ou* (ant.) **inconsequen'tial** (-si-kwè'n'te, -shal), *adj.*, illogique, mal déduit; peu important.

inconsequen'tially, *adv.*, illogiquement.

inconsid'erable (-'eur'a-b'l), *adj.*, peu important; de peu de considération; sans importance; peu considérable; peu sensible; petit; insignifiant.

inconsid'erableness, *n.*, manque d'importance, m.; petitesse, f.; peu de valeur, m.

inconsid'erate (-sid'eur'-), *adj.*, inconsidéré, irréfléchi.

inconsid'erately, *adv.*, inconsidérément; sans réflexion, imprudemment.

inconsid'erateness *ou* **inconsidera'tion**, *n.*, irréflexion ; inconsidération, imprudence, *f.*

inconsis'tence *ou* **inconsis'tency** (-sist'è'n'-), *n.*, inconséquence ; contradiction ; incompatibilité ; versatilité, inconstance, *f.*

inconsis'tent, *adj.*, inconséquent ; peu conséquent ; incompatible **avec** ; contradictoire à ; inconstant, changeant.

inconsis'tently, *adv.*, contradictoirement ; incompatiblement ; inconséquemment.

inconsol'able (-sôl'a-b'l), *adj.*, inconsolable **de**.

inconsol'ably, *adv.*, inconsolablement.

incon'sonance *ou* **incon'sonancy**, *n.*, (ant.) discordance, *f. ;* manque de conformité, *m.*

incon'sonant, *adj.*, discordant ; peu conforme.

inconspic'uous (-spik'iou-), *adj.*, qui n'est pas en vue ; peu marquant ; peu remarquable ; (bot.) mal défini.

incon'stancy, *n.*, inconstance ; diversité, *f. ;* caractère changeant, *m.*

incon'stant, *adj.*, inconstant, volage, changeant, incertain.

incon'stantly, *adv.*, inconstamment ; avec inconstance.

inconsu'mable (-sioum'a-b'l), *adj.*, (ant.) inconsumable ; indestructible ; (not eatable) inconsommable.

incontes'table (-tès'ta-b'l), *adj.*, incontestable, irrécusable.

incontes'tably, *adv.*, incontestablement, sans contredit.

incon'tinence *ou* **incon'tinency** (-ti-nè'n'-), *n.*, (med. and fig.) incontinence, *f.*

incon'tinent, *adj.*, (fig.) incontinent.

incon'tinently, *adv.*, (fig.) avec incontinence ; immédiatement ; incontinent ; aussitôt ; sur le champ.

incontrol'lable, *adj.*, ingouvernable, indomptable, irrésistible ; qu'on ne peut maîtriser.

incontrol'lably, *adv.*, irrésistiblement.

incontrover'tible (-tro-veurt'i-b'l), *adj.*, incontestable, indisputable.

incontrover'tibly, *adv.*, incontestablement.

inconve'nience *ou* **inconve'niency** (-vî'n'-iè'n'-), *n.*, incommodité, gêne ; disconvenance, *f. ;* inconvénient, embarras, dérangement, *m.*

inconve'nience (-vî-ni-è'n'ce), *v.a.*, déranger ; incommoder ; gêner.

inconve'nient (-vî'n'-), *adj.*, incommode ; gênant. If it is — to you ; *si cela vous gêne, si l'heure ne vous va pas.* You come at an — time ; *vous venez dans un mauvais moment.*

inconve'niently, *adv.*, incommodément.

inconver'tible (-veurt'i-b'l), *adj.*, non convertible ; (finances) inconvertible.

inconvin'cible (-ci-b'l), *adj.*, (ant.) incapable de conviction ; qui n'est pas à convaincre.

inconvin'cibly, *adv.*, (ant.) sans possibilité de conviction.

incor'poral, *adj.*, (ant.) incorporel ; immatériel.

incorporal'ity, *n.*, incorporalité, immatérialité, *f.*

incor'porally, *adv.*, d'une manière incorporelle ; immatériellement.

incor'porate (-ré-), *v.a.*, incorporer ; constituer en corps ; former en corporation ; (com.) constituer en compagnie, constituer en société.

incor'porate, *v.n.*, s'incorporer.

incorpora'tion (-ré-), *n.*, incorporation, *f.*

incorpo'real (-pô-ri-), *adj.*, incorporel, immatériel.

incorpo'really, *adv.*, d'une manière incorporelle ; immatériellement.

incorpore'ity (-pô-rî-î-), *n.*, (ant.) immatérialité ; nature spirituelle, *f.*

incorrect' (i'n-cor-rècte), *adj.*, incorrect, inexact.

incorrec'tion, *v.*, (ant.). *V.* **incorrectness**.

incorrect'ly, *adv.*, incorrectement ; inexactement.

incorrect'ness, *n.*, incorrection ; inexactitude, *f.*

incorrigibil'ity *ou* **incor'rigibleness** (-cor-ri-dji-), *n.*, incorrigibilité, *f.*

incor'rigible (-dji-b'l), *adj.*, incorrigible.

incor'rigibly, *adv.*, incorrigiblement.

incorrupt' *ou* **incorrup'ted** (-cor-reupt, -'ède), *adj.*, non corrompu ; pur ; intègre.

incorruptibil'ity *ou* **incorrup'tibleness** (-cor-reup-ti-), *n.*, incorruptibilité, intégrité, *f.*

incorrup'tible (-ti-b'l), *adj.*, incorruptible.

incorrup'tion (-reup'-), *n.*, incorruptibilité ; intégrité, *f.*

incorrup'tive, *adj.*, (ant.) incorruptible.

incorrupt'ness, *n.*, incorruptibilité ; pureté, intégrité, *f.*

incras'sate (-cras'séte), *v.a.* and *n.*, épaissir ; s'épaissir.

incras'sate *ou* **incras'sated** (-cras'séte, -'ède), *adj.*, épaissi.

incrassa'tion (-sé-), *n.*, épaississement, *m.*

incras'sative (-sa-tive), *adj.*, qui épaissit.

increas'able, *adj.*, (ant.) susceptible d'augmentation, augmentable.

in'crease (-crîce), *n.*, crue, augmentation, *f. ;* accroissement, surcroît ; (fig.) produit, rejeton ; (of the moon) croissant, *m. ;* (of rivers) crue, *f.*

increase', *v.a.*, augmenter, faire croître, grossir ; accroître. To — to ; *porter* à.

increase', *v.n.*, croître ; accroître ; s'accroître ; grossir ; augmenter ; s'augmenter ; prendre de l'accroissement.

increas'ing, *adj.*, croissant, augmentant. To go on — ; *aller toujours croissant.*

increas'ingly, *adv.*, de plus en plus, en augmentant.

in'create *ou* **in'created** (-cri-éte, -'ède), *adj.*, (ant.) incréé.

incredibil'ity *ou* **incred'ibleness** (-crèd'-), *n.*, caractère incroyable, *m. ;* incrédibilité, *f.*

incred'ible (-crèd'i-b'l), *adj.*, incroyable.

incred'ibly, *adv.*, incroyablement (fam.) ; d'une manière incroyable.

incredu'lity (-cri-diou-), *n.*, incrédulité, *f.*

incred'ulous (-crèd'iou-), *adj.*, incrédule.

incred'ulousness, *n.*, incrédulité, *f.*

in'crement (-cri-), *n.*, accroissement, produit, fruit, *m. ;* augmentation ; (math.) différentielle, quantité différentielle, *f.*

incrim'inate (-cri'm'-i-), *v.a.*, incriminer.

incrim'inating, *adj.*, tendant à incriminer.

incrim'inatory, *adj.*, tendant à incriminer.

incrust' *ou* (ant.) **incrus'tate** (-creust, -téte), *v.a.*, incruster **de**. *v.n.*, s'incruster **de**.

incrusta'tion (-té-) *ou* (ant.) **incrust'ment**, *n.*, incrustation ; croûte, *f.*

in'cubate (-kiou-), *v.a.*, couver.

incuba'tion (-bé-), *n.*, incubation, *f.*

in'cubator, *n.*, couveuse artificielle, *f. ;* couvoir, *m.*

in'cubus (-kiou-beusse), *n.*, cauchemar, (fig.) grand poids ; lourd fardeau, *m. ;* lourde charge ; oppression, *f. ;* (folk-lore) incube, *m.*

incul'cate (-keul-), *v.a.*, inculquer à.

inculca'tion (-ké-), *n.*, action d'inculquer, *f. ;* enseignement, *m.*

incul'pate (-keul-), *v.a.*, (ant.) blâmer ; censurer ; inculper ; incriminer.

inculpa'tion (-pé-), *n.*, (ant.) blâme, *m. ;* censure, inculpation, *f.*

incul'patory (-pa-teuri), *adj.*, (ant.) qui blâme, qui tend à incriminer.

incult' (-keulte) *ou* **incul'tivated** (-vét'ède), *adj.*, (ant.) inculte, grossier, impoli, sans éducation.

incultiva'tion (-keul-ti-vé-) *ou* **incul'ture** (-tioure), *n.*, (ant.) inculture, *f. ;* manque d'éducation, *m.*

incum'bency (-keu'm'-), n., état d'un objet couché sur un autre ; devoir, m. ; charge ; (ecc.) possession d'un bénéfice, f.

incum'bent, n., titulaire ; bénéficier, m.

incum'bent, adj., couché ; appuyé ; enjoint; obligatoire. To be — on ; incomber à. To feel it — on one to do . . . ; se faire un devoir de . . .

incum'ber (-keu'm'-), v. V. encumber.

incur' (-keur), v.a., encourir, s'attirer, contracter, s'exposer à ; (of debts) se créer, faire.

incurabil'ity ou **incu'rableness** (-kiou-ra-), n., incurabilité, f.

incu'rable (-kiou-ra-b'l), adj., incurable, irrémédiable ; sans remède.

incu'rable, n., incurable, m.f. Hospital for —s; les Incurables, m.pl.

incu'rably, adv., incurablement, sans remède.

incu'rious (-kiou-), adj., (ant.) peu curieux ; sans curiosité ; (not wishing to know) incurieux.

incu'riously, adv., sans curiosité ; avec incuriosité.

incurios'ity (-rioss'i-), n., incuriosité, f.

incur'sion (-keur-), n., (hostile inroad) incursion, irruption, f.

incur'sive, adj., incursif.

incur'vate (-keur-), v.a., courber.

incur'vate, adj., courbé.

incurva'tion (-vé-), n., (ant.) courbure, f.

incurve' (-keurve), v.a., courber.

in'cus, n., (anat.) enclume (ossicle of the ear), f.

in'dagate (-da-ghéte), v.a., (ant.) rechercher.

indaga'tion (-ghé-), n., (ant.) recherche, f.

in'dagator, n., (ant.) investigateur, m.

indart' (-dârte), v.a., (ant.) darder.

indebt'ed (-dèt'éde), adj., endetté ; redevable. — for ; redevable de. — to; redevable à.

indebt'edness, n., état de dette, m. ; dette, f. — to ; dette ou obligation à, f.

inde'cency (-dî-), n., indécence ; action indécente, f., propos indécent, m.

inde'cent (-dî-), adj., indécent ; déshonnête.

inde'cently, adv., indécemment.

indecid'uous (-di-cid'iou-), adj., (bot.) persistant.

indeci'sion (-di-sij'-), n., indécision, irrésolution, f.

indeci'sive (-di-çaï-cive), adj., peu décisif ; indécis, irrésolu.

indeci'sively, adv., d'une manière indécise.

indeci'siveness, n., état indécis, m.

indecli'nable (-di-claï'n'a-b'l), adj., indéclinable.

indecompo'sable (-dî-co'm'pôz'a-b'l), adj., indécomposable ; (chem.) simple.

indecompo'sableness, n., nature indécomposable, f.

indec'orous (-dèk'o- ou -di-cô-), adj., contraire au décorum ; qui blesse le décorum ; indécent ; inconvenant ; messéant, incongru.

indec'orously, adv., avec inconvenance ; incongrûment.

indec'orousness, n., manque de décorum, m. ; messéance ; inconvenance, f.

indeco'rum (-di-cô-), n., manque de décorum, m. ; messéance ; inconvenance, f.

indeed' (-dîde), adv., en effet, en vérité ; vraiment ; réellement ; il est vrai ; à dire vrai ; à la vérité. — ! vraiment! allons donc! comment! (iron.) par exemple ! (surprise) bah ! ah bah !

indefat'igable (-di-fat'i-ga-b'l), adj., infatigable.

indefat'igableness, n., caractère infatigable, m.

indefat'igably, adv., infatigablement ; sans relâche.

indefeasibil'ity (-di-fî-zi-), n., inaliénabilité; imprescriptibilité ; inprescriptibilité, f.

indefea'sible (-di-fî-zi-b'l), adj., inaliénable ; imprescriptible, indestructible.

indefea'sibly, adv., avec inaliénabilité ; avec imprescriptibilité ; d'une manière indestructible.

indefectibil'ity (-di-fèct'i-), n., indéfectibilité, f.

indefec'tible (-di-fèct-i-b'l), adj., indéfectible ; qui ne peut défaillir, ou cesser d'être.

indefec'tive (-di-fèk'tive), adj., non défectueux ; sans défaut.

indefen'sible (-di-fè'n'si-b'l), adj., indéfendable ; insoutenable ; inexcusable.

indefen'sibly, adv., d'une manière inexcusable.

indefin'able (-di-faï'n'a-b'l), adj., indéfinissable.

indef'inite (-dèf'i-), adj., indéfini.

indef'initely, adv., indéfiniment, vaguement; (fig.) à perte de vue.

indef'initeness, n., nature indéfinie, f.

indelib'erate (-di-lib'eur'-), adj., indélibéré.

indelib'erately, adv., d'une manière indélibérée ; sans délibération.

indelibil'ity ou **indel'ibleness** (-dèl'i-), n., (theol.) indélébilité, f.

indel'ible (-dèl-i-b'l), adj., indélébile, ineffaçable.

indel'ibly, adv., d'une manière indélébile ; d'une manière ineffaçable ; (fig.) en caractères ineffaçables.

indel'icacy (-dèl'i-), n., indélicatesse, f. ; procédé indélicat, m.

indel'icate (-dè'l'i-kéte), adj., indélicat, grossier.

indel'icately, adv., avec indélicatesse ; d'une manière indélicate ; indélicatement.

indemnifica'tion (-dè'm'ni-fi-ké-), n., indemnisation ; indemnité, f. ; dédommagement, m.

indem'nify (-dè'm'ni-faïe), v.a., dédommager de, indemniser de.

indem'nity (-dè'm'ni-ti), n., dédommagement, m. ; indemnité, f. Act of —; bill d'indemnité, m. ; (reign of Charles II.), amnistie, f.

indemon'strable (-di-mo'n'stra-b'l), adj., (ant.) qui ne peut être démontré.

indent' (-dè'n'te), n., denteleure ; échancrure, coupure, (stamp) empreinte, f.

indent', v.a., denteler ; ébrécher; échancrer ; (to bind out by indentures) mettre en apprentissage ; (print.) rentrer.

indent', v.n., denteler le bord de papier, de parchemin ; (to contract) passer contrat.

indenta'tion (-té-), n., denteleure ; échancrure, f.

indent'ed (-'ède), adj., dentelé ; bossué ; (bound out by indentures) obligé par un contrat d'apprentissage.

inden'ture (-'ioure), n., (jur.) titre, m. pl., contrat d'apprentissage, m.sing.

inden'ture, v.a., mettre en apprentissage.

indepen'dence ou **indepen'dency** (-di-), n., indépendance, f.

indepen'dent (-di-), adj., indépendant de. — firing; (mil.) feu à volonté, m.

indepen'dent, n., indépendant, m.

indepen'dently, adv., indépendamment ; dans l'indépendance ; avec indépendance.

indescri'bable (-di-scraïb'a-b'l), adj., indicible, indescriptible.

indestructibil'ity (-di-streuk'ti-), adj., indestructibilité, f.

indestruc'tible (-di-streuk'ti-b'l), adj., indestructible.

indeter'minable (-di-teur-mi-na-b'l), adj., (math.) indéterminable ; interminable.

indeter'minably, adv., d'une manière indéterminable.

indeter'minate (-di-teur-mi-), adj., (math.) indéterminé, indécis.

indeter'minately, adv., indéterminément.

indeter'minateness, n., nature indéterminée, f. ; manque de précision, m.

indetermina′tion (-né-), *n.*, indétermination, indécision, *f.*

indevo′tion, *n.*, indévotion, *f. ;* absence de dévouement, *f.*

indevout′ (-di-vaoute), *adj.*, indévot.

indevout′ly, *adv.*, indévotement, *m.*

in′dex, *n.*, indice, indicateur, *m. ; (of books)* table des matières ; (a hand of a watch) aiguille, *f. ;* (of Latin books) index ; (anat.) index, doigt indicateur, *m. ;* (of a globe) index ; (alg., arith.) exposant, *m.* Expurgatory — ; *index expurgatoire ; index, m.* — of refraction ; *indice de réfraction, m.*

in′dex-plate, *n.*, plaque à index, *f. ;* indicateur, *m.*

indexter′ity (-tèr′-), *n.*, manque de dextérité, *m. ;* maladresse, *f.*

In′dian, *adj.*, indien ; des Indiens. — fire ; *feu de Bengale, m.* —, *ou* India, ink ; *encre de Chine, f.* —, *ou* India, paper ; *papier de Chine, m.*

In′dian, *n.*, Indien, *m.*, Indienne, *f.*

In′dian-like (-laïke), *adj.*, comme l'Indien ; en Indien.

in′dicant, *adj.*, (med.) indicatif.

in′dicate, *v.a.*, indiquer ; annoncer ; désigner, marquer.

indica′tion (-di-ké-), *n.*, indication, marque, *f. ;* signe ; symptôme ; indice, *m.*

indic′ative, *adj.*, indicatif. — mood ; *mode indicatif, m.*

indic′ative, *n.*, indicatif, *m.* In the —; *a l'indicatif.*

in′dicator (-ké-teur), *n.*, indicateur, indice ; (orni.) coucou indicateur, *m.*

in′dicatory (-ké-to-ri), *adj.*, qui indique, qui montre.

indict′ (i'n′dite), *v.a.*, (jur.) poursuivre, attaquer, traduire en justice, mettre en accusation.

indict′able (-daït′a-b'l), *adj.*, (jur.) attaquable en justice ; (of things) qualifié crime, qualifié délit.

indic′tion (-dik′-), *n.*, indiction ; proclamation, *f.*

indict′ment (-daït′-), *n.*, accusation, charge ; mise en accusation ; plainte, *f.* Bill of — ; *acte d'accusation, m.* To find a bill of —; *prononcer une mise en accusation.*

indif′ference *ou* **indif′ferency** (-dif-feur′-), *n.*, indifférence, impartialité, neutralité, apathie, *f.*

indif′ferent (-dif′feur-), *adj.*, indifférent, impartial ; passable ; assez mauvais, médiocre.

indif′ferently, *adv.*, indifféremment ; impartialement ; passablement ; médiocrement.

in′digence *ou* **in′digency** (-di-djè′n′-), *n.*, indigence, pauvreté, *f.*

indig′enous (-didj′i-), *adj.*, du pays, indigène.

in′digent (-di-djè′n′te), *adj.*, nécessiteux, indigent.

indigest′ *ou* **indigest′ed** (-di-djèst, -′ède), *adj.*, indigeste, non digéré ; informe.

indiges′tible (-djèst′i-b'l), *adj.*, indigeste, difficile à digérer.

indiges′tion (-di-djèst′ieune), *n.*, (med.) indigestion, dyspepsie, *f.*

indig′nant (-dig-na′n′te), *adj.*, indigné **de** ; plein d'indignation, irrité **de** (things), **contre** (pers.).

indig′nantly, *adv.*, avec indignation.

indigna′tion (-dig-né-), *n.*, indignation, *f.* To give vent to one's —; *faire éclater son indignation.*

indig′nity (-dig-ni-ti), *n.*, indignité, avanie, *f. ;* outrage, affront, *m.*

in′digo (-di-gô), *n.*, (bot.) indigo, *m.*

in′digo-plant, *n.*, (bot.) indigotier, *m.*

indirect′ (-di-rècte), *adj.*, indirect, oblique, détourné ; (fig.) insidieux. — demonstration ; *réduction à l'absurde, f.* — **taxes**; *contributions indirectes, f.pl.*

indirec′tion (-di-rèk′-) (ant.) *ou* **indirect′ness** (-rèct′-), *n.*, voie détournée ; obliquité ; mauvaise foi, fraude, *f.*

indirect′ly, *adv.*, indirectement ; (fig.) insidieusement.

indiscern′ible (-diz-zeur-ni-b'l), *adj.*, imperceptible.

indis′ciplinable (-pli′n′a-b'l), *adj.*, indisciplinable.

indis′cipline (-pline), *n.*, indiscipline, *f.*

indiscov′erable (-dis-keuv′eur-a-b'l), *adj.*, qu'on ne peut découvrir.

indiscreet′ (-dis-crîte), *adj.*, indiscret, peu judicieux, irréfléchi, imprudent.

indiscreet′ly, *adv.*, indiscrètement.

indiscre′tion (-dis-krèsh′-), *n.*, indiscrétion, imprudence, *f.*

indiscrim′inate (-dis-cri′m′i-), *adj.*, confus ; indistinct ; sans distinction ; qui ne fait pas de distinction ; sans discernement.

indiscrim′inately, *adv.*, sans distinction, confusément, indistinctement ; sans discernement, au hasard, aveuglément.

indiscrim′inating (-nét′-), *adj.*, qui ne fait pas de distinction, aveugle.

indiscrimina′tion, *n.*, manque de discernement, *m.*

indispen′sable (-dis-pè′n′sa-b'l), *adj.*, indispensable, nécessaire ; de rigueur.

indispen′sableness, *n.*, nécessité, *f.*

indispen′sably, *adv.*, indispensablement, nécessairement.

indispose′ (-dis-pôze), *v.a.*, indisposer **contre**, déranger, incommoder ; (to make disinclined) détourner **de**, éloigner **de.**

indisposed′ (-pôz′de), *adj.*, souffrant, indisposé **contre** ; dérangé. Not to be — to ; *être assez disposé à.*

indisposi′tion (-dis-po-zish′-), *n.*, indisposition, répugnance, *f. ;* éloignement, *m.*

indis′putable (-dis-piou-ta-b'l), *adj.*, incontestable, indisputable, évident.

indis′putableness *ou* **indisputabil′ity**, *n.*, caractère incontestable, *m. ;* incontestabilité, *f.*

indis′putably, *adv.*, incontestablement, sans contredit, évidemment.

indisput′ed (-′ède), *adj.*, incontesté, reconnu.

indissolubil′ity (-dis′so-liou-bi-), *n.*, indissolubilité, *f.*

indis′soluble (-liou′b'l), *adj.*, indissoluble.

indis′solubly, *adv.*, indissolublement.

indistinct′ (-dis-ti′gn′cte), *adj.*, indistinct, confus, peu précis, vague.

indistinc′tion *ou* **indistinct′ness**, *n.*, confusion, *f. ;* défaut de netteté, *m.*

indistinct′ly, *adv.*, indistinctement, sans ordre, confusément.

indistin′guishable (-dis-tign′gwish-a-b'l), *adj.*, indistinct, qui ne peut être distingué.

indite′ (-daïte), *v.a.*, rédiger ; composer, dicter.

indite′ment, *n.*, (ant.) rédaction, composition ; dictée, *f. V.* **indictment.**

individ′ual (-di-vid′iou-), *n.*, individu ; particulier, *m.*

individ′ual, *adj.*, individuel, seul, unique.

individual′ity, *n.*, individualité, *f.*

individ′ualize (-aïze), *v.a.*, individualiser.

individ′ually, *adv.*, individuellement, isolément.

indivisibil′ity *ou* **indivis′ibleness** (-dis-viz′i-), *n.*, indivisibilité, *f.*

indivis′ible (-viz′i-b'l), *adj.*, indivisible.

indivis′ibly, *adv.*, indivisiblement.

indoc′ible (-doss-i-b'l) *ou* **indoc′ile** (-doss′il), *adj.*, indocile **à** (things).

indocil′ity, *n.*, indocilité, *f.*

indoc′trinate (-doc-tri′n′-), *v.a.*, (iron.) instruire, endoctriner.

indoctrina′tion (-tri′n′é-), *n.*, instruction, *f.*

in'dolence *ou* **in'dolency**, *n.*, indolence, paresse, fainéantise, *f.*

in'dolent, *adj.*, indolent, nonchalant, paresseux. — tumor ; (med.) *tumeur indolente*, *f.*

in'dolently, *adv.*, nonchalamment, indolemment, avec indolence.

indom'itable (-ta-b'l), *adj.*, indomptable.

indom'itably, *adv.*, indomptablement.

indor'sable (-'a-b'l), *adj.*, (com.) transférable par endossement.

indorse', *v.a.*, écrire au dos ; (com.) endosser.

indorsee' (-sî), *n.*, (com.) porteur, *m.* ; personne à laquelle une lettre de change est transférée, *f.*

indorse'ment, *n.*, endossement, endos, *m.*

indor'ser *ou* **indors'or** (-'eur), *n.*, (com.) endosseur, *m.*

indu'bitable (-diou-bi-ta-b'l), *adj.*, indubitable, incontestable.

indu'bitably, *adv.*, indubitablement.

induce' (-diouce), *v.a.*, porter à, engager à, amener à, décider à, déterminer à ; induire à, entraîner à ; (a thing) causer, produire, faire naître. To — the belief ; *donner lieu de penser*.

induce'ment, *n.*, incitation, raison, séduction, tentation, *f.* ; motif, mobile, stimulant, attrait, appât, encouragement, *m.*

indu'cer, *n.*, instigateur, séducteur, *m.*

indu'cible (-diou-ci-b'l), *adj.*, (ant.) qui peut être induit, inféré, causé, produit.

induct' (-deuk'te), *v.a.*, (ecc.) mettre en possession, installer, établir.

induc'tile (-til), *adj.*, (ant.) (phys.) inductile.

inductil'ity, *n.*, (ant.) (phys.) inductilité, *f.*

induc'tion (-deuk'-), *n.*, installation ; prise de possession, (philos., phys.) induction, *f.*

induc'tive (-deuk'tive), *adj.*, qui amène, qui décide ; par induction ; (philos.) (phys.) inductif. —-method ; *méthode par induction, f.*

indue' (-diou). *V.* **endue'.**

indulge' (-deuldje), *v.a.*, tolérer, favoriser, encourager, permettre, accorder ; se permettre, satisfaire, écouter ; se laisser aller à, se livrer à, (pers.) avoir trop d'indulgence **pour.** To — any one with a thing ; *accorder, permettre quelque chose à quelqu'un.* To — one's self ; *s'écouter, se soigner ; s'en donner.* To — in ; *se donner ; se permettre ; se laisser aller à (manger, boire).*

indulge', *v.n.*, se laisser aller à, se livrer à, s'abandonner à, s'adonner à.

indul'gence *ou* **indul'gency** (-deul-djè'n'-), *n.*, plaisir, *m.* ; faveur, *f.* ; abandon, *m.* ; indulgence ; clémence ; (c.rel.) indulgence, *f.*

indul'gent *ou* **indulgen'tial** (-deul-djè'n'te, -shal), *adj.*, indulgent à, **pour, envers,** facile à ; patient, qui se laisse aller à ; qui se livre à.

indul'gently, *adv.*, avec douceur, avec indulgence.

in'durate (-diou-), *v.a.*, (ant.) endurcir, durcir ; (med.) indurer.

in'durate, *v.n.*, s'endurcir, durcir ; (med.) s'indurer.

in'durate, *adj.*, (ant.) endurci ; (med.) induré.

indura'tion (-diou-ré-), *n.*, durcissement, endurcissement, *m.* ; (med.) induration, *f.*

indus'trial (-deus'-), *adj.*, industriel ; de l'industrie.

indus'trious (-deus'-), *adj.*, laborieux ; appliqué ; diligent ; qui aime le travail ; industrieux.

indus'triously, *adv.*, laborieusement, assidûment, diligemment, industrieusement.

in'dustry (-deus'tri), *n.*, travail ; amour du travail, *m.* ; assiduité, *f.* ; (fig.) empressement, *m.*, ardeur, (manufactures) industrie, *f.*

in'dweller (-dwèl'-), *n.*, habitant, *m.*, habitante, *f.*

in'dwelling, *adj.*, qui réside dans le cœur, dans l'âme ; intérieur.

ine'briant (-î-bri-) (ant.) *ou* **inebria'ting** (-î-bri-ét'-), *adj.*, enivrant.

ine'briate (-i-bri-), *v.a.*, (ant.) enivrer ; stupéfier.

ine'briate, *adj.*, ivre. *n.*, ivrogne, ivrognesse.

inebria'tion (-î-bri-é-) *ou* **inebri'ety** (-î-braï-i-ti), *n.*, ivresse, *f.*

ined'ited (-èd'it'ède), *adj.*, inédit.

ineffabil'ity *ou* **inef'fableness** (-èf-fa-), *n.*, ineffabilité, *f.*

inef'fable (-èf'fa-b'l), *adj.*, ineffable.

inef'fably, *adv.*, d'une manière ineffable.

inefface'able, *adj.*, ineffaçable, indélébile.

inefface'ably, *adv.*, ineffaçablement, d'une manière ineffaçable.

ineffec'tive (-èf-fèk'tive), *adj.*, inefficace, sans effet.

ineffec'tual (-èf-fèk'tiou-), *adj.*, inefficace, inutile, vain.

ineffec'tually, *adv.*, inutilement, sans efficacité.

ineffec'tualness, *n.*, inefficacité, *f.*

ineffica'cious (i'n-èf-fi-ké-sheusse), *adj.*, inefficace.

ineffica'ciously, *adv.*, inefficacement.

inef'ficacy (-èf-fi-ca-ci), *n.*, inefficacité, *f.*

ineffi'ciency (-èf-fi-shè'n'ci), *n.*, inefficacité, incapacité, *f.*

ineffi'cient (-èf-fi-shè'n'te), *adj.*, inefficace ; insuffisant ; impuissant ; incapable ; (mil.) un soldat qui n'a pas passé à l'école de bataillon, *m.*

ineffi'ciently, *adv.*, inefficacement, sans efficacité, d'une manière incapable.

inelas'tic (-i-las-), *adj.*, (ant.) non élastique.

inelastic'ity (-i-las-ti-ci-ti), *n.*, (ant.) manque d'élasticité, *m.*, inélasticité, *f.*

inel'egance (-èl-i-, -ci), *n.*, inélégance, *f.*

inel'egant (-èl-i-), *adj.*, sans élégance ; sans goût, inélégant, grossier.

inel'egantly, *adv.*, sans élégance.

ineligibil'ity (-èl'i-dji-), *n.*, inaptitude ; (pol.) inéligibilité, *f.*

inel'igible (-èl-i-dji-b'l), *adj.*, peu propre à ; (pol.) inéligible.

inel'oquent (-èl'o-kwè'n'te), *adj.*, (ant.) sans éloquence, indisert.

inel'oquently, *adv.*, sans éloquence.

inept' (-èpte), *adj.*, (ant.) inepte, faible ; sot ; absurde, peu propre à, inutile.

inep'titude (-ti-tioude) *ou* **inept'ness** (-èpt-'), *n.*, ineptie, inaptitude, *f.*

inept'ly, *adv.*, sottement, ineptement, absurdement.

inequal'ity (-i-kwol'i-ti), *n.*, inégalité ; insuffisance, incompétence, disparité, *f.*

ineq'uitable (-èk'wi-ta-b'l), *adj.*, (ant.) peu équitable, inéquitable.

ineq'uitably, *adv.*, inéquitablement.

inerad'icable, *adj.*, inéradicable, inextirpable, indestructible.

inert' (-curte), *adj.*, inerte.

iner'tia (-eur-shi-a), *n.*, (phys.) inertie, force d'inertie, *f.*

inert'ly (-eurt-), *adv.*, lourdement, d'une manière inerte.

inert'ness (-eurt'-), *n.*, inertie, *f.*

iner'udite (-èrioudaïte), *adj.*, inérudit.

in es'se (-ès'si), *adj.*, positif, réel.

ines'timable (-ès-ti-ma-b'l), *adj.*, inestimable ; incalculable.

ines'timably, *adv.*, incalculablement.

inevas'ible (-véz'-), *adj.*, inéludable.

inev'ident (-èv'i-), *adj.*, caché, qui n'est pas évident.

inevitabil'ity *ou* **inev'itableness** (-èv'i-), *n.*, impossibilité d'être évité, *f.*, caractère inévitable, *m.*

inev'itable (-èv'i-ta-b'l), *adj.*, inévitable, inéluctable.

inev'itably, *adv.*, inévitablement.

inexact' (-ègz'-), *adj.*, inexact.

inexact'ness, *n.*, inexactitude, *f.*

inexcu'sable (-kiou-za-b'l), *adj.*, inexcusable.

inexcu'sableness, *n.*, tort inexcusable; caractère inexcusable, *m.*

inexcu'sably, *adv.*, inexcusablement.

inexecut'able, *adj.*, inexécutable.

inexecu'tion (-èks'i-kiou-), *n.*, inexécution, *f.*

inexhaust'ed (-ègz'haust'ède), *adj.*, inépuisé.

inexhaust'ible (-ti-b'l), *adj.*, inépuisable.

inexhaust'ibleness, *n.*, nature inépuisable, *f.*

inexhaust'ibly, *adv.*, inépuisablement.

inexhaust'ive *ou* **inexhaust'less** (ant.), *adj.*, inépuisable.

inexist'ence (i'n-ègz'-), *n.*, (philos.) non-existence, *f.*

inexist'ent, *adj.*, non existant.

inexorabil'ity *ou* **inex'orableness** (-èks'o-), *n.*, caractère inexorable, *m.* ; inflexibilité, inexorabilité, *f.*

inex'orable (-èks'o-ra-b'l), *adj.*, inexorable, inflexible.

inex'orably, *adv.*, inexorablement.

inexpe'dience *ou* **inexpe'diency** (-èks'pî-), *n.*, inopportunité, *f.*

inexpe'dient, *adj.*, inopportun, mal à propos, désavantageux. To deem it — to; *ne pas juger convenable* de.

inexpe'diently, *adv.*, inopportunément, mal à propos.

inexpen'sive, *adj.*, peu coûteux, pas cher, bon marché ; peu dispendieux.

inexpen'sively, *adj.*, à peu de frais, à bon marché.

inexpe'rience (-èks'pî-), *n.*, inexpérience, *f.*

inexpe'rienced (-è'n'ste), *adj.*, inexpérimenté, sans expérience.

inexpert' (-èks'peurte), *adj.*, (ant.) inexpérimenté, maladroit, inhabile.

inex'piable (-èks'pi-a-b'l), *adj.*, inexpiable.

inex'piably, *adv.*, (ant.) d'une manière inexpiable.

inex'plicable (-èks'pli-ca-b'l), *adj.*, inexplicable.

inex'plicably, *adv.*, d'une manière inexplicable.

inexplic'it (-èks'pli-ci'te), *adj.*, (ant.) qui n'est pas explicite ; obscur.

inexplor'able, *adj.*, inexplorable.

inexplo'sive, *adj.*, inexplosif, inexplosible.

inexplo'siveness, *n.*, inexplosibilité, *f.*

inexpo'sure, *n.*, état de ce qui n'est pas exposé, *m.*

inexpres'sible (-si-b'l), *adj.*, inexprimable ; inouï.

inexpres'sibly, *adv.*, d'une manière inexprimable.

inexpres'sive, *adj.*, dénué d'expression, inexpressif.

inexpug'nable (-peug-na-b'l), *adj.*, (ant.) imprenable ; inexpugnable.

inextinct' (-èks'ti'gn'k'te), *adj.*, qui n'est pas éteint.

inextin'guishable (-èks'tign'gwish'a'b'l), *adj.*, inextinguible.

inex'tricable (-ca-b'l), *adj.*, inextricable ; qu'on ne peut pas débrouiller.

inex'tricableness, *n.*, nature inextricable, *f.*

inex'tricably, *adv.*, d'une manière inextricable.

infallibil'ity *ou* **infal'libleness**, *n.*, infaillibilité, *f.*

infal'lible (-fal'li-b'l), *adj.*, infaillible, immanquable.

infal'libly, *adv.*, infailliblement, immanquablement.

in'famous (-fé-), *adj.*, infâme, indigne ; (jur.) infamant.

in'famously, *adv.*, d'une manière infâme ; indignement, affreusement.

in'famousness *ou* **in'famy** (-fé-), *n.*, infamie, *f.*

in'fancy, *n.*, enfance, *f.* ; bas âge, *m.* ; (jur.) minorité, *f.*

in'fant, *n.*, enfant en bas âge, petit enfant ; (jur.) mineur, *m.*, mineure, *f.* — school ; *salle d'asile, f.*

in'fant, *adj.*, en bas âge, dans l'enfance ; (fig.) naissant, à sa naissance, qui commence. — colony ; *colonie naissante, f.*

infan'ta, *n.*, infante (of Spain, Portugal), *f.*

infan'te, *n.*, infant (of Spain, Portugal), *m.*

infan'ticide (-caïde), *n.*, infanticide, *m.*

in'fantile *ou* **in'fantine** (-taïl, -taïne), *adj.*, (ant.) enfantin, d'enfant.

in'fant-like (-laïke), *adj.*, enfantin.

in'fantry, *n.*, infanterie, *f.* — of the line ; *infanterie de ligne.* Light — ; *infanterie légère.*

infat'uate (-fat'iou-), *v.a.*, infatuer, entêter, tourner la tête à, engouer, enivrer, enorgueillir ; troubler l'esprit **de.** To become —d with ; *s'engouer* de, *s'enticher* de.

infatua'tion (-fat'iou-é-), *n.*, entêtement ; engouement ; enivrement ; vertige, *m.* ; infatuation, folie, *f.*

infeasibil'ity *ou* **infea'sibleness** (-fî-zi-), *n.*, (ant.) nature impraticable, impraticabilité, *f.*

infea'sible (-fî-zi-b'l), *adj.*, (ant.) impraticable, infaisable.

infect' (-fèk'te), *v.a.*, infecter **de**, empester ; gâter, corrompre.

infect'er, *n.*, (ant.) personne, *ou* chose, qui infecte, corrupteur, corruptrice.

infec'tion (-fèk'-), *n.*, infection, (fig.) corruption ; contagion, *f.*

infec'tious (-fèk-sheusse), *adj.*, contagieux, infect, pestilentiel.

infec'tiously, *adv.*, par infection, par contagion.

infec'tiousness, *n.*, nature contagieuse ; nature infecte ; contagion, infection, *f.*

infec'tive (-fèk-tive), *adj.*, (ant.) contagieux.

infe'cund (-fèk'eu'n'de), *adj.*, (ant.) stérile, infécond.

infecun'dity, *n.*, (ant.) stérilité, infécondité, *f.*

infelic'itous (-fi-liss'i-), *adj.*, (ant.) malheureux.

infelic'ity, *n.*, infortune, *f.* ; malheur, *m.*

infer' (-feur), *v.a.*, inférer, conclure **de** ; déduire de ; (fig.) supposer. I — from that . . . ; *je suppose* par *cela* . . .

infer'able (-a-b'l) *ou* **infer'rible** (-feur-ri-b'l), *adj.*, qui peut être inféré ; à inférer ; qui peut se déduire de.

in'ference (-feur'-), *n.*, conséquence, conclusion, déduction, *f.*

inferen'tial, *adj.*, déductif.

inferen'tially, *adv.*, par déduction.

infe'rior (-fî-rior), *adj.*, inférieur ; subalterne, subordonné.

infe'rior, *n.*, inférieur, subalterne, subordonné, *m.*

inferior'ity, *n.*, infériorité, *f.*

infe'riorly, *adv.*, inférieurement.

infer'nal (-feur-), *adj.*, infernal, d'enfer ; diabolique, détestable. — machine ; *machine infernale, f.*

infer'nal, *n.*, (ant.) habitant de l'enfer, *m.*

infer'no, *n.*, enfer, *m.*

infer'nally, *adv.*, infernalement.

infer'tile (-feur-til), *adj.*, (ant.) stérile, infertile.

infertil'ity (-feur-til'-), *n.*, (ant.) infertilité, stérilité, *f.*

infest' (-fèste), *v.a.*, infester ; attaquer, tourmenter.

infeuda'tion (-fiou-dé-), *n.*, (ant.) inféodation, *f.*

in'fidel (-dèle), *adj.*, infidèle, incrédule, impie.

in'fidel, *n.*, infidèle ; incrédule, impie, *m.f.*

infidel'ity (-dèl'-), *n.*, infidélité; incrédulité, *f.*

infil'trate, *v.n.*, s'infiltrer **dans**.

infiltra'tion (-tré-), *n.*, infiltration, *f.*

in'finite (-fi-nite), *adj.*, infini.

in'finitely, *adv.*, infiniment ; fort, à l'infini.

in'finiteness, *n.*, infinité ; immensité, *f.*

infinites'imal (-fi'n'i-tèss'i-), *adj.*, infinitésimal, infiniment petit.

infin'itive, *n.*, infinitif, *m.*

infin'itive, *adj.*, infinitif.

infin'itude (-tioude), *n.*, infinité, *f.*

infin'ity, *n.*, infinité ; immensité, *f.*

infirm' (-feurme), *adj.*, infirme, faible ; maladif ; (fig.) inconstant, irrésolu. — of purpose ; *irrésolu, à l'âme irrésolue.*

infirm'ary (-feurm'-), *n.*, infirmerie, *f.*

infirm'ity ou **infirm'ness** (-feurm'-), *n.*, infirmité ; faiblesse, *f. ;* (fig.) irrésolution, *f.*

infirm'ly (-feurm'-), *adv.*, débilement, faiblement.

infix' (-fikse), *v.a.*, fixer, inculquer, graver ; implanter, enfoncer.

inflame' (-fléme), *v.a.*, enflammer, embraser ; exciter, irriter. *v.n.*, s'enflammer.

inflammabil'ity ou **inflam'mableness** (-fla'm'-), *n.*, inflammabilité, *f.*

inflam'mable (-fla'm'ma-b'l), *adj.*, inflammable.

inflamma'tion (-flam'mé-), *n.*, inflammation; fluxion, *f.* — of the lungs ; *pneumonie, f.* — of the chest ; *fluxion de poitrine ; pleurésie, f.*

inflam'matory (-flam-ma-), *adj.*, inflammatoire ; incendiaire. — speeches ; *discours incendiaires, m.pl.*

inflate' (-fléte), *v.a.*, enfler, gonfler, bouffir.

inflat'ed, *part.*, enflé, gonflé ; (style) boursouflé.

infla'tion (-flé-), *n.*, enflure, *f. ;* gonflement, *m.*

inflect' (-flèk'te), *v.a.*, fléchir ; varier ; détourner ; (the voice) moduler ; (opt.) infléchir ; (gram.) décliner (un substantif), conjuguer (un verbe).

inflec'tion, *n.*, (opt.) inflexion;(gram.) flexion, *f. ;* (of the voice) modulation, *f.*

inflexibil'ity ou **inflex'ibleness** (-flèks'-), *n.*, inflexibilité, *f.*

inflex'ible (-flèks'i-b'l), *adj.*, inflexible.

inflex'ibly, *adv.*, inflexiblement.

inflict' (-flik'te), *v.a.*, infliger à ; (pain) faire à ; imposer à ; causer à, occasionner à.

inflict'er, *n.*, personne qui inflige, *f. ;* auteur (d'un mal), *m.*

inflic'tion (-flik'-), *n.*, infliction, peine, *f. ;* châtiment, *m.*

inflic'tive, *adj.*, (ant.) qui peut s'infliger.

inflores'cence (-rès'-), *n.*, (bot.) inflorescence, *f.*

in'fluence (-flou-), *n.*, influence **sur**, *f.* Undue — ; (jur.) captation, *m.*

in'fluence, *v.a.*, influer **sur** ; influencer.

influen'tial (-flou-è'n'shal), *adj.*, influent, qui a de l'influence, qui a le bras long.

influen'tially, *adv.*, avec influence.

influen'za (-flou'è'n'-), *n.*, grippe, influenza, *f.*

in'flux (-fleukse) ou **influx'ion** (i'n-fleuk'-sheune), *n.*, affluence ; abondance, *f. ;* influx, *m.*

infold' (-fôlde), *v.a.*, envelopper ; entourer.

inform', *v.a.*, instruire, informer, avertir ; renseigner; apprendre à, faire savoir à ; annoncer **à**. To — one's self ; *s'instruire, s'éclairer ;* (of a fact) *s'informer* **de**. To — against ; *dénoncer, accuser.*

inform', *v.n.*, dire, montrer ; (against) faire une dénonciation **contre**, dénoncer.

infor'mal, *adj.*, non en forme ; irrégulier ; insolite, fautif ; sans cérémonie.

informal'ity, *n.*, défaut de formalité, vice de forme, manque de cérémonie, *m.*

infor'mally, *adv.*, irrégulièrement ; sans les formalités voulues.

infor'mant, *n.*, correspondant, *m.*, personne qui fait savoir, qui informe, *f.*, (ant.) accusateur, dénonciateur, *m.*

informa'tion (-mé-), *n.*, nouvelle, information, *f. ;* avis ; renseignement, *m. ;* instruction, *f. ;* lumières, connaissances, *f.pl. ;* savoir, *m. ;* (jur.) dénonciation, révélation, délation ; enquête, *f.* To get — on ; *se procurer des renseignements* **sur**. To seek — ; *aller aux renseignements*. To lay an — against ; *dénoncer.* Appetite for — ; *vif désir de savoir*, *m.*

inform'er, *n.*, délateur, dénonciateur, révélateur, *m.*

infor'midable (-da-b'l), *adj.*, (ant.) qui n'est pas à craindre, peu formidable.

infor'mous, *adj.*, (ant.) informe.

infrac'tion (-frak'-), *a.*, infraction ; violation ; contravention, *f.*

infran'gible (-dji-b'l), *adj.*, (ant.) qui ne peut être brisé ; (fig.) qu'on ne peut enfreindre.

infre'quency ou **infre'quence** (-frî-), *n.*, rareté, *f.*

infre'quent (-frî-), *adj.*, rare.

infringe' (-fri'n'dje), *v.a.*, enfreindre, violer, transgresser. To — upon ; *empiéter* **sur** ; *porter atteinte* **à**.

infringe'ment, *n.*, infraction, violation, transgression, *f. ;* empiètement, *m. ;* (of a patent) contrefaçon, *f.*

infrin'ger, *n.*, infracteur, violateur, *m.*, violatrice, *f.*, (of a patent) contrefacteur, *m.*

infu'riate, *v.a.*, rendre furieux, mettre en fureur.

infu'riated, *adj.*, furieux, en fureur, furibond.

infuse' (-flouze), *v.a.*, infuser ; faire infuser ; verser, introduire ; (fig.) communiquer à, inspirer à, introduire. To be infused ; *s'infuser.*

infusibil'ity (-fiou-zi-), *n.*, infusibilité, *f.*

infu'sible (-fiou-zi-b'l), *adj.*, infusible ; (fig.) qui peut être communiqué ; qu'on peut introduire, ou faire entrer.

infu'sion (-fiou-jeune), *n.*, infusion ; suggestion ; inspiration, *f.*

infu'sive (-flou-zive), *adj.*, (ant.) absorbant.

infuso'ria (-flou-çô-), *n.pl.*, animalcules infusoires, infusoires, *m.pl.*

infu'sory (-flou-ço-), *adj.*, infusoire.

in'gathering (i'n'gath'eur-), *n.*, récolte, moisson, rentrée de la moisson, *f.*

inge'nious (-djî'n'-), *adj.*, ingénieux ; qui a du savoir ; qui a du talent ; de mérite ; de talent; spirituel ; savant.

inge'niously, *adv.*, ingénieusement ; spirituellement.

inge'niousness, **ingenu'ity**, *n.*, caractère ingénieux ; génie ; art ; mérite ; esprit ; talent, *m. ;* habileté, *f.*

ingen'uous (-djè'n'iou-), *adj.*, ingénu, naïf ; candide ; noble ; généreux ; (birth) honorable.

ingen'uously, *adv.*, ingénument ; naïvement.

ingen'uousness, *n.*, ingénuité, naïveté, *f.*

inglo'rious (-glô-), *adj.*, sans gloire ; inconnu ; déshonorant, honteux.

inglo'riously, *adj.*, sans gloire ; honteusement; avec déshonneur.

inglo'riousness, *n.*, absence d'éclat ; bassesse, obscurité, *f.*

in'goer, *n.*, entrant, *m.*

in'going, *n.*, entrée, *f. adj.*, entrant, nouveau. — tenant ; *nouveau locataire, m.*

in'got (i'n'gote), *n.*, lingot, *m.*

in'got-mold (-môlde), *n.*, lingotière, *f.*

ingraft' (-gráfte), *v.a.*, greffer, enter ; (fig.) graver, imprimer.

ingraft'ment, *n.*, (ant.) greffe ; ente, *f.*

ingrain' (-gréne), *v.a.*, teindre en laine.

ingrained', *adj.*, enraciné, invétéré.

in'grate, *n.*, (ant.) ingrat, *m.*, ingrate, *f.*
ingrate'ful (-foule), *adj.*, ingrat.
ingra'tiate (-gré-shi-), *v.n.* To — one's self with ; *s'insinuer dans les bonnes grâces* **de** ; *se concilier la faveur* **de** ; *se faire bien venir* **de**.
ingrat'itude (-tioude), *n.*, ingratitude, *f.*
ingre'dient (-grî-), *n.*, ingrédient; élément, *m.*
in'gress, *n.*, entrée, *f.*
in'growing, *n.*, (of the nails) incarnation, *f.*
in'growing, *adj.*, incarné.
ingulf' (-gheulfe), *v.a.*, (ant.) engouffrer ; engloutir.
ingur'gitate (-gheur'dji-), *v.a.*, ingurgiter.
ingur'gitate, *v.n.*, s'ingurgiter.
inhab'it, *v.a. and n.*, habiter ; habiter **dans** ; vivre **à**, demeurer **à**.
inhab'itable (-ta-b'l), *adj.*, habitable.
inhab'itance *ou* **inhab'itancy**, *n.*, habitation, *f.*
inhab'itant, *n.*, habitant, *m.*, habitante, *f.* (jur.) personne domiciliée, *f.*
inhabita'tion (-bi-té-), *n.*, habitation, *f.*
inhab'ited, *adj.*, habité.
inhab'iter, *n.*, (ant.) habitant, *m.*, habitante, *f.*
inhala'tion (-hél'é-), *n.*, inhalation, absorption des gaz ; inspiration, *f.*
inhale' (-héle), *v.a.*, aspirer; respirer ; humer.
inha'ler (-hél'-), *n.*, personne qui aspire, qui respire, *f.*
inharmon'ic *ou* **inharmon'ical**, *adj.*, (ant.) peu harmonieux ; discordant.
inharmo'nious (-mô-), *adj.*, peu harmonieux ; discordant, peu musical.
inharmo'niously, *adv.*, sans harmonie.
inharmo'niousness, *n.*, manque d'harmonie, *m.*
inhere' (-hîre), *v.n.*, être inhérent **à**, être inné **dans**.
inher'ence (-hî-), *n.*, inhérence, *f.*
inher'ent, *adj.*, inhérent **à** ; inséparable **de**.
inher'ently, *adv.*, par inhérence.
inher'it (-hèr'-), *v.a.*, hériter **de**. To — property ; *faire un héritage*.
inher'it, *v.n.*, hériter ; recueillir une succession.
inher'itable (-hèr'i-ta-b'l), *adj.*, héréditaire ; transmissible par héritage, inhéritable.
inher'itably, *adv.*, en héritage, par voie d'héritage.
inher'itance, *n.*, héritage, patrimoine, *m.* ; succession ; hérédité, *f.*
inher'itor, *n.*, héritier, *m.*
inher'itress, *n.*, héritière, *f.*
inhe'sion (-hî-jeune), *n.*, (ant.) inhérence, *f.*
inhib'it, *v.a.*, arrêter, prohiber, empêcher, interdire **à** ; défendre **à** ; (chancery) inhiber.
inhibi'tion, *n.*, interdiction ; défense ; prohibition ; (jur.) inhibition, *f.*
inhib'itory, *adj.*, inhibitoire.
inhos'pitable (-ta-b'l), *adj.*, inhospitalier.
inhos'pitableness *ou* **inhospital'ity**, *n.*, inhospitalité, *f.*
inhos'pitably, *adv.*, inhospitalièrement.
inhu'man (-hiou-), *adj.*, inhumain, cruel, insensible.
inhuman'ity, *n.*, inhumanité, *f.*
inhu'manly (-ma'n'-), *adv.*, inhumainement, avec inhumanité.
inhuma'tion (-mé-), *n.*, inhumation, *f.* ; enterrement, *m.*
inhume' (-hiou'me), *v.a.*, (ant.) inhumer, enterrer. [traire, **à**.
inim'ical, *adj.*, ennemi **de**, hostile, con-
inim'ically, *adv.*, (ant.) hostilement ; en ennemi.
inimitabil'ity, *n.*, caractère inimitable, *m.*
inim'itable (-ta-b'l), *adj.*, inimitable.
inim'itably, *adv.*, d'une manière inimitable ; au plus haut degré.

iniq'uitous (-ik'wi-), *adj.*, inique, injuste, abominable.
iniq'uity (-ik'wi-), *n.*, iniquité, *f.*
ini'tial (-ish'-), *adj.*, initial ; premier.
ini'tial, *n.*, initiale, *f.*
ini'tial, *v.a.*, mettre ses initiales **à** ; (to sign) parafer.
ini'tially, *adv.*, au premier degré ; au commencement.
ini'tiate (-ish'i-éte), *v.a.*, initier **à**, **dans**, **parmi** ; commencer.
ini'tiate, *v.n.*, prendre l'initiative.
initia'tion, *n.*, initiation, *f.*
ini'tiative, *adj.*, initiateur.
ini'tiative, *n.*, initiative, *f.* To take the—; *prendre l'initiative*.
ini'tiatory, *adj.*, initiateur.
inject' (-djèk'te), *v.a.*, injecter ; seringuer.
injec'tion (-djèk'-), *n.*, injection ; (med.) injection, *f.*, lavement, clystère, *m.*
injec'tor, *n.*, injecteur, *m.*
injudi'cial (-djiou-dish'-), *adj.*, (ant.) qui n'est pas dans les formes judiciaires.
injudi'cious (-djiou-dish'-), *adj.*, peu judicieux, imprudent, inconsidéré.
injudi'ciously, *adv.*, peu judicieusement, imprudemment.
injudi'ciousness, *n.*, manque de jugement, caractère peu judicieux, défaut de jugement, *m.*
injunc'tion (-djeu'gn'k'-), *n.*, injonction, *f.* ; commandement, (jur.) arrêt de sursis, *m.*
in'jure (-djeur), *v.a.*, nuire **à**, faire tort **à** ; léser ; endommager ; faire mal **à** ; blesser ; porter atteinte, *ou* préjudice, **à** ; outrager ; (a thing) faire du mal **à**, gâter ; (med.) léser ; faire une lésion **à**.
in'jurer, *n.*, personne qui nuit **à**, qui fait tort **à**, qui blesse, qui porte atteinte **à**, qui outrage, *f.* ; auteur d'un tort, d'un outrage, *m.*
inju'rious (-djiou-ri-), *adj.*, qui nuit **à**, qui fait tort **à**, qui blesse ; qui porte atteinte **à**, qui outrage; nuisible ; injurieux, outrageant, injuste ; préjudiciable **à**.
inju'riously, *adv.*, injustement ; **à** tort ; injurieusement ; outrageusement.
in'jury (-djiouri), injure, insulte, contrariété, *f.* ; tort, mal, préjudice, outrage, *m.* ; injustice, *f.* ; (to goods) dégât, dommage ; détriment, *m.* ; (med.) lésion, *f.* ; (nav.) avaries, *f. pl.* To the — of ; *au détriment* **de**. [injure, *f.*
injus'tice (-djeus'-), *n.*, injustice ; (offense)
ink, *n.*, encre, *f.* Indian- ; *encre de Chine*. Marking- ; *encre à marquer*. Printing- ; *encre d'impression*. Blot of — ; *pâté*, *m.* In red — ; *à l'encre rouge*. — eraser ; *gomme à l'encre*, *f.*
ink, *v.a.*, barbouiller, *ou* tacher, d'encre ; (print.) encrer ; (drawing) mettre à l'encre.
ink'bag, *n.*, (mol.) poche à encre, *f.*
ink'-bottle, *n.*, bouteille à encre, *f.*
ink'-box, *n.*, encrier, *m.*
ink'-case (-kéce), *n.*, écritoire, *f.* ; encrier, *m.*
ink'fish, *n.*, (mol.) seiche, sèche, *f.*
ink'horn, *n.*, écritoire, *f.*, encrier, *m.*
ink'iness, *n.*, noirceur d'encre, *f.*
ink'ing-pad, *n.*, tampon à impression, *m.*
ink'ing-roll'er (-rôl-), *n.*, (print.) rouleau, *m.*
ink'ing-ta'ble (-té-b'l), *n.*, (print.) table à encrer, *f.*
ink'ling, *n.*, avis, vent d'une affaire ; désir, *m.* ; envie, *f.*
ink'-maker, *n.*, fabricant d'encre, *m.*
ink'stand (-sta'n'de), *n.*, encrier, *m.* ; écritoire, *f.*
ink'-trough (-trofe), *n.*, (print.) encrier, *m.*
ink'y, *adj.*, d'encre ; taché d'encre ; noir comme de l'encre.
inlaid' (-léde), *adj.*, marqueté, incrusté. — work ; *marqueterie ; mosaïque*, *f.* ; *Boule*, *m.*
in'land (-la'n'de), *adj.*, intérieur ; de l'inté-

rieur ; (of letters of exchange) sur l'intérieur ; (geog.) méditerrané, dans l'intérieur des terres. —revenue ; *contributions directes et indirectes, f.pl.*

in'land, n., intérieur (d'un pays), m.

in'lander, n., habitant de l'intérieur (d'un pays), m.

in'lay (-lé), n., (ant.) marqueterie, incrustation ; (of clothes) élargissure, f., soufflet, m.

inlay', v.a., marqueter ; incruster **de**.

inlay'er (-lé-eur). n., parqueteur, marqueteur, m.

inlay'ing (-lé-igne), n., marqueterie, f.

in'let (-lète), n., entrée, f. ; passage, m. ; voie, f. ; (geog.) petit bras de mer, goulet, m. ; (of harbors) entrée, f.

in'mate (i'n'méte), n., habitant, m., habitante, f. ; (lodger) pensionnaire, interne, locataire, m.f. ; habitué, m.

in'most (-môste), adj., le plus intérieur ; intime, le plus profond, le plus secret ; dernier, le plus reculé.

inn, n., auberge, f. ; hôtel, m. ; taverne, f. — of court ; *école de droit, f.* To put up at an — ; *descendre à une auberge.*

inn, v.n., (ant.) loger.

inn, v.a., (ant.) loger ; (agri.) rentrer, engranger.

in'nate (i'n'néte), adj., inné, naturel. — ideas ; *idées innées ; notions premières, f.pl.*

in'nately, adv., d'une manière innée, naturellement.

in'nateness, n., qualité de ce qui est inné, innéité, f.

innav'igable (-nav'i-ga-b'l), adj., innavigable.

in'ner (i'n'neur), adj., intérieur, de l'intérieur ; (fig.) interne, secret.

in'nermost (-môste), adj., le plus intérieur ; intime ; dernier, le plus reculé.

in'ning, n., (agri.) rentrée, f. pl., (at cricket) tour, m. ; (lands abandoned by the sea) lais et relais de la mer, m.pl.

inn'keeper (-kî'p'-), n., aubergiste, hôtelier, hôte, m.

in'nocence ou **in'nocency**, n., innocence, f.

in'nocent, adj., innocent ; permis, légitime.

in'nocent, n., innocent ; (l.u.) idiot, m., idiote, f.

in'nocently, adv., innocemment.

innoc'uous (-nok'kiou-), adj., qui ne fait point de mal ; innocent, inoffensif.

innoc'uously, adv., innocemment, sans nuire.

innoc'uousness, n., innocuité, f.

innom'inate, adj., (anat.) innominé.

in'novate, v.a., innover.

in'novate, v.n., innover ; faire des innovations.

in'novating, adj., novateur.

innova'tion (-vé-), n., innovation, f., changement, m.

in'novator (-vét'eur), n., novateur, m.

innuen'do (-niou-è'n'dô), n., insinuation, allusion, f.

innu'merable (-niou-meur'a-b'l), adj., innombrable, infini.

innu'merably, adv., sans nombre ; innombrablement.

inobserv'able (-zeurv'a-b'l), adj., inobservable.

inobser'vance (-zeur-) ou **inobserva'tion** (-zeur-vé-), n., inobservation, f.

inoc'ulate (-ok'iou-), v.a., inoculer ; (hort.) écussonner.

inocula'tion (-ok'iou-lé-), n., inoculation ; (hort.) greffe en écusson, f.

inoc'ulator (i'n-ok'iou-lét'eur), n., inoculateur, m., inoculatrice ; (hort.) greffeur en écusson, m.

ino'dorous (i'n'ô-), adj., inodore.

inoffen'sive, adj., inoffensif.

inoffen'sively, adv., d'une manière inoffensive.

inoffen'siveness, n., caractère inoffensif, m.

inoffi'cial (-fish'al), adj., qui n'est pas officiel.

inoffi'cially, adv., d'une manière non officielle ; sans les formes usuelles.

inoffi'cious (-fish'eusse), adj., (jur.) inofficieux.

inop'erative (-'op'eur'-), adj., inefficace, sans effet.

inopportune' (-tioune), adj., inopportun, mal à propos.

inopportune'ly, adv., d'une manière inopportune.

inor'dinacy, n., nature désordonnée ; fureur, intempérance, f. ; dérèglement, excès, m.

inor'dinate, adj., déréglé, désordonné, démesuré.

inor'dinately, adv., d'une manière désordonnée ; démesurément ; déréglément.

inor'dinateness. V. **inor'dinacy**.

inorgan'ic ou **inorgan'ical**, adj., inorganique.

inorgan'ically, adv., d'une manière inorganique.

inor'ganized (-'aïz'de), adv., inorganique.

inos'culate (-os'kiou-), v.a., (anat.) unir.

inos'culate, v.n., s'anastomoser ; s'unir.

inoscula'tion (-os'kiou-lé-), n., anastomose, f.

inquest' (i'n'kwèste), n., enquête ; recherche, f. To hold an — on ; *faire une enquête en présence du cadavre.*

inqui'etude (i'n'kwaï-è-tioude), n., inquiétude, f.

inquir'able (-kwaïeur'a-b'l), adj., (ant.) qu'on peut examiner ; sujet à enquête.

inquire' (-kwaïeur), v.a.n., s'enquérir **de**, s'informer **de** ; demander ; s'adresser **à**. To —one's way ; *demander son chemin.* To — into ; *s'informer* **de** ; *faire une enquête* **sur**. To — after ; *demander des nouvelles* **de**. To send to — after anyone ; *envoyer savoir des nouvelles* **de**. I will —, I will — about it ; *je m'en informerai ou j'irai aux renseignements.* He —d after your health ; *il a demandé des nouvelles de votre santé.* — at the baker's, of the baker ; *adressez-vous chez le boulanger, au boulanger.* — within ! *s'adresser ici.*

inquir'er, n., personne qui s'enquiert, qui s'informe, f. ; investigateur, m., investigatrice, f.

inquir'ing, adj., investigateur, scrutateur. He is of an — disposition ; *il est d'un tempérament curieux.*

inquir'ingly, adv., d'un air scrutateur, sous forme d'interrogation.

inquir'y, n., demande ; investigation ; enquête, recherche, f. ; examen, m. pl., informations, f.pl., renseignements, m.pl., (jur.) enquête, f. — office ; *bureau de renseignements, bureau d'adresses, de placement, m.* On — ; *en allant aux informations, aux renseignements.* To make inquiries ; *aller aux informations, aux renseignements.* To make inquiries after ; *prendre des informations, des renseignements* **sur** ; *demander des nouvelles* **de** ; *s'informer* **de**. Without — ; *sans demander, sans prendre des renseignements.*

inquisi'tion (i'n'kwi-zish'-), n., inquisition ; recherche, investigation ; (jur.) enquête, f.

inquisi'tional ou **inquisi'tionary** (-kwi-zish'-), adj., (ant.) assidu dans ses recherches ; inquisitorial.

inquis'itive (-kwiz'-), adj., curieux ; (b.s.) indiscret.

inquis'itively, adv., avec curiosité ; (b.s.) indiscrètement.

inquis'itiveness, n., curiosité ; (b.s.) indiscrétion, f.

inquis'itor (-kwiz'i-teur), n., inquisiteur, m. ; (jur.) qui fait une enquête.

inquisito'rial (-kwiz'i-to-), *adj.*, inquisitorial; (jur.) d'enquête.

inquisito'rially (-kwiz'i-to-), *adv.*, d'une manière inquisitoriale.

inrail' (-réle), *v.a.*, griller, fermer avec une grille.

in'road (-rôde), *n.*, incursion, irruption, invasion, *f.*, empiètement, *m.*

insalu'brious (-liou-bri-) *ou* **insal'utary** (-sal'iou-), *adj.*, (ant.) insalubre, *f.*

insalu'brity (-liou-), *n.*, (ant.) insalubrité, *f.*

insane', *adj.*, fou, insensé, aliéné.

insane'ly, *adv.*, en aliéné ; en insensé ; follement.

insane'ness. *V.* **insan'ity**.

insan'ity (i'n'sa'n'-), *n.*, aliénation d'esprit, aliénation mentale, folie, démence, *f.*

insa'tiable (-sé-shi-a-b'l), *adj.*, insatiable.

insa'tiableness, *n.*, insatiabilité, *f.*

insa'tiably, *adv.*, insatiablement.

insa'tiate (-sé-shi-éte), *adj.*, insatiable.

insa'tiately, *adv.*, insatiablement.

insat'urable (-sat'iou-ra-b'l), *adj.*, (chem.) insaturable.

inscribe' (-scraïbe), *v.a.*, inscrire ; dédier ; graver ; (geom.) inscrire.

inscrib'er, *n.*, personne qui inscrit, *f.* ; auteur d'une inscription, d'une dédicace, *m.*

inscrip'tion (-skrip'-), **inscrib'ing**, *n.*, inscription, *f.* ; (title) titre, *m.* ; (dedication) dédicace, *f.*

inscrip'tive, *adj.*, (ant.) qui porte une inscription ; de la nature d'une inscription.

inscrutabil'ity *ou* **inscru'tableness** (-skrou-), *n.*, impénétrabilité, *f.*, caractère inscrutable, *m.*

inscru'table (-skrou-ta-b'l), *adj.*, inscrutable, impénétrable.

inscru'tably, *adv.*, impénétrablement.

inse'cable (-sî-ca-b'l), *adj.*, insécable, indivisible.

in'sect (-sèk'te), *n.*, insecte, *m.*

in'sect, *adj.*, vil, méprisable.

insec'tile, *adj.*, de la nature de l'insecte.

insectiv'ora, *n.pl.*, insectivores, *m.pl.*

insec'tivore, *n.*, insectivore, *m.*

insectiv'orous, *adj.*, insectivore.

insecure' (-si-kioure), *adj.*, sans sécurité ; exposé au danger ; en danger, chanceux ; hasardeux. To render —; *mettre en danger, en péril.*

insecure'ly, *adv.*, sans sécurité ; sans sûreté.

insecur'ity, *n.*, manque de sécurité ; défaut de sécurité ; le peu de sécurité **de** ; danger, péril, hasard, *m.* ; incertitude, *f.*

insen'sate, *adj.*, (ant.) insensé.

insensibil'ity, *n.*, insensibilité, *f.* ; évanouissement, *m.*

insen'sible (-si-b'l), *adj.*, insensible ; vide de sens.

insen'sibly, *adv.*, insensiblement, peu à peu.

insen'tient (-sèn'shè'n'te), *adj.*, (ant.) insensible, privé de sentiment.

insep'arable (-sèp'a-ra-b'l), *adj.*, inséparable.

insep'arableness, **inseparabil'ity**, *n.*, état de ce qui est inséparable, *m.*

insep'arably, *adv.*, inséparablement.

insep'arate, *adj.*, uni.

insert' (-seurte), *v.a.*, insérer, intercaler, introduire.

insert'ed, *adj.*, inséré, intercalé, introduit ; (bot.) inséré.

inser'tion, *n.*, insertion, intercalation, interpolation ; (bot.) insertion, *f.* ; (of lace) entre-deux, *m.*

inshrine' (-shraïne), *v.* *V.* **enshrine**.

in'side (-saïde), *n.*, dedans, intérieur, *m.*, entrailles, *f.pl.* — out ; *à l'envers.* To turn — out ; (of clothes) *retourner* ; (fig.) *mettre sens dessus dessous.*

in'side, *adj.*, intérieur, d'intérieur, de l'intérieur.

in'side, *adv.* or *prep.*, à l'intérieur ; en dedans.

insid'ious, *adj.*, perfide, traître ; insidieux ; fourbe, trompeur.

insid'iously, *adv.*, perfidement ; insidieusement.

insid'iousness, *n.*, perfidie, trahison ; (of things) nature insidieuse, *f.*

in'sight (i'n'saïte), *n.*, connaissance approfondie, inspection, *f.* ; éclaircissement, renseignement, *m.*

insig'nia (i'n'sig-ni-a), *n.pl.*, insignes, *m.pl.* ; marques distinctives, *f.pl.*

insignif'icance *ou* **insignif'icancy** (-sig-nif'i-), *n.*, insignifiance, *f.*

insignif'icant (-sig-nif'i-), *adj.*, insignifiant.

insignif'icantly, *adv.*, d'une manière insignifiante ; avec insignifiance.

insincere' (-cîre), *adj.*, peu sincère ; hypocrite, dissimulé, faux, trompeur.

insincere'ly, *adv.*, peu sincèrement ; sans sincérité ; faussement.

insincer'ity (-cèr'i-ti), *n.*, manque de sincérité, *m.* ; dissimulation, fausseté, hypocrisie, *f.*

insin'uate (-si'n'iou-), *v.a.*, insinuer ; glisser ; donner à entendre.

insin'uate (oneself), *v.n.*, s'insinuer ; se glisser.

insin'uating, *adj.*, insinuant.

insinua'tion (-si'n'iou-é-), *n.*, insinuation, *f.*

insin'uative, *adj.*, insinuant.

insip'id, *adj.*, insipide, fade.

insipid'ity *ou* **insip'idness**, *n.*, insipidité, fadeur, *f.*

insip'idly, *adv.*, insipidement ; fadement.

insist', *v.n.*, insister **sur**, *ou* à, ce que ; maintenir, persister **à** ; exiger, vouloir absolument.

insist'ence, **insist'ency**, *n.*, insistance, *f.*

insist'ent, *adj.*, (ant.) appuyé, insistant.

insnare', *v.a.*, faire tomber dans un piège, prendre au piège ; enlacer, surprendre.

insnar'er, *n.*, personne qui tend des pièges, *f.*

insobri'ety (-braï-è-ti), *n.*, manque de sobriété, *m.* ; intempérance, *f.*

insociabil'ity, *n.*, insociabilité, *f.*

inso'ciable (-shi-a-b'l), *adj.*, (ant.) insociable.

inso'ciably, *adv.*, d'une manière insociable.

in'solate, *v.a.*, (ant.) exposer au soleil.

insola'tion (-lé-), *n.*, (ant.) exposition au soleil ; (phys. med.) insolation, *f.* ; coup de soleil, *m.*

in'solence *ou* **in'solency**, *n.*, insolence, *f.*

in'solent, *adj.*, insolent.

in'solently, *adv.*, insolemment.

insolid'ity, *n.*, manque de solidité, *m.*

insolubil'ity *ou* **insol'ubleness** (-sol'iou-), *n.*, insolubilité, *f.*

insol'uble (-sol'iou-b'l), *adj.*, insoluble.

insolv'able (-va-b'l), *adj.*, insoluble, indissoluble ; qui ne peut être payé, insolvable.

insol'vency, *n.*, insolvabilité, faillite ; (of things) insuffisance, *f.* Act of —; *loi autorisant la cession de biens, f.*

insol'vent, *adj.*, insolvable ; (of things) insuffisant. — Act; *loi autorisant la cession de biens, f.* Benefit of the — Act ; *bénéfice de cession, m.* To become —; *faire faillite.*

insol'vent, *n.*, débiteur, *m.*, débitrice, *f.*, insolvable, failli, *m.*

insom'nia, *n.*, insomnie, *f.*

insom'nious, *adj.*, qui a des insomnies.

insomuch' (-sô-meutshe), *adv.*, au point que ; à un tel point que ; si bien que ; en tant que.

inspect' (-spèk'te), *v.a.*, inspecter, examiner, visiter ; surveiller ; vérifier.

inspec'tion (-spèk'-), *n.*, inspection, *f.* ; examen, *m.* ; visite ; vérification ; surveillance, *f.*

inspec'tor (-spèk'-), *n.*, examinateur, surveillant, vérificateur, inspecteur, *m.*

inspec'torship, *n.*, place d'inspecteur ; surveillance, inspection, *f.*

inspir'able (-spaïeur'a-b'l), *adj.*, (ant.) respirable ; (physiol.) qui peut être inspiré.

inspira'tion (-spi-ré-), *n.*, (inhaling air) **inspi-**

ration, aspiration ; (respiration) respiration ; (infusion of ideas into the mind) inspiration, *f.*

inspir'atory (-spaïeur'a-), *adj.*, inspirateur, respiratoire.

inspire' (-spaïeur), *v.a.*, (to breathe into) inspirer, souffler **dans** ; souffler ; (to draw into the lungs) aspirer ; (to infuse into the mind) inspirer **à**. To be —d with ; *être inspiré* **de**.

inspire', *v.n.*, aspirer.

inspir'er, *n.*, inspirateur, *m.*

inspir'ing, *adj.*, inspirateur ; inspirant.

inspir'it (-spir'ite), *v.a.*, animer, encourager.

inspis'sate, *v.a.*, épaissir.

inspissa'tion (-'sé-), *n.*, épaississement, *m.*

instabil'ity, *n.*, instabilité, *f.*

insta'ble (-sté-b'l), *adj.*, peu stable ; inconstant : instable.

install' (-stôl), *v.a.*, installer.

installa'tion (-stôl'lé-), *n.*, installation, *f.*

install'ment (-stôl'-), *n.*, installation, *f.*; (l.u.) siège ; (of money) versement partiel (de fonds), acompte, *m.*

in'stance, *n.*, demande, instance, *f.* ; exemple, *m.* ; occasion, circonstance, *f.* ; cas, *m.* For —; *par exemple.* In the first —; *dans le principe; pour la première fois; au préalable, préalablement, dès le début.*

in'stance, *v.a.*, citer, *ou* donner, pour exemple.

in'stant, *adj.*, instant, urgent, pressant, important ; immédiat, instantané ; (of the month) courant, présent.

in'stant, *n.*, instant, moment, *m.* This —; *à l'instant, tout de suite.* The — that . . .; *aussitôt que, dès que.*

instanta'neous (-té-ni-), *adj.*, instantané.

instanta'neously, *adv.*, instantanément.

instanta'neousness, *n.*, instantanéité, *f.*

instan'ter, *adv.*, immédiatement, sans délai ; séance tenante.

in'stantly, *adv.*, à l'instant ; tout de suite ; sur-le-champ ; (urgently) (ant.) instamment, avec instance.

instead' (-stède), *adv.*, à sa place, à la place, en place. — of ; *au lieu* **de**, *en place* **de**, *à la place* **de**. To be — of ; *tenir lieu* **de**. To stand, *ou* do, — of ; *remplacer, tenir lieu* **de**.

in'step (-stèpe), *n.*, cou-de-pied ; (anat.) tarse ; (of a horse) canon, *m.*

in'stigate, *v.a.*, exciter à, inciter à, entraîner à, pousser à, instiguer, provoquer.

instiga'tion (-ghé-), *n.*, instigation, *f.*

in'stigator (-ghét-eur), *n.*, instigateur, *m.*, instigatrice, *f.*

instill', *v.a.*, instiller ; (fig.) inspirer ; graver, inculquer, imprimer dans l'esprit.

instilla'tion (-stil'lé-), *n.*, instillation ; (fig.) action de graver, d'inculquer dans l'esprit, inspiration, *f.*

instil'ler (-stil'leur), *n.*, personne qui instille ; (fig.) personne qui grave, qui inculque, *f.*

in'stinct, *n.*, instinct, *m.*

instinct', *adj.*, animé, stimulé, poussé. — with life ; *respirant la vie.*

instinc'tive, *adj.*, instinctif, spontané ; de prime saut.

instinc'tively, *adv.*, instinctivement ; par instinct ; de prime saut.

in'stitute (-sti-tioute), *n.*, institution, *f.* ; principe, précepte, *m.*, maxime, *f.*; (learned society) institut, *m.*

in'stitute, *v.a.*, instituer, établir, fonder ; commencer ; (a lawsuit) intenter ; (an ecclesiastic) investir. To — proceedings against somebody ; *intenter un procès à quelqu'un ; commencer des poursuites judiciaires* **contre**.

institu'tion (-sti-tiou-), *n.*, institution, établissement, *m.*, (of an ecclesiastical) investiture, *f.*

in'stitutive, *adj.*, d'institution.

in'stitutor (-tiout'eur), *n.*, fondateur, *m.*, fondatrice, *f.*

instruct' (-streuk'te), *v.a.*, instruire, enseigner ; donner des instructions **à**, enjoindre **de**, charger **de**.

instruc'tion (-streuk'-), *n.*, instruction ; leçon, *f.* ; enseignement, *m.*

instruc'tive (-streuk'-), *adj.*, instructif.

instruc'tively, *adv.*, d'une manière instructive.

instruc'tor (-streuk'teur), *n.*, instituteur ; professeur, précepteur, maître, *m.*

instruc'tress, *n.*, institutrice, *f.*

in'strument (-strou-), *n.*, instrument ; (jur.) acte, titre, (fig.) agent, instrument, *m.*

instrumen'tal, *adj.*, instrumental ; d'instrument ; cause. To be —; *contribuer* **à***, servir* **à**.

instrumental'ity, *n.*, concours, moyen, *m.* ; action, *f.*

instrumen'tally, *adv.*, comme moyen ; (mus.) par des instruments de musique.

instrumen'talness. *V.* **instrumental'ity.**

insubjec'tion (-seub'djèk'-) *n.*, (ant.) révolte, désobéissance, *f.*

insubmis'sion (-seub'-), *n.*, manque de soumission, *m.* ; insoumission, *f.*

insubor'dinate (-seub'-), *adj.*, insubordonné.

insubordina'tion (-seub'or-di-né-), *n.*, insubordination, désobéissance, *f.* ; désordre, *m.*

insuf'ferable (-seuf'feur'a-b'l), *adj.*, insupportable, intolérable ; détestable.

insuf'ferably, *adv.*, insupportablement ; intolérablement ; détestablement.

insuffi'cience *ou* **insuffi'ciency** (-seuf-fish'-), *n.*, insuffisance, incompétence, *f.*

insuffi'cient, *adj.*, insuffisant, incapable, incompétent.

insuffi'ciently, *adv.*, insuffisamment.

insuffla'tion (-seuf-flé-), *n.*, insufflation, *f.*

in'sular *ou* **in'sulary** (-siou-), *adj.*, insulaire ; (fig.) étroit, rétréci, insulaire.

in'sular, *n.*, insulaire, *m.f.*

insular'ity, *n.*, insularité, *f.*

in'sulate (-siou-), *v.a.*, isoler.

in'sulated, *adj.*, isolé.

insula'tion (-siou-lé-), *n.*, action d'isoler ; (phys.) isolation, *f.* ; isolement, *m.*

in'sulator (-siou-lét'eur), *n.*, (phys.) isoloir, isolateur, mauvais conducteur, *m.*

in'sult (-seulte), *n.*, insulte, injure, *f.*, affront, outrage, *m.* To offer an — to any one ; *faire insulte, faire une insulte, un affront, à quelqu'un.*

insult', *v.a.*, faire insulte **à**, insulter, outrager, injurier.

insult', *v.n.*, triompher insolemment, se comporter insolemment ; insulter **à**.

insult'er, *n.*, insulteur, *m.*

insult'ing, *adj.*, insultant, outrageant, outrageux, injurieux.

insult'ingly, *adv.*, insolemment, outrageusement, injurieusement, d'une manière insultante.

insu'perable (-siou-peur'a-b'l), *adj.*, insurmontable, invincible.

insu'perableness *ou* **insuperabil'ity** (-siou-peur'-), *n.*, nature insurmontable, *f.*

insu'perably (-siou-peur'-), *adv.*, d'une manière insurmontable, invinciblement.

insupport'able (-seup-pôrt'a-b'l), *adj.*, insupportable, intolérable.

insupport'ableness, *n.*, nature insupportable, *f.*

insupport'ably, *adv.*, insupportablement, intolérablement.

insuppres'sible (-seup'près'i-b'l), *adj.*, qu'on ne peut supprimer ; (of laughter) inextinguible, irrésistible. — laughter; *fou rire, m.*

insur'able (-shour'a-b'l), *adj.*, susceptible d'être assuré, assurable.

insur'ance (-shour'-), *n.*, assurance, *f.* Life—; *assurance sur la vie.* Fire— ; *assurance contre l'incendie.* —broker ; *courtier d'assurances, m.* —company ; *compagnie d'assurances, f.* —

office ; *bureau d'assurances, m.* Marine — company ; *compagnie d'assurances maritimes, f.*

insure' (-shoure), *v.a.* and *n.*, assurer, faire assurer, garantir.

insured' (-shour'de), *n.*, assuré, *m.*, assurée, *f.*

insur'er (-shour'-), *n.*, assureur, *m.*

insur'gent (-seur-djè'n'te), *n.*, insurgé, *m.*

insur'gent, *adj.*, insurgé.

insurmount'able (-seur-maou'n't'a-b'l), *adj.*, insurmontable ; infranchissable.

insurmount'ably, *adv.*, d'une manière insurmontable.

insurrec'tion (-seur-rèk'-), *n.*, insurrection, *f.* ; soulèvement, *m.* To rise in — ; *s'insurger, se soulever.*

insurrec'tionary (-seur-rèk'sh'-), *adj.*, insurrectionnel.

insusceptibil'ity (-seus'cèp-), *n.*, manque de susceptibilité, *m.*, insensibilité à, *f.*

insuscep'tible (-seus-cèp'ti-b'l), *adj.*, qui n'est pas susceptible de, insensible à.

intact', *adj.*, intact.

intact'able *ou* **intact'ible** (-'i-b'l), *adj.*, (ant.) intangible.

intagl'iated (i'n'tal'yé-tède), *adj.*, gravé en creux.

intagl'io (i'n'tal'yō), *n.*, (arts) intaille ; gravure en creux, *f.*

intangibil'ity *ou* **intan'gibleness** (-dji-), *n.*, (ant.) intangibilité ; qualité de ce qui est intangible, *f.*

intan'gible (-dji-b'l), *adj.*, (ant.) intangible.

intan'gibly, *adv.*, d'une manière intangible.

in'teger (i'n'ti-djeur), *n.*, entier, nombre entier, *m.*

in'tegral (-ti-), *adj.*, entier ; intégral ; (chem.) intégrant ; (alg.) intégral.

in'tegral, *n.*, totalité, *f.* ; tout, *m.* ; (math.) intégrale, *f.*

in'tegrant (-ti-), *adj.*, intégrant.

in'tegrate (-ti-), *v.a.*, rendre entier ; (math.) intégrer.

integra'tion (-ti-gré-), *n.*, action de rendre entier ; (math.) intégration, *f.*

integ'rity (-tèg'-), *n.*, intégrité ; probité, rectitude ; pureté, *f.*

integ'ument (-tègh'iou-), *n.*, tégument, *m.*

in'tellect (-tèl'lèk'te), *n.*, intelligence, faculté intellectuelle, *f.* ; esprit ; intellect, entendement, *m.*

intellec'tion (-lèk'sheune), *n.*, (ant.) (log.) appréhension, intellective, compréhension, *f.*

intellec'tive, *adj.*, (ant.) intellectuel ; (philos.) intellectif.

intellect'ual (-lèk't'iou-), *adj.*, intellectuel ; intelligent.

intellect'ualist, *n.*, (ant.) personne qui exagère les facultés de l'intelligence, *f.*

intellect'ually, *adv.*, intellectuellement ; d'une manière intellectuelle ; dans l'intelligence.

intel'ligence (-'li-djè'n'ce), *n.*, intelligence, *f.* ; esprit, *m.* ; (information) nouvelle, *f.*, nouvelles, *f.pl.*, renseignements, *m.pl.*, avis ; (concord) accord, *m.*, intelligence, *f.* Piece of — ; *nouvelle, f.* — department ; *service des renseignements, m.* — office ; *bureau de renseignements, m.* Latest — ; *dernières nouvelles, f.pl.* To have — with ; *avoir des communications, des intelligences,* **avec.** To receive — that ; *apprendre que.*

intel'ligencer, *n.*, personne qui fournit des renseignements, *f.* ; donneur de nouvelles, *m.*, donneuse de nouvelles, *f.* ; messager, *m.* ; (newspaper) gazette, *f.*, moniteur, nouvelliste, messager, *m.*

intel'ligent (-'li-djè'n'te), *adj.*, intelligent.

intel'ligently, *adv.*, avec intelligence.

intelligibil'ity *ou* **intel'ligibleness** (-dji-), *n.*, intelligibilité, clarté, *f.*

intel'ligible (-dji-b'l), *adj.*, intelligible.

intel'ligibly, *adv.*, intelligiblement.

intem'perament (-tè'm'peur'a-), *n.*, (ant.) mauvais état, mauvais tempérament, *m.* ; mauvaise constitution, *f.*

intem'perance (-tè'm'peur'-), *n.*, intempérance, *f.*

intem'perate (-tè'm'peur-), *adj.*, déréglé, intempérant ; désordonné ; démesuré, immodéré ; (of language) violent, emporté ; peu mesuré ; (of the climate) non tempéré, (of the weather) orageux.

intem'perately (-tè'm'peur-ét'li), *adv.*, avec intempérance, démesurément, immodérément.

intem'perateness, *n.*, dérèglement, *m.* ; (of the weather) intempérie, *f.*

intend', *v.a.*, se proposer de ; avoir dessein de, avoir l'intention de, compter, vouloir ; (to reserve) destiner à.

intend'ant, *n.*, (ant.) intendant, *m.*

intend'ed, *adj.*, projeté ; intentionnel, prémédité, destiné à. To be — for ; *être destiné à.*

intend'ed, *n.*, (pop.) prétendu, futur époux, *m.*, prétendue, future épouse, *f.*

intend'edly, *adv.*, (ant.) à dessein.

intense', *adj.*, (strained) tendu ; (vehement) véhément, chaleureux, ardent ; (application) opiniâtre, acharné ; (of heat, cold) intense ; (of suffering, pain) vif, fort, aigu. — blue ; *bleu foncé* (invariable).

intense'ly, *adv.*, avec intensité ; avec opiniâtreté ; chaleureusement ; avec acharnement ; vivement ; fortement.

intense'ness, *n.*, tension, intensité ; force, violence ; ardeur, opiniâtreté, *f.*, acharnement, *m.* ; (of thought) contention, *f.*

inten'sity. *V.* **intense'ness.**

inten'sive, *adj.*, qui sert à rendre plus intense ; qui donne de la force.

intent', *n.*, dessein, but, objet ; sens, *m.*, intention, portée, signification, *f.* To all —s ; *dans tous les sens.* To all —s and purposes ; *à tous égards ; en réalité ; sous tous les rapports.* To the — that ; *afin que.*

intent', *adj.*, fort attentif, fort attaché, fort appliqué, déterminé à.

inten'tion, *n.*, intention, *f.* ; dessein, but, *m.* To heal by first —; *se cicatriser sans former de pus.*

inten'tional, *adj.*, intentionnel ; d'intention ; fait à dessein.

inten'tionally, *adv.*, avec intention, à dessein.

inten'tioned (-tè'n'sheu'n'de), *adj.*, (ant.) intentionné (only used with *bien, mal,* or *mieux*).

intent'ly, *adv.*, fort attentivement ; avec ardeur, avec zèle.

intent'ness, *n.*, forte attention, forte application, *f.*

inter' (-teur), *v.a.*, enterrer, inhumer, ensevelir.

interact' (-teur'-), *n.*, intermède ; entr'acte, *m.*

inter'calar *ou* **inter'calary** (-teur-), *adj.*, intercalaire.

inter'calate (-teur-), *v.a.*, intercaler.

intercala'tion (-lé-), *n.*, intercalation, *f.*

intercede' (-teur'cîde), *v.n.*, intercéder **auprès de.**

interced'er, *n.*, intercesseur, *m.*

interced'ing, *n.*, intercession, *f.*

intercept' (-teur-cèpte), *v.a.*, intercepter ; arrêter, interrompre, (the sight) dérober, surprendre.

intercept'er, *n.*, qui intercepte.

intercep'tion, *n.*, (ant.) interception ; interruption, *f.*

interces'sion (-teur-cèsh'-), *n.*, intercession, *f.*

interces'sor (-teur-cès'-), *n.*, intercesseur, *m.*

interchain' (-teur-tshéne), *v.a.*, (ant.) enchaîner.

in'terchange (-teur-tshé'n'dje), *n.*, échange, *m.*, succession, suite, *f.* ; (fig.) variété.

interchange', *v.a.*, donner par échange, échanger.

interchange'able (-teur-tshé'n'dj'a-b'l), *adj.*, échangeable ; qui se succède alternativement.

interchange'ableness, *n.*, nature échangeable ; succession alternative, *f.*

interchange'ably, *adv.*, alternativement, réciproquement.

intercolo'nial, *adj.*, intercolonial.

intercolumnia'tion (-teur-co-leu'm'-ni-é-), *n.*, (arch.) entre-colonne, entre-colonnement, *m.*

intercommu'nicate (-teur-co'm'miou-), *v.n.*, (ant.) communiquer ensemble.

intercommuni'cation, intercommu'nity, (-teur-co'm'miou-ni-ké'-), *n.*, communication réciproque, *f.*

intercos'tal, *adj.*, intercostal.

in'tercourse (-teur-côrse), *n.*, correspondance, *f.* ; commerce, *m.* ; relations, *f.pl.* ; rapports, *m.pl.*

interdict' (-teur'dik'te), *v.a.*, interdire, interdire à, défendre à, défendre.

in'terdict (teur-dik'te) *ou* **interdiction** (-dik'-), *n.*, interdiction, défense, prohibition, *f.* ; (canon law) interdit, *m.*

interdic'tory, *adj.*, d'interdiction.

in'terest (-teur'èste), *v.a.*, intéresser. To — one's self in ; *s'intéresser à*.

in'terest (i'n'teur'èste), *n.*, intérêt, *m.* ; intérêts, *m.pl.* ; (influence) pouvoir, crédit, *m.*, protection, *f.* Compound — ; *intérêt composé* ; *intérêt des intérêts, m.* Simple — ; *intérêt simple, m.* At —, upon — ; *à intérêt.* To one's — ; *dans son intérêt.* To promote any one's — ; *favoriser les intérêts de quelqu'un.* To have — with ; *avoir du crédit auprès de.* To give one's — to any one ; *accorder sa protection à quelqu'un.* To secure — (with any one) ; *mettre quelqu'un dans ses intérêts.* To bear — ; *porter intérêt.* To pay the — ; (fin.) *servir les intérêts.* To put out to — ; *placer à intérêt.* To pay with — ; *payer*, ou *rendre, avec usure.*

in'terested, *adj.*, intéressé.

in'teresting, *adj.*, intéressant.

in'terestingly, *adv.*, avec intérêt, d'une manière intéressante.

interfere' (-teur-fîre), *v.n.*, intervenir, se mêler **de**, s'entre-mettre ; s'ingérer, s'immiscer **dans** ; (to clash) être en conflit, s'entre-choquer ; (to hinder) mettre obstacle **à**, déranger, entraver.

interfer'ence (-teur-fîr'-), *n.*, intervention, ingérence, *f.* ; (collision) choc, *m.*, collision ; (man.) atteinte, *f.*

inter'fluent *ou* **inter'fluous** (-teur-flou-), *adj.*, (ant.) qui coule entre (deux).

interful'gent (-teur-feul-djè'n'te), *adj.*, (ant.) reluisant **entre**.

interfused' (-teur-fiou'z'de), *adj.*, (ant.) répandu **entre**.

in'terim (-teur-), *n.*, intérim, intervalle, *m.*, entrefaites, *f.pl.* In the — ; *en attendant ; sur ces entrefaites ; dans l'intérim.* Ad — ; *par intérim.* — functions ; *functions intérimaires, f.pl.*

inte'rior (-tî-), *adj.*, intérieur, interne.

inte'rior, *n.*, intérieur, *m.*

inte'riorly, *adv.*, (ant.) intérieurement.

interja'cent (-teur-djé-), *adj.*, situé entre, situé au milieu **de**, intermédiaire.

interject' (-teur'djèk'te), *v.a.*, interjeter ; jeter **entre** ; interposer ; insérer.

interjec'tion (-teur'djèk'-), *n.*, interjection, *f.*

interjec'tional, *adj.*, interjectif.

interjoin' (-teur'djoi'ne), *v.a.*, (ant.) unir, marier réciproquement.

interjoist' (-teur'djôïste), *n.*, (arch.) entrevous, *m.*

interlace' (-teur'-), *v.a.*, entremêler ; entrelacer.

interla'cing, *n.*, entrelacement, entremêlement, enchevêtrement, *m.*

interlard' (-teur-lârde), *v.a.*, entrelarder; (fig.) entrelarder **de**.

interlard'ing, *n.* entrelardement, *m.*

in'terleaf (-teur'lîfe), *n.*, feuillet intercalé, feuillet blanc, *m.*

interleave' (-teur-lîve), *v.a.*, interfolier.

interline' (-teur-laïne), *v.a.*, écrire entre les lignes, (l.u.) interlinéer, interligner, intercaler.

interlin'eal, interlin'ear, *ou* **interlin'eary** (-teur-li'n'i-), *adj.*, interlinéaire. — translation ; *traduction interlinéaire, f.*

interlinea'tion (-teur-li'n'i-é-), *n.*, (ant.) intercalation, *f.*

interlin'ing (-teur'laï'n'-), *n.*, action d'interligner, *f.* ; entrelignes, interlignes, *f.pl.*

interlink' (-teur-lign'ke), *v.a.*, (ant.) joindre les chaînons ; enchaîner ; lier.

interlocu'tion (-teur-lo-kiou-), *n.*, interlocution, discussion, *f.* ; dialogue, *m.*

interloc'utor (-teur-lok'iou-), *n.*, interlocuteur, (jur.) jugement interlocutoire, *m.*

interloc'utory, *adj.*, (jur.) interlocutoire ; de dialogue. — decree ; *jugement interlocutoire, m.*

interlope' (-teur'lôpe), *v.n.*, (ant.) être intrus ; s'introduire ; (com.) faire le commerce interlope.

in'terloper, *n.*, intrus, *m.*, intruse, *f.* ; (com.) courtier marron ; interlope, *m.*

in'terlude (-teur-loude), *n.*, intermède, entr'acte, *m.*

interlu'nar *ou* **interlu'nary** (-teur-lou-), *adj.*, interlunaire.

intermar'riage (-teur-mar'rèdje). *n.*, double mariage (entre deux familles), *m.*

intermar'ry (-teur'-), *v.n.*, faire un double mariage (entre deux familles) ; se marier les uns avec les autres.

intermed'dle (-teur-mèd'd'l), *v.n.*, se mêler **de**, s'immiscer **dans**, s'entremêler **de**.

intermed'dler, *n.*, personne qui se mêle des affaires d'autrui, *f.* ; médiateur officieux, *m.*, médiatrice officieuse, *f.* ; entremetteur, *m.*

intermed'dling, *n.*, intervention officieuse, *f.*

interme'diacy (-teur-mî-), *n.*, (ant.) intervention, *f.*

interme'dial (-teur-mî-), *adj.*, intermédiaire, *m.*

interme'diary (-teur-mî-), *n.*, intermédiaire, *m.*

interme'diate (-teur'mî-), *adj.*, intermédiaire.

interme'diately, *adv.*, d'une manière intermédiaire.

inter'ment (-teur-), *n.*, enterrement, *m.* sépulture, *f.*

intermigra'tion (-teur-maï-gré-), *n.*, émigration réciproque, *f.*

inter'minable (-teur-mi-na-b'l), *adj.*, interminable ; éternel.

inter'minably, *adv.*, d'une manière interminable.

inter'minate (-teur-mi-), *adj.*, (ant.) illimité ; sans bornes.

intermin'gle (-teur-mign'g'l), *v.a.*, mêler ; entremêler.

intermin'gle, *v.n.*, se mêler ; s'entremêler.

intermis'sion (-teur'mish'-), *n.*, intermission ; interruption, *f.* ; relâche, *m.* ; cessation, *f.* ; intervalle, *m.* ; (med.) intermission, *f.* Without — ; *d'arrache-pied.*

intermis'sive (-teur'-), *adj.*, intermittent.

intermit' (-teur-), *v.a.*, interrompre, discontinuer, cesser, arrêter.

intermit', *v.n.*, discontinuer, cesser, s'arrêter.

intermit'tent (-teur'-), *adj.*, intermittent.

intermix' (-teur-), *v.a.* V. **intermingle**.

intermix'ture (-teur-mixt'ieur), *n.*, mélange, *m.*

intermodil'lion (-teur-), *n.*, (arch.) entremodillon, *m.*

intermus'cular (-teur'meus'kiou-), *adj.*, intermusculaire.

intern', *v.a.*, interner.

inter'nal (-teur-), *adj.*, interne, intérieur ; (ant.) intrinsèque, intime.

inter'nally, *adv.*, intérieurement.

interna'tional (-teur'nash'-), *adj.*, international.

interne'cine, *adj.*, meurtrier ; mortel.

intern'ment, *n.*, internement, *m.*

in'ternode, *n.*, (bot.) entre-nœud, *m.*

internun'cio (-teur-neu'n'ci-ô), *n.*, (of the pope) internonce, *m.*

interpel'late, *v.a.*, interpeller.

interpella'tion (-teur-pèl'lé-), *n.*, appel, *m. ;* interpellation ; (ant.) interruption, *f.*

interplan'etary, *adj.*, situé entre les planètes.

inter'polate (-teur-), *v.a.*, interpoler ; intercaler, *f.*

interpola'tion (-lé-), *n.*, interpolation ; intercalation, *f.*

inter'polator (-lét'eur), *n.*, interpolateur, *m.*

interpose' (-teur-pôze), *v.a.*, interposer, placer entre ; faire intervenir, offrir.

interpose', *v.n.*, s'interposer ; intervenir ; interrompre.

interpo'ser, *n.*, médiateur, *m.*, médiatrice, *f.*

interposi'tion, *n.*, interposition ; intervention, médiation, *f.*

inter'pret (-teur-prète), *v.a.*, interpréter, expliquer, définir, traduire.

inter'pretable (-'a-b'l), *adj.*, explicable, interprétable.

interpreta'tion (-té-), *n.*, interprétation, *f.*

inter'pretative (-teur-pri-té-), *adj.*, interprétatif.

inter'pretatively, *adv.*, par interprétation.

inter'preter (-teur-prèt'eur), *n.*, interprète, *m.*

interreg'num (-teur-règ'-), *n.*, interrègne, *m.*

in'terrex, *n.*, interroi, régent, *m.*

inter'rogate (-tèr-ro-), *v.a.* and *n.*, interroger, questionner.

interroga'tion (-tèr-ro-ghé-), *n.*, interrogation, question, *f.* Note of — ; *point d'interrogation, m.*

interrog'ative (-teur-rogh'a-), *adj.*, interrogatif.

interrog'ative, *n.*, (gram.) terme interrogatif, *m.*

interrog'atively, *adv.*, par forme d'interrogation ; (gram.) interrogativement.

interrog'atory (-teur'ro-ghé-), *n.*, interrogations, *f.pl. ;* série de questions, *f.*

interrog'atory, *adj.*, interrogatif.

interrupt' (-teur'reupte), *v.a.*, interrompre.

interrupt'edly, *adv.*, avec interruption.

interrupt'er, *n.*, interrupteur, *m.*, interruptrice, *f.*

interrup'tion, *n.*, interruption ; intervention, *f.*, obstacle, *m.*

intersect' (-teur'sèk'te), *v.a.*, entrecouper ; croiser ; (geom.) couper.

intersect', *v.n.*, (geom.) se couper ; se croiser ; s'entre-croiser.

intersec'tion (-teur'sèk'-), *n.*, croisement, *m. ;* (geom.) intersection, *f.*

in'terspace (-teur-), *n.*, intervalle ; espacement, *m.*

intersperse' (-teur-speurse), *v.a.*, entremêler de ; parsemer de.

interstel'lar (-teur-stèl'-), *adj.*, (astron.) interstellaire.

inter'stice (-teur-), *n.*, interstice ; intervalle, *m.*

intersti'tial (-teur-stish'-), *adj.*, interstitiel.

intertex'ture (-teur-tèxt'ieur), *n.*, entrelacement, *m.*

in'tertie (-teur-taïe), *n.*, (carp.) entretoise ; (of a roof) sablière, *f.*

intertrop'ical (-teur-), *adj.*, intertropical.

intertwine' (-teur-twaïne), *v.a.*, (ant.) entrelacer. *v.n.*, s'entrelacer.

in'terval (-teur'-), *n.*, intervalle ; espacement,

(mus.) intervalle, *m.* At —s ; *par intervalles.* At long —s ; *à de longs intervalles.*

intervened' (-teur-vîne), *v.n.*, (of space, places) être, se trouver **entre** ; (pers.) intervenir, s'interposer ; (of circumstances) arriver, survenir, avoir lieu ; (of time) s'écouler, arriver.

interven'er, *n.*, personne qui intervient, *f.*, (jur.) intervenant, *m.* ; partie intervenante, *f.*

interven'ing, *adj.*, (pers.) intervenant ; (of space, places, time) intermédiaire. — party ; *intervenant, m., intervenante ; (jur.) partie intervenante, f.* — peace; *paix durant l'intervalle, f.*

interven'tion (-teur-vè'n'-), *n.*, intervention ; médiation ; (of things) interposition, action, *f.*

intervert' (-teur-veurte), *v.a.*, (ant.) intervertir ; tourner à un autre usage.

interver'tebral, *adj.*, (anat.) situé entre les vertèbres.

in'terview (-teur-viou), *n.*, entrevue, conférence, *f. ;* (journalism) interview.

in'terview, *v.a.*, visiter ; avoir une entrevue **avec** ; (journalism) interviewer.

in'terviewer, *n.*, personne qui visite, *f.*, qui a une entrevue **avec**, interviewer, *m.*

interweave' (-teur-wîve), *v.a.*, entrelacer, tresser, tisser ensemble, entremêler.

interweav'ing, *n.*, tissu ; entrelacement, *m.*

interwork'ing (-weurk'-), *n.*, (ant.) action réciproque, *f.*

interwreathed' (-teur-rîth'de), *adj.*, tissu en guirlande.

intest'able (-tès-ta-b'l), *adj.*, (jur.) incapable de tester.

intest'acy (-tès-taci), *n.*, (jur.) état de celui qui meurt intestat, *m.*

intes'tate (-tès-), *adj.*, (jur.) (of the deceased) intestat ; (of the heir) ab intestat.

intest'ate, *n.*, (jur.) intestat.

intes'tinal (-tès-), *adj.*, intestinal.

intes'tine (-tès-), *adj.*, intestin. — war ; *guerre intestine, f.*

intes'tine, *n.*, intestin, *m.*

inthrall' (-thrôl), *v.a. V. enthrall.*

inthrall'ment, *n.*, asservissement, esclavage, *m. ;* servitude, *f.*

inthrone' (-thrône), *v. V. enthrone.*

in'timacy, *n.*, intimité, liaison intime, *f.*

in'timate, *adj.*, intime ; intimement lié.

in'timate, *n.*, (ant.) ami intime, *m. ;* amie intime, *f.*

in'timate, *v.a.*, faire entendre ; donner à entendre **à** ; signifier **à** ; faire comprendre **à** ; déclarer **à** ; intimer **à**.

in'timately (-mét'li), *adv.*, intimement.

intima'tion (-mé-), *n.*, avis indirect, *m. ;* déclaration, *f.*

intim'idate, *v.a.*, intimider.

intimida'tion (-dé-), *n.*, intimidation, *f.*

in'to (i'n'tou), *prep.*, dans, en, à, entre ; (math.) par, multiplié par.

intol'erable (-tol'eur'a-b'l), *adj.*, intolérable, insupportable.

intol'erableness, *n.*, intolérabilité, *f.*

intol'erably, *adv.*, intolérablement, insupportablement.

intol'erance (-tol'eur'-), *n.*, intolérance, *f.*

intol'erant, *adj.*, intolérant. — of ; *incapable de supporter.*

intol'erantly, *adv.*, avec intolérance.

intolera'tion (-tol'eur'é-), *n.*, (ant.) intolérance, *f. ;* intolérantisme, *m.*

intomb' (-toume). *V. entomb.*

intonate, *v.n.*, (mus.) solfier, chanter.

intona'tion *ou* **inton'ing** (-tô'n'é-), *n.*, intonation, *f.*

intone' (-tône), *v.a.*, chanter ; (ecc.) entonner.

intox'icate, *v.a.*, enivrer ; enivrer **de.**

intox'icated (-toks'i-két'-), *adj.*, ivre ; (fig.) transporté, enivré **de.**

intox'icating, adj., enivrant. —gas; (chem.) gaz hilarant, protoxyde d'azote, m.

intox'ication (-toks'i-ké-), n., ivresse, f.; enivrement, m.

intractabil'ity ou **intract'ableness**, n., naturel intraitable, m.; indocilité, f.

intract'able (-ta-b'l), adj., intraitable; indocile.

intract'ably, adv., d'une manière intraitable.

intra'dos (-tré-doss), n., (arch.) intrados (ensemble des douelles intérieures), m.

intran'sitive, adj., (gram.) intransitif.

intran'sitively, adv., dans un sens intransitif.

intransmutabil'ity (-miou-), n., intransmutabilité, f.

intransmu'table (-miou-ta-b'l), adj., intransmuable.

intranspar'ency, n., intransparence, f.

in'trant, n., (fonctionnaire) entrant, m.

intrench' (-tré'n'she), v.a., (milit.) retrancher.

intrench', v.n., envahir; empiéter **sur**; creuser, fouiller, faire des tranchées; (milit.) se retrancher.

intrench'ment n., (milit.) retranchement, m.

intrep'id (-trèp'-), adj., intrépide.

intrepid'ity, n., intrépidité, f.

intrep'idly, adv., intrépidement, avec intrépidité.

in'tricacy, n., embrouillement, embarras, m.; perplexité, complication, difficulté, f.

in'tricate, adj., embrouillé; embarrassé; obscur; compliqué.

in'tricately, adv., d'une manière embrouillée, embarrassée, compliquée.

in'tricateness. V. **in'tricacy**.

intrigue' (-trîghe), n., intrigue, f.

intrigue', v.n., intriguer.

intrigu'er, n., intrigant, m., intrigante, f.

intrigu'ing (-trigh'igne), adj., intrigant.

intrigu'ingly, adv., par intrigue; en intriguant.

intrin'sic ou **intrin'sical**, adj., intrinsèque.

intrin'sically, adv., intrinsèquement.

introduce' (-diouce), v.a., introduire; faire entrer; (persons to one another) présenter à, faire connaître à. — him; faites-le entrer. — your friend to me; présentez-moi votre ami; faites-moi connaître votre ami. To — a fashion; introduire une mode.

introdu'cer, n., introducteur, m.

introduc'tion (-deuk'-), n., introduction; présentation; (letter) recommandation, f.

introduc'tive (-deuk'-), adj., qui sert d'introduction à.

introduc'tory (-deuk'-), adj., d'introduction; qui sert d'introduction à; préliminaire.

intro'it (-trô-), n., (ecc.) introit, m.

intromis'sion (-mish'-), n., introduction, admission; (phys.) intromission; (jur.) immixtion, ingérence, f.

introspec'tion (-trô-spèk'-), n.m., retour sur soi-même.

introvert' (-veurte), v.a., tourner en dedans; diriger intérieurement.

intrude' (-troude), v.n., se présenter sans être invité; se présenter; s'introduire; se faufiler; être intrus; être importun. To — one's self; se présenter sans être invité; se présenter; s'introduire; se faufiler dans; être intrus. To — on any one; importuner quelqu'un; déranger. To — on (any one's time); abuser de.

intrude', v.a., introduire (par importunité). To — on; imposer.

intrud'er, n., importun, m., importune, f.; intrus, m., intruse, f.; (ecc.) intrus, m.

intru'sion (-trou-jeune), n., intrusion, importunité; usurpation, f.; empiètement, m.; (geol.) intrusion, f. Why this —? pourquoi m'importuner ainsi?

intru'sive (-trou-cive), adj., importun, indiscret; (geol.) d'intrusion.

intru'sively, adv., indiscrètement; par intrusion; d'une manière importune.

intrust' (-treuste), v.a., confier. To — any one with anything; confier quelque chose à quelqu'un; charger quelqu'un de.

intui'tion (-tiou-ish'-), n., (philos., theol.) intuition, f.

intu'itive (-tiou-i-), adj., intuitif, d'intuition.

intu'itively, adv., par intuition; intuitivement.

intumes'cence, n., intumescence, excitation, agitation, f.

intussuscep'tion (-teus'seus'cèp'-), n., (physiol. surg.) intussusception, f.

intwine' (-twaï'ne), v.a. V. **entwine**.

inuen'do, n. V. **innuendo**.

in'ula (-iou-), n., (bot.) aunée, inule, f.

inun'date (-'eu'n'-), v.a., inonder, submerger, inonder de.

inunda'tion (-eu'n'dé-), n., inondation, f.; débordement, m.

inurban'ity (-'eur-ba'n'-), n., manque d'urbanité, de politesse, de civilité, m.

inure' (-'youre), v.a., accoutumer à, habituer à, endurcir, aguerrir, rompre à. To — to war; aguerrir.

inure'ment, n., habitude, f.

inutil'ity (-iou-), n., inutilité, f.

inut'terable, adj., indicible, inexprimable.

invade' (-véde), v.a., envahir; attaquer; (fig.) violer.

invad'er, n., envahisseur, agresseur, m.

invad'ing, adj., envahissant; d'invasion.

invaletu'dinary (-i-tiou-), adj., (ant.) valétudinaire.

in'valid (-va-lîd), adj., malade, infirme, faible.

inval'id, adj., (jur.) invalide, de nul effet.

in'valid (-lîde), n., malade, m., f.; personne malade, f.; (worn out soldier, sailor) invalide, m.

in'valid, v.a., (mil.) réformer; déclarer impropre au service; mettre à la réforme.

inval'idate, v.a., invalider, infirmer, casser; déclarer de nul effet.

invalid'ity, n., faiblesse; (jur.) invalidité, f.

inval'uable (-'iou-a-b'l), adj., inestimable, sans prix.

inval'uably, adv., d'une manière inestimable.

invariabil'ity ou **inva'riableness** (-vé-ri-), n., invariabilité, f.

inva'riable (-vé-ri-a-b'l), adj., invariable, constant, uniforme.

inva'riably, adv., invariablement, constamment, uniformément; toujours.

inva'sion (-vé-jeune), n., invasion, f.; envahissement, m.; violation, atteinte, attaque; (of territory) invasion, violation, f.

invec'tive, n., invective, f.

invec'tive, adj., satirique; injurieux.

invec'tively, adv., avec invective; injurieusement.

inveigh' (-vê), v.n., se déchaîner contre, invectiver, se récrier contre.

inveigh'er (-vê-eur), n., qui se répand en invectives, f.

invei'gle (-vî'g'l), v.a., séduire, attirer, capter, enjôler.

invei'glement, n., séduction, captation, f.

invei'gler, n., enjôleur, m., enjôleuse, f.; séducteur, m., séductrice, f.

invent', v.a., inventer, imaginer; (to contrive falsely) controuver, inventer.

inven'tion, n., invention; (faculty) invention, f.; génie de l'invention, m.; (fiction) invention; (forgery) chose controuvée, f.

inven'tive, adj., inventif, imaginatif.

inven'tor, n., inventeur, m.

invento'rially, adv., en forme d'inventaire.

in'ventory, n., inventaire, m.

in'ventory, *v.a.*, inventorier, inscrire dans un inventaire ; dresser l'inventaire **de**.

inven'tress, *n.*, inventriee, *f.*

inverse' (-veurse), *adj.*, inverse, en raison inverse.

inverse'ly, *adv.*, en sens inverse ; en raison inverse ; inversement.

inver'sion (-veur), *n.*, (gram., mil., nav.) inversion, *f.* ; (chem.) intervertissement, *m.* ; (fig., log., mus.) renversement, *m.*

invert' (-veurte), *v.a.*, tourner sens dessus dessous, renverser ; intervertir.

inver'tebrate (-veur-ti-), *n.*, (zoöl.) invertébré, *m.*

inver'tebrate *ou* **inver'tebrated** (-veur-ti-bréte, -'ède), *adj.*, invertébré.

invert'ed (-veurt'-), *adj.*, renversé ; inverse (of order of things) interverti.

invert'edly, *adv.*, dans un ordre renversé ; en sens inverse.

invest' (-vèste), *v.a.*, vêtir, revêtir ; (milit.) bloquer, investir ; (money) placer ; (to place in possession) mettre en possession ; investir (**de**).

inves'tigable (-vès'ti-ga-b'l), *adj.*, susceptible d'investigation.

inves'tigate (-vès'ti-), *v.a.*, rechercher, examiner ; faire une enquête **sur** ; faire des investigations **sur**.

investiga'tion (-vès'ti-ghé-), *n.*, investigation, recherche, enquête, *f.*

inves'tigative (-vès'ti-ghé-), *adj.*, investigateur.

inves'tigator (-vès'ti-ghé-teur), *n.*, investigateur, *m.*, investigatrice, *f.*

inves'titure *ou* **inves'ture** (-vès'ti-tioure, -vès'tioure), *n.*, (ecc.) investiture, (jur.) mise en possession, *f.* [vestit.

inves'tive (-vès'-), *adj.*, qui revêt ; qui in-

invest'ment (-vèst'-), *n.*, action de vêtir, de revêtir, *f.* ; vêtement ; (of money) placement ; (milit.) investissement, *m.*

inves'tor, *n.*, spéculateur ; celui qui place son argent, *m.*

invet'eracy *ou* **invet'erateness** (-vèt'eur-a-), *n.*, caractère invétéré ; acharnement, *m.*

invet'erate (-vèt'eur'-), *adj.*, invétéré ; acharné. To grow ; *s'invétérer*.

invet'erately, *adv.*, d'une manière invétérée ; avec acharnement.

invid'ious, *adj.*, odieux ; irritant ; désagréable, vexatoire.

invid'iously, *adv.*, odieusement.

invid'iousness, *n.*, odieux, *m.* ; nature irritante, *f.*

invig'orate, *v.a.*, renforcer, fortifier ; donner de la vigueur **à**.

invig'orating, *adj.*, fortifiant.

invigora'tion (-o-ré-), *n.*, action de fortifier, de donner de la vigueur, *f.* ; état de vigueur, accroissement de force, *m.*

invincibil'ity, *n.*, nature invincible, *f.*

invin'cible (-ci-b'l), *adj.*, invincible, insurmontable.

invin'cibleness, *n.*, nature invincible, invincibilité, *f.*

invin'cibly, *adv.*, invinciblement.

inviolabil'ity *ou* **invi'olableness**(-vaï-o-), *n.*, inviolabilité, *f.*

invi'olable (-vaï-o-la-b'l), *adj.*, inviolable.

invi'olably, *adv.*, inviolablement.

invi'olate (-vaï-o-), *adj.*, entier, pur, sans tache, intact.

invisibil'ity *ou* **invis'ibleness** (-viz'i-), *n.*, invisibilité, *f.*

invis'ible (-viz'i-b'l), *adj.*, invisible, imperceptible.

invis'ibly, *adv.*, invisiblement.

invita'tion (-vi-té-), *n.*, invitation, *f.*

invi'tatory (-vaï-ta-) *adj.*, d'invitation, invitatif ; (c.rel.) invitatoire.

invite' (-vaïte), *v.a.*, inviter **à**, engager **à** ; (fig.) appeler, provoquer.

invit'er (-vaït'-), *n.*, personne qui invite, *f.* ; hôte, amphitryon, *m.*

invit'ing (-vaït'-), *adj.*, engageant, attrayant, appétissant, tentant.

invit'ingly, *adv.*, d'une manière engageante, attrayante.

invit'ingness (-vaït'ign'nèce), *n.*, (ant.) nature engageante, vertu attractive, *f.*, attrait, *m.*

invoca'tion (-vo-ké-), *n.*, invocation, *f.*

in'voice (-voïce), *n.*, (com.) facture, *f.* — clerk ; *facturier, m.*

invoice', *v.a.*, (com.) facturer.

invoke' (-vôke), *v.a.*, invoquer, réclamer.

involu'crated (-liou-), *adj.*, (bot.) involucré.

in'volucre (-vo-liou-keur) *ou* **involu'crum** (-liou-creu-me), *n.*, (bot.) involucre, *m.*

invol'untarily (-vol'eu'n'-), *adv.*, involontairement.

invol'untariness (-vol'eu'n'-), *n.*, caractère involontaire, *m.*

invol'untary (-vol'eu'n'-), *adj.*, involontaire. *f.*

in'volute (-lioute), *n.*, (geom.) développante,

in'volute, **involut'ed**, **in'volutive**, *adj.*, (bot.) involutif, involuté.

involu'tion (-li'ou-), *n.*, enveloppement, *m.* ; complication ; (gram.) incise ; (arith., alg.) élévation aux puissances ; (jur.) complication, involution ; (bot.) involution, *f.*

involve', *v.a.*, (to envelop) envelopper ; (to comprise) comprendre, renfermer ; impliquer ; (to cause) entraîner, engager ; (to plunge) plonger ; (to entangle) embarrasser, entortiller ; (alg.) élever à une puissance. To — one's self ; *s'endetter*. To — one's self in ; *s'attirer*. To be — d ; *être endetté*. To — in difficulties ; *plonger dans des difficultés*. She has greatly —d him ; *elle l'a obéré de dettes*. That —s expense ; *cela entraîne de la dépense*.

involved', *adj.*, (of persons) accablé de dettes ; dans la gêne ; obéré ; (of things) grevé de dettes. The controversies in which he was — ; *les controverses dans lesquelles il était engagé*. To be in — circumstances ; *être dans un état de gêne*. — sentences ; *phrases entortillées, f.pl.* — estate ; *domaine grevé d'hypothèques, m.*

involve'ment, *n.*, (ant.) embarras pécuniaire, *m.* ; difficulté, gêne, *f.*

invulnerabil'ity *ou* **invul'nerableness** (-veul-neur'-), *n.*, invulnérabilité, *f.*

invul'nerable (-veul-neur'a-b'l), *adj.*, invulnérable, inattaquable.

inwall' (-wôl), *v.a.*, (ant.) entourer de murs.

in'ward (-worde), *adj.*, intérieur, interne.

in'ward *ou* **in'wards**, *adv.*, en dedans ; intérieurement.

in'wardly, *adv.*, intérieurement, mentalement, intimement.

in'wardness, *n.*, intimité, intériorité, *f.*

inweave' (-wîve), *v.a.*, (*preterite* Inwove ; *past part.*, Inwoven), enlacer, tresser.

inwrap' (-rape), *v.a.*, envelopper, entortiller ; (obsol. fig.) ravir.

inwreathe' (-rîthe), *v.a.*, couronner d'une guirlande ; ceindre, couronner.

inwrought' (-rôte), *adj.*, ciselé, orné de figures.

i'odide (aï-o-), *n.*, (chem.) iodure, *m.*

i'odine, *n.*, (chem.) iode, *m.*

iod'uret (aï-o-diou-rète), *n.*, (ant.) (chem.) iodure, *m.*

Ion'ic (aï-o'n'-), *adj.*, ionique ; ionien. — dialect ; *dialect ionien, m.* — order ; *ordre ionique.* [(gram.) *iota souscrit, m.*

io'ta (aï-o-), *n.*, iota ; rien, *m.* — subscript ;

I.O.U., *n.*, reconnaissance, *f.*

ipecacuan'ha (ip-i-kak'iou-), *n.*, (bot.) ipécacuana, *m.*

irascibil'ity, n., irascibilité, irritabilité, f.
iras'cible (-'ci-b'l), adj., irascible, irritable.
ire (aïeur), n., colère, ⊙ire, f.; courroux, m.
irid'ium (i-rid'ieume), n., (chem.) iridium, m.
i'ris (aï-rice), n., (irides) iris, m., (bot.) iris, f.m.
i'risated (aï-riss'ét'-) ou **i'rised** (aï-riste), adj., irisé.
I'rish (aïr'-), adj., irlandais. — bull; naïveté irlandaise, f.
I'rish, n., (language) irlandais, m.
I'rishism, n., locution irlandaise, f.
I'rishman, n., Irlandais, m.
I'rishwoman (-woum'-), n., Irlandaise, f.
i'ris-root (-route), n., racine d'iris, f.
irk'some (-seume), adj., pénible, ennuyeux; fatigant.
irk'somely, adv., d'une manière fatigante, ennuyeusement.
irk'someness, n., ennui, m.; fatigue, f.
i'ron (aï'eurne), n., fer; (tech.) ferrement, m. Flat- —; fer à repasser, m. Wrought —; fer forgé, m. Cast —; fonte, f. Old —; ferraille, f. Sheet- —; tôle, f. In —s; aux fers. To have many —s in the fire; courir plusieurs (ou deux) lièvres à la fois. —age; âge de fer, m. — crown; couronne de fer, couronne des rois Lombards, f. —fisted; serré, pingre, cupide, avide. —flint; silex ferrugineux, m. —heater; fer à chauffer, m. —sand; ménakanite, f. You must strike the — while it is hot; il faut battre le fer pendant qu'il est chaud.
i'ron, adj., de fer, en fer.
i'ron, v.a., ferrer; (linen) repasser; (to shackle) mettre les fers à.
i'ron-bound (-baou'n'de), adj., cerclé de fer; garni de fer, m.; (shackled) chargé de fers. — shore; côte rocheuse, f.
i'ron-brake, n., brimbale, f.
i'ron-clad, adj., cuirassé. —, n., navire cuirassé, m.
i'roner, n., (of linen) repasseuse, f.; (who furnishes with iron) ferreur, m.
i'ron-fil'ings (-faïl'ign'ze), n.pl., limaille de fer, f.sing.
i'ron-found'er (-faou'n'd'-), n., fondeur en fer, m.
i'ron-foun'dry, n., fonderie de fer, f.
i'ron-glance, n., (min.) fer spéculaire, fer oligiste, m., hématite, f.
i'ron-gray, adj., gris de fer.
i'ron-heart'ed (-hârt'-), adj., au cœur de fer.
iron'ic ou **iron'ical** (aï-ro'n'-), adj., ironique.
iron'ically, adv., ironiquement.
i'ron-manufac'tory (-'iou-fak'-), n., usine de fer, f.
i'ron-manufac'ture (-iou-fakt'ioure), n., fabrication du fer, f.
i'ron-mas'ter (-mâs'-), n., maître de forge, m.
i'ron-mon'ger (-meu'gn'gheur), n., quincaillier, m.
i'ron-mon'gery (-meu'gn'gheuri), n., quincaillerie, f.
i'ron-mold (-môlde), n., (stain) tache de rouille; (vessel) lingotière, f.
i'ron-ore (-ôre), n., minerai de fer, m.
i'ronside, n., soldat aguerri, vétéran, m.
i'ron-smith, n., ouvrier en fer, m.
i'ron-stone (-stône), n., minerai de fer, m.
i'ron-wire (-waïeur), n., fil de fer, m.
i'ron-wood (-woude), n., bois de fer, m.
i'ron-work (-weurke), n., ferrure, f.; ouvrage en fer, m.
i'ron-works (-weurkse), n.pl., forge, f.
i'ron-wort (-weurte), n., (bot.) sidéritis, m.; crapaudine, f.
i'rony (aï-ro'n'i), n., ironie, f.
i'rony (aï-eur'n'i), adj., de fer.
irra'diance ou **irra'diancy** (-'ré-di-', n., rayonnement; rayon, m.

irra'diate (-'ré-di-), v.a., rayonner sur; éclairer.
irra'diate, v.n., rayonner; resplendir.
irradia'tion (-'ré-di-é-), n., (phys., astron.) irradiation; splendeur, f.
irra'tional (ir-rash'eu'n'-), adj., irraisonnable; déraisonnable; (math.) irrationnel.
irrational'ity, n., déraison; nature irraisonnable, absurdité, f.
irra'tionally, adv., sans raison, déraisonnablement, absurdement.
irreclaim'able (ir-ri-clé'm-a-b'l), adj., incorrigible; indomptable; invétéré.
irreclaim'ably, adv., incorrigiblement.
irrec'oncilable (ir-rèk'o'n'çaïl'a-b'l), adj., irréconciliable avec; inconciliable avec; incompatible avec.
irrec'oncilableness, n., nature irréconciliable; incompatibilité, f.
irrec'oncilably, adv., irréconciliablement; d'une manière inconciliable.
irrec'onciled, adj., (ant.) qui n'a pas été expié; inexpié.
irreconcilia'tion, n., (ant.) incompatibilité, f.
irrecov'erable (ir-ri-keuv'eur-a-b'l), adj., irréparable; perdu sans ressource; (fin.) irrécouvrable.
irrecov'erableness, n., nature irréparable; perte sans ressource, f.
irrecov'erably, adv., irréparablement; sans ressource; sans remède.
irredeem'able (ir-ri-dî'm'a-b'l), adj., irrémédiable; (fin.) irrachetable.
irredu'cible (ir-ri-diou-ci-b'l), adj., irréductible.
irredu'cibleness, n., irréductibilité, f.
irreform'able, adj., inaltérable.
irrefragabil'ity ou **irref'ragableness** (ir-rèf'ra-ga-), n., nature irréfragable, f.
irref'ragable (ir-rèf-ra-ga-b'l), adj., irréfragable, irréfutable.
irref'ragably, adv., d'une manière irréfragable.
irrefu'table (ir-ri-fiout'a-b'l ou -rèf-), adj., irréfutable.
irrefu'tably, adv., d'une manière irréfutable.
irreg'ular (ir-règh'iou-), adj., irrégulier, déréglé, non uniforme; vicieux, désordonné.
irreg'ular, n., soldat de corps franc, irrégulier, m.
irregular'ity, n., irrégularité; déviation; conduite déréglée, (ecc.) irrégularité, f.
irreg'ularly, adv., irrégulièrement.
irrel'ative (ir-rèl'a-), adv., sans liaison; sans rapport.
irrel'evancy (ir-rèl-i-), n., nature étrangère, f.
irrel'evant (ir-rèl-i-), adj., inapplicable à; déplacé, hors de propos; étranger à.
irreli'gion (ir-ri-lidj'-),n., irréligion, impiété, f.
irreli'gious (ir-ri-lidj'-), adj., irréligieux, impie, contraire à la religion.
irreli'giously, adv., irréligieusement.
irreli'giousness, n., irréligion, f.
irreme'diable (ir-ri-mî-di-a-b'l), adj., irrémédiable; sans remède; incurable.
irreme'diableness, n., nature irrémédiable, f.
irreme'diably, adv., irrémédiablement.
irremis'sible (ir-ri-mis'si-b'l), adj., irrémissible, impardonnable.
irremis'sibleness, n., nature irrémissible ou impardonnable, f.
irremovabil'ity (ir-ri-mouv'-), n., fermeté inébranlable; inflexibilité; inamovibilité; immutabilité, f.
irremov'able (ir-ri-mouv'a-b'l), adj., immuable; inamovible; inflexible.
irremov'ably, adv., d'une manière immuable; immuablement, inflexiblement.
irreparabil'ity (ir-rèp'a-ra-), n., nature irréparable, f.

irrep'arable (ir-rèp'a-ra-b'l), *adj.*, irréparable; irrémédiable; irrécouvrable.

irrep'arably, *adv.*, irréparablement; sans remède.

irrepealabil'ity (ir-ri-pîl'-), *n.*, (ant.) irrévocabilité, *f.*

irrepeal'able (ir-ri-pîl'a-b'l), *adj.*, irrévocable.

irrepeal'ably, *adv.*, irrévocablement.

irreprehen'sible (ir-rèp'ri-hè'n'si-b'l), *adj.*, irrépréhensible, exempt de blâme; sans tache.

irreprehen'sibleness, *n.*, nature irrépréhensible, *f.*

irreprehen'sibly, *adv.*, d'une manière irrépréhensible, irréprochablement.

irrepres'sible (ir-ri-prèss'-i-b'l), *adj.*, irrépressible; (of laughter) inextinguible. — laughter; *fou rire, m.*

irreproach'able (ir-ri-prôtsh'a-bl'), *adj.*, irréprochable, irrépréhensible, innocent, sans tache.

irreproach'ableness, *n.*, nature irréprochable, *f.*

irreproach'ably, *adv.*, irréprochablement.

irreprov'able (ir-ri-prouv'a-b'l), *adj.*, irrépréhensible, irréprochable.

irreprov'ably, *adv.*, d'une manière irrépréhensible; irréprochablement.

irresist'ance (ir-ri-zist'-), *n.*, (ant.) soumission; obéissance passive, *f.*

irresistibil'ity *ou* **irresist'ibleness** (ir-ri-zist'-), *n.*, irrésistibilité, *f.*

irresist'ible (ir-ri-zist'i-b'l), *adj.*, irrésistible.

irresist'ibly, *adv.*, irrésistiblement.

irres'oluble (ir-rèz'o-liou-b'l), *adj.*, insoluble.

irres'olubleness, *n.*, insolubilité, *f.*

irres'olute (ir-rèz'o-lioute), *adj.*, irrésolu, indécis.

irres'olutely, *adv.*, irrésolument, avec hésitation.

irres'oluteness *ou* **irresolu'tion,** *n.*, irrésolution, hésitation, indécision, *f.*

irresolvabil'ity *ou* **irresol'vableness** (ir-ri-zol'-), *n.*, (chem.) irréductibilité, *f.*

irresolv'able (ir-ri-zol-va-b'l), *adj.*, (chem.) irréductible, indécomposable.

irrespect'ive (ir-ri-spèk'-), *adj.*, indépendant **de**; qui ne fait pas de distinction **entre**; (ant.) manquant de respect **pour.**

irrespect'ively, *adv.*, indépendamment, sans égard aux circonstances.

irres'pirable (ir-rès'-pi-ra-b'l), *adj.*, irrespirable.

irresponsibil'ity (ir-ri-spo'n'si-), *n.*, irresponsabilité, *f.*

irrespon'sible (ir-ri-spo'n'si-b'l), *adj.*, irresponsable; qui n'est pas digne de confiance.

irretriev'able (ir-ri-trîv'a-b'l), *adj.*, irréparable, irrémédiable.

irretriev'ably, *adv.*, irréparablement.

irrev'erence (ir-rèv'eur'-), *n.*, irrévérence, *f.*, manque de respect, *m.*

irrev'erent, *adj.*, irrévérent, irrévérencieux.

irrev'erently, *adv.*, irrévéremment, avec irrévérence.

irrever'sible (ir-ri-veur-si-b'l), *adj.*, irrévocable.

irrever'sibly, *adv.*, irrévocablement.

irrevocabil'ity *ou* **irrev'ocableness** (ir-rèv'-), *n.*, irrévocabilité, *f.*

irrev'ocable (ir-rèv'o-ca-b'l), *adj.*, irrévocable.

irrev'ocably, *adv.*, irrévocablement.

ir'rigate, *v.a.*, arroser, irriguer.

irriga'tion (-ghé-), *n.*, arrosement, *m.*; irrigation, *f.*

irritabil'ity, *n.*, irritabilité, irascibilité, *f.*

ir'ritable (-ta-b'l), *adj.*, irritable.

ir'ritant, *adj.*, irritant, qui cause de la colère.

ir'ritant, *n.*, (med.) irritant, *m.*

ir'ritate, *v.a.*, irriter; provoquer, ennuyer, exaspérer; énerver, agacer.

ir'ritating (-tét'igne), *adj.*, irritant.

irrita'tion (-ri-té-), *n.*, irritation, exaspération, colère, (med.) irritation, *f.*

irrup'tion (ir-reup'-), *n.*, irruption, attaque, invasion; violation de territoire, *f.*

irrup'tive (ir-reup'-), *adj.*, qui fait irruption.

is'abel-col'ored (-keul'leurde), *adj.*, isabelle (invariable).

is'chium (is-ki-), *n.*, (anat.) ischion, *m.*

ischuret'ic (is-kiou-rèt'-), *adj.*, (med.) ischurétique.

is'chury (is-kiou-), *n.*, (med.) ischurie, *f.*

Ish'maelite, *n.*, Ismaélite; (fig.) anarchiste, *m.*

i'singlass (aï'zign'glâce), *n.*, colle de poisson, *f.* — stone; *mica; talc, m.*

Is'lam *ou* **Is'lamism** (iz-, -iz'me), *n.*, islamisme, islam, *m.*

is'land (aï-la'n'de), *n.*, île, *f.*

is'lander (aï-la'n'd'-), *n.*, insulaire, *m.f.*

isle (aïl), *n.*, île, *f.*

is'let (aï-lète), *n.*, îlot, *m.*; petite île, *f.*

isoch'ronal *ou* **isoch'ronous** (aï-çok'-), *adj.*, isochrone.

i'solate (aïz'-), *v.a.*, isoler.

i'solated (aïz'o-lét'-), *adj.*, isolé.

isola'tion (aïz'o-lé-), *n.*, isolement, *m.*

isos'celes (aï-ços'ci-lize), *adj.*, isocèle.

Is'raelite (iz'ra-êl'aïte), *n.*, Israélite, *m.f.*

Israelit'ic *ou* **Israeli'tish,** *adj.*, israélite.

is'suable (ish'shiou-a-b'l), *adj.*, émissible.

is'sue (ish'shiou), *n.*, issue; (egress) sortie, *f.*, écoulement, *m.*; (sending out) distribution, expédition, *f.*; (ultimate result) résultat, *m.*, conclusion, issue, *f.*; (progeny) enfants, *m.pl.*, postérité; (fin.) émission; (jur.) question, *f.* At —; *en litige, en question.* To take, *ou* join, —; *discuter; engager une discussion, différer d'opinion* **avec.** To die without —; *mourir sans enfants, sans postérité.*

is'sue, *v.a.*, publier; expédier; (fin.) émettre; (jur.) donner, lancer. To — a writ; *lancer un mandat.*

is'sue, *v.n.*, sortir, jaillir, découler **de**; (to end) se terminer, être l'issue; (to accrue) provenir **de**; émaner **de**; (milit.) faire une sortie; (jur.) dépendre de la solution d'une question.

is'sueless, *adj.*, sans enfants, sans postérité.

is'sue-peas (-pîze), *n.pl.*, (med.) pois à cautère, pois de cautère, *m.pl.*

is'suer, *n.*, personne qui émet, *f.*; émetteur, *m.*

isth'mian, *adj.*, isthmique. — games; *jeux isthmiques, m.pl.*

isth'mus (isth-meusse *ou* is-), *n.*, isthme, *m.*

it (ite) *pron.*, il, *m.*, elle, *f.*; le, *m.*, la, *f.*; lui, *m.f.*; ce; cela. — is one thing; *autre chose est.* That's the truth of —; *c'est là la vérité.* I have heard — said; *j'ai entendu dire.* — must be; *il le faut.* — is over; *c'est fini.* — is I who said —; *c'est moi qui l'ai dit.* — is they who said —; *ce sont eux qui l'ont dit.* If — it be so; *s'il en est ainsi.* That is —; *c'est cela même.* That's not —; *ce n'est pas cela.* I have thought — necessary; *j'ai cru devoir (it* is not translated in these expressions). — rains; *il pleut.* Of —; *en.* At —, in —, to —; *y.*

Ital'ian (i-tal'ya'ne), *adj.*, italien.

Ital'ian, *n.*, Italien, *m.*, Italienne, *f.*; (language) italien, *m.*

ital'ic, *n.*, (print.) italique, *m.*

ital'ic, *adj.*, italique.

ital'icize (-çaïze), *v.a.*, imprimer en italiques.

itch (itshe), *n.*, démangeaison; (disease) gale, *f.*

itch, *v.n.*, avoir des démangeaisons; démanger **de.** My fingers are —ing to; *les doigts me démangent* **de.**

itch'ing, *n.*, démangeaison, *f.*

itch'y, *adj.*, galeux.

i'tem (aï-tème), *adv.*, item.

i'tem, *n.*, article, item, *m.*

it'erant (it'eur-), *adj.*, (ant.) qui répète.

it'erate (it'eur-), *v.a.*, (ant.) réitérer, répéter.

itera'tion (it'eur'é-), *n.*, réitération, répétition, *f.*

it'erative (it'eur'é-), *adj.*, répété, itératif.

itin'erant (aï-ti'n'eur-), *adj.*, ambulant.

itin'erant, *n.*, personne ambulante, *f.*; prédicateur ambulant, *m.*

itin'erary (aï-ti'n'eur'-), *n.*, itinéraire, *m.*

itin'erary, *adj.*, ambulant, ambulatoire.

its, *pron.*, son, *m.*, sa, *f.*; ses, *m.pl.*, *f.pl.*; le sien, *m.*, la sienne, *f.*; les siens, *m.pl.*, les siennes, *f.pl.*

itself', *pron.*, lui-même, *m.*, elle-même, *f.*; soi-même, *m.*; même, *m.f.* Virtue —; *la vertu même.* To go of —; *aller tout seul.*

i'vory (aï-vo-), *n.*, ivoire, *m.*

i'vory, *adj.*, d'ivoire.

i'vory-black, *n.*, noir d'ivoire, *m.*

i'vory-nut, *n.*, (bot.) noix de tagua, noix de palmier, *f.*; ivoire végétal, *m.*

i'vory-turn'er (-teurn'-), *n.*, tourneur en ivoire, *m.*

i'vory-work'er (-weurk'-), *n.*, sculpteur en ivoire; ivoirier, *m.*

i'vy (aï-vi), *n.*, lierre, *m.*

i'vy-berry (-bèr-ri), *n.*, baie de lierre, *f.*

i'vyed *ou* **i'vied** (aï-vide), *adj.*, couvert de lierre.

i'vy-man'tled (-ma'n't'l'de), *adj.*, couvert de lierre.

iz'ard, iz'zard, *n.*, (zoöl.) chamois, isard, *m.*

J

J, dixième lettre de l'alphabet, **j**, *m.*

jab'ber, *v.n.*, jaboter, jacasser; bredouiller, baragouiner.

jab'ber, *n.*, bredouillement; baragouinage, baragouin, *m.*

jab'berer, *n.*, bredouilleur, *m.*, bredouilleuse, *f.*; baragouineur, *m.*, baragouineuse, jacasse, *f.*

jab'bering, *n.*, bredouillement, baragouinage, baragouin, *m.*

jab'iru, *n.*, (orni.) savacou, jabiru, *m.*

jac'inth, *n.*, (bot.) jacinthe, *f.*

jack (djake), *n.*, (spit) tourne-broche; (ich.) brocheton; (frame for sawing wood on) chevalet, *m.*; (pitcher) broc, *m.*; (leather) outre, *f.*; (lifting jack) cric; (at bowls) cochonnet; (flag) pavillon, *m.*; (a boor) rustre; (sailor) matelot, *m.*; (measure) demi-pinte, *f.*; (for boots) tirebotte; (cards) valet, *m.*; (wedge) coin, *m.* Cheap —; *camelot*, *m.* — o' lantern; *feu follet*, *m.* — of all trades; *factotum, Michel Morin, Maître Jacques*, *m.* — of all trades and master of none; *propre à tout et bon à rien.* Every — has, *ou* must have, his Jill; *à un boiteux femme qui cloche*, *ou* il n'y a si méchant pot qui ne trouve son couvercle. — at a pinch; *bouche-trou*, *m.* —-by-the-hedge; (bot.) *alliaire*, *f.* —-in-office; *tyranneau, bureaucrate*, *m.* —-in-the-box; *surprise, boîte à surprise*, *f.* — of the clock-house; *jaquemart*, *m.* —-a-dandy; *petit-maître, dandy, gandin*, *m.* —-knife; *couteau de poche*, *m.* —-towel; *essuie-mains*, *m.*

jack'al, *n.*, chacal, *m.*

jack'alent (-a-lè'n'te), *n.*, (fig.) benêt, nigaud; (game) jaquemart, *m.*

jack'anapes (-épse), *n.*, singe; fat, *m.*

jack'ass, *n.*, âne, baudet, bourriquet, (fig.) âne, bête, imbécile, *m.*; bourrique, *f.*

jack'-boot (-boute), *n.*, botte à genouillère, *f.*

jack'daw (-dô), *n.*, (orni.) choucas, *m.*

jack'et, *n.*, veste, jaquette, *f.*; (for women) corsage, canezou, *m.*; (tech.) chemise, *f.* To beat, *ou* dust, one's —; *donner une roulée*, *ou* râclée, à quelqu'un.

Jack, *n.*, Jeannot.

Jack Ketch' (-kètshe), *n.*, le bourreau, Monsieur de Paris, *m.*

jack'-pudding (-poud'-), *n.*, pierrot, bouffon, paillasse, *m.* [*m.*

jack'sauce (-sôss), *n.*, impertinent; drôle,

jack'-straw, *n.*, épouvantail, *m.*

jack'-tar (-târ), *n.*, loup de mer, marin, matelot, *m.*

Jac'obin, *n.*, jacobin, *m.*

Jac'obin, *adj.*, jacobin; de jacobin.

Jacobin'ic *ou* **Jacobin'ical**, *adj.*, jacobin; de jacobin.

Jac'obinism (-iz'me), *n.*, jacobinisme, *m.*

Jac'obite (-baïte), *n.*, jacobite, partisan des Stuarts, *m.*

Ja'cob's-staff (djé-cob'z'stâfe), *n.*, bâton de pèlerin, bourdon de pèlerin, *m.*; canne à poignard, *f.*; bâton de Jacob; (astron.) astrolabe, *m.*

jaco'bus (djé-cô-), *n.*, jacobus, *m.*, pièce de 25 shillings, *f.*

jac'onet, *n.*, jaconas, *m.*

jade (jède), *n.*, haridelle, rosse; (woman) coquine, friponne; (min.) néphrite, *f.*

jade, *v.a.*, surmener, harasser; fatiguer.

jade, *v.n.*, se fatiguer; se décourager.

jad'ed, *adj.*, surmené, harassé; excédé de fatigue; usé.

jad'ish, *adj.*, de rosse, de haridelle; (fig.) coquin, fripon; (unchaste) incontinent.

jag, *n.*, dent de scie; (bot.) dentelure; (fig.) brèche, *f.*

jag, *v.a.*, ébrécher; denteler.

jag'gedness (djag'ghèd'-), *n.*, dentelure, *f.*

jag'ging-iron, *n.*, roulette à pâte, *f.*

jagged *ou* **jag'gy** (djag'ghi), *adj.*, dentelé, ébréché; (bot.) laciné.

jaguar' (djagh'ou'âr), *n.*, jaguar, *m.*

jail (djéle), *n.*, prison, geôle, *f.* — fever; *typhus*, *m.*

jail'-bird (-beurde), *n.*, gibier de potence, *m.*

jail'er *ou* **jail'-keeper** (-kîp'-), *n.*, geôlier, *m.*

jal'ap, *n.*, (pharm.) jalap, *m.*

jam, *n.*, conserve; confiture, *f.*

jam, *v.a.*, serrer, presser, fouler.

jamb (djame), *n.*, jambage; (of a chimney) chambranle, *m.* — post; *montant*, *m.*

jan'gle (djan'gn'g'l), *v.a.*, faire discorder.

jan'gle, *v.n. V.* **jingle** and **wrangle**.

jan'itor (-teur-), *n.*, portier, concierge, *m.*

jan'izary, *n.*, janissaire, *m.*

Jan'senism (dja'n'sè'n'iz'me), *n.*, jansénisme, *m.*

Jan'senist, *n.*, janséniste, *m.*

Jan'uary (dja'n'iou-), *n.*, janvier, *m.*

japan', *n.*, laque, vernis, *m.* — earth; *cachou*, *m.* — ink; *encre du Japon*, *f.* — ware; *japon*, *m.*

japan', *v.a.*, vernisser de laque; vernir; bronzer.

Japanese' (-ize), *adj.*, japonais.

Japanese', *n.*, Japonais, *m.*, Japonaise, *f.*; (language) japonais, *m.*

japan'ner, *n.*, vernisseur, *m.*

jar, *n.*, (djâr), *v.n.*, (of sound) (of a musical instrument) jurer; être discordant; (to quarrel) se disputer, se quereller; (to vibrate) vibrer; (to clash) être contraire à, heurter, choquer, se choquer; (of colors) jurer. Their interests —; *leurs intérêts sont contraires.*

jar (djâr), *v.a.*, remuer, secouer; faire trembler; faire vibrer; choquer, heurter; déplaire à, offenser.

jar (djâr), *n.*, (vessel) jarre, cruche, *f.*; pot, (glass) bocal, (harsh sound) son discordant, *m.*; (vibration) vibration; (dispute) contestation, *f.*, conflit, *m.* Family —s; *disputes de famille*, *f.pl.* Leyden —; (phys.) *bouteille de Leyde*, *f.* — of pickles; *pot de cornichons*, *m.* On the —; *entr'ouvert, entre-bâillé.*

jarde (djard), *n.*, (vet.) jardon, *m.*, jarde, *f.*

jardinière', *n.*, (stand) jardiniere, *f.*

jar'gon (djâr-), *n.*, jargon, argot; (min.) zircon, jargon, *m.;* hyacinthe, *f.*

jar'ring (djâr'-), *n.*, (dispute) querelle, contestation, *f.;* (harsh sound) bruit discordant, *m.*

jar'ring, *adj.*, en contestation; discordant; en conflit; jurant **avec.**

jar'ring, *adv.*, discordant; en conflit.

jar'vey, *n.*, cocher de fiacre; automédon, *m.*

jas'mine (djaz'-, *ou* djas'-), *n.*, jasmin, *m.*

jas'per, *n.*, jaspe, *m.*

jaun'dice (djâ'n'dice), *n.*, ictère, *m.*, jaunisse, *f.*

jaun'diced (-diste), *adj.*, qui a la jaunisse; (fig.) prévenu **pour, contre.**

jaunt (dj'ân'te), *n.*, tournée, promenade, excursion, partie, course, *f.;* tour, *m.*

jaunt, *v.n.*, courir çà et là; faire une promenade, faire une course, faire une partie, se promener.

jaun'tily, *adv.*, avec grâce, gracieusement, légèrement, avec enjouement, bravement, prétentieusement.

jaun'tiness, *n.*, gaieté; légèreté, grâce, *f.;* (showiness) étalage; (liveliness) enjouement, *m.*

jaun'ty, *adj.*, léger, enjoué; (showy) voyant.

jav'elin (djav'-), *n.*, javeline, *f.;* javelot, *m.* —men; escorte d'un juge, *f.*

jaw (djō), *n.*, mâchoire; (of a horse) ganache, *f.;* (talk) caquet, *m.;* (scolding) criaillerie, *f.;* (abuse) gueule, *f. pl.*, gueule; (fig.) porte, serre, *f.sing.;* bras, *m.pl.*, étreintes, *f.pl.* The —s of death; les étreintes, les bras, de la mort. Lock —; tétanos, *m.* (med.). —tooth; molaire, dent molaire, *f.*

jaw, *v.a.*, (pop.) crier **après;** dire des sottises à, criailler **contre.**

jaw, *v.n.*, (pop.) gueuler; bavarder; (to scold) bougonner.

jaw'bone (djō-bône), *n.*, mâchoire, *f.;* os maxillaire, *m.*

jaw'-fallen (-fōl'n). *V.* **chop-fallen**.

jay, *n.*, (orni.) geai, *m.*

jeal'ous (djèl'-), *adj.*, jaloux **de** (son honneur), **contre** (son amour-propre), **de** (before an infinitive), **sur** (une chose).

jeal'ously, *adv.*, jalousement; par jalousie.

jeal'ousness, *n.*, jalousie, *f.*

jeal'ousy (djèl'euss'i), *n.*, jalousie, *f.*

jean (djêne), *n.*, coutil satiné, *m.*

jears (djîrze), *n.pl.*, (nav.) drisse, *f.*

jeer (djîre), *n.*, raillerie, moquerie, *f.*

jeer, *v.a.*, railler, se moquer **de.**

jeer, *v.n.*, railler; se railler, se moqu **de,** goguenarder.

jeer'er, *n.*, railleur, *m.*, railleuse, *f.;* moqueur, *m.*, moqueuse, *f.*, goguenard, *m.*

jeer'ing, *adj.*, railleur, moqueur, goguenard.

jeer'ing, *n.*, raillerie, moquerie, *f.*

jeer'ingly, *adv.*, en raillant; par moquerie, d'un air goguenard.

Jeho'vah (dji-hô-), *n.*, Jéhovah, *m.*

je'hu, *n.*, cocher, automédon, *m.*

jejune' (dji-djioune), *adj.*, vide **de;** aride; pauvre **de;** maigre; sans intérêt.

jejune'ness, *n.*, vide, *m.;* aridité, pauvreté, *f.*

jel'ly (djèl'-), *n.*, gelée, *f.;* coulis, *m.* — fish; méduse, *f.* —mold; moule à gelées, *m.*

jel'lied, *adj.*, réduit en gelée.

jen'net (djè'n'nète), *n.*, genêt (cheval d'Espagne), *m.*

jen'ny (djè'n'ni), *n.*, métier à filer le coton, *m.* — ass; ânesse, *f.*

jeof'ail (djèf'al), *n.*, (jur.) erreur, omission, *f.*

jeop'ardize (djèp'ard, -'aïze), *v.a.*, hasarder, risquer, compromettre, mettre en danger.

jeop'ardy (djèp'ard'i), *n.*, péril, danger, risque, hasard, *m.*

jer'boa (djeur'-), *n.*, (mam.) gerboise, *f.*

jeremi'ad (djè-rî-maï-), *n.*, jérémiade, *f.*

jer'falcon (djeur-fô'k'n), *n.*, gerfaut, *m.*

jerk (djeurke), *n.*, saccade; secousse, *f.*, mouvement saccadé, *m.*

jerk, *v.a.*, donner une poussée, une saccade, à; pousser, jeter, lancer; (man.) saccader.

jerked-beef', *n.*, (South America) carne secca, *f.*, bœuf séché au soleil, *m.*

jer'kin (djeur-), *n.*, pourpoint, justaucorps; (orni.) gerfaut mâle, *m.*

jer'ry-built, *adj.*, bâti comme un château de cartes. This is a —house; c'est un vrai château de cartes que cette maison là.

jer'sey, *n.*, veste de laine, *f.*, suroît (V. H.), *m.*

Jeru'salem ar'tichoke, *n.*, topinambour, *m.*

jess, *n.*, (hawking) laisse, *f.;* ruban, *m.*

jes'samine (djès'sa-), *n.*, jasmin, *m.*

jest (djèste), *n.*, plaisanterie, facétie, *f.;* bon mot; mot pour rire, *m.;* (laughing-stock) risée, *f.* In —; par plaisanterie, pour badiner. To be in —; badiner. To take a —; entendre la raillerie, ou la plaisanterie.

jest, *v.n.*, plaisanter, badiner **sur.** To — at; rire de, railler de.

jest'-book (-bouke), *n.*, recueil de bons mots, *m.*

jest'er, *n.*, plaisant, farceur, diseur de bons mots, railleur, *m.*, railleuse, *f.;* (buffoon) bouffon, fou, *m.*

jest'ing, *adj.*, de plaisanterie; pour rire; badin.

jest'ing, *n.*, plaisanterie, *f.;* badinage, *m.*

jest'ingly, *adv.*, en riant; en plaisantant, pour rire.

Jes'uit (djèz'iou-ite), *n.*, jésuite, *m.* —'s bark; quinquina, *m.*

Jesuit'ic *ou* **Jesuit'ical**, *adj.*, jésuitique.

Jesuit'ically, *adv.*, jésuitiquement; en jésuite.

Jes'uitism, *n.*, jésuitisme, *m.*

jet (djète), *n.*, (min.) jais, jaïet; (of water) jet d'eau, jet, *m.* —black; jais, noir comme du jais.

jet, *v.n.*, s'élancer; (to strut) se pavaner, se carrer.

jet'sam, jet'som, jet'son, *ou* **jet'tison**, *n.*, (jur.) jet, jet de marchandises à la mer, *m.*

jet'ty (djèt'ti), *adj.*, couleur de jais.

jet'ty (djèt'-), *n.*, jetée, *f.* —head; (nav.) môle, musoir, *m.*, jetée, *f.*

Jew (djiou), *n.*, Juif, Israélite, *m.*

jew'el (djiou'èl), *n.*, joyau, bijou, *m.;* pierre précieuse, *f.;* (horl.) diamant, *m.* —case; écrin, *m.* —like; brillant, étincelant.

jew'el, *v.a.*, orner de bijoux; parer de pierreries; (horl.) monter sur rubis.

jew'eler, *n.*, joaillier, bijoutier, *m.*

jew'elry *ou* **jew'elery**, *n.*, joaillerie, bijouterie, *f.*

Jew'ess (djiou-èce), *n.*, Juive, *f.*

Jew'ish, *adj.*, juif, des Juifs; judaïque.

Jew'ishly, *adv.*, en juif; en juive.

Jew'ry, *n.*, juiverie, *f.*

jews'-harp (djiouz'hârpe), *n.*, guimbarde, *f.*

jez'ebel (djèz'i-bèl), *n.*, mégère, *f.*

jib (djibe), *n.*, (nav.) foc, *m.* —boom; bâton de foc, *m.* Flying —; clin de foc.

jib, *v.n.*, (of horses) s'acculer.

jig (djighe), *n.*, gigue (dance), *f.*

jig'ger (djig'gheur), *n.*, (print.) visorium, *m.*

jilt, *n.*, coquette, *f.*

jilt, *v.a.*, planter là; duper, tromper, jouer.

jilt, *v.n.*, faire la coquette; coqueter.

jin'gle (djign'g'l), *n.*, (of bells) tintement; (of glasses, metals) cliquetis; (little bell) grelot, *m.*, clochette, *f.;* (correspondence of sound in rhyme) consonance, concordance, *f.;* (doggerel) mauvais vers, *m.pl.;* (carriage) voiture à deux roues, *f.*

jin'gle, *v.n.*, (of bells) tinter; (of glasses)

s'entre-choquer ; (of chains) **retentir** ; (of verses) assoner, rimer.

jin'gle, *v.a.*, (bells) faire tinter ; (glasses) choquer ; (chains) faire retentir.

Jingo, *n.*, braillard, patriote de cabaret, chauvin, *m.* By —! *adv.*, sapristi !

Jin'goism, *n.*, chauvinisme, *m.*

job, *n.*, affaire, besogne, chose à faire, *f.* ; travail ; ouvrage, *m.* ; (among workmen) tâche, pièce, *f.* ; (print.) ouvrage de ville ; (b.s.) tripotage, coup ; mauvais coup, *m.* — hand ; *homme en conscience ; remiseur, m.* — lot ; *solde, m., occasion, f., lot à bon marché, m.* — master ; *loueur de chevaux, de voitures, m.* — printer ; *imprimeur de circulaires, de prix-courants, m.* By the — ; *à forfait ;* (among workmen) *à la tâche ; à la pièce.* To do the — for any one ; *tuer quelqu'un.* To do a thing by the — ; *travailler à la pièce.* It is a bad — for him ; *c'est bien malheureux pour lui.* It is a good — ; *c'est bien heureux.* He has got a good — ; *il a trouvé une bonne place.* To give it up as a bad — ; *y renoncer, en faire son deuil.* To be on the — ; *en être, être prêt à.*

job, *v.a.*, (to hire) louer ; (to let) louer ; (b.s.) tripoter.

job, *v.n.*, travailler à la tâche ; (in the public stocks) agioter, spéculer ; louer des chevaux, des voitures.

job'ber, *n.*, ouvrier à la tâche ; (in the public stocks) agioteur, spéculateur ; (b.s.) tripotier, faiseur, exploiteur, *m.*

job'bernowl (djob'beur'nôl), *n.*, benêt, butor, *m.*

job'bing, *n.*, ouvrage à la tâche ; (in the public stocks) agiotage ; (print.) ouvrage de ville ; (b.s.) tripotage, *m.*

Job's Com'forter, *n.*, *faux ami, m.*

jock'ey, *n.*, jockey ; (cheat) maquignon, fripon ; (horsedealer) maquignon, *m.*

jock'ey, *v.a.*, duper, tromper.

jock'eyship, *n.*, équitation, *f.*

jocose' (-côce), *adj.*, plaisant, badin, jovial.

jocose'ly, *adv.*, en plaisantant, en badinant.

jocose'ness, *n.*, enjouement, badinage, *m.*

joc'ular (djok'iou-), *adj.*, plaisant, gai, badin.

joc'ularly, *adv.*, en plaisantant, gaîment, plaisamment.

joc'und, *adj.*, joyeux, enjoué, gai.

joc'undly, *adv.*, joyeusement, gaîment.

joc'undness, *n.*, joie, gaîté, *f.* ; enjouement, *m.*

jog, *n.*, secousse légère, *f.* ; attouchement (pour éveiller l'attention) ; obstacle, *m.* — ; *lentement, cahin-caha.*

jog, *v.n.*, remuer ; se mouvoir, voyager, marcher, paresseusement, aller ; lourdement. To — on, *ou* along ; *aller doucement ; aller son petit bonhomme de chemin, aller cahin-caha.* To be —ging ; *être sur son départ ; s'en aller.*

jog, *v.a.*, toucher, pousser, secouer du coude, de la main.

jog'ging (djog'ghigne), *n.*, secousse légère ; mouvement saccadé, *m.*

jog'gle (djog'g'l), *v.a.*, secouer, remuer ; pousser tout à coup, mais légèrement.

jog'trot (djog'trote), *n.*, petit trot, *m.*

John, *n.*, Jean. —nie, Jack ; (fam.) *Jeannot.* — dory ; (ich.) *dorée, f.*

join (djoïne), *v.a.n.*, joindre, unir à ; (to overtake) rejoindre ; réunir ; se joindre à ; (to join in) prendre part à ; se toucher ; se réunir. He —ed in the plan ; *il fut de l'entreprise.* Will you — us ? *voulez-vous être des nôtres ?* To — battle ; *en venir aux mains.* To — issue ; *engager la discussion ; différer d'opinion* avec.

joined (djoï'n'de), *adj.*, (bot.) conné.

join'er (djoï'n'-), *n.*, menuisier, *m.*

join'ery, *n.*, menuiserie, *f.*

join'ing, *n.*, action de joindre ; jonction, *f.* ; (fig.) union, *f.*, assemblage, *m.*

joint (djôï'n'te), *n.*, jointure, *f.* ; joint ; (of a corslet) défaut, *m.* ; (hinge) charnière ; (anat.) articulation, *f.* ; (bot.) nœud, *m.*, articulation, *f.* — of meat ; *pièce de viande, f.* ; *rôti, m.* Out of — ; *disloqué, démis, luxé ;* (fig.) *dérangé.* To put one's arm out of — ; *se disloquer, se démettre le bras.* To put a person's nose out of — ; *supplanter quelqu'un ;* (fam.) *débusquer quelqu'un.*

joint, *v.a.*, couper dans la jointure ; (to join) joindre, rapporter.

joint, *adj.*, réuni ; commun. — guardian ; *cotuteur, m.* — heir ; *cohéritier, m.* With — consent ; *d'un commun accord.*

joint'ed, *adj.*, articulé ; jointé ; joint ; **séparé.**

joint'er *ou* **joint'ing-plane**, *n.*, varlope, *f.*

joint'ly, *adv.*, conjointement ; **d'accord,** de concert.

joint'-oil (-oïl), *n.*, synovie, *f.*

joint'-pin, *n.*, goupille, *f.*

joint-rack'ing (-rak'-), *adj.*, convulsif ; qui cause des douleurs dans les articulations ; articulaire.

joint'ress, *n.*, douairière, *f.*

joint'-stock, *n.*, fonds commun, *m.* —com-pany ; *société anonyme, f.* — bank ; *banque par actions, f.*

join'ture (djôï'n't'ioure), *n.*, douaire, *m.*

join'ture, *v.a.*, assigner un douaire à.

joist (djôïste), *n.*, solive, *f.* ; madrier, *m.*

joist, *v.a.*, poser des solives à, des madriers à.

joke (djô'ke), *n.*, bon mot ; mot pour rire, *m.* ; plaisanterie, *f.* A practical — ; *une attrape, f., un tour, m.* A dry — ; *un pince sans rire.* In — ; *par plaisanterie ; pour rire, en plaisantant.* To crack one's — ; *avoir le mot pour rire.* To crack a — ; *dire un bon mot.* To carry a — too far ; *pousser trop loin la plaisanterie.* Not to know how to take a — ; *prendre, ou entendre, mal la plaisanterie.* What a good — ! *la bonne plaisanterie !* ou (fam.) *en voilà une bonne.* To be no — ; *passer la plaisanterie.*

joke, *v.a.*, plaisanter **sur** ; railler **de.**

joke, *v.n.*, plaisanter ; badiner ; rire **de** ; faire le farceur.

jok'er, *n.*, diseur de bons mots, plaisant, farceur, *m.*

jok'ing, *n.*, plaisanterie, farce, *f.*

jok'ingly, *adv.*, en plaisantant ; pour rire.

jole (djôle), *n.* V. **jowl.**

jollifica'tion, *n.*, noce, jubilation, *f.* To have a — ; *faire la noce.*

jol'lily (djol'-), *adv.*, joyeusement ; gaillardement.

jol'liness *ou* **jol'lity**, *n.*, joie, gaieté, allégresse, gaillardise, *f.*

jol'ly, *adj.*, gai, joyeux, gaillard, aimable, jovial, réjoui.

jol'ly-boat (-bôte), *n.*, petit canot, *m.*

jolt (djôlte), *n.*, cahot, *m.*

jolt, *v.a.* and *n.*, cahoter.

jolt'head (djôlt'hède), *n.*, balourd, lourdaud, *m.*

jolt'ing, *n.*, cahotage, *m.*

jon'quil (djon'kwil), *n.*, (bot.) jonquille, *f.*

jor'dan, *n.*, pot de chambre, vase de nuit, *m.*

joss, *n.*, idole chinoise, *f.* — house ; *pagode chinoise, f.*

jos'tle (djos's'l) *ou* **jus'tle** (djeus's'l), *v.a.n.*, coudoyer, pousser, bousculer, heurter ; se heurter.

jos'tling, *n.*, poussade, poussée, *f.* ; coudoiement, *m.*

jot (djote), *n.*, iota, brin, *m.* No — ; *pas la moindre chose ; rien.*

jot (down), *v.a.*, noter ; prendre note **de.**

jour'nal (djeur-), *n.*, journal, *m.* ; feuille publique, *f.* ; (com.) journal, livre-journal, *m.*

jour'nalism, *n.*, journalisme, *m.*

jour'nalist, *n.*, journaliste, *m.*

jour'nalize (-'aïze), *v.a.*, insérer dans un journal ; (bookkeeping) porter au journal.

jour'ney (djeur-nè), *n.*, voyage (by land or

through life), *m.*; (ant.) (a day's work) journée, *f.* To take a —; *faire un voyage.* A pleasant — to you! *bon voyage!* By slow journeys; *à petites journées.* On the —; *en route.* —bated; *harassé de fatigue.* —woman sempstress; *couturière à la journée, f.*

jour'ney *v.n.,* voyager. I —ed many a land; *j'ai traversé maint pays.*

jour'neying, *n.,* voyage, *m.*

jour'neyman, *n.,* garçon; ouvrier, *m.* — tailor; *garçon tailleur, m.*

jour'ney-work (-weurke) *n.,* ouvrage à la journée, *m.*

joust (djouste) *n.,* joute, *f.*

joust, *v.a.,* jouter.

joust'er, *n.,* jouteur, *m.*

Jove, *n.,* Jupiter, (astron.) Jupiter, (fig.) air, *m.,* atmosphère, *f.;* (alchemy) étain, *m.* —'s beard; (bot.) *anthyllide, joubarbe, f.*

jo'vial (djô-), *adj.,* jovial, joyeux.

jovial'ity, *n.,* humeur joviale; jovialité, joie, *f.*

jo'vially, *adv.,* jovialement, joyeusement.

jo'vialness, *n.,* humeur joviale; joie, *f.*

jowl (djôle), *n.,* joue; (of a fish) hure, *f.* Cheek by —; *tête à tête; côte à côte.*

joy (djoè), *n.,* joie, *f.* To wish any one —; *féliciter quelqu'un; offrir ses félicitations à quelqu'un.* To leap for —; *tressaillir, ou sauter, de joie.*

joy, *v.n.,* se réjouir **de,** ou **avec.**

joy'ful (-foule) *adj.,* joyeux.

joy'fully, *adv.,* joyeusement.

joy'fulness, *n.,* allégresse, joie, *f.*

joy'less, *adj.,* sans joie; triste.

joy'lessly, *adv.,* sans joie; tristement.

joy'lessness, *n.,* absence de joie, tristesse, *f.*

joy'ous (djoè-yeusse), *adj.,* joyeux.

joy'ously, *adv.,* joyeusement.

joy'ousness, *n.,* joie, *f.*

jube, *n.,* (arch.) jubé, *m.*

ju'bilant (djiou-), *adj.,* qui pousse des cris de joie; triomphant; jubilant.

ju'bilate, *v.a.,* jubiler.

jubila'tion (djiou-bi-lé-), *n.,* réjouissances de triomphe, *f.pl.;* jubilation, *f.,* triomphe, *m.*

ju'bilee (djiou-bi-lî), *n.,* (of the Jews; c. rel.) jubilé, *m.;* réjouissance, jubilation, allégresse, *f.*

Juda'ic ou **Juda'ical** (-dé-), *adj.,* judaïque.

Juda'ically, *adv.,* judaïquement.

Ju'daism (djiou-dé-iz'me), *n.,* judaïsme, *m.*

Ju'daize (djiou-dé-aïze), *v.n.,* judaïser; donner une interprétation judaïque à.

Ju'daizing, *adj.,* judaïsant.

Ju'das-tree (djiou-dass-trî), *n.,* (bot.) gainier commun; arbre de Judée, *m.*

jud'cock (djeud'-), *n.,* (orni.) petite bécassine, *f.*

judge (djeudje), *n.,* juge; connaisseur, *m.* Assistant —; *assesseur, m.* — advocate; (dans un conseil de guerre) *officier rapporteur, m.* To be a — of; *se connaître à, se connaître* **en.** To be a —; *être juge; s'y connaître.*

judge, *v.a.* and *n.,* juger; discerner; distinguer; considérer. To — for one's self; *juger par soi-même.* Judging by, ou from; *à en juger* **par.** To — by appearances; *juger sur la mine.*

judge'ship, *n.,* fonctions de juge, *f.pl.;* dignité de juge; judicature, *f.*

judg'ment, *n.,* jugement; (of Heaven) châtiment, *m.,* punition, *f.;* avis, sens, *m.;* opinion, *f.;* (jur.) jugement, arrêt, *m.* In my —; *à mon avis.* To have a correct —; *avoir l'esprit juste.* —-debt; (jur.) *créance recouvrable par voie sommaire, f.*

judg'ment-day (-dé) *n.,* jour du jugement; jugement dernier, *m.*

judg'ment-hall (-hôl), *n.,* salle d'audience, *f.*

judg'ment-seat (-sîte), *n.,* tribunal, *m.*

ju'dicature (djiou-di-ca-tiour) *n.,* judicature, justice; cour de justice; juridiction, *f.*

judi'cial (djiou-dish'al), *adj.,* judiciaire, juridique. — separation; *séparation de corps et de biens, f.*

judi'cially, *adv.,* judiciairement, juridiquement.

judi'ciary (djiou-dish'i-a-ri), *adj.,* judiciaire.

judi'cious (djiou-dish'-), *adv.,* judicieux; sage; prudent.

judi'ciously, *adv.,* judicieusement.

judi'ciousness, *n.,* jugement, *m.;* sagesse, *f.;* bon sens, *m.*

jug (djeughe), *n.,* pot; broc, *m.;* cruche, *f.* Water —; *pot à eau, m.*

jug'gle, *n.,* jonglerie; imposture, *f.;* tour de gobelets; escamotage, tour de passe-passe, *m.*

jug'gle (djeug'g'l), *v.n.,* faire des tours de passe-passe; escamoter; tromper; jongler.

jug'gle, *v.a.,* jouer, duper, escamoter; tromper; en imposer **à.**

jug'gler, *n.,* jongleur, bateleur, joueur de gobelets, escamoteur; charlatan, *m.*

jug'glery, *n.,* tour de jongleur, d'escamoteur, *m.;* jonglerie, *f.*

jug'gling, *n.,* jonglerie, *f.;* batelage, escamotage, *m.*

jug'gling, *adj.,* qui fait des tours de passe-passe; qui escamote; trompeur.

jug'glingly, *adv.,* par jonglerie, en fourbe.

ju'gular (djiou-ghiou-), *adj.,* jugulaire.

ju'gular, *n.,* jugulaire, *f.*

juice (djiouce), *n.,* jus; suc, *m.*

juice, *v.a.,* humecter de jus, de suc.

juice'less, *adj.,* sans jus; sans suc.

jui'ciness, *n.,* abondance de jus, de suc, *f.*

jui'cy, *adj.,* juteux; succulent; plein de jus.

ju'jube (djiou-djioube), *n.,* (confectionery) jujube; (fruit) jujube, *m.* — tree; *jujubier, m.*

ju'lep (djiou-lèpe), *n.,* julep, *m.*

Ju'lian (djioul'ya'ne), *adj.,* (calendar) julien.

ju'lus (djiou-), *n.,* (bot.), chaton, *m.*

July' (djiou-laï), *n.,* juillet, *m.*

jum'ble (djeu'm'b'l), *v.a.,* jeter pêle-mêle, confondre, mêler, brouiller.

jum'ble, *v.n.,* se mêler confusément; se brouiller.

jum'ble, *n.,* pêle-mêle, brouillamini, fouillis, *m.;* confusion, *f.*

jump (djeu'm'pe), *n.,* saut, *m.*

jump, *v.a.n.,* sauter; cahoter; (pop.) (to agree) se rencontrer, s'accorder; (to rush on) se jeter, se précipiter **sur.** To — at; *accepter avec empressement; se jeter* **sur.** To — over; *sauter* **par dessus.** To — up; *monter en sautant; se lever précipitamment.* To — out of; *sauter* **hors de.** To — out of bed; *sauter à bas du lit.* Great wits — together; *les beaux esprits se rencontrent.*

jump'er, *n.,* sauteur, *m.,* sauteuse, *f.*

jump'ing, *n.,* saut. *adj.,* sauteur.

junc'tion (djeu'gn'k'-), *n.,* jonction; union; combinaison, *f.,* (of roads) croisement, carrefour, *m.;* (railways) bifurcation, *f.;* embranchement, *m.*

junc'ture (djeu'gn'k't'ioure), *n.,* joint, *m.;* jointure; (critical time) conjoncture, *f.,* moment critique, *m.*

June (djioune), *n.,* juin, *m.*

jun'gle (djeu'gn'g'l), *n.,* jungle, *f.;* fourré, *m.* — fever; *fièvre rémittente, f.*

ju'nior (djiou'n'ieur), *adj.,* jeune, cadet.

ju'nior, *n.,* cadet; inférieur en âge, *m.* — clerk; (jur.) *petit clerc, m.* — classes; (school) *classes élémentaires; classes de grammaire, f.pl.*

ju'niper (djiou-ni-), *n.,* (bot.) genièvre, *m.*

ju'niper-ber'ry (-bèr-ri), *n.,* baie de genièvre, *f.;* genièvre, *m.*

ju'niper-tree (-trî), *n.,* genévrier, (pop.) genièvre, *m.*

junk (djeu'gn'ke), *n.,* (ship) jonque, *f.;* (old cordage) bout de câble, de corde, vieux cordage; (salt beef) bœuf salé, *m.*

jun'ket (djeu'gn'kète), *n.*, régal en cachette, *m.; partie fine, f.*

jun'ket, *v.n.*, se régaler (en cachette); faire bonne chère.

jun'ta *ou* **jun'to** (djeu'n'ta, -tô), *n.*, junte; faction, cabale, *f.*

jurid'ical (djiou-), *adj.*, juridique.

jurid'ically, *adv.*, juridiquement.

juriscon'sult (djiou-ris'co'n'seulte), *n.*, jurisconsulte, *m.*

jurisdic'tion (djiou-ris-dik'-), *n.*, juridiction, *f.*

jurisdic'tional, *adj.*, juridictionnel.

jurisdic'tive, *adj.*, qui a juridiction.

jurispru'dence (djiou-ris'prou'-), *n.*, jurisprudence, *f.*

ju'rist (djiou-), *n.*, juriste, jurisconsulte, *m.*

ju'ror (djiou-), *n.*, juré, *m.* Petty —; *juré de jugement.* Grand —; *juré d'accusation.*

ju'ry (djiou-ri), *n.*, jury, *m.* Petty —; *jury de jugement.* Grand —; *jury d'accusation.* — process; *convocation de jury, f.* Foreman of the —; *chef du jury, m.*

ju'ry-box, *n.*, banc du jury, *m.*

ju'ryman, *n.*, juré, *m.*

ju'ry-mast, *n.*, (nav.) mât de rechange, de fortune, *m.*

just (djeuste), *adj.*, juste, exact; fidèle.

just, *adv.*, juste, justement; au juste; un peu; tout. To have —; *venir de.* He has — gone out; *il vient de sortir.* — let us see; *voyons un peu.* — by; *tout près.* — as; *de même que, au moment même où.* — now; *tout à l'heure, en ce moment.* — so; *précisément.* — out (of books); *vient de paraître.* This child is — like his father; *cet enfant est tout le portrait de son père.* — consider; *réfléchissez donc; voyez donc; considérez donc.* Excepting — one; *à l'exception d'un seul.* — at present; *en ce moment.* — in time; *juste à temps.* To have, *ou* be, but —; *ne faire que de.* — tell me what you saw; *dites-moi un peu ce que vous avez vu.* They have — the same opinion as you; *ils ont précisément la même opinion que vous.* I have — seen him; *je viens de le voir.* We had — started; *nous venions de partir.*

jus'tice (djeus-tice), *n.*, justice, *f.* — of the peace; *juge de paix, m.* Chief —; (in America) *premier juge*; (in France) *conseiller de cour, m.* Lord chief —; (in England) *président du banc du roi, ou premier président, ou Grand Juge, m.*

jus'ticeship, *n.*, dignité de juge, *f.*

justi'ciable (djeus'tish'i-a-b'l), *adj.*, justiciable.

justi'ciary (djeus'tish'i-), *n.*, justicier; (jur.) (in England) premier juge, (in France) président de cour, *m.* High court of —; *cour d'appel (en Ecosse), f.*

jus'tifiable (djeus-ti-fi-a-b'l), *adj.*, justifiable; légitime, permis.

jus'tifiableness, *n.*, caractère justifiable, *m.*

jus'tifiably, *adv.*, d'une manière justifiable; légitimement.

justifica'tion (djeus-ti-fi-ké-), *n.*, justification, *f.*; (jur.) moyens de défense, *m.pl.*

justif'icative *ou* **justif'icatory** (djeus-ti-fi-ka-), *adj.*, justificatif.

jus'tifier (djeus-ti-faï-eur), *n.*, justificateur, *m.*

jus'tify (djeus-ti-faïe), *v.a.*, justifier, motiver, autoriser à, permettre de; (print.) justifier, parangonner. To feel justified in; *se croire autorisé à; croire devoir.* To be justified in; *être autorisé à; être fondé à; avoir le droit de.*

jus'tify, *v.n.*, cadrer ensemble; (print.) (pers.) justifier; (of plates) être de la même justification.

jus'tifying, *n.*, (print.) justification, *f.*, parangonnage, *m.*

jus'tle, *v.a.* *V.* **jostle**.

just'ly (djeust'li), *adv.*, exactement, justement; à bon droit, à bon titre, à juste titre; avec justesse.

just'ness (djeust'-), *n.*, (equity) justice; (accuracy) justesse, exactitude, *f.*

jut (djeute), *v.n.*, avancer, déborder, faire saillie. To — out; *bomber, faire saillie; se projeter; s'avancer.*

jut, *n.*, saillie, *f.*

jute (djoute), *n.*, jute, chanvre de l'Inde, *m.*

jut'ting, *adv.*, en saillie, saillant. *n.*, saillie.

jut'ty (djeut'ti), *v.a.*, avancer, déborder, dépasser.

jut'ty, *n.*, saillie; jetée, *f.*

ju'venile (djou-vi-nil), *adj.*, (of things) juvénile, de jeunesse, de la jeunesse; (pers.) jeune. — ball; *bal d'enfants, m.*

juvenil'ity (djou-vi-nil'i-ti), *n.*, jeunesse, juvénilité, *f.*

juxtapos'ited (djeux-ta-poz'-), *adj.*, juxtaposé.

juxtaposi'tion (djeux'ta-po-zish'-), *n.*, juxtaposition, *f.* In —; *juxtaposé; à côté l'un de l'autre; vis à vis; en regard.*

K

k, onzième lettre de l'alphabet, k, *m.*

kale *ou* **kail** (kéle), *n.*, chou, chou frisé, *m.*

kalei'doscope (ka-laï-do-scôpe), *n.*, kaléidoscope, *m.*

kal'endar, *n.* *V.* **calendar**.

ka'li (ké-li), *n.*, (bot.) kali, *m.*, (chem.) potasse, *f.*; kali, *m.*

ka'lif, *n.* *V.* **ca'lif**.

kangaroo' (ka'gn'ga-rou), *n.*, (zoöl.) kanguroo, kangourou, *m.*

Kant'ian, *adj.*, de Kant.

Kant'ism, *n.*, kantisme, *m.*, philosophie de Kant, *f.*

ka'olin (ké-o-), *n.*, (min.) kaolin, *m.*

kaw (cô), *n.*, croassement, *m.*

kaw, *v.n.* *V.* **caw**.

keck'le (kèc'k'l), *v.a.*, (nav.) fourrer le câble.

kedge (anchor) (kèdje), *n.*, (nav.) ancre à touer, *f.*

kedge, *v.a.*, (nav.) touer.

keel (kîl), *n.*, quille; carène, (bot.) carène, *f.* On an even —; *de niveau; dans une position horizontale.*

keel, *v.a.* and *n.*, (to turn up the keel) montrer le dessous; tourner la quille en l'air, chavirer.

keel'age (kîl'èdje), *n.*, droit d'ancrage, quillage, *m.*

keeled, *adj.*, (nav.) à quille.

keel'haul, *v.a.*, (nav.) donner la cale à.

keel'hauling, *n.*, cale, *f.*

keel'ing, *n.*, morue franche, *f.*; cabillaud, *m.*

keel'son, *n.*, (shipbuilding) contre-quille, carlingue, *f.*

keen (kîne), *adj.*, (sharp) tranchant, affilé, aigu, acéré, aiguisé; (eager) vif, ardent, âpre; (bitter) sanglant, poignant, amer, mordant; (piercing) pénétrant, perçant, piquant, (deep) approfondi; (appetite) grand, féroce, dévorant; (cunning) fin. —edged; *bien affilé.* —eyed; *aux yeux perçants.* —sighted; *clairvoyant.* —witted; *à l'esprit perçant.*

keen'ly, *adv.*, avec un fil acéré; vivement, ardemment, âprement; d'une manière sanglante, poignante, mordante; amèrement; d'une manière pénétrante, piquante.

keen'ness, *n.*, (of edge) finesse; (of mind) subtilité; vivacité; (eagerness) ardeur, âpreté; (rigor) nature pénétrante, perçante, piquante; (asperity) aigreur, *f.*; mordant, *m.*, amertume; nature mordante, sanglante, (acuteness) nature pénétrante, *f.*

keep (kîpe), *v.a.*, (*preterit* and *past part.*,

Kept), tenir, retenir, garder, avoir; (to solemnize) observer, célébrer; (to preserve) entretenir, conserver; (to obey) observer; (to fulfill) tenir, remplir; (to continue) continuer; (to board) nourrir, entretenir; (to have in one's pay) avoir à son service; (to restrain) retenir; (a school, an inn, etc.,) tenir; (lodgers) prendre; (sheep, fowls, etc.) élever. To — doing, saying, telling, etc. ; *ne pas cesser de.* To — at it, to — hard at work; (school) *faire piocher; faire travailler sans relâche.* To — away; *tenir éloigné.* To — back; *écarter de; faire reculer; retenir; tenir en réserve.* To — down; *tenir en bas, modérer;* (fig.) *retenir, comprimer, contenir; tenir sous son grappin;* (com.) *maintenir à bas prix.* To — from danger; *préserver du danger.* To — any one from anything; *détourner quelqu'un de quelque chose.* To — any one from doing anything; *empêcher quelqu'un de faire quelque chose.* To — in; (to provide with) *fournir de, entretenir de;* (to shut in) *tenir enfermé;* (to repress) *retenir;* (at school) *mettre en retenue, consigner; priver de récréation.* To — off; *tenir éloigné.* To — on; (one's clothes) *garder;* (to feed on) *nourrir de.* To — out; *faire rester dehors;* (fig.) *écarter, éloigner.* To — out of; *tenir éloigné de; tenir à distance de.* To — to; *tenir fermé.* To — any one to it, to his work; *faire travailler, faire marcher quelqu'un.* To — under; *tenir dessous;* (fig.) *contenir, retenir, assujettir, maîtriser.* To — up; *tenir en haut; tenir en l'air; tenir levé; soutenir;* (to prolong) *prolonger, continuer;* (to maintain) *entretenir; maintenir un prix* (com.); (to prevent from going to bed) *faire veiller.* To — up a show of dignity; *sauver les apparences de la dignité.* To — one's bed, one's room; *garder le lit, la chambre.* To — house; *avoir une maison, tenir maison.* To — a secret; *garder un secret.* To — one's word; *tenir sa parole.* To — silent; *garder le silence; se taire.* To — a promise; *remplir une promesse.* To — a servant; *avoir un domestique.* To — a person company; *accompagner, escorter quelqu'un.* To — company with; *tenir compagnie à;* (to court) *courtiser, faire la cour à.* To — a great deal of company; *recevoir beaucoup de monde.* To — good hours; *se coucher de bonne heure.* To — bad hours; *se coucher à des heures indues.* To — one going; *tenir quelqu'un à l'ouvrage.* To — the pot boiling; *faire bouillir la marmite, faire aller le pot-au-feu.* To — one's hand in; *s'entretenir la main à.* To — in touch with; *rester en relation avec; se tenir au courant de.* To — in view; *ne pas perdre de vue.* To — open house; *tenir table ouverte.* To — a birthday; *célébrer une fête (de naissance), l'anniversaire de la naissance.* To — order; *maintenir le bon ordre.* To — any one waiting; *faire faire le pied de grue à quelqu'un; faire poser quelqu'un.* To — the peace; *s'abstenir de voies de fait envers; ne pas troubler l'ordre public.* To — any one at home; *faire rester quelqu'un à la maison.* Her father — s her at home; *son père la garde auprès de lui, la garde à la maison.* What! — a dog and bark thyself; *on ne prend pas un valet pour se servir soi-même.* To — the ball rolling; *tenir les gens en haleine.* To — the streets clear; *faire la police des rues.*

keep, v.n., se tenir; rester; se diriger; (to last) se garder, se conserver; (to dwell) demeurer. To — at it; *travailler d'arrache-pied.* To — away; *se tenir éloigné; s'absenter.* To — back; *se tenir en arrière;* (fig.) *se tenir à l'écart.* To — down; *rester en bas;* (fig.) *se contenir, se comprimer.* To — from; *s'abstenir de; se tenir de.* To — in; *rester dedans;* (at home) *rester à la maison;* (fig.) *se contenir, se retenir, se cacher.* To — in with; *rester bien avec.* To — off; *se tenir éloigné; s'éloigner;* (nav., milit.) *tenir le large.* To — on; *aller en avant; continuer*

de; *aller toujours, aller son train.* To — out; *rester dehors; s'éloigner.* To — out of the way; *s'absenter; se tenir caché.* To — to; *adhérer strictement à, rester fidèle à, tenir ferme à;* (to keep shut) *se tenir fermé.* To — to one's self; *faire bande à part.* To — to one's word, one's promise; *tenir sa parole, remplir sa promesse.* To — to the laws; *observer les lois.* To — under; *se tenir dessous;* (fig.) *se contenir.* To — up; *se tenir en haut, se tenir levé;* (fig.) *se soutenir, se maintenir;* (to continue) *se continuer, se prolonger;* (not to go to bed) *veiller, ne pas se coucher.* — there! *restez là!* To — it up; *aller toujours; s'en donner.* These apples — well; *ces pommes se gardent, sont de bonne garde.* Meat does not — well; *la viande ne se garde pas, n'est pas de bonne garde.* He — s on singing from morning till night; *il est toujours à chanter du matin au soir.* He — s telling me the same thing; *il me rabâche toujours la même chose.*

keep, n., (stronghold) donjon, m., (of a castle) cachot, m.; (support) nourriture, f., entretien; (condition) état, m., condition, f.; (l.u.) tutelle, contrainte, f. The — of a horse; *l'entretien d'un cheval.* The horse's—; *la nourriture de la bête* (V. Hugo).

keep'er, n., garde; gardien; surveillant, m. — of the Great Seal; *Garde des Sceaux,* m. — of a museum; *conservateur d'un musée,* m.

keep'ing, n., garde; surveillance; conservation; (fodder) nourriture; (congruity) harmonie, f., unisson, m.; (paint.) harmonie, f. In —; en harmonie **avec**; à l'unisson; à l'avenant **de.** In good —; *sons bonne garde; en bon entretien.*

keep'sake (kî'p'séke), n., souvenir d'amitié; album, souvenir, keepsake, m.

keg (kèghe), n., caque, f.; petit baril, m.

kelp (kèlpe), n., soude de varech, f.

kel'son (kèl-), n. V. keelson.

ken (kène), n., vue; portée de la vue, portée, f.

ken, v.a., voir de loin; apercevoir; savoir; comprendre.

ken'nel (kèn'nèl), n., (of a dog) chenil, m., niche, loge, f.; (of a fox) terrier; (of wild beasts) trou; (gutter) ruisseau, m., rigole, (pack of hounds) meute, f.

ken'nel, v.n., (of the dog) se coucher, se loger; (of the fox) se terrer.

ken'nel, v.a., mettre dans un chenil.

ken'nel-stone (-stône), n., (arch.) caniveau, m.; (mas.) culière, f.

kent'ledge (kèn'n't'lèdje), n., (nav.) gueuse, f.

kept (kèpte), adj., entretenu.

kerb, n., (arch.) cintre, m.; (of pavements) bordure de trottoir, f., parement, m., (of wells) margelle, f.

kerb, v.a., border, entourer d'une margelle.

kerb-stone, bordure de trottoir, f., parement, m.; (of a well) margelle, f.

ker'chief (keur'tshif), n., fichu.

ker'chiefed (-'tshif'te), adj., (ant.) habillé; coiffé.

kerf (keurfe), n., trait de scie, m., entaille, f.

ker'mes (keur-mize), n., kermès, m.

kern (keurne), v.n., durcir; se former en grain.

kern (keurne), n., fantassin irlandais, m.

ker'nel (keur-nèl), n., amande; (of fruit) graine, f., noyau, m.; (of pulpy fruit) pépin; (of corn) grain, m.; (med.) glande, f., (fig.) fond, fin mot, m., substance, (meat) noix, f. — fruit; *fruit à pépins, m.*

ker'nel, v.n., (ant.) se former en grain.

ker'nelly, adj., (ant.) de grains, de pépins.

ker'sey (keur-zè), n., gros drap, m.

ker'seymere (keur-zè-mîre), n., casimir, m.

kes'trel (kès-trèl), n., (orni.) crécerelle, f., émouchet, m.

ketch(kèt'she), n.,(nav.)quaiche, f., ketch, m.

ket'chup (kètsh'eupe), n. V. **cat'sup.**

ket'tle (kèt't'l), n., bouilloire, (large) chaudière, f. ; chaudron, m. Tea— ; bouilloire, f. A pretty — of fish ; un beau gâchis ; un joli tohu-bohu. The — sings when put on the fire (i.e., "innocence speaks out") ; la bouilloire chante devant le feu (V. Hugo).

ket'tle-drum (-dreume), n., timbale, f.

ket'tle-holder, n., poignée de bouilloire, f.

key (kî), n., clef, f. ; (book) corrigé, m., traduction, f., (bot.) chaton, m. ; (mus.) clef, tonique, f. ; ton, m. ; (in an organ, a harpsichord) touche, f. ; (on the side of rivers, etc.) quai, m. ; (for drawing teeth) clef ; (of mind) situation d'esprit, f. ; (railways) coin, m. Gold — ; clef de chambellan. Power of the —s ; (cath. rel.) puissance des clefs, f. To have the — of the street ; avoir la clef des champs ; n'avoir ni feu ni lieu. With a — ; à clef.

key'age (kî-èdje), n., quaiage, quayage, m.

key'-board (-bôrde), n., (mus.) clavier, m.

keyed (kî-de), adj., (mus.) à touches ; (ant.) adapté a une clef, à un ton.

key'-groove (-grouve), n., cannelure, f.

key'hole (-hôl), n., trou de serrure, m.

key'less, adj., (of watches) à remontoir.

key'-note (-nôte), n., (mus.) tonique, f.

key'-ring, n., clavier, m.

key'stone (-stône), n., clef de voûte, f.

khan (kâ'ne), n., kan ; caravansérail, m.

kibe (kaïbe), n., engelure, gerçure, f.

kibed (kaïb'de), adj., qui a des engelures ; gercé.

kick, n., coup de pied, m. ; (of animals) ruade, f., (recoil) recul, m.

kick, v.a., donner un coup de pied à ; donner des coups de pied à ; frapper du pied, pousser du pied. To — down ; renverser d'un coup de pied. To — out ; chasser à coups de pied. To — the bucket ; (colloq.) passer l'arme à gauche. To — up a row ; causer du tumulte.

kick, v.n., donner des coups de pied, (about) gigoter ; (of animals) ruer, regimber ; (of firearms) reculer ; repousser.

kick'er, n., personne qui donne des coups de pied, f. ; (man.) rueur, m., rueuse, f.

kick'ing, n., coups de pied ; coups, m.pl. ; (of animals) ruades, f.pl.

kick'ing-strap, n., (for horses) plate-longe, f.

kick'shaw (-shô), n., colifichet, m., bagatelle, niaiserie, f.

kick'-up (-eupe), n., (pop.) esclandre, tapage, grabuge, m.

kid, n., (zoöl.) chevreau, cabri ; (tub) petit baquet, m. ; (nav.) gamelle, f. ; (fagot) fagot ; fagot de bruyère, de genêt ; (fig.) enfant, bambim, marmot, môme ; gosse, m. (A. Daudet).

kid, adj., de chevreau. — gloves ; gants de chevreau, m.pl.

kid, v.n., (of the goat) chevroter, mettre bas ; (to form into a bundle) faire un fagot.

kid'der, n., regrattier, m.

kid'dow (kid'dô), n., (orni.) guillemot, m.

kid'nap, v.a., enlever un homme, une femme, un enfant.

kid'naper, n., auteur d'un enlèvement d'homme, de femme, d'enfant, m.

kid'ney (-'nè), n., rein ; (of animals) rognon, m,; (sort) trempe, sorte, espèce, f. A man of my — ; un homme de ma sorte, de ma trempe.

kid'ney-bean (-bîne), n., haricot, m.

kid'ney-potato, n., marjolin, vitelotte, f.

kid'ney-shaped (-shépte), adj., réniforme.

kid'ney-vetch (-vèt'she), n., (bot.) vulnéraire, f.

kil'derkin (-deur'-), n., demi-baril, m.

kill, v.a., tuer ; faire mourir ; abattre. To — time ; tuer le temps. To — two birds with one

stone ; faire d'une pierre deux coups. To — by inches ; faire mourir à petit feu. Killed on the spot ; tué sur place ; resté sur le carreau.

kill'er, n., tueur, m.

kill'ing, n., tuerie, boucherie, f. ; massacre, carnage, m. adj., mortel ; (of work) assommant, écrasant, tuant.

kiln (kile), n., four, m. Brick— ; four à briques. Lime— ; four à chaux.

kiln'-dry (-draïe), v.a., (preterite and past part., Kiln-dried) sécher au four.

kil'ogram, n., kilogramme, m.

kil'oli-ter ou **-tre** (-lî'teur), n., kilolitre, m.

kil'ome-ter ou **-tre** (-mî-teur),n.,kilomètre,m.

kilt ou **kelt** (kèlte), n., jupon (de montagnard écossais), m.

kim'bo (ki'm'bô), adj., crochu, courbé, plié. The arms a— ; les poings sur les hanches.

kin, n., parenté, f. ; parent, m. ; parente, f. ; allié, m., alliée ; famille, f. Next of — ; le plus proche parent, m., la plus proche parente, f.

kin, adj., parent, allié.

kind (kaï'n'de), adj., (pers.) bon ; plein de bonté, bienveillant, bienfaisant ; (obliging) obligeant, complaisant ; (of things) bon, bienfaisant. Will you be so — as to ; voulez-vous avoir la bonté de. My — regards to him ; faites-lui mes amitiés, dites-lui bien des choses de ma part.

kind (kaï'n'de), n., genre, m. ; sorte ; race, espèce, f. In — ; en nature. Nothing of the — ; rien de la sorte.

kin'dergarten, n., école maternelle, salle d'asile, f.

kind'hearted, adj., bon, plein de bonté, bienfaisant.

kind'heartedness, n., bonté (de cœur), f.

kin'dle (ki'n'd'l), v.a., allumer, enflammer ; (fig.) éveiller, réveiller, encourager, exciter.

kin'dle, v.n., s'allumer, s'enflammer ; (fig.) s'embraser, s'éveiller, se réveiller.

kin'dle-coal, kin'dle-fire, n., brandon de discorde, m.

kind'liness (kaï'n'd'-), n., bienveillance, bienfaisance, douceur, bonté, f.

kind'ly (kaï'n'd'li), adj., bienfaisant, bon, bienveillant, favorable, doux.

kind'ly (kaï'n'd'li), adv., avec bienveillance ; avec bonté ; complaisamment. To take — to ; affectionner, aimer bien, se prêter volontiers à.

kind'ness (kaï'n'd'-), n., bienveillance, bonté ; complaisance ; amitié, f. ; service ; acte de bienveillance, bienfait, m. Act of — ; acte de bienveillance, m. ; amitié, f.

kin'dred (ki'n'-), n., parenté ; affinité, f. ; parents, m.pl. ; (fig.) rapport, m.

kine (kaïne), n., (pl. de Cow) vaches, f.pl.

king, n., roi, m. ; (at draughts) dame damée ; dame, f. —-at-arms ; roi d'armes, m. —-befitting ; royal, digne d'un roi. —'s evidence ; témoin de la couronne, m. —'s yellow ; orpiment, m. —-killer ; régicide, m.

king, v.a., (at draughts) damer.

king'craft (-crâfte), n., art de régner, m. ; politique (de roi), f.

king'cup (-keupe), n., (bot.) bouton d'or, m.

king'dom (kign'deume), n., royaume ; (fig.) empire, m., région, f. ; (natur. hist.) règne, m United — ; Royaume-Uni.

king'fisher, n., (orni.) martin-pêcheur, m.

king'less (kign'-), adj., sans roi.

king'let (kign'lète), n., roitelet, m.

king'like (kign'laïke), adv., en roi ; comme un roi, royalement.

king'ling (kign'-), n., roitelet, m.

king'ly (kign'-), adj., royal, de roi.

king'ly, adv., royalement; en roi.

king's'-bench (kign'z'bèn'nshe), n., cour du banc du roi, f.

king's-e'vil (kign'z'î-vî'l), n.sing., écrouelles, f.pl.

king'ship (kign'-), *n.*, royauté, *f.*

king's'-spear (kign'z'spìre), *n.*, (bot.) asphodèle rameux, *m.*

ki'no (kaï-nŏ), *n.*, kino, *m. ;* résine kino ; gomme de Gambie, *f.*

kins'folk (ki'n'z'fôke), *n.*, parents, *m.pl.*, parenté, *f.*

kins'man (ki'n'z'-), *n.*, parent, allié, *m.*

kins'woman (ki'n'z'woum'-), *n.*, parente, alliée, *f.*

kiosk', *n.*, kiosque, *m.*

kirb (keurbe), *n.* V. **curb.**

kirb'-stone (keurb'stône), *n.* V. **curb-stone.**

kirk (keurke), *n.*, Eglise d'Ecosse, *f.*

kirschwas'ser (keursh'wŏs'seur), *n.*, kirschwasser ; kirsch, *m.*

kir'tle (keur't'l), *n.*, mante, *f.*, mantelet, jupon, *m.*

kirt'-roof (keurt'roufe), *n.*, toit pyramidal, *m.*

kish, *n.*, bourriche, *f.*

kiss, *n.*, baiser, *m. ;* (at billiards) contre, *m.*

kiss, *v.a.*, baiser, embrasser. To — the dust ; *mordre la poussière.* To — the ground ; *se prosterner à terre en signe de soumission.* To — the rod ; *se soumettre sans résistance au châtiment.* To — hands ; *baiser la main* (du roi *ou* de la reine). To — one's hand to ; *envoyer un baiser,* ou *des baisers,* à.

kiss'er, *n.*, baiseur, *m.*, baiseuse, *f.*

kiss'ing, *n.*, action de baiser, *f. ;* (of the Pope's slipper) baisement, *m. ;* baisers, embrassements, *m.pl.* — of hands ; (feudal) *baisemain, m.*

kiss'ing-crust (-creuste), *n.*, baisure, *f.*

kit, *n.*, (mus.) violon de poche, *m.*, pochette ; (tech.) tinette, *f. ;* (milit.) équipement ; attirail ; (nav.) sac, *m. ;* (of officers) effets, *m.pl. ;* seau ; baquet à poisson ; jeune chat, petit chat, chaton, *m.*, jeune chatte, petite chatte, *f.*

kitch'en (kit'shène), *n.*, cuisine, *f.* — garden ; *jardin potager, m.* —stuff ; *graisses de cuisine, f.pl.* — dresser ; *dressoir, m.* —latin ; *latin de cuisine, m.* — midden ; *tas d'ordures, m.*

kitch'ener, *n.*, fourneau de cuisine ; (ant.) cuisinier, *m.*

kitch'en-maid (-méde), *n.*, fille de cuisine, *f.*

kitch'en-range (-ré'n'dje), *n.*, cuisine anglaise, *f.*, fourneau de cuisine, *m.*

kitch'en-utensils,*n.pl.*, batterie de cuisine, *f.*

kitch'en-wench (-wè'n'she), *n.*, laveuse de vaisselle, *f.*

kitch'en-work (-weurke), *n.*, cuisine, *f.*

kite (kaïte), *n.*, (orni.) milan ; (toy) cerfvolant ; (rapacious person) vautour, *m.* To fly a —; *enlever un cerf-volant ;* (com.) *maintenir son crédit au moyen de billets de complaisance.*

kith, *n.*, parents, amis, *m.pl.*

kit'ten (kit't'n), *n.*, chaton, petit chat, *m. ;* petite chatte, *f.*

kit'ten, *v.n.*, chatter, mettre bas.

kit'tenish, *adj.*, (ant.) enjoué, folâtre.

klick, *n.*, cliquet, m.

klick, *v.n.*, faire un petit bruit aigu ; faire tic tac.

knab (nabe) *ou* **knab'ble** (nab'b'l), (ant.) *v.a.*, saisir, happer, ronger, mordre.

knack (nake), *n.*, (toy) colifichet, *m. ;* babiole ; (adroitness) adresse, *f. ;* talent, chic, truc, *m. ;* habitude, *f.*, tic, *m.*

knack'er (nak'-), *n.*, équarrisseur ; (maker of toys) (ant.) bimbelotier ; (saddler) sellier, harnacheur, *m.* —'s yard ; *écorcherie, voirie, f.*

knag (naghe), *n.*, nœud, *m. ;* cheville, *f.*

knag'gy (nag'ghi), *adj.*, noueux ; (fig.) hargneux.

knap (nape), *n.* V. **knob.**

knave (néve), *n.*, fripon, fourbe, coquin ; (at cards) valet. —bairn ; *enfant mâle, m.*

kna'very (név'ri), *n.*, friponnerie ; fourberie, coquinerie ; (waggishness) malice, *f.*

kna'vish (név'-), *adj.*, fripon, de fripon ; de coquin ; de fourbe ; (waggish) malin, malicieux. — trick ; *friponnerie, f.*

kna'vishly (név'-), *adv.*, en fripon ; en fourbe ; (waggishly) malicieusement, avec malice.

kna'vishness (név'-), *n.*, coquinerie ; friponnerie ; fourberie, improbité, *f.*

knead (nîde), *v.a.*, pétrir.

knead'ing (nîd'-), *n.*, pétrissage, *m.*

knead'ing-trough (nîd'ign'trofe), *n.*, pétrin, *m. ;* huche, *f.*

knee (nî), *n.*, genou, *m. ;* (nav.) courbe, *f. ;* (mec.) coude, *m.* On one's —s ; *à genoux.* — pad ; *genouillère, f.* Broken —s ; (of horses) *couronnement, m.* To break the —s ; (of horses) *couronner.* Down on your —s ! *à genoux !*

knee'-breeches, *n.pl.*, culotte courte, *f.*

knee'-cap (nî-cape), *n.*, genouillère ; (anat.) rotule, *f.*

kneed, *adj.*, (in compounds) à genoux . . . ; qui a les genoux . . . Knock —; *cagneux.*

knee'-deep (nî-dîpe), *adj.*, à la hauteur du genou ; jusqu'aux genoux.

knee'-high (nî-haïe), *adj.* V. **knee-deep.**

knee'-joint, *n.*, (anat.) joint du genou, *m.*, articulation du genou, *f.*

knee'-jointed, *adj.*, (bot.) géniculé, entrecoupé de nœuds.

kneel (nîl), *v.n.*, s'agenouiller. To — down ; *se mettre à genoux.*

kneel'er (nîl'-), *n.*, personne qui s'agenouille ; personne agenouillée, *f. ;* (stool) agenouilloir, *m.*

kneel'ing (nîl'-), *n.*, action de s'agenouiller ; génuflexion, *f. pres. part.* s'agenouillant ; agenouillé, à genoux. —stool ; *agenouilloir, m.*

knee'pan (nî-pa'ne), *n.*, rotule, *f.*

knell (nèl), *n.*, glas, *m.*

knicker-bockers, *n. plur.*, culotte, *f.*

knick'-knack (nik'nake), *n.*, brimborion, *m. ;* babiole, *f. ;* colifichet, bibelot, *m.*

knife (naïfe), *n.*, (knives) couteau ; (tech.) coupoir, *m. ;* (ant.) épée, *f.*, poignard ; (surg.) bistouri, *m.* Carving—; *couteau à découper.* Table—; *couteau de table.* Dessert—; *couteau à dessert.* — and fork ; *couvert, m.* Clasp—; *couteau pliant.* Pruning—; *serpette, f.* — basket ; *panier à couteaux, m.* War to the —; *guerre à mort, à outrance, f.* To have one's — in any one ; (fig.) *poursuivre quelqu'un avec acharnement.* [teau, *f.*

knife'-blade (naïfe-bléde), *n.*, lame de couteaux, *f.*

knife'-board (naïfe-bôrde), *n.*, planche à couteaux, *f.*

knife'-cleaning machine, *n.*, poli-couteaux, *m.*

knife'-grinder (naïfe-graï'n'd'-), *n.*, rémouleur, repasseur de couteaux ; gagne-petit, *m.*

knife'-handle, *n.*, manche de couteau, *m.*

knife'-rest (naïfe-rèste), *n.*, porte-couteau, *m.*

knife'-tray (naïfe-tré), *n.*, boîte à couteaux, *f.*

knight (naïte), *n.*, chevalier ; (at chess) cavalier, *m.* — of the shire ; *représentant d'un comté, m.* — of the shears ; *tailleur, m.*

knight (naïte), *v.a.*, créer chevalier ; armer chevalier, décorer.

knight-er'rant (naïte-èr'-), *n.*, chevalier errant, *m.*

knight-er'rantry (naïte-èr'-), *n.*, chevalerie errante, *f.*

knight'hood (naït'houde), *n.*, chevalerie, *f.*

knight'liness (naït'-), *n.sing.*, caractère chevaleresque, *m.*

knight'ly (naït'-), *adj.*, de chevalerie, de chevalier.

knit (nite), *v.a.*, tricoter ; (the brows) froncer ; (fig.) joindre, attacher ; lier ; nouer ; unir.

knit'ter (nit'-), *n.*, tricoteur, *m. ;* tricoteuse ; machine à tricoter, *f.*

knit'ting (nit'-), *n.*, tricotage, *m. ;* (fig.) union, *f.*

knit'ting-needle (nit'tign'nîd'l), n., aiguille à tricoter, f.

knob (nobe), n., bosse, protubérance, f. ; (of a door) bouton fixe, bouton ; (in wood) nœud, m.

knobbed (nob'b'de), adj., qui a des protubérances ; qui a des nœuds ; noueux.

knob'biness (nob'-), n., nature noueuse, f.

knob'by (nob'-), adj., plein de protubérances ; plein de nœuds ; noueux.

knock (noke), v.a., frapper, heurter, cogner. To — about ; frapper de tous côtés ; abîmer de coups ; chasser de côté et d'autre ; (fig.) ballotter. To — down ; faire tomber (par un coup) ; renverser ; assommer ; terrasser ; (at sales) adjuger. To — in ; enfoncer, cogner. To — off ; faire sauter ; (to get through) faire, achever. To — off a good deal of work ; abattre, débiter de l'ouvrage, ou de la besogne. To — on the head ; (fig.) déjouer ; faire échouer. To — out ; faire sortir (à force de coups) ; faire sauter. To — up ; (to awake) réveiller (en frappant à la porte) ; (to fatigue) éreinter.

knock (noke), v.n., frapper, heurter, cogner. To — about ; rouler sa bosse, aller de par le monde ; (the streets) se trimbaler par les rues. To — under ; se rendre ; mettre les pouces ; se soumettre. A —down argument ; argument décisif, m.

knock (noke), n., coup, m. To hear a — at the door, entendre frapper à la porte. There is a — at the door ; on frappe à la porte.

knock'er (nok'-), n., personne qui frappe, f. ; (of a door) marteau, m.

knock'ing (nok'-), n.sing., coups ; coups de marteau, m.pl.

knoll (nôl), n., monticule, tertre, m. ; butte, f.

knoll (nôl), v.a. and n., sonner, tinter.

knot (note), n., nœud ; (group of persons) groupe, cercle ; (group of things) groupe, m. ; (difficulty) difficulté, embarras ; (epaulet) aiguillette, f. ; (association) lien ; (nav., bot.) nœud, m. To make twelve —s an hour ; (nav.) filer douze nœuds à l'heure.

knot (note), v.n., faire des nœuds ; se nouer.

knot (note), v.a., nouer ; lier ; (fig.) embrouiller, embarrasser.

knot'grass (note'grâce), n., (bot.) renouée, centinode, trainasse, f.

knot'less (not'-), adj., sans nœuds.

knot'ted (not'-), adj., noueux.

knot'tiness (not'-), n., abondance de nœuds, f. ; (fig.) embrouillement, m. ; difficulté, f.

knot'ty (not-), adj., noueux ; (hard) dur ; (intricate) embarrassant, embrouillé, difficile, compliqué.

knout (naoute), n., knout, m.

know (nô), v.a. and n. (preterit, Knew ; past part., Known), (by the mind) savoir, posséder ; (by the senses) connaître ; (to recognize) reconnaître. To — by heart ; savoir par cœur. To — by sight ; connaître de vue. To — anything ; savoir quelque chose. To — any one ; connaître quelqu'un. To — one's lesson ; savoir sa leçon. To — two languages ; posséder deux langues. To let any one — anything ; faire savoir, faire connaître, faire part de, quelque chose à quelqu'un. To — again ; remettre, reconnaître. Not to — one from the other ; ne pouvoir distinguer l'un de l'autre. To — of ; connaître ; avoir connaissance de. To — how to read and write ; savoir lire et écrire. He —s ; il le sait. He has even been —n to ; on l'a même vu. You ought to — better at your age ; vous devriez être plus raisonnable à votre âge. You ought to have —n better ; vous n'auriez pas dû vous y laisser prendre. I — better ; je m'en garderai bien ; je ne suis pas si sot ; je sais tout le contraire. How do I — that ? (demonstrative) qu'est-ce qui me dit cela ? ; (conjunctive) qu'est-ce qui me dit que . . . Not that I —; pas que

je sache. I — how to deal with him ; je sais comment il faut le prendre. To make —n ; faire connaître ; démasquer ; exposer l'infamie de. Not to — from Adam ; ne connaître ni d'Eve ni d'Adam. To be in the — ; avoir vu le dessous des cartes.

know'able (nô-a-b'l), adj., qu'on peut savoir.

know'er (nô'-), n., connaisseur, m.

know'ing (no'-), adj., savant, intelligent ; instruit, éclairé ; (cunning) fin, rusé. A — fellow ; un rusé compère.

know'ingly (nô'-), adv., sciemment ; (cunningly) avec ruse, avec finesse.

know'ledge (nô-lèdje), n., savoir, m. ; connaissances, f.pl., science, f. To one's — ; à sa connaissance. To my — ; que je sache. Without my — ; à mon insu. — is power ; (prov.) de savoir vient savoir.

knuc'kle (neuk'k'l), n., articulation, jointure, f. ; (of meat) jarret, m. ; (of a hinge) jointure, f. ; (ham) demi-jambon, f. To rap any one on the —s ; donner sur les doigts à quelqu'un.

knuc'kle (neuk'k'l), v.n., se rendre ; mettre les pouces. To — down ; (at marbles) caler. To — to, under ; céder, se rendre ; mettre les pouces.

knuc'kle-bones, n.pl., osselets, m.pl.

knuc'kle-duster, n., coup de poing, m.

knuc'kled (neuk'k'lde), adj., articulé.

kop'je, n., colline, f.

koran' (kô-), n., Coran, Koran, m.

kreut'zer (krôit'zeur), n., kreutzer, m.

L

l, douzième lettre de l'alphabet, l, m., f.

la ! (lâ), int., là ! vois donc ! voyez donc ! tiens ! tenez !

la, n., (mus.) la, m.

la'bel (lé'b'l), n., étiquette, f. ; écriteau ; (jur.) codicille, m. ; (of a deed) queue, f. ; (her.) lambel, m. ; (bot.) lèvre, f.

la'bel, v.a., étiqueter ; désigner sous le nom de.

la'bial (lé-), adj., labial.

la'bial, n., (gram.) labiale, f.

la'biate ou **la'biated** (lé-bi-éte, -'ède), adj., (bot.) labié.

lab'oratory, n., laboratoire, m.

labo'rious (la-bô-), adj., laborieux ; (of things) pénible, laborieux. [ment.

labo'riously, adv., laborieusement, pénible-

labo'riousness, n., nature laborieuse, difficulté, f. ; labeur, m.

la'bor (lé-beur), n., travail, labeur, ouvrage, m. ; peine, f. ; (travail) travail d'enfant, m. The —s of Hercules ; les travaux d'Hercule. To lose one's — ; perdre sa peine. To be in — ; être en travail d'enfant. Hand — ; main d'œuvre, f. Hard — ; travail pénible ; (prison) travaux forcés, m. ; réclusion, f. Manual — ; ouvrage de manœuvre, m. To have one's — for one's pains ; en être pour ses frais, ou pour sa peine.

la'bor, v.a., travailler ; (to till) labourer ; (to urge) pousser, poursuivre ; (to beat) (l.u.) battre ; (fig.) élaborer, travailler.

la'bor, v.n., travailler ; (to be in distress) souffrir ; (to be in travail) être en travail d'enfant ; (to strive) chercher à, s'efforcer de, s'évertuer à. To — under a disease ; être travaillé par une maladie, souffrir d'une maladie. To — under an error ; être dans l'erreur.

la'bor-bureau, n., bureau de placement municipal.

la'borer, n., homme de peine, ouvrier, m. Bricklayer's — ; manœuvre, m. Day — ; journalier, m. [ouvrière.

la'boring, adj., qui travaille. — class ; classe

labur'num (la-beur-), n., (bot.) faux ébénier, m.

lab'yrinth (-ri'n'th), n., labyrinthe, dédale, m.

lac, n., laque (résine), gomme laque, f. — of rupees ; 250,000 francs.

lace (léce), n., dentelle, f. ; passement, galon ; (a snare) collet, filet ; (a string) ruban, lacet, cordon, m. Brussels —; dentelle de Bruxelles, f., point de Bruxelles, m. Gold, silver—; galon d'or, d'argent, m. Boot—; lacet de bottine. Stay—; lacet de corset.

lace, v.a., (to fasten) lacer ; (to beat) rosser, battre ; (to adorn with lace) garnir de dentelle, galonner ; (fig.) orner.

laced (léss-te), adj., lacé ; garni de dentelle ; galonné ; (of coffee) à l'eau-de-vie. — boot ; bottine lacée, f.

lace-embroid'erer (-è'm'broïd'-), n., brodeur en dentelle, m., brodeuse en dentelle, f.

lace'-frame, n., métier à dentelle, m.

lace'-hole, n., œillet, m.

lace'maker (-mék'-) ou **lace'-manufac'turer** (-ma'n'iou-fakt'iour'-), n., fabricant de dentelles, passementier, m.

lace'man, n., marchand de dentelles, passementier, m.

lace'-manufac'ture (-ma'n'iou-fakt'ioure),n., fabrication de dentelles, passementerie, f.

lace'-merchant (-meur'tsh'a'n'te), n., négociant en dentelles, m.

lace'-paper, n., papier dentelle, m.

la'cer, n., laceur, -euse, m.f.

lac'erable (lass'eur'a-b'l), adj., lacérable.

lac'erate (lass'eur'-), v.a., déchirer, lacérer.

lac'erate ou **lac'erated** (lass'eur'éte, -'ède), adj., déchiré ; (bot.) lacéré.

lacera'tion (lass'eur'é-), n., déchirure, f. ; lacération, f.

lace'-trade (-tréde), n., commerce des dentelles, m. ; passementerie, f.

lace'woman (-woum'-), n., marchande de dentelles ; passementière, f.

lace'-work (-weurke), n., dentelle ; passementerie, f.

lach'rymal (lak'ri-), adj., lacrymal.

lach'rymary, adj., lacrymatoire.

lach'rymatory, n., lacrymatoire, m.

lach'rymose, adj., larmoyant.

la'cing, n., lacement, m.

lacin'iate ou **lacin'iated**, adj., orné de franges ; (bot.) lacinié.

lack, n., besoin, manque, m. ; privation, f.

lack, v.a., manquer de, être dénué de. — land ; sans terre.

lack, v.n., manquer ; être dans le besoin.

lackadai'sical (-dé-zi-), adj., minaudier, sentimental, minaudière.

lackadai'sy ! (-dé-zi), int. V. lack-a-day.

lack-a-day'! (-dè), int., hélas ! ah !

lack'-beard, n., homme imberbe, m.

lack'brain (-bréne), n., homme sans tête, écervelé, m., tête sans cervelle, f.

lack'er ou **lac'quer**, n., laque, vernis, m.

lack'er ou **lac'quer**, v.a., enduire de laque ; laquer.

lack'ering ou **lac'quering**, n., vernissure en laque.

lack'ey, n., laquais, valet de pied, m.

lack'luster (-leusteur), adj., sans éclat ; sans brillant. terne.

lacon'ic ou **lacon'ical**, adj., laconique.

lacon'ically, adv., laconiquement.

lac'onism (-niz'me), n., laconisme, m.

lac'tary (-tary), adj., laiteux ; lacté ; lactaire.

lacta'tion (-té-), n., lactation, f.

lac'teal (-ti-), adj., lacté.

lac'tean ou **lac'teous** (-ti-), adj., de lait, laiteux.

lactif'erous, adj., lactifère.

lactom'eter (-to'm'i-), n., lactomètre, galactomètre, m.

lad, n., garçon, jeune homme ; gaillard, m.

Well, my — ; eh bien, mon garçon, mon ami, mon brave !

lad'der, n., échelle, f. Scaling—; échelle de siège. Rope—; échelle de corde. Rescuing —; échelle de sauvetage, f.

lade (léde), v.a., (water) puiser, tirer ; mettre ; (ant.) charger de. To — out ; vider.

la'den (léd'n), adj., (nav.) chargé ; (fig.) accablé de, oppressé de.

la'dies'-man, n., coqueluche (de femmes), m.

la'ding (léd'-), n., chargement, m. Bill of — ; (com.) connaissement, m.

la'dle (léd'l), n., cuiller à pot, cuiller à potage ; (of a water-mill) aube, palette, f. Soup — ; grande cuillère, f. To — out ; servir ; (speeches) débiter.

la'dy (lé-di), n., (ladies) dame, femme, f. Young —; demoiselle ; jeune personne, f. Yes, my — ; (to a countess) oui, madame la comtesse ; (a viscountess) oui, madame la vicomtesse, etc. Ladies ! mesdames ! mesdemoiselles ! She is a perfect — ; c'est une femme très comme il faut ou c'est une grande dame.

la'dy-bird (-beurde), **la'dy-bug** (-beughe), **la'dy-cow** (-cao), ou **la'dy-fly** (flaïe), n., (ent.) bête à bon Dieu, bête de la Vierge ; coccinelle, f.

La'dy-day (-dè), n., le vingt-cinq mars, m. ; fête de l'Annonciation, f.

la'dy-killer, n., lovelace, homme à bonnes fortunes, m.

la'dy-like (-laïke), adj., de bon ton ; comme il faut ; qui a l'air distingué ; (delicate) délicat. She is very — ; elle a très bon ton, l'air très comme il faut, un air très distingué.

la'dy-love (-leuve), n., dame de ses pensées, bien aimée, f.

la'dy's-comb (-di'z'côme), n., (bot.) aiguille de berger, f. ; peigne de Vénus, m.

la'dy's-compan'ion, n., dame, ou demoiselle, de compagnie, f.

la'dyship, n., madame, f. Her —, your — ; (of a countess) madame la comtesse ; (of a viscountess) madame la vicomtesse, etc.

lady's'-maid, n., femme de chambre, f.

la'dy's-man'tle (-di'z'ma'n't'l), n., (bot.) alchimille, f. ; pied-de-lion, m.

la'dy's-seal (-sîl), n., (bot.) sceau-de-Notre-Dame, sceau-de-Salomon, m.

la'dy's-slip'per (-slip'-), n., (bot.) sabot de Vénus, sabot des vierges, soulier de Notre-Dame, m.

la'dy's-smock (-di'z'-), n., (bot.) cardamine, f. ; cresson des prés, m.

lag, v.n., rester en arrière, se traîner, lambiner ; (of things) traîner !

lag, v.a., ralentir.

lag'ger ou **lag'gard** (lag'gheur), n., traînard, lambin, m.

lagoon' (lé-goune) ou **lagune'** (lé-ghioune), n., lagune, f.

la'ic (lé-ike), n., laïque, m.

la'ic ou **la'ical**, adj., laïque.

laid, past part. (of to lay), posé ; (nav.) désemparé, désarmé ; (of paper) vergé. New— eggs ; œufs frais, m.pl. — up ; alité. To be — up ; garder la chambre ; être alité. — bare ; (by the ebb) laissé à découvert ; (fig.) mis à nu. A well — plot ; un complot bien tramé.

lair (lére), n., repaire, antre, m. ; reposée, f. ; (of a wolf) liteau, m. ; (of a boar) bauge, f. ; (of a stag) fort, m.

laird (lérde), n., seigneur, hobereau, m.

laity (lé-), n.sing., laïques, m.pl.

lake (léke), n., lac, m. ; (color) laque, f.

lake'let, n., laquet, petit lac, m.

lake'like (-laïke), adj., en forme de lac.

Lake' school, n., école lakiste, f.

lake'-weed (-wîde), n., (bot.) renouée, persicaire, f. ; poivre d'eau, m.

La'kist, n., lakiste, m.

la'ma (la-), *n.*, (of the Tartars) lama ; (mam.) lama, llama, *m.*

laman'tin. *n.*, (mam.) lamantin, *m.*

lamb (lame), *n.*, agneau, *m.* With — ; (of ewes) *pleine.* God tempers the wind to the shorn — ; *à brebis tondue Dieu mesure le vent.*

lamb, *v.a.*, agneler.

lam'bative, *adj.*, (med.) à lécher.

lam'bent, *adj.*, qui effleure ; léger ; folâtre. — *light ; lumière étincelante, f.*

lamb'kin (la'm'kine), *n.*, agnelet, petit agneau, *m.*

lamb'-like (la'm'laïke), *adj.*, d'agneau, doux comme un agneau.

lamb's'-fry, *n.*, issues d'agnéau, *f.pl.*

lamb's'-let'tuce (la'm'z'lèt'teuce), *n.*, (bot.) doucette, mâche, valérianelle locuste, *f.*

lamb's'-skin (la'm's'skine),*n.*, peau d'agneau, *f.*

lamb's'-wool (la'm'z'woul),*n.*, laine d'agneau, laine agneline.

lame (léme), *adj.*, boiteux, estropié ; (of language) boiteux, qui cloche ; (fig.) défectueux, mauvais ; imparfait. To walk — ; *boiter, clocher.* A — excuse ; *une mauvaise excuse.* A — story ; *un conte borgne.* — verses; *des vers boiteux, m.pl.*

lame, *v.a.*, estropier.

lamel'la, *n.*, lamelle, *f.*

lam'ellar, *adj.*, lamelleux.

lam'ellate *ou* **lam'ellated**, *adj.*, lamellé.

lame'ly (lé'm'li), *adv.*, en boitant ; en clochant ; (fig.) imparfaitement, mal.

lame'ness (lé'm'-), *n.*, état d'une personne estropiée, boiteuse ; clochement, boitement, *m. ;* (of a horse) boiterie ; (fig.) imperfection, *f.*

lament' (la'-), *v.n.*, se lamenter. To — for ; *pleurer.* To — over ; *pleurer ; se lamenter* **sur**; *gémir* **de**, *s'affliger de.*

lament', *v.a.*, se lamenter **sur** ; pleurer ; s'affliger **de** ; gémir **sur** ; se désoler **de**.

lament', *n.*, lamentation, complainte, *f.*

lam'entable (la-mè'n't'a-b'l), *adj.*, lamentable ; pitoyable ; déplorable.

lam'entably, *adv.*, lamentablement ; déplorablement ; pitoyablement.

lamenta'tion (-mè'n'té-), *n.*, lamentation, jérémiade, *f.*

lament'ed, *adj.*, regrettable ; regretté.

lament'er, *n.*, personne qui se lamente, qui fait des lamentations, *f.*

lament'ing, *n.*, lamentation, *f.*, plaintes, *f.pl.*

la'mia (lé-mi-a), *n.*, (myth.) lamie, *f.*

lam'ina (la'm'i-na), *n.*, (*laminæ*) lame, *f. ;* (bot.) limbe, *m.*

lam'inar, *adj.*, composé de lames.

lam'inate, *v.a.*, laminer.

lam'inated (-né-tède), *adj.*, lamelleux, lamellé.

lam'mas, *n.*, le premier jour d'août, *m. ;* fête de saint Pierre-ès-Liens, *f.*

lamp, *n.*, lampe ; (fig.) lumière ; (carriage) lanterne, *f.* Street — ; *réverbère, m.* Argand —; *lampe d'Argant, f.* House — ; *quinquet, m.* Solar — ; *lampe solaire, f.* Illumination— ; *lampion, m.* Safety-—; *lampe de sûreté.* Foot —s ; (thea.) *rampe, f. sing.*

lam'pas, *n.*, (vet.) lampas, *m.*

lamp'black, *n.*, noir de fumée, *m.*

lamp'-chimney, *n.*, verre de lampe, *m.*

lamp'-lighter (-laït'-), *n.*, allumeur, *m.*

lamp'-maker (-mék'-), *n.*, lampiste, *m.*

lampoon' (-poune), *n.*, satire, *f.*, libelle, *m.*

lampoon', *v.a.*, écrire un libelle, *ou* une satire, contre.

lampoon'er, *n.*, libelliste, pamphlétaire, *m.*

lamp'-post (-pôste), *n.*, lampadaire, candélabre, *m. ;* colonne lampadaire, *f.*, réverbère, *m.* To hang up at the — ; *mettre à la lanterne.*

lam'prey, *n.*, (ich.) lamproie, *f.*

lamp'-room, *n.*, lampisterie, *f.*

lamp'-shade, *n.*, abat-jour, *m.*

lamp'-stand (la'm'p'-sta'n'd), *n.*, pied de lampe, *m.*

la'nate *ou* **la'nated** (lé-néte, -'ède), *adj.*, laineux.

lance (lâ'n'-), *n.*, lance, *f.*

lance, *v.a.*, percer d'un coup de lance ; (surg.) donner un coup de lancette **à** ; ouvrir avec une lancette, percer avec une lancette ; percer, ouvrir.

lan'ceolate *ou* **lan'ceolated** (-ci-o-léte, -'éde), *adj.*, (bot.) lancéolé.

lan'cer, *n.*, lancier, (plur.) (a dance) lancier, *m.*, lanciers, *m.pl.*

lan'cet (-ète), *n.*, lancette ; (arch.) ogive, *f.*

lanch (lâ'n'she). *V.* launch.

lanch'ing, *n. V.* launching.

lan'cinate, *v.a.*, déchirer.

lancina'tion (-né-), *n.*, déchirure, lacération, *f.*

land, *n.*, terre, *f. ;* pays ; (jur.) bien-fonds, *m.* —agent ; *agent foncier, m.* — measurer, — surveyor ; *arpenteur, m.* — of the leal ; *séjour des bienheureux, des fidèles trépassés, m.* Arable —; *terre labourable, f., terroir, m.* Promised —; *terre promise, terre de promission, f.* Holy — ; *Terre Sainte.* To make — ; (nav.) *atterrer.* To make the — ; *découvrir la terre.* To lose sight of —; (nav.) *perdre terre.*

land, *v.a.* and *n.*, débarquer **à** ; mettre à terre ; aborder ; aborder **à**.

land'-carriage, *n.*, transport par terre, *m.*

lan'dau, *n.*, landau (*pl.* landaus), *m.*

land'-chain (-tshéne), *n.*, (surveying) chaîne d'arpenteur, *f.*

land'ed, *adj.*, foncier ; territorial ; de biens-fonds. —property ; *propriété foncière, territoriale, f., bien-fonds, m.*

land'fall (-fôl), *n.*, succession inattendue de biens-fonds, *f. ;* (nav.) atterrage, *m.*

land'-flood (-fleude), *n.*, inondation, *f.*

land'-force (-fôrce), *n.*, troupes de terre, *f.pl.*

land'grave (-gréve), *n.*, landgrave, *m.*

landgra'viate (-grév-i-éte), *n.*, landgraviat, *m.*

land'holder (-hôld-), *n.*, propriétaire foncier, *m.*

land'ing, *n.*, débarquement ; (at the top of a staircase) palier, carré, *m.* —place ; (at which to disembark) *débarcadère ;* (arch.) *perron, m.* — net ; *épuisette, f.*

land'jobber, *n.*, spéculateur sur les biens fonciers, *m.*

land'lady (-lé-di), *n.*, (of houses) propriétaire ; (of a lodging house) maîtresse, principale locataire ; (of an inn, an hotel) maîtresse d'auberge *ou* d'hôtel, aubergiste, hôtesse ; (of a manor) dame de manoir, châtelaine, dame châtelaine, *f.*

land'less, *adj.*, sans terre.

land'locked (-lok'te), *adj.*, enfermé entre des terres.

land'loper (la'n'd-lôp'-), *n.*, vagabond, *m.*

land'lord (-lorde), *n.*, propriétaire ; (of an inn) hôte ; hôtelier, maître d'un hôtel, aubergiste, *m.*

land'lubber (-leub'-), *n.*, (nav.) marin d'eau douce, *m.*

land'man, *n.*, soldat de l'armée de terre, *m.*

land'mark (-mârke), *n.*, borne, limite, *f. ;* signal, point de repère, *m.*

land'measure, *n.*, mesure agraire, *f.*

land'-office, *n.*, bureau du cadastre, *m.*

land'-owner (-ô'n'-), *n.*, propriétaire foncier, *m.*

land'scape, *n.*, paysage ; point de vue, coup d'œil, *m.* —painter ; *paysagiste, m.* — gardener ; *architecte-paysagiste ; jardinier-paysagiste, m.*

land'-service, *n.*, service militaire, *m.*

land'slide (-slaïde) *ou* **land'slip** (-slipe), *n.*, éboulement de terre, *m.*

lands'man (la'n'd'z'ma'ne), *n.*, matelot sans expérience, *m.*

land'-tax, *n.*, impôt foncier, *m.* ; contribution foncière, *f.*

land'-waiter (-wét'-), *n.*, douanier, *m.*

land'ward (-worde), *adv.*, du côté de la terre ; vers la terre.

land'-wind, *n.*, vent de terre, *m.*

lane (lén'e), *n.*, petite rue, ruelle, *f.*, passage, *m.* ; (out of town) sentier, chemin, *m.*, allée, *f.*

lan'grage (laign'grèdje) *ou* **lan'grel-shot**,*n.*, (nav. artil.) mitraille, *f.*

lan'guage (laign'gwèdje), *n.*, langue ; (Bible) nation, *f.* ; (way of speaking) langage, style, *m.*, expression, *f.* Bad — ; *mauvais style, m.* ; (offensive language) *grossièretés, f.pl.* Good — ; *bon style, m. ; belles paroles, f.pl.* To use bad —; *dire des grossièretés.*

lan'guid (lai'gn'gwide), *adj.*, languissant, faible.

lan'guidly, *adv.*, languissamment, faiblement.

lan'guidness, *n.*, langueur, faiblesse, *f.*

lan'guish (lai'gn'gwishe), *v.n.*, languir.

lan'guishing, *adj.*, languissant, langoureux. — looks ; *regards langoureux, m.pl.*

lan'guishingly, *adv.*, d'une manière languissante, languissamment, langoureusement.

lan'guor, *n.*, langueur, *f.*

lan'iard *ou* **lan'yard**, *n.*, (nav.) garant, *m.* ; (of shrouds) ride, *f.* ; (mil.) tire-feu, *m.* ; (of stoppers) aiguillette, *f.*

lanif'erous *ou* **lanig'erous** (-eur-, -nidj'eur-), *adj.*, lanifère ; (zoöl.) lanigère.

lank, *adj.*, grêle, mince, maigre, décharné, fluet ; languissant ; flasque, mou, lâche. — hair ; *cheveux plats, m.pl.* To make — ; *amaigrir, décharner.* To grow — ; *s'amaigrir, maigrir.* — haired ; *à cheveux plats.*

lank'ly, *adv.*, mollement ; maigrement.

lank'ness, *n.*, maigreur ; mollesse, *f.*

lank'y, *adj.*, fluet. — fellow ; *grand flandrin, grand sec, m.*

lan'ner, *n.*, (orni.) lanier, *m.*

lan'neret, *n.*, (orni.) laneret, *m.*

lans'quenet (-ki-néte), *n.*, (milit. and cards) lansquenet, *m.*

lan'tern, *n.*, lanterne, *f.* ; (on a building) belvédère ; (nav.) fanal, phare, *m.* Dark- — ; *lanterne sourde.* Magic- — ; *lanterne magique.* Chinese — ; *lanterne chinoise, ou vénitienne, f.* — -fly ; *fulgore porte-lanterne, m.* — -Jack ; *feu follet, m.*

lan'tern-jaws (-djôze), *n.pl.*, joues creuses, *f.pl.* ; *visage maigre, m.*

lanu'ginous (-niou-dji-), *adj.*, lanugineux.

lap, *n.*, giron, *m.* ; genoux, *m.pl.* ; (fig.) sein ; (of a coat) pan ; (of the ear) bout, *m.* In the — of ; *au sein de.* In my — ; *sur mes genoux.* A child asleep on his mother's — ; *un enfant endormi dans le giron de sa mère.*

lap, *v.a.*, (animals) laper ; (to wrap) envelopper, plier, rouler. To — up ; *laper, avaler.*

lap, *v.n.*, laper ; avancer, s'étendre **sur**. To — over ; *retomber* **sur**, *recouvrir.*

lap'-board, *n.*, siffran, six francs, *m.*

lap'dog, *n.*, bichon, petit chien, chien de salon, *m.*

lapel', *n.*, revers d'habit, de redingote, *m.*

lap'idary, *n.*, lapidaire ; joaillier, *m.*

lap'idary, *adj.*, lapidaire. — style ; *style lapidaire, m.*

lap'idate, *v.a.*, (ant.) lapider.

lapida'tion (-dé-), *n.*, (ant.) lapidation, *f.*

lapides'cence, *n.*, pétrification, *f.*

lapid'ify (-faïe), *v.a.*, lapidifier.

lapid'ify, *v.n.*, se lapidifier, pétrifier.

la'pis-laz'uli (-la-ziou-laïe), *n.*, lapis-lazuli, *m.* ; lazulite, *f.*

Lap'lander, *n.*, Lapon, *m.*, Laponne, *f.*

lap'pet, *n.*, pan, *m.*

Lap'pic, *adj.*, de Laponie.

lap'ping, *n.*, lapement, *n.* ; (man.) recouvrement, *m.*

lapse (lapse), *n.*, (fault) faute, erreur, *f.* ; manquement ; (deviation) écart, manque ; (of time) laps, cours, *m.*, marche ; (fall) chute, *f.*

lapse, *v.n.*, s'écouler, passer ; tomber ; faillir ; faire un faux pas ; déchoir. The right of presentation — s to the King ; *le droit de patronage passe au roi.*

lapsed, *adj.*, (of legacies) caduc, périssé.

lap'-stone, *n.*, pierre à battre, *f.*

lap'wing, *n.*, (orni.) vanneau, *m.*

lap'work, *n.*, ouvrage à clin, *m.*

⊙**lar'board** (lâr-bôrde), *n.*, (nav.) bâbord, *m.*

lar'ceny (lâr-ci-), *n.*, larcin, vol, *m.*

larch (lârtshe), *n.*, (bot.) mélèze, *m.*

lard (lârde), *n.*, saindoux, *m.*

lard, *v.a.*, larder **de** ; piquer ; assaisonner **de.**

lard'er (lâr-), *n.*, offices, *f.pl.* ; dépense, *f.* ; garde-manger, *m.*

lard'ing-pin *ou* **lard'ing-needle** (-nî-d'l), *n.*, lardoire, *f.*

la'res (lé-rize), *n.pl.*, lares, dieux lares, *m.pl.*

large (lâr-dje), *adj.*, grand, gros ; étendu ; considérable, fort ; (nav.) largue. — sum ; *forte somme.* As — as life ; *de grandeur naturelle.* At — ; *en liberté ; libre ; en général ; au long ; au large ; amplement.* — sized ; *grand modèle ;* (of paper) *grand format.* To grow — ; *grossir, grandir.*

largely, *adv.*, amplement, largement, grandement ; libéralement ; au long.

large'ness, *n.*, grandeur ; grosseur, étendue, (width) largeur, *f.*

lar'gess (lâr-djèce), *n.*, largesse, libéralité, *f.*

lark (lârke), *n.*, alouette ; mauviette ; (trick) escapade, farce, *f.* To —, to have a — ; *rigoler.*

lark'spur (-speur), *n.*, (bot.) pied-d'alouette, *m.*

lar'va (lâr-dje), *n.*, (larvæ) (ent.) larve, *f.*

lar'ynx, *n.*, larynx, *m.*

las'car (-'câr), *n.*, matelot indien, lascar, *m.*

lasciv'ious, *adj.*, impudique, lascif.

lasciv'iously, *adv.*, lascivement.

lasciv'iousness, *n.*, impudicité, lasciveté, *f.*

lash, *n.*, lanière ; coup d'étrivière, coup de fouet, *m.* ; (ant.) (for dogs) laisse, *f.* ; (fig.) coup, trait ; (stroke of satire) trait, sarcasme ; coup de patte, *m.* ; (cord at end of whip) mèche, *f.* Eye- — es ; *cils, m.* To be under the — ; *être exposé aux coups de la critique.*

lash, *v.a.*, sangler, cingler, fouetter ; (nav.) amarrer ; (to tie) attacher ; (fig.) abîmer, censurer ; parler fortement **contre**, flageller ; châtier, battre. Insults which — him into fury ; *des insultes qui excitent sa fureur.*

lash, *v.n.*, faire claquer un fouet ; éclater ; s'emporter. To — out ; (horses) *ruer.*

lash'er, *n.*, fouetteur, *m.* ; (nav.) corde d'amarrage, *f.* ; (weir) barrage, *m.*

lash'ing, *n.*, coups de fouet, *m.pl.* ; châtiment, *m.* ; flagellation ; (nav.) ligne d'amarrage, *f.*

lass (lâce), *n.*, fillette, jeune fille, *f.*

las'situde (-tioude), *n.*, ennui, *m.* ; lassitude, *f.*

last (lâste), *n.*, dernier, dernier moment, bout, *m.*, fin ; dernière parole ; (for shoes) forme, *f.* ; (weight) last, laste, *m.* ; (endurance) résistance à la fatigue, *f.* At — ; *à la fin, enfin.* Till the —, to the — ; *jusqu'au bout, jusqu'à la fin, jusqu'au dernier moment.* To breathe one's — ; *rendre le dernier soupir.* — maker ; *formier, m.*

last, *adj.*, dernier, passé. — but one ; *avant-dernier.* — week ; *la semaine dernière*, ou *passée.* On one's — legs ; (money) *à bout de ressources ;* (health) *la santé ruinée,* ou *minée.* The — week ; (of a period) *la dernière semaine.* The — time ; *la dernière fois.* I have been waiting for you for the — two hours ; *il y a deux heures que je vous attends.* I have not been to Paris for the

— ten years ; *il y a dix ans que je ne suis allé à Paris.* This day — year ; *il y a aujourd'hui un an.* This day — week ; *il y a aujourd'hui huit jours.*

last, *v.n.,* durer ; se conserver ; se garder. To — out ; *surpasser en durée.* To — over ; *durer jusqu'à.*

last, *adv.,* dernièrement ; enfin ; pour la dernière fois, la dernière fois. — but not least ; *un dernier fait, mais ce n'est pas le moins important.*

last'ing, *adj.,* durable, permanent ; (of colors) bon teint. *n.,* lasting, *m.*

last'ingly, *adv.,* d'une manière durable.

last'ingness (lâst'ign'nèce), *n.,* durabilité, durée, *f.*

last'ly, *adv.,* en dernier, en dernier lieu ; enfin.

latch (lat'she), *n.,* loquet, *m. ;* cadole, *f.*

latch, *v.a.,* fermer au loquet. On the — ; *fermé au loquet.*

latch'et (-ète), *n.,* boucle, *f.,* cordon de soulier, *m.*

latch'key (-ky), *n.,* passe-partout, *m.*

late, *adj.,* (fruit, vegetables) tardif ; (of time) avancé ; (former) ancien, dernier, ci-devant, ex; (dead) feu ; (recent) récent, dernier. Of — years; *ces dernières années, f.pl.* The —st posterity ; *la postérité la plus reculée.*

late, *adv.,* tard ; sur la fin ; (of persons) en retard. At —st ; *au plus tard.* Of — ; *dernièrement, récemment ; depuis quelque temps ; depuis peu.* Very — ; *à une heure avancée.* To be — ; *être en retard.* — of London ; *dernièrement domicilié à Londres.* Better — than never ; *mieux vaut tard que jamais.* To be getting — ; *se faire tard* (used impersonally).

lateen'-sail (la-tîne-sél), *n.,* (nav.) voile latine, *f.*

late'ly, *adv.,* dernièrement, récemment, fraîchement, depuis peu.

late'ness, *n.,* arrivée tardive, *f. ;* retard, *m. ;* (of seasons) époque avancée ; (of the hour) heure avancée, *f.,* temps avancé, *m. ;* (hort.) tardiveté, *f.*

la'tent (lé-), *adj.,* caché, secret, latent. — period ; (of a disease) *incubation, f.*

lat'er (-lét'-), *adj.,* postérieur, ultérieur.

lat'er, *adv.,* plus tard.

lat'eral (lat'èr'-), *adj.,* de côté, latéral.

lat'erally, *adv.,* latéralement, de côté.

lath (lâth), *n.,* latte, *f.* — work ; *lattage, m.*

lath, *v.a.,* latter.

lathe (léthe), *n.,* tour (à tourner le bois, etc.), *m.*

lath'er (lâth'-), *n.,* mousse, écume, *f.*

lath'er (lâth'-), *v.a.,* savonner, couvrir de savon ; (pop.) rosser, battre, fouetter. I'd rather — father than father — me ; *j'aime mieux savonner mon père que d'être rossé par lui.*

lath'er (lâth'-), *v.n.,* mousser.

lath'y (lâth'i), *adj.,* de latte ; aussi mince qu'une latte, sec, décharné.

Lat'in (lat'ine), *adj.* and *n.,* latin.

Lat'inism (-'iz'me), *n.,* latinisme, *m.*

Lat'inist, *n.,* latiniste, *m.*

Latin'ity, *n.,* latinité, *f.*

Lat'inize (-'aïze), *v.a.,* latiniser.

lat'ish (lét'-), *adj.,* un peu tard ; un peu en retard.

lat'ish (lét'-), *adv.,* un peu tard.

lat'itude (lat'i-tioude), *n.,* latitude ; étendue, *f.*

latitudina'rian (-tiou-di-né-), *adj.* and *n.,* tolérant, (English church) latitudinaire.

la'tria (-tri-a), *n.,* (ecc.) latrie, *f.,* culte d'adoration (rendu à Dieu), *m.*

latrine', *n.,* (army, hospitals) latrines, *f. pl.*

lat'ten, *n.,* fer-blanc ; étain en feuille ; laiton, cuivre jaune fin, *n.*

lat'ten-brass (-brâce), *n.,* cuivre laminé, *m.*

lat'ter (lat'-), *adj.,* dernier ; moderne, récent. The — ; *ce dernier, ces derniers, celui-ci, ceux-ci, m. ; cette dernière, ces dernières, celle-ci, celles-ci, f.* The — end ; *la fin.* The — day ; *le jour du jugement.* —day Saints ; *mormons, m.pl.*

lat'terly, *adv.,* depuis peu, dernièrement.

lat'termath (-mâth), *n.,* regain, *m.*

lat'tice *ou* **lat'tice-work** (lat'ice, -weurke), *n.,* treillis, treillage, lattis, *m.*

lat'tice, *v.a.,* treillisser ; former en treillis.

laud, *n.,* louange, *f. ;* (c.rel.) laudes, *f.pl.*

laud, *v.a.,* louer, célébrer. To — to the skies ; *élever jusqu'aux nues.*

laud'able (-'a-b'l), *adj.,* louable, digne de louanges.

laud'ableness, *n.,* qualité louable, *f. ;* mérite, *m.*

laud'ably, *adv.,* louablement ; d'une manière louable.

lau'danum (lô-da-), *n.,* (pharm.) laudanum, *m. ;* teinture d'opium, *f.*

lau'datory *ou* **lau'dative,** *n.,* éloge, panégyrique, *m.*

lau'datory, *adj.,* laudatif, louangeur.

laud'er, *n.,* louangeur, panégyriste, *m.*

laugh (lâfe), *n.,* rire, ris, *m.,* risée, *f.* Loud — ; *gros rire, éclat de rire, m.* To burst into a loud — ; *partir d'un grand éclat de rire.* To have a good — at ; *se bien moquer de ; rire beaucoup de.* To force a — ; *rire du bout des dents, ou des lèvres.*

laugh (lâfe), *v.n.,* rire. To — at ; *se moquer de ; rire de, railler ; se jouer de.* To burst out —ing ; *rire aux éclats, éclater de rire.* To — out ; *partir d'un éclat de rire.* To — in any one's face ; *rire au nez de quelqu'un.* To — immoderately ; *rire à gorge déployée ou rire aux anges.* To — a scheme down ; *tourner un projet en ridicule.* To — a person out of a fancy ; *faire passer une fantaisie à quelqu'un en la tournant en dérision.* To — to scorn ; *tourner en dérision.* To — in one's sleeve ; *rire dans sa barbe ; rire sous cape.* To — on the wrong side of one's face ; *rire jaune.* They have most to — at who — last ; *rira bien qui rira le dernier.* — to-day and cry to-morrow ; *tel qui rit vendredi, dimanche pleurera.*

laugh'able (lâf'a-b'l), *adj.,* risible.

laugh'er (lâf'-), *n.,* rieur, *m.,* rieuse, *f.*

laugh'ing (lâf'-), *adj.,* rieur, enjoué, qui aime à rire. It is no — matter ; *il n'y a pas de quoi rire.*

laugh'ing (lâf'-), *n.,* rire, *m. ;* action de rire, *f.*

laugh'ingly (lâf'-), *adv.,* en riant, gaîment.

laugh'ing-stock (lâf'-), *n.,* risée, *f. ;* jouet, objet de risée, plastron, *m.*

laugh'ter (lâf'teur), *n.,* rire, ris, *m. ;* (b.s.) risée, moquerie, *f.* Burst of — ; *éclat de rire, m.* To break out into — ; *éclater de rire.* To move to — ; *faire rire, faire la risée de.* To split one's sides with — ; *se tordre de rire.* Up went a great shout of — from the crowd ! *et la foule de rire !* (V. Hugo).

launch (lâ'nshe), *v.n.,* se lancer, se jeter. To — out into ; *se jeter dans ; se lancer dans ; s'étendre sur.* To — out into long speeches ; *se jeter dans de grands discours.*

launch, *v.a.,* lancer ; (a ship) lancer ; lancer à l'eau ; mettre à l'eau, à la mer.

launch, *n.,* lançage, *m. ;* mise à l'eau ; (boat) chaloupe, *f.*

launch'ing, *n.,* (nav.) mise à l'eau, *f. ;* lançage, lancement, *m.*

laun'der (lâ'n-), *n.,* blanchisseuse ; (mines) auge, *f.*

laun'derer, *n.,* blanchisseur, *m.*

laun'dress, *n.,* blanchisseuse, *f.*

laun'dry, *n.,* buanderie, blanchisserie, *f.*

lau'reate (-ri-), *adj.,* couronné de lauriers, lauréat. Poet — ; *poète lauréat, m.*

lau′rel, n., laurier, m. —-wreath; *couronne de laurier*, f.

lau′reled (lor′èlde), adj., couronné de laurier.

laur′estine (-res′-), n., (bot.) viorne-tin,f.m.; laurier-tin, m.

la′va (lâ-va), n., lave, f.

lav′atory, n., lavoir, cabinet de toilette, urinoir, m.; (pharm.) lotion, f.

lave (léve), v.a., (l.u.) laver, arroser, baigner.

lave, v.n., (l.u.) se laver, se baigner.

lav′ender, n., (bot.) lavande, f.

lav′ender-cot′ton (-cot′t′n), n., (bot.) santoline, garde-robe, citronnelle, f.

lav′ender-wa′ter (-wô-), n., eau de lavande, f.

la′ver (lé-), n., lavoir, bassin, m., (bot.) laitue de mer,f.

lav′ish (lav′-), adj., prodigue; excessif.

lav′ish, v.a., prodiguer, dissiper.

lav′isher, n., prodigue, m. To be a — of; *être prodigue de*; prodiguer. God is not a — of his blessings; *Dieu ne prodigue pas ses bienfaits*.

lav′ishly, adv., prodigalement, avec prodigalité.

lav′ishness, n., prodigalité, f.

law (lō), n., loi, f.; droit, m.; jurisprudence, f. — Courts; *Palais de Justice*, m. Civil —; *droit civil*. Commercial —; *droit commercial*. Criminal —; *droit criminel*. — expenses; *frais de procédure*, m.pl. Roman —; *droit romain*. Ecclesiastical —; *droit canon*. International — ou — of nations; *droit des gens*. Maritime —; *droit maritime*. Military —; *code militaire*, m. Martial —; *état de siège*, m. To go to —; *recourir à la justice; plaider en justice*. To go to — with ou *to sue at* —; *citer en justice, poursuivre, intenter un procès à*. To study —; *étudier le droit*. To be at —; *être en procès*. To lay down the —; *expliquer la loi;* (fig.) *parler d'un ton tranchant*. To take the — into one's own hands; *se faire justice à soi-même*. He is very fond of going to —; *il aime beaucoup la chicane; il aime à plaider*.

law′-abiding, adj., qui observe la loi.

law′-book (-bouke), n., livre de jurisprudence, ou de droit, m.

law′-breaker (-brék′-), n., transgresseur de la loi, m.

law′ful (-foule), adj., légal; légitime; licite; permis.

law′fully, adv., légalement; légitimement.

law′fulness, n., légalité; légitimité, f.

law′giver (-ghiv′-), n., législateur, m.

law′less, adj., sans loi; arbitraire; illégal; (fig.) sans frein, déréglé.

law′lessly, adv., sans loi; illégalement.

law′lessness, n., illégalité, f.; (fig.) désordre, m.; licence, f.

law′-list, n., annuaire judiciaire, m.

law′maker (-mék′-), n., législateur, m.

lawn, n., (linen) linon, m.; (open space) pelouse, f.; tapis vert, gazon; boulingrin, m. The bishop's —; *rochet*, m.; *robe*, f. — mower; *tondeuse de gazon*, f.

lawn, adj., de linon.

lawn′y, adj., uni comme une pelouse; fait de linon.

law′suit (-sioute), n., procès, m.

law′-term (-teurme), n., terme de loi, terme de palais, m.; (sittings) session des tribunaux, f.

law′yer, n., légiste; homme de loi; jurisconsulte; avocat, avoué, m.

law′yer-like (-laïke), adj., en homme de loi.

lax, adj., relâché, lâche, mou, flasque; dissolu, licencieux; (of style) vague, obscur.

laxa′tion (laks′é-), n., action de relâcher, f.; relâchement, m.

lax′ative (laks′a-), adj., laxatif.

lax′ative, n., laxatif, m.

lax′ity, n., relâchement, état lâche; (med.)

relâchement, dévoiement, m.; flaccidité; (want of exactness) manque d'exactitude; (of style) obscurité, f. — of morals; *relâchement de mœurs*, m.

lax′ly, adv., mollement, avec nonchalance, sans vigueur; sans exactitude.

lax′ness, n. V. **lax′ity**.

lay, n. V. **lie**, v.

lay, v.a., (preterit and past part., Laid) placer, mettre, poser, déposer, coucher; (to beat down) abattre; (to calm) calmer, apaiser; (a bet) faire; (eggs) pondre; (a snare) tendre, dresser; (the cloth) mettre; (the dust) abattre; (an indictment) intenter; (a tax) imposer; (nav.) (cable) poser. To — aside; *mettre de côté, ôter, quitter; s'affranchir de*. To — before; *soumettre à; mettre sous les yeux de; exposer à*. To — by; *mettre de côté, garder, réserver*. To — down (arms); *mettre bas, poser, déposer (les armes);* (a principle, a foundation) *poser;* (to give up) *quitter, renoncer à*. To — down one's life for; *donner sa vie pour*. To — one's self down; *se coucher*. To — in; *faire une provision de, se procurer*. To — hold of; *s'emparer de, saisir*. To — on; *appliquer;* (blows) *porter;* (color) *étendre*. To — a fault on; *imputer une faute à*. To — open; *mettre à nu;* (fig.) *exposer*. To — out; *arranger;* (a garden, a road) *tracer;* (money) *dépenser, débourser;* (a corpse) *ensevelir*. To — over; *étendre, couvrir, incruster*. To — a spell; *enchanter;* *jeter un sort sur*. To — up; *mettre de côté, garder, amasser;* (to make ill) *faire garder le lit, ou la chambre, à;* (nav.) (of a ship) *tenir enfermé;* (nav.) (of a ship) *désarmer*. To — it on; (to beat) *étriller;* (to lie) *broder, exagérer;* (in price) *surfaire*. To — a ghost; *conjurer un revenant*. To — apart; *rejeter, mettre à part*. To — to heart; *prendre à cœur*. To — siege to; *assiéger*. To — in wait; *se mettre en embuscade; former un guet-apens pour* (infinitive), **contre** (person). To — violent hands on one's self; *se suicider; attenter à ses jours*. To — snares for any one; *tendre des pièges à quelqu'un*. He —s all the blame on me; *il en rejette toute la faute sur moi*.

lay, v.n., pondre. To — about; *frapper de tous côtés*. To — it on; *frapper fort; en découdre;* (of expenses) *y aller grand train*.

lay, n., (row) rangée; (layer) couche, f.; (wager) pari, m., mise, f.; (meadow) pré, m., prairie, f.; (song) chant, m.

ley, adj., lai, laïc, laïque. — brother; *frère lai*, m.

lay′-clerk (-clârke ou -cleurke), n., chantre, m.

lay′er (lé′eur), n., personne qui pose, f.; (tech.) poseur; (founder) fondateur, m., fondatrice; (a stratum) couche, f., lit, m.; (geol.) couche, assise, f., étage, m.; (hort.) marcotte, f.; (shoot of a plant) rejeton; (of vine) provin, m.; (hen) pondeuse, f.

lay′-figure, n., (paint.) mannequin; (fig.) type, caractère imaginaire, m.

lay′ing (lé-ìnge), n., mise, pose, f.; posage, m.; (of eggs) ponte, f.

lay′man, n., laïque; (paint.) mannequin; (in a cathedral) chantre, m.

lazaret′to, n., lazaret, m.

laze (léz′e), v.n., (ant.) paresser, fainéanter. To — about; *flâner*.

la′zily (lé-), adv., lentement, en paresseux, dans la paresse, dans la fainéantise.

la′ziness (lé-), n., fainéantise, paresse, f.

laz′ulite (laz′iou-laïte), n., (min.) lazulite, f.; lapis, lapis-lazuli, m.

la′zy (lé-), adj., fainéant, paresseux; (of a horse) mou, lent; (of life) indolent, de paresse. — fellow; *fainéant*, m. — people take most pains; *ce sont les paresseux qui font le plus de chemin*.

lea (lî) ou **ley** (lî), n., pré, clos, m.; prairie, plaine, f.

leach (lîtshe), *n.*, cendre de lessive, *f.*

leach, *v.a.*, lessiver.

leach'-tub (-teube), *n.*, cuve à lessive, *f.*; cuvier, *m.*

lead (lède), *n.*, (metal) plomb, *m.*; (print.) interligne, *f.*; (nav.) plomb de sonde, *m.*, sonde; (for pencils) mine de plomb, *f.* —s, *pl.*, (of a house) plombs (des toits) *m.pl.*; toit de plomb, *m.* —-wire; *fil de plomb*, *m.* — colic; *colique saturnine*, *f.* White——; *céruse*, *f.*; *blanc de céruse*, *m.* Sheet——; *plomb en feuille.* —-work; *plombage*, *m.* —-works, —-manufactory; *plomberie*, *f.sing.* To heave the —; *jeter la sonde.* Black —; *mine de plomb*, *f.*; *graphite*, *m.*

lead (lède), *v.a.*, plomber, couvrir de plomb; (print.) interligner.

lead (lîde), *n.*, conduite, direction, *f.*; commandement, *m.*; influence; préséance, *f.*; pas; (at billiards) acquit, *m.*; (at cards) main, *f.*; (at play) début, *m.*, ouverture, *f.* To take the —; *marcher en avant; dominer, primer, présider.* To have the —; (at cards) *avoir la main.* It's your —; *c'est à vous la main.*

lead (lîde), *v.a.*, (*preterit* and *past part.*, Led) mener, guider, conduire; donner le ton à; (to command) conduire, commander, diriger; (to induce) porter à, faire, induire à; (a life) mener. To — any one to believe; *faire croire à quelqu'un; porter quelqu'un à croire.* To — about; *mener de tous côtés, partout.* To — astray; *égarer; détourner de la bonne voie.* To — back; *ramener, reconduire.* To — in; *introduire.* — into; *entraîner dans.* To — off; *détourner; emmener.* To — out; *faire sortir, conduire dehors.* To — out of the way; *égarer.* To — on; *séduire; entraîner à.* To — up to; *pousser à; induire à.* To — the way; *ouvrir la marche; frayer, ou montrer, le chemin; marcher en tête.* —-ing his troops; *à la tête de ses troupes.*

lead (lîde), *v.n.*, conduire; mener; dominer; (at play) jouer le premier, avoir la main, débuter. To — off; *débuter; marcher en tête.*

lead'ed (lèd'ède), *adj.*, plombé; (print.) interligné.

lead'en (lèd'd'n), *adj.*, de plomb; (fig.) lourd.

lead'er (lîd'-), *n.*, conducteur, guide, chef, meneur, premier, commandant; (of a newspaper) article principal, article de fond, premier Paris, premier Londres, etc.; (man.) cheval de volée; (mus.) premier violin, chef d'orchestre, de musique; (in the courts) avocat principal; (in parliament) chef de la Chambre; (political party) chef de parti, *m.*

lead'ing (lîd'-), *adj.*, premier, principal. — card; *première carte, f.* — hand; *premier en carte, m.* — man; *chef, m.; personne influente; notabilité, f.* —-strings; *lisières, f.pl.* — word; *premier mot, m.* — note; (mus.) *note sensible, f.*

lead'ing (lîd'-), *n.*, conduite, direction, *f.*

leads'man (lèd'z'-), *n.*, (nav.) sondeur, *m.*

lead'y (lèd'î), *adj.*, couleur de plomb, *m.*

leaf (lîfe), *n.*, (*leaves*) feuille, *f.*; (of a book) feuillet, *m.*; (of a door) battant, *m.*; (of a table) rallonge, *f.*, pan, *m.* To turn over the leaves; *feuilleter.* To turn over a new —; (fig.) *changer de propos et de conduite*; (fam.) *changer de gamme.* To turn down the —; *faire une corne à la page.* To take a — out of one's book; *suivre l'exemple de; imiter.*

leaf, *v.n.*, porter des feuilles, feuiller.

leaf'age (lîf'èdje), *n.*, feuillage épais, *m.*

leaf'-gold (-gôlde), *n.*, or en feuille, *m.*

leaf'less, *adj.*, sans feuilles, effeuillé.

leaf'let, *n.*, petite feuille; (bot.) foliole, *f.*

leaf'stalk (-stôke), *n.*, (bot.) pétiole, *m.*

leaf'y, *adj.*, feuillé, feuillu, couvert de feuilles, touffu, ombragé.

league (lîghe), *n.*, ligue, *f.*; (measure) lieue, *f.*

league, *v.n.*, se liguer, se coaliser.

leagued (lîg'de), *adj.*, ligué, coalisé.

leagu'er (lîgh'eur), *n.*, confédéré, ligueur, *m.*

leak (lîke), *n.*, voie d'eau; perte d'eau; fuite (de gaz), *f.* To spring a —; *faire eau, faire une voie d'eau.*

leak, *v.n.*, couler, faire eau, fuir; (coal gas) s'échapper. To — out; (fig.) (of news) *s'ébruiter, s'éventer.* Then his name had —ed out; *puis on avait su son nom* (V. Hugo).

leak'age (lîk'èdje), *n.*, coulage, *m.*; fuite, *f.*; voies d'eau, *f.pl.*

leak'y, *adj.*, qui coule, qui fuit; (nav.) qui a des voies d'eau, qui fait eau.

lean (lîne), *n.*, maigre, *m.*

lean, *adj.*, maigre; stérile; chétif. To grow, to get —; *maigrir.* To make —; *amaigrir.*

lean (lîne), *v.n.*, pencher; s'appuyer, s'incliner; (to rest) reposer. To — against; *s'adosser contre.* To — over; *avancer.* To — to; *tendre à; incliner à; pencher vers.* To — towards; *favoriser.*

lean, *v.a.*, faire pencher, incliner; appuyer, reposer.

lean'ing, *n.*, penchement; penchant, *m.*; (fig.) tendance, partialité, *f.*, penchant, *m.*

lean'ly, *adv.*, maigrement, stérilement.

lean'ness, *n.*, maigreur, *f.*; amaigrissement, *m.*

leap (lîpe), *n.*, saut, *m.*; (of animals) monte, *f.* —-frog; *cheval fondu, saut de mouton, m.* — —year; *année bissextile, f.* To take a —; *faire un saut.* To take a — in the dark; (fig.) *faire un saut périlleux; faire une action hasardée.*

leap, *v.a.*, sauter, franchir; (of animals) saillir, couvrir.

leap, *v.n.*, sauter, s'élancer, se précipiter. To — for joy; *sauter de joie.*

leap'er, *n.*, sauteur, *m.*, sauteuse, *f.*

leap'ing, *adj.*, qui saute, qui fait des sauts.

leap'ing, *n.*, saut, sauts, *m.*

leap'ing-board, *n.*, tremplin, *m.*

leap'ingly, *adv.*, en sautant; par sauts.

learn (leurne), *v.a.*, apprendre; faire part de.

learn (leurne), *v.n.*, apprendre, s'instruire.

learn'ed (leurn'ède), *adj.*, savant, docte, instruit, érudit. — man; *savant, m.* — profession; *profession libérale, f.* — in the law; *versé dans le droit.*

learn'edly (leurn'èd'li), *adv.*, savamment.

learn'er (leurn'-), *n.*, écolier; apprenti; élève, *m.*; personne qui apprend, *f.*

learn'ing (leurn'-), *n.*, étude; belles-lettres, lettres, *f.pl.*; érudition, science, instruction, *f.*; savoir, *m.* Polite —; *belles-lettres, f.pl.* Man of —; *savant; homme instruit, m.*

lease (lî'ce), *n.*, bail, *m.* Long —; *bail à long terme.* — of ground; *bail à ferme.* Building—; *bail emphytéotique.* On a —; *à bail.*

lease (lî'ce), *v.a.*, louer, donner à bail; (land) affermer.

lease (lîze), *v.n.*, glaner.

lease'hold (lî'ce-hôlde), *n.*, tenure par bail, par bail emphytéotique, *f.*

lease'holder, *n.*, locataire à bail; propriétaire par bail emphytéotique,*m.f.*

leas'er (lîz'eur), *n.*, glaneur, glaneuse, *f.*

leash (lîshe), *n.*, laisse, attache, *f.*

leash, *v.a.*, mener en laisse, attacher.

least (lîste), *adj.*, moindre, le plus petit.

least, *adv.*, moins. At —; *au moins, du moins.* At the —; *pour le moins, tout au moins.* Not in the —; *point du tout, nullement, pas le moins du monde.* To say the — of it; *pour ne rien dire de plus; au bas mot, au moins.* — said, soonest mended; *trop gratter cuit, trop parler nuit.*

leath'er (lèth'eur), *n.*, cuir, *m.*, peau, *f.* Upper—; (de souliers) empeigne, *f.* — —dresser; *peaussier, corroyeur, mégissier, f.* —-seller; *marchand de cuir, m.* There is nothing like —;

tout marchand vante sa marchandise; (jest) *vous êtes orfèvre, monsieur Josse.*

leath'er (lèth'eur), *v.a.*, garnir de cuir; (to beat) (pop.) étriller, rosser, épousseter.

leath'ern (lèth'-), *adj.*, de cuir, de peau.

leath'ery (lèth'-), *adj.*, semblable à du cuir, coriace comme le cuir.

leave (live), *n.*, permission, liberté, *f.*; congé, permis, *m.* On —; *en congé.* To take — of; *prendre congé de, dire adieu* à. With your —; *avec votre permission.* To give —; *donner la permission de*; *permettre* à. To take French —; *prendre la permission sous son bonnet; filer,* ou *décamper, sans mot dire.* By any one's —; *par permission de quelqu'un.* —taking; *adieux, m.pl.*

leave (live), *v.n.*, partir; cesser. To — off; *cesser, s'arrêter* à; *en rester là, finir.* To — off work; *cesser de travailler.*

leave (live), *v.a.*, (*preterit* and *past part.*, Left) laisser; (to quit a person) quitter; (a place) quitter; partir de; (to discontinue) cesser de. I — that to you; *je m'en rapporte* à *vous.* To — about; *laisser traîner.* To — alone; *laisser seul, laisser tranquille; laisser.* To — off; *laisser, laisser de côté, quitter; cesser, cesser de porter, discontinuer.* To — out; *supprimer, omettre, oublier.* To be left; *rester.* There is some wine left; *il reste du vin.* To be left till called for; *poste restante, f.*; (of parcels) *bureau restant, m.* To have left; *avoir de reste, avoir encore.* I have nothing left; *il ne me reste rien.* To be left without; *être,* ou *rester,* **sans.** He had no choice left; *il ne lui restait plus à choisir.* The few looks that are left you; *les quelques cheveux qui vous restent.* There are about a hundred left; *il en reste une centaine.* I had nothing left to dispose of; *il ne me restait rien que je pusse vendre.* To — off a dress; *cesser de porter un habit.* To — no stone unturned; *remuer ciel et terre.* To — well alone; *le mieux est l'ennemi du bien.* To — without beat of drum; *déloger sans trompette* (Lafontaine). — it to me; *laissez-moi faire* (A. Daudet).

leaved (liv'de), *adj.*, feuillé, à feuilles; (doors) à battants.

leav'en (lèv'v'n), *n.*, levain, *m.*

leav'en (lèv'v'n), *v.a.*, fermenter, faire lever; (ant.) corrompre, gâter.

leav'ened (lèv'-), *adj.*, qui contient du levain; (fig.) corrompu, gâté. — bread; *pain au levain, m.*

leav'ings (liv'ign'z), *n.*, restes, *m.pl.*; bribes, *f.pl.*

lech'er (lètsh'-), *n.*, libertin, débauché, *m.*

lech'erous, *adj.*, lascif, débauché, libertin, lubrique.

lech'erously, *adv.*, lascivement, lubriquement, en libertin.

lech'erousness ou **lech'ery**, *n.*, lasciveté, *f.*; libertinage, *m.*

lec'tern (lèk'teurne), *n.*, lutrin, *m.*

lec'tion (lèk'-), *n.*, leçon, *f.*; texte d'auteur, *m.*

lec'ture (lèkt'ieur), *n.*, discours; sermon, *m.*; semonce, *f.*; conférence, leçon, *f.*; (fig.) mercuriale, semonce, *f.* Course of —s; *cours, m.* — hall; *salle des conférences, f.*; *amphithéâtre, m.*

lec'ture (lèkt'ieur), *v.a.*, donner des leçons à, faire un cours à; (fig.) sermonner, réprimander, semoncer, faire un sermon à; faire la morale à.

lec'ture (lèkt'ieur), *v.n.*, faire un cours de, faire une conférence **sur,** donner des leçons de, professer; (fig.) faire des sermons.

lec'turer, *n.*, professeur; maître de conférences; conférencier; orateur; (rel.) prédicateur, *m.*

lec'tureship, *n.*, chaire, *f.*; professorat, *m.*; fonctions de professeur, *f.pl.*

lec'turing, *n.*, cours publics, cours, *m.pl.*

led (lède), *past. part.* V. **lead**, *v.* — horse; *cheval de main, m.*

ledge (lèdje), *n.*, rebord, bord, *m.*; (nav.)

chaîne de rochers, saillie, *f.*; récif, *m.*; (layer) couche, *f.*; (of a window) appui, *m.*; (arch.) saillie, *f.*

ledg'er (lèdj'eur), *n.*, grand livre, *m.*

lee (li), *n.*, (nav.) côté de dessous le vent, côté opposé au vent, *m.*

lee, *adj.*, (nav.) sous le vent. — shore; *terre sous le vent, f.* — side; *côté sous le vent.*

lee'board (-bòrde), *n.*, (nav.) semelle, *f.*

leech (litsche), *n.*, sangsue, *f.*; (doctor) médecin, *m.* —rope; (nav.) *ralingue de chute, f.* —lines; *cargues-boulines, f.pl.* — craft; *art de guérir, m.*; *médecine, f.*

leech, *v.a.*, médicamenter, médeciner.

lee'-gauge (-ghédje), *n.*, (nav.) dessous du vent, *m.*

leek (like), *n.*, (bot.) poireau, porreau, *m.*

leer (lire), *n.*, œillade, *f.*; regard de côté, *m.*

leer, *v.n.*, lorgner, regarder de côté, du coin de l'œil.

leer'ingly, *adv.*, avec une œillade.

lees (lize), *n.pl.*, lie, *f.*; sédiment, *m.*

lee'ward (li-wòrde), *adv.*, (nav.) sous le vent.

lee'ward, *adj.*, (nav.) sous le vent; (of the tide) qui porte sous le vent.

lee'way (li-wé), *n.*, (nav.) dérive, *f.*

left (lèfte), *past part.* V. **leave,** *v.*

left (lèfte), *adj.*, gauche. On the —; à *gauche.* Eyes — ! (mil.) *tête à gauche.* To the — about; *par le flanc gauche.* — about face ! *demi-tour* à *gauche!*

left-hand'ed, *adj.*, gaucher; (fig.) gauche. — marriage; *mariage de la main gauche, mariage morganatique, m.*

left-hand'edness (-ha'n'dèd'-), *n.*, usage habituel de la main gauche, *m.*; gaucherie, *f.*

leg (lèghe), *n.*, jambe; (of birds, insects) patte; (of boots) tige; (of poultry) cuisse, *f.*; (of furniture) pied; (of mutton) gigot; (of beef) trumeau, *m.* — bail; *fuite, f.* Black —; *escroc, grec;* (workman) *gâte-métier, m.* On one —; à *cloche pied.* — guard; *jambière, f.* — rest; *appui pour la jambe, m.* To be on one's —s; *être sur pied, être debout.* To have sea —s; *avoir le pied marin.* He has not a — to stand upon; *il ne sait plus sur quel pied danser*; *il est à bout d'arguments.* To change the —s; *changer le pas.* To fall on one's —s; *l'échapper belle.* To feel one's —s; (of children) *commencer à marcher.* To give a — to, to give one a — up; *aider à* (monter à cheval). To set any one on his —s again; *remettre quelqu'un sur pied.* To put one's best — foremost; *se trémousser de son mieux.* To be on one's last —s; *ne battre que d'une aile, être aux abois.* To get on one's —s; *se lever pour parler.* To stand on one's own —s; *ne dépendre que de soi, être indépendant.*

leg'acy (lèg'-), *n.*, legs, héritage, *m.* To leave a — to; *faire un legs à.* To come into a —; *hériter d'un legs.*

le'gal (li-), *adj.*, légal, judiciaire, juridique, licite. — duty; *droits de succession, m.pl.* To be a — tender; (of money) *avoir cours.*

legal'ity (li-), *n.*, légalité, *f.*

le'galize (li-gal'aïze), *v.a.*, légaliser, autoriser, régulariser.

le'gally (li-), *adv.*, selon les lois, juridiquement, légitimement, légalement.

leg'atary (lèg'-), *n.*, légataire, *m.*

leg'ate (lèg'-), *n.*, légat; délégué, *m.*

legatee' (lèg'a-tî), *n.*, légataire, *m.*

lega'tion (li-ghé'-), *n.*, légation, *f.*

legator' (lèg'-), *n.*, testateur, *m.*, testatrice, *f.*

le'gend (li-djè'n'de, *ou* lèdj'-), *n.*, légende, *f.*; (ant.) chronique, *f.*

le'gendary (lèdj'-), *adj.*, légendaire, fabuleux.

le'gendary, *n.*, légende, *f.*; légendaire, *m.*

legerdemain' (ledj'eur'di-mène), *n.*, tour d'escamoteur, de passe-passe, d'adresse, de main, *m.*

le'ger-line, *n.*, (mus.) ligne postiche, *f.*

legged (lĕg'de) *ou* **leg'ged**, *adj.*, qui a des jambes. Two——; *à deux jambes*. Four——; *à quatre pattes*.

leg'ging (lĕg'ghigne), *n.*, grande guêtre, jambière, molletière, *f.*

legibil'ity *ou* **leg'ibleness** (lĕdj'-), *n.*, lisibilité, netteté d'écriture, *f.*, caractère lisible, *m.*

leg'ible (lĕdj'i-b'l), *adj.*, lisible.

leg'ibly (-), *adv.*, lisiblement.

le'gion (lĭ'djeune), *n.*, légion, *f.*

le'gionary, *adj.*, légionnaire; de légion.

le'gionary, *n.*, légionnaire; soldat légionnaire, *m.*

leg'islate (lĕdj'-), *v.n.*, faire des lois.

legisla'tion (lĕdj'is-lé-), *n.*, législation, *f.*

leg'islative (-lé-), *adj.*, législatif.

leg'islator (-lé-teur), *n.*, législateur, *m.*

leg'islature (lĕdj'is-lét'ieur), *n.*, législature, *f.*

legit'imacy (li-djit'-), *n.*, légitimité, *f.*

legit'imate, *adj.*, légitime; authentique, naturel, correct, exact.

legit'imate, *v.a.*, légitimer, déclarer légitime.

legit'imately, *adv.*, légitimement.

legitima'tion (-'i-mé-), *n.*, légitimation, *f.*

legit'imist, *n.*, légitimiste, *m.f.*

legit'imize (-maïze), *v.a.*, légitimer.

leg'ume (lĕgh'ioume) *ou* **legu'men** (li-ghioumène), *n.*, (bot.) légume, *m.*

legu'minous (lĕgh'iou-), *adj.*, (bot.) légumineux.

lei'surable (lĭ-jeur'a-b'l), *adj.*, fait à loisir.

lei'sure (lĭ-jeur), *n.*, loisir, *m.*; commodité, liberté d'esprit, *f.* At —; *de loisir.* To be at —; *être libre, être de loisir.* At one's —; *à sa convenance.*

lei'surely, *adv.*, à loisir, peu à peu.

lem'ma (lĕm'-), *n.*, (math.) lemme, *m.*

lem'on (lĕm'-), *n.*, citron, limon, *m.*

lemonade' (lĕ'm'o'n'éde), *n.*, limonade, *f.*

lem'on-grass (-grâce), *n.*, (bot.) schénanthe, jonc odorant, *m.*

lem'on-juice, *n.*, jus de citron, *m.*

lem'on-peel (-pîl), *n.*, écorce de citron, *f.*

lem'on-plant, *n.*, (bot.) verveine, *f.*

lem'on-sole, *n.*, sole lascaris,.*f.*

lem'on-tree (-trî), *n.*, citronnier, *m.*

le'mur (lî-meur), *n.*, (mam.) lémurien, maki, *m.*

lem'ures (lĕm-iou-rize), *n.pl.*, (Rom. antiq.) lémures, *m.pl.*, mânes, *m.pl.*

lend (lĕn'de), *v.a.*, prêter; (on hire) louer. To — a hand; *aider; donner la main à; donner un coup de main à.*

lend'er, *n.*, prêteur, *m.*, prêteuse, *f.*

lend'ing, *n.*, prêt, *m.*, location, *f.* — library; *location, f.; cabinet de lecture, m.*

length (lĕn'gth), *n.*, longueur; étendue, *f.*; (degree) degré, point, *m.*; (of time) durée, *f.*, espace, *m.* Full —; *en pied, de grandeur naturelle.* At full —; (not abridged) *tout au long;* (of writing) *en toutes lettres;* (pers.) *tout de son long.* At great —; *fort au long, longuement, en détail.* Two feet in —; *deux pieds de longueur.* To go to great —s; *aller bien loin.* To go the — of thinking; *aller jusqu'à penser.* At —; *enfin, à la fin;* (lengthily) *au long.* To fall full —; *tomber tout de son long.* Short —; (of silk, etc.) *coupon, m.* The whole —; (of silks) *toute la pièce.* To stretch one's body at full —; *se coucher,* ou *s'étendre, tout de son long.* Full —; (portraits) *en pied.* Half —; (portraits) *en buste.* To go the whole —; *aller jusqu'au bout.* To such —s; *si loin.*

length'en (lĕ'gn'th'n), *v.a.*, allonger, étendre; rallonger; (time) prolonger. To — out; *étendre, prolonger.*

length'en, *v.n.*, s'allonger, devenir plus long; s'étendre; (of time) se prolonger; (of days) grandir, croître.

length'ening, *n.*, prolongement, *m.;* (of time) prolongation, *f.;* (of days) accroissement; (piecing) rallongement, *m.*

length'ily (lĕ'gn'th'-), *adv.*, longuement.

length'iness, *n.*, longueur, prolixité (of speech), *f.*

length'ways *ou* **length'wise**, *adv.*, en longueur, de long, en long.

length'y, *adj.*, un peu long, prolongé, ennuyeux, prolixe.

le'niency (lî-), *n.*, douceur, (fig.) indulgence **pour**, *f.*

le'nient (lî-), *adj.*, doux, adoucissant; indulgent **à, envers, pour;** (med.) lénitif.

le'niently, *adv.*, avec douceur, avec indulgence.

len'itive (lè'n'-), *n.*, (med.) lénitif, calmant, émollient, adoucissant, *m.*

len'itive (lè'n'-), *adj.*, lénitif, calmant, émollient, adoucissant.

len'ity (lè'n'-), *n.*, douceur; indulgence **pour;** clémence, humanité, *f.* To show — to; *avoir de l'indulgence* **pour.**

lens (lè'n'ze), *n.*, (lenses) (opt.) lentille, loupe, *f.* — shaped; *lenticulaire;* (nat. hist.) *lenticulé.*

Lent (lè'n'te), *n.*, carême, *m.* Mid- —; *la mi-carême, f.* — lily; (bot.) *narcisse des prés, m.* To keep —; *faire carême.*

Lent'en, *adj.*, de carême.

lentic'ular (-tik'iou-) *ou* **len'tiform**, *adj.*, en forme de lentille, lenticulaire; (nat. hist.) lenticulé.

len'til (lè'n'tile), *n.*, (bot.) lentille, *f.*

Le'o (lî-ô), *n.*, (astron.) Lion, *m.*

le'onine (lî-o-naïne), *adj.*, de lion, léonin.

le'oninely, *adv.*, en lion, comme un lion.

leop'ard (lèp'arde), *n.*, (zoöl.) léopard, *m.*

lep'er (lèp'eur), *n.*, lépreux, *m.*

lepidop'tera (-ti-ra), *n.*, (ent.) lépidoptères, *m.pl.*

lepidop'teral, *adj.*, (ent.) lépidoptère.

lep'orine (lèp-o-raïne), *adj.*, de lièvre.

lep'rosy (lèp'ro-ci), *n.*, lèpre, *f.*

lep'rous (lèp'reusse), *adj.*, lépreux, ladre.

le'sion (lî-jeune), *n.*, (med.) lésion, *f.*

less (lèce), *adj.*, moindre, plus petit, inférieur. To grow —; *rapetisser, se rapetisser; diminuer.*

less, *adv.*, moins. The — . . . the more . . .; *moins . . . plus . . .* — and —; *de moins en moins.* No —; *rien moins; pas moins.* So much the —; *d'autant moins.* A man —; *un homme de moins.*

less, *n.*, moins; moindre, inférieur, *m.*

lessee' (lès'sî), *n.*, locataire à bail, *m.f.;* (jur.) preneur, *m.*

less'en, *v.a.*, rapetisser; diminuer, amoindrir; (to lower) rabaisser.

less'en, *v.n.*, diminuer, s'amoindrir, se rapetisser.

less'ening, *n.*, amoindrissement, *m.;* diminution, *f.*

less'er, *adj.*, moindre, plus petit; (geog.) mineur, petit; (mus.) mineur. *adv.*, à un moindre degré; moins.

les'son (lés's'n), *n.*, leçon; répétition, *f.*

lessor' (lès'sor), *n.*, (jur.) bailleur, *m.*, bailleresse, *f.*

lest (lèste), *conj.*, de peur que, de crainte que; (after To fear) que (subjunctive used in French).

let (lète), *v.a.*, (*preterit and past part.,* Let) (to permit) laisser; permettre de; souffrir que (with subjunctive); (to cause, make) faire; (a house) louer. To — alone (pers.); *laisser tranquille, laisser seul;* (a thing) *laisser, laisser là.* To — it alone; *n'en rien faire, ne pas s'en mêler.* To — blood; *saigner.* To — fly; *tirer, faire partir.* To — know; *faire savoir à.* To — loose; *lâcher; déchaîner.* To — see; *faire voir; montrer.* To be — with immediate possession; *à louer présentement.* House to —, to be —; *maison* *à louer.* To — fall, *ou* drop; *laisser tomber;* (of words) *proférer, prononcer, dire.* — him come; *qu'il vienne.* — us go; *allons.* To — in; *faire, laisser entrer; ouvrir la porte à;* (of water) *prendre l'eau;* (to insert) *insérer.* To — into; *faire, ou laisser, entrer; initier à, ou dans;* communiquer. To — off; *laisser partir, laisser échapper;* (of fire-arms) *tirer, faire partir, décharger;* (to forgive) *faire grâce de* (thing); *à* (person). To — down; *faire descendre; baisser, abattre.* To — out; *faire sortir, laisser échapper, laisser sortir;* (fig.) *ne pas tenir promesse à;* (of clothes) *élargir;* (of secrets) *ébruiter;* (a house) *louer;* (fire) *laisser éteindre;* (to divulge) *divulguer.* To — up, up-stairs; *faire, ou laisser, monter.* To — fall a remark; *faire une remarque en passant.* To — go; *lâcher; laisser aller; mettre en liberté.* To — into a secret; *révéler un secret à.* I will — you off the bargain; *je vous tiens quitte du marché.* To — have; (of goods) *donner, laisser, céder à.* To — sleeping dogs lie; *ne pas réveiller le chat qui dort.* — those laugh who win; (prov.) *marchand qui perd ne peut rire.* To — the cat out of the bag; *éventer la mèche; découvrir le pot aux roses.* To — slide; *ne pas s'inquiéter de.* — well alone; *le mieux est l'ennemi du bien.* To — an opportunity slip; *laisser échapper l'occasion.* — it be; *qu'il en soit ainsi.* — him have this book; *donnez lui ce livre.* — me see; *voyons.* — me hear you directly; *que je vous entende à l'instant.* — him go with me; *laissez-le venir avec moi.* — that child sleep; *laissez dormir cet enfant.* — no one go out of the house; *que personne ne sorte.* Do not — me disturb you; *que je ne vous dérange pas.* He was — off with a fine; *il en fut quitte pour une amende.*

let, *n.,* empêchement; obstacle, délai, *m.* Without — or hindrance; *sans entrave, en toute liberté.*

le'thal (lî-thal), *adj.,* mortel, fatal.

lethar'gic *ou* **lethar'gical** (lè-thâr-djike, -dji-cal), *adj.,* léthargique.

leth'argy (lèth'ar-dji), *n.,* léthargie, *f.*

Le'the (lî-thi), *n.,* (myth.) Léthé, *m.*

Lethe'an (li-thî'a'n), *adj.,* du Léthé, de l'oubli.

lethif'erous (li-thif'eur-), *adj.,* (ant.) léthifère, mortel.

let'ter (lèt'teur), *n.,* lettre, *f.* — of attorney; *procuration, f.* — of mark; *lettre de marque, f.* — of exchange; *lettre de change, f.* — -box; *boîte aux lettres, f.* — -case; *porte-lettres, m.;* (print.) *casse, f.* — clip; *serre-papier, pince-notes, m.* — copying-machine; *presse à copier, f.*

let'ter, *v.a.,* (a book) mettre le titre au dos.

let'ter-car'rier (-car'ri-eur), *n.,* facteur, *m.*

let'tered (let'teur'd), *adj.,* lettré, savant; littéraire; (bookbind.) avec le titre marqué au dos.

let'tering, *n.,* titre, *m.*

let'tern (lèt'teurne), *n.* (ant.). *V.* **lectern.**

let'ter-press, *n.,* impression typographique, *f.*

let'ter-rack, *n.,* semainier, porte-lettres, *m.*

let'ter-wri'ter (-raït'-), *n.,* personne qui aime à écrire des lettres, *f.;* auteur épistolaire, épistolier; (book) recueil de lettres, *m.*

let'ting, *n.,* (lèt'-), *n.,* louage, *m.,* location, *f.;* (of land) affermage, *m.*

let'tuce (lèt'tice), *n.,* laitue, *f.* Cabbage-—; *laitue pommée.* Cos-—; *laitue romaine.*

leu'corrhœa (liou-cor-rhi-a), *n.,* (med.) leucorrhée, *f.;* fleurs blanches, *f.pl.*

Levant' (lî-*ou* lè-), *n.,* Levant, Orient, *m.*

Levant', *adj.,* oriental, du Levant, de l'Orient.

levant', *v.n.,* décamper, s'enfuir; lever le pied.

levant', *v.a.,* tanner, corroyer.

Levant'ine (lî-va'n'tine *ou* lèv'a'n'taïne), *n.,* (native of the Levant) Levantin, *m.;* (stuff) levantine, *f.*

lev'ee (lèv'î), *n.,* lever, *m.;* réception, *f.* To hold a —; *recevoir.* A — will be held; *il y aura réception.*

lev'el (lèv'èl), *n.,* niveau, *m.;* surface unie; visée, *f.;* pays plat, *m.* On a —; *de niveau.* Dead —; *niveau parfaitement uni.*

lev'el, *adj.,* uni, de niveau, égal. — with; *au niveau de, de niveau avec; donnant du plein pied sur.* To do one's — best; *faire tous ses efforts, travailler de son mieux.* To have one's head —; *avoir la tête bonne.*

lev'el, *v.a.,* aplanir, niveler, mettre de niveau; (fire-arms) pointer, ajuster, viser, baisser; (a blow) porter, assener, lancer; (to throw down) renverser. To — to the ground; *raser, détruire, renverser.* To — at; *viser à; porter, assener, allonger, un coup à.* To — up; *élever au niveau de.* To — down; *abaisser au même niveau.*

lev'el, *v.n.,* viser, mettre en joue, pointer, ajuster; s'aplanir, se niveler.

lev'eler, *n.,* (politics) niveleur, égalitaire; aplanisseur, *m.*

lev'eling, *n.,* nivellement; aplanissement; pointage, *m.*

lev'eling-staff (-stâfe), *n.,* mire de nivellement, *f.,* jalon, *m.*

lev'elness, *n.,* niveau, *m.;* égalité, *f.*

lev'en (lèv'è'n), *n.,* levain, *m. V.* **leaven.**

lev'er (lî-veur), *n.,* levier, *m.;* bascule, *f.*

lev'eret (lè'veur'ète), *n.,* (zoöl.) levraut, *m.*

lev'iable (lèv'i-a-b'l), *adj.,* qui peut être levé.

levi'athan (lè-vaï-a-tha'n), *n.,* léviathan, *m.*

lev'igate (lèv'-), *v.a.,* (pharm.) broyer, pulvériser; (ant.) aplanir; polir.

leviga'tion (lèv'i-ghé-), *n.,* pulvérisation, *f.*

levita'tion (lèv'i-té-), *n.,* action de rendre léger; légèreté, *f.*

Le'vite (lî-vaïte), *n.,* lévite, *m.*

Levit'ical (lè-vit'i-), *adj.,* lévitique, des lévites.

Levit'icus (lè-vit'i-keusse), *n.,* Lévitique, *m.*

lev'ity (lèv'-), *n.,* légèreté, inconstance, *f.*

lev'y (lèv'i), *n.,* levée, *f.* — in mass; *levée en masse, f.*

lev'y, *v.a.,* lever; (a fine) imposer. To — a distress; *faire une saisie.*

lewd (lioude), *adj.,* dissolu, impudique, débauché, déréglé, licencieux, dépravé, luxurieux.

lewd'ly, *adv.,* licencieusement, impudiquement, dans la débauche, dans le débordement.

lewd'ness, *n.,* impudicité, luxure, débauche, dépravation, *f.;* libertinage, débordement, *m.*

lexicog'rapher (lèks'-), *n.,* lexicographe, *m.*

lexicograph'ic, *adj.,* lexicographique.

lexicog'raphy, *n.,* lexicographie, *f.*

lexicol'ogy (lèks'i-col-o-dji), *n.,* lexicologie, *f.*

lex'icon (lèks'i-), *n.,* lexique, dictionnaire, *m.*

ley (lî), *n.,* champ, *m.,* pâturage, *m.*

Ley'den-jar (laï-d'n-djâr) *ou* **Ley'den-phi'al** (-faï'al), *n.,* (phys.) bouteille de Leyde, *f.*

liabil'ity (laï'a-), *n.,* responsabilité, *f.;* tendance, danger, *m. pl.,* (com.) engagements, *m.pl.,* passif, *m.sing.* With limited —; *en commandite.* Their — to accidents; *comme ils sont exposés, ou sujets, à des accidents.*

li'able (laï'a-b'l), *adj.,* sujet à, exposé à, passible de, responsable de.

li'ar (laï'eur), *n.,* menteur, *m.,* menteuse, *f.*

li'as (laï'ace), *n.,* (geol.) liais, *m.*

liba'tion (laï-bé-), *n.,* libation, *f.*

li'bel (laï-bèl), *n.,* libelle, écrit diffamatoire, *m.;* publication diffamatoire, diffamation, *f.* Action for —; *plainte, f.,* ou *procès, m.,* en *diffamation.*

li'bel, *v.a.,* diffamer.

li'beler, *n.,* diffamateur, libelliste, pamphlétaire, *m.*

li'beling, *n.,* diffamation, *f.*

li'belous, *adj.,* diffamatoire.

lib'eral (lib'eur'-), *adj.,* libéral, généreux, prodigue, abondant ; copieux ; ample ; libre. — arts ; *arts libéraux, m.pl.*

lib'eral, *n.*, (politics) libéral, *m.*

lib'eralism (-'iz'me), *n.*, libéralisme, *m.*

liberal'ity, *n.*, libéralité, *f.*

lib'eralize ('-aïze), *v.a.*, (l.u.) rendre libéral.

lib'erally, *adv.*, libéralement, généreusement, largement.

lib'erate, *v.a.*, rendre libre, affranchir, mettre en liberté, élargir ; délivrer **de**, dégager **de** ; (jur.) libérer.

libera'tion (lib'eur'é-), *n.*, (of prisoners) mise en liberté, *f.*, élargissement ; affranchissement, *m.* ; libération, délivrance, *f.*

lib'erator ('-eur'éteur), *n.*, libérateur, *m.* ; libératrice, *f.*

lib'ertine (lib'eur-tine *ou* -taïne), *adj.*, libertin ; déréglé.

lib'ertine, *n.*, libertin, *m.*, libertine, *f.*

lib'ertinism (-ti'n'iz'me), *n.*, libertinage, *m.*

lib'erty (lib'eur'ti'), *n.*, liberté, *f. pl.*, privilèges, *m.pl.* ; franchises, *f.pl.* Cap of — ; *bonnet phrygien, m.* To be at — ; *être en liberté* ; *être libre* **de**. To set at — ; *mettre en liberté, donner la liberté* **à**. To take the — of ; *prendre la liberté* **de**. To take liberties ; *prendre des libertés avec, prendre des licences.*

libid'inous, *adj.*, libertin, libidineux.

libra'rian (laï-bré-), *n.*, bibliothécaire, *m.*

li'brary (laï-), *n.*, bibliothèque, *f.*

li'brate (laï-), *v.a.*, balancer.

li'brate, *v.n.*, balancer ; se tenir en équilibre.

libra'tion (laï-bré-), *n.*, balancement, équilibre, *m.* ; (astron.) libration, *f.*

li'bratory, *adj.*, de libration ; en équilibre.

lice (laïce), *n. V.* **louse**.

li'cense *ou* **li'cence** (laï-), *n.*, licence ; liberté ; permission, *f.* ; (fig.) déréglement ; (thea.) privilège, *m.* ; (of a preacher) autorisation ; (of tobacconists, vendors of excisable articles) licence, *f.* ; (of a bookseller, a printer) brevet, *m.* ; (com.) patente, *f.* Marriage— ; *dispense de bans, f.* Gun— ; *port d'arme* ; *permis de chasse, m.* Government— ; *licence accordée par le gouvernement.*

li'cense, *v.a.*, autoriser, accorder une autorisation **à** ; (a printer, a bookseller) breveter ; (theatre) accorder un privilège **à** ; (of tobacconists and vendors of excisable articles) accorder une licence **à** ; (com.) patenter.

li'censed (laï-cè'n'ste), *adj.*, autorisé ; (printers, booksellers) breveté ; (theatres) privilégié ; (com.) patenté. — victualer ; *aubergiste, cabaretier, m.*

li'censer (laï-), *n.*, agent qui accorde les autorisations ; (of plays) censeur, *m.*

licen'tiate (laï-cè'n'shi-éte), *n.*, licencié, *m.*

licen'tious (laï-cè'n'shi-eusse), *adj.*, licencieux, libertin, déréglé.

licen'tiously, *adv.*, licencieusement.

licen'tiousness, *n.*, licence, *f.* ; déréglement, libertinage, *m.*

li'chen (laï-kè'n *ou* litsh'è'n), *n.*, (bot.) lichen, *m.*

lich'-gate, *n.*, porte d'un cimetière, *f.*

lic'it, *adj.*, (ꜱɴᴛ.) licite, légal, permis.

lic'itly, *adv.*, (ant.) licitement.

lic'itness, *n.*, (ant.) légalité, *f.*

lick, *n.*, (pop.) coup, *m.* ; action de lécher ; la chose léchée, *f.* — on the head ; *taloche, f.* — in the face ; *gifle, f.*

lick, *v.a.*, lécher ; laper ; (to beat) (pop.) flanquer des coups **à**, rosser. To — into shape ; *faire prendre tournure* **à**. To — up ; *laper, avaler, dévorer.* To — the dust ; *mordre la poussière.* To — the spittle of ; *faire le chien couchant* **auprès de**. To — a dish ; *lécher un plat.*

lick'erish, *adj.*, friand ; avide.

lick'erishly, *adv.*, avec friandise ; lascivement.

lick'erishness, *n.*, friandise, *f.*

lick'ing, *n.*, (pop.) coups, *m.pl.* ; roulée raclée, rossée, *f.*

lick'-spittle, *n.*, parasite abject, chien couchant, *m.*

lic'orice *ou* **liqu'orice**, *n.*, réglisse, *f.*

lic'tor, *n.*, licteur, *m.*

lid, *n.*, couvercle, *m.* ; (of the eye) paupière, *f.* ; (bot.) opercule, *m.*

lie (laïe), *n.*, mensonge ; démenti, *m.* ; position, situation, *f.* ; état, *m.* To give the — to ; *donner un démenti* **à** ; *démentir.* To know the — of the land ; (fig.) *savoir où en sont les choses.*

lie (laïe), *v.n.*, (*preterit*, Lay ; *past part.*, Lain), être couché ; coucher ; se coucher ; rester couché ; être étendu ; reposer ; être ; être situé ; se trouver ; s'appuyer ; rester ; demeurer ; consister ; (nav.) être mouillé, être à l'ancre. To — about ; *traîner, être dispersé çà et là.* To — by ; (pers.) *se reposer* ; *se tenir* **en** *réserve* ; (of things) *être tenu* **en** *réserve.* To — down ; *coucher, être couché, se coucher, se reposer.* To — in ; *être en couches* ; *faire ses couches.* The town —s between two valleys ; *la ville est située, se trouve entre deux vallées.* He —s against the wall ; *il s'appuie* **contre** *le mur.* The whole —s in this ; *le tout repose* **sur** *ceci.* The difference —s in this ; *la différence consiste* **en** *ceci.* Here —s ; *ci-gît.* To let anything — ; *laisser là quelque chose.* To — under a mistake ; *se tromper* ; *être* **dans** *l'erreur.* It —s in my power to ; *il dépend de moi* **de**. To — heavy on ; *peser* **sur** ; *tourmenter.* My honor —s at stake ; *il y va* **de** *mon honneur.* To — alongside ; *être bord à bord.* To — at ; *importuner, tourmenter, agacer.* To — at one's door ; *être imputable* **à** *quelqu'un.* To — at one's heart ; *tenir* **au** *cœur.* To — at the root of ; *être la cause* **de**. To — between ; *être limité* **à** (of a choice). To — in a nutshell ; *être simple comme bonjour.* To — in the way ; *être un obstacle.* To — in wait ; *être* **en** *embuscade, être* **aux** *aguets.* To — on, *ou* upon ; *être du devoir* **de** ; *incomber* **à** ; *dépendre* **de**. To — on hand ; *ne pas trouver d'acheteur.* To — on one's oars ; *cesser de travailler* ; *être désœuvré.* To — over ; *être différé* ; *rester impayé.* To — to ; (nav.) *être en panne.* To — to one's work ; *travailler avec zèle.* To — under ; *être sujet,* ou *exposé,* **à** ; *être* **sous** ou **dans**. To — with ; *dépendre* **de**. To — dead (of money) ; *dormir* ; *rester sans emploi, être à découvert.* To — open ; (nav.) *être exposé* ; *être ouvert.* To — idle ; *chômer* ; (of money) *dormir.* He lay on his death-bed ; *il gisait sur son lit de mort.* The lion lay dead ; *le lion était étendu mort.*

lie (laïe), *v.n.*, mentir. To — unblushingly ; *mentir comme un arracheur de dents.*

lief (lîfe), *adj.*, (ant.) bien-aimé ; cher.

lief *ou* **lieve** (lîfe), *adv.*, volontiers. I had as — ; *j'aime autant.* I had as — not be, as to ; *j'aimerais autant ne pas exister que* **de**.

liege (lî'dje), *n.adj.*, lige, homme lige ; vassal. — lord ; *souverain* ; *suzerain, m.*

liege'-man, *n.*, homme lige, *m.*

lien (lî-è'n *ou* laï'è'n), *n.*, hypothèque, *f.* ; droit de recours ; (jur.) gage, nantissement, *m.*

lieu (liou), *n.*, lieu, remplacement, *m.* In — of ; *au lieu de* ; *en place de* ; *à la place de* ; *en remplacement* **de**. To —s'emploie qu'avec *in.*]

lieuten'ancy (liou-tè'n'- *ou* lèf'), *n.*, lieutenance, *f.*

lieuten'ant (liou-tè'n'- *ou* lèf'), *n.*, lieutenant, *m.* ; sub— ; *enseigne de vaisseau.*

lieuten'antship, *n.*, lieutenance, *f.*

life (laïfe), *n.*, (*lives*) vie, *f.* ; vivant, *m.* ; (fig.) vie, âme, vivacité, *f.* ; entrain ; mouvement ; (paint., sculpt.) naturel, *m.*, nature, *f.* I must give over this — ; *il faut que j'en finisse avec ce genre de vie.* He was the — of the party ; *c'est lui qui mettait tout en train* ou *il était le boute-*

en-train de la fête. He has no — in him; *il est dépourvu d'entrain.* Prime of —; *fleur de l'âge, f.* Fashionable —; *beau monde, m.* Single —; *célibat, m.* At that time of —; *à cet âge.* During his, her —; *de son vivant.* For —; *à vie ; pour toute la vie, sa vie durant.* Never in one's —; *jamais de sa vie.* From —; *d'après nature.* I cannot for the — of me ; *je ne peux pour tout au monde.* To the —; *exactement.* The streets are full of —; *les rues sont pleines de mouvement.* To depart this —; *mourir ; quitter cette vie.* To fly for one's —; *chercher son salut dans la fuite.* To give — to; *animer ; donner de la vie* **à,** *de l'âme* **à.** So this is called seeing —; *ainsi voilà ce qui s'appelle voir le monde !* To have a pension for —; *avoir une pension viagère.* Hard labor for —; *travaux forcés à perpétuité, m.pl.* Picture drawn to the —; *portrait d'une ressemblance frappante, m.* High —; *grand monde, m.* Low —; *le petit, ou bas, monde, m.* Manner of —; *manière de vivre, f.* Many lives were lost; *un grand nombre de personnes ont péri.* To swim for (one's) —; *chercher son salut dans la nage.* There's — in the old dog yet; (prov.) *petit bonhomme vit encore.*

life-annu'itant, *n.,* rentier viager, *m.*

life-annu'ity, *n.,* rente viagère, *f.*

life'belt, *n.,* ceinture de sauvetage, *f.*

life'-blood (-bleude), *n.,* le plus pur de son sang ; (fig.) sang, *m.,* vie, âme, *f.*

life'-boat (-bôte), *n.,* canot de sauvetage, *m.*

life'-buoy (-bou'é), *n.,* bouée de sauvetage, *f.*

life'-consum'ing (-siou'm'-), *adj.,* qui fait dépérir.

life-estate', *n.,* propriété à vie, *f. ;* usufruit, *m.*

life-everlast'ing, *n.,* (theol.) vie éternelle, *f. ;* (bot.) gnaphale, *m.*

life'giving (-ghiv'-), *adj.,* qui donne la vie; fortifiant ; vivifiant.

life'guard (-gârde), *n.,* garde du corps ; (railw.) chasse-pierres, *m.*

life'guards, *n.pl.,* garde du corps, *f.sing. ;* gardes du corps, *m.pl.*

life'guardsman (-gârd'z'ma'n), *n.,* garde du corps, *m.*

life'-insurance, *n.,* assurance sur la vie, *f.*

life-in'terest, *n.,* revenue viager ; viager, *m.*

life'less, *adj.,* sans vie ; inanimé, mort ; (fig.) sans âme, sans vigueur, sans mouvement.

life'lessly, *adv.,* sans vie ; sans âme, sans vigueur, sans mouvement.

life'lessness, *n.,* absence de vie ; absence de mouvement, *f.*

life'like (-laïke), *adj.,* comme un être vivant, vivant, animé ; d'après nature.

life'line (-laïne), *n.,* (nav.) garde-corps, garde-fou, *m.*

life'long, *adj.,* de toute la vie.

life'-policy, *n.,* police d'assurance sur la vie, *f.*

life'-preserver (-prî-ceur-), *n.,* appareil de sauvetage ; (truncheon) assommoir, casse-tête, *m.*

life'-rent, *n.,* rente viagère, *f.*

life'-size, *n.,* grandeur naturelle, *f.*

life'-string (-strigne), *n.,* nerf vital, *m.*

life'time (-taïme), *n.,* vie, *f. ;* vivant, *m.*

life'-weary (-wî-ri), *adj.,* las de la vie.

lift, *n.,* action de lever, de soulever, *f.,* effort; coup de main, *m. ;* charge, *f. ;* poids ; (hoisting machine) cric, treuil ; (elevator) ascenseur, *m.* To give a —; *donner un coup d'épaule* **à,** *un coup de main* **à** ; *faire monter avec soi.* To give a person a — (in a vehicle) ; *aider quelqu'un à monter en voiture.*

lift, *v.a.,* lever, élever, enlever, soulever, hausser ; (fig.) relever ; (rents) recevoir ; (cattle) voler.

lift'-gate, *n.,* pont-levis, *m.*

lift'ing, *n.,* action de lever, *f.* — **jack ;** *cric, m.*

lig'ament, *n.,* ligament ; lien, *m.*

lig'ature (lig'a-tioure), *n.,* (mus.) liaison; (print., surg.) ligature, *f.*

light (laïte), *n.,* lumière, clarté, *f. ;* jour, *m. ;* lueur, *f. ;* (paint.) jour, *m.,* lumière, *f. ;* (arch.) jour, *m. ;* (fig.) point de vue. Day—; *jour, m.* Moon—; *clair de lune, m.* By the — of ; *à la lumière* **de,** *à la clarté* **de.** It is —; *il fait jour ; il fait clair.* To give —; *éclairer.* By —; *à la lumière.* By the — of the moon ; *au clair de la lune.* By the — of the lamp; *à la lueur de la lampe.* This picture is not in the right —; *ce tableau n'est pas dans son jour.* To come to —; *se manifester, se produire, se découvrir.* Will you oblige me with a — ? (of smokers) *voulez-vous avoir la bonté de me donner du feu ?* To bring to —; *révéler ; mettre au jour ; faire connaître.* To see —; *voir la lumière.* To stand in one's own —; *nuire* **à** *ses propres intérêts ; se faire tort, se nuire.* To throw — on a subject; *jeter de la lumière sur un sujet.* — hair ; *cheveux blonds, m.pl.* Not to stand in any one's —; *ne pas se mettre sur les rangs* **contre,** *ne pas chercher à nuire* **à.**

light, *adj.,* léger ; (fig.) agile ; facile ; (of light and color) clair. To make — of; *traiter légèrement ; faire peu de cas* **de.** —-armed; *armé à la légère.* They are — as air ; (of threats, troubles) *autant en emporte le vent.*

light, *v.a.,* (preterit and past part., Lighted, Lit) allumer ; (of windows, etc.) illuminer, éclairer ; (to give light to) éclairer. To — a candle ; *allumer une chandelle.* To — the streets; *éclairer les rues.* To — a person (to his room); *éclairer à quelqu'un, éclairer quelqu'un.*

light, *v.n.,* s'abattre. To — upon ; *descendre, tomber* **sur** ; *retomber, rencontrer.* To — up ; *s'enflammer ; s'animer.*

light'-bearer (-bèr'-), *n.,* porte-flambeau, *m.*

light'en, *v.a.,* alléger ; (to alleviate) soulager, alléger ; (to cheer) égayer, réjouir ; (to dissipate darkness) éclairer.

light'en, *v.n.imp.,* faire des éclairs, éclairer.

light'ening, *n.,* (alleviation) soulagement, *m.* (of silver in cupellation) éclair, *m. ;* (act of brightening up) illumination, *f.*

light'er, *n.,* allumeur, *m.,* allumeuse ; (nav.) allège, gabare, *f.* Lamp —; *allumeur de réverbères, m.* — man; *gabarier, m.*

light'erage (laït'eur'èdje), *n.,* frais d'allège, *m.pl.*

light-fin'gered (-fi'gn'gheurde), *adj.,* qui a les doigts crochus ; à la main légère ; fripon.

light'-foot (-foute) *ou* **light-foot'ed** (-'ède), *adj.,* au pied léger ; agile.

light-head'ed (-hèd'-), *adj.,* qui a la tête légère ; étourdi ; en délire.

light-head'edness, *n.,* étourderie, *f. ;* délire, *m.*

light-heart'ed (-hârt'-), *adj.,* enjoué, gai, réjoui.

light-heart'edness, enjouement, *m.,* gaieté, *f.*

light'-horse, *n.,* cavalerie légère, *f.*

light'-house (-haouce), *n.,* phare, fanal, *m.*

light'-infantry, *n.,* infanterie légère, *f.*

light'ing, *n.,* éclairage, *m. ;* (metal.) recuite, *f.*

light'less, *adj.,* sans lumière ; sans clarté.

light'ly, *adv.,* légèrement ; avec légèreté ; à la légère ; lestement ; facilement, aisément ; gaîment *ou* gaiement. — come — go ; (prov.) *ce qui vient de la flûte s'en va,* ou *retourne, au tambour.*

light'-minded, *adj.,* à l'esprit léger ; inconstant; frivole.

light'ness, *n.,* légèreté ; agilité, *f.*

light'ning, *n.,* éclair, *m.,* foudre, *f.* —-rod, —-conductor ; *paratonnerre, m.* Flash of —; *éclair, m.* Fork —; *éclair en zigzag.* Sheet —; *éclair en nappe.* Struck by —; *frappé de la foudre.*

light'ning-glance (-glâ'n'ce), *n.,* éclair, *m.*

lights (laïtse), *n.pl.*, poumons (**of** animals) *m.pl.*; (of calves, etc.) mou, *m.*

light'ship, *n.*, bateau feu, bateau phare, *m.*

light'some (-seume), *adj.*, clair; éclairé; gai.

light'someness, *n.*, gaîté; légèreté, *f.*

lig'neous (lig-ni-), *adj.*, ligneux.

lig'nite, *n.*, (min. and geol.) lignite, *m.*

lig'num-vi'tæ (lig-neume-vaï-ti), *n.*, gaïac, bois de gaïac, *m.*

like (laïke), *n.*, chose pareille, *f.*; pareil, *m.*, pareille; même chose, *f.*; (liking) goût. Every-one his **—s** and dislikes; *chacun a son goût; des goûts et des couleurs il ne faut pas disputer.* To do the **—**; *en faire autant.* To give **—** for **—**; *rendre la pareille.* And the **—**; *et autres choses pareilles.*

like, *adj.*, semblable, tel, même, pareil, égal, enclin à, disposé à, ressemblant; vraisemblable. That is something **—**! *à la bonne heure!* To look, *ou* be, **—**; *avoir l'air* **de**; *ressembler* **à.** Does this portrait look **—** me? *est-ce que ce portrait me ressemble?* To be **—** unto; *ressembler* **à.** To be as **—** as two peas; *se ressembler comme deux gouttes d'eau.* **—** master, **—** man; *tel maître tel valet.* **—** sire **—** son; *bon chien chasse de race ou bon sang ne peut mentir.*

like, *adv.*, comme; en; tel que, telle que; pro-bablement. That is just **—** you; *c'est bien vous; je vous reconnais bien là.*

like, *v.a.*, aimer; trouver à son goût; trou-ver bien; prendre goût à; trouver convenable **de**; aimer à; convenir à; vouloir, vouloir bien; être curieux **de.** I begin to **—** it; *je commence à y prendre goût, à m'y faire.* As you **—**; *comme il vous plaira; comme vous jugerez convenable; comme vous voudrez.* I should **—** to go there; *je voudrais bien y aller.* If you **—**; *si vous voulez; si bon vous semble.* I should **—** to have been there; *j'aurais bien voulu m'y trouver.* I do not **—** it at all; *je ne le trouve pas bon du tout.* I should **—** to know; *je voudrais bien savoir.* Come when you **—**; *venez quand vous voudrez.* How do you **—** your tea? *comment trouvez-vous votre thé?* To **—** best; *aimer mieux, préférer.*

like'lihood (-houde) *ou* **like'liness**, *n.*, vrai-semblance, apparence, probabilité, *f.*

like'ly, *adj.*, vraisemblable; probable; capa-ble, dans le cas **de.** I am **—** to call on you; *j'irai probablement vous voir.* **—** to; *fait pour; propre* **à**; *de nature* **à.**

like'ly, *adv.*, probablement; vraisemblable-ment. He is **—** to come; *il viendra probable-ment; il est probable qu'il viendra.* To seem **—** to be; *sembler devoir être.* There was **—** to be some speechifying; *il était probable qu'il y aurait des discours.* He was most, *ou* very, **—** ignorant of it; *il est probable qu'il l'ignorait.*

li'ken (laïk'n), *v.a.*, comparer **à**; faire ressem-bler **à.**

like'ness, *n.*, ressemblance; apparence, *f.*; portrait, air, *m.*

like'wise (-waïze), *adv.*, également, pareille-ment, de même, aussi.

lik'ing, *n.*, gré; goût, *m.*; inclination; amitié, affection, *f.* To have a **—** for; *avoir du goût pour.* To take a **—** to; *prendre goût* **à**, *se faire* **à**; (pers.) *prendre en amitié.*

li'lac (laï-lake), *n.*, (bot.) lilas, *m.*

lilia'ceous (lil'i-é-sheusse), *adj.*, (bot.) liliacé.

lil'y, n., (bot.) lis, *m.* **—** of the valley; *mu-guet, m.*

li'mature (laï-ma-tioure), *n.*, (ant.) limaille, *f.*

limb (lime), *n.*, (of the body) membre; (edge) bord, *m.*; (of a tree) grosse branche, *f.*; (astron., bot.) limbe; (colloq.) enfant terrible, *m.* **—** of the Law; *homme de loi, robin, m.*

limbed (li'm'de), *adj.*, membré. Large **—**; *membru.*

lim'ber (li'm'beur), *adj.*, souple, flexible; (fig.) agile. *v.a.*; to **—** up; *amener l'avant train.*

lim'ber (li'm'beure), *n.pl.*, (artil.) caisson, avant-train, *m.*

lim'berness, *n.*, souplesse.

limb'less (li'm'-), *adj.*, sans membres.

lim'bo (li'm'bô) *ou* **lim'bus**, *n.*, limbes, *m.pl.*, prison, *f.*

lime (laï'me), *n.*, chaux; (for catching birds) glu, *f.*; (tree) limonier; (linden) tilleul; (fruit) citron, *m.* **—** quarry; *carrière de calcaire, f.* **—** water; *eau de chaux, f.*

lime, *v.a.*, (agri.) chauler; (ant.) gluer, en-gluer; prendre au gluau; (fig.) prendre dans un piège.

lime'-burner (-beurn'-), *n.*, chaufournier, *m.*

lime'-juice (-djiouce), *n.*, jus de citron, *m.*

lime'-kiln, *n.*, chaufour, four à chaux, *m.*

lime'-pit, *n.*, carrière de calcaire, *f.*

lime'stone (-stône), *n.*, (min.) pierre calcaire; pierre à chaux, *f.*; calcaire, *m.*

lime'-tree (-trî), *n.*, (bot.) limonier; tilleul, *m.*

lime'-twig, *n.*, gluau, *m.*

lim'it, *n.*, limite, *f.*; bornes, *f.pl.* **—s** of a for-tress; *limites de la garnison, f.pl.*

lim'it, *v.a.*, limiter, borner, restreindre. To **—** the meaning of a word; *limiter, ou restreindre, le sens d'un mot, ou la portée d'une expression.*

lim'itable (-'a-b'l), *adj.*, qu'on peut limiter.

limita'tion, *n.*, limitation, restriction; ré-serve, (jur.) prescription, *f.*

lim'ited, *adj.*, limité, borné; (math.) déter-miné. **—** monarchy; *monarchie constitution-nelle, f.* **—** liability; *responsabilité limitée, f.*

lim'itedly, *adv.*, avec des limites, avec des bornes.

limn (lime), *v.a.*, enluminer; peindre à l'aquarelle; (fig.) peindre.

lim'ner (li'm'neur), *n.*, enlumineur, *m.*, enlu-mineuse, *f.*; (fig.) peintre, *m.*

lim'ning (li'm'nigne), *n.*, enluminure; pein-ture à l'aquarelle, aquarelle; (fig.) peinture, *f.*

limp (li'm'pe), *adj.*, mou, flasque, flexible, souple.

limp, *v.n.*, clocher, boiter, clopiner. **—ing** verse; *vers boiteux, m.*

limp'er, *n.*, personne qui cloche, *f.*; boiteux, *m.*, boiteuse, *f.*

lim'pet (li'm'pète), *n.*, (zoöl.) lépas, *m.*; patelle, *f.*

lim'pid, *adj.*, limpide.

lim'pidness, limpid'ity, *n.*, limpidité, *f.*

limp'ingly (li'm'pign'li), *adv.*, en boiteux, en clochant.

li'my (laï'm'i), *adj.*, calcaire; (viscous) gluant, visqueux.

linch'pin (li'n'sh'pi'n), *n.*, esse; clavette (d'essieu), *f.*

lin'den *ou* **lin'den-tree** (-trî), *n.*, tilleul, *m.*

line (laïne), *n.*, ligne; (of steamers) message-ries, *f.pl.*; service de paquebots, *m.*; (string) corde, *f.*; cordeau; (building) alignement, *m.*; (series) suite, *f.*; (outline) contour; (conduct) genre, *m.*; (railways) ligne, voie; (family) lignée, race, *f.*; (of business) genre d'affaires, *m.*, spécialité, partie, *f.*; (poet.) vers; (short letter) mot, petit mot, *m.*; (limit) limite (fort., geog., geom., milit., tech.) ligne, *f.* **—s**, *pl.*, trans-parent, *m.* It is hard **—s**; *c'est dur, c'est bien rude.* **—** of battle; *ordre de bataille, m.* **—of-** battle ship; *vaisseau de ligne, m.* Ship of the **—**; *vaisseau de ligne, m.* Troops of the **—**; *troupes de ligne, f.pl.* **—** of business: *spécialité, profession, f., métier, m.* Single **—**; (rail.) *voie simple, f.* Double **—**; *voie double, f.* Up**—**; *voie montante, f.* Down**—**; *voie descendante, f.* In a **—**; *en ligne, aligné.* To draw the **—** somewhere; (fig.) *tracer la ligne de démarcation quelque part; savoir s'arrêter.* In the same **—**; (of business) *dans la même partie.* Send me a **—**; *écrivez-moi un mot.*

line, *v.a.*, garnir **de**; (garments) doubler,

garnir ; (fort.) fortifier ; (to trace) tracer ; (to border) border **de** ; (mas.) revêtir **de** ; (soldiers) ranger ; mettre en ligne.

lin'eage (li'n'i-édje), *n.*, lignée, race, fam'lle, *f.*

lin'eal (li'n'i'-), *adj.*, linéaire ; (genealogy) direct, en ligne directe ; (jur.) linéal.

lin'eally, *adv.*, en ligne droite ; en ligne directe.

lin'eament (li'n'i-a-), *n.*, trait, linéament, *m.*

lin'ear (li'n'i-), *adj.*, linéaire.

linea'tion (li'n'i-é-), *n.*, délinéation, *f.*

lin'en, *n.*, toile, toile de lin, *f.* ; lin ; (clothes) linge, *m.* — warehouse ; *magasin de blanc, m.* Clean — ; *linge blanc, m.* Dirty — ; *linge sale, m.*

lin'en, *adj.*, de toile, de lin ; de linge.

lin'en-cloth (-clôth), *n.*, toile de lin, *f.*

lin'en-dra'per (-dré-), *n.*, marchand de nouveautés ; marchand de toile ; linger, *m. ;* lingère, *f.*

lin'en-goods, *n.pl.*, lingerie, toilerie, *f.*

lin'en-press, *n.*, armoire à linge, *f.*

lin'en-warehouse, *n.*, magasin de blanc, *m.*

lin'en-yarn, *n.*, fil de lin, *m.*

lin'er, *n.*, paquebot transatlantique, *m.*

lin'ger (lign'gheur), *v.n.*, traîner, lambiner ; hésiter ; languir ; tarder. To — behind ; *rester en arrière.*

lin'gerer, *n.*, traînard, lambin, *m.*

lin'gering, *n.*, retardement, délai, *m. ;* hésitation ; lenteur, *f.*

lin'gering, *adj.*, qui tarde ; qui lambine ; qui traîne, lent ; languissant. — illness ; *maladie de langueur, f.*

lin'geringly, *adv.*, en traînant ; lentement ; avec langueur.

lin'go (lign'gô), *n.*, langage ; jargon, *m.*

lin'gual (li'gn'gwal), *adj.*, lingual.

lin'guist (li'gn'gwiste), *n.*, linguiste, *m.*

linguis'tic, *adj.*, linguistique.

lin'iment, *n.*, liniment, *m.*

li'ning (laï'n'igne), *n.*, (of garments) doublure ; garniture, *f. ;* (of hats) coiffe, *f. ;* (mas.) revêtement, *m.* Glazed — ; *lustrine, f.*

link (li'gn'ke), *n.*, chaînon, anneau, *m. ;* chaîne ; (torch) torche, *f.*, flambeau ; (fig.) lien, *m.*

link, *v.a.*, lier ; joindre ; enchaîner, unir.

link'boy (-boï) *ou* **link'man**, *n.*, porte flambeau, *m.*

lin'net (li'n'nète), *n.*, linotte, *f.*

lin'seed (-sîde), *n.*, graine de lin, *f.* — poultice ; *cataplasme de graine de lin, m.*

lin'seed-meal (-mîle), *n.*, farine de graine de lin, *f.*

lin'seed-oil (-oïl), *n.*, huile de lin, *f.*

lin'sey *ou* **lin'sey-wool'sey** (li'n'sè-woul'sè), *adj.*, de tiretaine ; (fig.) grossier, bas, vil.

lin'sey-wool'sey, *n.*, tiretaine, tartanelle, *f. ;* (ant.) galimatias, jargon, *m.*

lin'stock (li'n'stoke), *n.*, (ant.) (artil.) boutefeu, *m.*

lint (li'n'te), *n.*, filasse ; (surg.) charpie, *f.*

lin'tel (li'n'-), *n.*, linteau, *m.*

li'on (laï'o'n), *n.*, lion, *m. ;* (fig.) célébrité, *f.* — 's cub, *ou* whelp ; *lionceau, m.* To rush into the — 's mouth ; *se mettre dans la gueule du lion.*

li'oness (laï'o'n'-), *n.*, lionne, *f.*

li'on-hearted (-hârt'-), *adj.*, de lion ; cœur de lion.

li'on's-foot (-'z'foute), *n.*, (bot.) pied-de-lion, *m.*

li'on's-tail (-'z'téle), *n.*, (bot.) queue-de-lion, *f.*

lip, *n.*, lèvre, *f. ;* (of things) bord, *m.;* (of some beasts) babine ; (bot.) lèvre, *f.* To open one's —s ; *desserrer les dents.* To make a — ; *faire la moue* à ; *faire la grimace* à ; *faire sa lippe.* —reward ; *monnaie de singe ;* — salve ; *pommade pour les lèvres, f.* — strap ; *fausse gourmette, f.*

lip'less, *adj.*, sans lèvres.

lipped (lip'te), *adj.*, qui a des lèvres ; à lèvres ; (bot.) labié. Blubber — ; *lippu.*

lip'pitude (-tioude), *n.*, (med.) chassie, *f.*

liqua'tion (li-kwé-), *n.*, (metal.) liquation, *f. ;* ressuage, *m.*

liquefac'tion (lik'wè-fak'-), *n.*, liquéfaction, *f.*

liquefi'able (lik'wè-faï-a-b'l), *adj.*, liquéfiable.

liq'uefy (lik'wè-faïe), *v.a.*, liquéfier, fondre.

liq'uefy, *v.n.*, se liquéfier.

liques'cence (laï-kwès'-), *n.*, fusibilité, *f.*

liques'cent, *adj.*, fusible.

liq'uid (lik'wide), *n.*, (substance) liquide, *m.;* (gram.) liquide, *f.*

liq'uid, *adj.*, liquide, doux, coulant ; (of the letter L) mouillé.

liq'uidate (lik'wi-déte), *v.a.*, tirer au clair, (com.) liquider, solder, acquitter.

liquida'tion (-'wi-dé-), *n.*, liquidation, *f.*

liq'uidator, *n.*, liquidateur, *m.*

liquid'ity *ou* **liq'uidness**, *n.*, liquidité, *f.*

liq'uor (lik'eur), *n.*, liqueur, boisson, *f.* In — ; ivre. To be the worse for — ; *être ivre.* — stand ; *porte-liqueurs, m.* — traffic, *ou* trade ; *commerce des liqueurs, m.*

liq'uorice, *n.* V. **lic'orice**.

lisp, *n.*, zézaiement, *m. ;* (fig.) bégayement, *m.*

lisp, *v.a.* and *n.*, zézayer ; (fig.) bégayer.

lisp'er, *n.*, personne qui zézaye, *f.*

lisp'ing, *adj.*, qui zézaye. *n.*, bégayement, *m.*

lisp'ingly, *adv.*, en zézayant ; (fig.) en bégayant.

list, *n.*, liste, *f. ;* rôle, *m. ;* (arena) lice, arène, *f. ;* (nav.) faux côté, *m. ;* (selvage of cloth) lisière, *f. ;* (arch.) listel ; (limit) bord, *m.*, limite, barrière, *f.* Civil — ; *liste civile.* — of wines ; *carte des vins, f.* To enter the —s ; *entrer en lice ;* (fig.) *se mettre sur les rangs.*

list, *v.a.*, garnir de lisière ; (to enroll) enrôler, enregistrer ; disposer en arène.

list, *v.n.*, s'engager ; s'enrôler ; (to choose) vouloir, désirer ; (to listen) écouter ; faire attention à.

list'ed (list'ède), *adj.*, rayé, à raies.

lis'tel, *n.*, (arch.) listel, *m.*, listeaux, *m.pl.*

lis'ten (lis's'n), *v.a.* and *n.*, écouter.

lis'tener (lis's'neur), *n.*, auditeur ; (in a bad sense) écouteur, *m.*

list'less (list'less), *adj.*, nonchalant ; insouciant ; inattentif.

list'lessly (list'-), *adv.*, nonchalamment ; avec insouciance ; inattentivement.

list'lessness (list'-), *n.*, nonchalance, insouciance ; inattention, *f.*

list'-shoe (-shou), *n.*, chausson, *m.*

lit'any, *n.*, litanie, *f.*

li'ter *ou* **li'tre** (lî-teur), *n.*, litre, *m.*

lit'eral (lit'eur'-), *adj.*, littéral ; par des lettres.

literal'ity, *n.*, sens littéral, *m.*

lit'erally, *adv.*, littéralement ; à la lettre ; au pied de la lettre.

lit'eralness, *n.*, littéralité, *f.*

lit'erarily, *adv.*, littérairement.

lit'erary (lit'eur'-), *adj.*, (things) littéraire ; (pers.) lettré. — man ; *littérateur ; homme lettré ; homme de lettres, m.*

litera'ti (lit'eur'é-taïe), *n.pl.*, hommes de lettres, littérateurs ; savants, *m.pl.*

lit'erature (lit'eur'a'-tioure), *n.*, littérature, *f.*

lith'arge (lith'ardje), *n.*, litharge, *f.*

lithe (laïthe), *adj.*, pliant, flexible, souple ; doux, agréable.

lithe'ness (laïth'-), *n.*, flexibilité, souplesse, *f.*

lith'ograph (lith'-), *v.a.*, lithographier.

lith'ograph, *n.*, lithographie, *f.*

lithog'rapher, *n.*, lithographe, *m.*

lithograph'ic *ou* **lithograph'ical**, *adj.*, lithographique.

lithograph'ically, *adv.*, par la lithographie.

lithog'raphy, *n.*, lithographie, *f.*

lith'otome (lith'-), *n.*, (surg.) lithotome, *m.*

lithotom'ic, *adj.*, de, *ou* par, la lithotomie.

lithot'omist, *n.*, lithotomiste, *m.*

lithot'omy, *n.*, (surg.) lithotomie, cystotomie, *f.*

lithot'rity (li-thot- *ou* lith'o-traï-), *n.*, (surg.) lithotritie, *f.*

lit'igant, *n.*, litigant, plaideur, *m.*

lit'igant, *adj.*, (jur.) en litige ; litigant⊙.

lit'igate, *v.a.*, plaider, disputer.

lit'igate, *v.n.*, plaider, être en procès.

litiga'tion (-ti-ghé-), *n.*, (jur.) litige, procès, *m.*

liti'gious (-tidj'eusse), *adj.*, litigieux, contentieux ; (pers.) processif.

liti'giously, *adv.*, en chicaneur, (l.u.) contentieusement.

liti'giousness, *n.*, chicane; humeur processive, *f.* ; esprit litigieux, *m.*

lit'orn, *n.*, (orni.) grosse grive, litorne, *f.*

li'totes (laï-to-tize), *n.*, (rhet.) litote, *f.*

lit'ter, *n.*, (vehicle) brancard, *m.*, civière, litière ; (of a stable) litière, *f.* ; (b.s.) fumier, fouillis, désordre, *m.* ; (of animals) portée, ventrée, *f.*

lit'ter, *v.a.*, (a stable) pourvoir de litière, faire la litière **à** ; (fig.) mettre en désordre, éparpiller, jeter çà et là, mettre en fouillis ; salir ; (of animals) mettre bas.

lit'tle (lit't'l), *n.*, peu, *m.*

lit'tle, *adj.*, petit, faible, minime, exigu ; mesquin. — one ; *enfant, petit ; petit enfant, m.* — mind ; *petit esprit, m.* — fellows are often great wits ; (prov.) *dans les petites boîtes sont les bons onguents, dans les petits sacs sont les fines épices.* — pitchers have long ears ; *petit chaudron, grandes oreilles.* — rain lays much dust ; *petite pluie abat grand vent.* — strokes fell great oaks ; *petit à petit l'oiseau fait son nid.*

lit'tle, *adv.*, peu, un peu, pas beaucoup, peu de chose, peu **de**, guère **de**. Not a — ; *pas mal* **de**. — by — ; *petit à petit, peu à peu.* Be it ever so — ; *si peu que ce soit.* However — ; *pour peu que.* But — ; guère (with *ne* before a verb). A — ; *un peu.* As — as possible ; *le moins possible.* Ever so — ; *tant soit peu.*

lit'tleness, *n.*, petitesse, *f.*

lit'toral, *adj.*, maritime, littoral, riverain.

litur'gic (lit'eur'djike) *ou* **liturgical** (-djik'-), *adj.*, liturgique.

lit'urgy (lit'eur'dji), *n.*, liturgie, *f.*

live (laïve), *adj.*, en vie ; vivant ; (of coals) ardent, allumé, vif.

live (live), *v.n.*, vivre ; (reside) résider **à** ; demeurer **à** ; habiter. To — down a slander ; *faire taire la calomnie.* To — down ; (fig.) *survivre* **à**. To — up to one's income ; *dépenser, ou manger, tout son revenu ; dépenser tout ce qu'on gagne.* To — well ; *faire bonne chère.* To — away ; *avoir un grand train de maison ; faire bonne chère, mener joyeuse vie.* To — happily, *ou* unhappily ; (of married people) *faire bon, ou mauvais, ménage.* To — out of the house ; *ne pas coucher à la maison.* To — by ; *vivre* **de**. To — from hand to mouth ; *vivre au jour le jour, au jour la journée.* To — in London ; *demeurer* **à** *Londres, habiter Londres.* To — on, upon ; *vivre* **de**, *se nourrir* **de**, *subsister* **de**. To — up to ; *vivre selon.* Enough to — on ; *de quoi vivre.* Long — the Queen ! *vive la Reine !* To — happy days ; *couler des jours heureux.*

live (live), *v.a.*, mener (une vie).

lived (laïv'de), *adj.*, de vie. Long — ; *qui vit longtemps, de longue vie.* Short — ; *qui vit peu de temps, d'une courte vie ; (of things) passager, de courte durée.* High- — ; *de haut ton.* Low — ; *de mauvais ton.*

live'lihood (laïv'li-houde), *n.*, vie, existence, nourriture, subsistance, *f.* ; (means of) gagnepain, *m.*

live'lily, *adv.*, vivement, gaiement.

live'liness (laïv'-), *n.*, vivacité ; gaieté, *f.*

live'long (laïv'-), *adj.*, durable, permanent,

long, éternel, sans fin. The — day ; *toute la sainte journée.*

live'ly (laïv'-), *adj.*, vif, gai, enjoué, animé ; (of place) vivant, gai.

liv'er (liv'eur), *n.*, (anat.) foie ; (pers.) vivant, *m.* — complaint ; *maladie de foie, f.* Fast — ; *viveur, m., bon vivant, m., qui fait bonne chère.*

liv'er-col'ored (-keul'leurde), *adj.*, rouge foncé.

liv'ered, *adj.* White- — ; *qui a le foie blanc ;* (fig.) *peureux, poltron, irrésolu.*

liv'ery (liv'eur'i), *n.*, livrée ; (of horses) pension, *f.* ; (of the city of London) notables ; électeurs municipaux, *m.pl.* ; (jur.) mise en possession ; (of minors) émancipation, *f.* Full — ; *grande livrée.* Undress — ; *petite livrée.* To put out at — ; (of horses) *mettre en pension.* Out of — ; *sans livrée.*

liv'ery-man (-ma'n'), *n.*, homme qui porte la livrée ; (of the city of London) notable ; électeur municipal, *m.*

liv'ery-ser'vant (-seur'-), *n.*, domestique en livrée, *m.*

liv'ery-sta'ble (-sté-b'l), *n.*, écurie de chevaux de louage ; pension pour les chevaux, *f.* — keeper ; *loueur de chevaux, loueur de voitures, m.*

liv'id, *adj.*, livide, pâle.

livid'ity *ou* **liv'idness**, *n.*, lividité, *f.*

liv'ing (liv'-), *n.*, (ecc.) bénéfice, *m.*, cure, (livelihood) vie, subsistance, existence, *f.* ; (eating) chère, cuisine, *f.* For a — ; *pour vivre ; pour gagner sa vie.* To earn one's, *ou* get a, — ; *gagner sa vie, ou de quoi vivre.* To work for one's — ; *travailler pour vivre, ou pour gagner sa vie.* There are many — s in his gift ; *il a la présentation de plusieurs bénéfices.*

liv'ing (liv'-), *adj.*, vivant ; vif ; vivifiant ; (of coal) ardent. While — ; *de son vivant.* The — ; *les vivants, m.pl.* — force ; *force vive, f.* — or dead ; *mort ou vif.*

li'vre (lî-veur), *n.*, livre, *f.* ; franc, *m.*

lixiv'iate, *v.a.*, (chem.) lessiver.

lixiv'ium, *n.*, (solution) lessive, *f.*

liz'ard, *n.*, lézard, *m.*

lo ! (lô), *int.*, voici, voilà, voyez, regardez. — and behold ! *voilà que !*

loach (lôtshe), *n.*, (ich.) loche, dormille, *f.*

load (lôde), *n.*, charge, *f.* ; fardeau ; (mec.) travail, *m.* ; (cartful) voie, charretée ; quantité, *f.*, tas, *m.* He gives way under the — ; *il succombe sous le faix, ou le poids.* — line ; *ligne de flottaison, f.*

load (lôde), *v.a.*, charger **de** ; combler **de**, accabler **de**. To — dice ; *piper des dés.* To — wine ; *frelater du vin.* To — a stick ; *plomber une canne.* To — a man with insults ; *accabler un homme d'injures.* —ed stick ; *canne plombée, f.*

load'er, *n.*, chargeur, *m.*

load'ing, *n.*, charge, *f.* ; (com.) chargement, *m.*

load'stone (-stône), *n.*, aimant, *m.*

loaf (lôfe), *n.*, pain, *m.* — of bread ; *pain.* —sugar ; *sucre en pain, m.* — of sugar *ou* sugar — ; *pain de sucre, m.*

loaf, *v.a.n.*, flâner, fainéanter, vagabonder, badauder ; gaspiller (son temps) ; battre le pavé. To — one's time away ; *gaspiller son temps.* To — about town ; *battre le pavé.*

loaf'er, *n.*, fainéant, vagabond, *m.*

loam (lôme), *n.*, terre glaise, batteur de pavé, *m.*, marne argileuse, *f.*

loam (lôme), *v.a.*, marner, glaiser.

loam'y, *adj.*, argileux, glaiseux, marneux.

loan (lône), *n.*, prêt ; emprunt, *m.* — loses self and friend ; (prov.) *qui prête à l'ami perd au double.*

loan (lône), *v.a.*, prêter.

loan'-bank, *n.*, mont-de-piété, *m.*

loan'-fund, *n.*, caisse d'emprunt, *f.*

loan′ society, n., société de crédit, f.

loath (lôth), adj., fâché, peiné. To be —; avoir de la répugnance à; être fâché de; (imp.) répugner de. Nothing —; très volontiers.

loathe (lôthe), v.a., haïr, détester, abhorrer; avoir du dégoût pour, de l'aversion pour. I — meat; la viande me répugne.

loath′ful (lôth′foule), adj., dégoûtant.

loath′ing (lôth′-), adv., dégoût, m.; aversion, répugnance, horreur, f.

loath′ingly, loath′ly (lôth′-), adv., à contre-cœur, avec répugnance, avec dégoût, à regret.

loath′ness (lôth′-), n., répugnance, f.; dégoût, m.

loath′some (lôth′seume), adj., dégoûtant; détestable; horrible, odieux.

loath′someness (lôth′-), n., qualité dégoûtante, f.; dégoût, m.

lob, n., rustre, lourdaud, butor, m.

lob′by, n., antichambre, f.; couloir, m.; (waiting-room) salle d'attente, f.; (thea.) foyer, m.

lobe (lôbe), n., lobe, m.

lobed, adj., lobé.

lobe′lia, n., lobélie, f.

lob′ster, n., écrevisse de mer, f.; homard, m. — sauce; sauce homard, f.

lob′ule (lob′ioule), n., (anat.) lobule, m.

lo′cal (lô-), adj., local; topographique.

local′ity, n., localité, situation, f., endroit, m.; existence, f.

localiza′tion (-′aï′zé-), n., localisation, f.

lo′calize (lôcal′aï′ze), v.a., localiser.

lo′cally, adv., localement.

lo′cate (lô-), v.a., placer, établir, fixer.

loca′tion (lo-ké-), n., situation, f.; emplacement, placement, établissement, domicile, m.; (jur.) location, f.

loch (loke), n., (geog.) lac, m.

loch (loke) ou **lo′hock** (lô-hoke), n., (pharm.) looch, lok, m.

lo′chia (lo-ki-a), n.pl., (med.) lochies, f.pl.

lock, n., serrure; (of a canal) écluse; (of a fire-arm) platine, f., ressort, m.; (of a pond) bonde; (of hair) touffe, mèche, boucle, f.; (of wool) flocon, m. pl., cheveux, m.pl.; boucles de cheveux, f.pl. Dead—; impasse, m. — chamber; sas d'écluse, m. — keeper; éclusier, m. —out; fermeture (of workshops). Spring —; serrure à secret, f. — -up; (place of confinement) violon, m. Under — and key; sous clef, sous les verrous. Double —; serrure à double tour, f.

lock, v.a., fermer à clef; (print.) serrer; (step in marching) emboîter (le pas); (to clasp) serrer, presser; (a canal) écluser; (of wheels) accrocher; (with the drag) enrayer. To — in; enfermer, renfermer. To — any one out; fermer la porte à quelqu'un, (of workmen) renvoyer, fermer ses ateliers à. To — up; serrer, enfermer, tenir sous clef; (pers.) mettre au violon, mettre en prison, coffrer; conduire au dépôt; écrouer; (print.) serrer. To double —; fermer à double tour. To — the stable-door when the steed is stolen; (prov.) fermer l'écurie quand les chevaux sont dehors.

lock, v.n., fermer à clef; s'enfermer; (tech.) s'adapter.

lock′age (lok′èdje), n., écluses, f.pl.; péage d'écluse, m.

locked′-jaw (lok′te-djō) ou **lock′jaw** (-djō), n., (med.) tétanos, m.

lock′er, n., armoire, f.; placard, tiroir, coffre, m.

lock′et, n., (jewel) médaillon; fermoir, m.

lock′-gate, n., porte d'écluse, f.

lock′ram, n., toile grossière, f.

lock′smith (-smith), n., serrurier, m.

locomo′tion (lô-co-mô-), n., locomotion, f.

locomo′tive (lô-co-mô-), adj., mobile, locomotif.

locomo′tive (lô-co-mô-), n., locomotive, f.

lo′cust (lô-keuste), n., sauterelle, cigale, locuste, f.; (bot.) caroubier, m. —-tree; (bot.) faux acacia, robinier, f.

lode (lôde), n., filon, m.

lodge, n., maisonnette; loge; (of a stag) reposée; (of wild beasts) tanière; (of freemasons) loge, f. Hunting —; pied à terre, m.

lodge, v.a., loger; abriter; (to deposit) déposer; (to throw in) planter, enfoncer; (in the heart) implanter; (a complaint) déposer, porter; (an appeal) interjeter; (money) déposer.

lodge, v.n., loger, se loger, s'arrêter, se fixer. The ball —d in a hillock; la balle se logea dans un tertre. A spent ball —d in the folds of his black cravat; une balle morte s'arrêta dans les plis de sa cravate noire (Voltaire, Charles XII.).

lodg′er, n., locataire, m. and f.

lodg′ing, n., logis, logement, m.; chambre, f.; appartement, m. Furnished —s; chambres garnies, f.pl.; appartement meublé, m.sing. A night's —; logement pour la nuit. To let furnished —s; louer en garni. To live in furnished —s; loger en garni.

lodg′ing-house (-haouce), n., hôtel garni; logis, m. — keeper; propriétaire de maison garnie, m. and f.

lodg′ment (lodj′-), n., logement, (of cash) dépôt, m.

loft, n., étage; grenier, m.

loft′ily, adv., haut; (fig.) avec hauteur, pompeusement, fièrement, d'une manière sublime, avec sublimité.

loft′iness, n., élévation, f.; ordre élevé, m.; hauteur, fierté; pompe, sublimité, f.

loft′y, adj., haut, élevé, sublime; pompeux, fier, altier.

log (loghe), n., souche, bûche, solive, f.; (nav.) loch, m. To heave the —; jeter le loch.

log′arithm (-rithme), n., logarithme, m.

logarith′mic, logarithmet′ical, logarith′mic, ou logarith′mical (-rith-), adj., logarithmique.

log′-board (-bôrde), n., (nav.) table de loch, f.

log′book (-bouke), n., (nav.) livre de loch; journal de bord, m.

log′-cab′in, n., hutte au bois, f.

logged, adj., (nav.) engagé. Water—; engagé; rempli d'eau.

log′ger-head (-hède), n., sot, lourdaud, m., bûche, f. To fall, ou come, to —s; en venir aux mains; se prendre de querelle avec. To be at —; être aux prises aux, à couteaux tirés. To set at —; brouiller, mettre la discorde entre.

log′gerheaded (-hèd′-), adj., sot, lourd, stupide.

log′ic (lod′jike), n., logique, f.

log′ical, adj., logique; de la logique.

log′ically, adv., logiquement.

logi′cian (lod′jish′-), n., logicien, m.

log′man (log′-), n., porteur de bois; (in America) bûcheron, m.

logom′achy (-go′m′a-ki), n., logomachie, dispute de mots, f.

log′wood (-woude), n., campêche, bois de campêche, m.

loin (loïne), n., (of meat) longe, f. pl., (anat.) lombes, reins, m.pl.

loi′ter (loï-teur), v.n., tarder, traîner, muser, lambiner, flâner; (on the way) s'amuser en chemin. To — in the woods; flâner dans les bois.

loi′ter, v.a., perdre, gaspiller. To — away one's time; gaspiller son temps.

loi′terer, n., traînard, musard, flâneur, m.

loi′tering, n., négligence, flânerie, paresse, f.

loi′tering, adj., négligent, fainéant, paresseux, traînard, lambin.

loi′teringly, adv., en paresseux, en fainéant.

loll, v.n., s'étaler, s'étendre; se prélasser; se pencher, s'appuyer; (of the tongue) pendre.

loll, v.a., laisser pendre ; tirer.
Lol'lard, n., lollard ; sectateur de Wycliffe, m.
loll'ing, adj., étendu, penché, couché ; étalé (of the tongue) pendant.
lol'lipop, n., sucre d'orge, m.
Lon'doner, n., Londonien, m.
lone (lōne), adj., isolé, solitaire ; délaissé. V. **alone.**
lone'liness, n., solitude, f. ; isolement, m.
lone'ly, adj., solitaire ; isolé, délaissé.
lone'some (-seume), adj., solitaire.
lone'someness, n., solitude, f. ; ennui, m.
long (lo'gne), v.n., avoir bien envie **de** ; (imp.) tarder **de,** brûler d'envie **de** ; brûler **de.** I — to go there ; j'ai bien envie, ou il me tarde, d'y aller. To — for ; soupirer **après** ; avoir un grand désir **de.** We — to see the new play ; nous brûlons (ou il nous tarde, ou nous mourons d'envie) de voir la nouvelle pièce.
long, adj., long ; prolongé, allongé. Daddy — legs ; faucheur, faucheux, m. To be three feet — ; avoir trois pieds de long, être long de trois pieds. In the — run ; à la longue. — time ; longtemps, depuis longtemps, pendant longtemps. — tasseled ; aux longs glands. The — ; (Eng. Univ.) les vacances d'été, f.pl. The — and the short of the matter ; le court et le long de l'affaire. It is a — lane that has no turning ; (prov.) c'est un long jour qu'un jour sans pain ou tout à sa fin. Death will not be — in coming ; la mort ne tardera pas à venir.
long, adv., fort ; (of time) longtemps, longuement ; depuis longtemps ; pendant longtemps ; le long **de** ; durant. A — extended line ; une ligne fort étendue. How — have you been here ? combien de temps y a-t-il que vous êtes ici ? Have you been here — ? y a-t-il longtemps que vous êtes ici ? All night — ; tout le long de la nuit. Ere — ; bientôt, avant peu, dans peu, sous peu. — ago ; il y a longtemps, depuis longtemps. Not — ago ; il n'y a pas longtemps. All one's life — ; toute sa vie durant. Not — before ; peu de temps avant. Not — after ; peu de temps après. Before — ; avant peu, sous peu, bientôt. So — as ; tant que ; (since) du moment que. As — as ; aussi longtemps que. How — ; jusques à quand ?
longanim'ity, n., longanimité, f.
long'boat (-bôte), n., (nav.) chaloupe, f.
long'-bow, n., arc, m. To draw the — ; exagérer, blaguer ; gaber.
long'-dated, adj., (com.) à longue échéance.
longe (leu'n'dje), n., (man.) longe ; (fenc.) botte, f.
longe (leu'n'dje), v.n., (man.) mettre à la longe ; (fenc.) pousser une botte.
lon'ger, adj., plus long.
lon'ger, adv., plus longtemps, de plus, encore.
long-estab'lished (-ès-tab'lish'te), adj., établi depuis longtemps.
longe'val ou **longe'vous** (lon'-dji-), adj., qui vit longtemps.
longev'ity (-djè'v'-), n., longévité, f.
longe'-whip (leu'n'dj'houipe), n., (man.) chambrière, f.
long-forgot'ten, adj., oublié depuis longtemps.
long'-headed, adj., dolichocéphale ; (fig.) prudent, fin, rusé, à tête carrée.
long'-home', n., la dernière demeure, f.
long'ing (lo'gn'-), n., désir ardent, m. ; envie, passion, (physiol.) envie, f.
long'ingly (lo'gn'-), adv., avec ardeur ; passionnément.
long'ish (lo'gn'-), adj., passablement long, un peu long, longuet.
lon'gitude (lo'n-dji-tioude), n., longitude, f. — in ; (nav.) longitude arrivée. — by account ; longitude estimée. — by time-keeper ; longitude par le chronomètre. — by lunar observations ;

longitude observée. Board of — ; bureau des longitudes, m.
longitu'dinal (-dji-tiou-), adj., longitudinal.
longitu'dinally, adv., longitudinalement.
long'-legged (-lèg'de), adj., à longues jambes.
long'-lived (-laïv'de), adj., qui vit longtemps ; qui dure longtemps, de longue durée.
long'-lost, adj., perdu depuis longtemps.
long'-necked, adj., au long cou.
long'-nosed, adj., au long nez.
long'-saw, m., scie de scieur de long, f.
long'-sight'ed (-saït'-), adj., à longue vue ; qui a la vue longue ; (med.) presbyte. I am — ; j'ai la vue longue.
long'-sight'edness, n., vue longue ; presbytie, f.
long-suf'ferance (-seuf'-), n., patience, clémence, f.
long-suf'fering, n., longanimité, patience, f.
long-suf'fering, adj., endurant, patient.
long'-tailed, adj., à la queue longue.
long'ways (-wèze) ou **long'wise** (-waïze), adv., en long.
long'-wind'ed, adj., de longue haleine ; filandreux, traîné en longueur.
loo (lou), n., (card game) mouche, f. — table ; guéridon, m.
loo'bily (lou-), adj., niais, nigaud, gauche, maladroit.
loo'by (lou-), n., nigaud, niais, sot, m.
loof (loufe), n., (nav.) V. **luff.**
loof (loufe), v.n., (nav.) V. **luff.**
look (louke), n., regard, air, m. ; apparence, mine, f. ; coup d'œil, m. To give a — in ; faire une petite visite ; entrer en passant. Good — s ; bonne mine, f.sing. To give a — over ; jeter un regard, ou un coup d'œil, sur. To have a good — ; regarder bien. To take a last — at ; jeter un dernier regard sur. I mean to have a — in ; j'entends l'essayer, ou en faire l'essai ; ou (fam.) j'entends avoir ma part du gâteau. To give a — to ; avoir l'œil sur. One must not hang a man for his — s ; il ne faut pas juger les gens sur la mine. By the — of him ; à le voir. By the — of it ; à ce qu'il paraît.
look, v.a.n., regarder, sembler, (like) avoir l'air, paraître. To — to the north, the south ; être exposé au nord, au sud. To — back upon ; se souvenir de ; se reporter en arrière ; faire un retour sur. To — down ; contenir par des regards ; dompter par des regards. To — out ; chercher ; tâcher de trouver. To — over ; jeter un coup d'œil sur ; parcourir des yeux ; (a lesson) repasser ; (any one's shoulder) regarder par dessus les épaules. To — any one in the face ; regarder quelqu'un en face. To — about ; regarder autour de soi ; avoir l'œil ouvert. To — after ; regarder à ; chercher ; soigner ; veiller à. To — at ; regarder ; considérer, envisager. To — away ; détourner ses regards. To — back ; regarder en arrière ; (fig.) jeter un regard rétrospectif. To — down ; regarder en bas ; baisser les yeux. To — for ; chercher ; rechercher ; aller à la recherche **de** ; (to expect) s'attendre **à.** To — forward ; regarder devant soi ; (fig.) attendre avec impatience. To — forward to ; s'attendre **à** ; se promettre, espérer. To — in ; faire une petite visite, entrer en passant, dire un petit bonjour **à.** To — into ; regarder **dans** ; (fig.) examiner, s'informer **de.** To — on ; regarder ; être, ou rester, spectateur ; considérer. To — out upon ; donner **sur** ; (of aspect) donner sur, avoir voie **sur.** To — over ; chercher **dans** ; regarder **par dessus** ; (fig.) fermer les yeux **sur.** To — to ; veiller **à** ; avoir soin **de** ; prendre garde **à** ; s'adresser **à** ; surveiller ; avoir l'œil **sur.** To — through ; regarder **à travers** ; parcourir. To — up ; regarder en haut ; lever les yeux ; relever la tête ; (com.) être en voie de hausse. To — any one up ; aller voir quelqu'un.

To — **anything up** ; *chercher quelque chose.* To — **up to** ; *regarder ; mettre son espoir en* ; *compter* **sur** ; *se reposer* **sur.** To — **down upon any one** ; *regarder quelqu'un du haut en bas* ; *toiser quelqu'un.* To — **ill** ; *avoir mauvaise mine* ; *avoir l'air malade.* That — **s ill** ; *cela a mauvaise apparence, cela fait mauvais effet.* To — **well** ; *avoir bonne mine* ; *avoir l'air bien portant* ; (of things) *avoir une belle apparence, faire bon effet.* To — **like** ; *avoir l'air* **de** ; *ressembler* **à** ; *être ressemblant.* Our house — **s out on the river** ; *notre maison donne sur la rivière.* —**sharp** ; *dépêchez-vous.* To — **out** ; *être sur ses gardes* ; *avoir l'œil au guet* ; (milit.) *être en observation, en sentinelle* ; (nav.) *être en vigie.* To — **out of** ; *regarder* **par.** To — **upon** ; *regarder* ; *considérer.* They — **happy** ; *ils ont l'air heureux.* To — **very grave** ; *avoir la mine très grave.* Just to see how you'd — ; *juste pour voir quelle mine vous feriez.* How does it —? *quel effet cela fait-il ?* To — **askance** ; *regarder de travers, d'un œil méfiant.* The shopman — **ed over his books for the entry** ; *le commis de magasin chercha l'article dans ses livres.* He — **ed black at us** ; *il nous a fait la mine.* — **out for squalls** ; *attendez-vous à des bourrasques.* — **here!** *dites donc! gare les bombes!*

looked' for, *adj.,* attendu.

look'er(-on), *n.,* spectateur, témoin, assistant, *m.*

look'ing, *adj.,* (in compounds) à l'air . . ., à la mine . . . Dirty — ; *sale.* Ill — ; *laid, disgracié, peu avenant* ; *à mauvaise mine.*

look'ing-glass (-glâce), *n.,* miroir, *m.* ; glace, *f.*

look'-out (-aoute), *n.,* vue, *f.* ; guet, *m.* ; (nav.) découverte, vigie, *f.* To keep a — ; *avoir l'œil au guet* ; *veiller.* To keep a sharp — ; *guetter,* ou *observer, d'un œil attentif* ; *veiller attentivement.*

loom (loume), *n.,* métier de tisserand, métier à tisser ; (of an oar) manche, *m.*

loom, *v.n.,* paraître ; s'élever ; paraître sur l'horizon, se dessiner **sur.** The Apennines — afar off ; *les Apennines paraissent au loin sur l'horizon.*

loom'ing, *n.,* mirage, *m.*

loon (loune), *n.,* coquin, drôle, chenapan, *m.* ; coquine, drôlesse, *f.* ; (orni.) grand plongeon, *m.*

loop (loupe), *n.,* bride, *f.* ; (tech.) tenon; nœud coulant, *m.*

loop'hole (-hôl), *n.,* trou, *m.* ; ouverture ; (in a ship, in a wall) meurtrière ; (fig.) échappatoire, défaite, *f.* ; faux-fuyant, *m.*

loop'holed (-hôld), *adj.,* troué ; à meurtrières.

loose (louce), *n.,* liberté, licence, *f.* On the — ; *dissolu, dissipé.* To give a — to ; *donner carte blanche* **à,** *donner un libre cours* **à,** *s'abandonner* **à,** *se livrer* **à.**

loose (louce), *adj.,* délié, détaché, défait ; ample ; (of clothes) peu serré ; qui n'est pas ferme ; (fig.) (of morals) relâché, lâche ; large, ample ; vague, peu rigide, décousu, sans liaison ; (b.s.) licencieux, libre. — cash ; *monnaie, f.* He is a — fish ; *c'est un homme déréglé.* To set, ou let, — ; *lâcher, mettre en liberté* ; (fig.) *donner cours* **à** ; *déchaîner.* To get — ; *se détacher, s'échapper* ; (of teeth) *branler.*

loose (louce), *v.a.,* détacher ; délier ; relâcher ; délivrer, lâcher, (fig.) déchaîner.

loose'ly, *adv.,* librement ; lâchement ; nonchalamment ; négligemment ; vaguement ; (b.s.) licencieusement.

loo'sen (lous's'n), *v.a.,* détendre, lâcher, relâcher, délier ; détacher ; défaire ; desserrer ; ébranler.

loose'ness, *n.,* état desserré ; état détendu ; relâchement ; caractère vague ; caractère lâche, *m.* ; (b.s.) licence, *f.* ; (med.) dévoiement, cours de ventre, *m.*

loos'ening, *n.,* **desserrage, m., desserre** ; (fig.) relâchement, *f.*

loot, *v.a.,* piller, saccager.

loot, loot'ing, *n.,* pillage, *m.*

lop (lope), *n.,* élagage, ébranchement, *m.*

lop, *v.a.,* élaguer, émonder, ébrancher.

lop'-eared, *adj.,* aux oreilles pendantes ; (horses) oreillard.

lop'pard, *n.,* (tree) têtard, *m.*

lop'per, *v.n.,* (milk) se cailler. —ed milk ; *lait caillé, m.*

lop'per, *n.,* élagueur, *m.*

lop'-sided (-çaïd'-), *adj.,* qui a un côté plus lourd que l'autre.

loqua'cious (lo-kwé-), *adj.,* loquace.

loquac'ity (-kwass'-), *n.,* loquacité, *f.*

lord (lorde), *n.,* seigneur ; maître ; (title) lord, *m.* My — ; (to a prince of the royal blood, to a bishop) *Monseigneur* ; (to a nobleman) *Monsieur, Milord.* The —'s prayer ; *l'oraison dominicale, f.* ; *pater, m.* Our — ; *notre Seigneur, m.* —'s Supper ; *la Cène, f.* —'s day ; dimanche, *m.* —s and ladies ; (bot.) *gouet* ; *pied-de-veau, m.* The year of our — ; *l'an de grâce, m.* —lieutenant ; *vice-roi, m.* —lieutenancy, *vice-royauté, f.*

lord, *v.n.,* dominer, faire le maître. To — it over any one ; *tyranniser quelqu'un.*

lord'like (-laïke), *adj.,* de seigneur ; noble.

lord'liness, *n.,* dignité ; hauteur, *f.* ; orgueil, *m.*

lord'ling, *n.,* petit seigneur, hobereau, *m.*

lord'ly, *adj.,* de seigneur ; noble ; arrogant, hautain, altier, fier. [avec fierté.

lord'ly, *adv.,* en seigneur ; avec arrogance ;

lord'ship, *n.,* pouvoir, *m.* ; seigneurie, *f.* Your — ; *Monseigneur.*

lore (lôre), *n.,* **savoir, m.** ; science, doctrine, instruction, *f.*

lor'icate, *v.a.,* enduire.

lorica'tion, *n.,* action d'enduire, *f.*

lor'imer, *n.,* (ant.) sellier, harnacheur, *m.*

lo'riot, *n.,* (orni.) loriot, *m.*

los'able (louz'a-b'l), *adj.,* perdable.

lose (louze), *v.a.* and *n.,* (*preterit* and *past part.,* Lost) perdre. To — in people's estimation ; *baisser dans l'estime publique.* To make any one — anything ; *faire perdre quelque chose à quelqu'un.* To — by ; *perdre* **à** ; (in value) *perdre de sa valeur.* To — one's temper ; *s'emporter.* To — one's head ; (pop.) *perdre la boule.* To — one's way ; *s'égarer.* To be lost at sea ; *périr dans un naufrage.* The ship was lost on the coast of Africa ; *le vaisseau a péri sur la côte d'Afrique.* To — sight of ; *perdre de vue.*

los'er (louz'eur), *n.,* (at play) perdant, *m.* To be a — ; *être en perte.* To be a — by it ; *y perdre.*

loss, *n.,* perte, *f.* ; (hunt.) défaut, *m.* ; déperdition ; (of voice) extinction. At a — ; *dans l'embarras* ; *embarrassé* ; (to sell) *à perte* ; (hunt.) *en défaut.* To be at a — to ; *être en peine* **de.** To be at a — what to do ; *ne savoir que faire.* To bear a — ; *faire une perte.* To make good a — ; *réparer une perte.*

lost, *part.adj.,* perdu ; déchu ; (strayed) égaré ; (ruined) abîmé. To be — in public esteem ; *être déchu dans l'estime du public.*

lot, *n.,* sort, destin, *m.,* part, quote-part, destinée ; (quantity) quantité, grande quantité, *f.* ; (of persons) tas ; (at a sale) lot, *m.* ; (com.) partie, *f.* To draw ou cast — s ; *tirer au sort.* By — ; *par le sort* ; *au sort.* To fall to one's — ; *arriver* **à** *quelqu'un* ; *échoir* **à** ou *tomber en partage* **à.** To cast in one's — with — ; *partager la fortune de quelqu'un.* All the — of you ; *tous tant que vous êtes.* Bad — ; *tas de gredins, m.* ; *maudite engeance, f.* A — of good that will do you ; *cela ne vous rendra pas la jambe mieux faite.*

lot, v.a., assigner ; lotir.

lote (lôte), n., (bot.) jujubier ; lotus, lotos, m. ; (ich.) lotte, f.

lo'tion (lô-), n., lotion, f.

lot'tery, n., loterie, f. It is all a —; c'est une affaire de hasard ; c'est une loterie.

lot'ting, n., (com.) lotissement, m.

loud (laoude), adj., haut ; élevé, éclatant ; fort, grand ; bruyant, retentissant ; (b.s.) tapageur. In a — voice ; à haute voix.

loud'ly, adv., haut ; fort ; hautement, à haute voix ; avec grand bruit ; d'une manière éclatante ; à grands cris.

loud'ness, n., force, f. ; bruit ; retentissement ; éclat, m., (fig.) suffisance, f., ton tranchant, m.

lounge (laou'n'dje), v.n., badauder, flâner, rôder ; vivre dans la paresse ; être couché, être étendu. To — away the time ; passer le temps en flânant. To — about ; battre le pavé.

lounge, n., (stroll) promenade ; (gait) démarche nonchalante, f. ; (place) promenoir, rendez-vous ; (couch) sofa, m.

loun'ger, n., badaud, flâneur, m.

loun'ging-chair (-tshère), n., bergère ; chaise longue, f.

louse (laouce), n., (lice) pou, m.

louse'wort (laouss'weurte), n., (bot.) pédiculaire ; herbe aux poux, f.

lous'ily (laouz²-), adv., en pouilleux.

lous'iness (laouz'-), n., état pouilleux ; (bot.) état d'une plante attaquée par les pucerons, m.

lous'y (laouz'-), adj., pouilleux ; (bot.) couvert de pucerons ; (fig.) bas, vil, méprisable.

lout (laoute), n., rustre, benêt, butor, rustaud, m.

lout'ish, adj., benêt, rustre.

lout'ishly, adv., en benêt, en rustre.

lov'able (leuv'a-b'l), adj., digne d'être aimé ; aimable.

lov'age (leuv'adje), n., (bot.) angélique à feuilles d'ache, f.

love (leuve), v.a., aimer, chérir, affectionner.

love (leuve), n., amour, m. ; amitié, affection, sympathie, f. ; (term of endearment) amour, ami, m., amie, f. For —; par amour. To play for —; jouer pour rien, pour le plaisir de jouer, pour son plaisir, pour l'honneur. To be in —; être amoureux. To be in — with ; être amoureux de, être épris de. To make — to ; faire la cour à, conter fleurette à. To fall in — with ; devenir amoureux de, devenir épris de. To give one's — to ; faire ses amitiés à. — match ; mariage d'inclination, m. Labor of —; tâche, ou entreprise, sans espoir de récompense, f. My — to all ; mes amitiés à tous. True — dies hard ; (prov.) qui aime bien, tard oublie. — me, — my dog ; qui aime Bertrand, aime son chien. — laughs at locksmiths ; l'amour force toutes les serrures.

love'-affair, n., amourette, f.

love'-apple (-ap'p'l), n., tomate ; pomme d'amour, f.

love'-knot (-note), n., lacs d'amour, nœud, m.

love'less, adj., sans amour ; insensible.

love'-letter (-let'teur), n., billet doux, poulet, m.

love'lily, adv., avec amabilité, délicieusement.

love'liness, n., amabilité ; beauté, nature ravissante, f., charme, m.

love'lorn, adj., abandonnée de son amant ; abandonné de son amante ; délaissé.

love'ly, adj., aimable, charmant, ravissant, séduisant, gracieux, joli, beau ; digne d'amour.

love'-making (-mék'-), n., cour, f.

love'-potion (-pô-), n., philtre, m.

lov'er, n., amant, m., amante, f. ; ami, m., amie, f. ; amoureux ; amateur, m.

love'-secret (-sî-krète), n., secret d'amour, m.

love'sick, adj., malade d'amour.

love'-sickness, n., langueur amoureuse, f.

love'song, n., chanson d'amour, f. ; chansonnette, romance, f.

love'suit (-sioute), n., cour, f. ; assiduités, f.pl.

love'-tale (-téle), n., histoire galante, f., roman, m., fleurette, f.

love'-thought (-thôte), n., pensée d'amour ; pensée amoureuse, f.

love'-token, n., gage d'amour, m.

love'trick, n., amourette, f.

lov'ing, adj., aimant, affectueux, qui aime ; affectionné ; (of things) d'amour ; affectueux. — cup ; coupe de l'amitié, f.

lov'ing-kind'ness (-kaï'n'd'-), n., bonté, miséricorde, f.

lov'ingly, adv., avec amour ; tendrement, affectueusement.

low (lô), adj., bas ; peu élevé ; (of valleys) profond, bas, (of bows) profond ; petit ; (of diet) pauvre, peu substantiel ; (of dress) décolleté ; (of company) mal composé ; mauvais, faible ; commun, canaille ; vulgaire ; trivial ; (of fever) lent ; (in spirits) triste, abattu. — bodice ; corsage décolleté, m. — pressure, basse pression, f. In a — voice ; d'une voix faible ; à voix basse. To bring —; affaiblir ; (fig.) abattre, humilier. To lay —; abattre, coucher par terre ; ensevelir. To lie —; (fig.) attendre son occasion ; reposer ; être enseveli. My funds are —; les eaux sont basses chez moi. To get, ou run, —; baisser.

low, adv., bas ; profondément ; à voix basse ; à bas prix. — sized ; de petite taille.

low, v.n., beugler, mugir.

low'-born, adj., de basse naissance ou extraction.

low'-bred (-brède), adj., mal élevé ; vulgaire.

low'-built, adj., (nav.) de bas bord.

low'-crowned, adj., petit ; bas de forme (of hats).

low'er (lô-eur), adj., plus bas ; inférieur ; (geog.) bas, inférieur. — down ; plus bas.

low'er (laou-eur), v.n., (to frown) froncer les sourcils, se refrogner ; (of the weather) s'assombrir, s'obscurcir, se couvrir ; (of clouds) (fig.) s'amonceler, menacer. The sky —s ; le temps se couvre.

low'er (lô-eur), v.a., baisser, abaisser ; descendre ; (to humiliate) rabaisser, humilier, ravaler ; (to diminish) diminuer, affaiblir ; (com.) baisser. To — oneself ; s'abaisser jusqu'à ; se dégrader, se ravaler.

low'er-class, n., basse classe, f., peuple, m.

low'er-end, n., le bas bout, m.

low'ering (lô-eur'-), n., abaissement, m. ; diminution, f.

low'ering (laou-eur'-), adj., couvert, sombre ; menaçant, refrogné, rechigné. — look ; air refrogné, m. — weather ; temps couvert, m.

low'eringly (laou-eur'-), adv., d'un air refrogné, tristement ; d'une manière sombre, menaçante.

low'ermost (lô-eur-môste) ou **low'est** (lô-èste), adj., le plus bas, dernier.

low'ery (laou-euri), adj., nébuleux, triste ; sombre.

low'ing (lô'igne), n., mugissement, beuglement, m.

low'land (lô-), n., pays bas ; terrain bas, basfond, m. ; plaine, f. —er ; habitant des plaines, m. The Lowlands (of Scotland) ; les basses terres, f.pl.

low'liness (lô-), n., humilité ; bassesse, petitesse, f.

low'ly (lô-), adj., humble ; bas, vil.

low'ly (lô-), adv., humblement, bassement.

low'-mass, n., messe basse, f.

low'ness (lô-nèce), n., situation basse ; petitesse ; peu de profondeur ; (mus.) gravité ; (weakness) faiblesse ; (of funds) dépression, f. ; (of temperature) abaissement ; (of spirits) abattement, *m.;* (humility) humilité ; (vulgarity) vulgarité, bassesse, *f.* The — of the price ; *le bas prix.*

low'-priced' (-praïs'te), *adj.,* à bas prix, à bon marché.

low'-spir'ited, *adj.,* abattu, triste, découragé.

low'-spir'itedness, *n.,* tristesse, mélancolie, *f.*

Low'-Sunday, *n.,* dimanche de la Quasimodo, *m.*

low'-wa'ter (-wō-), *n.,* marée basse, *f.* — mark ; *étiage, niveau des basses eaux, m.*

loy'al (loïal), *adj.,* attaché au gouvernement, au souverain ; fidèle, loyal.

loy'alist, *n.,* personne attachée au gouvernement, au souverain, *f.*

loy'ally, *adv.,* fidèlement.

loy'alty, *n.,* attachement au gouvernement, au souverain, *m. ;* fidélité, (honesty) loyauté, *f.*

loz'enge (loz'è'n'dje), *n.,* pastille ; (pharm.) tablette, pastille, *f. ;* (geom., her.) losange, *m.*

loz'enged (-'è'n'dj'de), *adj.,* en losange.

lub'ber (leub'-), *n.,* lourdaud, rustre, manant, paltoquet ; (nav.) marin d'eau douce, *m.*

lub'berly, *adj.,* grossier, maladroit, gauche, lourd.

lub'berly, *adv.,* en lourdaud ; grossièrement.

lu'bric *ou* **lu'brical** (lou-), *adj.,* (slippery) glissant ; (unsteady) inconstant ; (lewd) lubrique.

lu'bricant (lou-), *n.,* lubrifiant, *f.*

lu'bricate (lou-), *v.a.,* lubrifier ; adoucir.

lubric'ity (lou-), *n.,* nature glissante ; inconstance ; lubricité, *f.*

lubrifac'tion (lou-bri-fak-) *ou* **lubrifica'tion** (-fi-ké-), *n.,* lubrification, *f.*

luce (liouce), *n.,* (ich.) brochet, *m.*

lucern' (lou-), *n.,* (bot.) luzerne, *f.*

lu'cid (lou-), *adj.,* lucide ; lumineux ; limpide, transparent. — interval ; *bon intervalle ; intervalle lucide, moment lucide, m.*

lu'cidly, *adv.,* lucidement, clairement.

lu'cidness *ou* **lucid'ity,** *n.,* transparence, limpidité, lucidité, clarté, *f. ;* éclat, *m.*

Lu'cifer (lou-), *n.,* (astron.) Lucifer, *m. ;* (match) allumette chimique, *f.*

Lucife'rian, *adj.,* de Lucifer.

lucif'erous, *adj.,* lucifère.

luck (leuke), *n.,* hasard ; bonheur, *m. ;* fortune, chance, *f.* Good— ; *bonne fortune, bonne chance, f. ; bonheur, m.* Ill— ; *mauvaise fortune, f.; malheur ;* (game) guignon, *m.* Good — to you ! *bonne chance !* To bring good — ; *porter bonheur.* To have a run of — ; *être en veine ; avoir un succès fou.* To be in —'s way ; *avoir du bonheur.* By good— ; *par bonheur.* By ill— ; *par malheur.* Pot— ; *la fortune du pot, f.*

luck'ily, *adv.,* heureusement, par bonheur.

luck'iness, *n.,* bonheur, *m.*

luck'less, *adj.,* malheureux, infortuné.

luck'y, *adj.,* heureux ; (of things) heureux, propice, favorable. To be — ; *avoir du bonheur, de la chance.*

lu'crative (lou-), *adj.,* lucratif.

lu'cratively, *adv.,* d'une manière lucrative, lucrativement.

lu'cre (lou-keur), *n.,* lucre, *m.*

lu'dicrous (lou-), *adj.,* plaisant, risible, comique, ridicule.

lu'dicrously, *adv.,* plaisamment, risiblement, comiquement.

lu'dicrousness, *n.,* plaisant, burlesque, *m. ;* plaisanterie, *f. ;* ridicule, *m.*

luff (leufe), *v.n.,* (nav.) venir au lof, lofer.

luff, *n.,* (nav.) lof, *m.*

lug, *v.a.,* traîner ; tirer ; (children) trimbaler. To — out ; *tirer, tirer dehors ; faire sortir ;* (a sword) *dégainer, mettre flamberge au vent.* To — away ; *entraîner, enlever de force.* To — in ; *faire entrer de force ;* (fig.) *introduire, faire entrer.*

lug'gage (leug'ghèdje), *n.,* bagage ; attirail, *m. ;* bagages, effets, *m.pl.* — van ; *voiture de bagages, f. ;* (railways) *wagon de bagages, m.* — office ; *bureau des bagages, m.* — porter ; *facteur, m.* —, *ou* goods, *ou* freight, train ; *train de marchandises, m.* — ticket ; *billet,* ou *bulletin, de bagages, m.*

lug'ger (leug'gheur), *n.,* (nav.) lougre ; chasse-marée, *m.*

lug'-sail, *n.,* voile de fortune, *f.*

lugu'brious (lou-ghiou-), *a:'j.,* lugubre.

lug'-worm, *n.,* laiche, ver rouge, *m.*

luke'warm (louk'wôrme), *adj.,* tiède ; (fig.) peu zélé. To get — ; *s'attiédir.*

luke'warmly, *adv.,* tièdement, avec tiédeur, avec peu de zèle.

luke'warmness, *n.,* tiédeur, *f. ;* manque de zèle.

lull (leule), *v.a.,* endormir ; bercer ; assoupir ; calmer. To — to sleep ; *endormir.* To — with false hopes ; *bercer de vaines espérances.*

lull, *v.n.,* se calmer, s'apaiser.

lull, *n.,* calmant ; (temporary calming down) moment de calme, *m. ;* intervalle de beau temps ; (nav.) accalmie, *f.*

lul'laby (leul'la-baïe), *n.,* berceuse, *f.*

lull'ing (leul'-), *adj.,* endormant, calmant.

lumba'go (leu'm'bé-go), *n.,* (med.) lumbago, *m. ;* courbature, *f.*

lum'bar (leu'm'-), *adj.,* (anat.) lombaire.

lum'ber (leu'm'-), *n.,* gros meubles, *m. ;* vieilleries, *f.pl. ;* rebut, fatras, (timber) bois de charpente, *m.*

lum'ber, *v.a.,* entasser sans ordre ; remplir de fatras.

lum'ber, *v.n.,* se traîner lourdement.

lum'ber-place (-pléce), **lum'ber-room** (-roume), *n.,* lieu, *m. ;* chambre de décharge, *f. ;* grenier ; hangar, *m.*

lum'bering, *n.,* action d'entasser sans ordre.

lum'bering, *adj.,* encombrant, lourd, pesant.

lu'minary (lou-), *n.,* corps lumineux ; luminaire ; flambeau, *m. ;* (fig.) illustration, *f.*

lu'minous (lou-), *adj.,* lumineux.

lu'minously, *adv.,* d'une manière lumineuse ; lumineusement.

lu'minousness, *n.,* luminosité ; clarté ; lucidité, *f.*

lump (leu'm'pe), *n.,* masse, *f. ;* morceau ; bloc ; monceau, tas, paquet, *m.* —sugar ; *sucre en pain, m.* — of sugar ; *morceau de sucre.* In the — ; *en gros, en bloc.* In one — ; *en tas.* A — sum ; *somme payée en une fois, f.*

lump, *v.a.,* mettre en bloc ; mettre en masse ; réunir ensemble. If he does not like it, he may — it; *si cela ne lui plaît pas, qu'il s'arrange.* —ed together ; *en bloc* (V. Hugo).

lump'er, *n.,* ouvrier déchargeur du port, *m.*

lump'ing, *adj.,* gros ; pesant.

lump'ish, *adj.,* gros, épais, lourd, grossier.

lump'ishly, *adv.,* lourdement ; grossièrement.

lump'ishness, *n.,* lourdeur ; grossièreté, *f.*

lump'y, *adj.,* grumeleux ; plein de grumeaux, en petites masses.

lu'nacy (liou-), *n.,* folie, démence ; aliénation mentale, *f.* Commission of — ; *conseil de famille, m. ; jury d'examen pour cas d'aliénation mentale, m.*

lu'nar, lu'nary (lou-), *adj.,* lunaire ; en forme de lune ; de la lune. — caustic ; *pierre infernale, f. ; nitrate d'argent, m.*

luna'rian (lou-), *n.,* habitant de la lune, *m.*

lu'nate *ou* **lu'nated** (lou-), *adj.,* en demi-lune.

lu'natic (lou-), *adj.,* de fou, d'aliéné ; (Bible) lunatique.

lu'natic (lou-), *n.,* aliéné, *m.,* aliénée, *f. ;* fou, *m.,* folle, *f. ;* (Bible) lunatique, *m.* — asylum ; *hospice d'aliénés, m. ; petites maisons, f.pl.*

luna'tion (lou-né-), *n.*, lunaison, *f.*

lunch (leu'n'sh) *ou* **lunch'eon** (leu'n'sh'eune), *n.*, second déjeuner, goûter ; lunch, *m.* — time; *heure du déjeuner, f.*

lunch, *v.n.*, faire son second déjeuner ; goûter ; luncher. —ing rooms ; *café-restaurant, m.*

lunette' (lou-), *n.*, lunette, *f.*

lung (leu'gne), *n.*, poumon, (of the calf, etc.) mou, *m.*

lunge (leu'n'dje), *n.*, (fenc.) botte, *f.*

lunge, *v.n.*, (fenc.) porter une botte.

lung'wort (-weurte), *n.*, (bot.) pulmonaire ; épervière des murailles, *f.*

lu'niform (lou-), *adj.*, en lune ; luniforme.

luniso'lar (lou-ni-cô-), *adj.*, luni-solaire.

lunt (leu'n'te), *n.*, (artil.) mèche, *f.*

lu'pine (lou-pine), *n.*, (bot.) lupin, *m.*

lu'pus, *n.*, lupus, *m.*

lurch (leurtshe), *n.*, embarras, *m. ;* (at trick-track) bredouille, partie double, (nav.) embardée, *f.* To leave in the — ; *faire faux bond* à ; *planter là ; laisser dans l'embarras.* To give a — ; (of a ship) *embarder.*

lurch (leurtshe), *v.n.*, jouer de ruse.

lurch'er, *n.*, (dog) chien qui guette le gibier, *f.*

lure (lioure), *n.*, leurre, appât, *m. ;* amorce, *f.*

lure (lioure), *v.a.*, leurrer, amorcer, attirer.

lu'rid (liou-), *adj.*, sombre, blafard ; lugubre ; d'une couleur jaune pâle *ou* rouge.

lurk (leurke), *v.n.*, être aux aguets ; être en embuscade ; être caché, se tenir caché ; se cacher ; couver.

lurk'er, *n.*, personne aux aguets, personne en embuscade, personne qui se cache, *f.*

lurk'ing, *adj.*, d'embuscade ; aux aguets.

lurk'ing (leurk'-), *n.*, aguets, *m.pl. ;* embuscade, *f.*

lurk'ing-place, *n.*, embuscade ; cachette, *f.*

lus'cious (leush'eusse), *adj.*, mielleux, très sucré ; succulent ; délicieux ; (wine) liquoreux.

lus'ciously, *adv.*, avec douceur ; délicieusement.

lus'ciousness, *n.*, nature succulente ; fadeur ; excessive douceur ; (of wine) saveur, *f.*

lust (leuste), *n.*, désir, *m.*, convoitise, impudicité, luxure, *f.*

lust (leuste), *v.n.*, convoiter ; désirer immodérément. To — after ; *convoiter, désirer avec passion ; avoir soif* de.

lus'ter *ou* **-tre** (leus'teur), *n.*, (gloss) lustre, brillant; (chandelier) lustre, candélabre ; (space of time) lustre; (fig.) lustre, éclat, *m.*, splendeur, *f.*

lust'ful (-foule), *adj.*, convoiteux, impudique, lascif, luxurieux.

lust'fully, *adv.*, avec convoitise, impudiquement ; avec luxure.

lust'ily (leust'-), *adv.*, vigoureusement, fort et ferme.

lust'iness, *n.*, vigueur, *f.*

lust'ing (leust'-) (ant.), *n.* V. lust.

lus'tral *ou* **lus'trical** (leus-), *adj.*, lustral.

lustra'tion (leus-tré-), *n.*, lustration, *f.*

lus'tring (leus'-), *n.*, (glossy silk) taffetas, *m.*, lustrine, *f.*

lus'trous (leus'-), *adj.*, brillant, lustré.

lust'y (leust'i), *adj.*, vigoureux, robuste, fort; copieux.

lute (loute), *n.*, (mus.) luth; (chem.) lut, *m.*

lute (loute), *v.a.*, (chem.) luter.

lute'-maker (-mék'-), *n.*, luthier, *m.*

Lu'theran (lou-theur-), *adj.*, luthérien.

Lu'theran (lou-theur-), *n.*, luthérien, *m.*

Lu'theranism (lou-theur'a'n'iz'me), *n.*, luthéranisme, *m.*

lu'ting (lout'-), *n.*, (chem.). V. lute.

lu'tist (lout'-), *n.*, joueur de luth, *m.*

lux *ou* **lux'ate** (leux'-), *v.a.*, luxer.

luxa'tion (leuks'é-), *n.*, luxation, *f.*

luxu'riance *ou* **luxu'riancy** (leux'ziou-), *n.*, exubérance, surabondance, luxuriance, *f.*

luxu'riant (leux'ziou-), *adj.*, exubérant, surabondant, fort riche, luxuriant.

luxu'riantly (leux'ziou-), *adv.*, avec exubérance; avec grande abondance ; richement, voluptueusement.

luxu'riate (leux'ziou-), *v.n.*, croître en abondance ; être en pleine fertilité, vivre dans l'abondance ; s'abandonner à, se livrer avec délices à, nager dans, se plaire dans (with article), en (without article). To — in; *se livrer avec abandon* à.

luxu'rious (leuks'iou-), *adj.*, de luxe, somptueux ; luxueux ; ami du luxe ; adonné au luxe ; voluptueux, luxurieux.

luxu'riously (leuks'iou-), *adv.*, avec luxe ; somptueusement ; voluptueusement ; luxurieusement.

luxu'riousness (leuks'iou-), *n.*, luxe, *m. ;* luxure, volupté, *f.*

lux'ury (leuks'iou-ri), *n.*, luxe, *m. ;* élégance, somptuosité ; volupté, luxure, *f. ;* (dainty) régal, fin morceau ; (superfluity) objet de luxe, *m.*

lyce'um (laï-cî-), *n.*, lycée, *m.*

Lyd'ian, *adj.*, lydien.

lye (laïe), *n.*, lessive, *f.* —washing; *lessive, f.*

lye'-trough (-trofe), *n.*, baquet à lessive, *m.*

ly'ing, *pres. part.* of To. To be — about ; *traîner.* To be — still ; *se reposer.*

ly'ing (laï'igne), *n.*, mensonge, *m.*

ly'ing (laï'igne), *adj.*, menteur ; (of things) mensonger.

ly'ing-in, *n.*, *sing.*, couches, *f.pl.* — hospital ; *hospice pour les femmes en couches ; hospice de la maternité, m.*

ly'ingly, *adv.*, mensongeusement.

ly'ing to (laï'ign'tou), *part.*, (nav.) en panne.

lymph (li'm'fe), *n.*, lymphe, *f. ;* vaccin, *m.*

lymphat'ic (-fat'-), *adj.*, lymphatique.

lymphat'ic, *n.*, vaisseau lymphatique, *m.*

lynch, *n.*, lynch, *m.* — law; *loi de Lynch, f.*

lynch, *v.a.*, exécuter sommairement.

lynch'ing, *n.*, exécution sommaire, *m.*

lynx (lign'kse), *n.*, lynx, *m.*

lynx'-eyed (-aïe'de), *adj.*, aux yeux de lynx.

lyre (laïeur), *n.*, lyre, *f.*

lyr'ic *ou* **lyr'ical** (lir'-), *adj.*, lyrique.

lyr'ic, *n.*, lyrique ; poème lyrique, *m.*

lyr'icism (-ciz'me), *n.*, ouvrage lyrique, *m.*

lyr'ist (laïeur'-), *n.*, joueur de lyre, *m.*

M

m, treizième lettre de l'alphabet, *m.f.*

mab, *n.*, Mab, reine des fées ; (b.s.) saligaude, salope, *f.*

macad'am, *n.*, macadam, *m.*

macad'amize (-'aïze), *v.a.*, macadamiser.

macaro'ni (-rô-), *n.*, macaroni; (fam.) (fop) fat, petit-maître, *m.*

macaron'ic, *adj.*, macaronique.

macaron'ic, *n.*, (piece of verse) macaronée, *f.*

macaroon' (-roune), *n.*, macaron, *m.*

macaw'-tree (-cô-trî), *n.*, cocotier du Brésil, *m.*

mace (méce), *n. ;* (staff) masse, *f. ;* (of the nutmeg) macis, *m. ;* (earnings in convict prisons) masse, *f.* (V. Hugo).

mace'-bear'er (-bèr'-), *n.*, massier, bedeau, *m.*, (univ.) appariteur, *m.*

ma'cerate, *v.a.*, amaigrir ; macérer.

macera'tion (-'eur'é-), *n.*, amaigrissement, *m. ;* macération, *f.*

Machiave'lian (mak'-), *adj.*, machiavélique.

Mach'iavelism, *n.*, machiavélisme, *m.*

machicola'tion (matsh'i-co-lé-), *n.*, (fort.) mâchicoulis, *m.*

mach'inate, *v.a.*, machiner, tramer.

machina'tion (mak'i-né-), *n.*, machination, *f.*

mach'inator (mak'i-né-), *n.*, machinateur, *m.*

machine' (ma-shîne), *n.*, machine ; mécanique, *f. ;* instrument ; (poet.) merve'lleux, *m.*

machine'-factory, *n.*, atelier de construction de machines, *m.*

machine'-gun', *n.*, mitrailleuse, *f.*

machine'-made, *adj.*, fait à la mécanique ; à la mécanique.

machine'-minder (-maï'n'd'-), *n.*, (print.) surveillant de machine, *m.*

machin'ery (ma-shï'n'euri), *n.*, mécanique, *f.* ; mécanisme, *m.* ; machines, *f.pl.* ; (poet.) merveilleux, *m.* Made by — ; *fait à la mécanique.*

machin'ist (ma-shï'n'-), *n.*, machiniste, *m.*

mack'erel (mak'eur'èl), *n.*, maquereau, *m.* — boat ; *maquilleur, m.* — breeze ; *frais coup de vent, m.* — sky ; *ciel pommelé, ciel bariolé, m.*

mack'intosh, *n.*, mackintosh, imperméable, *m.*

mac'ula (mak'iou-) *ou* **mac'ule** (mak'ioul), *n.*, (*maculæ*) tache ; (astron.) macule, *f.*

mac'ulate (mak'iou-), *v.a.*, tacher, gâter, maculer.

macula'tion (mak'iou-lé-), *n.*, maculage, *m.*

mad, *adj.*, fou, aliéné, en démence, insensé ; (of animals) enragé, furieux. — with any one ; *furieux contre quelqu'un.* — with pain ; *fou de douleur.* — for, after ; *fou de.* To drive — ; *faire devenir fou ; faire perdre la tête à.* To go —; *devenir fou ;* (of animals) *devenir enragé.* Raving — ; *fou à lier, fou furieux.* He is as — as a March hare ; *il est fou à courir les champs.* See how — he is ; *voyez comme il bisque.* — as a hatter ; *furieux, enragé.* To be — after anything ; *désirer violemment quelque chose ; être fou de quelque chose ; avoir la rage de.*

mad'am, *n.*, madame, *f.*

mad'-apple (-ap'p'l), *n.*, (bot.) morelle comestible, mélongène, *f.*

mad'cap, *n.*, fou, *m.*, folle, *f.* ; écervelé, *m.*, écervelée, *f.*

mad'cap, *adj.*, étourdi, écervelé ; fou.

mad'den, *v.a.*, rendre fou ; faire affoler ; faire devenir fou ; faire enrager.

mad'dening, *adj.*, à rendre fou.

mad'der (mad'deur), *n.*, garance, *f.*

mad'der, *v.a.*, garancer ; teindre en garance.

mad'der-col'ored (mad'deur-keul'leurde), *adj.*, garancé.

mad'der-dye'ing (-daï'igne), *n.*, garançage, *m.* ; teinture à la garance, *f.*

mad'der-dy'er (-daï'eur), *n.*, garanceur, *m.*

mad'dering, *n.*, garançage, *m.*

mad'der-root (-route), *n.*, alizari, *m.* ; garance, *f.*

made, *p.p.* and *adj.*, fait, confectionné. — so as to ; *fait de façon à.* — up ; *artificiel, faux ;* (of stories) *fait à plaisir, inventé ;* (of the face) *maquillé.* — up dishes ; *entremets ; m.pl., entrée, f.* A — man ; *homme dont la position est assurée.* A self- — man ; *l'architecte de sa propre fortune, m.*

Madei'ra (na-di-ra *ou* -dé-), *n.*, vin de Madère, *m.*

mad'house (-haouce), *n.*, maison de fous ; maison d'aliénés, *f.* ; petites-maisons, *f.pl.* Private —; *maison particulière de fous, d'aliénés, f.*

mad'ly, *adv.*, follement, furieusement ; en fou, à la folie.

mad'man, *n.*, aliéné, insensé, fou, *m.*

mad'ness, *n.*, aliénation mentale, démence, fureur, folie ; (of animals) rage, *f.* To drive to —; *boire à se rendre fou.* To drive to —; *rendre fou.*

madon'na, *n.*, madone, *f.*

mad'repore (mad'ri-pôre), *n.*, madrépore, *m.*

mad'rigal, *n.*, madrigal, *m.*

magazine' (-zine), *n.*, (milit.) magasin, *m.* ; (periodical) revue ; (nav.) soute aux poudres, *f.* Powder —; (mil.) *poudrière, f.*

magen'ta, *adj.*, (color) magenta.

mag'got, *n.*, larve, *f.* ; asticot ; (pop.) (whim) caprice, *m.*, lubie, quinte, *f.*

mag'goty, *adj.*, véreux ; plein de mites, de vers ; (pop.) (whimsical) quinteux, capricieux.

ma'gi (mé'djaïe), *n.pl.*, mages, *m.pl.*

ma'gian (mé-dji-), *n.*, mage, *m.*

ma'gian, *adj.*, des mages.

ma'gianism, *n.*, magisme, *m.*

ma'gic (madj'-), *n.*, magie, *f.* ; enchantement, *m.*

ma'gic *ou* **ma'gical** (madj'-), *adj.*, magique.

ma'gically, *adv.*, par magie, par enchantement.

magi'cian (ma-djish'-), *n.*, magicien, *m.*, magicienne, *f.*

magiste'rial (madj'is-tî-), *adj.*, magistral ; de maître ; de magistrat.

magiste'rially, *adv.*, en maître ; magistralement.

magiste'rialness, *n.*, air, *ou* ton, de maître, ton magistral, *m.*

mag'istracy (madj'-), *n.*, magistrature, *f.*

mag'istrate (madj'-), *n.*, magistrat, juge de paix, *m.* Police — ; *juge d'instruction* (examining), ou *du tribunal de police, m.*

Mag'na-Char'ta (mag-na-kâr-), *n.*, la Grande Charte ; loi fondamentale, *f.*

magnanim'ity (mag-na-), *n.*, magnanimité, *f.*

magnan'imous (mag-na'n'-), *adj.*, magnanime.

magnan'imously, *adv.*, magnanimement.

mag'nate (mag-néte), *n.*, magnat ; grand ; grand personnage ; homme influent ; puissance, *f.* ; (pop.) gros bonnet.

magne'sia (mag-nî-zi-a), *n.*, magnésie, *f.*

magne'sian (mag-nî-zi-), *adj.*, magnésien. — limestone ; *dolomie, f.* ; *calcaire magnésien, m.*

magne'sium, *n.*, magnésium, *m.* — light ; *lumière magnésique, f.*

mag'net (mag-nète), *n.*, aimant, *m.* ; pierre d'aimant, *f.*

magnet'ic *ou* **magnet'ical** (mag-), *adj.*, magnétique ; aimanté ; (fig.) attractif, attirant.

magnet'ically (mag-), *adv.*, par le magnétisme.

magnet'ics (mag-), *n.*, science du magnétisme, *f.*

mag'netism (mag-nèt'iz'me), *n.*, magnétisme, *m.* ; puissance attractive, *f.* Animal —; *magnétisme animal, m.*

mag'netize (mag-nèt'aïze), *v.a.*, aimanter ; (pers.) magnétiser.

mag'netize (mag-nèt'aïze), *v.n.*, s'aimanter.

magnif'icence (mag-), *n.*, magnificence, *f.*

magnif'icent (mag-), *adj.*, magnifique, superbe.

magnif'icently (mag-), *adv.*, magnifiquement.

magnif'ico (mag-), *n.*, grand patricien (à Venise) ; recteur (d'une université allemande), *m.*

mag'nified, *adj.*, grossi.

mag'nifier (mag-ni-faï'-), *n.*, verre grossissant, *m.* ; personne qui exalte, *ou* exagère, *f.* ; panégyriste, *m.*

mag'nify (mag-ni-faïe), *v.a.*, magnifier ; augmenter ; grossir ; exalter ; exagérer.

mag'nifying (mag-ni-faï'igne), *adj.*, qui grossit. —glass ; *verre grossissant, m.* ; loupe, *f.*

magnil'oquence (mag-), *n.*, emphase, *f.* ; style pompeux, *m.*

magnil'oquent (mag-), *adj.*, emphatique, pompeux.

mag'nitude (mag-ni-tioude), *n.*, grandeur ; grosseur ; importance, *f.*

magno'lia (mag-nô-), *n.*, (bot.) magnolia, magnolier, *m.*

mag'pie (-païe), *n.*, pie, *f.*

mahog'any, *n.*, acajou ; bois d'acajou, *m.*

mahog'any, *adj.*, d', *ou* en, acajou.

Mahom'edan *ou* **Mahom'etan** (-ho'm'è-), *n.* and *adj.*, mahométan, *m.*, mahométane, *f.*

Mahom'edanism *o u* **Mahom'etanism** (-iz'me), *n.*, mahométisme, *m.*

maid (méde), *n.*, vierge; fille, jeune fille; (servant) bonne, servante, domestique, fille, (of an upper class) demoiselle, *f.;* (ich.) ange de mer, *m.* — of honor; *demoiselle d'honneur.* — of Orleans; *la pucelle d'Orléans.* — of all work; *bonne à tout faire.* Nursery-—, nurse-—; *bonne d'enfant, f.* Lady's-—; *femme de chambre, f.* Chamber-—; *fille de chambre, f.* Kitchen-—; *fille de cuisine, f.* House-—; *servante, f.* To remain an old -—; *rester fille;* (pop.) *coiffer sainte Catherine.*

mai'den (méd'n), *n.*, fille, jeune fille, demoiselle; (pop.) guillotine, *f.*

mai'den (méd'n), *adj.*, de fille, de jeune fille; virginal; de vierge; non mariée; (fig.) pur, neuf, vierge; (of a speech) de début. — name; *nom de demoiselle, m.* — lady; *demoiselle, f.* — aunt; *une vieille fille de tante; une tante vieille fille, f.*

mai'den-hair, *n.*, capillaire, *m.*

mai'denhead (méd'n'hède) *ou* **mai'denhood** (-houde), *n.*, virginité, pureté, *f.*

maid'en-like (-laïke), *adj.*, en jeune fille; modeste; pudique.

maid'enliness, *n.*, tenue de jeune fille; pudeur, *ou* modestie, de jeune fille, *f.*

maid'enly, *adj.*, virginal; de jeune fille; modeste, chaste.

maid'enly, *adv.*, en jeune fille; modestement, avec pudeur; pudiquement.

maid'-servant (-seurv'-), *n.*, servante, *f.*

mail (méle), *n.*, (coat) maille; (coach) malle, malle-poste, *f.;* courrier, *m.;* (at the post-office) dépêche, *f.* Coat of —; *cotte de maille, f.*

mail (méle), *v.a.*, expédier (par le courrier); mettre une cotte de maille, cuirasser.

mail'-bag, *n.*, (ambassador's) valise; malle, *f., &pl.* dépêches, *f.pl.*

mail'-carriage, *n.*, wagon-poste, *m.*

mail'-coach (-kôtshe), *n.*, malle-poste, *f.;* courrier, *m.*

mailed, *adj.*, à mailles.

mail'-guard (-gârde), *n.*, courrier de la malle, *m.*

mail'-packet *ou* **steamer** (-pak'ète), *n.*, paquebot-poste, vapeur-poste, *m.*

maim (méme), *v.a.*, estropier, mutiler; (fig.) mutiler, tronquer; paralyser.

maim, *n.*, perte de l'usage d'un membre; perte; mutilation, *f.*

main (méne), *adj.*, principal, premier; général, régulier; vaste, grand; important, essentiel. — body; (of an army) *le gros.* — land; *continent, m.* — deck; *premier pont, m.* — mast; *grand mât, m.* —sail; *grande voile, f.* —sea; *haute mer, f.* —topmast; *grand mât de hune, grand hunier, m.* —yard; *grande vergue, f.* —shaft; *arbre moteur, m.* — sewer; *grand égout, égout collecteur, m.* (V. Hugo). — sheet; *grande écoule, m.* By—strength; *par force; de haute lutte.* The — thing, *ou* point; *l'essentiel, le principal, m.*

main (méne), *n.*, (gross) gros, principal; (ocean) océan; (continent) continent, *m.;* (strength) force, *f.;* (duct) grand conduit; (cockfight) combat de coqs, *m.* In the —; *pour la plupart; en général; en somme.* With might and —; *de toutes ses forces.*

main'ly, *adv.*, principalement; surtout, puissamment, grandement.

main'prise (mé'n'praïze), *n.*, (jur.) mise en liberté sous caution, *f.*

main'spring, *n.*, grand ressort, *m.;* (fig.) cheville ouvrière, *f.;* mobile, *m.*

maintain' (mé'n'té'n), *v.a.*, maintenir, entretenir; soutenir; alléguer, affirmer; conserver; (to keep in food) entretenir, nourrir.

maintain', *v.n.*, maintenir; soutenir.

maintain'able (-'a-b'l), *adj.*, soutenable; tenable.

maintain'er, *n.*, soutien, appui; (fig.) défenseur, *m.*

main'tenance (mé'n'tè'n'-), *n.*, maintien, entretien, soutien, *m.;* conservation, *f.;* moyen d'existence, *m.;* (jur.) pension alimentaire, *f.* Separate —; *séparation de biens, f.*

maize (méze), *n.*, maïs, blé de Turquie, *m.*

majes'tic *ou* **majes'tical** (ma-djès'-), *adj.*, majestueux.

majes'tically (ma-djès'-), *adv.*, majestueusement, avec majesté.

maj'esty (mad'jesté), *n.*, majesté, *f.* His, Her —; *Sa Majesté, f.*

ma'jor (mé-djeur), *adj.*, plus grand; majeur.

ma'jor (mé-djeur), *n.*, (log.) majeure; (jur.) personne majeure, *f.;* (of infantry) chef de bataillon; (of cavalry) chef d'escadron, *m.* —-general; *général de brigade, m.* Drum-—; *tambour major, m.*

ma'jor-do'mo (mé-djeur-dô'mô), *n.*, majordome, *m.*

major'ity (ma-djor'-), *n.*, majorité, *f.;* (milit.) grade de chef de bataillon; (cavalry) d'escadron, *m.;* majorité, *f.* To join, *ou* go over to, the —; *aller ad patres; mourir.*

make (méke), *n.*, façon, forme, nature, construction, structure; fabrique; tournure, *f.;* complément, *m.*

make (méke), *v.a.* (*preterit and past part.*, Made), faire, former, créer; façonner; (to render) rendre; (to force) faire, forcer, contraindre; (money) faire, amasser, gagner; (a pen) tailler; (to reach) gagner, atteindre; (nav.) découvrir; (to represent) représenter; (to fabricate) inventer. To — believe; *faire accroire à.* To — known; *faire connaître, faire savoir à.* To — one's self heard, understood, known; *se faire entendre, comprendre, connaître.* To — free with; (pers.) *traiter sans façon;* (things) *ne pas se gêner pour se servir de, pour prendre.* To — too free with; (pers.) *prendre des libertés avec;* (drink) *prendre trop de.* To — account of, *ou* much of; *faire grand cas de.* To — a great deal by; *profiter beaucoup de; tirer beaucoup de profit de.* To — nothing by; *ne tirer aucun parti de, aucun profit de.* To —out; (to understand) *venir à bout de comprendre;* (to discover the meaning of) *déchiffrer, découvrir;* (to furnish) *fournir, produire;* (to prove) *établir;* (to draw up) *rédiger;* (a bill) *dresser.* To — over to; *céder à; transférer à.* To — up; *compléter, combler;* (clothes) *façonner;* (a story) *inventer;* (to compose) *composer, constituer;* (medicine) *préparer;* (phar.) *façonner, former;* (to repair) *réparer;* (to dress an actor) *costumer;* (a quarrel) *accommoder, arranger;* (accounts) *faire régler, établir; balancer;* (print.) *mettre en pages.* To — up for; (to supply) *suppléer à, tenir compte de;* (to compensate) *dédommager de;* (of time) *rattraper.* To — it up; *se raccommoder; se réconcilier.* To — nothing of; *ne rien comprendre à; ne pas savoir à quoi s'en tenir;* (not to be scrupulous) *ne pas se faire un scrupule de;* (to find no difficulty in) *n'avoir aucune difficulté à.* He is not such a fool as you — him; *il n'est pas aussi bête que vous le représentez.* To — ill; *rendre malade.* To — sick; *faire vomir.* To — well; *faire bien;* (to restore to health) *guérir.* He —s clothes well; *il fait bien les habits; il travaille bien.* To — the bed; *faire le lit.* To — a lip; *faire la moue.* To — a fool of; *se jouer de.* To — a mistake; *se tromper.* To — land; *découvrir la terre.* To — one's escape; *se sauver.* To — angry; *fâcher.* To — good; *soutenir, prouver, défendre; réparer; dédommager de.* To — haste; *se dépêcher, se hâter.* To — less; *rapetisser, amoindrir.* To — ready; *préparer.* To — again; *refaire.* To — away one's property; *aliéner son bien.* To — shift with; *s'arranger* s'accommoder **de**. To — water; uriner; (nav.) faire eau. To — way; se frayer un chemin; avancer; faire des progrès. To — sail; mettre à la voile. To — sure of; considérer comme certain; se croire sûr **de**; compter **sur**; croire bien **que**; s'assurer **de**. To — sure; assurer. Things are made to go; on fait aller les choses. To — the most of; profiter **de**; tirer le meilleur parti **de**. To — fast; attacher. To — up one's mind; se décider; prendre une résolution, prendre son parti; s'arrêter à une décision. To — the best of; tirer le meilleur parti **de**. To — the best of a bad job, ou bargain; faire bonne mine à mauvais jeu, faire contre fortune bon cœur. To — the best of one's way; aller tout droit; aller droit; aller en toute hâte. To — amends for (a loss); réparer; dédommager **de**. To — fun of; se moquer **de**. To — an appointment with; donner un rendez-vous **à**; prendre rendez-vous **avec**. To — friends; réconcilier. To — head, headway; faire des progrès; avancer. To — light of; traiter légèrement. To — love to; courtiser; faire la cour **à**. To — more of; traiter avec plus de considération. To — much of; (use well) faire valoir; tirer bon parti **de**; (children) dorloter, câliner, choyer; (pers.) bien accueillir; traiter avec égard; (to think well of) faire grand cas **de**. To — no difference; être sans importance. To — no matter; n'être d'aucune importance; ne faire rien. To — of; comprendre. I don't know what to — of it; je ne sais ce qu'il en faut penser; j'y perds mon latin, je n'y comprends rien. To — a cat laugh; faire rire un tas de pierres. To — hay while the sun shines; prendre la balle au bond. To — the mouth water; faire venir l'eau à la bouche.

make (méke), v.n., (of the tide) monter. To — for; (person) s'avancer **sur**; courir **sur**; s'élancer **sur**. To — away with; se défaire **de**; tuer, détruire. To — away with one's self; se donner la mort, se suicider, se détruire. To — for; (place) s'avancer **à**; se rendre **à**; se diriger **vers**. To — for; tendre **à**; favoriser; (to sail to) faire voile **pour**. To — toward; se diriger **vers**. To — as if; faire semblant **de**, avoir l'air **de**. To — up to; s'approcher **de**; s'avancer **vers**; se diriger **vers**; (fig.) faire des avances **à**, faire la cour **à**. To — up for; tenir lieu **de**; suppléer **à**, dédommager **de**, compenser. To — against; nuire **à**; opérer, agir, contre; tendre **à** réfuter; tendre à prouver le contraire **de**. To — as if; prétendre; faire semblant **de**. To — nothing in; ne contribuer en rien **à**; ne prouver rien **en**. To — direct for; se diriger **sur**; se rendre tout droit **à**. To — believe; prétendre. To — friends; se réconcilier; se lier d'amitié **avec**. To — off; lever le pied; décamper; filer. To — up; (to dress, speaking of actors) se costumer, se grimer, se maquiller. This argument — nothing in his favor; cet argument ne prouve rien en sa faveur. This argument —s against his cause; cet argument nuit à sa cause.

mak'er, n., créateur, auteur; faiseur, fabricant; (of clothes) confectionneur, m.

mak'er-up (-eupe), n., (print.) metteur en pages, m.

make'shift, n., pis aller; expédient, m.

make'weight (-wête), n., supplément; (fig.) remplissage, m.

mak'ing (mék'-), n., création; façon; forme, construction; (of clothes) confection; fabrication; forme, f.

mak'ing-up (mék'ign'eupe), n., (of clothes) façon, confection; (print.) mise en pages, f.

Malac'ca cane, n., canne de jonc, f.

mal'achite (-kaïte), n., (min.) malachite, f.

maladministra'tion (-tré-), n., mauvaise administration, f.

mal'ady, n., maladie, f.

Mal'aga, n., vin de Malaga, m.

mal'apert (-peurte), adj., malappris, impertinent.

mala'ria, n., malaria; exhalaison malsaine; mofette, f., air malfaisant, air infect, m.

mal'content, n., mécontent, m.

mal'content, adj., mécontent.

male, adj., mâle; masculin.

male, n., mâle, m.

maledic'tion (mal'i-), n., malédiction, f.

malefac'tor (mal'i-fac-), n., malfaiteur, criminel, m.

malef'icence (-lèf-), n., malfaisance, f.

malef'icent (-lèf-), adj., malfaisant.

malev'olence (-lèv'-), n., malveillance, f.

malev'olent (-lèv'-), adj., malveillant; (astrol.) maléfique.

malev'olently (-lèv-), adv., avec malveillance.

malfea'sance (-fî-za'n'ce), n., (jur.) malfaisance, f.; méfait, m.

malforma'tion, n., malformation, f., vice de conformation, m.

malformed', adj., mal conformé.

mal'ice, n., malice; malveillance; méchanceté; (jur.) intention criminelle, f. To bear any one —; vouloir du mal à quelqu'un; en vouloir à quelqu'un; garder rancune **à**. With — prepense, ou aforethought; avec préméditation, avec intention criminelle.

mali'cious (ma-lish'eusse), adj., malveillant; malicieux; méchant; (jur.) criminel.

mali'ciously, adv., avec malveillance; méchamment; (jur.) criminellement.

mali'ciousness, n., malignité, malice, malveillance, f.

malign' (ma-laïne), adj., malin; méchant; pernicieux.

malign' (ma-laïne), v.a., diffamer; maltraiter; nuire **à**.

malig'nant (ma-lig-), adj., malin, méchant; malfaisant; (med.) malin.

malig'nantly (ma-lig-), adv., malignement; avec malignité; avec méchanceté.

malign'er (ma-laï'n'eur), n., personne maligne, f.; diffamateur, détracteur, m.

malig'nity (ma-lig-), n., malignité, malveillance, f.

malign'ly (ma-laï'n'-), adv. V. **malig'nantly**.

mal'kin (mô'-), n., écouvillon, m.

mall (môl), n., gros maillet, (promenade) mail, m.

malleabil'ity ou **mal'leableness** (mal'li-), n., (metal) malléabilité, f.

mal'leable (mal'li-a-b'l), adj., malléable.

mal'leate (mal'li-), v.a., marteler.

mallea'tion (mal'li-), n., malléation.

mal'let, n., maillet, mail, m.

mal'low ou **mal'lows** (-lô, -lôze), n., (bot.) mauve, f. Marsh-—; guimauve, f.

malm'sey (m'z'm'zè), n., malvoisie, f.; vin de Malvoisie, m.

malprac'tice, n., action illicite; menée; malversation, f.

malt (môlte), n., drèche, f.; malt, m.

malt'-distillery, n., distillerie de grains, f.

malt'-floor (-flôre), n., aire de germoir, f.; sol du germoir, m.

malt'-house (-haouce), n., germoir, m.

malt'ing (môlt'-), n., maltage, m.

malt'-kiln, n., touraille, f.; four à drèche, m.

malt-liq'uor (-lik'eur), n., (kind of) bière, f.

malt'man (môlt'ma'n), **malt'ster**, n., malteur, m.

Maltese', n., Maltais, m. adj.; — cross; croix de Malte, f. — dog; bichon, m.

Malthu'sian, adj., malthusien.

maltreat' (mal-trîte), v.a., maltraiter, malmener.

maltreat'ment (mal-trîte-), n., mauvais traitement, m.

malva'ceous (mal-vé-sheusse), *adj.*, (bot.) malvacé.

malversa'tion (-veur-sé-), *n.*, malversation, *f.*

Mam'aluke (-liouke) *ou* **Mam'eluke** (-'i-liouke), *n.*, mameluke, mamelouk, *m.*

mamma', *n.*, maman, mère, *f.*

mamma'lia (-'mé-li-a), *n.pl.*, (zoöl.) mammifères, *m.pl.*

mam'mary, *adj.*, (anat.) mammaire.

mam'mifer (-feur), *n.*, mammifère, *m.*

mammif'erous, *adj.*, mammifère.

mam'miform, *adj.*, mamillaire.

mam'millary, *adj.*, mamillaire.

Mam'mon, *n.*, (Bible) Mammon, *m.*

mam'monist, *n.*, adorateur de Mammon, *m.*

mam'moth (-moth), *n.*, mammouth, *m.*

man (ma'n), *n.* (*men*), homme, *m.*; (at chess) pièce ; (at draughts) dame, *f.*; pion ; (servant) domestique, valet ; (workman) ouvrier ; employé, garçon, *m.* Well, my — ! *eh bien, mon brave !* —servant ; *domestique, m.* — cook ; *cuisinier, m.* Head — ; *chef, m.* — and wife; *mari et femme.* —of-war ; *vaisseau de guerre, m.* —'s estate ; *âge viril, m.; virilité, f.* All to a — ; *tous sans exception, tous jusqu'au dernier.* No — ; *personne, nul ou aucun homme.* The — in the street ; *le premier venu.* — proposes and God disposes ; *l'homme propose et Dieu dispose ou l'homme s'agite et Dieu le mène.*

man, *v.a.*, garnir d'hommes ; (a ship) armer ; garnir de monde, fournir de monde, de marins ; équiper ; (of a gun) servir ; (a pump) armer ; (a prize) amariner ; (a hawk) apprivoiser ; (fig.) fortifier ; (mil.) mettre une garnison dans.

man'acle (-'a-k'l), *v.a.*, mettre les menottes à; emmenotter ; (fig.) garrotter.

man'acles (-a-k'l'ze), *n.pl.*, menottes, *f.pl.*

man'age (-'èdje), *v.a.*, conduire, gouverner, administrer, gérer ; (a machine or gun) manœuvrer ; régir, diriger ; (to spare) ménager ; (com.) gérer ; (a horse) manier, dresser, dompter ; (things) arranger. I know how to — him ; *je sais comment il faut le prendre.* I know how to — it ; *je sais comment m'y prendre.* Not one in four could — his piece at all; *sur quatre il n'y en avait pas un qui sût manœuvrer sa pièce.*

man'age, *v.n.*, s'arranger pour ; parvenir à, venir à bout de ; faire en sorte que (or de with inf.).

man'ageable (man'èdj'a-b'l), *adj.*, qui peut être conduit, dirigé, régi ; docile ; traitable ; maniable. A — child ; *un enfant docile, m.*

man'agement (-'èdj'-), *n.*, conduite, direction, administration ; (com.) gestion, *f.*; (contrivance) artifice ; savoir-faire, *m.*; prudence, adresse, *f.*

man'ager (-'èdj'-), *n.*, directeur ; gérant ; régisseur ; chef ; (thea.) directeur, *m.* Stage— ; *régisseur, m.* She is a good — ; *elle est bonne ménagère.* What a capital — you are! *comme vous vous entendez bien à arranger les choses !*

man'ageress, *n.*, directrice, gérante, *f.*

man'aging (-'èdj'-), *n.*, gestion, direction, *f.*

man'aging (-'èdj'-), *adj.*, qui conduit, qui dirige ; directeur ; gérant. —man ; *gérant ; chef, m.*

man'atee, *n.*, (mam.) lamentin, lamantin, *m.*

manchineel' (ma'n'sh-i-nîl), *n.*, (bot.) mancenillier, *m.*

man'ciple (-ci-p'l), *n.*; (of a college) économe, *m.*

manda'mus (-dé-) *n.*, (jur.) mandement, *m.*

mandarin' (-rîne), *n.*, mandarin, *m.*

man'datary *ou* **man'datory**, *n.*, mandataire, *m.*

man'date, *n.*, mandement ; mandat ; ordre, *m.*

man'datory, *n.*, mandataire, *m.*

man'dible (-di-b'l), *n.*, mandibule, *f.*

mandib'ular (-di-biou-), *adj.*, mandibulaire.

man'dolin, *n.*, mandoline, *f.*

man'dore (-dôre), *n.*, mandore, *f.*

man'drake (-dréke) *n.*, (bot.) mandragore, *f.*

man'drel (-), *n.*, mandrin, *m.*

man'drill, *n.*, (mam.) mandrill, *m.*

mane (méne), *n.*, crinière, *f.*

man'-eater (ma'n'ît'eur), *n.*, cannibale, anthropophage, *m.*

maned (mé'n'de), *adj.*, à crinière

manege' (ma-nèje), *n.*, manège, *m.*

ma'nes (mé-nize), *n.pl.*, mânes, *m.pl.*

man'ful. *V.* **man'ly.**

man'fully, *adv.*, en homme ; virilement, hardiment, vaillamment ; noblement, dignement.

man'fulness, *n.*, bravoure, *f.*

manganese' (-nize), *n.*, (chem.) manganèse, *m.*

mange (ma'n'dje), *n.*, (vet.) gale (de chien), *f.*

man'gel-wur'zel (ma'gn'g'l-weurz'l), **man'-gold-wur'zel**, *n.*, betterave, *f.*

man'ger (mé'n'djeur), *n.*, (for cattle) crèche; auge ; mangeoire, *f.* The dog in the — ; *le chien du jardinier.*

man'giness (ma'n'dji-), *n.*, (vet.) état galeux, *m.*

man'gle (ma'gn'g'l), *v.a.*, déchirer, déchiqueter ; mutiler, estropier ; (linen) calandrer, cylindrer ; (to carve badly) massacrer.

man'gle, *n.*, cylindre au linge, *m.*, calandre, *f.*

man'gler, *n.*, personne qui mutile, *f.*; (of linen) calandreur, *m.*

man'gling, *n.*, cylindrage, calandrage, *m.*; (fig.) mutilation, *f.*

man'go (ma'gn'gô), *n.*, mangue, *f.*

man'go-tree (-trî), *n.*, (bot.) manguier, *m.*

man'grove (ma'gn'grôve), *n.*, (bot.) (fruit) mangle, *f.*; (tree) manglier, palétuvier, *m.*

man'gy (ma'n'dji), *adj.*, (vet.) galeux.

man'-hater (ma'n'hét'eur), *n.*, misanthrope, *m.*

man'hole, *n.*, (of sewers) regard, *m.*

man'hood (-houde), *n.*, virilité, *f.*; âge viril, *m.*; nature humaine, *f.* — suffrage ; *suffrage universel, m.*

ma'nia (mé-), *n.*, folie ; rage ; manie, *f.*

ma'niac *ou* **mani'acal** (mé-), *adj.*, furieux ; fou ; enragé ; (fig.) maniaque.

man'iac (mé-), *n.*, fou furieux, *m.*, folle furieuse, *f.*; fou, *m.*, folle, *f.*; (fig.) maniaque, *m.*

Man'ichean (-ki-a'n), *adj.*, des manichéens.

Man'ichean *ou* **Man'ichee** (-kî), *n.*, manichéen, *m.*, manichéenne, *f.*

Man'icheism (-kî-iz'me), *n.*, manichéisme, *f.*

man'ichord *ou* **manichor'don** (-kord'-), *n.*, (mus.) manichordion ; manicorde, *m.*

man'ifest (-fèste), *v.a.*, manifester, témoigner, laisser voir ; montrer ; (custom-house) déclarer. To — a cargo; *déclarer une cargaison.*

man'ifest, *adj.*, manifeste, évident.

man'ifest, *n.*, (nav.) manifeste, *m.*

manifesta'tion (-fèst'é-), *n.*, manifestation, *f.*

man'ifestly, *adv.*, manifestement.

man'ifestness, *n.*, évidence, *f.*

manifes'to (-fès'tô), *n.*, manifeste, *m.*

man'ifold (-fôlde), *adj.*, nombreux, en grand nombre; divers; multiple ; varié. —writer ; (machine) *polygraphe, m.*

man'ifoldly, *adv.*, de diverses manières ; diversement.

man'ifoldness, *n.*, multiplicité, *f.*

man'iform, *adj.*, maniforme.

man'ikin, *n.*, bout d'homme ; nabot ; mannequin, homuncule, *m.*

ma'nioc (mé-), *n.*, manioc, *m.*

man'iple (-i-p'l), *n.*, manipule, *m.*

manip'ulate, *v.a.*, manipuler.

manipula'tion (-nip'iou-lé-), *n.*, manipulation, *f.*

manip'ulator (-lét'eur), *n.*, (pers.) manipulateur ; (instrument) manipulateur, *m.*

man'-killer, *n.*, homicide, assassin, tueur d'hommes, *m.*

man'kind (-kaï'n'de), *n.*, genre humain, *m. ;* espèce humaine, l'humanité, *f.*

man'-like (-laike), *adj.*, d'homme ; viril ; mâle, vigoureux; (of a woman) hommasse.

man'liness, *n.*, air d'homme ; air mâl~; caractère viril, *m. ;* bravoure ; vigueur ; dignité, *f.*

man'ly, *adj.*, d'homme ; viril ; mâle ; vigoureux, ferme.

man'ly, *adv. V.* **man'fully**.

man'-mid'wife (-waïfe), *n.*, (Byron) (l.u.) accoucheur, *m.*

man'na, *n.*, manne, *f.*

man'ner, *n.*, manière, *f. ;* genre, *m. ;* sorte, façon; espèce; coutume; habitude, *f. pl.*, mœurs, *f.pl. ;* politesse, *f.* By any — of means ; *à quelque prix que ce soit ; à toute force.* After the — of ; *à la manière* **de** ; *à la façon* **de** ; *d'après.* The — in which ; *la manière dont.* In a — ; *en quelque sorte, pour ainsi dire.* To have no —s ; *n'avoir pas de savoir vivre.* All —s of things ; *toutes espèces, toutes sortes de choses, f.pl.* Good —s ; *bonnes manières, f.pl. ; bon ton, m.sing.* Ill —s ; *mauvaises manières, f.pl. ; mauvais ton, m.sing.* In like — ; *de même.* In the same — as ; *de même que ; comme ; ainsi que.* To teach —s ; *apprendre à vivre.* One can easily see by your — that you are accustomed to good society ; *on voit facilement à votre air que vous avez l'habitude de la bonne société.* No — of; *aucune espèce* **de.** The — and the matter ; *la forme et le fond.* —s change with the times ; *autres temps, autres mœurs.* What — of man was; *quel homme c'était que* (V. Hugo).

man'nerism (-'iz'me), *n.*, air maniéré, maniérisme, *m.*

man'nerist, *n.*, personne maniérée, *f. ;* écrivain maniéré, *m.*

man'nerliness, *n.*, civilité, politesse, *f.*

man'nerly, *adj.*, poli, *adv.*, poliment.

man'ners (man'neurze), *n.*, (behaving in society) manières polies ; (morals) mœurs, *f.pl.* I shall have to teach you better — ; *il faudra que je vous apprenne à vivre. V.* **manner**.

man'ning, *n.*, armement, équipement, *m.*

man'nish, *adj.*, d'homme, mâle ; hommasse.

manœu'vre (ma-nou-veur), *n.*, manœuvre, *f. pl.*, manigances, *f.pl.*

manœu'vre, *v.n.*, manœuvrer ; (fig.) manigancer.

manœu'vre, *v.a.*, faire manœuvrer ; manœuvrer.

manœu'vrer, *n.*, conducteur de manœuvres, tacticien, manœuvrier ; (b.s.) intrigant, *m.*

manœu'vring, *n.*, manœuvres, *m.pl.*

manom'eter (-'èt'-), *n.*, (phys.) manomètre, *m.*

man'or, *n.*, manoir, château, *m. ;* seigneurie, *f.*

man'or-house (-haouce) *ou* **man'or-seat** (-sîte), *n.*, manoir seigneurial, château, *m.*

mano'rial, *adj.*, seigneurial.

mansard'-roof', *n.*, toit en mansarde, comble brisé, *m.*

manse, *n.*, presbytère, *m.*

man'sion (-sheune), *n.*, maison seigneuriale, *f. ;* (town) hôtel, (country) château, *m. ;* grande maison ; (fig.) habitation, *f. ;* séjour, *m.*

man'sion-house (-haouce), *n.*, hôtel, *m.*, grande maison, *f. ;* hôtel du lord-maire de Londres, de Dublin, *m. ;* mairie, *f. ;* hôtel de ville, *m.*

man'slaughter (ma'n'slô-teur), *n.*, homicide ; (jur.) homicide involontaire, *m.*

man'slayer (ma'n'slé-eur), *n.*, meurtrier, homicide, *m.*

man'suetude (ma'n'swît'ioude), *n.*, (ant.) mansuétude, *f.*

man'tel (ma'n'tl), *n.*, chambranle de cheminée, *m.*

man'telet *ou* **mant'let**, *n.*, mantelet, *m.*

man'telpiece, **man'tel-piece** (-pîce), *ou* **man'tel-shelf**, *n.*, manteau de cheminée, *m.*

mantil'la, *n.*, mantille, *f.*

man'tle, *n.*, mante, *f. ;* manteau ; (arch.) manteau; (her.) lambrequin ; (fig.) voile, manteau, *m.*

man'tle, *v.a.*, couvrir ; voiler, déguiser.

man'tle, *v.n.*, s'étendre ; se répandre ; (to revel) se réjouir ; (of blood, to rush to the face) monter à la figure. To — to the view ; *s'offrir à la vue.* The mantling bowl ; *le bol qui se couvre d'écume.*

man'tling, *n.*, (her.) manteau, lambrequin, *m.*

man'tua-maker (-mék'-), *n.*, couturière, *f.*

man'ual (-'iou-), *adj.*, manuel, de la main. — exercise ; *maniement des armes, m.*

man'ual, *n.*, (book) manuel, *m. ;* (fire engine) pompe à incendie, *f.*

man'ually, *adv.*, manuellement, à la main.

manufac'tory (ma'n'iou-fak'-), *n.*, manufacture, fabrique ; usine, *f. ;* ateliers, *m.pl.*

manufac'tural (-'iou-fakt'iou-),*adj.*, de manufacture; de fabrique; d'usine; manufacturier.

manufac'ture (-'iou-fakt'ieur), *n.*, manufacture, fabrique, industrie ; industrie manufacturière ; fabrication, *f. pl.*, industrie manufacturière, *f. ;* article, objet, tissu, *m. ;* produits des manufactures, *m.pl.*

manufac'ture, *v.a.*, manufacturer, fabriquer. To — wool ; *travailler, ou façonner, la laine.*

manufac'ture, *v.n.*, se livrer à la manufacture, à l'industrie.

manufac'turer, *n.*, manufacturier, fabricant ; industriel, *m.*

manufac'turing, *adj.*, manufacturier ; de manufacture ; de fabrique ; industriel, *m.*

manumis'sion (-'iou-mish'-), *n.*, (Rom. law) manumission, *f. ;* affranchissement, *m.*

manumit' (-'iou-mite), *v.a.*, (Rom. law) affranchir.

manur'able (-'iour'a-b'l), *adj.*, labourable, cultivable ; qui peut être engraissé, fumé.

manure' (-nioure), *n.*, engrais, fumier, *m.*

manure' (-nioure), *v.a.*, engraisser, amender ; fumer.

man'uscript (-'iou-scripte), *n.*, manuscrit, *m.*

man'uscript, *adj.*, manuscrit.

ma'ny (mè'n'i), *n.*, multitude, foule,*f.;* grand nombre, *m.* A great — ; *beaucoup ; un grand nombre; bon nombre* **de.** A very great — ; *un très grand nombre ; bien* **des**; *beaucoup* **de.** — think thus; *beaucoup de personnes pensent ainsi.* The — ; *la multitude ; la généralité du public, f.*

ma'ny (mè'n'i), *adj.*, nombreux ; beaucoup **de**; bien ; du, de la, des ; plusieurs, maint ; plus d'un. The — causes ; *les causes nombreuses, f.pl.* — more ; *maint autre ; beaucoup d'autres.* — persons ; *beaucoup de personnes ; bien des personnes.* — nations ; *de nombreuses nations, f.pl.* — a man ; *maint homme.* — a time; *mainte fois.* Full — a; *maint ; plus d'un ; bien des.* As —as ; *autant que ;* (before a numeral) *jusqu'à.* As — again ; *deux fois autant ; le double.* How — ? *combien ?* Too — ; *trop ; trop* **de.** So — ; *tant, tant* **de.** — a little makes a mickle ; *les petits ruisseaux font les grandes rivières* ou *goutte à goutte on emplit la cave.* There's — a true word spoken in jest ; *on dit souvent la vérité en riant.*

ma'ny-cleft (-clète), *adj.*, aux nombreuses fissures ; (bot.) multifide.

ma'ny-col'ored (-keull'eurde), *adj.*, de diverses couleurs; multicolore.

ma'ny-cor'nered (-cor'neur'de), *adj.*, qui a plusieurs coins; multangulaire; (geom.) polygone, polygonal.

ma'ny-flow'ered (-flaour'de), *adj.*, multiflore.

ma'ny-head'ed (-hèd'-), *adj.*, aux têtes nombreuses ; à plusieurs têtes.

ma'ny-leaved' (-lîv'de), *adj.*, à beaucoup de feuilles ; (bot.) polyphylle.

ma'ny-na'tioned (-né-sheu'n'de), *adj.*, de nations diverses.

ma'ny-peo'pled (-pî'p'l'de), *adj.*, fort populeux, très peuplé.

ma'ny-pet'aled (-pèt'alde), *adj.*, (bot.) poly-pétale.

ma'ny-sid'ed (-saïd'-), *adj.*, qui a à plusieurs côtés ; polygone ; (fig.) à considérer de plus d'un point de vue ; sujet à diverses influences, sympathique, libéral ; vaste.

ma'ny-toned (-tô'n'de), *adj.*, de divers sons; de sons variés.

map, *n.*, carte ; carte géographique, *f.* — of the world ; *mappemonde, f.* — of a town ; *plan d'une ville, m.* — maker ; *ingénieur-géographe, cartographe, m.*

map, *v.a.*, dessiner une carte ; tracer une carte, *ou* un plan, **de.**

ma'ple *ou* **ma'ple-tree** (mé-p'l-trî), *n.*, érable, *m.*

map'ping, *n.*, cartographie, *f.*

mar (mâr), *v.a.*, gâter, défigurer, abîmer ; (fig.) troubler, détruire. — joy ; *rabat-joie, trouble-fête ; m.* — plot ; *brouillon, m.*

marabou', *n.*, (orni.) marabout, *m.*

maraschi'no, *n.*, (liqueur) marasquin, *m.*

maras'mus (-raz'-), *n.*, (med.) marasme, *m.*

maraud', *v.n.*, marauder.

maraud'er, *n.*, maraudeur, *m.*

maraud'ing, *n.*, maraude, *f.*, maraudage, *m.*

marave'di, *n.*, maravédis (Spanish coin), *m.*

mar'ble (mâr'b'l), *adj.*, de marbre ; (veined) marbré.

mar'ble (mâr'b'l), *n.*, marbre, *m. ;* (toy) bille, *f.*

mar'ble, *v.a.*, marbrer.

mar'ble-cut'ter (-keut'-), *n.*, marbrier, *m.*

mar'bled (mâr'b'l'de), *adj.*, marbré.

mar'ble-heart'ed (-hârt-) *ou* **mar'ble-breast'ed** (-brèst-), *adj.*, inexorable ; cruel ; insensible; au cœur de marbre, de bronze.

mar'ble-quar'ry (-kwôr'-), *n.*, carrière de marbre ; marbrière, *f.*

mar'ble-works (-weurkse), *n.pl.*, marbrerie, *f.sing.*

mar'bling, *n.*, marbrure, *f.*

march (mârtshe), *n.*, marche ; course, *f. ;* pas ; progrès ; (month) mars, *m. ;* (frontier) frontière, *f.* Mad as a — hare ; *fou à lier.* To steal a — upon ; *dérober une marche* **à** ; *gagner une marche* **sur.** — man ; *habitant de la frontière, m.* —chick ; *enfant précoce, m.* Dead-— ; *marche funèbre, f.* — past ; *défilé, m.*

march (mârtshe), *v.n.*, marcher, se mettre en marche. To — off ; *se mettre en marche ; plier bagage, s'en aller.* To — in ; *entrer.* To — out ; *sortir.* To — on ; *marcher, avancer.* To — back ; *retourner ; revenir ; reculer.* To — down ; *descendre.* To — past ; *défiler* **devant.** To — round ; *tourner ; faire le tour* **de.**

march (mârtshe), *v.a.*, faire marcher; mettre en marche ; conduire, diriger. To — off ; *emmener ; mettre en marche ; faire décamper.* To — out; *faire sortir.* To — up ; *faire avancer ; faire monter.* To — down ; *faire descendre.* To — in ; *faire entrer.* To — back ; *faire revenir, faire retourner.* To — into ; *conduire* **à.**

march'es (mârtsh'èze), *n.pl.*, marche (frontiers), *f.sing.*

march'ing, *n.*, marche, *f.* — past ; *défilé, m.*

march'ing, *adj.*, en marche, de marche. — regiment ; *régiment de marche, m.*

mar'chioness (mâr'sheu'n'èce), *n.*, marquise, *f.*

mar'cid (mâr-), *adj.*, maigre, décharné, flétri.

mare (mère), *n.*, cavale, jument, *f.* —'s nest ; *merle blanc, m.* —'s tail ; (cloud) *cirrus, m. ;* (bot.) *pesse d'eau, f.*

mar'eschal (mâr'shal), *n.*, maréchal, *m.*

mar'garine, *n.*, margarine, *f.*

mar'gay (mâr-), *n.*, (mam.) margay, chat-tigre, *m.*

mar'gin (mâr'djine), *n.*, (of paper, etc.), marge, *f. ;* (of a river, a lake, etc.) bord, *m.,*

(of a well) margelle, *f.* In the — ; *en marge.* To have a sufficient — ; (fig.) *avoir de la marge.*

mar'gin, *v.a.*, border ; (books) marginer ; (printing) marger.

mar'ginal, *adj.*, de marge ; marginal ; de bord.

mar'grave (mâr'gréve), *n.*, (title) margrave, *m.*

margra'viate, *n.*, margraviat, *m.*

mar'igold (-gôlde), *n.*, (bot.) souci, *m.*

mar'inate, *v.a.*, mariner.

marine', *n.*, marine, *f. ;* (milit., nav.) soldat de marine, *m.* —s, *pl.*, infanterie de **marine,** *f.* Tell that to the —s ; *allez conter cela ailleurs.*

marine' (-rîne), *adj.*, marin, de mer ; naval. — stores ; *bric-à-brac, m.* — store dealer; *marchand de vieille ferraille, de chiffons, etc.* — painter ; *peintre de marines, mariniste, m.*

mar'iner, *n.*, marin, matelot, *m.* —'s card ; *rose des vents, f.* —'s compass ; *boussole, f.*

mariol'atry, *n.*, mariolâtrie, *f.*

mar'ital, *adj.*, marital.

mar'itally, *adv.*, maritalement.

mar'itime (-time) *ou* **marit'imal**, *adj.*, maritime. — court ; *cour de l'Amirauté, f.*

mar'joram (mâr'djor'-), *n.*, marjolaine, *f.*

mark (mârke), *n.*, marque, *f. ;* témoignage, *m. ;* empreinte, *f. ;* (at school) point ; (on the skin) signe ; (to aim at) but, blanc, *m.,* cible, *f. ;* (notice) avis, avertissement, *m. ;* (reprisal) marque, lettre de marque, *f. ;* (coin) marc ; (weight) marc, *m. ;* (signature) croix, marque, *f.* Near the — ; *près de la réalité, de la vérité.* Over the — ; *au-dessus de la réalité, de la vérité ; exagéré.* Under the — ; *au-dessous de la réalité, de la vérité.* To miss one's — ; *manquer son coup.* To come up to the — ; *atteindre à la hauteur voulue.* To make one's — ; *faire sentir son influence ; acquérir de l'influence, de la distinction.* To be hardly up to the — ; *laisser à désirer.* To be within the — ; *atteindre la limite.*

mark (mârke), *v.a. and n.*, marquer, remarquer; faire attention à. — ye ; *remarquez bien ; notez bien.* — my words ; *écoutez-moi bien, faites bien attention à ce que je dis.* — out ; *désigner.*

marked, *adj.*, marqué, (of accent) prononcé.

mark'er, *n.*, marqueur, *m. ;* (counter) jeton, (of a book) signet ; (at billiards, etc.) marqueur, *m.*

mar'ket (mâr'kète), *n.*, marché, *m. ;* halle, *f. ;* (com.) débouché, marché, *m.,* (exchange) place, *f. ;* (sale) débit, *m.,* vente ; (pers.) masse des acheteurs, *f. ;* (price) cours, prix, *m.* To be in — ; (com.) *sur notre place.* In the — ; *à la halle.* To find a — for ; *trouver un débouché* **pour.**

mar'ket, *v.a.*, acheter au marché ; vendre au marché. To go — ing ; *aller aux provisions.*

mar'ketable (-'a-b'l), *adj.*, propre à la vente, de bonne vente ; (com.) marchand ; (of price) courant.

mar'ket-day, *n.*, jour de marché, *m.*

mar'ket-gar'den (-gâr'd'n), *n.*, marais; jardin maraîcher, *ou* légumier, *m.*

mar'ket-gar'dener (-gâr'd'n'eur), *n.*, maraîcher, *m.*

mar'ket-gar'dening, *n.*, culture maraîchère, *f.*

mar'ket-house (-haouce), *n.*, marché, *m. ;* halle, *f.*

mar'keting, *n.*, marché, *m.*

mar'ket-place, *n.*, place du marché, *f.,* marché, *m.*

mar'ket-price (-praïce) *ou* **mar'ket-rate** (-réte), *n.*, cours du marché, prix courant, *m.*

mar'ket-town (-taoune), *n.*, ville à marché, *f. ;* bourg, *m.*

mar'ket-wom'an (woum'-), *n.*, femme, *ou* dame, de la halle, *f.*

mark'ing (mârk'-), *n.*, marquage, *m.* — ink ; *encre à marquer, f.* — iron ; *fer à marquer, m.*

marks'man (mârks'-), *n.*, tireur; bon tireur, *m.* —ship; *adresse au tir, f.*

marl (mârle), *n.*, (geol. agri.) marne, *f.*

marl (mârle), *v.a.*, marner.

mar'line (mâr-laïne), *n.*, (nav.) merlin, *m.*

mar'line-spike (-spaïke), *n.*, (nav.) épissoir, *m.*

mar'ling (mârl'-), *n.*, marnage, *m.*

marl'-pit, *n.*, marnière, *f.*

marl'stone (-stône) *n.*, marne dure, marne siliceuse, *f.*

mar'ly, *adj.*, marneux.

mar'malade (mâr-), *n.*, marmelade, *f.*

marmo'rean (mâr-mor-î-), *adj.*, de marbre.

marmoset', *n.*, (mam.) ouistiti, *m.*

mar'mot, *n.*, (mam.) marmotte, *f.*

Mar'onite, *n.*, (c.rel.) maronite, *m.*

maroon' (-roune), *n.*, nègre, nègre marron, fugitif, *m.*

marque (mârke), *n.*, marque; lettre de marque, *f.* Letter of —; *lettre de marque, f.*

marquee' (mâr-kî), *n.*, marquise (tente), *f.*

mar'quetry (mâr'kèt'ri), *n.*, marqueterie, *f.*

mar'quis (mâr'kwice) *ou* **mar'quess** (mâr'-kwè'ce), *n.*, marquis, *m.*

mar'quisate (-kwiss'éte), *n.*, marquisat, *m.*

mar'rer (mâr'-), *n.*, personne qui gâte, qui abîme.

mar'riage (mar'ridge), *n.*, mariage, *m.;* noces, *f.pl.*

mar'riageable (-ridj'a-b'l), *adj.*, mariable, nubile.

mar'riage-bed, *n.*, lit nuptial, *m.*

mar'riage-con'tract, *n.*, contrat de mariage, *m.*

mar'riage-li'cense (-laï-), *n.*, dispense de bans, *f.*

mar'riage-por'tion (-pôr-), *n.*, dot, *f.*

mar'riage-set'tlement (-sèt't'l'-mè'n't), *n.*, douaire, contrat de mariage, *m.*

mar'ried (ma-ride), *past part.*, marié; (of things) conjugal. — couple; *mari et femme, m. pl.*, *ménage, m.* Newly — couple; *nouveaux mariés, m.pl.* — life; *vie conjugale, f.* — state; *mariage, m.*

mar'row (mar-rô), *n.*, moelle; (fig.) essence, *f.*

mar'row-bone (-bône), *n.*, os à moelle, *m.* Upon one's —s; (fam.) *à genoux.*

mar'row-fat, *n.*, pois carré, *m.*

mar'rowless, *n.*, sans moelle.

mar'rowy (mar-rô-i), *adj.*, moelleux; (anat.) médullaire.

mar'ry, *v.a.*, (to give away; to perform the ceremony) marier; (to take as wife, as husband) se marier **avec**; épouser; (fig.) unir intimement, marier. To — below one's station; *se mésallier.*

mar'ry, *v.n.*, se marier. To — again; *se remarier.* To be married; *se marier, ou être marié.*

mar'ry, *int.*, vraiment, en vérité; parbleu.

marsh (mârshe), *n.*, marais, *m.* — gas; (chem.) *gas des marais; hydrogène protocarboné, m.* — land; *pays marécageux.*

mar'shal (mâr-), *n.*, maréchal; (nav.) prévôt, *m.* Field—; *maréchal, m.;* (in France) *maréchal de France, m.*

mar'shal, *v.a.*, ranger, régler, ordonner; placer *ou* mettre en ordre.

mar'shaler, *n.*, ordonnateur, régulateur, *m.*

Mar'shalsea (-sî), *n.*, maréchaussée, *f.*

mar'shalship, *n.*, dignité de maréchal, *f.*

marsh-mal'low (-mal'lo), *n.*, (bot.) guimauve, *f.*

marsh-mar'igold (-), *n.*, (bot.) populage, *m.*

marsh'y (mârsh'i), *adj.*, marécageux; de marais.

mart (mârte), *n.*, marché, entrepôt, *m.;* (auction) salle de vente, *f.;* (outlet) débouché, *m.*

martel'lo-tow'er (-taou'eur), *n.*, (fort.) tour d'observation, de vigie, *f.*

mar'ten (mâr-tène), *n.*, (mam.) martre, fouine, *f.*

mar'tial (mâr-shal), *adj.*, martial; de guerre, de bataille; militaire; guerrier, belliqueux. — law; *code militaire; état de siège, m.* — nation; *nation guerrière, belliqueuse, f.* Court —; *conseil de guerre, m.* — array; *ordre de bataille, m.*

mar'tially, *adv.*, en guerrier; bravement.

mar'tin (mâr'tine), *n.*, (orni.) martinet, *m.*

mar'tinet, *n.*, personne à cheval sur la discipline, *f.*; ratapoil, *m.;* (orni.) martinet, *m.*

mar'tingale (-ghéle), *n.*, martingale, *f.*

Mar'tinmas (mâr-), *n.*, la St.-Martin, *f.*

mart'let (mârt'-), *n.*, (orni.). *V.* **mar'tinet** (orni.).

mar'tyr (mâr-teur), *n.*, martyr, *m.*, martyre, *f.*

mar'tyr (mâr-teur), *v.a.*, martyriser.

mar'tyrdom (-deume), *n.*, martyre, *m.*

mar'tyrology (mâr-teur-ol'o-dji), *n.*, martyrologe, *m.*

mar'vel (mâr-), *n.*, merveille, chose merveilleuse, *f.*

mar'vel (mâr-), *v.n.*, s'émerveiller, s'étonner. To — at; *s'émerveiller* de; *s'étonner* de.

mar'velous, *adj.*, merveilleux, étonnant, étrange.

mar'velously, *adv.*, merveilleusement; à merveille.

mar'velousness, *n.*, caractère merveilleux; merveilleux, *m.*

mas'culine (mas-kiou-), *adj.*, mâle, d'homme; (gram.) masculin; (b.s.) hommasse.

mas'culine, *n.*, masculin. In the —; *au masculin.*

mas'culinely, *adv.*, virilement, en homme.

masculin'ity, *n.*, masculinité, *f.*

mash, *n.*, mélange, *m.;* tripotage; (in breweries) mélange de malt et d'eau chaude, brassin, (for horses) mélange de son et d'eau, *m.*

mash, *v.a.*, écraser, broyer, mêler, mélanger; (in breweries) brasser.

mash'ing, *n.*, mélange, fardeau, *m.*

mash'-tub (-teube), *n.*, (brewing) cuvematière, *f.*

mash'y, *adj.*, mêlé; mélangé; écrasé; broyé.

mask (mâske), *n.*, masque, *m.;* mascarade, *f.;* (arch.) mascaron; (woman's) loup, *m.* To throw off the —; *lever le masque.*

mask, *v.a.*, masquer; déguiser; (mil.) masquer.

mask, *v.n.*, se masquer.

mask'er, *n.*, masque (pers.), *m.*

ma'son (mé-s'n), *n.*, maçon, *m.* Free—; *franc-maçon, m.* Stone—; *maçon.* Master —; *maître maçon, m.* Journeyman —; *compagnon, m.*

mason'ic (mé-ço'n'-), *adj.*, maçonnique.

ma'sonry (mé-ço'n'-), *n.*, maçonnage, *m.;* maçonnerie, *f.* Free—; *franc-maçonnerie, f.*

masquerade (mas-keur'éde), *n.*, mascarade, *f.;* masque, déguisement, *f.*

masquerade' (mas-keur'éde), *v.n.*, se masquer; faire une mascarade.

masquerad'er, *n.*, masque (pers.), *m.*

mass (mâsse), *n.*, masse, *f.;* amas, gros, *m.;* (crowd) multitude, foule; (c.rel.) messe; (phys.) masse, *f.;* amas, monceau; (of smoke) tourbillon, *m.* A — of things; *une foule de choses.* High —; (c.rel.) *grand'messe, f.* Low —; (c.rel.) *messe basse, f.* —book; *livre de messe, missel, m.* The —es; *les masses, f.pl.; la foule, f.* To hear —; *assister à la messe. v.a.*, masser.

mass'-meeting, *n.*, assemblée en masse, *f.*

mas'sacre (mass'a-keur), *n.*, massacre, *m.*

mas'sacre, *v.a.*, massacrer.

mas'sacrer, *n.*, massacreur, *m.*

mas'sicot, *n.*, (chem.) massicot, oxide de plomb jaune, *m.*

mas'sive *ou* **mas'sy** (măs'-), *adj.*, massif, solide.

mas'sively, *adv.*, en masse, massivement.

mas'siveness, *n.*, nature massive ; solidité, *f.*

mast (măste), *n.*, (nav.) mât, *m. pl.*, mâts, *m.pl. ;* mâture, *f.sing.* Fore— ; *mât de misaine.* Main— ; *grand mât.* Spare — ; *mât de rechange.* Mizzen— ; *mât d'artimon.* Jury— ; *mât de fortune.* Before the — ; *sur le gaillard d'avant.* Half—high ; *à mi-mât.* —head; *tête de mât, f.*

mast, *v.a.*, (nav.) mâter.

mast, *n.*, (fruit) (of the chestnut) châtaigne, *f. ;* marron ; (of the oak) gland, *m. ;* (of the hazel) noisette ; (of the beech) faîne, *f.*

mast'ed, *adj.*, mâté.

mas'ter (măs'teur), *n.*, maître, directeur, chef ; (nav.) maître d'équipage ; (of clerks) chef, patron ; (of workmen) maître, patron, bourgeois ; (of a boat) patron ; (of a school) maître, maître de pension, chef d'institution, maître d'école, professeur ; (of a college) directeur ; (of ceremonies) maître des cérémonies ; (of fêtes) ordonnateur ; (appellation given to children) monsieur ; (possessor) possesseur : ☉ messire ; (of a merchantman) capitaine, *m. ;* (of a Masonic lodge) vénérable, *m.* — of arts ; *maître-ès-arts ;* *licencié-ès-lettres, m.* — of the Mint ; *directeur de la Monnaie, m.* — of the Rolls ; *garde des archives, m.* —s' degree ; *licence, f.* —passion ; *passion dominante, f.* To be — of ; *posséder ; être maître* **de.** To be thoroughly — of ; *posséder à fond ; savoir à fond ; être parfaitement maître* **de.** To be one's own — ; *s'appartenir, ne dépendre que de soi ; être libre de ses actions.* To make one's self — of ; *se rendre maître* **de ;** *acquérir ; se rendre familier* **avec.** Head— ; *principal ; proviseur, m.* —mind ; *esprit supérieur, m.*

mas'ter, *v.a.*, maîtriser ; dompter ; se rendre maître **de ;** vaincre ; l'emporter **sur ;** venir à bout **de ;** surmonter ; dominer ; apprendre, posséder.

mas'ter-build'er (-bild'-), *n.*, entrepreneur de bâtiments, *m.*

mas'terdom (-deume), *n.*, domination, autorité, *f. ;* pouvoir, *m. ;* puissance, *f.*

mas'terful (-foule), *adj.*, de maître ; impérieux ; habile.

mas'ter-hand, *n.*, main de maître, *f.* He is a — at it ; *il y est passé maître.*

mas'ter-key (-kî), *n.*, passe-partout, *m.*

mas'terless, *adj.*, sans maître.

mas'terliness, *n.*, talent de maître, *m. ;* grande habileté, *f.*

mas'terly, *adj.*, supérieur, de maître ; de main de maître ; magistral ; parfait ; (imperious) impérieux.

mas'terly, *adv.*, en maître.

mas'ter-piece (-pîce), *n.*, chef-d'œuvre, *m.*

mas'tership, *n.*, pouvoir de maître, *m. ;* autorité ; habileté ; supériorité, *f. ;* (office) fonctions de maître, de professeur, *f.pl. ;* (school) place de maître, de professeur, *f.*

mas'ter-string (-strigne), *n.*, corde principale, *f.*

mas'ter-stroke (-strôke), *n.*, coup de maître, *m.*

mas'ter-touch (-teutshe), *n.*, coup de maître, *m.*, touche de maître, *f.*

mas'ter-wort (-weurte), *n.*, (bot.) impératoire ; herbe aux goutteux, *f.*

mas'tery, *n.*, supériorité, puissance ; prééminence ; domination, *f.*, empire ; pouvoir, *m. ;* (knowledge) connaissance parfaite ; perfection ; (skill) grande habileté, *f.* To contend for the — of ; *le disputer* **à.** To get the — over ; *l'emporter* **sur.**

mas'tic *ou* **mas'tich** (-tike), *n.*, (resin) mastic, *m.* —tree ; *lentisque, m.*

mas'ticate, *v.a.*, mâcher.

mastica'tion (-ti-ké-), *n.*, mastication, *f.*

mas'ticatory, *n.* and *adj.*, masticatoire, *m.*

mas'ticot, *n.* V. **mas'sicot.**

mas'tiff, *n.*, dogue ; mâtin, *m.*

mast'less, *adj.*, sans mât.

mast'lin (maz'line), *n.*, méteil, *m.*

mast'-mak'er (-mék'-), *n.*, faiseur de mâts, *m.*

mas'todon, *n.*, mastodonte, *m.*

mat, *n.*, (of rush) natte, *f. ;* (of straw) paillasson ; (for lamps, dishes) dessous (de plat), *m. ;* (metal.) matte, *f.* Door— ; *paillasson, m.* Lamp — ; *dessous de lampe, m.* — maker; *nattier, m.* — scraper ; *décrottoir, m.*

mat, *v.a.*, couvrir de nattes ; couvrir de paillassons ; (press) aplatir ; natter, tresser ; (to stick) coller ensemble, coller. —ted hair ; *cheveux collés, m.pl.*

mat'adore (-dôre), *n.*, matador, *m.*

match (matshe), *n.*, (contest) lutte ; partie, *f. ;* concours, *m. ;* (in running, sailing, rowing, driving) course, joute, *f. ;* (in fighting) combat, *m.*, lutte, *f.*

match, *n.*, (an equal) pareil, égal ; (marriage) mariage, *m.*, alliance, *f. ;* (person to be married) parti, *m.* To meet with one's — ; *trouver son maître ; trouver à qui parler.* A set — ; *conspiration, f. ;* complot ; coup monté, *m.* To be a bad — ; *(of things) aller mal ensemble.* To be a good — ; *(of things) aller bien ensemble ; être bien assorti.* To make a good — ; *faire un bon mariage ; épouser un bon parti.* To make a bad — ; *faire un mauvais mariage ; épouser un mauvais parti.* Not to have one's — ; *n'avoir pas son pareil.* To be a — for ; *être de taille* **à ;** *pouvoir résister* **à ;** *pouvoir le disputer* **à.** To be more than a — for; *être trop fort* **pour.** You are not a — for him ; *vous n'êtes pas de taille à entrer en lice* **avec** *lui, à concourir* **avec** *lui,* ou *vous ne lui allez pas à la cheville.* Love— ; *mariage d'inclination, m.* Prudent — ; *mariage de raison, de convenance, m.*

match, *n.*, (combustible substance) allumette ; (artil.) mèche, *f.* Lucifer— ; *allumette chimique, f.*

match, *v.a.*, (to equal) égaler ; (to oppose as equal) tenir tête **à,** se mesurer **avec** ; (to proportion) proportionner ; (to marry) marier, allier, donner en mariage ; (colors, stuffs) assortir ; (pairs of things) apparier ; (horses, pictures, etc.) appareiller.

match, *v.n.*, (to be united in marriage) s'allier, se marier, s'unir ; (to correspond) assortir **à,** s'assortir ; (of pairs of things) être pareil ; être le pendant **de.**

match'able (-'a-b'l), *adj.*, comparable ; égal.

match'box, *n.*, porte-allumettes, *m. ;* boîte à allumettes, *f.*

match'less, *adj.*, incomparable, sans pareil, unique.

match'lessly, *adv.*, incomparablement.

match'lessness, *n.*, incomparabilité, *f. ;* grande supériorité, *f.*

match'lock, *n.*, platine à mèche, *f. ;* fusil à mèche, *m.*

match'-mak'er (-mék'-), *n.*, marieur, *m.*, marieuse, *f. ;* faiseur de mariages, *m.*, faiseuse de mariages, *f. ;* courtier de mariages, *m.*, courtière de mariages, *f. ;* fabricant d'allumettes, *m.*

match'-mak'ing (-mék'-), *n.*, action de faire des mariages ; fabrication des allumettes, *f.*

match'-tub (-teube), *n.*, (artil.) baril à mèches, *m.*

mate (méte), *n.*, camarade, *m.f.*, copain ; compagnon, *m.*, compagne, *f. ;* (nav.) second, lieutenant, aide, contre-maître ; (at chess) mat, *m.*

mate, *v.a.*, (to marry) marier ; (to equal) égaler, assortir, apparier ; (to oppose) résister **à,** s'opposer **à,** tenir tête **à ;** (to subdue) subjuguer, humilier ; (to crush) écraser, mater ; (at chess) mater.

ma'té (mâ-tè), n., (bot.) maté, m.

mate'less, adj., sans compagnon, sans compagne.

ma'ter (mé-teur), n., (anat.) mère, f. Dura —; (anat.) dure-mère, f. Pia —; pie-mère, f.

mate'rial (-tî-), adj., matériel; essentiel, important, sensible, considérable, sérieux.

mate'rial (-tî-), n., matière; étoffe, f.; tissu, (stores) matériel, m. —s, pl., matériaux, m.pl.; fournitures, f.pl. Raw —; matière première, f.

mate'rialism (-tî-ri-al-iz'me), n., matérialisme, m.

mate'rialist (-tî-), n., matérialiste, m.

material'ity (-tî-), n., matérialité; importance, f.

mate'rialize (-tî-ri-al-aïze), v.a., matérialiser.

mate'rially (-tî-), adv., matériellement; absolument; essentiellement.

mate'rialness (-tî-), n., matérialité; (fig.) importance, f.

mate'ria med'ica (ma-tî-ri-a-mèd'i-ca), n., (med.) matière médicale, f.

mater'nal (-teur-), adj., maternel.

mater'nally (-teur-), adv., maternellement.

mater'nity (-teur-), n., maternité, f.

mat'-grass (-grâce), n., nard, m.; barbe-de-vieillard, f.

mathemat'ic ou **mathemat'ical** (mathè-), adj., mathématique, de mathématique.

mathemat'ically (math-), adv., mathématiquement.

mathemati'cian (math-), n., mathématicien, m.

mathemat'ics (math-), n., mathématiques, f.pl.

mat'ins (-ti'n'ze), n.pl., matines, f.pl.

mat'rass (-), n., (chem.) matras, m.

matrica'ria (-ké-ri-a), n., (bot.) matricaire, f.

mat'ricide (-çaïde), n., matricide (l.u.); parricide, m.

matric'ulate (-trik'iou-), v.a., immatriculer. v.n., passer l'examen d'immatriculation, prendre ses inscriptions.

matric'ulate, adj., immatriculé.

matric'ulate, n., (bot.) matriculaire, m.

matricula'tion (-trik'iou-lé-), n., immatriculation, matricule, inscription, f. — book; registre matricule.

matrimo'nial (-mô-), adj., conjugal; matrimonial, de mariage.

matrimo'nially, adv., conjugalement.

mat'rimony, n., mariage, m.

ma'trix (mé-), n., matrice, f.

ma'tron (mé-), n., dame, femme; (of hospitals) directrice; mère de famille; (jur.) matrone, f.

ma'tronal ou **ma'tron-like** (-laïke), adj., respectable; sévère; maternel; de mère; de matrone.

ma'tronly (mé-), adj., qui tire sur l'âge; d'un âge mûr; d'un certain âge; respectable.

mat'ter (mat'teur), n., matière; chose; affaire, f.; fond; sujet; (med.) pus, m., matière purulente, f.; (jur.) moyen; (space of time) espace de temps, m.; (distance) distance; (suit) cause, f., sujet de plainte, m.; (import) importance, f. — of record; fait authentique, m. Upon the whole —; tout bien considéré. — of taste; affaire de goût, f. The — I speak of; le sujet dont je parle. It is a very easy —; c'est une chose bien facile. In —; dans le fond. What is the —? Nothing; qu'y a-t-il? de quoi s'agit-il? Il n'y a rien. What is the — with you? Nothing; qu'avez-vous? Je n'ai rien. What is the — in hand? de quoi s'agit-il? The — I have on hand cannot wait; l'affaire que j'ai ne peut attendre (V. Hugo). What —? qu'importe? No —! n'importe! It is no great —; ce n'est pas grand'chose. A small —; une bagatelle. For

that —, for the — of that; quant à cela. In —, ou —s, of; en fait de, en matière de. Something must be the —; il faut qu'il y ait quelque chose sous jeu. It is a small — after all; c'est bien peu de chose après tout. The manner and the —; la forme et le fond. —of-fact gossip; bavardage, commérage, m.; causerie terre à terre, f. — of course; chose toute naturelle; chose qui va sans dire, qui va de soi, f. As a — of course; comme de raison. It is no — whether you did it or not; il importe peu que vous l'ayez fait ou non. For the — of that; qu'à cela ne tienne; ce n'est pas l'embarras; pour ce qui est de ça; si ce n'est que cela. If nothing was the —; comme si de rien n'était. As a — of fact; le fait est que. As —s stand; au point où en sont les choses.

mat'ter, v.n.imp., importer. What—s? qu'importe? It —s; il importe. It —s not, it —s little; n'importe; il n'importe; peu importe.

mat'terless, adj., sans matière.

matter-of-fact', adj., pratique, positif.

mat'tery, adj., (med.) purulent.

mat'ting, n., (of straw) paillasson, m.; (of rush) natte, f.

mat'tock, n., pioche, f.

mat'tress (mat'trèce), n., matelas, m.

mat'tress-ma'ker (-mék'-), n., matelassier, m., matelassière, f.

matura'tion (-ré-), n., maturation, f. [fait.

mature' (-tioure), adj., mûr, mûri; (of wine)

mature', v.a., mûrir, faire mûrir.

mature'ly, adv., mûrement.

mature', v.n., mûrir; (com.) échoir, venir à échéance.

mature'ness ou **matu'rity**, n., maturité; (of bills) échéance, f. To come to —; (of bills) échoir.

matuti'nal, adj., matinal, du matin.

mat'-weed (-wîde), n. V. **mat'-grass**.

maud'lin, adj., à moitié ivre; (fig.) insipide, pleureur, larmoyant; affecté, sentimental.

maud'lin-wort, n., (bot.) grande marguerite, f., chrysanthème, m.

maul, v.a., rosser; rouer de coups, déchirer, meurtrir.

maul, n. V. **mall**.

maul'-stick, n., (painting) appui-main, m.

Maun'day-Thurs'day (mâ'n'dè-theur'z'dè), n., (c.rel.) jeudi saint.

mausole'an, adj., monumental.

mausole'um, n., mausolée, m.

mauve, adj., mauve.

maw (mô), n., (of birds) jabot, m.; (of animals) panse, f. —seed; graine de pavot, f. —worm; ver intestinal ou rongeur, m.

maw'kish (môk'-), adj., fade, dégoûtant, insipide.

maw'kishness, n., fadeur, insipidité, f.

max'illar, adj., (anat.) maxillaire.

max'im, n., maxime, f.

max'im-mon'ger (-meu'gn'gheur), n., débiteur de maximes, m.; débiteuse de maximes, f.

max'imum, n., maximum, m.

may (mé), v.auxil., pouvoir. — be; peut-être. It might be; cela se pourrait. It might happen that; il pourrait se faire que. You might have gone there; vous auriez pu y aller. One might as well; autant vaudrait. That — be; cela se peut. He — go; il peut sortir. — I! puis-je! puissé-je! — I die if . . . ; que je meure si . . . Any troops might have been expected to show signs of insubordination; on aurait pu s'attendre à voir les meilleures troupes montrer des signes d'insubordination. You — be humiliated; il se peut que vous soyez humilié. You — have seen; vous avez pu voir. You — not have seen; vous avez pu ne pas voir. It — be that; il se peut que (with subj.). [When **may** and **might** are auxiliary verbs they are the sign of the subjunctive or conditional.]

May, n., (month) mai, m. —-bloom ; aubépine, f.

May, v.a., célébrer le premier mai.

may'-bug (-beughe), n., hanneton, m.

may'-bush (-boushe), n., aubépine, f.

May'-day (mé-dé), n., premier mai, m., (fig.). — of life ; printemps de la vie, m.

may'-flower (-flaoueur), n., fleur d'aubépine, f.

May'-morn, n., (fig.) fraîcheur, vigueur, f.

may'or (mé-eur), n., maire, m.

may'oralty (mé-eur'-), n., mairie, f.

may'oress (mé-eur'-), n., femme du maire, f.

May'-pole (-pôl), n., mai, arbre du premier mai, m., plantation de mai, f. (V. Hugo).

May'-queen, reine du premier mai, f.

maze (méze), n., labyrinthe ; dédale ; (fig.) embarras, m., perplexité, f.

mazour'ka, n., mazourka, masurka, f.

ma'zy (méz'i), adj., de labyrinthe, sinueux ; (of a dance) pirouettant ; (fig.) confus ; embrouillé, compliqué.

me (mi), pron., me, moi. Of —, from — ; de moi. To — ; moi ; à moi ; me.

mead (mîde), n., hydromel ; (meadow) pré, m., prairie, f.

mead'ow (mèd'ô), n., prairie, f., pré, m.

mead'ow-grass, n., paturin, m.

mead'ow-land, n., prairie, f.

mead'ow-lark, n., étourneau, m.

mead'ow-saf'fron, n., colchique, m.

mead'ow-sweet (-swîte), n., spirée ; herbe aux abeilles, reine des prés, f.

mead'owy (mèd'ô-i), adj., de pré, de prairie.

mea'ger (mî-gheur), adj., maigre ; pauvre.

mea'gerly, adv., maigrement ; pauvrement.

mea'gerness, n., maigreur ; pauvreté, f.

meal (mîl), n., farine, f. ; (repast) repas, m.

meal'iness (mîl'-), n., propriété farineuse ; (fruit) nature cotonneuse, f., (fig.) douceur, f.

meal'man, n. (mealmen), farinier ; marchand de farine, m.

meal'-time (-taïme), n., heure du repas, f.

meal'-tub (-teube), n., farinière, huche, f.

meal'y (mîl'i), adj., farineux ; poudreux, (fruit) cotonneux, (fig.) doucereux.

meal'y-mouthed (-maouth'de), adj., qui a la bouche doucereuse ; qui a la langue dorée.

meal'y-mouthedness (-maouthd'-), n., bouche doucereuse ; langue dorée, f.

mea'ly-tree (-trî), n., (bot.) bourdaine blanche, f.

mean (mîne), adj., (wanting dignity) bas ; (despicable) bas, méprisable, vil, abject ; (of little value) médiocre ; (low-minded) mesquin, commun ; (humble) pauvre, petit, chétif ; (avaricious) sordide, avare, regardant ; (middle) moyen. — distance ; distance moyenne, f. Of — birth ; de basse extraction. A — affair ; une affaire mesquine, f.

mean, n., milieu, terme moyen ; (log.) moyen, terme moyen, m. ; (math.) moyenne proportionelle, moyenne ; (mediocrity) médiocrité. —s (sing.) ; moyen, m. ; voie, f. —s (pl.) ; moyens, revenus, m.pl. ; fortune, f.sing. By —s of ; au moyen de. Golden — ; juste milieu, m. By this —s ; par ce moyen. By some —s or other ; de manière ou d'autre. By all —s ; par tous les moyens ; absolument ; à toute force ; certainement. By no —s ; par aucun moyen ; en aucune manière ; aucunement ; nullement. To live on one's —s ; vivre de ses revenus, de sa fortune. By no manner of —s ; à aucun prix que ce soit ; nullement. By fair —s ; par des voies honnêtes, par des moyens légitimes. By foul —s ; par des voies injustes.

mean, v.a., (preterit and past part., Meant) (to signify) signifier, vouloir dire ; (to intend) se proposer de, avoir en vue, vouloir. To— for ; destiner à. What does that word —? que veut dire

ce mot ? What do you —? que voulez-vous dire ? I meant that for you ; je vous destinais cela. He never meant it ; il ne l'a pas fait exprès. Do you — it ? êtes-vous sérieux ? Do you — what you say ? entendez-vous réellement ce que vous dites ?

mean, v.n., avoir l'intention de ; se proposer de ; avoir en vue de ; vouloir ; entendre. To — well to ; vouloir le bien de. To — well ; avoir de bonnes intentions.

mean'der (mi-a'n'-), n., détour, méandre ; dédale, labyrinthe, m. ; sinuosité, f.

mean'der, v.n., serpenter ; aller en serpentant.

mean'dering, adj., qui serpente ; qui va en serpentant ; onduleux, sinueux, tortueux.

mean'ing (mî'n'-), adj., significatif ; (pers.) à intention. Ill— ; à mauvaises intentions, mal intentionné. Well— ; à bonnes intentions, bien intentionné.

mean'ing (mî'n'-), n., (signification) signification, f., sens, m. ; (intention) intention, f., dessein, m. ; (thought) pensée, f. What is the — of that ? que veut dire cela ? que signifie cela ? That is not my — ; ce n'est pas là ce que je veux dire, ce n'est pas là ma pensée. Double — ; double sens, m. To know the — of anything ; savoir ce que quelque chose signifie, veut dire.

mean'ingless, adj., vide de sens, dénué de sens.

mean'ly (mî'n'-), adv., bassement ; méprisablement, vilement, abjectement ; médiocrement ; mesquinement, pauvrement ; chétivement ; sordidement. To speak — of a person ; parler de quelqu'un avec peu de respect. To think — of ; avoir une triste opinion de, faire peu de cas de.

mean'ness (mî'n'-), n., bassesse, vilenie, f. ; caractère méprisable, caractère vil, caractère abject, m. ; médiocrité ; pauvreté ; mesquinerie, lésinerie, avarice, pingrerie, f.

mean-spir'ited, adj., sans cœur ; lâche. He was a — coward ; c'était un poltron dépourvu d'honneur.

mean'time ou **mean'while** (-taïme, -whaïle), adv., dans l'intervalle ; en attendant. In the — ; sur ces entrefaites.

mease (mîze), n., (of herrings) quantité de cinq cents, f.

mea'sled (mî'z'l'de), **mea'sly**, adj., atteint de rougeole ; couvert de taches de rougeole ; (pigs) atteint de ladrerie.

mea'sles (mî'z'l'ze), n.pl., rougeole, f.sing. ; (of swine) ladrerie, f.

mea'surable (mèj'eur'a-b'l), adj., mesurable ; (moderate) modéré, mesuré.

meas'urableness (mèj'eur'-), n., dimensions mesurables ; mensurabilité, f.

meas'urably (mèj'eur'-), adv., avec mesure ; modérément.

meas'ure (mèj'eur), n., mesure ; (of a number) division, partie aliquote, nombre, m., proportion, f. ; (mus., poet., dancing) mesure ; (fig.) capacité, portée, f. The — of my days ; le nombre de mes jours. To take —s ; prendre des mesures. To take legal —s ; avoir recours aux voies légales. To take any one's — for a coat ; prendre la mesure d'un habit à quelqu'un. In — ; avec mesure. In a great — ; en grande partie. In some — ; en quelque sorte, jusqu'à un certain point, en partie. Beyond all —, without — ; outre mesure, sans mesure, sans bornes. To — ; sur mesure. To have a coat made to — ; faire faire un habit sur mesure. There is — in everything ; il y a une limite à tout. To have no —s to keep ; n'avoir aucun ménagement à garder avec. To take a person's — ; (fig.) estimer à sa juste valeur. To have hard — ; être traité durement.

meas'ure (mèj'eur), v.a., mesurer ; (land) arpenter ; (pers.) prendre mesure à ; (solids)

métrer. To — other people's corn by one's own bushel ; *mesurer les autres à son aune.* To — one's length (on the ground) ; *tomber de son long.* To — strength ; *en venir aux mains.* To — swords with ; *se battre à l'épée* **avec.**

meas'ure (mèj'eur), *v.n.,* avoir. This —s ten feet ; *ceci a dix pieds de longueur.*

meas'ured (mèj'eur'de), *adj.,* mesuré ; égal, uniforme. He spoke in no — terms ; *il parla en termes peu mesurés.*

meas'ureless (mèj'eur'-), *adj.,* immense, infini, illimité.

meas'urement (mèj'eur'-), *n.,* mesurage, *m. ;* mesure, *f. ;* (of land) arpentage, *m.*

meas'urer (mèj'eur'-), *n.,* mesureur ; (of land) arpenteur ; (of buildings) toiseur, vérificateur, *m.*

meas'uring (mèj'eur'-) *v.n.,* mesurage, *m.*

meat (mîte), *n.,* viande ; (food) nourriture, *f.,* aliment, *m.* Roast — ; *rôti, m.* — tea ; *thé accompagné d'une collation, m.* — breakfast ; *déjeuner à la fourchette, m.* Boiled — ; *bouilli, m.* Broken — ; *graillons, m.pl.* Brown — ; *viande noire.* White — ; *viande blanche.* Butcher's — ; *viande de boucherie ; grosse viande.* Green — ; (for animals) *vert, m.* That is my — and drink ; *c'est ce qui me fait vivre.* Force— ball ; *boulette, f. ;* pl., *quenelles, f.pl.* — fly ; *mouche à viande, f.* — market ; *marché à la viande, m.* — salesman ; *chevillard, boucher en gros, m.*

meat'y, *adj.,* charnu.

mechan'ic (mi-ka'n'ike), *n.,* mécanicien ; artisan, ouvrier, *m.*

mechan'ic *ou* **mechan'ical** (mi-ka'n'-), *adj.,* mécanique ; d'ouvrier ; d'artisan ; de la classe ouvrière ; (done without intelligence) machinal.

mechan'ically (mi-ka'n'-), *adv.,* mécaniquement ; (without intelligence) machinalement.

mechan'icalness (mi-ka'n'-), *n.,* nature mécanique ; nature machinale, *f.*

mechani'cian (mèk'a-nish'a'n), *n.,* mécanicien, *m.*

mechan'ics (mi-ka'n'-ikse), *n.,* mécanique, *f.sing.*

mech'anism (mèk'a'n'iz'me), *n.,* mécanisme, *m. ;* mécanique, *f.*

mech'anist (mèk'a'n'-), *n.,* mécanicien.

mech'lin (mèk'line), *n.,* malines (dentelle), *f.*

med'al (mèd'-), *n.,* médaille, *f.*

medal'lic (mi-), *adj.,* de médaille.

medal'lion (mi-dal'ieune), *n.,* médaillon, *m.*

med'alist (mèd'-), *n.,* (engraver) médailleur ; (pers.) médailliste, *m. ;* (one rewarded) médaillé.

med'dle (mèd'd'l), *v.n.,* se mêler des affaires d'autrui. To — with ; *toucher* **à** ; *se mêler* **de** ; *s'occuper* **de** ; *intervenir* **dans** ; *s'immiscer* **dans.**

med'dler, *n.,* fâcheux ; intrigant ; fureteur, touche-à-tout. *m.*

med'dlesome (-seume) *ou* **med'dling,** *adj.* impertinent, indiscret, importun, intrigant ; qui touche à tout.

mediæ'val (mèd'i-i-), *adj.,* du moyen âge.

me'dial (mî-), *adj.,* moyen ; (gram.) médial.

me'dially, *adv.,* médialement.

me'diate (mî-), *v.n.* être médiateur **dans** ; s'interposer **dans,** s'entremettre, intervenir **en faveur de.**

me'diate, *adj.,* médiat, interposé, intermédiaire.

me'diately, *adv.,* médiatement.

media'tion (mî-di-é-), *n.,* médiation ; entremise ; intercession, *f. ;* intermédiaire, *m.*

mediatiza'tion (mî-di-a-taïzé-), *n.,* médiatisation, *f.*

me'diatize (mî-di-a-taïze), *v.a.,* médiatiser.

me'diator (mî-di-é-teur), *n.,* médiateur, *m.*

mediato'rial *ou* **me'diatory** (mî-), *adj.,* de médiateur.

me'diatorship, *n.,* office de médiateur, *m.*

me'diatrix (mî-di-é-), *n.,* médiatrice, *f.*

med'ic (mèd'-), *n.,* (bot.) luzerne, *f.*

med'icable (mèd'i-ca-b'l), *adj.,* guérissable, curable.

med'ical (mèd'-), *adj.,* médical ; de médecin, de médecine. — jurisprudence ; *médecine légale, f* — profession ; *la Faculté ; médecine, f.* — man' *médecin, m.* — student ; *étudiant en médecine, m. ;* (pop.) carabin, m. — officer ; *officier de santé, m.* — practitioner ; *médecin praticien.* —friend ; *ami médecin, m.* —advice ; consultation, *f.pl.* — attendance ; *visites (d'un médecin), f.pl.* To take — advice ; *consulter un médecin.*

med'ically, *adv.,* en médecine ; sous le rapport médical ; suivant les règles de la médecine.

medic'ament (mèd'-), *n.,* médicament, *m.*

medicamen'tal, *adj.,* médicamenteux.

medicamen'tally, *adv.,* en forme de médicament.

medicas'ter (mèd'-), *n.,* charlatan, *m.*

med'icate (mèd'-), *v.a.,* (to treat with medicine) médicamenter, traiter.

medica'tion (mèd'i-ké-), *n.,* médication, *f.*

medi'cinal (mè-diss'i-), *adj.,* médicinal.

medi'cinally, *adv.,* médicinalement.

med'icine (mèd'i-cine), *n.,* médecine, *f. ;* remède ; médicament, *m.*

med'icine-chest (-tshèste), *n.,* droguier, *m. ;* pharmacie, *f.*

medio'cre (mî-di-ô-keur), *adj.,* médiocre.

medioc'rity (mî-di-ok'-), *n.,* médiocrité, *f.*

med'itate (mèd'-), *v.n.* méditer ; avoir l'intention **de** ; se proposer **de** ; méditer, projeter. To — on ; *méditer* **sur** ; *méditer.*

med'itated (mèd'-), *adj.,* médité, projeté.

medita'tion (mèd'i-té-), *n.,* méditation, *f.*

med'itative, *adj.,* méditatif ; de méditation.

Mediterra'nean (mèd'i-teur-ré-ni-), *adj.,* méditerrané. — sea ; *mer Méditerranée, f.*

Mediterra'nean, *n.,* Méditerranée, *f.*

me'dium (mî-), *n.,* (media) milieu, terme moyen ; médium ; (log.) moyen terme, moyen, *m. ;* (math.) moyenne proportionnelle, moyenne, *f. ;* (agent) agent intermédiaire, organe ; véhicule ; (means) moyen, intermédiaire, *m. ;* voie, entremise, *f. ;* (spirit-rapping) médium, *m.* Circulating — ; *agent monétaire, agent de circulation, m.* Just — ; *juste milieu.* Through the — of ; *par l'intermédiaire* **de,** *par l'entremise* **de.**

med'lar (mèd'-), *n.,* (fruit) nèfle, *f. ;* (tree) néflier, *m.*

med'ley (mèd'li), *adj.,* mêlé, mixte, confus.

med'ley, *n.,* mélange, *m. ;* bigarrure, *f. ;* (mus.) pot pourri, *m.*

medul'la (mi-deul'la), *n.,* moelle, *f.*

medul'lar (mi-) *adj.* de moelle ; (anat.) médullaire.

Medu'sa, *n.,* méduse, *f. ;* (zool.) méduse, *f.*

meed (mîde), *n.,* récompense, *f. ;* prix, don, *m. ;* (share) part, *f.*

meek (mîke), *adj.,* doux, humble, soumis, débonnaire.

meek'-eyed (aïe'de), *adj.,* au regard doux.

meek'ly, *adv.,* avec douceur ; humblement.

meek'ness, *n.,* douceur ; humilité, *f.*

meer'schaum (mîr-), *n.,* écume de mer, *f.* — pipe ; *pipe en écume de mer, f.*

meet (mîte), *v.a.,* (*preterit* and *past part.,* Met) rencontrer ; faire la rencontre **de** ; (to find) trouver, recevoir ; (to join) joindre, rejoindre ; (to face) faire face **à,** affronter ; (to appear before) se présenter **devant** ; (in society) voir ; (a bill) faire honneur **à** ; (fig.) anticiper, aller **au devant de** ; (to foresee) prévoir ; (to satisfy) satisfaire, remplir, accommoder, arranger. Advancing to — them ; *s'avançant à leur rencontre.* To be met with ; *se rencontrer, se trouver.* To go to — ; *aller au devant* **de** (at the station) ; *aller trouver.* To — one's engagements ; *faire face* **à** *ses engagements.* Persons met together ; *des* *personnes réunies ensemble, f.pl.* Persons met from all parts; *des personnes réunies, rassemblées de toutes parts.* To — death; *affronter la mort.* To — with one's death; *trouver la mort; être tué.* More is meant than —s the ear; *il y a quelque chose de caché sous ces paroles.*

meet, *v.n.,* se rencontrer ; se voir; (to assemble) se réunir, s'assembler ; (to join) se joindre, se rejoindre, se toucher. To — half way; (fig.) *se faire des concessions mutuelles.* To — with; (a person) rencontrer, se trouver **avec**; (thing) rencontrer, trouver, découvrir; (misfortune) *éprouver, subir, essuyer ;* (good fortune) *éprouver;* (kindness, a reception) *recevoir.* When shall we — again ? *à quand notre prochaine réunion ? quand nous reverrons-nous ?* His father has met with a serious accident; *un grave accident est arrivé à son père.* Extremes — ; *les extrêmes se touchent.*

meet (mîte), *adj.,* propre, convenable, à propos. To be — with; *être quitte* **envers** ; *rendre la pareille à.*

meet, *n.,* rendez-vous de chasse, *m.*

meet'ing (mît'-), *n.,* rencontre; (interview) entrevue ; (assembly) assemblée, réunion, *f. ;* (of rivers) confluent, *m.,* jonction ; (of roads) jonction, *f. ;* (of dissenters) office, service, *m.* Right of —; *droit de réunion, m.*

meet'ing-house (-haouce), *n.,* maison de réunion, *f. ;* (of dissenters) temple, *m.*

meet'ly, *adv.,* convenablement, à propos ; comme il faut.

meet'ness, *n.,* convenance, propriété, *f.*

me'grim (mî-grime), *n.,* migraine, *f. ;* vertige, *m.*

melanchol'ic (mèl'a'n'kol'-), *adj.,* mélancolique, triste.

mel'ancholy, *n.,* hypocondrie, mélancolie, tristesse, *f.*

mel'ancholy, *adj.,* hypocondriaque, mélancolique, triste ; (of things) triste, cruel, lugubre, affligeant.

mel'ilot, *n.,* (bot.) mélilot, *m.*

mellif'erous (mèl'lif'eur'-) *ou* **mellif'ic** (mèl'-lif'-), *adj.,* (l.u.) mellifère.

mellifica'tion (-ik'é-), *n.,* mellification, *f.*

mellif'luence (-lif'líou-), *n.,* douceur constante, *f.*

mellif'luent *ou* **mellif'luous,** *adj.,* mellifiu, doux, plein de douceur ; suave.

mel'low (mèl'lô), *adj.,* mou ; mol ; (fruit) blet; (paint.) moelleux ; (in liquor) entre deux vins, en train, gai, gris ; (of land) meuble ; (fig.) doux, moelleux, mélodieux.

mel'low, *v.a.,* mûrir ; faire mûrir ; (fruit) rendre blet ; (paint.) donner du moelleux à ; (land) ameublir ; (fig.) rendre mélodieux, rendre doux ; adoucir, amollir.

mel'low, *v.n.,* mollir, mûrir ; (fruit) devenir blet ; (paint.) prendre du moelleux ; (of land) devenir meuble, ameublir ; (fig.) devenir mélodieux, s'adoucir, s'amollir.

mel'lowing, *n.,* amollissement, adoucissement; (of fruit) blettissement ; (of land) ameublissement, *m.*

mel'lowness, *n.,* maturité, *f. ;* état d'un fruit blet ; (paint.) moelleux ; état d'un terrain meuble, *m. ;* (fig.) mollesse, douceur, *f.,* moelleux, *m.*

melo'dious (mè-lô-di-), *adj.,* mélodieux.

melo'diously, *adv.,* mélodieusement.

melo'diousness, *n.,* mélodie, *f.*

mel'odrama (mèl-o-drâ-ma), *n.,* mélodrame, *m.*

melodramat'ic, *adj.,* mélodramatique.

melodramat'ically, *adv.,* mélodramatiquement.

melodra'matist, *n.,* mélodramaturge, *m.*

mel'ody (mèl'-), *n.,* mélodie, *f.*

mel'on (mèl'-), *n.,* melon, *m.* — **shaped ;** *melonné, en forme de melon.*

mel'on-bed (-bède), *n.,* melonnière, *f.*

melt (mèlte), *v.a.,* fondre, faire fondre ; résoudre ; (fig.) attendrir, fléchir ; faire faiblir.

melt, *v.n.,* fondre, se fondre ; se résoudre ; (fig.) fléchir, faiblir, s'attendrir. To — into tears; *fondre en larmes.* To — away; *fondre, disparaître ;* (fig.) *s'évanouir ; se dissiper.*

melt'er, *n.,* fondeur, *m.*

melt'ing, *adj.,* qui fond; (fruit) fondant ; (of the weather) étouffant ; (fig.) attendrissant, touchant.

melt'ing, *n.,* fusion, fonte, *f. ;* attendrissement, *m.* — point ; (phys.) *point de fusion, m.*

melt'ing-house (-haouce), *n.,* fonderie, *f.*

melt'ing-pot, *n.,* creuset, *m.*

mem'ber (mè'm'beur), *n.,* membre, député, membre du parlement, *m.*

mem'bered, *adj.,* membré ; qui a des membres. Big—; *membru.*

mem'bership, *n.,* qualité de membre ; société, *f.;* les membres d'une société, d'une association, *m.pl.*

mem'brane (mè'm'bréne), *n.,* membrane, *f.*

mem'branous (mè'm'bré-neusse), *adj.,* membraneux.

memen'to (mi-mè'n'tô), *n.,* souvenir, mémento, *m.*

mem'oir (mè'm'-), *n.,* mémoire, *m.*

mem'orable (mè'm'o-ra-b'l), *adj.,* mémorable.

mem'orably, *adv.,* d'une manière mémorable.

memoran'dum (mè'm'o-ra'n'deume), *n.,* (*memoranda, -dums*) note, *f. ;* (com.) bordereau, *m.* To make a — of ; *prendre note* **de,** *noter.*

memoran'dum-book (-bouke), *n.,* agenda ; (com.) carnet, *m.*

memo'rial (mi-mô-), *n.,* souvenir, *m. ;* commémoration ; (note) note, *f.,* mémoire, *m. ;* (petition) requête, pétition, demande, *f. ;* (scriptural) mémorial, *m.*

memo'rial, *adj.,* commémoratif ; de la mémoire.

memo'rialist (mi-mô-), *n.,* (memoirist) auteur de mémoires ; (petitioner) pétitionnaire, *m.*

memo'rialize (mi-mô-ri-al'aïze), *v.a.,* présenter une demande **à,** une requête **à** ; adresser un mémoire **à.**

mem'ory (mè'm'-), *n.,* mémoire, *f. ;* souvenir, *m.* In — of ; *en souvenir* **de.** To the best of my —; *autant qu'il m'en souvient.* From —; *de mémoire.* Within the —of man ; *de mémoire d'homme.* Good, bad —; *bonne, mauvaise mémoire.* This occurred within my own —; *ceci est arrivé de mon temps.*

men (mène), *n.pl. V.* **man.** — **die as they live ;** (prov.) *telle vie, telle fin.*

men'ace (mè'n'-), *n.,* menace, *f.*

men'ace, *v.a.,* menacer.

men'acer, *n.,* personne qui menace, *f.*

men'acing, *adj.,* menaçant.

mena'gerie (mi-nâ-ji-ri), *n.,* ménagerie, *f.*

mend (mè'n'de), *v.a.,* raccommoder ; réparer ; (a pen, pencil) tailler ; (one's pace) hâter ; (fig.) corriger, avancer, réformer, rétablir, améliorer. To — one's pace ; *hâter le pas.*

mend, *v.n.,* se corriger, s'améliorer, se réformer ; se rétablir ; (of the weather) se remettre au beau. My health is —ing ; *ma santé s'améliore, se rétablit.* The evil is past —ing ; *le mal est sans remède.*

mend'able (-a-b'l), *adj.,* réparable ; (fig.) corrigible.

menda'city (mè'n'-), *n.,* mensonge, *m. ;* habitude de mentir ; duplicité, fausseté, *f.* In him — was almost a disease ; *l'habitude de mentir était chez lui presque une maladie.*

mend'er (mè'n'd'-), *n.,* réparateur ; raccommodeur, *m.,* raccommodeuse, *f.* (fig.) correcteur, *m.*

men'dicant (mè'n'-), *adj.,* mendiant; de mendicité. — friar ; *frère mendiant, moine mendiant, m.*

men'dicant, *n.*, mendiant, *m.*, mendiante, *f.*

mendi'city (mè'n'-), *n.*, mendicité, *f.*

mend'ing, *n.*, raccommodage, *n.*; réparation, *f.*

me'nial (mî-), *n.*, domestique, *m.f.*; valet, laquais, subalterne, *m.*

me'nial, *adj.*, domestique, de domestique; (fig.) bas, avilissant, servile.

meningi'tis (mè-ni'n'djaï-tice), *n.*, méningite, *f.*

menis'cus (mi-nis'-), *n.*, (opt.) ménisque, *m.*

men'iver (mè'n'-) *ou* **min'iver** (mi'n'-), *n.*, petit-gris, ⊙vair, *m.*

menol'ogy (mi-nol'o-dji), *n.*, ménologe, *m.*

men'ses, *n.*, menstrues, *f.pl.*

men'struated, *adj.*, menstruée, réglée.

men'struum (mè'n'strou-), *n.*, dissolvant.

mensurabil'ity (mè'n's'iou-), *n.*, mesurabilité, *f.*

men'surable (mè'n's'iou-ra-b'l), *adj.*, mesurable.

mensura'tion (mè'n's'iou-ré-), *n.*, mesurage, *m.*; (math.) mensuration, *f.*

men'tal (mè'n'-), *adj.*, mental, intellectuel, moral. — arithmetic; *calcul mental, m.* — reservation; *restriction mentale, f.*

men'tally, *adv.*, mentalement, intellectuellement, moralement.

men'tion (mè'n'-), *n.*, mention, *f.*

men'tion (mè'n'-), *v.a.*, mentionner; faire mention **de**; parler **de**; rapporter, indiquer, constater. Do not — it ! *n'y faites pas attention ! il n'y a pas de quoi.* Not to —; (putting aside) *sans compter; sans parler* **de**. To — an instance; *pour citer un exemple.*

men'tor (mè'n'-), *n.*, mentor, guide, *m.*

mephit'ic, *adj.*, méphitique.

mephi'tis (mi-faï-) *ou* **meph'itism** (mèf'i-tiz'me), *n.*, méphitisme, *f.*

mer'cantile (meur-ca'n'taïl), *adj.*, mercantile, de commerce; commerçant, -e. — establishment; *maison de commerce, f.* — politics; *politique commerciale, f.* — law; *droit commercial, m.* — community; *classe commerçante, f.* — navy; *marine marchande, f.* In — circles; *dans le commerce.* — town; *ville marchande, f.* — nation; *nation commerçante, f.*

mer'cantilism, *n.*, mercantilisme, *f.*

Merca'tor's-chart, *n.*, carte, *ou* projection, de Mercator, *f.*

mer'cenarily (meur-ci-), *adv.*, d'une manière mercenaire, mercenairement.

mer'cenariness, *n.*, vénalité, *f.*

mer'cenary (meur-ci-), *adj.*, mercenaire, vénal.

mer'cenary, *n.*, mercenaire, *m.f.*

mer'cer (meur-ceur), *n.*, mercier, *m.*

mer'cery, *n.*, mercerie, *f.*

mer'chandise (meur'tsha'n'daize), *n.*, marchandise, *f.*

mer'chant (meur'tsha'n'te), *n.*, négociant, commerçant, (retailer) marchand, *m.*, marchande, *f.* Coal—; *marchand de charbon.*

mer'chant, *adj.*, commercial; marchand. Law —; *droit commercial, m.*

mer'chantable (-'a-b'l), *adj.*, marchand.

mer'chant-like (-laïke), *adj.*, en négociant, en marchand, en commerçant.

mer'chantman *ou* **mer'chant-ship**, *n.*, navire, vaisseau marchand, *m.*

mer'chant-sea'man, *n.*, marin de la marine marchande, *m.*

mer'chant-ser'vice (-seur-), *n.*, marine marchande, *f.*

mer'chant-tai'lor (-), *n.*, marchand-tailleur, *m.*

mer'ciful (meur'ci-foule), *adj.*, miséricordieux, enclin à la miséricorde; indulgent; compatissant.

mer'cifully, *adv.*, miséricordieusement; avec clémence.

mer'cifulness, *n.*, miséricorde, **clémence**, compassion, pitié, indulgence, *f.*

mer'ciless, *adj.*, sans pitié; sans clémence, cruel, implacable, impitoyable.

mer'cilessly, *adv.*, sans miséricorde; impitoyablement, sans pitié.

mercu'rial (meur-kiou-), *adj.*, de Mercure; de mercure; (fig.) ardent, vif; mercuriel. — bath; (chem.) *cuve à mercure, f.* — finger; *le petit doigt, m.*

mer'cury (meur-kiou-), *n.*, (astron., myth.) Mercure; (metal.) mercure, *m.*; (bot.) mercuriale; (fig.) ardeur, vivacité, activité, *f.*

mer'cy (meur-ci), *n.*, merci, miséricorde; (compassion) compassion; (clemency) clémence; (pardon) grâce, indulgence, *f.*, pardon, *m.* — ! *grâce !* For—'s sake; *par grâce.* At the — of; *à la discrétion* **de**; *à la merci* **de**; *au gré* **de**. To be at the — of; *être à la discrétion* **de**, *à la merci* **de**. To cry —; *demander grâce.* To have — on; *avoir pitié* **de**. Sisters of —; *sœurs de charité, f.pl.* — stroke; *coup de grâce, m.* With a recommendation to —; (jur.) *avec des circonstances atténuantes.*

mer'cy-seat (-sîte), *n.*, (Bible) propitiatoire, *m.*

mere (mîre), *n.*, étang, lac, *m.*; (boundary) borne, *f.*

mere (mîre), *adj.*, pur, simple, seul, rien que, pas autre chose que; (b.s.) vrai, franc. — right; *nu-propriété, f.*

mere'ly (mîr'-), *adv.*, simplement, seulement, purement; uniquement, rien que, pas autre chose que.

meretri'cious (mèr'i-trish'eusse), *adj.*, de courtisane, (fig.) d'emprunt, faux, de mauvais goût.

morgan'ser (meur'-), *n.*, (orni.) harle, *m.*

merge (meurdje), *v.a.*, laisser fondre; éteindre; fondre; absorber.

merge, *v.n.*, s'éteindre; se perdre **dans**. To — into; *se fondre* **dans**; *se perdre* **dans**; *se confondre* **avec**.

merid'ian (mi-), *n.*, méridien; midi; (fig.) apogée, *m.* In his —; *à son apogée.* In the — of his glory; *à l'apogée de sa gloire.*

merid'ian, *adj.*, méridien; midi.

merid'ional (mi-), *adj.*, méridional.

meridional'ity, *n.*, exposition au midi, *f.*

merid'ionally, *adv.*, dans la direction du midi; au midi, vers le sud.

meri'no, *n.*, mérinos, *m.* — breed; *race mérinos, f.*

mer'it (mè-), *n.*, mérite, *m.*

mer'it, *v.a.*, mériter. To — well of; *bien mériter de.*

merito'rious (mèr'i-tô-), *adj.*, (things) méritoire; (pers.) méritant.

merito'riously, *adv.*, méritoirement, d'une manière méritoire.

merito'riousness, *n.*, mérite, *m.*

mer'lin (meur-), *n.*, (orni.) émerillon, *m.*

mer'lon (meur-), *n.*, (fort.) merlon, *m.*

mer'maid (meur-méde), *n.*, (myth.) sirène, *f.*

mer'rily (mèr-), *adv.*, joyeusement, gaîment *ou* gaiement, avec allégresse.

mer'riment (mèr'-), *n.*, gaieté *ou* gaîté, joie, allégresse, réjouissance, *f.*

mer'riness (mèr'-), *n.*, gaîté, joie, *f.*

mer'ry (mèr'-), *adj.*, joyeux, allègre, gai; (b.s.) plaisant. — as a lark, *ou* as a grig; *gai comme un pinson.* —go-round; *chevaux de bois, m.pl.; manège, m.* To make —; *se divertir; se réjouir; être gai.* To make — with; *se réjouir de; se divertir* **de**; (b.s.) *plaisanter* **sur**. To make — at a person's mistakes; *se moquer des fautes de quelqu'un.* The more the merrier; *plus on est de fous, plus on rit.*

mer'ry, *n.*, (bot.) guigne, merise, *f.*

mer'ry-an'drew (-a'n'drou), *n.*, paillasse, bouffon, *m.*

mer'ry-an'drew, *adj.*, de paillasse, de bouffon.

mer'ry-making (-mék'-), *n.*, réjouissance ; fête ; gaieté, *f.* ; réjouissances, *f.pl.* ; divertissement, *m.*

mer'ry-thought (-thŏthe), *n.*, (of a fowl's breast) fourchette, lunette, *f.*

meseems', *v.imp.*, (l.u.) il me semble.

mesenter'ic (mèz'è'n'tèr'-), *adj.*, mésentérique.

mes'entery (mèz'è'n'tèr'i,, *n.*, (anat.) mésentère, *m.*

mesh (mèshe), *n.*, maille, *f.* ; (for netting) moule, *m.* ; (of brewers) marc, *m.*

mesh, *v.a.*, prendre au filet.

mesh'y, *adj.*, de mailles, en réseau.

mes'lin (mèz'-), *n.*, méteil, *m.*

mesmer'ic (mèz'mèr'-), *adj.*, mesmérique.

mes'merism (mèz'meur'iz'me), *n.*, mesmérisme, magnétisme animal, *m.*

mes'merize (-aïze), *v.a.*, magnétiser.

mes'merizer (-aïz'-), *n.*, magnétiseur, *m.*

mess (mèce), *n.*, (dish) mets, plat, *m.* ; (milit.) (of officers) pension, *f.* ; mess, *m.* ; (of non-commissioned officers) table, *f.* ; (of privates) ordinaire, *m.* ; (nav.) (of officers) table, *f.* ; (of seamen) plat, ordinaire, *m.* ; (medley) ripopée, potée, *f.* ; gâchis, *m.* ; (dirt) saleté ; (of animals) ration, *f.* To be in a —; *être dans le gâchis*, ou *le pétrin* ; *être sale*. To be in a fine — ; *être dans de beaux draps* ; *être dans un bel état*. What a —! *quel gâchis ! quelle saleté !* To make a — of; *gâcher, gâter* ; (fig.) embrouiller ; (fam.) *faire là une belle affaire*. To make a — of it ; *patauger* ; *faire manquer (une affaire)*; *donner en plein à gauche* ; *faire fiasco*. The soldiers are going to dine at the — ; *les soldats vont manger à la gamelle*. What a — you are making ! *quel gâchis vous faites là !* You make a pretty — of ; *vous les arrangez bien* (V. Hugo).

mess, *v.n.*, manger ; manger ensemble ; (to dirt) faire du gâchis. To — together ; *être à la même pension ; être du même ordinaire ; manger à la même gamelle* ; *faire plat ensemble*.

mess, *v.a.*, donner à manger à ; (to dirt) salir.

mes'sage (mès-sèdje), *n.*, message, *m.*, commission ; (telegram) dépêche, *f.*

mes'senger (mès-sè'n'djeur), *n.*, messager ; commissionnaire ; (fig.) avant-coureur, *m.*

Messi'ah (mès-saï'a), *n.*, Messie, *m.*

mes'sieurs (mé-syeu), *n.pl.*, messieurs, *m.pl.*

mess'mate, *n.*, camarade de pension, d'ordinaire, de gamelle, de table, de plat, *m.*

mess'-room, *n.*, chambrée, *f.*

mess'-tin, *n.* gamelle, *f.*

mes'suage (mès'wèdje), *n.*, (jur.) maison et dépendances, *f.pl.*

met'age (mî-tèdje), *n.*, mesurage de la houille ; prix de ce mesurage, *m.*

met'al (mèt'-), *n.*, métal ; (for roads) cailloutis, empierrement ; (railw.) rail, *m.*

met'al-bed (-bède), *n.*, encaissement de route, *m.*

met'al-dealer, *n.*, ferrailleur, *m.*

met'al-engrav'er (-gré-), *n.*, graveur sur métaux, *m.*

met'al-engrav'ing, *n.*, gravure sur métaux, *f.*

me'taled (mèt'al'de), *adj.*, (of roads) empierré, en empierrement ; ferré, caillouté.

metal'lic, *adj.*, métallique. — currency ; numéraire, *m.*

metallif'erous (-'if'eur'-), *adj.*, métallifère.

met'aling, *n.*, empierrement, *m.*

metalliza'tion (-laï-zé-), *n.*, métallisation, *f.*

met'allize (-laïze), *v.a.*, métalliser

metallog'raphy, *n.*, métallographie, *f.*

metallur'gic (-leur'djike) ou **metallur'gical** (-djik'-), *adj.*, métallurgique.

met'allurgist (-leur'djiste), *n.*, métallurgiste, *m.*

met'allurgy (-leur'dji), *n.*, métallurgie, *f.*

met'al-man, *n.*, ouvrier en métaux, *m.*

metamor'phose (mèt'a-mor-foce), *v.a.*, métamorphoser.

metamor'phosis (mèt'a-mor-fo-cice), *n.*, métamorphose, *f.*

met'aphor (mèt'-), *n.*, métaphore, *f.*

metaphor'ic ou **metaphor'ical**, *adj.*, métaphorique.

metaphor'ically, *adv.*, métaphoriquement.

met'aphorist, *n.*, personne qui emploie la métaphore, *f.*

met'aphrase (mèt'a-frèze) ou **metaph'rasis** (mi-taf'ra-cice), *n.*, métaphrase, *f.*

metaphys'ic ou **metaphys'ical** (mèt'a-fiz'-), *adj.*, métaphysique.

metaphys'ically, *adv.*, métaphysiquement.

metaphys'ics (-fiz'ikse), *n.pl.*, métaphysique, *f.sing.*

met'aplasm (mèt'a-plaz'me), *n.*, (gram.) métaplasme, *m.*

metas'tasis (mi-tas-ta-cice), *n.*, (med.) métastase, *f.*

metath'esis (mi-tath'i-cice), *n.*, (gram., med.) métathèse, *f.*

mete (out) (mîte), *v.a.*, mesurer. *n.*, mesure, *f.*

metempsycho'sis (-kô-cice), *n.*, métempsycose, *f.*

me'teor (mî-ti-), *n.*, météore, *m.*

meteor'ic, *adj.*, météorique.

me'teorite (-aïte) ou **me'teorolite** (-laïte), *n.*, (l.u.) aérolithe, *m.*

meteorolog'ical (-djik'-), *adj.*, météorologique.

meteorol'ogy (-ol-o-dji), *n.*, météorologie, *f.*

me'teorous, *adj.*, de météore.

me'ter (mît'-), *n.*, mesureur ; (ot gas) compteur, *m.*

me'ter ou **me'tre** (mî-teur), *n.*, (measure) mètre ; (poet.) vers, *m.*, mesure, *f.* ; (yard measure) mètre, *m.*

metheg'lin (mi-thèg'line), *n.*, hydromel, *m.*

methinks' (mi-thi'gn'kse), *v.imp.*, il me semble que ; (of anything previous) ce me semble, il me semble.

meth'od (mèth'-), *n.*, méthode ; manière ; voie, *f.* ; moyen ; ordre, *m.*

method'ic ou **method'ical**, *adj.*, méthodique.

method'ically, *adv.*, méthodiquement.

Meth'odism, *n.*, méthodisme, *m.*

Meth'odist, *n.*, méthodiste, *m.f.*

meth'odize (-aïze), *v.a.*, arranger avec méthode, arranger systématiquement.

methought' (mi-thôte), *v.imp.*, il me semblait, ou sembla, que.

metonym'ic ou **metonym'ical** (mèt'o'ni-), *adj.*, employé par métonymie.

metonym'ically, *adv.*, par métonymie.

meton'ymy (mi-to'n'-), *n.*, métonymie, *f.*

met'ope (mèt'o-pî), *n.*, (arch.) métope, *f.*

met'rical (mèt'-), *adj.*, métrique ; en vers, de mesure.

met'rically, *adv.*, d'une manière métrique, en vers.

metrol'ogy (mi-trol'o-dji), *n.*, métrologie, *f.*

metroma'nia, *n.*, métromanie, *f.*

metroma'niac, *n.*, métromane, *m.*

met'ronome (mèt'ro-nôme), *n.*, métronome, *m.*

metrop'olis (mi-), *n.*, capitale, métropole, *f.*

metropol'itan, *adj.*, de la capitale ; métropolitain.

metropol'itan, *n.*, (ecc.) métropolitain, archevêque, *m.*

met'tle (mèt't'l), *n.*, fougue, ardeur, vivacité, *f.* ; feu, *m.* ; (fig.) courage, cœur, *m.* To put (any one) upon his — ; *piquer (quelqu'un) d'honneur.*

met'tled (mèt't'l'de), *adj.*, vif, ardent ; fougueux ; courageux ; plein de cœur.

met'tlesome (-seume), *adj.*, fougueux, ardent ; vif.

mew (miou), *n.*, (orni.) mouette ; (cage) mue, cage ; prison, *f.* —s, *pl.*, écuries, *f.pl.*

mew (miou), *v.a.*, (to shut up) enfermer ; (to change) renouveler, changer.

mew (miou), *v.n.*, (of cats) miauler ; (to molt) muer ; (to change) changer.

mew'ing, *n.*, mue, *f.* ; (of a cat) miaulement, *m.*

mewl (mioule), *v.n.*, vagir.

mewl'ing, *n.*, vagissement, *m.*

meze'reon (mi-zĭ-ri-), *n.*, (bot.) mézéréon, garou, bois gentil, *m.*

mez'zanine (-nĭne), *n.*, (arch.) mezzanine, *f.*

mez'zo-relie'vo (-ri-lĭ-vô), *n.*, demi-relief, *m.*

mez'zotint *ou* **mezzotin'to** (-ti'n'te, -tô), *n.*, mezzo-tinto, *m.* ; gravure à la manière noire, *f.*

mi'asm (maï'az'me) *ou* **mias'ma** (mi-az'-), *n.*, (*miasmata*) miasme, *m.*

mi'ca (maï-), *n.*, (min.) mica, *m.*

mica'ceous (maï-ké-sheusse), *adj.*, (min.) micacé.

mice (maïce), *n.pl.* V. **mouse**.

Mi'chaelmas (maïk'èl'-), *n.*, la Saint-Michel.

mic'kle (mik'k'l), *adj.*, beaucoup. Many a little makes a — ; *les petits ruisseaux font les grandes rivières.*

mi'crocosm (maï-cro-coz'me), *n.*, microcosme, *m.*

microm'eter (maï-cro'm'-i-teur), *n.*, micromètre, *m.*

mi'croscope (maï-cro-scôpe), *n.*, microscope, *m.*

microscop'ic *ou* **microscop'ical**, *adj.*, microscopique.

microscop'ically, *adv.*, au microscope.

mid, *adj.*, du milieu ; moyen ; intérieur.

mid'-air, *n.*, milieu de l'air, haut des airs, *m.*

mid'-course (-côrse), *n.*, milieu du chemin ; milieu ; (middle course) parti moyen ; moyen terme, *m.*

mid'-day (-dè), *n.*, midi, *m.*

mid'-day, *adj.*, de midi.

mid'dle (mid'd'l), *n.*, milieu, centre, *m.* He was up to his — in water ; *il avait de l'eau par delà la ceinture.*

mid'dle, *adj.*, du milieu, du centre ; central ; (half) demi ; (fig.) intermédiaire, moyen ; (middling) médiocre ; moyen. —aged ; *d'âge moyen ; entre deux âges.* — ages ; *moyen-âge*, *m.sing.* —sized ; *de taille, de grandeur, moyenne.*

mid'dleman, *n.*, principal locataire ; intermédiaire, *m.*

mid'dlemost (-môste), *adj.*, le plus au milieu ; central.

mid'dling, *adj.*, médiocre, moyen ; (of health) passable ; (com.) bon, ordinaire, de moyenne qualité.

mid'dlingly, *adv.*, passablement ; médiocrement ; moyennement.

mid-heav'en (-hèv'v'n), *n.*, milieu du ciel, *m.*

mid'-land, *adj.*, méditerrané, intérieur, de l'intérieur.

mid'-leg (-lèghe), *n.*, mi-jambe, *f.*

Mid'-lent, *n.*, mi-carême, *f.*

mid'most (-môste), *adj.*, au milieu, au centre ; central.

mid'night (-naïte), *n.*, minuit, *m.*

mid'rib, *n.*, (bot.) nervure médiane, côte, *f.*

mid'riff, *n.*, (anat.) diaphragme, *m.*

mid'-sea (-sì), *n.*, pleine mer, *f.* ; milieu de la mer, *m.*

mid'ship, *n.*, (nav.) milieu du vaisseau, *m.* —frame ; (nav.) *maître couple*, *m.* —beam ; *maître bau*, *m.*

mid'shipman, *n.*, aspirant de marine, élève de marine, *m.*

mid'ships, *adv.*, (nav.) par le travers.

midst, *n.*, milieu ; fort ; cœur, *m.* In the — of winter ; *au cœur de l'hiver.* In the — of ; *au sein de ; dans le milieu de.*

midst, *adv.*, au milieu, parmi.

mid'-stream (-strîme), *n.*, milieu du courant ; milieu du fleuve ; thalweg, *m.* ; ligne médiane d'un cours d'eau, *f.*

mid'summer (-seum'-), *n.*, milieu de l'été, cœur de l'été, *m.* ; la Saint-Jean, *f.* —day ; *la Saint-Jean.*

mid'-watch (-wôtshe), *n.*, milieu de la veillée, *m.*

mid'way (-wé), *n.*, milieu du chemin ; milieu, *m.*

mid'way, *adj.*, à mi-chemin.

mid'way, *adv.*, à mi-chemin ; à moitié chemin ; (of a hill) à mi-côte.

mid'wife (-wife *ou* -waïfe), *n.*, sage-femme, accoucheuse, *f.*

mid'wifery (mid'wif'ri), *n.*, (surg.) art des accouchements, *m.* ; obstétrique, *f.* ; accouchement, *m.*

mid'winter (-wi'n'teur), *n.*, cœur de l'hiver, solstice d'hiver, *m.*

mid'-wood (-woude), *n.*, milieu du bois, des bois, *m.*

mien (mîne), *n.*, mine, *f.* ; air, *m.*

miff, *n.*, bouderie, fâcherie, brouille, *f.*

might, *v.* V. **may**. That — be ; *cela pourrait être.* Any troops — have been expected to show ; *on aurait pu s'attendre à voir les meilleures troupes montrer.* It — have added to their glory ; *cela aurait pu ajouter à leur gloire.* You — be humiliated ; *il se pourrait que vous fussiez, ou soyez, humilié.*

might (maïte), *n.*, puissance, force, *f.* With — and main ; *à corps perdu ; de toutes ses forces.* — is right ; *la force prime le droit, ou la raison du plus fort est toujours la meilleure* (Lafontaine).

might'ily, *adv.*, fortement, vigoureusement, grandement, puissamment, extrêmement, infiniment, bien.

might'iness, *n.*, grandeur, puissance, force, *f.*

might'y (maï-), *adj.*, fort, puissant, vigoureux ; vaste ; grand, important.

might'y, *adv.*, fort, très, bien.

mignonette' (mi'n'ieu'nète), *n.*, réséda, *m.*

mi'grate (maï-), *v.n.*, (zoöl.) émigrer. They —d in one body ; *ils émigrèrent en masse.*

migra'tion (maï-gré-), *n.*, (pers., zoöl.) migration, émigration, *f.*

mi'gratory (maï-gra-), *adj.*, (zoöl.) émigrant ; nomade ; migrateur. — birds ; *oiseaux de passage ou oiseaux voyageurs*, *m.pl.*

milch (milshe), *adj.*, à lait, laitière. — cow ; *vache laitière, vache à lait*, *f.*

mild (maïlde), *adj.*, doux ; (of drink, tobacco) léger, faible. — climate ; *climat doux, ou tempéré*, *m.* — efforts ; *efforts faibles*, *m.pl.*

mild'er, *adj.*, plus doux, moins rigoureux.

mil'dew (mil'diou), *n.*, tache d'humidité, *f.* ; (on plants) blanc, *m.*, rouille, *f.*

mil'dew (mil'diou), *v.a.*, frapper de blanc, de rouille ; gâter par l'humidité ; souiller ; tacher.

mil'dewed (mil'dioude), *adj.*, gâté par la rouille par l'humidité.

mild'ly (maïld'-), *adv.*, doucement, avec douceur ; modérément.

mild'ness (maïld'-), *n.*, douceur, *f.*

mile (maïle), *n.*, mille, *m.*

mile'age (maïl'èdje), *n.*, prix par mille ; péage par mille, *m.*

mile'-post (-pôste) *ou* **mile'-stone** (-stône), *n.*, borne milliaire, *f.*

mil'foil (-foïl), *n.*, (bot.) achillée ; millefeuille, *f.*

mil'iary, *adj.*, (med.) miliaire ; (bot.) granulé.

mil'itant, *adj.*, militant ; qui combat. — policy ; *politique militante*, *f.*

mil'itarily, *adv.*, militairement.

mil'itary, *adj.*, militaire. — law ; *code militaire*, *m.* — examination ; *concours d'admission aux écoles militaires.*

mil′itary, *n.*, militaires, *m.pl. ;* militaire, *m. sing. ;* troupe ; armée, *f.*

mil′itate, *v.n.*, militer **contre**.

mili′tia (mi-lish′ya), *n.*, milice, *f.* —**-man** ; *milicien, soldat de la milice, m.*

milk, *n.*, lait, *m.* — and water ; *lait coupé ;* (fig.) *fade, insipide ; flasque ; sans caractère.* Skimmed — ; *petit lait, m.* A land flowing with — and honey ; *un pays de cocagne* (Boileau).

milk, *v.a.*, traire ; (fig.) plumer, traire.

milk′-can, *n.*, pot à (ou au) lait, *m.*

milk′-diet (-daï′ète), *n.*, régime de laitage, *m. ;* diète lactée, *f.*

milk′er, *n.*, trayeur, *m.*, trayeuse, *f. ;* vache laitière, *f.*

milk′-fever, *n.*, fièvre de lait, *f.*

milk′-food, *n.*, laitage, *m.*

milk′iness, *n.*, nature laiteuse ; (fig.) douceur, *f.*

milk′-jug, *n.*, crémière, *f.*

milk′-livered (-liv′eurde), *adj.*, lâche, poltron.

milk′maid (-méde), *n.*, laitière, *f.*

milk′man (-ma′n), *n.*, laitier, *m.*

milk′pail (-péle), *n.*, seau à lait, *m.*

milk′pan (-pa′n), *n.*, jatte à lait, terrine à lait, *f.*

milk′-por′ridge, *n.*, bouillie d'avoine, *f.*

milk′-pot, *n.*, pot à lait, *m.*

milk′-pot′tage (-tèdje), *n.*, soupe au lait, *f.*

milk′sop, *n.*, poule mouillée (pers.), *f.*

milk′-sugar, *n.*, (chem.) sucre de lait, *m. ;* lactine, *f.*

milk′-tooth (-touth), *n.*, dent de lait, *f.*

milk′-van, *n.*, wagon à lait, *m.*

milk′-white (-hwaïte), *adj.*, blanc comme le lait.

milk′-woman (-woum′-), *n.*, laitière, *f.*

milk′wort (-weurte), *n.*, (bot.) herbe-au-lait, *f.*

milk′y, *adj.*, laiteux, doux.

Milk′y-Way (-wé), *n.*, (astron.) voie lactée, *f.*

mill, *n.*, moulin, *m. ;* (factory) filature, fabrique, usine, *f. ;* (coin.) balancier, *m. ;* (of cloth) croisure ; (fight) peignée, brossée, *f.* Wind— ; *moulin à vent, m.* Water— ; *moulin à eau, m.; roue hydraulique, f.* Cotton, silk— ; *filature de coton, de soie, f.* Flax— ; *manufacture de toile, f.* Saw— ; *scierie, f.* To bring grist to the — ; *faire venir l'eau au moulin.*

mill, *v.a.*, moudre ; (to full) fouler ; (coin.) estamper ; (chocolate) faire mousser ; (pop.) donner une volée de coups de poing à.

mill′-bar (-bâr), *n.*, barre laminée, *f.*

mill′-board (-bôrde), *n.*, carton, *m.*

mill′board-maker, *n.*, cartonnier, *m.*

mill′-course *ou* **race**, *n.*, coursier, bief, biez, *m.*

mill′-dam, *n.*, barrage de moulin, *m.*

mill′-dust (-deuste), *n.*, folle farine, *f.*

milled (milde), *adj.*, foulé. Double— ; *croisé.* — edge ; (coin) cordonnet, *m.*

millena′rian (mill′lè′n′-), *n.*, millénaire, *m.*

millena′rian, *adj.*, de mille ans ; du millénaire.

mil′lenary (mill′lè′n′-), *adj.*, millénaire, du millénaire.

millen′nial (mill′lè′n′-), *adj.*, millénaire, du millénaire.

millen′nium (mill′lè′n′-), *n.*, millénium, millénaire, *m.*, mille ans.

mil′leped (mill′li-pède), *n.*, mille-pieds ; myriapode, *m.*

mil′lepore (mil-li-pôre), *n.*, millépore, *m.*

mil′ler (mil′leur), *n.*, meunier, *m.* —**'s wife** ; *meunière, f.*

mil′ler's-thumb (mil′leur′z′theume), *n.*, (ich.) meunier, chabot, *m.*

milles′imal (mill′lèss′i-), *adj.*, (arith.) de millième.

mil′let (-lète) *ou* **mil′let-grass** (-grâce), *n.*, (bot.) millet, mil, *m.*

mill′-handle (-ha′n′d′l), *n.*, queue de moulin à bras, *f.*

mill′-hopper, *n.*, trémie, *f.*

mill′-horse, *n.*, cheval de moulin, *m.*

mill′-house (-haouce), *n.*, maison du moulin, *f. ;* atelier des meules, *m.*

mil′liard (mil-li-ârde), *n.*, milliard, billion, *m.*

mil′liary, *adj.*, milliaire.

mil′ligram, *n.*, milligramme, *m.*

mil′liliter (-lî-teur), *n.*, millilitre, *m.*

mil′limeter (-mî-teur), *n.*, millimètre, *m.*

mil′liner, *n.*, marchande de modes ; modiste, *f.* Man— ; *marchand de modes ; modiste, m.* (l.u.)

mil′linery, *n.sing.*, modes (parures de femmes), *f.pl.*

mil′lion, *n.*, million, *m.* The — ; *la multitude, les masses, f.pl. ; le peuple.*

millionaire′ (mill′ieun′ère), *n.*, millionnaire, *m.*

mil′lionary (adj.*), de millions, par millions.

mil′lionth (mill′ieu′n′th), *adj.*, millionième.

mil′lionth, *n.*, millionième, *m.*

mill′-moth (-moth), *n.*, (ent.) blatte, *f.*

mill′-owner (-ô′n′eur), *n.*, propriétaire de moulin ; chef de fabrique, manufacturier, *m.*

mill′-race. *V.* **mill-course**.

mill′-stone (-stône), *n.*, meule de moulin, *f. ;* (fig.) poids, *m.*, charge ; (min.) pierre meulière ; meulière, *f.* To have a — about one's neck ; *avoir un poids sur les épaules ; avoir la corde au cou.* To see through a — ; *pénétrer les choses les plus obscures ; voir à travers les murs.*

mill′-tooth (-touth), *n.*, dent molaire, *f.*

mill′wright (-raïte), *n.*, constructeur de moulins, *m.*

milt, *n.*, (anat.) rate ; (of fishes) laite, laitance, *f.* —**wort** ; doradille, *f.*

milt, *v.n.*, (ich.) féconder.

milt′er, *n.*, poisson laité, *m.*

mimet′ic (mi-mè-), *adj.*, d'imitation.

mim′ic *ou* **mim′ical**, *adj.*, imitateur ; (of things) imitatif, mimique ; (of animals) imitatif.

mim′ic, *v.a.*, contrefaire, imiter ; mimer.

mim′ic, *n.*, mime, imitateur, *m.*

mim′icking *ou* **mim′icry** (-crie), *n.*, mimique, imitation, *f.*

min′aret (-rète), *n.*, minaret, *m.*

min′atory, *adj.*, menaçant, comminatoire.

mince (mi′n′ce), *v.a.*, hacher menu ; (meat) émincer ; (fig.) atténuer, adoucir ; (to cut short in speaking) manger. Not to — matters ; *parler franchement ; ne pas tourner autour du pot ; ne rien cacher ; trancher le mot ; ne pas y aller par quatre chemins ; ne pas mâcher ses mots ; avoir son franc parler* **avec**. To — one's words ; *manger ses mots.*

mince, *v.n.*, (in walking) marcher à petits pas comptés ; (in speaking) minauder.

mince′-meat, *n.*, hachis, *m.* To make — of ; *hacher menu comme chair à pâté.*

mince′-pie (-païe), *n.*, pâté de fruits et de viande hachés, *m.*

min′cing, *adj.*, affecté, minaudier.

min′cing-knife (naïfe), *n.*, hachoir, *m.*

min′cingly, *adv.*, menu ; (fig.) avec minauderie, avec affectation.

mind (maï′n′de), *n.*, (understanding) esprit, *m.*, intelligence ; (intention) intention ; (inclination) envie, *f.*, désir, *m. ;* (opinion) opinion, pensée, idée, *f.*, avis, sentiment ; (memory) souvenir, *m.*, mémoire ; (heart, soul) âme, *f.*, moral ; (taste) goût, *m.* To have half a — to ; *avoir bonne envie de.* To tell any one your — ; *dire à quelqu'un son fait.* To have in — ; *se rappeler, avoir souvenance de.* I have a good — to report you ; *j'ai bonne envie de vous dénoncer.* Time out of — ; *de temps immémorial.* Bear in — that I expect you ; *n'oubliez pas que je vous attends.* To bear in — ; *se souvenir de, se rappeler, ne pas oublier, penser à.* To be in two —s;

hésiter ; être en suspens. To have one's — clear about ; *avoir le cœur net* **de.** Nobleness of — ; *noblesse d'âme, f.* To be of the same — ; *être du même avis que* ; *être d'accord* **avec.** To alter one's — ; *se raviser ; changer d'avis, d'idée.* To give one's — to ; *s'adonner* **à**, *s'appliquer* **à.** To find a thing to one's — ; *trouver une chose à son goût.* To speak one's — *dire sa pensée ; avoir son franc parler* **avec**, *dire sa façon de penser.* To make up one's — ; *se décider ; prendre son parti ; se résigner* **à**, *se résoudre* **à.** To call to — ; *rappeler.* To put any one in — of anything ; *rappeler quelque chose au souvenir de quelqu'un ; faire souvenir quelqu'un de quelque chose ; faire penser quelqu'un à quelque chose.* To set one's — upon ; *se mettre en tête.* To go out of one's —; *perdre la tête ; perdre la raison.* To be out of one's — ; *avoir perdu la tête, la raison ; être hors de son bon sens.* That went out of my —; *cela m'est sorti de la tête.* To know one's —; *savoir ce qu'on veut, savoir à quoi s'en tenir.* To be easy, uneasy, in one's — ; *avoir, n'avoir pas, l'esprit tranquille.* In my — ; *dans mon esprit ;* (opinion) *à mon avis.* Of sound — ; *sain d'esprit.* Of unsound — ; *qui n'est pas sain d'esprit.* A noble — ; *une belle âme.* A groveling — ; *une âme de boue.*

mind, *v.a.* and *n.,* (to attend to) prendre garde **à**, *s'occuper* **de**, songer **à**, faire attention **à** ; (to obey) obéir **à**, écouter ; (to nurse) soigner, garder ; (to watch) surveiller, observer ; (to care about) s'inquiéter **de**, regarder **à.** — what you are about ? *prenez garde à ce que vous faites !* I do not — going with you ; *je veux bien aller avec vous.* — your own business ; *mêlez-vous de ce qui vous regarde.* You do not — what I say ; *vous ne faites pas attention à ce que je dis ; vous ne vous inquiéz ez pas de ce que je dis.* Do not — it ; *ne f..tes pas attention à cela.* I do not — it ; *je n'y fais pas attention ; cela m'est égal.* If you don't — ; *si cela vous est égal ; si vous le voulez bien ; si cela ne vous fait de rien.* Never — him ; *ne faites pas attention à lui ; ne l'écoutez pas.* I do not — what they say ; *je ne m'inquiète pas de ce qu'on dit.* I do not — the money ; *je ne regarde pas à l'argent.* Never — ; *n'importe ; peu importe ; c'est égal ; ça ne fait rien ; ce n'est rien.*

mind'ed, *adj.,* disposé ; porté. High— ; *qui a l'esprit élevé ; noble, magnanime.* Low— ; *méprisable ; qui a l'esprit bas ; vil, commun.* Feeble— ; *qui a l'esprit faible.* Sober— ; *d'un esprit sobre ; sage, raisonnable.* Double— ; *irrésolu.* If you are so — ; *si le cœur vous en dit.*

mind'edness, *n.,* disposition, *f.*

mind'ful (-foule), *adj.,* attentif **à** ; soigneux **de** ; qui se souvient **de.**

mind'fully, *adv.,* attentivement ; soigneusement.

mind'fulness, *n.,* attention, *f. ;* soin, *m.*

mind'less, *adj.,* inattentif **à** ; insouciant **de** ; (without mind) sans facultés intellectuelles ; (stupid) stupide, sot. — of ; *oublieux* **de** ; *sans égard* **pour.**

mine (maïne), *pron.,* le mien, *m.,* la mienne, *f. ;* les miens, *m.pl. ;* les miennes, *f.pl. ;* à moi. This is — ; (belongs to) *cela,* ou *ceci, est* **à** *moi,* ou *m'appartient ;* (comes from) *est* **de** *moi.* A friend of — ; *un de mes amis ; un ami à moi* (fam.) ; *un mien ami* (l.u.). A favorite of — ; *un de mes favoris.* An old aunt of — ; *une vieille tante à moi.* That is no fault of — ; *ce n'est pas de ma faute ; je n'y suis pour rien.*

mine, *n.,* mine, *f.*

mine (maïne), *v.a.,* miner, creuser ; (fig.) saper.

mine'-burner (maï-ne-beurn'-), *n.,* (metal.) grilleur de minerai, *m.*

mine'-dial (-daï'al), *n.,* boussole de mineur, *f.*

mine'-digger (-dig'gheur), *n.,* mineur, *m.*

mi'ner (maï'n'-), *n.,* mineur, *m.*

min'eral (mi'n'eur-), *adj.,* minéral.

min'eral, *n.,* minéral, *m.*

mineraliza'tion (mi'n'eur'al-aïzé-), *n.,* minéralisation, *f.*

min'eralize (-aïze), *v.a.,* (chem.), minéraliser.

mineralog'ical (-'o-djik'-), *adj.,* minéralogique.

mineralog'ically (-'o-djik'-), *adv.,* en langage minéralogique.

mineral'ogist (-'o-djiste), *n.,* minéralogiste, *m.*

mineral'ogy (-'o-dji), *n.,* minéralogie, *f.*

min'ever (mi'n'i-veur), *n.,* (fur) petit-gris, *m.*

min'gle, *v.a.,* mêler, mélanger, mêler. To — with ; mêler, entremêler ; confondre **avec.**

min'gle, *v.n.,* se mêler **avec, dans,** *ou* **à** ; se mélanger ; s'entremêler ; se confondre (with **avec** *ou* **en**).

min'gling, *n.,* mélange, *m.*

min'iature, *n.,* miniature, *f.*

min'iature, *adj.,* en miniature.

min'iature-painter (-pé'n't'-), *n.,* miniaturiste ; peintre en miniature, *m.*

min'ikin, *n.,* (pin) camion ; (minion) mignon, *m.,* mignonne, *f.*

min'ikin, *adj.,* petit, minime, mignon.

min'im, *n.,* (dwarf) pygmée, nain, *m.,* naine *f. ;* (mus.) blanche, *f. ;* (ich.) véron, vairon, *f.* (Franciscan) minime, *m. ;* (med. pharm.) goutte, *f.*

min'imum, *n.,* minimum, *m.*

min'ing (maï'n'-), *adj.,* de mines ; de mineur.

min'ing, *n.,* exploitation des mines, *f. ;* travail dans les mines, *m.*

min'ion (mi'n'ieune), *n.,* mignon, *m.,* mignonne, *f. ;* favori, *m. ;* (print.) mignonne, *f.*

min'ister, *n.,* ministre ; (ecc.) ministre, pasteur, *m.* — of State ; *ministre d'Etat.* Prime — ; *premier ministre.*

min'ister, *v.a.* and *n.,* fournir ; donner ; administrer ; desservir ; servir ; (ecc.) officier ; (to take care of) soigner. To — to ; *favoriser, développer ;* (to relieve) *assister ; venir au secours* **de** ; (to contribute to) *contribuer* **à** ; (to humor) *se prêter* **à** ; (to provide for) *pourvoir* **à.**

ministe'rial (-is-tî'-), *adj.,* de ministère ; du pouvoir exécutif ; ministériel ; d'ecclésiastique, ecclésiastique.

ministe'rialist, *n.,* ministériel, *m.*

ministe'rially, *adv.,* ministériellement, dans la forme ministérielle.

ministra'tion (-tré-), *n.,* service ; office ; ministère, *m. ;* entremise, *f. ;* fonctions, *f.pl.*

mink, *n.,* vison, *m.*

min'now (-nô), *n.,* (ich.) véron, vairon, *m.*

mi'nor (maï-), *n.,* (jur.) mineur, *m.,* mineure, *f. ;* (friar) mineur, *m. ;* (log.) mineure, *f.*

mi'nor, *adj.,* moindre ; petit ; mince ; de second ordre, accessoire, secondaire ; (mus.,geog.) mineur. — Orders ; (ecc.) *ordres mineurs, m.pl.* — planet ; *planète télescopique, f.* In a — key ; *en mineur.*

minor'ity, *n.,* minorité, *f.*

Min'otaur, *n.,* (myth.) Minotaure, *m.*

min'ster, *n.,* cathédrale, église collégiale, *f.*

min'strel, *n.,* ménestrel, chanteur, musicien, (village fiddler) ménétrier, *m.*

min'strelsy, *n.,* chant des ménestrels, art du ménestrel, *m. ;* musique, *f. ;* chant, *m.*

mint (mi'n'te), *n.,* (bot.) menthe, *f.* Pepper— ; *menthe poivrée, f.*

mint, *n.,* monnaie, *f. ;* hôtel de la monnaie, *m. ;* (fig.) mine, *f. ;* trésor, *m. ;* (b.s.) fabrique, forge, *f.* Master of the — ; *directeur de la monnaie, m.* To have a — of money ; *être tout cousu d'or.*

mint, *v.a.,* monnayer ; frapper ; (fig.) forger, fabriquer, inventer, controuver.

mint'age (mi'n'tèdje), *n.,* objet monnayé ; (duty) droit de monnayage, *m.* [teur, *m.*

mint'er, *n.,* monnayeur, *f. ;* (fig.) forgeur ; inven-

mint'ing, *n.,* monnayage, *m.*

min'uet (mi'n'iou-ète), *n.,* menuet, *m.*

mi'nus (maï-neusse), *adv.,* moins ; (without) sans.

mi'nus, *n.*, (alg., print.) moins, *m.*

minute' (mi-nioute), *adj.*, menu, très petit ; minutieux ; mince.

min'ute (mi'n'ite *ou* mi'n'eute), *n.*, minute, instant, *m. ;* (astron., geom., arch.) minute ; (note) note, *f.* — -gun ; *canon de détresse, m.* —s (of a meeting) ; *procès-verbal, compte-rendu, m.* This —; *à l'instant.* This very —; *à l'instant même.* To expect some one every —; *attendre quelqu'un d'un instant à l'autre.* To make a — of ; *prendre note de.*

min'ute, *v.a.*, minuter, prendre note **de.**

min'ute-book (-bouke), *n.*, carnet, agenda ; journal ; (jur.) plumitif, *m.*

min'ute-glass (-glâce), *n.*, sablier **de** minute, *m.*

min'ute-hand (-ha'n'de), *n.*, aiguille des minutes ; grande aiguille, *f.*

min'utely, *adj.*, qui arrive à chaque minute ; de toutes les minutes. *adv.*, à chaque minute.

minute'ly (mi-niout'li), *adv.*, minutieusement ; exactement ; en détail.

minute'ness (mi-niout'-), *n.*, petitesse, exiguïté, *f. ;* détails minutieux, *m.pl.*

min'ute-watch (-wôtshe), *n.*, montre à minutes, *f.*

min'ute-wheel (-hwîle), *n.*, (horl.) roue des minutes, *f.*

minu'tiæ (mi-niou-shi-î), *n.pl.*, minuties, *f.pl.*

minx (mign'kse), *n.*, coquine, friponne, péronnelle, *f.*

mi'ny (maï-ni), *adj.*, riche en mines.

mir'acle (mir'a'k'l), *n.*, miracle, *m.* By a —; *par miracle.* —play ; *miracle, mystère, m.*

mir'acle-mon'ger (-meugn'gheur), *n.*, faiseur de miracles, imposteur, *m.*

mirac'ulous (-rak'iou-), *adj.*, miraculeux.

mirac'ulously, *adv.*, miraculeusement, par miracle.

mirac'ulousness, *n.*, caractère miraculeux, *m.*

mirage' (mi-raje), *n.*, mirage, *m.*

mire (maï'eur), *n.*, boue, bourbe, fange, vase, *f. ;* (place) bourbier, *m. ;* (ant.) fourmi, *f.* To sink in the —; *s'embourber, s'enfoncer dans la boue.*

mire, *v.a. V.* **bemire.**

mir'iness (maï'eur'-), *n.*, état boueux, état fangeux, *m. ;* saleté, *f.*

mirk'y (meurk'-), *adj. V.* **murky.**

mir'ror (-reur), *n.*, miroir, *m.*, glace, *f.*

mir'ror, *v.a.*, miroiter. To — back ; *réfléchir, refléter.*

mirth (meurth), *n.*, gaieté bruyante, réjouissance, joie, hilarité, allégresse, *f.*, rire, *m.*

mirth'ful (-foule), *adj.*, gai, joyeux, allègre.

mirth'fully, *adv.*, gaiement ; joyeusement ; avec allégresse.

mirth'fulness, *n.*, jubilation, allégresse, *f.*

mir'y (ma'ïeuri), *adj.*, fangeux, bourbeux, boueux.

mis, (in compounds) mé, més, mal, à tort.

misaccepta'tion (miss'ac-cèp-té-), *n.*, interprétation erronée, acception fausse, *f.*

misadven'ture (miss'ad-vè'n'tioure), *n.*, mésaventure, *f.*

misalli'ance (miss'al'laï'-), *n.*, mésalliance, *f.*

misallied' (-laïde), *adj.*, (l.u.) mésallié.

mis'anthrope (miz'a'n'thrôpe) *ou* **misan'thropist** (-thro-), *n.*, misanthrope, *m.*

misanthrop'ic *ou* **misanthrop'ical** (miss'-), *adj.*, (pers.) misanthrope ; (of things) misanthropique.

misan'thropy (miss'-), *n.*, misanthropie, *f.*

misapplica'tion (miss'ap-pli-ké-), *n.*, fausse application, *f.*, abus, mauvais usage, *m.*

misapply' (miss'ap'plaïe), *v.a.*, faire une mauvaise application **de**; appliquer mal à propos; mal appliquer, détourner.

misapprehend' (miss'ap-pri-hè'n'de), *v.a.*, mal entendre, comprendre mal; se méprendre

sur. He protested that he had been —ed; *il protesta qu'on l'avait mal compris.*

misapprehen'sion (miss'ap-pri-hè'n-), *n.*, malentendu, *m. ;* méprise, *f.*

misappro'priate, *v.a.*, distraire, détourner **de.**

misappropria'tion, *n.*, détournement, *m.*

misbecome' (miss'bi-keume), *v.a.*, messeoir à ; convenir mal **à.** Provided it were such drudgery as did not — an honest man ; *pourvu que ce ne fût pas une besogne trop vile pour un honnête homme.*

misbecom'ing, *adj.*, inconvenant, peu convenant, peu convenable, messéant.

misbecom'ingly, *adv.*, d'une manière inconvenante.

misbecom'ingness, *n.*, inconvenance, *f.*

misbegot'ten (miss'bi-), *adj.*, illégitime, bâtard.

misbehave' (miss'bi-héve), *v.n.*, se comporter mal, se conduire mal.

misbeha'vior (miss'bi-hév'ieur), *n.*, mauvaise conduite, inconduite, *f.*

misbelief' (miss'bi-lîfe), *n.*, fausse croyance, incrédulité, *f.*

misbeliev'er (miss'bi-lîv'-), *n.*, mécréant, infidèle, incrédule, *m.*

misbeliev'ing, *adj.*, infidèle, incrédule.

miscal'culate (miss'cal-kiou-), *v.a.*, calculer mal, mal calculer, se tromper, s'abuser.

miscalcula'tion (-kiou-lé-), *n.*, calcul erroné, faux calcul, *m. ;* supputation erronée, *f. ;* mécompte ; erreur de compte ou de calcul, *m.*

miscar'riage (miss'car'rèdge), *n.*, (failure) insuccès ; coup manqué, échec, *m. ;* affaire manquée ; (ill conduct) erreur, faute ; (of women) fausse couche, *f.* — of justice ; *erreur judiciaire, f.*

miscar'ry, *v.n.*, (to fail) ne pas réussir, manquer, échouer, avorter ; (not to arrive) faire fausse route ; ne pas arriver à sa destination, s'égarer ; (of women) faire une fausse couche.

miscella'neous (-lé-ni-), *adj.*, mêlé, varié ; divers ; général ; de mélange. — works ; *mélanges, m.pl.* —news ; *faits divers, m.pl.*

miscel'lanist, *n.*, auteur de mélanges, *m.*

mis'cellany, *n.*, (*miscellanea*) mélange, *m. ;* (book) mélanges, *m.pl.*

mischance' (mis'tshâ'n'ce), *n.*, mauvaise chance, *f. ;* malheur, accident fâcheux, revers, *m. ;* mésaventure, infortune, *f.*

mischarge' (mis'tshârdje), *v.a.*, porter à tort sur un compte.

mischarge', *n.*, somme portée à tort sur un compte.

mis'chief (mis'tshife), *n.*, mal ; dommage ; dégât ; tort, *m. ;* calamité, *f. ;* malheur, *m.* To do —; *faire du mal.* To be in —; *faire quelque mal.* To make —; *semer la discorde* **entre** ou **parmi** ; *ne chercher que plaie et bosse ; brouiller les gens.* Out of pure —; *par méchanceté, par pure malice.* To keep any one out of —; *empêcher quelqu'un de faire du mal, ou de songer à mal.* To intend —; *avoir de méchantes intentions ; préparer,* ou *méditer, un mauvais coup.* That child is always getting into —; *cet enfant est toujours dans le pétrin.*

mis'chief-mak'er (-mék'-), *n.*, semeur, *ou* brandon, de discorde; brouillon, *m.*

mis'chief-mak'ing, *adj.*, qui sème la discorde; qui brouille les gens. He delights in —; *il aime à semer la discorde, à brouiller les gens.*

mis'chievous (mis'tshè-veusse), *adj.*, (pers.) malicieux, méchant, porté au mal, malfaisant ; (of things) malfaisant, mauvais, nuisible, pernicieux, funeste, méchant; (of children) malicieux, méchant, enclin au mal.

mis'chievously, *adv.*, méchamment, mal, d'une manière nuisible ; malicieusement ; par méchanceté ; pernicieusement, nuisiblement, funestement.

mis′chievousness, *n.*, caractère malfaisant, *m.* ; nature malfaisante ; disposition au mal ; (of children) malice, méchanceté, *f.*

mischoose′ (mis′tshouze), *v.a.* (*preterit*, Mischose ; *past part.*, Mischosen), choisir mal.

mis′cible (mis-ci′b'l), *adj.*, miscible.

miscomputa′tion (-co′m′piou-té-), *n.*, erreur de calcul, *f.* ; mécompte, *m.*

miscompute′ (-pioute), *v.a.*, calculer mal.

misconceive′ (-cîve), *v.a.* and *n.*, concevoir mal ; juger mal ; se faire une fausse idée **de**.

misconceived′ (-cîv′de), *adj.*, mal conçu ; faux, erroné.

misconcep′tion (-cèp-), *n.*, fausse notion, méprise, *f.* ; malentendu, *m.*

miscon′duct (-deuk′te), *n.*, mauvaise conduite ; inconduite ; (management) mauvaise gestion, *f.*

misconduct′, *v.a.*, conduire mal ; (to manage) mal gérer. To — one's self ; *se conduire mal.*

misconjec′ture (-djèk′tioure), *n.*, fausse conjecture, *f.*

misconjec′ture, *v.a.* and *n.*, conjecturer à faux ; faire de fausses conjectures.

misconstruc′tion (-streuk′-), *n.*, interprétation fausse, *f.* ; contresens, *m.*

miscon′strue (-strou), *v.a.*, interpréter mal ; traduire mal ; dénaturer ; prendre à contresens.

miscon′struer, *n.*, personne qui interprète mal, *f.*

miscop′y, *v.a.*, copier mal, incorrectement.

miscount′ (-caou′n′te), *v.a.*, compter mal.

miscount′, *v.n.*, erreur de calcul, *f.*

mis′creant (-kri-), *n.*, mécréant ; misérable, vaurien, *m.*; canaille, *f.*

misdate′, *v.a.*, dater mal ; mettre une date fausse.

misdate′, *n.*, date erronée ; fausse date, *f.*

misdeal′, *v.a.*, maldonner. *n.*, maldonne, *f.*

misdeed′ (-dîde), *n.*, méfait, crime, *m.*

misdemean′ (-di-mîne), *v.a.*, se comporter (*used reflexively*). To — one's self ; *se conduire mal.*

misdemean′ant, *n.*, délinquant, *m.*, -e, *f.*

misdemean′or (-di-mî′n′eur), *n.*, mauvaise conduite, *f.* ; (jur.) délit, *m.* ; contravention, *f.*

misdirect′, *v.a.*, (letters, etc.) mettre une fausse adresse **à** ; adresser mal ; (pers.) renseigner mal ; diriger mal ; (misapply) mal appliquer, appliquer mal à propos ; employer mal.

misdo′ (-dou), *v.a.* and *n.* (*preterit*, Misdid ; *past part.*, Misdone), (l.u.) malfaire ; commettre des fautes.

misdo′er (-dou′-), *n.*, (ant.) auteur d'une faute ; malfaiteur, *m.*

misdo′ing (-dou′-), *n.*, faute, *f.*; méfait, *m.*

misemploy′ (miss′è′m′ploïe), *v.a.*, employer mal ; faire un mauvais emploi **de** ; mésuser **de**.

misemploy′ment, *n.*, mauvais emploi, *m.*

misen′try (miss′è′n′-), *n.*, inscription fausse, inscription erronée, (com.) contre-position, *f.*

mi′ser (maï-zeur), *n.*, avare, *m.*

mis′erable (miz′eur′a-b'l), *adj.*, misérable, pitoyable, malheureux, triste ; affreux ; (shabby) mesquin. To make any one's life — ; *rendre la vie dure* **à** *quelqu′un* ; (fam.) *en faire voir de belles* **à** *quelqu′un.*

mis′erableness, *n.*, (ant.) état malheureux, état misérable, délabrement, *m.*

mis′erably, *adv.*, misérablement, malheureusement, tristement ; pitoyablement ; affreusement ; mesquinement.

misere′re, *n.*, (c. rel.) miséréré, *m.*

mi′serly (maïz′eur′-), *adj.*, d'avare, avare, sordide. — father, spendthrift son ; (prov.) *à père avare, enfant prodigue.*

mis′ery (miz′eur′i), *n.*, misère, *f.* ; tourment, supplice, *m.* To put any one out of his —, *mettre fin aux souffrances* **de** *quelqu′un.* It is a — to . . . ; *c′est un supplice que de . . .*

mi′ser-like, *adj.*, en avare, comme un avare, d'avare.

mises′timate (miss′ès-), *v.a.*, estimer à tort ; juger, *ou* apprécier, mal.

misfash′ion, *v.a.*, former mal, mal façonner.

misfeas′ance (mis-fi-za′n′ce), *n.*, (jur.) dommage, *m.*

misfit′, *n.*, vêtement manqué, *m.*

misfor′tune (-fort′ioune), *n.*, malheur, *m.* ; infortune, *f.* —s never come singly ; *un malheur ne vient jamais seul.*

misgive′ (-ghive), *v.a.*, (*preterit*, Misgave ; *past part.*, Misgiven) faire craindre **à** ; inspirer des doutes, *ou* des craintes, **à** ; manquer **à** ; faire soupçonner **à**.

misgiv′ing (-ghiv′-), *n.*, crainte, *f.*; pressentiment de mal ; soupçon, doute, *m.*

misgov′ern (-gheuv′eurne), *v.a.*, gouverner mal, régir mal, mal gérer, mal administrer.

misgov′erned (-gheuv′eurn′de), *adj.*, mal gouverné, *ou* administré.

misgov′ernment, *n.*, mauvais gouvernement, *m.*; mauvaise administration, *f.*; (disorder) dérèglement, *m.*

misguid′ance (-gaïd′-), *n.*, fausse direction, *f.*

misguide′ (-gaïde), *v.a.*, mal guider, égarer, fourvoyer.

misguid′ed, *adj.*, mal guidé ; aveuglé ; égaré ; mal inspiré, abusé.

mishap′ (miss′hape), *n.*, accident ; contretemps ; malheur, *m.*, mésaventure, *f.*

mish′mash, *n.*, mélange ; micmac ; fatras ; salmigondis, pot-pourri, *m.*; galimafrée, *f.*

misinfer′ (miss′i′n′feur), *v.a.*, conclure à tort.

misinform′ (miss′-), *v.a.*, informer mal ; mal renseigner, donner de faux renseignements **à**.

misinforma′tion (-for-mé-), *n.*, faux renseignement, *m.* ; information inexacte, *f.*

misintel′ligence, *n.*, malentendu, désaccord, *m.*, mésintelligence, *f.*

misinter′pret (miss′i′n′teur-prète), *v.a.*, interpréter mal ; dénaturer.

misinterpreta′tion (-prè-té-), *n.*, fausse interprétation, *f.*; contresens, *m.*

misinter′preted, *adj.*, mal interprété.

misinter′preter, *n.*, personne qui interprète mal, *f.*; faux interprète, *m.*

misjoin′ (miss′djoïne), *v.a.*, joindre mal.

misjudge′ (-djeudje), *v.a.*, juger mal, mal juger, méjuger.

misjudge′, *v.n.*, se tromper **sur**.

misjudg′ment (-djeudj′-), *n.*, jugement erroné, *m.*

mislay′ (-lé), *v.a.* (*preterit* and *past part.*, Mislaid), égarer.

mislead′ (-lîde), *v.a.* (*preterit* and *past part.*, Misled), induire en erreur, égarer ; fourvoyer ; tromper.

mislead′er, *n.*, personne qui induit en erreur, *f.* ; trompeur, corrupteur, *m.*

mislead′ing, *adj.*, trompeur, décevant.

misman′age (-èdje), *v.a.*, gérer mal ; conduire mal ; diriger mal.

misman′age, *v.n.*, s'y prendre mal ; s'arranger mal **pour**.

misman′agement, *n.*, mauvaise gestion ; mauvaise administration ; mauvaise conduite, *f.*; mauvais arrangement, *m.*

mismatch′, *v.a.*, mal assortir, mal apparier.

misname′, *v.a.*, nommer improprement, mal nommer.

misno′mer (-nô-), *n.*, erreur de nom, *f.* ; faux nom, *m.* ; fausse appellation, *f.*

misog′amist (mi-ço-), *n.*, misogame, *m.*

misog′yny (mi-çodj′-), *n.*, haine des femmes, misogynie, *f.*

misplace′, *v.a.*, placer mal ; déplacer.

misplaced′ (-plés′te), *adj.*, mal placé ; déplacé.

mispoint', _v.a._, ponctuer mal.

misprint' (-pri'n'te), _n._, faute d'impression, erreur typographique, _f._

misprint', _v.a._, imprimer incorrectement.

mispri'sion (-prij'eune), _n._, (jur.) connivence ; non-révélation, _f._

misprize' (-praïze), _v.a._, (ant.) se méprendre **sur**, mépriser, dépriser.

misproceed'ing (-cîd'-), _n._, procédé irrégulier, _m._ ; irrégularité, _f._

mispronounce' (-naou'n'ce), _v.a._ and _n._, prononcer incorrectement.

mispronuncia'tion (-neu'n'cié-), _n._, fausse prononciation ; prononciation incorrecte, _f._

mispropor'tion (-pôr-), _v.a._, proportionner mal.

misquota'tion (-kwôt'é-), _n._, fausse citation, _f._

misquote' (-kwôte), _v.a._, citer à faux.

misreck'on (-rè'k'k'n), _v.a._, calculer mal.

misrelate' (-ri-léte), _v.a._, rapporter inexactement.

misrela'tion (-ri-lé-), _n._, rapport erroné, _m._

misreport' (-ri-pôrte), _v.a._, rapporter inexactement.

misreport' (-ri-pôrte), _n._, faux rapport ; rapport inexact, _m._

misrepresent' (-rèp'ri-zè'n'te), _v.a._, représenter sous de fausses couleurs ; dénaturer.

misrepresenta'tion (-zè'n'té-), _n._, faux rapport, faux exposé, _m._

misrepresent'er, _n._, qui dénature.

misrule' (-roule), _n._, confusion, _f._ ; désordre ; gouvernement tyrannique, mauvais gouvernement, _m._ ; tyrannie, _f._

miss, _n._, mademoiselle, demoiselle, _f._ — A. ; _mademoiselle A._

miss, _n._, (loss) perte, _f._, manque ; (at billiards) manque de touche, coup manqué, _m._ ; (mistake) erreur, méprise, _f._ ; pas de clerc, _m._

miss, _v.n._, manquer ; ne pas porter ; (at billiards) manquer de toucher. To be —ing ; (pers.) _être absent_ ; (of things) _manquer_. Many soldiers are —ing ; _un grand nombre de soldats manquent à l'appel._ To be —ing ; _être absent, manquer, faire défaut ; avoir disparu._ To — out ; _passer, omettre._ To — fire ; _rater_ (of a pistol, etc.)

miss, _v.a._, manquer ; (to omit) omettre, sauter ; (at billiards) manquer de touche ; (to perceive the want of) s'apercevoir de l'absence de, du manque **de** ; regretter vivement, ne plus trouver. To — one's mark ; _manquer, ou rater, son coup._ To — the mark ; _donner à côté._ I — my friend very much ; _mon ami me manque beaucoup._ I — you ; _vous me manquez ; je vous regrette._ He —ed the owl from the garden ; _il ne vit plus le hibou dans le jardin._ I — several books ; _il me manque plusieurs livres._ You have —ed your aim ; _vous avez manqué votre coup._ I —ed the train ; _j'ai manqué le train._

mis'sal, _n._, missel, _m._

missay'ing (-sé'igne), _n._, (ant.) expression incorrecte, _f._

missend', _v.a._, (preterit and _past part._, Missent), mal diriger, adresser mal. To —a parcel ; _envoyer un paquet à une fausse adresse._

misshape' (mis'shépe), _v.a._, former mal ; défigurer, déformer.

misshap'en (-shé-p'n), _adj._, difforme, contrefait.

mis'sile (mis's'l), _adj._, de jet, de trait ; lancé.

mis'sile (mis'sil), _n._, projectile, _m._ ; arme de trait, arme de jet, _f._

miss'ing, _adj._, absent, perdu, égaré. Killed, wounded, or — ; _tués, blessés, ou disparus._

mis'sion (mish'eune), _n._, mission, _f._

mis'sionary, _n._, missionnaire, _m._

mis'sive (mis'sive), _n.adj._, missive, _f._

misspell', _v.a._, épeler mal.

misspell'ing, _n._, orthographe vicieuse, _f._

misspend', _v.a._, dépenser mal à propos ; dépenser follement ; dissiper, gaspiller.

misstate' (mis'stéte), _v.a._, exposer inexactement ; rapporter inexactement.

misstate'ment, _n._, rapport inexact, rapport erroné, _m._

mist, _n._, brouillard, _m._ ; brume ; (drizzle) bruine, _f._ ; (fig.) nuage, _m._

mistak'able (-ték'a-b'l), _adj._, qui prête à erreur ; susceptible d'être mal compris.

mistake', _n._, erreur, méprise, faute, bévue, _f._ To make a — ; _faire une méprise ; se tromper._ To lie under a — ; _être dans l'erreur._ No — ! _sans aucun doute ; j'en réponds ; à coup sûr._ By — ; _par mégarde, par erreur._

mistake', _v.a._ (preterit, Mistook ; past part., Mistaken), se tromper de ; se tromper **sur** ; se méprendre à, **sur** ; prendre **pour**. He mistook me for you ; _il me prenait pour vous._

mistake', _v.n._, se tromper, se méprendre, s'abuser. If I — not ; _si je ne me trompe._ To be —n ; _se tromper, se méprendre, être dans l'erreur, s'abuser._

mistak'en (-ték'n), _adj._, (pers.) qui se trompe ; (of things) faux, mal entendu, erroné.

mistak'enly (-ték'n'li), _adv._, par méprise.

mistak'ing (-ték'-), _n._, méprise, erreur, _f._

mistak'ingly, _adv._, par méprise.

mistime' (-taïme), _v.a._, régler mal ; prendre mal son temps.

mistimed', _adj._, inopportun, déplacé.

mist'iness, _n._, état brumeux, _m._ ; obscurité, _f._

mis'tle-thrush, _n._, draine ; (pop.) lutrone, _f._

mis'tletoe (miz-z'l'tô), _n._, (bot.) gui, _m._

mist'-like (-laïke), _adj._, comme un brouillard ; brumeux.

mis'tral, _n._, mistral, _m._

mistranslate', _v.a._, traduire incorrectement.

mistransla'tion (-lé-), _n._, traduction incorrecte, _f._ ; contresens, _m._

mis'tress (-trèce _ou_ mis'sice), _n._, maîtresse ; madame ; (intended) prétendue, future ; (of a school) maîtresse, institutrice, _f._ — is not at home ; _madame n'y est pas._

mistrust' (-treuste), _n._, méfiance, défiance, _f._ ; soupçon, _m._

mistrust', _v.a._, se méfier **de** ; soupçonner ; se défier **de**.

mistrust'ful (-foule), _adj._, méfiant, défiant.

mistrust'fully, _adv._, avec méfiance.

mistrust'fulness, _n._, défiance, méfiance, _f._

mistrust'less (-treust'-), _adj._, sans défiance ; confiant.

mistune' (-tioune), _v.a._, (ant.) accorder mal ; désaccorder.

mist'y, _adj._, couvert de brouillards ; brumeux ; (of light) vaporeux ; (fig.) obscur.

misunderstand' (miss'eu'n'deur-), _v.a._ (preterit and past part., Misunderstood), comprendre mal ; mal comprendre, entendre mal ; se méprendre sur le sens (des paroles) de.

misunderstand'ing, _n._, conception erronée, _f._ ; (mistake) malentendu, _m._ ; (quarrel) mésintelligence, _f._

misus'age (miss'iou-zèdje), _n._, mauvais traitements, _m.pl._ ; abus, mauvais usage, mauvais emploi, _m._

misuse' (miss'iouce), _n._, abus ; mauvais usage, mauvais emploi, _m._ ; application erronée, _f._ ; mauvais traitements, _m.pl._

misuse' (-iouze), _v.a._, abuser **de** ; (to treat ill) maltraiter ; (to make an improper use) mésuser **de**.

mite (maïte), _n._, (money) denier ; (fig.) rien, _m._ ; obole, _f._ — a, _pl._, (ent.) mites, _f.pl._ ; acares, _m.pl._ The widow's — ; _le denier de la veuve._

mi'ter _ou_ **mi'tre** (maï-teur), _n._, mitre, _f._ ; (arch.) onglet, _m._

mi'ter _ou_ **mi'tre**, _v.a._, orner d'une mitre ; (arch.) assembler en onglet.

mi'tered *ou* **mi'tred** (maï-teurde), *adj.*, orné d'une mitre ; mitré ; (arch.) en onglet.

mit'igable (-ga-b'l), *adj.*, (ant.) susceptible de mitigation, susceptible d'adoucissement.

mit'igant, *adj.*, (ant.) qui mitige ; qui tempère ; adoucissant.

mit'igate, *v.a.*, mitiger, adoucir ; calmer, tempérer, modérer, apaiser.

mitiga'tion (-ghé-), *n.*, mitigation, *f.* ; adoucissement, *m.*

mit'riform, *adj.*, conique, en forme de mitre.

mit'ten, mitt, *n.*, mitaine,*f.*

mit'timus, *n.*, mandat de dépôt ; ordre de renvoi de pièces, *m.*

mit'y (maï-ti), *adj.*, plein de mites.

mix, *v.a.*, mêler ; mélanger (with, **de** *ou* **à**) ; (pharm.) mixtionner ; (a salad) retourner.

mix, *v.n.*, se mélanger ; se mêler ; fréquenter.

mixed (mix'te), *adj.*, mélangé ; mêlé **de** ; (math.) mixte, fractionnaire. The company is —; *la compagnie est mêlée.* — marriage ; *mariage mixte, m.*

mix'er, *n.*, qui mêle, qui mélange, ⚹

mixtilin'eal *ou* **mixtilin'ear**, *adj.*, (geom.) mixtiligne.

mix'tion (mixt'ieune), *n.*, (pharm. art.) mixtion,*f.* ; mélange, *m.*

mixt'ly, *adv.*, avec mélange ; d'une manière mixte.

mix'ture (mixt'ieur), *n.*, mélange, *m.* ; (pharm.) mixtion, potion, mixture,*f.*

miz'maze, *n.*, (pop.) labyrinthe, dédale, *m.*

miz'zen (miz-z'n), *n.*, artimon, *m.*

miz'zen-mast (-mâste), *n.*, mât d'artimon, *m.* — stay ; *étai d'artimon, m.* — top ; *hune d'artimon, f.* — yard ; *vergue d'artimon, f.*

miz'zle (miz-z'l), *v.a.*, bruiner.

mnemon'ic *ou* **mnemon'ical** (ni-mo'n'-), *adj.*, mnémonique.

mnemon'ics (ni-mo'n'-), *n.pl.*, mnémonique, mnémotechnie, *f.*

moan (mône), **moan'ing**, *n.*, gémissement, *m.* ; plainte, lamentation, *f.* The — of the wind ; *le sourd gémissement du vent.*

moan, *v.n.*, gémir, se lamenter.

moan, *v.a.*, gémir **de, sur** ; se lamenter **sur** ; pleurer, déplorer, lamenter.

moan'ful (-foule), *adj.*, lugubre, triste, lamentable, plaintif.

moan'fully, *adv.*, d'un ton plaintif, tristement, plaintivement.

moat (môte), *n.*, (fort.) fossé, *m.*

moat, *v.a.*, (fort.) entourer d'un fossé.

mob (mobe), *v.a.*, houspiller, harasser ; (to wrap up) coiffer, affubler.

mob, *n.*, foule ; populace ; cohue ; canaille, racaille, *f.* ; rassemblement, attroupement, *m.* ; (head-dress) cornette, *f.* Riotous —; *attroupement, rassemblement, m.* ; *masse confuse, f.* — law ; *justice populaire, f., gouvernement de la canaille, m.*

mob'bing, *n.*, houspillement, *m.*

mob'bish, *adj.*, tumultueux ; de la populace, de la foule.

mob'cap, *n.*, cornette (coiffure de femme),*f.*

mo'bile (mo-bîle), *adj.*, (ant.) mobile.

mobil'ity, *n.*, mobilité ; (activity) activité ; (inconstancy) légèreté,*f.*

mobiliza'tion, *n.*, mobilisation, *f.*

mo'bilize,*v.a.*, (mil. nav.) mobiliser.

mock, *v.a.*, se moquer **de**; se rire **de**, se jouer **de** ; railler ; tromper.

mock, *v.n.*, se moquer. To — at; *se moquer* **de**; *se rire* **de**; *se jouer* **de**; *railler.*

mock, *adj.*, dérisoire ; de moquerie ; burlesque ; (false) faux, imitation **de**, simulé, pour rire. — poem ; *poème burlesque, m.* — heroic; *héroï-comique.* The — doctor (of Molière) ; *le médecin malgré lui.* — prophet ; *faux prophète, m.* — style ; *style comique, m.* — sun ; (astron.) *par-*

hélie, parélie, m. — turtle ; (cook.) *soupe à la tête de veau, f.*

mock'er, *n.*, moqueur, *m.*, moqueuse, *f.* ; railleur, *m.*, railleuse, *f.* ; (impostor) imposteur, trompeur, *m.*

mock'ery, *n.*, moquerie, raillerie, dérision ; (sport) risée, *f.* ; jouet, *m.* ; (illusion) illusion, *f.* ; (imitation) semblant, *m.*

mock'ing, *n.*, moquerie ; dérision, *f.*

mock'ing-bird (-beurde), *n.*, oiseau moqueur, *m.*

mock'ingly, *adv.*, en se moquant ; d'un ton moqueur.

moc'main, *n.*, soie végétale, *f.*

mo'dal (mô-), *adj.*, (philos.) modal.

modal'ity (mo-), *n.*, (philos.) modalité, *f.*

mode (môde), *n.*, mode, façon, manière, *f.* ; genre, degré; (gram., music, philos.) mode, *m.*

mod'el, *n.*, modèle, *m.* ; (representation) représentation, *f.* ; (mold) moule ; plan, système, *m.*

mod'el, *v.a.*, modeler; faire, former d'après un modèle.

mod'eler (mod'èl'eur), *n.*, (art.) modeleur ; (planner) homme à projets; (contriver) inventeur, *m.*

mod'erate (mod'eur-), *adj.*, modéré ; modique, ordinaire ; passable ; raisonnable ; médiocre.

mod'erate, *v.a.*, modérer, adoucir, tempérer.

mod'erate, *v.n.*, se modérer.

mod'erately, *adv.*, modérément; modiquement; passablement ; raisonnablement ; médiocrement.

mod'erateness, *n.*, (l.u.) modération; modicité, *f.* ; état moyen, *m.*

modera'tion (-'eur'é-), *n.*, modération ; retenue, mesure, *f.* With, *ou* in, —; *modérément, avec mesure.* —s ; (Oxford Univ.) *premier examen du baccalauréat, m.*

mod'erating, *adj.*, modérateur.

mod'erator (-'eur'é-teur), *n.*, modérateur, *m.*, modératrice, *f.* ; (presbyt.) président, *m.* ; (Oxford Univ.) examinateur, *m.* ; (lamp) lampe à modérateur, *f.*

mod'eratorship, *n.*, fonctions de modérateur, *f.pl.* ; (presbyt.) présidence, *f.*

mod'ern (mod'eurne), *adj.*, moderne, nouveau, récent. — side ; (schools) *division de l'enseignement moderne, f.*

mod'ern, *n.*, moderne, *m.*

mod'ernism (-'iz'me), *n.*, forme moderne, tournure moderne,*f.*

mod'ernize (-'aïze), *v.a.*, moderniser ; rendre moderne ; rajeunir.

mod'ernizer, *n.*, personne qui modernise, *f.*

mod'ernly, *adv.*, modernement.

mod'ernness, *n.*, nouveauté,*f.*

mod'est (mod'èste), *adj.*, modeste ; pudique.

mod'estly, *adv.*, modestement, avec modestie.

mod'esty, *n.*, modestie; pudeur, *f.*

mod'icum, *n.*, petite portion, *f.* ; peu, *m.* ; *la moindre quantité* ; pitance,*f.*

mod'ifiable (-faï'a-b'l), *adj.*, modifiable.

modifica'tion (-fi-ké-), *n.*, modification, *f.*

mod'ificative, *adj.*, modificatif.

mod'ify (-faïe), *v.a.*, modifier, limiter, modérer, atténuer.

mod'ify, *v.n.*, faire des modifications à.

modil'lion (mo-dil'ieune), *n.*, (arch.) modillon, *m.*

mo'dish (mô-), *adj.*, (ant.) à la mode.

mo'dishly, *adv.*, (ant.) à la mode.

mo'dishness, *n.*, (aut.) asservissement à la mode; esclavage de la mode, *m.*

mod'ulate (mod'iou-), *v.a.*, (mus.) moduler ; proportionner, ajuster, adapter, régler.

modula'tion (mod'iou-lé-), *n.*, modulation ; (ant.) mélodie, *f.*

mod'ulator, *n.*, personne qui module; chose qui module, *f.* ; modulateur, *m.* ; modulatrice, *f.*

mod'ule (mod'ioule), n., (arch.) module, m.

mod'wall, mud'wall (-wôl), n., (orni.) abeiller, guêpier, m.

Mogul' (-gheule), n., Mogol, m.

mo'hair (mō-hère), n., poil de chèvre angora, m.

Moham'medan, n. and adj., mahométan, m., mahométane, f.

Moham'medanism, n., mahométisme, m.

Mo'hawk ou **Mo'hock** (mō-), n., tribu de peaux-rouges, f.

moi'ety, n., moitié, f.

moil, v.n., se fatiguer; travailler fort; s'échiner. To toil and —; suer sang et eau.

moire (moire), n., (silk) moire, f.

moist (moïste), adj., (of the skin, hands) moite; humide.

moist'en (moïs't'n), v.a., rendre humide; humecter, rendre moite.

moist'ness (moïs't'-) ou **mois'ture** (moïst'ioure), n., (of the skin, etc.) moiteur, humidité, f.

mo'lar (mō-), adj., (teeth) molaire.

molas'ses (-cize), n.pl., mélasse, f.

mold (môlde), n., (earth) terreau, m., terre végétale, terre, f.; (moldy part) moisi, m., moisissure, f.; (cast) moule, m., forme, f.; (fig.) modèle, calibre, m., trempe, f.; (arch.) panneau, m., moulure, f.; (nav.) gabari, gabarit, m.

mold, v.a., mouler, modeler, faire, former; (to knead, as bread) pétrir; (to make moldy) moisir.

mold, v.n., (to become moldy) moisir, se moisir.

mold'able (môld'a-b'l), adj., moulable.

mold'er (-), n., mouleur; (fig.) formateur, m.

mold'er, v.n., dépérir, fondre; se réduire en poudre, en poussière; se réduire, diminuer. To — away; tomber en poussière; dépérir, se dissiper.

mold'er, v.a., réduire en poussière.

mold'ering, adj., qui se réduit en poussière, qui dépérit, qui tombe en ruines.

mold'iness (môld'-), n., moisissure, f., moisi, m.

mold'ing, n., moulure, f.; panneau, m.

mold'ing-plane, n., (carp.) doucine, f.

mold'warp (-wôrpe), n., (zoöl.) taupe, f.

mold'y (môld'i), adj., moisi, chanci. To become (get) —; se moisir, se chancir. To smell —; sentir le moisi.

mole (môle), n., (mam.) taupe, f.; (on the skin) marque de naissance, f., signe, grain de beauté, m.; (med.) môle, f.; (mound) pile, digue; (of a port) jetée, f., môle, m.

mole'cast (-câste), n., taupinière, f.

mole'-catcher, n., taupier, m.

mole'-cricket (-ète), n., (ent.) taupe-grillon, m., courtilière, f.

molec'ular (-lèk'iou-), adj., (chem.) moléculaire.

mol'ecule (-'è-kioule), n., (chem.) molécule, f.

mole'-eyed (-aïe'-de), adj., qui a de très petits yeux; aveugle.

mole'hill, n., taupinière, f. To make a mountain out of a —; faire d'une mouche un éléphant; ou faire d'un œuf un bœuf.

mole'skin, n., (cotton cloth) futaine, f.

molest' (-lèste), v.a., molester, vexer; inquiéter; tourmenter; importuner.

molesta'tion (-lès-té-), n., molestation; vexation, contrariété, importunité, f.

molest'er (-), n., importun, m., importune, f.; fâcheux; perturbateur, m.

mole'-track, n., traînée de taupe, f.

mole'-trap, n., taupière, f.

Mo'linism (-'iz'me), n., (Church Hist.) molinisme, m.

Mo'linist, n., moliniste, m., f.

mol'lient. V. emol'lient.

mol'lifiable (-faï-a-b'l), adj., qui peut être amolli.

mollifica'tion (-fi-ké-), n., amollissement, adoucissement, m.

mol'lifier (-faï'-), n., adoucissant, calmant; (pharm.) émollient, m.

mol'lify (-faïe), v.a., amollir, calmer, adoucir; apaiser; (med.) mollifier (l.u.).

mol'lusc (-leuske), n., (mollusca) (zoöl.) mollusque, m.

molt (môlte), v.n., muer.

mol'ten (môl't'n), adj., fondu, de métal fondu, de fonte, de métal en fusion.

molt'ing, n., mue, f.

mo'ment (mō-), n., moment, instant, m.; importance, f.; (mec.; phys.) moment. In a —; dans un moment. He stops every —; il s'arrêt à tout moment, à tous moments. This —; à l'instant. This very —; à l'instant même. The — that; dès que, aussitôt que. At the present —; actuellement, à l'heure qu'il est.

mo'mentarily, adv., momentanément; à tous moments; à tout moment.

mo'mentary, adj., momentané; de peu de durée, passager.

momen'tous (mo-mè'n't'-), adj., important, de la dernière importance; (fig.) critique, difficile.

momen'tum (mo-mè'n'-), n., (mec.) moment, m., quantité de mouvement, f.

mon'achal (-kal), adj., monacal.

mon'achism (-kiz'me), n., monachisme, m.

mon'ad (-'ade), n., monade, f.

monad'ic ou **monad'ical**, adj., des monades.

mon'arch (mo'n'arke), n., monarque; roi, empereur, m.; reine, f.

monar'chic ou **monar'chical** (-'ark'-), adj., monarchique, de monarque, souverain.

monar'chically (-'ark'-), adj., monarchiquement, à la manière d'une monarchie.

mon'archist, n., monarchiste, m.

mon'archize (-'ark'aïze), v.n., faire le roi, monarchiser.

mon'archy (-'ark'i), n., monarchie, f.

mon'astery (-teur'i), n., monastère, m.

monas'tic ou **monas'tical**, adj., monastique.

monas'tically, adv., en moine.

monas'ticism (-ciz'me), n., monachisme, m.; vie monastique, f.

Mon'day (meu'n'dè), n., lundi, m. To keep Saint —; faire le (saint) lundi.

mon'etary (-'è-ta-), adj., monétaire.

monetiza'tion, n., monétisation, f.

mon'etize, v.a., monétiser.

mon'ey (meu'n'ni), n., argent, m.; monnaie, f.; pièces, f.pl.; deniers, m.pl. — down, ready —; argent comptant, m. Made of —; cousu d'or. Bad, base, counterfeit —; fausse monnaie. Odd —; appoint; compte borgne, m.; passe, f. Ready —; argent comptant. Pocket —; menus plaisirs, m.pl. In hard —; en espèces, en numéraire. Public —; deniers publics, m.pl. — dormant (lying dead); argent mort. Bank —; monnaie de banque; monnaie banco. Copper —; monnaie de cuivre, f.; billon, m. Even —; somme ronde, f.; compte rond, m. Paper —; papier-monnaie, m. Silver —; monnaie d'argent, argent blanc. Bag of —; sac d'argent; group, m. — article; bulletin financier, m. For —; au comptant. To coin —; battre monnaie. To earn —; gagner de l'argent. To get in —; faire rentrer des fonds. To make —; gagner, faire de l'argent. — makes —; l'eau va toujours au moulin. To put — out to interest; placer de l'argent. To receive —; recevoir, toucher de l'argent. To fetch —; rapporter de l'argent. To be worth —; valoir de l'argent, avoir du bien; (of things) avoir de la valeur, avoir du prix, valoir beaucoup. To have — with one, about one; avoir de l'argent sur soi. A man of —; un homme opulent. To take eggs for —; prendre des vessies pour des lanternes.

mon'ey-agent (-é-djè'n'te), *n.*, banquier, *m.*
mon'ey-bag, *n.*, sac à argent, *m. ;* sacoche, *f.*
mon'ey-bill, *n.*, budget des dépenses, *m. ;* loi des finances, *f.*
mon'ey-box, *n.*, tirelire, *f.*
mon'ey-bro'ker (-brô-), *n.*, courtier de change, *m.*
mon'ey-changer (-tshé'n'djeur), *n.*, changeur, *m.*
mon'eyed (meu'n'ède), *adj.*, riche, opulent, qui a de l'argent. — capital; *capital en espèces sonnantes, m.* — man ; *capitaliste, homme opulent, m.* The — interest ; *le parti de l'argent, m.*
mon'ey-getting (-ghèt'-), *adj.*, cupide ; intéressé.
mon'ey-grubber, *n.*, grippe-sou, *m.*
mon'ey-jobber (-djob'-), *n.*, agioteur, *m.*
mon'ey-lender, *n.*, prêteur d'argent ; bailleur de fonds, *m.*
mon'eyless, *adj.*, sans argent, sans le sou.
mon'ey-market, *n.*, Bourse, *f.*
mon'ey-matter, *n.*, affaire pécuniaire, affaire d'argent, *f.*
mon'ey-order, *n.*, (post) mandat, *m.*
mon'ey-spider, *n.*, (zoöl.) araignée aux écus ; araignée porte-bonheur, *f.*
money's-worth (-'i'z'weurth), *n.*, valeur de l'argent, *f. ;* objet de valeur, *m.* To have one's — ; *en avoir pour son argent.*
mon'ey-taker, *n.*, (cash-clerk) caissier, buraliste, *m.*
mon'ey-wort (-weurte), *n.*, (bot.) lysimaque, nummulaire, herbe aux écus, monnayère, *f.*
mon'ger (meu'gn'gheur), *n.*, (only used now as a suffix, as *fishmonger, ironmonger,* etc.), marchand, débitant, *m.*
mon'grel (meu'gn'-), *adj.*, métis ; mélangé. — dog ; *chien métis, m.*
mon'grel, *n.*, métis, *m.*, métisse, *f.*
moni'tion, *n.*, admonition, *f. ;* avertissement, avis, *m. ;* indication, *f.*
mon'itive, *adj.*, d'admonition, d'avis.
mon'itor (-teur), *n.*, moniteur, *m. ;* (ironclad) monitor, *m.*
monito'rial, *adj.*, (of instruction) par des moniteurs ; (of schools) qui a des moniteurs. — system ; *enseignement mutuel, m.*
mon'itory, *adj.*, d'admonition ; d'avertissement ; monitoire. — letters ; (ecc.) *lettres monitoires, f.pl.*
mon'itress, *n.*, monitrice, *f.*
monk (meu'gn'ke), *n.*, moine, religieux, *m.*
monk'ery, *n.*, moinerie, *f.*
mon'key (meu'gn'ki), *n.*, singe, *m. ;* (she —) guenon, *f. ;* (of piledrivers) mouton ; (children) babouin, *m.*, babouine, *f.* To get, *ou* have, one's — up ; *se mettre en colère, s'emporter.* —'s allowance ; *plus de coups que de caresses.* — trick ; *singerie, f.*
monk'-fish, *n.*, (ich.) ange de mer, *m.*
monk'hood (-houde), *n.*, moinerie, *f.*
monk'ish, *adj.*, de moine, monacal.
monk's'-hood, *n.*, (bot.) aconit, *m.*
mon'ochord (-korde), *n.*, (mus.) monocorde, *m.*
monochromat'ic (-krôm'-), *adj.*, monochrome.
monocotyle'don (-lî-), *n.*, (bot.) monocotylédone, *f.*
monocotyle'donous, *adj.*, monocotylédone.
monoc'ular (-ok'iou-), *adj.*, borgne, monoculaire. — vision; *vision avec un seul œil, f.*
mon'odist, *n.*, auteur d'une complainte, *m.*
mon'ody, *n.*, (song) complainte, monodie, *f.*
monog'amist, *n.*, monogame, *m.*
monog'amous, *adj.*, monogame.
monog'amy, *n.*, monogamie, *f.*
mon'ogram, *n.*, monogramme, *m.*
monog'raphy, *n.*, monographie, *f.*
mon'ologue (-loghe), *n.*, monologue, soliloque, *m.*

monoma'nia (-mé-nia), *n.*, (med.) monomanie, *f.*
monoma'niac (-nia), *n.*, monomane, *m.f.*
monoma'niac, *adj.*, monomane (pers.) ; monomaniaque (things).
mon'ome (-ôme), *n.*, (alg.) monôme, *m.*
monopet'alous, *adj.*, (bot.) monopétale.
monophyl'lous, *adj.*, (bot.) monophylle.
monop'olist, monop'olizer, *n.*, monopoleur, accapareur, *m.*
monop'olize (-laïze), *v.a.*, faire le monopole de ; monopoliser ; accaparer.
monop'oly, *n.*, monopole ; accaparement, *m.*
monop'teral (-teu-), *adj.*, (arch.) monoptère.
monosyllab'ic, *adj.*, monosyllabe, monosyllabique.
monosyl'lable, *n.*, monosyllabe, *m.*
monot'onous (-ot'o-), *adj.*, monotone.
monot'onously, *adv.*, avec monotonie ; d'une manière monotone.
monot'ony (-ot'o-), *n.*, monotonie, *f.*
monsoon' (-soune), *n.*, mousson, *f.*
mon'ster, *n.*, monstre, *m.*
mon'strance, *n.*, (cath. rel.) ostensoir, *m.*
monstros'ity, *n.*, monstruosité, *f.*
mon'strous, *adj.*, monstrueux ; horrible ; prodigieux. It is a — thing ; *cela passe les bornes.* It is — to think that . . . ; *il est horrible de penser que . . .*
mon'strously, *adv.*, monstrueusement ; horriblement ; prodigieusement, furieusement.
mon'strousness, *n.*, monstruosité, *f.*
Mon'teth, Mon'teith, *n.*, (vessel) verrière, *f.*
month (meu'n'th), *n.*, mois, *m.* Calendar —; *mois solaire.* Lunar —; *mois lunaire.* By the —; *au mois.* Twelve —s ; *un an, une année.* What is the day of the — ? *quel est le quantième du mois ?*
month'ly (meu'n'th'-), *adj.*, mensuel ; de tous les mois ; au mois. — newspaper ; *revue mensuelle, f.* — nurse ; *garde d'accouchée, f.*
month'ly, *adv.*, mensuellement, tous les mois ; par mois.
mon'ument (-iou-), *n.*, monument ; (tomb) tombeau, monument, *m.*, tombe, *f.*
monumen'tal, *adj.*, de monument ; monumental ; de la tombe, du tombeau.
monumen'tally, *adv.*, en monument.
mood (moude), *n.*, humeur, disposition, *f. ;* (gram., log., mus.) mode, *m.* To be in the — for ; *être d'humeur à ; être disposé à ; être en train de, ou en veine de.*
mood'iness, *n.*, humeur ; mauvaise humeur ; tristesse, *f.*
mood'y, *adj.*, de mauvaise humeur ; triste, morne, chagrin.
moon (moune), *v.n.*, (about) flâner ; muser, musarder.
moon, *n.*, lune, *f.* Full — ; *pleine lune.* New — ; *nouvelle lune.* By the light of the — ; *au clair, ou à la clarté, de la lune.* Beyond the — ; *hors d'atteinte.* Once in a blue — ; *tous les trente-six du mois* (V. Hugo). To believe the — is made of green cheese ; *prendre des vessies pour des lanternes.*
moon'-beam (-bîme), *n.*, rayon de lune ; rayon lunaire, *m.*
moon'-blindness (-blaï'n'd'-), *n.*, (vet.) ophtalmie périodique, *f.*
moon'-calf (-kâfe), *n.*, monstre ; (dolt) imbécile ; idiot, *m. ;* (med.) môle, *f.*
moon'-dial, *n.*, cadran lunaire, *m.*
mooned (mou'n'de), *adj.*, en forme de croissant. —horns ; *cornes en forme de croissant, f.pl.*
moonet' (-'ète), *n.*, (astron.) satellite, *m.*
moon'-eyed (-aïe'-de), *adj.*, myope ; qui voit peu ; aveugle ; (vet.) lunatique.
moon'ish, *adj.*, lunatique.
moon'less, *adj.*, sans lune ; sans clair de lune.
moon'light (-laïte), *n.*, clair de lune, *m. ;* (fig.)

eau de vie de contrebande, *f.* By —; *au clair de lune.*

moon'lit (-laïte), *adj.*, éclairé par la lune.

moon'-seed (-sîde), *n.*, (bot.) ménisperme, *m.*

moon'-shaped (-shép'te), *adj.*, en forme de lune, en forme de croissant ; (bot.) luné.

moon'shine (-shaïne), *n.*, clair de lune, *m. ;* (fig.) (rubbish) illusion, chimère, sornette, blague, *f. ;* vain projet, *m. ;* (smuggled spirit) eau de vie de contrebande, *f.*

moon'-struck (-streuke) *adj.*, lunatique.

moon'wort (-weurte), *n.*, (bot.) lunaire, *f.*

moon'y, *adj.*, de la lune ; en forme de lune.

Moor (moure), *n.*, More, Maure, *m.f. ;* lande, bruyère, *f. ;* marais, *m.*

moor, *v.a.*, amarrer. *v.n.*, s'amarrer.

moor'-berry (-bèr'-), *n.*, (bot.) canneberge, *f.*

moor'buzzard, *n.*, harpaye, *m.*

moor'-cock *ou* **moor'-fowl** (-faoul), *n.*, coq de bruyère, *m.*

moor'-hen, *n.*, (orni.) poule d'eau, *f.*

moor'ing, *n.*, (nav.) amarre, *f.*, amarrage, *m.*

moor'ings, *n.pl.*, mouillage, *m.sing.*

moor'ish *ou* **moor'y,** *adj.*, marécageux.

Moor'ish, *adj.*, (of the Moors) des Maures ; mauresque, moresque, more, maure.

moor'-land, *n.*, lande, bruyère, *f. ;* marais ; pays marécageux, *m.*

moose (mouce), *n.*, (zoöl.) élan d'Amérique, *m.*

moot, *v.a.*, discuter, débattre, soulever.

moot, *adj.*, discutable, sujet à contestation. — case, — point : *question discutable, question à décider, f.*

moot'ed, *adj.*, débattu, soulevé, discuté.

moot'er, *n.*, soutenant, *m.*

moot'ing, *n.*, conférence, discussion, *f. ;* débat, *m.*

mop, *n.*, balai à laver ; écouvillon ; (nav.) faubert, *m.*, (of hair) tignasse, *f.*

mop, *v.a.*, laver avec un balai ; essuyer avec un balai ; (nav.) fauberter ; (a gun, an oven) écouvillonner. To — one's face ; *s'éponger la figure.*

mope, *v.n.*, se séquestrer, être triste ; être mélancolique ; languir, s'ennuyer ; être hébété.

mope, *n.*, reclus, *m.*, recluse, personne triste ; personne qui s'ennuie toujours ; personne hébétée, *f.*

mop'ing, *adj.*, triste, mélancolique.

mop'ish (môp'-), *adj.*, triste ; abattu ; qui s'ennuie, hébété.

mop'ishly, *adv.*, tristement ; dans l'abattement.

mop'ishness, *n.*, tristesse ; stupidité, *f. ;* abattement ; ennui, *m.*

mop'pet *ou* **mop'sey,** *n.*, poupée ; marionnette ; (fondling name) pouponne, *f.*

mor'al, *adj.*, moral.

mor'al, *n.*, (mind) morale, (manners) moralité, *f.*

morale', *n.*, moral, *m.*

mor'alist, *n.*, moraliste, *m.*

moral'ity, *n.*, morale ; moralité, *f.*

moraliza'tion (-aïzé-), *n.*, moralisation, *f.*

mor'alize (-aïze), *v.a.*, (to render moral) rendre moral ; corriger les mœurs **de**, moraliser.

mor'alize, *v.n.*, moraliser, faire de la morale. To — on ; *moraliser* **sur**, *faire de la morale* **sur**.

mor'alizer, *n.*, personne qui moralise, qui fait de la morale, *f. ;* moraliseur, *m.*

mor'ally, *adv.*, moralement ; au moral, dans un sens moral. He was — and physically qualified for war ; *il avait les qualités physiques et morales requises pour la guerre.* He was far superior — and intellectually to Hume ; *au point de vue intellectuel et moral il était bien supérieur à Hume.* To live — ; *vivre selon les préceptes de la morale.* This is — certain ; *cela est certain à tous égards ; cela est moralement certain.*

mor'als (-'alze), *n.pl.*, mœurs, *f.pl. ;* moralité, morale, *f.*

morass', *n.*, marais, marécage, *m.*

moras'sy, *adj.*, marécageux.

Mora'vian, *adj.*, morave.

Mora'vian, *n.*, Morave, Hernute, *m.*

mor'bid, *adj.*, maladif, malsain, morbide.

mor'bidly, *adv.*, morbidement.

mor'bidness, *n.*, état maladif, état morbide, *m.*

morbose' (-bôce), *adj.*, malsain, morbeux.

morbos'ity, *n.*, (ant.) état maladif, *m.*

morda'cious (-dé-sheusse), *adj.*, mordant, caustique, piquant.

morda'ciously, *adv.*, d'une manière mordante, piquante, sarcastique, caustique.

mordac'ity (-dass'-), *n.*, mordacité, *f.*

mor'dant, *n.*, mordant, *m.*

more (môre), *adj.*, plus ; plus **de** ; encore ; plus nombreux ; davantage. — money ; *plus d'argent.* Give me one — ; *donnez-m'en encore un.* Some — ; *encore un peu ; encore quelques-uns ; davantage.* No — of that ! *assez de cela ! trêve à tout cela !* Give me some — ; *donnez-m'en encore.* Give me some — apples ; *donnez-moi encore des pommes.* It is — ; *c'est davantage.* They are — than we, there are — of them than of us ; *ils sont plus nombreux que nous.* One — ; *encore un ; un de plus.* — than ; *plus* **que** ; (followed by a number) *plus* **de**.

more (môre), *adv.*, plus ; davantage, encore. A great many — ; *beaucoup d'autres encore.* To be no — ; *être mort, n'être plus.* Once — ; *encore une fois.* Much — ; *beaucoup plus, bien plus, bien davantage.* Never — ; *jamais plus, plus jamais.* — and — ; *de plus en plus.* No —; *pas davantage.* No — ! *assez !* The —; *plus ; d'autant plus ; davantage.* So much the —; *d'autant plus ; d'autant mieux ; à plus forte raison.* The — that, *ou* because; *d'autant plus que.* To be — frightened than hurt ; *avoir plus de peur que de mal.* — haste less speed ; *qui trop se hâte, reste en chemin.* The — you speak the less you will learn ; *plus vous parlerez, moins vous apprendrez.* Nothing — than ; *pas plus que.*

moreen' (-rîne), *n.*, damas de laine, *m.*

mor'el, *n.*, (bot.) morille, *f.*

morel'lo, *n.*, (cherry) griotte, *f.* — tree, shrub; *griottier, m.*

moreo'ver (môr'ô-veur), *adv.*, de plus, outre cela, d'ailleurs, en outre.

moresque', *adj.*, moresque, mauresque.

moresque', *n.*, (paint.) moresque, mauresque, peinture moresque, *f.*

morganat'ic, *adj.*, morganatique, de la main gauche. —marriage ; *mariage morganatique, ou de la main gauche, m.*

mor'ibund (-beu'n'de), *adj.*, moribond.

mo'rion (mô-), *n.*, (helmet) morion, *m.*

morn, *n.*, matin, *m. ;* aurore, *f.*

morn'ing, *n.*, matin, *m. ;* matinée, *f.* Every —; *tous les matins.* All the —; *toute la matinée.* In the —; *le matin ; dans la matinée.* In the course of the —; *dans la matinée.* From — till night ; *depuis le matin jusqu'au soir.* Where have you been all this —? *où avez-vous passé la matinée ?* The next — ; *le lendemain matin.* The — before yesterday; *avant-hier matin.* The — after to-morrow ; *après demain matin.* The — before ; *la veille au matin.* Good — ; *bonjour.*

morn'ing, *adj.*, du matin ; matinier. —gown ; *robe de chambre, f.* — concert ; *matinée musicale, f.* — dress ; *déshabillé du matin, m.* — gun ; *coup de canon de diane, m.* —star ; *étoile du matin, f.*

moroc'co (-'cô), *n.*, maroquin, *m.*

moroc'co-leath'er (-lèth'eur), *n.*, maroquin, *m.*

moroc'co-pa'per (-pé'-), *n.*, papier maroquin, *m.*

morose' (-rôce), *adj.*, morose.

morose'ly, *adv.*, avec humeur.

morose'ness *ou* **moros'ity,** *n.*, morosité, humeur morose, *f.*

mor'phia *ou* **mor'phine**, *n.*, morphine, *f.*

mor'ris-dance, *n.*, danse moresque, *f.*

mor'ris-dancer, *n.*, danseur (de la moresque), *m.*

mor'row (mor'rô), *n.*, demain ; lendemain, *m.* On the —; *le lendemain.* Good-—; *bonjour.* To-—; *demain.* The day after to-—; *après demain.*

morse, *n.*, (zoöl.) morse, *m.;* vache marine, *f.;* cheval marin, *m.*

mor'sel, *n.*, morceau, *m.;* pièce, *f.*

mor'tal, *adj.*, (deadly) mortel, sujet à la mort, fatal, meurtrier, funeste; (human) des mortels, humain; (of combats) à outrance, à mort. Any — thing; *n'importe quoi, quoi que ce soit.*

mor'tal, *n.*, mortel, *m.*, mortelle, *f.* A mere —; *un simple mortel.*

mortal'ity, *n.*, mortalité; nature humaine; humanité; mort, *f.* Bills of —; *états de mortalité, m.pl.;* tables de mortalité, *f.pl.*

mor'tally, *adv.*, mortellement, à mort.

mor'tar, *n.*, (tech., artil., mas.) mortier, *m.* —board; *mortier, m.*

mort'gage (mor-ghèdje), *n.*, hypothèque, *f.* To pay off a —; *purger une hypothèque.*

mort'gage, *v.a.*, hypothéquer.

mortgagee' (-ghèdjî), *n.*, créancier hypothécaire, *m.*

mort'gager (-ghèdj'eur), *n.*, débiteur sur hypothèque, *m.*

mortif'erous (-eur'-), *adj.*, mortel, funeste; (med.) mortifère.

mortifica'tion (-fi-ké-), *n.*, mortification; (med.) gangrène, *f.*

mor'tified (-faïde), *adj.*, mortifié; affligé; (med.) gangrené.

mor'tify (-ti-faïe), *v.a.*, mortifier; (med.) déterminer la gangrène **dans**, faire gangrener.

mor'tify, *v.n.*, se mortifier; (med.) se gangrener.

mor'tise (-tice), *n.*, mortaise, *f.*

mor'tise, *v.a.*, emmortaiser; mortaiser.

mort'main (mort'méne), *n.*, mainmorte, *f.*

mor'tuary (mort'iou-a-ri), *n.*, (fee) droit mortuaire, *m.;* (dead house) morgue, *f.*

mor'tuary, *adj.*, mortuaire. — chambre; *chapelle ardente, f.*

mosa'ic (-zé-), *adj.*, en mosaïque; (pertaining to Moses) mosaïque. — work; *ouvrage en mosaïque, m.; mosaïque, f.*

mosque, *n.*, mosquée, *f.*

mosqui'to (-kî-), *n.*, moustique, *m.* — net; *moustiquaire, f.*

moss, *v.a.*, couvrir de mousse.

moss, *n.*, mousse, *f.;* (bog) marais, *m.*

moss'-clad *ou* **moss'-grown** (-grône), *adj.*, couvert de mousse; moussu.

mos'siness, *n.*, état moussu, *m.*

moss'-land, *n.*, dépôt tourbeux, *m.*

moss'-rose, *n.*, rose mousseuse, *f.*

moss'-trooper (-troup-'), *n.*, (Eng. hist.) maraudeur, bandit, *m.*

mos'sy, *adj.*, moussu, couvert de mousse.

most (môste), *adj.*, le plus; la plupart. The — part; *la plus grande partie, f.* — men; *la plupart des hommes.* — of us; *la plupart d'entre nous.*

most, *adv.*, le plus; très, fort; (extremely, highly, greatly) des plus, on ne peut plus, tout ce qu'il y a de plus, principalement. The — modest man in the world; *l'homme du monde le plus modeste.* The animals that man has — admired are . . .; *les animaux que l'homme a le plus admirés sont . . .* — vile; *très, fort, bien, excessivement, vil.* — laudable efforts; *des efforts des plus louables.* A — valuable book; *un livre des plus précieux, des plus importants.* To an extent which is — remarkable; *à un degré des plus remarquables.* A — marked curtsy; *une révérence des plus distinguées, des plus marquées.* — provokingly; *de la manière la plus*

impatientante. — likely; *très probablement.* To make the — of; *tirer tout le parti possible* **de.**

most, *n.*, la plupart, *f.;* le plus grand nombre, *m.* At —; *au plus; tout au plus.* To make the — of; *tirer le meilleur parti* **de.**

mos'tic, *n.*, appui-main, *m.*

most'ly (môst'-), *adv.*, pour la plupart; le plus souvent; la plupart du temps; ordinairement; principalement; presque tous.

mote (môte), *n.*, atome; (in the eye) fétu, *m.;* paille, *f.*

motet' (-tète), *n.*, (mus.) motet, *m.*

moth (moth), *n.*, *(moths)* papillon de nuit, *m.;* phalène; teigne, gerce, *f.;* (fig.) ver rongeur, *m.* The proverbial —; *le papillon qui veut absolument se brûler les ailes.*

moth'-eaten (-ît'-), *adj.*, rongé des vers.

moth'er (meuth'eur), *n.*, mère; (familiar term of address) bonne mère, bonne vieille, bonne femme, *f.;* (slimy substance in liquors) lie, moisissure; mère (de vinaigre), *f.* Grand-—; *grand'-mère.* Step-—; *belle-mère.* To be a — to; *être une mère* **pour.** — Carey's goose; *pétrel, m.*

moth'er, *adj.*, mère; maternel; national; (of churches) métropolitain. —-country; *mère patrie, f.* —-tongue; *langue maternelle, propre langue, f.*

moth'er, *v.a.*, servir de mère **à**; adopter.

moth'er, *v.n.*, (of liquors) se moisir.

moth'erhood (-houde), *n.*, maternité, *f.*

moth'er-in-law (-lô), *n.*, belle-mère, *f.*

moth'er-land, *n.*, mère patrie, *f.*

moth'erless, *adj.*, sans mère; orphelin de mère.

moth'erly, *adj.*, maternel, de mère; (in look) qui a l'air d'une mère de famille.

moth'erly, *adv.*, maternellement; en mère.

moth'er-of-pearl (-ov'peurle), *n.*, nacre de perle, *f.*

moth'er-wa'ter (-wô-teur), *n.*, (chem.) eau mère, *f.*

moth'er-wit, *n.*, esprit naturel, *m.*

moth'ery, *adj.*, (of liquids) moisi.

moth'-worm (-weurme), *n.*, (ent.) teigne des habits; teigne, *f.*

moth'wort (moth'weurte), *n.*, (bot.) agripaume, *f.*

moth'y (moth'i), *adj.*, plein de teignes, de gerces.

mo'tion (mô-), *v.n.*, (ant.) faire une proposition, faire une motion. To — to; *faire signe* **à.**

mo'tion, *v.a.*, (ant.) proposer. To — a person to a seat; *montrer un siège à quelqu'un.*

mo'tion, *n.*, mouvement, *m.;* motion, *f.;* (astron.) mouvement, *m.;* (proposal) motion, proposition; (med.) selle, *f.;* (signal) signe, *m.* The laws of —; *les lois du mouvement, f.pl.* Perpetual —; *mouvement perpétuel.* Diurnal —; *mouvement diurne.* To make a —; *faire une motion, une proposition.* To carry a —; *faire adopter une motion.* To put in —; *mettre en mouvement; imprimer le mouvement* **à.**

mo'tionless, *adj.*, immobile.

mo'tion-rod, *n.*, (mec.), bielle de parallélogramme, *f.*

mo'tive (mô-), *adj.*, moteur, qui fait agir. — power, — force; *force motrice, f.; moteur, m.*

mo'tive, *n.*, motif, mobile, *m.* To allege, to state a — for, the — of; *motiver; exposer le motif* **de.**

mot'ley (-'lè), *adj.*, bigarré, mêlé, varié, mélangé.

mo'tor (mô-teur), *n.*, moteur, *m.;* force motrice, *f.;* mobile, *m.* — car; *automobile, m.* — cycling; *automobilisme, m.* — cycler; *automobiliste, m.*

mo'tory (mô-), *adj.*, (ant.) moteur; (anat.) moteur. — muscles; *muscles moteurs, m.pl.*

mot'tle (mot't'l), *v.a.*, madrer, moirer; (soap) marbrer.

mot'tled (mot't'l'de), *adj.*, pommelé, saumoné, tacheté ; (of wood) madré, moiré ; (of soap) marbré.

mot'to (-'tô), *n.*, (*mottoes*) devise, *f.*

mould, mould'er, moult, *etc.* V. **mold, molder, molt,** *etc.*

mound (maou'n'de), *n.*, levée, digue, *f. ;* (natural elevation) butte, *f.*, tertre, exhaussement ; (fort.) rempart ; (arch.) remblai, *m.*

mound, *v.a.*, fortifier par un rempart, faire une digue à.

mount (maou'n'te), *n.*, mont, monticule, tertre, *m.*, colline, montagne, *f. ;* (of horses, etc.) monture, *f.*

mount, *v.a.*, monter ; monter **sur.** To — the throne ; *monter sur le trône.* To — a broom ; *aller à cheval sur un manche à balai.* To — a play ; (thea.) *monter une pièce.* To — guard ; (mil.) *monter la garde.* To — a drawing ; *monter un dessin.*

mount, *v.n.*, monter, s'élever ; (one's horse) monter à cheval, enfourcher son cheval.

mount'ain, *n.*, montagne, *f. ;* (fig.) monceau, *m.* Waves — high ; *des vagues hautes comme des montagnes.* To make —s of mole hills ; *faire d'un œuf un bœuf ; faire d'une mouche un éléphant.* The Old Man of the M— ; *le Vieux de la Montagne* (14th Century) — dew ; *whisky* (*d'Ecosse*), *m.*

mount'ain, *adj.*, de la montagne, des montagnes ; agreste ; (of scenery) montagneux ; vaste, énorme ; montagnard.

mountaineer' (-tén'ïre), *n.*, montagnard, *m.*

mount'ain-girl (-gheurle) *ou* **mount'ain-maid** (-mède), *n.*, jeune montagnarde, *f.*

moun'tainous, *adj.*, montagneux, de montagnes, montueux ; (fig.) énorme.

mount'ain-stream (-strïme), *n.*, ravin, torrent, *m.*

moun'tebank (maou'n'tè-), *n.*, charlatan, saltimbanque, *m.*

mount'ed, *adj.*, monté ; à cheval ; portant, armé de ; (*pl.*) pourvus de chevaux. — on ; *à cheval* **sur.** — police ; *gendarmerie à cheval,* *f.*

mount'er, *n.*, (tech.) monteur, *m.*, monteuse, *f.*

mount'ing, *n.*, (ascent) montée, *f. ;* (tech.) montage, *m. ;* (thing mounted) monture, *f. ;* (equipment) équipement, *m.*

mount'ingly, *adv.*, en montant.

mourn (môrne), *v.a.*, pleurer, déplorer.

mourn, *v.n.*, pleurer, se lamenter ; porter le deuil **de.** To — for ; *pleurer, se lamenter* **sur.**

mourn'er (-), *n.*, (hired) pleureur, *m.*, pleureuse, *f. ;* (in funerals) personne qui suit le convoi. Chief — ; *personne qui mène, ou conduit, le deuil, f.* To be a —, one of the —s ; *suivre le deuil, être du convoi.* To be chief — ; *mener, ou conduire, le deuil.*

mourn'ful (-foule), *adj.*, triste, lugubre, fatal ; lamentable, déplorable. —-widow ; (bot.) *veuve, fleur de veuve, f.*

mourn'fully, *adv.*, d'un air lugubre, d'une manière lugubre ; tristement, lamentablement, déplorablement.

mourn'fulness, *n.*, deuil, *m. ;* affliction, tristesse, douleur, *f.*

mourn'ing, *n.*, deuil, *m. ;* affliction, lamentation, *f.* Deep — ; *grand deuil.* To be in — for ; *être en deuil* **de,** *porter le deuil* **de.** To go into — for; *prendre le deuil, se mettre en deuil* **pour,** *ou porter le deuil* **de** (V. Hugo). To wear — ; *être en deuil.* To go out of — ; *quitter le deuil.* Court — ; *deuil de cour, m.* — garments ; *vêtements de deuil, m.pl.*

mourn'ing, *adj.*, affligé ; triste ; de deuil.

mourn'ingly, *adv.*, d'une manière lugubre, tristement, lugubrement.

mouse (maouce), *n.*, souris, *f. ;* (nav.) bouton, *m.*, pomme, *f.* Field— ; *mulot, m.* —-colored ;

couleur poil de souris (invariable). A man or **a** — ; *quelque chose ou rien.*

mouse (maouze), *v.n.*, prendre des souris.

mouse (maouze), *v.t.*, (nav.) aiguilleter.

mouse'-hole (-hôle), *n.*, trou de souris, *m.*

mous'er (maouz'eur), *n.*, preneur de souris, *m.*

mouse'-trap (-trape), *n.*, souricière, *f.*

moustache', *n.*, moustache, *f. ;* (fig.) vétéran, *m.*

mouth (maouth), *n.*, bouche ; (of things) ouverture, entrée, *f. ;* orifice ; (of a bottle) trou, goulot, *m. ;* (of a pistol) gueule ; (of ravenous beasts) gueule ; (of rivers, instruments) embouchure ; (of cannon) gueule, bouche ; (wry face) grimace ; (of a cave or harbor) entrée, *f.* To make any one's — water ; *faire venir l'eau à la bouche à quelqu'un.* By the — of ; (fig.) *par l'organe* **de.** With open — ; *la bouche béante.* To be in everybody's — ; *être dans toutes les bouches.* To shut any one's — ; *faire taire quelqu'un, fermer la bouche* **à** *quelqu'un.* To live from hand to — ; *vivre au jour le jour.* To be down in the — ; *être déconcerté, découragé ;* (fam.) *avoir la mine allongée ; être tout penaud.* To make —s ; *faire des grimaces.*

mouth (maouth), *v.a.*, crier, déclamer ; insulter ; (to take in the mouth) avaler, dévorer, gober ; saisir avec la bouche ; mettre dans la bouche.

mouth (maouth), *v.n.*, crier, brailler ; déclamer, pérorer, vociférer.

mouthed' (maouth'de), *adj.*, qui a une bouche, qui a la bouche ; à la bouche. Foul— ; *mal embouché.* Hard— ; (man.) *qui a la bouche dure, qui n'a point de bouche.* Hundred — ; *aux cent bouches.* Mealy— ; *doucereux.* Wide— ; *qui a la bouche large.*

mouth'er (maouth'eur), *n.*, braillard, criailleur ; péroreur, *m.*

mouth'-friend (-frè'n'de), *n.*, faux ami, *m.*

mouth'-ful (-foule), *n.*, bouchée, *f.* At a — ; *d'une seule bouchée.*

mouth'-honor (-o'n'or), *n.*, égards feints, *m. pl. ;* déférence feinte, eau bénite de cour, *f.*

mouth'ing (maouth'-), *n.*, criaillerie, déclamation, *f.*

mouth'less (maouth-), *adj.*, sans bouche.

mouth'-piece (-pïce), *n.*, embouchure, *f. ;* bocal ; (pers.) organe, orateur, interprète, *m.*

mov'able (mouv'a-b'l), *adj.*, mobile ; meuble, mobilier. — goods ; *biens meubles ; effets mobiliers, m.pl.* — feast ; *fête mobile, f.*

mov'ableness, *n.*, mobilité, *f.*

mov'ables (mouv'a-b'lze), *n.*, biens meubles ; effets mobiliers ; meubles, *m.pl.*

mov'ably, *adv.*, d'une manière mobile.

move (mouve), *v.a.*, (to shake, stir) remuer ; (to give motion to) mouvoir, faire mouvoir, mettre en mouvement, faire marcher, faire aller ; (to take, carry away) transporter, porter ; (to excite, induce) exciter à, pousser à, porter à, engager à ; (to inspire) inspirer ; (to affect) toucher, émouvoir ; (to produce) produire, faire naître, soulever ; (to propose) faire la motion **de,** proposer, demander ; (at chess) jouer. To — to pity ; *toucher, émouvoir.* To — to laughter ; *exciter la risée* **de.** To be — d by ; *se laisser émouvoir, toucher* **par.** To — away ; *éloigner, enlever, ôter.* To — back ; *remettre à sa place, rapporter.* To — backward ; *reculer.* To — down ; *baisser, descendre.* To — forward ; *avancer.* To — off ; *ôter, enlever ;* (off the pavement, etc.) *faire quitter* **à.** To — out ; *sortir.* To — round ; *tourner.* To — up ; *monter, hausser.* To — heaven and earth ; *remuer ciel et terre.*

move, *v.n.*, bouger, se remuer, se mouvoir ; (to go, advance) se mettre en mouvement, aller, partir, marcher, s'avancer, se transporter ; (of an army) s'ébranler ; (to stir) s'agiter, se remuer, bouger ; (to change residence) déménager ; (to turn) tourner ; (to propose) faire une motion, proposer, demander ; (at chess) jouer. To — in the highest circles ; *fréquenter le grand monde.* To — on; *passer son chemin ; avancer ; s'avancer.* To — about ; *se donner du mouvement ; se remuer, se trémousser ; aller et venir ; aller çà et là.* To — aside ; *s'écarter.* To — away ; *s'éloigner, s'en aller.* To — back ; *reculer, se reculer.* To — down ; *descendre.* To — forward, to — on; *avancer, s'avancer, marcher, circuler* ; (of coaches, etc.) *s'ébranler.* To — off; *s'éloigner, décamper, s'en aller, filer.* To — out ; *sortir, déloger* ; (of furniture) *déménager.* To — round; *se retourner, se tourner, tourner.* To — up; *monter, avancer.* To — in ; *emménager, entrer, rentrer.* The troops began to — ; *les troupes se mirent en marche.* — on, please ! *circulez, Messieurs !*

move, *n.,* mouvement ; coup, trait ; (at chess) trait, coup, *m.;* (progress) marche, *f.* The — s of the pieces ; (at chess) *la marche des pièces, f.* To be up to a — or two, to know a — or two; *en savoir long.* To be on the — ; *se remuer, s'agiter.* To make a — ; *se préparer à partir* ; *s'en aller ; faire un pas en avant.* To have the —, to play the first — ; *jouer le premier, avoir le trait.* Masterly — ; *coup de maître, coup de partie.* Lucky — ; *coup de bonheur.* To recall a — ; *rejouer.* Whose — is it ? *à qui est-ce à jouer ?* It is my — ; *c'est à moi à jouer.* What is to be the next — ? *que va-t-on faire maintenant ? quel nouveau parti va-t-on prendre ?*

move'ment (mouv'-), *n.,* mouvement, *m.; agitation, f.*

mov'er (mouv'-), *n.,* moteur ; mobile, *m.; force motrice, f.;* (proposer) auteur d'une motion, d'une proposition, *m.* First, *ou* prime, —; *principe moteur, m., force motrice, f.;* (fig.) *premier mobile, m.*

mov'ing (mouv'-), *adj.,* (having motion) mouvant, mobile ; (giving motion) moteur ; (affecting) touchant, émouvant, attendrissant, persuasif, pathétique, qui émeut. — power; *force motrice, f.; moteur, m.*

mov'ing, *n.,* mouvement, *m.;* impulsion, *f.;* (of furniture) déménagement ; (change from place) déplacement, *m.*

mov'ingly, *adv.,* d'une manière touchante, attendrissante ; pathétiquement.

mow (maou), *n.,* (a stack) monceau, tas de foin, de gerbes, *m.;* moue, grimace, *f.*

mow (mô), *v.a.* and *n.,* faucher ; (to heap up) mettre en tas, en meule ; (fig.) moissonner ; (ant.) grimacer. To — down ; *faucher, moissonner, abattre, faire tomber.*

mow'er, *n.,* faucheur, *m.;* (engine) faucheuse, *f.;* (for grass) tondeuse, *f.*

mow'ing, *n.,* (operation) fauchage, *m.;* (produce) fauche, *f.* — time ; *fauchaison, f.*

mox'a, *n.,* moxa, *m.*

Mr. (ab. of Mister), Monsieur ; M. (**Mons.** *is vulgar*) ; (before certain titles) Monsieur le président, Monsieur le général.

Mrs. (ab. of Mistress), Madame ; Mme.

much (meutshe), *adv.,* beaucoup **de**; beaucoup, bien, fort, très; (nearly) à peu près. — about the same; à peu près égal ; *passablement ; doucement ; comme ça.* — of a muchness ; *à peu près la même chose.* Thus — ; *autant.* This — ; *cela, ceci.* Nothing — ; *pas grand chose.* Pretty — ; *à peu près.* Read — ; *lisez beaucoup.* — more ; *bien plus.* So — ; *tant ; tant* **de.** So — so that ; *si bien que, à tel point que.* So — as ; *tant que, autant que ; assez* **pour.** In so — as ; *d'autant plus que.* So — the more . . . that ; *d'autant plus . . . que.* Too — ; *trop, de trop, trop* **de.** As —; *autant* **de.** How — ? *combien ? combien* **de ?** As — as ; *autant que ; jusqu'à.* To make — of ; *faire grand cas* **de,** *tirer grand parti* **de,** *faire valoir, estimer beaucoup.* So — for; *voilà* **pour.**

Rebecca's —-talked-of dinners ; *les dîners si célèbres de Rébecca, m.pl.* My work is too — for me ; *ma besogne est au-dessus de mes forces.* You are not — the wiser for it ; *vous n'en êtes pas plus avancé ; vous n'en savez pas plus long.* — ado about nothing ; *plus de bruit que de besogne, beaucoup de bruit pour rien.* So — the better; *tant mieux.* — coin, much care ; (prov.) *qui terre a, guerre a.* —-loved ; *fort aimé.*

mu'cilage (miou-cil'èdje), *n.,* mucilage, **m.**

mucilag'inous, *adj.,* mucilagineux.

muck (meuke), *n.,* fumier, *m.;* fiente, *f.;* objet méprisable, *m.*

muck, *v.a.,* fumer ; (to dirty) salir.

muck'hill, *n.,* tas de fumier, *m.*

muck'iness, *n.,* saleté, ordure, *f.*

muck'worm (-weurme), *n.,* ver de fumier ; (miser) ladre, *m.*

mucky, *adj.,* sale, malpropre.

mu'cous (miou-), *adj.,* (anat.) muqueux ; visqueux.

mu'culent (miou-kiou-), *adj.,* visqueux.

mu'cus (miou-), *n.,* mucosité, *f.;* (physiol., pathol.) mucus, *m.*

mud (meude), *n.,* boue, bourbe, vase, fange, *f.* —-cart ; *tombereau, m.* —-guard ; *garde-crotte, m.* —-lark ; *égoutier, ravageur, m.* To stick in the — ; *s'embourber.* —-building ; *bousillage, m.* —-wall ; *mur de terre, mur de bousillage, torchis, m.*

mud, *v.a.,* embourber, salir, couvrir de boue, crotter; (a liquid) troubler.

mud'dily, *adv.,* salement ; d'un air sombre.

mud'diness, *n.,* état boueux, état bourbeux, état trouble, *m.*

mud'dle (meud'd'l), *v.a.,* hébéter ; troubler, étourdir. He has —d the whole affair ; *il a gâté toute l'affaire.* He has —d away all his money ; *il a gaspillé tout son argent.*

mud'dle, *v.n.,* barboter, patauger, se salir ; faire du gâchis.

mud'dle, *n.,* confusion, *f. ;* désordre, gâchis, brouillamini, *m.* All in a — ; *tout brouillé.*

mud'dled (meud'd'l'de), *adj.,* trouble, troublé; hébété, lourd ; confus ; (of liquor) gris.

mud'dy, *adj.,* boueux, bourbeux, fangeux ; limoneux, vaseux ; crotté, couvert de boue; (stupid) lourd, borné, hébété ; (dark) couleur de boue; (of precious stones) nuageux; (of wine) trouble.

mud'dy, *v.a.,* troubler; salir, crotter.

mud'dy-head'ed (-hèd'ède), *adj.,* lourd, borné, bouché ; sot, hébété.

mud'-fish, *n.,* (ich.) limande, *f.*

mud'-lighter, *n.,* marie-salope, *f.*

mud'wort (-weurte), *n.,* (bot.) limoselle, *f.*

muff (meufe), *n.,* manchon ; (pers.) cornichon, serin, *m.,* huître, *f.*

muf'fin (meuf'-), *n.,* (espèce de) galette, *f.*

muf'fle (meuf'f'l), *v.a.,* emmitoufler ; envelopper; affubler ; (a bell) assourdir ; (a drum) voiler ; (the eyes) bander ; (fig.) couvrir, cacher, étouffer. To — up; *affubler, envelopper.*

muf'fle, *n.,* (chem.) moufle, *m.* (*f.* according to some); (mec.) moufle, *f.* (*m.* according to some).

muf'fler, *n.,* cache-nez, *m.*

muf'ti (meuf'-), *n.,* (Mahommedan) mufti, muphti ; (milit., nav.) habit bourgeois, *m.*

mug (meughe), *n.,* gobelet, *m. ;* timbale ; (mouth) gueule, *f.*

mug'gy (meug'ghi), *adj.,* couvert, humide, lourd, mou.

mug'house (-haouce), *n.,* cabaret borgne, *m.*

mug'wort (meug'weurte), *n.,*(bot.) armoise, *f.*

mulat'to (miou-lat'tô), *n.,* mulâtre, *m.f.,* mulâtresse, *f.*

mul'berry (meul'bèr'-), *n.,* mûre, *f.;* (tree) mûrier, *m.*

mulct (meulk'te), *n.,* amende, *f.*

mulct, *v.a.*, mettre à l'amende ; frapper d'une amende ; imposer une amende à ; (fig.) priver **de**.

mule (mioule), *n.*, mulet, *m.*, mule, *f. ;* (orni.) mulet, *m. ;* (for spinning) mule-jenny, *f.*, métier à filer un fin, *m.* As stubborn as a — ; *têtu comme un âne.*

mule'-driver (-draïv'-) *ou* **mul'eteer** (miou-lèt'ïre), *n.*, muletier.

mul'eteer, *n. V.* **mule-driver**.

mule'wort (-weurte), *n.*, herbe aux mulets, *f.*

mul'ish (mioul'-), *adj.*, de mulet, de mule ; (fig.) entêté, têtu, obstiné.

mull, *n.*, four, *m. ;* boulette, *f.* To make a — of ; *gâcher.*

mull (meul), *v.a.*, faire chauffer et épicer ; (fig.) gâcher, faire un gâchis **de**.

mulled (meul'de), *adj.*, (of wine) chaud et épicé.

mul'len (meul'line) *ou* **mul'lein** (meu'line), *n.*, (bot.) molène, *f.*, bouillon-blanc, *m.*

mul'ler (meul'-), *n.*, molette (à broyer), *f.*

mul'let (meul'-), *n.*, (ich.) mulet, surmulet, *m.* Gray —; *mulet, muge, m.* Red —; *rouget, m.*

mul'ligrubs (meul'li-greubze), *n.pl.*, colique, *f. ;* tranchées, *f.pl.*

mul'lion (meul'ïeune), *n.*, (arch.) meneau, *m.*

mul'lioned, *adj.*, en meneaux.

multan'gular (meult'a'gn'ghiou-), *adj.*, (geom.) polygonal.

mul'ti-colored, *adj.*, multicolore.

multifa'rious (meul-ti-fé-), *adj.*, varié, divers, différent, multiplié.

multifa'riously, *adv.*, diversement ; avec une grande diversité.

multifa'riousness, *n.*, diversité ; multiplicité, variété, *f.*

multiflo'rous (meul-ti-flô-), *adj.*, (bot.) multiflore.

mul'tifold (-fôlde), *adj.*, (ant.) nombreux, varié.

mul'tiform *ou* **multiform'ous** (meul-), *adj.*, (anat.) varié, multiforme.

multiform'ity, *n.*, diversité de formes, *f.*

multilat'eral (meul-), *adj.*, (geom.) à plusieurs côtés ; polygonal.

mul'tiple (meul'ti-p'l), *adj. and n.*, multiple, *m.*

mul'tipliable (meul-ti-plaï-a-b'l), *adj.*, multipliable.

multiplicand' (meul'-), *n.*, multiplicande, *m.*

mul'tiplicate (meul-), *adj.*, multiplié.

multiplica'tion (meul-ti-pli-ké-), *n.*, multiplication, *f.*

mul'tiplicator (meul-ti-pli-ké-), *n.*, multiplicateur, *m.*

multipli'city (meul-), *n.*, multiplicité, *f.*

mul'tiplied (meul-ti-plaïde), *adj.*, multiplié ; réitéré, nombreux.

mul'tiplier (meul-ti-plaï'-), *n.*, (arith.) multiplicateur, *m.*

mul'tiply (meul-ti-plaïe), *v.a.*, multiplier.

mul'tiply, *v.n.*, multiplier, se multiplier.

mul'tiplying, *adj.*, multipliant. — -glass ; *multipliant ; verre multipliant, m.*

mul'titude (meul-ti-tioude), *n.*, multitude, *f.*

multitu'dinous (meul-ti-tiou-), *adj.*, très-nombreux, diversifié, en grand nombre, vaste, immense.

mul'tivalve, *n.*, (conch.) multivalve, *f.*

mum (meume), *adj.*, silencieux, muet. To be —; *avoir la bouche close, la bouche cousue.*

mum ! *int.*, bouche close ! chut ! motus !

mum'ble (meu'm'b'l), *v.n.*, marmotter ; mâchonner.

mum'bler, *n.*, grogneur ; marmotteur, *m. ;* grogneuse, marmotteuse, *f.*

mum'blingly, *adv.*, en marmottant ; en mâchonnant.

mumm (meume), *v.n.*, se masquer.

mum'mer, *n.*, masque, *m.*

mum'mery, *n.*, mascarade ; momerie, *f. ;* momon, *m.*

mummifica'tion (-mi-fi-ké-), *n.*, momification, *f.*

mum'miform, *adj.*, en forme de momie.

mum'mify (meum'mi-faïe), *v.a.*, momifier.

mum'ming, *n.*, mascarade, *f.*

mum'my, *n.*, momie, *f.* To beat to a — ; *rouer de coups.*

mump (meu'm'pe), *v.a.* and *n.*, marmotter ; (to chatter) jacasser, jaboter ; (to cheat) attraper, duper ; (to nibble) grignoter, mâchonner ; (to beg) mendier, gueuser ; (to be sulky) bouder, se refrogner.

mump'er, *n.*, gueux, *m.*, gueuse, *f.*

mump'ing, *n.*, ruse de gueux ; grimace, *f.*

mump'ish, *adj.*, de mauvaise humeur, rechigné, chagrin, maussade.

mumps (meu'm'pse), *n.pl.*, (med.) oreillons, *m.pl. ;* (ord. lang.) mauvaise humeur, *f.*

munch (meu'n'she), *v.a.* and *n.*, mâcher, manger à grosses bouchées.

mun'dane (meu'n'-), *adj.*, mondain, du monde.

mundan'ity (meu'n'-), *n.* (ant.), mondanité, *f.*

mun'dify (meu'n'di-faïe), *v.a.*, (ant.) (med.) mondifier, nettoyer, déterger.

mun'grel, *n.* and *adj. V.* **mongrel**.

munic'ipal (miou-), *adj.*, municipal. — law ; *droit municipal, ou civil, m.*

municipal'ity, *n.*, municipalité, *f.*

munif'icence (miou-), *n.*, munificence, *f.*

munif'icent, *adj.*, libéral, généreux.

munif'icently, *adv.*, libéralement, avec munificence.

mu'niment (miou-), *n.*, fortification, place forte, *f. ;* fort, *m. ;* défense ; (jur.) charte, *f.*, document, titre, *m.* — -room ; *archives, f.pl.*

muni'tion (miou-), *n.*, munition ; fortification, *f.*

muni'tion-ship, *n.*, (nav.) transport, vaisseau de transport, *m.*

mu'ral, *adj.*, mural, de mur.

mur'der (meur-), *n.*, meurtre, assassinat, homicide ; (fig.) meurtre, grand dommage, *m.* —! *à l'assassin !* Willful —; *homicide volontaire, m.* The — is out ; *la mèche est éventée.* — will out ! *la vérité se sait toujours.* To cry out — ; *crier à l'assassin.*

mur'der, *v.a.*, assassiner, tuer ; (to do badly) massacrer, estropier ; (a language) écorcher. To — a name ; *estropier un nom.* To — the King's English ; *donner un soufflet à Vaugelas.*

mur'derer, *n.*, meurtrier, assassin, *m.*

mur'deress, *n.*, femme homicide, (l.u.) meurtrière, *f.*

mur'dering, *adj.*, assassin, meurtrier.

mur'derous, *adj.*, homicide, meurtrier, assassin, sanguinaire.

mur'derously, *adv.*, par le meurtre, par l'assassinat, en assassin.

mu'rex (miou-rèkse), *n.*, (zoöl.) murex, *m.*

muriat'ic, *adj.*, muriatique.

mu'rine (miou-raïne), *adj.*, (zoöl.) de souris, des souris.

murk'iness (meurk'-), *n.*, obscurité, *f. ;* ténèbres, *f.pl.*

murk'y, *adj.*, sombre, obscur, ténébreux, noir.

mur'mur (meur-meur), *n.*, murmure, *m.*

mur'mur, *v.n.*, murmurer.

mur'murer, *n.*, murmurateur (l.u.), *m.*, personne qui murmure, *f.*

mur'muring, *adj.*, murmurant, murmurateur.

mur'muring, *n.*, murmure, *m. ;* murmures, *pl.*

mur'muringly, *adv.*, en murmurant.

mur'rain (meur-rène), *n.*, (med.) épizootie, *f.*

murre (meurre), *n.*, (orni.) pingouin, *m.*

mus'cadel, **mus'cadine**, *ou* **mus'catel** (meus-), *n.*, muscat, vin muscat, raisin muscat ; (pear) muscat royal, muscat vert, *m.*

mus′cadel *ou* **mus′catel** (meus-), *adj.*, muscat.

mus′cat (meus-), *n.*, vin muscat ; raisin muscat, *m.*

mus′cle (meus′s′l), *n.*, (anat.) muscle, *m.*

mus′cular *ou* **mus′culous** (meus-kiou-), *adj.*, musculaire ; musculeux.

muscular′ity, *n.*, constitution musculaire, *f.*

mus′cularly, *adv.*, par l'action musculaire ; vigoureusement.

mus′culous, *adj.* *V.* **muscular**.

muse (miouze), *n.*, muse, rêverie, méditation, *f.* In a — ; *rêveur, pensif.*

muse (miouze), *v.n.*, méditer, rêver ; être distrait, rêveur, pensif. To — on ; *rêver à, songer à, méditer sur, réfléchir à, sur.*

muse, *v.a.*, penser à, réfléchir à, méditer.

muse′ful (-foule), *adj.*, taciturne, rêveur, pensif.

muse′fully, *adv.*, pensivement, d'une manière rêveuse.

mus′er, *n.*, rêveur ; penseur ; distrait, *m.*

muse′um (miou-zi-), *n.*, musée, muséum, *m.*

mush′room (meush′roume), *n.*, champignon, (upstart) parvenu, *m.*

mush′room-bed (-bède), *n.*, couche de champignons, champignonnière, *f.*

mush′room-house (-haouce), *n.*, serre à champignons, *f.*

mu′sic (miou-zic), *n.*, musique ; harmonie, *f.* Rough — ; *charivari, m.* To set to — ; *mettre en musique.* To face the — ; (pop.) *affronter ses opposants ; affronter ses adversaires ; défendre sa position.*

mu′sical (miou-zi-), *adj.*, musical, harmonieux, mélodieux. – instrument ; *instrument de musique, m.* —-box ; *boîte à musique, f.*

mu′sically, *adv.*, en musique, musicalement, harmonieusement, avec harmonie.

mu′sicalness, *n.*, harmonie ; mélodie, *f.*, caractère musical, *m.*

mu′sic-book (-bouke), *n.*, cahier de musique, *m.*

mu′sic-composer, *n.*, compositeur de musique, *m.*

mu′sic-copyist, *n.*, noteur, (l.u.) copiste de musique, *m.*

mu′sic-desk, *n.*, pupitre à musique, *m.*

mu′sic-hall, *n.*, salle de concert, salle de variétés, *f.*

musi′cian (miou-zish′-), *n.*, musicien, *m.*, musicienne, *f.* —s, *pl.*, musiciens, *m.pl. ;* musique, *f.sing.*

music-mad, *adj.*, mélomane.

mu′sic-pen, *n.*, griffe (à graver la musique), *f.*

mu′sic-publisher (-peub′-), *n.*, éditeur de musique, *m.*

mu′sic-room (-roume), *n.*, salle de musique, de concert, *f.*

mu′sic-seller, *n.*, marchand de musique, *m.*

mu′sic-stand, *n.*, pupitre à musique ; lutrin, *m.*

mu′sic-stool (-stoul), *n.*, tabouret de piano, *m.*

mu′sing (miouz′-), *n.*, méditation, contemplation ; rêverie, *f.*

musk (meuske), *n.*, musc. — deer ; (mam.) *chevrotain, porte-musc, musc, m.*

musk, *v.a.*, musquer.

musk′-cat, *n.*, (zoöl.) rat musqué, ondatra, *m.*

mus′ket (meus′kète), *n.*, mousquet, fusil, fusil de munition, *m.*

mus′ket-ball, *n.*, balle de fusil, *ou* de mousquet, *f.*

musketeer′ (-′tre), *n.*, mousquetaire ; fusilier, *m.*

musketoon′ (-′oune), *n.*, mousqueton, *m.*

mus′ketry, *n.*, mousqueterie, *f. ;* fusils, *m.pl.* Discharge of — ; *fusillade, f.* School of — ; *école de tir, f.*

mus′ket-proof, *adj.*, à l'épreuve des balles.

musk′iness (meusk′-), *n.*, odeur de musc, *m.*

musk′-melon (meusk′mèl′-), *n.*, melon muscat, *m.*

musk′-pear (-père), *n.*, poire musquée, *f.*

musk′-rose (-rôze), *n.*, rose musquée, *f.*

musk′-seed (-sîde), *n.*, (bot.) graine d'ambrette, *f.*

musk′y (meusk′-), *adj.*, musqué, de musc.

mus′lin (meuz′-), *adj.*, de mousseline.

mus′lin, *n.*, mousseline, *f.*

mus′lin-manufacturer, *n.*, mousselinier, brodeur en mousseline, *m.*

mus′lin-printer, *n.*, imprimeur de mousseline, *m.*

mus′rol (meuz′rôle), *n.*, (of a bridle) muserolle, *f.*

mus′sel (meus′s′l), *n.*, moule, *f.*

Mus′sulman (meus′seul′-), *n.*, musulman, *m.*, musulmane, *f.*

Mus′sulman, *adj.*, en musulman ; musulman.

must (meuste), *v.n.*, falloir ; devoir. I — ; *il le faut.* It — be so ; *il le faut ; il le faut absolument ;* (must be the case) *cela doit être ainsi.* I — dine ; *il me faut dîner ; il faut que je dîne.* I — do it ; *il faut que je le fasse.* You — return to Paris ; *il faut que vous retourniez à Paris.* Had all his men fought with a like ardor, our army — infallibly have been repulsed ; *si tous ses soldats avaient combattu avec la même ardeur, notre armée était* (ou *aurait été) infailliblement repoussée.* The peasants — have been supplied with ; *les paysans ont dû se procurer.* These causes — have arisen ; *ces causes ont dû naître.* What — it be ? *qu'est-ce que cela doit être ?* Something — be done ; *il faut (il fallait) faire quelque chose.* He — have lost his way ; *il se sera égaré ; il faut qu'il se soit égaré.* You — know ; *vous saurez ; vous devez savoir, il faut que vous sachiez.* You — have known ; *vous avez dû savoir.* It — be done ; *il faut le faire absolument.*

must (meuste), *v.a.* and *n.*, moisir, se moisir.

must (meuste), *n.*, moût, *m.*

mustache′ (meus′tâshe) *ou* (ant.) **musta′chio** (-tâ-shiô), *n.*, moustache, *f.*

musta′chioed (-ôde), *adj.*, qui porte des moustaches ; à moustaches.

mus′tard (meus-tarde), *n.*, (bot.) moutarde, *f. ;* sénevé, *m.*

mus′tard-pot (-pote), *n.*, moutardier, *m.*

mus′tard-seed (-sîde), *n.*, graine de moutarde, *f.*

mus′tee (meus-tî), *n.*, métis, *m.*, métisse, *f.*

mus′teline (meus-tî-laïne), *adj.*, (zoöl.) de belette.

mus′ter (meus-), *n.*, appel, *m. ;* réunion ; revue, *f. ;* rassemblement, *m. ;* foule ; troupe, bande, *f. ;* contrôles, *m.pl.* To pass — ; *passer à la revue, être admis, être toléré, passer à l'inspection ;* (fig.) *passer.* To call over the — roll ; *faire l'appel.*

mus′ter, *v.a.* and *n.*, faire l'appel **de** ; réunir ; rassembler, se procurer ; s'assembler ; se réunir ; (milit.) faire l'appel, répondre à l'appel. How many do we — ? *combien sommes-nous ?* We could only — a few shillings between us ; *nous n'avions entre nous tous que quelques schellings tout comptés.* To — up courage ; *prendre son courage à deux mains.*

mus′ter-book (-bouke), *n.*, rôle ; contrôle ; (nav.) rôle d'équipage, *m. ;* (milit.) matricule, *f.*, registre matricule d'un régiment, *m.*

mus′ter-mas′ter (meus-teur-mâs-teur), *n.*, (milit.) adjudant ; sergent-major, *m.*

must′ily (meus-), *adv.*, avec un goût moisi ; avec un goût de renfermé.

must′iness (meus′ti-), *n.*, moisi ; (closeness) relent, renfermé, *m.*

must′y, *adj.*, moisi ; (close) qui sent le relent, qui sent le renfermé.

mutabil′ity (miou-) *ou* **mu′tableness** (miou-ta-b'l-), *n.*, mutabilité ; instabilité ; inconstance, *f.*

mu'table (miou-ta-b'l), *adj.*, changeant, inconstant, peu stable.

muta'tion (miou-té-), *n.*, mutation, *f.* ; changement, *m.*

mute (mioute), *adj.*, muet ; silencieux.

mute, *n.*, muet, *m.*, muette, *f.* ; (mus.) sourdine (de violon) ; (gram.) lettre muette ; (at a funeral) pleureur, *m.* ; (ant.) (of birds) fiente, *f.*

mute, *v.n.*, fienter.

mute'ly, *adv.*, en muet ; silencieusement ; en silence.

mute'ness, *n.*, mutisme, silence, *m.*

mu'tilate (miou-), *v.a.*, mutiler, tronquer.

mu'tilate *ou* **mu'tilated**, *adj.*, mutilé ; (bot.) incomplet.

mutila'tion (miou-ti-lé-), *n.*, mutilation, *f.*

mu'tilator (-ti-lé-teur), *n.*, mutilateur, *m.*, mutilatrice, *f.*

mutineer' (miou-ti-nîre), *n.*, mutin, rebelle, révolté, *m.*

mu'tinous (miou-), *adj.*, mutin, séditieux, mutiné (of soldiers, sailors).

mu'tinously, *adv.*, en mutin (in the army, navy) séditieusement.

mu'tinousness, *n.*, mutinerie, *m.*

mu'tiny, *n.*, mutinerie, sédition, révolte, *f.* Indian —; *la révolte de l'Inde.*

mu'tiny, *v.n.*, se mutiner ; s'insurger ; se révolter.

mut'ter, *v.a.n.*, marmotter, marmonner ; gronder, grommeler, murmurer.

mut'terer, *n.*, murmurateur, *m.* ; marmotteur ; mécontent, *m.*

mut'tering, *adj.*, murmurant, marmotteur. *n.*, murmure, *f.*, marmottement, marmottage, *m.*

mut'teringly, *adv.*, en marmottant, en murmurant.

mut'ton (meut't'n), *n.*, mouton, *m.* Leg of —; *gigot, m.*

mut'ton-chop (-tshope), *n.*, côtelette de mouton, *f.*

mu'tual (miout'iou-), *adj.*, mutuel, réciproque, commun. On — terms ; *au pair.*

mutual'ity, *n.*, réciprocité, *f.*

mu'tually, *adv.*, mutuellement, réciproquement.

mu'tule (miout-ioule), *n.*, (arch.) mutule, *f.*

muz'zle (meuz'z'l), *n.*, (of animals) museau, *m.* ; (of cannon) bouche, *f.* ; (of rifles, pistols) bout, *m.*, bouche, *f.* ; (of bellows) canon, bec, tuyau, *m.* ; (fastening for the mouth) muselière, *f.* — loader ; *arme à feu, f.*, ou *fusil, m., se chargeant par la bouche.*

muz'zle, *v.a.*, museler.

my (maïe), *pron.*, mon, *m.*, ma, *f.* ; mes, *pl.m.f.*

myog'raphy (maï-og'-), *n.*, myographie, *f.*

myolo'gical (maï-ol-o-dj'-), *adj.*, myologique.

myol'ogy (maï-ol-o-dji), *n.*, myologie, *f.*

my'opy (maï-o-pi), *n.*, myopie, *f.*

myoso'tis (maï-ô-çô-), *n.*, (bot.) myosotis, *m.*

myr'iad, *n.*, myriade, *f.*

myr'iameter (-mî-teur), *n.*, myriamètre, *m.*

myr'midon (meur-mi-), *n.*, myrmidon, *m.*

myrrh (meur), *n.*, myrrhe, *f.*

myr'tiform (meur-), *adj.*, (anat.) myrtiforme.

myr'tle (meur't'l), *n.*, (bot.) myrte, *m.*

myr'tle-berry (-bèr'-), *n.*, baie de myrte, ..

my'self (maïe-cèlfe), *pron.*, moi-même ; moi.

mys'tagogue (-goghe), *n.*, mystagogue, *m.*

myste'rious (mis-tî-), *adj.*, mystérieux.

myste'riously, *adv.*, mystérieusement.

myste'riousness, *n.*, mystère, *m.* ; nature mystérieuse, *f.* ; caractère mystérieux, *m.*

mys'tery (-teuri), *n.*, mystère, secret, *m.*

mys'tic, *n.*, mystique, *m.*

mys'tic *ou* **mys'tical**, *adj.*, mystique ; emblématique.

mys'tically, *adv.*, mystiquement.

---

mys'ticism (-ciz'me), *n.*, mysticisme, *m.*, mysticité, *f.*

mystifica'tion (-fi-ké-), *n.*, mystification, *f.*

mys'tify (-faïe), *v.a.*, envelopper de mystère ; (pers.) mystifier ; embarrasser, dérouter.

myth (mith), *n.*, mythe, *m.*

myth'ic *ou* **myth'ical** (mith'-), *adj.*, de mythe ; fabuleux ; mythique.

mytholog'ic *ou* **mytholog'ical** (-thol'-o-dj'-), *adj.*, mythologique.

mytholog'ically, *adv.*, mythologiquement.

mythol'ogist, *n.*, mythologue, mythologiste, *m.*

mythol'ogy (-o-dji), *n.*, mythologie, *f.*

N

n, quatorzième lettre de l'alphabet, n, *f.*

nab, *v.a.*, gripper, happer ; gober ; saisir ; pincer, attraper.

na'bob (né-), *n.*, nabab, *m.*

nac'arat, *n.adj.*, nacarat, *m.*

na'cre (né-keur), *n.*, nacre, *f.*

na'creous (né-kri-), *adj.*, nacré.

na'dir (né-), *n.*, (astron.) nadir, *m.*

nag, *n.*, bidet, petit cheval, *m.*

nag, *v.a.n.*, critiquer, clabauder, gronder.

nai'ad (né-), *n.*, (myth.) naïade, *f.*

nail (nèle), *n.*, clou, *m.* ; (of claws, fingers, toes) ongle ; (measure) un seizième de yard (centimèt. 5.50), *m.* To cut one's —s ; *se couper, se tailler, les ongles.* To bite one's —s ; *se ronger les ongles.* To drive in a —; *enfoncer, ficher un clou.* To pay down on the —; *payer écus sonnants, payer comptant, payer rubis sur l'ongle.* To hit the — on the head ; *découvrir le fin mot d'une chose ; mettre le doigt dessus, frapper juste.* On the —; *sur le champ ; sans tarder.* To work (at anything) tooth and —; *s'y mettre de toutes ses forces.* One — drives out another ; *un clou chasse l'autre.*

nail, *v.a.*, clouer ; clouter ; (a cannon) enclouer. To — any one (to an argument or bargain) ; *prendre quelqu'un au mot ; y prendre quelqu'un.* To — up ; *clouer ; fermer avec des clous ;* (a window, a door, etc.) *condamner.*

nail'-brush (-breushe), *n.*, brosse à ongles, *f.*

nail'or, *n.*, cloutier, *m.*

nail'ery, *n.*, clouterie, *f.*

nail'-file, *n.*, lime à ongles, *f.*

nail'-head (-hède), *n.*, tête de clou, *f.*

nail'-headed (-hèd'ède), *adj.*, à tête de clou.

nail'ing, *n.*, clouage, clouement, *m.*

nail-mak'er (-mék'-), *n.*, cloutier, *m.*

nail-manufac'tory (-ma'n'iou-fac-), *n.*,(trade, works, making) clouterie, *f.*

nail'-scissors, *n.pl.*, ciseaux à ongles, *m.pl.*

nail'-shank, *n.*, tige de clou, *f.*

naive' (né-ive), *adj.*, naïf.

naive'ly, *adv.*, naïvement.

naive'te (né-iv'té), *n.*, naïveté, *f.*

na'ked (né'kède), *adj.*, (not covered) nu, à nu ; (open to view) à découvert, ouvert, dégarni ; (defenceless) sans défense, exposé sans défense ; (evident) évident, manifeste ; (simple) simple, pur ; (print.) dégarni ; (bot.) dépouillé. With the — eye ; *à l'œil nu.* Stark —; *tout nu ; nu comme la main, nu comme un ver.*

na'kedly, *adv.*, à nu ; sans défense ; simplement, purement ; manifestement, ouvertement ; à découvert ; nûment.

na'kedness, *n.*, nudité, *f.* ; état sans défense, *m.*, (plainness) évidence, clarté, simplicité, *f.* ; (fig.) dénûment, *m.*

namby-pam'by, *adj.*, prétentieux, musqué, minaudier, sentimental.

name, *n.*, nom, *m.* ; (fame) renom, *m.*, renommée, réputation, *f.* Christian —; *prénom, nom de baptême, petit nom, m.* Maiden —; *nom de demoi-*

selle, m. Nick—; *nom de guerre, m.* **—sake**;
homonyme, m. **—day;** *fête, f.* What is your —?
comment vous appelez-vous? What is that gentleman's —? *comment s'appelle ce monsieur?* By
—; *de nom; nommé.* To go by the — of; *être
nommé; être connu sous le nom* **de.** In the — of;
au nom **de;** *sous le nom* **de;** *de la part* **de.** The
house is in the — of; *la maison est sous le nom*
de. He came in my —; *il est venu de ma part.*
Assumed —; *nom d'emprunt, pseudonyme, nom
de guerre, m.* (nom de plume is an English neologism). Another — for; *synonyme* **de.** Family
—; *nom de famille.* In —; *de nom.* To call
—s; *dire des injures, des sottises,* **à;** *injurier.*
To mention a person's —; *se servir du nom de
quelqu'un; nommer quelqu'un.* To mention no
—s; *ne nommer personne.*

name, *v.a.,* nommer, appeler; intituler; (to
point out) indiquer, mentionner, désigner; (Engl.
Parliament) censurer. To — the day; *fixer le
jour de la cérémonie* (du mariage). To be —d;
s'appeler, se nommer; (of things) *être appelé,
nommé, intitulé; s'appeler, se nommer.* Do not
— it; *n'en parlez pas;* (in answering thanks)
il n'y a pas de quoi.

named (né'm'de), *adj.,* nommé, désigné, mentionné. Above —; *ci-dessus nommé.*

name'less, *adj.,* sans nom, anonyme; inconnu. — crime; *crime qui outrage la nature;
crime qui n'a pas de nom* (Bossuet). — man;
homme sans nom, sans crédit, sans réputation.

name'ly, *adv.,* savoir, nommément; c'est à
dire.

nankeen' (-kīne), *n.,* nankin, m.

nap, *n.,* (of cloth, hats) poil; (of plants) duvet;
(sleep) somme; (top of a hill) haut, m.; (protuberance) éminence, touffe, f., bouton, m.;
(game) napoléon, m. Afternoon —; *sieste, f.*

nap, *v.n.,* faire un somme; sommeiller; (fig.)
s'endormir, manquer de vigilance. To catch
—ping; *prendre au dépourvu, prendre en défaut;
prendre à l'improviste.*

nape (népe), *n.,* nuque, f.

naph'tha (nap'tha), *n.,* naphte, m.

nap'kin, *n.,* serviette, f.; (of babies) couche,
f. — ring; *rond de serviette, m.*

nap'less, *adj.,* sans poil; râpé.

nap'piness, *n.,* (of cloth) état poilu, m.

nap'py, *adj.,* (wine, etc.) capiteux; (downy)
poilu; (of plants) duveteux.

narcis'sus, *n.,* (bot.) narcisse, m.

narcot'ic, *adj.,* narcotique.

narcot'ic, *n.,* narcotique, m.

narcot'ically, *adv.,* avec un effet narcotique.

nard (nârde), *n.,* nard; (bot.) **nard,** m.;
barbe-de-vieillard, f.

nar'dine (nâr'd'aïne), *adj.,* de nard.

nar'gileh, *n.,* narguilé, m.

narrate', *v.a.,* raconter, narrer, conter.

narra'tion (nar-ré-), *n.,* narration, f.; récit, m.

nar'rative, *n.,* récit, narré, m.

nar'rative, *adj.,* narratif.

nar'ratively, *adv.,* (l.u.) sous forme de narration.

narra'tor (-rét'eur), *n.,* narrateur, conteur, m.

nar'row (-rô), *adj.,* étroit, resserré, gêné;
(contracted, of confined views) rétréci, limité,
borné, étroit; (accurate) exact, soigneux, scrupuleux, attentif; (near) de près; (not liberal)
mesquin. — brimmed; *à petits bords.* To be
in — circumstances; *être à l'étroit; vivre à
l'étroit.* To have a — escape, *ou* shave; *l'échapper
belle.* — mind; *esprit borné, m.* **—minded**;
à l'esprit borné. It was a — shave; *il s'en fallut
de bien peu.*

nar'row, *n.* (generally used in the plural),
(between two seas) détroit, pas, m.; (through a
mountain) défilé, passage, m.

nar'row, *v.a.,* rendre étroit, rétréci, limiter,
resserrer, restreindre.

nar'row, *v.n.,* devenir étroit; se rétrécir.

nar'rowing (-rô-igne), *n.,* rétrécissement, m.

nar'rowly, *adv.,* étroitement; à l'étroit;
(fig.) d'une manière rétrécie, bornée; exactement,
soigneusement, scrupuleusement, attentivement;
de près; (sparingly) mesquinement. We — escaped being killed; *nous avons failli être tués,* ou
peu s'en est fallu que nous ne fussions tués.

nar'rowness, *n.,* étroitesse, f.; manque
d'étendue, rétrécissement, m.; petitesse, mesquinerie, f.; (of means) exiguïté, modicité, f.

nar'wal ou **nar'whal** (når-), *n.,* (mam.) narval, m.; licorne de mer, f.

na'sal (né-zal), *adj.,* nasal, du nez.

na'sal, *n.,* (gram.) nasale, f.; (med.) errhin, m.

nasal'ity, *n.,* nasalité, f.

na'salize, *v.n.,* nasaliser.

na'sally, *adv.,* nasalement.

nas'cent, *adj.,* naissant.

nas'tily, *adv.,* salement, malproprement;
(fig.) grossièrement; vilainement.

nas'tiness, *n.,* saleté, malpropreté, obscénité,
grossièreté, f.

nastur'tium (nas-teur-shi-eume), *n.,* (bot.)
capucine; graine de capucine, f.

nas'ty, *adj.,* sale, malpropre; (fig.) sale,
vilain, dangereux, mauvais, désagréable. —
boy; *vilain enfant; vilain, vilain sale, m.* To
smell —; *sentir mauvais.* — weather; *vilain,* ou
sale, temps, m. — cold; *vilain rhume, m.* —
wound; *blessure grave, f.*

na'tal (né-), *adj.,* natal; de naissance.

nata'tion (na-té-), *n.,* natation, f.

natato'rial (né-ta-tô-) ou **na'tatory** (-to-),
adj., natatoire.

na'tion (né-), *n.,* nation, f.; peuple, m. Law
of **—s;** *droit des gens, m.*

na'tional (nash'-), *adj.,* national. — debt;
dette publique, f. — navy; *marine de l'État, f.*
— school; *école communale, f.*

national'ity, *n.,* nationalité, f.

na'tionalize (-aïze), *v.a.,* rendre national,
nationaliser.

na'tionally, *adv.,* nationalement.

na'tionalness, *n.,* (ant.) caractère national, m.

na'tive (né-), *adj.,* naturel, natif; natal; du
pays, de son pays; de naissance; paternel,
maternel; indigène; primitif; (min.) natif. —
genius; *le génie naturel, m.* — oyster; *huître
parquée, f.* — soil; *sol natal, m.* — place; *pays,
lieu de naissance, m.* — tongue; *propre langue,
langue maternelle, f.* — productions; *productions indigènes, f.pl.*

na'tive, *n.,* natif (of a town); naturel (of
savage tribes); habitant, insulaire (of an island);
indigène (of a continent, of plants, etc.), m. A
— of Paris; *né à Paris, natif de Paris.* A — of
England; *Anglais de naissance; né en Angleterre.* — of; *originaire* **de.**

nativ'ity, *n.,* nativité; naissance, f.; lieu de
naissance, m. To cast any one's —; *tirer l'horoscope* **de.**

na'tron (né-), *n.,* (min.) natron, natrum, m.

nat'ty, *adj.,* gentil, pimpant, avenant.

nat'ural, *adj.,* naturel; réel; naïf; simple;
(mus.) bécarre; (paint.) au naturel. — philosophy; *physique, f.* — selection; (Darwin) *sélection naturelle, f.*

nat'uralism (-'iz'me), *n.,* naturalisme, m.;
religion de la nature, f.

nat'uralist, *n.,* naturaliste, m.

naturaliza'tion (-'aïze-), *n.,* naturalisation,
acclimatation, f.

nat'uralize (-aïze), *v.a.,* naturaliser, acclimater.

nat'urally, *adv.,* naturellement.

nat'uralness, *n.,* naturel; caractère naturel,
m.; naïveté, parfaite simplicité, f.

na'ture (né't'-), *n.,* nature, f.; naturel, m.
Good—; *bon naturel, m.; bonté, bonhomie, f.*

Ill-— ; *mauvais naturel, m. ; méchanceté, f.* To pay the debt of —; *payer sa dette à la nature ; payer la dette de la nature.* In a state of —; *dans l'état de pure nature ;* (theol.) *dans l'état de nature.* From —; (paint., etc.) *d'après nature.* Of a — to ; *de nature* à.

na′tured (nét′ieur′de), *adj.*, de nature ; de naturel. Good-— ; *d'un bon naturel ; bon.* Ill-— ; *d'une mauvaise naturel ; méchant ;* (of things) *mauvais ; ingrat.*

na′turedly, *adv.* Good-— ; *avec bonté ; avec bonhomie, sans se fâcher.* Ill-— ; *méchamment ; avec méchanceté.*

naught (nōte), *n.*, néant, rien ; (arith.) zéro, *m.* To set at —; *ne faire aucun cas* **de**, *ne tenir aucun compte* **de** ; *mépriser ; braver ; défier.* To come to — ; *échouer, avorter, faire fiasco.*

naught, *adv.*, nullement ; aucunement.

naught′ily, *adv.*, par méchanceté.

naught′iness, *n.*, méchanceté, *f.*

naught′y, *adj.*, méchant. — boy! *vilain! méchant!* — trick ; *méchanceté, f. ; vilain tour, m.*

nau′sea (nō-shi-a), *n.*, nausée, *f. ;* soulèvement de cœur, *m.*

nau′seate (nō-shi-éte), *v.n.*, avoir des nausées ; (fig.) être dégoûté **de**, avoir du dégoût **pour**.

nau′seate, *v.a.*, donner des nausées ; avoir des nausées de ; dégoûter.

nau′seating, *adj.*, nauséabond ; dégoûtant.

nausea′tion, *n.*, dégoût, *m.*

nau′seous (nō-sheusse), *adj.*, nauséabond ; répugnant ; dégoûtant.

nau′seously, *adv.*, d'une manière nauséabonde ; d'une manière dégoûtante.

nau′seousness, *n.*, nature nauséabonde, *f. ;* (fig.) dégoût, *m.*

nau′tic *ou* **nau′tical**, *adj.*, nautique, de marin.

nau′tilus, *n.*, (zool.) nautile, argonaute, *m.*

na′val (né-), *adj.*, naval, maritime ; de la marine, de marine. — officer ; *officier de marine, m.* — architect ; *constructeur de vaisseaux, m.* — station ; *station navale, f.*

nave, *n.*, (of a church) nef, *f. ;* (of a wheel) moyeu, *m.*

na′vel (né-v′l), *n.*, (anat.) nombril ; (fig.) centre, cœur, *m.*

na′vel-string (-strigne), *n.*, cordon ombilical, *m.*

na′vel-wort (-weurte), *n.*, (bot.) cotylédon, *m.*

nav′igable (-ga-b′l), *adj.*, navigable.

nav′igableness, *n.*, navigabilité, *f.*

nav′igate, *v.a. and n.*, naviguer, naviguer **sur** ; gouverner. To — a vessel ; *gouverner un navire ;* (by means of oars) *naviguer un bateau.*

naviga′tion (-ghé-), *n.*, navigation, *f.* Inland — ; *navigation intérieure.* Aerial — ; *navigation aérienne.*

naviga′tion-laws (-lōze), *n.pl.*, code maritime, *m. ;* législation maritime, *f.*

nav′igator (-ghé-teur), *n.*, navigateur, *m.*

nav′vy, *n.*, terrassier, manœuvre, *m.*

na′vy (né-), *n.*, marine, *f.* Mercantile — ; *marine marchande, f.* Royal — ; *marine de l'Etat.*

na′vy-a′gency (-é-djè′n′-), *n.*, agence maritime, *f.*

na′vy-a′gent (-é-djè′n′te), *n.*, agent maritime, agent pour la marine, *m.*

na′vy-bills (-bil′ze), *n.pl.*, lois et ordonnances maritimes, *f.pl.*

na′vy-board (-bôrde), *n.*, conseil de la marine, conseil d'amirauté, *m.*

na′vy-list, *n.*, annuaire de la marine, *m.*

na′vy-office, *n.*, bureaux de la marine, *m.pl.*

na′vy-sur′geon, *n.*, chirurgien de marine, *m.*

na′vy-yard, *n.*, arsenal maritime, *m.*

nay, *adv.*, bien plus, non, nenni ; même ; qui plus est ; en vérité. To say — ; *refuser.* I cannot say him — ; *je ne puis le lui refuser.*

Naz′arene (-rîne), *n.*, Nazaréen, *m.*

Naz′arite (-raïte),*n.*, (Jews) nazaréen, *m.*

Neapol′itan, *adj.*, napolitain ; de Naples.

Neapol′itan (nî-a-), *n.*, Napolitain, *m.*, Napolitaine, *f.*

neap′ tide (-taïde), *n.*, (nav.) morte eau, *f.* — tides ; *eaux mortes, marées mortes, f.pl.*

near (nîr), *adj.*, proche ; près ; près **de** ; rapproché ; (parsimonious) serré, parcimonieux, très regardant ; (stingy) chiche ; (intimate) précieux, chéri, cher ; (faithful) exact, fidèle. — relation ; *proche parent, m., proche parente, f.* — side ; *côté gauche, m.* — horse ; *cheval de gauche, m.* To be — and dear to ; *toucher de près.* He lived in a — way ; *il vivait chichement.*

near, *adv.*, près ; près **de** ; **de** près ; presque. To draw — ; *s'approcher.* To draw, *ou* go, — to ; *s'approcher* **de**. Nothing — ; *à beaucoup près.*

near, *prep.*, près de, auprès de.

near, *v.a. and n.*, s'approcher **de**, s'approcher ; approcher **de**.

near′ly, *adv.*, de près ; à peu près ; environ ; près **de**, presque ; (parsimoniously) chichement, mesquinement. He copied it as — as possible ; *il le copia aussi exactement que possible.* He is not — so mean as his brother ; *il n'est pas à beaucoup près aussi ladre que son frère.* He was — hanged ; *peu s'en est fallu qu'il ne fût pendu.* They are — related ; *ils sont très proches parents.* It is — five o'clock ; *il est près de cinq heures.*

near′ness, *n.*, proximité, *f. ;* (close union) proche parenté, union étroite ; (parsimony) parcimonie, mesquinerie, *f.*

near-sight′ed (-saït′-), *adj.*, qui a la vue basse, myope.

neat (nîte), *n.*, gros bétail ; *m.*, vache, *f.* —'s foot oil ; *huile de pieds de bœuf, f.* — 's tongue ; (bot.) *langue de bœuf, f.*

neat (nîte), *adj.*, (clean) net, propre, soigné, rangé ; (unadulterated) pur ; (unadorned) propre, simple ; de bon goût ; joli, élégant ; (pers.) pimpant ; (of drinks) sec ; (of compliments) joli ; bien tourné. A — trick ; *un tour adroit.*

neat′herd (-heurde), *n.*, bouvier, vacher, *m.*

neat′ly, *adv.*, proprement ; nettement ; d'une manière soignée, purement, simplement ; (dexterously) adroitement ; avec bon goût. An idea — expressed ; *une idée élégamment exprimée.*

neat′ness, *n.*, propreté, netteté ; pureté ; simplicité, *f.* — of a drawing ; *élégance, netteté, pureté, d'un dessin, f.* — of a repartee ; *finesse d'une repartie, f.*

neb′ula (nèb′iou-), *n.*, nébuleuse, *f.*

nebulos′ity, *n.*, état nébuleux, *m. ;* nébulosité, *f.*

neb′ulous, *adj.*, nébuleux, nuageux, obscur.

nec′essaries (nèss′ès-sa-rize), *n.pl.*, nécessaire, *m. ;* nécessités, *f.pl. ;* objets de nécessité, *m.pl.*, commodités, *f.pl.*

nec′essarily, *adv.*, nécessairement, de nécessité, forcément.

nec′essary (nèss′ès-sa-ri), *adj.*, nécessaire ; (unavoidable) obligé, forcé, péremptoire. If —; *s'il le faut ; au besoin.* To be — ; *falloir, être nécessaire.*

neces′sitate (niss′ès-si-), *v.a.*, nécessiter, obliger, contraindre.

necessita′tion (-si-té-), *n.*, obligation, contrainte, *f.*

neces′sitous (ni-cès-si-teusse), *adj.*, indigent, nécessiteux, dans le besoin.

neces′sitousness, *n.*, nécessité, *f. ;* besoin, *m.*

neces′sity (ni-cès-si′-), *n.*, nécessité ; (indigence) nécessité, *f. ;* besoin, *m.* From —; *par nécessité ; par besoin.* To make a virtue of —; *faire de nécessité vertu.* — is the mother of invention ; *de tout s'avise à qui pain faut.* To be under the — of ; *se trouver dans la nécessité* **de**, *ou forcé* **de**. Of —; *nécessairement, forcément.*

neck (nèke), *n.*, cou ; (of bottles, etc.) cou, goulot ; (of musical instruments) manche ; (of meat) collet ; (of a mountain) col, *m.* ; (of land) langue, *f.* To harden the — ; *s'obstiner, s'entêter à.* To lay on the — of ; *imputer à.* Best end — ; (of mutton) *carré, m.* Stiff-— ; *torticolis, m.* — and shoulders ; (of animals) *encolure, f.* To break one's — ; *se casser le cou.* To break any one's — ; *casser le cou à quelqu'un.* — and crop ; *complètement.* — or nothing ; *à tout hasard ; tout ou rien.* — and — ; *de très près.* By a — ; (racing) *d'une demi-encolure, f.*

neck'-chain, *n.*, chaîne de cou, *f.*

neck'cloth (-clŏth) *ou* **neck'tie**, *n.*, cravate, *f.*

necked (nèk'te), *adj.*, qui a un cou. Stiff-— ; *au cou raide* ; (fig.) *altier, arrogant.* Long-— ; *au long cou.* Short-— ; *au cou court.*

neck'erchief (nèk'èr-tshif), *n.*, fichu, *m.*

neck'lace, *n.*, collier, *m.*

neck'laced (-lésste), *adj.*, marqué comme d'un collier ; ayant un collier.

necrol'ogist (nèk'rol-o-djiste), *n.*, nécrologue, *m.*

necrol'ogy (nèk'rol-o-dji), *n.*, nécrologie, *f.*

nec'romancer (nèk'-), *n.*, nécromancien, *m.*, nécromancienne, *f.* ; ⊙nécromant, *m.*

nec'romancy (nèk'-), *n.*, nécromancie, *f.*

necroman'tic, *adj.*, nécromantique.

necrop'olis, *n.*, nécropole, *f.*

necro'sis (ni-crŏ-cice), *n.*, (med.) nécrose, *f.*

nec'tar, *n.*, nectar, *m.*

nectar'eal *ou* **nectar'ean** (-ri-), *adj.*, de nectar ; nectaréen ; nectaré.

nec'tarine, *n.*, (peach) brugnon, *m.*

nec'tary, *n.*, (bot.) nectaire, *m.*

need (nîde), *n.*, besoin, *m.* ; nécessité, *f.* ; (indigence) besoin, *m.*, nécessité, misère, *f.* In case of — ; *au besoin ; en cas de nécessité ; le cas échéant.* What — is there of that ? *quel besoin y a-t-il de . . . ? quelle nécessité y a-t-il pour cela ?* There is no — of that ; *il n'y a pas besoin de cela.* To be in — of, to stand in — of, to have — of ; *avoir besoin de.* To be in — ; *être dans le besoin, dans la misère.*

need (nîde), *v.n.*, avoir besoin ; devoir ; avoir ; (imp.) falloir, être nécessaire. You— not come ; *vous pouvez vous dispenser de venir.* It —s the pen of ; *il faudrait la plume de.*

need, *v.a.*, avoir besoin de ; exiger. I —ed no second permission ; *je ne me le fis pas dire deux fois.* That —s much care ; *cela exige beaucoup de soin.*

need'ful (-foule), *adj.*, nécessaire. The — ; *le nécessaire ;* (pop.) *le quibus, m.*

need'fully, *adv.*, nécessairement.

need'fulness, *n.*, besoin, *m.* ; nécessité, *f.*

need'ily, *adv.*, dans le besoin ; par besoin.

need'iness, *n.*, indigence, nécessité, *f.* ; besoin, *m.*

nee'dle (nî-d'l), *n.*, aiguille, *f.*, (compass) boussole, *f.* To thread a — ; *enfiler une aiguille.* Netting— ; *navette, f.* Sewing— ; *aiguille à coudre, f.* Darning-— ; *aiguille à repriser, f.* Eye of a — ; *trou d'aiguille, m.* To look for a — in a bundle of hay ; *chercher une aiguille dans une botte de foin.*

nee'dle-case (-kéce), *n.*, étui, étui à aiguilles, *m.*

nee'dleful (-foule), *n.*, aiguillée, *f.*

nee'dle-gun, *n.*, fusil à aiguille, *m.*

nee'dle-mak'er (-mék'-), *n.*, aiguillier, *m.*

need'less, *adj.*, inutile. It is — to say that ; *il va sans dire que.*

need'lessly, *adv.*, inutilement.

need'lessness, *n.*, inutilité, *f.*

nee'dlewoman, *n.*, couturière, *f.*

nee'dle-work (-weurke), *n.*, ouvrage à l'aiguille, *m.* To do — ; *travailler à l'aiguille.*

needs (nîdze), *adv.*, nécessairement, absolument ; de toute nécessité, forcément, inévitable-ment. I must — ; *je dois nécessairement* (with inf.). . . ; *il faut absolument que je* (with subj.) . . . He must — ; *il doit nécessairement* (with inf.) . . . ; *il faut nécessairement qu'il* (with subj.) . . . — must when the devil drives ; *il le faut bien quand le diable s'en mêle.*

need'y (nîd'-), *adj.*, indigent, nécessiteux, pauvre.

nefa'rious (ni-fé-), *adj.*, exécrable, atroce, abominable, infâme.

nefa'riously, *adv.*, exécrablement, atrocement, abominablement ; avec infamie.

nega'tion (ni-ghé'-), *n.*, négation, *f.*

neg'ative (nèg'a-), *n.*, négative, *f.*, (photo.) négatif, *m.* ; (plate) cliché, *m.* In the — ; négativement.

neg'ative, *adj.*, négatif.

neg'ative, *v.a.*, décider négativement ; (in parliament) rejeter.

neg'atively, *adv.*, négativement.

neglect' (nèg-), *n.*, négligence, *f.* ; oubli, *m.*

neglect', *v.a.*, négliger.

neglect'ful (-foule), *adj.*, négligent, oublieux de ; nonchalant.

neglect'fully, *adv.*, négligemment ; nonchalamment.

negligée' (nèg-li-jé), *n.*, (undress) négligé, *m.*

neg'ligence (nèg-li-djè'n'ce), *n.*, négligence ; nonchalance, *f.* ; oubli, *m.*

neg'ligent (nèg-li-djè'n'te), *adj.*, négligent. — of ; *oublieux de.*

neg'ligently (nèg-li-djè'n'te), *adv.*, négligemment ; par négligence.

negotiabil'ity (ni-gô-shi-), *n.*, négociabilité, *f.*

nego'tiable (ni-gô-shi-a-b'l), *adj.*, négociable.

nego'tiate (ni-gô-shi-), *v.a.*, négocier.

nego'tiate, *v.n.*, négocier, être en négociation.

negotia'tion (ni-gô-shi-é-), *n.*, négociation, *f.*

nego'tiator (ni-gô-shi-ét'eur), *n.*, négociateur, *m.*

ne'gress (nî-grèce), *n.*, négresse, *f.*

ne'gro (nî-), *n.*, nègre, *m.* — boy ; *jeune nègre ; négrillon, m.* — girl ; *jeune négresse ; négrillonne, f.*

ne'gus (nî-), *n.*, vin chaud ; (sovereign of Abyssinia) Négus, *m.*

neigh (né), *v.n.*, hennir.

neigh, *n.*, hennissement, *m.*

neigh'bor (né-), *n.*, voisin, *m.*, voisine, *f.* ; (biblically) prochain, *m.* Next-door — ; *plus proche voisin.* To be next-door —s ; *demeurer porte à porte.*

neigh'bor, *adj.*, voisin.

neigh'bor, *v.a.*, avoisiner.

neigh'borhood (né-beur'houde), *n.*, voisinage, *m.* ; alentours, environs, *m.pl.* ; district, quartier, *m.*

neigh'boring, *adj.*, voisin ; du voisinage ; des alentours ; approximatif. To go — ; *voisiner.*

neigh'borly, *adj.*, de voisin. — act ; *trait de bon voisin, m.*

neigh'borly, *adv.*, en voisin ; en bon voisin.

neigh'ing (né-igne), *n.*, hennissement, *m.*

nei'ther (nî-*theur*), *pron.*, ni l'un ni l'autre, *m.*, ni l'une ni l'autre, *f.* ; ni les uns ni les autres, *m.pl.*, ni les unes ni les autres, *f.pl.*

nei'ther, *conj.*, ni ; non plus ; du reste, d'ailleurs (*with a negative sentence in French*).

nem. con. (nème-) (*ab.* of Nemine contradicente), à l'unanimité.

Neme'an (ni-mî-), *adj.*, néméen ; de Némée.

nen'uphar (nè'n'iou-fâr), *n.*, nénufar, (bot.) lis d'eau, *m.*

neolog'ic *ou* **neolog'ical** (ni-ô-lodj'-), *adj.*, néologique.

neol'ogism (ni-ol'o-djiz'me), *n.*, néologisme, *m.*

neol'ogist (ni-ol-o-djiste), *n.*, néologue ; néologiste, *m.*

neol'ogy (ni-ol-o-dji), *n.*, néologie, *f.*

ne'ophyte (nĭ-o-faïte), *n.*, néophyte, *m.f.*

neph'ew (nèv'viou), *n.*, neveu, *m.* Grand—; *petit-neveu, m.*

nephrit'ic (nè-), *adj.*, (med.) néphrétique.

nephrit'ic, *n.*, (med.) néphrétique, *m.*

nephri'tis (nè-fraï-), *n.*, (med.) néphrite, *f.*

ne'potism (nĭ-po-tizme), *n.*, népotisme, *m.*

Ne'reid (nĭr-e-id), *n.*, néréïde, *f.*

ner'oli (nèr-), *n.*, néroli, *m.*

nerve (neurve), *n.*, nerf ; (fig.) courage, sang froid, *m. ;* (arch., bot.) nervure, *f.*

nerve, *v.a.*, donner du nerf **à**, de la force **à**, fortifier.

nerved (neurv'de), *adj.*, fortifié, vigoureux ; (bot.) nervé.

nerve'less, *adj.*, sans nerf ; sans vigueur, sans force.

nerv'ine, *n.*, (med.) nervin, *m.*

nerv'ose (neur-vôce), *adj.*, (bot.) nervé.

nerv'ous (neur-), *adj.*, nerveux, vigoureux ; timide, impressionnable ; intimidé, troublé ; (med.) nerveux ; (bot.) nervé.

nerv'ously, *adv.*, nerveusement, timidement ; avec vigueur.

nerv'ousness, *n.*, nerf, *m. ;* vigueur ; inquiétude, timidité, *f.*, trouble ; (med.) état nerveux, *m.*

nest (nèste), *n.*, nid, *m. ;* (brood of birds) nichée ; (fig.) nichée, *f.*, repaire, *m. ;* (of boxes, cases, etc.) caisse à tiroirs, *f.*, casier, *m.* To have found a mare's —; *croire avoir trouvé la pie au nid.* To feather one's —; *faire son nid ; faire ses orges.* A — of thieves; *un repaire de voleurs.* — egg ; *nichet, m.*

nest, *v.n.*, nicher, faire un nid.

nes'tle (nès's'l), *v.n.*, nicher ; se nicher ; se cacher. To — close to; *se serrer* **contre.**

nes'tle, *v.a.*, nicher, loger ; chérir, choyer.

nes'tling (nès's'l-), *adj.*, encore au nid.

nest'ling (nès'ligne), *n.*, petit oiseau encore au nid, *m.*

net (nète), *n.*, filet, rets ; réseau ; (for the hair) résille, *f. ;* (textile fabric) tulle, tricot, *m.* In a — (*i.e.*, caught); *pris dans un rets.*

net, *v.a.*, (com., fin.) rapporter net, produire *ou* donner un bénéfice net **de** ; (gain) gagner net ; (to catch) prendre dans un filet ; (to inclose) couvrir d'un filet. I —ted a thousand pounds ; *j'ai gagné mille livres net.*

net, *v.n.*, faire du filet.

net, *adj.*, net ; pur. — profit ; *profit net, m.*

neth'er. *V.* **lower.**

neth'ermost (-môste), *adj.*, le plus bas.

net'-mak'ing, *n.*, fabrication de filets, *f. ;* (of stuffs) tullerie, *f.*

net'ting, *n.*, réseau, rets ; filet, *m.* — needle; *navette, f.* — silk ; *cordonnet, m.*

net'tle (nèt't'l), *n.*, (bot.) ortie, *f.* —-butterfly ; (ent.) vanesse, *f.* — in, dock out; *changer de métier comme de chemise.*

net'tle, *v.a.*, piquer ; aigrir ; irriter, vexer.

net'tle-rash, *n.*, (med.) urticaire, *f.*

net'work (-weurke), *n.*, réseau, lacis, *m.*

neural'gia (niou-ral-djia), *n.*, (med.) névralgie, *f.*

neural'gic, *adj.*, névralgique.

neurol'ogy (niou-rol-o-dji), *n.*, névrologie, *f.*

neurot'ic (niou-), *adj.*, nervin ; (l.u.) névritique.

neurot'ic, *n.*, (disease) névrite, *f.*

neurot'omy, *n.*, (anat.) névrotomie, *f.*

neu'ter (niou-), *adj.*, neutre.

neu'ter, *n.*, neutre, *m. ;* personne neutre, *f. ;* (gram., ent.) neutre, *m.*

neu'tral (niou-), *adj.*, neutre ; indifférent.

neutral'ity, *n.*, neutralité ; indifférence, *f.*

neutraliza'tion (-aïzé-), *n.*, neutralisation, *f.*

neu'tralize (-aïze), *v.a.*, neutraliser.

neu'trally, *adv.*, (gram.) neutralement.

nev'er (nèv'-), *adv.*, jamais ; ne . . . jamais ;

pas ; ne . . . aucunement ; ne . . . nullement; quelque . . . que ce soit. —! *jamais!* (indeed) *bah ! allons donc !* I have — seen it ; *je ne l'ai jamais vu.* — a word ; *pas un mot.* Be — so idle ; *ne soyez jamais si paresseux.* —ending ; *qui n'en finit point.* —failing ; *toujours prêt ; infaillible.*

nev'ertheless (-*thi*-), *adj.*, néanmoins, toutefois, cependant, pourtant.

new (niou), *adj.*, neuf, nouveau, nouvel ; (of bread) tendre, frais ; (unaccustomed) neuf, novice ; frais, récent ; (recently commenced, recently appeared) nouveau, nouvel. Bran—; brand—; *battant neuf.* Spick and span —; *tout battant neuf.* —from ; *frais* **de.** A —hat ; *un chapeau neuf.* —wine ; *du vin nouveau.* The — moon ; *la nouvelle lune.* A — work ; *un nouvel ouvrage.* A — book ; (not used) *un livre neuf ;* (newly out) *un livre nouveau ;* (a different one) *un nouveau livre.* A — word ; *un mot nouveau.* —-comer ; *nouveau venu, m.* —-laid eggs ; *œufs frais, m.pl.* — year ; *nouvel an, m.* — year's-day ; *le jour de l'an, m.* — year's-gifts ; *étrennes, f.pl.* — milk ; *lait du jour, m.* — bread ; *pain frais, m.* A — man ; (not of ancient extraction) *un homme nouveau.* A — fashion ; *une nouvelle mode.* A — metal ; *un nouveau métal.* To lead a — life ; *s'amender ; venir à résipiscence.* — to the plow ; *peu habitué à la charrue.* — to the trade ; *nouveau au métier.* As good as —; *presque neuf.* To make as good as —; *remettre à neuf.*

new'el (niou-èl), *n.*, noyau d'escalier, *m.*

new-fan'gled (niou-fa'gn'g'l'de), *adj.*, nouvellement inventé, d'invention nouvelle, de nouveau genre.

new-fash'ioned, *adj.*, de nouvelle mode.

New'gate-bird, *n.*, gibier de potence, *m.*

New'gate calendar, *n.*, annuaire des causes célèbres, *m.*

new'ing (niou'igne), *n.*, levure, *f.*

new'ish (niou'ishe), *adj.*, assez neuf ; assez nouveau ; assez récent, assez frais ; (of bread) assez tendre, assez frais.

new'ly (niou-), *adv.*, nouvellement, fraîchement, récemment, de nouveau.

new'ness (niou-), *n.*, nouveauté ; (want of practice) inexpérience ; (innovation) innovation, *f.*

news (niouze), *n.*, nouvelle, *f. ;* nouvelles, *f.pl.* What —s ? *quelles nouvelles? qu'y a-t-il de nouveau?* —agent ; *marchand de journaux, m.* No — is good —; *point de nouvelles, bonnes nouvelles.*

news'-boy (-boï), *n.*, marchand, porteur de journaux, *m.*

news'man, *n.*, commissionnaire pour les journaux ; marchand de journaux, *m.*

news'-monger (-meu'gn'gheur), *n.*, débitant de nouvelles, *m.*

news'paper (-pé-), *n.*, journal, *m. ;* feuille, gazette, *f.* — wrapper ; *bande timbrée, f.*

news'-room, *n.*, cabinet de lecture, *m.*

news'-vendor, *n.*, commissionnaire pour les journaux ; marchand de journaux, *m.*

newt (nioute), *n.*, (zoöl.) triton, *m.*

Newto'nian (niou-tô-), *adj.*, newtonien.

next (nèkste), *adj.*, (in degree) le plus proche, voisin ; (in place) le plus près ; (in succession) suivant, premier ; (of past time) suivant ; (of future time) prochain ; (fig.) voisin, rapproché, suivant, prochain, futur. The — interview ; *la prochaine entrevue.* The — world ; *l'autre monde, m. ; la vie future ; la vie à venir.* He will come — month ; *il viendra le mois prochain.* He came — day ; *il est venu le jour suivant, le lendemain.* — of kin ; (jur.) *le plus proche parent, m.* —door to ; *très voisin* **de** ; (fig.) ressemblant fort **à.** Monday —; *lundi prochain.* The — Monday ; *le lundi suivant, le lundi d'après.* To know what to do —; *savoir ce qu'il faut faire* *ensuite.* I will take the — train; *je prendrai le train suivant.* — to that, the best course to follow will be . . . ; *à défaut de cela, la meilleure marche à suivre sera de . . . .*

next (nèkste), *adv.,* auprès **de**, à côté **de**; après; bientôt après, immédiatement après; ensuite; le premier, *m.,* la première, *f.;* les premiers, *m.pl.,* les premières, *f.pl.* — to; à côté **de**; *après;* (nearly) *à peu près, presque.* — to nothing; *presque rien.* — to impossible; *à peu près, ou presque, impossible.* He sat — to me; *il était assis à côté de moi.* He came —; *il vint immédiatement après.* What —? *après? et après? ensuite?* He sat down — to him; *il s'assit à côté, ou auprès,* **de** *lui.*

nib, *n.,* (of a bird, a pen) bec, *m. ;* (point) pointe, *f.,* bout, *m.;* (cocoa) casson, *m.*

nibbed (nib'de), *adj.,* à bec; à pointe. Hard— ; *qui a le bec dur.* Soft— ; *qui a le bec flexible.*

nib'ble (nib'b'l), *n.,* coup de dent, de bec, *m.*

nib'ble, *v.a.,* mordiller; grignoter; ronger; (of fish) mordiller à l'hameçon; (of birds) becqueter; (the grass, etc.) brouter.

nib'ble, *v.m.,* mordiller; grignoter; brouter; mordre. To — at; *mordiller, grignoter, brouter;* *mordre;* (to carper at) *gloser* **sur,** *faire la critique* **de,** *épiloguer* **sur.**

nib'bler, *n.,* grignoteur, *m.,* grignoteuse, *f.;* rongeur; (carper) gloseur, *m.,* gloseuse, *f.;* critique, épilogueur, *m.,* épilogueuse, *f.*

nice (naïce), *adj.,* (to the taste) bon, délicieux, agréable, friand; (delightful) joli; (delicate) délicat, fin; (tidy) propre, soigné; (exact) exact, juste; (scrupulous) scrupuleux; (fastidious) difficile, sévère, exigeant, rigide, prude; (refined) recherché, subtil; (acute) subtil, pénétrant; (well-behaved) (of children) sage, gentil; (amiable) gentil, aimable, charmant, bon; (jest.) joli; (punctilious) pointilleux; (particular) difficile, exigeant. To make — of; *être scrupuleux* **sur;** *être délicat* **sur.** A — dinner; *un bon dîner.* A — child; *un enfant gentil, sage.* A very — girl; *une demoiselle bien aimable, bien gentille; une petite fille très sage.* A — little wife; *une bonne petite femme.* A — man; *un homme aimable.* You're a — person! (jest.) *vous êtes une jolie personne!* A — looking man; *un bel homme.* You are a — fellow! a — man! *vous êtes un joli garçon!* I hear — goings on of you; *j'en entends de belles sur votre compte.*

nice'ly, *adv.,* bien; agréablement; délicatement; finement; exactement; justement; scrupuleusement; difficilement; sévèrement, rigidement; avec recherche; subtilement; avec pénétration; gentiment; avec amabilité, aimablement; joliment; (jest.) joliment; (of dressing) d'une manière recherchée.

nice'ness, *n.,* goût agréable, *m.;* délicatesse, finesse; exactitude, justesse, *f.;* soin scrupuleux, *m.;* sévérité, rigidité, pruderie; recherche, *f.;* raffinement, *m.;* subtilité; pénétration; gentillesse; amabilité, *f.* — of taste; *délicatesse du goût.*

ni'cety, *n.,* délicatesse, finesse, *f.;* (delicate management) soin scrupuleux, *m.;* (of dress) recherche, précision, exactitude, justesse, *f.* Niceties; *friandises, délicatesses, douceurs, f.pl.* To a —; *exactement; parfaitement; à point; très bien; avec une exactitude rigoureuse.* The niceties of a language; *les délicatesses d'une langue.*

niche (nishe), *n.,* niche, *f.*

nick, *n.,* moment précis; moment critique; (northern myth.) esprit malfaisant, *m.;* (notch) entaille, *f.;* (print.) cran, *m.* Old Nick; *le diable, m.* In the — of time; *juste à point; à propos; à point nommé; tout à point.* To come just in the — of time; *arriver comme marée en carême.*

nick, *v.a.,* (to hit) rencontrer juste; (to notch) faire une entaille **dans;** (a horse) anglaiser.

nick'el (-'èl), *n.,* (min.) nickel, *m.* — silver, *maillechort, m. v.a.,* nickeler.

nick'-nack, *n.,* rien, colifichet, bibelot, *m.*

nick'name, *n.,* sobriquet, *m.*

nick'name, *v.a.,* donner un sobriquet **à.**

nico'tian (ni-kô-sha'n), *n.,* nicotiane, *f.*

nidifica'tion (-fi-ké-), *n.,* construction d'un nid, *f.*

nidoros'ity (naï-dor-o-ci-), *n.,* (ant.) (med.) rapport nidoreux, *m.*

niece (nîce), *n.,* nièce, *f.* Grand- —; *petite-nièce.*

nig'gard, *adj.,* chiche, avare, vilain, ladre.

nig'gard, *n.,* avare, ladre, vilain, lésineur, *m.*

nig'gardliness, *n.,* mesquinerie, ladrerie, avarice sordide, lésinerie, *f.*

nig'gardly, *adv.,* avec avarice, en avare, en ladre.

nig'gardly, *adj.,* mesquin, ladre, chiche, lésineur. — doings; *vilenies, lésineries, f.pl.*

nig'ger (nig'gheur), *n.,* (pop.) nègre, *m.,* négresse, *f.;* moricaud (pop.).

nigh (naïe), *adv.,* presque, de près; près **de.** To draw —; *approcher; s'approcher* **de.**

nigh, *adj.,* proche, rapproché; près; près **de.** Well —; *presque, à peu près.*

night (naïte), *n.,* nuit, *f.;* soir, *m.;* (thea.) représentation, *f.* It is —; *il fait nuit.* At —; *pendant la nuit, la nuit, de nuit.* Dark —; *nuit noire, nuit close.* First —; *première, f.* Good — ! *bon soir !* A good —'s rest to you ! *bonne nuit !* All —; *toute la nuit.* Every —; *toutes les nuits, tous les soirs.* — after —; *plusieurs nuits de suite; tous les soirs.* Last —; *la nuit dernière; hier au soir.* The — before last; *avant hier soir.* To— ; *ce soir.* Twelfth— ; *le jour des Rois, m., l'Epiphanie, f.* To turn — into day; *faire de la nuit le jour.*

night'-bird, *n.,* oiseau de nuit, *m.*

night'-brawler (-brôl'-), *n.,* tapageur de nuit, *m.*

night'-cart (-cârte), *n.,* voiture de vidange, *f.*

night'-dress, *n.,* chemise de nuit, *f.*

night'-fall (-fôl), *n.,* tombée de la nuit, chute du jour, *f.;* déclin du jour, *m.*

night'-fire (-faï'eur), *n.,* feu de nuit; feu follet, *m.*

night'-gown, *n.,* chemise de nuit, *f.*

night'-hawk (-hôke), *n.,* (orni.) hulotte, huette, *f.*

night'ingale (naït'i'n'ghéle), *n.,* (orni.) rossignol, *m.*

night'-light, *n.,* veilleuse, *f.*

night'-long, *adj.,* de toute la nuit.

night'ly, *adj.,* nocturne, de nuit.

night'ly, *adv.,* de nuit; pendant la nuit; chaque nuit, toutes les nuits; (till midnight) tous les soirs.

night'man, *n.,* vidangeur, *m.*

night'mare, *n.,* cauchemar, *m.*

night'-piece (-pîce), *n.,* (paint.) tableau, *ou* effet, de nuit, *m.*

night'shade (-shéde), *n.,* (bot.) solanum, *m.;* morelle, *f.* Deadly —; *belladone, f.*

night'-shirt, *n.,* chemise de nuit, *f.*

night'-soil (-soïle), *n.sing.,* vidanges, *f.pl.*

night's rest', *n.,* nuit. To have a good —; *faire* (V. Hugo), *ou passer, une bonne nuit.*

night'-time (-taïme), *n.,* nuit (temps), *f.* In the —; *pendant la nuit.*

night'-walk (-wôke), *n.,* promenade nocturne, *f.*

night'-walker, *n.,* rôdeur nocturne; coureur de nuit; somnambule, *m.*

night'-walking, *adj.,* qui rôde la nuit; qui court la nuit; somnambule.

night'-watch (-wôtshe), *n.,* garde de nuit, sentinelle, *f.*

night'-watchman, *n.,* veilleur, gardien de nuit, veilleur de nuit, *m.*

night'-work (-weurke), *n.*, veille, *f.*, travail de nuit, *m. ;* vidange (de fosses), *f.*

nigres'cent (naï-grès'-), *adj.*, (ant.) noirâtre.

ni'hilism (naï-hil'iz'me) *ou* **nihil'ity**, *n.*, néant ; (philos. polit.) nihilisme, *m.*

nil, *n.*, rien, néant, *m. adj.*, (com.) nul.

nilom'eter (naï-lom'i-), *n.*, nilomètre, *m.*

nim'ble (ni'm'b'l), *adj.*, agile, actif, ingambe, léger, leste, vif, dispos ; (of the tongue) délié, affilé. —-fingered ; (b.s.) *qui a les doigts crochus.*

nim'ble-footed (-fout'-), *adj.*, au pied léger ; leste.

nim'bleness, *n.*, légèreté ; agilité ; vivacité, *f.*

nim'ble-witted, *adj.*, à l'esprit vif.

nim'bly, *adv.*, agilement ; lestement.

nim'bus (-beusse), *n.*, (paint., sculpt.) nimbe, (meteorol.) nimbus, *m.*

nin'compoop (ni'n'keu'm'poupe), *n.*, niais, sot, nicodème, *m.*

nine (naïne), *n.* and *adj.*, neuf. A — days' wonder ; *une affaire de huit jours.* He is —; *il a neuf ans.* The —; *les Muses, f.pl.* (Dressed) to the —s ; *mis à la perfection, tiré à quatre épingles.* To look — ways ; *loucher.*

nine'fold (-fôlde), *adj.*, neuf fois autant.

nine'holes (-hôl'ze), *n.pl.*, balle au pot, *f.*

nine'pins (-pi'n'ze), *n.pl.*, quilles, *f.pl.*

nine'score (-scôre), *n.* and *adj.*, cent quatre-vingts.

nine'teen (-tîne), *adj.*, dix-neuf.

nine'teenth (-ti'n'th), *adj.*, dix-neuvième.

nine'tieth (naïn'ti-èth), *adj.*, quatre-vingt-dixième.

nine'ty, *adj.*, quatre-vingt-dix.

nin'ny (-n, nigaud, *m.*, nigaude, *f. ;* benêt, niais, *m. ;* niaise, *f.*

ninth (naïnth), *adj.*, neuvième ; (of the month ; of a dynasty) neuf.

ninth'ly, *adv.*, neuvièmement.

nip, *n.*, (with the nails, the teeth) coup d'ongle, coup de dent, *m. ;* (cut) coupure ; (of plants) brûlure (par le froid), *f. ;* (sarcasm) sarcasme, trait piquant, lardon ; (sip) petit coup, *m.*

nip, *v.a.*, pincer ; pincer le bout **de** ; couper le bout **de** ; mordre ; (plants) brûler (par le froid); (to blast) flétrir; (fig.) piquer ; (nav.) amarrer; saisir. To — off ; *couper ; couper le bout* **de**; *pincer ; pincer le bout* **de**. To — in the bud ; (fig.) *détruire dans son germe.* She was —ped in the bud ; *la mort la frappa au berceau, ou dans sa plus tendre enfance.*

nip'per, *n.*, pince, *f. pl.* pincettes, pinces, *f.pl. ;* (nav.) garcette de tournevire, *f.*

nip'ping, *adj.*, mordant, piquant ; (of cold) perçant.

nip'ple (nip'p'l), *n.*, mamelon, tetin, bout de sein, *m. ;* (of fire-arms) cheminée, *f.*

nip'ple-wort (-weurte), *n.*, lampsane, *f.*

nit, *n.*, (ent.) lente, *f.*

ni'ter *ou* **ni'tre** (naï-teur), *n.*, nitre, *m.*

ni'ter-works (-weurkse), *n.pl.*, salpêtrière, *f.*

ni'trate (naï-), *n.*, nitrate, *m.*

ni'triary (naï-), *n.*, (min.) nitrière, *f.*

ni'tric (naï-), *adj.*, (chem.) nitrique, azotique.

ni'trify (naï-tri-faïe), *v.a.*, nitrifier.

ni'trogen (naï-tro-djène), *n.*, azote, *m.*

nitrog'enous (naï-tro-djè'n-), *adj.*, azoté.

ni'trous *ou* **ni'try** (naï-), *adj.*, (chem.) nitreux, azoteux.

nit'ty, *adj.*, couvert de lentes.

no (nô), *adj.* and *adv.*, nul, aucun ; pas, point ; pas **de**; ne . . . pas **de**; ne . . . point **de** ; non, ne pas, ne point. He has — money about him; *il n'a pas d'argent sur lui.* He has — money (at all); *il n'a point d'argent.* —where; *nulle part.* There is — means to ; *il n'y a pas moyen* **de**. — fear of that ; *il n'y a pas de danger.* — pay — piper ; (prov.) *point d'argent, point de suisse.* — sooner said than done ; *aussitôt dit, aussitôt*

fait. — matter ; *n'importe.* There is — raising her ; *il n'y a pas moyen de l'élever.* — matter how unruly the House ; *si agitée que soit la Chambre.* Have you — friends ? (reproach) *n'avez-vous pas des amis ?* Have you — friends ? (query) *n'avez-vous pas* (ou *point*) *d'amis ?* There is — hesitating about it ; *il n'y a pas à hésiter.* There is — avoiding it ; *il n'y a pas moyen de l'éviter.* — more ; *pas davantage.* — living man all things can ; *à l'impossible nul n'est tenu.*

nob, *n.*, caboche, boule, *f.; ;* (pop.) gros bonnet, *m.*

nobil'iary, *n.*, nobiliaire, *m.*

nobil'ity, *n.*, noblesse, *f.*

no'ble (nô-b'l), *n.*, gentilhomme, noble, *m.*

no'ble, *adj.*, noble, illustre, grand; généreux.

no'bleman, *n.*, noble, gentilhomme, *m.*

no'bleness, *n.*, noblesse, grandeur, *f.*

no'bles (nô-b'l'ze), *n.pl.*, noblesse, *f. ;* corps des nobles, *m.*

no'blewoman (-wou-m'a'n), *n.*, femme noble, *f.*

no'bly, *adv.*, noblement ; honorablement; de noble rang ; de noble condition.

no'body (nô-), *n.*, personne, *f.; ;* rien; (a person of no worth) pleutre, *m.* — knows it ; *personne ne le sait.* I know — ; *je ne connais personne.* Who is there ? — ; *qui est là ? Personne.* To be — ; *n'être rien du tout.*

noc'turn (-teurne), *n.*, (c.rel.) nocturne, *m.*

noctur'nal, *adj.*, nocturne, de nuit.

nod, *n.*, signe de tête, salut, *m. ;* inclination de tête, *f. ;* balancement, *m.* The land of —; *les bras de Morphée, m.pl.* To give a —; *faire signe que oui.*

nod, *v.n.*, faire un signe de tête; incliner la tête; s'incliner ; (to be drowsy) s'assoupir ; (of things) se plier, se balancer. To — to; *faire un signe de tête* **à** ; *saluer.*

nod, *v.a.*, exprimer par une inclination de tête, montrer par une inclination de tête. To — assent ; *faire signe que oui.*

nod'dle (nod'd'l), *n.*, caboche, boule, *f.*

nod'dy, *n.*, sot, benêt, niais, *m.*

node (nôde), *n.*, nœud ; (med.) nodus, *m.*

nodose' (no-dôce), *adj.*, noueux.

nodos'ity (no-dô-ci-ti), *n.*, nœud, *m. ;* nodosité, *f.*

nod'ular (nod'iou-), *adj.*, en forme de nœud.

nod'ule (nod'ioule), *n.*, nodule, *m.*

nog'gin (nog-ghine), *n.*, petit pot, godet, bidon, *m.*

noise (noïze), *n.*, bruit ; tapage ; fracas, vacarme ; (in the ears) tintement, bourdonnement ; (fig.) éclat, retentissement, *m.* To make a —; *faire du bruit.* To hold one's —; *se taire.* What a —! *quel fracas ! quel tapage !*

noise, *v.a.*, publier, répandre, ébruiter. To — abroad ; *répandre au loin; faire circuler; crier sur les toits.* It is —d abroad ; *le bruit court.* To be —d abroad ; *s'ébruiter, se répandre au loin.*

noise'less, *adj.*, sans bruit ; silencieux ; tranquille, calme.

noise'lessly, *adv.*, sans bruit ; silencieusement.

noise'lessness, *n.*, tranquillité, *f.*, silence, *m.*

noise'-maker (-mék'-), *n.*, tapageur, *m.*

nois'ily, *adv.*, bruyamment.

nois'iness, *n.*, grand bruit ; tumulte, tapage, *m.*, clameur, *f.*

noi'some (noï-ceume), *adj.*, dégoûtant ; malsain ; infect; nuisible; malfaisant, insalubre, malsain.

noi'somely, *adv.*, d'une manière infecte.

noi'someness, *n.*, nature nuisible, *f.*

noi'sy (noï-zi), *adj.*, bruyant, turbulent, tumultueux ; (pers.) tapageur.

no'lens-vo'lens (nô-lè'n'ze-vô-lè'n'ze), *adv.*, de gré ou de force ; bon gré, mal gré.

no'li me tan'gere, *n.*, (bot., med.) noli me tangere, *m.*

nom'ad *ou* **nomad'ic**, *adj.*, nomade.

nom'ad, *n.*, nomade, *m.*

no'menclator (nō-mè'n'clé-teur), **-tress**, *n.*, nomenclateur, *m.*

no'menclature (-klét'ieur), *n.*, nomenclature, *f.*

nom'inal, *adj.*, nominal ; de nom.

nom'inally, *adv.*, de nom ; nominalement.

nom'inate, *v.a.*, nommer ; désigner ; (a candidate to the electors) présenter, proposer.

nomina'tion (-né-), *n.*, nomination ; présentation, *f.*

nom'inative, *adj.*, au nominatif ; du nominatif, nominatif.

nom'inative, *n.*, (gram.) nominatif, *m.*

nom'inator (-né-teur), *n.*, nominateur, *m.*

nominee' (-nî), *n.*, personne nommée, présentée, *f. ;* (by the king to a benefice) nominataire, *m.f.;* candidat, *m.*, (in a bad sense) créature, *f.*

non, *adv.*, non ; défaut, manque, *m.;* absence, *f.*

non-abil'ity, *n.*, inhabilité, incapacité, *f.*

non-acquaint'ance (-ak'kwé'n't'-), *n.*, défaut de connaissance, *m. ;* ignorance, *f.*

non-admit'tance, *n.*, refus d'admettre, *m.*

non'age (no'n'èdje), *n.*, minorité, *f.*

non-appear'ance (-pîr'-), *n.*, (jur.) absence, contumace, *f. ;* défaut de comparution, *m.*

non-attend'ance, *n.*, absence, *f.*, manque de service, *m.*

nonce, *n.*, (ant.) dessein, effet, but, *m.* For the — ; *à cet effet ; pour cette fois-ci.*

non'-claim (-cléme), *n.*, défaut de réclamation, *m.*

non-com'batant, *n.*, non-combattant, *m.*

non-commis'sioned, *adj.*, sans brevet. — officier ; *sous-officier.*

non-compli'ance (-plaï'-), *n.*, (jur.) non-acquiescement, refus d'acquiescer, *m.*

non-comply'ing (-plaï'igne), *adj.*, qui refuse d'acquiescer, qui ne se conforme pas.

non com'pos men'tis, *adj.*, atteint d'aliénation mentale.

non-conduct'ing (-deuk't'-), *adj.*, non-conducteur, *m.*

non-conduc'tor (-deuk't'eur), *n.*, non-conducteur, *m.*

non-conform'ist, *n.*, non-conformiste, *m.*

non-conform'ity, *n.*, défaut de conformité, *m. ;* non-conformité, *f.*

non-conta'gious (-té'djeusse), *adj.*, (med.) non-contagieux.

non-conta'giousness, *n.*, caractère non contagieux, *m.*

non'-content, *n.*, voix contre, *f.*, opposant, *m.*

non-deliv'ery, *n.*, manque de livraison, (of letters) non-distribution, *f.*

non'descript, *adj.*, qui n'a pas encore été décrit, indéfinissable ; inclassable, déclassé ; innommé.

non'descript, *n.*, chose sans nom ; chose indéfinissable, *f. ;* (pers.) original, *m.*

none, *adj.pron.*, nul, *m.*, nulle, *f. ;* aucun, *m.*, aucune, *f. ;* pas un, *m.*, pas une, *f. ;* personne, *m. ;* rien ; pas ; point. — the less, *ou* more ; *pas moins . . . pour cela ; pas plus . . . pour cela.* I will have — ; *je n'en veux pas.* I have — ; *je n'en ai pas.*

non-elec'tric, *n.*, substance non électrique, *f.*

non-emphat'ic *ou* **non-emphat'ical**, *adj.*, peu énergique.

non-en'tity, *n.*, non-existence ; chose qui n'existe pas, *f. ;* (pers.) pleutre, *m.*, nullité, *f.*

non-epis'copal, *adj.*, non épiscopal.

non-essen'tial (-shal), *n.*, chose non essentielle, *f.*

none'such (neu'n'seutshe), *n.*, (bot.) croix de Jérusalem ; (apple) nonpareille, *f.*

none'-such, *adj.*, nonpareil ; sans pareil.

non-execu'tion (-ègz'é-kiou-), *n.*, inexécution, *f.*

non-exist'ence, *n.*, non-existence ; chose qui n'existe pas, *f.*

no'nius (nō-ni-), *n.*, (astron.) nonius, vernier, *m.*

non-metal'lic, *adj.*, non métallique.

non-observ'ance (-zeurv'-), *n.*, inobservation, *f.*

nonpareil' (-rèl), *n.*, (apple, print.) nonpareille, *f.*

nonpareil', *adj.*, nonpareil ; sans égal.

non-pay'ment, *n.*, non-payement ; défaut de payement, *m.*

non-perform'ance, *n.*, inexécution, *f.*

non'plus (-pleusse), *n.*, embarras, quia, bout, *m.* At a — ; *à quia.*

non'plus, *v.a.*, mettre au pied du mur ; mettre à quia ; embarrasser ; dérouter.

non-pres'sure (-prèsh'eur), *n.*, absence de pression, *f.*

non-produc'tion (-deuk'-), *n.*, non-production, *f.*

non-profi'ciency (-fish'è'n'-), *n.*, défaut de force ; manque de savoir, *m. ;* faiblesse, absence de progrès, *f.*

non-profi'cient (-fish'è'n'te), *adj.*, peu fort, peu savant ; faible, arriéré.

non-resem'blance (-ri-zè'm'-), *n.*, dissemblance, *f.*, manque de ressemblance, *m.*

non-res'idence (-rèz'-), *n.*, non-résidence, *f.*

non-res'ident, *adj.*, non résident ; externe ; (of landlords) forain.

non-res'ident, *n.*, non résident, *m.*

non-resis'tance (-ri-zist'-), *n.*, obéissance passive, *f.*

non-resis'tant, qui ne résiste pas.

non'sense, *n.*, nonsens, *m. ;* bêtise, sottise, *f. ;* galimatias, *m. ;* absurdité, baliverne, *f.* — ! *allons donc ! laissez donc ! quelle sottise !*

nonsen'sical, *adj.*, vide de sens ; bête, sot, absurde, qui n'a pas le sens commun.

nonsen'sically, *adv.*, contre le bon sens, contre le sens commun ; bêtement, sottement, absurdement.

nonsen'sicalness, *n.*, absurdité, bêtise, sottise, *f.*

non-sen'sitive, *adj.*, sans perception.

non'suit (-sioute), *n.*, (jur.) désistement, *m.*

non'suit, *v.a.*, (jur.) mettre hors de cour ; débouter de.

non-u'sance (-you-za'n'ce), *n.*, non-usage, *m.*

non-u'ser (-youz'-), *n.*, non-exercice de fonctions ; non-usage, *m.*

noo'dle (noud'l), *n.*, nigaud, benêt, sot, *m.*

nook (nouke), *n.*, coin, recoin ; réduit ; enfoncement, *m.* —s and corners ; *coins et recoins.*

noon (noune), *n.*, midi ; (fig.) milieu, *m.* — of night ; *minuit, m.* Real — ; (astron.) midi vrai, *m.*

noon'day, *adj.*, méridional, de midi.

noon'day, *n.*, plein jour ; midi, *m.* At — ; *en plein midi.*

noon'tide (-taïde), *n.*, heure de midi, *f. ;* midi, *m.*

noose (nouce *ou* nouze), *n.*, nœud coulant, *m.*, (fig.) piège, lacet, *m.*

noose, *v.a.*, attacher par un nœud coulant ; (fig.) prendre dans un piège, attraper.

no'pal (nō-), *n.*, (bot.) nopal, *m.*

nope, *n.*, (orni.) bouvreuil, *m.*

nor, *conj.*, ni ; ni . . . ne ; pas . . . non plus, d'ailleurs, du reste, de plus, en outre, d'autre part, d'un autre côté (with a negative sentence in French). —was this caution unnecessary ; *et vraiment (ou d'ailleurs) cette recommandation ne fut pas inutile.* — was he to ; *et il ne devait pas non plus.* ⌐ could any soldier venture beyond ;

*aucun soldat ne pouvait d'ailleurs s'aventurer au
delà.* — I either; *ni moi non plus.* — you
either; *ni vous non plus.* — was this all; *et ce
n'était pas tout.*

nor'mal, *adj.,* normal; (geom.) perpendiculaire.

nor'mal, *n.,* (geom.) normale, *f.*

Nor'man, *adj.,* normand.

Nor'man, *n.,* Normand, *m.,* Normande, *f.*

north (north), *n.,* nord, septentrion, *m.*

north, *adj.,* du nord, de nord, septentrional.

north, *adv.,* au nord.

north'-east (-îste), *n.,* nord-est, *m.*

north'erly *ou* **north'ern** (north'-), *adj.,* septentrional, du nord.

north'erly (north'-), *adv.,* au nord; vers le nord.

north'ern lights', *n.pl.,* aurore boréale, *f.*

north' star' (north-), *n.,* étoile polaire, *f.*

north'ward (north'wŏrde), *adj.,* vers le nord; au nord.

north'ward *ou* **north'wards** (-wŏrd'ze), *adv.,* vers le nord, au nord.

north'-west (north'wèste), *n.,* nord-ouest, *m.*

north' wind' (-wî-dji-), *n.,* vent du nord, *m.*

Norwe'gian (-wî-dji-), *adj.,* norvégien.

Norwe'gian, *n.,* Norvégien, *m.,* Norvégienne, *f.*

nose (nŏze), *n.,* nez; (of animals) museau; (of bellows) tuyau, *m.* To blow any one's —; *moucher quelqu'un.* To blow one's (own) —; *se moucher.* He scarcely sees what passes under his —; *c'est à peine s'il voit ce qui se passe sous son nez.* To put any one's — out of joint; *supplanter quelqu'un; couper l'herbe sous le pied à quelqu'un; mortifier quelqu'un.* Roman —; *nez aquilin, m.* To speak through one's —; *parler du nez.* Pug-—, snub-—, turned-up —; *nez épaté, camus, retroussé.* To bleed at the —; *saigner du nez.* My — is bleeding; *je saigne du nez.* To lead by the —; *mener par le nez.* To take pepper in the —; *prendre la mouche; s'offenser de.* To thrust, *ou* put, one's — into the affairs of others; *fourrer son nez où l'on n'a que faire; se mêler des affaires d'autrui.* To turn up the nose (at); *faire fi de; faire la petite bouche, faire le difficile.* To wipe a person's —; (fig.) *duper, filouter quelqu'un.* To hold any one's — to the grindstone; *rendre la vie dure à quelqu'un.*

nose'-bag, *n.,* (for horses, etc.) musette, *f.*

nose'-band, *n.,* (for horses, etc.) muserolle, *f.*

nose'-cap, *n.,* (of a rifle) bouchon, *m.*

nosed (nŏz'de), *adj.,* au nez; qui a le nez. Pug-—, snub-—; *qui a le nez épaté.* Flat-—; *camus, camard.*

nose'gay (-ghé), *n.,* bouquet, *m.*

nose'less, *adj.,* sans nez.

nostal'gia (-djia), *n.,* nostalgie, *f.; mal du pays, m.*

nos'tril, *n.,* narine, *f.; (of a horse)* naseau, *m.*

nos'trum, *n.,* élixir merveilleux, *m.; panacée, f.; remède secret, m.*

not, *adv.,* ne . . . pas; ne . . . point; non; pas; non pas; (expressing surprise) vraiment. — at all; *point du tout.* It is — so with; *il n'en est pas ainsi de.* — but that; *non que; non pas que; ce n'est pas que* (with subjunctive in French). I do — see; *je ne vois pas.* Good or —; *bon ou non.* — here; *pas ici.* — the more; *pas davantage.* — the less; *pas moins néanmoins.* Is it — ? *n'est-ce pas?* That is — in my line; *ce n'est pas de mon ressort.* It is — any use my talking; *j'ai beau dire.*

notabil'ity, *n.,* notabilité, éminence, *f.*

not'able (nŏt'a-b'l), *adj.,* notable; insigne; manifeste; remarquable; entendu, habile.

not'able, *n.,* notable, *m.; chose digne d'être notée, f.; personnage notable, m.*

not'ably, *adv.,* notablement; remarquablement; (specially) notamment.

nota'rial (-té-), *adj.,* de notaire, notarial, (done by a notary) notarié.

no'tary (nŏ-) *ou* **no'tary-pub'lic** (-peub'-), *n.,* notaire, *m.* — 's business; *notariat, m.*

nota'tion (no-té-), *n.,* notation; (arith.) numération écrite, *f.; (mus. alg. chem.)* notation, *f.*

notch, *n.,* coche, entaille; dent, *f.; (tech.)* cran, *m.; (of the back-sight of a gun)* cran de mire, *ou* de hausse.

notch, *v.a.,* entailler; tailler inégalement; ébrécher; faire une coche à, une entaille à.

notch'board (-bŏrde), *n.,* (arch.) limon d'escalier, *m.*

notch'wheel (-hwîl), *n.,* (horl.) roue de compte, *f.*

note (nŏte), *n.,* note, marque, *f.; signe, m.;* (letter) billet, *m.,* lettre; (reputation) remarque, marque, distinction, *f.; (com.)* billet, *m.; (mus.)* note, *f.,* ton; accent, accord; (gram.) point, *m.* Bank-—; *billet de banque, m.* — of exclamation; *point d'admiration, point d'exclamation, m.* To take a — of; *prendre note de.* Leading —; (mus.) *note sensible, f.* — of hand; *billet à ordre, m.* — paper; *papier à lettres, m.*

note, *v.a.,* noter; prendre note de, marquer, remarquer. To — a bill; (com.) *protester un billet.*

note'-book (-bouke), *n.,* cahier de notes; carnet, *m.*

not'ed, *adj.,* distingué, remarquable, fameux, célèbre; (b.s.) noté, insigne, bien connu, fieffé.

not'edly, *adv.,* exactement, parfaitement.

note'less, *adj.,* peu distingué; peu remarquable; obscur.

note'worthy, *adj.,* remarquable, digne de remarque.

noth'ing (neuth'-), *n.,* rien, néant; zéro, *m.* — of that sort, I assure you; *il n'en est rien, je vous assure.* Next to —; *presque rien, rien qui vaille.* That is — to me; *cela ne me regarde pas, ne m'intéresse pas.* - This pupil does — but talk; *cet élève ne fait que causer.* — else; *pas autre chose.* — done; *rien de fait.* A mere —; *un rien; une bagatelle.* Good for —; *bon à rien.* — at all; *rien du tout.* To make — of; *ne rien comprendre à; (not to be scrupulous) ne pas se faire scrupule de; (to find no difficulty in) n'avoir aucune difficulté à.* To come to —; *n'aboutir à rien.* To do — but; *ne faire que.* To go for —; *compter pour rien.* There is — to laugh at; *il n'y a pas de quoi rire.* There is — to boast of; *il n'y a pas de quoi se vanter.* — ask — have; (prov.) *il n'y a que les honteux qui perdent.* There — succeeds like success; *qui perd pèche.* There's — like leather! *vous êtes orfèvre, Monsieur Josse!* (Molière, *L'Amour Médecin*). — venture — have; *qui ne risque rien n'a rien.* That is — new! (fam.) *je la connais celle-là!* A good-for-— ; *un vaurien, m.*

noth'ing, *adv.,* en rien; nullement; aucunement. Worth —; *vil; bas; sans valeur; sans mérite.*

noth'ingness, *n.,* néant, rien, *m.*

no'tice (nŏ-tice), *n.,* connaissance; attention; notice (article in newspaper); revue (books); notice (pers.), *f.; (warning)* avis; (to quit) congé, *m.; (jur.)* notification, *f.* Biographical —; *notice biographique.* Take —; *avis!* To take — of; *avoir des attentions pour; prendre connaissance de; faire attention à; remarquer; s'apercevoir de.* At short —; *à court délai.* At the shortest —; *dans le plus bref délai.* Until further —; *jusqu'à avis contraire.* To rise to —; *se faire connaître.* To attract —; *attirer l'attention.* To bring into —; *produire; faire connaître.* To bring to the — of; *porter à la connaissance de.* You are beneath our —; *vous ne valez pas que l'on vous réponde.* — to quit;

congé, m. Without a moment's — ; *immédiatement*. To give — ; *donner avis, avertir, prévenir*.

no'tice, v.a., prendre connaissance **de**, remarquer, noter ; faire connaître ; faire attention **à** ; avoir des attentions **pour**.

no'ticeable (-a-b'l), adj., perceptible ; remarquable, sensible, visible.

no'ticeably, adv., visiblement, sensiblement, perceptiblement.

notifica'tion (-fi-ké-), n., notification, f. ; avis, avertissement.

no'tify (nô-ti-faïe), v.a., faire connaître, faire savoir ; notifier, déclarer, annoncer.

no'tion (nô-), n., notion, idée, pensée, opinion, f. ; sentiment, m. ; prétention ; teinture, f. He has no — of going away ; *il n'a pas l'intention de s'en aller* ; *il n'a pas envie de s'en aller*. The extravagant — they entertain of themselves ; *la haute opinion qu'ils ont d'eux-mêmes*.

no'tionist, n., songe-creux, m.

notori'ety (nô-to-raï-è-), n., notoriété, f.

noto'rious (no-tô-), adj., notoire, évident, manifeste ; fieffé ; (b.s.) insigne, fameux. A — rogue ; *un fameux coquin*.

noto'riously, adv., notoirement.

noto'riousness, n., notoriété, f. ; (ant.) enormité, f.

noto'riously, adv., notoirement, foncièrement.

no'tus (nô-teusse), n., vent du sud, m.

notwithstand'ing (-with'-), conj., malgré que, quand même, nonobstant.

notwithstand'ing, prep., malgré ; nonobstant ; en dépit de.

nought (nôte), n. V. **naught**.

noun (naou'ne), n., (gram.) nom, substantif, m.

nour'ish (neur'-), v.a., nourrir ; entretenir, encourager, fomenter.

nour'ishable (-a-b'l), adj., nourrissable.

nour'ishing, adj., nourrissant, nutritif.

nour'ishment, n., nourriture, f.

nov'el, adj., neuf ; nouveau, neuf ; étrange.

nov'el, n., roman, m. ; (short) nouvelle, f.

nov'elist, n., (writer of fiction) romancier ; (ant.) (writer of news) nouvelliste, m.

nov'elty, n., nouveauté, f.

nov'el-writ'er (-raït'-), n., romancier, m.

Novem'ber, n., novembre, m.

nover'cal (-veur-), adj., de marâtre.

nov'ice, n., novice, m.f.

novi'tiate, n., noviciat, m.

now (nao), adv., maintenant, à présent, actuellement ; (of the past) alors, pour lors, or ; donc. — the state of affairs was critical ; **or** *la situation était critique*. Till — ; *jusqu'ici* ; *jusqu'alors*. Just — ; *tout à l'heure* ; *à l'instant*. — and then ; *de temps en temps* ; *de temps à autre*. — . . . . — ; *tantôt . . . tantôt*. Before — ; *déjà* ; *auparavant*. — then are you going to be quiet ? *eh bien ! allez-vous rester tranquille ?* —'s the time ; *voici le moment*. —! *ah ça, enfin !*

now'adays (nao-a-dèze), adv., aujourd'hui, de nos jours, par le temps qui court.

no'where (nô-hwère), adv., nulle part.

no'wise (nô-waïze), adv., en aucune manière ; nullement.

nox'ious (nok-sheusse) adj., nuisible, pernicieux, malfaisant.

nox'iously, adv., d'une manière nuisible ; pernicieusement.

nox'iousness, n., qualité nuisible, f.

noz'zle (noz'z'l), n., nez ; museau ; groin ; bec, tuyau, bout, m. — mouth ; *tuyère*, f.

nu'cleus (niou-kli-), n., noyau, m.

nude (nioude), adj., nu ; (jur.) nul.

nude, n., (sculpt. paint.) nu, m.

nudge, n., coup de coude. v.a., donner un coup de coude à ; pousser du coude.

nu'dity (niou-), n., nudité, f.

nu'gatory (niou-ga-), adj., futile, frivole ; insignifiant, inefficace ; nul ; de nul effet.

nui'sance (niou-ça'n'ce), n., (jur.) dommage aux propriétés, m. ; peste, plaie, f. ; fléau, ennui, désagrément, tourment, m., scie, corvée, f., cauchemar, tourment, m. What a —! *quel ennui ! comme c'est ennuyeux !* He is a — to every one ; *c'est une peste pour tout le monde*. Inspector of —s ; *officier de salubrité, m.* Commit no — ; *il est défendu de déposer*, ou *de faire, aucune ordure ; défense d'uriner.*

null (neul), adj., nul. — and void ; (jur.) *nul et de nul effet.*

nul'lify (neul'li-faïe), v.a., rendre nul ; annuler, casser.

nul'lity (neul'li-ti), n., nullité, f. The sentence was treated as a — ; *la sentence fut regardée comme nulle et de nul effet.*

numb (neume), adj., engourdi, transi.

numb, v.a., engourdir, transir.

num'ber (neu'm'beur), n., nombre, m. ; quantité, f. ; (of things in succession, as houses, etc.) numéro, m. ; (of publications) livraison, f. ; (gram., math., rhet.) nombre, m. ; (harmony) harmonie, j. ; (ant.) (poet.) vers, m. pl. (Bible) Nombres, m.pl. Cardinal, ordinal, odd, even — ; *nombre cardinal, ordinal, impair, pair.* In great —s ; *en grand nombre.* The superiority of —s ; *la supériorité*, ou *l'avantage, du nombre.* Twelve in — ; *au nombre de douze.*

num'ber, v.a., nombrer, compter **parmi** ; supputer ; mettre au nombre **de** ; (things in succession, as houses, etc.) numéroter. He was —ed with the transgressors ; *il fut mis au nombre des transgresseurs*. The army —ed 50,000 men ; *l'armée se composait de*, ou *s'élevait à,* ou *montait à,* ou *se montait à, 50,000 hommes.* I — him among my friends ; *je le mets au nombre de mes amis*, ou *je le compte parmi mes amis.*

num'berer, n., qui suppute, qui compte, qui numérote, f., numérateur, m.

num'bering, n., supputation, f. ; numérotage, calcul, m. — machine ; *machine à numéroter, f.*

num'berless, adj., sans nombre ; innombrable.

numb'ness (neu'm'nèce), n., engourdissement, m. ; torpeur, f.

nu'merable (niou-meur'a-b'l), adj., (ant.) qui peut être compté, nombrable.

nu'meral (niou-meur'-), n., lettre numérale, f. ; chiffre, m.

nu'meral, adj., numéral, numérique.

nu'merally, adv., numériquement.

nu'merary (niou-meur'-), adj., numéral.

numera'tion (niou-meur'é-), n., numération, f.

nu'merator (niou-meur'é-), n., numérateur, m.

numer'ic ou **numer'ical**, adj., numérique.

numer'ically, adv., numériquement.

nu'merous (niou-meur'-), adj., nombreux.

nu'merously, adv., en grand nombre.

numismat'ic ou **numismat'ical** (niou-miz-), adj., numismatique.

numismat'ics, n.pl., numismatique, f.

numis'matist ou **numismatol'ogist** ('-o-djiste), n., numismate, numismatiste, m.

numismatog'raphy, n., numismatographie, f.

num'mulite (neu'm'miou-laïte), n., (palæont.) nummulite, f.

num'skull (neu'm'skeul), n., benêt, lourdaud, nigaud, balourd, m. ; bûche, f.

num'skulled (neu'm'skeul'de), adj., imbécile, nigaud, balourd.

nun (neune), n., religieuse ; nonne, (jest.) nonnain, nonnette, f.

nun'ciature (neu'n'shi-a-tiour), n., (ant.) nonciature, f.

nun'cio (neu'n'shi-ô), n., nonce, m.

nun'nery (neu'n'n'-), n., couvent de religieuses, ou de femmes, m.

nup'tial (neup'shal), adj., nuptial, de noces.

nup'tials (-shalze), n.pl., noces, f.pl.

nurse (neurse), n., (for infants) nourrice ; (for

children) bonne d'enfant ; (for the sick) garde-
malade, garde, *f.* ; (in hospitals) infirmier, *m.*,
infirmière ; (fig.) mère, *f.* —-maid ; *bonne
d'enfant.* —-child ; *nourrisson, m.* To put out
to —; *mettre en nourrice.*

nurse, *v.a.*, nourrir, allaiter, garder, élever ;
(the sick) soigner, garder ; (fig.) alimenter, soigner, entretenir, ménager ; (to encourage) fomenter, chérir ; (to fondle) dorloter, choyer.

nur'sery (neurs'-), *n.*, chambre des enfants ;
(public) crèche ; (gard., fig.) pépinière ; (of silk-
worms) magnanerie, *f.* — governess ; *gouvernante, f.* — rhymes ; *contes de nourrice, m.pl.*

nur'sery-gar'den (-gâr'd'n), *n.*, pépinière, *f.*
nur'sery-maid (-méde), *n.*, bonne d'enfant, *f.*
nur'sery-man, *n.*, pépiniériste, *m.*

nurs'ling (neurs'-), *n.*, nourrisson ; (fig.) mignon, *m.*, mignonne, *f.*

nur'sy, *n.*, (children's talk) nounou, *f.*

nur'ture (neurt'ieur), *n.*, nourriture ; instruction, éducation, *f.*

nur'ture, *v.a.*, nourrir, alimenter ; élever.

nut (neute), *n.*, noisette, *f.* ; (of a screw)
écrou, *m.* ; (of a fiddle-bow) hausse, *f.* ; (of
stringed instruments) sillet, *m.* —s (of coal)
grêle, *m.* A —to crack ; *un problème à résoudre ;
une énigme à deviner.* To be —s on ; (fam.)
raffoler de. —-tree ; *noisetier, m.*

nut, *v.n.*, cueillir des noisettes. To go nutting ;
aller cueillir la noisette.

nuta'tion (niou-té-) *n.*, (astron., bot.) nutation, *f.*

nut'brown (-braoune), *adj.*, châtain.
nut'cracker, *n.*, casse-noisette, casse-noix, *m.*
nut'gall (-gôl), *n.*, noix de galle, *f.*
nut'hook (-houke), *n.*, croc, crochet aux noix.
nut'meg, *n.*, muscade, *f.* —-tree ; *muscadier, m.*

nu'trient (niou-), *n.*, (ant.) aliment, *m.*
nu'trient, *adj.*, (ant.) nourrissant, nutritif.
nu'triment (niou-), *n.*, nourriture, *f.* ; aliment, *m.*

nutri'tious (niou-tri-sheusse) *ou* **nu'tritive**
(niou-tri-tive), *adj.*, nutritif, nourrissant.

nut'-shell, *n.*, coquille de noix, *f.* To lie in
a — ; *être simple comme bonjour ; se résumer en
un mot, être facile à comprendre.*

nut'ty, *adj.*, qui a un goût de noisette.
nux-vom'ica (neuks'vo-), *n.*, noix vomique, *f.*
nuz'zle (*v.a.*, (to ring) anneler, ferrer, boucler ;
(to root) fouiller ; se cacher.

nye (naïe), *n.* (of pheasants) nichée, *f.*
nymph (ni'm'fe), *n.*, nymphe, *f.*
nymphe'an (-phî-), *adj.*, de nymphe.
nymph'-like (-laïke), *adj.*, comme une
nymphe.

nymphoma'nia *ou* **nym'phomany**, *n.*, érotomanie, fureur utérine, *f.*

O

O, quinzième lettre de l'alphabet, o, *m.*

oaf (ôfe), *n.*, enfant de fée ; (dolt) benêt,
idiot, imbécile, *m.*

oaf'ish, *adj.*, stupide, idiot.
oaf'ishness, *n.*, stupidité, *f.*

oak (ôke), *n.*, chêne ; chêne rouvre ; (wood)
chêne, bois de chêne, *m.* —-tree ; *chêne.* Holm-
— ; *yeuse, f. ; chêne vert, m.* —-bark, *n.*, écorce
du chêne, *f.* ; (in powder) tan, *m.* Heart of — ;
cœur ferme, m.

oak'-apple (-ap'p'l), *n.*, noix de galle, *f.*
oak'en, *adj.*, de chêne.
oak'-grove (-grôve), *n.*, chênaie, *f.*
oak'ling (-), *n.*, jeune chêne, chêneau, *m.*
oa'kum (ôk'eume), *n.*, étoupe, *f.* —-boy ;
(nav.) *mousse de calfat, m.* To pick — ; *faire
de la filasse ou de l'étoupe.*

oak'y, *adj.*, de chêne ; dur comme le chêne.

oar (ôre), *n.*, rame, *f.* ; aviron, *m.* The blade
of the — ; *le plat, ou la pale, de l'aviron.* To ply
the — ; *faire force de rames.* To be a good — ;
manier bien l'aviron. Will you take an — ?
voulez-vous être de notre équipage ? To boat, *ou*
ship, the —s ; *armer.* To unship the —s ; *désarmer.* Let us take a pair of —s ; *prenons un
canot à deux rames.* Stroke — ; *chef de nage,
m.* To put one's — in ; *se fourrer où l'on n'a
que faire.* To lie on one's —s ; *se reposer ; cesser
de travailler.*

oar, *v.n.*, ramer.

oared (ôr'de), *adj.*, à rames, à avirons.
Eight-— boat ; *bateau à huit rames, m.*

oars'man (ôrz'-), *n.*, rameur, *m.* —-ship; *art
de ramer, talent de rameur, m.*

oar'y, *adj.*, en forme de rame.
oa'sis (ô-é-cice), *n.*, oasis, *f.*
oast (ôste), *n.*, four à houblon, *m.*
oat'cake (ôt'kéke), *n.*, gâteau d'avoine, *m.*
oa'ten (ôt'ène), *adj.*, d'avoine.
oat'-grass (ôt'grâce), *n.*, avoine, *f.*

oath (ôth), *n.*, serment ; (b.s.) juron, jurement, serment, *m.* On —, on one's — ; *sous
serment ; sous la foi du serment.* To put any one
on his — ; *faire prêter serment à quelqu'un.* To
take an, *ou* the, — ; *prêter serment.* To break
one's — ; *manquer à ; fausser son serment.* To
administer an — ; *faire prêter serment à.* Tremendous — ; *gros juron, m.* Volley of —s ; *bordée de jurements, f.* To rap out an — ; *lâcher un
jurement.* To swear an — ; *faire un serment.*
To take one's — of it ; *en mettre la main au feu ;
en lever la main.*

oath'-breaking (-brèk'-), *n.*, violation de
serment, *f.* ; parjure, *m.*

oath'-taking, *n.*, prestation de serment, *f.*
oat'-malt (-môlt), *n.*, drêche d'avoine, *f.*
oat'-meal (-mîl), *n.*, gruau d'avoine, *m.* ;
farine d'avoine, *f.*

oats (ôtse), *n.pl.*, avoine, *f.sing.* To sow one's
wild — ; *jeter sa gourme, faire des folies, faire
des fredaines.*

obliga'to, *adj.*, obligé.
ob'duracy (-diou-), *n.*, endurcissement, *m.* ;
impénitence, *f.*

ob'durate (-diou-), *adj.*, endurci, impénitent ;
inflexible, obstiné, opiniâtre.

ob'durately, *adv.*, opiniâtrément, obstinément, avec endurcissement, avec impénitence.

obe'dience (-bî-), *n.*, obéissance ; soumission,
(of monks and nuns) obédience, *f.* In — to ; *pai
obéissance à.* To give — to ; *obéir à.*

obe'dient, *adj.*, obéissant, soumis.
obedien'tial, *adj.*, respectueux, de soumission ;
(ecc.) obédientiel.

obe'diently, *adv.*, avec obéissance ; avec
soumission. Yours — ; *votre très humble et très
obéissant serviteur.*

obei'sance (o-bé- *ou* o-bî-), *n.*, révérence, *f.* ;
salut, *m.*

obelis'cal, *adj.*, en forme d'obélisque.
ob'elisk (ob-è-), *n.*, obélisque, *m.* ; (print.)
croix, *f.*

obese'ness *ou* **obe'sity** (o-bî-), *n.*, obésité, *f.*
obey' (o-bé), *v.a.*, obéir à ; écouter ; (jur.)
obtempérer à.

obey', *v.n.*, obéir.
obfus'cate (-feus'-), *v.a.*, offusquer, obscurcir.
obfusca'tion (-feus'-), *n.*, obscurcissement, *m.*,
offuscation, *f.*

o'bit (ô-), *n.*, (c.rel.) obit, *m.*
obit'ual (o-bit'iou-), *adj.*, de l'obit.
obit'uary, *adj.*, obituaire ; nécrologique.
obit'uary, *n.*, obituaire, nécrologe, *m.* ; (notice of the decease) nécrologie, *f.* — notice ; *notice nécrologique, f.*

ob'ject, *n.*, objet ; but, *m.* ; considération, *f.* ;
(gram.) complément, régime ; (milit.) objectif,
m. ; (pop.) personne ridicule, effroyable, *f.* ;

objet effrayant, *m.*, horreur, *f.* That — is of some consequence ; *c'est important.* He will not gain his — ; *il n'atteindra pas son but ; il ne réussira pas dans son dessein.* What an — you are ! *comme vous voilà fait !* Money is no — to us ; *nous ne regardons pas à la dépense.*

object', *v.a.*, objecter ; opposer.

object', *v.n.*, objecter **à** ; s'opposer **à**, refuser **de** ; se refuser **à** ; répugner **à**. The king's mother —ed to his marriage ; *le mariage du roi répugnait à sa mère ; la mère du roi élevait des objections contre son mariage.* Do you — to having the door shut ? *vous opposez-vous à ce que la porte soit fermée ?*

ob'ject-glass (-glâce), *n.*, verre objectif, objectif, *m.*

objec'tion (-jèk'-), *n.*, objection, difficulté, *f.* Have you any — to ? *vous opposez-vous à ?* I have no — ; *je ne m'y oppose nullement ; je le veux bien.* I have a great — to that man ; *cet homme me répugne.* I have not the slightest — ; *je ne demande pas mieux.*

objec'tionable (-a-b'l), *adj.*, répréhensible ; inadmissible. — language ; *langage répréhensible, m.*

objec'tive, *adj.*, objectif ; (gram.) du complément, du régime.

objec'tive, *n.*, (gram.) complément, régime, *m.*, (milit.) objectif, *m.*

objec'tively, *adv.*, objectivement ; (gram.) comme un régime.

objec'tiveness *ou* **objectiv'ity**, *n.*, (philos.) objectivité, *f.*

ob'jectless, *adj.*, sans but, sans objet.

objec'tor, *n.*, personne qui fait une objection, *f.*

objurga'tion (-jeur-ghé-), *n.*, vive réprimande ; objurgation, *f.*

objur'gatory (-jeur-ga-), *adj.*, objurgatoire, de réprimande, de reproche.

ob'late, *adj.*, (geom.) aplati (vers les pôles).

ob'late, *n.*, (c.rel.) oblat, *m.*

ob'lateness, *n.*, (geom.) aplatissement, *m.*

obla'tion (ob-lé-sheune), *n.*, (ecc.) oblation, offrande, *f.*

obliga'tion (-ghé-), *n.*, obligation, *f.* ; engagement, *m.* Under an — to ; *dans l'obligation* **de** ; tenu **de.** To be under an — to any one ; *avoir de l'obligation à quelqu'un.* To lay any one under an — ; *obliger quelqu'un.*

ob'ligatory, *adj.*, obligatoire.

oblige' (-blaïdje), *v.a.*, obliger ; faire plaisir **à** ; (to force) obliger, astreindre **de** *ou* **à.** — me by not saying anything about it ; *obligez-moi de n'en rien dire.* — me with ; *ayez l'obligeance* **de** (*ou veuillez*) *me donner* (*ou me passer*).

obligee' (-bli-djî), *n.*, (jur.) créancier, *m.*, créancière, *f.* ; obligataire, *m.f.*

obli'ger, *n.*, personne qui oblige ; (jur.) personne qui souscrit une obligation, *f.*

obli'ging, *adj.*, obligeant, complaisant, serviable.

obli'gingly, *adv.*, obligeamment ; complaisamment.

obli'gingness (-blaïdj'ign-nèce), *n.*, obligeance, complaisance, *f.*

obligor' (ob-li-), *n.*, (jur.) obligé, *m.*, obligée, *f.* ; débiteur, *m.*, débitrice, *f.*

oblique', *adj.*, oblique ; indirect, détourné. — dealings ; *procédés détournés, m.pl.*

oblique'ly, *adv.*, obliquement ; indirectement, d'une manière détournée.

oblique'ness (-blîk'-) *ou* **obliq'uity** (-lik-wi-), *n.*, obliquité ; (fig.) irrégularité, *f.* ; défaut de droiture, *m.* ; obliquité, *f.*

oblit'erate (-eur-), *v.a.*, effacer ; faire oublier ; oblitérer.

oblitera'tion, *n.*, action d'effacer ; rature ; oblitération, *f.*

obliv'ion, *n.*, oubli, *m.* Act of — ; *amnistie, f.*

obliv'ious, *adj.*, d'oubli, oublieux **de.**

ob'long, *adj.*, oblong.

ob'long, *n.*, figure oblongue, *f.* ; (geom.) rectangle, *m.*

ob'longly, *adv.*, d'une forme oblongue.

ob'longness, *n.*, (ant.) forme oblongue, *f.*

ob'loquy (-kwi), *n.*, reproche ; blâme, déshonneur, *m.* ; censure, honte, *f.*

obnox'ious (-nok'sheusse), *adj.*, (hurtful) dangereux, nuisible ; (odious) odieux, désagréable, offensant ; (reprehensible) répréhensible, blâmable ; (liable) sujet, exposé, soumis **à.**

obnox'iously, *adv.*, d'une manière offensante, d'une manière répréhensible ; odieusement.

obnox'iousness, *n.*, odieux, caractère répréhensible, *m.*

ob'olus *ou* **ob'ole** (-ôle), *n.*, obole, *f.*

obrep'tion (-rèp-), *n.*, (jur.) surprise ; obreption, *f.*

obrepti'tious (-rèp-ti-sheusse), *adj.*, (jur.) fait par surprise ; obreptice.

obscene' (-sîne), *adj.*, obscène, sale ; grossier.

obscene'ly, *adv.*, d'une manière obscène ; avec obscénité.

obscene'ness *ou* **obscen'ity**, *n.*, obscénité, *f.*

obscura'tion (-skiou-ré-), *n.*, obscurcissement, *m.* ; (astron.) obscuration, *f.*

obscure' (-skioure), *adj.*, obscur ; de la nuit ; des ténèbres ; caché.

obscure', *v.a.*, obscurcir ; offusquer ; cacher ; éclipser.

obscure'ly, *adv.*, obscurément ; dans l'obscurité.

obscure'ness *ou* **obscur'ity**, *n.*, obscurité, *f.*

ob'secrate (-si-), *v.a.*, (ant.) supplier, conjurer, implorer.

ob'sequies (-si-kwize), *n.pl.*, obsèques, *f.pl.*

obse'quious (-sî-kwi-eusse), *adj.*, soumis ; obéissant ; obséquieux ; officieux.

obse'quiously, *adv.*, avec soumission ; avec obéissance ; obséquieusement.

obse'quiousness, *n.*, soumission ; obéissance servile, basse complaisance, soumission obséquieuse, *f.*

observ'able (-zeurv'a-b'l), *adj.*, remarquable ; digne de remarque ; appréciable ; observable ; sensible.

observ'ably, *adv.*, remarquablement ; d'une manière appréciable ; d'une manière observable.

observ'ance (-zeurv'-), *n.*, (theol.) observance ; pratique, *f.* ; accomplissement ; (respect) respect, *m.* ; observation, *f.* Duties more honored in their breach than in their — ; *devoirs plus souvent négligés que remplis.*

observ'ant (-zeur-), *adj.*, observateur, exact, attentif. — of ; *attentif* **à** ; *attentif à observer,* **à** *pratiquer.* We know how — he was of his master ; *on sait avec quel profond respect il traitait son maître* (*son précepteur*).

observa'tion (-zeur-vé-), *n.*, observation, *f.*

observa'tor (-zeur-vé-), *n.*, observateur, *m.*, observatrice, *f.*

observ'atory (-zeurv'a-), *n.*, observatoire, *m.*

observe' (-zeurve), *v.a.*, observer, remarquer ; (to persons) faire observer, faire remarquer.

observ'er, *n.*, observateur, *m.*

observ'ing, *adj.*, observateur ; attentif.

observ'ingly, *adv.*, attentivement.

obses'sion, *n.*, obsession, *f.*

obsid'ian, *n.*, (miner.) obsidiane, obsidienne, *f.*

obsid'ional, *adj.*, obsidional (of sieges).

obsoles'cence, *n.*, état de ce qui vieillit, *m.*

obsoles'cent, *adj.*, vieillissant, qui vieillit ; (jur.) (of laws) qui tombe en désuétude.

ob'solete (-lîte), *adj.*, vieilli, suranné, vieux ; inusité ; tombé en désuétude.

ob'soleteness, *n.*, état de désuétude, *m.* ; désuétude, *f.*

ob'stacle (-sta-k'l), *n.*, obstacle, empêchement, *m.*

obstet′rio *ou* **obstet′rical** (-stèt′-), *adj.*, (surg.) d'accouchement ; obstétrical.

obstetri′cian (-trish′-), *n.*, accoucheur, *m.*

obstet′rics (stèt′rikse), *n.pl.*, obstétrique, *f. sing.*

ob′stinacy, *n.*, obstination, opiniâtreté, *f. ;* entêtement ; acharnement, *m. ;* (med.) résist-ance, *f. ;* caractère presque incurable, *m.*

ob′stinate, *adj.*, opiniâtre, obstiné ; entier ; acharné ; têtu, entêté ; (med.) rebelle. An — complaint; *une maladie chronique, rebelle.*

ob′stinately, *adv.*, obstinément ; opiniâtré-ment ; avec entêtement ; avec acharnement.

ob′stinateness. *V.* ob′stinacy.

obstipa′tion (-pé-), *n.*, action de boucher ; (med.) constipation, *f.*

obstrep′erous (-strèp′eur′-), *adj.*, turbulent ; tapageur ; très bruyant ; étourdissant.

obstrep′erously, *adv.*, avec turbulence; d'une manière étourdissante ; à grand bruit.

obstrep′erousness, *n.*, grand bruit, *m. ;* tur-bulence, *f.*

obstruct′ (-streuk′te), *v.a.*, empêcher, encom-brer ; fermer ; obstruer ; boucher; barrer ; (fig.) mettre obstacle **à.** A cloud —s the light of the sun ; *un nuage intercepte la lumière du soleil.* To become —ed ; *s'obstruer, s'encombrer, se bou-cher.*

obstruct′er, *n.*, qui met obstacle **à.**

obstruc′tion (-streuk′-), *n.*, empêchement ; encombrement ; embarras ; obstacle, *m. ;* (med.) (parliam.) obstruction, *f.* To cause an — ; (in streets) *gêner la circulation.*

obstruc′tive (-streuk′-), *adj.*, qui empêche, qui obstrue, qui bouche, qui barre ; qui met obstacle **à** ; embarrassant ; (med.) obstructif, opilatif.

obtain′ (-téne), *v.a.*, obtenir **à** ; procurer **à** ; acquérir **pour,** se procurer ; recevoir, gagner ; posséder, tenir. Easily —ed ; *facile à obtenir, à se procurer.*

obtain′, *v.n.*, exister, régner, prévaloir ; s'éta-blir ; s'accréditer, exister, se maintenir ; être gé-néralement reçu, admis.

obtain′able (-′a-b′l), *adj.*, qu'on peut se pro-curer ; à obtenir ; accessible **à.**

obtain′er, *n.*, obtenteur, *m. ;* personne qui ob-tient, *f.*

obtain′ment, *n.*, action d'obtenir ; obtention (l.u.), *f.*

obtrude′ (-troude), *v.a.*, imposer, présenter de force.

obtrude′, *v.n.*, s'imposer ; s'introduire de force ; être importun.

obtrud′er, *n.*, importun, *m.*

obtru′sion (-trou-jeune), *n.*, intrusion, intro-duction forcée ; importunité, *f.*

obtru′sive (-trou-cive), *adj.*, importun.

obtru′sively, *adv.*, d'une manière importune ; avec importunité.

obtuse′ (-tiouce), *adj.*, obtus ; émoussé ; (of sound) sourd.

obtuse′-angled (-tiouce-agn′g′l′de) *ou* **obtus-an′gular** (-agn′ghiou-), *adj.*, (geom.) obtus-angle.

obtuse′ly, *adv.*, d'une manière obtuse ; (stu-pidly) stupidement ; (dully) sourdement.

obtuse′ness, obtu′sion, *n.*, état émoussé, *m.;* stupidité ; (of sound) nature sourde, *f.*

ob′verse (-veurse), *adj.*, (bot.) obcordé, en forme de cœur renversé.

ob′verse, *n.*, (of medals, coins) **face,** *f.;* (print.) recto, *m.*

ob′viate, *v.a.*, obvier **à** ; prévenir.

ob′vious, *adj.*, évident, sensible, clair ; qui saute aux yeux ; qui tombe sous les sens ; visible. It is quite — that he has altered his mind; *il est évident qu'il a changé d'avis.* It is not quite so — as you imagine ; *la chose est loin d'être aussi claire que vous l'imaginez.*

ob′viously, *adv.*, évidemment, clairement.

ob′viousness, *n.*, évidence, clarté, *f.*

occa′sion (-ké-jeune), *n.*, occasion, rencontre; (cause) cause, occasion, *f. ;* sujet, motif ; (need) besoin, *m.*, nécessité, *f.* There is no — for ; *il n'y a pas besoin* **de** ; *il n'est pas besoin* **de.** To profit by the — ; *profiter de l'occasion.* On — ; *dans l'occasion, au besoin.* For the — ; *pour la circonstance.* On this — ; **à** ou **en** *cette occasion, dans cette circonstance.* On the first — ; *à la première occasion.* On another — ; *une autre fois.* On all —s ; *en toute occasion ; en toute rencontre.* What — is there for so much secrecy ? *quelle nécessité y a-t-il d'un si grand secret ?* By — ; *par hasard ; accessoirement.*

occa′sion, *v.a.*, occasionner ; donner lieu **à**, causer, produire; déterminer.

occa′sional, *adj.*, occasionnel, d'occasion ; intermittent, accidentel, casuel, fortuit. Not-withstanding his — prolixity and tediousness, B. is an orator in every sense of the word ; *quoiqu'il soit parfois prolixe et ennuyeux, B. est un orateur dans toute la force du mot.* — visitor ; *personne qui rend visite de temps à autre, f.* — chair ; *chaise de fantaisie, f.* — table ; *table de fantaisie, f.*

occa′sionally, *adv.*, quand l'occasion s'en pré-sente ; par occasion, parfois ; de temps en temps.

occa′sioner, *n.*, cause, *f. ;* auteur, *m.*

oc′cident, *n.*, occident, *m.*

occident′al, *adj.*, occidental.

occip′ital, *adj.*, (anat.) occipital.

oc′ciput (-peute), *n.*, occiput, *m.*

occult′ (-keulte), *adj.*, occulte.

occulta′tion (-té-), *n.*, (astron.) occultation, *f.*

occult′ly, *adv.*, occultement.

occult′ness (-keult′-), *n.*, secret, *m.*

oc′cupancy (ok′kiou-), *n.*, occupation, *f.*

oc′cupant, *n.*, personne qui occupe un lieu, *f.;* possesseur, occupant, *m.*

occupa′tion (ok′kiou-pé-), *n.*, occupation, *f.;* emploi, état, métier, *m.;* (possession) occupation, possession, *f.*

oc′cupier, *n.*, possesseur ; (of houses) habi-tant, *m.*, habitante, *f. ;* (tenant) locataire, *m.f.* First — ; *premier occupant, m.*

oc′cupy (ok′kiou-païe), *v.a.*, occuper ; em-ployer. To be occupied in, with ; *s'occuper* **de, à.**

occur′ (ok′keur), *v.n.*, se présenter, se rencon-trer, s'offrir ; venir à l'esprit, à l'idée ; sur-venir, arriver. A thought —red to me ; *une pen-sée me vint à l'esprit.* An accident has —red to me ; *il m'est arrivé un accident.* Proofs — of public robberies perpetrated by noblemen; *il existe des preuves d'actes de brigandage commis par des nobles.* It —red to me that ; *l'idée m'est venue que; il m'est venu à l'idée que.* It —s to me that ; *j'ai dans l'idée que.* To — again ; *se re-nouveler, se reproduire.* That won't — again ; *cela n'arrivera plus.*

occur′rence (-keur′-), *n.*, occurrence, rencon-tre, *f. ;* événement, incident, fait, accident, *m.* It is of common, ou daily, —; *cela se voit tous les jours.*

o′cean (ô-sha′n), *n.*, océan, *m. ;* (fig.) immen-sité, *f.* He has —s of money ; *il est tout cousu d'or.*

o′cean, *adj.*, de l'océan. — steamer ; *long-courrier transatlantique, m.*

Ocea′nian, *adj.*, océanien, -ne.

ocean′ic (-shî-), *adj.*, océanique.

ocher (ô-keur), *n.*, ocre, *f.*

o′chrea (ô-kri-a), *n.*, (bot.) gaine, *f.*

o′chreous (ô-keur′eusse), *adj.*, ocreux.

oc′tagon, *n.*, octogone, *m.*

octag′onal *ou* **octan′gular**, *adj.*, octogone, octogonal.

octahe′dron (-hî-), *n.*, (geom.) octaèdre, **m.**

octan′dria, *n.*, (bot.) octandrie, *f.*

octan′drian, *adj.*, (bot.) octandre.

oc′tant, *n.*, (astron., opt.) octant, *m.*

oc′tave (-téve), *n.*, octave, *f.*

octa'vo (-té-vô), n., in-octavo, m.

octen'nial, adj., (ant.) de huit ans.

octen'nially, adv., tous les huit ans.

Octo'ber (-tô-beur), n., octobre, m.

octogena'rian (-djè-né-), n., octogénaire, m.f.

oc'togenary, adj., octogénaire.

oc'tosyllable (-cil'la-b'l), n., mot de huit syllabes, mot octosyllabe, m.

oc'tuple (-tiou'p'l), adj., octuple.

oc'ular (ok'iou-), adj., oculaire.

oc'ularly, adv., de ses propres yeux.

oc'ulate (ok'iou-) ou oc'ulated (-lét'-), adj., qui a des yeux ; (fig.) tacheté.

oc'ulist (ok'iou-), n., oculiste, m.

odd, adj., impair ; (surplus) de surplus, de reste, quelques ; (of money) d'appoint ; de reste ; (singular) étrange, singulier ; (droll) bizarre, drôle, original, baroque ; (leisure) perdu ; (not fellows) déparié ; (of books, etc.) dépareillé. — looking ; à la mine bizarre. — moments ; moments perdus, moments de loisir, m.pl. — fish ; drôle de corps, m. Thirty pounds — ; trente et quelques livres.

odd'ity, n., singularité ; bizarrerie, f. ; (pers.) original, m., originale, f. ; travers, m. He is a great — ; c'est un original s'il en fut jamais.

odd'ly, adv., étrangement, singulièrement ; bizarrement.

odd'ness, n., singularité ; étrangeté ; bizarrerie, f.

odds (odze), n., (inequality) inégalité, disparité, f. ; (advantage) avantage, m., supériorité ; (probability) probabilité, f. ; chances, chances contraires, f.pl. ; (quarrel) dispute, querelle, f., différend, m. At — ; en querelle. To set at — ; brouiller. To have the — against one ; avoir affaire à plus fort que soi ; avoir toutes les chances contre soi. — and ends ; petits bouts, fragments, m.pl. ; bribes, f.pl. Little — and ends ; petites choses sans valeur. The — are ; il y a à parier (que with indicative). In the face of such — ; avec toutes les chances contre lui. Against such tremendous — ; contre des forces si supérieures.

ode (ôde), n , ode, f.

ode'on (ô-dî-), n., odéon, m.

o'dious (ô-di-), adj., odieux, détestable.

o'diously, adv., odieusement.

o'diousness, n., nature odieuse, f. ; odieux, m. The — of the thing ; l'odieux de la chose.

o'dium (ô-), n., odieux, m., fiel, haine, f. To cast, ou throw, — upon ; rendre odieux.

odom'eter (-'i-teur), n., odomètre, compte-pas, m.

odontal'gia ou odontal'gy (ô-do'n-tal'dji-a, -dji), n., (med.) odontalgie, f.

odontal'gic, adj., odontalgique, m.

odon'toid (-toïde), adj., (anat.) odontoïde.

odontol'ogy (-tol'o-dji), n., (anat.) odontologie, f.

odorif'erous, adj., odorant, odoriférant.

odorif'erously, adv., avec une odeur suave.

odorif'erousness, n., parfum, m.

o'dorous, adj., odorant.

o'dor (ô-deur), n., odeur, senteur, f. ; parfum ; (of wine) bouquet ; (of meat, etc.) fumet, m. In bad — ; en mauvaise odeur, en défaveur.

o'dorless, adj., inodore ; sans odeur.

œcon'omy. V. econ'omy.

œcumen'ical (êk'iou-mè'n-), adj., œcuménique, œcuménique.

œcumen'ically (-'îk-), adv., œcuméniquement, œcuméniquement.

œde'ma (î-dî-), n., (med.) œdème, m.

œsoph'agus (î-çof'-), n., (anat.) œsophage, m.

of (ove), prep., de. — late ; dernièrement. — all things ; entre, par-dessus toutes choses. On the first — July ; le premier juillet. To consist —; consister en. That 's — course ; cela va sans dire. The Gauls — old ; les Gaulois des anciens temps ; les anciens Gaulois. It is very stupid —

you ; c'est bien sot de votre part. It is very good — you ; c'est bien aimable à vous, ou de votre part. — old ; autrefois. The best — men ; le meilleur des hommes. — one's self ; de soi même.

off (ôf), adv., adj., loin ; de distance ; (paint.) avec relief ; (broken off) rompu, manqué, cessé ; (separated) de dessus, séparé, enlevé ; (nav.) au large. We are but poorly — ; nous ne sommes guère à l'aise. The house is a mile — ; la maison est à un mille de distance. — and on ; avec interruption ; de temps à autre ; par boutades. — with that ; ôtez, ou enlevez, cela. — with him ; emmenez-le. I am — ; je m'en vais, je file. Hats —! chapeaux bas! To be well, badly — ; être bien, mal, dans ses affaires, heureux, malheureux. To be — color ; (fig.) n'être pas dans son assiette. Fifty yards — ; à cinquante pas. — goes B. ; voilà B. parti. They're — ; les voilà partis ; ils sont partis. He lives two miles — ; il demeure à deux milles d'ici. I'll go farther — ; j'irai plus loin. To put — ; remettre, ajourner. To tear — ; arracher. To cut — ; trancher ; amputer. The pain goes — ; le mal s'en va. — and on ; à bâtons rompus ; par intervalles. The engagement is — ; l'engagement est rompu. The match is — ; le mariage est rompu. To come — ; s'échapper. To go — ; partir. To take — ; jouer, imiter, contrefaire. Hands—! à bas les mains! n'y touchez pas! — with you ; allez vous promener ; allez vous coucher. You come — cheap ; vous en êtes quitte à bon marché.

off, adj., le plus éloigné ; (man.) hors main. — day ; jour de liberté, m. — time ; temps libre, m. — side ; côté droit ; (riding) hors montoir.

off, prep., (nav.) à la hauteur de, devant, au large de. All this he did — the said farm ; tout cela il le fit des revenus de la dite ferme. One must not take one's eye — one's book ; il ne faut pas ôter les yeux de dessus son livre. The ship was — the port ; le vaisseau était devant le port, ou au large du port. — one's head ; éperdu, fou, détraqué. To dine — boiled beef ; dîner de bouilli. Take the cloth — the table ; ôtez la nappe de dessus la table. — the hinges ; hors des gonds.

of'fal, n., abattis, m. ; issues, f.pl. ; reste de viande, m. ; chair grossière, f. ; (refuse) rebut, m. ; (carrion) charogne, f.

off'cut (-keute), n., (print.) petit carton de feuilles, m.

offend', v.a., offenser, choquer ; outrager, violer, blesser ; scandaliser, fâcher, déplaire à ; (to transgress) violer, enfreindre, transgresser.

offend', v.n., déplaire ; commettre une offense ; commettre un péché ; se scandaliser. To — against ; nuire à.

offend'er, n., offenseur, coupable ; pécheur ; (jur.) contrevenant, délinquant, criminel, m. An old — ; coutumier du fait ; repris de justice, récidiviste, m.

offense', n., offense, f. ; outrage, m. ; injure, infraction, f. ; (jur.) atteinte, contravention, violation de la loi et du droit, f., délit, crime ; (scandal) scandale, m. ; (attack) attaque, agression, f. Indictable — ; fait qualifié crime, ou délit, m. Capital — ; crime capital, m. Arms of — ; armes offensives, f.pl. To commit an — against ; faire outrage à ; (jur.) porter atteinte à. To take — ; se formaliser, s'offenser de. To give — ; choquer, offenser, blesser ; déplaire à ; faire outrage à.

offen'sive, adj., offensant ; injurieux ; désagréable ; choquant, blessant ; (assailant) offensif. — weapons ; armes offensives, f.pl.

offen'sive, n., offensive, f. To act on the — ; prendre l'offensive.

offen'sively, adv., d'une manière offensante, injurieuse, blessante ; (attack) offensivement.

offen'siveness, n., nature offensante, blessante, choquante, injurieuse, f.

of'fer, v.a., offrir, présenter, proposer à. To — violence ; faire violence à. To — one's self, itself ; *s'offrir, se présenter.* To — resistance ; *résister* à, *faire résistance* à.

of'fer, *v.n.*, s'offrir, se présenter à ; faire l'offre **de** ; offrir **de** ; (to attempt) essayer **de**, vouloir. To — to ; *faire l'offre* **de**, *offrir* **de**.

of'fer, *n.*, offre, *f.* ; propositions de mariage, *f.pl.* ; (attempt) tentative, *f.* ; essai, *m.* On — ; *à vendre* ; *en vente.*

of'ferable (of'feur-a-b'l), *adj.*, que l'on peut offrir, présentable ; qui peut s'offrir.

of'ferer, *n.*, personne qui offre, *f.* ; (worship) sacrificateur, *m.*

of'fering, *n.*, offrande, *f.*, présent ; sacrifice, *m.*

of'fertory (-feur-), *n.*, (prayer) offertoire, *m.*, offerte ; (collection) quête, *f.*

off'-hand, *adv.*, d'abord ; au premier abord, d'abondance, sans réflexion, sur-le-champ, sans préparation, couramment, sans peine ; cavalièrement.

off'-hand, *adj.*, tranchant, cru, brusque, sans cérémonie, dégagé, libre, cavalier.

off'-handed, *adj.*, sans façon, sans gêne, grossier.

off'-handedness, *n.*, grossièreté, sans façon, sans gêne.

of'fice, *n.*, (service) office, service ; (duty) devoir ; (employment) emploi, ministère, *m.*, charge, *f.*, fonctions, *f.pl.* ; (power) pouvoir, *m.*, place, *f.* ; (apartment) bureau, (private) cabinet, *m.* ; (of lawyers) étude, *f.* ; (rel.) office, *m.* pl. (of a house) offices, *f.pl.* ; (out-houses) communs, *m.pl.* The cares of — ; *le souci des affaires.* A jack in — ; *un petit employé.* In — ; *en place.* Holy — ; *le Saint-Office*, *m.*, *l'Inquisition*, *f.* — bell ; *sonnette de table*, *f.* —holder ; *fonctionnaire*, *m.* — hours ; *heures de bureau*, *f.pl.* — requisites ; *fournitures de bureau*, *f.pl.*

of'ficer, *n.*, officier ; (of state) dignitaire ; (of the government) fonctionnaire ; (of justice, of police) agent ; (of a court) huissier. Staff — ; *officier d'état-major*, *m.* Field — ; *officier supérieur*, *m.* Non-commissioned — ; *sous-officier*, *m.*

of'ficer, *v.a.*, fournir des officiers à.

of'ficered (of'fi-ceurde), *adj.*, commandé ; pourvu d'officiers. His army was better — than that of the allies ; *son armée était mieux commandée*, ou *pourvue de meilleurs officiers, que celle des alliés.*

offi'cial (-fish'al), *n.*, fonctionnaire ; (ecc.) official, *m.*

offi'cial, *adj.*, officiel, public.

offi'cially, *adv.*, officiellement.

offi'cialty, *n.*, officialité, *f.*

offi'ciate (of-fish'i-), *v.n.*, exercer ses fonctions ; exercer ; (in place of worship) officier.

offi'ciate, *v.a.*, donner, conférer.

offi'ciating, *adj.*, qui fait ses fonctions ; (ecc.) officiant, desservant.

offici'nal, *adj.*, (pharm.) officinal.

offi'cious (-sheusse), *adj.*, officieux ; importun ; (kind) bienveillant.

offi'ciously (-sheus'-), *adv.*, officieusement ; d'une manière importune, importunément ; (kindly) avec bienveillance ; complaisamment.

offi'ciousness, *n.*, empressement ; zèle officieux, *m.*

off'ing, *n.*, (nav.) large, *m.* In the —; *au large, dans la rade.*

off'scouring (-skaour'-), *n.*, rebut, *m.*

off'scum, *n.*, rebut, *m.* ; écume, *f.*

off'set, *n.*, (hort.) rejeton, œilleton, *m.* ; (com.) compensation, *f.*

off'shoot, *n.*, rejeton, *m.* ; (of trees) œilleton, *m.*

off'-side (-saïde), *n.*, (man.) hors main ; côté droit, *m.*

off'spring, *n.*, enfant, *m.* ; enfants, *m.pl.* ; descendant, *m.* ; descendants, *m.pl.* ; progéniture, race, postérité, *f.* ; (fig.) fruit, produit, *m.*

off'-take (-téke), *n.*, (mines) galerie d'écoulement, *f.*

---

off'ward (-wŏrde), *adv.*, vers le large, vers la mer.

oft, **of'ten** (of'f'n), **of'tentimes** (-taï'm'ze), *ou* **oft'times**, *adv.*, souvent.

ogee' (o-djî), *n.*, (arch.) cymaise, *f.*, talon, *m.*

o'gival, *adj.*, ogival.

o'give (o-djive), *n.*, (arch.) ogive, *f.*

o'gle (ô-g'l), *n.*, œillade, *f.*

o'gle, *v.a.*, lorgner ; lancer des œillades à ; reluquer ; faire les yeux doux à.

o'gler, *n.*, lorgneur, *m.*, lorgneuse, *f.*

o'gling, *n.*, lorgnerie, *f.* ; œillades, *f.pl.*

o'gre (ô-gheur), *n.*, ogre, *m.*

o'gress, *n.*, ogresse, *f.*

oh ! *int.*, oh !

oil (oïl), *n.*, huile, essence, *f.* —cruet ; *burette à l'huile, f.* In —s ; (paint.) *à l'huile.*

oil, *v.a.*, huiler ; (fig., of the tongue) délier.

oil'bag, *n.*, (orni.) glande oléifère, *f.*

oil'-baize, *n.*, toile cirée, *f.*

oil'cake, *n.*, (agri.) tourteau, *m.*

oil'-case (-kéce), *n.*, toile cirée (pour vêtement), *f.*

oil'-cloth (-cloth), *n.*, toile cirée (pour meuble), *f.*

oil-col'or (-keul'eur), *n.*, couleur à l'huile, *f.*

oil'iness, *n.*, onctuosité ; nature huileuse, *f.*

oil'-lamp, *n.*, lampe à huile, *f.*

oil'man, *n.*, marchand d'huile, *m.*

oil'-mill, *n.*, huilerie, *f.*

oil'nut (-neute), *n.*, (bot.) noix de ben, *f.*

oil'nut-tree (-trî), *n.*, ricin, palmachristi, *m.*

oil'-plant, *n.*, plante oléagineuse, *f.*

oil'-press, *n.*, pressoir à l'huile, *m.*

oil'-shop, *n.*, boutique de marchand de couleurs, *f.*

oil'-silk, *n.*, taffetas gommé, *m.*

oil'-skin, *n.*, toile vernie, *f.* ; (of a hat) coiffe en toile, *f.*

oil'-spring, *n.*, source de pétrole, *f.*

oil'-trade, *n.*, commerce des huiles, *m.*

oil'-works, *n.*, huilerie, *f.*

oil'y, *adj.*, huileux, (fig.) oléagineux, onctueux.

oint'ment (oï'n't'-), *n.*, onguent, *m.*

old (ôlde), *adj.*, vieux, vieil ; âgé ; ancien, antique. How— are you ? *quel âge avez-vous ?* I am ten years — ; *j'ai dix ans*. At ten years — ; *à l'âge de dix ans.* —enough to ; *en âge de, d'âge* à. Ten years — ; *âgé de dix ans.* The — world ; *l'ancien monde, m.* An — man ; *un vieillard, un vieux, un vieil homme* ; *un homme vieux.* — people ; *vieillards, m.pl.* ; *vieilles gens, f.pl.* An — shoe ; *un vieux soulier.* To grow — ; *vieillir.* The —est ; *le plus âgé* ; *le doyen d'âge.* Of — ; *anciennement.* The brave days of — ; *le bon vieux temps.* A perfect specimen of — ; *un parfait spécimen du bon vieux temps.* That story is as — as the hills ; *cette histoire-là est vieille comme les rues.* — book ; *bouquin, m.* How— do you take me to be ? *quel âge me donnez-vous ?* —as the hills ; *vieux comme le monde, comme le Pont-Neuf, comme les rues.* — birds are not to be caught with chaff ; (prov.) *on ne prend pas les vieux merles à la pipée.* — dog will learn no tricks ; (prov.) *qui jeune n'apprend, rien ne saura.* — wives' tales ; *des contes à dormir debout.*

old'en (ôld'n), *adj.*, vieux, ancien.

old-estab'lished, *adj.*, ancien, fondé depuis longtemps.

old-fash'ioned, *adj.*, suranné ; du bon vieux temps ; à l'ancienne mode, passé de mode, démodé ; (pers.) de vieille roche. An — spring ; *un ressort vieux modèle.*

old'ish, *adj.*, un peu vieux, d'un certain âge, vieillot, -te.

old'ness, *n.*, vieillesse, *f.* ; âge avancé, *m.*, antiquité ; ancienneté ; vétusté, *f.*

oleag'inous (ô-li-adj'-), *adj.*, oléagineux.

oleag'inousness, *n.*, nature oléagineuse, *f.*

olean'der (ô-li-), n., (bot.) laurier-rose, oléandre, m.

olfac'tory, adj., olfactif.

olib'anum, n., oliban, encens, m.

oligarch'al, **oligarch'ic**, ou **oligarch'ical** (-gărk'-), adj., oligarchique.

ol'igarchy (-gărki), n., oligarchie, f.

o'lio (ô-li-ô), n., (cook.) oille, olla podrida, f. ; (mus.) recueil d'airs, m. ; (fig.) pot-pourri, m., macédoine, olla podrida, f.

oliva'ceous, adj., olivacé.

ol'ivary, adj., olivaire, en forme d'olive.

ol'ive, n., olive, f. — -tree ; olivier, m. — -yard, ou garden ; jardin des olives, m. Mount of —s ; Mont des Oliviers, m. — complexion ; teint olivâtre, m. — color ; couleur olive, f. — grove ; olivaie, f. — green ; vert olive, m. — season ; olivaison, f. — shaped ; oliviforme.

olym'piad, n., olympiade, f.

Olym'pian, adj., olympien ; Olympique.

olym'pic, adj., Olympique.

olym'pics, n.pl., jeux Olympiques, m.pl.

Olym'pus, n., Olympe, m.

om'bre (ô'm'beur), n., (game) hombre, m.

omeg'a (ô-mè-), n., oméga, m.

om'elet (o'm'léte), n., omelette, f.   [tic, m.

o'men (ô-mè'ne), n., augure, présage, pronos-**o'mened** (ô-mè'n'de), adj., d'augure. Ill—; de mauvais augure.

omen'tum (o'mè'n'-), n., (anat.) épiploon, m.

om'inous (o'm'-), adj., de mauvais présage ; de mauvais augure ; sinistre.

om'inously, adv., de mauvais augure.

om'inousness, n., mauvais augure, caractère sinistre.

omis'sible (-si-b'l), adj., qui peut être omis.

omis'sion (-mish'-), n., omission, f., oubli, m.

omis'sive, adj., qui commet des omissions, oublieux.

omit', v.a., omettre ; négliger, oublier.

omit'tance, n., (ant.) omission, f. But that 's all one ; — is no quittance ; mais c'est tout un ; silence n'est pas quittance.

om'nibus (-beusse), n., (omnibuses) omnibus, m. — conductor ; conducteur d'omnibus, m. — driver ; cocher d'omnibus, m. Motor —; autobus, m.

omnifa'rious (-fé-), adj., de toutes sortes ; varié.

omnip'otence, n., omnipotence, toute-puissance, f.

omnip'otent, adj., tout-puissant, omnipotent.
Omnip'otent, n., Tout-Puissant, m.

omnip'otently, adv., avec omnipotence, avec toute-puissance.

omnipres'ence (-prèz'-), n., présence universelle ; ubiquité, f.

omnipres'ent (-prèz'-), adj., universellement présent ; ubiquitaire.

omnis'cience (-nish'-), n., (theol.) omniscience, f.

omnis'cient, adj., (theol.) omniscient ; qui sait tout.

om'nium, n., (stock-exch.) omnium, m. — gatherum ; (of things) fouillis, fatras ; (of persons) ramassis, m.

omniv'orous, adj., omnivore.

o'moplate, n., (anat.) omoplate, f.

on, prep., sur ; à; de ; en ; lors **de**, en conséquence **de**. — foot ; à pied. — high ; en haut, là haut. — horseback ; à cheval. — purpose ; à dessein, exprès, de parti pris. — that day ; ce jour-là. — the left ; à gauche. — the right ; à droite. — the table ; sur la table. — my honor ; sur mon honneur. Loss — loss ; perte sur perte. — credit ; à crédit. A ring — the finger ; une bague au doigt. — one ; sur soi. To play — the piano (etc.) ; jouer du piano. — Monday ; lundi. — such journeys ; à l'occasion de pareils voyages. — a fine day ; par un beau jour.

— further inquiry ; après plus ample information, ou plus amples renseignements. To deliberate — it ; en délibérer. — the whole ; au total ; en somme, à tout prendre. — such an occasion ; en pareille circonstance ou à une telle occasion. To rely — a person for help ; compter sur l'assistance de quelqu'un. Peace was settled — favorable terms ; la paix fut conclue à des conditions favorables. — thy life ; au péril de ta vie. A curse — him ; qu'il soit maudit ou maudit soit-il. To have pity — a person ; avoir pitié d'une personne. He was — the Times ; il appartenait à la rédaction du Times ; il écrivait pour le Times. — fire ; en flammes. — hand ; entre les mains ; (com.) en magasin. — the way ; en chemin ; chemin faisant. — the wing ; au vol ; en train de voler ou de partir. — my arrival in Paris, à mon arrivée à Paris. — entering ; en entrant. — examination ; après examen.

on, adv., dessus ; (forward) en avant, avant, avancé ; (continuation) toujours ; (succession) de suite. Read —; lisez toujours. — ! en avant ! Far — in the night ; bien avant dans la nuit. And so —; et ainsi de suite. Play —; continuez de jouer. To live —; exister encore ; continuer d'exister. To be —; avoir fait un pari ; (of drink) être lancé. He entered with his hat —; il entra le chapeau sur la tête. With one's shoes, boots, gloves —; chaussé, botté, ganté.

on'ager (o'n'a-djeur), n., (mam.) onagre, m.

once (weu'n'ce), adv., une fois ; autrefois ; jadis. At —; sur le champ, tout de suite. — upon a time ; une fois. — for all ; une fois pour toutes. — in a way ; une fois par hasard ; de temps à autre. — for all ; une fois pour toutes ; une bonne fois. — before ; une première fois. This —; pour cette fois. All at —; tout d'un coup, tout à coup. — I knew how to sing ; autrefois je savais chanter. — bit twice shy ; (prov.) bien fin qui me rattrapera. When —; quand, lorsque, une fois, une fois que.

one (weu'ne), adj., un, m., une, f. ; un seul, m. ; unique ; seul, un certain, un nommé, un sieur. — man ; un homme. Like — man ; comme un seul homme. — man ; — vote ; un suffrage, une voix par personne. He has but — child ; il n'a qu'un seul enfant. There is — Charles ; il y a un certain Charles. — by —; un à un. At —; uni, d'accord, réconcilié(s). It is all —; c'est la même chose ; cela revient au même ; c'est tout un ; c'est égal. It is all — to me what he does or says ; peu m'importe ce qu'il fait ou dit ; ce qu'il fait ou dit m'est bien égal. — and all; tous jusqu'au dernier.

one, pron., on, l'on ; celui, m., celle, f. ; quelqu'un ; un homme, m., une femme, f. — sees that every day ; on voit cela, cela se voit, tous les jours. He is — who ; c'est un homme qui. He is the — who ; c'est celui qui. A good thing and a bad —; une bonne chose et une mauvaise. Any —; quelqu'un ; le premier venu, tout le monde ; qui que ce soit ; personne ; n'importe qui. Some —; quelqu'un. No —; personne. Every —; chacun ; tout le monde. Every — of you ; tous tant que vous êtes. — another ; l'un l'autre, l'une l'autre ; les uns les autres, les unes les autres. The great —s of the earth ; les grands de la terre. — of themselves ; un des leurs. It is —; c'en est un (ou une). The inspiration fell upon — in whom . . . ; l'inspiration tomba sur un homme chez qui . . . That makes — shudder ; cela fait frémir (V. Hugo). To talk about — thing and another ; causer de choses et d'autres. The little —s ; les petits, m.pl. — by one ; l'un après l'autre. — with another ; l'un dans l'autre. It does — good to hear him ; cela fait du bien de l'entendre. — with another ; (average) l'un dans l'autre, l'un portant l'autre.

one-armed', adj., manchot.

one-eyed' (weu'n'aïe'de), adj., borgne.

one'ness (weu'n'-), *n.*, unité ; individualité, *f.*

on'erous (-'eur'-), *adj.*, onéreux.

on'erousness, *n.*, poids, *m.*, charge, *f.*

one's self' (weu'n'ze-), *pron.*, soi-même ; se.

one'-sid'ed, *adj.*, à un seul côté, qui n'a qu'un côté ; (fig.) partial, exclusif.

one-sid'edness, partialité, *f.*, exclusivisme, *m.*

on'ion, *n.*, ognon, oignon, *m.* — bed; *oignon-nière, f.* —peel; *pelure d'ognon, f.* — sauce; *sauce Soubise, f.* — seed ; *graine d'ognon, f.*

on'ly (ô'n'-), *adj.*, seul ; unique.

on'ly, *adv.*, seulement ; uniquement ; ne . . . que ; mais ; avec cette différence **que**. — yesterday; *hier encore ; pas plus tard que hier.* — think ! *songez un peu !* — see ! *voyez un peu ! voyez donc !* If —; *pour peu que (subj.).* He — sleeps when he is sleepy ; *il ne dort que quand il a sommeil.* It — angers him the more ; *cela ne fait que l'irriter davantage.*

onomatopœ'ia (-pi-ya), *n.*, (gram.) onomatopée, *f.*

on'set, *n.*, commencement, début ; abord ; premier choc ; (attack) assaut, *m.*, attaque, charge, *f.* At the first —; *d'emblée.*

on'slaught (-slôte), *n.*, attaque, *f.* ; assaut, *m.*

ontolog'ic *ou* **ontolog'ical** (-o-dj'-), *adj.*, ontologique.

ontol'ogist (-djiste), *n.*, ontologiste, *m.*

ontol'ogy (-dji), *n.*, ontologie, *f.*

o'nus (ô-), *n.*, (onera) fardeau, poids ; devoir, *m.* ; obligation, *f.*

on'ward (-wôrde), *adv.*, en avant ; plus loin ; progressivement.

on'ward, *adj.*, qui conduit en avant ; avancé ; progressif. To go —; *avancer, s'avancer.*

o'nyx (ô-nikse), *n.*, (min.) onyx, *m.*

o'olite (ô-o-laïte), *n.*, (geol.) oolithe, *f.*

oolit'ic (ô-o-lit'-), *adj.*, oolithique.

ooze (ouze), *n.*, vase, *f.* ; limon, *m.*, vase, *f.* Atlantic —; *vase de l'Atlantique, f.*

ooze, *v.n.*, suinter, s'écouler, filtrer ; (fig.) transpirer, s'ébruiter. A secret —s out ; *un secret s'ébruite.* His courage —d out at his fingers' ends ; *son courage s'évanouit, disparut.* His name had —d out ; *on avait su son nom* (V. Hugo).

ooz'ing, *n.*, suintement, *m.* ; filtration, *f.* ; (fig.) ébruitement, *m.*

ooz'y, *adj.*, vaseux, limoneux.

opac'ity, *n.*, opacité ; (fig.) obscurité, *f.*

o'pal (ô-), *n.*, (min.) opale, *f.*

o'paline, *adj.*, d'opale, opalin.

opaque' (-péke), *adj.*, opaque ; (fig.) obscur.

opaque'ness, *n.*, opacité, *f.*

o'pen (ô-p'n), *v.a.*, ouvrir ; (a bottle) déboucher ; (to explain) expliquer, entamer ; (to reveal) révéler, exposer ; (a letter) ouvrir, décacheter ; déplier ; (a package) défaire ; (a street) percer. To — one's legs; *écarter les jambes.* To — the pleadings; *ouvrir les débats.* To — fire; *commencer le feu.*

o'pen, *v.n.*, s'ouvrir ; (to begin to appear) se découvrir. These flowers are beginning to —; *ces fleurs commencent à s'épanouir.* This door —s on the garden ; *cette porte donne sur le jardin, ouvre sur le jardin.*

o'pen, *adj.*, ouvert ; à découvert ; nu, à nu, (of the weather) doux; (print.) blanc; (frank) franc, sincère, ouvert ; (fig.) exposé, en butte à ; (of a question) non résolu, à décider; (mus.) vide. — -handed ; *libéral, généreux.* — -hearted ; *qui a le cœur sur la main ; franc, sincère.* — heartedly ; *franchement.* — -heartedness ; *franchise, f.* — weather ; *temps doux, m.* — -eyed ; *vigilant.* — -mouthed ; *la bouche ouverte, bouche béante.* — to an engagement ; *libre pour un engagement, en position d'accepter.* — ; *disposé à écouter.* — work ; *ouvrage à claire-voie, ouvrage à jour.* Half —; *entr'ouvert.* Wide —; *tout grand ouvert.* The — air ; *le grand air.* In the — ; (of

country) *en pleine, ou rase, campagne.* In the — air ; *en plein air ; à la belle étoile.* In the — sea; *en pleine mer.* I am — to any reasonable offer ; *je suis prêt à accepter toute offre raisonnable.* I am — to argument ; *je suis disposé à écouter les raisons contraires.*

o'pener, *n.*, personne qui ouvre, qui entame la discussion, *f.*; ouvreur, *m.*, ouvreuse, *f.*; interprète, *m.*

o'pening, *adj.*, premier. The — chapter; *le premier chapitre.*

o'pening, *n.*, ouverture, *f.* ; commencement ; début, *m.* ; chance de réussite ; (in clouds, fogs, forests, etc.) éclaircie, *f.*; (at play) début ; (com.) débouché, *m.*

o'penly, *adv.*, ouvertement ; sincèrement, franchement, sans détour.

o'penness, *n.*, situation ouverte; (of the weather) douceur ; (frankness) franchise, sincérité, candeur, *f.*; (unreservedness) abandon, *m.*; (clearness) clarté, évidence, *f.*

op'era (o'peur'a), *n.*, opéra, *m.* — -goer; *habitué de l'opéra, m.* — -glass ; *lorgnette, jumelle de théâtre, f.* — -hat ; *claque, m.* — -house ; *opéra, m.*, *salle d'opéra, f.* — -cloak ; *sortie de bal, f.* — night ; *jour d'opéra, m.* — -writer ; *parolier, librettiste, m.*

op'erate (op'eur'-), *v.n.*, opérer, agir ; avoir son effet. To — for a rise, for a fall ; (com:) *jouer à la hausse, à la baisse.*

operat'ic, *adj.*, d'opéra ; lyrique.

op'erating, *adj.*, qui opère, opératif. — room ; (hospitals) *amphithéâtre, m.* — surgeon ; *chirurgien opérant ; opérateur, m.*

opera'tion (op'eur'â-), *n.*, opération ; action, *f.* ; effet, *m.*

op'erative (op-eur'a-), *adj.*, manuel ; ouvrier ; des ouvriers ; (efficacious) actif, efficace.

op'erative, *n.*, artisan, ouvrier, *m.*

op'erator (op'eur-é-teur), *n.*, personne qui opère ; chose qui opère, *f.* ; agent ; (com.) (for a rise, for a fall) joueur à la hausse, à la baisse ; (surg.) opérateur, *m.*

oper'cular (o-peur-kiou-), *adj.*, (bot.) operculé.

oper'culate *ou* **oper'culated**, *adj.*, (bot.) operculé.

oper'culum (-peur-kiou-), *n.*, (bot.) opercule, *m.*

oph'ite (ô-faïte), *n.*, (geol.) ophite, marbre ophite, marbre serpentin, *m.* ; serpentine, *f.*

ophthal'mia *ou* **oph'thalmy** (-thal-), *n.*, (med.) ophtalmie, *f.*

ophthal'mic (-thal-), *adj.*, (med.) ophtalmique.

o'piate (ô-), *n.*, opiat, électuaire, *m.*

o'piate (ô-), *adj.*, (med.) narcotique, soporifique ; (fig.) qui endort.

opine' (-païne), *v.n.*, opiner ; être d'avis ; penser.

opin'ion (-pi'n'yeune), *n.*, opinion, *f.*, avis, sentiment ; jugement, *m.* ; idée, pensée ; (counsel's) consultation, *f.* That's a matter of —; *c'est une affaire d'opinion.* To give one's —; *donner son opinion, son avis* **sur.** To have a high — of ; *avoir une haute opinion, ou idée,* **de.** To be of — that ; *être d'avis que.* To be of the — of ; *être de l'avis* **de.** To be entirely of the — of ; *être entièrement de l'avis* **de** ; *abonder dans le sens* **de.** To state one's —; *dire son avis, son sentiment, sa pensée.* In the — of ; *selon l'opinion* **de.** In my —; *à mon avis.* To take counsel's —; *consulter un avocat.*

opin'ionated, *adj.*, opiniâtre, entêté, obstiné ; suffisant.

opin'ionative, *adj.*, (l.u.) opiniâtre, entêté, obstiné ; suffisant.

opin'ionatively, *adv.*, opiniâtrément, obstinément ; avec suffisance.

opin'ionativeness, *n.*, (l.u.) opiniâtreté, *f.* ; entêtement, *m.* ; suffisance, *f.*

opin'ioned (-pi'n'yeu'n'de), *adj.*, plein de soi-même ; suffisant.

opin'ionist, *n.*, (ant.) personne suffisante, *f.*

o'pium (ô-), *n.*, opium, *m.*

opobal'sam (-bôl-), *n.*, baume de la Mecque, *m.*

opodel'doc, *n.*, opodeldoch, *m.*

opos'sum, *n.*, (mam.) opossum, *m.; sarigue, m.* and *f.*

oppo'nent (-pô-), *n.*, antagoniste, opposant, adversaire ; concurrent, rival, *m.*

opportune' (-tioune), *adj.*, opportun ; à propos.

opportune'ly, *adv.*, à propos; en temps opportun.

opportune'ness, *n.*, opportunité, *f. ;* à propos, *m.*

op'portunist, *n.*, opportuniste, *m.*

opportu'nity, *n.*, occasion, opportunité, *f.* To take, *ou* seize, an — ; *saisir, profiter d'une occasion favorable.* — makes the thief ; *l'occasion fait le larron.*

oppose' (op-pôze), *v.a.*, opposer, s'opposer à; résister à; combattre; arrêter; empêcher. To — a rival for a prize ; *concourir avec un rival pour un prix.*

oppose', *v.n.*, s'opposer ; faire des objections.

oppos'er, *n.* *V.* **opponent**.

op'posite (op-po-zite), *adj.*, opposé; vis-à-vis **de**; en face **de**; (contrary) opposé, contraire. On the — side of the river ; *de l'autre côté de la rivière.* The — sex; *l'autre sexe, m.*

op'positely, *adv.*, en face **de** ; à l'opposite **de**; (adversely) en sens opposé.

op'positeness, *n.*, situation opposée, *f.; état opposé ou contraire, m.*

opposi'tion (-zish'eune), *n.*, situation opposée ; opposition ; (competition) concurrence, *f.;* (obstacle) obstacle, empêchement, *m.; (resist-ance)* résistance ; (repugnance) répugnance, *f.* In — to ; *par opposition à.* To be in the — ; *être de l'opposition.*

oppress', *v.a.*, opprimer ; oppresser ; écraser ; accabler ; (of heat) suffoquer ; (med.) oppresser.

oppres'sion (-prèsh'-), *n.*, oppression, *f.;* (suppression) accablement, abattement, *m.;* (med.) oppression, *f.* — of the heart; *serrement de cœur, m.*

oppres'sive, *adj.*, accablant, oppressif.

oppres'sively, *adv.*, oppressivement, d'une manière oppressive ; avec accablement.

oppres'siveness, *n.*, caractère oppressif, *m.;* nature accablante, *f.*

oppres'sor, *n.*, oppresseur, *m.*

oppro'brious (-prô-), *adj.*, infamant ; injurieux ; outrageant ; d'opprobre.

oppro'briously, *adv.*, avec opprobre ; d'une manière outrageante.

oppro'briousness, *n.*, nature infamante, infamie, *f.;* opprobre, *m.*

oppro'brium (-prô-), *n.*, opprobre, *f.*

op'tative (op-té-), *adj.*, (gram.) optatif. — mood ; (gram.) *optatif, m.*

op'tic, *n.*, œil, *m.*

op'tic *ou* **op'tical**, *adj.*, optique ; d'optique.

op'tically, *adv.*, par l'optique.

opti'cian (-tish'-), *n.*, opticien, *m.*

op'tics, *n.pl.*, optique, *f.*

op'timism, *n.*, optimisme, *m.*

op'timist, *n.*, optimiste, *m.,f.*

op'tion (op'sheune), *n.*, option, faculté, *f. ;* choix, *m. ;* faculté d'opter ; (com.) différence de report (on Change), *f.*

op'tional, *adj.*, laissé au choix ; facultatif ; loisible.

op'tionally, *adv.*, facultativement.

op'ulence (op'iou-), *n.*, opulence ; richesse, *f.*

op'ulent, *adj.*, opulent, riche.

op'ulently, *adv.*, opulemment, avec opulence.

opus'cle (ô-peus's'l) *ou* **opus'cule** (-kioule), *n.*, opuscule, *m.*

or, *conj.*, ou ; (negatively) ni. — **else** ; *ou, ou bien, autrement.* **Either you — he ; *ou vous ou lui.***

or, *n.*, (her.) or, *m.*

or'ache, *n.*, (bot.) arroche, *f.*

or'acle (or'a-k'l), *n.*, oracle, *m.* To work the — ; (fig.) *savoir manœuvrer ; faire agir son influence, arriver à ses fins (par stratagème).*

orac'ular, *adj.*, qui rend des oracles ; d'un ton d'oracle ; d'oracle ; dogmatique ; magistral.

or'al (ô-), *adj.*, oral.

or'ally, *adv.*, oralement.

or'ange (- a'n'dje), *n.*, orange, couleur orange, *f.* —**tree**; *oranger, m.* —**house**; *orangerie, f.* —**peel** ; *écorce d'orange, f.* Seville — ; *bigarade ; orange amère, f.*

or'angeade, *n.*, orangeade, *f.*

or'ange-col'ored (-keul'leurde), *adj.*, orange; couleur d'orange, orangé.

or'ange-flow'er (-flaour), *n.*, fleur d'oranger, fleur d'orange, *f.* — water; *eau de fleur d'oran-ger, f.*

or'ange-man, *n.*, marchand d'oranges ; (Eng. Hist.) Orangiste, *m.*

or'ange-musk (-meuske), *n.*, (pear) orange musquée, *f.*

or'angery (-djeur'i), *n.*, orangerie, *f.*

or'ange-woman (-woum'a'n), *n.*, marchande d'oranges, *f.*

orang'-outang (ô-ra'gne-ou-ta'gne), *n.*, (mam.) orang-outang, *m.*

ora'tion (ô-ré-), *n.*, discours, *m.; harangue, oraison, f.*

or'ator (-teur), *n.*, orateur, *m.*

orator'ical, *adj.*, oratoire.

orator'ically, *adv.*, oratoirement.

orator'ian, *n.*, oratorien, *m.*

orator'io (-tô-), *n.*, (chapel) oratoire ; (mus.) oratorio, *m.*

or'atory (-teuri), *n.*, art oratoire, *m.; élo-quence, f.;* (chapel) oratoire, *m.*

orb, *n.*, globe ; corps sphérique ; orbe, *m.; or-bite ;* sphère, *f.;* cercle, *m.;* (of time) révolution, période, *f.*

orbed (orb'de), *adj.*, rond, circulaire, sphérique.

orbic'ular (-bik'iou-), *adj.*, circulaire, sphérique ; orbiculaire.

orbic'ularly, *adv.*, orbiculairement, sphériquement ; en rond.

orbic'ularness, *n.*, sphéricité, *f.*

orbic'ulate *ou* **orbic'ulated**. *V.* **orbicular**.

or'bit, *n.*, orbite, *f. ;* orbe, *m. ;* (anat.) orbite, *m.*

or'bital, *adj.*, (anat.) orbitaire.

orc, *n.*, (ich.) épaulard, *m.; orque, f.*

or'chal (-kal) *ou* **or'chel** (-kèl), *n.*, (bot.) or-seille (des teinturiers), *f.*

or'chanet (-ka-), *n.*, orcanète, *f.*

or'chard (-tsharde), *n.*, verger, *m.*

or'charding, *n.*, culture des arbres fruitiers, fructiculture, *f.*

or'chardist, *n.*, fructiculteur, *m.*

or'chestra (-kès-), *n.*, orchestre, *m.*

or'chestral, *adj.*, d'orchestre ; de l'orchestre.

or'chid (-kide), *n.*, (bot.) orchis, *m.*, orchide, *f.* — house; *serre à orchides, f.*

ordain' (-déne), *v.a.*, ordonner, décréter, prescrire ; établir, instituer, destiner ; (ecc.) ordonner; (biblically) élire, choisir.

ordain'able (-'a-b'l), *adj.*, que l'on peut ordonner.

ordain'er, *n.*, ordonnateur, (ecc.) ordinant, *m.*

ordain'ing, *adj.*, ordonnateur ; (ecc.) ordinant.

or'deal (-di-), *n.*, (hist.) (jur.) ordalie ; (fig.) épreuve, *f.*, jugement de Dieu, *m.*

or'der, *n.*, ordre ; règlement, *m. ;* règle, *f.;* arrêté ; (arch., her., milit.) ordre, *m.;* décoration ; (fin.) ordonnance, *f.;* (thea., etc.) billet de faveur ; (class) rang, *m.*, classe ; (for goods) commande, demande, *f.;* (draft) mandat, *m.* Postal —; bon de poste, *m.* Post office —; mandat-poste, *m.* —s, *pl.*, (ecc.) ordres, *m.pl.* In very good —; *en très bon état.* —! *à l'ordre!* In — to; *pour, afin* **de**; *dans le but* **de**; *dans le dessein* **de**; *dans l'intention* **de**. In — that ; *afin* **que** ; *pour* **que**. To —; (of bills) *à ordre ;* (of clothes, etc.) *de commande*. Made to —; *sur commande*. By —; *par ordre ;* (com.) *d'ordre.* In —; *en règle ; en bonne forme ;* (alphabetical, etc.) *par ordre.* Till further —s ; *jusqu'à nouvel ordre.* Out of —;*dérangé; détraqué; indisposé, malade.* In —s ; (ecc.) *dans les ordres.* — of the day ; *ordre du jour.* To call to —; *rappeler à l'ordre.* To get out of —; *se détraquer.* To keep in —; *tenir dans l'ordre ; tenir dans le devoir.* To keep —; *maintenir l'ordre.* To put out of —; *déranger ; mettre en désordre ; détraquer.* To set in —; *mettre en ordre ; mettre de l'ordre* **dans**, *régulariser.* Higher —s ; *classes élevées ; hautes classes, f.pl.* Lower —s ; *basses classes ; classes inférieures, f.pl.*

or′der, *v.a.* ordonner, ordonner **à** ; donner l'ordre **à** ; (to regulate) régler, arranger, disposer ; (to conduct) diriger, conduire, guider ; (things, as clothes, etc.) commander, demander. The dinner is —ed ; *le dîner est commandé.* To — a coat ; *commander un habit.* They —ed him to be set free ; *ils ordonnèrent qu'on le mit en liberté* ou *ils le firent mettre en liberté.* To — about ; *mener à la baguette.* To — along; *faire avancer, faire circuler.* To — **away**, *ou* to — off ; *ordonner de s'en aller.* To — in ; *ordonner d'entrer.* To — out; *ordonner de sortir.* To be —ed to ; *recevoir l'ordre* **de**. — arms ! (milit.) *reposez vos armes!*

or′derer, *n.*, ordonnateur, régulateur, *m,*

or′dering, *n.*, ordonnance, disposition, *f. ;* ordre, arrangement, *m.*

or′derless, *adj.*, sans ordre ; désordonné.

or′derliness, *n.*, ordre, *m. ;* méthode ; régularité ; bonne conduite, *f.*

or′derly, *n.*, (milit.) officier d'ordonnance, *m.;* ordonnance, *f. ;* planton ; (ant.) balayeur de rues, *m.*

or′derly, *adj.*, réglé, régulier ; en bon ordre ; méthodique ; tranquille ; rangé. — officer ; *officier de corvée, m.* Hospital —; *infirmier, m.*

or′derly, *adv.*, dans l'ordre, avec ordre, en ordre.

or′dinal, *n.*, nombre ordinal ; (ecc.) rituel, *m.*

or′dinal, *adj.*, ordinal.

or′dinance, *n.*, ordonnance ; loi, *f. ;* ordre ; (protest. rel.) sacrement, *m.*

or′dinarily, *adv.*, ordinairement ; d'ordinaire.

or′dinary, *n.*, ordinaire, *m. ;* chose ordinaire, *f. ;* (meal) ordinaire, *m.*, table d'hôte, *f. ;* (of a prison) aumônier ; (of a diocese) évêque, ordinaire, *m.*

or′dinary, *adj.*, ordinaire.

or′dinate, *adj.*, régulier.

or′dinately, *adv.*, régulièrement.

ordina′tion (-né-), *n.*, (ecc.) ordination, *f.*

ord′nance, *n.*, artillerie, *f.* Piece of — ; *pièce d'artillerie, f.* — yard ; *polygone, m.* — map ; *carte du dépôt de la guerre, f.*

or′donnance, *n.*, (paint.) ordonnance, *f.*

or′dure (ord′yeur), *n.*, ordure, *f.*

ore (ôre), *n.*, minerai, *m.*

ore′-hearth (-hârth), *n.*, (metal.) fourneau de fusion, *m.*

or′gan, *n.*, organe ; (mus.) orgue, *m.sing. ;* orgues, *m.* ou *f.pl.*

or′gan-blow′er (-blô′eur), *n.*, souffleur d'orgue, *m.*

or′gan-build′er (-bild′-), *n.*, facteur d'orgues, *m.*

or′gan-case (-kéce), *n.*, buffet d'orgue, *m.*

organ′ic, *adj.*, organique ; des organes.

organ′ically, *adv.*, organiquement.

organ′icalness, *n.*, état organique, *m.*

or′ganism (-′iz′me), *n.*, organisme, *m.*

or′ganist, *n.*, organiste, *m.*

organiza′tion (-′aïzé-), *n.*, organisation, *f.*

or′ganize (-aïze), *v.a.*, organiser, constituer.

or′gan-loft, *n.*, tribune d'orgue, *f.*

organog′raphy, *n.*, (nat. hist.) organographie, *f.*

or′gan-pipe (-païpe), *n.*, tuyau d'orgue, *m.*

or′gan-stop, *n.*, jeu d'orgue, *m.*

or′gan-tuner, *n.*, accordeur d'orgues, *m.*

or′ganzine, *n.*, organsin, *m.*

or′ganzine, *v.a.*, organsiner.

or′gies (-djïe), *n.pl.*, orgies, *f.pl.*

or′ient (ô-), *n.*, orient, est, *m.*

or′ient, *adj.*, levant ; naissant ; d'orient ; oriental; (fig.) brillant, étincelant, éclatant.

orien′tal, *adj.*, oriental ; d'Orient.

orien′tal, *n.*, natif de l'Orient, Oriental, *m.*

orien′talist, *n.*, orientaliste, *m.*

or′ifice, *n.*, orifice, trou, *m. ;* ouverture, *f.*

or′igin (-djïne), *n.*, origine, source ; (produce) provenance, *f.*

orig′inal (o-ridj′-), *n.*, original, *m.*

orig′inal, *adj.*, original, originel, primitif.

original′ity, *n.*, originalité, *f.*

orig′inally, *adv.*, originairement ; dans, ou à, l'origine ; d'une manière originale ; originalement.

orig′inate, *v.a.*, faire naître, produire, donner naissance à ; (fig.) créer, concevoir, inventer.

orig′inate (o-ridj′-), *v.n.*, provenir **de** ; dériver **de** ; tirer son origine **de** ; avoir son origine **dans**.

origina′tion (o-ridj′i-né-), *n.*, génération, origine, *f.*

orig′inator (-teur), *n.*, cause première, *f. ;* mobile; auteur, *m.*

oril′lon, *n.*, (fort.) orillon, *m.*

or′iole (ô-ri-ôl), *n.*, (orni.) loriot, *m.*

Ori′on (o-raï′-), *n.*, (astron.) Orion, *m.*

or′ison (or′i-zeune), *n.*, (l.u.) oraison, **prière,** *f.*

orle, *n.*, (her.) orle, *m.*

or′let, *n.*, (arch.) orle, *m.*

or′lop (*deck*), *n.*, (nav.) faux pont, **m.,** entre pont (V. Hugo).

or′nament, *n.*, ornement, *m.*, parure, *f.*

or′nament, *v.a.*, orner, décorer ; ornementer ; parer (with) **de**.

ornamen′tal, *adj.*, ornemental, d'ornement ; (fig.) artificiel, agréable, d'agrément. — water; *pièce d'eau, f.*

ornamen′tally, *adv.*, pour servir d'ornement, pour ornement.

ornamenta′tion, *n.*, ornementation, décoration, *f. ;* embellissement, *m.*

or′namenter, *n.*, décorateur, *m.*

or′nate, *adj.*, orné, beau, élégant, paré.

or′nately, *adv.*, avec ornement.

or′nateness, *n.*, élégance, *f.*

ornitholog′ic (-thol′o-djïk), *adj.*, **ornitholo-**gique.

ornithol′ogist (-thol′o-djist), *n.*, **ornitholo-**giste, ornithologue, *m.*

ornithol′ogy (-thol′o-dji), *n.*, ornithologie, *f.*

orol′ogist (-djiste), *n.*, personne versée dans l'orographie, *f.*

orol′ogy (-dji), *n.*, orographie, *f.*

or′phan, *n.*, orphelin, *m.*, orpheline, *f.* — asylum; *orphelinat, m.*

or′phan, *adj.*, orphelin.

or′phan, *v.a.*, rendre orphelin.

or′phanage (-′èdje), *n.*, état d'orphelin; orphelinat, *m.*

orphe′an, *adj.*, d'Orphée.

Or′phic, *adj.*, orphique.

or′phrey, *n.*, orfroi, *m.*

or′piment, *n.*, orpiment, *m.*

or′pine (-païne), *n.*, (bot.) (paint.) orpin, *m.*

or'rery (or-eur'ie), *n.*, planétaire, *m.*

or'ris, *n.*, passement; (bot.) iris, *m.*

ort, orts, *n.*, fragment, débris, rebut, *m. ;* épluchures, *f.pl.*

or'thodox (-tho-), *adj.*, orthodoxe.

or'thodoxly (-tho-), *adv.*, d'une manière orthodoxe.

or'thodoxy (-tho-), *n.*, orthodoxie, *f.*

or'thoepist (-tho-è-), *n.*, personne qui prononce bien, *f.*

or'thoepy (-tho-è-), *n.*, prononciation correcte, *f.*

orthog'rapher, *n.*, orthographiste, *m.*

orthograph'ic *ou* **orthograph'ical** (-tho-), *adj.*, d'orthographe ; bien orthographié ; orthographique ; (draw., geom.) orthographique.

orthograph'ically (-tho-), *adv.*, orthographiquement, selon les règles de l'orthographe.

orthog'raphy (-tho-), *n.*, orthographe, ⊙orthographie ; (arch., fort., geom., persp.) orthographie, *f.*

or'thopedist (-thop'i-), *n.*, orthopédiste, *m.*

orthope'dic (-thop'i-), *adj.*, orthopédique.

or'thopedy (-thop'i-), *n.*, orthopédie, *f.*

or'tive, *adj.*, (astron.) ortive (adj. fem.).

or'tolan, *n.*, (orni.) ortolan, *m.*

or'val, *n.*, (bot.) orvale, *f.*

os'cillate, *v.n.*, osciller ; balancer, hésiter ; (fig.) osciller, vaciller.

oscilla'tion (-cil-lé-), *n.*, oscillation, *f.*

os'cillatory, *adj.*, oscillatoire.

oscula'tion (-kiou-lé-), *n.*, (geom.) osculation, *f.*

os'culatory (-kiou-lé-), *adj.*, (geom.) osculateur.

os'culatory, *n.*, (ecc.) paix, patène, *f.*

o'sier (ô-jeure), *n.*, osier, *m.*

o'sier-ground (-graou'n'de), *n.*, oseraie, *f.*

os'mund (oz'meu'n'de), *n.*, (bot.) osmonde, *f.*

os'prey, *n.*, (orni.) orfraie, *f. ;* aigle de mer, huard, *m.*

os'seous (osh'i-), *adj.*, osseux.

os'sicle (os'si-k'l), *n.*, (anat.) osselet, *m.*

ossifica'tion (-fi-ké-), *n.*, ossification, *f.*

os'sify (-faïe), *v.n.*, s'ossifier.

os'suary (os-shiou-), *n.*, charnier ; ossuaire, *m.*

ostensibil'ity, *n.*, caractère ostensible, *m.*

osten'sible, *adj.*, ostensible.

osten'sibly, *adv.*, ostensiblement.

osten'sive, *adj.*, évident.

ostenta'tion (-tè'n'-té-), *n.*, ostentation, *f. ;* faste, étalage, *m.*

ostenta'tious (-té-sheusse), *adj.*, plein d'ostentation; fastueux; de parade; vain.

ostenta'tiously, *adv.*, fastueusement, avec ostentation, avec étalage.

osteog'raphy (-ti-), *n.*, (anat.) ostéographie, *f.*

os'teolite (os-ti-o-laïte), *n.*, (min.) ostéolithe, *m.*

osteol'oger *ou* **osteol'ogist** (-odj'-), *n.*, ostéologue, *m.*

osteolog'ic *ou* **osteolog'ical** (-o-dj'-), *adj.*, ostéologique.

osteolog'ically, *adv.*, selon l'ostéologie.

osteol'ogy (-o-dji), *n.*, (anat.) ostéologie, *f.*

osteot'omy (-ti-o-to-), *n.*, (anat.) ostéotomie, *f.*

ost'ler (os'leur), *n.*, valet *ou* garçon d'écurie, *m.*

os'tracism (-ciz'me), *n.*, ostracisme, *m.*

os'tracize (-caïze), *v.a.*, frapper d'ostracisme.

os'trich (-tritshe), *n.*, (orni.) autruche, *f.* — feather ; *plume d'autruche, f.*

otal'gia *ou* **o'talgy** (-dj'-), *n.*, (med.) otalgie (douleur d'oreille), *f.*

oth'er (euth'-), *pron.*, autre ; autrui. Every —; *tous les deux ; de deux . . . l'un.* Of all —s ; *entre tous.* Each —; *l'un l'autre ; les uns les autres.* The — day ; *l'autre jour.*

oth'erwise (-waïze), *adv.*, autrement ; d'ailleurs.

ot'tar *ou* **ot'to** (-tô), *n.*, essence de roses, huile essentielle, *f.*

ot'ter, *n.*, loutre, *f.*

Ot'toman, *adj.*, ottoman.

Ot'toman, *n.*, (Turk) Ottoman, *m. ;* ottomane, *f. ;* divan, sofa, *m.*

ought (ōte), *n.* *V.* **aught**.

ought (ōte), *v.* *defective*, devoir. It is as it — to be ; *c'est bien comme cela ;* c'est comme il *faut.* You — to do it ; *vous devriez le faire.* These things — not so to be ; *il ne devrait pas en être ainsi.* You — to have done this ; *vous auriez dû faire ceci.* You — to have (should have) seen ; *il aurait fallu voir.*

ounce (aou'n'ce), *n.*, (weight) once, *f. ;* (mam.) once, *f.*

our (aou'eur), *adj.*, notre, *sing. ;* nos, *pl.* — self ; *nous-même.* —selves ; *nous-mêmes.*

ours (aoueurze), *pron.*, le nôtre, *m.*, la nôtre, *f. ;* les nôtres, *pl.m.f. ;* à nous ; de nous.

ourselves' (aou'eur-cèlv'ze), *pron.*, nous-mêmes ; nous.

ous'el (ou-z'l), *n.*, (orni.) merle d'eau, cincle plongeur, *m.*

oust (aouste), *v.a.*, débusquer, déloger ; supplanter ; (jur.) évincer, déposséder.

oust'er (aoust'-), *n.*, (jur.) éviction, dépossession, *f.*

out (aoute), *n.*, (print.) bourdon, *m.*

out (aoute), *adv.*, (on the outside) dehors ; (abroad) sorti ; (milit.) sur pied ; (disclosed) découvert, connu ; (extinct) éteint ; (at an end) épuisé, usé, fini ; (without) sans ; (to the end) jusqu'au bout, jusqu'à la fin ; (loudly, without restraint) haut, hautement, ouvertement, à haute voix ; (not in the hands of the owner) loué, prêté ; (puzzled) embarrassé, dans l'embarras ; (in error) dans l'erreur ; (of clothes, shoes, etc.) percé, troué ; (of books) paru ; (not in power) non au pouvoir, ne . . . plus au pouvoir, non en fonctions, ne . . . plus en fonctions. —! *dehors !* — with him ! *à la porte !* — with it ! *dites ce que c'est !* finissez ! donnez ! voyons ! — of ; *hors de; sans ; dans ; par.* Take the horses —! *détélez !* To be — of ; *être* **sans** *; manquer* **de**. To be — of pocket ; *perdre.* I was fifty pounds — of pocket by it ; *j'y ai perdu cinquante livres.* — of friendship ; *par amitié.* To read — of a book; *lire dans un livre.* To come —; *débuter.* — of money ; *sans argent.* — and — ; (of a rascal) *achevé, fieffé.* — of hatred ; *par haine.* — of charity ; *par charité.* — of hand ; *tout de suite.* — of measure ; *outre mesure.* — of hope ; *sans espérance.* — of favor ; *disgracié.* — of place ; (unbecoming) *déplacé ;* (of situations) *sans place ; hors de place.* — of sight ; *à perte de vue ; hors de vue.* — at sea ; *en mer ; dans la haute mer.* — of humor ; *de mauvaise humeur.* Where are you going ? — ; *où allez-vous ? Je vais sortir.* The truth must — ; *il faut que la vérité sorte ; disons la vérité.* To be — with ; (a person) *être brouillé* **avec**. To squeeze — ; *exprimer.* To throw — of the window ; *jeter par la fenêtre.* To be — in one's reckoning ; *être loin du compte.* I wish I were — **of it** ; *je voudrais bien en être débarrassé(e),* ou *m'en être tiré.* — of doors ; *dehors ; hors de la maison.* — of temper ; *en colère ; excité.* Get — of that ; *va-t'en ; ôte-toi de là.* — of tune ; (singing) *faux.* — of number; *innombrable, sans nombre.* — of sight — of mind ; *loin des yeux, loin du cœur.* The fire is — ; *le feu est éteint.* The cask is — ; *le tonneau est vide.* Hear me — ; *entendez-moi jusqu'au bout.* Speak — ; *parlez plus haut.* — of ammunition ; *à bout de munitions.* You put me quite — ; *vous me déroutez ; vous me poussez à bout.* The book is — of print ; *l'édition est épuisée.* — of use ; *inusité, vieilli.* I shall not be — of the way ; *je ne serai pas loin.* She laughed right — ; *elle rit tout haut.* I found you — ; *je vous ai deviné* ou *je vous y prends ; je vous ai découvert.* To be — of sorts ; *être indisposé ; n'être pas dans son assiette.* I am

— of sorts ; *je suis tout je ne sais comment* (fam.).
— of the way; (price paid) *excessif* ; (secluded) *retiré.* To drink — of a glass ; *boire dans un verre.* To drink — of a bottle ; *boire à même une bouteille.* Time — of mind ; *de temps immémorial.* The sun is — ; *il fait du soleil tout chose.* To — -Herod Herod ; *être plus royaliste que le roi,* ou *être plus catholique que le Pape.* — of debt — of danger ; *qui ne droit rien n'a rien à craindre.* To fall — of the frying-pan into the fire ; *tomber de la poêle dans la braise,* ou *de Charybde en Scylla.* One had as well be — of the world as — of the fashion ; *il vaut mieux être fou avec tous que sage tout seul.*

outbal'ance, *v.a.,* l'emporter **sur,** surpasser.

outbid', *v.a.* and *n.,* (*preterit,* Outbid, Outbade; *past part.,* Outbidden, Outbid) enchérir, surenchérir ; enchérir **sur** ; renchérir **sur.**

outbid'der, *n.,* enchérisseur, *m.*

out'bound. *V.* **outward.**

out'break (-brék'), *n.,* explosion ; émeute, insurrection ; débordement, déchaînement ; soulèvement, *m. ;* (of epidemics) invasion, *f. ;* (of fire) incendie, *m.*

out'building, *n.,* bâtiment extérieur, *m.,* dépendance, *f. ;* hangar, *m.*

out'cast (-câste), *n.,* proscrit, banni, exilé, maudit, *m.*

out'cast, *adj.,* expulsé, proscrit, exilé, abandonné.

out'crop, *n.,* (geol.) affleurement, *m.*

out'cry (-craïe), *n.,* grand cri, *m. ;* hauts cris, *m.pl. ;* clameur, *f.,* clameurs, *f.pl. ;* tollé, *m. ;* (sale) (ant.) criée, *f.*

outdare', *v.a.,* surpasser en audace ; défier ; braver ; affronter.

outdo' (-dou), *v.a.,* (*preterit,* Outdid ; *past part.,* Outdone) surpasser ; exceller ; renchérir **sur** ; l'emporter **sur.**

out'er, *adj.,* extérieur, du dehors ; externe.

out'ermost (-môste), *adj.,* le plus en dehors ; le plus extérieur ; le plus avancé.

out-face' (-féce), *v.a.,* faire baisser les yeux **à** ; déconcerter, dévisager, affronter, défier, braver.

out'fall (-fôl), *n.,* embouchure, chute d'eau, *f.*

out'fit, *n.,* armement, équipement ; trousseau, *m.* — allowance; *frais d'équipement, m. pl.*

out'fitter, confectionneur ; fabricant d'équipements, *m.*

out'fitting, *n.,* confection, *f. ;* équipement, *m.*

outflank', *v.a.,* (milit.) déborder, tourner.

outflank'ing, *n.,* débordement, *m.*

out'flow' (aout'flô), *v.n.,* découler, provenir, venir.

out'flow, *n.,* émigration, *f.*

outfly' (-flaïe), *v.a.* (ant.), (*preterit,* Outflew ; *past part.,* Outflown) surpasser dans son vol ; dépasser ; échapper **à.**

outgen'eral, *v.a.,* surpasser en tactique ; l'emporter **sur.**

out'goer, *n.,* sortant ; ancien locataire, *m.*

out'going, *n.,* sortie, *f. ;* (ant.) extrême limite, *f. pl.,* (com.) déboursés, frais, *m.pl.*

out'going, *adj.,* sortant, qui sort.

outgrow' (-grô), *v.a.,* (*preterit,* Outgrew ; *past part.,* Outgrown) grandir plus que ; surpasser en croissance ; dépasser, surpasser. He —s his clothes ; *ses habits deviennent trop petits.*

out'growth, *n.,* excroissance, *f.*

out'-guard (-gârde), *n.,* garde avancée, *f.*

out-Her'od (-hèr'-), *v.a.,* dépasser en cruauté. That —s Herod ; *cela dépasse tout.*

out'house (-haouce), *n.,* pavillon, hangar, *m. ;* dépendance, *f.* —s, *pl.,* communs, *m.pl.*

out'ing, *n.,* excursion, promenade, *f.*

outland'ish, *adj.,* étranger ; grossier ; curieux ; bizarre ; extraordinaire.

outlast', *v.a.,* surpasser en durée ; survivre **à.**

out'law (-lô), *n.,* personne mise hors la loi, *f. ;* proscrit, *m.*

out'law (-lô), *v.a.,* mettre hors la loi ; proscrire, bannir.

out'lawry, *n.,* mise hors la loi, proscription, *f.*

out'lay, *n.,* dépense, *f. ;* déboursés, *m.pl.*

out'let, *n.,* issue ; sortie, *f. ;* passage ; (com.) débouché, *m. ;* voie d'écoulement ; (of a roof shoot) gargouille, *f.*

outlie' (-laïe), *v.a.,* surpasser en mensonge.

out'lier (-laïeur), *n.,* non-résident ; (geol.) portion détachée, *f.*

out'line (-laï'ne), *n.,* contour, *m. ;* esquisse, ébauche, *f. ;* premier jet, aperçu, *m.*

out'line, *v.a.,* dessiner le contour **de** ; esquisser.

outlive', *v.a.,* survivre **à** ; vivre plus longtemps que.

out'look (-louke), *v.a.,* faire baisser les yeux **à** ; affronter ; braver ; mater ; observer, veiller ; regarder, choisir.

out'look, *n.,* vigilance, garde ; tour d'observation; (fig.) vue, perspective, *f.*

out'lying (-laïgne), *adj.,* éloigné ; extérieur ; isolé, détaché ; (mil.) avancé. — parts (of a town) ; *pays perdus, m.pl.* (V. Hugo).

outmanœu'vre (-), *v.a.,* surpasser en manœuvre.

outmarch' (-mârtshe), *v.a.,* devancer; marcher plus vite que ; laisser en arrière.

out'most (-môste), *adj.,* le plus en dehors ; extrême, le plus éloigné.

outpace' (-péce), *v.a.,* devancer, dépasser.

out'-parish, *n.,* paroisse extérieure, *f.*

out'-part (-pârte), *n.,* partie extérieure, *f.*

outpass', *v.a.,* dépasser ; devancer.

out'-porch, out'er-porch (-pôrtshe), *n.,* (ant.) portique extérieur ; parvis, *m.*

out'-port, out'er-port, *n.,* port éloigné ; port à quelque distance du centre commercial, *m.*

out'post (-pôste), *n.,* (milit.) avant-poste, *m.,* garde avancée, *f.*

outpour' (-pôre), *v.a.,* épancher, verser à flots.

out'pouring, *n.,* effusion, *f. ;* épanchement, *m.*

out'rage (-rédje), *n.,* outrage, affront, *m. ;* violence; (jur.) atteinte, *f.* — on common decency; *outrage à la pudeur, m.*

out'rage, *v.a.,* outrager.

outra'geous (-ré'djeusse), *adj.,* outrageux, scandaleux, atroce; outrageant ; furieux, violent; (tumultuous) tumultueux, turbulent; (excessive) exorbitant; abominable ; outré, exagéré; (enormous) énorme.

outra'geously, *adv.,* outrageusement ; violemment, furieusement ; avec turbulence ; d'une manière outrée ; énormément ; abominablement.

outra'geousness, *n.,* nature outrageuse, nature outrageante; violence, fureur, turbulence, énormité, *f.*

outride' (-raïde), *v.a.,* (*preterit,* Out-rode ; *past part.,* Outridden) (ant.) dépasser, devancer à cheval.

out'rider (-raïd'-), *n.,* piqueur, *m.*

out'rigger, *n.,* (of a sailing boat) bout-dehors ; (of a rowing boat) porte-rame, outrigger, *m.*

out'right (-raïte), *adv.,* sur-le-champ; sur le coup; tout de suite; (completely) entièrement, complètement ; (without constraint) sans gêne, sans contrainte, net, carrément. To laugh — ; *partir d'un grand éclat de rire.*

outri'val (-raï-), *v.a.,* (ant.) l'emporter **sur.**

outrun' (-reune), *v.a.,* (*preterit,* Outran; *past part.,* Outrun) devancer à la course ; devancer ; dépasser ; gagner de vitesse. To — an amount ; *dépasser, excéder une somme.* To — the constable ; *dépenser au delà de son revenu.*

outsail' (-séle), *v.a.,* dépasser à la voile ; gagner de vitesse ; dépasser.

outsell', *v.a.,* (*preterit* and *past part.,* Outsold) vendre plus que, plus vite que ; obtenir de plus hauts prix que.

out'set, *n.,* début, commencement ; principe, *m.*

outshine' (-shaïne), v.a., (preterit and past part., Outshined ou Outshone) surpasser en éclat; surpasser; éclipser.

out'side (-saïde), n., dehors, extérieur, m. ; (of a diligence) impériale, banquette, f. ; (of cabs) dessus; (of roast meat) rissolé, m. At the —; tout au plus.

out'side, adj., extérieur, externe, du dehors. The — passengers; les voyageurs de l'impériale, m.pl. — shutter; contrevent, m.

out'side, adv., en dehors, à l'extérieur, sur le dessus; (of a diligence) sur l'impériale, sur la banquette.

outsid'er, n., étranger; qui n'a rien à faire avec; (on Exchange) coulissier. —s, pl., le public.

outsit', v.a., (preterit and past part., Outsat) (ant.) être assis plus longtemps que.

out'skirt (-skeurte), n., extrémité, f. ; bord ; (of a town) faubourg, m. ; (of a wood) lisière, f.

outsleep' (-slîpe), v.a., (preterit and past part., Outslept) dormir plus longtemps que, dormir au-delà **de**.

outspok'en, adj., franc, clair, explicite ; qui a son franc-parler **avec**.

outspread' (-sprède), v.a., (preterit and past part., Outspread) étendre, déployer ; répandre.

outstand', v.a., (preterit and past part., Outstood) (ant.) rester au-delà **de** ; durer plus que ; (to withstand) soutenir ; résister à.

outstand'ing, adj., en saillie ; (of bills) non payé, encore dû ; (com.) en suspens, courant.

outstare', v.a., (l.u.) faire baisser les yeux à ; décontenancer, déconcerter, dévisager.

outstep' (-stèpe), v.a., devancer ; dépasser ; excéder.

out'-street (-strîte), n., rue écartée ; rue de faubourg, f.

out'stretch (-strètshe), v.a., étendre.

out'stretched (-strètsch'te), adj., étendu ; ouvert.

outstrip', v.a., gagner de vitesse ; devancer ; surpasser.

outvote' (-vôte), v.a., l'emporter à la pluralité des voix **sur**, obtenir la majorité **sur**.

outwalk' (-wôke), v.a., (l.u.) marcher plus vite que ; devancer.

out'-wall, out'er-wall (-wôl), n., mur extérieur, avant-mur, m.

out'ward (-worde), adj., extérieur, externe ; superficiel.

out'ward, n., extérieur, dehors, m.

out'ward ou **out'wards** (-wordze), adv., à l'extérieur ; au dehors, extérieurement ; (of ships) pour l'étranger. An —-bound ship ; un navire à destination pour l'étranger, en cours de voyage. — voyage ; voyage d'aller, m.

out'wardly, adv., extérieurement, à l'extérieur ; au dehors ; (fig.) à la surface, en apparence.

outweigh' (-wé), v.a., peser plus que ; l'emporter **sur**, avoir plus de poids que.

outwit', v.a., surpasser en finesse ; duper, attraper, (pop.) mettre dedans ; en revendre **à**.

out'work (-weurke), n., (fort.) ouvrage avancé, m.

o'val (ô-), adj., ovale.

o'val, n., (geom.) ovale, m. — in a wall ; œil-de-bœuf, m.

ova'rious (ô-vé-), adj., d'œufs.

o'vary (ô-), n., ovaire, m.

o'vate ou **o'vated** (ô-vét'-), adj., (bot.) ovale.

ova'tion, n., ovation, f.

ov'en (euv'v'n), n., four, m. — fork ; fourgon, râble, m. — full ; fournée, f. Dutch — ; rôtissoire, cuisinière, f. — baked ; cuit au four. — maker ; constructeur de fours, m. — peel ; pelle de four, f. To be in the same —, ou boat ; être dans le même état, dans le même pétrin.

o'ver (ô-veur), prep., (above) au-dessus **de** ; par-dessus ; sur ; (during) durant, pendant ;

(upon) sur ; sur la surface **de** ; (across) à travers ; au travers **de** ; (on the other side) de l'autre côté ; au delà **de** ; (about) dans, par. — the water ; de l'autre côté de l'eau. — hill and dale; par monts et par vaux. To walk — the field ; marcher dans, à travers, le champ. — the table; sur la table. — winter ; pendant l'hiver. The water is — one's shoes ; l'eau est au-dessus des souliers. To be placed — any one ; être placé au-dessus **de**, surveiller quelqu'un. To watch — a person's interest ; veiller aux intérêts de quelqu'un. To hand — ; livrer à. He lost — a hundred pounds ; il a perdu plus de cent livres sterling. — the left ; à gauche. — head and ears in debt ; criblé de dettes.

o'ver, adv., (from side to side) d'un côté à l'autre ; (on the opposite side) de l'autre côté ; (on the surface, above the top) par-dessus, au-dessus ; (throughout) partout, tout, entièrement ; (ended) fini, passé ; (more than the quantity assigned) de reste. — ! (of a sheet of paper) tournez ! — ! (com.) à reporter ! A task — difficult ; une tâche par trop difficile, très difficile. I have heard it — ; je l'ai entendu du commencement jusqu'à la fin. A brief interval — ; après un court intervalle. The danger is — ; le danger est passé. All the world — ; dans le monde entier, par toute la terre. The business is not — yet ; l'affaire n'est pas encore finie. There is nothing — ; il n'y a rien de reste. — again ; de nouveau, encore une fois. — and above ; en outre, en sus. A table ten feet — ; une table de dix pieds de large. He is — ; il est de l'autre côté. To walk — ; marcher par-dessus. To give — ; cesser **de**. You are splashed all — ; vous êtes couvert d'éclaboussures. To have something — ; avoir de reste. — and — ; mille fois, sans cesse, incessamment. To be all — ; être fini. All — ; des pieds jusqu'à la tête. Red all — ; tout rouge. To be all — with ; en être fait **de**. I am glad it is — ; je suis content que ce soit fini.

overabound' (-abaou'n'de), v.n., surabonder.

overact', v.a. and n., outrer, exagérer, charger, un rôle.

over-ag'itate, v.a., discuter trop ; agiter trop.

o'verall (-ôl), **o'vercoat**, n., surtout, pardessus, m. —s, pl., pantalon de voyage ; (of workmen) pantalon de travail, m. ; cotte, salopette, f.

overarch' (-ârtshe), v.a., voûter.

overawe' (ô-veur-ô), v.a., imposer le respect à ; intimider ; imposer à ; tenir en respect.

over-baked', adj., trop cuit.

o'verbalance, n., excédent, m. ; prépondérance, f.

overbal'ance, v.a., l'emporter **sur** ; excéder. To — one's self ; perdre l'équilibre ; faire la bascule.

overbal'ancing, n., prépondérance, f.

over'bear (-bère), v.a., (preterit, Overbore ; past part., Overborne) subjuguer, dompter, maîtriser ; (fig.) accabler, vaincre ; surmonter.

overbear'ing, adj., dominateur ; impérieux ; arrogant ; tyrannique ; autoritaire ; dogmatique.

overbend', v.a., (preterit and past part., Overbent), plier trop, courber trop.

overbid', v.a., (preterit, Overbade ; past part., Overbidden), offrir trop **pour** ; enchérir **sur**.

overblack'en, v.a., trop décrier, trop diffamer, trop noircir.

o'verboard (-bôrde), adv., pardessus bord ; à la mer.

overboil', v.a., faire trop bouillir ; bouillir trop longtemps.

overboiled', adj., trop bouilli.

overbuilt' (-bilte), adj., chargé de bâtiments, chargé. To be — ; avoir plus de maisons qu'il n'en faut.

overbur'den (-beur-d'n), v.a., surcharger.

overbus'y (-biz'zi), adj., trop affairé ; trop occupé ; trop officieux.

overbuy' (-baïe), v.a., (preterit and past part., Overbought) (ant.) acheter trop cher ; faire trop d'achats.

overcare'ful, adj., (over-attentive) soigneux à l'excès ; (over-solicitous) soucieux à l'excès.

overcast' (-câste), adj., couvert, nuageux ; sombre ; obscur.

overcast' (-câste), v.a., (preterit and past part., Overcast) assombrir, obscurcir ; (to compute) porter trop haut ; (needlework) surjeter.

overcau'tious (-cô-sheusse), adj., par trop prudent.

overcharge' (-tshârdje), v.a., surcharger ; (in price) survendre, prendre trop cher, faire payer trop cher, surfaire, rançonner ; (fire-arms) mettre une charge trop forte dans ; exagérer.

o'vercharge, n., charge excessive, f. ; (in price) prix trop élevé, m. ; (of taxes) surtaux, m.

overcloud' (-claoude), v.a., couvrir de nuages ; obscurcir.

o'vercoat, n. V. **overall**.

overcol'or (-keul'leur), v.a., charger de couleur ; colorer trop ; (fig.) charger ; exagérer ; outrer.

overcome' (-keume), v.a., (preterit, Overcame ; past part., Overcome) subjuguer ; accabler ; dompter ; triompher **de** ; vaincre ; surmonter.

overcome', v.n., vaincre ; être victorieux ; l'emporter. I am quite —; je n'en puis plus.

overcom'er, n., vainqueur, m.

overcon'fidence, n., trop grande confiance, confiance excessive, f.

overcon'fident, adj., par trop sûr ; trop plein de confiance.

overcount' (-caou'n'te), v.a., (ant.) évaluer trop ; priser trop.

overcred'ulous (-crèd'iou-leusse), adj., par trop crédule.

overcrowd', v.a., encombrer à l'excès.

overcrowd'ing, n., encombrement excessif, m.

overcu'rious, adj., par trop curieux.

overdate', v.a., (ant.) postdater.

overdo' (-dou), v.a., (preterit, Overdid ; past part., Overdone) faire trop ; exagérer ; outrer ; (eatables) faire trop cuire ; (to fatigue) harasser, fatiguer.

overdo' (-dou), v.n., faire trop ; trop travailler.

overdone', adj., (cook.) trop cuit.

o'verdose, n., dose trop forte, f.

overdraw' (-drô), v.a., (preterit, Overdrew ; past part., Overdrawn) excéder ; tirer trop. To — one's account ; (com.) dépasser le montant de son crédit ; dépasser son actif. —n account ; compte découvert, m.

overdraw'ing (-drô-igne), n., (com.) action de dépasser, d'excéder son crédit, f.

overdress', v.a., habiller trop ; trop charger de parure, parer avec excès.

overdrink', v.n., (preterit, Overdrank ; past part., Overdrunk) boire à l'excès.

overdrive' (-draïve), v.a., (preterit, Overdrove ; past part., Overdriven) faire marcher trop vite ; pousser trop loin ; (of animals) surmener.

overdry' (-draïe), v.a., sécher trop.

o'verdry, adj., trop sec.

o'verdue (-diou), adj., (of a bill) échu, non payé, en souffrance ; périmé ; (of a ship, etc.) en retard.

overea'ger (-î-gheur), adj., trop empressé.

overea'gerly (-î-gheur-), adv., avec trop d'empressement.

overea'gerness (-î-gheur-), n., excès d'empressement, m.

overeat', v.n., manger trop, manger avec excès.

overes'timate, v.a., surestimer ; estimer trop ; évaluer trop haut.

overexcite', v.a., surexciter, exciter trop.

overexcite'ment, n., surexcitation, f.

overfatigue', n., excès de fatigue, m.

overfatigue', v. a., excéder de fatigue.

overfeed', v.a., nourrir trop ; gorger.

overflow' (-flô), v.n., déborder ; se déborder ; se répandre ; (fig.) regorger.

overflow', v.a., faire déborder ; inonder ; se répandre **sur**.

o'verflow, n., inondation, f. ; débordement, m. ; (fig.) surabondance, f., excès, trop plein, m.

overflow'ing (-flô-igne), adj., qui déborde ; (fig.) surabondant ; qui regorge ; trop plein.

overflow'ing, n., débordement ; épanchement, m. ; effusion, surabondance, f. The hall was filled to —; il y avait salle comble.

overflow'ingly, adv., à l'excès ; surabondamment.

overfond', adj., trop passioné **pour** ; trop tendre ; fou **de**.

overfond'ness, n., trop grande passion ; tendresse excessive, f.

overfor'ward (-worde), adj., trop empressé ; trop hardi, trop présomptueux.

overfor'wardness, n., empressement excessif, m. ; hardiesse excessive, f. ; (hort.) hâtiveté excessive.

overfraught' (-frôte), adj., (ant.) surchargé.

overfree', adj., trop libre ; trop libéral, prodigue **de**.   [trop fécond.

overfruit'ful (-frout'foule), adj., trop fertile.

overglance', v.a., parcourir des yeux, voir à la hâte.

overgo' (-gô), v.a., (preterit, Overwent ; past part., Overgone), dépasser.

overgrow' (-grô), v.a., (preterit, Overgrew ; past part., Overgrown) (of plants) couvrir, tapisser de ; croître au-dessus **de** ; s'élever au-dessus **de** ; (pers., animal) grandir au-dessus **de**.

overgrow', v.n., croître trop ; (pers.) grandir trop ; (animal) grossir trop.

overgrown' (-grône), adj., (with plants) couvert, plein ; trop grand ; trop développé ; énorme.

o'vergrowth (-grôth), n., (ant.) accroissement excessif, m., croissance excessive, f.

o'verhand, n., dessus, m.

overhan'dle (-ha'n'd'l), v.a., manier trop ; toucher trop souvent ; discuter trop.

overhang' (-haï'gne), v.n., (preterit and past part., Overhung) pencher, surplomber, avancer.

overhang', v.a., pencher **sur** ; être suspendu **sur**, surplomber, avancer ; (fig.) menacer.

overhang'ing (-igne), adj., en surplomb, en saillie ; suspendu **sur**.

overhard'en, v.a., endurcir trop.

o'verhaste, **overhast'iness** (-héste), n., précipitation ; trop grande hâte, f.

overhast'ily (-hést'-), adv., avec précipitation ; trop à la hâte.

overhast'y (-hést'-), adj., précipité ; trop vif ; trop emporté.

overhaul', v.a., examiner de nouveau ; revoir ; visiter ; revenir **sur** ; inspecter ; (nav.) (a rope) affaler, larguer ; (overtake) gagner, atteindre.

overhead' (-hède), adv., au-dessus de la tête ; au-dessus ; en l'air ; en haut, au ciel.

overhear' (-hîr), v.a., (preterit and past part., Overheard) entendre par hasard, ou sans le vouloir ; surprendre ; saisir.

overheat' (-hîte), v.a., échauffer trop ; surchauffer. To — one's self ; s'échauffer.

overhon'est, adj., trop honnête.

over-is'sue, n., surémission, f.

overjoyed', adj., transporté de joie ; ravi.

overkind', adj., trop bon.

overkind'ness, n., bonté excessive, f.

overlade' (-lède), v.a., (preterit, Overladed ; past part., Overladen) surcharger (with, **de**).

o'verland, *adj.*, par voie de terre. By — mail; *par voie de terre.* — route; *voie de terre, f.*

overlap', *v.a.*, recouvrir, dépasser, enchevaucher. *v. n.*, se recouvrir, chevaucher.

o'verlap, *n.*, recouvrement, *m.*

overlap'ping, *n.*, recouvrement, chevauchement, *m.*

overlarge' (-lârdje), *adj.*, trop gros; trop grand.

overlarge'ness, *n.*, grosseur excessive; grandeur excessive; largeur excessive, *f.*

overlay', *v.a.*, (*preterit and past part.*, Overlaid) couvrir; étouffer; (fig.) obscurcir; (ant.) accabler, surcharger de. To — a child; *étouffer un enfant.*

overleap' (-lîpe), *v.a.*, sauter par-dessus; sauter; franchir. To — one's self; *sauter trop loin*, ou *trop haut*; *faire de trop grands efforts*; *aller trop loin.*

overlearn'ed, *adj.*, trop savant.

o'verleather (-lèth'-), *n.*, (ant.) empeigne, *f.*

overlib'eral, *adj.*, trop libéral; trop généreux.

o'verlight (-laïte), *adj.*, trop clair, trop léger.

o'verlighted, *adj.*, trop éclairé.

overload' (-lôde), *v.a.*, surcharger.

o'verlong (-lo'ngue), *adj.*, trop long.

overlook' (-louke), *v.a.*, (to view from on high, applied to persons) avoir vue sur, planer sur; (applied to things) dominer, commander; (to see from behind) regarder, regarder pardessus l'épaule de; (to view fully) parcourir en entier, voir en entier; (to superintend) surveiller; avoir l'œil sur; (to review) examiner, revoir, retoucher; (to excuse) fermer les yeux sur, avoir de l'indulgence pour, passer sur, pardonner, ne vouloir pas voir; (to pass by, to neglect) laisser échapper, ne pas remarquer, négliger; perdre de vue; (to despise) dédaigner, mépriser. —ing; *qui a vue sur, donnant sur.*

o'verlooker, *n.*, inspecteur, surveillant; (of factories) contre-maître, *m.*

overlook'ing, *n.*, surveillance, *f.*

overly'ing, *adj.*, superposé; qui recouvre.

overmast'ed (-mâst'-), *adj.*, trop haut mâté.

overmas'ter (-mâs-), *v.a.*, (ant.) maîtriser.

o'vermatch, *n.*, (ant.) force supérieure, *f.*; vainqueur, *m.*

overmatch' (-matshe), *v.a.*, opposer une force supérieure à; surmonter; être trop fort pour, accabler; maîtriser, vaincre. They were —ed; *ils n'étaient pas de force.*

o'vermeasure (-mèj'eur), *n.*, (ant.) trop bonne mesure, *f.*, surplus, *m.*

overmer'ry (-mèr'-), *adj.*, (ant.) par trop gai.

overmix', *v.a.*, (ant.) mêler trop.

overmod'est, *adj.*, trop modeste.

o'vermuch (-meutshe), *n.*, trop; excès, *m.*

o'vermuch, *adj.*, excessif; trop grand; trop de; à l'excès.

o'vermuch, *adv.*, trop, excessivement.

overneat', *adv.*, excessivement propre; recherché.

overnice', *adj.*, trop délicat, trop difficile.

o'vernight, *adv.*, durant la nuit, la veille au soir. He stayed —; *il passa la nuit.*

over-offi'cious (-fish'eusse), *adj.*, trop officieux, trop empressé.

overpaid', *adj.*, trop payé; payé trop cher.

overpaint' (-pé'n'te), *v.a.*, surcharger de couleur.

overpass' (-pâce), *v.a.*, passer sur; passer, franchir; omettre; ne pas remarquer.

overpay', *v.a.*, surpayer; payer trop; payer libéralement; payer trop cher.

overpay'ment, *n.*, surpaye, *f.*

overpeo'pled (-pî'p'l'd), *adj.*, trop peuplé; surchargé de population.

o'verplus (-pleusse), *n.*, surplus; excédent; trop-plein, *m.*

overpoise', *v.a.*, (ant.). *V.* outweigh.

o'verpoise (-poïze), *n.*, poids plus fort, *m.*; (fig.) prépondérance, *f.*

overpol'ish, *v.a.*, polir trop ou à l'excès.

overpon'derous (-dèur'-), *adj.*, trop pesant, trop lourd.

overpop'ulated, *adj.*, trop peuplé, trop populeux.

overpow'er (-paou'eur), *v.a.*, être trop fort pour; vaincre; subjuguer; venir à bout de, accabler de (by, par); (with fatigue) excéder; (to dazzle) éblouir.

overpow'ering, *adj.*, accablant; écrasant.

overpow'eringly, *adv.*, excessivement.

overpraise', *v.a.*, louer à l'excès.

overprais'ing, *n.*, louange excessive, *f.*

overpress', *v.a.*, (ant.) presser vivement; vaincre (à force d'instances); accabler; opprimer.

overprize' (-praïze), *v.a.*, évaluer trop, estimer trop, priser trop.

overprompt', *adj.*, trop prompt; trop vif.

overprompt'ness, *n.*, promptitude excessive; précipitation, *f.*

overproud', *adj.*, trop fier.

overrank' (-ra'gn'ke), *adj.*, trop rance; trop luxuriant, trop fertile, trop fort; surabondant.

overrate' (-réte), *v.a.*, évaluer trop, priser trop, estimer trop, s'exagérer; (fig.) présumer de, présumer trop de. —d; (of taxes) *surtaxé.*

overreach', *v.a.*, aller au-delà de; dépasser; (to deceive) tromper; jouer; duper; (of horses) forger. To — oneself; *se faire tort à soi-même*; *trop entreprendre*; *aller trop loin.*

overreach'ing, *n.*, duperie, tromperie, *f.*

overreach'ing, *adj.*, trompeur.

override' (-raïde), *v.a.*, (*preterit*, Overrode; *past part.*, Overridden) surmener; excéder de fatigue; annuler; se défaire de; (to supersede) primer. Might —s right; *la force prime le droit.*

overripe' (-raïpe), *adj.*, trop mûr.

overrip'en (-raï-p'n), *v.a.*, mûrir trop.

overroast' (-rôste), *v.a.*, rôtir trop.

overrule' (-roule), *v.a.*, dominer; gouverner; régir; maîtriser; l'emporter sur; (jur.) rejeter.

overrul'ing, *adj.*, qui gouverne; qui régit; dominant; souverain.

overrun' (reune), *v.a.n.*, (*preterit*, Overran; *past part.*, Overrun), couvrir; (to infest) envahir, faire une irruption dans; infester; ravager; (to outrun) devancer, passer; (print.) remanier; (to overflow) déborder, se dégorger.

overrun'ning, *n.*, envahissement, *m.*; incursion, *f.*; (print.) remaniement, *m.*

overscru'pulous, *adj.*, méticuleux, par trop scrupuleux.

o'versea (-sî), *adj.*, d'outre-mer.

oversee' (-sî), *v.a.*, (*preterit*, Oversaw; *past part.*, Overseen) surveiller; avoir l'œil sur.

overseer' (-sî-eur), *n.*, surveillant; (of the poor) administrateur de la taxe des pauvres; (print.) prote; (of a factory, etc.) contremaître, *m.*

overset', *v.a.*, (*preterit* and *past part.*, Overset) renverser; (a vehicle) verser; (a boat) faire chavirer; (fig.) renverser, bouleverser.

overset', *v.n.*, se renverser; (of vehicles) verser; (of boats) chavirer, faire capot.

overshad'ow (-shad'ô), *v.a.*, ombrager; protéger; jeter dans l'ombre; éclipser; obscurcir.

o'vershoes (-shouze), *n.pl.*, claques; galoches, *f.pl.*

overshoot' (-shoute), *v.a.n.*, (*preterit* and *past part.*, Overshot) porter trop loin, aller trop avant; dépasser le but. To — one's self; *aller trop loin*; *affirmer trop.*

overshot' (-shote), *adj.*, en dessus; dépassé.

o'vershot-wheel (-), *n.*, (mec.) roue en dessus, *f.*

o'versight (-saïte), *n.*, méprise, inadvertance, *f.*; oubli, *m.*; (superintendence) surveillance, *f.*

overskip', *v.a.*, sauter par-dessus; (fig.) passer, sauter.

oversleep' (-slîpe), *v.a.*, (*preterit* and *past part.*, Overslept) dormir au-delà de son heure. To — one's self ; *dormir trop longtemps ; se réveiller trop tard, s'oublier.*

oversoon' (-soune), *adv.*, trop tôt, de trop bonne heure.

overspent', *adj.*, (ant.) harassé, épuisé ; extenué, excédé, éreinté ; rendu.

overspread' (-sprède), *v.a.*, (*preterit* and *past part.*, Overspread) couvrir ; se répandre **sur.**

overstand' (-sta'n'd), *v.a.*, (*preterit* and *past part.*, Overstood) (ant.) insister trop **sur ;** tenir trop **à.**

overstate' (-stéte), *v.a.*, exagérer.

overstep' (-stèpe), *v.a.*, passer ; dépasser ; violer ; excéder.

o'verstock, *n.*, surabondance, *f.*

overstock', *v.a.*, remplir trop ; encombrer **de.**

overstrain' (-stréne), *v.n.*, faire de trop grands efforts.

overstrain', *v.a.*, forcer trop ; pousser trop loin ; outrer, forcer.

overstrew' (-strou *ou* -strô), *v.a.*, (ant.) répandre **sur ;** joncher.

o'vert (ô-veurte), *adj.*, ouvert, évident, manifeste. Market —; *marché public, m.*

overtake' (-téke), *v.a.*, (*preterit*, Overtook ; *past part.*, Overtaken) atteindre, rattraper, rejoindre ; surprendre.

overtask' (-tâske), *v.a.*, surcharger de travail ; imposer une tâche difficile **à.**

overtax', *v.a.*, surtaxer, (fig.) surmener.

o'vertime, *n.*, travail en sus, *m.*

overthrow' (-thrô), *v.a.*, (*preterit*, Overthrew ; *past part.*, Overthrown) renverser ; bouleverser ; défaire, détruire, mettre en déroute.

o'verthrow, *n.*, renversement ; bouleversement, *m. ;* défaite ; ruine, destruction, *f.*

o'verthrower, *n.*, renverseur, *m.*

overtire' (-taïeur), *v.a.*, fatiguer trop.

o'vertly (ô-veurt'-), *adv.*, ouvertement ; manifestement.

overtop', *v.a.*, dépasser le sommet **de ;** être plus grand que ; surpasser, éclipser ; s'élever au-dessus **de.**

overtrust' (-treuste), *v.a.*, (ant.) se fier trop **à.**

o'verture (ô-veur-tioure), *n.*, ouverture, *f. ;* (mus.) prélude, *m.*, ouverture, *f.*

overturn' (-teurne), *v.a.*, renverser ; bouleverser ; (a vehicle) verser ; (a boat) faire chavirer.

overturn'er, *n.*, renverseur, destructeur, *m.*

overturn'ing, *n.*, renversement ; bouleversement, *m. ;* (of a carriage) versade, *f.*

overvalua'tion (-val'iou-é-), *n.*, estimation trop élevée, surestimation, *f.*

overval'ue (-val'iou), *v.a.*, priser trop ; estimer trop ; faire trop de cas **de ;** évaluer trop haut.

o'verweak (-wîke), *adj.*, trop faible.

overwea'ry (-wî-rè), *adj.*, excédé de fatigue, épuisé.

overween'ing, *adj.*, présomptueux, outrecuidant. *n.*, présomption, outrecuidance, *f.*

overween'ingly, *adv.*, présomptueusement.

overweigh' (-wé), *v.a.*, (ant.) *V.* **outweigh.**

o'verweight (-wéte), *n.*, excédent, surpoids, *m.*

overwhelm' (ô-veur-hwèlme), *v.a.*, accabler **de,** écraser ; (with kindness) combler **de.**

overwhelm'ing, *adj.*, accablant, écrasant.

overwhelm'ingly, *adv.*, d'une manière irrésistible, accablante.

o'verwise (-waïze), *adj.*, par trop sage.

overwork' (-weurke), *v.a.*, (*preterit* and *past part.*, Overworked, Overwrought) faire travailler au-delà de ses forces ; accabler de travail ; fatiguer ; (a horse) surmener, travailler. To — one's self ; *travailler trop, s'excéder de travail.*

o'verwork, *n.*, travail excessif, excès de travail ; (extra) travail en sus, surplus de travail, *m.*

overworn', *adj.*, accablé de fatigue, usé.

overwrought' (ô-veur-rôte), *adj.*, (l.u.) trop travaillé, trop élaboré.

overzeal', *n.*, excès de zèle, trop de zèle, *m.*

overzeal'ous (-zèl'leusse), *adj.*, trop zélé.

o'vine (ô-vine), *adj.*, ovine. *adj.f.*, de la brebis.

ovip'arous, *adj.*, ovipare.

o'void (ô-voïde), *adj.*, ovoïde, en forme d'œuf.

o'volo (ô-vo-lô), *n.*, (arch.) ove, *m.*

owe (ô), *v.n.*, devoir ; être redevable **à . . . de.** You must — it me ; *nous me devrez cela.*

ow'ing (ô-igne), *adj.*, dû **à.** — to ; *à cause* **de ;** *grâce* **à,** *par suite* **de ;** *qui tient* **à.**

owl (aoul), *n.*, (orni.) hibou, *m.*

owl'er, *n.*, contrebandier, *m.*

owl'et, *n.*, (orni.) hulotte, *f.*

owl'ish, *adj.*, de hibou.

owl'-light (-laïte), *n.*, (ant.) tombée de la nuit, *f.*, crépuscule, *m.*

own (ô'ne), *adj.*, propre (à soi). Of my —; *à moi.* My —; *à moi ; le mien.* At his — house ; *chez lui.* There is not much of his — in that book ; *il n'y a pas beaucoup du sien dans ce livre.* It is a trick of his —; *c'est un tour de sa façon.* To hold one's —; *ne pas lâcher pied ; ne pas perdre de terrain ; tenir sa place ; se maintenir.*

own, *v.a.*, avouer, confesser, convenir **de ;** (to possess) être propriétaire **de ;** avoir ; jouir **de,** posséder ; réclamer, s'attribuer.

own'er, *n.*, propriétaire, possesseur, *m.* Ship- —; *armateur, m.*

own'ership, *n.*, propriété, *f.*

ox, *n.*, (*oxen*) bœuf, *m.*

oxal'ic, *adj.*, (chem.) oxalique.

ox'-calf, *n.*, veau mâle, *m.*

ox'-driver (-draïv'-), *n.*, bouvier, *m.*

ox'eye (-aïe), *n.*, (bot.) buphthalme, œil de bœuf, *m. ;* (orni.) mésange charbonnière, *f.* — **-daisy ;** (bot.) grande marguerite, *f.*

ox'-eyed (-aïe'de), *adj.*, aux yeux de bœuf.

ox'fly (-flaïe), *n.*, taon, *m.*

ox'-goad, *n.*, aiguillon (de bouvier), *m.*

ox'idable (-a-b'l), *adj.*, oxydable.

ox'idate, *v.a.*, oxyder.

oxida'tion, *n.*, oxydation, *f.*

ox'ide (oks'ide), *n.*, (chem.) oxyde, *m.*

ox'idize (-'aïze), *v.a.*, oxyder.

ox'idizement (-aïz'-), *n.*, oxydation, *f.*

Oxo'nian (-ô-ni-), *n.*, étudiant, membre, de l'université d'Oxford, *m.*

ox'-stall (-stôl), *n.*, étable à bœufs, *f.*

ox'tail, *n.*, queue de bœuf, *f.*

ox'-tongue (-teu'gn'e), *n.*, (bot.) buglosse, langue-de-bœuf, *f.*

ox'ygen (-djène), *n.*, (chem.) oxygène, *m.*

ox'ygenate (-djè'n'-), *v.a.*, oxygéner.

oxygena'tion (-djè'n'é-), *n.*, oxygénation, *f.*

ox'ygenize (-djè'n'aïze), *v.a.*, oxygéner.

oxyg'enous (-djè'n'-), *adj.*, d'oxygène.

ox'ygon, *n.*, (ant.) (geom.) triangle oxygone, triangle acutangle, *m.*

ox'ytone (-tône), *n.*, (gram.) oxyton, *m.*

o'yer (ô-yeur), *n.*, (jur.) audition, *f.* — and terminer ; *audition et jugement, m.*

o'yez ! (ô-yèsse), *int.*, oyez ! écoutez ! faites silence !

oys'ter (oïs-teur), *n.*, huître, *f.* — -shell ; *écaille d'huître, f.*

oys'ter-bed (-bède), *n.*, banc d'huîtres, *m.*

oys'ter-brood *ou* **oyster-spawn** (-broude), *n.*, frai d'huîtres, *m.*

oys'ter-fishery, *n.*, pêche des huîtres, *f.*

oy'ster-knife, *n.*, ouvre-huîtres, *m.*

oys'ter-plant, *n.*, salsifis, *m.*

oys'ter-woman (-woum-a'n), *n.*, marchande d'huîtres ; écaillère, *f.*

o'zone, *n.*, (chem.) ozone, *m.*

ozonif'erous, *adj.*, ozonifère.

o'zonize, *v.a.*, ozoniser.

ozonom'eter, *n.*, ozonomètre, *m.*

P

p, seizième lettre de l'alphabet, p, *m.* To mind one's P's and Q's ; *être sur son bien dire ; mettre les points sur les i ; se tenir bien.* To be — and q ; *être de première qualité ; être de la première eau.*

pab'ular *ou* **pab'ulous** (pab'iou-), *adj.,* (ant.) alimentaire.

pab'ulum (pab'iou-leume), *n.,* aliment, nourriture, *m.*

pace (péce), *n.,* pas ; (man.) pas, *m.* At a great —; *à grands pas, à grand train.* At a foot's —; *au pas.* At a slow —; *au petit pas.* To mend, to hurry one's —; *hâter, presser le pas.* To keep — with; *marcher de front avec ; suivre ;* (fig.) *marcher de pair avec.*

pace, *v.n.,* aller au pas ; aller; marcher. To — up and down ; *se promener de long en large.*

pace, *v.a.,* mesurer ; arpenter ; toiser ; faire marcher ; faire aller au pas.

paced (péste), *adj.,* qui a le pas . . . ; au pas ; (broken in) dressé, exercé. Slow— ; *qui a le pas lent.* Easy —; *doux au montoir.* Thorough- —; *consommé.* Thorough- —rascal ; *une franche canaille ; un fameux coquin.*

pa'cer, *n.,* cheval qui va bien au pas, *m.*

pacha' (pa-shō), *n.,* pacha, *m.*

pacha'lic, *n.,* pachalik, *m.*

pach'yderm (pak'i-deurme), *n.,* (mam.) pachyderme, *m.*

pachyder'matous (pak'i-deur-), *adj.,* pachyderme.

pacifi'able, *adj.,* pacifiable.

pacif'ic, *adj.,* pacifique ; calme, paisible ; (geog.) Pacifique.

pacifica'tion (-fi-ké-), *n.,* pacification, *f.*

pacif'icator (-ké'teur), *n.,* pacificateur, *m.*

pacif'icatory, *adj.,* pacificateur, conciliatoire.

pac'ifier (-faï'eur), *n.,* pacificateur, *m.*

pac'ify (-faïe), *v.a.,* pacifier, apaiser, calmer.

pack, *n.,* paquet ; ballot ; fardeau, *m.* ; balle, *f.* ; (heap) tas, *m.* ; (band) bande ; (of hounds) meute, *f.* ; (of cards) jeu, *m.* — cloth ; *toile d'emballage, f.* What a — of nonsense ! *quel tas de bêtises !*

pack, *v.a.n.,* emballer ; encaisser ; (fish, meat) mettre en baril ; (herrings) encaquer ; (cards) préparer ; (jury, etc.) trier subrepticement ; (persons) entasser, ramasser, se tasser ; s'emballer ; s'encaisser ; faire sa malle. To — off ; (of things) *expédier* ; (of persons) *se débarrasser de*; *décamper ; plier bagage.* To send —ing ; *envoyer paître, envoyer promener.* To — up ; *faire sa malle, emballer, empaqueter, encaisser.* A —ed meeting ; *un ramassis de gens corrompus, de partisans.* To — cards ; *tricher.*

pack'age (-'èdje), *n.,* emballage ; (packet) colis, ballot ; paquet, *m.*

pack'er, *n.,* emballeur, *m.*

pack'et, *n.,* paquet, *m.*

pack'et *ou* **pack'et-boat,** *n.,* paquebot, *m.*

pack'horse, *n.,* cheval de bât, *m.*

pack'-ice, *n.,* embâcle, *m.*

pack'ing, *n.,* emballage, *m.* ; (tech.) garniture, *f.* —case ; *caisse d'emballage, f.* —case-maker ; *layetier, emballeur, m.* —needle ; *aiguille d'emballage,* ou *à emballer, f.*

pack'ing-plate, *n.,* plateau de garniture, *m.*

pack'ing-press, *n.,* presse à empiler, *f.*

pack'saddle (-sad'd'l), *n.,* bât, *m.*

pack'thread (-thrède), *n.,* fil d'emballage, *m.* ; ficelle, *f.*

pact, *n.,* (ant.) pacte, *m.*

pad, *n.,* coussinet, bourrelet ; tampon, *m.* ; (of a saddle) sellette, *f.* ; (man.) cheval dressé au pas ; (thief) voleur de grand chemin, *m.* ; (fencing) plastron, *m.*

pad, *v.n.,* (to travel) aller lentement, voyager doucement.

pad, *v.a.,* ouater ; garnir, rembourrer. To — the hoof ; *aller à pied, marcher.*

pad'ding, *n.,* ouate ; garniture, *f.*

pad'dle (pad'd'l), *n.,* rame courte ; (of a canoe) pagaie ; (of a wheel) palette, aube ; (tech.) rame ; (of a lock-gate) pale, *f.* — board ; *palette, f.*

pad'dle, *v.a.n.,* ramer ; aller à la pagaie ; patrouiller, barboter ; patauger ; faire aller à la pagaie ; (like the Indians) pagayer ; (to scull) gabarer. To — on ; *continuer de ramer.* To — about ; *s'amuser à ramer.*

pad'dle-beam (-bîme), *n.,* grand bau de roue à aubes, *m.*

pad'dle-boat, *n.,* vapeur à roues, *m.*

pad'dle-box, *n.,* tambour (de roue), *m.*

pad'dle-door (-dôre), *n.,* vanne, *f.*

pad'dler, *n.,* pagayeur, *m. ;* personne qui barbote, qui patauge, *f. ;* rameur, *m.*

pad'dle-shaft (-shâfte), *n.,* arbre de pale, arbre de roue, *m.*

pad'dle-wheel (-hwîl), *n.,* roue à pales, roue à aubes, *f.*

pad'dling, *n.,* nage à la pagaie ; nage, *f. ;* barbotage, *m.*

pad'dock, *n.,* enclos, pré, pâturage ; (l.u.) gros crapaud ; (of a race-ground) promenoir, *m.*

pad'lock, *n.,* cadenas, *m.*

pad'lock, *v.a.,* cadenasser, fermer au cadenas.

pæ'ony (pî-), *n.,* (bot.) pivoine, *f.*

pa'gan (pé-), *adj.,* païen.

pa'gan, *n.,* païen, *m.,* païenne, *f.*

pa'ganish, *adj.,* païen.

pa'ganism (-ga-n'iz'm'), *n.,* paganisme, *m.*

pa'ganize (-aïze), *v.a.,* (ant.) rendre païen, convertir au paganisme.

page (pédje), *n.,* (pers.) page, *m. ;* (of a book) page, *f.*

page, *v.a.,* (print.) paginer.

pa'geant (pédj'è'n'te), *n.,* spectacle, appareil, *m. ;* parade, pompe, *f.*

pa'geant, *adj.,* de spectacle ; de parade ; d'apparat ; pompeux.

pa'geantry, *n.,* parade, *f. ;* spectacle, *m. ;* pompe, *f. ;* faste, apparat, faux éclat, *m.*

page'-paper, *n.,* (print.) porte-page, *m.*

pag'inal (padj'-), *adj.,* composé de pages ; des pages.

pa'ging (pédj'-), *n.,* (print.) pagination, *f.*

pago'da (-gô-), *n.,* pagode, *f.*

paid, *adj.,* acquitté ; pour acquit ; payé ; (of letters) affranchi ; (of capital) versé. Carriage —; *port payé.* Carriage not —; *port dû.*

pail, *n.,* seau, *m.,* (nav.) baille, *f.*

pail'ful (pél-foule), *n.,* seau, seau plein, *m.*

pain (pé'n'), *n.,* douleur, peine, *f.,* mal, *m. pl.* (care) peine, *f.* In — ; *souffrant.* On — of ; *sous peine de.* To give any one — ; (mental) *faire de la peine à quelqu'un ;* (physical) *faire mal à, causer des douleurs à quelqu'un.* To suffer — ; *souffrir.* To take —s ; *se donner de la peine.* To take —s with ; *soigner.* To have one's labor for one's —s ; *en être pour sa peine.* Where do you feel the — ? *où sentez-vous le mal ?* He has a — in his finger ; *il a mal au doigt.* To be at — s to ; *se donner la peine de.*

pain, *v.a.,* faire mal à ; causer de la douleur à ; faire de la peine à ; attrister, tourmenter ; peiner, affliger.

pain'ful (-foule), *adj.,* douloureux, pénible, laborieux ; (fig.) fâcheux.

pain'fully, *adv.,* douloureusement ; péniblement.

pain'fulness, *n.,* douleur, nature douloureuse, peine, fatigue, *f.*

pain'less, *adj.,* sans douleur, sans peine.

pains'taker (pé'n'z'ték'-), *n.,* travailleur, *m.*

pains'taking, *adj.,* qui se donne de la peine ; laborieux.

paint (pé'n'te), *n.,* couleur ; peinture, *f. ;* (for the face) fard, rouge, *m.* — brush ; *pinceau, m.*

paint, *v.a.,* peindre ; (fig.) peindre, dépeindre ; (the face) farder, se grimer, se maquiller.

paint, *v.n.,* peindre ; (fig.) peindre ; se farder. To — white, red, blue ; *peindre en blanc, en rouge,* **en** *bleu.*

paint'er, — *n.,* peintre ; (nav.) câbleau, *m.* House— ; *peintre en bâtiments, m.*

paint'ing, *n.,* peinture, *f.* ; tableau, *m.*

pair, *n.,* paire, couple, *f.* ; (married people) couple, *m.* A carriage and —; *une voiture à deux chevaux.* — oar ; *à deux avirons.*

pair, *v.a.,* accoupler ; (pers.) unir ; (birds) accoupler ; (colors) marier ; (fig.) assortir.

pair, *v.n.,* (of birds) s'accoupler, s'apparier ; (fig.) s'assortir, se convenir. To — off ; (in parliament) *s'abstenir (de voter) par compensation de votes contraires.*

pair'ing, *n.,* accouplement ; apparîment, *m.* ; (of partridges) pariade, *f.* — , — off ; (in parliament) *absence convenue d'un membre ministériel et d'un membre de l'opposition, f.* — time ; *saison de l'accouplement, f.*

pal, *n.,* compère, camarade, copain, copin ; (b.s.) acolyte, complice, *m.* ; *copine, f.*

pal'ace (pal'ĕce), *n.,* palais, *m.* Bishop's — ; *évêché, m.* Archbishop's — ; *archevêché, m.*

pal'adin, *n.,* paladin, *m.*

palanquin' (-kîne), *n.,* palanquin, *m.*

pal'atable ('-a-b'l), *adj.,* agréable **au goût** ; bon ; de bon goût.

pal'atableness, *n.,* goût agréable, *m.* ; saveur agréable, *f.*

pal'atal, *adj.,* (gram.) palatale, *adj.f.*

pal'atal, *n.,* palatale, *f.*

pal'ate (pal'ate), *n.,* palais (de la bouche), *m.* ; (taste) goût, *m.*

pala'tial (pa-lé-shal), *adj.,* du palais, palatial.

palat'inate, *n.,* palatinat, *m.*

pal'atine, *adj.,* palatin.

pal'atine, *n.,* palatin, *m.*

pala'ver (-lă-), *n.,* flagornerie, *f.* ; verbiage, *m.* ; sornettes, *f.pl.* (pop.) ; conférence, délibération, *f.*

pala'ver, *v.a. and n.,* flagorner, faire des phrases (pop.) ; conférer, délibérer.

pala'verer, *n.,* flagorneur, *m.,* flagorneuse, *f.*

pale, *adj.,* pâle, blême ; (fig.) (of light) blafard, faible. To grow, *ou* turn, pale ; *pâlir.* — as a ghost ; *blanc comme un linge.* — as death ; *d'une pâleur mortelle ou pâle comme la mort.*

pale, *v.a.,* pâlir, faire pâlir.

pale, *v.n.,* pâlir, se ternir ; s'effacer, s'éclipser.

pale, *n.,* pieu ; pais ; (punishment) pal, *m.* ; (bounds) limites, *f.pl.* ; (inclosure) enceinte, sphère, *f.* ; (fig.) (of the church) giron, sein, *m.* To leap the —; *manger son fonds et son revenu.*

pale, *v.a.,* entourer de palis ; palissader ; renfermer. To — up ; (hort.) *palisser.*

pale'-eyed (-aïe'de), *adj.,* aux yeux ternes.

pale'-faced (-féste), *adj.,* au teint pâle.

pale'ly, *adv.,* avec pâleur.

pale'ness, *n.,* pâleur, *f.*

paleog'raphy (pé-li-), *n.,* paléographie, *f.*

pal'etot, *n.,* paletot, *m.*

pal'frey (pâl'-), *n.,* palefroi ; cheval de parade, *m.,* haquenée, *f.*

pal'freyed, *adj.,* monté sur un palefroi.

palifica'tion (-fi-ké-), *n.,* (arch.) palification, *f.* ; pilotis, *m.*

pal'ing (pél'-), *n.,* palissade, *f.*

pal'inode ('-ôde), *n.,* palinodie, *f.*

palisade' (-céde), *n.,* palissade, *f.*

palisade', *v.a.,* palissader.

pal'ish (pél'-), *adj.,* (l.u.) un peu pâle ; pâlot.

pall (pôl), *n.,* poêle ; drap mortuaire ; (of an archbishop) pallium ; (mantle) manteau, *m.* ; (of a ratchet wheel) palette, *f.* —bearer ; *personne qui porte un coin du drap mortuaire, qui tient un cordon du poêle.*

pall, *v.n.,* (of liquors) s'**éventer** ; (to become

insipid) devenir fade, insipide ; (fig.) s'affaiblir, s'affadir, perdre sa force, diminuer, baisser.

pall, *v.a.,* (to cloak) couvrir d'un manteau de parade ; revêtir ; envelopper ; (to make vapid) affadir, éventer ; (to weaken) affaiblir ; (to cloy) rassasier, blaser ; (to dispirit) décourager.

palla'dium (pal-lé-), *n.,* palladium, *m.*

pal'let, *n.,* lit de veille ; grabat, *m.* ; (paint., surg.) palette, *f.* —-knife ; *spatule, f.*

pal'liasse, *n.,* paillasse, *f.*

pal'liate, *v.a.,* pallier.

pallia'tion (-li-é-), *n.,* palliation, *f.*

pal'liative, *adj.,* qui pallie ; palliatif.

pal'liative, *n.,* palliatif, *m.*

pal'lid, *adj.,* pâle, blême, blafard.

pallid'ity *ou* **pal'lidness,** *n.,* pâleur, *f.*

pal'lidly, *adv.,* avec pâleur.

pal'lium, *n.,* (c.rel.) pallium, *m.*

pall-mall' (pèl-mèl), *n.,* mail, *m.*

palm (pâme), *n.,* (of the hand) paume, *f.* ; (bot.) palmier, *m.* ; (branch) palme ; (nav.) patte, *f.* ; (measure) palme, *m.* —Sunday ; *dimanche des Rameaux, m., Pâques fleuries, f.pl.* —-tree ; *palmier, m.* To bear the —; *remporter la palme.* With open — ; *la main ouverte.*

palm, *v.a.,* cacher dans la paume de la main ; glisser ; couler ; escamoter ; (to impose) imposer ; (to handle) manier ; (fig.) attribuer **à.** To — off a thing upon any one for; *faire passer à quelqu'un une chose* **pour.**

pal'ma-chris'ti (-kris'-), *n.,* (bot.) palma-christi, ricin, *m.*

pal'mate *ou* **pal'mated** (-mét'-), *adj.,* palmé.

pal'mer (pâ-meur), *n.,* pèlerin ; croisé, *m.*

pal'miped, *adj.,* (orni.) palmipède.

pal'mistry, *n.,* chiromancie, *f.* ; escamotage, *m.*

pal'my (pâ'm'é), *adj.,* chargé de palmiers ; (fig.) beau, glorieux, victorieux, triomphant (prosperous) beau, heureux, joyeux. In the — days of ; *dans les jours heureux* **de.**

palp, *n.,* (ent.) palpe, *f.*

palpabil'ity *ou* **pal'pableness,** *n.,* nature palpable, palpabilité, *f.*

pal'pable (-pa-b'l), *adj.,* palpable.

pal'pably, *adv.,* palpablement.

palpa'tion (-pé-), *n.,* attouchement, *m.* ; (med.) palpation, *f.*

pal'pebral (pal-pè-), *adj.,* (anat.) palpébral.

pal'pitate, *v.n.,* palpiter.

palpita'tion (-pi-té-), *n.,* palpitation, *f.*

pal'sical (pôl-zi-), *adj.,* paralytique ; paralysé.

pal'sied (pôl-zide), *adj.,* frappé de paralysie ; paralysé.

pal'sy (pôl-zi), *n.,* paralysie, *f.*

pal'ter (pôl-), *v.n.,* tergiverser ; biaiser ; (trifle) jouer avec, plaisanter.

pal'terer (pôl-), *n.,* tergiversateur, biaiseur, *m.*

pal'tering, *n.,* tergiversation, *f.,* biaisement, *m.*

pal'triness (pôl-), *n.,* mesquinerie ; nature chétive, petitesse, *f.*

pal'try (pôl-), *adj.,* insignifiant, chétif ; méchant, mesquin ; qui fait pitié ; pitoyable ; pauvre ; misérable. His verses are of the most — description ; *ses vers sont des plus pitoyables.* A — excuse ; *une misérable excuse.* A — sum ; *une somme insignifiante.*

pa'ly (pé-), *adj.,* (her.) divisé par pals, palé.

pam'per, *v.a.,* gorger, rassasier, nourrir à l'excès ; (to indulge) choyer ; bien traiter, flatter, dorloter ; caresser.

pam'pered (-peur'de), *adj.,* trop nourri ; choyé ; riche ; abondant.

pam'perer, *n.,* pourvoyeur, *m.,* -euse, *f.*

pam'phlet, *n.,* brochure, *f.* ; pamphlet, *m.*

pam'phlet, *v.n.,* écrire des brochures, des pamphlets.

pamphleteer' (-flèt'îre), *n.,* auteur de brochures, (b.s.) pamphlétaire, *m.*

pan, *n.,* terrine ; casserole ; bassine ; poêle, *f.* ;

(of a gun) bassinet, *m.* Foot—; *bain de pieds, m.* His gun flashed in the —; *son fusil rata.* Warming —; *bassinoire, f.* Preserving —; *bassine, f.* A flash in the —; *un feu de paille.* To savor of the frying —; *sentir le fagot.*

panace'a (-cî-a), *n.*, panacée, *f.*

pan'cake (-kéke), *n.*, crêpe, *f.* — Tuesday ; Mardi gras, *m.*

pan'creas (pa'gn'kri-ace), *n.*, (anat.) pancréas, *m.*

pan'dect, *n.*, traité complet, *m. pl.*, pandectes (de Justinien), *f.pl.*

pandemo'nium (-di-mô-),*n.*,pandémonium, *m.*

pan'derer, *n.*, complaisant ; entremetteur, *m.*

pan'der, *v.a.*, favoriser ; se prêter à, se faire complaisant de.

pan'der, *v.n.*, être le complaisant de, être le ministre complaisant de (en amours, en galanteries).

pan'derism, *n.*, métier de complaisant (en amours, en intrigues) ; métier d'entremetteur, *m.*

pane, *n.*, carreau, *m. ;* vitre, *f.* — of glass ; *carreau, m.*

panegyr'ic, *adj.*, de panégyrique.

panegyr'ic, *n.*, panégyrique, *m.*

panegyr'ist (-i-djir'-), *n.*, panégyriste, *m.*

pan'egyrize (pa'n-i-djir'aize), *v.a.*, faire le panégyrique de ; louer ; faire l'éloge de.

pan'egyrize, *v.n.*, faire un panégyrique.

pan'el, *n.*, (arch.) panneau ; (jur.) tableau, *m.*, liste, *f. ;* (ant.) jury, *m.*

pan'el, *v.a.*, faire des panneaux à ; diviser par panneaux ; (to wainscot) lambrisser.

pane'less (pé'n'-), *adj.*, sans carreau, sans vitres.

pan'eling, *n.*, panneaux, lambris, *m.pl. ;* lambrissage, *m.*

pang, *n.*, angoisse ; douleur, *f. ;* saisissement, serrement de cœur, *m.*

pan'ic, *n.*, panique ; terreur panique, frayeur subite,*f.* —-stricken; *saisi d'une terreur panique.*

pan'ic, *adj.*, panique.

pan'ic-grass (-grâce), *n.*, (bot.) panis, *m.*

pan'icle (pa'n'i-k'l), *n.*, (bot.) panicule,*f.*

panic'ulate (-'ik-iou-) *ou* **pan'icled**, *adj.*, (bot.) paniculé, en panicule.

panifica'tion (-fi-ké-), *n.*, panification,*f.*

pan'nade, *n.*, (man.) courbette,*f.*

pan'nage (-nèdje), *n.*, glandée, *f. ;* panage, *m.*

pan'nel, *n.*, (saddle) bât ; (of a hawk) gésier, *m.*

pan'nier (pa'n-nier), *n.*, cacolet, *m. ;* hotte, *f.* On—ed mule ; *en cacolet* (V. Hugo).

pan'oply, *n.*, panoplie, armure complète, *f.*

panora'ma (-râ-), *n.*, panorama, *m.*

panoram'ic, *adj.*, panoramique.

pansla'vism, *n.*, panslavisme, *m.*

pan'sy (-zi), *n.*, (bot.) pensée,*f.*

pant, *n.*, palpitation,*f. ;* battement, *m.*

pant, *v.n.*, battre, haleter, palpiter. To — after ; *soupirer après.* To — for breath; *haleter.*

pantaloons' (-lou'n'ze), *n.*, pantalon à pieds ; (*pl.*) pantalon ; (thea.) pantalon, *m.*

pantech'nicon, *n.*, bazar ; garde-meuble, *m.*

pan'theism (-thi-iz'me), *n.*, panthéisme, *m.*

pan'theist (-thi-), *n.*, panthéiste, *m.*

pantheis'tic *ou* **pantheis'tical** (-thi-), *adj.*, panthéiste.

Panthe'on (-thî-), *n.*, panthéon, *m.*

pan'ther (-theur), *n.*, panthère, *f.*

pan'tile (-taïl), *n.*, tuile faîtière; faîtière,*f.*

pant'ing, *n.*, battement de cœur, *m. ;* palpitation, respiration courte,*f. ;* (fig.) désir ardent, *m.*

pant'ingly, *adv.*, en palpitant, en haletant.

pant'ler, *n.*, panetier, *m.*

pantom'eter, *n.*, (geom.) pantomètre, *m.*

pan'tomime (-tô-maïme), *n.*, pantomime, *f. ;* (ant.) (pers.) pantomime, *m.*

pantomim'ic, *adj.*, de pantomime ; pantomime.

pan'tomimist, *n.*, pantomime, *m.*

pan'ton-shoe (-shou), *n.*, (of horses) fer à pantoufle, *m.*

pan'try, *n.*, garde-manger, *m. ;* office, dépense, *f.*

pap, *n.*, tétin, téton, *m. ;* mamelle, *f. ;* mamelon, *m. ;* (food) bouillie ; (of fruit) pulpe, *f.*

papa' (-pâ), *n.*, papa, père ; (Greek church) papa, *m.* (Voltaire).

pa'pacy (pé-pa-), *n.*, papauté,*f.*

pa'pal (pé-), *adj.*, papal, du pape. The — States ; *Les Etats de l'Eglise*, ou *du Pape*, *m.pl.*

papa'verous (-pé-veur'-), *adj.*, de pavot.

papaw' (-pō), *n.*, (bot.) papaye, *f.* —-tree ; *papayer*, *m.*

pa'per (pé-peur), *n.*, papier, *m. ;* feuille de papier ; (newspaper) feuille, *f. ;* journal, papiernouvelles, papier public ; (article) article, morceau ; (fin.) papier-monnaie, (com.) papier, *m. ;* billets,*m.pl. ;* valeurs,*f.pl. ;* (document) mémoire, écrit, bulletin, document, *m. ;* (schools) copie, (examinations) composition,*f.*, questions d'examen,*f.pl. pl.*, papiers, titres, mémoires, manuscrits, *m.pl.* Brown — ; *papier gris.* Public —s ; *journaux, m.pl. ;* *feuilles publiques, f.pl.* Foreign —; *papier pelure ; papier pelure d'oignon.* Gilt-edged —; *papier doré sur tranche.* Imperial —; *papier jésus.* Stained —; *papier peint.* Stamped —; *papier timbré.* Waste —; *papier de rebut, m. ;* (print.) *maculature, f.* Whitybrown —, *papier bulle.* Blotting—; *papier brouillard.* Foolscap—; *papier écolier.* Letter—, note—; *papier à lettres.* Petition—; *papier ministre.* Printing—; *papier à imprimer; papier d'impression.* Tissue—; *papier de soie ; papier joseph ; papier serpente.* —-clip, — holder; *serre-papiers, m.* — weight ; *presse-papier, m.* Fossil —; *papier fossile.* To set down on —; *coucher par écrit.*

pa'per, *adj.*, de papier ; (fig.) faible. A — army; *une armée sur le papier.* — blockade; *blocus ineffectif, m.* — currency; *papier-monnaie, m.*

pa'per, *v.a.*, (a room) décorer de papier ; tapisser (de papier) ; (to wrap) mettre dans du papier.

pa'per-collar, *n.*, faux col en papier, *m.*

pa'per-credit (-crèd'-), *n.*, crédit sur effets; papier-monnaie, *m.*

pa'pered (-peur'de), *adj.*, décoré de papier ; tapissé.

pa'per-faced (-fés'te), *adj.*, à figure de papier mâché.

pa'per-folder, *n.*, plioir, *m.*

pa'per-hanger (-ha'gn'eur), *n.*, colleur, décorateur, *m.*

pa'per-hangings, *n.pl.*, papier de tenture, papier peint, *m.*

pa'per-knife (-naïfe), *n.*, couteau à papier ; plioir, coupe-papier, *m.*

pa'per-maker (-mék'-), *n.*, fabricant de papier, papetier, *m.*

pa'per-making (-mék'-), *n.*, fabrication du papier, *f.*

pa'per-manufactory (-'iou-fak-), *n.*, papeterie ; fabrique de papier, *f.*

pa'per-manufacturer (-'iou-fak-tiour'-), *n.*, fabricant de papier, papetier, *m.*

pa'per-mill, *n.*, moulin à papier, *m. ;* papeterie,*f.*

pa'per-money (-meu'n-nè), *n.*, papier-monnaie, *m.*

pa'per-rush (-reushe), *n.*, (bot.) papyrus, *m.*

pa'per-stainer (-sté'n'-), *n.*, fabricant de papier peint; dominotier, *m.*

pa'per-staining (-sté'n'-), *n.*, fabrication du papier peint ; dominoterie,*f.*

pa'per-trade (-tréde), *n.*, papeterie,*f.*

pa'per-war (-wor), *n.*, guerre de plume,*f.*

papes'cent (-pèss'-), *adj.*, pulpeux.

pa′pess, *n.*, papesse, *f.*

pa′pier-mâché (pap'i-é-mâ-shé), *n.*, papier mâché, *m.*

papiliona′ceous (-né-sheusse), *adj.*, (bot.) papilionacé, papilionacé.

papil′la (pa-pil-la), *n.*, (anat.) papille. *f.*

pap′illary, pap′illose, *ou* pap′illous, *adj.*, papillaire.

pap′illate, *v.n.*, (anat.) se former en papille.

pa′pism (pé-piz′m), *n.*, (ant.) papisme, *m.*

pa′pist (pé-), *n.*, papiste, *m.*

pa′pistry (pé-), *n.*, (ant.) papisme, *m.*

pap′pose *ou* pap′pous, *adj.*, (bot.) duveteux.

pap′pus, *n.*, (bot.) aigrette, *f.*

pap′py, *adj.*, comme de la bouillie ; mou ; succulent.

papy′rus (pa-païl-), *n.*, (*papyri*) (bot.) papyrus, *m.*

par (pâr), *n.*, égalité, *f.* ; (com.) pair, *m.* At —; *au pair.* On a —; *sur un pied d'égalité* **avec** ; *de pair* **avec**. Above —; *à prime* ; *en prime* ; *au-dessus du pair.* Below —; *au-dessous du pair* ; *(fig.) au-dessous du médiocre.*

par′able (par′a-b′l), *n.*, (gospel) parabole, *f.*

par′able, *v.a.*, représenter par une parabole.

parab′ola, *n.*, (math.) parabole, *f.*

parab′ole (-bô-lî), *n.*, (rhet.) similitude ; comparaison, *f.*

parabol′ic *ou* parabol′ical, *adj.*, par parabole ; parabolique ; allégorique ; (geom.) parabolique.

parabol′ically, *adv.*, paraboliquement.

parab′oloid (-loïde), *n.*, (solid) paraboloïde, *m.*

par′achute (-shioute), *n.*, parachute, *m.*

par′aclete (-clîte), *n.*, (Gospel) Paraclet, *m.*

parade′ (pa-réde), *n.*, parade, *f.* ; étalage, faste, *m.* ; (fenc., milit.) parade, (drill ground) place d'armes, (public walk) esplanade, avenue, terrasse, *f.* To make a — of ; *faire parade* **de**.

parade′, *v.a.*, faire parade **de** ; (milit.) faire faire la parade **à**.

parade′, *v.n.*, se donner en spectacle **à** ; marcher ; (milit.) faire la parade.

par′adigm (-dime), *n.*, paradigme, *m.*

par′adise (-daïce), *n.*, paradis, *m.* To live in a fool's —; *vivre dans une fausse sécurité.*

paradisi′acal (-di-saï-), *adj.*, du paradis.

par′adox, *n.*, paradoxe, *m.*

paradox′ical, *adj.*, paradoxal.

paradox′ically, *adv.*, d'une manière paradoxale.

paradox′icalness (-doks′-), *n.*, caractère paradoxal, *m.*

par′affine, *n.*, paraffine, *f.*

paragog′ic *ou* paragog′ical (-godj′-), *adj.*, paragogique.

par′agon, *n.*, parangon, phénix, modèle ; modèle parfait, chef-d'œuvre ; (print.) parangon, *m.*

par′agram, *n.*, jeu de mots, calembour, *m.*

par′agram′matist, *n.*, faiseur de jeux de mots, faiseur de calembours, *m.*

par′agraph, *n.*, paragraphe ; (break in a) alinéa, *m.* ; (poet.) strophe, *f.* ; (in newspapers) entrefilet, petit article, *m.*

par′agraph, *v.a.*, diviser en paragraphes.

paragraph′ic *ou* paragraph′ical, *adj.*, composé de, *ou* divisé en, paragraphes.

paragraph′ically, *adv.*, par paragraphes.

Para′ grass, *n.*, piassava, *m.*

paralipom′ena (-po′m′i-), *n.pl.*, Paralipomènes, *m.pl.*

parallac′tic *ou* parallac′tical, *adj.*, parallactique.

par′allax, *n.*, (astron.) parallaxe, *f.*

par′allel, *adj.*, parallèle ; (fig.) semblable, pareil. To run — with; *être parallèle* **à** ; *aller parallèlement* **à** ; (fig.) *se conformer* **à**.

par′allel, *n.*, ligne parallèle ; direction parallèle ; (fort., geom.) parallèle, *f.* ; (geog.) parallèle, *m.* ; **(fig.)** comparaison, conformité, *f.*,

parallèle, *m.* To draw a — between ; *établir un parallèle, une comparaison*, **entre**.

par′allel, *v.a.*, mettre dans une ligne parallèle **à** ; placer parallèlement ; (fig.) correspondre **à**, ressembler **à**, mettre en parallèle ; comparer **à** ; être pareil **à**. Never —ed ; *qui n'a jamais eu son pareil.*

par′allelism (-′iz′m), *n.*, parallélisme, *m.* ; (fig.) ressemblance, comparaison, conformité, *f.*

par′allelly, *adv.*, parallèlement.

parallel′ogram, *n.*, parallélogramme, *m.*

parallelopi′ped (-′o-paï-) *ou* parallelopi′pedon (-pip′i-), *n.*, (geom.) parallélépipède, parallélipipède, *m.*

par′alogism (-djiz′m) *ou* paral′ogy (-dji), *n.*, (log.) paralogisme, *m.*

par′alogize (-djaïze), *v.n.*, faire de mauvais raisonnements.

paral′ysis (-cice), *n.*, paralysie, *f.*

paralyt′ic *ou* paralyt′ical, *adj.*, paralytique.

paralyt′ic, *n.*, paralytique, *m.*, *f.* — stroke ; *attaque de paralysie*, *f.*

par′alyze (-laïze), *v.a.*, paralyser. To be —d ; *être frappé de paralysie.*

par′amount (-maou′n′te), *adj.*, souverain, dominant ; en chef ; suprême, principal. — to; *supérieur* **à**. Lord — ; *suzerain, seigneur*, *m.*

par′amount, *n.*, souverain, chef, *m.*

par′amour, *n.*, amant, *m.* ; maîtresse, *f.*

par′apet, *n.*, parapet, *m.*

parapher′nal, *adj.*, (jur.) paraphernal.

parapherna′lia (-feur-né-), *n.pl.*, (jur.) les biens paraphernaux ; paraphernaux, *m.pl.* ; équipement, équipage, paraphernal ; (trappings, etc.) attirail, *m.sing.* ; ornements, atours, colifichets, falbalas, *m.pl.*

par′aphrase (-fréze), *n.*, paraphrase, *f.*

par′aphrase, *v.a.*, paraphraser.

par′aphrast, *n.*, paraphraste, *m.*

paraphras′tic *ou* paraphras′tical, *adj.*, en forme de paraphrase.

paraphras′tically, *adv.*, en forme de paraphrase.

par′aplegy (-plèdj′i), *n.*, (med.) hémiplégie, *f.*

parasele′ne (-sè-lî-ni), *n.*, (astron.) parasélène, *f.*

par′asite (-çaïte), *n.*, parasite, *m.* ; (bot.) plante parasite, *f.*

parasit′ic *ou* parasit′ical (-cit′-), *adj.*, de parasite ; (bot., ent.) parasite ; parasitique.

parasit′ically, *adv.*, en parasite.

par′asitism (-cit′-iz′m), *n.*, parasitisme, *m.*

par′asol (-çol), *n.*, ombrelle, *f.* ; parasol, *m.*

par′boil (pâr-boïl), *v.a.*, faire bouillir, *ou* faire cuire, à demi, *ou* trop ; (nav.) bouillir, *ou* cuire, à demi, *ou* trop.

par′buckle, *n.*, trévire, *f.* *v.a.*, trévirer.

Par′cæ (pâr-ci), *n.pl.*, (myth.) Parques, *f.pl.*

par′cel, *n.*, (bundle) paquet, *m.* ; (a part) parcelle, pièce, portion, partie, *f.* ; (a number, in contempt) tas, *m.* ; (com.) partie, *f.* ; envoi, *m.* Bill of —s ; *facture*, *f.* To be part and — of ; *faire partie intégrante* **de**. — post ; *poste des petits colis, or des colis postaux*, *f.* —s delivery (company); *service du petit roulage* ; *factage*, *m.*

par′cel *ou* par′cel out, *v.a.*, (land) morceler ; diviser ; partager ; distribuer par parcelles.

par′cenary (pâr-cè-), *n.*, (jur.) succession indivise, *f.* In — ; *par indivis.*

par′cener (pâr-cè′n-), *n.*, (jur.) propriétaire indivis (par succession), *m.*

parch (pârtshe), *v.a.*, brûler, rôtir ; dessécher (par la chaleur). To be —ed up ; *être desséché, brûlé.* To be —ed with thirst; *être dévoré de soif.* My lips are —ed with thirst; *la soif m'a desséché les lèvres.* To jump about like a —ed pea in a frying pan; *ne pas tenir en place* ; *ne faire que se remuer.*

parch, *v.n.*, se brûler ; se rôtir ; se dessécher (par la chaleur).

parch'edness (pắrtsh'èd-), *n.*, état brûlé, état rôti, état desséché, *m. ;* aridité, *f.*

parch'ing (pắrtsh'-), *adj.*, brûlant, dévorant.

parch'ment (pắrtsh'-), *n.*, parchemin, *m.* — maker ; *parcheminier, m.* —works ; *parcheminerie, f.sing.* — paper ; *parchemin végétal, m.*

pard (pắrde),*n.*,(mam.)léopard,*m.*,panthère,*f.*

par'don (pắr'd'n), *n.*, pardon, *m. ;* grâce, *f.* To ask any one's —; *demander pardon à quelqu'un.* I beg your —; *je vous demande pardon.*

par'don, *v.a.*, pardonner, pardonner à ; faire grâce **de** ; gracier. — us, me ! *pardon ! permettez !*

par'donable (pắr-d'n'a-b'l), *adj.*, (of things) graciable, pardonnable; (of persons) digne de pardon.

par'donableness, *n.*, nature pardonnable, *f.*

par'donably, *adv.*, d'une manière pardonnable.

par'doner (pắr'd'n'-), *n.* V. **forgiver.**

par'doning (pắr'd'n'-), *adj.*, qui pardonne ; clément ; miséricordieux.

pare, *v.a.*, rogner ; ébarber ; (fruit) peler ; (turf) tondre ; (man.) rogner. To — one's nails ; *se rogner, se couper, les ongles.* To — away, to — off ; *couper ; enlever ; ôter.*

paregor'ic (par-ĭ-), *adj.*, parégorique, anodin.

paregor'ic, *n.*, parégorique, anodin, *m.*

paren'chyma (-rĕn'n'ki-), *n.*, (anat., bot.) parenchyme, *m.*

pa'rent (pèr'-),*n.*, père,*m.*, mère,*f.* *pl.*, père et mère, parents, *m.pl.* *adj.*; mère, principal.

pa'rentage (pèr'è'nt'édje), *n.*, parentage, *m. ;* naissance, extraction, *f.*

paren'tal, *adj.*, de père, de mère ; paternel, maternel.

paren'thesis (-rĕn'n'thi-cice),*n.*, (*parentheses*) parenthèse, *f.* In a —; *entre parenthèses.* By way of —; *par parenthèse.*

parenthet'ic *ou* **parenthet'ical** (-thèt'-), *adj.*, par parenthèse ; (pers.) qui emploie souvent des parenthèses.

parenthet'ically (-thèt'-), *adv.*, par parenthèse.

parent'icide (-çaïde) *n.*, parricide, *m.*

pa'rentless (pèr'-), *adj.*, sans père ni mère.

pa'rer (pèr'-), *n.*, personne qui rogne, qui ébarbe, qui pèle, *f. ;* (thing) ébarboir, rognoir, *m. ;* (farrier's, currier's, tool) boutoir, *m.*

par'get (pắr-djète), *n.*, pierre à plâtre, *f. ;* gypse ; (mas.) crépi, *m.*

par'get, *v.a.*, (mas.) crépir.

par'geter, *n.*, (mas.) ouvrier qui crépit ; plâtrier, *m.*

par'geting, *n.*, crépi, *m.*

parhe'lion *ou* **parhe'lium** (-hĭ-), *n.*, (*parhelia*) (astron.) parélie, parhélie, *m.*

par'iah (pè-rĭ-â), *n.*, paria, *m.*

Pa'rian (pé-), *adj.*, de Paros.

pari'etal (pa-raï-èt'-), *adj.*, de mur ; (anat.) pariétal.

pari'etary (-raï-è-ta-), *n.*, (bot.) pariétaire, *f.*

pa'ring (pèr'igne), *n.*, (of fruits, etc.) pelure; rognure; (of vegetables) épluchure, *f.* — knife; *tranchet, épluchoir, m.*

par'ish, *adj.*, de la commune ; (of roads, rates, etc.) communal, vicinal ; (ecc.) de la paroisse, paroissial. — priest (in France) ; *curé ;* (in England) *ministre, m.* — record ; *registres de la paroisse, m.pl.* — church ; *paroisse, église paroissiale, f.* — clerk ; *clerc de l'œuvre, m.* — relief ; *secours du bureau de bienfaisance, m.* — school ; *école communale,* ou *paroissiale, f.*

par'ish, *n.*, commune ; (ecc.) paroisse, *f.* To come on the —; *être réduit à l'hôpital,* ou *tomber à la charge de la commune.*

parish'ioner, *n.*, habitant de la commune ; (ecc.) paroissien, *m.*

Paris'ian (-rish'ĭ-), *adj.*, de Paris, parisien.

Paris'ian, *n.*, Parisien, *m.*, Parisienne, *f.*

parisyllab'ic *ou* **parisyllab'ical**, *adj.*, parisyllabique.

par'itor, *n.*, (ant.) appariteur, huissier, *m.*

par'ity, *n.*, parité, *f. ;* rapport, *m.*

park (pắrke), *n.*, parc ; (artil.) parc, *m.* — keeper ; *gardien de parc, m.*

park, *v.a.*, enfermer dans un parc ; parquer.

par'lance (pắr-), *n.*, conversation, *f. ;* langage, *m.* In common —; *dans le langage ordinaire.*

par'ley (pắr-), *n.*, pourparler, *m. ;* conférence, *f.* To beat a —; *battre la chamade.*

par'ley, *v.n.*, s'entretenir, converser, conférer **avec** ; être en pourparler **avec** ; (mil.) parlementer.

par'liament (pắr-lè-), *n.*, parlement, *m. ;* chambre, *f. ;* chambres, *f.pl.* House of —; *palais du parlement, m. ; Chambre, f.* Act of —; *loi, f. ; acte du parlement, m.*

parliamenta'rian (-té) *ou* (ant.) **parliamenteer'** (-tîre), *n.*, (English hist.) parlementaire, *m.*

parliamen'tary, *adj.*, parlementaire ; du parlement, de la tribune.

par'lor (pắr-leur), *n.*, petit salon ; (convents, schools) parloir, *m. ;* (of inns) salle, salle commune, *f.* — boarder ; *élève en chambre, m.f.*

par'lous (pắr-), *adj.*, fin, rusé ; hardi, téméraire.

Parmesan' (pắr-mè-za'n), *adj.*, de Parme. —cheese ; *parmesan, m.*

Parnas'sian, *adj.*, du Parnasse.

paro'chial (-rô-ki-), *adj.*, de la commune ; communal ; (ecc.) de la paroisse, paroissial.

paro'chially, *adv.*, par commune ; par paroisse.

parod'ic *ou* **parod'ical**, *adj.*, parodié, travesti.

par'ody, *n.*, parodie, *f.*

par'ody, *v.a.*, parodier, travestir.

parol' *ou* **parole'** (-rôle), *n.*, (jur.) parole, déclaration de vive voix, *f. ;* plaidoyer, *m.*

parol' *ou* **parole'** (-rôle), *adj.*, oral ; verbal ; de vive voix.

parole', *n.*, (milit.) parole, *f.* To be on —; *être prisonnier sur parole.*.

paronoma'sia (-mé-zi-), *n.*, (rhet.) paronomase, *f.*

paronomas'tic, *adj.*, (l.u.) par forme de paronomase.

par'onym, *n.*, paronyme, *m.*

paron'ymous, *adj.*, (gram.) paronyme.

paroquet' (-kète), *n.*, perruche, *f.*

parot'id (-rô-), *n.*, (anat.) parotide, *f.*

par'oxysm (-iz'm), *n.*,(med.)(fig.) paroxysme, accès, *m.*

parquet', *n.*, parquet, *m.* *v.a.*, parqueter. — flooring ; *parquetage, m.*

par'quetry, *n.* parqueterie, *f.*

parrakeet', *n.*, perruche, *f.*

par'rel, *n.*, (nav.) racage, *m.*

parrici'dal (-çaïd'-), *adj.*, parricide.

par'ricide (-çaïde), *n.*, parricide, *m.*

par'rot, *n.*, perroquet, *m. ;* perruche, *f. ;* (fig.) moulin à paroles, *m.*, jacasse, *f.*, imitateur, singe, *m.* —coal ; *anthracite, m.*

par'ry, *v.a.*, parer ; (fig.) éluder ; éviter. To — and thrust ; *riposter.* To — a question ; *éluder une question. v.n.*, riposte, *f.*

parse (pắrse), *v.a.*, (gram.) analyser.

Parsee', *n.*, Parse, Guèbre, Gaure, *m.*

parsimo'nious (pắr-si-mô-), *adj.*, parcimonieux.

parsimo'niously, *adv.*, avec parcimonie.

parsimo'niousness *ou* **par'simony**, *n.*, parcimonie, *f.*

pars'ing (pắrs'-), *n.*, (gram.) analyse, *f.*

pars'ley (pắrs-), *n.*, (bot.) persil, *m.*

pars'nip (pắrs-), *n.*, (bot.) panais, *m.*

par'son (pắr-s'n), *n.*, curé, pasteur, *m.*

par'sonage (pắr-s'n-èdje), *n.*, presbytère, *m. ;* cure, *f.* —house; *presbytère, m.*, *maison curiale, f.*

part (pârte), *n.*, partie; (portion) portion, part, *f.* ; (thea.) rôle ; (side, defense) parti, *m.*, défense ; (of a book) livraison, *f.* ; (quarter) quartier, *m.* ; (mus.) partie, *f. pl.*, (talent) talent, *m.*, moyens, *m.pl.* ; intelligence, *f.* ; (country) pays, *m.*, pays, *m.pl.* ; contrées, *f.pl.* In — ; *en partie.* From all —s ; *de tous côtés.* In —s ; *par livraisons.* In a great — ; *en grande partie.* For my — ; *pour ma part, pour moi.* To take any one's — ; *prendre le parti, la défense de quelqu'un ; prendre fait et cause* **pour**. On any one's — ; *de la part de quelqu'un.* In good — ; *en bonne part.* In ill — ; *en mauvaise part.* That is too much presumption on your — ; *c'est une trop grande présomption de votre part.* Do your — and do not trouble about the rest ; *faites votre devoir, et ne vous inquiétez pas du reste.* To be, *ou* form, — of ; *faire partie* **de**. In the early — ; *dans les premiers (jours ou mois) ; au commencement* **de**. To play a — ; *jouer, ou ac- complir, un rôle.* To be the — of ; *être du de- voir* **de**. For the most — ; *pour la plupart.* — music ; *morceaux d'ensemble, m.pl.* — owner ; *copropriétaire, m. & f.* — and parcel ; *partie essentielle, partie intégrante, f.* — of speech ; (gram.) *partie du discours, f.*

part, *v.a.*, partager ; séparer ; diviser ; (nav.) casser ; (chem.) faire le départ **de**.

part, *v.n.*, se séparer (from *ou* with, **de**) ; se quitter ; (nav.) aller en dérive ; (of cables) se casser, se rompre. To — with ; *se défaire* **de** ; *abandonner, céder ; se dessaisir* **de** ; *se séparer* **de** ; *vendre.*

partake', *v.n.*, (preterit, Partook ; *past part.*, Partaken) participer **à** ; prendre part **à** ; avoir part **à**. To — of ; *prendre part* **à** ; *participer* **à** ; *goûter* **à** ; *manger* **de** ; (to have something of the nature of) *participer* **de**, *tenir* **de**.

partak'er (-ték'-), *n.*, participant, *m.* To be a — of ; *participer* **à** ; *avoir, ou prendre, part* **à**.

partak'ing, *n.*, participation, *f.*

parterre' (pâr-tère), *n.*, (hort.) parterre, *m.*

par'tial (pâr-shal), *adj.*, (biased) partial ; (not total) partiel ; particulier. To be — to; (to like) *aimer ; avoir un faible* **pour** ; *affectionner.*

partial'ity (pâr-shi—), *n.*, partialité ; prédi- lection, *f.* ; goût, *m.* ; affection, préférence, *f.* ; faible, *m.* ; faiblesse, *f.*

par'tially (pâr-shal-), *adv.*, (with a bias) par- tialement ; avec partialité ; (in part) partielle- ment, en partie.

part'ible (pârt'i-b'l), *adj.*, divisible, séparable.

partic'ipant, *adj.*, participant **à** ; qui par- tage ; qui prend part **à**.

partic'ipant, *n.*, participant, *m.*

partic'ipate, *v.a.*, participer à, partager.

partic'ipate, *v.n.*, avoir une part **à**. To — in ; *prendre part* **à** ; *participer* **à** ; *s'associer* **à**. To — of ; *participer* **de**.

participa'tion (pâr-ti-ci-pé-), *n.*, participation, part, *f.*

partic'ipative (-pét'-), *adj.*, (ant.) capable de participer.

particip'ial, *adj.*, de la nature du participe ; participial. — noun ; *substantif participial, m.*

particip'ially, *adv.*, comme participe.

par'ticiple (pâr-ti-cip'l), *n.*, (gram.) parti- cipe, *m.*

par'ticle (pâr-ti-k'l), *n.*, particule ; molécule, *f.* ; grain, *m.* ; la plus petite partie, parcelle, *f.* (gram.) particule, *f.* He has not a — of honor in him ; *il n'a pas un grain d'honneur.*

partic'ular (par-tik'iou-leur), *adj.*, particulier ; spécial ; précis, exact, minutieux, pointilleux ; (scrupulous) scrupuleux ; (over nice) difficile, exi- geant ; (singular) singulier, remarquable, étrange. — in one's dress ; *recherché dans sa toilette.* To be — in choosing things ; *bien choisir, faire un bon choix.* A — friend of mine ; *un de mes amis intimes.* A — account ; *un récit détaillé.* To be

— about it ; *y tenir ; y regarder de près.* I am not — to a day ; *je ne regarde pas à un jour.*

partic'ular, *n.*, particularité, *f.* ; détail ; point circonstancié, *m.* ; circonstance, *f.* Further —s ; *de plus amples détails.* For further —s address . . . ; *pour tous renseignements s'adresser* **à . . .** In — ; *particulièrement ; en particulier.*

particular'ity, *n.*, particularité, *f.* ; détail ; point circonstancié, *m.*

partic'ularize (-aïze), *v.a.*, particulariser, détailler, exposer, spécifier.

partic'ularize (-aïze), *v.n.*, entrer dans des détails minutieux.

partic'ularly (-leur'li), *adv.*, particulièrement ; principalement, surtout, individuellement.

part'ing (pârt'-) *adj.*, de séparation ; d'adieu ; dernier. — shot ; *la flèche du Parthe, f.* — cup ; *coup de l'étrier, m.*

part'ing, *n.*, séparation, *f.* ; départ ; adieu, *m.* ; (hair) raie, *f.*

par'tisan (pâr-ti-z'n), *n.*, partisan, homme de parti ; (staff) bâton de commandement, *m.* ; (hal- bert) pertuisane, *f.* ; (milit.) partisan, *m.*

parti'tion (par-tish'-), *n.*, (division) partage, *m.*, répartition ; division ; séparation ; (bot., carp.) cloison, paroi, *f.* ; (separated part) (ant.) endroit à part, *m.* ; (of a leaf) partition ; (mus.) partition, *f.* — wall ; *refend, mur de refend, m.* ; *cloison, f.*

parti'tion, *v.a.*, partager, diviser, morceler ; (carp.) séparer par une cloison.

par'titive (pâr-), *adj.*, (gram.) partitif.

par'titively, *adv.*, dans un sens partitif.

part'ly (pârt'-), *adv.*, en partie ; partie.

part'ner (pârt'-), *n.*, (com.) associé, *m.*, as- sociée, *f.* ; (mate) compagnon, *m.*, compagne, *f.* ; sociétaire, *m.f.* ; (in dancing) danseur, *m.*, danseuse, *f.* ; cavalier, partenaire, *m.*, dame, *f.* ; (at cards) partenaire, partner, *m.* Sleeping— ; *associé commanditaire ; commanditaire, m.*

part'nership, *n.*, association, société ; (arith.) règle de société, *f.* Dissolution of— ; *dissolution de société, f.* To enter into— with ; *s'associer* **avec**.

par'tridge (pâr-), *n.*, (orni.) perdrix, *f.* Young — ; *perdreau, m.*

partu'rient (-tiou-), *adj.*, (ant.) prête à enfanter ; (of animals) prête à mettre bas, *f.*

parturi'tion (pâr-tiou-rish'-), *n.*, enfantement, *m.*, parturition, *f.*

par'ty (pâr-), *n.*, parti, *m.*, partie, *f.* ; (milit.) détachement, parti, *m.* ; (pers.) partie, personne, *f.*, individu, *m.* ; (of pleasure) partie ; (company) réunion, société, *f.*, monde, *m.* ; (one concerned) partie intéressée, *f.*, intéressé, complice, *m.* — allegiance ; *fidélité à son parti, f.* Attacking — ; (milit.) *troupe d'attaque ; colonne d'attaque, f.* Storming — ; *colonne d'assaut, f.* Fatigue — ; *corvée, f.* Firing — ; *peloton d'exécution, m.* Hunting — ; *partie de chasse, f.* To go on a — ; *faire une partie* **de**. — spirit ; *esprit de parti, m.* Evening— ; *soirée, f.* Leader of a — ; *chef de parti, m.* To be a — to a contract ; (jur.) *être partie contractante.* To go to a — ; *aller en soirée.* To go to a dinner — ; *aller dîner en ville.* To be of the — ; *être de la partie.* To be a — to ; *prendre part* **à** ; *être complice* **de**, *tremper* **dans**. Will you join our — ? *voulez-vous être des nôtres ?* We have a small dancing — this evening ; will you join us ? *nous aurons une sauterie ce soir ; voulez-vous en être ?*

par'ty-col'ored (-keul'leurde), *adj.*, bigarré, bariolé, multicolore.

par'ty-man, *n.*, factieux ; homme de parti, *m.*

par'ty-wall (-wôl), *n.*, mur mitoyen, *m.*

par'venu (pâr-vi-niou), *n.*, parvenu, *m.*

pas'chal (pas-kal), *adj.*, pascal. — eggs ; *œufs de Pâques, m.pl.*

pasch'-flower *ou* **pasque'-flower** (pask- fiaoueur), *n.*, (bot.) pulsatille, coquelourde, herbe au vent, *f.*

pas'quinade (-kwi'n'-), *v.a.n.*, faire des pasquinades **sur**.

pas'quinade (-kwi'n'-), *n.*, pasquinade, *f.*

pass, *v.n.*, passer ; se passer ; (to occur) se passer ; (to die) mourir ; (of time) passer, se passer, s'écouler ; (ant.) (to give judgment) prononcer un jugement. To — away, off ; *passer, se passer, s'écouler, s'évanouir, disparaître ; mourir*. To — by ; *passer à côté* **de** ; *passer devant ; passer*. To — on ; *passer son chemin ; se passer*. To — for ; *passer* **pour**. To — out ; *sortir*. To — over ; *franchir ; passer, traverser ; s'écouler*. To come to — ; *arriver*. To bring to — ; *effectuer, accomplir, amener ; faire arriver*. Words —ed between them ; *il y a eu quelques paroles entre eux ; il y eut un échange d'aménités entre eux*. To be brought to — ; *arriver, s'accomplir, avoir lieu, se faire*.

pass, *v.a.*, passer ; passer **par** ; (to transfer) transférer, faire passer ; (to pronounce) prononcer ; (a law) faire, voter ; (compliment) faire ; (one's word) engager ; (accounts) approuver ; (fig.) passer, surpasser. To — ; (a coin) *donner en payement*. To — round ; *faire circuler*. To — a trick on ; *jouer un tour* **à**. To — away ; *passer ;* (time) *employer, dépenser*. To — by ; (near) *passer à côté* **de** ; (beyond) *passer au delà* **de** ; (to omit) *omettre, oublier, sauter ; ne pas faire attention* **à** ; (to forgive) *pardonner*. To — for ; *faire passer* **pour**. To — over ; *franchir, passer, traverser ;* (to pardon) *pardonner ;* (to omit) *passer ; sauter, omettre ; ne pas voir ; laisser de côté ; négliger ; glisser* **sur**. To — an examination ; *passer un examen*. To — the news along ; *communiquer, ou faire circuler, les nouvelles*. To — a person (in a theater) ; *laisser entrer une personne*. To — a candidate ; *recevoir un candidat*. To — muster ; *passer ; souffrir examen*.

pass, *n.*, (entrance) passage, défilé ; (permission) permis, laissez-passer ; (passport) passeport ; (for vagrants and impotent persons) ordre de transporter les vagabonds et des infirmes à leur demeure respective ; (state) état, *m.*, extrémité, *f.;* (nav.) congé, *m.*, lettres de mer, *f.pl.;* (fenc.) passe, botte, *f.;* (thea.) billet de faveur, billet gratuit ; (excise) laissez-passer, sauf-conduit, *m.* He knows enough to get a — ; (universities) *il sait tout juste ce qu'il faut pour passer l'examen*. — book ; *livre de compte, m.* — key ; *passe-partout, m.* — word ; *mot de passe ; mot d'ordre, mot de ralliement, m.*

pass'able (-a-b'l), *adj.*, praticable ; pénétrable ; (of water) navigable ; (tolerable) passable, tolérable.

pass'ably, *adv.*, passablement ; tolérablement.

passade' (-çâde), **passa'do** (-çâdô), *n.*, (fenc.) botte, passe, *f.*

passade' (-çâde), *n.*, (man.) passade ; (fenc.) passe, botte, *f.*

pas'sage (-cèdje), *n.*, (passing over) passage, *m.*, traversée, *f. ;* (road) chemin, accès, *m. ;* (entrance) entrée, *f. ;* (arch.) couloir, corridor ; (man., mus., and of a book) passage ; (at dice) (ant.) passe-dix, *m.* — boat ; *bac, bateau, m.* — money ; *prix de la traversée, m.* Bird of — ; (orni. fig.) *oiseau de passage, m.* To take — *s'embarquer* **pour**. To force a — ; *s'ouvrir un passage*.

pas'sage (-cèdje), *v.a.* and *n.*, (man.) passager, passéger.

pas'senger (-djeur), *n.*, (on boats) passager, *m.*, passagère, *f.;* (in the street) passant, *m.;* (in vehicles) voyageur, *m.*, voyageuse, *f.*

pass'er *ou* **pass'er-by** (pâss'eur, -baïe), *n.*, passant, *m.*

pas'serine (pass'eur'ine), *adj.*, (orni.) de passereau.

passibil'ity *ou* **pas'sibleness**, *n.*, (ant.) passibilité, *f.*

pas'sible (-si-b'l), *adj.*, (ant.) passible **de**.

pass'ing, *adj.*,(exceeding) extrême, supérieur, éminent ; (ephemeral) passager, éphémère.

pass'ing, *adv.*, extrêmement, éminemment, étonnamment, fort.

pass'ing, *n.*, passage ; cours, (death) trépas, *m.* — of a bill ; *discussion et vote d'un projet de loi.*

pass'ing-bell, *n.*, glas, *m.*

pass'ing-place, *n.*, (railways) gare d'évitement ; voie supplémentaire, *f.*

pas'sion (pash'-), *n.*, passion , (anger) colère, *f.*, courroux, emportement ; (zeal) zèle, *m.*, ardeur, *f.* In a — ; *en colère*. To fly into, to put one's self into a — ; *se mettre en colère ; s'emporter*. His — is music ; *la musique est sa passion.*

pas'sionate (pash'-), *adj.*, colère, colérique, irascible, vif, emporté ; (of things) passionné, ardent.

pas'sionately (pash'-), *adv.*, à la passion ; à la folie ; passionnément ; avec emportement, avec colère ; ardemment ; extrêmement.

pas'sionateness (pash'-), *n.*, caractère passionné ; caractère irascible, colérique, *m. ;* véhémence ; ardeur, *f.*

pas'sion-flower (-flaoueur), *n.*, (bot.) passiflore, grenadille, fleur de la passion, *f.*

Pas'sion-play, *n.*, mystère (de la passion de Notre-Seigneur), *m.*

Pas'sion-week (-wîke), *n.*, semaine sainte, *f.*

pas'sive, *adj.*, passif.

pas'sively, *adv.*, passivement.

pas'siveness, *n.*, nature passive ; passibilité, *f.*

pass'less (pâss'-), *adj.*, sans passage, impassable.

pass'over (pâss'ô-), *n.*, Pâque, *f.* (of the Jews).

pass'port (pâss-), *n.*, passeport, *m.*

past (pâst), *adj.*, passé. — a child ; *qui a passé l'enfance*. These — days ; *ces jours derniers, m.pl.*

past, *adv.*, près, par là. He ran — ; *il passa près de là en courant.*

past, *prep.*, au delà **de** ; au-dessus **de** ; à côté **de** ; près **de** ; devant ; sans ; hors **de** ; (of age) plus **de** ; (of the hour) passé, sonné, et. — feeling ; *sans sentiment*. — cure ; *incurable*. — dispute ; *incontestable ;* — remedy ; *sans remède*. In times — ; *autrefois, par le passé*. It is — ten ; *il est dix heures passées, sonnées*. It is — twelve ; *il est midi sonné, passé*. Half — twelve ; *midi et demi*. It is ten minutes — three ; *il est trois heures dix.*

past, *n.*, passé, *m.*

paste (péste), *n.*, (dough) pâte ; (cement) colle ; (paint.) maroufle, *f. ;* (imitation gem) stras, *m.*

paste, *v.a.*, coller. To — up ; *poser, afficher.*

paste'board (-bôrde), *n.*, carton, *m.* — maker ; *cartonnier, m.*

paste'board, *adj.*, de carton.

paste'-brush, *n.*, doroir, *m.*

pas'tel, *n.*, (art, dyeing) pastel, *m. ;* (bot.) guède, *f.*

paste'-pot, *n.*, pot à colle, *m.*

pas'tern (pâs-teurne), *n.*, (horse) paturon, *m.*

pastic'cio (pas-tit'shi-ô), *n.*, mélange ; (mus., paint.) pastiche, *m.*

pas'til (pâs-), *n.*, pastel, crayon de pastel, *m. ;* (pharm.) pastille, *f.*

pas'time (pâs'taïme), *n.*, passe-temps, amusement, *m. ;* récréation, distraction, *f.*

pas'tor (pâs-teur), *n.*, (Protest. minister) pasteur, *m.*

pas'toral (pâs-), *adj.*, pastoral. — staff ; *crosse, f.* — ring ; *anneau pastoral, m.*

pas'toral, *n.*, pastorale, églogue, *f.*

pas'torally, *adv.*, pastoralement.

pas'torless, *adj.*, sans pasteur.

pas'torly, *adj.*, pastoral ; de pasteur.

pas'torship, *n.*, fonctions pastorales, *f.pl.*
pas'try (pés'-), *n.*, pâtisserie, *f.*
pas'try-cook (-couke), *n.*, pâtissier, *m.*
pas'turable (pâst'ieur'a-b'l), *adj.*, propre au pâturage ; de pâturage, pâturable.
pas'turage (-èdje), *n.*, pâturage, *m.*
pas'ture (pâst'ieur), *n.*, pâture, *f.*, pâturage, *m. ;* (hunt.) viandis, *m.* — ground; *pâturage*, *m.*
pas'ture, *v.n.*, paître.
pas'ture, *v.a.*, faire paître, nourrir.
pas'ture-land, *n.*, pâturage, *m.*
pas'tureless, *adj.*, sans pâture, sans pâturage.
pas'ty (pés'ti), *n.*, pâté, *m.*
past'y, *adj.*, pâteux.
pat, *adj.* and *adv.*, à propos, tout juste ; sans tortiller.
pat, *n.*, tape, *f. ;* (for butter) moule à beurre, *m.* Pat ; (Irish) *Patrice*, *m.* — of butter ; *rond de beurre, m.*
pat, *v.a.*, donner une tape à, des coups de patte à ; caresser. To — on the back; (fig.) *flatter à l'excès.*
patache' (-tâshe), *n.*, (small vessel ; stage-coach) patache, *f.*
patch, *n.*, pièce, *f. ;* morceau, *m. ;* (for the face) mouche, *f. ;* (of land) coin, morceau, *m. ;* (of plants) touffe, *f.* Cross — ; (pers.) *bourru, grognon*, *m.* Little cross — ; *petit grognon, m.* —work ; *rapiécetage, replâtrage*, *m.*, pièces de rapport, *f.pl. ;* assemblage disparate ; (medley) *mélange*, *m.*, mosaïque, *f.*
patch, *v.a.*, mettre des pièces à ; rapiécer, rapiéceter, raccommoder ; (the face) mettre des mouches à. To — up ; *plâtrer, replâtrer ;* (fig.) bâcler, bousiller. Not to be a — on ; *n'être pas digne d'être comparé à.*
patch'er, *n.*, ravaudeur, *m.*, ravaudeuse, *f. ;* savetier, gâcheur, *m.*
patch'ing, *n.*, rapiécetage, ravaudage, replâtrage, *m.*
patch'y, *adj.*, fait de pièces et de morceaux ; bariolé.
pate, *n.*, caboche, boule, tête ; (of a calf) peau de tête de veau, *f. ;* (fort.) pâté, *m.*
pa'ted (pét'-), *adj.*, (l. u.) à caboche. Shallow-—; *à caboche vide.*
pat'en, *n.*, (ecc.) patène, *f.*
pa'tent (pét'- *ou* pat'-), *adj.*, patent; breveté; (fig.) apparent, évident. — leather ; *cuir verni, m.* — office ; *bureau pour les brevets d'invention*, *m.*
pa'tent, *n.*, lettres patentes, *f.pl. ;* privilège ; brevet, brevet d'invention, *m.* To take out a — ; *prendre un brevet.*
pa'tent, *v.a.*, accorder par lettres patentes ; breveter.
pa'tentable (-a-b'l), *adj.*, brevetable.
patentee' (-tî), *n.*, concessionnaire ; breveté, *m.*, brevetée, *f.*
paterfamil'ias, *n.*, père, *ou* chef, de famille, *m.*
pater'nal (-teur-), *adj.*, paternel. — grand-father; *aïeul paternel, m.* — grandmother; *aïeule paternelle, f.*
pater'nally, *adv.*, paternellement.
pater'nity (-teur-), *n.*, paternité, *f.*
pa'ter noster, *n.*, Pater, *m. ;* patenôtre, *f.*
path (pâth), *n.*, chemin, sentier, *m. ;* (in gardens) allée, *f. ;* (astron.) route, *f.*, cours, *m. ;* (fig.) voie, *f.* Beaten — ; *sentier battu*, *m.* By- — ; *sentier détourné*, *m.* Foot- — ; (in towns) trottoir, *m. ;* (rural) sentier, *m. ;* bas-côté, accotement, *m.*
pathet'ic (-thèt'-), *adj.*, pathétique.
pathet'ic (-thèt'-), *n.*, pathétique, *m.*
pathet'ically (-thèt'-), *adv.*, pathétiquement.
path'less (pâth'-), *adj.*, sans sentier, sans chemin frayé ; (fig.) inconnu, désert.
patholog'ical (-thol'o-dj'-), *adj.*, pathologique.
patholog'ically (-thol'-), *adv.*, pathologiquement.
pathol'ogist (-thol'-), *n.*, pathologiste, *m.*
pathol'ogy (-thol'o-dji), *n.*, pathologie, *f.*

pa'thos (pé-thoss), *n.*, pathétique ; (rhet.) pathos, *m.*
path'way (pâth'wé), *n.*, sentier ; chemin, *m. ;* (fig.) sentier, *m.*
patib'ulary (-tib'iou-), *adj.*, patibulaire.
pa'tience (pé-shè'n'ce), *n.*, patience ; (bot.) patience, parelle ; (game of cards) réussite, *f.* To lose, *ou* to be out of, — ; *perdre patience ; être à bout de patience.* To have — ; *patienter, prendre patience.* To put out of — ; *impatienter ; faire perdre patience à.* To get out of — ; *s'impatienter.* I am quite out of — with him ; *il a mis ma patience à bout.*
pa'tient (pé-shè'n'te), *n.*, malade, *m., f.*
pa'tient, *adj.*, patient.
pa'tiently, *adv.*, patiemment.
pat'in, *n.* *V.* pat'en.
pat'ly, *adv.*, juste, à propos, à point; sans tortiller, carrément.
pat'ness, *n.*, justesse, *f. ;* à-propos, *m.*
pa'triarch (pé-tri-ârke), *n.*, patriarche, *m.*
patriar'chal, *adj.*, patriarcal.
pa'triarchate *ou* pa'triarchship, *n.*, patriarcat, *m.*
patri'cian (-trish'-), *adj.*, patricien.
patri'cian, *n.*, (Rom. Hist.) patricien, *m.*, patricienne, *f. ;* (Rom. Empire) patrice, *m.*
patrimo'nial (-mô-), *adj.*, patrimonial, de patrimoine.
patrimo'nially, *adv.*, comme patrimoine ; par héritage.
pat'rimony, *n.*, patrimoine, *m.*
pa'triot (pé-), *n.*, patriote, *m.f.*
patriot'ic, *adj.*, (of things) patriotique ; (of persons) patriote.
patriot'ically, *adv.*, patriotiquement ; en patriote.
pa'triotism (-'iz'm), *n.*, patriotisme, *m.*
patrol', *n.*, (milit.) patrouille, ronde, *f.*
patrol' (-trôl), *v.n.*, (milit.) faire la patrouille dans ; patrouiller.
pa'tron (pé-), *n.*, patron ; protecteur, *m.* — saint ; *patron, m.*, *patronne, f.*
pat'ronage (-'èdje), *n.*, patronage, appui, *m. ;* protection, *f.*
pa'troness (pé-), *n.*, patronne, protectrice ; (of charities) dame patronnesse, patronnesse, *f.*
pat'ronize (-'aïze), *v.a.*, favoriser, protéger, patronner, soutenir, défendre ; (a shop) fréquenter.
pat'ronizer (-'aïzeur), *n.*, protecteur, *m.*, protectrice, *f.*
pat'ronizingly, *adv.*, d'un air de protection.
pa'tronless, *adj.*, sans protecteur.
patronym'ic, *adj.n.*, patronymique, *m.*
pat'ten, *n.*, socque ; (arch.) soubassement, *m.*
pat'ter, *v.n.*, grésiller, frapper avec bruit (comme la grêle, la pluie) ; fouetter ; (to talk) caqueter.
pat'tering, *n.*, (of hail, rain) grésillement ; (of feet) petit bruit, *m. ;* caquet, *m.*
pat'tern, *n.*, patron, modèle ; (specimen, sample) échantillon ; (design) dessin ; (fig.) modèle, exemple, *m.* — drawer ; *dessinateur*, *m.* — card ; *carte d'échantillons*, *f.* To have made to — ; *faire faire sur échantillon, sur modèle.* To take — by ; *se modeler sur.*
pat'ty, *n.*, petit pâté, *m.*
pat'ty-pan, *n.*, moule à pâtés, *m.*
pat'ulous (pat'iou-), *adj.*, (bot.) étalé.
pau'city, *n.*, petit nombre, *m.*, petite quantité, *f. ;* manque de, *m.*, disette de, *f.*
paunch (pâ'n'sh *ou* pô'n'sh), *n.*, panse, *f. ;* ventre, *m. ;* (nav.) baderne, *f.*
pau'per, *n.*, pauvre, indigent, mendiant, *m.*
pau'perism, *n.*, paupérisme, *m.*
pau'perize, *v.a.*, réduire à l'indigence.
pause (pôze), *n.*, pause, *f. ;* intervalle ; silence, moment de silence ; (poet.) repos, *m. ;* césure, *f. ;* (mus.) point d'orgue, *m.* Awful — ; *silence de mort, m.*

pause, *v.n.*, faire une pause, s'arrêter ; délibérer ; attendre, hésiter ; réfléchir. To — upon ; *bien considérer*. I — for a reply ; *j'attends votre réponse.*

pave, *v.a.*, paver (with, **de**). To — a way for ; *frayer, préparer, un chemin* à.

pave'ment, *n.*, pavé ; trottoir ; (of tiles) carreau, *m. ;* (of flagstones) dalles, *f.pl.*

pa'ver, pa'vier *ou* **pa'vior** (pé-), *n.*, paveur, *m.*

pavil'ion, *n.*, pavillon, *m. ;* tente, *f.*

pavil'ion, *v.a.*, munir de pavillons, de tentes ; abriter sous un pavillon, une tente.

pav'ing (pév'-), *n.*, pavement, pavage, *m.* — tile, — brick ; *carreau, m.*

pav'ing-beetle (-bīt't'l), *n.*, hie, demoiselle,*f.*

pav'ing-stone (-stōne), *n.*, pavé, *m. ;* (flag) dalle, *f.*

pav'onine (-naïne), *adj.*, irisé, gorge-de-pigeon.

pav'onine (-naïne), *n.*, (min.) sulfure de cuivre irisé, *m.*

paw (pō), *n.*, patte ; (jocul.) main, patte, *f.*

paw (pō), *v.a.*, frapper du pied ; (to handle) manier, manier rudement, patiner ; (to scratch) griffer ; (to fawn) flatter, caresser. To — the ground ; *piaffer.* —ed, *adj.*, à pattes.

paw (pō), *v.n.*, trépigner ; (of horses) piaffer.

pawn (pō'n), *n.*, gage ; nantissement ; (at chess) pion, *m.* In — ; *en gage ; engagé.* — ticket ; *reconnaissance, f.* To put in — ; *mettre en gage, engager.* To take out of — ; *dégager.*

pawn, *v.a.*, engager ; mettre en gage ; mettre au mont-de-piété.

pawn'broker (-brōk'-), *n.*, (in England) prêteur sur gage ; (in France) commissionnaire du mont-de-piété, *m.*

pawnee' (pō'n'ī), *n.*, (ant.) prêteur sur gage, *m.*

pawn'er, *n.*, emprunteur sur gage, *m.*

pawn'ing, *n.*, engagement, *m.*

pawn'shop, *n.*, (in France) mont-de-piété, *m. ;* (in England) boutique de prêteur sur gage, *f.*

pax, *n.*, (ecc.) paix, *f.*

pay, *n.*, paye, solde, *f. ;* salaire, *m. ;* (salary) appointements, *m. ;* (of a servant) gages, *m.pl. ;* (mil.) (privates) prêt, *m. ;* (officers) solde, *f.* Full — ; *paye entière, solde entière, f.* Half— ; *demi-solde, f.* Extra — ; *supplément de solde, m. ; surpaye, f.* To be on half — ; *être en demi-solde ; être à la suite.* To be in the — of ; *être à la solde* **de** ; *aux gages* **de**. To be a bad — ; *être une mauvaise paye.*

pay, *v.a.*, payer, acquitter ; s'acquitter **de** ; (fin.) verser ; (bring in) rapporter ; (compliments, attention) faire ; (attentions) avoir des attentions **pour** ; (honor) rendre ; (visits) rendre, faire. To — back ; *rendre, rembourser, restituer.* To — down ; *payer argent comptant.* To — off ; *payer ; liquider.* To — on, over ; (nav.) *espalmer, goudronner, solder, suiffer.* To — away ; *payer ;* (nav.) (of cable) *filer.* To — out ; *lâcher ; ralentir ; étendre ; laisser courir ;* (fig.) *donner son fait* à, *rendre la pareille* à ; *rembarrer.* To — in ; *verser.* To — homage ; *rendre hommage* à. To — one's addresses to ; *faire sa cour* à, *courtiser.* To — a visit ; *faire une visite* à. To — an account ; *solder un compte.* You will — dearly for this insolence ; *cette insolence vous coûtera cher.* This does not — ; *le jeu n'en vaut pas la chandelle ; je n'y trouve pas mon compte ; cela ne fait pas mon affaire.* To — for ; *payer ;* (fig.) *payer cher.* To — a person ; *payer quelqu'un.* To — a person something ; *payer quelque chose à quelqu'un.* To — one's addresses (to a lady) ; *faire la cour* **a**. To — off a crew ; *licencier un équipage ;* (a mortgage) *purger une hypothèque.* To — out ; *donner une roulée* à, *rosser.* To — the piper ; *payer les violons ; payer l'amende.* Carriage paid ; *port payé.* Carriage not paid ; *port dû.*

pay'able (pé-a-b'l), *adj.*, payable. — to order ; *à l'ordre* **de**. — to bearer ; *au porteur.*

pay'-bill, *n.*, (milit.) feuille de prêt, *f.*

pay'-day, *n.*, jour de payement, jour de paye, *m.*

payee' (pé-ī), *n.*, (com.) porteur, *m.*

pay'er (pé-eur), *n.*, payeur, *m.*

pay'master (-mâs-), *n.*, payeur ; (milit.) trésorier ; (nav.) agent comptable, *m.*

pay'ment, *n.*, payement, paiement, *m.* — in full of all demands ; *pour solde de tout compte, f.* — on account, *ou* in part ; *acompte, m.*

pea (pī), *n.*, pois, *m.* Green —s ; *petits pois ; pois verts, m.pl.* — gun, *ou* — shooter ; *sarbacane, f.* — soup ; *purée de pois, f.*

peace (pīce), *n.*, paix ; tranquillité, *f. ;* (jur.) ordre public, *m.* —-officer ; *officier de police, officier de paix, m.* Breach of the — ; *délit contre l'ordre public, m.* — establishment ; *pied de paix, m.* Justice of the — ; *juge de paix, m.* At — ; *en paix.* To keep the — ; *ne pas troubler l'ordre public ; s'abstenir de voies de fait* **envers**. To hold one's — ; *se taire.* To make one's — with ; *se réconcilier* **avec**. — of God and the Church ; (Medieval Hist.) *trève de Dieu, f.* —-offering ; (Bible) *sacrifice de propitiation, m.*

peace'able (-'a-b'l), *adj.*, paisible, tranquille.

peace'ably, *adv.*, paisiblement, tranquillement, avec calme.

peace'ful (-foule), *adj.*, paisible ; tranquille, calme.

peace'fully, *adv.*, paisiblement, tranquillement.

peace'fulness, *n.*, tranquillité, *f.*, calme, *m.*

peace'less, *adj.*, sans paix ; sans tranquillité.

peace'-maker (-mék'-), *n.*, pacificateur, *m.*

peace'-making, *n.*, pacification, *f.*

peach (pît-she), *n.*, (hort.) pêche, *f. ;* (tree) pêcher, *m.* —-color, colored ; *couleur fleur de pêcher, f.* — house ; *serre à pêchers, f.* — stone ; *noyau de pêche, m.*

pea'-chick (-tshike), *n.*, (orni.) paonneau, *m.*

pea'cock, *n.*, (orni.) paon, *m.* In —'s feathers ; *paré des plumes du paon.*

pea'-green, *adj.*, vert pois.

pea'hen (pî-hène), *n.*, (orni.) paonne, *f.*

peak (pîke), *n.*, pointe, *f. ;* sommet ; (geog.) pic, *m. ;* (of a mountain) cime, *f. ;* piton, *m. ;* (of a cap) visière, *f.*

peaked, *adj.*, pointé, à visière.

peak'y, peak'ing, *adj.*, maigre, pâle ; malingre ; aux os saillants.

peal (pîle), *n.*, bruit ; retentissement ; (of thunder) éclat, coup ; grondement ; (of bells) carillon, *m. ;* volée ; (of cannon) salve ; (of applause) salve, *f. ;* (of laughter) éclat, *m.*

peal, *v.n.*, retentir, résonner ; gronder ; carillonner.

peal, *v.a.*, faire retentir, faire résonner.

pea'-pod, *n.*, gousse, *ou* cosse, de pois, *f.*

pear (père), *n.*, poire, *f.*

pearl (peurle), *n.*, perle, *f. ;* (print.) parisienne, sédanoise ; (med.) taie perlée de la cornée, *f. ;* (her.) argent, *m.* Mother-of— ; *nacre, f.* It is casting —s before swine ; *c'est du bien perdu.*

pearl, *v.a.n.*, perler.

pearl'-ash, *n.*, (chem.) perlasse ; potasse d'Amérique, *f.*

pearl'-diver, *n.*, pêcheur de perles, *m.*

pearled (peurlde), *adj.*, perlé (ant.) ; orné de perles ; (her.) perlé. — barley ; *orge perlé, m., orge perlée, f.*

pearl'-eyed (-aïe-de), *adj.*, qui a une taie sur l'œil.

pearl'-fishery, *n.*, pêche de perles, *f.*

pearl'-grass (-grâce), *n.*, (bot.) grémil, *m.*, herbe aux perles, *f.*

pearl'-gray, *adj.*, gris perle, gris de perle, *m.*

pearl'-oyster, *n.*, (zoöl.) huître perlière, *f.*

pearl'-powder (-paou-), *ou* **pearl'-white** (-hwaïte), *n.*, blanc de perle, *m.*

pearl'-shell, *n.*, nacre, *f.*

pearl'-white, *n.* V. **pearl'-powder.**

pearl'-wort, *n.*, (bot.) sagine, *f.*

pearl'y, *adj.*, de perle.

pear'main (pèr-méne), *n.*, (hort.) pomme-poire, *f.*

pear'-tree (-trî), *n.*, poirier, *m.*

peas'ant (péz'-), *n.*, paysan, *m.*, paysanne, *f.*

peas'ant, peas'ant-like (-laïke), *adj.*, de paysan ; rustique.

peas'antry, *n.*, paysans, gens de la campagne, *m.pl.*

pease (pîze), *n.pl.* V. **pea.**

peat (pîte), *n.*, tourbe, *f. ;* (mines) dépôt tourbeux, *m. ;* (for fuel) motte à brûler, *f.*

peat'-moss, *n.*, tourbe, *f.*

peb'ble (pèb'b'l), *n.*, caillou ; (for spectacles) cristal de roche, *m.*

peb'ble-work (-weurke), *n.*, blocage, cailloutage, *m.*

peb'bly, *adj.*, plein de cailloux ; caillouteux.

pec'cable (pèk'ka-b'l), *adj.*, peccable.

peccadil'lo (pèk'ka-dil-lô), *n.*, peccadille, *f.*

pec'cancy (pèk'-), *n.*, vice, défaut, *m.*

pec'cant, *adj.*, pécheur ; coupable.

pecca'vi (pèk'ké-vi), *n.* To cry —; *dire son meâ culpâ.*

peck (pèke), *n.*, (of oats) picotin, *m. ;* (quantity) quantité, *f.*

peck, *v.a.*, becqueter ; percer à coups de bec ; picoter. To — at ; *gloser sur ; critiquer.* To — a hole ; *faire un trou* (à coup de bec). A hen——ed husband ; *un mari mené par sa femme ; un jocrisse.*

peck'er, *n.*, (orni.) pivert, *m.* To keep up one's — ; *ne pas perdre courage.*

peck'ing, *n.*, coups de bec, *m.pl.*

peck'ish, *adj.*, en appétit.

pec'toral (pèk'-), *n.*, pectoral, *m.*

pec'toral, *adj.*, pectoral.

pec'ulate (pèk'iou-), *v.n.*, être coupable de péculat.

pecula'tion (pèk'iou-lé-), *n.*, péculat, *m.*

pec'ulator (-lé-teur), *n.*, auteur d'un péculat, concussionnaire, *m.*

pecu'liar (pi-kiou-li-eur), *adj.*, particulier, propre, spécial ; singulier ; bizarre, original.

pecu'liar, *n.*, propriété particulière ; (canon law) chapelle privilégiée, *f.*

peculiar'ity, *n.*, propriété particulière ; chose particulière ; singularité, particularité, originalité, *f.*

pecu'liarly, *adv.*, particulièrement ; spécialement ; singulièrement.

pecu'niary (pi-kiou-), *adj.*, pécuniaire.

pedagog'ic (-go-djike), *adj.*, pédagogique.

ped'agogue (pèd'a-goghe), *n.*, pédagogue, *m.*

ped'agogy (-godj'i), *n.*, pédagogie, *f.*

ped'al (pèd'-), *n.*, pédale, *f.* — board ; *marche de pédale, f.* — note ; *note soutenue, f.* — stop ; *pédale, f.*

ped'al, *adj.*, du pied.

ped'ant (pèd'-), *n.*, pédant, *m.*

pedan'tic (pèd'-), *adj.*, pédant, (of things) pédantesque.

pedan'tically, *adv.*, pédantesquement.

ped'antry (pèd'-), *n.*, pédanterie, *f.*, pédantisme, *m.*

ped'dle (about) (pèd'd'l), *v.a.*, colporter.

ped'dle, *v.n.*, s'occuper de bagatelles ; baguenauder, niaiser ; faire le colportage.

ped'dler, *n.* V. **ped'lar.**

ped'dling, *adj.*, futile, mesquin, de peu de valeur.

ped'dling, *n.*, colportage, *m.*

ped'estal (pèd'-), *n.*, piédestal, *m.*

pedes'trian (pi-dès-), *adj.*, à pied ; pédestre.

pedes'trian, *n.*, piéton ; marcheur, *m.*

ped'icel (pèd'i-cèl) *ou* **ped'icle** (pèd'i-k'l), *n.*, (bot.) pédicelle, pédoncule, *m.*

pedic'ular (pi-dik'iou-), *adj.*, (med.) pédiculaire.

ped'igree (pèd'i-grî), *n.*, généalogie, *f.*

ped'igree, *adj.*, généalogique.

ped'iment (pèd'-), *n.*, fronton, *m.*

ped'lar *ou* **ped'dler** (pèd'-), *n.*, colporteur, *m.*, colporteuse, *f. ;* chipotier, tatillon, *m.*

ped'lary, ped'dlery, *n.*, marchandise de colporteur, *f. ;* colportage, *m.*

pedom'eter (pi-deum'i-), *n.*, pédomètre, odomètre, compte-pas, *m.*

pedomet'rical, *adj.*, de pédomètre.

pedun'cle (pi-deu'gn'k'l), *n.*, (bot.) pédoncule, *m.*

pedun'cular (pi-deu'gn'k'iou-), *adj.*, (bot.) pédonculé.

pedun'culate, *adj.*, (bot.) pédonculé.

peel (pîl), *n.*, peau ; pelure ; (of oranges, lemons) écorce, *f. ;* (print.) étendoir, *m. ;* (shovel) pelle de four, *f.*

peel, *v.a.*, peler ; ôter l'écorce de ; (fig. ant.) dépouiller, piller ; (barley) monder.

peel, *v.n.*, se peler ; s'écailler.

peel'er, *n.*, personne qui pèle, *f. ;* (London) (pop.) sergent de ville, sergot, agent, *m.*

peep (pîpe), *n.*, (of day) point, *m.*, pointe, aube, *f. ;* (look) coup d'œil, regard, *m.* — -hole ; *judas, m.* — show ; *optique, f.* — -o'-day ; *point du jour, m.* Bo- — ; *cache-cache, m.* To take a — at ; *donner un coup d'œil à, ou regarder, furtivement.*

peep, *v.n.*, (to look) regarder ; (to appear) (of the day) paraître, poindre, percer, se montrer ; (of flowers) éclore ; (of chickens, etc.) pépier, piper. To — slily ; *regarder à la dérobée.*

peep'er, *n.*, curieux, -se, *m.f. ;* (chicken) poussin, *m.*

peer (pîr), *n.*, pair ; égal, pareil ; compagnon, *m.*

peer, *v.n.*, paraître ; poindre. To — into ; (to look) *regarder.* —ing eyes ; *regards scrutateurs, m.pl.*

peer'age (pîr'èdje), *n.*, pairie, *f. ;* pairs, *m.pl.* To raise to the — ; *anoblir, élever à la pairie.* Life — ; *pairie personnelle, f.*

peer'ess, *n.*, pairesse, *f.*

peer'less, *adj.*, incomparable ; sans égal ; sans pareil ; unique ; hors de pair.

peer'lessly, *adv.*, sans pareil ; sans égal.

peer'lessness, *n.*, supériorité incomparable, *f.*

pee'vish (pî'-), *adj.*, chagrin, bourru, maussade, hargneux, acariâtre, grincheux.

pee'vishly, *adv.*, maussadement, avec mauvaise humeur.

pee'vishness, *n.*, maussaderie ; humeur chagrine, mauvaise humeur, humeur acariâtre, *f.*

pee'wit (pî-), *n.*, (orni.) vanneau, *m.*

peg (pèghe), *n.*, cheville, patère, *f. ;* point ; (for hats) patère, *f. ;* champignon, *m.*, (for hanging linen on a rope) épingle de bois, *f. ;* (ventpeg) (of casks) fausset, *m. ;* (of ladders) ranche, *f. ;* (of violins) cheville, *f.m.* To take one down a — ; *rabattre l'orgueil de quelqu'un, rabattre le caquet à quelqu'un.* To come down a — ; *baisser d'un cran.* To rise a — higher ; *monter d'un cran.* Not to stir a — ; *ne pas bouger d'une semelle.*

peg, *v.a.*, cheviller ; marquer ; restreindre, assujettir ; jeter. To — away ; *travailler sans relâche ; piocher toujours.*

Peg'asus (pèg'a-ceusse), *n.*, Pégase, *m.*

pelf (pèlf), *n.*, (b.s.) argent, gain, lucre, *m. ;* richesses mal acquises, *f.pl.*

pel'ican (pèl'-), *n.*, (orni.) pélican, *m.*

pelisse' (pè-lîce), *n.*, pelisse, *f.*

pel'let (pèl'-), *n.*, balle, boulette, *f.*

pel'licle (pèl-li-k'l), *n.*, pellicule, *f.*

pell'-mell, *adv.*, pêle-mêle.

pellu'cid (pèl-liou-), *adj.*, transparent ; clair, pellucide.

pellucid'ity *ou* **pellu'cidness**, *n.*, transparence ; clarté, *f.*

pelt (pèlte), *n.*, peau, *f.* —-monger ; *peaussier*, *m.* Full—; *ventre à terre.*

pelt (pèlte),*v.a.n.*, assaillir, jeter, lancer, lapider, battre. To — any one with anything ; *lancer quelque chose à quelqu'un.* To — with stones ; *assaillir à coups de pierres.* The rain —ed down; *la pluie tombait à torrents.*

pelt'ing *adj.*, (of rain) battant.

pelt'ing, *n.*, attaque,*f. ;* assaut, *m.*

pel'try, *n.*, pelleterie, peausserie, *f.*

pel'vic, *adj.*, (anat.) pelvien.

pel'vis, *n.*, (anat.) bassin, *m.*

pen (pè'n), *n.*, plume, *f. ;* (for poultry) poulailler ; (for cattle) parc, enclos, *m. ;* (fig.) plume, *f.* (speaking of style or of a prose-writer). To mend a quill — ; *tailler une plume.* To put — to paper ; *mettre la main à la plume ; prendre la plume pour.* —-and-ink drawing ; *dessin à la plume, m.* Fountain—; *porte plume réservoir.*

pen, *v.a.*, écrire ; rédiger ; coucher par écrit ; (cattle) parquer, enfermer. To — up ; *enfermer, parquer.*

pe'nal (pî-), *adj.*, passible d'une amende ; punissable ; pénal. — statute ; *loi pénale, f.* —-settlers ; *colonie pénale, f.* —servitude ; *travaux forcés, m.pl.*

pen'alty (pè'n'-), *n.*, peine, amende. To pay the — of ; *porter la peine de ;* (fam.) *payer la folle enchère, f.*

pen'ance (pè'n'-), *n.*, pénitence, *f.* To do —; *faire pénitence.*

pence (pè'n'ce), *n.pl.* V. **penny.** St. Peter's —; *denier de St. Pierre, m.*

pen'cil (pè'n'-), *n.*, pinceau ; crayon ; (opt.) faisceau, *m.* Drawing—; *crayon à dessin.* —-case ; *porte-crayon, m.* —mark ; *marque au crayon, f.*

pen'cil, *v.a.*, peindre ; dessiner ; écrire au crayon.

pen'cil-shaped (-shép'te), *adj.*, en forme de pinceau ; (bot.) pénicillé.

pen'-cutter (-keut'-), *n.*, taille-plumes, *m.*

pend'ant (pè'n'-), *n.*, pendant, *m.*, breloque, pendeloque, *f. ;* mousqueton, *m. ;* (nav.) banderole, flamme, *f.* Broad —; *guidon, m.*

pen'dency, *n.*, (ant.) (jur.) litispendance, *f.*

pend'ent, *adj.*, pendant ; (jutting) saillant ; (hanging) suspendu.

penden'tive, *n.*, (arch.) pendentif, *m.*

pend'ing, *adj.*, pendant, non décidé.

pend'ing,*prep.*, pendant ; (until) en attendant.

pen'dulous (-diou-), *adj.*, pendant ; oscillant.

pen'dulum (-diou-leume), *n.*, pendule, balancier, *m.* —-clock ; *pendule, f.* —-bob ; *lentille de pendule, f.* —-rod ; *verge de pendule, f.*

penetrabil'ity (pè'n'l-), *n.*, pénétrabilité, *f.*

pen'etrable (pè'n'i-tra-b'l), *adj.*, pénétrable, (impressible) impressionnable.

penetra'lia, *n.pl.*, sanctuaire, *m.*

pen'etrant, *adj.*, pénétrant.

pen'etrate (pè'n'i-), *v.a.* (de) and *n.*, pénétrer dans, jusqu'à.

pen'etrating, *adj.*, pénétrant.

penetra'tion (pè'n'i-tré), *n.*, pénétration, *f.*

pen'etrative, *adj.*, pénétrant.

pen'ful (-foule), *n.*, plumée d'encre, *f.*

pen'guin (pè'n'gwine), *n.*, (orni.) pingouin, *m.*

pen'-holder (-hôld'-), *n.*, porte-plume, *m.*

penin'sula (pè'n'i'n-siou-), *n.*, péninsule, presqu'île, *f.* The Peninsula ; *la Péninsule* (l'Espagne et le Portugal).

penin'sular, *adj.*, en forme de péninsule ; péninsulaire. The — war ; (1808-1813) *la guerre d'Espagne, f.*

pen'itence, *n.*, pénitence, *f. ;* repentir, *m.*

pen'itent, *adj.*, pénitent, repentant.

pen'itent, *n.*, pénitent, *m.*, pénitente, *f.*

peniten'tial (-tè'n'shal), *adj.*, de pénitence ;

pénitentiel, pénitentiaux, *m.pl.*, **pénitentielles,** *f.pl.* —psalms ; *psaumes pénitentiaux.* —works; *œuvres pénitentielles, f.pl.*

peniten'tial, *n.*, (a guide-book for priests in c.rel.) pénitentiel, *m.*

peniten'tiary (-tè'n'sha-), *adj.*, pénitentiaire.

peniten'tiary, *n.*, pénitencier, *f. ;* (house of correction) maison pénitentiaire, maison centrale, *f.*

pen'itently, *adv.*, avec pénitence, repentie.

pen'knife (pè'n'naïfe), *n.*, canif, *m.*

pen'man (pè'n'ma'n), *n.*, calligraphe ; auteur, écrivain, *m.*

pen'manship, *n.*, écriture, calligraphie, *f.*

pen'nant (pè'n'-), *n.*, (nav.) banderole, flamme, *f.*

pen'nate *ou* **pen'nated** (pè'n'nét'-), *adj.*, (bot.) penné, pinné ; (ant.) ailé.

penned, *adj.*, à plumes.

pen'ner, *n.*, écrivain, rédacteur, *m.*

pen'niless, *adj.*, sans le sou ; pauvre. To be —; (*prov.) loger le diable dans sa bourse* (Lafontaine).

pen'ning, *n.*, écriture ; rédaction, *f. ;* (of cattle) parcage, *m.*

pen'non (-), *n.*, (nav.) banderole, flamme,*f.*

penny (pè'n'-), *n.*, (*pence ou pennies*) deux sous, dix centimes, *m.pl. ;* penny, *m.* —royal ; (bot.) pouliot, *m.* —weight ; *denier de poids* (gramme 1·5545), *m.* —-worth ; *pour deux sous ; pour son argent.* —wort ; *hydrocotyle, m.* Not to be worth a — ; *n'avoir pas le sou.* A — saved is a — gained ; (prov.) *il n'y a pas de petites économies ; ou qui épargne, gagne.* To earn, *ou* turn, an honest — ; *gagner honnêtement sa vie.* — a liner; *journaliste à dix centimes la ligne.*

pen'ny-wise (-waïze), *adj.*, ménager de bouts de chandelle. To be — and pound-foolish ; *faire des économies de bouts de chandelle.* — and pound foolish; *économe dans les petites choses et prodigue dans les grandes.*

pen'sile (pè'n'sil), *adj.*, suspendu ; pendant.

pen'sileness, *n.*, suspension, *f.*

pen'sion (pè'n'sheune), *n.*, pension, rente ; (of officers, etc.) retraite, *f.* Retiring —; *pension de retraite, f.*

pen'sion, *v.a.*, pensionner. To — off ; *mettre à la retraite.*

pen'sionary, *n.*, (ant.) pensionnaire, *m.*

pen'sionary, *adj.*, (ant.) pensionné ; (of things) par pension.

pen'sioner, *n.*, pensionnaire ; (Cambridge) étudiant ordinaire ; (milit., nav.) invalide, *m.*

pen'sive, *adj.*, pensif, triste, préoccupé ; rêveur, morose.

pen'sively, *adv.*, d'un air pensif ; tristement.

pen'siveness, *n.*, air pensif, air triste, air préoccupé, *m. ;* tristesse,*f.*

pen'stock, *n.*, (sluice) vanne, porte écluse, *f.*

pent, *adj.* (up) renfermé ; (fig.) étouffé. —-roof ; *toit incliné, m.*

pen'tagon, *n.*, pentagone, *m.*

pentam'eter (pè'n'ta'm'i-), *adj.*, pentamètre.

pentam'eter, *n.*, (poet.) pentamètre, *m.*

pentan'dria, *n.*, (bot.) pentandrie, *f.*

Pen'tateuch (-teuke), *n.*, Pentateuque, *m.*

Pen'tecost (-tî-côste), *n.*, Pentecôte, *f.*

pentecost'al, *adj.*, de la Pentecôte.

pentecost'als (-talze), *n.pl.*, (c.rel.) offrandes de la Pentecôte, *f.pl.*

pent'house (-haouce), *n.*, appentis ; abat-vent, auvent, *m.*

pen'tile (-taïle), *n.*, tuile faîtière ; faîtière, *f.*

pe'nult (pî-neulte), **penul'tima, penul'timate** (pî-neul-), *n.*, (gram.) pénultième,*f.*

penum'bra (pi-neu'm-), *n.*, (astron.) pénombre, *f.*

penu'rious (pi-niou-), *adj.*, avare ; sordide ; ladre ; (of things) pauvre ; dans l'indigence.

penu'riously, adv., avec pénurie, parcimonieusement.

penu'riousness, pen'ury (pè'n'-), n., pénurie, disette, extrême pauvreté, misère, f.

pen'-wiper (-waïp'-), n., essuie-plume, m.

pe'ony (pî-), n., (bot.) pivoine, f.

peo'ple (pî-p'l), n., peuple; (the vulgar) le vulgaire, la foule, f.; (persons in general) on, monde, m., personnes, f.pl.; habitants, gens, m.pl. — say; on dit. Old —; de vieilles gens. The little —; les petites personnes, f.pl.; les petits personnages, m.pl. Bad —; de méchantes gens. There were a great many — in the park; il y avait beaucoup de monde dans le parc.

peo'ple, v.a., peupler.

pep'per (pèp'-), n., poivre, m. Cayenne —; poivre de Guinée; poivre d'Inde; piment, m. — -tree; poivrier, m. —wort; passerage, f.

pep'per, v.a., poivrer; (to beat) cribler de coups.

pep'per-box ou **pep'per-cast'er** (-càst'-), n., poivrier, m.; poivrière, f.

pep'per-corn, n., grain de poivre, m.; (fig.) bagatelle, f. — rent; loyer nominal, m.

pep'permint (-mi'n'te), n., menthe poivrée, f.

pep'per-vine (-vaïne), n., vigne vierge, f.

per (peur), prep., par; (com.) le, m., la, f., les, pl.; (pers.) par l'entremise de, par. A shilling — hundred; un schelling le cent. — cent; pour cent. As —; (com.) suivant.

peradven'ture (pèr'ad-vè'n'tieur), adv., par hasard, d'aventure, peut-être.

peram'bulate (peur'am-biou-), v.a., parcourir à pied; visiter.

perambula'tion (-biou-lé-), n., inspection; tournée, f., voyage, m.

peram'bulator (-biou-lé-teur), n., odomètre, pédomètre, compte-pas, m.; voiture d'enfant, f.

perceiv'able (-cîv'a-b'l), adj., apercevable, perceptible, sensible.

perceiv'ably, adv., perceptiblement; d'une manière perceptible; sensiblement.

perceive' (-cîve), v.a., apercevoir, découvrir; (mentally) s'apercevoir de; remarquer; sentir; (phil.) percevoir.

percent'age (-cè'n't'èdje), n., intérêt de . . . pour cent; taux, m.; remise, commission, f. A —; tant pour cent.

perceptibil'ity, n., perceptibilité.

percept'ible (-cèp-ti-b'l), adj., perceptible; apercevable.

percept'ibly, adv., perceptiblement; d'une manière perceptible.

percep'tion (-cèp'-), n., sensibilité, découverte, observation, f.; (philos.) perception, f.

percept'ive (-cèp-), adj., perceptif.

perceptiv'ity, n., faculté de perception, f.

perch (peurtshe), n., perche, f.; (of birds) perchoir, m.; (ich.) perche; (measure) ⊙perche (mètre 5·0291), f. To tip over the —; (colloq.) passer l'arme à gauche. To get any one off his —; déloger, dégommer quelqu'un.

perch (peurtshe), v.a. and n., percher; se percher.

perchance' (-tshà'n'ce), adv., par hasard; peut-être; par aventure.

perch'ing (peurtsh'-), adj., qui perche, percheur.

percip'ient, adj., doué de perception.

per'colate (peur-), v.a. and n., filtrer, passer.

percola'tion (peur-co-lé-), n., filtration, f.

per'colator, n., filtre, percolateur, m.

percus'sion (-keush'-), n., percussion, f. — cap; capsule, f. — -gun; fusil à piston, m.

percus'sive (-keus'-) ou **percu'tient** (kioush'-), adj., qui frappe.

perdi'tion (-dish'-), n., perdition, ruine, f.

per'egrinate (pèr'i-), v.n., habiter à l'étranger, voyager.

peregrina'tion (pèr'i-gri-né-), n., pérégrination, f.; voyage; séjour à l'étranger, m.

per'egrine (pèr'i-grine), n., (orni.) pèlerin, faucon pèlerin, m.

peremp'tion (peur-), n., (ant.) (jur.) péremption, f.

per'emptorily (pèr'-), adv., péremptoirement, absolument, d'une manière tranchante.

per'emptoriness (pèr'-), n., caractère péremptoire; ton tranchant, m.

per'emptory (pèr'-), adj., péremptoire, tranchant, absolu; (jur.) péremptoire.

peren'nial (pèr'è'n'-), adj., qui dure l'année; perpétuel; (bot.) vivace.

peren'nial, n., (bot.) plante vivace, f.

peren'nially, adv., continuellement; perpétuellement.

peren'nity (pèr'è'n-), n., (ant.) perpétuité, f.

per'fect (peur-fèkte), adj., parfait; achevé, fini; complet, accompli. — tense; parfait, m.

per'fect, v.a., rendre parfait; achever; perfectionner; accomplir, compléter.

per'fecter, n., qui perfectionne, (b.s.) perfectionniste, m.

perfectibil'ity, n., perfectibilité, f.

perfect'ible (-fèk-ti-b'l), adj., perfectible.

perfec'tion (-fèk'-), n., perfection, f. To —; en perfection; dans la perfection, parfaitement.

per'fectly, adv., parfaitement, à fond.

per'fectness, n., perfection, excellence, f.

perfid'ious, adj., perfide.

perfid'iously, adv., perfidement.

perfid'iousness ou **per'fidy**, n., perfidie, f.

perfo'liate (-fô-), adj., (bot.) perfolié.

per'forate, v.a., percer (d'outre en outre); perforer.

perfora'tion (-fo-ré-), n., percement, m.; ouverture, perforation, f.

per'forative, adj., (ant.) perforatif.

per'forator, n., (surg.) trépan perforatif, m.

perforce', adv., forcément, par force; de force.

perform', v.a., exécuter, accomplir; faire, opérer, effectuer; (thea.) donner, jouer, représenter; (to fulfill) remplir; s'acquitter de; (of actors) jouer; (of musicians) exécuter, jouer. To — a piece of music; exécuter un morceau de musique. To — one's part; remplir son rôle; faire son devoir. To — a vow; accomplir un vœu.

perform'able (-'a-b'l), adj., (l.u.) faisable, exécutable, praticable; (thea.) jouable.

perform'ance, n., exécution, f.; acte, accomplissement; exercice; (thing done) ouvrage, m., œuvre, f.; (thea.) représentation, f.; (way of acting) jeu, m. Promises are not binding where the — is impossible; à l'impossible nul n'est tenu. No —; (thea.) relâche. Morning —; matinée, f. Evening —; représentation du soir, f.

perform'er, n., auteur, m.; personne qui peut, qui accomplit, f.; (thea.) artiste, m., f., acteur, m., actrice, f.; comédien, m., comédienne, f.; (mus.) artiste, m.f., exécutant, musicien, m.

per'fume (-fioume), n., parfum, m.; (of wine) bouquet, m.

perfume', v.a., parfumer, embaumer.

perfum'er, n., parfumeur, m., parfumeuse, f.

perfum'ery, n., parfumerie, f.

perfunc'torily (-feu'gn'k-), adv., par manière d'acquit; négligemment; légèrement.

perfunc'toriness, n., négligence, f.

perfunc'tory, adj., négligent, léger; fait par manière d'acquit.

perhaps' (-hàps'), adv., peut-être. — so; peut-être bien; peut-être que oui. —not; peut-être que non.

per'i (pî-), n., (Persian Mythol.) péri, m., f.

per'ianth (pèr-i-an'th) ou **perian'thium** (-thi-), n., (bot.) périanthe, m.

perib'olus (pè-), n., (ant.) (arch.) péribole, m.

per'icar'dium (pèr'i-câr-), n., (anat.) péricarde, m.

per'icarp ou **pericar'pium** (pèr-i-câr-), n., (bot.) péricarpe, m.

pericra'nium (pèr-i-cré-ni-eume), *n.*, (anat.) péricrâne, *m.*

per'igee (-djî), *n.*, (astron.) périgée, *m.*

perihe'lion *ou* **perihe'lium** (pèr-i-hî-), *n.* (astron.) périhélie, *m.*

per'il (pèr'-), *n.*, péril, danger, *m.* At one's —; *à ses risques et périls; à ses périls.* At the — of; *au péril de.*

per'ilous, *adj.*, périlleux, dangereux.

per'ilously, *adv.*, périlleusement.

per'ilousness, *n.*, nature périlleuse, *f.;* danger, péril, *m.*

perim'eter (pè-ri'm'i-), *n.*, périmètre, *m.*

pe'riod (pî-), *n.*, période, *f.;* temps, espace, *m.;* (portion of time) durée, *f.;* temps, *m.;* (epoch) époque; (end) fin, limite, *f.*, terme, *m.;* (astron., chron., gram.) période, *f.;* (in punctuating) point, *m.;* (degree) degré, période, *m.;* (indefinite portion of time) période, *m.* (according to French Academy), *f.* (according to some writers); (gram. rhet.) période, *f.* To put a — to; *mettre fin à.* At a later —; *plus tard.*

period'ic, *adj.*, (chem.) périodique.

period'ical, *n.*, périodique, ouvrage périodique, journal, magasin, *m.*, revue, *f. adj.*, périodique.

period'ically, *adv.*, périodiquement.

periodic'ity, *n.*, périodicité, *f.*

perios'teum (pèr-i-os-ti-), *n.*, (anat.) périoste, *m.*

peripatet'ic (pè'ri-pa-tèt-), *adj.*, péripatéticien, péripatétique.

peripatet'ic, *n.*, péripatéticien, *m.*

peripatet'icism, *n.*, péripatétisme, *m.;* philosophie péripatéticienne, *f.*

periph'ery (pi-rif'i-), *n.*, circonférence, *f.*

per'iphrase (pèr-i-fréze), *v.n.*, périphraser.

periph'rasis (pi-rif'ra-cice), *n.*, (*periphrases*) périphrase, *f.*

periphras'tic (pèr'-), *adj.*, de périphrase; périphrastique; indirect; verbeux.

periphras'tically, *adv.*, par périphrase, verbeusement.

Peris'cii (pè-rish'i-aïe), *n.*, (geog.) périsciens, *m.pl.*

per'ish (pèr'-), *v.n.*, périr (with, **de**); dépérir. To — with hunger; *mourir de faim.* To be —ed with cold; *être tout transi de froid*, ou *être presque mort de froid.* To perish by the sword; *périr par le fer.*

per'ishable (-a-b'l), *adj.*, périssable.

per'ishableness, *n.*, nature périssable, éphémère, *f.*

per'istyle (pèr-i-staïl), *n.*, (arch.) péristyle, *m.*

peritoni'tis (pèr'it'o-näi-), *n.*, péritonite, *f.*

per'iwig (pèr'-), *n.*, perruque, *f.*

periwin'kle (pèr'i-wign'k'l), *n.*, (bot.) pervenche, *f.;* (mol.) bigorneau, vigneau, vignot, *m.*

per'jure (peur-djioure), *v.a.*, parjurer (mostly used reflexively). To — one's self; *se parjurer.*

per'jurer, *n.*, parjure; faux témoin, *m.*

per'jury (peur-djiouri), *n.*, parjure; (jur.) faux témoignage, faux serment, *m.* Willful —; *parjure prémédité.*

perk (peurke), *adj.*, vif, éveillé; coquet; fier; pimpant.

perk (**up**), *v.n.*, se rengorger, porter le nez au vent; porter la tête haute.

per'kin (peur-), *n.*, petit cidre, *m.*

per'manency (peur-), *n.*, permanence; (jur.) inamovibilité, *f.* For a —; *pour un terme, pour un temps fixe.*

per'manent, *adj.*, permanent; en permanence. A — situation; *une place inamovible, f.* The — way; (rail.) *la voie permanente.*

per'manently, *adv.*, en permanence; d'une manière permanente.

permeabil'ity (peur-mi-), *n.*, (phys.) perméabilité, *f.*

per'meable (-mi-a-b'l), *adj.*, (phys.) pénétrable, perméable.

per'meate (peur-mi-), *v.a.*, (phys.) pénétrer; (fig.) remplir; être répandu **dans**; se répandre **dans.**

permea'tion (peur-mi-é-), *n.*, pénétration, *f.*

permis'sible (peur-mis'si-b'l), *adj.*, qui peut être permis *ou* se permettre.

permis'sion (peur-mish'-), *n.*, permission, *f.;* permis, *m.*

permis'sive (peur-), *adj.*, qui permet, tolérant; toléré; facultatif.

permis'sively, *adv.*, avec permission; sans empêchement, par tolérance.

permit' (peur-), *v.a.*, permettre; permettre **à** quelqu'un **de.** You are —ted to speak; *on vous permet de parler; vous avez la permission de parler.* As circumstances —; *ainsi que les circonstances le permettront.*

per'mit, *n.*, permission, *f.*, permis, laissez-passer; congé, *m.;* (excise) licence, *f.*

permut'able (peur-miou-ta-b'l), *adj.*, (gram.) permutable.

permuta'tion (peur-miou-té-), *n.*, (math. gram.) permutation, *f.*

permute', *v.a.*, permuter. *v.n.*, se permuter.

perni'cious (peur-nish'-), *adj.*, pernicieux.

perni'ciously, *adv.*, pernicieusement.

perni'ciousness, *n.*, nature pernicieuse, *f.*

perora'tion (pèr-o-ré-), *n.*, (speech) péroraison, *f.*

perox'ide (peur'-), *n.*, (chem.) peroxyde, *m.*

perpend', *v.a.*, peser, examiner.

perpendic'ular (peur-pè'n-dik'iou-), *adj.*, (geom.) perpendiculaire.

perpendic'ular, *n.*, (geom.) ligne perpendiculaire; perpendiculaire, *f.*

perpendicular'ity, *n.*, perpendicularité, *f.*

perpendic'ularly, *adv.*, perpendiculairement.

per'pend-stone (-stône), *n.*, parpaing, *m.;* pierre faisant parpaing, pierre parpaigne, *f.*

per'petrate (peur-pi-), *v.a.*, commettre; exécuter; (jur.) perpétrer. To — a crime; *perpétrer, commettre, un crime.* To — a pun; *faire un mauvais calembour.*

perpetra'tion (-pi-tré-), *n.*, (jur.) perpétration, exécution, *f.*

per'petrator, *n.*, auteur d'un crime; coupable, criminel, *m.*

perpet'ual (peur-pèt'iou-), *adj.*, perpétuel, continuel; constant.

perpet'ually, *adv.*, perpétuellement, continuellement.

perpet'uate (peur-pèt'iou-), *v.a.*, perpétuer.

perpetua'tion (peur-pèt'iou-é-), *n.*, perpétuation, *f.*

perpetu'ity (peur-pi-tiou-), *n.*, perpétuité, *f.*

perplex' (peur-), *v.a.*, embarrasser, intriguer; embrouiller, brouiller; rendre perplexe, jeter dans la perplexité.

perplex'edly, *adv.*, d'une manière embrouillée; avec embarras.

perplex'ity, *n.*, embrouillement; embarras, *m.;* perplexité, *f.*

per'quisite (peur-kwi-zite), *n.*, revenant-bon, émolument, *m.* —s, *pl.*, revenants-bons; profits éventuels; émoluments, *m.pl.;* casuel, revenu casuel, *m.;* (illicit) tour du bâton, *m.;* anse du panier, *f.;* (tip) pourboire, *m.*, gratification, *f.*

perquisi'tion (peur-kwi-zish'-), *n.*, (jur.) perquisition, recherche, *f.*

per'roquet (pè-ro-kète), *n.*, (orni.) perruche, *f.*

per'ry (pèr'-), *n.*, poiré, *m.*

per'secute (peur-si-kioute), *v.a.*, persécuter.

per'secuting, *adj.*, persécuteur.

persecu'tion, *n.*, persécution, *f.*

per'secutor, *n.*, persécuteur, *m.*, persécutrice, *f.*

persever'ance (peur-si-vîr'-), *n.*, persévérance, *f.*

persevere' (peur-si-vîre), *v.n.*, persévérer (in, **dans**).

persever'ing, *adj.*, persévérant.

persever'ingly, *adv.*, avec persévérance.

Per'sian (peur-shi-), *adj.*, de Perse; persan. — Gulf; *golfe Persique, m.*

Per'sian, *n.*, Persan, *m.*, Persane, *f. ;* (antiq.) Perse, *m.f. ;* (language) perse, *m. ;* (stuff) marceline, *f.* — carpet; *tapis de Perse, m.*

persica'ria (peur-), *n.*, (bot.) persicaire, *f.*

persist' (peur-), *v.n.*, persister (in, **dans**; in doing, **à**).

persist'ence *ou* **persist'ency**, *n.*, persistance; opiniâtreté; (phys.) persistance, *f.*

persist'ent, *adj.*, (bot.) persistant.

per'son (peur-), *n.*, personne, *f. ;* personnage, caractère, *m. ;* (gram.) personne, *f. pl.*, personnes, *f.pl. ;* gens, *pl.m.*, *f. ;* monde, *m.* A —; *une personne; quelqu'un, quelqu'une.* —s say so; *on dit.* Young —s; *les jeunes gens.* In —; *en personne.* No —; *personne, m.* Respecter of —s; *qui est influencé par la position, le rang, des personnes.* To attend in —; *assister, être présent en personne.* I know no such —; *je ne connais personne de ce nom.*

per'sonable (peur-ceu'n'a-b'l), *adj.*, de bonne mine; beau de sa personne.

per'sonage (peur-ceu'n'èdje), *n.*, personnage, *m.*, personne, *f.*

per'sonal, *adj.*, personnel. — property; *mobilier, m.; biens meubles, m.pl.* — action; (jur.) *action personnelle, action mobilière, f.*

personal'ity, *n.*, personnalité, *f.*

per'sonalization, *n.*, personnalisation, *f.*

per'sonalize, *v.a.*, personnaliser.

per'sonally, *adv.*, personnellement.

per'sonalty, *n.*, (jur.) biens meubles, *ou* mobiliers, *m.pl.*

per'sonate, *v.a.*, passer **pour**, se faire passer pour un autre; représenter; contrefaire; feindre; jouer; jouer le rôle **de**; ressembler **à**.

persona'tion (peur-ceu'n'é-), *n.*, impersonation, *f.*

per'sonator, *n.*, personne qui passe pour une autre, *f. ;* (ant.) acteur, *m.*

personifica'tion (-so'ni-fi-ké-), *n.*, personnification, *f.*

person'ify (-i-faïe), *v.a.*, personnifier.

perspec'tive (peur-spèk'-), *adj.*, perspectif.

perspec'tive, *n.*, perspective, *f.* —glass; *lunette d'approche, f. ; verre optique, m.*

perspec'tively, *adv.*, par une lunette; selon les règles de la perspective; en perspective.

perspica'cious (peur-spi-ké-sheusse), *adj.*, pénétrant, clairvoyant, perspicace; (of the sight) perçant.

perspicac'ity (peur-), *n.*, vue pénétrante, perspicacité; pénétration; sagacité; clarté, *f.*

perspicu'ity *ou* **perspic'uousness** (peur-spi-kiou-), *n.*, clarté, perspicuité, netteté, *f.*

perspic'uous, *adj.*, clair, net.

perspic'uously, *adv.*, nettement, avec clarté.

perspira'tion (peur-spi-ré-), *n.*, transpiration, sueur, *f.* To be covered with —; *être tout en nage, ou tout en eau.*

perspire' (peur-spaïeur), *v.n.*, transpirer, suer.

persuade' (peur-swéde), *v.a.*, persuader; persuader (à quelqu'un) **de**; déterminer, décider **à.** To — from; *dissuader de.* To — one's self; *se plaire à croire.*

persuas'ible (-ci-b'l), *adj.*, que l'on peut persuader; à qui l'on peut persuader.

persua'sion (-swé-jeune), *n.*, persuasion; croyance; opinion; (creed) croyance, religion, opinion religieuse, *f. ;* culte, *m.*

persua'sive (-swé-cive), *adv.*, persuasif, persuadant.

persua'sively, *adv.*, d'une manière persuasive.

persua'siveness, *n.*, force persuasive, *f. ;* talent de persuader, *m.*

pert (peurte), *adj.*, éveillé; pétulant; sémillant; (saucy) impertinent, insolent.

pertain' (peur-téne), *v.n.*, appartenir; concerner; se rapporter à, avoir rapport à.

pertina'cious (peur-ti-né-sheusse), *adj.*, persévérant; opiniâtre; obstiné.

pertina'ciously, *adv.*, avec persévérance; obstinément; opiniâtrément.

pertina'ciousness *ou* **pertinac'ity**, *n.*, persévérance; obstination, opiniâtreté, pertinacité, *f. ;* entêtement, *m.*

pert'inence *ou* **pert'inency** (peur-), *n.*, convenance; justesse, *f. ;* à-propos, *m.*

pert'inent (peur-), *adj.*, pertinent, convenable, à propos.

pert'inently, *adv.*, pertinemment, convenablement; à propos.

pert'ly (peurt'-), *adv.*, avec vivacité; avec pétulance; (saucily) impertinemment, insolemment.

pert'ness (peurt'-), *n.*, vivacité; pétulance; (sauciness) impertinence, insolence, *f.*

perturba'tion (peur-teur-bé-), *n.*, bouleversement, trouble, *m. ;* agitation; perturbation, *f.*

per'turbator *ou* **perturb'er**, *n.*, perturbateur, *m.*

perturbed' (peur-teurb'de), *adj.*, troublé, inquiet, agité.

peruke' (pèr-ouke), *n.*, perruque, *f.*

peruke'-maker (-mék'-), *n.*, perruquier, *m.*

peru'sal (pi-riou-zal), *n.*, lecture, *f. ;* (ant.) examen, *m.* Worthy of —; *digne d'être lu.*

peruse' (pi-riouze), *v.a.*, lire attentivement; lire, parcourir; (ant.) examiner, étudier.

perus'er, *n.*, lecteur, lectrice, *m.f.*

Peru'vian (pi-riou-), *adj.*, péruvien.

pervade' (peur-), *v.a.*, pénétrer; pénétrer **dans**; régner **dans**; se répandre **dans**; être répandu **dans.**

perverse' (peur-veurse), *adj.*, pervers, méchant; mauvais; (jur.) contraire.

perverse'ly, *adv.*, avec perversité; méchamment; opiniâtrément.

perverse'ness *ou* **perver'sity**, *n.*, perversité; méchanceté, opiniâtreté, *f.*, entêtement, *m.*

perver'sion, *n.*, perversion, *f. ;* (in England) conversion à la religion catholique, *f.*

per'vert, *n.* *V.* **convert.**

pervert' (peur-veurte), *v.a.*, pervertir.

pervert'er, *n.*, corrupteur, *m.*, corruptrice, *f.*, pervertisseur, *m.*, pervertisseuse, *f.*

pervert'ible, *adj.*, pervertissable.

per'vious (peur-), *adj.*, pénétrable; perméable; (fig.) abordable, accessible.

per'viousness, *n.*, pénétrabilité; perméabilité, *f.*

pesade' (pi-zâde), *n.*, (man.) pesade, *f.*

pes'sary (pès'-), *n.*, (med.) pessaire, *m.*

pes'simist (pès-), *n.*, pessimiste, *m.*

pest (pèste), *n.*, peste, *f. ;* (ant.) (plague) peste; (a bore) scie, *f.* — house; *lazaret, m.*

pes'ter (pès'-), *v.a.*, tourmenter, ennuyer, importuner, assommer; (pop.) scier; scier le dos **à.**

pes'terer, *n.*, importun, fâcheux, *m. ;* scie, *f.*

pestif'erous (pès-tif'eur'-), *adj.*, pestifère, pestilentiel; pestiféré; malfaisant, funeste; pernicieux.

pes'tilence (pès-), *n.*, peste, pestilence, *f.*

pes'tilent (pès-), *adj.*, pestilentiel, contagieux; (troublesome) méchant; malfaisant; pernicieux; funeste; malicieux.

pestilen'tial (-lè'n'shal), *adj.*, pestilentiel; malfaisant, funeste, pernicieux.

pes'tilently, *adv.*, fatalement, mortellement, pernicieusement.

pes'tle (pès-t'l), *n.*, pilon, *m.* *v.a.*, piler.

pet (pè't), *n.*, boutade, *f. ;* dépit; accès d'humeur; (lamb) agneau élevé à la cuiller; (fondling) favori, *m.*, favorite, *f.*, chère, *m.*, chérie, *f.*, enfant gâté, *m.* To be in a —; *être piqué, être dépité; se dépiter; être de mauvaise humeur.* To be a great —; *être très aimé.*

pet, *adj.*, favori, gâté. — name ; *petit nom*, *m.* — aversion ; *bête noire, f.*

pet, *v.a.*, choyer, dorloter, gâter.

pet'al (pèt'- *ou* pi'-), *n.*, (bot.) pétale, *m.*

pet'aled (pèt'alde) *ou* **pet'alous**, *adj.*, à pétales, pétalé.

petard' (pi-târde), *n.*, (milit.) pétard, *m.* Hoist with his own —; *pris dans son propre traquenard.*

pet'-cock, *n.*, robinet d'essai, *m.*

pe'tersham (pî-teur-), *n.*, ratine, *f.*

pet'iole (pèt'i-ôle), *n.*, (bot.) pétiole, *m.*

peti'tion (pi-tish'-), *n.*, requête, pétition, demande, *f.* ; placet, *m.* ; supplication, supplique, prière, *f.* Right of —; *droit de pétition, m.* — paper ; *papier-ministre, papier-tellière, m.*

peti'tion, *v.a.*, supplier ; présenter une pétition à ; (jur.) présenter une requête à ; pétitionner.

peti'tionary, *adj.*, suppliant ; de supplication.

petitionee', *n.*, personne contre laquelle on a présenté une pétition, *f.*

peti'tioner, *n.*, pétitionnaire, *m.f.* ; suppliant, *m.*, suppliante, *f.* ; (jur.) requérant, *m.*, requérante, *f.*, demandeur, *m.*, demanderesse, *f.*

peti'tioning, *n.*, pétitionnement, *m.*, pétitions, *f.pl.*

peti'tio princip'ii, *n.*, pétition de principe, *f.*

pet'rel (pèt-rèl), *n.*, (orni.) pétrel, *m.* Stormy —; *pétrel-tempête.*

petrifac'tion (pèt-ri-fak'-), *n.*, pétrification, *f.*

petrif'ic (pi-), *adj.*, pétrifiant.

pet'rify (pèt-ri-faïe), *v.a. and n.*, pétrifier ; se pétrifier.

petro'leum (pi-trô-li-), *n.*, huile de pétrole, *f.*

petro-si'lex (pî-tro-çaï-lèkse), *n.*, pétrosilex, *m.*

pe'trous (pî-), *adj.*, (ant.) pierreux.

pet'ticoat (pèt'ti-côte), *n.*, jupe, *f.* ; jupon, cotillon, *m.* ; (of little boys) jaquette, *f.* — —government ; *régime du cotillon, m.*

pet'tifogger (-gheur), *n.*, (b.s.) petit avoué, petit avocat ; avocassier, chicaneur, *m.*

pet'tifoggery (-gheri), *n.*, chicane, avocasserie, *f.*

pet'tifogging (-ghigne), *adj.*, avocassier, chicaneur ; chicanier.

pet'tiness (pèt'-), *n.*, petitesse ; mesquinerie, *f.*

pet'tish (pèt'-), *adj.*, qui a des boutades ; maussade ; bourru.

pet'tishly, *adv.*, par boutade ; d'une manière bourrue ; de dépit, par dépit.

pet'tishness, *n.*, aigreur ; humeur bourrue, *f.*

pet'titoes (pèt'ti-tôze), *n.pl.*, pieds de cochon de lait, *m.pl.* ; (jest.) pattes, *f.pl.*, (children) petons, *m.pl.*

in **pet'to**, *adv.*, in petto, en secret. Cardinal in —; *cardinal in petto, m.*

pet'ty (pèt'-), *adj.*, petit ; mesquin, chétif ; subalterne ; (jur.) inférieur. — —officer ; (nav.) *sous-officier*, *m.* — charges ; (com.) *menus frais, m.pl.* — cash ; *argent pour menus frais, m.* — jury ; (jur.) *jury de jugement, m.*

pet'ulance, *n.*, pétulance, *f.*

pet'ulant, *adj.*, pétulant ; impertinent, insolent.

pet'ulantly, *adv.*, avec pétulance ; insolemment, impertinemment.

petu'nia, *n.*, pétunia, *m.*

pew (piou), *n.*, banc d'église ; banc, *m.* Churchwarden's —; *banc de l'œuvre, banc d'œuvre, m.*

pe'wet (pî-wète) *ou* **pe'wit** (pi-wite), *n.*, (orni.) vanneau, *m.*

pew'ter (piou-), *n.*, vaisselle d'étain, *f.* ; alliage d'étain, métal britannique, *m.* ; (polishing material) potée d'étain, *f.* — pot ; *broc d'étain, m.*

pew'terer, *n.*, potier d'étain, *m.*

pew'ter-wort, *n.*, (bot.) prêle-d'hiver, *f.*

pha'eton (fé-i-), *n.*, (open four-wheeler) phaéton, *m.*, victoria, *f.* ; (orni.) paille-en-queue, *m.*

phal'anx, *n.*, (*phalanges*) (Greek antiq., bot.) phalange, (anat. *pl. phalanxes*) phalange, *f.*

phan'tasm (-taz'm) *ou* **phantas'ma** (-taz'-), *n.*, vision, illusion, hallucination, *f.*

phantasmago'ria (-taz'ma-gô-), *n.*, fantasmagorie, *f.*

phantasmagor'ical, *adj.*, fantasmagorique.

phan'tom, *n.*, fantôme, *m.*

phar'aon (fé-), *n. V.* **fa'ro.**

pharisa'ic *ou* **pharisa'ical** (-cé-ïk, -cé-i-cal), *adj.*, pharisaïque.

pharise'an, *adj.*, pharisaïque ; hypocrite.

Phar'isee (-cî), *n.*, pharisien, *m.*, pharisienne, *f.*

pharmaceu'tic *ou* **pharmaceu'tical** (fâr-maciou-), *adj.*, pharmaceutique.

pharmaceu'tically, *adv.*, suivant la pharmaceutique.

pharmaceu'tics, *n.pl.*, pharmaceutique, *f. sing.*

pharmacol'ogist (-djiste), *n.*, qui traite de la pharmacologie, *m.*

pharmacol'ogy (-dji), *n.*, pharmacologie, *f.*

pharmacopœ'ia (-pî-ia), *n.*, pharmacopée, *f.*, codex, *m.*

pharmacop'olist, *n.*, pharmacien, apothicaire, (jest.) pharmacopole, *m.*

phar'macy, *n.*, pharmacie, *f.*

phar'os (fé-), phare, *m.*

phar'ynx (fé-), *n.*, (anat.) pharynx, *m.*

phase (féze) *ou* **pha'sis** (fé-cice), *n.*, (*phases*) phase, face, *f.*, aspect, *m.*

pheas'ant (fèz'-), *n.*, faisan, *m.* Cock- —; *coquard*, *m.* Hen- —; *faisande, faisane, coquarde, f.* Young — ; *faisandeau, m.* —-keeper ; *faisandier, m.* — shooting ; *chasse au faisan, f.*

pheas'antry (fèz'-), *n.*, faisanderie, *f.*

phenom'enon (fi-no'm'i-), *n.*, (*phenomena*) phénomène, *m.*

phi'al (faï-), *n.*, fiole, *f.*

philanthrop'ic *ou* **philanthrop'ical**, *adj.*, philanthropique.

philan'thropist, *n.*, philanthrope, *m.f.*

philan'thropy, *n.*, philanthropie, *f.*

philharmon'ic, *adj.*, philharmonique.

philhel'lenist (-hèl'lè'n'-), *n.*, philhellène, *m.*

philip'pic, *n.*, philippique, *f.*

phil'ippize (-païze), *v.n.*, faire des philippiques, invectiver **contre.**

philolog'ical (-o-dj'-), *adj.*, philologique.

philol'ogist (-djiste), *n.*, philologue, linguiste, *m.*

philol'ogy (-dji), *n.*, philologie, linguistique, *f.*

phil'omel *ou* **philome'la** (-mî-la), *n.*, philomèle, *f.*, rossignol, *m.*

philos'opher (-loss'-), *n.*, philosophe ; savant ; moraliste ; physicien, *m.* —'s stone ; *pierre philosophale, f.* Natural — ; *physicien, m.*

philosoph'ical (-çof'-), *adj.*, philosophique ; de morale ; de physique.

philosoph'ically, *adv.*, philosophiquement.

philos'ophize (-faïze), *v.n.*, philosopher.

philos'ophy, *n.*, philosophie ; morale ; physique, *f.* Natural — ; *physique, f.*

phil'ter, *n.*, philtre, *m.*

phiz, *n.*, visage, *m.* ; trogne, binette, frimousse, *f.*

phlebot'omist (fli-), *n.*, phlébotomiste, *m.*

phlebot'omize (fli-bot'o-maïze), *v.a.*, saigner ; (jest.) phlébotomiser.

phlebot'omy (fli-bot'-), *n.*, phlébotomie, saignée, *f.*

phlegm (flème), *n.*, flegme, phlegme, glaire, *m.* ; mucosité, pituite, *f.* ; (fig.) flegme, sang-froid, *m.*

phlegmat'ic *ou* **phlegmat'ical** (flèg-), *adj.*,

flegmatique, phlegmatique. — disposition ; *caractère flegmatique, m.*

phlegmat'ically, *adv.,* flegmatiquement.

phleg'mon (flég-), *n.,* (med.) phlegmon, *m.*

phleg'monous (flég-), *adj.,* (med.) phlegmoneux, flegmoneux.

pho'ca (fô-), *n.,* (mam.) phoque, *m.*

Phœ'bus (fî-), *n.,* Apollon; Phébus ; soleil, *m.*

phœ'nix (fî-), *n.,* phénix, *m.* — *like; comme le phénix.*

phon'ics, *n.pl.,* phonétique, *f.*

phonog'raphy, *n.,* phonographie, *f.*

phonol'ogy (-dji), *n.,* phonétique, *f.*

phos'phate, *n.,* (chem.) phosphate, *m.*

phos'phor, *n.,* phosphore ; (astron.) Lucifer, *m.*

phosphoresce' (-rès'ce), *v.n.,* être phosphorescent.

phosphores'cence (-rès'-), *n.,* phosphorescence, *f.*

phosphores'cent (-rès'-), *adj.,* (chem.) phosphorescent.

phosphor'ic, *adj.,* (chem.) phosphorique.

phos'phorus, *n.,* (chem.) phosphore, *m. ;* (astron.) étoile du matin, *f. ;* Lucifer, *m.* — box ; *briquet phosphorique, m.* — paste ; *pâte phosphorée, f.*

phos'phuret (-fiou-), *n.,* (chem.) phosphure, *m.*

phos'phureted (-fiou-), *adj.,* (chem.) phosphoré.

photogen'ic (-todj'-), *adj.,* photogénique.

pho'tograph, *n.,* photographie, *f.*

pho'tograph, *v.a.,* photographier. *v.n.,* faire de la photographie.

photog'rapher, *n.,* photographe, *m.*

photograph'ic, *adj.,* photographique.

photog'raphy, *n.,* photographie, *f.*

photom'eter (-to'm'i-), *n.,* photomètre, *m.*

photomet'ric *ou* **photomet'rical,** *adj.,* photométrique.

photom'etry (-to'm'i-) *n.,* photométrie, *f.*

phrase (fréze), *n.,* phrase ; locution, *f.* As the — is ; *comme on dit.*

phrase, *v.a.,* exprimer ; appeler, nommer, phraser, désigner.

phraseolog'ic *ou* **phraseolog'ical** (fré-zi-ol-o-dj'-), *adj.,* phraséologique.

phraseol'ogist, *n.,* phraseur, *m.*

phraseol'ogy (fré-zi-ol-o-dji), *n.,* phraséologie, *f.*

phrenet'ic (fri-nèt'-), *adj.,* fou, frénétique.

phren'ic (frè'n'-), *adj.,* (anat.) phrénique.

phreni'tis (fri-naï-), *n.,* inflammation du cerveau, *f.*

phrenolog'ical (fri-nol-odj'-), *adj.,* phrénologique.

phrenol'ogist, *n.,* phrénologiste, phrénologue, *m.*

phrenol'ogy (fri-nol-o-dji), *n.,* phrénologie, *f.*

phren'sy (frè'n'zi) *ou* **fren'zy,** *n.,* frénésie, *f.*

phthis'ical (tiz-ik'-), *adj.,* phtisique.

phthi'sis (taï-cisse), *n.,* phtisie, *f.*

phylac'tery, *n.,* (Judaism) phylactère, *m.*

phyl'lite (fil'laïte), *n.,* (min.) phyllithe, *m.*

phys'ic, *n.,* médecine, *f. ;* médicament, remède, *m.*

phys'ic, *v.a.,* médicamenter ; médeciner ; droguer ; (to cure) guérir.

phys'ical, *adj.,* physique ; (med., ant.) médical, médicinal, de médecine.

phys'ically, *adv.,* physiquement.

physi'cian (fi'zish'-), *n.,* médecin, *m.* Head — ; *médecin en chef.*

phys'ics (fiz'-), *n.pl.,* physique, *f.*

physiognom'ic (fiz'i-on-o-), *adj.,* de la physionomie ; physiognomonique.

physiog'nomist (fiz'i-og-no-), *n.,* physionomiste, *m.*

physiog'nomy (fiz'i-og-no-mi *ou* -o'n'o-), *n.,* physionomie; physiognomonie, *f.*

physiograph'ical (fiz'-), *adj.,* physiographique.

physiog'raphy (fiz'-), *n.,* physiographie, *f.*

physiolog'ical (fiz'i-ol-odj'-), *adj.,* physiologique.

physiolog'ically, *adv.,* de, par la physiologie.

physiol'ogist (fiz'i-ol-odj'-), *n.,* physiologiste, *m.*

physiol'ogy (fiz'i-ol'o-dji), *n.,* physiologie, *f.*

phytog'raphy (faï-), *n.,* phytographie, *f.*

phytol'ogy (faï-tol'o-dji), *n.,* phytologie, *f.*

pi'a ma'ter (paï-a mé-teur), *n.,* (anat.) pie-mère, *f.*

pi'anet (paï-a-), *n.,* (orni.) petit pivert, *m.*

piani'no, *n.,* (mus.) pianino, *m.*

pian'ist, *n.,* pianiste, *m.f.*

pia'no *ou* **pia'no-forte** (pi-â-no-fôr-té), *n.,* piano, *m.* Grand— ; *piano à queue.* Semi-grand — ; *petit piano à queue.* Cabinet — ; *grand piano droit.* Cottage — ; *piano droit.* Square, upright — ; *piano carré, droit.* — maker ; *facteur de pianos, m.* — tuner ; *accordeur de pianos, m.* To play on the — ; *jouer du piano.*

pias'ter, *n.,* piastre, *f.*

piaz'za, *n.,* arcade, galerie ; place, *f.;* passage, *m.*

pi'broch, *n.,* pibroch, *m.,* cornemuse écossaise ; musique de cornemuse, *f.*

pi'ca (paï-), *n.,* (print.) cicéro, *m.;* (orni.) pie, *f.;* (med.) pica, *m.*

picaroon' (-roune), *n.,* pilleur, voleur, pirate, forban, *m.*

pick, *n.,* (a tool) pic, *m. ;* (print.) ordure, *f. ;* (choice) choix, *m.* The — of the basket; *la crème ; la fleur, la fine fleur.*

pick, *v.a.,* (to pull off) enlever, ôter ; (to gather) cueillir ; (to choose) prendre, choisir, trier ; (a bone) ronger ; (a quarrel) chercher ; (a fowl, etc.) plumer ; (a pocket) voler à la tire ; (a lock) crocheter ; (to clean) éplucher. To — a quarrel with ; *chercher querelle à.* To — oakum ; *démêler des étoupes.* To — the salad ; *éplucher la salade.* To — up acquaintance ; *faire la connaissance de, raccrocher quelqu'un.* To have a bone to — with ; *avoir maille à partir avec.* To — a hole in any one's coat; *trouver à redire à quelqu'un ; blâmer quelqu'un.* You can — and choose, as you like ; *choisissez et prenez ce que vous voudrez.* To — to pieces ; *déchirer à belles dents.* To — one's nose ; *se nettoyer le nez ; tourmenter son nez.* To pick one's teeth, one's nails ; *se curer les dents, les ongles.* To — off, to — out ; *enlever, ôter ;* (to choose) trier, choisir. To — up; *ramasser, relever ; raccrocher.*

pick, *v.n.,* faire avec délicatesse et soin ; (to eat) grignoter, pignocher. To — up again ; *reprendre ses forces ; se refaire, repiquer à la vie.*

pick'aback, *adv.,* sur le dos.

pick'ax (pik'akse), *n.,* pioche, *f.;* pic, *m.*

picked (pikte), *adj.,* épluché ; (pointed) pointu; (choice) d'élite, choisi. — men; *hommes d'élite ; hommes de choix* (V. Hugo).

pick'er, *n.,* cueilleur, *m.,* cueilleuse, *f. ;* éplucheur, *m.,* éplucheuse ; (tool) pioche, *f. ;* (of quarrels) chercheur, *m.,* chercheuse, *f.*

pick'erel, *n.,* (ich.) brocheton, filardeau, *m.*

pick'et, *n.,* pieu, piquet ; (cards, milit.) piquet, *m.*

pick'et, *v.a.,* enfermer de piquets ; (milit.) former en piquet ; (of horses) attacher à un piquet.

pick'ing, *n.,* action de cueillir, d'ôter, d'enlever, de choisir, *f. ;* épluchement, cueillage ; glanage ; (choosing) triage ; (of oakum) décordage, *m.* —s, *pl.,* épluchures, *f.pl. ;* choses à recueillir, *f.pl. ;* (b.s.) le tour du bâton, *m. ;* petits profits, *m.pl.* —pockets; *filouterie, f.* —s, *vol à la tire, m.*

pic'kle (pick'l), *n.,* saumure, *f.* —s, *pl.,* conserves au vinaigre, *f.pl. ;* marinade, *f.* Little —;

petit polisson, *m.* To be in a fine — ; *être dans un bel état, dans de beaux draps.* To have a rod in — for any one ; *la garder bonne à quelqu'un ; apprêter une sauce à quelqu'un.*

pic′kle, *v.a.*, mariner, saler ; confire au vinaigre, conserver dans du vinaigre.

pic′kled (pick′lde), *adj.*, salé ; mariné ; confit au vinaigre.

pick′lock, *n.*, crochet à serrures ; rossignol ; (pers.) crocheteur de serrures, *m.*

pick′pocket, *n.*, filou, voleur à la tire ; coupeur de bourses, pickpocket, *m.*

pick′thank (-tha′gn′k), *n.*, flagorneur, *m.*

pic′nic, *n.*, pique-nique, *m.* To go for, *ou* get up, a — ; *faire, arranger un pique-nique.*

picto′rial (-tō-), *adj.*, de peintre ; illustré ; pittoresque.

picto′rially, *adv.*, avec illustrations.

pic′ture (pikt′ieur), *n.*, peinture, *f.* ; tableau, portrait, *m. ; image, f.* — book ; *livre d'images, m.* — card ; *figure, f.* — cleaning ; *nettoyage de tableaux, m.* — frame ; *cadre, m.* — framemaker ; *encadreur, m.* — gallery ; *galerie de tableaux, f.* Dark side of the — ; *revers de la médaille.*

pic′ture, *v.a.*, peindre, dépeindre, représenter, décrire. To — to one's self ; *se figurer, se représenter ; se faire une idée de.*

picturesque′ (pikt′iou-rèske), *adj.*, pittoresque.

picturesque′ *ou* **picturesque′ness**, *n.*, pittoresque, *m.*

picturesque′ly, *adv.*, d'une manière pittoresque, pittoresquement.

pid′dle (pid′d′l), *v.n.*, s'occuper de bagatelles, pignocher, niaiser ; uriner.

pid′dler, *n.*, chipotier, *m.*

pid′dling, *adj.*, futile, frivole, chipotier.

pie (pāïe), *n.*, (of meat) pâté, *m. ;* (fruit) tourte ; (orni., ant.) pie, *f. ;* (print.) pâté, *m.*, pâte, *f.* To eat humble — ; *filer doux ; avaler des couleuvres.* To have a finger in the — ; *avoir part au gâteau ; y être pour quelque chose.*

pie′bald (pāïe-bōld), *adj.*, (of horses) pie.

pie′-crust, *n.*, croûte de pâté, *f.*

pie′-dish, *n.*, tourtière, *f.*

piece (pìce), *n.*, (of large dimensions) pièce, *f. ;* (a portion, a bit, a hunch) morceau ; (fragment) fragment, bout ; (action) acte, exemple, *m. ;* (of money, of poetry, etc.) pièce ; (artil.) pièce ; bouche à feu, *f. ;* (paint.) scène, *f.*, tableau, *m. ;* (for mending) pièce ; (of dress goods) pièce, *f.* — of information ; *fait, point, m.* I'll give him a — of my mind ; *je lui dirai son fait.* A — of news ; *une nouvelle, f.* A — of business ; *une affaire, f.* A — of wit ; *un trait d'esprit, m.* A — of impertinence ; *une impertinence, f.* — goods ; *étoffes qui se vendent à la pièce, f.pl.* A — of water ; *une pièce d'eau.* The —s of a machine ; *les pièces d'une machine.* A — of soap, of bread ; *un morceau de savon, de pain.* A theatrical — ; *une pièce de théâtre.* Broken — ; *fragment, tronçon, m.* To break to —s ; *mettre en morceaux, en pièces ; tomber en morceaux, en pièces.* To fall to —s ; *se démonter ; tomber en pièces.* To take to —s ; *démonter ; se démonter.* To fly to —s ; *voler en éclats.* To cut to —s ; (mil.) *écharper.* All of a — ; *d'une seule pièce ; d'un seul morceau ; tout d'une pièce ;* (fig.) *du même acabit ; de la même espèce ; à l'avenant de.* So much a — ; *chacun ; par personne ; par tête ; la pièce.* What a — of a man! *quel bout d'homme!*

piece, *v.a.*, rapiécer, rapetasser ; mettre une pièce à ; allonger. To — out ; *allonger ; mettre une pièce à.* To — up ; *plâtrer.*

piece, *v.n.*, se joindre ; s'unir.

piece-goods, *n.*, marchandises à la pièce, *f.pl.*

piece′hand, *n.*, (print.) paquetier, *m.*

piece′less, *adj.*, entier.

piece′meal (pìss′mîl), *adv.*, en pièces, par pièces, pièce à pièce ; par morceaux ; peu à peu.

pie′cer, *n.*, ravaudeur, *m.*, ravaudeuse, *f.*

piece′work (-weurke), *n.*, ouvrage fait à la pièce, *ou* à la tâche, *m.*

pied (pāïe′de), *adj.*, bariolé, bigarré ; (of horses) pie.

pier (pîre), *n.*, jetée. *f. ;* (of wharves) embarcadère, *m. ;* (of harbors) jetée, *f.*, môle, *m. ;* (of a bridge) pile, *f. ;* (arch.) contrefort, trumeau, entre-deux, *m.*

pier′-dues (pîr′-), *n.*, droits de jetée, *m.pl.*

pierce (pîr-ce), *v.a.* and *n.*, percer, pénétrer ; pénétrer **dans** ; toucher. To — through ; *transpercer.* To — through and through ; *percer de part en part.*

pierced (pîr′ss′te), *adj.*, (open-work) à jour.

pier′cer, *n.*, (a tool) perçoir, *m. ;* (mines) épinglette, *f. ;* (pers.) perceur, *m.*

pier′cing, *adj.*, perçant ; pénétrant ; (of sound) perçant, aigu.

pier′cingly, *adv.*, d'une manière perçante, d'une manière pénétrante.

pier′cingness, *n.*, pénétration, *f. ;* son aigu, *m.*

pier′-glass (-glâce), *n.*, glace en trumeau, *f.*, trumeau, *m.*

pier′head, *n.*, môle, musoir (V. Hugo), *m.*

pier′-shaft (-shâfte), *n.*, fût vertical de pile, *m.*

pier′-table (-té-b'l), *n.*, console, *f.*

pi′etist (paï-èt-), *n.*, piétiste, *m.f.*

pi′ety (paï-è-), *n.*, piété, *f.*

pig, *n.*, cochon, *m.*, cochonne, *f. ;* porc, pourceau ; (metal.) lingot, saumon, *m.* Sucking-— ; *cochon de lait, m.* To buy a — in a poke ; *acheter chat en poche.* To drive one's —s to market ; *ronfler comme quatre.*

pig, *v.a.* and *n.*, cochonner ; mettre bas. To — it ; *vivre en pourceau.*

pig′-driver (-draïv′-), *n.*, porcher, *m.*

pig′eon (pidj′-), *n.*, pigeon, *m. ;* (pers.) dupe, *f.* To pluck a — ; *plumer un pigeon.*

pig′eon-breasted, *adj.*, bossu par devant.

pig′eon-dung (-deu′gne), *n.*, colombine, *f.*

pig′eon-fancier, *n.*, colombophile, *m.*

pig′eon-hearted (-hârt′-), *adj.*, timide, craintif.

pig′eon-hole (-hôl), *n.*, boulin, *m. ;* (for papers, etc.) case, *f.* Set of —s ; *casier, m.* To be —d ; *rester dans les cartons.*

pig′eon-house (-haouce), *n.*, pigeonnier, colombier, *m.*

pig′eon-livered (-liv′eur′de), *adj.*, sans fiel, doux.

pig′eon-shooting, *n.*, tir aux pigeons, *m.*

pig′eon-toed (-tôde), *adj.*, qui a les pieds en dedans.

pig′gery (pig′gheur′i), *n.*, étable à porcs, *f.*

pig′-headed (-hèd′ède), *adj.*, à grosse tête ; entêté, têtu ; stupide.

pig′-iron, *n.*, fonte en saumon, gueuse, *f.*

pigme′an (-mî-), *adj.*, de pygmée.

pig′ment, *n.*, couleur, *f. ;* (physiol.) pigment, *m.*

pig′my, *n.*, pygmée, *m.*

pig′my, *adj.*, de pygmée ; très petit.

pig′-nut (-neute), *n.*, (bot.) terre-noix, châtaigne de terre, *f.*

pig′-sty (-staïe), *n.*, toit à cochons, *m.*, étable à porcs, *f.*

pig′-tail (-téle), *n.*, queue (de cheveux), *f. ;* (tobacco) tabac en corde, *m.* —ed ; *à queue.*

pike (païke), *n.*, (milit. weapon) pique, *f. ;* (ich.) brochet, *m. ;* (of mountains ; a tool) pic, *m. ;* (a point) (ant.) pointe ; (turnpike) barrière, *f.*

piked (païk′te), *adj.*, pointu, en pointe.

pike′man (païk′-), *n.*, (soldier) piquier, *m.*

pike′staff (païk′stâf), *n.*, bois de pique ; bâton pointu, *m.* Plain as a — ; *clair comme le jour, ou comme le soleil en plein midi.*

pilas′ter, *n.*, pilastre, *m.*

pilch′ard (piltsh′-), *n.*, (ich.) pilchard, célan, *m.*, sardine, *f.*

pile (païl), n., pile, f.; tas, monceau ; (of fire-arms) faisceau, m. ; (building) construction, f., édifice, bâtiment, m. ; (of churches) basilique ; (of shot) pile, f. ; (arch.) pieu, pilotis, pilot, m. ; (phys.) pile, f.; (nap of cloth) poil, m. Funeral —; bûcher, m. — of wood ; bûcher, m. To make one's —; faire fortune. — of buildings ; pâté de maisons, m. To drive a —; enfoncer un pieu, un pilotis.

pile (païl), v.a., entasser, empiler, amonceler ; (milit.) mettre, ou ranger, en faisceau. To — it on ; (fig.) exagérer.

pile, v.n., piloter ; enfoncer des pieux.

pil'eate ou **pil'eated** (pil-i-), adj., (bot.) en forme de chapeau.

pile'-bridge, n., pont sur pilotis.

pile'-driver (-draiv'-), n., (mec.) sonnette, f.

pile'-engine (-è'n'dji'n), n. V. **pile-driver**.

pile'-planking, n., plancher sur pilotis, m. ; plate-forme sur pilotis, f.

pil'er (païl'-), n., personne qui empile, qui entasse, f. ; empileur, m.

piles (païl'ze), n.pl., (med.) hémorroïdes, f.pl. Blind —s ; hémorrhoïdes sèches.

pile'-work (-weurke), n., pilotage, m. ; pilotis, m.

pil'fer, v.a., dérober, voler, chiper, grapiller.

pil'fer, v.n., voler, dérober ; commettre un larcin, un petit vol.

pil'ferer, n., petit voleur ; larron, fripon, chipeur, m.

pil'fering, n., petit vol ; larcin, m.

pil'feringly, adv., par vol, par larcin.

pil'grim, n., pèlerin, m., pèlerine, f.

pil'grimage (-'èdje), n., pèlerinage, m.

pil'ing (païl'-), n., empilement ; amoncellement ; (arch.) ouvrage en pilotis, pilotage, m.

pill, n., pilule, f. To swallow many a bitter —; en avaler de dures.

pil'lage (pil-lèdje), n., pillage, sac, saccagement, m.

pil'lage, v.a., saccager, piller.

pil'lager, n., pillard, m.

pil'lar, n., pilier, m. ; colonne, f. ; (support) support, soutien, m., fondation, f. ; (monument) monument, m. From — to post ; çà et là. To send from — to post ; renvoyer de Caïphe à Pilate. — post-box ; borne-boîte, f.

pil'lared (pil-larde), adj., soutenu par des colonnes ; à colonnes ; en forme de colonne.

pil'lar-plate, n., (horl.) platine, f.

pil'lau, n., pilau, m.

pil'lion (pil'ieune), n., coussinet, m. ; selle de femme, f.

pil'lory, n., pilori, m.

pil'lory, v.a., pilorier, mettre au pilori.

pil'low (pil'lô), n., oreiller ; (nav.) coussin du mât de beaupré ; (of a plow) (tech.) coussinet, m. —case ; taie d'oreiller, f. To smooth the —; lisser l'oreiller.

pil'low, v.a., poser, reposer, coucher (comme sur un oreiller) ; servir d'oreiller à, soutenir.

pil'ose (paï-lôce) ou **pil'ous** (paï-), adj., poilu, velu ; (bot.) capillaire.

pilos'ity (pi-loss'-), n., (ant.) abondance de poils, f.

pi'lot (paï-), n., pilote ; nocher, m. —-boat; bateau-pilote, m. —-coat, ou jacket; vareuse, f. ; paletot-pilote, m. —-cloth; drap-pilote, m. — engine ; machine-pilote, f. —-fish ; pilote, m.

pi'lot, v.a., piloter ; servir de pilote à ; conduire, diriger.

pi'lotage (paï-lot'èdje), n., droit de pilotage, pilotage, lamanage, m.

pi'loting (paï-lot'-), n., pilotage, m.

pimen'ta ou **pimen'to** (-tô), n., (bot.) piment, m.

pimp, n., entremetteur, maquereau, m.

pim'pernel ou **pimpinel'la**, n., (bot.) pimprenelle, f.

pim'ple (pi'm'p'l), n., (med.) bouton, m. ; pustule, f. ; (in the face) bourgeon, m.

pim'pled (pi'm'p'l'de), adj., bourgeonné, pustuleux.

pin, n., épingle ; (peg) cheville ; (linchpin) esse, clavette ; (of a hinge) fiche, f. ; (of a pulley) essieu, m. ; (bolt, tree-nail) cheville, f. ; (center) centre ; (valueless thing) fétu, rien, m., bagatelle, valeur d'une épingle ; (of watches) goupille, f. Rolling-—; rouleau, m. Not to care a— for ; se moquer pas mal de ; se soucier comme de l'an quarante de. To be upon —s and needles ; être sur des charbons ; être dans ses petits souliers. To hear a — drop ; entendre trotter une souris, ou voler une mouche. I have —s and needles in my hand ; la main me fourmille.

pin, v.a., attacher avec une épingle ; attacher avec une cheville ; attacher ; clouer ; arrêter ; cheviller. To — down ; attacher avec une épingle ; (tech.) cheviller. To — any one down to ; lier quelqu'un à ; tenir quelqu'un à. To — up ; attacher avec une épingle, trousser avec une épingle. To — one's faith to ; avoir confiance en ; se reposer sur ; se régler sur l'opinion de.

pin'afore, n., blouse ; blouse d'enfant, f. ; tablier, m.

pinas'ter, n., (bot.) pinastre, pin sauvage, m.

pin'case (-kéce), n., étui à épingles, m.

pin'cers (pi'n'ceurze), n.pl., pince, f.sing. ; tenailles, f.pl.

pinch (pi'n'sh), n., (of salt, etc.) pincée ; (of snuff) prise ; (straits) embarras, m. ; difficulté, gêne, extrémité, nécessité, f., besoin ; (gripe) pinçon, m., meurtrissure faite en pinçant ; (distress) angoisse, f. At, ou on, a —; au besoin ; en cas de nécessité. With a — of salt ; sous bénéfice d'inventaire (Lafontaine).

pinch, v.a., pincer ; (of clothes) serrer, gêner ; (of cold) pincer ; (to deprive) priver; refuser à ; (to press hard) serrer de près ; (to distress) faire pâtir ; (to straiten) gêner, mettre dans la gêne, mettre à l'étroit. To — one's self ; se priver du nécessaire ; vivre chichement. To — off ; arracher, emporter. This shoe —es me ; ce soulier me gêne. —ed for money ; court d'argent.

pinch, v.n., pincer ; (to be straitened) se gêner, être dans la gêne ; (to live close) se priver du nécessaire. To know where the shoe —es ; savoir où le bât blesse.

pinch'beck, n., similor, m.

pinch'er, n., pinceur, m., pinceuse, f.

pinch'fist ou **pinch'penny**, n., pince-maille, fesse-mathieu, ladre, m.

pinch'ing, adj., pressant ; (of cold) piquant.

pinch'ing, n., pincement, m.

pin'cushion (-keush'ieune), n., pelote à épingles, f.

Pindar'ic, adj., pindarique.

Pindar'ic, n., ode pindarique, f.

pin'dust (-deuste), n., limaille d'épingles, f.

pine (païne), n., (tree) pin ; (fruit) ananas ; (wood) bois de pin, m.

pine, v.n., languir, dépérir. To — after ; languir après, soupirer après. To — away ; languir, dépérir.

pin'eal, adj., (anat.) pinéal (only used in the phrase glande pinéale, f.).

pine'apple (-ap'p'l), n., ananas, m.

pine'-nut (-neute), n., (l.u.) pomme de pin, f.

pin'ery (païn'euri), n., serre à ananas, f.

pin'-feather (pi'n'fèth'-), n., petite plume, f. ; duvet, m.

pin'feathered (-fèth'eur'de), adj., dont les plumes commencent à naître.

pin'fold, n., (ant.) fourrière, f.

ping, n., (of a bullet) sifflement, m.

pin'ion (pi'n'ieune), n., aileron, bout d'aile, m. ; (feather) plume, f. ; (quill) bout d'aile ; (tech.) pignon, m. ; (fetters) liens (pour les bras), m.pl.

pin'ion, v.a., lier les ailes à ; couper le bout de

l'aile à ; lier les bras à ; lier, attacher ; garrotter, enchaîner.

pin'ioned (pi'n'ieu'n'de), adj., ailé ; les bras liés, attachés.

pin'ioning, n., (of criminals) saisissement, garrottage, m.

pink, n., (bot.) œillet ; (ich.) véron, m. ; (nav.) flûte, pinque, f. ; (model) modèle ; perfection ; (fig.) perle, fleur, crême, f. ; (color) rose, m. He, she, ou it, is the — of fashion ; c'est la fleur des pots. In the — of condition ; (of a horse) dressé à point ; (pers.) on ne peut mieux.

pink, adj., couleur de rose ; rose. —-eyed ; qui a de petits yeux.

pink, v.a., travailler à jour ; percer ; découper ; faire des œillets à.

pink'er, n., découpeur, m., découpeuse, f.

pink'ing, n., decoupage, m. ; découpure, f.

pink'ish, adj., rosâtre.

pin'-maker (-mék'-), n., épinglier, fabricant d'épingles, m.

pin'-money, n., argent pour menus plaisirs, m.

pin'nace (pi'n'néce), n., barque ; pinasse, f. ; grand canot (du capitaine), m.

pin'nacle (-na-k'l), n., tour, tourelle, f. ; pinacle ; faîte, sommet, m. — of glory ; faîte de la gloire, m.

pin'nacle, v.a., pourvoir de tourelles, de pinacles ; (fig.) élever.

pin'ner, n., cornette, f. ; bonnet, m.

pin'nock, n., (orni.) mésange, f.

pint (paï'n'te), n., (Eng. measure) pinte (litre 0·5679) ; (old Fr. measure) chopine, f. — bottle ; demi-bouteille, f.

pin'tail, n. (orni.) pilet ; canard à longue queue, m.

pin'tle (pi'n't'l), n., petite épingle ; (artil.) cheville ouvrière, f.

pin'y, adj., couvert de pins.

pioneer' (paï-o-nieur), n., pionnier, sapeur, m.

pi'ony (pï'o-), n., (bot.) pivoine, f.

pi'ous (paï-), adj., pieux, dévot.

pi'ously, adv., pieusement.

pip, n., pépie, f. ; (on cards) point ; (fruit) pépin, m.

pip, v.n., crier ; (of sparrows) pépier ; (of little birds) piper, pipier.

pipe (païpe), n., (mus.) pipeau, chalumeau ; (long tube, tech.) tuyau, conduit, m. ; (to smoke out of) pipe ; (of the voice) voix, organe, f. ; son de la voix ; (windpipe) larynx, m. ; (of organs) tuyau, m. ; (of syringes, etc.) canule ; (measure) pipe, pièce anglaise (477 liters), f. ; (mines) amas horizontal ; (nav.) sifflet, m. Main —; tuyau principal. Cutty —; brûle-gueule, m. The — of peace ; le calumet de paix.

pipe (païpe), v.a., jouer du chalumeau, de la flûte ; jouer d'un instrument à vent ; (of birds) siffler ; (nav.) appeler d'un coup de sifflet. To — one's eye ; pleurer.

pipe, v.n., jouer d'un instrument à vent ; siffler.

pipe'-case, n., étui à pipe, m.

pipe'-clay, n., terre de pipe, f.

piped (païp'te), adj., à tuyau ; tubulaire, (of keys) foré.

pi'per (païp'-), n., joueur de flûte ; joueur d'instrument à vent, m. As drunk as a —; soûl comme une grive. To pay the —; payer les violons.

pi'perine, n., (chem.) pipérin, m.

pi'ping (païp'-), adj., qui joue du chalumeau ; sifflant, qui siffle ; (of the voice) criard, flûté. — hot ; (pop.) tout bouillant, tout chaud.

pi'ping (païp'-), n., liséré, passepoil, m.

pip'kin, n., pot de terre, poêlon, coquemar, m.

pip'pin, n., (bot.) reinette, rainette, f. Normandy —s ; pommes tapées, f.pl.

pi'quancy (pï-ka'n'-), n., goût piquant ; piquant, m.

pi'quant (pï-ka'n'te), adj., piquant.

pi'quantly, adv., d'une manière piquante.

pique (pïke), n., pique, brouille, brouillerie, f. ; (punctilio) point, m. To take a —; se piquer, s'offenser.

pique (pïke), v.a., piquer, offenser. To — one's self on ; se piquer de ; se glorifier de.

piq'uet (pi-kète), n., (cards, milit.) piquet, m.

pi'racy (paï-), n., piraterie ; (liter.) contrefaçon, f. ; plagiat, m.

pi'rate (paï-), n., pirate, forban, écumeur de mer ; (liter.) contrefacteur, plagiaire, m.

pi'rate, v.a., (lit.) contrefaire, piller.

pi'rate, v.n., pirater ; exercer la piraterie ; (lit.) faire la contrefaçon ; commettre un plagiat.

pi'rated, adj., de contrefaçon ; de plagiat.

pirat'ical, adj., de pirate ; (lit.) de contrefaçon.

pirat'ically, adv., en pirate ; en contrefaçon.

pi'rating, adj., de piraterie, de contrefaçon.

pirogue (pi-rôghe), n., pirogue, f.

pirouette', n., pirouette, f.

pirouette', v.n., pirouetter.

pis'catory ou piscato'rial (-tô-), adj., de la pêche ; de pêcheur.

Pisces (pï-cize), n.pl., (astron.) les Poissons, m.pl.

piscicul'ture, n., pisciculture, f.

piscicul'turist, pisciculteur, m.

pisci'na, n., piscine, f.

pis'cine, adj., de poisson.

pisciv'orous, adj., ichtyophage, piscivore.

pish ! int., bah !

pis'mire (-maïre), n., (ent.) fourmi, f.

piss, v.a.n., pisser.

piss'abed, n., (bot.) pissenlit, m.

pissas'phalt, n., (min.) asphalte, m.

piss'ing, n., (med.) pissement, m.

piss'ing-place, n., pissoir, m.

pista'chio (-tâ-shiô), n., pistache, f.

pis'til, n., (bot.) pistil, m.

pis'tol, n., pistolet, m. —-case ; boîte à pistolets, f. —-shot ; coup de pistolet, m. Within —-shot ; à portée de pistolet.

pis'tol, v.a., tuer d'un coup de pistolet.

pistole' (-tôle), n., pistole, f.

pis'tol-gal'lery, n., tir au pistolet, m.

pis'ton, n., piston, m. — rod ; tige de piston, f.

pit, n., fosse ; cavité, f. ; creux ; (thea.) parterre ; (mines) puits ; (of the stomach) creux, m. ; (of the arm) aisselle ; (for cock-fighting) arène ; (mark) marque, empreinte ; (of the small-pox) marque, trace ; (grave) fosse ; (biblically) citerne, f. ; abîme, m. ; (quarry) carrière, f. Coal —; mine de houille, f.

pit, v.a., creuser ; marquer de petits creux. To — with ; marquer de. To — against ; opposer à ; mettre aux prises avec.

pit'apat, n., palpitation, f. ; battement de cœur, m.

pit'apat, adv., en palpitant, en battant ; d'un pas léger. To go —; palpiter, battre. Her heart went —; le cœur lui battait, ou palpitait.

pit'-box, n., (thea.) baignoire, f.

pitch, n., (degree) point, degré ; (highest rise) plus haut point, faîte, plus haut degré, comble, m. ; (slope) pente, f., penchant, versant, m. ; (stature) taille, stature ; (elevation) élévation, hauteur ; (arch., tech.) portée, f. ; (mus.) ton, diapason, m. ; (of a roof) pente ; (of the belt of a wheel) épaisseur ; (substance) poix, f. ; (of the voice) portée, étendue, f. — dark ; noir comme dans un four ; (of night) nuit noire, f. To play — and toss ; jouer à pile ou face. One cannot touch — without soiling one's fingers ; (prov.) ou ne peut manier le beurre qu'on ne se graisse les doigts.

pitch, v.a., lancer, jeter ; précipiter ; (with a fork) jeter avec la fourche ; (to plant) planter ; (a net) tendre ; (to fix) asseoir, fixer ; (a tent) dresser ; (camp) asseoir ; (mus.) donner le ton, le diapason **à** ; (to smear with pitch) enduire de poix, poisser. To — a yarn ; *conter une histoire.* To — it strong ; *parler avec beaucoup de véhémence.* To — out of the window ; *jeter par la fenêtre.*

pitch, *v.n.*, (of vehicles) plonger ; (of ships) plonger, tanguer ; (of birds) s'abattre ; (a camp) camper ; (to fall) tomber ; (of a horse) se cabrer. To — into ; *se jeter* **dans**, *se précipiter* **dans**, *plonger* **dans** ; (to fall foul of) *tomber* **dessus** ; *déblatérer* **contre** ; *dire des injures* **à**. To — upon ; *choisir ; faire choix* **de** ; *s'arrêter* **à** ; *jeter son dévolu* **sur**. To — upon the right person ; *tomber juste sur la personne qu'il faut.* To — out of the window ; *tomber par la fenêtre.* — and pay ; *argent comptant, m.*

pitch'-coal (-côle), *n.*, jais, jaïet, *m.*

pitched (pitsh'tè), *adj.*, (sloping) en pente, à pente. — battle ; *bataille rangée, f.*

pitch'er, *n.*, cruche, *f.* —s have ears ; *les murs ont des oreilles.* The — goes to the well once too often ; *tant va la cruche à l'eau qu'à la fin elle se casse.*

pitch'-farthing (-fàr-*t*hígne), *n.*, (game) fossette, *f.*

pitch'fork, *n.*, fourche, *f. v.a.;* to — any one into a position ; *lancer, ou pousser quelqu'un* **a**, ou **dans**, *un poste, un emploi, sans rime ni raison.*

pitch'ing, *n.*, (of vehicles) plongement ; (of ships) tangage, *m.*

pitch'-penny, *n.* V. **pitch'-farthing**.

pitch'-pine, *n.*, pin à trochets, picéa, *m.*

pitch'y, *adj.*, poissé ; de poix ; enduit de poix ; (fig.) sombre.

pit'-coal (-côle), *n.*, charbon de terre, *m. ;* houille, *f.*

pit'-door, *n.*, entrée du parterre, *f.*

pit'eous (pit'i-), *adj.*, digne de pitié ; piteux ; (compassionate) compatissant ; (pitiful) pitoyable.

pit'eously, *adv.*, de manière à exciter la pitié ; avec compassion ; pitoyablement ; piteusement.

pit'eousness, *n.*, tristesse ; pitié, compassion, *f.*

pit'fall (-fôl), *n.*, trappe, *f. ;* piège, *m. ;* fosse, *f.*

pith (pith), *n.*, sève, moelle ; (force) force, vigueur, énergie ; (quintessence) quintessence ; (importance) importance, substance, *f.*, essentiel, poids, *m.*

pith'ily (pith'-), *adv.*, fortement, avec force, vigoureusement, énergiquement, avec énergie.

pith'iness (pith'-), *n.*, force, vigueur, énergie, *f.*

pith'less (pith'-), *adj.*, sans sève, sans moelle ; (fig.) sans énergie, sans force.

pith'y (pith'-), *adj.*, plein de sève ; moelleux ; (fig.) fort, énergique, vigoureux.

pit'iable (pit'i-a-b'l), *adj.*, (pers.) digne de pitié ; (of things) pitoyable, à faire pitié.

pit'iableness, *n.*, état pitoyable, *m.*

pit'iful (-foule), *adj.*, pitoyable ; (compassionate) compatissant.

pit'ifully, *adv.*, pitoyablement ; avec compassion.

pit'ifulness, *n.*, caractère, *ou* état, pitoyable, *m. ;* (pity) pitié, compassion, *f.*

pit'iless, *adj.*, impitoyable, sans pitié, sans compassion, dur, insensible.

pit'ilessly, *adv.*, impitoyablement ; sans pitié.

pit'ilessness, *n.*, caractère impitoyable, *m. ;* cruauté, *f.*

pit'man, *n.*, scieur de long de dessous ; (mines) mineur, *m.*

pit'-saw, *n.*, scie de scieur de long, *f.*

pit'tance, *n.*, pitance ; légère portion ; légère dose, *f.*

pit'ted, *adj.*, (with smallpox) grêlé ; marqué (de la petite vérole). — against ; *opposé* **à**.

pit'uite (pit'iou-aïte), **n.**, (med.) pituite, *f.*

pitu'itous (pit'iou-it'-), *adj.*, (med.) pituiteux.

pit'y, *n.*, pitié, compassion, *f. ;* (regret) dommage, *m.* For —'s sake ; *par pitié.* It is a — ; *c'est dommage.* What a — ! *quel dommage !* It is a thousand pities he did not do so ; *c'est bien dommage, ou il est à regretter, ou c'est bien regrettable, qu'il n'ait pas agi de la sorte.* To have — on ; *avoir pitié* **de**. The more 's the — ; *c'est d'autant plus dommage ; tant pis.*

pit'y, *v.a.*, avoir pitié **de**, prendre en pitié ; plaindre. He is to be pitied ; *il est à plaindre.*

piv'ot, *n.*, pivot, *m.* — man ; (milit.) *guide, m. v.a.*, faire pivoter. *v.n.*, pivoter.

pla'cable (plé-ca-b'l), *adj.*, facile à apaiser.

pla'card (-cârde), *n.*, placard, *m.*, affiche, pancarte, *f. v.a.*, afficher, placarder **de**.

place, *n.*, place, *f. ;* endroit, lieu, *m. ;* localité ; (rank) position, *f.*, rang, *m. ;* (dwelling) demeure, résidence, *f. ;* logis, *m. ;* (employment) place, *f.*, emploi, *m.*, condition, *f. ;* (priority) pas, *m.*, préséance ; (milit.) place, place de guerre ; (space) place, *f.*, espace ; (for a house, etc.) emplacement, *m.* Come to my — ; *venez chez moi.* In — of ; *à la place* **de**; *au lieu de.* In one's —, in its — ; *à sa place.* In the first — ; *en premier lieu ; d'abord.* In — ; (office) *en place.* In high —s ; *en haut lieu.* To give — ; *faire place* **à**, *céder* **à**, *céder le pas* **à**. To give — to ; *succéder* **a**, *succéder.* In the next — ; *en second lieu ; ensuite.* Louis XI. came in his time and — ; *Louis XI vint en son temps et lieu.* To take the — of ; (of medicaments) *servir de succédané* **à** ; (of persons) *prendre la place* **de**, *arriver, se passer ; succéder* **à**, *remplacer ; prendre le pas* **sur**. To take — ; *avoir lieu.* Out of — ; *déplacé ;* (of time) *inopportun, intempestif.*

place, *v.a.*, placer, mettre ; (money) verser, déposer, placer.

place'man, *n.*, fonctionnaire public ; homme en place, *m.*

placen'ta, *n.*, (anat., bot.) placenta, *m.*

pla'cer (plé-), *n.*, placeur, *m.f. ;* (gold-digging) (pron. pla-) placer, *m.*

plac'id, *adj.*, placide, doux, tranquille ; calme, serein, paisible.

plac'idly, *adv.*, placidement, doucement, tranquillement, avec calme, paisiblement.

plac'idness, *n.*, placidité, *f.*, calme, *m.* douceur, sérénité, tranquillité, *f.*

pla'gal (plé-), *adj.*, (mus.) plagal.

pla'giarism, *n.*, plagiat, *m.*

pla'giarist, *n.*, plagiaire, contrefacteur, *m.*

pla'giarize, *v.a.*, s'approprier par plagiat, piller, contrefaire. *v.n.*, commettre un plagiat, faire la contrefaçon.

pla'giary, *adj.*, plagiaire.

plague (pléghe), *n.*, peste ; (fig.) plaie, *f.*, fléau, tourment, *m.* He is the — of my life ; *il fait le tourment de ma vie.* — on ! *peste de !* — spot ; *foyer d'infection, ulcère, m.*

plague (pléghe), *v.a.*, infecter de la peste ; (fig.) être une peste **pour**, un fléau **pour**, un tourment **pour** ; tourmenter ; ennuyer ; harceler, importuner ; (pop.) assommer, taonner. To — to death ; *assommer.*

pla'guily (plé-ghi-), *adv.*, furieusement, terriblement.

plag'uy (plé-ghi), *adj.*, maudit ; méchant.

plaice (plèce), *n.*, (ich.) plie, *f. ;* carrelet, *m.*

plaid (plade), *n.*, étoffe écossaise, *f. ;* (garment) manteau écossais, plaid, *m.*

plain (plène), *n.*, plaine, *f.*

plain, *adj.*, (level) uni, plat, plain ; (simple) (pers.) simple, sans façon ; (of things) simple ; (frank) franc, sincère ; (evident) évident, clair ; (undisguised) pur, franc ; (ordinary) commun, ordinaire ; (ugly) laid ; (of stuffs) uni ; (of language) intelligible, bon ; (cook.) (without sauce) au naturel. — truth ; *pure vérité, franche vérité, f.* He used very — language ; *il parla sans détour.*

In — English ; (fig.) *en bon français.* It was all — sailing ; *toutes les difficultés avaient été aplanies.* — hair ; *cheveux en bandeaux, m.pl.* — as a pikestaff; *clair comme le jour, comme bon jour.* In — clothes ; *en bourgeois.*

plain, *adv.* *V.* **plainly.**

plain, *v.a.,* aplanir.

plain'-chant *ou* **plain'-song,** *n.,* plain-chant, *m.*

plain'-cooking, *n.,* cuisine bourgeoise, *f.*

plain'-dealing (-dîl'-), *n.,* droiture, probité, bonne foi, franchise, *f.* *adj.,* loyal, franc.

plain'ly, *adv.,* franchement, sincèrement, ouvertement, bonnement ; évidemment, clairement ; simplement; distinctement; sans déguisement ; (with a level surface) de niveau.

plain'ness, *n.,* (levelness) surface plane, unie ; égalité; (fig.) franchise, sincérité ; simplicité ; évidence, clarté ; nature ordinaire ; laideur, *f. ;* air commun, *m.*

plain'-speaking, *n.,* franchise, *f.,* clarté, *f.*

plain'-spoken, *adj.,* qui parle à cœur ouvert; franc, clair, explicite.

plaint (plé'n'te), *n.,* plainte ; lamentation; (jur.) plainte, *f.*

plain'tiff, *n.,* (jur.) demandeur, *m.,* demanderesse, *f.;* plaignant, *m.,* plaignante, *f.;* (crim. law) partie civile, *f.*

plain'tive, *adj.,* plaintif.

plain'tively, *adv.,* plaintivement, d'une voix plaintive.

plain'tiveness, *n.,* ton plaintif, *m.,* tristesse, *f.*

plain'-work (-weurke) *ou* **plain'-sewing,** *n.,* ouvrage à l'aiguille uni, *m. ;* couture, *f.*

plait (pléte) *n.,* pli, *m. ;* (of hair) natte, tresse, *f.*

plait, *v.a.,* plisser ; (hair) tresser, natter.

plait'ed, *adj.,* à plis, plissé ; (of the hair) natté, à nattes ; tressé, à tresses.

plait'ing, *n.,* action de plisser ; plissure, *f. ;* plissement, tressage, *m.*

plan, *n.,* plan ; (project) plan, dessein, projet, système ; moyen ; (course) parti, *m.* Raised — ; *élévation, f.* To raise, to take a — ; *lever un plan.*

plan, *v.a.,* tracer un plan ; faire le plan de ; (fig.) projeter, préparer, arranger.

plane (pléne) *n.,* (geom.) plan, *m.,* surface plane, *f. ;* (persp.) plan ; (carp.) rabot ; (print.) taquoir, *m.*

plane, *v.a.,* raboter ; (print.) taquer ; (fig.) aplanir.

plane *ou* **plane'-tree** (-trî) *n.,* platane, *m.*

plan'er, *n.,* raboteur ; (print.) taquoir, *m.*

plan'et (pla-nète), *n.,* planète, *f.*

plan'etary, *adj.,* planétaire.

planim'etry (-ni'm'è-), *n.,* (geom.) planimétrie, *f.*

plan'ing (plé'n'-), *n.,* rabotage, *m.* — -machine ; *machine à raboter, f.*

plan'ish (pla'n'-), *v.a.,* (tech.) planer.

plan'isher, *n.,* planeur, *m.*

plan'isphere (-sfîre), *n.,* planisphère, *m.*

plank, *n.,* planche, *f.;* madrier ; ais ; (nav.) bordage, *m. ;* (in politics) programme politique, *m.* To walk the — ; *faire le tremplin.* To tread the — ; (at sea) *faire le quart.* To — down ; (money) *déposer ;* (fam.) *abouler.*

plank, *v.a.,* planchéier, plancheyer ; (a ship) border.

plank'ing, *n.,* planchéiage ; (of a ship) bordage, *m.*

plan'ner, *n.,* auteur d'un plan, d'un projet ; projeteur, *m.*

plan'ning, *n.,* tracé d'un plan, *m. ;* (fig.) conception, invention, *f.*

plant, *v.n.,* planter, semer.

plant, *n.,* (bot.) plante, *f.,* plant ; (tech.) matériel, outillage, *m. ;* (rail.) matériel, *m.*

plant, *v.a.,* planter ; (to found) fonder, établir ; (to place) poser, placer, déposer ; (cannon) pointer, braquer.

plan'tain (-tine), *n.,* (bot.) plantain, *m.*

plan'tain *ou* **plan'tain-tree** (-trî), *n.,* (bot.) bananier, musa, *m.*

planta'tion (-té-), *n.,* plantation ; (colony) colonie, *f. ;* (in America) plantage ; (establishment) établissement, *m.,* fondation, *f.*

plant'er, *n.,* planteur, colon ; (fig.) propagateur, *m.*

plant'ing, *n.,* plantage, *m.;* plantation ; (arch.) pose; (fig.) fondation, *f.,* établissement, *m.*

plant'let, *n.,* (bot.) plantule, *f.*

plash, *n.,* flaque d'eau, *f.*

plash, *v.n.,* patauger, barboter. *V.* **splash.**

plash, *v.a.,* éclabousser ; jeter de l'eau sur ; entrelacer.

plash'y, *adj.,* gâcheux, boueux, bourbeux.

plas'ter (plâs-), *n.,* plâtre ; (pharm.) emplâtre, *m.* — of Paris ; *plâtre cuit, gypse, m.* — -work ; *plâtrage, m.* Old — ; *plâtras, m.* — stone ; *gypse, m.* Court — ; *taffetas d'Angleterre, taffetas gommé, m.* Diachylon — ; *diachylon, m.* Sticking — ; *sparadrap, m.*

plas'ter, *v.a.,* plâtrer ; (med.) mettre un emplâtre à.

plas'terer, *n.,* plâtrier ; (in figures) mouleur, *m.*

plas'tering, *n.,* plâtrage, *m.*

plas'tery, *adj.,* plâtreux.

plas'tic, *adj.,* plastique.

plastic'ity, *n.,* nature plastique, plasticité, *f. ;* (ant.) courbure, *f.*

plat, *n.,* petite pièce de terre, *f.*

plat *ou* **plat'ting,** *n.,* tresse, natte, *f.*

plat, *v.a.,* tresser, natter.

plat'ane, *n.,* (bot.) platane, *m.*

plate, *n.,* assiette ; (metal) plaque ; (gold and silver articles) vaisselle plate, argenterie, *f. ;* (prize) prix en vaisselle plate, *m. ;* (of a lock, tech.) platine ; (phot.) plaque, *f. ;* cliché ; (print.) cliché, *m. ;* (engr.) planche ; (armor) armure de plaques de fer, *f.* Dinner— ; *assiette plate.* Soup— ; *assiette à soupe.* Piece of — ; *pièce d'argenterie, f.* Silver-— ; *vaisselle d'argent, argenterie.* Gold-— ; *vaisselle d'or.* — -basket ; *panier à l'argenterie, m.* — -warmer ; *chauffe-assiettes, m.*

plate, *v.a.,* plaquer ; (to beat into thin pieces) réduire en plaques, en lames ; laminer ; (to arm) revêtir d'une armure de plaques, cuirasser, blinder ; (to adorn with plate) orner de plaques ; (mirrors) étamer ; (to cover with gold or silver) plaquer, dorer, argenter.

plateau' (pla-tô), *n.,* plateau, *m.*

plate'-cover (-keuv'-), *n.,* cloche d'assiette, *f.*

plat'ed (plét'ède), *adj.,* plaqué. — goods ; *plaqué, m.*

plate'ful (-foule), *n.,* assiettée, *f.*

plate'-glass, *n.,* glace, *f.,* cristal, verre poli, *m.*

plate'-layer (-lé-eur), *n.,* (railways) poseur de rails, *m.*

plate'-mark, *n.,* contrôle, *m.*

plat'en (plat'-), *n.,* (print.) platine, *f.*

plate'-rack (plét'-), *n.,* porte-assiettes, *m.*

plate'-stand, *n.,* porte-assiettes, *m.*

plat'form (plat'-), *n.,* plate-forme ; estrade ; tribune, *f.;* (railways) quai ; (fig.) plan, modèle, *m. ;* (of a bridge) tablier, *m. ;* (arch.) plate-forme, *f. ;* (politics) programme, *m. ;* profession de foi (politique). Arrival —; *débarcadère, m.* Leaving — ; *embarcadère, m.*

plat'ina *ou* **plat'inum,** *n.,* platine, *m.*

plat'ing (plét'-), *n.,* opération de plaquer, *f.* art de plaquer, *m.*

Platon'ic, *adj.,* platonicien ; platonique.

platon'ically, *adv.,* d'une manière platonique.

Pla'tonism (plé-to-niz'm), *n.,* platonisme, *m.*

platoon' (pla-toune), *n.,* (milit.) peloton, *m.*

— exercise ; *école de peloton. f* — firing ; *feu de peloton, m.*

plat'ter, *n.,* grand plat, *m. ;* (milit. nav.) ganelle, *f. ;* (pers.) tresseur, *m.,* tresseuse, *f.*

plaud'it, *n.,* applaudissement, *m.*

plausibil'ity *ou* **plaus'ibleness** (plô-zi-), *n.,* plausibilité, *f.*

plaus'ible (-zi-b'l), *adj.,* plausible ; (pers.) à langue dorée.

plaus'ibly (-zi-), *adv.,* plausiblement, d'une manière plausible.

play, *v.a.,* (to put in motion) faire jouer ; (to act) jouer, représenter, faire, feindre ; (sportive) déployer gaîment ; (a game) jouer, faire ; (a trick) jouer, faire ; (mus.) jouer **de** ; (the piano, the organ) jouer **de** ; toucher **de** ; (the harp, the guitar) pincer **de**. To — cards ; *jouer aux cartes.* To — the fool ; *badiner ; folâtrer ; faire la bête ; faire le singe, faire l'enfant.* To — off ; *déployer, faire voir ;* (tricks) *faire, jouer ;* (fig.) (against) *opposer* à. To — truant ; *faire l'école buissonnière.* To — one's cards well ; (fig.) *jouer bien son jeu.* To — a deep game ; *jouer de finesse.* To — fast and loose ; *agir avec duplicité ; agir avec imprudence, avec témérité ; être volage, inconstant.* To — into a person's hands ; *donner beau jeu à quelqu'un.* To — into each other's hands ; *être de connivence, d'intelligence.* To — on words ; *jouer sur les mots.* To — possum ; *faire le mort, feindre, dissimuler.* To — with a person ; *se jouer de quelqu'un, le tromper ; se moquer de.*

play, *v.n.,* jouer ; (to move) se mouvoir ; (to frolic) folâtrer, s'amuser, badiner ; (tech.) travailler ; (mus.) jouer, exécuter ; (of precious stones) briller, chatoyer, étinceler. To — against ; *jouer, jouer contre.* To — at ; *jouer* à. To — on, upon ; (mus.) *jouer de* ; (the piano, organ) *jouer de ; toucher ;* (the harp, the guitar) *pincer de* ; (to mock) *se jouer de, s'amuser de.* To — with ; *jouer avec* ; (to trifle with, to mock) *se jouer de.* To — fair ; *jouer bon jeu.* To — false ; *jouer faux ; tricher, tromper.* To — high, low ; *jouer gros jeu, jouer petit jeu.* To — for love ; *jouer pour l'honneur, pour le plaisir.* To — upon a person ; *faire un tour, une niche, à quelqu'un ; se jouer de quelqu'un.* To — at sight ; (mus.) *déchiffrer, jouer (un morceau) à première vue.* To — away ; *perdre au jeu.*

play, *n.,* jeu ; badinage, *m. ;* (recreation) récréation, *f. ;* (scope) essor, *m.,* carrière ; (mus.) exécution, *f. ;* (tech.) jeu ; (playhouse) spectacle, théâtre, *m. ;* (book) comédie, pièce de théâtre ; (representation) représentation, *f.,* spectacle, *m.* In —; *pour badiner, pour rire ;* (busy) occupé. At —; *en jouant, en récréation ;* (gambling) *au jeu.* To be lucky at — ; *jouer de bonheur.* To be unlucky at — ; *jouer de malheur.* To — first ; *jouer le premier ;* (at cards) *avoir la main.* Whose turn is it to —? *Mine ; à qui est-ce à jouer? A moi.* It is not your turn to — ; *ce n'est pas à vous à jouer.* To have full — ; *avoir libre essor, pleine carrière.* To give — to ; *donner essor* à, *carrière* à. To give full — to ; *donner un libre essor* à, *ou libre carrière* à. Full of — ; *badin.* By — ; *jeu de scène, jeu muet.* Fair — ; *franc jeu ; bon jeu ; de bonne guerre ;* (fig.) *la justice, f.* Foul — ; *mauvais jeu ; mauvais tour, m. ; perfidie, f. ; trait de perfidie, m. ; trahison, f.* I will hold the foe in — ; *j'occuperai l'ennemi.* To give fair — to ; *donner beau jeu* à *; jouer cartes sur table avec* ; *jouer franc jeu avec.* — of colors ; *le jeu de la lumière.* A — on, *ou* upon, words ; *un jeu de mots.*

play'able, *adj.,* jouable.

play'bill, *n.,* affiche de spectacle, *f. ;* programme de spectacle, *m.*

play'book (-bouke), *n.,* recueil de pièces de théâtre, livre de comédies, *m. ;* pièce de théâtre, *f.*

play'-day, *n.,* jour de congé, *m.*

play'-debt (-dète), *n.,* dette de jeu, *f.*

play'er, *n.,* joueur, *m.,* joueuse, *f. ;* (thea.) acteur, *m.,* actrice, *f.,* comédien, *m.,* comédienne, *f.,* artiste, *m.f. ;* (mus.) exécutant, *m.,* artiste, *m.f.,* (b.s.) joueur, *m.,* joueuse, *f.* (**de**, on ; à, at).

play'fellow (-lô) *ou* **-mate,** *n.,* compagnon, *m.,* compagne, *f.,* camarade de jeu, *m.f.*

play'ful (-foule), *adj.,* qui aime à jouer ; folâtre, badin.

play'fully, *adv.,* d'une manière badine ; en badinant ; avec enjouement.

play'fulness, *n.,* badinage, enjouement, *m. ;* gaîté, *f.*

play'-game, *n.,* jeu d'enfant, *m.*

play'-goer (-gô-eur), *n.,* habitué de spectacle, *m. ;* coureur de spectacles, *m.*

play'-going, *adj.,* qui va souvent au spectacle ; qui court les spectacles.

play'ground (-graou'n'de), *n.,* cour de récréation, *f.*

play'-hour (-aoueur), *n.,* heure de récréation ; récréation, *f.*

play'house (-haouce), *n.,* salle de spectacle, *f. ;* théâtre, *m. ;* comédie, *f.*

play'-night (-naïte), *n.,* jour de spectacle, *m.*

play'-room (-roume), *n.,* salle de récréation, *f.*

play'thing (-thigne), *n.,* jouet, joujou, *m.*

play'-time (-taïme), *n.,* heures de récréation, *f.pl. ;* récréation, *f.sing.*

play'wright *ou* **play'writer** (-raït'-), *n.,* faiseur, *ou* auteur, de pièces de théâtre, *m.*

plea (plî), *n.,* (jur.) moyen, ⊙plaid, *m.,* exception, *f. ;* (lawsuit) procès, *m. ;* (fig.) cause ; pretexte ; (justification) justification, excuse, défense ; (urgent prayer) supplication, *f.* Court of Common —s ; (ant.) *cour des plaids communs, f.* — for mercy ; *appel à la clémence (de la Cour,* etc.), *m.*

plead (plîde), *v.n.,* plaider ; se défendre ; (jur.) se déclarer ; (to allege) déclarer, alléguer, soutenir, faire valoir. To — for ; *parler en faveur de.* To — with ; *intervenir auprès de.* To — guilty ; (jur.) *se déclarer coupable.* To — not guilty ; (jur.) *se déclarer innocent.*

plead (plîde), *v.a.,* plaider, défendre ; (to maintain) soutenir ; (to allege) déclarer, alléguer, faire valoir ; (to offer in excuse) s'excuser **sur.** To — against ; *opposer* à.

plead'able (-a-b'l), *adj.,* allégable ; (jur.) plaidable.

plead'er (plîd'-), *n.,* avocat ; défenseur ; (fig.) intercesseur, *m.*

plead'ing (plîd'-), plaidoirie, *f.* —s, *pl.,* débats, *m.pl. ;* plaidoyer, *m.*

pleas'ant (plèz'-), *adj.,* agréable à, charmant **pour** ; aimable **pour** ; gracieux ; gai.

pleas'antly, *adv.,* agréablement ; d'une manière charmante, aimable ; gaîment ; (ludicrously) (ant.) plaisamment.

pleas'antness, *n.,* agrément, charme, *m. ;* humeur plaisante, gaîté, *f.*

pleas'antry, *n.,* plaisanterie, *f.*

please (plîze), *v.a.,* plaire à ; faire plaisir à ; charmer ; contenter. I — ; *je plais* à. I — (choose) to ; *il me plaît de.* To be —d ; *être content ;* (with) *être content de ;* (to) *se plaire* à, *se faire un plaisir de, daigner, vouloir bien.* You are —d to say so ; *cela vous plaît à dire.* To — one's self ; *se contenter ; faire son choix ;* (in) *se plaire* à *; faire comme on veut.* To be —d in ; *prendre plaisir* à. We are —d to think ; *il nous plaît de penser.* To be —d to do a thing ; *daigner, avoir la bonté de, vouloir bien, se faire un plaisir de, faire une certaine chose.*

please, *v.n.,* plaire. To — to ; *plaire à ; vouloir bien ; vouloir ; daigner.* If you — ; *s'il vous plaît.* As you — ; *comme il vous plaira ; comme bon vous semblera ; comme vous voudrez.* If I — ; *si cela me plaît.* — God ; *s'il plaît à Dieu.* — lift up your hand ; *veuillez lever la main.* May it — the Court ; (jur.) *plaise à la cour.*

May it — your Majesty ; *n'en déplaise à votre Majesté.*

pleased, *adj.,* (of pers. and things) charmé **de,** content **de,** heureux **de** ; (with things only) satisfait **de.** — as Punch ; *enchanté.*

pleas'ing (plîz'-), *adj.,* agréable, charmant, aimable, gracieux ; (of things) riant, agréable.

pleas'ingly, *adv.,* agréablement, avec amabilité ; gracieusement ; d'une manière riante.

pleas'ingness, *n.,* agrément, charme, *m.* ; amabilité, nature gracieuse ; nature riante, *f.*

pleas'urable (plèj'eur'a-b'l), *adj.,* agréable, charmant.

pleas'urably, *adv.,* agréablement.

pleas'ure (plèj'eur), *n.,* plaisir ; agrément, charme ; (will) gré, *m.,* volonté, *f.* At — ; *à volonté, à plaisir.* At my — ; *à mon gré ; quand bon me semble.* What is your — ? *qu'y a-t-il pour votre service ?* To afford — to ; *faire plaisir* à. To have the — of ; (acquaintance) avoir *l'avantage, le plaisir,* de. To take — in ; *prendre plaisir* à. To make a — of ; *mettre son plaisir* à. To esteem it a — to ; to make a — of ; *se faire un plaisir* de. — boat ; *canot de plaisance, m.* — trip ; *partie de plaisir, f. ; voyage d'agrément, m.* — van ; *char à bancs, m. ; carriole, f.* To request the — of ; *prier . . . de vouloir bien venir.*

pleas'ure, *v.a.,* plaire à, contenter.

pleas'ure-ground (-graou'n'de), *ou* **pleas'ure-garden.** *n.,* parc, *ou* jardin, d'agrément ; jardin anglais, *m.*

pleas'ure-house (-haouce), *n.,* maison de plaisance, *f. ;* château (à la campagne), *m.*

pleas'ure-seeking, ami du plaisir, *m. ;* qui cherche le plaisir.

plebe'ian (plè-bi-ya'n), *n.,* plébéien, *m.,* plébéienne, *f.,* roturier, *m.,* roturière, *f.*

plebe'ian, *adj.,* plébéien, vulgaire, roturier.

pledge, *n.,* gage, garant, *m. ;* garantie, *f. ;* nantissement ; (toast) toast ; toste, *m. ;* (promise) assurance, promesse, *f. ;* (temperance) vœu de tempérance ; (milit.) (ant.) otage, *m. ;* (jur.) caution,*f.* To give, *ou* put, in — ; *mettre en gage ; engager.* To take the — ; *promettre de s'abstenir de spiritueux.* Unredeemed — ; (pawnbroking) *effet non dégagé, m.* To hold in — ; *tenir en gage.*

pledge, *v.a.,* engager ; engager la parole, *ou* la foi, *ou* la responsabilité, **de** ; mettre en gage ; (to vouch for) garantir ; se porter garant **de** ; (toast) faire raison à, boire à la santé **de.**

pledgee' (plèd'jî), *n.,* créancier, nanti d'un gage, *m.*

pledg'er, *n.,* personne qui met en gage, *f. ;* débiteur ; garant, *m. ;* personne qui boit à la santé **de,** *f.*

Ple'iades (pli-ya-dize), *n.pl.,* Pléiades, *f.pl.*

ple'narily (plî-), *adv.,* pleinement, complètement.

ple'nary (plî-), *adj.,* plein, complet, entier ; (indulgence) plénière, *f.*

plenipoten'tiary (-tè'n'shia-), *adj.,* plénipotentiaire ; (of things) plein et entier.

plenipoten'tiary, *n.,* plénipotentiaire, *m.*

plen'itude (plè'n'i-tioude), *n.,* plénitude, *f. ;* état complet, *m.* The moon in her — ; *la lune en son plein.* In the — of her glory ; *à l'apogée de sa gloire.*

plen'teous (plè'n'ti-), *adj.,* abondant.

plen'teously, *adv.,* abondamment.

plen'teousness, *n.,* abondance, fertilité, *f.*

plen'tiful (plè'n'ti-foule), *adj.,* abondant, en abondance.

plen'tifully, *adv.,* abondamment.

plen'tifulness, *n.,* abondance, fertilité, *f.*

plen'ty (plè'n'ti), *n.,* abondance ; *f.* Horn of — ; *corne d'abondance, f.* There is — of it ; *il y en a bien assez.* There are — of them ; *il y en y en a bien assez.* There are a — of them, *il y en a un grand nombre, il y en a à foison.* To have

— of time ; *avoir largement du temps, avoir tout le temps.*

plen'ty, *adj.,* abondant ; en abondance.

ple'onasm (pli-o-naz'm), *n.,* pléonasme, *m.*

pleonas'tical, *adj.,* pléonastique.

pleonas'tically, *adv.,* par pléonasme ; d'une manière pléonastique.

pleth'ora (plèth'-), *n.,* (med., fig.) pléthore, *f.* — of wit ; *surabondance d'esprit, f.*

plethor'ic *ou* **plethoret'ic,** *adj.,* (med.) pléthorique.

pleu'risy (pliou-ri-ci), *n.,* (med.) pleurésie, *f.*

pleurit'ic *ou* **pleurit'ical,** *adj.,* (med.) pleurétique.

plex'us, *n.,* (anat.) plexus, *m.*

pliabil'ity (plaï-), *n.* *V.* **pli'ableness.**

pli'able (plaï-a-b'l), *adj.,* pliable ; pliant, souple, flexible.

pli'ableness, *n.,* souplesse, flexibilité, *f.*

pli'ancy, pli'antness (plaï-), *n.,* flexibilité, souplesse, *f.*

pli'ant (plaï-), *adj.,* pliant, souple, flexible.

pli'ers (plaï-eurze), *n.pl.,* pinces, *f.pl.*

plight (plaïte), *n.,* état, *m. ;* condition, *f. ;* (pledge) (ant.) gage, *m.* To be in a sore — ; *être mal loti ; être dans une triste condition.*

plight, *v.a.,* engager. To — one's faith ; *engager sa foi.*

plight'er, *n.,* personne qui engage, *f.*

plinth (pli'n'th), *n.,* (arch.) plinthe, *f. ;* (of a wall) bandeau, *m.*

Pli'ocene, *n.,* (geol.) pliocène, *m.*

plod, *v.n.,* marcher avec peine ; marcher à pas pesants ; aller clopin-clopant ; (to study) s'appliquer à, piocher ; travailler assidûment.

plod'der, *n.,* piocheur, *m.* A mere — ; *un bon bouleux.*

plod'ding, *adj.,* laborieux, d'un travail soutenu.

plod'ding, *n.,* travail laborieux, travail soutenu, pénible, *m.*

plot, *n.,* (stratagem, conspiracy) stratagème, *m.,* ruse, *f.,* complot, *m.,* trame ; (of a dramatic piece) intrigue ; (of ground) petite pièce de terre, *f.,* petit terrain, petit champ ; (fam.) lapin de terre ; (in surveying) plan de terrain, *m.* To lay a — ; *ourdir, tramer un complot, ourdir une trame.*

plot, *v.n.,* comploter, conspirer.

plot, *v.a.,* comploter, tramer ; machiner ; former le plan **de** ; (in surveying) rapporter.

plot'ter, *n.,* personne qui forme des plans, des projets ; conspirateur, comploteur, *m.*

plot'ting, *n.,* stratagèmes, *m.pl. ;* machinations, *f.pl. ;* complot, *m. ;* (in surveying) action de rapporter, *f.*

plot'ting-scale, *n.,* échelle à rapporter, *f.*

plow (plaou), *n.,* charrue ; terre labourée, *f. ;* (astron.) la Grande Ourse, *f. ;* (fig.) culture, agriculture, *f. ;* (bookbind.) rognoir ; (carp.) bonnet de deux pièces, *m.* To put one's hand to the — ; *mettre la main à la pâte ; mettre la main à l'œuvre.*

plow (plaou), *v.a.,* labourer ; passer la charrue **sur** ; (bookbind.) rogner ; (carp.) creuser ; (fig.) sillonner, fendre ; (exams.) refuser ; (pop.) bouler, couler, retoquer. To — in ; *enfouir à la charrue.* To — up, *ou* out ; *défoncer à la charrue ; déterrer, découvrir en labourant ;* (fig.) *soulever.*

plow, *v.n.,* labourer.

plow'able (a-b'l), *adj.,* labourable, arable.

plow'-boy (-boï), *n.,* valet de charrue ; garçon de charrue ; jeune laboureur, *m.*

plow'er (plaou'eur), *n.,* laboureur, cultivateur, *m.*

plow'ing (plaou-igne), *n.,* labourage, labour, *m.*

plow'-land (-la'n'de), *n.,* terre de labour, terre labourable, *f.*

plow'man, n., valet de charrue ; laboureur ; paysan, m.

plow'share, n., soc de charrue, m.

plow'-tail (-téle), n., manche de charrue, m.

plover (pleuv'-), n., (orni.) pluvier, m.

pluck (pleuke), v.a., tirer ; (flowers, fruit) cueillir ; (poultry) plumer ; (at examinations) refuser, (pop.) bouler, couler. To — away, off ; arracher, enlever. To — up ; arracher, déraciner ; (courage) reprendre courage. To be —ed ; (at final examinations of a military college, etc.) être fruit sec, être retoqué. To — down ; faire crouler.

pluck, n., action de tirer ; (of animals) fressure, f. ; (courage) cœur, courage, m.

pluck'ily, adv., courageusement, bravement.

pluck'y, adj., courageux, brave.

plug (pleughe), n., tampon ; bouchon, m.; cheville, f. ; (of a water-cock) piston, m.; (of a waterpipe) crapaudine, f., robinet ; (of a pipe) culot, m. — hole ; bouche d'eau, f.

plug, v.a., tamponner, boucher. To — with a peg ; cheviller.

plum (pleume), n., prune, f. ; (raisin) raisin sec ; ($500,000) cent mille livres sterling. — cake ; baba, m. —-pudding ; plum-pudding ; pouding au raisin de Corinthe, m. —-tree ; prunier, m. Dried — ; pruneau, m. —-stone ; noyau de prune, m. — tart ; tourte aux prunes, f. Sugar —s ; dragées, f.pl.

plu'mage (pliou-mèdje), n., plumage ; (of birds of prey) pennage, m.

plumb (pleume), **plumb'-line** (-laïne), ou **plumb'-rule** (-roule), n., plomb, fil à plomb, m.

plumb (pleume), adv., à plomb, perpendiculairement.

plumb (pleume), v.a., mettre à plomb.

plumbag'incus (-badj'-), adj., de plombagine.

plumba'go (-bé-gô), n., (min.) plombagine, f.

plum'bean ou **plum'beous** (-bi-), adj., de plomb.

plumb'er (pleum'eur), n., plombier, m.

plumb'ery (pleum'eur'i), n., plomberie, m.

plumbif'erous (pleu'm'bif'eur'-), adj., plombifère.

plumb'ing (pleu'm'igne), n., plombage, f.; (the art of sounding) sondage, m.

plumb'-level, n., niveau à plomb, m.

plumb'-line (-laïne), n., fil à plomb, m. ; (nav.) ligne de sonde, f.

plume (ploume), n., plume, f. ; panache, plumet ; (pride) orgueil, m. ; (ant.) (token of honor) palme, marque d'honneur, f. — plucked ; humilié ; l'oreille basse.

plume (ploume), v.a., plumer ; orner d'un plumet, d'un panache, d'une plume ; (of birds) nettoyer. To — itself ; (of birds) nettoyer ses plumes. To — one's self on; se piquer de, se glorifier de, faire parade de. To — (deck) oneself with ; se paver de.

plume'less (plou'm'-), adj., sans plumes ; sans plumet, sans panache, sans plume.

plume'let (plou'm'-), n., (bot.) plumule, f.

plum'met (pleum'-), n., (for sounding) sonde, f.; plomb ; (tech.) plomb, fil à plomb ; (weight) contrepoids, m.

plum'ming (pleum'-), n., (mines) sondage, m.

plu'mose (plou-môce) ou **plu'mous** (plou-), adj., de plumes ; plumeux ; cotonneux.

plump (pleu'm'pe), adj., dodu, potelé, gros et gras ; replet ; (blunt) (downright) (ant.) net. A — lie ; un mensonge pur et simple, ou tout cru, m.

plump, adv., tout d'un coup ; tout à coup ; droit, lourdement ; comme une pierre.

plump, v.a. To — down ; (money) jeter son argent sur la table ; payer rondement.

plump, v.n., tomber comme une masse ; tomber lourdement ; (at elections) voter en masse **pour.**

plump'er, n., (lie) bourde, mensonge, f. ; (vote) double vote, vote entier, m.

plump'ish, adj., (l.u.) grasset, grassouillet.

plump'ly, adv., nettement ; rondement ; carrément.

plump'ness, n., état potelé ; embonpoint, m.; rondeur ; (bluntness) brusquerie, f.

plu'my (pliou-), adj., couvert de plumes ; orné d'un plumet, d'un panache, d'une plume.

plun'der (pleu'n'-), n., pillage ; sac ; saccagement ; butin, m. ; (personal luggage in America) (fam.) effets, m.pl., bagage, m., nippes, f.pl.

plun'der, v.a., piller, saccager, voler ; faire main basse sur.

plun'derer, n., pillard, pilleur, maraudeur, m.

plunge (pleu'n'dje), n., action de plonger, f. ; (ant.) plongeon ; (difficulty) embarras, m., difficulté, f. To take the — ; se décider, ne plus hésiter ; faire le plongeon.

plunge, v.a., plonger, précipiter.

plunge, v.n., se plonger, se précipiter, se jeter. To — into debt ; s'endetter jusqu'aux yeux.

plun'geon (pleu'n'djeune), n., (orni.) plongeon, m.

plun'ger (pleu'n'dj'-), n., plongeur ; (hydr.) piston plongeur, plongeur ; (betting) parieur à outrance, pante, m.

plu'perfect (plou-peur-fek'te), adj., (gram.) plus-que-parfait.

plu'ral (plou-), adj., (ant.) de plus d'un ; (gram.) pluriel. n., pluriel, m.

plu'ralism, n., cumul, m.

plu'ralist (plou-), n., ecclésiastique qui jouit de plus d'un bénéfice ; (b.s.) cumulard, m.

plural'ity (plou-), n., pluralité, f.; (of emoluments, etc.) cumul, m. ; pluralité de bénéfices, f.

plu'rally (plou-), adv., dans un sens de pluralité ; (gram.) au pluriel.

plus (pleuss), adv., (math.) plus.

plush (pleushe), n., peluche ; futaine ; panne. — breeches ; culotte de panne, f.

plush'y, adj., peluché.

plutoc'racy, n., plutocratie, f.

plutocrat'ic, adj., plutocratique.

pluto'nian, adj., plutonien, -ne.

plu'vial (plou-), adj., pluvieux ; pluvial.

pluviam'eter (plou-vi-am'i-), n., (phys.) udomètre, pluviomètre, m.

ply (plaïe), v.a., s'appliquer à, s'attacher à ; manier ; (to practice) exercer, employer, appliquer ; (to urge) presser, solliciter. To — any one with questions ; presser, talonner, bourrer, quelqu'un de questions. To — any one with drink; presser quelqu'un de boire. To — an oar ; manier la rame ; (the oar) ramer avec force.

ply (plaïe), v.n., plier, céder ; (to work steadily) travailler ferme ; (to go in haste) se rendre à la hâte ; (to busy oneself) s'occuper ; (nav.) aller à la bouline, bouliner, louvoyer ; (of vehicles) faire le service. To — ; (of carriages, etc. between two points) faire le service, le parcours de ; desservir la ligne de. To — for hire ; faire la maraude, marauder. To — for ; tâcher d'obtenir, chercher, solliciter. He was forced to — in the streets as a porter for his livelihood ; il fut forcé de faire le métier de commissionnaire pour gagner sa vie. To — for hire ; marauder.

ply'er (plaïeur), n., personne qui travaille, chose qui travaille, f. pl., (fort.) bascule, f.sing.

ply'ing, n., importunité, sollicitation, f. ; (of carriages, steamers) service, m.

P. M., de l'après-midi, du soir ; (in time-tables) soir, m.

pneumat'ic ou **pneumat'ical** (niou-mat'-), adj., (phys.) pneumatique.

pneumat'ics, n.pl., (phys.) pneumatique, f. sing.

pneumo'nia (niou-mô-), n., (med.) pneumonie, f.

pneumon'ic, *n.,* (med.) pneumonique, *m.f.*

poach (pôtshe), *v.a.,* (to begin) commencer, entamer ; (upon) (to steal) voler, piller ; (to spear) harponner ; (eggs) pocher.

poach, *v.n.,* (game) braconner ; (of the earth) être boueux, marécageux. To — on any one's preserves ; *aller sur les brisées de quelqu'un.*

poach'ard (pôtsh'-), *n.,* (orni.) millouin, *m.*

poach'er (pôtsh'-), *n.,* braconnier, *m.*

poach'iness (pôtsh'-), *n.,* humidité, *f.*

poach'ing (pôtsh'-), *n.,* braconnage, *m.*

poach'y (pôtsh'-), *adj.,* humide, mou, boueux.

pock, *n.,* grain de petite vérole, *m.* — mark ; *marque de petite vérole, f.* — marked ; *marqué de la petite vérole, grêlé.*

pock'et, *n.,* poche, *f.;* (fob) gousset, *m.;* (of a billiard-table) blouse, *f.* To spare any one's — ; *ménager la bourse de quelqu'un.* To be out of — by ; *perdre* à. To be in — by ; *gagner* à. To have in one's — ; *avoir en poche ; tenir, ou avoir, ... dans sa manche.* To pick —s ; *voler à la tire, filouter.* To pay out of one's — ; *payer de sa poche.*

pock'et, *v.a.,* empocher, mettre en poche ; soustraire, dérober ; (affront) avaler, digérer ; (billiards) blouser. To — an insult ; *avaler un affront.*

pock'et-book (-bouke), *n.,* portefeuille, carnet, *m.*

pock'et-flap, *n.,* patte de poche, *f.*

pock'etful, *n.,* poche pleine, *f.*

pock'et-glass (-glâce), *n.,* miroir de poche, *m.*

pocket'-hand'kerchief, *n.,* mouchoir de poche, *m.*

pock'et-hole (-hôle), *n.,* ouverture de la poche, *f.*

pock'et-knife, *n.,* couteau de poche, *m.*

pock'et-money (-meu'n'nè), *n.,* argent pour les menus plaisirs, *m.;* menus plaisirs, *m.pl.;* (of children) semaine, *f.*

pock'et-pick'ing, *n.,* vol à la tire, *m.*

pock'et-volume, volume portatif, *m.*

pod, *n.,* cosse ; gousse, *f.*

pod, *v.n.,* produire des cosses, des gousses.

pod'agra, *n.,* podagre, *f.*

podag'rical, *adj.,* podagre, goutteux ; (of things) de la goutte.

pod'ded, *adj.,* muni de cosse, de gousse ; à cosse, à gousse. *rondeau*

po'em (pô-ème), *n.,* poëme, *m. ;* vers, *m.pl.*

po'esy (pô-è-ci), *n.,* poésie, *f.*

po'et (pô-ète), *n.,* poëte, *m.* Minor — ; *poète de second ordre ; poétereau.*

poetas'ter (pô-èt'-), *n.,* (l.u.) poëtereau, rimailleur, rimeur de balle, *m.*

po'etess (pô-èt'-), *n.,* poète, femme poète, *f.*

poet'ic ou **poet'ical,** *adj.,* poétique.

poet'ically, *adv.,* poétiquement.

poet'ics, *n.pl.,* poétique, *f.sing.*

po'etize (pô-èt'aïze), *v.n.,* poétiser (l.u.).

po'etry (pô-è-), *n.,* poésie, *f.*

poig'nancy (pôï-na'n'-), *n.,* piquant ; (wit) sel, *m.;* pointe ; (grief) nature poignante, violence, *f.*

poig'nant (pôï'na'n'te), *adj.,* piquant, mordant ; poignant, cuisant.

poig'nantly, *adv.,* d'une manière piquante, cuisante, poignante.

point (pôï'n'te), *n.,* point, *m. ;* (sharp end) pointe ; (aiglet) aiguillette ; (character) trait saillant, *m. ;* (of an epigram) pointe ; (engr.) pointe, pointe sèche, *f. ;* (astron., geom., gram., mus.) point, *m. ;* (geog.) pointe, *f. ;* (at cards) point, *m. ;* (print.) pointure ; (railways) aiguille, *f.,* rail mobile ; (of the compass) quart de vent, *m.,* aire de vent, *f. ;* (of a sail) garcette de ris ; (of a cable) queue de rat, *f. ;* (in falconry) point, *m. ;* (quality) qualité, *f. ;* (aim, purpose) but, *m.,* fins, *f.pl.* — of distance, sight ; *point de vue.* — of sight ; (of firearms) *point de mire.* To — ; *exactement,*

minutieusement. Brussels — ; *point de Bruxelles.* Self-acting — ; (Eng. railways) *aiguille à contre-poids.* Chief, *ou* main, — ; *essentiel, point capital, m.* In — of fact ; *par le fait, au fait.* That is not the — ; *ce n'est pas là la question.* At the — of ; *au point* de. At the — of death ; *à l'article de la mort.* On the — of ; *sur le point* de. In — ; (case) *en question, ad hoc.* In — of ; *sous le rapport* de ; *en fait* de ; *en matière* de. In all —s ; *en tout point ; de tous points.* To go to the — ; *aller au fait.* To come to the — ; *venir au fait, arriver au fait ; aborder la question.* To make a — of ; *se faire un devoir* de, *une loi* de, *une règle* de ; *s'arranger* pour ; *prendre à tâche* de. To gain one's — ; *arriver, venir, à ses fins ; atteindre son but.* —-blank ; *de but en blanc ; directement ; à brûle-pourpoint ; à bout portant ; droit au but, sans tortiller, nettement, carrément.* To maintain, *ou* press, one's — ; *maintenir son dire.* To stretch a — ; *forcer ses moyens.* There are some good —s in his disposition ; *il y a d'excellents traits dans son caractère.* Armed at all —s ; *armé de toutes pièces.* Armed at — ; *armé de pied en cap.* To come to —s ; *se battre à l'épée ; mettre flamberge au vent ; tirer son épée.*

point, *v.a.,* (to sharpen) aiguiser, affiler ; (to make pointed) tailler ; signaler, constater, faire une pointe à ; (to direct) indiquer ; montrer ; faire remarquer ; diriger ; (fire-arms) pointer, braquer, mettre en joue ; (to punctuate) ponctuer ; (to mark with vowel points) marquer de points-voyelles ; (a sail) garnir de garcettes de ris ; (cable) garnir de queues de rat ; (mas.) jointoyer. To — out ; *montrer au doigt ; signaler ; faire remarquer ; désigner, indiquer, appeler l'attention* de ... à. To — the finger at any one ; *montrer quelqu'un au doigt.* To be, to get, —ed at ; *se faire montrer au doigt.*

point, *v.n.,* pointer ; (mas.) jointoyer ; (of dogs) arrêter ; tomber, être en arrêt ; (nav.) prendre un ris. To — at ; *montrer du doigt ;* (b.s.) (in contempt) *montrer au doigt.* To — to ; *indiquer, montrer, signaler, constater ;* (of things) *indiquer ; se tourner* vers.

point'ed, *adj.,* (sharp) à pointe, pointu, acéré ; (epigrammatic) épigrammatique, mordant, piquant ; (personal) personnel, direct, évident. — style ; (arch.) *style gothique, m. ; architecture ogivale, f.*

point'edly, *adv.,* d'une manière piquante ; positivement, expressément ; directement.

point'edness, *n.,* forme pointue ; aspérité ; pointe ; épigramme ; tournure épigrammatique, *f. ;* esprit, *m.*

point'er, *n.,* index, *m. ;* aiguille, *f. ;* (dog) chien d'arrêt, *m. ;* (railways) aiguille, *f.*

point'ing, *n.,* (artil.) pointage ; pointement ; (mas.) jointoiement, *m. ;* (gram.) ponctuation, *f.*

point'less, *adj.,* sans pointe ; fade ; plat.

points'man, *n.,* (railways) aiguilleur, *m.*

poise, *n.,* poids, *m. ;* pondération, gravité, importance, *f. ;* équilibre, *m.*

poise, *v.a.,* peser ; balancer ; équilibrer, tenir en équilibre, pondérer.

poised, *adj.,* pesé ; en équilibre.

poi'son, *n.,* poison, *m.* —ed wound ; *plaie envenimée, f.*

poi'son, *v.a.,* empoisonner.

poi'soner, *n.,* empoisonneur, *m.,* empoisonneuse, *f.*

poi'soning, *n.,* empoisonnement, *m.*

poi'son-nut (-neute), *n.,* noix vomique, *f.*

poi'sonous, *adj.,* toxique ; (plants) vénéneux ; (anim.) venimeux ; (poisoned) empoisonné, (fig.) venimeux ; funeste.

poi'sonously, *adv.,* avec venin.

poi'sonousness, *n.,* nature vénéneuse, *f. ;* poison, *m. ;* (of plants) vénénosité ; (of animals) venimosité, *f.*

poi'son-tree (-trî), *n.,* (bot.) upas de Java, *m.*

poke (pôke), *n.*, sachet, *m.* ; poche, *f.* ; coup de coude, de poing, *m.* ; (haycock) meule de foin, *f.* To buy a pig in a —; *acheter chat en poche.*

poke, *v.a.* and *n.*, fourrer ; (to push) pousser ; donner un coup de coude, de poing; (the fire) attiser, remuer, fourgonner ; (of cattle) donner des cornes **contre** ; (ant. ; to fumble) fouiller ; (to feel) tâtonner. To — about; *pousser, talonner.* To — after, for; *chercher; chercher à tâtons.* To — fun at ; *se rire* **de**, *se moquer* **de**. To — one's nose into ; (things) *fourrer son*, ou *le, nez* **dans** ; *se mêler indiscrètement* **de**. To — about ; *fureter, rôder.* —ing about where we had no business ; *fourrant le*, ou *notre, nez où nous n'avions que faire.*

pok'er, *n.*, tisonnier ; fourgon, *m.*

poke'-weed (-wîde), *n.*, (bot.) herbe à la laque, *f.* ; raisin d'Amérique, *m.*

pok'ing *or* **poky,** *adj.*, (colloquial) servile ; obscur; sale ; petit, mesquin. —hole; *taudis, m.*

pok'ing, *n.*, action de pousser, *f.* ; (of the fire) remuage, *m.*

polac'ca *ou* **pola'cre,** *n.*, (nav.) polacre, polaque, *f.*

po'lar (pô-), *aaj.*, polaire.

polar'ity, *n.*, (phys.) polarité, *f.*

polariza'tion (pô-lar-aïzé-), *n.*, (phys.) polarisation, *f.*

po'larize (pô-lar'aïze), *v.a.*, (phys.) polariser.

pole (pôle), *n.*, perche, *f.* ; (staff) bâton ; (of a carriage) timon ; (of a dancer) balancier, *m.* ; (of a stable) barre ; (of a mast) flèche ; (measure) perche (mètres 5·02911), *f.* ; (astron. geog.) pôle ; (for hops, vines) échalas, *m.* Under bare —s ; (nav.) *à voiles ferlées, à mâts et à cordes.* Greasy —; *mât de cocagne, m.* May— ; *mai, m.* — pin ; *cheville de timon, f.* — ring ; *porte-barres, m.* — socket ; *têtard, m.*

pole (pôle), *v.a.*, mettre des perches à ; (to bear) porter sur une perche ; (to impel) faire avancer au moyen d'une perche.

Pole (pôle), *n.*, Polonais, *m.*, Polonaise, *f.*

pole'-ax (pôl'akse), *n.*, hache d'armes, *f.* ; (of butchers) merlin, *m.*

pole'cat (pôl'cate), *n.*, (mam.) putois, *m.*

polem'ic *ou* **polem'ical** (-lè'm'-), *adj.*, polémique.

polem'ic (-lè'm'-), *n.*, écrivain polémique, *m.*

polem'ics (po-lè'm'-), *n.pl.*, polémique, *f.sing.*

pole'-star, *n.*, étoile polaire, *f.*

polian'thes (po-li-a'n'thize), *n.*, (bot.) tubéreuse, *f.*

police' (-lîce), *n.*, police, *f.* —court; *tribunal de simple police, m.* —officer; *sergent de ville* ; *agent de police, m.* —man; V. *policeman.* —spy ; *espion de police; mouchard, m.* —station; *poste de polic ; commissariat de police, poste.* — regulations ; *règlements de police, m.pl.* —sergeant ; *brigadier de police, de gendarmes.* —sheet ; *feuille de consignation, f.* — ! *à la garde* ! Cycling —; *agents-cyclistes, m.pl.* Diving —; *agents-scaphandriers, m.pl.* Military, *ou* county, —; *gendarmerie, f.* Skating —; *agents-patineurs, m.pl.* Swimming —; *agents-plongeurs, m.pl.*

policed' (po-liste), *adj.*, (ant.) policé.

police'man, *n.*, agent de police, sergent de ville, gardien de la paix, *m.*

pol'icy, *n.*, politique, *f.* ; système, plan; utilité, prudence, *m.* ; vues, *f.pl.* ; (com.) police, *f.* — of insurance ; *police d'assurance.* Fire—; *police d'assurance sur la vie.* Fire—; *police d'assurance contre l'incendie.* — holder ; *assuré, m.*

Po'lish (pô-), *adj.*, polonais. *n.*, le polonais, *m.*

pol'ish (pol'-), *n.*, poli, luisant, *m.* ; (fig.) élégance, politesse, *f.*, vernis, *m.* French —; *vernis.*

pol'ish (pol'-), *v.a.*, polir ; (furnit.) vernir ; (shoes) cirer ; (fig.) policer ; civiliser. To — up; *polir, dérouiller* ; (pers.) *façonner, dégourdir.*

To — off (to get rid of) *se débarrasser* **de** ; (to kill) *tuer, donner le coup de grâce* **à** ; (to eat) *avaler, faire une bouchée* **de**.

pol'ish, *v.n.*, se polir ; se façonner.

pol'ishable (pol'ish-a-b'l), *adj.*, polissable.

pol'ished (po-lish'te), *adj.*, poli ; (pers.) de manières élégantes ; distingué, de bon ton ; policé.

pol'isher, *n.*, polisseur ; (thing) polissoir, *m.* French —; *vernisseur en meubles, m.*

pol'ishing, *n.*, poli ; polissage, *m.* ; (French) vernissage de meubles ; (of boots) cirage, (fig.) policement, *m.*

polite' (-laïte), *adj.*, poli, élégant, courtois. — literature ; *belles-lettres, f.pl.*

polite'ly, *adv.*, poliment.

polite'ness (-laït'-), *n.*, politesse, *f.*

pol'itic (pol'i-tike), *adj.*, politique ; fin, avisé, prudent.

polit'ical, *adj.*, politique.

polit'ically, *adv.*, politiquement.

politi'cian (pol'i-tish'-), *n.*, politique, politicien, homme politique, *m.*

pol'itics, *n.pl.*, politique, *f.*

pol'ity, *n.*, constitution politique, *f.* ; gouvernement, régime politique, *m.* ; forme de gouvernement, *f.*

poll (pôl), *n.*, (head) tête ; (register of persons) liste de personnes ; (register of electors) liste électorale, liste d'électeurs, inscription des votes, *f.* ; collège électoral, *m.* ; élection, *f.* ; (place) lieu de l'élection ; (parrot) jacquot, *m.* To go to the —; *aller aux votes, briguer les suffrages.* To ask for, *ou* demand, a —; *demander le scrutin.* The — is open ; *le scrutin est ouvert.*

poll, *v.a.* and *n.*, (to clip) tondre ; (trees) étêter ; (electors) inscrire ; se faire inscrire; (to vote) donner son vote, voter; obtenir (des voix).

pol'lack, *n.*, (whiting) merlan jaune, *m.*

pol'lard, *n.*, (hort.) têtard ; (meal) **recoupe**, repasse, *f.*

pol'lard, *v.a.*, (hort.) étêter.

polled (pôl'd), *adj.*, sans cornes ; étêté.

pol'len (pol'lène), *n.*, (fine bran) recoupe, *f.* ; (bot.) pollen, *m.*

poll'er (pôll'-), *n.*, (voter) votant, *m.* ; (hort.) qui étête les arbres, *f.*

poll'ing, *n.*, vote, *m.*, élection, *f.* ; (hort.) étêtement, *m.*

poll'-tax, *n.*, capitation, *f.*

pollute' (pol-lioute), *v.a.*, polluer, souiller (with) **de** ; profaner ; flétrir, corrompre, pervertir ; rendre impur.

pollut'edness (-liout'èd'-), *n.* V. **pollution**.

pollut'er (-liou-), *n.*, corrupteur, *m.*, corruptrice, *f.* ; profanateur, *m.*, profanatrice, *f.*

pollu'tion (-liou-), *n.*, pollution ; profanation ; souillure, impureté, *f.*

polonaise' (-néze), *n.*, (garment) polonaise, *f.*

polonese' (-na), (language) le polonais, *m.*

poltroon' (-troune), *n.*, poltron, *m.*, poltronne, *f.*

poltroon'ery, *n.*, poltronnerie, *f.*

polyan'dria, *n.*, (bot.) polyandrie, *f.*

polyg'amist, *n.*, polygame, *m.f.*

polyg'amous, *adj.*, polygame.

polyg'amy, *n.*, polygamie, *f.*

pol'yglot, *adj.*, polyglotte.

pol'yglot, *n.*, polyglotte, *f.*

pol'ygon, *n.*, polygone, *m.*

polyg'onal, *adj.*, (geom.) polygone, polygonal.

polyhe'dral (-hî-), *adj.*, (geom.) (à plusieurs faces, à plusieurs côtés) polyédrique.

polyhe'dron (-hî-), *n.*, (geom.) polyèdre, *m.*

pol'ynome (-nôme), *n.*, (alg.) polynôme, *m.*

polypet'alous (-pèt'a-), *adj.*, (bot.) polypétale.

polyp'ier (-pié), *n.*, (zoöl.) polypier, *m.*

pol'ypus, *n.*, (zoöl. med.) polype, *m.*

polysyllab'ic, *adj.*, polysyllabique, polysyllabe.

polysyl'lable, *n.*, polysyllabe, *m.*
polytech'nic (-tèk'-), *adj.*, polytechnique.
pol'ytheism (-thi-iz'me), *n.*, polythéisme, *m.*
pol'ytheist (-thi-), *n.*, polythéiste, *m.*
polytheist'ic, *adj.*, polythéiste.
pom'ace (peu'm'èce), *n.*, marc de pommes ; petit cidre, *f.*
pomade', *n.*, pommade, *f.*
poma'tum (-mé-), *n.*, pommade, *f.* — jar ; *pot à pommade*, m.
poma'tum, *v.a.*, pommader.
pome'granate (peu'm'gra'n'ète), *n.*, grenade, *f.;* (tree) grenadier, *m.*
pom'mel (peu'm'mèl), *n.*, (of beds, canes) pomme ; pommette, *f.;* (of a saddle, a sword) pommeau, *m.*
pom'mel, *v.a.*, rosser, frotter.
pomp, *n.*, pompe, *f.;* éclat, faste, *m.*
pompos'ity (-poss'-), *n.*, pompe ; ostentation ; (of language) emphase, *f.;* pathos, *m.*
pom'pous, *adj.*, pompeux, fastueux, emphatique ; prétentieux.
pom'pously, *adv.*, pompeusement ; fastueusement.
pom'pousness, *n.* *V.* **pomposity**.
pond, *n.*, étang, vivier, *m.;* (pool) mare, *f.;* (for cattle) abreuvoir, *m.*
pon'der, *v.a.*, peser, considérer, méditer ; réfléchir à.
pon'der, *v.n.*, méditer, réfléchir, faire réflexion.
ponderabil'ity (-deur'-), *n.*, pondérabilité, *f.*
pon'derable (-deur'a-b'l), *adj.*, pondérable.
pondera'tion (-deur'é-), *n.*, (ant.) pondération, *f.*
pon'derer, *n.*, personne qui pèse, qui considère, qui médite, *f.*
pon'deringly, *adv.*, avec méditation ; avec réflexion.
pon'derous, *adj.*, lourd, pesant ; important ; fort.
pon'derously, *adv.*, pesamment.
pon'derousness, *n.*, (ant.) poids, *m.; pesanteur*, gravité, *f.*
pond'-weed (-wîde), *n.*, (bot.) potamot, épi d'eau, *m.*
pon'go (po'gn'gô), *n.*, (mam.) pongo, *m.*
pon'iard, *n.*, poignard, *m.*
pon'iard, *v.a.*, poignarder.
pont'age (-tèdje), *n.*, pontonage, *f.*
pon'tiff, *n.*, pontife, *m.*
pontif'ical, *adj.*, pontifical.
pontif'ical, *n.*, (c. rel. ordinal) pontifical, *m.*
pontif'icals, *n.pl.*, habits pontificaux, *m.pl.*
pontif'ically, *adv.*, pontificalement, en pontife.
pontif'icate, *n.*, pontificat, *m.*
pon'tine, *adj.*, pontin.
pontoon' (-toune), *n.*, ponton, *m.* —-bridge; *pontons*, *m.pl.* —-train ; *équipage de pont*, m.
po'ny (pô-), *n.*, poney, petit cheval, *m.* — chaise ; *chaise à poney*, *f.*
poo'dle (pou-d'l), *n.*, caniche, chien caniche, *m.*
pooh, *int.*, bah ! allons donc !
pool (poul), *n.*, étang, *m. ;* mare ; (at cards, billiards) poule, *f.*
poop (poupe), *n.*, dunette, poupe, *f.;* arrière, *m.*
poor (pour), *adj.*, pauvre ; indigent ; misérable; (unhappy) malheureux ; (trifling, paltry) méchant, triste ; (bad) mauvais. The — *(pl.); les indigents*, *m.pl.* — man's herb ; (bot.) *herbe-au-pauvre-homme ; gratiole, f.* — health ; *petite santé, f.* A — man ; *un homme pauvre.* — little fellow ; *pauvre petit.* The — fellow ; *le malheureux.* To have a — opinion of ; *avoir une triste opinion de.* The patient has passed a — night ; *le malade a passé une mauvaise nuit.* A — excuse; *une mauvaise excuse.* —fare ; *mauvaise chère, f.* As — as a church mouse ; *gueux comme un rat d'église.*

poor'-box, *n.*, tronc des pauvres, *m.*
poor'-house, *n.*, asile des indigents ; dépôt de mendicité, *m.*
poor'-law (-lō), *n.*, loi sur les pauvres ; assistance publique, *f.*
poor'-law-board, *n.*, conseil de l'assistance publique, *m.*
poor'ly, *adj.*, indisposé, souffrant.
poor'ly, *adv.*, pauvrement ; mal, tristement.
poor'ness, *n.*, pauvreté ; indigence ; (mediocrity) médiocrité ; (meanness) bassesse ; (barrenness) stérilité ; (bad quality) mauvaise qualité, *f.*
poor'-rate, *n.*, taxe des pauvres, *f.*
poor-spir'ited, *adj.*, lâche ; sans cœur, pusillanime, *m.*
poor-spir'itedness, *n.*, lâcheté, pusillanimité, *f.;* manque de cœur, *m.*
pop, *n.*, son vif, aigu, sec, *m.* — gun ; *canonnière, f.* — shop ; *mont de piété ; clou, m.*
pop, *v.n.*, entrer, sortir, subitement, précipitamment. Off he —s ; *le voilà parti.* To — in ; *entrer subitement, précipitamment.* To — off ; *s'en aller subitement, précipitamment ; partir allégrement ; partir, sauter.* To — out ; *sortir subitement, précipitamment ; s'esquiver.* To — up ; *se lever subitement, précipitamment.* To — at ; *tirer* **sur**.
pop, *v.a.*, pousser subitement, précipitamment ; mettre vivement. To — corn; *griller du maïs.* To — off ; *renvoyer subitement, lancer.* To — up ; *faire monter subitement.* To — the question ; *faire une demande (en mariage) ; lâcher le grand mot tout à coup.*
pop, *adv.*, soudain, tout à coup ; crac ! — goes his pate; *voilà sa tête (ou caboche) qui part.*
pope (pôpe), *n.*, pape ; (of the Greek church) papas, pope, *m.* —'s eye ; (meat) *noix, f.* —'s head ; *balai à long manche, m.*
pope'dom (pôp'deume), *n.*, papauté, *f.*
pope'-joan (pôp'djône), *n.*, (game) nain jaune, *m.*
pop'ery (pôp'-), *n.*, (b.s.) papisme, *m.*
pop'injay (-djé), *n.*, perroquet, papegai ; (fop) freluquet, fat, damoiseau, *m.*
pop'ish, *adj.*, papiste ; (of things) de papiste.
pop'ishly, *adv.*, en papiste.
pop'lar, *n.*, (bot.) peuplier, *m.*
pop'lin, *n.*, popeline, *f.*
pop'py, *n.*, (bot.) pavot, *m. ;* œillette, *f.* —oil ; *huile d'œillette, f.* — color ; *ponceau, m.*
pop'py-head (-hède), *n.*, tête de pavot, *f.*
pop'ulace (pop'iou-), *n.*, populace, *f.*
pop'ular, *adj.*, aimé, populaire, en **vogue** ; couru.
popular'ity, *n.*, popularité, *f.*
pop'ularize (-aïze), *v.a.*, populariser, vulgariser.
pop'ularly, *adv.*, populairement.
pop'ulate, *v.a.*, peupler.
pop'ulate, *v.n.*, se peupler.
popula'tion (pop'iou-lé-), *n.*, population, *f.*
pop'ulous, *adj.*, populeux.
pop'ulously, *adv.*, d'une manière populeuse.
pop'ulousness, *n.*, populosité, *f.*
por'celain (-ci-léne), *n.*, porcelaine, *f.* — painter ; *peintre sur porcelaine, f.*
porch (pôrtshe), *n.*, porche, portique ; (phil.\ Portique, m., doctrine du Portique, *f.*
por'cine (-çaïne), *adj.*, de porc, du porc.
por'cupine (-kiou-païne), *n.*, porc-épic, *m.*
pore, *v.n.*, regarder avec grande attention. To — on, over ; *fixer les yeux* **sur**; *avoir les yeux fixés* **sur**, *collés* **sur**; *pâlir* **sur**; (a book) *dévorer.*
pork (pôrke), *n.*, porc, *m.*
pork'-butcher (-bout'sheur), *n.*, charcutier, *m.* —'s shop ; *charcuterie, f.*
pork'-chop (-tshope), *n.*, côtelette de porc, *f.*
pork'er, *n.*, (mam.) porc ; cochon, *m.*

pork'et *ou* **pork'ling** (pôrk'-), *n.*, (mam.) jeune porc, jeune cochon, *m.*

pork'-pie, *n.*, pâté de porc, *m.*

poros'ity (pô-ross'-) *ou* **por'ousness** (pô-), *n.*, porosité, *f.*

por'ous (pô-), *adj.*, poreux.

porphyrit'ic, *adj.*, porphyrique, porphyritique.

por'phyry, *n.*, porphyre, *m.*

por'poise (por-peusse), *n.*, marsouin, pourceau de mer, *m.*

por'ridge, *n.*, potage, *m.; pâtée, bouillie, soupe, f. —-pot; pot, m.; marmite, f.* Oatmeal —; *bouillie d'avoine, f.*

por'ringer (-djeur), *n.*, écuelle, *f.*

port (porte), *n.*, (harbor) port; (carriage) port, maintien, air, *m.,* tenue, *f.;* (of a steam engine) lumière, *f.;* (nav.) sabord; (side) bâbord; (wine) Porto, vin d'Oporto, *m.* To put into —; (nav.) *relâcher.*

port, *v.a.,* porter. To — the helm; (nav.) *mettre la barre à bâbord.* —! bord bas! Hard *a* —! *bord bas tout !*

port'able (-'a-b'l), *adj.*, portatif, portable.

port'ableness, *n.*, nature, forme portative, *f.*

port'-admiral, *n.*, amiral, *ou* commandant, de port, *m.*

port'age (pôrt'èdje), *n.*, portage, port, *m.*

port'al (pôr-), *n.*, portail, *m.* — vein; (physiol.) *veine porte, f.*

portamen'to, portamen'to-voice, *n.*, (mus.) port de voix, *m.*

port'-charges (-tshârdjize), *n.pl.*, frais de port, *m.pl.*

portcul'lis (pôrt'keul-lice), *n.*, (fort.) herse, *f.*

portcul'lis, *v.a.*, défendre par une herse; fermer, barrer, obstruer. —ed; *à herse.*

port'-dues, *n.pl.* V. **port-charges.**

Porte (pôrte), *n.*, Porte, *f.* Sublime —; *Sublime Porte.*

porte-monnaie', *n.*, porte-monnaie, *m.*

portend', *v.a.,* présager; augurer; annoncer.

por'tent, *n.*, présage sinistre, mauvais augure, *m.*

porten'tous, *adj.*, de mauvais augure; de sinistre présage; monstrueux, prodigieux, effroyable; sinistre.

porten'tously, *adv.*, sinistrement, effroyablement, prodigieusement.

port'er (pôr-), *n.*, porteur, commissionnaire; crocheteur, portefaix; (door-keeper) portier, concierge, *m.;* (market-porter) fort de la halle; porteur; (railways) facteur; (warehouse) garçon de magasin; (com.) garçon de bureau, *m.* —'s knot; *crochet de portefaix, m.* The —'s knot; (thea. piece) *les crochets du Père Martin, m.pl.*

port'er, *n.*, (liquor) porter, *m.*

port'erage (-'èdje), *n.*, port; portage; factage; crochetage, *m.*

portfo'lio (pôrt'fô-liô), *n.*, portefeuille, *m.*

port'hole (-hôl), *n.*, sabord, *m.*

por'tico (-cô), *n.*, portique, *m.*

por'tion (pôr-), *n.*, portion, partie, part; (dowry) dot, *f.*

por'tion, *v.a.,* partager, distribuer; (to dower) doter. — out; *répartir, distribuer.*

por'tioner, *n.*, répartiteur, *m.*

por'tionless, *adj.*, sans dot.

port'last (pôrt'lâste) *ou* **port'oise** (pôr-toïze), *n.*, (nav.) plat-bord, *m.*

port'-lid, *n.*, (nav.) mantelet de sabord, *m.*

port'liness (pôrt-), *n.*, port majestueux, noble maintien, *m.; prestance, corpulence, f.*

port'ly (pôrt-), *adj.*, de noble port; d'un port majestueux; (corpulent) corpulent.

portman'teau (pôrt'ma'n'tô), *n.*, valise, *f.;* portemanteau, *m.*

por'trait (pôr-tréte), *n.*, portrait, *m.;* (fig.) tableau, *m.* Full-length —; *portrait en pied.* Half-length —; *portrait en buste.* To have one's

— taken; *se faire peindre; faire faire son portrait.*

por'trait-paint'er (-pé'n't'eur), *n.*, peintre de portraits, portraitiste, *m.*

por'traiture (-tioure), *n.*, portrait, tableau, *m.; peinture, description, f.*

portray' (pôr-), *v.a.*, peindre; dépeindre; représenter, décrire.

portray'er (pôr-tré-eur), *n.*, peintre, *m.*

port'ress (pôr-), *n.*, portière, concierge, *f.*

Portuguese' (pôr-tiou-ghize), *adj.*, portugais.

Portuguese', *n.*, Portugais, *m.*, Portugaise, *f.; (language) portugais, m.*

pose (pôze), *v.a.,* embarrasser, confondre; mettre au pied du mur; fermer la bouche à; poser des questions difficiles à; (at dominoes) poser; (to attitudinize) poser. *n.,* pose, *f.*

pos'er (pôz'-), *n.*, personne qui embarrasse; (at Eton and Winchester) examinateur, *m.;* qui confond; (thing) question embarrassante, qui ferme la bouche, qui met à quia, *f.;* (painting) poseur, *m.,* -se, *f.*

posi'tion (-zish'-), *n.*, situation, position; (state) position, condition, *f.,* état; (principle laid down) principe avancé, principe posé, principe, *m.;* assertion, *f.;* (advancement of a principle) position; (gram., milit.) position; (nav.) point, emplacement, *m.;* (arith.) fausse position, règle de fausse position, *f.* In a — to; *en position de; en état de; à même de.* In a false —; *dans une fausse position.*

pos'itive (poz'-), *adj.*, positif; absolu; précis, exact; (confident) sûr, certain; (decisive) décisif, tranchant; (determined) résolu; (obstinate) entier, entêté, obstiné. — philosophy; *positivisme, m.; philosophie positive, f.*

pos'itive, *n.*, (reality) positif; (gram., photo.) positif, *m.*

pos'itively, *adv.*, positivement; absolument; précisément, exactement; décisivement, d'une manière tranchante.

pos'itiveness, *n.*, (ant.) réalité; nature positive; nature absolue, *f.; caractère positif; caractère absolu, m.; précision, exactitude, f.; ton décisif, ton tranchant, m.; opiniâtreté, f.; entêtement, m.*

pos'se (pos'sè), *n.*, force publique d'un comté; (crowd) cohue, foule, *f.*

possess' (poz'zèss), *v.a.*, posséder; jouir de; être possesseur de; être en possession de; (to occupy) occuper; (to obtain possession of) rendre maître de; s'emparer de, se rendre maître de. To — one's self of; *se rendre maître de; s'emparer de, se saisir de, prendre possession de.* To — one's self; *être maître de soi.* To be —ed of; *être possesseur de; être en possession de; être muni de;* (jur.) *être saisi, ou nanti, de; être doué de.* —ed with the devil; *possédé du démon.*

posses'sion (poz'zèsh'-), *n.*, possession; (thing possessed) possession, *f.,* bien, *m.;* (jur.) possession, *f.,* (of real property) possessoire, *m.* — is nine-tenths of the law; *possession vaut titre.* To put in —; *mettre en possession; préposer à la garde de.* To enter in —; *entrer en possession de.* To take — of; *prendre possession de; entrer en jouissance de;* (to seize) *s'emparer de;* (jur.) *se saisir de.*

posses'sive (poz'zès'-), *n.*, possessif, *m.*

posses'sive, *adj.*, qui possède; (gram.) possessif. — case; *le génitif, m.*

posses'sor (poz'zès'-), *n.*, possesseur; (of a bill) porteur, *m.*

posses'sory, *adj.*, qui possède; (jur.) possessoire.

pos'set, *n.*, lait caillé au vin, *m.; piquette, f.*

pos'set, *v.a.*, faire cailler.

possibil'ity, *n.*, possibilité, *f.* (means) moyen, *m.* Possibilities are infinite; *le possible est immense.*

pos'sible (-si-b'l), *adj.*, possible.

pos'sibly, *adv.*, possiblement, peut-être ; en quelque manière ; le moins du monde, absolument. When I — can, I will return ; *je reviendrai quand je le pourrai.* How can I — help it ? *comment puis-je l'éviter, dites-moi ?*

post (pôste), *n.*, poteau ; (of a door) montant ; (milit.) poste ; (nav.) étambot ; (employment) poste, *m.*, place ; (post-office) poste, *f.* ; (paper) écu, *m.*, coquille, *f.* By the —; *par la poste, par le courrier.* By return of —; *par le retour du courrier.* To travel —; *voyager en poste.* Deaf as a —; *sourd comme un pot.* To ride —; *courir la poste.* —-captain ; (nav.) *capitaine de vaisseau*, *m.* — paper ; *papier à lettres*, *m.* The — is gone ; *la levée est faite.* When is the next — out ; *à quand le prochain départ ?*

post, *v.a.*, coller sur un poteau, etc. ; afficher ; (letters) jeter à la poste, mettre à la poste, (milit.) poster ; (in book-keeping) porter au grand livre. To — up ; (bills) *poser, afficher ;* (bookkeep.) *porter au grand livre ;* (to inform) *renseigner ; tenir au courant.* To be —ed up in ; *être ferré* **sur.**

post, *v.n.*, voyager en poste ; aller, *ou* se rendre, en poste ; courir la poste ; marcher rapidement ; voler. To — off ; *s'en aller en poste ; s'en aller à la hâte.*

post'age (pôst-èdje), *n.*, port de lettre, port, *m.* Extra —; *supplément de port*, *m.* ; (admin.) surtaxe, *f.* To pay the — of ; *payer le port de ; affranchir.*

post'age-stamp (-sta'm'p),*n.*, timbre-poste,*m.*

post'al, *adj.*, postal. — order ; *bon de poste*, *m.* — union ; *union postale, convention postale,f.*

post'boy (-boï), *n.*, postillon, *m.*

post'-card, *n.*, carte postale, *f.*

post'chaise (-tshéze) *ou* **post'-coach** (-côtsh), *n.*, chaise de poste, *f.*

post'date, *v.a.*, postdater.

post'day, *n.*, jour de courrier, *m.*

postdilu'vial *ou* **postdilu'vian** (pôst'di-liou-), *adj.*, (geol., archæol.) postdiluvien.

post'er (pôst'-), *n.*, (bill) affiche, pancarte, *f.*, placard, *m.* Bill —; *colleur d'affiches, afficheur,* *m.* — bearer ; *homme-affiche, porte-affiches,* *m.*

poste'rior (-ti-rieur), *adj.*, postérieur.

posterior'ity, *n.*, postériorité, *f.*

poste'riors (-ti-ri-eurze), *n.pl.*, parties postérieures, *f.pl.* ; postérieur, derrière, *m.*

poster'ity (-tér'-), *n.*, postérité, *f.* The remotest —; *la postérité la plus reculée.*

post'ern (pôs-), *n.*, porte de derrière ; porte dérobée ; (fort.) poterne, *f.*

post'ern, *adj.*, de derrière ; dérobé.

post'-existence(pôst'-),*n.*,(ant.) vie future,*f.*

post'-haste (-héste), *adj.*, fait avec toute la diligence possible.

post'-haste, *adv.*, train de poste, en grande diligence *ou* hâte.

post'-horse, *n.*, cheval de poste, *m.*

post'-house (-haouce), *n.*, poste aux chevaux, *f.* ; bureau de poste, *m.*

post'humous (post'hiou-), *adj.*, posthume.

post'humously, *adv.*, après la mort, après décès.

postil'ion (-lieune), postillon, *m.*

post'ing (pôst'-), *n.*, voyage en poste ; louage de chevaux de poste ; (of bills) collage, affichage, *m.* — house ; *poste aux chevaux, f.* — (up) ; (com.) *inscription au grand livre, f.*

pos'tique, *adj.*, postiche ; fait et ajouté après coup.

post'man (pôst'-), *n.*, (*postmen*) facteur de la poste, facteur, *m.*

post'mark (-märke), *n.*, timbre de la poste, *m.*

post'master (-mâst'-), *n.*, (in France) receveur des postes, *m.* —-general ; (in France) *directeur général des postes ; ministre des postes et des télégraphes, m.*

post-merid'ian (-mi-), *adj.*, post-méridien, de l'après-midi.

post'mortem, *n.*, après déces,*f.* — examination ; *autopsie, f.*

post'-natal, *adj.*, postérieur à la naissance.

post'-obit (-ôbite), *n.*, (jur.) contrat exécutoire après décès, *m.*

post'-office, *n.*, bureau de poste, *m.* ; poste ; poste aux lettres ; boîte aux lettres ; administration des postes, *f.* To be left at the — till called for ; *poste restante.* — order ; *mandat-poste, mandat sur la poste,* *m.* General — ; (in France) *direction générale des postes,f.; ministère des postes et des télégraphes, m.* — directory ; *almanach des adresses ;* (in France) *almanach Bottin, m.*

post'-paid (-péde), *adj.*, affranchi, franc de port ; port payé. *adv.*, franco.

postpone' (pôst'pône),*v.a.*, ajourner ; différer ; remettre ; (to esteem less) estimer moins ; subordonner **à** ; faire passer, placer **après.**

postpone'ment, *n.*, ajournement, *m.* ; remise, *f.*

post'road, *n.*, route de poste, route postale, *f.*

post'script, *n.*, postscriptum, *m.* ; apostille, *f.*

post'-stage (-stédje), *n.*, relais de poste, *m.*

post'-time, *n.*, heure de la poste, *f.*

post'-town (-taoune), *n.*, ville à bureau de poste ; (for horses) ville où il y a une poste aux chevaux, *f.*

pos'tulant (-tiou-), *n.*, postulant, *m.*, postulante, *f.*

pos'tulate (post'iou-), *v.a.*, postuler, solliciter ; (assume) s'arroger ; supposer ; (geom.) admettre comme évident.

pos'tulate, *n.*, (geom.) postulat, *m.*

postula'tion (post'iou-lé-), *n.*, supposition ; (ant.) cause ; demande ; supplication, *f.*

pos'tulatory (post'iou-lé-), *adj.*, supposé, sans preuves.

postula'tum (-tiou-lé-), *n.*, (geom.) postulatum, *m.*

pos'ture (post'ieur), *n.*, posture, position, pose, *f.* ; état, *m.* ; (paint.) attitude, pose, *f.*

pos'y (pô-zi), *n.*, devise, inscription, *f.* ; (of flowers) petit bouquet, *m.*

pot, *n.*, pot, *m.* ; marmite, *f.* ; (for preserved game, etc.) terrine, *f.* ; (smelting) creuset ; (measure) litre, *m.* To go to — ; (pop.) *s'en aller au diable, faire fiasco.* To keep the — boiling ; *faire bouillir la marmite ; faire aller le pot-au-feu.* —-hanger *ou* -hook ; *crémaillère, f.* The — calls the kettle black ; (prov.) *la pelle se moque du fourgon.* A little — is soon hot ; *petite cervelle, prompte colère.*

pot, *v.a.*, (hort.) empoter, mettre en pot ; (cook.) mettre en terrine.

pot'able (pô-ta-b'l), *adj.*, potable.

pot'ash *ou* **potas'sa**, *n.*, (chem.) potasse, *f.*

potas'sium, *n.*, (chem.) potassium, *m.*

pota'tion (po-té-), *n.*, débauche, *f.* ; libations, *f.pl.* ; (beverage) boisson, *f.* ; breuvage, *m.*

pota'to (-té-tô), *n.*, (*potatoes*) pomme de terre, *f.* Sweet — ; *patate, f.* Kidney — ; *vitelotte, f.*

pot'bellied (-bèl'li'de), *adj.*, pansu, ventru.

pot'belly, *n.*, grosse panse, bedaine, *f.* ; gros ventre, *m.*

pot'-boy (-boï), *n.*, garçon de cabaret, *m.*

pot-compan'ion (-pa'n'ieune), *n.*, camarade de bouteille ; compagnon de débauche, *m.*

pot'-cover, *n.*, cache-pot, *m.*

po'tency (pô-), *n.*, puissance, autorité ; force, vigueur, *f.* ; pouvoir, *m.* —of a medicine ; *puissance, ou efficacité, d'un remède, f.*

po'tent (pô-), *adj.*, puissant, fort ; (fig.) efficace, puissant.

po'tentate (pô-), *adj.*, potentat, *m.*

poten'tial (pô-tè'n'shal), *adj.*, virtuel, efficace ; (math., gram., med.) potentiel.

poten'tial, *n.*, chose possible, *f.* ; (elec. mag.) potentiel ; (gram.) potentiel, conditionnel, *m.*

potential'ity, *n.*, virtualité, *f.*

poten'tially, *adv.*, virtuellement.

po'tently, *adv.*, puissamment, efficacement.

pot'ful, *n.*, potée, *f.* ; pot plein, *m.*

poth'er (poth'-), *n.*, confusion, *f.* ; tumulte ; tourment ; bruit ; vacarme ; tintamarre ; ennui, *m.*

poth'er, *v.a.*, tourmenter, ennuyer, tracasser.

poth'er, *v.n.*, se trémousser, s'agiter.

pot'herb (-eurbe), *n.*, herbe potagère, *f.*

pot'hook (-houke), *n.*, (pot.) crémaillère, *f.* ; (in writing) jambage ; (scrawl) griffonnage, *m.*

pot'house (-haouce), *n.*, cabaret, bouchon ; (b.s.) cabaret borgne, *m.*

po'tion (pô-), *n.*, potion, *f.* ; breuvage, *m.*

pot'-lid, *n.*, couvercle, *m.*

pot'luck (-leuke), *n.*, fortune du pot, *f.* To take —; *partager,* ou *accepter, la fortune du pot.*

pot'man, *n.*, garçon de cabaret, *m.*

pot'-metal, *n.*, potin, *m.*

pot'sherd, *n.*, tesson, *f.*

pot'stone (-stône), *n.*, (min.) pierre ollaire, *f.*

pot'tage (pot'tèdje), *n.*, potage, *f.*

pot'ted, *adj.*, en pot, en terrine : —meat ; *conserve de viande, f.*

pot'ter, *n.*, potier, *m.* —'s clay ; *argile plastique, f.* —'s wheel ; *tour du potier, m.*

pot'ter, *v.n.* To — about ; *s'amuser* **à,** *ou des riens ;* (walking) *flâner.*

pot'tery, *n.*, poterie, *f.*

pot'ting, *n.*, (hort.) mise en pot, *f.*, empotage, *m.*

pot'tle (pot't'l), *n.*, quatre pintes, *f.pl.* ; (for fruit) petit panier, pot, *m.*

pot'-valiant, *adj.*, brave le verre en main, *ou* après boire.

pouch (paoutshe), *n.*, poche, *f.* ; sachet, sac, *m. ;* (belly) grosse panse : bedaine ; (of animals) bourse ; (of monkeys) abajoue ; (of sportsmen) gibecière, carnassière ; (tobacco) blague, *f.* —belt ; *(Mil.)* porte-giberne, *m.*

pouch, *v.a.*, (of birds) avaler.

pouched (paoutshte), *adj.*, (zoöl.) à bourse, marsupial ; (orni.) à poche.

poult, *n.*, jeune volaille, *f.* ; jeune oiseau, *m.*

poul'terer (pôl-teur'-), *n.*, marchand de volaille, *m.*

poul'tice, *n.*, cataplasme, *m.* Mustard — ; *sinapisme, m.*

poul'tice (pôl-tice), *v.a.*, appliquer un cataplasme à.

poul'ticing, *n.*, application de cataplasmes, *f.*

poul'try (pôl-tri) *n.*, volaille, *f.* ; oiseaux de basse-cour, *m.pl.* —house ; *poulailler, m.* —yard ; *basse-cour, f.*

pounce (paou'n'ce), *n.*, (for paper) sandaraque ; poudre de sandaraque ; (for drawing) ponce ; (of birds) griffe, serre, *f.* —box ; *poudrier, m.*

pounce, *v.n.*, fondre **sur.**

pounce, *v.a.*, poudrer (de sandaraque) ; (for drawing) poncer ; (to perforate) perforer ; (of birds) saisir avec les serres.

pound (paou'n'de), *n.*, (weight) livre ; (coin) livre sterling (fr. 25) ; livre ; (inclosure) fourrière, *f.* ; (apothecaries' weight) livre (grammes 373.233) ; (avoirdupois weight) livre (grammes 450.544). By the —; *à la livre.* So much in the —; *tant pour cent.*

pound, *v.a.*, piler, broyer, concasser ; battre ; frapper ; (animal) mettre en fourrière ; (metal.) bocarder.

pound'age (-'èdje), *n.*, commission, *f.* ; pondage, *m.*

pound'er, *n.*, pilon, *m.* A twenty-four- — ; (artil.) *une pièce de vingt-quatre, f.* ; (ball) *boulet de vingt-quatre,* **m.**

pound'ing, *n.*, broiement, broyage ; pilage ; (metal.) bocardage, *m.*

pound'-keeper (-kîp'-), *n.*, gardien de fourrière, *m.*

pour (pore), *v.a.*, verser ; répandre. To — forth ; *verser ; répandre, lancer ;* (a broadside) *lâcher.* To — in ; *verser* **dans** ; *lancer.* To — out ; *verser ; répandre ; décharger ;* (fig.) *épancher.*

pour, *v.n.*, couler ; se précipiter ; (to rush) fondre **sur** ; (of the rain) pleuvoir à verse. To — in ; (fig.) *entrer, arriver en foule ; entrer de tous côtés.* To — down ; *tomber à verse, descendre en foule.*

pour'ing, *adj.*, (rain) torrentiel.

pout (paoute), *n.*, bouderie, moue ; (ich.) lotte, *f. ;* tacaud ; (orni.) francolin, *m.*

pout, *v.n.*, bouder ; faire la mine, faire la moue ; (to jut) déborder, saillir. To — at ; *bouder.* To — one's lip ; *faire la moue.*

pout'er, *n.*, tondeur, *m.*, tondeuse, *f.* ; (orni.) pigeon grosse gorge, boulant.

pout'ing, *adj.*, qui fait la miue, qui fait la moue ; (jutting) saillant.

pout'ing, *n.*, bouderie, moue, mine, *f.*

pov'erty, *n.*, pauvreté, misère, indigence, *f.* To come to— ; *tomber dans la misère.* —stricken ; *réduit à la misère.* — is no crime ; (prov.) *pauvreté n'est pas vice.*

pow'der (paoudeur), *n.*, poudre, *f.* Tooth— ; *poudre dentifrice, f.* Gun— ; *poudre à canon, f.* To waste — and shot ; *tirer sa poudre aux moineaux.* Worth — and shot ; *valant la peine.* It is not worth — and shot ; *le jeu ne vaut pas la chandelle.* To fall to — ; *se réduire en poudre, tomber en poussière.*

pow'der, *v.a.*, réduire en poudre ; piler ; pulvériser ; (the hair) poudrer ; (to sprinkle with salt) saupoudrer de sel, saupoudrer.

pow'der-box, *n.*, (for hair-powder) boîte à poudre, *f.*

pow'der-cart (-cârte), *n.*, caisson, *m.*

pow'der-chest (-tshèste), *n.*, caisson à poudre, *m.*

pow'dered, *adj.*, pulvérisé, réduit en poudre ; (of the hair) poudré ; (sprinkled) saupoudré. — sugar ; *sucre en poudre, sucre pilé, m.*

pow'der-flask *ou* **pow'der-horn**, *n.*, poire à poudre, *f.*

pow'dering, *n.*, pulvérisation ; action de poudrer les cheveux ; salaison, *f.*

pow'dering-tub (-teube), *n.*, saloir, *m.*

pow'der-magazine (-zîne), *n.*, poudrière, (nav.) soute aux poudres, *f.*

pow'der-mill, *n.*, poudrière, *f.*

pow'der-mon'key, *n.*, gargoussier, *m.*

pow'der-puff (-peufe), *n.*, houppe à poudrer, *f.*

pow'der-room (-roume), *n.*, (nav.) soute aux poudres, *f.*

pow'dery, *adj.*, poudreux ; friable.

pow'er (paou'eur), *n.*, pouvoir, empire, *m. ;* force, autorité, puissance, *f. ;* (ability) talent, *m.*, moyens, *m.pl.*, forces, *f.pl. ;* (faculty) faculté ; (military force) armée, puissance militaire, *f.*, forces, *f.pl. ;* (mec.) effet, travail, *m.*, puissance ; force ; (math.) puissance, *f.* To the utmost of one's — ; *de tout son pouvoir ; autant que possible ; autant que faire se peut.* To have it in one's —; *être en pouvoir* **de** ; *avoir en son pouvoir* **de** ; *être à même* **de.** It is not in my — to ; *je n'ai pas le pouvoir* **de** ; *je ne suis pas à même* **de.** A machine of eight-horse — ; *une machine de la force de huit chevaux.* To be in — ; *être au pouvoir.* The Great —s ; (of Europe) *les grandes puissances, f.pl.* The —s that be ; *les autorités constituées.* Full —s ; *pleins pouvoirs, m.pl.* — of attorney ; *procuration, f.* —press ; (print.) *presse mécanique, f.* Balance of — ; *équilibre européen, m.*

pow'erful (-foule), *adj.*, puissant ; fort ; efficace ; actif.

pow'erfully, *adv.*, puissamment, fortement, efficacement.

pow'erfulness, *n.*, puissance, force, énergie ; efficacité, *f.*

pow'erless, *adj.*, impuissant, faible ; inefficace.

pow'erlessness, *n.*, impuissance ; faiblesse, *f.*

pow'er-loom (-loume), *n.*, métier à tisser, métier mécanique, *m.*

pox, *n.*, vérole, *f.* Chicken---; *petite vérole volante*, *f.* Small---; *petite vérole*, *f.* Cow---; *vaccine*, *f.*

poy (poï), *n.*, (for rope-dancers) balancier, *m.*

practicabil'ity *ou* **prac'ticableness**, *n.*, nature praticable ; possibilité, praticabilité, *f.*

prac'ticable (-ca-b'l), *adj.*, praticable, faisable.

prac'tical, *adj.*, pratique. --- joke ; *mauvais tour*, *m.; mauvaise plaisanterie, mauvaise farce*, *f.*

prac'tically, *adv.*, pratiquement ; en pratique, dans la pratique ; à tous égards ; réellement, en effet. To look at things ---; *considérer les choses au point de vue pratique.* To be --- acquainted with ; *avoir une connaissance pratique* **de**.

prac'ticalness, *n.*, nature, qualité pratique, *f.*

prac'tice, *n.*, pratique, (custom) habitude, coutume, *f.*, usage ; (exercise) exercice, *m.; (of doctors, barristers) clientèle, *f.; (artifice) artifice, stratagème, *m.; menée, intrigue, *f.; (arith.) méthode des parties aliquotes ; (jur.) pratique, *f.* Rifle ---; *exercice du tir*, *m.* To get out of ---; *se perdre la main; se rouiller.* To make it one's --- to; *se faire une habitude, une règle* **de.** --- makes perfect ; (prov.) *on ne peut faire qu'en faisant; ou à force de forger, on devient forgeron; ou usage rend maître.*

prac'tice (-tice), *v.a.*, pratiquer, mettre en pratique ; (to commit) commettre, exercer ; (profession) exercer, pratiquer ; (mus.) étudier. To --- what one preaches ; *prêcher d'exemple.*

prac'tice, *v.n.*, pratiquer ; exercer ; (to try artifices) employer des pratiques, employer des menées ; (mus.) étudier ; s'exercer à. To --- upon; *en imposer* **à**, *tromper; abuser* **de**, *spéculer* **sur.**

prac'ticed, *adj.*, exercé **à**, expérimenté ; versé **dans** ; habile, émérite.

prac'ticer, *n.*, personne qui pratique, qui met en pratique, *f.; praticien*, *m.*

prac'ticing, *adj.*, praticien; en exercice, exerçant.

practi'tioner (-tish'eu'n'eur), *n.*, praticien ; médecin exerçant, médecin praticien, *m.* General ---; *médecin-chirurgien.*

prætex'ta (prī-), *n.*, (antiq.) prétexte, *f.*

præ'tor (prī-teur), *n.*, (Rom. Hist.) préteur, *m.*

prætor'ial, *adj.*, de préteur ; des préteurs.

præto'rian, *adj.*, prétorien.

prætor'ium (prī-), *n.*, (antiq.) prétoire, *m.*

præ'torship, *n.*, préture, *f.*

pragmat'ic, *adj.*, pragmatique. --- sanction ; *pragmatique sanction; pragmatique*, *f.*

pragmat'ic *ou* **pragmat'ical**, *adj.*, officieux, impertinent ; importun.

pragmat'ically, *adv.*, pragmatiquement ; avec importunité.

pragmat'icalness, *n.*, importunité, *f.*

prag'matist, *n.*, importun, *m.*

prair'ie, *n.*, prairie ; (in America) savane, *f.* --- dog ; *écureuil fouisseur, écureuil d'Amérique*, *m.*

praise (préze), *n.*, louange, *f.; éloge*, *m.* In --- of ; *à la louange* **de.** To bestow --- on ; *donner des louanges* **à**, *des éloges* **à.** To speak in --- of ; *faire l'éloge* **de.**

praise, *v.a.*, louer, vanter, faire l'éloge **de** ; (biblically) louer ; célébrer les louanges **de**, glorifier ; louanger.

praise'less, *adj.*, sans louange ; sans éloge.

prais'er, *n.*, distributeur d'éloges ; approbateur ; louangeur, panégyriste, *m.*

praise'worthily (préz'weur-*thi*-), *adv.*, d'une manière louable, louablement.

praise'worthiness (-weur-*thi*-), *n.*, mérite, *m.*

praise'worthy (préz'weur-*thi*), *adj.*, louable ; digne d'éloges.

pram *ou* **prame**, *n.*, (nav.) prame, *f.*

prance, *v.n.*, se cabrer ; bondir ; piaffer ; (pers.) se carrer, se pavaner.

pran'cer, *n.*, cheval qui se cabre, piaffeur, *m.*

pran'cing, *n.*, action de se cabrer, *f.*, piaffement, *m.*

prank, *n.*, escapade ; folie ; fredaine ; farce ; niche, *f.; tour*, *m.* To play ---s on ; *faire une farce* **à**, *une niche* **à**, *un tour* **à.** To play one's ---s ; *faire des siennes.*

prank'ish, *adj.*, (ant.) badin ; espiègle ; malin.

prate, *v.n.*, jaser, babiller, bavarder (about, **de**).

prate, *v.a.*, débiter ; dire sottement.

prate, *n.*, babil, caquet, caquetage, bavardage, *m.*

prat'er (prét'-), *n.*, jaseur, *m.*, jaseuse, *f.; caqueteur, *m.*, caqueteuse, *f.; bavard, *m.*, bavarde, *f.; babillard, *m.*, babillarde, *f.*

prat'ingly (prét'-), *adv.*, en bavard, en babillard.

pra'tique (prat'ike), *n.*, (nav.) pratique, *f.; (in reference to vessels subjected to quarantine).

prat'tle (prat't'l), *n.* *V.* **prate.**

prat'tle, *v.n.*, babiller, jaser, caqueter, bavarder ; (of brooks) murmurer.

prat'tler, *n.*, bavard, *m.*, bavarde, *f.; babillard, *m.*, babillarde, *f.; caqueteur, *m.*, caqueteuse, *f.; jaseur, *m.*, jaseuse, *f.*

prat'tling, *n.*, bavardage, caquet, *m.; (of streams) murmure, babil, *m.*

prawn (pro'n), *n.*, grosse crevette, salicoque, *f.*

prax'is, *n.*, exercice ; exemple, *m.*

pray (pré), *v.a.*, prier **de**, supplier ; (jur.) demander, requérir. I --- you ; *je vous prie, je vous en prie.* ---! *de grâce; dites moi!* --- be seated ; *veuillez vous asseoir.*

pray, *v.n.*, prier. To --- for ; *prier* **pour** ; *demander.* To --- to God ; *prier Dieu.*

prayer (prère), *n.*, prière ; supplication ; (jur.) demande, *f.* ---book ; *livre de prières*, *m.; (Anglican) liturgie*, *f.* The Lord's ---; *l'oraison dominicale, f.* To say one's ---s ; *faire la prière.*

prayer'ful (-foule), *adj.*, porté à la prière.

prayer'fully, *adv.*, à force de prières.

pray'ing, *n.*, prière, *f.*

pray'ingly, *adv.*, en priant, par la prière.

preach (prītshe), *v.n.*, prêcher.

preach, *v.a.*, prêcher. To --- up ; *prêcher ; vanter, prôner.* To --- down ; *dénigrer, prêcher contre.* To --- up ; *prôner.* ---ing friars ; *dominicains*, *m.pl.*

preach'er, *n.*, prédicateur ; (b.s.) prêcheur, *m.*

preach'ing, *n.*, prédication, *f.; sermons*, *m.pl.*

pre-acquaint'ance (prī-ac-kwé'n't'-), *n.*, connaissance préalable, *f.*

pre-acquaint'ed (prī-ac-kwé'n'tède), *adj.*, familier d'avance **avec.**

pre-adam'ic *ou* **pre-adamit'ic** (-'it'ike), *adj.*, préadamite.

pre-ad'amite (prī-ad'a'm'aïte), *n.*, préadamite, *m.f.*

pre-administra'tion (prī-ad-mi'n'is-tré-), *n.*, administration antérieure, *f.*

pre-admon'ish (prī-), *v.a.*, avertir au préalable ; prévenir préalablement, *ou* d'avance.

pre-admoni'tion (prī-), *n.*, avertissement préalable, avertissement antérieur, *m.*

pre'amble (prī-a'm'b'l), *n.*, préambule, avant-propos ; (of an act of parliament) exposé des motifs, *m.*

pre-appoint' (pri-ap-poï'n'te), *v.a.*, nommer, *ou* arrêter, *ou* fixer, auparavant, *ou* d'avance.

pre-au'dience (prī-o-), *n.*, (jur.) préséance d'avocats aux audiences, *f.*

preb'end (prèb'-), *n.*, prébende, *f.*

prebend'al, *adj.*, de prébende.

preb'endary, *n.*, chanoine **prébendé** ; prébendier, *m.*

preca'rious (pri-ké-), *adj.*, précaire, peu solide ; (of the weather) incertain.

preca'riously, *adv.*, précairement.

preca'riousness, *n.*, nature précaire, *f.* ; état précaire, *m.* ; incertitude, *f.*

pre'cative (prī-) *ou* **pre'catory** (-teuri), *adj.*, suppliant, de supplication ; (gram.) précatif.

precau'tion (pri-cō-), *n.*, précaution, *f.* By way of — ; *par précaution, par prudence.*

precau'tion, *v.a.*, (ant.) précautionner **contre**, avertir **de**, prémunir **contre**.

precau'tional *ou* **precau'tionary**, *adj.*, de précaution.

precede' (pri-cîde), *v.a.*, précéder ; faire précéder ; avoir le pas, la préséance **sur**.

preced'ence, *n.*, priorité ; (superiority) supériorité ; (in rank) préséance, *f.*, pas, *m.* To have — of ; *avoir le pas* **sur**, *la préséance* **sur**.

preced'ent, *adj.*, précédent, antécédent.

preced'ent, *n.*, précédent, *m.* ; (jur.) décision de la cour, *f.*

preced'ing, *adj.*, précédent.

precen'tor (pri-cè'n'teur), *n.*, (in cathedrals, collegiate churches) chantre ; (in chapels) maître de chapelle ; (presbyter.) chantre, *m.*

precen'torship, *n.*, maîtrise, *f.*

pre'cept (prī-cèpte), *n.*, précepte, *m.*

precep'tor, *n.*, précepteur, instituteur, (Knight Templar) commandeur, *m.*

precepto'rial (prī-cèp-tō-), *adj.*, de précepteur, d'instituteur.

pre'ceptory (pri-cèp-teuri), *adj.*, de préceptes.

pre'ceptory, *n.*, (hist.) commanderie de l'ordre du Temple ; maison religieuse d'éducation, *f.*

precep'tress, *n.*, institutrice, *f.*

preces'sion (pri-cèsh'-), *n.*, (astron.) précession, *f.*

pre'cinct (prī-), *n.*, limite, borne, enceinte, *f.*

pre'cious (prèsh'eusse), *adj.*, précieux ; de prix ; (b.s.) fameux, fier, fichu. — near it ; *il ne s'en faut, il ne s'en fallait guère.* They are a — pair ; *le couvercle est digne du chaudron.*

pre'ciously, *adv.*, précieusement ; (b.s.) fameusement, fièrement, furieusement, diablement.

pre'ciousness, *n.*, prix, *m.* ; valeur, *f.*

pre'cipe (prī-ci-pi), *n.*, (jur.) sommation, *f.*

prec'ipice (prèss'i-), *n.*, précipice, *m.*

precip'itable (pri-cip'i-ta'-b'l), *adj.*, (chem.) précipitable.

precip'itance *ou* **precip'itancy** (pri-), *n.*, précipitation, *f.* ; empressement excessif, *m.*

precip'itant, *adj.*, qui se précipite ; précipité.

precip'itant (pri-), *n.*, (chem.) précipitant, *m.*

precip'itantly, *adv.*, précipitamment.

precip'itate (pri-), *adj.*, précipité ; qui se précipite.

precip'itate, *n.*, (chem.) précipité, *m.*

precip'itate, *v.a.*, précipiter. To be —d ; (chem.) *se précipiter.*

precip'itate, *v.n.*, (chem.) précipiter ; se précipiter.

precip'itately, *adv.*, précipitamment.

precipita'tion (pri-cip-i-té-sheune), *n.*, précipitation, *f.*

precip'itous (pri-), *adj.*, escarpé ; de précipice ; (fig.) (hasty) précipité, rapide.

precip'itously, *adv.*, à pic, en précipice ; (fig.) précipitamment.

precip'itousness, *n.*, escarpement, *m.* ; nature escarpée ; précipitation, *f.*

precis' (pré-ci), *n.*, (abstract) précis, *m.*

precise' (pre-saïsse), *adj.*, précis, exact ; affecté, pointilleux, vétilleux, cérémonieux, scrupuleux ; formaliste.

precise'ly, *adv.*, précisément ; exactement ; au juste ; scrupuleusement. At 3 p.m. — ; *à trois heures de relevée* ; *à trois heures précises.*

precise'ness, *n.*, précision, exactitude, *f.* ; scrupule, *m.* ; formalité ; raideur, *f.*

preci'sion (pri-cij'eune), *n.*, précision, exactitude, *f.*

preclude' (pri-cloude), *v.a.*, exclure ; (prevent) empêcher ; écarter.

preclu'sion (pri-clou-jeune), *n.*, exclusion, *f.* ; empêchement, *m.*

preclu'sive (pri-clou-cive), *adj.*, qui exclut ; (preventive) qui empêche, qui écarte.

preclu'sively, *adv.*, avec exclusion.

preco'cious (pri-cō-sheusse), *adj.*, précoce.

preco'ciousness *ou* **precoc'ity**, *n.*, précocité, *f.*

precogni'tion (prī-cog-), *n.*, (ant.) connaissance antérieure, *f.* ; examen préliminaire, *m.* ; (Scotch Law) enquête préliminaire, *f.*

preconceive' (prī-co'n'cîve), *v.a.*, concevoir d'avance ; juger d'avance ; (philos.) préconcevoir.

preconceived' (-cîv'de), *adj.*, formé d'avance ; (philos.) préconçu.

preconcep'tion (prī-), *n.*, opinion préconçue ; prévention, *f.* ; préjugé, *m.*

preconcert' (prī-co'n'ceurte), *v.a.*, concerter d'avance.

preconsign' (prī-co'n'caïne), *v.a.*, consigner d'avance ; faire une consignation préalable.

precon'stitute (prī-co'n'sti-tioute), *v.a.*, constituer préalablement.

precontract', *v.a.* and *n.*, contracter préalablement.

precor'dial (prī-), *adj.*, (anat.) précordial.

precur'sor (pri-keur-seur), *n.*, précurseur, avant-coureur, *m.*

precur'sory, *adj.*, précurseur.

pred'atory (prèd'-), *adj.*, de pillard ; de pillage ; de rapine ; de vol ; pillard ; déprédateur.

predecease' (prī-de-cîce), *v.a. ou v.n.*, (jur.) prédécéder.

predeces'sor (prèd'e-cès'seur), *n.*, prédécesseur, devancier, *m.* —s ; *pl.*, ancêtres, pères, *m.pl.*

predesign' (prī-dè-zaïne), *v.a.*, projeter d'avance.

predestina'rian (pri-dès-ti-né-), *n.*, fataliste, *m.*

predes'tinate (pri-dès-), *adj.*, prédestiné.

predes'tinate *ou* **predes'tine** (pri-dès-), *v.a.*, prédestiner, vouer d'avance à.

predestina'tion (pri-dès-ti-né-), *n.*, (theol.) prédestination, *f.*

predes'tinator (pri-dès-ti-né-teur), *n.*, celui qui prédestine ; celui qui croit à la prédestination, *m.*

predetermina'tion (pri-di-teur-mi-né-), *n.*, (theol.) prédétermination, *f.*

predeter'mine (pri-de-teur-), *v.a.*, (theol.) arrêter d'avance ; prédéterminer.

pred'icable (prèd'i-ca-b'l), *adj.*, (log.) prédicable.

pred'icable, *n.*, (log.) universel, *m.* *pl.*, universaux, *m.pl.*

predic'ament (pri-dik'-) *n.*, catégorie, *f.* ; ordre ; (state) état, *m.*, passe, position, situation difficile, *f.* ; (log.) prédicament, *m.*, catégorie, *f.* You put me in a fine — ; *vous me mettez dans de beaux draps, ou dans une singulière position.*

pred'icate (prèd'-), *n.*, (log.) prédicat, attribut, prédicament, *m.*

pred'icate (prèd'-), *v.a. and n.*, (log.) affirmer.

predica'tion (prèd'-), *n.*, affirmation.

pred'icatory (prèd'-), *adj.*, affirmatif.

predict' (pri-), *v.a.*, prédire.

predic'tion (pri-), *n.*, prédiction, prévision, *f.*

predic'tive (pri-), *adj.*, (l.u.) qui prédit ; prophétique.

predic'tor (pri-dic-teur), *n.*, prophète, préviseur, *m.* This false — ; *ce faux prophète.*

predilec'tion (prī-di-lèk'sheune), *n.*, prédilection, *f.*

predispose' (prī-dis-pôze), *v.a.*, (med.) prédisposer. To be —d in favor of ; *être disposé, ou prédisposé, en faveur de.*

predisposi'tion, *n.*, (fig.) (med.) prédisposition ; disposition, tendance naturelle, *f.*

predom'inance *ou* **predom'inancy** (pri-), *n.*, prédominance, *f.* ; ascendant, pouvoir, *m.* ; prépondérance ; (med.) prédominance, *f.*

predom'inant (pri-), *adj.*, prédominant.

predom'inantly, *adv.*, d'une manière prédominante.

predom'inate, *v.n.*, prédominer, l'emporter, prévaloir ; régner.

predomina'tion (pri-do'm'i-né-), *n.*, influence supérieure, prédominance, *f.*

pre-elect' (prî-i-lèk'te), *v.a.*, préélire ; (theol.) élire d'avance.

pre-elec'tion (prî-i-lèk'-), *n.*, (theol.) élection antérieure ; élection faite d'avance, *f.*

pre-em'inence (prî-è'm'-), *n.*, prééminence, supériorité, *f.*

pre-em'inent (prî-è'm'-), *adj.*, prééminent, supérieur, extraordinaire, remarquable.

pre-em'inently (prî-), *adv.*, d'une manière prééminente ; supérieurement ; par excellence ; souverainement ; entre tous.

pre-empt', *v.a.*, préempter.

pre-emp'tion (prî-è'm'-), *n.*, (jur. customs) préemption, *f.*

preen (prî'n), *v.a.*, (of birds) nettoyer les plumes **de**.

pre-engage' (prî-è'n'ghédje), *v.a.*, engager d'avance.

pre-engage'ment (prî-è'n'ghédj'-), *n.*, engagement antérieur, *f.*

pre-estab'lish (prî-ès'-), *v.a.*, préétablir.

pre-estab'lishment, *n.*, établissement antérieur, *m.*

pre-examina'tion (prî-ègz'a'm'i-né-), *n.*, examen préalable, *m.*

pre-exam'ine (prî-ègz'a'm'-), *v.a.*, examiner préalablement.

pre-exist' (prî-ègz'-), *v.n.*, préexister.

pre-exist'ence (prî-ègz'ist'-), *n.*, préexistence, *f.*

pre-exist'ent, *adj.*, préexistant.

pref'ace (prèf-), *n.*, préface, *f.* ; avant-propos, *m.*

pref'ace, *v.a.*, faire une préface **à** ; faire précéder ; dire comme préface ; dire en forme de préface.

pref'atory (prèf'-) *ou* **prefato'rial** (-tô-), *adj.*, qui sert de préface ; préliminaire, introductif.

pre'fect (prî-fèkte), *n.*, préfet, *m.*

prefecto'rial, *adj.*, préfectoral.

pre'fecture (pri-fèk-tioure) *ou* **pre'fectship**, *n.*, préfecture, *f.*

prefer', *v.a.*, préférer ; aimer mieux ; (to advance) avancer, élever ; (to offer) présenter **à**, offrir ; (to make) présenter, former. To — a complaint, an accusation ; *former, ou formuler, une plainte, une accusation ; porter plainte ; déposer une plainte* contre. —red stock ; (com.) actions privilégiées, *f.pl.*

pref'erable (-'a-b'l), *adj.*, préférable **à**.

pref'erableness, *n.*, avantage, *m.*

pref'erably, *adv.*, préférablement, de préférence.

pref'erence (prèf'eur'-), *n.*, préférence, *f.*

prefer'ment (pri-feur'-), *n.*, avancement, *m.* ; élévation, promotion ; (superior place) place supérieure, *f.*

prefigura'tion (pri-figh'iou-ré-), *n.*, (theol.) figure, *f.* ; symbole, *m.*

prefig'urative (pri-figh'iou-ré-), *adj.*, (theol.) symbolique, typique.

prefig'ure (pri-figh'ieure), *v.a.*, (theol.) figurer d'avance.

prefix' (pri-), *v.a.*, mettre en tête, mettre devant ; (ant.) arrêter d'avance.

pre'fix (prî-), *n.*, (gram.) préfixe, *m.*

preg'nancy (prèg-), *n.*, grossesse ; (fig.) fécondité, *f.*

preg'nant (prèg-), *adj.*, enceinte, grosse ; (fig.) (with) gros **de**, plein **de**, fertile **en**, fécond **en**.

preg'nantly (prèg-), *adv.*, avec fertilité ; clairement, évidemment.

prehen'sile *ou* **prehen'sory** (pri-hè'n'-), *adj.*, préhensile. — tail ; *queue préhensile, prenante*, *f.*

prehistor'ic, *adj.*, préhistorique.

prejudge' (prî-djeudje), *v.a.*, condamner d'avance, préjuger.

prejudg'ment (prî-djeudj'-), *n.*, jugement par avance, *m.*

preju'dicative (-két'-), *adj.*, (ant.) qui préjuge.

prej'udice (prèd'jiou-dice), *v.a.*, (to bias) prévenir ; donner des préventions **à**, des préjugés **à** ; (to injure) préjudicier **à**, faire tort **à**, nuire **à**, porter préjudice **à**, porter dommage **à**. This did not — me much in his favor ; *cela ne me prévint pas beaucoup en sa faveur.*

prej'udice (prèd'jiou-dice), *n.*, (bias) prévention, *f.* ; préjugé ; (injury) préjudice, tort, dommage, *m.* To my — ; *à mon préjudice ; à mon détriment.* To do any one a — ; *faire tort, porter préjudice à quelqu'un.* Without — ; *sans préjudice* **de**, *sans faire tort* **à**, *sans renoncer* **à**, *sans préjudice de mes droits.*

prej'udiced (-diste), *adj.*, prévenu ; à préjugés ; à préventions ; qui a des préjugés.

prejudi'cial (prèd'jiou-dish'-), *adj.*, préjudiciable, nuisible.

prejudi'cially. V. detrimentally.

pre-knowl'edge (prî-nol'èdje), *n.*, connaissance antérieure ; (theol.) prescience, *f.*

prel'acy (prèl'-), *n.*, prélature, *f.* ; épiscopat, *m.*

prel'ate (prèl'-), *n.*, prélat, *m.*

prel'ateship (prèl'èt'shipe), *n.*, prélature, *f.*

prelat'ic *ou* **prelat'ical** (pri-lat'-), *adj.*, de prélat.

prelat'ically, *adv.*, en prélat.

prelec'tion (pri-lèk'-), *n.*, discours lu en public, ou devant une classe d'étudiants, *m.*

prelec'tor (pri-lèkt'eur), *n.*, professeur, lecteur, *m.*

prelim'inarily, *adv.*, préliminairement.

prelim'inary (pri-), *adj.*, préliminaire ; préalable.

prelim'inary, *n.*, préliminaire, *m.*

prel'ude (prèl'ioude), *n.*, prélude, *m.*

prel'ude, *v.a.* and *n.*, préluder, préluder **à**.

prelu'sive (pri-liou-cive) *ou* **prelu'sory** (-ço-) (ant.), *adj.*, préliminaire, préparatoire.

pre'mature (prî-ma-tioure), *adj.*, prématuré.

pre'maturely, *adv.*, prématurément, avant le temps.

pre'matureness *ou* **prematu'rity**, *n.*, prématurité, *f.*

premed'itate (pri-mèd'-), *v.a.* and *n.*, préméditer ; méditer d'avance.

premed'itated (-tét'ède), *adj.*, prémédité.

premed'itately (-tét'-), *adv.*, avec préméditation.

premedita'tion (-té-sheune), *n.*, préméditation, *f.*

pre'mier (prî-mi-eur), *adj.*, premier (de rang).

pre'mier (prî-mi-eur), *n.*, premier ministre ; (France) président du conseil (des ministres), *m.*

pre'miership, *n.*, dignité de premier ministre ; présidence du conseil (des ministres), *f.*

premise' (pri-maïze), *v.a.*, exposer d'avance ; commencer par dire ; (log.) poser les prémisses **de**.

premise', *v.n.*, poser des prémisses.

prem'ises (prè'm'iss'ize), *n.pl.*, lieux, *m.pl.* ; lieu, établissement, local, *m.sing.* ; propriété, terre, *f.* ; bien-fonds, *m.* ; (jur.) intitulé (d'un acte, d'un jugement), *m.sing.* ; (log.) prémisses, *f.pl.* Large — ; *vaste local*, *m.* On the —, *dans l'établissement ; sur les lieux.*

pre'miss, *n.*, (log.) prémisse, *f.*

pre'mium (prî-), *n.*, prix ; prix d'encouragement, *m.; récompense;* (com., fin.) prime, *f.;* (a bonus) pot-de-vin, *m.* High —; *forte prime, f.* At a —; *à prime.*

premon'ishment *ou* **premoni'tion** (prî-), *n.,* avis préliminaire, avertissement.

premon'itory (prî-mo'n'i-teuri), *adj.,* qui avertit d'avance; (med.) prémonitoire, précurseur.

premo'tion (prî-mô-), *n.,* (theol.) prémotion, *f.*

preno'men (prî-nô-mène), *n.,* prénom, *m.*

prenom'inate (prî-), *v.a.,* (ant.) nommer d'avance.

prenom'inate, *adj.,* (ant.) déjà nommé, susnommé; (jur.) prénommé.

prenomina'tion (-mi-né-), *n.,* (ant.) privilège d'être nommé le premier, *m.*

preno'tion (prî-nô-), *n.,* (philos.) prénotion, *f.*

preobtain' (prî-ob-téne), *v.a.,* (ant.) obtenir d'avance.

preoc'cupancy (prî-), *n.,* (jur.) préoccupation, occupation antérieure, *f.;* droit d'occupation, *m.*

preoccupa'tion (prî-oc-keu-pé-), *n.,* (anticipation) préoccupation, anticipation; (ant.) occupation antérieure; (of the mind) préoccupation, *f.*

preoc'cupy (prî-oc-keu-païe), *v.a.,* occuper avant un autre; occuper le premier; (fig.) préoccuper.

preordain' (prî-or-déne), *v.a.,* ordonner d'avance; prédéterminer; arranger d'avance.

preor'dinance (prî-), *n.,* préordonnance, *f.*

preordina'tion (prî-or-di-né-), *n.,* préordination, *f.*

prepaid' (prî-), *adj.,* affranchi, franc de port.

prepara'tion (prèp'a-ré-), *n.,* préparation, *f.;* (for a journey, etc.) préparatifs, apprêts, *m.pl.;* (state) état, *m.,* condition; (anat., mus., pharm.) préparation, *f.* To make —s for; *faire des préparatifs, des apprêts* pour.

prepar'ative (pri-par-é-), *adj.,* préparatoire; qui prépare.

prepar'ative, *n.,* préparatif; apprêt, préparatoire, *m.*

prepar'atively, *adv.,* d'une manière préparatoire, préalablement.

prepar'ator, *n.,* (in museums) préparateur, *m.*

prepar'atory, *adj.,* préparatoire. *adv.* comme préparation, préalablement. — to; *avant* de.

prepare', *v.a.,* préparer; (to set) disposer; apprêter; (to provide) se pourvoir de, fournir; (food) apprêter.

prepare', *v.n.,* se préparer à; se disposer à; s'apprêter à.

prepar'edly, *adv.,* par des mesures préparatoires.

prepar'edness, *n.,* état de préparation, *m.*

prepar'er, *n.,* préparateur, *m.;* (of food) apprêteur, *m.*

prepay' (prî-pé), *v.a.,* payer d'avance; (letters) affranchir.

prepay'ment (prî-pé-), *n.,* payement d'avance; (of letters) affranchissement, *m.*

prepense', *adj.,* (jur.) prémédité.

prepon'derance (pri-po'n'deur-), *n.,* (of weight) supériorité de poids; excès de poids; prépondérance, *f.*

prepon'derant, *adj.,* qui surpasse en poids; prépondérant.

prepon'derate, *v.a.,* surpasser en poids; (fig.) l'emporter sur; avoir la prépondérance sur.

prepon'derate, *v.n.,* peser le plus; (fig.) avoir la prépondérance, l'emporter.

prepon'derating (pri-po'n'deur'é-), *adj.,* prépondérant.

preposi'tion (prèp'o-zish'-), *n.,* (gram.) préposition, *f.*

preposi'tional, *adj.,* prépositif.

prepos'itive (prî-poz'-), *adj.,* prépositif.

prepos'itive, *n.,* mot prépositif, *m.;* particule prépositive, *f.;* prépositif, *m.*

prepos'itor (prî-poz'i-teur), *n.,* moniteur, *m.*

prepossess' (prî-poz'zèss), *v.a.,* occuper antérieurement; (fig.) préoccuper, prévenir; (the mind, the heart) gagner. This speech did not — them in his favor; *ce discours ne les prévint pas en sa faveur, ne lui gagna pas leurs suffrages.*

prepossess'ing, *adj.,* prévenant; engageant; qui prévient en sa faveur; avenant, agréable.

prepossess'sion, *n.,* possession antérieure; (fig.) prévention, *f.,* préjugé, *m.*

prepos'terous (pri-pos-teur'-), *adj.,* dont l'ordre est renversé; absurde, déraisonnable. It is —; *c'est le monde renversé.*

prepos'terously, *adv.,* dans un ordre renversé; à rebours; absurdement, déraisonnablement.

prepos'terousness, *n.,* ordre renversé, *m.;* absurdité, déraison, *f.*

prerequire' (prî-ri-kwaïeur), *v.a.,* demander préalablement; requérir *ou* exiger, d'avance. Some things are—d of us; *certaines choses sont requises de nous au préalable.*

prereq'uisite (prî-rèk'wi-zite), *adj.,* (ant.) nécessaire auparavant.

prereq'uisite, *n.,* (ant.) chose nécessaire au préalable, *f.*

prerog'ative (pri-), *n.,* prérogative, *f.*

pre'sage (près'èdje), *n.,* présage, *m.*

presage' (pri-cédje), *v.a.* and *n.,* présager; indiquer; être le signe de. The weather —s a storm; *le temps annonce une tempête.*

pres'byter (prèz'-), *n.,* ancien; prêtre; (presbyterian) ministre presbytérien, *m.*

presbyte'rial *ou* **presbyte'rian** (prèz-bi-tî-), *adj.,* de presbytère; presbytérien.

Presbyte'rian (prèz-bi-tî-), *n.,* presbytérien, *m.,* presbytérienne, *f.*

Presbyte'rianism, *n.,* presbytérianisme, *m.*

pres'bytery, *n.,* presbytère, *m.*

pre'science (prî-shi-), *n.,* prescience, *f.*

pre'scient (prî-shi-), *adj.,* doué de prescience.

prescribe' (pri-scraïbe), *v.a.,* prescrire, ordonner; (med.) prescrire, ordonner.

prescribe', *v.n.,* faire la loi; (med.) faire, écrire, une prescription, une ordonnance; (jur.) gagner la prescription; prescrire contre.

pre'script, *n.,* précepte, *m.;* (med.) ordonnance, *f.*

prescrip'tible (prî-script'i-b'l), *adj.,* (jur.) prescriptible.

prescrip'tion (pri-), *n.,* ordonnance, *f.;* précepte, *m.;* prescription; (med.) ordonnance; (jur.) prescription, *f.*

prescrip'tive (pri-), *adj.,* (jur.) établi, acquis par la prescription.

pres'ence (prèz'-), *n.,* présence, *f.;* (mien) port, air, maintien, *m.,* mine; (persons assembled) assemblée, réunion, société; (apartment) salle d'audience, *f.;* (pers.) personnage supérieur, *m.* — of mind; *présence d'esprit.* A dignified —; *un air, ou un port, majestueux.* In — of; *en présence de.* In such a —; *devant une telle assemblée; devant un si auguste personnage.* Saving your —; *sauf votre respect.*

pres'ence-chamber (-tshé'm'beur) *ou* **pres'ence-room** (-roume), *n.,* salle de réception, *f.*

pres'ent (prèz'-), *adj.,* présent; actuel; (of the month) courant; (ant.) (attentive) attentif. In the — tense; *au présent.* At the — moment; *à présent; actuellement; à l'heure qu'il est.* To be —at; *assister* à, *être présent* à, *se trouver* à.

pres'ent, *n.,* (gram.) présent; (time) présent; (gift) présent; cadeau, don, *m.* —s, *pl.,* (jur.) présentes, *f.pl.* At—; *à présent; actuellement; présentement.* In the —; (gram.) *au présent.* Know all men by these —s; *à tous ceux qui ces présentes verront ou orront.* To make a —; *faire un cadeau.* To make any one a — of anything; *faire don, faire cadeau,* de *quelque chose* à *quelqu'un.* For the —; *pour le moment; quant à présent;* (colloq.) *pour le quart d'heur—*

present' (pri-zè'n'te), *v.a.*, présenter, offrir à ; (to a benefice) présenter, nommer à ; (jur.) déférer au tribunal compétent. To — somebody with something ; *faire présent de, faire don de, faire cadeau de quelque chose à quelqu'un.* — arms ! (milit.) *présentez armes !* —l (milit.) en joue ! joue ! To — at ; (fire-arms) *coucher en joue, viser.*

present'able (-a-b'l), *adj.*, présentable.

presenta'tion (prèz'è'n'té-), *n.*, présentation ; (representation) représentation ; (ecc.) présentation, *f.* On—; à présentation. — copy ; *exemplaire donné par l'auteur ou l'éditeur ; exemplaire dont on a fait hommage, m.* Feast of the Presentation ; (c.rel.) *la Chandeleur ; la Présentation de la Vierge.*

presentee' (prèz'è'n'tî'), *n.*, (ecc.) prêtre présenté à un bénéfice, *m.*

present'er (pri-zè'n't'-), *n.*, présentateur, collateur, *m.*

presen'timent (pri-cè'n't'-), *n.*, pressentiment, *m.*

pres'ently (prèz'-), *adv.*, tout à l'heure ; bientôt ; tantôt ; tout à coup ; peu de temps après.

present'ment (pri-zè'n't-), *n.*, présentation ; conduite, *f.* ; tableau, *m.*, représentation ; apparence ; (jur.) dénonciation spontanée, *f.*

preserv'able (pri-zeurv'a-b'l), *adj.*, (l.u.) qui peut se conserver.

preserva'tion (prèz'eur-vé-), *n.*, salut, *m.*, conservation ; préservation **de** ; protection **contre.** Instinct of —; *instinct de conservation, m.*

preserv'ative *ou* **preserv'atory** (pri-zeur-), *n.*, préservatif, *m.*

preserv'ative *ou* **preserv'atory**, *adj.*, préservateur ; préservatif ; conservateur.

preserve' (pri-zeurve), *n.*, (fruit) confiture, *f.* ; fruits confits, *m.pl.*, conserve de fruits ; (vegetables, etc.) conserve, conserve alimentaire, *f.* ; conserves de viande, *f.pl.* ; (inclosure) réserve, *f.*, parc pour la conservation du gibier, *m.*, chasse, *f.* pl., plaisirs, *m.pl.*

preserve', *v.a.*, préserver ; conserver, garder ; (fruit) confire. —d land ; *chasse gardée, f.* —d meat ; *conserves de viande, f.pl.*

preserv'er, *n.*, conservateur, *m.*, conservatrice, *f.* ; préservatif, sauveur, bienfaiteur, *m.* ; confiseur, *m.* Eye—s ; *conserves (lunettes), f.pl.* Life—; *porte-respect, m.*

preside' (pri-zaïde), *v.n.*, présider à. To — at a meeting ; *présider une assemblée.* To — at the assizes ; *présider les assises.* Ceres —d over harvests; *Cérès présidait aux moissons.*

pres'idency (prèz'-), *n.*, présidence, *f.*

pres'ident (prèz'-), *n.*, président, *m.* ; présidente, *f.* Vice—; *vice-président, m.*

presiden'tial (prèz'i-dè'n'shal), *adj.*, présidentiel; de président. — angel ; (ant.) *ange gardien, imposant tutélaire, m.* —chair; *fauteuil, m.*

pres'identship, *n.*, présidence, *f.*

presid'ing, *adj.*, présidant. — angel ; *ange gardien, m.* — judge ; *président, m.*

presignifica'tion (pri-cig-), *n.*, (ant.) (theol.) prédiction, *f.* ; type, symbole, *m.*, figure, *f.*

presig'nify (pri-cig-ni-faïe), *v.a.*, (ant.) signifier d'avance, présager.

press (prèce), *v.a.*, presser ; serrer ; (to urge) presser, pousser ; (to embrace) serrer, presser, étreindre ; (sailors) exercer la presse **contre,** presser, enrôler de force ; (paper) glacer, satiner ; (fruit) pressurer ; (manu.) mettre en presse. To — upon ; *appuyer* **sur** ; *insister* **sur** ; *faire sentir* à ; (pers.) *attaquer violemment ; poursuivre, serrer de près.* To — a thing on any one ; *imposer une chose à quelqu'un.* To — down ; *presser ; appuyer fortement sur.* To — forward ; *pousser, faire avancer.* To — out ; *exprimer ; pressurer.* To—hard ; *presser fort ;* (on the heels of) *serrer de près.* To cold—; to hot—; *satiner à froid, à chaud.* To be —ed for time ; *être pressé.*

press, *v.n.*, presser ; pousser ; (to encroach) empiéter ; envahir ; (to approach) approcher, s'approcher ; avancer ; (to crowd) se presser, affluer. To — upon ; *serrer.* To — forward ; *se hâter ; avancer rapidement, se porter en avant ; hâter le pas.* To — on; *pousser en avant ; poursuivre son chemin.*

press, *n.*, (for fruit) pressoir, *m.* ; presse ; (print.) presse ; (crowd) presse, foule ; (closet) armoire ; (urgency) urgence, presse ; (levy of men for service) presse, *f.* — of sail ; (nav.) *force de voiles, f.* Printing—; *presse d'imprimerie.* —error ; *faute d'impression, erreur typographique, f.* In the —; *sous presse.* To go to —; *mettre sous presse.* Too late for —; *trop tard pour l'impression.* In time for —; *à temps pour l'impression.*

press'-bed (-bède), *n.*, lit en armoire, *m.*

pressed (près-te), *adj.*, satiné.

press'er, *n.*, (of fabrics) presseur, *m.* ; (of a wine-press) pressureur ; (of a printing-press) pressier, *m.*

press'-gang, *n.*, presse, *f.*

press'-house, *n.*, pressoir, *m.*

press'ing, *adj.*, urgent ; pressant, qui presse, pressé. —roller ; *rouleau à satiner, m.*

press'ing, *n.*, action de presser, *f.* ; (tech.) pressage ; (fruit) pressurage, *m.* ; (paper) satinage, *m.* To require —; *se faire prier ; se faire tirer l'oreille* **pour.**

press'ingly, *adv.*, d'une manière urgente ; d'une manière pressante ; instamment.

pres'sion, *n.*, pression, *f.*

press'man, *n.*, (pressmen) (wine) pressureur ; (print.) pressier, imprimeur, *m.* ; (journalist) journaliste, reporter, *m.*

press'-money (-meu'n'nè), *n.*, gratification à un homme enrôlé par la presse, *f.*

press'-revise, *n.*, (print.) tierce, *f.*

pres'sure (prèsh'eur), *n.*, action de presser ; (phys.) (of the air) pression ; (impulse) impulsion, force ; (urgency) urgence ; presse ; (calamity) calamité ; oppression, misère, *f.* ; (weight) poids, *m.* ; (impression) impression, *f.* ; (fruit) pressurage, *m.* High, low, mean —; *haute, basse, moyenne pression.* The — of business ; *l'urgence des affaires, f.*

pres'sure-gauge (-ghédje), *n.*, (phys.) manomètre, *m.*

press'-warrant (-wor'-), *n.*, autorisation de presser, d'exercer la presse, *f.*

press'work (-weurke), *n.*, ouvrage fait à la presse ; (print.) tirage, *m.*

presta'tion (près-té-), *n.*, prestation, redevance, *f.*

presta'tion-money (-meu'n'ni), *n.*, prestation (en argent) payée aux évêques, *f.*

prestidigita'tion, *n.*, prestidigitation, *f.*

prestidigita'tor, *n.*, presdidigitateur, *m.*

pres'tige, *n.*, prestige, *m.*

pres'to (près-tô), *adv.*, preste, prestement ; (mus.) presto.

presum'able (pri-ziou'm'a-b'l), *adj.*, présumable.

presum'ably, *adv.*, probablement.

presume' (pri-zioume), *v.a.*, présumer.

presume', *v.n.*, présumer trop **de** ; compter trop **sur** ; se permettre, oser, prendre la liberté. To — upon ; *s'aviser de, présumer trop* **de** ; *se flatter* **de** ; *compter trop* **sur.** — not that I am the thing I was ; *n'allez pas croire que je sois ce que j'étais autrefois.*

presum'er, *n.*, arrogant, présomptueux, *m.*

presum'ing, *adj.*, présomptueux.

presum'ingly, *adv.*, présomptueusement.

presump'tion (-zeu'm'-), *n.*, présomption, *f.*

presump'tive (pri-zeu'm'-), *adj.*, présumé ; (presumptuous) présomptueux ; (jur.) (of heirs) présomptif ; (of evidence) indirect ; (of arrests) préventif.

presump'tively, adv., par présomption ; (of arrests) préventivement.

presump'tuous (pri-zeu'm'pt'iou-), adj., présomptueux.

presump'tuously, adv., présomptueusement.

presump'tuousness, n., présomption, f.

presuppose' (pri-ceup'poze), v.a., présupposer.

presupposi'tion, n., présupposition, f.

pretend' (pri-), v.a., prétexter ; affecter ; feindre ; faire semblant de ; prétendre. To — ignorance ; *prétexter l'ignorance, faire l'ignorant.*

pretend' (pri-), v.n., prétendre **de** ; avoir la prétention **de** ; feindre **de**. To — to be dead ; *feindre d'être mort ; faire le mort.* To — to be ill ; *feindre, ou faire semblant, d'être malade ; faire le malade.*

pretend'ed, adj., prétendu, soi-disant, supposé, faux, feint.

pretend'er (pri-), n., personne qui prétexte, qui feint, qui fait semblant **de**, f. ; prétendant, m., prétendante, f. ; (hist.) prétendant, m.

pretense' (pri-), n., prétexte ; faux semblant, m. ; défaite, feinte ; (claim) prétention, f. To make — to, ou of ; *faire semblant de.* Under — of ; *sous prétexte* **de** ; *sous couleur* **de.** Under — of friendship ; *sous couleur d'amitié.* Under false —s ; *par moyens frauduleux.*

preten'sion (pri-), n., prétention, f. ; (a claim) titre, droit, m., prétention, f. To have —s to ; *avoir des prétentions* **à.** To have —s (to beauty) ; (of women) *avoir des prétentions.* Of great —s ; *à prétentions.* Of no —s ; *sans prétentions.*

preten'tious, adj., prétentieux, ambitieux.

preten'tiously, adv., ambitieusement, prétentieusement.

preten'tiousness, n., air prétentieux, m., prétention, f.

pret'erit (prèt'eur'-), n., (gram.) prétérit, m. In the — ; *au prétérit.*

pretermis'sion (prî-teur-mish'-), n., omission ; (rhet.) prétermission, prétérition, f.

preternat'ural (prî-teur-nat'iou-), adj., surnaturel ; contre nature.

preternat'urally, adv., surnaturellement.

preternat'uralness, n., état surnaturel ; état contre nature, m.

pre'text (prî-), n., prétexte ; faux semblant, m. ; couleur ; feinte, défaite, f. Under — of ; *sous prétexte* **de** ; *sous couleur* **de.**

pret'tily (prit'-), adv., joliment ; gentiment ; avec grâce.

pret'tiness (prit'-), n., gentillesse, élégance, grâce, beauté, f. ; agrément, m.

pret'ty (prit'-), adj., joli ; gentil ; (b.s., jest.) joli, beau. — little fellow ; *joli petit garçon, m.* — fellow ; (b.s.) *joli garçon, m.*

pret'ty, adv., assez ; passablement. — well ; *assez bien.* — much ; *presque, à peu près.* I am — sure of that fact ; *je suis presque certain du fait.*

pret'ty-spoken (-spôk'ène), adj., gentil ; qui parle joliment.

prevail' (pri-vél), v.n., prévaloir ; régner, dominer ; avoir du pouvoir ; avoir de l'influence ; avoir de l'effet, avoir du poids ; (to succeed) réussir. To — on ; *obtenir* **de** ; *décider* **à**, *persuader* **de**, *entraîner* **à**, *convaincre* **de.** To — over ; *prévaloir* **sur**, *l'emporter* **sur.** To — with ; *avoir de l'empire* **sur**, *avoir de l'influence* **sur** ; *prévaloir* **auprès de** ; *prédominer* **auprès de.** To be — ed on ; *se laisser persuader* **à** ; *se laisser entraîner* **à** ; *consentir* **à.** To — upon one's self to ; *se résoudre* **à**, *se persuader* **de.** To — on any one to ; *décider quelqu'un* **à.** Easterly winds — here during the month of March ; *le vent d'est règne ici pendant le mois de mars.* Try to — upon him to come ; *tâchez de l'engager à venir.*

prevail'ing, adj., dominant, régnant ; général ; (efficacious) efficace. The — opinion ; *l'opinion générale,* f.

prev'alence (prèv'a-), n., règne, ascendant, empire, pouvoir, m. ; influence ; efficacité ; (of weather, disease, etc.) durée, existence, f.

prev'alent, adj., régnant, dominant, général ; (victorious) victorieux ; (efficacious) efficace.

prev'alently, adv., efficacement, puissamment, fortement, avec force.

prevar'icate (pri-var'i-), v.n., prévariquer ; tergiverser ; (jur.) user de collusion.

prevarica'tion (pri-var'i-ké-), n., prévarication ; tergiversation, f.

prevar'icator (pri-var'i-ké-teur), n., prévaricateur ; auteur d'une collusion, m.

prevent' (pri-), v.a., prévenir ; empêcher **de**, détourner **de.**

prevent'er, n., personne qui prévient, qui empêche ; chose qui prévient, qui empêche, f.

prevent'ible, **-able** (-'i-b'l), adj., empêchable, évitable.

preven'tion (pri-), n., empêchement, obstacle, m.

prevent'ive (pri-), n., préventif, m., chose qui prévient, qui empêche, f. ; préservatif, m.

prevent'ive, adj., préventif ; propre à empêcher, propre à prévenir.

prevent'ively, adv., pour prévenir, pour empêcher ; préventivement.

pre'vious (pri-), adj., précédent, antérieur, préalable. — question ; (parliament) *question préalable,* f. To be — ; (coll.) *anticiper.* — to ; *avant.*

pre'viously, adv., précédemment, antérieurement ; préalablement ; auparavant ; d'avance. — to ; *avant, avant* **de.**

pre'viousness, n., antériorité, priorité, f.

previ'sion (pri-vij'eune), n., prévision, f.

prey (prê), n., proie, f. To be a — to ; *être en proie* **à,** *être la proie* **de.** To fall a — to ; *devenir la proie* **de.** Beast of — ; *animal carnassier, m.* Bird of — ; *oiseau de proie, m.*

prey (prê), v.n., butiner, piller ; faire sa proie **de** ; (fig.) miner, ronger. To — on ; *voler, piller, victimer* ; (on the mind) *tourmenter, obséder.*

prey'er (prê-eur), n., (an.) spoliateur, m.

price (praïce), n., prix, m. ; (com.) cote, f. Trade — ; *prix marchand, m.* Market — ; *cours ; prix courant, m.* Cost — ; *prix coûtant.* Low — ; *bas prix.* The lowest — ; *le dernier prix ; le plus juste prix.* Under — ; *à vil prix, au rabais.* At greatly reduced —s ; *au grand rabais.* To set a — on ; (fig.) *mettre à prix.* To rise, ou fall, in — ; *hausser, baisser de prix.* Half — ; *à moitié prix.* All at one — ; *au choix.* High — ; *prix élevé.* At any — ; *coûte que coûte ; à tout prix.*

price, v.a., marquer, coter, tarifer.

price'-current (-keur'-), n., prix courant, m.

price'less, adj., (invaluable) sans prix, inappréciable, inestimable, impayable.

price'-list, n., prix courant, tarif, m.

prick, n., pointe, f. ; piquant ; (goad) aiguillon, m. ; (puncture) piqûre ; (remorse) douleur cuisante, f., remords ; (mark) but, blanc, m. ; (fixed place) place marquée, f., point, m. ; (of a hare) trace, f.

prick, v.a., piquer ; (the ears) dresser ; (to fix) enfoncer par la pointe ; (to designate by a puncture) désigner, marquer, piquer ; (to spur) piquer ; (to goad) aiguillonner ; (to incite) pousser, exciter ; (to sting with remorse) tourmenter de remords ; (to affect with pain) faire éprouver une douleur poignante **à** ; (liquors) rendre piquant ; (mus.) noter ; (nav.) pointer. To — off ; *piquer, marquer, désigner.* To — up the ears ; *dresser les oreilles.* To — on ; *piquer, aiguillonner.* To — out ; (hort.) *transplanter.*

prick, v.n., piquer ; piquer des deux ; (to dress one's self out) se parer ; (to become acid) devenir piquant. To — on ; *s'avancer au galop ; piquer des deux.*

prick'er, n., (thing) pointe, f. ; piquant, m. ; (tech.) épinglette, f.

prick'ing, n., action de piquer, f. ; picotement, m., piqûre, f. ; (nav.) pointage, m.

prick'ing, adj., qui pique ; piquant.

pric'kle (prik'k'l), n., aiguillon, piquant, m. ; épine, f.

pric'kle-back, n., (ich.) épinoche, f.

prick'liness, n., abondance de piquants, f.

prick'ly, adj., plein de piquants ; (bot.) armé d'aiguillons, armé d'épines, épineux.

prick'song (-so'gne), n., air noté, air modulé, m.

prick'wood (-woude), n., (bot.) fusain, m.

pride (praïde), n., orgueil, m. ; fierté, f. ; (ostentation) faste ; (ornement) ornement, m. Honest —; *noble orgueil*. Puffed up with —; *bouffi d'orgueil*. To humble any one's —; *rabatre, rabaisser l'orgueil, la fierté de quelqu'un*. London —; (bot.) *désespoir des peintres*, m.

pride, v.n. To — one's self on; *être fier* **de**; *se faire gloire* **de**; *s'enorgueillir* **de**; *se glorifier* **de**; *se faire une gloire* **de**; *tirer vanité* **de**; *se piquer* **de**. To take — in ; *tenir à gloire*; *mettre sa gloire* **à**, *tenir à honneur* **de**.

pri'er (praï'eur), n., curieux, espion, m.

priest (prîs'te), n., prêtre, m. High — ; *grand prêtre*.

priest'craft, n., intrigues de prêtres, f.pl.

priest'ess, n., prêtresse, f.

priest'hood (-houde), n., prêtrise, f., sacerdoce, clergé, m. ; (b.s.) prêtraille, f.

priest'like (-laïke), adj., de prêtre, sacerdotal.

priest'liness, n., air de prêtre, m.

priest'ly, adj., de prêtre, sacerdotal.

priest'ridden (-rid'd'n), adj., gouverné par les prêtres.

prig, v.a., escamoter ; chiper ; voler ; dérober.

prig, n., freluquet, faquin, fat ; pédant, m. ; chipeur, voleur, m.

prig'ging, n., filouterie, f. ; escamotage, m.

prig'gish, adj., suffisant, vaniteux, pédant.

prig'gishly, adv., avec suffisance.

prill, n., (ich.). *V.* **brill**.

prim, adj., affecté, précieux, collet monté, tiré à quatre épingles.

pri'ma (praï-), n., (print.) réclame, f.

pri'macy (praï-), n., primatie, primauté (supremacy), f.

pri'mage (praï-mèdje), n., (nav.) allocation, f., primage, chapeau, m.

pri'marily (praï-), adv., primitivement ; originairement, dans le principe.

pri'mary (praï-), adj., primitif ; premier ; principal ; primaire, élémentaire.

pri'mate (praï-), n., primat, m.

pri'mateship (praï-), n., primatie, f.

prima'tial (praï-ma-shal), adj., primatial.

prime (praïme), adj., principal ; premier ; de premier rang, de premier ordre ; (first in quality) de première qualité, excellent ; florissant ; (early) précoce ; (arith.) premier. — cost ; *prix de revient*, m. — minister ; *premier ministre*, m.

prime (praïme), n., (dawn) aurore, aube, f., point du jour ; (beginning) commencement, m., premiers temps, m.pl., origine, naissance, f. ; (spring) printemps, m. ; (best part) meilleure partie, fleur, élite, f., meilleur choix, m. ; (perfection) comble de perfection, m. ; (fenc.) prime, f. ; (chem.) rapport le plus simple, m. ; (c.rel.) prime ; (fig.) beauté, force, fraîcheur, fleur, première jeunesse, f., printemps, m. — of life ; *fleur de l'âge, la force de l'âge*; *le matin des jours*, m. (V. Hugo). To be in one's —; *être à, ou dans, la fleur de l'âge*. To be in its, their —; *être dans toute sa beauté, dans toute sa fleur, dans toute sa fraîcheur* ; (of fruit, flowers) *être en pleine saison*.

prime (praïme), v.a., (of fire-arms) amorcer ; (nav.) abreuver ; (paint.) préparer, imprimer. To — a pump; *amorcer une pompe*.

prime'ly (praï'm'-), adv., (originally) en premier lieu, primitivement ; (most excellently) parfaitement, on ne saurait mieux.

prime'ness (praï'm'-), n., excellence, f.

prim'er (pri'm'-), n., (spelling-book) abécédaire, syllabaire, premier livre de lecture ; (c.rel.) livre d'heures, m., heures canoniales, f.pl. ; (print.) romain, m. ; (milit.) épinglette, f.

prime'ro (pri-mî-), n., (game) prime, f.

prime'val (praï-mî-), adj., primitif, premier ; primordial.

prim'ing (praï'm'-), n., amorce ; (action of priming) amorçage ; (paint.) impression, empreinte, f.

prim'ing-horn, n., corne d'amorce, f.

prim'ing-pan, n., (of fire-arms) bassinet, m.

prim'ing-powder (-paou-), n., pulvérin, m., poudre fulminante, f.

prim'ing-wire (-waïeur), n.,(artil.) épinglette, f. ; dégorgeoir, m.

prim'itive (pri'm'-), adj., primitif. The — Church ; *la primitive Eglise*.

prim'itive, n., (philol.) primitif, mot primitif, mot radical, m.

prim'itively, adv., primitivement.

prim'itiveness, n., nature primitive, antiquité, f. ; caractère primitif, m.

prim'ness (pri'm'-), n., affectation, afféterie, f.

primoge'nial (praï-mo-djî-), adj., premier-né ; primordial ; primitif.

primogen'itor (praï-mo-djè'n'i-teur), n., premier père, m.

primogen'iture (praï-mo-djè'n'i-tioure), n., primogéniture, f.

primogen'itureship, n., droit de primogéniture, droit d'aînesse, m.

primor'dial, adj., primordial.

primor'dial, n., origine, f.

prim'rose (-rôze), n., (bot.) primevère, f. — bed ; *planche de primevères*, f.

prince, n., prince, m. —'s feather ; (bot.) *amarante*, f.

prince'dom, n., principat, m.

prince'let, **-ling**, n., princillon, m.

prince'like (-laïke), adj., digne d'un prince ; de prince.

prince'liness, n., caractère de prince, m. ; munificence de prince, f.

prince'ly, adj., de prince, de princesse ; princier ; digne d'un prince, d'une princesse ; royal, auguste ; magnifique, riche.

prince'ly, adv., en prince, en princesse, magnifiquement.

prin'cess, n., princesse, f.

prin'cipal, adj., principal, premier, en chef ; (of staircases) grand ; (of courtyards) d'honneur ; (mus.) fondamental.

prin'cipal, n., (chief) partie principale, f., chef ; (main point) principal, essentiel ; (leader) chef ; (master) patron ; (of a college) proviseur, principal, directeur, m. ; (lady) directrice, f. ; (of a school) maître ; (com.) associé principal ; commettant ; (jur.) auteur principal ; (capital) capital, m., capitaux, m.pl., principal, m. — and agent ; *commettant et agent*, m.

principal'ity, n., principauté, f.

prin'cipally, adv., principalement ; surtout.

prin'cipalship, n., provisorat, principalat, m.

prin'ciple (-ci-p'l), n., principe, m. To be a man of —; *avoir des principes*. Of no —; *sans principes*. On —; *par principe*. Proximate —; (chem.) *principe immédiat*, m.

prin'cipled (-ci-p'l'de), adj., qui a des principes. High —; *qui a des sentiments nobles*. Ill —; *qui a de mauvais principes*. Well- —; *qui a de bons principes*.

print, v.a., imprimer ; (to mark) faire une empreinte **sur**, laisser une trace **sur**. —ed by ; *imprimé* **par** ; (on books) *imprimerie* **de**. —ed for; *imprimé* **pour**; (on books) *librairie de*; *chez*. To — off a thousand copies; *tirer mille exemplaires*.

print, *v.n.*, imprimer; se faire imprimer.

print, *n.*, (mark) empreinte, trace, marque; (of books) impression, *f.*; (printed book) imprimé, *m.*; (engraving) estampe, gravure, *f.*; (newspaper) journal, *m.*, feuille, *f.*; (print) caractère; (mold) moule, *m.*; (stuff) indienne, toile peinte, *f.* This book is out of —; *l'édition de ce livre est épuisée*. In —; *imprimé*. To rush into, *ou* appear, in —; *se faire imprimer*; *avoir la manie de se faire imprimer*.

print'-dress, *n.*, robe d'indienne, *ou* de toile peinte, *f.*

print'ed, *adj.*, imprimé.

print'er, *n.*, imprimeur, *m.* Letter-press —; *typographe*, *m.* Lithographic —; *imprimeur lithographe.* —'s ink; *encre d'imprimerie, f.* —'s reader; *correcteur d'épreuves*, *m.*

print'ing, *n.*, impression; imprimerie, *f.* — house; *imprimerie, f.* — off; *tirage*, *m.*

print'ing-machine (-ma-shīne), *n.*, presse mécanique, *f.*

print'ing-office, *n.*, imprimerie, *f.*

print'ing-paper, *n.*, papier à imprimer, *ou* d'impression, *m.*

print'ing-press, *n.*, presse à imprimer, *f.*

print'ing-type, *n.*, caractères, *m.pl.*

print'less, *adj.*, qui ne laisse point de trace.

print'seller, *n.*, marchand d'estampes, *m.*

print'-shop, *n.*, magasin d'estampes, *m.*

print'-works, *n.*, imprimerie d'étoffes, *f.*

pri'or (praï'-), *n.*, (of convents) prieur, *m.*

pri'or (praï'-), *adj.*, antérieur.

pri'or, *adv.*, antérieurement à. — to; *avant de*.

pri'oress (praï'-), *n.*, (of a convent) prieure, *f.*

prior'ity (praï-), *n.*, priorité, *f.*

pri'orship (praï-), *n.*, prieuré, *m.*

pri'ory (praï-), *n.*, prieuré, *m.*

prise, *n.*, levier, *m.* *v.a.* To — open; *ouvrir avec un levier, forcer à l'aide d'un levier*. To — up; *soulever (à l'aide d'un levier).*

prism (priz'm), *n.*, prisme, *m.*

prismat'ic *ou* **prismat'ical** (priz'-), *adj.*, prismatique.

prismat'ically (priz'-), *adv.*, en forme de prisme.

pris'moid (priz'moïde), *n.*, prismoïde, *m.*

pris'on (priz'z'n), *n.*, prison, *f.* To be in —; *être en prison.* To break out of —; *forcer sa prison; s'évader.* To take out of —; *retirer de prison.* To take out of —; *hors de prison.*

pris'on, *v.a.*, emprisonner; captiver.

pris'on-bars (-bärze) *ou* **pris'on-base** (-béce), *n.*, (game) barres, *f.pl.*

pris'oner, *n.*, prisonnier, *m.*, prisonnière, *f.*; détenu, (jur.) prévenu, *m.*, prévenue, *f.*; accusé, *m.*, accusée, *f.* To take —; *faire prisonnier.* — at the bar; *accusé, prévenu, m.* Witness for the —; *témoin à décharge, m.* To be kept a close —; (fig.) *être forcément retenu à la maison.*

pris'on-house (-haouce), *n.*, prison, *f.*

pris'on-van, *n.*, voiture cellulaire, *f.*

pris'on-yard, *n.*, préau de prison, *m.*

pris'tine, *adj.*, primitif; ancien; (fig.) premier, de jeunesse.

prith'ee! (prith'ï), *int.*, de grâce! je vous en prie!

pri'vacy (praï-), *n.*, retraite, solitude, *f.*; secret; intime, *m.*; intimité, *f.* In —; *dans son intérieur, en son particulier.*

pri'vate (praï-), *adj.*, privé; (retired) retiré; (secret) secret; (personal) particulier; (of dress) bourgeois, civil, de ville; (jur.) à huis clos. — individual; *simple particulier, m.* — gentleman; *simple particulier, rentier, m.* A — staircase; *escalier dérobé, m.* — soldier; *simple soldat, m.*

They live in a very — way; *ils mènent une vie bien retirée.* — carriage; *voiture de maître, ou bourgeoise, f.* — asylum; *maison de santé, f.* — room; *cabinet particulier; cabinet; salon de société, m.* — tutor; *précepteur, m.* — tuition; *enseignement libre, m.* — school; *pensionnat, m.; institution, f.* — student; *étudiant sans maître, m.* — pupil; *élève particulier, m.* — lessons; *leçons particulières, répétitions, f.pl.* — hotel; *maison meublée, f.* — room; (in restaurants) *salon particulier; cabinet particulier;* (for business) *cabinet, m.*

pri'vate, *n.*, (soldier) simple soldat, *m.* In —; *en secret; en particulier; en son particulier; dans son intérieur;* (jur.) à *huis clos.*

privateer' (praï-vé-tîre), *n.*, corsaire, *m.*

privateer', *v.n.*, (nav.) faire la course, aller en course.

privateer'ing, *n.*, (nav.) course, *f.*

pri'vately (praï-vét'-), *adv.*, en particulier; en secret; secrètement; sans aucun appareil; (jur.) à huis clos; (of sales) de gré à gré, à l'amiable; (of living) en bourgeois, en rentier.

priva'tion (praï-vé-), *n.*, privation; perte, absence, *f.*

priv'ative (priv'a-), *adj.*, qui prive; négatif; (gram.) privatif; (jur.) privatif.

priv'ative (priv'a-), *n.*, négation, *f.*; (gram.) privatif, *m.*

priv'atively (priv'a-), *adv.*, négativement.

priv'et, *n.*, (bot.) troène, *m.*

priv'ilege (-lèdje), *n.*, privilège, *m.*

priv'ilege (-lèdje), *v.a.*, privilégier.

priv'ileged (-lèdj'de), *past part.*, privilégié.

priv'ily (priv'-), *adv.*, secrètement, en secret.

priv'ity (priv'-), *n.*, connaissance, *f.*, assentiment, *m.*

priv'y (priv'-), *adj.*, privé, secret, caché; dérobé, retiré. — to; *instruit de, qui a connaissance de, initié à.* — council; *conseil privé, m.* — councilor; *membre du conseil privé, m.* Keeper of the — purse; *trésorier de la maison du roi, m.* — purse; *cassette, f.* — seal; *petit sceau;* (pers.) *garde des sceaux, m.* — chamber; *chambre du conseil, f.*

priv'y (priv'-), *n.*, lieux, lieux d'aisance, *m.pl.*, garde-robe, *f.*, latrines, commodités, *f.pl.*; (jur.) ayant droit, ayant cause, *m.*

prize (praïze), *n.*, (things taken) prise, capture, *f.*; (reward) prix; (in a lottery) lot, *m.*; bonne fortune, aubaine, *f.*; (nav.) bâtiment pris, *m.*, prise, *f.* It is a lawful —; *c'est de bonne prise.* The vessel returned to port with her —; *le vaisseau rentra au port avec sa prise.* To win a —; *remporter, gagner un prix.*

prize, *v.a.*, priser, évaluer, estimer, apprécier; tenir à; faire cas de.

prize'-essay, *n.*, ouvrage couronné (par l'Académie, etc.), *ou* qui a remporté un prix, *m.*

prize'-fighter (-faït'-), *n.*, pugiliste, boxeur de profession, *m.*

prize'-list, *n.*, palmarès, *m.*

prize'-man, *n.*, lauréat, *m.*

prize'-medal, *n.*, médaille d'honneur, *f.*

prize'-money (-meu'n'nè), *n.*, part de prise, *f.*

prize'-ox, *n.*, le bœuf gras, *m.*

prize'-taker, **-winner**, *n.*, lauréat, médaillé, *m.*

pro, *prep.* V. **pour**. — and con; *pour et contre, le pour et le contre.*

probabil'ity, *n.*, probabilité, *f.*

prob'able (-'a-b'l), *adj.*, probable.

prob'ably, *adv.*, probablement.

pro'bang (prô-bai'gne), *n.*, (surg., vet.), sonde, *f.*; poussoir, *m.*

pro'bate (prô-), *n.*, (jur.) vérification, légalisation, d'un testament, *f.* — duty; *droit de succession, m.*

proba'tion (pro-bé-), *n.*, (religious orders) probation, *f.*, noviciat, *m.*; (trial) épreuve, *f.*;

essai, examen ; (in France, for barristers) stage, *m.* On —; *à l'essai.*

proba'tionary (pro-bé-), *adj.*, d'épreuve, qui sert d'épreuve ; de probation.

proba'tioner (pro-bé-), *n.*, personne admise à l'examen, *f.*, candidat, stagiaire ; (novice) novice, *m.*

proba'tionership, *n.*, candidature, *f.* ; noviciat, *m.*

probe (prôbe), *n.*, (surg.) stylet, *m.* ; sonde, *f.*

probe (prôbe), *v.a.*, (surg.) sonder ; (fig.) sonder, approfondir, examiner à fond. — scissors ; *ciseaux boutonnés, m.pl.*

prob'ity (prŏb'-), *n.*, probité, *f.* Of —; *de probité ; probe.*

prob'lem, *n.*, problème, *m.*

problemat'ical, *adj.*, problématique.

problemat'ically, *adv.*, problématiquement.

probos'cis, *n.*, (*proboscides*) trompe, proboscide, *f.*, (fig. and jest.) nez, *m.*

proce'dure (-cîd'ieur), *n.*, procédé, *m.* ; manière de procéder ; (jur.) procédure, *f.*

proceed' (-cîde), *v.n.*, (to go on) poursuivre ; continuer ; (to act) agir, procéder, s'y prendre ; (to make progress) avancer, marcher ; faire des progrès ; passer outre ; (to come from) provenir **de**, naître **de**, venir **de**, procéder **de**. To — against ; (jur.) *procéder* **contre**, diriger des poursuites **contre**. To — from ; *procéder* **de**, *passer* **de**, *tirer son origine* **de**, *provenir* **de**, *naître* **de**, To — on ; (to continue) poursuivre, continuer ; *procéder* **d'après**, *agir* **d'après**. To — to ; *se mettre* **à** ; *passer* **à** ; *commencer* **à** ; (to go to) *se rendre* **à**, *aller* **à**, *se porter* **vers** ; (to begin) *se mettre* **à**, *s'occuper* **de**, *se mettre en devoir* **de**. To — with ; *continuer*, *poursuivre* ; (to act towards) *en agir* **avec** ; *en user* **avec**. To — to blows ; *en venir aux mains, aux coups*. To — to extremities ; *se porter à des excès, à des extrémités* **envers**. I thought how I had best —; *je songeai à ce qu'il y avait de mieux à faire*. They have threatened to — against him ; *on a menacé de lui intenter un procès.*

proceed'ing (-cîd'-), *n.*, procédé, *m.* ; manière d'agir, de faire, *f.* —s, *pl.*, procédés, *m.pl.* ; démarches, mesures, *f.pl.* ; moyens, actes, *m.pl.* ; (jur.) procédure, *f.*, poursuites, *f.pl.* The —s of the Royal Society ; *les comptes rendus de la Société Royale, m.pl.* To take —s against ; (jur.) *diriger des poursuites* **contre**.

pro'ceeds (-cîd'ze), *n.pl.*, produit, rapport ; (of a sale) produit, bénéfice, *m.*

pro'cess, *n.*, (progress) progrès ; — (course) cours, *m.*, marche ; (of time) suite ; (operation) opération, *f.* ; procédé, *m.* ; (anat.) apophyse, *f.* ; (jur.) procès, exploit judiciaire, *m.* ; (writ) sommation de comparaître, assignation, *f.* In — of time ; *avec le temps*. —server ; (France) *huissier, m.*

proces'sion (-cèsh'-), *n.*, cortège, *m.* ; marche, *f.* ; procession, *f.*, convoi, *m.* ; (theol.) procession, *f.* Torch-light — ; *promenade, retraite aux flambeaux, f.* To walk in — ; *défiler.*

proces'sional (-cèsh'-), *adj.*, de cortège ; processionnel.

proclaim' (-cléme), *v.a.*, proclamer, déclarer, publier, annoncer ; (to outlaw) (ant.) mettre hors la loi ; (Ireland) interdire le port d'armes **dans** un district.

proclaim'er (-clé'm'-), *n.*, proclamateur, *m.*

proclama'tion (-cla-mé-), *n.*, proclamation, publication, déclaration ; ordonnance, *f.* ; édit, *m.*

procliv'ity, *n.*, inclination **à**, *f.* ; penchant **à**, **pour**, **vers**, *m.* ; (facility of learning) disposition pour l'étude, facilité à apprendre, *f.*

procon'sul (-seul), *n.*, proconsul, *m.*

procon'sular (-seul'-), *adj.*, proconsulaire.

procon'sulship, procon'sulate, *n.*, proconsulat, *m.*

procras'tinate, *v.a.*, remettre de jour en jour ; différer de jour en jour, retarder.

procras'tinate, *v.n.*, temporiser.

procrastina'tion (-ti-né-), *n.*, retardement, délai, *m.* ; remise, temporisation, *f.*

procras'tinator (-ti-né-), *n.*, temporisateur, temporiseur, *m.*

pro'create (prô-cri-), *v.a.*, procréer ; produire.

pro'creating, *adj.*, procréateur, productif.

procrea'tion (prô-cri-é-), *n.*, procréation, *f.* ; engendrement, *m.*

pro'creative, *adj.*, de procréation ; de production ; productif, générateur.

pro'creativeness, *n.*, faculté de procréer, *f.*

proc'tor (-teur), *n.*, homme d'affaires ; agent ; avoué ; (in universities) censeur ; (in ecclesiastical courts) procureur, *m.* —s of the clergy ; (Eng. Church) *représentants du clergé (au synode provincial), m.pl.*

proctor'ial, *adj.*, de censeur.

proc'torship, *n.*, fonctions de censeur, *f.pl.*

procum'bent (-keu'm'-), *adj.*, couché.

procur'able (-kiour'a-b'l), *adj.*, facile à se procurer, à trouver ; qu'on peut se procurer.

procura'tion (prok'iou-ré-), *n.*, procuration ; gestion des affaires d'autrui, *f.* —fee ; *commission prélevée par un agent d'affaires, f.*

proc'urator (prok'iou-ré-teur), *n.*, agent d'affaires ; (jur.) procureur, *m.* ; (Scotland) procureur fiscal, *m.*

procure' (-kioure), *v.a.n.*, procurer ; faire avoir ; obtenir, se procurer ; (to cause) causer, amener, occasionner.

procure'ment, *n.*, action de procurer ; entremise, obtention, *f.*

procur'er (-kiour'-), *n.*, (b.s.) maquereau (l. ex.), entremetteur, *m.*

procur'ess (-kiour'-), *n.*, (b.s.) procureuse, entremetteuse, *f.*

prod, *v.a.*, piquer, percer, enfoncer ; (fig.) éperonner, aiguillonner.

prod'igal, *adj.*, prodigue. The — son ; *l'enfant prodigue, m.*

prod'igal, *n.*, prodigue, *m.*

prodigal'ity, *n.*, prodigalité, *f.*

prod'igally, *adv.*, prodigalement ; avec prodigalité.

prodi'gious (-didj'eusse), *adj.*, prodigieux, énorme.

prodi'giously (-didj'-), *adv.*, prodigieusement, énormément.

prodi'giousness (-didj'-), *n.*, nature prodigieuse ; énormité, *f.*

prod'igy (prod'i-dji), *n.*, prodige, *m.*

prod'uce (-diouce), *n.*, produit, *m.* ; (provisions) denrées, *f.pl.*

produce', *v.a.*, produire ; exhiber, montrer ; (geom.) prolonger.

produ'cer, *n.*, qui produit, *f.* ; producteur, *m.*

produ'cible (-diou-ci-b'l), *adj.*, qui peut être produit, productible.

produ'cibleness, *n.*, productibilité, *f.*

prod'uct (prod'eukte), *n.*, produit ; (effect) effet, résultat ; (math.) produit, *m.*

produc'tion (-deuk'-), *n.*, production, *f.* ; (chem. manu.) produit, *m.*

product'ive (-deuk-), *adj.*, productif ; d'un bon rapport. To be — of ; *produire, donner naissance* **à** ; *causer, occasioner.*

product'iveness, *n.*, nature productive, productivité, *f.* ; bon rapport, *m.*

pro'em (prô-è'm), *n.*, préface, introduction, *f.* ; préambule, *m.*

proe'mial, *adj.*, de préface ; introductoire ; préliminaire.

profana'tion (-né-) *ou* **profan'ity**, *n.*, profanation, *f.*

profane', *adj.*, profane.

profane', *v.a.*, profaner.

profane'ly (-fé'n'-), *adv.*, avec profanation.

profane'ness (-fé'n'-), *n.*, conduite profane, impiété, *f.* ; langage profane, *m.*

profan'er (-fé'n'-), *n.*, profanateur, *m.*

profan'ity. *V.* **profana'tion.**

profess', *v.a.*, professer ; faire profession **de** ; déclarer, dire, se piquer **de**, avoir la prétention **de**. To — one's self ; *se dire ; se déclarer.*

profess', *v.n.*, se déclarer ; se dire.

professed' (pro-fèste), *adj.*, déclaré, avoué ; de profession ; (ecc.) profès.

profess'edly (-fèss'èd'-), *adv.*, ouvertement ; ostensiblement ; de profession ; par son propre aveu.

profes'sion (-fèsh'-), *n.*, profession ; déclaration ; (calling) profession, *f.*, état, métier, *m.* ; (ecc.) profession, *f.* Military —; *métier des armes, m.* By —; *de profession.*

profes'sional (-fèsh'-), *adj.*, de sa profession ; de la profession ; du métier ; qui a rapport à une profession ; professionnel. — man ; *homme de profession libérale ; homme de l'art, m.*

profes'sional, *n.*, homme du métier, homme de l'art ; (at games, etc.) professeur, *m.*

profes'sionally (-fèsh'-), *adv.*, de profession ; (by calling) par profession, par état ; dans l'exercice de sa profession.

profes'sor, *n.*, personne qui professe, *f.* ; (teacher) professeur, *m.*

professor'ial, *adj.*, de professeur, professoral.

profes'sorship, *n.*, professorat, *m.* ; chaire de professeur, place de professeur, *f.*

prof'fer, *n.*, offre ; proposition ; (essay) tentative, épreuve, *f.*, essai, *m.*

prof'fer, *v.a.*, offrir, proposer, faire offre **de**.

prof'ferer, *n.*, personne qui offre, *f.*

profi'ciency (-fish'-), *n.*, progrès, *m.* ; talents, *m.pl.* ; force, *f.* To have attained great—; *avoir fait de grands progrès.*

profi'cient, *adj.*, fort **en**, avancé **en**, expert **dans, en** ; à (*before an infinitive*) ; habile **dans**, versé **dans**. In —; *entendre bien* (*le, la, les*). Practice makes —; *la pratique rend habile.*

pro'file (prô-faïle), *n.*, profil, *m.* In —; **en, de,** *profil.*

pro'file (prô-faïle), *v.a.*, profiler.

pro'file, *v.n.*, se profiler.

prof'it, *n.*, profit ; (advantage) avantage, *m.*, utilité, *f.* ; (com.) bénéfice, profit, rapport, *m.* On half —s ; *de compte à demi ; de moitié dans les bénéfices.* Gross —; *bénéfice brut.* Net —; *bénéfice net.* To make a — by ; *faire son profit* **de** ; (com.) *bénéficier* **sur**. — and loss ; (com.) *profits et pertes, m.pl.*

prof'it, *v.n.*, profiter à ; faire du bien à ; (to improve) améliorer, perfectionner. To be —ed by ; *gagner* à ; *profiter* **de**. It might — me to ; *il pourrait m'être utile* **de**.

prof'it, *v.n.*, (to improve) faire des progrès **dans** ; (to be of use) être utile à, servir à. To — by ; *profiter* **de** ; *profiter* à ; *tirer du profit* **de**. Things that — not ; *des choses qui ne servent à rien.* What will it — me to ? *à quoi me servira* **de** ? To — by reading ; *gagner* à *lire.*

prof'itable (-a-b'l), *adj.*, profitable, utile ; avantageux ; (lucrative) lucratif.

prof'itableness, *n.*, avantage ; profit, *m.* ; utilité ; nature profitable ; nature lucrative, *f.*

prof'itably, *adv.*, avantageusement, utilement ; avec profit.

prof'itless, *adj.*, sans profit ; sans avantage.

prof'ligacy, *n.*, dérèglement, abandonnement, *m.* ; licence, débauche, dissolution ; atrocité, scélératesse, *f.*

prof'ligate, *adj.*, abandonné au vice ; sans mœurs ; scélérat ; déréglé, débauché, dissolu ; atroce, vicieux.

prof'ligate, *n.*, scélérat, abandonné, *m.*, abandonnée, *f.* ; mauvais sujet, libertin, *m.*

prof'ligately (-ghét'-), *adv.*, sans mœurs ;

dans la licence ; sans honte ; sans principes ; dissolument.

pro for'ma, pour la forme ; (com.) simulé.

profound' (-faou'n'de), *adj.*, profond. In most — earnest ; *très sérieusement ; on ne peut plus sérieusement.*

profound'ly, *adv.*, profondément. — learned ; *profondément instruit.*

profound'ness *ou* **profund'ity** (-feu'n'-), *n.*, profondeur, *f.* — of learning ; *profondeur du savoir.*

profuse' (-fiouce), *adj.*, prodigue ; (of things) extravagant, abondant, excessif.

profuse'ly (-fious'-), *adv.*, profusément ; avec profusion ; avec prodigalité ; abondamment.

profuse'ness (-fious'-), *n.*, profusion ; prodigalité, abondance, *f.*

profu'sion (-fiou-jeune), *n.*, profusion ; prodigalité, abondance, *f.*

prog, *v.n.*, (ant.) rôder çà et là à la recherche de vivres ; gueuser, voler, piller.

prog, *n.*, vivres mendiés ; vivres, *m.pl.* ; (pers.) mendiant, *m.*, mendiante, *f.*

progen'itor (-dje'n'i-teur), *n.*, aïeul, ancêtre, premier père ; (jur.) ascendant, *m.*

prog'eny (prodj'i-), *n.*, race, lignée, postérité, famille, *f.* ; descendants, *m.pl.*

prognos'tic (prog-nos-), *adj.*, (med.) pronostique.

prognos'tic, *n.*, pronostic ; (med.) pronostic, *m.*

prognos'ticable (-ca-b'l), *adj.*, que l'on peut pronostiquer.

prognos'ticate (prog-), *v.a.*, pronostiquer ; présager, prédire.

prognostica'tion (-ti-ké-), *n.*, présage ; pronostic, *m.*

prognos'ticator (-ti-ké-teur), *n.*, (fam.) pronostiqueur, *m.*

pro'gramme (prô-), *n.*, programme, *m.*

prog'ress (prô-), *n.*, progrès ; cours, *m.* ; course, marche, *f.* ; (state journey) voyage, *m.* ; (of a judge) tournée, *f.* ; (advance in knowledge) progrès, *m.pl.* To report —; (in parliament) *faire un rapport à la chambre du travail du comité ; ajourner la discussion* (*d'un projet de loi*) ; (generally) *faire son rapport.* To make —; (in knowledge) *faire des progrès.*

progress', *v.n.*, s'avancer ; continuer son cours, *ou* son chemin ; s'étendre progressivement ; progresser ; (in knowledge) faire des progrès, avancer. The business is —ing ; *l'affaire est en train ; l'affaire marche.* How is your work —ing ? *où en êtes-vous de votre travail ?*

progres'sion (-grèsh'-), *n.*, progression, *f.* ; cours, progrès, voyage, *m.* ; (math.) progression, *f.*

progres'sionist (-grèsh'-), **progres'sive**, *n.*, progressiste, *m.*

progres'sive, *adj.*, progressif.

progres'sively, *adv.*, progressivement.

progres'siveness, *n.*, marche progressive, *f.*

prohib'it, *v.a.*, défendre à ; interdire à ; défendre ; (jur.) prohiber.

prohib'iter, *n.*, qui défend, *ou* interdit, à.

prohibi'tion (-bish'-), *n.*, prohibition ; défense, interdiction ; (jur.) défense de statuer, prohibition, *f.* Writ of —; *défense de statuer.*

prohib'itive *ou* **prohib'itory**, *adj.*, (customs) prohibitif ; (general) de défense, d'interdiction ; qui défend, qui interdit.

proj'ect (prodj'è'te), *n.*, projet, dessein, *m.*

project' (-djèk'te), *v.a.*, projeter.

project', *v.n.*, se projeter ; avancer ; saillir ; faire saillie ; être en saillie ; (arch.) ressauter.

projec'tile, *n.*, projectile, *m.*

project'ing, *adj.*, saillant, en saillie.

projec'tion (-djèk'-), *n.*, projection ; saillie, *f.* ; (arch.) ressaut, *m.*

project'or (-djèkt'eur), *n.*, homme à projets ; rêveur ; projeteur, *m.*

projec'ture (-djèkt'ieur), *n.*, (arch.) projecture, *f.*

prolap'sus, *n.*, (surg.) prolapsus ; renversement, *m. ;* (med.) chute, procidence, *f.*

pro'late, *adj.*, (geom.) allongé.

prolegom'ena, *n.pl.*, prolégomènes, *m.pl.*

proleta'rian *ou* **pro'letary**, *adj.* and *n.*, prolétaire, *m.*

proleta'riat, *n.*, prolétariat, *m.*

prolif'ic, *adj.*, fécond ; fertile ; prolifique.

prolif'ically, *adv.*, (ant.) avec fécondité, avec fertilité.

prolif'icness, *n.*, (ant.) fécondité, fertilité, *f.*

prolix' (pro-), *adj.*, prolixe.

prolix'ity *ou* **prolix'ness**, *n.*, prolixité, *f.*

prolix'ly, *adv.*, avec prolixité ; prolixement.

proloc'utor (-lok'iou-teur), *n.*, (Engl. Church) président (d'une assemblée du clergé), *m.*

proloc'utorship, *n.*, (Engl. Church) présidence (d'une assemblée du clergé), *f.*

pro'logue (prol'oghe), *n.*, prologue, *m.*

prolong' (-lo'gne), *v.a.*, prolonger ; (to delay) retarder, différer. To be —ed ; *se prolonger ; être prolongé ; traîner en longueur.*

prolonga'tion (prô-lo'gn'ghé-), *n.*, (geom., anat., bot.) prolongement, *m. ;* (of time, mus.) prolongation, *f.*

prolong'er (-lo'gn'eur), *n.*, personne qui prolonge, chose qui prolonge, *f.*

promenade' (-nâde *ou* -néde), *n.*, promenade ; (place) promenade, *f.*

promenade', *v.n.*, se promener.

promenad'er, *n.*, promeneur, *m.*

Prome'thean (-mî-thi-), *adj.*, de Prométhée.

prom'inence *ou* **prom'inency**, *n.*, proéminence ; saillie ; (fig.) distinction ; (astron.) protubérance, *f.*

prom'inent, *adj.*, proéminent, saillant, qui fait saillie ; (pronounced) (eminent) éminent, marquant, distingué ; (principal) principal ; (conspicuous) marquant, remarquable ; (paint.) prononcé. — **features**: *traits prononcés, traits saillants, m.pl.* — **eyes** ; *yeux à fleur de tête, m.pl.* In a — position ; (of pers.) *en évidence, en vue.*

prom'inently, *adv.*, d'une manière proéminente ; en saillie ; d'une manière distinguée ; d'une manière frappante ; d'une manière marquée ; d'une manière prononcée ; (conspicuously) en évidence, en vue.

promis'cuous (-kiou-), *adj.*, mêlé ; en commun ; général ; confus, sans ordre, sans méthode.

promis'cuously, *adv.*, généralement, en général ; en commun ; confusément, pêle-mêle, indistinctement.

promis'cuousness, *n.*, mélange confus ; caractère général, *m. ;* promiscuité, confusion, *f.*

prom'ise (-ice), *n.*, promesse, *f. ;* (hope) espérances, *f.pl. ;* avenir, *m. ;* (biblically) promission, *f.*, espérances, *f.pl.* To make a —; *faire une promesse.* Of great — ; *de beaucoup d'avenir ; qui donne de grandes espérances.* To break one's —; *manquer à sa promesse.* To keep one's —; *tenir promesse, tenir sa promesse.* The Land of —; *la Terre de promission, la Terre promise, f.* Breach of —; *violation de promesse, f.* To pay any one with —s; *payer (quelqu'un) en monnaie de singe.*

prom'ise, *v.a.* and *n.*, promettre. I — you ! *je vous le promets !*

prom'ise-break'er (-brèk'-), *n.*, qui viole sa promesse, *f.*

prom'ised (-miste), *adj.*, promis ; (biblically) promis, de promission.

prom'iser, *n.*, prometteur, *m.*, grand faiseur de promesses, *n.*

prom'ising (-miss'-), *adj.*, qui promet ; qui donne des espérances ; plein d'avenir, plein de moyens.

prom'isor (-miss'eur *ou* -or), *n.*, (jur.) promettant, *m.*

prom'issorily, *adv.*, par manière, *ou* forme, de promesse.

prom'issory, *adj.*, qui contient une promesse. — note; *billet à ordre, m.*, obligation, *f.*

prom'ontory, *n.*, promontoire, *m.*

promote' (-môte), *v.a.*, favoriser, encourager, servir, protéger ; avancer ; donner de l'avancement à ; élever ; promouvoir (only used in infin. and compound tenses) ; (to excite) provoquer ; (an action) provoquer ; (a company) former (une société en commandite). To be —d ; *obtenir de l'avancement.* He was —d to the rank of general ; *il fut promu au grade de général.* To — any one's interests ; *avancer les intérêts de quelqu'un.*

promot'er (-môt'-), *n.*, personne qui favorise, qui encourage, *f. ;* protecteur, *m.*, protectrice, *f. ;* promoteur, *m.*, promotrice, *f. ;* lanceur d'affaires, *m.*

promo'tion (-mô-), *n.*, promotion, *f. ;* avancement, *m. ;* protection ; élévation, *f.*, encouragement, *m.*

prompt (pro'm'te), *v.a.*, exciter, porter, pousser à ; dicter, inspirer ; suggérer ; (thea.) souffler.

prompt (pro'm'te), *adj.*, prompt, empressé ; (com.) comptant.

prompt'-book (-bouke), *n.*, (thea.) livre du souffleur, *m.*

prompt'er, *n.*, (thea.) souffleur, *m.*

promp'titude (pro'm'ti-tioude), *n.*, promptitude, *f. ;* empressement, *m.*

prompt'ly (pro'm't'-), *adv.*, promptement ; avec empressement.

prompt'ness (pro'm't'-), *n.*, promptitude, *f. ;* empressement, *m.*

promul'gate (pro-meul-), *v.a.*, promulguer ; publier ; divulguer.

promulga'tion (-ghé-), *n.*, promulgation ; publication ; divulgation, *f.*

prom'ulgator (-ghét'eur), *n.*, qui promulgue, qui publie ; promulgateur, *m.*

prone (prône), *adj.*, (not erect) courbé, penché, incliné ; (declivous) incliné, penché, en pente ; (disposed) disposé, enclin, porté à ; (lying with the face downward) couché le visage contre terre, couché.

prone'ness, *n.*, position courbée, penchée, inclinée ; (declivity) inclinaison, pente ; (disposition) disposition, inclination, *f.*, penchant, *m. ;* (bending) position renversée, *f.*

prong (pro'gne), *n.*, (fork) fourche, *f. ;* (of a fork) fourchon ; (of a dinner-fork) fourchon, *m.*, dent, *f.*

pronged (pro'gn'de), *adj.*, à fourchons, à dents.

pronom'inal, *adj.*, pronominal.

pronom'inally, *adv.*, pronominalement.

pro'noun (prô-naou'n), *n.*, pronom, *m.*

pronounce' (-naou'n'ce), *v.a.*, prononcer ; déclarer, annoncer, dire.

pronounce', *v.n.*, prononcer ; se prononcer pour.

pronoun'cable (-'a-b'l), *adj.*, prononçable.

pronoun'cer, *n.*, prononceur, *m.*

pronoun'cing, *adj.*, de prononciation, qui donne la prononciation. *n.*, prononciation, *f.*

pronuncia'tion (-neu'n'shi-é-), *n.*, prononciation, *f. ;* (rhet.) débit, *m.*

pronun'ciative (-shi-é-), *adj.*, dogmatique.

proof (proufe), *n.*, preuve, *f. ;* (trial) essai, *m.*, épreuve ; (alg., arith.) preuve ; (of spirit) preuve ; (print.) épreuve ; (in bankruptcy) affirmation de créances, *f.* — against ; *à l'épreuve de.* Water— ; *imperméable à l'eau ; imperméable.* In — of ; *pour preuve de.* To come to the — ; *en venir à la preuve.* Above — ; *au-dessus de preuve.* Below — ; *au-dessous de preuve.* In — of, *ou* as a — of ; *en, ou pour, preuve de.*

proof'less, *adj.*, sans preuve.

proof'-puller (-poul'-), *n.*, (print.) tireur d'épreuves, *m.*

proof'-sample (proof-sa'm'p'l), *n.*, (com.) preuve, *f.*

proof'-sheet, *n.*, (print.) épreuve, *f.*

prop, *n.*, appui, soutien, étai, support; (carp.) étai, étançon; (hort.) tuteur, échalas; (nav.) accore; (fig.) appui, soutien, *m.*

prop, *v.a.*, appuyer, soutenir, étayer; (carp.) étayer, étançonner; (nav.) accorer; (hort.) échalasser. To — up against; *adosser*. To — one's self up against; *s'adosser* à, ou **contre**. To be —ped up against; *être adossé* à.

prop'agable (-ga-b'l), *adj.*, susceptible de propagation.

propagan'da, *n.*, propagande, *f.*

propagan'dism (-diz'me), *n.*, système de propagande, *m.*

propagan'dist, *n.*, membre de la propagande, *m.*

prop'agate, *v.a.*, propager; accroître; (to spread) étendre, répandre, porter au loin; (news, etc.) répandre; (to produce) produire, créer, enfanter.

prop'agate, *v.n.*, se propager.

propaga'tion (-pa-ghé-), *n.*, propagation, *f.*

prop'agator (pro-pa-ghét'eur), *n.*, propagateur, *m.*

propel', *v.a.*, pousser en avant, mouvoir; faire marcher; faire avancer; mettre en mouvement; (to cast) lancer.

propel'ler, *n.*, propulseur, moteur, *m.* Screw —; *hélice propulsive, propulseur à hélice, m.*

propel'ling, *adj.*, propulseur, moteur. — power; *force motrice, f.*

propense' (-pè'n'sé), *adj.*, enclin, porté, disposé à.

propen'sity ou **propen'sion**, *n.*, penchant, *m.*; propension, tendance, inclination, *f.*; goût, *m.*

prop'er, *adj.*, (peculiar) propre, particulier; (natural) propre, naturel; (one's own) propre, à soi; (fit) propre, convenable, à propos; (correct) propre, juste, exact; (not figurative) propre; (handsome) beau. — name; *nom propre, m.* — sense; *sens propre, m.* The — way to do it, is to; *le vrai moyen de s'y prendre, c'est de.* To deem it — to; *juger convenable de ; juger à propos de.* It is — to; *il est bien de ; il convient de.*

prop'erly, *adv.*, proprement; particulièrement, justement; naturellement; exactement; convenablement; bien; comme il faut; (by rights) pour bien faire, à la rigueur. — speaking; *à proprement parler ; proprement parlant.* — so called; *proprement dit.* More — speaking; *pour mieux dire.* He acted —; *il a bien agi, il a agi comme il faut.*

prop'erty, *n.*, (ownership) propriété; (thing owned) propriété, *f.*, bien, *m.*, biens, *m.pl.*; (quality) propriété, qualité, vertu, *f.*; (characteristic) propre; (disposition) caractère; (thea.) accessoire, *m.* Funded —; *biens en rentes, ou en consolidés.* Landed —; *biens fonciers; bien-fonds.* Real —; *biens immeubles.* Personal —; *biens mobiliers, biens meubles.* Literary —; *propriété littéraire.* Man of —; *homme qui a du bien, de la fortune, qui a des biens au soleil ; propriétaire, m.* —qualification; *cens électoral, m.* To become public —; (of books, etc.) *tomber dans le domaine public.* These books are my —; *ces livres m'appartiennent.*

prop'erty-man, *n.*, fournisseur de théâtre, *m.*

prop'erty-tax, *n.*, impôt sur les propriétés, impôt foncier, *m.*

proph'ecy (prof'i-ci), *n.*, prophétie, prédiction, *f.*

proph'esier (-i-caï-eur), *n.*, prophète, *m.*

proph'esy (prof'i-çaïe), *v.a.*, prophétiser, prédire.

proph'esy, *v.n.*, prononcer des prophéties.

proph'esying (-i-caï-igne), *n.*, prophétie, *f.*

proph'et, *n.*, prophète, *m.* — of evil; *prophète de malheur.*

proph'etess, *n.*, prophétesse, *f.*

prophet'ic ou **prophet'ical**, *adj.*, prophétique.

prophylac'tic, *adj.n.*, prophylactique, *n.m.*

propin'quity (-pi'gn'kwi-), *n.*, proximité; (of persons) parenté, *f.*

propi'tiable (-pish'i-a-b'l), *adj.*, que l'on peut rendre propice.

propi'tiate (pro-pish'i-), *v.a.*, propitier, rendre propice, rendre favorable; apaiser.

propitia'tion (-pish'i-é-), *n.*, propitiation, *f.*

propi'tiator (-pish'i-é-teur), *n.*, propitiateur, *m.*

propi'tiatory, *adj.*, propitiatoire.

propi'tiatory, *n.*, (mercy-seat) propitiatoire, *m.*

propi'tious (-pish'eusse), *adj.*, propice, favorable.

propi'tiously, *adv.*, favorablement, d'une manière propice.

propi'tiousness, *n.*, bonté, disposition favorable; (of things) nature favorable, nature propice, *f.*

propor'tion, *n.*, proportion, partie, quantité, *f.*; rapport, *m.*; (arith., math.) proportion; (geom.) raison, *f.* In — to; *en proportion* **de**, *proportionné* à. In — as; *à mesure que, à proportion que.*

propor'tion (-pôr-), *v.a.*, proportionner.

propor'tionable (-a-b'l), *adj.*, qui peut être proportionné; à proportion; proportionné; en proportion.

propor'tionably, *adv.*, proportionnément, à proportion, en proportion.

propor'tional, *adj.*, en proportion; proportionnel.

proportional'ity, *n.*, proportionnalité, *f.*

propor'tionally, *adv.*, proportionnellement.

propor'tionate, *v.a.*, proportionner.

propor'tionate, *adj.*, proportionné.

propor'tionately, *adv.*, en, ou à, proportion; proportionnellement.

propor'tionateness, *n.*, proportion; (math.) proportionnalité, *f.*

propor'tionless, *adj.*, (ant.) sans proportion.

propos'able, *adj.*, proposable, que l'on peut avancer.

propo'sal (-pô-zal), *n.*, proposition, offre, *f.*

propose' (-pôze), *v.a.*, proposer; offrir, présenter. To — a toast; *porter un toste* ou *toast; porter la santé* **de**, *boire à la santé* **de**.

propose', *v.n.*, se proposer. He —d to her; *il lui offrit sa main ; il la demanda en mariage.* To — (to one's self) to; *se proposer* **de**.

propos'er, *n.*, proposant, auteur d'une proposition, *m.*

proposi'tion (-pô-zish'-), *n.*, proposition, *f.*

proposi'tional, *adj.*, de proposition.

propound' (-paou'n'de), *v.a.*, proposer, exposer; mettre en avant; avancer; soumettre; (a legal document) produire; (a will) soumettre à la vérification; livrer à l'examen.

propound'er, *n.*, personne qui propose, qui expose, qui met en avant, *f.*; (of a will) vérificateur, *m.*

prop'ping, *n.*, appui, soutien; (carp.) étayement; (hort.) échalassement, *m.*

propræ'tor (-prî-teur), *n.*, propréteur, *m.*

propri'etary (-praï-è-), *n.*, actionnaires, *m.pl.*

propri'etary, *adj.*, de propriété; de propriétaire, par actions.

propri'etor (-praï-è-teur), *n.*, propriétaire, maître, *m.*

propri'etress, *n.*, propriétaire, maîtresse, *f.*

propri'ety (-praï-è-), *n.*, convenance, *f.*, convenances, *f.pl.*; bienséance, décence, *f.*; bienséances, *f.pl.*; (gram.) propriété, *f.* To keep within the bounds of —; *garder les convenances, les bienséances.*

propul'sion (-peul-), *n.*, propulsion, *f.*

propul'sive (-peul-), *adj.*, (mec.) propulseur.

prop'-wood (-woude), *n.*, (mines) étai vertical, *m.*

pro ra'ta, à proportion ; au prorata **de**.

proroga'tion (prô-ro-ghé-), *n.*, prorogation, *f.*

prorogue' (-rôghe), *v.a.*, proroger.

prosa'ic (-zéïke), *adj.*, prosaïque.

prosa'icism (-zéï-ciz'm) *ou* **prosa'ism** (-zéïz'm), *n.*, prosaïsme, *m.*

prosa'ist (-zéïste), *n.*, prosateur, *m.*

prosce'nium (-cî-), *n.*, proscenium, *m.*, avant-scène, scène, *f.*

proscribe' (-scraïbe), *v.a.*, proscrire.

proscrib'er (-), *n.*, proscripteur, *m.*

proscrip'tion, *n.*, proscription, *f.*

proscrip'tive, *adj.*, de proscription.

prose (prôze), *n.*, prose, *f.* — -writer ; *prosateur, m.*

prose (prôze), *v.a.n.*, proser, écrire en prose ; raconter ennuyeusement.

pros'ecutable, *adj.*, poursuivable.

pros'ecute (pross'i-kioute), *v.a.*, poursuivre, continuer ; persévérer **dans** ; (jur.) poursuivre, diriger des poursuites **contre**, intenter un procès **à**, poursuivre en justice ; (claims) revendiquer. We intend to — our claims; *nous avons l'intention de revendiquer nos droits.*

prosecu'tion (-kiou-), *n.*, poursuite ; continuation ; (jur.) poursuite, *f.*, poursuites, *f.pl.* ; accusation, *f.* Witness for the —; *témoin à charge, m.*

pros'ecutor (-kiout'eur), *n.*, personne qui poursuit, qui continue, *f.* ; (jur.) poursuivant, plaignant, *m.* Public —; (France) *ministère public, m.* ; (the crown) *partie publique, f.* ; *procureur de la république, m.*

pros'ecutrix, *n.*, poursuivante, plaignante, *f.*

pros'elyte (pross'i-laïte), *n.*, prosélyte, *m.f.*

pros'elytism (pross'i-laï-tiz'm), *n.*, prosélytisme, *m.* (very often used disparagingly).

pros'elytize, *v.a.n.*, convertir, faire des prosélytes.

pros'er (prôz'-), *n.*, (b.s.) conteur ennuyeux, conteur fastidieux, *m.*

pro'sily, *adv.*, prosaïquement, ennuyeusement, *m.*

pro'siness, *n.*, prosaïsme, verbosité, *f.* ; terre à terre, *m.*

prosod'ical (-çod'-), *adj.*, prosodique.

pros'odist (pross'o-), *n.*, personne versée dans la prosodie, *f.*

pros'ody (pross'o-), *n.*, prosodie, *f.*

prosopopœ'ia (pross'o-po-pî-ya), *n.*, prosopopée, *f.*

pros'pect, *n.*, vue, perspective, *f.* ; point de vue, coup d'œil, *m.* ; (expectation) espoir, *m.*, espérance, perspective, *f.*, avenir, *m.* To have fine —s before one; *avoir devant soi un bel avenir.*

prospec'tive, *adj.*, en perspective ; (of glasses) d'approche ; (of extensive prospect) d'une vue étendue ; (viewing at a distance) de longue vue. — glass; *lunette d'approche, f.*

prospec'tively, *adv.*, en perspective ; pour l'avenir.

prospec'tor, *n.*, explorateur ; (of gold) orpailleur, *m.*

prospec'tus (-spèk-), *n.*, prospectus, *m.*

pros'per, *v.a.*, faire prospérer ; faire réussir ; favoriser.

pros'per, *v.n.*, prospérer, être florissant, réussir.

prosper'ity (-pèr'-), *n.*, prospérité, *f.*

pros'perous (-peur-), *adj.*, prospère ; (of things) florissant ; heureux ; favorable.

pros'perously, *adv.*, avec prospérité ; heureusement ; avec bonheur.

pros'perousness, *n.*, prospérité, *f.*

pros'tate, *adj.*, (anat.) prostatique. — gland; *prostate, f.*

pros'thesis (-thi-cice), *n.*, (gram.) prosthèse, (surg.) prothèse, *f.*

pros'titute (-ti-tioute), *n.*, prostituée, *f.*

pros'titute, *v.a.*, prostituer.

pros'titute, *adj.*, prostitué, prostituée.

prostitu'tion (-ti-tiou-), *n.*, prostitution, *f.*

pros'titutor, *n.*, prostituteur, qui prostitue, *f.*

pros'trate, *v.a.*, (to lay flat) coucher ; (to throw down) abattre, renverser ; (to overthrow) détruire, ruiner, perdre ; (to reduce) réduire entièrement, jeter dans l'abattement, dans l'anéantissement, anéantir. To — one's self before ; *se prosterner devant.*

pros'trate, *adj.*, prosterné, couché ; (fig.) abattu. To be utterly —; *être dans l'anéantissement ; être abattu ; être épuisé de fatigue.* To lie —; *être prosterné, couché.*

prostra'tion (-tré-), *n.*, (throwing down) renversement, *m.* ; (bowing) prosternation, *f.* ; prosternement ; (dejection) abattement, anéantissement, *m.* ; (med.) prostration, *f.*

pro'style (prô-staïle), *n.*, prostyle, *m.*

pro'sy (prô-zi), *adj.*, lourd, ennuyeux, assommant, terre à terre, verbeux.

protag'onist, *n.*, protagoniste, *m.*

Pro'tean (prô-ti-), *adj.*, de Protée.

protect' (-tèkte), *v.a.*, protéger (from) **contre** ; défendre (with) **de**, garantir **de**, abriter ; (interests) sauvegarder.

protec'tion (-tèk-), *n.*, protection ; défense, garantie, *f.*, abri, *m.*, (safeguard) sauvegarde, *f.*, passeport, sauf-conduit ; (exemption) privilège contre les arrestations, *m.*

protec'tionism, *n.*, (polit. econ.) protectionnisme, *m.*

protec'tionist, *n.*, (polit. econ.) protectionniste, *m.*

protec'tive, *adj.*, protecteur.

protec'tor (-teur), *n.*, protecteur, *m.*, gardien, (jur.) tuteur, curateur d'un bien substitué, *m.*, (c.rel.) protecteur, *m.*

protec'torate *ou* **protec'torship**, *n.*, protectorat, *m.*

protec'tress, *n.*, protectrice, gardienne, *f.*

pro'test (prô-), *n.*, protestation, *f.* ; (com.) (of billet) protêt ; (of a skipper) rapport énonçant les avaries, *m.* Under — ; (com.) *protesté.* — for non-payment ; *protêt faute de paiement.*

protest' (pro-), *v.a.*, protester ; attester ; (ant.) prendre à témoin ; (com.) protester, faire protester.

protest', *v.n.*, protester **contre** ; (jur.) protester **de**.

Prot'estant, *n.*, protestant, *m.*, protestante, *f.*

Prot'estantism, *n.*, protestantisme, *m.*

protesta'tion (prot'ès-té-sheune), *n.*, protestation, *f.*

protest'er, *n.*, protestateur, *f.* ; (com.) créancier qui fait faire un protêt, *m.*

pro'tocol (prô-), *n.*, protocole, *m.*

pro'tomartyr (prô-to-mâr-teur), *n.*, (ecc. hist.) premier martyr, *m.*

pro'totype (prô-to-taïpe), *n.*, prototype, *m.*

protox'ide, *n.*, (chem.) protoxyde, *m.*

protract', *v.a.*, prolonger ; faire durer ; traîner en longueur ; (to defer) ajourner, différer.

protrac'tion, *n.*, prolongation, *f.*

protrac'tive, *adj.*, qui prolonge, qui diffère.

protrac'tor, *n.*, (instrument) rapporteur, *m.*

protrude' (-trioude), *v.a.*, pousser en avant, pousser dehors, chasser.

protrude', *v.n.*, s'avancer, se projeter, sortir, faire saillie.

protru'sion (-triou-jeune), *n.*, action de pousser en avant ; saillie, *f.*

protru'sive (-triou-cive), *adj.*, qui pousse en avant, qui pousse dehors.

protu'berance (-tiou-beur-), *n.*, saillie, éminence, proéminence ; protubérance, bosse ; (knoll) éminence, hauteur ; (anat., astron.) protubérance, *f.*

protu'berant, adj., en saillie, saillant, proéminent, protubérant ; (of swellings) enflé.

protu'berate, v.n., s'enfler ; faire saillie, être en saillie ; ressortir, s'avancer.

proud (pra-oude), adj., fier ; (arrogant) hautain, orgueilleux, superbe, arrogant ; (fam.) rogue ; (magnificent) beau, magnifique, superbe ; (grand) noble, beau, grand ; (animal) en chaleur ; (med.) fongueux, baveux. To be — of ; *être fier de, s'enorgueillir de.* — flesh; *bourgeons charnus, m.pl., chair baveuse, f., ulcère fongueux, m.* As — as a peacock ; *fier comme Artaban.*

proud'ly, adv., fièrement, orgueilleusement, d'un air rogue.

prov'able (prouv'a-b'l), adj., qui peut se prouver, prouvable.

prove, v.a., (to try, to experience) mettre à l'épreuve, éprouver ; faire l'épreuve **de** ; (to establish, to confirm) prouver, démontrer ; (arith.) faire la preuve **de** ; (a debt) produire des titres **de,** affirmer (une créance) ; (a will) vérifier, légaliser. To — one's self, itself ; *se montrer.* To — a sum ; (arith.) *vérifier un calcul.*

prove, v.n., (to be found to be) se montrer, se trouver, se trouver être ; (of things) se trouver, se trouver être ; (to be) être ; devenir ; être démontré par l'expérience. The change of king —d no remedy ; *le changement de roi ne fut nullement un remède.* As it —d ; *comme l'expérience le démontra.*

proved, adj., prouvé, démontré, reconnu ; (of pers.) expérimenté. Of — capacity ; *d'une habileté reconnue.*

prov'en (prouv'n), adj., prouvé, démontré.

Provençal', adj., provençal ; de Provence. — rose, Provence rose ; *rose de Provence, f.*

prov'ender, n., fourrage, m. ; nourriture (for animals), f.

prov'erb (prov'eurbe), n., proverbe, m.

prover'bial (-veur-), adj., proverbial, qui fait proverbe.

prover'bially, adj., proverbialement.

provide' (-vaïde), v.a., pourvoir **de,** fournir ; (to foresee) préparer, prévoir ; stipuler. To — one's self with ; *se pourvoir de, se procurer.* To be —d for ; *être pourvu ; avoir son avenir assuré.* To — for ; *pourvoir, nourrir, pourvoir aux besoins de, à l'entretien de.*

provide', v.n., pourvoir. To — for one's self ; *se suffire.* To — against ; *se prémunir contre* ; *se pourvoir contre, prendre des mesures contre,* parer **à,** obvier **à.** To — for ; *pourvoir à.*

provid'ed, conj., pourvu que. — that ; *pourvu que* (with subj.).

prov'idence, n., prévoyance ; (theol.) Providence ; (foresight) prévoyance ; prudence ; (economy) économie, f. But this is where — steps in ; *mais voici ce qui est de la providence* (V. Hugo).

prov'ident, adj., prévoyant ; prudent, frugal ; économe. — society ; *société de secours mutuels, f.*

providen'tial (-shial), adj., providentiel, de la providence.

providen'tially, adv., d'une manière providentielle ; providentiellement.

prov'idently, adv., prudemment, avec prévoyance.

provid'er (-vaïd'-), n., pourvoyeur, fournisseur, m.

prov'ince, n., province, f. ; (business) département, ressort, domaine, m. ; occupation, affaire, compétence, f. ; devoir, m. ; fonctions, attributions, f.pl. It is not in my — ; *ce n'est pas de ma compétence, ou de mon ressort.*

provin'cial (-shal), adj., provincial ; de province.

provin'cial, n., provincial, m., provinciale, f.

provin'cialism (pro-vin'shal'iz'm), n., provincialisme, m.

prov'ing, n., vérification, épreuve, f.

provi'sion (-vij'eune), n., action de pourvoir, stipulation, précaution, mesure de prévoyance ; (stock) provision ; (jur.) disposition, f. —s, pl., vivres, comestibles, m.pl., denrées, munitions de bouche, f.pl. To lay in a — of ; *faire provision de.* To make — against, for ; *prendre des précautions contre, ou pour.* To make a — for any one ; *pourvoir aux besoins de quelqu'un ; assurer l'avenir de quelqu'un ; faire une rente à quelqu'un, faire un sort, un avenir à quelqu'un.* — dealer; *marchand de comestibles, m.* — warehouse ; *magasin de comestibles, m.*

provi'sion, v.a., approvisionner de vivres ; (milit., nav.) avitailler.

provi'sional *ou* **provi'sionary** (-vij'-), adj., provisoire ; provisionnel.

provi'sionally, adv., provisoirement, par provision ; provisionnellement.

provi'sionary, adj. V. **provisional.**

provi'sion-mer'chant (-meur-tsha'n't), n., négociant en comestibles, m.

provi'so (-vaï-zô), n., condition, clause, f. With that —, with the — that ; *pourvu que ; à condition que.*

provi'sorily, adv., provisoirement ; (jur.) conditionnellement.

provi'sory (-vaï-ço-), adj., provisoire ; conditionnel.

provoca'tion (-ké-), n., provocation, f.

provoc'ative, n., provocation, f. ; aiguillon, stimulant, m.

provoc'ative (-vô-ka-), adj., qui provoque ; provocant ; provocateur.

provoke' (-vôke), v.a., provoquer ; exciter, inciter **à** ; (to enrage) vexer, impatienter, agacer, fâcher, irriter, contrarier ; (to challenge) défier. To — laughter ; *faire rire.* To — a smile ; *faire sourire.*

provok'er, n., provocateur, m.

provok'ing, adj., provocant ; (vexing) irritant, contrariant, ennuyeux, fâcheux, agaçant.

provok'ingly, adv., d'une manière provocante, irritante, contrariante.

prov'ost (prov'oste), n., prévôt ; (of a college) proviseur, recteur, président ; (in Scotland) maire, m.

prov'ost (-vô), n., (milit.) prévôt, m. —-marshal ; (milit.) *grand prévôt.*

prov'ostship (-vô-shipe), n., prévôté, f. ; proviserat, m. ; (Scotland) mairie, f.

prow (praou), n., proue, f.

prow'ess (praou-èss), n., bravoure, valeur ; (jest) prouesse, f.

prowl (praoul), v.n., rôder. To — about ; *rôder çà et là.* To — about the wood ; *rôder dans la forêt.* To — about town ; *flâner par la ville, battre le pavé.*

prowl'er, n., rôdeur, m.

prox'imate, adj., proche, prochain ; (chem.) immédiat.

prox'imately, adv., immédiatement.

proxim'ity, n., proximité, f., voisinage, m.

prox'imo, adv., du mois prochain.

prox'y, n., (pers.) fondé de pouvoir, mandataire, délégué, m. ; (thing) procuration, délégation, f. By — ; *par procuration.*

prox'yship, n., fonctions d'un fondé de pouvoir, f.pl.

prude (proude), n., prude, f.

pru'dence (prou-), n., prudence, sagesse, f.

pru'dent, adj., prudent, sage. — marriage ; *mariage de convenance, ou de raison, m.*

pruden'tial (-shal), adj., de prudence ; dicté par la prudence.

pruden'tials (-shalze), n.pl., maximes de sagesse, f.pl.

pru'dently, adv., prudemment, sagement.

prud'ery (prou-), n., pruderie, f.

prud'ish (prou-), adj., prude ; de prude.

prud'ishly, *adv.*, en prude ; avec pruderie.
prune (proune), *n.*, pruneau, *m.* ; prune sèche, *f.*

prune, *v.a.*, (hort.) élaguer, tailler, émonder ; rogner ; (to trim) parer, arranger, ajuster.

prune, *v.n.*, (jest.) s'ajuster, s'attifer.
prunel'lo (prou-nèl-lô), *n.*, (woolen stuff ; fruit) prunelle, *f.*

prun'er (prou'n'-), *n.*, élagueur, émondeur (V. Hugo), *m.*

prunif'erous, *adj.*, qui porte des prunes.
prun'ing (prou'n'-), *n.*, (hort.) taille, *f.* ; élagage, émondage, *m.*

prun'ing-hook (-houke) ou **prun'ing-knife** (-naïfe), *n.*, serpe, serpette, *f.* ; croissant, *m.*

prun'ing-shears (-shîrze), *n.pl.*, sécateur, *m.sing.*

pru'rience ou **pru'riency** (prou-), *n.*, (med.) démangeaison, *f.* ; prurit ; (fig.) désir immodéré, violent, *m.*, démangeaison, *f.*

pru'rient (prou-), *adj.*, qui démange ; (fig.) qui brûle de désir.

prurig'inous (-ridj'-), *adj.*, (med.) prurigineux.

Prus'sian (preush'a'n), *adj.*, prussien ; de Prusse. — blue ; *bleu de Prusse, m.*

Prus'sian, *n.*, Prussien, *m.*, Prussienne, *f.*
prus'sic (preus'-), *adj.*, (chem.) prussique.

pry (praïe), *v.n.*, scruter, fureter. To — into ; *scruter ; fouiller* **dans** ; *fourrer le nez* **dans** ; *se mêler* **de** ; *épier, chercher à pénétrer.* To — about ; *fourrer le nez partout.*

pry, *n.*, regard scrutateur ; regard indiscret, *m.* Paul Pry ; *brouillon ; homme qui se mêle de tout, curieux indiscret, m.*

pry'ing (praï-igne), *adj.*, scrutateur, curieux ; indiscret.

pry'ing, *n.*, curiosité ; indiscrétion, *f.*
pry'ingly, *adv.*, curieusement ; indiscrètement.

psalm (sâme), *n.*, psaume, *m.* — -book ; *livre de psaumes ; psautier, m.* — -singing ; psalmodie, *f.*

psalm'ist (sâ'm'iste ou sal'-), *n.*, psalmiste, *m.*
psalm'ody (sâ'm-), *n.*, psalmodie, *f.*
psalm'odize, *n.*, psalmodier.
psal'ter (sôl'-), *n.*, psautier, *m.*
psal'tery (sôl'-), *n.*, (mus.) psaltérion, *m.*
pseu'do (siou-dô), *adj.*, pseudo, faux.
pseudon'ymous (siou-), *adj.*, pseudonyme.
pshaw ! (shô), *int.*, bah ! baste !
psor'a, *n.*, psore, *f.*
psor'ic, *adj.*, psorique.
psycholog'ic ou **psycholog'ical** (saï-kol-odj'-), *adj.*, psychologique.
psychol'ogist (saï-kol'odj'iste), *n.*, (philos.) psychologiste, psychologue, *m.*
psychol'ogy (saï-kol'o-dji), *n.*, (philos.) psychologie, *f.*
ptar'migan (tar-), *n.*, ptarmigan, tétras, *m.*
ptis'an (tiz'-), *n.*, tisane, *f.*
Ptolema'ic (tol'i-mé-), *adj.*, de Ptolémée, ptoléméen.
pu'berty (piou-beur-), *n.*, puberté, *f.*
pubes'cence (piou-bès'-), *n.*, puberté ; (bot.) pubescence, *f.*
pubes'cent (piou-bès-), *adj.*, pubère ; (bot.) pubescent.
pub'lic (peub'-), *adj.*, public, *m.* ; publique, *f.* — accounts ; *budget, m.* — -house ; *cabaret, m.* ; *auberge, f.* — spirit ; *esprit public, m.* — spiritedness ; *amour du bien public, m.*
pub'lic, *n.*, le public, le peuple.
pub'lican (peub'-), *n.*, (Bible) publicain ; (inn-keeper) cabaretier, aubergiste, *m.*
publica'tion (peub'li-ké-), *n.*, publication, *f.*
pub'licist (peub'-), *n.*, publiciste, *m.*
public'ity (peub'-), *n.*, publicité, *f.*
pub'licly (peub'-), *adv.*, publiquement ; en public.

pub'lic-spir'ited, *adj.*, qui s'occupe du bien général ; dévoué au bien public, dévoué aux intérêts généraux, animé de l'esprit public.
pub'lish (peub'-), *v.a.*, publier.
pub'lisher, *n.*, personne qui publie, *f.* ; éditeur ; libraire-éditeur, *m.* ; (of a newspaper) directeur, gérant, *m.*
puce (piouce) ou **puce-col'ored** (-keulleurde), *adj.*, puce.
puck (peuke), *n.*, esprit follet ; lutin, *m.*
puck'er (peuk'-), *v.a.*, rider ; (needlework) faire boire ; faire goder ; (clothes) plisser, faire grimacer.
puck'er, *v.n.*, grimacer, goder.
puck'er (peuk'-), *n.*, ride ; (in needlework) poche, *f.* ; (clothes) fronce, *f.* ; mauvais pli, *m.*
puck'ering, *n.*, froncement, froncis, *m.*, mauvais plis, *m.pl.*
pud'dening, *n.*, bourrelet, *m.*
pud'ding (poud'-), *n.*, pouding, *m.* Black-—; *boudin noir, m.*
pud'ding-pie (-païe), *n.*, pâté, *m.*
pud'ding-sleeve (-slîve), *n.*, grande manche, manche pagode, *f.*
pud'ding-stone, *n.*, (min.) poudingue, *m.*
pud'dle (peud'd'l), *n.*, flaque d'eau ; mare, *f.* ; gâchis ; (mas.) corroi, *m.*
pud'dle, *v.a.*, troubler ; rendre bourbeux ; remplir de boue ; embourber, crotter ; (metal.) puddler ; (mortar) corroyer ; (a wall) remblayer.
pud'dling, *n.*, (mas.) corroi ; (metal.) puddlage, *m.* ; (fam.) ribote, *f.*
pud'dly, *adj.*, bourbeux, trouble, boueux.
pudic'ity (piou-), *n.*, pudicité, *f.*
pu'erile (piou-eur'il), *adj.*, puéril.
pu'erilely, *adv.*, puérilement.
pueril'ity (piou-eur'il'-), *n.*, puérilité, *f.*
puer'peral (piou-eur-peur'-), *adj.*, (med.) puerpéral. — fever ; *fièvre de lait, f.*
puff (peuf), *n.*, (breath) souffle, *m.* ; (of wind, smoke) bouffée, *f.* ; (pastry) feuilletage, *m.* ; (for powdering the hair) houppe à poudrer, *f.* ; (on dresses) bouillon ; (of sleeves) bouffant ; (advertisement) pouf, *m.* ; réclame, *f.*
puff ou **puff-ball** (-bôl), *n.*, (bot.) vesse-de-loup, *f.*
puff, *v.a.*, souffler ; (to swell) bouffir, enfler ; (to praise) faire mousser, louer d'une façon excessive. To — away ; *dissiper ; chasser.* To — up ; *enfler ; bouffir.* To be —ed up with ; *être bouffi,* ou *gonflé,* **de.**
puff, *v.n.*, souffler ; (to swell) boursoufler, bouffir ; (to swell the cheeks) bouffer ; (to breathe with vehemence) haleter ; (fig.) faire des poufs, faire de la réclame ; faire l'article. To — away ; *fumer rageusement ; lancer des bouffées de tabac.*
puff'er, *n.*, personne qui souffle, *f.* ; faiseur de poufs, faiseur de réclames, *m.*
puf'fin (peuf'-), *n.*, (orni.) plongeon de mer, *m.*
puff'iness (peuf'-), *n.*, enflure, *f.* ; (med.) empâtement, *m.*
puff'ingly (peuf'-), *adv.*, en haletant ; avec enflure ; par des poufs.
puff'y (peuf'-), *adj.*, bouffi, enflé ; (style) boursouflé.
puff'-paste, *n.*, feuilletage, *m.* ; pâte feuilletée, *f.*
puff'-ic, *n.*, vol-au-vent, *m.*
pug (peughe), *n.*, (ant.) (monkey) petit singe, *m.* — -nose ; *nez épaté, nez camus, m.* — -nosed ; *camus.*
pug (peughe), *v.a.*, (mas.) hourder ; (tech.) pilonner.
pug ou **pug'-dog**, *n.*, roquet, carlin, bichon, *m.*
pug'ging (peug-ghigne), *n.*, (mas.) hourdage, hourdis, *m.* ; aire de plancher, *f.*
pug'ging-mor'tar, *n.*, bauge, *f.*
pugh ! (pou), *int.*, nargue ! fi donc !
pu'gilism (piou-djil'iz'm), *n.*, pugilat, boxe, *m.*

pu'gilist, *n.*, boxeur, pugiliste, *m.*

pugilis'tic, *adj.*, de pugilat.

pug'-mill, *n.*, (brick-making) pétrin, *m.*

pugna'cious (peug-né-sheusse), *adj.*, enclin à se battre ; querelleur ; batailleur.

pugna'ciously, *adv.*, d'un air batailleur.

pugna'ciousness, **pugna'city**, *n.*, humeur batailleuse, querelleuse ; pugnacité, *f.*

puis'ne (piou-ni), *adj.*, inférieur ; cadet. — judge ; *juge assesseur, conseiller, m.*

puke (piouke), *n.*, vomitif, émétique ; vomissement, *m. v.n.*, vomir.

pule (pioule), *v.n.*, piauler, piailler ; gémir ; (to whine) pleurnicher.

pul'ing, *n.*, cri ; piaulement ; pleurnichement, *m.*

pul'ingly, *adv.*, en piaulant ; en pleurnichant.

pull (poule), *n.*, action de tirer, *f. ;* coup de main ; (rowing) coup de rame, *m.*, coups de rame, *m.pl.;* (effort) effort, assaut, coup de main, *m.*, tâche ; (violence) secousse, *f. ;* (advantage) avantage ; (draught) coup, trait, *m. ;* (contest) lutte, *f. ;* (of bells) cordon, *m. ;* (print.) impression, *f.* A — on the water ; *une promenade sur l'eau.* Hard — ; *rude effort, m. ; rude tâche, f.*

pull (poule), *v.a.*, tirer ; (to gather) cueillir ; (to tear) déchirer ; arracher ; (print.) tirer. To — the trigger ; *presser la détente.* To — aside ; *tirer de côté.* To — asunder, apart ; *déchirer en deux.* To — away ; *arracher.* To — back ; *faire reculer ; tirer en arrière.* To — down ; *faire descendre ;* (to demolish) *démolir, abattre ;* (of illness) *amaigrir, maigrir ;* (to abase) *abaisser, rabattre.* To — off ; *arracher, enlever ; ôter ;* (one's clothes) *ôter ; retirer ;* (one's boots) *tirer, ôter.* To — in ; *tirer dedans ; rentrer.* To — in, ou to, pieces ; *mettre en pièces.* To — on (as boots, etc.) ; *mettre.* To — open ; *ouvrir.* To — out ; *tirer dehors ; tirer ; arracher ; faire sortir ; sortir ;* (hair, teeth) *arracher.* To — up ; *tirer en haut ;* (hoist) *hisser ;* (root up) *arracher ; déraciner ; extirper ;* (fig.) *stimuler, remonter ;* (before a magistrate) *traduire, citer ; gronder.* To — up; (a horse) *retenir, arrêter.* To — a long face ; *avoir le visage allongé d'une aune.* To — a match off ; *arranger un mariage ;* (a game) *enlever une partie.* To — a wry face ; *faire la grimace.* To — up stakes ; *changer de logis ; déménager.*

pull, *v.n.*, tirer ; (to row) ramer. To — through ; *réussir, en sortir, s'en tirer.* To — up ; (of horses, carriages, etc.) *arrêter ; s'arrêter ; descendre.* To — away ; (at the oars) *nager de toutes ses forces.* To — off ; (nav.) *démarrer, partir.* To — together ; *s'accorder, s'entendre.* — up,driver ! *arrêtez, cocher !*

pull'er, *n.*, tireur ; arracheur ; (rower) rameur, *m.*

pul'let (poul'-), *n.*, poulette, *f.* Fat — ; *poularde, f.*

pul'ley (poul'-), *n.*, poulie, *f.* [*m.*

pull'ing (poul'-), *n.*, tirage ; (agri.) arrachage, **Pull'man-car**, *n.*, wagon salon, *m.*

pul'lulate (peu'liou-), *v.n.*, germer ; bourgeonner ; pousser ; pulluler.

pullula'tion (peul-liou-lé-), *n.*, germination ; pullulation, *f.*

pul'monary (peul-), *adj.*, pulmonaire.

pulmon'ic (peul-), *adj.*, pulmonaire ; (pers.) phtisique, pulmonique.

pulp (peulpe), *n.*, substance molle ; (of fruit) chair, pulpe ; (marrow) moelle ; (bot.) pulpe, *f.*, parenchyme, *m. ;* (for making paper) pâte, bouillie, *f.*

pulp (peulpe), *v.a.*, enlever la chair de, enlever l'enveloppe de ; pulper, réduire en pâte ; décortiquer.

pulp'iness (peulp'-), *n.*, nature molle ; nature pulpeuse, *f.*

pul'pit (poul-), *n.*, (ecc.) chaire ; (pol.) tribune, *f.;* (for auctioneers) bureau, *m.* — oratory ; *éloquence de la chaire, f.*

pulp'ous *ou* **pul'py** (peul-), *adj.*, pulpeux, mou.

pul'sate (peul-), *v.n.*, battre ; palpiter.

pul'satile (peul-), *adj.*, (mus.) de percussion, (med.) pulsatif.

pulsa'tion (peul-sé-), *n.*, (med.) pulsation, *f.*

pul'satory (peul-sa-), *adj.*, (med.) pulsatif.

pulse (peulse), *n.*, pouls, *m. ;* (phys.) pulsation ; (bot.) plante légumineuse, *f.*, légume, *m.* High, low — ; *pouls élevé, faible.* Irregular, regular — ; *pouls déréglé, réglé.* Strong, weak — ; *pouls élevé, faible.* Quick — ; *pouls fréquent.* Wiry — ; *pouls sec.* To feel any one's — ; *tâter le pouls à quelqu'un ;* (fig.) *sonder quelqu'un sur une affaire.*

pul'verizable (peul-veur-aïz-a-b'l), *adj.*, pulvérisable.

pulveriza'tion (-veur-aïz-é-), *n.*, pulvérisation, *f.*

pul'verize (peul-veur'aïze), *v.a.*, pulvériser ; réduire en poudre.

pul'verous (peul-veur'-), *adj.*, poudreux.

pum'ice (peu-mice) *ou* **pum'ice-stone** (-stône), *n.*, ponce, pierre ponce, *f.*

pum'ice, *v.a.*, poncer.

pumi'ceous (piou-mish'eusse), *adj.*, ponceux.

pum'mel. *V.* **pom'mel.**

pump, *n.*, pompe, *f.;* (shoe) escarpin, *m.* Fire- — ; *pompe à incendie.* Stomach- — ; *pompe stomacale.* Sucking- —, suction- — ; *pompe aspirante.* Forcing- — ; *pompe foulante.* Air- — ; *machine pneumatique, f.* Chain- — ; *noria, pompe à chapelet, f.* To fetch the — ; *amorcer la pompe.*

pump, *v.a.*, pomper ; (fig.) sonder, tirer les vers du nez à. To — anything out of any one ; *tirer quelque chose de quelqu'un ; tirer à quelqu'un les vers du nez.* — ship ! (nav.) *à la pompe !*

pump, *v.n.*, pomper.

pump'-bore, *n.*, âme de pompe, *f.*

pump'-brake, *n.*, brimbale de pompe, *f.*

pump'er, *n.*, personne qui pompe, *f.*

pump'-gear (-ghîre), *n.*, garniture de pompe, *f.*

pump'-hose, *n.*, manche de pompe, *f.*

pump'kin, *n.*, citrouille, courge, *f. ;* potiron, *m.*

pump'-room, *n.*, buvette, *f.*

pump'-spear (-spîre), *n.*, tige de pompe, *f.*

pump'-water, *n.*, eau de pompe, *f.*

pump'-well, *n.*, puits à bras, *m.*

pun (peune), *n.*, calembour, jeu de mots, *m.*

pun, *v.n.*, faire des calembours ; jouer sur les mots.

punch (peu'n'she), *n.*, (instrument) emporte-pièce ; poinçon ; (buffoon) polichinelle ; (beverage) punch ; (blow) coup de poing ; (short man) courtaud ; (horse) cheval ramassé, *m. ;* (newspaper) Punch ; (in France) Charivari, *m.* — and Judy show ; *théâtre de Guignol, m.*

punch, *v.a.*, percer, perforer, poinçonner ; (to hit) donner un coup de poing à. To — out ; *enlever à l'emporte-pièce.*

punch'-bowl (-bôl), *n.*, bol à punch, *m.*

punch'eon (peu'n'she), *n.*, poinçon ; (carp.) montant, *m. ;* (of beer) pièce (litres 332·6876); (of wine) pièce (litres 318), pièce anglaise, *f.*, poinçon, *m.*

punch'er, *n.*, poinçonneur, *m. ;* (thing) emporte-pièce, poinçon, *m.*

punchinel'lo (peu'n'shi-nèl'lô), *n.*, polichinelle, *m.*

punch'ing-machine, *n.*, poinçonneuse, *f.*

punch'y, *adj.*, ramassé, trapu, courtaud.

punc'tiform (peu'gn'k-), *adj.*, en forme de pointe.

punctil'io (peu'gn'k-til'iô), *n.*, exactitude scrupuleuse ; vétille, pointillerie ; formalité, *f. ;* cérémonie, étiquette, *f.* To stand upon —s ; *être méticuleux, cérémonieux, pointilleux.*

punctil′ious (peu′gn′k-), *adj.*, d'une exactitude scrupuleuse ; pointilleux, méticuleux, qui tient aux formes, à l'étiquette.

punctil′iously, *adv.*, avec une exactitude scrupuleuse ; d'une manière pointilleuse ; minutieusement.

punctil′iousness, *n.*, exactitude scrupuleuse, pointilleuse ; pointillerie, *f.*

punc′tual (peu′gn′kt′iou-), *adj.*, ponctuel, exact. To be — to time ; *être exact à l'heure ; être à l'heure.*

punctual′ity, *n.*, ponctualité, exactitude, *f.*

punc′tually, *adv.*, ponctuellement, exactement.

punc′tuate (peu′gn′kt′iou-), *v.a.*, ponctuer.

punctua′tion (peu′gn′k-tiou-é-), *n.*, ponctuation, *f.*

punc′ture (peu′gn′kt′ieur), *n.*, piqûre ; (surg.) ponction, *f.*

punc′ture, *v.a.*, piquer ; faire une piqûre à ; faire une ponction à.

pun′dit, *n.*, pundit, *m.*

pun′gency (peu′n′djè′n′-), *n.*, nature piquante, acrimonie ; âcreté ; aigreur, *f.* ; (of sarcasm, style) piquant, mordant, *m.*

pun′gent (peu′n′djè′n′te), *adj.*, piquant, mordant ; acrimonieux ; (of sarcasm, style) âcre ; cuisant ; poignant.

Pu′nic (piou-), *adj.*, punique.

pu′niness (piou-), *n.*, petitesse ; nature chétive, *f.*

pun′ish (peu′n′-), *v.a.*, punir, châtier (for, **de**) ; corriger ; (an enemy) maltraiter.

pun′ishable (peu′n′ish-a-b′l), *adj.*, punissable ; (jur.) passible (by, **de**).

pun′ishableness, *n.*, caractère punissable, *m.*

pun′isher, *n.*, personne qui punit, *f.* ; punisseur, correcteur, *m.*

pun′ishment, *n.*, punition ; peine, *f.* ; châtiment, supplice, *m.* Capital — ; *peine de mort, peine capitale, f.*

pu′nitive, *adj.*, (ant.) pénal, punitif, *f.*

pun′net, *n.*, maniveau, *m.*

pun′ning, *n.*, calembours, jeux de mots, *m.pl.*

pun′ster (peu′n′-),*n.*, faiseur de calembours, *m.*

punt (peu′n′te), *v.a.*, (boat) conduire un bachot (à la gaffe).

punt, *v.n.*, (at play) ponter.

punt, *n.*, bateau plat, bâtiment ras, bachot, *m.* — gun ; *canardière, f.*

punt′er, *n.*, (at play) ponte, *m.*

pu′ny (piou-), *adj.*, petit ; faible ; mesquin, chétif.

pup (peupe), *v.n.*, chienner ; mettre bas.

pup, *n.*, petit chien, petit, *m.* ; petite chienne ; (pers.) (b.s.) freluquet, fat ; drôle, *m.* With —; *pleine.*

pu′pa (piou-) *ou* **pupe** (pioupe), *n.*, (*pupæ*) (ent.) nymphe ; (of butterflies) chrysalide, *f.*

pu′pil (piou-), *n.*, (scholar) élève, *m.f.* ; écolier, *m.*, écolière, *f.* ; (ward) pupille, *m.f.* ; (of the eye) pupille, prunelle, *f.* — teacher ; *maître-* ou *maîtresse-élève.*

pu′pilage (-èdje), *n.*, état d'élève, *m.* ; pupillarité, minorité, *f.*

pu′pilary (piou-), *adj.*, (of a ward, a pupil, the pupil of the eye) pupillaire.

pup′pet (peup′-), *n.*, marionnette ; poupée, *f.* ; poupard, *m.* ; *bamboche, f.*

pup′pet-man, *n.*, joueur de marionnettes, *m.*

pup′pet-show (-shô), *n.*, marionnettes, *f.pl.*

pup′py (peup′-), *n.*, petit chien, *m.*, petite chienne, *f.* ; petit ; (pers.) fat, faquin, drôle, roquet, freluquet, *m.*

pup′pyism, *n.*, fatuité, impertinence, *f.*

pur *ou* **purr** (peur), *v.n.*, (of the cat) filer son rouet ; faire ronron ; ronronner.

pur *ou* **purr,** *n.*, ronron, *m.*

pur′blind (peur-blaï′n′de), *adj.*, qui a la vue basse (*ou* courte) ; myope ; (animal) qui ne voit pas clair, presque aveugle.

pur′blindly, *adv.*, à l'aveuglette.

pur′blindness, *n.*, vue basse ; myopie, *f.*

pur′chasable (peur′tshèss′a-b′l), *adj.*, achetable, qu'on peut acheter, qui peut s'acheter.

pur′chase (peur-tchèce), *n.*, achat, *m.* ; acquisition, emplette ; (mec.) puissance, prise ; (jur.) obtention, *f.* ; (nav.) apparaux, *m.pl.* — money ; *prix d'achat, m.* — system ; (abolished in 1871 in Engl.) achat des grades (dans l'armée). To make —s ; *faire des emplettes.*

pur′chase (peur-tchèce), *v.a.*, acheter, acquérir ; faire l'achat **de** ; (to obtain) obtenir, gagner.

pur′chase-deed, *n.*, contrat d'acquisition, *m.*

pur′chase-money, *n.*, prix d'achat, *m.*

pur′chaser (peur-tchèss′-), *n.*, acquéreur ; acheteur, chaland, *m.*

pure (pioure), *adj.*, pur ; (b.s.) vrai, franc. — from ; *exempt* **de.**

pure′ly, *adv.*, purement.

pure′ness, *n.*, pureté, *f.*

purga′tion (peur-ghé-), *n.*, purgation, *f.*

pur′gative, *n.adj.*, purgatif, *m.*

purgator′ial, *adj.*, du purgatoire.

Pur′gatory (peur-), *n.*, purgatoire, *m.*

pur′gatory, *adj.*, qui purifie ; expiatoire.

purge (peurdje), *n.*, purgation, *f.* ; purgatif, *m.*

purge, *v.a.*, purger ; nettoyer, purifier ; clarifier ; épurer ; (jur.) purger.

pur′ger, *n.*, personne *ou* chose qui purge, qui épure, qui nettoie, qui purifie.

pur′ging, *n.*, diarrhée ; purgation ; (fig.) épuration, *f.*

purifica′tion (piou-ri-fi-ké-), *n.*, purification ; épuration, *f.*

pu′rificative *ou* **pu′rificatory** (piou-ri-fi-ké-), *adj.*, qui purifie.

pu′rifier (piou-ri-faï-), *n.*, personne *ou* chose qui purifie, qui épure, *f.* ; purificateur, *m.*

pu′rify (piou-ri-faïe), *v.a.*, purifier ; épurer.

pu′rify, *v.n.*, se purifier ; s'épurer.

pu′rism (piou-riz′m), *n.*, purisme, *m.*

pu′rist, *n.*, puriste, *m.*

Pu′ritan (piou-), *adj.*, puritain.

Pu′ritan, *n.*, puritain, *m.*, puritaine, *f.*

Puritan′ical, *adj.*, de puritain, puritain.

Pu′ritanism (-′iz′m), *n.*, puritanisme, *m.*

pu′rity (piou-), *n.*, pureté, *f.*

purl (peurle), *n.*, bordure en broderie ; (of lace) engrêlure ; (beverage) bière à l'absinthe, *f.* ; (of brooks) doux murmure, gazouillement, *m.*

purl, *v.a.*, orner de broderie, engrêler.

purl, *v.n.*, murmurer, gazouiller.

pur′lieu (peur-liou), *n.*, alentours, confins, *m.pl.* ; limites, *f.pl.* —s, *pl.*, pays perdus, *m.pl.*

pur′lin (peur-), *n.*, (carp.) ventrière, *f.*

purl′ing (peurl′-), *adj.*, murmurant.

purl′ing (peurl′-), *n.*, murmure, gazouillement, *m.*

purloin′ (peur-lôïne), *v.a.*, soustraire, dérober, voler, détourner.

purloin′er, *n.*, voleur, *m.*, voleuse ; personne qui soustrait, qui dérobe, *f.*

purloin′ing, *n.*, soustraction, *f.* ; vol, détournement, *m.*

pur′ple (peur-p′l), *adj.*, pourpre, de pourpre ; (med.) pourpré.

pur′ple (peur-p′l), *n.*, pourpre, *m.* ; (dye, fig.) pourpre, *f.*

pur′ple, *v.a.*, teindre en pourpre ; empourprer ; rougir.

pur′ples (peur-p′l′ze), *n.pl.*, (med.) fièvre pourprée, *f.* ; pourpre, *m.*

pur′plish, *adj.*, tirant sur le pourpre ; purpurin.

pur′port (peur-), *n.*, but, objet ; (sense) sens,

contenu, *m.*, teneur, *f.;* (import) portée, force, valeur, *f.*

pur'port, *v.a.*, tendre **à**; montrer; signifier; donner à entendre, faire voir, indiquer.

pur'port, *v.n.*, avoir pour but de; avoir la prétention de, être censé de.

pur'pose (peur-poss), *n.*, but, effet, *m.*, fin, *f.;* dessein, projet, *m.*, intention, vue, *f.;* besoin, usage, intérêt, *m.;* utilité, *f.* Or — ; exprès; à dessein. Of set — ; exprès; à propos (V. Hugo). To no — ; sans effet; inutilement; en vain; en pure perte. For the — of; dans le but de. To good — ; avantageusement, avec fruit. To little — ; à peu d'effet; en vain. To the — ; à propos. To some — ; utilement, bien. Foreign to the — ; étranger au but. To what — ? à quoi bon? à quoi sert? à quel effet? For one — only; (man.) à une main; pour un seul usage. To answer, to suit one's — ; faire son affaire; arranger quelqu'un. To answer a — ; remplir un but. To answer no — ; être inutile; ne servir de rien. To come to the — ; venir au fait. To gain one's — ; en venir à ses fins. To answer the — of; faire l'office de, servir à la fois de. That is nothing to the — ; cela ne fait rien à l'affaire; cela ne veut rien dire. For a double — ; à deux fins (V. Hugo).

pur'pose (peur-poss), *v.a.*, se proposer, avoir le dessein, avoir l'intention, avoir le projet de; se décider à.

pur'posed, *adj.*, projeté, proposé, voulu.

pur'posely, *adv.*, à dessein, exprès; de propos délibéré.

pur'pura (peur-piou-), *n.*, (ich.) pourprier; (med.) pourpre, *m.*

pur'pure (peur-piour), *n.*, (her.) pourpre, *m.*

purpu'ric (peur-piou-), *adj.*, (chem.) purpurique.

purr, *v.n.* *V.* **pur.**

purr'ing, *n.* *V.* **pur**, *n.*

purr'ing (peur'-), *adj.*, (of the cat) qui file son rouet, qui fait ronron.

purse (peurse), *n.*, bourse, *f.*, porte-monnaie, *m.* Privy — ; cassette, *f.* Long, *ou* well-lined, — ; bourse bien garnie, *f.* To hold the — strings; tenir les cordons de la bourse. To loosen the — strings; délier les cordons.

purse, *v.a.*, (fig.) plisser, froncer.

purse'-maker, *n.*, boursier, *m.*, boursière, *f.*

purse'-net, *n.*, filet en bourse, *m.*

purse'-proud (-praoude), *adj.*, fier de son argent, de ses écus.

pur'ser, *n.*, agent comptable, commissaire, *m.* —'s steward; distributeur des vivres, *m.*

pur'siness (peur-), *n.*, boursouflure, enflure; (of breath) courte haleine, *f.*

purs'lane (peurs'léne), *n.*, (bot.) pourpier, *m.*

pursu'able (peur-siou-a-b'l), *adj.*, qu'on peut poursuivre, poursuivable; (jur.) actionnable.

pursu'ance (peur-siou-), *n.*, poursuite; suite, conséquence, *f.* In — of; en conséquence de; en vertu de, conformément à. In the — of his duty; dans l'exécution de son devoir.

pursu'ant (peur-siou-), *adj.*, en conséquence de; par suite de; conforme à; aux termes de. — to; conformément à.

pursue' (peur-siou), *v.a.*, poursuivre; suivre; chercher; (fig.) persécuter.

pursu'er, *n.*, personne qui poursuit, *f.;* poursuivant, *m.*

pursuit' (peur-sioute), *n.*, poursuite; recherche; occupation, profession, *f.* —s, *pl.*, travaux, *m.pl.;* occupations, *f.pl.;* carrière, *f.*, études, *f.pl.* In — of; à la poursuite de, à la recherche de. Maritime —s; commerce maritime, *m.*

pur'suivant (peur-swi-), *n.*, poursuivant d'armes, *m.* — at arms; poursuivant d'armes.

purs'y (peur-), *adj.*, bouffi; (short-breathed) poussif.

pu'rulence *ou* **pu'rulency**, *n.*, purulence, *f.*

pu'rulent, *adj.*, purulent.

purvey' (peur-), *v.a.*, **faire provision de**; pourvoir; fournir; procurer.

purvey', *v.n.*, faire ses provisions; se pourvoir; pourvoir à.

purvey'ance (peur-vé-), *n.*, provisions, *f.pl.;* approvisionnement, *m.*

purvey'or (peur-vé-eur), *n.*, pourvoyeur, fournisseur, *m.* — to his Majesty; fournisseur de sa Majesté.

pus (peuss), *n.*, (med.) pus, *m.*

Pu'seyism, *n.*, puséisme, *m.*

Pu'seyite, *n.*, puséiste, *m.*

push (poush), *n.*, coup, *m.;* impulsion; poussée, poussade; (attack) attaque, *f.;* (critical moment) moment critique, *m.*, conjoncture, extrémité, *f.;* (ant.) effort, *m.* At a —, on a —; dans un moment critique, à l'extrémité; comme un pis aller. To be put to the — ; être mis à l'épreuve.

push (poush), *v.n.*, pousser; faire un effort; se pousser; attaquer. To — at; pousser; attaquer. To — away; pousser toujours. To — off; (nav.) pousser au large. To — on, forward; pousser en avant; s'avancer; se pousser dans le monde. To — on to; pousser jusqu'à. At one —; d'un seul coup. To have plenty of —, ou go; aller de l'avant, être fort entreprenant.

push, *v.a.n.*, pousser; (to urge) presser, importuner. To — away; repousser, éloigner. To — back; repousser; faire reculer. To — down; faire tomber, renverser. To — any one down the stairs; faire dégringoler l'escalier à quelqu'un; faire descendre l'escalier à quelqu'un. To — forward; avancer, faire avancer, pousser. To — in; faire entrer. To — off; repousser; lancer; pousser au large. To — in; faire entrer, pousser dedans. To — on; *v.a.*, pousser, faire avancer, activer, hâter, pousser en avant; *v.n.*, avancer, continuer son chemin. To — out; pousser dehors; faire sortir. To — up; faire monter, élever, pousser. To — open; ouvrir, pousser. To be —ed for money; être à court d'argent. To be —ed for an answer; être embarrassé pour répondre. To be —ed for time; être pressé.

push'er, *n.*, pousseur, *m.*

push'ing, *adj.*, qui se pousse; qui pousse; (enterprising) entreprenant.

push'ing, *n.*, poussée, poussade; impulsion, *f.;* effort, *m.;* (fig.) caractère entreprenant, *m.;* hardiesse, *f.;* (b.s.) toupet, *m.*

push'ingly, *adv.*, vigoureusement, hardiment; avec toupet.

push'pin, *n.*, (game) poussette, *f.*

pusillanim'ity (piou-cil'-), *n.*, pusillanimité, *f.*

pusillan'imous, *adj.*, pusillanime.

pusillan'imously, *adv.*, avec pusillanimité.

puss (pouss), *n.*, (cat) minon, minet, *m.*, minette, *f.;* (hare) lièvre, *m.* — in boots; le chat botté. To play at — in the corner; jouer aux quatre coins.

pus'tular *ou* **pus'tulous** (peust-'iou-), *adj.*, couvert de pustules; pustuleux.

pus'tule (peust'ioule), *n.*, pustule, *f.*

put (poute), *v.a.* (preterit and past part., Put), mettre; poser; placer; (to suppose) supposer, poser; (to offer) offrir, proposer. If I may — it so; si je puis m'exprimer ainsi. To — a restraint upon; restreindre, réprimer. To — about; faire passer, faire circuler; (fig.) gêner, troubler, embarrasser. To — again; répéter; remettre. To — aside; mettre de côté; (fig.) écarter. To — away; serrer, cacher; (to take away) ôter; (a wife) répudier. To — back; reculer; faire reculer; (to replace) replacer, remettre. To — by; mettre de côté, serrer, ranger. To — down; déposer, poser; mettre par terre; (to suppress) supprimer, réprimer; (to writedown) mettre ou coucher par écrit, inscrire; (to confound) réduire au silence, confondre. To

— down as; *considérer* comme, *qualifier* de, *traiter* de. To — forth; *mettre en avant ; étendre, tendre, avancer ;* (to display) *déployer ;* (leaves, flowers) *pousser ;* (a book) *publier, éditer, faire paraître.* To — forward; *pousser en avant ;* (of opinions) *avancer ;* (of arguments) *susciter.* To — in; *mettre* dedans; *mettre, passer ;* (to insert) *insérer.* To — off; *ôter, quitter ;* (to defer) *remettre, retarder, différer.* To — on; (to advance) *avancer ;* (to assume) *prendre ;* (to attribute to) *mettre sur le compte* de, *attribuer* à, *imputer* à; (clothes) *mettre.* To — out; *mettre dehors ; mettre à la porte ;* (to extinguish) *éteindre ;* (to confuse) *embarrasser, déranger, troubler ;* (money) *placer ;* (flowers, leaves) *pousser ;* (to display) *déployer.* To — over ; *mettre* dessus; *mettre au-dessus* de. To — to; *mettre* à; (to refer to) *s'en référer* à; (to harness) *atteler.* To — up; *mettre en haut; réduire* à; *contraindre ; mettre* à; *engager* à; (to replace) *remettre ;* (to pack) *empaqueter, emballer ;* (a prayer) *faire, offrir ;* (to lodge) *loger, caser.* To — up any one ; (at a house) *caser, loger ;* (a carriage) *remiser.* To — any one up to anything ; *donner le mot à quelqu'un ; mettre quelqu'un au courant de quelque chose, mettre quelqu'un au fait* de ; *pousser* à. To — to the sword ; *passer au fil de l'épée.* To be — to it; *être embarrassé ; avoir du fil à retordre ; avoir fort à faire.* To — together; *mettre ensemble ; rapprocher ; réunir ;* (a piece of mechanism) *assembler, monter, fixer, poser.* To — any one on his trial ; *mettre quelqu'un en jugement, en cause.* To — an affront on any one ; *faire affront à quelqu'un.* To — a question to ; *faire une question* à. To — upon the right track ; *mettre sur la voie, sur la piste.* To — one's self forward ; *se mettre en évidence, se pousser, se mettre en avant, se produire.* To — in mind of ; *rappeler* à; *faire penser* à. To be — upon ; *être trompé ; être exploité.* You have — your foot in it ; *vous avez fait de belle besogne ; vous avez pataugé en plein ; vous avez mis le pied dans le plat.* Dinner was — back an hour ; *le dîner fut retardé d'une heure.* To — by something for a rainy day ; (prov.) *garder une poire pour la soif.* To — one's shoulder to the wheel; *mettre la main à l'œuvre* ou *y mettre du sien* (Daudet). To — in force ; (a law) *faire exécuter, faire observer.* To — on a job ; (work) *faire travailler* (*à la pièce*) *; donner du travail* à. To — on steam ; *chauffer.* To — on airs ; *se donner des airs.*

put (poute), *v.n.,* (to germinate) germer, pousser; (nav.) se mettre. To — forth ; *annoncer, déclarer, publier ;* (to bud) *germer, pousser.* To — in; (nav.) *entrer au port, relâcher ;* (at play) *mettre au jeu.* To — into; (nav.) *relâcher* à, *faire escale* à. To — in for; *se mettre sur les rangs* pour, *se porter candidat* pour. To — off; *pousser au large.* To — on; *aller vite.* To — to sea; *mettre à la voile, prendre la mer.* To — up; *loger, donner un lit* à. To — up at; *descendre* à. To — up for; *se mettre sur les rangs* pour. To — up with; *souffrir, endurer, supporter, avaler, digérer ;* (to make shift with) *se contenter* de, *s'accommoder de, s'arranger* de.

put (poute), *n.,* nécessité, extrémité, *f.*

pu'tative (piou-té-), *adj.,* supposé, réputé ; (of fathers) putatif.

pu'tatively, *adv.,* censément.

put'log (peut'-), *n.,* (build.) boulin, *m.*

put'-off (pout'ôfe), *n.,* défaite, excuse, échappatoire, *f.,* faux-fuyant, *m.*

putrefac'tion (piou-tri-fak'-), *n.,* putréfaction, *f.*

putrefac'tive (piou-tri-fak-), *adj.,* de putréfaction.

pu'trefy (piou-tri-faïe), *v.a.,* putréfier ; corrompre.

pu'trefy, *v.n.,* se putréfier, pourrir.

putres'cence (piou-très'-), *n.,* état de putréfaction, *m.,* putrescence, *f.*

putres'cent (piou-très'-), *adj.,* en état de putréfaction ; putride ; putréfié.

pu'trid (piou-), *adj.,* putride.

pu'tridness ou **putrid'ity** (piou-), *n.,* pourriture, putridité, *f.*

put'ter (pout'-), *n.,* personne qui met, qui pose, qui place, *f.* ; faiseur, *m.,* faiseuse, *f.* — off ; *temporisateur, temporiseur, lanternier, m.* — on ; *instigateur, m.*

put'ting (pout'-), *n.,* action de mettre, de placer ; mise, pose, *f.* — asunder ; *écartement, m., séparation, f.* — back ; *reculement ;* (nav.) *retour,* m. — off ; *délai, retardement, m. ;* remise, *f.* — up ; *candidature, f.,* (mec.) *installation, f.*

put'ty (peut'-), *n.,* potée d'étain, *f.* ; (for glaziers) mastic ; ciment, *m.* *v.a.,* mastiquer.

puz'zle (peuz'z'l), *n.,* embarras, *m.,* difficulté, énigme, *f. ;* (toy) jeu de patience, casse-tête, *m.*

puz'zle (peuz'z'l), *v.a.,* intriguer, embarrasser, démonter, alambiquer. To — one's brains ; *s'alambiquer l'esprit, la cervelle.* To be much — d how to ; *être fort en peine de savoir comment ; être fort intrigué ; être fort embarrassé* de. To — out ; *découvrir à force d'efforts (de l'esprit).*

puz'zle (peuz'z'l), *v.n.,* être embarrassé.

puz'zle-headed (-hèd'ède), *adj.,* plein d'idées creuses.

puz'zler, *n.,* personne qui embarrasse ; chose qui embarrasse, *f.* That's a —; (fam.) *cela donne diablement à penser.*

pygme'an (-mi-), *adj.,* de pygmée.

pyg'my, *n.,* pygmée, *m.*

pylor'ic (-lô-), *adj.,* (anat.) pylorique.

pylo'rus (-lô-), *n.,* (anat.) pylore, *m.*

pyr'acanth (pir'a-ca'n'th), *n.,* (bot.) buisson ardent, *m.*

pyr'amid, *n.,* pyramide, *f.*

pyram'idal, pyramid'ic, ou **pyramid'ical,** *adj.,* pyramidal.

pyramid'ically, *adv.,* en pyramide.

pyre (païeur), *n.,* bûcher, *m.*

pyr'iform, *adj.,* piriforme.

pyri'tes (-raï-tize), *n. sing.* and *pl.,* (min.) pyrite, *f.*

pyr'itous, *adj.,* (min.) pyriteux.

pyrolig'neous (-lig-ni-), *adj.,* pyroligneux.

pyrom'eter (-ro'm'i-), *n.,* pyromètre, *m.*

pyroph'orus, *n.,* pyrophore, *m.*

pyrotech'nic, *adj.,* pyrotechnique.

pyrotech'nics (-tèk'-), *n.pl.,* pyrotechnie, *f.sing.*

pyrotech'nist (-tèk'-), *n.,* personne versée dans la pyrotechnie, *f.,* artificier, *m.*

pyrotech'ny (-tèk'-), *n.,* pyrotechnie, *f.*

pyr'oxene (pir'oks'ïne), *n.,* (min.) pyroxène, *m.*

pyr'rhic, *n.,* pyrrhique; danse pyrrhique, *f. ;* (poet.) pyrrhique, *m.*

pyrrhon'io, *adj.,* pyrrhonien.

Pyr'rhonism (-niz'm), *n.,* pyrrhonisme, *m.*

Pyr'rhonist, *n.,* pyrrhonien, *m.*

Pythagore'an (-thag-o-rî-), *n.,* pythagoricien, *m.,* pythagoricienne, *f.*

Pythag'orism (-thag-o-riz'm), *n.,* pythagorisme, *m.*

Pyth'ian (pith'-), *adj.,* pythien ; pythique, de la pythie.

py'thon (paï-theune), *n.,* python, devin, *m.*

py'thoness, *n.,* pythonisse, *f.*

pyx, *n.,* (anat.) acétabule; (c.rel.) ciboire, *m. ;* (com.) boîte où l'on dépose des échantillons des monnaies, *f.*

Q

q, dix-septième lettre de l'alphabet, q, *m.*

quack (kwake), *n.*, charlatan ; empirique ; marchand, d'orviétan, (mus.) (false note) canard, couac, *m.*

quack, *v.n.*, faire le charlatan ; faire le gascon ; hâbler ; (of ducks) nasiller ; (mus.) canarder, faire la cane ; faire un plongeon.

quack, *adj.*, de charlatan ; d'empirique.

quack'ery (kwak'ri), *n.*, charlatanisme, empirisme, *m. ;* charlatanerie, *f.*

quack'ish, *adj.*, de charlatan ; d'empirique ; charlatanesque ; faux.

Quadrages'ima (kwŏd-ra-djèss-), *n.*, (ecc.) Quadragésime, *f.* — Sunday; *dimanche de la Quadragésime, m.*

quadrages'imal, *adj.*, (ecc.) quadragésimal.

quad'rangle (kwŏd-ragn'g'l), *n.*, quadrangle, *m.*, place, cour, *f.*

quadran'gular (-ghiou-), *adj.*, quadrangulaire.

quad'rant (kwŏd'-), *n.*, (astron.) quart ; quart de cercle ; (trig.) quadrant, (of towns) rondpoint, carrefour, *m.* — of altitude; *quart de cercle mural, m.*

quad'rat (kwŏd'-), *n.*, (print.) cadrat, *m.*

quad'rate (kwŏd'-), *adj.*, carré ; (astrol.) quadrat.

quad'rate, *n.*, carré ; (astrol.) quadrat aspect, *m.*

quad'rate, *v.n.*, cadrer.

quadrat'ic (kwad'-), *adj.*, (alg.) du second degré.

quad'rature (kwŏd'ra-tioure), *n.*, (geom.) (astron.) quadrature, *f.*

quadren'nial (kwŏd'-), *adj.*, quatriennal, quadriennal.

quadren'nially, *adv.*, tous les quatre ans.

quadrilat'eral (kwŏd'ri-lat'eur'-), *adj.*,(geom.) quadrilatéral.

quadrilat'eral, *n.*, (geom.) quadrilatère, *m.*

quadrille' (ka-drile), *n.*, (cards) quadrille ; (mus., danc.) quadrille, *m.*, contre-danse, *f.*

quadrino'mial (kwŏd-ri-nô-), *n.*, (alg.) quadrinôme, *m.*

quadripart'ite (kwa-dri-par-taïte), *adj.* (bot.) quadriparti.

quadrisyl'lable (kwŏd-ri-cil-la-b'l), *n.*, quadrisyllabe, *m.*

quadroon' (kwŏd-roune), *n.*, quarteron, *m.*, quarteronne, *f.*

quad'rumane (kwŏd-rou-), *n.*, quadrumane, *m.*

quadru'manous, *adj.*, quadrumane.

quad'ruped (kwŏd-rou-), *n.*, quadrupède, *m.*

quad'ruple (kwŏd-rou-p'l), *n.*, quadruple, *m.*

quad'ruple, *adj.*, quadruple.

quad'ruple, *v.a.*, quadrupler.

quadru'plicate (kwŏd-rou-), *v.a.*, quadrupler.

quadru'plicate, *adj.*, quadruplé.

quadruplica'tion (-pli-ké-), *n.*, quadruplication, *f.*

quaff (kwaf), *v.a.* and *n.*, boire copieusement ; boire à longs traits ; boire à grands coups ; vider (en buvant) ; (pop.) lamper.

quaff'er, *n.*, buveur, grand buveur, *m.*

quag'gy (kwag-ghi), *adj.*, marécageux.

quag'mire (kwag-maïeur) *ou* **quag**, *n.*, fondrière, *f.*

quail (kwéle), *n.*, (orni.) caille, *f.*

quail (kwéle), *v.n.*, perdre courage, faiblir ; fléchir, être abattu ; reculer, se troubler ; trembler ; (to coagulate) se cailler, se coaguler.

quail'-pipe (-païpe), *n.*, courcaillet, appeau, *m.*

quaint (kwén-te), *adj.*, (odd) singulier, bizarre, original ; (unusual) extraordinaire, étrange ; (affected) affecté, prétentieux ; (fine spun) recherché, apprêté ; (pretty) gentil, joli ; (clever) adroit.

quaint'ly, *adv.*, singulièrement, bizarrement, originalement ; extraordinairement, étrange-

ment ; d'une manière affectée, d'une manière prétentieuse ; d'une manière recherchée, d'une manière apprêtée ; gentiment ; adroitement.

quaint'ness, *n.*, singularité, bizarrerie, originalité ; nature extraordinaire, nature étrange ; gentillesse, *f.*

quake (kwéke), *v.n.*, trembler ; trembloter.

quake, *n.*, tremblement, *m.* Earth—; *tremblement de terre, m.*

Qua'ker, *n.*, (relig. sect) quaker, quakre ; trembleur, *m.*

Quak'eress, *n.*, quakeresse, *f.*

Quak'erism (-iz'm), *n.*,(ecc. hist.) quakerisme, *m.*

quak'erly, *adv.*, de quaker.

quak'ing (kwék'-), *n.*, tremblement, *m. ;* terreur, *f.*

quak'ing, *adj.*, tremblant ; tremblotant. — grass ; *amourette, brize, f.*

quak'ingly, *adv.*, en tremblant.

qual'ifiable, *adj.*, qualifiable.

qualifica'tion (kwŏl'-i-fi-ké-), *n.*, qualité, qualité requise ; capacité, *f.*, talent, titre, *m.;* (diminution) diminution, *f.*, affaiblissement, *m.;* (modification) modification, restriction ; (denomination) dénomination, désignation, qualification, *f.*

qual'ificative, *adj.* and *n.* qualificatif.

qual'ified (kwŏl'i-faïde), *adj.*, qui a les qualités requises ; apte à, capable de, propre à, autorisé à, modifié ; tempéré ; (jur.) qui a qualité pour.

qual'ify (kwŏl'i-faïe), *v.a.* and *n.*, donner les qualités requises à ; rendre apte à, rendre capable de, rendre propre à, préparer à ; autoriser à, donner le droit de ; qualifier de ; (to modify) modifier ; (to soften) adoucir, modérer ; (to regulate) déterminer, fixer ; (intrans.) se préparer à ; (at an exam.) obtenir le nombre de points requis.

qual'ifying (kwŏl'i-faï-igne), *adj.*, (gram.) qualificatif.

qual'ity (kwŏl'-), *n.*, qualité, *f. ;* (acquirement) talent, *m.*

qualm (kwâme), *n.*, mal, *ou* soulèvement, de cœur, *m. ;* nausée; envie de vomir, *f. ;* (scruple) scrupule, remords, *m.*

qualm'ish (kwâm'-), *adj.*, qui a mal au cœur ; qui a des nausées ; qui a envie de vomir.

qualm'ishness, *n.*, envie de vomir ; nausée, soulèvement de cœur, *f.*

quan'dary (kwo'n'da-), *n.*, embarras, *m. ;* incertitude ; difficulté, impasse, *f.*

quan'titative, *adj.*, (chem.) quantitatif.

quan'tity (kwo'n-), *n.*, (math.) quantité, grandeur ; (gram. prosody) quantité, *f.* In —; in quantities; *en grande quantité, en grand nombre.*

quan'tum (kwo'n-), *n.*, montant, total, *m. ;* quantité, *f.* — sufficit ; *quantité suffisante, f.*

quar'antine (kwor'a'n-tîne), *n.*, (com., nautical) quarantaine, *f.* To perform — ; *faire quarantaine.*

quar'antine, *v.a.*, faire faire quarantaine à, mettre en quarantaine.

quar'rel (kwor'rèl), *n.*, querelle, dispute, brouille, *f. ;* démêlé ; (cause of dispute) sujet de querelle, *m.*, cause de querelle, *f. ;* (pane of glass) carreau, *m.* To fasten a — on any one ; *chercher querelle, chercher noise, à quelqu'un.* To take up any one's — ; *embrasser* (ou *épouser*) *la querelle de quelqu'un.* To have a — with ; *avoir noise avec* (V. Hugo).

quar'rel, *v.n.*, quereller ; se quereller ; disputer, se brouiller ; (to cavil) trouver à redire à. To — with ; *se quereller avec.* To — about nothing ; *chercher une querelle d'Allemand.* To want to — with, *ou* to pick a — with ; *chercher querelle à.* To have —ed with ; *être en querelle avec ; être brouillé avec.*

quar'reler, *n.*, querelleur, *m.*, querelleuse, *f.*

quar'reling, *n.*, querelle ; dispute, *f.*, démêlé, désaccord, *m.*

quar′relsome, *adj.*, querelleur. — man ; *querelleur, m.* — woman ; *querelleuse, f.*

quar′relsomely, *adv.*, en querelleur.

quar′relsomeness, *n.*, humeur querelleuse, *f.*

quar′ry (kwŏr′-), *n.*, carrière de pierre ; (hunt.) curée ; (prey) proie, *f.*

quar′ry, *v.a.*, tirer, *ou* extraire, d'une carrière.

quar′rying, *n.*, exploitation d'une carrière, *f.*

quar′ryman, *n.*, carrier, *m.*

quart (kwŏrte), *n.*, quart (litre 1·11), *m.* — bottle ; *bouteille entière, f.*

quar′tan (kwŏr-), *n.*, fièvre quarte, *f. ;* (of a measure) quart, *m.*

quar′tan, *adj.*, (med.) quarte, *f.*

quarta′tion (kwŏr-té-), *n.*, (metal.) quartation, inquartation, *f.*, inquart, *m.*

quar′ter (kwŏr-), *v.a.*, partager en quarts ; diviser en parties, diviser en parties distinctes ; (her.) écarteler ; (to lodge) loger. To draw and — ; *écarteler ;* (in barracks) caserner.

quar′ter, *v.n.*, loger ; (milit.) être en quartier.

quar′ter, *n.*, (fourth part) quart ; (of a hundred-weight) quart de quintal (kilo. 12·699) ; (astron.) her., milit., vet.) quartier ; (of a city, of a shoe, of lamb) quartier ; (region) endroit, parage, *m.*, contrée, *f. ;* (particular part) endroit, côté ; (of the year, of schooling) trimestre ; (of rent) terme ; (mercy) quartier ; (of a ship) arrière, *m.*, hanche, *f.* Head—s ; *quartier général, m.sing.* False — ; (vet.) *faux quartier, m.* Fore—s ; *avant-main, avant-train, m.* Hind—s ; *arrière-main, arrière-train, m.* There is nothing to hope from that — ; *il n'y a rien à espérer de ce côté-là.* From all —s ; *de tous côtés ; de toutes parts ; de tous les points.* Four —s of the globe ; *quatre parties (f.), ou quatre coins (m.), du globe.* In high —s ; *en haut lieu.* At free —s ; *à discrétion.* To give — ; *faire quartier.* To come to close —s ; *en venir aux mains, ou aux prises.* To give no — ; *ne pas faire de quartier.* To ask for — ; *demander quartier, ou quartier.* In the proper — ; *à qui de droit.*

quar′ter-bill, *n.*, (nav.) rôle d'équipage, *ou* de combat, *m.*

quar′ter-cask, *n.*, demi-pièce, *f.*

quar′ter-day, *n.*, terme, *m.*

quar′ter-deck, *n.*, gaillard d'arrière, *m.*

quar′terer, *n.*, qui écartèle, bourreau, *m.*

quar′tering, *n.*, division par quarts, *f. ;* (milit.) logement militaire ; (punishment) écartèlement ; (her.) écartèlement, *m.*, écartelure, *f.*

quar′terly, *adj.*, trimestriel ; de quart.

quar′terly, *adv.*, par trimestre.

quar′termaster (-mâs-), *n.*, (nav.) quartiermaître ; (cav.) maréchal des logis ; (infantry) fourrier, *m.* — general ; *chef d'état-major-général.*

quar′tern (kwŏr-teurne), *n.*, quart de pinte (litre 0·14), *m.* A — loaf ; *un pain de quatre livres.*

quar′ter-pace, *n.*, (arch.) quartier tournant, repos, *m.*

quar′ter-ses′sions (-sèsh′eu′n′ze), *n.*, session trimestrielle, *f.*

quar′ter-staff (-stâf), *n.*, bâton ; bâton de garde forestier ; bâton ferré, *m.*

quartet′ (kwŏr-tète) *ou* **quartet′to** (-tèt′tô), *n.*, (mus.) quatuor, *m.*

quar′tile (kwŏr-), *n.*, (astrol.) quartile aspect, *m. ;* quadrature, *f.*

quar′to (kwŏr-tô), *adj.*, in-quarto.

quar′to, *n.*, in-quarto, *m.*

quartz (kwŏrtz), *n.*, (min.) quartz, *m.*

quartz′y (-zi), *adj.*, quartzeux.

quash (kwŏshe), *v.a.*, briser, écraser ; (to repress) réprimer, étouffer ; (to subdue) subjuguer, dompter ; (jur.) annuler, casser, infirmer.

qua′si (kwé-çaïe), *adv.*, quasi.

Quasimo′do (kwa-ci-mô-dô), *n.*, (c. rel.) Quasimodo, *f.*

quas′sia (kwŏsh′i-a), *n.*, quassia ; (tree) quassier, *m.*

quater′nary, *adj.*, (bot., chem., geol.) quaternaire.

quater′nion (kwa-teur-), *n.*, nombre quatre, *m. ;* série de quatre, *f. ;* (math.) quaternion, *m.*

quat′rain (kwŏt′ra′n), *n.*, quatrain, *m.*

qua′ver (kwé-), *n.*, tremblement de la voix ; (mus.) croche, *f.*, trille, *m.* — rest ; *demi-soupir, m.*

qua′ver, *v.n.*, faire trembler sa voix ; trembler ; (mus.) triller, cadencer.

qua′vering, *n.*, trille, *m. ;* cadence, *f.*, tremblement de voix, *m.*

quay (kî), *n.*, quai, *m.*

quay, *v.a.*, garnir de quais.

quay′age, *n.*, quayage, droit de quai, *m.*

quean (kwî′n), *n.*, femme de mauvaise vie, coquine, guenipe, *f.*

queen (kwî′n), *n.*, reine ; (at cards, at draughts) dame ; (at chess) dame, reine, *f.* — Anne is dead ; *c'est vieux comme le Pont Neuf.* — bee ; *mère ou reine-abeille, f.* — mother ; *reine-mère, f.* As a — ; *en reine.*

queen, *v.a.*, faire la reine ; trôner ; (at chess) aller à dame.

queen′like (-laïke) *ou* **queen′ly**, *adv.*, de reine ; comme une reine ; semblable à une reine.

queer (kwîr), *adj.*, bizarre, étrange, singulier ; original ; drôle **de**. A — fellow, *ou* fish ; *un drôle de corps, un original.* I feel very — ; *je ne me sens pas bien ; je suis tout chose, ou tout je ne sais comment.* Things look very — ; *les choses ont (une) mauvaise tournure.* To be in — street ; *branler dans le manche, ou au manche.*

queer′ish, *adj.*, assez drôle ; (fam.) cocasse.

queer′ly, *adv.*, étrangement ; bizarrement ; originalement, singulièrement, drôlement.

queer′ness, *n.*, étrangeté, bizarrerie, originalité, singularité, *f.*

quell (kwèl), *v.a.*, réprimer, étouffer, dompter, apaiser.

quell, *v.n.*, s'éteindre.

quell′er, *n.*, personne qui réprime, qui étouffe, *f. ;* dompteur, *m.*

quench (kwè′n′she), *v.a.*, éteindre ; (to check) amortir ; (to repress) étouffer ; (to still) apaiser. To — one's thirst ; *étancher ou éteindre sa soif, se désaltérer.*

quench′able (-′a-b'l), *adj.*, extinguible.

quench′er, *n.*, personne qui éteint ; chose qui éteint, *f.*

quench′less, *adj.*, inextinguible, inapaisable.

quercit′ron (kwèr-), *n.*, (bot.) quercitron, chêne jaune ; (chem.) quercitron, *m.*

quer′ist (kwî-), *n.*, personne qui fait une question, *f. ;* questionneur, *m. ;* questionneuse, *f.*

quer′ulous (kwèr-iou-), *adj.*, plaintif, maussade.

quer′ulousness, *n.*, habitude de se plaindre, *f.*

quer′y (kwi-), *n.*, question, demande, *f.*, point d'interrogation, *m.*

quer′y (kwi-), *v.a.n.*, faire une question, des questions ; marquer d'un point d'interrogation ; s'informer **de** ; questionner, interroger ; demander, faire, dire ; mettre en doute ; douter **de**.

quest (kwèste), *n.*, enquête, recherche ; (request) demande, sollicitation, *f.* In — of ; *à la recherche* **de**. In — of him ; *à sa recherche.* In — of us ; *à notre recherche.*

ques′tion (kwèst′-), *n.*, question, interrogation, demande ; (discussion) discussion ; (subject of debate) question, proposition, *f.*, sujet, *m. ;* (in parliament) interpellation ; (math.) question, *f.*, problème, *m. ;* (torture) question, torture, *f.* A pretty — ! *belle question! la belle demande!* An unfair — ; *une question indiscrète ; une indiscrétion, f.* That is out of the — ; *c'est impossible, il ne faut pas y songer, c'est hors de cause, c'est hors de doute.* To ask a — ; *faire* *une question.* To put a —; (parl., etc.) *faire,* ou *adresser, une interpellation* **à.** To call in —; *mettre en question ; révoquer en doute.* Without a —; *sans aucun doute, sans contredit.* Beyond all —; *hors de doute.* Previous —; *question préalable, f.* To beg the —; *supposer la question résolue ; faire une pétition de principe ; tourner dans un cercle vicieux.* To put to the —; *mettre à la question,* ou *à la torture.* Leading —; *question qui indique la réponse désirée.* If it is a — of ; *s'il agit de.* If it was a — of charity; *s'il s'agissait de charité* (V. Hugo). That is not the —; *il ne s'agit pas de cela.*

ques'tion, *v.a.,* questionner, interroger ; (to doubt) mettre en question, mettre en doute, révoquer en doute, douter **de.**

ques'tion, *v.n.,* interroger ; questionner ; faire des questions ; douter (**si**) ; se demander (**si**). I — whether it would not be better to . . . ; *je ne sais pas s'il ne vaudrait pas mieux* ou *je me demande s'il . . .*

ques'tionable (-'a-b'l), *adj.,* contestable, douteux, incertain ; suspect, équivoque.

ques'tionableness, *n.,* caractère douteux, caractère incertain, *m.* ; nature douteuse, suspecte, équivoque.

ques'tioner, *n.,* questionneur, *m.,* questionneuse, *f.* ; interrogateur, *m.,* interrogatrice, *f.*

ques'tioning, *n.,* questions, *f.pl.* ; interrogation, *f.*

ques'tionless, *adj.,* sans doute, certain, incontestable.

ques'tor (kwès-teur), *n.,* (Rom. antiq.) questeur, *m.*

ques'torship, *n.,* (Rom. antiq.) questure, *f.*

quib (kwibe), *n.,* (ant.) sarcasme ; mot piquant, *m.*

quib'ble (kwib'b'l), *n.,* argutie, chicane, *f.* ; jeu de mots, faux-fuyant ; (in univers. of old) quolibet ; (pun) jeu de mots, calembour, *m.*

quib'ble, (*v.n.*) ergoter ; chicaner sur les mots ; jouer sur les mots ; faire des calembours ; turlupiner.

quib'bler, *n.,* ergoteur, *m.,* ergoteuse, *f.* ; chicaneur, *m.,* chicaneuse, *f.*

quib'bling, *n.,* chicanes de mots, *f.pl.*

quick (kwike), *n.,* vif, *m.* ; chair vive, *f.* The —; (*pl.*) les vivants. Stung to the —; *piqué au vif.* An incision in the —; *une incision dans la chair vive* (V. Hugo).

quick, *adj.,* (living) vif, vivant ; (of flesh) vif ; (rapid) rapide, prompt; agile, leste ; (brisk) vif, ardent ; (intelligent) intelligent ; (of the pulse, the breath) fréquent. — ear; *oreille fine, f.* — sale ; *prompt débit, m.* Be — ! *dépêchez-vous ! * — step, march ! *pas accéléré ! pas de charge !* — hedge; *haie vive, f.* — wit; *esprit vif, m.* To be —; *se dépêcher.*

quick, *adv.,* vite, promptement, rapidement, lestement.

quick, *v.a.,* étamer; mettre le tain **à.**

quick'beam (-bîme), *n.,* (bot.) sorbier, *m.*

quick'en (kwik'k'n), *v.a.,* animer, vivifier ; exciter ; accélérer, hâter. To — one's pace ; *hâter le pas.*

quick'en, *v.n.,* prendre vie, s'animer.

quick'ener, *n.,* être qui vivifie ; principe vivifiant, *m.* ; chose qui accélère, *f.*

quick'ening, *adj.,* vivifiant, excitant; qui vivifie ; qui ranime.

quick'lime (-laïme), *n.,* chaux vive, *f.*

quick'ly (kwik'-), *adv.,* vite, rapidement, promptement ; vivement ; bientôt.

quick'ness, *n.,* vitesse ; promptitude ; vivacité ; (perception) facilité ; pénétration, sagacité ; activité, finesse ; (of the pulse, the breath) fréquence, *f.*

quick'sand (-ça'n'de), *n.,* sable mouvant, *m.*

quick'set, *n.,* plante vive, aubépine, *f.* — hedge ; *haie vive, f.*

quick'set, *v.a.,* entourer d'une haie vive.

quicksight'ed (-saït'-), *adj.,* qui a la vue bonne ; clairvoyant, pénétrant.

quick-sight'edness, *n.,* vue perçante ; (fig.) sagacité, *f.*

quick'silver, *n.,* vif-argent, mercure, *m.*

quick'silvered (-verde), *adj.,* étamé.

quick'silvering, *n.,* étamage, *m.*

quick'-tempered, *adj.,* emporté, vif, colérique.

quick'witted, *adj.,* à l'esprit vif.

quid (kwide), *n.,* chique, *f.* ; (pop.) louis d'or, *m.* ; livre, *f.*

quid'dity, *n.,* (philos.) quiddité, essence, *f.*

quid'nunc (kwid'neu'gn'ke), *n.,* curieux insatiable, colporteur de nouvelles, *m.*

quid pro quo', *n.,* (jur.) équivalent.

quies'cence, *n.,* quiétude, tranquillité, *f.,* repos, *m.* ; (Hebr. gram.) être quiescent (of letters).

quies'cent (kwaï-ès'-), *adj.,* paisible, en repos, calme, serein, tranquille.

qui'et (kwaï-eute), *n.,* tranquillité, *f.* ; repos ; calme, *m.* ; paix ; quiétude, *f.* On the —; *sans bruit, en silence ;* (fig.) *secrètement ; à la dérobée ; clandestinement.*

qui'et, *adj.,* tranquille, en repos, calme, paisible, serein ; sans éclat ; modeste. To keep —; *tenir tranquille ; se tenir tranquille,* ou *coi.* To be —; *être tranquille ; rester tranquille ; se taire.* Be — ; *silence ! taisez-vous ! laissez-moi tranquille !*

qui'et, *v.a.,* tranquilliser, apaiser, calmer ; adoucir ; faire taire.

qui'et, *v.n.* To — down ; *s'apaiser, se calmer.*

qui'eter, *n.,* qui tranquillise, qui calme.

qui'eting, *n.,* action d'apaiser, *f.*

qui'eting, *adj.,* calmant ; tranquillisant.

qui'etism (kwaï-eut'-), *n.,* quiétisme, *m.*

qui'etist, *n.,* quiétiste, *m.*

qui'etly (kwaï-eut'-), *adv.,* tranquillement ; paisiblement ; doucement ; en silence.

qui'etness (kwaï-eut'-), *n.,* tranquillité ; paix, *f.* ; calme ; repos, *m.*

qui'etude (kwaï-eut'ioude), *n.,* quiétude, tranquillité, *f.*

qui'e'tus (kwaï-i-), *n.,* repos, *m.* ; tranquillité ; mort ; satisfaction ; (fig.) coup de grâce, coup mortel, *m.* ; (discharge) libération, *f.* ; (fin.) quitus, *m.* To give any one his — ; *river son clou à quelqu'un ; faire passer le goût du pain à quelqu'un ; donner le coup de grâce à quelqu'un.*

quill (kwile), *n.,* plume, plume d'oie, *f.* ; (of a porcupine) piquant, *m.*

quill, *v.a.,* plisser ; tuyauter ; (needlework) rucher.

quill'-driver (-draïv'-), *n.,* (b.s.) gratte-papier ; (jest.) plumitif, *m.*

quill'-driving, *n.,* métier de gratte-papier, *m.*

quill'ing (kwil'igne), *n.,* plissement, tuyau, tuyautage, *m.* ; (needlework) ruche, *f.*

quilt (kwilte), *n.,* couvre-pied piqué, couvre pied, *m.,* courte-pointe, *f.*

quilt, *v.a.,* piquer ; (nav.) garnir.

quilt'ing, *n.,* piqué, *m.* ; (nav.) garniture, *f.*

quilt'-maker (-mék'-), *n.,* courtepointier, *m.*

quin'ary, *adj.,* quinaire.

quince (kwi'n'ce), *n.,* coing, *m.* Wild —; *cognasse, f.* — tree ; *cognassier, m.*

quincen'tenary, *adj.,* de cinq siècles, *n.,* cinquième centenaire, *m.*

quin'cunx (kwi'n'keu'gn'kse), *n.,* quinconce, *m.*

quindecen'nial, *adj.,* quindécennial.

quinde'cagon (kwi'n'dèk'-), *n.,* (geom.) quindécagone, *m.*

quinine' (kwi-nîne ou -naïne), *n.,* (chem.) quinine, *f.*

quinquages'ima (kwi'n'kwa-djèss'-), n., (ecc.) quinquagésime, f.

quinquen'nial (kwi'n'kwè'n'-), adj., quinquennal.

quin'quina (kwi'n'kwaï-), n., (pharm.) quinquina, m.

quin'sy (kwi'n'zi), n., (med.) esquinancie, f.

quint (kwi'n'te), n., quinte, f.

quin'tal (kwi'n'-), n., quintal, m.

quintes'sence (kwi'n'tèss'-), n., quintessence, f.

quintet'to (kwi'n'tèt-), n., (mus.) quintette, m.

quin'tuple (kwi'n'tiou-p'l), adj., quintuple.

quin'tuple, v.a., quintupler.

quip (kwipe), n., mot piquant, lardon, badinage, m. ; raillerie, f.

quip, v.a., railler amèrement.

quire (kwaïeur), n., (of paper) main, f. ; (ant. ecc.) chœur, m. In —s; en feuilles.

quirk (kweurke), n., sarcasme ; mot piquant, m., pointe, (quibble) argutie, subtilité, f. ; détour, subterfuge, air irrégulier ; (arch.) contour, m.

quirk'ish (kweurk'-), adj., de détour ; de subterfuge, d'argutie.

quit (kwite), v.a., quitter ; sortir de ; abandonner ; (to pay) payer, acquitter ; (to remit) tenir quitte de. To — oneself ; s'acquitter de. Notice to —; congé, m. To — costs ; payer les frais. To — scores ; être quitte à quitte. — rent ; redevance, f.

quit, adj., quitte.

quitch'-grass (kwitsh'grâce), n., (bot., agri.) chiendent, m.

quite (kwaïte), adv., tout à fait, entièrement, parfaitement, complètement, tout, bien. It is — three years ago ; il y a bien trois ans de cela. — as well ; tout aussi bien. — differently ; tout autrement. — another thing ; tout autre chose. — enough ; bien assez ; tout ce qu'il faut. — good enough ; bien assez bon. — right ; parfaitement juste, très juste, très bien. — hot; tout chaud. To be — right ; (of watches) être bien à l'heure ; (of pers.) avoir bien raison, être dans le vrai. To have — done ; avoir tout-à-fait fini.

quit'-rent, n., (feudal) cens, m. ; redevance, f.

quits (kwitse), adv., quitte. To be —; être quitte ; être quitte à quitte. Double or —; quitte ou double. We'll cry —; nous voilà quittes.

quit'ter (kwit'-), n., personne qui quitte, f.

quiv'er (kwiv'-), n., carquois, (shaking) frisson, frissonnement, m.

quiv'er (kwiv'-), v.n., trembler ; frissonner ; (of flesh) palpiter.

quiv'ered (kwiv'eurde), adj., armé d'un carquois.

quiv'ering, n., tremblement, frissonnement, frisson, m.

quixot'ic (kwiks'-), adj., de don Quichotte, extravagant.

quix'otism (kwiks'ot'iz'm) ou **quix'otry**, n., don-quichottisme, m. ; extravagance, f.

quiz (kwize), n., énigme, f. ; (pers.) persifleur, loustic, railleur, m., railleuse, f.

quiz, v.a., railler, persifler ; berner ; (to look at) lorgner.

quiz'zical, adj., railleur, comique, qui aime le persiflage ; de persiflage.

quiz'zing, n., raillerie, f., persiflage, m. ; lorgnerie, f.

quiz'zing-glass (-glâce), n., lorgnon, m.

quod, n., bloc, violon, m. ; prison, f. To put in —; coffrer, mettre au bloc.

quod'libet (kwod-li-), n., subtilité, raison subtile, f.

quoin (kôïne), n., coin, m. ; encoignure, encognure ; (arch.) arête, f. ; (print.) coin, m.

quoin'-post (-pôste), n., poteau cornier, m.

quoit (kôïte), n., palet ; (antiq.) disque, m. To play at —s ; jouer au palet.

quon'dam (kwo'n-), adj., ci-devant, ancien, d'autrefois, de jadis.

quo'rum (kwô-), n., nombre suffisant, nombre compétent, m. ; (of justices) commission de juges de paix, f.

quo'ta (kwô-), n., quote-part ; quotité, f. ; contingent, m.

quot'able, adj., citable.

quota'tion (kwo-té-), n., citation ; (com.) cote, f. ; (of stock exchange) cours, m.

quote (kwôte), v.a., citer, alléguer ; (com.) coter.

quot'er (kwôt'-), n., citateur, m.

quoth (kwôth), v.n., dire. V. **say.**

quotid'ian (kwô-), adj., quotidien, journalier.

quo'tient (kwô-shè'n'te), n., (arith., alg.) quotient, m.

R

r, dix-huitième lettre de l'alphabet, r, m.f.

rab'bet, n., (arch.) feuillure ; saillie ; rainure, f. ; chanfrein, m.

rab'bet, v.a., (arch.) faire une saillie dans ; faire une rainure, ou feuillure, à ; chanfreiner.

rab'bet-plane, n., guillaume, m.

rab'bi (rab-baïe ou -'bi), n., rabbin, m. Chief —; grand rabbin, m.

rabbin'ic, n., dialecte rabbinique, m., langue rabbinique, f.

rabbin'ical, adj., rabbinique.

rab'binism (-'iz'm), n., construction propre à la langue rabbinique, f.

rab'binist, n., rabbiniste, rabbaniste, m.

rab'bit, n., lapin, m., lapine, f. Young —; lapereau, m. Tame —; lapin de clapier, m. Wild —; lapin de garenne, m. — burrow, ou hole ; rabouillère, f., terrier, m. — hutch ; clapier, m. — warren ; garenne à lapins, f. Welsh —, ou rarebit ; rôtie au fromage, f.

rab'ble (rab'b'l), n., populace, canaille ; foule tumultueuse, cohue, f. — rout ; assemblée tumultueuse, f.

Rab'elaisian, adj., rabelaisien, de Rabelais.

rab'id, adj., (pers.) forcené, furieux ; (of the appetite) canin, dévorant ; (of animals) enragé, qui a la rage, hydrophobe.

rab'idly, adv., rageusement (A. Daudet), furieusement. To be — hungry ; (fam.) avoir une faim de tous les diables.

rab'idness, n., rage ; fureur, f.

ra'bies (rab'i-èss), n., (med.) rage, hydrophobie, f.

raccoon', n., raton, m.

race, n., (breed) race ; (root) (ant.) racine, f. ; (of wine) goût de terroir, goût âpre, m. ; (running contest) course ; (course) course, carrière, f. ; (tide) ras, raz de marée ; (of a mill) bief, m. Horse— ; course de chevaux, f. Boat— ; régate, course de bateaux, f. Foot — ; course à pied, f. Hurdle — ; course de haies, f. Flat — ; course plate, f. — ground ; champ de courses, m.

race, v.n., courir, courir de toute sa force, à toutes jambes, à bride abattue.

race'-course (-côrse), n., terrain de course, hippodrome, m. ; arène, piste, f.

race'-horse, n., cheval de course, m.

ra'cer (ré-), n., coureur ; cheval de course, m.

ra'ces (ré-cize), n.pl., courses de chevaux, f.pl.

race'-stand, n., tribunes (de courses), f.pl.

ra'ciness (ré-), n., (fig.) caractère distinctif, piquant, m. ; verve, f. ; (of wine) goût de terroir, fumet, bouquet, m. ; vinosité, f.

ra'cing (ré-), adj., qui court ; de course ; hippique. Horse — ; course de chevaux, f.

rack, n., (of a stable) râtelier ; (instrument for stretching) chevalet, m. ; (instrument for torture) roue, question, *f.* ; (horl.) rochet, *m.* ; (tech.) crémaillère ; (torture) question, torture, *f.* ; (for plates, bottles, etc.) dressoir, râtelier, *m.*, planche ; (of a cart) échelette, *f.* ; (liquor) rack, arack, *m.* To put to the —; *mettre à la torture, à la question.* To live at — and manger; *être à bouche que veux-tu.*

rack, *v.a.*, mettre sur la roue ; (to torment) mettre à la torture, torturer, tourmenter ; (to harass by exaction) commettre des exactions **sur,** pressurer, opprimer ; (nav.) aiguilleter ; (liquor) soutirer. To — off; (liquor) soutirer. To — one's brains; *se creuser la cervelle.*

rack, *v.n.*, commettre des exactions.

rack'et, *n.*, fracas, tapage, tintamarre, *m.*, crierie, *f.* ; caquet, *m.* ; (at tennis) raquette, *f.*, battoir, *m.* ; (game) paume, *f.* To be on the —; *être dissipé.* To stand the —; *être responsable* **de** ; *subir les conséquences* **de** ; (pop.) *payer les pôts cassés.*

rack'et, *v.a.*, relancer à coups de raquette.

rack'et, *v.n.*, faire un tintamarre ; faire du tapage ; (to frolic, to knock about) s'amuser ; faire la vie ; courir. —ing noise ; *tapage, m.*

rack'ety (rak'ĕt'-), *adj.*, de tapage, de tintamarre.

rack'ing, *adj.*, de torture ; (of pain) atroce ; (drifting) qui fuit.

rack'ing, *n.*, torture, *f.* ; (tech.) étendage ; (of liquors) soutirage, *m.*

rack'ing-pace, *n.*, (man.) traquenard, *m.*

rack'-rent, *n.*, loyer excessif, égal au produit annuel de l'immeuble; loyer porté au maximum,*m.*

rack'-rented, *adj.*, qui paye un loyer excessif, le maximum du loyer (égal au produit annuel de l'immeuble).

rack'-renter, *n.*, personne qui paye un loyer excessif, un maximum du loyer, *f.*

ra'cy (ré-), *adj.*, (of wine) qui a un goût de terroir, qui a du bouquet; (fig.) vif, attrayant, piquant, original, plein de verve (of the style, of the language).

rad'dle (rad'd'l), *v.a.*, tresser.

ra'dial (ré-), *adj.*, (anat.) radial.

ra'diance *ou* **ra'diancy** (ré-), *n.*, rayonnement ; éclat, lustre, *m.* ; splendeur, *f.*

ra'diant (ré-), *adj.*, rayonnant (with **de**) ; radieux; éclatant; (bot.) radiant, radié;(her.) radié. — heat; *chaleur rayonnante, f.*

ra'diant (ré-), *n.*, point lumineux ; point radieux ; point rayonnant, *m.*

ra'diantly, *adv.*, en rayonnant ; d'une manière radieuse, splendidement.

ra'diate (ré-), *v.n.*, rayonner, émettre des rayons.

ra'diate, *adj.*, (bot.) radié.

ra'diating (ré-diét'-), *adj.*, rayonnant.

radia'tion (ré-di-é-), *n.*, rayonnement, *m.*, radiation, *f.*

rad'ical, *adj.*, radical ; fondamental.

rad'ical, *n.*, radical ; primitif, *m.*

rad'icalism (-iz'm), *n.*, (polit.) radicalisme, *m.*

rad'ically, *adv.*, radicalement ; essentiellement.

rad'icle (rad'i-k'l) *n.*, (bot.) radicule, *f.*

rad'ish, *n.*, radis, *m.* ; rave, *f.* Turnip-—; *petite rave.* Horse-—; *raifort, m.* — bed ; *ravière, f.* — dish ; *ravier, m.*

ra'dius (ré-), *n.*, rayon, parcours ; rais ; (anat.) radius, *m.* In a — of ; *dans un rayon, ou parcours,* **de.**

ra'dix (ré-), *n.*, (*radices*) racine, *f.*

raff, *n.*, (mob) populace, canaille, *f.* ; rebut ; (jumble) fatras, *m.* Riff-—; *canaille, lie, f.*

raf'fle (raf'f'l), *n.*, loterie, *f.*

raf'fle, *v.a.*, mettre en loterie.

raf'fle, *v.n.*, faire une loterie. To — for ; *mettre en loterie.*

raf'fler, *n.*, personne qui met à la loterie, *f.*

raft (râfte), *n.*, radeau, train de bois, *m.*

raft'er, *n.*, poutre, *f.* ; chevron, *m.*

raft'er, *v.a.*, chevronner.

raf'tered (râf-teurde), *adj.*, à poutres ; à chevrons.

raft'ing (râft'-), *n.*, flottage en train, *m.*

rafts'man (râfts'-), *n.*, flotteur, *m.*

rag, *n.*, (piece of cloth torn off) chiffon ; (tatter) haillon, lambeau, *m.*, guenille, loque, *f.* In —s ; *en haillons, en loques, en guenilles, déguenillé.* Meat boiled to —s ; *de la viande en charpie, en compote.* To tear to —s ; *mettre en lambeaux.* — and bone man ; *chiffonnier, m.*

ragamuf'fin (-meuf'fine), *n.*, gueux, maroufle, polisson, va-nu-pieds, *m.*

rag'-bolt (-bôlte), *n.*, cheville à fiche, *f.*

rag'-doll, *n.*, poupée de chiffons, *f.*

rage (rédje), *n.*, (anger) fureur, rage, *f.*, emportement, *m.* ; (violent desire) passion, furie, rage, manie ; (of things) fureur, force, violence, *f.* To fly, *ou* to get, into a —; *se mettre en colère, entrer en colère* ; *s'emporter.* To put into a —; *mettre en colère, faire enrager.* To be all the —, to be quite the —; *faire fureur, faire rage.* In a —; *furieux; en colère, en fureur.*

rage, *v.n.*, (pers.) être furieux, être en fureur, enrager, jeter feu et flamme ; se courroucer, être courroucé, s'emporter ; (of things) se courroucer, être en fureur ; (of wind) se déchaîner ; (of war) sévir, régner ; (of fire, famine, etc.) faire des ravages. War was raging in Europe ; *la guerre sévissait en Europe.*

rage'ful (-foule), *adj.*, furieux, violent.

rag'-fair, *n.*, foire aux chiffons ; friperie, *f.*

rag-gath'erer (-gath'-), *n.*, chiffonnier, *m.*

rag'ged (rag-ghède), *adj.*, (pers.) en haillons, en guenilles, déguenillé ; (of things) en lambeaux, en loques, déchiré, délabré ; (jagged) ébréché ; (uneven) inégal.

rag'gedly (-ghèd'-), *adv.*, en lambeaux, en guenilles.

rag'gedness (-ghèd'-), *n.*, délabrement, déguenillement, *m.* ; guenilles, *f.pl.*, lambeaux, haillons, *m.pl.* ; (roughness) inégalité, rudesse, *f.*

ra'ging (rédj'-), *adj.*, courroucé, furieux ; en fureur ; (of tempests, war, etc.) déchaîné, violent, destructeur. — fever ; *fièvre ardente, f.*

ra'ging, *n.*, fureur ; rage, violence, *f.*

ra'gingly, *adv.*, avec fureur ; furieusement, rageusement (A. Daudet).

rag'man, *n.*, marchand de chiffons; chiffonnier, *m.*

ragout' (râ-gou), *n.*, ragoût, *m.*

rag'-picker, *n.*, chiffonnier, *m.*

rag'stone (-stône), *n.*, tuf, *m.*

rag'-wheel (-hwîle), *n.*, (tech.) hérisson, *m.*

rag'wort (-weurte), *n.*, (bot.) jacobée, herbe de Saint-Jacques, *f.* ; séneçon jacobée, *m.*

rail (réle), *n.*, (bar of wood, of metal) barre, *f.*, barreau, *m.* ; (of a staircase) rampe, *f.* ; (of bridges) parapet ; (carp.) traverse, balustrade, *f.*, garde-fou, garde-corps, *m.*, grille, barrière ; (nav.) lisse, *f.* ; (railways) rail ; (orni.) râle, *m.pl.*, garde-fou, garde-corps, *m.*, grille, *f.* Hand-—; *lisse,f.* To run off the —s ; *dérailler* ; *sortir de la voie, quitter les rails.* To throw off the —; *dérailler* ; *faire quitter les rails, ou la voie,* **à.**

rail (réle), *v.a.*, garnir d'un garde-fou ; garnir d'une grille, griller. To — in; *fermer avec une grille* ; *griller.* To — round ; *entourer d'une grille* ; *entourer d'un garde-fou.*

rail (réle), *v.n.*, (followed by "at") dire des injures à ; injurier, outrager ; médire de.

railed (rél'de), *adj.*, à voie. Double-—; *à double voie.*

rail'er (rél'-), *n.*, personne qui injurie, qui outrage, *f.* ; frondeur, médisant, *m.*

rail'ing (rél'-), *n.*, injures, *f.pl.* ; outrage, *m.*

rail'ing, *adj.*, injurieux ; outrageant.

rail'ing, *n.*, grille, *f.* ; garde-fou, garde-corps, *m.* ; rampe, balustrade, *f.*

rail′ingly, *adv.*, injurieusement, outrageusement.

rail′lery (rél′leur′i), *n.*, raillerie, *f.*

rail′road (rél-rôde) *ou* **rail′way** (rél′wé) *n.*, chemin de fer, *m.* ; voie, *ou* ligne, ferrée, voie, *f.* — contractor ; *entrepreneur de chemins de fer*, *m.* — debentures ; *obligations de chemin de fer*, *f.pl.* — guide ; *indicateur (des chemins de fer)*, *m.* — plant ; *matériel de chemin de fer*, *m.* — porter ; *facteur*, *m.* — shares, *ou* stock ; *actions de chemin de fer*, *f.pl.* — terminus ; *gare*, *f.* — rug ; *couverture de voyage*, *f.*

rai′ment (ré-), *n.*, vêtement, *m.* ; vêtements, *m.pl.*

rain (ré′ne), *n.*, pluie, *f.* Fine —; (drizzle) *pluie fine*, *f.* Heavy —; *forte pluie*, *f.* Pelting —; *pluie battante.* It looks like —; *le temps est à la pluie.* To pour with —; *pleuvoir à verse.*

rain (ré′ne), *v.n.*, pleuvoir ; tomber de l'eau ; (fig.) tomber en pluie. It —s; *il pleut ; il tombe de l'eau.* To — hard; *pleuvoir à verse.*

rain, *v.a.*, faire pleuvoir ; faire tomber, répandre à foison. To — shot ; *faire pleuvoir des projectiles.* To — cats and dogs; *pleuvoir des hallebardes.*

rain′bow (-bô), *n.*, arc-en-ciel, *m.*

rain′fall, *n.*, quantité de pluie, *f.* Heavy —; *pluie abondante*, *f.*

rain′-gauge (-ghédje), *n.*, (phys.) udomètre, pluviomètre, *m.*

rain′iness, *n.*, temps pluvieux, *m.*

rain′-water (-wô-), *n.*, eau de pluie, eau pluviale, *f.*

rain′y (ré-), *adj.*, pluvieux, de pluie. To lay by something for a — day ; (prov.) *garder une poire pour la soif.*

raise (réze), *v.a.*, lever ; élever ; hausser ; soulever ; (to build) élever, bâtir, fonder ; (to produce) produire, faire naître ; (to enlarge) grandir, augmenter, accroître ; (suspicions) faire naître ; (to excite) soulever, exciter, provoquer ; (a cry) pousser ; (to propagate) semer, propager, faire courir ; (the dead) ressusciter ; (troops, taxes, a siege) lever ; (a quarrel) susciter ; (dough) faire lever ; (evil spirits) évoquer ; (courage) faire reprendre à, relever ; (prices) hausser ; (money) trouver, se procurer ; (live stock) élever ; (hopes) donner, redonner, faire naître. To — up; *lever ;* *élever ; soulever ; hausser.* To — a statue ; *ériger une statue.* To — the wind; *se procurer de l'argent.* To — the blockade; *lever le blocus.* To — one's hat ; *tirer son chapeau.* To — to the peerage ; *anoblir.*

raised, *adj.*, levé ; (embossed) en relief.

rais′er (réz′-), *n.*, personne *ou* chose qui lève, qui élève, qui soulève, qui hausse, *f.* ; auteur ; fondateur, *m.*, fondatrice, *f.* ; (agri.) cultivateur ; (of live stock) éleveur, *m.*

rai′sin (ré-z′n), *n.*, raisin sec, *m.*

rais′ing (réz′-), *n.*, action de lever, d'élever, de hausser, de soulever ; soulèvement, *m.* ; (foundation) fondation ; production, *f.* ; agrandissement, *m.*, augmentation, *f.*, accroissement, *m.* ; excitation ; (of taxes, of troops, of sieges) levée ; (of spirits) évocation, *f.* ; (of live stock) élevage, *m.*, élève ; (of plants, etc.) culture ; (of ores) extraction, *f.*

rais′ing-piece (-pîce), *n.*, (carp.) sablière, *f.*

ra′ja *ou* **ra′jah** (râ-dja *ou* ré-djâ), *n.*, raja, rajah, *m.*

rake, *n.*, (garden) râteau ; (ovens) fourgon, *m.* ; (nav.) quête ; (of masts) inclinaison, *f.* ; (libertine) mauvais sujet, libertin, dissolu, abandonné, débauché, roué, *m.* —ful (râ′te), *râtelée*, *f.*

rake, *v.a.*, (to gather with a rake) râteler ; (hort.) ratisser ; (to scrape) gratter, ratisser, râcler ; (to collect) rassembler, ramasser ; (to search) fouiller **dans** ; (milit.) enfiler, prendre d'enfilade. To — off ; *enlever au râteau.* To — out; *dégager ;* (the fire) *éteindre.* To — together;

ramasser. To — up ; *ramasser ; ramasser au râteau ;* (fig.) raviver, exhumer. To — up the fire ; (to stir) *remuer ; couvrir le feu de cendre.* To — up an old grievance ; *raviver un vieux grief, réveiller le chat qui dort.*

rake, *v.n.*, (to scrape) gratter ; (to search) fouiller ; (to lead a dissolute life) libertiner.

rak′er, *n.*, râteleur, *m.*

rak′ing (rék′-), *n.*, ratissage ; râtelage, *m.* ; (quantity raked) râtelée, *f.* ; (fig.) ramassis ; (ground raked) terrain râtelé, *m.* — out ; (of fires) *extinction*, *f.*

rak′ing, *adj.*, (milit.) d'enfilade.

rak′ish (rék′-), *adj.*, dissolu, débauché, libertin ; (nav., of ships) élancé.

rak′ishly, *adv.*, en libertin.

rak′ishness, *n.*, débauche, *f.* ; libertinage, *m.*

ral′ly, *v.a.*, rallier, rassembler ; (to banter) railler (pers.).

ral′ly, *v.n.*, se rallier, se rassembler ; (to banter) railler, railler **de**, se railler ; (stock exchange, com.) reprendre ; (to gain strength) reprendre des forces, se remettre.

ral′ly, *n.*, ralliement, *m.* ; (bantering) raillerie, *f.* ; (gaining strength) mieux, *m.*, amélioration, *f.*

ral′lying, *n.*, ralliement, *m.* ; (bantering) raillerie, *f.* — point, *ou* sign ; *point, ou signe, ou mot, de ralliement*, *m.*

ram, *n.*, (mam., astron.) bélier, *m.* ; (for paving-stones) hie, demoiselle, *f.* ; (pile-driver) mouton ; (of a man-of-war) éperon, *m.* Battering-— ; *bélier*, *m.*

ram, *v.a.*, enfoncer ; battre à la hie, tasser ; (to stuff) fourrer ; (artil.) bourrer ; (fig.) faire pénétrer, *ou* entrer, de force **dans**.

ra′madan, *n.*, ramadan, ramazan, *m.*

ram′ble (ra′m′b′l), *n.*, course, excursion, promenade ; (fig.) divagation, *f.*

ram′ble, *v.n.*, courir çà et là ; errer ; rôder ; se promener ; (fig.) (in mind) divaguer. To — about ; *errer* **par**, *errer* **partout**, *courir de tous côtés, battre la campagne.*

ram′bler, *n.*, vagabond, *m.*, vagabonde, *f.* ; rôdeur ; promeneur, *m.*, promeneuse, *f.*

ram′bling, *n.*, courses, excursions, promenades ; (fig.) divagations, *f.*

ram′bling, *adj.*, qui erre çà et là ; errant, vagabond ; plein de divagations ; vague ; (fig.) (of speech, style, etc.) décousu, sans suite, incohérent. — tour ; *excursion, course vagabonde*, *f.*

ram′blingly, *adv.*, en rôdant ; (fig.) (in mind) en divaguant ; (of talk, etc.) d'une manière décousue.

ramifica′tion (-fi-ké-), *n.*, ramification, *f.*

ram′ify (-faïe), *v.n.*, se ramifier.

ram′ify, *v.a.*, diviser en ramifications, diviser en branches.

ram′mer, *n.*, personne qui enfonce, qui bat à la hie, *f.* ; (artil.) refouloir ; (pile-driver) mouton, *m.* ; (of a gun) baguette ; (for driving stones, etc.) hie, demoiselle, *f.*

ram′mish, *adj.*, rance.

ram′mishness, *n.*, rancidité, *f.*

ra′mous, *adj.*, rameux, branchu.

ramp′age, *n.*, vacarme, désordre, tumulte, *m.* To be on the — ; *faire les cent coups ; ne plus connaître de bornes.*

ramp′ancy, *n.*, exubérance ; influence, *f.* ; pouvoir, empire, *m.*

ramp′ant, *adj.*, dominant, régnant ; prédominant ; exubérant ; effréné ; surabondant ; (her.) rampant.

ram′part, *n.*, (fort.) rempart, *m.*

ram′pion, *n.*, (bot.) raiponce, *f.*

ram′pire, *n.*, (fort.) rempart, *m.*

ram′rod, *n.*, baguette, *f.* ; (of a cannon) refouloir, *m.*

ram′shackle, *adj.*, décrépit, qui tombe en ruines, délabré.

ran'cid, *adj.*, rance. To become —; *devenir rance, rancir*.

rancid'ity *ou* **ran'cidness**, *n.*, rancissure, rancidité, *f.*

ran'cor (rai'gn'keur), *n.*, haine, rancune, *f.*

ran'corous (rai'gn'-), *adj.*, rancunier, haineux.

ran'corously, *adv.*, avec, *ou* par, rancune.

ran'dom (-deume), *n.*, aventure, *f.*, hasard, *m.* At —; *au hasard ; à l'aventure, à l'abandon.* To speak at —; *parler à tort et à travers.*

ran'dom (-deume), *adj.*, au hasard ; fait au hasard ; (artil.) à toute volée, tiré à toute volée, perdu.

ran'dom-shot, *n.*, coup perdu, *m.*

range (ré'n'dje), *n.*, (row) rangée, *f.*, rang, *m.* ; (class) classe, *f.*, ordre, *m.* ; (excursion) excursion, course ; (extent) étendue, distance, portée, *f.*, essor ; (space) champ, espace, *m.* ; (reach) portée, *f.* ; (of a ladder) échelon, *m.* ; (kitchen grate) grille de cuisine, *f.*, fourneaux, *m.pl.* ; (sieve) sas à farine, bluteau, blutoir, *m.* ; (of mountains) chaîne, *f.*; (firing ground) tir, *m.*; (of firearms) (reach) portée, *f.* —finder ; *télémètre, m.* Within —; *à portée.*

range (ré'n'dje), *v.a.*, (arch., print.) aligner ; (to sift) bluter ; (nav.) ranger ; (to rove over) parcourir ; rôder **à travers** ; errer ; (to pass over) franchir ; (to arrange) arranger, ranger.

range, *v.n.*, errer; s'aligner ; (to lie) être situé ; (nav.) ranger la côte ; (to vary) varier ; s'étendre ; se vendre à un prix variant de . . . à.

ran'ger (ré'n'dj'-), *n.*, conservateur ; (dog) chien courant ; (ant.) corps de cavalerie légère, *m.*

ran'gership, *n.*, fonctions d'officier forestier, *f.pl.*, charge de conservateur, *f.*

ran'ging (ré'n'dj'-), *n.*, action de ranger ; action de franchir, *f.* ; rangement, arrangement ; (arch., print.) alignement, *m.*; excursion, *f.*; vagabondage, *m.* ; vie errante, *f.*

rank (raignke), *n.*, (row, class, dignity) (milit.) rang, grade, *m.*; (of cabs) place, station, *f.* To rise from the —s; *de simple soldat passer officier.* To close the —s; *serrer les rangs.* — and file ; *la ligne, f., les rangs ; hommes, soldats, m.pl.* To leave, *ou* quit, the —s ; *sortir des rangs, se débander.* To take from the —s ; *tirer des derniers rangs.* An officer of high — ; *un officier supérieur, un officier général.* An officer risen from the —s ; *un officier de fortune.* Cab — ; *station de voitures de place, f.* A person of — ; *une personne de condition ; une personne de haut rang ; une personne de qualité.* To take — of ; *avoir la préséance, ou le pas, sur.* To reduce to the —s ; *casser.* To take — ; *avoir, ou prendre, rang* **parmi**, *ou* **avec** ; *marcher de pair* **avec**.

rank, *adj.*, rance ; (strong) fort ; (gross) grossier, rude ; (excessive) violent, excessif, extrême ; (downright) vrai ; (fertile) fertile, fécond ; (of vigorous growth) vigoureux, fort, luxuriant.

rank, *v.a.*, ranger, classer. To — among one's friends ; *compter*, *ou* *mettre, au rang, ou au nombre, de ses amis.*

rank, *v.n.*, se ranger, être rangé ; prendre rang, occuper un rang ; avoir un rang ; avoir rang. To — high ; *occuper un rang élevé, prendre une place élevée.* To — after ; *prendre*, ou *avoir, rang* **après** ; *venir* **après**.

rank'ish, *adj.*, un peu rance.

ran'kle (rai'gn'k'l), *v.n.*, s'envenimer, s'enflammer. Hatred —s in his breast ; *la haine lui ronge le cœur, ou ronge son cœur.*

rank'ly, *adv.*, avec rancidité ; fortement ; grossièrement, rudement ; excessivement, extrêmement ; fertilement, avec fécondité ; vigoureusement.

rank'ness, *n.*, rancissure, rancidité, *f.* ; goût fort, *m.* ; abondance, *f.* ; excès, *m.* ; (of vegetation) vigueur, surabondance, exubérance, *f.*

ran'sack (ran-), *v.a.*, saccager ; piller ; fouiller ; fouiller **dans** ; mettre à contribution.

ran'sacking, *n.*, saccagement, sac, pillage, *m.*; (search) perquisition, *f.*

ran'som (-ceume), *n.*, rançon, délivrance, *f.* ; rachat, *m.*

ran'som (-ceume), *v.a.*, rançonner ; racheter.

ran'somer, *n.*, personne qui rachète, qui délivre, *f.*

ran'somless, *adj.*, sans rançon.

rant, *n.*, déclamation extravagante, *f.*; paroles ampoulées, *f. pl.* ; phébus, clabaudage, galimatias, *m.*

rant, *v.n.*, déclamer avec extravagance ; extravaguer ; clabauder ; tempêter ; parler phébus.

rant'er, *n.*, déclamateur extravagant, *m.*

rant'ing, *adj.*, d'une déclamation extravagante, extravagant.

ran'ula (ra'n'iou-), *n.*, (med.) ranule, grenouillette, *f.*

ranun'culus (ra-neu'n'kiou-), *n.*, (bot.) renoncule, *f.*

rap, *n.*, tape, *f.*; coup sec ; (ant. coin) liard, *m.* Not worth a — ; *qui ne vaut pas le diable, les quatre fers d'un chien.* I don't care a — ; *je m'en soucie comme de l'an quarante, je m'en moque.*

rap, *v.n.*, frapper. To — out ; (an oath) *lâcher, laisser échapper (un juron)* ; (general) *dire étourdiment.*

rap, *v.a.* To — and rend ; *faire main basse* **sur**.

rapa'cious (ra-pé-sheusse), *adj.*, rapace.

rapa'ciously, *adv.*, avec rapacité.

rapa'ciousness *ou* **rapac'ity**, *n.*, rapacité, *f.*

rape, *n.*, rapt, enlèvement ; (jur.) viol, *m.* ; (bot.) navette, *f.*, colza, *m.*

rape'-cake, *n.*, tourteau de colza, *m.*

rape'-oil, *n.*, huile de colza, *f.*

rape'-wine, *n.*, piquette, *f.*, râpé, *m.*

rap'id, *n.*, (rapids) rapide, *m.*

rap'id, *adj.*, rapide.

rapid'ity, **rap'idness**, *n.*, rapidité, *f.*

rap'idly, *adv.*, rapidement.

ra'pier (ré-pieure), *n.*, rapière, *f.*

rap'ine (rap'ine), *n.*, rapine, *f.*

rappee' (-pî), *n.*, tabac râpé ; râpé, *m.*

rap'per, *n.*, personne qui frappe, *f.* ; (thing) marteau, *m.*

rapt, *past part.*, ravi, transporté, extasié, en extase.

raptor'ial, *adj.*, (orni.) de proie.

rap'ture (rapt'ieur), *n.*, ravissement, transport ; enthousiasme, *m.* ; extase, joie, ivresse,*f.*

rap'tured (rapt'ieurde), *adj.* V. **rapt**.

rap'turous (rapt'ieur'-), *adj.*, ravissant ; enivrant ; enthousiaste ; joyeux ; (of applause) frénétique.

rap'turously, *adv.*, avec transport ; avec enthousiasme ; avec frénésie.

rare, *adj.*, rare ; (thinly scattered) épars, clairsemé ; excellent, exquis, beau ; (phys.) rare, raréfié ; (thorough) fameux, furieux, fier.

rar'ee-show (rè-rî-shô) *ou* **rare'-show**, *n.*, spectacle ambulant, *ou* forain, *m.* ; curiosité, *f.*

rarefac'tion (rèr-i-fak-), *n.*, raréfaction, *f.*

rarefi'able (rèr-i-faï-a-b'l), *adj.*, raréfiable.

rar'efy (rèr'i-faïe), *v.a.*, raréfier.

rar'efy, *v.n.*, se raréfier.

ra'refying, *adj.*, raréfiant.

rare'ly (rèr'-), *adv.*, rarement.

rare'ness *ou* **rar'ity** (rèr'-), *n.*, rareté ; (phys.) raréfaction, *f.*

ras'cal (râs'-), *n.*, coquin, fripon, polisson, drôle, gredin, *m.*

rascal'ity, *n.*, friponnerie, gredinerie, coquinerie ; (populace) canaille, *f.*

rascal'lion (-cal'ieune), *n.*, malotru, drôle, faquin, polisson, *m.* ; canaille,*f.*

ras'cally (râs-), *adj.*, de coquin, de fripon ; (worthless) misérable, vil.

rase (réze *ou* réce), *v.a.*, (to graze) raser,

friser, effleurer ; (to erase) rayer, effacer ; (to overthrow) raser, extirper, renverser, détruire, démolir.

rash, n., (med.) éruption, f.

rash, adj., téméraire ; irréfléchi, inconsidéré ; imprudent. It is very — of you ; c'est très imprudent de votre part.

rash'er, n., tranche, barde, f. — of bacon ; tranche de lard, f.

rash'ly, adv., témérairement ; inconsidérément ; sans réflexion ; imprudemment.

rash'ness, n., témérité ; précipitation ; imprudence ; nature irréfléchie, f.

rasp (râspe), n., (tool) râpe ; (surg.) rugine, f.

rasp, v.a., râper ; (bread) chapeler ; (surg.) ruginer.

ras'patory, n., rugine, f.

rasp'berry, n., framboise, f.

rasp'berry-bush (-boushe), n., framboisier, m. — jam ; confiture de framboises, f. — vinegar ; vinaigre framboisé, m.

rasp'er, n., râpeur, m., râpeuse ; râpe, f.

rasp'ing, n., râpage, m. —s, pl., râpure, f.sing. ; (of bread) chapelure, f.sing. —-mill ; moulin à râper, m.

rat (rate), n., rat ; (pers.) transfuge ; (workman) gâte-métier, m. To smell a — ; se douter de quelque chose.

rat, v.n., tourner casaque ; (workman) gâter le métier.

rat'able (ré-ta-b'l), adj., qui peut être évalué ; (liable to taxation) imposable, sujet aux impôts.

rat'ably (ré-ta-), adv., à proportion.

ratafi'a, n., ratafia, m.

ratan', n., rotin, rotang, m.

rat'-catcher, n., preneur de rats, m.

ratch, n., (horl.) rochet, m. ; (mec.) crémaillère, f.

ratch'et, n., (horl.) guide-chaîne, m. ; (tech.) dent d'engrenage, f. ; (of a lock) rochet, m.

ratch'et-en-gine (-è'n'djine), n., machine à tailler les dents d'engrenage, f.

ratch'et-wheel (-hwîle), n., roue d'engrenage, roue à dents ; (horl.) roue d'échappement, roue à rochet, f.

rate (réte), n., (standard) prix, taux, m. ; proportion, f.; (degree of value) taux, cours ; (price) prix ; (of exchange) cours ; (degree) degré, rang, ordre, m. ; classe, mesure, f. ; (allowance) quantité ; (degree of speed) vitesse, f.; (pace) train, m., vitesse, f.; (nav.) rang, m. ; (tax) contribution, taxe, f., impôt, m. First— ; de première force ; (of rank) de première classe ; de premier ordre ; (of quality) de première qualité. At any — I will come ; de toute façon je m'y trouverai. At any —; de toute façon ; coûte que coûte ; à tout prix ; à quelque prix que ce soit ; quoi qu'il en soit ; à tout événement. At a great — ; grand train. At a tremendous — ; ventre à terre, à bride abattue. At the — of ; au taux de ; à raison de ; (of speed) à la vitesse de. At the — you are going, you will soon be ruined ; au train dont vous allez, vous vous ruinerez bientôt. She was talking away at a great — ; elle parlait avec une volubilité extrême. At a cheap — ; à bon compte, à bon marché. At this — ; sur ce pied-là ; à ce compte-là ; à ce train ; de cette façon.

rate, v.a., évaluer ; tarifer ; coter ; estimer ; apprécier ; (to place in a class, as a ship) classer ; donner un rang à, donner un ordre à ; (to assess) imposer, taxer ; (to chide) gronder vertement, réprimander, tancer ; faire une mercuriale à, semoncer, sermoner.

rate, v.n., faire une estimation. To — as ; être classé comme ; être estimé à ; compter comme ; avoir le rang de.

rate'-book (-bouke), n., registre (pour l'assiette et la perception d'une taxe), m.

rate'-payer (-pé-eur), n., contribuable, m. f.

rat'er, n., estimateur, priseur, m.

ra'ther (râth'-), adv., (in preference) plutôt ; mieux ; un peu ; quelque peu ; assez, passablement. —! un peu! I would — ; j'aimerais mieux, je voudrais plutôt. — ill ; un peu malade. Or — ; ou plutôt ; ou pour mieux dire. Anything — than ; rien moins que. — pretty ; assez joli. With — a lisp ; avec quelque chose comme un zézaiement. The — for ; the — because ; d'autant plus que. I — think ; j'ai idée, je suis porté à croire, je soupçonne. To have, ou choose, — ; préférer, aimer mieux.

ratifica'tion (-fi-ké-), n., ratification, f.

rat'ifier (-faï'-), n., qui ratifie, f.

rat'ify (-faïe), v.a., ratifier.

rat'ifying, adj., ratificatif.

rat'ing (rét'-), n., estimation ; évaluation ; (assessment) répartition de l'impôt ; (chiding) gronderie, semonce, f.; (pop.) savon, m.

ra'tio (ré-shi-ô), n., proportion, raison, f.; rapport, m. In the — of ; dans le rapport de, à raison de.

ratiocina'tion (rash'i-oss'i-né-), n., ratiocination, logique, f. ; raisonnement, m.

ra'tion (ré-), n., ration, f. v.a., rationner.

ra'tional (rash'eu'n'-), adj., (endowed with reason) doué de raison ; raisonnable ; (agreeable to reason, judicious) raisonnable ; (arith., astron.) rationnel.

rationa'le (rash'i-o-né-li), n., analyse raisonnée, f.

rat'ionalism (rash'eu'n-al-iz'm), n., rationalisme, m.

rat'ionalist, n., rationaliste, m.

rational'ity, n., faculté de raisonner, f.; raisonnement, m. ; raison, justesse, f. ; (philos.) caractère rationnel, m.

ra'tionally, adv., raisonnablement ; (philos.) rationnellement.

rat's'-bane, n., mort aux rats, f. [de-rat, f.

rat'-tail ou **rat's'-tail** (-téle), n., (vet.) queue-**rattan'**, n., rotin, rotang, m.

ratteen' (rat'tîne), n., ratine, f.

rat'ten, v.a., intimider, priver de ses outils.

rat'tery, **rat'ting**, n., apostasie, tergiversation, désertion, f.; nid à rats, m.

rattinet', n., petite ratine, f.

rat'tle (rat't'l), v.a., faire résonner, faire retentir ; faire sonner ; (chains) secouer ; (to scold) gronder vertement.

rat'tle, v.n., faire du bruit ; résonner, retentir ; crier, grincer ; (to speak) bavarder. To — along ; rouler. To — on ; aller toujours. To — over ; résonner sur. To — past ; passer avec fracas. To — away ; dégoiser.

rat'tle (rat't'l), n., (noise) bruit ; (of metals) cliquetis, m. ; (empty talk) bavardage ; (med.) râle ; (toy) hochet, grelot, m. ; (for a policeman) crécelle ; (scolding) réprimande, mercuriale, f. Death-— ; râle de la mort, m.

rat'tle-brained (-brè'n'de) ou **rat'tle-head'ed** (-hèd'ède), adj., étourdi, écervelé.

rat'tles (rat't'l'ze), n.pl., (med.) croup, m.

rat'tlesnake, n., serpent à sonnettes ; crotale, m.

rat'tle-traps, n.pl., effets, m.pl.; affaires, choses, f.pl.; (pop.) bataclan, m., bagages, m.pl.

rat'tling, adj., bruyant ; (fig.) excellent ; (pop.) fier. A — breakfast ; un fier déjeuner. At a — pace ; au grand trot (V. Hugo). — tongue ; langue bien pendue, f.

rat'tling, n., bruit, cliquetis, bruissement, m.

rat'-trap, n., ratière, f.

rau'city, n., son rauque, m., raucité, f.

rau'cous, adj., rauque.

rav'age (rav'èdje), n., ravage, m.

rav'age, v.a., ravager.

rav'ager, n., ravageur ; dévastateur, m.

rave (réve), v.n., délirer, avoir le délire, être surexcité ; se désespérer, se lamenter ; (fig.)

extravaguer, divaguer ; battre la campagne (A. Daudet). To — at ; *s'emporter*, ou *être furieux*, contre. To — about ; *raffoler de* ; *être fou de*.

rav'el, *v.a.*, entortiller ; (fig.) embrouiller. To — out ; *effiler, effiloquer, démêler, débrouiller*.

rav'el (rav-v'l), *v.n.*, s'embrouiller ; s'entortiller. To — out ; *s'effiler, s'effiloquer, se débrouiller*.

rave'lin (rav'line), *n.*, (fort.) ravelin, *m.*, demi-lune, *f.*

rav'elings (rav'èl'lign'z), *n.pl.*, effilures, *f.pl.*

ra'ven (ré-v'n), *n.*, (orni.) corbeau, *m.*

rav'eners, *n.pl.*, rapaces, ravisseurs, *m.pl.*

rav'ening, *n.*, rapacité, *f.*

rav'enous (rav'v'n'-), *adj.*, vorace, dévorant ; carnassier.

rav'enously, *adv.*, avec voracité, *f.*

rav'enousness, *n.*, voracité, rapacité, *f.*

ravine' (ra-vîne), *n.*, ravin, *m.* ; ravine, *f.*

rav'ing (rév'-), *adj.*, en délire, délirant ; furieux, frénétique ; fou. — mad ; *fou à lier ; fou furieux*.

rav'ing, *n.*, délire, *m.* ; frénésie, divagation, *f.*

rav'ingly, *adv.*, furieusement ; avec frénésie ; en frénétique.

rav'ish (rav'-), *v.a.*, ravir ; enlever ; (to delight) ravir, transporter ; (to violate) violer.

rav'isher, *n.*, ravisseur, *m.* ; personne qui ravit, qui transporte, *f.*

rav'ishing, *adj.*, ravissant.

rav'ishingly, *adv.*, à ravir ; d'une manière ravissante.

rav'ishment, rav'ishing, *n.*, ravissement ; enlèvement ; viol, ravissement, *m.*

raw (rō), *adj.*, (not cooked) cru ; (bare) vif, ulcéré, écorché ; (unripe) vert, peu mûr ; (inexperienced) sans expérience, inexpérimenté, novice, neuf ; (untried) nouveau, non essayé ; (of liquors) pur, sans eau ; (of the weather) froid et humide ; (of silk) grège ; (of hides) brut ; (of sugar, of materials) brut ; premier. — material ; *matière première, f.* To touch one on the —; *piquer, toucher quelqu'un au vif*.

raw'bone (-bōne) *ou* **raw'boned** (-bō'n'de), *adj.*, qui n'a que la peau et les os ; maigre, décharné.

raw'-flesh, *n.*, chair vive, *f.*

raw'-hand, *n.*, novice, *m.f.*

raw'head (-hède) *n.*, loup-garou, *m.*

raw'-hide, *n.*, cuir brut, *m.*

raw'ly, *adv.*, crûment, sans expérience ; sans avenir assuré, sans provision.   [*f.pl.*

raw' mate'rials, *n.pl.*, matières premières,

raw'ness, *n.*, crudité, *f.* ; (of the weather) froid humide ; (soreness) état ulcéré, *m.* ; inexperience) inexpérience, ignorance, *f.*

raw' silk, *n.*, soie grège, ou crue, *f.*

ray (ré), *n.*, rayon ; (fig.) éclat, rayon, *m.* ; (ich.) raie, *f.*

ray'-grass, *n.*, ivraie vivace, *f.*

ray'less, *adj.*, sans rayon ; sans lumière.

raze (réze), *v.a.*, raser, abattre ; déraciner.

razee' (ra-zî), *n.*, (nav.) vaisseau rasé, *m.*

ra'zor (ré-zeur), *n.*, rasoir, *m.* ; (of a boar) défense, *f.*

ra'zor-bill (ré-), *n.*, (orni.) pingouin commun, *m.*

ra'zor-cloth, *n.*, linge à barbe, *m.*

ra'zor-fish (ré-), *n.*, (ich.) rasoir, rason, *m.*

ra'zor-strap, *or* **-strop**, *n.*, cuir à barbe, *m.*, raz'zia, *n.*, razzia, *m.*   [cuir à rasoir.

reabsorb' (rî-), *v.a.*, absorber de nouveau.

reabsorp'tion (rî-), *n.*, absorption nouvelle, *f.*

reac'cess (rî-), *n.*, retour, *m.* ; visite renouvelée, *f.*

reach (rîtshe), *n.*, (extent) étendue ; (power of extending to) portée, *f.* ; (power) pouvoir, *m.* ; (intellectual power) portée, capacité, étendue ; (artifice) ruse, *f.* ; (of a canal) bief, *m.* Out of any one's —; *hors de la portée de quelqu'un*,

hors d'atteinte. Within any one's —; *à la portée de quelqu'un*.

reach, *v.a.*, atteindre ; (to hand) passer, donner ; (to touch) toucher ; (to attain) arriver à, parvenir à, atteindre ; (to extend) étendre. To — down ; *descendre*. The letter will — you to-morrow ; *la lettre vous parviendra demain*. — me that book ; *descendez ; passez-moi ce livre*.

reach, *v.n.*, s'étendre à ; (to penetrate) pénétrer dans ; (of firearms) porter à. To — after ; *s'efforcer d'atteindre*.

reach'able, *adj.*, accessible.

react' (rî-), *v.a.*, jouer de nouveau ; représenter de nouveau ; rejouer.

react', *v.n.*, réagir ; résister.

reac'tion (rî-), *n.*, réaction, *f.*

read (rède), *past part.*, qui a de la lecture ; qui a profité de ses lectures. To be well —; *avoir beaucoup de lecture ; avoir lu beaucoup ; être savant, ou instruit ; être versé dans*.

read (rîde), *v.a.* (*preterit* and *past part.*, Read), lire ; faire la lecture de. To — again ; *relire, étudier de nouveau*. To — aloud ; *lire à haute voix*. To — on ; *continuer à*, ou *de, lire*. To — to one's self ; *lire tout bas*. To — out ; *lire tout haut*. To — over ; *parcourir*. To — over and over again ; *lire et relire*. To — between the lines ; *lire entre les lignes*. To — up ; *faire une étude spéciale de*. To — music ; (at sight) *déchiffrer un morceau*. To — one's self in ; (Engl. Church) *déclarer son adhésion aux articles de religion*. To — to a person ; *faire la lecture à quelqu'un*. To — of ; *lire l'histoire de*. The passage —s thus ; *voici les termes textuels du passage*. Which we — of ; *dont on fait mention dans les livres*. Not to — well ; (of a passage) *ne pas faire bon effet*. To — out the names ; (of prize-winners) *proclamer les noms*.

read'able (rîd'a-b'l), *adj.*, lisible, qui se lit avec plaisir.

read'ableness, *n.*, lisibilité, *f.*

read'er (rîd'-), *n.*, lecteur, *m.*, lectrice, *f.* ; (print.) correcteur, *m.* ; (person fond of reading) personne qui aime la lecture, *f.*, liseur, *m.*, liseuse, *f.* ; (church) lecteur ; (of a book) livre de lecture, livre de traduction, *m.*

read'ership, *n.*, fonctions d'ecclésiastique qui lit les prières, *m.* ; (univ.) chaire, *f.*

read'ily (rèd'-), *adv.*, tout de suite, promptement, aisément ; (willingly) volontiers, avec plaisir, avec empressement ; de bonne grâce, sans hésiter.

read'iness (rèd'-), *n.*, promptitude ; facilité ; (willingness) bonne volonté, *f.* ; empressement, *m.* — of mind ; *présence d'esprit, f.* — of wit ; *talent de repartie, m.* In —; *tout prêt*.

read'ing (rîd'-), *n.*, lecture ; (in criticism) teneur ; (lecture) leçon ; interprétation, explication ; (study) étude ; (variation in a text) variante, leçon ; (of the barometer) variation, indication, *f.*

read'ing-book (-bouke), *n.*, livre de lecture, *m.*

read'ing-boy (-boï), *n.*, (print.) teneur de copie, *m.*

read'ing-clos'et (-clôz'-), *n.*, (print.) cabinet de correcteur, *m.*

read'ing-desk, *n.*, pupitre ; (church) lutrin, *m.*

read'ing-lamp (-), *n.*, lampe de travail, *f.*

read'ing-man, *n.*, travailleur, piocheur, *m.*

read'ing-room (-roume), *n.*, cabinet de lecture, *m.* ; salle de lecture, *f.*

readjourn' (rî-ad-jeurne), *v.n.*, ajourner de, ou à, nouveau ; réajourner.

readjust' (rî-ad-jeuste), *v.a.*, rajuster.

readjust'ment (ri-ad-jeust'-), *n.*, rajustement, *m.*

readmis'sion *ou* **readmit'tance** (rî-), *n.*, réadmission, *f.*

readmit' (rî-), *v.a.*, admettre de nouveau.

readopt' (rî-), *v.a.*, adopter de nouveau.

readorn' (rî-), *v.a.*, orner de nouveau.

read'y (rèd'-), *adj.*, (quick) prompt; (dexterous) qui a de la facilité; (quick of apprehension) vif; (of money) comptant; (prepared) prêt; (willing) prêt à, prompt à, disposé à, empressé à; (inclined) porté à; (near at hand) le premier venu, sous la main; (easy, short) facile, court. To make —; *préparer, apprêter, tenir prêt.* To get —; *se préparer; se tenir prêt.* Now —; (of books) *vient de paraître, en vente.* —! fire! (mil.) *en joue! feu!*

read'y (rèd'-), *adv.*, tout. — -armed; *tout armé.* — -formed; *tout formé.*

read'y-made (-méde), *adj.*, tout fait; confectionné. — clothier; *confectionneur, m.*

read'y-money, *n.*, argent comptant, comptant, *m.*

read'y-reckoner, *n.*, barème, *f.*

read'y-witted, *adj.*, spirituel; à l'esprit vif.

reaffirm' (rî-af'feurme), *v.a.*, affirmer de nouveau.

reaffirm'ance (rî-af'feurm'-), *n.*, nouvelle affirmation, *f.*

rea'gent (rî-é-djè'n'te), *n.*, (chem.) réactif, *m.*

re'al (rî-), *adj.*, réel; vrai; véritable; effectif; (jur.) réel, immeuble, immobilier.

re'al (rî-), *n.*, réal (Spanish coin), *m.*

re'algar (rî-), *n.*, (min.) réalgar, *m.*

re'alist (rî-), *n.*, réaliste, *m.*

real'ity (rî-), *n.*, réalité, *f.*; réel, *m.* In —; *réellement, en réalité.*

re'alizable, *adj.*, réalisable.

realiza'tion (rî-al-aï-zé-), *n.*, réalisation, *f.*; (of money) conversion en bien-fonds, immobilisation, *f.*

re'alize (rî-al-aïze), *v.a.*, réaliser; effectuer; (to believe as real) regarder comme réel; croire à la réalité **de**; se rendre compte **de**; sentir dans toute sa force; bien comprendre; concevoir; se représenter; se faire une idée juste **de**; se figurer; (to fetch) rapporter; produire; se vendre à; (money, property) immobiliser; convertir en bien-fonds; (to obtain) obtenir; (to derive) tirer, recueillir. To be —d; *se réaliser.*

reallege' (rî-al'lèdje), *v.a.*, alléguer de nouveau.

re'ally (rî-), *adv.*, réellement, en réalité, en effet, effectivement, vraiment, véritablement, franchement, en vérité, ma foi.

realm (rèl'm), *n.*, royaume, pays, domaine, *m.*, région, *f.*

re'alty (rî-), *n.*, (jur.) caractère immobilier, *m.*; biens immeubles, *m.pl.*

ream (rîme), *n.*, rame, *f.*

rean'imate (rî-), *v.a.*, ranimer.

reanima'tion (rî-a'n'i-mé-), *n.*, action de ranimer, *f.*

reannex' (rî-), *v.a.*, annexer de nouveau.

reannexa'tion (rî-a'n'nèks'é-), *n.*, action d'annexer de nouveau, *f.*

reap (rîpe), *v.a.*, moissonner; récolter; (to obtain) retirer, recueillir. To — the harvest; *faire la moisson.*

reap, *v.n.*, moissonner; faire la moisson.

reap'er, *n.*, moissonneur, *m.*; moissonneuse, *f.*

reap'ing, *n.*, moisson, *f.* — machine; *moissonneuse, f.*

reap'ing-hook (-houke), *n.*, faucille, *f.*

reap'ing-time (-taïme), *n.*, moisson, *f.*, temps de la moisson, *m.*

reappar'el (rî-), *v.a.*, rhabiller.

reappear' (rî-ap-pîr), *v.n.*, reparaître.

reappear'ance (rî-ap-pîr'-), *n.*, réapparition; (of an actor) rentrée; (jur.) comparution nouvelle, *f.*

reappease', *v.a.*, rapaiser.

reappease'ment, *n.*, rapaisement, *m.*

reapplica'tion (ri-ap-pli-ké-), *n.*, nouvelle application, *f.*; nouvel emploi, *m.*; nouvelle demande, nouvelle sollicitation, *f.*

reapply' (rî-ap-plaïe), *v.a.*, appliquer de nouveau; adresser de nouveau.

reapply', *v.n.*, s'appliquer de nouveau; s'adresser de nouveau.

reappoint' (rî-ap-pôï'n'te), *v.a.*, arrêter de nouveau; instituer de nouveau; rétablir; désigner de nouveau; indiquer, fixer de nouveau; renommer à des fonctions.

reappoint'ment, *n.*, nouveau rendez-vous, *m.*; nouvelle nomination, *f.*

reappor'tion (rî-ap-), *v.a.*, répartir de nouveau.

reappor'tionment (rî-), *n.*, nouveau partage, *m.*; nouvelle répartition, *f.*

rear (rîre), *n.*, dernier rang, *m.*; queue, *f.*; (milit.) arrière-garde, *f.*; derrière, *m.*; (of buildings, etc.) derrière, *m.* At, *ou* in, the —; *par derrière.* In the — of; *derrière.* To attack in the —; *attaquer par derrière, en queue.* To bring up the —; *fermer la marche.*

rear (rîre), *v.a.*, élever; relever.

rear, *v.n.*, se cabrer.

rear-ad'miral, *n.*, contre-amiral, *m.*

rear'-guard, *n.*, (milit.) arrière-garde, *f.*

re-arm', *v.a.*, réarmer.

re-arm'ament, *n.*, réarmement, *m.*

rear'-rank, *n.*, dernier rang, *m.*

rear'ward (-wôrde), *n.*, arrière-garde, queue, *f.*

reascend' (rî-), *v.a. and n.*, remonter.

reascent', *n.*, nouvelle montée, *f.*

rea'son (rî-z'n), *n.*, raison, *f.* By — of; *en raison de*; *à cause de.* For — s best known to myself; *pour des raisons à moi connues.* For the very — that; *par cela même que, précisément parce que.* To speak —; *parler raison.* That stands to —; *cela va sans dire*; *cela tombe sous le sens.* To have — to believe; *avoir lieu de croire.* To bring to —; *amener à la raison.* To listen to —; *entendre raison.* It stands to — that; *le bon sens dit que.* There is every — to believe; *il y a tout lieu de croire.*

rea'son (rî-z'n), *v.n.*, raisonner.

rea'son, *v.a.*, raisonner. To — into; *entraîner à.* To — out of; *détourner* **de**.

rea'sonable (ri-z'n'a-b'l), *adj.*, raisonnable.

rea'sonableness, *n.*, caractère raisonnable, *m.*; raison, modération, justice, justesse, *f.*

rea'sonably, *adv.*, raisonnablement.

rea'soner (rî-z'n'-), *n.*, raisonneur, *m.*; raisonneuse, *f.*; logicien, dialecticien, *m.*

rea'soning (ri-z'n'-), *n.*, raisonnement, *m.*

rea'sonless, *adj.*, sans raison.

reassem'blage (rî-as'sè'm'blèdje), *n.*, assemblage nouveau, *m.*

reassem'ble (ri-as'sè'm'b'l), *v.a.*, assembler de nouveau.

reassem'ble, *v.n.*, s'assembler de nouveau.

reassert' (rî-as'seurte), *v.a.*, soutenir de nouveau; déclarer de nouveau; avancer de nouveau; affirmer de nouveau; (rights) revendiquer de nouveau.

reassess', *v.a.*, réimposer, imposer de nouveau.

reassess'ment, *n.*, réimposition, *f.*

reassign' (rî-as'saïne), *v.a.*, assigner de nouveau; réassigner.

reassign'ment, *n.*, réassignation, *f.*

reassim'ilate (rî-), *v.a.*, assimiler de nouveau.

reassume' (rî-as-sioume), *v.a.*, prendre de nouveau; reprendre.

reassur'ance (rî-a-shiour'-), *n.*, nouvelle assurance, (com.) réassurance, *f.*

reassure' (rî-a-shioure), *v.a.*, rassurer; (com.) réassurer.

reassur'er, *n.*, (com.) réassureur, *m.*

reattach' (rî-at'tatshe), *v.a.*, rattacher; (jur.) arrêter, saisir de nouveau.

reattach'ment, *n.*, nouvel attachement, *m.*; (jur.) nouvelle contrainte; nouvelle saisie, *f.*

reattempt' (rî-), *v.a.*, essayer de nouveau, tenter de nouveau; faire une nouvelle tentative.

reattempt', *n.*, nouvelle tentative, *f.*

rebap'tism (rî-bap-tiz'm), *n.*, nouveau baptême, *m.*

rebaptize' (rî-bap-taïze), *v.a.*, rebaptiser.

rebate' (rî-), *n.*, diminution, *f.*; (com.) rabais, *m.*; réfaction, réduction ; (arith.) règle d'escompte, *f.*

rebate', *v.a.*, émousser ; diminuer.

rebate'ment, *n.* *V.* rebate.

re'bec (rî-bèke), *n.*, (mus.) rebec, *m.*

reb'el (rèb'èl), *n.*, rebelle, révolté, insurgé, *m.*

rebel', *v.n.*, se révolter, se soulever, se rebeller, s'insurger.

rebel'lion (ri-bel'ieune), *n.*, rébellion, *f.*

rebel'lious (ri-bèl'-), *adj.*, rebelle, révolté, insurgé.

rebel'liously, *adv.*, en rebelle.

rebel'liousness, *n.*, rébellion, *f.*

reblos'som (rî-blos'seume), *v.n.*, refleurir.

reboil', *v.n.*, rebouillir.

rebound' (rè-baou'n'de), *n.*, rebondissement, rejaillissement, contre-coup, *m.*

rebound', *v.n.*, rebondir ; rejaillir ; (of sound) retentir.

rebound', *v.a.*, faire rebondir ; (sound) répercuter, renvoyer.

rebreathe' (rî-brî*th*e), *v.n.*, respirer de nouveau.

rebuff' (rî-beuf), *n.*, rebuffade, *f.*; échec ; refus, *m.*

rebuff', *v.a.*, rebuter, repousser, rebuffer.

rebuild' (rî-bilde), *v.a.*, (*preterit* and *past part.*, Rebuilt) rebâtir, reconstruire.

rebuild'er, *n.*, reconstructeur, *m.*

rebuk'able (rè-biouk'a-b'l), *adj.*, répréhensible, blâmable.

rebuke' (rè-biouke), *n.*, réprimande, *f.*; reproche, blâme, *m.*; rebuffade, *f.*

rebuke', *v.a.*, réprimander, blâmer, reprendre, censurer ; faire des reproches à ; (in Scripture) châtier, réprimander.

rebuk'er, *n.*, personne qui réprimande, qui censure, qui fait des reproches, *f.*; censeur, *m.*

rebuk'ingly, *adv.*, avec une réprimande.

re'bus (rî-), *n.*, rébus, *f.*

rebut' (rè-beute), *v.a.*, rebuter ; repousser ; réfuter.

rebut', *v.n.*, riposter ; (jur.) dupliquer.

rebut'ter (rè-beut'-), *n.*, (jur.) duplique, *f.*

recal'citrant, *adj.*, récalcitrant, insoumis.

recal'citrate, *v.n.*, récalcitrer, regimber.

recall' (rè-côl), *n.*, rappel, *m.*; révocation ; rétractation, *f.*

recall', *v.a.*, rappeler ; rétracter ; retirer ; révoquer ; (to remember) se rappeler.

recall'able (rè-côl'a-b'l), *adj.*, révocable, rappelable.

recane', *v.a.*, (chairs) recanner.

recant' (rè-), *v.n.*, se rétracter ; se dédire **de** ; chanter la palinodie.

recant', *v.a.*, rétracter, désavouer ; abjurer.

recanta'tion (rî-ca'n'té-), *n.*, rétractation, abjuration, palinodie, *f.*

recant'er, *n.*, personne qui se rétracte, qui se dédit, qui abjure, *f.*

recapit'ulate (rî-ca-pit'iou-), *v.a.*, récapituler, résumer.

recapitula'tion (rî-ca-pit'iou-lé-), *n.*, récapitulation, *f.*; résumé, *m.*

recapit'ulatory, *adj.*, récapitulatif.

recap'tion (rî-), *n.*, (jur.) reprise, *f.*

recap'tor, *n.*, repreneur, *m.*

recap'ture (rî-capt'ieur), *n.*, reprise ; (l.u.) recousse, rescousse, *f.*

recap'ture (rî-capt'ieur), *v.a.*, reprendre.

recar'ry (rî-), *v.a.*, reporter, rapporter.

recast' (rî-câste), *v.a.*, (*preterit* and *past part.*, Recast) refondre ; (metal.) couler de nouveau ; (arith.) additionner, calculer, **compter** de nouveau.

recede' (rè-cîde), *v.n.*, reculer ; s'éloigner ; se retirer ; (to desist) se désister **de**, se rétracter **de**.

receipt' (rè-cîte), *n.*, (act of receiving) réception ; (place) recette, *f.*; bureau de recette, *m.*; (recipe) recette, *f.*; (com.) reçu, *m.*, quittance, *f.*, acquit, *m.* *pl.* (money received) recette, *f.sing.*, recettes, *f.pl.*; (admin.) récépissé, *m.* Acknowledgment of — ; *accusé de réception, m.* To acknowledge the — of ; *accuser réception* **de**. To put a — to ; *acquitter ; mettre un acquit à.* — in full of all demands ; *quittance pour solde de tout compte.* On — of ; *au reçu* **de** ; (stamps, etc.) *contre envoi* **de** ; (news, etc.) *en recevant.* To be in — of ; (letters, etc.) *avoir reçu* ; (fig.) *jouir* **de**.

receipt', *v.a.*, donner un reçu **pour** ; donner une quittance **pour** ; acquitter ; mettre un acquit à, acquitter.

receipt'ed, *adj.*, acquitté. Bill — ; *mémoire acquitté, m., note acquittée, f.*

receiv'able (rè-cîv'a'b-l), *adj.*, recevable, admissible ; (com.) à recevoir.

receive' (rè-cîve), *v.a.*, recevoir; accueillir ; (money) recevoir, toucher ; (stolen goods) recéler. —d ; *reçu ; pour acquit.*

receiv'er (rè-cîv'-), *n.*, percepteur, receveur, *m.*, receveuse, *f.*; (of stolen objects) receleur, *m.*, receleuse, *f.*; (sharer) distributaire ; (of letters) destinataire ; (com.) réceptionnaire ; (chem.) récipient, *m.* The — is as bad as the thief ; (prov.) *autant vaut celui qui tient que celui qui écorche.*

receiv'ership, *n.*, recette ; charge, *f.*, ou emploi, *m.*, de receveur.

receiv'ing (rè-cîv'-), *n.*, réception, *f.* ; (jur.) recel, recèlement, *m.*

receiv'ing-house (-haouce), *n.*, petite poste, boîte aux lettres ; (of the Royal Humane Society) maison de secours pour les noyés, *f.* ; (of parcels delivery companies) dépôt de paquets pour les petites messageries ; bureau de factage, *m.*

re'cency (rî-cè'n'-), *n.*, nouveauté ; date récente, *f.*

recense' (rè-cè'n'se), *v.a.*, reviser.

recen'sion (rè-), *n.*, énumération ; recension ; revue, *f.*

re'cent (rî-), *adj.*, récent, frais, nouveau. — intelligence ; *nouvelles fraîches, f.pl.*

re'cently, *adv.*, récemment, fraîchement, nouvellement.

recep'tacle (rè-cèp'ta-k'l), *n.*, asile, refuge ; réceptacle ; (anat.) réservoir ; (bot., hydraul.) réceptacle, *m.*

recep'tion (rè-cèp-), *n.*, réception, *f.*; accueil, *m.*; (readmission) rentrée ; (opinion generally admitted) opinion reçue, *f.* For the — of ; *pour recevoir.*

recep'tive (rè-cèp-tive), *adj.*, réceptif.

recess' (rè-), *n.*, retraite, *f.*; (holidays) vacances, *f.pl.*; (secret) secret ; (of the heart) repli ; (arch.) renfoncement, *m.*, embrasure, niche ; (for a bed) alcôve, *f.*

reces'sion (rè-cèsh-), *n.*, retraite, *f.*; (from a claim) désistement, *m.* ; (of things given back) restitution, *f.*

recharge' (rî-tshârdje), *v.a.*, renvoyer l'accusation à ; (milit.) recharger, attaquer de nouveau.

recheat' (rî-tshîte), *n.*, (hunt.) rappel, *m.*

recheat', *v.n.*, (hunt.) sonner le rappel.

rec'ipe (rèss'-i-pî), *n.*, récipé, *m.*; recette ; ordonnance de médecin, *f.*

recip'ient, *n.*, personne qui reçoit, *f.*; recevant ; (of a diploma) impétrant ; réceptacle ; (chem.) récipient, *m.*

recip'rocal, *adj.*, réciproque, mutuel ; (of contracts) synallagmatique, bilatéral.

recip'rocal, *n.*, (math.) réciproque, *f.*

recip'rocally, *adv.*, réciproquement, mutuellement.

recip'rocate, *v.a.*, échanger réciproquement ; échanger ; rendre, rendre la pareille à. I —

your sentiments ; *j'éprouve de mon côté les mêmes sentiments à votre égard.*

recip'rocate, *v.n.,* agir réciproquement, alterner, se succéder.

recip'rocating (rè-cip-ro-két'-), *adj.,* alternatif ; de va-et-vient.

reciproca'tion (rè-cip-ro-ké-), **reciproc'ity** (-prosse-), *n.,* réciprocité, *f.;* contre-échange, *m.*

reci'sion (rè-cij'eune), *n.,* (jur., surg.) rescision, *f.*

reci'tal (rè-caï-), *n.,* récit, narré, exposé, *m. ;* (of music) séance musicale, *f.;* (jur.) exposé, *m.;* répétition ; narration, relation ; (enumeration) énumération, *f.*

recita'tion (rèss'i-té-), *n.,* récit ; narré ; exposé, *m. ;* répétition ; narration, relation ; (in schools) récitation,*f.*

recitative' (rèss'i-ta-tîve) *ou* **recitati'vo** (-tî-vô), *n.,* récitatif ; récit, *m.*

recitative'ly, *adv.,* (mus.) en récitatif.

recite' (rè-çaïte), *v.a.,* réciter ; faire le récit de ; raconter ; rapporter ; exposer ; répéter ; (to enumerate) énumérer.

recit'er, *n.,* récitateur ; réciteur, *m.,* réciteuse, *f.;* narrateur, *m.,* narratrice, *f.*

reck (rèke), *v.a.,* (ant.) se soucier de, faire cas de, s'inquiéter de.

reck, *v.n.,* (ant.) se soucier de ; importer. What —s it ? *qu'importe ?* It —s me not ; *peu m'importe.*

reck'less (rèk'-), *adj.,* insouciant de ; indifférent à ; téméraire, imprudent, insensé.

reck'lessly, *adv.,* témérairement ; avec insouciance ; imprudemment, furieusement.

reck'lessness, *n.,* insouciance, témérité, imprévoyance, imprudence, *f.*

reck'on (rèk'k'n), *v.a.,* calculer, compter ; considérer comme ; estimer, évaluer, juger. To — up ; *additionner.* To — again ; *recompter.* To — off ; *défalquer ; faire la part de.* —ing from to-day ; *à compter, à partir d'aujourd'hui, ou dès aujourd'hui.*

reck'on, *v.n.,* compter, s'imaginer. To — on ; *compter sur ; faire fond sur.*

reck'oner, *n.,* calculateur, chiffreur, *m.* Ready — ; *prompt calculateur.* Ready-—; (book) *barême, m.*

reck'oning, *n.,* calcul ; compte ; (at an inn) écot, *m. ;* (at a restaurant) addition ; (nav.) estime,*f.* To be out of one's — ; *se tromper de,* ou *être loin du compte.* The pilot made a mistake in his — ; *le pilote s'est trompé dans son estime.* Short —s make long friends ; *les bons comptes font les bons amis.*

reclaim' (rè-cléme), *v.a.,* (to claim back) réclamer, redemander ; revendiquer ; (to restrain) retenir, arrêter ; (to tame) apprivoiser ; (to reform) amender, corriger, ramener au bien, réformer ; (a hawk) apprivoiser, dresser. To — from ; *faire revenir de.* To — one from error ; *tirer, faire revenir quelqu'un de son erreur.* To — land ; *mettre un terrain en culture, défricher un terrain.*

reclaim'able (-'a-b'l), *adj.,* qui peut être réclamé ; réformable, corrigible ; (of land) cultivable, défrichable.

reclaim'less, *adj.,* incorrigible.

reclama'tion (rèk-la-mé-), **reclaim'ing,** *n.,* réclamation, demande ; (of land) mise en culture ; (of criminals) réforme,*f.*

reclina'tion (rèk-li-né-), *n.,* position inclinée, *f.;* (surg.) abaissement de la cataracte, *m.*

recline' (rè-claïne), *v.a.,* incliner, pencher, reposer, appuyer.

recline', *v.n.,* s'incliner, se pencher, s'appuyer, se reposer, se coucher.

reclin'ing (rè-claï'n'-), *adj.,* incliné, penché, appuyé, couché. — chair ; *fauteuil à la Voltaire, m.*

reclose' (rî-clôze), *v.a.,* refermer.

reclose', *v.n.,* se refermer.

recluse' (rè-cliouce), *adj.,* reclus ; (of things) de reclus ; solitaire ; retiré.

recluse' (rè-cliouce), *n.,* reclus, *m.;* recluse,*f.*

recluse'ly, *adv.,* en reclus.

reclu'sion (rè-cliou-jeune), *n.,* réclusion, retraite,*f.*

recogni'tion (rèk'og-ni-), *n.,* reconnaissance.

recog'nitory, *adj.,* récognitif.

recogniz'able (rèk-og-naï-za-b'l), *adj.,* reconnaissable.

recog'nizance (rè-cog-ni-za'n'ce), *n.,* reconnaissance ; (jur.) obligation authentique (de faire quelque acte particulier),*f.* To enter into —s ; *s'engager à comparaître.*

rec'ognize (rèk'og-naïze), *v.a.,* reconnaître.

recoil' (rè-coïl), *n.,* recul, *m.;* (fig.) répugnance, *f.*

recoil', *v.n.,* reculer ; retomber. To — from ; *reculer devant.* To — with ; *reculer de.* To — upon ; *retomber sur.*

recoil'ing, *n.,* recul, *m. ;* (fig.) répugnance, *f.*

recoin' (rî-coïne), *v.a.,* refondre.

recoin'age (-'èdje), *n.,* refonte ; monnaie de refonte,*f.*

recollect' (rèk'-), *v.a.,* se souvenir de ; se rappeler ; se ressouvenir de ; se remettre ; recueillir, rassembler. — it ; *souvenez-vous-en.* Do you — my face ? *me remettez-vous ?* To — one's self, *v.n., se recueillir ; se réunir de nouveau.*

recollec'tion (rèk'-), *n.,* souvenir, ressouvenir, *m.;* mémoire, *f.* To have no — of ; *ne pas se rappeler ; n'avoir aucun souvenir de.* To have some — of ; *avoir quelque souvenir de.* To the best of my — ; *autant que je puis m'en souvenir.* Out of — ; *dont on a perdu le souvenir.*

rec'ollet (rèk'-), *n.,* récollet, *m.*

recoloniza'tion (rî-col-o-ni-zé-), *n.,* nouvelle colonisation,*f.*

recol'onize (rî-col-o-naïze), *v.a.,* coloniser de nouveau.

recombina'tion (rè-co'm'bi-né-), *n.,* combinaison nouvelle, *f.*

recombine' (rî-co'm'baïne), *v.a.,* combiner de nouveau.

recom'fort (rî-keu'm'feurte), *v.a.,* réconforter ; consoler de nouveau, ranimer.

recommence' (rî-), *v.a.,* recommencer.

recommend' (rèk'-), *v.a.,* recommander. He has nothing else to — him ; *il n'a pas d'autre recommandation ; il n'a que cela pour lui,* ou *en sa faveur.*

recommend'able (-'a-b'l), *adj.,* recommandable.

recommenda'tion (rèk'om'mè'n'dé-), *n.,* recommandation (a petition) apostille,*f.*

recommend'atory, *adj.,* de recommandation ; d'éloge.

recommis'sion (rî-), *v.a.,* renommer à une charge ; déléguer de nouveau à une commission. To — a ship of war ; *armer de nouveau un vaisseau de guerre.*

recommit' (rî-), *v.a.,* (a prisoner) renvoyer en prison ; (a bill) renvoyer devant une commission.

recommit'ment *ou* **recommit'tal** (rî-), *n.,* nouvelle incarcération,*f.;* (of a bill) renvoi à une commission, *m.*

recommu'nicate (rî-co'm'miou-), *v.a.,* communiquer de nouveau.

rec'ompense (rèk'-), *n.,* récompense ; réparation, compensation, *f. ;* dédommagement ; retour, *m.*

rec'ompense (rèk'-), *v.a.,* récompenser ; donner en retour ; dédommager ; compenser ; réparer.

recompile'ment (rî-co'm'païl'-), *n.,* nouvelle compilation,*f.*

recompose' (rî-co'm'pôze), *v.a.,* recomposer ; calmer de nouveau ; tranquilliser, remettre ; (print.) recomposer.

rec'oncilable (rèk'o'n'çaïl'a-b'l), adj., réconciliable ; (of things) conciliable, compatible **avec**.

rec'oncilableness (-çaïl'-), n., possibilité de réconciliation, de conciliation, d'arrangement ; compatibilité, f.

rec'oncile (rèk'o'n'çaïle), v.a., réconcilier ; mettre d'accord, raccommoder, concilier ; (of things) arranger ; apaiser, accorder ; (to accustom) habituer, accoutumer. To be —d with ; être réconcilié **avec**. To — one's self to a thing ; s'accoutumer à, s'habituer à ; se faire à une chose, se résigner à une chose.

rec'oncilement (-çaïl'-), n., réconciliation, f.; raccommodement, m.

rec'onciler (-çaïl'-), n., réconciliateur, m., réconciliatrice, f. ; conciliateur, m., conciliatrice, f.

reconcilia'tion (rèk'o'n'cil-i-é-), n., réconciliation, f. ; raccommodement, m. ; (of things) conciliation ; (biblically) expiation, f.

reconcil'iatory (-cil'-), adj., conciliateur.

rec'ondite (rèk'o'n'daïte), adj., secret, profond, caché ; abstrus, abstrait, profond, mystérieux.

reconduct' (rî-co'n'deuk'te), v.a., reconduire.

reconfirm' (rî-co'n'feurme), v.a., confirmer de nouveau.

recon'naissance, n.,(milit.) reconnaissance,f.

reconnoi'tre (rèk'o'n'noï-teur), v.a., (milit.) reconnaître, faire la reconnaissance **de**.

reconnoi'tre, v.n., reconnaître, faire une reconnaissance, pousser une reconnaissance **jusqu'à**.

reconnoi'tring, adj., (milit.) de reconnaissance. — expedition ; reconnaissance, f. — party ; détachement envoyé en reconnaissance, m.

recon'quer (rî-ko'gn'keur), v.a., reconquérir.

recon'secrate (rî-co'n'si-), v.a., consacrer de nouveau.

reconsecra'tion (rî-co'n'si-), n., consécration nouvelle, f.

reconsid'er (rî-), v.a., considérer de nouveau ; (a decision) revenir **sur**.

reconsidera'tion (rî-), n., reconsidération, nouvelle réflexion, f.; nouvel examen, m.

recon'stitute, v.a., reconstituer.

reconstitu'tion, n., reconstitution, f.

reconstruct', v.a., reconstruire.

reconstruc'tion, n., reconstruction, f.

reconvene' (rî-co'n'vîne), v.a., réunir de nouveau ; assembler de nouveau.

reconver'sion (rî-co'n'veur-), n., nouvelle conversion, f.

reconvert' (rî-co'n'veurte), v.a., convertir de nouveau.

reconvey' (rî-co'n'vê), v.a., transporter de nouveau ; reporter, ramener ; (jur.) rétrocéder.

reconvey'ance (rî-co'n'vê-), n., nouveau transport, m. ; (jur.) rétrocession, f.

rec'ord (rè-), n., registre, m. ; marque, trace, mention, f. ; souvenir, signe, monument, m. pl., archives ; annales ; notes, f.pl. Public —s ; archives, f.pl. On — ; dans les annales de l'histoire ; inscrit, enregistré. To beat, ou break, the — ; surpasser ce qui a été fait auparavant. It is on — that . . . ; il est fait mention dans l'histoire que . . . To make a — of ; tenir registre **de**. Keeper of the —s ; archiviste, greffier, m. —-office ; archives, f.pl. ; greffe, m.

record' (rè-), v.a., enregistrer ; inscrire ; consigner ; (to imprint) graver, imprimer ; (to celebrate) célébrer ; (in history) rapporter, mentionner, indiquer. To — one's vote ; voter.

record'er, n., receveur de l'enregistrement ; archiviste ; (jur.) premier officier judiciaire d'une ville, juge, m.

record'ership, n., charge d'archiviste, f. ; fonctions de juge, f.pl.

recount' (rè-), v.a., raconter, réciter ; rapporter ; compter de nouveau.

re-count' (rî-), n., (at elections) nouvelle addition des voix, f.

recoup' (rè-), v.a., rembourser **de** ; dédommager **de** ; indemniser **de**. To — one's self ; se rattraper **sur**. To — one's expenses ; rentrer dans ses fonds.

recoup'ment, n., indemnité, reprise, f. ; dédommagement, m.

recourse', n., recours, m. To have — to ; recourir à ; avoir recours à.

recov'er, v.a., recouvrer, retrouver, ravoir, reprendre ; reconquérir ; (to reach) parvenir à, atteindre ; (a loss) réparer ; (health) recouvrer, rétablir ; (jur.) obtenir ; (to cover again) recouvrir ; (com.) recouvrer, récupérer. To — one's self ; se remettre ; revenir à soi.

recov'er, v.n., (from illness) se rétablir, guérir, se guérir ; se relever, se remettre, se refaire ; (jur.) gagner son procès, avoir gain de cause. To — ; (from surprise, fright) se remettre **de**, revenir **de**.

recov'erable (-'a-b'l), adj., qui peut être recouvré ; recouvrable ; réparable ; (of invalids) guérissable.

recov'ery, n., recouvrement, m. ; reprise, f. ; (of one's health) recouvrement, m., guérison, f., rétablissement, m. ; (jur.) adjudication, f. Past — ; incurable, désespéré ; (of things) sans remède.

rec'reant (rèk'ri-), n., lâche, poltron ; (ant.) apostat, m.

rec'reant, adj., lâche, poltron ; faux, traître ; (ant.) apostat.

rec'reate (rèk'ri-), v.a., récréer, réjouir, divertir, distraire.

recreate' (rî-cri-), v.a., (to create again) recréer.

recrea'tion (rèk'ri-é-), n., récréation ; distraction, f. ; divertissement, m.

rec'reative (rèk'ri-), adj., récréatif, divertissant, amusant.

rec'reatively, adv., d'une manière récréative.

recrim'inate (rè-), v.n., récriminer contre.

recrimina'tion (rè-cri'm'i-né-), n., récrimination, f.

recrim'inatory, adj., récriminatoire.

recross' (rî-), v.a., traverser de nouveau ; repasser. To cross and — ; traverser en tous sens.

recrudes'cence (rî-crou-dès'-), n., recrudescence, f.

recrudes'cent, adj., (med.) recrudescent.

recruit' (rî-), n., recrue, f. ; conscrit ; (fig.) renfort, m. —-school ; école du soldat, f.

recruit', v.a., recruter, rétablir ; (to strengthen) renforcer, réparer. To — one's self ; se remettre, se refaire ; reprendre des forces.

recruit', v.n., se recruter ; se refaire, se remettre, reprendre.

recruit'ing ou **recruit'ment** (rè-crout'-), n., recrutement, m.

recruit'ing, adj. — sergeant ; sergent recruteur, m.

rect'angle (rèk'ta'ng'g'l), n., rectangle, m.

rect'angled (rèk'ta'gn'g'l'de), adj., rectangle.

rectan'gular (-ghiou-), adj., rectangulaire, rectangle, à angle droit.

rectan'gularly, adv., avec des angles droits.

rec'tifiable (-faï-a-b'l), adj., susceptible de rectification ; rectifiable.

rectifica'tion (-fi-ké-), n., rectification.

rec'tifier (-faï-eur), n., rectificateur.

rec'tify (rèk-ti-faïe), v.a., rectifier ; redresser, corriger ; (chem., geom.) rectifier.

rectilin'eal, adj., rectiligne.

rec'titude (rèk'ti-tioude), n., rectitude ; (in a moral sense) droiture, f.

rec'tor (rèk'teur), n., (of a parish) curé ; (of a university) recteur ; (of religious orders) directeur, supérieur ; (of a Jesuits' college) recteur, m.

recto'rial, adj., rectoral ; de curé.

rec'torship, n., cure, f. ; (of a university) rectorat, m.

rec'tory, n., cure, f. ; presbytère; (of universities) rectorat, m.

rec'tum, n., (anat.) rectum, m.

recum'bence ou recum'bency (rè-keum-), n., (ant.) état d'une personne couchée, repos, m.

recum'bent, adj., couché ; étendu ; appuyé ; (idle) en repos, oisif.

recup'erate, v.n., récupérer.

recupera'tion (rè-kiou-peur'é-), n., recouvrement, m.

recu'perative ou recu'peratory, adj., récuperatif, récuperative.

recur' (rè-keur), v.n., revenir; se représenter ; reparaître ; revenir à l'esprit ; se reproduire ; (to happen again) se répéter.

recur'rence, n., retour; recours; renouvellement, m. ; répétition ; (anat.) récurrence,f. Of frequent —; qui revient souvent, qui arrive souvent.

recur'rent, recur'ring (rè-keur'-), adj., périodique, qui revient de temps en temps ; (anat., alg.) récurrent.

recurv'ate (rè-keur-) ou recurve' (-keurve), v.a., recourber.

recurv'ate ou recurved', adj., recourbé.

recurva'tion (rî-keurv'é-), n., courbure, f.

recurv'ous (rè-), adj., recourbé.

rec'usancy (rèk'iou-za'n'-), n., non-conformité,f.

rec'usant (rèk'iou-za'n'te), n.adj., non-conformiste, dissident, sectaire, m.

recusa'tion (rèk'iou-zé-), n., (jur.) récusation, f.

recuse' (rè-kiouze), v.a., (jur.) récuser.

red (rède), n., rouge, m.

red, adj., rouge ; (of the hair) roux.   —-hot ; tout rouge, tout chaud ; (of coals) ardent.   —-coat ; soldat, m.   —-deer ; cerf, m.   —-face ; visage enluminé, m.   —-berried ; à baies rouges.   — herring ; hareng saur, m.   — heat ; rouge, m. At a — heat ; chauffé au rouge.   —-lead ; minium, m.   — hair; cheveux roux, m.pl.   —-letter day ; jour propice, m.

redan' (rè-), n., (fort.) redan, m.

red'breast (-brèste), n., (orni.) rouge-gorge, m.

red'den (rèd'd'n), v.a. and n., rougir.

red'dish (rèd'-), adj., rougeâtre.

red'dishness, n., couleur, ou teinte, rougeâtre, f.

reddi'tion (rèd'dish'-), n., reddition ; restitution ; (explanation) explication, traduction, f.

red'dle (rèd'd'l), n., rubrique (craie rouge), sanguine ; (min.) ocre rouge, f.

redeem' (rè-dîme), v.a., racheter ; (fin.) racheter, rembourser, amortir ; (things pawned) dégager, retirer ; (fig.) dégager, délivrer, compenser. To — a promise ; remplir, ou accomplir, une promesse. To — a fault ; réparer une faute.

redeem'able (-'a-b'l), adj., rachetable ; remboursable; (fig.) amortissable.

redeem'er (rè-dî'm'-), n., Rédempteur ; racheteur ; libérateur, m., libératrice, f.

redeem'ing, adj., qui rachète, qui compense, réparateur.   n., rachat, m.   A — quality ; qualité qui rachète des défauts, f.

redelib'erate (rî-dé-lib'eur'-), v.n., délibérer de nouveau.

redeliv'er (rî-dè-), v.a., restituer ; (to deliver again) délivrer de nouveau.

redeliv'ery (rî-dè-), n., restitution ; nouvelle délivrance, f.

redemand' (rî-dè-), v.a., redemander.

redemand', n., demande en restitution, f.

redemand'able (-'a-b'l), adj., redemandable.

redemise' (rî-dè-maïze),v.a., (jur.) rétrocéder.

redemise', n., (jur.) rétrocession, f.

redemp'tion (rè-dè'm'sheune), n., rachat, m. ;

délivrance,f.; (fin.) amortissement ; (jur.) rachat, réméré, m., rédemption ; (theol.) rédemption, f.

redemp'tory (rè-dè'm'-), adj., rédempteur.

redescend' (rî-), v.n., redescendre.

redin'tegrate (rè-di'n'ti-), adj., réintégré, rétabli, renouvelé.

redin'tegrate (rè-di'n'ti-), v.a., réintégrer, rétablir ; renouveler.

redintegra'tion (-ti-gré-), n., réintégration, f.; renouvellement ; rétablissement, m.

rediscount' (rî-dis-caou'n'te), v.a., escompter de nouveau.

redissolve' (rî-diz-zolve), v.a., dissoudre de nouveau.

redistill' (rî-), v.a., distiller de nouveau.

redistilla'tion (rî-), n., nouvelle distillation,f.

redistrib'ute (rî-dis-trib'ioute), v.a., distribuer de nouveau.

redistribu'tion, n., nouvelle distribution, f.

red'ness, n., rougeur, f.; rouge, m. ; (of the hair) rousseur, couleur rousse, f.

red'olence, n., parfum, m.; odeur agréable, senteur, f.

red'olent, adj., qui a un parfum de, odoriférant, parfumé.   — of . . . ; qui sent le, ou la, cu les . . .

redou'ble (rî-deub'b'l), v.a. and n., redoubler. To — one's efforts ; redoubler d'efforts.

redoubt' (rè-daoute), n., (fort.) redoute, f.

redoubt'able (-'a-b'l), adj., redoutable, formidable.

redoubt'ed, adj., redouté.

redound' (rè-daou'n'de), v.n., rejaillir sur, revenir à ; (to contribute) tendre à, contribuer à; (to result) résulter.   This action —s to his credit; cette action est à son honneur.

red'pole ou red'poll (-pôle), n., (orni.) linotte, f., linot, m.

redraft' (rî-drâfte),v.a., dessiner de nouveau ; rédiger de nouveau.

redraft', n., (com.) nouveau dessein ; nouveau brouillon, m. ; (com.) retraite,f.

redraw' (rî-drô), v.a., retirer ; faire un nouveau brouillon ; (com.) faire retraite.

redress' (rè-), v.a., redresser, rectifier, réparer ; faire justice à ; (to relieve) secourir, soulager, réformer, corriger.

redress', n., redressement, m. ; justice, réparation, satisfaction ; réformation, f.; soulagement, secours, remède, m.

redress'er, n., redresseur, réparateur, m.

redress'ible (-'i-b'l), adj., réparable.

red'shank, n., montagnard écossais, m. ; (orni.) bécasseau, m.

red'shanks, n., (bot.) renouée persicaire, persicaire ; herbe à Robert, f.

red'tail (-téle), n., (orni.) rouge-queue, m.

red' tape, n., bureaucratie, routine administrative, f.

red-tap'ism, n., bureaucratie, routine, f.; formalisme, m.

red-tap'ist, n., bureaucrate, routinier, m.

reduce' (rè-diouce),v.a., réduire à, ou en; convertir ; diminuer ; rabaisser ; (in flesh) maigrir ; (impoverish) appauvrir ; (classify) classer; (degrade) dégrader.   A person —d in circumstances ; une personne tombée dans la gêne.   To — to the ranks; casser. To — ; (a figure, design, or draught) réduire en petit, réduire. To — to rule; soumettre à des règles fixes.   To — to practice ; mettre en pratique.

redu'cer, n., réducteur, m.

redu'cible (-'i-b'l), adj., réductible, f.

redu'cibleness, n., réductibilité, f.

reduct' (rè-deukte), n., (arch.) réduit, m.

reduc'tion (rè-deuk-), n., réduction, diminution ; (com.) remise, f. ; rabais, m. ; (to the ranks) cassation, f.

reduc'tive, adj., réductif.

reduc'tive, n., agent réductif, m.

reduc'tively, *adv.*, par réduction.

redun'dance *ou* **redun'dancy** (rè-deu'n'-), *n.*, (style) redondance, surabondance, *f.*

redun'dant (rè-deu'n'-), *adj.*, (style) redondant; surabondant.

redun'dantly, *adv.*, avec superfluité, (of style) d'une manière redondante.

redu'plicate (rè-diou-), *v.a.*, redoubler.

redu'plicate, *adj.*, double.

reduplica'tion (rè-diou-pli-ké-), *n.*, réduplication, *f.*; redoublement, *m.*

redu'plicative (rè-diou-pli-ké-), *adj.*, réduplicatif, double.

red'wing, *n.*, (orni.) mauvis, *m.*, grive mauvis, *f.*

re-ech'o (rî-èk'o), *v.a.*, répéter; redire; renvoyer.

re-ech'o, *v.n.*, résonner, retentir; répondre.

re-ech'o, *n.*, écho répété, *m.*

reed (rîde), *n.*, roseau, *m.*; canne, *f.*; (musical pipe) chalumeau, *m.*; (of wind instruments) anche, (anat.) caillette, *f.*; (used by weavers) peigne, *m.* To trust to a broken —; *s'appuyer sur un roseau*.

reed, *v.a.*, canneler (en relief).

reed'ed (rîd'-), *adj.*, couvert de roseaux.

reed'-grass (-grâce), *n.*, roseau, rubanier, *m.*

re-edifica'tion (rî-èd'i-fi-ké-), *n.*, réédification, *f.*

re-ed'ify (rî-èd'i-faïe), *v.a.*, réédifier, rebâtir.

reed'less, *adj.*, sans roseaux.

reed'-pipe, *n.*, tuyau d'orgue; chalumeau, *m.*

reed'y, *adj.*, plein de roseaux, couvert de roseaux.

reef (rîfe), *n.*, récif, écueil; (of a sail) ris; (of coral) banc, *m.*

reef, *v.a.*, (nav.) prendre un ris, des ris, à; carguer. To let out a —; (nav.) *larguer un ris*.

reefed, *adj.*, qui a pris ses ris.

reef'-line (-laîne), *n.*, (nav.) garcette de ris, *f.*

reef'-tackle, *n.*, palan de ris, *m.*

reef'y, *adj.*, plein de récifs.

reek, *v.n.*, fumer; s'exhaler. —ing with; *tout fumant* **de**.

reek'y, *adj.*, enfumé, noirci, sale. Auld Reeky; *Edimbourg*, *m.*

reel (rîle), *n.*, dévidoir; (of rope-makers) touret, *m.*; (of cotton) bobine, *f.*; (dance) branle; (fishing) moulinet, *m.* Scotch —; *branle écossais*, *m.* Off the —; *d'arrache-pied, sans interruption*.

reel (off), *v.a.*, dévider.

reel, *v.n.*, chanceler; aller en zigzag; vaciller; tourner. To — out; *sortir en trébuchant, en chancelant*.

re-elect' (rî-i-), *v.a.*, réélire.

re-elec'tion (rî-î-lèk-), *n.*, réélection, *f.*

re-eligibil'ity (rî-èl'i-dji-), *n.*, (l.u.) rééligibilité, *f.*

re-el'igible (rî-èl'i-dji-b'l), *adj.*, rééligible.

re-embark' (rî-è'm'bârke), *v.a.*, rembarquer.

re-embark', *v.n.*, se rembarquer; (nav.) rembarquer.

re-embarka'tion (rî-è'm'bâr-ké-), *n.*, rembarquement, *m.*

re-embod'y (rî-), *v.a.*, réincorporer.

re-em'igrate, *v.n.*, réémigrer.

re-employ', *v.a.*, remployer.

re-enact' (rî-è'n'-), *v.a.*, ordonner, décréter; promulguer de nouveau; remettre en vigueur.

re-enact'ment, *n.*, remise en vigueur, *f.*; rétablissement, *m.*

re-engage' (rî-è'n'ghédje), *v.a.*, rengager.

re-engage', *v.n.*, se rengager.

re-enlist' (rî-è'n'-), *v.a.*, enrôler de nouveau.

re-enlist', *v.n.*, se rengager.

re-en'ter (rî-è'n'-), *v.a.* and *n.*, rentrer; rentrer **dans**, *ou* **à**.

re-en'tering, *adj.*, (of an angle) rentrant.

re-en'trance (rî-è'n'-), *n.*, rentrée, *f.*

re-equip', *v.a.*, équiper de nouveau.

re-estab'lish (rî-ès-), *v.a.*, rétablir; réintégrer.

re-estab'lishment, *n.*, rétablissement, *m.*; réintégration, *f.*

reeve (rîve), *v.a.*, (nav.) passer un cordage dans. To — out; *éfaufiler*.

reeve, *n.*, bailli, *m.*

re-examina'tion (rî-ègz'a'm'i-né-), *n.*, nouvel examen, *m.*; (jur.) nouvel interrogatoire, *m.*

re-exam'ine (rî-ègz'-), *v.a.*, examiner de nouveau; revoir; (a prisoner or witness) interroger de nouveau.

re-exchange' (rî-èks'tschè'n'dje), *n.*, nouvel échange; (com.) rechange, *m.*

re-export' (rî-èks'-), *v.a.*, réexporter.

re-ex'port, *n.*, marchandise réexportée, *f.*

re-exporta'tion (rî-èks-pôr-té-), *n.*, réexportation, *f.*

refec'tion (rè-fèk'-), *n.*, repas, *m.*; collation; (convents) réfection, *f.*

refec'tive, *adj.*, restaurant.

refec'tory (rè-), *n.*, (convents, schools) réfectoire, *m.*

refer' (rè-feur), *v.a.*, référer, renvoyer, rapporter, adresser **à**; adresser pour des renseignements **à**; remettre à la décision **de**.

refer', *v.n.*, (of things) se référer, référer, se rapporter, avoir trait à, avoir rapport à; faire allusion **à**; (pers.) s'en rapporter, se référer, s'adresser **à**; en référer **à**; se reporter à; renvoyer un témoignage **de**.

refer'able (rè-feur'a-b'l), *adj.*, qui peut être référé, rapporté à; rapportable, attribuable **à**.

referee' (rèf'eur'î), *n.*, arbitre, *m.*

ref'erence (rèf'eur'-), *n.*, (direction) renvoi; (respect) regard, rapport, *m.*; (allusion) allusion; (recommendation) recommandation, *f.*; (for character) renseignement, *m.*, garantie, *f.*, répondant, *m.*; référence, *f.*; (print.) renvoi, *m.*, lettrine, *f.*; (jur.) renvoi, *m.* Book of —; *ouvrage à consulter, ouvrage de référence, m.* For —; *à consulter.* In — to; *à l'égard* **de**; *par rapport* **à**, *quant* **à**; *en ce qui concerne.* To have — to; *se rapporter* **à**; *faire allusion* **à**. To make — to; *citer, faire allusion* **à**. To give a — to any one; *donner une référence, indiquer quelqu'un pour fournir des renseignements.* To go for a —; *aller aux renseignements.* To have good —s; *avoir de bonnes recommandations, de bonnes références.*

referend'ary (rèf'-), *n.*, (ant.) référendaire, arbitre, *m.*

refine' (rè-faîne), *v.a.*, (fig.) épurer; purifier; polir; (metal.) affiner; (liquids) épurer, clarifier; (sugar, saltpeter) raffiner.

refine', *v.n.*, s'épurer, se purifier; s'affiner, se raffiner; (of liquids) s'épurer, se clarifier; (to affect nicety) raffiner (sur).

refined' (rè-faî'n'de), *adj.*, épuré; pur; affiné; poli; raffiné; cultivé, recherché; subtil; affecté.

refin'edly (-èd'-), *adv.*, avec raffinement.

refine'ment (rè-faî'n'-), *n.*, raffinement; poli, *m.*; pureté; politesse; affectation, recherche, *f.*; (of sugar, saltpeter) raffinage; (metal.) affinage, *m.*; (of liquids) épuration, *f.*

refin'er (-faï'n'-), *n.*, personne qui épure, qui purifie, *f.*; (of sugar, saltpeter) raffineur; (metal.) affineur, *m.*

refin'ery (rè-faï'n'-), *n.*, (metal.) affinerie; (of sugar) raffinerie, *f.*

refin'ing (rè-faï'n'-), *n.*, raffinage, affinage, *m.*; (of liquids) épuration; (fig.) affectation, épuration, subtilisation, *f.*; raffinement, *m.*

refit' (rî-), *v.a.*, réparer; (nav.) radouber.

reflect' (rè-), *v.a.*, réfléchir; faire rejaillir **sur**; refléter; procurer, valoir **à**; (to discredit) faire tort **à**; (to blame) blâmer, critiquer; (to think) songer à, songer **que**. That —s no credit on you; *cela ne vous fait pas honneur.* To be —ed; *être réfléchi; se réfléchir.*

reflect', *v.n.*, réfléchir ; faire réflexion ; faire ses réflexions. To — on ; (to bring reproach to) *retomber* **sur**, *rejaillir* **sur** ; (to censure) *censurer*, *fronder*, *critiquer* ; *jeter le blâme* **sur**. To be —ed on ; *être un sujet de blâme*, *être un sujet de censure* **pour**.

reflect'ed, *adj.*, réfléchi ; reflété.

reflect'ent, *adj.*, qui se réfléchit.

reflect'ing (-flèkt'-), *adj.*, réfléchi, méditatif ; réflecteur, réfléchissant.

reflect'ingly, *adv.*, avec réflexion ; (censure) avec blâme.

reflec'tion (rè-flèk'-), *n.*, (of light) réflexion,*f.*; reflet, *m.*; (of the mind) réflexion ; (censure) censure, critique,*f.*, reproche, blâme, *m.* To cast —s on ; *censurer, critiquer, blâmer.* On — ; *en y réfléchissant* ; *réflexion faite, tout bien considéré, décidément.*

reflec'tive, *adj.*, qui réfléchit ; réfléchissant ; réflecteur ; méditatif, réfléchi.

reflec'tor,*n.*, personne qui réfléchit, *f.*; (phys.) réflecteur, *m.*

re'flex (rî-flèkse), *adj.*, réfléchi ; (paint.) reflété ; (phys., physiol.) réflexe.

re'flex, *n.*, (paint.) reflet, *m.*

reflexibil'ity (rè-), *n.*, (phys.) réflexibilité, *f.*

reflex'ible (-'ĭ-b'l), *adj.*, (phys.) réflexible.

reflex'ion, *n.* V. **reflection.**

reflex'ity, *n.*, réflexibilité,*f.*

reflex'ive, *adj.*, réflexif ; (gram.) réfléchi, pronominal.

reflex'ively, *adv.*, réflexivement.

reflores'cence (rè-), *n.*, nouvelle floraison,*f.*

reflour'ish (rî-fleur'-), *v.n.*, refleurir.

reflow' (rî-flô), *v.n.*, refluer, retourner en arrière.

reflow'er, *v.n.*, refleurir.

ref'luent, *adj.*, qui reflue.

re'flux (rî-fleukse), *n.*, reflux, *m.*

re'flux, *adj.*, de reflux.

reform' (rè-), *n.*, réforme,*f.*

reform', *v.a.*, réformer ; (criminals) moraliser.

reform', *v.n.*, se réformer, se corriger.

re-form' (rî-), *v.a.*, reformer.

re-form', *v.n.*, se reformer.

reforma'tion (rèf'or-mé-), *n.*, réformation, réforme, moralisation,*f.*

re-forma'tion (rî-form'-é-), *n.*, formation nouvelle,*f.*

reform'er (rè-), *n.*, réformateur,*m.*

reform'ing (rè-), *adj.*, qui réforme, qui conduit à la réformation.

refortifica'tion (rî-for-ti-fi-ké-), *n.*, nouvelle fortification,*f.*

refor'tify (rî-for-ti-faïe), *v.a.*, refortifier.

refound' (rî-faou'n'de), *v.a.*, refondre ; fonder de nouveau, refonder.

refound'ing, *n.*, refonte,*f.*

refract' (ri-), *v.a.*, (phys.) réfracter.

refract'ing (rè-), *adj.*, (phys.) réfringent ; à réfraction, de réfraction.

refrac'tion (rè-), *n.*, (phys.) réfraction,*f.*

refrac'tive (rè-), *adj.*, (phys.) réfractif. — index ; *index de réfraction, m.*

refrac'toriness (rè-), *n.*, résistance, opiniâtreté ; obstination, insoumission ; mutinerie,*f.*

refrac'tory (rè-), *adj.*, mutin, revêche, indocile, insoumis, intraitable, rebelle ; réfractaire ; (chem.) réfractaire ; (of horses), rétif.

refrain' (rè-fréne), *v.a.*, retenir ; contenir, réprimer.

refrain', *v.n.*, se retenir **de** ; se contenir ; s'abstenir ; se garder, s'empêcher **de**. To — from tears ; *retenir ses larmes.*

refrain' (rè-fréne), *n.*, refrain, *m.*

refrangibil'ity (rè-fra'n'dji-), *n.*, (phys.) réfrangibilité,*f.*

refran'gible (rè-fra'n'dji-b'l), *adj.*, (phys.) réfrangible.

refresh' (rè-frèshe), *v.a.*, rafraîchir ; ranimer ;

soulager ; délasser ; refaire ; récréer. To — one's self ; *se rafraîchir* ; *se délasser, se remettre, se refaire.*

refresh'er, *n.*, personne qui rafraîchit, qui délasse ; chose qui rafraîchit, qui délasse, *f.* ; (extra fee) supplément d'honoraires, *m.pl.*

refresh'ing, *adj.*, rafraîchissant ; qui délasse ; récréatif, délassant, réparateur, calmant, qui repose.

refresh'ment (rè-frésh'-), *n.*, rafraîchissement ; délassement, repos, *m.* ; récréation, *f.* — booth ; (on a race-course) *buvette, f.* — room ; (rail.) *buffet, m.*

refrig'erant (rè-fridj'eur-), *n.*, (pharm.) réfrigérant, *m.*

refrig'erant (rè-fridj'eur'-), *adj.*, réfrigérant.

refrig'erate, *v.a.*, rafraîchir ; réfrigérer.

refrigera'tion (rè-fridj'eur'é-), *n.*, réfrigération,*f.*

refrig'erative *ou* **refrig'eratory** (rè-fridj'-eur'-), *n.*, (med.) réfrigératif, rafraîchissant.

refrig'erative *ou* **refrig'eratory** (rè-fridj'-eur'-), *adj.*, (med.) rafraîchissant, réfrigératif ; (chem.) réfrigérant.

ref'uge (rèf'ioudje), *n.*, refuge, *m.* (from, **contre.** To take — ; *se réfugier, prendre refuge.*

refugee' (rèf'iou-djî), *n.*, réfugié, *m.*, réfugiée,*f.*

reful'gence *ou* **reful'gency** (rè-feul-dj'-), *n.*, éclat, *m.* ; splendeur,*f.*

reful'gent (rè-feul-djè'n'te), *adj.*, éclatant, resplendissant.

refund' (rè-feu'n'de),*v.a.*, rembourser, rendre, restituer.

refur'nish (rî-feur-), *v.a.*, remeubler.

refus'able (rè-fiou-za-b'l), *adj.*, qui peut être refusé.

refus'al (rè-fiou-zal), *n.*, refus ; choix de refuser ou d'accepter, *m.* To meet with a — ; *éprouver un refus.* To have the — of ; *avoir le choix de refuser ou d'accepter* ; *avoir la première offre* **de.** On his — ; *sur son refus.*

ref'use (rèf'iouze), *n.*, rebut, *m.*

ref'use, *adj.*, de rebut.

refuse' (rè-fiouze), *v.a.*, refuser. That is not to be —d ; *cela n'est pas de refus.* To — point-blank ; *refuser net.*

refuse', *v.n.*, refuser.

re-fuse' (rî-fiouze), *v.a.*, fondre de nouveau, refondre.

refus'er (rè-), *n.*, personne qui refuse, *f.* ; refusant, *m.*

refut'able (rè-fiout'a-b'l), *adj.*, réfutable.

refuta'tion (rè-fiou-té-), *n.*, réfutation,*f.*

refute' (rè-fioute), *v.a.*, réfuter.

refut'er, *n.*, réfutateur, *m.*

regain' (rè-ghéne), *v.a.*, regagner, reprendre, recouvrer, rattraper ; ressaisir, reconquérir.

re'gal (rî-), *adj.*, royal ; régalien.

regale' (rè-ghéle), *n.*, (feast) festin, *m.*, fête,*f.*

regale', *v.a.*, régaler ; (fig.) réjouir ; charmer.

regale' (rè-ghéle), *v.n.*, se régaler.

regale'ment (rè-ghél'-), *n.*, festin, banquet, *m.*

rega'lia (rè-ghé-), *n.*, insignes de la royauté ; diamants de la couronne ; (jur.) droits régaliens, *m.pl.*

re'gally (rî-), *adv.*, royalement, en roi.

regard' (rè-gârde), *n.*, égard, *m.* ; (esteem) considération, *f.*, respect ; (reference) égard, rapport, *m.* ; (in the forest laws) inspection, *f.* ; (eminence) distinction,*f.* *pl.*, amitiés,*f.pl.*; compliments, *m.pl.* Give my —s to your brother ; *dites mille choses de ma part à votre frère* ; *faites mes amitiés à votre frère.* With — to ; *par rapport* **à** ; *relativement* **à** ; *à l'égard* **de** ; *quant* **à.** Out — for ; *par égard* **pour.** To pay — to ; *avoir égard* **à** ; *faire attention* **à** ; *écouter.* In — to ; *quant* **à.** As —s ; *pour ce qui est* **de.**

regard' (rè-gârde), *v.a.*, regarder, considérer ;

(to mind) avoir égard **à**, prendre garde **à**, regarder **à**, faire attention **à**, estimer, faire cas **de**. I shall — it as a favor; *je l'estimerai comme une faveur.*

regard'ful (-foule), *adj.*, soigneux **de**; attentif **à**; plein d'égards **pour**; qui songe **à**, qui s'inquiète **de**.

regard'fully, *adv.*, attentivement; avec égard.

regard'ing (rè-gârd'-), *prep.*, touchant, concernant; à l'égard **de**, quant **à**.

regard'less, *adj.*, peu soigneux **de**; inattentif **à**; insouciant **de**; sans égard **pour**. — of; *sans se soucier* **de**; *sans avoir aucun égard* **à**; (expense, money) *sans regarder* **à**; *sans faire aucun cas* **de**; *indifférent* **à**; *sans considération* **pour**.

regard'lessly, *adv.*, avec indifférence.

regard'lessness, *n.*, insouciance; indifférence, *f.*

regat'ta (rè-), *n.*, régate, *f.*

re'gency (rî-djè'n'-), *n.*, régence, *f.*

regen'erate (rè-djè'n'eur'-), *adj.*, régénéré.

regen'erate (rè-djè'n'eur'-), *v.a.*, régénérer.

regen'erating, *adj.*, régénérateur.

regenera'tion (rè-djè'n'eur'é-), *n.*, régénération, *f.*

regen'erator, *n.*, régénérateur, *m.*, régénératrice, *f.*

re'gent (rî-djè'n'te), *n.*, régent, *m.*

reger'minate (rî-djeur-), *v.n.*, germer de nouveau.

reg'icidal, *adj.*, régicide.

reg'icide (rèdj'i-caïde), *n.*, régicide, *m.*

reg'imen (rèdj'i-mène), *n.*, régime; (med.) régime, *m.*, diète, *f.*; (gram.) régime, *m.*

reg'iment (rèdj'-), *n.*, régiment, *m.*

regiment'al, *adj.*, du régiment, de régiment; (of clothes) d'ordonnance, d'uniforme.

regiment'als (-talze), *n.pl.*, uniforme, habit d'ordonnance, *m.*

re'gion (rî-djeune), *n.*, région; contrée, *f.*

reg'ister (rèdj'-), *n.*, registre; (of voters) liste électorale; (print., of organs) registre; (of furnaces, etc.) registre, *m.*, trappe; (of vessels) jauge officielle, plaque, *f.*

reg'ister, *v.a.*, enregistrer; enrôler; porter sur les rôles, inscrire; (print.) pointer; (a letter) charger, recommander; (a trademark, etc.) déposer. —ed letter; *lettre chargée*, ou *recommandée, f.*

reg'istership, *n.*, fonctions d'archiviste, de greffier, *f.pl.*

reg'istrar, *n.*, gardien, teneur, des registres; (jur.) greffier; archiviste, secrétaire, (Engl.) (births, etc.,) officier de l'état civil, *m.*

reg'istrarship, *n.*, place de secrétaire, *f.*

registra'tion (rèdj'is-tré-), *n.*, enregistrement, *m.*; inscription, *f.*, (of letter) chargement; (of a trademark, etc.) dépôt, *m.*

reg'istry (rèdj-), *n.*, enregistrement, *m.*; inscription, *f.*; greffe, secrétariat, *m.* — office; (for servants) *bureau de placement*; (for inquiries) *bureau de renseignements*; (general) *bureau d'enregistrement, m.*

reg'istry-book (-bouke), *n.*, matricule, *f.*

reg'let (règ'-), *n.*, (print.) réglette, *f.*; (arch.) réglet, *m.*

regorge' (ri-gordje), *v.a.*, vomir; (to swallow again) ravaler.

regraft' (rî-), *v.a.*, (ant.) greffer de nouveau, réenter.

regrate' (rè-), *v.a.*, (to engross) accaparer, regratter; (to sell) revendre; (mas.) regratter.

regrat'er, *n.*, revendeur, *m.*, revendeuse, *f.*

regrat'ing, *n.*, revente, *f.*, revendage; (mas.) regrattage, *m.*

regres'sion (rè-grèsh'eune), *n.*, retour, *m.*; (astron.) mouvement rétrograde, *m.*

regres'sive, *adj.*, rétrograde, qui retourne.

regres'sively, *adv.*, (ant.) par rétrogradation.

regret' (rè-), *n.*, regret, *m.* To feel —; *éprou-*

ver, *avoir du regret*. With —; *avec regret*; (reluctantly) *à regret, à contre cœur.*

regret' (rè-), *v.a.*, regretter, avoir regret. It is to be —ted; *il est regrettable*, ou *à regretter.*

regret'ful (-foule), *adj.*, plein de regrets; regrettable.

regret'fully, *adv.*, avec regret, à regret.

regret'table, *adj.*, fâcheux.

reg'ular (règh'iou-), *adj.*, régulier; réglé; en règle; (geom., gram., milit.) régulier; (real) vrai, véritable; (downright) franc, fieffé, parfait; (usual) accoutumé, ordinaire; (character) suivi; (of rhymes) plat, suivi. As — as clockwork; *réglé comme un papier de musique.*

reg'ular (règh'-), *n.*, (milit., c.rel.) régulier, *m.*

regular'ity (règh'iou-), *n.*, régularité, *f.*

regulariza'tion, *n.*, régularisation, *f.*

reg'ularize, *v.a.*, régulariser.

reg'ularly, *adv.*, régulièrement; réglément; dans les règles; véritablement; vraiment, franchement.

reg'ulate (règh'iou-), *v.a.*, régler; réglementer; ordonner, diriger; mettre en ordre; (horl.) régler.

regula'tion, *adj.*, réglementaire, d'ordonnance.

regula'tion (règh'iou-lé-), *n.*, règlement, *m.*, ordonnance, *f.*

reg'ulator (règh'iou-lé-teur), *n.*, régulateur, *m.*

rehabil'itate (rî-), *v.a.*, réhabiliter.

rehabilita'tion (rî-ha-bil'i-té-), *n.*, réhabilitation, *f.*

rehear' (rî-hîr), *v.a.*, entendre de nouveau.

rehear'ing (rî-hîr'-), *n.*, nouvelle audition, *f.*

rehear'sal (rè-heurs'-), *n.*, récit, *m.*; récitation; (thea.) répétition, *f.* Dress —, *répétition générale, f.*

rehearse' (rè-heurse), *v.a.*, réciter; répéter; (to narrate) raconter, rapporter; (thea.) répéter.

reign (rêne), *n.*, règne; royaume, *m.*; (authority) souveraineté, *f.* In the — of; *sous le règne* **de**.

reign (rêne), *v.n.*, régner; (prevail) dominer.

reign'ing, *adj.*, régnant; (prevailing) dominant.

reimburs'able (rî-i'm'beurs'a-b'l), *adj.*, remboursable.

reimburse' (rî-i'm'beurse), *v.a.*, rembourser.

reimburse'ment, *n.*, remboursement, *m.*

reimburs'er (rî-), *n.*, personne qui rembourse, *f.*

reimport' (rî-), *v.a.*, réimporter.

reimporta'tion (rî-i'm'por-té-), *n.*, réimportation, *f.*

reimpose', *v.a.*, réimposer.

reimposi'tion, *n.*, réimpositiom, *f.*

reimpres'sion (rî-i'm'prèsh'-), *n.*, réimpression, *f.*

reimpris'on (-priz'eune), *v.a.*, remettre en prison, remprisonner.

reimpris'onment, *n.*, remprisonnement, *m.*

rein (rêne), *n.*, rêne, bride, *f.* To keep a tight — over any one; *tenir la bride courte, tenir la bride serrée, la bride haute, à quelqu'un.* To give the — to; *rendre la bride* **à**; *lâcher la bride* **à**; (fig.) *laisser déchaîner, donner libre cours* **à**. To take the —s; *prendre les rênes*, ou (fig.) *la direction.*

rein, *v.a.*, conduire à la bride, conduire, gouverner; brider; (to restrain) brider, contenir. To — in; *retenir, maintenir.*

rein'deer (rê'n'dîr), *n.*, renne, *m.*

reinforce' (rî-i'n'fôrce), *v.a.*, (milit.) renforcer; (fig.) fortifier.

reinforce'ment, *n.*, (fig.) secours, appui; (milit.) renforcement, (of troops) renfort, *m.*

reingra'tiate (rî-i'n'gré-shi-), *v.a.*, faire rentrer en grâce; remettre en faveur. To — one's self; *rentrer en grâce.*

reinhab'it (rî-), *v.a.*, habiter de nouveau.

reinscribe', *v.a.*, réinscrire.

rein'less (rê'n'-), *adj.*, sans rênes; sans frein.

reinsert′ (rî-i'n'seurte), *v.a.*, insérer de nouveau, réinsérer.

reinser′tion (rî-i'n'seur'-), *n.*, insertion nouvelle, réinsertion, *f.*

reinspect′ (rî-), *v.a.*, inspecter de nouveau.

reinspec′tion, *n.*, nouvelle inspection, *f.*

reinstall′ (rî-i'n'stôl), *v.a.*, réinstaller ; rétablir.

reinstall′ment, reinstallation (rî-), *n.*, réinstallation, *f.* ; rétablissement, *m.*

reinstate′ (rî-), *v.a.*, rétablir ; réintégrer.

reinstate′ment, *n.*, rétablissement, *m.* ; réintégration, *f.*

reinsur′ance, *n.*, réassurance, *f.*

reinsure′, *v.a.*, réassurer.

reinsur′er, *n.*, réassureur, *m.*

rein′tegrate (rî-i'n'ti-), *v.a.*, réintégrer.

reinter′rogate (rî-i'n'tèr-), *v.a.*, interroger de nouveau, réinterroger.

reintroduce′ (rî-i'n'tro-diouce), *v.a.*, introduire de nouveau, réintroduire.

reinvest′ (rî-i'n'vèste), *v.a.*, investir de nouveau ; revêtir de nouveau ; (money) replacer.

reinvest′ment (rî-), *n.*, nouvel investissement ; (money) replacement, *m.*

reinvig′orate (rî-), *v.a.*, rendre de la vigueur à ; ranimer.

reinvite′, *v.a.*, réinviter.

reis′sue (rî-ish'iou), *n.*, nouvelle émission ; (print.) réimpression, republication, nouvelle édition, *f.*

reis′sue (rî-ish'iou), *v.a.*, émettre de nouveau, réémettre, republier.

reit′erate (rî-it'eur-), *v.a.*, réitérer.

reitera′tion (rî-it'eur'é-), *n.*, réitération, *f.*

reit′erative, *adj.*, réitératif.

reit′eratively, *adv.*, réiterativement.

reject′ (rè-djèk'te), *v.a.*, rejeter.

reject′able (-'a-b'l), *adj.*, rejetable, à rejeter.

reject′er, *n.*, personne qui rejette, *f.*

rejec′tion, *n.*, rejet, *m.* ; réjection, *f.*

reject′ive, *adj.*, qui rejette.

rejoice′ (rè-djôîce), *v.a.*, réjouir.

rejoice′, *v.n.*, se réjouir de.

rejoin′ (rè-djôîne), *v.a.*, rejoindre.

rejoin′, *v.n.*, (reply) répliquer, répondre, repartir.

rejoin′der, *n.*, repartie, réponse ; (jur.) réplique, *f.*

rejoint′ (rè-djôî'n'te), *v.a.*, rejoindre ; (mas.) rejointoyer.

rejoint′ing, *n.*, (mas.) rejointoiement, *m.*

rejudge′ (rî-djeudje), *v.a.*, rejuger.

reju′venate (ri-djiou-vi-) *ou* **reju′venize** (-vè'n'aïze), *v.a.*, rajeunir.

rejuvenes′cence (rî-djiou-vè-nès'-), *n.*, rajeunissement, *m.*

rekin′dle (rî-ki'n'd'l), *v.a.*, enflammer de nouveau ; rallumer.

rekin′dling, *v.*, nouvel embrasement, *m.* ; nouvelle flamme, *f.*

reland′ (rî-), *v.a.* and *n.*, débarquer de nouveau.

relapse′ (rè-), *n.*, rechute, *f.* ; (pers.) relaps, *m.*, relapse, *f.* ; (into crime) récidive, *f.*

relapse′, *v.n.*, retomber ; (into crime) récidiver.

relapsed′, *adj.*, relaps.

relate′ (rè-), *v.a.*, raconter ; rapporter ; réciter ; conter. Strange to —; *chose étonnante à dire.*

relate′, *v.n.*, se rapporter, avoir rapport à, être relatif à.

relat′ed, *adj.*, qui a relation, qui a un rapport à ; relatif à ; (by blood) allié à, parent de.

relat′er, *n.*, raconteur, conteur, narrateur, *m.*

relat′ing, *adj.*, relatif, qui a rapport à ; qui a trait à, qui se rapporte à.

rela′tion, *n.*, (recital) relation, *f.*, récit, rapport ; (analogy) rapport, *m.*, relation ; (alliance) parenté, *f.* ; (pers.) parent, *m.*, parente, *f.* pl.,

(intercourse) relations, *f.pl.* ; rapports, *m.pl.* In — to ; *quant à* ; *par rapport à* ; *à l'égard* de. Near —s ; *proches parents, m.pl.* Distant —s ; *parents éloignés, m.pl.*

rela′tionship (rè-lé-), *n.*, parenté ; relation, *f.*

rel′ative (rèl′-), *n.*, parent, *m.*, parente, *f.* ; (gram.) relatif ; (log.) relatif, *m.*

rel′ative (rèl′-), *adj.*, relatif à.

rel′atively, *adv.*, relativement.

rel′ativeness (rèl′-), *n.*, relation, *f.* ; rapport, *m.* ; (log.) relativité, *f.*

relax′ (rè-), *v.a.*, relâcher, détendre, débander ; lâcher ; se relâcher de ; (fig.) relâcher, délasser, reposer, distraire. To — the mind ; *détendre l'esprit.* To — one's mind ; *se distraire, se délasser.*

relax′, *v.n.*, se relâcher ; se délasser ; céder, s'adoucir ; faiblir, fléchir ; se ralentir ; (of the weather) se radoucir.

relaxa′tion, *n.*, relâchement, relâche ; (med.) relâchement, *m.* ; relaxation (l.u.), *f.* ; (fig.) relâchement, délassement, repos, *m.*, distraction ; (jur. canon law) relaxation, *f.*

relax′ing, *adj.*, (of climate) énervant, mou ; qui relâche ; (med.) relâchant, laxatif.

relay′, *n.*, relais, *m.* *v.a.*, reposer, replacer.

release′, *n.*, (from prison) élargissement, *m.* ; délivrance ; libération, mise en liberté, *f.* ; (jur.) abandon, renoncement, *m.* ; cession, *f.* ; (from an obligation) décharge, *f.*, dégagement ; (from pain) soulagement ; (rest) relâche, repos, *m.*

release′, *v.a.*, relâcher, lâcher, (a prisoner) élargir ; libérer, mettre en liberté ; dégager, débarrasser ; délivrer, relever, abandonner ; (from an obligation) décharger, délier ; tenir quitte de.

releas′er, *n.*, libérateur, *m.*, libératrice, *f.*

rel′egate (rèl′-), *v.a.*, reléguer.

relega′tion, *n.*, relégation, *f.*

relent′, *v.n.*, s'amollir ; se ramollir ; (pers.) se radoucir, fléchir, céder, s'adoucir, s'attendrir ; (to repent) se repentir ; (things) se ralentir.

relent′ing, *n.*, ramollissement ; (pers.) radoucissement, attendrissement, *m.*

relent′less, *adj.*, inflexible, sans pitié, impitoyable, inexorable, implacable, acharné.

relent′lessly, *adv.*, implacablement, avec acharnement.

relent′lessness, *n.*, rigueur, dureté, *f.*

relessee′ (rî-lès'sî), *n.*, (jur.) abandonnataire, *m.f.*

relessor′ (rî-lès'sor), *n.*, (jur.) personne qui donne une décharge, qui abandonne, *f.*

rel′evancy, *n.*, dépendance, convenance, relation, *f.* ; à propos, *m.* ; applicabilité, *f.*

rel′evant, *adj.*, relatif ; applicable ; convenable ; à propos ; pertinent.

reli′able (rè-laï-), *adj.*, (pers.) à qui l'on peut se fier, sur lequel on peut compter ; digne de confiance, digne de foi, croyable, sérieux ; (of information) sûr, exact, positif, certain, bien fondé.

reli′ableness *ou* **reliabil′ity**, *n.*, crédibilité, certitude, foi ; véracité, *f.*

reli′ance, *n.*, confiance, *f.* To place — on ; *avoir confiance* dans, en ; *se fier à* ; *compter* sur ; *mettre sa confiance* dans, en.

rel′ic (rèl′-), *n.*, reste, *m.* ; (saint, martyr) relique, *f.* —s, *pl.*, restes, *m.pl.* ; dépouille mortelle, *f.* ; cendre, *f.* ; cendres, *m.pl.*

rel′ict (rèl′-), *n.*, veuve, *f.*

relief′ (rè-), *n.*, (from pain, etc.) soulagement, adoucissement, allégement ; (assistance) secours, *m.*, aide ; (milit.) action de relever une sentinelle, *f.* ; (milit.) (of sentries) pose, *f.* ; (redress) redressement, *m.*, réparation, justice, *f.* ; (feudalism, paint., sculpt.) relief, *m.* Demi — ; (paint., sculpt.) demi-relief. Out-door —; *secours à domicile, m.* — ticket ; *bon de secours, m.* To afford, to give —; *donner du soulagement ;* (assistance) *donner des secours.* Parish —; *secours du bureau de bienfaisance.* To stand out in —; *ressortir*. To bring out in strong —; *faire vivement ressortir*.

relieve', *v.a.*, (from pain, etc., to give ease to) soulager ; (to alleviate) adoucir, alléger ; (to deliver) délivrer **de** ; (to assist) secourir, aider ; subvenir aux besoins **de** ; (milit.) relever ; (to right) redresser ; (to abate) adoucir, tempérer ; (to set off) relever ; donner du relief **à**, faire ressortir, mettre en relief.

reliev'er, *n.*, personne qui soulage, qui adoucit, qui secourt, qui aide ; chose qui soulage, qui adoucit, qui secourt, qui aide, *f.*

reliev'ing, *n.*, soulagement, allégement, adoucissement ; secours, *m.* ; aide, *f.*

reliev'ing-officer, *n.*, employé chargé de distribuer les secours ; commissaire des pauvres, *m.*

relie'vo (rè-li-vô), *n.*, relief, *m.*

relight' (ri-laïte), *v.a.*, rallumer ; éclairer de nouveau.

reli'gion (rè-), *n.*, religion, *f.*

reli'gionist, *n.*, bigot, fanatique, *m.*

reli'gious, *adj.*, religieux ; de religion ; de piété. — book ; *livre de dévotion, ou de piété, m.*

reli'giously, *adv.*, religieusement ; (piously) pieusement ; avec piété.

reli'giousness, *n.*, piété ; religiosité, *f.*

relin'quish, *v.a.*, abandonner ; quitter ; renoncer à.

relin'quisher, *n.*, personne qui abandonne ; personne qui renonce à, *f.*

relin'quishment, *n.*, renonciation, *f.* ; abandon, désistement, *m.*

rel'iquary (rèl'i-kwa-), *n.*, reliquaire, *m.*

rel'ish (rèl'-), *n.*, goût, *m.*, saveur, *f.* ; (fig.) parfum ; (charm) charme, plaisir ; (titbit) morceau friand, *m.*, friandise, *f.* ; (inclination) appétit, *m.* To give a — to ; *relever le goût* **de**. To eat with — ; *manger de bon appétit*.

rel'ish (rèl'-), *v.a.*, (to give a taste to) donner du goût à, relever le goût **de** ; (to like) trouver goût à, goûter, savourer, trouver bon, aimer. I do not — his jokes ; *ses plaisanteries ne sont pas du tout de mon goût*.

rel'ish, *v.n.*, avoir bon goût, (fig.) plaire **à**, faire plaisir **à** ; (to have a flavor) avoir un parfum **de**, une saveur **de** ; sentir le, *ou* la, *ou* les.

rel'ishable, *adj.*, savoureux.

relive' (ri-liv'), *v.n.*, revivre.

reload', *v.a.*, recharger.

reluct'ance *ou* **reluct'ancy** (rè-leuk-), *n.*, répugnance, *f.*

reluct'ant (-leuk'-), *adj.*, qui a de la répugnance à ; qui balance ; qui agit à contre-cœur ; peu disposé à ; (of things) qui résiste, forcé. I am, *ou* feel, — to ; *j'ai de la répugnance* **à** ; *je répugne* **à** ; *il me répugne* **de** ; *j'éprouve de la répugnance* **à**.

reluct'antly (-leuk'-), *adv.*, avec répugnance, à contre-cœur, à regret.

rely', *v.n.*, compter **sur**, se reposer **sur**, se fier **à**, faire fond **sur**, se fonder **sur**, avoir confiance **dans, en**.

remain' (-mé'n'), *v.n.*, rester, demeurer, survivre ; (ant.) séjourner. It only —s for him to ; *il ne lui reste plus qu'à*. It —s to be seen whether ; *reste à savoir si*. That —s to be seen ; *c'est ce que nous verrons*. That —s to be proved ; *cela n'est pas certain* ; *cela n'est pas encore prouvé*. There —, there —s ; *il reste*. To have —ing ; *avoir de reste*. It —s for me to ; *il me reste* **à**. To — till called for ; (of letters) *poste restante*, *f.*

remain'der, *n.*, reste, restant, *m.* ; (jur.) réversibilité à terme fixe, *f.*

remain'der, *adj.*, de reste.

remain'ing, *adj.*, de reste ; restant.

remains' (-mé'n'ze), *n.pl.*, restes ; vestiges, débris, *m.pl.* ; traces, *f.pl.* ; cendres, *f.pl.*, cendre, dépouille mortelle, *f.* Mortal — ; *restes mortels, m.pl.* ; *cendres, f.pl.* ; *cendre* ; *dépouille mortelle, f.*

remake' (ri-), *v.a.* (preterit and past part., Remade), refaire.

reman' (ri-), *v.a.*, remettre du monde **dans** ; (nav.) armer de nouveau.

remand' (rè-mâ'n'd), *v.a.*, rappeler ; contremander ; (jur.) renvoyer à une autre audience. —ed for a week ; *renvoyé à huitaine*.

remand', *n.*, renvoi à une autre audience, *m.*

remark', *n.*, remarque, observation, *f.*

remark', *v.a.*, remarquer, observer ; (to a person) faire remarquer, faire observer.

remark'able (-'a-b'l), *adj.*, remarquable.

remark'ableness, *n.*, caractère remarquable, *m.*, singularité, *f.*

remark'ably, *adv.*, remarquablement.

remar'ry (ri-), *v.a.*, remarier.

remar'ry, *v.n.*, se remarier.

reme'diable (-mi-di-a-b'l), *adj.*, à quoi l'on peut remédier, réparable, remédiable.

reme'dial (-mi-), *adj.*, curatif, réparateur ; (jur.) récusoire.

rem'edy (rèm-), *n.*, remède ; (jur.) recours, *m.* Past — ; *sans remède*.

rem'edy, *v.a.*, remédier **à**, porter remède **à**.

remem'ber (rè-), *v.a.*, se souvenir **de**, se ressouvenir **de** ; se rappeler ; rappeler au souvenir. If I — rightly ; *s'il m'en souvient bien, si je m'en souviens bien* ; *si j'ai bonne mémoire*. — me to him ; *rappelez-moi à son souvenir* ; *dites-lui mille choses de ma part*.

remem'brance, *n.*, souvenir, ressouvenir, *m.*, mémoire, *f.* ; (token) souvenir ; (memorandum) mémento, mémorandum, *m.*, note, *f.* In — of ; *en souvenir* **de** ; *en mémoire* **de**. To bring a thing to any one's — ; *rappeler une chose au souvenir de quelqu'un*. Give him my kind —s ; *rappelez-moi à son souvenir* ; *dites-lui mille choses de ma part*. My kind —s to ; *mes amitiés* **à**.

remem'brancer, *n.*, personne qui fait souvenir, *f.* ; (thing) souvenir ; (of the exchequer) secrétaire, archiviste, *m.*

remind' (-maï'n'de), *v.a.*, rappeler ; rappeler au souvenir ; faire penser **à** ; remettre dans l'esprit, faire souvenir **de**, faire ressouvenir **de**. — him of that ; *rappelez-lui cela, faites-le souvenir de cela*. That —s me of ; *cela me fait l'effet* **de**. I do not want —ing ; *je n'ai pas besoin qu'on m'y fasse penser*.

remind'er, *n.*, souvenir, aide-mémoire, mémento ; avis, *m.* Send me a — ; *faites m'y penser* ; *avisez-moi* ; *envoyez-moi un petit mot*.

reminis'cence (rè'm'-), *n.*, réminiscence, *f.*

remiss' (-sî), *adj.*, nonchalant ; négligent, lent, inexact ; sans soins ; mou.

remis'sible (-'si-b'l), *adj.*, rémissible ; graciable, pardonnable.

remis'sion, *n.*, rémission, *f.*, relâchement, radoucissement, adoucissement, *m.* ; (pardon) remise, grâce, *f.*, pardon, *m.* — of sins ; *rémission des péchés*.

remiss'ly, *adv.*, négligemment, nonchalamment, lentement, sans soin.

remiss'ness, *n.*, nonchalance, lenteur, négligence, inexactitude, *f.*

remit', *v.a.*, (to relax) se relâcher **de**, calmer, diminuer, affaiblir ; (to forgive) faire grâce **de**, faire remise **de**, pardonner, remettre ; (to give up) livrer, remettre ; (to refer) renvoyer ; (to restore) remettre **dans**, rendre **à** ; (to send back) renvoyer ; (money) remettre ; faire une remise **de**.

remit', *v.n.*, se relâcher ; se calmer ; diminuer ; s'affaiblir ; s'apaiser.

remit'tal, *n.*, (forgiveness) pardon, *m.* ; (remittance) remise, *f.*

remit'tance, *n.*, (com.) remise, *f.*, envoi de fonds, *m.*

remit'tent, *adj.*, (med.) rémittent.

remit'ter, *n.*, personne qui pardonne, qui fait grâce ; (of money) remetteur de fonds, *f.*

rem'nant (rè'm'-), *n.*, reste, *m.* ; restes, débris, *m.pl.* ; (of stuff) coupon, *m.*

remod'el (rî-mod'èl), *v.a.*, refondre ; (fig.) remanier, refondre.

remod'eling, *n.*, remodelage, *m.* ; (fig.) refonte, remaniement, *f.*

remon'strance (rè-), *n.*, remontrance, *f.* ; (c. rel.) ostensoir, *m.*

remon'strant, *n.*, (hist.) remontrant, *m.*

remon'strate, *n.*, remontrer, représenter. To — with ; *faire des remontrances* à.

remon'strator (-stré-teur), *n.*, remontreur, *m.*

rem'ora (rè'm'-), *n.*, (ich.) rémora, *m.*

remorse' (rè-), *n.*, remords, *m.*

remorse'ful (-foule), *adj.*, rempli de remords, déchiré, *ou* dévoré, de remords.

remorse'less, *adj.*, sans remords ; sans pitié, impitoyable.

remorse'lessly, *adv.*, sans remords.

remorse'lessness, *n.*, cruauté, inhumanité, barbarie, *f.*

remote', *adj.*, éloigné, lointain ; reculé, écarté, retiré.

remote'ly, *adv.*, au loin, de loin ; d'une manière éloignée ; légèrement, faiblement.

remote'ness, *n.*, éloignement, *n.;* époque reculée ; distance, *ou* nature éloignée, *f.* ; degré éloigné, *m.* ; faiblesse, *f.*

remold' (rî-môlde), *v.a.*, mouler de nouveau ; (fig.) refondre.

remount' (rî-maou'n'te), *v.a.* and *n.*, remonter.

remount', *n.*, (milit.) remonte, *f.* ; cheval de remonte, *m.* — officer ; *capitaine de remonte, m.*

remount'ing, *n.*, (milit.) remonte, *f.*

removabil'ity (rè-mouv'-), *n.*, amovibilité, *f.*

remov'able (rè-mouv'a-b'l), *adj.*, (pers.) amovible ; (things) transportable.

remov'al, *n.*, (of residence) changement de domicile, déménagement ; éloignement ; départ ; (from office) déplacement, renvoi, *m.*, destitution, *f.* ; (of a grievance) redressement, *m.* ; abolition, suppression, *f.* ; (of a disease) guérison ; (of bandages) levée, *f.* ; (change of place) changement de place ; déplacement ; enlèvement, *m.* Three —s are as bad as a fire ; *trois déménagements valent un incendie.*

remove', *n.*, (change of place) changement de place, *m.* ; (translation) translation, *f.*, transport ; (removal) déménagement ; (departure) départ ; (at chess, draughts) coup ; (step) degré, *m.* ; (distance) distance ; (dish) entrée, *f.*, relevé, *m.* ; (in Eng. public schools) classe de rhétorique, *f.*

remove', *v.a.*, (to place at a distance) éloigner ; écarter ; (to put out of its place) déplacer ; (a grievance) redresser ; abolir, supprimer ; (to set aside) ôter, enlever, écarter ; (to take away) ôter, enlever ; (to transport) transporter ; (from office) déplacer, démettre, destituer ; (furniture) déménager ; (bandages) lever ; (obstacle) lever ; (a disease) chasser ; extirper ; (jur.) porter à une autre cour ; (by death) enlever ; (from school) retirer. To be far —d from ; *être bien éloigné* de.

remove', *v.n.*, s'éloigner ; s'ôter, s'écarter ; se déplacer ; se transporter ; (to change residence) changer de domicile, déménager.

remov'er, *n.*, personne qui ôte, qui éloigne, qui déplace, *f.*, déménageur, *m.*

remu'nerable (-miou-neur'a-b'l), *adj.*, rémunérable.

remu'nerate (-miou-neur'-), *v.a.*, rémunérer ; rétribuer ; salarier, payer.

remu'nerated (-miou-neur'ét'-), *adj.*, rémunéré ; rétribué ; salarié, payé.

remu'nerating (-miou-neur'ét'-), *adj.*, qui rétribue ; de rémunération, lucratif.

remunera'tion (-miou-neur'é-), *n.*, rémunération ; rétribution, *f.*

remu'nerative (-neur'é-), *adj.*, qui rétribue ; rémunérateur ; lucratif ; (jur.) rémunératoire.

re'nal (rî-), *adj.*, (anat.) rénal.

rename', *v.a.*, renommer.

ren'ard (rè'n'-), *n.*, renard, maître renard, *m.*

renas'cence (rè-), *n.*, renaissance, *f.*

renas'cent, *adj.*, renaissant.

renas'cible (-ci-b'l), *adj.*, (ant.) qui peut renaître.

renav'igable (rî-), *adj.*, renavigable.

renav'igate (rî-), *v.a.*, naviguer de nouveau sur.

renav'igate, *v.n.*, naviguer de nouveau.

rencoun'ter (rè'n'caou'n'-), *n.*, rencontre, *f.* ; choc, *m.* ; (combat) rencontre, *f.*, combat, *m.*

rencoun'ter, *v.a.*, rencontrer hostilement.

rencoun'ter, *v.n.*, se rencontrer, se heurter ; se choquer ; (to fight) se rencontrer hostilement, se battre.

rend, *v.a.* (*preterit* and *past part.*, Rent), déchirer ; (fig.) déchirer à belles dents ; fendre. To — the heart ; *fendre le cœur.* To — asunder ; *déchirer en deux, fendre en deux.* To — the air with ; *faire retentir l'air* de. — -rock ; (chem.) lithofracteur, *m.*

ren'der, *v.a.*, rendre ; (mas.) appliquer, enduire.

ren'der, *n.*, (pers.) fendeur, *m.*, fendeuse, *f.*, déchireur, *m.*, déchireuse, *f.*

ren'derable (-a-b'l), *adj.*, qui peut être rendu, rendable.

rend'ering, *n.*, traduction, *f.* ; (mas.) enduit, *m.*

ren'dezvous, *n.*, rendez-vous, *m.* To give — ; *donner rendez-vous* à ; *se donner rendez-vous ; se réunir, se rassembler.*

rendi'tion (rè'n'dish'-), *n.*, reddition ; interprétation, reproduction, *f.*

ren'egade *ou* **renega'do** (-ghé-dô), *n.*, rénégat, transfuge ; vagabond, *m.* To turn — ; *renier.*

renew' (rè-), *v.a.*, renouveler ; renouer.

renew'able (-a-b'l), *adj.*, renouvelable.

renew'al, *n.*, renouvellement, *m.* ; rénovation ; (fig.) reprise, *f.*

renew'er, *n.*, rénovateur, *m.*, rénovatrice, *f.*

renew'ing, *adj.*, rénovateur.

renew'ing, *n.*, renouvellement, *m.*

ren'iform (rè'n'-), *adj.*, (bot.) réniforme.

reni'tence (rè-naï-), *n.*, (med.) rénitence ; résistance, *f.*

reni'tent (rè-naï-), *adj.*, (med.) rénitent ; résistant.

ren'net, *n.*, présure, caillette, *f.*

ren'net, *n.*, (apple) reinette, *f.*

renounce', *v.a.* and *n.*, renoncer, désavouer ; renoncer à ; abjurer ; renier.

renounce'ment, *n.*, renoncement, *m.* ; renonciation, *f.*

renoun'cer, *n.*, renégat, *m.*

ren'ovate (rè'n'-), *v.a.*, renouveler ; rajeunir ; faire renaître.

ren'ovating (rè'n'o-vét'-), *adj.*, rénovateur.

renova'tion (rè'n'o-vé-), *n.*, rénovation, *f.*, renouvellement, rajeunissement, *m.*

renown' (rè-), *n.*, renommée, *f.* ; renom, *m.*

renowned', *adj.*, renommé.

rent, *n.*, (fissure) déchirement, *m.*, déchirure, fente, *f.* ; (in garments) accroc, *m.*, déchirure, *f.* ; (schism) schisme, *m.* ; (mint.) fente, fissure ; rente, redevance, *f.* ; (of farms) fermage, (of houses, rooms) loyer, *m.* Heavy — ; *gros loyer.* High, low — ; *loyer élevé, faible.* — -free ; *exempt de loyer, sans payer de loyer.*

rent, *v.a.*, (to let out) louer, donner à louage, donner à ferme, donner à loyer ; (to take) louer, prendre à louage, prendre à ferme, prendre à loyer ; arrenter.

rent, *v.n.*, se louer.

rent'able (-a-b'l), *adj.*, affermable.

rent'al, *n.*, état de revenus, état de rentes ; livre censier, *m.*

rent'er, *n.*, bailleur ; propriétaire qui donne à loyer, à ferme ; (lessee) locataire ; (of a farm) fermier, *m.*

ren'ter, *v.a.*, faire des reprises perdues à.

ren'terer, *n.*, ouvrier en reprises perdues, *m.*, ouvrière en reprises perdues, *f.*

rent'-roll, *n.*, état de revenus, livre censier, *m.*

renuncia'tion (rè-neu'n'shi-é-), *n.*, renonciation, *f.* ; renoncement, *m.*

reobtain' (rî-), *v.n.*, obtenir de nouveau.

reoccupa'tion, *n.*, réoccupation, *f.*

reoc'cupy, *v.a.*, réoccuper.

reo'pen (rî-ô-), *v.a.*, rouvrir, ouvrir de nouveau. *v.n.*, rouvrir, se rouvrir.

reo'pen, *v.n.*, (of schools, theaters, law courts) rentrer.

reo'pening, *n.*, réouverture; (of schools, etc.) rentrée, *f.*

reoppose' (rî-op-pôze), *v.a.*, opposer de nouveau.

reordain' (rî-or-dé'n), *v.a.*, (ecc.) réordonner.

reordina'tion (rî-or-di-né-), *n.*, (ecc.) réordination, *f.*

reorganiza'tion (rî-or-ga'n'aïzé-), *n.*, réorganisation, *f.*

reor'ganize (rî-or-ga'n'aïze), *v.a.*, réorganiser.

reor'ganizer, *n.*, réorganisateur, *m.*

reor'ganizing, *adj.*, réorganisateur.

reor'ganizing, *n.*, réorganisation, *f.*

rep, repp, *n.*, (fabric) reps, *m. adj.*, de reps.

repac'ify (rî-pa-ci-faïe), *v.a.*, pacifier de nouveau.

repack', *v.a.*, rempaqueter, remballer ; rencaisser.

repack'ing, *n.*, rempaquetage, remballage ; rencaissage.

repaint', *v.a.*, repeindre.

repair' (rè-père), *v.a.*, réparer ; raccommoder ; restaurer, rétablir ; (nav.) radouber ; (an injury) réparer, indemniser.

repair', *n.*, réparation, *f.* ; entretien ; (of clothes, etc.) raccommodage, rétablissement, entretien ; (nav.) radoub ; (place) séjour, *m.*, demeure, *f.* To be out of —; *être en mauvais état ; avoir besoin de réparation.* To be in good —; *être en bon état ; être bien entretenu.* To keep in —; *entretenir en bon état.*

repair', *v.n.*, aller; se rendre à ; se transporter dans.

repair'er, *n.*, réparateur, *m.*, réparatrice, *f.* ; (of clothes, etc.) raccommodeur, *m.*, -euse, *f.*

repand', *adj.*, (bot.) godronné.

rep'arable (rèp'a-ra-b'l), *adj.*, réparable.

rep'arably, *adv.*, d'une manière réparable.

repara'tion (rèp'a-ré-), *n.*, action de réparer ; (for an injury) satisfaction, réparation, *f.* ; rétablissement, *m.*

rep'arative (-par-a-), *adj.*, qui répare ; réparateur.

repartee' (rèp'ar-tî), *n.*, repartie, riposte, *f.*

repass' (rî-pàss), *v.a.* and *n.*, repasser.

repass'ing, *n.*, repassage, *m.*

repast' (rè-), *n.*, repas, *m.*

repave' (rî-), *v.a.*, repaver.

repav'ing, *n.*, repavage, *m.*

repay' (rè-pé), *v.a.* (*preterit* and *past part.*, Repaid), rembourser ; payer, rendre ; récompenser; payer de retour ; (for) payer de ; (to return like for like) revaloir. To —; (reading, inspection, etc.) *valoir la peine, ou mériter, d'être lu, examiné, etc.*

repay'able (-pé-a-b'l), *adj.*, payable, remboursable.

repay'ment (-pé-), *n.*, payement, remboursement, *m.*

repeal' (-pîl), *v.a.*, révoquer, abolir, abroger, rapporter.

repeal' (-pîl), *n.*, révocation, abrogation, abolition, *f.* ; rappel, *m.*

repeal'able (-'a-b'l), *adj.*, révocable.

repeal'er, *n.*, personne qui révoque, qui abroge, *f.* ; (Eng. Hist.) partisan de la révocation ; (Ireland) autonomiste, *m.*

repeat' (-pîte), *v.a.*, répéter, redire ; réitérer ; (by heart) réciter.

repeat' (-pîte), *n.*, répétition ; (mus.) reprise, *f.*

repeat'ed, *adj.*, répété, réitéré ; (redoubled) redoublé.

repeat'edly (-pît'èd'-), *adv.*, à plusieurs reprises ; souvent, bien des fois.

repeat'er, *n.*, rediseur, *m.*, rediseuse ; (arith.) fraction périodique, *f.* ; (nav.) répétiteur, *m.* ; (horl.) montre à répétition, *f.* ; (fire-arm) revolver, *m.*

repeat'ing, *adj.*, qui répète ; (horl.) à répétition. — decimal ; *fraction périodique, f.*

repel', *v.a.*, repousser, combattre ; (med.) répercuter.

repel'lency, *n.*, force répulsive, *f.*

repel'lent, *n.*, (med.) répercussif, révulsif, *m.*

repel'lent, *adj.*, répulsif ; (med.) répercussif, révulsif.

repel'ler, *n.*, personne, chose qui repousse, *f.*

repent', *v.a.* and *n.*, se repentir de (of a thing); se repentir. To — at leisure ; *se repentir trop tard.*

re'pent (rî-), *adj.*, rampant.

repent'ance (rè-, *n.*, repentir, *m.* ; repentance (l.u.), *f.*

repent'ant, *adj.*, repentant.

repent'ant, repent'er, *n.*, pénitent, *m.*

repent'ing, *n.*, repentir, *m.*

repent'ingly, *adv.*, avec repentir.

repeo'ple (ri-pî-p'l), *v.a.*, repeupler.

repeo'pling (ri-pî-), *n.*, repeuplement, *m.*

repercuss' (rî-peur-keuss), *v.a.*, (ant.) répercuter.

repercus'sion (rî-peur-keush'-), *n.*, répercussion, *f.*

repercus'sive (rî-peur-keuss'-), *adj.*, répercussif ; répercutant.

rep'ertory (rèp'eur-), *n.*, répertoire, recueil, *m.*

reperu'sal (rî-), *n.*, deuxième lecture, *f.*

rep'etend (rèp-), *n.*, (arith.) période, *f.*

repeti'tion (rèp'è-tish'-), *n.*, répétition; (mus.) reprise, répétition ; (recital) récitation, *f.*

repine', *v.n.*, se plaindre de, se chagriner de ; murmurer contre, de ; s'affliger, gémir de.

repin'er, *n.*, mécontent, *m.*, mécontente, *f.*

repin'ing, *adj.*, disposé à s'affliger, à gémir ; disposé à se plaindre, à murmurer. *n.*, murmure, regret, chagrin, mécontentement, *m.*

repin'ingly, *adv.*, en murmurant.

replace' (rè-), *v.a.*, replacer ; remettre en place ; (to make good, by a substitute) remplacer ; (to supersede) remplacer.

replace'ment, *n.*, remise en place; remplacement, *m.* ; (surg.) réduction, *f.*

replait' (rî-pléte), *v.a.*, replisser ; replier ; tresser, natter de nouveau.

replant' (rî-), *v.a.*, replanter; (of forests) reboiser.

replanta'tion (ri-pla'n'té-), *n.*, replantation, *f.* ; (of forests) reboisement, *m.*

replate', *v.a.*, replaquer.

replen'ish (rè-), *v.a.* and *n.*, remplir (with, de) ; se remplir.

replete', *adj.*, plein, rempli de.

reple'tion (rè-), *n.*, plénitude ; (med.) réplétion, *f.*

replev'in (-plèv'-), *n.*, mainlevée (sur caution), *f.*

rep'lica, *n.*, double, *m.* ; répétition, *f.*

replica'tion (rèp'li-ké-), *n.*, réplique, *f.*

repli'er (-plaï-), *n.*, personne qui réplique, *f.*

replunge' (rî-), *v.a.*, replonger.

reply' (rè-plaïe), *n.*, réplique, réponse, *f.*, dernier mot, *m.*

reply' (-plaïe), *v.a.*, and *n.*, répliquer, repartir, répondre. — post-card ; *carte postale réponse, f.*

repol'ish (rī-), *v.a.*, repolir.

repol'ishing, *n.*, repolissage, *m.*

report' (rè-pôrte), *v.a.*, rapporter, **signaler** ; raconter, dire, réciter ; faire le rapport **de**, faire un rapport **sur** ; rendre compte **de**. It is —ed ; *on rapporte que ; on dit que ; le bruit court que.* To — one's self ; *se présenter (à la place, à l'état-major ; au bureau de police) ; faire viser ses papiers.*

report', *v.n.*, faire un rapport.

report' (-pôrte), *n.*, (account) rapport, compte rendu ; (rumor) rapport, bruit, ouï-dire ; (of meetings) compte rendu ; (story) récit, *m.* ; (re-pute) réputation ; (of fire-arms) détonation, *f.*, coup ; (jur.) procès-verbal, rapport, *m.* Of good —; *bien vu, considéré.*

report'er, *n.*, rapporteur ; auteur d'un récit, auteur d'un compte rendu ; (short-hand writer) sténographe ; (correspondent) correspondant ; (of a newspaper) reporter, *m.* —s' gallery ; *tribune des journalistes, des sténographes, f.*

report'ing, *n.*, comptes rendus, *m.* ; sténographie ; correspondance, *f.* Parliamentary —; *comptes-rendus des chambres, m.pl.*

repos'al (-pô-zal), *n.*, action de reposer, *f.*

repose' (-pôze), *v.n.*, se reposer ; reposer. To — on ; *se reposer* **sur** ; *se fier* à ; *se confier* à ; *s'en remettre* à.

repose', *v.a.*, reposer ; (to confide) mettre sa confiance **en** *ou* **dans**, confier.

repose' (-pôze), *n.*, repos, *m.*

repos'edness (-pôz'èd'-), *n.*, repos, *m.*

repos'it (-poz'-), *v.a.* *V.* **deposit.**

repos'itory (-poz'i-teuri), *n.*, dépôt, magasin **(de)**, *m.* ; boutique, *f.*

repossess' (rî-poz'zèss), *v.a.*, rentrer en possession **de**, posséder de nouveau.

reposses'sion (rî-poz-zèsh'-), *n.*, rentrée en possession, *f.*

repot', *v.a.*, repoter.

reprehend' (rèp'rè-), *v.a.*, reprendre ; réprimander ; censurer, blâmer.

reprehend'er, *n.*, censeur, critique, *m.*

reprehen'sible (rèp-rè-hè'n'sī-bl), *adj.*, répréhensible, blâmable.

reprehen'sibleness, *n.*, répréhensibilité, *f.*, caractère répréhensible, *m.*

reprehen'sibly, *adv.*, d'une manière répréhensible.

reprehen'sive (rèp'rè-), *adj.*, de reproche.

represent' (rèp-rè-zè'n'te), *v.a.*, représenter.

representa'tion (rèp'rè-zè'n'té'-), *n.*, représentation, *f.*

represent'ative (rèp'rè-zè'n'ta-), *adj.*, représentatif ; qui représente.

represent'ative, *n.*, représentant, député, *m.* ; (of things) représentation, *f.*

represent'atively, *adv.*, d'une manière représentative ; par représentation.

represent'er, *n.*, représentant, *m.*

repress' (rè-prèss), *v.a.*, réprimer.

repress'er, *n.*, réprimeur, *m.*

repres'sion (rè-prèsh'-), *n.*, répression, *f.*

repres'sive (rè-près'-), *adj.*, répressif.

repres'sively, *adv.*, d'une manière répressive.

reprieve' (rè-prîve), *n.*, sursis, répit, *m.*

reprieve', *v.a.*, accorder un sursis à ; surseoir à l'exécution de ; accorder un répit, du répit à.

rep'rimand (rèp'-), *n.*, réprimande, *f.*

reprimand' (-mà'-), *v.a.*, réprimander ; blâmer ; faire la morale à ; sermonner, semoncer.

re'print (rî-), *n.*, réimpression, *f.*

reprint', *v.a.*, réimprimer.

repri'sal (rè-praï-zal), *n.*, représaille ; (jur.) reprise, *f.* To make, *ou* have recourse to, —; *user de représailles.*

reproach' (rè-prôtshe), *n.*, reproche, *m.* ; (shame) honte, *f.*, opprobre, *m.* To be a — to ; *être la honte de.*

reproach', *v.a.*, reprocher ; faire un reproche à ; blâmer, réprimander, accuser. To — a person with having done, etc.; *reprocher à quelqu'un d'avoir fait, etc.* To be —ed with ; *recevoir des reproches* **de**. He is —ed with having done ; *on lui reproche d'avoir fait.*

reproach'able (-a-b'l), *adj.*, reprochable, qui mérite des reproches, digne de reproche.

reproach'ful (-foule), *adj.*, plein de reproches ; digne de reproche ; injurieux ; outrageant, offensant ; honteux, d'opprobre.

reproach'fully, *adv.*, avec reproche ; d'un ton, d'un air, de reproche ; injurieusement, avec insulte ; avec honte ; honteusement.

rep'robate (rèp'-), *n.*, vaurien, mauvais garnement, (theol.) réprouvé, *m.*

rep'robate, *v.a.*, réprouver.

rep'robateness (rèp'ro-bét'-), *n.*, état de réprobation, *m.*

reproba'tion (-bé-), *n.*, réprobation, *f.*

reproduce' (rî-pro-diouce), *v.a.*, reproduire.

rep'robative, *adj.*, réprobatif, réprobateur.

reprodu'cer, *n.*, reproducteur, *m.*

reproduc'tion (-deuk-), *n.*, reproduction, *f.*

reproduc'tive (-deuk'-), *adj.*, reproducteur ; reproductif.

reproof' (rè-proufe), *n.*, répréhension, réprimande, *f.* ; reproche, *m.*

reprov'able (rè-prouv'a-b'l), *adj.*, répréhensible, blâmable.

reprove' (rè-prouve), *v.a.*, censurer ; blâmer, reprendre, réprimander.

reprov'er, *n.*, censeur, répréhenseur, *m.*

reprov'ing, *adj.*, réprobateur.

reprune' (rî-proune), *v.a.*, élaguer de nouveau.

rep'tile (rèp'-), *n.*, reptile, *m.*

rep'tile, *adj.*, reptile ; rampant, bas, **vil**. The — press ; *la presse rampante, f.*

repub'lic (rè-peub'-), *n.*, république, *f.*

repub'lican (-peub'-), *adj.n.*, républicain.

repub'licanism (-ca'n'iz'm), *n.*, républicanisme, *m.*

republica'tion (rè-peub'li-ké-), *n.*, (of a book) nouvelle édition, réimpression, *f.* ; (of a will) renouvellement, *m.*

repub'lish (rî-peub'-), *v.a.*, publier de nouveau, republier ; publier une nouvelle édition **de** ; (a will) renouveler.

repu'diable (rè-piou-di-a-b'l), *adj.*, qui peut être répudié.

repu'diate (-piou-), *v.a.*, répudier.

repudia'tion (-piou-), *n.*, répudiation, *f.*

repug'nance, *n.*, répugnance ; (ant.) résistance, opposition, (contrariety) contrariété, *f.*

repug'nant (-peug-), *adj.*, répugnant, qui répugne, contraire à ; incompatible **avec**. It is — to me to ; *il me répugne* **de**.

repug'nantly, *adv.*, avec répugnance.

repulse' (-peulse), *v.a.*, repousser ; rebuter ; refuser ; rejeter.

repulse', *n.*, échec, refus, *m.* ; rebuffade, *f.* ; désappointement, *m.*

repuls'er, *n.*, personne qui repousse, *f.*

repul'sion (-peul-), *n.*, répulsion ; action de rebuter, *f.*

repuls'ive (-peul-) *ou* **repuls'ory** (-seuri), *adj.*, rebutant ; (forbidding) repoussant ; (phys.) répulsif. A — appearance ; *une figure répulsive ; une laideur repoussante.*

repuls'iveness, *n.*, caractère repoussant, caractère rebutant, *m.*

repump', *v.n.*, repomper.

repur'chase (rî-peur-tshéce), *v.a.*, racheter.

repur'chase, *n.*, rachat, *m.*

rep'utable (rèp'iou-ta-b'l), *adj.*, (pers.) honorable, en bonne réputation, bien vu, considéré ; (things) honorable, compatible avec la bonne réputation ; estimable.

rep'utably, *adv.*, avec honneur ; honorablement.

reputa'tion (rèp'iou-té-), *n.*, réputation, renommée, *f.* To get a — ; *se faire une réputation.*

repute' (rè-pioute), *v.a.*, réputer ; estimer. He is —d to be very rich; *il passe pour être très riche.*

repute' (-pioute), *n.*, réputation, renommée, *f.;* renom, *m.* Of — ; *de renom ; renommé.* Of good — ; *qui jouit d'une bonne réputation.* To bring into — ; *mettre en réputation, mettre en vogue.* Good — is better than wealth ; *bonne renommée vaut mieux que ceinture dorée.*

reput'ed (-piout'-), *adj.*, réputé, censé, qui passe pour ; (of fathers) putatif.

reput'edly, *adv.* suivant l'opinion commune ; censément.

repute'less, *adj.*, sans réputation.

request' (-kwèste), *n.*, requête, demande, prière, *f.* In —; *en crédit, en vogue ;* (pers.) *répandu, recherché ;* (com.) *demandé, recherché, répandu, couru.* At the — of ; *à la demande* **de**; *sur la demande* **de** ; *à la prière* **de** ; *à la requête* **de.**

request' (-kwèste), *v.a.*, demander ; prier ; solliciter. To — any one to; *prier quelqu'un* **de**, *demander à quelqu'un* **de** ; *inviter . . . à.* To — a thing ; *demander, solliciter une chose.*

request'er, *n.*, demandeur, *m.*, demandeuse, *f.;* solliciteur, *m.*, solliciteuse, *f.*

requick'en (rî-kwik'k'n), *v.a.*, raviver, ranimer.

re'quiem (rî-kwi-è'm), *n.*, requiem, *m.*

requir'able (rè-kwaïeur'a-b'l), *adj.*, que l'on peut exiger, exigible.

require' (-kwaïeur), *v.a.*, exiger, requérir ; demander, réclamer; (to want) avoir besoin **de**, falloir. To be —d ; *falloir.* It —s; *il faut.* It is —d of me ; *il faut que je ; on demande, on exige que je.* Two are —d ; *il en faut deux.* You will not — your umbrella ; *vous n'aurez pas besoin de votre parapluie.* That is all that is —d ; *c'est tout ce qu'il faut.*

required'. *V.* **requisite.**

require'ment, *n.*, exigence ; condition requise ; nécessité, *f.;* besoin, *m.;* condition essentielle, *f.*

requir'er, *n.*, personne qui requiert, qui demande, qui exige, *f.*

req'uisite (rèk'wi-zite), *adj.*, requis, exigé, voulu ; demandé ; nécessaire, indispensable. It is — to ; *il faut.*

req'uisite (rèk'wi-zite), *n.*, qualité requise, condition requise ; chose requise ; chose indispensable, *f.*, article nécessaire, *m.*

req'uisitely, *adv.*, nécessairement.

req'uisiteness, *n.*, nécessité absolue, *f.*

requisi'tion (rèk'wi-zish'-), *n.*, réquisition ; demande, requête, convocation, invitation, *f.*

requisi'tion, *v.a.*, réquisitionner, mettre en réquisition, convoquer, inviter.

requit'al (rè-kwaï-), *n.*, récompense, *f.;* retour, *m. ;* (b.s.) revanche, *f.* In — of ; *en récompense* **de** ; *en retour* **de.**

requite' (-kwaïte), *v.a.*, récompenser ; payer **de** ; reconnaître ; rendre, rendre la pareille **à** ; payer de retour.

requit'er, *n.*, personne qui récompense, qui rend, *f.*

rere'dos (rîr'dos), *n.*, retable, arrière-dos, *m.*

resad'dle, *v.a.*, reseller.

resail' (rî-céle), *v.n.*, retourner à la voile ; remettre à la voile.

resale' (rî-céle), *n.*, revente, *f.*

resalute' (rî-ça-lioute), *v.a.*, saluer de nouveau ; rendre le salut **à.**

rescind' (rè-cinde), *v.a.*, rescinder ; abolir ; (jur.) casser ; annuler ; révoquer.

rescis'sion (-cij'eune), *n.*, (jur.) rescision ; annulation ; révocation, abrogation, *f.*

rescis'sory, *adj.*, rescisoire.

re'script (rî-), *n.*, rescrit, *m.*

rescrip'tively (rè-), *adv.*, par rescrit.

res'cue (rès'kiou), *n.*, délivrance, *f.;* secours, *m. ;* délivrance par force, *f.*, sauvetage, *m.* To the — ; *au secours ! à la rescousse !*

res'cue (rès'kiou), *v.a.*, sauver, délivrer **de**; arracher **à** ; tirer **de** ; reprendre ; secourir, délivrer par force ; (jur.) ressaisir.

res'cuer, *n.*, sauveur ; libérateur, *m.*

research' (rè-ceurtshe), *n.*, recherche, *f.;* examen, *m.*

research', *v.a.*, rechercher ; examiner.

reseat' (rî-cîte), *v.a.*, rasseoir, replacer (of members of parliament) rétablir, réélire ; (with seats) régarnir de sièges ; (of chairs, etc.) remettre un fond à.

reseize' (rî-cize), *v.a.*, ressaisir ; (jur.) séquestrer.

reseiz'ure (rî-cî-jour), *n.*, seconde saisie, *f.*

resell' (rî-), *v.a.* (*preterit* and *past part.*, Resold), revendre, vendre de nouveau.

resem'blance (rè-zè'm'-), *n.*, ressemblance ; image, *f. ;* (fig.) rapport, *m.*

resem'ble (-zè'm-b'l), *v.a.*, ressembler **à**. To — each other ; *se ressembler.*

resent', *v.a.*, ressentir ; sentir vivement ; se ressentir **de** ; se venger **de** ; (fig.) s'offenser **de** ; prendre en mauvaise part ; s'indigner **de.**

resent'ful (-foule), *adj.*, plein de ressentiment ; haineux, rancunier, vindicatif. — of ; *qui se ressent vivement* **de** ; *qui se venge* **de.**

resent'fully *ou* **resent'ingly**, *adv.*, avec ressentiment.

resent'ment, *n.*, ressentiment, *m.*

reserva'tion (rèz'eur-vé-), *n.*, réserve ; restriction, arrière-pensée ; (jur.) réserve, réservation, (ecc.) réservation, *f. ;* (in America) terrain réservé, *m.* Mental — ; *restriction mentale.*

reserve' (rè-zeurve), *n.*, réserve ; (modesty, caution) réserve, retenue, prudence ; (exception) restriction ; (thought withheld) arrière-pensée ; (jur.) réserve, réservation ; (milit.) réserve, *f.* Body of — ; (milit.) *corps de réserve, m.* — fund ; *fonds de réserve, m.* To place on the — ; *mettre en disponibilité.*

reserve' (-zeurve), *v.a.*, réserver, conserver, garder. To — oneself ; *se réserver, se contenir.*

reserved' (-zeurv'de), *adj.*, réservé ; qui a de la retenue. — price ; *prix minimum, m.*

reserv'edly (-zeurv'èd'-), *adv.*, avec retenue, avec réserve.

reserv'edness (-zeurv'èd'-), *n.*, réserve, retenue, discrétion, *f.*

reserv'ist, *n.*, réserviste, *m.*

res'ervoir (rèz'eur-voir), *n.*, réservoir ; puisard, *m.*

reset' (rî-cète), *v.a.*, (*preterit* and *past part.*, Reset), (print.) recomposer, composer de nouveau ; (a gem, etc.) monter, replacer, poser, fixer de nouveau.

reset' (rî-cète), *n.*, (print.) recomposition, *f.*

reset'ting, *n.*, (of gems) remontage, *m.;* (print.) recomposition.

reset'tle (rî-cèt't'l), *v.a.*, rétablir, arranger de nouveau, installer de nouveau.

reset'tle (rî-cèt't'l), *v.n.*, s'installer de nouveau ; s'établir de nouveau ; (of lees) se rasseoir, se reposer.

reset'tlement (rî-), *n.*, rétablissement, *m. ;* réinstallation ; (of lees) nouvelle formation, *f.*

reship' (rî-), *v.a.*, rembarquer, *m.*

reship'ment (rî-), *n.*, rembarquement, *m.*

reside' (rè-zaïde), *v.n.*, résider, demeurer.

res'idence (rèz'-), *n.*, résidence, demeure, *f. ;* séjour ; (jur.) domicile, *m.* Board and — ; *la table et le logement.*

res'idency, *n.*, hôtel d'un ministre résident, *m.*

res'ident (rèz'-), *n.*, habitant, *m.*, habitante, *f. ;* résident, ministre résident, *m.* — master ; *maître interne, m.* — mistress ; *institutrice interne, f.*

res'ident, *adj.*, résidant.

residen'tiary (rèz'i-dè'n'shi-), *adj.*, en résidence ; résidant.

residen'tiary (rèz'i-dè'n'shi-), *n.*, ecclésiastique obligé à la résidence, *m.*

resid'ual (rèz'i-diou-eul), *adj.*, résiduel ; qui reste.

resid'uary (rèz'i-diou-), *adj.*, pour le reste ; du reste ; (of legatees) universel, *ou* bénéficiaire.

res'idue (rèz'i-diou), *n.*, reste ; restant ; résidu ; (of debts) reliquat, *m.*

resid'uum (rè-zid'iou-eume), *n.*, (chem.) résidu ; (jur.) résidu, reste, *m.*

resign' (rè-zaïne), *v.a.*, résigner ; (to submit) soumettre ; (to yield) renoncer à ; (functions) se démettre **de**, donner sa démission **de** ; abandonner, céder. To be —ed ; *se résigner ; être résigné.* To be —ed ; (to the inevitable) *faire son deuil* **de**.

resign', *v.n.*, donner sa démission, démissioner.

re-sign' (rî-çaïne), *v.a.*, resigner ; signer de nouveau.

resigna'tion (rèz'ig-né-), *n.*, résignation ; soumission ; cession, *f. ;* abandon, *m. ;* (of functions) démission, *f.* To send in one's —; *donner sa démission.*

resigned' (rè-zaïnde), *adj.*, résigné ; (from a post) démissionnaire.

resign'edly, *adv.*, avec résignation.

resign'er, *n.*, démissionnaire ; résignant, *m.*

resil'ience, *n.*, (ant.) rebondissement, *m.*

resil'ient (-cil'-), *adj.*, rebondissant.

res'in (rèz'i'n), *n.*, résine ; colophane, *f.*

res'inous (rèz'-), *adj.*, résineux.

res'inousness (rèz'-), *n.*, nature résineuse ; propriété résineuse, *f.*

resipis'cence (rèss'-), *n.*, (ant.) résipiscence, *f.*

resist' (rè-ziste), *v.a.*, résister à ; se raidir **contre** ; se refuser à.

resist' (-ziste), *v.n.*, résister.

resist'ance (-zist'-), *n.*, résistance ; (jur.) rébellion, *f.*

resist'ant (-zist'-), *adj.*, résistant.

resist'er, *n.*, personne qui résiste, *f.*

resistibil'ity (-zist'-), *n.*, résistibilité, *f.*

resist'ible (-zist'i-b'l), *adj.*, à quoi l'on peut résister, résistible.

resist'ing (-zist'-), *adj.*, résistant.

resist'less (-zist'-), *adj.*, irrésistible ; sans défense.

res'oluble ((rèz'o-liou-b'l), *adj.*, dissoluble, réductible.

res'olute (rèz'o-lioute), *adj.*, déterminé à, résolu **de, à**.

res'olutely, *adv.*, résolument.

res'oluteness, *n.*, résolution, fermeté, *f.*

resolu'tion (rèz'o-liou-), *n.*, résolution ; (of deliberative bodies) décision ; (math.) résolution, solution, *f.*

res'olutive (rèz'o-liou-), *adj.*, résolutif, résolvant.

resolv'able (rè-zolv'a-b'l), *adj.*, résoluble. — nebula ; *nébuleuse résoluble, f.*

resolve' (-zolve), *n.*, résolution ; décision, *f.*

resolve' (-zolve), *v.a.*, résoudre ; (to melt) dissoudre, fondre ; (to inform) informer, instruire ; (med., math.) résoudre ; (of deliberative bodies) arrêter, décider ; (doubts) éclaircir, lever, dissiper.

resolve', *v.n.*, (to determine) résoudre, décider, se résoudre, se décider ; (to melt) se résoudre, se dissoudre, se fondre, fondre. To — upon ; *prendre la résolution* **de** ; *décider* **de** ; *se résoudre* **à**. Tc fully — upon ; *se promettre bien* **de**. To — oneself into — ; *se constituer* **en**, *se former* **en**.

resolv'ent (-zolv'-), *n.*, dissolvant ; (med.) résolvant, résolutif, *m.*

resolv'ing, *n.* *V.* resolution.

res'onance (rèz'o-), *n.*, résonance, *f.*, retentissement, *m.*

res'onant (rèz'-), *adj.*, résonnant, retentissant.

resort' (rè-), *n.*, (application) ressource, *f. ;* recours, *m. ;* (visiting) fréquentation, *f. ;* (concourse) concours, *m.*, affluence ; (assembly) assemblée, *f. ;* (place) rendez-vous ; (jur.) ressort, *m.* In the last — ; *en dernier ressort.* — of thieves ; *repaire de voleurs, m.*

resort', *v.n.*, (to apply) recourir **à**, avoir recours **à** ; (to go) se rendre **à**, aller **à**, fréquenter.

resort'er, *n.*, fréquentateur, *m.*

resound' (-zaou'n'de), *v.n.*, retentir ; résonner ; avoir du retentissement. To — with ; *résonner* **de**, *retentir* **de**.

resound', *v.a.*, renvoyer le son **de** ; faire résonner ; faire retentir ; célébrer ; répéter.

resound', *v.n.*, résonner ; retentir **de**, avoir du retentissement.

resound'ing, *n.*, retentissement ; résonnement, *m.*

resound'ing, *adj.*, retentissant.

resource', *n.*, ressource, *f.* Beyond — ; *sans remède.*

resource'ful, *adj.*, de ressource, plein de ressources.

resource'less, *adv.*, sans ressource.

resow' (rî-çô), *v.a.* (*preterit,* Resowed ; *past part.,* Resown), ressemer ; (land) réensemencer.

respect' (rè-), *n.*, respect, *m. ;* considération, estime, *f. ;* égards, *m.pl. ;* (reference) égard, rapport, *m.* —s, *pl.*, respects, hommages, devoirs, *m.pl.* In — to ; *par rapport* **à** ; *à l'égard* **de**. In every — ; *sous tous les rapports ; à tous égards.* In some —s ; *sous quelques rapports.* In some — ; *en quelque sorte.* Out of — to ; *par égard* **pour**, *par respect* **pour**. To pay — to ; *avoir des égards* **pour**, *avoir du respect* **pour**. To pay one's — to ; *offrir ses hommages* **à**. With — to ; *quant* **à** ; *à l'égard* **de** ; *sous le rapport* **de**. In no — ; *sous aucun rapport, à aucun prix.* In other —s ; *sous d'autres rapports, d'ailleurs.* In this — ; *en cela, à cet égard.* Give him my —s ; *présentez lui mes hommages, mes respects.* To have — of persons ; *faire acception de personnes.*

respect', *v.a.*, respecter, considérer, estimer ; avoir de la considération **pour** ; honorer ; (of things) se rapporter **à**, regarder, concerner. To — the person ; *faire acception de personnes ; avoir égard au rang des personnes.*

respectabil'ity, *n.*, position honorable, honorabilité, *f. ;* caractère honorable ; crédit, *m.*, considération ; (com.) notabilité ; (of external appearance, of dress, etc.) décence, *f.*, extérieur décent, *m.* Of — ; *dans une position honorable ; de considération dans le monde ; comme il faut ; honorable, respectable.* Of no — ; *sans considération dans le monde.*

respect'able (-'a-b'l), *adj.*, respectable, honorable, honnête ; notable, dans une position honorable, de considération dans le monde, comme il faut ; (of things) respectable, passable, qui n'est pas mal.

respect'ably, *adv.*, honorablement ; décemment ; comme il faut ; très bien ; passablement, pas mal.

respect'er, *n.* To be a — of persons ; *faire acception de personnes.*

respect'ful (-foule), *adj.*, respectueux, honnête.

respect'fully, *adv.*, respectueusement, avec respect, honnêtement.

respect'fulness, *n.*, respect, caractère respectueux, *m.*

respect'ing, *prep.*, par rapport **à**, à l'égard **de**, quant **à**, au sujet **de**.

respect'ive, *adj.*, respectif ; relatif. They were conveyed to their — hor·es ; *on les transporta chacun à son domicile.*

respect'ively, *adv.*, respectivement, relativement.

respir'able (rè-spaïeur'a-b'l), *adj.*, respirable.

respira'tion (rès-pi-ré-), *n.*, respiration, *f.*

res′pirator (rès-pi-ré-teur), *n.*, (device for breathing) respirateur, *m.*

res′piratory, *adj.*, (anat.) respiratoire.

respire′ (rè-spaïeur), *v.a.n.*, respirer.

res′pite (rès-pite), *v.a.*, donner du répit **à** ; suspendre, remettre, différer ; (jur.) surseoir, surseoir **à**, accorder un sursis **à**.

res′pite (rès-pite), *n.*, répit, relâche ; (jur.) sursis, *m.*

resplend′ence, resplend′ency, *n.*, resplendissement ; éclat, *m. ;* splendeur, *f.*

resplend′ent (-splè′n′-), *adj.*, resplendissant (with, **de**).

resplend′ently, *adv.*, d′une manière resplendissante ; avec éclat, avec splendeur.

respond′ (rè-spo′n′de), *v.a. and n.*, répondre ; s′accorder ; répondre **à**.

respond′ent (-spo′n′-), *n.*, répondant ; (jur.) défendeur, *m.*, défenderesse, *f.*

respond′ent (-spo′n′-), *adj.*, qui répond, correspondant **à**.

respon′den′tia (-spo′n′dè′n′shia), *n.pl.*, (com.) prêt à la grosse, *m.*

response′ (-spo′n′se), *n.*, réponse, *f. ;* (fig.) écho, *m. ;* (ecc.) répons, *m.*

responsibil′ity (rè-spo′n′-), *n.*, responsabilité ; (jur.) solidarité, *f.* On my own — ; *de mon chef, sous ma propre responsabilité.*

respons′ible (-spo′n′si-b′l), *adj.*, responsable (for, **de**) ; solidaire **de**.

respons′ibleness, *n.*, responsabilité, *f.*

respons′ive, *adj.*, qui répond, qui correspond ; (jur.) responsif.

respons′ory, *adj.*, responsif. *n.*, répons, *m.*

res′sault (rès′sôlte), *n.*, (arch.) ressaut, projection, saillie, *m.*

rest (rèste), *n.*, (remainder) reste, restant, *m. ;* (the others) les autres, *m.pl.* Among the — ; *entre autres.*

rest (rèste), *n.*, (repose) repos ; (support) appui ; (poet.) repos, *m.*, césure ; (mus.) pause, *f.*, silence ; (of a lance) arrêt ; (of a rifle) chevalet ; (tech.) support, *m.* At — ; *en repos, tranquille ;* (of a lance) *en arrêt.* Among the —; *entre autres.* A good night′s rest ; *une bonne nuit.* To set at — ; *mettre en repos ; décider, vider, régler, mettre fin* **à**, *en finir* **avec**. To go to — ; *se retirer, aller se reposer, se coucher.* Quarter— ; *soupir, m.* Eighth-— ; *demi-soupir, m.* Sixteenth- — ; *quart de soupir, m.* Half- — ; *demi-pause, f.*

rest, *v.n.*, se reposer, reposer ; dormir ; (to lean) se reposer, s′appuyer, s′arrêter ; (to rely) se reposer **de** (things), **sur** (pers.) ; se fier **à** ; se confier **à** ; s′en remettre **à** (pers.), **pour** (things) ; (to be satisfied) s′en tenir **à**, s′arrêter **à** ; (to be) demeurer, se tenir **pour**, (to remain) demeurer, rester. It — s with me to . . . ; *c′est à moi qu′il appartient* **de** . . . To —assured ; *être assuré.* It —s entirely with you ; *la chose dépend entièrement de vous.*

rest, *v.a.*, reposer ; faire reposer ; (fig.) appuyer, poser, fonder.

restem′ (rî-stème), *v.a.*, (the tide or current) rebrousser.

rest′ful (-foule), *adj.*, en repos, paisible.

rest′fully, *adv.*, en repos, paisiblement.

rest′-harrow, *n.*, (bot.) arrête-bœuf, *m.*

rest′ing, *adj.*, se reposant ; (leaning) appuyant ; (fig.) fondant ; (in a neuter sense) s′appuyant, appuyé. — on ; *se couchant* **sur** ; (in a neuter sense) *couché* **sur**.

rest′ing, *n.*, repos. — -place ; *abri, gîte, m. ;* lieu de repos, *m.* Last — -place ; *dernière demeure, f.*

rest′ing-stick, *n.*, appui-main, *m.*

res′titute, *v.a.*, restituer.

restitu′tion (rès-ti-tiou-), *n.*, restitution, *f.*

restitu′tor, *n.*, restituteur.

res′tive (rès-), *adj.*, rétif ; (obstinate) opiniâtre, entêté.

res′tiveness, *n.*, naturel rétif, *m. ;* rétiveté, opiniâtreté, obstination, indocilité, *f.*

rest′less, *adj.*, sans repos ; inquiet ; agité ; turbulent, remuant. I have had a — night ; *j′ai passé une nuit agitée.*

rest′lessly (rèst′-), *adv.*, sans repos ; avec inquiétude ; avec turbulence.

rest′lessness, *n.*, absence de repos, insomnie ; inquiétude ; agitation ; turbulence, *f. ;* caractère remuant, *m.*

restock′ (rî-), *v.a.*, (a shop, a farm) remonter ; (a gun, a pond) rempoissonner ; (a preserve) repeupler.

restock′ing, *n.*, remontage ; rempoissonnement, *m.*

restor′able (rè-stôr′a-b′l), *adj.*, qui peut être rendu ; susceptible de restauration.

restora′tion (rès-tô-ré-), *n.*, (re-establishment) rétablissement, *m. ;* (of a church, etc.) restauration, *f. ;* (of health) rétablissement, *m. ;* (giving back) restitution, *f.*

restor′ative (-stô-ra-), *n.*, (med.) restaurant, *m.*

restor′ative, *adj.*, (med.) restaurant ; fortifiant.

restore′ (-stôre), *v.a.*, (to return) restituer, rendre ; (to bring back) ramener ; faire revenir ; (to cure) rétablir, restaurer ; (to make restitution) restituer ; (to replace) remettre ; (to recover) restituer, rétablir ; (to rebuild) restaurer, rétablir ; (paint., sculpt.) restaurer.

re-store′ (rî-), *v.a.*, approvisionner, emmagasiner de nouveau.

restor′er (rè-), *n.*, restaurateur, *m.*, restauratrice, *f. ;* rénovateur, *m.*, rénovatrice, *f. ;* (of a text) restituteur.

restrain′ (-stréne), *v.n.*, retenir ; contenir ; arrêter ; empêcher ; restreindre ; réprimer ; gêner. To — from ; *éloigner* **de** ; *détourner* **de** ; *empêcher* **de** ; *interdire* **de**. To — to ; *restreindre* **à**.

restrain′able (-stré′n′a-b′l), *adj.*, qui peut être retenu, contenu, réprimé.

restrain′edly (-′èd′-), *adv.*, (ant.) d′une manière restreinte.

restrain′er, *n.*, personne, *ou* chose, qui retient, qui contient, qui réprime, *f.*

restrain′ing, *adj.*, qui restreint, restrictif.

restraint′, *n.*, contrainte, gêne ; entrave ; restriction, *f. ;* frein, empêchement, *m.*

restrict′ (-strikte), *v.a.*, restreindre **à**.

restric′tion (-strik′-), *n.*, restriction, *f.*

restrict′ive, *adj.*, restrictif.

restrict′ively, *adv.*, avec restriction.

restrin′gency (-stri′n′dj′-), *n.*, (med.) astringence, *f.*

restrin′gent (-stri′n′dj′-), *adj.*, (med.) restringent, astringent.

restrin′gent, *n.*, (med.) restringent, astringent, *m.*

result′ (rè-zeulte), *n.*, conséquence, *f. ;* résultat, *m.* In the—; *finalement.* The — was that . . . ; *la conséquence en fut que* . . ., ou *il en résulta que*, ou *il s′ensuivit.*

result′, *v.n.*, résulter. To — in ; *aboutir* **à**. To — in nothing ; *n′aboutir à rien.*

result′ant (rè-zeul-), *n.*, (mec.) résultante, *f.*

resum′able (-ziou′m′a-b′l), *adj.*, qui peut être repris, que l′on peut reprendre.

resume′ (-zioume), *v.a.*, reprendre ; (acquaintance) renouer ; continuer ; poursuivre.

resum′mon (rî-ceu′m′meune), *v.a.*, réassigner ; citer de nouveau.

resum′mons, *n.*, réassignation, *f.*

resump′tion (rè-zeu′m′p-), *n.*, reprise, continuation, *f.*

resurrec′tion (rèz′eur-rèk′-), *n.*, résurrection, *f.* — pie ; *pâté de restes de viande, m.*

resurrec′tionist (l.u.), **resurrec′tion-man**, *n.*, déterreur de cadavres, *m.*

resurvey' (rî-ceur-vé), *v.a.*, arpenter de nouveau ; revoir ; lire et examiner de nouveau.

resur'vey, *n.*, (fig.) révision, *f. ;* nouvel examen ; nouvel arpentage ; réarpentage, *m.*

resus'citate(rè-ceus-ci-),*v.a.*,ressusciter,faire revivre, rappeler à la vie ; ranimer.

resus'citate, *v.n.*, revivre, renaître ; ressusciter.

resuscita'tion (rè-ceus-ci-té-), *n.*, résurrection,*f. ;* retour à la vie, *m. ;* (of the arts, etc.) renaissance,*f. ;* (chem.) renouvellement, *m.*

ret, *v.a.*, rouir.

re'tail (rî-tél), *n.*, détail, *m. ;* vente en détail, *f. ;* commerce de détail, *m.* — -dealer ; *marchand en détail ; détaillant,* m.

re'tail, *adj.*, en détail. — price ; *prix de détail,* m.

retail' (ri-téle) *v.a.*, vendre en détail, détailler ; (fig.) débiter, redire ; (news) colporter.

re'tailer, *n.*, détaillant, *m.*, détaillante, *f. ;* débitant, *m.*, débitante, *f. ;* (fig.) débiteur, *m.*, débiteuse,*f. ;* (of news) colporteur, *m.*, colporteuse,*f.*

retain' (rî-téne),*v.a.*,retenir, garder ; conserver ; (by a fee) engager ; (to hire) prendre à son service.

retain'able (-'a-b'l), *adj.*, qui peut être retenu.

retain'er, *n.*, personne qui retient, qui garde, qui conserve, *f. ;* (attendant) suivant, *m.*, suivante,*f. ;* personne de la suite **de** ; (adherent) adhérent, partisan, dépendant, *m. ;* (fee) honoraires donnés d'avance, *m.pl.* —s, *pl.*, suite, *f.sing. ;* personnes de la suite,*f.pl. ;* gens, *m.pl.*

retain'ing, *adj.*, qui retient, qui garde, qui conserve, qui engage ; (of bandages) contentif. — -wall; *mur de soutènement.* — -fee ; *honoraires donnés d'avance, m.pl.*

retake' (rî-) *v.a.* (*preterit,* Retook; *past part.,* Retaken), reprendre.

retak'ing, *n.*, reprise, *f.*

retal'iate (rè-),*v.a.*, rendre ; rendre la pareille **de** ; prendre sa revanche ; user de représailles **pour.**

retal'iate, *v.n.*, rendre la pareille ; prendre sa revanche ; user de représailles. To — upon; *user de représailles* **envers** ; *rendre la pareille* **à.**

retalia'tion (rè-tal-i-é-), *n.*, pareille,*f. ;* représailles, *f.pl. ;* revanche, peine du talion,*f.* By way of — ; *en revanche, par représailles.*

retal'iatory, *adj.*, de représailles.

retard' (rè-tärde), *v.a.*, retarder ; ralentir ; différer ; apporter des délais **à,** remettre. To — negotiations ; *prolonger les négociations, faire traîner les négociations.*

retarda'tion (-dé-),*n.*, retardement, *m.;* (mec.) retardation, *f.*

retard'ing, *adj.*, retardateur.

retch (rîtshe *ou* rètshe),*v.n.*, faire des efforts pour vomir, avoir des haut-le-cœur.

retch'ing, *n.*,efforts pour vomir, *m.pl. ;* (med.) vomiturition,*f.*, haut-le-cœur, *m.*

re-tell' (rî-), *v.a.*, (*preterit* and *past part.,* Retold), redire, répéter.

reten'tion (rè-), *n.*, conservation; mémoire,*f.;* souvenir, *m. ;* (med., philos.) rétention, *f.*

reten'tive (rè-), *adj.*, qui retient ; (med.) rétentif, contentif ; (of the memory) tenace, fidèle, sûr.

reten'tiveness, *n.*, faculté de retenir, *f. ;* (of the memory) fidélité, ténacité, sûreté, *f.*

ret'icence (rèt'-), *n.*, réticence, *f.*

ret'icent, *adj.*, réservé, taciturne.

ret'icle (rèt'-k'l), *n.*, petit filet, *m.*

retic'ular (rè-tik'iou-), *adj.*, réticulaire.

retic'ulate (rè-tik'iou-)*ou* **retic'ulated**(-lét'-), *adj.*, réticulé.

reticula'tion (rè-tik'iou-lé-), *n.*, disposition en forme de réseau *ou* rétiforme,*f.*

ret'icule (rèt'-i-kioule), *n.*, sac à ouvrage, ridicule, ⊙réticule, *m.*

ret'iform (rèt'-), *adj.*, en forme de réseau.

ret'ina (rèt'-), *n.*, (anat.) rétine, *f.*

ret'inue (rèt'i-niou),*n.*, suite, *f. ;* cortège, *m.*

retire' (rè-taïeur), *v.n.*, se retirer, s'en aller.

retire', *v.a.*, retirer.

retired' (rè-taïeur'de), *adj.*, retiré, secret, caché; (of places) écarté, retiré; (superannuated) en retraite, retraité; (former) ancien. On the — list ; *en retraite, retraité.* To put on the — list ; *mettre à la retraite, retraiter.*

retir'edly, *adv.*, dans la retraite.

retire'ment (rè-taïeur'-),*n.*, retraite,solitude, *f. ;* isolement, *m.*

retir'ing, *adj.*, qui se retire, qui fuit le monde; réservé, timide, modeste; (leaving office) sortant. — -pension; *pension de retraite, f.* — -fund ; *caisse de retraites, f.*

retold' (rî-tôlde), *adj.*, répété ; redit.

retort', *n.*, riposte, réplique, repartie; (chem.) cornue, *f.* To give the — courteous ; *donner poliment un démenti.*

retort',*v.n.*, riposter, répliquer. To — on, *ou* upon ; *rembarrer (quelqu'un).*

retort', *v.a.*, renvoyer ; (an argument) rétorquer.

retort'er, *n.*, personne qui rétorque, qui riposte, qui renvoie,*f.*

retort'ing, *n.*, renvoi, *m. ;* (of an argument) rétorsion,*f.*

retor'tion, *n.*, (int. law) rétorsion, *f.*

retoss' (rî-), *v.a.*, rejeter, relancer.

retouch' (rî-teutshe), *v.a.*, retoucher.

retouch', *n.*, retouche, *f.*

retrace', *v.a.*, retracer ; reprendre ; revenir **sur** ; remonter à ; rechercher ; examiner ; (one's steps) revenir **sur,** retourner **sur** ; (one's way) rebrousser chemin. To — one's steps ; *revenir sur ses pas.*

retract' (rè-), *v.a.*, rétracter ; retirer.

retract', *v.n.*, se rétracter, se dédire.

retract'able (-'a-b'l), *adj.*, qui peut se rétracter.

retracta'tion, *n.*, rétractation, *f.*

retrac'tile, *adj.*, rétractile.

retrac'tion,*n.*, rétractation ; (med., zoöl.) rétraction,*f.*

retranscribe' (rî-), *v.a.*, retranscrire.

retranslate', *v.a.*, retraduire.

retrax'it (rè-), *n.*, (jur.) désistement, *m.*

retreat', *n.*, retraite, *f.*

retreat', *v.n.*, se retirer (into, **à** *ou* dans) ; (milit.) se retirer, battre en retraite.

retreat'ing, *adj.*, qui bat en retraite ; (of the forehead) fuyant.

retrench',*v.a.*,retrancher; (things) retrancher **de**; (persons) retrancher à. — *v.n.*, se retrancher.

retrench'ment, *n.*, retranchement, *m.;* réduction des dépenses, économie, *f.;* (milit.) retranchement, *m.*

ret'ribute (rèt-), *v.a.*, récompenser, rétribuer.

retrib'uter (rè-), *n.*, qui rétribue.

retribu'tion (rèt'ri-biou-), *n.*, récompense, rémunération, rétribution,*f.;* (b.s.) châtiment, *m.;* vengeance,*f.*, représailles, *f.pl.*

retrib'utive *ou* **retrib'utory** (rè-), *adj.*, qui récompense, qui punit.

retriev'able, *adj.*, qui peut être réparé, réparable.

retrieve',*v.a.*, (to restore) rétablir; (to repair) réparer, racheter ; (to regain) regagner, recouvrer, retrouver, récupérer ; (to rehabilitate) réhabiliter, corriger; (one's losses) se récupérer **de.**

retriev'er, *n.*, chien de remise, chien rapporteur, épagneul écossais, *m.*

retroac'tion (rî-), *n.*, rétroaction, *f.*

retroac'tive (rî-), *adj.*, rétroactif.

retroac'tively, *adv.*, rétroactivement.

retrocede' (rî-tro-cîde),*v.a.*, rétrocéder.

retrocede', *v.n.*, reculer, rétrograder.

retroces'sion (-cèsh'-), *n.*, rétrocession,*f.*

retrograda'tion (rèt'ro-gra-dé-), n., rétrogradation, f.

ret'rograde (rèt'ro-gréde), v.n., rétrograder.

ret'rograde, adj., rétrograde, en arrière.

retrogres'sion (rè'tro-grès'-), n., mouvement rétrograde, m.; rétrogradation, f.

ret'rospect, retrospec'tion (rèt'-), n., regard en arrière; coup d'œil, rétrospecte; examen, m.; revue, f.

retrospect'ive (rèt'-), adj., rétrospectif; qui regarde en arrière; rétroactif.

retrospect'ively, adv., rétrospectivement, rétroactivement.

retrover'sion (-ro-veur-), n., renversement, m.

re'trovert (rî-), v.a., renverser.

ret'ting (rèt'-), n., (of flax, hemp) rouissage, m.

ret'ting-pit, n., routoir; rutoir, m.

return' (rè-teurne), v.n., (to come back) revenir, rentrer; (to go back) retourner; rentrer; (to answer) répondre, répliquer. To — to one's subject; (fam.) revenir à ses moutons. To — to the subject; reprendre le récit, revenir au sujet.

return' (rè-teurne), v.a., (to give back) rendre; (to send back) renvoyer; (to repay) rendre, restituer; (to give in recompense) rendre; (an answer) rendre, faire; (to render an account) faire un rapport de, rapporter, rendre compte de; (to report officially) faire l'état de; (verdict) rendre; (candidates) élire, nommer, envoyer. The money—s interest; l'argent rapporte intérêt. To — thanks; remercier; faire un discours de remerciments.

return', n., (coming back, going back) retour, m.; (coming back) rentrée, f.; (sending back) renvoi, m.; (putting back) remise en place, f.; (revolution, periodical renewal) retour; (profit) profit, gain, produit, m.; (restitution) restitution, f.; (retribution) retour; (reimbursement) remboursement; (milit.) état, m.; (election) élection, f.; (jur.) renvoi; (arch.) retour; (of carriages) de renvoi; (report) rapport, compte rendu, relevé, état, m.; (of funds) rentrée, f.; (of health) retour; (com.) montant des opérations, montant des remises, m.; (of a bank) bilan, m. pl., produit, m. sing. On —; (com.) en dépôt; en commission. In — for; en retour de. By — of post; par retour du courrier. Small profits and quick —s; petits profits, promptes ventes. To make some — for; payer de retour. — ticket; billet d'aller et retour, m. — journey; retour, m. — match; revanche, f. The official —s; les relevés officiels, m.pl. — shock; (elec.) choc en retour, m.

return'able (-'a-b'l), adj., restituable; qui doit être rendu; qui doit être renvoyé; (elections) éligible; (com.) en commission; (jur.) de renvoi.

returned', adj., retourné, revenu, rentré. To have —; être de retour. — convict; repris de justice, m.

return'ing-of'ficer, n., rapporteur du procès-verbal des élections; fonctionnaire chargé de renvoyer les actes officiels, m.

return'-side (-saïde), n., (arch.) côté en retour, m.

reu'nion (rî-you'n'yeune), n., réunion, f.

reunite' (rî-you-naïte), v.a., réunir.

reunite', v.n., se réunir.

revac'cinate, v.a., revacciner.

revaccina'tion, n., revaccination, f.

reveal' (rè-vîle), v.a., révéler.

reveal', n., (arch.) jouée, f.

reveal'er, n., révélateur, m., révélatrice, f.

reveille' (ri-vèl'ié), n., (milit.) réveil, m.; diane, f.

rev'el (rèv'èl), n., divertissement, m.; réjouissances, f.pl., ébats, m.pl.; fête, fête bruyante, orgie, ripaille, bombance, f.

rev'el (rèv'èl), v.n., se réjouir; se divertir; s'ébattre; faire bombance; (pop.) riboter. To — in; se livrer à; s'abandonner à; se plaire à, faire ses délices de.

revela'tion (rèv'è-lé-), n., révélation; (New Testament) Apocalypse, f.

rev'eler (rèv'èl'-), n., convive, joyeux convive, viveur, riboteur, noceur, ripailleur, m.

rev'eling ou **rev'elry** (rèv'èl'-), n., fêtes, réjouissances, f.pl.; divertissements, ébats, festins, m.pl.; orgie, f.

reven'dicate (rî-), v.a., revendiquer.

revendica'tion, n., revendication.

revenge' (rè-), n., vengeance; (at play) revanche, f.

revenge', v.a., venger; se venger de. To be —d; se venger. To be —d on, to — one's self on; se venger de.

revenge'ful (-foule), adj., qui respire la vengeance; vindicatif; vengeur.

revenge'fully, adv., par vengeance; vindicativement.

revenge'fulness, n., caractère vindicatif; esprit de vengeance, m.

revenge'less, adj., sans vengeance.

reven'ger, n., vengeur, m., vengeresse, f.

reven'gingly, adv., par vengeance.

rev'enue (rèv-), n., revenu; (of the state) revenu, fisc, trésor, m. Public —; revenus publics, revenus de l'Etat, m.pl. — cutter; patache de la douane), f.

rev'enue-board (-bôrde), n., administration des revenus publics, f.

rever'berant (rè-veur-beur'-), adj., qui renvoie; réverbérant.

rever'berate (rè-veur-beur'-), v.a., réverbérer; réfléchir; (of sound) répercuter; renvoyer.

rever'berate, v.n., réverbérer; se répercuter.

rever'berate (rè-veur-beur'-), adj., qui réverbère, qui répercute, qui réfléchit, qui renvoie; réverbéré, réfléchi, répercuté.

reverbera'tion (rè-veur-beur'é-), n., réverbération; répercussion, f.

rever'beratory (-a-teuri), adj., à réverbère.

rever'beratory, n., four à réverbère, fourneau à réverbère, foyer à réverbère, m.

revere' (rè-vîre), v.a., révérer, respecter.

rev'erence (rèv'eur'-), n., révérence, f.; respect, m.; (title, bow) révérence, f. Your —; Monsieur le curé, Monsieur l'abbé.

rev'erence (rèv'eur'-), v.a., révérer, respecter.

rev'erencer, n. V. reverer.

rev'erend (rèv'eur'-), adj., vénérable, respectable; (of the clergy) révérend. Most —; révérendissime. Right —; très révérend. — Sir; monsieur l'abbé, m. The — gentleman; le révérend père.

rev'erent (rèv'eur'-), adj., révérencieux; respectueux.

reveren'tial, adj., de révérence, de respect; (of fear) révérencielle (only used in the feminine).

reveren'tially ou **rev'erently**, adv., avec révérence, avec respect; révérencieusement, respectueusement.

rever'er (rè-vîr'-), n., personne qui révère, qui respecte, f.

rev'erie (rèv-), n., rêverie, f.

rever'sal (rè-veur-), n., annulation; révocation; cassation, f.; changement, renversement, m. — gear; leviers de renversement, m.pl. — handle; manette de renversement, f.

reverse' (rè-veurse), n., (change) vicissitude, f.; (misfortune) revers; (contrary) opposé, contraire; (of a page) revers, verso; (of a medal) revers, m. The very, ou quite the, —; tout l'opposé, tout le contraire de.

reverse' (rè-veurse), adj., contraire, opposé.

reverse' (rè-veurse), v.a., renverser; mettre en sens inverse; (jur.) infirmer, casser, annuler; réformer. To — the engine; faire machine arrière; renverser la vapeur, ou la marche.

reversed' (rè-veurs'te), adj., renversé; (jur.) cassé, infirmé.

reverse'less, *adj.*, qui ne peut être renversé.
reverse'ly, *adv.*, en sens inverse, inversement.
revers'ible (rè-veurs'i-b'l), *adj.*, réformable, révocable, annulable ; réversible.
rever'sion (rè-veur'-), *n.*, réversion, *f. ;* retour ; bien qui fait retour, *m. ;* (of offices) survivance ; (succession) succession, *f.*
rever'sionary, *adj.*, réversible ; (of offices) de survivance.
rever'sioner, *n.*, (of offices) survivancier, *m.*
revert' (rè-veurte), *v.n.*, revenir (to, **sur**) ; retourner ; faire retour ; (jur.) retourner **à**.
revert'ible, *adj.*, réversible.
revert'ive, *adj.*, (ant.) qui retourne ; qui change.
revet'ment, *n.*, (fort.) revêtement, *m.*
revi'brate (rî-vaï-), *v.n.*, (ant.) vibrer en retour.
revibra'tion (rî-vaï-bré-), *n.*, (ant.) vibration en retour, *f.*
revict'ual (rî-vit't'l), *v.a.*, ravitailler.
revict'ualing, *n.*, ravitaillement, *m.*
review' (rè-), *n.*, revue ; (revision) revision ; (periodical) revue ; (of a book) analyse, critique, *f.*, compte rendu, examen critique, *m. ;* (milit.) revue ; (jur.) revision, *f.* The period under our — ; *la période que nous passons en revue.*
review', *v.a.*, (to see again) revoir, reviser ; (to examine) revoir, repasser ; passer en revue ; faire la revue **de** ; (a book) analyser ; rendre compte **de** ; (milit.) passer en revue ; faire la revue **de**.
review'er, *n.*, personne qui passe en revue, *f. ;* auteur d'une analyse, **d'une** critique ; rédacteur de revue ; critique, *m.*
revile', *v.a.*, injurier, insulter, outrager.
revile'ment, *n.*, injure, insulte, *f.*
revil'er, *n.*, personne qui injurie, qui insulte, *f.*
revil'ing (rè-vaïl'-), *n.*, insulte, injure, *f.*
revil'ing, *adj.*, diffamatoire, outrageant.
revil'ingly, *adv.*, injurieusement, outrageusement.
revi'sal, *n.*, revision, *f. ;* (print.) relute, *f.*
revise', *n.*, (print.) deuxième épreuve, *f.* Second — ; *troisième épreuve d'auteur, f.*
revise', *v.a.*, revoir, reviser ; faire la revision **de**.
revis'er, *n.*, personne qui revoit, *f. ;* reviseur, *m.*
revi'sion, *n.*, revision, *f.*
revi'sional *ou* **revi'sionary**, *adj.*, de revision.
revis'it (rè-), *v.a.*, revisiter ; revoir ; retourner **à**.
revi'val (rè-vaï-), *n.*, retour à la vie, renouvellement, rétablissement, *m. ;* (of arts and letters) renaissance ; remise en vigueur, *f. ;* (of a play) reprise, *f.*
revive', *v.a.*, faire revivre ; rappeler à la vie ; ressusciter ; renouveler ; ranimer ; raviver ; faire renaître, remettre en vigueur ; (chem.) revivifier.
revive', *v.n.*, revivre, ressusciter ; se ranimer ; se raviver ; (of arts) refleurir, renaître.
reviv'er, *n.*, personne *ou* chose qui fait revivre, qui ranime, qui ravive, qui ressuscite ; restaurateur, *m.*, restauratrice, *f.*
revivifica'tion (rî-viv'i-fi-ké-), *n.*, revivification, *f.*
reviv'ify (rî-viv'i-faïe), *v.a.*, revivifier.
revivis'cence, *n.*, retour à la vie, *m. ;* résurrection ; renaissance, *f.*
revi'vor, *n.*, (jur.) reprise de procès, *f.* Roll of — ; *demande en reprise de procès, f.*
revoc'able (rè-vo-ca-b'l), *adj.*, révocable.
revoc'ableness, **revocabil'ity**, *n.*, révocabilité, *f.*
revoca'tion (rèv'o-ké-), *n.*, révocation ; abjuration, *f. ;* (jur.) rappel, *m.*
revoke' (rè-), *v.a.*, révoquer.
revoke', *v.n.*, (at cards) renoncer, faire renonce.
revoke', *n.*, (at cards) renonce, *f.*

revolt', *n.*, révolte, soulèvement, *m.*
revolt', *v.n.*, se révolter, se soulever. To — at ; *se révolter* **contre**.
revolt', *v.a.*, (to cause to) révolter, soulever.
revolt'ed, *adj.*, révolté ; en révolte ; soulevé.
revolt'er, *n.*, révolté, rebelle, *m.*
revolt'ing, *adj.*, révoltant.
revolu'tion (rèv'o-lou-), *n.*, révolution, *f. ;* (of a wheel) tour, *m.*, révolution, *f.*
revolu'tionary, *adj.*, révolutionnaire. —- calendar ; *calendrier républicain, m.*
revolu'tionist, *n.*, révolutionnaire, *m.*
revolu'tionize (rèv'o-lou-sheu'n'aïze), *v.a.*, révolutionner, mettre en révolution.
revolve' (rè-), *v.a.*, tourner ; (in the mind) retourner, repasser, rouler ; penser à, méditer.
revolve', *v.n.*, tourner ; retourner ; revenir ; (astron.) tourner, faire sa révolution.
revolv'ency, *n.*, mouvement de révolution, *m.*
revolv'ing, *adj.*, tournant ; qui retourne ; (astron.) qui fait sa révolution, qui tourne. — light ; *feu tournant, m.* — pistol ; *pistolet tournant, révolver.*
revom'it (rî-), *v.a.*, revomir.
revul'sion (rè-veul-), *n.*, révulsion, *f.*
revuls'ive (rè-veul-), *adj.*, (med.) révulsif.
reward' (rè-wôrde), *n.*, récompense, *f. ;* prix, *m.*
reward', *v.a.*, récompenser (for, **de**).
reward'able (-'a-b'l), *adj.*, digne de récompense.
reward'er, *n.*, rémunérateur, récompenseur, *m.*
reward'ing, *n.*, action de récompenser, *f.*
reward'ing, *adj.*, rémunérateur.
reware'house (rî-wèr'haouce), *v.a.*, (com.) remettre en magasin.
rewrite' (rî-raïte), *v.a.*, récrire.
rey'nard (rèn-eurde), *n.*, (med.) maître renard, *m.*
rham'adan, *n.* *V.* **ramadan**.
rhap'sodical, *adj.*, de rapsodie.
rhap'sodist, *n.*, rapsodiste ; (antiq.) rapsode, *m.*
rhap'sodize, *v.n.*, rapsoder.
rhap'sody, *n.*, rapsodie, *f.*
Rhen'ish (rèn'-), *adj.*, du Rhin ; (geog.) rhénan.
Rhe'tian (rî-shi-), *adj.*, rhétien.
rhe'tor (rî-), *n.*, rhéteur, *m.*
rhet'oric (rèt'-), *n.*, rhétorique ; (fig.) éloquence, *f.*
rhetor'ical, *adj.*, de rhétorique.
rhetor'ically, *adv.*, suivant les règles de la rhétorique ; en rhétoricien.
rhetori'cian (rèt'o-rish'a'n), *n.*, rhétoricien ; rhéteur, *m.*
rhe'torize (rî-), *v.n.*, faire de la rhétorique.
rheum (roume), *n.*, (med.) rhume, catarrhe, *m. ;* pituite, *f. ;* (Shakespeare) crachat, *m.*
rheumat'ic (rou-), *adj.*, (med.) rhumatismal, rhumatique. — fever ; *rhumatisme articulaire, m.* — gout ; *rhumatisme goutteux, m.*
rheu'matism (rou-ma-tiz'm), *n.*, (med.) rhumatisme, *m.*
rhi'no (raï-nô), *n.*, (pop.) écus, jaunets, *m.pl.*, quibus, *m.*
rhinoc'eros (raï-noss'i-), *n.*, (zoöl.) rhinocéros, *m.*
Rho'dian (rô-), *adj.*, de Rhodes.
rho'dium (rô-), *n.*, (chem.) rhodium, *m.*
rhododen'dron (rô-), *n.*, (bot.) rhododendron, *m.*
rhom'boid (-boïde), *n.*, (geom.) rhomboïde, *m.*
rhomboid'al (-boïd'-), *adj.*, (geom.) rhomboïdal.
rhom'bus, rhomb, *n.*, (geom.) rhombe, *m.*
rhon'chus (ro'gn'keusse), *n.*, (med.) râle, *m.*
rhu'barb (rou-bârbe), *n.*, (bot. pharm.) rhubarbe, *f.*
rhumb (reu'm'e), *n.*, (nav.) rumb, *m.*
rhumb'-line (-laïne), *n.*, (nav.) loxodromie, ligne de rumb, *f.*

rhyme (raïme), *n.*, rime, *f.* ; vers, *m.* Neither — nor reason ; *ni rime ni raison.* In — ; *rimé.* To put in — ; *mettre en rimes, rimer.*

rhyme, *v.a.* and *n.*, rimer ; (b.s.) rimailler.

rhyme'less, *adj.*, sans rime.

rhym'er, rhyme'ster, *n.*, rimeur ; rimailleur, versificateur, *m.*

rhythm (rith'm) *ou* **rhyth'mus** (rith-), *n.*, rythme, *m.*

rhyth'mical, *adj.*, rythmique.

rib, *n.*, côte ; (of an umbrella) branche ; (bot.) nervure, côte ; (carp.) entretoise, *f.*, tirant, étançon, *m.* ; (of a roof) fermé ; (arch.) nervure, *f.* ; (nav.) membre, *m.*, membrure, côte ; (in cloth) côte ; (of land) bande, *f.* —grass ; (bot.) *plantain lancéolé, m.*

rib, *v.a.*, garnir de côtes ; (cloth, etc.) faire des côtes à.

rib'ald (-l'de), *n.*, débauché ; libertin ; (pop.) ribaud, *m.*, ribaude, *f.*

rib'ald, *adj.*, licencieux ; vil, bas ; (pop.) ribaud.

rib'aldish, *adj.*, (ant.) licencieux, déshonnête ; (pop.) ribaud.

rib'aldry, *n.*, langage licencieux, *ou* obscène, *m.*, ribauderie, *f.*

rib'and, *n.* *V.* **rib'bon**.

ribbed (rib'de), *adj.*, muni de côtes ; (of cloth, etc.) à côtes.

rib'bon (-beune), *n.*, ruban ; ruban de soie ; (of orders) cordon, ruban ; (shred) lambeau, *m.* ; (nav.) lisse, *f.* —trade ; *rubanerie, f.* —weaver ; *rubanier, m.* —grass ; (bot.) *herbe-à-ruban, f.* To —s ; *en lambeaux.*

rib'bon, *v.a.*, enrubaner, garnir de rubans.

rib'bonism, *n.*, ribbonisme, *m.*

rib'-wall (-wôl), *n.*, (mines) compartiment, *m.*

rice (raïce), *n.*, riz, *m.* —plantation ; *rizière, f.* Ground — ; *farine de riz, f.*

rice, *adj.*, de riz (as rice-cakes, etc.).

rich (ritsh), *adj.*, riche ; (opulent) riche, opulent ; (fertile) fertile, fécond ; (succulent) succulent, savoureux ; (highly seasoned) de haut goût ; (costly, valuable) précieux ; (splendid) magnifique, superbe, beau ; (of colors) vif, brillant, voyant ; (fig.) délicieux, exquis ; (of wine) velouté, corsé. A — treat ; *un fameux régal.* To grow — ; *s'enrichir.* To be — ; *avoir de la fortune.*

rich'es, *n.pl.*, richesse, *f.sing.*, richesses, *f.pl.* A good name is better than — ; (prov.) *bonne renommée vaut mieux que ceinture dorée.*

rich'ly, *adv.*, richement ; (truly) grandement, amplement, largement, bien ; abondamment.

rich'ness, *n.*, richesse ; opulence ; fécondité ; fertilité ; nature succulente, *f.* ; haut goût, *m.* ; qualité précieuse ; magnificence, *f.* ; goût délicieux, goût exquis ; prix, *m.*

ric'inus, *n.*, (bot.) ricin, *m.*

rick, *n.*, meule, *f.* ; monceau, *m.* — cloth ; *bâche de meule, f.*

rick'ets, *n.pl.*, (med.) rachitis, rachitisme, *m.* To have the — ; *être rachitique, noué.*

rick'ety (-êt'i), *adj.*, (med.) noué, rachitique ; (fig.) détraqué, dérangé, en mauvais état, (of furniture) boiteux.

ric'ochet (rik'o-shé), *n.*, (artil.) ricochet, *m.* —fire ; (artil.) *tir à ricochets, m.*

rid, *v.a.*, (preterit, Rid ; past part., Rid, Ridden) défaire, délivrer, débarrasser. To — one's self of ; *se défaire de.* To get — of ; *se débarrasser de ; se défaire de.* To have got — of ; *être débarrassé de.*

rid'dance, *n.*, délivrance, *f.*, débarras, *m.* A good — ! *bon débarras !*

rid'dle (rid'd'l), *n.*, énigme, *f.* ; (sieve) crible, *m.* To speak in —s ; *parler énigmatiquement.*

rid'dle, *v.a.*, (to perforate) cribler ; (wheat) cribler ; (to solve) résoudre, expliquer. To be —d with bullets ; *être criblé de balles.*

rid'dling, *n.*, (metal.) lavage au crible, *m.*

ride (raïde), *v.n.*, (preterit, Rode ; past part., Ridden) (on horseback) aller à cheval, être à cheval, se promener à cheval, monter à cheval ; (in a vehicle) aller en voiture, être en voiture, se promener en voiture ; (print.) chevaucher ; (man.) monter ; (to be borne on a fluid) être porté sur, flotter, voguer. To be riding ; *être à cheval.* To — on ; *monter* **sur** ; *être monté* **sur**. To — at anchor ; *être à l'ancre.* To — easy ; *ne pas fatiguer (à cheval) ;* (nav.) *ne pas fatiguer à l'ancre.* To — hard ; (nav.) *fatiguer à l'ancre.* The vessel —s on the sea ; *le vaisseau vogue sur la mer.* To — over ; *venir à cheval, aller à cheval ; parcourir (à cheval) ;* (pers.) *passer* **sur**, *renverser.* To — rough-shod over a person ; *sauter à pieds joints sur quelqu'un.* To — out a gale ; *tenir bon sur ses ancres (dans un coup de vent).* To — on an elephant ; *aller à dos d'éléphant.* Riding party ; *excursion à cheval, f.* Shall you walk or — ? *irez-vous à pied ou à cheval ?* A horse good to — or drive ; *un cheval à deux fins.* To — the high horse ; *monter sur ses hauts chevaux.* To — the wild mare ; *jouer à la balançoire.* To — on the top, *ou* outside ; *aller sur l'impériale.* To — well ; *monter bien à cheval.* To — with one's back to the engine ; *avoir le dos tourné à la locomotive ; aller à reculons.* To — on an ass ; *monter, ou être, à âne.* Riding on an ass ; *monté sur un âne.* To — on a stick ; *monter, ou être, à cheval sur un bâton.* To — part of the way ; *faire une partie du chemin (à cheval, en voiture, en chemin de fer).* To — away ; *partir, s'en aller, ou se sauver, à cheval.* To — back ; *revenir, ou s'en retourner, à cheval.* To — off ; *partir, ou se sauver, à cheval.* To — on ; *poursuivre son chemin.* To — up ; *s'avancer, arriver, ou venir, (à cheval).*

ride, *v.a.*, monter ; (to take to, to lead) mener. To — a race ; *faire une course à cheval.*

ride (raïde), *n.*, (on horseback) promenade à cheval ; (in a vehicle) promenade en voiture ; (in an omnibus, a cab) course ; trajet, parcours, *m.* ; (place) promenade, allée, *f.* ; cours, *m.* To give a — to any one ; *faire monter quelqu'un* **avec** *soi ; promener quelqu'un (en voiture).*

rid'er, *n.*, personne à cheval, personne en voiture, *f.* ; cavalier ; écuyer, *m.* ; écuyère, *f.* ; (at horse-races) jockey, *m.* ; (document) annexe, *f.*, renvoi, *m.* ; (com.) allonge ; (fly-sheet) feuille volante ; (of an ore) matrice, *f.* ; (geom.) problème ; (ant., com.) commis-voyageur, *m.* Gentleman— ; *écuyer amateur.* Rough — ; *casse-cou, m.*

ridge, *n.*, (top) sommet, *m.* ; cime ; (elevation) élévation, hauteur ; (of mountains) chaîne ; (of a mountain) crête, *f.* ; (of a roof) faîte ; (agri.) sillon, billon ; (nav.) récif, banc de rochers, *m.*

ridge, *v.a.*, sillonner ; surmonter ; (agri.) faire des sillons **dans**, billonner, butter.

ridge'-piece (-pîce) *ou* **ridge'-plate** *ou* **ridge'-pole**, *n.*, (carp.) faîtage, faîte, *m.*

ridg'ing, *n.*, billonnage, buttage, *m.*

rid'icule (-kioule), *n.*, ridicule, *m.* To bring into — ; *rendre ridicule.*

rid'icule, *v.a.*, tourner en ridicule, ridiculiser.

ridic'ulous (-dik'iou-), *adj.*, ridicule ; (laughable) risible. — thing ; *chose ridicule, f.* ; *ridicule, m.*

ridic'ulously, *adv.*, ridiculement.

ridic'ulousness, *n.*, ridicule, *m.*

rid'ing (raïd'-), *n.*, action de monter à cheval, *f.* ; art de monter à cheval, exercice à cheval ; (horsemanship) manège, *m.*, équitation ; promenade en voiture, à cheval ; (place) promenade, *f.* ; (print.) chevauchage ; (of Yorkshire) arrondissement, *m.* ; (at anchor) à l'ancre. To like — ; *aimer à monter à cheval.*

rid'ing-boots, *n.pl.*, bottes à l'écuyère, *f.pl.*

rid'ing-coat (-côte), *n.*, habit de cheval, *m.*, redingote de voyage, *f.*

rid'ing-habit (raïd'-), *n.*, habit d'amazone, *m.* ; amazone, *f.*

rid'ing-hood (-houde), *n.*, (for ladies) mante, capote, *f.* Little red —; *petit chaperon rouge, m.*

rid'ing-horse, *n.*, cheval de selle, *m.*

rid'ing-master (-mâs-), *n.*, maître d'équitation, *m.*

rid'ing-school (-skoul), *n.*, école d'équitation, *f.* ; manège, *m.*

rid'ing-whip, *n.*, cravache, *f.*

ridot'to (-tô), *n.*, (assembly) redoute, *f.*

rife (raïfe), *adj.*, qui règne, qui domine ; abondant ; commun ; répandu ; général ; régnant. To be —; *régner, dominer*, (of rumors) *courir*.

riff'raff, *n.*, (of things) rebut, *m.*, racaille, *f.* ; (pers.) gens de rien, *m.pl.*, lie du peuple, racaille, canaille, *f.*

ri'fle (raï-f'l), *v.a.*, piller ; dévaliser, voler ; (of fire-arms) carabiner, rayer.

ri'fle, *n.*, fusil à balle forcée, *m.* ; carabine, *f.* —s, *pl.*, (men) (milit.) tirailleurs ; (France) chasseurs à pied, *m.pl.* —butt ; *butte de tir, f.*, —gallery, —range, —practice, —shooting ; *tir à la carabine, m.* Within — range ; *à portée de carabine.* — shot ; *coup de carabine, m.*

ri'fleman, *n.*, (*riflemen*) carabinier, *m.* ; ⊙tirailleur ; chasseur à pied, *m.*

ri'fler (raï-), *n.*, pillard, *m.*

ri'fling, *n.*, pillage, *m.* ; (of guns) rayage, *m.*

rig, *n.*, (dress) accoutrement, harnachement, affublement, *m.* ; (trick) farce, *f.* ; tour, (nav.) gréement, *m.*

rig, *v.a.*, équiper, accoutrer, attifer, harnacher ; (nav.) garnir, gréer. To — the market ; *faire hausser, ou faire baisser, les prix.*

rigadoon' (-doune), *n.*, (dance) rigodon, *m.*

rigged, *adj.*, équipé ; (nav.) gréé ; (with sails) voilé.

rig'ger (-gheur), *n.*, (nav.) gréeur ; (mec.) tambour, *m.*

rig'ging (-ghigne), *n.*, (of dress) attifement, accoutrement, *m.* ; (nav.) agrès, *m.pl.*, gréement, grément, *m.*, manœuvres, manœuvres de gréement, *f.pl.* Standing, running — ; *manœuvres dormantes, courantes.*

rig'ging-loft, *n.*, (nav.) atelier de garniture, *m.*

rig'gle (rig-g'l), *v.n. V. wriggle.**

right (raïte), *adj.*, (straight) droit ; (direct) direct, en ligne droite ; (becoming) convenable ; (lawful) légitime ; (true) vrai, véritable, bon ; (equitable) droit, juste, bon ; propre, convenable ; (side) droit ; (com.) régulier ; en règle ; (that which is meant) qu'il faut. —hand man ; *le bras droit.* The — thing to do ; *ce qu'il y a de mieux à faire.* Is it — so? *est-ce que c'est bien comme ça?* This is the — book ; *voici le livre qu'il faut.* The — train ; *le bon train, le train qu'il faut.* To be — ; *avoir raison* ; (of things) *convenir* ; (of an account) *être juste, être bien le compte.* To be in the — ; *être dans son droit.* That is — ; *c'est bien ; c'est cela.* The — road ; *la route directe* ; (fig.) *le bon chemin.* Is it — ? *est-ce bien?* All —! *en route! allez! c'est bon! c'est bien! bon! bien!* All 's — ; *tout va bien.* To go the — way to work ; *s'y prendre bien.* That is not the — thing ; *ce n'est pas là ce qu'il faut.* To set — ; *mettre en bon ordre, mettre en règle* ; (to rectify) *corriger, rectifier* ; (a watch) *régler* ; (pers.) *éclairer, mettre sur la bonne voie ; mettre à la raison, redresser.*

right, *adv.*, (straight) droit, tout droit ; (justly) juste, justement, droit, droitement ; (properly) comme il faut, bien ; (before titles) très ; (very) très, furieusement. —away! *allez! partez! tout droit!* —! *Sir ; on y va* ; (done) *ça y est, monsieur.* It served you — ; *c'est bien fait.* To send to the —about ; *envoyer promener.* Did I not say — ? *n'ai-je pas dit vrai?* — or wrong ; *à*

tort et à travers ; à tort ou à raison. By — ; *de droit.* By —s ; *pour bien faire, à la rigueur.*

right, *n.*, droit, *m.* ; (justice) justice, raison, *f.*, droit ; (property) bien ; (interest) intérêt ; (right side) côté droit, *m.*, droite, *f.* — and wrong ; *le bien et le mal, le juste et l'injuste.* — of way ; *droit de passage.* Bill of —s ; *déclaration des droits et privilèges politiques d'un peuple, f.* In — of ; *par le droit de ; du chef de.* Of — ; *de droit, de plein droit.* In one's own — ; *de son chef ; en propre.* To be within one's — ; *être dans son droit.* To have the — to ; *avoir le droit de* ; *avoir droit à, avoir des droits à.* On the — ; *à droite.* On one's — ; *à sa droite.* To set to —s ; *mettre en bon ordre, mettre en règle* ; (pers.) *mettre à la raison, faire voir à.* To know the —s of ; *savoir le fin mot de ; en avoir le cœur net.*

right, *v.a.*, (pers.) faire droit à, rendre justice à ; (things) redresser, arranger, remettre ; corriger ; (a ship) redresser ; (the helm) dresser.

right, *v.n.*, (itself) se redresser, se relever.

right'eous (raït'i'eusse), *adj.*, juste, droit, saint.

right'eously, *adv.*, justement.

right'eousness, *n.*, droiture, justice, *f.*

right'er, *n.*, (of wrongs) redresseur, *m.*

right'ful (-foul), *adj.*, légitime, véritable.

right'fully, *adv.*, légitimement.

right'fulness, *n.*, justice, légitimité ; rectitude, équité, *f.*

right'-handed, *adj.*, droitier.

right'-hearted (-hârt'-), *adj.*, qui a le cœur bien placé.

right'ly, *adv.*, droitement, bien, justement ; à juste titre ; (properly) convenablement, comme il faut ; (not erroneously) juste ; (exactly) bien.

right'-minded (-maï'n'd'-), *adj.*, qui a l'esprit juste, droit.

right'-mindedness, *n.*, justesse d'esprit, droiture d'esprit, *f.*

right'ness, *n.*, rectitude ; droiture ; équité ; justesse ; (straightness) direction droite, *f.*

rig'id (ridj'-), *adj.*, rigide ; (stiff) raide.

rigid'ity, *n.*, rigidité ; raideur, *f.*

rig'idly, *adv.*, rigidement ; avec raideur.

rig'idness, *n.*, rigidité ; raideur, *f.*

rig'let, *n.*, (print.) réglet, *m.*, réglette, *f.*

rig'marole (-rôle), *n.*, amphigouri, rabâchage ; conte à dormir debout, galimatias, *m.*

rig'or, *n.*, (med.) rigidité, *f.* —mortis ; *rigidité cadavérique, f.*

rig'or (righ'eur), *n.*, rigueur, sévérité, dureté, *f.* ; (of weather) froid, *m.*

rig'orous, *adj.*, rigoureux ; sévère, dur ; de rigueur.

rig'orously, *adv.*, rigoureusement ; avec rigueur, à la rigueur.

rig'orousness, *n.*, rigueur, *f.*

rile, *v.a.*, vexer, faire enrager, faire endêver.

rill, *n.*, (petit) ruisseau, *m.*

rim, *n.*, bord, rebord, *m.* ; (of wheels) jante, *f.*

rim, *v.a.*, mettre un bord à.

rimmed, *p.p. & adj.*, à bord, à rebord, à cercle de.

rime (raïme), *n.*, givre, *m.* ; gelée blanche, *f.*

rime, *v.n.*, geler blanc (Lit.) ; geler à blanc.

ri'mose (raï-môce) *ou* **ri'mous** (raï-), *adj.*, (bot., zoöl.) crevassé.

rim'ple, *n. V. ripple.*

rim'ple (ri'm'p'l), *v.a. V. ripple.*

rim'pling, *n. V. rippling.*

rim'y (raï-), *adj.*, couvert de givre, couvert de gelée blanche.

rind (raï'n'de), *n.*, écorce, peau, pelure ; (of cheese) croûte ; (of bacon) couenne, *f.*

ring (rigno), *n.*, (circle) cercle, rond ; (of metal, etc.) anneau, *m.* ; (for the fingers) bague, *f.*, anneau ; (round a wound) cerne ; (bot.) cerne ; (for napkins) rond, *m.* ; (nav.) anneau ; (of an anchor) organeau, *m.*, boucle ; (of a wheel) jante, *f. ;* (astron.) anneau ; (of a bottle, an animal) collier, *m. ;* (on a coin) cordon, filet, *m. ;* (to a handle) virole, *f. ;* (for fighting) terrain, *m.,* arène, *f. ;* (fig.) ligue, condition ; clique, coterie, *f.* —-dove ; *pigeon ramier, m.* —-finger ; *annulaire, m.* In a —; *en rond.* Wedding —; *alliance, f.,* anneau nuptial, *m.* Split —; *anneau brisé, m.*

ring, *v.a.,* mettre un anneau **à.** To — a mare; *boucler une jument.*

ring, *n.,* (sound) son, tintement, retentissement ; (on a bell) coup de sonnette, *m. ;* (chime) sonnerie, *f.* Give a —; *sonnez.* To have a —; *entendre sonner.* There 's a — at the door ; *on sonne.*

ring, *v.n.,* (*preterit,* Rang ; *past part.,* Rung) résonner, retentir ; sonner, tinter ; (of the ears) tinter. — away ; *cavillonner.* To — with ; *résonner de ; retentir de.* To — for the chambermaid ; *sonner la femme de chambre.*

ring, *v.a.,* sonner, faire sonner. To — a coin ; *faire sonner une pièce.* To — the changes upon ; (of words) *employer en sens divers.* To — the bees ; *carillonner les abeilles.* To — down the curtain ; *tirer le rideau.*

ring'-bone (-bône), *n.,* (vet.) forme, *f.*

ring'er, *n.,* sonneur, *m.*

ring'-fence, *n.,* clôture continue, *f.*

ring'ing (rign'igne), *n.,* action de sonner, *f. ;* tintement ; retentissement ; (of bells) son, *m. ;* sonnerie, *f.* — in the ears ; *tintement d'oreilles, m.*

ring'leader (rign'lîd'-), *n.,* chef d'émeute, meneur, chef de bande, *m.*

ring'let (rign'lète), *n.,* petit anneau, *m. ;* (of hair) boucle de cheveux, *f.,* tire-bouchon, *m.*

ring'-shaped (-shép'te), *adj.,* annulaire.

ring'-stand, *n.,* baguier, *m.*

ring'-streaked (-strîk'te), *adj.,* annelé.

ring'-tail (-tél), *n.,* (orni.) paille-en-queue, paille-en-cul ; (nav.) tapecu, *m.*

ring'-worm (-weurme), *n.,* impétigo, *m. ;* teigne ; dartre à la tête, *f.*

rinse, *v.a.,* rincer.

rins'er, *n.,* rinceur, *m.,* rinceuse, *f.*

rins'ing, *n.,* rinçage, rincement ; (slops) rinçure, *m.*

ri'ot, (raï'ote), *n.,* émeute, *f. ;* rassemblement tumultueux ; attroupement ; (uproar) vacarme, tumulte, *m. ;* (feasting) festins, *m.pl.,* orgies, *f. pl. ;* dissipation ; intempérance, *f. ;* excès, *m. ;* (fam.) bagarre, *f.* To run — ; *faire le diable à quatre ; faire les cent coups ; se dévergonder, ne plus connaître de frein.* To run — with fancy and imagination ; *se laisser aller à tous les écarts de l'imagination.*

ri'ot, (raï'ote), *v.n.,* faire une émeute ; faire du vacarme, faire du tumulte ; se réjouir, se divertir ; faire des orgies, faire des excès ; riboter.

ri'ot-act, *n.,* loi contre les émeutes, contre les attroupements, *f.* To read the — ; *faire les trois sommations.*

ri'oter, *n.,* séditieux, mutin ; émeutier ; débauché ; (noisy) tapageur, *m.*

ri'otous (raï'ot'-), *adj.,* séditieux, tumultueux ; (luxurious) déréglé, dissipé, intempérant, débauché ; (noisy) tapageur, *m.*

ri'otously, *adv.,* tumultueusement, séditieusement ; licencieusement ; avec excès, avec intempérance ; dans les plaisirs, dans les orgies.

ri'otousness, *n.,* caractère tumultueux, caractère séditieux ; dérèglement, désordre, *m. ;* intempérance, dissipation, débauche, *f.*

rip, *v.a.,* ouvrir, fendre, déchirer ; (med.) découdre. To — from ; *arracher de.* To — off ; *arracher, enlever.* To — open ; *ouvrir, éventrer ;* (in needlework) *découdre.* To — up ; *ouvrir, fendre, déchirer, labourer ;* (man or animal) *éventrer ;* (to search) *pénétrer, exhumer ;* (fig.) (of stories, old sores) *remettre sur le tapis, rabâcher.*

rip, *n.,* ouverture en long ; déchirure, fente ; (blackguard) vaurien, polisson, mauvais garnement, *m.,* canaille, *f.*

ripa'rian (ri-pé-), *adj.,* riverain.

ripe (raïpe), *adj.,* mûr ; (consummate) parfait, consommé, accompli.

ripe'ly, *adv.,* mûrement ; à temps, à propos.

rip'en (raï'p'n), *v.a.,* mûrir, faire mûrir.

rip'en, *v.n.,* mûrir ; venir à maturité.

ripe'ness (raïp'-), *n.,* maturité ; (fitness) à-propos, *m.,* opportunité, *f.*

rip'ening (raïp'-), *n.,* maturation, *f.*

rip'per, *n.,* qui ouvre, qui fend ; éventreur ; (nav.) déchireur, *m.*

rip'ping, *n.,* fendage, déchirement ; ouverture en long, *f.*

rip'ple (rip'p'l), *v.n.,* se rider ; bouillonner, clapoter.

rip'ple, *v.a.,* rider ; faire bouillonner.

rip'ple, *n.,* (of water) ride, *f.,* bouillon, *m.*

rip'pling, *n.,* action de rider, *f. ;* bouillonnement ; clapotage, clapotis (of a stream) murmure ; (nav.) remous de courant, *m.*

rise (raïze), *v.n.* (*preterit,* Rose ; *past part.,* Risen), se lever ; (after a fall, a misfortune, etc.) se relever ; (to swell) s'élever, monter ; se soulever ; (to augment) s'augmenter, s'agrandir, s'accroître ; (of waters) s'accroître, s'élever, monter, hausser ; (of price) hausser, monter, s'élever, augmenter ; (of bread, etc.) renchérir ; (to rebel) se lever, se soulever ; (of courts) se lever ; (of assemblies) se séparer ; (of sound) s'élever, monter ; (of the dead) ressusciter ; (to gain elevation, rank) s'élever ; (to grow) s'élever, hausser ; (to ascend) s'élever, monter ; (to have its source in, to spring) avoir sa source (**en, dans**) ; naître, venir, s'élever. The funds are —ing ; *les fonds sont à la hausse.* To — again ; *se relever ; renaître ;* (Script.) *ressusciter.* To — out of ; *sortir de ;* naître **de** ; *provenir* **de.** To — to view ; *s'offrir à la vue, se présenter à la vue.* To — up ; *se lever ; se soulever, s'élever.* To — early ; *se lever matin.* I — with the sun ; *je me lève avec le soleil.*

rise (raïze), *n.,* lever, *m. ;* (elevation) élévation ; (ascent) ascension ; (of a hill, etc.) montée ; (of waters) crue ; (in price) hausse, augmentation, *f.,* renchérissement, *m. ;* (source) source, naissance, origine ; (increase) augmentation, *f. ;* (promotion) avancement, *m. ;* (in power) élévation, grandeur, *f.* The —and fall of the Roman Empire ; *Grandeur et décadence des Romains* (Montesquieu). To get a — out of M. ; *pour faire rager M. ; pour mettre M. en colère ; tourner M. en ridicule.* To give — to ; *donner naissance* **à** ; *faire naître ; donner lieu* **à,** *provoquer.* To take its — ; *prendre naissance ;* (of rivers & fig.) *avoir sa source.* On the — ; (com.) *en hausse.*

ris'er (raïz'-), *n.,* (of a stair) degré, *m.,* marche, contremarche, *f.* Early — ; *personne matineuse, f.* Late — ; *qui se lève tard.* To be an early — ; *être matineux.*

risibil'ity (riz'-), *n.,* risibilité, *f.*

ris'ible (riz'i-b'l), *adj.,* risible.

ris'ing (raïz'-), *adj.,* levant ; qui s'élève ; naissant ; (promising) d'avenir, qui a de l'avenir ; (tide) montant.

ris'ing (raïz'-), *n.,* action de se lever, de se relever, *f. ;* (from bed ; of the sun) lever, *m. ;* (act of ascending) ascension ; (of a hill) montée ; (elevation) élévation ; (of waters) crue ; (of assemblies, a court) levée, clôture ; (resurrection) résurrection ; (med.) tumeur, *f. ;* (resurrection) soulèvement, *m.,* insurrection, *f.* I like early — ; *j'aime me lever de bon matin.*

risk, *n.,* risque, péril, *m.* At the — of ; *au risque* **de,** *au péril* **de.** At one's — ; *à ses risques et périls.*

risk, *v.a.,* risquer, hasarder.

risk'y, *adj.,* risqué, hasardeux, chanceux, dangereux.

rite (raïte), *n.,* rite, *m. ;* cérémonie, *f.*

ritornel'lo (rî-tor-nèl-lô), *n.,* (mus.) ritournelle, *f.*

rit'ual (rit'iou-), *n.,* rituel, *m.*

rit'ual, *adj.*, rituel, du rite.

rit'ualist, *n.*, ritualiste, *m.*

rit'ually, *adv.*, selon le rite.

ri'val (raï-), *n.*, rival, *m.*, rivale, *f.*; émule, *m.f.*

ri'val, *adj.*, rival.

ri'val (raï-), *v.a.* and *n.*, rivaliser **avec**, rivaliser, surpasser.

ri'valry *ou* **ri'valship** (raï-), *n.*, rivalité, *f.*

rive (raïve), *v.a.* and *n.*, fendre; se fendre.

riv'er (raï'ver), *n.*, fendeur, *m.*

riv'er (riv'er), *n.*, rivière, *f.*; (large) fleuve, *m.* Down the —; *en descendant le fleuve; en aval.* Up the —; *en remontant le fleuve; en amont.* —side; *bord de l'eau, m.*

riv'er, *adj.*, de rivière, fluvial.

riv'er-dragon, *n.*, crocodile, *m.*

riv'er-god, *n.*, dieu de rivière; fleuve, *m.*

riv'er-horse, *n.*, hippopotame, *m.*

riv'et, *n.*, rivet, *m.*; rivure; (shoemaker's) pointe, cheville, *f.*; (for china) attache, *f.*

riv'et, *v.a.*, river; (fig.) river, fixer, clouer, affermir, consolider.

riv'eting, *n.*, rivement, *m.* — hammer; *rivoir, m.* — machine; *machine à river, f.*

riv'ulet (riv'iou-), *n.*, ruisseau, *m.*

rix'-dollar, *n.*, rixdale, risdale, *f.*

roach (rôtsh), *n.*, (ich.) gardon, *m.*

road (rôde), *n.*, route, *f.*; chemin, *m.*; chaussée, voie, *f.*; (nav.) rade; (fig.) voie, route, *f.*, chemin, *m.* Carriage- —; *voie charretière.* High —; *grand chemin, grand'route.* Rail— —; *chemin de fer.* Turnpike- —; *chemin à barrière.* By- —; *chemin détourné.* Beaten —; *chemin battu.* Heavy —; *chemin rompu.* Cross- —; *chemin de traverse.* On the —; *en route, en chemin.* On the — to; *sur la route de; en route pour.* —s and bridges; (France) *ponts et chaussées, m.pl.* By —; *à pied; à cheval.* To take the —; *prendre le chemin de; se diriger vers.* To take to the —; *avoir recours au brigandage; se faire voleur de grand chemin.*

road-embank'ment, *n.*, remblai de route, *m.*

road-engineer' (-è'n'dji-nîre), *n.*, ingénieur des routes, *m.*

road'er, *n.*, vaisseau en rade, *m.*

road'-fence, *n.*, clôture de route, *f.*

road-la'borer (-léb'eur'-), *n.*, cantonnier, *m.*

road'-maker (-mék'-), *n.*, constructeur de routes, *m.*

road'-making, *n.*, construction de routes, *f.*

road'-map, *n.*, carte routière, *f.*

road'-metal, *n.*, cailloutis, empierrement, *m.*

road'-scraper (-scrép'-), *n.*, racloir; rabot; (pers.) boueur, *m.*

road'-side (-saïde), *n.*, bord de la route, bas côté, *m.* By, ou on, the —; *au bord de la route, ou du chemin.*

road'stead (-stède), *n.*, (nav.) rade, *f.*

road'ster, *n.*, cheval de route; (nav.) navire en rade, *m.*

road'way, *n.*, chaussée, *f.*; (of a bridge) voie, *f.*; pavé, *m.*

roam (rôme), *v.a.* and *n.*, errer, rôder; rôder **dans, parmi.**

roam'er, *n.*, promeneur, *m.*

roam'ing (rô'm'-), *n.*, course vagabonde, *f.*

roan (rône), *adj.*, rouan. — leather; *peau maroquinée, f.*

roan'-tree (-trî), *n.*, (bot.) sorbier des oiseaux, *m.*

roar (rôre), *n.*, (of the lion) rugissement; (of the bull, etc.) mugissement; cri; bruit, fracas; (of laughter) éclat, grand éclat; (of horses) cornage, (of thunder) grondement, *m.*

roar, *v.n.*, (of the lion) rugir; (of the bull, etc.) mugir; (of thunder, cannon) gronder; (to cry aloud) crier; pousser des cris; tempêter; **(of horses)** corner. To — with laughter; *rire*

aux larmes, rire aux éclats. To set in a —; *faire rire aux éclats; faire pâmer de rire quelqu'un.*

roar'er, *n.*, animal qui rugit; animal qui mugit; (of horses) corneur, cornard; (pers.) crieur, criard, *m.*, crieuse, criarde, *f.*

roar'ing, *n.* *V.* roar.

roar'ing (rôr'-), *adj.*, mugissant, rugissant, qui gronde. To drive a — trade; (fig.) *faire des affaires d'or.*

roar'ingly, *adv.*, en rugissant, avec bruit, avec éclat.

roast (rôste), *v.a.*, rôtir; faire rôtir; griller, faire cuire; (metal.) griller; (to banter) railler, plaisanter vivement.

roast, *adj.*, rôti. — meat; *rôti, m.*

roast, *n.*, rôti, *m.*; (fig.) haute main, *f.* To rule the —; *avoir la haute main* ou *gouverner.*

roast'er, *n.*, rôtisseur, *m.*; (pig) cochon de lait pour rôtir, *m.*; (thing) rôtissoire, cuisinière, *f.*; (for coffee) brûloir, *m.*

roast'ing (rôst'-), *n.*, cuisson, *f.*; (metal.) rôtissage, grillage, *m.*; (coffee) brûlage, *m.*, torréfaction, *f.*; (bantering) raillerie mordante, *f.* —jack; *tournebroche, m.* —furnace; (metal.) *fourneau à réverbère, m.*

rob, *v.a.*, voler; voler à main armée; piller; dépouiller de; dérober à; frustrer de; priver **de.** To — an orchard; *piller un verger.* To — a person of anything; *voler, dérober quelque chose à quelqu'un; fruster quelqu'un de quelque chose.* To — Peter to pay Paul; *décoiffer St. Pierre pour coiffer St. Paul, ou boucher un trou pour en ouvrir un autre.* He would — a church; *il en prendrait sur l'autel.* I have been — bed of everything; *on m'a dévalisé; on m'a tout pris.*

rob'ber, *n.*, voleur, *m.*; voleuse, *f.*; voleur à main armée; brigand, bandit, *m.* Highway —; *voleur de grand chemin.*

rob'bery, *n.*, vol; (highway) vol à main armée; brigandage; larcin, *m.*; soustraction, *f.*

robe (rôbe), *n.*, robe, *f.* —s, *pl.*, robes, *f.pl.*, vêtements; ornements, *m.pl.*

robe, *v.a.*, vêtir d'une robe; vêtir **de**; revêtir **de.**

robe, *v.n.*, (one's self) se revêtir de sa robe.

rob'in *ou* **rob'in-red'breast** (-rèd'brèste), *n.*, (orni.) rouge-gorge, *m.* — good-fellow; *lutin domestique, m.*

robin'ia, *n.*, (bot.) robinier, *m.*

robust' (ro-beuste), *adj.*, robuste, vigoureux, rude.

robust'ly, *adv.*, robustement, vigoureusement.

robust'ness, *n.*, vigueur, force, *f.*

roc, rock, *ou* **rukh** (reuke), *n.*, (fabulous bird of Eastern tales) rouc, rock, *m.*

roc'ambole (-bôl), *n.*, échalote d'Espagne, *f.*

roche'-alum (rotsh'al'eume) *n.*, alun de roche, *m.*

roch'et (rotsh'-), *n.*, rochet (surplis), *m.*

rock, *n.*, roche, *f.*; rocher, roc; (sugar) sucre d'orge, sucre de pomme; (geol.) terrain, *m.*, roche, *f.*; (at sea) écueil, brisant, *m.pl.*, (shoals) récif, *m.sing.*; (flax around a distaff) poupée, quenouillée, *f.* —crystal; *cristal de roche, m.* — bound; *entouré de rochers.*

rock, *v.a.*, bercer, remuer; balancer.

rock, *v.n.*, se balancer, branler; (to quake) trembler.

rock'-basin (-bé's'n), *n.*, bassin de roche, *m.*

rock'er, *n.*, personne qui berce; berceuse; (thing) bascule, *f.*

rock'et, *n.*, fusée volante; (bot.) julienne des jardins, *f.*

rock'-fish, *n.*, labre; bar rayé, *m.*

rock'-head (-hède), *n.*, (geol.) crête de roche, *f.*

rock'iness, *n.*, nature rocailleuse, *f.*

rock'ing, *n.*, ébranlement, balancement; (of a child) bercement, *m.*

rock'ing-chair (-tahére), *n.*, chaise à bascule, chaise berceuse, *f.*

rock'ing-horse, *n.*, cheval à bascule, *m.*

rock'less, *adj.*, sans rochers.

rock'-oil, *u.*, pétrole, *m.*

rock'-rose (-rōze), *n.*, (bot.) ciste, *m.*

rock'-salt. *n.*, sel gemme, *m.*

rock'-work (-weurke), *n.*, rocaille, *f.;* mur de rocher, cailloutage, *m.*

rock'y, *adj.*, plein de rochers; de rocher; de roche; rocheux; rocailleux.

rocou'. *V.* **arnotto.**

rod, *n.*, verge; baguette; (of curtains, etc.) tringle; (of a pump) tige; (for fishing) canne à pêcher; (tech.) verge; (measure) perche (mètres 5·0291); (birch) verge, *f.*, verges, *f.pl.;* (of a shepherd) houlette, *f.;* (of mach., etc.) bielle, tige, *f.* — and line; *ligne à pêcher, f.* With — and line; *à la ligne.* To have a — in pickle for any one; *la garder bonne à quelqu'un.* To kiss the —; *se soumettre (à un châtiment) sans rien dire.* Spare the — and spoil the child; (prov.) *qui aime bien, châtie bien.*

ro'dents (rō-), *n.pl.*, (mam.) rongeurs, *m.pl.*

rodomontade', *n.*, rodomontade, *f.*

rodomontade', *v.n.*, (ant.) faire le rodomont.

roe (rō), *n.*, (deer) chevreau, *m.*, chevrette; (hind) biche, *f.;* (of fish) œufs de poisson, *m.pl.* Hard —; *œufs de poisson, m. pl.* Soft —; *laite, laitance, f.*

roe'buck (rō-beuke), *n.*, chevreuil, *m.*

roed (rōde), *adj.*, œuvé; à laite.

rogue (rōghe), *n.*, coquin, fripon, fourbe; (jest) malin, espiègle, farceur; (jur.) vagabond, *m.*

rog'uery (rōgh'-), *n.*, coquinerie, friponnerie, fourberie; malice, espièglerie, *f.;* (jur.) vagabondage, *m.*

rog'uish (rōgh'ishe), *adj.*, coquin, fripon, fourbe; (jest.) malin, espiègle.

rog'uishly (rōgh'ish'-), *adv.*, en coquin; en fripon, en fourbe; (jest.) malicieusement, avec espièglerie.

rog'uishness (rōgh'-), *n.*, coquinerie, friponnerie, fourberie; malice, espièglerie, *f.*

roist'er *ou* **roist'erer** (roïs'-), *n.*, (ant.) tapageur, fanfaron, *m.*

roist'er *ou* **roist** (roïst), *v.n.*, (ant.) faire du tapage; faire le fanfaron.

roist'ering, *n.*, tapage, *m.;* (boasting) fanfaronnade, *f. adj.*, tapageur, bruyant; (boasting) fanfaron.

Ro'land, *n.*, Roland, *m.* A — for an Oliver; *à bon chat, bon rat;* ou *un prêté pour un rendu.* To give a — for an Oliver; *rendre pois pour fève.*

roll (rōl), *n.*, rouleau; (act of rolling) roulement, *m.*, roulade, *f.;* (round mass) rouleau; (of a ship) roulis; (of a drum) roulement; (loaf petit pain; (of tobacco) rouleau, *m.*, carotte, *f.;* (metal.) laminoir; (list) rôle, tableau, contrôle, *m.* —s, *pl.*, rôle, *m.*, rôles, *m.pl.*, contrôle, *m.*, contrôles, *m.pl.;* (annals) annales, archives, *f.;* (fig.) suite, succession, *f.* —call; (milit.) *appel, m.* To call the —; *faire l'appel.* To strike off the —s; *raser du tableau, du contrôle.*

roll, *v.a.*, rouler; (metal.) laminer; (a garden walk) passer le rouleau **sur** *ou* passer au rouleau. To — down; *rouler en bas.* To — up; *rouler en haut;* (to enwrap) *rouler, enrouler.* To — one's self up; *s'enrouler, se pelotonner; se ramasser.* To — back; *faire refluer, faire reculer, repousser.* To — round; *peloter, rouler en boule.*

roll, *v.n.*, rouler, se rouler; (to revolve) faire sa révolution; (milit.) faire un roulement. To — away; *s'éloigner en roulant;* (of time) *s'écouler.* To — off; *tomber de.* To — up; *se rouler, s'enrouler.* To — by; *passer en roulant.* A —ing stone gathers no moss; *pierre qui roule n'amasse pas de mousse.*

roll'er, *n.*, rouleau; cylindre, *m.;* (caster) roulette, *f.;* (print.) rouleau; (tech.) tambour; (metal.) cylindre, laminoir; (bandage) rouleau, *m.*, bande roulée, *f.;* (of a lock) galet; (orni.) rollier, *m.* Garden—; *rouleau, cylindre de jardin, m.* — blind; *store, m.* — skate; *patin à roulettes, m.*

roll'ing, *n.*, roulement; roulage; (of a ship) roulis; (metal.) laminage, *m.*

roll'ing-mill, *n.*, (metal.) laminoir, *m.;* machine à cingler le fer, *f.*

roll'ing-pin, *n.*, rouleau, *m.*

roll'ing-press, *n.*, presse à cylindres, calandre, *f.*

roll'ing-stock, *n.*, matériel roulant, *m.*

rolls'-court (rōlz'cōrte), *n.*, cour des rôles, *f.*

ro'ly-po'ly, *n.*, (game) balle au pot, *f.*

Ro'man (rō-), *n.*, Romain, *m.*, Romaine, *f.;* (print.) romain, *m.*

Ro'man, *adj.*, des Romains, romain; (print.) romain; (of the nose) aquilin.

romance', *n.*, roman de chevalerie, roman, *m.;* (mus.) romance, *f.* — writer; *romancier, m.*

Romance', *adj.*, roman. — languages; *langues romanes, f.pl.*

romance', *v.n.*, faire des romans; broder.

roman'cing, *adj.*, de roman (fiction).

Romanesque', *adj.*, (linguist.) roman; (arch.) roman.

Ro'manism (-'iz'm), *n.*, religion catholique (romaine), *f.*

Ro'manist, *n.*, catholique (romain), *m.*, catholique (romaine), *f.*

ro'manize (-'aïze), *v.a.*, latiniser; convertir au catholicisme (romain).

Ro'man-like (-laïke), *adj.*, à la romaine.

roman'tic, *adj.*, romanesque; (scenery, style) romantique.

roman'tically, *adv.*, romanesquement; (of scenery) romantiquement.

roman'ticist, *n.*, romantique, *m.*

roman'ticness, *n.*, caractère romanesque, *m.*, nature romantique, *f.*

Rome, *n.*, Rome, *f.* — was not built in a day; (prov.) *l'arbre ne tombe pas au premier coup; Paris ne s'est pas fait en un jour.*

Rom'ish, *adj.*, (b.s.) romain.

romp, *n.*, gamine, garçonnière, *f.;* (play) jeu rude *ou* grossier, tapage, *m.*

romp, *v.n.*, jouer rudement; folâtrer; gambader, batifoler, faire du tapage.

romp'ing, *n.*, jeux rudes, *m.pl.*

romp'ish, *adj.*, rude; folâtre.

romp'ishness, *n.*, folâtrerie, *f.;* batifolage, *m.*

rood (roude), *n.*, le quart d'une acre, *m.;* (10.12 ares) (c.rel.) crucifix, *m.*

rood'-loft, *n.*, galerie du crucifix, *f.*, ambon, *m.* — screen; *jubé, m.*

roof (rouf), *n.*, toit; (of the mouth) palais, *m.;* (of a coach) impériale; (of omnibuses, cabs) impériale, *f.;* dessus, *m.;* (fig.) voûte, *f.* — timber; *faîtage, m.* —tile; *faîtière, tuile faîtière, f.* —work; *toiture, f.*

roof, *v.a.*, couvrir d'un toit; couvrir; (to shelter) abriter.

roof'ing, *n.*, toiture, *f.*

roof'less, *adj.*, sans toit; (unsheltered) sans abri.

roof'y, *adj.*, couvert d'un toit.

rook (rouke), *n.*, (orni.) grolle, corneille, *f.;* freux; (cheat) tricheur, capon, filou, *m.;* (at chess) tour, *f.*

rook, *v.a.* and *n.*, friponner, filouter; tricher.

rook'ery, *n.*, lieu habité par des freux, des corneilles; (close assemblage of dirty buildings) ramassis de taudis; (fig.) nid à rats, repaire de voleurs, lupanar, *m.*

room (roume), *n.*, (apartment) chambre, salle; (of a suite of apartments) pièce, *f.;* (space) espace, *m.*, place; (place) place; (stead) place, *f.*, lieu; (fig.) (reason) lieu, sujet, motif, *m.*, matière ; (fig.) latitude, marge, *f.* ; (workshop) atelier, *m.* Powder-—; (nav.) *soute aux poudres,* *f.* Bed-—; *chambre à coucher.* Dining-—; *salle à manger.* There is no —; *il n'y a pas de place.* To make — for; *faire de la place à* ; *faire place à.* In —of; *au lieu* **de** ; *à la place* **de.** There is — for improvement; *cela laisse à désirer.* To have a — not big enough to swing a cat in ; *avoir une chambre grande comme la main.*

room′ful (-foule), *n.*, chambre pleine ; chambrée, *f.*

room′iness, *n.*, nature vaste, nature spacieuse, grandeur, *f.*

room′y, *adj.*, spacieux, vaste, grand.

roost (rouste), *n.*, juchoir, perchoir, *m.* Hen-—; *poulailler, m.*

roost, *v.n.*, jucher, se percher, se jucher. To go to —; (fam.) *aller se coucher.* Curses, like chickens, come home to —; (prov.) *à qui mal veut, mal arrive.* To rule the —; *V.* roast.

roost′er, *n.*, coq, *m.*

root (route), *n.*, racine ; (first ancestor) souche ; (original cause) source ; (mus.) base; (lower part) fondation, *f.*, fondement, *m.* ; (alg., arith., bot., gram.) racine, *f.*, radical, *m.* To take —, to strike —; *prendre racine.* —cutter ; *coupe-racine, m.*

root, *v.a.*, enraciner ; fixer en terre ; laisser enraciner ; (to turn up the earth) (of swine) fouiller la terre avec le groin. To — out; to — up; *déraciner, extirper ;* (to ferret out) *découvrir.*

root, *v.n.*, s'enraciner ; prendre racine, fouiller avec le groin.

root′-bound (-baou'n'de), *adj.*, attaché par la racine.

root′-crop, *n.*, racinage, *m.*

root′ed, *adj.*, enraciné ; (fig.) invétéré. — out ; *déraciné, extirpé.*

root′edly, *adv.*, profondément.

root′ing, *n.*, enracinement, *m.* — out, up ; *extirpation, extermination, f., arrachement, m.*

root′let, *n.*, (bot.) radicule, *f.*

root′-stock, *n.*, (bot.) rhizome, *m.* ; souche, *f.*

rope (rôpe), *n.*, corde, *f.*, cordage, *m.* ; (nav.) manœuvre, *f.*, cordage ; (of birds) intestin, *m.* ; (of onions) glane, *f.* ; (string) rang ; (row) fil, *m.* ; (fig.) latitude, *f.*, coudées franches, *f.pl.* Tight-—; *corde tendue ; corde raide, f.* Slack —; *voltige, corde lâche, f.* Running —s ; (nav.) *manœuvres courantes, f.pl.* A —of sand ; *une union précaire, une chaîne de paille, f.* To give a person —; *lâcher la bride à quelqu'un ; mettre à quelqu'un la bride sur le cou.* To give (any one) plenty of —; *donner toute latitude à ; donner ses franches coudées à.* To be on the high —s ; *être monté sur ses grands chevaux* ou *prendre ses grands airs.*

rope, *v.n.*, filer. *v.a.*, attacher, lier.

rope′-barrel (-′rèl), *n.*, tambour, *m.*

rope′-dancer, *n.*, danseur, *m.*, ou danseuse, *f.*, de corde ; funambule, acrobate, *m.f.*

rope′-ladder, *n.*, échelle de corde, *f.*

rope′-maker (-mék′-), *n.*, cordier, *m.*

rope′-making (-mék′-), *n.*, corderie, fabrication de cordes, *f.*

rope′-roll (-rôl), *n.*, (mec.) tambour, *m.*

rop′ery, *n.*, corderie, *f.* ; (trick) tour pendable, *m.*

rope′-trick, *n.*, tour pendable, *f.*

rope′-walk (-wôke), *n.*, corderie, *f.*

rope′-walker, *n.*, acrobate, *m.*

rope′-yarn, *n.*, fil de caret, *m.*

rop′iness (rô-), *n.*, viscosité, *f.*

rop′ish ou **rop′y** (rô-), *adj.*, qui file ; visqueux ; filant.

rosa′ceous (-zé-sheusse), *adj.*, (bot.) rosacé.

ro′sary (rô-za-ri), *n.*, roseraie, *f.* ; (c.rel.) rosaire, *m.*

rose (rôze), *n.*, rose ; (of ribbon) rosette ; (arch.) rosace, *f.* ; (of a watering pot) pomme d'arrosoir. He is not on a bed of —; *il n'est pas sur un lit*

---

de roses, ou *il est loin d'être à son aise.* **There is** no — without a thorn, *ou* every rose has its thorn ; *il n'y a pas,* ou *il n'est pas, de rose sans épines.* Under the —; (fig.) *sous la cheminée, sous le manteau ; en secret, confidentiellement.* Guelder —; *obier, m.* ; *boule de neige, f.*

ro′seate (rô-ji-), *adj.*, de rose ; rosé ; vermeil ; orné de roses.

rose′-bay, *n.*, laurier-rose, oléandre, épilobe, *m.* Dwarf —; *rhododendron, m.*

rose′-bed, *n.*, massif de rosiers, *m.*

rose′-bud (-beude), *n.*, bouton de rose, *m.*

rose′-bush (-boushe), *n.*, rosier, *m.*

rose′-campion, *n.*, lychnide coronaire, coquelourde ; coquelourde des jardiniers, *f.*

rose′-cheeked (-tshîk′te), *adj.*, aux joues de rose.

rose′-color (-keul′leur), *n.*, rose, *m.*

rose′-colored (-keul′leurde), *adj.*, couleur de rose ; rose ; vermeil.

rose′-gall (-gôl), *n.*, (bot.) bédegar, bédeguar, *m.*

rose′-garden, *n.*, roseraie, *f.*

rose′-grower, *n.*, rosiériste, *m.*

rose′-laurel, *n.*, laurier-rose, *m.*

rose′-like (-laïke), *adj.*, en rose.

rose′-mallow (-lô), *n.*, (bot.) rose trémière ; passe-rose, *f.*

rose′mary, *n.*, (bot.) romarin, *m.*

rose′-quartz (-kwôrtze), *n.*, quartz rosé, *m.*

rose′-show, *n.*, exposition de roses, *f.*

rose′-tribe (-traïbe), *n.sing.*, rosacées, *f.pl.*

rose′-water (-wô-), *n.*, eau de rose, *f.*

rose′-window (-dô), *n.*, rosace, *f.*

rose′wood (-woude), *n.*, (bot.) bois de Chypre, palissandre, *m.*

rose′-work (-weurke), *n.sing.*, rosaces, *f.pl.* *m.*

Rosicru′cian (rôz′i-crou-shi-), *n.*, rose-croix, *m.*

Rosicru′cian, *adj.*, de rose-croix.

ros′in (roz′-), *n.* *V.* resin.

ros′in, *v.a.*, frotter, *ou* enduire, de résine ; frotter de colophane.

ros′iness (rô-zi-), *n.*, rose, vermillon, *m.* ; couleur rose, *f.*

ros′iny (roz′-), *adj.*, résineux.

ros′land, *n.*, bruyère (place), *f.* ; terrain marécageux, *m.*

rosset′, *n.*, (mam.) roussette, rougette, *f.*

ros′ter, *n.*, (milit.) règlement, rôle, *m.* ; liste, *f.* ; cadres, *m.pl.*

ros′trum, *n.*, (of a ship) bec, éperon, *m.* ; (platform) rostres, *m.pl.*, tribune aux harangues ; (of auctioneers) tribune aux enchères, *f.* ; (of an alembic) bec ; (nat. hist.) rostre, *m.*

ro′sy (rô-zi), *adj.*, rose, rosé, de rose ; vermeil.

ro′sy-bosomed (-bou-zeu′m′de), *adj.*, au sein de rose.

ro′sy-colored (-keul′leurde), *adj.*, couleur de rose (*invariable*).

ro′sy-crowned (-craou′n′de), *adj.*, couronné de roses.

ro′sy-fingered (-fi′gn′gheurde), *adj.*, aux doigts de rose.

ro′sy-lipped, *adj.*, aux lèvres rosées.

ro′sy-tinted, *adj.*, rosé.

rot, *n.*, pourriture ; (vet.) clavelée, *f.*, claveau, tac, *m.* Dry —; *pourriture sèche ;* (fig.) (fam.) *galimatias, m.*

rot, *v.a.*, pourrir ; faire pourrir ; (of teeth) carier.

rot, *v.n.*, pourrir, se pourrir ; (of teeth) se carier.

rotang (ro-taï′gne), *n.*, rotang, rotin, *m.*

ro′tary (rô-), *adj.*, rotatoire.

rota′tion (ro-té-), *n.*, rotation ; succession, *f.* ; roulement, *m.* — of crops; *assolement, m.* By —, in —; *à tour de rôle.*

ro′tatory (rô-ta-teuri), *adj.*, de rotation ; alternatif ; (anat.) rotateur ; (mec.) rotatoire.

rote (rôte), *n.*, routine, *f.* By —; *par cœur.*

rote, v.n., rouler, alterner.

rot'ten (rot'r'n), adj., pourri, carié ; (of teeth) gâté ; (insolvent) véreux. To smell —; sentir le pourri.

rot'tenness, n., pourriture ; carie, f. ; pourri, m. ; (fig.) fausseté, f.

rot'ten-stone (-stône), n., terre pourrie, f. ; tripoli, m.

rot'ting, adj., qui pourrit, qui se carie.

rot'ting, n., putréfaction.

rotund' (-teu'n'de), adj., rond, arrondi.

rotun'da ou **rotun'do**, n., rotonde, f.

rotund'ity, n., rondeur ; rotondité, f.

rou'ble, n. V. **ru'ble**.

roucou', n., (bot.) roucouyer ; roucou, m.

rouge (rouje), n., rouge, fard, m.

rouge, v.n., mettre du rouge.

rouge, v.a., mettre du rouge à ; farder.

rough, adj., rude ; (harsh to the taste) âpre ; (rugged) rude, raboteux ; (shaggy) hérissé, ébouriffé ; (of features) rude ; (of roads) raboteux ; (of the sea) agitée, grosse, houleuse ; (of the weather) orageux, gros ; (of precious stones) brut ; (violent) violent ; (coarse in manners) brusque, brutal, grossier ; (not exact) approximatif ; (of glass) dépoli. — copy; brouillon, m. — estimate ; appréciation en gros, f. A — diamond ; un diamant brut. In the —; brut, en gros. Very — usage ; traitement très dur, m., mauvais procédés, m.pl. Very — weather ; très mauvais temps, m. — sea ; mer houleuse, f. — tools for — work ; (prov.) à gens de village, trompette de bois. We must take the — with the smooth ; à la guerre comme à la guerre. To be — with ; brutaliser, rudoyer.

rough, v.a., rendre rude ; ébaucher, dégrossir. To — shoe ; ferrer à glace. To — it ; manger de la vache enragée ; coucher sur la dure.

rough', n., voyou, polisson, m. —s, pl., canaille, racaille, f.

rough'cast (-câste), v.a., ébaucher ; (mas.) crépir.

rough'cast, n., ébauche, f. ; (mas.) crépi, m.

rough'casting, n., crépissage, ravalement, m.

rough'-coat (-côte), v.a. (mas.) crépir, ravaler.

rough'-coating, n., crépissage, ravalement, m.

rough'-down, v.a., dégrossir.

rough'-draught (-drâfte), n., ébauche, f. ; brouillon, m., minute, f.

rough'-draw (-drô), v.a., ébaucher, esquisser.

rough'en (reuf'f'n), v.n., devenir rude. v.a., rendre rude.

rough'ening, n., action de rendre rude, f.

rough'-footed (-fout'-), adj., pattu.

rough'-hew (-hiou), v.a., ébaucher; dégrossir.

rough'-hewn, adj., ébauché ; dégrossi.

rough'ing (reuf'-), n., ébauchage, m.

rough'ly (reuf'-), adv., rudement ; grossièrement ; âprement, durement, brutalement, brusquement ; approximativement, à peu près.

rough'ness (reuf'-), n., aspérité ; rudesse ; (austereness to the taste) âpreté ; (of the sea) agitation ; (of the wind) violence ; (of the weather) rigueur ; (of features) rudesse ; (coarseness of manners) grossièreté, rudesse, f., manières impolies, manières grossières, f.pl., brusquerie, f. ; sans-façon, (of roads) mauvais état, m.

rough'-rider, n., écuyer, piqueur, dresseur de chevaux, m.

rough'-shod, adj., ferré à glace.

rough'-work, n., grosse besogne, f.

rough'-wrought (-rôte), adj., travaillé grossièrement, fait grossièrement.

rounce (raou'n'ce), n., (print.) manivelle.

round (raou'n'de), n., (circle) rond, cercle, m. ; (tech.) rondelle, f. ; (of a ladder) échelon, m. ; (of beef) rouelle, f. ; cimier, m. ; (of applause) salve; (milit.) décharge, f. ; (fenc.)

assaut, m., attaque ; (milit.) ronde, inspection ; (draw.) bosse ; (sculp.) ronde bosse ; (of watchmen, police, etc.) ronde, f. ; (revolution) tour ; (walk round) tour, m., tournée, (dance) ronde, f. — of ammunition ; cartouche, f. In a —; en rond. To go the —s; faire la tournée, la ronde. To fire a —; tirer une volée.

round (raou'n'de), v.a., arrondir ; (to encircle) environner, entourer ; (to walk round) faire le tour de, contourner ; (nav.) haler ; (a cape) doubler ; (an island) contourner, arrondir. To — off ; arrondir, finir, compléter, achever. To — on; (any one) dénoncer, injurier, tancer, réprimander.

round, v.n., s'arrondir, s'achever ; (to go round) faire la ronde.

round, adj., rond ; en rond ; (large) rond, grand, joli, bon ; (full) rond, arrondi ; (candid) rond, facile, coulant ; (positive) absolu. With a rope — one's neck ; la corde au cou. To tie a rope — one's neck ; se mettre une corde au cou. — numbers ; chiffres ronds, m.pl. To make —; arrondir.

round, adv., (circularly) en rond ; (on all sides) autour, tout autour, à l'entour, à la ronde. All —; tout autour. To hand —; passer à la ronde. To go —; faire le tour de; faire un détour. To get —; tourner ; (of the health) se rétablir, se refaire; se remettre. All the year —; pendant tout le cours de l'année, pendant toute l'année. To go — to ; aller voir ; visiter.

round, prep., autour de. To go — the garden ; faire le tour du jardin. To get — any one ; circonvenir, entortiller, quelqu'un.

round'about (-'aboute), adj., détourné; (fig.) indirect, vague.

round'about, n., jeu de bagues, manège, m.

round'elay (raou'n'di-), n., rondeau, m.

round'ers, n., (at a game, sort of) balle au camp, f.sing.

round'head, n., (hist.) tête ronde, f.

round'-headed, adj., à tête ronde.

round'house (-haouce), n., corps de garde, violon, poste, m. ; (in a ship) dunette, f.

round'ing (raou'n'd'-), n., (nav.) fourrure de câble, f.

round'ish (raou'n'd'-), adj., arrondi, presque rond ; (pers.) rondelet.

round'ishness, n., forme arrondie.

round'let, n., petit rond, petit cercle, m.

round'ly, adv., (circularly) en rond ; (plainly) rondement, franchement ; (completely) rondement, complètement ; (briskly) rondement, bon train.

round'-man, n., homme de tournée, m.

round'ness, n., rondeur ; (fig.) franchise, f.

round'-robin, n., pièce, ou pétition, revêtue de signatures en rond, ou en cercle, f.

round-shoul'dered, adj., voûté.

roup, n., pépie, f., (disease in poultry).

rouse (raouze), v.a., réveiller, éveiller ; animer ; exciter ; soulever ; (nav.) haler ; (animal) faire lever ; lancer. To — the sleeping lion; réveiller le chien qui dort.

rous'ing (raouz'-), adj., qui réveille, qui éveille ; (of fire) grand, bon.

rout (raoute), n., (party) assemblée, réunion ; partie, f., rout, raout, m. ; (multitude) cohue, foule, multitude ; (milit.) déroute, f. To put to —; mettre en déroute. To — out ; découvrir, déterrer ; (to turn out) faire décamper.

rout (raoute), v.a., mettre en déroute.

route (route), n., route, f. ; itinéraire, parcours, m. ; (milit.) feuille de route, f.

routine (rou-tîne), n., routine ; manière routinière, f. To return to the old —; reprendre le collier de misère.

rove (rôve), v.n., rôder ; courir.

rove, v.a., errer dans ; parcourir, courir ; (in spinning) passer dans une maille, boudiner.

rov'er, n., coureur, rôdeur, vagabond, m. ;

(fickle person) inconstant, *m.*, inconstante, *f. ;*
(pirate) écumeur de mer, pirate, corsaire ; (in
spinning) boudineur, *m.* [bond.

rov'ing (rôv'-), *adj.*, errant, qui court ; vaga-
rov'ing, *n.*, (spinning) boudinage, *m.*
rov'ing-frame, *n.*, boudinoir, *m.*
rov'ingly, *adv.*, en rôdant. *V.* **ramblingly**.

row (raou), *n.*, (tumult) tapage, vacarme, *m. ;*
querelle, *f. ;* chamaillis, *m.*, batterie, rixe, scène,
f. To get into a —; *se faire, s'attirer, une mauvaise affaire.* To kick up a — ; *faire du tapage,
du train.*

row (raou), *v.a.*, blâmer ; *v.n.*, quereller.

row (rô), *n.*, (rank) rang, *m.*, rangée ; (of figures) colonne ; (on the water) promenade sur
l'eau, promenade en bateau, (street) rue, ruelle,
f. In a — ; *en rang, en ligne.* In —s ; *par
rangs ;* (hort.) en rayons. In three — ; *sur trois
rangs* (V. Hugo). All of a — ; *en rang d'oignon.*

row (rô), *v.a.*, conduire, transporter, faire
aller, à la rame ; (nav.) nager.

row (rô), *v.n.*, ramer ; (nav.) nager. To —
in the same boat : *courir même fortune.*

row'-boat, *n.*, bateau à rames, *m.*

row'dy, *adj.*, tapageur, turbulent, canaille.

row'dy, *n.*, voyou, gredin, émeutier, *m.*

row'dyism, **row'dyness**, *n.*, tapage, *m.*,
polissonnerie, turbulence, gredinerie, *f.*

row'el (raou-èl), *n.*, (of a spur) molette ; (of a
bit) bossette, *f. ;* (vet.) séton, *m.*, ortie, *f.*

row'el, *v.a.*, (vet.) appliquer un séton à.

row'er (rô-eur), *n.*, rameur ; (nav.) nageur,
canotier, *m.*

row'ing (rô-), *adj.*, (nav.) qui va à la nage ; à
rames. — club ; *cercle des rameurs, m.* —
-match ; *course à l'aviron, f.* To be fond of — ;
aimer à ramer.

row'lock (rô-), *n.*, (nav.) tolétière, *f.*

row'-port (rô-), *n.*, (nav.) sabord d'aviron,
m.

roy'al (roi-ial), *adj.*, royal, de roi ; (of paper)
grand raisin. — assent ; *sanction royale, f.* —
navy ; *marine de l'Etat, marine royale, f.* — blue ;
bleu de roi. —sail ; (nav.) *cacatois, m.* — yard ;
vergue de cacatois, f.

roy'alism (-'iz'm), *n.*, royalisme, *m.*

roy'alist, *n.*, royaliste, *m.*

roy'ally, *adv.*, royalement, en roi.

roy'alty, *n.*, royauté, *f. ;* (money paid) droit,
tantième, *m.*, redevance, commission, *f. ;* (on
books) droit sur la vente, droit d'auteur.

rub (reube), *v.a.*, frotter ; (med.) frictionner ;
(to tease) contrarier. To — away ; *enlever par
le frottement.* To — down ; *frotter ;* (a horse)
bouchonner. To — off ; *enlever par le frottement ;
faire disparaître.* To — out ; *enlever, effacer.*
To — up ; *frotter, dérouiller ;* (to polish) *polir ;*
(to excite) *exciter, réveiller.*

rub (reube), *v.n.*, frotter ; (med.) faire une
friction. To — through ; *se frayer un chemin à
travers, faire son chemin, se tirer d'affaire.* To
— on, *ou* along ; *aller son petit bonhomme de
chemin.* To — off ; *s'user ; s'enlever ; s'effacer.*

rub (reube), *n.*, frottement ; frottage, coup de
brosse, *m. ;* (difficulty) difficulté, *f.*, point difficile, obstacle ; (sarcasm) lardon, coup de patte,
m. At the — ; *au fait et au prendre.* There's
the — ; *c'est là le diable,* ou *c'est là que gît le
lièvre ; c'est là la question.* A — down ; (to a
horse) *un coup de bouchon ;* (with a cloth) *coup
de torchon, m.*

rub'ber (reub'-), *n.*, (pers.) frotteur ; fric-
tionneur ; (thing) frottoir ; (file) carreau, *m. ;*
(whetstone) pierre à aiguiser ; (at cards) partie
liée ; belle, *f. ;* (at whist) rob, robre, *m.* India-
— ; *caoutchouc, m.* ; *gomme élastique, f.*

rub'bing (reub'-), *n.*, frottement ; frottage ;
(hunt.) frayoir, *m. ;* (med.) friction, *f. ;* (professional) frictionnement, *m.*

rub'bish (reub'-), *n.*, décombres ; débris, dé-

blais ; gravois, gravats, *m.pl. ;* ordures, *f.pl. ;*
(nonsense) fatras, *m. ;* bêtises, fadaises, *f.pl. ;*
(anything worthless) drogue, *f.*, fumier, rebut,
m. ; (mingled mass) masse informe, *f.*

rub'bish-cart (-cârte), *n.*, tombereau, *m.*

rub'bishing (reub'-), *adj.*, de rebut ; de rien.

rub'bish-pan, *n.*, panier aux ordures, *m.*

rub'bishy, *adj.*, de rebut, sans valeur, mauvais,
méchant.

rub'ble-stone (reub'b'l-stône), *n.*, pierre
brute ; blocaille, *f. ;* moellon brut, blocage, *m.*

rub'ble-work (-weurke), *n.*, maçonnerie brute
de moellons, maçonnerie de blocaille, *f.*

rubes'cent (riou-bès-), *adj.*, (ant.) rubescent.

ru'bican (rou-), *adj.*, rubican.

ru'bicund (rou-bi-keu'n'de), *adj.*, rubicond.

ru'bied (rou-bid), *adj.*, rouge, de rubis.

rubifica'tion (rou-bi-fi-ké-), *n.*, (med.) rubéfaction, *f.*

ru'bify (rou-bi-faïe), *v.a.*, rubéfier.

ru'ble (rou-b'l), *n.*, rouble, *m.*

ru'bric (rou-), *n.*, rubrique, *f.*

ru'brical, *adj.*, contenu dans les rubriques.

ru'bricate (rou-), *v.a.*, tacher, *ou* marquer, de
rouge.

ru'bricate, *adj.*, taché, *ou* marqué, de rouge.

ru'by (rou-), *adj.*, vermeil, de rubis. — lips ;
lèvres de corail, f.pl.

ru'by (rou-), *n.*, (min.) rubis, *m. ;* (chem.)
rubine, *f. ;* (color) teinte rouge, *f.*, incarnat, *m.*,
couleur rouge, *f. ;* (blain) rubis, *m.*

ruck, *n.*, pli ; sillon, *m.* Out of the common
— ; *hors du commun des martyrs.*

rud'der (reud'-), *n.*, gouvernail, *m.*

rud'der-case (-kéce), *n.*, boîte de gouvernail,
f.

rud'diness (reud'-), *n.*, rougeur, *f. ;* teint rouge,
m., fraîcheur de teint, *f. ;* incarnat, *m.*

rud'dy (reud'-), *adj.*, rouge, vermeil ; (pers.)
au teint vermeil, couperosé, frais.

rude (roude), *adj.*, (uneven) rude, grossier ;
(impolite) impoli, malhonnête ; impertinent ;
(violent, impetuous) rude, violent, sévère, dur ;
(harsh, inclement) rude, rigoureux ; (barbarous)
barbare, grossier, rustique.

rude'ly, *adv.*, rudement ; grossièrement ; insolemment, impoliment, malhonnêtement ; violemment ; sévèrement, durement ; rigoureusement.

rude'ness (roud'-), *n.*, rudesse ; grossièreté ;
insolence, impertinence ; violence ; sévérité, dureté ; rigueur, *f.*

ru'diment (rou-), *n.*, rudiment, *m.*

rudiment'al *ou* **rudiment'ary**, *adj.*, rudimentaire ; élémentaire.

rue (rou), *v.a.*, se repentir de ; regretter, déplorer. He will — it ; *il en pâtira.* I — the
day when ; *je regrette le jour où.*

rue (rou), *n.*, (bot.) rue, *f.*

rue'ful (rou-foule), *adj.*, triste, lamentable,
déplorable.

rue'fully, *adv.*, tristement, déplorablement.

rue'fulness, *n.*, tristesse, *f.*

rue'ing, *n.*, regrets, *m.pl. ;* lamentations, *f.pl*

ruff (reuf), *n.*, (collar) fraise, *f.* (ich.) ; paon
de mer, *m. ;* (milit.) rappel, roulement de tambour, *m.*

ruff (reufe), *v.a.*, (at cards) jouer atout.

ruf'fian (reuf'ya'n), *n.*, brigand, bandit ; gredin, scélérat, chenapan ; (brute) brutal, *m.*

ruf'fianism (-'iz'm), *n.*, brigandage, *m. ;*
scélératesse, brutalité, *f.*

ruf'fianly, *adj.*, de brigand, de bandit ; brutal.

ruf'fle (reuf'f'l), *n.*, manchette, *f. ;* (agitation)
trouble, *m.*, agitation, *f. ;* (milit.) rappel, roulement de tambour, *m.*

ruf'fle (reuf'f'l), *v.a.*, (to wrinkle) froncer,
froisser, chiffonner ; (to agitate) irriter ; troubler,
agiter ; (the feelings) froisser ; (to throw into
disorder) mettre en désordre, déranger ; (the

hair) ébouriffer, rebrousser ; (sleeves) mettre des manchettes à ; (milit.) battre le rappel.

ruf'fle, v.n., se troubler, s'agiter ; s'ébouriffer ; (mil.) battre aux champs.

ruf'fling, n., plissement, froncement, m. ; (of the feelings) froissement, m.

rug (reughe), n., (for beds) **descente de lit ;** couverture de bure, f. ; (for rooms) tapis de pied, tapis de foyer, m. Traveling —; couverture de voyage, f. —work ; tapisserie, f.

rug'ged (reug'ghède), adj., (rough) tempétueux, rude ; (uneven) raboteux ; (harsh) âpre ; (surly) refrogné ; rechigné.

rug'gedly, adv., rudement; âprement.

rug'gedness, n., aspérité ; nature raboteuse; âpreté ; (temper) rudesse, âpreté, f.

rugine' (rou-djîne), n., (surg.) rugine, f.

ru'gose (rou-gôce) ou **ru'gous** (rou-), adj., ridé ; rugueux.

rugos'ity (rou-gôss'i-), n., rugosité, f.

ru'in (rou-), n., ruine; perte, f. To go to —; s'en aller, tomber en ruine ; (pers.) courir à sa perte.

ru'in (rou-), v.a., ruiner; perdre.

ruina'tion (rou-i'n'é-), n., (l.u.) ruine, perte, f.

ru'iner, n., destructeur ; fléau, m.

ru'inous, adj., (decayed) ruineux, en ruine ; destructif, ruineux. To prove — to ; être la ruine de.

ru'inously, adv., ruineusement.

rule (roule), n., règle, f. ; règlement ; (government) gouvernement, pouvoir, empire, m., autorité, domination, f. ; (instrument) règle ; (print.) filet, tiret, réglet, m., réglette, f. ; (jur.) ordonnance, f. To make it a — to ; se faire une règle de. There is no — without exception; il n'y a point de règle sans exception. To lay out by — and line; tirer au cordeau. To live by —; vivre de régime. As a —; en général, en thèse générale. By — of thumb; à vue de nez, empiriquement. Home —; autonomie, f.

rule (roule), v.a., (to govern) gouverner, régir; (to determine) régler, décider, déterminer ; (to conduct) régler, diriger ; (paper, etc.) régler; To — men with a rod of iron; mener les gens à la baguette.

rule, v.n., gouverner ; (to decide) décider. To — over; régner sur.

rul'er, n., gouverneur ; gouvernant, souverain, arbitre, m. ; (instrument) règle, f. ; (workman) régleur, m. ; régleuse, f.

rul'ing (roul'-), adj., dominant, régnant. — machine ; machine à régler, f.

rul'ing, n., (jur.) ordonnance de juge, décision, f.

rum (reu'm), adj., drôle ; (fam.) cocasse ; drôle de; original. A — fellow, a — one ; un drôle de corps, un original.

rum, n., rhum, rum, m. — punch ; punch au rhum, m.

rum'ble (reu'm'b'l), v.n., gronder, murmurer, bruire ; (of vehicles) résonner, retentir ; (of the stomach) grouiller.

rum'ble, n., (seat of a carriage) siège de derrière, m.

rum'bling, n., bruit sourd, grondement ; roulement ; (of vehicles) roulement, retentissement, bruit ; (of the stomach) grouillement, m.

rum'bling, adj., qui bruit, qui gronde ; (of vehicles) retentissant; (of sound) sourd.

ru'minant (rou-), adj.m., ruminant, m.

ru'minate (rou-), v.a. and n., (of animals) ruminer. To — on, ou over ; (fig.) méditer sur, réfléchir à, ruminer.

rumina'tion (rou-mi-né-), n., rumination, f. méditation, réflexion, f.

rum'mage (reum'mèdje), v.a., chercher en fouillant, fouiller, remuer ; farfouiller. v.n., faire un remue-ménage.

rum'mage (reum'mèdje), n., remuement, remue-ménage, m., fouille, f.

rum'mer (reu'm'-), n., grand verre à pied, m. (mil.) battre aux champs.

ru'mor (rou-meur), n., rumeur, f. ; bruit, m. There is a —; le bruit court.

ru'mor, v.a., faire courir le bruit **de** ; ébruiter. It is —ed that; le bruit court que.

rump (reu'm'pe), n., croupe ; (of meat) culotte, f. ; (pers., birds) croupion ; (hist.) croupion ; (cook.) (of meat) contre-filet, m. —steak; bifteck, m.

rum'ple (reu'm'p'l), n., pli, m. ; froissure, f.

rum'ple (reu'm'p'l), v.a., chiffonner, froisser.

rum'pus (reu'm'-), n., chamaillis, grabuge, m. ; bagarre, f. ; grave différend, m.

rum'wort (-weurte), n., moût de rhum, m.

run (reune), v.n., [preterit, Ran ; past part., Run) courir ; marcher ; (to hasten up to) accourir; (to flee) se sauver ; (to extend) courir, s'étendre ; (to leak) fuir ; (to flow) couler ; (to melt) fondre; (to turn) tourner ; (to be) être ; (to be circulated) courir, circuler ; (to slide) glisser; (to be wheeled) rouler ; (of public coaches, boats) aller, faire le service ; (of the eyes) couler, pleurer ; (of time) s'écouler, passer ; (of writings) être conçu ; (of paper) boire ; (of prices) aller ; (of bills) courir; (of ships) filer ; (of ulcers) couler, suppurer; (of candles) couler ; (of meteors) filer. — for your lives ! sauve qui peut ! To be hard —; être serré de près; être aux abois. To — about ; courir çà et là. To — after ; chercher ; rechercher ; poursuivre. To — against; courir contre ; se précipiter sur, se jeter sur ; se heurter contre. To — aground ; échouer, se mettre à la côte. To — at; courir sur; attaquer. To — away ; s'enfuir; fuir ; se sauver ; (of horses) s'emporter, prendre le mors aux dents ; s'emballer ; (of time, liquids) s'écouler. To — away with ; se sauver avec; emporter ; enlever. To — away with the idea; se mettre dans la tête, s'imaginer. To — back ; retourner en courant ; retourner vite. To — down; courir en bas ; descendre ; (fig.) (to disparage) déprécier, dénigrer. My watch is — down ; ma montre ne va plus, ou n'est pas montée. To — for; courir chercher. To — from ; fuir de; s'enfuir de ; s'échapper de. To — headlong into a trap; donner tête baissée dans un piège. To — in; entrer ; entrer précipitamment. To — into; entrer dans ; (danger) se jeter dans ; (rail) tamponner ; (dissipation) se livrer à ; (of colors) se fondre. To — off ; s'enfuir ; fuir ; se sauver, s'échapper. To — off the line; (of trains) dérailler, quitter la voie. To — on ; continuer ; aller toujours ; (to talk) parler sans cesse, parler toujours ; (to refer to) rouler sur ; porter sur ; s'attacher à. To — out ; courir dehors ; sortir ; (to expire) expirer, finir ; tirer à sa fin ; (extend) s'étendre, s'allonger, se prolonger ; (of the tide) descendre. To — out of ; être à sec de, n'avoir plus de, épuiser. To — over ; passer dessus, passer sur ; parcourir ; (pers.) passer sur, écraser ; (a book) parcourir ; (a piece of music) jouer à première vue ; (a street, etc.) passer, traverser ; (of glasses, etc.) déborder. To — through ; passer à travers, parcourir, traverser ; (to dissipate) manger, dissiper, gaspiller ; (of trains) aller directement à. To — up ; courir en haut ; monter précipitamment ; arriver en courant. To — up to ; courir à ; (to amount to) s'élever à, monter à. To — upon ; rouler sur ; porter sur; s'attacher à ; (strike) donner sur. To — to seed ; monter en graine. To — into debt ; s'endetter ; faire (ou contracter) des dettes. To — into money ; coûter de l'argent. To — out only for an instant; ne faire que sortir et rentrer. To — down with wet ; ruisseler, dégoutter. It —s in the blood; cela est dans le sang. To —, ou be, on all fours with; être en tous points comparable à. To — across; traverser (en courant) ; (of persons) rencontrer par hasard. To — high (of

the sea) *être en fureur, être agitée, être haute.*
Words ran high between them ; (fig.) *ils en vinrent*
aux gros mots. To — ashore ; *échouer.* To —
with the hare and hunt with the hounds ; (prov.)
ménager la chèvre et le chou. To keep —ning into
one's head ; *trotter dans la tête.* So —s the legal
maxim ; *ainsi est conçue la maxime légale.*

run (reune), *v.a.,* (to incur) *courir, encourir ;*
(to melt, to cast) *fondre, couler ;* (to smuggle)
faire entrer par contrebande ; (to pursue) *pour-*
courir, suivre, poursuivre ; (to drive, to thrust)
pousser, enfoncer, fourrer ; (to mark, as a line)
tirer ; (to cause to fly) *faire marcher ;* (to cause
to pass) *passer, faire courir ;* (to wheel) *rouler.*
To — down ; *lasser à la course ;* (a ship) *couler,*
couler bas, couler à fond ; (pers.) *réduire au*
silence, fermer la bouche à ; (to decry) *ravaler ;*
(hunt.) *forcer.* To — for ; *courir chercher.* To
— hard ; *presser ; serrer de près.* To — in ; *en-*
foncer. To — a thorn into one's foot ; *s'enfoncer*
une épine dans le pied. To — into difficulties ;
jeter, précipiter dans des difficultés. To — into
debt ; *endetter.* To — foul of ; (nav.) *aborder ;*
(fig.) *se heurter contre.* To — in close ; (of ships)
serrer ; ranger la côte. To — in ; (nav.) *entrer au*
port. To — any one in ; *arrêter, coffrer.* To
— out ; *faire sortir ;* (to exhaust) *épuiser ;* (to
waste) *dissiper ;* (to extend) *étendre ;* (print.)
composer en alinéa. To — over ; *passer rapide-*
ment **sur** ; *examiner rapidement ; parcourir.* To
— through ; *percer de part en part ; passer*
d'outre en outre ; transpercer ; (to peruse) *par-*
courir. To — a sword through any one ; *passer*
une épée à travers le corps de quelqu'un. To —
up ; *monter en courant ;* (to build) *élever, bâtir ;*
(an account) *faire monter.* To — the risk ; *cou-*
rir le risque. To — a race ; *faire une course.*
He was — over ; *une voiture lui passa sur le*
corps. I ran my head against the wall ; *je don-*
nai (je cognai) la tête contre le mur.

run (reune), *n.,* (act of running) course, *f. ;*
(series) cours, *m.,* suite, *f. ;* (process) cours, *m.,*
marche, *f. ;* (course) courant ; (success) succès ;
(censure) cri, *m.,* clameur, opposition ; (on a
bank, etc.) descente, irruption, invasion, *f. ;*
(voyage) voyage ; (generality) commun, *m. ;* (of
millstones) paire ; (at play) veine, *f. ;* (of lodes)
gisement, *m.* In the long — ; *à la longue, à la fin,*
en fin de compte, avec le temps. To go for a — ;
faire une course, une promenade. To have a good
—, a great ; *être très couru ; avoir beaucoup de*
succès. To get the — upon ; *faire un plastron de ;*
tourner en ridicule. The common —, ou ruck ; *le*
commun, m. ; la généralité, f. To have had their
— ; (of books, etc.) *avoir eu leur temps.*

run'away (reu'n'a-wé), *n.,* fuyard, *m.,* fuyarde,
f. ; fugitif, *m.,* fugitive, *f. ;* déserteur, *m.* — slave ;
esclave fugitif, m. — horse ; *cheval échappé, m.*
— match ; *mariage d'enlèvement, m.*

run'dle (reu'n'd'l), *n.,* cylindre ; (of a ladder)
échelon, *m.*

rung (reu'gne), *n.,* (of a ladder) échelon, *m.* (of
a chair, etc.) bâton, *m.*

ru'nic (rou-), *adj.,* runique.

run'ner (reu'n'-), *n.,* coureur ; messager, courrier ; (racer) coureur ; (of an umbrella) coulant ;
(bot.) rejeton ; (of a strawberry plant) filet, *m. ;*
(nav.) itague, *f. ;* (tech.) anneau mobile, *m. ;* (of
a mill) meule supérieure, *f.* Scarlet — ; *haricot*
à rame, haricot d'Espagne.

run'ning (reu'n'-), *n.,* course, *f. ;* écoulement,
m. ; (of wounds) suppuration, *f. ;* (of the nose)
écoulement ; (of the pen) courant ; (of needle-
work) point devant ; (of trains, etc.) service,
m. — away ; *désertion, fuite, f.* — off ; (the rails)
déraillement, *m.* — foul ; *abordage, m.* —
aground, ashore ; *échouement ; échouage, m.*

run'ning (reu'n'-), *adj.,* courant ; (consecutive) consécutif, de suite ; (print., nav.) courant ;
(of water) courant, vif ; (of accounts) courant ;

(of bills) à échoir ; (of wounds) en suppuration.
—-horse ; *cheval de course, m.* —-knot ; *nœud*
coulant, m. He came three days — ; *il vint trois*
jours de suite. A — fire ; *un feu roulant, m.* —
fight ; *combat en chasse, m.* — account ; (com.)
compte courant, m.

runt (reu'n'te), *n.,* animal rabougri ; (pers.)
avorton, nabot, nain, *m.*

rupee' (rou-pî), *n.,* roupie, *f.*

rup'ture (reupt'ieur), *n.,* rupture ; (med.)
rupture, hernie, descente, *f.*

rup'ture (reupt'ieur), *v.a.,* rompre. To be
—d ; *avoir une hernie.*

rup'ture, *v.n.,* se rompre.

rup'turing, *n.,* rupture, *f.*

rup'ture-wort (-weurte), *n.,* (bot.) herniaire,
herniole, turquette, *f.*

ru'ral (rou-), *adj.,* champêtre, rural, rustique,
agreste. — postman ; *facteur rural, m.* — district ; commune rurale, *f.*

ru'ralist (rou-), *n.,* habitant de la campagne,
m., habitante de la campagne, *f.*

ru'rally, *adv.,* d'une manière rurale ; rustiquement.

rush (reushe), *n.,* jonc ; (thing of trivial value)
fétu, rien, *m. ;* (crowd) foule, *f. ;* (motion) élan,
choc, *m. ;* violence, impétuosité, *f.* There is a
— for the papers ; *on s'arrache les journaux.* Not
to be worth a — ; *ne pas valoir un centime.* There
was a — (to ou for) ; *on se précipita* **vers** . . .

rush (reushe), *v.n.,* se lancer, s'élancer ; se
jeter ; se ruer ; se précipiter ; fondre ; (of the wind
in chimneys) s'engouffrer ; courir à. To — on ;
se précipiter **sur.** To — forward ; *s'élancer*
en avant ; se précipiter en avant. To — in ; *se*
précipiter **dans,** *s'élancer* **dans.** To — upon ; *se*
précipiter **sur.** To — out ; *s'élancer dehors ; se*
précipiter dehors ; sortir brusquement. To —
through ; *s'élancer à travers.*

rush'-broom (-broume), *n.,* (bot.) genêt jonciforme, genêt d'Espagne, *m.*

rush'ing, élan, *m. ;* précipitation, impétuosité, violence, *f.*

rush'light (-laïte), *n.,* chandelle de veille, *f.*

rush'-like (-laïke), *adj.,* comme un jonc ; faible comme un jonc.

rush'-nut (-neute), *n.,* (bot.) souchet comestible, *m.*

rush'y (reush'-), *adj.,* plein de joncs ; fait de
jonc ; de jonc.

rusk (reuske), *n.,* biscotin, *m. ;* biscotte, *f.*

rus'set, *adj.,* roussâtre, roux ; d'un brun
rouge ; (rustic) grossier, rustique.

rus'set (reus'-), *n.,* roux, *m.*

rus'set (reus'-), *n.,* (apple) reinette grise, *f.*

rus'sety, *adj.,* roussâtre.

Rus'sian (reush'a'n), *adj.,* russe, de Russie.
—, ou Russia, leather ; *cuir de Russie, m.*

Rus'sian, *n.,* Russe, *m. ;* (language) russe, *m.*

rust (reuste), *n.,* rouille ; rouillure ; moisissure ; (in grain) rouille, *f.* Black — ; *nielle, f. ;*
charbon, m. Brown — ; *carie, f., noir, m.* To
rub, ou get, the — off ; *dérouiller.*

rust, *v.n.,* se rouiller.

rust, *v.a.,* rouiller.

rus'tic (reus'-), *adj.,* rustre ; rustique ; rude.

rus'tic, *n.,* rustaud, rustre, paysan, *m.*

rus'tically, *adv.,* rustiquement.

rus'ticate (reus-), *v.n.,* demeurer à, ou habiter,
la campagne.

rus'ticate, *v.a.,* reléguer à la campagne ; (at
universities) expulser, ou renvoyer, temporairement. To be —ing ; *être en villégiature.*

rus'ticated (reus-ti-két'-), *adj.,* relégué à la
campagne ; (univ.) renvoyé temporairement.

rustica'tion (reus-ti-ké-), *n.,* vie de campagne ;
(at universities) expulsion temporaire, *f.,* renvoi,
m.

rustic'ity (reus-tiss'-), *n.,* simplicité rustique ;
rusticité, *f.*

rust′iness, *n.*, rouillure, rouille, *f.*

rus′tle (reus's'l), *v.n.*, bruire ; (of trees) frémir, frôler ; (of dresses) faire frou-frou. To — against ; *frôler.*

rus′tle *ou* **rus′tling**, *n.*, frôlement ; bruissement, frémissement ; (of dresses) frou-frou, *m.*

rus′tling, *adj.*, qui bruit, qui frôle, qui fait frou-frou.

rust′y (reust'-), *adj.*, rouillé ; (worn out) usé, vieilli, délabré ; (angry) fâché ; (voice) rauque ; (musty) rance, moisi ; (color) couleur de rouille, roux. To become, *ou* get, — ; (pers.) *se rouiller ; roussir ; s'user, vieillir.*

rut (reute), *n.*, (in a road) ornière, *f.;* (of deer, etc.) rut, *m.*

rut, *v.n.*, être en rut.

rut, *v.a.*, sillonner d'ornières ; creuser des ornières **dans**.

ruth′ful (routh′foule), *adj.*, compatissant.

ruth′fully, *adv.*, avec compassion.

ruth′less (routh′-), *adj.*, impitoyable, implacable; sans pitié; insensible.

ruth′lessly, *adv.*, sans pitié, sans merci.

ruth′lessness, *n.*, dureté de cœur, cruauté, inhumanité, *f.*

rut′ted, rut′ty (reut′-), *adj.*, coupé d'ornières.

rut′ting, *n.*, rut, *m.* — season; *temps du rut, m.*

ry′der (raïd′-), *n.* *V.* **rider** (com.).

rye (raïe), *n.*, seigle, *m.* — bread ; *pain de seigle, m.*

rye′-grass (-grâce), *n.*, ivraie vivace, *f. ;* ray-grass, *m.*

ry′ot (raï-ott), *n.*, ryott, *m. ;* paysan de l'Inde.

S

s, dix-neuvième lettre de l'alphabet, **s**, *m.f.*

Sabbata′rian (-té-), *n.*, rigide observateur du dimanche, *m.*

Sab′bath (-bath), *n.*, (Jews) sabbat ; (fig.) repos ; (Christians) dimanche, *m.*

Sab′bath-break′er (-brèk′-), *n.*, violateur du sabbat, *m.*

Sab′bath-break′ing, *n.*, violation du sabbat, *f.*

sabbat′ic *ou* **sabbat′ical**, *adj.*, sabbatique ; du sabbat.

sa′ber (sé-beur), *n.*, sabre, glaive, *m.* — cut, *ou* thrust ; *coup de sabre, m.* — fish ; (ich.) *trichiure, f.* —tache ; *sabretache, f.*

sa′ber, *v.n.*, sabrer.

Sa′bian *ou* **Sabæ′an** (-bî-), *n.*, Sabéen, *m.*, Sabéenne, *f.*

Sa′bian, *adj.*, sabéen ; (geog.) de Saba (modern Mareb), sabéen.

Sa′bianism (-′iz′m), *n.*, sabéisme, sabisme, sabaïsme, *m.*

sab′ine (-′aïne), *n.*, (bot.) sabine, *f.*

sa′ble (sé-b'l), *n.*, (mam.) martre zibeline ; zibeline, *f. ;* (her.) sable ; (garment) vêtement de deuil, *m.*

sa′ble, *adj.*, de zibeline, de martre zibeline ; (her.) de sable ; (fig.) noir, sombre, de deuil.

sac, *n.*, sac, *m. ;* (anat.) bourse, *f.*

saccade (sak′kéde), *n.*, (man.) saccade, *f.*

sac′charine (-rine), *adj.n.;* saccharin.

sacerdo′tal (sass′eur-dô-), *adj.*, sacerdotal.

sacerdo′talism, *n.*, sacerdotalisme, *m.*

sack, *n.*, sac ; (measure) sac (hectolitre 1·09), *m.;* (of an abscess) poche, *f.;* (wine) vin de Xérès ; vin d'Espagne ; (of a town) sac, saccagement, *m.* To give the — to; (fam.) *renvoyer, congédier ;* (pop.) *donner du balai* **à**. To get the — ; (fam.) *être renvoyé, congédié.* — coat ; *paletot sac, m.* — race ; *course en sac, f.*

sack, *v.a.*, (to pillage) saccager, piller, mettre à sac ; (to put in a sack) ensacher ; (to discharge) renvoyer, remercier.

sack′age (sak′èdje), *n.*, saccagement, sac, *m.*

sack′cloth (-cloth), *n.*, toile à sac, *f. ;* (biblically) sac, *m.*

sack′er, *n.*, saccageur, *m.*

sack′ful (-foule), *n.*, sachée, *f.*

sack′ing, *n.*, (of a town) sac, saccagement, *m.;* (cloth) toile à sac ; (of a bed) sangle, *f.*

sa′cral (sé-), *adj.*, (anat.) du sacrum.

sac′rament, *n.*, sacrement, *m.* To receive the — ; *communier.* To receive the last — ; *être administré.* To administer the last — to; *administrer les derniers sacrements* **à**.

sacrament′al, *adj.*, sacramentel.

sacrament′ally, *adv.*, sacramentellement.

sacramenta′rian *ou* **sacrament′ary**, *n.adj.*, sacramentaire, *f.*

sa′cred (sé-crède), *adj.*, sacré ; saint. — to ; *consacré* **à**.

sa′credly, *adv.*, saintement ; religieusement.

sa′credness, *n.*, sainteté, *f. ;* caractère sacré, *m.*

sac′rifice (-faïze), *v.a.* and *n.*, sacrifier.

sac′rifice (-faïce), *n.*, sacrifice, *m.;* victime, *f.* To sell one's stock at a — ; *vendre ses marchandises au dessous du cours, au grand rabais.* To fall a — to; *être victime* **de**.

sac′rificer (-faïss′-), *n.*, sacrificateur, *m.*

sacrifi′cial (-fish′ial) *ou* **sac′rificatory**, *adj.*, des sacrifices, sacrificatoire.

sac′rilege (-lèdje), *n.*, (thing) sacrilège, *m.*

sacrile′gious (-lîdj′-), *adj.*, sacrilège.

sacrile′giously, *adv.*, sacrilègement ; d'une manière sacrilège ; avec sacrilège.

sacrile′giousness, *n.*, caractère sacrilège, *m.*

sac′ristan, *n.*, sacristain, *m.*

sac′risty, *n.*, sacristie, *f.*

sad, *adj.*, triste ; pitoyable, déplorable ; (of losses) cruel. —iron ; *fer à repasser, m.* To make— ; *rendre triste ; attrister.* To become, get, *ou* grow— ; *s'attrister, devenir triste.* He is a —, *ou* sorry, fellow ; *c'est un triste sire.*

sad′den, *v.a.* and *n.*, attrister; s'attrister.

sad′dle (sad′d'l), *n.*, selle, *f. ;* (of a bowsprit) taquet ; (of a yard) croissant, *m. ;* (of mutton) selle, *f.* Side—; *selle de dame.* To put the — on the wrong horse ; *accuser quelqu'un à faux.*

sad′dle, *v.a.*, seller ; (to load) charger, accabler, embarrasser ; mettre sur le dos **de**. To — with ; *charger* **de**, *mettre sur le dos* **à**. To be —d with ; *avoir sur le dos.* — back; *dos ensellé ;* (tech.) *dos d'âne, m.* — my nag ; (game) *cheval fondu, m.*

sad′dle-backed (-bak′te), *adj.*, ensellé; (arch.) en dos d'âne ; (of chairs) en sacoche.

sad′dle-bags (-bag′ze), *n.pl.*, sacoche, bourse, *f.*

sad′dle-bow (-bô), *n.*, arçon, *m.*

sad′dle-cloth (-cloth), *n.*, housse de cheval, *f.*

sad′dle-horse, *n.*, cheval de selle, *m.*

sad′dle-maker (-mék′-), *n.*, sellier; bourrelier, *m.*

sad′dler, *n.*, sellier, *m.*

sad′dle-room, *n.*, sellerie, *f.*

sad′dlery, *n.*, sellerie, *f.*

sad′dle-tree (-trî), *n.*, bois de selle ; pontet ; (bot.) tulipier, *m.*

Sad′ducee′an (sad-diou-ci-), *adj.*, saducéen.

Sad′ducee (sad-diou-cî), *n.*, saducéen, *m.*, saducéenne, *f.*

Sad′ducism (-ciz′m) *ou* **Sad′duceeism** (-cî-îz′m), *n.*, saducéisme, *m.*

sad′ly, *adv.*, tristement, d'une manière pitoyable ; mal ; déplorablement, cruellement ; (a great deal) beaucoup ; grandement, très, bien. — hurt ; *grièvement blessé.* To be — in want of; *avoir grand besoin* **de**.

sad′ness, *n.*, tristesse, *f.*

safe, *adj.*, sauf ; sain et sauf ; (trustworthy) sûr ; (secure) sûr, intact ; (fig.) prudent ; convenable. —from ; *à l'abri* **de** ; *en sûreté* **contre**.

Your money is — in his hands ; *votre argent est en sûreté entre ses mains, votre argent ne court aucun danger.* — and sound ; *sain et sauf.* — bind — find ; *la méfiance est mère de la sûreté.* It is not — to ; *il n'est pas prudent* **de** ; *il y a un certain danger* **à.**

safe, n., garde-manger ; (for money) coffre-fort, m.

safe'-conduct (-co'n'deuk'te), n., sauf-conduit, m. ; escorte, f.

safe'guard (-gârde), n., sauvegarde ; protection, f. ; (railw.) chasse-pierres, m.

safe'guard, v.a., sauvegarder, protéger.

safe'-keeping (-kîp'-), n., bonne garde ; sûreté, f.

safe'ly, adv., sain et sauf ; sans accident, sans encombre ; sûrement ; en sûreté ; sous bonne garde ; (without fear) sans danger, en toute sécurité.

safe'ness, n., sûreté, f.

safe'ty, n., sûreté, f. ; (preservation) salut, m. To seek — in flight ; *chercher son salut dans la fuite.* Committee of public — ; *comité du salut public,* m. The — of the republic is at stake ; *il y va du salut de la république.* Public — ; *la sûreté publique.*

safe'ty, adj., de sûreté.

safe'ty-lamp, n., lampe de sûreté, f.

safe'ty-pin, n., épingle de nourrice, f.

safe'ty-valve, n., soupape de sûreté, f.

saf'flower (saf'flaoueur), n., carthame, m.

saf'fron (saf'reune), n., (bot., chem., pharm.) safran, m. — flower ; *crocus,* m. Meadow — ; *colchique,* m.

saf'fron, adj., safrané ; couleur de safran ; de safran.

saf'fron, v.a., safraner.

saf'fron-planta'tion (-pla'n'té-), n., safranière, f.

saf'frony, adj., safrané.

sag, v.n., plier, pencher, incliner ; (to sink) s'affaisser ; (nav.) tomber ; fléchir, être courbé.

saga'cious (sa-ghé-shieusse), adj., sagace ; fin, intelligent, pénétrant.

saga'ciously, adv., avec pénétration, avec sagacité.

saga'ciousness ou **sagac'ity,** n., sagacité ; pénétration, f. [sauge, f.

sage (sédje), n., sage, philosophe, m. ; (herb) sage, adj., sage ; prudent.

sage'ly, adv., sagement ; prudemment.

sag'ging (sag-ghigne), n., courbure, f., affaissement, m.

sag'ittal (sadj'-), adj., sagittale (f.).

Sagitta'rius (sadj-it'té-), n., (astron.) le Sagittaire, m.

sag'ittary, adj., sagittale, (f.).

sag'ittate (sadj'-), adj., (bot.) sagitté.

sa'go (sé-gô), n., (food) sagou, m.

sa'goin (sa-goïne), n., (mam.) sapajou, m.

sa'go-tree (-trî), n., (bot.) sagouier ; sagoutier, m.

sa'gy (sé-dji), adj., plein de sauge ; qui a un goût de sauge.

said (sèd'), adv., dit, susdit.

sail (séle), n., voile ; (of a windmill) aile ; (ship) voile ; (on the water) course, ou promenade, à la voile, f. ; (ship) vaisseau, m. ; voile, f. Fore- — ; *misaine ; voile de misaine,* f. Main- — ; *grande voile.* Top- — ; *hunier,* m. Gallant- — ; *voile de perroquet,* f. To set — ; *mettre à la voile ; faire voile, appareiller.* To crowd all — ; *faire force de voiles.* To shorten — ; *diminuer de voiles.* Under — ; *à la voile, sous voiles.* To strike — ; *baisser pavillon ; amener,* ou *saluer,* les voiles. Full — ; *à voiles déployées.*

sail, v.n., faire voile ; cingler, naviguer ; mettre à la voile ; appareiller ; aller ; voguer, se promener en bateau. To — along the coast ; *côtoyer.* To — twelve knots an hour ; *filer douze*

nœuds à *l'heure.* To — round the world ; *faire le tour du monde.* To be about to —, *ou* on the point of —ing ; *être en partance.* To — close to the wind ; *serrer le vent ;* (fig.) *friser l'indécent.* To — under false colors ; *se faire passer pour ce qu'on n'est pas.* To — in company with ; *aller,* ou *naviguer, de conserve* **avec.** To — about ; (cruise) *croiser ; se promener en bateau.* To — down ; (a river) *descendre.* To — up ; *remonter.*

sail, v.a., naviguer **sur,** voguer **sur** ou **dans.**

sail'able (sél'a-b'l), adj., navigable.

sail'-cloth (-cloth), n., toile à voile, f.

sail'er, n., voilier, m. Fast, heavy — ; *bon, mauvais voilier.*

sail'ing, n., navigation ; marche, f. ; (setting sail) appareillage, m. ; (departure) partance, f. ; (flight) vol, m., course ; (excursion) promenade à la voile, f.

sail'ing, adj., à voiles. —-ship ; *bâtiment à voiles,* m. Fast- — ship ; *bâtiment d'une marche rapide ; fin voilier,* m.

sail'ing-boat, n., bateau à voiles, m.

sail'ing-match, course à (la) voile, f.

sail'ing-orders, n., ordre de marche, m.

sail'ing-vessel, n., navire à voiles, m.

sail'-loft, n., voilerie, f. ; magasin à voiles, m.

sail'-maker (-mék'-), n., voilier, m.

sail'-making (-mék'-), n., voilerie, f.

sail'or, n., marin ; matelot, m. Fresh-water —; *marin d'eau douce.* To be a good — ; *avoir le pied marin.*

sail'-yard (-yârde), n., vergue, f.

sain'foin (sé'n'foïne), n., (bot.) sainfoin, m.

saint (sé'n't), n., saint, m., sainte, f. One's —'s day ; *sa fête,* f. All —s' day ; *jour de la Toussaint,* m. ; *la Toussaint,* f. — Swithin's day ; *le jour de la St. Médard.*

saint'ed, adj., saint ; sacré ; canonisé.

saint'-like (-laïke) ou **saint'ly,** adj., saint ; semblable à un saint. To put on a — look ; *faire le bon apôtre.*

saint'ly, adv., saintement, en saint.

saint'ship, n., sainteté, f.

sake, n., égard ; but, m. ; cause, amour, f. For your — ; *par égard pour vous ; à cause de vous ; pour vous.* For my — ; (remembrance) *en mémoire de moi.* For the — of annoying me ; *pour le plaisir de me vexer.* For pity's — ; *par pitié, de grâce.* For God's — ; *pour l'amour de Dieu ; je vous en supplie.* For charity's — ; *par charité, pour l'amour de Dieu.* For the — of appearances ; *pour sauver les apparences.* For the — of going there ; *dans le but, pour le plaisir d'y aller.* For the — of health ; *pour cause de santé.* For the — of money ; *pour l'amour de l'argent.* For their — ; *pour eux-mêmes, pour l'amour d'eux, par égard pour eux.* For conscience' —; *pour l'acquit de sa conscience.* For brevity's — ; *rien que pour la brièveté.* For form's — ; *pour la forme.* For mercy's — ; *pour goodness' —; par grâce, pour l'amour de Dieu.* For argument's — ; *pour un instant, par manière d'argument.*

sa'ker (sé-keur), n., (orni.) sacre, m.

sak'eret (sak'eur'-), n., (orni.) sacret, m.

sal, n., sel, m.

sal'able (sél'a-b'l), adj., vendable ; de bonne vente.

sal'ableness, n., facilité de vente, f.

sal'ad, n., salade, f.

sal'ad-basket, n., panier à salade, m.

sal'ad-bowl (-bôl), n., saladier, m.

sal'ad-mixture, n., assaisonnement pour salades, m.

sal'ad-oil, n., huile d'olive, f.

sal'amander, n., (zoöl.) salamandre, f. ; (cook.) fer à gratiner, four de campagne, m.

salaman'drine (-drine), adj., de salamandre.

sal'aried (-ride), adj., salarié.

sal'ary (-ri), *n*., appointements, *m.pl.* ; traitement ; (of high functionaries) traitement ; (fig.) salaire, *m*.

sal'ary, *v.a.*, salarier, appointer.

sale, *n*., vente, *f.* ; débit, *m.* ; mise en vente, *f.* Deed of —; *contrat de vente, m. ; lettre de vente, f.* — by auction ; *vente aux enchères.* Private —; *vente à l'amiable.* To put up for —; *mettre en vente.* Dull —; *vente difficile.* Quick —; *vente facile.* Ready —; *prompt débit, m.* To command a ready —; *être de bonne vente, f.* For —, on —; *en vente.* For —; (of houses, etc.) *à vendre.* On — or return; *en dépôt, à condition.* — room; *salle de vente, f.*

sale'-goods, *n.pl.*, marchandises de pacotille, *f.pl.*

sal'ep (sa-), *n.*, (food, drink) salep, *m*.

sales'man (sélz'-), *n.*, commis vendeur ; (of clothes) fripier, marchand d'habits ; (of cattle) marchand de bestiaux, *m. ;* (wholesale dealer) marchand en gros; (agent) courtier de commerce, *m. ;* (at market) facteur de la halle, *m.* Dead —: *boucher qui vend à la criée, m.*

sale'work (-weurke), *n.*, ouvrage de pacotille, *m. ;* camelote, pacotille, *f.*

sal'ic (sa-lik'), *adj.*, salique.

sa'lient (sé-), *adj.*, qui saute ; bondit, bondissant ; (projecting) saillant.

sa'liently, *adv.*, d'une manière saillante.

salif'erous (-lif'eur-), *adj.*, qui produit du sel.

sal'ifiable (-faï-a-b'l), *adj.*, (chem.) salifiable.

salifica'tion (-fi-ké-), *n.*, salification, *f.*

sal'ify (sal'i-faïe), *v.a.*, (chem.) salifier.

salina'tion (-né-), *n.*, salaison, *f. ;* salage, *m*.

saline' (-laïne), *adj.*, salin.

saline' (-laïne), *n.*, (spring) source salée, *f.*

sali'va (-laï-), *n.*, salive, *f.*

sali'val (-laï-) *ou* **sali'vary**, *adj.*, salivaire.

sal'ivate (sal'i-), *v.a.*, faire saliver.

saliva'tion (sal'i-vé-), *n.*, salivation, *f.*

sali'vous (-laï-), *adj.*, saliveux.

sal'low (sal'lô), *adj.*, blême, terne, blafard ; jaunâtre, jaune.

sal'lowness, *n.*, couleur blême, *f. ;* teint blême, *m*.

sal'ly, *n.*, excursion ; (arch., of wit) saillie, *f. ;* trait d'esprit, *m. ;* (of youth) écart, *m. ;* boutade; excursion ; (milit.) sortie, *f.*

sal'ly, *v.n.*, (milit.) sortir ; faire une sortie.

sal'ly-port, *n.*, (milit.) poterne, *f. ;* (nav.) sabord de fuite (in a fire-ship), *m*.

salmagun'di (-gheu'n'-), *n.*, salmigondis, *m*.

salm'on (sa'm'eune), *n.*, saumon, *m.* Young —; *saumoneau, m.*

salm'on-fishery *ou* **fishing**, *n.*, pêche du saumon, *f.*

salm'on-trout (-traoute), *n.*, truite saumonée, *f.*

saloon' (sa-loune), *n.*, salle de réception, *f. ;* salon ; (thea.) foyer, *m. ;* (nav.) chambre de première classe, *f.*, premières, *f.pl.* — carriage ; (Eng.) *wagon-salon, m.*

salop', **saloop'**, *n.* *V.* **salep**.

sal'sify (-fi), *n.*, (bot.) salsifis, *m*.

salt (sôlt), *n.*, sel, *m. ;* (fig.) marin, loup de mer, *m.* —**s**, *pl.*, (chem.) sel, *m.sing.* Epsom —s; *sel anglais, sel d'Epsom.* Attic —; *sel attique.* Not to be worth one's —; *ne pas valoir le pain qu'on mange.* To put — on a bird's tail; *mettre du sel sous la queue d'un oiseau.*

salt, *adj.*, salé ; d'un goût salin; (abounding with salt) qui abonde en sel ; à sel.

salt, *v.a.*, saler ; saupoudrer de sel. To — down; *saler.* To — an invoice; *saler une facture.*

salta'tion (sal-té-), *n.*, (leaping) action de sauter; (palpitation) palpitation, *f.*

salt'-box, *n.*, salière de cuisine, *f.*

salt'-cat, *n.*, salignon, *m*.

salt'-cellar, *n.*, salière, *f.*

salt'ed, *adj.*, salé ; (fig.) aguerri.

salt'er (sôlt'-), *n.*, saunier ; (drysalter) saleur, marchand de salaisons, *m*.

salt'ern (sôlt'-), *n.*, saunerie ; saline, *f.*

salt'-fish, *n.*, poisson salé, *m. ;* saline, salaison, *f.*

salt'ier *ou* **sal'tire** (sal-tîre), *n.*, (her.) sautoir, *m.* —wise ; *en sautoir.*

salt'ing (sôlt'-), *n.*, salaison, *f. ;* salage, *m*.

salt'ing-tub (-teube), *n.*, saloir, *m*.

salt'ish (sôlt'-), *adj.*, un peu salé ; saumâtre.

salt'ishness, *n.*, goût salin, *m*.

salt'-lake, *n.*, lac salé, *m*.

salt'less (sôlt'-), *adj.*, sans sel ; fade.

salt'-maker (-mék'-), *n.*, saunier, *m*.

salt'-marsh, *n.*, marais salant ; pré salé, *m*.

salt'-meat (-mîte), *n.*, viande salée ; salaison, *f. ;* salé, *m*.

salt'-mine (-maïne) *ou* **salt'-pit**, *n.*, saline ; mine de sel, *f.*

salt'ness (sôlt'-), *n.*, salure, *f.*

salt'peter (sôlt'pî-teur), *n.*, salpêtre, *m*.

salt'peter-maker (-mék'-), *n.*, salpêtrier, *m*.

salt'peter-pit, *n.*, nitrière, *f.*

salt'peter-works (-weurks), *n.pl.*, salpêtrière, *f.sing.*

saltpe'trous (-pît'-), *adj.*, salpêtreux.

salt'-springs (-sprign'ze), *n.pl.*, sources salées, *f.pl.*

salt'-water (-wôs'-), *n.*, eau de mer; saumure ; eau salée, *f.* — fish ; *poisson de mer, m.*

salt'-works (-weurkce), *n.*, saline, saunerie, *f.*

salt'wort (-weurte), *n.*, (bot.) soude ; herbe au verre ; salicorne, *f. ;* salicor, *m*.

salt'y (sôlt'-), *adj.*, salé ; qui a un goût de sel.

salu'brious (-liou-), *adj.*, salubre.

salu'briously, *adv.*, d'une manière salubre.

salu'brity (-liou-), *n.*, salubrité, *f.*

sal'utary (sal'iou-), *adj.*, salutaire.

saluta'tion (sal'iou-té-), *n.*, salut, *m. ;* salutation, *f.*

salute' (sa-lioute), *n.*, salut ; (kiss) baiser ; (milit., nav.) salut, *m. ;* (of guns) salve, *f.* To fire a —; *tirer une salve ;* (nav.) *saluer.*

salute', *v.a.*, saluer ; (to kiss) baiser, embrasser ; (milit., nav.) saluer (fig.) s'offrir aux regards.

salut'er, *n.*, personne qui salue, *f.*

sal'vage (-vèdje), *n.*, sauvetage; (due) droit de sauvetage, *m.* —money ; *prix du sauvetage, m*.

salva'tion (sal-vé-), *n.*, salut, *m.* — army ; *armée du salut, f.*

salva'tionist, *n.*, membre de l'armée du salut, *m*.

salve (sâve), *n.*, onguent ; (remedy) remède, baume, *m.* Lip —; *pommade pour les lèvres, f.*

salve, *v.a.*, guérir avec des onguents ; (to remedy) secourir ; remédier à.

sal'ver (sal-veur), *n.*, plateau, *m. ;* soucoupe, *f.*

sal'vo (sal-vô), *n.*, réserve ; restriction ; (of artillery) salve, *f.*

sal'vor (sal-veur), *n.*, sauveteur, *m*.

Samar'itan, *n.*, *adj.*, Samaritain, *m.*, Samaritaine, *f.*

same, *adj.*, même. It is all the —; *c'est égal ; c'est tout un ; c'est tout de même ; c'est la même chose.* It is all the — to me; *cela m'est égal, ou parfaitement égal.* Much about the —; *à peu près de même.* The — to you ; *et moi de même.* To do, *ou* say, the —; *faire de même ; en faire, ou en dire, autant.* The very —; *le même.* Just the —; *tout de même.* The — ; *ledit, ladite,* etc. ; *la même chose.* All the —; *néanmoins ; malgré cela ; quand même.* One and the —; *un seul et même.* To come to the —; *revenir au même.* It is the — as saying ; *cela revient à dire.* It's the — old story ; *c'est toujours la même rengaine.*

same'ness, n., identité ; similitude ; ressemblance ; (uniformity) uniformité, monotonie, f.

sam'let, n., saumoneau, m.

sam'phire (-faï'eur), n., (bot.) bacile, fenouil marin, m. ; passe-pierre, perce-pierre, christemarine, f.

sam'ple (sa'm'p'l), n., échantillon, modèle, m. ; montre, f., exemple, m.

sam'ple, v.a., échantillonner.

sam'ple-bottle (-bot't'l), n., bouteille d'échantillon, f.

sam'pler, n., modèle, patron ; (for needle-work) canevas ; (pers.) échantillonneur, m.

sam'pling, n., échantillonnage, m.

san'ative (san-a-tive) (ant.) ou **san'atory**, adj., curatif, sanitaire.

sanator'ium, n., infirmerie ; maison de santé, f.

sanctifica'tion (sai'gn'k-ti-fi-ké-sheune), n., sanctification, f.

sanc'tified (-faïde), adj., sanctifié ; (b.s.) béat. A — air ; une mine béate.

sanc'tifier (-faï'-), n., sanctificateur, m.

sanc'tify (-faïe), v.a., sanctifier.

sanc'tifying (-faï-igne), adj., sanctifiant.

sanctimo'nious (-mô-), adj., saint ; dévot ; (b.s.) béat, hypocrite.

sanctimo'niously, adv., d'un air béat, sous le manteau de la religion.

sanctimo'niousness, n., dévotion affectée, f., air de sainteté, m.

sanc'tion (-sheune), n., sanction, autorité, f.

sanc'tion, v.a., sanctionner, autoriser, approuver.

sanc'titude (-ti-tioude), n., sainteté, f.

sanc'tity (sai'gn'k-ti-té), n., sainteté, f.

sanc'tuary (sai'gn'kt'iou-), n., sanctuaire ; asile ; refuge, m. To take —; se réfugier dans un asile (hist.). Right of — ; droit de sanctuaire, ou d'asile, m. —! —! asile ! asile ! (V. Hugo, Notre Dame de Paris).

sanc'tum, n., sanctuaire ; (pers.) cabinet de travail, cabinet particulier, m. ; retraite, f. — sanctorum ; le saint des saints.

sand, n., sable ; (fine sand) sablon, m. To be embedded in the —; (nav.) être engravé ; être ensablé.

sand, v.a., sabler.

san'dal, n., sandale, espadrille, f. ; (wood) santal, m.

san'dal ou **san'dal-wood** (-woude), n., sandal, santal, bois de santal, de sandal, m.

sand'-bag, n., (milit.) sac à terre, (for windows) bourrelet, m.

sand'-bank, n., banc de sable, m.

sand'-bath, n., (chem.) bain de sable, m.

sand'-blind (-blaï'n'de), adj., qui a la vue trouble.

sand'-box, n., poudrière, f., sablier ; [bot.] sablier, poudrier, m. [sable.

sand-col'ored (-keul'leurde), adj., couleur de

sand'-crack, n., (vet.) bleime, seime, f.

sand'-drift, n., amas de sable, m.

sand'ed, adj., sablé ; (sandy) sablonneux.

sand'-eel, n., lançon, m., équille, f.

sand'-flood (-fleude), n., mer de sable, f.

sand'-glass, n., sablier, m.

sand'-hill, n., dune, f.

sand'-hopper, n., talitre, m.

sand'iness, n., nature sablonneuse, f. ; (color) blond ardent, m. ; couleur vive, f.

sand'ish, adj., sablonneux.

sand'-martin, n., hirondelle de rivage, f.

sand'-paper (-pé-), n., papier de verre, papier sablé, m.

sand'-piper (-païp'-), n., (orni.) bécasseau, m.

sand'-pit, n., sablière ; sablonnière, f.

sand'stone (-stône), n., grès, m. — quarry ; grésière, carrière de grès, f.

sand'-storm, n., ouragan de sable, m.

sand'wich (-'wit'che), n., sandwich, f.

sand'-worm, n., ver arénicole, m.

sand'y, adj., sablonneux ; de sable ; (of color) d'un blond ardent, roux.

sane, adj., sain, sain d'esprit.

sang-froid (saï'gn-froi), n., sang-froid, m.

san'guinary (-gwi'n'-), adj., sanguinaire.

san'guine (sai'gn'gwine), adj., sanguin ; (ardent) ardent, vif ; (confident) plein de confiance, confiant. — hopes ; de vives espérances, f.pl. Beyond my most — hopes ; au-delà de mes plus vives espérances. — temperament ; tempérament sanguin, m. — temper ; caractère ardent, vif, m. He is — of success ; il se fait sûr de réussir ; il s'attend à réussir. I am not very — as to the result ; je n'ai pas grand espoir que l'affaire réussisse.

san'guinely, adv., ardemment ; avec confiance.

san'guineness, n., nature sanguine ; (ardor) ardeur ; (confidence) confiance, assurance, f. ; grand espoir, m.

sanguin'eous (-gwi'n'i-), adj., sanguin.

san'hedrim (-hi-), n., (Jew. ant.) sanhédrin, m.

san'itary, adj., sanitaire, hygiénique. — inspector ; inspecteur de salubrité, m.

san'ity, **sane'ness**, n., état d'un esprit sain, jugement sain, m.

San'scrit, n.adj., sanscrit, m.

sap, n., (bot.) sève ; (milit.) sape, f.

sap, v.a., saper.

sap, v.n., saper ; aller à la sape.

sap'an ou **sap'an-wood** (-woude), n., sapan, bois de sapan, m.

sap'an-tree (-trî), n., (bot.) sapan, m.

sap'-color (-keul'leur), n., couleur végétale, f.

sap'-green (-grîne), n., (paint.) vert de vessie, m.

sap'id, adj., sapide.

sapid'ity ou **sap'idness**, n., sapidité, f.

sa'pience (sé-), n., (l.u.) sagesse, f.

sa'pient (sé-), adj., (l.u.) sage ; doué de sagesse.

sapien'tial (sé-piè'n-shal), adj., (rel.) sapientiaux, adj.m.pl.

sap'less, adj., sans sève ; sec ; desséché.

sap'ling, n., plant ; (of willow, etc.) plantard, m.

sapodil'la, n., (bot.) sapote, sapotille, f.

sapona'ceous (-né-sheusse), adj., saponacé.

saponifica'tion (-fi-ké-), n., saponification, f.

sapon'ify (-faïe), v.a. and n., saponifier ; se saponifier.

sap'per, n., (milit.) sapeur, m. —s and miners ; corps du génie, m.

sap'phic, n., (prosody) saphique, m.

sap'phire (saf'ir), n., (min. orni.) saphir, m.

sap'phirine (-'ine), adj., de saphir, ressemblant au saphir.

sap'piness, n., abondance de sève, f.

sap'py, adj., plein de sève ; de sève ; (foolish) sot.

sap'-wood, n., (bot.) aubier, m.

sar'aband, n., sarabande, f.

Sar'acen, n., Sarrasin, m.

Sar'acen, adj., sarrasin. —wheat, — corn ; sarrasin ; blé noir, m.

Saracen'ic, adj., sarracénique ; (arch.) sarrasin.

sar'casm (sâr-caz'm), n., sarcasme, m.

sarcas'tic ou **sarcas'tical**, adj., sarcastique.

sarcas'tically, adv., avec sarcasme ; d'une manière, ou d'un ton, sarcastique.

sarce'net (sârs'nète), n., florence, taffetas, m.

sarcoph'agus (-gheusse), n., (coffin) sarcophage, m.

sarcot'ic, adj., (med.) sarcotique.

sarcot'ic, n., (med.) sarcotique, m.

sard (sârde) ou **sar'doin** (-doïne), n., (min.) sardonyx, sardoine, f.

sar'dine (sâr-dine), *n.*, (ich.) sardine, *f.*

Sardin'ian, *n.*, Sarde, *m.,f. adj.*, sarde.

sardon'ic, *adj.*, sardonique. A — smile ; *ris sardonique, m.*

sardon'yx (sâr-), *n.*, sardonyx, sardoine, *f.*

Sarma'tian (-mé-), *n.adj.*, sarmate, *m.f.*

sarmen'tose (sâr-mè'n-tôce) *ou* **sarmen'tous** (-teusse), *adj.*, (bot.) sarmenteux.

sar'plier (sâr-plîre), *n.*, (canvas) serpillière, *f.*

sarsaparil'la (sâr-), *n.*, (bot., pharm.) salsepareille, *f.*

sash, *n.*, ceinture ; (mark of distinction) écharpe, *f.*, cordon ; (of a window) châssis, *m.*

sash, *v.a.*, parer d'une ceinture ; (carp.) munir d'un châssis.

sash'-door, *n.*, porte vitrée, *f.*

sash'-frame, *n.*, (carp.) châssis dormant, *m.*

sash'-line, *n.*, corde de châssis, *f.*

sash'-window (-dô), *n.*, fenêtre à châssis, fenêtre à coulisse, fenêtre à guillotine, *f.*

sas'safras, *n.*, (bot.) sassafras, *m.*

Sa'tan (sé-), *n.*, Satan, *m.*

satan'ic *ou* **satan'ical** (sa-), *adj.*, satanique.

satan'ically (sa-), *adv.*, d'une manière satanique.

satch'el, *n.*, sachet, petit sac, sac d'écolier, *m. ;* gibecière, *f.;* (of lawyers) sac de procès, sac, *m.*

sate (séte), *v.a.*, rassasier (with, **de**).

sate'less, *adj.*, insatiable.

sat'ellite (sa-tèl'laïte), *n.*, satellite, *m.*

sa'tiate (sé-shi-éte), *v.a.*, rassasier (with, **de**).

sa'tiated, *adj.*, rassasié **de**.

sa'tiating, *n.*, assouvissement, *m.*

sati'ety (sa-taï-è-), *n.*, satiété, *f.*

sat'in, *n.*, satin, *m.*

sat'in, *adj.*, de satin ; satiné. —-ribbon ; *ruban de satin, m.* —-wood ; (timber) *bois de citron, m.*

satinet', *n.*, satinade, *f.*

sat'ining, *n.*, satinage, *m.*

sat'iny, *adj.*, satiné.

sat'ire (sat'aïeur *ou* sat'eur), *n.*, satire, *f.*

satir'ic *ou* **satir'ical** (-tir'-), *adj.*, satirique.

satir'ically, *adv.*, satiriquement.

sat'irist (sat'ir'-), *n.*, satirique, satiriste, *m.*

sat'irize (sat'ir'aïze), *v.a.*, satiriser.

satisfac'tion, *n.*, satisfaction, *f.;* contentement, plaisir ; (discharge) acquittement, *m.;* (amends) réparation ; (concession, apology) satisfaction, raison, réparation, *f.* To give — ; (to please, to suit) *donner de la satisfaction ;* (to apologize) *donner satisfaction à ;* (to fight) *rendre raison à.*

satisfac'torily, *adv.*, d'une manière satisfaisante, suffisamment.

satisfac'toriness, *n.*, caractère satisfaisant, *m.*

satisfac'tory, *adj.*, satisfaisant.

sat'isfied (-faï'-), *n.*, qui satisfait.

sat'isfy (-faïe), *v.a.*, satisfaire ; satisfaire à ; (passions) assouvir ; contenter ; (to convince) convaincre ; persuader ; (to assure) assurer ; (a debt) acquitter ; (the appetite) rassasier. To — one's vengeance ; *assouvir sa vengeance.* To — one's appetite ; *se rassasier.* To be satisfied of ; *être persuadé, sûr, convaincu* **de**. To be satisfied with ; *être satisfait* **de** ; *être content* **de**. To be rather more than satisfied; *en avoir plus qu'assez.* To be satisfied about ; *être fixé* **sur**.

sat'isfy, *v.n.*, satisfaire à.

sat'isfying, *adj.*, rassasiant, qui rassasie.

sa'trap (sé-), *n.*, satrape, *m.*

sa'trapy (sé-tra-pi), *n.*, satrapie, *f.*

sat'urable (sat'iou-ra-b'l), *adj.*, saturable.

sat'urant, *adj.*, saturant.

sat'urate (sat'iou-), *v.a.*, saturer.

satura'tion (sat'iou-ré-), *n.*, saturation, *f.*

Sat'urday (sat'eur-), *n.*, samedi, *m.*

Sat'urn (sat'eurne), *n.*, (myth., astron., old chem.) Saturne, *m.*

Saturna'lia (-'eur-né-), *n.pl.*, saturnales, *f.pl.*

Saturna'lian, *adj.*, des saturnales.

Satur'nian, *adj.*, de Saturne, (prosody) saturnien.

sat'urnine (sat'eur-naïne), *adj.*, sombre ; taciturne, mélancolique ; (old chem.) de Saturne, de plomb.

sat'yr (sa-teur *ou* sé-teur), *n.*, (myth., ent.) satyre, *m.*

sauce (sôss), *n.*, sauce ; (insolence) insolence, impertinence, *f.* Butter- — ; *sauce blanche.* Sweet- — ; *sauce douce.* To serve any one with the same — ; *rendre la pareille à quelqu'un ; rendre à quelqu'un la monnaie de sa pièce.*

sauce, *v.a.*, assaisonner ; (the palate) flatter ; (to be impudent to) dire des insolences **à**, dire des sottises **à**.

sauce'-boat (-bôte), *n.*, saucière, *f.*

sauce'-box, *n.*, insolent, impertinent, *m.*

sauce'pan, *n.*, casserole, marmite, *f.;* poêlon, *m.* —ful; *casserolée, f.*

sau'cer, *n.*, soucoupe, *f.* —ful; *soucoupe pleine ou plein une soucoupe.*

sauce'-tureen, *n.*, saucière, *f.*

sau'cily (sô-), *adv.*, insolemment ; avec impertinence.

sau'ciness (sô-), *n.*, insolence ; impertinence, *f.*

sau'cy (sô-), *adj.*, insolent ; impertinent. A — fellow ; *un insolent, un impertinent.*

sauer kraut (saour-kraoute), *n.*, choucroute, *f.*

saun'ter (sô'n'-), *v.n.*, flâner ; badauder ; se promener sans objet.

saun'ter, *v.a.*, perdre, dissiper, gaspiller. To — away the time ; *perdre son temps à flâner ; user son temps sans profit.*

saun'terer, *n.*, flâneur, *m.*, flâneuse, *f.;* badaud, *m.*, badaude, *f.*

saun'tering, *n.*, flânerie ; badauderie, *f.*

saun'tering, *adj.*, de flâneur, de badaud.

sau'rians (sô-), *n.pl.*, sauriens, *m.pl.*

sau'sage (sô-cèdje), *n.*, saucisse, *f.;* saucisson, *m.* — meat ; *chair à saucisse, f.*

sav'age (sav'èdje), *adj.*, sauvage ; féroce ; barbare ; farouche, furieux.

sav'age (sav'èdje), *n.*, sauvage, *m., f.*

sav'agely, *adv.*, sauvagement, d'une manière sauvage ; en sauvage ; (brutally) brutalement ; d'une manière féroce.

sav'ageness, *n.*, état sauvage, *m. ;* férocité ; brutalité ; sauvagerie, *f.*

sav'agery, *n.*, férocité ; barbarie, *f.*

savan'na *ou* **savan'nah**, *n.*, savane, *f.*

save, *v.a.*, sauver ; (to spare) épargner, éviter, sauver ; (to prevent) prévenir ; (to put by) mettre de côté ; amasser ; réserver ; (to economize) économiser, ménager, épargner ; (not to lose) ne pas manquer, ne pas perdre, profiter **de**, arriver à temps **pour**. In order to — the post ; *pour ne pas manquer la poste, le courrier.* God — the King! *Dieu sauve le roi ! Vive le roi !* To — trouble ; *épargner de la peine.* To — appearances ; *sauver les apparences, ou les dehors.* I — five pounds by it ; *j'y gagne cinq livres.*

save, *v.n.*, économiser. To — up ; *faire des économies.*

save, *prep.*, hormis ; excepté ; sinon ; si ce n'est ; sauf. — reverence ; *sauf votre respect, sauf respect.*

save'-all (-ôl), *n.*, brûle-tout, *m.*

sav'eloy (sav'-), *n.*, cervelas, *m.*

sav'er (sév'-), *n.*, (liberator) sauveur, libérateur, *m.*, libératrice, *f. ;* (economiser) économe, ménager, *m.*, ménagère, *f.*

sav'in (sav'-) *ou* **sav'ine** (sav'ine), *n.*, (bot.) sabine, *f.*

sav'ing (sév'-), *n.*, épargne ; économie ; (jur.) (reservation) réserve ; exception, *f.*

sav'ing (sév'-), *adj.*, (pers.) économe, ménager ; (of things) économique ; (fig.) de réserve ; (salutary) salutaire. — grace ; *grâce justifiante, f.* — clause ; *réservation, f.*

sav'ing (sév'-), *prep.*, sauf ; excepté. — your reverence ; *sauf votre respect.*

sav'ingly (sév'-), *adv.* V. **sparingly.**

sav'ingness (sév'-), *n.*, épargne ; économie, *f.* ; (biblically) salut, *m.*

sav'ings-bank (sév'ign'z'-), *n.*, caisse d'épargne, *f.*

Sav'ior (sév'ior), *n.*, Sauveur, *m.*

savonette', *n.*, savonnette, *f.*

sa'vor (sé-vor), *n.*, saveur, *f.* ; goût, fumet, *m.* ; odeur, *f.*

sa'vor (sé-vor), *v.a.*, goûter avec plaisir ; savourer.

sa'vor, *v.n.*, avoir le goût **de** ; sentir. To — of ; *sentir* le, la, les . . .

sa'vorily (sé-vor'-), *adv.*, savoureusement ; avec goût ; avec plaisir.

sa'voriness, *n.*, goût agréable, *m.* ; bonne saveur, odeur agréable, *f.*

sa'vory (sé-vori), *adj.*, savoureux ; qui a de la saveur, du fumet ; délicieux ; aromatique. A — tongue ; *une langue fourrée.*

sa'vory (sé-), *n.*, (bot.) sarriette, *f.*

saw (sô), *n.*, scie, *f.*

saw (sô), *n.*, (saying) proverbe ; adage ; dicton, *m.* An old — ; *un vieux dicton.*

saw (sô), *v.a.* and *n.*, scier ; se scier.

saw'-bones (-bô'n'ze), *n.*, carabin, *m.*

saw'-dust (-deuste) *ou* **saw'der**, *n.*, sciure, sciure de bois, *f.*

saw'-file, *n.*, lime à scier, *f.*, tiers-point, *m.*

saw'-mill, *n.*, scierie, *f.*

saw'-pit, *n.*, fosse de scieurs de long, *f.*

saw'-yard (-yârde), *n.*, scierie, *f.*

saw'yer (sô-yeur), *n.*, scieur ; scieur de long, *m.* — 's block ; *chantier, m.*

sax'atile (saks'a-), *adj.*, saxatile ; de rocher.

sax'horn, *n.*, (instr.) saxhorn, *m.*

sax'ifrage (sak'ci-frèdje), *n.*, (bot.) saxifrage, *f.*

Sax'on, *adj.*, saxon, de Saxe.

Sax'on, *n.*, Saxon, *m.*, Saxonne, *f.* ; (language) saxon, anglo-saxon, *m.*

say, *v.a.* (*preterit* and *past part.*, Said), dire, parler ; marquer ; réciter. I —! *dites donc! dis donc!* Let us — no more about it ; *n'en parlons plus.* They — ; *on dit.* That is saying a good deal ; *c'est beaucoup dire.* My watch —s one o'clock ; *ma montre marque une heure.* To — right ; *dire vrai.* It —s, it is said ; *on dit.* — ou that is to — ; *c'est à dire ; en d'autres termes ; autrement.* Be it said ; *soit dit.* It is hard to —; *on ne sait pas* ou *c'est difficile à dire.* It is hard to — whether ; *il est difficile de dire si.* That is said every day ; *cela se dit tous les jours.* To — nay ; *refuser.* I cannot — nay to you ; *je ne sais rien vous refuser.* What — you to B.? *que pensez-vous de B.?* I must — that ; *je dois avouer que.* To — nothing of ; *sans parler* **de.** You don't — so! *ah bah! pas possible!* — $1000 ; *disons,* ou *mettons, mille dollars.* To — again ; *répéter, redire.*

say, *n.*, dire ; mot ; mot à dire ; ce qu'on a à dire, *m.* To have one's — ; *dire son mot.*

say'ing (sé-igne), *n.*, mot, proverbe, dicton, (statement) dire, *m.* ; sentence, maxime, expression, *f.* As the — is ; *comme on dit.* —s and doings ; *faits et dires, faits et gestes, m.pl.*

scab, *n.*, (med.) croûte ; (vet.) gale, rogne, *f.*

scab'bard, *n.*, fourreau, *m.* ; gaine, *f.* — maker ; *gainier,* **m.**

scabbed (scab'de), **scab'by**, *adj.*, couvert de gale ; galeux ; (vile) vil.

scab'biness, *n.*, état galeux, *m.* ; (fig.) vilenie, bassesse, *f.*

sca'bious (ské-), *adj.*, scabieux.

scaf'fold, *n.*, échafaud, *m.* To ascend the —; *monter sur l'échafaud.*

scaf'fold, *v.a.*, échafauder.

scaf'folding, *n.*, échafaudage, *m.* ; estrade ; (fig.) charpente, *f.* —-pole ; *perche d'échafaudage, f.*

scaglio'la (scal'yi-ô-), *n.*, stuc, *m.*

scal'able (ské-la-b'l), *adj.*, que l'on peut escalader.

scalade' (sca-lâde), *n.*, escalade, *f.*

scald (scôlde), *n.*, brûlure ; (med.) teigne, *f.* — weed ; (bot.) cuscute, teigne, *f.* — head ; *teigne.*

scald (scôlde), *v.a.*, échauder ; (meat) blanchir ; brûler ; faire bouillir. To — one's self ; *s'échauder ; se brûler.* To — one's hand ; *s'échauder la main.*

scald'ing (scôld'-), *n.*, échaudage ; brûlure, *f.* — -house, — -tub ; *échaudoir, m.*

scald'ing (scôld'-), *adj.*, bouillant. — -hot ; *tout bouillant.*

scale, *n.*, échelle, *f.* ; (balance) bassin, plateau, *m.* ; (gradation, mus., math., geog.) échelle ; (of a fish) écaille ; (bot.) écaille, *f.* —s, pair of —s ; (for weighing) *balance, f. sing.* —s ; (mus.) *gammes, f.pl.* Sliding- — ; *échelle mobile.* Drawn to the — of ; *dressé à l'échelle* **de.** On a large, small — ; *sur une grande, petite échelle ; en grand, en petit.*

scale, *v.a.*, (to climb) escalader ; (to pick off) écailler ; (a cannon) souffler, flamber ; (to weigh, measure, compare, estimate) peser, mesurer, comparer, estimer ; atteindre le poids **de.** To — teeth ; *enlever le tartre des dents.*

scale, *v.n.*, s'écailler.

scaled (skélde), *adj.*, écaillé, écailleux, à écailles.

scale'less (skél'-), *adj.*, sans écailles.

scale'-maker (-mék'-), *n.*, balancier, fabricant de balances, *m.*

scalene' (sca-lîne), *adj.*, (geom.) scalène ; (cone) oblique.

sca'liness (skél'-), *n.*, nature écailleuse, *f.* ; (fig.) mesquinerie, ladrerie, *f.*

scal'ing, *n.*, (climbing) escalade, *f.* ; (peeling off) écaillage, *m.* ; (of a gun) flambage, *m.* — ladder ; *échelle de siège, f.*

scal'lion (scal'lieune), *n.*, (bot.) échalote, *f.*

scal'lop (skol'leupe), *n.*, (mollusc.) pétoncle ; coquille ; pèlerine, *f.* ; peigne, *m.* ; (notching) denteleure, *f.* ; (in needlework) feston, *m.*

scal'lop (skol'leupe), *v.a.*, denteler ; (in needlework) festonner.

scalp, *n.*, cuir chevelu ; crâne ; os frontal ; (fig.) front, sommet, *m.* — wound ; *blessure à la tête, f.*

scalp, *v.a.*, scalper. *v.n.*, s'entrescalper.

scal'pel, *n.*, (surg.) scalpel, *m.*

scalp'er, *n.*, (surg.) rugine, *f.*

scalp'ing, *n.*, action de scalper, *f.*

scalp'ing-knife (-naïfe), *n.*, couteau à scalper, *m.*

sca'ly (skél'i), *adj.*, écaillé ; (bot.) écailleux à écailles ; (pop.) (stingy) chiche, mesquin ladre.

scam'mony, *n.*, (bot.) scammonée, *f.*

scamp, *n.*, chenapan, mauvais sujet, vaurien, *m.* ; canaille, *f.* Young — ; *petit polisson, m.*

scam'per, *v.n.*, courir ; jouer des talons ; s'enfuir. To — off, to — away ; *détaler ; décamper lestement ; prendre ses jambes à son cou.*

scan, *v.a.*, examiner minutieusement ; scruter ; mesurer des yeux ; éplucher ; (verses) scander.

scan'dal, *n.*, scandale, *m.* ; honte ; médisance, *f.* ; opprobre, *m.* To raise a — ; *faire du scandale.* To be a — to ; *être la honte* **de** ; *faire la honte* **de.**

scan'dalize (-'aïze), *v.a.*, scandaliser, choquer ; (to defame) médire **de**, diffamer, calomnier.

scan'dalizing (-'aïz'-), *adj.*, scandaleux.

scan'dal-mon'ger (-meu'gn'gheur), *n.*, médisant ; colporteur de médisances, *m.*

scan'dalous, *adj.*, scandaleux ; honteux ; calomnieux ; diffamatoire, médisant.

scan'dalously, *adv.*, scandaleusement ; honteusement ; avec médisance.

scan'dalousness, *n.*, caractère scandaleux, scandale, *m.*

scan'dent *adj.*, (bot.) grimpant.

scan'ning, *n.*, examen minutieux, *m. ;* (in poetry) action de scander, scansion, prosodie, *f.*

scan'sion (-sheune), *n.*, scansion, *f.*

scant, *v.a.*, restreindre, borner, resserrer ; distribuer chichement ; donner à contre-cœur.

scant, *v.n.*, (nav.) (of the wind) refuser ; diminuer, faiblir.

scant. *V.* **scanty.**

scant'ily, *adv.*, (narrowly) étroitement, d'une manière rétrécie ; (insufficiently) faiblement, d'une manière insuffisante, chétivement, mesquinement.

scant'iness, *n.*, (narrowness) étroitesse, *f.*, état rétréci, *m.*, limites étroites, *f.pl. ;* (insufficiency) faiblesse, insuffisance, mesquinerie, *f.*

scan'tle (sca'n't'l), *v.a.*, couper en morceaux, morceler.

scant'ling, *n.*, faible quantité, *f. ;* fragment ; (nav.) échantillon, *m. ;* (carp.) volige, *f.*

scant'y, *adv.*, (narrow) étroit, rétréci, étriqué ; (poor, insufficient) modique, faible, peu abondant, insuffisant, chétif, mesquin ; (of the hair) clairsemé. — of ; *sobre* **de** ; *avare* **de** ; *économe* **de** ; *ménager* **de.**

scape, *n.*, (bot.) hampe ; (arch.) apophyge, *f. ;* fût, *m.*

scape'-goat (-gôte), *n.*, bouc émissaire ; souffre-douleur, *m.*

scape'-grace, *n.*, vaurien, mauvais garnement, mauvais sujet, *m.*

scape'ment, *n.*, (horl.) échappement, *m.*

scape'-wheel, *n.*, (horl.) roue à échappement ; roue de rencontre, *f.*

scap'ula, *n.*, (anat.) omoplate, *f.*

scap'ular, *adj.*, (anat.) scapulaire.

scap'ulary, *n.*, (c.rel.) scapulaire, *m.*

scar (scăr), *n.*, cicatrice ; balafre, *f.*

scar (scăr), *v.a.*, cicatriser ; balafrer.

scar'ab, scar'abee, *n.*, (ent.) scarabée, *m.*

scar'amouch (-maoutshe), *n.*, scaramouche, *m.*

scarce (skèrce), *adj.*, rare. To make one's self — ; *disparaître ; décamper ; filer.*

scarce'ly, *adv.*, à peine ; presque pas ; guère ; pas trop ; difficilement ; rarement. — ever ; *presque jamais.* — any one ; *presque personne.* — anything ; *presque rien.* — anywhere ; *presque nulle part.*

scarce'ness *ou* **scar'city** (skèr'-), *n.*, rareté ; disette, *f.*

scare (skère), *n.*, panique, frayeur subite, *f.*

scare, *v.a.*, effrayer, épouvanter, effaroucher ; effarer.

scare'crow (skèr'crô), *n.*, épouvantail, *m.*

scarf (scărfe), *n.*, (*scarfs*) écharpe ; cravate longue, (for ladies) châtelaine, *f. ;* (carp.) assemblage, *m.* — pin ; *épingle de cravate, f.* —wise, *adv.*, en écharpe.

scarf, *v.a.*, nouer en écharpe ; (carp.) assembler.

scarfed (scărf'te), *adj.*, paré d'une écharpe ; (carp.) assemblé.

scarf'ing, *n.*, (carp.) assemblage, *m.*

scarf'skin, *n.*, (anat.) épiderme, *m.*

scarifica'tion (-fi-ké-), **scar'ifying,** *n.*, (surg.) scarification, *f.*

scar'ificator (-fi-ké-teur), *n.*, (surg.) scarificateur, *m.*

scar'ifier (-faï'-), *n.*, scarificateur, *m.*

scar'ify (-faïe), *v.a.*, scarifier.

scarlati'na (scăr-la-tî-), *n.*, (med.) fièvre scarlatine ; scarlatine, *f.*

scar'let (scăr-), *n.*, écarlate, *f.*

scar'let, *adj.*, écarlate ; vermeil.

scar'let-fe'ver (-fî-), *n.*, fièvre scarlatine, *f.*

scar'let-run'ner (-reun'-), *n.*, haricot à rame, haricot d'Espagne, *m.*

scarp (scârpe), *n.*, (fort.) escarpe ; (her.) écharpe, *f.*

scathe'less (scath'-), *adj.*, sans dommage ; sans perte. *V.* **unhurt.**

scath'ing (skéth'-), *adj.*, écrasant, sévère, qui porte coup. A — fire ; *un feu écrasant.*

scat'ter, *v.a.*, disperser ; répandre ; dissiper ; éparpiller, disséminer.

scat'ter, *v.n.*, se disperser ; se répandre, s'éparpiller ; (of fire-arms) écarter.

scat'tered (scat'teurde) *adj.*, dispersé ; répandu ; dissipé ; éparpillé, épars ; (of the hair) clair-semé.

scat'tering, *n.*, éparpillement, *m. ;* dispersion, *f.*

scat'teringly, *adv.*, éparsement, de loin en loin, çà et là.

scav'enge (sca-vè'n'dje), *v.a.*, ébouer, balayer.

scav'enger (sca-vè'n'djeur), *n.*, boueur ; balayeur, *m.*

scav'enging, *n.*, ébouage, balayage, *m.*

scene (cîne), *n.*, scène, *f. ;* (place) théâtre, *m. ;* (thea.) scène, décoration, *f.* —s, *pl.*, (thea.) décors, *m.pl.* Behind the —s ; (thea.) *derrière le rideau ; dans la coulisse.* To get up, *ou* make, a — ; *faire une scène.* The — is laid in ; *la scène se passe à.*

sce'nery (cî'n'ri), *n.*, scène ; vue ; perspective, *f. ;* paysage, *m. ;* (thea.) scène, *f.*, décorations, *f.pl.*, décors, *m.pl.*

sce'nic (cî'n'-), *adj.*, scénique.

scenograph'ic *ou* **scenograph'ical** (ci-no-), *adj.*, scénographique.

scenograph'ically (ci-no-), *adv.*, scénographiquement.

sceno'graphy (ci-nog'-), *n.*, scénographie, *f.*

scent (sè'n'te), *n.*, odeur ; senteur, *f. ;* parfum, *m. ;* (track) piste ; (of the boar) trace, *f. ;* (of the dog) nez, *m. ;* (of the stag) voie, *f.* Upon the right — ; *sur la voie.* On the wrong — ; *en défaut.* To put on the wrong —, to put off the — ; *mettre sur la fausse voie, mettre en défaut ;* (fig.) *donner le change à, dépister.* To get — of ; *avoir vent de ; découvrir.*

scent (sè'n'te), *v.a.*, parfumer (with, **de**) ; (of animals) sentir, flairer.

scent'-bag, *n.*, sachet, sachet d'odeurs, *m.*

scent'-bottle (-bot't'l), *n.*, flacon d'odeur, *m.*

scent'-box, *n.*, cassolette ; boîte à parfums, *f.*

scent'less, *adj.*, inodore ; sans odeur, sans parfum ; (of animals) qui n'a pas de nez.

scep'tic (skèp'-), *n.*, sceptique, *m.f.*

scep'tic *ou* **scep'tical** (skèp'-), *adj.*, sceptique.

scep'tically (skèp'-), *adv.*, sceptiquement ; d'une manière sceptique ; avec scepticisme.

scep'ticism (skèp'ti-ciz'm), *n.*, scepticisme, pyrrhonisme, *m.*

scep'ter, *n.*, sceptre, *m.*

scep'ter (sèp'teur), *v.a.*, revêtir d'un sceptre.

scep'tered (sèp'teurde) *adj.*, portant le sceptre.

sched'ule (skèd'youle), *n.*, rouleau, *m. ;* liste, *f. ;* inventaire ; (com.) bilan, *m.* To file a — ; (in bankruptcy) *déposer son bilan.*

sched'ule, *v.a.*, enregistrer, **inventorier,** inscrire.

scheik, *n.*, cheik, scheik, *m.*

scheme (skî'me), *n.*, plan ; projet, système, *m. ;* (b.s.) intrigue, *f.*

scheme (skî'me), *v.a.* and *n.*, projeter ; faire des projets, (b.s.) intriguer, ruser.

schem'er (skî'm'-), *n.*, faiseur de projets ; rêveur ; homme à projets, (b.s.) intrigant, exploiteur, *m.*

schem'ing (skî'm'-), *adj.*, à projets ; intrigant ; rusé.

schism (ciz'm), n., schisme, m.

schismat'ic (ciz'mat'ik), n., schismatique, m.f.

schismat'ic ou **schismat'ical** (ciz'-), adj., schismatique.

schismat'ically (ciz'-), adv., en schismatique.

schol'ar (skol'-), n., écolier, m., écolière, f.; disciple, m.; élève, m.f.; (learned person) érudit, m., érudite, f., homme instruit, savant, m.; savante, f.; (at public schools, on a foundation) boursier, m. Day—; externe, m. Good Latin —; bon latiniste, m. Greek —; helléniste, m. To be a good French —; savoir bien le français, posséder à fond le français. —s differ on that point; les érudits ne sont pas d'accord là-dessus.

schol'ar-like (-laïke), schol'arly, adj., d'écolier; d'érudit, de savant; savant. A scholarly speech; un savant discours; un discours plein d'érudition.

schol'ar-like (-laïke), adv., en écolier.

schol'arship, n., érudition, f.; savoir, m.; (at public schools) bourse, f.

scholas'tic ou **scholas'tical**, adj., scolastique.

scholas'tic, n., scolastique, m.

scholas'tically, adv., scolastiquement.

scholas'ticism (-ciz'm), n., scolastique, f.

scho'liast (skô-), n., scoliaste, m.

scho'lium (skô-), n., (scholia ou scholiums) scolie, f.; (math.) scolie, m.

school (skoule), n., école; pension; institution, f.; pensionnat, m.; classe, salle, f. Boarding—; pension; pensionnat. Private —; pensionnat. Fencing—; salle d'armes. Day—; externat, m. —-room; classe. Infant—; salle d'asile, maison d'éducation, école maternelle, institution. National —; école communale. At —; en pension; à l'école. In —; en classe. Charity —; école gratuite. Board —; école primaire. Of the old —; de la vieille roche.

school, v.a., instruire, enseigner; (to reprimand) réprimander; faire la leçon à. To — one's self; se faire à, savoir supporter, endurer; s'aguerrir contre.

school'-agent, m., agent scolastique, m.

school'-apparatus ou **school'-fittings**, n., matériel d'école, m.

school'-assistant, n., sous-maître, maître d'étude, m.; maîtresse d'étude, f.

school'-board, n., comité scolaire, m.

school'-boy (-boï), n., écolier, m. Still a —; encore sur les bancs, encore au collège. In our —-days; quand nous étions sur les bancs du collège.

school'-day, n., jour de classe, m. —s, pl., temps des études, m.sing.; études, f.pl.

school'-fellow (-fèl'lô), n., camarade de collège, de pension, de classe, d'école, m.f.; condisciple, m.

school'-girl (-gheurle), n., écolière, f.

school'ing (skoul'-), n., instruction, enseignement; (reprimand) réprimande, f.

school'man (skoul'-), n., savant; philosophe; (Mid. Ages) scolastique, m.

school'master (skoul-mâs-teur), n., maître d'école, maître de pension; chef d'institution, m.

school'mistress (skoul-mis-trèce), n., maîtresse d'école, maîtresse de pension, f.

school'-ship, n., vaisseau-école, m.

school'-time (skoul-taïme), n., classe, f.; temps de la classe, m.; heures de classe, f.pl.

schoon'er (skou'n'-), n., (nav.) goélette, f.

schot'tishe, n., (dance) schotisch, f.

sciat'ic (saï-), adj., (anat.) sciatique.

sciat'ica (saï-), n., (med.) sciatique, f.

sci'ence (saï-é'n'ce), n., science, f.

scientif'ic ou **scientif'ical** (saï-), adj., (pers.) de science, savant; (of things) scientifique. — man; homme de science, savant, m.

scientif'ically (saï-), adv., scientifiquement.

sci'entist, n., homme de science, savant, m.

scim'iter, n., cimeterre, m.

scin'tillant, adj., scintillant.

scin'tillate, v.n., scintiller.

scintilla'tion (ci'n'til'lé-), n., scintillation, .

sci'olist (saï-), n., demi-savant, m.

sci'on (saï-), n., (bot.) scion, m.

scir'rhous, adj., (med.) squirreux.

scir'rhus, n., (med.) squirre, m.

scis'sible (-ci'b'l) ou **scis'sile** (-cile), adj., scissile; sécable.

scis'sion (sij'eune), n., scission; séparation, division, f.

scis'sors (ciz'zeurze), n.pl., ciseaux, m.pl. Pair of —; paire de ciseaux, f. —-sheath, ou case; étui à ciseaux, m.

Sclavo'nian ou **Sclavon'ic**, adj., slave, slavon.

scobs, n.pl., râpure, scorie, f.sing.

scoff, n., raillerie; moquerie, f.

scoff, v.a., railler; se moquer de; se rire de, tourner en dérision.

scoff, v.n., railler; se moquer. Why do you — at me? pourquoi vous moquez-vous de moi?

scoff'er, n., railleur, moqueur, m.

scoff'ing, n., raillerie, moquerie, f.

scoff'ing, adj., railleur, moqueur.

scoff'ingly, adv., avec raillerie, par moquerie.

scold (scôlde), v.n., gronder; crier; bougonner (Daudet).

scold, v.a., gronder; crier, criailler après.

scold (scôlde), n., (virago) grondeuse, criailleuse; harpie; mégère; (scolding) gronderie, f.

scold'ing (scôld'-), n., gronderie, criaillerie, f. To give a — to; gronder; (fam.) laver la tête à.

scold'ing, adj., grondeur; criailleur.

scold'ingly, adv., en grondant; en criaillant.

scol'lop, n. V. **scallop**.

scolopen'dra, n., (ent.) scolopendre, f.

scolopen'drium, n., (bot.) doradille, f.

sconce, n., chandelier à bras, candélabre; (bracket) bras de lumière, m.; (head) caboche, boule, f.

scoop (scoupe), n., grande cuiller; (nav.) écope; (for cheese) sonde; (for coal) seau à charbon; (shovel) pelle à main, f.; (of brewers) fourquet; (stroke) coup, m.

scoop, v.a., vider; ôter, évider; (nav.) écoper. To — out; enlever, ôter (en creusant, en puisant); creuser; évider.

scoop'ing (out), n., évidement, enlèvement, m.

scope (scôpe), n., (aim) but, objet, m., visée, fin; dessein, m., vue, f.; (space) espace, m., place, f.; (liberty) liberté, carrière, f., essor, cours; avenir, m. To have — enough; avoir assez de place, d'espace. To give full — to; donner libre carrière, libre essor à. To have full —; avoir libre carrière, liberté entière; (fam.) avoir ses franches coudées.

scorbu'tic (-biou-), adj., scorbutique.

scorbu'tically (-biou-), adv., par le scorbut.

scorch (scortshe), v.a. and n., roussir, brûler, rôtir, griller.

scorch'ing (scortsh-), adj., brûlant, ardent, très chaud. —-hot; tout brûlant. At a — pace; à tout briser, à tout casser.

score (scôre), n., (notch) entaille, coche; (mus.) partition; (line) ligne, f., trait; (motive) motif, m., raison, cause, f.; chapitre; compte; (bill) compte, écot; (twenty) vingt, m., vingtaine, f.; (games) nombre de points, m. On, ou upon, a new —; sur nouveaux frais. On that —; sur ce chapitre, à cet égard. On the — of; sur l'article de; à titre de; en raison, en considération de; à cause de; au sujet de. Upon what —? à quel titre? en vertu de quoi? Three—; soixante. Four—; quatre-vingts. What is the —? comment va la partie ou où en sommes-nous?

score, v.a., faire une coche à, entailler; marquer; (as a debt) porter en compte; (mus.) orchestrer. To — over; avoir le dessus, gagner

la partie; l'emporter sur. To — out; *effacer*. To
— up; *marquer, compter*. Have you —d? (at
billiards) *avez-vous carambolé*, ou *fait quelque
chose?* Who will —? *qui veut marquer?*

scor'er (scôr'-), *n.*, marqueur, *m.*

sco'ria (scô-), *n.*, (*scoriæ*) scorie, *f.*

scorifica'tion (-ri-fi-ké-), *n.*, scorification, *f.*

scor'ify (scô-ri-faïe), *v.a.*, scorifier.

scor'ing (scôr'-), *n.*, (mus.) orchestration, *f.*;
(at billiards) marque, action de marquer, *f.*

scorn, *v.a.*, dédaigner; mépriser, railler.

scorn, *v.n.*, dédaigner, mépriser. To — at;
montrer du mépris pour; *traiter avec mépris*;
railler. To — to fiy; *dédaigner de fuir*. Which
—s to tell a lie; *qui jamais ne ment* (V. Hugo).

scorn, *n.*, mépris, dédain; (subject of contempt) objet de dédain, *m.*; raillerie, dérision, *f.*
To laugh to —; *couvrir de honte et de mépris*.

scorn'er, *n.*, qui méprise; railleur, *m.*, railleuse, *f.* Thou — of the ground; (Shelley) *toi
qui méprises la terre*.

scorn'ful (-foule), *adj.*, méprisant; railleur;
dédaigneux.

scorn'fully, *adv.*, dédaigneusement; avec mépris; avec dédain.

scorn'fulness, *n.*, caractère méprisant, caractère dédaigneux, *m.*

scorn'ing, *n.*, mépris; dédain, *m.*

scor'pion, *n.*, (zoöl.) scorpion, *m.*

scor'pion-grass (-grâce), *n.*, myosotis, *m.*

scot, *n.*, écot, *m.*; quote-part, *f.* To pay — and
lot; *payer les contributions communales*.

scot, *v.a.*, enrayer.

Scot, *n.*, Ecossais, *m.*, Ecossaise, *f.*

Scotch (scotshe), *adj.*, écossais. —man; *Ecossais, m.* —woman; *Ecossaise, f.*

Scotch, *n.*, langue écossaise, *f.* Broad —;
patois écossais, m.

scotch (scotshe), *v.a.*, (tech.) arrêter; (a
wheel) enrayer, accorer; (to cut) entamer, taillader. To — the serpent; *blesser, sans tuer* . . .

scotch (scotshe), *n.*, (of a wheel) enrayure, *f.*

scotch'-hoppers, *n.pl.*, (game) marelle, *f.*

Scotch-kale, *n.*, chou frisé, *m.*

Scotch'-mist, *n.*, bruine écossaise, *f.*

Scotch'-terrier, *n.*, terrier-griffon, *m.*

sco'ter, *n.*, (orni.) macreuse, *f.*

scot'-free (-frî), *adj.*, exempt de payement;
exempt de contribution; sans frais; (unhurt) sain
et sauf.

sco'tia (scô-shi-a), *n.*, (arch.) scotie, *f.*

Scot'ticism (-ciz'm), *n.*, idiotisme écossais, *m.*

Scot'tish, *adj.*, écossais.

scoun'drel (scaou'n'-), *n.*, misérable; gredin;
scélérat; mauvais drôle; gueux, *m.*; canaille, *f.*

scoun'drelism (-'iz'm), *n.*, scélératesse, *f.*

scoun'drelly, *adj.*, scélérat; misérable; infâme.

scour (scaour), *v.a.*, écurer, récurer; nettoyer;
décrasser; (articles of dress) dégraisser; (to
purge) purger; (to roam) parcourir; (to pass
quickly over) raser; (the sea) écumer; (a room)
nettoyer; (copper) écurer. To — the country;
*courir la campagne, courir le pays, battre l'es-
trade* (Regnier, Scarron). To —; (with artillery)
balayer.

scour, *v.n.*, écurer; nettoyer; (to rove) courir.

scour'er, *n.*, écureur, nettoyeur; (of articles
of dress) dégraisseur; (runner) coureur; (purgation) violent purgatif, *m.*

scourge (skeurdje), *n.*, fouet; fléau, *m.*

scourge, *v.a.*, fouetter; flageller; châtier;
affliger.

scour'ger, *n.*, flagellateur; (fig.) châtieur;
(ecc. hist.) flagellant, *m.*

scour'ging, *n.*, flagellation, *f.*

scour'ing (scaour'-), *n.*, écurage; nettoyage;
(of articles of dress) dégraissage, *m.* Off—s;
(fig.) *rebut, m.* — brick; *brique anglaise, f.* —
paper; *papier de verre, m.*

scout (scaoute), *n.*, éclaireur, *m.*; vedette, *f.*;
(Eng. college servant) garçon, *m.*

scout, *v.n.*, aller en éclaireur; aller à la découverte; battre l'estrade.

scout, *v.a.*, rejeter; repousser avec indignation, *ou* avec mépris; (pers.) traiter avec dédain.

scout'ing-party, *n.*, troupe d'éclaireurs, *f.*

scov'el (skeuv'v'l), *n.*, écouvillon (de four), *m.*

scowl (scaoul), *v.n.*, se refrogner; froncer le
sourcil; avoir l'air menaçant.

scowl, *n.*, refrognement; froncement de sourcil; air refrogné; sombre regard; aspect sombre;
aspect menaçant, *m.*

scowl'ing, *adj.*, refrogné, renfrogné, menaçant.

scowl'ingly, *adv.*, d'un air refrogné; avec un
aspect menaçant.

scrag, *n.*, corps décharné, squelette, *m.* —
end; (of meat) *bout saigneux, m.*

scrag'ged (-ghède) *ou* **scrag'gy** (-ghi), *adj.*,
décharné; abrupt; rude; raboteux, rocailleux.

scrag'gily (-ghi-), *adv.*, avec maigreur; avec
rudesse.

scrag'giness (-ghi-), *n.*, état raboteux, rocailleux, *m.*; anfractuosité; inégalité; rudesse,
maigreur, *f.*

scram'ble (scra'm'b'l), *v.n.*, se traîner; avancer à l'aide des pieds et des mains; (of children)
jouer à la gribouillette. To — for; *chercher à
attraper, à saisir, tâcher d'empoigner, se battre
pour avoir, se disputer*. To — up; *grimper* (à
quatre pattes).

scram'ble, *n.*, mêlée; dispute pour avoir; (fig.)
lutte; (among children) gribouillette, *f.*

scram'bled, *adj.* — eggs; *œufs brouillés,
m.pl.*

scram'bling. *V.* scramble.

scram'blingly, *adv.*, en se traînant, en grimpant (à quatre pattes), en se disputant.

scranch, scraunch (scra'n'she), *v.a.*, broyer
avec les dents; croquer.

scrap, *n.*, morceau; fragment; (of paper)
chiffon, bout, *m.* —s, *pl.*, (remains) restes,
m.pl.; bribes, *f.pl.* —s of Greek and Latin;
des bribes de Grec et de Latin.

scrap'-book (-bouke), *n.*, album, *m.*

scrape (scrépe), *v.a.*, gratter; décrotter; râcler; ratisser; (chem.) décaper; (engr.) décrotter;
(the fiddle) râcler. To — acquaintance with any
one; *faire connaissance avec quelqu'un*. To —
the dirt off; *décrotter, enlever la boue* de. To
— the mud off one's shoes; *décrotter ses souliers*.
To — up, together; *ramasser*; (by small savings)
amasser petit à petit. To — off; *gratter, enlever,
râcler*.

scrape, *v.n.*, gratter; (to play the fiddle) râcler.
To bow and —; *faire des salamalecs, des courbettes* à; *ramper* devant. To — along; (fig.)
vivoter, boulotter.

scrape (scrépe), *n.*, coup de grattoir; grattage;
frottement, *m.*; (difficulty) difficulté, mauvaise
affaire, *f.*; embarras, mauvais pas; guêpier, bourbier, *m.*; (bow) révérence, *f.* To get into a —;
*s'attirer une affaire; se mettre dans l'embarras;
se mettre dans le pétrin, donner dans un guêpier*.
To get any one into a —; *engager* (*faire tomber*) *quelqu'un dans une mauvaise affaire*.

scrape'-penny, *n.*, grippe-sou, *m.*

scrap'er (scrép'-), *n.*, grattoir; râcloir, *m.*;
(agr.) ratissoire; (tech.) curette, *f.*; (engr.) ébarboir; (for shoes) décrottoir; (on a fiddle) râcleur
(miser) grippe-sou, *m.*

scrap'ing (scrép'-), *n.*, (of vegetables) ratissure, *f.*; (ordinary sense) grattage; (rubbing)
frottement; râclage, *m.*; (of ivory, etc.) râclure, *f.* —s, *pl.* (of things collected together)
ramassis, *m.*; (of money) petits profits, *m.pl.*;
boursicaut, *m.*; (of the roads) immondices, *f.pl.*
Bowing and —; *courbettes, f.pl.*

scrap'-iron, *n.*, ferraille, *f.*; riblons, *m.pl.*

scratch (scratshe), *n.*, égratignure, *f. ;* coup de griffe, *ou* d'ongle, *m. ;* (on a smooth surface) raie, rayure, *f.* To come to the —; *en venir au fait et au prendre.* It is a mere —; *ce n'est qu'une égratignure.* He didn't get a —; *il n'a rien reçu ; il n'a pas eu la plus légère blessure.*

scratch, *v.a.*, gratter ; égratigner ; (a smooth surface) rayer. She —ed out his eyes ; *elle lui arracha les yeux avec ses ongles.* To — out ; *raturer ; rayer ; barrer, effacer.*

scratch, *v.n.*, gratter ; égratigner. To — one's head ; *se gratter la tête.*

scratch'er, *n.*, (pers.) égratigneur ; (instrument) grattoir, *m.*

scratch'ing, *n.*, grattage, *m. ;* égratignure, rayure, *f. ;* (of horses, in a race) retrait, *m.* —s, *pl.*, rayures, *f.pl.*

scrawl (scrōl), *n.*, griffonnage ; barbouillage, *m. ;* pattes de mouche, *f.pl.*

scrawl, *v.a.* and *n.*, griffonner ; barbouiller, faire des pattes de mouche.

scrawl'er, *n.*, griffonneur, barbouilleur, *m.*

scray (scré), *n.*, (orni.) hirondelle de mer, *f.*

scream (scrîme), *n.*, cri ; cri perçant, aigu, *m.* To give a —; *jeter, ou pousser, un cri.*

scream (scrîme), *v.n.*, crier ; pousser un cri. To — out ; *pousser un cri, des cris; jeter les hauts cris.*

scream'er, *n.*, crieur, *m.*, crieuse, *f. ;* (orni.) kamichi, *m.*

scream'ing (scrî'm'-), *adj.*, aigu ; perçant ; (pers.) qui crie.

scream'ing, *n.*, cris, *m.pl.*

screech (scrîtshe), *n.*, cri ; cri aigu, *m.*

screech, *v.n.*, crier ; jeter un cri ; pousser un cri ; (to sing badly) glapir.

screech'-owl (-aoul), *n.*, (orni.) chat-huant, *m.*, chouette, *f.*

screen (scrîne), *n.*, paravent ; écran, *m. ;* rideau, voile ; (of an altar) retable, *m. ;* (sieve) claie ; (arch.) boiserie, grille ; (fig.) défense, *f.* Folding-— ; *paravent à feuilles, m.* Fire-—, hand-— ; *écran, m.* — wall ; *avant-mur, m.*

screen, *v.a.*, mettre à couvert ; abriter **contre** ; mettre à l'abri, *ou* à couvert **de** ; (to sift) passer à la claie *ou* au crible ; (a fault *ou* a person) pallier, excuser. To — a man from punishment ; *soustraire quelqu'un au châtiment.*

screen'ings, *n.pl.*, criblures, *f.pl.*

screw (scrou), *n.*, vis, *f. ;* (hollow) écrou, *m. ;* (pers.) pince-maille, pingre, fesse-mathieu, *m. ;* (nav.) hélice, *f.* Archimedean — ; *vis d'Archimède, f.* To put the — on some one ; *serrer le bouton, la vis, les pouces, à quelqu'un.* Endless — ; *vis sans fin, f.* There is a — loose somewhere ; *il y a quelque chose qui cloche, qui va de travers, qui branle dans le manche.*

screw, *adj.*, à hélice.

screw, *v.a.*, visser ; (to press) presser, serrer ; (to oppress) opprimer, pressurer ; (to distort) déformer. To — up one's courage to the sticking point ; *prendre son courage à deux mains ; prendre son grand courage.* To — up one's face ; *faire une grimace.* To — up one's lips ; *pincer les lèvres.* To — one's workmen ; *écraser ses ouvriers.* To — money out of ; *forcer à payer ; faire rendre gorge à.* To — up ; (an instrument) *monter.* To — down ; *visser ; fermer à vis ;* (to oppress) *opprimer, pressurer.* To — in ; *faire entrer en vissant.* To — one's self in ; *se glisser dedans.* To — up ; *fermer à vis ; visser.*

screw'-arbor, *n.*, axe de vis, *m.*

screw'-bolt (-bôlte), *n.*, boulon à vis, *m.*

screw'-cap, *n.*, bouchon à vis, *m.*

screw'driver (-draïv'-), *n.*, tournevis, *m.*

screwed (scrou'de), *adj.*, à vis ; (tipsy) gris. To be — ; *être dans les vignes du Seigneur.*

screw'-handle, *n.*, poignée à vis, *f.*

screw'-jack (-djack), *n.*, (tech.) cric, *m.*

screw'-making (-mék'-), *n.*, fabrication des vis, *f.*

screw'-nail (-néle), *n.*, clou à vis, *m.*

screw'-nut (-neute), *n.*, écrou de vis, *m.*

screw'-plate, *n.*, filière, *f.*

screw'-plug (-pleughe), *n.*, cheville vissée, *f. ;* tampon à vis, *m.*

screw'-shank, *n.*, tige de vis, *f.*

screw'-steamer (-stî-meur), *n.*, bâtiment, vapeur à hélice, *m.*

screw'-worm (-weurme), *n.*, filet de vis, *m.*

screw'-wrench, *n.*, clé anglaise, *f.*

scrib'ble (scrib'b'l) *ou* **scrib'bling**, *n.*, griffonnage ; barbouillage, *m. ;* (of writings) écrivasserie, *f.*

scrib'ble (scrib'b'l), *v.a.* and *n.*, griffonner ; barbouiller.

scrib'bler, *n.*, griffonneur, barbouilleur ; (writer) écrivassier, *m.*

scribe (scraïbe), *n.*, scribe ; écrivain, *m.*

scribe (scraïbe), *v.a.*, (carp.) étriquer.

scrim'mage, *n.*, lutte ; bagarre ; rixe, grabuge, *f.*

scrimp, *adj.*, court, serré ; étriqué.

scrip, *n.*, (fin.) action provisoire ; inscription, *f. ;* titres, *m.pl.*, valeurs, *f.pl. ;* (of paper) chiffon ; (wallet) petit sac, *m.*

script, *n.*, (print.) anglaise, *f.*

scrip'tural (script'ieu-ral), *adj.*, de l'Ecriture Sainte ; biblique ; scriptural.

Scrip'ture (script'ieur), *n.*, Ecriture Sainte ; Ecriture, *f.* — history ; *histoire sainte, f.*

scriv'ener (scriv'neur), *n.*, notaire ; courtier, agent d'affaires, *m.*

scrof'ula (scrof'iou-), *n.*, (med.) scrofules ; écrouelles, *f.pl.*

scrof'ulous (scrof'iou-), *adj.*, scrofuleux.

scroll (scrôle), *n.*, rouleau, rôle ; (arch.) enroulement, *m.*

scrub (screube), *n.*, souffre-douleur, pauvre diable, *m.* A mean — ; *un fesse-mathieu.*

scrub, *v.a.*, frotter fort ; laver, écurer, récurer, décrasser.

scrub, *v.n.*, travailler fort ; s'éreinter. To — hard for a living ; *gagner sa vie péniblement.*

scrub'bing, *n.*, frottage, écurage, récurage, *m.* To give a good — ; *laver bien ; frotter ferme.*

scrub'bing-brush (-breushe), *n.*, brosse à récurer, *f.*

scrub'by (screub'-), *adj.*, mauvais ; méchant ; misérable ; (stunted) rabougri, chétif.

scru'ple (scrou-p'l), *n.*, scrupule ; (weight) scrupule, *m.* Without a — ; *sans scrupule.*

scru'ple (scrou-p'l), *v.n.*, se faire scrupule **de** ; se faire un scrupule **de** ; balancer, hésiter **à**.

scru'pulous (scrou-piou-), *adj.*, scrupuleux. Over — ; *trop scrupuleux ; méticuleux, difficile.*

scru'pulously, *adv.*, scrupuleusement.

scru'pulousness, *n.*, scrupule, doute, *m.*, scrupules, *m.pl. ;* hésitation ; humeur scrupuleuse, *f.*

scru'table (scrou-ta-b'l), *adj.*, qu'on peut scruter.

scruta'tor (scrou-té-teur), *n.*, scrutateur, *m.*

scru'tinize (scrou-ti-naïze), *v.a.*, scruter ; examiner à fond ; rechercher.

scru'tinizer, *n.*, scrutateur, *m.*

scru'tinizing, *adj.*, scrutateur, inquisiteur.

scru'tiny, *n.*, examen sévère, *m. ;* recherche minutieuse, enquête rigoureuse, *f.*

scud (skeude), *n.*, (thin cloud) léger nuage chassé par le vent, *m. ;* (flight) course rapide ; fuite précipitée ; (shower) ondée, *f.*

scud (skeude), *v.n.*, s'enfuir ; se sauver ; (of clouds) courir. To — before the wind ; (nav.) *se courir, fuir devant le vent.* To — under bare poles ; *courir à sec, courir à mâts et à cordes.* It was a full moon over which —ded heavy clouds driven by the wind ; *c'était une pleine lune sur laquelle couraient de larges nuées chassées par le vent* (V. Hugo).

scuf'fle (skeuf-f'l), *n.*, lutte, bagarre, rixe, querelle, *f.*

scuf'fle (skeuf'f'l), *v.n.*, lutter, se battre, se houspiller, se quereller.

scuf'fler, *n.*, lutteur, *m.;* (agri.) scarificateur, *m.*

scuf'fling, *n.*, lutte, rixe, bagarre, *f.*

sculk (skeulk). *V.* **skulk.**

sculk'er, *n. V.* **skulker.**

sculk'ing. *V.* **skulking.**

scull (skeule), *n.*, (oar) aviron de couple, *m.;* (stern oar) godille, *f.;* (brainpan) *V.* **skull.**

scull (skeule), *v.a.*, godiller; (with one oar at the stern) gabarer.

scull'er, *n.*, godilleur; nageur (ant.), *m.*

scull'ery, *n.*, lavoir de cuisine, *m.* — -maid; *fille de cuisine; souillon, f.*

scull'ing, *n.*, nage à l'aviron de couple; godillage, *m.*

scull'ion, *n.*, marmiton; laveur de vaisselle, *m.*, laveuse de vaisselle, *f.*, souillon, *m.*

sculp'tor (skeulp'teur), *n.*, sculpteur, *m.*

sculp'ture (skeulpt'ieur), *n.*, sculpture; ciselure, *f.*

sculp'ture (skeulpt'ieur), *v.a.*, sculpter; ciseler.

sculp'tured (skeulpt'ieurde), *adj.*, sculpté; ciselé.

scum (skeume), *n.*, écume; (metal.) scorie, crasse, *f.;* (refuse) rebut, *m.;* (fig.) lie, *f.*, rebut, *m.* The — of the people; *la lie du peuple, f.* — of the earth; *excrément de la terre* (Lafontaine).

scum, *v.a.*, écumer.

scum'mer (skeu'm'-), *n.*, écumoire, *f.*

scum'ming (skeu'm'-), *n.*, action d'écumer, *f.;* écumage, *m. pl.*, écume, *f.sing.*

scum'my, *adj.*, écumeux.

scup'per (skeup'-) *ou* **scup'per-hole** (-hôle), *n.*, (nav.) dalot, trou de dalot, *m.*

scup'per-hose (-hôze), *n.*, cuir des dalots, *m.*

scurf (skeurfe), *n.*, (on the skin) croûte; (on the head) crasse; teigne, *f.*

scurf'iness (skeurf'-), *n.*, état dartreux, encroûtement, *m.*

scurf'y (skeurf'-), *adj.*, dartreux; crasseux, teigneux.

scurril'ity (skeur'-), *n.*, grossièreté; indécence; raillerie grossière, *f.*

scur'rilous (skeur'-), *adj.*, grossier; indécent, bas, insultant.

scur'rilously, *adv.*, grossièrement; indécemment.

scur'rilousness. *V.* **scurril'ity.**

scur'vily (skeur-), *adv.*, bassement, indignement, vilement; (stingily) avec ladrerie.

scur'viness (skeur-), *n.*, état scorbutique; (fig.) caractère vil, *m.;* bassesse; (stinginess) ladrerie, mesquinerie, *f.*

scur'vy (skeur-), *n.*, scorbut, *m.*

scur'vy (skeur-), *adj.*, atteint du scorbut; scorbutique; (fig.) (vile, mean) vil, méprisable; vilain; (stingy) ladre.

scur'vy-grass (-grâce), *n.*, (bot.) cochléaria, cranson, *m.;* herbe-au-scorbut, *f.*

scut (skeute), *n.*, queue (de lièvre, de cerf), *f.*

scu'tage (skiou-tèdje), *n.*, (feudal) écuage, *m.*

scutch, *v.a.*, teiller; tiller.

scutch'eon (skeutsh'eune), *n. V.* **escutcheon.**

scu'tiform (skiou-), *adj.*, en forme de bouclier, d'écu.

scut'tle (skeut't'l), *n.*, panier, seau; (quick pace) pas précipité, *m.;* (nav.) écoutille, *f.* Coal— —; *seau, panier à charbon.* — -ful; *seau plein, panier plein.*

scut'tle, *v.a.*, (nav.) couler bas, saborder.

scut'tle, *v.n.*, aller à pas précipités. To — away; *s'enfuir précipitamment, décamper, détaler.*

scut'tling, *n.*, sabordement, *m.*

scythe (saï*th*e), *n.*, (agri.) faux, *f.*

Scyth'ian (ci-thi-), *adj.*, des Sythes; scythe.

Scyth'ian (ci-thi-), *n.*, Scythe, *m.f.*

sea (sî), *n.*, mer, *f.;* (billow, wave) coup de mer, *m.*, lame, *f.;* paquet de mer, *m.;* (large quantity) multitude, infinité, *f.*, déluge, *m.;* (of blood)mer. *adj.*, de mer, marin, maritime, naval. Beyond the —s; *outre mer; au delà des mers.* Half— —s over; *à demi ivre; dans les vignes du Seigneur; entre deux vins.* To ship a —; *embarquer un coup* ou *un paquet de mer.* Heavy —, rough —; *grosse mer; mer houleuse.* Deep —; *pleine mer, haute mer.* On the high —s; *sur la haute mer.* On the main —, on the open —; *en pleine mer.* At —; *en mer; sur mer.* Narrow —; *détroit, m.* To go to —, to follow the —; *se faire marin.* To put to —; *mettre en mer.* To be at —; (fig.) *ne savoir quel parti prendre; être perdu, confondu, dérouté.* To stand out to —; *se tenir au large, gagner le large.*

sea'-acorn, *n.*, (zoöl.) balane, *m.*

sea'-adder, *n.*, (ich.) couleuvre de mer, *f.*

sea-anem'one (-a-né'm'o-ni), *n.*, (zoöl.) anémone de mer, *f.*

sea'-ape (-épe), *n.*, (ich.) singe de mer, *m.*

sea'-bank, *n.*, rivage de la mer; môle, brise-lames, *m.*

sea'-bat, *n.*, (ich.) poisson volant, *m.*

sea'-bathing, *n.*, bains de mer, *m.pl.*

sea'-bear (-bère), *n.*, (zoöl.), ours blanc, ours polaire, ours marin, *m.*

sea'-beard (-bîrde), *n.*, (bot.) barbe de mer, *f.*

sea'-boat (-bôte), *n.*, embarcation, *f.* Good —; *navire qui tient bien la mer, m.*

sea'-born, *adj.*, né de la mer; né sur mer.

sea'-borne, *adj.*, porté par la mer; (of coals) transporté par mer, *ou* par eau.

sea'-bound (-baou'n'de), *adj.*, borné par la mer.

sea'-boy (-boï), *n.*, novice; mousse, *m.*

sea'-breach (-brîtshe), *n.*, irruption de la mer, *f.*

sea'-breeze (-brîze), *n.*, brise de mer, *f.*

sea'-built (-bilte), *adj.*, bâti, *ou* construit, pour la mer.

sea'-calf (-kâfe), *n.*, (zoöl.) veau marin, *m.*

sea'-card (-cârde), *n.*, rose des vents, *f.;* compas de mer, *m.*

sea'-chart (-tshârte), *n.*, carte marine, *m.*

sea'-chest (-tshèste), *n.*, coffre de bord, *m.*

sea'-coast (-côste), *n.*, côte de la mer, *f.*, littoral, *m.*

sea-cor'morant, *n.*, (orni.) corbeau de mer; cormoran, *m.*

sea'-cow, *n.*, lamantin, *m.*, vache marine, *f.;* (walrus) morse, *m.*

sea'-devil (-dèv'v'l), *n.*, (ich.) baudroie, *f.*

sea'-dog, *n.*, (mam.) phoque, veau marin, *m.*

sea'-eel, *n.*, anguille de mer, *f.*, congre, *m.*

sea-encir'cled (-cir-k'l'de), *adj.*, entouré par la mer.

sea'farer (-fèr'-), *n.*, homme de mer, marin, *m.*

sea'faring (-fèr'-), *adj.*, marin; de marin. — -man; *marin, m.*

sea'-fennel (-fè'n'-), *n.*, (bot.) fenouil marin, *m. V.* **samphire.**

sea'-fight (-faïte), *n.*, combat naval, *m.*

sea'-fish, *n.*, poisson de mer, *m.*

sea'-fog, *n.*, brume, *f.*

sea'-fowl (-faoule), *n.*, oiseau de mer, *m.*

sea'-fox, *n.*, (ich.) renard marin, *m.*

sea'-front, *n.*, digue, promenade, terrasse, *f.*

sea'-gauge (-ghédje), *n.*, tirant d'eau, *m.*

sea'-girt (-gheurte), *adj.*, entouré par la mer.

sea'-god, *n.*, dieu marin, *m.*

sea'-grass (-grâce), *n.*, herbe marine, *f.*

sea'-green (-grîne), *n.*, vert de mer, *m.*

sea'-green, *adj.*, vert de mer, vert d'eau.

sea'-gull (-gheule), *n.*, (orni.) mouette, *f.*

sea-hedge'hog (-hèdj'-), *n.*, (zoöl.) oursin, hérisson de mer, *m.*

sea'-hog, *n.*, marsouin, *m.*

sea'-holm (-hôlme), *n.*, petite île inhabitée, *f.*

sea'-horse, *n.*, (ich.) hippocampe, cheval marin; (mam.) hippopotame; morse, *m.*

sea'-kale, *n.*, chou marin, *m.*

sea'-king (-kigne), *n.*, roi des pirates, *m.*

seal (sîl), *n.*, cachet, sceau; (jur.) scellé, *m.*; scellés, *m.pl.*; (mam.) veau marin, phoque, *m.* The —s of state; *les sceaux de l'Etat.* Privy—; *petit sceau.* Great—; *grand sceau.* To affix the —s; *apposer les scellés.* Under one's —; *sous seing privé.* His writings bear the — of genius; *ses écrits sont marqués du sceau*, ou *au coin, du génie.*

seal, *v.a.*, sceller; (letters, parcels, etc.) cacheter; (to shut) fermer, clore; (arch.) sceller, (to ratify) ratifier. To — up; *mettre le sceau* à; *sceller*; (letters, etc.) *cacheter.* His fate is —ed; *c'(en) est fait de lui; son sort est décidé ; sa porte est certaine.*

seal, *v.n.*, mettre un sceau à.

sea'-legs (-lèg'ze), *n.pl.*, pied marin, *m.sing.*

seal'er, *n.*, cacheteur; scelleur, *m.*

seal'ing, *n.*, action de sceller, de cacheter, *f.*; (arch.) scellement, *m.*; (pisc.) pêche du, *ou* chasse au, phoque, *f.*

seal'ing-wax, *n.*, cire à cacheter, *f.*

sea'-lion (-laï-o'n), *n.*, lion marin, *m.*

seal'-ring, *n.* *V.* **signet-ring.**

seam (sîme), *n.*, couture, *f.*; (of a mast) joint, *m.*; (mines) couche; (geol.) veine; (scar) cicatrice, *f.*; (measure) huit boisseaux, *m.pl.*; (anat.) suture, *f.*

seam, *v.a.*, joindre; faire une couture à; cicatriser, couturer. —ed with the small-pox; *marqué, couturé de la petite vérole.*

sea'-maid (-méde), *n.*, nymphe océanique; sirène, *f.*; (zoöl.) lamantin, *m.*

sea'man, *n.*, marin, matelot, *m.*

sea'manship, *n.*, navigation; habileté à manœuvrer un vaisseau, *f.*; habile manœuvre, *f.*

sea'-marks, *n.pl.*, (nav.) amers, *m.pl.*

sea'-mew (-miou), *n.*, (orni.) mouette, *f.*

seam'less, *adj.*, sans couture; (of metals) sans soudure, *f.*

seam'-rent, *n.*, décousure, *f.*

seam'ster, *n.*, couturier, tailleur, *m.*

seam'stress, *n.*, couturière; lingère; ouvrière en linge, *f.*

seam'y, *adj.*, à couture; plein de coutures.

sea'-nettle (-nèt't'l), *n.*, (zoöl.) méduse, ortie de mer, *f.*

sea'-nymph, *n.*, nymphe de l'océan, néréide, sirène, *f.*

sea'-owl (-aoul), *n.*, (ich.) cycloptère, *m.*

sea'-pad, *n.*, (zoöl.) astérie, étoile de mer, *f.*

sea'-piece (-pîce), *n.*, (paint.) marine, *f.*

sea'-plant, *n.*, plante marine, *f.*

sea'port (-pôrte), *n.*, port de mer, *m.* —town; *port de mer, m.; ville maritime, f.*

sear (sîre), *adj.*, sec; séché, fané, flétri; mort. —leaf; *feuille morte, f.*

sear (sîre), *v.a.*, brûler; cautériser; dessécher; faner; flétrir; (vet.) mettre le feu à, appliquer un cautère à. —ing iron; *fer à cautériser, m.*

search (seurtshe), *n.*, recherche; (jur.) descente, visite, perquisition; (at the customs) visite, *f.* To go in — of; *aller à la recherche* **de.** A vain —; *d'inutiles recherches.* To be in — of; *être à la recherche* **de.** Right of —; *droit de visite, m.*

search (seurtshe), *v.a.*, faire une recherche; (to probe) sonder; (to examine) examiner, fouiller; (pers.) visiter, fouiller; (jur.) faire

une perquisition **dans**, visiter; (at the customs) visiter; fouiller **dans.** To — about; *fureter.* To — out; *découvrir.*

search, *v.n.*, chercher; fouiller. To — after; *rechercher.* To — for; *chercher.* To — into; *faire des recherches* **sur**; *approfondir.*

search'er, *n.*, personne qui cherche, qui recherche, qui fouille, *f.*; (inquirer) investigateur, *m.*, investigatrice, *f.*; (b.s.) chercheur, *m.*, chercheuse, *f.*; (trier) sondeur, scrutateur; (at the customs) visiteur, *m.*, visiteuse, fouilleuse; (instrument) sonde, *f.*

search'ing (seurtsh'igne), *n.*, examen, *m.*; recherche, *f.*

search'ing, *adj.*, (of the eye) scrutateur; pénétrant, minutieux; (of the wind) vif, perçant, pénétrant.

search'ingly (seurtsh'ign'-), *adv.*, avec pénétration; d'un regard scrutateur; minutieusement.

search'ingness (seurtsh'ign'nèce), *n.*, subtilité, *f.*; examen profond, minutieux, *m.*

search'less, *adj.*, impénétrable; inscrutable.

search'-warrant (-wŏr'-), *n.*, (jur.) mandat de perquisition, *m.*

sear'-cloth (cîre-cloth), *n.*, toile cirée, *f.*; (plaster) emplâtre, *m.*

sear'edness (sîr'èd-), *n.*, sécheresse; (fig.) insensibilité, *f.*; endurcissement, *m.*

sea'-risk, *n.*, (insur.) risques et périls de la mer, *m.pl.*, risque de mer, *m.*

sea'-robber, *n.*, pirate; corsaire, *m.*

sea'-room (-roume), *n.*, eau à courir, *f.*; le large, *m.*

sea'-route, *n.*, voie de mer, *f.*

sea'-rover (-rov'-), *n.*, écumeur de mer, *m.*

sea'-serpent (-seur-), *n.*, serpent de mer, *m.*

sea'-service (-seur-vice), *n.*, service de la marine, *f.*

sea'-shell, *n.*, coquillage, *m.*; coquille de mer, *f.*

sea'-shore, *n.*, rivage de la mer, rivage, littoral, *m.*; côte, *f.*

sea'-sick, *adj.*, qui a le mal de mer. To be —; *avoir le mal de mer.*

sea'-sickness, *n.*, mal de mer, *m.*

sea'-side (-saïde), *n.*, bord de la mer, *m.*

sea'son (sî-z'n), *n.*, saison, *f.*; (fig.) temps, moment opportun, *m.*; époque, *f.* — ticket; *billet*, ou *abonnement, de saison, m.* In —; *de saison*; (in time) *à temps, en temps opportun, au bon moment.* Out of —; *hors de saison*; (fig.) *mal à propos.* For a—; *pendant une saison; pour un temps.* In due —; *en temps et saison.* Summer is the — of warmth; *l'été c'est la saison de feu* (V. Hugo).

sea'son, *v.a.*, (cook.) assaisonner; (to give a zest to) relever le goût **de**; (to temper) tempérer, modérer; (to imbue) imprégner (with, **de**); (to fit) accoutumer, endurcir, aguerrir; (to make) faire; (to prepare for a climate) acclimater; (wood) préparer, sécher.

sea'son, *v.n.*, s'acclimater; (of wood) se préparer, se sécher.

sea'sonable (-'a-b'l), *adj.*, de saison; (fig.) à propos; opportun; convenable.

sea'sonableness, *n.*, opportunité, *f.*; à-propos, *m.*

sea'sonably, *adv.*, de saison; à propos.

sea'soned, *adj.*, (of meats) assaisonné; (fig.) endurci, aguerri, acclimaté.

sea'soning, *n.*, assaisonnement, *m.*; (of wood) préparation, *f.*, séchage, *m.*

seat (sîte), *n.*, chaise, *f.*, siège; (bench, form) gradin, banc; (abode) séjour, *m.*, demeure, *f.*; (of war) théâtre, *m.*; (mansion) château; maison de campagne, *f.*; (of chairs) siège, fond, *m.*; (place where anything is established) siège; (site) emplacement, *m.*, situation, *f.*; (tribunal) tribunal, *m.*; (place) place; (riding) assiette, *f.*;

(of trousers) fond, *m.* ; (of a water-closet) lunette, *f.*, siège, *m.* To have a — in parliament; *siéger au parlement.* To take one's — at a board; *prendre place au conseil.* To vacate one's — in parliament; *donner sa démission.* To put a — to a pair of trousers ; *mettre un fond à un pantalon.* To take a — ; *s'asseoir, prendre un siège.* To take one's — at table ; *prendre sa place à table.* To keep one's — ; *rester assis ;* (on horseback) *rester en selle.* To have a good — ; *avoir une bonne assiette ; se tenir bien à cheval.* The — of war ; *le théâtre de la guerre.*

seat (sîte), *v.a.*, asseoir; faire asseoir ; (to fix) fixer, établir ; (to place) placer ; (to fit up with seats) garnir de sièges ; (trousers) mettre un fond à. To — one's self ; *s'asseoir.* Pray be —ed ; *donnez-vous la peine de vous asseoir ; veuillez vous asseoir.* This hall —s a thousand persons ; *il y a place dans cette salle* **pour** *mille personnes.*

seat'ed, *adj.*, assis, placé. Double — ; *à deux places.* Cane — ; (of chairs) *à fond de canne.* Low — ; (of chairs) *à siège bas.*

seat'ing, *n.*, (of trousers) fond, *m.*

sea'-tossed (-tos'te), *adj.*, ballotté sur la mer.

sea'-trout, *n.*, truite saumonée, *f.*

sea'-urchin (-eur-tshine), *n.*, (ich.) oursin, *m.*

sea'-walled (-wôl'de), *adj.*, entouré de la mer.

sea'ward (-wôrde), *adj.*, tourné vers la mer.

sea'ward, *adv.*, vers la mer, du côté de la mer.

sea'-water, *n.*, eau salée ; eau de mer, *f.*

sea'-weed (-wîde), *n.*, algue ; plante marine, *f.* ; varech, *m.*   [navigabilité, *f.*

sea'-worthiness (-weur-*thi*-), *n.*, (of a ship)

sea'worthy (-weur-*thi*), *adj.*, (of a ship) qui peut tenir la mer ; en bon état de navigation.

se'cant (sî-), *n.*, (geom.) sécante, *f.*

se'cant (sî-), *adj.*, sécant.

secede' (si-cîde), *v.n.*, séceder, se séparer ; faire scission ; se retirer de.

seced'er, *n.*, scissionnaire, *m.f.* ; dissident, *m.* ; (in the civil war) sécessioniste, *m.*

seced'ing, *adj.*, scissionnaire.

seces'sion (si-cèsh'-), *n.*, sécession ; séparation, scission, *f.*

seclude' (si-clioude), *v.a.*, séparer ; écarter, éloigner ; renfermer ; retirer ; exclure. To — one's self ; *se retirer ; se renfermer.*

seclud'ed, *adj.*, retiré, solitaire.

seclu'sion (si-cliou-jeune), *n.*, retraite, solitude, *f.*

seclu'sive (si-cliou-cive), *adj.*, qui tient dans la retraite.

sec'ond (sèk'eu'n'de), *adj.*, second; deuxième; (of the month) deux ; (inferior) inférieur. Every — day ; *tous les deux jours.* — floor ; *second, m., deuxième (étage), m.* A — Nero ; *un autre Néron.* —cousin; *cousin issu de germain, m.* — captain *ou* — in command ; *capitaine en second, m.* — class ; (rail.) *en seconde.* —lieutenant ; *lieutenant en second ; sous-lieutenant ; enseigne, m.* In the — place ; *en second lieu.* At — hand ; (hearsay) *de seconde main.* —s hand ; (of watches) *aiguille des secondes, f.* To be — to none ; *n'être inférieur à personne ; ne le céder à personne.* To come off — best ; *avoir le dessous.* —hand ; *d'occasion.*

sec'ond, *n.*, (in a duel) témoin ; second ; (supporter) second, *m.* ; (of time) seconde ; (mus.) seconde, *f.* —s ; *deuxième qualité ;* (of meal, flour) *recoupe, f.*

sec'ond, *v.a.*, seconder, aider ; appuyer. To — a motion ; *appuyer une motion.*

sec'ondarily, *adv.*, secondairement.

sec'ondary, *adj.*, secondaire ; accessoire ; subordonné ; subalterne. — cause ; *cause seconde, f.*

sec'onder, *n.*, personne qui seconde, qui appuie, *f.*   [de seconde main.

sec'ond-hand, *adj.*, d'occasion ; de hasard ;

sec'ondly, *adv.*, secondement.

sec'ond-rate, *adj.*, de second ordre, inférieur.

sec'ond-sight (-saïte), *n.*, seconde vue, *f.*

sec'ond-sight'ed, *adj.*, doué de seconde vue.

se'crecy (sî-cri-ci), *n.*, secret, *m.* ; (solitude) solitude ; (closeness) discrétion, *f.* I rely upon your — ; *je compte sur votre discrétion.*

se'cret (sî-crète), *adj.*, secret ; (secluded) retiré. To keep — ; *tenir secret.* — drawer ; *tiroir à secret, m.* —service funds ; *fonds secrets, m.pl.*

se'cret, *n.*, secret, *m.* In — ; *en secret ; secrètement, à la dérobée.* To keep a — ; *garder un secret.* To tell a — to ; *confier un secret à.* An open — ; *le secret de Polichinelle.* No — but between two ; *secret de deux, secret de Dieu, secret de trois, secret de tous.*

sec'retary (sèk'ri-), *n.*, secrétaire, ministre, *m.* —'s office ; *secrétariat, m. ; secrétairerie, f.* — of state ; *secrétaire d'Etat.* Home — ; *ministre de l'Intérieur, m.*

sec'retaryship (sèk'ri-), *n.*, secrétariat, ministère, *m.*

secrete' (si-crîte), *v.a.*, cacher ; tenir secret ; celer; (physiolog.) (to secern) sécréter.

secret'ing, *adj.*, sécréteur.

secre'tion (si-crî-), *n.*, sécrétion, *f.*

secre'tiveness (si-crî-tiv'-), *n.*, (phrenology) sécrétivité, *f.*

se'cretly (si-crèt'-), *adv.*, secrètement, en secret ; (inwardly) intérieurement.

se'cretness (si-crèt'-), *n.*, fidélité à garder un secret, *f.* ; caractère secret, *m.* ; discrétion, *f.*

secre'tory (-crî-teuri), *adj.*, sécrétoire.

sect, *n.*, secte, *f.*

secta'rian (sèc-té-), *adj.*, de sectaire.

secta'rian, *n.*, sectaire, sectateur, *m.*

secta'rianism (-'iz'm), *n.*, esprit de secte, *m.*

sec'tary (-ta-), *n.*, sectaire, *m.*

secta'tor (sèc-té-), *n.*, sectateur, *m.*

sec'tile (-til'), *adj.*, (min.) sécable.

sec'tion, *n.*, section, partie ; coupe, *f.* ; profil ; (mil.) peloton, *m.* Cross — ; *coupe transversale.*

sec'tional, *adj.*, sectionnel, de section.

sec'tor, *n.*, (geom.) secteur ; (instrument) compas de proportion, *m.*

sec'ular (sèk'iou-), *adj.*, séculier, temporel ; (mus.) profane ; (of years) séculaire.

secular'ity, *n.*, sécularité, mondanité, *f.*

seculariza'tion (-'i-zé-), *n.*, sécularisation, *f.*

sec'ularize (-'aïze), *v.a.*, séculariser ; rendre séculier.

sec'ularly, *adv.*, séculièrement.

sec'ularness, *n.*, sécularité, mondanité, *f.*

se'cundine (sî-keu'n'dîne), *n.*, (bot.) secondine, *f.* —s, *pl.*, (in obstetrics) secondines, *f.pl.* ; délivre, *m.*

secure' (si-kioure), *adj.*, (pers.) dans la sécurité, en sûreté ; (of things) sûr, assuré. — against, — from ; *en sûreté* **contre** ; *à couvert de ; à l'abri de.* — of ; *sûr de.*

secure' (si-kioure), *v.a.*, (to make safe) mettre en sûreté, défendre, protéger ; (make certain) assurer, s'assurer ; (payments) assurer, garantir ; (to make fast) fermer ; barrer ; (fig.) consolider, assurer, affermir ; (to seize and confine) mettre en lieu de sûreté, s'assurer **de**, s'emparer **de** ; (a place in a coach, etc.) retenir ; (to procure for) valoir **à**. *V.* To win (for), *under* **win**.

secure'ly, *adv.*, en sûreté ; sûrement, bien ; dans la sécurité ; avec sécurité ; sans danger ; (strongly) fortement, solidement.

secure'ness, *n.*, sécurité, *f.*

secur'er, *n.*, défenseur, *m.*

secur'ities, *n.pl.*, (fin.) effets, titres, *m.pl.* ; valeurs, *f.pl.* Government — ; *effets publics ; fonds publics, m.pl. ; rente sur l'état, f.*

secur'ity (si-kiou-), *n.*, sécurité ; sûreté, assurance ; certitude, *f.* ; (pledge) nantissement, *m.*, garantie ; (jur.) caution, *f*. To give —; *fournir un cautionnement ; donner des garanties ;* (jur.) *fournir caution.*

sedan'-chair (si-da'n'tshère), *n.*, chaise à porteurs, *f.*

sedate' (si-), *adj.*, posé ; calme, rassis.

sedate'ly, *adv.*, posément ; tranquillement.

sedate'ness, *n.*, calme, *m. ;* tranquillité, *f.*

sed'ative (sèd'-), *adj.*, sédatif, calmant.

sed'ative, *n.*, sédatif, calmant, *m.*

sed'entarily (sèd'-), *adv.*, sédentairement.

sed'entary (sèd'-), *adj.*, sédentaire ; (inactive) inactif, inerte.

sedge (sèdje), *n.*, laîche, *f.*, carex, jonc, *m.*

sedged (sèdj'de), *adj.*, de laîche, de carex.

sedg'y, *adj.*, plein de laîche, de joncs.

sed'iment (sèd'-), *n.*, sédiment ; dépôt ; résidu, *m.*, lie, *f.*

sedi'tion (si-dish'-), *n.*, sédition, *f.*

sedi'tious (si-di-sheusse), *adj.*, séditieux.

sedi'tiously, *adv.*, séditieusement.

sedi'tiousness, *n.*, esprit séditieux ; caractère séditieux, *m.*

seduce' (si-diouce), *v.a.*, séduire.

sedu'cer, *n.*, séducteur, *m.*, séductrice, *f.*

sedu'cible (-'i-b'l), *adj.*, séductible, corruptible.

sedu'cing, *adj.*, séduisant.

seduc'tion (si-deuk'-), *n.*, séduction, *f.*

seduc'tive, *adj.*, séducteur ; séduisant.

sedu'lity, sed'ulousness (si-diou-), *n.*, assiduité, diligence ; application, *f.*

sed'ulous (sèd'iou-), *adj.*, assidu ; diligent ; appliqué.

sed'ulously, *adv.*, assidûment ; diligemment ; avec application.

see (sî), *n.*, siège, *m.* Holy —; *saint-siège.*

see (sî), *v.a.*, (preterit, Saw ; past part., Seen) voir. He —s nobody ; *il ne voit personne.* To be seen ; *être vu ; se voir.* To — any one off ; *accompagner quelqu'un à la gare, au bateau, le voir partir.* To — any one out ; *reconduire quelqu'un.* To — any one home, to the door ; *conduire quelqu'un jusque chez lui, jusqu'à la porte.* To — a thing out ; *voir finir une chose, voir la fin d'une chose.* I will — to it ; *je m'en occuperai, j'y veillerai ; j'y aviserai.* I saw him through his difficulties ; *je l'ai tiré de son embarras.* Fit to be seen ; *présentable.*

see (sî), *v.n.*, voir. To — about ; *penser à ;* s'occuper de. To — to ; *avoir soin de ; veiller à ; prendre garde à ; s'occuper de.* To — that; *avoir soin que ; veiller à ce que.* I shall — that all be ready ; *j'aurai soin que tout soit prêt.* — to it ; *veillez-y ; prenez-y garde, avisez-y.* Let us —; *voyons.* You —; *voyez-vous.* —! *voyez !* To — into ; (a thing) *voir le fond* de; *pénétrer.* To — through ; (a thing) *comprendre, deviner, pénétrer.* —ing is believing ; *voir c'est croire.*

seed (sîde), *n.*, semence ; (of vegetables) graine ; (silk-worms) graine, *f.*, œufs, *m.pl. ;* (fig.) semence, race, *f.* To run to —; *monter en graine.* To sow the — of ; *semer.* To cast its —; (of a plant) *s'égrener.*

seed, *v.n.*, grener ; produire de la graine ; monter en graine.

seed, *v.a.*, semer.

seed'-bearing, *adj.*, séminifère.

seed'-bed, *n.*, semis, *m.*

seed'-bud (-beude), *n.*, germe ; (bot.) ovule, *m.*

seed'-cake, *n.*, gâteau anisé ; (of colza, linseed, etc.) tourteau, *m.*

seed'-coat (-côte), *n.*, (bot.) épisperme, *m.*, arille, *f.*

seed'-corn, *n.*, grain pour semis, *m.*

seed'-leaf (-lîfe), *n.*, (bot.) feuille séminale, *f. ;* cotylédon, *m.*

seed'ling, *n.*, plante semée, *f. ;* sauvageon, *m.*

seed'-lip *ou* **seed'-lop**, *n.*, semoir, *m.*

seed'-pearl (-peurle), *n.*, semence de perle, *f.*

seed'-plot, *n.*, semis, *m.*

seeds'man (sîdz'-), **seed'-merchant**, *n.*, grainier, grènetier, grainetier ; (sower) semeur, *m.*

seed'-time (-taïme), *n.*, semailles, *f.pl.*

seed'-trade, *n.*, grèneterie, *f.*

seed'-vessel, *n.*, (bot.) péricarpe, *m.*

seed'y (sîd'-), *adj.*, grenu ; (of brandy) aromatisé ; (worn out) râpé ; (pers.) éreinté, fatigué, mal à son aise, malade, souffrant. — clothes ; *habits râpés, m.pl.*

see'ing (sî-), *n.*, vue ; vision, *f.*

see'ing, *conj.*, (that) vu que ; puisque. — the state of things, *ou* matters ; *vu l'état de choses.*

seek (sîke), *v.a.*, (preterit and past part., Sought) chercher ; demander ; (one's life, property) en vouloir à. To — out ; *chercher ; rechercher ; quêter.* To — the life of ; *en vouloir, ou attenter, aux jours, ou à la vie* de.

seek, *v.n.*, chercher. To — for, after ; *poursuivre ; chercher ; rechercher, tâcher de trouver.* To — from ; *demander à.* To — to ; *faire tout son possible* **pour** ; *chercher* **à** ; (to apply to) *s'adresser* à.

seek'er, *n.*, chercheur, *m.*, chercheuse, *f.*

seek'ing, *n.*, recherche, poursuite, *f.*

seem (sî'm), *v.n.*, sembler ; paraître ; avoir l'air de. To — to ; *faire semblant* de; *feindre* de. It —s to me ; *ce me semble, il me semble.* Without —ing to ; *sans faire semblant* de. It —s *ou* it would —; (as the story goes) *à ce qu'il paraît.* So it —s ; *cela en a tout l'air.*

seem'ing, *n.*, semblant ; extérieur, *m. ;* apparence, *f. ;* dehors, *m. ;* (opinion) opinion, *f.*

seem'ing, *adj.*, apparent ; (sham) feint, faux ; (of things) spécieux.

seem'ingly, *adv.*, en apparence ; apparemment.

seem'ingness, *n.*, apparence spécieuse, *f.*

seem'liness, *n.*, bienséance ; convenance, grâce, *f.*

seem'ly, *adj.*, bienséant ; convenable.

seem'ly, *adv.*, avec bienséance ; convenablement.

seer (sî-eur), *n.*, spectateur, *m.*, spectatrice, *f.*, (prophet) prophète, voyant ; mage (V. Hugo), (weight in India), kilogramme, *m.* Sight—; *amateur de spectacles, m.*

see'saw (sî-çô), *n.*, bascule, balançoire, *f. ;* va-et-vient, *m.* — motion; *mouvement de va-et-vient, m.*

see'saw, *v.n.*, faire la bascule, basculer.

seethe (sîthe), *v.a.* and *n.*, faire bouillir ; bouillonner, cuire ; bouillir. The —ing crowd ; *la foule bouillonnante, ameutée.*

seeth'er (sîth'-), *n.*, marmite, *f.*

segar' *ou* **cigar'**, *n.*, cigare, *m.*

segar'- *ou* **cigar'-case**, *n.*, porte-cigare, *m.*

seg'ment (sèg'-), *n.*, segment, *m. ;* portion, *f. ;* morceau, *m.*

so'gregate (sî-grè-), *v.a.*, séparer.

sogrega'tion (sî-grè-ghé-), *n.*, séparation ; ségrégation, *f. ;* isolement, *m.*

seign'ior (sîn'ieur), *n.*, seigneur, *m.*

seine (séne), *n.*, (net) seine, *f.*

seiz'able (sîz'a-b'l), *adj.*, saisissable.

seize (sîze), *v.a.*, saisir ; (upon) se saisir de; s'emparer de; (nav.) aiguilleter ; (jur.) saisir. To — again ; *ressaisir, reprendre.* To be —d of ; *être en possession* de.

seized, *adj.*, saisi ; (with) saisi de, (illness, madness, etc.) atteint de, attaqué de ; (jur.) en possession de.

seiz'er, *n.*, (jur.) saisissant, *m.*

seiz'in (sîz'-), *n.*, (jur.) saisine, *f.*

seiz'ing, *n.*, action de saisir, *f.;* (nav.) aiguilletage, *m.;* (jur.) saisie, *f.*

seiz'ure (sîj'eur), *n.*, saisie ; prise ; (taking possession) prise de possession ; (jur.) capture, arrestation, saisie, saisie-arrêt ; (med.) attaque, *f.*, accès, *m.*

sel'dom (sèl-deume), *adv.*, rarement ; peu souvent.

sel'domness, *n.*, rareté, *f.*

select' (sè-lèkte), *adj.*, choisi ; d'élite ; distingué, bien composé. The — few ; *l'élite de la société, l'élite, f. ; le petit nombre des élus, m.*

select', *v.a.*, choisir.

select'ed, *adj.*, choisi.

select'edly, *adv.*, avec choix.

selec'tion (sè-lèk'-), *n.*, choix ; recueil, *m.* Natural —; *sélection naturelle, f.* Excellent —; *excellent choix, m. ; (of extracts) recueil choisi, m.*

select'ness, *n.*, bon choix, *m. ;* excellence ; excellente composition, *f.*

select'or, *n.*, qui choisit, qui fait un recueil.

sele'nium (sè-lî-), *n.*, (chem.) sélénium, *m.*

self (sèlfe), *pron.*, *(selves)* soi ; soi-même ; même. My—, thy—, him—, her—, it—; *moi-même, toi-même, lui-même, elle-même, se.* Our-selves, yourselves, themselves ; *nous-mêmes, vous-mêmes, eux-mêmes, elles-mêmes, se.* One's —; *se, soi-même.* Another —; *un autre soi-même ; un sosie* (Molière). I shave my—; *je me rase moi-même.* He knows how to enrich him—; *il sait s'enrichir.* By one's —; *seul ; tout seul ; de soi-même.* I dine by my—; *je dîne seul.* For my own —; *pour ma part.* Her gracious —; *sa gracieuse personne.* Her own dear —; *sa chère personne.*

self, *n.*, le moi, individu, *m. ;* personne, *f.*

self-abased' (-a-bés'te), *adj.*, humilié (par le sentiment de sa honte).

self-abase'ment (-a-bés'-), *n.*, humiliation volontaire, *f.*

self-abas'ing (-a-bés'-), *adj.*, qui s'humilie ; (of things) humiliant.

self-abuse' (-a-biouss), *n.*, abus de soi-même, dénigrement de ses propres talents, *m.*

self-accus'ing (-ak'kiouz'-), *adj.*, qui s'accuse soi-même.

self-act'ing, *adj.*, automoteur ; automobile ; automatique.

self-admira'tion (-mi-ré-), *n.*, admiration de soi-même, *f.*

self-admir'ing (-ad-maïeur'-), *adj.*, qui s'admire soi-même.

self-ador'ing, *adj.*, qui s'adore soi-même.

self-aggrand'izement (-daïz'-), *n.*, agrandissement de soi-même, *m.*

self-applause' (-plôze), *n.*, applaudissement de soi-même, *m.*

self-approv'ing (-prouv'-), *adj.*, qui s'approuve soi-même.

self-asser'tion (as-seur-), *n.*, défense (revendication) de sa propre dignité *ou* de ses droits, présomption, *f.*

self-assumed' (-as'sioum'de), *adj.*, de sa propre autorité.

self-begot'ten (-bi-got't'n), *adj.*, créé par soi-même ; produit par soi-même.

self'-born, *adj.*, né de soi-même.

self-cen'tred, *adj.*, fixé sur son centre.

self-command', *n.*, empire sur soi-même, sang-froid, *m. ;* retenue, *f.*

self-compla'cency, *n.*, suffisance, présomption, *f.*

self-conceit' (-co'n'sîte), *n.*, suffisance ; vanité, *f. ;* amour-propre, *m.*

self-conceit'ed, *adj.*, suffisant ; vain, rempli d'amour-propre.

self-conceit'edness. *V.* **self-conceit.**

self-condemna'tion (-dè'm'né-), *n.*, condamnation de soi-même, *f.*

self-con'fidence, *n.*, confiance en soi-même, assurance, *f.*

self-con'fident, *adj.*, confiant, *ou* plein de confiance, en soi-même ; sûr de soi.

self-con'scious (-co'n'sheusse), *adj.*, qui a la connaissance de soi-même, *f.*

self-con'sciousness (-sheus'-), *n.*, connaissance de soi-même, *f.*

self-con'sequence, *n.*, importance personnelle, *f.*

self-con'stituted, *adj.*, constitué par l'initiative de ses propres membres.

self-consum'ing (-sioum'-), *adj.*, qui se consume ; qui s'épuise ; qui se détruit soi-même.

self-contradic'tion, *n.*, contradiction avec soi-même, *f.*

self-contradic'tory, *adj.*, qui se contredit, contradictoire.

self-control', *n.*, empire sur soi-même, *m.*

self-convict'ed, *adj.*, convaincu, condamné par soi-même.

self-convic'tion (-vik'-), *n.*, conviction par soi-même, condamnation de soi-même, *f.*

self-creat'ed (-cri-ét'-), *adj.*, créé par soi-même.

self-deceit' (-dè-cîte), **self-decep'tion**, *n.*, illusion, *f.*

self-deceived' (-dè-cîv'de), *adj.*, qui se trompe soi-même, dupe de ses propres illusions.

self'-defense' (-dè-), *n.*, défense personnelle ; légitime défense, *f.* In —; *pour se défendre.* The art of —; *boxe, f. ; pugilat, m.*

self-delu'sion (-dè-liou-jeune), *n.*, illusion, *f.*

self-deni'al (-dè-naï-), *n.*, abnégation de soi-même, *f. ;* renoncement à soi-même ; désintéressement, dévouement, *m.*

self-deny'ing (-dè-naï-yigne), *adj.*, qui fait abnégation de soi-même ; qui s'oublie soi-même ; de dévouement, de désintéressement.

self-depend'ent (-dè-), *adj.*, qui dépend de soi-même ; indépendant.

self-destroy'er (-dè-stroï-yeur), *n.*, suicide, *m.*

self-destruc'tion (-dè-streuk'-), *n.*, suicide, *m.*

self-destruc'tive, *adj.*, qui tend à se détruire.

self-determina'tion (-dè-teur-mi-né-), *n.*, détermination par soi-même, *f.*

self-deter'mining (-dè-teur-mi'n'-), *adj.*, qui se détermine de soi-même.

self-devot'ed (-dè-vot'-), *adj.*, dévoué volontairement.

self-devour'ing (-dè-vaour'-), *adj.*, qui se dévore soi-même.

self-ed'ucated (-èd'iou-két'-), *adj.*, qui s'est instruit, ou formé de lui-même.

self-educa'tion, *n.*, instruction sans maîtres, *f.*

self-elect'ed (-è-lèkt'-), *adj.*, élu par soi-même.

self-elect'ive, *adj.*, qui a le droit de s'élire soi-même, *ou* d'élire ses membres.

self-enjoy'ment (-è'n'djoï-), *n.*, satisfaction intérieure, *f.*

self-esteem' (-ès-tîme), *n.*, estime de soi-même, *f.*

self-ev'ident, *adj.*, évident en soi ; évident de soi ; clair comme le jour, qui tombe sous le sens.

self-exalta'tion (-ègz-al-té-), *n.*, élévation de soi-même, *f.*

self-exalt'ing (-ègz-ôlt'-), *adj.*, qui s'exalte soi-même.

self-examina'tion (-ègz'a'm'i-né-), *n.*, examen de conscience, *m.*

self-excus'ing (-èks'kiouz'-), *adj.*, qui s'excuse soi-même.

self-exist'ence (-ègz'ist'-) *n.*, existence indépendante, *f.*

self-exist'ent, *adj.*, qui existe par soi-même.

self-flat'tering, *adj.*, qui se flatte soi-même.

self-flat'tery, *n.*, flatterie de soi-même, *f.*

self-gov'erned (-gheuv'eurn'de), *adj.*, gouverné par soi-même, indépendant, autonome.

self-gov'ernment (-gheuv'eurn'-), *n.*, empire sur soi-même, *m. ;* indépendance, *f. ;* gouvernement du peuple par le peuple, *ou* de la nation par la nation, *m.*, autonomie, *f.* The right to —; *le droit de se gouverner soi-même.*

self'-heal (-hîl), *n.*, (bot.) brunelle, *f.*

self-heal'ing, *adj.*, qui se guérit soi-même.

self-impor'tance, *n.*, égoïsme, *m.*

self-impor'tant, *adj.*, égoïste.

self-improve'ment, *n.*, instruction sans maîtres, culture de soi-même, *f.*

self-in'terest (-teur'èste), *n.*, intérêt personnel, égoïsme, *m.*

self-in'terested, *adj.*, intéressé, égoïste.

self-invit'ed (-vaït'-), *adj.*, invité par soi-même ; qui est venu sans invitation.

self'ish (sèlf'-), *adj.*, égoïste.

self'ishly, *adv.*, en égoïste, avec égoïsme, d'une manière égoïste.

self'ishness, *n.*, égoïsme, *m.*

self-judg'ing (-djeudj'-), *adj.*, qui se juge soi-même.

self-kin'dled, *adj.*, enflammé spontanément.

self-knowl'edge (-no-lèdje), *n.*, connaissance de soi-même, *f.*

self'-love (-leuve), *n.*, amour de soi ; égoïsme ; amour-propre, *m.*

self-lov'ing, *adj.*, égoïste.

self'-made, *adj.*, qui s'est fait ce qu'il est. He is a — man ; *il est l'artisan de sa fortune ; il est fils de ses œuvres.*

self-moved' (-mouv'de), *adj.*, mû spontanément.

self-mov'ing (-mouv'-), *adj.*, qui se meut de soi-même ; automoteur.

self-mur'der (-meur-), *n.*, suicide, *m.*

self-mur'derer, *n.*, suicide, *m.*

self-neglect' (-nèg-lèkte), *n.*, oubli de soi-même, *m.*

self-neglect'ing, *adj.*, qui s'oublie soi-même.

self-opin'ioned (-o-pi'n'ieu'n'de), *ou* **self-opin'ionated**, *adj.*, prévenu en faveur de soi-même ; vain ; entier dans ses opinions.

self-orig'inated, *adj.*, né spontanément.

self-pleas'ing (-plîz'-), *adj.*, qui se plaît à soi-même.

self-posses'sion (-poz'zèsh'-), *n.*, empire sur soi-même ; calme ; sang-froid ; aplomb, *m.*

self'-praise (-préze), *n.*, éloge de soi-même, *m.* — is no recommendation ; (prov.) *qui se loue, s'emboue.*

self-preserva'tion (-prè-zeur-vé-), *n.*, conservation de soi-même, *f.*

self-preserv'ing (-prè-zeurv'-), *adj.*, qui se conserve soi-même ; (of things) qui se conserve de soi-même.

self-reg'istering, *adj.*, à registre.

self-reg'ulating (-règh'iou-lét'-), *adj.*, automoteur ; agissant de soi-même.

self-reli'ance, *n.*, confiance en soi-même, indépendance, *f.*

self-repel'ling (-rè-pèl'-), *adj.*, d'une répulsion spontanée.

self-reproach' (-rè-prôtshe), *n.*, reproche de soi-même, *m. ;* condamnation de soi-même, *f.*

self-reproached' (-rè-prôtsh'te), *adj.*, qui se fait des reproches à soi-même.

self-reproved' (-rè-prouv'de), *adj.*, réprouvé par soi-même.

self-reprov'ing (-rè-prouv'-), *adj.*, qui se réprouve soi-même.

self-reprov'ing, *n.*, réprobation de soi-même, *f.*

self-restrained' (-rè-stré'n'de), *adj.*, contenu, retenu.

self-restrain'ing (-rè-stré'n'-), *adj.*, qui se contient (soi-même).

self-restraint' (-rè-stré'n'te), *n.*, retenue, *f.*

self-sac'rifice, *n.*, abnégation, *f.*

self'-same, *adj.*, le même ; exactement le même.

self-sat'isfied, *adj.*, content de soi.

self-secur'ity, *n.*, suffisance, infatuation, *f.*

self-seek'er, *n.*, égoïste, *m.f.*

self-seek'ing (-sîk'-), *adj.*, intéressé ; égoïste.

self-seek'ing, *n.*, égoïsme, *m.*

self-slaugh'ter (-slô-), *n.*, suicide, *m.*

self-styled' (-staïl'de), *adj.*, soi-disant, prétendu.

self-suffi'ciency (-seuf'fish'è'n'ci), *n.*, suffisance, *f.*

self-suffi'cient (-seuf'fish'è'n'te), *adj.*, suffisant.

self-support'ing, **self-support'ed**, *adj.*, subvenant (pourvoyant) lui-même (elle-même) à ses besoins ; se suffisant à lui-même (elle-même), indépendant.

self'-taught (-tôte), *adj.*, instruit par soi-même, qui s'est instruit seul.

self-torment'ing, *adj.*, qui se tourmente.

self-upbraid'ing (-eup'bréd'-), *adj.*, qui se fait des reproches à soi-même.

self-will', *n.*, obstination, opiniâtreté, *f.*

self-willed' (-wil'de), *adj.*, obstiné, volontaire, opiniâtre.

self-wor'ship (-weur-), *n.*, adoration de soi-même, *f.*

sell, *n.*, attrape, *f.* What a — for him ! *quelle attrape pour lui !*

sell, *v.a.*, (preterit and past part., Sold) vendre. To—any one up ; *vendre les marchandises,* ou *les meubles,* ou *les biens, de quelqu'un.* To— one's life dearly; *vendre chèrement sa vie.* To be sold ; *à vendre ;* (fig.) être attrapé, être mis dedans; *être exploité.* The papers sold like wild-fire ; *on enleva les journaux comme du pain.* To — out ; *vendre ; vendre tout ;* (mil.) *vendre son grade.* To — off ; *liquider, solder, vendre son fonds de commerce.*

sell, *v.n.*, se vendre. To — off ; *se liquider, se solder ;* (of goods) *s'écouler.* To — well ; *être de bonne vente.* To — by auction ; *vendre à l'encan, aux enchères.*

sel'landers *ou* **sel'lenders**, *n.pl.*, (vet.) solandre, *f.*

sell'er, *n.*, vendeur, *m.*, vendeuse, *f. ;* marchand, *m.*, marchande, *f.* (of, **de**).

selling-off', *n.*, liquidation, vente au rabais, *f.*

selling-out' (-aoute), *n.*, vente totale ; (ant.) (of the army) vente de son grade, *f.* — price; *prix de vente, m.*

seltz'er-water, *n.*, eau de seltz, *f.* A bottle of —; *une bouteille,* ou *un siphon, d'eau de Seltz.*

sel'vage (sèl-vèdje) *ou* **sel'vedge** (-vèdje), *n.*, lisière, *f.*

sel'vaged (-vèdj'de), *adj.*, à lisière.

sem'aphore (sè'm'a-fôre), *n.*, sémaphore, *m.*

sem'blance, *n.*, ressemblance ; image, *f. ;* (show) semblant, *m.*, apparence, *f.*

se'men (sî-mè'n), *n.*, (bot.) semence, *f.*

sem'i (sè'm'i), *adj.*, semi, demi, à demi, à moitié.

sem'i-an'nual, *adj.*, semi-annuel, semestriel.

sem'i-an'nular (-a'n'niou-), *adj.*, semi-annulaire.

sem'i-barba'rian (-bar-bé-), **sem'i-bar'barous** (-bar-beu), *adj.*, semi-barbare.

sem'i-breve (-brîve), *n.*, (mus.) ronde, *f.*

sem'i-circle (-cir-k'l), *n.*, demi-cercle, *m.*

sem'i-colon (-cô-), *n.*, point et virgule, *m.*

sem'i-cylin'drical, *adj.*, semi-cylindrique.

sem'i-detached', (of a house) contiguë à une autre. — houses ; *maisons jumelles, f. pl.*

sem'i-diaph'anous (-daï-), *adj.*, semi-transparent ; à moitié diaphane.

semi-floret', *n.*, demi-fleuron, *m.*

semi-lu'nar (-liou-), *adj.*, en demi-lune; semilunaire.

sem'i-metal, *n.*, demi-métal, *m.*

sem'i-metal'lic, *adj.*, semi-métallique.

sem'inal (sè'm'-), *adj.*, (bot.) séminal. — leaf ; *cotylédon, m.*

sem'inarist (sè'm'-), *n.*, séminariste, *m.*

sem'inary, *n.,* pépinière, *f.;* (ecc.) séminaire, *m.;* (school) institution, *f.,* pensionnat, *m.,* école, *f.;* (seminary priest) (ant.) séminariste *;* (fig.) pépinière, *f.*

semina'tion (sè'm'i'né-), *n.,* (bot.) sémination *;* (fig.) propagation, *f.*

sem'i-offi'cial, *adj.,* demi-officiel.

sem'i-offi'cially, *adv.,* demi-officiellement.

sem'i-opaque', *adj.,* demi-opaque.

sem'iped (-pède), *n.,* (prosody) demi-pied, *m.*

sem'iquaver (-kwé-), *n.,* (mus.) double croche, *f.* — rest *; quart de soupir, m.*

semi'-savage (-sav-èdge), *n.,* homme à demi-sauvage, *m.*

sem'i-spher'ical (-sfèr'-), *adj.,* demi-sphérique.

sem'itone (-tône), *n.,* (mus.) demi-ton, *m.*

sem'itonic (-tô'n'-), *adj.,* de demi-ton.

sem'i-transpar'ency, *n.,* demi-transparence, *f.*

sem'i-transpar'ent, *adj.,* demi-transparent.

sem'i-vowel (-vaou-èl), *n.,* demi-voyelle, *f.*

sempiter'nal (-teur-), *adj.,* éternel, sempiternel.

sempiter'nity (-teur-), *n.,* éternité, *f.*

semp'stress (sè'm'strèss), *n.,* couturière *;* lingère, *f.*

sen'ary (sè'n'-), *adj.,* senaire.

sen'ate (sè'n'-), *n.,* sénat, *m.*

sen'ate-chamber (-tchém-beur), *n.,* sénat, *m.*

sen'ate-house (-haouce), *n.,* sénat, *m.*

sen'ator (sè'n'-), *n.,* sénateur *;* (biblically) ancien, *m.*

senator'ial *ou* **senator'ian,** *adj.,* sénatorial *;* sénatorien *;* du sénat.

sen'atorship, *n.,* dignité de sénateur, *f.*

sena'tus consul'tum (sĭ-né-teus'co'n'seul-), *n.,* sénatus-consulte, *m.*

send (sè'n'de), *v.a.,* (*preterit and past part.,* Sent) envoyer *;* faire partir *;* expédier *;* adresser à *;* (to bestow) accorder *;* donner *;* (to inflict) infliger *;* (to diffuse) répandre. To — away *; renvoyer; congédier, faire partir.* To — back *; renvoyer.* To — down *; faire descendre, envoyer;* (at universities) *renvoyer temporairement.* To — forth *; produire; lancer; jeter;* (a cry) *pousser;* (of trees, etc.) *pousser;* (to emit) *émettre, répandre, exhaler.* To — for *; envoyer chercher, faire venir.* To — in *; faire entrer; introduire;* (to deliver) *livrer, déposer;* (to serve up) *servir;* (to publish) *annoncer.* To — off *; faire partir, renvoyer, expédier.* To — out *; envoyer dehors; faire sortir;* (to send on an errand) *envoyer en course;* (newspapers) *faire demander; faire appeler.* To — any one about his business *; envoyer promener (quelqu'un).* To — to health to *; donner la santé à.* To — on *;* (letters, etc.) *faire suivre.* To — word to *; envoyer dire à; faire dire* à *; envoyer un mot à.* To — up *; jeter, lancer, élever; lancer en l'air;* (to serve up) *servir.* To be in danger of being sent flying *; en danger de sauter.* To — on a fool's errand *; charger d'une commission ridicule.*

send, *v.n.,* envoyer *;* (nav.) tanguer. To — after any one, for any one, anything *; envoyer chercher quelqu'un, quelque chose; faire venir quelqu'un, quelque chose.* They have sent for me *; on m'a envoyé chercher.*

send'er, *n.,* envoyeur, *m.,* envoyeuse, *f.;* (com.) expéditeur, *m.*

send'ing, *n.,* envoi, *m.;* (com.) expédition, *f.*

sen'eschal (sè'n'ès-shal), *n.,* sénéchal, *m.*

sen'green (sè'n'grî'n), *n.,* (bot.) joubarbe, *f.*

se'nile (sĭ-naïle), *adj.,* de vieillard *;* sénile.

se'nilely, *adv.,* en vieillard

senil'ity (sĭ-nil'-), *n.,* vieillesse, sénilité, *f.*

sen'ior (sî'n'ieur), *adj.,* aîné *;* (in office) plus ancien, *m.;* (of classes, studies) élevé, supérieur. Mr. A. — *; M. A. aîné; M. A. père.*

sen'ior, *n.,* aîné, *m.,* aînée, *f.;* (in office)

ancien, *m.,* ancienne, *f.;* (in a firm) associé principal *;* (of societies) doyen, *m.*

senior'ity, *n.,* supériorité d'âge *;* ancienneté, *f.* By, *ou* by right of, — *; par droit d'ancienneté* (V. Hugo).

sen'na (sè'n'-), *n.,* (bot., pharm.) séné, *m.*

sen'night (sè'n'naïte), *n.,* huit jours, *n.pl.;* huitaine, *f.*

sen'nit (sè'n'nite), *n.,* tresse, *f.,* paillet, *m.;* (nav.) tresse, garcette, *f.*

sensa'tion (sè'n'sé-), *n.,* sensation, *f.;* sentiment, *m.* To make, *ou* create, a — *; faire sensation.*

sensa'tional, *adj.,* à sensation, à effet *;* qui vise à l'effet, qui fait sensation. — drama *; drame à effet, à sensation, saisissant, m.*

sense (sè'n'se), *n.,* bon sens *;* sens droit et délicat *;* (perception) sens *;* (understanding) sens, esprit, bon sens, *m.,* raison, intelligence *;* (sensibility) sensibilité, *f.;* (opinion) sens, sentiment, avis, *m.,* opinion, *f.;* (consciousness) sentiment *;* (signification) sens, *m.,* signification, force, acception *;* (reason) raison, *f.* Common — *; sens commun, m.* Good — *; bon sens.* A man of — *; un homme de bon sens, sensé.* In a good, a bad — *; en bonne, en mauvaise, part.* In the full — of the word *; dans toute l'acception du mot; dans toute la force du terme.* To be in one's right —s *; être dans son bon sens.* To be out of one's —s *; être hors de son bon sens.* To lose one's —s *; perdre la raison; perdre la tête;* (to swoon) *perdre connaissance.* To bring any one to his —s *; mettre, ou ramener, quelqu'un à la raison.* To drive any one out of his —s *; faire perdre la tête à quelqu'un.* To come to one's —s *; reprendre ses sens; reprendre connaissance;* (fig.) *revenir à la raison.* To take the — of an assembly *; prendre l'avis d'une assemblée, consulter une assemblée.* Against all — *; contre le sens commun.* To talk — *; dire des choses sensées; parler raison.* You are not in your right — *; vous avez perdu le sens.* The deep — of my obligation to you *; le sentiment profond de l'obligation que je vous ai.* To have a — of *; avoir le sentiment de; sentir.* There is no — in that *; cela ne signifie rien; cela n'a pas le sens commun.* To make sense *;* (of words) *faire un sens.* To take the — of a meeting *; mettre une question aux voix.*

sense'less, *adj.,* sans connaissance *;* (insensible) insensible, privé de sentiment *;* (unreasonable) insensé, déraisonnable, absurde *;* (meaningless) vide de sens.

sense'lessly, *adv.,* d'une manière insensée *;* déraisonnablement.

sense'lessness, *n.,* déraison, *f.;* manque de bon sens, *m.;* sottise *;* absurdité, *f.*

sensibil'ity, *n.,* sensibilité, *f.;* sentiment, *m.* False — *; sensiblerie, f.*

sen'sible (sè'n'si-b'l), *adj.,* (perceptible by the senses, having moral perception, intelligence) sensible à *;* (mus.) sensible *;* (intelligent) sensé, raisonnable *;* (conscious) avec toute sa connaissance, en pleine connaissance, conscient. To be — of *; être sensible à; avoir le sentiment de; avoir connaissance de.* A — man *; un homme intelligent, sensé.* A — answer *; une réponse sensée.* — to cold *; sensible au froid.* — of injury *; sensible aux injures.* He was not — *; il était sans connaissance.* — balance *; balance sensible, f.* — thermometer *; thermomètre sensible, m.* That is a — deed *; voilà une action sensée.* She is ostentatiously — to her inferiority *;* (Charles Lamb) *elle sent son infériorité, et ne s'en cache pas.*

sen'sibleness, *n.,* (sensibility) sensibilité *;* (possibility of being perceived by the senses) perceptibilité, perception *;* (intelligence) intelligence, *f.,* sens, bon sens, esprit, *m.,* raison, *f.*

sen'sibly, *adj.,* sensiblement *;* (intelligently) sensément, sagement, raisonnablement.

sen'sitive (se'n'si-tive), adj., sensible ; sensitif ; délicat, impressionable ; (touchy) susceptible, ombrageux.

sen'sitively, adv., d'une manière sensible, sensiblement.

sen'sitiveness, n., sensibilité; susceptibilité, f.

sen'sitive-plant, n., (bot.) sensitive, f.

sensor'ial (se'n'sō-), adj., sensorial, des sens.

sensor'ium ou sen'sory (se'n'sō-), n., sensorium ; organe des sens, m.

sen'sual (se'n'shiou-), adj., sensuel ; des sens.

sen'sualism (se'n'shiou-al'iz'm), n., (philos.) sensualisme, m.

sen'sualist, n., (philos.) sensualiste, m.f.

sensual'ity, n., sensualité, f.

sen'sually, adv., sensuellement ; d'une manière voluptueuse.

sen'tence (se'n'te'n'ce), n., (gram.) phrase, période ; (maxim) maxime, sentence ; (opinion) opinion, f., avis, m. ; (judgment) sentence, f., jugement, arrêt, m. To pass — of death on; condamner à mort; prononcer une sentence de mort contre.

sen'tence, v.a., prononcer une sentence, un jugement, un arrêt contre ; condamner.

senten'tious (se'n'te'n'sheusse), adj., sentencieux ; laconique.

senten'tiously, adv., sentencieusement ; laconiquement.

senten'tiousness, n., caractère sentencieux, laconisme, m.

sen'tient (se'n'shi-e'n'te), adj., sensitif ; capable de percevoir par les sens, sensible.

sen'timent, n., sentiment ; avis, m. ; opinion, pensée, f. ; (sensibility) sentiment, m.

sentiment'al, adj., sentimental.

sentiment'alist, n., personne sentimentale, f.

sentimental'ity, n., sensiblerie ; vive sensibilité, f.

sen'tinel ou sen'try, n., sentinelle, f. ; factionnaire, m. To stand — ; faire sentinelle, être de sentinelle, faire faction, être de faction.

sen'try-box, n., guérite ; (on a rampart) vedette, f.

separabil'ity, n., divisibilité, f.

sep'arable (-ra-b'l), adj., séparable, divisible.

sep'arate (sep'a-rét), adj., séparé ; disjoint ; (distinct) distinct ; (disunited) désuni ; à part ; seul ; (jur.) dotal. — estate ; biens dotaux, m.pl.

sep'arate, v.a., séparer ; disjoindre ; désunir.

sep'arate, v.n., se séparer ; se disjoindre.

sep'arated (sep'a-rét'éde), adj., séparé ; divisé.

sep'arately (-rét'li), adv., séparément ; à part.

separa'tion (sep'a-ré-), n., action de séparer ; séparation ; dissolution ; désunion, f.

sep'aratist (sep'a-ra-), n., séparatiste, m.

sep'aratory, adj., séparateur, qui sépare.

sepawn', sepon', n., (native food) gaude, f.

se'pia (si-), n., (pigment) sépia, f.

se'poy (si-pōi), n., cipaye ; (in Algeria) spahi, m.

seps (sèpse), n., (lizard) seps, m.

sept, n. V. sect.

septan'gular (-tai'gn'ghiou-), adj., (geom.) à sept angles.

Septem'ber, n., septembre, m.

septem'vir, n., septemvir, m.

septem'virate, n., septemvirat, m.

septen'ary (sèp-tè'n'-), adj., septénaire.

septen'nate, n., septennat, m.

septen'nial (sèp-tè'n'-), adj., septennal.

septen'nially, adv., tous les sept ans.

septen'trional, adj., septentrional.

septet', septette', n., sept. or, m.

sept'foil (sèpt'foil), n., (bot.) tormentille, f.

sep'tic, adj., (med.) septique.

sep'tic, n., (med.) poison septique, m.

septin'sular (-siou-leur), adj., (ant.) aux sept

îles. The — republic ; la république des îles Ioniennes, f.

septuagena'rian ou septuag'enary (sèp-tiou-a-dji-né-, -adj'i-na-), n., septuagénaire, m.f.

septuag'enary, adj., de soixante-dix ans ; septuagénaire.

septuages'ima (sèp-tiou-a-djèss'-), n., (ecc.) Septuagésime, f.

Sep'tuagint (sèp-tiou-a-djï'n'te), n., (Script.) version des Septante, f.

sep'tuple (sèp-tiou-p'l), adj., septuple.

sepul'chral (si-peul-kral), adj., sépulcral.

sep'ulchre (sèp'eul-keur), n., sépulcre, m.

sep'ulture (sèp'eul-tioure), n., sépulture, f.

se'quel (si-kwèl), n., suite ; conséquence, f. In the —; par la suite; dans la suite.

se'quence (si-kwè'n'ce), n., suite ; série, f. ; ordre de succession, m. ; (c.rel. ; at cards) séquence, f.

seques'ter (si-kwès'teur), v.a., séquestrer. To — one's self ; se séquestrer ; se retirer.

seques'ter, v.n., se séquestrer ; (jur.) (of widows) renoncer à la succession de son mari.

seques'tered (-teurde) adj., retiré, écarté ; (jur.) en séquestre.

seques'trable (-'ra-b'l), adj., sujet à séquestre.

seques'trate, v.a., séquester.

sequestra'tion (-tré-), n., prise de possession, f. ; séquestre, m. ; (retirement) retraite, f., isolement, m.

seq'uestrator (-tré-teur), n., (jur.) séquestre, m.

se'quin (si-kwi'n), n., sequin, m.

seragl'io (si-ral'iō), n., sérail, m.

ser'aph (sèr'-), n., (seraphim) séraphin, m.

seraph'ic ou seraph'ical, adj., séraphique.

ser'aphim, n.pl., séraphins, m.pl.

seras'kier, n., sérasquier, m.

Serb, n., Serbe, m.f.

sere (sîre), adj. V. sear.

serenade', n., sérénade, f.

serenade', v.a., donner une sérénade à, sérénader.

serene' (si-rîne), adj., serein ; calme ; (bright) clair ; brillant ; (title) sérénissime. All —! (int.) tout va bien ! ça y est ! parfait !

serene'ly, adv., avec sérénité.

serene'ness (si-rî'n'-) ou seren'ity (si-rè'n'-), n., sérénité, f. ; calme parfait, m. ; (title) Sérénité, f.

serf (seurfe), n., (feudal law) serf, m.

serf'dom, n., (feudal law) servage, m.

serge (seurdje), n., serge, f. —maker ; serger, sergier, m. — manufactory, — trade ; sergerie, f.

ser'geant (sâr-dje'n'te), n., huissier ; (of infantry) sergent ; (of cavalry) maréchal des logis ; (of police) brigadier de gendarmerie (V. Hugo); (jur.) (ant.) avocat de premier rang, m. — major ; (of infantry) sergent-major ; (of cavalry) maréchal des logis chef, m. — at arms ; sergent d'armes.

ser'geancy, ser'geantship, n., fonctions d'huissier, f.pl. ; (of infantry) grade de sergent; (of cavalry) grade de maréchal des logis ; (of police) grade de brigadier de gendarmerie, m.

ser'ial, adj., sérial, paraissant par série ou par livraisons.

ser'ial, n., publication périodique, f.

ser'io-comic, adj., héroï-comique.

ser'ially, adv., par série.

ser'iated, adj., en série.

seria'tim, adv., régulièrement, par ordre.

ser'ies (si-rize), n., suite ; succession ; série, f.

ser'ious (si-), adj., sérieux, grave. To take for — ; prendre au sérieux. Is he — ? parle-t-il sérieusement ?

ser'iously, adv., sérieusement, grièvement, gravement. To take — ; prendre au sérieux.

ser'iousness, n., sérieux, m., gravité, f.

ser'jeant. V. **ser'geant.**

ser'mon (seur-), n., sermon ; prône ; prêche, m.

ser'monize (-'aïze), v.n., prêcher ; sermonner ; faire des sermons.

ser'monizer (-'aïz'-), n., sermonneur, m.

seros'ity (sî-ross'-), n., sérosité, f.

ser'ous (sî-), adj., séreux.

ser'pent (seur-), n., (reptile, astron., mus., fig.) serpent ; (firework) serpenteau, m.

Serpenta'rius, n., (astron.) Serpentaire, m.

ser'pent-fish, n., (ich.) serpent d'eau, m.

ser'pentine (-pè'n'taïne), adj., serpentin, de serpent ; qui serpente ; qui va en serpentant ; sinueux ; tortueux ; (marble) serpentin. **—-worm**, (of a still) serpentin, m.

ser'pentine, n., (min.) serpentine, f.

ser'pent-like (-laïke), adj., de, ou en, serpent.

ser'pent's-tongue, n., (bot.) langue-de-serpent, ophioglosse, f.

ser'rate ou **ser'rated** (sèr-), adj., en scie ; (of machines) à engrenage, dentelé ; serraté.

ser'ried, adj., compact, serré, pressé.

serrula'tion (sèr-riou-lé-), n., dentelure, f.

ser'um (sî-), n., sérum, m.

ser'vant (seur-), n., serviteur, m., servante, f. ; (of companies, etc.) employé, m. ; (domestic) domestique, m.f., servante, bonne, fille, femme de service, f. ; (of officers) brosseur, (bondman) esclave ; (of God) serviteur, m., servante, f. **—-s'** hall ; office, f. Your **—!** votre serviteur ! votre servante ! Man—; domestique, m. Woman—; domestique, servante, bonne, f. Maid—; servante, bonne, f. **—-boy** ; petit domestique, m. General—; bonne à tout faire ; domestique, f. **—** of **—s** ; (title assumed by the Pope) serviteur des serviteurs de Dieu, m.

serve, v.a., servir ; (to treat) traiter, en user avec, en agir avec, agir à l'égard de ; (to fulfill) servir à, remplir ; (to satisfy) satisfaire, contenter ; (to comply with) s'accommoder à ; (to obey) obéir à ; (to be a slave to) être esclave de ; (an apprenticeship) faire ; (a gun) servir ; (a battery) desservir ; (a trick) jouer ; (a church) desservir ; (a rope) fourrer, garnir ; (a writ) (upon) signifier à. Dinner was **—**d in . . . ; on servit à dîner dans . . . Dinner is **—**d ! Monsieur, Madame, est servi, servie ! To **—** out ; (to distribute) distribuer ; (to be revenged on) rendre la monnaie de sa pièce à, payer, rendre la pareille à, arranger (quelqu'un) ; (time) finir, achever. I will **—** him out ; je lui revaudrai cela ; il me le paiera, ou payera. To **—** up ; servir. It **—**ed you, him, etc., right ; c'est bien fait ; vous n'avez (il n'a, etc.) que ce que vous méritez (que ce qu'il mérite, etc.) ; vous ne l'avez pas volé. To **—** a writ of attachment ; (jur.) faire une saisie-exécution. To **—** a writ, a process (upon) ; signifier un exploit à. To **—** a warrant (upon) ; signifier un mandat d'arrêt ou d'amener.

serve, v.n., servir ; (in the army, etc.) servir, être au service ; (the purpose of) servir de ; (to be convenient) être convenable, être favorable, (to be in subjection) être esclave ; (to suffice) suffire. To **—** as ; servir de. To **—** for nothing ; ne servir de rien ; ne servir à rien.

ser'vice (seur-vice), n., service ; (favor) service, office, m., faveur, f. ; (use) avantage, m., utilité, f. ; (bidding) ordres, m.pl. ; (worship) service, office ; (duty) devoir, hommage, m. ; obéissance, f. ; (nav., milit.) service, m. ; (of a rope) fourrure, f. ; (of a writ) signification, f. ; (of china, of plate, etc.) service, m. ; (of a rope) fourrure, f. Divine **—** ; office divin. Tea— ; cabaret à thé ; service à thé, m. Secret **—** money ; (police, etc.) fonds secrets, m.pl. In **—**, out at **—** ; (of servants) en service, en condition. Out of **—** ; (of servants) sans place. The **—** ; l'armée, la marine, f. Of **—** ; utile. On **—** ; (on duty) de service. On active **—** ; en activité. In the **—** of ;

au service de. To do, ou be of, **—** to ; être utile à ; faire du bien à. To do any one a **—** ; rendre un service à quelqu'un. In the **—** ; (army) au service. To be in the **—** of ; être au service de. To go to **—** ; se mettre en service, entrer en condition.

ser'viceable (-a-b'l), adj., (pers.) utile à, (obliging) serviable ; (of things) avantageux à, utile à, qui peut servir.

ser'viceableness, n., (pers.) (obligingness) disposition serviable, disposition à rendre service, f. ; (of things) avantage, m., utilité, f.

ser'viceably, adv., utilement, d'une manière utile.

ser'vice-book (-bouke), n., rituel, m.

ser'vice-pipe, n., tuyau de service, m.

ser'vice-tree, n., (bot.) sorbier domestique ; cormier, m.

ser'vile (seur-vaïl), adj., servile ; (in subjection) asservi.

ser'vilely, adv., servilement, avec servilité.

ser'vileness ou **servil'ity**, n., (slavery) servitude, f. ; esclavage, m. ; (baseness) servilité, bassesse, f.

ser'ving, adj., servant ; qui sert.

ser'ving-maid (-méde), n., servante, f.

ser'ving-man, n., serviteur, m.

ser'vitor (seur-vi-teur), n., serviteur, m. ; (at Oxford University) étudiant servant, boursier, m.

ser'vitorship, n., bourse, f.

ser'vitude (seur-vi-tioude), n., servitude, f. ; asservissement, m. Penal **—** ; travaux forcés, m.pl. ; (for life) à perpétuité.

ses'ame, n., (bot.) sésame, m. Open **—** ; sésame, ouvre-toi.

ses'eli, n., (bot.) séséli, m.

ses'quitone (-koui-tône), n., (mus.) tierce mineure, f.

ses'sile (sès'sile), adj., sessile.

ses'sion (sèsh'-), n., session ; (sitting) séance, f. **—s**, pl., assises, f.pl. Quarter-**—s** ; assises trimestrielles ; audiences trimestrielles, f.pl.

ses'terce (sès-teurce), n., sesterce, m.

ses'tet, n., (mus.) sextuor, m.

set, v.a., (preterit and past part., Set) poser ; (to put) mettre ; (to place) placer ; (to fix) fixer ; (to plant) planter ; (to appoint) indiquer ; (to regulate) régler, déterminer ; (to sharpen) repasser, affiler ; (tools) affûter ; (to begin to sing) entonner ; (to spread) déployer ; (to oppose) opposer ; (an example) donner ; (to music) mettre en ; (a bone) remettre, remboîter ; (precious stones) monter, enchâsser ; (a hen) faire couver ; (a clock, etc.) mettre à l'heure, régler ; (the land) (nav.) relever ; (a task) donner, imposer ; (milk) laisser reposer ; (a trap) dresser, tendre ; (of dogs) arrêter, tomber en arrêt sur ; (print.) composer. To **—** against ; opposer à. To **—** a-going ; faire aller ; mettre en mouvement ; mettre en marche (Bert.). To **—** in motion ; mettre en mouvement, faire aller. To **—** apart, aside ; mettre à part ; mettre de côté. To **—** aside ; mettre de côté ; écarter ; (to annul) casser, infirmer ; (to reject) rejeter. To **—** at ; exciter, agacer contre, exciter après. To **—** a dog at ; haler un chien après, contre. To **—** by ; mettre de côté ; (to reject) rejeter. To **—** a watch by the right time ; mettre une montre à l'heure. To **—** by the ears ; brouiller. To **—** down ; poser ; mettre à terre, mettre par terre ; (to establish) établir, arrêter ; (to register) coucher par écrit, mettre par écrit, inscrire, désigner ; (to relate) rapporter ; (from a vehicle) descendre ; (fig.) mettre à sa place. To **—** down as ; considérer (comme), estimer, appeler. To **—** forth ; manifester, montrer ; faire paraître ; (to publish) publier, énoncer ; (to display) déployer, relever, rehausser ; faire ressortir ; (to explain) expliquer, développer. To **—** forward ; avancer ; (to promote) favoriser ; pousser, faire avancer. To **—** off ;

(to adorn) *orner*, *parer*, *embellir*, *relever ;* (to eulogize) *rehausser ; mettre en relief*, *faire ressortir ;* (to place against as an equivalent) *compenser* par. Her clothes — off her figure ; *ses vêtements dessinaient avantageusement sa taille.* To — on ; *exciter* à, *pousser* à ; (to employ) *employer* à, *pousser* à. To — on edge ; (teeth) *agacer.* To — on fire ; *mettre le feu* à, *incendier ;* (fig.) *enflammer*, *mettre en feu.* To — out ; (to assign) *assigner*, *allouer ;* (to mark) *marquer*, *tracer ;* (to adorn) *orner*, *embellir ;* (to set off) *rehausser.* To — over ; *établir* sur ; *préposer* à. To — up ; (to erect) *ériger*, *élever*, *dresser ;* (to establish) *établir ;* (at auctions) *mettre à prix ;* (to found) *fonder*, *établir ;* (to exalt) *élever*, *exalter ;* (to place in view) *mettre en évidence ;* (to utter loudly) *pousser*, *jeter ;* (to advance) *mettre en avant*, *avancer ;* (print.) *composer ;* (a carriage) *se donner*, *se payer.* To — up its back ; (of a cat) *faire le gros dos.* To — up in business ; *établir.* To — up a laugh ; *se mettre à rire.* To be hard — ; *être bien embarrassé.* To — at ease ; *mettre* à *l'aise ; rendre tranquille.* To — to music ; *mettre en musique.* To — sail ; *mettre à la voile*, *appareiller.* To — the sails ; *hisser*, *déferler les voiles.* To — one's self about ; *se mettre* à ; *s'occuper* de. To — free ; *mettre en liberté.* All sails — ; *toutes voiles dehors*, *toutes voiles déployées.* To — in order ; *arranger*, *ranger.* To — eyes upon ; *jeter les yeux* sur. To — one's face ; *se diriger ; diriger ses regards* sur *(un objet)*, vers *(un endroit).* To — one's heart upon ; *convoiter*, *désirer vivement ; avoir envie* de. To — one's self to ; *s'appliquer*, *s'ingénier* à. To —, ou put, the, ou one's, shoulder to the wheel ; *se mettre* à *l'œuvre ; pousser* à *la roue ; y mettre du sien* (Daudet). To — on foot ; *mettre en branle*, ou *en vogue.* To — right ; *redresser ; corriger.* To — the fashion ; *mettre en marche ; régir la mode.* He has not — the Thames on fire ; *il n'a pas inventé la poudre.* To — at defiance ; *défier*, *braver.* To — at naught ; *ne faire aucun cas* de ; *ne compter pour rien ; ne tenir aucun compte* de ; *braver*, *mépriser.* To — a trap, ou snare ; *tendre*, *dresser un piège* à. To — at work ; (trans.) *mettre* à *l'œuvre.* To — eyes on ; *regarder*, *contempler ; apercevoir.* I have never so much as — eyes on him ; *je ne l'ai même pas aperçu de loin.* To — in ; *planter*, *fixer*, *établir ; mettre en train.* To — little, ou much (store), by ; *avoir une pauvre ou haute opinion* de, *faire peu ou grand cas* de. To — at variance ; *mettre mal* avec ; *brouiller.* — a thief to catch a thief ; (prov.) à *corsaire*, *corsaire et demi.* To — the fox to keep the geese ; (prov.) *renfermer le loup dans la bergerie.*

set, *v.n.*, (of the sun) se coucher ; (to be fixed) *se fixer ;* (to congeal) *se coaguler*, *se figer*, *se prendre ;* (to plant) *planter ;* (of the tide) *se diriger ;* (of plants) *prendre racine*, *prendre ;* (arch., mas.) *prendre*, *prendre du corps ;* (hunt.) *chasser au chien d'arrêt ;* (of dogs) *arrêter*, *tomber en arrêt.* The sun is —ting ; *le soleil se couche.* To — forth ; *s'avancer ; partir.* To — about ; *s'occuper* de ; *s'appliquer* à ; *se mettre* à. To — forward ; *se mettre en marche ; se mettre en chemin.* To — in ; *commencer ;* (of the weather) *se mettre* à ; (to flow) *se diriger* vers ; (of a storm) *s'élever ;* (to be felt) *se faire sentir.* Winter has — in ; *l'hiver a commencé.* It — in wet ; *le temps se mit à la pluie.* To — off ; *se mettre en route*, *se mettre en chemin*, *partir.* To — on ; (to begin) *commencer ;* (to assault) *attaquer.* To — out ; *partir ;* (to begin) *commencer*, *débuter.* To — to ; *se mettre* à. To — up ; (in business for one's self) *s'établir* à, ou pour, *son compte.* To — up for ; *se donner* pour ; *avoir des prétentions* à.

set, *adj.*, mis, posé, placé ; (regular) régulier ; (fixed) arrêté, fixe, immobile ; (firm) ferme, résolu ; (prescribed) prescrit, établi ; (of battles) rangé ; (of speech) d'apparat, préparé ; (of phrases) d'usage, tout fait, fixe. — square ; *équerre*, *f.* — purpose ; *dessein arrêté*, à *propos*, *m.* Of — purpose ; *exprès*, à *dessein*, *de propos délibéré.* — fair ; (barometer) *au beau.*

set, *n.*, (collection) collection, réunion, *f. ;* (of china or other ware) service, *m. ;* (of ornaments, ribbons, etc.) garniture ; (of precious stones) parure, *f. ;* (of chairs, tables, etc.) assortiment ; (of trees, etc.) rang, *m.*, rangée, *f. ;* (opinions) système, *m. ;* (of studs) garniture ; (pers.) réunion, *f.*, assemblage, corps, *m.*, (b.s.) clique, bande, troupe, *f. ;* (of horses) attelage, *m. ;* (of harness) paire, *f. ;* (young plant) plant, *m. ;* (game) partie, *f. ;* (bet at dice) pari ; (of the sun, etc.) coucher, *m.* — of furniture ; *ameublement*, *m.* To come to a dead — ; *être stationnaire ; être* à *quia ; rester court.* To make a dead — upon ; *mettre au pied du mur ; attaquer vivement*, *combattre avec acharnement.* — of teeth ; *denture*, *f.*, *râtelier*, *m.*

set'-down (-daoune), *n.*, semonce, *f. ;* savon, *m.*

se'tiform (sî-ti-), *adj.*, en forme de soie, filiforme.

set'-off, *n.*, compensation, déduction ; contrepartie, *f. ;* (decoration) embellissement ; ornement, relief, *m. ;* (in a wall) retraite ; (jur.) reconvention, *f.* As a — against ; *par contre ; en compensation* de.

set'-out (-aoute), *n.*, attirail ; appareil ; étalage ; commencement, début ; (departure) départ, *m. ;* (bustle) confusion, vie, *f.*

settee' (sèt'tî), *n.*, canapé, tête-à-tête, *m. ;* causeuse, *f.*

set'ter (sèt'teur), *n.*, (dog) chien d'arrêt ; chien couchant ; (mus.) compositeur ; (of gems) monteur, *m. ;* (fig.) embaucheur, *m.*

setter-on', *n.*, instigateur, *m.*, instigatrice, *f.*

set'ting, *n.*, mise, pose, *f. ;* placement, *m. ;* fixation, *f.*, établissement ; (of the sun, etc.) coucher, *m. ;* (of mus.) mise en musique, *f. ;* (of a bone) emboîtement, remboîtement ; (of precious stones) montage, *m.*, enchâssure ; (of plastering) prise, *f. ;* (of the compass) relèvement ; (of razors) repassage, *m. ;* (of a stone) pose, *f.* — free ; *élargissement*, *m. ; mise en liberté*, *f.* — sun ; *soleil couchant*, *m.* — of the sun ; *coucher du soleil*, *m.* — in ; *commencement*, *début*, *m.* — off ; *départ*, *m.* — on ; *instigation*, *incitation*, *f.* — out ; *départ ;* (commencement) *début*, *commencement*, *m.* — rule ; *filet* à *composer*, *m.* — stick ; *compositeur*, *m.* — up ; *établissement*, *m. ;* (print.) *composition*, *f.*

set'tle (sèt'ti'l), *n.*, banc, *m.*

set'tle (sèt'ti'l), *v.a.*, (to fix) fixer, établir ; (to establish, to marry) établir ; (to determine) déterminer, décider, arrêter ; (to colonize) coloniser ; (to tranquilize) tranquilliser, calmer ; (to adjust) accommoder, arranger ; (questions, etc.) résoudre ; (a minister) installer ; (to pay) payer ; (a quarrel) arranger, ajuster ; (lees) faire déposer ; (accounts) régler, arrêter, solder ; (to make close ; arch., mas.) tasser, faire tasser. To — up ; *régulariser.* To — a pension on ; *assigner une pension* à ; *constituer une rente* à. To — a country ; *coloniser un pays.* To — any one ; *donner son compte* à *quelqu'un*, *dire son fait* à *quelqu'un.*

set'tle, *v.n.*, (to sink to the bottom) se rasseoir ; reposer ; déposer ; (to fix one's residence) s'établir, se fixer ; (of birds) se poser ; (to marry) s'établir ; faire une fin, se mettre en ménage ; (to become fixed after change, as of the wind) se fixer ; (to repose) reposer ; (to become calm) se calmer, se tranquilliser ; (of the weather) se remettre, se remettre au beau ; (to determine) se déterminer, se décider ; (to become compact) (arch., mas.) tasser, se tasser ; (to come to an agreement) prendre des arrangements, s'arranger, s'organiser. To — down; *se fixer, s'établir*. To — down to; *s'appliquer* à. To — into; *devenir; finir par former; se faire* à. To — with; *régler avec*. To let —; *laisser reposer*.

set'tled, *adj.*, fixe, établi; calme, tranquille, permanent. — price; *prix fait, m.* — idea; *idée fixe, f.* — habit; *habitude faite, enracinée, f.*

set'tlement, *n.*, (act of settling) établissement; (subsidence) dépôt, *m.*, action de former au fond; (act of giving possession) mise en possession; (jur.) institution, *f.*; (jointure) douaire, *m.*; (of an annuity) constitution, *f.*; (marriage and housekeeping) établissement, *m.*; (a becoming stationary) fixation; (colonization) colonisation; établissement, *m.*; (colony) colonie, *f.*, établissement; (of disputes, etc.) ajustement; arrangement; accommodement; (of accounts) règlement, *m.*; (of a question, etc.) solution; (of a minister) installation, *f.*; (legal residence) domicile légal, *m.*; (liquidation) liquidation, *f.*, (arch., mas.) tassement, *m.* Act of —; *acte de succession (au trône), m.* Deed of —; *acte, ou contrat, de constitution, m.* Marriage- —; (jointure) *douaire; contrat de mariage, m.*

set'tler, *n.*, colon, *m.*

set'tling, *n.*, (act of settling) établissement, *m.*; (subsidence) précipitation, *f.*; (marriage and housekeeping) établissement; (of an annuity) constitution; (a becoming stationary) fixation; (colonization) colonisation, *f.*; (of disputes, etc.) ajustement, arrangement, accommodement, *m.*; (of questions) solution, *f.*; (of accounts) règlement; (arch., mas.) tassement, *m. pl.*, (of liquids) sédiment, dépôt, *m.*, lie, *f.* — day; (fin.) *jour de liquidation, m.*

set'-to (-tou), *n.*, dispute, *f.*; chamaillis, *m.*; batterie, brossée, *f.*; (fenc.) assaut, *m.*

sev'en (sèv'n), *adj.*, sept.

sev'enfold (-fôlde), *adj.* and *adv.*, septuple, de sept fois; sept fois.

sev'en-hilled (-hilde), *adj.*, aux sept collines.

sev'ennight (sè'n'naïte), *n.* V. **sennight**.

sov'enscore (-scôre), *adj.*, cent quarante.

sev'enteen (-tîne), *adj.*, dix-sept.

sev'enteenth (-tî'n'th), *adj.*, dix-septième.

sev'enth (sèv'n'th), *adj.*, septième; (of kings) sept.

sev'enth, *n.*, septième, *m.*; (mus.) septième, *f.*; (of the month) sept, *m.*

sev'enthly, *adv.*, septièmement.

sev'entieth (-tièth), *adj.*, soixante-dixième.

sev'enty, *adj.*, soixante-dix. The —, the Septuagint; (Script.) *les Septante, m.pl.*

sev'er (sèv'eur), *v.a.*, séparer; diviser; désunir; (cut) couper, trancher; disjoindre. To — one's connection with; *rompre toutes relations avec.*

sev'er, *v.n.*, faire une séparation; se séparer.

sev'eral (sèv'reul), *adj.*, plusieurs; (divers) divers; (different) différent; (distinct) distinct, séparé; (particular) particulier; respectif.

sev'erally, *adv.*, séparément; individuellement; en particulier, respectivement; distinctement; à part.

sev'erance (sèv'-), *n.*, séparation, désunion; disjonction, *f.*

severe' (sè-vîre), *adj.*, sévère; (cruel) cruel; (rigorous) rigoureux, rude; (violent) violent, grand; (acute) aigu, vif. A — winter; *un hiver rigoureux.* A — cold; *un gros rhume.*

severe'ly (sè-vîr'-), *adv.*, sévèrement; cruellement; rigoureusement.

sever'ity (sè-vèr'-), *n.*, sévérité; (rigor) rigueur, violence, gravité, *f.*

sew (sô), *v.a.* and *n.*, coudre; (of books) brocher.

sewed (sôd'), *adj.*, (of books in paper wrappers) broché.

sew'age (siou-èdje), *n.*, immondices des égouts; eaux des égouts; curures, *f.pl.*; gadoue, *f.*

sew'er (sô-eur), *n.*, couseur, *m.*; couseuse, *f.*

sew'er (siou-eur), *n.*, (subterranean channel) égout; cloaque; conduit pour les eaux, *m.*

sew'erage (siou-eur-èdje), *n.*, égout; système d'égouts, *m.*; égouts, *m.pl.*; immondices des égouts, *f.pl.*

sew'ing (sô-igne), *n.*, couture, *f.* — machine; *machine à coudre, f.* — press; (print.) *cousoir, m.*

sew'ing-cotton, *n.*, cotton à coudre, *m.*

sew'ing-silk (sô-ign'-), *n.*, soie à coudre, *f.*

sex, *n.*, sexe, *m.* The fair —; *le sexe, le beau sexe, m.*

sex'less, *adj.*, sans sexe.

sexagena'rian (sèks-a-dji-né-), *n.*, sexagénaire, *m.f.*

sexag'enary (sèks-adj'i-), *adj.*, sexagénaire.

Sexages'ima (sèks-a-djèss'-), *n.*, (ecc.) Sexagésime, *f.*

sexages'imal, *adj.*, sexagésimal.

sex'angle (sèks-ai'gn'g'l), *n.*, hexagone, *m.*

sex'angled (-g'l'de) *ou* **sexan'gular** (-ghiou-), *adj.*, hexagone.

sexen'nial (sèks-'è'n-), *adj.*, sexennal.

sexen'nially, *adv.*, tous les six ans.

sex'tain (sèks'tine), *n.*, sixain, sizain, *m.*

sex'tant, *n.*, (astron.) sextant, *m.*

sex'ton (-teu'ne), *n.*, fossoyeur; (ant.) sacristain, *m.*

sex'tonship, *n.*, charge de fossoyeur, *f.*

sex'tuple (sèks-tiou-p'l), *adj.*, sextuple, *m.*

sex'ual (sèk'shiou-eule), *adj.*, sexuel.

sexual'ity (-al'i-), *n.*, sexualité, *f.*, sexualisme, *m.*

shab, *v.a.*, jouer un mauvais tour (à un amant).

shab'bily, *adv.*, (of dress) mal mis, mal vêtu; avec des habites râpés; (meanly) mesquinement.

shab'biness, *n.*, (of dress) état râpé, *m.*; pauvreté; (meanness) bassesse, mesquinerie, *f.*

shab'by, *adj.*, (of clothes) usé, râpé, qui montre la corde; (of hats) pelé, usé; (clothed shabbily) mal vêtu, mal mis; (mean) mesquin, bas, petit, vilain, ignoble. That is very — of you; *c'est bien mal à vous; c'est bien petit, ou vilain, de votre part.* — fellow; *drôle mal brossé* (V. Hugo); *homme mesquin, m.; un ladre, un crasseux.* To play a — trick to; *jouer un tour ignoble* à. — genteel; *assez mal vêtu.* — looking; *de pauvre apparence.*

shac'kle (shak'k'l), *v.a.*, enchaîner; garrotter; (fig.) entraver, embarrasser, empêtrer.

shac'kles (shak'k'l'ze), *n.pl.*, fers, liens, *m.*; chaînes; (fig.) entraves, *f.pl.*

shad, *n.*, (ich.) alose, *f.*

shad'dock, *n.*, (bot.) pamplemousse, *f.* and *m.*

shade, *n.*, ombre, *f.*; ombrage; (of a lamp, etc.) abat-jour, *m.*; (of color) nuance; (spirit) ombre; (paint.) ombre, (degree) idée, *f.*; (of a clock) globe, cylindre, *m.*; (of a cap) visière, *f.*; (for the eyes) garde-vue, *m.* —s, *pl.*, (wine vaults) caveaux; (abode of spirits) enfers, *m.pl.* The —s of night; *les ombres de la nuit, f.pl.*; (of an hotel, public-house) *estaminet, m., buvette, f.* To throw into the —; *éclipser.* In, *ou* under, the —; *à l'ombre.* Prices are a — higher; *les prix sont une idée plus élevés.*

shade, *v.a.*, ombrager (with, **de**); couvrir d'ombre; (to obscure) obscurcir, cacher, masquer; (to protect) abriter, protéger, mettre à l'ombre; (paint.) ombrer; (to mark with gradations of color) nuancer.

shad'ed (shéd'-), *adj.*, à l'ombre; (paint.) ombré; (of places) ombragé **de**.

shad'ed, *p.p.*, abrité **de**, *ou* **contre**.

shade'less, *adj.*, sans ombre; privé d'ombre.

shad'iness (shéd'-), *n.*, ombrage; état ombreux, *m.*; ombre; (fig.) nature suspecte, *f.*

shad'ing (shéd'-), *n.*, ombrage, *m.*

shad'ow (shad'ô), *n.*, ombre; (type) figure, *f.*, type, signe, *m.*; (protection) ombre, *f.*, abri, *m.* Under the — of; *à l'ombre* **de**. The great —s of a picture; *les grandes ombres d'un tableau.* To pass like a —; *passer comme une ombre.* May your — never grow less; *puissiez-vous ne jamais essuyer les revers de la fortune.* He is but a —; *il n'est plus que son ombre,* ou *que l'ombre de lui-même.*

shad'ow, *v.a.,* ombrager; couvrir de son ombre; (colors) nuancer; (to protect) protéger, abriter; (to represent faintly) esquisser, ébaucher; (to hide) cacher, couvrir; (paint.) ombrer; (to follow closely) espionner. To — forth; (to represent typically) *représenter; figurer.*

shad'owing (shad'ô-igne), *n.,* ombrage, *m.,* action d'ombrer, de nuancer, *f.;* (fig.) espionnage, *m.*

shad'owless, *adj.,* sans ombre.

shad'owy (shad'ô-i), *adj.,* couvert d'ombre; ombragé; (gloomy) sombre, ténébreux; (typical) typique, figuré; (unreal) chimérique; (obscure) obscur.

shad'y (shéd'i), *adj.,* couvert d'ombre; ombragé; ombreux; (cool) frais; (dark) sombre, obscur; (sheltered) à l'ombre. The — side (of the street); *le côté ombragé, où il y a de l'ombre.*

shaft (shâf'te), *n.,* (arrow) flèche, dard, trait; (mines) puits; (of a carriage) timon; (of a chimney stack) souche, *f.;* (of a cart) brancard; (of a quill) tuyau; (of a lance) bois; (of a column) fût; (of a weapon) manche; (mec.) arbre; (of a chimney) tuyau, *m.* To sink a —; *percer un puits.* Main —; (mec.) *arbre moteur, m.*

shaft'ed, *adj.,* à manche; (her.) à tête de lance.

shaft'-horse, *n.,* limonier, cheval de brancard; (of a two-wheeled post-chaise in France) mallier, brancardier, *m.*

shag, *n.,* (cloth) peluche, panne, *f.;* (hair) poil rude; (tobacco) caporal, *m.*

shag'ged (-ghède) *ou* **shag'gy** (-ghi), *adj.,* poilu; velu; (rugged) raboteux; inégal. A — dog; *un barbet, m.*

shag'giness (-ghi-), *n.,* état poilu; état hérissé, *m.,* rudesse de poil, *f.*

shagreen' (-grîne), *n.,* peau de chagrin, *f.*

shagreen' *adj.,* de peau de chagrin.

shah, *n.,* schah, *m.*

shake, *n.,* secousse; (agitation) agitation, *f.,* tremblement, *m.;* (in wood) fente, gerçure, *f.;* (mus.) trille, trill, tril, *m.* — of the hand *ou* hand- —; *poignée de main, f.* To give a — down; *héberger; donner le coucher à.* No great —s; *rien d'extraordinaire; pas grand'chose; rien qui vaille; des gens tels quels.*

shake, *v.a.,* (*preterit,* Shook; *past part.,* Shaken) secouer; ébranler; branler, remuer; agiter; (to weaken, to move) ébranler, affaiblir; (to rouse) réveiller, tirer **de**; (mus.) cadencer. To — hands with; *serrer la main* **à**; *donner une poignée de main* **à**. To — one's head; *hocher la tête.* To — to pieces; *faire tomber en pièces.* This carriage has shaken me to pieces; *cette voiture m'a tout brisé.* To — off; *secouer; faire tomber;* (to get rid of) *se débarrasser* **de**; *se défaire* **de**. To — up; *remuer.* To — the table; *remuer* **la** *table.* To — one's sides with laughter; *se tenir les côtes* **de** *rire.* Let us — hands; *donnons-nous la main.* To — down; *faire tomber;* (to settle one's self) *s'établir; se caser.* To — off the yoke; *secouer le joug.* To — the dust off one's feet; *secouer la poussière de ses souliers.* To — oneself free from; *s'affranchir* **de**.

shake, *v.n.,* s'ébranler; trembler (with, **de**); (of trains) ballotter; trembloter; (of the teeth) branler. To — with cold; *trembler de froid.* His hand —s; *la main lui tremble.* To — together; *faire bon ménage ensemble.* To — in one's shoes; *avoir une peur de tous les diables,* ou *une peur de chien.*

shak'en (shék'n), *adj.,* ébranlé, secoué; (of wood) fendillé.

shak'er (shék'-), *n.,* secoueur, *m.*

Shakers, *pl.,* (sect) trembleurs, *m.pl.*

shak'ing (shék'-), *n.,* secousse, *f.;* ébranlement; tremblement; (rail.) ballottement, *m.* Hand- —; *serrement de main, m.* To give a good — to; *secouer bien.*

sha'ko, *n.,* (milit.) shako, schako, *m.*

sha'ky (shék'i), *adj.,* infirme; débile; faible; qui branle dans le manche, branlant; (of things) peu solide; (of wood) éclaté, fendillé. With — step; *à pas chancelants.* He is rather —; *il branle au,* ou *dans le, manche; il est sujet à caution.*

shale, *n.,* (min.) argile schisteuse, *f.*

shall, *v.* auxil., (*preterit,* Should) devoir; vouloir. I — go; *j'irai.* — I go? *irai-je? dois-je aller? faut-il que j'aille?* You — do it; *je veux que vous le fassiez.* But he —; *mais je l'y forcerai.* But I — not; *mais je n'en ferai rien.* They have a notion that their children — ou should be taught gratis; *ils ont dans l'idée,* ou *ils s'imaginent, qu'on devrait instruire leurs enfants gratis.*

shal'loon (-loune), *n.,* serge fine, *f.*

shal'lop, *n.,* chaloupe, pinasse, *f.*

shal'low (-lô), *adj.,* peu profond; superficiel; (slight) léger; frivole, futile; (silly) borné; (of water) bas, peu profond.

shal'low-brained (-lô-bré'n'de), *adj.,* à cervelle creuse; borné.

shal'low-hearted, *adj.,* au cœur léger, vide.

shal'lowly, *adv.,* de peu de profondeur; (fig.) superficiellement.

shal'lowness, *n.,* (of intellect) peu de profondeur, manque de profondeur, *m.;* nature superficielle, *f.;* esprit superficiel, borné, *m.*

shal'lows (-lôz), *n.pl.,* haut-fonds, bas-fonds, écueil, *m.*

sham, *n.,* feinte, *f.,* prétexte, *m.;* imposture; (fam.) frime, *f.*

sham, *adj.,* feint; faux; simulé; prétendu; postiche, pour rire. — fight; *petite guerre, f.; combat simulé, m.*

sham, *v.a.,* feindre, simuler; tromper; faire (le, la, les). To — upon; *faire accroire à.* To — lameness, illness; *feindre d'être boiteux, malade, faire le malade, etc.* To — Abraham; *jouer l'innocence patriarcale; feindre d'être malade, faire la sainte nitouche, faire le bon apôtre; faire le sinure* (V. Hugo).

sham, *v.n.,* user de feintes, feindre, faire la comédie.

sham'ble (along) (-b'l-), *v.n.,* marcher lourdement, gauchement.

sham'bles (-b'l'ze), *n.pl.,* boucherie, *f.;* charnier, *m.* (V. Hugo); (mines) niche, retraite, *f.*

sham'bling, *adj.,* traînant, à démarche lourde. — gait; *marche traînante, f.*

sham'bling, *n.,* démarche lourde, *f.;* pas lourd, *m.*

shame, *n.,* honte; pudeur; (dishonor) honte, *f.,* opprobre, *m.* From —, for —, out of —; *de honte.* For —! *fi donc!* — *! quelle honte! c'est honteux! c'est infâme! honte!* To cry —; *crier à l'infamie, crier au scandale.* To be the — of; *être, faire, la honte* **de**. To be lost to all —; *avoir perdu toute honte.* The more — to him; *c'est d'autant plus honteux pour lui.* To put to —; *faire honte* **à**.

shame, *v.a.,* faire honte **à**; (to mock at) se moquer de; (to disgrace) déshonorer.

shame'faced (-féste), *adj.,* honteux; timide.

shame'facedly (-fést'li), *adv.,* avec mauvaise honte; timidement.

shame'facedness (-fést'nèce), *n.,* mauvaise honte; timidité, *f.*

shame'ful (-foule), *adj.,* honteux; (indecent) indécent, déshonnête.

shame'fully, *adv.,* honteusement; indécemment.

shame'fulness, *n.,* opprobre, *m.,* honte, infamie, ignominie, *f.*

shame'less, _adj._, éhonté, effronté ; impudent.
shame'lessly, _adv._, sans honte ; effronté-ment ; impudemment.
shame'lessness, _n._, effronterie ; impudence, _f._
shammed (sha'm'de), _adj._, faux ; prétendu, feint, simulé.
sham'mer (sha'm'-), _n._, trompeur, imposteur, farceur, _m._
sham'oy _ou_ **sham'my**, _n._, (zoöl.) chamois, _m._
shampoo' (-pou), _v.a._, masser, frictionner ; (of the head) nettoyer.
shampoo'er, _n._, masseur, _m._, masseuse, _f._
shampoo'ing (-pou-igne), _n._, massage, fric-tionnement ; (of the head) nettoyage, _m._
sham'rock, _n._, (bot.) trèfle blanc, _m._
shank (sha'gn'ke), _n._, jambe ; (jest.) gigue, quille, _f._ ; (tibia) tibia, os de la jambe ; (of a horse) canon, _m._ ; (of instruments) tige, branche, _f._ ; (of a pipe) tuyau, _m._ ; (of a button) queue ; (of an anchor) tige, verge ; (of a key) tige, _f._ ; (of a column) fût, _m._ — painter ; (nav.) serre-bosse, _m._ To ride —'s mare, _ou_ nag ; aller à pied (fam. à pattes), voyager par la diligence d'Adam.
shanked (sha'gn'k'te), _adj._, à jambe ; à tige ; a queue.
shan'ty, _n._, baraque, hutte, _f._
shape (shépe), _n._, forme ; figure ; (pers.) tour-nure, taille ; (idea) idée ; (of a bonnet) forme, car-casse, _f._ In the — of ; en forme de ; sous la forme de. To take —; prendre tournure ; (fig.) s'ébau-cher (V. Hugo). To get out of —; se déformer. To put out of —; déformer.
shape, _v.a._, former ; façonner ; (to regulate) régler, modeler sur ; (to direct) diriger. To — one's course for ; (nav.) mettre le cap sur (V. Hugo) ; faire route pour. —d like ; en forme de, en . . .
shape, _v.n._, (with) cadrer à, _ou_ avec ; conve-nir à.
shape'less, _adj._, informe, sans forme.
shape'lessness, _n._, absence de forme, diffor-mité, _f._
shape'liness, _n._, symétrie, belle forme, _f._
shape'ly, _adj._, bien fait ; bien formé.
shard (shârde), _n._, têt ; tesson, _m._ ; (bot.) carde, _f._ ; (of an insect) étui, élytre, _m._ ; (of a snail) coquille, _f._
share (shère), _n._, (portion) part, portion ; (part allotted) part, _f._ ; (interest) intérêt, _m._ ; (in a railway, a mine, etc.) (com.) action, _f._ ; (of a plow) soc ; (quota) contingent, _m._ To have a — in ; avoir part à ; avoir un intérêt dans. To fall to any one's —; échoir, ou tomber, en par-tage à quelqu'un, devenir le partage de, être donné à. To go —s ; partager. In half —s ; de compte à demi.
share, _v.a._, partager, diviser ; prendre part à ; avoir part à.
share, _v.n._, partager ; avoir part à. To — in ; avoir part à ; participer à.
share'-broker, _n._, courtier d'actions, _m._
share'-certif'icate, _n._, titre d'actions, _m._
share'holder (-hôld'-), _n._, actionnaire, _m.f._
share'-list, _n._, cote des actions, _f._
shar'er, _n._, participant, _m._ ; (jur.) partageant, _m._ Joint-— ; copartageant, _m._ To be a — in ; participer à, prendre part à.
shar'ing (shèr'-), _n._, partage, _m._, participa-tion, _f._
shark (shârke), _n._, (ich.) requin ; (sharper) chevalier d'industrie, escroc, filou, écornifleur, _m._
sharp (shârpe), _adj._, tranchant, affilé, qui coupe bien ; (pointed) pointu, aigu, à pointe acérée ; (of angles) saillant ; (acute of mind) vif, intelligent, pénétrant, fin ; (of children) éveillé, dégourdi ; (piercing) perçant, pénétrant ; (of features) anguleux, saillant ; (acid) acide, piquant ; (biting) mordant, piquant, vif, amer, **acerbe**, aigre ; (rigid) rigide, sévère ; (subtle)

subtil, fin, délié ; (ardent) vif, ardent ; (violent) violent ; (fierce) vif, vigoureux, rude ; (keen) aigu, vif ; (of sound) aigre, aigu, perçant ; (mus.) dièse. A — edge ; un fil tranchant. A — appetite ; un appétit dévorant. A — pain ; douleur vive, aiguë, _f._ A — contest ; une contestation vive, violente. A — tongue ; une langue bien affilée. To look —; se dépêcher. As — as a needle ; (pers.) (pop.) fin comme tout ; fin comme l'ambre.
sharp, _adv._, (of the hour) précise. At one o'clock — ; à une heure précise. At four o'clock — ; à quatre heures précises. To look — after ; surveiller attentivement ; avoir l'œil sur. Look —! vivement ! alerte ! remuez-vous !
sharp, _n._, (mus.) dièse, _m._
sharp'-edged (-èdj'de), _adj._, bien affilé ; (carp., etc.) à vive arête.
sharp'en (shârp'n), _v.a._, aiguiser, affiler ; (to point) rendre pointu, rendre aigu ; (to make active) rendre vif ; (to make acid) aigrir, rendre acide, rendre piquant ; (the intellect, the sight) aiguiser ; (the appetite) aiguiser, ouvrir ; (pain) rendre vif, rendre aigu ; (desire) exciter ; (mus.) diéser. To — (up) ; (pers.) dégourdir.
sharp'ener, _n._, affiloir, _m._
sharp'er, _n._, aigrefin ; escroc ; filou ; chevalier d'industrie, _m._
sharp'ly, _adv._, avec un fil tranchant ; avec une pointe aiguë ; (rigorously) rigoureusement ; (vigorously) vigoureusement, rudement, vive-ment, âprement, avec âpreté ; (distinctly) nette-ment, vivement ; (roughly) vivement, vertement, avec aigreur ; (violently) violemment, fortement ; (acutely) d'une manière pénétrante, d'une ma-nière perçante. To answer —; répondre avec aigreur, vivement ; spirituellement. — outlined ; nettement dessiné, ou profilé.
sharp'ness, _n._, (keenness of an edge) tran-chant, _m._ ; pointe, _f._ ; (acidity) acidité ; (of pain, grief) force, violence ; (of language) aigreur, amertume, _f._, piquant, _m._ ; (clearness) netteté ; (acuteness of intellect) intelligence, _f._, (of chil-dren) esprit éveillé, _m._, vivacité, _f._ ; (quickness of perception) pénétration, subtilité, finesse ; (of the weather) rigueur, _f._ ; (of sound) éclat, _m._, acuité, _f._
sharp prac'tice, _n._, filouterie, rouerie, _f._
sharp'-sauce, _n._, sauce piquante, _f._
sharp'-set, _adj._, affamé ; vorace ; avide (on, de), qui a les dents longues.
sharp'-shooter, _n._, (milit.) tirailleur, _m._
sharp'-sighted (-saït'-), _adj._, pénétrant ; qui a la vue perçante.
sharp'-witted, _adj._, qui a l'esprit pénétrant.
shat'ter, _v.a._, briser, fracasser ; mettre en pièces ; faire voler en éclats ; (to rend) déchirer ; (to derange) déranger ; (to impair) altérer ; abîmer, délabrer. To be —ed into spray ; éclater en poussière d'eau.
shat'ter, _v.n._, se briser ; se fracasser.
shat'ters, _n.pl._, pièces, _f.pl._ ; éclats, _m.pl._
shave (shéve), _v.a._, raser ; faire la barbe à ; (animal) tondre ; (just to touch) raser ; (to fleece) plumer, écorcher ; (tech.) planer ; (carp.) raboter ; (in price) rogner. To — one's self ; se raser, se faire la barbe. To get —d ou to have a —; se faire raser, se faire faire la barbe.
shave, _v.n._, se raser, se faire la barbe.
shave, _n._, action de raser ou de se raser ; (in-strument) plane, _f._ It was a narrow —; il s'en est fallu d'un cheveu. To have a narrow —; l'échapper belle.
shave'-grass (-grâce), _n._, prêle d'hiver, _f._
shave'ling, _n._, (b.s.) tonsuré, calotin, _m._
shav'er (shév'-), _n._, barbier ; (plunderer) usu-rier, écorcheur, fripon ; (sharp man to deal with) fin matois ; (youngster) blanc-bec, moutard, _m._
shav'ing (shév'-), _n._, action de raser, _f._ ; (of wood) copeau, _m._ ; (of paper) rognure, _f._
shav'ing-box, _n._, boîte à savonnette, _f._

shav'ing-brush (-breushe), *n.*, blaireau, *m.*

shav'ing-cloth (-cloth), *n.*, linge à barbe, *m.*

shav'ing-soap, *n.*, savon à barbe, *m.*

shawl (shôl), *n.*, châle, *m.*

shawm (shô'm), *n.*, (ant.) hautbois, *m.*

she (shî), *pron.*, elle, *f.*; (of some animals) femelle. — -ass; *ânesse*. — -bear; *ourse*. — -cat; *chatte*. — -devil; *diablesse*. — -fox; *renarde*. — -goat; *chèvre*. — -monkey; *guenon*. — -wolf; *louve*, *f.* — is, *ou* will be; *c'est*, ou *ce sera*, *elle*.

sheaf (shîf), *n.*, gerbe; (loose) javelle, *f.*; (of arrows) faisceau, *m.*

sheaf, *v.a.*, engerber; mettre en gerbe;(loose) javeler.

sheaf'y, *adj.*, de gerbes; en forme de gerbes.

shear (shîr), *v.a.*, (*preterit*, Sheared; *past part.*, Sheared, Shorn) tondre; couper; (of corn) scier; (fig.) dépouiller **de**; frustrer; plumer.

shear'-bill, *n.*, (orni.) coupeur d'eau, *m.*

shear'er, *n.*, tondeur, *m.*; (machine) tondeuse, *f.*; (of wheat) scieur, *m.*, tondeuse, *f.*

shear'ing (shîr-), *n.*, tonture; tonte, tondaison, *f.*

shear'ing-machine (-ma-shîne), *n.*, tondeuse mécanique, *f.*

shear'ing-time, *n.*, tonte, tondaison, *f.*

shear'man (shîr-), *n.*, tondeur (de drap), *m.*

shears (shîrze), *n.pl.*, grands ciseaux, *m.pl.*; (for met.) cisailles, *f.pl.*

sheath (shîth), *n.*, (*sheaths*) étui, *m.*; gaine, *f.*; (scabbard) fourreau, *m.*; (ent.) étui, *m.*, élytre, *m.f.*; (anat., bot.) gaine, *f.* — -maker; gainier, *m.*

sheathe (shîthe), *v.a.*, mettre dans un étui; (a sword, etc.) mettre dans le fourreau, rengainer; (to cover) couvrir, revêtir; (to fit with a sheath) munir d'un fourreau; (fig.) plonger, enfoncer; (a ship) doubler. To — the sword; *poser l'épée : cesser la guerre*.

sheath'ing (shîth'-), *n.*, bordage; (nav.) doublage, *m.*

sheath'less, *adj.*, sans étui; sans gaîne.

sheath'-winged (shîth-wign'de), *adj.*, (ent.) à étui; à élytre.

shed (shède), *n.*, hangar; appentis; (building) atelier; chantier, *m.*; (hovel) bicoque, hutte, *f.* Cow—; *étable à vaches, f.*

shed, *v.a.*, (*preterit* and *past part.*, Shed) répandre, verser; faire couler; (of trees) laisser tomber, se dépouiller **de**, perdre; (of animals) jeter, changer, quitter; (to emit) répandre, exhaler; (tears) verser. To — over; *répandre* **sur**; *verser* **sur**.

shed'der, *n.*, personne qui répand, qui verse, qui fait couler, *f.*

shed'ding, *n.*, action de répandre; (loss) perte; (of blood) effusion, *f.*

sheen (shîne), *n.*, splendeur, *f.*; éclat, lustre, brillant, *m.*

sheen *ou* **sheen'y**, *adj.*, éclatant; brillant; luisant, étincelant.

sheep (shîpe), *n.*, brebis, *f.*; mouton; (silly fellow) sot, *m.*; (fig.) (theo.) brebis, *f.*; (skin) (binding) mouton, *m.*, basane, *f.* Lost, *ou* stray, —; *brebis perdue*, ou *égarée*. The black —; *la brebis galeuse*.

sheep'-bell, *n.*, bélière, *f.*

sheep'-breeding (-brîd-), *n.*, élevage des moutons, *m.*

sheep'-farmer, *n.*, éleveur de moutons, *m.*

sheep'fold (-fôlde), *n.*, bercail, *m.*; bergerie, *f.*

sheep'hook (-houke), *n.*, houlette, *f.*

sheep'ish, *adj.*, penaud; bête, niais.

sheep'ishly, *adv.*, en penaud; d'un air bête; d'un air penaud.

sheep'ishness, *n.*, timidité, niaise, *f.*, air penaud, *m.*

sheep'-market, *n.*, marché aux moutons, *m.*

sheep'-pen, *n.*, parc à moutons, *m.*

sheep's-eye (-aïe), *n.*, œillade, *f.*; yeux doux, *m.pl.* To cast — s on; *faire les yeux doux* à, *lancer des œillades* à.

sheep'-run, *n.*, parc, *ou* pâturage, à moutons, *m.*

sheep'-shearer (-shîr'-), *n.*, tondeur de moutons, *m.*

sheep'-shearing (-shîr'-), *n.*, tonte, *f.*

sheep'-skin, *n.*, peau de mouton; (leather) basane, *f.*; mouton, *m.*

sheep'-stealer (-stîl'-), *n.*, voleur de moutons, *m.*

sheep'-stealing, *n.*, vol de moutons, *m.*

sheep'walk, *n.*, pâturage à moutons, *m.*

sheer (shîr), *adj.*, pur; (of rocks) escarpé, perpendiculaire. — up; *à pic*. — nonsense; *pure sottise, f.*

sheer, *adv.*, tout d'un coup, complètement, tout net.

sheer, *n.*, (nav.) tonture; embardée, *f.* *pl.*, V. **sheers**.

sheer, *v.n.*, (nav.) embarder, faire des embardées. To — off; *fuir, filer, se sauver, s'esquiver*; (nav.) *démarrer, pousser au large*. To — up (to); *accoster*.

sheer'-hooks (-houkse), *n.*, grappin, *m.*

sheer'-hulk (-heulke), *n.*, machine à mâter flottante, mâture flottante, *f.*

sheers (shîrze), *n.pl.*, (nav. build.) bigue, *f.*; bigues, *f.pl.*; machine à mâter, *f.sing.*

sheet (shî'te), *n.*, drap, *m.*; (of paper, of metals) feuille, lame; (of water, etc.) nappe, pièce; (nav.) écoute, *f.* As white as a —; *blanc comme un linge*. Winding-—; *linceul, m.* — -lightning; *éclair en nappe, m.* Three —s in the wind; *entre deux vins*; *lancé, pris de vin*.

sheet (shî'te), *v.a.*, garnir de draps; couvrir; envelopper; (building) blinder.

sheet, *v.n.*, (nav.) border une écoute.

sheet'-anchor (-ai'gn'k'eur), *n.*, ancre de miséricorde, maîtresse ancre; grande ancre; (fig.) planche de salut; ancre de salut, *f.*

sheet'-cable, *n.*, maître câble, *m.*

sheet'-copper, *n.*, cuivre en planches, *ou* feuilles, *m.*

sheet'-glass, *n.*, verre à vitres, *m.*

sheet'ing, *n.*, toile pour draps de lit, *f.*; (lining) blindage, *m.*

sheet'-iron (-aï-eur'n), *n.*, tôle, *f.*

sheet'-lead (-lède), *n.*, plomb en feuilles, *m.*

sheet'-piles *ou* **sheet'ing-piles** (-païlze), *n.pl.*, madriers, *m.pl.*

shelf (shèlfe), *n.*, tablette, planche, *f.*; (of a book-case) rayon; (ledge) bord; (nav.) banc de sable, écueil, récif, brisant, *m.*; (min.) couche, *f.* On the —; (fig.) *mis de côté*. To lay, *ou* put, on the —; *reléguer au grenier*; *mettre de côté*; (of a boat) *mettre au rancart* (A. Daudet).

shelf'y, *adj.*, (nav.) plein d'écueils.

shell, *n.*, (of eggs, of fruit) coque, coquille, écaille; (of peas) cosse, écale; (of oysters) écaille; (mol.) coquille; (coffin) bière, *f.*, cercueil de sapin; (artil.) obus, *m.*, bombe; (of a drum) caisse, *f.*, fût; (outer part) extérieur, *m.*, écorce; (of a house) charpente, carcasse; (mus.) lyre, *f.* In the —; (of eggs) *à la coque*.

shell, *v.a.*, écaler, ôter la coque **de**, la coquille **de**; (peas) écosser; (of seeds) égrener; (of shrimps) éplucher; (mil.) bombarder, lancer des obus.

shell, *v.n.*, (of fruits) s'écaler; (of fish) s'écailler; (of seeds) s'égrener. To — out; (colloq.) *s'exécuter*; *payer*; *rendre gorge*.

shell'er, *n.*, (of peas, etc.) écosseur (de pois); (machine) écossoir, *m.*

shell'-fish, *n.*, coquillage; mollusque, *m.*; crustacés, *m.pl.*

shell'ing, *n.*, égrenage; (mil.) bombardement, *m.*

shell'-proof, *adj.*, à l'épreuve des bombes.

shell'-work (shèl'weurke), *n.*, coquillage ; ouvrage en coquillage, *m.*

shell'y, *adj.*, couvert de coquillages ; de coquilles.

shel'ter (shèl-), *n.*, abri ; couvert ; (protection) abri, refuge, asile, gîte, *m.*, protection, *f.* To take —; *s'abriter ; se mettre à l'abri.* Under — from; *à l'abri* **de**, *à couvert* **de**.

shel'ter, *v.a.*, abriter ; mettre à l'abri ; protéger, garantir.

shel'ter, *v.n.*, s'abriter. To — oneself (behind), *se réfugier* **derrière** ; (from) se réfugier **contre**.

shel'tered, *adj.*, abrité, à l'abri.

shel'terer, *n.*, protecteur, *m.*

shel'terless, *adj.*, sans abri ; sans asile.

shelve (shèlve), *v.a.*, mettre sur une planche, *ou* sur un rayon ; (fig.) mettre de côté ; se débarrasser **de** ; planter là.

shelve, *v.n.*, aller, *ou* être, en pente ; incliner.

shelv'ing, shelf'y, *adj.*, en pente ; en talus ; incliné. A — bed (in a garden) ; *ados*, *m.*

shep'herd (shèp'eurde), *n.*, berger ; pâtre ; (fig.) pasteur, *m.* — kings ; *rois pasteurs*, *n.pl.*

shep'herdess, *n.*, bergère, *f.*

shep'herd's-purse (-peurse), *n.*, (bot.) tabouret, *m.* ; bourse-à-pasteur, *f.*

sher'bet (sheur-), *n.*, (drink) sorbet, *m.*

sher'iff (shèr'-), *n.*, shérif, *m.*

sher'ry, *n.*, vin de Xérès, *m.* — cobbler ; *punch américain à la glace*, *m.*

shew'-bread (shô-), *n.* V. **show-bread**.

shib'boleth (-lèth), *n.*, schibboleth, *m.*, marque distinctive d'un parti, *f.* ; mot d'ordre, *m.*

shield (shîlde), *n.*, bouclier, *m.* ; (of Minerva) égide, *f.* ; (fig.) bouclier, *m.*, égide, *f.* ; (hort.) écusson ; (her.) écu, écusson, *m.*

shield, *v.a.*, couvrir d'un bouclier. To — from ; *couvrir* **de** ; *mettre à l'abri* **de** ; *défendre* **de**, *protéger* **contre** ; *garantir* **de**.

shield'-bearer (-bèr'-), *n.*, écuyer, *m.*

shift, *n.*, (change) changement ; (expedient) expédient, *m.*, ressource, *f.* ; (mean refuge) biais, détour ; (trick to escape detection) fauxfuyant, *m.*, défaite, *f.* ; (mus.) démanché, *m.* ; (chemise) chemise de femme, *f.* To use —s ; *user de biais.* To be reduced to —s ; *en être aux expédients.* To make — to ; *s'arranger* **pour** ; *trouver moyen* **de** ; (to do with difficulty) *avoir de la peine* **à**. Not to know what — to make ; *ne savoir à quel saint se vouer.* My last — ; *ma dernière ressource.* To — off ; *secouer, se débarrasser* **de** ; *éviter, détourner.* To make — with ; *s'arranger* **de** ; *s'accommoder* **de**.

shift, *v.a.*, changer ; transporter. To — off ; *secouer ; éviter ; se délivrer* **de** ; *différer, remettre.*

shift, *v.n.*, (to change place) changer de place ; (to vary) changer ; (to resort to expedients) trouver des expédients, s'arranger ; (to change dress) changer de vêtements ; (to practice indirect methods) user de faux-fuyants, biaiser. To — for one's self ; *s'arranger.* To make — without ; *se passer* **de**. To — about ; *vaciller ; passer d'un parti à l'autre ; changer d'opinion, de parti ; tourner casaque ; tourner à tous les vents comme une girouette.*

shift'er, *n.*, personne qui change, *f.* ; (person who uses artifice) biaiseur, *m.*, biaiseuse, *f.* ; (nav.) aide-coq, *m.* Scene- — ; *machiniste*, *m.*

shift'ing, *n.*, changement, changement de place, *m.* ; (of cargo, etc.) déplacement, transbordement ; (evasion) défaite, *f.*, subterfuge, détour, biais, (mus.) démanchement, *m.*

shift'ing, *adj.*, changeant ; (deceitful) qui use de détours. —sand ; *sable mouvant*, *m.*

shift'ingly, *adv.*, en changeant ; (deceitfully) par des détours.

shift'less, *adj.*, sans ressource ; sans expédient.

shift'y, *adj.*, plein d'expédients ; retors. He's a — customer ; *c'est un retors.*

shilla'lah (-lé), *n.*, gourdin, assommoir, *m.*

shil'ling, *n.*, schelling, shilling, *m.* A —'s worth ; *la valeur d'un*, ou *pour un*, *schelling.*

shil'ly-shal'ly, *n.*, hésitation ; irrésolution, lanternerie, barguignage, *f.*

shil'ly-shal'ly, *v.n.*, lanterner, barguigner ; hésiter, être irrésolu.

shin *ou* **shin'-bone** (-bône), *n.*, tibia, os de la jambe, (of beef) trumeau, *m.*

shin'dy, *n.*, tapage, bousin, boucan, *m.* To kick up a —; *faire du bousin*, ou *le diable et son train.*

shine (shaîne), *n.*, splendeur, clarté, *f.*, éclat, lustre, (of the weather) beau temps, *m.* To take the — out of; *éclipser, exceller, surpasser*, (to settle) *remettre à sa place.*

shine, *v.n.*, (preterit *and* past part., Shone) luire ; reluire ; briller. The sun —s ; *il fait du soleil ; le soleil luit, brille.* The moon —s ; *il fait clair de lune.* To — forth ; *éclater.* To — at the wrong end ; (prov.) *avoir l'esprit aux talons.*

shin'gle (shin'g'l), *n.*, galet ; caillou ; (carp.) bardeau, *m.*

shin'gle, *v.a.*, couvrir de bardeaux.

shin'gles (shin'g'lze), *n.pl.*, (med.) zona, *m.*

shin'gly, *adj.*, couvert de galets.

shin'ing (shaî'n'-), *adj.*, luisant ; reluisant ; éclatant, brillant.

shin'ing, shin'iness, *n.*, brillant ; luisant ; éclat, *m.*

shin'y (shaî'n'-), *adj.*, luisant ; reluisant ; éclatant, brillant.

ship, *n.*, navire ; vaisseau ; bâtiment, *m.* Merchant- —; *navire, vaisseau marchand.* — of war ; *vaisseau de guerre.* Store- —; *vaisseau de transport.* First-class — ; *vaisseau de premier rang.* — of the line ; *vaisseau de ligne.* His Majesty's —; *vaisseau de la marine royale.* To take — ; *s'embarquer, prendre la mer.*

ship, *v.a.*, embarquer ; charger ; mettre à bord ; expédier ; (a sea) recevoir, embarquer (un paquet de mer) ; (the rudder) monter ; (oars) armer. To — the oars ; *armer*, ou *border, les avirons.* To — off ; (goods) *embarquer des marchandises, transporter par eau ;* (any one) *embarquer quelqu'un.*

ship, *v.n.*, s'engager dans la marine ; **s'embarquer.**

ship'-biscuit, *n.*, biscuit de bord, *m.*

ship'-board (-bôrde), (on) *n.*, à bord.

ship'-boy (-boï), *n.*, mousse, *m.*

ship'-broker (-brôk'-), *n.*, courtier maritime, agent maritime, *m.*

ship'builder (-bild'-), *n.*, constructeur de vaisseaux, *ou* de navires, *m.*

ship'building, *n.*, construction de vaisseaux ; architecture navale, *f.*

ship'-carpenter, *n.*, charpentier de navire, *m.*

ship'-chan'dler (tshà'n'd'-), *n.*, fournisseur de navires, *m.*

ship'-load (-lôde), *n.*, chargement, *m.* ; cargaison, *f.*

ship'master (-mâs-), *n.*, capitaine *ou* patron de navire, *m.*

ship'mate, *n.*, camarade de bord, *m.*

ship'ment, *n.*, chargement ; embarquement, *m.* ; expédition, mise à bord, *f.*

ship'-money (-meu'n'nè), *n.*, impôt pour la construction des vaisseaux, *m.*

ship'-owner (-ô'n'-), *n.*, armateur, *m.*

ship'per, *n.*, expéditeur, chargeur, *m.*

ship'ping, *n.*, vaisseaux ; navires, *m.pl.* ; forces navales, *f.pl.* ; (loading) chargement, embarquement, *m.* ; mise à bord, *f.* — agent ; *commissionnaire-expéditeur*, *m.* — intelligence ; *nouvelles maritimes*, *f.pl.* The —interest ; *le commerce maritime*, *m.*

ship'ping, adj., maritime ; naval.

ship's'-boat, n., chaloupe, f.

ship's-carpenter, n. maître charpentier, m.

ship'-shape (-shépe), adv., bien ; en ordre ; proprement, comme il faut ; bien arrangé ; (of sails) bien orienté.

ship's'-papers (-pé-peurze), n.pl., papiers de bord, m.pl.

ship'wreck (-rèke), n., naufrage, m. To make — of ; (fig.) ruiner.

ship'wreck, v.a., faire faire naufrage à ; (fig.) faire échouer, faire périr. To be —ed ; faire naufrage, être naufragé.

ship'wrecked (-rèk'te), adj., naufragé ; (fig.) ruiné.

ship'wright (-raïte), n., constructeur de vaisseaux, m.

ship'-yard, n., chantier de construction, m.

shire (shîre ou shaïeur), n., comté, m.

shirk (sheurke), v.a., éviter, éluder, manquer à ; se soustraire à. Never to — one's work ; être franc du collier.

shirk, v.n., finasser. He —ed it ; il recula ; il refusa de venir au fait, au prendre.

shirt (sheurte), n., chemise d'homme ; chemise, f. Night—; chemise de nuit, f. Clean —; chemise blanche, f. To sell the — off one's back ; vendre jusqu'à sa chemise. — button ; bouton de chemise, m. — collar ; col, m. —front ; chemisette, f.

shirt (sheurte), v.a., couvrir, ou vêtir, d'une chemise.

shirt'ing, n., toile, f., calicot, m. ; toile pour chemises, f.

shirt'less, adj., sans chemise.

shive (shaïve), n., morceau, fragment, m.

shiv'er (shiv'eur), n., (min.) schiste ; (nav.) rouet ; (fragment) fragment, morceau, éclat ; (trembling) frissonnement, frisson, tremblement, m. To break to—s ; faire voler en éclats, briser en éclats. To have the —s ; avoir le frisson.

shiv'er, v.a., briser en morceaux ; fracasser ; faire voler en éclats; (a sail) faire fasier ; (a mast) casser.

shiv'er, v.n., se briser en morceaux ; voler en éclats, se fracasser ; (of sails) fasier ; (to tremble) trembler, tressaillir ; (with cold) grelotter ; (with cold, fear) frissonner.

shiv'ering, adj., tremblant ; tremblotant ; frissonnant.

shiv'ering, n., brisement ; (severance) démembrement ; (trembling) frissonnement, frisson, tremblement, m.

shiv'eringly, adv., en tremblant, en grelottant, en frissonnant.

shiv'ery, adj., qui vole en éclats ; cassant, friable. I have a — feeling about me ; il me prend des frissons.

shoal (shôle), n., (multitude) multitude, foule, f. ; (shallow) bas-fond, haut-fond ; (of fish) banc, m. ; (of a river) barre, f. In —s ; en troupes, en foule.

shoal, v.n., affluer ; s'attrouper ; (of fish) se réunir en banc ; (of water) baisser, diminuer en profondeur.

shoal, adj., bas ; peu profond.

shoal'iness, n., manque de profondeur ; grand nombre de hauts-fonds, m.

shoal'y, adj., plein de hauts-fonds, d'écueils.

shock, n., choc ; (impression) dégoût, coup, saisissement, m. ; (in electricity) secousse, f. ; (of corn) tas, m., moyette ; (of hair) tignasse, f. —-dog ; barbet, m.

shock, v.a., choquer, heurter ; (to strike with horror, disgust) révolter, scandaliser ; saisir ; frapper d'horreur, dégoûter ; (to offend) choquer, offenser, blesser ; (corn, sheaves) mettre en tas, en moyettes.

shock'-headed (-hèd'-), adj., à épaisse chevelure ; aux cheveux ébouriffés.

shock'ing, adj., (frightful) affreux, horrible ; (offensive) blessant, offensant, choquant ; (disgusting) repoussant, révoltant, dégoûtant. —! fi ! quelle horreur !

shock'ingly (-'ign-li), adv., affreusement, horriblement.

shock'ingness (-'ign-nèce), n., horreur ; nature affreuse, f.

shod, past part., (of horses) ferré ; (of pers.) chaussé.

shod'dy, adj., d'effilochage ; (very poor) de camelote, de pacotille. — goods ; pacotille, camelote, f. — wool ; laine d'effilochage, f.

shod'dy, n., effilochage, f.

shoe (shou), n., (shoes) soulier ; (of animals) fer, sabot, m. ; (of a sleigh) semelle, f., sabot ; (of a carriage) sabot, m. ; (of an anchor) semelle, f. ; (tech.) coussinet, m. List-—s ; chaussons, m.pl. Over—s ; claques, galoches, f.pl. Snow-—s ; raquettes, f.pl. Wooden—s ; sabots, m.pl. A — loose ; (of horses) un fer qui lâche. To stand in any one's —s ; être à la place de quelqu'un. To step into any one's —s ; prendre la place de quelqu'un. To walk in any one's —; (fig.) aller sur les brisées de quelqu'un. To be waiting for any one's old —s ; attendre après la défroque de quelqu'un. To take off one's —s and stockings ; se déchausser. To buy one's — of ; acheter ses souliers à ; se faire chausser par, chez. To make —s for any one ; chausser quelqu'un. To die in one's — ; (pop.) épouser la fille du cordier. To shake in one's —s ; avoir la venette. To put the — on the right foot ; deviner juste ; mettre le doigt dessus. That's where the — pinches ; c'est là que le mât me blesse ; c'est là que le soulier me pince. For want of a nail the — was lost ; (prov.) faute d'un point Martin perdit son âme. V. trifles.

shoe, v.a., (preterit and past part., Shod) chausser ; (animal) ferrer ; (an anchor) garnir les pattes de, brider ; (tech.) saboter.

shoe'-black, n., décrotteur, m.

shoe'-brush, n., brosse à souliers, f.

shoe'-buckle (-beuk'l), n., boucle de soulier, f.

shoe'-horn, n., chaussepied, m., corne, f.

shoe'ing (shou-igne), n., ferrage, m.

shoe'ing-forge, n., forge, f.

shoe'ing-hammer, n., brochoir, m.

shoe'-latchet, n., cordon de soulier, m.

shoe'-leather (-lèth-'), n., cuir de soulier, m. To save — ; pour épargner ses souliers.

shoe'less, adj., sans souliers.

shoe'maker (-mék'-), n., cordonnier, m. The —'s wife goes the worst shod ; (prov.) le cordonniers sont les plus mal chaussés.

shoe'making, n., cordonnerie, f.

shoe'-smith, n., maréchal, maréchal ferrant, m.

shoe'-string, n., cordon de soulier, m.

shoot (shoute), v.a., (preterit and past part., Shot) (with fire-arms) tirer, décharger, faire partir ; (an arrow) tirer, décocher, lancer ; (to dart) lancer, jeter, darder ; (to strike) frapper, atteindre ; (to push forth) pousser ; (to push out) faire sortir ; (to traverse rapidly) traverser rapidement, percer, pénétrer ; (carp.) ajuster ; (to kill) tuer ; (to kill with a gun) (fig.) fusiller ; (a bolt) tirer, mettre, pousser ; (the contents of anything) décharger, verser. To — at any one with a gun, to — a gun at any one ; tirer un coup de fusil à quelqu'un, sur quelqu'un. To — any one with a gun ; tuer quelqu'un d'un coup de fusil, d'un coup de feu ; (by a succession of shots) à coups de fusil. To — dead ; tuer raide. To — oneself ; se tuer, se tirer un coup de fusil, de pistolet. Ney was shot ; Ney a été fusillé. He has shot me ; il m'a atteint. I shot him in the leg ; je lui ai logé une balle dans la jambe. Trees — branches; les arbres poussent des branches. To

— forth; *pousser ;* (to dart) *lancer, darder.* To
— off; *tirer, décharger ;* (to carry away) *emporter.* The ball shot his leg off; *le boulet lui
emporta la jambe.* He was shot through the
leg; *il eut la jambe traversée,* ou *fracassée, par
une balle.* To — out; *lancer.* To — through;
*traverser, transpercer, percer d'outre en outre,
de part en part.* The ball shot him through the
heart; *la balle lui traversa le cœur.* To — the
rapids; *traverser, s'élancer* **sur,** *les rapides.* To
be shot through the back with a pistol bullet;
être tué d'un coup de pistolet tiré dans le dos. To
— one's bolt; *épuiser ses ressources, avoir dit
son dernier mot.* To — the moon; (fam.) *faire
un trou à la lune ;* (to decamp without paying)
déménager à la cloche de bois. I'll be shot, if; *le
diable m'emporte si.* Well! I'll be shot; *eh bien,
par exemple !* To be shot (*ou* scot-free) of;
(fam.) *être quitte* **de.**

shoot, *v.n.,* (to bud) *pousser, croître ;* (to run
along) *s'élancer, courir,* **s'avancer ;** (to feel a
quick darting pain) *éprouver des élancements* **à ;**
élancer ; (of stars, ships) *filer.* To — ahead;
courir en avant ; se précipiter en avant. To —
ahead of; *devancer, dépasser.* To — at; *tirer*
sur ; *tirer un coup de fusil* **à.** To — by, *ou* past;
*passer rapidement, passer comme une flèche,
comme un trait.* To — forth; *s'avancer, s'élancer ;* (of plants) *croître, pousser ;* (of light) *jaillir.* To — up; *croître, pousser.* To — forward; *s'élancer en avant.* To — into; *se former*
en, *se développer* **en,** *se projeter en ; se précipiter*
dans. To — out; *s'élancer dehors ;* (to project)
se projeter, s'avancer ; faire saillie ; (of plants)
pousser. To — through; *traverser, pénétrer.*
To — true; *tirer juste.* To — up; *croître, grandir ; devenir ; s'élancer, monter ;* (of light) *jaillir.*
My temples —; *j'éprouve des élancements aux
tempes.* To go out —ing; *aller à la chasse,
chasser.*

shoot (shoute), *n.,* coup; (of plants) jet, rejeton, *m. ;* pousse, *f. ;* (young pig) goret, *m. ;* (of
an arch) poussée, *f. ;* (spout) gouttière, *f. ;* (for
rubbish) dépôt de décombres, *m. ;* (slide) descen-
seur, *m. ;* (of water) chute, *f.*

shoot'er, *n.,* tireur; chasseur; archer, *m.*

shoot'ing, *n.,* (of fire-arms) tir, *m. ;* décharge,
f. ; (of an arrow) décochement, *m. ;* (hunt.)
chasse au tir, chasse au fusil, *f. ;* (of pain) élancement, *m. ;* (of plants) pousse, *f. ;* (of rubbish)
décharge, *f. ;* voirie ; (of a criminal) exécution,
f., fusillement, *m.* To practice —; *s'exercer
au tir.*

shoot'ing, *adj.,* (of pain) qui élance; lancinant; (of a star) filante (*adj.f.*); (projecting)
saillant. — pains; *des élancements de douleur.*

shoot'ing-box (-bokse), *n.,* muette; pavillon
de chasse, *f.*

shoot'ing-coat (-côte), **-jacket,** *n.,* veste de
chasse, *f.*

shoot'ing-gal'lery, *n.,* tir, *m.*

shoot'ing-license, *n.,* permis de chasse, port
d'armes, *m.*

shoot'ing-match, *n.,* concours de tir, *m.*

shoot'ing pain, *n.,* élancement, *m. ;* douleur
lancinante, *f.*

shoot'ing-pouch, *n.,* gibecière, *f.*

shoot'ing-star, *n.,* étoile filante, *f.*

shoot'ing-stick, *n.,* (print.) décognoir, *m.*

shop, *n.,* magasin, *m. ;* boutique, *f. ;* (workshop) atelier, *m.* To keep a —; *tenir un magasin, une boutique.* To keep —; *garder le magasin, la boutique.* To talk —; *parler métier.* To
smell of the —; *sentir le métier.* To —; *courir
les magasins, faire des emplettes.*

shop'-bill, *n.,* prospectus, imprimé, *m.*

shop'-board (-bôrde), *n.,* établi, *m.*

shop'-book (-bouke), *n.,* livre de comptes, *m.*

shop'-boy (-boï), *n.,* garçon de magasin, *ou*
de boutique, *m.*

shop'-girl (-gheurle) *ou* **-wom'an,** *n.,* fille de
boutique; dame, demoiselle de magasin, *f.*

shop'keeper (-kîp'-), *n.,* marchand, *m.,* marchande, *f. ;* boutiquier, *m.,* boutiquière, *f.*

shop'lifter, *n.,* voleur à la détourne, *m. ,* voleuse
à la détourne, *f.*

shop'lifting, *n.,* vol à la détourne, *m.*

shop'man, *n.,* commis de magasin, de boutique; commis, *m.*

shop'-marker, *n.,* inspecteur de magasin, *m.*

shop'-window, *n.,* devanture de boutique,
f. ; étalage de magasin, *m. ;* montre, *f.*

shop'ping, *n.,* emplettes, *f.pl.* To go —;
aller faire des emplettes.

shop'py, *adj.,* qui sent le magasin; (pers.)
qui sent le boutiquier ; (fig.) vulgaire, commun.

shor'age (shôr'èdje), *n.,* droit de rivage, *m.*

shore (shôre), *n.,* (of the sea), rivage, *m.,*
plage, *f. ;* côte; (of a river) rive, *f. ;* (carp.) étai,
étançon; (nav.) accotoir, accore, *m.* On —; *à
terre.* To go on —; *aller à terre; aborder.*
Along the —; *le long de la côte ; près de la terre.*
To follow, *ou* hug, the —; *serrer la côte.*

shore (up), *v.a.,* (carp.) étayer; étançonner;
(nav.) accorer.

shore'less, *adj.,* sans côte; sans rivage.

shorl, *n.,* (min.) schorl, *m.*

shorn. *V.* **shear.**

short, *adj.,* court; (insufficient) insuffisant;
(abrupt) brusque; (brief) bref; (stature) petit;
(of earth, marl) friable; (of pastry) croquant;
(gram., mus.) bref; (limited) étroit; borné;
(of time) de courte durée; (brittle) cassant; (of
the sea) clapoteux. To be taken —; *être pris
d'un besoin pressant.* To turn —; *se retourner
brusquement, tourner court.* It falls far — of
it; *il s'en faut de beaucoup.* It does not fall
far — of it; *il ne s'en faut guère.* Nothing —
of murder; *rien au-dessous du meurtre.* To be
— of; (pers.) *être* **sans ;** *être à court* **de ;** (of
things) *être au-dessous* **de.** To fall —; *être à
court ; manquer ; être insuffisant.* To fall — of;
être au-dessous **de ;** *être loin* **de,** *ne pas répondre*
à. To fall — of my expectations; *ne pas répondre à mon attente.* To fall — in; *manquer* **à.**
To cut —; *couper court* **à ;** *couper la parole* **à ;**
abréger ; retrancher, réduire. To stop —; *s'arrêter tout court ;* (fig.) *rester court.* In —; *bref,
en un mot, enfin.* The long and the — of it; *le fin
mot de la chose.* To become, *ou* get, —; *se raccourcir.* To make —er; *raccourcir.* To make
— work of; *en avoir bientôt fait* **avec.** (fam.)
n'en faire ni une ni deux. To cut the matter —;
en finir ; pour le trancher net. The sum is — of
ten pounds; *il manque dix livres à la somme* ou
la somme n'y est pas, il y manque dix livres. To
live a — life and a merry one; *la faire bonne et
courte,* ou *après nous le déluge.*

short, *n.,* court, *m.* To know the long and the
— of; *savoir le court et le long* **de,** *en avoir le
cœur net.*

short, *adv.,* court; peu; tout court; en moins;
vivement, brusquement.

short'-breathed (-brêth'de), *adj.,* qui a l'haleine courte.

short'coming (-keum'-), *n.,* insuffisance, faute,
f. ; déficit, *m. ;* erreur, omission, *f. ;* manquement au devoir, *m.*

short'-dated (-dét'-), *adj.,* à courte date; à
courte échéance.

short'en (short'n), *v.a.,* raccourcir; accourcir;
(to abridge) abréger ; (to diminish) diminuer ; (to
deprive) priver **de ;** (to contract) resserrer.

short'en, *v.n.,* (of the days) se raccourcir; décroître ; diminuer ; se resserrer, s'abréger.

short'ening, *n.,* raccourcissement; accourcissement; (contraction) resserrement, *m. ;* diminution, *f.*

short'hand, *n.,* sténographie, *f.* — writer; *sténographe, m.* To take down in —; *sténographier*

short'-hand'ed, *adj.*, à court de monde ; qui n'a pas tout son personnel.

short'-horn, *n.*, bétail à courtes cornes, *m.*

short'-jointed (-djŏï'n't'-), *adj.*, (of a horse) court-jointé.

short'-lived (-liv'de), *adj.*, d'une courte vie ; qui vit peu ; de courte durée ; passager.

short'ly, *adv.*, bientôt ; sous peu ; dans peu de temps ; (briefly) brièvement, en peu de mots.

short'-necked, *adj.*, au cou court.

short'ness, *n.*, court ; (of space) peu d'étendue, *m.;* (stature) petitesse ; (brevity) brièveté ; (imperfection) faiblesse, imperfection ; (mus., gram.) brièveté, *f.* — of breath; *courte haleine, f.* — of waist; *courte taille, f.* — of memory ; *faiblesse de la mémoire, mémoire courte, f.*

short'-rib, *n.*, fausse côte, *f.*

shorts (shortze), *n.pl.*, son, *m.sing.*

shorts, *n.pl.*, culotte courte, *f.*

short'sight (-saïte), *n.*, vue courte, myopie, *f.*

short'-sighted (-saït'ède), *adj.*, qui a la vue courte, myope ; (fig.) peu prévoyant, peu clairvoyant, peu sagace. To be —; *avoir la vue basse ; être myope.*

short'-sightedness, *n.*, vue courte, myopie, *f.;* (fig.) manque de clairvoyance, *m.*

short'-tempered, *adj.*, vif, pétulant ; brusque, revêche.

short'-waisted, *adj.*, à courte taille.

short'-winded, *adj.*, à courte haleine.

short'-witted, *adj.*, qui a peu d'esprit, borné.

shot, *n.*, (of a fire-arm) coup ; (from a bow) trait, *m.;* (for a rifle) balle, *f.;* (for cannon) boulet ; (for a fowling-piece) grain de plomb, plomb, plomb de chasse, *m. ;* (artil.) charge, *f. ;* (reach) portée, *f. ;* (reckoning) écot ; (a man) tireur, *m.* A — in the locker ; *argent disponible, m. ; somme disponible, f.* Small —; *menu plomb, m. ; dragée, f.* Grape—, canister- —; *mitraille, f.* Bar— ; *boulet ramé, m.* Chain- —; *boulets enchaînés, m.pl.* Random- —; *coup perdu, m.* Round —; *boulet de canon, m ; boulets, m.pl.* Spent —; *balle morte, f.* To waste powder and —; *tirer sa poudre aux moineaux.* To be a good —; *être bon tireur.* To fire a —; *tirer un coup.* To fire a — at; *tirer sur.* Without firing a —; *sans coup férir ; sans brûler une cartouche,* ou *une amorce.* Within —; *à portée de.* Within ear- —; *à la portée de l'oreille.* Within cannon —; *à portée de canon.* At a —; *d'un seul coup.* Like a —; *comme un trait.* To be a dead —; *ne manquer jamais son coup ; avoir un tir infaillible* (V. Hugo). That's not a bad —; *ce n'est pas mal tiré ;* (fig.) (guess) *ce n'est pas mal deviné.*

shot, *adj.*, changeant, chatoyant, gorge-de-pigeon ; (of stuffs) glacé. To be — dead ; *être tué raide.* To be shot ; (militarily) *être fusillé.*

shot, *v.a.*, charger à boulet; (bottles) laver avec du plomb.

shot'-belt, *n.*, ceinture de chasse, *f. ;* sac à plomb, *m.*

shot'-casting (-câst'-), *n.*, fonte de plomb de chasse, *f.*

shot'-free (-frî), *adj.* V. **scot-free**.

shot'-hole (-hôle), *n.*, trou de balle, *m.*

shot'-locker, *n.*, (nav.) caisson ; (mil.) parc à boulets, *m.*

shot'-proof, *adj.*, à l'épreuve des balles, ou du boulet.

shot'ten (shot't'n), *adj.*, en saillie ; (of a bone) disloqué ; (of fish) qui a déchargé son frai ; (dried) saur. As thin as a — herring ; *maigre comme un hareng saur.*

shot'-tower, *n.*, tour à plomb de chasse, *f.*

should (shoude), *v.*, (as the sign of the conditional). I — speak ; *je parlerais.* — I, *ou* if I —, meet him ; *si je le rencontre,* ou *rencontrais.* Whom — I meet but his sister; *qu'est-ce que je vois ? Sa sœur.* (For — meaning **ought**, V. **ought**.)

shoul'der (shŏl'deur), *n.*, épaule ; (tech.) languette, *f.* To shrug one's —s ; *hausser les épaules.* Round —s ; *dos rond, m.sing.* To lay one's — to the wheel ; *pousser à la roue.* — to —; *de concert ; d'intelligence ; d'accord.* Over the left —; (fam.) *par-dessus l'épaule.* To put one's — to the wheel ; *mettre la main à la pâte ; y mettre du sien ; se mettre à l'œuvre.* To show any one the cold —; *battre froid à quelqu'un.* Across, *ou* over, the —; *en sautoir, en bandoulière.* To fire from the —; (mil.) *tirer à bras francs.*

shoul'der, *v.a.*, charger sur les épaules ; (to push) pousser avec violence ; (arms) porter, épauler.

shoul'der-belt, *n.*, baudrier, *m. ;* bandoulière, *f.*

shoul'der-blade, *n.*, omoplate, *f.*

shoul'dered (shôl-deurde), *adj.*, à épaules. Broad—; *qui a les épaules larges ; aux larges épaules.* Round—; *qui a le dos rond.*

shoul'der-high, *adv.*, sur les épaules ; à hauteur d'épaules.

shoul'der-knot (-note), *n.*, nœud d'épaule, *m.; aiguillette, f.*

shoul'der-shot'ten (-shot't'n), *adj.*, épaulé.

shoul'der-strap, *n.*, (of a game-bag) bretelle, *f. ;* (mil.) patte de collet, *f. ;* (of porters) bricoles, *f.*

shout (shaoute), *v.n.*, crier, vociférer ; pousser, *ou* jeter, des cris ; faire des acclamations. To — at ; *huer* (trans.). He was —ed at ; *il fut hué.* To — down ; *faire taire à force de cris.*

shout, *n.*, cri ; cri de joie, *m.;* (applause) acclamations, *f.pl. ;* (of laughter) éclat, *m.* —s of applause ; *tonnerre d'applaudissements, d'acclamations, m.*

shout'er, *n.*, criard ; (hired) acclamateur à gages, *m.*

shout'ing, *n.*, acclamation, *f. ;* cris, *m.pl.*

shove (sheuve), *v.a.*, pousser ; (one's nose anywhere, anything in one's pocket) fourrer. To — away ; *repousser, éloigner.* To — from ; *repousser de, éloigner de.* To — back ; *faire reculer ; repousser.* To — down ; *pousser en bas ; faire tomber ; renverser.* To — forward ; *faire avancer.* To — from ; *éloigner de, repousser de.* To — off; *repousser ;* (a boat) *lancer, pousser à l'eau.* To — out ; *pousser dehors ; faire sortir.*

shove, *v.n.*, pousser. To — away ; *pousser toujours ;* (to push off) *s'éloigner.* To — by ; *bousculer.* To — off ; (nav.) *s'éloigner ; pousser au large.*

shove, *n.*, coup, *m. ;* poussée, *f.* To give a — to; *pousser ; donner une poussée à, prêter un coup de main à.*

shov'el (sheuv'v'l), *n.*, pelle ; (of bricklayers) gâche, *f.* Fire— ; *pelle à feu.*

shov'el, *v.a.*, ramasser avec la pelle ; jeter avec la pelle ; amasser ; pelleter. To — away ; *déblayer.* To — in ; *ramasser avec la pelle ; jeter avec la pelle.* To — out ; *vider par pelletées.*

shov'elful (-foule), *n.*, pelletée, *f.*

shov'eler, *n.*, (orni.) spatule, *f.*

shov'eling, *n.*, pelletage, *m.*

show (shŏ), *v.a.*, (*preterit*, Showed ; *past part.*, Showed, Shown) montrer ; faire voir ; exposer à la vue ; (to prove) démontrer ; (to manifest) manifester, témoigner, montrer ; (to make known) faire connaître ; (to explain) expliquer ; (attention, kindness, etc.) témoigner, avoir. To — any one how to do a thing ; *montrer à quelqu'un comment il faut faire.* To — any one in ; *introduire quelqu'un ; faire entrer quelqu'un.* To — any one out ; *reconduire quelqu'un ;* (to get rid of) *éconduire.* To — any one up ; *faire monter quelqu'un ;* (to unmask) *démasquer,* ou *pilorier, quelqu'un ; montrer quelqu'un dans ses vraies couleurs.* To — off ; *étaler ; faire valoir ; faire ressortir ; faire parade de ; faire montre de.* To

— over ; *faire visiter* **à.** To — the white feather ; *faire la cane ; montrer le bout de l'oreille.*

show, *v.n.,* se montrer. To — off ; *poser ; se donner des airs, se donner du relief ; se faire remarquer.*

show, *n.,* (superficial appearance) apparence, *f. ;* (spectacle) spectacle ; (ostentatious parade) étalage, *m.,* ostentation, montre, parade ; (pomp) pompe, *f.,* apparat, *m. ;* (semblance) semblance, apparence, figure ; (exhibition) exposition,*f. ;* (external appearance) extérieur ; (phantom) fantôme, *m.* Cattle-— ; *exposition de bétail, f.* Dumb-— ; *jeu muet,* m. ; *pantomime, f.* To make a — of ; *faire parade* **de** ; *faire étalage* **de** ; *étaler ;* (to pretend) *faire semblant* **de** ; *faire mine* **de,** *faire profession* **de.** For —; *pour les apparences ; pour faire parade.*

show'-board, *n.,* enseigne, *f.*

show'-bottle (-bot't'l),*n.,* (of chemists) flacon de montre, *m.*

show'-bread (-brède), *n.,* (Script.) pain de proposition, *m.*

show'-case (-kéce), *n.,* montre, vitrine, *f.*

show'er (shô-eur), *n.,* montreur, *f.*

show'er (shaou-eur), *n.,* (slight) ondée ; (copious) averse, pluie ; (of blows, stones, etc.) pluie, grêle,*f. ;* (of arrows) nuée, *f.* April —; *giboulée de mars, f.* Heavy — ; *forte averse, f.*

show'er (shaou-eur), *v.a.,* inonder (de pluie) ; arroser ; (to bestow liberally) verser, faire pleuvoir. To — down ; *répandre ; faire pleuvoir* **sur.**

show'er-bath (shaou-eur-bâth), *n.,* douche,*f.*

show'eriness (shaou-eur-), *n.,* état pluvieux, *m.*

show'ery (shaou-euri), *adj.,* pluvieux.

show'-glass (shô-glâce), *n.,* montre, vitrine, *f.*

show'ily (shô-ili), *adv.,* avec éclat ; d'une manière voyante ; pompeusement ; fastueusement.

show'ing, *n.,* aveu, *m. ;* représentation, *f.* By one's own — ; *de son propre aveu.*

show'iness (shô-i-), *n.,* ostentation ; pompe,*f. ;* faste, étalage, éclat, *m. ;* couleur voyante, *f.*

show'man (shô-), *n.,* directeur de spectacle forain, saltimbanque, *m.*

show'-room, *n.,* salon de montre, magasin, *m.*

show'-window (-ôuin-dô), *n.,* montre, *f. ;* étalage, *m.*

show'y (shô-i), *adj.,* éclatant ; voyant ; fastueux.

shrap'nel, *n.,* obus à balles, *m.*

shred (shrède), *n.,* bande, rognure, *f. ;* (fig.) lambeau ; fragment, bout. To tear to —s ; *déchirer en lambeaux.*

shred, *v.a.,* couper en lambeaux, déchiqueter ; (cut small) hacher menu.

shrew (shrou), *n.,* mégère ; grondeuse ; piegrièche ; femme acariâtre, *f.* —-mouse ; *musaraigne, f.* Taming the — ; *la mégère mise à la raison.*

shrewd (shroude), *adj.,* sagace ; clairvoyant, pénétrant, malin, fin, rusé ; (of things) fin, adroit, subtil, malin.

shrewd'ly, *adv.,* avec sagacité ; avec pénétration, avec malice, avec finesse ; finement ; adroitement ; subtilement ; avec adresse ; avec ruse. To — suspect ; *soupçonner fort.*

shrewd'ness, *n.,* sagacité ; pénétration, malice, finesse, ruse, adresse, *f.*

shrew'ish (shrou-ish), *adj.,* grondeur ; acariâtre.

shrew'ishly (shrou-ish'-), *adv.,* en mégère ; en grondeuse ; en pie-grièche.

shrew'ishness (shrou-ish'-), *n.,* h..meur acariâtre, humeur de mégère, *f.*

shriek (shrîke), *n.,* cri ; cri perçant, *m.*

shriek, *v.n.,* crier ; jeter un cri perçant ; jeter des cris. To — out ; *crier, jeter les hauts cris.*

shriek'ing, *n.,* cris perçants, *m.pl.*

shriev'alty (shrîv'-), *n.,* fonctions de **shérif,** *f.pl. ;* charge de shérif, *f.*

shrift, *n.,* confession, *f.*

shrift'less, *adj.,* sans confession.

shrike (shraïke), *n.,* (orni.) lanier, laneret, *m. ;* pie-grièche, *f.*

shrill, *adj.,* aigu ; perçant ; aigre, grêle.

shrill, *v.n.,* produire un son aigu ; glapir. To — forth ; *chanter d'une voix aiguë.*

shrill'ness, *n.,* son aigu, ton aigu ; éclat, *m.*

shrill'ly, *adv.,* d'un ton aigu, d'une voix perçante.

shrimp (shrimpe), *n.,* (zoöl.) crevette, salicoque,*f. ;* (pers.) bout d'homme, avorton, crique nain, *m.,* naine,*f. ;* nabot, *m.* *v.n.,* pêcher des crevettes.

shrimp'er, *n.,* pêcheur de crevettes, *m.*

shrimp'ing, *n.,* pêche à la crevette,*f.*

shrine (shraïne), *n.,* châsse, *f. ;* reliquaire, (fig.) autel, temple, sanctuaire, *m.*

shrink (shrign'ke),*v.n.,*(*preterit* and *past part.,* Shrunk) rétrécir, se rétrécir, s'étrécir ; (recoil) reculer, se retirer ; (to shrivel) se rider ; se ratatiner ; (to diminish) diminuer, baisser ; (of wood) se contracter, se resserrer. To — back ; *reculer.* To — from ; *reculer* **devant** ; *trembler* **devant** ; *avoir horreur* **de.** To — up ; *rétrécir ; se rétrécir ; s'étrécir ;* (pers.) *se recoquiller.* He —s at the sight of danger ; *il recule à la vue du danger.* To — in awe ; *être saisi d'une crainte respectueuse.* To — away ; *reculer, s'effacer ; disparaître ; se dérober, s'évanouir.*

shrink, *v.a.,* rétrécir ; contracter, diminuer ; rider. To — to ; *diminuer ; se réduire* **à.** To — one's self ; *se retirer, s'écarter* **de.**

shrink'age (shri'gn'k'èdge), *n.,* rétrécissement, étrécissement, *m. ;* contraction, *f. ;* (pers.) recoquillement ; (of metals, earth) retrait, *m.*

shrink'er, *n.,* personne qui recule devant le danger,*f.*

shrink'ing, *n.,* rétrécissement, *m. ;* contraction ; (act of running back) action de reculer, de se retirer ; (of timber) contraction, *f.*

shrive (shraïve), *v.a.,* (*preterit,* Shrove ; *past part.,* Shriven) confesser ; entendre à confesse ; donner l'absolution **à.**

shriv'el (shriv'v'l), *v.n.,* se rider ; se ratatiner ; se recroqueviller, se recoquiller.

shriv'el (up), *v.a.,* faire ratatiner, faire recroqueviller ; rider, racornir, grésiller.

shroud (shraoude), *n.,* (winding-sheet) drap mortuaire ; linceul, suaire ; (shelter) abri, couvert, *m.* —s, *m.pl.,* (nav.) haubans, *m.pl.*

shroud (shraoude), *v.a.,* (to shelter) mettre à l'abri, mettre à couvert, abriter, couvrir ; (to dress for the grave) ensevelir, mettre dans un linceul, dans un suaire ; (to conceal) cacher, couvrir, dérober à la vue.

shroud'less, *n.,* sans linceul. *V.* **unhonored.**

shroud'y (shraoud'-), *adj.,* qui abrite ; qui sert d'abri.

Shrove'-tide (shrov'taïde), *n.,* les jours gras, les jours de carnaval, *m.pl.*

Shrove'-Tuesday (-tiouz'dè), *n.,* mardi gras, *m.*

shrub (shreube), *n.,* (bot.) arbrisseau ; arbuste ; (drink) grog, *m.*

shrub (shreube), *v.a.,* tailler en forme d'arbrisseaux, d'arbustes.

shrub'bery, *n.,* plantation d'arbrisseaux, *f. ;* bosquet, *m. ;* arbustes, arbrisseaux, *m.pl.*

shrub'by, *adj.,* plein d'arbrisseaux, touffu ;(resembling a shrub) qui ressemble à un arbuste ; (consisting of shrubs) d'arbrisseaux.

shrug (shreughe), *n.,* haussement' d'épaules, *m.*

shrug (shreughe), *v.a.,* hausser. To — one's shoulders ; *hausser les épaules.*

shud'der (sheud-), *v.n.,* frissonner ; frémir (with, **de**).

shud'der (sheud-), *n.*, frissonnement; frémissement, *m.*

shuf'fle (sheuf'f'l), *v.a.*, mettre en confusion; brouiller; mêler; (cards) mêler, battre; (dominoes) remuer; (to cheat) duper, tromper. To — off; *éluder; se débarrasser de; éconduire; éluder, planter là.* To — in, into; *glisser adroitement* dans; *introduire adroitement* dans. To — any one out of anything; *escamoter quelque chose à quelqu'un.* To — up; *faire à la hâte; bâcler.* To — away; *escamoter.*

shuf'fle, *v.n.*, (at cards) battre les cartes; (to change position) changer de position; (to prevaricate) tergiverser, chicaner, biaiser; équivoquer; (to shift) se tirer d'affaire, s'arranger; (to shove the feet) battre des pieds; (to move with an irregular gait) traîner les jambes. To — along; *traîner les jambes,* ou *les pieds.* To — off; *reculer honteusement.*

shuf'fle (sheuf'f'l), *n.*, (pushing) poussée, action de pousser; (confusion) confusion, *f.,* mélange; (artifice) artifice, tour, *m.;* (evasion) défaite, échappatoire, *f.,* faux-fuyant, subterfuge, *m.*

shuf'fler, *n.*, biaiseur, chicaneur, *m.,* chicaneuse; fourbe; (of cards) personne qui bat, *ou* qui fait, les cartes, *f.*

shuf'fling, *adj.,* (pers.) chicaneur, biaiseur; (of things) évasif; (of the gait) traînant. With — gait; *à la démarche traînante.*

shuf'fling, *n.,* confusion; (of gait) marche traînante, *f.;* (of cards) battement des cartes, *m.;* (artifice) ruses, *f.pl.,* détours, artifices, *m.pl.,* chicane, équivocation, *f.*

shuf'flingly, *adv.,* d'une manière évasive; en biaisant; par chicane, par artifice; (of the gait) en traînant les pieds, d'un pas traînant.

shun (sheune), *v.a.,* éviter; fuir.

shun'less, *adj.,* inévitable.

shunt (sheu'n'te), *v.a.,* changer de voie, garer.

shunt, *v.n.,* se garer, changer de voie.

shunt'ing, *n.,* (railways) ligne, gare d'évitement, voie de garage, *f.;* (action of) garage, *m.*

shut (sheute), *v.a.,* fermer; (inclose) enfermer. To — again; *refermer.* To — close, *ou* down; *fermer bien.* To — out from; *exclure* **de.** To — in; *enfermer.* To — off; *intercepter;* (of steam) *couper.* To — out; *exclure;* (to intercept) *intercepter; séparer, éloigner;* (to shut the door against) *fermer la porte* **à;** *interdire l'entrée* **à.** To be — out all night; *trouver la porte fermée et être obligé de coucher dehors.* To — out from; *exclure* **de.** To — up; *fermer;* (to confine) *enfermer, mettre sous les verrous;* (a door, a window) *condamner;* (to end) *terminer, finir;* (pers.) *faire taire; imposer silence* **à;** *fermer la bouche* **à.** To — up shop; *fermer boutique; cesser d'exister.*

shut, *v.n.,* fermer; se fermer. — up! *taisez-vous! en voilà assez! finissez! assez comme cela!*

shut'ter, *n.,* (of a window) volet, *m.,* persienne, *f.;* (door) guichet; (of a shop) volet brisé; (outside) contrevent, *m.* To put up the —s; *mettre les volets.*

shut'ting (up), *n.,* fermeture; clôture, *f.*

shut'tle (sheut't'l), *n.,* navette, *f.*

shut'tle, *adj.,* à navette.

shut'tle-cock, *n.,* volant, *m.* Battledore and —; *volant, m.*

shy (shaïe), *adj.,* craintif; timide; honteux; sauvage, farouche; difficile à aborder; (reserved) réservé; (suspicious) soupçonneux, ombrageux; (cautious) circonspect, prudent; défiant; (of horses) ombrageux. To be — of using; *craindre d'employer; regarder à deux fois* **pour;** *hésiter* **à.** To fight — of; *se défier* **de,** *éviter.*

shy (shaïe), *v.n.,* (of horses) faire un écart; se jeter de côté; être ombrageux.

shy, *v.a.,* jeter, lancer; flanquer.

shy'ly, *adv.,* timidement; avec réserve; avec prudence, avec circonspection.

shy'ness (shaïe-nèce), *n.,* timidité; sauvagerie; retenue; réserve; fausse honte; (of horses) nature ombrageuse, *f.*

Sibe'rian (si-bî-), *adj.,* sibérien; de la Sibérie.

sib'ilant, *adj.,* (gram.) sifflant; (med.) sibilant.

sib'ilant, *n.,* (gram.) lettre sifflante, *f.*

sibila'tion (-lé-), *n.,* sifflement, *m.;* (med.) sibilance, *f.*

sib'yl, *n.,* sibylle, *f.*

sib'ylline (-laïne), *adj.,* sibyllin.

sic'cative, *adj.,* siccatif.

sic'cative, *n.,* siccatif, *m.*

sic'city (sik-ci-), *n.,* (chem.) siccité, *f.*

sice (saïze), *n.,* (at dice) six, *m.*

Sicil'ian, *adj.,* sicilien. The — Vespers; *les Vêpres siciliennes, f.pl.*

sick, *adj.,* (ill) malade; (affected with nausea) qui a des nausées, qui a mal au cœur. — of; *dégoûté* **de;** *las,* ou *fatigué,* **de.** — of a fever; *malade de la fièvre.* To feel —; *avoir mal au cœur; avoir des nausées.* To be — at heart; *avoir la mort dans le cœur, dans l'âme; être navré.* To feel —; *avoir des nausées, des envies de vomir.* To make —; *donner mal au cœur* **à,** *faire vomir;* (fig.) *écœurer, soulever le cœur* **à.** — unto death; *malade* **à** *la mort.* — room; *chambre de malade;* (schools) *infirmerie, f.* — headache; *migraine, f.* —bed; *lit de douleur, m.* To be sea-—; *avoir le mal de mer.*

sick, *n.pl.,* malades, *pl.m.f.*

sick'-berth (-beurth), *n.,* (nav.) poste des malades, *m.;* infirmerie, *f.*

sick'-brained (sik-bré'n'de), *adj.,* malade d'esprit, qui a le cerveau malade. To be — and tired of anything; (fam.) *en avoir plein le dos.*

sick'en (sik'k'n), *v.a.,* rendre malade; (to disgust) lasser, ennuyer, dégoûter; (to make squeamish) faire soulever le cœur **à.** To be —ing for; (an illness) *couver une maladie.*

sick'en, *v.n.,* tomber malade; (to be satiated) se rassasier; (to languish) languir. To — of; *se dégoûter* **de.** To — at; *éprouver des maux de cœur* **à.** I —ed at the sight of that thing; *la vue de cette chose me souleva le cœur* ou *le cœur me souleva à la vue de . . .*

sick'ener, *n.,* ennui, *m.;* chose ennuyeuse, *f.* To give any one a —; *ennuyer quelqu'un;* (fam.) *embêter quelqu'un.*

sick'ening, *adj.,* nauséabond, à soulever le cœur; (fig.) dégoûtant.

sick'-fund, *n.,* caisse de secours mutuels (pour les malades), *f.*

sick'ish, *adj.,* un peu malade, indisposé; (nauseating) nauséabond, fadasse. To feel —; *avoir un léger mal de cœur.*

sic'kle (sik'k'l), *n.,* faucille, *f.*

sick'-leave, *n.,* congé de convalescence, *m.*

sick'liness, *n.,* mauvaise santé; état maladif, *m.;* (of places) insalubrité, *f.*

sick'-list, *n.,* (milit., nav.) rôle des malades, *m.* On the —; *indisposé.*

sick'ly, *adj.,* (pers.) maladif, d'une mauvaise santé; (of things) maladif; (producing disease) insalubre, malsain; (languid) languissant; (of plants) étiolé. To grow —; *devenir maladif; languir.*

sick'ly, *adv.,* d'une manière maladive.

sick' man (woman), *n.,* malade, *m.f.*

sick'ness, *n.,* maladie, *f.;* (nausea) mal de cœur, *m.,* nausées, *f.pl.* Sea-—; *mal de mer, m.*

sick'-nurse, *n.,* garde-malade, *f.*

sick'-ward, *n.,* infirmerie; salle des malades, *f.*

side (saïde), *n.,* côté; flanc; (edge, border) bord; (of a mountain) versant; (party) parti; (in games, matches) camp, *m.;* (of bacon) flèche, *f.* Along-—; *bord à bord.* Blind-—; *côté faible,*

Off-—; (man.) *hors montoir, m.* Near-—; (man.) *montoir, m.* Wrong —; *mauvais côté;* (of stuffs) *envers, m.* — by —; *côte à côte.* On, *ou* from, all —s; *de tous côtés; de toutes parts.* On the other —; *de l'autre côté.* By my —; *à côté de moi, à mes côtés.* On whose — are you? *de quel parti êtes-vous?* On my —; *de mon côté,* (fig.) (in my favor) *pour moi.* On neither —; *d'aucun côté.* On one —; *d'un côté, d'une part.* On this —; *de ce côté-ci; en deça.* On that —; *de ce côté-là; au delà.* On the —; (of rocks, etc.) *sur le côté, couché.* This — up; (of cases) *dessus.* On this — of Easter; *bien avant Pâques.* On the wrong — of; (of age) *avoir plus de* . . . To change —s; *changer de parti.* To choose —s; (for games) *choisir les partenaires.* To hold one's —s for laughter, to shake one's —s with laughter; *se tenir les côtes de rire.* To put on—; *se donner des airs.* The wrong — outwards; *à l'envers.* On both —s; *des deux côtés; de part et d'autre.* The right —; (of stuffs) *l'endroit, m.;* (opposed to left) *le côté droit;* (party) *le bon côté.* The wrong —; (of stuffs) *l'envers; le mauvais côté.* By the — of; (a road) *sur le bord* **de** ; (a river) *au bord* **de.** To take —s; *s'attacher à un parti.* To hear both —s; *entendre le pour et le contre.* To lash one's —s; (of animals) *se battre les flancs.*

side, *adj.,* de côté; latéral; (indirect) indirect, oblique, de profil. — way ; *sentier détourné, chemin de traverse, m.* — face ; de profil.

side, *v.n.,* (to lean on one side) pencher d'un côté; (pers.) s'engager dans un parti. To — with ; *se ranger du côté* **de,** *prendre parti* **pour,** *prendre fait et cause* **pour.**

side'-alley (-al'ly), *n.,* contre-allée, *f.*
side'-arms, *n.,* (mil.) armes blanches, *f.pl.*
side'-board (-bôrde), *n.,* buffet, *m.*
side'-box, *n.,* loge de côté, *f.*
sid'ed, *adj.,* à-côtés, à-faces. Two —; *à deux faces, ou côtés.*
side'-door, *n.,* porte latérale; porte dérobée, *f.*
side'-face, *n.,* figure de côté, profil, *f.*
side'long (saïd'lo'gne), *adj.,* de côté; oblique. To cast — glances at; *regarder du coin de l'œil ;* *faire les yeux en coulisse* **à.**
side'long, *adv.,* de côté; latéralement.
side'-look, *n.,* regard oblique, *m.*
side'-note, *n.,* note marginale, *f.*
side'-path, *n.,* sentier détourné, *f.*
sid'eral (sid'eur'-) *ou* **side'real** (saï-dî-ri-), *adj.,* des astres; sidéral.
side'-saddle (-sad'd'l), *n.,* selle de femme, *f.*
sides'man (saïd'z'-), *n.,* marguillier adjoint, *m.*
side'-stick, *n.,* (print.) biseau de côté, *m.*
side'-table (-té-b'l), *n.,* table portefeuille ; (for children) petite table, *f.*
side'-view, *n.,* vue de côté ; vue de profil, *f.*
side'walk, *n.,* contre-allée, *f.;* trottoir, *m.*
side'ways (saïd'wèze) *ou* **side'wise** (-waïze), *adv.,* de côté ; latéralement ; obliquement.
sid'ing, *n.,* (railways) gare d'évitement, *f.;* voie de garage, (of a single line) croisière, *f.*
si'dle (saïd'l), *v.n.,* marcher de côté ; (to be on the side) être sur le côté.
siege (sîdje), *n.,* siège, *m.* To lay — to; *mettre le siège* **devant,** *faire le siège* **de,** *assiéger.* To raise the —; *lever le siège.* Regular —; *siège en règle, m.*
siege'-piece, *n.,* pièce de siège, *f.*
siege'-train, *n.,* équipage de siège, *m.*
sies'ta (ci-èss-), *n.,* sieste, *f.* To take one's —; *faire sa sieste.*
sieve (sive), *n.,* crible ; sas ; tamis, *m.*
sieve'-box, *n.,* caisse à crible, *f.*
sift, *v.a.,* cribler ; sasser ; tamiser ; passer au crible, au sas, au tamis ; (fig.) sonder, examiner. To — out ; *venir à bout de découvrir ;* (to scrutinize) *examiner scrupuleusement, approfondir.*
sift'er, *n.,* cribleur, *m.,* **cribleuse,** *f.;* (sieve) tamis, sas, crible, *m.*

sift'ing, *n.,* tamisage ; sassement ; (fig.) examen, approfondissement, *m. pl.,* criblure, *f.sing. adj.,* (fig.) minutieux.
sigh (saïe), *n.,* soupir, *m.* To fetch, *ou* utter, a —; *jeter, ou pousser, un soupir.*
sigh (saïe), *v.n.,* soupirer. To — over ; *gémir* **sur.** To — after ; *soupirer* **après.**
sigh, *v.a.,* se lamenter **sur** ; pleurer ; (to express by sighs) exprimer par des soupirs.
sigh'er (saïeur), *n.,* soupirant, *m.*
sigh'ing (saï-igne), *n.,* soupirs, *m.pl.*
sight (saïte), *n.,* (faculty of vision) vue; (act of seeing) vue, vision ; (view) vue; (eye) vue, *f.;* regards, yeux, *m.pl.;* (of a quadrant) lumière ; (of fire-arms) (fore-sight) mire, (back-sight) hausse, *f.;* (spectacle) spectacle, *m.,* vue ; (quantity) quantité, *f.;* tas, *m.;* curiosité, caricature ; (looks) yeux, regards, *m.pl.* A fine —; *un beau spectacle.* Long —; *presbytie, f.* Near —; *myopie, vue basse, f.* At —; *à première vue ;* (of reading) *à livre ouvert ;* (com.) *à vue.* Three days after —; *à trois jours de vue.* At first —; *à première vue ; de prime abord.* By —; *de vue.* In—; *en vue ; à la portée de la vue.* Out of —; *hors de vue.* Out of —, out of mind ; *loin des yeux, loin du cœur.* In — of ; *à la vue* **de ;** *devant.* Within —; *à portée de la vue.* Within — of ; *en vue* **de.** To come in —; *commencer à paraître, paraître.* To lose — of ; *perdre de vue.* Not to lose — of, not to let out of one's —; *ne pas perdre de vue.* To take —; *pointer ; prendre son point de mire.* To take a — of ; *jeter un coup d'œil* **sur.** To get — of ; *voir, apercevoir.* To know by —; *connaître de vue.* To keep out of —; *se tenir éloigné, caché.* I hate the — of him, her, etc. ; *sa présence m'est odieuse ; je l'ai en horreur ; c'est ma bête noire.* To lose, to recover one's —; *perdre, recouvrer la vue.* To vanish out of —; *disparaître.* To go —seeing ; *aller voir les curiosités.* —seer, *n.,* curieux, *m.* Field of —; *champ, m. ; étendue qu'embrasse une lunette, f.* To keep in —; (intrans.) *ne pas s'éloigner ;* (trans.) *ne pas perdre de vue.* To come in —; *paraître.*
sight, *v.a.,* (nav.) reconnaître, apercevoir.
sight'ed, *adj.,* en vue.
sight'less, *adj.,* privé de la vue ; aveugle.
sight'lessness, *n.,* cécité, *f.;* aveuglement, *m.*
sight'liness, *n.,* beauté, *f.;* charme, *m.*
sight'ly, *adj.,* beau ; beau à voir ; charmant ; qui plaît à l'œil ; (open to view) visible, en vue.
sign (saïne), *n.,* signe, *m.;* (sign-board) enseigne, *f. ;* (alg., med., astron.) signe, *m.* To give —s of ; *donner signe* **de.** —manual ; *seing, m., signature, f.*
sign (saïne), *v.a.,* signer.
sign, *v.n.,* faire signe à.
sig'nal (sig-nal), *n.,* signal ; (to start; of trains) coup de sifflet, *m.*
sig'nal (sig-nal), *adj.,* signalé, insigne.
sig'nal-box, *n.,* guérite (de signaliste), *f.*
sig'nal-chest, *n.,* coffre aux signaux, *m.*
sig'nal-gun, *n.,* coup de canon de signal, *m.*
sig'naling flag, *n.,* fanion, *m.*
sig'nalize (-aïze), *v.a.,* signaler ; (oneself) se distinguer.
sig'nal-light (-laïte), *n.,* fanal, *m.*
sig'nally, *adv.,* d'une manière signalée.
sig'nalman, *n.,* signaliste, *m.*
sig'nal-post, *n.,* sémaphore, *m.*
sig'nal-word (-weurde), *n.,* signal, mot d'ordre, *m.*
sig'natory (sig-na-teuri), *adj.,* de sceau.
sig'nature (sig-na-tioure), *n.,* signature, *f.;* (stamp) cachet, *m.,* marque, empreinte ; (mus.) armure, *f.* Joint —; *signature collective.*
sign'-board (-bôrde), *n.,* enseigne, *f. ;* (giving directions) écriteau, *m.*
sign'er (saï'n'eur), *n.,* signataire, *m.f.*
sig'net (sig-nète), *n.,* sceau ; cachet *privé du*

souverain, *m.* —-ring; *bague à cachet, chevalière, f.* Writer to the —; (in Scotland) *avoué, m.*

signif'icance *ou* **signif'icancy** (sig-nif'-), *n.*, (meaning) signification, *f.*, sens, *m.; (*force) force, énergie, *f.; (*importance) poids, *m.*, importance, portée, *f.*

signif'icant (sig-nif'-), *adj.*, significatif; signifiant; (fig.) (of gesture, etc.) énergique.

signif'icantly, *adv.*, d'une manière significative.

significa'tion (sig-ni-fi-ké-), *n.*, signification, *f.*

signif'icative (sig-nif'i-ca-), *adj.*, significatif; signifiant, expressif; important.

signif'icatively, *adv.*, significativement, d'une manière significative.

sig'nify (sig-ni-faïe), *v.a.*, (to mean) vouloir dire, signifier; faire signe à; (to make known) faire connaître; (to import) importer. To — to; *signifier* à, *déclarer* à, *notifier* à, *annoncer* à, *communiquer* à. What does it —? *qu'importe?* It does not —; *cela ne signifie rien, cela ne veut rien dire; cela importe peu; n'importe.*

sign'ior (sî'n'ieur), *n.*, seigneur, *m.*

sign'-painter (saïn'-), *n.*, peintre d'enseignes, *m.*

sign'-post (-pôste), *n.*, poteau d'enseigne; (of roads) poteau indicateur, *ou* guide, *m.*

si'lence (saï-), *n.*, silence, *m.; (*taciturnity) taciturnité, *f.* To keep —; *faire silence, garder le silence; faire faire silence.* To reduce to —; *réduire au silence; imposer silence* à. —! *silence!* To pass over in —; *passer sous silence.* — gives consent; *qui ne dit mot consent.* — is golden; *le silence est d'or.*

si'lence (saï-), *v.a.*, réduire au silence; faire taire; imposer silence à; interdire la parole à; (to stop) mettre un terme à, arrêter, faire cesser, étouffer. To —complaints; *étouffer les plaintes.* To — a battery; *éteindre (faire cesser) le feu d'une batterie.*

si'lent (saï-), *adj.*, silencieux; muet; (taciturn) taciturne; (calm) calme, tranquille; (of letters) muet. To be —; *faire silence, garder le silence; se taire.* Keep those children —; *faites taire ces enfants.* To remain —; *garder l silence.* Real grief is —; *le vrai chagrin est muet.* The — system; *le système cellulaire, m.*

si'lently (saï-), *adv.*, silencieusement; en silence; sans bruit.

si'lentness (saï-), *n.*, silence, *m.*

Sile'sian (si-lî-shi-), *adj.*, de Silésie.

si'lex (saï-lèkse) *ou* **sil'ica**, *n.*, (min.) silice, *f.*

silhouette' (sil'ou-ète), *n.*, silhouette, *f.*

sili'cious, *adj.*, siliceux. [silicium, *m.*

sili'cium (si-lish'i-) *ou* **sil'icon**, *n.*, (min.)

silk, *n.*, soie, *f.*, taffetas; (for sewing) fil de soie, *m.*, soie à coudre, *f.* —s, *pl.*, soieries, *f.pl.* Floss— ; *soie plate; filoselle, f.* Raw —; *soie crue; soie grège.* Twisted —; *soie torse.* Unbleached —; *soie écrue.* Bleached —; *soie blanchie.* One cannot make a — purse out of a sow's ear; (prov.) *on ne saurait faire d'une buse un épervier.* —s and satins put out the kitchen fire; *habit de velours, ventre de son.* Japanese —; *peau de soie.*

silk, *adj.*, de soie, en soie; de fil de soie; (of silk-growing) séricicole. — handkerchief; *foulard, m.*

silk'-cotton, *n.*, soie végétale, *f.*

silk'-culture, *n.*, sériciculture, *f.*

silk'-district, *n.*, pays séricole, *m.*

silk'en (silk'n), *adj.*, de soie; soyeux; (soft) soyeux, doux, moelleux.

silk'-engine (-è'n'djine), *n.*, moulin à organsiner, *m.*

silk'-goods (-goudze) *ou* **-stuffs**, *n.pl.*, soierie, *f.; soieries, f.pl.*

silk'-grower, *n.*, sériciculteur, *m.*

silk'-growing, *n.*, sériciculture, *f.* — industry; *industrie séricicole, f.*

silk'iness, *n.*, nature soyeuse, *f.; douceur, f.*

silk'-mercer (-meur-ceur), *n.*, marchand de soieries, *m.*, marchande de soieries, *f.*

silk'-merchant, *m.*, négociant en soieries, *m.*

silk'-mill, *n.*, fabrique de soie, *f.*

silk'-spinner, *n.*, filateur de soie, *m.*

silk'-spinning, *n.*, filature de soie, *f.*

silk' thread (-thrède), *n.*, fil de soie, *m.*

silk'-thrower (-thrô-) *ou* **silk'-throwster** (-thrôst'-), *n.*, moulineur; moulinier, organsineur, *m.*

silk'-throwing (-thrô-igne), *n.*, moulinage de la soie, organsinage, *m.*

silk'-trade, *n.*, commerce de la soierie, *m.*

silk'-twist, *n.*, cordonnet de soie, *m.*

silk'-wares (-wèr'ze), *n.*, soieries, *f.pl.*

silk'-weaver (-wîv'-), *n.*, tisserand en soie; (in Lyons) canut, *m.*

silk'-worm (-weurme), *n.*, ver à soie, *m.* —breeding; *sériciculture, f.*

silk'y, *adj.*, de soie; soyeux; (soft) soyeux, moelleux, doux.

sill, *n.*, seuil; (of wood) racinal; (of a door) seuil, *m.; (*of a window) allége; appui, *f.* Ground —; *semelle, f.*

sil'labub (-beube), *n.* V. **syllabub.**

sil'lily, *adv.*, sottement; bêtement; niaisement.

sil'liness, *n.*, sottise, nigauderie; niaiserie; bêtise, *f.*

sil'ly, *adj.*, sot, nigaud; niais; bête, bêta. He is —; (idiotic) *c'est un idiot.* — thing; *chose sotte, sottise, nigauderie; (*pers.) bête, *f.*, nigaud, *m.*, nigaude, *f.*, sot, *m.*, sotte, *f.* To be —; (play the fool) *faire la bête.* A — billy; *un nicodème.*

silt, *v.a.*, envaser, atterrir. *v.n.*, s'envaser.

silt, *n.*, vase, boue, *f.*, limon, *m.*

silt'ing, *n.*, envasement, limonage, *m.*

sil'van, **syl'van**, *adj.*, des bois; des forêts.

sil'ver, *n.*, (metal.) argent; (money) monnaie d'argent; argent blanc, *m.; (*plate) argenterie, vaisselle d'argent, *f.* German —; *maillechort, m.*

sil'ver, *adj.*, d'argent; (of color) argenté, argentin; (of sound) argentin. To be born with a — spoon in one's mouth; *être né coiffé.*

sil'ver, *v.a.*, argenter; (a mirror) étamer.

sil'ver-beater (-bît'-), *n.*, batteur d'argent, *m.*

sil'ver-bush, *n.*, (bot.) anthyllide, *f.*

sil'verer, *n.*, argenteur, *m.*

sil'ver-eyed (-aïe-de), *adj.*, (of needles) à tête d'argent; (of horses) vairon.

sil'ver-fir, *n.*, sapin blanc, argenté, *m.*

sil'ver-fish, *n.*, (ich.) cyprin doré, poisson rouge, *m.*, athérine, *f.*

sil'ver-gilt (-ghilte), *n.*, vermeil, argent doré, *m.*

sil'ver-glance, *n.*, (min.) argent rouge, *m.*

sil'ver-gray, *adj.*, gris argenté.

sil'ver-haired, *adj.*, aux cheveux argentés, aux cheveux blancs.

sil'ver-headed (-hèd'-), *adj.*, (of things) à pomme d'argent.

sil'ver-hilted, *adj.*, à poignée, *ou* à garde d'argent.

sil'vering, *n.*, argenture, *f.; (*of mirrors) étamage, *m.*

sil'ver-lace, *n.*, galon d'argent, *m.*

sil'ver-leaf (-lîfe), *n.*, argent battu, *m.sing.;* feuilles d'argent, *f.pl.*

sil'verly, *adv.*, comme l'argent.

sil'ver-mounted (-maou'n't-), *adj.*, monté en argent.

sil'ver-paper, *n.*, papier joseph, *m.*

sil'ver-plate, *n.*, argenterie; vaisselle d'argent, *f.*

sil'ver-shaft'ed (-shâft'-), *adj.*, au carquois d'argent.

sil'versmith (-smith), *n.*, orfèvre, *m.*

sil'ver spoon, *n.*, cuiller d'argent, *f.*

sil'ver-tongue, *n.*, langue dorée, *f.* —d; *à la langue dorée.*

sil′ver-trade, *n.*, orfèvrerie, *f.*
sil′ver-wedding, *n.*, noces d'argent, *f.pl.*
sil′ver-weed (-wîde), *n.*, (bot.) argentine, *f.*
sil′ver-winged (-wign′de), *adj.*, aux ailes argentines.
sil′very, *adj.*, d'argent; (of color) argenté, argentin; (of sound) argentin.
sim′ilar, *adj.*, semblable; pareil; (of same nature) similaire.
similar′ity, *n.*, ressemblance, similitude; (same nature) similarité, *f.*
sim′ilarly, *adv.*, de la même manière; pareillement; d'une manière semblable.
sim′ile (-lî), *n.*, (rhet.) comparaison; similitude, *f.*
simili′tude (-tioude), *n.*, similitude; comparaison, ressemblance, *f.*
sim′mer, *v.a.n.*, bouillir lentement; mitonner; mijoter; commencer à bouillir.
sim′mering, *n.*, (cook.) mitonnage; mijotement, *m.*
sim′nel, *n.*, gâteau de Pâques (sans levain), *m.*
si′mon, *n.*, simon. A — pure; *un nicodème.*
simo′niac (-mô-) *ou* **sim′onist**, *n.*, simoniaque, *m.*
sim′ony, *n.*, simonie, *f.*
simoom′ (-moume), *n.*, simoun, *m.*
sim′per, *n.*, sourire niais, *m.*; minauderie, *f.*
sim′per, *v.n.*, sourire niaisement; minauder.
sim′perer, *n.*, minaudier, grimacier, *m.*
sim′pering, *n.*, sourire niais, *m.*, minauderie, *f.*
sim′peringly, *adv.*, en minaudant.
sim′ple (si′m′p′l), *adj.*, simple; (of contracts) (jur.) non scollé.
sim′ple, *n.*, simple; (pharm.) simple, *m.*
sim′ple-hearted *ou* **-minded** (-hârt′-), *adj.*, ingénu, candide, naïf.
sim′ple-mind′edness (-maï′n′d′-), *n.*, ingénuité, candeur, simplicité, naïveté, *f.*
sim′pleness, *n.*, simplicité, *f.*
sim′pleton, *n.*, niais, nigaud; jobard, gobemouches, *m.*
simpli′city, *n.*, simplicité, *f.*
simplifica′tion (-fi-ké-), *n.*, simplification, *f.*
sim′plify (-faïe), *v.a.*, simplifier. To become —ied; *se simplifier.*
sim′ply, *adv.*, simplement; bonnement; (merely) simplement, tout bonnement; (foolishly) avec simplicité; (of itself) de soi-même.
sim′ulate (si′m′iou-), *v.a.*, feindre; contrefaire, simuler.
simula′tion (si′m′iou-lé-), *n.*, simulation; feinte, *f.*; déguisement, *m.*
sim′ulator, *n.*, simulateur, *m.*
simulta′neous (-meul-té-ni-), *adj.*, simultané.
simulta′neously, *adv.*, simultanément.
simulta′neousness (-meul-té-ni-) *ou* **simultane′ity** (-meul-ta-nî-i-), *n.*, simultanéité, *f.*
sin, *n.*, péché, vice, *m.* Original —; *péché originel.* —offering; (Script.) *sacrifice expiatoire, m.* As ugly as —; *laid comme les sept péchés capitaux; laid à faire peur.* Poverty is no —, *ou* crime; (prov.) *pauvreté n'est pas vice.*
sin, *v.n.*, pécher.
since, *conj.*, puisque; depuis que. — you like it; *puisque vous l'aimez.* — I saw him; *depuis que je ne l'ai vu.* How long is it — the doctor died? *combien de temps y a-t-il que le médecin est mort?*
since, *prep.*, depuis. — then; *depuis ce temps, depuis lors.*
since, *adv.*, depuis. Ever —; *depuis ce temps là; depuis lors.* Long —; *il y a longtemps.* It is not long — I was there; *il n'y a pas longtemps que j'y étais.* Two years —; *il y a deux ans.* It happened —; *cela est arrivé depuis.*
sincere′ (-cîre), *adj.*, sincère; de bonne foi.
sincere′ly, *adv.*, sincèrement. Yours —; *tout à vous d'amitié; votre tout dévoué.*

sincere′ness *ou* **sincer′ity**, *n.*, sincérité; bonne foi, *f.*
sine (saïne), *n.*, (trigon.) sinus, *m.*
si′necure (saï-ni-kioure *ou* si′n'i-kioure), *n.*, sinécure, *f.*
si′necurist (saï-ni-kiour′-), *n.*, sinécuriste, *m.*
sine die (saï-nî-daï′î), *adv.*, indéfiniment.
sin′ew (si′n'iou), *n.*, nerf; (anat.) tendon, *m. pl.*, (fig.) nerf, *m.sing.* The —s of war; *le nerf de la guerre.*
sin′ewed (si′n'iou'de), **sin′ewy**, *adj.*, nerveux; vigoureux.
sin′ewless, *adj.*, sans nerf; sans vigueur; énervé.
sin′ew-shrunk (-shreugn′ke), *adj.*, (vet.) efflanqué.
sin′ful (-foule), *adj.*, (pers.) pécheur; criminel; coupable de péché; (of things) criminel, coupable.
sin′fully, *adv.*, criminellement; en pécheur.
sin′fulness, *n.*, méchanceté; criminalité, *f.*
sing (signe), *v.a.n.*, (*preterit*, Sang; *past part.*, Sung) chanter; (the praises of) célébrer; (of the wind) siffler; (to make a shrill sound) siffler; (of a kettle) chanter; (of ears) tinter. To — small; *déchanter, filer doux.* To make any one — small; *rembarrer quelqu'un; rabattre le caquet à.* To — to a person; *chanter une chanson à quelqu'un.* To — (a child) to sleep; *endormir en chantant.* To — in tune; *chanter juste.* To — out of tune; *chanter faux.* To — out; (to halloo) *crier.*
singe (si′n'dje), *v.a.*, flamber; roussir; brûler.
singe, *n.*, (slight burn) légère brûlure, *f.*
singe′ing, *n.*, flambage; (tech.) grillage, *m.*
sing′er (sign′eur), *n.*, chanteur, *m.*, chanteuse; (professional) cantatrice, *f.*; (in a church) chantre; (bird) oiseau chanteur, *m.*
sing′ing (sign′igne), *adj.*, qui chante; (of birds) chanteur.
sing′ing (sign′igne), *n.*, chant; (of the cat) ronron; (of the wind) sifflement; (of ears) tintement, bourdonnement, *m.*
sing′ing-bird (-beurde), *n.*, oiseau chanteur, *m.*
sing′ing-book (-bouke), *n.*, livre de chant, *m.*
sing′ing-boy (-boî), *n.*, enfant de chœur, *m.*
sing′ing-class, *n.*, classe de chant, *f.*
sing′ingly, *adv.*, en chantant.
sing′ing-master (-mâs-), *n.*, maître de chant, *m.*
sing′ing-mistress, *n.*, maîtresse de chant, *f.*
sing′ing-school (-skoule), *n.*, école de chant, *f.*; (for choristers) maîtrise, *f.*
sin′gle (si′gn'g′l), *adj.*, (one) seul, simple, unique; (individual) individuel, particulier; (uncompounded, not double) simple; (of combat) singulier; (unmarried) non marié, célibataire; (bot.) simple; (in Scripture) simple, sincère. — combat; *combat singulier.* — man; *homme non marié; célibataire; garçon, m.* — woman; *femme non mariée; fille, f.* — life; *célibat, m.* To remain —; *coiffer sainte Catherine.* — blessedness; *célibat, m.* To be —; (of man) *être garçon;* (of women) *être fille.*
sin′gle (out) (si′gn'g′l-), *v.a.*, choisir; (to separate) séparer. To — out; *choisir; remarquer; distinguer de la foule, du nombre.*
sin′gle-armed, *adj.*, manchot.
sin′gle-bar′reled, *adj.*, à un coup, simple.
sin′gle-gen′tleman, *n.*, vieux garçon, célibataire, *m.*
sin′gle-handed, *adj.*, seul; tout seul, sans aide.
sin′gle-hearted (-hârt′-), *adj.*, sincère; honnête, franc.
sin′gle-heart′edness (-hârt′èd′-), *n.*, sincérité, *f.*
sin′gleness, *n.*, unité; sincérité, simplicité, *f.*

sin'gle-railway, *n.*, chemin de fer à une seule voie, *m.*

sin'gle-stick, *n.*, bâton, gourdin; jeu du bâton, *m.*

sin'gle-ticket, *n.*, billet d'aller seulement, *m.*

sin'gle-woman, *n..*, demoiselle, fille, *f.*

sin'gly, *adv.*, (individually) individuellement, un à un; (sincerely) sincèrement; (by one's self) seul, à part.

sing'song (sign'so'gne), *n.*, chant monotone, *m.;* psalmodie, *f.*

sing'song, *adj.*, traînant, monotone.

sin'gular (sign'ghiou-), *n.*, singulier, *m.*

sin'gular (sign'ghiou-), *adj.*, singulier; (remarkable) singulier; (not compound) simple; (gram.) singulier, au singulier.

singular'ity, *n.*, singularité, *f.*

sin'gularize, *v.a.*, singulariser.

sin'gularly, *adv.*, singulièrement; (gram.) au singulier.

sin'ister, *adj.*, sinistre; (pers.) méchant, pervers; (her.) sénestre, gauche.

sin'isterly, sin'istrously, *adv.*, sinistrement; d'une manière sinistre.

sink, *n.*, cloaque (sewer) égout, *m.;* (of ancient Rome) cloaque, *f.;* (of kitchens) évier, *m.;* (print.) tremperie, *f.* A — of iniquity; *un cloaque d'iniquité.*

sink, *v.n.*, (*preterit* Sank, Sunk; *past part.*, Sunk) aller au fond; tomber au fond; s'enfoncer; (to decrease) diminuer, baisser, s'abaisser; (to decline) décliner, s'affaiblir; (to decay) périr; (to be overwhelmed) succomber; (to fall) se laisser tomber; (of vessels) couler à fond; (of price) baisser; (of courage, of the spirits) être abattu; (of patients) décliner, s'affaiblir; (of the sun) descendre; (of buildings, etc.) tasser, se tasser; (to be reduced to) dégénérer **en**. To — back; *retomber.* To — down; *aller au fond, s'enfoncer;* (to fall prostrate) *s'affaisser, tomber;* (of the sun) *descendre, se coucher; se plonger* **dans**. To — down on; *se laisser tomber*, ou *s'affaisser*, **sur**. To — down to; *s'habituer* **à**, *se faire* **à**; (to decrease to) *s'abaisser* **jusqu'à**, *diminuer* **jusqu'à**. To — into; *s'enfoncer* **dans**; (to penetrate) *pénétrer* **dans**, *entrer* **dans**; (to fall into) *tomber* **dans**; (to degenerate into) *dégénérer* **en**. To — low; *s'affaisser.* To — under; *succomber* **à** ou **sous**. To — to rest; *s'abandonner au sommeil;* (to die) *entrer dans la mort.* To — ing; (dying) *baisser rapidement.*

sink, *v.a.*, faire tomber au fond; enfoncer; plonger **dans**; (to degrade) abaisser; (to diminish) diminuer, faire baisser; (to depress) abattre; (to plunge into destruction) perdre; (to cause to decline) affaiblir; (to waste) dissiper; (to diminish) diminuer, réduire; (fin.) amortir; (a ship) couler à fond, couler bas; (a well, a shaft) percer, creuser; (engr.) graver en creux; (money) placer à fonds perdus. —ing the others; *non compris les autres.*

sink'er, *n.*, poids, (on a fish-line) plomb, *m.*

sink'hole (-hôle), *n.*, trou d'évier, *m.;* ouverture d'égout, *f.*

sink'ing, *n.*, (of money) placement à fonds perdus; déboursés; (fin.) amortissement; (of wells, shafts) percement, creusage; (of buildings) tassement; (fig. and med.) affaissement, *m.;* défaillance, *f.*

sink'ing-fund (-feu'n'de), *n.*, fonds d'amortissement, *m.;* (of a public debt) caisse d'amortissement, *f.*

sink'stone (-stône), *n.*, pierre d'évier, *f.*

sink'-trap, *n.*, valve de puisard, *f.*

sin'less, *adj.*, sans péché; innocent; pur de tout péché; impeccable.

sin'lessly, *adv.*, purement, innocemment; sans péché.

sin'lessness, *n.*, innocence; pureté, *f.*

sin'ner, *n.*, pécheur, *m.*, pécheresse, *f.* Oh! you —! (fig.) *mauvais sujet que vous êtes!* He is a great — in that respect; *il pèche beaucoup de ce côté-là.*

sinuos'ity (si'n'iou-oss'-), *n.*, sinuosité, *f.*

sin'uous (si'n'iou-), *adj.*, sinueux; tortueux.

si'nus (saï-), *n.*, ouverture; cavité; (geog.) baie, *f.;* (anat.) sinus, *m.*

sip, *n.*, (of drinking) petit coup, *m.;* gorgée, *f.*

sip, *v.a.*, buvoter; (to extract) extraire, sucer.

sip, *v.n.*, buvoter, siroter, déguster.

si'phon (saï-), *n.*, siphon, *m.*

sip'per (sip-peur), *n.*, siroteur, *m.*

sir (seur), *n.*, monsieur; (before the name of a baronet or knight) Sir, *m.;* (in addressing sovereigns) Sire, *m.* — count; *seigneur comte, m.* Did you ring, sir? (of servants to masters) *monsieur a-t-il sonné ?*

sire (saïeur), *n.*, père; (in addressing the king) Sire, *m.* —s, *pl.*, pères, aïeux, *m.pl.* Grand- —; *grand-père, m.*

sir'en (saï-), *n.*, sirène, *f.*

sir'en-(like), *adj.*, de sirène.

Sir'ius (si-), *n.*, (astron.) Sirius, *m.*

sir'loin (seur-loï'n), *n.*, aloyau, *m.;* surlonge, *f.*

siroc'co, *n.*, siroco, siroc, *m.*

sir'rah (sir-), *n.*, coquin; fripon, *m.*

sis'kin, *n.*, (orni.) tarin, *m.*

sis'sy, *n.*, petite sœur, sœurette, *f.*

sis'ter, *n.*, sœur, *f.* The fatal —s; *les Parques, f.pl.*

sis'ter, *adj.*, (of ships) construit sur les mêmes lignes; du même gabarit.

sis'terhood (-houde), *n.*, communauté de sœurs, *f.*, sœurs, *f.pl.*

sis'ter-in-law (-lô), *n.*, belle-sœur, *f.*

sis'terly, *adj.*, de sœur, en sœur, comme une sœur.

sit, *v.n.*, (*preterit* and *past part.*, Sat) s'asseoir; (be seated) être assis; (to stay) rester, demeurer; (of assemblies, courts, judges, etc.) siéger, tenir séance, se réunir; (of clothes) aller; (of birds) couver; se percher; (for one's portrait) poser. To be —ting; *être assis;* (fig.) (of assemblies) *être en séance, siéger.* To — down; *s'asseoir.* To — down to table; *se mettre à table, s'attabler.* (To be seated at table; *être attablé.*) To — down before the town; (milit.) *mettre le siège devant la ville.* To be —ting down; *être assis.* To — in judgment on; *juger.* To — in parliament; *siéger au parlement.* Congress is now —ting; (at this moment) *les Chambres sont maintenant en séance;* (has met) *les Chambres sont assemblées.* To — on; (to be imprinted on) *être empreint* **sur**, *s'imprimer* **sur**, *se peindre* **sur**; (of eggs) *couver* **sur**; (to become) *seoir* **à**, *convenir* **à**, *aller* **à**. To — heavy on; *peser* **sur**. To — up; *se tenir droit;* (to rise from a recumbent position) *se mettre sur son séant;* (not to go to bed) *passer la nuit, veiller.* To — up with; *veiller, garder.* To make any one — up; *étonner, épater quelqu'un.* To — close; *se serrer, se tasser.* To — loose, tight; (of clothes) *être large; être étroit, être serré.* Money —s crowned as a queen; *l'argent trône partout.* To — for one's picture; *donner séance à un peintre.* To — through the night; (at cards) *ne pas jouer, faire galerie;* (of Parliament) *rester en séance toute la nuit.* To — for; (in Parliament) *représenter.* To — up for; *attendre.*

sit, *v.a.*, asseoir; (a horse) se tenir **sur**, monter. To — one's self down; *s'asseoir.* To — out; *rester jusqu'à la fin de.* To — a horse well; *monter, ou se tenir, bien à cheval; avoir une bonne assiette.* To want to — it out; *vouloir en voir la fin.*

sit-at-home', *n.adj.*, homme casanier, sédentaire, *m.*

site (saïte), *n.*, situation, assiette, *f.;* (spot) emplacement, *m.;* (of a landscape) site, *m.*

sit'fast (sit-fâste), *n.*, (vet.) cor; durillon, *m*

sit′ter, n., homme sédentaire; (paint.) personne qui pose, f., modèle, m.; (hen) couveuse, f.

sit′ting, n., séance; (of a court) audience; (incubation) incubation; (in a church) place; (paint.) séance, f. — up; veille, veillée, f.

sit′ting, adj., assis; (of birds) perché, au posé; qui couve; (bot.) sessile. In a — posture; sur son séant.

sit′uate ou **sit′uated** (sit′iou-), adj., situé; (jur.) sis; (pers.) placé. Awkwardly —d; dans une position embarrassante, délicate. This is how I am —; voici la position dans laquelle, où où, je me trouve; voici comme je suis placé; voici ma position.

situa′tion (sit′iou-é-), n., situation, f., état, m.; (place) place, f., emploi, m.; (condition) place, position, f. To have a good —; avoir une bonne place, un emploi lucratif. To hold a good —; occuper une place importante. In a —; en place. Out of a —; sans place. I should be sorry to find myself in such a —; je serais fâché de me trouver dans un cas, ou état, pareil.

six (sikse), adj., six.

six, n., six, m. To be at —es and sevens; être sens dessus dessous; être en désordre, à l'abandon; aller à la débandade. It is — of one and half a dozen of the other; c'est bonnet blanc et blanc bonnet. — foot; de six pieds. — foot way; (rail.) entre-voie, f., entre-rails, m.

six′fold (-fôlde), adj., sextuple; six fois.

six′pence, n., six pence; pièce de 60 centimes, f.

six′penny, adj., de six pence.

six′score (-scôre), adj., cent vingt.

six′teen (-tîne), adj., seize.

six′teenth (-tî'n'th), adj., seizième; (of kings, days of the month) seize. On the —; le seize. Lewis the —; Louis seize.

sixth (siks′th), adj., sixième; (of kings, etc.) six.

sixth, n., sixième, m.; (mus.) sixte, f.

sixth′ly (siks′th-'), adv., sixièmement.

six′tieth (siks-ti-éth), adj., soixantième.

six′ty, adj., soixante.

siz′able, adj., d'une bonne grosseur; de la grosseur voulue (par les règlements).

siz′ar (saï-), n., étudiant servant (of Cambridge university), m.

size (saïze), n., grandeur; taille; (bulk) grosseur, f., volume, m., dimension, f.; (caliber) calibre, m.; (portion) portion, f.; (of a book, of paper) format; (general term) modèle, m.; (of shoes) pointure, f.; (com.) numéro, m.; (glue) colle; colle forte, f.; (tech.) encollage; (of shoemakers) compas, m. Large, small —; grand, petit modèle; (of paper) grand, petit format, m. A man of his —; un homme de sa taille. What is your —? (for gloves, etc.) quel est votre numéro? (for boots) quelle est votre pointure?

size, v.a., ajuster; calibrer; (to cover with size) coller; encoller.

size′able (saïz′a-b'l), adj. V. **sizable**.

sized (saïz′de), adj., de grosseur; de taille; de volume; de grandeur. Middle— —; de moyenne taille, de grandeur moyenne.

size′stick (saïz′-), n., (of shoemakers) compas de cordonnier, m.

siz′ing (saïz′-), n., collage, encollage, m.

siz′y (saïz′-), adj., glutineux, visqueux; gluant.

skate (skéte), n., (ich.) raie, raie blanche, f.; (for sliding) patin, m.

skate, v.n., patiner.

skat′er, n., patineur, m.

skat′ing, n., patinage, m. To be fond of —; aimer à patiner. — club; cercle des patineurs, m.

skedad′dle, v.n., décamper, filer; prendre ses jambes à son cou.

skeet (skîte), n., (nav.) écope, escope, f.

skeg (skèg′), n., (bot.) prune sauvage, f.

skeg′ger (skèg′gheur), n., saumoneau, m.

skein (ské'n′), n., écheveau, m.

skel′eton (skél-è-), n., (anat.) squelette, m.; (fig.) charpente; carcasse; (tech.) carcasse, monture, (of an umbrella) carcasse, f.; (of a speech, etc.) canevas; (mil.) cadre, m. — -key; crochet, rossignol, m. — map; carte muette, f. — regiment; cadres d'un régiment, m.pl. — in the cupboard; (fig.) secret désagréable, m. One must not allude to the — in the cupboard; il ne faut pas parler de corde dans la maison d'un pendu. He is a mere —; il n'a que la peau et les os.

sketch (skètshe), n., esquisse, f.; croquis, m.; ébauche, f.; (fig.) plan; aperçu de, m.; étude sur, f.

sketch, v.a., esquisser; ébaucher. To — out; esquisser; faire le croquis de; (fig.) tracer le plan de.

sketch′-book (-bouke), n., album; cahier de croquis, m.

skew, (a-) (a-skiou), adv., obliquement; en biais.

skew, adj., oblique; de biais.

skew′-back, n., (arch.) imposte, f.

skew′-bridge, n., pont oblique, de biais, m.

skew′er (skiou-eur), n., brochette, f.

skew′er, v.a., brocheter.

skid (skide), n., chaîne à enrayer; enrayure, f.; frein, sabot, m.; (nav.) défense, f.

skid, v.a., enrayer.

skiff (skife), n., esquif, m.

skill, n., habileté; dextérité; adresse, industrie, f.; savoir-faire, talent, m.

skilled (skilde), adj., habile; adroit. — in; versé dans; habile à.

skil′let, n., casserole, f., coquemar, m.

skil′ful (skil-foul), adj., adroit; habile, entendu; expérimenté.

skil′fully, adv., adroitement; habilement.

skil′fulness, n., adresse; habileté, f.; talent, m.

skim, v.a., écumer; (milk) écrémer; (fig.) raser, effleurer.

skim, v.n., passer légèrement sur; glisser sur. To — over; effleurer, raser; voler, courir.

skim, n., écume; (of milk) crème, f.

skim′mer, n., écumoire, f.; (orni.) bec-enciseaux, m.

skim′-milk ou **skimmed′-milk** (ski′m'de-), n., lait écrémé, m.

skim′ming, n., écumage; (milk) écrémage, m.

skim′mings, n.pl., écume, f.sing.

skin, v.a., écorcher; (to cover with skin) couvrir de peau. To — a flint; tondre sur un œuf.

skin (over), v.a., couvrir superficiellement; (potatoes, etc.) peler, éplucher. v.n., se couvrir de peau; se cicatriser.

skin, n., peau, f.; (of certain animals) cuir; (bot.) épiderme, m. To have a fair —; avoir la peau blanche. To be nothing but — and bone; n'avoir que la peau et les os. Next to one's —; sur la peau. Wet to the —; trempé jusqu'aux os. To come off with a whole —; s'en tirer sain et sauf, sans une égratignure. I would not be in his — for worlds; je ne voudrais être lui, ou dans sa peau, pour rien au monde. To escape by the — of one's teeth; l'échapper belle, ou d'un cheveu.

skin′-deep (-dîpe), adj., de l'épaisseur de la peau; (fig.) superficiel, léger, peu profond.

skin′-disease, n., maladie de la peau, f.

skin′-dresser, n., peaussier, m.

skin′-eruption, n., éruption cutanée, f.

skin′flint, n., pince-maille, fesse-mathieu; pingre, ladre, m.

skink (skign′k), n., (zoöl.) scinque, m.

skin′less, adj., sans peau; qui a peau mince.

skin′ner, n., écorcheur; (dealer in skins) peaussier, m. — 's trade; pelleterie, f.

skin'niness, *n.*, maigreur, *f.*; décharnement, *m.*

skin'ny, *adj.*, de peau ; (thin) maigre ; décharné.

skip, *n.*, saut ; bond, *m.*

skip, *v.n.*, sauter, sautiller, bondir. To —; (with a rope) *sauter à la corde.*

skip, *v.a.*, sauter ; omettre, passer, lire du ponce. To — over ; *sauter par-dessus, passer.*

skip'-jack (-djake), *n.*, parvenu, *m.*

skip'-kennel (-kè'n'-), *n.*, galopin, sauteruisseau, *m.*

skip'per, *n.*, (of a merchant vessel) patron ; (dancer) danseur, *m.*, danseuse, *f.*, sauteur, *m.*, sauteuse, *f.*; (ent.) ver de fromage, *m.*

skip'ping, *n.*, action de sauter, de danser; (fig.) omission, *f.*

skip'pingly, *adv.*, en sautant ; par sauts ; par bonds.

skip'ping-rope (-rôpe), *n.*, corde ; corde à sauter, *f.*

skir'mish (skeur-), *n.*, escarmouche ; lutte, contestation, querelle, *f.*

skir'mish (skeur-), *v.n.*, escarmoucher.

skir'misher, *n.*, tirailleur, *m.*

skir'mishing, *n.*, escarmouche, *f.*

skir'ret (skir-), *n.*, (bot.) berle, *f.*, chervis, *m.*

skirt (skeurte), *n.*, (of a coat) pan, *m.*, basque ; (of a gown) jupe, *f.*; (of animals) diaphragme, *m.*; (of a forest, etc.) lisière, extrémité, *f.*, bord, *m.*; (of a town) extrémité, *f.* Out—s ; *faubourgs, m.pl.*

skirt (skeurte), *v.a.*, border, garnir ; (to go alongside) longer.

skirt, *v.n.*, être sur les bords.

skirt'ing *ou* **skirt'ing-board** (-bôrde), *n.*, bordure, garniture ; (arch.) plinthe, *f.*; (stuff for skirts) étoffes pour jupes, *ou* pour robes, *f.pl.*

skit (skit'), *n.*, raillerie, *f.*; (on a play) burlesque, *m.*

skit'tish, *adj.*, (fickle) capricieux, volage, inconstant ; (of horses) ombrageux, quinteux.

skit'tishly, *adv.*, (changeably) avec inconstance, capricieusement.

skit'tishness, *n.*, (fickleness) légéreté, inconstance ; (of horses) nature ombrageuse, *f.*

skit'tle, *n.*, quille (jouet), *f.*

skit'tle-ground (-graou'n'de), **-alley**, *n.*, quillier, jeu de quilles, *m.*

sko'lezite (skol'èz'aïte), *n.*, (min.) scolézite, *f.*

skulk (skeulke), *v.n.*, se cacher, se tenir caché, s'enfermer, caponner. To — in ; *entrer furtivement, à la dérobée.* To — out ; *sortir furtivement, à la dérobée.*

skulk'er, *n.*, capon, cagnard, *m.*

skull (skeul), *n.*, crâne, *m.*

skull'cap, *n.*, calotte ; (bot.) toque, *f.*

skunk (skeugn'ke), *n.*, (zoöl.) chinche, *m.*; moufette, *f.*; putois d'Amérique, *m.* Mean — ; *chafouin, ladre, m.*

sky (skaïe), *n.*, ciel, *m.*; (climate, weather) climat, air, *m.*

sky' color (-keul'leur), *n.*, azur, bleu de ciel, *m.*

sky'-colored (-keul'leurde), *adj.*, azuré, bleu de ciel.

sky'-dyed (-daï-de), *adj.*, teint en azur, en bleu de ciel.

sky'ey, *adj.*, du ciel ; éthéré.

sky'-high, *adj.*, qui touche aux cieux. To blow up any one — ; (fig.) *tancer vertement.*

sky'lark (-lârke), *n.*, alouette (des champs), *f.*

sky'lark, *v.n.*, polissonner ; folâtrer.

sky'larking, *n.*, polissonneries ; mauvaises plaisanteries ; (toying) folâtreries, *f.pl.*

sky'light (-laïte), *n.*, lucarne en tabatière, *f.*; vasistas, abat-jour, *m.*; (nav.) claire-voie, écoutille vitrée, *f.*

sky'rocket, *n.*, fusée volante, *f.*

sky'sail, *n.*, (nav.) contre-cacatois, *m.*

sky'-scraper, *n.*, (nav.) papillon, *m.*; (of high houses in America) qui touche aux nues, qui se perd dans les nues.

sky'ward, *adv.*, vers le ciel.

slab, *n.*, (metal.) plaque ; (of stone) dalle, plaque, table, pierre plate, *f.*; (print.) marbre, *m.*; (carp.) planche ; (for an epitaph) pierre sépulcrale, (tablet) tablette, *f.*

slab'ber, *v.n.*, baver.

slab'ber, *v.a.*, couvrir de bave ; barbouiller.

slab'berer, *n.*, baveur, *m.*, baveuse, *f.*; (fig.) idiot, *m.*

slab'bering, *adj.*, baveux.

slack, *n.*, (small coal) petit charbon ; (of ropes) mou, *m.*

slack, *adj.*, lâche ; (slow) lent ; (remiss) négligent, nonchalant ; (weak) faible, mou ; (com.) faible, languissant. The — season ; *la morte saison.* Trade, *ou* business, is — ; *les affaires ne vont pas ; le commerce est presque nul* (V. Hugo).

slack *ou* **slack'en**, *v.a.*, relâcher, détendre ; (to relax) relâcher de, se relâcher ; (to mitigate) affaiblir, adoucir ; (to make slower) ralentir ; (to repress) retenir, arrêter ; (fire) amortir ; (lime) éteindre. To — out ; (nav.) *mollir.*

slack *ou* **slack'en** (slak'k'n), *v.n.*, se relâcher, se détendre ; (to be remiss) se relâcher ; (to become more slow) se ralentir ; (to lose cohesion) mollir ; (to abate) diminuer, baisser ; (to become less violent) diminuer d'intensité ; (to flag) pendre ; se relâcher ; (of lime) s'éteindre.

slack'ening (slak'k'n-), *n.*, relâchement, ralentissement, *m.*; diminution, *f.*

slack'ing, *n.*, (of lime) extinction, *f.*

slack'ly, *adv.*, mollement ; lâchement ; (negligently) négligemment, nonchalamment.

slack'ness, *n.*, relâchement, *m.*; (remissness) négligence, nonchalance, *f.*, relâchement, *m.*, (slowness) lenteur ; (weakness) faiblesse, mollesse, *f.*

slag, *n.*, scorie, *f.*

slake (sléke), *v.a.*, éteindre ; (thirst) éteindre, étancher ; (lime) éteindre.

slak'ing, *n.*, (of thirst) étanchement, *m.*; (of lime) extinction, *f.*

slam, *n.*, action de fermer bruyamment une porte ; (at cards) vole, *f.*; chélem, *m.*

slam, *v.a.*, fermer bruyamment, avec violence, claquer (une porte) (A. Daudet) ; (at cards) faire la vole.

slam'ming, *n.*, claquement (de porte), *m.*

slan'der, *n.*, médisance ; calomnie ; (jur.) diffamation, *f.*

slan'der, *v.a.*, médire de ; calomnier ; (jur.) diffamer.

slan'derer, *n.*, médisant, *m.*, médisante, *f.*; calomniateur, *m.*, calomniatrice, *f.*; (jur.) diffamateur, *m.*, diffamatrice, *f.*

slan'dering, *adj.*, médisant.

slan'derous, *adj.*, (of things) calomnieux, calomniateur ; diffamatoire, diffamant ; (pers.) médisant.

slan'derously, *adv.*, avec médisance ; calomnieusement.

slan'derousness, *n.*, caractère diffamatoire, *m.*

slang, *n.*, argot; langue verte, *f.* A — word ; *terme d'argot, m.*

slang'y, *adj.*, trivial, d'argot.

slant, *v.a.*, rendre oblique, faire biaiser, incliner, mettre en pente.

slant, *v.n.*, être oblique, en pente, de biais ; biaiser.

slant *ou* **slant'ing**, *adj.*, (of rays) oblique; de biais, incliné, en pente ; (fort.) en écharpe. Cut — ; *coupé en biais, en talus.*

slant *ou* **slant'ing**, *n.*, direction oblique, *f.*; biaisement, biais, talus, *m.*

slant'ingly, slant'ly, *ou* **slant'wise** (-waïze), *adv.*, obliquement ; en biais, en talus.

slap, *n.*, tape, claque, *f. ;* coup ; (on the face) soufflet, *m. ;* (pop.) calotte, gifle, *f.*

slap, *adv.*, voilà que ; pan ! raide comme balle, en plein. I told him — out ; *je lui ai dit en plein, de but en blanc, sans tortiller.*

slap, *v.a.*, taper ; claquer ; frapper ; (any one's face) souffleter. He —ped my face ; *il m'a donné une gifle, il m'a souffleté ;* (fam.) *il m'a calotté.*

slap'dash, *adv.*, tout d'un coup ; raide comme balle, d'emblée ; (anyhow) bredi-breda, n'importe comment ; brelique-breloque.

slap'per, *n.*, personne qui soufflette, *f.* That's a — ! *en voilà un fameux ! en voilà une bonne !*

slap'ping, *n.*, coups ; (on the face) soufflets, *m.pl. adj.*, fameux, bon. *V.* **spanking.**

slap'-up, *adj.*, (fam.) fameux, soigné.

slash, *n.*, taillade, coupure ; (on the face) balafre, *f.*

slash, *v.a.*, taillader ; sabrer ; frapper d'estoc et de taille ; (the face) balafrer ; (a whip) faire claquer ; (to lash) fouetter ; (to criticize) éreinter. To — right and left ; *taillader à droite et à gauche.*

slash'ing, *adj.*, (fam.) bien tapé ; (of a story) fameux, huppé ; (fig.) mordant, sanglant.

slate (sléte), *n.*, ardoise, *f. ;* (min.) schiste, *m.* To have a — loose ; *avoir les idées quelque peu brouillées, avoir le cerveau fêlé.*

slate, *v.a.*, couvrir d'ardoises; (fig.) (pers.) tancer ; (a book) éreinter.

slate'-ax (-akse), *n.*, hache à ardoise, assette, *f.*

slate'-clay, *n.*, schiste argileux, *m.*

slate'-colored (-keul'leurde), *adj.*, ardoisé.

slate'-knife (-naïfe), *n.*, couperet à ardoise, *m.*

slate'-pencil, *n.*, crayon d'ardoise, *m.*

slate'-quarry (-kwŏr-), *n.*, carrière d'ardoise, ardoisière, *f.*

slat'er (-slét'-), *n.*, couvreur en ardoise, *m.*

slat'ing (-slét'-), *n.*, toiture en ardoise ; (fig.) semonce, *f.*

slat'ter (slat'-), *v.n.*, s'habiller négligemment, malproprement.

slat'tern, *n.*, femme malpropre, souillon, saligaude, salope, *f.*

slat'ternly, *adj.*, négligent, malpropre, sale.

slat'ternly, *adv.*, négligemment ; malproprement, salement.

sla'ty (slé-ti), *adj.*, ardoiseux ; (of color) ardoisé.

slaugh'ter (slŏ-), *n.*, tuerie ; boucherie, *f.*, (massacre) massacre ; (of animals) abatage, *m.*

slaugh'ter, *v.a.*, tuer, égorger ; massacrer; (animal) abattre.

slaugh'ter-house (-haouce), *n.*, abattoir, *m.*

slaugh'terman, **slaugh'terer**, *n.*, abatteur ; équarrisseur, *m.*

slaugh'terous, *adj.*, meurtrier, destructif.

slave (sléve), *n.*, esclave, *m.f.* He is a — to ; *il est esclave* **de.**

slave, *v.n.*, travailler comme un nègre, comme un forçat ; s'échiner.

slave'-born, *adj.*, né dans l'esclavage.

slave'-dealer, *n.*, négrier, *m.*

slave'-driver (-draïv'-), *n.*, surveillant d'esclaves, *m. ;* (fig.) maître sévère et cruel, *m.*

slave'-like (-laïke), *adj.*, d'esclave ; comme un esclave.

slave'-owner (-ô'n'-), *n.*, propriétaire d'esclaves, *m.*

slav'er (slév'-), *n.*, négrier ; bâtiment négrier; bâtiment de traite, *m.*

slav'er (slav'-), *v.a.n. V.* **slabber.**

slav'erer (slav'-), *n. V.* **slabberer.**

slav'ery (slév'-), *n.*, esclavage, *m.* This work is perfect — ; (fig.) *c'est un travail tuant.*

slave'-ship, *n. V.* **slaver.**

slave'-trade, *n.*, traite des noirs, traite des nègres ; traite, *f.*

slav'ish (slév'-), *adj.*, d'esclave ; servile, bas, assujettissant.

slav'ishly (slév'-), *adv.*, en esclave ; servilement.

slav'ishness (slév'-), *n.*, servilité, *f.*

Slavon'ic (sla-), *adj.*, slave ; slavon.

Slavon'ic, *n.*, (lang.) slave, *m.*

slay (slé), *v.a.*, (preterit, Slew ; *past part.*, Slain) tuer, égorger ; massacrer.

slay'er (slé-eur), *n.*, tueur **de**, meurtrier, *m.*

slay'ing, *n.*, massacre, *m. ;* tuerie, *f.*

sledge, *n.*, traîneau. — hammer; *marteau à deux mains ; marteau de forgeron, m., masse, f.*

sledge'-driver (-draïv'-), *n.*, conducteur de traîneau, *m.*

sleek (slîke), *adj.*, lisse ; luisant ; poli ; (of horses) d'un beau poil ; (fig.) doux, délicat ; doucereux.

sleek, *v.a.*, lisser, lustrer, rendre luisant.

sleek'ly, *adv.*, doucement, délicatement.

sleek'ness, *n.*, surface lisse ; (fig.) douceur, délicatesse, *f.*

sleek'y, *adj.*, lisse ; doux ; luisant ; (fig.) rusé, hypocrite.

sleep (slîpe), *n.*, sommeil, *m.* Want of — ; *défaut de sommeil, m. ;* insomnie, *f.* Sound, deep — ; *profond sommeil.* Restless — ; *sommeil agité.* To go to — ; *s'endormir.* To go to — again ; *se rendormir.* He did not get a wink of — all night ; *il n'a pu fermer l'œil de la nuit.* To startle any one out of his — ; *réveiller quelqu'un en sursaut.* To start (up) out of one's — ; *se réveiller en sursaut.* To be dying with — ; *n'en pouvoir plus de sommeil ; tomber de sommeil.* To have a — ; *faire un somme.* To send to — ; (of drugs, etc.) *faire dormir.* To get an hour or two's sleep ; *dormir une heure ou deux.* To get no — ; *ne pas dormir.* Overcome with — ; *accablé de sommeil.* — at-noon ; (bot.) *salsifis-des-prés, m. ;* barbe-de-bouc, *f.* —walker ; *somnambule, m.f.*

sleep (slîpe), *v.n.*, (preterit and past part., Slept) dormir ; (to stay for the night, as at an inn) coucher. He slept at my house last night ; *il a couché chez moi cette nuit.* I can — you to-night ; *je puis vous donner le coucher.* To — out ; *découcher.* To — like a top ; *dormir comme une marmotte,* ou *comme un sabot,* ou *les* (ou **à**) *poings fermés.* To — like a log ; *dormir comme une souche.* To — in peace ; *reposer en paix.* To — till late in the day ; *dormir fort avant dans la journée ;* faire la grasse matinée. To — at night, in the day ; *dormir la nuit, le jour.* To — out ; *découcher.* To — soundly ; *dormir profondément,* ou *sur les deux oreilles.* To — off the effects of wine, to — one's self sober ; *cuver son vin.* To — one's life away ; *passer sa vie à dormir.* — upon it ; (prov.) *la nuit porte conseil.*

sleep'er, *n.*, dormeur, *m.*, dormeuse ; (arch.) lambourde, traversine, semelle de bois; (in ships) guirlande de genou ; (railways) traverse, longuerine, *f. ;* (animal) animal hibernant, *m.* To be a heavy — ; *avoir le sommeil lourd,* ou *dur.*

sleep'ily, *adv.*, d'un air endormi ; (heavily) lourdement ; (stupidly) bêtement.

sleep'iness, *n.*, assoupissement, *m. ;* envie de dormir ; (heaviness) pesanteur ; (of pears) blet-tissure, *f.*

sleep'ing, *n.*, sommeil ; repos, *m.*

sleep'ing, *adj.*, endormi, dormant ; (of partners) commanditaire. — partner ; *commanditaire, m.* —room ; *chambre à coucher ;* (in schools) dortoir, *m. ;* (in barracks) *chambrée, f.* —car ; *wagon-lit, coupé-lit, m.*

sleep'ing-berth, *n.*, couchette, *f.*

sleep'ing-draught, *n.*, potion calmante, *f.*

sleep'ing-place, *n.*, abri, gîte, *m.*

sleep'less, *adj.*, sans sommeil ; sans repos — nights ; *nuits sans sommeil, f.pl.*

sleep'lessness, *n.*, insomnie, *f.*

sleep'y, *adj.*, qui a sommeil ; qui a envie de dormir ; (asleep) endormi ; (somniferous) somnifère, soporifique ; (lazy) inactif ; (heavy) lourd ; (of pears) blet. To be, to feel—; *avoir sommeil ; avoir envie de dormir.*

sleep'y-head (-hède),*n.*, paresseux, *m.*, paresseuse, *f.* ; (fam.) endormi, *m.*, endormie, *f.*

sleep'y-looking (-louk'-), *adj.*, qui a l'air endormi.

sleet (slîte), *n.*, grésil, givre, frimas, *m.* ; neige fondue, *f.* — is falling ; *il grésille.*

sleet'y, *adj.*, de grésil.

sleeve (slîve), *n.*, manche, *f.* To laugh in one's — ; *rire dans sa barbe ; rire sous cape.* To hang on the — of ; *être sous la tutelle* **de.**

sleeve, *v.a.*, mettre des manches **à.**

sleeve'-board (-bôrde), *n.*, passe-carreau, *m.*

sleeve'-button (-beut't'n), **-link**, **-stud**, *n.*, bouton de manche, *m.*

sleeved(slîv'de), *adj.*, à, *ou* garni **de,**manches.

sleeve'less, *adj.*, sans manches.

sleigh (slé), *n.*, traîneau, *m.* — chair ; *chaise-traîneau, f.*

sleigh'ing (slé-igne), *n.*, transport par traîneau, *m.*

sleight (slaïte), *n.*, ruse, *f.* ; tour d'adresse, escamotage, *m.* — of hand ; *passe-passe ; tour de passe-passe, m. ; prestidigitation, f.*

slen'der (slè'n'-), *adj.*, mince ; svelte, délié, grêle ; élancé ; (slight, weak) faible, léger ; (not amply supplied) pauvre, chétif, exigu, maigre ; (small) petit. — waist ; *taille svelte, taille élancée, f.* — blade ; *lame mince, f.* — stalk ; *tige déliée, f.* — repast ; *léger repas, m.* — hopes ; *faibles espérances, f.pl.*

slen'derly,*adv.*, d'une manière élancée, d'une forme svelte ; légèrement, pauvrement, chétivement ; médiocrement.

slen'derness, *n.*, finesse, *f.* ; légèreté ; (weakness) faiblesse, légèreté ; (spareness) pauvreté ; (want of plenty) exiguïté, petitesse, *f.*

sleuth'-hound (slouth-haounde), *n.*, chien limier, *m.*

sley (slé), **slay**, *n.*, peigne de tisserand, *m.*

slice (slaïce), *n.*, tranche ; (of poultry) aiguillette ; (of a melon) côte ; (utensil) écumoire, (round slice) rouelle ; (spatula) spatule,*f.* Fish—; *truelle, f.* — of bread, of meat; *tranche de pain, de viande, f.* — of bread and butter; *tartine de beurre ; beurrée, f.* — of bread and jam ; *tartine de confitures, f.*

slice (slaïce), *v.a.*, couper par tranches ; couper par aiguillettes : (to divide) couper, partager.

slick, *adv.*, tout de suite ; d'emblée.

slide (slaïde), *n.*, glissoire ; glissade, *f.* ; (of umbrellas, parasols) coulant, (of a wheel) patin, *m.* ; (tech.) coulisse, *f.*, chariot ; (of a steam-engine) tiroir, *m.* ; (inclined plane) plan incliné, couloir ; (of a magic lantern) verre ; (dancing) coulé, *m.* ; glissé, *m.* ; (of a microscope) porte-objet, *m.* — of rock, etc. ; *éboulement de rocher, m.*

slide, *v.n.*, (*preterit*, Slid ; *past part.*, Slidden) glisser ; couler ; (mec.) mouvoir en coulisse. To — away; *glisser toujours ;* (to pass) *glisser, s'écouler.* To — down ; *glisser en bas ; descendre en glissant.* To — in ; *se glisser* **dans,** *se faufiler* **dans.** To — into; *tomber* **dans,** *passer insensiblement* **dans.** To let things —; *laisser faire, laisser aller les choses (ne pas s'en occuper).*

slide, *v.a.*, glisser. To — in ; *glisser* **dans.**

slid'er (slaïd'-), *n.*, glisseur, *m.* ; (mec.) coulisse, *f.* ; coulant, *m.*

slide'-rest,*n.*, support à coulisse, à chariot,*m.*

slide'-rod, *n.*, tige de tiroir, *f.*

slide'-valve, *n.*, soupape à tiroir, *f.*

slid'ing, *n.*, glissade, *f.* ; glissement, *m.*

slid'ing, *adj.*, glissant, à coulisse ; coulant ; mobile.

slid'ing-door, *n.*, porte à coulisse, *f.*

slid'ing-rule (-roule), *n.*, (math.) règle à calcul, règle logarithmique, règle à coulisse, *f.*

slid'ing-sash, *n.*, châssis à coulisse, *m.*

slid'ing-scale, *n.*, (corn laws) échelle mobile ; (math.) règle à calcul, *f.*

slight (slaïte), *adj.*, mince ; léger ; faible ; peu considérable; (of no consequence) peu important, insignifiant. A — wound ; *une légère blessure,f.* Not in the —est; *pas le moins du monde.*

slight, *n.*, manque d'égards, manque de respect, mépris, dédain, *m.* ; insulte, *f.* To put a — upon any one; *manquer de respect,* ou *d'égards,* **à** *quelqu'un ; insulter.*

slight (slaïte), *v.a.*, manquer d'égards **à** ; manquer **à**; traiter sans égard ; négliger ; mépriser, insulter ; faire peu de cas **de** ; dédaigner.

slight'er, *n.*, qui fait peu de cas **de**, qui méprise, contempteur, *m.*

slight'ing, *n.*, mépris ; manque d'égards, *m.*

slight'ingly, *adv.*, avec peu d'égards ; avec mépris, avec dédain.

slight'ly, *adv.*, légèrement, négligemment ; à la légère ; faiblement, (little) peu, un peu.

slight'ness, *n.*, légèreté ; faiblesse,*f.*

sli'ly (slaï'-), *adv.*, en sournois ; avec malice, avec ruse ; sournoisement ; finement. To look — at ; *regarder en dessous, à la dérobée ; lorgner.*

slim, *adj.*, svelte, mince ; délié, élancé, grêle ; (slight) léger, faible ; (fig.) fin, rusé.

slime (slaïme), *n.*, vase, *f.* ; limon, *m.* ; (of snails) bave, *f.* ; (asphalt) asphalte, bitume, *m.*

slime-pit, *n.*, bassin d'asphalte, de bitume ; (metal.) labyrinthe, *m.*

slim'iness (slaï'm'-), *n.*, viscosité ; nature limoneuse, *f.*

slim'ness (sli'm'-),*n.*, forme svelte, minceur ; légèreté, faiblesse, *f.*

sli'my (slaï'm'-), *adj.*, vaseux ; limoneux, visqueux, gluant ; (bot.) muqueux.

sli'ness (slaï-), *n.* V. **slyness.**

sling, *n.*, fronde ; (for a broken limb) écharpe; (nav.) élingue; (for horses) sangle ; (of muskets) bretelle, *f.* ; (blow) coup de fronde ; coup, *m.* To carry one's arm in a — ; *porter, avoir le bras en écharpe.*

sling, *v.a.*, (*preterit* and *past part.*, Slung) lancer avec une fronde ; (to suspend) suspendre ; (nav.) élinguer. To — the hammocks ; *tendre les hamacs.* To — over one's shoulder ; *mettre,* ou *porter, en bandoulière, en sautoir.*

sling'er (slign'eur), *n.*, frondeur, *m.*

slink (slign'ke), *v.a.*, (*preterit* and *past part.*, Slunk) s'échapper ; se dérober. To — away; *s'échapper à la dérobée, se dérober, s'esquiver, se retirer.* To — in ; *entrer furtivement, se glisser* **dans.** To — out; *sortir à la dérobée ; s'esquiver.* To — off ; *s'esquiver.*

slip, *v.n.*, glisser; couler ; faire un faux pas. To — away; *s'échapper, s'esquiver ; se dérober, s'en aller furtivement ;* (to err) *faillir, faire un faux pas ;* (of the tongue) *fourcher, tourner ;* (of wheels) *patiner.* To — down; *tomber.* To — in; *glisser dedans ; entrer furtivement.* To — into; *se glisser* **dans.** To — off; *s'échapper, s'esquiver, se dérober, s'en aller furtivement.* To — off from ; *glisser* **de.** To — over ; *glisser* **sur,** *passer* **sur,** *sauter.* To — out ; *glisser dehors ;* *s'échapper, s'esquiver, sortir furtivement.* To — out of; *sortir* **de** . . . *à la dérobée ; s'échapper* **de**; (to throw off) *se dégager* **de.** My foot —ped ; *mon pied glissa, le pied me glissa.* To let —; *laisser échapper ; lâcher.*

slip, *v.a.*, glisser ; couler ; (to lose) perdre, laisser échapper ; (to escape from) quitter à la dérobée ; (to let loose) lâcher ; (to throw off) se dégager **de**; (to tear off) arracher, enlever, (of clothes) ôter; (cable) filer. To — in ; *introduire; glisser* **dans;** *couler* **dans.** To — into; *glisser* **dans.** To — off ; *enlever, ôter.* To —

on ; *passer, mettre*. To — the collar ; *se dégager de ses liens ; s'affranchir*. To — on one's clothes ; *s'habiller à la hâte, passer, mettre ses habits*. To — the leash ; (fig.) *s'affranchir de sa tutelle, secouer son long*.

slip, *n*., (sliding) action de glisser, glissade ; (fault) erreur, méprise, (fam.) bévue, *f*. ; faux pas, oubli, *m*., faute ; (long piece) bande ; (of herbs) brin, (of turf) parterre, tapis vert, *m*. ; (leash) laisse, *f*. ; (twig) brin, plant, *m*., bouture, *f*. ; (print.) placard, *m*. ; (thea.) coulisse ; (of a river, a harbor) cale, *f*. ; (writing-copy) exemple ; (petticoat) jupon de dessus ; (bodice) cache-corset ; (geol.) déplacement de strates, *m*. — of land ; *bande de terre, f.* Land — ; *éboulement de terre, m.* There 's many a — 'twixt the cup and the lip ; *de la main à la bouche se peut souvent la soupe ; n'épouse pas toujours qui fiance*. To give any one the — ; *faire faux bond à quelqu'un ; fausser compagnie à quelqu'un ; planter quelqu'un là*. To make a — ; *glisser ;* (fig.) *faire un faux pas*. It is a — of the tongue ; *c'est un mot échappé, un lapsus linguæ*. He made a — of the tongue ; *la langue lui a fourché*. — of the pen ; *faute d'inattention, erreur de plume, f. ; lapsus calami, m.*

slip'-board (-bôrde), *n*., coulisse, *f*.

slip'-carriage, *n*., wagon détaché en route, *m*.

slip'-knot (-note), *n*., nœud coulant, *m*.

slip'per, *n*., pantoufle ; (of the pope) mule, *f*. ; (bot.) soulier de Notre-Dame, *m*. To hunt the — ; *jouer à la savate*.

slip'pered (slip'peurde), *adj*., en pantoufles.

slip'perily, *adv*., en glissant, d'une manière glissante.

slip'periness, *n*., nature glissante ; (uncertainty) incertitude ; (of the tongue) volubilité, liberté de langue, *f*.

slip'pery, *adj*., glissant ; (not easily held) difficile à tenir ; (uncertain) incertain, peu sûr ; (unstable) peu stable, variable, inconstant ; (of the tongue) indiscret ; (lubricious) scabreux, lubrique. It is very — out of doors ; *il fait très glissant ; le pavé est très glissant, très gras.* — customer ; *rusé compère.* To be as — as an eel ; *échapper comme une anguille.* — promises ; *des promesses peu sûres, f.pl.*

slip'shod, *adj*., chaussé en pantoufles ; (fig.) négligé, désordonné, débraillé ; (of style) décousu. To go about — ; *traîner la savate*.

slip'slop, *n*., ripopée, lavasse, *f*.

slip'slop, *adj*., mou, lâche ; décousu ; désordonné.

slit, *v.a.*, (*preterit* and *past part.*, Slit) fendre.

slit, *v.n.*, se fendre.

slit, *n*., fente ; (grafting) enture, *f*. — iron ; *fer fendu, m.*

slit'ter, *n*., fendeur, *m*., fendeuse, *f*.

slit'ting, *n*., fendage, *m*. ; (of iron) fenderie, *f*.

slit'ting-mill, *n*., fenderie, *f*.

sli'ver (sli-veur), *v.a.*, couper par tranches.

sli'ver, *n*., tranche, *f*. ; (of wood) éclat, fragment, *m*.

slob'ber, *v.n.* V. **slabber**.

sloe (slô), *n*., (bot.) prunelle, *f*.

sloe'-tree (trî), *n*., prunier épineux ; prunellier, *m*.

sloop (sloupe), *n*., (nav.) sloop, *m*. ; corvette, *f*.

slop, *v.a.*, renverser ; répandre ; laisser tomber ; tacher, salir, avec un liquide.

slop, *n*., gâchis, *m*. ; (bad liquor) ripopée, *f*. —s, *pl.*, rinçure. V. **slops**.

slop'-basin (-béss'n) *ou* **slop'-bowl** (-bôl), *n*., bol (à rinçure), rince-tasse, *m*.

slope (slôpe), *n*., pente, rampe, inclinaison, *f*. ; talus, penchant, versant, *m*. ; (in a garment) échancrure, *f*., biais, *m*.

slope, *v.a.*, incliner ; couper en biais ; taluter ; échancrer.

slope, *v.n.*, pencher ; aller en pente, aller en talus, incliner ; biaiser, aller en biais.

slop'-goods, *n*., marchandises de pacotille, *f.pl.*

slop'ing, *adj*., de biais ; échancré ; (of land) en talus, en pente.

slop'ing, *n*., pente, *f*. ; biais ; (of land) talus, *m*., rampe, pente, obliquité, *f*.

slop'ingly (slôp'-), *adv*., obliquement ; en biais ; avec échancrure ; en talus.

slop'-pail (-péle), *n*., seau aux eaux sales, *m*.

slop'piness (slop'-), *n*., état bourbeux, état boueux, *m*.

slop'py, *adj*., gâcheux ; humide, bourbeux.

slop'-room, *n*., (nav.) soute aux hardes, *f*.

slops, *n.pl.*, habits de pacotille, de camelote ; pantalons ; caleçons, *m.pl.* ; literie, *f.* ; eaux sales, *f.pl.* ; (drink) lavasse, *f*.

slop'seller (slop'sèl'eur), *n*., confectionneur d'habits de pacotille, *m*.

slop'shop, *n*., boutique d'habits de pacotille, *f*.

slot, *n*., barre de bois, *f*. ; (ant.) (of a deer) foulées, abattures, *f.pl.*, voie, *f*. ; (mach.) fente, ouverture ; (theat.) trappe, *f*. ; trappillon, *m*.

sloth (slôth), *n*., (idleness) paresse, fainéantise ; oisiveté ; (slowness) lenteur, *f*. ; (mam.) paresseux, *m*.

sloth'ful (slôth'foule), *adj*., paresseux ; fainéant ; indolent.

sloth'fully, *adv*., d'une manière paresseuse, en fainéant ; avec paresse ; en paresseux.

sloth'fulness, *n*., paresse ; fainéantise ; indolence, *f*.

slot'-hole (-hôle), *n*., rainure, *f*.

slouch (slaoutshe), *n*., (of the head) inclinaison ; inclination ; (gait) démarche lourde, gauche, *f*. ; (pers.) gros manant, paysan, *m*.

slouch, *v.n.*, marcher des épaules ; avoir une démarche lourde, de paysan, de manant ; (fam.) bouliner. To — along ; *marcher en se dandinant*.

slouch, *v.a.*, rabattre ; rabaisser.

slouched (slaoutsh'te), *adj*., rabattu. — hat ; *chapeau rabattu, m.*

slouch'ing, *adj*., incliné ; rabattu ; rabaissé. — gait ; *démarche lourde, ou pesante, f.*

slough (sleufe), *n*., (of a snake) peau ; dépouille ; (of a boar) bauge ; (med.) exfoliation gangreneuse, escarre, *f*.

slough (slaou), *n*., fondrière, *f*., bourbier ; (fig.) abîme, *m*. — of despond ; *abîme de désespoir, m.*

slough, *v.n.*, (med.) s'exfolier.

slough'y (slaou-i), *adj*., bourbeux.

slov'en, *n*., sagouin ; saligaud, *m*.

slov'enliness (sleuv'n'-), *n*., malpropreté ; saleté ; négligence, *f*.

slov'enly, *adj*., malpropre, sale ; négligent.

slov'enly, *adv*., malproprement ; salement ; négligemment.

slow (slô), *adj*., lent ; (late) tardif ; (tedious) monotone, ennuyeux ; (dull) lourd, stupide ; (inactive) indolent, paresseux ; (of clocks, watches) en retard ; (of the pulse) faible. A — train ; *un train de petite vitesse.* That clock is ten minutes too — ; *cette horloge est en retard de, ou retarde de, dix minutes.* He was not — to take advantage of it ; *il ne tarda pas à en profiter.* To be — of speech ; *parler lentement, avoir la parole lente.* — and sure wins the race ; (prov.) *qui va doucement, va loin ; on en va mieux quand on va doux* (Lafontaine) ; *qui trop se hâte reste en chemin.*

slow, *v.a.* and *n.*, ralentir ; se ralentir. To — down ; (rail.) *ralentir la marche.*

slow'-coach, *n*., lambin, *m*., lambine, *f*. ; clampin, *m*., clampine, *f*.

slow'-going, *adj*., qui lambine, qui va lentement.

slow'ly, *adv*., lentement ; doucement ; avec lenteur ; tardivement.

slow'ness, n., lenteur; paresse; (dullness) lourdeur, f.; (dilatoriness) naturel lent; (of clocks, watches) retard, m.

slow-paced' (-pés'te), adj., qui a le pas lent.

slow'-worm (-weurme), n., (zoöl.) orvet, m.

slub'ber (sleub'-), v.a., bousiller.

slub'bing, n., bousinage, m.

slue (sliou), v.a., (nav.) faire pivoter.

slue, v.n., pivoter, tourner.

slug (sleughe), n., (mol.) limace, f.; limaçon (lazy fellow) fainéant, paresseux; (hindrance) obstacle; (for a gun) lingot, m., chevrotine, f.

slug'gard (sleug-garde), n., fainéant, m., fainéante, f.; paresseux, m., paresseuse, f.; dormeur, m., dormeuse, f.

slug'gish (sleug-ghishe), adj., paresseux, indolent, lourd, apathique; (of a stream) lent, qui coule lentement.

slug'gishly, adv., avec paresse; avec fainéantise; avec apathie; avec indolence; avec inertie, nonchalamment.

slug'gishness, n., paresse; fainéantise; inertie; apathie; (of a stream) lenteur, f.

sluice (sliouce), n., écluse; vanne, f., clapet, m.; (opening) issue; (of ponds) bonde, f. — gate; écluse, vanne, f. — keeper; éclusier, m.

sluice, v.a., lâcher par une écluse; lâcher par une vanne; lâcher les chasses; débonder; (to pour over) verser à flots **sur**; répandre à flots **sur**, inonder d'eau.

slui'cy (sliouss'i), adj., à flots; torrentiel.

slum (sleume), n., impasse, ruelle (dans un quartier pauvre), f. —s, pl., bas quartiers, m.pl.

slum, v.n., visiter les quartiers pauvres, les bas quartiers (d'une ville).

slum'ber (sleu'm'beur), n., sommeil; assoupissement; repos, m. [somme.

slum'ber, v.n., sommeiller; dormir; faire un

slum'berer, n., dormeur, m., dormeuse, f.

slum'bering, n., sommeil, assoupissement, m.

slum'bering, adj., qui sommeille, endormi, assoupi. [meillant.

slum'beringly, adv., en dormant, en sommeillant.

slur (sleur), n., tache, f.; (print.) barbouillage; (mus.) coulé, m., liaison; (blame) flétrissure, atteinte, tache, f., stigmate, m. To cast a — upon; déverser le blâme **sur**; dénigrer, diffamer.

slur, v.a., (to soil) tacher, salir; souiller; (to pass lightly) glisser une tache **sur**, passer légèrement **sur** (to conceal) cacher, voiler; (mus.) lier; couler; (print.) barbouiller. To — over; passer légèrement **sur**, faire bon marché **de**.

slur'ring (sleur'-), n., (mus.) liaison, f.

slush, n., gâchis, m.; neige à moitié fondue, f.

slut (sleutè), n., saligaude; salaude; souillon; coquine; friponne; (b. s.) coureuse, f.

slut'tish, adj., salaude; (b.s.) sale, malpropre.

slut'tishly, adv., malproprement, salement.

slut'tishness, n., malpropreté; saleté, f.

sly (slaïe), adj., sournois (cunning); en dessous; rusé; fin; (arch.) malin, matois. — dog; rusé compère, fin matois, m., fine mouche, f. — puss; sournoise, finaude, f. On the —; à la sourdine, à la dérobée, en cachette.

sly'-boots (-boutse), n., sournois; (child) petit malin, m., petite maligne, f., espiègle, m.f.; sournois, finaud, fin matois, m.

sly'ly (slaïe-li), adv., finement, avec ruse, en sournois; (archly) avec malice; sournoisement, en tapinois (Molière).

sly'ness, n., adresse, ruse; finesse, f.

smack, n., (boat) bateau de pêche; (kiss) gros baiser; (taste) goût, m., saveur; (smattering) connaissance superficielle, teinture, f.; (of a whip) claquement, m.; (slap) tape, claque; (in the face) gifle, f.

smack, v.n., (to kiss) baiser; (of whips, of the lips) claquer. To — one's lips; (pop.) se lécher les babines; se lécher les lèvres. To — of; avoir un goût **de**; sentir le, la, les.

smack, v.a., (to slap) donner une claque **à**; (a whip, the lips) faire claquer.

smack'ing, adj., qui claque; (of kisses) retentissant, bruyant.

small (smôl), adj., petit; (slender) délié; (fine) fin, menu; (minute) minime, exigu; (weak) faible, léger; (not considerable) peu considérable, peu important, insignifiant; (narrow) étroit. — improvement; légers progrès, m.pl. — hand; écriture en fin, f. — arms; armes portatives, f.pl. — beer; de la petite bière. To think no — beer of one's self; avoir haute opinion de soi-même. — card; (at whist) basse carte, f. — cattle; menu bétail, m. —-coal; menu charbon, m., menues houilles, f.pl. — fry; menu fretin, m. — shot; menu plomb, m. — talk; conversation banale, f., commérage, m., menus propos, m.pl. — hours; heures indues, f.pl. — change; petite monnaie, f. — craft; petits bâtiments, m.pl. To look — ; avoir l'air penaud. To cut — ; hacher menu; couper en petits morceaux. — parcels; fine hold wares; (prov.) dans les petits sacs sont les fines épices.

small, n., partie mince; (of an anchor) tige, f.; (of the leg) bas, m. — of the back; chute des reins, f.

small'age (-'èdje), n., (bot.) ache, f.

small'-clothes (-clôthze), n.pl., culotte, f.sing.

small'ish, adj., un peu petit, un peu fin, un peu menu.

small'ness, n., petitesse; (fineness) finesse, ténuité, f.; peu de volume, m.; (inconsiderableness) peu d'importance, m., faiblesse, exiguïté; (of income) modicité, f.

small'-pox, n., petite vérole, f.

smalt (smôlte), n., smalt; bleu d'azur, m.

smart (smârte), adj., (pricking) cuisant, douloureux, vif, aigu; (severe) mordant, poignant, piquant; (vigorous) vigoureux, vif, rude; (of intellect) intelligent, éveillé; (brisk) bon, fort; (pertinent) bon, fameux; vif, subtil, fin, à propos; (of horses) fringant; (spruce) beau, élégant, pimpant, coquet.

smart, n., cuisson; douleur aiguë, f.; (anguish) douleur poignante, f. To feel the — of; sentir l'aiguillon **de**.

smart, v.n., cuire; (to feel pain of mind) éprouver une vive douleur, souffrir cruellement. To — for; porter la peine **de**. To — under; sentir l'aiguillon **de**. To make any one — for any-thing; faire payer cher quelque chose **à** quelqu'un. My hand —s; la main me cuit. He shall — for it; il lui en cuira. Some of us will — for it; il en cuira à quelques-uns d'entre nous. You may — for it; il pourra vous en cuire.

smart'en (smârt'n), v.a., faire beau, attifer. To — one's self up; se faire beau, s'attifer.

smart'ing, n., cuisson, douleur vive, ou cuisante, f.

smart'ing, adj., cuisant; poignant.

smart'ly, adv., (with pain) d'une manière cuisante, douloureusement; (sharply) d'une manière mordante, d'une manière piquante, vivement; (vigorously) vigoureusement, rudement; (showily) coquettement, avec recherche, élégamment.

smart'-money (-meu'n'nè), n., indemnité, f.; dédit, m.; gratification pour blessure, f.

smart'ness, n., (poignancy) nature poignante, nature cuisante; force, finesse; (vigor) vigueur, rudesse; (vivacity) vivacité; (of dress) coquetterie, élégance, f., éclat, m.; intellig :ce, f.; savoir faire, m.

smart'-ticket, n., certificat de blessure, m.

smart'-weed (-wîde), n., (bot.) poivre d'eau, m.; persicaire âcre, f.

smash, n., déconfiture, faillite, banqueroute, f.; fracas, m.; (railway) catastrophe, f. To come to — ; faire faillite.

smash, *v.a.*, (mil.) briser ; écraser ; ruiner. To — to pieces ; *briser en morceaux.*

smat'ter, *v.n.*, parler en ignorant. To — of ; *parler en ignorant* **de**.

smat'terer, *n.*, demi-savant, bavard ignorant, homme superficiel, *m.*

smat'tering, *n.*, connaissances superficielles, *f.pl.*, teinture, teinte, *f.* To have a — of ; *n'avoir qu'une connaissance superficielle* **de**.

smear (smîre), *v.a.*, enduire ; couvrir ; barbouiller.

smell, *n.*, (faculty) odorat ; (of a dog) flair, *m. ;* (odor) odeur, senteur, *f.*, parfum ; (of meat, etc.) fumet, *m.* To be offensive to the — ; *blesser l'odorat.*

smell, *v.a.*, (*preterit* and *past part.*, Smelt, Smelled) sentir ; respirer ; flairer. To — out ; *flairer, découvrir.* To — a rat ; *se défier de quelque chose, soupçonner anguille sous roche.*

smell, *v.n.*, sentir ; (to emit a bad odor) sentir, sentir mauvais ; (of animals) sentir, flairer. To — — bad, nasty ; *sentir mauvais.* To — good, nice ; *sentir bon.* To — of smoke ; *sentir la fumée.* To — of the lamp ; (of literary work) *sentir l'huile.* To — stuffy ; *sentir le renfermé.* To — at ; *sentir, flairer.* To — a rat ; *se douter de quelque chose.* Nasty —ing ; *qui sent mauvais.* Sweet —ing ; *qui sent bon ; odoriférant.*

smell'er, *n.*, flaireur ; (the nose) nez.

smell'ing, *n.*, odorat, *m.*

smell'ing-bottle (-bot't'l), *n.*, flacon d'essence, de senteur, *m.*

smell'ing-salts, *n.pl.*, sels, *m.pl.*

smelt, *n.*, éperlan, *m.*

smelt, *v.a.*, fondre.

smelt'er, *n.*, (metal.) fondeur, *m.*

smelt'ery, *n.*, (metal.) fonderie, *f.*

smelt'ing, *n.*, (metal.) fonte, *f.* — furnace ; *haut fourneau, m.*

smew (smiou), *n.*, (orni.) plongeon, *m.*

smick'er (smi-keur), *v.n.*, minauder, lancer des œillades **à**.

smile (smaïle), *n.*, sourire ; (poet.) souris, *m.*

smile, *v.n.*, sourire. To — on ; *sourire à.* To — at ; (a person) *sourire à* ; (a thing) *sourire* **de**.

smil'er, *n.*, sourieur, *m.*

smil'ing, *adj.*, souriant ; (of things) riant.

smil'ingly, *adv.*, en souriant, d'un air riant.

smil'ingness, *n.*, air souriant, *m.*

smirch (smeurtshe), *v.a.*, salir, barbouiller ; (fig.) noircir, salir.

smirk (smeurke), *v.n.*, sourire avec affectation ; affecter un air de bonté, minauder.

smirk (smeurke), *n.*, sourire affecté, *m. ;* minauderies, *f.pl.*

smirk'ing, *adj.*, affecté, minaudier.

smite (smaïte), *v.a.*, (*preterit*, Smote ; *past part.*, Smitten) frapper ; (to destroy) détruire ; (to punish) châtier, frapper ; (to affect with passion) passionner, embraser, charmer. To be smitten with ; *être épris, être amoureux,* **de**. To be desperately smitten with ; *être extrêmement épris* **de**, *éperdument amoureux* **de**, *raffoler* **de**. To — hip and thigh ; *frapper d'estoc et de taille.*

smite (smaïte), *v.n.*, se heurter ; se choquer.

smit'er (smaït'-), *n.*, qui frappe fort ; (fig.) grand batailleur, *m.*

smith (smith), *n.*, forgeron, *m.*

smith'ery (smith'euri), *n.*, forge, *f. ;* (work) ouvrage de forge, de forgeron, *m.*

smith'y, *n.*, forge, *f. ;* (man.) forgeron, *m.*

smit'ten (smit't'n), *frappé.* — with ; *épris* **de**, *amoureux* **de**.

smock (frock), *n.*, blouse, souquenille, vareuse, sarrau, *f.*

smoke (smôke), *v.n.*, fumer.

smoke (smôke), *v.a.*, fumer ; (to cover with . . .) enfumer ; (tobacco) fumer. To — out ; *enfumer ; chasser par la fumée.* To — out ; (a cigar) *fumer jusqu'au bout.*

smoke (smôke), *n.*, fumée ; (vapor) vapeur, *f.* To end in — ; *s'en aller en eau de boudin ; s'en aller en fumée ;* (fig.) *n'aboutir à rien.*

smoke'-box, *n.*, (steam engine) boîte à fumée, *f.*

smoke'-consumer (-co'n'sioum'-), *n.*, fumivore, *m.*

smoke'-consuming, *adj.*, fumivore.

smoke'-dried (-draïde), *adj.*, fumé, boucané.

smoke'-dry (-draïe), *v.a.*, fumer, boucaner.

smoke'-jack (-djake), *n.*, tournebroche à courant d'air, *m.*

smoke'less, *adj.*, sans fumée.

smoke'-preventer, *n.*, fumifuge, *m.*

smok'er (smôk'-), *n.*, fumeur, *m.*

smok'iness, *n.*, état enfumé, *m.*

smok'ing, *adj.*, fumant. — -hot ; *tout chaud.* — -room, — -divan ; *fumoir, salon-fumoir, m.* — -carriage ; *compartiment pour fumeurs, m.* — -cap ; *fez, m. ; calotte, f.*

smok'ing, *n.*, habitude de fumer ; action de fumer ; (fam.) fumerie, *f.* To be fond of — ; *aimer la pipe ; aimer à fumer.* No — allowed ; *défense de fumer.*

smok'y, *adj.*, qui fume ; plein de fumée ; de fumée ; (black) enfumé, noir. — chimney ; *cheminée qui fume, f.*

smol'der (smôld'-), *v.n.*, couver ; brûler sans fumée ni flamme, charbonner ; (fig.) couver.

smol'dering (smôld'-), *adj.*, qui couve.

smooth (smouth), *adj.*, uni ; (even) égal ; (of the sea) calme, unie, de glace ; (not rough) doux ; (glossy) poli, lisse ; (gently flowing) bland) doux ; facile ; (bot.) glabre. — spoken *ou* — tongued ; *au doux parler ; à langue dorée ;* (b.s.) *mielleux, doucereux.*

smooth (smouth), *v.a.*, (wood) aplanir ; (hair) lisser ; polir ; (to flatter) flatter ; (to calm) calmer, adoucir ; (to make even) aplanir, unir, adoucir ; (to make easy, to free) faciliter ; (difficulties) aplanir ; (the brow) dérider. To — down ; *unir, adoucir ; aplanir ;* (to cajole) *cajoler.*

smooth'-bored, *adj.*, à canon lisse ; non rayé.

smooth'-faced (smouth'fés'te), *adj.*, imberbe ; (fig.) qui a l'air doux ; (b.s.) papelard.

smooth'ing (smouth'-), *n.*, action d'unir, *f. ;* adoucissement ; aplanissement, *m.*

smooth'ing-iron (smouth'igne-aï-eur'n), *n.*, fer à repasser, *m.*

smooth'ly (smouth'-), *adv.*, uniment, doucement ; (with even flow) doucement ; (easily) aisément, facilement ; sans difficulté ; (blandly) doucement, avec douceur.

smooth'ness (smouth'-), *n.*, égalité ; douceur, *f. ;* poli ; (of the sea) calme, *m. ;* accalmie, accalmée, *f.*

smoth'er (smeuth'-), *v.a.*, suffoquer ; asphyxier ; étouffer ; (to suppress) étouffer, éteindre.

smoth'er, *n.*, grande fumée ; nuée de poussière ; grande poussière, *f.*

smoth'ering, *n.*, suffocation, *f. ;* étouffement, *m. ;* asphyxie, *f.*

smoth'ering, *adj.*, étouffant, suffocant.

smoth'ering, *part.pres.*, suffoquant.

smudge (smeudge), *v.a.*, barbouiller, salir, noircir ; tacher de noir, d'encre.

smudge, *n.*, barbouillage, *m. ;* tache de noir, tache d'encre, *f.*

smud'gy, *adj.*, noir de suie, noir, barbouillé.

smug (smeug'), *adj.*, pimpant, propret, coquet ; (affectedly nice) recherché, requinqué.

smug'gle (smeug'g'l), *v.n.*, faire la contrebande.

smug'gle, *v.a.*, passer en contrebande ; faire passer par contrebande. To — in ; *faire entrer en contrebande ; introduire par fraude ;* (fig.) *introduire clandestinement.*

smug'gled (-g'l'de), *adj.*, de contrebande. — goods ; *marchandises de contrebande, f. pl.*

smug'gler, *n.*, contrebandier, *m.*

smug'gling, *n.*, contrebande, fraude, *f.*

smut (smeute), *n.*, noir; (in corn) charbon, *m.*, nielle, *f.*; (obscenity) graveleté, saleté, *f.*

smut, *v.a.*, noircir; tacher; salir; (corn) nieller, *v.a.*

smut, *v.n.*, se noircir; (of corn) se carier.

smut'-ball (-bōl), *n.*, (bot.) noir, *m.*, carie, *f.*

smutch (smeutshe), *v.a.*, noircir; barbouiller.

smut'tily (smeut'-), *adv.*, salement.

smut'tiness, *n.*, noirceur, *f.*; (obscenity) saleté, obscénité, *f.*

smut'ty, *n.*, noir; enfumé; (of corn) carié, niellé; (obscene) graveleux, obscène; (ribald) grivois.

snack, *n.*, portion; part, *f.*; (hasty repast) morceau sur le pouce, *m.* To go —s; partager le gâteau, être de moitié. To take a —; manger un morceau sur le pouce; casser une croûte.

snaf'fle (snaf'f'l), *n.*, bridon; filet, *m.* — bit; mors brisé, *m.*

snaf'fle, *v.a.*, mettre un bridon à.

snag, *n.*, nœud, *m.*; bosse, *f.*; (branch) branche, *f.*, jet; (old tooth) croc, *m.*

snag'ged ou **snag'gy**, *adj.*, noueux.

snail (snél), *n.*, limaçon; colimaçon; escargot; (pers.) lambin, *m.*, lambine, tortue, *f.* Edible —; escargot des vignes, *m.*

snail'-clover (-klô-) ou **snail'-trefoil** (-trī-foïl), *n.*, (bot.) luzerne, *f.*

snail'-like (-laïke), *adj.*, de limaçon, comme un limaçon; de tortue, lent.

snail'-like, *adv.*, en limaçon; (slowly) comme une tortue.

snail's'-pace, *n.*, pas de tortue, *m.*

snake (snéke), *n.*, serpent, *m.* A — in the grass; quelque anguille sous roche. Rattle—; serpent à sonnettes, *m.* Common —; couleuvre, *f.*

snake'root (-route), *n.*, (bot.) serpentaire; bistorte, *f.*

snake's'-head (-'hède), *n.*, (bot.) fritillaire, *f.*

snake'weed (-wîde), *n.*, (bot.) renouée, bistorte, *f.*

snake'wood (-woude), *n.*, (bot.) bois de couleuvre, *m.*

sna'ky, **sna'kish** (snék'-), *adj.*, de serpent; (having serpents) hérissé de serpents, à serpents; (sly) de serpent, rusé; (winding) tortueux, sinueux; (sly) rusé.

snap, *v.n.*, se casser, se rompre; craquer. To — at; tâcher de mordre, de happer; (fig.) gourmander, rudoyer; (fam.) rembarrer, brusquer. To — in two; se casser en deux. To — off; se casser net. The thread he thought he held had —ped in two; le fil qu'il croyait tenir s'était rompu (V. Hugo).

snap, *v.a.*, casser, rompre, éclater; (a whip, one's fingers) faire claquer; (to seize suddenly) happer, empoigner. To — in two; casser en deux. To — off; casser. To — up; happer; se saisir de; (to reprimand) brusquer, gourmander; relever vivement. They are —ped up; on se les arrache, se les dispute. To — one's fingers at; se moquer; (fam.) se ficher de.

snap, *n.*, cassure, *f.*; rupture; éclat, *m.*; (bite) coup de dent; (of a whip, the fingers) claquement; (of noise) bruit sec; (greedy fellow) glouton, *m.*; (theft) prise, *f.*; (catch) crochet d'arrêt, *m.*; (clasp) fermoir, *m.* — fastening; agrafe, *f.* Not to care a —; s'en battre l'œil.

snap'dragon, *n.*, (bot.) muflier, *m.* To play at —; jouer à attrape-dragon.

snap'pers, *n.pl.*, cliquettes, *f.pl.*

snap'pish, *adj.*, disposé à happer; hargneux; (peevish) bourru, hargneux, acariâtre.

snap'pishly, *adv.*, d'une manière bourrue; d'une manière hargneuse.

snap'pishness, *n.*, humeur bourrue; humeur hargneuse, acariâtre; aigreur, *f.*

snare (snère), *n.*, piège, collet, lacet, *m.*

snare, *v.a.*, prendre dans un piège.

snarl, *v.n.*, grogner; gronder; montrer les dents.

snarl'er, *n.*, grognard, *m.*, grognarde, *f.*; bourru, grogneur, grognon, *m.*

snarl'ing, *adj.*, bourru; hargneux.

snar'y (snèr'-), *adj.*, insidieux.

snatch, *n.*, effort pour saisir; prise, *f.*; (fragment) petit morceau, fragment; (short fit of vigor) éclair, accès passager, moment, *m.*; échappée, *f.* By —es; par accès; par échappées; par boutades, à bâtons rompus.

snatch, *v.a.*, saisir avidement; se saisir de; gripper. To — from; arracher à, dérober à. To — up; se saisir de, s'emparer de, ramasser, empoigner. To — at; se jeter sur, chercher à saisir; (to cling) se raccrocher à.

snatch'-block, *n.*, (nav.) poulie coupée, *f.*

snatch'er, *n.*, personne qui saisit avidement, *f.* Body- —; voleur de cadavres, *m.*

snatch'ingly, *adv.*, avidement; brusquement, par accès, par boutades.

sneak (snîke), *v.n.*, (to truckle) ramper; (to steal away) s'en aller furtivement; (to tell) rapporter; cafarder. To — away; s'en aller à la dérobée, s'en aller furtivement; s'esquiver; s'en aller la tête baissée; (of a dog) s'en aller la queue entre les jambes. To — in; se glisser furtivement dans; se faufiler dans. To — off; s'échapper furtivement; s'en aller tout penaud.

sneak, *n.*, homme rampant; pied plat, mouchard, rapporteur, cafard; sournois, *m.*

sneak'ing, *adj.*, rampant; bas; servile, sournois, hypocrite; (niggardly) ladre, chiche.

sneak'ingly, *adv.*, furtivement, à la dérobée; servilement; bassement.

sneak'ingness, *n.*, bassesse, *m.*; servilité, *f.*

sneer (snîre), *n.*, rire moqueur, ris moqueur, sarcasme, ricanement, *m.*; raillerie, *f.*

sneer, *v.n.*, ricaner; se moquer de, railler. To — at; se moquer de, se railler de.

sneer'er, *n.*, ricaneur, railleur, *m.*

sneer'ing, *n.*, ricanement, *m.*

sneer'ing, *adj.*, ricaneur, moqueur, ironique.

sneer'ingly, *adv.*, en ricanant, d'un air moqueur.

sneeze (snîze), *n.*, éternuement, *m.*

sneeze, *v.n.*, éternuer; (vet.) s'ébrouer. That is not to be —d at; ce n'est pas à dédaigner, ou à mépriser; ce n'est pas de refus.

sneez'ing, *n.*, éternuement, *m.*

snick'er ou **snig'ger** (snig'gheur), *v.n.*, rire sous cape, rire en dessous, ricaner.

sniff, *v.n.*, renifiement, *m.* To get a — of the sea; prendre un air de mer.

sniff, *v.a.*, aspirer.

sniff, *v.n.*, renifler.

sniff'er, *n.*, renifleur, *m.*, renifleuse, *f.*

sniff'ing, *n.*, renifiement, *m.*

snig'gle, *v.n.*, pêcher des anguilles.

snig'gling, *n.*, pêche aux anguilles, *f.*

snip, *n.*, coup de ciseaux; (shred) morceau coupé, *m.*; (share) portion; (a tailor) chevalier de la coupe, *f.* To go —; partager le gâteau.

snip, *v.a.*, couper (d'un coup de ciseaux).

snipe (snaïpe), *n.*, (orni.) bécassine; (of a person) bécasse, *f.*, oison, *m.*

snipe'-fish, *n.*, bécasse de mer, *f.*

snip'per, *n.*, coupeur, *m.*, coupeuse, *f.* A — snapper; une chétive créature; un fat, un impertinent; un faiseur d'embarras.

snip'pet, *n.*, tantinet, petit morceau, *m.*

snip'snap, *n.*, dialogue piquant, *m.*

sniv'el (sniv'v'l), *n.*, roupie, *f.*

sniv'el, *v.n.*, avoir la roupie; (to cry) pleurnicher.

sniv'eler (sniv'èl'-), *n.*, pleurnicheur, *m.*, pleurnicheuse, *f.*

sniv'eling, **sniv'ely** (sniv'èl'-), *adj.*, pleurnicheur; roupieux, morveux.

sniv'eling (sniv'èl'-), *n.*, pleurnicherie, *f.*

snob, *n.*, personne de mauvais ton, *f.; ;* goujat ; malotru ; petit-maitre, poseur, *m.*

snob'bish, *adj.*, de mauvais ton, commun, vulgaire ; prétentieux.

snob'bishness, *n.*, vulgarité ; fierté prétentieuse, *f.*

snooze, *n.*, somme, *m.* To have a —; *faire un somme.*

snore (snôre), *v.n.*, ronfler.

snore, *n.*, ronflement, *m.*

snor'er, *n.*, ronfleur, *m.*, ronfleuse, *f.*

snor'ing, *n.*, ronflement, *m.*

snort, *v.n.*, ronfler.

snort'ing, *n.*, ronflement, *m.*

snot, *n.*, roupie, morve, *f.*

snot'ty, *adj.*, roupieux ; morveux.

snot'ty-nosed (-nôz'de), *adj.*, roupieux ; morveux.

snout (snaoute), *n.*, museau ; (of a pig) groin ; (of a wild boar) boutoir ; (of things) bout, bec ; (of a pipe, of a pair of bellows) tuyau, *m.*

snout'ed (snaout'-), *adj.*, à museau, à groin, à bout, à bec, à tuyau.

snout'y, *adj.*, qui ressemble à un museau.

snow (snô), *n.*, neige, *f.* There has been a fall of —; *il est tombé de la neige.*

snow, *v.n.*, neiger ; tomber de la neige.

snow'-ball (-bôl), *n.*, boule de neige, pelote de neige, *f.* —, —-tree ; (bot.) *boule de neige, rose de Gueldre, viorne, f.* To — anybody ; *lancer des boules de neige à ; attaquer à coups de boules de neige.*

snow'-capped (-cap'te), *adj.*, couronné de neige.

snow'-drift, *n.*, monceau, *ou* amas, de neige, *m.*

snow'-drop, *n.*, perce-neige, galantine, *f.*

snowed'-up, *adj.*, pris par les neiges.

snow'-flake, *n.*, flocon de neige, *m.;* (bot.) nivéole printanière, *f.*

snow'-fleck, *n.*, bruant de neige, *m.*

snow'-like (-laïke), *adj.*, de neige ; comme la neige.

snow'-line, *n.*, limite des neiges, *f.*

snow'-plow, *n.*, chasse-neige, *m.*

snow'-shoe (-shou), *n.*, raquette, *f.*

snow'-slip, *n.*, avalanche, *f.*

snow'-storm, *n.*, orage, *m.*, tempête de neige, *f.*

snow'-water (-wô-), *n.*, eau de neige, *f.*

snow'-white (-hwaïte), *adj.*, blanc comme neige, blanc de neige.

snow'y (snô-i), *adj.*, de neige ; neigeux ; (white like snow) blanc comme neige ; (pure) pur, sans tache. — weather ; *un temps de neige.*

snub (sneube), *n.*, nœud (in wood), *m.;* (rebuke) réprimande, *f.;* (tobacco) leçon ; coup de patte, *m.*

snub (sneube), *v.a.*, (to nip) couper le bout de ; (to rebuke) brusquer ; relancer, rembarrer ; manquer à ; traiter cavalièrement, *ou* de haut en bas.

snub'-nose (-nôze), *n.*, nez camus, *m.*

snub'-nosed (-nôz'de), *adj.*, au nez camus.

snuff (sneufe), *n.*, (of a wick) lumignon, *m.;* (of a candle snuffed off) mouchure, *f.;* (tobacco) tabac à priser, tabac, *m.* Pinch of —; *prise de tabac, f.* To take —; *priser, prendre du tabac.* To be up to —; *ne pas se moucher du pied, s'y connaître.* To put up to —; *dégourdir ; donner l'éveil à.*

snuff, *v.a.*, aspirer ; humer ; (to scent) flairer ; (a candle) moucher. To — out ; *éteindre ;* (fig.) exterminer.

snuff, *v.n.*, renifler.

snuff'box, *n.*, tabatière, *f.*

snuff'-color, -col'ored, *n.adj.*, marron, *m.*

snuff'er, *n.*, moucheur, *m.*

snuff'ers, *n.pl.*, mouchettes, *f.pl.*

snuff'ers-stand (-feurze-), *n.*, porte-mouchettes, *m.*

snuf'fle (sneuf'f'l), *v.n.*, parler du nez ; nasiller, nasillonner.

snuf'fler, *n.*, (pers.) nasilleur, nasillard, *m.*

snuf'fles (sneuf'f'l'ze), *n.pl.*, enchifrènement, *m.*

snuf'fling, *n.*, nasillement, *m.*

snuff'-taker (-ték'-), *n.*, priseur, *m.*

snuff'-taking, *n.*, habitude de priser, *f.*, usage du tabac à priser, *m.*

snuff'y, *adj.*, barbouillé de tabac.

snug (sneughe), *v.n.*, se serrer ; se presser.

snug, *adj.*, (convenient) commode et petit ; (neat) gentil, agréable ; (lying close) serré, compact ; (of income) aisant, joli petit ; (quiet) tranquille, retiré. He has a — place ; *il a une bonne petite place.* We are very — here ; *nous sommes on ne peut mieux ici.* A — house ; *une petite maison bien commode.* A — little dinner ; *un dîner en petit comité.* To have a — little income ; *avoir un joli petit revenu.*

snug'gery (sneug'gheuri), *n.*, endroit petit et commode, *m.; ;* bonbonnière, *f.* (Bescherelle).

snug'gle (sneug'g'l), *v.n. V.* **cuddle.**

snug'ly, *adv.*, petitement et commodément ; à son aise. To live —; *vivre agréablement, à son aise.*

snug'ness (sneug-), *n.*, commodité, *f.; ;* confortable, *m.*

so (sô), *adv.*, (thus) ainsi, en conséquence ; (in such a degree) si, tellement, tant ; (in this manner) ainsi, de cette manière, comme cela, comme ça ; (in the same manner) de même ; (therefore) donc, aussi ; (about) environ, à peu près ; (be it so) soit. — as to ; *de manière à.* —, you are here at last ! *eh bien ! vous voici, enfin !* I think —; *je le pense.* — , he went ; *ainsi, il est parti.* He is — obstinate ; *il est si entêté ;* il est tellement entêté. — many, — much ; *tant.* — much the better ; *tant mieux.* Nearly —; *à peu près.* Do it —; *faites-le ainsi, faites-le de cette manière.* Make it —; *disons comme cela.* — true it is ; *tant il est vrai.* — good an opportunity ; *une si bonne occasion.* As . . . — . . . ; *de même que . . . ainsi . . . — ni trop mal ni trop bien ; passablement ; comme ça.* — that ; *de sorte que ; si bien que ; de manière que.* I fear —, I am afraid —; *je le crains, j'en ai peur.* I do not say —; *je ne dis pas cela.* I thought —; *c'est ce que je pensais.* If —, if it is —; *s'il en est ainsi.* Not —; *il n'en est rien ; il n'en est pas ainsi ; non pas.* And — on ; *et ainsi de suite ; et ainsi du reste.* — then ; *ainsi donc.* — it is ; *il en est ainsi ; c'est ainsi, c'est comme cela.* — saying ; *à ces mots.* You don't say —? *pas possible !* Mr. — and —; *Monsieur un tel.* — long as ; *aussi longtemps que ; tant que.* — far ; *jusqu'ici ; jusque là.* Why —? *pourquoi cela ?* — . . . as ; *assez . . . pour.* — do I, — can I, — shall I ; *et moi aussi.* He tilled — much ground as kept half a dozen men ; *il cultivait autant de terrain qu'il en fallait pour entretenir six hommes.* — old that he might have been at Agincourt ; *assez vieux pour avoir assisté à la bataille d'Agincourt.* He was standing —; *il se trouvait là ; il était là tout auprès.* — many men — many minds ; (prov.) *autant de têtes, autant d'avis.* It is — much to the good ; *c'est autant de pris sur l'ennemi.*

so, *conj.*, pourvu que. — that ; *de sorte que ; si bien que ;* (provided that) *pourvu que.*

soak (sôke), *v.a.*, tremper ; abreuver, baigner ; faire tremper ; pénétrer, imbiber. To — in ; *absorber, pénétrer ; boire.* I am — ed through ; *je suis tout trempé ; mouillé jusqu'aux os.*

soak, *v.n.*, tremper ; s'imbiber ; (to drink intemperately) pomper, lamper. To — into ; *s'infiltrer dans ;* pénétrer dans.

soak (sôke), *n.*, trempage, *m.* To put in —; *mettre tremper.*

soak'age (sôk'èdje), *n.*, action de tremper, *f.*; trempage, *m.*

soak'er, *n.*, (hard drinker) buveur, biberon, ivrogne, *m.*; (of rain) averse, *f.*

soak'ing, *adj.*, qui trempe; qui s'infiltre; qui pénètre. A — rain; *une pluie battante*, ou *trempante*.

soak'ing, *n.*, (drinking) ivrognerie; (with rain) trempée, *f.*

soap (sôpe), *n.*, savon, *m.* Mottled —; *savon marbré*; *savon madré*. Soft —; *savon noir*; *f.*; (of a lamp) bec, *m.*; (of a candlestick, etc.) (cajolery) *flagornerie, cajolerie*; *eau bénite de cour*, *f.* Shaving-—; *savon pour la barbe.* Scented —; *savon de toilette*; *savon parfumé.*

soap, *v.a.*, savonner; (fig.) flagorner.

soap'-ball (-bôl), *n.*, savonnette, *f.*

soap'berry-tree (-bèr'ri-trî), *n.*, (bot.) savonnier, *m.*

soap'-boiler (-boïl'-), *n.*, savonnier, *m.*

soap'-bubble, *n.*, bulle de savon, *f.*

soap'-dish, *n.*, boîte à savon, *f.*

soap'-house (-haouce), *n.*, savonnerie, *f.*

soap'stone (-stône), *n.*, (min.) stéatite, *f.*

soap'-suds (-seudze), *n.pl.*, eau de savon, *f.*

soap'-tablet, *n.*, pain de savon, *m.*

soap'-works, *n.pl.*, savonnerie, *f.*

soap'wort (-weurte), *n.*, (bot.) saponaire, *f.*

soap'y, *adj.*, savonneux, savonné; (fig.) douce-reux.

soar (sôre), *n.*, essor; élan, *m.*

soar (sôre), *v.n.*, prendre l'essor, son essor; s'élever. To — over, *ou* above; *planer sur.*

soar'ing, *n.*, essor, élan, *m.*

soar'ing, *adj.*, qui plane, qui s'élève; trans-cendant.

soar'ingly, *adv.*, avec élan, en prenant l'essor.

sob, *v.n.*, sangloter. *n.*, sanglot, *m.*

sob'bing, *n.sing.*, sanglots, *m.pl.* The — of the sea; *le sanglot de la mer* (V. Hugo).

so'ber (sô-beur), *adj.*, sobre, tempérant; (not intoxicated) pas ivre; (not mad) sensé, raison-nable; (not visionary) sobre, modéré, tempéré; (grave) grave, sérieux; (calm) calme, posé, rassis. To sleep one's self — ; *cuver son vin.* To be —; *être sobre;* (not to be drunk) *n'être pas ivre, n'avoir pas bu; être à jeun.* To appeal from Philip drunk to Philip — ; *en appeler de Philippe ivre à Philippe à jeun.*

so'ber (sô-), *v.a.*, dégriser; désenivrer; (fig.) rendre raisonnable, calmer, désillusionner, rame-ner à la raison.

so'berly, *adv.*, sobrement, avec tempérance, sensément; raisonnablement; modérément; gravement, sérieusement; avec calme.

so'ber-minded (-maï'n'd'-), *adj.*, modéré; sage, raisonnable, sérieux.

so'ber-mindedness, *n.*, modération; sa-gesse, *f.*

so'berness (sô-) *ou* **sobri'ety** (so-braï-i-), *n.*, sobriété, tempérance; (moderation) sagesse, modération, *f.*; (calmness) calme, sang-froid, *f.* (seriousness) sérieux, *m.*, gravité, réserve, *f.*

sociabil'ity (sô'shi-), *n.*, sociabilité, *f.*

so'ciable (sô-shi-a-b'l), *adj.*, sociable; qui aime la société.

so'ciable, *n.*, calèche à bateau, *f.*; tricycle à deux cavaliers, *m.*; (sofa) tête à tête, *m.*

so'ciableness, *n.*, sociabilité, *f.*

so'ciably (sô-shi-), *adv.*, sociablement, d'une manière sociable.

so'cial (sô-shal), *adj.*, social; sociable; com-municatif.

so'cialism (sô-shal'iz'm), *n.*, socialisme, *m.*

so'cialist (sô-shal'-), *n.*, socialiste, *m.f.*

social'ity (sô-shal'-), *n.*, sociabilité, *f.*

so'cially (sô-shal'-), *adv.*, socialement; d'une manière sociale; d'une manière sociable.

soci'ety (sô-çaï-i-), *n.*, société, *f.*; monde, *m.*; réunion, *f.* Fashionable —; *beau monde.* Lon-don —; *le monde de Londres.* To go into — ;

aller dans le monde. Charitable — ; *société de bienfaisance.* Learned — ; *société littéraire.*

Socin'ian, *n.*, socinien, *m.*, socinienne, *f.*

Socin'ian, *adj.*, socinien.

Socin'ianism ('iz'm), *n.*, socinianisme, *m.*

sock, *n.*, chaussette, *f.*; (of a plow) soc; (shoe) socque; (inner sole) semelle, *f.*; (comedy) socque, brodequin, *m.*, (fig.) comédie, *f.*

sock'et, *n.*, emboîture, *f.*; (of a tooth) alvéole, *m.*; (of the eye) orbite, cavité; (of tools) douille, *f.*; (of a lamp) bec, *m.*; (of a candlestick, etc.) bobèche, *f.*

sock'less, *adj.*, sans chaussettes.

so'cle (sok'l), *n.*, (arch.) socle, *m.*

Socrat'ic *ou* **Socrat'ical**, *adj.*, socratique.

Soc'ratist, *n.*, disciple de Socrate, *m.*

sod, *n.*, gazon, *m.*; motte de gazon, *f.*

sod, *v.a.*, gazonner.

so'da (sô-), *n.*, (min.) soude, *f.*

so'da-water (-wô-), *n.*, eau de Seltz, *f.*

sod'den, *v.a.*, imprégner d'eau.

sod'den, *past part.*, imprégné d'eau, détrempé; pâteux, mollasse; (of bread) pâteux.

sod'dy, *adj.*, gazonneux, revêtu de gazon.

sod'omy, *n.*, sodomie, *f.*

soev'er (so-èv'-), *adj.*, ... que ce soit; ... qui soit ... How—; *quelque ... que.* What things — ; *quelques choses que ce soient.*

so'fa (sô-), *n.*, canapé, sofa. — bed; *lit-canapé, m.*

sof'fit, *n.*, (arch.) soffite; plafond de cor-niche, *m.*

soft, *adj.*, mou, mol, mollet; (to the touch) doux; (delicate) délicat; (yielding) doux, facile, coulant; (tender) tendre; (mild) doux; (effemi-nate) mou, efféminé; (still) calme, paisible, doux; (easy) facile, coulant, délié; (weak) faible; (foolish) sot, niais; (gram.) doux. The —er pas-sions; *les passions plus douces.*

soft, *adv.*, mollement; doucement.

soft! *int.*, doucement! tout doux!

soft'en (sof'f'n), *v.a.*, amollir, ramollir; (to make less harsh, to palliate) adoucir; (to make easy) rendre facile; (to calm) calmer, adoucir, apaiser, radoucir; (to make less glaring) adoucir; (to enervate) efféminer, amollir, affaiblir; (to move) attendrir, adoucir, fléchir; (paint.) adoucir.

soft'en (sof'f'n), *v.n.*, s'amollir, se ramollir; s'adoucir; devenir facile; se calmer, s'adoucir; s'apaiser, se radoucir, devenir efféminé, s'affai-blir; (of the heart) s'attendrir, fléchir.

soft'ening (sof'f'n'-), *n.*, amollissement; adou-cissement; (weakening) affaiblissement; (of the heart) attendrissement; (paint.) adoucissement, *m.* — of the brain; (med.) *ramollissement du cerveau, m.*

soft'-headed (-hèd'-), *adj.*, niais; sot.

soft'-hearted (-hârt'-), *adj.*, tendre, compa-tissant.

soft'ly (soft'-), *adv.*, mollement; (of sound) bas, doucement; (placidly) avec calme, paisible-ment, doucement; (tenderly) tendrement, douce-ment, avec tendresse; (gently) doucement, déli-catement.

soft'ener (sof'n'eur), *n.*, personne *ou* chose qui amollit, qui adoucit, (paint.) brosse à adoucir, *f.*, blaireau, *m.*

soft'ish, *adj.*, mollet, un peu mou; (fig.) doucereux; (silly) un peu simple.

soft'ness (soft'-), *n.*, mollesse; (to the touch) douceur; (mildness) douceur; (effeminacy) déli-catesse efféminée, mollesse; (weakness) fai-blesse; (silliness) niaiserie; (gentleness) douceur, facilité; (timorousness) timidité, *f.*

soft'-sawder, *n.*, eau bénite de cour; monnaie de singe; blague, *f.* [la langue dorée.]

soft'-spoken, *adj.*, à la voix douce; (iron.) à

so'ho! (so-hô), *int.*, holà! ho!

soil (soïl), *n.*, (stain) tache, souillure; (dirt)

ordure, saleté, *f.* ; (manure) engrais, fumier ; (land) sol, terroir, terrain, *m.*, glèbe, terre, *f.* To take —; (of a deer) *se réfugier dans l'eau, dans un marécage.*

soil (soïl), *v.a.*, salir ; souiller ; (to defile) profaner, souiller ; (to manure) engraisser, fumer ; (cattle) nourrir de vert.

soil'-bound (-baou'n'de), *adj.*, attaché à la glèbe, au sol.

soil'less (soïl-lèce), *adj.*, sans terre.

so'journ (sô-djeurne), *n.*, séjour, *m.*

so'journ (sô-djeurne), *v.n.*, séjourner.

so'journer, *n.*, habitant temporaire, oiseau de passage, *m.* We are only —s on this earth ; *nous ne faisons que passer sur cette terre.*

so'journing, *n.*, séjour, *m.*

so'journment, *n.*, séjournement, *m.*

sol'ace, sol'acement (sol'-), *n.*, consolation, *f.* ; soulagement, adoucissement, *m.*

sol'ace, *v.a.*, consoler ; égayer, réjouir ; (to allay) soulager, adoucir. To — one's self with ; *se consoler* par, ou à.

so'lar, *adj.*, solaire ; du soleil ; (anat. bot.) solaire. — spots ; *taches du soleil, f.pl.*

sol'der, *n.*, soudure, *f.*

sol'der, *v.a.*, souder ; joindre.

sol'derer, *n.*, soudeur, *m.*

sol'dering, *n.*, soudure, *f.* ; (action of) soudage, *m.* —iron ; *soudoir ; fer à souder, m.*

sold'ier (sôl-djeur), *n.*, soldat ; militaire, *m.* Foot—; *fantassin, m.* Private —; *simple soldat.* A great —; *un grand capitaine ; un grand soldat.* What would that great — of France say, who is lying there at the Invalides ; *que dirait ce grand soldat de la France qui est couché là aux Invalides* (Victor Hugo, *Discours oratoires*).

sold'ier-like (-laïke) *ou* **sold'ierly**, *adj.*, de soldat, de militaire ; militaire, martial.

sold'iership, *n.*, qualités militaires, *f.pl.* ; talents militaires, *m.pl.* ; bravoure, *f.*

sold'iery, *n.*, troupes, *f.pl.* ; soldats, militaires, *m.pl.* ; (b.s.) soldatesque, *f.*

sole (sôle), *adj.*, seul ; unique ; (jur.) non marié ; (of a legatee) universel.

sole (sôle), *n.*, (of the foot) plante ; (of a shoe) semelle ; (of a hoof) sole ; (ich.) sole, *f.* ; (of a rudder) talon ; (tech.) châssis, *m.*

sole (sôle), *v.a.*, mettre des semelles à ; ressemeler.

sol'ecism (sol'è-ciz'm), *n.*, solécisme, *m.*

soled (sôlde), *adj.*, à semelles.

sole'ly (sôl'-), *adv.*, seulement ; uniquement.

sol'emn (sol'è'm), *adj.*, solennel ; (grave) grave, sérieux.

solem'nity, sol'emnness (sol'è'm'-), *n.*, solennité ; (gravity) gravité, *f.* ; air, *ou* ton, solennel.

solemniza'tion (sol'è'm'naïzé-), *n.*, solennisation ; célébration solennelle, *f.*

sol'emnize (sol'è'm'naïze), *v.a.*, solenniser ; célébrer solennellement.

sol'emnly (sol'è'm'-), *adv.*, solennellement.

sole'ness (sôl'-), *n.*, caractère unique, *m.* ; nature unique ; unité, *f.*

sol-fa' (-fâ), *v.n.*, solfier. *n.*, gamme, *f.*

solfeg'gio (-fè-dji-ô), *n.*, solfège, *m.*

soli'cit (so-li-cite), *v.a.*, solliciter ; briguer ; demander ; postuler, rechercher ; (to invite) inviter, attirer, importuner ; (jur.) essayer de corrompre.

solicita'tion (-'i-té-), *n.*, sollicitation, instance ; (excitement) excitation, *f.* ; appel, *m.* ; (jur.) corruption, *f.*

soli'citor (-teur), *n.*, solliciteur ; (jur.) avoué, procureur, *m.* — general ; *avocat général, m.*

soli'citous, *adj.*, désireux. — about ; *qui a de la sollicitude* pour ; *soigneux de* ; *attentif* à. — for ; *inquiet* de ; *qui s'intéresse à.* — of, — to ; *désireux, ou avide,* de ; *qui tient à.*

soli'citously, *adv.*, avec sollicitude.

soli'citude (-tioude), **soli'citousness**, *n.*, sollicitude, *f.*

sol'id, *adj.*, solide ; massif, plein ; (firm) ferme ; (grave) grave, sérieux, posé ; (of measure) de capacité. To become —; *se solidifier.* — rock ; *roc vif, m.* Of — oak ; *en chêne massif.*

sol'id, *n.*, solide, *m.*

solidar'ily, *adv.*, solidairement.

solidar'ity, *n.*, solidarité, *f.*

sol'idary, *adj.*, solidaire.

solidifica'tion (-fi-ké-), *n.*, solidification, *f.*

solid'ify (-faïe), *v.a.*, solidifier.

solid'ify (-faïe), *v.n.*, se solidifier.

solid'ity, sol'idness, *n.*, solidité, *f.* ; état massif ; (pers.) caractère posé, *m.*, gravité, *f.*

sol'idly, *adv.*, solidement.

solil'oquize (-o-kwaïze), *v.n.*, faire un soliloque, monologuer.

solil'oquy (-o-kwi-), *n.*, soliloque, monologue, *m.*

sol'ing, *n.*, ressemelage, *m.*

sol'itarily, *adv.*, solitairement.

sol'itariness, *n.*, solitude ; retraite, *f.* ; isolement, *m.*

sol'itary, *adj.*, solitaire ; retiré ; isolé ; désert ; (gloomy) triste, sombre ; (single) seul, unique. — confinement ; *emprisonnement cellulaire ; secret, m.*

sol'itude (-tioude), *n.*, solitude, *f.*

so'loist, *n.*, soliste, *m.*

Sol'omon's-seal' (-mo'n'z'sîle), *n.*, (bot.) sceau-de-Salomon, *m.*

sol'stice, *n.*, (astron.) solstice, *m.* Summer —; *solstice d'été.*

solubil'ity (sol'iou-), *n.*, solubilité, *f.*

sol'uble (-'iou-b'l), *adj.*, soluble, résoluble.

solu'tion (-liou-), *n.*, solution, *f.*

sol'utive, *adj.*, dissolvant.

solvabil'ity, *n.*, (of a person) solvabilité, *f.*

sol'vable, *adj.*, soluble, résoluble ; (that can be paid) qui peut être payé.

solve, *v.a.*, résoudre ; expliquer, éclaircir.

sol'vency, *n.*, (of a person) solvabilité, *f.*

sol'vent, *n.*, (chem.) dissolvant, *m.*

sol'vent, *adj.*, solvable ; dissolvant.

som'bre (sô'm'beur), *adj.*, sombre.

some (seume), *adj.*, du, *m.* ; de la, *f.* ; de l', *m.f.* ; des, *pl.m.,f.* ; quelque ; un peu de, une partie de ; certain ; à peu près, environ. — six or seven persons ; *quelque six ou sept personnes, environ six ou sept personnes.* — persons say ; *quelques personnes disent, on dit.* — persons who were there said ; *des personnes qui y étaient ont dit.* — thirty years ago ; *il y a quelques trente ans.* He has — wit ; *il a quelque peu d'esprit.* — one ; *quelqu'un, m., quelqu'une, f.* — scrape or other ; *quelque mauvaise affaire, f.* — few ; *quelques-uns ; quelques personnes ; un petit nombre* de.

some, *pron.*, en ; quelques-uns, *m.pl.*, quelques-unes, *f.pl.* ; les uns, *m.pl.*, les unes, *f.pl.* ; qui . . . qui ; une partie, *f.* — say yes, — say no ; *les uns disent oui, les autres disent non.* — went one way and — another ; *les uns allèrent d'un côté, et les autres d'un autre.* They went — one way — another ; *ils s'en allèrent qui d'un côté, qui de l'autre.* Have you received all your books ? No, but I have received — of them ; *avez-vous reçu tous vos livres ? Non, mais j'en ai reçu une partie, quelques-uns.* Give me — ; *donnez m'en.* Give him — ; *donnez-lui-en.* — of them ; *quelques-uns d'entre eux.*

some'body, *n.*, quelqu'un, *m.*, quelqu'une, *f.* — else ; *quelque autre.* To be — ; *être quelque chose ; être un personnage.* To think oneself — ; *se croire quelqu'un, quelque chose, un personnage.*

some'how (-haou), *adv.*, d'une façon ou d'une autre ; de manière ou d'autre ; de façon ou d'autre ; d'une façon quelconque, tant bien que mal.

som'ersault (seum'eur-sôlte) *ou* **som'erset** (seum'eur-cète), *n.*, saut périlleux, *m.* ; culbute, *f.* To turn a — ; *faire la culbute, faire le saut périlleux.*

some'thing (-thigne), *n.*, quelque chose ; (before an *adj.*) quelque chose **de**, *m.* ; (at a small distance) à peu de distance ; (adverbially) un peu, quelque peu, tant soit peu. There is — to boast of ; *il y a de quoi se vanter.* He has a — about him which pleases every one ; *il a un je ne sais quoi qui plaît à tout le monde.* — good ; *quelque chose de bon.* There is — in that ; *c'est assez plausible ; c'est une idée ; cela mérite considération.* To be — between . . . and ; *tenir le milieu entre . . . et.* — else ; *autre chose, m.*

some'time (-taïme), *adv.*, un de ces jours ; (formerly) autrefois, ci-devant. — or other ; *un de ces jours, un beau jour ; quelque jour ; une fois ou une autre.* My — general ; *mon ancien général.*

some'times (-taï'm'ze), *adv.*, quelquefois ; parfois ; tantôt. — rich, — poor ; *tantôt riche, tantôt pauvre.*

some'what, *n.*, quelque chose, *m. ;* quelque peu ; tant soit peu ; un peu, *m.*

some'what, *adj.*, un peu ; quelque peu ; tant soit peu ; assez.

some'where, *adv.*, quelque part. — else ; *ailleurs, autre part.*

some'while (-hwaïle), *adv.*, pendant un temps ; pendant quelque temps.

somnam'bulism (-biou-liz'm), *n.*, somnambulisme, *m.*

somnam'bulist (-biou-liste), *n.*, somnambule, *m.f.*

somnif'erous (-if'eur'-), *adj.*, somnifère.

som'nolence, *n.*, envie de dormir ; somnolence, assoupissement, *m.f.*

som'nolent, *adj.*, enclin au sommeil ; somnolent, assoupi.

son (seune), *n.*, fils ; (fig.) descendant, *m.* — in-law ; *beau-fils, gendre, m.* Grand— ; *petit-fils, m.* God— ; *filleul, m.*

sona'ta (so-nâ-ta), *n.*, sonate, *f.*

song (so'gne), *n.*, romance, *f. ;* chant ; (hymn) chant, cantique ; (poet.) poème, *m.*, poésie, *f.* ; vers, *m.pl.* ; (lay) chanson, *f.*, couplet ; (of birds) chant ; (trifle) rien, *m.*, bagatelle, *f.* Old —, mere — ; (trifle) *rien, m., bagatelle, f.* To buy for a mere — ; *acheter à vil prix, ou pour un rien, ou pour une bagatelle.* No — no supper ; (prov.) *nul bien sans peine.* Drinking— ; *chanson à boire.*

song'-book (-bouke), *n.*, chansonnier, *m.*

song'less, *adj.*, sans voix, muet.

song'ster, *n.*, chanteur ; (bird) oiseau chanteur ; (writer) chansonnier, *m.*

song'stress, *n.*, chanteuse, *f.*

song'-writer (-raït'-), *n.*, chansonnier, *m.*

sonif'erous (-'if'eur'-), *adj.*, résonnant.

son'net, *n.*, sonnet, *m.*

sonneteer' (-nèt'îre), *n.*, auteur de sonnets ; (b.s.) poétereau, *m.*

sonor'ous (so-nô-), *adj.*, sonore, résonnant.

sonor'ously, *adv.*, d'une manière sonore.

sonor'ousness, *n.*, sonorité, *f. ;* son éclatant, *m.*

son'ship (seu'n'-), *n.*, qualité de fils, *f.*

soochong' *ou* **souchong'** (sou-sho'gne), *n.*, (tea) souchong, thé noir, *m.*

soon (soune), *adv.*, bientôt ; (early) tôt, prochainement, de bonne heure ; (willingly) volontiers, aisément. Too — ; *trop tôt.* — after ; *bientôt après.* How — ? *quand ?* So — ; *si tôt.* Very — ; *bientôt, dans très peu de temps, très prochainement.* Too — by an hour ; *trop tôt d'une heure.* As — as ; *aussitôt que, dès que ;* le plus tôt que. I would as — remain as go ; *j'aime-*

rais autant rester que de m'en aller. —er ; *plus tôt ;* (rather) *plutôt.* —er than ; *plus tôt que ;* (rather than) *plutôt que.* —er or later ; *tôt ou tard.* The —er the better ; *le plus tôt sera le mieux.* No —er said than done ; *aussitôt dit, aussitôt fait.* No —er had he spoken ; *à peine eut-il parlé que* (with indic.).

soon'est, *adv.*, le plus tôt. At the — ; *au plus tôt.*

soot (soute), *n.*, suie, *f.*

soot, *v.a.*, couvrir de suie.

soot'-bag, *n.*, sac à suie, *m.*

sooth (south), *n.*, (ant.) vérité ; réalité, *f.* In — ; *en vérité, à vrai dire.*

soothe (south*e*), *v.a.*, (to flatter) flatter, caresser ; (to assuage) adoucir, apaiser, calmer ; (to please) charmer, satisfaire.

sooth'er (south'-), *n.*, personne *ou* chose qui calme, qui adoucit, *f. ;* calmant, adoucissant ; (flatterer) flatteur, *m.*, flatteuse, *f.*

sooth'ing (south'-), *adj.*, (assuaging) adoucissant ; calmant ; (of thought) consolant ; (flattering) flatteur.

sooth'ingly, *adv.*, doucement ; d'un ton consolant.

sooth'say (south'sé), *v.n.*, prophétiser ; prédire (l'avenir).

sooth'sayer (south'sé-eur), *n.*, devin, *m.*, devineresse, *f. ;* prophète ; augure, *m.*

sooth'saying, *n.*, divination, *f.*

soot'iness (sout'-), *n.*, fuliginosité, *f.*

soot'y (sout'-), *adj.*, (producing soot) qui produit de la suie ; (consisting of soot) de suie, fuligineux ; (foul with soot) plein, *ou* couvert, de suie ; (black) noir ; (dusky) sombre, obscur.

sop, *n.*, morceau trempé ; (present) présent, *m. ;* (small gratuity) douceur, *f. ;* (something given to pacify) os à ronger, *m.*

sop, *v.a.*, tremper, saucer.

so'phi (sô-fî), *n.*, (shah) sophi, sofi, *m.*

soph'ism (sof'iz'm), *n.*, sophisme, *m.*

soph'ist, *n.*, sophiste, *m.*

sophist'ic *ou* **sophist'ical**, *adj.*, sophistique.

sophist'ically, *adv.*, d'une manière trompeuse ; d'une manière sophistique ; sophistiquement.

sophist'icate, *v.a.*, sophistiquer ; falsifier ; frelater, travailler.

sophistica'tion (-ti-ké-), *n.*, sophistication ; falsification ; frelaterie, *f. ;* frelatage, *m.*

sophist'icator (-ti-ké-tor), *n.*, sophistiqueur, frelateur, *m.*

soph'istry, *n.*, sophismes, *m.pl. ;* sophistiquerie (l. u.) ; excessive subtilité, *f.*

sopor'iferous (-rif'eur'-), *adj.*, soporifère.

sopor'iferousness (-rif'eur'-), *n.*, propriété soporifère, *f.*

soporif'ic, *adj.n.*, soporifique ; soporatif.

sop'py, *adj.*, trempé.

sopra'no (so-prâ-nô), *n.*, soprano, sopraniste, *m.f.*

sorb, *n.*, (bot.) sorbier ; cormier, *m.*

sor'cerer, *n.*, sorcier ; magicien, *m.*

sor'ceress, *n.*, sorcière ; magicienne, *f.*

sor'cery, *n.*, sorcellerie, *f. ;* sortilège ; enchantement, *m. ;* magie, *f.*

sor'did, *adj.*, sale ; sordide ; vil ; bas, méprisable.

sor'didly, *adv.*, sordidement.

sor'didness, *n.*, (dirtiness) saleté ; (meanness) bassesse ; (niggardliness) sordidité, avarice sordide, *f.*

sore (sôre), *n.*, plaie, *f. ;* (in Scripture) ulcère ; (mam.) chevreuil de quatrième année, *m. ;* (fig.) douleur, *f.*, mal, *m.*

sore (sôre), *adj.*, (tender) sensible ; douloureux, endolori ; (susceptible) susceptible, sensible ; (affected with inflammation) malade ; (afflictive) douloureux, cruel ; (violent) violent, grand, rude ; (vexed) vexé, tourmenté. To have — eyes, ears ;

avoir mal aux yeux, un mal d'yeux, mal aux oreilles, un mal d'oreille. — fingers; *mal aux doigts.* To have a — foot; *avoir mal au pied.* To make —; *rendre sensible, rendre malade;* (to irritate) *irriter.* A — trial; *une cruelle épreuve.* —throat; *mal de gorge, m.*

sore, *adv.,* douloureusement, grièvement; (greatly) grandement, fortement, gravement, profondément.

sore'ly (sôr-), *adv.,* douloureusement, grièvement, vivement, fortement, cruellement, rudement, sévèrement.

sore'ness, *n.,* sensibilité; douleur, *f.;* mal, *m.;* sensation pénible; (susceptibility) susceptibilité, sensibilité, *f.*

sor'rel, *n.,* (bot.) oseille; (color) couleur alezan, *ou* saure, *f.* — soup; *soupe à l'oseille, f.*

sor'rel, *adj.,* alezan, saure.

sor'rily, *adv.,* tristement, pauvrement, chétivement; pitoyablement.

sor'row (sor-rô), *n.,* chagrin, *m.;* douleur; affliction, peine, tristesse, *f.,* déplaisir, déboire, *m.* In —; *dans le chagrin.* To one's —; *à son grand chagrin; à sa grande douleur.*

sor'row (sor-rô), *v.n.,* être affligé; avoir du chagrin; s'affliger, s'attrister, pleurer.

sor'rowful (-foule), *adj.,* triste; affligé; chagrin; mélancolique; (of things) affligeant, attristant, funeste, pénible, douloureux.

sor'rowfully, *adv.,* avec chagrin; avec douleur; tristement.

sor'rowfulness, *n.,* chagrin, *m.;* tristesse, douleur, *f.*

sor'rowing (sor-rô-igne), *n.,* chagrin, *m.*

sor'rowless, *adj.,* sans chagrin.

sor'ry, *adj.,* fâché (for, **de** (of a thing), **pour** (of a person)); contrarié, affligé, peiné; (melancholy) mélancolique; triste; (poor, worthless) triste, pauvre, méchant, pitoyable; (of meals) maigre. A — poet; *un méchant poète.* A — meal; *un triste, ou maigre, repas.* A — jest; *une mauvaise plaisanterie.* I am — for you; (pity) *je vous plains;* (sympathy) *je prends part à votre douleur; je suis désolé de votre mésaventure.* I am unable to help you, I am — to say; *à mon grand regret,* ou *malheureusement, je ne puis vous venir en aide.* To be — for anything; *être fâché de quelque chose.* I am — for it; *j'en suis fâché, peiné.* I am — to say that . . . ; *je regrette d'avoir à dire que . . .*

sort (sorte), *n.,* (species) sorte, *f.,* genre, *m.,* espèce; (manner) manière, sorte, façon; (class) classe, condition; (pair) paire, *f.* To be out of —s; *n'être pas dans son assiette, être de mauvaise humeur.* To put out of —s; déranger, bouleverser, détraquer, mettre de mauvaise humeur. In some —; *en quelque sorte, en quelque manière, en quelque façon.* Nothing of the —; *rien de semblable; il n'en est rien.* You will do nothing of the —; *vous n'en ferez rien.* A woman of the right —; *une bonne pâte de femme.* I am out of —s; (fam.) *je suis tout chose.* A strange — of a fellow; *un homme étrange, singulier;* (fam.) *un drôle de corps.*

sort (sorte), *v.a.,* classer, distribuer; séparer; assortir; réunir; (letters) trier; (cards) appareiller. To — out; *assortir, trier, séparer.* To — from; *séparer* **de.** To — with; (to be joined with) *se joindre* **à,** *s'unir* **à,** *se lier* **avec;** (to suit) *s'accorder* **avec,** *convenir* **à.**

sort'able (-a-b'l), *adj.,* qui peut être classé, distribué, trié; (ant.) (fitting) convenable, sortable.

sort'ably, *adv.,* (ant.) convenablement, sortablement, d'une manière sortable.

sort'ed, *adj.,* assorti; trié, arrangé, séparé.

sort'er, *n.,* trieur, *m.,* trieuse, *f.*

sor'tie (-tî), *n.,* (milit.) sortie, *f.*

sort'ing, *n.,* triage, assortiment, *m.*

sot (sote), *n.,* sot, *m.,* sotte, bête, *f.;* imbécile, *m.f.;* (drunkard) ivrogne, *m.,* ivrognesse, *f.*

sot'tish, *adj.,* (stupid) sot, stupide, hébété; (drunken) abruti par l'ivrognerie.

sot'tishly, *adv.,* (stupidly) sottement; stupidement; (drunkenly) en ivrogne.

sot'tishness, *n.,* sottise; bêtise; stupidité, *f.;* (drunkenness) abrutissement, *m.*

sou, *n.,* sou, *m.*

souchong', *n.* *V.* **soochong**.

sough (seuf), *v.n.,* (of the wind) bruire, murmurer, soupirer.

sough'ing, *n.,* bruissement, murmure, soupir, *m.*

soul (sôle), *n.,* âme; (creature) âme, *f.,* être, *m.,* créature; (fig.) essence, *f.,* principe, *m.* With all my —; *de toute mon âme.* The — of honor; *l'honneur même, m.* Poor —; *pauvre chère âme.* Simple —; *bonhomme, m., bonne femme, f.* Good —; *bonne créature; bonne pâte d'homme, bonne âme, f.* The life and — of; *l'âme, f.; le boute en train de.* There was not a — about; *il n'y avait âme qui vive dans les rues,* ou (fam.) *pas un chat dans les rues.* All —'s day; *jour des morts, m.*

souled (sôlde), *adj.,* à l'âme.

soul'-destroying (-dè-stroï-yigne), *adj.,* qui perd l'âme.

soul'-felt, *adj.,* senti dans l'âme, intime.

soul'less, *adj.,* sans âme; apathique.

soul'-saving (-sév'-), *adj.,* qui sauve l'âme.

soul'-searching (-seurtsh'-) *ou* **-stirring,** *adj.,* qui remue, ou qui émeut, l'âme.

soul'-sick, *adj.,* malade d'esprit.

soul'-vexed (-vèks'te), *adj.,* tourmenté d'esprit.

sound (saou'n'de), *n.,* (strait) détroit, *m.;* (surg.) sonde, *f.;* (noise) son, bruit, *m.* The Sound; *le Sund.* —wave; (physics) *onde sonore, f.* Not a —; *pas le moindre bruit.*

sound, *adj.,* sain; en bon état; (of the mind) sain; (of principles) bon; (of the health) bon, solide; parfait; (of sleep) profond; (of blows) bon, fort, vigoureux; (valid) valide; (correct) légitime; (well founded) bien fondé. — doctrine; *doctrine saine, f.* Safe and —; *sain et sauf.* — thrashing; *bonne raclée, f.* To give a — thrashing; *fouetter d'importance.* The firm is —; *la maison (de commerce) est solvable.*

sound, *v.n.,* sonner; rendre un son; retentir (with, **de**); résonner; (to search the depth of water) sonder, jeter la sonde; (to appear) sembler; avoir l'air **de;** faire un (*ou* l')effet **de.** To — like; *avoir le son* **de.** To — well; *sonner bien, faire bon effet.* To — to horse; *sonner le boute-selle.* The praises — ed in him like reproaches; *les éloges lui semblaient autant de reproches,* ou *lui faisaient l'effet de reproches.*

sound, *v.a.,* sonner **de;** faire sonner; faire résonner; (proclaim) proclamer, publier, faire retentir; (to try the depth of, to examine) sonder; (a person) sonder. To be —ed; (of letters) *se prononcer.*

sound'able (-'a-b'l), *adj.,* qu'on peut sonder.

sound'-headed (-hèd'-), *adj.,* qui a la tête saine; qui a une bonne tête.

sound'-hearted (-hârt'-), *adj.,* qui a le cœur bien placé; sincère.

sound'ing, *adj.,* à son; résonnant; retentissant; (fig.) pompeux, ronflant.

sound'ing, *n.,* action de sonner, *f.;* retentissement, résonnement, *m.,* résonance, *f.;* (of wounds, water, etc.) action de sonder, *f.,* sondage, *m.;* (nav.) fond, *m.* To take —s; *faire des sondages.*

sound'ing-board, *n.,* (mus.) table d'harmonie, *f.;* (of a pulpit) abat-voix; (of an organ) sommier, *m.*

sound'ing-lead (-lède), *n.,* sonde, *f.;* plomb de sonde, *m.*

sound'ing-line (-laïne), *n.,* ligne de sonde, *f.*

sound'ing-post (-pôste), *n.,* (mus.) âme, *f.*

sound'less, *adj.,* (unfathomable) insondable,

que l'on ne peut sonder; (having no sound) sans son ; sans bruit.

sound'ly, *adv.*, (healthily) avec santé; (lustily) vigoureusement, rudement, d'importance, ferme ; bien, comme il faut ; (without fallacy) sainement ; (firmly) solidement, profondément; (of sleeping) profondément, d'un profond sommeil. — *beaten; bien, joliment battu; rossé d'importance.*

sound'ness, *n.*, état sain; bon état, *m.;* solidité; (strength) force, vigueur ; (rectitude) rectitude, droiture, justesse, pureté ; (of the body) santé, *f.*

soup (soupe), *n.*, **potage,** *m.;* soupe, *f.* Gravy— ; *consommé, m.* Vegetable— ; *potage à la julienne.* Turtle— ; *potage à la tortue.* Mockturtle— ; *potage à la tête de veau; soupe, potage à la financière.* —ladle ; *louche, f.* —plate; *assiette creuse, assiette à soupe, f.* —ticket ; *bon de soupe, m.* —tureen ; *soupière, f.*

sour (saour), *adj.*, aigre ; sur; acide ; (of milk) tourné ; (fig.) aigre, âpre, morose. To make — ; *aigrir.* To turn —; *s'aigrir.* The grapes are —; *les raisins sont trop verts*

sour (saour), *v.a.*, aigrir; (chem.) acidifier ; (fig.) aigrir, empoisonner.

sour, *v.n.*, s'aigrir. To — into; *tourner en; dégénérer en.*

source (sörce), *n.*, source, *f.*

sour'ing, *n.*, aigrissement, *m.*

sour'ish (saour'-), *adj.*, aigret; suret; aigrelet.

sour'krout, *n.*, choucroute, *f.*

sour'ly (saour-), *adv.*, avec aigreur; (fig.) aigrement, âprement, avec aigreur.

sour'ness (saour-), *n.*, aigreur, acidité ; (fig.) âpreté, aigreur, *f.*

souse (saouce), *n.*, marinade, *f.*

souse (saouce), *v.a.*, mariner ; plonger dans l'eau ; tremper, mouiller, doucher; administrer une douche à ; saucer.

souse (saouce), *adv.*, tout à coup.

south (saouth), *n.*, sud, midi, *m.*

south, *adj.*, sud, du sud ; méridional, austral.

south, *adv.*, vers le midi ; vers le sud, au sud.

south'down (-daoune), *n.*, (mutton) mouton de pré salé, *m.*

south'east (-îste), *n.*, sud-est, *m.*

south'east, *adj.*, sud-est, du sud-est.

southeast'er, *n.*, vent du sud-est, *m.*

southeast'ern (-îst'eur'n), *adj.*, du sud-est.

south'erly (seu*th*'eur'-), *adv.*, vers le sud.

south'ern (seu*th*'eur'n), *adj.*, du sud; du midi; méridional. The — Cross; *la Croix du Sud.*

south'ernly (seu*th*-eur'n'-), *adj.*, sud, du sud ; méridional.

south'ernmost (-môste), *adj.*, le plus au sud, à l'extrême sud.

south'ern-wood (-woude), *n.*, citronnelle, *f.*

south' pole, *n.*, pôle sud, *m.*

South' Sea, *n.*, mer du Sud, *f.*

south'ward (saouth'weurde), *adv.*, vers le sud ; au sud.

south'west (-wèste), *n.*, sud-ouest, *m.*

south'west, *adj.*, sud-ouest; du sud-ouest.

southwest'erly (-wèst'eur-), *adj.*, de sud-ouest; du sud-ouest.

southwest'ern (-wèsteur'n),- *adj.*, de sud-ouest ; du sud-ouest ; sud-ouest.

sou'venir (souv'nîr), *n.*, souvenir, *m.*

sou'wester, *n.*, suroît, *m.*

sov'ereign (sov'eur'ine), *n.*, souverain, *m.;* souveraine, *f.;* (gold coin) souverain (20 shil. = 25 f.), *m.* Half —; *demi-souverain, 12 f. 50 c.*

sov'ereign, *adj.*, souverain.

sov'ereignly, *adv.*, souverainement, *f.*

sov'ereignty, *n.*, souveraineté, *f.*

sow (saou), *n.*, truie; (metal.) gueuse, *f.;* (of lead) saumon, *m.* Wild —; *laie, f.* To have the right — by the ear; (fam.) *deviner juste.* You

---

cannot make a silk purse out of a —'s ear; (prov.) *on ne saurait faire d'une buse un épervier* (Boileau). To have hold of the — by the wrong ear; *tenir le loup par la queue.*

sow (sō), *v.a.*, (preterit, Sowed; past part., Sown) semer, ensemencer ; (to scatter) répandre; parsemer. To — one's wild oats ; *jeter ses premiers feux; faire ses farces, ses fredaines; jeter sa gourme.*

sow (sō), *v.n.*, semer; faire les semailles.

sow'er (sō-eur), *n.*, semeur, *m.*

sow'ing (sō-igne), *n.*, semailles, *f.pl.;* ensemencement, *m.;* (fig.) propagation, *f.* —time; *temps de semer;* (agri.) *temps des semailles, m. ;* (bot.) *semaison, f.*

sow'-thistle (saou-this's'l), *n.*, laiteron, *m.*

spa (spâ), *n.*, source d'eau minérale, *f.*

space (spésse), *n.*, espace, *m.;* étendue, *f.;* (space between) entre-deux; (quantity of time) espace de temps ; (short time) court espace de temps; intervalle ; (mus.) espace, interligne, *m.* The limited — at our disposal ; *le peu d'espace dont nous disposons.*

space, *v.a.*, (print.) espacer.

spa'cing, *n.*, espacement, *m.;* (print.) interligne, *f.*

space'-line (-laîne), *n.*, interligne, *f.*

spa'cious (spé-sheusse), *adj.*, spacieux ; d'une grande étendue; vaste.

spa'ciously, *adv.*, amplement, spacieusement.

spa'ciousness, *n.*, nature spacieuse ; immensité ; vaste étendue ; grandeur, *f.*

spad'dle (spad'd'l), *n.*, petite bêche, *f.*

spade, *n.*, bêche, *f.;* (at cards) pique ; (hunt.) daim de trois ans, *m.* — husbandry ; *petite culture, f.* To call a — a —; *appeler les choses par leur nom; appeler un chat un chat.*

spade, *v.a.*, bêcher.

spade'ful (-foule), *n.*, pelletée.

spadille (spa-dil) *ou* **spadil'lo** (-dil-iô), *n.*, spadille, as de pique, *m.*

spahi' *ou* **spahee'** (spâ-hî), *n.*, spahi, *m.*

span, *n.*, empan, *m.;* main, *f.;* (short space of time) moment, instant, *m.;* (duration) durée ; (of wings) envergure ; (arch.) ouverture ; (of an arch) corde ; (of horses, oxen) paire, *f.* Short —; *courte durée.*

span, *v.a.*, mesurer par empan ; mesurer de la main ; embrasser ; (to cross) traverser ; (nav.) saisir, brider. His career —s half a century ; *sa carrière embrasse un demi-siècle.* A bridge —s the river ; *un pont traverse la rivière, ou le fleuve est traversé par un pont.*

span'drel, *n.*, (of an arch) naissance, *f.;* (of a bridge) tympan, *m.*

span'gle (spai'gn'g'l), *n.*, paillette, *f.*

span'gle (spai'gn'g'l), *v.a.*, pailleter (with, **de**) ; parsemer de paillettes, orner de paillettes ; (fig., of flowers) émailler; (of stars) étoiler. The —d vault (or skies); *la voûte étoilée.*

Span'iard, *n.*, Espagnol, *m.;* Espagnole, *f.*

span'iel, *n.*, épagneul, *m.*

Span'ish, *adj.*, espagnol ; d'Espagne. — white ; *blanc d'Espagne, m.* — wines ; *vins d'Espagne, m.pl.* — wool ; *laine d'Espagne, f.*

Span'ish-broom (-broume), *n.*, (bot.) genêt d'Espagne, *m.*

Span'ish-fly (-flaîe), *n.*, (ent.) cantharide, *f.*

spank (spai'gn-ke), *v.a.*, (pop.) claquer, fesser.

spank, *v.n.*, filer vite ; arpenter le terrain.

spank'er, *n.*, gros gaillard, gros luron; rapide marcheur, *m.;* (nav.) basse voile d'artimon, *f.* That 's a —; (fam.) (a lie) *en voilà une bonne*, ou *un fameux.*

spank'ing, *adj.*, fort; vigoureux, de première force; (of pace) rapide. To go at a — pace; *aller à grands pas; aller bon train.*

span'-long (-lo'gne), *adj.*, de la **longueur** d'un empan; longue d'une panne.

span'ner, n., personne qui mesure par empan, (of a carbine) platine, (mec.) clef à boulon, clef à levier, f.

span'-new (-niou), adj. V. **brand-new**.

spar (spår), n., (nav.) espar, mâtereau, pièce de bois; (min.) spath, m. — deck; (nav.) faux pont, pont volant, m.

spar (spår), v.n., se quereller; se disputer, se chamailler; se battre, boxer, s'escrimer; (fig.) tâcher de gagner du temps, tergiverser.

spare, v.a., épargner; ménager; (to economize) économiser; (to do without) se passer de, se dispenser de; (to omit) s'épargner, s'éviter; (to let have) donner, céder; (to forbear to punish, destroy, etc.) épargner; (to trouble) épargner à; (to remit) faire grâce de; remettre. To — any one trouble; épargner de la peine à quelqu'un. To — oneself; se ménager. To — oneself trouble; s'épargner, s'éviter de la peine. To have to —; avoir de reste, avoir de trop. To have money to —; avoir de l'argent de reste, de trop. It cannot be —d; on ne saurait s'en passer. I have not a moment to —; je n'ai pas un moment dont je puisse disposer. I have not ten minutes to —; je n'ai pas dix minutes à moi. Can you — me a pound of sugar? pouvez-vous me céder une livre de sucre? To — the time; trouver le temps. We have no time to —; nous n'avons pas de temps à perdre. I can't — the time; je n'ai pas le temps. Can you — the time? êtes-vous libre? We have some to —; nous en avons à revendre. We have enough and to —; nous en avons à revendre; nous en avons plus qu'il n'en faut. — your brains; dispensez-vous de penser. — the rod, and spoil the child; (prov.) qui aime bien, châtie bien.

spare, v.n., économiser; épargner; vivre frugalement; faire des économies; (to forbear) s'abstenir de; (to use mercy) être clément.

spare, adj., (scanty) modique, faible, pauvre; (superfluous) de reste, de trop; (lean) maigre, chétif, sec; (of time) de loisir, libre; (nav.) de rechange. — time; heures libres, heures de loisir, f.pl. — moments; moments perdus, m.pl. — of; sobre de; économe de; ménager de. — bed; lit de reste; lit au service des amis, m. — room; chambre d'ami, f. —anchor; ancre de rechange, f. A tall — man; un grand homme sec.

spare'ness (spèr'-), n., maigreur, f.

spar'er (spèr'-), n., personne économe, f.

spare'rib, n., côte de porc, f.

spar'ing (spèr'-), adj., (little) peu de; (scanty) modique, faible, pauvre, peu abondant; (saving) économe, ménager, épargnant, frugal, sobre; (parsimonious) parcimonieux, chiche, avare. — of; sobre de, économe de.

spar'ingly (spèr'-), adv., sobrement; frugalement, avec parcimonie; modérément; économiquement; (seldom) rarement, peu souvent.

spar'ingness (spèr'ign'nèce), n., économie; frugalité; épargne; modération; parcimonie, f.

spark (spårke), n., étincelle, f., (fig.) étincelle, lueur, f.; éclair; (gay man) galant, petit-maître, mirliflore, m.

spark'ish (spårk'-), adj., vif; brillant; élégant, fringant, pimpant.

spark'le (spårk'l), n., étincelle, f.

spark'le (spårk'l), v.n., étinceler; pétiller; briller; (of beverages) mousser, pétiller.

spark'let, n., petite étincelle, (fig.) bluette, f.

spark'ling, adj., pétillant; étincelant; (of beverages) mousseux. n., étincellement, éclat; pétillement, m.

spark'lingly, adv., d'une manière étincelante; avec éclat; en pétillant.

spar'ling (spår-), n., (ich.) éperlan, m.

spar'ring (spår'-), n., querelle; dispute, chamaillis, f.; (in boxing) prélude de combat, m.

spar'row (-rô), n., (orni.) moineau; passereau, m. Hedge- —; fauvette d'hiver, des haies, f.

spar'row-grass, n. V. **asparagus**.

spar'row-hawk (-hôke), n., épervier, m.

spar'row-wort (-weurte), n., passerine, f.

sparse (sparse), adj., épars, éparpillé; clairsemé.

sparse'ly (spårs'-), adv., d'une manière éparse, de loin en loin, à de rares intervalles.

sparse'ness, n., rareté, f.; (scattered) éparpillement, m.

Spar'tan (spär-), n., Spartiate, m.f.

Spar'tan, adj., spartiate. — dog; limier, m.

spasm (spaz'm), n., spasme, m.

spasmod'ic ou **spasmod'ical** (spaz'-), adj., spasmodique.

spat, n., frai (des mollusques), naissain; jeune mollusque; (blow) coup, m.; taloche; (of a shoe) guêtre, f.

spathe (spéthe), n., (bot.) spathe, f.

spath'ic (spath-), adj., (min.) spathique.

spat'ter, v.a. V. **bespatter**.

spat'terdashes (-dash'ize), n.pl., houseaux, m.pl.; jambières, f.pl.

spat'ula (-'iou-), n., (surg., pharm., paint., zoöl.) spatule, f.

spav'in, n., (vet.) éparvin; épervin, m.

spav'ined (spav'i'n'de), adj., (vet.) qui a des éparvins.

spawl (spôl), v.n., cracher en parlant.

spawn (spô'n), n., frai; (fig.) produit, m.

spawn (spô'n), v.n., frayer; (fig.) naître.

spawn, v.a., engendrer par du frai; engendrer.

spawn'er, n., poisson femelle, m.

spawn'ing, n., frai, m. — place; frayère, f. —-time; temps du frai, m.

speak (spîke), v.n., (preterit, Spoke; past part., Spoken) parler; dire. To — with; s'entretenir avec, causer avec, parler avec. So to —; pour ainsi dire. Worth —ing; qui vaille, d'aucune importance. To — ill of; dire du mal de; médire de; déconsidérer. To — highly, ou well, of; dire du bien de; parler avantageusement de, faire l'éloge de. To — up; parler plus haut; parler hardiment; (fig.) s'expliquer; dire franchement, ou hardiment, sa pensée; parler ouvertement. To — out; parler tout haut, à haute voix, crier. To — up for; parler en faveur de, louer; parler hautement pour. To — with; s'entretenir avec, causer avec. To — loud; parler haut. To — well for; être un signe favorable, faire honneur à. That —s well for him; cela lui fait honneur. It —s for itself; cela en dit assez.

speak, v.a., parler; dire; (to proclaim) proclamer, publier; (to celebrate) célébrer; (to express) montrer; manifester, exprimer, dire; (to accost) accoster; (to communicate) communiquer, parler; (nav.) héler. To — the truth; dire la vérité. To — one's mind; dire sa pensée. To — a language; parler une langue. To — English; parler anglais. To his shame be it spoken; soit dit à sa honte. Ships spoken; vaisseaux hélés. I beg leave to —; je demande la parole. French spoken here; ici on parle français. — of angels and you hear their wings; (prov.) quand on parle du loup on en voit la queue, ou il sort du bois; V. **devil**.

speak'able (-'a-b'l), adj., exprimable; que l'on peut dire.

speak'er, n., personne qui parle, f., orateur; parleur, diseur; (in a dialogue) interlocuteur; (of the House of Commons) président, m. Eternal —; parleur sempiternel. The previous —; le préopinant.

speak'ing, n., action de parler; parole, f.; langage; discours, parler, m.; (in college) déclamation, f. adj., parlant, qui parle. To be on — terms; se connaître un peu; se parler.

speak'ing, adj., parlant.

speak'ing-pipe (-païpe), *n.*, cordon acoustique, *m.*

speak'ing-trumpet (-treu'm'-), *n.*, portevoix ; cornet acoustique, *m.*

speak'ing-tube, *n.*, tube acoustique, *m.*

spear (spîre), *n.*, lance, *f.* ; (for fish) harpon, *m.* ; (for hunting) épieu ; (for eels) trident, *m.*

spear (spîre), *v.a.*, percer d'un coup de lance, d'un coup d'épieu ; harponner.

spear'-foot (-foute), *n.*, (of a horse) pied droit de derrière, *m.*

spear'-grass (-grâce), *n.*, (bot.) folle-avoine, *f.*

spear'-hand, *n.*, main droite, *f.*

spear'-head, *n.*, pointe, *f.*, *ou* fer, *m.*, de lance.

spear'man, *n.*, lancier, *m.*

spear'mint, *n.*, (bot.) menthe verte, *f.*

spear'wort (-weurte), *n.*, grande douve, *f.*

spe'cial (spèsh'al), *adj.*, spécial ; (peculiar) particulier, exprès ; (extraordinary) extraordinaire, remarquable ; (uncommon) peu commun ; (chief) premier. In a — case ; *dans un cas particulier.* — constable ; *constable spécial, temporaire, m.* — department, etc. ; *spécialité, f.*

spe'cialist, *n.*, spécialiste, *m.*

special'ity. *V.* **spec'ialty.**

spe'cialize (spèsh'al'aïze), *v.a.*, spécifier ; particulariser.

spe'cially, *adv.*, particulièrement ; spécialement ; principalement ; surtout.

spe'cialty, *n.*, spécialité, *f.* ; (jur.) contrat sous seing privé, *m.*

spe'cie (spî-shi), *n.*, numéraire, *m.* ; espèces, *f.pl.*

spe'cies (-shize), *n.*, espèce, *f.* ; genre, *m.* ; sorte ; (representation) image ; (appearance) apparence, *f.*

specif'ic (spè-), *n.adj.*, spécifique, *m.*

specif'ically, *adv.*, spécifiquement.

specifica'tion (spè-ci-fi-ké-), *n.*, spécification ; (thing specified) chose spécifiée ; (of patents) description, *f.* ; (estimate) devis, *m.* —s, *pl.*, cahier des charges, *m.sing.*

specify (spèss'i-faïe), *v.a.*, spécifier ; particulariser, determiner ; (of time) fixer d'avance. Kindly — the time ; *ayez la bonté de fixer l'heure.*

spec'imen (spèss'i-mè'n), *n.*, spécimen ; modèle ; échantillon, *m.*

spe'cious (spî-sheusse), *adj.*, spécieux ; agréable à la vue, à l'œil.

spe'ciously, *adv.*, spécieusement.

spe'ciousness, *n.*, nature spécieuse ; apparence spécieuse, nature plausible, *f.*

speck (spèk), *n.*, tache ; marque, *f.* ; point, *m.* ; (med.) taie, *f.*

speck, *v.a.*, tacher ; marquer.

spec'kle (spèk'k'l), *n.*, petite tache ; (on animals) moucheture, grivelure, *f.*

spec'kle, *v.a.*, tacheter ; marqueter ; moucheter.

spec'kled (spèk'k'l'de), *adj.*, tacheté ; marqueté ; moucheté ; (of a trout ; of iron) truité ; (of a tiger) tigré.

spec'kledness, *n.*, tacheture, moucheture, *f.*

spec'tacle (spèk'ta-k'l), *n.*, spectacle, *f.*

spec'tacle-case, *n.*, étui à lunettes, *m.*

spec'tacled (-tak'l'de), *adj.*, qui porte des lunettes ; à lunettes ; chaussé de lunettes (J. de Saint Victor).

spec'tacle-glasses (-glâcize), *n.pl.*, verres de lunettes, *m.pl.*

spec'tacle-maker (-mék'-), *n.*, lunetier, *m.*

spec'tacles (-tak'l'ze), *n.pl.*, lunettes, besicles, *f.pl.*

spectac'ular (-tak'iou-), *adj.*, théâtral, de spectacle.

specta'tor (-té-teur), *n.*, spectateur, *m.* ; spectatrice, *f.* ; assistant ; curieux, *m.*

specta'tress (spèk-té-), *n.*, spectatrice, *f.*

spec'ter (spèk-teur), *n.*, spectre ; fantôme, *m.*

spec'tral, *adj.*, de spectre, spectral.

spec'trum (spèk-treume), *n.*, (*spectra*) (opt.) spectre solaire, *m.* — analysis ; (phys., chem.) *analyse spectrale, f.*

spec'ular (spèk'iou-), *adj.*, spéculaire.

spec'ulate, *v.n.*, spéculer **sur**; méditer **sur**; conjecturer ; (com.) spéculer ; (stock exchange) (rise) jouer à la hausse ; (fall) à la baisse ; agioter.

specula'tion (spèk'iou-lé-), *n.*, spéculation ; méditation ; contemplation, réflexion ; (com.) spéculation, *f.* I came on speck ; *je suis venu dans la chance de vous voir.*

spec'ulative, *adj.*, spéculatif ; (com.) spéculateur, qui spécule, (of things) de spéculation.

spec'ulatively, *adv.*, en théorie ; spéculativement.

spec'ulativeness, *n.*, caractère spéculatif, *m.*

spec'ulator (-lé-teur), *n.*, spéculateur ; (com.) spéculateur, *m.*

spec'ulum (spèk'iou-), *n.*, (*specula*) miroir ; (optique) (bot.) prismatocarpe ; miroir de Vénus, *m.* ; doucette, *f.* ; (surg.) speculum, *m.* — metal ; *métal de miroirs, m.*

speech (spîtshe), *n.*, parole, *f.* ; (oration) discours, *m.*, harangue, allocution ; (language) langue, *f.* ; langage ; (talk) discours, langage, *m.*, paroles, *f.pl.*, propos, *m.pl.*, entretien ; (gram.) discours, *m.*, oraison, *f.* ; (of a barrister) plaidoyer, *m.* Figure of — ; *figure de rhétorique, f.* —day ; (in schools) *distribution des prix, f.* The parts of — ; *les parties du discours, f.pl.* Maiden— ; *discours de début.* Extempore — ; *improvisation, f.* Such — is improper ; *ce langage est indécent.* To be slow of— ; *parler lentement.* — is silvern, silence is golden ; (prov.) *trop gratter cuit, trop parler nuit.*

speech'ifier (-faï-eur), *n.*, péroreur, *m.*

speech'ify (spîtsh'i-faïe), *v.n.*, pérorer ; faire de beaux discours.

speech'ifying, *n.*, beaux discours, *m.pl.* To be fond of — ; *aimer à pérorer.*

speech'less, *adj.*, privé de la parole, sans voix ; muet, interdit. To be — ; *avoir perdu la parole.* To be rendered — ; *perdre la parole.* To stand — ; *rester, ou demeurer, interdit.*

speech'lessness, *n.*, mutisme, *m.*

speech'-maker (-mék'-), *n.*, faiseur de discours, *m.*

speed (spîde), *n.*, vitesse ; rapidité ; célérité ; vélocité ; hâte ; diligence, promptitude, *f.* ; (success) succès, *m.*, réussite, *f.* At full — ; (of horses) *à franc étrier ; à bride abattue ; à toute bride* ; *ventre à terre* ; (of trains, steamers) *à toute vapeur* ; (of sailing vessels) *à toutes voiles* ; (of birds) *à tire d'aile* ; (of vehicles) *à grande vitesse* ; (pers.) *à toutes jambes ; à fond de train.* God—! *bon succès! bonne chance!* With all possible — ; *en toute hâte, au plus vite.* At the top of one's — ; *de toute sa vitesse.* More haste less — ; (prov.) *qui trop se hâte reste en chemin ; ou plus on se presse, moins on arrive.*

speed, *v.a.*, faire partir à la hâte, dépêcher, expédier ; (to hurry) hâter, accélérer ; (to prosper) favoriser, protéger, faire prospérer, faire réussir ; (to furnish in haste) fournir à la hâte. To — the parting guest ; *souhaiter " bon voyage " à l'hôte qui part.* God — you! *Dieu vous garde!*

speed, *v.n.*, (to make haste) se hâter, se dépêcher, venir en toute diligence ; (to succeed) réussir, avoir du succès, prospérer ; (to fare) être, se trouver.

speed'ily, *adv.*, vite ; rapidement, promptement ; en toute hâte, avec diligence.

speed'iness, *n.*, rapidité ; vitesse ; célérité, promptitude ; hâte, diligence, *f.*

speed'well, *n.*, (bot.) véronique, *f.m.*

speed'y, *adj.*, rapide ; vite ; prompt ; expéditif.

spell, *n.*, charme ; sort ; (turn of work) tour ; coup de main ; (nav.) temps ; (period) intervalle, *m.* To cast a — upon ; *jeter un sort* **sur** ; *ensorce-*

ler. To break a —; *rompre un charme.* To take a — at; *prendre son tour* **à.**

spell, *v.a.*, (to name the letters) épeler; (to write with the proper letters) orthographier, écrire; (to charm) charmer, mettre sous le charme; (nav.) relever. To — out; *déchiffrer, découvrir, lire.* To — in full; *écrire en toutes lettres.* To learn to —; *apprendre à épeler*, ou à *mettre l'orthographe.* This —s ruin; *c'est la ruine complète.* To — the difference between success and failure; *faire toute la différence* **entre** *le succès et l'insuccès.*

spell, *v.n.*, épeler; orthographier correctement, écrire correctement; (to read unskillfully) lire mal, ânonner.

spell'-bound (-baou'n'de), *adj.*, sous le charme; retenu par un charme, *ou* fasciné.

spell'er, *n.*, personne qui épèle, *f.* To be a bad —; *ne pas savoir l'orthographe.*

spell'ing, *n.*, épellation; orthographe, *f.*

spell'ing-bee, *n.*, concours orthographique, *m.*

spell'ing-book (-bouke), *n.*, syllabaire, *m.*

spelt, *adj.*, épelé. — in full; *écrit en toutes lettres.*

spel'ter, *n.*, (metal.) zinc, *m.*

spen'cer, *n.*, (dress) spencer, *m.*

spend, *v.a.*, (*preterit* and *past part.*, Spent) dépenser; (to waste) prodiguer, gaspiller, perdre, dissiper, manger; (to consume, to exhaust) épuiser; (time) passer; (a mast) casser; (to flow) couler. The ball had spent its force; *la balle avait perdu sa force.* To — money on; *dépenser son argent* **à.**

spend, *v.n.*, dépenser; faire de la dépense; (to be lost) se perdre; (to be consumed) se consumer, s'épuiser.

spend'er, *n.*, dépensier, *m.*, dépensière, *f.*; dissipateur, *m.*, dissipatrice, *f.*

spend'ing, *n.*, action de dépenser; dépense, *f.*

spend'thrift (-thrif'te), *n.*, dépensier, *m.*, dépensière, *f.*; prodigue; mange-tout; dissipateur; bourreau d'argent, *m.*

spent, *adj.*, (of balls) morte; (of masts) cassé.

sperm (speurme), *n.*, sperme; (of fish, frogs) frai, *m.* — candle; *bougie diaphane, f.* — oil; *huile de baleine, f.* — whale; *cachalot, m.*

spermace'ti (speur-ma-cî-ti), *n.*, blanc de baleine, *m.*

spew (spiou), *v.a.n.*, vomir, dégobiller.

spew'ing (spiou-igne), *n.*, vomissement, *m.*

sphere (sfîre), *n.*, sphère, *f.*; élément, *m.* Limited —; *cadre limité, m.*

sphere (sfîre), *v.a.*, arrondir en sphère.

spher'ical (sfèr'-), *adj.*, sphérique.

spher'ically, *adv.*, sphériquement.

spher'icity, *n.*, sphéricité, *f.*

spher'ics, *n.pl.*, théorie de la sphère, *f.sing.*

spher'oïd (sfî-roïde), *n.*, sphéroïde, *m.*

spheroid'al, *adj.*, sphéroïdal.

spherom'eter, *n.*, sphéromètre, *m.*

sphinx, *n.*, (myth. fig.) sphinx, *m.*

spi'ca-bandage (-ba'nd'èdje), *n.*, spica, *m.*

spice (spaïce), *n.*, épice, *f.*; épices, *f.pl.*; (small quantity) teinte, nuance, idée, *f.*, grain, *m.*

spice (spaïce), *v.a.*, épicer.

spi'cily, *adv.*, crânement, fameusement.

spi'ciness (spaï-), *n.*, goût épicé, goût aromatisé, *m.*; (fig.) piquant, *m.*

spick'-and-span, *adj.*, brillant. — new; *tout battant neuf; tout neuf, flambant neuf.*

spi'cy (spaï-), *adj.*, fertile en épices; épicé; (fragrant) aromatique, parfumé; (showy) pimpant, flambant; (pungent) piquant; (fig.) épicé, fameux, huppé; (of a story) grivois.

spi'der (spaï-), *n.*, araignée, *f.* —'s web; *toile d'araignée, f.*

spi'der-like (-laïke), *adj.*, d'araignée; comme une araignée.

spi'der-monkey, *n.*, atèle, *m.*

spig'ot (spi-gheutte), *n.*, fausset, *m.*

spike (spaïke), *n.*, pointe, *f.*; (a nail) clou, *m.*; (of wood) cheville, *f.*; (of corn) épi; (of a plant) aspic, *m.* Marline —; (nav.) *épissoir, m.*

spike, *v.a.*, clouer; (a cannon) enclouer. To — a gate; *hérisser une grille de pointes.*

spiked (spaïk'te), *adj.*, à pointes, armé, garni **de** pointes; (of a gun) encloué. — helmet; *casque à pointe, m.*

spike'let (spaïk'-), *n.*, (bot.) épillet, *m.*

spike'-nail (-néle), *n.*, clou barbelé, *m.*; **che**ville barbelée, *f.*

spike'nard (spaïk'-), *n.*, nard indien, *m.*

spik'y (spaïk'-), *adj.*, à pointe aiguë; pointu.

spill, *n.*, cheville; goupille, *f.*; fausset; pieu, *m.*; (for lighting) allumette de papier, *ou* (chip) en copeau; (fig.) (upset) culbute, *f.* To have a —; *verser, culbuter.*

spill, *v.a.*, (*preterit* and *past part.*, Spilt, Spilled) répandre; verser; renverser; (nav.) carguer; (of a sail) carguer.

spill, *v.n.*, se verser, se répandre.

spin, *v.a.*, (*preterit* and *past part.*, Spun) filer; (to unroll) dérouler; (a top) faire tourner; (hay) tordre. To — a yarn; *raconter une longue histoire.* To — out; *allonger; prolonger; étendre; faire durer, tirer en longueur.* To — round; *tourner, tournoyer; traîner.*

spin'ning, *adj.*, tournoyant, tournant.

spin'age *ou* **spin'ach** (spi'n'èdje), *n.*, (bot.) épinard, *m.*; (cook.) épinards, *m.pl.*

spin'al (spaï-), *adj.*, (anat.) spinal; (of the spinal cord) épinière; (of the backbone) rachidien. — -column; *colonne vertébrale, f.* — cord, — -marrow; *moelle épinière, f.* — curvature; *déviation de la colonne vertébrale, f.* — complaint; *maladie de la moelle épinière, f.*

spin'dle (spi'n'd'l), *n.*, fuseau; (rod on which a thing turns) pivot, *m.*; (horl.) fusée; (of a compass) aiguille, *f.*; (mec.) essieu; (of a vane) fer; (tech.) axe, *m.*; (in spinning-mills) broche, *f.*; (nav.) pivot du cabestan, *m.*

spin'dleful, *n.*, fusée, *f.*

spin'dle-legs (-lèg'ze) *ou* **spin'dle-shanks**, *n.pl.*, jambes de fuseau, *f.pl.*

spin'dle-shanked (-sha'gn'k'te), *adj.*, à jambes de fuseau.

spin'dle-shaped (-shép'te), *adj.*, fusiforme.

spin'dle-tree (-trî), *n.*, fusain, bonnet de prêtre, bonnet carré, *m.*

spine (spaïne), *n.*, épine dorsale, *f.*

spin'et (spi-nette), *n.*, (mus.) épinette, *f.*

spinif'erous (spaï-nif'eur-), *adj.*, épineux.

spin'iness, *n.*, nature épineuse, *f.*

spin'ner, *n.*, fileur, *m.*, fileuse, *f.*; (proprietor of spinning mill) filateur, *m.*

spin'ning, *n.*, filature, *f.*; filage, *m.*

spin'ning-factory, *n.*, filature, *f.*

spin'ning-frame, *n.*, métier à filer, *m.*

spin'ning-jenny (-djè'n'-), *n.*, métier à filer, *m.*; mule-jenny, *f.*

spin'ning-machine (-ma-shîne), *n.*, machine à filer, *f.*

spin'ning-mill, *n.*, filature, *f.*

spin'ning-top, *n.*, sabot, *m.*

spin'ning-wheel (-hwîle), *n.*, rouet à filer, *m.*

spin'ny, *n.*, petit bois, taillis, bosquet, *m.*

spinos'ity (spaï-noss'-), *n.*, nature épineuse; (fig.) matière épineuse, *f.*

spin'ous (spaï-), *adj.*, épineux.

Spi'nozism (-ziz'm), *n.*, spinosisme, *m.*

Spi'nozist, *n.*, spinosiste, *m.f.*

spin'ster, *n.*, fileuse; (unmarried) demoiselle; (jur.) femme non mariée, *f.*

spin'y (spaï-), *adj.*, épineux; plein d'épines; (perplexing) difficile, épineux.

spi'racle (spaï-ra-k'l), *n.*, pore; (bot.) stomate, *m.*

spiræ'a, *n.*, spirée, *f.*

spi'ral (spaï-), *adj.*, spiral; (of staircases) tournant, à vis, en limaçon.

spi'rally, *adv.*, en spirale.

spire (spaïeur), *n.*, spirale; (of a steeple) aiguille, flèche, *f.*; (top) sommet; (of grass) brin; (of plants) germe, *m.*

spire (spaïeur), *v.n.*, s'élever en flèche; (of grain) germer.

spired (spaïeur'de), *adj.*, à flèche.

spir'it (spi-rite), *n.*, (breath) souffle; (soul of man) esprit, *m.*, âme; (ardor, fire) ardeur, force, vigueur, verve, *f.*, feu, entraînement; élan, entrain; (courage) courage, caractère, cœur; (genius) génie; (vigor of intellect) esprit, *m.*, intelligence, *f.*; (temper) caractère, *m.*, nature, disposition, *f.*, esprit; (immaterial substance) esprit; (immaterial being) esprit, *m.*; (turn of mind) disposition, *f.*, esprit, sentiment, *m.*; (animation) vivacité, gaieté, *f.*, entrain, *m.*; (perception) perception, *f.*, sentiment; (eager desire) esprit, *m.*, ardeur, rage, *f.*; (person of activity) esprit entreprenant, *m.*; (essence) essence; (energy) énergie, *f.*; (of troops) moral; (apparition) esprit, fantôme, spectre; (liquor) spiritueux, *m.*, liqueur spiritueuse, *f.*; (chem., com.) esprit, *m. pl.*, verve, gaîté, bonne humeur, *f.sing.*; entrain, courage, *m.sing.* In good —s; *gai*; *en train*; *de bonne humeur*. Party-—; *esprit de parti.* Ardent —; *esprit ardent*; *caractère ardent.* Ardent —s; *liqueurs fortes,f.pl.*; *spiritueux, m.pl.* Depressed —s, low —s; *abattement*; *accablement, m.sing.* Good —s, high —s; *gaîté, f.sing.*; *entrain, m.sing.*; *bonne humeur, f.sing.* Evil-—; *mauvais génie, malin esprit, esprit malfaisant, m.* Raw —s; *liqueurs pures, sans eau, f.pl.* To labor under depression of —s; *être abattu*; *être dans l'abattement.* To raise any one's —s, *ou* put any one into good —s; *égayer quelqu'un, remonter le courage* ou *le moral à quelqu'un*; *mettre quelqu'un de bonne humeur, mettre en train.* To raise a —; *évoquer un esprit.* Proof-—; *esprit de preuve.* A man of —; *un homme de cœur, de caractère.* He is in better —s now; *il est maintenant de meilleure humeur.* To keep up one's —s; *ne pas perdre courage, ne pas se laisser abattre, ne pas se décourager.* To recover one's —s; *reprendre courage.*

spir'it, *v.a.*, animer; encourager; exciter; transporter. To — away; *faire disparaître, enlever, entraîner*; *escamoter.*

spir'ited, *adj.*, animé, plein de cœur, plein de courage, plein de caractère; plein d'ardeur; ardent; chaleureux; entraînant; plein de force, plein de vigueur; vigoureux; fort; vif; plein de verve; (of horses) fougueux, vif, ardent. Bold-—; *hardi.* High-—; *de caractère*; *plein de cœur, de courage*; *ardent, fougueux*; *fier.* Low-—; *abattu*; *dans l'abattement.* Mean-—; *sans cœur, sans caractère.* Poor-—; *sans cœur, sans caractère, lâche.*

spir'itedly, *adj.*, avec cœur, avec caractère, avec courage; courageusement; avec ardeur; ardemment; (of speeches or writings) chaleureusement; avec force, avec vigueur; vivement; fortement; vigoureusement.

spir'itedness, *n.*, cœur; courage; caractère; feu, *m.*; ardeur; chaleur, *f.*; entraînement, *m.*; (of speech) verve; force; vigueur; (of horses) fougue, ardeur, *f.*

spir'itless, *adj.*, inanimé, sans âme; (destitute of vigor) languissant, sans vigueur, sans caractère, sans ardeur, sans force; mou, énervé; (without courage) sans cœur, sans courage; (of speech) sans verve; (dejected) abattu, accablé, dans l'abattement, dans l'accablement.

spir'itlessly, *adj.*, sans cœur, sans courage.

spir'itlessness, *n.*, manque de caractère; manque de cœur; manque d'ardeur; manque de force, de courage; (of speech) manque de verve, *m.*

spir'it-lamp, *n.*, lampe à esprit de vin, *f.*

spir'it-level (-lèv'-), *n.*, niveau à bulle d'air, *m.*

spir'it-me'dium, *n.*, médium, *m.*

spir'it-rapper, *n.*, médium, *m.*

spir'it-rapping, *n.*, spiritisme, *m.*

spir'it-room (-roume), *n.*, (nav.) cale à vin, *f.*

spir'it-stirring (-steur'-), *adj.*, qui transporte, qui excite le cœur, émouvant.

spir'it-trade, *n.*, commerce des spiritueux, *m*

spir'itual (-'iou-), *adj.*, spirituel.

spir'itualism (-'iou-al'iz'm), *n.*, (philos.) spiritualisme; (spirit-rapping) spiritisme, *m.*

spir'itualist, *n.*, (philos.) spiritualiste, *m.f.*; (spirit-rapping) spirite, *m.*

spiritual'ity, *n.*, spiritualité, *f.*; spirituel, *m.*

spiritualiza'tion (-'aï-zé-), *n.*, spiritualisation, *f.*

spir'itualize (-'iou-al'aïze), *v.a.*, spiritualiser.

spir'itually, *adv.*, spirituellement.

spir'ituous (-'iou-), *adj.*, spiritueux.

spir'ituousness, *n.*, propriété spiritueuse, *f.*

spirt (speurte), *n.*, jaillissement; rejaillissement; (sudden effort) effort, accès, *m.*, boutade, saillie, *f.*

spirt (speurte), *v.a.*, faire jaillir; faire rejaillir.

spirt, *v.n.*, saillir; jaillir; s'élancer; (of pens) cracher.

spir'y (spaïeur'-), *adj.*, spiral; pyramidal; en spirale; en flèche, élancé.

spit, *n.*, broche; (depth of earth pierced by the spade) terre bêchée; pelletée, *f.*; (geog.) cap; (saliva) crachat, *m.*, salive, *f.* To put upon the —; *mettre à la broche.* He is the dead — of his father; *c'est son père tout craché*; *c'est le vrai portrait de son père.*

spit, *v.a.*, (preterit and past part., Spit) embrocher; mettre à la broche; (to eject from the mouth) cracher, rejeter.

spit, *v.n.*, cracher; saliver; (of cats) félir. To — out; *cracher.* To — in any one's face; *cracher au visage à quelqu'un.* To — on, upon; *traiter avec mépris, ravaler.*

spite (spaïte), *n.*, dépit, *m.*; haine; rancune, *f.* In —of; *en dépit* de, *malgré.* Out of —; *par dépit.* To have a — against any one; *garder rancune à quelqu'un*; *en vouloir à quelqu'un, avoir une dent* contre.

spite (spaïte), *v.a.*, (to vex) dépiter; blesser, outrager; avoir du dépit, ou une dent, contre.

spite'-fire, *n.*, rageur, *m.*

spite'ful (-foule), *adj.*, plein de rancune, haineux; rancunier; (of animals) méchant.

spite'fully, *adv.*, par dépit; par haine; par rancune, par méchanceté.

spite'fulness, *n.*, dépit, *m.*; rancune; méchanceté; haine, *f.*

spit'ter, *n.*, (deer) daguet; (pers.) cracheur, *m.*, cracheuse, *f.*

spit'ting, *n.*, crachement, *m.*

spit'tle (spit't'l), *n.*, salive, *f.*; crachat, *m.*

spittoon' (-toune), *n.*, crachoir, *m.*

splash, *v.a.*, éclabousser; (of waves) clapoter. *V.* **plash.** *v.n.*, tomber avec fracas. —ed all over; *tout couvert d'éclaboussures.*

splash, *n.*, éclaboussure, *f.*; bruit que fait un corps en tombant ... (V. Hugo). *V.* **plash.**

splash'-board (-bôrde), *n.*, splash'er, *n.*, garde-crotte, *m.*

splash'ing, *n.*, (act of splashing) éclaboussement, *m.*; (the outcome of it) éclaboussure, *f.*

splash'y, *adj.*, gâcheux; bourbeux.

splat, *n.*, (of a chair) barre, *f.*

splay, *v.a.*, épauler (a horse); (arch.) ébraser.

splay, *n.*, écartement; (arch.) ébrasement, *m.*

splay, *adj.*, écarté, en dehors.

splay'-foot ou **splay'-footed** (-fout'-), *adj.*, qui a les pieds plats, ou tournés en dehors; cagneux, panard.

splay'-mouth (-maouth), *n.*, grande bouche, *f.*

spleen (splîne), *n.*, rate; (anger) haine, *f.*,

fiel, *m.*, animosité, bile, *f.* ; (melancholy) spleen, *m.*, mélancolie, humeur noire, *f.* To have the —; *avoir le spleen, broyer du noir.* — wort; *scolopendre, f.*

spleened (splî'n'de), *adj.*, dératé.

spleen'ful (-foule), **spleen'y**, *ou* **spleen'ish**, *adj.*, irrité, chagrin ; (melancholy) mélancolique, atrabilaire.

splen'did, *adj.*, (shining) resplendissant, éclatant ; (brilliant) brillant, éclatant ; (sumptuous) somptueux, splendide ; (magnificent) magnifique.

splen'didly, *adv.*, d'une manière resplendissante ; avec éclat ; brillamment ; somptueusement, splendidement; magnifiquement.

splen'dor (splè'n'deur), *n.*, splendeur, magnificence, *f.* ; éclat, *m.*

splenet'ic, *adj.*, atrabilaire; chagrin.

sple'nic *ou* **sple'nical**, *adj.*, (anat.) splénique.

splent, *n.*, (vet.) suros, *m.*

splice (splaïce), *n.*, (nav.) épissure, *f.*

splice (splaïce), *v.a.*, (nav.) épisser ; (carp.) joindre à onglet ; (fam.) (to marry) marier. To get —d ; (fam.) *se marier.*

spli'cing-fid (splaïss'-), *n.*, épissoir, *m.*

splint *ou* **splin'ter**, *n.*, éclat, éclat de bois, *m.* ; (of a bone) esquille ; (surg.) attelle, éclisse, *f.* ; (vet.) suros, *m.* ; (small) écharde, épine, *f.* To fly into —s; *voler en éclats.*

splint *ou* **splin'ter**, *v.a.*, faire éclater, briser en éclats ; (surg.) éclisser ; mettre une attelle à.

splint'-bone (-bône), *n.*, péroné, *m.*

splin'ter, *v.n.*, éclater, se briser, voler en éclats.

splin'ter-bar, *n.*, barre d'appui ; (of springs) volée de timon, *f.*

splin'tery, *adj.*, (min.) écailleux, en esquilles.

split, *v.a.*, (*preterit* and *past part.*, Split) fendre ; briser, diviser, partager ; (a sail) crever ; déchirer. To — one's sides with laughing; *crever de rire.* To — asunder; *fendre en deux.* To — into; *diviser* en. To — hairs; *épiloguer ;* (fam.) *chercher du poil aux œufs.* To — a hair; *epiloguer ; couper un cheveu en quatre.* To — words; *chicaner* sur *les mots.* To — votes; *partager.* To — off ; *se détacher, se séparer* de. To — the difference ; *partager le différend ; couper la poire en deux.*

split, *v.n.*, se fendre, se briser ; (to quarrel) se quereller, se brouiller. To — into; *se fendre* en. To — with laughter; *crever de rire, se tordre de rire ;* (fam.) *rire comme un bossu.*

split'ter, *n.*, fendeur, *m.*, fendeuse, *f.*

split'ting, *n.*, fendage, *m.* adj. A — headache ; *un mal de tête fou.*

splotch, *n.*, tache, *f.*, barbouillage, *m.*

splut'ter (spleut'teur), *n.*, tracas ; tapage, vacarme, *m.*

splut'ter (spleut'-), *v.n.*, bredouiller ; (to scatter) s'éparpiller ; (of pers.) cracher. To — against; *dénoncer, trahir.*

splut'tering, *n.*, bredouillement, *m.* ; éclaboussure, *f.*

spoil (spoïl), *n.*, dépouille, *f.* ; butin, *m.* ; (of animals) dépouille, *f.* ; (plundering) pillage, *m.*

spoil *ou* **spoil'-bank**, *n.*, déblai ; dépôt de décombres, *m.*

spoil (spoïl), *v.a.*, (to corrupt) corrompre ; (to destroy) détruire, ruiner ; (to injure) gâter, abîmer ; (to plunder) ravager, dévaster ; (to seize by violence) se saisir de, s'emparer de, piller. To — a child ; *gâter un enfant.* To — sport ; *troubler la fête.* — sport ; *trouble-fête, m.* To — the Egyptians ; *dépouiller, ou voler, ou piller, l'ennemi.* Spare the rod and — the child ; (prov.) *qui aime bien, châtie bien.*

spoil, *v.n.*, se corrompre ; se gâter ; s'abîmer.

spoiled (spoïl'de), *adj.*, gâté ; abîmé.

spoil'er, *n.*, personne qui gâte, qui abîme, *f.* ; (plunderer) spoliateur, *m.*, spoliatrice, *f.*, corrupteur, destructeur, *m.*

spoil'ing, *n.*, spoliation ; action de gâter, détérioration, *f.*

spoil'-sport, *n.*, trouble-fête, *m.*

spoke (spôke), *n.*, rais, rayon, *m.* ; (of a ladder) échelon, *m.* To put a — in one's wheel; *mettre des bâtons dans les roues* à *quelqu'un.*

spok'en (spôk'n), *past part.* V. **speak.** (In compounds) au parler . . . , au langage . . . Well — of ; *dont on dit du bien.* Ill — of; *dont on dit du mal.*

spoke'-brush, *n.*, passe-partout, *m.*

spoke'-shave, *n.*, (carp.) plane, *f.*

spokes'man (spôks'-), *n.*, orateur, *m.* ; personne qui porte la parole, *f.*, organe, *m.*

spo'liate (spô-), *v.a.*, dépouiller ; spolier; piller.

spolia'tion (spô-li-é-), *n.*, spoliation, *f.*

sponda'ic (dé-), *adj.*, spondaïque.

spon'dee (-dî), *n.*, spondée, *m.*

sponge (speu'n'dje), *n.*, éponge, *f.* ; (artil.) écouvillon, *m.* ; (for cakes) pâte molle, *f.* To throw up the — ; *s'avouer vaincu.*

sponge, *v.a.*, (to cleanse) éponger ; (artil.) écouvillonner, (cloth) décatir. To — out; *effacer.* To — up; éponger.

sponge, *v.n.*, boire ; pomper; (to gain things by mean acts) (fam.) piquer l'assiette ; écornifler (Montaigne). To — on ; *vivre aux dépens* de ; *faire le métier de parasite auprès* de ; *attraper un dîner.*

sponge'-bath, *n.*, bain anglais ; bain de siège, *m.*

sponge'-cake, *n.*, gâteau de Savoie, *m.*

spon'ger, *n.*, pique-assiette, écornifleur, *m.*, écornifleuse, *f.* ; parasite, *m.*

spon'giness, *n.*, nature spongieuse, *f.*

spon'ging, *n.*, épongement ; (mil.) écouvillonnement ; (fig.) écorniflerie, *f.*

spon'ging-house (-haouce), *n.*, (ant.) maison d'huissier, prison provisoire (pour dettes), *f.*

spon'gy, *adj.*, spongieux.

sponk, *n.* V. **spunk.**

spon'sor (-seur), *n.*, parrain, *m.*, marraine, *f.* ; (surety) garant, répondant, *m.*

spon'sorship, *n.*, parrainage, *m.*

spontane'ity (-nî-i-), *n.*, spontanéité, *f.*

sponta'neous (-té-ni-), *adj.*, spontané.

sponta'neously, *adv.*, spontanément.

sponta'neousness, *n.*, spontanéité, *f.*

spontoon' (-toune), *n.*, (milit.) esponton, *m.*

spool (spoul), *n.*, (tech.) bobine, *f.* ; espoulin, *m.*

spool, *v.a.*, bobiner, espouliner.

spoom (spoume), *v.n.*, (nav.) courir, *ou* fuir, vent arrière.

spoon (spoune), *n.*, cuiller, cuillère, *f.* ; (simpleton) niais, sot, *m.* Table— ; *cuiller à soupe, à bouche.* Dessert— ; *cuiller à dessert.* Tea— ; *cuiller à thé, à café.* Gravy— ; *cuiller à ragoût.* To be born with a silver — in one's mouth ; *être né coiffé.* To be —s on; *être amoureux fou* de. — and fork ; *couvert, m.* Salt —; *pelle à sel, f.*

spoon, *v.n.*, faire les amoureux.

spoon'bill, *n.*, (orni.) palette, *f.*

spoon'drift, *n.*, (nav.) embrun, *m.*

spoon'ful (-foule), *n.*, cuillerée, *f.*

spoon'meat (-mîte), *n.*, aliment liquide, *m.*

spoon'wort (-weurte), *n.*, (bot.) cochléaria, *m.; herbe aux cuillers, f.*

spoon'y, **spoon'ey**, *adj.*, niais, sot. — on; *amoureux* de, *épris* de.

sporad'ic, *adj.*, (med., bot., geol.) (fig.) sporadique.

sport (spôrte), *n.*, sport, jeu, divertissement, amusement, *m.;* récréation ; (mockery) moquerie, raillerie, *f.;* (plaything) jouet ; (of words) jeu, *m.;* (hunt., shooting) chasse ; (fishing) pêche, *f.* Good, poor —; (of game) bonne, pauvre chasse ; (of fish) bonne, mauvaise pêche ou *prise.* Field —s ; *plaisirs de la chasse,* m.pl. In —; *pour rire, par plaisanterie ; en se jouant.* To be the — of ; *être le jouet* de. To make a — of ; *s'amu-*

ser **de** ; *se jouer* **de** ; *se rire* **de**. To spoil —; *troubler la fête.*

sport, *v.a.*, (to divert) divertir ; (to represent) représenter ; (to exhibit) étaler, faire parade **de** ; (to wear) porter.

sport, *v.n.*, se divertir, s'amuser ; se récréer ; folâtrer, badiner, s'ébattre. To — with ; (to trifle with) *se jouer* **de** ; *se faire un jeu* **de**.

sport'ing, *n.*, divertissement, *m.* ; (hunt., shooting) chasse ; (fishing) pêche, *f.* ; (le) sport, *m.* — character ; *amateur du sport, m.* — dog ; *chien de chasse, m.* — gun ; *fusil de chasse, m.*

sport'ive, *adj.*, enjoué ; gai ; badin, folâtre ; amusant.

sport'ively, *adv.*, avec enjouement, en badinant, en plaisantant.

sport'iveness, *n.*, enjouement, *m.* ; gaieté, folâtrerie, humeur badine, *f.* ; badinage, *m.*

sports'man, *n.*, chasseur ; amateur de la chasse, amateur de la pêche ; sportsman, *m.*

spot, *n.*, tache ; (stain on character, etc.) tache, souillure, *f.* ; (place) endroit, lieu, *m.*, place ; (of ground) coin *ou* morceau (de terre), *m.* ; (fam.) lopin (de terre) ; (astron.) tache, *f.* On the —; *sur les lieux* ; *sur la place* ; (immediately) *sur-le-champ*. To be killed on the —; *être tué raide, ou tué sur le coup*. Dead on the —; *raide mort.*

spot, *v.a.*, tacher, tacheter ; moucheter ; tigrer ; (to blemish) (ant.) tacher, souiller. I —ted him ; (fam.) *je l'ai bien reconnu.*

spot'less, *adj.*, sans tache ; (without sin) immaculé ; pur ; (fig.) irréprochable.

spot'lessness, *n.*, pureté, *f.*

spot'ted, *adj.*, tacheté ; moucheté ; (of horses) tigré.

spot'tedness, *n.*, tacheture ; moucheture, *f.*

spot'ter, *n.*, personne qui fait des taches, *f.*

spot'ty, *adj.*, couvert de taches ; moucheté ; taché, tacheté.

spouse (spaouze), *n.*, époux, *m.*, épouse, *f.* ; mari, *m.*, femme, *f.*

spouse'less, *adj.*, sans époux ; sans épouse.

spout (spaoute) *n.*, tuyau ; tuyau de décharge ; canal ; (of a pitcher, etc.) bec, goulot, *m.* ; (of a house) gouttière ; (mines) ouverture, *f.* ; (at sea) typhon, *m.*, trombe, *f.* Up the —; (in pawn) *en gage* ; (pop.) *chez ma tante* ; *au clou* ; (slang) (pers.) *ruiné, flambé.*

spout, *v.n.*, jaillir, rejaillir, s'élancer ; (to declaim) déclamer ; faire des phrases, pérorer ; (of whales) rejeter l'eau par les narines.

spout, *v.a.*, lancer, jeter ; (to declaim) déclamer ; (of whales) rejeter l'eau par les narines.

spout'er, *n.*, déclamateur, péroreur, *m.*

spout'ing, *n.*, jaillissement, *m.* ; déclamation, *f.*

sprain (sprē'n), *n.*, entorse ; foulure, *f.*

sprain, *v.a.*, donner une entorse **à** ; fouler ; se fouler ; se donner une entorse **à**. I have —ed my wrist ; *je me suis foulé le poignet.* He has —ed his ankle ; *il s'est donné une entorse à la cheville.*

sprat, *n.*, (ich.) sprat, harenguet, *m.* To give a — to catch a herring ; *donner un œuf pour avoir un bœuf ou donner un pois pour avoir une fève.*

sprawl (sprôl), *v.n.*, s'étendre ; s'étaler ; (to move when lying down) s'agiter, se débattre. To send any one —ing ; *étendre quelqu'un à terre* (*tout de son long*). To lie —ing ; (on the ground) *être étendu tout de son long.*

spray, *n.*, (branch) brin, *m.*, brindille, ramille, *f.* ; (of the sea), embrun, *m.* ; (of water) poussière d'eau, *f.* ; panache ; brouillard, pulvérin, *m.*

spread (sprède), *v.a.*, (preterit and past part., Spread) étendre ; déployer ; (to cover) couvrir ; (to propagate) répandre, propager ; (to emit) répandre ; exhaler ; (to scatter, publish) répandre ; (a sail) déferler, déployer ; (a net) tendre ; (a tent) dresser ; (a disease) répandre, propager ; (sails) tendre, déployer. To — the table ; *mettre*

le couvert ; *dresser la table.* To — abroad ; *répandre au loin, divulguer.* To — over ; *répandre* **sur**. To — out ; *étendre, étaler*. To — the report of ; *répandre, faire courir, propager le bruit* **de**.

spread, *v.n.*, s'étendre ; se déployer ; se répandre ; se propager ; s'exhaler ; s'épandre. To — forth ; *se dérouler, se déployer*. To — over ; *s'étendre* **sur**.

spread, *n.*, étendue ; (expansion) expansion ; (propagation) propagation, *f.* ; progrès, *m.* ; (feast) régal, festin, *m.* To give a — ; *traiter.*

spread'-eagle, *n.*, aigle aux ailes déployées ; (her.) aigle éployée, *f.*

spread'er, *n.*, propagateur, *m.* ; (of news) débiteur, colporteur, *m.* ; (of a garden engine) arrosoir, *m.* ; pomme, *f.*

spread'ing, *n.*, propagation, extension, *f. adj.*, étendu, qui s'étend, qui se répand.

spree (sprī), *n.*, bamboche, bombance, fredaine, *f.* To have a — ; *rigoler* ; *faire bamboche*. To be out on the — ; *faire la noce.*

sprig, *n.*, brin, *m.* ; brindille, *f.* ; rejeton, surgeon, scion, *m.* ; (in embroidery) branche, *f.* ; (fig.) rejeton, *m.* — of nobility ; *hobereau, m.*

spright (sprā'te), *n.* *V.* **sprite**.

spright'liness, *n.*, vivacité ; gaieté, *f.* ; enjouement, feu, entrain, *m.*

spright'ly, *adj.*, enjoué, vif, animé, gai, sémillant, égrillard.

spring, *v.n.*, (preterit, Sprung, Sprang ; past part., Sprung) (to begin to grow) pousser, croître ; (to spurt out) jaillir, rejaillir ; (to begin to appear) surgir, commencer ; (of the day) paraître, poindre ; (to issue into sight) venir au jour, naître ; (to be descended) descendre ; (to thrive) prospérer, s'élever ; (to leap, to shoot) se lancer, s'élancer ; (to rise from a covert) se lever, partir ; (to warp) se déjeter ; (of a mast, a yard) (nav.) consentir. To — at ; *lâcher de saisir* ; *s'élancer* **à** ; *sauter à la gorge* **à**. To — back ; *s'élancer en arrière* ; *reculer* ; (of a gun) *faire recul* ; (of things) *faire ressort*. To — forth ; *pousser, croître* ; (to spurt out) *jaillir, rejaillir* ; (fig.) *naître, surgir*. To — forward ; *s'élancer en avant*. To — from ; (to issue from) *être issu* **de** ; *sortir* **de**, *naître* **de**, *provenir* **de**, *découler* **de**, *dériver* **de** ; *avoir sa source* **dans**. To — in ; *se précipiter* **dans**, *sauter* **dans**. To — on ; *se précipiter* **sur**, *s'élancer* **sur**, *sauter* **sur**. To — out ; *s'élancer dehors*. To — over ; *sauter, franchir, enjamber*. To — up ; (to rise up) *se lever précipitamment* ; (to grow) *pousser, croître* ; (of young persons) *grandir*.

spring, *v.a.*, (to rouse) faire lever, faire partir ; (to produce quickly) produire ; (to cause to explode) faire sauter ; (nav.) a leak) faire une voie d'eau ; (a mast, a yard) faire consentir ; (a trap) faire jouer ; (a rattle) sonner ; agiter ; (a mine) faire jouer. To — anything upon ; *présenter à l'improviste . . .* **à**.

spring, *n.*, (leap) saut, bond, élan ; (resilience) ressort ; (elastic power) ressort, *m.*, élasticité, *f.* ; (of braces, etc.) élastique ; (elastic plate, wire, etc.) ressort ; (active power) ressort, *m.* ; (fountain, source) source ; (cause) cause, origine, *f.* ; mobile ; (season) printemps, *m.* ; (nav.) fente, *f.* ; (of a trigger) gâchette, *f.* — of an arch ; *naissance de voûte, f.* — balance ; *dynamomètre, m.* — blind ; *store, m.* — day ; *jour de printemps, m.* — grass ; (bot.) *flouve, f.* — mattress ; *sommier élastique, m.* Main — ; *grand ressort, m.* With —s ; (of boots) *à ressorts* ; *à élastiques* ; (of carriages) *suspendu*. —s with pump action ; *ressorts à pompe, m.pl.* Without —s ; *posé à cru sur l'essieu* (V. Hugo). With a —; *d'un bond.* Hot —; *source d'eau chaude* ; (pl.) *station thermale, f.* To take a — ; *prendre son élan.* In the —; *au printemps.* The —s of action ; (fig.) *les mobiles qui font agir les hommes.*

spring'-board, *n.*, tremplin, *m.*

spring'bok *ou* **spring'buck** (-beuke), *n.*, gazelle africaine, *f.*

spring'-box, *n.*, (horl.) barillet, *m.*

spring'-carriage (-kar'ridje), *n.*, voiture suspendue, *f.*

spring'-cart, *n.*, tapissière, *f.*

spring'-cleaning, *n.*, grand nettoyage, *m.*

springe (spri'n'dje), *n.*, lacet, *m.;* lacs, *m.pl.*

springe, *v.a.*, prendre au lacet, prendre aux lacs.

sprin'ger (spri'n'djeur), *n.*, (hunt.) traqueur, rabatteur, *m. ;* (arch.) imposte, *f.*

spring'-gun (-gheune), *n.*, fusil à ressort, *m.*

spring'-head (-hède), *n.*, grande source, *f.*

spring'iness (sprign'i-), *n.*, élasticité ; (abundance of springs) abondance de sources, *f.*

spring'ing (sprign'-), *n.*, action de s'élancer, de lancer, *f.;* élan, saut, *m. ;* (arch.) naissance de voûte, *f.*

spring'ing-lev'el (sprign'igne-lèv'èl), *n.*, (arch.) niveau des naissances, *m.*

spring'ing-line (-laïne), *n.*, (arch.) ligne de naissance, *f. ;* montant, *m.*

spring'-like, *adj.*, printanier.

spring'-lock, *n.*, houssette, *f. ;* bec de cane, *m.*

spring'-morning, *n.*, matinée de printemps, *f.*

spring'-tide (-taïde), *n.*, (nav.) grande marée, *f.*

spring'-time (-taïme), *n.*, printemps, *m.*

spring'-water (-wô-), *n.*, eau de source, *f.*

spring'-wheat (-hwîte), *n.*, (agri.) blé de mars, froment de mars, *m.*

spring'y (sprign'i), *adj.*, élastique ; (abounding in springs) plein de sources.

sprin'kle, *v.imp.*, pleuvoir un peu.

sprin'kle (spri'gn'k'l), *v.a.*, répandre ; parsemer **de** ; saupoudrer ; (with water) arroser **de** ; (with holy-water) asperger **de**. To — with salt ; *saupoudrer* **de**. —d with gold ; *parsemé d'or*.

sprin'kler, *n.*, aspersoir, goupillon, *m.*

sprin'kling, *n.*, action de répandre, de saupoudrer ; aspersion, *f. ;* arrosement, arrosage ; (of salt) saupoudrage, *m. ;* (small quantity) petite quantité ; (fig.) teinte, teinture, *f. ;* petit nombre, *m.* A — of rain ; *quelques gouttes de pluie*, *f.pl.*

sprit, *n.*, (nav.) livarde, *f.*

sprite (spraïte), *n.*, spectre ; esprit ; fantôme, sylphe, lutin, follet, *m.*

sprit'-sail (-séle), *n.*, voile à livarde, *f.*

sprout (spraoute), *n.*, jet, rejeton ; germe, pousse, *f. ;* chou vert, *m.* Brussels—s ; *choux de Bruxelles*, *m.pl.*

sprout (spraoute), *v.n.*, pousser ; germer ; (of flowering plants) bourgeonner.

sprout'ing, *n.*, germination, *f.*

sprout'ing, *adj.*, qui germe.

spruce (sprouce), *adj.*, paré ; orné ; requinqué ; pimpant.

spruce, *v.n.*, se parer, se faire beau ; se requinquer, se bichonner. *v.a.* To — up any one ; *attifer*, *afistoler*, *bichonner*, *requinquer quelqu'un*.

spruce, *n.*, (bot.) sapin, *m. ;* épinette, *f.*

spruce'ly, *adv.*, d'une manière pimpante, avec recherche.

spruce'ness, *n.*, recherche, *f.;* air pimpant, air requinqué, *m. ;* recherche, élégance (de toilette), *f.*

spud (speude), *n.*, petit couteau, *m. ;* (agri.) béquille, (pop. in Ireland) pomme de terre, *f.*

spume (spioume), *n. V.* **foam**.

spunge. *V.* **sponge**.

spun'ging-house. *V.* **sponging-house**.

spunk (speu'gn'ke), *n.*, amadou ; (pop.) (spirit) cœur, courage, feu, *m. ;* fougue, *f.*

spun'yarn (speun'yârne), *n.*, (nav.) bitord, *m.* —winch ; *moulinet*, *m.*

spur (speur), *n.*, éperon, aiguillon ; (of cocks) ergot ; (in grain) ergot ; (carp.) arc-boutant ; (bot., fort.) éperon ; (incitement) aiguillon, stimulant, *m.* On the — of ; *sous le feu de*. On the — of the moment ; *sous l'impulsion du moment, dans l'ardeur du moment*. To win one's —s ; *faire ses preuves*. To put —s to one's horse ; *piquer des deux*. To put on the — ; *chausser l'éperon*.

spur (speur), *v.a.*, éperonner, donner de l'éperon **à** ; (to incite) stimuler, aiguillonner, exciter, pousser, presser, encourager ; (to put spurs on) armer d'éperons, mettre des éperons **à**. To — on ; *presser, aiguillonner*.

spur, *v.n.*, jouer des éperons ; avancer ; piquer des deux.

spur'gall (-gôl), *n.*, blessure d'éperon, *f.*

spurge (speurdje), *n.*, (bot.) euphorbe, *f.* Caper-— ; *épurge*, *f.* — laurel ; *lauréole, f.; bois gentil*, *m.* — olive ; *mézéréon, m.* — flax ; *malherbe*, *f.*

spu'rious (spiou-), *adj.*, faux ; (adulterated) falsifié, sophistiqué ; (of writings) apocryphe ; (med., bot.) faux ; (jur.) illégitime. — edition ; *édition de contrefaçon*, *f.*

spu'riously, *adv.*, faussement ; (of books) par, *ou* en, contrefaçon.

spu'riousness, *n.*, falsification ; sophistication ; (fig.) fausseté ; (of books) nature, *f.*, *ou* caractère, *m.*, apocryphe ; (jur.) illégitimité, *f.*

spur'-leather, *n.*, monture d'éperon, *f.*

spur'-maker (-mék'-), *n.*, éperonnier, *m.*

spurn (speurne), *n.*, mépris, dédain, *m. ;* insulte, *f.*

spurn (speurne), *v.a.*, pousser du pied ; (to reject with disdain) rejeter avec mépris, rejeter, repousser, dédaigneusement ; (to treat with disdain) traiter avec mépris, mépriser.

spurn, *v.n.*, gigoter, se débattre des pieds. To — at ; *repousser dédaigneusement ; rejeter dédaigneusement ; dédaigner, mépriser*.

spurned, *adj.*, rejeté, méprisé **de**.

spurn'er, *n.*, personne qui méprise, qui dédaigne, *f.;* contempteur, *f.* Thou — (or scorner) of the ground (Shelley) ; *toi qui méprises la terre*.

spurred (speurde), *adj.*, éperonné ; (of rye, of cocks) ergoté.

spur'rer (speur'-), *n.*, cavalier qui use de l'éperon, *m. ;* (on) (fig.) instigateur, *m.*

spur'rier (speur'-), *n.*, éperonnier, *m.*

spurt (speurte), *v.a. V.* **spirt**.

spur'-wheel (-hwîle), *n.*, (tech.) hérisson, *m.*

sput'ter (speut'-), *n.*, salive, *f. ;* (noise) vacarme ; (stammering) bredouillement, *m.*

sput'ter, *v.n.*, cracher en parlant ; (to utter indistinctly) bredouiller ; (of pens) cracher ; (of things burning) siffler, pétiller, cracher. To — out ; (excuses) *bredouiller, laisser échapper*.

sput'terer, *n.*, personne qui crache en parlant, *f. ;* bredouilleur, *m.*, bredouilleuse, *f.*

sput'tering, *n.*, bredouillement ; (noise) vacarme, tintamarre, *m.*

spu'tum, *n.*, crachat, *m.*

spy (spaïe), *n.*, espion, *m.*, espionne, *f.*

spy (spaïe), *v.a.*, épier, espionner. To — out ; *trouver, découvrir ;* (a person) *apercevoir ;* (to explore) *reconnaître*. *V.* **espy**.

spy, *v.a.*, scruter, épier.

spy'-boat (-bôte), *n.*, (nav.) aviso, **m.**

spy'-glass (-glâce), *n.*, longue-vue, lunette d'approche, *f.*

spy'-system, *n.*, espionnage, *m.*

squab (skwôbe), *n.*, coussin, coussinet ; sofa ; (young pigeon) pigeonneau, *m.*

squab (skwôbe), **squab'by**, *adj.*, dodu ; potelé ; (of birds) sans plumes.

squab, *adv.*, lourdement ; avec violence ; rudement.

squab'ble (skwab'b'l), *n.*, dispute ; bagarre ; querelle, *f.*, chamaillis, *m.*

squab'ble, *v.n.*, se quereller ; se chamailler.

squab'bler, *n.*, querelleur, *m.*, querelleuse, *f.*

squab'bling, *n.*, querelle, *f. ;* chamaillis, *m.*

squad (skwŏde), n., (milit.) escouade; (set) clique, f. — drill; école de peloton, f. An awkward —; Jean-Jeans, m.pl. To appear an awkward — (Macaulay); (fig.) faire bien mauvaise figure.

squad'ron (skwŏd'reune), n., (of cavalry) escadron, m.; (nav.) escadre, division, f.

squad'roned (skwŏd'reu'n'de), adj., formé en carré; rangé en escadron.

squal'id (skwŏl'-), adj., crasseux; sale; malpropre. — poverty; pauvreté abjecte, f.

squal'idly, adv., salement, malproprement.

squal'idness, squal'or, n., malpropreté; crasse; saleté, f.

squall (skwŏl), n., cri; (of wind) coup de vent, grain, m., rafale, bourrasque, f. To look out for —s; se tenir sur ses gardes. Look out for —s! gare la bombe!

squall (skwŏl), v.n., crier; brailler; piailler.

squall'er, n., brailleur, m., brailleuse, f.; braillard, m., braillarde, f.

squall'ing, n., criaillerie, f.; cris, m.pl.

squall'ing, adj., criard, braillard.

squall'y, adj., venteux, tempétueux; à rafales.

squa'mous, adj., squameux; écailleux.

squan'der (skwo'n'-), v.a., dissiper; gaspiller; dépenser follement, prodiguer, manger.

squan'derer (skwo'n'-), n., dissipateur, gaspilleur, m., prodigue, m.f.

squan'dering, n., dissipation, f.; gaspillage, m.

square (skwère), n., carré; (on stuffs; of glass) carreau; (equality) niveau, pied d'égalité, m., égalité; (rule) règle, équerre; (of measure) superficie, f.; (carp.) équarrissage; (arith.) carré, m.; (on a chessboard) case; (place) place, f., square, m.; (in garrison towns) place d'armes, f. Set; équerre, f. To cut on the —; couper à angles droits. To act on the —; agir de bonne foi; jouer cartes sur table. To be — with; être quitte envers.

square (skwère), v.a., carrer; (to regulate) régler; (to fit) adapter, proportionner; (carp.) équarrir; (arith.) carrer; (accounts) balancer, solder; (a yard) (nav.) brasser carré; (fig.) mesurer, régler, adapter, ajuster.

square, v.n., cadrer; s'accorder; (to quarrel) se quereller. To — up; régler ses comptes. To — up to any one; s'avancer vers quelqu'un en posture de combat (à coups de poing), se mettre en posture de boxe **devant**.

square, adj., carré; (leaving no balance) balancé, soldé, égalisé; (true) vrai; conforme, exact; (fair) équitable, juste; (honest) honnête; (carp.) d'équarrissage; (math., nav.) carré; (of measure) de superficie. To make an account —; balancer, égaliser un compte.

square, adv., à angles droits, en carré; (fig.) de bonne foi, honnêtement, justement.

square'-built (-bilte), adj., bâti en carré; taillé carrément; trapu.

square'-cornered, adj., aux coins coupés carrément.

square'ly, adv., carrément; (fairly) honnêtement, justement, équitablement.

square'ness (skwèr'-), n., forme carrée, f.; équarrissage, m.

square'-rigged (-rig'de), adj., (nav.) mâté à carré, gréé en carré.

square'-sail (-séle), n., voile carrée, f.

squar'ing, n., équarrissage. — of the circle; quadrature du cercle, f.

squar'ish (skwèr'-), adj., à peu près carré.

squash (skwosh), v.a., écraser; (jur., ant.) casser. V. **quash**.

squash, n., chose molle; (fall) chute lourde, f.; (crushing) écrasement, m.; (at play) presse; foule serrée, f.; (bot.) gourde, courge, f. Lemon —; limonade à l'eau de Seltz, f.

squash'er, n., écraseur, m.

squash'ing, n., (of crowds) écrasement; (of fruits, etc.) écrasage, m.

squash'y, adj., mou, mollasse.

squat (skwote), adj., accroupi; blotti; tapi; (short and thick) trapu, ramassé. To lie, ou sit, —; se blottir, se tapir, s'accroupir; être accroupi, être tapi, être blotti. To be quite —; (fig.) (fam.) ne pas souffler mot.

squat (skwote), v.n., se tapir; s'accroupir; se blottir.

squat (skwote), n., accroupissement, m.

squat'ter, n., personne accroupie, blottie, f.; (settler) colon, m.

squat'ting, n., accroupissement, m.

squaw (skwŏ), n., femme; épouse (among the savages of Northern America), f.

squeak (skwîke), n., cri; cri aigu, m.

squeak (skwîke), v.n., crier; (of musical instruments) jurer.

squeak'er, n., personne qui crie, f.; criard, m., criarde, f.; animal qui crie, m.; pigeonneau; jeune perdreau, m.

squeak'ing, adj., qui crie; criard; (of musical instruments) qui jure.

squeal (skwîle), v.n., crier. n., cri, m.

squeam'ish (skwî-), adj., (of the stomach) qui se soulève; (fastidious) bégueule, trop délicat, trop difficile; dégoûté, délicat, difficile; (scrupulous) scrupuleux, délicat. To be —; faire le difficile; faire le dégoûté. She is —; elle fait la bégueule.

squeam'ishly, adv., trop délicatement, avec dégoût.

squeam'ishness, n., (fastidiousness) délicatesse exagérée, outrée; bégueulerie, f.

squeeze (skwîze), n., étreinte, compression, f.; (of the hand) serrement, m.

squeeze (skwîze), v.a., serrer; presser. To — into; comprimer **dans**, faire entrer de force **dans**. To — out; exprimer. To — out of; (money) extorquer **à**, faire cracher **à**. To — through; forcer à travers.

squeeze, v.n., serrer, presser. To — through; se forcer à travers. To — out of; sortir de . . . en pressant, en poussant.

squeez'ing, n., étreinte; compression, f.; (of the hand) serrement, m.

squelch, v.a., écraser, aplatir.

squib (skwibe), n., (fireworks) pétard, serpenteau, m.; (lampoon) satire personnelle, pasquinade, f.; pamphlet, m.

squill (skwil), n., (bot.) scille; (zoöl.) squille, f.

squint (skwi'n'te), adj., louche.

squint (skwi'n'te), n., regard louche, m.

squint (skwi'n'te), v.n., loucher, bigler.

squint'er, n., loucheur, bigle, m.

squint'-eyed (-aï'e'de), adj., louche.

squint'ing, n., action de loucher, f.; strabisme, m.

squint'ingly, adv., en louchant.

squire (skwaï'eur), n., seigneur de village; propriétaire foncier; (lord of a manor) châtelain, hobereau; écuyer; (of a lady) cavalier, chevalier, (in fables) sire, maître, m. The Squire of Dames; (play) L'ami des femmes (Dumas fils).

squire (skwaï'eur), v.a., servir d'écuyer **à**; (to a lady) servir de cavalier **à**; escorter.

squireen' (skwaïr'îne), n., hobereau, m.

squire'ly, adv., d'écuyer, en écuyer, en cavalier.

squire'ship, n., qualité d'écuyer, de cavalier, f.

squirm (skweurme), v.a.n., grimper; grimper **sur**; s'agiter, frétiller, se tortiller.

squir'rel (skwir'rèl), n., écureuil, m. — monkey; sagouin, m.

squirt (skweurte), n., seringue, f.; jet (d'eau), m.

squirt (skweurte), *v.a.*, seringuer, faire jaillir, lancer.

squirt, *v.n.*, jaillir.

stab, *n.*, coup ; coup mortel ; coup de poignard, coup d'épée, coup de couteau, *m.*

stab, *v.a.* and *n.*, poignarder ; percer ; frapper ; porter un coup de poignard **à**, un coup d'épée **à**, un coup mortel **à** ; donner un coup de couteau **à** ; faire une blessure mortelle **à**. To — to the heart ; *percer le cœur* **à**, *porter un coup mortel* **à**. To — eels ; *prendre des anguilles à la fouine.*

stab'ber, *n.*, assassin, *m.*

stab'bing, *n.*, coup d'épée, coup de poignard, *m.*

stabil'ity *ou* **sta'bleness** (sté-b'l'nèce), *n.*, stabilité ; solidité ; fixité ; (pers.) constance, fermeté, *f.*

sta'ble (sté-b'l), *adj.*, stable ; fixe ; solide ; (pers.) constant, ferme.

sta'ble (sté-b'l), *v.a.*, (cattle) établer ; (horses) loger.

sta'ble (sté-b'l), *n.*, (for horses) écurie ; (for cattle) étable, *f.*

sta'ble-boy (-boï) *ou* **sta'ble-man**, *n.*, valet, *ou* garçon d'écurie, *m.*

sta'ble-dung (-deugn'e), *n.*, fumier, *m.*

sta'ble-keep'er, *n.*, loueur de chevaux, *m.*

sta'ble-room, *n.*, place **dans** une écurie ; place **pour** des écuries, *f.*

sta'ble-yard (-yârde), *n.*, cour d'écurie, *f.*

sta'bling (sté-), *n.*, action d'établer, *f.* ; (for horses) écuries, (for cattle) étables, *f.pl.* — -stand ; (for hay, etc.) support de meule, *m.*

sta'bly (sté-), *adv.*, d'une manière stable.

stack, *n.*, (of chimneys) souche, *f.*, corps ; (of arms) faisceau, *m.* ; (of hay, etc.) meule ; (of wood) pile, *f.* ; (of houses) bloc, *m.*

stack, *v.a.*, (wood) empiler ; (hay, etc.) emmeuler, mettre en meule ; (arms) mettre en faisceau.

stack'-pipe, *n.*, tuyau de chute, *m.*

stack'-yard (-yârde), *n.*, cour de ferme, *f.*

stack'ing (stac-), *n.*, empilage, entassement ; (of hay) emmeulage, *m.*

stad'dle (stad'd'l), *n.*, (young tree) baliveau ; (support) appui ; (of hay) support, *m.*

stad'dle (stad'd'l), *v.a.*, laisser des baliveaux **dans** ; (hay) faire un support à une meule.

stad'dle-roof (-roufe), *n.*, toit de meule, *m.*

sta'dium (sté-), *n.*, (Greek antiq.) stade, *m.*

stadt'holder (-hôld'-), *n.*, stathouder, *m.*

stadt'holderate, *n.*, stathoudérat, *m.*

staff (stâf), *n.*, bâton ; (pilgrims) gourdin ; bourdon ; (milit.) état-major, *m.* ; (mus.) portée ; (nav.) bâton, mâtereau ; (crosier) crosse, *f.* ; (support) soutien, appui ; (of a chair) bâton, barreau ; (badge of office) bâton de commandement, *m.* ; (pole) perche, *f.* ; mât, (pers.) corps, personnel, *m.* ; (newspapers) rédaction ; (of a flag) hampe, *f.* Flag-— ; *bâton de pavillon, m.* Field-marshal's — ; *bâton de maréchal, m.* To be on the — ; *être attaché* **à**, ou *faire partie de, l'état-major* ; (at schools, colleges) *faire partie du personnel de*. Medical — ; (milit.) *service de santé, m.* Bread is the — of life ; *le pain est le soutien de la vie.*

staff'-officer, *n.*, officier d'état-major, *m.*

stag, *n.*, cerf, *m.*

stag'-beetle, *n.*, (ent.) cerf-volant, *m.*

stage (stédje), *n.*, (platform) estrade ; (thea.) scène, *f.* ; théâtre ; (degree of advance) degré, *m.*, période, phase, *f.* ; (relay) relais, *m.* ; étape, *f.* ; (of a press) établi, *m.* ; (for a mountebank) tréteaux, *m.pl.* ; (nav.) échafaud, plancher ; (arch.) échafaud, échafaudage, *m.* To come on, to go on the — ; *entrer en scène.* Front of the —; *avant-scène, m.* By short —s ; *à petites étapes, à petites journées.* By easy —s ; (fig.) *en grand seigneur.* At this — of the disease, of the busi-

ness, matter ; *au point où en est la maladie, au point où en sont les choses.* To go on the — (to turn actor) ; *se faire acteur.* To quit the — (the profession) ; *quitter le théâtre.* To go off the — ; *quitter la scène.*

stage *ou* **stage'-coach** (-côtshe), *n.*, diligence ; voiture publique, *f.*

stage'-box, *n.*, (thea.) loge d'avant-scène, *f.*

stage'-carpenter, *n.*, machiniste, *m.*

stage'-dancer, *n.*, baladin, *m.*, danseuse d'opéra, *f.*

stage'-directions (-di-rèk'-), *n.pl.*, indications scéniques, *f.pl.*

stage'-door, *n.*, entrée des acteurs, *f.*

stage'-effect, *n.*, effet scénique, coup de théâtre, *m.*

stage'-manager, *n.*, (thea.) régisseur de la scène, *m.*

stage'-play, *n.*, pièce de théâtre, *f.*

stage'-player (-plé-eur), *n.*, acteur, *m.*, actrice, *f.*, comédien, *m.*, comédienne, *f.*

stage'-properties, *n.pl.*, accessoires de théâtre, *m.pl.*

sta'ger (stédj'-), *n.*, routier, *m.* Old — ; *vieux routier, vieux retire, m.*

stag'-evil (stagh'-i-v'l), *n.*, (vet.) tétanos, *m.*

stag'gard, *n.*, cerf de quatre ans, *m.*

stag'ger (stag-gheur), *v.a.*, faire chanceler ; faire vaciller ; (to cause to waver) faire chanceler, faire fléchir, faire hésiter ; (to shock) (fig.) saisir, émouvoir, ébranler, étonner.

stag'ger (stag-gheur), *v.n.*, chanceler, vaciller ; (to fail) chanceler, faiblir, fléchir ; (to hesitate) hésiter, balancer. To — to one's feet ; *se lever en chancelant.* To — back ; *reculer en chancelant.* To — away ; *s'éloigner en chancelant.*

stag'gering (-gheur'-), *n.*, chancellement, *m.* ; hésitation, *f.*, ébranlement, étonnement, *m.*

stag'gering (-gheur'-), *adj.*, chancelant ; vacillant ; incertain ; saisissant. A — blow ; *un coup étourdissant, foudroyant.*

stag'geringly (-gheur'-), *adv.*, en chancelant ; (with hesitation) avec hésitation.

stag'gers (-gheurze), *n.*, (vet.) vertigo, *m.*

stag'-horn, *n.*, (bot.) herbe-aux-massues, *f.*

stag'-hound, *n.*, limier, *m.*

stag'-hunt *ou* **-hunting**, *n.*, chasse au cerf, *f.*

stag'nancy (stag'-), *n.*, stagnation, *f.*

stag'nant (stag'-), *adj.*, stagnant ; dormant ; croupissant, dans un état de stagnation ; (fig.) inactif, mort ; (of trade) nul (V. Hugo).

stag'nate (stag'-), *v.n.*, être stagnant ; être dans un état de stagnation ; croupir.

stagna'tion (stag-né-), *n.*, stagnation, *f.*

stag'-worm (-weurme), *n.*, (ent.) œstre des cerfs, *m.*

staid (stéde), *adj.*, rassis ; sérieux ; grave, posé.

staid'ly, *adv.*, gravement, posément ; sérieusement.

staid'ness (stéd'-), *n.*, gravité, *f.* ; sérieux ; caractère rassis, caractère posé, *m.*

stain (sté'n), *n.*, tache ; (colored spot) tache ; (disgrace) tache, flétrissure, souillure ; (shame) honte, *f.*, opprobre, *m.* Without a — on his character ; *sans atteinte à sa réputation.*

stain (sté'n), *v.a.*, tacher ; (fig.) tacher, souiller, flétrir, ternir, entacher ; (paint.) colorier, mettre en couleur, imprimer ; (dy.) teindre.

stained (sté'n'de), *adj.*, taché ; (fig.) souillé, terni, entaché ; (paint.) mis en couleur ; (dy.) teint ; (of glass) de couleur ; (of paper) peint, de couleur. — glass ; *vitraux peints, m.pl.*

stain'er (sté'n'-), *n.*, teinturier, *m.*

stain'less, *adj.*, sans tache.

stair, *n.*, degré, *m.* ; marche, *f.* —s, *pl.*, escalier, *m.sing.* One pair, two pairs of —s ; *au premier, au second.* Go up one pair of —s ; *montez un étage.* Back— ; *escalier de service, m.* To be up —s ; *être en haut.* To be down —s ; *être*

en bas. Below —s; *dans la cuisine, à l'office.*
Above —s; *dans le salon.* Flight of —s; *escalier ;*
étage, m. To go up —s; *monter l'escalier, ou les*
escaliers. To come down —s; *descendre l'esca-*
lier, ou les escaliers. To fall down —s; *rouler en*
bas de l'escalier. To run, ou tumble, down the
—s; *dégringoler les escaliers.*

stair'-carpet, n., tapis d'escalier, m.

stair'-case (-kéce), n., cage d'escalier, f. ;
escalier, m. Back-—; *escalier de service, m.*
Private —; *escalier dérobé, m.* Winding —;
escalier en limaçon, m.

stair'-head (-hède), n., haut de l'escalier, m.

stair'-rod, n., tringle de marche d'escalier, f.

stake (stéke), v.a., (to wager) parier, gager ;
(to risk) hasarder, exposer, risquer, jouer, parier ;
(at play) jouer, mettre au jeu ; (to defend with
stakes) garnir de pieux ; (to pierce with a stake)
percer avec un pieu ; (to sharpen) faire une
pointe à un pieu. To — out ; *jalonner.*

stake, n., pieu ; poteau, piquet ; jalon ; (at
cards) enjeu, m., mise, f. ; (funeral pile) bûcher ;
(martyr's) poteau, m. To be at —; *y aller de,*
s'agir de ; être en jeu. My life is at —; *il y va*
de ma vie. To perish at the —; *mourir sur le*
bûcher. If the destinies of mankind were at —;
s'il y allait des destinées de l'humanité. There
are many interests at —; *il y a plus d'un intérêt*
en jeu. — holder ; *qui tient les enjeux.*

stal'der (stôl-), n., (for casks) porte-fût, m.

stale (stéle), adj., vieux, vieil, vieille ; (worn
out, trite) suranné ; vieilli, passé, usé ; (of bread)
rassis ; (of liquors) plat, éventé. —mate ; (chess)
pat, m. To draw —; *faire pat.*

stale, n., urine, f. ; (handle) long manche ;
(at chess) pat, m.

stale, v.n., (of animals) uriner.

stale'ness (stél'-), n., vieillesse ; (triteness)
état suranné, banalité, f. ; (of liquor) évent ; (of
bread) état rassis, m., dureté, f.

stal'ing (stél'-), n., (of animals) action d'uriner, f.

stal'ish, adj., un peu vieux.

stalk (stôke), n., tige ; (of a plant) tige, f. ;
(of a shoot) pied, m. ; (of a flower) queue, f., pédoncule ; (of a leaf) pétiole ; (of a quill) tuyau ;
(of a cabbage) trognon, m. ; (walk) démarche
fière, hautaine, f.

stalk (stôke), v.n., marcher fièrement ; (of
animals) se carrer, se prélasser, se pavaner ; (to
go behind a cover) aller à la dérobée ; (hunting)
se mettre à l'affût. To — over ; *arpenter, par-*
courir. She came—ing out ; *elle sortit marchant*
à pas comptés.

stalked (stôk'te), adj., à tige.

stalk'er (stôk'-), n., chasseur à l'affût, m.

stalk'ing (stôk'-), n., (hunt.) traque, chasse
à l'affût, f.

stalk'ing-horse (stôk'igne-), n., cheval factice, cheval d'abri ; (fig.) prétexte, masque, m.

stalk'y (stôk'-), adj., comme une tige ; dur.

stall (stôl), n., (church) stalle ; (for cattle)
étable ; (for horses) écurie, f. ; (in a stable) compartiment, m., case ; (shed) échoppe, f. ; (of a
butcher) étal ; (for the sale of things in the open
air) étalage, m. ; échoppe, f. ; (in theaters) fauteuil d'orchestre ; (in a market) boutique, f.

stall (stôl), v.a., établer ; mettre à l'étable.
To — off ; *déjouer, dépister ; repousser, éloigner.*

stall'age (stôl'édje), n., étalage, droit d'étaler,
d'emplacement, m.

stalled, adj., (used in compounds) à . . . stalle.
Four- — stable ; *écurie, ou étable, à quatre stalles.*

stall'-feed (-fîde), v.a., nourrir à l'étable, ou au
fourrage. —-fed ; *nourri à l'étable.*

stal'lion (stal'ieune), n., étalon, m.

stall'-keeper (-kîp'-), n., étalagiste, m.

stal'wart (stôl'-), adj., intrépide, vaillant ;
fort ; vigoureux, robuste.

sta'men (sté-), n., (stamens) (bot.) étamine, f.

sta'mened (sté-mè'n'de), adj., (bot.) staminé.

sta'min (sté-), n., (stuff) étamine, f.

stam'ina (sta-mi-na), n.pl., force vitale ; (fig.)
nerf, énergie, vigueur, m.

sta'min-maker (sté-min-mék'eur), n., étaminier, m.

stam'mer, v.a. and n., bégayer, balbutier.
To — through ; *balbutier.*

stam'merer, n., bègue, m., f. ; (stutterer)
(fig.) bredouilleur, m.

stam'mering, n., bégaiement, bégayement ;
balbutiement, bredouillement, m.

stam'mering, adj., qui bégaie ; qui balbutie ;
bègue.

stam'meringly, adv., en bégayant ; en balbutiant.

stamp, v.a., frapper du pied ; (to impress)
poinçonner, marquer, imprimer ; (to imprint)
empreindre, imprimer, graver ; (coin.) monnayer,
frapper ; (gold, silver) contrôler ; (coin.) estamper ; (paper, parchment) timbrer ; (metal.)
bocarder ; (goods) estampiller ; (letters) affranchir, mettre un timbre à ou **sur** ; (tickets) poinçonner ; (weights, etc.) étalonner ; (to complete) mettre le sceau à. On —ed paper ; *sur*
papier timbré. To — one's reputation ; *mettre*
le sceau à sa réputation. That —s him ; *cela*
montre ce qu'il est. His manners — him a gentleman ; *ses manières indiquent, ou révèlent, l'homme*
comme il faut. —ed with genius ; *marqué au*
coin, ou au sceau (V. Hugo), *du génie.* The company he keeps —s a man ; *on juge d'un homme*
par la société qu'il fréquente. He has had his
plate —ed ; *il a fait contrôler sa vaisselle.* To —
out ; (fire) *éteindre* ; (fig.) *étouffer, extirper, écra-*
ser, détruire. To — a letter ; *affranchir une*
lettre.

stamp, v.n., piétiner, trépigner, frapper du pied.

stamp, n., (instrument) estampe, f., coin,
poinçon, m. ; (impression) empreinte, marque,
f. ; (on gold, on silver) contrôle ; (on paper,
parchment) timbre ; (metal.) bocard ; (coin.)
coin, poinçon, m. ; (on goods) estampille, f. ;
(character) calibre, caractère, genre, m., trempe ;
(character of reputation) marque, empreinte, f.,
coin, sceau, cachet ; (of the foot) coup de pied,
piétinement, trépignement ; (postage-stamp)
timbre-poste ; (for pounding) pilon, m. Post-
office-— ; *timbre de la poste, m.* Postage-—;
timbre-poste. On receipt of —s ; *contre envoi*
de timbres-poste. To be of the right — ; *être*
marqué au bon coin. Men of that — are rare ;
les hommes de cette trempe, ou de ce calibre, sont
rares.

stamp'-act, n., loi sur le timbre, f.

stamp'-duty (-diou-ti), n., droit de timbre, m.

stamp'er, n., poinçon, m., estampe, f. ; pilon ;
(metal.) bocard ; (pers.) timbreur, m.

stamp'ing, n., action d'empreinte, d'imprimer, f. ; (of gold, of silver) contrôlage ; (of
paper, parchment) timbrage ; (coin.) monnayage ;
(metal.) bocardage, m. ; (with the feet) piétinement, trépignement, m.

stamp'ing-machine, n., poinçonneuse, f.

stamp'ing-mill, n., (metal.) bocard, m.

stamp'ing-press, n., presse à percussion, f.

stamp'-laws (-lôze), n.pl., lois sur le timbre,
f.pl.

stamp'-mill, n., (metal.) bocard, m.

stamp'-office, n., bureau de timbre ; bureau
de papier timbré, m.

stanch ou **staunch** (stâ'n'she), adj., (strong)
solide, fort ; (firm) ferme ; (zealous) zélé.

stanch (stâ'n'she), v.a., étancher ; arrêter.

stanch, v.n., s'arrêter.

stanch'er, n., personne qui étanche ; chose
qui étanche, f.

stanch'ing, n., étanchement, m.

stan'chion (stâ'n'sheune), n., étançon, m. ;
(nav.) épontille, f.

stanch'less, *adj.*, impossible à étancher ; (fig.) insatiable.

stanch'ness, staunch'ness, *n.*, solidité ; (fig.) fermeté, force, constance, *f.*, zèle, *m.*

stand, *v.n.*, (*preterit* and *past. part.*, Stood) être debout ; se tenir debout ; rester debout ; (to keep on one's legs) se soutenir ; (to place one-self) se placer, se mettre ; (to resist) résister à, faire force à ; (to be still on its foundation) être debout, se trouver, être ; (to be, to remain) se tenir, rester, demeurer, être ; (to be placed or situated) se trouver, être ; (to become erect, as the hair) se dresser ; (to stop) s'arrêter, arrêter, rester, demeurer, faire halte ; (to be stationary) rester stationnaire ; (to continue) durer ; sub-sister ; (to maintain a posture of defense) se défendre ; (to be placed with regard to order or rank) se trouver, être ; (to consist) consister ; (to maintain one's ground) se maintenir ; (to continue living) vivre ; (to offer one's self as a candidate) se présenter comme candidat, se porter candidat ; (to place one's self) se mettre, se tenir ; se placer ; (to stagnate) être stagnant ; (of liquids) reposer ; (to remain, to make delay) rester ; (to persevere) persévérer, persister ; (to adhere) s'attacher à, adhérer à ; (nav.) porter ; (milit.) faire halte ; (of cabs) stationner ; (at cards) s'y tenir ; (of color) être bon teint, ne pas passer. I stood gazing at the sun ; *j'étais occupé à contempler le soleil.* No human being ever stood in such a position ; *aucun être humain ne se trouva jamais,* ou *ne fut jamais placé, dans une telle position.* We — or fall by this bill ; *nous resterons debout ou nous tomberons avec le projet de loi.* I left him —ing at the garden-gate ; *je le laissai planté à la porte du jardin.* To — looking ; *rester à regarder.* To — firm ; *tenir ferme, tenir bon.* To — still ; *rester au repos, s'arrêter.* Trade is —ing still ; (com.) *le commerce ne va pas ; le commerce est nul* (V. Hugo). Prisoner at the bar, you — convicted of ; *accusé, le jury vient de vous déclarer coupable de.* To — up against ; *résister* à ; *tenir* **contre.** To — aside ; *se ranger* ; (aloof) *se tenir à l'écart.* To — back ; *reculer ; se tenir en arrière ; se tenir à l'écart.* — back ! (int.) *arrière !* To — by ; *se trouver à côté de ; assister à ; être auprès ;* (to support) *soutenir, défendre, assister ;* (to rest on for confirmation) *reposer* **sur** ; (to abide by) *s'en tenir à ;* (nav.) *se tenir près de ;* (to be ready) *être prêt, se tenir prêt.* To — by one's self ; *être tout seul.* To — close ; *se serrer.* — close ! *serrez-vous !* To — down ; *descendre.* To — for ; (to support) *soutenir ;* (to be in lieu of) *tenir lieu de, être à la place de ;* (to signify) *signifier, représenter ; être considéré comme ;* (nav.) *faire route* **pour** ; (to be a candidate) *se porter candidat* **pour,** *se mettre sur les rangs* (**pour**) ; *postuler* (*une charge*) ; (for rights, liberty) *se déclarer* **pour, en faveur de.** To — for nothing ; *ne compter pour rien.* To — at nothing ; *ne reculer devant rien ; ne s'arrêter à rien ; ne s'effrayer de rien.* To — fast ; *tenir ferme ; tenir bon.* To — forth ; *se mettre en avant ; s'avancer.* To — from ; *venir de.* To — good ; *être valide.* To — in, at ; *rentrer ;* (to cost) *revenir* **à,** *coûter ;* (nav.) *donner dedans.* To — in for ; *se diriger* **vers.** To — in fear of ; *craindre ; avoir peur de.* To — in any one's light ; *se tenir au jour de quelqu'un.* To — in the way ; *barrer le passage ; faire obstacle.* To — off ; *se tenir éloigné, se tenir à l'écart ;* (nav.) *porter au large ; passer au large ;* (nav.) *être à la hauteur de.* — off ! *au large !* To — on ; *se tenir* **sur,** (to rely on) *s'appuyer* **sur,** *compter* **sur,** *se baser* **sur.** To — on ceremony ; *faire des façons.* To — out ; *être en saillie, être en relief, être mis en relief ; ressortir, se dessiner ;* (to resist) *résister, tenir ferme ;* (nav.) *porter au large.* To — out from , *se distinguer* **parmi.** To — out against ; *tenir tête* **à,** *résister* **à,** *s'opposer*

à. To — out of the way ; *s'ôter du chemin, se garer.* — out of my light ; *ôtez-vous de mon jour.* To — over ; *être en suspens, attendu ;* (jur.) *être ajourné, être remis.* To — with ; *s'accorder* **avec.** To — still ; *se tenir tranquille.* To — to ; *persister* **dans** ; *s'appliquer* **à** ; *persévérer* **dans** ; (to abide by) *s'en tenir* **à,** *adhérer* **à,** *rester fidèle* **à.** To — out to sea ; *porter au large.* To — to it ; *s'y tenir.* To — together ; *se tenir ensemble, s'accorder.* To — up ; *se lever, se tenir debout.* To — up against ; *opposer ; s'attaquer* **à.** To — up for ; *se lever* **pour** ; *défendre ; soutenir ; prendre le parti* **de.** To — upon ; (to concern) *concerner, regarder ;* (to value) *estimer ; faire cas* **de** ; (to insist upon) *insister* **sur.** How does the price of wheat — ? *quel est le prix du blé ?* How do these things — ? *où en sont ces affaires ?* How do you — with him ? *quelle est votre position vis-à-vis de lui ? comment vous trouvez-vous placé à son égard ?* As matters — ; *au point où en sont les choses ; sur le pied où sont les choses ; dans l'état actuel des choses.* Let us see how the matter —s ; *voyons ce qui en est.* He asked himself how matters stood ; *il se demanda où il en était* (V. Hugo). It —s to reason ; *cela va sans dire ; la raison le veut ainsi.* It —s to reason that ; *la raison, ou le bon sens, dit que ; il est évident, il va sans dire que.* How do we — ? *où en sommes-nous ?* (at school) *quelles sont nos places ?* Were he to — for consul ; *dût-il se présenter au consulat,* ou *postuler pour la charge de consul.*

stand, *v.a.*, (to endure) endurer, essayer, souffrir, supporter, soutenir ; (to abide by) subir ; (to treat to) payer. To — fire ; *soutenir le feu.* To — the enemy's fire ; *essuyer le feu de l'ennemi.* To — cold ; *supporter le froid.* To — fatigue ; *soutenir la fatigue.* To — one's ground ; *défendre son terrain ; se maintenir sur son terrain.* To — it ; *le souffrir ; y tenir.* What are you going to — ? *qu'allez-vous nous payer ?* I will — you a drink ; *je vous paierai à boire.* To — the racket ; *payer les pots cassés.* To — the risk ; *courir le risque.* To — a joke ; *entendre raillerie.* To — the test ; *subir l'épreuve.* To — one's ground ; *tenir bon.* Not to — one's ground ; *céder.* To — water ; *résister à l'eau.* To — a fair chance ; *avoir une bonne chance.* To — a chance of succeeding ; *être en passe de réussir.* He will — no nonsense ; *il ne permet pas qu'on prenne des libertés avec lui.*

stand, *n.*, (halt) arrêt, *m.*, halte, pause ; (place) place, position, *f.* ; (stall) étalage, *m.* ; (act of opposing) résistance, *f.* ; (highest point) point culminant ; (young tree) jeune arbre, *m.* ; (platform) estrade, tribune, *f.* ; (race-stand) tribunes, *f.pl.* ; (of a telescope) affût ; (bonnet stand) champignon, *m.* ; (for vases, busts, etc.) socle ; (of rest for anything) dessous, pied, porte- . . . ; (tech.) support, *m.* ; (of cabs) place, station, *f.* ; (for umbrellas) porte-parapluie ; (for a lamp) dessous, pied, *m.* —still ; *arrêt, m.* To come to a —still ; *s'arrêter ; ne pouvoir plus avancer.* At a —still ; *arrêté, suspendu, inactif.* To come to a — ; *s'arrêter ; ne pouvoir plus avancer ;* (fig.) *ne savoir que faire ;* (of commerce) *être nul* (V. Hugo). To make a — ; *s'arrêter, faire halte.* To take one's — ; *prendre position ; se placer.* To take one's — upon ; *s'en tenir* **à.** To make a — against ; *se soulever* **contre** ; *résister* **à** ; *faire une levée* **contre.**

stand'ard, *n.*, étendard, drapeau ; (nav.) pavillon ; (of weights, measures) étalon, type ; (coin.) titre légal ; (bot.) étendard ; (tree) arbre en plein vent ; (regulator) régulateur ; (fig.) type, degré, modèle, régulateur, *m.* — of knowledge ; *degré de connaissances, d'instruction.*

stand'ard, *adj.*, qui sert de modèle ; (coin.) au titre ; (of books) classique ; (of weights, measures) qui sert d'étalon ; (of trees) en plein vent ; (of price) régulateur ; (fig.) régulateur.

stand'ard-bearer (-bèr'-), n., porte-étendard ; porte-drapeau, m.

stand'ing, adj., (established) établi ; de tous les jours ; (lasting) durable, solide ; (permanent) fixe, permanent ; (stagnant) stagnant, dormant ; (of colours) bon teint, solide ; (fixed) fixé, à demeure ; (not cut down) debout, sur pied ; (of rigging) dormant ; (fig.) constant, fixe, invariable. — rules ; règles fixes, f.pl. — account ; compte courant, m. Long- — account ; compte d'ancienne date, m. —-orders ; (parl.) règlement ; (mil.) cadre permanent, m. —-room ; place pour se tenir debout, f. — army ; armée permanente, f. — stones ; menhirs, pelvans (V. Hugo), cromlechs, m.pl. — dish ; plat de tous les jours ; plat de fondation, m. — joke ; plaisanterie reconnue, établie, f.

stand'ing, n., action de se tenir debout ; (continuance) durée, dane ; (station) place, f.; exercice, service, m.; (posture) pose, f.; (rank) position, place, f., rang ; (stall) étalage, m., boutique, f. Of long — ; d'ancienne date ; de vieille date ; ancien. — out ; résistance, f. There is no — out against him ; impossible de lui résister. An officer of twenty years — ; un officier de vingt années de service. A gentleman of high — ; un personnage de haut rang, ou haut placé.

stand'ish, n., écritoire, f.

stand'-point (-pôï'n'te), n., point d'arrêt, m.; base, f.; principe ; point de vue, m.

stand'-up (-eupe), adj., montant. — collar ; col droit, m. — fight ; combat en règle, m.

stan'za (stan-za), n., stance ; strophe, f.; couplet, m.

sta'ple (sté-p'l), n., (emporium) marché, entrepôt ; (of goods, commodities, etc.) produit principal, m., denrée principale, f.; (of trades) article principal, premier article ; (of wool, flax, etc.) brin, m.; (of cotton) soie ; (of land) qualité, f.; (loop of iron) crampon de fer, m.; (of a lock) gâche ; (nav.) boucle, f.; (fig.) objet principal, m.

sta'ple, adj., (established) établi, fixe ; (principal) principal ; (fit to be sold) marchand, de commerce.

star (stâr), n., étoile, f.; astre ; (pers.) astre, m., célébrité, f.; grand artiste ; (print.) astérisque, m.; étoile, f.; (decoration) crachat, m., décoration, croix, f. North- — ; Pole- — ; étoile du nord, étoile polaire, f. The seven —s ; les Pléiades, f.pl. —-of-Bethlehem ; (bot.) ornithogale, m.

star (stâr), v.a., étoiler ; parsemer d'étoiles ; parsemer. v.n., briller (au premier rang).

star'board (stâr'bôrde), n., tribord, m.

star'board, adj., de tribord.

star'board, adv., tribord. Hard a — ! tribord tout !

starch (stârtshe), n., amidon ; empois, m. ; (fig.) raideur, f. —-hyacinth ; (bot.) ail-des-chiens, m. —-corn ; (bot.) épeautre, f. —-sugar ; (tech. chem.) glucose, glycose, f.

starch (stârtshe), v.a., empeser.

star'-chamber (-tshé'm-), n., chambre étoilée, f.

starched (stârtsh'te), adj., empesé ; (fig.) empesé, raide, guindé.

starch'edness (stârtsh'èd'-), n., raideur, f.

starch'er, n., empeseur, m., empeseuse, f.

starch'-maker (-mék'-), n., amidonnier, m.

starch'-works (-weurkse), n.pl., amidonnerie, f.sing.

starch'y, adj., empesé ; (fig.) empesé, guindé.

stare (stère), n., regard fixe ; regard ébahi ; (orni.) étourneau, m.

stare, v.a. and n., regarder fixement ; (astonished) ouvrir de grands yeux ; (to be prominent) avancer, s'avancer. To — at ; regarder fixement, regarder d'un air ébahi ; contempler ; considérer ; fixer ses regards **sur** ; ouvrir de

grands yeux **à**. To — any one in the face ; regarder quelqu'un en face ; (of things) sauter aux yeux à quelqu'un ; crever les yeux à quelqu'un. To — any one out ; faire baisser les yeux à quelqu'un ; faire perdre contenance **à**. To — right in the face ; regarder dans le blanc des yeux. To — out ; (intrans.) se montrer, se trahir. To — hard at ; regarder fixement, dévisager. Ruin —s him in the face ; la ruine est à sa porte, ou le menace de près.

star'fish, n., (zoöl.) astérie, étoile de mer, f.

star'flower (-floueur), n., (bot.) ornithogale, m.

star'-gazer (-ghéz'-), n., astrologue, m.

star'-gazing (-ghéz'-), n., astrologie, f. To be always — ; (fig.) être toujours dans les nuages.

star'ing (stèr'-), n., action de regarder fixement, f.

star'ing, adj., qui regarde fixement ; (of things, colors) voyant, tranchant ; (of stuffs) à grande ramages, aux couleurs éclatantes.

star'ingly, adv., fixement ; entre les deux yeux.

stark (stârke), adv., tout, tout à fait ; entièrement. — naked ; tout nu ; nu comme la main, comme un ver.

stark (stârke), adj., vrai, pur, franc ; (strong) fort ; (stiff) raide. — staring mad ; fou à lier.

star'less (stâr-), adj. sans étoiles.

star'light (-laïte), n., lumière ou clarté, des étoiles, lumière stellaire, f.

star'like (-laïke), adj., qui ressemble à une étoile ; étoilé ; brillant.

star'ling (stâr-), n., (orni.) étourneau, sansonnet ; (of a bridge) avant-bec, brise-glace, m.

star'lit (-lite), adj., étoilé.

star'-paved (-pév'de), adj., parsemé d'étoiles ; étoilé.

starred (stâr'de), adj., étoilé ; parsemé d'étoiles. Ill- — ; né sous une mauvaise étoile ; voué au malheur.

star'ry (stâr'-), adj., étoilé ; (fig.) étincelant, brillant.

star'-thistle, n., chausse-trappe, f.

start (stârte), v.n., tressaillir (with, **de** ; at, **à**) ; (to set out) partir, se mettre en route ; (of persons, horses, etc., racing) partir ; (to begin) commencer, débuter ; (of a plank) se disjoindre ; (of horses) être ombrageux. To — horses ; donner le signal du départ. To — aside ; se jeter de côté ; faire un écart, s'écarter. To — back ; se jeter en arrière ; reculer ; faire un écart en arrière (V. Hugo). To — from ; partir **de** ; (to get up from) se lever précipitamment **de**. To — off ; partir. To — out ; se jeter dehors ; sortir précipitamment. To — out of ; sortir **de**. To — out of one's sleep ; se réveiller en sursaut. To — up ; se lever précipitamment, se dresser ; (fig.) naître, surgir. To — again ; se lancer de nouveau ; se relancer dans les affaires ; rentrer aux affaires.

start, v.a., (to alarm) alarmer ; (to rouse) lever ; (of game) faire lever, débucher ; (to send off) faire partir ; (a person) lancer dans le monde, ou dans les affaires ; (to invent) inventer, découvrir ; (to establish) établir ; (to bring into notice) faire naître ; soulever, mettre en avant ; (question) soulever ; (opinion) émettre, avancer ; (machinery) mettre en marche ; (a bone) déboîter ; (to broach a cask) défoncer.

start (stârte), n., tressaillement ; (spring) saut, bond ; (sally, sudden fit) élan ; (a swerving from) écart ; (first motion) premier pas, premier mouvement ; (beginning) commencement, début ; (departure) départ ; (advance on) avance **sur**, m. False — ; faux départ, m. By fits and —s ; à bâtons rompus, par boutades ; par sauts et par bonds. To give a — ; faire un soubresaut. To give a — ; (in life) lancer, pousser. To get the — ; prendre les devants. To get the — of ;

prendre les devants **sur**; devancer. To wake with a —; se réveiller en sursaut.

start′er, n., personne qui tressaille; (of a question, etc.) personne qui soulève, qui met en avant, f.; (founder) fondateur, inventeur, auteur; (dog) chien qui lève le gibier; (at races) starter, m.

start′ing, n., tressaillement; mouvement subit, élan; (departure) départ; (beginning) commencement, début, m.; (of engines) mise en train, mise en marche, f.

start′ingly, adv., par élans; (fig.) par boutades, à bâtons rompus.

start′ing-point, n., point de départ, m.

start′ing-post (-pôste), n., poteau de départ, m.; barrière, f.

star′tle (stär-t'l), n., alarme, f.; tressaillement · saisissement; (fig.) effroi, m.

star′tle (stär-t'l), v.n., tressaillir; frémir.

star′tle, v.a., faire tressaillir; effrayer; faire frémir; faire peur à.

star′tling, adj., effrayant; étonnant, foudroyant, étourdissant, saisissant.

starva′tion, n., inanition; faim, f.; besoin, dénûment, m.

starve (stärve), v.a., faire mourir de faim; affamer; réduire par la faim. To — with cold; faire mourir de froid. To — to death; faire, ou laisser, mourir de faim. To — out; réduire, ou vaincre, par la faim.

starve, v.n., mourir de faim. To — with cold; mourir de froid. To — to death; mourir de faim; (fig.) languir.

starve′ling, n., animal affamé, m.; (plant) plante affamée, f.; (pers.) affamé, meurt-de-faim, famélique, m.f.

starv′ing (stärv-'), adj., affamé; famélique, mourant de faim, qui meurt de faim.

star′wort (-weurte), n., (bot.) aster, m.

state (stéte), n., (condition) état, m., condition, situation, disposition, f.; (political body, government) Etat; (body of men united by profession) ordre; (rank) rang, m., classe; (pomp) pompe, grande cérémonie, parade, f., apparat, m.; (grandeur) grandeur, dignité, f.; (canopy) dais, m. —s-general; états généraux, m.pl. Bed of —; lit de parade, m. Chair of —; trône, m. Robes of —; habits de cérémonie, m.pl. Married —; vie conjugale, f. In —; en grande cérémonie. In a —; dans un état de. Lying in —; exposition sur un lit de parade, f. To lie in —; être exposé sur un lit de parade.

state, adj., d'état, d'apparat, de cour, d'honneur, de gala; (of dinners, etc.) officiel.

state, v.a., (to set) régler, fixer, arrêter; (to express) exposer, énoncer, déclarer, avancer, affirmer, rapporter, dire; (math.) poser; (an account) établir, dresser.

state′-apartments, n.pl., grands appartements; appartements de gala, m.pl.

state′-ball, n., grand bal officiel, de cour, m.

state′-cabin, n., grand salon, salon de premières, m.

state′-carriage, n., voiture de gala, f.

state′-church, n., église d'état, f.

state′craft (-crâfte), n., politique, f., ruses de la politique, f.pl.

state′-criminal, n., criminel politique, m.

stat′ed (stét'-), adj.part., exposé, réglé; fixé, établi, déterminé, certain.

stat′edly, adv., régulièrement.

state′less, adj., sans apparat, sans pompe.

state′liness, n., majesté, noblesse, grandeur, f.; caractère imposant, air imposant, m.; (dignity) dignité, f., (b.s.) faste, m., pompe, ostentation, f., grands airs, m.pl.

state′ly, adj., plein de grandeur; imposant; pompeux, grand; majestueux; (magnificent) magnifique, superbe; (elevated in sentiment) plein de dignité, noble, élevé; (b.s.) fastueux.

state′ly, adv., majestueusement, avec dignité.

state′ment, n., exposé; énoncé; compte rendu, récit, dire, rapport, m., assertion, déclaration, f.; (of an account) relevé, m.; (act of stating) exposition, f. Verbal —; rapport verbal, m. According to the — of; au dire de, ou à ce que dit.

state′-monger (-meu'gn'gheur), n., personne qui se mêle de politique, f.

state′-paper, n., document officiel, m.

state′-prison (-priz'z'n), n., prison d'Etat, f.

state′-prisoner (-priz'z'neur), n., prisonnier d'Etat, m.

state′-room, n., salle de réception; (nav.) cabine de luxe, f.

states′man (stéts'-), n., homme d'Etat, m.

states′manlike (-laïke), adj., d'homme d'Etat.

states′manship, n., science du gouvernement; connaissances de l'homme d'Etat, f.pl.; politique, f.

states′woman (stéts′woum'-), n., femme politique, f.

state′-trial (-traï-), n., procès politique, m.

stat′ic ou **stat′ical** (sta-), adj., de la statique.

stat′ics, n.pl., statique, f.sing.

sta′tion (stéo-), n., station; place, f.; (office) poste; (character) caractère; (rank) rang, m., position, condition; (railways) station, f., (chief one) embarcadère, débarcadère, m., gare, f. Fire —; caserne, f., ou poste, m., de sapeurs-pompiers. — in life; position sociale, f. Freight —; gare de marchandises, f. To take one's —; se placer, se porter.

sta′tion, v.a., placer; poser; poster; (mil.) caserner. To be —ed at; être caserné à; être en garnison à. To — sentries; poser des sentinelles.

sta′tional (sté-), adj., de station; (c. rel.) stationnale, f.

sta′tionary (sté-), adj., stationnaire; (of engines) fixe, à demeure.

sta′tioner (sté-), n., papetier; petit libraire, m. —s' hall; dépôt de la librairie, m. Entered at —s' hall; déposé à la librairie centrale.

sta′tionery (sté-), n., papeterie, f.; (com.) fournitures de bureau, f.pl. — case; papeterie, f.

sta′tion-house (-haouce), n., poste de police, m.

sta′tion-master (-mâs-), n., chef de gare, chef de station, m. Deputy —; sous-chef de gare, m.

sta′tion-staff (-stâfe), n., (survey.) jalon, m., perche d'arpenteur, f.; (rail.) personnel, m.

sta′tism, n., politique, f.

statis′tical ou **statis′tic**, adj., statistique.

statisti′cian (-tish'a'n), n., statisticien, m.

statis′tics, n., statistique, f.

stat′uary (stat'iou-), n., statuaire, sculpture, f.; (pers.) statuaire, m.

stat′ue (stat'iou), n., statue, f.

stat′ure (stat'iour), n., stature; taille, f.

sta′tus (sté-), n., position; condition, f.; rang, état, m.; position sociale, f.

stat′utable (stat'iou-ta-b'l), adj., statué, conforme aux statuts; (jur.) prévu par la loi.

stat′utably, adv., conformément aux statuts; conformément aux lois.

stat′ute (stat'ioute), n., statut, m.; loi, f. — of bankruptcy; déclaration de faillite, f. — book; bulletin des lois, m. — of limitation; loi de prescription, f. — mile; mille légal, m. — labor; (for repair of highways) corvée, f. — law; droit écrit, m.

stat′utory (stat'iou-), adj., établi par des statuts; établi par la loi; statutaire.

stave (stéve), n., (of a cask) douve; (mus.) portée, f.; (of a song) couplet; (of a psalm) verset, m. — wood; merrain, m.

stave, v.a., (preterit and past part., Stove, Staved) briser; crever; (a cask) défoncer. To — in; crever, briser, enfoncer. To — off; chasser, repousser, éloigner, avec un bâton; (fig.) repousser, écarter, tenir éloigné, (to defer) retarder, remettre. To — and tail; arrêter, suspendre le combat.

stay, v.n., (preterit and past part., Staid, Stayed) rester, demeurer; séjourner, s'arrêter; (to continue) continuer, rester; (to wait) attendre (of a horse) endurer. To — at; rester à, demeurer à. To — at any one's; rester, être, demeurer chez quelqu'un. To — away; s'éloigner, s'absenter. To — for; attendre. To — in; rester chez soi, à la maison; (at schools) être en retenue. To — up; veiller. To — up for; attendre. To — out (all night); découcher.

stay, v.a., (to stop) arrêter, retenir; (to restrain) réprimer, retenir, contenir; (to support) soutenir, fortifier; (to hinder) empêcher **de,** détourner **de;** (to prop up) étayer; (nav.) donner vent devant. To — one's stomach; étourdir la grosse faim.

stay, n., (abode) séjour, m.; visite; (stability) stabilité, f.; (support) soutien, appui; (arch., nav.) étai; (tech.) arrêt, m.; (carp.) entretoise, f.; (obstacle) obstacle; (mec.) support, m.; (a brace) bride, f. Main—; (nav.) grand étai; (fig.) principal soutien, m.

stay'-at-home, adj., casanier.

stay'er (stè-eur), n., soutien; appui, m.; (of a horse) qui endure, de longue haleine.

stay'lace, n., lacet, m.

stay'-maker (-mék'-), n., fabricant de corsets; corsetier, m., corsetière, f.

stays (stéze), n.pl., corset, m.sing., (more than one pair) corsets, m.pl.

stay'-sail (-sél) n., (nav.) voile d'étai, f.; foc, m.

stay'-supporter (-seup-pôrt'-), n., étançon, m.

stead (stède), n., lieu, m.; place; (fig.) utilité, f., profit, avantage, m. To stand in — of; tenir lieu **de.** In any one's —; au lieu de, ou à la place de, quelqu'un. In his —; à sa place. To stand in good — to; être très utile à; (fig.) être d'un grand secours à.

stead (stède), v.a., servir; rendre service à; être utile à; aider; tenir lieu **de,** remplacer; prendre la place **de.**

stead'fast (-fâste), adj., ferme; solide; (resolute) ferme, résolu; (constant) constant, fixe, stable.

stead'fastly, adv., fermement; avec constance, résolument.

stead'fastness, n., stabilité; fermeté; solidité; (fig.) constance, f.

stead'ily (stèd'-), adv., fermement; (without irregularity) posément, d'une manière rangée, posée; (without inconstancy) avec constance, avec persistance, avec fermeté; (resolutely) avec assurance, fermement, avec fermeté.

stead'iness, n., fermeté; (of conduct) conduite rangée; (constancy) constance; (resolution) assurance, fermeté, f.

stead'y, adj., ferme; assuré; sûr; (in conduct) rangé, posé; sérieux; (assiduous) assidu; (regular) régulier; (fastened) assujetti; (constant) constant, ferme; (of the wind) fait; (of the sea) étale. —! (of hoisting sails, etc.) restez tranquille! (nav.) doucement! (of steering) comme ça! (milit.) fixe! To have a — hand; avoir la main sûre. To keep —; ne pas bouger, rester en place; (fig.) ne pas faire de fredaines.

stead'y, v.a., affermir; assurer; (to fasten) assujétir, assujettir.

steak (stéke), n., (of pork) côtelette, f.; (beef-steak) bifteck, m.

steal (stîle), v.a., (preterit, Stole; past part., Stolen) voler, dérober, soustraire (from a person, à); (to abduct) enlever; (to gain, to win) gagner, séduire. To — one's self into; s'insinuer dans. To — a march on; gagner une marche sur; dérober une marche à. To — all hearts; gagner tous les cœurs. To — a glance; dérober un regard.

steal, v.n., voler. To — away; s'en aller à la

dérobée, furtivement; s'esquiver; se dérober. To — down; descendre à la dérobée, furtivement. To — from; se dérober à. To — in; entrer à la dérobée, furtivement, se glisser dans. To — into; se glisser furtivement dans. To — on; avancer insensiblement, lentement. To — out; sortir à la dérobée, furtivement. To — up; monter furtivement, à la dérobée. To — upon; surprendre; s'approcher doucement de.

steal'er, n., voleur, m., voleuse, f.

steal'ing, n., vol, m.

stealth (stèlth), n., vol, m. By —; à la dérobée; furtivement, en cachette.

stealth'ily, adv., à la dérobée; en cachette; furtivement.

stealth'y (stèlth'-), adj., fait à la dérobée; dérobé; furtif.

steam (stîme), n., vapeur; (of a little liquid) fumée, f. By —, ou by — power; à la vapeur. With its — on; en vapeur. With all its — on; à toute vapeur, à pleine vapeur. To put on —; mettre en vapeur, chauffer; (fig.) se trémousser, se presser; se mettre en train. The — is up; la machine est en pleine vapeur. To get up —; chauffer la vapeur, chauffer. To shut off the —; stopper; arrêter la machine.

steam (stîme), v.n., émettre de la vapeur; fumer. To — away; s'évaporer; (of a steamer) s'éloigner. To — back; (to go back) retourner; (to come back) revenir au port. To — down; descendre. To — in; entrer au port. To — off; s'éloigner. To — up; remonter.

steam, v.a., passer à la vapeur; (cook.) cuire à la vapeur.

steam'-boat (-bôte), n., bateau à vapeur, m.

steam'-boiler (-boïl'-), n., chaudière à vapeur, f.

steam'-carriage (-car'ridje), n., voiture à vapeur, f.

steam'-casing (-késs'-), n., chemise, f.

steam'-engine (-è'n'djine), n., machine à vapeur, f. Double-acting, single-acting —; machine à vapeur à double effet, à simple effet.

steam'er, n., bateau à vapeur; navire à vapeur; vapeur; steamer, m.; (cook.) marmite de Pepin, f.

steam'-gauge (-ghédje), n., manomètre, m.

steam'ing, n., navigation à la vapeur; (cook.) cuisson à la vapeur. adj., fumant. — hot; bouillant, fumant.

steam'-navigation (-vi-ghé-), n., navigation à la vapeur, f.

steam'-packet, n., paquebot à vapeur, m.

steam'-pipe (-païpe), n., tuyau à vapeur, tuyau de prise de vapeur, m. Waste —; tuyau de dégagement de la vapeur, m.

steam'-piston, n., piston de machine à vapeur, m.

steam'-roller, n., rouleau à vapeur, m.

steam'-ship, n., bâtiment à vapeur, m.

steam'-tight (-taïte), adj., imperméable à la vapeur, étanche.

steam'-tug (-teug), n., remorqueur à vapeur, m.

steam'-vessel (-vès's'l), n., bâtiment à vapeur, m.

steam'-whistle (-hwis's'l), n., sifflet à vapeur; sifflet d'alarme, m.

steed (stîde), n., coursier, m.

steel (stîle), n., acier; (phar.) fer, m.; (to sharpen knives on) fusil; (to strike a light on) briquet; (weapon) fer, m., épée, lame, f.; (hardness) fer, m. Heart of —; cœur de fer, m.

steel, adj., d'acier, de fer. —pen, plume d'acier; plume métallique, f.

steel, v.a., acérer; garnir d'acier; (to make obdurate) endurcir; (to arm) armer, fortifier, endurcir. To — one's heart against; s'endurcir, ou s'armer, le cœur contre.

steel'-clad, adj., revêtu d'acier.

steel'-engraver, n., graveur sur acier, m.

steel'-engraving, n., gravure sur acier, f.

steel'iness, n., dureté d'acier ; (fig.) dureté de fer, insensibilité, f.

steel'-pills, n.pl., pillules ferrugineuses, f.pl.

steel'-wire (-waïeur), n., fil d'acier, m.

steel'-works (-weurkse), n.pl., aciérie, f. sing.

steel'y, adj., d'acier ; (fig.) dur, de fer.

steel'yard ('-yârde), n., (mec.) romaine, f. ; (small one) peson, m.

steep (stîpe), adj., escarpé ; à pic ; (of stairs) raide. —-grass ; (bot.) grassette, f.

steep (stîpe), n., pente rapide, f. ; précipice, escarpement, m.

steep (stîpe), v.a., tremper ; (plants, drugs) infuser ; (of hemp) rouir ; (fig.) plonger dans ; abreuver de.

steep'ing, n., action de tremper, f.; trempage, m.

steep'ing-place, steep'ing-vat, n., (for flax, hemp) routoir, m.

stee'ple (stî'p'l), n., clocher, m.

stee'ple-chase (-tshéce), n., course au clocher, f. ; steeple-chase, m.

stee'pled (stîp'l'de), adj., à clocher.

steep'ly, adv., en pente rapide.

steep'ness, n., raideur ; pente rapide, f. ; escarpement, m.

steep'y, adj., escarpé, raide.

steer, n., bouvillon, jeune bœuf, m.

steer (stîre), v.a., (nav.) gouverner, diriger ; (fig.) conduire, guider.

steer (stîre), v.n., (nav.) gouverner ; manœuvrer ; (fig.) se conduire, se diriger, manœuvrer.

steer'age (stîr'èdje), n., timonerie, f. ; (in merchant ships) logement des matelots ; entrepont ; (fig.) gouvernement, m., conduite, f. — passenger ; passager de bord, de troisième classe, m.

steer'age-way, n., (nav.) vitesse, f., sillage, m., erre, f.

steer'er, steers'man, n., timonier, m.

steer'ing, n., gouvernement, m. ; direction, f.

steer'ing-wheel (-hwîle), n., roue du gouvernail, f. ; (of a tricycle) roue directrice, f.

steganog'raphy (stèg'a-), n., stéganographie, f.

stel'lar, adj., stellaire ; étoilé ; astral.

stel'late (stèl'-) ou **stel'lated** (-lét'-), adj., en étoile, étoilé ; (bot.) radié ; (min.) radié, rayonnant.

stel'liform, adj., en forme d'étoile, radié.

stel'lion (stèll'ieune), n., (zoöl.) stellion.

stem (stème), n., tige ; (of a flower) queue, f. ; pédoncule ; (of a leaf) pétiole ; (stock of a family) tronc, m., souche ; (branch of a family) branche, f., rejeton, m. ; (mus.) queue, f. ; (of a pen) tuyau, m. ; (of a glass) jambe ; (nav.) proue, étrave, f. ; avant, m. From — to stern ; de l'avant à l'arrière.

stem (stème), v.a., arrêter ; refouler ; (to resist) résister à, s'opposer à ; lutter contre. To — the tide ; aller contre la marée, refouler la marée.

stem'-leaf (-lîfe), n., feuille caulinaire, f.

stem'less, adj., sans tige.

stench (st'èn'she), n., mauvaise odeur ; odeur infecte ; puanteur, f. — trap ; valve contre les émanations, f.

sten'cil (stè'n'-), n., (plate of metal, cardboard, etc.) patron, poncis, m.

sten'cil, v.a., peindre, ou marquer, au patron ; poncer.

sten'ograph, v.a., sténographier.

stenog'rapher, n., sténographe, m.

stenograph'ic ou **stenograph'ical**, adj., sténographique.

stenog'raphy, n., sténographie, f.

stento'rian, adj., de stentor.

step (stèpe), v.n., faire un pas ; marcher pas à pas ; passer ; (to come) venir ; (into a carriage)

monter **dans** ; (out of) descendre **de**. To — short ; (mil.) raccourcir le pas. To — after ; courir **après** ; suivre. To — aside ; s'écarter, se ranger. To — back ; faire un pas en arrière, reculer ; rebrousser chemin. To — down ; descendre ; venir. Just — down to my house ; venez chez moi pour un instant. To — forward, ou forth ; faire un pas en avant ; s'avancer. To — in ; entrer ; entrer pour un instant ; faire une petite visite ; (fig.) intervenir. To — into ; entrer **dans** ; entrer dans . . . pour un instant. To — into an estate, a good place ; entrer en possession d'une terre ; entrer dans une bonne place. To — on ; marcher **sur**, fouler. To — out ; sortir ; sortir pour un instant ; (to quicken one's pace) allonger le pas. To — over ; traverser, franchir, enjamber. To — round ; faire le tour **de** ; (to go and see) passer **chez**. To — up ; monter. To — up to ; s'avancer **vers** ; s'approcher **de**.

step, v.a., mesurer en comptant les pas ; arpenter ; (nav.) fixer le pied **de** (un mât).

step (stèpe), n., pas ; (of stairs) degré, gradin, m., marche, f. ; (progression) progrès, acheminement, m. ; (gait) marche, démarche ; (measure) démarche, f., pas, m.; (of a capstan, a mast) carlingue, emplanture, f. ; (of a door) pas, seuil ; (of a ladder) échelon ; (of a carriage, a bicycle) marchepied; (of a shaft, a wheel) piédestal, m. pl., (ladder) marchepied, m. A good — ; un bon bout de chemin. Pair of —s ; échelle double, f. — by — ; graduellement ; pas à pas. By his, ou her, —; à son pas. —-ladder ; échelle double, f. To take a — ; faire un pas ; (fig.) faire une démarche ; prendre un parti. To keep — ; être au pas. A — in the right direction ; une bonne démarche. To take —s to ; prendre des mesures **pour**. Within a — of ; à deux pas **de**. A few — s off ; à deux pas d'ici. To retrace one's —s ; revenir sur ses pas ; rebrousser chemin. To tread in any one's foot—s ; aller sur les brisées de quelqu'un.

step'-board, n., banquette, f.

step'-brother (-breu*th*'eur), n., beau-frère, m.

step'-child (-tshaïlde), n., beau-fils, m., belle-fille, f.

step'-daughter (-dô-teur), n., belle-fille, f.

step'-father (-fâ-theur), n., beau-père, m.

step'-mother (-meu*th*'eur), n., belle-mère ; (b.s.) marâtre, f.

steppe (stèpe), n., (plain) steppe, m.f.

step'per (stèp'-), n., (man.) cheval qui a de l'action, m. Bad — ; sans action.

step'ping, n., marche, allure, f.

step'ping-stone (-stône), n., marchepied, m. ; (fig.) introduction, préparation, f.

steps, n., (leading up to house) perron, m.

step'-sister, n., belle-sœur, f.

step'-son (-seune), n., beau-fils, m.

stercora'ceous (steur-co-ré-sheusse), adj., stercoraire ; stercoral.

stere (stîre), n., (measure) stère, m.

stereograph'ic ou **stereograph'ical** (stèr'è-), adj., stéréographique.

stereograph'ically, adv., stéréographiquement.

stereog'raphy (stèr'è-), n., stéréographie, f.

stereomet'rical (stèr'è-), adj., stéréométrique.

stereom'etry (stèr'è-), n., stéréométrie, f.

stereotom'ical (stèr'è-), adj., stéréotomique.

stereot'omy (stèr'è-), n., stéréotomie, f.

ster'eotype (stèr'è-o-taïpe), n., cliché, m.

ster'eotype, adj., stéréotype ; cliché. — printing, — printing-office ; stéréotypie, f.

ster'eotype, v.a., clicher ; stéréotyper.

ster'eotype-plate, n., cliché, m.

ster'eotyper, n., clicheur, stéréotypeur, m.

ster'eotyping, n., clichage ; stéréotypage, m.

ster'ile (stèr'île), adj., stérile ; (bot.) stérile.

steril'ity, n., stérilité, f.

ster'ilize, v.a., stériliser.

ster′let (steur-lète), n., (ich.) sterlet, m.

ster′ling (steur-) ou **star′ling** (stâr-), n., (of a bridge) avant-bec, brise-glace, m.

ster′ling (steur-), adj., sterling ; (fig.) pur, vrai, de bon aloi.

stern (steurne), adj., sévère ; austère ; (harsh) dur, rigide ; (cross) rébarbatif ; (afflictive) rigoureux, rude.

stern (steurne), n., (nav.) poupe, f.; arrière, m.

stern′-chaser (-tshéss′-), n., (nav.) canon de retraite, m.

sterned (steurn′de), adj., à poupe.

stern′-frame, n., (nav.) arcasse, f.

stern′ly, adv., sévèrement ; austèrement.

stern′most, adj., le dernier. — ship ; vaisseau serre-file, m.

stern′ness, n., sévérité ; austérité ; rigidité ; dureté ; rigueur, f.

stern′-oar, n., aviron de gouverne, m. ; godille, f.

stern′post (-pôste), n., (nav.) étambot, m.

stern′-sheets, n.pl., arrière, m.

stern′-way, n., (nav.) culée, f.

stet (stète), v.n., (print.) bon.

stethom′eter (stèth′o-), n., stethomètre, m.

steth′oscope (-scôpe), n., stéthoscope, m.

stew (stiou), n., (of meat) étuvée, f., ragoût ; (of hare) civet, m.; (of rabbit) gibelotte ; (of fish) matelote ; (fruit) compote, f.; (fig.) embarras, m., venette, f.; trac, m. To be in a —; être sur le gril ; être sur les charbons ; avoir la venette, ou le trac.

stew (stiou), v.a., étuver ; faire un ragoût de ; (fruit) mettre en compote. To — in one's own juice ; cuire dans son jus.

stew, v.n., cuire à l'étuvée ; cuire en ragoût ; (fruit) cuire en compote ; (pers.) cuire dans sa peau.

stew′ard (stiou-), n., maître d'hôtel ; régisseur ; intendant ; (of a college) économe ; (of a ball) commissaire ; (nav.) commis aux vivres ; (in Scripture) dispensateur, m. —'s mate cambusier, m. —'s pantry ; office, cambuse, f.

stew′ardess, n., femme de chambre (de bord), f.

stew′ardship, n., intendance, f.; office de maître d'hôtel ; office de régisseur, d'intendant ; (in a college) économat, m. ; (fig.) gestion, administration, m. To give an account of one's — ; rendre compte de la gestion, de son administration, des affaires.

stewed (stioude), adj., étuvé, en ragoût ; en compote. — fowl ; fricassée de poulet, f. — pigeon ; pigeon en compote, m. — rabbit ; gibelotte de lapin, f. — pears ; compote de poires, f.

stew′pan, n., casserole, f.

stib′ial, adj., antimonial.

stib′iated (stib′i-ét′-), adj., (pharm.) stibié.

stick, n., bâton, m.; trique, canne, f. ; (for walking) (of a tree) tronc, m., tige ; (for peas, beans) rame, f. ; (for vines) échalas, m.; (fig.) (one who perseveres) celui qui s'attache à un parti ; (b.s.) lourdaud, maladroit ; (thrust with a pointed instrument) coup ; (of sealing-wax, chocolate, etc.) bâton, m.; (of vanilla) gousse, f. ; (of a fiddle) archet, m. ; (small stick) baguette, f. —s, pl., menu bois, bois sec, m. — peas ; pois ramés, m.pl. Blow with a — ; coup de bâton, ou de canne, m. To pick up —s ; ramasser du bois sec. To beat all to —s ; surpasser en tous points. To get hold of the wrong end of the — ; brider l'âne par la queue.

stick, v.a., (preterit and past part., Stuck) (to pierce) percer ; (with paste, etc.) coller, attacher ; (to fix in) fixer, planter ; (a sheep) saigner ; (peas) ramer. — no bills ; défense d'afficher. To — into ; piquer dans, enfoncer dans ; ficher dans. To — on ; fixer ; (with paste, etc.) coller, attacher ; afficher ; (to overcharge) surfaire. To — out ; faire ressortir, mettre en saillie. To — up ; dresser ; mettre droit ; mettre ; (to paste up)

coller, afficher. To — round with ; garnir tout autour de, armer de, hérisser de. Stuck-up people ; parvenus, m.pl., parvenues, f.pl. ; gens qui se donnent des airs, m.pl.

stick, v.n., (to adhere) se coller, coller, s'attacher, tenir, adhérer à ; (to remain) rester, demeurer ; (to get embedded) être engagé, pris, demeurer engagé, pris ; (to get embarrassed) s'embarrasser, s'empêtrer ; (to stop short) s'arrêter, rester court. To — in the mud ; être embourbé, s'embourber ; (fig.) s'arrêter court. To — at ; s'arrêter devant ; reculer devant ; hésiter devant, se faire scrupule de. To — by ; rester fidèle à ; soutenir ; s'en tenir à. To — close, fast ; s'attacher fortement ; adhérer fortement ; s'arrêter court, s'embarrasser ; rester pris ; rester engagé dans la boue, etc. To — close ; ne pas lâcher, ne pas quitter ; (to work) travailler d'arrache-pied. To — fast ; tenir bien, rester collé. To — on ; s'attacher ; se coller, tenir. To — it on ; saler, surfaire. To — out ; faire saillie ; ressortir ; bomber ; (not to give in) tenir bon, ferme, tenir toujours bon, ferme ; persister ; insister ; ne pas lâcher d'une semelle. To — to ; s'attacher à, ne pas quitter ; (to persevere in) persévérer dans, ne pas démordre de ; (to abide by) s'en tenir à ; (to be constant to) s'attacher à, rester fidèle à. To — up ; se dresser ; se redresser, être planté. To — up for ; prendre fait et cause pour, prendre le parti de (quelqu'un). The name will — to him ; le nom lui restera.

stick′iness, n., nature gluante ; viscosité ; ténacité, f.

stick′ing-plaster (-plâs-), n., taffetas d'Angleterre, m.

stic′kle (stik′l), v.n., prendre le parti de ; (to contend) se débattre ; se disputer ; batailler ; (to pass from one side to the other) flotter entre deux opinions. To — for ; insister pour avoir.

stic′kle-back (stik′l-), n., (ich.) épinoche, f.

stic′kler, n., (in a duel) second, témoin ; partisan ; (contender) disputeur obstiné, champion, formaliste, m. He is a great — for ; il tient beaucoup à. He is a great — for etiquette ; il est toujours à cheval sur l'étiquette.

stick′up, adj., droit, montant.

stick′y, adj., gluant, collant ; glutineux ; visqueux, poisseux, poissé.

stid′dy, n., enclume, f.

stiff, adj., raide ; rigide ; inflexible ; (not liquid) dur, ferme ; (constrained) raide, gêné, contraint ; (stubborn) opiniâtre, obstiné, rude, dur ; (strong) fort ; (of style) raide, guindé ; (from fatigue) courbaturé, engourdi ; (nav.) (of wind) carabiné. A — price ; un prix élevé. As — as a poker ; raide comme un bâton ; raide comme une barre de fer. To grow — ; devenir raide ; se raidir. — gale ; brise carabinée, f.

stiff′en, v.a., raidir ; (fig.) endurcir ; (to make torpid) engourdir ; (paste) durcir, rendre ferme ; (sauces) lier.

stiff′en, v.n., se raidir ; raidir ; (fig.) s'endurcir ; s'engourdir ; (of paste) durcir, devenir ferme ; (of sauces) se lier.

stiff′ener (stif′neur), n., (of boots) contrefort ; (of shoes) cambrillon ; (of a cravat) col, m.

stiff′ening (stif′nigne), n., raidissement ; (support) soutien, m.

stiff′ly, adv., avec raideur ; avec opiniâtreté ; obstinément ; inflexiblement ; fortement.

stiff′-neck, n., torticolis, m.

stiff′-necked (-′nèk′te), adj., raide ; au cou raide ; obstiné ; opiniâtre ; entêté.

stiff′ness, n., raideur, f.; engourdissement, m.; (of paste, liquids) consistance ; (constraint) raideur, gêne, contrainte ; (harshness) dureté ; (obstinacy) opiniâtreté, raideur, f.; (not natural) air guindé ; style guindé, m.

stiff'-starched (-stârt'sh'te), adj., empesé ; (fig.) raide, à cheval sur.

sti'fle (staï-f'l), v.a.n., étouffer ; suffoquer. To — a report ; étouffer un bruit. We are stifling here ; nous étouffons ici.

sti'fle (staï-f'l), n., rotule, f. ; (vet.) grasset ; (disease) vessigon du grasset, m.

sti'fle-joint, n., (vet.) grasset, m.

sti'fling (staï-), adj., étouffant ; suffocant. The heat is — ; la chaleur est accablante. It is — hot ! on étouffe !

sti'fling, n., suffocation, f.

stig'ma, n., (stigmas) (mark of infamy) stigmate, m. ; note d'infamie ; (fig.) tache, flétrissure, f.

stig'matize (-taïze), v.a., stigmatiser ; marquer d'un stigmate ; flétrir.

sti'lar (staï-), adj., de style de cadran solaire.

stile (staïl), n., (of hedges) barrière, f. ; échalier ; (of a dial) style, m., aiguille, f. Turn—; tourniquet, m.

stilet'to (sti-lèt'tô), n., stylet ; (for needlework) poinçon, m.

still, n., alambic, m.

still, adj., tranquille ; calme ; paisible ; (silent) silencieux, taciturne ; en repos ; immobile ; (of wine) non mousseux. — water ; eau dormante, f. — waters run deep ; (prov.) il n'y a pire eau que l'eau qui dort. A — tongue shows a wise head ; qui plus sait, plus se tait. Be —; restez tranquille. To be —; rester tranquille, rester en place ; ne pas bouger. To stand —; se tenir, ou rester, tranquille ; (stop) s'arrêter ; rester immobile ; (of commerce) être nul (V. Hugo).

still, adv., encore ; toujours ; (nevertheless) cependant, néanmoins, toutefois, malgré cela. — less ; encore moins ; à plus forte raison. — more ; encore plus ; à plus forte raison.

still, v.a., arrêter ; calmer ; apaiser.

still'born, adj., mort-né ; (fig.) avorté.

still'burn (-beurne), v.a., brûler (en distillant ou par la distillation).

still'house (-haouce), n., distillerie, f.

still'ing, n., apaisement ; (stand for casks) chantier, m.

still'-life (-laïfe), n., (paint.) nature morte, f.

still'ness, n., tranquillité, f. ; calme ; silence, repos, m. ; (taciturnity) taciturnité, f.

still'-room (-roume), n., distillerie, f., laboratoire, m.

still'y, adj., siencieuse ; calme.

stil'ly, adv., silencieusement.

stilt, n., échasse, f. ; (of a bridge) pilotis, pieu, m. To be on —s ; être monté sur des échasses.

stilt'-bird (-beurde), n., (orni.) grand pluvier, courlis, courlieu, arpenteur, m.

stilt'ed, adj., (fig.) (of style, manners) guindé ; ampoulé ; pompeux.

stim'ulant, stim'ulative (stim'iou-), n.adj., stimulant, m.

stim'ulate (stim'iou-), v.a., stimuler ; aiguillonner, piquer ; exciter.

stim'ulating (stim'iou-lét'-), adj., stimulant, excitant.

stimula'tion (-'iou-lé-), n., stimulation, f.

stim'ulus (-'iou-), n., stimulant ; aiguillon (med.) stimulus ; (bot.) dard, aiguillon, m.

sting (stigne), n., aiguillon ; dard, m. ; (thrust of a sting into the flesh) piqûre, f. ; (of conscience) remords ; (fig.) aiguillon, m., morsure ; (of an epigram) pointe, f. The —s of remorse ; les aiguillons du remords. The — is in the tail ; (prov.) à la queue gît le venin.

sting (stigne), v.a., (preterit and past part., Stung) piquer ; (fig.) piquer, fâcher, irriter ; navrer, déchirer. Stung with remorse ; bourrelé, tourmenté, de remords. Stung to the quick ; piqué au vif.

sting'er (stign'eur), n., chose qui pique, qui

blesse, qui irrite, f. ; (a blow) coup bien appliqué, m. He gave him a blow, a regular —; il lui appliqua un coup, mais un fameux.

stin'gily (sti'n'dji-), adv., chichement ; sordidement, mesquinement.

stin'giness (sti'n'dji-), n., mesquinerie ; ladrerie ; avarice, lésinerie, f.

sting'ing, n., piqûre, f. adj., piquant ; (of a blow) fameux, bien appliqué.

sting'less (stign'-), adj., sans aiguillon ; sans dard.

stin'gy (sti'n'dji), adj., avare ; mesquin ; ladre ; chiche ; pingre. A — old fellow ; un vieux crasseux. A — old woman ; une vieille avare.

stink (stign'ke), n., puanteur ; mauvaise odeur, odeur infecte, f. What a — there is here ! comme il sent mauvais ici !

stink (stign'ke), v.n., (preterit and past part., Stunk) puer ; sentir mauvais. To — of ; puer (le, la, les). He—s of wine ; il pue le vin. It —s in one's nostrils ; c'est écœurant. To — in the nostrils of ; puer au nez à.

stink'ard (stign'kârde), n., (mam.) puant ; (fig.) goujat, m.

stink'ing (stign'k'-), adj., puant.

stink'ing, n., puanteur, f.

stink'ingly (stign'k'-), adv., en puant.

stink'pot, n., (artil.) pot à feu, m.

stink'stone (-stône), n., (min.) pierre puante, f. ; calcaire puant, m.

stink'-trap, n., valve contre les émanations, f.

stint, n., (limit) borne, limite, restriction ; (portion) part, portion, f. Without — ; sans restriction, sans bornes ; à volonté, à discrétion.

stint, v.a., limiter ; borner ; restreindre ; (in food) compter les morceaux à ; (retrench) rogner. To — one's self ; se refuser le nécessaire. To — one's self of ; se priver de.

sti'pend (staï-), n., appointements, émoluments, m.pl. ; salaire, traitement, m.

stipen'diary (staï-), adj., salarié, appointé ; (b.s.) stipendié. — magistrate ; juge salarié, m.

stipen'diary (staï-), n., (a magistrate) magistrat à traitement fixe ; (b.s.) stipendié, stipendiaire, m.

stip'ple (stip'p'l), v.a., pointer ; pointiller.

stip'pling, n., (act of) pointillage ; (result of) pointillé, m.

stip'ulate (stip'iou-), v.n., stipuler que ; convenir de. To — for ; stipuler.

stipula'tion (stip'iou-lé-), n., contrat, m. ; convention ; (jur.) stipulation.

stip'ulator (stip'iou-lét'-), n., partie contractante ; partie stipulante, f.

stir (steur), n., remuement, remue-ménage ; mouvement, m. ; agitation, rumeur, f. ; bruit, (disturbance) tumulte, trouble, bruit, mouvement séditieux, m. There was a great — in the town ; toute la ville était en rumeur (V. Hugo).

stir (steur), v.a., remuer ; (to agitate) agiter ; (to incite) exciter, pousser ; irriter ; (to excite) exciter à ; (the fire) fourgonner, attiser, remuer ; pousser à. To — round ; tourner, remuer. To — up ; remuer ; (to incite) exciter, pousser à ; (to excite) exciter, irriter ; (to enliven) animer, réveiller. There is no air —ring ; il ne fait pas un souffle, ou une bouffée, de vent (E. Pouvillon). To — the fire ; attiser, fourgonner le feu.

stir, v.n., remuer, se remuer ; se mouvoir ; bouger. Do not — ; ne bougez pas. To — abroad, out ; bouger de chez soi, sortir de chez soi. To be —ring ; être debout, être levé ; être sur pied. He is not —ring yet ; il n'est pas encore levé ; il ne fait pas encore jour chez lui.

stir'rer (steur'-), n., (instigator) agitateur, instigateur, m.

stir'ring (steur'-), adj., remuant ; actif, agissant ; éclatant ; (of spectacles) émouvant.

stir′ring, n., agitation, f. In the — up; (raking up of) à remuer (V. Hugo).

stir′rup (stir-reupe) ou **stir′rup-iron** (-aïeur′n), n., étrier; (of a shoemaker) tire-pied, m.

stir′rup-cup, **stir′rup-glass**, n., coup de l'étrier, m.

stir′rup-leather (-lèth′-), n., étrivière, f.

stir′rup-oil (-oïl), n., huile de cotret, f.

stitch, n., point, m.; (in knitting) maille, f. — in the side; point de côté, m. To put a — to; faire un point à. Back— ; arrière-point. Cross— ; point croisé. Open-work — ; point à la turque, point à jour. A — in time saves nine ; (prov.) un point à temps en épargne cent.

stitch, v.a., piquer; coudre ; (books) brocher. To — up; coudre ; faire un point à.

stitch, v.a., piquer; coudre.

stitched (stitsh′te), adj., piqué; (of books) broché.

stitch′er, n., couseuse, f.; piqueur, m., piqueuse, f.; (of books) brocheur, m., brocheuse, f.

stitch′ing, n., arrière-point, m.; points, m.pl.; piqûre, f.; (of books) brochage, m.

sti′ver (staï-), n., (Dutch coin) stiver (10 centimes) ; (fig.) liard, sou, centime, m. Not to have a — ; n'avoir pas le sou, ou être pauvre comme un rat d'église, m.

stoat (stôte), n., (mam.) hermine d'été, f.

stoccade′ (stok′kéde), n., estocade, f.

stock, n., (race) souche, f., race, famille, f.; (of a tree) tronc, (store) fonds, approvisionnement, m., provision, réserve, f. ; (of wood, stone) bloc ; (cravat) col ; (at cards) talon, m. ; (bot.) girofiée ; (print.) fonte; (of firearms) monture, f., bois, m.; (handle) manche ; (of an anchor) jas; (of a tree) tronc, m.; (stupid person) bûche, f.; (hort.) sujet, m., ente, f.; (on a farm) bétail, m., bestiaux, m.pl.; (log) bûche, f.; (capital) capital, fonds, m., capitaux, m.pl.; (goods on hand) marchandises en magasin, f.pl.; (manu.) matériel, m., monture, f.; (center-bit) cintre, m., mèche anglaise, f.; (tech.) fût, m., souche, f.; (in book-keeping) capital, m. ; (fin.) fonds, fonds publics, m.pl., rentes, f.pl., effets, effets publics, m.pl.; (for shipbuilding) chantier, m.sing., cale de construction, f.sing.; (punishment) bloc, m.sing. — of plays; répertoire, m. Dead — ; (agri.) mobilier mort; matériel ; (com.) fonds de boutique, m. Live — ; (agri.) mobilier vif; bétail, m., bestiaux, m.pl. Rolling —; matériel roulant, m. Working — ; matériel, m. To take — ; faire l'inventaire des fonds en magasin. To take in — ; recevoir des marchandises. To lay in a — of ; faire une provision de. In — ; en magasin. On the —s; sur le chantier; (fig.) sur le métier. In the —s; (punishment) au bloc. — in trade ; marchandises disponibles, f.pl.; fonds de commerce, m. — on hand ; marchandises en magasin, f.pl.; approvisionnement, m. India — ; fonds de la compagnie des Indes. To put a ship on the —s ; mettre un bâtiment sur la cale.

stock, v.a., fournir de; pourvoir de ; monter de, en; approvisionner de ; (a farm) pourvoir de bétail ; (a country) peupler ; (a warren) peupler ; (a fish-pond) empoissonner ; (cards) rassembler ; (a hop) monter ; (the mind) meubler.

stockade′, n., (fort.) palissade f.; (of canals) estacade, f.

stockade′, v.a., (fort.) palissader, estacader.

stock′-account, n., compte de capital, m.

stock′-book (-bouke), n., livre de magasin, m.

stock′broker (-brô-), n., agent de change, m.

stock′-broking, n., profession d'agent de change, f. He has gone in for — ; il s'est fait agent de change.

stock′dove (-deuve), n., pigeon ramier, m.

stock′-exchange (-èks′tshé′n′dje), n., bourse (pour les fonds publics); compagnie des agents de change, f.

stock′fish, n., stockfisch, m.; morue séchée à l'air, f.

stock′holder (-hôld′-), n., rentier, m., rentière, f.; actionnaire, m.f.; détenteur de fonds publics, m.

stock′ing, n., bas, m. Silk-—s; bas de soie. To have a long — ; avoir du foin dans les bottes. Blue — ; bas bleu. Elastic — ; bas élastique.

stock′ing-frame, n., métier à bas, m.

stock′ing-stitch, n., tricot au crochet, m.

stock′ing-trade, n., bonneterie, f.

stock′jobber (-djob′-), n., agioteur, m.

stock′jobbing (-djob′-), n., agiotage, m.

stock′-loom (-loume), n., métier à bas, m.

stock′-piece, n., (thea.) pièce de répertoire, f.

stock′-still, adj., immobile.

stock′-taking, n., inventaire, m.

stock′y, adj., trapu.

stoic (stoïke), n., stoïcien, m., stoïcienne, f.

sto′ic ou **sto′ical** (stoïk′-), adj., stoïcien; (of things) stoïque.

sto′ically, adv., stoïquement.

sto′icism (stoï-ciz′m), n., stoïcisme, m.

stok′er (stô-), n., chauffeur, m.

stok′ing, n., chauffage, m.; chauffe, f.

stole (stôle), n., (ecc.) étole, f. Groom of the — ; premier gentilhomme de la chambre, m.

stol′en, adj.part., volé; dérobé. — looks, ou glances ; regards dérobés, m.pl. — joys are sweet ; (prov.) pain dérobé réveille l'appétit.

stol′id (stol′-), adj., lourd; stupide.

stolid′ity ou **stol′idness** (stol′-), n., pesanteur, stupidité, f.

stom′ach (steum′ake), n., estomac, ventre ; (appetite) appétit, m., faim, f. On an empty — ; à jeun. To turn one's — ; soulever le cœur. It goes against his — ; le cœur ne lui en dit pas. To stay any one's — ; apaiser la faim à quelqu'un.

stom′ach (steum′ake), v.a., se fâcher de ; s'estomaquer de ; (to brook) endurer, digérer, souffrir. I cannot — that; je ne peux pas digérer cela.

stom′ach-ache (-éke), n., mal à l'estomac, m.; douleur d'estomac, f.

stom′ached (steum′ak′te), adj., fâché; en colère ; irrité.

stom′acher (steum′a-keur), n., corsage lacé, devant de corsage, m.

stomach′ic (sto-mak′ike), n., stomachique, m.

stomach′ic, adj., stomachique.

stom′ach-pump (-peu′m′pe), n., (surg.) pompe stomacale, f.

stone (stône), n., pierre, f. ; (pebble) caillou; (of fruit) noyau ; (of grapes) pépin; (med.) calcul, m., pierre ; (of a mill) meule ; (gem) pierre précieuse, pierre, f.; (min.) grès; (weight) stone (kilog. 6·348), m. ; (fig.) pierre, f., rocher, m. Meteoric — ; aérolithe, m. — age; (geol.) âge de pierre, m. Precious —s ; pierres précieuses, pierreries, f.pl. Philosopher's — ; pierre philosophale. To leave no — unturned ; remuer ciel et terre ; employer le vert et le sec, mettre tout en œuvre (pour parvenir). Not to leave a — standing ; ne pas laisser pierre sur pierre. A heart of — ; un cœur de rocher, ou de pierre. He is of — ; rien ne le touche.

stone (stône), adj., de pierre ; de grès. — bottle ; bouteille de grès, f.

stone (stône), v.a., lapider ; assaillir, poursuivre à coups de pierres; (mas.) garnir de pierres, maçonner ; (to harden) endurcir; (fruit) vider ; (roads) empierrer, caillouter.

stone′-blind (-blaï′n′de), adj., complètement aveugle.

stone′-borer (-bôr′-), n., (zoöl.) lithophage, m.

stone′-bottle, n., cruchon, m.; bouteille de grès, f.

stone′-bridge, n., pont de pierre, m.

stone'-chat (-tshat'), *n.*, (orni.) traquet, *m.*

stone'-color, *n.*, couleur de pierre, *f.*

stone'-crop, *n.*, (bot.) orpin, *m.*

stone'-cutter (-keut'-), *n.*, tailleur de pierres, *m.*

stone'-cutting (-keut'-), *n.*, taille, *ou* coupe, des pierres, *f.*

stone'-dead, *adj.*, raide mort.

stone'-deaf, *adj.*, complètement sourd.

stone'-fruit (-froute), *n.*, fruit à noyau, *m.*

stone'-horse, *n.*, cheval entier, *m.*

stone'-jug, *n.*, pot, *m.*, *ou* cruche, *f.*, de grès.

stone'-mason (-mé-s'n), *n.*, maçon ; (for tombstones) marbrier, *m.*

stone'-pit *ou* **-quarry**, *n.*, carrière de pierre, *f.*

stone'-post, *n.*, borne, *f.*

stone's'-throw (-thrô), *n.*, jet de pierre, *m.* Within a —; *à un jet de pierre ; à deux pas.*

stone'-wagon, *n.*, fardier, *m.*

stone'-wall, *n.*, mur de pierre, *m.*

stone'-ware, *n.*, grès, *m.* ; poterie de terre, *f.*

stone'-work (-weurke), *n.*, ouvrage de maçonnerie, *m.* ; maçonnerie, *f.*

stone'-yard (-yârde), *n.*, chantier de pierre, *m.*

ston'iness, *n.*, nature pierreuse ; (fig.) dureté, insensibilité, *f.*

ston'ing, *n.*, lapidation ; (of roads, etc.) empierrement, caillloutage, *m.* ; chaussée ; partie empierrée, *f.* ; (of fruit) vidage, *m.*

ston'y (stō'n'i), *adj.*, de pierre ; (abounding in stones) pierreux ; (fig.) de rocher, dur, cruel, insensible ; (petrifying) pétrifiant. — **hearted**, *au cœur de pierre.*

stook, *n.*, (of corn) tas, *m.* ; meule de blé, *f.*, (containing 12 sheaves).

stook, *v.a.*, mettre en gerbes.

stool (stoule), *n.*, tabouret ; escabeau, *m.* ; sellette ; (med.) selle ; (hort.) plante mère, *f.* Foot — ; *tabouret*, *m.* Camp — ; *pliant*, *m.* Close — ; *chaise percée*, *f.* — of repentance ; *sellette*, *f.*

stoop (stoupe), *v.n.*, se pencher ; se baisser ; se courber ; (from age) se voûter ; (of birds) se poser ; (of birds of prey) s'abattre, fondre **sur** ; (fig.) s'abaisser ; s'incliner ; descendre ; se soumettre ; s'humilier ; s'avilir ; (to acknowledge inferiority) céder. To — down ; *se baisser.* Carthage —ed to Rome ; *Carthage se soumit à Rome.* She —s to conquer ; *elle s'abaisse pour vaincre.* To — to ; *se baisser*, *ou se courber*, **vers** ; (fig.) *s'abaisser* **jusqu'à.**

stoop, *v.a.*, pencher, incliner, baisser.

stoop (stoupe), *n.*, inclination ; (of birds of prey) action de s'abattre, de fondre ; (vessel) cruche, *f.* ; (fig.) abaissement, *m.* He has a slight — ; *il a le dos légèrement voûté.* To make a — at ; *fondre* **sur.**

stoop'ing (stoup'-), *adj.*, penché, courbé, qui se soumet. In a — posture ; *dans une posture courbée.*

stoop'ingly (stoup'-), *adv.*, en se baissant ; en se courbant ; en baissant la tête.

stop, *n.*, (halt) halte ; pause, *f.* ; (interruption) retard, *m.*, interruption, *f.* ; retardement ; (hindrance) obstacle, empêchement, *m.* ; (prohibition of sale) vente prohibée, *f.* ; (of an organ) jeu, registre ; (of a clock) détente, *f.* ; (of a lute) touche, *f.* ; (of a flute) trou ; (gram.) signe de ponctuation ; (nav., tech.) heurtoir, butoir, *m.* ; (of trains, vessels, etc.) arrêt, *m.* To put a — to ; *arrêter ; suspendre ; empêcher ; mettre fin* **à** ; *s'opposer* **à** ; *mettre un terme* **à**. Full — ; *point*, *m.* To come to a dead — ; *s'arrêter court*, *net.* Put the —s ; *ponctuez.*

stop, *v.a.*, arrêter ; suspendre ; (to hinder) empêcher, entraver, gêner ; (mus.) presser ; (gram.) ponctuer ; (a hole) boucher ; (the breath) couper ; (to intercept) intercepter, supprimer ; faire cours, interrompre ; (a tooth) plomber ; (wages) retenir. To — the wages of ; *retenir les*

gages **de.** To — payment ; *suspendre*, *cesser ses payements.* To — any one's salary ; *faire une retenue sur*, *ou retenir*, *les appointements de quelqu'un.* To — any one from ; *empêcher quelqu'un* **de.** To — up ; *boucher*, *fermer*, *condamner* ; (to obstruct) *obstruer ;* (a street) *encombrer*, *barrer.* — thief ! *au voleur !*

stop, *v.n.*, s'arrêter ; arrêter ; (nav.) parer ; (com.) cesser ses payements. — there (leave off) ; *restez-en là.* To — for any body ; *attendre quelqu'un.* To — up with any one ; *veiller quelqu'un.*

stop'-chain, *n.*, chaînette d'arrêt, *f.*

stop'-cock, *n.*, robinet d'arrêt, *m.*

stop'-gap, *n.*, bouche-trou, *m.*

stop'page (-pèdje), *n.*, interruption ; fermeture ; obstruction ; pause, halte, *f.* ; (of salary) retenue ; (of payment) suspension, cessation, *f.* ; (in the streets) embarras, encombrement, *m.* ; obstruction, *f.* ; (of work) chômage ; (of a train) arrêt, *m.* ; (of teeth) plombage, *m.* ; (in streets) stationnement, *m.*

stop'per, *n.*, (of a bottle) bouchon, *m.* ; (nav.) bosse, *f.* ; tampon, *m.*

stop'per, *v.a.*, boucher ; (nav.) bosser.

stop'ping, *n.*, (of teeth) matière à plomber, *f.* — up ; *fermeture*, *f.* ; (at night) *veillée*, *f.*

stop'-plank, *n.*, (carp.) poutrelle, *f.*

stop'ple (stop'p'l), *n.*, bouchon, *m.*

stop'-valve, *n.*, soupape d'arrêt, *f.*

stop'-watch (-wôtshe), *n.*, montre à arrêt, *f.*

stor'age (stôr'èdje), *n.*, magasinage, *m.*

store (stôre), *n.*, provision ; quantité ; abondance, *f.* ; approvisionnement, *m.* ; (warehouse) magasin, dépôt, *m.* ; boutique, *f.* ; arsenal ; (fig.) fonds, trésor, *m.* —s, *pl.*, matériel, *m.sing.* ; (milit., nav.) vivres, *m.pl.* ; munitions, *f.pl.* ; matériel de guerre, *m.* In — ; *en réserve.* To lay in a — of ; *faire une provision* **de.** What is in — for us ; *ce qui nous est réservé.* — is no sore ; *abondance de biens ne nuit pas.* To set — by ; *faire grand cas* **de** ; *attacher beaucoup de prix* **à.** To keep in — ; *tenir en réserve ; réserver ; avoir en réserve.*

store, *v.a.*, (with, **de**), pourvoir ; munir ; approvisionner ; (to warehouse) emmagasiner ; (fig.) (the mind) enrichir, orner ; meubler. To — up ; *amasser*, *accumuler.*

store'-house (-haouce), *n.*, magasin ; dépôt ; grenier public, *m.*

store'-keeper (-kîp'-), *n.*, garde-magasin ; magasinier ; (nav.) cambusier, garde-magasin, *m.* ; (dealer in) marchand, *m.*

stor'er, *n.*, personne qui amasse, *f.*

store'ship, *n.*, (nav.) gabare, *f.* ; transport, bâtiment de transport, *m.*

stor'ied (stō-rîde), *adj.*, historié ; á inscriptions ; rapporté par l'histoire ; à étage. A one-house ; *une maison à un seul étage.*

stork, *n.*, (orni.) cigogne, *f.*

stork's'-bill, *n.*, (bot.) bec-de-grue, *m.* ; herbe à Robert, *f.* ; géranium, *m.*

storm, *n.*, (on land) orage, *m.* ; (at sea) tempête, *f.* ; (milit.) assaut ; (fig.) orage, *m.* To take by — ; *prendre d'assaut.* — in a tea-cup ; *grand fracas à propos de rien*, ou *à propos de bottes*, *m.* A — is brewing ; *une tempête se dessine* (V. Hugo).

storm, *v.a.*, donner l'assaut **à** ; prendre d'assaut, attaquer.

storm, *v.n.*, faire de l'orage ; (pers.) tempêter, s'emporter.

storm'-beaten (-bît'n), *adj.*, battu par la tempête.

storm'-bell, *n.*, tocsin, *m.*

storm'ily, *adv.*, orageusement, tempétueusement.

storm'iness, *n.*, état orageux, *m.*

storm'ing, *n.*, (milit.) assaut, *m.* ; prise d'assaut, *f.* ; (fig.) violence, rage, *f.* —**-party** ; (milit.) *colonne d'assaut*, *f.*

storm'-jib (-djibe), n., (nav.) tourmentin, m.

storm'-signal, -drum, n., signal de tempête; cylindre de tempête, m.

storm'y, adj., orageux; à l'orage. — petrel; (orni.) pétrel, m.

sto'ry (stô-), n., histoire, f.; (tale) conte, m.; historiette, f.; (falsehood) conte, mensonge; (of a house) étage, m. As the — goes; à ce que dit l'histoire, comme dit la chanson. The best of the —; le plus beau de l'histoire. Always the old —; toujours la même chanson. That is quite another —; c'est une autre paire de manches. There is a — that; on raconte que. To tell stories (falsehoods); dire des mensonges. On the first, second, third —; au premier, au second, au troisième; ou au premier étage, etc.

'sto'ry-book (-bouke), n., livre de contes, m.

sto'ry-rod, n., (carp.) perche d'étage, f.

sto'ry-teller, n., (narrator) conteur, m., conteuse, f.; (liar) menteur, m.; menteuse, f.

stoup, n., cruche, f.; (for holy water) bénitier, m.

stout (staoute), n., bière brune, f.; porter, m.

stout (staoute), adj., (strong) vigoureux, fort; robuste; (brave) brave, courageux, vaillant; (resolute) ferme, décidé, résolu; (large) gros, fort, corpulent, qui a de l'embonpoint; (of things) vigoureux, fort, ferme, solide. — -built; trapu. —-hearted; vaillant, courageux, au cœur intrépide. To have a — heart; avoir du cœur. To grow —; engraisser; prendre de l'embonpoint.

stout'ly, adv., vigoureusement; courageusement, vaillamment; fortement; bravement, fermement; résolument; fort et ferme.

stout'ness, n., (strength) vigueur; (bulk) corpulence, f., embonpoint, m.; (boldness) intrépidité, bravoure; fermeté, résolution, f.

stove (stôve), n., poêle; (for washing, cookery) fourneau, calorifère, m.; (for the feet) chauffe-rette; (drying-room) étuve; (hort.) serre chaude, f. Hot air —; calorifère, m.

stove'-room (-roume), n., étuve, f.

stow (stô), v.a., arranger; placer; déposer; mettre; mettre en place; entasser; serrer; (nav.) arrimer. To — away; emmagasiner. — away; voyageur à fond de cale, m.

stow'age (stô-èdje), n., mise en place, f.; arrangement, magasinage; emmagasinage; (nav.) arrimage, m.

stra'bism (-biz'm), n., (med.) strabisme, m.

strad'dle (strad'd'l), v.a., enfourcher; être à califourchon sur.

strad'dle, v.n., écarter les jambes; marcher les jambes écartées.

strag'gle (strag'g'l), v.n., s'écarter; se détacher; errer; rôder; être écarté, être éloigné; (milit.) traîner.

strag'gler, n., rôdeur, m., rôdeuse, f.; retardataire, m.; (milit.) traînard; (ant.) vagabond, m.

strag'gling, adj., écarté; séparé; éloigné; égaré; (scattered) éparpillé; épars; irrégulier; (bot.) divariqué.

strag'glingly, adv., en traînard; à l'aventure; (of hours) de loin en loin; çà et là.

straight (stréte), adj., droit; (upright) droit, équitable, juste; de mœurs irréprochables. The — road; le droit chemin. — hair; cheveux plats, m.pl. To make —; dresser, rendre droit; (fig.) arranger. To make things —; arranger les choses. To make — again; redresser, réajuster. — as an arrow; droit comme un I. To let a person have it —; dire son fait à quelqu'un; n'y pas aller par quatre chemins avec.

straight, adv., droit; tout droit; (immediately) sur-le-champ, aussitôt, tout de suite, immédiatement; incontinent. — on; tout droit. To keep — on; aller tout droit. — forward; droit devant soi. — from the shoulder; (fig.)

nettement, carrément, sans tortiller. I tell you —; je vous dis nettement.

straight'en (stré-t'n), v.a., rendre droit; redresser.

straight'ener, n., redresseur, m.

straight'forward (-fôr-worde), adj., droit, loyal, franc.

straight'forwardly, adv., avec droiture, avec franchise, carrément, nettement.

straight'forwardness, n., droiture, loyauté; franchise, f.

straight'ly, adv., droit; en ligne droite.

straight'ness, n., ligne directe, (rectitude) droiture, f.

straight'way, adv., sur-le-champ; à l'instant; immédiatement, directement.

strain (stré'n), v.a., tendre trop; forcer; (to constrain) contraindre, forcer; (to sprain) se fouler; (to make tighter) serrer, resserrer; (animal) forcer, outrer; (liquids) filtrer, passer; (fig.) forcer, outrer; faire violence à. To — a point; excéder son pouvoir; faire une exception à. To — one's self; se forcer, se donner un effort. To — every nerve to; faire tous ses efforts possibles pour, se mettre en quatre pour, faire feu des quatre pieds; (fam.) suer sang et eau. To — out; exprimer, extraire. To — one's eyes; écarquiller les yeux (pour); (by reading) se gâter la vue (en lisant).

strain, v.n., s'efforcer; (of liquids) passer, filtrer. To — at; faire des efforts pour avaler. To — at a gnat and swallow a camel; s'arrêter à des vétilles et avaler de grosses bourdes, ou rejeter le moucheron et avaler le chameau. There is no —ing at a point; il ne force rien.

strain (stré'n), n., grand effort, m.; fatigue, f.; (stretching) tension, f.; (sprain) effort, m., entorse, foulure, f.; (style) style, caractère, m., manière, f.; (song) chant, m., (note) accords, accents, chants, m.pl.; (disposition) disposition naturelle, f.; (manner of speech) ton; (nav.) effort; (fig.) élan, essor, m.; (race) race, lignée, f. In a lower —; d'un ton plus bas. To speak of any one in lofty —s; parler de quelqu'un avec enthousiasme, avec exaltation.

strained, adj., (of language, style) forcé; pas naturel.

strain'er, n., passoire, f.; filtre, m.

strain'ing, n., tension excessive, f.; grand effort, m.; violence, exagération; (filtration) filtrage, m.; (of limbs) foulure, f. — after; grands efforts pour produire, m.pl.

strait (stréte), adj., étroit; serré; (strict) strict, rigide, rigoureux; (intimate) étroit, intime; (difficult) difficile, embarrassé, gêné; (straight) droit.

strait, n., (geog.) détroit, m.; (distress) gêne, difficulté, f.; embarras; (on land) défilé, m.; gorge, f. To be in great —s; être très gêné; être dans la gêne; être à bout de ressources.

strait'en, v.a., (narrow) rétrécir; (contract) resserrer; (tighten) tendre; (fig.) embarrasser, gêner. In —ed circumstances; gêné dans ses affaires; gêné; dans la gêne.

strait'laced (-lés'te), adj., lacé étroitement; (fig.) bégueule; prude; collet monté; raide; (constrained) raide, contraint; (strict) rigide, sévère.

strait'ly, adv., étroitement; (strictly) rigoureusement, strictement; (intimately) étroitement, intimement.

strait'ness, n., étroitesse, f.; (difficulty) embarras, m., gêne; (tightness) tension; (strictness) rigueur, f.; (scarcity) manque, besoin, m.

straits, n.pl., (geog.) détroit, m.sing.

strait'-waistcoat (-wést'côte) ou **strait'-jacket** (-djak'kète), n., camisole de force, f.

stram'ony, n., (bot.) pomme épineuse, f.

strand, n., rivage, m.; plage, grève, f.; (of a rope) toron, cordon, m.

strand, v.a., jeter à la côte; échouer.

strand, v.n., échouer. —**ed**; échoué; (fig.) ruiné, à bout de ressources.

strand'ing, n., échouement, échouage, m.

strange (stré'n'dje), adj., étrange ; singulier ; bizarre ; extraordinaire ; (unknown, foreign) étranger, inconnu. — to say ; chose étrange ! It is not — that ; il n'est pas étonnant que ; (wonder) on ne doit pas s'étonner si.

strange'ly, adv., étrangement ; singulièrement.

strange'ness, n., (singularity) singularité, étrangeté, bizarrerie ; (novelty) nouveauté, f.

stran'ger (stré'n'djeur), n., étranger, m., étrangère, f., inconnu ; (guest) hôte, m., hôtesse, f. I am a — to that ; je suis étranger à cela. To make a — of ; traiter en étranger. He is a — to me ; je ne le connais pas du tout ; il m'est inconnu. To become quite a —; devenir rare comme les beaux jours ; devenir bien rare. You are quite a —; on ne vous voit plus.

stran'gle (stra'gn'g'l), v.a., étrangler.

stran'gler, n., étrangleur, m.

stran'gles (stragn'g'l'ze), n.pl., (vet.) étranguillon, m.sing. ; (of horses) gourme, f.

stran'gling, n., étranglement, m. ; strangulation, f.

stran'gulated (stragn'ghiou-), adj., (surg.) étranglé.

strangula'tion (-ghiou-lé-), n., strangulation, f. ; (surg.) étranglement, m.

stran'gury (-ghiou-), n., strangurie, f.

strap, n., courroie, f. ; (of iron) lien, m., bande, f. ; (for trousers) sous-pied ; (of boots) tirant, m. ; (of a carriage window) courroie, bricole ; (of a stirrup) étrivière, f. Razor-—; cuir à rasoir, m. —oil ; huile de cotret, f. Chin-—; (mil.) jugulaire, f. Shoulder-—; patte, f.

strap, v.a., attacher avec une courroie ; boucler ; lier ; (a razor) repasser ; (to beat) donner les étrivières à.

strappa'do (-pé-dô), n., (ant.) estrapade, f.

strappa'do (-pé-dô), v.a., estrapader.

strap'per, n., gaillard bien découplé, grand gaillard, m.

strap'ping, adj., bien découplé, grand, bien bâti. A — woman ; une femme bien découplée.

strat'agem (-'a-djè'm), n., stratagème, m.

strate'gic (-î-djîke), adj., stratégique.

strat'egist, n., stratégiste, m.

strat'egy (-'è-dji), n., stratégie, f.

strat'ify (-'î-faïe), v.a., stratifier.

stratoc'racy, n., stratocratie, f.

stratog'raphy, n., stratographie, f.

stra'tum (stré-), n., (strata) couche, f.

straw (strô), n., paille, f. ; (fig.) fétu, m. adj., de paille. In the —; (animals) sur la litière. On the —; en couches. Not to be worth a —; ne pas valoir un fétu ; ne pas valoir un zeste. Not to care a — for ; se soucier comme d'un fétu de, comme de l'an quarante de. To pick —s ; enfiler des perles. Man of—; homme de paille, m.

straw'-bed ou **-mattress**, n., paillasse, f.

straw'berry, n., (fruit) fraise, f. ; (plant) fraisier, m.

straw'berry-tree (-trî), n., arbousier, m.

straw'-bonnet, n., chapeau de paille, m.

straw'-bottomed, adj., à fond de paille.

straw'-built (-bîlte), adj., fait de paille.

straw'-color (-keul'leur), n., couleur paille, f. ; paille, m.

straw'-colored (-keul'leurde), adj., paille, couleur paille.

straw'-cutter (-keut'-), n., hache-paille, m.

straw'-hat, n., chapeau de paille, m.

straw'-mat, n., paillasson, m.

straw'-platter, n., nattier, m.

straw'-stuffed (-steuf'te), adj., rembourré de paille.

straw'y (strô-i), adj., de paille, comme la paille.

stray, v.n., errer ; vaguer ; s'éloigner (de) ; s'écarter (de) ; s'égarer.

stray, adj., égaré ; (jur.) épave ; (fig.) (of thoughts) détaché ; exceptionnel, fortuit. — sheep ; brebis égarée, m.

stray, n., bête épave, f.

stray'er (stré-eur), n., personne qui erre, qui vague ; personne errante, égarée, f.

stray'ing (stré-igne), n., égarement, m.

streak (strîke), n., raie ; ligne ; (of light) bande, traînée, f. ; sillon, m. ; (variegation) panachure, bigarrure, f. ; (nav.) bordage, m.

streak (strîke), v.a., rayer, barioler, bigarrer, panacher.

streaked, adj., rayé (with, de) ; (variegated) bariolé, panaché, bigarré.

streak'y, adj., rayé ; (of meat) entrelardé. — bacon ; petit lard, lard maigre, m.

stream (strîme), n., courant ; (of a river) fil, courant ; (river) fleuve, cours d'eau, ruisseau, m., rivière, f. ; (fig.) cours ; (of light) jet, flot ; (of words) torrent, flux ; (of people) flot, m. Mountain—; torrent, m. Against the —; contre le courant. Down —; à vau l'eau. Up —; en amont. To go down —; aller en aval. To go up —; aller en amont.

stream (strîme), v.n., couler ; ruisseler ; (to issue in streaks) jaillir ; (of a flag, etc.) flotter. To — with ; ruisseler de.

stream'-anchor, n., ancre de touée, f.

stream'-cable, n., câble de touée, m.

stream'er, n., drapeau, m. ; bannière ; (nav.) banderole, f.

stream'ing (with), adj., ruisselant de.

stream'let, n., petit ruisseau ; filet d'eau, m.

street (strîte), n., rue ; (mil.) haie, f. The high —, Main —; la grande rue. He went down the high —; il prit la grand'rue (V. Hugo). By-—; rue écartée. In the open —; en pleine rue. —-organ ; orgue de Barbarie, m. To turn into the —; mettre sur le pavé. To walk the —s; courir les rues, battre le pavé. The —s are crowded ; il y a foule dans les rues.

street'-arab, n., gamin, voyou, enfant des rues, m.

street'-band, n., musiciens ambulants, m.pl.

street'-door (-dôre), n., porte sur la rue, porte d'entrée, f.

street'-lamp, n., réverbère, m.

street'-rob'bery, n., vol sur la voie publique, m.

street'-sweep'er, n., balayeur de rues, m.

street'-sweeping-machine, n., balayeuse, f.

street'-walker (-wôk'eur), n., coureuse, fille publique, f.

strength (strègn'th), n., force, f. ; (pers.) forces, f.pl. ; (of numbers) effectif, m. ; (of materials) résistance, solidité, f. With all my —; de toutes mes forces. On the — of ; sous l'influence de ; sur la foi de ; sur. By sheer —; de haute lutte ; à force de bras. To regain —; reprendre des forces, recouvrer ses forces.

strength'en (strègn'th'n), v.a., fortifier ; affermir ; raffermir ; renforcer ; (ant.) encourager.

strength'en, v.n., se fortifier ; s'affermir ; se raffermir, se renforcer.

strength'ener, n., contrefort, m. ; (med.) fortifiant, m.

strength'less (strègn'th'-), adj., sans force.

stren'uous (strè'n'iou-eusse), adj., zélé ; ferme ; ardent ; (bold) intrépide, courageux, vaillant, ardent ; (of things) vif, ardent, vigoureux.

stren'uously, adv., avec zèle ; ardemment ; intrépidement, courageusement, vaillamment, vigoureusement.

stren'uousness, n., zèle, m. ; ardeur ; vigueur ; activité, f.

stress, n., importance ; force, f. ; poids ; (gram.) accent prosodique ; accent tonique, accent, m. ; (of the weather) violence, f. ; (mec.)

effort, *m.* By — of weather ; *par le gros temps.* We were forced by — of weather to put back into port ; *le vent, la violence du vent, nous força de relâcher, de regagner le port.* To lay a — upon ; *s'appuyer* **sur** ; *insister* **sur**. To lay — on ; *attacher de l'importance* à ; *appuyer* **sur**.

stretch, *v.a.*, (to extend in a line) tendre, bander ; (to extend in breadth) étendre, étirer ; (to spread as wings) étendre, déployer ; (to strain) forcer ; (to enlarge, as gloves) élargir ; (fig.) exagérer, forcer, outrer ; (to relieve numbness) dégourdir. To — one's self out full length ; *s'étendre tout de son long.* To — one's self ; *s'étirer.* To — one's limbs ; *se dégourdir.* To — forth the hand ; *tendre, ou avancer, la main.* To — a point ; *forcer les choses ; faire une exception en* **faveur** *de.*

stretch, *v.n.*, s'étendre ; s'étirer ; se déployer ; (to become larger) s'élargir ; (of gloves) prêter ; (to become tense) se tendre ; (nav.) s'étendre ; (to exaggerate) exagérer, gasconner. To — from ; *s'étendre* **de**. To — over ; *s'étendre* **sur**. To — away to ; *s'étendre* **vers**. To — forth into ; *s'avancer* **dans** ; *s'allonger* **dans**.

stretch, *n.*, tension ; extension ; (force of body) force, vigueur, *f.* ; (strain) effort ; (widening) élargissement, *m.* ; (min.) direction ; (nav.) bordée ; (fig.) étendue, portée, *f.* At a — ; *d'un trait ; tout d'une haleine ; d'arrache-pied* ; (of a horse without stopping) *d'une traite* (V. Hugo). A — of imagination ; *un effort d'imagination.* On the — ; (of the mind) *tendu.* To put upon the — ; *forcer.*

stretch'er, *n.*, (arch.) carreau, *m.* ; (of a boat) barre de pied, *f.* ; traversin, *m.* ; (gloves) baguette ; (to carry a person on) civière, *f.*, brancard, *m.* ; (beam, bedstead) traverse ; (fig.) blague, *f.* — bearer ; *brancardier, m.*

stretch'ing, *n.*, tension, *f.* ; élargissement, *m.*

strew (strô), *v.a.*, répandre ; semer. To — with ; *parsemer* **de** ; *couvrir* **de** ; *joncher* **de** ; *disperser, éparpiller.*

strew'ing (strô'-), *n.*, jonchée, *f.*

stri'a (straï-a), *n.*, (*striæ*) strie, *f.* ; (arch.) cannelure, *f.*

stri'ate, **stri'ated** (straï-ét'-), *adj.*, strié.

stri'ature (straï-a-tioure), *n.*, striure, *f.*

stric'kle (strik'k'l), *n.*, racloire, radoire, *f.*

strict, *adj.*, (exact) exact, strict ; précis ; (precise) exprès, formel ; (rigorous) rigide, rigoureux, sévère, strict.

strict'ly, *adv.*, (exactly) exactement, strictement ; (rigorously) rigoureusement, sévèrement ; strictement ; formellement. — speaking ; *à la rigueur ; à vrai dire ; rigoureusement parlant ; à proprement parler.*

strict'ness, *n.*, (exactness) exactitude rigoureuse ; (rigor) rigueur, sévérité.

strict'ure, *n.*, (strikt'ieur), *n.*, (censure) remarque, observation critique, *f.* ; (med.) étranglement, *m.*

stride (straïde), *n.*, pas ; grand pas, *m.* ; enjambée, *f.* With rapid —s ; *à grands pas.* With giant —s ; *à pas de géant.* With one — ; *d'une enjambée.* To make rapid —s ; *avancer à grands pas.*

stride (straïde), *v.a.n.*, (*preterit*, Strode ; *past part.*, Stridden) marcher à grands pas ; à grandes enjambées ; (to straddle) se mettre à califourchon ; (a horse) enfourcher. To — over ; *enjamber.* To — along ; *marcher à grandes enjambées.*

stri'dent (straï-), *adj.*, strident ; perçant.

strife (straïfe), *n.*, lutte ; querelle, contestation ; dispute, *f.* ; (opposition) contraste, *m.*, guerre, *f.* To be at —; *être en contestation, en querelle.*

strike (straïke), *v.a.*, (*preterit* and *past part.*, Struck) frapper ; (to dash) jeter ; (coin.) frapper ; (to affect) frapper, saisir ; (to produce) produire ; (metal.) battre ; (a bargain) faire ; conclure ;

(a mast) abaisser ; (a flag) amener ; (ground) toucher ; atteindre ; (a measure) rader ; (a blow) porter ; assener ; (root) prendre ; (balance) établir ; prendre ; (a musical instrument) jouer **de**, toucher ; (a tent) lever, plier ; (of clocks, etc.) sonner ; (coin) frapper ; (to erase) rayer **de**. To — down ; *abattre, renverser, faire tomber.* To — in ; *enfoncer.* To — off ; *enlever ; retrancher* ; (to erase) *effacer, rayer, biffer* ; (print.) *tirer.* To — out ; *faire jaillir* ; (to erase) *effacer* **de**, *rayer* **de**, *biffer* ; (to devise) *former, imaginer, inventer, créer.* To — up ; *entonner ; commencer à jouer ; contracter.* To — any one in the face ; *frapper quelqu'un à la figure.* To — with astonishment ; *frapper d'étonnement.* To — blind ; *frapper de cécité, rendre aveugle.* To — with horror ; *frapper, ou saisir, d'horreur.* To — dead ; *frapper de mort.* To — dumb ; *rendre muet* ; (fig.) *interdire, réduire au silence.* The clock is striking nine ; *la pendule sonne neuf heures.* It — s me ; *il me semble ; j'ai l'idée,* ou *idée.* It did not — me that ; *il ne m'est pas venu à l'idée que.* To — the feet ; *battre la semelle.* To — a bargain ; *conclure un marché.* To — a rate ; *établir une taxe.* To — off the rolls ; (jur.) *rayer de la matricule ; rayer du tableau des avoués.* To — oil ; *forer un puits d'huile de pétrole* ; (fig. and fam.) *déterrer une mine d'or.* To — out a new line ; *inventer une nouvelle méthode ; entreprendre une nouvelle spécialité ; se frayer un nouveau chemin.* To — soundings ; *sonder une rivière, une côte,* etc. To — up acquaintance with ; *faire connaissance* **avec**. To — work ; *faire grève.* To — a light ; *battre le briquet ; allumer une allumette.* To — asunder ; *séparer, diviser ; fendre.* Struck all of a heap ; *atterré, abasourdi.* To be struck all of a heap ; *tomber des nues* ; (fam.) *tomber les quatre fers en l'air.* Without striking a blow ; *sans coup férir.*

strike, *v.n.*, frapper ; (to be stranded) toucher ; échouer ; (to lower a ship's flag) baisser pavillon, amener ; (of clocks, etc.) sonner ; (hort.) prendre racine, pousser ; (of workmen) faire grève, se mettre en grève. It has just struck five ; *cinq heures viennent de sonner.* To — while the iron is hot ; *battre le fer pendant qu'il est chaud.* To — against ; *frapper* **contre**, *donner* **contre**, *heurter* **contre**. To — at ; *tâcher de frapper, vouloir frapper* ; (fig.) *s'attaquer* **à**, *attenter* **à**. To — in ; *interrompre ; arriver tout à coup.* To — in with ; *se conformer* **à** ; (to join with) *se joindre* **à**, *s'unir* **à**. To — out ; *se lancer.* To — out into ; *se lancer* **dans** ; *se jeter* **dans**. To — up ; *commencer à jouer ; commencer à chanter.* To — home ; *frapper juste ; porter coup.* To — out for land ; *nager vers le rivage.*

strike, *n.*, radoire, racloire ; (geol.) inclinaison de couche ; (of workmen) grève, *f.* To be on —; *être en grève.* To go on —; *se mettre en grève.* On —; *en grève.*

strik'er (straïk'-), *n.*, frappeur ; (hammer) marteau ; (workman on strike) gréviste, *m.*

strik'ing, *adj.*, frappant ; remarquable ; imposant, surprenant ; (of color) marquant, tranchant ; (of clocks) sonnant, à sonnerie.

strik'ing, *n.*, frappement, *m.* ; (of clocks, etc.) sonnerie, *f.* — off, *ou* out ; *radiation, f.*

strik'ing-clock, *n.*, pendule à sonnerie, *f.*

strik'ingly, *adv.*, d'une manière frappante, remarquablement.

strik'ingness (straïk'ign'nèce), *n.*, caractère frappant, *m.* ; nature remarquable ; (of resemblance) exactitude, ressemblance frappante, *f.*

string, *n.*, ficelle ; corde, *f.* ; (of a purse, of shoes) cordon ; (of beads) fil, chapelet ; (of onions) chapelet, *m.* ; (of a bonnet, cap) bride, *f.*, ruban, *m.* ; (mus.) corde ; (of a bow) corde, *f.* ; (of the tongue) filet ; (of plants) filet, fil, *m.* ; fibre, *f.* ; (of meat, of leguminous plants) filandres, *f.pl.* ; (list) kyrielle, enfilade ; (series) file, suite, série, *f.* ;

enchaînement ; (fig.) fil, *m.*, tirade, *f.* To harp upon one — ; *chanter toujours la même antienne* ; ou *frapper toujours sur la même enclume.* To have two — s to one's bow ; *avoir deux cordes à son arc* ; ou *manger à plus d'un râtelier.*

string, *v.a.*, (*preterit* and *past part.*, Strung) garnir de ficelle ; munir de cordes ; (to strengthen) fortifier ; (mus.) accorder ; (beads) enfiler ; (leguminous plants) effiler ; (to make tense) bander, tendre. To — up ; *pendre.*

string'-board (-bôrde), *n.*, (of a staircase) limon intérieur, *m.*

string'-course (-côrse), *n.*, (arch.) cordon, *m.*

stringed (strign'de), *adj.*, à cordes.

strin'gent (stri'n'djè'n'te), *adj.*, (fig.) rigoureux, strict, sévère.

strin'gently, *adv.*, strictement, rigoureusement.

string'halt (-hôlte), *n.*, (vet.) éparvin sec, *m.*

string'less (strign'-), *adj.*, sans cordes.

string'-roller, string'-reel, *n.*, ficelier, *m.*

string'y (strign'i), *adj.*, filamenteux ; fibreux ; filandreux.

strip, *n.*, bande, *f.*, ruban ; (of land) morceau, coin, *m.*

strip, *v.a.*, dépouiller ; (to undress) déshabiller ; (to take off) se dépouiller **de** ; (a tree) écorcer ; (hemp, etc.) teiller ; (nav.) dégréer ; (to rob) dévaliser. To — of ; *dépouiller* **de**. To — from ; *enlever* **à** ; *ôter* **à**. To — off ; *enlever*, *ôter, arracher.*

strip, *v.n.*, se déshabiller.

stripe, *n.*, raie ; barre ; (long piece) bande, *f.*; (with a whip) coup de fouet, de cravache, *m.*; (weal) marque, empreinte, *f.*; (milit.) galon ; chevron ; (punishment) châtiment, *m.*

stripe, *v.a.*, rayer ; barrer.

striped (straïp'te), *adj.*, rayé ; à raies.

strip'ling (strip'-), *n.*, tout jeune homme ; adolescent ; (fam.) gamin, blanc-bec, *m.* He is a mere — ; *il est encore tout jeune ; ce n'est encore qu'un enfant, un blanc bec.*

strive (straïve), *v.n.*, (*preterit* and Strove ; *past part.*, Striven) s'efforcer **de**, tâcher **de** ; faire des efforts **pour** ; se donner du mal **pour** ; (to vie) le disputer **à**. To — against, with ; *lutter* **contre**, *lutter* **avec** ; *se disputer* **avec**, *rivaliser* **avec** ; *se débattre* **contre**. To — hard to ; *faire tous ses efforts* **pour**.

striv'ing, *n.*, lutte, *f.* ; efforts, *m.pl.*

striv'ingly, *adv.*, avec effort ; à l'envi.

stroke, *n.*, coup ; (dash) trait ; (of a brush) coup de pinceau ; (of a pen) trait de plume ; (of an oar) coup d'aviron, *m.* ; (in swimming) brasse, *f.*; (of a piston) coup, mouvement ; (effort) effort, *m.*; (touch) touche, *f.*, trait, coup, *m.* At a — ; *d'un coup, d'un trait.* On the — of two ; *sur le coup de deux heures.* Who has n't done a — of work ; *qui n'a pas fait œuvre de ses dix doigts.* — of paralysis ; *attaque de paralysie, f.* Returning — ; (physics) *choc en retour, m.* Master — ; *coup de maître, m.* Bold — ; *coup hardi, m.* Great — of business ; *grande affaire, f.* To pull a long — ; *nager de long.* To pull — ; *donner,* ou *régler, la nage.* Back— ; *coup de revers.* Down— ; (in writing) *jambage, plein, m.* Up— ; (in writing) *délié, m.* Straight— ; (in writing) *bâton, m.* Little — s fell great oaks ; (prov.) *petit à petit l'oiseau fait son nid ;* ou *peu à peu la vieille file sa quenouille.*

stroke (strôke), *v.a.*, passer la main **sur** ; caresser ; flatter avec la main ; frotter doucement. To — the wrong way ; *frotter à contre-poil, à rebrousse-poil.* To — any one the wrong way ; (fig.) *prendre quelqu'un à contre-poil.*

stroke'-engraving, *n.*, gravure au burin, *f.*

stroke'-oar (strôk'-), *n.*, (nav.) chef de nage, *m.*

strok'ing, *n.*, caresses, *f.pl.* ; action de caresser, *f.*

stroll (strôle), *n.*, promenade ; flânerie, *f.*,

tour, *m.* Will you come for a — ? *voulez-vous faire un tour (de promenade) ?*

stroll (about), *v.n.*, errer ; flâner ; se promener à l'aventure ; rôder ; courir le pays.

stroll'er (strôl'-), *n.*, coureur ; flâneur, *m.*, flâneuse, *f.*; (vagabond) vagabond ; (actor) comédien ambulant, *m.*, comédienne ambulante, *f.*

stroll'ing, *adj.*, qui erre ; de flâneur ; ambulant. — actor, ou player ; *comédien ambulant, m.*

strong (stro'gne), *adj.*, fort ; (robust) énergique, vigoureux, solide ; (gram.) fort ; (firm) ferme ; (ardent) ardent, chaud ; (of the memory) tenace ; (vehement) véhément, violent ; puissant, grand. — light ; *vive lumière, f.* To be — in the arm ; *avoir le bras fort.* To muster — ; *s'assembler en grand nombre.* To smell — of ; *avoir une forte odeur* **de**. An army a hundred thousand — ; *une armée forte de cent mille hommes.* With a — hand ; *avec énergie, énergiquement.*

strong'-backed (-bak'te), *adj.*, fort des reins, qui a les reins forts.

strong'-box, *n.*, coffre-fort, *m.*

strong'-fisted, *adj.*, qui a le poignet solide.

strong'-hand, *n.*, main vigoureuse ; (fig.) force, énergie.

strong'-handed, *adj.*, qui a les mains fortes.

strong'hold (-hôlde), *n.*, forte prise ; (mil.) place forte ; forteresse, *f.* ; fort, *m.*

strong'ly (stro'gn'li), *adv.*, fortement ; (firmly) fermement ; (vehemently) véhémentement.

strong'-minded (maï-), *adj.*, à esprit fort ; résolu.

strong'-room, *n.*, cave aux caisses, resserre, *f.*

strong'-voiced, *adj.*, à la voix forte.

strong'-set, *adj.*, solidement bâti.

strop, *n.*, cuir à repasser ; cuir à rasoir, *m.* ; (nav.) élingue, estrope, *f.* Razor— ; *cuir à rasoir.*

strop, *v.a.*, repasser sur le cuir.

strophe (strô-fi), *n.*, stance, strophe, *f.*

struc'tural (streuk'tiou-), *adj.*, de structure.

struc'ture (streuk't'ieur), *n.*, construction, structure ; (of verses) façon, *f.* ; (building) édifice, monument, *m.*, construction, *f.* ; (anat.) tissu, *m.*

strug'gle (streug-g'l), *n.*, lutte, *f.* ; violent effort, combat, *m.* — for existence ; (Darwin) *combat pour la vie, m.*

strug'gle, *v.n.*, lutter ; faire de violents efforts ; se débattre ; se démener ; lutter **contre** (with), ou **pour** (to).

strug'gler, *n.*, personne qui lutte, qui fait de violents efforts, qui se débat, *f.*

strug'gling, *n.*, lutte, *f.*; effort, *m.*

strum, *v.a.*, taper sur ; (mus.) massacrer.

stru'ma (strou-), *n.*, (bot.) renflement, *m.* ; (med.) scrofules ; (pop.) écrouelles, humeurs froides, *f.pl.*

stru'mous (strou-), *adj.*, (med.) scrofuleux.

strum'pet (streum'-), *n.*, prostituée, *f.*

strut (streute), *n.*, démarche fière, *f.* ; (carp.) étai, *m.*

strut (streute), *v.n.*, se pavaner ; se carrer.

strut'tingly, *adv.*, en se carrant ; en se pavanant.

strych'nia ou **strych'nine**, *n.*, strychnine, *f.*

stub (steube), *n.*, (of a tree) souche, *f.*; chicot, tronçon, *m.*

stub, *v.a.*, déraciner, arracher.

stub'ble (steub'b'l), *n.*, chaume, *m.* ; éteule, esteuble, *f.* — field ; *chaume, m.*

stub'bly, *adj.*, plein de chaumes ; (of the beard) buissonneux.

stub'born (steub'-), *adj.*, obstiné ; opiniâtre ; têtu ; entêté ; (inflexible) inflexible ; (stiff) raide, inflexible ; (of metals) réfractaire ; (constant) opiniâtre. — ass ; (fam.) *âne entêté, têtu, m.*

stub'bornly, *adv.*, obstinément ; opiniâtrement.

stub'bornness (steub'-), *n.*, opiniâtreté, *f.* ;

entêtement, *m.; * obstination; (inflexibility) inflexibilité; (stiffness) raideur, inflexibilité, *f.*

stub'by (steub'-), *adj.*, plein de chaume; plein d'éteule; (short and thick) gros et petit; (pers.) trapu, ramassé; (of stubby build, of a ship) ramassé; (of beards) hérissé, en brosse.

stuc'co (steuk'kô), *n.*, stuc, *m.*

stuc'co, *v.a.*, revêtir de stuc.

stuck, *adj.*, (over with) garni **de**. — up; *prétentieux; *(conceit) *suffisant.*

stud (steude), *n.*, clou, *m.; *(on harness) bossette, *f.; *(of a shirt) bouton de chemise; (carp.) montant; (ornamental knob) bouton, clou; (of horses) chevaux, *m.pl.; *écuries, *f.pl.* —-farm; *haras, m.*

stud, *v.a.*, garnir de clous, clouter; (fig.) semer **de**; parsemer **de**.

stud'-book (-bouke), *n.*, registre des chevaux de pur sang, *m.*

stud'ding-sail (steun's'l), *n.*,(nav.) bonnette, *f.*

stu'dent (stiou-), *n.*, étudiant, *m.*, élève, *m.f.;* personne studieuse, *f.* Law-—; *étudiant en droit.* Medical —; *étudiant en médecine.*

stud'-groom (-grou'm), *n.*, piqueur, *m.*

stud'horse, *n.*, étalon de haras, *m.*

stud'ied (steud'ide), *adj.*, (learned) savant, instruit; érudit; (of style) étudié, apprêté, recherché; (premeditated) prémédité, calculé.

stu'dio (stiou-diô), *n.*, atelier, *m.*

stu'dious (stiou-), *adj.*, studieux; adonné à l'étude; (diligent) diligent; (careful) soigneux; (deliberate) délibéré; (contemplative) contemplatif; (favorable to study) favorable à l'étude. — of: *adonné à l'étude* **de**; (attentive to) *attentif* **à**, *soigneux* **de**. To be — to; *s'étudier* **à**, *chercher* **à**; *travailler* **à**; *être empressé* **de**. He is very — to please; *il cherche, il s'étudie beaucoup à* plaire.

stu'diously, *adv.*, studieusement; (carefully) soigneusement; attentivement; avec empressement; (of style) avec affectation.

stu'diousness, *n.*, attachement à l'étude, *m.;* application, *f.*

stud'y (steud'i), *n.*, étude, *f.*; (attention) attention, *f.*, soin, *m.*, application, *f.; *(apartment) cabinet d'étude; cabinet, *m.; *(paint.) étude; (reverie) rêverie, méditation, *f.* To make it one's — to; *s'étudier* à, *chercher* à, *s'appliquer* à. To be in a brown —; *songer creux.* — table; *table de travail, f.*

stud'y, *v.a.*, étudier. To — one's comfort; *rechercher ses aises.* To — economy; *viser à l'économie.*

stud'y, *v.n.*, étudier; travailler; (to endeavor) s'étudier, chercher, s'appliquer, viser **à**; (to muse) méditer. To — hard; *travailler ferme,* piocher.

stuff (steufe), *n.*, (matter indefinitely) matière; (fabric) étoffe, *f.*, tissu; (manu.) stoff, *m.; *(materials) matériaux, *m.pl.*, étoffe, *f.; *(nav.) suif, doublage, *m.; *(essence) essence, *f.; *(mas.) mortier, *m.; *(rubbish) drogue, *f.*, fatras; (fig.) bois, *m.* Has she got the —? (is she rich?) *a-t-elle des monacos?* (fam.) (*est-elle riche?*). — ! bah! quelle *bêtise! laissez donc! allons donc!* What —! *quelles sottises!* Old —; *vieillerie, f.* Wretched —; *méchante drogue.* Nasty —; *saleté, cochonnerie, f.* Silly —; *des sottises; des sornettes.* That is all — and nonsense; *c'est de la bêtise! balivernes,* ou *histoire, que tout cela! niaiseries que tout cela!* He is of the — of which statesmen are made; *il est du bois dont on fait les hommes d'État.*

stuff (steufe), *v.a.*, remplir **de**; (cram) bourrer **de**; gorger **de**; farcir **de**; (a hole) boucher; (cook.) farcir; (dead animals) empailler; (furniture) rembourrer. To — in; *bourrer.* To — up; *bourrer;* (to crowd) *encombrer;* (a hole) *boucher;* (the nose) *enchifrener.* —ed up with

nonsense; *plein d'affectation.* My nose is —ed up; *je suis enchifrené* ou *je suis pris du nez.* To — out; *rembourrer.*

stuff, *v.n.*, se bourrer; se gorger.

stuff'er, *n.*, empailleur, *m.*

stuff'ing, *n.*, (material for) bourre; (cook.) farce, farcissure, *f.; *(act of) rembourrage; (of dead animals) empaillage, *m.; *(eating) mangeaille, *f.*

stuff'ing-box, *n.*, boîte à étoupe, *f.*

stuff'y, *adj.*, privé d'air, mal aéré; renfermé. To be —; *sentir le renfermé.*

stul'tify (steul-ti-faïe), *v.a.*, hébéter; abrutir; (jur.) (to render void) infirmer, annuler, rendre nul; (to neutralize) neutraliser. To — one's self; *se rendre ridicule; se dédire; se contredire.*

stum (steume), *n.*, moût; râpé, *m.*

stum (steune), *v.a.*, passer par le râpé; (with brimstone) soufrer.

stum'ble (steu'm'b'l), *n.*, faux pas, *m.; *(blunder) bévue, *f.*

stum'ble (steu'm'b'l), *v.n.*, trébucher; broncher; faire un faux pas; (to err) faillir; (of animals) broncher. To — upon; *rencontrer par hasard; tomber* **sur**; *trouver par hasard.*

stum'bling, *n.*, trébuchement, *m.; *(fig.) bronchement; faux pas.

stum'bling, *adj.*, qui bronche; qui fait des bévues.

stum'bling-block ou **stum'bling-stone**, *n.*, pierre d'achoppement, *f.; *écueil, *m.*

stump (steu'm'pe), *n.*, tronçon; (of a limb) moignon; (of a tooth) chicot; (of a cabbage) trognon; (of a pen) bout; (of a tree) tronçon, chicot, *m.; *(in drawing) estompe, *f. * *pl.* (at cricket) guichet, *m.* —s were drawn at . . . ; *on a enlevé les guichets* **à** . . . Stir your —s; (fam.) *alerte! remuez-vous, trémoussez-vous! * On the —; *en tournée;* (of M. C.'s) *haranguant ses constituants.*

stump (steu'm'pe), *v.a.*, (to lop) ne laisser qu'un tronçon **de**; (in drawing) estomper; (to take all from) mettre à sec; (to canvass) haranguer; (to puzzle) réduire au silence; (to nonplus) embarrasser, coller. To — out; *mettre à sec.* To — up; (pop.) *dégainer ses écus; rendre gorge;* (fam.) *abouler, cracher.*

stump'-orator (-or'a-teur), *n.*, orateur de carrefour, péroreur, *m.*

stump'y, *adj.*, plein de tronçons; (pers.) trapu.

stun (steune), *v.a.*, étourdir; (fig.) étourdir, ébouriffer, abasourdir.

stun'ning (steu'n'-), *adj.*, étourdissant, ébouriffant; (big, grand) fameux.

stunt (steu'n'te), *v.a.*, empêcher de croître; rendre rabougri, rabougrir.

stunt'ed, *adj.*, (of trees) rabougri; (pers.) atrophié, chétif. To become —; *se rabougrir.*

stunt'edness, *n.*, rabougrissement, *m.; *atrophie, *f.*

stupe (stioupe), *n.*, (pers.) (fam.) imbécile, *m.f.*, bête, *f.*

stupefac'tion, *n.*, stupéfaction, *f.; *étonnement, *m.*

stu'pefier (stiou-pè-faï-), *n.*, stupéfiant, *m.*

stu'pefy, *v.a.*, hébéter; abrutir; stupéfier; (to make torpid) engourdir.

stupen'dous (stiou-), *adj.*, étonnant; prodigieux, foudroyant; (fam.) épatant.

stupen'dously, *adv.*, prodigieusement; étonnamment.

stupen'dousness, *n.*, grandeur prodigieuse, *f.*

stu'pid (stiou-), *adj.*, stupide; sot; bête; engourdi; lourd. To become —; *devenir stupide; s'abêtir.* — thing; *stupidité, f.; *(pers.) *bêta, m.*, bête, *f.*

stupid'ity, *n.*, stupidité; bêtise; sottise, *f.*

stu'pidly, *adv.*, stupidement; sottement; bêtement.

stu'por (stiou-peur), *n.*, stupeur, *f.*

stur'dily (steur-), *adv.*, hardiment, fortement, vigoureusement.

stur'diness, *n.*, hardiesse, résolution; vigueur; force, *f.*

stur'dy (steur-), *adj.*, hardi; vigoureux; fort.

stur'dy (steur-), *n.*, (vet.) tournis, *m.*

stur'geon (steur-djeune), *n.*, esturgeon, *m.*

stut'ter, (steut'-), *v.a.n.* V. **stammer.**

stut'terer, *n.*, bègue, *m.f.*

stut'tering, *n.*, bégaiement, *m.*

stut'teringly, *adv.*, en bégayant; en balbutiant.

sty (staïe), *n.*, étable à cochons, *f.*

sty, *v.a.*, mettre dans une étable à cochons.

stye, *n.*, orgelet, *m.*

styg'ian (stidj'i-), *adj.*, du styx.

style (staïle), *n.*, style; genre, goût, *m.*; manière, *f.*; ton; (probe) (surg.) stylet; (bot.; of a dial; in chronology; graver) style; (of beauty) élégance, grâce, *f.*; (title) titre, nom, *m.*; (of a firm) raison sociale, *f.* In —; *comme il faut*; (of a thrashing) *d'importance.* In good —; *dans le bon genre; de bon goût.* In grand —; *dans le grand genre, en grand seigneur.* In bad —; *dans le mauvais genre, de mauvais goût.* To live in —; *avoir un train de maison.* The — in which they live; *le train qu'ils mènent.* To live in first-rate —; *avoir un grand train de maison, mener grand train.* To go on in fine —; *aller grand train.* He gave it me in fine —; *il m'en a dit d'une belle manière; il m'a arrangé d'une belle façon; il m'a tancé vertement.* She has no — about her; *elle n'a pas de ton.* His — is bad; *son style est mauvais, il n'a pas de style.* — is the man himself; *le style est l'homme* (Buffon).

style (staïle), *v.a.*, appeler; qualifier **de**; donner le titre de . . . à . . . To — one's self; *s'appeler; se faire appeler; se donner le titre de, se dire; s'intituler* (V. Hugo).

styl'ish (staï-), *adj.*, élégant; de bon ton; de haut ton; dans le bon genre; comme il faut; huppé, *f.*

styp'tic (stip-), *n.*, styptique, *m.*

styp'tic, *adj.*, (med.) styptique.

styptic'ity, *n.*, (med.) propriété styptique, *f.*

su'able, *adj.* poursuivable.

suave, *adj.*, suave.

suav'ity, *n.*, suavité, *f.*

subac'id (seub'-), *adj.*, acidule.

subac'rid (seub'-), *adj.*, un peu âcre.

sub'-agent (seub'é-djè'n't), *n.*, sous-agent, *m.*

sub'-almoner (seub'al-meu'n'-), *n.*, sous-aumônier, *m.*

subal'tern (seub'al-teurne), *adj.*, subalterne.

subal'tern, *n.*, subalterne; sous-lieutenant, *m.*

subalter'nate, *adj.*, successif, alternatif.

subalterna'tion (seub'al-teur-né-), *n.*, subalternité, subordination, sujétion, *f.*

subaquat'ic (seub'a-kwat'-), **suba'queous** (-é-), *adj.*, subaquatique.

subas'tral (seub'-), *adj.*, terrestre.

subceles'tial (seub-ci-lèst'-), *adj.*, terrestre.

sub-chant'er (-tshâ'n'teur), *n.*, sous-chantre, *m.*

sub-commis'sioner (seub-com'mish'-), *n.*, sous-commissaire, *m.*

sub-commit'tee (seub-), *n.*, sous-comité, *m.*

sub-contrac'tor (seub-co'n'trac-teur), *n.*, sous-entrepreneur, *m.*

subcos'tal (seub-), *adj.*, sous-costal.

sub-dea'con (seub-dî-k'n), *n.*, sous-diacre, *m.*

sub-dea'conry *ou* **sub-dea'conship**, *n.*, sous-diaconat, *m.*

sub-dean' (seub-dîne), *n.*, sous-doyen, *m.*

sub-dean'ery, *n.*, sous-doyenné, *f.*

sub-del'egate, *n.*, sous-délégué, subdélégué, *m. v.a.*, sous-déléguer, subdéléguer.

sub-direct'or, *n.*, sous-directeur, *m.*

sub'-district, *n.*, canton; (of towns) quartier, *m.*

subdivide' (seub-di-vaïde), *v.a.*, subdiviser.

subdivide', *v.n.*, se subdiviser.

subdu'able (seub-diou-a-b'l), *adj.*, domptable.

subduce' (seub-diouce) *ou* **subduct'** (seub-deuk'te), *v.a.*, soustraire; retirer, enlever.

subduc'tion (seub-deuk'-), *n.*, soustraction, *f.*; enlèvement, *m.*

subdue' (seub-diou), *v.a.*, subjuguer; soumettre; réduire; dompter; assujettir; vaincre; maîtriser; (sound) étouffer, adoucir. —d light; *demi-jour, m.* In a —d voice; *d'une voix étouffée.* In a —d tone; *d'un ton soumis;* ou *en baissant la voix.*

subdu'er, *n.*, vainqueur, dompteur, *m.*

subdu'plicate (seub-diou-), *adj.*, (math.) sous-doublé.

sub'-editor, *n.*, sous-gérant, rédacteur gérant, *m.*

sub'-editorship, *n.*, sous-gérance, *f.*

sub-inspect'or, *n.*, sous-inspecteur, *m.*

subja'cent (seub-djé-), *adj.*, subjacent, sous-jacent.

sub'ject (seub-djèkte), *adj.*, assujetti à; soumis à; sujet à; exposé à. The — nations; *les peuples asservis, m.pl.* — to; *sous la condition de; sauf.*

sub'ject (seub-djèkte), *n.*, sujet, individu, *m.*; personne, *f.*; (gram.) sujet; (mus.) motif, *m.*

subject' (seub-djèkte), *v.a.*, assujettir à; soumettre à; (to make liable) rendre sujet à, exposer à. To — one's self to; *s'exposer à.*

subjec'tion (seub-djèk'-), *n.*, sujétion; soumission, *f.*; assujétissement, *m.* To bring under —; *assujettir; soumettre.*

subject'ive (seub-djèkt'-), *adj.*, subjectif.

subject'ively, *adv.*, subjectivement.

sub'ject-matter, *n.*, sujet, *m.*, matière, *f.*

subjoin' (seub-djôine), *v.a.*, ajouter à; joindre à; (com.) remettre ci-contre. —ed; *ci-joint, ci-contre.*

sub'jugate (seub-djiou-), *v.a.*, subjuguer; assujettir; soumettre; réduire; asservir.

subjunc'tion (seub-djeu'gn'k'-), *n.*, adjonction, *f.* In — to; *joint à.*

subjunc'tive (seub-djeu'gn'k'-), *n.*, (gram.) subjonctif, *m.* In the —; *au subjonctif.*

subjunc'tive, *adj.*, joint, ajouté.

sub'let (seub-), *v.a.*, (preterit and past part., Sublet) sous-louer.

sub-libra'rian (seub-laï-bré-), *n.*, sous-bibliothécaire, *m.*

sublieuten'ancy, *n.*, sous-lieutenance, *f.*

sub-lieuten'ant (seub-liou-tè'n'-), *n.*, (artil.) sous-lieutenant; (nav.) enseigne de vaisseau, *m.*

subli'mable (seub'laï-), *adj.*, sublimable.

sub'limate (seub'li-), *v.a.*, (fig.) élever; (chem.) sublimer.

sub'limate, *n.adj.*, (chem.) sublimé, *m.*

sublime' (seub'laïme), *adj.*, élevé; haut; (fig.) sublime, imposant, majestueux, élevé.

sublime', *n.*, sublime, *m.*

sublime'ly, *adv.*, d'une manière sublime; sublimement, avec sublimité.

sublime'ness, *n.*, sublimité, *f.*; sublime, *m.*

sublim'ing-pot (seub'laïm'-), *n.*, (chem.) sublimatoire, *m.*

sublim'ity (seub'li'm'-), *n.*, élévation, hauteur; (fig.) sublimité, *f.*, sublime, *m.*, grandeur, élévation, *f.*

sublu'nar, *adj.*, sublunaire.

sub'-manager, *n.*, sous-directeur, *m.*

submarine' (seub'ma-rîne), *adj.*, sous-marin.

submerge' (seub-meurdje), *v.a.*, submerger.

submerge', *v.n.*, s'enfoncer sous.

submis'sion (seub-mish'-), *n.*, soumission; obéissance; résignation, déférence, *f.*

submis'sive (seub-), *adj.*, soumis; humble; obéissant; résigné,

submis'sively, *adv.*, humblement ; avec soumission, avec déférence.

submis'siveness, *n.*, soumission, humilité ; déférence, *f.*

submit' (seub-), *v.a.*, soumettre à ; déférer à.

submit', *v.n.*, se soumettre à ; se résigner à.

submul'tiple (-meul-), *n.*, sous-multiple, *m.*

subnor'mal (seub-), *n.*, (geom.) sous-normale, *f.*

sub'-officer, *n.*, sous-officier, *m.*

subor'dinate (seub-), *adj.*, inférieur à ; subordonné à.

subor'dinate, *n.*, subordonné, subalterne, *m.*

subor'dinate, *v.a.*, subordonner à ; (to make subject) assujettir à.

subor'dinately, *adv.*, subordonnément ; en sous-ordre ; (in descending) en descendant, par gradation.

subordina'tion (seub-or-di-né-), *n.*, subordination ; soumission, *f.* ; rang inférieur, *m.*

suborna'tion (seub-or-né-), *n.*, subornation ; corruption ; séduction, *f.*

suborn'er, *n.*, suborneur, *m.*, suborneuse, *f.*

subpœ'na (seub-pî-), *n.*, (jur.) citation ; assignation, *f.*

subpœ'na, *v.a.*, (jur.) citer, assigner.

sub'-prefect, *n.*, sous-préfet, *m.*

sub-pri'or (seub-praï-), *n.*, sous-prieur, *m.*

sub-rec'tor (seub-rèk'teur), *n.*, vice-recteur, *m.*

subrep'tion (seub-rèp-), *n.* V. **surreption.**

subsalt' (seub-sôlte), *n.*, (chem.) sous-sel, *m.*

subscribe' (seub-scraïbe), *v.a.*, souscrire ; signer. To — five francs to ; *souscrire pour la somme de cinq francs* à. To — one's self ; *se dire.*

subscribe', *v.n.*, souscrire (à, to ; for or towards, **pour**). To — to a newspaper, etc. ; *s'abonner, prendre un abonnement, à un journal ; être abonné à un journal.* To — one's self ; (in letters) *se dire.*

subscrib'er, *n.*, souscripteur ; signataire ; (to a newspaper, etc.) abonné, *m.*, abonnée, *f.*

subscrip'tion (seub-scrip'-), *n.*, souscription ; signature, *f.* ; (to a newspaper, etc.) abonnement, *m.* — library ; *cabinet de lecture,* m.

sub-sec'tion (seub'sèk'-), *n.*, subdivision, *f.*

sub'sequence *ou* **sub'sequency**, *n.*, postériorité, subséquence, *f.*

sub'sequent, *adj.*, subséquent ; postérieur.

sub'sequently, *adv.*, ensuite ; par la suite ; après ; (jur.) subséquemment, ultérieurement.

subserve' (seub-seurve), *v.a.*, servir subordonnément ; être dépendant de ; aider à, contribuer à ; favoriser ; servir d'instrument à.

subser'vience *ou* **subser'viency** (seub-seur-), *n.*, concours, *m.* ; utilité ; dépendance, obéissance, *f.*

subser'vient, *adj.*, utile à ; (subordinate) subordonné à ; secondaire ; inférieur à. To make — to ; *faire servir* à.

subser'viently, *adv.*, en sous-ordre, utilement.

subside' (seub-saïde), *v.n.*, tomber au fond ; (to become tranquil) se calmer, s'apaiser ; (to sink) s'affaisser ; (of buildings) tasser ; (to abate) baisser, s'abaisser. To — into ; *descendre* **dans** ; *devenir ; se changer en.*

subsid'ence (seub-saï-), *n.*, affaissement, *m.* ; (of liquids) action de tomber au fond, *f.*, dépôt ; (of buildings) tassement, *m.* ; (fig.) apaisement, *m.* ; cessation, *f.*

subsid'iarily, *adv.*, subsidiairement.

subsid'iary (seub-si-), *adj.*, subsidiaire ; auxiliaire.

subsid'iary, *n.*, auxiliaire, *m.*

sub'sidize (seub-si-daïze), *v.a.*, subventionner ; donner des subsides à.

sub'sidy, *n.*, subside, *m.* ; subvention, *f.*

subsist' (seub-), *v.n.*, exister ; subsister. To — on ; *subsister* **de** ; *vivre* **de.** To make any one

— ; *faire subsister quelqu'un ; pourvoir aux besoins de.*

subsist'ence, *n.*, (being) existence ; (means of support) subsistance, *f.*, entretien, *m.*, moyens d'existence, *m.pl.* ; (inherence) inhérence, *f.*

subsist'ent, *adj.*, existant, qui existe ; (inherent) inhérent.

sub'soil (seub-soïle), *n.*, (agri.) sous-sol, *m.* ; (jur.) tréfonds, *m.* — plowing ; *défoncement, m.* To sell both soil and —; (i.e. everything) *vendre le fonds et le tréfonds.*

sub-spe'cies (seub-spî-shîze), *n.*, sous-espèce, *f.*

sub'stance (seub-), *n.*, substance, *f.* ; fond, *m.* ; (means of living) moyens d'existence ; (goods) biens, *m.pl.* ; (fig.) matière, réalité, corps, *m.* ; (summary) résumé, *m.*

substan'tial (seub-sta'n'shal), *adj.*, (belonging to substance) de substance, qui existe, essentiel, substantiel ; (real) réel, vrai ; (solid, stout) solide, fort, substantiel ; (material) vital, important, matériel, corporel ; (well off) aisé, à l'aise, cossu. — proof ; *preuve matérielle, f.* — meal ; *repas solide, m.* — speech ; *discours substantiel, f.* — food ; *nourriture substantielle, f.* — man ; *homme à son aise, cossu, m.*

substantial'ity, **substan'tialness**, *n.*, existence réelle ; réalité, force, solidité, *f.*

substan'tially, *adv.*, (solidly) solidement, fortement ; (really) essentiellement, matériellement, réellement, vraiment ; (in substance) en substance ; (at one's ease) à l'aise, dans l'aisance ; (theol.) substantiellement.

substan'tials (-shalze), *n.pl.*, parties essentielles, *f.pl.*

substan'tiate (seub-sta'n'shi-), *v.a.*, faire exister ; (to establish by proof) prouver, établir ; confirmer, appuyer.

sub'stantive (seub-), *adj.*, (gram. ; of colors) substantif.

sub'stantive, *n.*, (gram.) substantif, *m.*

sub'stantively, *adv.*, substantivement.

sub'stitute (seub-sti-tioute), *v.a.*, substituer (for) à.

sub'stitute (seub-sti-tioute), *n.*, substitut ; suppléant ; délégué ; remplaçant ; représentant, mandataire ; (milit.) remplaçant, *m.* ; (professors, judges) professeur, juge, suppléant ; (thing) chose qui remplace ; (of an actor) doublure, *f.* ; double, *m.* That is a — for ; *cela remplace ; cela peut remplacer, sert* à **ou** **pour** *remplacer.* As a — for ; *pour remplacer ; en remplacement* **de.**

substitu'tion (seub-sti-tiou-), *n.*, (jur., alg., chem., ordinary language) substitution, *f.*

sub'stitutive, *adj.*, substitutif.

substract' (seub-), *v.a.* V. **subtract.**

substra'tum (seub-stré-), *n.*, (*substrata*) (min.) couche inférieure, sous-couche ; (philos.) substance, *f.* ; (agri.) sous-sol, *m.* There is a — of truth in this *ou* that ; *il y a un fond de vérité en cela.*

substruc'tion (seub-streuk-) *ou* **substructure** (-streukt'ieur), *n.*, substruction, *f.* ; fondement, sous-œuvre, *m.*

subtan'gent (seub-ta'n'djè'n'te), *m.*, (geom.) sous-tangente, *f.*

subtend' (seub-), *v.a.*, sous-tendre.

subtense' (seub-), *n.*, (geom.) sous-tendante ; corde, *f.*

sub'terfuge (seub-tèr-fioudje), *n.*, subterfuge ; détour, faux-fuyant, *m.*, échappatoire, *f.*

subterra'nean *ou* **subterra'neous** (seub-tèr-ré-ni-), *adj.*, souterrain.

subterra'neously, *adj.*, souterrainement.

sub'tilize (seub-til-aïze), *v.n.*, subtiliser ; (fig.) subtiliser, raffiner.

sub'tilize, *v.a.*, rendre subtil ; (fig.) subtiliser.

sub'tle (seut't'l), *adj.*, (cunning) subtil ; rusé ; (fine) fin, délié ; (cunning) subtil, **fin.**

sub'tleness, sub'tility, *ou* **sub'tlety** (soub-), *n.*, subtilité ; (slyness) finesse, ruse, *f. ;* artifice, *m.*

sub'tly (seut't'li), *adv.*, finement, avec finesse ; artificieusement, avec artifice.

subtract' (seub-), *v.a.*, soustraire ; **défalquer** ; retrancher ; ôter ; déduire.

subtract'er, -or, *n.*, soustrayeur, *m.*

subtrac'tion, *n.*, soustraction, *f.*, retranchement, *m.*, défalcation ; (arith.) soustraction, *f.*

subtrac'tive, *adj.*, qui tend à soustraire, à retrancher ; (math.) négatif ; soustractif.

sub'trahend, *n.*, (arith.) nombre à retrancher, *m.*

sub'-tutor (seub-tiou-teur), *n.*, sous-précepteur, *m.*

su'bulate (siou-biou-), *adj.*, (bot.) subulé, en forme d'alène.

sub'urb (seub'eurbe), *n.*, faubourg, *m.* —**s,** *pl.*, alentours, environs, *m.pl. ;* banlieue, *f.*

suburb'an (seub-eur-), *adj.*, (admin.) suburbain, de faubourg, des faubourgs ; de la banlieue. A — residence ; *une villa dans les environs, dans la banlieue.*

sub'-vari'ety, *n.*, sous-variété, *f.*

subven'tion (seub-), *n.*, subvention, *f.*

subven'tion-al, -ary, *adj.*, subventionnel.

subver'sion (seub-veur-), *n.*, subversion, *f. ;* renversement, *m.*

subver'sive (seub-veur-), *adj.*, subversif.

subvert' (seub-veurte), *v.a.*, subvertir, renverser, bouleverser.

subvert'er, *n.*, destructeur, *m.*, destructrice, *f.*

sub'way, *n.*, passage souterrain, *m.*

sub'worker (seub-weurk'-), *n.*, auxiliaire ; aide, *m.*

succeda'neous (seuk-ci-dé-ni-), *adj.*, qui remplace, succédané.

succeed' (seuk-cîde), *v.n.*, succéder ; (to prosper) réussir, succéder. He —s in everything ; *il réussit en tout ; tout lui réussit ; ⊙tout lui succède* (La Bruyère).

succeed' (seuk'cîde), *v.a.*, succéder **à** ; suivre ; (to supersede) remplacer ; (to inherit) hériter **de** ; (to prosper) faire réussir, faire prospérer. To — each other ; *se succéder.* To — in ; *réussir* **dans, en** (before a noun) ; (before a verb) *réussir* **à,** *parvenir* **à.**

succeed'ing, *adj.*, (of the past) suivant ; (of the future) à venir, futur ; (successive) successif.

success' (seuk'cèss), *n.*, réussite, *f. ;* (luck) bonne chance, *f.* To have —; *avoir du succès ; réussir.* I wish you —! *bonne chance !* — justifies the means ; *la fin justifie les moyens.*

success'ful (-foule), *adj.*, qui réussit ; heureux, couronné de succès, victorieux. To be —; *avoir du succès ; réussir.* To be — in doing ; *réussir* **à** (with inf.).

success'fully, *adv.*, heureusement **;** avec succès, victorieusement.

success'fulness, *n.*, (of things) réussite, *f. ;* succès ; (of pers.) succès, *m.*

succes'sion (seuk'cèsh'-), *n.*, (series) succession ; suite, *f. ;* (to the throne) avènement, *m. ;* (lineage) postérité ; (inheritance) succession, *f. ;* (right to inherit) droit de succession ; héritage, *m. ;* (mus.) succession ; (agri.) rotation, *f.* In —; *successivement, tour à tour ; de suite.* — of crops ; *rotation, f., assolement, m.* — act, duty, war ; *acte,* ou *droit, m.,* ou *guerre, f., de succession.*

succes'sive (seuk'-), *adj.*, successif, consécutif.

succes'sively, *adv.*, successivement.

succes'siveness, *n.*, nature successive, *f.*

succes'sor (seuk'cèss'eur), *n.*, successeur, *m.*

succinct' (seuk'cignk'te), *adj.*, succinct, concis.

succinct'ly, *adv.*, succinctement ; avec concision.

succinct'ness, *n.*, concision ; brièveté, *f.*

suc'cor (seuk'keur), *v.a.*, secourir ; aider ; assister ; (a mast) renforcer ; (cable) fortifier.

suc'cor (seuk'keur), *n.*, secours, *m. ;* aide ; assistance, *f.*

suc'corer, *n.*, personne qui donne du secours, qui apporte du secours, *f.*

suc'corless, *adj.*, sans secours, privé de secours.

suc'culence *ou* **suc'culency** (seuk'kiou-), *n.*, abondance de suc, succulence, *f.*

suc'culent, *adj.*, succulent ; plein de jus, plein de suc. — plants ; (bot.) *plantes grasses, f.pl.*

succumb' (seuk'keu'me), *v.n.*, succomber (under, **sous** : fig., **à**); céder **à** ; (to circumstances) se soumettre **à.**

succus'sion (-keush'-), *n.*, secousse ; (med.) succussion, *f.*

such (seutshe), *adj.*, tel ; certain ; pareil, semblable. — an one ; *un tel, m., une telle, f.* — an one as ; *tel que.* — as you ; *tel que vous.* — as do not like ; *ceux qui n'aiment pas ; tels qui n'aiment pas.* — as it is ; *tel quel, m., telle quelle, f.* — and —; *tel et tel.* These verses are cf — a poet ; *ces vers sont de tel poète.* On — occasions ; *dans ces occasions,* ou *à des occasions pareilles.* We have walked — a way that ; *nous avons tellement marché que.* He remained — a time that ; *il est resté si longtemps que.* It is — a way ; *c'est si loin.* He is — a bore ; *il est si ennuyeux, si assommant.* Take — as are there ; *prenez ceux,* ou *celles, qui sont là.* Continue —; *continuez ainsi, tel.* Give me — things as . . . ; *donnez-moi des choses que . . .* At — a time ; *à un tel moment.* You are — a man ! *vous êtes si galant, si brave, si farceur, etc.* It is no — thing ; *il n'en est rien.* No — thing ; *rien de semblable, rien de pareil.* There is no — thing as ; *il n'y a pas* **de.** There is no — thing as that ; *cela n'existe pas.* Never was there a man — as he ; *il n'y eut jamais son pareil.* Did any one ever see — a war ? *a-t-on jamais vu une guerre pareille ?* — an honor ; *un si grand honneur.* It eats and sleeps, and has — senses as we have ; *il boit et mange, et a les mêmes sens que nous.* If you repay me not on — a day in — a place, — sum or sums as are expressed, etc. ; *si vous ne me remboursez pas tel et tel jour, dans tel et tel endroit la somme ou les sommes spécifiées, etc.* (Shakespeare, " Merchant of Venice "). — a kind man ; *un homme si bon, si aimable.* Tears — as angels weep ; *des larmes comme en pleurent les anges.* With —; *pour de telles personnes.* In — weather ; *par le temps qu'il fait.* In — times as these ; *par le temps qui court.* — a profusion of flowers ! *quelle profusion de fleurs !* — papers as he submitted for the consideration of the Cabinet ; *les pièces qu'il soumettait à l'examen du Cabinet.* — like ; *de ce genre, de même espèce.* They offer us their protection. Yes, — protection as vultures give to lambs ; *ils nous offrent leur protection. Oui, la protection* **que** *les vautours accordent aux agneaux.*

suck (seuke), *v.a.*, sucer ; (the teat) téter ; (to inhale) aspirer, pomper ; (to absorb) absorber, boire. To — down ; *sucer* ; (fig.) *engloutir, entraîner au fond.* To — in ; *sucer ;* (to absorb) *absorber ;* (to inhale) *aspirer ;* (to believe) *gober.* To — in with one's milk ; *sucer avec le lait.* To — out ; *sucer ; tirer, vider (en suçant).* To — up ; *aspirer ;* (to absorb) *absorber.* To — out of ; *puiser* **dans,** *tirer* **de.** It is teaching one's grandmother how to — eggs ; *c'est Gros Jean qui en remontre à son curé ;* ou *ce n'est pas à un vieux singe qu'on apprend à faire des grimaces.*

suck, *v.n.*, sucer ; (of young things) téter ; (to draw in) aspirer.

suck (seuke), *n.*, sucement, *m. ;* aspiration, *f. ;* (milk) lait ; (sugar-stick) sucre d'orge, *m.* To give — **to** ; *donner le sein* **à,** *donner à téter* **à,** *allaiter.*

suck'er, *n.*, suceur, *n. ;* (of a pump) piston ; (ent.)

suçoir ; (bot.) drageon, surgeon ; (ich.) disco-bole, *m.*

suck'ing, *n.*, sucement, *m.*; succion ; (of liquids) aspiration ; absorption, *f.*

suck'ing, *adj.*, qui suce ; qui tette ; qui absorbe ; aspirant, d'aspiration. — child ; *enfant à la mamelle, m.*

suck'ing-bottle (bot't'l), *n.*, biberon, *m.*

suck'ing-fish, *n.*, rémora, *m.*; rémore, *f.*; sucet, *m.*

suck'ing-pig, *n.*, cochon de lait, *m.*

suck'ing-pipe, *n.*, tuyau d'aspiration, *m.*

suck'ing-pump (-peu'm'p), *n.*, pompe aspirante, *f.*

suc'kle (seuk'k'l), *v.a.*, allaiter ; nourrir ; donner le sein à.

suc'kling, *n.*, (act of) allaitement, *m.*

suck'ling (seuk'-), *n.*, enfant à la mamelle ; nourrisson ; (animal) animal qui tette encore.

suc'tion (seuk'-), *n.*, succion ; aspiration ; absorption, *f.*; sucement, *m.*

sucto'rial (seuk'tô-), *adj.*, suceur.

suda'tion (siou-dé-), *n.*, (med.) sudation, *f.*

su'datory (siou-), *n.*, sudatoire, *m.*

sud'den (seud'-), *adj.*, subit ; soudain ; inopiné ; imprévu. — death ; *mort subite, f.*

sud'den, *n.*, événement soudain, *m.* On a —, all of a —; *tout à coup.* All on a —; *tout d'un coup.*

sud'denly, *adv.*, subitement ; soudainement ; tout à coup, soudain.

sud'denness, *n.*, soudaineté, *f.*

sudorif'ic (siou-), *n.*, sudorifique, *m.*

sudorif'ic, *adj.*, sudorifique ; (l.u.) sudorifère.

suds (seudze), *n.pl.*, eau de savon ; lessive, *f.sing.* In the —; *dans le pétrin, dans l'embarras ; de mauvaise humeur.*

sue (siou), *v.a.*, poursuivre ; poursuivre en justice ; demander en mariage ; (of a hawk) s'essuyer. To — out; *obtenir par pétition.* To — for; *poursuivre en.* To — for damages ; *poursuivre en dommages-intérêts.* To — for libel; (jur.) *attaquer en diffamation.* To — for separation, divorce ; (jur.) *plaider en séparation, en divorce.*

sue, *v.n.*, poursuivre en justice. To — for ; *solliciter, demander, implorer.*

su'et (siou-ète), *n.*, graisse, *f.*

suf'fer (seuf'-), *v.a.*, souffrir (by, with, from, **de**) ; supporter ; endurer ; (to undergo) subir ; (to permit) souffrir, laisser, permettre ; (to sustain) éprouver, essuyer ; (to lose) perdre (by, **à**). To — losses ; *éprouver des pertes.* To — punishment ; *subir, souffrir une peine.* — me to tell you ; *permettez moi de vous dire, souffrez que je vous dise.* To — one's self to be deceived ; *se laisser tromper,* etc., etc. He was —ed (allowed) to go; *on lui permit de partir ; on le laissa aller.*

suf'fer, *v.n.*, souffrir. To — for ; *souffrir de ; pâtir de, porter la peine de.* He will — for it ; *il ne le portera pas en paradis ;* (fam.) *il en portera la peine ; il s'en mordra les pouces ; il en pâtira.*

suf'ferable (seuf'feur'a-b'l), *adj.*, supportable ; tolérable ; permis.

suf'ferably, *adv.*, d'une manière supportable.

suf'ferance (seuf'feur'-), *n.*, (toleration) tolérance, permission ; (endurance) souffrance ; (patience) patience, modération, *f.* Bill of — ; (customs) *lettre d'exemption des droits de la douane, f.* You are here only on — ; *vous n'êtes ici que par tolérance.* On — ; (jur.) *par tolérance.* To exist only upon — ; *n'exister que par tolérance.*

suf'ferer, *n.*, personne qui souffre ; victime (by, **de**), *f.*; malade, *m.f.*, patient, *m.* Fellow---; *compagnon d'infortune, m.* To be a — by ; *être victime de ; perdre à.* To be a heavy — by ; *perdre beaucoup à.* Yes, but I am the — ; *oui, mais c'est moi qui en souffre, ou qui en pâtis.*

suf'fering, *n.*, souffrance, douleur, *f.*

suf'feringly, *adv.*, avec douleur, en souffrant ; péniblement.

suffice' (seuf'faïze), *v.a.*, suffire à ; satisfaire.

suffice', *v.n.*, suffire. — it to say ; *qu'il suffise de dire ; suffit que.*

suffi'ciency (seuf'fish'è'n'-), *n.*, suffisance ; (ability) capacité, aptitude ; (competence) fortune suffisante, aisance ; (vanity) suffisance, *f.* A — of ; *suffisamment de, assez de.* — is a compound of vanity and ignorance ; *la suffisance est un composé de la vanité et de l'ignorance.*

suffi'cient (seuf'fish'è'n'te), *adj.*, suffisant ; assez ; (fit) capable. — for ; *suffisant pour, qui suffit à.* That is — ; *cela suffit, c'est assez.* — unto the day is the evil thereof ; *à chaque jour suffit sa peine.* —reason ; (philos.) *raison suffisante, f.* It is not — for us to know . . . ; *il ne nous suffit pas de savoir . . .*

suffi'ciently, *adv.*, suffisamment, assez.

suf'fix (seuf'-), *n.*, (gram.) terminaison, *f.*; suffixe, *m.*

suf'focate (seuf'-), *v.a.*, suffoquer ; étouffer ; asphyxier.

suf'focating (seuf'fo-két'-), *adj.*, suffocant, étouffant. *part.*, suffoquant. *adj. & part.*, asphyxiant.

suf'focatingly, *adv.*, d'une manière suffocante, de manière à suffoquer.

suffoca'tion (seuf'fo-ké-), *n.*, suffocation, asphyxie, *f.*; étouffement, *m.*

suf'focative (-fo-ké-), *adj.*, suffocant ; étouffant.

suf'fragan (seuf'-), *n.*, (ecc.) suffragant, *m.*

suf'fragan, *adj.*, (ecc.) suffragant. —bishop ; *évêque suffragant, m.*

suf'frage (seuf'frèdje), *n.*, suffrage, *m.* Manhood---; *suffrage universel, m.*

suffuse' (seuf'fiouze), *v.a.*, couvrir **de** ; répandre ; remplir **de** ; se répandre **sur**, s'épancher **sur**. Her face was —d with blushes ; *une rougeur lui était montée au visage.* Tears —d his cheeks ; *des larmes coulaient sur ses joues.* His eyes —d with tears ; *les yeux gonflés de larmes.*

suffu'sion (seuf'fiou-jeune), *n.*, épanchement ; (med.) épanchement, *m.*, suffusion ; (surg.) cataracte, *f.*; (fig.) voile, *m.*; rougeur, *f.*

sug'ar (shoug'-), *n.*, sucre, *m.* Brown — ; *cassonade, f.*; sucre brut. Moist — ; *cassonade, f.* Raw — ; *sucre brut.* Barley---; *sucre d'orge.* Loaf of — ; *pain de sucre, m.* Lump of — ; *morceau de sucre, m.* Lump---, loaf---; *sucre en pain.* Caster — ; *sucre en poudre.* — and water ; *eau sucrée, f.* To sweeten with — ; *sucrer.* Help yourself to — ! *sucrez-vous !*

sug'ar, *v.a.*, sucrer ; (fig.) adoucir.

sug'ar-baker (-bak'-), *n.*, raffineur de sucre, *m.*

sug'ar-bak'ing, raffinage du sucre, *m.*

sug'ar-basin (-bé-s'n), *n.*, sucrier, *m.*

sug'ar-beet, *n.*, (bot.) betterave, poirée, *f.*

sug'ar-candy, *n.*, sucre candi, *m.*

sug'ar-cane, *n.*, canne à sucre, *f.*

sug'ar-chop'per, *n.*, casse-sucre, *m.*

sug'ar-crush'er, *n.*, pilon à sucre, *m.*

sug'ared (shough'eurde), *adj.*, sucré ; **doux** ; (fig.) mielleux.

sug'ar-house (-haouce), *n.*, sucrerie ; raffinerie de sucre, *f.*

sug'ar-loaf (-lôfe), *adj.*, en forme de pain de sucre.

sug'ar-loaf, *n.*, pain de sucre, *m.*

sug'ar-maple, *n.*, (bot.) érable à sucre, *m.*

sug'ar-mill, *n.*, moulin à cannes (à sucre), *m.*

sug'ar-mite (-maïte), *n.*, (ent.) lépisme du sucre, *m.*

sug'ar-mold (-môlde), *n.*, forme à sucre, *f.*

sug'ar-nippers, *n.pl.*, pinces à sucre, *f.pl.*

sug'ar-orchard, *n.*, plantation d'érables à sucre, *f.*

sug'ar-planta'tion (-pla'n'té-), *n.*, plantation de cannes à sucre, *f.*

sug′ar-planter, *n.*, planteur de cannes à sucre, *m.*

sug′ar-plum (-pleu′me), *n.*, dragée, *f.*

sug′ar-refin′er (-ri-faï′n′-), *n.*, raffineur de sucre, *m.*

sug′ar-refin′ery (-ri-faï′n′-), *n.*, raffinerie de sucre, *f.*

sug′ar-refin′ing, *n.*, raffinage du sucre, *m.*

sug′ar-sifter, *n.*, cuiller à sucre, *f.*

sug′ar-tongs (-to′gn′ze), *n.pl.*, pinces à sucre, *f.pl.*

sug′ar-trade, *n.*, commerce des sucres, *m.*

sug′ar-works (-weurkce), *n.pl.*, sucrerie, *f.*

sug′ary (shoug′-), *adj.*, sucré ; (of melons) sucrin ; (fond of sugar) qui aime le sucre.

suggest′ (seud′jèste), *v.a.*, suggérer ; inspirer ; faire naître ; faire penser à ; insinuer ; proposer ; donner à entendre. To be —ed ; *se suggérer.* To — itself to the mind ; *se présenter à l'esprit.*

sugges′tion (seud′jèst′ieu′ne), *n.*, suggestion, proposition ; inspiration ; idée ; impulsion ; (b.s.) instigation ; (jur.) déposition (sans serment), *f. ;* avis, *m.* On my — ; *à ma suggestion.*

suggest′ive (seud′jèst′-), *adj.*, suggestif, qui inspire ; qui suggère ; qui fait penser à ; qui met dans l'idée. — of ; *qui nous rappelle.*

suicid′al (siou-i-caï-), *adj.*, de suicide, fatal. It is — to think of it ; *c'est fatal d'y penser.*

su′icide (siou-i-caïde), *n.*, suicide, *m.* To commit — ; *se suicider, se donner la mort.*

suit (sioute), *n.*, collection, *f. ;* nombre complet ; assortiment, *m. ;* (at cards) couleur ; (solicitation) sollicitation, demande ; (petition) pétition, requête ; (courtship) recherche en mariage, cour ; (pursuit) poursuite ; (jur.) action, poursuite, *f.*, procès, *m.* To bring a — against ; (jur.) *intenter une action,* ou *un procès, à.* — of armor ; *armure complète, f.* — of clothes ; *habillement complet, m.* To follow — ; (at cards) servir, donner de la couleur jouée, (fig.) *faire de même, en faire autant.*

suit (sioute), *v.a.*, (to adapt) adapter, approprier ; (to become) convenir à, aller à, arranger ; (to please) plaire à ; (to clothe) revêtir. That just —s me ; *cela me convient, me va, m'arrange, fait mon affaire.* To — the action to the word ; *mettre ses actions d'accord avec ses paroles, faire répondre ses actions à ses discours.* If that — you ; *si cela vous convient, vous plaît,* (fam.) *si cela vous va.* Are you —ed with a servant ? *avez-vous trouvé un (une) domestique ?*

suit, *v.n.*, s'accorder ; convenir ; cadrer **avec**, être d'accord.

suit′able (siout′a-b′l), *adj.*, convenable à ; conforme à ; approprié à ; qui convient à ; en rapport **avec**. — to ; *adapté à ; suffisant pour.*

suit′ableness, *n.*, convenance, *f. ;* accord, *m. ;* conformité, *f.* (to, **avec**).

suit′ably, *adv.*, convenablement ; conformément.

suite (sioûte), *n.*, suite, *f. ;* cortège, *m. ;* (series) suite ; (of rooms) enfilade, *f.* — of furniture ; *ameublement complet, m.* Bedroom — ; *ameublement de chambre à coucher, m.* Drawing-room — ; *ameublement de salon, m.* — of apartments ; *appartement, m.*

suit′or (siout′eur), *n.*, pétitionnaire, *m.f. ;* solliciteur, *m.*, solliciteuse, *f. ;* suppliant, *m.*, suppliante, *f. ;* (lover) amant, prétendant, soupirant ; (jur.) plaideur, *m.*, plaideuse, *f.*

sulk (seulke), *v.n.*, bouder ; faire la mine. To — with ; *bouder.*

sulks, *n.pl.*, mauvaise humeur ; bouderie, *f.* To be in the —s ; *être de mauvaise humeur, bouder.*

sulk′ily, *adv.*, en boudant ; en faisant la mine.

sulk′iness, *n.*, bouderie ; humeur boudeuse, *f.*

sulk′ing, *n.*, bouderie, *f.*

sulk′y (seulk′-), *adj.*, boudeur ; maussade ; qui fait la mine. To be — ; *être bouâeur ; bouder.*

sulk′y (seul′ki), *n.*, (carriage) désobligeante, *f.*

sul′len (seul′-), *adj.*, maussade, morose, bourru, chagrin ; (malignant) malfaisant ; (intractable) obstiné, revêche, refrogné, intraitable ; (gloomy) sombre, triste ; d'humeur chagrine ; (sorrowful) affligeant, funeste.

sul′lenly, *adv.*, maussadement ; (intractably) d'un air refrogné ; (gloomily) tristement.

sul′lenness (seul′-), *n.*, maussaderie ; morosité ; (intractableness) humeur intraitable, acariâtre ; (gloominess) humeur sombre, tristesse, *f.*

sul′ly (seul′-), *v.a.*, souiller (with, **de**) ternir.

sul′ly, *v.n.*, se ternir. *n.*, souillure, tache, *f.*

sulph′ate (seul-), *n.*, (chem.) sulfate, *m.*

sulphat′ic, *adj.*, (chem.) sulfaté.

sulph′ite (seul-faïte), *n.*, (chem.) sulfite, *m.*

sul′phur (seul-feur), *n.*, (chem.) soufre, *m.* — bath ; *bain sulfureur, m.* — mine ; *soufrière, f.* — ore ; *pyrite de fer, f. ; fer sulfuré, m.* — stick ; *soufre en canon.*

sul′phur, *v.a.*, soufrer.

sul′phurate, *adj.*, sulfuré.

sul′phurate, *v.a.*, sulfurer, soufrer.

sulphura′tion (seul-feu-ré-), *n.*, sulfuration, *f.*

sulphu′reous, *adj.*, sulfureux.

sul′phuret, *n.*, (chem.) sulfure, *m.*

sul′phureted, *adj.*, (chem.) sulfuré.

sulphu′ric, *adj.*, (chem.) sulfurique.

sul′phuring, *n.*, soufrage, *m.*

sul′phurous, *adj.*, (chem.) sulfureux.

sul′phur-wort (-weurte), *n.*, (bot.) peucédane, *f.*, fenouil de porc, *m.*

sul′tan (seul- ou soul-), *n.*, sultan, *m.*

sulta′na (seul-tâ-nâ ou -té-), *n.*, sultane ; (orni.) poule sultane, *f.* —s ; *raisins de Damas, m.pl.*

sul′tanship, *n.*, sultanat, *m.*

sul′triness (seul-), *n.*, chaleur étouffante, *f.*

sul′try (seul-), *adj.*, d'une chaleur étouffante ; lourd, étouffant, suffocant. It is very — ; *il fait une chaleur étouffante, un temps très lourd.*

sum (seu′me), *n.*, somme, *f. ;* (compendium) résumé, sommaire ; (height) comble, sommet ; (arith.) problème, calcul, *m. ;* règle, *f. ;* (in Scripture) dénombrement, *m.* To set any one a — ; (arith.) *poser un problème (une règle) à quelqu'un.* To work out a — ; *résoudre un problème ; faire un calcul.* — total ; *somme totale, f. ; total, m.* A stated — ; *une somme de.* In — ; *en somme.*

sum, *v.a.*, additionner ; (to condense) résumer. To — up ; (arith.) *additionner ; faire l'addition de, le total de, la somme de, prendre la somme de, le total de ;* (figur.) *récapituler.* —ming up ; *addition, f. ;* (jur.) *résumé, m.* To — up the case ; *résumer les débats.*

su′mac ou **su′mach** (sou-make), *n.*, sumac, *m.*

sum′less, *adj.*, incalculable.

sum′marily (seu′m′-), *adv.*, sommairement ; sans délai ; sans enquête, sans explication aucune ; rondement.

sum′mary (seu′m′-), *n.*, sommaire, abrégé, précis, résumé, *m.*

sum′mary, *adj.*, sommaire ; prompt, expéditif, inmédiat.

sum′mer (seu′m′-), *n.*, été, *m.* In — ; *l'été, en été. adj.*, estival, d'été. — weather ; *un temps d'été.*

sum′mer, *v.n.*, passer, ou rester, l'été.

sum′mer, *n.*, (arch.) sommier ; (carp.) poitrail, *m.*

sum′mer-freckle (-frèk′k′l), *n.*, tache de rousseur, *f.* [*f.pl.*]

sum′mer-hol′idays, *n.pl.*, vacances d'été, *f.*

sum′mer-house (-haonce), *n.*, pavillon, kiosque, *m. ;* (residence) habitation d'été, *f.*

sum′mersault. *V.* **somersault.**

sum′mer-sea′son, *n.*, saison d'été, *f.*

sum′mer-tree (-trî), *n.*, (carp.) lambourde, *f.*

sum′mer-wheat, *n.*, blé de mars, *m.*

sum'mit (seu'm'-), n., sommet, m. ; cime, f. ; (fig.) comble, faîte, m.

sum'mit-level (-lèv'v'l), n., point de partage, m.

sum'mon (seu'm'meu'n), v.a., convoquer à ; sommer de ; adjurer de ; (jur.) citer, assigner ; (to call) appeler à, demander, réclamer ; inviter à. To — away ; appeler, réclamer, rappeler. To — up ; (to excite) exciter ; (to call up) rassembler (son courage). To — a meeting ; convoquer une assemblée. To — the rioters to disperse ; sommer les émeutiers de se disperser. I could not — up courage to tell her the sad news ; le courage m'a manqué ; je n'ai pas pu lui dire la triste nouvelle.

sum'moner, n., personne qui convoque, qui cite, qui somme, f. ; sommateur ; (jur.) huissier, m.

sum'mons (seu'm'meu'n'ze), n., sommation ; convocation ; invitation, f. ; appel, m. ; (jur.) assignation, citation, f., mandat de comparution, m. To take out a — against ; envoyer une assignation à. To grant, ou issue, a — ; lancer un mandat de comparution, une assignation.

sump (seu'm'pe), n., (mines) puisard, m.

sump'ter-horse (seu'm'teur-), n., cheval de somme, sommier, m.

sump'tuary (seu'm'p-tiou-é-ri), adj., somptuaire.

sump'tuous (seu'm't'iou-eusse), adj., somptueux.

sump'tuously, adv., somptueusement.

sump'tuousness, n., somptuosité, f.

sun (seu'n), n., soleil ; (fig.) éclat, m. The — is down, up ; le soleil est couché, levé. The — is high up ; il fait grand soleil. The — shines ; il fait du soleil, le soleil luit. To worship the rising — ; (fig.) adorer le soleil levant. To sit in the — ; être assis au soleil. In the — ; dans le soleil ; (in the sunshine) au soleil. There is no new thing under the — ; il n'y a rien de nouveau sous le soleil.

sun, v.a., chauffer, ou exposer, au soleil. To — one's self ; se chauffer au soleil.

sun'beam (-bî'me), n., rayon de soleil, rayon solaire, m.

sun'-blind (-blaïnde), n., abat-jour, m.

sun'-bright (-braïte), adj., radieux.

sun'burn (-beurne), n., hâle, m.

sun'burnt, adj., brûlé par le soleil ; hâlé, basané.

sun'clad, adj., radieux, baigné de soleil.

Sun'day, n., dimanche, m. On —s ; le dimanche. adj., du dimanche. In — best, ou clothes ; endimanché. To put on one's — clothes ; s'endimancher. When two —s come together ; la semaine des trois jeudis.

sun'der, v.a., séparer de ; diviser ; couper ; rompre.

sun'der, n., séparation en deux parties, f. In — ; en deux.

sun'dew (-diou), n., (bot.) rossolis, m.

sun'dial (-daï-al), n., cadran solaire, m.

sun'-dried (-draïde), adj., séché au soleil.

sun'dries (-drize), n., diverses choses, f.pl. ; faux frais ; (com.) divers, m.pl.

sun'dry, adj., divers.

sun'fish, n., (ich.) molle, lune de mer, f.

sun'flower (-flaoueur), n., hélianthe ; soleil ; tournesol, m.

sun'less, adj., sans soleil.

sun'light (-laïte), n., lumière du soleil, f.

sun'like (-laïke), adj., semblable au soleil.

sun'lit, adj., ensoleillé.

sun'ny, adj., de soleil ; (bright) brillant comme le soleil ; (exposed to the sun) exposé au soleil, ensoleillé ; (colored by the sun) coloré du soleil ; vermeil ; (fig.) riant, heureux. — side of a hill ; côté d'une colline exposé au soleil. — side of nature ; le beau côté de la nature. It is — ; il fait du soleil.

sun'proof (-proufe), adj., impénétrable aux rayons du soleil.

sun'rise (-raize) ou **sun'rising** (-raiz'-), n., lever du soleil ; soleil levant, m.

sun'-rose, n., (bot.) hélianthème, m.

sun'set ou **sun'setting**, n., coucher du soleil ; soleil couchant, m.

sun'-shade, n., abat-jour ; parasol, en-tout-cas, m.

sun'shine (-shaïne), n., clarté du soleil, f. ; soleil ; (fig.) bonheur, éclat, m. In the — ; au soleil. In the broad — ; au grand soleil.

sun'shine ou **sun'shiny**, adj., ensoleillé ; plein de soleil ; inondé de lumière.

sun'stroke (-strôke), n., (med.) coup de soleil, m. ; insolation, f.

sun'-wor'ship, n., culte du soleil, m.

sup (seupe), n., petit coup, m. ; goutte légère, gorgée, f.

sup (seupe), v.a., (to sip) boire à petits coups, humer, siroter ; (to give supper to) donner à souper à. To — up ; boire.

sup, v.n., souper (on, de).

super. V. supernumerary.

su'perable (siou-peur'a-b'l) adj., surmontable.

superabound' (siou-peur'a-baou'n'de), v.n., surabonder (with, de).

superabun'dance (siou-peur'a-beu'n'-), n., surabondance, f.

superabun'dant, adj., surabondant.

superabun'dantly, adv., surabondamment.

superadd' (siou-peur'-), v.a., surajouter, joindre.

superaddi'tion, n., surcroît, m. ; addition, f.

superan'nuate (siou-peur'a'n-niou-), v.a., rendre suranné ; affaiblir par l'âge ; (to pension off) mettre à la retraite.

superan'nuated, adj., suranné ; (pensioned off) mis à la retraite, retraité, en retraite.

superannua'tion (siou-peur'a'n'niou-é-), n., (pensioning off) mise à la retraite ; pension de retraite, f. — fund ; caisse de retraites, f.

superb' (siou-peurbe), adj., superbe.

superb'ly, adv., superbement.

supercar'go (siou-peur'câr-gô), n., subrécargue, m.

supercil'iary (siou-peur'-), adj., (anat.) sourcilier.

supercil'ious, adj., hautain, arrogant, impérieux, fier.

supercil'iously, adv., avec hauteur ; arrogamment, fièrement.

supercil'iousness, n., hauteur, fierté, arrogance, f. ; dédain, m.

superem'inence (siou-peur'è'm'-), n., prééminence, supériorité, f.

superem'inent (siou-peur'è'm'-), adj., suréminent, prééminent, très supérieur.

superem'inently, adv., très éminemment.

superer'ogate (siou-peur'èr'-), v.n., faire plus qu'on n'est obligé, faire plus que son devoir.

supereroga'tion (-'èr'o-ghé-), n., (theol.) surérogation, f.

superer'ogatory (siou-peur'-), adj., (theol.) surérogatoire.

superex'cellence (siou-peur'-), n., excellence supérieure, f.

superex'cellent, adj., excellent, parfait ; surfin.

superfi'cial (siou-peur-fish'al), adj., (measure) de superficie ; superficiel ; (fig.) superficiel, léger, peu profond.

superficial'ity, n., peu de profondeur, m. ; caractère superficiel, m.

superfi'cially, adv., superficiellement.

superfi'cies (siou-peur-fish'ize), n., superficie, aire, f.

superfine' (siou-peur-faïne), adj., superfin, surfin.

superflu'ity, super'fluousness (siou-peur-flou-), n., superfluité, f. ; superflu, m.

super'fluous (siou-peur-flou-eusse), *adj.*, superflu.

super'fluously, *adv.*, avec superfluité; au delà du nécessaire, inutilement.

superhu'man (siou-peur-hiou-), *adj.*, surhumain.

superimpose' (siou-peur'i'm'pôze), *v.a.*, superposer, surimposer.

superimposi'tion, *n.*, superposition, surimposition, *f.*

superincum'bent (siou-peur-i'n'keu'm-), *adj.*, superposé.

supe'rior (siou-pî-), *adj.*, supérieur.

supe'rior, *n.*, supérieur, *m.*, supérieure, *f.*

superior'ity, *n.*, supériorité, *f.*

superja'cent (-djé-), *adj.*, superposé, surimposé.

super'lative (siou-peur-), *adj.*, au suprême degré; suprême; le plus haut; (gram.) superlatif.

super'lative, *n.*, (gram.) superlatif, *m.*

super'latively, *adv.*, (gram.) au superlatif; au suprême degré, superlativement.

super'lativeness, *n.*, suprême degré, *m.*

supermun'dane (siou-peur-meu'n'-), *adj.*, au-dessus du monde.

super'nal (siou-peur-), *adj.*, supérieur; céleste.

super'nally, *adv.*, par en haut, d'en haut.

supernat'ural (siou-peur-nat'iou-), *adj.*, surnaturel.

supernat'uralism, *n.*, surnaturalisme, *m.*

supernat'urally, *adv.*, surnaturellement. [*m.*

supernat'uralness, *n.*, caractère surnaturel,

supernu'merary (siou-peur-niou-meur'a-ri), *adj.*, surnuméraire; (of things) supplémentaire. — -**tooth;** *surdent, f.*

supernu'merary, *n.*, surnuméraire; (thea.) (substitute) doublure, *f.;* (super) figurant, comparse, *m.*

su'perplus (siou-peur-pleusse), *n.*, surplus, excédent, *m.*

su'perpose (siou-peur-pôze), *v.a.*, superposer.

superposi'tion, *n.*, superposition, *f.*

superroy'al (siou-peur-), *adj.*, (paper) jésus.

superscribe' (siou-peur-scraïbe), *v.a.*, mettre une suscription, une adresse, une inscription à.

superscrip'tion (siou-peur-), *n.*, adresse, suscription; inscription; (coin.) légende, *f.*

supersede' (siou-peur-cîde), *v.a.*, (to set aside) faire abandonner; supplanter, remplacer; (to suspend) différer, arrêter, suspendre; (jur.) rejeter, annuler; (to come in the room of) se substituer à, remplacer; (to be put in the room of) remplacer.

supersed'ed, *adj.*, supprimé; (of dress) démodé.

supersti'tion (siou-peur-), *n.*, superstition, *f.*

supersti'tious (siou-peur-stish'eusse), *adj.*, superstitieux.

supersti'tiously, *adv.*, superstitieusement.

supersti'tiousness, *n.*, caractère superstitieux, *m.*

superstra'tum (siou-peur-stré-), *n.*, couche supérieure, *ou* superposée, *f.*

su'perstruct (siou-peur-streukte), *v.a.*, bâtir sur; surélever un bâtiment.

superstruc'ture (-streukt'ieur), **superstruc'tion,** *n.*, édifice, *m.;* construction; superstructure, superstruction, *f.*

supervene' (siou-peur-vîne), *v.n.*, survenir.

superve'nient, *adj.*, qui survient; survenant, additionnel.

superven'tion, *n.*, arrivée inopinée; (jur.) survenance, *f.*

supervise' (siou-peur-vaïze), *v.a.*, surveiller; inspecter; contrôler; veiller à; (of books) reviser.

supervi'sion, *n.*, surveillance, inspection, *f.;* contrôle, *m.;* (of the Police) surveillance; (of books) révision, *f.*

supervi'sor (-vaï-zeur), *n.*, inspecteur, surveillant; (of books) reviseur, *m.*

su'pine (siou-païne), *adj.*, couché sur le dos; renversé; incliné; (fig.) nonchalant, oisif, indolent, insouciant.

su'pine (siou-païne), *n.*, (gram.) supin, *m.*

su'pinely, *adv.*, couché sur le dos; (fig.) nonchalamment, avec négligence.

su'pineness, *n.*, supination; (fig.) indolence, nonchalance, négligence, *f.*

sup'per (seup-peur), *n.*, souper, soupé, *m.* Lord's —; (ecc.) Cène; sainte Cène, *f.*

sup'perless, *adj.*, sans souper.

sup'per-ta'ble (-té-b'l), *n.*, table mise pour le souper, *f.*

sup'per-time (-taïme), *n.*, heure du souper, *f.*

supplant' (seup'-), *v.a.*, supplanter. To — a rival (in a woman's affection) ; *faire perdre à un rival l'affection d'une femme; s'établir sur les ruines de (son rival)* (Fontenelle).

supplanta'tion (-pla'n't'é-), *n.*, supplantation, *f.*

supplant'er, *n.*, supplantateur, *m.*

sup'ple (seup'p'l), *adj.*, souple, flexible.

sup'ple (seup'p'l), *v.a.*, assouplir.

sup'ple, *v.n.*, s'assouplir.

sup'plement, *v.a.*, suppléer; compléter; remplir les lacunes dans.

sup'plement (seup-pli-), *n.*, supplément, *m.*

supplement'al *ou* **supplement'ary,** *adj.*, supplémentaire.

supplement'arily, *adv.*, d'une manière supplémentaire.

sup'pleness (seup'p'l'-), *n.*, souplesse, flexibilité, *f.*

sup'pliant (seup-), *adj.*, suppliant.

sup'pliant (seup-), *n.*, suppliant, *m.*, suppliante, *f.;* (jur.) requérant, *m.*, requérante, *f.*

sup'pliantly, *adv.*, en suppliant.

sup'plicant (seup-), *n.*, suppliant, *m.*, suppliante, *f.;* (jur.) requérant, pétitionnaire, *m.*

sup'plicate (seup-), *v.a.*, supplier; implorer.

sup'plicatingly, *adv.*, en suppliant; d'un ton, *ou* d'un air, suppliant.

supplica'tion (-pli-ké-), *n.*, supplication; supplique; prière, *f.*

sup'plicatory (-ké-teuri), *adj.*, suppliant, de supplication.

suppli'er (seup-plaï-), *n.*, personne qui fournit, *f.;* fournisseur, *m.*

supply' (seup-plaïe), *n.*, provision, fourniture, *f.;* approvisionnement, *m.;* (reinforcements) renfort, secours; (of parliament) subsides, *m.pl.*, budget des dépenses, *m.sing.* The demand and —; (pol. econ.) *l'offre et la demande.* Commissioners of —; (Scotland) *commissaires du cadastre, m.pl.* To vote the supplies; *voter les subsides, le budget, les fonds.* To cut off the supplies of; *couper les vivres à.* To stop supplies; (parl.) *refuser de voter les fonds, refuser les subsides.* To take in a — of; *faire une provision de.* Bill of —; *projet de loi de finance, m.* Committee of —; *comité de subsides et dépenses, m.*

supply' (seup-plaïe), *v.a.*, (to furnish) fournir; offrir, procurer; (to serve instead of) suppléer à, remplacer; (a vacancy) remplir; (wants) pourvoir **à**, subvenir **à**; satisfaire; (com.) être fournisseur **de**. To — with; *fournir* **à**, ou **de**; *pourvoir* **de**; *approvisionner* **de**; *alimenter* **de**. To — what is wanting; *suppléer à ce qui manque*. To — the poor with food; *fournir de la nourriture, de quoi manger*, **aux** *pauvres*. The tradesmen who — him; *ses fournisseurs, m.pl.* I — him with goods; *je lui fournis des marchandises*. I — him; *je suis son fournisseur*.

supply'ing (seup-plaï-igne), *n.*, fourniture, *f.*; approvisionnement, *m.*

support' (seup-porte), *n.*, action de supporter, de soutenir, *f.*; (prop) soutien, support, appui; (upholding) maintien; (subsistence) entretien, soutien, *m.*, nourriture, subsistance, *f.*; (fig.) soutien, appui, *m.*, protection, *f.* In — of; *à l'appui* **de**; (for the benefit of) *au profit* **de**. For my —; *pour mon entretien*. With the favor of your —; *à la faveur de votre appui, de votre protection*.

support' (seup-porte), *v.a.*, soutenir; supporter; porter; (to endure) supporter, endurer, souffrir; (to sustain, to uphold) soutenir; (to second) appuyer; soutenir; (to keep up) soutenir, entretenir; (to provide with the necessaries of life) entretenir, nourrir, faire vivre; soutenir; pourvoir **à**. — arms! (mil.) *arme au bras!* To — one's self; *se soutenir*; (to keep one's self) *s'entretenir; se suffire à soi-même*.

support'able (-'a-b'l), *adj.*, supportable; tolérable; (that can be maintained) soutenable.

support'ably, *adv.*, supportablement.

support'er, *n.*, (prop) support, soutien; (her.) support; (adherent) adhérent, partisan; (sustainer) appui, soutien; (in a rebellion) fauteur, soutien; (defender) défenseur, *m.*

support'less, *adj.*, sans soutien; sans appui.

suppos'able (seup-pôz'a-b'l), *adj.*, supposable.

suppose' (seup-pôze), *v.a.*, supposer; présumer; s'imaginer, penser, croire. I — it was an accident; *mettons que c'était un accident; je veux bien croire que c'était un accident.* — we went (*i.e.* what do you say to our going; *si nous allions.* — they came (*i.e.* what if they should come); *si par hasard ils venaient.* That being —d; *cela supposé.* —d to be; *supposé être; censé être.* We are not —d to know it; *nous ne sommes pas censés le savoir.*

suppos'ing, *conj.*, en supposant 'que; supposons, *ou* supposé, que.

supposi'tion (seup-po-zish'-), *n.*, supposition; hypothèse, *f.*

supposi'tional, *adj.*, hypothétique.

suppositi'tious (seup-poz'i-tish-), *adj.*, supposé; faux; contrefait.

suppositi'tiously, *adv.*, par une supposition, hypothétiquement; faussement.

suppositi'tiousness, *n.*, nature fausse, *ou* supposée, *f.*

suppos'itively, *adv.*, par supposition, par hypothèse.

suppos'itory (seup-poz'i-teuri), *n.*, (med.) suppositoire, *m.*

suppress' (seup'press), *v.a.*, (to overpower) réprimer; étouffer; (to withhold from publicity) taire, supprimer; (to check) contenir, retenir; (to stifle) étouffer; (to stop) arrêter. In a —ed voice; *d'une voix étouffée.* A —ed laugh; *un rire étouffé.*

suppress'ible, *adj.*, supprimable; répressible.

suppres'sion (seup-presh'-), *n.*, suppression; répression; (med.) rétention, *f.*

suppress'ive, *adj.*, suppressif; répressif.

suppress'or, *n.*, personne qui réprime, etc., *f.*

sup'purate (seup-piou-), *v.n.*, (med.) suppurer.

suppura'tion (-piou-ré-), *n.*, suppuration, *f.*

sup'purative, *adj.*, (med.) suppuratif.

supputa'tion (-piou-té-), *n.*, supputation, *f.*

suprem'acy (siou-prè'm'-), *n.*, suprématie, *f.*; ascendant, *m.*

supreme' (siou-prî'me), *adj.*, suprême, souverain.

supreme'ly, *adv.*, au suprême degré; (of authority) avec une autorité suprême; souverainement.

sur'base (seur-béss), *n.*, (arch.) corniche (de lambris d'appui), *f.*

sur'based (seur-bés'te), *adj.*, (arch.) surbaissé; à corniche.

sur'basement, *n.*, surbaissement, *m.*

surbed' (seur-bède), *v.a.*, (a stone) déliter.

sur'charge (seur-tshàrdje), *n.*, surcharge, demande exorbitante (d'argent); charge excessive; (admin. *and* finan.) surtaxe, *f.*

surcharge', *v.a.*, surcharger; (of goods) surfaire, faire payer trop cher; (fin.) surtaxer.

surcin'gle (seur-cign'g'l), *n.*, ceinture, *f.*; (of a horse) surfaix, *m.*

surcin'gled (-cigu'g'lde), *adj.*, lié avec un surfaix.

surd (seurde), *adj.*, (math.) irrationnel; (linguist.) sourd, fort.

surd (seurde), *n.*, (math.) quantité irrationnelle; (linguist.) consonne forte, sourde, *f.*

sure (shoure), *adj.*, sûr, certain; (not liable to failure) sûr, assuré; (permanent) permanent; (secure, steady) sûr; (stable) stable. — enough! *à coup sûr!* To be — of; *être sûr* **de**, *certain* **de**. His income is —; *son revenu est sûr, assuré.* A — man; *un homme sûr.* To have a — eye; *avoir le coup d'œil sûr.* To be —; *sûrement, assurément, certainement, à coup sûr.* As — as a gun; *sûr comme père et mère.* To be — to; *ne pas manquer de.* To be —; *soyez sûr* **de**. To be — not to; *se garder* **de**; *être sûr de ne pas.* To make — of; (to secure) *s'assurer* **de**, *s'emparer* **de**; (to think one is sure to) *se croire sûr* **de**; (to rely on) *compter sur.* I am — I don't know; *je n'en sais vraiment rien; ou parole d'honneur! je ne sais pas.*

sure (shoure), *adv.*, sûrement, à coup sûr.

sure'-footed, *adj.*, qui a le pied sûr.

sure'ly, *adv.*, sûrement, assurément; certainement, à coup sûr; en vérité.

sure'ness, *n.*, certitude; sûreté, *f.*

sure'ty (shour-), *n.*, (certainty) certitude; (safety) sûreté, sécurité, *f.*; (support) soutien, appui; (evidence) témoignage, *m.*, confirmation, *f.*; (jur.) garant, répondant, *m.*; (bail) caution, *f.* Of a —; *pour sûr.* To be — for; *se porter garant* **de**, ou *répondre* **de**.

sure'tyship (shour-), *n.*, cautionnement, *m.*

surf (seurfe), *n.*, (nav.) ressac, *m.*; houle, *f.*

sur'face (seur-), *n.*, surface, *f.*

sur'feit (seur-fite), *n.*, excès de table; rassasiement; dégoût, *m.*; réplétion, *f.*; satiété, indigestion, *f.* To have a — of; *être rassasié* **de**.

sur'feit (seur-fite), *v.a.*, rassasier; (fig.) dégoûter, fatiguer; blaser **sur**. To — one's self; *se gorger.* To be —ed with; *être rassasié, ou gorgé, ou repu,* **de**.

sur'feiter, *n.*, glouton, *m.*, gloutonne, *f.*

sur'feiting, *n.*, gloutonnerie, *f.*; excès, *m.*

surf'y, *adj.*, plein de ressac, de brisants.

surge (seurdje), *n.*, lame, vague, houle, *f.*

surge (seurdje), *v.n.*, s'enfler, s'élever.

surge, *v.a.*, (nav.) larguer.

sur'geon (seur-djeune), *n.*, chirurgien; médecin, *m.* Military —; *chirurgien militaire,* Assistant- —; (milit. nav.) aide-major, *m.* Field —; *chirurgien d'ambulance, m.* — dentist; *dentiste, m.* — major; *chirurgien-major, m.*

sur'geoncy, *n.*, poste de chirurgien, *m.*

sur'gery (-djeu-ri), *n.*, chirurgie, *f.*; (apartment) laboratoire; cabinet de consultation, *m.*

sur'gical (seur-djic'-), *adj.*, chirurgical.

sur'gy (seur-dji), *adj.*, houleux, agité.

sur'lily (seur-), *adv.*, d'une manière hargneuse; d'un air rechigné, maussade.

sur'liness, *n.*, morosité, *f.*; caractère, *ou* naturel, hargneux, bourru, *m.*

sur'ly (seur-), *adj.*, morose; hargneux; maussade; bourru; (of dogs) hargneux.

surmise' (seur-maïze), *n.*, soupçon, *m.*; conjecture; supposition, *f.*

surmise' (seur-maïze), *v.a.*, se douter de; supposer, conjecturer, soupçonner.

surmis'ing, *n.*, soupçon, *m.*; conjecture, *f.*

surmount' (seur-maou'n'te), *v.a.*, surmonter; vaincre; s'élever au dessus de.

surmount'able (-'a-b'l), *adj.*, surmontable.

surmount'er, *n.*, personne qui surmonte, *f.*

sur'mullet (seur-meul'-), *n.*, (ich.) surmulet, rouget, *m.*

sur'mulot (seur-miou-), *n.*, (mam.) surmulot, *m.*

sur'name (seur-), *n.*, nom de famille; (name added to the original name) surnom, *m.* Give your Christian names and —s; *donnez vos noms et prénoms.*

surname' (seur-), *v.a.*, surnommer.

surpass' (seur-pâss), *v.a.*, surpasser; exceller, l'emporter sur.

surpass'able (-'a-b'l), *adj.*, qui peut être surpassé, surpassable.

surpass'ing, *adj.*, éminent, supérieur, éclatant, rare.

surpass'ingly, *adv.*, éminemment, supérieurement, avec éclat.

sur'plice (seur-plice), *n.*, (ecc.) surplis, *m.*

sur'pliced (seur-plis'te), *adj.*, à surplis.

sur'plice-fees (-fîze), *n.pl.*, (ecc.) casuel, *m.s.*

sur'plus (seur-pleuss), *n.*, surplus, excédent; (jur.) actif net, *m.* — stock; *solde*, *m.* — stock for sale at reduced prices; *solde au rabais, m.*

sur'plusage (-'èdje), *n.*, surplus, *m.*; excédent; (jur.) superfluité, *f.*

surpris'al (seur-praï-zal), *n.*, surprise, *f.*

surprise' (seur-praïze), *n.*, surprise, *f.*; étonnement, *m.*; (unexpected event) surprise, *f.*, coup de main, *m.* To take by —; (a town, etc.) *surprendre;* (a person) *prendre au dépourvu.* To be taken by —; *être surpris; être pris par surprise; être pris au dépourvu.* To recover from one's —; *revenir de sa surprise.*

surprise' (seur-praïze), *v.a.*, surprendre, prendre par surprise; prendre au dépourvu; étonner. Surprising to say; *chose surprenante.* To be —d at, with; *être surpris de.* I am —d at your going there; *je suis étonné que vous y alliez.* I am not —d at it; *je n'en suis pas surpris.*

surpris'ing, *adj.*, surprenant, étonnant.

surpris'ingly, *adv.*, d'une manière surprenante; étonnamment.

surren'der (seur-rè'n'-), *n.*, (milit.) reddition; (of a claim) renonciation, *f.*, abandon, *m.*; (com.) cession; (of an estate for life or years) reddition, *f.* — of property; *cession de biens, f.*

surren'der (seur-), *v.a.*, rendre, livrer; (to resign) abandonner; renoncer à; (jur.) rendre. To — one's self; *se rendre; se livrer;* (jur.) *se constituer prisonnier;* (of a bankrupt) *se mettre à la disposition de ses syndics.*

surrenderor', *n.*, (jur.) redditionnaire, *m.*

surrep'tion (seur-), *n.*, subreption, *f.*

surrepti'tious (seur-rèp-tish'eusse), *adj.*, subreptice, clandestin, frauduleux.

surrepti'tiously, *adv.*, subrepticement, clandestinement; à la dérobée.

sur'rogate (seur-), *n.*, (ecc.) délégué (d'un évêque), *m.*

sur'rogate (seur-), *v.a.*, (jur.) substituer; subroger.

surround' (seur-raou'n'de), *v.a.*, environner de; entourer de; cerner; ceindre de.

surround'ing, *adj.*, environnant, voisin.

surround'ings, *n.pl.*, (personal) entourage, milieu, *m.*; (places) alentours, environs, *m.pl.*

surtout' (seur-toute), *n.*, pardessus, *m.*

sur'vey (seur-vé), *n.*, vue, *f.*; coup d'œil; (examination) examen, *m.*, inspection, expertise, *f.*; (math.) levé, *ou* lever, des plans; levé, *ou* lever, topographique; arpentage, *m.* Trigonometrical —; *triangulation, f.* Official —; (of property) *cadastre, m.* To make, ou take, a — of; (fig.) *contempler,* ou *embrasser, dans son ensemble.*

survey' (seur-vé), *v.a.*, promener sa vue sur, considérer; contempler; (to examine) examiner, inspecter; (math.) lever le plan de; arpenter.

survey'ing, *n.*, arpentage; levé, lever des plans, *m.*

survey'ing-wheel (-hwîl), *n.*, pédomètre, odomètre, compte-pas, *m.*

survey'or (seur-vé-eur), *n.*, (of land) arpenteur, arpenteur-géomètre; (of buildings, etc.) inspecteur; commissaire voyer; (examiner) examinateur; (overseer) inspecteur, surveillant; (of taxes) contrôleur des contributions directes; (post office) inspecteur; (law) expert, *m.* — general; *inspecteur général, m.*

survey'orship, *n.*, inspection; place d'inspecteur, *ou* de contrôleur, etc., *f.*

survi'val (seur-vaï-), *n.*, survie, *f.* — of the fittest; *sélection naturelle, f.*

survi'vance (seur-vaï-), *n.*, survivance, *f.*

survive' (seur-vaïve), *v.a.* and *n.*, survivre à; survivre; (to remain, to escape death, etc.) rester, rester debout.

surviv'ing, *adj.*, survivant.

surviv'or (seur-vaïv'-), *n.*, survivant, *m.*

surviv'orship, *n.*, survivance, *f.* You will have my — (ie., you will step into my shoes); *vous aurez ma survivance* (V. Hugo, *Quatrevingt-Treize*).

susceptibil'ity (seus'cèp'-), *n.*, susceptibilité, sensibilité, *f.*

suscep'tible (seus'cèp-ti-b'l), *adj.*, susceptible de; (fig.) sensible à.

suscep'tibly, *adv.*, d'une manière susceptible.

suscep'tive (seus-), *adj.*, susceptible de.

suspect' (seus-pèk'te), *v.a.*, soupçonner; (to doubt) douter de, se défier de, soupçonner; tenir pour suspect; (to imagine to be guilty) soupçonner, suspecter; (to conjecture) se douter de, soupçonner, conjecturer. I —ed as much; *je m'en doutais, je m'y attendais.*

suspect', *v.n.*, soupçonner. I — he has...; *je le soupçonne d'avoir...;* ou *je soupçonne qu'il a...*

suspect'able, *adj.*, soupçonnable.

suspect'ed, *adj.*, suspect.

suspect'edly (-pèkt'èd'-), *adv.*, de manière à exciter les soupçons.

suspect'er, *n.*, personne qui soupçonne, *f.*

suspect'ful (-foule), *adj.*, soupçonneux; suspect.

suspect'less, *adj.*, sans soupçon.

suspend' (seus-), *v.a.*, suspendre; (payments) cesser, *ou* suspendre, ses payements.

suspend'er, *n.*, personne qui suspend, *f.*; (bandage) suspensoire, suspensoir, *m.*; (brace) bretelle, *f.*; (stockings) jarretelle, *f.*

suspense' (seus-), *n.*, suspens, doute, *m.*; incertitude, indécision; (jur.) suspension, cessation, *f.* In —; *en suspens, dans l'incertitude.*

suspens'ible (seus-pè'n'si-b'l), *adj.*, qui peut être suspendu.

suspen'sion (seus-pè'n'sheune), *n.*, suspension, (ecc.) suspense; interdiction; (of a bank) suspension de payements, *f.*

suspen'sion-bridge, *n.*, pont suspendu, *m.*

suspen'sion-pier, *n.*, jetée suspendue, *f.*

suspen'sor (seus'-), *n.*, suspensoir, *m.*

suspi′cion (seus-pish′eune), *n.*, soupçon, *m.*; (jur.) suspicion, *f.* Imprisonment on —; *détention préventive, f.* To be taken up on —; *être détenu préventivement.*

suspi′cious (seus-pish′eusse), *adj.*, soupçonneux; (liable to suspicion) suspect, louche, équivoque. —-looking; *à la mine suspecte, à l'air suspect.* That looks — to me; *cela me paraît suspect, louche.*

suspi′ciously, *adv.*, avec soupçon; d'une manière suspecte.

suspi′ciousness, *n.*, caractère soupçonneux, *m.*; défiance; méfiance; (liability to be suspected) nature suspecte, *f.*

sustain′ (seus-té′n), *v.a.*, soutenir, supporter; (to feed) entretenir, nourrir, soutenir; sustenter; (to endure) endurer, souffrir, soutenir; (to assist) soutenir, appuyer; (to maintain) soutenir, maintenir; (to hold suspended) tenir, retenir; (mus.) soutenir; (a loss) éprouver, essuyer, faire; (to bear out) justifier, prouver.

sustain′able (seus-té′n'-), *adj.*, soutenable.

sustain′er, *n.*, appui, soutien, *m.*

sustain′ing (seus-té′n'-), *adj.*, fortifiant, nourrissant.

sus′tenance (seus-té′n'-), *n.*, (support) soutien, *m.*; alimentation, subsistance; (food) nourriture, *f.*, aliments, *m.pl.*

sustenta′tion (seus-tè′n'té-), *n.*, soutien, *m.*; (med.) sustentation, *f.*

susurra′tion (siou-ceur-ré-), *n.*, (ant.) murmure, doux murmure, *m.*

sut′ler (seut′-), *n.*, vivandier, *m.*, vivandière, *f.*; cantinier, *m.*, cantinière, *f.*

suttee′ (seut′tî), *n.*, suttee, suttie, *f.*

sut′tle (seut′t'l), *adj.*, (of weight) net.

su′ture (siout′ieur), *n.*, (surg.) suture, *f.*

su′zerain (siou-zi-ré′n), *n.*, suzerain, *m.*, suzeraine, *f.*

su′zerainty, *n.*, suzeraineté, *f.*

swab (swôbe), *n.*, (nav.) balai de chiffons, torchon, *m.*; grosse éponge, *f.*; (nav.) faubert; (for a gun) écouvillon. *V.* mop.

swab (swôbe), *v.a.*, récurer; laver, nettoyer; (nav.) fauberter. — decks! *faubertez le pont!* The deck was —bed; *le pont était fauberté.*

swab′ber, *n.*, faauberteur, *m.*

swad′dle (swod′d'l), *v.a.*, emmailloter.

swad′dle (swod′d'l), *n.*, maillot, *m.*; langes, *m.pl.*

swad′dling, *n.*, emmaillotement, *m.*

swad′dling-clothes (-clôth′ze), *n.*, maillot, *m.sing.*; langes, *m.pl.*

swag (swag), *v.n.*, s'affaisser. *V.* sag.

swag′-bellied (-bèl′lide), *adj.*, à gros ventre; pansu, ventru.

swag′ger (swag-gheur), *v.n.*, faire le rodomont, faire le fanfaron, faire le crâne; (to boast) se vanter, gasconner. To — along; *marcher d'un air fanfaron, se pavaner, se carrer.*

swag′gerer, *n.*, rodomont, fanfaron, bravache, crâne; fier-à-bras, tapageur; (boaster) vanteur, vantard, gascon, *m.*

swag′gering, *n.*, rodomontade, fanfaronnade, crânerie; (boasting) vanterie, gasconnade, *f.*

swag′gering, *adj.*, fanfaron, de fanfaron, de crâne; (boasting) vantard, de gascon.

swag′gy (swag-ghi), *adj.*, pendant. *V.* saggy.

swain (swé′ne), *n.*, berger; pastoureau; jeune homme; villageois; jeune paysan; amant, *m.*

swal′low (swol′lô), *n.*, gosier, *m.*; arrière-bouche; (what is swallowed at once) gorgée; (voracity) voracité, *f.*; (orni.) hirondelle, *f.* What a —! (jest.) *quelle avaloire!* One — does not make a summer; (prov.) *une hirondelle ne fait pas le printemps.*

swal′low (swol′lô), *v.a.*, avaler; (to ingulf) engloutir; (to absorb, to occupy) absorber; (to consume) consumer; (to believe) avaler, gober. To—down; *avaler*; (fig.) *avaler, gober.* To—the wrong way; *avaler de travers.* To — up;

avaler; (to ingulf) *engloutir*; (to absorb) *absorber, consumer.* To be —ed up by the waves; *être englouti dans les vagues.*

swal′lower, *n.*, avaleur, *m.*

swal′low-fish, *n.*, (ich.) hirondelle de mer, *f.*

swal′lowing, *n.*, déglutition; absorption, *f.*; avalement; engloutissement, *m.*

swal′low-stone (-stône), *n.*, pierre d'hirondelle, *f.*

swal′low-tail (swol′lô′téle), *n.*, (carp.) queue d'aronde, *f.*; (coat) habit à queue d'hirondelle, à queue de morue, *m.* — butterfly; *grand porte-queue, m.*

swal′low-wort (-wurte), *n.*, (bot.) chélidoine; asclépiade, *f.*, dompte-venin, *m.*

swamp, *n.*, marais, marécage, *m.*

swamp, *v.a.*, enfoncer dans; submerger; (a boat) faire submerger, faire chavirer; (fig.) plonger dans de graves difficultés. To be —ed; (of boats) *chavirer, couler à fond; s'emplir d'eau.*

swamp′y, *adj.*, marécageux.

swan, *n.*, cygne, *m.* The song of the dying —; *le chant du cygne.*

swan′-like, *adj.*, de cygne; semblable au cygne.

swan′s-down (swa′n'z′daou′ne), *n.*, duvet de cygne; (cloth) drap de vigogne, *m.*

swan′-shot, *n.*, plomb à cygne, *m.*

swan′-skin (-ski′n), *n.*, molleton, *m.*

swap, *v.a.*, échanger, troquer. Let us go —s; (fam.) *troquons.*

sward (sworde), *n.*, gazon, *m.*; pelouse, *f.*

sward (sworde), *v.a.*, (to cover with sward) couvrir de gazon, gazonner.

sward′y, *adj.*, couvert de gazon.

swarm (swôrme), *n.*, (of bees; fig.) essaim, *m.*; (crowd) multitude, nuée, *f.* — of ants; *fourmilière, f.*

swarm (swôrme), *v.n.*, essaimer; (fig.) s'attrouper, accourir en foule. To — with; *fourmiller de.* To — up; *se presser en foule sur*, ou *dans*; *grimper en foule à*, ou *sur.*

swarm′ing, *n.*, essaimage, *m.*; *adj.*, pullulant.

swarth′iness (sworth′-), *n.*, teint basané, *m.*

swarth′y (sworthi), *adj.*, basané, hâlé; bistré.

swash (swôsh), *n.*, grand flux d'eau; clapotis, clapotage, *m.* —-buckler; *fanfaron, matamore, m.*

swath (swôth), *n.*, (agri.) andain, *m.*

swathe (swéthe), *v.a.*, emmailloter; (fig.) envelopper de.

sway, *n.*, (swing of a weapon) course; (anything moving with bulk and power) masse; (preponderance) prépondérance, *f.*; (power) pouvoir, empire, sceptre, *m.*, puissance; domination; autorité; (influence) influence, *f.* To bear —; *dominer, prédominer; porter le sceptre.*

sway, *v.a.n.*, manier, porter; (to and fro) balancer; (to bias) influencer; influer sur; (to rule) gouverner, régir, diriger, conduire; (to lean) pencher, incliner; brandir, ballotter; secouer. To — from; *détourner de.* To — on; *pousser en avant.* To — to and fro; *chanceler, se balancer, aller et venir.* To — up; (nav.) *guinder*; *hisser.*

sway′ing, *n.*, (swé-igne) *n.*, balancement, *m.*

swear (swère), *v.a.*, (preterit, Swore; past part., Sworn) (witnesses, a jury) faire prêter serment à, déférer le serment à; (an oath) prêter. To — in; *assermenter.* To be sworn in; *prêter serment*; (of judges, etc.) *être assermenté.* To — off; *renoncer solennellement à.*

swear (swère), *v.n.*, jurer; prêter serment; faire serment; déclarer sous la foi du serment, affirmer sur serment; (to blaspheme) jurer, blasphémer. To— falsely; *se parjurer*; (jur.) *porter faux témoignage.* To — to; *jurer de.* To— like a trooper; *jurer comme un charretier.* To curse and —; *jurer et sacrer.* To— by all that is sacred, by all the powers; *jurer ses grands dieux.* To — by; *avoir grande confiance* **en**; *jurer* **par.** To — at; *jurer* **après.**

swear'er, *n.,* (blasphemer) jureur, blasphémateur, *m.* What a — he is! *comme il jure!*

swear'ing, *n.,* serments; (blaspheming) jurements, jurons, *m.pl.* — in; *prestation de serment;* (of judges, etc.) *assermentation, f.*

sweat (swète), *n.,* sueur; (fig.) sueur, fatigue, *f.;* sueurs, *f.pl.* By the — of one's brow; *à la sueur de son front.* All in a —; *tout en nage, tout en sueur.*

sweat (swète), *v.n.,* **suer**; (fig.) travailler comme un nègre, comme un forçat. *v.a.,* faire suer. To — out; *faire passer par la sueur.*

sweat'er, *n.,* (garment) vareuse, *f.,* tricot; (grinder of workmen) exploiteur, marchandeur, *m.* This hill is a —! *ouf! cette côte est rude!*

sweat'iness, *n.,* sueur, *f.;* état de sueur, *m.*

sweat'ing, *n.,* sueur, fatigue, *f.*

sweat'ing, *adj.,* en sueur; tout en sueur.

sweat'ing-bath, *n.,* bain de vapeur, *m.*

sweat'ing-house (-haouce), *n.,* étuve, *f.*

sweat'ing-iron (-aïeur'n), *n.,* strigile, *m.*

sweat'ing-room (-roume), *n.,* (med.) étuve, *f.;* (agri.) séchoir, *m.*

sweat'ing-sickness, *n.,* suette miliaire, *f.*

sweat'y (swét'-), *adj.,* en sueur; couvert de sueur.

Swede (swîde), *n.,* Suédois, *m.,* Suédoise, *f.;* (turnip) rutabaga, navet de Suède, *m.*

Swed'ish (swîd'-), *adj.,* suédois, de Suède.

sweep (swîpe), *v.a.,* (*preterit* and *past part.,* Swept) balayer; (a chimney) ramoner; (to sweep over) glisser **sur,** raser; (the lyre) frapper; (a river) draguer; (to view rapidly) parcourir; parcourir des yeux. To — away, off; *balayer; emporter, enlever.* To — up; *balayer.* To — a room; *balayer une chambre.* Her dress —s the ground; *sa robe balaie la terre.* To — the board; *faire rafle.* To — the board of honors; (at universities) *tout enlever, tout remporter.*

sweep, *v.n.,* passer rapidement; (to pass with pomp) passer avec pompe, marcher pompeusement. To — along, over; *passer rapidement* **sur**; *brûler.* To — round; *faire le tour* **de**; *se tourner rapidement, décrire une courbe.* The train swept past; *le train passa comme la foudre, comme un trait.* The procession swept past; *la procession,* ou *le cortège, défila au grand galop.*

sweep (swîpe), *n.,* balayage; (stroke with a broom) coup de balai; (metal.) fourneau de coupelle; (oar) aviron de galère; (chimney-sweep) ramoneur, *m.;* (the compass of any turning body) courbe décrite; (the carrying off) razzia, rafle, *f.;* (the compass of anything flowing) cours, *m.,* course, *f.;* (the compass of a stroke) coup, *m.,* ligne; (tech.) point, cambrure, courbe; (extent) étendue; (reach) portée, *f.* At one —; *d'un seul coup; tout d'un trait; d'un coup de filet.* To give a —; *donner un coup de balai* **à.** To take a —; *décrire une courbe.* To make a clean — of; *faire table rase* **de.**

sweep'er, *n.,* balayeur, *m.,* balayeuse, *f.;* (of chimneys) ramoneur, *m.*

sweep'ing, *n.,* balayage; (of chimneys) ramonage, *m.* —s, *pl.,* balayures, ordures, *f.pl.*

sweep'ing, *adj.,* rapide, irrésistible; destructeur; (fig.) complet, vaste, étendu; général, qui ne ménage personne.

sweep'ingly, *adv.,* rapidement; (fig.) en masse, sans ménagement, sans distinction.

sweep'-net, *n.,* épervier, *f.*

sweep'stake ou **sweep'stakes,** *n.,* (horse-races; billiards) poule, *f.*

sweep'y (swîp'-), *adj.,* qui passe rapidement; rapide; (wavy) onduleux, ondoyant, ondulé.

sweet (swîte), *n.,* (sweet substance) chose douce, chose sucrée, sucrerie, *f.;* (perfume) parfum; (word of endearment) chéri, *m.,* chérie, *f.,*

doux ami, *m.,* douce amie, *f.;* (something pleasing) plaisir, *m.,* douceur, *f.*

sweet (swîte), *adj.,* (to the taste) doux, sucré; succulent, délicieux; (fragrant) doux, odoriférant; (melodious) doux, suave, mélodieux; (to the eye) qui flatte les yeux; (beautiful) beau; joli, gentil; (fresh) doux, frais; (mild) doux; (not stale) bon, frais; (of wine) liquoreux, sucré; (charming) charmant; (jest.) joli. You're a — youth! (jest.) *vous êtes un joli garçon!* What a — child! *quel charmant enfant!* To be — upon; *être amoureux* **de.** To smell —; *sentir bon.* How — of you! *que vous êtes aimable!* —, —! (to a bird) *petit, petit!* To have a — tooth; *aimer les douceurs, les friandises.* To keep a house —; *tenir une maison propre, bien aérée.* — herbs; *fines herbes, f.pl.* —-acorn; *gland doux, m.* —-calabash; (bot.) *grenadille, passiflore, fleur de la passion, f.* —-chervil; (bot.) *myrrhis; cerfeuil musqué, m.* —-chestnut; (bot.) *châtaignier, m.* —-potato; (bot.) *patate, f.* —-apple; *pomme douce, f.*

sweet'-bread (-brède), *n.,* ris de veau, *m.*

sweet'-brier (-braï'-), *n.,* églantier odorant, *m.*

sweet'en (swît't'n), *v.a.,* sucrer; (to make mild, to soften) adoucir; (to make pleasing) adoucir, rendre agréable; (a room, the air) purifier, désinfecter; (to perfume) embaumer, parfumer; (the soil) fertiliser; (water, butter, etc.) rafraîchir; (with sugar) sucrer; (medicine) édulcorer; (paint.) adoucir.

sweet'ener, *n.,* adoucissant, *m.;* (fig.) qui adoucit.

sweet'ening, *n.,* action de sucrer, purification, désinfection; (of medicine) édulcoration, *f.;* (of pain) adoucissement, *m.*

sweet'heart (-hârte), *n.,* amoureux, *m.,* amoureuse, *f.;* amant, *m.,* amante, *f.;* bon ami, *m.,* bonne amie, *f.*

sweet'ish, *adj.,* douceâtre.

sweet'ishness, *n.,* goût douceâtre, *m.*

sweet'ly, *adv.,* doucement; agréablement, mélodieusement; avec douceur.

sweet-mar'joram (-mâr-djo-), *n.,* (bot.) marjolaine commune, *f.*

sweet'meat, *n.,* sucrerie, *f.;* bonbon, *m.*

sweet'ness, *n.,* douceur; saveur; (melody) douceur, mélodie; (fragrance) douceur, *f.,* parfum, *m.;* (mildness) suavité, douceur; (freshness) fraîcheur; (of eatables) bonté; (fig.) douceur, *f.,* charme, attrait, *m.*

sweet' nothings, *n.pl.,* douceurs, *f.pl.* To say —; *dire des douceurs* **à.**

sweet'-oil, *n.,* huile d'olives, *f.*

sweet'-pea (-pî), *n.,* pois de senteur, *m.*

sweet'-scented ou **sweet'-smelling,** *adj.,* odoriférant, odorant, parfumé.

sweet'-stuffs, *n.pl.,* sucreries, *f.pl.,* bonbons, *m.pl.*

sweet'-tempered (-tè'm'peurde), *adj.,* d'un caractère doux.

sweet' things, *n.pl.,* douceurs, *f.pl.*

sweet'-toned (-tô'n'de), *adj.,* d'un son doux, au son doux.

sweet'-tongued, *adj.,* doucereux, mielleux.

sweet'-toothed, *adj.,* qui aime les sucreries.

sweet'-water (grape), *n.,* chasselas, *m.*

sweet'-weed (-wîde), *n.,* (bot.) capraire théiforme, *f.*

sweet'-william, *n.,* œillet barbu, œillet velu, œillet de poète, bouquet parfait, *m.*

swell (swèl), *v.n.,* (*preterit,* Swelled; *past part.,* Swelled, Swollen) enfler, s'enfler; se gonfler; (to increase by any addition) grossir, croître, augmenter; (to bulge out) faire ventre (V. (Hugo) ou le ventre (Littré), bomber; (to become larger) grandir; (to strut) se carrer, s'enfler; (of sound) augmenter; (to rise) s'élever, se soulever. To — along; *se carrer en marchant.* To — into; *s'élever* **en**; *grandir* **en**; *se conver-*

tir **en**, *devenir ;* (b.s.) *dégénérer* **en**. To — to ; *s'élever* **à**. To — out ; *bomber ; faire ventre ; bouffer*. To — with pride ; *bouffir d'orgueil*. To — with rage ; *bouffer, bouffir de colère*.

swell, *v.a.*, enfler, gonfler ; (to aggravate) aggraver ; (to raise to arrogance) bouffir, faire bouffer ; (to enlarge) grandir, grossir, élever ; (mus.) enfler. To be —ed with pride ; *être bouffi d'orgueil*.

swell (swèl), *n.*, bombement, *m. ;* (elevation) élévation, montée ; (of sound) renflement, *m. ;* (of the sea) houle ; (mus.) pédale d'expression, *f. ;* (of an organ) récit ; vibration sonore ; (of sound) ampleur ; (pers.) fashionable, freluquet, gandin, élégant, muscadin ; faraud, *m*. Ground —; *houle de fond, f*. What a — she is ! *quelle toilette elle a !* To cut a —; *faire des embarras*.

swell'ing, *n.*, (tumor) enflure ; (morbid enlargement) bouffissure, *f. ;* (arch.) galbe ; (protuberance) gonflement, bombement, *m.*, bosse, grosseur ; (of rivers) crue, *f. ;* (of the waves) soulèvement ; (of anger, grief, pride) mouvement, transport, *m*.

swell'ing, *adj.*, qui enfle ; qui s'enfle, qui se gonfle ; qui bouffe ; qui grossit ; (turgid) enflé, ampoulé ; (growing larger) grandissant, croissant ; (of sound) augmentant, grossissant.

swell'ish, *adj.*, élégant, à la mode ; recherché, affecté, prétentieux.

swell'-mob, *n.*, pickpockets, chevaliers d'industrie, *m.pl.*

swel'ter, *v.n.*, griller, étouffer de chaleur, être accablé de chaleur. It is —ing hot ; *on grille* ou *il fait une chaleur étouffante*.

swel'try (swèl-), *adj.*, étouffant, accablant.

swerve (sweurve), *v.n.*, errer ; (to incline) incliner ; (milit.) obliquer ; (of horses) faire un écart. To — from ; *s'écarter* **de**, *s'éloigner* **de**, *dévier* **de**.

swerv'ing (sweurv'-), *n.*, (of horses) écart, déviation, *f*.

swift, *adj.*, rapide ; (prompt) prompt, vif ; (in running) vite ; léger, léger à la course ; (of a ship) bon marcheur, rapide.

swift, *n.*, bobine, *f. ;* (orni.) martinet, *m*.

swift'er, *n.*, (nav.) ceinture, *f. ;* (of the capstan) garde-corps, *m*.

swift'-footed, *adj.*, léger à la course.

swift'ly, *adv.*, vite, vîtement, rapidement, promptement, vivement, agilement.

swift'ness, *n.*, rapidité ; promptitude, vitesse, *f*.

swift'-sailing (-sél'-), *adj.*, fin voilier, bon marcheur, de marche rapide.

swift'-winged (-wign'de), *adj.*, à l'aile rapide.

swig, *v.a.* and *n.*, boire à longs traits, *ou* à grands coups ; (pop.) flûter. To — at ; *humer*.

swig, *n.*, long trait (en buvant) ; (of liquor) grand coup, coup sur coup, *m*.

swill, *n.*, lavure de vaisselle, lavure, *f. ;* (of liquor) grand coup, coup sur coup, *m.*, lampée, *f*.

swill, *v.a.*, boire avidement ; (to inebriate) enivrer, griser.

swill, *v.n.*, s'enivrer ; (pop.) pomper, lamper.

swill'er, *n.*, ivrogne ; grand buveur, *m*.

swill'ings (swill'ign'ze), *n.pl.*, lavure de vaisselle, *f.sing*.

swill'-tub (-teube), *n.*, baquet à cochon, *m*.

swim, *v.n.*, (*preterit*, Swam ; *past part.*, Swum) nager ; (to float) flotter, surnager ; (to glide along) glisser, filer ; (to be dizzy) avoir des vertiges ; (of the head) tourner ; (to be overflowed) être inondé **de**. To — across ; *traverser à la nage*. To — out of one's depth ; *perdre pied*. To — over ; *passer à la nage*. To — with ; *suivre ; se laisser aller* **à**. To — with the tide ; *nager avec le courant*. To — against the tide ; *remonter le courant en nageant ; nager contre le courant*. To be —ming in riches ; *nager dans l'abondance,*

ou *en pleine eau*. My head is —ming ; *la tête me tourne ; j'ai le vertige*.

swim, *n.*, bout de nage, *m.*, nage, *f. ;* (bath) bain, *m*. In the —; *dans le secret ; dans le courant ; au courant de toutes les circonstances*.

swim'mer, *n.*, nageur, *m.*, nageuse, *f. ;* (orni.) palmipède, *m*.

swim'ming, *n.*, natation, nage, *f. ;* (dizziness) vertige, étourdissement, *m*. By —; *en nageant,* à *la nage*.

swim'ming-bath, *n.*, bain de natation, *m*.

swim'ming-belt, *n.*, ceinture de natation, *f*.

swim'ming-bladder, *n.*, vessie natatoire, *f*.

swim'mingly, *adv.*, aisément ; d'emblée ; à merveille, tout seul ; comme sur des roulettes.

swim'ming-match, *n.*, course à la nage, *f*.

swim'ming-school (-skoule), *n.*, école de natation, *f*.

swim'ming-tub (-teube), *n.*, baquet, *m*.

swin'dle (swi'n'd'l), *v.a.*, escroquer, flouer. To — out of ; *escroquer* à.

swin'dle (swi'n'd'l), *n.*, escroquerie, flouerie, *f*.

swin'dler, *n.*, escroc ; chevalier d'industrie ; floueur, *m*.

swin'dling, *n.*, escroquerie, flouerie, *f*.

swine (swaï'ne), *n.sing.* and *pl.*, cochon, pourceau, porc, *m*. To cast pearls before —; *semer des perles, des marguerites, devant les pourceaux*.

swine'-herd (-heurde), *n.*, porcher, *m*.

swine'-pipe (-païpe), *n.*, (orni.) mauvis, *m*.

swine'-pox, *n.*, (med.) varicelle, *f*.

swine'-stone (-stône), *n. V.* **stink-stone**.

swine'-sty (-staïe), *n.*, étable à cochons, *f*.

swing (swigne), *n.*, (oscillation) oscillation, vibration, *f. ;* (motion from one side to the other) va et vient, balancement, *m. ;* (apparatus to swing in) balançoire, *f. ;* (of bells) branle, *m. ;* (free course) libre carrière, *f.*, libre essor, libre cours, élan, *m. ;* (influence) force, action, influence ; (sweep of a moving body) courbe décrite, ligne parcourue, *f*. In full —; *en pleine opération,* (fig.) *en pleine activité*.

swing (swigne), *v.a.*, faire vibrer ; balancer ; faire aller ; (to wave) agiter ; (to brandish) brandir, brandiller.

swing, *v.n.*, vibrer ; se balancer ; (of a ship) éviter ; (to be hanging) pendiller ; (in walking) se dandiner ; (of a pendulum) osciller ; (to be hanged) pendre.

swing'-bar, *n.*, palonnier, *m*.

swing'-bed, *n.*, hamac, *m*.

swing'-bridge, *n.*, pont tournant, *m*.

swing'-cot, *n.*, barcelonnette, *f*.

swing'-door, *n.*, porte battante, *f*.

swinge (swi'n'dje), *v.a.*, rosser, étriller, battre.

swing'er (swign-eur), *n.*, personne qui se balance, *f. ;* (fig.) frondeur, *m*.

swing'-gate, *n.*, porte, *ou* barrière, à bascule, *f*.

swing'ing (swign'-), *n.*, vibration, *f. ;* balancement, branlement, (nav.) évitage, *m*.

swing'ing (swign'-), *adj.*, énorme.

swing'ingly (swign'-), *adv.*, énormément.

swin'gle (swign'g'l), *v.a.*, macquer (le lin, etc.). *v.n.*, gambiller.

swin'gle-tree (-trî),*n.*, volée,*f. ;* palonnier, *m*.

swin'ish (swaï'n'-), *adj.*, de cochon ; grossier ; malpropre, sale, bestial.

swin'ishly (swaï'n'-), *adv.*, salement, comme un cochon, malproprement.

swipe (swaïpe), *n.*, coup fort, *m*.

swipes (swaïp'ce), *n.pl.*, mauvaise *ou* petite bière,*f.sing. ;* (in colleges) abondance, *f*.

Swiss, *n.*, Suisse, *m.*, Suissesse, *f*.

Swiss, *adj.*, suisse.

switch (switshe), *n.*, badine, houssine, gaule ; (railways) aiguille, *f.*, rail mobile, *m*. — -back railway ; *montagne russe, f. ; chemin de fer canadien, m*.

switch, *v.a.*, houssiner, cingler, sangler ; (railways) aiguiller ; garer (teleg.). To — on, off ; *ouvrir, fermer le circuit.*

switch'man, *n.*, (railways) aiguilleur, *m.*

swiv'el, *n.*, tourniquet ; (mil.) porte-mousqueton ; (artil.) pierrier, *m.* — bridge ; *pont tournant, m.* — gun ; *pierrier, m.*

swoon (swoune), *v.n.*, s'évanouir, se trouver mal ; tomber en défaillance.

swoon (swoune), *n.*, évanouissement, *m. ;* syncope, défaillance, *f.*

swoon'ing, *n.* V. **swoon.**

swoop (swoupe), *v.a.n.*, fondre **sur** ; (to seize) s'emparer **de**, enlever. To — down upon ; (of birds of prey) *s'abattre* **sur** ; (fig.) *se précipiter* **sur**, *fondre* **sur.** Seeing him from afar — down on the waters ; " *en le voyant de loin s'abattre sur les eaux* " (A. de Musset).

swoop (swoupe), *n.*, (of birds of prey) action de fondre sur la proie, *f. ;* coup, *m.* At one fell —; *d'un seul coup.*

swop, *v.a.*, troquer, échanger.

sword (sôrde), *n.*, épée, *f. ;* (broad) sabre ; (harlequin's sword) batte, *f. ;* (fig.) fer, glaive, *m.* — in hand ; *l'épée à la main.* At the point of the — ; *à la pointe de l'épée.* To cross —s ; *croiser l'épée.* To fight with —s ; *se battre à l'épée.* To put to the — ; *passer au fil de l'épée.* To put to fire and — ; *mettre à feu et à sang.* — of justice ; *glaive de la justice, m.*

sword'-bayonet, *n.*, sabre-baïonnette, *m.*

sword'-bearer (-bèr'-), *n.*, porte-épée, *m.*

sword'-belt, *n.*, ceinturon, porte-épée, *m.*

sword'-blade, *n.*, lame d'épée, *f.*

sword'-cane, *n.* V. **sword-stick.**

sword'-cutler (-keut'-), *n.*, fourbisseur, *m.*

sword'-fight (-faïte), *n.*, combat à l'épée, *m.*

sword'-fish, *n.*, espadon, *m.*

sword'-hanger, *n.*, porte-épée, *m.*

sword'-hilt, *n.*, poignée d'épée, *f.*

sword'-knot (-note), *n.*, nœud d'épée, *m. ;* dragonne, *f.*

sword'-player (-plé-eur), *n.*, tireur d'épée, *m.*

sword'-shaped (-shép'te), *adj.*, (bot.) ensiforme.

swords'man (sôrd'z'-), *n.*, tireur d'armes, *m. ;* lame, *f. ;* sabreur, *m.*

sword'-stick, *n.*, canne à épée, *f.*

sword'-thrust, *n.*, coup d'épée, *m.*

sworn (swôrne), *adj.*, juré ; assermenté ; (of enemies) juré, acharné ; (of friends) intime, dévoué. To be —, *ou* — in; *prêter serment, être assermenté.* — to ; (do a thing) *obligé par serment à.*

syb'arite (-raïte), *n.*, sybarite, *m.*

sybarit'ic, *adj.*, sybaritique.

syc'amore (-môre), *n.*, (bot.) sycomore, érable blanc, *m.*

syc'ophancy, **syc'ophantry**, *n.*, adulation, flagornerie, *f.*

syc'ophant (-fa'n'te), *n.*, sycophante, flagorneur, *m.*, flagorneuse, *f. ;* adulateur, *m.*, adulatrice, *f.*

syc'ophant, *v.n.*, flagorner, aduler.

sycophan'tic, *adj.*, de flagorneur, de parasite, adulateur.

syllab'ic, *adj.*, syllabique.

syllab'ically, *adv.*, syllabiquement, par syllabes.

syllabica'tion (-bi-ké-), *n.*, division des mots en syllabes, syllabisation (Bescherelle), *f.*

syl'lable (sil'la-b'l), *n.*, syllabe, *f.*

syl'labus, *n.*, extrait, résumé ; abrégé, sommaire ; (c.rel.) syllabus ; (univ.) programme, *m.*

syllep'sis, *n.*, syllepse, *f.*

syl'logism (-lo-djiz'm), *n.*, syllogisme, *m.*

syllogis'tic, *adj.*, syllogistique.

syllogis'tically (-lo-djist'-), *adv.*, par un syllogisme.

syllogiza'tion (-lo-djaï-zé-), *n.*, raisonnement par syllogismes, *m.*

syl'logize (-lo-djaïze), *v.n.*, raisonner par syllogismes.

syl'logizer (-lo-djaïz'-), *n.*, personne qui raisonne par syllogismes, *f.*

sylph, *n.* sylphe, *m. ;* sylphide, *f.*

sylph'id, *n.*, sylphide, *f.*

syl'van, *adj.*, champêtre, agreste, des bois.

syl'vanite (-va'n'aïte), *n.*, (min.) tellurure d'or et d'argent, *m. ;* sylvane, *f.*

sylves'trian, *adj.*, sylvestre.

syl'via, *n.*, (orni.) sylvie, *f.*

sym'bol, *n.*, symbole ; signe symbolique ; (alg.) symbole, signe, *m.*

symbol'ic *ou* **symbol'ical**, *adj.*, symbolique.

symbol'ically, *adv.*, d'une manière symbolique, par symbole.

symboliza'tion (-bol'aïzé-), *n.*, symbolisation, *f.*

sym'bolize (-'aïze), *v.n.*, symboliser.

sym'bolize, *v.a.*, faire accorder.

symbol'ogy (-'o'dji), *n.*, art d'exprimer par des symboles, *m. ;* symbolisation, *f.*

symmet'rical (-mèt'-), *adj.*, symétrique.

symmet'rically, *adv.*, symétriquement.

sym'metrize (-mét'raïze), *v.a.*, symétriser, rendre symétrique.

sym'metry (-mè-), *n.*, symétrie, *f.*

sympathet'ic, *adj.*, sympathique.

sympathet'ically (-thèt'-), *adv.*, sympathiquement ; par sympathie.

sym'pathize (-thaïze), *v.n.*, sympathiser **avec**, compatir à **ou** avec.

sym'pathy (-thi), *n.*, sympathie, *f.*

sympho'nious (-phô-) *ou* **symphon'ic**, *adj.*, harmonieux.

sym'phonist, *n.*, symphoniste, *m.*

sym'phony, *n.*, (harmony) harmonie ; (instrument, composition) symphonie, *f.*

sympo'sium (-pô-zi-), *n.*, banquet, *m.*

symp'tom (si'm-to'm), *n.*, symptôme, indice, *m.*

synær'esis (-'ïr'i-cice), *n.*, synérèse, *f.*

synagog'ical (-go-djic'-), *adj.*, de la synagogue.

syn'agogue (-goghe), *n.*, synagogue, *f.*

syn'chronal *ou* **synchron'ical** (sign-kro-), *adj.*, synchronique, synchrone, contemporain.

synchron'ically (sign'kro-), *adv.*, d'une manière synchronique.

syn'chronism (sign'kro-niz'm), *n.*, synchronisme, *m.*

syn'chronize (sign'kro-naïze), *v.n.*, être contemporain (with, **avec**).

syn'chronous (-kro-), *adj.* V. **syn'chronal.**

syn'copate, *v.a.*, (gram.) élider ; (mus.) syncoper.

syncopa'tion (-pé-), *n.*, élision ; (mus.) syncope, *f. ;* contre-temps, *m.*

syn'cope (sign'ko-pi), *n.*, syncope, *f.*

syn'dic (sin-), *n.*, syndic, *m.*

syn'dicate, *n.*, syndicat, *m.*

syn'dicate, *v.a.*, syndiquer ; juger, censurer.

synec'doche (-nèk'do-ki), *n.*, synecdoche, synecdoque, *f.*

synneuro'sis (si'n'niou-rô-cice), *n.*, (anat.) synévrose, *f.*

syn'od, *n.*, synode, *m. ;* (astron.) conjonction, *f.*

syn'odal, *adj.*, synodal.

synod'ic *ou* **synod'ical**, *adj.*, synodique.

synod'ically, *adv.*, synodalement, synodiquement.

syn'onym, *n.*, synonyme, *m.*

synon'ymize (-maïze), *v.a.*, exprimer par des synonymes.

synon'ymous, *adj.*, synonyme.

synon'ymously, *adv.*, comme synonyme.

synon'ymy, *n.*, synonymie, *f.*

synop'sis, *n.*, (*synopses*) sommaire, résumé, *m.*, vue générale, *f. ; tableau synoptique, m.*

synop'tical, *adj.*, synoptique.

synop'tically, *adv.*, d'une manière synoptique.

syntac'tical, *adj.*, (gram.) syntaxique, conforme aux règles de la syntaxe.

syn'tax, *n.*, (gram.) syntaxe, *f.*

syn'thesis (-thi-cice), *n.*, (*syntheses*) (chem., philos., surg.) synthèse, *f.*

synthet'ic *ou* **synthet'ical** (-thèt'-), *adj.*, (chem., philos., geom.) synthétique.

synthet'ically (-thèt'-), *adv.*, (geom.) synthétiquement.

Syr'acusan, *n.*, Syracusain, *m.*

Syr'iac, *n.*, syriaque, *m.*

Syr'iac, *adj.*, syriaque.

Syr'ian, *adj.*, syrien.

Syr'ian, *n.*, Syrien, *m.*, Syrienne, *f.*

syrin'ga (si-rign'ga), *n.*, (bot.) syringa, lilas, *m.*

syr'inge (sir'i'n'dje), *n.*, seringue, *f.*

syr'inge (sir'i'n'dje), *v.a.*, seringuer ; injecter.

syr'inging, *n.*, seringage, seringuement, *m.*

syr'up (sir'eupe), *n.*, sirop, *m.*

syr'upy, *adj.*, sirupeux.

sys'tem, *n.*, système ; régime ; organisme, *m. ;* constitution ; faiseur de systèmes, *f. ;* (railway system) réseau, *m.* — monger ; *systématiste, m.* (Bescherelle).

systemat'ic *ou* **systemat'ical**, *adj.*, systématique.

systemat'ically, *adv.*, systématiquement.

sys'tematist *ou* **sys'tematizer** (-taïz'-), *n.*, auteur, *ou* faiseur, de systèmes, *m.*

systematiza'tion (-taï-zé-), *n.*, réduction en système, systématisation, *f.*

sys'tematize (-taïze), *v.a.*, systématiser, réduire en système.

sys'tole, *n.*, (gram., physiol.) systole, *f.*

sys'tyle, *n.*, (arch.) systyle, *m.*

sy'zygy (saï-zi-dji), *n.*, (astron.) syzygie, *f.*

T

t, vingtième lettre de l'alphabet, **t**, *m.* Marked with a —; *marqué d'un V. ; voleur.* That fits me to a —; *cela me va comme un gant, parfaitement, on ne peut mieux.*

tab, *n.*, patte, *f.*

tab'ard (-bârde) *ou* **tab'erd** (-beurde), *n.*, (of heralds) tabard, *m. ;* cotte d'armes, *f.*

tab'aret, *n.*, satin rayé (pour rideaux), *m.*

tab'by, *n.*, tabis ; (cat) chat tigré, *m.*

tab'by, *adj.*, tacheté, moucheté, tavelé, tigré.

tab'by, *v.a.*, (tech.) tabiser.

tabefac'tion (-i-fak'-), *n.*, dépérissement, marasme, *m.*

tab'efy, *v.n.*, amaigrir, dépérir.

tabel'lion, *n.*, tabellion, *m.*

tab'ernacle (-eur-na-k'l), *n.*, **tabernacle** ; sanctuaire, *m.*

tabernac'ular (-nak'iou-), *adj.*, treillissé.

ta'bes (té-bîze), *n.*, marasme, *m.*

tab'id (ta-bide), *adj.*, (med.) tabide ; consumé par le marasme.

tab'idness, *n.*, dépérissement, marasme, *m.*

tab'lature (-tioure), *n.*, (mus.) tablature ; (paint.) peinture murale, *f.*

ta'ble (té-b'l), *n.*, table ; (loo table) guéridon, *m. ;* (tablet) tablette, table, *f. ;* (paint.) tableau, *m. ;* (arch.) tablette, *f. ;* (persp.) plan perspectif, *m. ;* (anat.) table ; (catalogue) table, *f.*, catalogue, *m. ;* (synopsis) table synoptique ; (among jewelers) table ; (index) table des matières, *f. pl.* The Lord's —; *la sainte table ; la table du Seigneur.* Astronomical, chronological —s ; *tables astronomiques, chronologiques.* Office—; *bureau, m.* Folding—; *table brisée.* Dining-, tea-, work-, card-, writing—; *table à manger, à thé, à ouvrage, à jouer, à écrire.*

Kitchen—; *table de cuisine.* Night—; *table de nuit.* Raised —; (sculpt.) *abaque, m.* To keep open —; *tenir table ouverte.* Good, poor —; *bonne, pauvre table.* Frugal —; *table frugale.* Side—; (for children) *petite table.* To keep a good —; *avoir, tenir, bonne table.* To sit down to —; *se mettre à table.* To be seated at —; *être attablé.* To remain long at —; *rester longtemps à table.* To be left under the —; (of persons intoxicated) *rester sous la table.* To rise from —; *se lever, sortir, de table.* To put upon the —; *servir.* To clear the —; *desservir.* To lay the —, *mettre le couvert.* To turn the —s upon ; *tourner les chances contre ; renvoyer la balle à.* The —s are turned ; *les choses ont changé de face, les rôles sont intervertis.* To lay, to be laid upon the —; (in Parliament) *déposer, être déposé sur le bureau.* The pleasures of the —; *les plaisirs, m.pl., les délices, f.pl., de la table.* Occasional —; *table de fantaisie.* To bring, ou to put on, the table ; *servir.* To turn the —s ; (fig.) *intervertir les rôles.*

ta'ble, *v.a.*, (to form catalogues) cataloguer ; (to board) donner la table à, nourrir ; (carp.) assembler.

ta'ble-apple, *n.*, pomme à couteau, *f.*

tableau' (tab'lô), *n.*, tableau, *m.*

ta'ble-beer (-bîr), *n.*, petite bière, bière ordinaire, *f.* [table.

ta'ble-bell, *n.*, sonnette, *f.*, *ou* timbre, *m.*, de

ta'ble-book (-bouke), *n.*, tablettes, *f.pl.*

ta'ble-center, *n.*, chemin de table, *m.*

ta'ble-cloth (-cloth), *n.*, nappe, *f.*

ta'ble-companion, *n.*, ami de table, *m.*

ta'ble-cover (-keuv'-), *n.*, tapis de table, *m.*

ta'ble-d'hôte (tâ-b'l-dôte), *n.*, table d'hôte, *f.*

ta'ble-fruit (té-), *n.*, fruit à couteau, *m.*

ta'ble-full, *n.*, tablée, *f.*

ta'ble-land, *n.*, (geog.) plateau, *m.*

ta'ble-linen, *n.*, linge de table, *m.*

ta'ble-mat, *n.*, garde-nappe, *m.*

ta'ble-shore, *n.*, rivage plat, *m.*

ta'ble-spoon (-spoune), *n.*, cuiller à soupe, *f.*

ta'ble-spoon and fork, *n.*, couvert de table, *m.*

ta'ble-spoonful (-foule), *n.*, grande cuillerée, *f.*

tab'let (ta'blète), *n.*, plaque ; tablette, *f.*

ta'ble-talk (-tôke), *n.*, propos de table, *m.pl.*

ta'ble-turning, *n.*, tables tournantes, *f.pl.*

ta'ble-wine, *n.*, vin ordinaire, *m.*

ta'bling (té-), *n.*, classification, *f. ;* assemblage, *m.*

ta'bor (té-bor), *n.*, tambourin, *m.*

ta'boret (téb'eur'-), *n.*, petit tambourin, *m.*

tab'ular (tab'iou-), *adj.*, en forme de table ; (having the form of plates) en forme de plaque ; (set in squares) disposé en carrés ; (set down in tables) disposé en tables.

tab'ulate (tab'ou-léte), *v.a.*, disposer en forme de tables, cataloguer.

tab'ulated (tab'iou-), *adj.*, en table.

tabula'tion (tab'iou-lé-sheune), *n.*, arrangement en tableaux, *m.*

tace (té-ci) *ou* **ta'cet** (té-cète), *n.*, (mus.) tacet, *m.*

tac'it (ta-cite), *adj.*, tacite, implicite.

tac'itly, *adv.*, tacitement, implicitement.

tac'iturn (-teurne), *adj.*, taciturne, morose.

tacitur'nity (-teur-ni-), *n.*, taciturnité, morosité, *f.*

tac'iturnly, *adv.*, taciturnement.

tack (take), *n.*, (nail) broquette, **pointe**, *f. :* petit clou ; (nav.) bord, *m.*, bordée ; (of a sail) amure, *f.*, point du vent ; (of a flag) œillet, *m.* To make a —; (nav.) *courir une bordée.* To be on the right —; (fig.) *être en bonne voie.* To be on the starboard —; *avoir les amures à tribord.* To stand on the same —; *courir le même bord.*

tack, *v.a.*, attacher ; joindre ; accoupler ; (to

fasten slightly) clouer légèrement; mettre une point à ; (to sew slightly) coudre légèrement, bâtir, faufiler.

tack, *v.n.,* (nav.) virer vent devant, courir une bordée. To — about ; (nav.) *virer de bord ; louvoyer.*

tack'ing, *n.,* addition ; (needle-work) faufilure, *f.;* (nav.) virement de bord, louvoyage, *m.*

tac'kle (tak'k'l), *n.,* poulie moufle, *f. ;* (for fishing, etc.) attirail ; (nav.) na. n, *n. m.* cordages, *m. pl.* Fishing —; *engins de pê he, m. pl.*

tac'kle, *v.a.,* (to supply with ackl) pourvoir de poulies, de palans ; (to seize) empoig ie ; saisir ; s'emparer de. To — (to) work ; *se mettre* à, *attaquer l'ouvrage.*

tac'kle-block, *n.,* moufle ; (nav.) poulie de palan, *f.*

tac'kling, *n.,* (seizing) empoignement, *m.*

tact, *n.,* tact, toucher : (skill) tact, savoir faire, *m.*

tac'tical, *adj.,* tactique . de la tactique.

tac'tically, *adv.,* par la tactique.

tacti'c'ian (-tish'i 'n), *n.,* + col ien, *m.*

tac'tics, *n.pl.,* tactique, *f.*

tac'tile, *adj.,* (anat., physiol.) tactile.

tact'less, *adj.,* sans tact, sans savoir faire.

tac'tion, *n.,* tact ion, (g m." tangence, *f.*

tad'pole (-pôle), *n.,* têtard, *m.*

tæ'nia (ti-), *n.,* t.n.a, v˜ solitaire, *m.*

taf'feta *ou* **taf'fety** (-.. n., taffetas, *m.*

taf'frail, *n.,* couron.ement de la poupe, *m.*

taf'fy, *n.,* homme :u Pays de Galles, *m.*

tag, *n.,* fer, ferret, b ut ferré, *m.* — lace, *aiguillette, f.* — -rag *eople ; racaille, canaille, f.* — rag and bobtail ; *quatre pelés et un tondu.* All the — -rag and .obtail ; *toute la racaille ou toute la lie du peuple.*

tag, *v.a.,* (a la e) ferrer ; (to join) indre à, lier, attacher, cordre. To — with ; *joindre à, faire suivre de.*

tag'-sore, *n.,* (vet.) clavelée, *f.,* clav .u, *m.*

tail (téle), *n.,* que e · (extremity) ex.rémité *f.;* bout ; (of a coat) pan, *m.,* basque, *f.;* (of a cart) derrière ; (of a plow) manche ; (nav.) fouet, *m.;* (mus.) queue ; (of a comet, a pasha, a letter) queue ; (of a storm) fin ; (of a coin) pile, *f.* In —; (jur.) *par substitution.* To turn —; *s'enfuir ; prendre la fuite ; montrer les talons.* With his — between his legs ; *serrant la queue, oreille basse.*

tail'board (-bôrde), *n.,* derrière de charrette, *m.*

tailed (tél'de), *adj.,* à queue.

tail'-end, *n.,* queue, *f. ;* bout, *m.*

tail'ing, *n.,* (arch.) corbeau, *m. ;* queue, *f.*

tail'ings, *pl.,* (of wheat) grenailles, *f. pl.*

tail'less, *adj.,* sans queue.

tail'or (té-), *n.,* tailleur, *m.*

tail'oress, *n.,* culottière, tailleuse, *f.*

tail'oring, *n.,* état de tailleur ; ouvrage de tailleur, *m.*

tail'piece (-pîce), *n.,* queue ; (of a violin) queue, *f. ;* (print.) cul-de-lampe, fleuron, *m. ;* (mus.) touche, *f. ;* cordier, *m.*

tail'-pointed (-poï'n't'-), *adj.,* (bot.) caudé.

tail'-rope (-rôpe), *n.,* corde de remorque, *f.*

taint (té'n'te), *v.a.,* corrompre, altérer ; (to infect) infecter ; (to sully) ternir, souiller ; (meat) gâter. — ed meat ; *viande gâtée, f.*

taint, *v.n.,* se corrompre ; (of meat) se gâter.

taint, *n.,* corruption ; infection ; souillure ; (blemish) tache, *f.* Free from —; *sans tache ;* (of meat) *bon, qui n'est pas gâté.*

taint'less, *adj.,* sans infection, sans tache, pur de toute souillure.

taint'ure (té'n't'ieur), *n.,* souillure, tache, *f.*

take, *v.a.,* (*preterit,* Took ; *past part.,* Taken) prendre ; (a person to) mener à, conduire à ; (a thing to) porter à ; (to consider) considérer, regarder comme ; (to understand) comprendre, concevoir ; (to arrest) arrêter ; (to lead away) emme-

ner; (of things) enlever, ôter, emporter; (to adopt) adopter ; (to suppose) supposer, s'imaginer ; présumer, croire ; (to fascinate) fasciner, séduire ; (opportunity) saisir ; profiter de ; (to choose) choisir ; adopter, prendre ; (to admit) admettre ; (to require) falloir, prendre ; (to endure) endurer, souffrir ; (to copy) copier, saisir ; (portrait) faire ; (a walk, a run, a stroll, etc.) faire ; (prisoner) aire ; (impression) recevoir ; (revenge, satisfaction) voir, tirer ; (affront) recevoir, essuyer, subir ; (to bespeak) retenir, arrêter ; (to have) pr ndr (to deduct) retrancher, ôte , (a bet) tenir. T— ~ny one's life ; *ôter la vie à quelqu'un* To tak ne'..yes off, *ou* from · *détourner les yeux* e. "o — some trouble ; *prendre de la peine, du mal.* To — about ; *conduire partout.* To — again ; *reprendre.* To — away *emmener ;* (things) *emporter ;* (to deprive .) *priver* de, *ôter ;* (to remove) *ôter ;* (dinnerthings, etc.) *desservir.* .o — away from ; *prendre* à, *ôter* à. To — back · *reprendr ;* (to carry back) *remmener,* (things) *remporter.* To — down; *de.cendre · · ;* (to humble) *humilier, abaisser, raba"re ;* (to swallow) *prendre, avaler ;* (to pull uown) *abattre, démolir ;* (to write down) *prendre note* de, *coucher par écrit ;* (at school) *prendre lu place* de; (to consult) *consulter, ouvrir, prendre.* To — for ; *prendre* pour ; *regarder* comme ; (a walk, etc.) *mener faire (une promenade) ; mener promener.* To — from ; *prendre* de, *accepter* de ; (to deprive of) *prendre* à, *enlever* à, *ôter* à, *dérober* à ; (to subtract) *soustraire* à, *retrancher* de ; (to detract) *enlever* à, *diminuer* de. To — in ; *faire entrer, rentrer, faire rentrer ;* (to inclose) *enclore ;* (to comprise) *comprendre, renfermer, embra er ,* (to contract) *resserrer, rétrécir, rentrer ;* (to receive) *recevoir, prendre ;* "o receive in one's house' *loger, recevoir chez soi ;* (to hold) *contenir ;* (to cheat) *tromper, duper,* mettre de*dans ;* (garments) *rendoubler, remplier ;* (sails) *carguer, ferler, serrer ;* (a periodical) *recevoir ; être abonné* à ; (lodgers) *prendre, recevoir ;* (washing, needlework, etc.) *faire, prendre ; s'occuper* de, *travailler* à ; (provisions, a stock, etc.) *faire sa provision* de ; (shop goods) *recevoir ;* (to see) *remarquer.* To — in hand ; *se charger* de ; *prendre en main ; se mettre* après. To — into ; *admettre* dans, à. To — off, away ; *enlever, ôter ;* (to cut off) *couper, trancher ;* (to destroy) *détruire ; enlever ;* (to invalidate) *affaiblir ;* (to swallow) *avaler ;* (to purchase) *prendre, acheter ;* (to copy) *copier ;* (to mimic) *contrefaire ;* (to lead away) *emmener ;* (a mask) *lever ;* (clothes) *ôter ;* (to withdraw) *retirer.* To — off the stage ; *retirer du théâtre.* To — off from ; *détourner* de ; (to lessen) *diminuer.* To — off one's eyes from; *détourner les yeux* de ; *quitter des yeux.* To — off the mind from ; *détourner l'esprit* de. To — one's self off ; *s'en aller, décamper, filer, se sauver, s'esquiver.* Death has — n him off ; *la mort nous l'a enlevé.* To — out ; *faire sortir ;* (things) *sortir ;* (from pawn) *dégager ; retirer ;* (teeth) *arracher ;* (stains) *ôter, enlever ;* (for a walk) *promener ;* (horses from a carriage) *dételer ; détacher les chevaux d'une voiture.* To — out of ; *sortir* de ; *tirer* de. To — it out (in); se *payer* en. To — over ; *prendre en main, se charger* de ; (business) *prendre la succession* de; (to pass any one) *faire traverser* à ; *passer ; mener* à, *emmener* à ; (warehouse) *faire parcourir* à. To — up ; *porter en haut ;* (to raise) *lever, soulever ;* (to pick up) *relever, ramasser ;* (to buy) *acheter ;* (to borrow) *emprunter ;* (to begin) *commencer, entamer ;* (to engross, to occupy) *prendre, occuper ;* (to arrest) *prendre, arrêter, empoigner ;* (to reprimand) *réprimander, relancer, relever, reprendre, tancer ;* (to begin where another leaves off) *continuer, reprendre ;* (to extend over) *embrasser ;* (to adopt) *adopter ;* (to espouse) *épouser;* (to take in hand) *prendre en main, se charger* de; (to collect) *lever, prélever;* (to carry up) *monter;* (to lead up) *faire monter;* (a bill) *payer, acquitter, faire honneur* à; (surg.) *attacher avec une ligature, lier.* To — up one's quarters; *s'établir* à, en; *élire domicile, se fixer* à. To — up into; *faire monter* dans. — my trunk into my bed-room; *portez ma malle dans ma chambre à coucher.* To — upon one's self to; *prendre sur soi* de, *se charger* de. What will you — for that clock? *combien voulez-vous de cette pendule?* To — any one's opinion; *consulter quelqu'un.* To give and —; *faire des concessions mutuelles.* To — aback; *surprendre, étonner, confondre.* To — a back seat; *en rabattre.* To — aim; *viser.* To — up arms; *prendre les armes; commencer les hostilités.* To — sight; *viser.* To — breath; *prendre haleine.* To — earth; *se réfugier dans sa tanière; se cacher.* To — effect; *porter coup; faire effet.* To — advantage of; *profiter* de. To — care of; *épargner; prendre soin* de. To — care; (beware) *prendre garde* de. To — the lead; *diriger; prendre la direction* de; *marcher en tête* de; *donner le ton* à. To — notice; *remarquer; s'apercevoir* de. To — no verbal notice; *ne faire aucune observation.* To — place; *avoir lieu.* To — a run to; *faire une excursion* à. To — stock of; *faire l'inventaire* de; *inventorier.* To — walks; *faire des tournées, des promenades; se promener.* To — up (a certain line after another); *suivre les traces* de; *marcher sur les traces* de. To — the cake; *lever la paille.* To — farewell of; *prendre congé* de; *faire ses adieux* à. To — fire; *s'enflammer, prendre feu.* To — care; *prendre garde; avoir l'œil au guet; faire attention.* To — heart; *reprendre courage.* To — heed; *prendre garde* à. To — into consideration, *ou* notice of; *tenir compte* de. To — in water; *faire de l'eau, faire provision d'eau douce.* I cannot — that story in; *je ne puis admettre la vérité de cette histoire.* To — in vain; *prendre en vain.* To — out a summons against; *envoyer une assignation* à. To — out a patent; *prendre un brevet.* To — leave; *prendre congé* de; *faire ses adieux* à; *se permettre* de; *prendre la liberté* de. To — French leave; *décamper sans mot dire.* To — the oath; *prêter serment.* To — any one's part; *prendre fait et cause pour quelqu'un.* To — on, *ou* upon, one's self; *prendre sur soi; se charger* de. You — too much upon yourself; *vous présumez trop de vous-même; vous affichez de trop hautes prétentions.* He took the value out in money; *il reçut (il se fit payer) la valeur en argent.* To — pains; *se fatiguer* à, *se donner du mal.* To — root; *prendre racine.* To — the air (an airing); *prendre l'air.* To — the field; *se mettre en campagne.* To — the law into one's own hands; *se faire raison* à *soi-même.* To — the wall; *prendre le haut du pavé.* To — thought of; *s'inquiéter* de. To — time; *prendre son temps;* (require time) *prendre du temps.* To — to heart; *ressentir vivement.* To — to task; *réprimander; gronder, prendre à partie.* To — prisoner; *faire prisonnier.* To — refuge in; *se réfugier* dans. To — it into one's head to, that; *se mettre dans la tête de,* ou *que; s'aviser* de. It —s . . . to go; *il faut . . .* pour *aller.* To — any one to be; *prendre quelqu'un* pour. To — n with; *être enchanté* de; *être épris* de; *être charmé* de; *être entiché* de. To be —n ill; *se trouver mal; tomber malade.* To be —n with illness; *tomber malade.* To be —n with cholera; *être attaqué du choléra.* To be —n giddy; *être pris de vertiges.* To be —n with pains in the stomach; *éprouver des tiraillements d'estomac.* How old do you — me for? *quel âge me donnez-vous?* I — you to be thirty; *je vous donne trente ans.* Whom, *ou* what, do you — me for? *pour qui me prenez-vous?* — care of the pence and the pounds will — care of themselves; (prov.) *il n'y a pas de petites économies.* You must — it or leave it; *c'est à prendre ou à laisser.* To — time by the forelock; (prov.) *prendre la balle au bond, prendre l'occasion aux cheveux.* It —s a wise man to be a fool; (prov.) *qui ne sait pas être fou n'est pas sage.*

take, *v.n.,* (to please) *plaire;* (to succeed) *avoir du succès, réussir, prendre;* (to catch) *prendre, opérer.* To — after; *imiter;* (to resemble) *ressembler* à; *tenir* de. She —s after you, *elle a . . . . chose de . . . otre air.* To — on; *se lamenter, s'affliger;* (of anger) *s'emporter.* To — to; (' go towards) *se diriger* vers; (to take refuge in) *se réfugier* dans; (to resort to) *avoir recours* à; (to apply to) *s'appliquer* à, *se livrer* à, *se mettre* à; (to be fond of persons) *s'attacher* à, *prendre amitié;* (to be fond of things) *prendre du goût* à, *mordre* à; *adopter, embrasser, choisir; faire usage* de. To — to (any profession); *se faire* à. To — to horse; *monter à cheval; sauter en selle.* To — to fainting; *tomber en syncope.* To — to running; *se mettre à courir.* To — up with; *s'associer* à, ou avec; *s'attacher* à; *prendre en amitié.* To — with; *plaire* à.

take, *n.,* prise, *f.;* (of fish) pêche, quantité, *f.* Have you had a good —? *avez-vous fait bonne pêche?*

take'-in, *n.,* duperie, attrape, volerie, *f.;* (trick) tour; (pers.) voleur, charlatan, fripon, *m.*

take'-off, *n.,* caricature, charge, *f.*

tak'er (ték'-), *n.,* preneur, *m.,* preneuse, *f.*

tak'ing (ték'-), *n.,* prise; arrestation, *f.;* (stealing) soustraction, *f.* —s, *pl.,* (receipts) recettes, *f.pl.*

tak'ing (ték'-), *adj.,* attrayant; séduisant; (infectious) contagieux.

tak'ingly, *adv.,* d'une manière attrayante.

tak'ingness (ték'-), *n.,* charme, attrait, *m.*

tal'bot, *n.,* chien de Saint-Hubert, *m.*

talc, *n.,* (min.) talc, *m.*

talc'ose (-côce), *adj.,* talqueux.

tale, *n.,* conte, récit, *m.;* histoire; historiette, n uvelle, *f.;* (reckoning) compte, *m.;* (telling) ppor' *m.;* (number) nombre, chiffre, *m.* To ell —; *rapporter; mentir.* His — is told; *c'en est f ' à lui.* A — never loses in the telling; (prov.) *on fait toujours le loup plus gros qu'il n'est.* That tells a —; *cela dit beaucoup.*

tale'-bearer (-bèr'-), *n.,* rapporteur, *m.,* mauvaise langue, *f.*

tale'-bearing (-bèr'-), *n.,* rapportage, cancan; bavardage, *m.*

tale'-bearing (-bèr'-), *adj.,* rapporteur.

ta'led (té-lède), *n.,* (Jewish) tald, *m.*

tale'ful (tél'foule), *adj.,* riche de contes; riche en récits.

tal'ent (tal'-), *n.,* talent; (coin) talent, *m.*

tal'ented, *adj.,* de talent, habile, savant, lettré.

tale'-teller, *n.,* conteur, *m.,* conteuse, *f.*

tal'isman (tal'iz'-), *n.,* talisman, *m.*

talk (tôke), *v.n.* and *a.,* parler (of, about, over) de; *converser; causer;* (to prate) *bavarder, jaser;* (of persons) *parler* à; (of things) *dire.* Now you speak, you were only — ing before; *voilà ce qui s'appelle parler, vous ne faisiez que bavarder auparavant.* To — at; *haranguer.* To — away from the point; *s'éloigner de la question en parlant.* To — any one down; *réduire quelqu'un au silence (par une conversation incessante).* To — any one into; *persuader* à *quelqu'un* de. To — any one out of; *dissuader quelqu'un* de. To — out a bill; *continuer la discussion de manière à faire ajourner indéfiniment l'adoption d'un projet de loi.* To — of; *parler* de, *causer* de; *parler, causer.* To — to; (to advise) *faire des reproches* à; *reprendre doucement; faire la morale* à. To — to one's self; *parler à son bonnet, se parler à soi-même.* To — of politics, to — politics; *parler politique.* To — nonsense; *dire des sottises, dire des bêtises.* To — away; *parler toujours, ne pas cesser de parler.* To — small; *dire des banalités; parler "pluie et beau temps;"* (fig.) *s'effacer, se faire petit.* To — away the time; *passer le temps à causer.* To — any one into; *persuader à quelqu'un de.* To — any one out; *l'emporter par la parole sur quelqu'un.* To — over; *parler de; causer de;* (to cajole) *cajoler.* What are you —ing about? *de quoi parlez-vous?* (you are out of your senses) *vous n'y songez-pas!* ou *y songez-vous?*

talk (tōke), n., conversation, f.; entretien, m.; causerie; (prattling) jaserie, f., bavardage; (report) bruit; (conversation) entretien, sujet de conversation, m., propos, m.pl. Small — ; *banalités, f.pl.; lieux communs, propos insignifiants, m.pl.* It is the — of the town; *on ne parle que de cela dans toute la ville.* That his arrival would soon be the — of the town; *qu'avant peu son arrivée serait l'événement de toute la ville* (V. Hugo, *Les Misérables*). There is a — of; *on parle* **de,** *il est question* **de;** *le bruit court* **que.** She is full of, ou all, —, *elle aime beaucoup à causer; elle a la langue bien pendue.* He is all —; *ce n'est qu'un bavard.*

talk'ative (tōk'a-), adj., causeur; bavard.

talk'ativeness (tōk'a-), n., loquacité, f.; caquet, bavardage, m.

talk'er (tōk'-), n., causeur; parleur; (b.s.) bavard; (boaster) vantard, m.

talk'ing (tōk'-), n., conversation; causerie, f.; (b.s.) bavardage, m. I hear — in the next room; *j'entends un bruit de conversation dans la chambre d'à côté.* It is like — to the air (preaching in the desert); *c'est comme si je chantais.*

talk'ing (tōk'-), adj., causeur; bavard. That's a — story; *en voilà d'une bonne, par exemple!*

tall (tōl), adj., (pers.) grand; haut (things) grand. — man; *un homme grand.* A — fellow; *un grand gaillard.* A — hat; *un chapeau à haute forme.*

tal'lage (-lèdje), n., (ant.) taille, f.; impôt, m.

tall'ness (tōl'-), n., (pers.) haute taille, grandeur; (of things) grandeur, hauteur, f.

tal'low (-lō), n., suif, m.

tal'low, v.a., suiffer.

tal'low-candle, n., chandelle de suif, f.

tal'low-chandler (-tsha'n'd'-), n., fabricant, ou marchand, de chandelles, m.

tal'low-faced (-fés'te), adj., à figure maladive; pâle.

tal'low-grease (-grîce), n., suif, m.

tal'low-trade, n., commerce des suifs, m.

tal'low-tree (-trî), n., (bot.) arbre à suif, m.

tal'lowy (-lō-i), adj., de suif; graisseux.

tal'ly, v.a., faire des coches, ou marquer sur une taille; (to fit) ajuster, adapter; (nav.) border.

tal'ly, v.n., s'accorder. To — with; *s'accorder* **avec;** *s'ajuster à; cadrer* **avec;** *correspondre à; s'adapter* **à.**

tal'ly, n., taille (petit bâton), f.; (com.) tempérament; (fellow) pendant, m.

tal'ly-ho! (-hō), exc., (hunt.) taïaut.

tal'ly-man, n., personne qui marque la taille, f.; (com.) marchand qui vend à tempérament, m.

tal'ly-shop, n., boutique où l'on paie à tempérament, f.

tal'ly-trade, n., commerce à tempérament, m.

Tal'mud (-meude), n., (Jewish Lit.) talmud, m.

tal'on, n., serre; (arch.) talon, m.; cymaise, f.

tam'able (té'm'a-b'l), adj., apprivoisable; domptable.

tam'ableness, n., nature apprivoisable, nature domptable, f.

tam'arind, n., (fruit) tamarin, m.

tam'arind ou **tam'arind-tree,** n., (bot.) tamarinier, m.

tam'arisk. n., (bot.) tamaris, tamarisc, m.

tambour' (ta'm'-), n., (arts, fort.) tambour, m.

— frame; *métier à broder,* m. — work; *broderie au tambour,* f.

tam'bour (ta'm'bour), v.a., broder au tambour.

tambourine' (-bo-rîne), n., tambour de basque, m.

tame (téme), v.a., apprivoiser, dompter; rendre domestique; (fig.) subjuguer, dompter.

tame, adj., apprivoisé; privé, domestique; (spiritless) traitable; (of style, etc.) insipide; fade, pâle, plat, sans couleur; (subdued) soumis. To grow — ; *s'apprivoiser.*

tame'ly, adv., avec soumission; sans résistance, tranquillement; servilement; (without force) sans force, sans couleur; (cowardly) lâchement, sans cœur.

tame'ness, n., état apprivoisé, apprivoisement, m.; domesticité, f.; (want of force) manque de force, manque de couleur, m.; (submission) soumission, servilité; faiblesse, f.

tam'er (té'm'-), n., apprivoiseur; (of wild beasts) dompteur, m.

Tam'il (ta-mile), n., Tamoul; (language) tamoul, le dialecte tamoul, m.

tam'iny, n., étamine, f.; tamis, filtre, m.

tam'o'shanter, n., (cap) béret, m.

tam'per, v.a., (to practice secretly) machiner, agir dans l'ombre, tâtonner. To — with; (of things) *faire de petites expériences; employer de petits moyens* **pour;** *jouer* **avec;** (a lock, etc.) *fausser; se mêler* **de;** *prendre des libertés* **avec;** (a witness) *pratiquer suborner, travailler, tâcher de gagner; transiger* **avec;** (objects) *toucher à, déranger, abîmer, corrompre, gâter.*

tam'pering, n., menées secrètes, pratiques secrètes ou sourdes, f.pl. There must be no — with; *il ne faut pas toucher à.* There must be no — with the witnesses; *toute tentative de gagner, ou de corrompre, ou de suborner, les témoins sera punie par la loi.*

tamp'ing-bar (-bâr), n., bourroir, m.

tam'pion, n., tampon de canon, m.

tam'tam, n., tam-tam, m.

tan, n., tan, m. Waste — ; *tannée,* f.

tan, v.a., tanner; (to sunburn) basaner, hâler.

tan'-color (-keul'leur), n., tanné, m.

tan'dem, n., tandem; attelage en flèche, m.

tan'gent (-djè'n'te), n., tangente, f. To go, ou fly, off at a —; (lit.) *s'échapper, par le tangente;* (fig.) *prendre feu comme la poudre; passer subitement à un autre sujet.*

tan'gerine (-djeurîn), n., orange de Tanger, mandarine, f.

tangibil'ity (-dji-), n., tangibilité, f.

tan'gible (-dji-b'l), adj., tangible; palpable; sensible; réel.

tan'gle (ta'gn'g'l), n., confusion, f.; embarras, embrouillement, enchevêtrement, m.; (brake) fourré, m.; hautes herbes, f.pl. It is in a —; *c'est tout embrouillé.* To be in a —; *être dans le pétrin.*

tan'-house (-haouce) ou **-yard,** n., tannerie, f.

tank, n., réservoir, m.; citerne; cuve; (of a pump) bâche, f.

tan'kard, n., hanap, m.

tan'ner, n., tanneur, m.

tan'nery, n., tannerie, f.

tan'ning, n., tannage, m.

tan'ning-liquor (-lik'eur), n., (tech.) jusée, f.

tan'-pit, n., fosse à tan, f.

tan'sy (-zi), n., tanaisie, herbe aux vers, f.

tantaliza'tion (-laï-zé-), **tan'talism,** n., action de torturer, f.; torture, f.; tentation, f.; supplice de Tantale, m.

tan'talize (-laïze), v.a., tantaliser (Bescherelle); se jouer **de,** torturer, tourmenter, tenter; faire subir le supplice de Tantale **à;** (pop.) faire venir l'eau à la bouche **à.**

tan'talizer (-laïz'-), n., personne qui torture, f.

tan'talizing (laïz'-), adj., tentant, torturant.

tan'tamount (-maou'n'te), *adj.*, équivalent à. To be — to; *équivaloir* à; *revenir* à. That is — to saying; *c'est comme si l'on disait;* cela *revient à dire.*

tantiv'y, *adv.*, à fond de train; à bride abattue. To ride —; *galoper ventre à terre.*

tan'trum (-treu'm), *n.*, mauvaise humeur, *f.;* accès de rage, de colère, *m.* To be in a —; *prendre la mouche; tempêter, être en colère.*

tan'-vat, *n.*, fosse à tan, *f.*

tan'-waste (-wéste), *n.*, tannée, *f.*

tap, *n.*, (blow) tape, *f.*, coup; (of an inn, etc.) comptoir, *m.;* estaminet, buvette, *f.;* (gas, water) robinet, *m.;* (of a cask) cannelle, cannette, *f.;* (tech.) taraud, *m.* — room; *salle de cabaret;* (of an hotel) *buvette, f., estaminet, m.* On —; *en perce.* A fresh —; *un nouveau baril en perce.* We have a good —; *nous avons de bonne bière en perce.*

tap, *v.a.*, (to strike) taper; frapper; (surg.) ponctionner, faire la ponction à; (wine, etc.) tirer; (a cask) mettre en perce; (a tree) inciser; (tech.) tarauder; (metal.) faire la coulée à. He —ped me on the shoulder; *il me toucha l'épaule.*

tap, *v.n.*, taper; frapper. To — at the door; *frapper légèrement à la porte; frapper un petit coup très faible* (V. Hugo).

tap'-borer (-bôr'-), *n.*, taraud, *m.*

tape (tépe), *n.*, ruban de fil, ruban de coton, *m.* Red —; (fig.) *routine administrative, bureaucratie, f.*

ta'per (té-), *n.*, petite bougie, *f.;* (church) cierge; (fig.) flambeau, *m.*

ta'per (té-), *v.a.*, tailler en pointe, effiler.

ta'per, *v.n.*, se terminer en pointe, s'effiler. To — up; *s'élancer* vers, *s'enfoncer* dans (*le ciel*) (V. Hugo).

ta'pering (té-), *adj.*, terminé en pointe; effilé; (conical) en forme de cône, conique; (of the waist) élancé. — fingers; *doigts effilés, m.pl.*

ta'peringly, *adv.*, en pointe.

tap'estried (tap'ès-tride), *adj.*, tapissé.

tap'estry (tap'ès-), *n.*, tapisserie, *f.*

tap'estry, *v.a.*, tapisser.

tap'estry-carpet, *n.*, tapis bouclé, *m.*

tap'estry-maker (-mék'-), *n.*, tapissier, *m.*

tape'-worm (tép'weurme), *n.*, ténia; ver solitaire, *m.*

tap'-hole (tap'-), *n.*, (metal.) trou de coulée, *m.*

tapio'ca, *n.*, tapioca, *m.*

tapis' (tap-pi), *n.*, tapis, *m.* To be on the —; *être sur le tapis.*

tap'-maker, *n.*, robinetier, *m.*

tap'ping (tap-pigne), *n.*, (surg.) ponction; (metal.) coulée; (of a cask) mise en perce; (of a tree) incision, *f.*

tap'room, *n.*, estaminet, buvette, *f.*

tap'root (-route), *n.*, (bot.) pivot, *m.;* racine pivotante, *f.*

tap'-rooted, *adj.*, à racine pivotante.

tap'ster, *n.*, garçon de cabaret, *m.*

tar (târ), *n.*, goudron; (sailor) loup de mer, *m.*

tar (târ), *v.a.*, goudronner.

tarantel'la, *n.*, (dance) tarentelle, *f.*

tar'-barrel, *n.*, baril (de ou à) goudron, *m.*

tar'dily (târ-), *adv.*, lentement; tardivement.

tar'diness (târ-), *n.*, lenteur; (reluctance) répugnance, *f.;* (lateness) retard, *m.;* tardiveté, *f.*

tar'dy (târ-), *adj.*, lent; paresseux, indolent; (late) en retard, tardif; (unwilling) qui a de la répugnance, mal disposé.

tare (tére), *n.*, (Script.) ivraie; (com.) tare; (bot.) vesce, *f.;* ers, *m.*

tare, *v.n.*, (com.) tarer; prendre la tare de.

tar'get (târ-ghète), *n.*, cible, *f.;* but, blanc, *m.;* (shield) targe; (antiq.) pelte, *f.* — firing, ou practice; *tir à la cible, m.*

tar'iff, *n.*, tarif, *m.* *v.a.*, tarifer.

tar'in, *n.*, (orni.) tarin, *m.*

tar'-lake (târ-léke), *n.*, lac d'asphalte, *m.*

tar'latan, *n.*, tarlatane, *f.*

tarn, *n.*, (lake) lac, *m.;* mare, *f.;* (marsh) bourbier, marais, *m.*

tar'nish, *v.a.*, ternir; (fig.) souiller, flétrir.

tar'nish, *v.n.*, se ternir.

tar'-paper, *n.*, papier goudronné, *m.*

tarpau'lin *ou* **tarpau'ling** (-pō-), *n.*, prélart, *m.*, toile goudronnée, *f.*

Tarpe'ian (-pî-), *adj.*, Tarpéien. The — rock; *la roche tarpéienne.*

tar'-pit, *n.*, puits à goudron, *m.*

tar'ragon, *n.*, (bot.) estragon, *m.*

tar'rier, *n.*, personne qui tarde, *f.*

tar'ry, *v.n.*, (to stay) rester en arrière, s'arrêter; s'attarder; (to delay) tarder, différer, attendre.

tar'ry (târ'-), *adj.*, de goudron.

tar'rying, *n.*, retard; séjour, *m.*

tar'sal (târ-), *adj.*, ᵗarsien, du tarse.

tar'sel (târ-), *n.*, tiercelet, *m.*

tar'sus (târ-), *n.*, tarse, *m.*

tart (târte), *n.*, tarte, tourte, *f.* —-dish; *tourtière, f.*

tart (târte), *adj.*, aigre, âcre; acide; (fig.) aigre, mordant, piquant, âcre.

tar'tan (târ-tane), *n.*, tartan, *m.;* (vessel) tartane, *f.*

tar'tar (târ-tare), *n.*, (chem., of the teeth) tartre, *m.*

Tar'tar, *n.*, Tartare, *m.f.;* (fig.) bourru, Turc, *m.* To catch a —; *s'attaquer à plus fort que soi; trouver à qui parler; trouver son maître.*

tarta'rean (târ-té-), *adj.*, (myth.) du Tartare.

tarta'reous, *adj.*, (chem.) tartreux.

tartar'ic (târ-ta-), *adj.*, tartrique, tartarique.

tar'tarous (târ-), *adj.*, tartreux, tartareux.

tart'ish (târ-), *adj.*, aigrelet.

tart'let, *n.*, tartelette, tourtelette, *f.*

tart'ly (târt-), *adv.*, avec âcreté; avec aigreur; (fig.) vertement, avec aigreur, sévèrement.

tart'ness (târt-), *n.*, acidité, aigreur, âcreté; (fig.) aigreur, sévérité, *f.*

tar'trate (târ-), *n.*, tartrate, *m.*

tartuffe' (târ-teufe), *n.*, hypocrite, cafard, *m.*

tartuff'ish (târ-teuf'-), *adj.*, de tartufe.

tar'-water, *n.*, eau goudronnée; eau de goudron, *f.*

task (tâske), *n.*, tâche, *f.;* travail, ouvrage, *m.;* besogne; charge, *f.;* emploi; (lesson) devoir; (punishment) pensum, *m.* To take to —; *réprimander; sermonner; blâmer; gronder; prendre à partie.*

task, *v.a.*, donner une tâche à; charger de travail; (fam.) tailler de la besogne à; éprouver, mettre à l'épreuve, exiger, réclamer. To — with; *accuser* de; *reprocher* à.

task'master (-mâs-), *n.*, surveillant, maître; maître oppresseur, *m.*

task'work (task'weurke), *n.*, ouvrage à la tâche, *f.*

tas'sel, *n.*, gland, *m.;* (large one) houppe, *f.;* (arch.) tasseau; (of flags) cravate, *f.;* (hawk) tiercelet d'autour, *m.*

tas'seled, *adj.*, à glands; orné de glands.

tast'able (tést'a-b'l), *adj.*, qu'on peut goûter; savoureux.

taste, *v.a.*, goûter; (liquids) déguster; (fig.) goûter, goûter de, sentir, savourer.

taste, *v.n.*, goûter. To — of; *goûter* de, *goûter;* (to have a smack of) *avoir un goût* de, *sentir le, la, les;* (just to taste) *effleurer;* (to experience) *sentir, éprouver, goûter, subir;* (to be tinctured with) *avoir une odeur* de, *sentir le, la, les.* To — good, bad; *avoir un bon, un mauvais goût.*

taste, *n.*, goût, *m.;* (small quantity) idée, *f.*, soupçon; (specimen) échantillon, spécimen, *m.;* (of beverages) dégustation, *f.* There is no disputing about —s; *il ne faut pas disputer des goûts.* To have a — of; *avoir un goût* de; *sentir* *le, la, les.* A wee —; (pop.) *un petit peu ; un soup-çon, une idée.* Every one to his —; *chacun à son goût.* To one's —; *à son goût.* To dress with —; *s'habiller avec goût.* That is good, bad —; *c'est de bon, de mauvais goût.* From, out of —; *par goût.* —s differ; *chacun à son goût.* There is no disputing about —s ; *des goûts et des couleurs il ne faut (pas) disputer* (La Fontaine).

taste'ful (tést'foule), *adj.*, savoureux ; (having good taste) de bon goût; arrangé, *ou* fait, avec goût.

taste'fully (-foul'-), *adv.*, avec goût.

taste'fulness, *n.*, bon goût, *m.*

taste'less, *adj.*, fade, insipide, sans goût.

taste'lessly, *adv.*, insipidement. fadement.

taste'lessness, *n.*, manque de goût, *m. ;* insipidité, fadeur, *f.*

tast'er (tést'-), *n.*, (of beverages) dégustateur; (instr.) sonde, pipette, *f.*

tast'ing (tést'-), *n.*, goût, *m. ;* gustation ; (of beverages) dégustation, *f.*

tast'y (tést'-), *adj.*, de bon goût, savoureux.

tat'ter, *n.*, haillon, lambeau, *m. ;* guenille, *f.*

tat'ter, *v.a.*, (only used in past part.) déchirer.

tatterdemal'ion (-dè-), *n.*, déguenillé, va-nu-pieds, gueux, *m.*

tat'tered (tat'teurde), *adj.*, (pers.) déguenillé ; (of garments) en lambeaux, en guenilles, en haillons, en loques ; tout déchiré, délabré.

tat'ting, *n.*, (lace) frivolité, *f.* To do —; *faire de la frivolité.*

tat'tle (tat't'l), *n.*, babil, caquet, bavardage, *m. ;* cancans, *m.pl.*

tat'tle (tat't'l), *v.n.*, babiller, jaser, caqueter, bavarder ; cancaner.

tat'tler, *n.*, bavard, *m. ;* babillard, *m. ;* cancanier, *m.*

tat'tling, *adj.*, babillard, bavard.

tat'tling, *n.*, bavardage, *m.*

tattoo' (tat'tou), *v.a.*, tatouer.

tattoo' (tat'tou), *n.*, tatouage, *m. ;* (milit.) retraite, *f.* To beat the devil's —; *tambouriner avec les doigts.*

tattoo'ing (tat'tou-), *n.*, tatouage, *m.*

taught, *past.part.* V. **teach.**

taunt (tâ'n'te *ou* tô'n'te), *n.*, injure, insulte, *f. ;* (bitter reproach) reproche sanglant, reproche amer, *m. ;* réprimande ; (invective) invective, raillerie, *f. ;* sarcasme, *m.*

taunt (tâ'n'te *ou* tô'n'te), *v.a.*, reprocher vivement à; outrager; injurier, insulter ; dire des injures à, railler, censurer, critiquer.

taunt'er, *n.*, qui injurie, qui outrage ; railleur, *m.*, railleuse, *f.*

taunt'ingly, *adv.*, injurieusement, avec raillerie ; d'une manière insultante.

Tau'rus, *n.*, (astron.) le Taureau, *m.*

taut *ou* **taught** (tôte), *adj.*, raide, tendu, *ou* à la serre (V. Hugo); (of sails) enflé, plein. To haul —; *raidir, mettre à la serre.*

tautolog'ic *ou* **tautolog'ical** (-lodj'-), *adj.*, tautologique.

tautol'ogize (-djaïze), *v.n.*, se répéter.

tautol'ogy (-dji), *n.*, tautologie, *f.*

tav'ern (tav'eurne), *n.*, taverne, *f. ;* cabaret, restaurant, *m.*

tav'ern-haunter, *n.*, pilier de cabaret, *m.*

tav'ern-keeper (-kîp'-), *n.*, aubergiste, cabaretier, *m.*

taw (tô), *n.*, grosse bille, *f. ;* calot, *m.*

taw (tô), *v.a.*, passer en mégie, mégisser.

taw'drily (tô), *adv.*, avec un faux éclat ; d'une manière voyante, sans goût.

taw'driness (tô), *n.*, faux éclat; clinquant, *m.*; mauvais goût, *m.*

taw'dry (tô), *adj.*, de clinquant ; éclatant; voyant ; de faux éclat, de mauvais goût (fig.) prétentieux.

taw'er (tô-), *n.*, mégissier, *m.*

taw'ing (tô-), *n.*, mégisserie, *f.*

taw'ny (tô-ni), *adj.*, basané, tanné, hâlé; (animal) fauve.

tax, *n.*, impôt, *m. ;* contribution, imposition, taxe; (fig.) taxe, *f.*, impôt, fardeau, *m. ;* (censure) censure, *f.* Assessed —es; *contributions directes, f.pl.* Income- —; *impôt sur le revenu, m.* Land —; *taxe foncière, f.* —-collector, —-gatherer ; *percepteur des contributions, percepteur, m.*

tax, *v.a.*, imposer; frapper d'un impôt; taxer; (to accuse) taxer **de**, accuser **de** ; (to censure) blâmer ; (fig.) taxer, mettre à contribution ; (jur.) taxer. The country's resources were —ed to the utmost ; *toutes les ressources du pays furent mises à contribution.* To —; (friendship, any one's patience, etc.) *mettre à l'épreuve.*

tax'able (taks'a-b'l), *adj.*, imposable ; qui peut être taxé.

taxa'tion (taks'é-), *n.*, taxation ; (jur.) taxation, taxe, *f. ;* impôt, *m.*

tax'er (taks'-), *n.*, (jur.) taxateur, *m.*

tax'-free (-frî), *adj.*, exempt d'impôts.

taxid'ermy (taks'i-deur-), *n.*, taxidermie, *f.*

tax'ing-master, *n.*, taxateur, *m.*

tax'-payer (-pé-eur), *n.*, contribuable, *m.*

tax'-paying, *adj.*, imposé.

tea (tî), *n.*, thé ; (broth) bouillon, *m. ;* (infusion) eau, tisane, infusion, *f.* Beef- —; *bouillon, consommé, m.* To come to —; *venir prendre le thé.*

tea'-board (-bôrde), *n.*, cabaret à thé, plateau, *m.*

tea'-broker, *n.*, courtier en thés, *m.*

tea'-caddy *ou* **tea-can'ister,** *n.*, boîte à thé, *f.*

teach (tîtshe), *v.a.*, (*preterit* and *past part.*, Taught) (pers.) enseigner, instruire ; (things) enseigner, apprendre à ; (any manual labor) montrer ; (to lecture on) professer ; (to accustom) apprendre à, habituer à ; (to suggest to the mind) communiquer; (to signify) indiquer. To — any one French ; *enseigner,* ou *apprendre, le français à quelqu'un.* To — a lesson; *donner une leçon à.* That will — you to be more . . . ; *cela vous apprendra à être plus . . .*

teach, *v.n.*, enseigner ; professer ; donner des leçons.

teach'able (tîtsh'a-b'l), *adj.*, disposé à apprendre ; (docile) docile; (of things) enseignable.

teach'ableness, *n.*, disposition à apprendre ; (docility) docilité, *f.*

teach'er, *n.*, maître, *m.*, maîtresse, *f. ;* instituteur, *m. ;* institutrice, *f. ;* professeur ; (preacher) prédicateur ; prédicateur laïque, *m.*

tea'-cake, *n.*, brioche, madeleine, *f.*

teach'ing, *n.*, enseignement, *m. ;* instruction, *f.*

tea'-cup, *n.*, tasse à thé, *f.* A storm in a —; *beaucoup de bruit pour rien.* A — -ful ; *plein une tasse à thé.*

tea'-dealer (-dîl'-), *n.*, marchand de thé, *m.*

tea'-drinker, *n.*, buveur, *m.*, buveuse, *f.*, de thé.

tea'-drinking, *n.*, l'usage du thé, *m.*

tea'-dust (-deuste), *n.*, poudre, *ou* poussière, de thé, *f.*

tea'-equipage (-èk'wi-pèdje), *n.*, cabaret à thé, *m.*

tea'-grower (-grô-), *n.*, cultivateur de thé, *m.*

teak (tîke), *n.*, (bot.) teck, tek, *m.*

tea'-kettle (-kèt't'l), *n.*, bouilloire, bouillotte, *f.*

teal (tîle), *n.*, (orni.) sarcelle, *f.*

team (tîme), *n.*, attelage, *m. ;* ligne, file, *f. ;* (in games) camp, *m.*, équipe, *f.*

tea'-merchant, *n.*, marchand de thé, *ou* négociant en thés, *m.*

team'ster, *n.*, conducteur d'attelage, *m.*

tea'-pot, *n.*, théière, *f.*

tear (tîre), *n.*, larme, *f. ;* pleur (V. Hugo), *m.* To shed —s; *verser des larmes.* To shed bitter —s; *pleurer à chaudes larmes.* To burst into —s;

fondre en larmes. To be drowned in —s ; *avoir les yeux noyés de larmes.* To affect (any one) to —s ; *toucher jusqu'aux larmes.* With —s in one's eyes ; *les larmes aux yeux.* All in —s ; *tout en pleurs ; tout éploré.*

tear (tère), *v.a.,* (*preterit,* Tore ; *past part.,* Torn) déchirer ; (the hair) arracher **à** ; (fig.) arracher, déchirer, abîmer. To — up ; (a railway) *détruire ; enlever les rails d'un chemin de fer.* To — asunder ; *déchirer en deux, arracher l'un de l'autre.* To — away, down, off, out ; *arracher.* To — from ; *arracher* **à**. To — up ; *arracher ; (to tear to pieces) mettre en morceaux, en pièces ; déchirer, abîmer.*

tear (tère), *v.n.,* s'agiter ; se démener. To — along ; *aller ventre à terre, brûler le pavé.* To —away ; *partir au grand galop,* ou *comme un trait.* To — down(stairs) ; *descendre quatre à quatre ; descendre précipitamment.* To — up(stairs) ; *monter quatre à quatre.* To — into ; *entrer précipitamment.*

tear (tère), *n.,* déchirure ; (injury done to things in use) détérioration, *f.* Wear and —; *usure, f.*

tear'er (tèr'-), *n.,* personne qui déchire ; (one that rages) personne qui se démène, *f.*

tear'-drop (tîre-), *n.,* larme, *f.*

tear'-falling (tîre-fôl'-), *adj.,* qui répand des larmes, tendre.

tear'ful (tîre-foule), *adj.,* tout en larmes ; rempli de larmes, en pleurs, éploré.

tear'fully, *adv.,* les larmes aux yeux.

tear'ing (tèr'-), *n.,* déchirement ; arrachement, *m.*

tear'less (tîre-), *adj.,* sans larmes, sec, insensible.

tea'-rose, *n.,* rose thé, *f.*

tear'-shaped (tîre-shép'te), *adj.,* (tech.) en forme de larme.

tease (tîze), *v.a.,* tracasser, tourmenter ; contrarier ; agacer, taquiner ; chicaner ; (to card) carder ; (cloth) lainer.

teas'er, tease (tîz'-), *n.,* tracassier, *m.f. ;* taquin, *m. ;* chicaneur, *m.*

tea'sel (tî-zèl), *n.,* (bot.) cardère, *f. ;* chardon à foulon, à bonnetier, *m. ;* cardère à foulon, à bonnetier, *f.*

tea'seler (tî-zèl'-), *n.,* laineur, *m.,* laineuse, *f.*

tea'-service (-seur-vice), *n.,* cabaret, service à thé, *m.*

tea'-set, *n.,* service à thé, *m.*

tea'sling (tîz'-), *n.,* lainage ; ratinage, *m.*

tea'-spoon (tî-spoune), *n.,* cuiller à thé, *f.* —ful ; *petite cuillerée, cuillerée à café, f.*

tea'-strainer, *n.,* passe-thé, *m.*

teat (tîte), *n.,* mamelon, tétin ; bout de sein ; (of animals) mamelon, *m.,* tette, *f.*

tea'-table (-té-b'l), *n.,* table à thé, *f.*

tea'-things (-thign'ze), *n.pl.,* service à thé, *m.sing.*

tea'-trade, *n.,* commerce des thés, *m.*

tea'-tray, *n.,* plateau, *m.*

tea'-tree (-trî), *n.,* thé ; arbre à thé, *m.*

tea'-urn (-eurne), *n.,* fontaine à thé, *f.*

tech'ily (tètsh'-), *adv.,* maussadement ; d'une manière hargneuse.

tech'iness (tètsh'-), *n.,* maussaderie ; humeur hargneuse, *f.*

tech'nical (tèk-), *adj.,* technique ; de l'art. — education ; *enseignement professionnel, m.* — school ; *école professionnelle, f.*

technical'ity, *n.,* caractère technique ; (term) terme technique, *m. ;* (fig.) formalité, *f.*

tech'nically (tèk-), *adv.,* techniquement ; suivant l'art.

tech'nics (tèk-), *n.pl.,* technique, *f.*

technolog'ical (tèk-nol-o-dj'-), *adj.,* technologique ; des arts.

technol'ogy (tèk-nol'o-dji), *n.,* technologie ; terminologie, *f.*

tech'y (tètshi), *adj.,* maussade ; bourru.

ted, *v.a.,* (agri., hay, etc.) étendre, faner.

Te De'um (ti-dî-), *n.,* Te Deum, *m.*

te'dious (tîd'-), *adj.,* ennuyeux, fastidieux, fatigant ; (slow) lent, trop long.

te'diously (tîd'-), *adv.,* ennuyeusement ; fastidieusement.

te'diousness (tîd'-), *n.,* ennui, *m. ;* fatigue, nature fastidieuse ; (slowness) lenteur fatigante ; (prolixity) prolixité, longueur, *f.*

te'dium (tî-), *n.,* ennui, *m. ;* fatigue, lenteur, longueur, *f.*

teem (tî'me), *v.n.,* enfanter ; être fécond **en.** To — with ; *être plein* **de** ; *abonder* **en** ; *fourmiller* **de** ; *regorger* **de.**

teem, *v.a.,* enfanter ; produire.

teem'ing, *adj.,* fécond, fertile, surabondant ; plein jusqu'au bord **de.**

teens (tî'nze), *n.pl.,* l'âge de treize à dix-neuf ans, *m.sing.* To be in one's — ; *n'avoir pas vingt ans, être encore " au matin des jours "* (V. Hugo).

teeth (tîth), *n.pl.* V. **tooth.**

teethe (tîthe), *v.n.,* faire ses dents.

teeth'ing (tîth'-), *n.,* dentition, *f.* To be — ; *faire ses dents.*

teeth'-range (tîth-ré'n'dje), *n.,* denture, *f.*

teeto'tal (tî-tô-), *adj.,* de tempérance.

teeto'taler (tî-tô-), *n.,* buveur d'eau, *m. ;* abstème, *m.f.*

teeto'talism (tî-tô-tal'iz'm), *n.,* abstinence absolue ; tempérance, *f.*

teeto'tum (tî-tô-), *n.,* toton, *m.*

teg'ular (tègh'iou-), *adj.,* de tuile.

teg'ularly, *adv.,* en tuile.

teg'ument (tègh'iou-), *n.,* tégument, *m.*

tegument'ary, *adj.,* tégumentaire.

teil'-tree (tîle-), *n.,* tilleul, *m.*

tel'egram, *n.,* télégramme, dépêche, *f.*

tel'egraph (tèl'î-), *n.,* télégraphe, *m.* — clerk ; *employé du télégraphe, m.*

tel'egraph, *v.a.,* télégraphier. I —ed to say that . . . ; *j'ai télégraphié que . . .*

telegraph'ic, *adj.,* télégraphique.

teleg'raphy, *n.,* télégraphie, *f.*

tel'ephone, *n.,* téléphone, *m.*

tel'ephone, *v.n.,* téléphoner. I —d to say that . . . ; *j'ai téléphoné que . . .*

tel'escope (tèl'è-scôpe), *n.,* télescope, *m. ;* lunette d'approche, longue vue, *f.*

tel'escope-table, *n.,* table à rallonges, *f.*

telescop'ic, *adj.,* télescopique.

tell, *v.a.,* (*preterit* and *part part.,* Told) dire ; (to express) exprimer ; faire part **de** ; (to narrate) raconter, conter ; (to teach) apprendre, dire ; (to disclose) révéler, dévoiler, rapporter ; (to count) compter, énumérer ; (to confess) avouer ; (to publish) publier, proclamer ; (to discover) découvrir, trouver ; (to explain) expliquer, dire ; (to confess) avouer ; (to publish) proclamer, annoncer, publier ; (to know) savoir. To — by ; *juger* **à** *ou* **par.** To — off ; *énumérer ; désigner ;* (of troops) *détacher, envoyer.* Don't — me ! *laissez donc !* — that to others, *ou* to the marines ; *à d'autres* ou *allez conter cela à d'autres.* I have been told ; *on m'a dit ; j'ai entendu dire.* It is told of ; *on dit* **de.** To — any one anything ; *dire quelque chose à quelqu'un ; faire part* **de**, ou *faire savoir, quelque chose* **à** *quelqu'un.* He is very fond of —ing tales ; *il aime beaucoup à rapporter.* He told you to stay here ; *il vous a commandé de rester ici.* I cannot — ; *je ne saurais dire, je ne sais pas.* I cannot — how much I regret . . . ; *je ne saurais vous dire combien je regrette . . .* I cannot — one from the other ; *je ne puis pas distinguer l'un de l'autre.* I can — you ; (colloq.) *allez ! je vous en réponds !* To — one's beads ; *dire son chapelet.* To — up ; *compter.*

tell, *v.n.,* dire ; raconter ; (to take effect)

faire son effet; se faire sentir; porter ; porter coup; (to tell by) juger **par**, *ou* **à**. Every shot told ; *chaque coup porta.* To — upon ; *affecter ;* *influer* **sur**; *agir* **sur**, *modifier.* To — of ; (pers.) *dénoncer ;* (things) *dire ; parler* **de**. To — up; *monter.*

tell′er, *n.*, diseur, *m.*, diseuse, *f. ;* raconteur, *m.*, raconteuse, *f.;* conteur ; (in parliament) scrutateur ; (of the exchequer) (ant.) agent comptable ; (thing) compteur, *m.*

tell′ing, *adj.*, qui porte ; (of speech) expressif, énergique, puissant ; (striking) frappant; efficace; puissant, à effet.

tell′-tale, *n.*, rapporteur, *m.*, rapporteuse, *f. ;* (mec.) compteur ; (nav.) indicateur, *m.*

tell′-tale, *adj.*, bavard ; (fig.) révélateur.

tellu′rium (tèl-liou-), *n.*, (chem.) tellure, *m.*

temer′ity (ti-mèr′-), *n.*, témérité, *f.*

tem′per, *n.*, caractère ; naturel, *m.;* (humor) humeur, *f.*, caractère, *m. ;* (anger) colère, *f.;* (calmness of mind) sang-froid, calme, *m. ;* (of steel, etc.) trempe ; (mixture) combinaison, *f.*, mélange, *m.*, (in sugar-works) matière à défécation, *f.* Out of —; *de mauvaise humeur ; en colère.* In a good —; *de bonne humeur.* To lose one′s —, to get out of —; *se mettre en colère ; s'emporter ; perdre son sang-froid, perdre patience.* To put out of —; *mettre de mauvaise humeur.* To keep one's —; *garder son sang-froid; ne pas s'emporter.* A man of a violent —; *un homme d'un caractère emporté.* He has a bad — but a good heart; *il a mauvaise tête, mais bon cœur.* To show —; *montrer de l'humeur.*

tem′per, *v.a.*, (to mix) mélanger, combiner ; (colors) délayer, détremper ; (to adjust) ajuster, proportionner ; mesurer, ménager ; ajuster, adapter ; (to modify) tempérer ; (to soften) adoucir ; (mus.) tempérer ; (steel, etc.) tremper. Ill— ed ; *qui a mauvais caractère, qui a le caractère mal fait.* Good— ed ; *d'un bon caractère, qui a le caractère bien fait ; aimable, doux, pas méchant.* —ed ; (of steel) *trempé.*

tem′perament (-peur′-), *n.*, constitution, disposition, *f. ;* tempérament ; caractère, *m.*

tem′perance (-peur-), *n.*, tempérance ; sobriété, modération, patience, *f.* — society ; *société de tempérance, f.*

tem′perate (-peur′-), *adj.*, tempéré ; modéré ; (pers.) tempérant, sobre ; (calm) calme ; (in speech) réservé ; (geog., of climates) tempéré. — zone ; *zone tempérée, f.*

tem′perately, *adv.*, avec sobriété, avec tempérance ; modérément ; avec calme ; avec réserve.

tem′perateness, *n.*, modération ; (mildness) douceur, *f. ;* (calmness) calme, sang-froid, *m.*

tem′perature (-tioure), *n.*, température, *f.*

tem′pest (-pèste), *n.*, (at sea) tempête, *f.;* (on land) orage, *m.* —beaten; *battu par la tempête.* —tossed; *ballotté par la tempête.*

tempes′tuous (-pèst′iou-), *adj.*, orageux ; tempétueux.

tempes′tuously, *adv.*, d'une manière orageuse, tempétueusement.

tempes′tuousness, *n.*, état orageux, tempétueux, *m.*

tem′plar, *n.*, templier ; (law-student) étudiant en droit, *m.*

tem′ple (tè′m′p′l), *n.*, temple, *m. ;* (anat.) tempe, *f.*

tem′ple-bone (-bône), *n.*, (anat.) os temporal, *m.*

tem′plet, *n.*, (mas.) panneau, patron, *m.*

tem′poral *adj.*, temporel ; (anat.) temporal.

temporal′ity, *n.*, (*temporalities,* *temporals*) bien temporel, revenu temporel, *m.*

tem′porally, *adv.*, temporellement.

tem′porarily, *adv.*, temporairement, momentanément, provisoirement.

tem′porariness, *n.*, état temporaire, *ou* provisoire, *m.*

tem′porary, *adj.*, temporaire, provisoire.

temporiza′tion (-raï-zé-), *n.*, temporisation, *f.*

tem′porize (-raïze), *v.n.*, temporiser ; transiger **avec** ; s'accommoder aux circonstances.

tem′porizer (-raïz′-), *n.*, temporisateur, temporiseur, *m. ;* qui s'accommode **à**.

tem′porizing (-raïz′-), *adj.*, temporisateur, qui temporise ; accommodant.

tempt (tè′m′te), *v.a.*, tenter ; (to incite) exciter, pousser **à**, provoquer ; (to draw) entraîner : (in Scripture) tenter, éprouver.

tempt′able (-′a-b′l), *adj.*, sujet à la tentation.

tempta′tion (tè′m′té-), *n.*, tentation, *f. ;* entraînement, *m.* To lead into — ; *induire en tentation.* To resist — ; *résister à la tentation.* To yield to — ; *céder à la tentation.* I feel a great — to ; *j'ai grande envie* **de** ; (to answer him) *les doigts me démangent* **de** . . .

tempt′er (tè′m′t′-), *n.*, tentateur, *m.*, tentatrice, *f.* The— ; (Script.) *le tentateur, le démon.*

tempt′ing (tè′m′t′-), *adj.*, tentant, séduisant, attrayant; (of food) appétissant, ragoûtant.

tempt′ingly, *adv.*, d'une manière tentante.

tempt′ress (tè′m′t′-), *n.*, tentatrice, *f.*

ten, *adj.*, dix, dizaine, *f.* About —, some — ; *une dizaine ; une dizaine* **de**. —fold ; *décuple ; dix fois.* To increase —fold ; (of population) *décupler.*

ten, *n.*, dix, *m. ;* dizaine, *f.*

ten′able (tè′n′a-b′l), *adj.*, soutenable ; (milit.) tenable.

tena′cious (tè-né-sheusse), *adj.*, tenace. — of ; *qui tient à ; fortement attaché* **à**. To be — of life ; *avoir la vie dure.*

tena′ciously, *adv.*, d'une manière tenace, obstinément.

tena′city (ti-nass′-), *n.*, ténacité, opiniâtreté, *f.*

ten′ancy (tè′n′-), *n.*, location, jouissance, possession, *f.* Joint — ; *copropriété, f.* In joint — ; *par indivis.*

ten′ant, *n.*, locataire, *m., f. ;* (who underlets) principal locataire, *m. ;* habitant ; (feudal law) tenancier, *m.*, habitante, *f. ;* (of a farm) fermier, *m.* — farmer ; *fermier à bail.* Co— ; *copropriétaire, colocataire, m.*

ten′antable (-′a-b′l), *adj.*, logeable ; habitable.

ten′antless, *adj.*, sans locataire ; sans habitant; vide ; inhabité.

ten′antry, *n.*, locataires, (of farms, land) fermiers ; (feud.) tenanciers, *m.pl.*

tench, *n.*, (ich.) tanche, *f.*

tend, *v.a.*, garder ; soigner ; avoir soin **de**; veiller **sur**.

tend, *v.n.*, (nav.) éviter. To — upon ; *servir.* To — to ; *se diriger* **vers** ; (fig.) *aboutir* **à** ; (to aim at) *viser* **à**, *tendre* **à** ; (to contribute to) *tendre* **à**, *contribuer* **à**.

tend′ency, *n.*, tendance, disposition, *f. ;* penchant, *m.*

tend′er, *n.*, (nurse) garde, *f. ;* (nav.) aviso ; bâtiment de transport ; bâtiment de servitude, *m. ;* allège, gabare, *f. ;* (railways) tender, *m.*

ten′der, *n.*, (offer) offre ; (for contracts) soumission ; (of an oath) action de déférer, délation (du serment), *f.* Legal — ; *monnaie légale, monnaie de cours, f.* To be a legal —; *avoir cours légal.* The lowest — ; *la soumission la moins élevée.*

ten′der, *v.a.*, offrir, présenter ; (an oath) déférer. To —for; (contracts) *soumissionner* **pour**. To — one's services ; *offrir ses services ; faire l'offre* **de**.

ten′der, *adj.*, tendre ; (easily pained) tendre, sensible ; (effeminate) délicat, mou ; (young) tendre ; (mild) doux ; (compassionate) tendre, compatissant ; (dear) cher, tendre ; (of flowers) délicat, de serre ; (ticklish) délicat, scabreux. — of ; *soucieux* **de**; *jaloux* **de**. To be — of ; *craindre* **de**, *se faire scrupule* **de**.

ten'derer, n., soumissionnaire, m.

ten'der-heart'ed (-härt'-), adj., compatissant, sensible, au cœur tendre.

ten'der-heart'edness, n., sensibilité, f.

ten'derling, n., enfant chéri, enfant gâté ; (of a deer) premier bois, m.

ten'derly, adv., tendrement ; doucement ; délicatement ; (with pity) avec compassion.

ten'derness, n., tendresse ; (soreness, sensibility) sensibilité ; (softness) mollesse, délicatesse ; (kind attention) sollicitude, f., égards, m.pl. ; (scrupulousness) scrupule ; (care) soin, m. ; (expression) douceur, f.

tend'ing, n., (nav.) évitage, m.

ten'dinous, adj., (anat.) tendineux.

ten'don, n., (anat.) tendon, m.

ten'dril, n., vrille, main, f. ; cirre, m.

ten'dril, adj., (bot.) grimpant.

ten'ebrous (tè'n-è-), adj., ténébreux.

tenebros'ity, n., ténèbres, f.pl. ; obscurité, f.

ten'ement (tè'n-è-), n., habitation, maison, f. ; appartement, logement ; local ; (feudal law) tènement, m.

ten'et (tè'n'-), n., dogme, principe, m. ; doctrine, f.

ten'nis, n., paume, f. ; jeu de paume, m.

ten'nis-court (-côrte), n., jeu de paume, m.

ten'on (tè'n'-), n., tenon, m.

ten'or (tè'n'-), n., (mus.) ténor ; (instrument) alto, m., viole, f. — key ; clé d'ut, f.

ten'or, n., (strain) style, ton, m. ; portée ; teneur, f. ; (character) caractère ; (sense) sens, esprit ; cours, m. ; substance, f.

tense (tè'n'ce), n., (gram.) temps, m.

tense, adj., tendu, raide.

ten'sile (-sile), adj., extensible.

ten'sion, n., tension, raideur ; (physics) tension, f.

tens'ive, adj., qui tend, qui raidit, tensif.

ten'sor (tè'n'seur), n., (anat.) extenseur, m.

tent, n., tente, f. ; pavillon, m. ; (surg.) tente, f. — bed ; lit d'ange, m. — cloth ; coutil, m. — wine ; vin d'Alicante, m.

tent, v.a., (surg.) sonder.

ten'tacle (tè'n-ta-k'l), n., (zoöl.) tentacule, m.

ten'tative (tè'n-ta-), adj., tentatif, d'essai, expérimental.

ten'tatively (tè'n'ta-), adv., expérimentalement.

tent'ed, adj., couvert de tentes. The — field ; le champ couvert de tentes.

tent'er, n., crochet à étendre les draps ; (drying-room) séchoir, étendoir, m. To be on — hooks ; être dans des transes ; être sur les épines ; être sur le gril.

tent'er, v.a., (of cloth) ramer ; courroyer, étendre.

tent'er-frame, n., (to stretch cloth) métier, châssis, m. ; rame, f.

tent'er-hook (-houke), n., clou à crochet, m.

tent'ering, n., ramage ; courroyage ; étendage, m.

tenth (tè'n'th), adj., dixième ; (of the month, a dynasty, etc.) dix.

tenth (tè'n'th), n., dixième, m. ; (tithe) dîme ; (mus.) dixième, f.

tenth'ly (tè'n'th-), adv., dixièmement.

tenu'ity (tè-niou-i-), n., ténuité.

ten'uous (tè'niou-), adj., délié, mince, ténu.

ten'ure (tè'n'iour), n., possession, redevance ; jouissance, occupation ; (right) droit de redevance ; (state) état, m. ; (feudal law) mouvance, tenure, f. — of office ; administration, f. During his — of office ; pendant son ministère.

tep'id (tèp'-), adj., tiède.

tepid'ity ou tep'idness (tèp'-), n., tiédeur, f.

terce (teurce), n., (cask) tiers (d'une pipe), m.

ter'cel (teur-), n., (of a bird) tiercelet, m.

tercen'tenary, adj., de trois siècles.

tercen'tenary, n., troisième centenaire, m.

terce'-major (teurs'mé-djeur), n., tierce majeure, f.

ter'ebinth, n., térébinthe, m.

tere'do, m., (mollusk worm) taret, m.

tergiversa'tion (teur-dji-veur-sé-), n., tergiversation ; (fickleness) inconstance, évasion, f.

term (teurme), n., (limit) terme, m., limite, f. ; (time) temps ; (duration) durée, f. ; (math.) terme, m. ; (jur.) session ; (in universities) (partie de l') année scolaire, f. ; (gram., log., arch.) terme, m. ; (jur.) session, f. ; (school) trimestre, m. —s, pl., conditions, f.pl. ; (price) prix, m. To make —s ; composer, transiger, avec. To bring to —s ; soumettre ; faire capituler ; forcer à un arrangement. To come to —s, to make —s ; s'accorder ; s'arranger ; tomber d'accord ; prendre des arrangements avec ; s'entendre avec ; (submit) céder, se rendre. To be on good —s with ; être bien avec ; vivre en bonne intelligence avec ; être sur un bon pied avec. To be on bad, ill —s with ; être mal avec ; être brouillé avec. To be on familiar —s with ; être sur un pied de familiarité avec. Are you on good —s with ? êtes vous bien avec ? We are not on good —s ; nous sommes très mal ensemble. To live on good, ou bad, —s with ; vivre en bonne, ou mauvaise, intelligence avec. To keep one's —s ; (in univ. ou law) prendre ses inscriptions ; (at an inn of court) faire son stage. The lowest — ; (math.) la plus simple expression. What are your —s ? quels sont vos prix ? quelles sont vos conditions ? On those —s ; à ce prix ; à ces conditions. In plain —s ; en termes précis. On moderate —s ; à un prix modéré. For a — of years ; pour un temps limité.

term (teurme), v.a., nommer, appeler, dire.

ter'magant (teur-), n., mégère, f. ; dragon, m.

ter'magant, adj., acariâtre.

ter'minable (teur-mi-na-b'l), adj., terminable, limitable. — annuity ; rente, ou annuité, terminable, f.

ter'minal (teur-), adj., dernier, extrême ; terminal. — station ; gare, f.

ter'minally (teur-), adv., chaque session ; (schools) chaque trimestre.

ter'minate (teur-), v.a., terminer, finir ; mettre un terme à.

ter'minate, v.n., se terminer en, finir ; cesser, s'arrêter ; (fig.) aboutir à ; finir par.

termina'tion (teur-mi-né-), n., limitation, (limit) extrémité, bout ; (end) fin, terminaison ; (result) conclusion, f., résultat ; (last purpose) but final, m. ; (gram.) désinence, terminaison, f.

terminol'ogy (-ol'o-dji), n., terminologie, f.

ter'minus (teur-), n., gare, tête de ligne, f. ; embarcadère, m. ; gare de départ, f. ; débarcadère, m. ; gare d'arrivée, f.

ter'mite (teur-), n., (ent.) termite, m.

term'less, adj., illimité, infini.

tern (teurne), n., (orni.) sterne, m.

ter'nary (teur-), adj., ternaire.

ter'race (tèr-), n., terrasse, f.

ter'race (tèr'-), v.a., former en terrasse.

ter'ra-cotta, n., terre cuite, f.

ter'ra firma (tèr'ra-feur-), n., terre ferme, f. ; (fam.) le plancher des vaches, m.

terra'queous (tèr-ré-kwi'-), adj., terraqué.

terres'trially (tèr-), adv., d'une manière terrestre.

ter'rible (tèr-ri-b'l), adj., terrible ; redoutable ; formidable ; (severe) terrible, horrible, épouvantable.

ter'ribleness, n., horreur, nature terrible, f.

ter'ribly, adv., terriblement ; (greatly) terriblement, diablement.

ter'rier (tèr-ri-eur), n., (hole ; dog) terrier, chien terrier, m. ; (wimble) tarière, f. ; registre, cadastre ; terrier, papier terrier, m. — bitch ; chienne terrier, f.

terrif'ic (tèr'-), adj., affreux, terrible, épouvantable.

terrif'ically, adj., terriblement, épouvantablement.

ter'rify (tèr-ri-faïe), v.a., terrifier, épouvanter.

territor'ial, adj., territorial; (local) limité.

territor'ially, adv., territorialement.

ter'ritory, n., territoire, état, m.; Etats, m.pl.

ter'ror, n., terreur, f.; effroi, m.; épouvante, f. The reign of —; la Terreur; le règne de la terreur. He is my —; c'est ma bête noire que cet homme. He is a perfect —; (of a child) c'est un petit diable que cet enfant là. To go in — of one's life; craindre **pour** sa vie, **pour** sa sûreté personnelle.

terse (teurse), adj., poli, net, concis, élégant.

terse'ly, adv., nettement; élégamment; d'une manière concise.

terse'ness, n., netteté, pureté; élégance; verve, f.

ter'tian (teur-sha'n), adj., (med.) tierce. — fever; fièvre tierce, f.

ter'tiary (teur-shi-a-ri), adj., (geog.) de troisième ordre; (geol. med.) tertiaire.

tes'sellate (tès-sèl-), v.a., marqueter.

tes'sellated (tès-sèl-lét'-), adj., marqueté, tessellé; en mosaïque; (bot.) en damier. — pavement; mosaïque, f.

tessella'tion (tès-sèl-lé-), n., mosaïque, f.

test, n., essai, m., épreuve; (standard) pierre de touche, f.; degré de comparaison; criterium, m.; (proof) preuve, f.; (characteristic) caractère distinctif, m.; (distinction) distinction, f.; (chem.) réactif; (cupel) têt; (hist.) test, m. To put to the —; mettre à l'épreuve. To stand the —; subir l'épreuve. — paper; papier réactif, m. — tube; (chem.) tube à essai, m.

test, v.a., éprouver; faire l'épreuve **de**; faire l'essai **de**; vérifier; (metal.) coupeller; (jur.) attester, légaliser.

test'able (tèst-a-b'l), adj., (jur.) qui peut être légué.

testa'cea (tès-té-shi-a), n.pl., testacés, m.pl.

testa'ceous (tès-té-sheusse), adj., testacé.

test'ament, n., testament, m.

testament'ary, adj., testamentaire; (given in a testament) légué, hérité.

test'ate, adj., (jur.) qui a testé.

testa'tor (tès-té-teur), n., (jur.) testateur, m.

testa'trix, n., (jur.) testatrice, f.

tes'ter, n., ciel de lit, baldaquin, m. — bed; lit à baldaquin, m.

test'icle, n., testicule, m.

testifica'tion (-fi-ké-), n., témoignage, m.

tes'tifier (-faï-eur), n., témoin, déposant, m.

tes'tify (tès-ti-faïe), v.a., attester, certifier; témoigner **de**; rendre témoignage **de**; (to publish) proclamer; (jur.) déposer **de**.

tes'tify, v.n., rendre témoignage; (jur.) déposer. To — against; déposer **contre**.

test'ily (tès-ti-li), adv., maussadement, d'une manière bourrue, avec humeur.

testimo'nial (-mô-ni-eule), n., témoignage; certificat, m.; attestation, f.; (a gift) témoignage d'estime, de reconnaissance, m.

testimo'nials, n.pl., certificats, m.pl.

tes'timony (-mo-), n., (declaration, evidence) témoignage, m.; (proof) preuve, f.; (authority) témoignage, m., autorité, f.; (jur.) témoignage, m., déposition; (open attestation) proclamation; (the ark) arche, f.; (tables of the law) tables de la loi, f.pl.; (word of God) parole de Dieu, f. In — whereof; en foi de quoi. To bear — to; rendre témoignage à.

test'iness, n., maussaderie; pétulance, f.

test'ing, n., épreuve, f.; (metal.) essai, m.

test'y, adj., bourru; maussade; susceptible.

tet'anus (tèt'-), n., (med.) tétanos, m.

tête-à-tête, n., tête-à-tête, m.

teth'er (tèth'-), n., attache, courroie, longe; (fig.) chaîne, f.; limites, bornes, f.pl. To be at

the end of one's —; être au bout de sa corde, de son rouleau.

teth'er (tèth'-), v.a., lier par une longe; mettre à l'attache; (mil.) mettre au piquet; (fig.) enchaîner.

tet'rachord (tèt'ra-korde), n., tétracorde, m.

tet'ragon (-gone), n., tétragone, m.

tetrag'onal, adj., tétragone.

tetrahe'dron (-hî-dreune), n., (geom.) tétraèdre, m.

tetrapet'alous (tèt'ra-pèt'-), adj., (bot.) tétrapétale, à quatre pétales.

te'trarch (tî-trârke), n., tétrarque, m.

tet'rarchy (tèt-rar-ki), n., tétrarchie, f.

tet'ter (tèt'teur), n., (med.) dartre, f., herpès, m.

Teu'ton, n., Teuton, m., Teutonne, f.

Teuton'ic (tiou-), adj., teutonique.

tew'el (tiou-èl), n., tuyère, f.

text (tèks'te), n., texte, m.; (handwriting) écriture, f. Large —; gros, m., écriture grosse, ou en gros, f. Middle —; écriture moyenne, f., moyen, m. Small —; écriture fine, f., fin, m.

text'-book (-bouke), n., livre de texte; manuel; guide, livre de classe, m.

text'-hand, n., écriture grosse, ou en gros, f.

tex'tile (tèks'tile), adj., textile. — fabric; tissu, m.

textor'ial (-tô-), adj., du tissage; textile. — arts; industries textiles, f.pl.

tex'tual (tèkst'iou-), adj., textuel.

tex'tually, adv., textuellement.

tex'ture (tèkst'iour), n., tissage; (stuff, anat.) tissu, m.; (of writings) texture, contexture, f.

Thames (tèmze), n., Tamise, f. He will never set the — on fire; il n'a pas inventé la poudre.

than (tha'n), conj., que; (between more or less and a number) **de**; (before a verb in a finite mood) **que . . . ne** (when the principal clause is affirmative), **que** (when the principal clause is interrogative or negative); (before a verb in the infinitive) **que de**. More — a hundred; plus de cent. Rather —; plutôt que. No other —; personne autre que; (of things) rien autre que. He is younger — I am; il est plus jeune que je ne suis. The house is more — three miles from here; il y a plus de trois milles d'ici à la maison. He does not speak otherwise — he acts; il ne parle pas autrement qu'il agit. Napoleon — whom no one ever better understood war, thought . . . ; Napoléon, et jamais personne n'entendit mieux la guerre que lui, pensait que . . . ; I prefer to do without it rather — to ask for it; j'aime mieux m'en passer que **de** le demander.

thank (tha'gn'ke), v.a., remercier (for, of a thing) **de**, (for, of a person) **pour**; faire des remercîments à; rendre grâces à. — God! grâce à Dieu! Dieu merci! God be —ed! grâces en soient rendues à Dieu! Dieu soit loué! No, I — you; je vous remercie; merci. I will — you to shut the door; veuillez bien fermer la porte. I will — you for; je vous demanderai; veuillez me donner, ou bien me passer. To have only oneself to — for; ne s'en prendre qu'à soi-même. You have only yourself to — for it; c'est à vous seul qu'il faut vous en prendre.

thank'ful (-foule), adj., reconnaissant (for, **de**). I am — to say that . . . ; je suis heureux, ou content, **de** dire que . . .

thank'fully, adv., avec reconnaissance.

thank'fulness, n., gratitude, reconnaissance, f.; remercîments, m.pl.

thank'less, adj., ingrat; (not thanked) oublié, méconnu.

thank'lessness, n., ingratitude, f.

thank'-offering, n., sacrifice d'actions de grâces, m.

thanks, n., remercîments, m.pl.; grâces, f.pl. Many —; mille, ou bien des, remercîments. To return, ou to give, — to; faire des remercîments à ; *remercier*. To give — to God ; *rendre grâces à Dieu, au ciel.* Give him my best — ; *remerciez-le bien de ma part.*

thanksgiv'er (-ghiv'-), *n.*, personne qui rend des actions de grâces, *f.*

thanksgiv'ing (-ghiv'-), *n.*, actions de grâces, *f.pl. ;* remercîments, *m.pl.*

that (*thate*), *demonstrative adj.*, (*those*) ce, ce . . . là, cet, cet . . . là, *m. ;* cette, cette . . . là, *f. ;* (*pronoun*) celui-là, *m.*, celle-là, *f. ;* cela, ça, le, *m.* I do not like — man ; *je n'aime pas cet homme-là.* This is good ; I prefer — ; *celui-ci est bon ; je préfère celui-là.* On — ; *sur cela ; là-dessus.* In — ; *en cela ; là dedans,* y. Upon — ; *sur cela, là-dessus.* With — ; *avec cela ;* (thereupon) *là-dessus.* By — ; *par cela, par là.* — he, I, etc., will not ! *oh, pour cela non !* You have not seen him ? — I have ; *vous ne l'avez pas vu ? Si fait.* — you are not ; *pour ça non ; bien sûr.* What of — ? *qu'est-ce que cela prouve ? qu'est-ce que cela fait ?* You saw the ceremony ? — I did ; *vous avez vu la cérémonie ? Oui, vraiment.* To have come to — ; *en être là ; en être venu là.* Has it come to — ? *est-ce là l'état de choses ?* It will not come to — ; *il n'en sera pas ainsi ; cela n'arrivera sûrement pas.* — is the question ! (Hamlet) ; *c'est là,* ou *voilà,* la question. — crowns all ; *il ne manquait plus que cela.* In — ; *vu que ; parce que ; en cela ;* y ; *là dedans.* For all — ; *en dépit de cela ; malgré cela.* — much ; *cela.*

that (*thate*), *relative pron.*, qui, *m., f. ;* lequel, *m.*, laquelle, *f. ;* lesquels, *m.pl.*, lesquelles, *f.pl. ;* (object) que.

that (*thate*), *conj.*, que ; (in order that) afin que, pour que ; (because) de ce que, parce que ; (so that) de sorte que. Than — ; *que,* ou *que si,* ou *que de voir.* Oh ! — I had his talent ; *que n'ai-je son talent !* ou *si seulement j'avais.* Oh ! — I were with you ; *que ne suis-je avec vous !*

thatch (*thatshe*), *n.*, chaume, *m.*

thatch (*thatshe*), *v.a.*, couvrir de chaume.

thatch'er, *n.*, couvreur en chaume, *m.*

thaw (*thô*), *n.*, dégel, *m.*

thaw (*thô*), *v.a.* and *n.*, dégeler ; (fig.) fondre.

the (*thi* ou *theu*), *art.*, le, *m.*, la, *f. ;* les, *pl.m.f.* At —, to — ; *au, m., à la, f. ; aux, pl.m.f.* From — of — ; *du, m., de la, f. ; des, pl.m.f.* — dear boy ; *ce cher enfant.* — more . . . — less ; *plus . . . moins.* — more . . . be- cause ; *d'autant plus que.* — sooner — better; *plus tôt ce sera, mieux ça vaudra.*

the'ater (thi-a-teur), *n.*, théâtre, *m. ;* salle de spectacle, *f. ;* spectacle ; (lecture-room) amphi- théâtre, *m.* To go to the — ; *aller au spectacle.* The — will be closed to-night ; *il y aura relâche ce soir.* The French — ; *le théâtre français.* Minor — ; *petit théâtre.*

theat'rical (thi-), *adj.*, de théâtre ; théâtral ; scénique. — piece ; *pièce de théâtre, f.* — writ- er ; *dramaturge, auteur dramatique, m.*

theat'rically, *adv.*, théâtralement.

theat'ricals (thi-at-ri-calze), *n.pl.*, spectacle, *m.sing.* Private — ; *comédie d'amateurs ; comé- die de société, comédie de salon, f.*

thee (*thî*), *pron.*, toi ; te.

theft (*thêfte*), *n.*, larcin ; vol, *m.*

their (*thère*), *pron.*, leur, leurs.

theirs (*thèr'ze*), *pron.*, à eux, *m.pl.*, à elles, *f.pl. ;* le leur, *m.*, la leur, *f. ;* les leurs, *pl.m.f.*

the'ism (thî-iz'm), *n.*, théisme, *m.*

the'ist (thî-iste), *n.*, théiste, *m.*

theist'ic (thî-ist'-), *adj.*, théiste.

them (*thème*), *pron.*, eux, *m.pl.*, elles, *f.pl. ;* les, leur, *pl.m.f.* To — ; *à eux, à elles ; leur ;* (of things) *y, leur.* Of, from — ; *d'eux, d'elles ; en.* I have seen — ; *je les ai vus.* I have spoken to — : *je leur ai parlé.* I have given — three ; *je leur en ai donné trois.*

theme (thîme), *n.*, thème, sujet, *m. ;* (in schools) narration, dissertation, *f. ;* discours ; (mus., gram.) thème, *m.*

themselves' (*thè*'m'sèlv'ze), *pron.*, eux- mêmes, *m.pl.*, elles-mêmes, *f.pl. ;* se, *pl.m.f.* They think — ; *ils se croient.*

then (*thè*'ne), *adv.*, alors, pour lors ; (after- ward) ensuite, puis ; (in that case) alors, dans ce cas ; (in consequence) alors, en conséquence. Now — ! *voyons ?* What — ? *quoi donc ? et après ? et puis ?* Now and — ; *de temps en temps.* The — government ; *le gouvernement d'alors.* Till — ; *jusqu'alors.* Since — ; *depuis ce temps là ; depuis.* By — ; *alors, déjà.* But — ; *d'un autre côté ; par contre.* First one — the other ; *d'abord l'un, puis l'autre.*

then (*thè*'n), *conj.*, donc.

thence (*thè*'n'ce), *adv.*, de là, par là, en ; (of time) depuis ce temps ; dès lors, depuis lors ; (for that reason) par cette raison, de là, partant, c'est pourquoi.

thence'forth (*thè*'n'ce-forth), *adv.*, dès lors, dès ce moment-là ; depuis ce temps, désormais.

thence'forward (*thè*'n'ce-for-worde), *adv.*, depuis lors, dès ce moment, désormais.

theoc'racy (thî-), *n.*, théocratie, *f.*

theocrat'ic, *adj.*, théocratique.

theocrat'ically, *adv.*, théocratiquement.

Theodo'sian, *n.*, théodosien.

theod'olite (thî-od'o-laïte), *n.*, (astron., surv.) théodolite, *m.*

theog'ony (thi-), *n.*, théogonie, *f.*

theolo'gian (thî-o-lô-dji-), *n.*, théologien, *m.*

theolo'gical (thî-o-lo-dj'-), *adj.*, théologique.

theolo'gically, *adv.*, théologiquement.

theol'ogy (thî-ol'o-dji), *n.*, théologie, *f.*

theor'bo (thi-or-bô), *n.*, téorbe, théorbe, tuorbe, *m.*

the'orem (thî-o-rè'm), *n.*, théorème, *m.*

theoret'ic ou **theoret'ical** (thi-o-rèt'-), *adj.*, théorique ; spéculatif.

theoret'ically, *adv.*, théoriquement.

the'orist (thî-o-) *and* **the'orizer** (-raïz'eur), *n.*, théoricien, *m.*

the'orize (thî-o-raïze), *v.n.*, théoriser.

the'ory (thî-), *n.*, théorie, *f.*

theos'ophist (thi-oss'-), *n.*, théosophe, *m.*

theos'ophy (thi-oss'-), *n.*, théosophie, *f.*

therapeu'tic (thèr'a-piou-), *adj.*, thérapeu- tique.

therapeu'tics (thèr'a-piou-), *n.pl.*, thérapeu- tique, *f.sing.*

there (*thère*), *adv.*, (place) là, y. —'s a kiss ; don't fret ; *allons ! embrasse-moi ; et ne pleure pas.* — and back ; *aller et retour.* Here and — ; *çà et là.* — he is ! *le voilà !* — they are ! *les voilà !* — is, — are ; *il y a.* Down — ; *là-bas.* Off — ; *de là.* Out — ; *là dehors.* In — ; *là dedans.* On — ; *là-dessus.* Over — ; *là-bas.* Under — ; *là-dessous.* Up — ; *là-haut.* — and then ; *séance tenante ; sur place, sur le champ ; pendant qu'on y est.* — exists . . . ; *il existe . . .* — I have him ; *c'est par là que je le tiens.* —'s many a slip 'twixt the cup and the lip ; (prov.) *il y a loin de la coupe aux lèvres ;* ou *n'épouse pas toujours qui fiance.*

there'about (*thèr*'abaoute) ou **there'abouts** (-baoutse), *adv.*, par-là ; près de là ; (nearly) à peu près, environ.

thereaf'ter (*thèr*'âf-), *adv.*, ensuite ; là-dessus, après cela.

thereat' (*thèr*'-), *adv.*, par là ; à cet endroit ; (at that) à cela, à ce sujet.

thereby' (*thèr*'-baïe), *adv.*, par là ; par ce moyen, ainsi, de cette manière ; (consequence) par conséquent.

there'fore (*thèr*'-), *adv.*, c'est pourquoi, aussi ; (consequently) donc, par conséquent, ainsi.

therefrom' (*thèr*'-), *adv.*, de là ; en ; de cela.

therein' (*thèr*'i'n), *adv.*, là dedans ; en cela ; y.

thereinto′ (*thèr′*i′*n′*tou), *adv.*, là dedans, en cela.

thereof′ (*thèr′*ove), *adv.*, de cela, en.

thereon′ (*thèr′*-), *adv.*, là-dessus, sur cela ; à ce sujet.

thereout′ (*thèr′*aoute), *adv.*, de là.

thereto′ (*thèr*-tou) *ou* **thereunto′** (-eu′*n′*tou), *adv.*, à la ; à quoi, y.

thereupon′ (*thèr′*eup′-), *adv.*, là-dessus, sur cela, sur ce.

therewith′ (*thèr′*with), *adv.*, avec cela, de cela ; en ; y.

ther′mæ (theur-mî), *n.pl.*, thermes, *m.pl.*

ther′mal *ou* **ther′mic** (theur-), *adj.*, thermal ; (med.) thermique. — baths; *thermes, m.pl.*

thermom′eter, *n.*, thermomètre, *m.*

thermomet′rical, *adj.*, thermométrique.

thermomet′rically, *adv.*, au moyen d'un thermomètre.

these (*thîze*), *pron.*, ces, ces . . . ci, *pl.m.f.* ; ceux-ci, *m.pl.*, celles-ci, *f.pl.* — are ; *ce sont là ; tels sont ; voilà.* Are not these shoes yours ? *ne sont-ce pas là vos souliers ?* Dinner has been waiting for —, *ou* the last, two hours ; *il y a deux heures que le dîner attend.*

the′sis (thi-cice), *n.*, thèse, *f.*

Thes′pian, *adj.*, tragique, de la tragédie.

thew (thiou), *n.*, (ant.) nerf, muscle, *m.* —s and sinews ; *nerfs et muscles.*

thew′y, *adj.*, nerveux ; musculeux.

they (*thê*), *pron.*, ils, *m.pl.*, elles, *f.pl.*, (followed by a relative) ceux, *m.pl.*, celles, *f.pl.* ; (standing alone) eux, *m.pl.*, elles, *f.pl.* ; (people) on. — say; *on dit.* —are silly people ; *ce sont de sottes gens.* — sin who tell us love can die ; *ceux là pèchent qui nous disent que l'amour peut mourir.*

thick (thick), *adj.*, épais ; gros ; (turbid) trouble ; (close) dru, serré ; (frequent) fréquent, nombreux ; (paint.) gras, épais ; (of the pronunciation) gras ; (of hearing) dur ; (of shot) dru ; (intimate) intime ; (dull) lourd. They are very — together ; *ils sont très liés* ou *ils sont inséparables.* They are as — as thieves together ; *ils s'entendent comme larrons en foire.*

thick (thick), *n.*, partie la plus épaisse, *f.* ; fort, *m.* In the — of ; *au plus épais* **de**. In the — of the fight ; *au plus fort de la mêlée.* Through — and thin ; *à travers tous les obstacles ;* (fig.) *envers et contre tous ; en dépit de tout, quoi qu'il arrive.*

thick, *adv.*, épais ; (fast) dru ; (closely) épais ; tout près les uns des autres ; en troupe, en foule; dru ; (deeply) profondément. To speak — ; *parler gras.*

thick′en (thik′k′n), *v.a.*, épaissir ; (to make more numerous) grossir, épaissir ; (to make close) serrer, resserrer ; (a sauce) lier.

thick′en (thik′k′n), *v.n.*, épaissir ; s'épaissir ; se grossir; (to become obscure) s'obscurcir ; (to become close) se serrer, se resserrer ; (to become animated) s'animer, s'échauffer ; (to be crowded) se presser ; (of sauces) se lier. The plot —s ; *l'intrigue s'embrouille, ou s'épaissit.*

thick′ening, *n.*, épaississement, *m. ;* (of a sauce) liaison, *f.*

thick′et, *n.*, taillis ; fourré ; hallier ; buisson ; bosquet ; (clump of trees) bouquet d'arbres, *m.*

thick′-headed (-hèd′ède), *adj.*, lourd, épais.

thick′ish, *adj.*, un peu épais ; un peu gros.

thick′ly, *adv.*, d'une manière épaisse ; (in quick succession) dru ; (deeply) profondément. — clad ; *vêtu chaudement.*

thick′ness, *n.*, épaisseur ; (consistence) consistance, *f.*, épaississement ; (closeness of the parts) état serré, état dru, *m.*

thick′-set, *adj.*, épais, serré ; touffu, (pers.) trapu.

thick′-skinned, *adj.*, à peau **dure** ; (fig.) (pers.) dur à cuire, coriace.

thick′-skull (-skeule), *n.*, balourd, lourdaud, *m.*

thick′-soled (-sôlde), *adj.*, à semelles épaisses.

thick′-sown, *adj.*, épais.

thief (thîf), *n.*, voleur, *m.*, voleuse, *f.* ; auteur de vol ; (in Scripture) larron ; (in a candle) champignon, *m. ;* (bot.) ronce, *f.* Stop — ; *au voleur ! arrêtez !* Opportunity makes the — ; *l'occasion fait le larron.* Set a — to catch a — ; (prov.) *à corsaire, corsaire et demi.*

thief′-catcher *ou* **thief′-taker**, *n.*, agent de police, *m.*

thieve (thi′ve), *v.n.*, voler.

thiev′ing, *n.*, vol, *m.* To live by — ; *vivre de vol,* ou *de larcins.*

thiev′ish, *adj.*, adonné au vol ; de voleur.

thiev′ishly, *adv.*, en voleur ; par le vol.

thiev′ishness, *n.*, penchant au vol, *m. ;* habitude du vol, *f.*

thigh (thaïe), *n.*, cuisse ; (of a horse) jambe, *f.* —-bone ; *fémur ; os de la cuisse, m.* — -piece; *cuissard, m.*

thill (thil), *n.*, limon, timon, brancard, *m.* — horse; *limonier, cheval de brancard, m.*

thim′ble (thi′m′b′l), *n.*, dé, *m.*

thim′bleful, *n.*, plein un dé. A — of wine ; *un doigt de vin.*

thim′blerig, **thim′blerigging**, *n.*, tour de gobelets, *m.*

thim′blerigger, *n.*, joueur de dé ; escamoteur, escroc, *m.*

thin (thi′n), *adj.*, mince ; (lean) maigre ; (slender) mince, délié ; fluet ; (not crowded) peu nombreux ; (slight) léger, mince ; (of liquids) clair ; (of animals) maigre, efflanqué; (of the air) rare ; (of trees, plants, hair) clairsemé, rare; (of voice) grêle, faible. — as a lucifer; *maigre comme un clou.* To grow — ; (pers.) *maigrir, s'amincir, s'éclaircir.* To make — ; *amaigrir.* There was a — attendance ; *il y avait peu de monde ; la salle était presque vide.* There was a — house; (parl.) *la chambre était presque vide.*

thin, *adv.*, d'une manière éparse ; clair. — -skinned ; (fig.) irritable, pointilleux, susceptible. To lay paint — ; *donner une couche légère.* To sow too — ; *semer trop clair.*

thin, *v.a.*, éclaircir ; (to rarefy) raréfier ; réduire. To — out a forest ; *éclaircir une forêt.* To — the air ; *raréfier l'air.*

thine (thaïne), *pron.*, le tien, *m.*, la tienne, *f. ;* les tiens, *m.pl.*, les tiennes, *f.pl. ;* à toi.

thing (thigne), *n.*, chose, *f. ;* objet, *m. ;* affaire ; (event) affaire, chose, *f. ;* (creature) être, *m.*, créature ; (animal) créature, bête ; (trash) drogue, *f.* —s, *pl.*, chose, *f.*, affaires, *f.pl.*, effets, *m. ;* (clothes) affaires, *f.pl.*, habits, effets, *m.pl.* That is the very — ! *c'est cela même ! c'est ce qu'il faut !* Poor little — ! *pauvre petit !* Good —; (fig.) *bonne chose;* (com.) (fin.) *bonne affaire.* It is a bad — for her ; *c'est une mauvaise affaire pour elle ; c'est une chose bien pénible pour elle.* No such —; *point du tout.* That is quite another — ; *c'est tout autre chose ; c'est une autre paire de manches.* For one — ; *d'abord.* Above all —s ; *avant tout, par-dessus tout.* Not to do an earthly — ; *ne faire œuvre de ses dix doigts.* Any—; *quelque chose ; quoi que ce soit.* Not any—; *rien.* Any— but ; *rien moins que ; tout excepté.* It is a very good —; *cela se trouve bien.* It is a very good — that ; *c'est,* ou *il est, fort heureux que.* A — of a . . . ; *un mauvais . . . ; une dérision de . . .* What a — of a hat it was you sold me ! *quel mauvais chapeau vous m'avez vendu !* It is not quite the — ; *ce n'est pas précisément cela ; ce n'est pas tout à fait ce qu'il faut,* ou (of propriety) *comme il faut.* Mr. — -a-bob ; *Monsieur chose, machin.* Poor — ! *pauvre femme ! pauvre enfant ! pauvre bête ! etc.*

thing′ummy, *n.*, machin, chose, *m.* Little — ; *petit chose.*

think (thign'ke), *v.a.n.*, (*preterit* and *past part.*, Thought) penser ; (to fancy) croire, penser ; s'imaginer ; (to believe) croire ; (to judge) trouver, juger. To — to oneself ; *penser en soi-même*. To — over ; *songer* à ; *réfléchir* sur, *ou* à ; *examiner*. — of me what you please ; *pensez de moi ce que vous voudrez*. To — much of ; *faire beaucoup de cas*, ou *grand cas*, de ; *avoir une haute opinion* de. I thought he would have died of convulsions ; *je voyais le moment où il allait mourir dans les convulsions*. I can't — of it ; *je ne peux pas me le rappeler*. Little did I — that ; *je ne m'imaginais guère que* (Burke). Little did I — that he would fail, *ou* disappoint me ; *je ne me doutais guère qu'il me fît faux bond*. That he would do well to — twice before he sent such poltroons into a breach defended by English soldiers (Macaulay) ; *qu'il ferait bien d'y regarder* à *deux fois avant de lancer de tels poltrons dans une brèche défendue par des soldats anglais*. I — I'll go too ; *ma foi, j'y vais aussi*. I — so ; *je crois que oui*. I — not ; *je crois que non*. To — of ; *penser* à, *songer* à, *réfléchir* à ; (to light on) *s'aviser* de ; (to intend) *avoir l'intention* de. To — to ; *avoir l'intention* de. To — ill of, well of ; *avoir une mauvaise*, ou *une bonne opinion*, de ; *penser du mal* de, *du bien* de. What do you — of him ; *que pensez-vous de lui ?* I will — it over ; *j'y réfléchirai*. I told him what I thought of him ; *je lui ai dit son fait*.

think'er, *n.*, penseur, *m.*

think'ing, *n.*, pensée, *f.* ; jugement, avis, sens, *m.* In my — ; *à mon avis*. Way of thinking ; *façon de penser*, *opinion*, *f.*

think'ing, *adj.*, pensant, intelligent, raisonnable, réfléchi, sérieux.

thin'ly (thi'n'-), *adv.*, faiblement ; peu ; légèrement ; (sparsely) de loin en loin. The performance was — attended ; *l'assistance était peu nombreuse* ; ou *il n'y avait pas salle comble, tant s'en faut*.

thin'ness (thi'n'-), *n.*, peu d'épaisseur, *m.* ; (tenuity) ténuité ; (fluidity) fluidité ; (paucity) rareté, *f.* ; petit nombre, *m.* ; (leanness) maigreur ; (exility) finesse, *f.* ; état délié, *m.*

thin'-soled, *adj.*, à minces semelles.

thin'-sown (-sô'n), *adj.*, clairsemé.

third (theurde), *n.*, tiers, *m.* ; (mus.) tierce, *f. adj.*, troisième.

third'-estate, *n.*, (hist.) tiers-état, *m.*

third'ly, *adv.*, troisièmement.

thirst (theurste), *n.*, soif ; altération, *f.* — for ; *soif* de.

thirst, *v.n.*, avoir soif de, être altéré de, soupirer après.

thirst'ily, *adv.*, avidement.

thirst'iness, *n.*, soif ; altération, *f.*

thirst'y, *adj.*, qui a soif ; altéré. To be —; *avoir soif*. To make —; *altérer*.

thir'teen (theur-tî'n), *adj.*, treize.

thir'teenth (theur-tî'n'th), *adj.* and *n.*, treizième ; (mus.) treizième, *f.*

thir'tieth (theur-tièth), *n.* and *adj.*, trentième ; (of the days of the month) trente, *m.*

thir'ty (theur-ti), *adj.*, trente.

this (*th*iss), *pron.*, (*these*) ce ; ce . . . ci ; cet ; cet . . . ci, *m.* ; cette ; cette . . . ci, *f.* ; celui-ci, *m.*, celle-ci, *f.* ; ceci, *m.* — is one which, *ou* who ; *en voici un qui*. — is Miss Trotwood's ; *voici la maison de Miss Trotwood*. — once ; *cette fois*. — or that ; *tel ou tel*. — moment ; *à l'instant* ; *ce moment, maintenant*. At — moment ; *à présent* ; *à l'heure qu'il est*. — is what I fear ; *c'est ce que je crains*. I have been waiting — last hour ; *il y a une heure que j'attends*.

this'tle (this's'l), *n.*, (bot.) chardon, *m.*

this'tly (this's'l), *adv.*, plein de chardons.

thith'er (*th*ith'eur), *adv.*, là ; y ; (to that end) dans ce but. Hither and — ; *çà et là*.

thith'erward (*th*ith'eur-worde), *adv.*, vers ce lieu *ou* cet endroit.

thole (thôle), *n.*, (nav.) tolet, *m.* ; (of a scythe) poignée, *f.*

thong (tho'gne), *n.*, sangle, courroie, lanière, *f.*

thora'cic (tho-ra-), *adj.*, thoracique.

thor'ax (tho-), *n.*, thorax, *m.*

thorn (thorne), *n.*, (bot.) épine ; (prickle) épine, *f.*, piquant, *m.* ; (anything troublesome) épine, *f.*, souci, *m.* ; (in Scripture) écharde, épine, *f.* ; (fig.) remords, aiguillon, *m.* To be upon —s ; *être sur des* ou *les épines*, ou *brûler à petit feu* ; *être sur la braise*. To run a — into one's finger ; *s'enfoncer une épine dans le doigt*. — in one's side ; (fig.) *une épine au pied* ; (pers.) *un sujet de trouble, d'inquiétude*. There are no roses without —s ; *il n'y a point de plaisir sans peine*.

thorn'-apple (-ap'p'l), *n.*, (bot.) pomme épineuse, *f.* ; stramonium, *m.*

thorn'-back, *n.*, (ich.) raie bouclée, *f.*

thorn'-bush (-boushe), *n.*, buisson épineux, *m.*

thorn'less, *adj.*, sans épines.

thorn'y, *adj.*, épineux ; pénible.

thor'ough (theur'rô), *adj.*, (complete) entier, complet ; (perfect) achevé, parfait ; (b.s.) franc, fieffé ; fameux.

thor'ough-bass (-béce), *m.*, (mus.) basse continue ; harmonie, *f.*

thor'ough-bred (-brède), *adj.*, (of horses, etc.) pur sang, de pur sang ; (colloq.) vrai, accompli, parfait, consommé.

thor'oughfare, *n.*, lieu de passage, chemin passant, passage, *m.* Great — ; *rue très passante, f., chemin très passant, m.* ; *rue commerçante, f.* No — ; *on ne passe pas* ; *rue barrée, f.* ; *passage interdit au public*.

thor'ough-going, *adj.*, prêt à tout, résolu, entreprenant ; transcendant, achevé ; complet, consommé.

thor'oughly (theur'rô-li), *adv.*, entièrement ; complètement ; à fond, parfaitement, soigneusement.

thor'ough-paced (-pés'te), *adj.*, achevé, franc, fieffé.

thor'ough-pin, *n.*, (vet.) vessigon, *m.*

those (*th*ôze), *pron.*, ces ; ces . . . là, *pl.m., f.* ; ceux, *m.pl.*, celles, *f.pl.* ; ceux-là, *m.pl.*, celles-là, *f.pl.* — are ; *ce sont, ce sont là* ; *voilà*. — are the very words ; *voilà les mots mêmes* ; *voilà* (ou *ce sont* là) *les propres expressions*. — who lose pay ; (prov.) *les battus payent l'amende*.

thou (*th*aou), *pron.*, tu ; toi.

thou and thee (*th*aou), *v.a.* and *n.*, tutoyer.

though (*th*ô), *conj.*, quoique, bien que ; (even if) (*always* with subj.) quand même ; quand ; (yet) cependant, pourtant, malgré cela. As — ; *comme si*. Even — ; *quand, quand même* (with conditional). — it cost me a franc ; *quand cela me coûterait un franc*.

thought (thô-te), *n.*, pensée ; (idea) idée ; (opinion) pensée, opinion, façon de penser, *f.*, sentiment, *m.* ; (care) inquiétude, *f.* To read any one's —s ; *lire dans la pensée de quelqu'un*. A — better ; *un peu mieux*. A — ; (small quantity) *un petit brin* ; *une idée*. On second —s ; *réflexion faite* ; *tout bien considéré* ; *décidément*. To collect one's — ; *se recueillir*. I speak my —s ; *je dis ce que je pense, ou je dis ma pensée*. To take — of, for ; *s'inquiéter* de, *se soucier* de, *se préoccuper* de.

thought'ful (thôt'foule), *adj.*, pensif ; rêveur ; méditatif ; (anxious) inquiet ; (kind) attentif, prévenant ; soigneux, soucieux ; (provident) prévoyant. — of ; *qui pense* à ; *attentif* à ; *occupé* de.

thought'fully, *adv.*, pensivement ; d'un air rêveur ; (with solicitude) avec sollicitude, avec prévenance.

thought'fulness, *n.*, méditation profonde,

f. ; recueillement, *m. ; (*solicitude) sollicitude, attention, prévenance ; (anxiety) anxiété, *f.*

thought'less (thŏt'-), *adj.*, irréfléchi ; insouciant ; étourdi, léger ; (stupid) stupide, bête.

thought'lessly, *adv.,* avec insouciance ; avec étourderie ; étourdiment ; (stupidly) stupidement, bêtement.

thought'lessness, *n.,* insouciance ; légèreté, étourderie, indiscrétion, inadvertance, *f.*

thou'ing and thee'ing, *n.,* tutoiement, *m.*

thou'sand (thaou-za'n'd), *n.,* mille ; millier, *m.*

thou'sand, *adj.,* mille ; (date) mil. The year one — ; *l'an mille, m.* It is a — to one . . . ; *il y a mille à parier contre un . . .*

thou'sands, *n.,* milliers, *m.pl. By* — ; *par milliers.* — of ; *des milliers* de.

thou'sandth (thaou-za'n'dth), *n.* and *adj.,* millième.

Thra'cian (thré-), *adj.,* Thrace.

thral'dom (thrŏl-deume), *n.,* esclavage, asservissement, *m.*

thrall (thrŏl), *n.,* esclave, *m.f.*

thrash (thrashe), *v.a.,* battre, rosser, rouler, étriller ; (wheat, walnuts) battre. To — out ; (a question) *discuter à fond, sous toutes ses faces.*

thrash (thrashe), *v.n.,* battre en grange.

thrash'er, *n.,* batteur en grange, *m.*

thrash'ing, *n.,* rossée, roulée, raclée, *f. ;* (of wheat) battage, *m.*

thrash'ing-floor, *n.,* aire, *f.*

thrash'ing-machine (-ma-shîne), *n.,* machine à battre ; batteuse (à blé), *f.*

thread (thrède), *n.,* fil ; (of flowers, of a screw) filet ; (of plants) filament, *m.,* fibre ; (of a skein) centaine, sentène, *f. ;* (fig.) fil, *m.* Air—s ; *fils de la Vierge, m.pl.* To lose the — ; (fig.) *perdre le fil.* To resume the — ; *reprendre le fil.*

thread (thrède), *v.a.,* enfiler ; (to pass through) passer par, traverser, enfiler.

thread'bare, *adj.,* qui montre la corde, usé ; râpé ; (fig.) usé, épuisé, rebattu.

thread'bareness, *n.,* état râpé, usé, *m. ;* (fig.) trivialité, *f.*

thread'-shaped (-shép'te), *adj.,* (bot.) filiforme.

thread'y (thrèdi), *adj.,* plein de fils ; (filamentous) filamenteux, fibreux.

threat (thrète), *n.,* menace, *f.* To utter —s ; *faire des menaces.*

threat'en (thrèt't'n), *v.a.,* menacer ; faire des menaces à (with, de). To — a man with a stick ; *menacer un homme d'un bâton.* It —s to rain ; *le temps est à la pluie, ou il va pleuvoir.*

threat'ener, *n.,* qui menace, *f.*

threat'ening (thrèt't'n'igne), *n.,* menace, *f.*

threat'ening, *adj.,* menaçant ; de menaces. The weather is — ; *le temps est à la pluie ;* (of a storm) *un orage se prépare ; une tempête se dessine* (V. Hugo).

threat'eningly, *adv.,* avec menace ; d'un air, *ou* d'un ton, menaçant.

three (thrf), *adj.,* trois. Rule of — ; *règle de trois, f.* — o'clock ; *trois heures.* He is — ; *il a trois ans.*

three, *n.,* trois, *m.* Number — ; *numéro trois.*

three'-angled, *adj.,* triangulaire.

three'-cap'suled (-cap-sioul'de), *adj.,* (bot.) tricapsulaire.

three'-cleft, *adj.,* (bot.) trifide.

three-cor'nered (-cor-neurde), *adj.,* à trois cornes. — hat ; *tricorne, m.*

three'-decker (a), *n.,* un trois-ponts, *m.*

three'-edged (-èdj'de), *adj.,* triangulaire.

three'-flowered (-flaoueurde), *adj.,* (bot.) triflore.

three'fold (-fŏlde), *adj.,* triple, trois fois autant.

three'-headed (-hèd'-), *adj.,* à trois têtes.

three'-leaved (-lîv'de), *adj.,* à trois feuilles.

three'-lobed (-lob'de), *adj.,* (bot.) trilobé.

three'-masted, *adj.,* à trois mâts.

three'-master (a), *n.,* un trois-mâts.

three'pence, *n.pl.,* trente centimes, *m.pl.*

three'penny, *adj.,* de trente centimes.

three'score (-scôre), *adj.,* soixante.

three'-valved (-valv'de), *adj.,* (bot.) trivalve.

thresh. *V.* **thrash.**

thresh'old (thrèsh'ôlde), *n.,* seuil (de porte) ; pas ; (fig.) début, commencement, *m. ;* entrée, *f.*

thrice (thraïce), *adv.,* trois fois.

thrift (thrif'te), *n.,* (gain) gain, profit, *m. ;* (prosperity) prospérité, richesse ; (frugality) frugalité, épargne, économie, *f. ;* (bot.) gazon d'Olympe, *m.,* statice, *f.*

thrift'ily, *adv.,* avec économie.

thrift'iness, *n.,* épargne ; économie, frugalité, *f.*

thrift'less, *adj.,* dépensier, prodigue.

thrift'lessly, *adv.,* sans profit, follement.

thrift'lessness, *n.,* prodigalité, *f. ;* folles dépenses, *f.pl.*

thrift'y, *adj.,* ménager, frugal, économe.

thrill (thril), *v.a.,* percer ; pénétrer ; faire tressaillir de. —ed with remorse ; *dévoré de remords.*

thrill, *v.n.,* pénétrer ; (to shiver) frémir de, tressaillir de.

thrill (thril), *n.,* frémissement, tressaillement, saisissement, *m.*

thrill'ing, *adj.,* saisissant, pénétrant ; (of cries) perçant.

thrive (thraïve), *v.n.,* (*preterit,* Throve ; *past part.,* Thriven) prospérer, réussir, faire ses affaires ; (of things, of animals) prospérer, croître, grandir, se développer, venir bien ; profiter, réussir.

thriv'ing (thraïv'-), *n.,* florissant, qui prospère, qui réussit ; (of plants) qui vient bien, vigoureux.

thriv'ingly (thraïv'-), *adv.,* d'une manière florissante ; heureusement, avec succès.

thriv'ingness (thraïv'-), *n.,* prospérité, *f. ;* état florissant, succès, *m.*

throat (thrôte), *n.,* gorge, *f. ;* (the swallow) gosier ; (of a chimney) gueulard ; (of an anchor) diamant, *m. ;* (of things) gorge ; entrée, voie, *f.* To seize by the — ; *saisir, ou prendre, à la gorge.* To cut one's — ; *se couper la gorge.* To cut one another's —s ; (fig., com.) *se faire une concurrence ruineuse ;* (ord.) *s'égorger l'un l'autre.* To lie in one's — ; *mentir par la gorge, par sa gorge ; mentir effrontément.* To give any one the lie in his — ; *donner le démenti à quelqu'un.* A sore — ; *un mal de gorge.* To have a fish-bone (sticking) in one's — ; *avoir une arête dans le gosier.*

throat'-band (-ba'n'de), *n.,* (saddlery) sousgorge, *f.*

throat'ed, *adj.,* (in compounds) à gorge.

throat'-pipe, *n.,* trachée-artère, *f.*

throat'wort (-weurte), *n.,* (bot.) gantelée, *f. ;* gant de Notre-Dame, *m.*

throb (throbe), *v.n.,* battre ; palpiter. My thumb —s ; *le pouce me bat.*

throb'bing, *n.,* battement, *m. ;* palpitation, *f. ;* (of the pulse) battement, *m.,* pulsations, *f.pl.*

throe (thrô), *n.,* douleur de l'enfantement ; (fig.) angoisse, torture, agonie, *f.*

throne (thrône), *n.,* trône, *m.*

throned (thrôn'de), *adj.,* assis sur le trône.

throne'less, *adj.,* sans trône.

throne'-room (-roume), *n.,* salle du trône, *f.*

throng (thro'gne), *v.n.,* accourir en foule, se presser, affluer.

throng, *v.a.,* fouler, remplir, encombrer.

throng (thro'gne), *n.,* foule, presse, *f.*

throng'ing (thro'gn'ghigne), *n.,* encombrement, *m. ;* foule, presse, *f.*

thros'tle (thros's'l), *n.,* (orni.) grive commune, *f.*

thros'tle-frame, n., métier continu, m.

thros'tle-twist, n., chaîne filée, f.

throt'tle (throt't'l), v.a., étrangler ; étouffer, suffoquer.

throt'tle, v.n., étouffer ; prendre à la gorge.

throt'tle (throt't'l), n., trachée-artère, f. ; larynx, m.

throt'tle-valve, n., soupape à gorge, f. ; registre de vapeur, m.

through (throu), prep., à travers ; au travers **de** ; (passage, means of conveyance) par ; (over the whole extent) d'un bout à l'autre ; (denoting passage among) dans ; en ; (without stopping) directement, droit ; (in consequence of) en conséquence **de**, par suite **de**, par. — him ; (fig.) par son entremise. To pass — a gate ; passer par une porte. To see —; (a door) voir à travers, au travers **de** ; (a person) savoir à quoi s'en tenir sur le compte **de**. To read —; (a person) pénétrer la pensée **de**. To run (any one) — and —; percer de part en part. To go — the whole ceremony ; passer par tous les détails de la cérémonie. To sit a play — ; rester jusqu'au bout (d'une représentation). To be wet — ; être mouillé, trempé, jusqu'aux os.

through, adj., (of trains, tickets) direct.

through, adv., d'outre en outre ; de part en **part** ; (from beginning to end) d'un bout à l'autre ; (to the end) jusqu'à la fin, à bonne fin. To carry, **ou** see, anything — ; mener à bonne fin. To drop, **ou** fall, — ; (of a project) ne pas aboutir ; manquer ; (fam.) rater. To go — with anything ; mener une entreprise à bonne fin, jusqu'au bout. To book (one's luggage) — ; faire enregistrer (ses bagages) directement **pour**.

throughout' (throu-aoute), prep. and adv., d'un bout à l'autre **de** ; partout ; dans, **ou** par, tout, toute, etc. ; (entirely) entièrement, en entier. — the course of his long life ; dans tout le cours de sa longue vie.

throw (thrô), v.a., (preterit, Threw ; past part., Thrown) jeter ; lancer, précipiter ; (to prostrate) jeter, renverser, terrasser ; (to send) lancer ; (silk) organsiner ; (at dice) jeter, amener ; (a horseman) démonter, désarçonner ; (of serpents, etc.) jeter, **se** dépouiller **de** ; (at dice) mettre au jeu. To — **at** ; jeter **à**, **contre** ; lancer **à**, **contre**. To — aside ; jeter de côté. To — away ; jeter, rejeter ; (to lose) perdre ; (to waste) gaspiller, jeter par la fenêtre ; (one's life) prodiguer. To — back ; **renvoyer** ; réfléchir ; rejeter, refuser ; renverser ; (to delay) retarder. To — down ; jeter en bas ; abattre ; renverser ; (pers.) renverser, terrasser. To — down on ; jeter **sur**. To — in ; jeter dedans ; (to give in) donner par-dessus le marché. To — off ; chasser ; se défaire **de** ; (garments) ôter ; (the mask) lever ; (to shake off) secouer. To — off the scent ; dépister. To — open ; ouvrir subitement. To — wide open ; ouvrir à deux battants. To — out ; jeter dehors ; chasser ; (to utter carelessly) parler mal ; (to insinuate) insinuer ; donner à entendre ; (to distance) distancer, devancer ; (to reject) rejeter ; (to emit) lancer ; (words) émettre, mettre en avant ; (a hint) donner à entendre ; lancer un mot. To — — one's self into ; (the work) se mettre avec acharnement **à** ; (into pleasures) s'abandonner **à**. To — out of work ; priver de travail. To be thrown out of work ; être privé de travail ; chômer. To — out of ; (a window) jeter par. To — up ; jeter en haut, jeter en l'air ; (to resign) se démettre **de** ; renoncer **à** ; (to vomit) vomir, rejeter ; (to give up) renoncer **à**, abandonner. To — up earthworks ; construire, ou élever, des ouvrages en terre. To — one's self on ; se jeter **sur** ; s'élancer **sur** ; s'abandonner **à** ; (to appeal to) en appeler **à** ; (to rely on) se reposer **sur**. To — one's self on the ground ; se jeter par terre. To be thrown (from a horse) ; vider les arçons.

throw (thrô), n., jet ; coup, m. ; (fig.) saillie, f. ; élan, m. ; (of dice) coup de dé, m.

throw'er, n., personne qui jette, qui lance, f. ; (of silk) organsineur, m. V. **throwster**.

throw'ing, n., lancement ; jet ; (of silk) organsinage, moulinage, m.

throw'ing-mill, n., moulin à organsiner, m.

throw'ing-wheel, n., tour, m.

throw'ster (thrôs-), n., organsineur, moulineur, m.

thrum (threume), n., bout de fil, m.

thrum (threume), v.a., tisser ; franger ; (a sail) larder.

thrum, v.n., jouer mal, jouailler, tapoter ; (on a fiddle) râcler. V. **drum**.

thrush (threushe), n., (orn.) grive ; (vet.) teigne, f. ; (med.) aphte (Littré), m.

thrust (threuste), v.a.n., (preterit and past part., Thrust) pousser ; fourrer ; serrer, presser. To — away, back ; repousser ; (to reject) rejeter, écarter. To — down ; pousser en bas ; jeter **dans**. To — in ; pousser dedans ; fourrer ; introduire de force ; (a stick, etc.) enfoncer. To — into ; jeter **dans** ; forcer **à**. To — on ; pousser en avant ; (to urge) pousser, exciter. To — out ; pousser dehors, mettre dehors. To — under ; pousser **sous**, mettre **sous**, passer **sous**. To — through ; passer à travers ; (to pierce) transpercer. To — back ; repousser, écarter. To cut and — ; frapper d'estoc et de taille.

thrust (threuste), n., coup, m., poussée, f. ; (assault) assaut, m., attaque, f. ; (fenc.) coup, m., botte ; (arch.) poussée, f. Home- — ; coup qui porte ; (fenc.) coup de fond. To make a —; (fenc.) porter, pousser une botte **à** ; porter un coup **à**. To give a home — ; piquer au vif.

thud, n., bruit sourd **ou** mat ; coup sourd, m.

thu'ja (thiou-dja) **ou** **thu'ya** (thiou-ya), n., (bot.) thuia, thuya, m.

thumb (theume), n., pouce, m. Tom —; Tom Pouce, petit Poucet, m. —-stall ; poucier, m. Rule of — ; règle empirique, f., procédé empirique, m. Under one's — ; en son pouvoir ; sous son autorité, ou sa domination. To bite the — at ; faire la nique **à**.

thumb, v.a., manier gauchement ; (to soil) salir avec les pouces, fatiguer. To — over (a tune) ; écorcher.

thumb (theume), v.n., tambouriner.

thumb'-mark, n., marque de pouce. v.a., marquer, ou salir, avec le pouce.

thumb'-piece, n., poucier, m.

thumb'-screw, n., vis de pression, f., (torture) poucettes, f.pl.

thumb'-stall, n., poucier, m. ; (nav.) dé de voilier, m.

thump (theum'pe), v.a.n., frapper du poing ; frapper lourdement, cogner.

thump (theum'pe), n., grand coup, coup de poing, m. ; bourrade, taloche, f.

thump'er, n., personne d'une grosseur extraordinaire, roulée de coups, f.

thump'ing, adj., gros, énorme ; (heavy) lourd, pesant.

thun'der (theu'n'-), n., tonnerre, m. ; (lightning and) foudre, f. ; (fig.) foudre, f.

thun'der, v.n., tonner ; (fig.) gronder, retentir, fulminer. It —s ; il tonne.

thun'der (theu'n'-), v.a., fulminer ; crier d'une voix de tonnerre.

thun'derbolt (-bôlte), n., foudre, f. ; coup de foudre, m. ; (daring person) foudre, m. Struck down by —; frappé de la foudre.

thun'der-clap **ou** **peal**, n., coup de tonnerre, éclat de tonnerre, m.

thun'der-cloud (-claoude), n., nuage orageux, ou chargé d'électricité, m.

thun'derer, n., qui lance la foudre, m.

thun'dering, adj., tonnant, foudroyant ; de

tonnerre ; (fam.) énorme, terrible. — Jove;
Jupiter tonnant. A — fool; *un furieux*, ou *fameux, imbécile*. — voice; *voix de tonnerre, f.*
To go — past; *passer comme la foudre*.

thun'dering, *n.*, tonnerre, *m. ;* (fig.) commotion, *f.*

thun'deringly, *adv.*, avec un bruit de tonnerre.

thun'der-shower (-shaoueur), *n.*, pluie d'orage, *f.*

thun'der-stone (-stône), *n.*, aérolithe, *m.*

thun'der-storm, *n.*, tempête, *f.*, orage accompagné de tonnerre, *m.*

thun'der-strike (-straïke), *v.a.*, (*preterit* and *past part.*, Thunder-struck) foudroyer ; frapper de la foudre ; (fig.) foudroyer, atterrer.

thun'der-struck (-streuke), *adj.*, foudroyé; (fig.) atterré, anéanti.

thun'dery, *adj.*, orageux. It is — weather; *le temps est à l'orage.*

Thurs'day (theurz'-), *n.*, jeudi, *m.* On —s; *le jeudi.*

thus (*theuss*), *adv.*, ainsi, si, tant. — far; *jusqu'ici.* — much; *autant.*

thwack (thwake), *n.*, coup, sec, *m. ;* taloche, *f.*

thwack, *v.a.*, frapper, rosser, étriller.

thwack'ing, *n.*, roulée de coups ; râclée, *f.*

thwart (thwôrte), *v.a.*, traverser, croiser ; (fig.) opposer à, contrarier, traverser, contrecarrer. He keeps on —ing him ; *il ne cesse de le contrecarrer, l'opposer.*

(*a*)**thwart**, *adv.*, en travers.

thwart (thwôrte), *n.*, banc de rameurs, banc de nage, *m.*

thwart'ing (thwôrt'-), *adj.*, contrariant.

thwart'ing, *n.*, contrariété, *f.*

thwart'ingly, *adv.*, d'une manière contrariante.

thwart'ship, *adv.*, par le travers (du vaisseau).

thy (*thaïe*), *adj.*, ton, *m.*, ta, *f. ;* tes, *pl.m.f.*

thyme (taï'm), *n.*, (bot.) thym, *m.* Wild — ; *serpolet ; thym sauvage, m.*

thy'my (taï'mi), *adj.*, qui a l'odeur du thym ; qui abonde en thym ; odoriférant.

thyr'sus (theur-ceuss), *n.*, (antiq., bot.) thyrse, *m.*

thy'self (*thaïe'-*), *pron.*, toi, toi-même ; te, toi (reflexive).

tia'ra (taï-), *n.*, tiare, *f.*

tib'ia, *n.*, tibia, os de la jambe, *m.*

tic-douloureux' (-dou-lou-rou), *n.*, tic douloureux, *m.*

tick (tike), *n.*, (for beds) toile à matelas, *f.*, coutil ; (credit) crédit ; (noise) tic-tac ; (ent.) acarus, *m.*, tique, *f.* On —; *à crédit;* (pop.) *à l'œil.*

tick, *v.n.*, prendre à crédit ; (to give on credit) faire crédit ; (of clocks) faire tic tac, battre.

tick, *v.a.*, pointer, marquer. To — off; *effacer, rayer.*

tick'er, *n.*, (fam. for **watch**) tocante, toquante, *f.*

tick'et, *n.*, (com.) marque, étiquette, *f. ;* (thea., lottery, etc.) billet ; (omnibus) carton; (of a series) cachet, *m. ;* (pawn) reconnaissance, *f. ;* (luggage) bulletin ; (for soup, etc.) bon, *m. ;* (mark, label) étiquette, marque; (badge) plaque, *f.* Return —; *billet d'aller et retour.* Single —; *billet simple.* Season —; *billet de saison, d'abonnement.* Season — holder ; *abonné à l'année.* Yearly —; *billet d'abonnement à l'année.* — of leave; (thing) *passeport jaune* (V. Hugo); (pers.) *forçat libéré, m.* To be out on — of leave ; *être en libération conditionnelle.*

tick'et, *v.a.*, (com.) étiqueter, numéroter.

tick'et-collector, *n.*, contrôleur, *m.*

tick'et-office, *n.*, bureau des billets, *m.*

tick'ing, *n.*, tic tac, battement; (for beds) coutil, *m.*, toile à matelas, *f.*

tic'kle (tik'k'l), *v.a.*, chatouiller ; (to please) plaire à. That —d my fancy ; *cela me fit sourire.*

tic'kler, *n.*, personne qui chatouille, *f. ;* flatteur, *m.*

tic'kling, *n.*, chatouillement, *m.*

tic'klish, *adj.*, chatouilleux ; (critical) critique, délicat, difficile, scabreux ; (tottering) chancelant, mal assuré.

tic'klishly, *adv.*, d'une manière critique, d'une manière délicate.

tic'klishness, *n.*, nature chatouilleuse, *f. ;* état critique, état difficile, *m. ;* difficulté, nature scabreuse, *f.*

tick'tack, *n.*, tic tac.

tid'al, *adj.*, de marée, à marée. — harbor; *port à marée, m.* — wave; *rapport, m.* (Bescherelle).

tide (taïde), *n.*, marée, *f.;* (stream) courant, *m.*, marche, *f.;* flux, flot ; (ebb and flow) flux et jusant; (course) cours, *m. ;* (among miners) période de travail de douze heures, *f. ;* (fig.) fort, *m.*, plénitude, *f.;* flux, *m.;* saison, époque, *f.* Christmas —; *saison de Noël, f. ;* fêtes de Noël, *f.pl.* High —; *marée haute, f., flot, m.* Half —; *mi-marée.* Low —; *marée basse.* Ebb —; *jusant, m. ;* marée descendante, *f.* Rising —; *marée montante.* At low —, *ou* water ; *à marée basse.* Neap —; *morte eau, f.* Spring —; *grande marée.* To go with the —; *suivre le courant.* Carried away by the —; *emporté, ou entraîné, par le courant.* The — of human affairs; *le cours des affaires humaines.*

tide, *v.n.*, aller avec la marée. To — on; *durer.* To — over ; *venir à bout de; surmonter ; passer par-dessus ; se tirer de.*

tide'-gate (-ghéte), *n.*, écluse à marée montante, *f. ;* goulet à forte marée, *m.*

tide'-gauge (-ghédje), *n.*, échelle de marée, *f.*

tide'less, *adj.*, sans marée.

tide'-mill, *n.*, moulin à marée, *m. ;* roue à flux et à reflux, *f.*

tides'-man (taïd'z'-) *ou* **tide'-waiter**, *n.*, matelot de douane, *m.*

tide'-surveyor, *n.*, chef des préposés de la douane, *m.*

tide'-table, *n.*, établissement des marées, *m.*

tide'-way, *n.*, ras, *ou* lit, de marée, *m.*

ti'dily (taïd'-), *adv.*, proprement; en bon ordre.

ti'diness (taïd'-), *n.*, propreté, netteté ; bonne tenue, *f. ;* bon ordre, *m.*

ti'dings (taïdign'ze), *n.pl.*, nouvelles, *f.pl.*

ti'dy (taïd'-), *adj.*, rangé, bien arrangé, bien tenu, en ordre, propre, net. A — sum ; *une bonne petit somme* ou *un bon petit magot.*

ti'dy, *n.*, dessus de fauteuil ; (for rubbish) videpoches, *m.*

ti'dy, *v.a.*, mettre en ordre ; (of a room) ranger; (of papers) arranger. To — one's self up; *faire un bout de toilette.*

tie (taïe), *v.a.*, (to bind) attacher, lier ; (mus.) couler, lier ; (an artery) lier ; (ribbons, etc.) nouer ; (a knot) lier, serrer ; (fig.) lier, attacher, enchaîner. To — down; *lier;* (fig.) *lier, enchaîner ; astreindre, assujetir, obliger à.* To — in; *attacher; serrer.* To — up; *lier, attacher ; nouer ; (a parcel) ficeler ; (an artery) lier ;* (animal) *mettre à l'attache.* —d for time; *pressé.*

tie, *v.n.*, s'attacher ; se nouer ; se her.

tie (taïe), *n.*, lien, *m. ;* attache, *f. ;* (of hair, knot) nœud ; (of a shoe) cordon, *m. ;* (mus.) barre de jonction ; (cravat) cravate ; (in games) partie égale, *ou* nulle ; (political) égalité de voix, *f. ;* (fig.) lien ; (bond) assujettissement, engagement, *m.*

tie'-beam (taïe-bî'm), *n.*, (carp.) entrait ; tirant, *m.*

tier (tîre), *n.*, rangée, *f. ;* gradin, rang ;

(thea.) rang, *m. ;* (of guns) batterie, rangée, *f. ;* (cable) rang, *m.* Boxes on the first, second — ; *premières, deuxièmes loges, f.pl.* — upon — ; *étage sur étage; en s'étageant.* In —s ; *étagé.*

tierce (tîrse *ou* teurce), *n.,* tierce, *f.*

tier'cet (tîr-sète), *n.,* (poet.) tercet, *m.*

tie'-rod (taïe-rode), *n.,* (arch.) tirant, *m.*

tiff, *n.,* pique, querelle, boutade, bisbille, *f. ;* (of liquor) petit coup, *m.* To be in a — ; *bisquer.* To get into a — ; *prendre la mouche.* To have a — with; *avoir une bisbille* **avec.**

tiff, *v.n.,* se piquer, se fâcher; (pop.) bisquer.

tiff'any, *n.,* (fabric) gaze de soie, *f.*

ti'ger (taï-gheur), *n.,* (zoöl.) tigre; (fig.) tigre ; (groom) petit laquais, groom, *m.* — cat; *chat tigré, m.* — lily ; *lis tigré, m.*

tight (taïte), *adj.,* serré ; (parsimonious) serré, parcimonieux ; (not admitting much air) clos, fermé ; (not leaky) (nav.) étanche ; (not slack) raide, tendu ; (well closed) bien, *ou* hermétiquement, fermé ; (phys.) imperméable ; (of clothes) étroit, serré ; (tipsy) gris, à moitié ivre. — -fitting ; (of trousers, etc.) *collant.* Air —, water — ; *imperméable à l'air, à l'eau.* To hold — ; *tenir bien.* To sit — ; *ne pas en démordre.* To keep a — hand on (a person); *tenir la bride courte à.*

tight'en (taï-t'n), *v.a.,* serrer; tendre ; (fig.) resserrer.

tight'-fitting, *adj.,* serré.

tight'-lace, *v.n.,* se lacer serré.

tight'-laced, *adj.,* lacé serré.

tight'ly (taït'-), *adv.,* d'une manière serrée, raide, tendue; étroitement; (ant.) proprement.

tight'ness (taït'-), *n.,* tension ; parcimonie, *f. ;* état de ce qui est bien fermé ; état serré, *m. ;* (phys.) raideur ; imperméabilité; (in the chest) oppression, *f. ;* (of clothes) étroitesse, *f.*

tights, *m.pl.,* (for acrobats) maillot, *m.*

ti'gress (taï-), *n.,* tigresse, *f.*

tile (taïle), *n.,* tuile, *f. ;* (for flooring) carreau, *m. ;* (hat) couvre-chef, gibus, *m.* To have a — loose ; (fam.) *être un peu toqué.*

tile (taïle), *v.a.,* couvrir de, *ou* en, tuiles; (of floors) carreler.

tile'-field (-fîlde), *n.,* tuilerie, *f.*

tile'-kiln (-kil'n), *n.,* four à tuiles, *m.*

tile'-maker (-mék'-), *n.,* tuilier, *m.*

til'er (taïl'-), *n.,* couvreur en tuiles, *m.*

til'ing (taïl'-), *n.,* (action) recouvrement en tuiles, *f. ;* (roof) toit couvert en tuiles, *m. ;* (tiles) tuiles, *f.pl.*

till, *prep.,* jusqu'à ; (before) quand, jusques à ; (before a verb) jusqu'à ce que (with *subjunctive*).

till, *v.a.,* labourer, cultiver.

till, *n.,* tiroir (de comptoir), *m. ;* petite caisse, *f.*

till'able (til'a-b'l), *adj.,* labourable, arable.

till'age (-èdje), *n.,* labourage, labour, *m. ;* culture, *f.*

till'er, *n.,* laboureur ; cultivateur, *m. ;* (of a rudder) barre du gouvernail, *f. ;* (sprout) bourgeon, rejeton, *m.*

till'ing, *n.,* labourage, *m.*

tilt, *n.,* (awning, tent) tente, *f. ;* (of a cart, a boat) bâche, banne, *f. ;* (thrust) coup ; tournois, *m. ;* (incline) pente, inclinaison ; (ant.) joute, *f. ;* (hammer) martinet, *m.* Full —; (headlong) *à tête baissée ;* (of a horse) *au grand galop, ventre à terre, à toute bride.*

tilt, *v.a.,* (to incline casks) incliner, pencher ; (to thrust) pousser ; (to hammer) marteler ; (to cover with an awning) couvrir d'une tente ; (a carriage) bâcher ; (a cart) vider, décharger. With his hat —ed on one side ; *le chapeau sur l'oreille.*

tilt, *v.n.,* jouter; pousser ; poindre ; (to lean) incliner, pencher; (to float) flotter ; (to fight with rapiers) ferrailler. To — at ; *fondre* **sur.**

tilt'-cart (-cârte), *n.,* charrette à bâche, *f.*

tilt'ed, *adj.,* (of a boat *ou* carriage) à couvert.

tilt'er, *n.,* jouteur, *m.*

tilth (tilth), *n.,* labour, *m. ;* culture, *f.*

tilt'-hammer, *n.,* martinet de forge, *m.*

tilt'ing, *n.,* joute, *f. ;* tournoi ; (tech.) martelage au martinet, *m.*

tilt'-yard, *n.,* lice, *f.,* champ clos, *m.*

tim'bal, *n.,* (mus.) timbale, *f.*

tim'ber, *n.,* bois de haute futaie; bois de construction; bois de charpente; bois ; (nav.) couple, membre, *m.* — -work ; *charpente, f.* — -yard ; *chantier de bois de construction, m.*

tim'ber, *v.a.,* munir de bois de charpente ; boiser.

tim'bered (ti'm'beurde), *adj.,* à charpente ; construit en bois ; boisé ; couvert d'arbres de haute futaie.

tim'ber-head (-hède), *n.,* (nav.) bitton, *m.*

tim'bering, *n.,* boisage, *m.*

tim'ber-merchant, *n.,* marchand de bois de construction, *m.*

tim'ber-tree (-trî), *n.,* arbre de haute futaie, *m.*

tim'brel, *n.,* tambour de basque, tambourin, *m.*

time (taï'me), *n.,* temps ; (specified space of time) temps, terme, *m. ;* (repetition) fois, *f. ;* (age) temps, *m. ;* (in history) époque, *f.,* siècle, *m. ;* (of day and night) heure, *f. ;* (moment) moment; (mus.) temps, *m.,* mesure; (drilling) cadence, *f. ;* (hour of travail) terme, *m.* At —s ; *parfois ; de temps à autre.* At all —s ; *dans tous les temps ; de, ou en, tout temps.* In —; *avec le temps ;* (in good season) *à temps ;* (mus.) *en mesure, en cadence.* In good —; *à temps.* In —, *ou* —s, to come ; *à l'avenir.* This — last year ; *l'année dernière à pareille époque.* Behind one's — ; *en retard.* Before one's — ; *en avance ; avant l'heure ;* (of childbirth) *avant terme.* In proper — and place ; *en temps et lieu.* In no —; *en aucun temps ;* (in a short time) *en peu de temps, en moins de rien, en un clin d'œil.* Once upon a — there was; *il y avait une fois.* After a — ; *quelque temps après ;* (hence) *dans quelque temps.* Out of — ; (mus.) *à contretemps, contre-mesure.* Next — ; *la prochaine fois.* At such a — ; *à un tel moment ; à une telle époque.* (So many) at a — ; *à la fois.* At a — when ; *dans un temps où ; dans un moment où.* At any — ; *n'importe quand ; à toute heure, à tout moment.* At different —s ; *à diverses reprises.* At no —; *dans aucun temps.* One — or another ; *un jour ou l'autre.* At the present — ; *à présent, actuellement, à l'heure qu'il est.* As —s go ; *par le temps qui court.* Up to the present — ; *jusqu'à présent.* In the — of ; *du temps* **de** *; à l'époque* **de.** Another — ; *une autre fois.* At the same —; *en même temps ;* (on the other hand) *d'autre part, en revanche, d'un autre côté.* Some — or other ; *un jour ou l'autre.* In a week's, a fortnight's —; *dans une huitaine, une quinzaine de jours.* Three —s ; *trois fois.* Hundreds of —s; *des centaines de fois.* In the nick of — ; *à point nommé.* To keep — ; (mus.) *aller en mesure;* (of clocks, etc.) *être à l'heure.* To serve one's —; *faire son temps.* What — is it? *quelle heure est-il?* — out of mind ; *de temps immémorial.* Till the end of — ; *jusqu'à la fin des siècles.* He is almost out of his —; *il a presque fini son apprentissage.* In course of —; *avec le temps.* In due —; *en temps opportun.* To lose —; (of persons) *perdre du temps ;* (of clocks, etc.) *retarder.* To beat — ; *battre la mesure.* To kill —; *tuer le temps.* True —; (astron.) *temps vrai, m.* Every —; *chaque fois.* To keep one's —; *être exact ; arriver à l'heure.* To have a fine, *ou* a high old, —; *s'en donner.* To have a bad, hard, *ou* unpleasant, —; *en voir de dures,* ou (fam.) *de grises.* — is money ; *le temps vaut,* ou *est, de l'argent.* I had a bad —; (for the moment) *j'ai passé un bien mauvais quart d'heure.* This — six months ; *dans six mois.* This — last year ; *il y a un an.*

time' (taï'me), *v.a.*, adapter, *ou* accommoder, au temps, faire à propos; fixer l'heure **de**, calculer; régler; (clocks, etc.) régler; (mus.) cadencer.

time'-bargain, *n.*, marché à terme, *m.*

timed (taïm'de), *adj.* Ill —; *inopportun, mal à propos, hors de saison; intempestif;* (improper) *déplacé, hors de saison.* Well —; *opportun, à propos; bien réglé.*

time'-honored (-o'n'orde), *adj.*, honoré de tout temps; depuis longtemps en honneur; séculaire.

time'-keeper (-kîp'-), *n.*, chronomètre; (pers.) surveillant, contrôleur, *m.* To be a good —; (oi a watch) *être toujours à l'heure; ne pas varier.*

time'lessly, *adv.*, mal à propos.

time'liness, *n.*, opportunité, *f.;* à-propos, *m.*

time'ly, *adj.*, opportun, à propos, de saison.

time'ly, *adv.*, à propos, à temps; en temps opportun.

time'-piece (-pîce), *n.*, pendule, *f.*

time'-server (-seurv'-), *n.*, serviteur complaisant du pouvoir, opportuniste, *m.*, girouette, *f.*

time'-serving (-seurv'-), *adj.*, complaisant envers le pouvoir, opportuniste.

time'-serving, *m.*, servilité (envers le pouvoir), *f.*, opportunisme, *m.*, lâche complaisance, *f.*

time'-sheet, *n.*, feuille de présence, *f.*

time'-stroke (-strôke), *n.*, (mus.) temps, *m.*

time'-table, *n.*, (mus.) division du temps; (railways) tableau des heures (de départ et d'arrivée); indicateur, horaire, *m.*

time'-worn, *adj.*, usé par le temps.

tim'id, *adj.*, timide; craintif; peureux.

timid'ity, *n.*, timidité, *f.*

tim'idly, *adv.*, timidement.

tim'ing, *n.*, horaire, règlement des heures, *m.*

tim'ist (taï'm'-), *n.*, (mus.) musicien qui va bien en mesure, *m.*

timoneer' (taï-mo-nîre), *n.*, timonier, *m.*

tim'orous, *adj.*, (theol.) timoré. *V.* **timid**.

tim'orously, *adv.*, timidement, craintivement.

tim'orousness, *n.*, timidité; (theol.) nature timorée, *f.*

Tim'othy-grass, *n.*, fléole, *f.*

tin, *n.*, (chem.) étain; (sheet iron coated with tin) fer-blanc; (of looking-glasses) tain; (pop.) quibus, *m.*

tin, *v.a.*, étamer.

tin'cal (ti'gn-kal), *n.*, (min., chem.) borax brut, tinkal, *m.*

tinc'ture (ti'gn'kt'ieur), *n.*, teinte, *f.;* (slight taste) léger goût, *m.;* (pharm.) teinture; (fig.) teinture, nuance, *f.;* émail, *n.m.* (her.)

tinc'ture (ti'gn'kt'ieur), *v.a.*, teindre légèrement; colorer **de**, teindre **de**; (fig.) empreindre, imprégner **de**. To be —d with; *avoir une teinture* **de**.

tin'der, *n.*, mèche, *f.;* amadou, *m.*

tin'der-box, *n.*, boîte à amadou, *f.*, briquet, *m.*

tine (taïne), *n.*, fourchon, *m.;* dent de fourche, de herse, *f.*

tin'-foil (-foïl), *n.*, étain en feuille, *m.*, feuille d'étain, *f.*

tinge (ti'n'dje), *n.*, teinte, nuance, *f.;* (slight taste) léger goût, *m.*

tinge (ti'n'dje), *v.a.*, teindre légèrement; (fig.) empreindre, imprégner **de**.

tin'gle (ti'gn'g'l), *v.a.*, fourmiller, picoter, démanger; (of the hands, feet) brûler, cuire; (of pain) se faire sentir; (of the ears) tinter; (fig.) tressaillir, frémir **de**.

tin'gling (ti'gn'g'li'gne), *n.*, fourmillement, picotement; (of the ears) tintement; (fig.) frémissement, tressaillement, *m.*

tin'ker (ti'gn'keur), *n.*, rétameur, raccommodeur, *m.*

tin'ker, *v.a.n.*, rétamer; raccommoder, *ou* réparer, maladroitement.

tin'kerly, *adv.*, en rétameur; maladroitement.

tin'kle (ti'gn'k'l), *v.n.*, tinter, résonner.

tin'kle, *v.a.*, faire tinter, faire résonner.

tin'kling, *n.*, tintement; (pop.) drelin, *m.*

tin'-lode (-lôde), *n.*, filon d'étain, *m.*

tin'man, *n.*, ferblantier, *m.*

tin'ning, *n.*, étamage, *m.*

tin'ny, *adj.*, qui abonde en étain; stannifère.

tin'-plate, **n.**, fer-blanc, *m.* —s,*n.pl.*,plaques, feuilles en fer-blanc, *f.pl.*

tin'sel, *n.*, clinquant; oripeau; (fig.) faux éclat, brillant, *m.*

tin'sel, *adj.*, de clinquant; d'un faux éclat.

tin'sel, *v.a.*, orner de clinquant; donner un faux éclat à.

tin'-stone (-stône), *n.*, (min.) cassitérite, *f.;* étain oxydé, *m.*

tin'-tack, *n.*, broquette étamée, *f.*

tin'-trade, *n.*, ferblanterie, *f.*

tint (ti'n'te), *n.*, teinte, nuance, *f.*

tint (ti'n'te), *v.a.*, donner une teinte à; (in drawing) laver; (to shade) ombrer; (paint.) teinter, nuancer.

tint'ing, *n.*, (of an architectural drawing) lavis, *m.*

ti'ny (taï-), *adj.*, tout petit; mignon. A — bit; *un tout petit peu.*

tip, *n.*, extrémité, *f.;* bout, *m.;* (tap) tape, *f.;* (gratuity) pourboire; (of a cue) procédé, *m.;* (metal) virole, *f.*

tip, *v.a.*, garnir le bout; ferrer; (of a cue) mettre un procédé **à**; (to tap) taper; donner un pourboire à *ou* graisser la patte **à**. To — the porter; *graisser le marteau.* To — the wink; *faire signe de l'œil.* To — off; *v.a., faire tomber, verser, culbuter. v.n.*, tomber, se détacher. To — over; *v.a., culbuter, renverser. v.n.*, basculer, verser, culbuter, faire la culbute; (of boats) *chavirer.*

tip'-cat, *n.*, bâtonnet, *m.*

tipped (tip-te), *adj.*, à bout (**de** *ou* **en . . .**).

tip'pet, *n.*, pèlerine; (fur) palatine, *f.*

tip'ping, *n.*, la manie du pourboire, *f.*

tip'ple (tip'p'l), *n.*, boisson, goutte, *f.*

tip'ple (tip'p'l), *v.n.*, (pop.) ivrogner; pomper, pinter, godailler; se griser.

tip'pler, *n.*, buveur, biberon, *m.*

tip'pling, *n.*, ivrognerie, gobelotterie, *f.*

tip'sily, *adv.*, en ivrogne.

tip'staff (-stâfe), *n.*, huissier, *m.;* (staff) verge, *f.*

tip'sy, *adj.*, gris, ivre. To get —; *se griser; s'enivrer.* — cake; *gâteau au madère, m.*

tip'toe (-tô), *n.*, pointe du pied, *f.* To be, *ou* stand, on —; *se tenir,* ou *se dresser,* ou *se hausser, sur la pointe des pieds.* To be on the — of expectation; *être sur le qui-vive; avoir l'oreille au guet.*

tip'-top, *n.*, le plus haut degré; comble, faîte, *m.*

tip'-top, *adj.*, suprême; excellent; de premier ordre; (fam.) huppé; (of the upper ten) de la haute volée.

tirade' (ti-réde), *n.*, tirade, *f.*

tire (taïre), *n.*, (of a wheel) bande, *f.*, bandage, *m.*

tire (taïre), *v.a.*, lasser, fatiguer, éreinter; (to bore) ennuyer. To — of; *degoûter* **de**. To get —d; *se lasser* **de**, *se fatiguer* **de**; (in mind) *s'ennuyer* **de**. To — out; *excéder, éreinter;* (to bore) *assommer.* I am quite —d out; *je suis éreinté; je n'en peux plus.* To —; (any one's patience) *mettre à bout.*

tire, *v.n.*, se fatiguer, se lasser.

tired'ness (taïr'd'-), *n.*, fatigue, lassitude, *f.*

tire'some (taïr'-ceume), *adj.*, fatigant; (tedious) ennuyeux, ennuyant, fatigant.

tire'someness, *n.*, nature fatigante, *f.;* (tediousness) ennui, *m.*

tis'sue (tish-shiou), *n.*, tissu d'or, tissu d'argent; (anat.) tissu; (fig.) tissu, *m.*, suite, *f.*

tis'sue (tish-shiou), *v.a.*, tisser, broder ; (to interweave) entrelacer, entremêler.

tis'sue-paper (-pé-peur), *n.*, papier de soie, papier joseph, *m.*

tit, *n.*, bidet, poney, *m.* ; (orni.) mésange, *f.* — for tat ; *un prêté pour un rendu; à bon chat bon rat.* To give — for tat; *rendre la pareille à* ou *rendre pois pour fève.*

titan'ic (taï-), *adj.*, titanique.

Ti'tan-like (taï-), *adj.*, comme un Titan.

tit'bit (tit-), *n.*, morceau friand, *m.* As a — ; *pour la bonne bouche.*

tith'able (taïth'a-b'l), *adj.*, décimable, dîmable.

tithe (taïthe), *n.*, dîme ; dixième partie, *f.*

tithe (taïthe), *v.a.*, dîmer **sur** (un vignoble) ; dîmer **dans** (un champ).

tithe'-collector (-lèk-teur), *n.*, dîmeur, *m.*

tithe'-free (-frî), *adj.*, exempt de la dîme.

tithe'-owner (-ô'n-), *n.*, décimateur, *m.*

tithe'-paying (-pé-igne), *adj.*, assujetti à la dîme.

tith'ing (taïth'-), *n.*, dizaine ; dîmée, *f.*

tit'illate, *v.a.*, chatouiller, tiller.

titilla'tion (-'il-lé-), *n.*, titillation, *f.; chatouillement, m.*

tit'ivate, *v.a.*, s'attifer ; faire de la toilette.

tit'lark (-lârke), *n.*, farlouse, alouette des prés, *f.*

ti'tle (taï-t'l), *n.*, titre ; nom ; (com.) document, *m.* Running — ; *titre courant.*

ti'tle (taï-t'l), *v.a.*, intituler ; nommer, appeler ; titrer ; qualifier **de** ; donner un titre **à**.

ti'tled (taï-t'l'de), *adj.*, titré.

ti'tle-deed (-dîde), *n.*, titre, titre de propriété, *m.*

ti'tle-page (-pédje), *n.*, titre, *m.*

tit'mouse (tit'maouce), *n.*, (*titmice*) (orni.) mésange, *f.*

tit'ter, tit'tering, *n.*, rire du bout des lèvres ; rire étouffé ; demi rire, ricanement, *m.*

tit'ter, *v.n.*, rire du bout des lèvres ; rire tout bas.

tit'tle, *n.*, point, iota, rien, *m.; ombre, f.* Not to abate one jot or — ; *ne pas démordre d'un point, d'un pouce.*

tit'tle-tat'tle (tit't'l-tat't'l), *n.*, caquetage, cancan, bavardage, *m.*

tit'tle-tat'tle (tit't'l-tat't'l), *v.n.*, jaser, bavarder ; caqueter.

tit'tle-tat'tler, *n.*, bavard, jaseur, *m.*

tit'ular (tit'iou-), *adj.*, titulaire.

tit'ular *ou* **tit'ulary** (tit'iou-), *n.*, titulaire, *m.*

tit'ularly, *adv.*, par le titre.

tit'ulary, *adj.*, de titre.

to, *particle* (*used before an infinitive*) **à, de.**

to (tou), *prep.*, à ; (before names of countries) **en**; (opposition) contre ; (amount) jusqu'à concurrence **de**; (possession) pour; (in comparison of) en comparaison **de**, auprès **de**; (as far as) jusqu'à; (obligation) envers; (inclination, dislike) pour, envers ; (direction) vers, de ; (before an infinitive) à, de ; (in order to) afin **de**, pour. — this day ; *jusqu'à ce jour ; depuis ce temps là ;* (events) *même à ce jour ; même de nos jours.* A quarter — four ; *quatre heures moins un quart.* Ten minutes — four ; *quatre heures moins dix.* To go — Rome ; *aller à Rome.* The road, *ou* way, —; *le chemin,* ou *la route, qui mène,* ou *qui conduit,* à . . . The way — London; *le chemin de Londres.* To apply — ; *s'adresser* **à**. To write —; *écrire* **à**. To go — Italy ; *aller en Italie.* — any one's face ; *à la face* **de** ; *au nez de quelqu'un.* Ten — one ; *dix contre un.* Let us keep it — ourselves; *gardons-le pour nous ;* (fig.) *gardons-nous d'en parler ; n'en soufflons pas mot.* He is nothing — her ; *il ne lui est rien.* That is nothing — me ; *cela ne me fait rien, m'est parfaitement égal* ou *indifférent, ne m'intéresse pas.* To count — ten ; *compter jusqu'à dix.* Our duty — God ;

notre devoir envers Dieu. His kindness — **me; sa bonté pour moi,** ou *envers moi.* To stretch one's arms — heaven; *tendre les bras vers le ciel.* The way — the bank ; *le chemin de la banque.* The heir — the throne ; *l'héritier du trône.* Purveyor — ; *fournisseur* **de**, *m.* To go — any one, to any one's house ; *aller chez quelqu'un.* From street — street ; *de rue en rue.* From one street — another; *d'une rue à l'autre.* To bet twenty francs — one ; *parier vingt francs contre un.* It is ten — one that . . . ; *il y a dix à parier* **contre** *un que* . . . To fall — ruins ; *tomber en ruine.* To put — flight ; *mettre en fuite.* His conduct — me ; *sa conduite envers moi.* Reserved . . . almost — stiffness ; *réservé . . . presque jusqu'à la raideur ; d'une réserve qui frise la raideur.* — and fro; *çà et là ; de long en large.*

toad (tôde), *n.*, crapaud, *m.*

toad'eater (-ît'-), *n.*, flagorneur, chien couchant, parasite, *m.*

toad'-flax, *n.*, (bot.) linaire, *f.* ; lin sauvage, *m.*

toad'ish (tôd'-), *adj.*, de crapaud.

toad'-stone (-stône), *n.*, crapaudine, *f.*

toad'-stool (-stoule), *n.*, champignon bâtard, *m.*

toad'y (tôd'-), *n.*, flagorneur, *m.*

toad'y (tôd'-), *v.a.*, flagorner, aduler; ramper **auprès de**.

toad'yism, *n.*, flagornerie, servilité, *f.*

toast (tôste), *n.*, rôtie ; grillade; (health) santé, *f.*, toste, toast, *m.* — water ; *eau panée, f.* — in wine ; *rôtie au vin.*

toast (tôste), *v.a.*, faire rôtir, faire griller; (to drink a health) porter la santé **de**, toaster.

toast, *v.n.*, porter un toast.

toast'er (tôst'-), *n.*, (instrument) gril, grille pain, *m.*

toast'ing-fork, *n.*, fourchette à rôtie, *f.*

toast'-master (-mâs-), *n.*, directeur des toasts, *m.*

toast'-rack, *n.*, porte-rôties (pour la table), *m.*

tobac'co (-cô), *n.*, tabac, tabac à fumer, *m.*

tobac'co-box, *n.*, boîte à tabac, *f.*

tobac'co-jar, *n.*, pot à tabac, *m.*

tobac'co-manufacturer, *n.*, fabricant de tabacs, *m.*

tobac'co-manufactory, *n.*, manufacture de tabacs, *f.*

tobac'conist, *n.*, marchand de tabac ; débitant de tabac, *m.*

tobac'co-pipe (-païpe), *n.*, pipe, *f.*

tobac'co-pouch, *n.*, blague à tabac, *f.* [*m.*

tobac'co-shop, *n.*, débit, *ou* bureau, de tabac,

tobac'co-stopper (-peur), *n.*, fouloir, bourre-pipe, *m.*

toc'sin, *n.*, tocsin, *m.*

to-day' (tou-dé), *adv.*, aujourd'hui.

tod'dle (tod'd'l), *v.n.*, trottiner ; marcher à petits pas, en chancelant. I must — (be off) ; (fam.) *il faut que je file.*

tod'dy, *n.*, grog, *m.*

toe'-do, *n.*, scène, *f. ; éclat, m.* There was a fine — ; *il y eut une fameuse scène,* ou *un fameux éclat,* ou *un fameux esclandre.*

toe (tô), *n.*, orteil; doigt du pied ; (of horses) devant du sabot, *m.*, pince, *f.; (of animals)* doigt ; (of a stocking) bout, *m.* On tip— ; *sur la pointe du pied.* To step, *ou* tread, on any one's —s; *marcher sur le pied* **à** *quelqu'un ;* (fig.) *froisser quelqu'un.*

toe'-clip, *n.*, (bicycle) calepied, *m.*

tof'fy, *n.*, caramel au beurre, *m.*

to'ga, *n.*, toge, *f.*

togeth'er (tou-ghèth'-), *adv.*, ensemble ; **(in** the same time) en même temps ; (in concert) conjointement **avec**; (in succession) de suite. — with ; joint à ; *ainsi que ;* en combinaison **avec**.

tog'gel, tog'gle (tog-g'l), *n.*, (nav.) éperon, cabillot, *m.*

tog'gery (tog-gheuri), *n.sing.*, (pop.) hardes, nippes, *f.pl.*; attifement, *m.*

toil (toïl), *n.*, travail fatigant, labeur, *m.*; peine, fatigue, *f.*; (net) filet, piège, rets, *m.* In the —s; *dans les toiles.*

toil (toïl), *v.n.*, travailler fort; fatiguer. To — and moil; *s'échiner, peiner,* (pop.) *s'esquinter, suer sang et eau.* To — up; *franchir,* ou *gravir, laborieusement, avec peine.* To — along; *avancer péniblement, avec difficulté.*

toil'er (toïl'-), *n.*, travailleur, *m.*, travailleuse, *f.*; piocheur, *m.*

toil'et (toïl'-), *n.*, toilette, *f.* — cover; *dessus de toilette, m.* — set; *garniture de toilette, f.* —-glass; *miroir de toilette, m.* —-table; *toilette, f.*

toil'ing, *n.*, labeur, peine, *f.*; travail fatigant, *m.*

toil'some (toïl'ceume), *adj.*, pénible, laborieux, fatigant.

toil'someness, *n.*, difficulté, *f.*

Tokay', *n.*, (wine) tokai, tokay, *m.*

to'ken (tô-), *n.*, signe, *m.*; marque, *f.*; (memorial) témoignage, gage, *m.*; (med.) tache; (of paper) demi-rame, *f.*; (coin) jeton, *m.*

tol-de-rol-lol, *n.*, flonflon, turlututu, *m.*; faridondon, faridondaine, *f.*

tol'erable (tol'eur'a-b'l), *adj.*, tolérable; supportable; (pretty good) passable.

tol'erableness, *n.*, nature passable, *f.*; état passable, *m.*; médiocrité, *f.*

tol'erably, *adv.*, tolérablement; (so-so) passablement, assez.

tol'erance, *n.*, tolérance, *f.*

tol'erant, *adj.*, tolérant.

tol'erate, *v.a.*, tolérer.

tolera'tion (tol'eur'é-), *n.*, tolérance, *f.*

toll (tôl), *n.*, pontonage; péage; droit; (town due) octroi; (for grinding) droit de mouture; (of a bell) tintement, glas, *m.*

toll (tôl), *v.a.*, prélever; (a bell) sonner, tinter.

toll, *v.n.*, (of bells) tinter, sonner le glas.

toll'-bar (-bâr), *n.*, barrage, péage, *m.*

toll'-bridge, *n.*, pont à péage, *m.*

toll'-gate, *n.*, barrière de péage, *f.*

toll'-gatherer (-gath'-), *n.*, péager, *m.*

toll'-house (-haouce), *n.*, péage, bureau de péage *ou* d'octroi, *m.*

toll'ing, *n.*, tintement, glas, *m.*

toll'ing, *adj.*, qui tinte, *ou* qui dit le glas.

toll'-money, *n.*, péage, *m.*

Tom, *n.*, (abbreviation) Thomas. —, Dick and Harry; *le tiers et le quart.*

tom'ahawk (to'm'a-hôke), *n.*, casse-tête, *m.*

toma'to, *n.*, tomate, pomme d'amour, *f.* — sauce; *sauce tomate; sauce aux tomates, f.*

tomb (toume), *n.*, tombeau, sépulcre, *m.*; tombe; (grave) tombe, fosse, *f.*; (monument) tombeau, *m.*

tom'boy (-boï), *n.*, gros gaillard, luron, *m.*; (girl) garçonnière, *f.*

tomb'stone (-stône), *n.*, pierre tumulaire, tombe, *f.*

tom'cat, *n.*, matou, chat, *m.*

tome (tô'm), *n.*, tome, volume, *m.*

tomen'tose (tô-mè'n'tôce), *adj.*, (bot.) tomenteux.

tomen'tum (tô-), *n.*, (bot.) duvet cotonneux, *m.*

tomfool' (-foule), *n.*, nigaud, sot, bêta, niais, *m.*

tomfool'ery, *n.*, nigauderie, sottise, bêtise, niaiserie, *f.*

tom'-noddy, *n.*, nigaud, dadais, *m.*

Tom'my Atkins, *m.*, le pioupiou (anglais).

to-mor'row (tou-mo-rô), *adv.*, demain. The day after —; *après-demain.* The — that never comes; *la semaine des trois jeudis.*

tom'tit, *n.*, (orni.) mésange, *f.*

tom'-tom, *n.*, tam tam, *m.*

ton (teune), *n.*, (weight) tonne, *f.*, tonneau, *m.* (kilogrammes 1016·48).

ton (togne), *n.*, (fashion) ton, *m.*; mode, *f.*

tone (tône), *n.*, ton; (med., mus.) ton; (whine) accent plaintif; (of the voice) ton, accent, timbre, *m.* In a — of voice; *d'un ton de voix.* To speak in a low —; *parler à voix basse.* To give — to; (to invigorate) *donner du ton* à; (to add luster to) *de l'éclat* à.

tone (tône), *v.a.*, donner un ton affecté à; (to tune) donner le ton à, régler; (piano, etc.) accorder; (phot.) virer. To — down; *adoucir, pallier.*

tone'less, *adj.*, peu harmonieux.

tongs (tognze), *n.pl.*, pincettes; (tech.) tenailles, pinces, *f.pl.*

tongue (teugne), *n.*, langue; (language) langue, *f.*, langage, idiome, *m.*; (of land) langue de terre, *f.*; promontoire, *m.*; (tech.) languette, *f.*; (of a buckle) ardillon, *m.* To hold one's —; *se taire.* To have on the tip of the —; *avoir sur le bout de la langue.* To have a glib —; *avoir la langue bien pendue.* To give —; (of hounds) *donner de la voix.* To be — valiant; *être brave en paroles.* It was a slip of the —; *la langue m'a, ou lui a, fourché.*

tongued (teugn'de), *adj.*, à langue; (tech.) à languette. A hundred- —; *aux cents voix.*

tongue'less, *adj.*, sans langue; (speechless) muet.
[langue, *m.*

tongue'-scraper (-scrép'-), *n.*, cure-*ou* gratte-

tongue'-shaped (-shép'te), *adj.*, (anthropology) en forme de langue; (bot.) en languette.

tongue'-tie (-taïe), *v.a.*, nouer la langue à; (fig.) lier la langue à.

tongue'-tied (-taïde), *adj.*, qui a le filet; (fig.) qui a la langue liée; (fig.) obligé (*ou* réduit) au silence.

ton'ic, *adj.*, tonique, incitant.

ton'ic, *n.*, (med.) tonique, *m.*; (mus.) tonique, *f.*

to-night' (tou-naïte), *n.*, cette nuit, *f.*; ce soir, *m.*

ton'nage (teu'nè'dje), *n.*, tonnage; droit de tonnage, *m.*

ton'sil, *n.*, (anat.) amygdale, *f.*

ton'silar, *adj.*, (anat.) tonsillaire.

ton'sure (to'n'sheur), *n.*, (c.rel.) tonsure, *f.*

tontine' (-tîne), *n.*, tontine, *f.*

to'ny (tô-), *n.*, imbécile, niais, *m.*

too (toû), *adv.*, trop, par trop; (also) aussi, de même, également, encore. — much, —many; *trop;* (before a noun) *trop* de. — heavy a burden; *une charge trop lourde.* This task is — much for you; *cette tâche est au-dessus de vos forces.* He is — much for you; *vous n'êtes pas de force à lutter avec lui.* — many cooks spoil the broth; (prov.) *trop de cuisiniers gâtent la sauce.* — much of a good thing is good for nothing; *jeu qui trop dure ne vaut rien* (Charles d'Orléans).

tool (toule), *n.*, outil; instrument; (pers.) instrument, jouet, agent, *m.* Set of —s; *affûtage, m.*

tool'-chest (-tshèste), *n.*, boîte à outils, *f.*

tool'-house, *n.*, hangar aux outils, *m.*

tooth (touth) *n.*, (*teeth*) dent, *f.*; (palate) palais, goût, *m.* Set of teeth; *râtelier, m.* To cast in the teeth; *reprocher* à; *jeter au nez* à ou *à la face* de. In spite of one's teeth; *malgré quelqu'un.* To set the teeth on edge; *agacer les dents.* To have a — out; *se faire arracher une dent.* To show one's teeth; *montrer les dents.* To have a sweet —; *aimer les douceurs.* In any one's teeth; *à la figure, au nez de quelqu'un.* To go at it — and nail; *s'y prendre de toutes ses forces, être aux prises.* — and nail; *bec et ongles;* (fig.) *à belles dents; comme un enragé.* They are at it — and nail; *ils y sont bec et ongles.* In the teeth of the gale; *au plus fort de la tempête.* In the teeth of; *malgré, en dépit* de; *à l'encontre* de ; *en opposition directe* avec ; *en face* de. To cut one's teeth; (of a child) *faire ses dents.* First teeth ; *dents de lait.* False —; *fausse dent ; dent postiche.* — -powder ; *poudre dentifrice, f.*

tooth, *v.a.,* (to indent) denteler ; (to lock into each other) engrener.

tooth′ache (-'éke), *n.,* mal de dents, *m.* My —; *mon mal* de *dents.* To have a —; *avoir mal* aux *dents.*

tooth′brush (-breushe), *n.,* brosse à dents, *f.*

tooth′-drawer (-drō′-), *n.,* arracheur de dents, dentiste, *m.*

tooth′-drawing (-drō-igne), *n.,* extraction de dents, *f.*

toothed (touth′te), *adj.,* à dents ; (bot., tech.) denté, dentelé, à dents.

tooth′ing, *n.,* (arch.) arrachement, *m.*

tooth′less, *adj.,* sans dents ; édenté.

tooth′-pick, *n.,* cure-dents, *m.*

tooth′-rash, *n.,* feu de dents, *m.*

tooth′some, *adj.,* agréable au goût, savoureux, friand.

tooth′someness, *n.,* goût agréable, *m. ;* saveur agréable, *f.*

tooth′wort (-weurte), *n.,* dentaire, *f.*

tooth′y, *adj.,* muni de dents, à dents.

top, *n.,* haut, sommet, *m. ;* (of a mountain, a tree, a rock) cime, *f. ;* (of a building) haut, faîte ; (of the head) sommet, dessus, haut, *m. ;* (of a hat) fond, *m. ;* (of a cap) calotte ; (of water) surface, *f. ;* (cover) couvercle, *m. ;* (nav.) hune, *f. ;* (highest person) chef, *m.,* tête ; (highest rank) tête, *f. ;* (arch.) couronnement ; (of boots) revers, *m. ;* (of plants) tête ; (of a pole) bout, haut bout ; (of a table) dessus, *m. ;* (of a piano) table ; (of coaches) impériale, banquette, *f. ;* (further end) haut, haut bout, *m. ;* (plaything) toupie, *f.,* sabot ; (fig.) sommet, comble, faîte, *m. pl.,* (of turnips, etc.) fane, *f. ;* (boots) bottes à revers, *f.pl.* From — to bottom ; *du haut en bas ;* (fig.) *de fond en comble.* From — to toe ; *de la tête aux pieds.* Humming-— ; *toupie d'Allemagne, f.* Whipping-— ; *sabot, m.* At the — of ; *en haut* de. At the — of the house ; *tout en haut de la maison.* — of the tree ; (fig.) *tête, f. ; sommet ; premier rang, m.*

top, *adj.,* premier, principal, extrême.

top, *v.a.,* couronner de, surmonter de ; (to raise above) dépasser ; (to surpass) surpasser ; (to lop) étêter ; (to rise to the top of) atteindre le sommet de ; (nav.) apiquer. To — off ; (a stack of hay) *achever, compléter.*

top, *v.n.,* dominer ; (to predominate) dominer, prédominer, primer ; (to excel) dominer, exceller, s'élever, monter.

to′paz (tô-), *n.,* topaze, *f.*

top′-coat, *n.,* pardessus, *m.*

tope (tôpe), *v.n.,* (pop.) pinter, ivrogner, godailler.

tope (tôpe), *n.,* (ich.) squale ; milandre, *m.*

top′er (tôp′-), *n.,* biberon, ivrogne, *m.*

top′et, *n.,* (orni.) mésange huppée, *f.*

top′ful (-foule), *adj.,* tout plein.

topgal′lant, *adj.,* (nav.) de perroquet.

topgal′lant (sail *ou* mast), *n.,* (nav.) voile de perroquet, *f. ;* mât de perroquet, *m.*

top′-heavy (-hèv′-), *adj.,* trop lourd du haut.

top′ic, *n.,* matière, *f. ;* sujet ; argument ; (rhet., med.) topique, *m.*

top′ic *ou* **top′ical,** *adj.,* local ; (pertaining to a topic) qui développe un sujet, une matière.

top′ically, *adv.,* localement.

top′knot (-note), *n.,* (of women) fontange ; (of birds) huppe, aigrette, *f.*

top′-lantern, *n.,* fanal de hune, *m.*

top′less, *adj.,* d'une hauteur infinie.

top′man, *n.,* scieur de long (de dessus); (nav.) gabier, *m.*

top′-mast (-mâste), *n.,* mât de hune ; hunier, *m.*

top′most (-môste), *adj.,* le plus haut, le plus élevé.

topog′rapher, *n.,* topographe, *m.*

topograph′ic *ou* **topograph′ical,** *adj.,* topographique.

topog′raphy, *n.,* topographie, *f.*

top′ple (top′p′l), *v.n.,* tomber en avant. To — over ; *dégringoler ; s'écrouler ; faire la bascule ;* (of a carriage) verser.

top′-sail (-séle), *n.,* hunier, *m.* — yard ; *vergue de hune, f.*

top′-shaped (-shép′te), *adj.,* (bot.) turbiné ; en forme de toupie.

top′-sides, *n.,* œuvres mortes, *f.pl. ;* hauts, *m.pl.*

topsy-tur′vy (-teur-), *adv.,* sens dessus dessous.

torch (tortshe), *n.,* torche, *f. ;* flambeau, *m.* — -light procession ; *promenade,* ou *retraite, aux flambeaux ;* (Church) *procession aux flambeaux, f.*

torch′-bearer, *n.,* porte-flambeau, *m.*

torch′-thistle (-this's'l), *n.,* (bot.) cactus vierge ; cierge du Pérou, *m.*

toreador′, *n.,* toréador, *m.*

tor′ment, *n.,* tourment, *m. ;* (torture) torture, *f.,* supplice, *m. ;* souffrance ; (that which torments) cause de tourments, *f.*

torment′, *v.a.,* tourmenter, harasser, vexer ; faire souffrir.

tor′mentil, *n.,* (bot.) tormentille, *f.*

torment′ing, *adj.,* tourmentant, harassant, vexant.

torment′or (-mè′n′t′eur), *n.,* tourmenteur, bourreau, *m.*

torna′do (-né-dō), *n.,* tourbillon, tornado, *m.*

tor′ose (-rôce) *ou* **tor′ous,** *adj.,* (bot.) bosselé, finement bosselé.

torpe′do (-pî-dô), *n.,* (ich., milit., nav.) torpille, *f.* — -boat ; (nav.) *torpilleur, m.* — destroyer ; *contre-torpilleur, m.*

tor′pid, *adj.,* engourdi ; torpide ; (fig.) inerte, lourd, apathique.

torpid′ity, tor′pidness, *ou* **tor′por,** *n.,* torpeur ; (fig.) torpeur, apathie, lourdeur, *f.*

torrefac′tion (-ri-fak′-), *n.,* torréfaction, *f.*

tor′refy (-ri-faïe), *v.a.,* torréfier ; griller.

tor′rent, *n.,* torrent, *m.* In —s; (of rain) à, ou par, *torrents ; à verse.*

tor′rent(like), *adj.,* torrentueux.

torren′tial, *adj.,* torrentiel.

tor′rid, *adj.,* (burning) brûlant, de la zone torride ; (parched) brûlé ; (geog.) torride.

tor′ridness, torrid′ity, *n.,* chaleur brûlante, *f.*

tor′sel, *n.,* (arch.) sablière, *f.*

tor′sion, *n.,* (mec., phys., surg.) torsion, *f.* — balance ; (phys.) *balance de torsion, f.*

tor′so (-sô), *n.,* (sculp.) torse, *m.*

tor′toise (tor-tize *ou* -tiss), *n.,* tortue, *f.*

tor′toise-shell, *n.,* écaille de tortue, écaille, *f.*

tortuos′ity *ou* **tor′tuousness** (tort′iou-), *n.,* tortuosité, *f.*

tor′tuous (tort′iou-euss), *adj.,* (winding) tortueux, sinueux ; (fig.) clandestin, secret, caché.

tor′ture (tort′iour), *v.a.,* torturer ; mettre à la torture ; (fig.) tourmenter, faire souffrir.

tor′ture (tort′iour), *n.,* torture, douleur, *f. ;* supplice, tourment, *m.*

tor′turer, *n.,* bourreau, *m.*

tor′turingly, *adv.,* de manière à torturer.

tor′y (tô-), *adj.,* tory.

tor′y, *n.,* tory, conservateur, *m.*

tor′yism (-iz′m), *n.,* torysme, *m.*

toss, *n.,* secousse, *f. ;* jet, ballottement ; (with horns) coup de corne, *m.* — of the head ; *coup de tête en arrière, m.* To win the —; *gagner à pile ou face.*

toss, *v.a.n.,* lancer, jeter ; jeter, *ou* lancer, en l'air ; (to cause to rise and fall) ballotter, secouer ; (to agitate) agiter, remuer ; (of horned cattle) lancer en l'air. To — off; (throw off) *jeter loin de soi ;*

(drink) *avaler d'un trait,* ou *d'un coup, lamper.*
To — up ; *jeter en l'air ;* (oars) *mâter ;* (the head)
relever ; (to play) *jouer à croix ou pile.* To — in
a blanket ; *berner.* To — off (a glass of wine) ;
avaler d'un trait, d'une gorgée. To — in bed ;
être agité ; changer sans cesse de position. Let
us — for sides; *décidons à croix ou pile qui jouera
des deux côtés.*

toss'er, n., (of money) joueur à pile ou face, m.

toss'ing, n., secousse, f.; ballottement; (of the
head) mouvement, coup de tête, m. ; coups de
corne, m.pl. We had a fine —; (at sea) *nous avons
été rudement secoués,* ou *ballottés.*

to'tal (tô-), n., total ; montant, m. ; somme, f.

to'tal (tô-), adj., total ; complet ; entier.

total'ity, n., totalité, f. ; montant ; total, m.

to'tally, adv., totalement ; tout à fait ; entièrement ; complètement.

to'to-cœlo, adv., du tout en tout.

tot'ter, v.n., chanceler ; branler ; vaciller ;
menacer ruine. To — to one's feet ; *se lever en
chancelant.* To — away ; *s'éloigner d'un pas
tremblant.*

tot'tering, adj., chancelant, tremblant, mal
assuré.

tot'tering, n., chancellement ; branlement, m.

tot'teringly, adv., d'une manière chancelante.

tot'tery, adj., chancelant.

touch (teutshe), v.a., toucher ; (to meddle,
disturb, break into (money)), toucher à ; (to
reach) toucher à, atteindre; (to concern) toucher,
concerner, regarder ; (to move) toucher, émouvoir ; (to delineate) tracer ; (to make an impression on, as of a file) entamer ; (to try metals)
toucher, essayer ; (mus.) toucher. To — one's
hat to ; *saluer.* To — up ; *retoucher ; raviver ;*
(fig.) *relever, rehausser.* To — up . . . into ; *retoucher . . . pour le convertir en.* To — off ;
ébaucher, esquisser ; retoucher. —pot, —penny;
crédit est mort.

touch, v.n., toucher ; se toucher. To — at ;
(of ships) *toucher à, aborder à ; faire escale à.*
To — upon ; (to take effect on) *entamer ;* (to
treat of slightly) *toucher, effleurer ; faire allusion
à.* Not to — it ; (of merchandise, etc.) *n'en pas
vouloir ; ne pas s'y risquer.*

touch (teutshe), n., (sense of feeling) toucher ;
(contact) contact, attouchement ; (test) criterium, m., pierre de touche ; (proof) preuve, f. ;
qualités éprouvées, f.pl. ; (arts) coup de crayon,
de pinceau ; trait, m., touche ; (at billiards)
touche, f.; (feature) trait ; (stroke, as of raillery)
trait ; (animadversion) reproche, blâme, m. ; (of
disease) légère attaque, f.; (trial) essai ; (sample)
échantillon, m. ; (very small quantity) idée, f. ;
soupçon ; (metal.) essai, m., touche, f. ; (mus.)
toucher, m. To give the last — ; *mettre la dernière main à.* To have a near —, a close — *ou*
shave; *l'échapper belle.* It was — and go; *il s'en
est fallu de bien peu,* ou *de l'épaisseur d'un cheveu.*
To be in — (with others) ; *être au courant des
sentiments et des opinions de.* To lose — ; *ne
plus être en sympathie avec ;* (milit.) *ne plus
maintenir de communications avec.*

touch'able (teutsh'a-b'l), adj., tangible, palpable.

touched, adv., touché ; (fig.) ému, affecté ;
(in the head) un peu toqué ; timbré.

touch'-hole (-hôle), n., (artil.) lumière, f.

touch'ily, adv., avec humeur ; avec susceptibilité.

touch'iness, n., irascibilité, humeur chagrine ;
susceptibilité, f.

touch'ing, adj., (moving) touchant, émouvant.

touch'ing, prep., (concerning) touchant, concernant ; au sujet de.

touch'ingly, adv., d'une manière touchante.

touch'-me-not (teutshe-mi-), n., (med., bot.)
noli me tangere, m.; (bot.) balsamine des bois, f.

touch'-needle (-nîd'd'l), n., touchau, m.

touch'-paper (-pé-peur), papier d'amorce, m.

touch'-stone (-stône), n., pierre de touche,
f. ; criterium, m.

touch'-wood (-woude), n., amadou, m.

touch'y, adj., irascible; irritable, chatouilleux;
susceptible.

tough (teufe), adj., (of things) inflexible, rigide, raide, résistant; (viscous) visqueux, tenace;
(of meat) dur, coriace ; (strong) fort, solide,
robuste, vigoureux, épineux, difficile ; (formidable) rude ; (fig.) dur. A — job ; (colloq.) *une rude
tâche.*

tough'en (teuf'f'n), v.a. and n., durcir, raidir,
s'endurcir.

tough'ish (teuf'-), adj., un peu dur.

tough'ly (teuf'-), adv., durement, avec raideur *ou* ténacité, vigoureusement.

tough'ness (teuf'-), n., (of things) raideur,
inflexibilité, rigidité, ténacité ; (viscosity) viscosité, ténacité ; (of meat) dureté, nature coriace ;
(firmness) vigueur, solidité ; (fig.) difficulté, f.

toupee' (tou-pî) *ou* **toupet'** (tou-pé), n., toupet, m.

tour, n., (journey) tour, voyage, m.

tour'ist, n., touriste, voyageur, m.

tour'nament *ou* **tour'ney,** n., tournoi, m.

tout (taoute), v.n., racoler ; courir après les
pratiques ; pousser à la consommation. To — for ;
*lâcher d'obtenir (solliciter) la clientèle de ; pister,
racoler.*

tout, n., placier, solliciteur, pisteur, rabatteur ;
(in racing) espion, m.

tout'ing, n., sollicitation, f. ; racolage, m.;
(fig.) importunité, f.

tow (tô), n., (hemp) filasse, étoupe ; (rope)
touée; (fig.) remorque, f. In —; (fig., nav.) *à
la remorque ; à la touée.*

tow, v.a., remorquer; (from the shore) touer ;
haler ; haler à la cordelle.

tow'age (tô-èdje), **tow'ing,** n., remorque,
f. ; (from the shore) touage, halage, remorquage, m.

toward *ou* **towards,** adv., près.

toward (tôrde) *ou* **towards** (tôrd'ze), prep.,
vers ; du côté de ; (with respect to) à l'égard de,
envers, pour ; (of time) vers, sur, environ.

to'ward *ou* **to'wardly** (tô-), adj., docile.

to'wardliness *ou* **to'wardness,** n., docilité, f.

tow'-boat (-bôte), n., (tug) bateau remorqueur;
(from the shore) bateau halé, m.

tow'el (taou-èl), n., essuie-mains, m.; serviette, f.

tow'eling, n., toile pour serviettes, f.

tow'er (taou'eur), n., tour; citadelle, f. A
— of strength ; *un puissant appui.* To be a —
of strength ; *valoir à soi (tout) seul toute une
armée.*

tow'er (taou-eur), v.n., s'élever **au-dessus de;**
planer ; dominer.

tow'ered (taou-eurde), adj., à tours, défendu
par des tours.

tow'ering, adj., élevé comme une tour ; qui
plane; (fig.) élevé, grand, sublime ; dominant.

tow'ery, adj., flanqué de tours.

tow'ing (tô-igne), n., halage, m. ; remorque,
f. **—path** ; *chemin de halage,* m. **—rope** ;
corde de halage; cordelle, f. **—boat** *ou* tow-
boat ; *bateau remorqueur,* m.

tow'line (-laïne), n., corde de halage ; haussière, cordelle, f.

town (taou'ne), n., ville ; capitale, f. To go to
— ; (Eng.) *aller à Londres.* In —, *en ville ;* (Eng.)
à Londres. Out of — ; *à la campagne.* To live
upon the — ; *battre le pavé.* A man about — ; *un
batteur de pavé,* m. The talk of the — ; *l'événement de toute la ville,* m. (V. Hugo).

town'-band, n., musique municipale, f.

town'-clerk, n., secrétaire de la mairie, m.

town'-council, n., conseil municipal, m.

town'-councillor, m., conseiller municipal, m.

town'-crier (-craï-), *n.*, crieur public, *m.*
town'-due (-diou), *n.*, droit d'entrée, *m. pl.*, octroi, *m.*
town'-hall (-hōl), *n.*, hôtel de ville, *m.*
town'-house (-haouce), *n.*, hôtel de ville, *m.*, mairie; (residence) maison de, *ou* en, ville, *f.*; (Engl.) hôtel à Londres, *m.*
town'ish, *adj.*, de ville, *m.*
town'-major, -commandant, *n.*, commandant, *ou* major, de place, *m.*
town'-rate, *n.*, taxe communale, *f.*
town'ship, *n.*, commune; étendue territoriale d'une ville, *f.*
towns'man (taou'n'z'-), *n.*, citadin; habitant de ville; bourgeois; (of the same town) concitoyen, *m.*
towns'-people, *n.*, habitants, citadins, bourgeois, *m.pl.*
town'-surveyor, *n.*, inspecteur des travaux publics, *m.*
town'talk (-tōke), *n.*, bruit de ville; propos de ville; entretien de toute la ville, *m.*
tow'-path (-pâth), *n.*, chemin de halage, *m.*
toxicolo'gical (-lodj'-), *adj.*, toxicologique.
toxicol'ogy (-'odji), *n.*, toxicologie, *f.*
toy (toïe), *n.*, jouet, joujou; (com.) bimbelot; (bauble) brimborion, colifichet, *m.*, babiole; bagatelle, *f.*, rien, *m.*; (folly) niaiserie, futilité, *f. pl.*, jouets, *m.pl.*; (com.) bimbeloterie, *f.*
toy (toïe), *v.n.*, jouer; badiner, folâtrer; jouer **avec**; s'amuser **avec**.
toy'-book (-bouke), *n.*, livre d'images, *m.*
toy'-box, *n.*, boîte à joujoux, *f.*
toy'er (toïeur), *n.*, joueur, badin, *m.*
toy'ish (toïish), *adj.*, futile; (wanton) badin, folâtre.
toy'ishness, *n.*, humeur badine, folâtre; folâtrerie, *f.*
toy'man *ou* **toy'-dealer**, *n.*, marchand de jouets, de joujoux, tabletier, bimbelotier, *f.*
toy'-shop, *n.*, magasin de jouets, de joujoux, *m.*
toy'-terrier, *n.*, bichon; petit épagneul, *m.*
toy'-trade, *n.*, bimbeloterie, tabletterie, *f.*
trace, *n.*, trace, *f.*; (of harness) trait, *m.*; (geom.) trace, *f.* — bearer; *porte-trait, m.*
trace, *v.a.*, tracer; (in drawing) calquer; (to track) suivre à la trace, à la piste; suivre la trace **de**; remonter à l'origine **de**; remonter à. To — to; *reporter, faire remonter* **à**. To — out; *tracer, faire le tracé* **de**; (to track out) *tracer, découvrir la trace* **de**. To — the origin of; *découvrir l'origine* **de**. To — back; *faire remonter* **à**; *remonter à l'origine* **de**.
trace'able (tréss'a-b'l), *adj.*, que l'on peut tracer; dont on peut suivre les traces; (fig.) attribuable **à**.
tra'cer (tréss'-), *n.*, traceur; (inst.) traçoir, *m.*
tra'cery (tré-ceur'i), *n.*, (arch.) réseau, *m.*; broderie (en pierre), *f.*
tra'chea (tré-ki-), *n.*, (anat.) trachée-artère, *f.* (bot.) trachée, *f.*
tracheot'omy (tré-ki-), *n.*, (surg.) trachéotomie, *f.*
tra'cing, *n.*, tracé; cours; tracement; (drawing) calque, *m.* — paper; *papier à calquer, m.*
track, *n.*, trace; voie; (hunt.) piste; voie; (hunt., railways) voie; (of a comet) route, *f.*; cours; (of a ship) sillage, *m.*, eaux, *f.pl.*; (fig.) trace, voie, route, ornière, *f.*; (road) chemin, sentier, *m.* Beaten —; *sentier battu, m.* To make —s; *s'en aller précipitamment, filer.*
track, *v.a.*, suivre à la trace, à la piste; (to tow) haler, remorquer.
track'-boat (-bôte), *n.*, coche, *m.*
track'ing, *n.*, action de suivre à la trace, poursuite, *f.*; (towing) halage, *m.*
track'less, *adj.*, sans trace; non frayé; sans chemins, impraticable.
track'road (-rôde), *n.*, chemin de halage, *m.*

tract, *n.*, étendue; (region) contrée, région, *f.*, district, *m.*; (of time) espace, *m.*, durée, *f.*; (book) opuscule, traité; (religion) petit livre de dévotion, *m.*, brochure, *f.*
tractabil'ity. *V.* **tractableness**.
tract'able (-ta-b'l), *adj.*, traitable; maniable; doux; docile.
tract'ableness, *n.*, nature traitable; docilité, douceur, *f.* [docilement.
tract'ably, *adv.*, d'une manière traitable,
tracta'rian (trak-té-), *n.*, tractarien, *m.*
trac'tile, *adj.*, ductile.
tractil'ity, *n.*, ductilité, *f.*
trac'tion (trak'sheune), *n.*, tension; attraction; (mec.) attraction; traction, *f.* —engine; *locomotive routière, locomobile à vapeur, f.*
trac'tive, *adj.*, (mec.) de traction, tractif.
trade, *n.*, commerce, trafic, négoce; (calling) état, métier, *m.*; profession, industrie; (habit) habitude, coutume; (of slaves) traite, *f.*; (employment) emploi, *m.*, occupation, *f.*; (men engaged in the same occupation) corps de métier; (b.s.) métier, commerce, *m.* By —; *de son état, de son métier.* In —; *dans les affaires, dans le commerce.* In the —; *dans le commerce.* — is slack; *le commerce ne va pas; les affaires ne marchent, ou ne vont, pas.* — is at a standstill; *le commerce est nul* (V. Hugo). To learn a —; *apprendre un métier.* To carry on the — of; *faire le commerce* **de**. To drive a roaring —; *faire d'excellentes affaires.* To be good for —; *faire aller le commerce.* The — supplied; *on vend en gros et en détail.* A Jack of all —s; *un homme de tous les métiers.* Every one to his —, and all will go well; (prov.) *chacun son métier, et les vaches seront bien gardées.* —-wind; *vent alizé, m.* Free —; *libre-échange, m.*
trade, *v.n.*, trafiquer, commercer, faire le commerce **de**. To — in; *faire le commerce* **de**. To — on, upon; *exploiter; spéculer* **sur**.
trade'-allowance, *n.*, remise, *f.*
trad'er (tréd'-), *n.*, négociant, *m.*, négociante, *f.*; commerçant, *m.*, commerçante, *f.*; (ship) vaisseau marchand, *m.* Free——; *libre-échangiste, m.*
trade'-mark, *n.*, marque de fabrique, *f.*
trade'-sale, *n.*, vente publique, *f.*
trades'man (tréd'z'-), *n.*, marchand; débitant; (com.) fournisseur, *m.*
trades'people (tréd'z'pl'p'l) *ou* **trades'folk** (-fōke), *n.pl.*, commerçants; marchands, fournisseurs, *m.pl.*
trades'woman (tréd'z'woum'-), *n.*, commerçante, marchande, *f.*
trad'ing (tréd'-), *n.*, négoce, commerce, trafic, *m.*
trad'ing (tréd'-), *adj.*, commercial; commerçant; marchand; de commerce.
tradi'tion, *n.*, tradition, *f.*
tradi'tional, *adj.*, traditionnel.
tradi'tionally, *adv.*, traditionnellement.
traduce' (tra-diouce), *v.a.*, censurer, critiquer; (to calumniate) diffamer, calomnier; médire **de**.
tradu'cer (-diouss'-), *n.*, calomniateur, *m.*, calomniatrice, *f.*; diffamateur, *m.*, diffamatrice, *f.*
traf'fic, *n.*, trafic; commerce, négoce, *m.*; (railw.) transport, mouvement, *m.*, circulation; (going and coming) circulation, *f.*; roulage; (of streets) mouvement, *m.*; (commodities) marchandises, *f.pl.* —-manager; (railw.) *chef du mouvement, m.* —-return; (railw.) *état des recettes, m.* Opened for —; *livré à la circulation.* There is much — in the streets; *il y a beaucoup de mouvement dans les rues.*
traf'fic, *v.n.*, trafiquer, commercer.
traf'ficker, *n.*, marchand, négociant, commerçant, trafiquant; (b.s.) trafiqueur, *m.*
trag'acanth (-ca'n'th), *n.*, (bot.) tragacanthe; (gum) gomme adragante, *f.*

trage'dian (tra-djî-), *n.*, tragédien, *m.*; tragédienne, *f.*; (writer) tragique, auteur tragique, *m.*

tra'gedy (tra-dji-), *n.*, tragédie, *f.*

tra'gic (tra-djike) *ou* **tra'gical** (tra-dji-), *adj.*, tragique.

tra'gically, *adv.*, tragiquement.

tra'gicalness, *n.*, tragique; caractère tragique, *m.*

tragi-com'edy (tradj'i-), *n.*, tragi-comédie, *f.*

tragi-com'ical, *adj.*, tragi-comique.

tragi-com'ically, *adv.*, d'une manière tragicomique.

trail (tréle), *n.*, traînée; (hunt.) trace, piste, voie; (of a meteor) queue, traînée lumineuse, *f.*; (fig.) voie, trace, *f.* In the — of; *à la suite de.* On the —; *sur la piste.* —-boards; (nav.) *frise de l'éperon, f.*

trail (tréle), *v.n.*, traîner; passer lentement.

trail, *v.a.*, suivre à la piste; (to drag) traîner; (to lower) baisser.

train (tréne), *n.*, (retinue) suite, *f.*, cortège, *m.*, (series) suite, série, *f.*; (of ideas) enchaînement; (course) cours, *m.*; (of a watch, etc.) marche, *f.*, mouvement, *m.*; (of gunpowder) traînée; (of a bird, of a dress) queue, *f.*; (of insects, etc.) arrière-train, *m.*; (of a gun-carriage) derrière, (artil.) train; (of boats) convoi, *f.*; (railways) convoi, train; (artifice) artifice, *m.* Freight —; *train de marchandises.* Passenger —; *train de voyageurs.* Fast, express —; *train de grande vitesse.* The fast —; *le rapide, le train-éclair.* Mixed —; *train mixte.* Down —; (railw.) *train descendant, train s'éloignant* **de.** Up —; (railw.) *train montant, ou se dirigeant* **vers.** Excursion —; (railw.) *train de plaisir.* Return —; *train de retour.* Military —; *soldats du train.* Siege —; *équipage de siège, m.* Armored —; *train blindé.* Tidal —; (railw.) *train de marée.* Parliamentary, *ou* slow, —; *train omnibus.* Next —; *le prochain train, le train suivant.* In the — of; (fig.) *à la suite* **de.** Corridor —; *train à couloirs.*

train, *v.a.*, dresser, former, exercer; élever; instruire; (to draw along) traîner; (to entice) entraîner, séduire; (hort.) dresser; (man.) entraîner; dresser. To — up; élever, instruire, former. To — (soldiers) *discipliner; faire faire l'exercice* à. To —; (a gun) *pointer.*

train'-band, *n.*, milice bourgeoise, *f.*

train'-bearer (-bèr'-), *n.*, porte-queue, *m.*; (of a cardinal) caudataire, *m.*

train'er, *n.*, dresseur; instructeur; (of racehorses) entraîneur, *m.*

train'ing, *n.*, éducation, instruction; discipline, *f.*; exercice, *m.*; (of horses) dressage; (of race-horses) entraînement, *m.* —-ship; *vaisseau-école, m.* — college; *école normale primaire, f.*

train'-oil (-oïl), *n.*, huile de baleine, *f.*

train'-service, *n.*, service des trains, *m.*

traipse (trépse), *v.n.*, traîner, trimer, battre la semelle.

trait (tréte *ou* tré), *n.*, trait, *m.*

trai'tor (tré-teur), *n.*, traître; perfide, conspirateur, *m.*

trai'torous (tré-teur'-), *adj.*, traître; (perfidious) traître, perfide.

trai'torously, *adv.*, en traître; (perfidiously) traîtreusement, perfidement.

trai'tress (tré-), *n.*, traîtresse; perfide, *f.*

trajec'tion (tra-djèk-), *n.*, passage, *m.*; transposition, *f.*

trajec'tory (tra-djèk-teuri), *n.*, (mec., geom., astron., mil.) trajectoire, *f.*

tram, *n.*, chariot de roulage; (railways) rail plat, *ou* à ornière; (in the streets) tramway, *m.* — service; *service de tramways, m.*

tram'mel, *v.a.*, entraver, empêtrer; embarrasser (with, **de).**

tram'mel, *n.*, (net) tramail, traîneau, *m.*; (for animals) entrave; (iron hook) crémaillère, *f.*; (elliptic compasses) compas à ellipse, *m.*; (fig.) entrave, *f.*, obstacle, *m.*

tram'ontane (-téne), *n.adj.*, (in France) ultramontain, *m.* — wind; *la tramontane, f.*

tramp, *v.n.*, errer, rôder; (to go on foot) aller à pied, cheminer; battre la semelle.

tramp, *v.a.*, faire à pied, faire.

tramp, *n.*, marche à pied, *f.*; (stamp) piétinement; bruit de pas; (a person) vagabond, truand, ouvrier ambulant, chemineau, *m.*

tram'ple (tra'm'p'l), *v.a.n.*, fouler aux pieds; marcher **sur,** piétiner. To — down; *écraser.* To — under foot; *fouler aux pieds.*

tram'pling, *n.*, piétinement, bruit de pas, *m.*

tram'-rail (-réle), *n.*, rail plat, *m.*

tram'-road *ou* **tram'-way** (-wé), *n.*, chemin de fer américain, tramway, *m.*

trance, *n.*, extase; (med.) catalepsie, *f.*

tranced (trâ'n'ste), *adj.*, en extase.

tran'quil (tra'n'kwile), *adj.*, tranquille.

tranquil'lity *ou* **tran'quilness** (-kwil-li-), *n.*, tranquillité, quiétude, *f.*, calme, *m.*

tran'quillize (-kwil-laïze), *v.a.*, tranquilliser, rassurer, calmer.

tran'quilly (-kwil'-), *adv.*, tranquillement.

transact', *v.a.*, faire; faire exécuter; traiter; expédier. To — business; *être en affaires; travailler.*

transac'tion, *n.*, (management) conduite, gestion, négociation; (act) transaction, affaire, *f.*, acte, événement, *m.*; (com.) transaction, affaire, opération, *f.* The —s of the Royal Society; *les comptes-rendus de la Société royale, m.pl.*

transac'tor, *n.*, négociateur, agent, *m.*

transal'pine, *adj.*, transalpin.

transatlan'tic, *adj.*, transatlantique.

transcend', *v.a.*, dépasser; (fig.) surpasser, dépasser, excéder.

transcend'ence *ou* **transcend'ency,** *n.*, excellence, transcendance, *f.*

transcend'ent, *adj.*, transcendant.

transcenden'tal, *adj.*, (metaph.) transcendantal; (math.) transcendant.

transcenden'tally, *adv.*, d'une manière transcendante.

transcribe' (-scraïbe), *v.a.*, transcrire, copier.

transcrib'er (-scraïb'-), *n.*, copiste, transcripteur, *m.*

tran'script, *n.*, transcription; copie, *f.*

transcrip'tion, *n.*, transcription, *f.*

tran'sept, *n.*, (arch.) transept, *m.*

trans'fer (-feur), *n.*, translation, *f.*; transport; (fin.) transfert, *m.*, assignation, *f.*; (jur.) transfert, transport; (com.) transfert, *m.*, cession, *f.*

transfer' (-feur), *v.a.*, transférer; transporter; (jur.) transférer, céder; transmettre.

transfer'able (-feur'a-b'l), *adj.*, transportable; (jur.) cessible; (com.) cessible, négociable. Not —; (of tickets) *personnel.*

transferee' (-feur'î), *n.*, cessionnaire, *m.*

transfer'ence, *n.*, transférement, *m.*

transfer'rer (-feur'-), *n.*, cédant, *m.*

transfigura'tion (-figh'iou-ré-), *n.*, (c. rel.) Transfiguration; (ant.) transformation, *f.*

transfig'ure (-figh'ioure), *v.a.*, transfigurer; transformer.

transfix', *v.a.*, transpercer.

transform', *v.a.*, transformer **en**; changer; (metals) convertir, transmuer.

transform', *v.n.*, se transformer **en.**

transforma'tion (-form'é-), *n.*, transformation, *f.*; changement, *m.*; conversion; (ent.) métamorphose; (of metals) conversion, transmutation, *f.* — scene; *changement à vue, m.*

transform'ing, *adj.*, qui transforme; qui change.

transfuse' (-fiouze), *v.a.*, transvaser; transfuser; instiller; (surg.) transfuser; (fig.) communiquer à; faire passer **dans.**

transfu'sion (-fiou-jeune), *n.*, (of a liquor) action de transvaser; (of blood) transfusion, *f.*

transgress', *v.a.*, dépasser ; (to infringe) trangresser, enfreindre, violer ; contrevenir **à**.

transgress', *v.n.*, transgresser ; pécher.

transgres'sion (-grèsh'-), *n.*, transgression, violation, infraction ; contravention **à**, *f. ;* péché, *m.*

transgres'sive, *adj.*, transgressif ; coupable.

transgres'sor, *n.*, transgresseur ; violateur, *m.*, violatrice, *f. ;* (rel.) pécheur, *m.*, pécheresse, *f.*

tranship', *v.a.*, transborder ; transférer **à** bord **de**.

tranship'ment, *n.*, transbordement, *m.*

tran'sient (tra'n'shè'n'te), *adj.*, passager ; transitoire ; fugitif, éphémère ; (hasty) rapide, momentané.

tran'siently, *adv.*, en passant, légèrement, rapidement.

tran'sientness, *n.*, brièveté ; nature transitoire ; rapidité ; courte durée, *f.*

tran'sit, *n.*, passage ; (at the customs) transit ; (astron.) passage, *m.*

tran'sit-duty, *n.*, droit de transit, *m.*

tran'sit-instrument (-strou-), *n.*, (astron.) lunette méridienne, *f.*

transi'tion (-cij'eune), *n.*, transition, *f.*

transi'tional (-cij'eu'n'-), *adj.*, de transition.

tran'sitive, *adj.*, qui passe ; (gram.) transitif.

tran'sitory (-teuri), *adj.*, transitoire, passager, fugitif.

translat'able (-lét'a-b'l), *adj.*, traduisible.

translate' (-léte), *v.a.*, (from one language) traduire ; (to convey to heaven) enlever au ciel ; (a bishop) transférer.

transla'tion (-lé-), *n.*, traduction ; (removal) translation, *f.*, déplacement ; (as a school-task) version, *f. ;* (to heaven) enlèvement, *m. ;* (of a bishop) translation, *f.*

transla'tor (-lé-teur), *m.*, traducteur, *m.*

transla'tress (-lé-tresse), *f.*, traductrice, *f.*

translu'cence *ou* **translu'cency** (-liou-), *n.*, transparence, diaphanéité ; translucidité, *f.*

translu'cent (-liou-), *adj.*, transparent ; diaphane ; translucide.

transmarine' (-rîne), *adj.*, d'outre-mer, transmarin.

trans'migrant, *adj.n.*, émigrant.

trans'migrate, *v.n.*, émigrer ; (of souls) transmigrer, passer d'un corps dans un autre.

transmigra'tion (-gré-), *n.*, transmigration ; (of souls) transmigration, métempsycose, *f.*

transmissibil'ity, *n.*, transmissibilité, *f.*

transmis'sible (-si-b'l), *adj.*, transmissible.

transmis'sion (-mish'-), *n.*, transmission, *f.*

transmis'sive, *adj.*, transmis, de transmission.

transmit', *v.a.*, transmettre ; envoyer ; (phys.) transmettre, conduire, laisser passer.

transmit'tal, *n.*, transmission, *f.*

transmit'ter, *n.*, personne qui transmet, *f. ;* (phys.) transmetteur, *m.*

transmutabil'ity (-miou-ta-), *n.*, transmutabilité, *f.*

transmu'table (-miou-ta-b'l), *adj.*, transmuable.

transmu'tably, *adv.*, de manière à pouvoir être transformé.

transmuta'tion (-miou-té-), *n.*, transmutation ; transformation, *f. ;* (of colors) changement, *m.*

transmute' (-mioute), *v.a.*, transmuer ; transformer.

transmut'er, *n.*, transmutateur, *m.*

tran'som (-ceume), *n.*, traverse de fenêtre ; (of a ship) barre d'arcasse, *f.*

transpa'rence (-pér'-), **transpar'ency**, *n.*, transparence, *f.*

transpar'ent (-pér'-), *adj.*, transparent, diaphane.

transpar'ently, *adj.*, avec transparence ;

clairement, évidemment. He is so — honest ; *il est si évidemment, ou clairement, honnête.*

transpierce' (-pîrce), *v.a.*, transpercer ; pénétrer.

transpira'tion (-spi-ré-), *n.*, transpiration ; exhalation, *f.*

transpire' (-spaïeure), *v.n.*, transpirer ; (to become public) transpirer ; (to happen) arriver, se passer, avoir lieu.

transplant', *v.a.*, transplanter ; déplacer, transporter.

transplanta'tion (-pla'n'té-), *n.*, transplantation, *f. ;* déplacement, *m.*

transplant'er, *n.*, transplanteur ; (thing) transplantoir, *m.*

transplant'ing, *n.*, transplantation, *f.*

trans'port (-pôrte), *n.*, transport ; (ship) transport ; (rapture) transport ; (of anger) transport, accès ; (convict) (ant.) forçat, déporté, *m.*

transport' (-pôrte), *v.a.*, transporter, transplanter ; (convicts) déporter. To — with ; *transporter* **de**. To be —ed with joy ; *être transporté* **de** *joie ; être dans le ravissement.*

transport'able (-pôrt'a-b'l), *adj.*, transportable ; (jur.) punissable de la déportation.

transporta'tion (-pôr-té-), *n.*, transport, *m. ;* transmission ; (of plants) transplantation ; (of convicts) déportation, *f. ;* (ecstasy) extase, *f.*

transport'edly, *adv.*, en extase, *f.*

transport'ing (-pôrt'-), *adj.*, ravissant, transportant.

transpos'al (-pôz'-), *n.*, transposition, *f.*

transpose' (-pôze), *v.a.*, transposer.

transpos'ing, *n.*, transposition, *f.*

transpos'ing, *adj.*, transpositeur.

transpos'itive (-poz'-), *adj.*, transpositif.

transubstan'tiate (-shi-éte), *v.a.*, (theol.) transsubstantier.

transubstantia'tion (-sta'n'shi-é-), *n.*, (theol.) transsubstantiation, *f.*

transuda'tion (-sioud'é-sheune), *n.*, transsudation, *f.*

transude' (-sioude), *v.n.*, transsuder.

transver'sal (-veur-), *adj.*, transversal.

transver'sally, *adv.*, transversalement, en travers.

trans'verse (-veurse), *adj.*, transverse ; oblique, transversal.

trans'versely, *adv.*, en travers ; transversalement.

trap, *n.*, trappe, *f. ;* traquenard, traquet ; (fig.) piège, *m.*, embûche ; (milit.) chausse-trape ; (game) balle à la volée ; (of a drain) valve, *f. ;* (mines) rejet, *m. ;* (carriage) carriole, petite voiture, *f. pl.*, effets, *m.pl.*, affaires, *f.pl.*, bagage, *m.* To be caught in the — ; *se laisser prendre au piège, donner dans le panneau.*

trap, *v.a.*, prendre au piège, attraper.

trap, *v.n.*, tendre, *ou* dresser, un piège à.

trapan', *n.*, piège, panneau, *m.*

trap'-ball, *n.*, balle à la volée, *f.*

trap'-door (-dôre), *n.*, trappe, *f. ;* (theat.) trapillon, *m.*

trapes (trépse), *n.*, souillon, *m f.*

trapeze' (-pîze), *n.*, (gymnastics) trapèze, *m.*

trape'zium (-pî-zi-), *n.*, (geom.) trapèze ; (anat.) os trapèze, *m.*

trapezoid'al (-zoïd'-), *adj.*, trapézoïde.

trap'pings (-pign'ze), *n.pl.*, harnachement, harnais, *m.sing. ;* ornements (du harnais), *m.pl. ;* (dress) parure, *f.s.*, ornements, atours, *m.pl.* The — of courts ; *la livrée des cours.* The — of woe ; *les vêtements de deuil.*

trap'-stick, *n.*, crosse (pour jouer), *f. ;* battoir, *m. ;* (of carts) clé, *ou* clef, de tombereau, *f. ;* (fig.) jambe grêle, *f.*

trash, *n.*, rebut, *m. ;* drogue, camelote ; (of eatables) drogue, cochonnerie, *f. ;* (loppings of trees) émondes, *f.pl. ;* (writings) fatras, *m.*, fadaises, *f.pl. ;* (bruised canes) bagasse, *f.*

trash'y, *adj.*, de rebut, de camelote ; méchant ; de nulle valeur ; de rien.

trav'ail (trav'il), *n.*, travail pénible, *m.* ; fatigue, *f.* ; (of women) travail d'enfant, *m.*

trave (tréve), *n.*, (arch.) traverse, *f.* ; (for a horse) travail, *m.* (pl. *travails*).

trav'el, *v.n.*, voyager ; être en voyage ; (to walk) cheminer, marcher ; (to pass) passer, marcher, aller ; (of news) circuler, voyager. To — over ; *parcourir* ; *voyager* **dans** ; *faire*. We —ed thirty miles in one day ; *nous fîmes trente milles en un jour*. To — on foot, on horseback ; *voyager à pied, à cheval.*

trav'el, *n.*, voyage, *m.* — stained ; *les vêtements souillés par le voyage, m.pl.*

trav'eled, *adj.*, qui a beaucoup voyagé ; (of a country) exploré.

trav'eler, *n.*, voyageur, *m.*, voyageuse, *f.* ; (com.) commis voyageur, *m.* —s tell fine tales ; (prov.) *a beau mentir qui vient de loin.*

trav'eler's-joy (-leur'z'djoè), *n.*, (bot.) clématite commune, herbe aux gueux, *f.*

trav'eling, *n.*, voyage, *m.* ; voyages, *m.pl.*

trav'eling, *adj.*, voyageur ; ambulant ; (of things) de voyage. —requisites ; *articles de voyage, m.pl.* — bag ; *sac de nuit*, ou *de voyage, m.* —case ; *nécessaire de voyage, m.* — expenses ; *frais de voyage, m.pl.* — post-office ; *bureau de poste ambulant, m.* — rug ; *couverture de voyage, f.*

trav'ersable (-veurs'a-b'l), *adj.*, (jur.) niable ; (able to be crossed) qui peut être traversé.

trav'erse (trav'eurse), *n.*, traverse ; (cross accident) traverse, *f.*, obstacle, *m.* ; (jur.) dénégation ; (nav.) bordée, route oblique ; (fort.) traverse, *f.*

trav'erse, *adj.*, oblique ; transversal.

trav'erse, *prep.*, à travers.

trav'erse, *adv.*, à travers, en travers.

trav'erse (-veurse), *v.a.*, traverser ; (to survey) scruter, examiner ; (jur.) nier, dénier ; (artil.) pointer.

trav'erse, *v.n.*, tourner, pivoter ; (fenc.) se tenir en garde.

trav'erser, *n.*, (jur.) défendeur, *m.*

trav'estier, *n.*, travertisseur, *m.*

trav'esty, *n.*, travesti, *m.* ; traduction burlesque ; parodie, *f.*

trav'esty, *v.a.*, travestir, parodier.

trawl, *n.*, (net) chalut, *m.* ; traille, *f.* *v.n.*, pêcher au chalut, à la traille, chaluter.

trawl'er, *n.*, (pers.) chalutier, pêcheur à la traille ; (boat) bateau chalutier, chalutier, *m.*

trawl'ing, *n.*, pêche au chalut, *f.*

tray (tré), *n.*, plateau, *m.* ; (trough) auge, *f.* ; baquet, *m.* ; (of a wardrobe) coulisse, *f.* Ash — ; *petit cendrier, m.*

treach'erous (trètsh'eur'-), *adj.*, traître, perfide, déloyal.

treach'erously (trètsh'eur'-), *adv.*, en traître ; perfidement ; traîtreusement.

treach'erousness *ou* **treach'ery** (trètsheur'-), *n.*, trahison, perfidie, *f.*

trea'cle (trî-k'l), *n.*, mélasse, *f.*

tread (trède), *v.n.*, (*preterit*, Trod ; *past part.*, Trodden) poser le pied ; marcher **sur** ; (of the feet) se poser ; (of birds) cocher. To — on ; *marcher* **sur** ; *fouler aux pieds*. To — in any one's footsteps ; *marcher sur les traces* **de**, *sur les pas* **de**.

tread, *v.a.*, marcher **sur** ; fouler ; fouler aux pieds; écraser. To — under foot ; *fouler aux pieds*. To — the stage ; *parcourir la scène*. To — the boards ; *être acteur* ; *monter sur les planches*.

tread (trède), *n.*, pas, *m.* ; (of a stair) marche, *f.* ; giron, *m.* ; (man.) allure, *f.* ; poser, *m.* ; (of birds) accouplement, *m.*

tread'ing, *m.*, foulement, pas, *m.* ; marche, *f.* — out ; *écrasement, m.* ; (of corn) dépiquage, *m.*

trea'dle (trèd-d'l), *n.*, marche ; pédale, *f.* ; (of an egg) cordon albumineux, germe, *m.*

tread'-mill, *n.*, moulin de discipline, *m.*

trea'son (trî-z'n), *n.*, trahison, *f.* High-— ; *haute trahison* ; *lèse-majesté* ; (against the nation) *lèse-nation, f.*

trea'sonable (trî-z'n'a-b'l), *adj.*, de traître ; de trahison ; (of a speech) séditieux.

trea'sonably, *adv.*, en traître, traîtreusement.

treas'ure (trèj'eur), *n.*, trésor, *m.*

treas'ure *ou* **treas'ure up** (trèj'eur-), *v.a.*, amasser, accumuler ; garder, conserver précieusement.

treas'ure-house (-haouce), *n.*, trésor, *m.* ; trésorerie, *f.*

treas'urer (trèj'eur'-), *n.*, trésorier, caissier ; (bursar) économe, *m.*

treas'urership, *n.*, charge de trésorier, *f.*

treas'ure-trove (-trôve), *n.*, (jur.) trésor, *m.*

treas'ury (trèj'euri), *n.*, trésor ; (building) trésor, trésor public, *m.* ; trésorerie, *f.* First lord of the — ; *Président du Conseil* (*des ministres*). The — ; *le Ministère des finances.*

treat (trîte), *v.a.*, traiter ; (to regale) traiter, régaler (with, **de**) ; (med.) traiter, soigner. To — one to ; *régaler quelqu'un* **de** ; *payer à boire à quelqu'un*. To — of ; *traiter* **de** ; (in a lecture or speech) *discourir* **sur**. To — with ; (negotiate) *traiter* **avec**.

treat, *v.n.*, traiter.

treat (trîte), *n.*, régal ; festin, banquet, *m.* ; fête, *f.* ; (pleasure) charme, délice, plaisir, grand plaisir, *m.* To stand — ; *régaler* ; *payer à boire.*

treat'er (trît'-), *n.*, personne qui traite, *f.* ; (regaler) amphitryon, *m.*

treat'ise (trî-tize), *n.*, (book) traité, *m.*

treat'ment (trît'-), *n.*, traitement, *m.* ; manière d'agir, *f.*

treat'y (trî-), *n.*, traité ; pacte, *m.* ; convention ; négociation, *f.* By private — ; *à l'amiable*. To be in — for ; *être en négociation* **pour** ; *être en pourparlers* **pour**.

treb'le (trèb'b'l), *v.a.* and *n.*, tripler.

treb'le, *adj.*, triple ; (mus.) de dessus ; (of sound) aigu, perçant.

treb'le (trè'b'l), *n.*, triple ; (mus.) dessus, *m.* Shrill, *ou* high, *ou* false — ; *fausset*, m., ou *voix de tête, f.*

treb'ling (trèb'-), *n.*, triplement, *m.*

treb'ly (trèb'-), *adv.*, triplement, trois fois.

tree (trî), *n.*, (bot.) arbre ; arbrisseau ; (of a saddle) pontet ; (for boots) embauchoir, *m.* ; (rel.) croix, *f.* ; (nav.) gournable, *m.* Axle-— ; essieu, *m.* At the top of the — ; *au haut de l'échelle*. To be up a — ; (fig., fam.) *être à bout de ressources* ; *être au bout de son rouleau*. To be at the top of the — ; *tenir le haut du pavé*. Genealogical — ; *arbre généalogique*.

tree'less, *adj.*, sans arbre.

tree'-nail, *n.*, cheville, *f.*

tree'-nail, *v.a.*, cheviller ensemble.

tree'-sparrow, *n.*, moineau des bois, *m.*

tre'foil (trî-foïl), *n.*, (bot.) trèfle, (arch.) trèfle, *m.*

treil'lage (trèl'èdje), *n.*, treillage, *m.*

trel'lis, *n.*, treillis, treillage, *m.*

trel'lis, *v.a.*, treillisser.

trel'lised (trèl'liste), *adj.*, treillissé.

trem'ble (trèm'b'l), *v.n.*, trembler ; (of sound) trembloter.

trem'bler, *n.*, trembleur, *m.*, trembleuse, *f.*

trem'bling, *n.*, tremblement, *m.*

trem'bling, *adj.*, tremblant ; tremblotant.

trem'blingly, *adv.*, en tremblant ; en tremblotant.

tremen'dous, *adj.*, redoutable ; formidable ; terrible ; imposant ; (violent) terrible, épouvantable, horrible.

tremen'dously, *adv.*, terriblement ; (with violence) terriblement, furieusement.

tremen'dousness, n., caractère terrible, caractère formidable, m., nature terrible, f.

trem'or (trè'm'eur), n., tremblement, m.

trem'ulous (trè'm'iou-), adj., tremblant; tremblotant; (mus.) chevrotant.

trem'ulously, adv., en tremblant; en tremblotant; (mus.) en chevrotant.

trem'ulousness, n., tremblotement; tremblement; (of the voice) chevrotement, m.

trench, n., (agri.) tranchée; rigole, f., fossé, m.; (milit.) tranchée, f.

trench, v.a., (to cut short) trancher; (to cut) trancher, tailler, couper; creuser, ouvrir; (to furrow) sillonner; (milit.) retrancher.

trench (upon), v.n., empiéter **sur**.

trench'er, n., tranchoir, tailloir, m.; (table) table; (food) bonne chère, f. — board; bonnet carré, m.; toque universitaire, f.

trench'er-friend (-frè'n'de) ou **-knight**, n., ami de table, parasite, pique-assiette, écornifleur, m.

trench'er-man, n., gros mangeur, m.

trend, n., direction; tendance, f. The — of public opinion; la direction de l'opinion publique.

trend, v.n., (nav.) courir; fuir; (to go towards) se diriger, tendre; (to extend) s'étendre.

tren'dle (trè'n'd'l), n., roulette, f.

trepan' (tri-), n., (surg.) trépan, m.

trepan' (tri-), v.a., trépaner.

trepan'ning (tri-), n., (surg.) trépan, m.; trépanation, f.

trepida'tion (trèp'i-dé-), n., trépidation; vibration, f.; (trembling) tremblement, m.; (hurry) hâte; (terror) terreur, f., effroi, m.

tres'pass (très-), n., injure; (jur.) violation de propriété, f., délit contre la personne, m.; (in Scripture) offense, f., péché, m., transgression, f.

tres'pass (très-), v.n., abuser **de**; (jur.) violer la propriété; (in Scripture) pécher, faillir. To — against; violer, enfreindre; (pers.) nuire à, léser. To — on; empiéter **sur**; abuser **de**.

tres'passer, n., personne qui empiète, f.; intrus; (jur.) violateur du droit de propriété; délinquant; (rel.) pécheur, m., pécheresse, f., transgresseur, m. —s will be prosecuted; défense d'entrer sous peine d'amende.

tres'pass-of'fering (-of'feur'-), n., sacrifice expiatoire (pour le péché), m.

tress, n., tresse; boucle, f.

tressed (très'te), adj., tressé; bouclé; en tresses.

tres'sel ou **tres'tle** (très's'l), n., tréteau; (of a table) châssis, m., pl., échelle double, f. — bed; lit de sangle, m. — bridge; pont sur chevalets, m.

tress'ing, n., (arch.) armature, f.

tret (trète), n., (com.) réfaction (sur le poids), f.

trev'et (trèv'-), n. V. **triv'et**.

trey (trè), n., (at cards) trois, m.

tri'able (traï-a-b'l), adj., qu'on peut essayer, qu'on peut éprouver; (jur.) justiciable, du ressort **de**.

tri'ad (traï-ade), n., triade, f.

tri'al (traï-al), n., tentative, f.; essai, m.; (experiment) expérience, épreuve, f.; essai, m.; (temptation) épreuve; (jur.) cause, f.; débats, m.pl.; procès, jugement, m.; (suffering) épreuve, f. To bring to —; mettre en jugement. To make a — of; faire l'essai **de**. To take one's —; passer en jugement; être jugé. To grant a new —; (jur.) accorder l'appel. To move for a new —; demander à interjeter appel. By way of —; pour essayer; pour essai. On —; à l'essai; (of things) pour essai. A sad —; une grande épreuve. It is a — to me to have to do it; c'est une grande épreuve pour moi que d'avoir à le faire. — trip; voyage d'essai, m.

tri'angle (traï-a'gn'g'l), n., triangle, m.

tri'angled (traï-a'gn'g'l'de), adj., triangulé.

trian'gular (traï-a'gn-ghiou-), adj., triangulaire.

trian'gularly, adv., triangulairement.

tribe (traïbe), n., tribu; peuplade; (b.s.) race, famille; (natur. hist.) tribu, famille, classe, f., ordre, m.

trib'let ou **trib'olet**, n., (forge) mandrin, m.

tribula'tion (trib'iou-lé-), n., tribulation, f.

tribu'nal (tri-biou-), n., tribunal, m.

trib'une (trib'ioune), n., (Rom. antiq.) tribun, m.; (pulpit) tribune, galerie, f.

trib'utary (trib'iou-), adj., tributaire; (subordinate) inférieur, subordonné.

trib'utary (trib'iou-), n., tributaire, m.; (a stream) affluent, tributaire, m.

trib'ute (trib'ioute) ou **trib'ute-money**, n., tribut, m.

trice (traïce), n., instant, moment, clin d'œil, m. In a —; en un clin d'œil.

trice (traïce), v.a., (nav.) hisser; mettre à la serre.

tricen'nial, adj., tous les trente ans.

trichino'sis, n., trichinose, f.

tri'cing-line (traï-cign'laïne), n., (nav.) aiguillette, f.

trick, n., (cheat) supercherie, duperie, tricherie, f.; (dexterous artifice) artifice, m., ruse, finesse, f., tour, m.; (jest.) malice, niche, f.; (of a juggler) tour, m.; (of children) espièglerie; (habit) habitude, f., tic, m.; (of cards) levée, f. To know a — or two; en savoir plus d'une. To be at one's —s again; faire encore des siennes. I know a — worth two of that; j'ai quelque chose de meilleur à vous proposer; je connais un meilleur expédient. To play any one a —; faire une niche à; jouer un tour à quelqu'un. To have the —; (at cards) faire la levée. The —s of the trade; les ruses, ou les tours, du métier. Nasty —; vilain tour, m.; (habit) vilaine habitude, f. Shabby —; vilenie, f.

trick, v.a., duper; tricher; (to play a trick on) faire une niche à; (to dress) orner, ajuster, parer, (jest.) atourner; (to draw) esquisser. To — out; parer, orner; (jest.) atourner. —ed out; paré **de**, attifé **de**; dessiné **sur**.

trick'ery, n., tromperie, duperie; tricherie, f.

trick'ing, n., tromperie, duperie, supercherie; (ornament) parure, f., atours, m.pl.

trick'ish, adj., artificieux, astucieux; trompeur; fourbe; fin, subtil, captieux.

tric'kle, v.n., couler; découler, ruisseler, dégoutter, s'épancher. To — down; couler le long de, dégoutter **de**, ruisseler **de**.

trick'ling, n., écoulement, murmure, m.

trick'ster, n., fourbe, m. f.; trompeur, farceur, mauvais plaisant; tricheur, m.

trick'track, n., (game) trictrac, m.

trick'y, adj., (of light) incertain, changeant. V. **trick'ish**.

tri'color (traï-keul'eur), n., drapeau tricolore, m.

tri'colored (traï-keul'leurde), adj., tricolore.

tri'cycle, n., tricycle, m.

tri'cyclist, n., tricycliste, m.

tri'dent (traï-), n., trident, m.

tri'dented (traï-), adj., (bot.) tridenté.

tried (traïde), adj., éprouvé.

trien'nial (traï-), adj., triennal.

trien'nially (traï-), adv., tous les trois ans.

tri'er (traï-), n., expérimentateur, essayeur, ajusteur, m.; (test) pierre de touche, épreuve, f.

tri'fid (traï-), adj., (bot.) trifide.

tri'fle (traï-f'l), n., bagatelle; vétille; babiole, f.; rien, m.; (small quantity) idée, f.; soupçon, m. To stand upon —s; s'arrêter à des vétilles, à des riens. To dispute about —s; disputer sur la pointe d'une aiguille. I gave him a —; je lui ai donné quelque chose pour lui.

tri'fle (traï-f'l), v.n., s'amuser à des riens, niaiser; badiner; baguenauder; (to act or talk with levity) être frivole, être léger. To — away, v.a., gaspiller, perdre. To — with; (things) jouer avec, plaisanter avec ou sur; (pers.) amuser; (to mock) se moquer de, se rire de. He is not the man to be —d with; ce n'est pas un homme qu'on mène tambour battant, ou dont on se moque.

tri'fler (traï-), n., personne frivole, f.; baguenaudier, lanternier, m.

tri'fling (traï-), adj., de rien; insignifiant; petit; (playful) badin; (trivial) futile, oiseux; (frivolous) frivole, léger. — but troublesome debt; dette criarde, f. A — matter; peu de chose.

tri'fling, n., légèreté, frivolité; plaisanterie, f.; bagatelles, f.pl.; badinage, m.

tri'flingness, n., petitesse, insignifiance, f.

triform' (traï-), adj., ayant une triple forme.

trig'amy, n., trigamie, f.

trig'ger (trig-gheur), n., enrayure; (of firearms) détente, f. —-guard; pontet, m.

trigonomet'rical (-mèt'-), adj., trigonométrique.

trigonom'etry (-no'm-i-), n., trigonométrie, f.

trihe'dral (traï-hî-), adj., (geom.) trièdre.

trilat'eral (traï-lat'eur'-), adj., trilatéral.

trill, n., (mus.) trille, m. v.a.n., triller.

trill'ion (tril'ieune), n., quintillion, m.

trilo'bate (traï-), adj., (bot.) trilobé.

trim, v.a., arranger; ajuster; (to decorate) orner, parer de; (to dress) habiller; (to lop) émonder; (to clip) tailler, rafraîchir; (to finish off) achever; (to scold) gronder; savonner, arranger; (nav.) (the hold) arrimer; (the sails) orienter; (the yards) brasser carré (when not sailing); (a boat) dresser; asseoir; (a lamp) arranger, préparer; (carp.) dégrossir, planer; (a garment) garnir; (a horse) panser, faire le poil à; (timber) équarrir. To — in; (carp.) assembler. To — up; arranger, ajuster; (to decorate) garnir de; (to dress) parer, orner de. To know how to — one's sails; (fig.) savoir ménager la chèvre et le chou, ou nager entre deux eaux.

trim, v.n., hésiter; balancer entre deux partis; tergiverser.

trim, adj., propre, gentil, coquet; bien ajusté; bien arrangé; (of sails) bien orienté.

trim, n., parure, toilette, f., ornement; (state) état, m.; (of a ship) assiette, f.; (of sails) orientement; (of the hold) arrimage, m. To be in proper —; être en bon ordre; en bon état. In good —; bien arrangé, bien tenu, bien soigné, à sa place. Out of —; dérangé, hors de place.

trim'eter, n., (prosody) trimètre, m.

trim'ly, adv., bien, gentiment, proprement.

trim'mer, n., garnisseur; ajusteur, décorateur; (time-server) girouette, homme de tous les partis; (of trees) émondeur; (arch.) bande de trémie, f.

trim'ming, n., garniture; passementerie; arrangement, ornement, m.; (scolding) danse, semonce, f.; savon, m.; (of trees) émondage, m.; (nav.) (of the hold) arrimage, m.; (of the sails) orientation; (fig.) tergiversation, vacillation, hésitation, f.

trim'ness, n., netteté, propreté, f.; bon ordre, m.; (of appearance) coquetterie, f.

trine, **tri'nal**, adj., triple.

trin'gle (trin'g'l), n., (arch.) tringle, f.

trinita'rian (tri'n'i-té-), n., trinitaire, m.

Trin'ity, n., Trinité, f. — Sunday; dimanche de la Trinité, m.

trin'ket (trin'gn'-), n., bijou, m.; breloque, f.; (thing of little value) colifichet, brimborion, m.

trino'mial (traï-nô-), n., (alg.) trinôme, m.

tri'o (traï-ô), n., (mus.) trio, m.

tri'olet (traï-), n., (poet.) triolet, m.

trip, n., croc-en-jambe; (stumble) faux pas, m.; (error) méprise, boulette; (journey) excursion, tournée, f., tour, petit voyage, partie; (voyage) voyage, m.; (nav.) bordée, f.

trip, v.a., donner un croc-en-jambe à, renverser; faire trébucher, tomber; (to supplant) supplanter; couper l'herbe sous le pied de; (to detect) découvrir, surprendre, démasquer; (an anchor) faire déraper; (to dance) danser.

trip, v.n., trébucher, faire un faux pas; tomber; (to err) errer, se tromper; (of the tongue) fourcher, tourner; (to run lightly) courir avec légèreté; (to step lightly) marcher avec légèreté; (to take a journey) faire un petit voyage.

tripart'ite (traï-par-taïte), adj., triparti; tripartite.

tripe (traïpe), n., tripes, f.pl.; gras-double, m. —-man, -woman; tripier, m., tripière, f. — shop; triperie, f.

triph'thong (trip'thogne), n., triphtongue, f.

triphyl'lous (traï-fil-), adj., (bot.) triphylle.

trip'le (trip'p'l), adj., triple. v.a., tripler.

trip'let, n., trio; (poet.) tercet; (mus.) triolet, m.

trip'licate, adj., (math.) triplé. — ratio; (math.) raison triplée, f.; (copy) triplicata, m. In —; en triplicata.

triplica'tion (-pli-ké-), n., triplication, f., triplement, m.

triplic'ity, n., triplicité, f.

trip'ly, adv., triplement, trois fois.

tri'pod (traï-), n., trépied, m.

trip'oli, n., (min.) tripoli, m.

tri'pos (traï-), n., (univ.) grand concours, concours général, m.

trip'per, n., danseur; (pop.) excursionniste, m.

trip'ping, n., bronchade, f.; faux pas, m.; faute, erreur, f.; pas léger, m., danse légère, f. — up; croc en jambe, m.

trip'ping, adj., (nimble) agile, léger, leste; (quick) rapide.

trip'pingly, adv., agilement; légèrement; vivement, lestement, d'un pas léger.

tri'reme (traï-rîme), n., trirème, f.

trisect' (traï-cèkte), v.a., diviser en trois parties, couper en trois.

trisyllab'ic ou trisyllab'ical (tri-cil'-), adj., trissyllabe; trissyllabique.

trisyl'lable (tri-cil'-), n., trissyllabe, m.

trite (traïte), adj., usé, banal, rebattu, trivial, commun.

trite'ly (traït'-), adv., banalement, trivialement.

trite'ness (traït'-), n., nature banale, trivialité, f.

tri'ton (traï-), n., (myth., zoöl.) triton, m.

trit'urable (trit'iou-ra-b'l), adj., triturable.

trit'urate (trit'iou-), v.a., triturer.

tritura'tion (trit'iou-ré-), n., trituration, f.

tri'umph (traï-eu'm'fe), n., triomphe, m.; (exultation) joie triomphante, f.

tri'umph (traï-eu'm'fe), v.n., triompher; (to flourish) prospérer. To — over; triompher de, insulter à. To — over (it or them); en triompher; (to surmount) surmonter, l'emporter sur.

trium'phal (traï-eu'm'-), adj., triomphal; de triomphe. — arch; arc de triomphe, m.

trium'phant (traï-eu'm'-), adj., triomphant; triomphal, triomphateur; de triomphe.

trium'phantly, adv., en triomphe, triomphalement; d'un air de triomphe.

tri'umpher, n., triomphateur, vainqueur, m.

trium'vir (traï-eu'm'veur), n., (triumviri) (Rom. hist.) triumvir, m.

trium'virate (-veur'-), n., triumvirat, m.

triv'et (tri-), n., trépied; (kitchen utensil) trépied, trois-pieds, m. To be as right as a —; (pop.) être on ne peut mieux portant.

triv'ial, n., trivial, vulgaire; insignifiant; sans importance.

triv'ially, adv., trivialement, vulgairement; d'une manière insignifiante.

triv'ialness, **trivial'ity**, n., trivialité; vulgarité, f.; (unimportance) nullité, f.

troat (trôte), *v.n.*, (of the buck) bramer, raire, réer.

troat (trôte), *n.*, (of the buck) bramement, *m.*

trocha′ic *ou* **trocha′ical** (tro-ké-), *adj.*, (prosody) trochaïque.

tro′chee (trô-kî), *n.*, (prosody) trochée, *m.*

Tro′jan (tro-dja′ne), *n.*, Troyen, *m.*, Troyenne, *f.*

Tro′jan, *adj.*, troyen. — war ; *la guerre de Troie.*

troll (trôl), *v.n.*, rouler, tourner ; pêcher à la ligne.

troll′ing, *n.*, pêche au brochet (à la ligne).

trol′lop, *n.*, salope, souillon, *f.*

trol′ly, trol′ley, *n.*, fardier, binard, *m.*

trombone′ (-bône), *n.*, (mus.) trombone, *m.*

troop, *n.*, troupe, *f. ;* (of cavalry) corps ; peloton, *m.*, compagnie, *f.* A — of horse ; *un détachement de cavalerie.*

troop (troupe), *v.n.*, s'attrouper ; s'assembler ; (to march in a body) marcher en corps.

troop′er (troup′-), *n.*, cavalier, soldat de cavalerie ; troupier ; (troopship) transport, *m.*

tro′phied (trô-fide), *adj.*, orné de trophées.

tro′phy (trô-fi), *n.*, trophée, *m.*

trop′ic, *n.*, (geog.) tropique, *m.*

trop′ical, *adj.*, tropical ; du tropique ; des tropiques ; (rhet.) figuratif, symbolique, emblématique, métaphorique.

trop′ically, *adv.*, figurativement.

trop′ic-bird (-beurde), *n.*, (orni.) oiseau des tropiques ; phaéton ; paille-en-queue, *m.*

tropolo′gical (-′o-djic′-), *adj.*, (rhet.) tropologique, figuré.

trot, *n.*, trot, *m.* Jog — ; *petit trot.* Full — ; *grand trot.* At a gentle — ; *au petit trot.* At a jog- — pace ; *cahin-caha.*

trot, *v.n.*, trotter, aller le trot, au trot ; courir. To — out ; *faire marcher, montrer l'allure ;* (fig.) *avancer, mettre en avant.*

troth (troth), *n.*, foi, fidélité ; vérité, *f.* By my — ! *ma foi !* To plight one's — ; *engager sa foi.* In — ; *en vérité.*

trot′ter, *n.*, cheval de trot ; trotteur ; (sheep's foot) pied de mouton, *m. ;* (pigs) pied de cochon.

trot′ting, *n.*, trot, *m.*

trot′ting, *adj.*, trotteur. — match, *ou* race ; *course au trot, f.*

trou′badour (trou-ba-dour), *n.*, troubadour, *m.*

troub′le (treub′b′l), *v.a.* (with, about, de) troubler, inquiéter ; (to disturb) déranger, importuner ; (to perplex) tourmenter, agiter ; (to distress) chagriner, affliger ; (to busy) préoccuper, occuper ; (to vex) ennuyer, tracasser ; (to give occasion for labor to) donner de la peine à ; donner la peine de ; charger de, prier de ; (a debtor) importuner. I will — you to pass me that; *auriez-vous la bonté de me passer cela ?* I will not — you with it; *je ne veux pas vous en embarrasser.* I will not — you in this affair; *je ne veux pas vous déranger (importuner) pour cette affaire.* I will not — you ; *je ne veux pas vous donner cette peine.* May I — you to move ? *auriez-vous la bonté de me laisser passer ?* May I — you for a light ? *puis-je vous demander du feu ? voulez-vous avoir la bonté de me donner une allumette ?* May I — you to ? *puis-je vous prier de ?* May I — you to post this letter ? *voulez-vous avoir la bonté de jeter cette lettre à la poste ?* To — one's self ; *se déranger ; se donner la peine de ; s'embarrasser de ; s'inquiéter de ; se mettre en peine de.*

troub′le (treub′b′l), *n.*, (disturbance) trouble, *m. ;* (fatigue, work) peine ; (uneasiness) inquiétude ; (affliction) affliction, peine, *f.*, souci, chagrin, *m. ;* (annoyance) importunité, tracasserie, *f.*, ennui, dérangement, *m. ;* (pains) peine, *f.* To be in — ; *être dans la peine, dans le chagrin ; avoir de la peine, du chagrin, des soucis.* To **give, to** save any one — ; *donner, épargner de la*

peine à quelqu'un. I gave myself all the — in the world ; *je me suis donné toutes les peines du monde,* ou *un mal infini.* I got into no end of — ; *je me suis attiré une foule de désagréments.* To take the — to ; *prendre, se donner la peine de.* Out of one's — ; *hors de peine.* It is not worth the — ; *ce n'est pas la peine ; cela n'en vaut pas la peine.* To get into — ; *se faire une mauvaise affaire ; s'attirer des désagréments ;* (fam.) *se mettre dans le pétrin ;* (to be detected and punished) *se faire pincer ; tomber dans la nasse.*

troub′led, *adj.*, inquiet ; agité, troublé ; (of water) trouble, fangeux. To be — about ; *s'inquiéter de, se préoccuper de.*

troub′ler, *n.*, perturbateur, *m.*

troub′lesome (treub′b′l′ceume), *adj.*, ennuyeux ; incommode ; gênant, embarrassant ; (tiresome) fatigant, ennuyeux, tracassier, tourmentant ; (importunate) ennuyeux, fâcheux, importun ; (burdensome) à charge à. Children are very — ; *les enfants donnent beaucoup de peine.*

troub′lesomely, *adv.*, d'une manière ennuyeuse ; avec importunité.

troub′lesomeness, *n.*, ennui ; embarras ; désagrément, *m. ;* (importunity) importunité, *f.*

troub′lous, *adj.*, (l.u.) troublé, agité, orageux ; plein de troubles, de désordres.

trough (trofe), *n.*, auge ; huche, *f. ;* (kneading-trough) pétrin ; (for a bird, etc.) auget ; (metal.) creuset ; (of the sea) entre-deux des lames *ou* creux des vagues, *m.; (*of a mill) auge, *f.*

trounce (traou′n′ce), *v.a.*, rosser, étriller.

tron′sering, *n.*, étoffe pour pantalons, *f.*

trou′sers *ou* **trow′sers** (traou-zeurze), *n.pl.*, pantalon, *m.sing.* A pair of — ; *un pantalon.* — pocket ; *poche de pantalon, f.* — strap ; *sous-pied, m.*

trout (traoute), *n.*, (ich.) truite, *f.*

trout′-colored (-keul′leurde), *adj.*, truité.

trout′-fishing, *n.*, pêche de la truite, *f.*

trout′-net, *n.*, étave, *f.*

trout′-stream (-strîme), *n.*, vivier à truites, *m.*

tro′ver (trôv′-), *n.*, (jur.) demande en restitution d'une chose trouvée, *f.*

trow (trô), *v.n.*, (ant.) penser, croire, s'imaginer.

trow′el (traou′èl), *n.*, truelle, *f. ;* (gard.) déplantoir, *m.*

trow′sers, *n.pl.* V. **trousers.**

troy′-weight (troï-wéte), *n.*, poids de douze onces à la livre, *m.*

tru′ant (trou-), *adj.*, fainéant, paresseux, flâneur, vagabond.

tru′ant (trou-), *n.*, fainéant, paresseux, flâneur ; vagabond, *m.* To play —, ou the — ; *faire l'école buissonnière.*

tru′antcy, *n.*, fainéantise, paresse, flânerie, *f.*

tru′antly, *adv.*, en fainéant, en paresseux.

truce (trouce), *n.*, trêve, *f.* A — to ; *trêve de ; trève à.* Flag of — ; *pavillon parlementaire, m.*

truce′-breaker (-brèk′-), *n.*, violateur de trêve, *m.*

truck (treuke), *n.*, (barter) troc, échange ; (manu.) paiement en marchandises, *m. ;* (wooden wheel) roue de bois, *f. ;* (cart) camion, binard, *m. ;* charrette à bras, brouette, *f. ;* (artil.) roue d'affût ; (nav.) cosse de bois ; (on topmasts, etc.) pomme ; (railways) plate-forme, *f.*, truc, truck, wagon, *m.* —-system ; *système de payer les ouvriers en marchandises, m.* — man ; *camionneur, m.*

truck (treuke), *v.a.* and *n.*, troquer.

truck′age (treuk′èdje), *n.*, troc, échange ; (transport) camionnage, *m.*

truck′er (treuk′-), *n.*, troqueur, trafiquant, *m.*

truc′kle (treuk′l), *n.*, roulette, *f.*

truc′kle (treuk′l), *v.n.*, céder, se soumettre à ; s'abaisser **devant** ; ramper, s'humilier **devant** ; faire le chien couchant.

truc'kle-bed (-bède), n., lit à roulettes, grabat, m.

truc'kling, n., soumission, humiliation, f., abaissement, m.

truc'ulence (treu-kiou-), n., barbarie, férocité, cruauté ; truculence, f.

truc'ulent, adj., barbare, brutal, féroce ; (destructive) meurtrier, cruel ; d'un aspect terrible.

trudge (treudje), v.n., aller à pied, cheminer ; faire route à pied ; marcher péniblement, se traîner ; (pop.) trimer, battre la semelle.

true (trou), adj., vrai ; (real) vrai, réel, véritable ; (faithful) fidèle ; (free from falsehood) vrai, exact, fidèle ; (speaking truth) véridique, sincère ; (honest) honnête, intègre, loyal ; (exact) exact, conforme ; (straight) droit ; (rightful) légitime. — to; fidèle à.

true, int., c'est vrai ! c'est juste !

true'-born, adj., de naissance légitime ; vrai ; véritable.

true'-bred (-brède), adj., de bonne race ; pur sang ; (fig.) accompli, achevé, véritable, vrai.

true'-hearted (-hârt'-), adj., au cœur sincère.

true'-heartedness, n., sincérité de cœur, f.

true'-love (-leuve), n., bien-aimé, m., bien-aimée ; (bot.) parisette, f. ; raisin-de-renard, m.

true'ness, n., vérité ; sincérité ; fidélité ; (genuineness) vérité, authenticité, f.

truf'fle (treu-f'l), n., truffe, f. v.a., truffer.

truf'fle-ground ou **-bed** (-graou'n'de), n., truffière, f.

tru'ism (trou-iz'm), n., vérité évidente, f., truisme, m.

tru'ly (trou-li), adv., vraiment ; (exactly) vraiment, réellement, véritablement ; (sincerely) vraiment, fidèlement ; (ironically) ma foi ! Yours —; tout à vous, bien à vous.

trump (treu'm'pe), n., trompe, trompette, f. ; (at cards) atout ; (pers.) brave garçon, brave cœur, m. — card ; atout, m. ; retourne, f.

trump (treu'm'pe), v.a., jouer atout, couper. To — over ; surcouper. To — up ; inventer, forger, imaginer, machiner, manigancer. It is a —ed up story ; c'est une histoire inventée.

trum'pery (treu'm'p'-), n., éclat trompeur ; faux brillant ; (rubbish) rebut, m., pacotille, friperie ; (nonsense) farce, blague, f.

trum'pery, adj., faux, sans valeur ; (of goods) de camelote ; (fig.) méchant, pitoyable, mesquin ; ridicule, insignifiant. A — thing ; une drogue. A — affair ; une vétille.

trum'pet (treu'm'-), n., trompette ; trompe ; (praiser) louangeur ; prôneur, f. ; (trumpeter) trompette, m. Speaking——, porte-voix, m. To blow one's own — ; chanter ses propres louanges ; faire claquer son fouet.

trum'pet, v.a., publier à son de trompe ; proclamer ; trompeter, prôner.

trum'pet, v.n., (of elephants) barrir.

trum'pet-blast, -call, coup de trompette, m.

trum'peter (-'èt'eur), n., trompette ; (orni.) agami, oiseau trompette, m. ; (fig.) trompette, f.

trum'pet-flower (-flaoueur), n., (bot.) bignone, f.

trum'pet-shaped (-shép'te), adj., en trompette ; (bot.) tubulé, tubuleux.

trum'pet-tongued (-teugn'de), adj., à voix de stentor.

trun'cate (treugn'-), v.a., tronquer, mutiler.

trun'cated (treugn'két'-), adj., tronqué.

trunca'tion, n., mutilation, f.

trun'cheon (treu'n'sheune), n., gourdin, rondin ; gros bâton, m.

trun'dle (treu'n'd'l), n., roulette, f. ; (cart) camion, m.

trun'dle (treu'n'd'l), v.a., rouler ; (a hoop) faire courir, faire aller, faire rouler.

trun'dle-bed, n., lit à roulettes, m.

trunk (treugn'ke), n., tronc ; (box) coffre, m.,

maille, f. ; (long tube) long tube, m., sarbacane, f. ; (anat., arch.) tronc ; (sculpt.) torse ; (of elephants, of insects) trompe, f. — -hose ; chausses, f.pl. — line ; (rail.) grande ligne, f. — -maker ; coffretier, m.

trun'nion (treu'n'ieune), n., tourillon, axe, m.

truss (treusse), n., trousse ; (bot.) touffe ; (of hay, straw) botte ; (nav.) drosse (de racage) ; (surg.) bandage herniaire, m. ; suspensoir ; (carp.) nœud, m., ferme (triangulaire), f., lien, m. ; (of bridges) travée ; console, f.

truss (treusse), v.a., empaqueter ; serrer ; attacher ; lier ; (poultry) trousser, brider.

truss'er, n., trousseur, f.

truss'-maker (-mék'-), n., bandagiste, m.

trust (treuste), n., (confidence) confiance ; (ground of confidence) espérance ; (charged, received in confidence) confiance, f. ; (something committed to a person's care) dépôt, m. ; (care) garde ; (state of one to whom something is intrusted) place de confiance, f. ; (credit) crédit ; (jur.) fidéicommis, m. On — ; de confiance ; (com.) à crédit. To hold in — ; avoir en dépôt ; (jur.) tenir par fidéicommis. To put — in ; mettre confiance en. I resign my — into your hands ; je vous rends le dépôt que vous m'avez confié (Racine). To give any one — ; (com.) faire crédit à quelqu'un.

trust (treuste), v.a., se fier à ; se confier à ; mettre sa confiance en ; (to believe) ajouter foi à, croire ; (to commit to the care of) confier ; (to give credit to) faire crédit à ; (to give credit for, de) ; donner à crédit à. To — with ; confier à ; (to give credit to) faire crédit à. I dare not — myself in it ; je n'ose m'y hasarder. He is not to be —ed ; il est sujet à caution ; on ne peut pas s'en rapporter à lui, se fier à lui.

trust, v.n., (to be credulous) être crédule ; (expect) se flatter de ; aimer à croire que ; espérer ; s'attendre à ; (venture) s'aventurer, se hasarder, se risquer. To — to ; se fier à ; mettre sa confiance en ; se confier à ; compter sur ; croire à. To — to ; (before an infinitive) espérer, compter ; s'attendre à. I sincerely — ; j'espère bien.

trust'-deed, n., acte fiduciaire, m.

trust'ed, adj., intime, de confiance.

trustee' (treus-tî), n., curateur, dépositaire, gardien ; directeur, administrateur ; (jur.) fidéicommissaire ; (in bankruptcy) syndic ; (of orphans) tuteur, m., tutrice, f. In the hands of —s ; en régie. Board of —s ; conseil d'administration, m.

trustee'ship, n., curatelle, direction ; administration, f. ; (jur.) fidéicommis, m. ; (of orphans) tutelle, f.

trust'ily, adv., fidèlement ; loyalement.

trust'iness, n., fidélité ; probité, loyauté, f.

trust'ingly, adv., avec confiance.

trust'less, adj., faux ; infidèle, déloyal.

trust'worthy (-weurthi), adj., digne de confiance ; (of news) exact.

trust'y (treust'i), adj., sûr, fidèle, loyal, sincère ; (firm) fidèle, sûr.

truth (trouth), n., vérité, f. ; vrai, m. ; (honesty) probité, loyauté ; (fidelity) fidélité ; (veracity) véracité, f. The real, ou honest, — ; la pure vérité. To distinguish — from falsehood ; distinguer le vrai d'avec le faux. There's some — in it ; il y a du vrai dans cela. There's not a word of — in it ; c'est absolument faux ; ou il n'y a pas un mot de vrai dans cela. Sooner or later the — will out ; tôt ou tard la vérité se fait jour ; ou la vérité comme l'huile vient au-dessus. — is sometimes stranger than fiction ; le vrai peut quelquefois n'être pas vraisemblable (Boileau : Art Poétique). To tell the — ; à dire la vérité ; (adverbial) à vrai dire. In — ; en vérité ; à vrai dire ; vraiment.

truth'ful (-foule), adj., véridique, vrai.

truth'fully, *adv.*, véridiquement ; avec vérité.
truth'fulness, *n.*, véracité, *f.*
truth'less, *adj.*, faux ; mensonger ; (faithless) sans foi, déloyal.
try (traïe), *v.n.*, essayer ; tâcher ; (nav.) être à la cape.
try (traïe), *v.a.*, essayer, éprouver ; faire l'épreuve de ; mettre à l'épreuve ; (to attempt) tenter, entreprendre, essayer ; (to experience) éprouver, faire l'expérience de ; (to strain) fatiguer ; (to use as means) essayer ; faire l'essai de ; (to search carefully into) sonder ; (metals) essayer ; faire l'essai de ; (to refine) affiner, purifier, épurer ; (weights, measures) contrôler, vérifier ; (jur.) juger ; (pers.) traduire en justice, mettre en jugement. To — on ; *essayer*. To — it on with; *chercher à rançonner, chercher à mettre dedans*. To — the eyes; *fatiguer la vue, les yeux*. To — for; *tâcher d'obtenir ; concourir pour ; se porter candidat pour ; postuler*. To — hard; *s'efforcer de, s'évertuer à*. To — (one's hand); *s'essayer (la main)*.
try (traïe), *n.*, essai, *m.*
try'ing (traï-igne), *adj.*, d'épreuve, difficile, critique ; (straining) pénible, dur, rude, fatigant ; (nav.) à la cape. A — experience ; *une pénible expérience*. That is very — ; *c'est très contrariant, fatigant*.
try'-sail (-séle), *n.*, voile de senau, *f.*
tryst (triste *ou* traïste), *n.*, rendez-vous, *m.*
tryst'ing-place, *n.*, rendez-vous, *m.*
tub (teube), *n.*, cuve, *f.*; baquet ; (small cask) tonneau, baril, *m.*; (for vegetables) caisse, *f.*; (of Diogenes) tonneau, *m.*; (nav.) galiote, *f.* (V. H.). A tale of a — ; *un coq-à-l'âne ; une histoire ridicule*. An old — ; (nav.) *un vieux sabot*.
tub, *v.a.*, encuver ; (gard.) encaisser.
tub'bing, *n.*, encuvage ; (of plants) encaissage, *m.*
tube (tioube), *n.*, tube ; conduit, canal, vaisseau, *m.*; (of cannon) âme, *f.*; (railway) métro, *m.*
tube (tioube), *v.a.*, tuber.
tu'ber (tioub'-), *n.*, (bot.) tubercule, *m.*
tu'bercle (tiou-beur'k'l), *n.*, tubercule, *m.*
tu'bercled (-beur'k'l'de), *adj.*, tuberculeux.
tuber'cular *ou* **tuber'culous** (tiou-beur'kiou-), *adj.*, tuberculeux.
tuberculo'sis, *n.*, (med.) tuberculisation, *f.*
tube'rose (tiou-b'rôze), *n.*, (bot.) tubéreuse, *f.*
tu'berous (tiou-beur-), *adj.*, tubéreux.
tub'-fish (teube-), *n.*, (ich.) perlon, *m.*
tu'bular (tiou-), *adj.*, tubulaire. — bridge ; *pont tubulaire, pont-tube, m.*
tuck (teuke), *n.*, (rapier) estoc ; (in garments) rempli, pli, *m.*; (nav.) fesses, *f.pl.*
tuck (teuke), *v.a.*, trousser, retrousser, relever. To — in; *rentrer*. To — in the bed-clothes ; *border le lit*. To — into bed ; *bien envelopper avec des couvertures*. To — up; *trousser, retrousser, relever ; envelopper, couvrir ;* (to fold) *remplier*. To — in; (fam.) *avaler, gober*.
tuck'er (teuk'-), *n.*, chemisette ; collerette, *f.*; tour de gorge, *m.*
tuck'-out, *n.*, (fam.) bombance, *f.*
tuck'-shop, *n.*, échoppe de marchand de gâteaux, *f.*
Tues'day (tiouz'-), *n.*, mardi, *m.* On —s ; *les mardis*. Every — ; *tous les mardis*.
tu'fa-stone (-stône), *n.*, tuffeau, *m.*
tuft (teuf'te), *n.*, (of hair) touffe, houppe ; (of a bird) huppe, aigrette ; (of trees, of flowers) touffe, *f.*, bouquet ; (milit.) pompon ; (bot.) corymbe, *m.* — hunter ; *plat valet, m.*
tuft (teuf'te), *v.a.*, diviser en touffes.
tuft'ed, *adj.*, touffu ; en touffe ; semé de touffes ; (of birds) huppé.
tug (teughe), *v.a.* and *n.*, tirailler ; tirer bien fort; (tow) remorquer ; (to struggle) lutter. To — away at ; *s'évertuer à ; faire un grand effort, donner un rude coup de collier*.

tug (teughe), *n.*, tiraillement, effort ; (boat) remorqueur, *m.* To give a — ; *tirer*. To give a good —; *tirer bien fort ;* (in drawing teeth) *donner une forte secousse*. The — of war ; *le grand coup, le grand effort, la grande lutte ;* (sports) *la lutte à la corde*.
tug'gingly (teug'ghign'-), *adv.*, en tirant.
tui'tion (tiou-ish'eune), *n.*, (instruction) instruction, *f.*, enseignement, *m.*, leçons, *f.pl.*; (fig.) direction, conduite, *f.* — fees; *honoraires, m.pl.; prix de la pension, f.*
tu'lip (tiou-), *n.*, tulipe, *f.* —-tree; *tulipier, m.* —-wood; *bois de rose, m.*
tulle, *n.*, tulle, *m.* — maker; *tulliste, m.* — making; *tullerie, f.*
tum'ble (teu'm'b'l), *n.*, chute; culbute, *f.*
tum'ble (teu'm'b'l), *v.n.*, tomber ; (to roll) rouler, se rouler ; (to roll down) descendre en roulant, rouler, dégringoler ; (to pieces) tomber en ruines, s'écrouler ; (of mountebanks) faire la culbute, culbuter. To — down ; *tomber par terre ;* (of things) tomber ; of (buildings) *s'écrouler*. To — into a cab ; *se jeter dans un fiacre*. To — down stairs ; *dégringoler l'escalier*. To — out ; *se précipiter dehors (en se bousculant) ;* (of bed) *sauter à bas du lit*. To — over; *tomber, faire une chute*.
tum'ble, *v.a.*, tourner, retourner, remuer ; déranger ; (to rumple) chiffonner, bouchonner. To — down stairs ; *faire dégringoler l'escalier à*. To — (things) over ; *tourner et retourner*.
tum'ble-down, *adj.*, croulant, délabré, qui menace ruine ; (pers.) caduc.
tum'bler, *n.*, bateleur ; saltimbanque, sauteur, *m.* ; (glass) grand verre ; (orni.) pigeon culbutant, *m.* ; (firearms) noix, *f.*
tum'blerful, *adj.*, le contenu d'un grand verre ; plein un grand verre. — *n.*, rasade, *f.*
tum'brel, tum'bril (teu'm'-), *n.*, tombereau ; (mil.) fourgon, caisson, *m.*
tumefac'tion (tiou-mi-fak-), *n.*, tuméfaction, *f.*
tu'mefy (tiou-mi-faïe), *v.a.*, tuméfier, enfler.
tu'mefy, *v.n.*, s'enfler, se tuméfier.
tu'mid (tiou-), *adj.*, enflé, gonflé, renflé ; (fig.) boursouflé, ampoulé, bouffi.
tu'midly, *adv.*, avec enflure.
tu'midness, tumid'ity, *n.*, enflure ; turgescence, *f.* ; gonflement, *m.*
tu'mor (tiou-meur), *n.*, tumeur ; (fig.) boursouflure, enflure, *f.*
tu'mored (tiou-meurde), *adj.*, à tumeur.
tump (teu'm'pe), *n.*, motte, butte, *f.*
tump (teu'm'pe), *v.a.*, (agri.) chausser, entourer de terre, butter.
tu'mular (tiou-miou-), *adj.*, en monticule.
tu'mult (tiou-meulte), *n.*, tumulte ; trouble, *m.*
tumul'tuary, *adj.*, tumultuaire ; agité.
tumul'tuous (tiou-meult'iou-eusse), *adj.*, tumultueux ; (turbulent) turbulent ; (agitated) agité, troublé.
tumul'tuously, *adv.*, tumultueusement.
tumul'tuousness, *n.*, disposition tumultueuse ; turbulence, *f.*
tu'mulus (tiou-miou-), *n.*, tumulus, *m.*
tun (teune), *n.*, (cask) tonneau, *m.*, tonne, *f.* ; (of wine) tonneau (litres 953·8); (of round timber) environ mètre cube 1·124 ; (of square timber) environ mètre cube 1·517 ; (drunkard, large quantity) tonneau, *m.* He is a regular — at it ; *c'est un vrai tonneau que cet ivrogne-là*.
tun (teune), *v.a.*, entonner.
tun'able (tiou'n'a-b'l), *adj.*, harmonieux ; musical ; (mus.) accordable.
tun'ableness, *n.*, harmonie, *f.*
tun'ably, *adv.*, harmonieusement ; (mus.) d'accord.
tun'-bellied (-bèl'lide), *adj.*, pansu, ventru.
tune (tioune), *n.*, air ; (concert of parts) ton, accord ; (note) son, *m.*, note ; (harmony) harmonie ; concorde ; (fit temper) humeur, veine, *f.*

To sing to another —; *changer de ton, de gamme.*
To sing in —; *chanter juste.* To sing out of —;
chanter faux. To get out of — ; *se désaccorder.*
To put out of — ; *fausser, désaccorder.* In — ;
d'accord. Out of —; *faux.* To the — of ; *au
montant* **de**, *jusqu'au chiffre* **de** ; *pour la somme*
de. To make any one change his — ; *faire changer de ton, de gamme* **à.**

tune (tioune), *v.a.,* accorder, mettre d'accord.
To — a piano ; *accorder un piano.*

tune'ful (-foule), *adj.,* mélodieux, harmonieux ;
aux accents mélodieux.

tune'less (tiou'n'-), *adj.,* sans harmonie ; discordant ; (mute) muet.

tun'er (tiou'n'-), *n.,* accordeur, *m.*

tu'nic (tiou-), *n.,* tunique ; (anat.) tunique ;
membrane ; (of the eye) tunique, enveloppe, *f.*

tu'nicated (tiou-ni-két'-), *adj.,* (bot., zoöl.)
recouvert de tuniques.

tun'ing (tiou'n'-), *n.,* action d'accorder, *f.*

tun'ing-fork (tiou'n'-), *n.,* diapason, *m.*

tun'ing-hammer, *n.,* accordoir ; clef d'accordeur, *f.*

tun'nage (teu'n'nèdje), *n. V.* **tonnage.**

tun'nel (teu'n'nèle), *n.,* tunnel ; souterrain ; (of
a chimney) tuyau ; (funnel) entonnoir, *m.*

tun'nel (teu'n'-), *v.a.,* faire un souterrain,
faire un tunnel ; former en entonnoir ; (hunt.)
tonneler.

tun'neling, *n.,* construction de tunnels, *f.*

tun'nel-net, *n.,* (fishing) tonnelle, *f.*

tun'nel-shaft (-shâfte), *n.,* puits de tunnel, *m.*

tun'ning (teu'n'-), *n.,* entonnage, *n.*

tun'ny-fish (teu'n'-), *n.,* (ich.) thon, *m.*

tup (teupe), *n.,* (mam.) bélier, *m.*

tup, *v.a.,* and *n.,* (of rams) cosser.

tur'ban (teur-), *n.,* turban, *m.*

tur'baned (teur-ba'n'de), *adj.,* coiffé du turban.

tur'bid (teur-), *adj.,* trouble, bourbeux.

tur'bidly, *adv.,* dans un état trouble.

tur'bidness, *n.,* état bourbeux, état trouble, *m.*

tur'binate *ou* **tur'binated** (teur-bi-nét'-), *adj.,*
(bot., zoöl.) turbiné, en toupie.

tur'bine, *n.,* turbine, *f.*

tur'bot (teur-beute), *n.,* turbot, *m.* Young — ;
turbotin, m. —kettle ; *turbotière, f.*

tur'bulence *ou* **tur'bulency** (tour-biou-), *n.,*
(insubordination) turbulence, insubordination ;
(agitation) agitation, *f. ;* (tumult) trouble, désordre, tumulte, *m.*

tur'bulent (teur-biou-), *adj.,* en tumulte ;
tumultueux ; bruyant ; (refractory) turbulent.

tur'bulently, *adv.,* en tumulte, tumultueusement ; (with refractoriness) d'une manière tur-
bulente, turbulemment.

tur'cism (teur-ciz'm), *n.,* mahométisme, *m.*

tureen' (teu-rîne), *n.,* (for soup) soupière ;
(for sauce) saucière, *f.*

turf (teurfe), *n.,* gazon, *m. ;* (peat) tourbe, *f. ;*
(raceground) hippodrome, terrain de course,
turf, *m.;* (lawn) pelouse, *f.* To be on the — ; (of
racing) *faire courir* (*des chevaux*).

turf (teurfe), *v.a.,* gazonner.

turf'iness, *n.,* abondance de gazon, nature du
gazon ; nature de la tourbe, *f.*

turf'ing, *n.,* gazonnement, *m.*

turf'-moss, *n.,* tourbière, *f. ;* terrain marécageux, *m.*

turf'ite (-aïte), *n.,* homme qui fréquente les
courses ; habitué du turf, *m.*

turf'-pit, *n.,* tourbière, *f.*

turf'y, *adj.,* herbeux, gazonneux ; (turfed)
gazonné ; (formed of turf) tourbeux.

turges'cence *ou* **turges'cency** (teur-djès'-),
n., turgescence, *f. ;* gonflement, *m. ;* (fig.) bours-
souflure, emphase, enflure, *f.*

tur'gid, *adj.,* enflé ; gonflé ; turgescent ; (style)
boursouflé, ampoulé, bouffi.

turgid'ity (teur-djid'-), *n.,* enflure, *f. ;* gonflement, *m.*

tur'gidly, *adv.,* avec enflure, avec bouffissure

tur'gidness, *n.,* turgescence ; (of the style)
boursouflure, enflure, emphase, *f.*

Tur'inese, *n.adj.,* Turinois, *m.,* Turinoise, *f.*

Turk (teurke), *n.,* Turc, *m.,* Turque, *f. ;* (of a
woman) mégère, *f.* A young — ; (of a boy) *un
petit diable.*

tur'key (teur-ki), *n.,* dindon, coq d'Inde, *m.*
Young — ; *dindonneau, m.* Hen — ; *dinde, f.*
— carpet ; *tapis de Turquie, m.*

tur'meric (teur-meur'-), *n.,* curcuma ; (dy.)
safran des Indes, *m.*

tur'moil (teur-moïl), *n.,* vacarme, tumulte ;
trouble ; tracas, *m. ;* agitation, *f.*

turn (teurne), *v.a.,* tourner ; (to shift sides)
tourner, retourner ; (to alter) changer ; (of a
balance) faire pencher, emporter ; (to bring the
inside out) retourner ; (to form on a lathe) tourner ; (to cause to deviate) fausser ; (to shape)
tourner, façonner ; (to change, to transform)
changer, convertir, transformer ; (to translate)
traduire ; (to convert) convertir ; (to alter from
one effect to another) faire tourner ; (to sour)
tourner, faire tourner ; (to revolve) rouler, retourner ; (to transfer) transférer ; (prose into poetry)
mettre, traduire **en** ; (the stomach) soulever, faire
soulever ; (one's head) tourner, faire tourner,
troubler ; (the edge of anything) ôter, émousser ;
(print.) bloquer ; (com.) convertir. To — to
account ; *tirer parti* **de**, *profiter* **de**. To be —ed
thirty, forty, etc. ; *avoir passé la trentaine, la
quarantaine, etc.* To — about; *tourner, retourner.*
To — aside ; *détourner* **de**, *éloigner* **de**, *écarter*
de. To — away ; *renvoyer, congédier, chasser,
éloigner* ; (to turn aside) *détourner* **de**. To —
back ; *faire retourner ; renvoyer ;* (print.) *débloquer.* To — down ; *retourner ;* (a leaf, etc.) *plier ;
faire un pli* **à** ; (a collar) *rabattre.* To — from ;
détourner **de**. To — in ; *tourner en dedans ; rentrer, faire rentrer ;* (dress-making) *remplier.* To
— into ; *changer* **en**, *transformer* **en**, *convertir*
en ; (writing) *traduire* **en**, *mettre* **en**. To — off ;
renvoyer, chasser, congédier ; (steam) *supprimer ;*
(a cock) *fermer.* To — on ; *tourner* **contre** ; *diriger*
sur ; (the eyes) *tourner* **vers**, *diriger* **sur** ; (steam)
donner ; faire fonctionner ; (a cock) *ouvrir.* To —
out ; *mettre dehors ; renvoyer, chasser, mettre à la
porte ;* (cattle) *renvoyer aux champs ;* (work) *faire.*
To — over ; *tourner, retourner ;* (a book) *feuilleter.*
To — over and over (again) ; *tourner et retourner.
retourner en tous sens.* To — over to ; *envoyer*
à ; *adresser* **à** ; *abandonner* **à** ; *passer* **à** ; *transférer* **à** ; (nav.) *transborder.* To — round ; *tourner,
retourner.* To — up ; *tourner, retourner, trousser, retrousser ;* (in needle-work) *remplier ; faire
un rempli* **à** ; (at cards) *retourner.* To — upside down ; *mettre sens dessus dessous.* To be
—ed twenty ; *avoir plus de vingt ans.* To — an
honest penny ; *faire un profit légitime.* — him,
her, them out! *à la porte!* To — out of doors ;
mettre à la porte, chasser, expulser. To — out
to grass ; *mettre au vert.* To — adrift ; *mettre à
la porte ; abandonner à ses propres ressources.*
To — up one's nose at ; *dédaigner, mépriser ;
faire le dégoûté.* A — ed up nose ; *un nez
retroussé.* To — a cold shoulder to, *ou* on ;
traiter avec dédain ; battre froid **à**. To — a somersault ; *faire un saut périlleux.* To — one's
hand to ; *s'appliquer* **à**. He —s over, *ou* has a
turnover of, $2500 a week ; *ses recettes montent à
2500 dollars par semaine.* To — over a new
leaf ; *changer de conduite, faire peau neuve.* To
— tail ; *prendre la fuite ; s'enfuir honteusement ;
tourner le dos.*

turn, *v.n.,* tourner ; se tourner ; se retourner ;
(to deviate) se détourner **de**, dévier ; (to be
changed) se changer **en**, se transformer **en**, se
convertir **en** ; (to become) devenir, se faire ; (to
change to acid) tourner ; (to become giddy) tourner, se troubler ; (of the tide) changer ; (conduct)

revenir **de** ; (to direct one's steps) se diriger **vers**, se porter **vers** ; (fig.) se reporter **sur**. To — about : *se tourner*, *se retourner*. To — again ; *tourner de nouveau* ; *se retourner* ; (to become again) *redevenir*. To — aside ; *se détourner*. To — away ; *se détourner* ; *s'en aller*. To — back ; *se retourner en arrière* ; (to return) *rebrousser chemin*, *retourner sur ses pas*. To — down ; *se retourner* ; *se recourber*. To — down a street ; *entrer dans une rue* ; *prendre une rue*. To — from ; *s'éloigner de* ; *se détourner* **de** ; (of the stomach) *se soulever* **à**. To — in ; *se tourner en dedans* ; (to enter) *entrer* ; (to go to bed) *se coucher* ; (nav.) (of sailors) *coucher dans son fourreau*. — in ! (nav.) *dans le sac !* To — into ; *se changer* **en**, *se convertir* **en**, *se transformer* **en**. To — off ; *tourner*, *faire un détour* ; (pers.) *se détourner*. To — on ; (of conversation) *tourner* **sur**, *rouler* **sur** ; (to be given to) *se porter* **sur**, *se reporter* **sur**. To — out ; *tourner en dehors* ; *se retourner* ; (to go out) *sortir* ; (to rise from bed) *quitter le lit*, *se lever* ; (to happen) *arriver* ; (to end ill, ou well) *tourner*, *finir* ; (to become) *devenir* ; *se montrer* ; (of plants, etc.) *venir* ; (of workmen) *faire grève*. The guards —ed out ; *la garde prit les armes*. To — over ; *se tourner*, *se retourner* ; (to upset) *verser*, *se renverser* ; (to tumble) *culbuter* ; (to change sides) *changer de parti* ; *passer* **à**. To — round ; *tourner* ; *se tourner* ; *se retourner* ; (to change sides) *changer de parti*. To — round and round ; *tournoyer*. To — coat ; *tourner casaque*. To — to ; *tourner en* ; *se changer* **en** ; (to apply to) *s'adresser* **à**, *avoir recours* **à** ; (to set about) *se mettre* **à** ; *se résoudre* **à**, *prendre un parti*. What is it that I should — to ? (Tennyson) *à quoi me résoudre*, *quel parti prendre* ? To — under ; *tourner en dessous*. To — up ; *tourner en haut* ; *être relevé* ; *être retroussé* ; (to happen) *arriver* ; *se trouver* ; *se présenter* ; *être* ; (to be found again) *se retrouver* ; (pers.) *se montrer* ; *se trouver* ; *être* ; *venir*, *revenir* ; (of events) *survenir* ; (at cards) *retourner*. To — upside down ; *se renverser*. To — soldier ; *se faire militaire*. To — to the left, to the right ; *prendre à gauche*, *à droite*.

turn (teurne), *n.*, (circular movement) tour ; (winding) tournant, coude, détour, *m.*, courbe, *f.* ; (walk) tour ; (service) office, service ; (vicissitude) changement, *m.*, vicissitude, *f.* ; (successive course) tour, tour de rôle ; (course) cours, *m.*, direction, tournure ; (chance) occasion, opportunité, chance, *f.* ; (action of kindness or malice) trait, office ; (reigning inclination) goût, *m.*, fantaisie, *f.* ; (purpose) projet, *m.*, vue, affaire ; (direction) forme, tournure, *f.*, contour, *m.* ; (of thought, style) tournure, *f.*, tour, *m.* ; (change) phase, *f.* ; (of the tide) changement ; (of a rope) tour, rond ; (of scale) trait ; (mines) puits ; (mus.) double, *m.* It is your — ; *à vous le dé* ; (at cards) *vous avez la main* ; *c'est votre tour* ; *c'est à vous* **de**. It is your — to play ; (at cards) *vous avez la main*. Whose — is it ? *à qui le tour ? à qui est-ce à . . . ?* In —s ; *tour à tour* ; *à tour de rôle*. In one's — ; *à son tour*. The books we read give a — to our thoughts ; *les livres que nous lisons donnent le ton à nos pensées*. To take it in —s ; (of nurses, etc.) *se relayer*, *procéder à tour de rôle*. To take a — ; (of events) *prendre une tournure* ; (in garden, etc.) *faire un tour* **de**. That fashion has had its — ; *cette mode a eu son temps*. One good — deserves another ; *à beau jeu, beau retour*. Cooked **to a** — ; *cuit à point*. It is your — to read ; *c'est à vous à lire*. This news has given me quite a — ; *cette nouvelle m'a tout bouleversé*. At every — ; *à tout moment* ; *à tout propos* ; *à tout bout de champ*. By —s ; *à tour de rôle* ; *tour à tour*. A good — ; *un bon office*. A bad — ; *un mauvais office, un mauvais tour*. He did me a good — ; *il m'a*

rendu un grand service. He did me a bad — ; *il m'a joué un mauvais tour* ; ou *il a usé de mauvais procédés* **envers** *moi*.

turn'bench, *n.*, tour à pointes, *m.*
turn'coat (-côte), *n.*, renégat, tourne-casaque ; transfuge, *m.* ; girouette, *f.*
turn'-cock, *n.*, fontainier, *m.*
turn'-down, *adj.*, (of caps, etc.) rabattu ; plié.
turn'er (teurn'-), *n.*, tourneur, *m.*
turn'ery (teurn'-), *n.*, art du tourneur, *m.* ; (things) objets faits au tour, *m.pl.*
turn'ing (teurn'-), *n.*, action de tourner, *f.* ; (of a road, etc.) détour, tournant, coude ; (print.) blocage, *m.*
turn'ing-chisel, *n.*, plane, *f.*
turn'ing-engine, *n.*, tour à la mécanique, *m.*
turn'ing-lathe (-léthe), *n.*, tour, *m.*
turn'ing-off, *n.*, détour ; (rail.) embranchement, *m.*
turn'ing-point, *n.*, (fig.) point décisif, moment critique, *m.*
tur'nip (teur-), *n.*, navet, *m.* ; rave, *f.*
tur'nip-cabbage (-cab-bèdje), *n.*, (bot.) chou-rave, *m.*
turn'key (teurn'kî), *n.*, guichetier, porte-clefs, *m.*
turn'out (teurn'aoute), équipage, train, *m.* ; (of workmen) grève.
turn'-over, maximum d'affaires ; (pastry) chausson, *m.*
turn'pike (-païke), *n.*, tourniquet, *m.* ; barrière de péage, *f.*
turn'plate *ou* **turn'table**, *n.*, (railways) plate-forme tournante, plaque tournante, *f.*
turn'screw (-scrou), *n.*, tournevis, *m.*
turn'sick, *n.*, (vet.) tournis, tournoiement, *m.*
turn'sole (-sôle), *n.*, (bot.) tournesol, *m.*
turn'spit, *n.*, tournebroche ; (dog) tourne-broche, *m.*
turn'stile (-staïle), *n.*, tourniquet, *m.*
turn'stone (-stône), *n.*, (orni.) tournemotte, *m.*
turn'-up, *adj.*, (of the nose) retroussé ; (fig.) dédaigneux, impertinent.
tur'pentine (teur-pè'n'taïne), *n.*, (chem.) térébenthine, *f.*
tur'pitude (teur-pi-tioude), *n.*, turpitude, infamie, bassesse, *f.*
tur'quoise (teur-koïze), *n.*, (min.) turquoise, *f.*
tur'rel (teur-), *n.*, (a tool) tire-fond, *m.*
tur'ret (teur-), *n.*, tourelle, *f.* ; (bot.) laîche. — ship ; *navire à tourelles*.
tur'reted (teur-), *adj.*, en forme de tour ; garni de tourelles.
tur'tle (teur't'l), *n.*, tortue. To turn — ; (of a ship) *culbuter*, *faire la culbute*.
tur'tle-dove (-deuve), *n.*, (orni.) tourterelle, *f.*
tur'tle-shell. V. **tortoise-shell**.
tus'can (teus-), *adj.*, toscan.
tush ! (teushe), *int.*, bah ! allons donc !
tusk (teuske), *n.*, dent canine, canine, *f.* ; croc, *m.* ; (of elephants, boars) défense, *f.*
tusked (teusk'te) *ou* **tusk'y** (teus-), *adj.*, muni de canines, de crocs, de défenses.
tus'sle (teus's'l), *n.*, lutte, bagarre, *f.*
tut ! (teute), *int.*, ta, ta, ta ; fi ! fi donc !
tu'telage (tiou-ti-lèdje), *n.*, tutelle, minorité, *f.* ; état de pupille, *m.*
tu'telary (tiou-ti-), *adj.*, tutélaire.
tu'tor (tiou-teur), *n.*, précepteur, instituteur ; (jur.) tuteur ; (at college) répétiteur ; (private) préparateur, *m.*
tu'tor (tiou-teur), *v.a.*, instruire ; enseigner ; (to correct) corriger, reprendre ; faire la leçon à ; (to treat with authority) dominer, commander.
tu'torage (tiou-teur-èdje), *n.*, tutelle, *f.*
tuto'rial, *adj.*, de précepteur.
tu'toring, *n.*, instruction, *f.* ; enseignement, *m.* ; éducation, *f.*

tu′torship, *n.*, préceptorat, *m. ;* place de professeur, *f.*

tut′ty (powder), *n.*, (metal.) tutie, *f.*

twad′dle (twod′d′l) *ou* **twad′dling** (twod′-), *n.*, babil, bavardage, caquetage, *m.*

twad′dler, *n.*, bavard ; péroreur, *m.*

twain (twéne), *adj.*, deux.

twang (twa′gne), *n.*, ·son aigu ; (nasal voice) nasillement, accent nasillard ; (after-taste) arrière-gout désagréable, *m.*

twang (twa′gne), *v.n.*, nasiller.

tweak (twîke), *v.a.*, tirer, pincer.

tweez′ers (twîz′eurze), *n.pl.*, pincettes ; (for the hair) petites pinces à épiler, *f.pl.*

twelfth (twĕlf′th), *adj.* and *n.*, douzième. —-night ; *jour des Rois, m.* —-night cake, —-cake ; *gâteau des Rois, m.* To celebrate —-night ; *célébrer,* ou *faire, les Rois.*

twelve (twĕl′ve), *adj.* douze ; (of age) douze ans. — *ou* — o′clock ; (noon) *midi ;* (midnight) *minuit, m.*

twelve′month (twĕlv′meu′n′th), *n.*, an, *m. ;* année, *f.* This day —; (past) *il y a aujourd′hui un an ;* (future) *à un an d′ici.* Last Easter — ; *il y a un an à Pâques dernier.*

twen′tieth (twĕn′tièth), *n.* and *adj.*, vingtième.

twen′ty (twĕn′-), *adj.*, vingt. —-first ; *vingt et unième.* The —-first ; (of the month) *le vingt et un . . .*

twice (twaïce), *adv.*, deux fois. — as much ; *le double* ou *deux fois autant.* To — one′s thumbs ; *tourner ses pouces.*

twig, *n.*, ramille, brindille, *f.*

twig′gy (twig′ghi), *adj.*, plein de ramilles.

twi′light (twaï-laïte), *n.*, crépuscule ; demi-jour, déclin du jour, *m. ;* (fig.) aurore, *f.*, crépuscule, *m.*

twill, *v.a.*, plisser ; croiser.

twill, *n.*, étoffe croisée, *f. ;* tissu croisé, *m.*

twin, *n.*, jumeau, *m.*, jumelle, *f. ;* (fig.) jumeau, frère, *m.*, sœur, *f.* The —s ; (astron.) *les Gémeaux, m.pl.*

twin, *adj.*, jumeau ; (bot.) double, géminé.

twin′-born, *adj.*, né jumeau, née jumelle.

twine (twaïne), *n.*, ficelle, *f. ;* (embrace) embrassement ; (twist) entrelacement, enveloppement, entortillement ; (arch.) entrelacs, *m.*

twine (twaïne), *v.a.*, retordre ; dévider ; tisser ; (fig.) enlacer, entortiller ; lier.

twine, *v.n.*, tourner ; serpenter ; s′enrouler ; (to unite closely) s′unir, se lier, s′entrelacer.

twinge (twi′n′dje), *n.*, élancement ; tiraillement ; (fig.) tourment ; (of conscience) remords, *m.*

twinge (twi′n′dje), *v.a.*, torturer, tourmenter; (to pinch) pincer, tirer.

twinge, *v.n.*, élancer, causer des élancements.

twin′ging (twi′n′dj′-), *n.*, douleur aiguë et subite, *f. ;* élancement, *m.*

twin′kle (twign′k′l), *v.n.*, étinceler ; scintiller ; briller ; (of the eyes) cligner, clignoter.

twin′kling, *n.*, scintillement, *m. ;* scintillation, *f. ;* (of the eyes) clignotement, clin d′œil, *m.* In the — of an eye ; *en un clin d′œil.*

twirl (tweurle), *v.n.*, tournoyer ; tourner ; pirouetter.

twirl, *v.a.*, tourner, faire tourner ; faire faire le moulinet à. He —s him round his little finger; *il lui fait faire tout ce qu′il veut ; il l′a complètement sous sa main.*

twirl (tweurle), *n.*, mouvement circulaire, *m.*, rotation, pirouette, *f. ;* (twist) tortillement, *m.*

twist, *v.a.*, tordre, retordre ; (to form into a thread) filer ; (to contort) contourner, tortiller, tordre ; (to encircle) cercler, entourer ; (to unite by intertexture) entrelacer, enlacer ; (to pervert) tordre, torturer, pervertir, défigurer.

To — round one′s finger; *tenir* (ou *avoir*) *dans sa manche ; entortiller.* To — one′s self into ; *s′insinuer dans, se glisser dans.*

twist, *v.n.*, s′entrelacer, s′enlacer, s′enrouler, se nouer.

twist, *n.*, tortis, cordon, *m. ;* corde, *f. ;* cordonnet ; (of a cord) cordon, fil, *m. ;* (contortion) contorsion ; spirale, *f. ;* entortillement, tordage, tortillement ; (of tobacco) rouleau, *m.*, carotte; (prejudice) préjugé, *m. ;* (arch.) nervure, *f.* To give a — ; *tordre.* To give one′s self a — ; *se tordre.*

twist′ed, *adj.*, tordu ; (arch.) tors ; (bot.) tors, tordu ; (fig.) perverti, défiguré, dénaturé.

twist′er, *n.*, tordeur, *m.*, tordeuse, *f. ;* cordier, *m.*

twist′ing, *n.*, tordage ; tortillement, *m.* — machine ; *machine à tordre* (*quelque chose*), *f.*

twit, *v.a.*, blâmer ; jeter une chose au nez **de** ; reprocher, accuser. To — with ; *reprocher à.*

twitch, *n.*, élancement ; tiraillement, *m.*

twitch, *v.a.*, tirer brusquement ; arracher.

twitch, *v.n.*, se contracter, se crisper.

twitch′ing, *n.*, saccade, secousse ; (contraction) crispation, *f. ;* (of pain) tiraillement, élancement ; (of conscience) remords, *m.*

twit′ter, *v.n.*, gazouiller ; (to titter) rire du bout des lèvres.

twit′ter, *n.*, censeur, critique ; (of birds) gazouillement ; (titter) rire du bout des lèvres, *m.*

twit′tingly, *adv.*, avec reproche, en censurant.

two (tou), *n.adj.*, deux, *m.* — can play at that game ; *nous sommes à deux de jeu.* — heads are better than one ; *deux avis valent mieux qu′un.* — of a trade seldom agree ; *deux moineaux sur même épi ne sont pas longtemps amis.* — ′s company, three is none ; *deux s′amusent, trois s′embêtent.*

two′-celled (tou-cèl′de), *adj.*, (bot.) biloculaire.

two′-cleft (-clèf′te), *adj.*, (bot.) bifide.

two′-cornered, *adj.*, bicorne.

two′-decker, *n.*, un vaisseau à deux ponts.

two′-edged (-èdj′de), *adj.*, à deux tranchants.

two′-fold (-fôlde), *adj.*, double ; (of screens) à deux feuilles.

two′-fold, *adv.*, doublement, deux fois autant.

two′-footed, *adj.*, à deux pieds.

two′-handed, *adj.*, bimane ; à deux mains ; (bot.) à deux faces.

two′-horned (-horn′de), *adj.*, bicorne, à deux cornes.

two′-leaved (-lîv′de), *adj.*, à deux feuilles; (bot.) bifolié ; (of doors) à deux battants.

two′-lobed (-lob′de), *adj.*, (bot.) bilobé.

two′-masted (-mâst′-), *adj.*, à deux mâts.

two′-pence, *n.pl.*, vingt centimes, quatre sous, *m.pl.*

two′penny, *adj.*, de quatre sous.

two′-valved (-valv′de), *adj.*, (zoöl.) bot.) bivalve.

tycoon′, *n.*, (Japan) taïcoun, *m.*

tym′bal (tim′bale), *n.*, (mus.) timbale, *f.*

tym′pan (tim′pane), **tym′panum**, *n.*, tambour, tympan, *m.*

type (taïpe), *n.*, type ; (print.) caractère, *m.* To be in — ; *être composé.* To set up in — ; *composer.*

type′-metal (-mèt′al), *n.*, métal pour caractères d′imprimerie, *m.*

type′-writer, *n.*, machine à écrire, *f.*

type′-written, *adj.*, écrit à la machine.

ty′phoid (taï-foïde), *adj.*, (med.) typhoïde.

typhoon′ (-foune), *n.*, typhon, *m. ;* trombe, *f.*

ty′phus (taï-), *n.*, (med.) typhus, *m.*

typ′ic *ou* **typ′ical** (tip′-), *adj.*, typique, figuratif.

typ'ically, adv., d'une manière typique; figurativement.

typ'icalness, n., nature typique, f.

typ'ify, typ'efy (tip'i-faïe), v.a., offrir le type de ; figurer, symboliser, représenter d'une manière typique.

typ'ified, adj., typifié ; dont on a fait un type.

typ'ist, n.m. and f., dactylographe.

typog'rapher (taï-), n., typographe, m.

typograph'ic ou **typograph'ical**, adj., typographique ; (emblematic, ant.) emblématique, typique, figuratif.

typograph'ically, adv., typographiquement ; (emblematically, ant.) figurativement, symboliquement.

typog'raphy (to-), n., typographie ; (emblematical representation ; ant.) écriture symbolique, f. : [nique.

tyran'nic ou **tyran'nical** (taï-), adj., tyran-

tyran'nically, adv., tyranniquement.

tyran'nicide (taï-ran'ni-çaïde), n., tyrannicide, m.

tyr'annize (tir-an-naïze), v.n., faire le tyran. To — over ; tyranniser.

tyr'anny, n., tyrannie, f.

ty'rant (taï-), n., tyran, m.

tyre. V. tire.

Ty'rian (tir'-), n., Tyrien. adj., de Tyr.

ty'ro (taï-rô), n., novice, commençant ; (mil.) conscrit, m.

Tyr'olese (tir'-), n., Tyrolien.

tyrtæ'an (teur-tî-), adj., tyrtéen.

tzar (tzâr), n., tzar, czar, m.

tzari'na (tzâr'-), n., tzarine, czarine, f.

U

u, vingt et unième lettre de l'alphabet, u, m.

ubi'quitary, ubi'quitous (you-bik'wi-), adj., présent partout, ubiquitaire.

ubi'quitary, n., ubiquitaire, m.

ubi'quity (you-bik'wi-), n., ubiquité, f.

ud'der (eud'-), n., pis, m. ; (cook.) tetine, f.

ud'dered (eud-deur'de), adj., à pis, à mamelles.

udom'eter, n., udomètre, m.

ugh (eu'), inter., pouah !

ug'lily (eug'li-li), adv., vilainement, avec laideur.

ug'liness (eug'-), n., laideur, f.

ug'ly (eug'-), adj., laid, vilain. To grow —; en-laidir. As — as sin ; laid comme les sept péchés capitaux. — words ; de vilaines paroles, f.pl.

uh'lan (ou-), n., uhlan, m.

u'kase (you-kéce), n., ukase, m.

ul'cer (eul-), n., (med.) ulcère, m., (in the mouth) aphte, f.

ul'cerate (eul-), v.a., ulcérer.

ul'cerate (eul-), v.n., s'ulcérer.

ulcera'tion (eul-ceur'é-), n., ulcération, f.

ul'cered (eul-ceurde), adj., ulcéré.

ul'cerous (eul-ceur-), adj., ulcéreux.

ule'ma, n.pl., (amongst Turks) uléma, m.pl.

uli'ginous (iou-lidj'-), adj., vaseux, boueux.

ul'lage (eul-lèdje), n., (com.) vidange, f.

ul'nage (eul-nèdje), n., aunage, m.

ulte'rior (eul-tî-), adj., ultérieur, postérieur.

ul'timate (eul-tî-), adj., dernier ; extrême ; (final) final, extrême, définitif.

ul'timately, adv., finalement, à la fin, définitivement, en résultat.

ulti'matum (eul-ti-mé-), n., ultimatum, m.

ul'timo (eul-ti-mô), adv., du mois dernier.

ultramarine' (eul-tra-ma-rîne), adj., d'outre-mer ; d'au delà des mers.

ultramarine' (eul-tra-ma-rîne), n., (chem.) outremer, bleu d'outremer ; (min.) outremer, lazulite, m.

ultramon'tane (eul-), adj.n., ultramontain, m.

ultramun'dane (eul-tra-meu'n'-), adj., ultra-mondain.

um'bel (eu'm'-), n., (bot.) ombelle, f.

umbel'lar (eu'm'-), adj., (bot.) ombellé.

umbellif'erous (eu'm'-), adj., (bot.) ombellifère.

um'ber (eu'm'-), n., (min.) terre d'ombre, f. ; (ich.) umble, ombre, m.

um'ber (eu'm'-), v.a., ombrer.

umbil'ic ou **umbil'ical** (eu'm'-), adj., ombilical ; (geom.) de foyer.

umbil'icate ou **umbil'icated** (eu'm'bil'i-két'-), adj., (bot.) ombiliqué.

umbil'icus (eu'm'-), n., ombilic, m.

um'brage (eu'm'brèdje), n., ombrage, m. ; ombre, f. ; (fig.) ombrage, m. To give — to; donner de l'ombrage à ; faire, ou porter, ombrage à. To take — at ; prendre de l'ombrage, ou ombrage, de ; s'offusquer de.

umbra'geous (eu'm'brédj'-), adj., ombreux ; (shady) ombragé, ombreux ; (obscure) obscur.

umbra'geousness, n., nature ombreuse ; ombre, f.

umbrel'la (eu'm'-), n., parapluie, m. — — case ; fourreau de parapluie, m. — —stand ; porte-parapluie, m. — stick ; manche de parapluie, m. — —tree ; (bot.) magnolier parasol, m.

um'pire (eu'm'païeur), n., tiers arbitre ; arbitre ; (com.) prud'homme, m.

un, prefix, non, in, pas, peu, dé, mal, é.

unabashed' (eu'n'a-bash'te), adj., non confus ; sans honte.

unabat'ed (eu'n'a-bét'-), adj., non diminué ; sans diminution ; toujours égal ; toujours le même.

unabet'ted (eu'n'-), adj., sans aide ; seul ; sans encouragement.

una'ble (eu'n'é-b'l), adj., incapable de ; inhabile à ; hors d'état de ; impuissant à (before inf.), pour (before noun) ; (not having adequate skill) incapable de. To be — to ; ne pas pouvoir ; être incapable de ; ne pas être à même de, n'être pas en état de.

unabridged' (eu'n'a-bridj'de), adj., non abrégé ; non raccourci ; complet, en entier.

unaccent'ed (eu'n'ak'cèpt'a-b'l), adj., sans accent ; (syllable) atone.

unaccept'able (eu'n'ak'cèpt'a-b'l), adj., inacceptable. — to ; déplaisant, ou désagréable, à. refusé.

unaccept'ed (eu'n'-), adj., inaccepté ; rejeté, refusé.

unaccli'matized, adj., inacclimaté.

unaccom'modating, adj., peu accommodant.

unaccom'panied, adj., seul, sans suite.

unaccom'plished (eu'n'ak-ko'm'plish'te), adj., inachevé ; incomplet ; (fig.) sans talent ; sans connaissances.

unaccount'able (eu'n'ac-caou'n't-a-b'l), adj., inexplicable, inconcevable ; bizarre, étrange ; (not responsible) irresponsable.

unaccount'ableness, n., bizarrerie ; étrangeté ; nature inexplicable ; (irresponsibility) irresponsabilité, f.

unaccount'ably, adv., d'une manière inexplicable ; inconcevablement, étrangement.

unaccred'ited, non autorisé ; sans pouvoirs définis.

unaccus'tomed (eu'n'ak'keus-teu'm'de), adj., inaccoutumé ; peu habitué ; extraordinaire.

unacknowl'edged (eu'n'ak'nol'èdjde), adj., non reconnu, non avoué ; non accrédité ; (of letters) sans réponse. — letter ; lettre à laquelle on n'a pas répondu.

unacquaint'ed (eu'n'ak'kwè'n't'-), adj., qui ignore ; qui ne connaît pas ; étranger à ; peu familier avec, peu versé dans. To be — with ; (pers.) ne pas connaître ; (things) ignorer, ne pas savoir.

unacquir'able, adj., inacquérable.

unacquired', adj., naturel ; non acquis.

unacquit'ted (eu'n'ak'kwit'-), *adj.*, non acquitté.

unac'tionable, *adj.*, (jur.) inattaquable.

unadjust'ed, *adj.*, non ajusté, non arrangé ; (jur.) en litige.

unadmin'istered (eu'n'ad-mi-nis'teurde), *adj.*, non administré.

unadorned' (eu'n'-), *adj.*, sans ornements ; naturel, simple.

unadul'terated (eu'n'a-deul-teur'ét'-), *adj.*, non frelaté, non falsifié ; naturel, pur ; (fig.) candide.

unadvis'able (eu'n'ad-vaïz'a-b'l), *adj.*, peu sage, peu judicieux, peu prudent ; peu convenable ; inopportun.

unadvis'ableness, *n.*, imprudence ; inutilité, *f.*

unadvised' (eu'n'ad'vaïz'de), *adj.*, malavisé ; inconsidéré ; (rash) irréfléchi, téméraire, imprudent.

unadvis'edly (eu'n'ad-vaïz'èd'-), *adv.*, inconsidérément ; imprudemment.

unadvis'edness, *n.*, imprudence, *f.*

unaffect'ed (eu'n'-), *adj.*, non affecté ; naturel, simple, naïf ; sans affectation ; franc ; sincère ; (not moved) impassible, insensible.

unaffect'edly, *adv.*, sans affectation, sans prétention ; simplement, naturellement ; sincèrement, franchement.

unaffect'edness, *n.*, simplicité ; sincérité, franchise, *f. ;* naturel, *m.*

unaffect'ing, *adj.*, peu touchant, peu pathétique.

unaid'ed, *adj.*, seul ; sans aide.

una'lienable (eu'n'él'yè'n'a-b'l), *adj.*, inaliénable.

unallayed' (eu'n'al'léde), *adj.*, non apaisé, qui dure toujours ; toujours vivace.

unallow'able, *adj.*, non permis.

unalloyed', *adj.*, pur ; sans alliage, sans mélange.

unal'terable (eu'n'al'teur'a-b'l), *adj.*, inaltérable, invariable.

unal'terableness, *n.*, nature inaltérable ; invariabilité, *f.*

unal'terably, *adv.*, d'une manière inaltérable.

unal'tered, *adj. V.* **unchanged.**

unambig'uous (-a'm-bi-ghiou-eusse), *adj.*, clair ; sans ambiguïté ; non équivoque.

unambig'uously, *adv.*, sans ambiguïté ; clairement.

unambi'tious, *adj.*, peu ambitieux ; sans ambition, sans prétention, simple.

unambi'tiously, *adv.*, sans prétention, sans ambition ; simple.

una'miable (eu'n'é-mi-a-b'l), *adj.*, peu aimable.

una'miableness, *n.*, défaut d'amabilité, *m.*

unanim'ity (you-na-), *n.*, unanimité, *f.* With — ; *à l'unanimité.*

unan'imous (you-na-), *adj.*, unanime.

unan'imously (you-na-), *adv.*, unanimement, à l'unanimité. Carried — ; *voté à l'unanimité.*

unan'swerable (eu'n'an'seur'a-b'l), *adj.*, sans réplique ; incontestable.

unan'swerableness, *n.*, nature irréfutable, *f.*

unan'swerably, *adv.*, sans réplique ; d'une manière irréfutable, incontestablement.

unan'swered (eu'n'a'n'seurde), *adj.*, sans réponse ; sans réplique.

unappalled' (eu'n'ap-pôlde), *adj.*, sans être ému, sans s'émouvoir, sans éprouver de crainte, sans pâlir ; intrépide.

unappar'ent (eu'n'-), *adj.*, non apparent ; invisible, inapercevable.

unappeal'able (-pîl'a-b'l), *adj.*, sans appel.

unappeas'able (eu'n'ap-pîz'a-b'l), *adj.*, qu'on ne peut apaiser ; implacable.

unappeased' (eu'n'ap-pîz'de), *adj.*, non apaisé, non assouri ; inapaisé.

unapplied' (eu'n'ap-plaïde), *adj.*, inappliqué ; (fin.) non engagé.

unappre'ciated (eu'n'ap-pri-shi-ét'-), *adj.*, incompris, inapprécié.

unapprehen'sive, *adj.*, sans appréhension ; qui ne saisit pas.

unapprised' (eu'n'ap-praïz'de), *adj.*, ignorant **de** ; sans être prévenu **de.**

unapproach'able (eu'n'ap-prôtsh'a-b'l-), *adj.*, inaccessible, inabordable.

unapproached', *adj.*, inaccessible.

unappro'priated (eu'n'ap-prô-pri-ét'), *adj.*, sans emploi ; sans application ; libre.

unapproved' (eu'n'ap-prouv'de), *adj.*, non approuvé.

unapt' (eu'n'-), *adj.*, impropre ; (dull) incapable, inepte ; (improper) peu convenable ; inapte.

unapt'ly, *adv.*, mal ; hors de propos, mal à propos.

unapt'ness, *n.*, incapacité ; inaptitude ; disconvenance ; ineptie, *f.*

unar'guable, *adj.*, indiscutable.

unarmed' (eu'n'ârm'de), *adj.*, sans armes ; (bot.) inerme ; (of animals) sans défenses.

unar'mored, *adj.*, non blindé, non cuirassé.

unarrayed' (eu'n'ar-réde), *adj.*, non vêtu ; sans ornements, sans fard ; (of armies) non rangé.

unascertain'able, *adj.*, qu'on ne peut déterminer, vérifier.

unascertained', *adj.*, non déterminé, inconnu ; non vérifié, non constaté.

unasked' (eu'n'âsk'te), *adj.*, non sollicité ; non demandé ; sans être invité ; spontané, spontanément.

unaspir'ing (-païeur'igne), *adj.*, sans ambition, modeste.

unassail'able (-sél'a-b'l), *adj.*, hors d'atteinte ; inattaquable.

unassailed', unassault'ed, *adj.*, inattaqué, non assailli.

unassist'ed, *adj. V.* **unaided.**

unassort'ed, *adj.*, inassorti.

unassum'ing (-as'siou'm'-), *adj.*, sans prétention ; simple ; modeste.

unassured' (eu'n'as-sheurde), *adj.*, non assuré, inassuré.

unatoned' (eu'n'a-tô'n'de), *adj.*, non expié ; sans expiation.

unattached' (eu'n'at'tatsh'te), *adj.*, non attaché **à** ; indépendant **de** ; (without affection) sans affection **pour** ; (milit.) en disponibilité ; en non-activité, à la suite.

unattain'able (eu'n'at'té'n'a-b'l), *adj.*, inaccessible ; impossible à atteindre.

unattain'ableness, *n.*, impossibilité d'atteindre.

unattempt'ed (eu'n'-), *adj.*, non essayé, non tenté.

unattend'ed, *adj.*, seul, sans suite ; (med.) laissé sans soins, privé de soins, négligé.

unattest'ed (eu'n'-), *adj.*, non attesté, sans attestation.

unattired', *adj.*, sans parure, sans ornements ; sans vêtements.

unattract'ive, *adj.*, peu attrayant ; sans attrait.

unauthen'tic (eu'n'o-thè'n'-), *adj.*, inauthentique, apocryphe.

unauthen'ticated, *adj.*, non constaté, non authentique ; (jur.) non légalisé.

unau'thorized (eu'n'o-theur'aïz'de), *adj.*, non autorisé ; sans autorisation ; (of things) illicite, illégal.

unavail'able (eu'n'a-vél'a-b'l), *adj.*, inefficace, infructueux, inutile, vain ; (not holding good) non valable.

unavail'ableness, *n.*, inefficacité, inutilité, *f.*

unavail'ing (eu'n'a-vél'-), *adj.*, inutile, inefficace.

unavenged' (eu'n'a-vè'n'dj'de), *adj.*, impuni, non vengé.

unavoid'able (-voïd-a-b'l), *adj.*, inévitable.

unavoid'ableness, *n.*, nécessité inévitable, *f.*

unavoid'ably, *adv.*, inévitablement.

unaware' (eu'n'a-wère), *adj.*, inattentif, ignorant. To be — of ; *ignorer ; n'être pas instruit* **de**, ou *au courant* **de** ; *être ignorant* **de**.

unawares' (eu'n'a-wèrze), *adv.*, inopinément, à l'improviste ; par mégarde ; (unconsciously) à son insu. To be taken — ; *être pris au dépourvu*.

unawed' (eu'n'ôde), *adj.*, sans crainte, sans être intimidé ; hardi ; audacieux.

unbacked', *adj.*, (unsupported) non secondé, sans appui.

unbal'anced (eu'n'bal'a'n'ste), *adj.*, non balancé, instable, sans contrepoids.

unbal'last (eu'n'-), *v.a.*, délester.

unbaptized' (-taïz'de), *adj.*, non baptisé.

unbar' (eu'n'-), *v.a.*, débarrer.

unbear'able, *adj.*, insupportable, intolérable.

unbeat'en, *adj.*, (of roads) non frayé, non battu ; invaincu (Corneille).

unbecom'ing (eu'n'bi-keu'm'-), *adj.*, inconvenant ; déplacé ; malséant ; (of clothes) qui ne va pas **à**.

unbecom'ingly, *adv.*, d'une manière inconvenante ; avec inconvenance ; (ungracefully) sans grâce.

unbecom'ingness, *n.*, inconvenance, *f.*

unbefit'ting, *adj.*, qui ne convient pas ; peu propre ; qui s'accorde mal **avec**.

unbefriend'ed, *adj.*, sans amis.

unbelief' (eu'n'bi-lîfe), *n.*, incrédulité, *f.* ; manque de foi, scepticisme, *m.*

unbeliev'er (eu'n'bi-lîv'-), *n.*, incrédule, infidèle, *m.f.* ; mécréant, sceptique, *m.*

unbeliev'ing, *adj.*, incrédule ; sans croyance ; infidèle.

unbend' (eu'n'-), *v.a.*, détendre, relâcher ; (to enervate) affaiblir, énerver ; (fig.) délasser, détendre ; (nav.) détalinguer, démarrer ; (a sail) désenverguer ; (a bow) débander. To — the brow ; *dérider le front*. To — one's self ; *se délasser*.

unbend'ing, *adj.*, qui ne se courbe pas ; qui ne fléchit pas ; inflexible.

unbend'ingly, *adv.*, inflexiblement.

unben'eficed, *adj.*, (of clergymen) sans bénéfice.

unbenefi'cial (eu'n'bè'n'i-fish'-al), *adj.*, infructueux, sans profit, sans avantage.

unbesiege'able, *adj.*, inassiégeable.

unbewailed', *adj.*, non pleuré, non regretté.

unbi'ased (eu'n'baï-aste), *adj.*, sans prévention ; impartial.

unbid'den (eu'n'-), *adj.*, non sollicité ; non invité, spontanément ; sans invitation ; spontané, non prié.

unbig'oted, *adj.*, exempt de bigoterie.

unbind' (eu'n'baï'n'de), *v.a.*, délier ; détacher ; (to loose) desserrer.

unblam'able (-blé'm'a-b'l), *adj.*, irréprochable, irréprehensible, exempt de blâme, sans reproche.

unbleached' (eu'n'blîtsh'te), *adj.*, écru.

unblem'ished (eu'n'blé'm'ish'te), *adj.*, sans tache, pur ; (free from deformity) beau, parfait, sans difformité.

unblend'ed, *adj.*, pur, sans mélange.

unblest' (eu'n'-), *adj.*, non béni ; (unhappy) malheureux, infortuné ; (cursed) maudit.

unblight'ed (-blaï-tède), *adj.*, non flétri, non broui ; (fig.) dans toute sa fraîcheur. — happiness ; *félicité pure, f.*

unblock', *v.a.*, décaler.

unblown', *adj.*, en bouton ; non épanoui.

unblush'ing (eu'n'bleush'-), *adj.*, qui ne rougit point, effronté ; éhonté, déhonté.

unblush'ingly, *adv.*, sans rougir, effrontément, sans honte.

unbolt' (eu'n'bôlte), *v.a.*, déverrouiller ; ouvrir, tirer les verrons **de**.

unbolt'ed, *adj.*, déverrouillé ; (unsifted, of flour) non bluté.

unbolt'ing, *n.*, déverrouillement, *m.*

unborn' (eu'n'-), *adj.*, encore à naître ; (of things) futur, à venir. Innocent as a babe — ; *innocent comme l'enfant qui vient de naître.*

unbor'rowed (eu'n'bor-rôde), *adj.*, non emprunté ; (of style) original ; naturel.

unbos'om (eu'n'beuz'eume), *v.a.*, ouvrir, découvrir, révéler, confier. To — one's self ; *ouvrir son cœur* **à** ; *s'ouvrir* **à**.

unbought' (eu'n'bôte), *adj.*, non acheté.

unbound', *adj.*, délié, détaché, non attaché ; (of books) non relié ; (free) libre.

unbound'ed (eu'n'baou'n'd'-), *adj.*, illimité, infini, sans bornes ; (unrestrained) démesuré ; effréné.

unbound'edly, *adv.*, sans bornes ; démesurément, infiniment.

unboun'teous (eu'n'baou'n'ti-), *adj.*, peu libéral.

unbrace' (eu'n'bréce), *v.a.*, délier ; détacher ; desserrer ; débander, détendre ; (to weaken) affaiblir, énerver ; relâcher.

unbreak'able (-bré-ka-), *adj.*, incassable.

unbred' (eu'n'-), *adj.*, mal élevé ; grossier.

unbreech' (-britshe), *v.a.*, déculotter ; (of guns) déculasser.

unbrewed' (-broude), *adj.*, non brassé ; (fig.) pur, sans mélange.

unbribed' (eu'n'braïb'de), *adj.*, non corrompu, non acheté, non séduit.

unbri'dle (eu'n'braïd'l), *v.a.*, débrider ; (fig.) déchaîner.

unbri'dled, *adj.*, débridé ; (fig.) effréné, déchaîné ; sans frein.

unbrok'en (-brôk'n), *adj.*, non rompu ; non cassé ; (uninterrupted) ininterrompu, continuel, continu ; (not subdued) non dompté, indompté ; (not violated) non violé, non enfreint, intact ; (of animals) non rompu, non dressé.

unbroth'erly (-li), *adj.*, peu fraternel, indigne d'un frère.

unbruised' (-brouz'de), *adj.*, sans meurtrissure ; intact.

unbuc'kle (eu'n'beuk'k'l), *v.a.*, déboucler.

unbuilt', *adj.*, pas encore bâti ; à bâtir, à construire.

unbung', *v.a.*, (a cask) débonder.

unbuoyed', *adj.*, qui n'est pas soutenu. — by vain hopes ; *qui ne se berce pas de vaines espérances.*

unbur'den (eu'n'beur-), *v.a.*, décharger ; débarrasser d'un fardeau; (fig.) décharger, soulager, alléger.

unbur'ied, *adj.*, sans sépulture.

unburnt', *adj.*, non consumé, non brûlé.

unbur'y (-bè-ri), *v.a.*, déterrer.

unbus'inesslike (-biz'nèce-), *adj.*, peu pratique, impropre aux affaires.

unbut'ton (eu'n'beut't'n), *v.a.*, déboutonner.

uncage' (eu'n'kédje), *v.a.*, faire sortir d'une cage ; délivrer ; lâcher.

uncaged' (-kédj'de), *adj.*, sorti de sa cage ; délivré, en liberté ; lâché.

uncalled' (eu'n'côl'l'de), *adj.*, sans être appelé. — for ; *sans être demandé ;* (unnecessary) *peu nécessaire ; gratuit ; inutile ;* (unbecoming) *déplacé, peu convenable ;* (undeserved) *non mérité, immérité.*

uncan'cellable (eu'n'ca'n'cèl-la-b'l), *adj.*, qu'on ne peut biffer, *ou* annuler ; ineffaçable.

uncan'celed (eu'n'ca'n'cèl'de), *adj.*, non biffé, non barré, non rayé ; non annulé.

uncan'did (eu'n'-), *adj.*, peu sincère ; faux, sans franchise.

uncan'ny, *adj.*, (of shape) disgracieux ; (awkward) maladroit ; (of the time) indu ; intempestif ; dangereux, peu prudent ; (weird) fantastique, surnaturel.

uncap', *v.a.*, découvrir ; (bottles) décoiffer ; (fire-arms) désamorcer.

uncapsiz'able, *adj.*, inchavirable.

uncared'-for (eu'n'kèrde'-), *adj.*, dont on ne se soucie pas ; négligé, dans l'abandon.

uncar'peted, *adj.*, sans tapis.

uncaught' (eu'n'côte), *adj.*, non pris. He is still — ; *on ne l'a pas encore pris, il est encore en liberté ; on n'a pas encore mis les mains dessus.*

unceas'ing (eu'n'cîss'-), *adj.*, incessant, sans relâche, continuel.

unceas'ingly, *adv.*, incessamment, sans cesse.

uncen'sured (eu'n'cè'n'sheurde), *adj.*, non censuré ; sans censure.

unceremo'nious (eu'n'cèr'i-mô-), *adj.*, peu cérémonieux ; sans cérémonie ; sans gêne ; sans façon ; cavalier.

unceremo'niously, *adv.*, sans cérémonie, sans façon, sans gêne ; cavalièrement.

unceremo'niousness, *n.*, sans-façon, sans-gêne, *m.*

uncer'tain (eu'n'ceur'-), *adj.*, incertain, irrésolu, peu sûr ; (of steps) mal assuré, chancelant.

uncer'tainly, *adv.*, avec incertitude.

uncer'tainty (eu'n'ceur-), *n.*, incertitude, *f. ;* (something unknown) l'incertain, *m. ;* (contingency) éventualité, *f.*

uncertif'icated, *adj.*, (teacher) sans diplôme, non diplômé ; non breveté ; (bankrupt) qui n'a pas obtenu un concordat.

unchain' (eu'n'tshé'ne), *v.a.*, déchaîner ; briser les chaînes **de** ; lâcher ; délivrer.

unchange'able (eu'n'tshé'n'dj'a-b'l), *adj.*, inaltérable, invariable, immuable.

unchange'ableness, *n.*, immutabilité ; inaltérabilité, invariabilité, *f.*

unchange'ably, *adv.*, immuablement ; d'une manière inaltérable ; invariablement.

unchanged' (eu'n'tshé'n'dj'de), *adj.*, qui n'est pas changé ; qui est toujours le même ; (of things) dans le même état ; (not alterable) inaltérable.

unchan'ging, *adj.*, qui ne change pas ; invariable, constant.

uncharged' (eu'n'tshârdje), *adj.*, (unloaded) non chargé. — for ; *gratis, qu'on ne fait pas payer, exempt de frais ; franco, gratuit.*

unchar'itable (eu'n'tshar'i-ta-b'l), *adj.*, peu charitable.

unchar'itableness, *n.*, manque de charité, *m.*

unchar'itably, *adv.*, sans charité.

unchaste' (eu'n'tshéste), *adj.*, incontinent ; impudique.

unchaste'ly, *adv.*, impudiquement.

unchas'tity (eu'n'tshas'-), *n.*, impudicité, incontinence, *f.*

unchecked' (eu'n'tshèk'te), *adj.*, non réprimé ; sans retenue ; effréné, sans frein. Abuses go on — ; *les abus continuent sans qu'on cherche à les réprimer.*

unchewed' (eu'n'tshioude), *adj.*, non mâché.

unchiv'alrous, *adj.*, peu chevaleresque.

unchiv'alrously, *adv.*, d'une manière peu chevaleresque.

unchrist'ened (-kris'n'de), *adj.*, non baptisé ; sans baptême.

unchrist'ian *ou* **unchrist'ianly** (eu'n-krist'-), *adj.*, peu chrétien ; anti-chrétien.

unchrist'ianly, *adv.*, peu chrétiennement.

uncir'cumcised (eu'n'ceur-keu'm'çaïz'de), *adj.*, incirconcis.

uncircumci'sion (eu'n'ceur-keu'm'cij'eune), *n.*, incirconcision, *f.*

uncir'cumscribed (eu'n'ceur-keu'm'scraïbde), *adj.*, illimité.

uncir'cumspect (eu'n'-seur-keum'-), *adj.*, peu circonspect, imprudent.

uncir'cumspectly, *adv.*, imprudemment.

unciv'il, *adj.*, malhonnête, incivil, impoli, grossier.

unciv'ilizable, *adv.*, incivilisable.

unciv'ilized (eu'n'civ'il'aïz'de), *adj.*, non civilisé, barbare ; rude ; sauvage ; grossier.

unciv'illy (eun'-), *adv.*, malhonnêtement, impoliment, grossièrement.

unclad', *adj.*, nu ; sans vêtements.

unclaimed' (eu'n'clé'm'de), *adj.*, non réclamé. — dividend ; *dividende non réclamé, m.*

unclar'ified (eu'n'clar-i-faïde), *adj.*, non clarifié.

unclasp' (eu'n'clâspe), *v.a.*, ouvrir le fermoir **de** ; détacher ; dégrafer ; défaire.

unclas'sical (eu'n'-), *adj.*, peu classique.

un'cle (eugn'k'l), *n.*, oncle, *m. ;* (pop.) (pawnbroker) tante, *f.*

unclean' (eu'n'clîne), *adj.*, malpropre, sale ; (lewd) impudique ; (in Scripture) impur, immonde.

unclean'liness, *n.*, malpropreté ; saleté ; (fig.) impureté, impudicité, *f.*

unclean'ly, *adj.*, sale, malpropre ; (obscene) impur, impudique. *V.* **unclean**.

unclean'ness, *n.*, saleté ; malpropreté ; (lewdness) impureté, impudicité, *f.*

uncleans'able, *adj.*, innettoyable.

uncleansed' (eu'n'clè'n'zde), *adj.*, non nettoyé ; (of drains, etc.) non curé ; (not purified) non purifié.

uncleared', *adj.*, (of land) indéfriché.

uncler'ical (eu'n'clèr-), *adj.*, peu clérical ; qui ne convient pas à un ecclésiastique.

unclinch', *v.a.*, ouvrir, desserrer.

unclipped' (eu'n'clip'te), *adj.*, non taillé, non coupé ; (of animals) non tondu ; (of coins) non rogné.

unclog' (eu'n'-), *v.a.*, ôter les entraves **de** (*ou* à) ; (fig.) dégager.

unclois'ter (eu'n'cloïs'-), *v.a.*, tirer du cloître.

unclose' (eu'n'clôze), *v.a.*, ouvrir.

unclosed' (-clôz'de), *adj.*, non fermé, ouvert ; (not sealed) ouvert ; (not fenced in) non clôturé ; (not finished) inachevé, non conclu.

unclothe' (eu'n'clôthe), *v.a.*, déshabiller ; (fig.) dépouiller ; mettre à nu.

uncloud'ed *ou* **uncloud'y** (eu'n'claoud'-), *adj.*, sans nuage, serein, pur.

uncloud'edness, *n.*, sérénité, pureté ; (fig.) clarté, sérénité, *f.*

uncocked' (eu'n-cok'te), *adj.*, (agri.) non mis en meule ; (of fire-arms) désarmé.

uncof'fined, *adj.*, (Byron) sans linceul (Lamartine).

uncoil' (eu'n'coïl), *v.a.*, dérouler.

uncoined', *adj.*, non monnayé.

uncollect'ed (eu'n'-), *adj.*, non rassemblé ; non recueilli ; non recouvré ; dispersé ; (fin.) (of money) non perçu, à percevoir.

uncollect'ible (eu'n'col-lèk-ti-b'l), *adj.*, non recouvrable, irrécouvrable.

uncol'onized, *adj.*, non colonisé.

uncol'ored (eu'n'keul'leurde), *adj.*, non coloré, incolore ; sans couleur ; (fig.) (of style) naturel, simple, vrai.

uncombed' (eu'n'cô'm'de), *adj.*, non peigné ; mal peigné.

uncombin'able (eu'n'co'm'baï'n'a-b'l), *adj.*, qui ne peut se combiner.

uncombined' (-baï'n'de), *adj.*, non combiné.

uncome'liness (eu'n'keu'm'li-), *n.*, manque, *ou* défaut, de grâce, *m. ;* forme disgracieuse, laideur ; (of behavior) inconvenance, *f.*

uncome'ly, *adj.*, sans grâce ; déplaisant ; disgracieux ; désagréable ; (unseemly) malséant.

uncom'fortable (eu'n'keu'm-fort'a-b'l), *adj.*, incommode ; gênant, fâcheux, désagréable ; pénible ; (pers.) gêné, mal à son aise ; (gloomy) triste, malheureux.

uncom'fortableness, *n.*, incommodité, *f.* ; malaise ; désagrément, *m.* ; gêne, *f.*

uncom'fortably, *adv.*, incommodément, peu confortablement ; (in an uneasy state) dans le malaise, dans la gêne, désagréablement ; (sadly) tristement.

uncommend'able (eu'n'co'm'mè'n'd'a-b'l), *adj.*, peu louable.

uncommend'ed, *adj.*, non loué ; sans éloge.

uncommer'cial (eu'n'co'm'meur-shale), *adj.*, peu commercial ; peu commerçant ; contraire, *ou* peu conforme, aux règles du commerce.

uncommis'erated, *adj.*, sans commisération, qui n'est pas plaint ; qui ne reçoit pas de pitié. *V.* **unpitied.**

uncommit'ted (eu'n'-), *adj.*, non commis ; qui n'est pas engagé à ; (parl.) qui n'a pas été référé (à un comité).

uncom'mon (eu'n'-), *adj.*, peu commun ; peu ordinaire ; rare, extraordinaire, inouï.

uncom'monly, *adv.*, rarement ; extraordinairement ; (greatly) extrêmement, infiniment.

uncom'monness, *n.*, rareté, *f.*

uncommu'nicable, *adj.* *V.* **incommunicable.**

uncommu'nicated (-miou-ni-két'-), *adj.*, non communiqué, incommuniqué.

uncommu'nicative (-miou-ni-ca-), *adj.*, peu communicatif, réservé, taciturne ; (stingy) parcimonieux, mesquin.

uncompan'ionable, *adj.*, peu sociable.

uncompared', *adj.*, non comparé.

uncompas'sionate (eu'n'co'm-pash'eu'n'-), *adj.*, incompatissable ; sans compassion.

uncompel'lable (eu'n'co'm'pèl-la-b'l), *adj.*, qu'on ne peut contraindre.

uncompelled' (-pèlde), *adj.*, sans contrainte, volontaire, spontané.

uncom'pensated (eu'n'co'm'pè'n'sét-), *adj.*, sans compensation *ou* récompense.

uncomplain'ing (eu'n'co'm'plé'n'-), *adj.*, sans se plaindre ; sans plainte ; sans murmure.

uncomplais'antly (-plés-), *adv.*, sans complaisance.

uncomplet'ed (eu'n'co'm'plît'-), *adj.*, incomplet ; inachevé.

uncomply'ing (eu'n'co'm'plaï-yigne), *adj.*, peu complaisant ; désobéissant ; inflexible.

uncompound'ed (eu'n'co'm'paou'n'd'-), *adj.*, non composé, simple.

uncomprehend'ed (eu'n'co'm'pri-), *adj.*, incompris.

uncompressed' (eu'n'co'm'prèste), *adj.*, non comprimé.

uncom'promised, *adj.*, non compromis.

uncom'promising (eu'n'co'm'pro-miz'-), *adj.*, peu accommodant ; qui ne transige pas ; entier ; opiniâtre ; irréconciliable ; inflexible. An — attitude ; *une attitude inflexible.*

unconcealed' (eu'n'co'n'cîlde), *adj.*, non caché ; ouvert, à découvert.

unconceived' (-co'n'cîv'de), *adj.*, inconçu.

unconcern' (eu'n'co'n'ceurne), *n.*, insouciance ; indifférence, *f.*

unconcerned' (-ceur'n'de), *adj.*, indifférent à, insouciant de ; insensible à ; (having no interest in) désintéressé dans ; indifférent, étranger à.

unconcern'edly (-nèd'-), *adv.*, avec indifférence, avec insouciance ; indifféremment.

unconcil'iating, *adj.*, inconciliable, irréconciliable.

uncondemned' (eu'n'co'n'dè'm'de), *adj.*, non condamné ; (of things) non défendu, non interdit.

uncondi'tional (eu'n'co'n'dish'eu'n'-), *adj.*, sans conditions ; absolu ; pur et simple.

uncondi'tionally, *adv.*, sans condition ; absolument ; sans réserve.

unconfessed' (eu'n'co'n'fèste), *adj.*, non avoué, inavoué ; (of sins) non confessé.

unconfined' (eu'n'co'n'faï'n'de), *adj.*, pas gêné ; libre ; (illimitable) illimité.

unconfin'edly (-faï'n'èd-), *adv.*, sans bornes ; sans contrainte ; librement, sans limites.

unconfirmed' (eu'n'co'n'feurm'de), *adj.*, non confirmé.

unconform'able (eu'n'co'n'form'a-b'l), *adj.*, non conforme à ; inconciliable ; incompatible avec.

unconform'ity (eu'n'-), *n.*, non-conformité ; incompatibilité, *f.*

unconfused' (eu'n'co'n'fiouz'de), *adj.*, non confus, non troublé.

unconfus'edly (-fiouz'èd'-), *adv.*, sans confusion.

uncongeal'able (-djîl'a-b'l), *adj.*, non congelable.

uncongealed' (-djîl'de), *adj.*, non congelé.

uncongen'ial (eu'n'co'n'djî-), *adj.*, désagréable ; peu sympathique ; peu conforme à ; impropre à.

unconnect'ed (eu'n'-), *adj.*, non lié ; détaché de ; séparé de ; étranger à ; isolé de ; sans rapport avec ; sans liaison ; (fig.) décousu, sans suite, sans liaison.

uncon'querable (eu'n'cogn'keur'a-b'l), *adj.*, invincible, indomptable ; insurmontable.

uncon'querably, *adv.*, invinciblement.

uncon'quered (eu'n'cogn'keurde), *adj.*, indompté, insoumis, inconquis ; (poet.) invaincu.

unconscien'tious, *adj.*, peu consciencieux.

uncon'scionable (eu'n'co'n'sheu'n'a-b'l), *adj.*, déraisonnable ; (enormous) énorme, démesuré. You have an — time ; *vous avez pris largement votre temps.*

uncon'scionableness, *n.*, déraison ; extravagance, exorbitance, *f.*

uncon'scionably, *adv.*, déraisonnablement ; sans conscience.

uncon'scious (eu'n'co'n'sheusse), *adj.*, qui n'a pas la conscience de, qui n'a pas conscience de ; (ignorant) ignorant ; (insensible) sans connaissance, insensible ; (philos.) inconscient. To be — of ; *n'avoir pas la conscience de ; ignorer.* To be —; *avoir perdu connaissance ; être sans connaissance.* He lay — on the ground ; *il était étendu à terre sans connaissance.*

uncon'sciousness, *n.*, (philos.) inconscience, *f.*, manque de conscience de ; manque de connaissance ; (swoon) évanouissement, *m.* ; (ignorance) ignorance ; (insensibility) insensibilité, *f.*

uncon'sciously, *adv.*, à son insu, insciemment, sans le savoir ; par inadvertance, sans y penser.

uncon'secrated (eu'n'co'n'si-crét'-), *adj.*, non consacré ; (of kings, of bishops) non sacré ; (of ground) non bénit.

unconsent'ing (eu'n'-), *adj.*, (jur.) non consentant ; qui ne consent pas.

unconsid'ered (-sid'eurde), *adj.*, non considéré ; (not seen) inaperçu.

unconsoled' (eu'n'-), *adj.*, inconsolé ; inconsolable.

unconstitu'tional (eu'n'co'n'sti-tiou-), *adj.*, inconstitutionnel.

unconstitu'tionally, *adv.*, inconstitutionnellement.

unconstrained' (eu'n'co'n'strè'n'de), *adj.*, sans contrainte ; (voluntary) volontaire, libre, spontané ; (of style) naturel, aisé.

unconstrain'edly (-'èd'-), *adv.*, sans contrainte ; volontairement, librement, sans gêne.

unconstraint' (eu'n'co'n'strè'n'te), *n.*, absence de contrainte, *f.* ; laisser aller, *m.* ; liberté, aisance, *f.*

unconsumed' (eu'n'co'n'siou'm'de), *adj.*, (not burnt) non consumé ; (of food) non consommé.

uncontam'inated (eu'n'co'n'ta'm'i-nét'éde), *adj.*, sans souillure ; pur ; non corrompu **par**.

uncontest'ed (eu'n'-), *adj.*, incontesté.

uncontradict'ed (eu'n'-), *adj.*, non contredit, sans contradiction ; non démenti.

uncontrol'lable (eu'n'co'n'trôl-la-b'l), *adj.*, incontrollable ; indomptable ; irrésistible ; ingouvernable ; qu'on ne peut maîtriser ; (of laughter) inextinguible, fou.

uncontrol'lably, *adv.*, irrésistiblement.

uncontrolled' (-trôl'de), *adj.*, sans contrôle ; sans opposition ; sans frein, irrésistible.

uncontrol'ledly (-'èd'-), *adv.*, sans contrôle ; sans frein, irrésistiblement.

uncon'troverted (eu'n'co'n'tro-veurt'-), *adj.*, incontesté, reconnu.

unconvers'able (eu'n'co'n'veurs'a-b'l), *adj.*, peu propre à la conversation ; réservé ; insociable.

unconvert'ed (-veurt'-), *adj.*, inconverti.

unconvert'ible. *V.* **inconvertible.**

unconvinced' (eu'n'co'n'vi'n'ste), *adj.*, non convaincu.

unconvin'cing, *adj.*, peu convaincant.

uncord' (eu'n'-), *v.a.*, ôter la corde **de.** To — a trunk ; *décorder*, ou *défaire, une malle.*

uncork' (eu'n'-), *v.a.*, déboucher.

uncorrect'ed (eu'n'-), *adj.*, non corrigé ; non réformé.

uncorrupt'ed, *adj.*, non corrompu ; intègre.

uncoup'le (-keup'l), *v.a.*, découpler, détacher ; (of machinery) désengrener.

uncourt'eous, *adj.* *V.* **discourt'eous.**

uncourt'liness (eu'n'côrt'-), *n.*, manque de politesse, *m.;* inélégance, impolitesse, gaucherie, *f.*

uncourt'ly, *adj.*, étranger au grand monde, à la cour ; inélégant, incivil, impoli ; (of manners) rustique.

uncouth' (eu'n'couth), *adj.*, bizarre ; singulier, baroque, étrange, rude, grossier.

uncouth'ly, *adv.*, rudement, grossièrement ; gauchement ; singulièrement, étrangement.

uncouth'ness, *n.*, rudesse ; grossièreté ; gaucherie ; singularité, étrangeté, *f.*

uncov'er (eu'n'keuv'-), *v.a.*, découvrir. To — one's head ; *se découvrir.*

uncreat'ed (-cri-ét'-), *adj.*, à créer, à naître ; (not produced by creation) incréé.

uncred'ited, *adj.*, qui n'est pas cru.

uncrip'pled, *adj.*, qui a plein usage de ses membres. The chip came out of action — ; *le vaisseau sortit du combat sans avoir reçu d'avaries.*

uncrit'ical, *adj.*, peu judicieux ; sans discernement ; non conforme aux règles de la critique.

uncropped', *adj.*, (land) non cultivé ; (not gathered) non moissonné, non récolté ; (of the ears of a dog) non coupé.

uncrossed' (-cros'te), *adj.*, non traversé ; (not cancelled) non rayé, non biffé ; (not thwarted) non contrarié.

uncrowd'ed (eu'n'craoud'-), *adj.*, non serré, non encombré par la foule.

uncrown' (eu'n'craou'ne), *v.a.*, détrôner.

uncrowned' (-craou'n'de), *adj.*, détrôné ; sans couronne.

unc'tion (eugn'k'sheune), *n.*, onction, *f.*

unctuos'ity (eugn'kt'iou-oss'-), *n.*, onctuosité, *f.*

unc'tuous, *adj.*, onctueux, huileux.

uncul'tivable (eu'n'keul-ti-va-b'l), *adj.*, incultivable.

uncul'tivated (-vét'-), *adj.*, inculte, sans culture.

uncurbed' (eu'n'keurb'de), *adj.*, indompté, effréné, sans frein.

uncured' (eu'n'kiourde), *adj.*, non guéri.

uncurl' (eu'n'keurle), *v.a.*, dérouler ; (of hair) défriser ; déboucler.

uncurl', *v.n.*, se dérouler ; (of hair) se défriser, se déboucler.

uncurtailed' (eu'n'keur-télde), *adj.*, inabrégé ; non raccourci.

uncus'tomary (eu'n'keus-teu'm'-), *adj.*, rare, pas habituel.

uncut' (eu'n'keute), *adj.*, entier ; non entamé ; (of the leaves of a book) non coupé.

undam'aged (eu'n'da'm'-èdjde), *adj.*, non endommagé ; en bon état ; (nav.) non avarié ; (of reputation) intact.

undamped' (eu'n'da'm'p'te), *adj.*, non découragé, ferme ; qui n'est pas abattu.

undaunt'ed (eu'n'dâ'n't'-), *adj.*, intrépide, qui ne se laisse pas abattre.

undaunt'edly, *adv.*, intrépidement.

undaunt'edness, *n.*, intrépidité, *f.*

undaz'zled, *adj.*, non ébloui ; sans se laisser éblouir.

undebarred', *adj.*, non empêché ; sans être retenu.

undebased' (-di-bés'te), *adj.*, non avili.

undebat'able, *adj.*, indiscutable.

undecayed' (eu'n'di-kéde), *adj.*, intact ; en bon état.

undecay'ing (-ké-igne), *adj.*, impérissable.

undeceiv'able (eu'n'di-cîv'a-b'l), *adj.*, qu'on ne peut tromper.

undeceive' (-di-cîve), *v.a.*, désabuser, détromper, désillusionner.

undecid'ed (-caï-dède), *adj.*, indécis ; incertain ; irrésolu ; vacillant.

undeci'pherable, *adj.*, indéchiffrable.

undeck', *v.a.*, déparer.

undecked', *adj.*, sans ornements ; (nav.) non ponté.

undefaced', *adj.*, non défiguré.

undefend'ed (eu'n'di-fè'n'd'-), *adj.*, sans défense ; non défendu ; (of a prisoner) sans défenseur, sans avocat ; (of a case) non contesté.

undefiled' (eu'n'di-faïl'de), *adj.*, sans tache ; immaculé ; pur.

undefi'nable (eu'n'di-faï'n'a-b'l), *adj.*, indéfinissable.

undefined' (-faï'n'de), *adj.*, indéfini.

undeliv'ered (eu'n'di-liv'eurde), *adj.*, non délivré ; non affranchi ; (not sent in) non livré.

undelud'ed, *adj.*, qui n'est pas déçu ; désabusé.

undemon'strable, *adj.*, qui ne peut être démontré.

undemon'strated, *adj.*, indémontré.

undemon'strative, *adj.*, réservé ; froid ; peu démonstratif.

undeni'able (-naï-a-b'l), *adj.*, incontestable ; indéniable ; irrécusable.

undeni'ably, *adv.*, incontestablement, irrécusablement.

undeplored' (eu'n'di-plôrde), *adj.*, non déploré.

un'der (eu'n'deur), *adv.*, dessous ; au-dessous ; (fig.) dans la sujétion. To keep — ; *retenir, maîtriser.* To go — ; *faire fiasco.* To be back — the hour ; *être rentré en moins d'une heure.*

un'der, *prep.*, sous ; dessous ; (in a rank inferior to, in a less degree than, less than, for less than) au-dessous **de** ; (in a state of subjection to, in) dans. — discussion ; *en discussion.* — consideration ; *à l'examen.* — the breath ; *à demivoix.* — age ; *mineur.* — favor of ; *à la faveur* **de** ; *aux soins* **de.** — cover of ; *sous prétexte* **de.** — cover of the batteries ; *sous la protection des batteries.* — cover of a tree ; *à l'abri d'un arbre.* — cover of the darkness ; *à la faveur de l'obscurité.* — the law of ; *en vertu de la loi de.* — the impression that ; *dans l'idée que.* To be — water ; (of land) *être inondé.* To be — sail ; (nav.) *être sous voiles.* To be — way ; *être en marche.* To be — the land ; *raser la côte ; être à l'abri de la côte.* — these circumstances ; *dans ces circonstances.* — the doctor's hands ; *entre les mains du médecin.* To be — obligations to; *avoir des obligations* **à**. They will not sell it — five francs ; *ils ne veulent pas le vendre à moins de cinq francs.* To sell — price ; *vendre à perte ; vendre au rabais.*

un'der (eu'n'deur), *prefix*, sous, aide.

un'der (eu'n'deur), *adj.*, de dessous ; (lower) inférieur ; (less than the usual quantity) inférieur, léger ; (of rank) sous, inférieur, subalterne, subordonné.

un'derbaked, *adj.*, pas assez cuit.

underbid', *v.a.*, (*preterit*, Underbid ; *past part.*, Underbidden) offrir moins que, offrir à plus bas prix.

un'derbred, *adj.*, mal élevé, malappris, commun, vulgaire.

un'derbutler, *n.*, aide-sommelier, *m.*

underbuy', *v.a.*, acheter à bas, à vil prix.

un'derchaplain, *n.*, sous-aumônier, *m.*

un'derclerk, *n.*, sous-commis ; petit clerc, *m.*

un'derclothing (-clôth'-), *n.*, vêtements de dessous, *m.pl.*, linge, *m.*

un'dercrust, *n.*, croûte de dessous, *f.*

un'dercurrent, *n.*, courant inférieur, *ou* sous marin ; (fig.) influence secrète, *f.*

un'dercut, *n.*, (of meat) filet, *m.*

un'derdealing (eu'n'deur'dîl'-), *n.*, menée, manœuvre secrète, *f.*

un'derdeck, *n.*, entrepont, faux pont, *m.*

underdone', *adj.*, (of meat) pas assez cuit, mal cuit, saignant, peu cuit.

un'derdrain (eu'n'deur-dré'ne), *n.*, fossé d'écoulement souterrain, *m.*

underdrain', *v.a.*, dessécher.

underfoot' (eu'n'deur-foute), *adv.*, sous les pieds, à terre, en bas, dans la rue, dans la sujétion.

un'der-gardener, *n.*, aide-jardinier, *m.*

un'der-governess, *n.*, sous-maîtresse, *f.*

undergo', *v.a.*, (*preterit*, Underwent ; *past part.*, Undergone) subir ; supporter, endurer ; (to experience) subir, éprouver, essuyer.

undergrad'uate (-grad'iou-), *n.*, étudiant, *m.*

un'derground (eu'n'deur-graou'n'de), *n.*, lieu souterrain ; (railway) chemin de fer souterrain ; (in Paris) Métropolitain, *m.*

un'derground, *adv.*, sous terre, en forme de souterrain.

un'derground, *adj.*, souterrain. — story ; *sous-sol, m.*

un'dergrowth (eu'n'deur-grôth), *n.*, broussailles, *f.pl. ;* taillis, *m.*

un'derhand, **un'derhandedly**, *adv.*, sous main ; sourdement, en cachette ; en secret.

un'derhand, *adj.*, fait sous main, clandestin ; sourd ; (pers.) caché, sournois.

un'der-housemaid, *n.*, deuxième bonne, *f.*

underived', *adj.*, non dérivé ; (fig.) qui n'est pas emprunté ; indépendant **de**.

under-keep'er, *n.*, sous garde-chasse, *m.*

underlay', *v.a.*, (*preterit and past part.*, Underlaid) mettre **sous** ; soutenir **par** ; étayer.

un'derlayer (eu'n'deur-lé-eur), *n.*, (mec.) étai, étançon, *m. ;* sous-couche, *f.*

un'derlease, *n.*, sous-bail, *m.*

underlease', *v.a.*, sous-affermer.

underlet', *v.a.*, sous-louer ; (a farm) sous-affermer ; (to let below the value) louer au-dessous de sa valeur.

underline' (eu'n'deur-laïne), *v.a.*, souligner.

un'derling (eu'n'deur-ligne), *n.*, subalterne ; (tool) instrument, suppôt, *m.*

undermen'tioned, *adj.*, mentionné ci-dessous, plus loin ; ci-dessous.

undermine' (eu'n'deur-maïne), *v.a.*, miner ; (fig.) miner, détruire ; nuire **à**.

undermin'er, *n.*, mineur ; (fig.) destructeur, ennemi secret, *m.*

un'dermost (eu'n'deur-môste), *adj.*, le plus bas.

underneath' (eu'n'deur-nîth), *adv.*, dessous ;

au-dessous ; par-dessous ; en dessous. From —; *de dessous.*

underneath', *prep.*, sous ; au-dessous **de**.

underpaid', *adj.*, mal payé, mal rétribué.

un'derpart (eu'n'deur-pârte), *n.*, dessous ; (fig.) petit rôle, accessoire, *m.*

underpay', *v.a.*, payer mal, payer trop peu.

underpeo'pled, *adj.*, peu populeux, pas assez peuplé.

under-pet'ticoat, *n.*, jupe, *f.*, *ou* jupon, *m.*, de dessous.

underpin', *v.a.*, reprendre en sous-œuvre ; étayer.

underpin'ning, *n.*, reprise en sous-œuvre ; étayement, étayage, *m.*, sous-œuvre, *f.*

un'derplot, *n.*, menée secrète ; (thea.) sous-intrigue, *f.*

underprop', *v.a.*, étançonner, étayer, soutenir.

underrate', *v.a.*, estimer au-dessous de sa valeur ; ne pas apprécier à sa juste valeur ; (fig.) dépriser, déprécier, rabaisser, mépriser ; faire trop peu de cas **de**.

underripe', *adj.*, vert, pas assez mûr.

undersec'retary (eu'n'deur-sèk-ri-), *n.*, sous-secrétaire, *m.*

undersell', *v.a.*, (*preterit and past part.*, Undersold) vendre à plus bas prix que ; vendre à meilleur marché que ; (too cheap) vendre à trop bas prix.

undersell'er, *n.*, gâte-métier, *m.*

under-serv'ant, *n.*, domestique inférieur, *m.*

un'derset, *n.*, (nav.) courant sous-marin, *m.*

under-sher'iff (eu'n'deur-shèr-), *n.*, sous-shérif, *m.*

un'dershot-wheel (eu'n'deur-shot'hwil), *n.*, (hydraulics) roue à aubes, à palettes, *f.*

un'dershrub (eu'n'deur-shreube), *n.*, (bot.) sous-arbrisseau, *m.*

un'derside (eu'n'deur-saïde), *n.*, dessous, côté de dessous, *m.*

undersigned' (eu'n'deur-saï'n'de), *n.*, sous-signé, *m.*, soussignée, *f.* I, the — ; *Je soussigné.*

un'dersized, *adj.*, au-dessous de la moyenne.

un'derskirt, *n.*, jupe de dessous ; sous-jupe, *f.*

un'dersoil. *V.* **subsoil.**

understand', *v.a.*, (*preterit and past part.*, Understood) entendre, comprendre ; (to be informed) apprendre, entendre dire, être informé ; (to mean without expressing) sous-entendre ; (to know how to set about anything) s'entendre **à**, **en**. We thought that was understood ; *nous supposions qu'on était convenu de cela.* To make one's self understood ; *se faire comprendre.* To give any one to — ; *donner à entendre à quelqu'un.* It is understood that ; *il est entendu que.* To — one another ; *se comprendre ;* (to be in agreement) *s'entendre.* To give to — ; *donner à entendre, faire entendre.* There is no —ing what they mean ; *il n'y a pas moyen de comprendre ce qu'ils veulent dire.* Something understood ; *quelque chose de sous-entendu.* That must be understood to mean a refusal ; *il faut entendre cela comme signifiant un refus.* I do not — it at all ; *je n'y comprends rien.*

understand', *v.n.*, comprendre ; (to learn) apprendre.

understand'able, *adj.*, intelligible.

understand'ing, *n.*, intelligence, *f. ;* entendement, esprit, jugement, *m. ;* compréhension ; (knowledge) connaissance, intelligence ; (agreement of minds) entente ; intelligence, harmonie, *f.*, accord, *m.* Good — ; *bonne intelligence.* Friendly, *ou* amicable, — ; *entente cordiale.* To come to an — with ; *s'entendre avec.* There is an — between them ; *ils sont d'intelligence, ils s'entendent.*

understand'ingly, *adv.*, avec intelligence ; sciemment, en connaissance de cause.

understate', v.a., amoindrir, diminuer, atténuer ; dire moins que.

understat'ed, adj., amoindri, atténué.

un'dersteward, n., sous-intendant, m.

un'derstrapper, n., subalterne, suppôt, m.

un'derstratum (eu'n'deur-stré-), n., (understrata) (geol.) couche inférieure, f.

un'derstudy, n., doublure, f.

undertak'able, adj., entreprenable.

undertake', v.a.n., (preterit, Undertook ; past part., Undertaken) entreprendre ; se charger de ; s'engager à ; promettre de ou que ; se faire fort de. To — to say ; ne pas craindre d'affirmer, oser dire. To — to convince ; se faire fort de convaincre.

undertak'er (eu'n'deur-ték'-), n., entrepreneur, m. ; (of funerals) entrepreneur des pompes funèbres, m. [prise, f.

undertak'ing (eu'n'deur-ték'-), n., entre-

un'dertenant (eu'n'deur-tè'n'-), n., sous-locataire, m.f.

un'dertone, n., ton bas, n. In an —; à voix basse, à demi-voix.

undervalua'tion (eu'n'deur-val'iou-é-), n., sous-évaluation, f.

underval'ue (-val'iou), n., bas prix, trop bas prix, m.

underval'ue, v.a., estimer au-dessous de sa valeur, sous-évaluer; (fig.) déprécier, rabaisser, dépriser.

un'derwaistcoat (eu'n'deur-wèst'côte), n., gilet de dessous, m.

un'derwood (eu'n'deur-woude), n., taillis, m.; broussailles, f.pl.; sous-bois, m.; (bot.) arbrisseaux, m.pl.

underwrite' (eu'n'deur-raïte), v.a., (preterit, Underwrote ; past part., Underwritten) souscrire ; (an insurance policy) assurer.

underwri'ter, n., souscripteur de police d'assurance ; assureur, m.

underwri'ting, n., (com.) assurance, f.

undescribed' (eu'n'di-scraïb'de), adj., non décrit.

undescried', adj., non découvert, inaperçu.

undeserved' (eu'n'di-zeurv'de), adj., immérité ; non mérité ; injuste.

undeserv'edly (-zeurv'èd'-), adv., à tort ; injustement.

undeserv'edness (-zeurv'èd'-), n., injustice, f.

undeserv'ing, adj., (pers.) sans mérite ; indigne de ; (of things) peu méritoire.

undeserv'ingly, adv., sans avoir mérité ; injustement.

undesigned' (eu'n'di-zaï'n'de), adj., sans dessein, involontaire.

undesign'edly (-'èd'-), adv., sans intention ; involontairement, par mégarde.

undesign'edness (-'èd'-), n., absence de dessein ; nature fortuite, f.

undesign'ing (eu'n'di-zaï'n'-), adj., sans dessein ; sans artifice ; loyal, sans mauvais dessein ; sans malice ; sans intention.

undesir'able (eu'n'di-zaïeur'a-b'l), adj., peu désirable ; peu convenable ; désagréable.

undesired' (eu'n'di-zaïeurde), adj., non sollicité, non désiré.

undesir'ous, adj., peu enclin, peu disposé à. I am — to ; je n'ai aucun désir de.

undespair'ing, adj., qui ne se laisse pas abattre, qui espère toujours.

undetect'ed (eu'n'di-tèk-), adj., non découvert.

undeter'mined (eu'n'di-teur-mi'n'de), adj., indéterminé, indécis, irrésolu ; indéfini.

undeterred', adj., sans être épouvanté par.

undevel'oped, adj., non développé.

unde'viating (eu'n'di-vi-ét'-), adj., qui ne dévie pas ; droit ; constant ; qui ne se dément pas ; ferme, sans détour.

undigest'ed (eu'n'di-djèst'-), adj., qui n'est pas digéré, indigéré ; (fig.) indigeste, informe.

undig'nified, adj., peu digne, sans dignité ; bas, grossier.

undimin'ished (eu'n'di-mi'n'ish'te), adj., non diminué ; soutenu, infatigable, qui ne se ralentit pas.

undiplomat'ic, adj., peu diplomatique.

undirect'ed, adj., sans direction ; (of letters, etc.) sans adresse.

undiscerned' (eu'n'di-zeur'n'de), adj., inaperçu, caché.

undiscern'ible (-'i-b'l), adj., invisible, imperceptible.

undiscern'ibly, adv., imperceptiblement.

undiscern'ing, adj., qui manque de discernement, sans discernement.

undis'ciplined (eu'n'dis-ci-pli'n'de), adj., indiscipliné, sans discipline.

undisclosed', adj., non découvert ; caché, voilé.

undiscount'able, adj., (com.) inescomptable.

undiscov'erable (eu'n'dis-keuv'eur'a-b'l), adj., qu'on ne peut découvrir.

undiscov'ered (-keuv'eurde), adj., non découvert ; inconnu.

undiscussed', adj., indiscuté.

undisfig'ured, adj., non défiguré.

undisguised' (eu'n'diz'gaïz'de), adj., sans déguisement ; sincère ; ouvert ; sans fard.

undismayed' (eu'n'diz'méde), adj., sans peur, sans terreur. — by ; sans se laisse • effrayer par.

undispu'ted (eu'n'dis-piout'-), adj., incontesté, sans conteste.

undissem'bled (eu'n'dis'sè'm'b'l'de), adj., non simulé ; sincère ; sans déguisement.

undissem'bling, adj., franc, ouvert, honnête, qui ne dissimule pas.

undissolv'able (eu'n'diz'zolv'a-b'l), adj., indissoluble ; (chem.) insoluble.

undissolved', adj., non dissous, non fondu.

undistin'guishable (eu'n'dis-tign'gwish-a-b'l), adj., qu'on ne saurait distinguer ; indistinct, confus, imperceptible ; (unrecognizable) méconnaissable.

undistin'guishably, adv., indistinctement.

undistin'guished (-'gwish'te), adj., non distingué ; (indistinct) indistinct, sans distinction.

undistin'guishing, adj., qui ne fait point de distinction ; sans discernement.

undisturbed' (eu'n'dis-teurb'de), adj., non troublé ; tranquille, calme ; sans interruption.

undisturb'edly (-'èd'-), adv., sans trouble ; tranquillement.

undivert'ed (eu'n'di-veurt'-), adj., non détourné ; (not amused) non diverti.

undivid'able (eu'n'di-vaïd'a-b'l), adj., indivisible.

undivid'ed (-vaïd'-), adj., entier, sans partage, tout entier ; (jur.) indivis; (bot.) entier.

undivorced', adj., non séparé, non désuni ; non divorcé.

undivulged' (eu'n'di-veul-dj'de), adj., non divulgué, secret.

undo' (eu'n'dou), v.a., (preterit, Undid ; past part., Undone) défaire ; (to untie) défaire, délier, détacher ; (to untangle) débrouiller ; (to ruin) ruiner, perdre ; (reputation) perdre de réputation.

undock', v.a., faire sortir des docks.

undo'er (eu'n'dou-eur), n., défaiseur, destructeur, m.

undo'ing (eu'n'dou-igne), n., ruine, perte, f.

undone', adj., inexécuté ; à faire, qui reste à faire ; (ruined) ruiné, perdu. To leave —; négliger de faire. To come —; se délier ; se défaire. What is done cannot be —; ce qui est fait, est fait.

undoubt'ed (eu'n'daout'-), adj., indubitable, incontestable, incontesté, certain.

undoubt'edly, *adv.*, indubitablement ; sans aucun doute, incontestablement.

undoubt'ing, *adj.*, qui ne doute pas ; convaincu ; inébranlable.

undramat'ic, *adj.*, peu dramatique.

undrawn' (eu'n'drô'n), *adj.*, non tiré ; non attiré ; (not portrayed) qui n'est pas peint ; qui n'est pas décrit.

un'dress, *n.*, déshabillé, négligé, *m. ;* (milit.) petite tenue, *f.* — cap ; *képi de petite tenue, bonnet de police, m.*

undress', *v.a.*, déshabiller ; (a wound) lever l'appareil **de**.

undress', *v.n.*, se déshabiller.

undressed' (eu'n'drèste), *adj.*, déshabillé ; en négligé ; sans parure ; (manu.) non préparé, non apprêté ; écru ; (hort.) non taillé ; (fig.) nu ; (cook.) non apprêté, au naturel.

undried' (eu'n'draïde), *adj.*, non séché ; vert.

undrink'able (eu'n'drign'k'a-b'l), *adj.*, imbuvable ; (of water) qui n'est pas potable.

undue' (eu'n'diou), *adj.*, non dû ; (not legal) illégal ; injuste ; (excessive) excessif, outré ; (of bills) non échu ; (improper) indu. — influence ; (jur.) *captation, f.*

un'dulate (eu'n'diou-), *v.a.* and *n.*, onduler, ondoyer ; flotter.

un'dulate *ou* **un'dulated** (-lét'-), *adj.*, (of hair, bot.) ondulé ; (of a river) onduleux ; (of ground) accidenté.

un'dulating (-lét'-), *adj.*, (crops) ondoyant ; (river) onduleux ; (ground) accidenté.

un'dulatingly, *adv.*, d'une manière ondoyante.

undula'tion (eu'n'diou-lé-), *n.*, ondulation, *f.*

un'dulatory (-lat'-), *adj.*, ondulatoire.

undu'ly (eu'n'diou-), *adv.*, irrégulièrement, indûment ; à tort ; (excessively) trop ; à l'excès.

undu'teous (eu'n'diou-ti-) *ou* **undu'tiful** (-foule), *adj.*, désobéissant ; irrespectueux ; indocile ; qui manque à ses devoirs **envers**.

undu'tifully, *adv.*, indocilement, irrévéremment, irrespectueusement.

undu'tifulness, *n.*, désobéissance, irrévérence, *f. ;* manque de respect, *m.*

undyed' (eu'n'daïde), *adj.*, non teint.

undy'ing (eu'n'daï-yigne), *adj.*, qui ne périt point ; impérissable ; immortel.

unearned' (eu'n'eur'n'de), *adj.*, non gagné ; non mérité, immérité.

unearth' (eu'n'eurthe), *v.a.*, déterrer.

unearth'ly, *adj.*, qui n'est pas de ce monde ; céleste ; surnaturel, surhumain ; (of noise, row) infernal, d'enfer ; (of the countenance) blême, d'une pâleur de mort.

uneas'ily (eu'n'îz'-), *adv.*, dans l'inquiétude ; mal à son aise ; (with difficulty) difficilement, péniblement, avec gêne.

uneas'iness, *n.*, (discomfort) malaise, *m. ;* peine ; (of mind) inquiétude ; (want of comfort) gêne, *f. ;* (annoyance) déplaisir, ennui, *m.*

uneas'y (eu'n'îz'i), *adj.*, (in mind) inquiet ; (constraining) gênant, incommode ; (constrained) mal à son aise, gêné ; (disagreeable) désagréable. To make one's self — about ; *se mettre en peine de, s'inquiéter de.*

uneat'able (eu'n'ît'a-b'l), *adj.*, immangeable.

unedi'fying (eu'n'èd'i-faï-yigne), *adj.*, peu édifiant. [cation ; sans instruction.

uned'ucated (eu'n'èd'iou-két'-), *adj.*, sans éducation ; sans instruction.

uneffaced' (-féste), *adj.*, ineffacé.

unembar'rassed (eu'n'è'm'bàr-raste), *adj.*, non embarrassé ; non gêné ; (of property) clair, net, libre **de** ; (of pers.) à l'aise.

unembel'lished, *adj.*, sans embellissement.

unembod'ied (eu'n'è'm'bod'ide), *adj.*, incorporel ; (milit.) non incorporé.

unemployed' (eu'n'è'm'ploïde), *adj.*, non employé ; sans occupation ; inoccupé ; (capital) dormant, inactif, oisif.

unemployed', *n.m.pl.*, les sans-travail.

unenclosed', *adj.*, ouvert, sans clôture.

unencum'bered (-keu'm'beurde), *adj.*, non encombré ; dégagé **de**, débarrassé **de** ; libre, à l'aise ; (of property) non grevé ; qui n'est grevé d'aucune charge ; libre de toute hypothèque.

unendowed' (eu'n'è'n'daoude), *adj.*, non doué ; non doté ; (fig.) dénué **de**.

unendur'able, *adj.*, insupportable, intolérable.

unendur'ing, *adj.*, qui ne dure pas, de courte durée.

unenga'ging, *adj.*, peu attrayant ; sans charmes.

un-En'glish, *adj.*, pas anglais ; pas digne d'un Anglais.

unenlight'ened (eu'n'è'n'laït'n'de), *adj.*, peu éclairé, ignorant.

unenslaved', *adj.*, libre, inasservi.

unen'terprising, *adj.*, peu entreprenant.

unen'viable, *adj.*, peu à envier, peu enviable.

unentertain'ing (eu'n'è'n'teur-té'n'-), *adj.*, peu divertissant ; peu amusant ; ennuyeux.

unen'vied (eu'n'è'n'vide), *adj.*, non envié, peu envié.

une'quable (eu'n'î-kwa-b'l), *adj.*, variable ; changeant ; inégal ; qui n'est pas uniforme.

une'qual (eu'n'î-kwal), *adj.*, inégal ; insuffisant, disproportionné ; au-dessous **de** ; inférieur **à** ; (bot.) irrégulier. He is — to that ; *il n'est pas capable de le faire.* He is — to the task ; *il n'est pas à la hauteur de la tâche.*

une'qualed (-kwal'de), *adj.*, sans égal ; sans pareil ; hors de pair ; unique.

une'qually, *adv.*, inégalement.

unequiv'ocal (eu'n'i-kwiv'-), *adj.*, clair, non équivoque.

unequiv'ocally, *adv.*, sans équivoque.

unerr'ing, *adj.*, infaillible, sûr.

unerr'ingly, *adv.*, infailliblement.

unevangel'ical (eu'n'î-va'n'djèl'-), *adj.*, non évangélique.

une'ven (eu'n'î'v'n), *adj.*, inégal ; (rough) raboteux ; (of numbers) impair ; (fig.) inégal.

une'venly, *adv.*, inégalement.

une'venness, *n.*, inégalité, *f.*

unevent'ful, *adj.*, (of life) monotone ; ordinaire, peu fécond en événements.

unexag'gerated, *adj.*, nullement exagéré.

unexam'ined (eu'n'èg-za'm'i'n'de), *adj.*, non examiné ; non visité ; (jur.) non interrogé.

unexam'pled (eu'n'èg-za'm'p'l'de), *adj.*, sans exemple, sans égal, sans pareil, unique.

unexcep'tionable (eu'n'èks-cèp-sheu'n'a-b'l), *adj.*, irréprochable ; irrécusable ; sans défaut.

unexcep'tionableness, *n.*, nature irréprochable, irréprochabilité, *f.*

unexcep'tionably, *adv.*, irréprochablement.

unex'ecuted (-èg-zi-kiout'-), *adj.*, inexécuté.

unex'emplary, *adj.*, peu exemplaire.

unexem'plified (eu'n'èg-zè'm'pli-faïde), *adj.*, non appuyé d'exemple, sans exemple.

unexempt', *adj.*, non exempt.

unexhaust'ed, *adj.*, inépuisé.

unexpand'ed, *adj.*, non dilaté.

unexpect'ed, *adj.*, inopiné, inattendu ; imprévu ; subit ; soudain ; (unhoped for) inespéré ; (pers.) qu'on n'attendait pas. The — usually happens ; *c'est l'imprévu qui arrive toujours.* His — arrival ; *son arrivée soudaine, inopinée.*

unexpect'edly, *adv.*, inopinément, subitement ; à l'improviste.

unexpect'edness, *n.*, soudaineté, *f.*

unexpen'sive, *adj.*, V. **inexpensive**.

unexpend'ed, *adj.*, non dépensé ; en main.

unexper'ienced, *adj.*, V. **inexperienced**.

unex'piated, *adj.*, inexpié.

unexpired' (eu'n'èks'païeurde), *adj.*, non expiré ; (of bills) non échu.

unexplained', *adj.*, resté sans explication ; inexpliqué.

unexplored' (eu'n'èks-plôrde), *adj.*, inexploré.

unexposed' (eu'n'èks-pôz'de), *adj.*, non exposé ; secret ; caché ; à l'abri de tout danger.

unexpressed' (eu'n'èks-prèste), *adj.*, inexprimé, sous-entendu.

unextin'guished (eu'n'èks-tign'gwish'te), *adj.*, non éteint.

unfad'ed (eu'n'féd'-), *adj.*, non fané, non flétri ; frais.

unfad'ing, *adj.*, qui ne se fane pas ; qui ne se flétrit pas ; (fig.) impérissable, immortel.

unfail'ing (eu'n'fél'-), *adj.*, inépuisable, intarissable ; (certain) infaillible, immanquable.

unfail'ingly, *adv.*, infailliblement, immanquablement.

unfail'ingness, *n.*, infaillibilité, *f.*

unfair' (eu'n'fère), *adj.*, injuste ; déloyal ; de mauvaise foi ; (at games) pas du jeu.

unfair'ly, *adv.*, injustement ; déloyalement.

unfair'ness, *n.*, injustice ; improbité, déloyauté, partialité, *f.*

unfaith'ful (eu'n'féth'foule), *adj.*, infidèle.

unfaith'fully, *adv.*, infidèlement.

unfaith'fulness, *n.*, infidélité, *f.*

unfal'tering, *adj.*, ferme, hardi, assuré ; (of actions, etc.) décidé, résolu.

unfamil'iar, *adj.*, peu familier ; inconnu ; peu connu.

unfamiliar'ity, *n.*, manque de familiarité, *m.*

unfash'ionable (eu'n'fash'eu'n'a-b'l), *adj.*, qui n'est pas de mode, démodé ; (pers.) pas à la mode.

unfash'ionableness, *n.*, inélégance, *f.*

unfash'ionably, *adv.*, contre la mode.

unfash'ioned (eu'n'fash'eu'n'de), *adj.*, non façonné ; informe ; simple.

unfas'ten (eu'n'fâs's'n), *v.a.*, délier, détacher ; défaire ; desserrer, relâcher ; (a door) débarrer ; ôter la chaîne, *ou* la barre, **de**.

unfa'therly (eu'n'fâ-*th*eur), *adj.*, peu paternel ; contre nature ; dénaturé.

unfath'omable (eu'n'fa*th*o'm'a-b'l), *adj.*, sans fond ; insondable ; impénétrable.

unfath'omableness, *n.*, impénétrabilité, *f.*

unfath'omably, *adv.*, d'une manière insondable ; impénétrablement.

unfath'omed (-fa*th*'eu'm'de), *adj.*, insondable.

unfa'vorable (eu'n'fé-veur'a-b'l), *adj.*, défavorable ; contraire, fâcheux.

unfa'vorableness, *n.*, nature défavorable, *f.*

unfa'vorably, *adv.*, défavorablement.

unfa'vored (eu'n'fé-veurde), *adj.*, non favorisé. — by nature ; *disgracié de la nature.*

unfeared' (eu'n'ffrde), *adj.*, non craint.

unfeas'ible (eu'n'ff'z'i-b'l), *adj.*, impraticable ; infaisable.

unfeath'ered (-fè*th*'eurde), *adj.*, sans plumes ; déplumé.

unfeat'ured (-fît'ieurde), *adj.*, difforme, laid, disgracieux.

unfed' (-fède), *adj.*, non nourri ; sans nourriture ; (of machinery) non alimenté.

unfeed' (-fîd), *adj.*, non rétribué ; non payé.

unfeel'ing (-fîl'-), *adj.*, insensible ; dur, cruel.

unfeel'ingly, *adv.*, cruellement.

unfeel'ingness, *n.*, insensibilité, dureté, *f.*

unfeigned' (eu'n'fé'n'de), *adj.*, non feint ; vrai ; sincère, réel.

unfeign'edly (-'èd'-), *adv.*, sans feinte ; sans hypocrisie ; sincèrement, de bonne foi.

unfeign'edness (-'èd'-), *n.*, sincérité, *f.*

unfelt' (eu'n'fèlte), *adj.*, qu'on ne sent, *ou* ne ressent, pas ; inconnu.

unfenced' (eu'n'fè'n'ste), *adj.*, sans clôture ; sans défense ; ouvert.

unferment'ed, *adj.*, non fermenté ; sans levain.

unfer'tile (eu'n'feur-til), *adj.*, infertile, stérile.

unfet'ter, *v.a.*, ôter les fers **à** ; déchaîner ; (fig.) délivrer **de**, affranchir **de**, débarrasser **de**.

unfet'tered (eu'n'fèt'teurde), *adj.*, n—n gêné ;

non entravé ; libre, sans entraves ; avec pleins pouvoirs.

unfil'ial, *adj.*, indigne d'un fils ; peu filial.

unfilled' (eu'n'fil'de), *adj.*, non rempli ; non plein ; (of a post) vacant.

unfil'tered, *adj.*, non filtré.

unfind'able, *adj.*, introuvable.

unfin'ished (eu'n'fi-nish'te), *adj.*, inachevé ; incomplet ; imparfait.

unfit', *adj.*, peu propre **à** ; impropre **à** ; qui n'est pas fait **pour** ; (unqualified) incapable **de** ; (unsuitable) déplacé, inopportun. — for food ; *impropre à la consommation.* — for service ; *hors d'état de servir ;* (mil.) *impropre au service.* — for use ; *inutile, qui ne sert à rien ; d'aucun usage.*

unfit', *v.a.*, rendre incapable **de**, mettre hors d'état **de**, rendre impropre **à**.

unfit'ly, *adv.*, mal ; peu convenablement ; mal à propos, à tort.

unfit'ness, *n.*, inaptitude **à** ; incapacité ; (unbecomingness) inconvenance, *f.*

unfit'ting, *adj.*, inconvenant.

unfix', *v.a.*, détacher, délier ; rendre fluide. To become —ed ; *se détacher.* — bayonets ! (mil.) *remettez la baïonnette !*

unfixed' (eu'n'fiks'te), *adj.*, mobile, errant ; inconstant, indécis ; irrésolu ; incertain.

unflag'ging (eu'n'flag-ghigne), *adj.*, qui ne languit pas ; persévérant ; soutenu ; infatigable.

unfledged' (eu'n'flèdj'de), *adj.*, sans plumes ; (fig.) novice ; jeune, inexpérimenté.

unflinch'ing (eu'n'fli'n'thigne), *adj.*, ferme, déterminé, résolu, qui ne recule pas.

unfold' (eu'n'fôlde), *v.a.*, déployer ; déplier ; (to disclose) exposer, développer, dérouler ; (to display) déployer, montrer ; (to tell) déclarer ; (to reveal) révéler ; expliquer ; dévoiler ; découvrir ; (sheep) déparquer.

unfold', *v.n.*, se déployer, se déplier ; se dévoiler ; se découvrir ; (of scenery) fuir se dérouler.

unfold'ing, *n.*, révélation, *f. ;* développement, *m.*

unforbear'ing, *adj.*, impatient, intolérant.

unforbid'den, *adj.*, non défendu ; permis.

unforced' (eu'n'fôrste), *adj.*, libre ; non forcé ; non contraint ; spontané ; (natural) naturel ; (easy) aisé, facile.

unfor'cible (eu'n'fôr-ci-b'l), *adj.*, sans force, sans vigueur.

unford'able, *adj.*, inguéable *ou* impassable.

unforesee'ing, *adj.*, qui ne prévoit pas ; imprévoyant.

unforeseen' (eu'n'fôr-sîne), *adj.*, imprévu.

unfor'feited (eu'n'for-fit'ède), *adj.*, non confisqué ; non perdu.

unforget'table, *adj.*, inoubliable, qui ne s'oublie pas.

unforgiv'en (eu'n'for-ghiv'n), *adj.*, à qui on n'a pas pardonné ; (of things) non pardonné.

unforgiv'ing (eu'n'for-ghiv'-), *adj.*, inexorable, implacable.

unforgot'ten, *adj.*, inoublié.

unformed' (eu'n'for'm'de), *adj.*, informe ; non formé.

unforsak'en (eu'n'for-sék'n), *adj.*, non délaissé.

unfor'tified (-for-ti-faïde), *adj.*, non fortifié ; sans défense, ouvert. — town ; *ville ouverte, f.*

unfor'tunate (eu'n'fort'iou-), *adj.*, infortuné ; malheureux.

unfor'tunate, *n.*, malheureux, *m.*, malheureuse ; prostituée, *f.*

unfor'tunately, *adv.*, malheureusement ; par malheur.

unfought' (eu'n'fô-te), *adj.*, non combattu ; (of battles) non livré.

unfound'ed (eu'n'faou'n'dède), *adj.*, sans fondement ; mal fondé ; dénué de fondement.

unframed' (eu'n'fré'm'de), *adj.*, non façonné; (of timber) non équarri ; (without a frame) sans cadre.

unfre'quency (eu'n'frî-kwè'n'-), *n.*, rareté, *f.*

unfre'quent, *adj.*, rare, peu fréquent.

unfrequent'ed, *adj.*, infréquenté, peu fréquenté ; (of places) écarté, solitaire, retiré.

unfre'quently, *adv.*, rarement ; peu souvent. Not —; *assez souvent.*

unfriend'ed (eu'n'frè'n'd'-), *adj.*, sans protection, sans amis, sans soutien.

unfriend'liness, *n.*, froideur ; disposition peu amicale, *f.*

unfriend'ly, *adj.*, peu amical ; mal disposé; peu bienveillant ; (of things) hostile ; malveillant. — to ; (to things) *nuisible* à ; *contraire* à.

unfrock', *v.a.*, défroquer.

unfroz'en (eu'n'frô-z'n), *adj.*, non gelé.

unfruit'ful (eu'n'frout'foule), *adj.*, infertile, infécond, stérile; (fig.) infructueux.

unfruit'fully, *adv.*, (without success) infructueusement ; stérilement, infertilement.

unfruit'fulness, *n.*, infertilité, stérilité, infécondité, *f.*

unfulfilled' (eu'n'foul-filde), *adj.*, non accompli, non exécuté.

unfund'ed, *adj.*, non consolidé. — debt ; *dette flottante, f.*

unfurl' (eu'n'feurl'), *v.a.*, déployer ; déplier ; dérouler ; (nav.) déferler.

unfur'nish (eu'n'feur-), *v.a.*, (a house) démeubler ; dégarnir ; dépouiller.

unfur'nished (-nish'te), *adj.*, non garni ; (fig.) dépourvu de ; dénué de ; (of houses, rooms) non garni, non meublé, démeublé.

ungain'able, *adj.*, ingagnable.

ungain'ful (eu'n'ghé'n'foule), *adj.*, sans profit ; ingrat.

ungain'ly (eu'n'ghé'n'-), *adj.*, maladroit, gauche ; mal bâti.

ungallant', *adj.*, peu galant ; peu courtois.

ungar'nished (eu'n'gar-nish'te), *adj.*, non garni ; sans ornements.

ungar'risoned (eu'n'gar-ri-s'n'de), *adj.*, sans garnison.

ungartered (eu'n'gâr-teurde), *adj.*, sans jarretières.

ungath'ered (eu'n'gath'eurde), *adj.*, non cueilli ; non recueilli ; (of crops) pas récolté.

ungauged' (eu'n'ghédj'de), *adj.*, non jaugé ; non mesuré.

ungen'erous (eu'n'djè'n'eur-), *adj.*, peu généreux ; (mean) mesquin.

ungen'erously, *adv.*, peu généreusement ; mesquinement.

ungen'ial (eu'n'dji-), *adj.*, peu propice ; défavorable; (of climate) rude, malsain ; (of a person) froid, raide.

ungenteel' (eu'n'djè'n'tîle), *adj.*, peu distingué; mal élevé ; pas comme il faut ; de mauvais ton ; de mauvais goût, de mauvais genre ; peu poli ; commun, vulgaire.

ungenteel'ly, *adv.*, d'une manière peu distinguée ; peu poliment.

ungen'tle (eu'n'djè'n't'l), *adj.*, rude, dur ; indocile ; impoli.

ungen'tlemanly *o u* **ungen'tlemanlike** (-djè'n'-), *adj.*, peu distingué, peu comme il faut ; (pers.) qui ne sait pas vivre, de mauvais ton, sans formes ; (things) indélicat, grossier ; indigne d'un homme comme il faut.

ungen'tlemanliness, *n.*, impolitesse ; vulgarité, *f.*

ungen'tleness, *n.*, rudesse, dureté ; brusquerie ; (incivility) incivilité, *f.*

ungen'tly, *adv.*, rudement ; durement.

ungild' (eu'n'ghilde), *v.a.*, dédorer.

ungild'ing, *n.*, dédorure, *f.* ; dédorage, *m.*

ungird' (eu'n'gheurde), *v.a.*, ôter la ceinture à ; détacher ; dessangler.

ungirt' (eu'n'gheurte), *adj.*, sans ceinture ; détaché; (of horses, etc.) dessanglé.

unglor'ified, *adj.*, qu'on ne loue pas, inglorifié.

unglove', *v.a.*, déganter.

unglue' (eu'n'glou), *v.a.*, décoller ; détacher.

ungod'lily, *adv.*, en impie.

ungod'liness, *n.*, impiété, *f.*

ungod'ly, *adj.*, impie.

ungov'ernable (eu'n'gheuv'eurn'a-b'l), *adj.*, ingouvernable; effréné; sans frein, déréglé, violent, emporté.

ungov'ernably, *adv.*, désordonnément, sans frein.

ungrace'ful (eu'n'grés'foule), *adj.*, peu gracieux, sans grâce, disgracieux.

ungrace'fully, *adv.*, peu gracieusement ; sans grâce ; sans élégance.

ungrace'fulness, *n.*, absence, *f.*, *ou* manque, *m.*, de grâce.

ungra'cious (eu'n'gré-sheusse), *adj.*, disgracieux, déplaisant ; désagréable ; (not favored) mal vu ; (wicked) méchant. — answer ; *réponse blessante, défavorable, f.*

ungra'ciously, *adv.*, disgracieusement; d'une manière peu gracieuse ; d'une manière déplaisante ; de mauvaise grâce.

ungrammat'ical, *adj.*, incorrect.

ungrammat'ically, *adv.*, incorrectement.

ungrant'ed, *adj.*, non accordé.

ungrate'ful (eu'n'grét'foule), *adj.*, ingrat envers ; (unpleasant) désagréable **pour**.

ungrate'fully, *adv.*, avec ingratitude ; désagréablement.

ungrate'fulness, *n.*, ingratitude, *f.* ; nature désagréable, *f.*

unground'ed (eu'n'graou'n'd'-), *adj.*, sans fondement. *V.* **groundless**.

unground'edly, *adv.*, sans fondement.

ungrudged' (eu'n'greudj'de), *adj.*, donné de bon cœur.

ungrudg'ing, *adj.*, qui ne donne pas à contrecœur, qui donne de bon cœur.

ungrudg'ingly, *adv.*, volontiers ; de bon cœur.

unguard'ed (eu'n'gârd'-), *adj.*, non gardé ; (pers.) sans protection, sans garde ; (of a position) sans défense, découvert ; (fig.) où l'on n'est pas sur ses gardes ; (not cautious) peu mesuré, peu réservé, peu sage ; imprudent ; inconsidéré, irréfléchi. In an — moment ; *dans un moment d'imprudence, d'absence, d'oubli.*

unguard'edly, *adv.*, étourdiment ; imprudemment ; sans mesure, sans réserve.

un'guent (eu'n'gwè'n'te), *n.*, onguent, *m.*

unguess'able, *adj.*, indevinable.

unguessed' (eu'n'gu-èste), *adj.*, non deviné.

ungu'iculate *ou* **ungu'iculated** (eu'n'-gwik'-iou-lét'-), *adj.*, onguiculé ; à onglet.

unguid'ed (eu'n'gaïd'-), *adj.*, sans guide.

un'gulate (eu'n'ghiou-), *adj.*, ongulé.

ungum' (-gheume), *v.a.*, (silk) dégommer ; décruser.

ungum'ming, *n.*, (of silk) dégommage ; décrusement (result of), *m.*, ou décrusage (act of), *m.*

unhal'low (eu'n'hal-lô), *v.a.*, profaner.

unhal'lowed (-lôde), *adj.*, non sanctifié; non consacré ; profane ; (fig.) profané, impie.

unhand', *v.a.*, lâcher.

unhand'ily, *adv.*, maladroitement, gauchement.

unhand'iness, *n.*, (pers.) maladresse, gaucherie, *f.* ; (of things) incommodité, *f.*

unhand'some (eu'n'han'd'seume), *adj.*, (illiberal) peu libéral, vilain, indélicat ; (uncivil) malhonnête ; impoli ; (ungraceful) laid, disgracieux.

unhand'somely, *adv.*, (illiberally) peu libéralement, vilainement, peu indélicatesse ; (uncivilly) impoliment ; malhonnêtement ; (ungracefully) d'une manière disgracieuse.

unhand'someness, *n.*, indélicatesse ; (incivility) impolitesse ; (want of beauty) laideur, nature disgracieuse, *f.*

unhand'y, *adj.*, maladroit, gauche ; (inconvenient) gênant, incommode.

unhang', *v.a.*, descendre, dépendre ; (a door, etc.) retirer des gonds ; (paper in a room) tirer les tentures.

unhap'pily, *adv.*, malheureusement ; par malheur.

unhap'piness, *n.*, malheur ; mal, *m.*

unhap'py, *adj.*, malheureux ; (calamitous) malheureux, funeste.

unhar'assed (eu'n'har'aste), *adj.*, non harassé; non tourmenté.

unhar'bored, *adj.*, sans port, sans abri ; découvert ; (fig.) qu'on n'entretient pas.

unharmed' (eu'n'hârm'de), *adj.*, intact ; sain et sauf.

unhar'ness, *v.a.*, déharnacher ; (to take from a vehicle) dételer ; (of armor) ôter l'armure à ; désarmer.

unhatched' (eu'n'hatsh'te), *adj.*, non éclos.

unheath'ful. *V.* **unhealthy.**

unhealth'fulness, *n.*, insalubrité, *f.*

unhealth'ily (eu'n'hélth'-), *adv.*, (of places) insalubrement.

unhealth'iness, *n.*, défaut de santé ; (want of vigor) état maladif, *m. ;* (insalubrity) insalubrité, *f.*

unhealth'y, *adj.*, maladif, malsain ; (insalubrious) insalubre, malsain ; (morbid) maladif ; (wanting vigor of growth) maladif.

unheard' (eu'n'heurde), *adj.*, non entendu ; sans être entendu ; (not celebrated) inconnu, obscur, ignoré ; (of prayers) inexaucé. — of ; *in-connu ;* (extraordinary) *inouï.*

unheed'ed (eu'n'hîd'-), *adj.*, inaperçu, négligé ; à qui (auquel) on ne fait pas attention ; (of advice) méconnu.

unheed'edly, *adv.*, sans être remarqué.

unheed'ful (-foule), *adj. V.* **unmindful.**

unheed'ing, *adj.*, insouciant ; inattentif, distrait, négligent.

unhelped' (eu'n'hèlp'te), *adj.*, sans secours ; sans aide ; (at dinner) non servi.

unhelp'ful (-foule), *adj.*, qui n'est d'aucun secours, qui ne sert à rien, inutile.

unhes'itating (eu'n'hèz'i-tét'-), *adj.*, qui n'hésite pas ; décidé ; déterminé, ferme, résolu.

unhes'itatingly, *adv.*, sans hésiter.

unhewn' (eu'n'hioune), *adj.*, brut ; non travaillé ; (of stone) non taillé ; (of wood) de brin, en brin.

unhinge' (eu'n'hi'n'dje), *v.a.*, faire sortir des gonds, mettre hors des gonds ; (fig.) bouleverser, troubler, démonter.

unhitch', *v.a.*, décrocher.

unho'liness (eu'n'hô-), *n.*, impiété, *f.*

unho'ly (-hô-), *adj.*, profane ; impie.

unhon'ored (eu'n'o'n'eurde), *adj.*, sans honneur ; dédaigné, méprisé.

unhood' (eu'n'houde), *v.a.*, (a falcon) déchaperonner.

unhook' (eu'n'houke), *v. a.*, décrocher ; (clothes) dégrafer.

unhoop' (eu'n'houpe), *v.a.*, décercler.

unhoped' (eu'n'hôp'te) *ou* **unhoped for**, *adj.*, inespéré, inattendu.

unhorse', *v.a.*, désarçonner, démonter. To be —d ; *vider les arçons.*

unhouse' (-'haouce), *v.a.*, déloger, chasser.

unhung' (-heugne), *adj.*, à pendre. The greatest rascal — ; *le plus grand pendard imaginable.*

unhurt' (eu'n'heurte), *adj.*, sain et sauf ; intact, indemne.

u'nicorn (you-ni-), *n.*, licorne, *f.* — team ; *attelage en arbalète, m.*

u'nicorn-fish, *n.*, (zoöl.) narval, *m. ;* licorne de mer, *f.*

unicorn'ous (you-ni-), *adj.*, unicorne.

unide'al (eu'n'aï-di-), *adj.*, non idéal ; réel ; positif ; (not having ideas) dépourvu d'idées ; (senseless) absurde.

unidiomat'ic, *adj.*, qui n'est pas idiomatique.

unif'lorous (you-ni-flô-), *adj.*, uniflore.

u'niform (you-ni-), *adj.*, uniforme.

u'niform (you-ni-), *n.*, uniforme, *m.* In full —; *en grande tenue ; en grand uniforme.* In undress — ; *en petite tenue.*

uniform'ity (you-ni-), *n.*, uniformité, *f.*

u'niformly (you-ni-), *adv.*, uniformément.

unilat'eral, *adj.*, unilatéral.

unima'ginable (eu'n'i-madji'i'n'a-b'l), *adj.*, inimaginable, inconcevable.

unima'ginably (eu'n'i-madj'-), *adv.*, d'une manière inimaginable.

unima'ginative (eu'n'-), *adj.*, non imaginatif.

unima'gined (eu'n'i-madji'i'n'de), *adj.*, non imaginé.

unimpair'able (eu'n'i'm'pér'a-b'l), *adj.*, inaltérable.

unimpaired' (-pérde), *adj.*, non altéré, inaltéré ; intact ; entier ; non affaibli ; non diminué ; endommagé, avec toute sa vigueur.

unimpas'sioned (eu'n'i'm'pash'eu'n'de), *adj.*, sans passion ; calme ; tranquille.

unimpeach'able (eu'n'i'm-pîtsh'a-b'l), *adj.*, inattaquable ; irréprochable ; incontestable.

unimpeached' (-pîtsh'te), *adj.*, incontesté.

unimped'ed (eu'n'i'm-pîd'-), *adj.*, sans empêchement ; sans obstacle.

unim'plicated (eu'n'i'm'pli-ké-), *adj.*, non impliqué ; non compromis.

unimplied' (eu'n'i'm'plaîde), *adj.*, exprimé, non sous-entendu.

unimplored' (eu'n'i'm'plôrde), *adj.*, non imploré ; non supplié.

unimport'ance, *n.*, peu d'importance, *m. ;* insignifiance, *f.*

unimport'ant (eu'n'-), *adj.*, sans importance ; insignifiant, indifférent ; peu important ; sans prétention ; léger.

unimportuned' (eu'n'i'm'por-tiou'n'de), *adj.*, non importuné.

unimposed' (eu'n'i'm'poz'de), *adj.*, non imposé ; volontaire.

unimpos'ing, *adj.*, peu imposant.

unimpressed' (-prèste), *adj.*, non empreint ; non imprimé ; (not penetrated) non pénétré.

unimpres'sive, *adj.*, peu frappant ; froid, peu touchant ; peu émouvant.

unimprov'able (eu'n'i'm'prouv'a-b'l), *adj.*, non susceptible d'amélioration ; incorrigible ; (of land) non exploitable.

unimprov'ableness, *n.*, nature incorrigible ; (of land) nature non exploitable, *f.*

unimproved' (-prouv'de), *adj.*, non corrigé ; non amélioré ; (not advanced) peu avancé ; qui n'a pas fait de progrès, sans progrès, arriéré, mal développé, peu avancé ; (of land) non exploité.

unimprov'ing, *adj.*, qui ne corrige pas ; qui n'améliore pas ; qui ne fait pas faire de progrès.

uninclosed' (eu'n'i'n'clôz'de), *adj.*, sans clôture, ouvert.

unincum'bered (-'keu'm'beurde), *adj.*, non encombré ; (jur.) non grevé ; libre.

unindebt'ed (eu'n'i'n'dèt'-), *adj.*, non endetté.

unindorsed' (eu'n'i'n'dorste), *adj.*, non endossé ; sans endossement.

unindul'gent (eu'n'i'n'deuldj'-), *adj.*, peu indulgent ; sans indulgence.

unindus'trious (eu'n'i'n'deus-), *adj.*, peu laborieux ; peu assidu.

uninflamed' (eu'n'i'n'flé'm'de), *adj.*, non enflammé.

uninflam'mable (eu'n'i'n'fla'm'ma-b'l), *adj.*, non inflammable.

unin'fluenced (eu'n'i'n'flou-è'n'ste), *adj.*, non influencé ; impartial.

uninfluen'tial (-shal), *adj.*, peu influent ; sans influence.

uninformed' (eu'n'i'n'form'de), *adj.*, non cultivé, sans culture ; (pers.) ignorant, sans instruction, non instruit. To be — of ; *être ignorant de*; *ignorer*.

uninform'ing, *adj.*, qui n'instruit pas.

uninfringed' (eu'n'i'n'fri'n'dj'de), *adj.*, (jur.) non enfreint.

uninhab'itable (eu'n'i'n'hab'i-ta-b'l), *adj.*, inhabitable.

uninhab'ited, *adj.*, inhabité.

unini'tiated (-'ish-i-ét'-), *adj.*, non initié.

uninjured' (-djeurde), *adj.*, auquel on n'a pas fait tort ; (safe) en sûreté, sain et sauf, sans blessure, sans mal (of things) non endommagé, intact.

uninquis'itive (eu'n'i'n'kwiz'-), *adj.*, peu curieux.

uninscribed' (eu'n'i'n'scraïb'de), *adj.*, non inscrit ; sans inscription.

uninspired' (eu'n'i'n'spaïeurde), *adj.*, non inspiré ; sans inspiration.

uninstruct'ed (eu'n'i'n'streukt'-), *adj.*, non instruit, ignorant, sans instruction ; (without authority) sans instructions.

uninstruct'ive, *adj.*, non instructif, peu instructif.

uninsured', *adj.*, non assuré, inassuré.

unintellec'tual (eu'n'i'n'tèl-lèkt'iou-), *adj.*, peu intellectuel.

unintellec'tually, *adv.*, peu intellectuellement.

unintel'ligent (eu'n'i'n'tèl-li-djè'n'te), *adj.*, inintelligent ; sans intelligence.

unintelligibil'ity (eu'n'i'n'tèl-li-dji-), *n.*, caractère inintelligible, *m.*

unintel'ligible (-li-dji-b'l), *adj.*, inintelligible.

unintel'ligibly, *adv.*, inintelligiblement ; d'une manière inintelligible.

uninten'tional *ou* **unintend'ed** (eu'n'-), *adj.*, sans dessein, involontaire, sans intention.

uninten'tionally, *adv.*, involontairement ; sans le vouloir, sans intention, sans dessein.

unin'terested, *adj.*, désintéressé, non intéressé **dans**, indifférent **à**.

unin'terestedly, *adv.*, d'une manière désintéressée.

unin'teresting, *adj.*, peu intéressant, dénué d'intérêt.

unin'terestingly, *adv.*, d'une manière peu intéressante.

unintermit'ting *ou* **unintermit'ted** (eu'n-i'n'-teur-), *adj.*, incessant, continu, continuel, non interrompu.

unintermit'tingly, *adv.*, sans cesse, sans intermission.

uninterred' (-teurde), *adj.*, sans sépulture.

uninterrupt'ed (eu'n'i'n'teur-reupt'-), *adj.*, ininterrompu ; continuel ; sans interruption.

uninterrupt'edly, *adv.*, sans interruption.

unintrenched' (eu'n'i'n'trè'n'sh'te), *adj.*, (milit.) sans retranchements, non retranché.

uninured', *adj.*, non aguerri ; non endurci.

uninvad'ed (eu'n'i'n'véd'-), *adj.*, non envahi. Leave the province of the professor — ; *n'empiétez pas sur le domaine du professeur*.

uninvent'ed, *adj.*, non inventé.

uninvent'ive, *adj.*, peu inventif.

uninvest'ed, *adj.*, (of towns) non **investi** ; (of money) non placé.

uninvest'igable (eu'n'i'n'vès-ti-ga-b'l), *adj.*, non susceptible d'investigation ; inscrutable.

uninvest'igated (-ti-ghét'-), *adj.*, que l'on n'a pas scruté, examiné ; sans investigation.

uninvit'ed (eu'n'i'n'vaït'-), *adj.*, non invité ; non engagé, sans invitation ; sans être invité.

uninvit'ing (-vaït'-), *adj.*, peu attrayant, peu engageant ; (of food) peu appétissant, peu ragoûtant ; repoussant.

u'nion (you'n'ieune), *n.*, union ; réunion, *f.*; (concord) accord, *m.*, concorde, harmonie ; (states united) union ; (of parishes) union, *f.* — cloth ; *toile métisse*, *f.* — is strength ; *l'union fait la force.*

u'nionist (you'n'ieun'-), *n.*, unioniste, *m.*

U'nion-jack (-djake), *n.*, pavillon anglais, *m.*

unip'arous (you-ni-), *adj.*, (biology) unipare.

unique' (you-nîke), *adj.*, unique.

unique'ly, *adv.*, d'une manière unique.

unisex'ual (you-ni-cèks'iou-), *adj.*, (bot.) unisexuel.

u'nison (you-ni-ceune), *n.*, unisson, *m.*

u'nison (you-ni-), **in**, *adv.*, à l'unisson.

unis'onance (you-niss'-), *n.*, consonance parfaite, *f.*, unisson, *m.*

unis'onant, *adj.*, à l'unisson.

u'nit (you-nite), *n.*, unité, *f.*

Unita'rian (you-ni-té-), *n.*, (theol., philos.) unitaire, *m.f.*

Unita'rianism, *n.*, unitarisme, *m.*

unite' (you-naïte), *v.a.*, unir **à**, *ou* **avec** ; (one's efforts) joindre, réunir ; joindre **à**.

unite', *v.n.*, s'unir, se réunir, se joindre **à**.

unit'ed, *adj.*, uni ; réuni ; joint.

unit'edly, *adv.*, avec union ; conjointement ; ensemble ; en harmonie, d'accord.

u'nity (you-ni-), *n.*, unité ; union ; concorde, harmonie, *f.*

univer'sal (you-ni-veur-), *adj.*, universel.

univer'sals, *n.pl.*, universaux, *m.pl.*

universal'ity, *n.*, universalité, *f.*

univer'sally, *adv.*, universellement.

u'niverse (you-ni-veurse), *n.*, univers, *m.*

univer'sity (you-ni-veur-), *n.*, université, *f.* — man ; *universitaire*, *m.* — degree ; *grade universitaire*, *m.*

unjoin' (eu'n'djoïne), *v.a.*, déjoindre, disjoindre, séparer.

unjoy'ful (eu'n'djo-è-foule) *ou* **unjoy'ous** (-djo-yeuss'e), *adj.*, peu joyeux ; triste.

unjudged' (eu'n'djeudj'de), *adj.*, non jugé.

unjust' (eu'n'djeuste), *adj.*, injuste ; faux.

unjust'ifiable (eu'n'djeust'i-faï-a-b'l), *adj.*, inexcusable, injustifiable.

unjust'ifiableness, *n.*, nature injustifiable, *ou* inexcusable, *f.*

unjust'ifiably, *adv.*, d'une manière injustifiable.

unjust'ified (-faïde), *adj.*, sans justification, sans excuse.

unjust'ly (eu'n'djeust'-), *adv.*, injustement.

unken'nel, *v.a.*, sortir de son trou ; (a dog) sortir du chenil ; lancer ; (a fox) lancer ; (a stag) débucher.

unkind' (eu'n'kaï'n'de), *adj.*, peu obligeant, peu complaisant ; malhonnête, méchant ; dur, peu bienveillant, désobligeant ; peu aimable ; mauvais, cruel.

unkind'liness, *n.*, désobligeance, dureté, malveillance, *f.*

unkind'ly, *adj.*, peu propice ; contraire, nuisible ; défavorable ; désobligeant, dur ; cruel ; malfaisant.

unkind'ly, *adv.*, sans complaisance, sans bienveillance ; désobligeamment ; durement ; cruellement ; mal. To take (anything) — ; *prendre en mauvaise part, prendre mal*. Don't take it — on my part, if . . . ; *ne me sachez pas mauvais gré, si . . .*

unkind'ness, *n.*, manque de complaisance, défaut de bienveillance ; mauvais vouloir, *m.*; malveillance, désobligeance, cruauté, dureté, *f.*

unking'ly, *adj.*, indigne d'un roi.

unknelled' (eu'n'nèlde), *adj.*, (Byron) privé de tombeau (Lamartine).

unknit' (eu'n'nète), *v.a.*, défaire ; dénouer ; délier ; (the brow) dérider, défroncer. To — one's brows ; *se dérider le front.*

unknow'able (eu'n'nô-a-b'l), *adj.*, **qu'on ne**

peut savoir ; (pers.) méconnaissable ; impénétrable.

unknow'ing (eu'n'nô-igne), *adj.*, ignorant, qui ne sait pas; ignorant.

unknow'ingly, *adv.*, sans le savoir ; à son insu ; insciemment ; sans en avoir conscience ; par ignorance ; par inadvertance, sans y penser.

unknown' (eu'n'nône), *adj.*, inconnu **à** ; ignoré **de**. — to me ; (without my knowledge) *à mon insu ;* (unheard of) *inouï.*

unla'bored (eu'n'lé-beurde), *adj.*, non travaillé ; naturel; spontané, facile, aisé.

unlace', *v.a.*, délacer; détacher.

unlade', *v.a.*, (*preterit*, Unloaded; *past part.*, Unladen) décharger.

unlad'ing, *n.*, déchargement, *m.*

unla'dylike (eu'n'lédi-laïke), *adj.*, commun, de mauvais ton; indélicat ; indigne, *ou* peu digne, d'une dame.

unlaid', *adj.*, non posé ; (fig.) non apaisé.

unlament'ed, *adj.*, non regretté ; sans laisser de regrets.

unlatch', *v.a.*, lever le loquet **de** ; ouvrir.

unlaw'ful (eu'n'lô-foule), *adj.*, illégal ; illicite; (of birth) illégitime.

unlaw'fully, *adv.*, illégalement ; illicitement; illégitimement.

unlearn' (eu'n'leurne), *v.a.*, désapprendre.

unlearn'able, *adj.*, inapprenable.

unlearn'ed (eu'n'leurn'ède), *adj.*, ignorant ; illettré; (of things) désappris, non appris.

unleav'ened (eu'n'lèv'n'de), *adj.*, sans levain ; (Script.) azyme.

unless', *conj.*, à moins **que** . . . ne (with subjunctive) ; à moins **de** (followed by infin.) ; si ce n'est, excepté que, sinon. — I send for you ; *à moins que je ne vous envoie chercher.* — sent for ; *à moins d'être appelé.*

unlet'tered (eu'n'lèt'teurde), *adj.*, illettré.

unlev'eled (eu'n'lèv'èlde), *adj.*, non nivelé.

unlev'eling, *n.*, dénivellement, *m.*

unli'censed (eu'n'laï-cèn'ste), *adj.*, non autorisé ; sans autorisation ; sans privilège ; (of trades) sans patente, sans brevet ; (of sportsmen) sans permis (de chasse). — broker ; *courtier marron, m.*

unlicked' (eu'n'lik'te), *adj.*, mal léché ; grossier. — bear ; *ours mal léché, m.*

unlight'ed (eu'n'laït'ède), *adj.*, non allumé ; inéclairé.

unlike' (eu'n'laïke), *adj.*, dissemblable **à**, *ou* **de** ; différent **de** ; qui ne ressemble pas **à** ; (improbable) invraisemblable, improbable. To be — each other ; *ne pas se ressembler.* Not — a . . . ; *qui ne ressemble pas mal,* ou *qui ressemble assez,* **à** . . .

unlike', *prep.*, à l'inverse **de**, tout au contraire **de**.

unlike'lihood (eu'n'laïk'li-houde) *ou* **unlike'liness** (-laïk'-), *n.*, invraisemblance, improbabilité, *f.*

unlike'ly, *adj.*, improbable, invraisemblable ; peu sûr, peu certain ; (not promising success) inefficace ; qui ne promet pas de réussir. That is not at all — ; *cela se pourrait bien, c'est bien possible.* It is very — that ; *il est peu probable que.*

unlike'ly, *adv.*, invraisemblablement.

unlike'ness, *n.*, différence, dissemblance, *f.*

unlim'ber, *v.a.*, (mil.) désatteler ; mettre en batterie.

unlim'ited, *adj.*, illimité ; indéfini, indéterminé.

unlim'itedly, *adv.*, sans limites, sans bornes.

unlim'itedness, *n.*, illimitation, immensité, *f.*

unlink' (eu'n'lign'ke), *v.a.*, défaire ; (to uncoil) dérouler.

unli'quidated (eu'n'lik'wi-dét'-), *adj.*, non réglé, non soldé.

unload' (eu'n'lôde), *v.a.*, décharger ; alléger.

unload'ed, *adj.*, déchargé ; (not charged) non chargé.

unload'ing, *n.*, déchargement, *m.*

unlock', *v.a.*, ouvrir (ce qui était fermé à clef) ; (print.) desserrer ; (fig.) découvrir, révéler, épancher.

unlooked'-for (eu'n'louk'te-), *adj.*, inattendu, imprévu, inopiné, inespéré.

unloved' (eu'n'leuv'de), *adj.*, pas aimé.

unlove'liness, *n.*, défaut d'amabilité, *m. ;* laideur, *f.*

unlove'ly, *adj.*, peu aimable.

unlov'ing, *adj.*, peu affectueux, insensible.

unluck'ily (eu'n'leuk'-), *adv.*, malheureusement, par malheur.

unluck'iness, *n.*, malheur, *m. ;* infortune, *f.*

unluck'y, *adj.*, malheureux ; infortuné; malencontreux ; (ill-omened) sinistre ; de mauvais augure ; (mischievous) malin, méchant. To be — ; (at cards) *avoir du guignon, être en guignon ; n'avoir pas de chance.*

unmade' (eu'n'méde), *adj.*, pas fait; défait ; informe, non confectionné.

unmaintain'able (eu'n'mé'n'té'n'a-b'l), *adj.*, insoutenable.

unmake', *v.a.*, (*preterit* and *past part.*, Unmade) défaire ; anéantir ; détruire ; ruiner.

unman', *v.a.*, dégrader ; (to deprive of men) dégarnir d'hommes ; (to deject) abattre, décourager, ôter le courage **à** ; (to dispeople) dépeupler ; (fig.) énerver, amollir. To — a ship ; *désarmer un vaisseau.*

unman'ageable (eu'n'ma'n'édj'a-b'l), *adj.,* impossible à conduire, *ou* à diriger ; indocile, ingouvernable, difficile à gouverner ; intraitable ; rebelle. To become — ; (of horses) *s'emporter, s'emballer.*

unman'ageableness, *n.*, (of persons) indocilité, *f.*, caractère intraitable, *m. ;* (of things) impossibilité, difficulté de diriger, *f.*

unman'liness, *n.*, conduite indigne d'un homme ; lâcheté ; (of things) indignité, *f.*

unman'ly, *adj.*, inhumain ; (base, cowardly) lâche, vil, indigne d'un homme ; (effeminate) mou, efféminé.

unman'nered (eu'n'ma'n'neurde), *adj.* V. **unmannerly.**

unman'nerliness, *n.*, grossièreté, *f. ;* mauvais ton, *m.*

unman'nerly, *adj.*, grossier, malappris ; malhonnête ; de mauvais ton.

unman'nerly, *adv.*, grossièrement, malhonnêtement, avec mauvais ton.

unmanufac'tured (-ma'n'iou-fak'tieurde), *adj.*, non manufacturé, non fabriqué, brut.

unmanured' (-ma-niourde), *adj.*, sans engrais.

unmarked' (-mârk'te), *adj.*, non marqué ; inaperçu, inobservé.

unmar'ketable, *adj.*, invendable.

unmar'riageable (eu'n'mar'ridj'a-b'l), *adj.*, non mariable ; qui n'est pas libre de se marier.

unmar'ried (en'n'mar'ride), *adj.*, non marié, dans le célibat. — man ; *homme non marié;* célibataire ; *garçon, m.* — woman ; *femme non mariée, demoiselle, fille, f.*

unmarred', *adj.*, non troublé, non gâté.

unmar'ry, *v.a.*, démarier; dissoudre le mariage **de**.

unmask' (eu'n'mâske), *v.a.*, démasquer ; dévoiler. *v.n.*, se démasquer.

unmasked', *adj.*, sans masque ; démasqué ; (fig.) sans déguisement.

unmast' (eu'n'mâste), *v.a.*, démâter.

unmas'terable, *adj.*, qu'on ne peut maîtriser, *ou* dompter.

unmas'tered (eu-n'mâs-teurde), *adj.*, indompté ; fougueux ; (fig.) non maîtrisé.

unmatch', *v.a.*, désassortir, dépareiller, déparier.

unmatched' (eu'n'matsh'te), *adj.*, désassorti,

dépareillé, déparié ; (fig.) sans pareil, incomparable, unique.

unmean'ing (eu'n'mī'n'-), *adj.*, qui ne signifie rien ; insignifiant ; vide de sens.

unmean'ingly, *adv.*, d'une manière insignifiante.

unmean'ingness, *n.*, insignifiance, *f. ;* manque de signification, *m.*

unmeant' (eu'n'mè'n'te), *adj.*, involontaire, sans intention.

unmeas'ured (eu'n'mèj'eurde), *adj.*, non mesuré ; immense ; infini ; démesuré, sans mesure, peu mesuré. In — terms ; *de manière à ne pas s'y méprendre.*

unmed'itated (eu'n'mèd'i-tét'-), *adj.*, non médité ; improvisé ; sans préméditation.

unmelo'dious (eu'n'mi-lô-), *adj.*, discordant ; sans mélodie.

unmelo'diously, *adv.*, d'une manière discordante, peu mélodieuse.

unmelt'ed, *adj.*, non fondu ; non résous ; (fig.) non attendri, inexorable.

unmen'tionable (-sheu'n'a-b'l), *adj.*, dont on ne doit pas parler ; (phil.) innommable.

unmen'tionables, *n.pl.*, pantalon, *m.*, culotte, *f.;* inexpressible, *m.*

unmen'tioned(eu'n'mè'n'sheu'n'de), *adj.*, non mentionné, dont on ne parle pas ; (fig.) ignoré.

unmer'cenary, *adj.*, désintéressé.

unmer'ciful (eu'n'meur-ci-foule), *adj.*, sans miséricorde ; impitoyable; barbare ; cruel.

unmer'cifully, *adv.*, sans miséricorde ; impitoyablement, cruellement, sans pitié. To beat —; *rouer (quelqu'un) de coups.*

unmer'cifulness, *n.*, nature impitoyable ; barbarie, dureté, cruauté, *f.*

unmer'ited, *adj.*, non mérité, immérité.

unmethod'ical, *adj.*, sans méthode; confus.

unmethod'ically, *adv.*, confusément, sans méthode.

unmil'itary, *adj.*, non militaire.

unmilked', *adj.*, non traite.

unmind'ed, *adj. V.* **unheeded**.

unmind'ful (eu'n'maï'n'd'foule), *adj.*, oublieux **de**, insouciant **de**, peu soucieux **de**. — of ; *inattentif* à ; *insouciant* **de** ; *oublieux* **de** ; *peu soigneux* **de** ; *négligent* **de**.

unmind'fully, *adv.*, avec insouciance ; négligement, inattentivement, sans soin.

unmind'fulness (eu'n'-), *n.*, négligence, insouciance, inattention, *f.*, oubli, *m.*

unmin'gled (eu'n'mign'g'l'de), *adj.*, pur, sans mélange.

unmissed' (eu'n'mis'te), *adj.*, dont on ne remarque pas l'absence ; qu'on ne regrette pas.

unmistak'able, *adj.*, à ne pas s'y méprendre ; évident ; manifeste ; clair.

unmistak'ably, *adv.*, clairement ; de manière à ne pas s'y méprendre ; évidemment.

unmit'igable (eu'n'mit'i-ga-b'l), *adj.*, non susceptible de mitigation, impossible à adoucir ; inflexible, implacable.

unmit'igated (eu'n'mit'i-ghét'-), *adj.*, non mitigé ; implacable ; complet, absolu, positif ; (of scoundrels, etc.) franc, fieffé, dans toute la force du terme.

unmixed' (-miks'te), *adj.*, sans mélange ; pur.

unmob'ilized, *adj.*, non mobilisé.

unmod'ifiable (eu'n'mod'i-faï'a-b'l), *adj.*, non susceptible de modification.

unmod'ified (-faïde), *adj.*, non modifié.

unmolest'ed, *adj.*, sans être molesté ; sans obstacle, *ou* empêchement ; en paix.

unmoor' (eu'n'moure), *v.a.*, lever l'ancre **de** ; démarrer.

unmoor'ing, *n.*, démarrage, *m.*

unmort'gaged (eu'n'mor-ghèd'j'de), *adj.*, non hypothéqué, libre d'hypothèques.

unmoth'erly, *adj.*, indigne d'une mère, peu maternel.

unmourned'. *V.* **unlamented**.

unmount'ed, *adj.*, (on foot) à pied ; (of game) non monté.

unmoved' (eu'n'mouv'de), *adj.*, immobile ; fixe ; (fig.) non touché, non ému, impassible, ferme ; calme, inébranlable, insensible.

unmuf'fle(eu'n'meuf'f'l), *v.a.*, découvrir ; (of garments) désaffubler ; (a drum) découvrir.

unmu'sical (eu'n'miou-zi-), *adj.*, peu musical ; sans harmonie, discordant.

unmu'tilated (eu'n'miou-ti-lét'-), *adj.*, non mutilé ; intact.

unmuz'zle (eu'n'meuz'z'l), *v.a.*, démuseler ; (fig.) déchaîner.

unnail' (eu'n'néle), *v.a.*, déclouer.

unnamed'(eu'n'né'm'de), *adj.*,innommé; anonyme. Who shall be — ; *dont je tairai le nom.*

unnat'ural (eu'n'nat'iou-), *adj.*, contraire à la nature ; peu naturel ; forcé ; (pers.) dénaturé. An — mother ; *une marâtre.*

unnat'uralize (-aïze), *v.a.*, dénaturer.

unnat'uralized, *adj.*, non naturalisé.

unnat'urally, *adv.*, contre nature ; d'une manière dénaturée ; d'une manière forcée, factice. I was not — surprised to see ; *j'étais assez naturellement surpris,* ou *j'avais tout lieu d'être surpris de voir.*

unnat'uralness, *n.*, état de ce qui est contre nature ; défaut, *ou* manque, de naturel, *m.*

unnav'igable, *adj.*, innavigable.

unnav'igated, *adj.*, qu'on n'a pas parcouru ; inconnu à la navigation.

unnec'essarily, *adv.*, sans nécessité ; inutilement.

unnec'essariness, *n.*, inutilité, *f.*

unnec'essary ou **unneed'ful** (eu'n'nîd'-foule), *adj.*, peu nécessaire ; inutile.

unneed'ed (eu'n'nîd'-), *adj.*, dont on n'a pas besoin ; inutile.

unneigh'borly (eu'n'nè-beur-), *adj.*, de mauvais voisin ; peu obligeant.

unneigh'borly, *adv.*, en mauvais voisin.

unnerve' (eu'n'neurve), *v.a.*, énerver ; affaiblir ; faire perdre contenance à ; décourager.

unnot'ed (eu'n'nôt'-) ou **unno'ticed** (-nô-tiste), *adj.*, inaperçu ; négligé, passé sous silence, inobservé ; méconnu ; dédaigné ; (of persons) traité sans égards.

unnum'bered (-neu'm'beurde), *adj.*, non numéroté; (innumerable)innombrable, sans nombre.

unobjec'tionable (eu'n'ob-jèk'sheu'n'a-b'l), *adj.*, irréprochable ; inattaquable ; irrécusable.

unobjec'tionably, *adv.*, irréprochablement, irrécusablement.

unobli'ging, *adj.*, désobligeant, peu complaisant ; inserviable (Bescherelle).

unoblit'erated (eu'n'-), *adj.*, ineffacé.

unobnox'ious (eu'n'ob-nok-sheusse), *adj.*, qui n'est pas sujet à ; peu offensant ; inoffensif.

unobscured' (eu'n'ob-skiourde), *adj.*, non obscurci ; non éclipsé, clair, brillant.

unobserv'able (eu'n'ob-zeurv'a-b'l), *adj.*, qu'on ne peut observer ; imperceptible.

unobserv'ance (-zeurv'-), *n.*, inattention ; inobservation; inobservance, *f.*

unobserv'ant (-zeurv'-), *adj.*, inattentif, qui n'observe pas.

unobserved' (-zeurv'de), *adj.*, inaperçu ; inobservé.

unobserv'ing, *adj.*, peu observateur, inattentif.

unobtain'able (é'n'a-b'l), *adj.*, qu'on ne peut obtenir, impossible à obtenir.

unobstruct'ed (eu'n'ob-streukt'-), *adj.*, non obstrué ; (fig.) sans empêchement, sans obstacle.

unobtru'sive (-trou-cive), ou **unobtrud'ing**, *adj.*, discret, réservé, modeste.

unobtru'sively, *adv.*, discrètement, sans importunité, avec modestie.

unobtru'siveness, *n.*, discrétion, réserve, *f.*

unoc'cupied (eu'n'ok'kiou-païde), *adj.*, (idle) inoccupé ; oisif ; (of time, etc.) libre, disponible, (houses) inhabité.

unoffend'ing, *adj.*, inoffensif ; innocent; sans péché.

unof'fered (eu'n'of'feurde), *adj.*, non offert.

unoffi'cial (eu'n'of'fish'-), *adj.*, non officiel.

unoffi'cially, *adv.*, non officiellement.

uno'pened (eu'n'ô-p'n'de), *adj.*, fermé ; qui n'est pas ouvert ; (of letters, etc.) non décacheté.

unopposed' (eu'n'op'pôz'de), *adj.*, sans être opposé ; sans opposition ; (of elections) non contesté.

unor'ganized (eu'n'or-ga'n'aïz'de), *adj.*, non organisé, dépourvu d'organisation.

unornament'al, *adj.*, qui ne sert pas d'ornement.

unor'namented, *adj.*, sans ornements, simple.

unor'thodox (eu'n'or-tho-), *adj.*, peu orthodoxe ; hétérodoxe.

unostenta'tious (eu'n'os-tè'n'té-sheusse), *adj.*, sans ostentation, sans faste, sans éclat ; modeste.

unostenta'tiously, *adv.*, sans ostentation.

unostenta'tiousness, *n.*, simplicité, *f.*

unowed' (eu'n'ôde), *adj.*, non dû.

unowned' (eu'n'ô'n'de), *adj.*, sans possesseur *ou* propriétaire, non avoué, non reconnu ; (not claimed) non réclamé.

unpacif'ic, *adj.*, peu pacifique ; belliqueux.

unpa'cified (eu'n'pass'i-faïde), *adj.*, non pacifié ; non apaisé.

unpack', *v.a.*, (goods) déballer ; (parcels) dépaqueter. To come —ed ; *se dépaqueter, se défaire.*

unpack'ing, *n.*, déballage ; (of small parcels) dépaquetage, *m.*

unpaid' (eu-n'péde), *adj.*, impayé, non payé, non acquitté; non rétribué; (of armies) sans paye, sans solde; (of letters, etc.) non affranchi.

unpaint'ed (eu'n'pé'n't'-), *adj.*, non peint ; non fardé.

unpaired' (eu'n'pèr'de), *adj.*, non assorti ; non uni ; non apparié ; (of color) non marié ; (parl.) non pairé.

unpal'atable (eu'n'pal'a-ta-b'l), *adj.*, désagréable au goût ; (fig.) désagréable.

unpar'alleled (eu'n'par-al-lèlde), *adj.*, incomparable ; sans pareil ; sans exemple, sans précédent ; unique.

unpar'donable (eu'n'pâr-d'n'a-b'l), *adj.*, impardonnable, irrémissible.

unpar'donably, *adv.*, d'une manière impardonnable.

unpar'doned (-d'n'de), *adj.*, non pardonné ; sans pardon.

unpared' (eu'n'pèrde), *adj.*, non pelé.

unparliamen'tary (eu'n'pâr-li-), *adj.*, contraire aux usages du parlement ; non parlementaire, peu parlementaire.

unpart'ed, *adj.*, non séparé.

unpaste', *v.a.*, décoller.

unpa'tented, *adj.*, non patenté, non breveté.

unpathet'ically, *adv.*, peu pathétiquement.

unpatriot'ic (eu'n'pé-), *adj.*, peu patriotique.

unpatriot'ically, *adv.*, peu patriotiquement.

unpat'ronized (eu'n'pat'ro'n'aïz'de), *adj.*, sans patron, sans protecteurs, sans protections ; (of a shop) mal achalandé.

unpave' (eu'n'péve), *v.a.*, dépaver ; (of tiles) (of flagstones) dédaller.

unpaved', *adj.*, (not paved) non pavé ; (taken décarreler ; up) dépavé, dédallé, décarrelé.

unpav'ing, *n.*, dédallage ; dépavage ; décarrelage.

unpeg', *v.a.*, ôter la cheville à ; décheviller.

unpen'sioned, *adj.*, sans retraite.

unpeo'ple (eu'n'pî-p'l), *v.a.*, dépeupler.

unperceiv'able (eu'n'peur-cîv'a-b'l), *adj.*, imperceptible.

unperceiv'ably, *adv.*, imperceptiblement.

unperceived' (-peur-cîv'de), *adj.*, inaperçu.

unper'fected, *adj.*, incomplet, imparfait ; inachevé, inaccompli.

unperformed' (-peur-form'de), *adj.*, inachevé ; inexécuté ; inaccompli.

unpermit'ted, *adj.*, non permis ; illicite.

unphilosoph'ical, *adj.*, peu philosophique.

unphilosoph'ically, *adv.*, peu philosophiquement.

unpick'able, *adj.*, (of locks) incrochetable.

unpicked' (eu'n'pik'te), *adj.*, (of fruits, flowers) non cueilli ; (of rags, etc.) non épluché ; (of locks) non crocheté.

unpin', *v.a.*, ôter les épingles **de** ; défaire ; détacher ; (tech.) décheviller.

unpit'ied (eu'n'pit'ide), *adj.*, que l'on ne plaint pas ; dont on n'a pas pitié ; qu'on ne regrette pas ; sans être plaint.

unpit'ying (-ti-yigne), *adj.*, sans pitié ; impitoyable.

unplant'ed, *adj.*, non planté (with, **de**) ; de croissance spontanée ; (not settled) non colonisé.

unplait' (-pléte), *v.a.*, déplisser, détresser.

unplaus'ible (eu'n'plô-ci-b'l), *adj.*, peu plausible.

unpleas'ant (eu'n'plèz'-), *adj.*, déplaisant, désagréable, fâcheux.

unpleas'antly, *adj.*, désagréablement.

unpleas'antness, *n.*, nature désagréable, *f.* ; désagrément, *m.*

unpleased', *adj.*, *V.* **displeased**.

unpleas'ing (-plïz'-), *adj.*, qui ne plaît pas ; déplaisant ; désagréable ; fâcheux.

unpledged' (eu'n'plèdj'de), *adj.*, non engagé.

unpli'able (eu'n'plaï-a-b'l), *adj.*, peu pliable ; inflexible.

unplow'able, *adj.*, illabourable.

unplowed' (eu'n'plaoude), *adj.*, non labouré ; inculte.

unplucked' (eu'n'pleuk'te), *adj.*, (of flowers) non cueilli ; (of birds) non plumé.

unplume', *v.a.*, déplumer ; (fig.) humilier ; dégrader, avilir.

unpoet'ical (eu'n'po-èt'-), *adj.*, prosaïque, peu poétique.

unpoet'ically, *adv.*, peu poétiquement, prosaïquement.

unpoint'ed (-poï'n't'-), *adj.*, sans pointe; peu piquant ; (gram.) non ponctué.

unpoised' (-poïz'de), *adj.*, qui n'est pas en équilibre.

unpol'ished (eu'n'pol'ish'te), *adj.*, non poli ; (of gold, etc.) mat ; (of marble) brut ; (of boots) non ciré; (of glass) dépoli ; (fig.) inculte, grossier, rude, sans éducation.

unpolite' (eu'n'po-laïte), *adj.*, *V.* **impolite**.

unpollut'ed (-pôl-liout'-), *adj.*, non souillé ; pur, sans souillure, sans tache.

unpop'ular (eu'n'pop'iou-), *adj.*, impopulaire.

unpopular'ity, *n.*, impopularité, *f.*

unpop'ularly, *adv.*, impopulairement.

unport'able, *adj.*, non portatif.

unpossessed' (eu'n'poz'zèste), *adj.*, non possédé ; non occupé. — of ; *qui ne possède pas ; privé* **de**.

unpot', *v.a.*, dépoter.

unprac'tical, *adj.*, peu pratique.

unprac'ticed (eu'n'prak'tiste), *adj.*, inexpérimenté ; sans expérience ; peu habitué ; sans pratique, novice.

unpre'cedented (-prèss'i-), *adj.*, sans exemple, sans antécédent, sans précédent ; unique.

unprecise' (eu'n'pri-çaïce), *adj.*, peu précis.

unpreferred' (eu'n'pri-feurde), *adj.*, non préféré ; non avancé.

unpre'judiced (eu'n'prèdj'eu-diste), *adj.*, non prévenu, sans préjugé, sans prévention, exempt de préjugés, impartial.

unpremed'itated (eu'n'pri-mèd'i-tét'-), *adj.*, non médité ; irréfléchi, spontané, improvisé ;

(not previously intended) non prémédité, sans préméditation.

unprepared' (eu'n'pri-pèrde), *adj.*, non préparé ; sans préparation ; à l'improviste ; au dépourvu. To be — for ; *ne pas s'attendre à.* He was — for such an event ; *il était loin de s'attendre à un tel événement.*

unprepar'edly (-pèr'èd'-), *adv.*, sans préparation.

unprepar'edness (-pèr'èd'-), *n.*, manque de préparation, *m.*

unprepossessed'. *V.* **unprejudiced.**

unprepossess'ing (-poz'zèss'-), *adj.*, peu prévenant, peu engageant, disgracieux de figure, laid.

unpressed' ('prèste), *adj.*, non pressuré ; (not enforced) volontaire, non forcé.

unpretend'ing (eu'n'pri-) *ou* **unpresum'ing**, *adj.*, sans prétention *ou* présomption, simple, modeste.

unprevail'ing (eu'n'pri-vél'-), *adj.*, impuissant.

unprevent'ed (eu'n'pri-), *adj.*, non prévenu ; non empêché.

unprince'ly, *adj.*, indigne d'un prince.

unprin'cipled (eu'n'pri'n'ci-p'l'de), *adj.*, sans principes, immoral, sans mœurs, dénué de principes.

unprint'ed, *adj.*, non imprimé, inimprimé ; (of stuffs) uni ; (of calico) blanc.

unpriv'ileged (eu'n'priv'i-lèdj'de), *adj.*, non privilégié, sans privilège.

unpriz'able (eu'n'praïz'a-b'l), *adj.*, sans prix ; sans valeur.

unprized' (eu'n'praïz'de), *adj.*, peu estimé, dont on fait peu de cas.

unproclaimed' (eu'n'pro-clé'm'de), *adj.*, non proclamé.

unprodu'cible (-diou-ci-), *adj.*, improductible.

unproduc'tive (eu'n'pro-deuk'-), *adj.*, peu productif, infertile, de mauvais rapport ; stérile, improductif ; (of trade) peu lucratif ; (of money) qui ne rapporte pas ; (fig.) inefficace, stérile, impuissant. — of any real benefit ; *ne produisant aucun avantage, résultat.*

unproduc'tiveness, *n.*, stérilité ; infertilité ; nature improductive ; inefficacité ; impuissance, *f.*

unprofaned' (eu'n'pro-fé'n'de), *adj.*, non profané ; non souillé.

unprofes'sional (-fèsh'eu'n'-), *adj.*, étranger à une profession ; non professionnel ; indigne, *ou* contraire, aux règles, *ou* aux devoirs, d'une profession.

unprofi'ciency, *n.*, défaut, *ou* manque, de progrès, *m.* ; faiblesse, *f.*

unprofi'cient, *adj.*, faible, peu avancé.

unprof'itable (eu'n'prof'it'a-b'l), *adj.*, peu profitable, peu lucratif ; sans profit ; ingrat ; inutile ; impuissant ; vain.

unprof'itableness, *n.*, nature peu profitable ; stérilité ; inutilité, *f.*

unprof'itably, *adv.*, inutilement ; sans profit.

unprohib'ited, *adj.*, non prohibé ; permis, licite.

unprolif'ic, *adj.*, non prolifique ; stérile, infécond.

unprom'ising (eu'n'pro'm'i-cigne), *adj.*, qui promet peu ; qui s'annonce mal ; stérile ; ingrat.

unprompt'ed (eu'n'pro'm'tède), *adj.*, sans y être poussé ; de son propre chef ; de son plein gré ; (of speech) non soufflé.

unpromul'gated, *adj.*, non promulgué.

unpronounce'able, *adj.*, imprononçable.

unpronounced' (eu'n'pro-naou'n'ste), *adj.*, non prononcé ; inarticulé.

unprophet'ic *ou* **unprophet'ical** (pro-fèt'-), *adj.*, non prophétique.

unpropi'tious (eu'n'pro-pish'eusse), *adj.*, peu propice à ; défavorable à, contraire à, peu favorable à.

unpropi'tiously, *adv.*, d'une manière peu propice.

unpropor'tioned (-pôr-sheu'n'de), *adj.*, disproportionné.

unpros'perous (eu'n'pros-peur'-), *adj.*, peu prospère ; malheureux.

unpros'perously, *adv.*, d'une manière peu prospère ; malheureusement, sans succès.

unpros'perousness, *n.*, état peu prospère ; insuccès, *m.*

unprotect'ed, *adj.*, non protégé ; sans protection, seul, sans défense. — from the rain; *sans abri* contre *la pluie.*

unproved' (eu'n'prouv'de), *adj.*, non prouvé, sans preuve ; (not tried) non éprouvé, non essayé.

unprovid'ed (eu'n'pro-vaïd'-), *adj.*, dépourvu de ; dénué de ; non pourvu ; (not prepared) pris au dépourvu ; non préparé. — for ; *non pourvu ; non prévu.* We were —, *ou* unprepared, for that ; *nous ne nous attendions pas à cela ; nous étions loin de nous y attendre.*

unprovoked' (-pro-vôk'te), *adj.*, non provoqué ; sans provocation ; (not incited) non irrité, non fâché ; (fig.) immérité, gratuit. An — insult ; *une insulte gratuite.*

unprovok'ing, *adj.*, qui ne provoque pas ; inoffensif.

unprovok'ingly, *adv.*, sans provocation.

unpruned' (eu'n'prou'n'de), *adj.*, non élagué ; non taillé, non émondé.

unpub'lishable, *adj.*, impubliable.

unpub'lished (eu'n'peub'lish'te), *adj.*, (of books) non publié, inédit ; secret, inconnu.

unpunc'tual (eu'n'peu'gn'kt'iou-), *adj.*, inexact.

unpunctual'ity, *n.*, irrégularité, inexactitude, *f.*, manque de ponctualité, *m.*

unpun'ished (-peu'n'ish'te), *adj.*, impuni. To go — ; *rester impuni.*

unpur'chasable (-peur-tshèss'-), *adj.*, qu'on ne peut acheter ; inachetable.

unpur'chased, *adj.*, non acheté ; inacheté (La Harpe).

unpu'rified (eu'n'piou-ri-faïde), *adj.*, non purifié; impur.

unqual'ified (eu'n'kwol'i-faïde), *adj.*, peu propre à ; inhabile à, incapable de ; sans talent pour ; (not modified) sans réserve, sans restriction, absolu, positif, entier ; inadmissible ; (jur.) inhabile à ; (of practitioners, etc.) sans diplôme, non diplômé.

unquelled' (eu'n'kwèl'de), *adj.*, non réprimé ; non étouffé ; indompté.

unquench'able (eu'n'kwè'n'tsh'a-b'l), *adj.*, inextinguible, insatiable.

unquenched' (-kwè'n'tsh'te), *adj.*, non éteint, non étanché ; (fig.) insatiable.

unques'tionable (-kwèst'ieu'n'a-b'l), *adj.*, incontestable, indubitable.

unques'tionably, *adv.*, incontestablement ; indubitablement, sans contredit.

unques'tioned (-kwèst'ieu'n'de), *adj.*, (pers.) sans être questionné ; (indubitable) incontesté, hors de doute, incontestable.

unquick'ened (eu'n'kwik'k'n'de), *adj.*, inanimé, non vivifié.

unqui'et (eu'n'kwaï-eute), *adj.*, inquiet ; agité.

unqui'et, *n.*, agitation, inquiétude ; turbulence, *f.*

unqui'etly, *adv.*, avec inquiétude.

unqui'etness, *n.*, inquiétude ; agitation, *f.*

unran'somed (eu'n'ra'n'œu'm'de), *adj.*, non racheté ; non rançonné.

unrav'el, *v.a.*, démêler, débrouiller ; (of threaded stuffs) effiler, défaire ; (intrigue) dénouer ; (fig.) démêler, débrouiller, éclaircir.

unrav'el, *v.n.*, se démêler, se débrouiller, s'effiler, se défaire ; (fig.) se débrouiller.

unreached' (-rītsh'te), *adj.*, non atteint, qui n'a pas été atteint.

unread' (eu'n'rède), *adj.*, qui n'a pas été lu ; qu'on ne lit pas, sans être lu ; sans lecteurs ; (illiterate) peu lettré, illettré, ignorant, sans instruction. To leave ... — ; *laisser ... sans* (*le, la, les*) *lire*.

unread'able (eu'n'rîd'a-b'l), *adj.*, illisible ; indigne d'être lu.

unread'ableness, *n.*, illisibilité, *f.*

unread'ily (-rèd'-), *adv.*, lentement ; sans préparation ; (against the grain) à contre-cœur.

unread'iness (eu'n'rèd'-), *n.*, lenteur, *f.* ; (want of promptitude) défaut de promptitude ; (want of dexterity) défaut de facilité ; (reluctance) manque de bonne volonté, *m.*, répugnance, *f.*

unread'y (eu'n'rèd'i), *adj.*, lent, non préparé ; qui n'est pas prêt à, peu prompt ; peu vif ; peu facile ; peu disposé à, peu empressé à ; (awkward) gauche.

unre'al (eu'n'rî-), *adj.*, non réel ; faux ; incorporel, immatériel ; vain ; chimérique, fantastique, imaginaire.

unreal'ity, fausseté ; (philos.) incorporalité ; vision, chimère, *f.*

unre'alizable (-), *adj.*, irréalisable.

unreaped' (-rîpte), *adj.*, non moissonné.

unreas'on (-rî-z'n), *n.*, déraison, *f.*

unreas'onable (eu'n'rî-z'n'a-b'l), *adj.*, déraisonnable ; (exorbitant) extravagant, excessif, exorbitant.

unreas'onableness, *n.*, déraison, *f.* ; absurdité ; (exorbitance) caractère déraisonnable, *m.*, extravagance ; exigence, *f.*

unreas'onably, *adv.*, déraisonnablement ; sans raison ; à l'excès ; contre la raison.

unreas'oned, *adj.*, non raisonné.

unreas'oning, *adj.*, qui ne raisonne pas.

unrebuk'able (eu'n'rî-biouk'a-b'l), *adj.*, irrépréhensible.

unrebuked', *adj.*, (pers.) non censuré, sans être réprimandé ; (of things) sans être relevé.

unrecall'able (eu'n'rî-kōl'a-b'l), *adj.*, irrévocable.

unrecalled' (eu'n'rî-cōl'de), *adj.*, non rappelé.

unreceived' (eu'n'rî-cîv'de), *adj.*, non reçu, qui n'est pas reçu.

unreclaimed' (eu'n'rî-klé'm'de), *adj.*, non réclamé ; (not reformed) non amendé ; non corrigé ; non réformé ; (of land) inculte.

unrec'ognizable, *adj.*, méconnaissable.

unrec'ognized, *adj.*, sans être reconnu ; (fig.) (ignored) méconnu ; (not tolerated) qui n'est pas accepté, qui n'a pas cours.

unrecommend'ed (eu'n'rèk'-), *adj.*, non recommandé ; sans être recommandé.

unrec'ompensed (-o'm'pè'n'ste), *adj.*, sans récompense.

unrec'onciled (-çaïl'de), *adj.*, irréconcilié.

unrecord'ed (eu'n'rî-), *adj.*, non enregistré ; oublié.

unrecov'erable (-keuv'eur'a-b'l), *adj.* V. **irrecoverable**.

unrecov'ered (-rî-keuv'eurde), *adj.*, non recouvré ; (not cured) non guéri, non rétabli.

unredeem'able (eu'n'rî-dî'm'a-b'l), *adj.*, (of moneys) irrachetable, irremboursable ; irrémédiable, irréparable.

unredeemed' (eu'n'rî-dî'm'de), *adj.*, non racheté ; non remboursé ; (of things pawned) non dégagé, non retiré ; (financial) non amorti. — *loan ; emprunt non amorti.*

unredressed' (eu'n'rî-drèste), *adj.*, non réformé ; (of wrongs) non redressé.

unreduced' (eu'n'rî-diouste), *adj.*, non réduit.

unrefined' (-faï'n'de), *adj.*, non purifié, non épuré ; (of sugar) non raffiné, brut ; (of metals) non affiné, (of manners) peu poli, peu délicat, grossier, indélicat.

unreform'able (eu'n'rî-form'a-b'l), *adj.*, incorrigible ; irréformable.

unreformed' (-form'de), *adj.*, non réformé.

unrefreshed' (-frèsh'te), *adj.*, non rafraîchi ; (of fatigue) non délassé, toujours fatigué.

unrefut'ed (-fiou-), *adj.*, irréfuté.

unregard'ed (eu'n'rî-gård'-), *adj.*, oublié, négligé, dédaigné, méprisé ; méconnu.

unregard'ful (-foule), *adj.*, négligent.

unregard'fully, *adv.*, négligemment.

unregen'erate *ou* **unregen'erated** (-djè'n'-eur'ét'-), *adj.*, (theol.) non régénéré ; (fig.) endurci.

unreg'istered (eu'n'rèdj'is-teurde), *adj.*, non enregistré ; non inscrit ; dont on n'a pas conservé le souvenir ; (of letters, etc.) non chargé, non recommandé.

unreg'ulated (-règh'iou-lét'-), *adj.*, non réglé.

unrelat'able, *adj.*, incontable, inénarrable.

unrelat'ed (eu'n'rî-lét'-), *adj.*, sans rapport, qui n'a aucun rapport **avec** ; sans parenté **avec**. Who is — to ; *qui n'est pas parent* **de**.

unrelent'ing (eu'n'rî-), *adj.*, inflexible ; implacable ; inexorable ; cruel ; impitoyable, acharné ; sans retour.

unrelent'ingly, *adv.*, inflexiblement, inexorablement, implacablement.

unreli'able (-laï-), *adj.*, (pers.) sur qui on ne peut pas compter ; à qui on ne peut pas se fier ; indigne de confiance ; (things) qui ne mérite pas créance ; mal fondé.

unreli'ableness, *n.*, incrédibilité ; (of things) inexactitude, fausseté, *f.*

unreliev'able (eu'n'rî-lîv'a-b'l), *adj.*, qu'on ne peut secourir, perdu sans ressource.

unrelieved' (-lîv'de), *adj.*, non soulagé, non secouru ; (milit.) non relevé, non secouru, resté sans secours.

unremark'able (eu'n'rî-mårk'a-b'l), *adj.*, non remarquable ; (fig.) tout à fait ordinaire.

unremarked' (-mårk'te), *adj.*, inobservé, inaperçu.

unrem'edied (eu'n'rè'm'i-dide), *adj.*, auquel on n'a pas remédié ; irrémédiable.

unremem'bered (-ri-mè'm'beurde), *adj.*, oublié ; (of things) méconnu.

unremem'bering (-beur'-), *adj.*, oublieux **de**.

unremit'ted (eu'n'rî-), *adj.*, non remis, non pardonné ; (continual) continuel, incessant.

unremit'ting, *adj.*, incessant, persévérant, infatigable, continuel.

unremit'tingly, *adv.*, sans relâche ; sans cesse ; sans en démordre.

unremov'able (eu'n'rî-mouv'a-b'l), *adj.*, fixe ; qui ne peut être déplacé ; (of judges) inamovible.

unremoved' (-mouv'de), *adj.*, non écarté ; non éloigné ; non déplacé, non ôté, non enlevé ; (of furniture) non déménagé.

unremu'nerated, *adj.*, non rétribué ; sans rétribution.

unremu'nerative, *adj.*, qui ne rapporte guère ; peu lucratif.

unrenewed' (eu'n'ri-nioude), *adj.*, non renouvelé ; (theol.) non régénéré.

unrepaid' (-ri-péde), *adj.*, (of money) non remboursé ; non rendu ; non dédommage **de** ; non récompensé **de** ; (of love) non payé de retour, méconnu.

unrepaired' (-pèrde), *adj.*, non réparé.

unrepeal'able (-pîl'a-b'l), *adj.*, irrévocable.

unrepealed' (-pîl'de), *adj.*, non révoqué ; (of a law) non abrogé.

unrepent'ed (eu'n'ri-), *adj.*, dont on ne s'est pas repenti.

unrepent'ing *ou* **unrepent'ant**, *adj.*, sans repentir ; impénitent.

unrepin'ing (-paï'n'-), *adj.*, qui ne se plaint pas, qui ne murmure pas. Silent she passed and — ; *elle passa en silence et sans murmurer.*

unrepin'ingly, *adv.*, sans gémir, sans murmurer, sans se plaindre.

unreplen'ished, *adj.*, (qui est) resté vide.

unrepresent'ed (-rèp-ri-zè'n't'-), *adj.*, non représenté.

unrepressed', *adj.*, non réprimé.

unreprieved' (-prîv'de), *adj.*, à qui l'on n'a pas accordé de sursis.

unreproached' (eu'n'ri-prôtsh'te), *adj.*, sans reproche.

unreproved' (-prouv'de), *adj.*, non blâmé ; non repris.

unrequest'ed, *adj.*, non sollicité ; spontané. *adv.*, spontanément ; sans sollicitation.

unrequired' (-kwaïeurde), *adj.*, qui n'est pas nécessaire ; dont on n'a pas besoin.

unrequit'ed (-kwaït'-), *adj.*, sans être récompensé ; méconnu ; (of love) qui n'est pas payé de retour.

unres'cued, *adj.*, non secouru.

unreserve' (-zeurve), *n.*, absence de réserve, *f.*; abandon, *m.* ; franchise, expansion, *f.*

unreserved' (-zeurv'de), *adj.*, sans réserve ; expansif ; (complete) absolu, illimité ; (of a sale) non réservé ; sans réservation. — sale; *liquidation, f.* Full and — powers; *autorité pleine et entière, f. ; pleins pouvoirs, m.pl.*

unreserv'edly (-zeurv'èd'-), *adv.*, sans réserve; franchement, absolument.

unreserv'edness (-zeurv'èd'-), *n.*, abandon, *m.* ; nature expansive ; franchise, *f.*

unresist'ed (eu'n'ri-zist'-), *adj.*, sans résistance ; sans rencontrer de résistance ; (ant.) irrésistible.

unresist'ing, *adj.*, qui ne résiste pas ; soumis.

unresist'ingly, *adv.*, sans résistance.

unresolv'able (-zolv'a-b'l), *adj.*, insoluble.

unresolved' (-zolv'de), *adj.*, non résolu ; sans solution; (not determined) irrésolu ; indécis.

unrespect'ed (eu'n'ri-spèkt'-), *adj.*, non respecté ; dont on ne tient pas compte ; négligé ; méconnu.

unrest', *n.*, inquiétude, agitation, *f.;* malaise ; (of sleep) sommeil agité, *m.*, insomnie, *f.*

unrestored' (-stôrde), *adj.*, non rendu ; non restitué ; non restauré ; (of health) non rétabli.

unrestrained' (eu'n'ri-strê'n'de), *adj.*, non retenu ; non restreint, sans contrainte ; non réprimé ; effréné ; déréglé ; sans frein.

unrestrict'ed, *adj.*, sans restriction.

unreten'tive (eu'n'ri-), *adj.*, peu tenace, qui retient peu ; (of the memory) peu sûr, peu fidèle.

unretract'ed, *adj.*, non rétracté ; non révoqué.

unretrieved', *adj.*, irréparé.

unrevealed' (eu'n'ri-vîl'de), *adj.*, non révélé.

unrevenged' (-vè'n'dj'de), *adj.*, non vengé.

unreversed' (-veurste), *adj.*, non renversé ; irrévoqué ; non annulé, non révoqué.

unrevised' (eu'n'ri-vaïz'de), *adj.*, non revu ; non revisé.

unrevoked', *adj. V.* **unrepealed.**

unreward'ed (eu'n'ri-word'-), *adj.*, sans récompense.

unrid'dle (eu'n'rid'd'l), *v.a.*, expliquer, résoudre.

unri'fled (-raï-f'l'de), *adj.*, non dévalisé ; (of cannon) lisse, non rayé.

unrig', *v.a.*, dépouiller ; enlever les vêtements à ; (nav.) dégréer.

unright'eous (eu'n'raït'ieusse), *adj.*, injuste, impie, inique.

unright'eously, *adv.*, injustement, iniquement.

unright'eousness, *n.*, injustice ; iniquité ; impiété, *f.*

unright'ful (eu'n'raït'foule), *adj.*, injuste ; illégitime.

unring' (-rigne), *v.a.*, ôter les anneaux de.

unrip', *v.a.*, (needlework) découdre ; fendre, ouvrir.

unripe' (raïpe), *adj.*, qui n'est pas mûr ;`vert ; (fig.) prématuré.

unrip'ened (-raïp'n'de), *adj.*, qui n'est pas mûr; imparfait.

unripe'ness, n_w verdeur ; immaturité, *f.*

unri'valed (-raï-valde), *adj.*, sans rival ; sans pareil, sans égal ; unique.

unriv'et, *v.a.*, limer la rivure de ; détacher.

unrobe' (eu'n'rôbe), *v.n.*, ôter sa robe (de cérémonie).

unroll' (eu'n'rôle), *v.a.*, dérouler; déployer.

unroll', *v.n.*, se dérouler; se déployer.

unroman'tic, *adj.*, peu romanesque ; (of places) peu romantique.

unroof' (eu'n'roufe), *v.a.*, enlever le toit de.

unroot' (eu'n'route), *v.a.*, déraciner, extirper.

unrout'ed (eu'n'raout'-), *adj.*, qui n'a pas été mis en déroute ; invaincu (Corneille).

unruf'fle (eu'n'reuf'f'l), *v.n.*, se calmer ; s'apaiser.

unruf'fled (-reuf'f'l'de), *adj.*, tranquille, calme; (of materials) uni, lisse.

unruled' (-roul'de), *adj.*, non gouverné.

unrul'iness (-roul'-), *n.*, dérèglement, *m.;* fougue; nature indisciplinable ; turbulence, mutinerie, indiscipline, *f.*

unrul'y, *adj.*, déréglé ; mutin, insoumis ; revêche ; intraitable, indomptable, indisciplinable ; rebelle ; fougueux.

unrum'ple, *v.a.*, défricher ; lisser.

unsad'dle (-sad'd'l), *v.a.*, desseller ; (of an ass) débâter ; (to throw from a horse) désarçonner.

unsafe', *adj.*, peu sûr ; dangereux ; hasardeux; périlleux ; imprudent, incertain ; (pers.) sur qui on ne peut compter.

unsafe'ly, *adv.*, peu sûrement ; dangereusement ; sans sûreté.

unsafe'ly, *n.*, défaut de sûreté ; danger, *m.;* insécurité, *f.*

unsaid', *adj.*, non dit, non prononcé. To leave —; *taire, ne pas dire.* It had better been left —; *il aurait mieux valu le taire.*

unsale'able (eu'n'sél'a-b'l), *adj.*, invendable.

unsalt'ed (-sôlt'-), *adj.*, non salé, sans sel.

unsalut'ed (eu'n'sa-liout'-), *adj.*, non salué.

unsal'utary, *adj.*, peu salutaire.

unsanc'tified (eu'n'sa'gn'k'ti-faïde), *adj.*, non sanctifié ; profane, impie.

unsanc'tioned (eu'n'sa'gn'k'sheu'n'de), *adj.*, non sanctionné.

unsapped', *adj.*, non miné, non sapé.

unsat'ed (-sé-), *adj.*, inassouvi ; non rassasié.

unsatisfac'torily, *adv.*, d'une manière peu satisfaisante.

unsatisfac'toriness, *n.*, nature peu satisfaisant, *m.* ; impuissance, insuffisance, *f.* The — and barrenness of the school-philosophy; *l'impuissance et la stérilité de la scolastique.*

unsatisfac'tory, *adj.*, peu satisfaisant ; insuffisant, peu convaincant.

unsat'isfied (eu'n'sat'is-faïde), *adj.*, non satisfait de ; mécontent de ; (com.) non acquitté.

unsa'vorily (-sé-veur'-), *adv.*, sans saveur, désagréablement.

unsa'voriness, *n.*, nature désagréable ; insipidité, fadeur ; (bad smell) mauvaise odeur ; (b.s.) obscénité, *f.*

unsa'vory (eu'n'sé-veuri), *adj.*, sans saveur, fade, insipide ; (disgusting) désagréable, dégoûtant, repoussant.

unsay' (-sé), *v.a.*, (*preterit* and *past part.*, Unsaid) se dédire de ; rétracter.

unscanned', *adj.*, inconnu ; (unexamined) non scruté, non examiné. — by mortal eyes ; *que l'œil humain n'a jamais vu.*

unscared' (eu'n'skèrde), *adj.*, qui n'est pas épouvanté, non effrayé.

unscarred' (eu'n'skârde), *adj.*, sans cicatrices ; sans blessure.

unscathed' (eu'n'skéth'de), *adj.*, intact ; sans blessure ; sain et sauf.

unschol'arly (-sko-), *adj.*, illettré, ignorant.

unschooled' (-skoul'de), *adj.*, illettré ; sans éducation ; inexpérimenté, sans expérience.

unscientif'ic (eu'n'saï-è'n'-), *adj.*, peu scientifique ; (pers.) étranger à la science.

unscientif'ically, *adv.*, peu scientifiquement.

unscorched' (-scortsh'te), *adj.*, non roussi ; non brûlé.

unscoured' (-scaourde), *adj.*, non écuré ; non nettoyé.

unscratched' (-scratsh'te), *adj.*, non égratigné, sans égratignure.

unscreened' (eu'n'skrî'n'de), *adj.*, non abrité ; non défendu ; (not sifted) non passé au crible.

unscrew' (eu'n'scrou), *v.a.*, dévisser. To become —ed ; *se dévisser*.

unscrip'tural (eu'n'script'iou-), *adj.*, contraire à l'Écriture, antibiblique.

unscru'pulous (-scrou-piou-), *adj.*, sans scrupule ; sans conscience ; sans principes. *n.*, (man.) arriviste. [conscience.

unscru'pulously, *adv.*, sans scrupule ; sans

unscru'pulousness, *n.*, improbité, indélicatesse, *f.* ; manque de scrupule, *m.*

unseal' (eu'n'sîle), *v.a.*, décacheter ; desceller ; (custom house) déplomber ; (fig.) dessiller (les yeux à).

unsealed', *adj.*, (that have been opened) décacheté ; (left open) ouvert, non cacheté.

unsearch'able (eu'n'seurtsh'a-b'l), *adj.*, inscrutable ; incompréhensible ; impénétrable.

unsearch'ableness, *n.*, incompréhensibilité, inscrutabilité, *f.*

unsea'sonable (eu'n'sî-z'n'a-b'l), *adj.*, hors de saison ; (untimely) hors de propos, intempestif, inopportun ; (of time) incommode, indu ; (of weather) peu de saison ; (improper) déplacé. — hours ; *heures indues,f.pl.*

unsea'sonableness, *n.*, inopportunité, *f.*

unsea'sonably, *adv.*, hors de saison ; mal à propos, à contretemps.

unsea'soned (eu'n'sî-z'n'de), *adj.*, (of wood) non préparé, non séché ; (not accustomed) non accoutumé, non fait, non endurci ; (to a climate) non acclimaté ; (cook.) non assaisonné.

unseat' (eu'n'sîte), *v.a.*, renverser d'un siège ; (from horseback) désarçonner ; (a member of parliament) faire annuler, *ou* invalider, l'élection de.

unsea'worthiness, *n.*, innavigabilité, *f.*

unsea'worthy (eu'n'sî-weur-*thi*), *adj.*, incapable de tenir la mer, innavigable.

unsec'onded (eu'n'sèk'-), *adj.*, mal secondé ; non secondé ; non appuyé.

unsecured' (-kiourde), *adj.*, non garanti, sans garantie ; mal assuré ; (of a door) pas fermé, mal fermé.

unsee'ing (eu'n'sî-igne), *adj.*, aveugle.

unseem'liness (eu'n'sî'm'-), *n.*, inconvenance ; messéance, malséance ; indécence, *f.*

unseem'ly (eu'n'sî'm'-), *adj.*, inconvenant ; messéant, malséant ; indécent.

unseen' (eu'n'sî'ne), *adj.*, sans être vu ; invisible ; (by stealth) inaperçu, à la dérobée. The — ; *le monde invisible.*

unsent', *adj.*, non envoyé ; non expédié. — for ; *qu'on n'a pas envoyé chercher ; qu'on n'a pas invité ; qu'on n'a pas fait appeler ; sans invitation ; sans être appelé ; sans être mandé.*

unserved' (eu'n'seurv'de), *adj.*, non servi.

unser'viceable (eu'n'seur-viss'a-b'l), *adj.*, inutile, bon à rien ; hors de service, impropre au service.

unser'viceableness, *n.*, inutilité, *f.*; mauvais état, *m.*

unser'viceably, *adv.*, inutilement.

unset', *adj.*, non posé ; non mis ; (mas.) non posé ; (of the sun, etc.) qui n'est pas couché ; (of tools) non affûté ; (of precious stones) non enchâssé, non monté ; (of bones) non remis, non emboîté. *v.a.*, démonter, dessertir.

unset'tle (eu'n'sèt't'l), *v.a.*, déranger ; ébranler ; désorganiser, détraquer ; faire mouvoir ; (fig.) déranger, troubler, bouleverser, agiter, rendre incertain.

unset'tled, *adj.*, non fixé ; non établi ; (not firm) chancelant ; (in mind) dérangé, troublé ; (of things) désorganisé, troublé ; (not determined) indéterminé, incertain, irrésolu ; (not paid) non payé, non liquidé ; (of liquids) qui n'a pas déposé ; (of the weather) variable, changeant, inconstant ; (changeable) inconstant, changeant ; (having no fixed abode) non fixé, sans domicile, sans résidence ; comme l'oiseau sur la branche.

unset'tledness, *n.*, instabilité, agitation, *f.*, trouble ; défaut de fixité ; état chancelant, état dérangé, *m.*; (uncertainty) incertitude, inconstance, instabilité, irrésolution, *f.*; (of the weather) état variable, état inconstant, *m.*, incertitude, *f*

unsev'ered (-eurde), *adj.*, non séparé, uni.

unsew' (eu'n'sô), *v.a.*, découdre. To —, *ou* become —ed ; *se découdre.*

unsew'able, *adj.*, indécousable.

unsex', *v.a.*, priver de sexe.

unshac'kle (eu'n'shak'k'l), *v.a.*, briser les fers **de** ; affranchir **de**, délivrer **de** ; déchaîner.

unshac'kled (-shak'k'l'de), *adj.*, sans chaînes; sans entrave ; delivré (by, **de**), affranchi **de** ; libre. — by party connections and prejudices ; *libre des entraves et des préjugés de parti.*

unshad'ed (eu'n'shéd'-), *adj.*, sans ombrage ; sans ombre ; (drawing) non ombré.

unshak'able, *adj.*, inébranlable ; qu'on ne saurait ébranler.

unshak'en (eu'n'shék'n), *adj.*, inébranlable, ferme, non ébranlé, à toute épreuve.

unshap'en (eu'n'shép'n), **unshape'ly** (eu'n'shép'n), *adj.*, difforme, informe.

unshaved' (eu'n'shév'de), **unshav'en**, *adj.*, non rasé, sans être rasé.

unsheathe' (eu'n'shî*the*), *v.a.*, dégainer, tirer du fourreau, tirer. To — the sword ; *tirer l'épée.*

unshelled' (eu'n'shèlde), *adj.*, en cosse, sans cosse, non écossé ; (grain) non égrené.

unshel'tered (eu'n'shèl-teurde), *adj.*, sans abri ; exposé, découvert. — from ; *exposé* **à** ; *non protégé* **contre**.

unshield'ed (eu'n'shîld'-), *adj.*, sans défense, sans abri. — from ; *exposé* **à**.

unship', *v.a.*, (merchandise) débarquer, décharger ; (the rudder, etc.) (nav.) démonter ; (the oars) désarmer.

unshod', *adj.*, déchaussé ; sans chaussure ; (of a horse) déferré, non ferré.

unshoe' (-shou), *v.a.*, (of a horse) déferrer.

unshorn', *adj.*, non tondu ; non coupé.

unshrink'able, *adj.*, irrétrécissable.

unshrink'ing, *adj.*, inébranlable ; intrépide, sans reculer ; qui ne recule pas.

unshut' (-sheute), *adj.*, non fermé, non clos.

unsift'ed, *adj.*, non criblé, non tamisé ; (fig.) qui n'a pas été scruté, examiné, approfondi.

unsight'liness (eu'n'saït'-), *n.*, laideur, *f.*

unsight'ly, *adj.*, disgracieux, laid.

unsig'nalized (-aïz'de), *adj.*, non signalé.

unsil'ver, *v.a.*, désargenter.

unsil'vered (eu'n'sil-veurde), *adj.*, non argenté ; (of mirrors) non étamé ; désargenté.

unsil'vering, *n.*, désargentage, *m.*

unsinged' (eu'n'si'n'dj'de), *adj.*, non flambé ; non roussi.

unsin'ning, *adj.*, qui ne pèche pas.

unsis'terly, *adj.*, peu digne, *ou* indigne, d'une sœur.

unskil'ful (eu'n'skil-foule), *adj.*, inhabile ; maladroit, ignorant.

unskil'fully, *adv.*, malhabilement, maladroitement.

unskill'fulness, *n.*, inhabileté, maladresse, *f.*

unskilled', *adj.*, inexpérimenté, inexpert, inhabile, maladroit. — labor ; *travail manuel,m.*

unslacked' (eu'n'slak'te) *ou* **unslaked'** (eu'n'slék'te), *adj.*, non éteint ; (of thirst) non étanché ; (of lime) vive.

unsized', *adj.*, non collé.

unsleep'ing, *adj.*, vigilant ; toujours éveillé ; (fig.) toujours vivace.

unsling' (eu'n'sligne), *v.a.*, (*preterit* and *past part.*, Unslung) ôter les élingues **de**.

unsmirched' (-smeurtsh'te), *adj.*, non souillé, pur de toute souillure.

unsmok'able, *adj.*, infumable.

unsmoked' (eu'n'smôk'te), *adj.*, non fumé.

unso'ciable (-sô-sha-b'l), *adj.*, insociable.

unso'ciableness *ou* **unsociabil'ity** (-sô-sha-), *n.*, insociabilité, *f.*

unso'ciably, *adv.*, insociablement.

unso'cial (eu'n'sô-shal), *adj.*, peu social ; insociable.

unsoiled' (eu'n'soïl'de), *adj.*, non sali ; sans tache ; propre ; pur (by, **de**).

unsold' (eu'n'sôlde), *adj.*, invendu.

unsol'der (eu'n'sol-deur), *v.a.*, dessouder.

unsol'derable (eu'n'sol-djeur-), *adj.*, insoudable.

unsold'ierly (eu'n'sôl-djeur-) *ou* **unsold'ier-like** (-laïke), *adj.*, peu martial, indigne d'un soldat.

unsoli'cited, *adj.*, sans être sollicité, sans sollicitation.

unsoli'citous, *adj.*, peu désireux **de**, peu soucieux **de**.

unsol'id, *adj.*, non solide, sans consistance.

unsolved' (eu'n'solv'de), *adj.*, non résolu, resté, sans solution.

unsophis'tical (eu'n'so-fis-ti-cale), *adj.*, simple ; ignorant.

unsophis'ticated (eu'n'so-fis-ti-két'-) *ou* **unsophis'ticate**, *adj.*, non sophistiqué ; pur ; vrai ; non altéré ; non frelaté (unsophistical) simple, ignorant.

unsort'ed, *adj.*, non trié ; non assorti.

unsought' (eu'n'sôte), *adj.*, non recherché ; spontané, sans qu'on le cherche.

unsound' (eu'n'saou'n'de), *adj.*, en mauvais état ; (defective) défectueux, vicieux ; (sickly) maladif, malsain ; (of mind) qui n'est pas sain **d'esprit** ; (not orthodox) hétérodoxe, non orthodoxe ; (deceitful) trompeur, déloyal ; (not real) trompeur, illusoire ; (not compact) non ferme, non solide ; (not sincere) faux ; (not material) immatériel ; (erroneous) erroné, faux ; (cracked) fêlé ; (credit) mal établi ; (of sleep) peu profond.

unsound'ed (eu'n'saou'n'd'-), *adj.*, non sondé.

unsound'ly, *adv.*, sans solidité ; défectueusement ; (of sleeping) mal, peu profondément ; (of reasoning) faussement.

unsound'ness (eu'n'saou'n'd'-), *n.*, (defectiveness) mauvais état, *m.*, mauvaise condition, nature défectueuse, imperfection, *f.* ; (of body) état maladif, état malsain, *m.* ; (of principles) absence de rectitude, *f.* ; défaut de solidité, *m.* ; fausseté, erreur, *f.* ; (want of solidity) manque de solidité, de fermeté, *m.* ; (fig.) infirmité, *f.* ; vice, *m.*, impureté, corruption, *f.*

unsoured' (eu'n'saourde), *adj.*, non aigri.

unsown' (eu'n'sône), *adj.*, non semé ; (of land) non ensemencé.

unspar'ing (eu'n'spèr'-), *adj.*, libéral, prodigue ; (not merciful) impitoyable, cruel.

unspar'ingly, *adv.*, avec prodigalité ; avec profusion ; (fig.) sans ménagement, impitoyablement.

unspar'ingness, *n.*, prodigalité ; (fig.) nature impitoyable, cruauté, *f.*

unspeak'able (-spîk'a-b'l), *adj.*, inexprimable, inénarrable ; (rapturous) indicible, ineffable.

unspeak'ably, *adv.*, d'une manière inexprimable ; ineffablement, indiciblement.

unspe'cified (eu'n'spèss'i-faïde), *adj.*, non spécifié.

unspec'ulative (eu'n'spèk'iou-), *adj.*, peu spéculatif ; pratique.

unspent', *adj.*, non dépensé ; (not exhausted) non épuisé ; non affaibli.

unspoiled' (eu'n'spoïl'de), *adj.*, non corrompu, non gâté ; (not plundered) non spolié, non dépouillé.

unspok'en, *adj.*, qui n'est pas dit ; qui n'est pas raconté ; non mentionné.

unsports'manlike, *adj.*, indigne d'un chasseur ; (fig.) indigne d'un homme d'honneur.

unspot'ted, *adj.*, sans tache ; pur.

unspot'tedness, *n.*, pureté, *f.*

unsta'ble (eu'n'sté-b'l), *adj.*, non stable, mal assuré ; (irresolute) irrésolu, indécis ; (inconstant) inconstant ; (pers.) étourdi, volage ; (mec.) instable ; (fig.) instable, irrésolu.

unsta'bleness (-sté-b'l-), *n.*, instabilité ; (fig.) irrésolution, inconstance, *f.*

unstained' (eu'n'stén'de), *adj.*, non souillé, pur, sans tache ; (not dyed) non teint ; (of glass) blanc.

unstamped', *adj.*, (of paper) non timbré ; (of postal packets) non affranchi ; sans timbre.

unstanched' (eu'n'stâ'n'tsh'te), *adj.*, non étanché, non arrêté.

unstarch', *v.a.*, désempeser.

unstarched', *adj.*, mou, non empesé.

unstead'fast (eu'n'stèd'fâste), *adj.*, non stable, instable ; (inconstant) inconstant, indécis.

unstead'fastly, *adv.*, sans fermeté ; sans stabilité.

unstead'fastness, *n.*, instabilité ; (inconstancy) inconstance, *f.*

unstead'ily (eu'n'stèd'-), *adv.*, en chancelant ; (waveringly) irrésolument ; sans fixité ; (inconstantly) d'une manière inconstante ; (badly) mal.

unstead'iness, *n.*, inconstance, légèreté ; indécision, irrésolution, *f.* ; manque d'aplomb, de fermeté, *m.* ; (misconduct) inconduite, *f.*

unstead'y (eu'n'stèd'-), *adj.*, chancelant ; incertain, mal assuré ; (irresolute) irrésolu, indécis ; (changeable) changeant, variable, inconstant ; (of furniture) boiteux ; (of bad conduct) qui se conduit mal ; irrégulier.

unsteeped' (eu'n'stîp'te), *adj.*, non trempé ; non infusé.

unstemmed', *adj.*, (tobacco) non écôté.

unstim'ulated (eu'n'sti'm'iou-lét'-), *adj.*, non stimulé ; non excité.

unstint'ed, *adj.*, non restreint ; abondant, copieux ; illimité ; à discrétion.

unstirred' (eu'n'steurde), *adj.*, non remué, qui n'est pas agité **par**.

unstitch', *v.a.*, découdre, défaire.

unstock', *v.a.*, dégarnir ; (of animals) dépeupler ; (of goods) désassortir.

unstocked' (eu'n'stok'te), *adj.*, dégarni, dépeuplé, désassorti.

unstop', *v.a.*, déboucher ; ouvrir ; (a tooth) déplomber.

unstopped', *adj.*, débouché ; (fig.) sans être arrêté, sans se laisser arrêter.

unstrained', *adj.*, non filtré ; (fig.) naturel, aisé.

unstrait'ened (eu'n'stré-t'n'de), *adj.*, non rétréci ; non resserré ; (fig.) non resserré, non gêné.

unstrength'ened (eu'n'strègn'th'n'de), *adj.*, non fortifié, non raffermi, non renforcé.

unstring' (eu'n'strigne), *v.a.*, (*preterit* and *past part.*, Unstrung) détendre, relâcher ; ôter les cordes **de** ; (beads) défiler, désenfiler ; (to untie) délier ; détacher.

unstrung' (-streugne), *adj.*, détendu, relâché.

unstud'ied (eu'n'steud'ide), *adj.*, non étudié ; sans apprêt ; naturel.

unstu'dious (eu'n'stiou-), *adj.*, peu studieux.

unstuffed' (eu'n'steuf'te), *adj.*, non rempli ; vide ; non rembourré ; (cook.) non farci ; (of animals, birds) non empaillé.

unsubdued' (eu'n'seub'dîoude), *adj.*, non subjugué; indompté; inassujetti; inasservi; insoumis.

unsubmis'sive (eu'n'seub'-), *adj.*, insoumis.

unsubmis'siveness, *n.*, insoumission, *f.*

unsuborned' (eu'n'seub'orn'de), *adj.*, non suborné; non corrompu.

unsubstan'tial (eu'n'seub-sta'n'shal), *adj.*, sans substance; (of food) creux; sans réalité; immatériel; peu substantiel; peu solide; (fig.) chimérique, idéal.

unsuccess'ful (eu'n'seuk'cèss'foule), *adj.*, qui n'a pas réussi; malheureux; sans succès, infructueux, vain. To be —; *échouer, ne pas réussir*.

unsuccess'fully, *adv.*, sans succès, malheureusement.

unsuccess'fulness, *n.*, insuccès, *m.*

unsuc'cored (eu'n'seuk'eurde), *adj.*, non secouru; sans secours; sans aide.

unsuit'able (eu'n'siout'a-b'l), *adj.*, non convenable **à**; peu propre **à**; peu fait **pour**; peu approprié **à**; (unbecoming) malséant, inconvenant; (out of season) inopportun.

unsuit'ableness, *n.*, disconvenance; incongruité; inconvenance; (incapacity) incapacité, inaptitude; inopportunité, *f.*

unsuit'ably, *adv.*, d'une manière peu convenable; avec inconvenance, inconvenablement; improprement; (badly) mal; (unseasonably) mal à propos.

unsuit'ed (eu'n'siout'-), *adj.*, peu approprié, peu adapté **à**; peu fait **pour**; peu convenable **à**.

unsuit'ing, *adj.*, qui ne convient pas.

unsul'lied (eu'n'seul'ide), *adj.*, sans souillure, sans tache.

unsum'moned (eu'n'seu'm'eu'n'de), *adj.*, non convoqué; non assigné; sans être mandé.

unsung' (eu'n'seugne), *adj.*, non chanté; que les poètes n'ont pas célébré.

unsupplied' (eu'n'seup-plaïde), *adj.*, non pourvu **de**; non approvisionné **de**; dépourvu **de**; non alimenté; non satisfait.

unsupport'ed (eu'n'seup'-), *adj.*, sans support; sans moyens d'existence; non soutenu, non entretenu; (fig.) sans appui.

unsuppressed', *adj.*, non supprimé.

unsure', *adj.*, *V.* **unsafe.**

unsurpas'sable, *adj.*, insurpassable.

unsurpassed' (eu'n'seur-pâste), *adj.*, non surpassé; (fig.) transcendant.

unsurren'dered (eu'n'seur'rè'n'd'eurde), *adj.*, non rendu, non livré.

unsurround'ed (eu'n'seur'raou'n'd'-), *adj.*, non entouré, non ceint.

unsuspect'able, *adj.*, insoupçonnable.

unsuspect'ed (eu'n'seus-pèk't'-), *adj.*, non soupçonné; non suspecté; non suspect.

unsuspect'edly, *adv.*, sans exciter le soupçon.

unsuspect'ing (eu'n'seus-pèk'-), *adj.*, qui ne soupçonne rien; sans soupçon; confiant, sans méfiance.

unsuspi'cious (eu'n'seus-pish'eusse), *adj.*, confiant; non soupçonneux; sans soupçon; sans méfiance; (not to be suspected) à l'abri du soupçon.

unsuspi'ciously, *adv.*, sans soupçon, sans méfiance.

unsustain'able (-té'n'a-b'l), *adj.*, insoutenable, insupportable.

unsustained' (-té'n'de), *adj.*, sans soutien; sans être soutenu; qu'on ne peut soutenir.

unswathe' (eu'n'swéthe), *v.a.*, démailloter.

unswayed' (eu'n'swéde), *adj.*, non influencé; non dirigé; qui ne se laisse pas influencer.

unswept', *adj.*, non balayé; (of chimneys) non ramoné.

unsworn', *adj.*, qui n'a pas prêté serment; non assermenté; qui n'a pas été donné sous la foi du serment.

unsyllogis'tical (eu'n'sil-lo-djis-), *adj.*, non syllogistique; contraire aux règles du syllogisme.

unsymmet'rical (eu'n'si'm'mèt'-), *adj.*, peu symétrique; sans symétrie.

unsymmet'rically, *adv.*, sans symétrie.

unsym'pathizing (eu'n'si'm'pa-thaïz'-), *adj.*, sans sympathie, peu sympathique.

unsystemat'ical, *adj.*, peu systématique; sans système.

unsystemat'ically, *adv.*, sans système.

untack', *v.a.*, détacher; défaire; (needlework) débâtir.

untaint'ed (eu'n'té'n't'-), *adj.*, non corrompu; (of meat) frais; non gâté; (fig.) intact, pur, sans tache.

untak'en (eu'n'ték'n), *adj.*, qu'on n'a pas pris.

untam'able (-té'm'a-b'l), *adj.*, indomptable; qu'on ne peut apprivoiser; inapprivoisable.

untam'ably, *adv.*, indomptablement.

untamed' (eu'n'té'm'de), *adj.*, indompté; non apprivoisé.

untan'gle, *v.a.* *V.* **disentangle**.

untar'nished (eu'n'târ-nish'te), *adj.*, non terni; sans tache.

untast'ed (eu'n'tést'-), *adj.*, qu'on n'a pas goûté.

untaught' (eu'n'tôte), *adj.*, ignorant, illettré, sans éducation; (of things) qu'on n'a pas appris, naturel.

untaxed' (eu'n'taks'te), *adj.*, exempt d'impôt, exempt d'imposition; (jur.) non taxé; (not accused) qu'on n'accuse pas.

unteach' (eu'n'titshe), *v.a.*, faire désapprendre.

unteach'able (-'a-b'l), *adj.*, que l'on ne saurait enseigner; incapable d'apprendre; bouché.

untear'able (-a-b'l), *adj.*, indéchirable.

untem'pered (-tè'm'peurde), *adj.*, (of metals) non trempé; (fig.) non tempéré; non adouci.

unten'able (eu'n'tè'n'a-b'l), *adj.*, pas tenable; insoutenable, intenable.

unten'antable (eu'n'tè'n'a'n't'a-b'l), *adj.*, non logeable; inhabitable.

unten'anted, *adj.*, sans locataire; sans fermier; inhabité; vide.

untend'ed, *adj.*, non gardé; non soigné.

unter'rified (-faïde), *adj.*, non épouvanté, non terrifié.

untest'ed, *adj.*, non éprouvé, qu'on n'a pas éprouvé.

unthanked' (eu'n'thagn'k'te), *adj.*, qui ne reçoit pas de remercîments; sans être remercié; sans remercîment; méconnu.

unthank'ful (-foule), *adj.*, ingrat envers.

unthank'fully, *adv.*, avec ingratitude, ingratement.

unthank'fulness, *n.*, ingratitude, *f.*

unthawed' (eu'n'thôde), *adj.*, non dégelé; toujours gelé.

unthink'ing (eu'n'thign'k'-), *adj.*, étourdi, irréfléchi; inconsidéré.

unthink'ingly, *adv.*, sans y penser, par distraction; étourdiment, sans réflexion.

unthought'ful (-foule), *adj.*, irréfléchi, étourdi.

unthought' of (eu'n'thôt'ov), *adj.*, auquel on ne pense pas; négligé, oublié; (unexpected) inattendu, imprévu.

unthread' (eu'n'thrède), *v.a.*, défiler; séparer, détacher. To — a needle; *désenfiler une aiguille*.

unthrift'ily (eu'n'thrif'-), *adv.*, avec prodigalité.

unthrift'iness *ou* **unthrift'**, *n.*, prodigalité, *f.*

unthrift'y, *adj.*, prodigue, dépensier.

unti'dily, *adv.*, sans ordre, en désordre; malproprement.

unti'diness (eu'n'taï-), *n.*, désordre; mauvais arrangement; (pers.) manque d'ordre, *m.*; malpropreté, *f.*

unti'dy (eu'n'taï-di), *adj.*, mal arrangé, en

désordre ; malpropre, qui a une mauvaise tenue ; négligé, débraillé.

untie' (eu'n'taïe), *v.a.*, détacher, délier ; dénouer ; (a knot) défaire.

until', *prep.*, jusque, jusqu'à ; jusques (before a vowel) jusques **à** ; en attendant ; avant, d'ici là ; qu'après ; ne . . . que. — now, — this day ; *jusqu'à ce jour, jusqu'à présent, jusqu'ici.* — then ; *jusqu'alors, jusque là ;* (meanwhile) *en attendant.* — the break of day ; *jusqu'au point du jour.* — to-morrow ; *d'ici à demain.* I shall not go out — this afternoon ; *je ne quitterai la maison que l'après-midi.* He will not return — very late this evening ; *il ne rentrera que très tard ce soir.* He does not return from the country — Monday night ; *il ne reviendra pas de la campagne avant lundi soir,* ou *il ne reviendra de la campagne que . . .*

until', *conj.*, jusqu'à ce que, jusqu'à tant que, en attendant que, avant que (with *subj.*) *ou* avant **de** (with *inf.*), jusqu'au moment où. He will not start — I have seen him ; *il ne partira pas avant que je le voie.* He will not start — he sees me ; *il ne partira pas avant de me voir.* I will not desist — I have persuaded him ; *je ne cesserai pas que je ne l'aie persuadé. V.* **till.**

untile' (eu'n'taïle), *v.a.*, ôter les tuiles **de**, découvrir.

until'lable (eu'n'til-la-b'l), *adj.*, non labourable ; incultivable.

untilled' (eu'n'til'de), *adj.*, inculte ; en friche.

untime'liness, *n.*, prématurité ; inopportunité, *f.*

untime'ly (eu'n'taï'm'-), *adv.*, avant le temps ; avant terme, prématurément ; mal à propos, inopportunément.

untime'ly, *adj.*, avant terme ; hâtif, précoce, prématuré ; intempestif.

untinged' (eu'n'ti'n'dj'de), *adj.*, non teint ; non empreint ; pur **de**. Neither is he — with it ; *et du reste il ne laisse pas d'en être infecté.*

unti'ring (eu'n'taïeur'-), *adj.*, infatigable ; (of work) soutenu.

untir'ingly, *adv.*, sans relâche ; infatigablement.

unti'tled (-taï'-), *adj.*, sans titre. —, *ou* unentitled, to ; *n'ayant pas droit* **à**.

un'to (eu'n'tou), *prep. V.* **to.**

untold' (eu'n'tôlde), *adj.*, non raconté, non conté ; non exprimé ; passé sous silence ; non révélé ; non compté ; sans nombre, immense, énorme ; indicible, inouï ; impossible à énumérer.

untouched' (eu'n'teutsh'te), *adj.*, non touché, non atteint ; intact ; (not moved) non ému **de**, insensible à ; peu touché **de**. To leave — ; *laisser* (quelque chose) *sans y toucher ; ne pas toucher* **à**.

unto'ward (eu'n'tô-worde), *adj.*, insoumis ; indocile ; (troublesome) fâcheux ; désagréable ; malencontreux ; (awkward) gauche, maladroit.

unto'wardly, *adv.*, d'une manière insoumise ; malencontreusement ; maladroitement.

unto'wardness, *n.*, indocilité, *f.* ; caractère fâcheux, *m.* ; maladresse, gaucherie, *f.*

untrace'able (eu'n'tréss-a-b'l), *adj.*, qu'on ne peut tracer ; (not to be discovered) qu'on ne peut découvrir.

untraced', *adj.*, non tracé, non frayé ; (of drawings) non calqué.

untracked', *adj.*, non suivi, non frayé, non battu.

untrac'table, *adj. V.* **intractable.**

untrained' (eu'n'tré'n'de), *adj.*, inexercé ; inexpérimenté ; indiscipliné ; sans discipline ; (of animals) non dressé.

untram'meled (-tram'mèlde), *adj.*, sans entraves, sans être entravé.

untransfer'able (eu'n'tra'n's-feur'a-b'l), *adj.*, non transférable ; non transmissible ; incessible ; inaliénable.

untransferred' (-feur'de), *adj.*, non transféré ; non cédé, inaliéné.

untranslat'able (eu'n'tra'n's-lét'a-b'l), *adj.*, intraduisible.

untranslat'ed, *adj.*, non traduit.

untrav'eled (eu'n'trav'èlde), *adj.*, inexploré ; (pers.) qui n'a pas voyagé.

untried' (eu'n'traïde), *adj.*, non essayé ; non éprouvé ; (jur.) qui n'a pas été mis en jugement, non jugé.

untrimmed' (eu'n'tri'm'de), *adj.*, (of clothes) sans garniture ; (without finery, ant.) sans ornement ; (of horses, mules, etc.) auquel on n'a pas fait la toilette ; (of trees) non taillé, non émondé.

untrod'den (eu'n'tro'd'n), *adj.*, non foulé, non frayé ; non battu ; (of snow) vierge, immaculée, qui n'a pas été foulée.

untroub'led (eu'n'treub'l'de), *adj.*, calme ; paisible ; tranquille ; non tracassé ; (of liquids) clair, limpide.

untrue' (eu'n'trou), *adj.*, dénué de vérité, faux, inexact ; (pers.) infidèle ; déloyal ; (inconstant) inconstant, infidèle. To be — to ; *trahir.*

untru'ly, *adv.*, sans vérité, faussement ; inexactement.

untrust'worthiness, *n.*, (of news) inexactitude, fausseté, *f.* ; manque de confiance, de foi, *m.*

untrust'worthy (eu'n'treust'weur-*thi*), *adj.*, indigne de confiance ; infidèle ; (of news, etc.) inexact, mensonger.

untruth' (eu'n'trouth), *n.*, mensonge, *m.* ; inexactitude, fausseté, *f.*

untruth'ful, *adj.*, qui ne dit pas la vérité ; perfide, faux ; déloyal, menteur ; (of news, etc.) mensonger.

untruth'fulness, *n.*, fausseté, *f.*

untuck' (eu'n'teuke), *v.a.*, détrousser ; déplier ; (a bed) déborder.

untun'able (eu'n'tiou'n'a-b'l), *adj.*, inaccordable ; discordant.

untune' (eu'n'tioune), *v.a.*, désaccorder ; (to disorder) déranger, troubler.

unturf', *v.a.*, dégazonner.

unturned' (eu'n'teurn'de), *adj.*, non tourné, non renversé, non retourné. To leave no stone —; *remuer ciel et terre.*

untu'tored (eu'n'tiou-teurde), *adj.*, peu instruit ; ignorant ; inculte ; sans instruction.

untwine' (-twaï'ne), *v.a.*, détordre ; dérouler.

untwist', *v.a.*, détordre, détortiller ; défaire ; délier ; décorder.

untwist'ed, *adj.*, détordu, détortillé ; détors.

unurged' (eu'n'eurdj'de), *adj.*, sans être pressé ; spontané.

unused' (eu'n'iouz'de), *adj.*, non employé ; inaccoutumé ; (of words) inusité. — to; *inac. coutumé* **à**, *étranger* **à**.

unu'sual (eu'n'iou-jiou-), *adj.*, peu commun ; rare ; inaccoutumé ; extraordinaire ; insolite.

unu'sually, *adv.*, plus que d'habitude ; rarement ; extraordinairement.

unu'sualness, *n.*, rareté ; étrangeté, *f.* ; caractère étrange, *m.*

unut'terable (eu'n'eut'teur-a-b'l), *adj.*, inexprimable, ineffable, indicible.

unut'tered, *adj.*, non proféré, non exprimé ; non articulé ; (of coin, etc.) non émis.

unval'ued (eu'n'val'ioude), *adj.*, non estimé ; non évalué ; méprisé ; dédaigné, peu estimé.

unvan'quished (eu'n'vagn'kwish'te), *adj.*, indompté ; (poet.) invaincu.

unva'riable (-vé-), *adj.*, invariable ; qui ne manque, ne rate jamais.

unva'ried (eu'n'vé-ried), *adj.*, qui ne varie pas ; uniforme ; toujours le même.

unvar'nished (eu'n'vâr-nish'te), *adj.*, non verni ; (fig.) simple, naturel, pur et simple.

unva'rying, *adj.*, invariable ; uniforme.

unveil' (eu'n'vél), *v.a.*, dévoiler ; découvrir.

unven'erable (-vè'n'eur'a-b'l), *adj.*, peu vénérable ; méprisable.

unven'tilated, *adj.*, non aéré ; sans ventilation, mal aéré ; (fig.) (of a subject) non discuté, non examiné, pas approfondi.

unversed' in (eu'n'veurste-), *adj.*, peu versé **dans.**

unvi'olated (eu'n'vaï-o-lét'-), *adj.*, non violé, intact. The — wood ; *la forêt vierge.*

unvis'ited, *adj.*, non visité, non fréquenté.

unvi'tiated, *adj.*, non corrompu, non gâté ; (jur.) non vicié.

unvis'ored (eu'n'viz'eurde), *adj.*, sans visière ; démasqué.

unwak'ened (eu'n'wék'n'de), *adj.*, non réveillé, endormi.

unwalled' (eu'n'wolde), *adj.*, non muré ; sans murailles, sans murs.

unwa'rily (eu'n'wé-ri-li), *adv.*, avec imprévoyance ; sans précaution, imprudemment, inconsidérément.

unwa'riness, *n.*, imprévoyance ; étourderie ; imprudence, *f.*

unwar'like, *adj.*, pacifique, peu belliqueux.

unwarmed' (-worm'de), *adj.*, non échauffé ; froid.

unwarned' (-worn'de), *adj.*, non averti ; non prémuni **de.**

unwarped', *adj.*, non déjeté.

unwar'rantable (-wor-ra'n't-a-b'l), *adj.*, inexcusable, injustifiable, impardonnable.

unwar'rantableness, *n.*, nature inexcusable, *f.*

unwar'rantably, *adv.*, inexcusablement ; sans excuse ; injustement.

unwar'ranted, *adj.*, non garanti ; non autorisé ; incertain ; injustifiable ; gratuit, sans motif ; (com.) sans garantie. An — insult ; *une insulte gratuite.*

unwa'ry (eu'n'wé-), *adj.*, imprévoyant ; inconsidéré ; étourdi, imprudent.

unwa'ry, *n.* The — ; *ceux qui ne sont pas sur leurs gardes.*

unwashed' (eu'n'woshte), *adj.*, non lavé, sale ; crasseux, malpropre. The Great Unwashed ; *le prolétariat ; la populace, la canaille ; la vile multitude.*

unwast'ed (eu'n'wést'-), *adj.*, non perdu, non gaspillé ; non consumé ; non ravagé, non dévasté.

unwaste'fully, *adv.*, sans perte, avec économie.

unwatched' (eu'n'wotshte), *adj.*, qu'on ne surveille point ; non gardé, nou surveillé.

unwa'tered (eu'n'wo-teurde), *adj.*, non arrosé ; (of spirits) non étendu d'eau ; (of silk) non moiré.

unwa'vering, *adj.*, ferme, résolu, inébranlable.

unweak'ened (-wîk'n'de), *adj.*, non affaibli.

unwear'able (-wêr'-), *adj.*, non portable, qu'il est impossible de porter.

unwear'ied (eu'n'wîr'ide), *adj.*, non lassé ; (things) infatigable, inépuisable.

unwear'iedly, *adv.*, sans relâche.

unweave' (eu'n'wîve), *v.a.*, (*preterit*, Unwove ; *past part.*, Unwoven) détisser ; effiler ; défaire ; (fig.) démêler.

unwed'ded, *adj.*, non marié.

unweed'ed (eu'n'wîd'-), *adj.*, non sarclé.

unweighed' (eu'n'wéde), *adj.*, non pesé ; (fig.) non examiné.

unwel'come (eu'n'wèl'keume), *adj.*, qui n'est pas bien venu ; mal reçu ; mal accueilli ; mal vu ; (of things) mal accueilli ; (disagreeable) déplaisant, désagréable, fâcheux, malencontreux.

unwell', *adj.*, malade, indisposé, souffrant, mal portant, mal à son aise.

unwept, *adj.*, non pleuré, **non regretté** ; sans laisser de regrets.

unwhole'some (eu'n'hôl'seume), *adj.*, malsain, insalubre ; (pernicious) nuisible, pernicieux.

unwhole'someness, *n.*, insalubrité ; (of food) nature malsaine, *f.*

unwield'ily (eu'n'wîld'-), *adv.*, lourdement, pesamment.

unwield'iness, *n.*, lourdeur, pesanteur, *f.*

unwield'y (eu'n'wîld'-), *adj.*, lourd, pesant ; maladroit.

unwill'ing, *adj.*, mal disposé ; de mauvais vouloir ; de mauvaise volonté. To be — to ; *n'être pas disposé* à ; *ne pas vouloir ; ne pas vouloir prendre sur soi* **de.**

unwill'ingly, *adv.*, avec mauvaise volonté ; à contre-cœur ; à regret, avec répugnance ; sans le vouloir. Not — ; *d'assez bonne grâce, assez volontiers, sans trop se faire prier.*

unwill'ingness (eu'n'will'ign-nèce), *n.*, mauvaise volonté, *f.* ; mauvais vouloir, *m.* ; répugnance, *f.*

unwind' (eu'n'waï'n'de), *v.a.*, (*preterit* and *past part.*, Unwound) dévider ; dérouler ; (fig.) démêler, débrouiller.

unwiped' (eu'n'waïp'te), *adj.*, non essuyé.

unwis'dom, *n.*, folie, déraison, *f.*

unwise' (eu'n'waïze), *adj.*, peu sage, malavisé, insensé, sot.

unwise'ly, *adv.*, peu sagement ; d'une manière insensée ; sottement, imprudemment.

unwished' (for) (eu'n'wish'te-), *adj.*, non souhaité, non désiré.

unwith'ered (eu'n'with'eurde), *adj.*, non desséché, non flétri.

unwith'ering (-with'eur'-), *adj.*, qui ne se dessèche pas, qui ne se flétrit pas.

unwit'nessed (-wit'nèste), *adj.*, sans témoins ; inaperçu.

unwit'tily, *adv.*, sans esprit, sottement.

unwit'tingly, *adv.*, sans le savoir, à son insu.

unwit'ty, *adj.*, sans esprit ; sot, peu spirituel.

unwo'manly (-wou'm'-), *adj.*, indigne d'une femme, peu séant à une femme ; peu féminin.

unwont'ed, *adj.*, inaccoutumé, rare, extraordinaire.

unwont'edly, *adv.*, rarement.

unwont'edness, *n.*, rareté, *f.*

unwooed' (eu'n'woû'de), *adj.*, que l'on ne recherche pas ; dédaigné, méprisé.

unwork'able (-weurk'-), *adj.*, impraticable ; (of mines, etc.) inexploitable.

unwork'ableness, *n.*, impraticabilité, *f.*

unworked', *adj.*, (of mines, etc.) inexploité.

unworld'liness (eu'n'weurl'd'-), *n.*, absence de mondanité, *f.*

unworld'ly, *adj.*, qui n'a rien de ce monde ; étranger au monde ; étrange ; peu mondain.

unworn', *adj.*, (not in fashion) qui n'est pas porté ; non usé ; (not put on) qui n'a pas été porté.

unwor'thily (eu'n'weur-ïhi-), *adv.*, indignement ; sans le mériter.

unwor'thiness, *n.*, manque de mérite, *m.* ; indignité, *f.*

unwor'thy, *adj.*, indigne, vil ; sans mérite.

unwot'ting, *adj.*, ne se doutant, *ou* qui ne se doute, de rien.

unwound'ed, *adj.*, sans blessure, intact.

unwov'en (eu'n'wôv'n), *adj.*, non tissu ; effilé.

unwrap' (eu'n'rap), *v.a.*, défaire, développer ; (fig.) révéler, découvrir.

unwreath' (eu'n'rîthe), *v.a.*, dérouler ; détordre ; défaire.

unwrin'kle (eu'n'rign'k'l), *v.a.*, dérider.

unwrin'kled, *adj.*, uni, sans rides.

unwrit'ten (eu'n'rit't'n), *adj.*, non écrit ; en blanc ; (fig.) verbal, traditionnel. — law ; (jur.) *droit coutumier, m.*

unwrought' (eu'n'rôte), *adj.*, non travaillé, brut ; non ouvré ; (fig.) naturel, sans effort.

unwrung' (eu'n'rugue), *adj.*, non tordu ; (fig.) non navré.

unyield'ing (eu'n'yïld'-), *adj.*, qui ne cède pas ; dur ; (fig.) inflexible, entêté, entier.

unyoke' (eu'n'yôke), *v.a.*, ôter le joug à ; dételer ; (fig.) séparer, rendre à la liberté.

unzeal'ous, *adj.*, peu zélé, sans zèle.

unzoned' (-zô'n'de), *adj.*, sans ceinture.

up (eupe), *adv.*, haut, en haut ; en l'air ; (out of bed) levé, sur pied; (above the horizon) levé, sur l'horizon ; (on one's legs) debout ; sur pied ; (excited) excité ; (in revolt) en révolte, en insurrection ; (over) fini ; écoulé ; (in a state of elevation, of ascending) haut ; (of the tide) haut, monté ; (of shutters) fermé ; (of the wind) être levé ; (of prices) élevé ; (of stocks and shares) en hausse ; (of navigation) en amont. — to here ; *jusqu'ici.* — to there; *jusque là.* — and down ; *en haut et en bas ; çà et là ; de long en large ; de haut en bas ; de tous côtés.* — from ; *de ; du fond de.* He is — ; *il est levé, ou sur pied.* — and doing ; *à l'ouvrage ; à la besogne, occupé.* Hard — ; *vivement pressé ;* (without money) *gêné.* To make — to any one ; *faire des avances à.* To be — ; (of wine) *mousser.* — in arms; *en armes.* To be — in arms ; *prendre les armes;* (fig.) *prendre la mouche ; s'emporter.* It is all — ; *tout est fini ; c'en est fait.* To be — to ; *être au fait,* ou *au courant, de ; être à la hauteur de.* To come — with ; *rattraper.* To have any one — ; *traduire quelqu'un en justice.* Well — in ; *fort en, ferré sur.* The —train; (rail.) *convoi montant, train montant, m.* — there; *là-haut.* — to ; *jusqu'à ; jusqu'à la hauteur de ;* (conformably to) *selon, conformément à ;* (conversant with) *au fait de, au courant de.* To live — to one's fortune ; *dépenser tout son revenu.* To be — to snuff; *ne pas se moucher du pied ; avoir le fil.* To be — to all manner of tricks ; *en savoir plus d'une.* To be — to one's ears in work ; *avoir de la besogne par-dessus la tête,* ou *ne savoir où donner de la tête.* To be — to one's knees in water ; *avoir de l'eau jusqu'au genou.* — ! *levez-vous !* (go up) *montez !* — with ; *levez ! montez !* — comes a fox ; *voilà que survient un renard.* To be — to date; *être fin de siècle, être à jour, au courant du jour.* — to-day, down to-morrow ; (prov.) *cent ans bannière, cent ans civière ;* ou *aujourd'hui chevalier, demain vacher.* To get — a play ; *monter une pièce.* To get — by heart ; *apprendre par cœur.* A made — dinner ; *un dîner de pièces et de morceaux.* — line ; *ligne de retour, f.* — went the King's cane ; (Macaulay) *et le roi de lever sa canne.* — went a shout of laughter from the crowd ; *et la foule de rire !* (V. Hugo).

up, *prep.*, en haut *de,* au haut *de ;* (of motion) en montant. — hill, — stream ; *en amont.* To go — stream ; *aller en amont, remonter.* Praised — hill and down dale ; *loué de toutes les façons.* To go — country ; *aller dans l'intérieur.* To be all —hill work ; *avoir tout à faire.* To run — to town ; *faire une course,* ou *un petit voyage, à la cité.*

up (eupe), *n.*, haut, *m.* The —s and downs; *les vicissitudes, f.pl.; les hauts et les bas; les succès et les revers, m.pl.*

u'pas (you-pass), *n.*, (bot., toxicology) upas, *m.*

upbear' (eup'bère), *v.a.*, (*preterit* Upbore; *past part.* Upborne) élever ; soutenir ; soulever ; supporter.

upbraid' (eup'brède), *v.a.*, reprocher **à ;** faire des reproches à ; réprimander ; réprouver.

upbraid'ing, *n.*, reproche, *m. ;* réprimande, *f.*

upbraid'ingly, *adv.*, avec reproche, d'un ton de reproche.

up'cast (eup'câste), *n.*, jet ; coup, *m.*

upcast', *adj.*, lancé en l'air ; levé. —-shaft (*pron.* eup'câste-) ; (mines) *puits de sortie, n.*

upheav'al (-), *n.*, (geol.) soulèvement, *m.*

upheave' (eup'hîve), *v.a.*, soulever, lever.

upheld' (-'hèlde), *adj.*, soutenu, maintenu.

n'pher, *n.*, (arch.) échasse, *f.*

up'hill (eup'-), *adj.*, qui va en montant, en

pente ; (fig.) ardu, dur, pénible, difficile. — work ; *travail fatigant, éreintant, m.*

uphold' (eup'hôlde), *v.a.*, (*preterit and past part.*, Upheld) lever, élever ; soutenir, maintenir ; (to keep up) entretenir.

uphold'er, *n.*, soutien, appui, partisan, *m.*

uphol'ster, *v.a.*, tapisser, meubler.

uphol'sterer (eup-hôl-), *n.*, tapissier, *m.*

uphol'stery, *n.*, commerce de tapissier, *m. ;* tapisserie, *f. ;* meubles, *m.pl.*

up'land (eup'-), *n.*, terrain élevé, *m. ;* haute terre, *f.*, plateau, *m.*

up'land, *adj.*, montagneux, des hautes terres.

up'lander (eup'-), *n.*, montagnard, *m.*

uplift' (eup'-), *v.a.*, lever, élever, soulever.

uplift'ing, *n.*, soulèvement ; (moral) relèvement, *m.*

upon' (eup'-), *prep.*, sur ; (on occasion of) dans, à l'occasion **de ;** (before a present participle) en ; (denoting exposure) sous ; (engaged in) occupé **à.** — the whole ; *en somme ; à tout prendre; au total.* — those terms; *à ces conditions-là.* To come — the parish ; *aller à l'hôpital, à l'hospice.* To live — ; *vivre de ; se nourrir* **de.** — pain of ; *sous peine de.* — it ; *dessus.* — that; *là-dessus.* — the death of ; *à la mort de.*

up'per (eup'-), *adj.*, supérieur ; d'en haut ; de dessus ; au-dessus ; haut ; (geog.) haut. The Upper House ; *la chambre haute.* The — ten ; *la haute volée, l'aristocratie, f. ; le grand monde.*

up'per-boxes, *n.pl.*, troisièmes loges, *f.pl.*

up'per-deck, *n.*, pont supérieur, *m.*

up'per-end, *n.*, (of a table) le haut bout, *m.*

up'per-form, *n.*, (in schools) classe des grands, classe supérieure, *f.*

up'per-hand, *n.*, avantage, dessus, *m. ;* supériorité, *f.* To get, ou gain, the — ; *l'emporter* **sur**, *avoir l'avantage* **sur.**

up'per jaw, *n.*, mâchoire supérieure, *f.*

up'per-leather (eup'peur-lèth'-), *n.*, empeigne, *f.*

up'per lip, *n.*, lèvre supérieure, *f.* To keep a stiff — ; *tenir son courage à deux mains.*

up'permost (eup'peur-môste), *adj.*, supérieur, le plus élevé ; (fig.) le plus fort ; dominant. To be — ; *prédominer.* To stand — ; *être le premier.* To stand — in any one's thoughts ; *occuper entièrement les pensées* **de**, ou *être le principal objet des pensées* **de.**

up'per part, *n.*, le haut, le dessus, *m.*

up'pers, *n.pl.*, (of boots) empeignes, *f.pl.*

up'per story, *n.*, étage supérieur ; (the last) dernier étage ; (fam.) (of the head) caboche, *f.* He is cracked in the — ; *il a le timbre fêlé.*

up'per-town, *n.*, haute ville, *f.* [*f.pl.*

up'per-works, *n.pl.*, (nav.) œuvres mortes,

up'pish, *adj.*, fier, arrogant.

up'pishness, *n.*, fierté, arrogance, *f.*

upraise' (eup'réze), *v.a.*, lever, élever; (fig.) exalter.

uprear' (eup'rîre), *v.a.*, élever, soulever, lever, dresser.

up'right (eup'raïte), *adj.*, droit ; debout ; à plomb, vertical ; (honest) droit, honnête, loyal, intègre.

up'right, *n.*, élévation, *f.; (mech.)* montant, *m.*

up'rightly (eup'raït'-), *adv.*, droit, debout, à plomb, de champ ; (honestly) avec droiture, loyalement, avec probité.

up'rightness (eup'raït'-), *n.*, aplomb, *m. ;* (honesty) droiture, loyauté, intégrité, *f.*

uprise' (eup'raïze), *v.n.*, (*preterit* Uprose; *past part.*, Uprisen) se lever.

upris'ing (eup'raïs'-), *n.*, lever ; (rebellion) soulèvement, *m. ;* révolte, *f.*

up'roar (eup'rôre), *n.*, tumulte, désordre ; tapage, vacarme, *m.*

uproar'ious (eup'rôr'-), *adj.*, bruyant ; tumultueux.

uproar'iously, *adv.*, avec un grand vacarme.

uproar'iousness, *n.*, turbulence, *f.*, désordre, *m.*

uproot' (eup'roûte), *v.a.*, déraciner, extirper.

uproot'ing, *n.*, déracinement, *m.*; (fig.) extirpation, *f.*

upset' (eup'sète), *v.a.*, (*preterit* and *past part.*, Upset) renverser ; (fig.) bouleverser ; (a vehicle) faire verser ; (a boat) faire chavirer.

upset', *v.n.*, (*preterit* and *past part.*, Upset) se renverser ; (of vehicles) verser ; (of boats) chavirer, faire capot. — price; *mise à prix*, *f.*

upset'ting, *n.*, renversement, *m.*; (of a vehicle) versade, *f.*; (of a boat) chavirement, *m.*

up'shot (eup'-), *n.*, résultat, *m.*; issue, fin, conclusion, *f.*; résultat définitif, fin mot, *m.* On the —; *en définitive.*

up'side (eup'saïde), *n.*, dessus, *m.*

up'side-down (-daoune), *adv.*, sens dessus dessous. To turn —, *v.a.*, *mettre sens dessus dessous*; bouleverser ; *v.n.*, *se renverser sens dessus dessous.*

upsoar', *v.a.*, s'envoler, prendre son essor vers.

up'standing, *adj.*, droit, debout.

up'start (eup'stârte), *n.*, parvenu, nouveau riche, *m.*

up'start, *adj.*, qui croît soudainement; subit ; (b.s.) parvenu, vain, fanfaron.

upstay' (eup'-), *v.a.*, étayer ; appuyer.

uptear' (eup'tère), *v.a.*, arracher.

upturn' (eup'teurne), *v.a.*, tourner; retourner; lever ; (of land) labourer.

up'wafted, *adj.*, porté sur la brise.

up'ward (eup'worde) *ou* **up'wards** (-'wordze), *adv.*, en haut ; en remontant ; (over) au-delà ; (nav.) en amont. **—s** of ; *plus* **de.** **—s** and downwards; *en haut et en bas*; *par haut et par bas.*

up'ward, *adj.*, levé, dirigé en haut ; ascensionnel ; de bas en haut; droit. To show an — tendency; (of shares) *tendre à la hausse.*

uranog'raphy (you-ra-), *n.*, uranographie, *f.*

U'ranus (you-ra-), *n.*, (astron.) Uranus, *m.*

u'rate (you-), *n.* (chem.) urate, *m.*

ur'ban (eur-), *adj.*, urbain.

urbane' (eur-), *adj.*, qui a de l'urbanité, poli.

urbane'ly, *adv.*, poliment, avec urbanité.

urban'ity (eur-ba-), *n.*, urbanité, *f.*

ur'chin (eur-tshi'ne), *n.*, gamin, moutard, polisson; mioche, môme ; gosse (Daudet). *m.*

ure'thra (you-rî-thra), *n.*, (anat.) urètre, *m.*

urge (eurdje), *v.a.*, presser ; pousser, exciter, porter, hâter, avancer; (a battle) engager; (to exasperate) provoquer, irriter, exciter; (to follow closely) suivre de près, presser ; (to press with eagerness) prier instamment **de,** presser vivement **de** ; exhorter **à** ; (to importune) importuner ; (petition, etc.) présenter, produire; (argument) avancer, émettre ; mettre en avant ; (the necessity of) faire valoir; insister **sur** ; (to allege) alléguer ; (to object) objecter, représenter. To — on ; *pousser* **à,** *exciter* **à,** *porter* **à,** *pousser en avant; activer.*

ur'gency (eur-djè'n'-), *n.*, urgence ; nécessité urgente, *f.*; besoin pressant, *m.*; (earnest solicitation) sollicitation urgente, *f.*; instances, *f.pl.*

ur'gent (eur-djè'n'te), *adj.*, urgent; instant ; pressant; (impending) imminent ; (of letters) pressé.

ur'gently, *adv.*, avec urgence ; instamment ; avec instance ; avec importunité.

ur'ging (eurdj'-), *adj.n.*, pressant ; importun. No — on your part will avail ; *aucune sollicitation de votre part n'y fera rien ; ou toute sollicitation de votre part restera sans effet.*

u'ric (you-), *adj.*, (chem.) urique.

u'rinal (you-), *n.*, urinal ; (public) urinoir, *m.*

u'rinary (-ri-na-), *n.*, réservoir d'urine, *m.*

u'rinary (you-), *adj.*, (anat.) urinaire.

u'rine (you-ri'ne), *n.*, urine, *f.*

urn (eurne), *n.*, urne, *f.* ; vase, *m.* ; (for tea, coffee) fontaine, *f.*

ur'sa (eur-), *n.*, (astron.) Ourse, *f.* Ursa Major ; *grande Ourse.* Ursa Minor ; *petite Ourse.*

ur'sine (eur-saïne), *adj.*, d'ours, oursin.

Ur'suline (eur-siou-), *n.*, ursuline, *f.*

us (euss), *pron.*, nous, nous outres. For — Frenchmen; *pour nous outres Français.*

us'able, *adj.*, dont on peut se servir ; utile ; employable.

us'age (you-zèdje), *n.*, usage ; procédé ; traitement, *m.* By bad or ill — on the part of the court of Vienna (Macaulay) ; *a cause des mauvais procédés* **de . . .**

us'ance (you-za'n'ce), *n.*, (com.) usance, *f.*

use (youce), *n.*, usage, emploi, *m.*; (utility) utilité, *f.* ; (advantage) avantage, profit; (interest) intérêt; (custom) usage ; (jur.) usage, usufruit, *m.*, jouissance ; coutume, habitude, *f.* ; (need) besoin, *m.* For the — of ; *à l'usage* **de** ; *au profit* **de.** Of —; *utile.* Of great — ; *très utile* ; *d'une grande utilité.* Of no — ; *inutile* ; *d'aucune utilité* ; *qui ne sert à rien* ; *bon à rien.* In — ; *d'usage*, *en usage*, *employé*; (of words) *usité.* Out of —; *hors d'usage* ; *inusité*, *passé*, *vieilli*, *tombé en désuétude.* In general —; *d'un usage général.* What is the — of doing it ; *à quoi sert de le faire?* To make — of ; *profiter* **de** ; *faire usage* **de** ; *se servir* **de.** To have no further — for ; *n'avoir plus besoin* **de.** It is of no — for one to . . . ; *on a beau . . .* — is a second nature ; (prov.) *l'habitude est une seconde nature.*

use (youce), *v.a.*, faire usage **de** ; user **de** ; se servir **de** ; employer ; utiliser ; (to consume) user, consommer ; (up) finir, achever; (to accustom) accoutumer, habituer ; (to treat) en user *ou* agir **avec,** agir **envers** ; traiter. To — forbearance towards ; *user d'indulgence*, ou *de ménagements*, **envers.**

use (youze), *v.n.*, avoir coutume, avoir l'hab.-tude ; (of things) être ordinairement. **Used to** (followed by infinitive) is often the sign of the imperfect, *e.g.* he —d to admire ; *il admirait.* To get —d to ; *s'accoutumer* **à,** *s'habituer* **à** ; *se faire* **à.** To have been —d; (of plate, linen, clothes, etc.) *avoir servi.*

used (youz'de), *adj.*, (of words) usité. Not — ; *inusité* ; *hors d'usage.* Much — ; *très usité.* Very little — ; *très peu usité* ; *d'un usage restreint* ; (of linen, plate, clothes, etc.) *presque neuf.* — up ; *usé* ; (of an edition) *épuisé* ; (pers.) *blasé.*

use'ful (yous'foule), *adj.*, utile ; avantageux.

use'fully, *adv.*, utilement ; avec profit ; avantageusement.

use'fulness, *n.*, utilité, *f.* ; profit, avantage, *m.*

use'less (yous'-), *adj.*, inutile ; sans avantage ; (fig.) vain.

use'lessly, *adv.*, inutilement.

use'lessness, *n.*, inutilité ; vanité, *f.*

us'er (youz'eur), *n.*, personne qui se sert **de,** *f.* Right of — ; *droit d'usage*, *m.*

ush'er (eush'eur), *n.*, huissier ; (in schools) sous-maître, maître d'étude ; (among schoolboys) pion, *m.*

ush'er, *v.a.*, introduire **dans** ; faire entrer **dans** ; précéder, inaugurer, annoncer. The snow-drop —s in the spring ; *la perce-neige est l'avant-coureur du printemps.* To — out ; *reconduire (à la porte).*

u'sual (you-jiou-), *adj.*, ordinaire, commun ; fréquent ; habituel ; accoutumé ; usuel ; d'usage. As —; *comme d'ordinaire* ; *comme à l'ordinaire* ; *comme de coutume* ; *comme d'habitude.* With the — ceremonies ; *avec les cérémonies d'usage.* More than —; *plus qu'à l'ordinaire.*

u'sually, *adv.*, ordinairement, d'ordinaire ; usuellement ; habituellement.

u'sualness, *n.*, habitude, fréquence, *f.*

u'sufruct (you-ziou-freuk'te), *n.*, (jur.) usufruit, *m.*

usufruc′tuary (-′iou-), *n.*, (jur.) usufruitier, *m.*, usufruitière, *f.*

u′surer (you-jiou-reur), *n.*, usurier, *m.*

usu′rious (you-jiou-ri-eusse), *adj.*, qui fait l'usure ; usuraire.

usu′riously, *adv.*, usurairement.

usu′riousness, *n.*, nature usuraire, *f.*

usurp′ (you-zerp′), *v.a.*, usurper.

usurpa′tion (you-zeur-pé-), *n.*, usurpation, *f.*

usurp′er, *n.*, usurpateur, *m.*, usurpatrice, *f.*

usurp′ingly, *adv.*, par usurpation.

u′sury (you-jiou-), *n.*, usure, *f.*

ut (eute), *n.*, (mus.) ut, do, *m.*

uten′sil (you-), *n.*, ustensile, vase, *m.*

u′terine (you-teur′-), *adj.*, utérin.

u′terus (you-teur′-), *n.*, (anat.) utérus, *m.*, matrice, *f.*

utilita′rian (you-til′i-té-), *adj.*, utilitaire.

utilita′rianism, *n.*, utilitarisme, *m.*

util′ity (you-til′-), *n.*, utilité, *f.*; avantage, *m.*

u′tilizable, *adj.*, utilisable.

utiliza′tion (you-til′aïzé-), *n.*, utilisation, *f.*

u′tilize (you-til′aïze), *v.a.*, utiliser.

ut′most (eut′môste), *adj.*, extrême, dernier ; le plus haut ; le plus grand ; le plus imminent ; (com.) le plus haut (prix) ; (le prix) le plus élevé.

ut′most (eut′môste), *n.*, extrême, plus haut degré, comble, (all one can) possible, tout son possible, le plus possible, *m.* To the — ; *à l'extrême, au suprême degré.* To do one's — ; *faire tout son possible* pour, ou *tous ses efforts* pour. At the — ; *tout au plus.*

Uto′pia (you-tô-), *n.*, utopie, *f.*

Uto′pian (you-tô-), *adj.*, d'utopie, chimérique.

uto′pist (you-tô-), *n.*, utopiste *m.*

ut′ter (eut′teur), *v.a.*, énoncer, proférer, prononcer, articuler, dire ; (to disclose) révéler, dire, publier ; (to put in circulation) mettre en circulation, émettre ; (sighs, groans) pousser, jeter. He did not — a word ; (fam.) *il ne souffla pas mot.* To — notes ; *émettre des billets.*

ut′ter (eut′teur), *adj.*, (total) total, entier, complet ; (absolute) absolu, positif ; (extreme) le plus profond, le plus grand, le plus reculé ; (quite) tout à fait, parfaitement ; (downright) vrai, fieffé. To my — astonishment ; *à mon grand étonnement* ou *ébahissement ; à ma grande surprise.* — strangers to one another ; *tout à fait inconnus l'un à l'autre.*

ut′terable (eut′teur′a-b′l), *adj.*, qu'on peut prononcer ; exprimable.

ut′terance (eut′teur′-), *n.*, articulation, prononciation ; parole ; (com.) émission ; (of sounds) émission ; élocution ; expression, *f.*; débit, *m.* To deprive of — ; *priver de la parole.* To lose all power of — ; *perdre entièrement l'usage de la parole.* To give — to ; *prononcer, proférer.*

ut′terer, *n.*, personne qui articule, qui prononce, qui émet, *f.*; (issuer) émetteur, *m.* — of base coin ; *émetteur de fausse monnaie), m.*

ut′terly, *adv.*, de fond en comble ; tout à fait, complètement, entièrement.

ut′termost (eut′teur-môste), *adj.* V. **utmost.** At the —; *au plus.* To the — ends ; *au fin bout, aux confins.*

u′vula (you-viou-), *n.*, (anat.) luette, *f.*

u′vular, *adj.*, (anat.) uvulaire.

uxo′rious (eug-zô-ri-eusse), *adj.*, tendre à l'excès pour sa femme ; esclave de sa femme.

uxo′riously, *adv.*, avec une sotte, *ou* une excessive, complaisance pour sa femme.

uxo′riousness, *n.*, complaisance excessive pour sa femme, *f.*

V

v, vingt-deuxième lettre de l'alphabet, v, *m.*

va′cancy (vé-), *n.*, vide, *m.*; lacune, *f.*; (leisure) loisir, repos, *m.*; interruption, *f.*; (empti-

ness of thought) manque de réflexion, défaut de pensée, *m.* ; (place not occupied) place vacante, vacance, *f.*

va′cant (vé-), *adj.*, vide ; (free) libre ; (not occupied) vacant ; (of time) perdu, libre, de loisir ; (indicating want of thought) sans expression, insignifiant ; (thoughtless) qui ne réfléchit pas ; (jur.) vacant. — look ; *air hébété, air distrait, m.*

va′cate, *v.a.*, laisser vacant ; (jur.) vider ; (to annul) annuler, abolir ; (to resign) donner sa démission de ; quitter ; se démettre de.

vaca′tion (va-ké-), *n.*, vacation, *f.* ; (holidays) vacances ; (of courts of law) vacations, vacances, *f.pl.* ; (annulment) annulation, abolition, *f.*

vac′cinate (vak′si-), *v.a.*, vacciner.

vaccina′tion (vak′si-né-), *n.*, vaccination, vaccine, *f.*

vac′cine (vak-saïne *ou* -cine), *adj.*, de vache.

vac′cine-matter (-mat′teur), *n.*, vaccin, virus vaccin, *m.*

vac′cinist, vac′cinator, *n.*, vaccinateur, *m.*

va′cillate (vass′il-), *v.n.*, vaciller ; (fig.)balancer.

va′cillating (-′il-lét′-), *adj.*, vacillant ; indécis.

vacilla′tion (vass′il-lé-), *n.*, vacillation, hésitation, indécision, *f.*

vacu′ity (va-kiou-), *n.*, vide, *m.* ; vacuité, *f.*; (fig.) néant, *m.*

vac′uous (vak′iou-euss), *adj.*, (ant.) vide.

vac′uum (vak′iou-), *n.*, vide, *m.* To get a — ; *faire le vide.* —gauge ; (air-pump) *baromètre tronqué, m.*

vade-me′cum (vé-di-mî-), *n.*, vade-mecum, *m.*

vag′abond, *n.*, vagabond, *m.*, vagabonde, *f.*, va-nu-pieds, vaurien, mendiant, *m.* —s, *pl.*, gens sans aveu,*m.pl.*

vag′abond, *adj.*, errant, vagabond ; flottant.

vag′abondize (-′aïze), *v.n.*, vagabonder.

vaga′ries, *n.pl.*, divagations, *f.pl.*

vaga′ry (va-ghé-), *n.*, caprice, *m.* ; quinte, boutade, *f.*

vagi′na (va-djaï-na), *n.*, vagin, *m.*

va′grancy (vé-), *n.*, vagabondage, *m.*

va′grant, *adj.*, vagabond ; errant.

va′grant (vé-), *n.*, vagabond, *m.*, vagabonde, *f.*; homme sans aveu, *m.*

va′grantly, *adv.*, en vagabond.

vague (véghe), *adj.*, vague.

vague′ly, *adv.*, vaguement.

vague′ness, *n.*, vague, *m.*

vails (vélze), *n.pl.*, gratifications aux domestiques, *f.pl.* ; pourboire, *m.* ; (ant.) profits, *m.pl.*

vain (véne), *adj.*, vain ; (showy) fastueux, somptueux ; (false) faux, mensonger ; (conceited) vain, vaniteux, glorieux ; (proud) orgueilleux, superbe. — as a peacock ; *glorieux, ou fier, comme un paon.* It is in — for one to ; *on a beau.* It is in — you try ; *vous avez beau faire.* In — ; *en vain ; vainement ; en pure perte.* To take in — ; *prendre en vain.*

vainglo′rious (vé′n′-), *adj.*, vain, vaniteux ; orgueilleux, superbe.

vainglo′riously, *adv.*, vaniteusement.

vainglo′ry, vainglo′riousness (vé′n′-), *n.*, vaine gloire ; gloriole, *f.*; sot orgueil, *m.*

vain′ly, *adv.*, en vain ; vainement ; (foolishly) sottement ; (arrogantly) orgueilleusement, avec vanité.

vain′ness, *n.*, inutilité ; (empty pride) vanité, *f.*

vair (vére), *n.*, (her.) vair, *m.*

val′ance, *n.*, pente, cantonnière, draperie de bas de lit ; garniture de rideau, *f.*

vale (véle), *n.*, (poetic) vallon, *m.*; vallée, *f.*

valedic′tory (va-), *n.*, discours d'adieu, *m.*

valedic′tory, *adj.*, d'adieu.

val′entine (-taïne), *n.*, amant choisi le jour de la Saint-Valentin ; (letter) billet de la St.-Valentin, *m.* —'s-day ; *la St.-Valentin, f.*

vale′rian (-lî-), *n.*, (bot.) valériane, *f.*

val'et (-ète), *n.*, valet, valet de chambre, *m.*

valetudina'rian (val'i-tiou-di-né-), *n.* and *adj.*, valétudinaire, *m.f.*

val'iant, *adj.*, vaillant, valeureux, brave.

val'iantly, *adv.*, vaillamment, bravement.

val'iantness, *n.*, valeur, vaillance, bravoure, *f.*

val'id, *adj.*, valable, valide. To make —; *rendre valable, valider, rendre valide.*

val'idate, *v.a.*, valider, rendre valable.

valid'ity *ou* **val'idness**, *n.*, validité, *f.*

val'idly, *adv.*, validement, valablement.

valise' (va-lîce), *n.*, valise, *f.*, portemanteau, *m.*

valla'tion (val-lé-), *n.*, circonvallation, *f.*

val'ley (val-lé), *n.*, vallée, *f.*; vallon, *m.*

val'lum, *n.*, retranchement, *m.*

val'or (-eur), *n.*, valeur, vaillance, bravoure, *f.*

val'orous, *adj.*, vaillant, valeureux, brave.

val'orously, *adv.*, vaillamment, valeureusement.

val'uable (val'iou-a-b'l), *adj.*, précieux; de prix; de valeur.

val'uableness, *n.*, valeur, *f.*; prix, *m.*

val'uables (val'iou-a-b'l'ze), *n.*, choses de prix; choses précieuses, *f.pl.*; objets de luxe, objets de prix, *m.pl.*

valua'tion (val'iou-é-), *n.*, évaluation, estimation, appréciation, *f.*

val'uator (-é-teur), *n.*, estimateur, expert, *m.*

val'ue (val'iou), *n.*, valeur, *f.*; prix, *m.*; (precise signification) valeur, signification; (importance) valeur, importance, *f.* To set a — on; *estimer*; *mettre à haut prix*; *faire cas de*; *mettre du prix à*; *attacher de la valeur à.* For — received; (promissory notes) *valeur reçue.* To be of no —; *ne valoir rien, n'avoir aucune valeur.* The — of a thing is what it will fetch; *la valeur d'une chose est mesurée (ou se mesure) par le prix qu'on en obtient.*

val'ue (val'iou), *v.a.*, évaluer, estimer, apprécier; (to reckon) évaluer, estimer, calculer; (to esteem) estimer, priser, apprécier; faire cas de, tenir à; (to take account of) calculer; tenir compte de. [prisé; précieux, digne.

val'ued (val'ioude), *adj.*, estimé, apprécié,

val'ueless, *adj.*, sans valeur, sans prix.

val'uer, *n.*, estimateur, expert; (one who holds in esteem) appréciateur, *m.*

valv'ate, *adj.*, (bot.) valvé, valvaire.

valve, *n.*, soupape, valve, *f.*; clapet, *m.*; (of a lock-gate) ventelle, soupape, *f.*; (of a door) battant, *m.*; (anat.) valvule; (bot., conch.) valve, *f.* — -box; *boîte à soupape*; *boîte de tiroir, f.* — -casing; *boîte à tiroir, f.* — -door; *porte de soupape, f.* — -gear; *appareil de soupape, m.* Safety- —; *soupape de sûreté, f.*

valved (valv'de), *adj.*, à soupape; (bot.) valvé, à valves, à valvules. [à valves.

val'vular (valv'iou-), *adj.*, de soupape; (bot.)

vamp, *n.*, empeigne, *f.*, avant-pied, *m.*

vamp, *v.a.*, raccommoder, rapiécer; (of boots) remonter.

vam'pire (-païeur), *n.*, vampire, *m.*

van, *n.*, (milit.) avant-garde, *f.*; (agri.) van, *m.*; tarare; (wing) aile; (cart) charrette couverte, carriole, *f.*; (pleasure van) char à bancs; (rail.) wagon; (mil.) fourgon, *m.*; (spring van) tapissière, *f.* — -courier; *avant-coureur, précurseur*; (milit.) *éclaireur, m.* — -guard; *avantgarde, f.* Furniture —; *voiture de déménagements*; *tapissière, f.* To be in the —; (fig.) *être à l'avant-poste*; *au fort de la mêlée.* Luggage —; *fourgon de bagages.* Guard's —; *fourgon du chef du train.*

Van'dal, *n.*, Vandale, *m.f.*

Vandal'ic, *adj.*, vandale, de vandale.

Van'dalism (-'iz'm), *n.*, vandalisme, *m.*

vandyke', *n.*, col à la Van Dyck, *m.*

vandyke', *v.a.*, (to scollop the edges of) crêter.

vane, *n.*, (weather-cock) girouette, *f.*; (of a steam-engine) registre; (in mathematical instru-

ments) pinnule; (of a feather) barbe; (nav.) girouette, *f.*; (flag) guidon, *m.* — -spindle; *fer de girouette, m.*

vanil'la (-nil-la), *n.*, vanille, *f.* — -plant; *vanille, f.*; *vanillier, m.*

van'ish, *v.n.*, s'évanouir; disparaître; se dissiper, passer; (fam.) (to make off) déguerpir.

van'ished (-nish'te), *adj.*, évanoui, disparu.

van'ishing, *n.*, action de s'évanouir; disparition; (persp.) fuite, *f.* — -point; *point de fuite, m.*

van'ity, *n.*, vanité, *f.* — fair; (Thackeray) *la foire aux vanités.*

van'quish (-kwishe), *v.a.*, vaincre; dompter.

van'quishable (-kwish'a-b'l), *adj.*, que l'on peut vaincre, domptable; (neologism) vincible.

van'quisher (-kwish'-), *n.*, vainqueur, *m.*

van'tage (-tèdje), *n.*, occasion favorable, *f.* — -ground; *terrain avantageux*; *avantage, avantage du terrain, m.*; *haute position, position supérieure, supériorité, éminence, f.*

vap'id, *adj.*, fade; insipide; (unanimated) inanimé, inerte; (of liquors) plat, éventé.

vap'idly, *adv.*, insipidement.

vap'idness, vapid'ity, *n.*, fadeur; insipidité; (dullness) nature inanimée; inertie; (of liquor) évent, *m.*

va'porizable (-'aïz'a-b'l), *adj.*, qui peut être vaporisé, *ou* résous en vapeur.

vaporiza'tion (-'aïzé-), *n.*, vaporisation, *f.*

va'porize (-'aïze), *v.a.*, vaporiser.

va'porize, *v.n.*, se vaporiser.

va'porizer, *n.*, vaporisateur, *m.*

va'porous (vé-), *adj.*, vaporeux; (windy) venteux, flatueux; (vain) vain, chimérique.

va'por (vé-peur), *n.*, vapeur; fumée; (fig.) fumée, *f.* — s; *hystérie, f.sing.*; *vapeurs, f.pl.* — -bath; *bain de vapeur, m.*

va'porer (vé-peur'-), *n.*, vantard, *m.*

va'poring, *adj.*, glorieux; vantard.

va'porish *ou* **va'pory**, *adj.*, vaporeux.

var'ec (vâr'èke), *n.*, (bot.) varech, fucus, *m.*

va'riable (vé-ri-a-b'l), *adj.*, variable, changeant, variant; (inconstant) inconstant; (math.) variable; (of feasts) mobile; (of colour) changeant.

va'riableness, *n.*, variabilité; inconstance, *f.*

va'riably, *adv.*, d'une manière variable, variablement.

va'riance (vé-), *n.*, dissidence, discorde, *f.*; désaccord, *m.*; (jur.) modification, *f.* At —; *en désaccord*; *mal ensemble*; *en mésintelligence*; *brouillé avec, mal avec*; (of things) *en contradiction.* To set at —; *brouiller, mettre mal avec.*

varia'tion (vé-ri-é-), *n.*, variation, déviation, *f.*; changement, *m.*; (astron., math., mus.) variation; (gram.) inflexion; (of the needle) variation, déclinaison, *f.*

varicel'la, *n.*, (med.) varicelle, *f.*

var'icocele (vèr-i-cô-cîle), *n.*, (med.) varicocèle, *f.*, (*m.* according to some).

var'icose (-côce) *ou* **var'icous**, *adj.*, (med.) variqueux. — vein; *varice, f.*

va'ried, *adj.*, varié.

va'riegate, *v.a.*, varier, nuancer; panacher.

va'riegated (vé-ri-î-ghét'-), *adj.*, varié, nuancé; (bot.) varié, panaché; (of lamps) de couleurs diverses.

variega'tion (vèr-i-î-ghé-), *n.*, variété de nuances, diversité de couleurs; diaprure; bigarrure; panachure, *f.*

vari'ety (va-raï-é-), *n.*, variété; quantité; race, *f.*

vari'ola (va-raï-), *n.*, variole, petite vérole, *f.*

va'rious (vé-), *adj.*, divers, différent; (changeable) changeant, variable; (diversified) varié, différent. — readings; *variantes, f.pl.*

va'riously (vé-), *adv.*, différemment, diversement.

var'let (vâr-), *n.*, (hist.) **varlet**; page; (l.u.) coquin, drôle, *m.*

var'nish (vâr-), n., vernis, m.

var'nish (vâr-), v.a., vernir, **vernisser**; (fig.) farder, colorer.

var'nisher, n., vernisseur, m.

var'nishing, n., vernissure, f.; **vernissage**, m.

va'ry (vé-), v.a., varier; diversifier.

va'ry, v.n., varier; (to disagree) différer **sur**, être d'avis différent; (to deviate) dévier **de**, s'écarter **de**; (to change in succession) se suivre, se succéder. Not to — a minute; (of watches) ne pas varier d'une minute.

var'ying, adj., changeant, divers; qui varie.

vas'cular (vas-kiou-), adj., vasculaire.

vase (véce, vâze ou véze) n., vase, m. — shaped; vasiforme, évasé, en forme de vase.

vas'sal, n., vassal, m., vassale, f.; (ant.) esclave, m.f.

vas'salage (-'èdje), n., vasselage; esclavage, asservissement, m.; (fig.) sujétion, servitude, f.

vast (vâste), adj., vaste; immense.

vast (vâste), n., vaste espace, espace vide, m.; immensité, f.

vast'ly, adv., immensément; excessivement.

vast'ness, n., vaste étendue, grandeur, immensité; (importance) grande importance, f.

vat, n., cuve, f.; cuvier, m. —ful; cuvée, f.

Vat'ican, n., Vatican, m.

vaticina'tion (-i-né-), n., prophétie, prédiction, f.

vaudeville', n., vaudeville, m. Writer of —s; vaudevilliste, m.

vault (volte), n., voûte; caverne, f.; (cellar) cave, f., cellier; (for the dead) caveau, m., sépulture, f.; (leap) saut, m.; voltige, f.

vault (volte), v.a., voûter.

vault, v.n., sauter, voltiger.

vault'ed, adj., voûté, en voûte.

vault'er, n., (acrobat) voltigeur, sauteur, m.

vault'ing, n., (arch.) construction de voûtes, f.; (vaults) voûtes, f.pl.; (art of a vaulter) voltige, f.

vaunt (vô'n'te), n., vanterie, f.

vaunt (vô'n'te), v.n., se vanter; se glorifier.

vaunt, v.a., vanter, élever jusqu'aux nues.

vaunt'er, n., vantard, m.

vaunt'ful (-foule), adj., plein de jactance.

vaunt'ing, n., vanterie, jactance, f.

vaunt'ingly, adv., avec jactance.

veal (vîle), n., veau, m. —broth; bouillon de veau, m.

Ve'da (vî-dâ), n., véda, m.

vedette', n., vedette, f.

veer (vîre), v.n., tourner, changer de direction; (of ships) virer vent arrière; changer de bord; (of the wind) se ranger de l'arrière, adonner. To — round; (fig.) changer d'opinion. To — round to any one's opinion; devenir de l'avis de quelqu'un; se ranger à l'opinion de quelqu'in.

veer, v.a., virer; (a rope) filer.

veg'etable (vèdj'i-ta-b'l), **veg'etal**, adj., végétal.

veg'etable, n., végétal; (food) légume, m.

vegeta'rian, n., légumiste, m.f.

veg'etate (vè'dj'i-), v.n., végéter.

vegeta'tion (vè'dj'i-té-), n., végétation, f.

veg'etative, adj., végétatif; végétant.

ve'hemence (vî-), n., véhémence; force, violence; (fig.) ardeur, impétuosité, f.

ve'hement, adj., véhément; impétueux; violent.

ve'hemently, adv., avec véhémence; impétueusement; violemment; ardemment.

ve'hicle (-k'l), n., véhicule, m.; voiture, f.

veil (véle), n., voile, m.; (lady's) voilette, f.; (fig.) voile, rideau, m.; apparence, f., déguisement, m.

veil (véle), v.a., voiler; (fig.) voiler, masquer, cacher, déguiser, dissimuler.

veil'less (vél-lèce), adj., sans voile.

vein (vé'n), n., (anat., in marble, etc.) veine; (bot.) nervure; (geol., min.) veine, f., filon, m.; (humor) veine, humeur; (turn of mind) veine, disposition; (current) veine, source, f.

vein (vé'ne), v.a., veiner.

veined' (vé'n'de) ou **vein'y**, adj., veineux, veiné.

vein'ing, n., (paint.) veinage, m.

vein'less, adj., (bot.) sans nervures.

velle'ity (vèl-lî-i-), n., velléité, f.

vel'lum (vèl'-), n., vélin; (of note paper) papier vélin, m.

veloc'ipede (vi-loss'i-pîde), n., vélocipède, m.

veloc'ity (vi-), n., vélocité, vitesse, rapidité, f.

vel'vet (vèl'-), n., velours; (bot.) velouté, m.

vel'vet (vèl'-), adj., de velours; (fig.) doux. — -down; velouté, m. —flower; (bot.) amarante, f. — pile; moquette, f. — -powder; bourre tontisse; tonture, f.

vel'vet, v.n., peindre du velours; velouter.

vel'veted, adj., de velours; velouté, doux.

velveteen' (vèl-vèt'îne), n., velours de coton croisé, m.; (fig., colloq.) garde-chasse, m.

vel'veting, n., velouté, m.

vel'vety ou **vel'vet-like** (-laïke), adj., velouté.

ve'nal (vî-), adj., vénal.

venal'ity, n., vénalité; corruption, f.

ve'nally, adv., vénalement.

ve'nary (vè'n'-), adj., de vénerie; de chasse.

vend, v.a., vendre; débiter.

vendee' (vè'n'dî), n., (jur.) acquéreur, m.

vend'er, n., vendeur, m., vendeuse, f.; débitant; (jur.) vendeur, m., venderesse, f.

vend'ible (vè'n'dî-b'l), adj., vendable.

ven'dor, n. V. **vender**.

veneer' (vi-nîre), v.a., plaquer.

veneer' (vi-nîre), n., feuille à plaquer, f.

veneer'ing, n., placage, m.

veneer'ing-web, n., scie de placage, f.

ven'erable (vè'n'eur'a-b'l), adj., vénérable.

ven'erableness, n., caractère vénérable, m.

ven'erably, adv., vénérablement.

ven'erate (vè'n'eur'-), v.a., vénérer, révérer.

venera'tion (vè'n'eur'é-), n., vénération, f.

ven'erator (vè'n'eur'é-), n., vénérateur.

ven'ery (vè'n'i-), n., coït, m.; (hunt.) chasse, vénerie, f.

Vene'tian (vi-nî-shi-a'n), adj., vénitien, de Venise. — blind; jalousie, f. — shutter; persienne, f.

Vene'tian, n., Vénitien, m., Vénitienne, f.

venge'ance (vè'n'dja'n'ce), n., vengeance, f. Out of —; par vengeance. With a —; excessivement, terriblement, furieusement, vigoureusement, à outrance. I gave it him with a —; (scolding) je l'ai tancé d'importance; (beating) je l'ai rossé d'importance. This is what I call raining with a —; c'est ce que j'appelle pleuvoir.

venge'ful (vè'n'dj'foule), adj., vindicatif.

ve'nial (vî-), adj., véniel, pardonnable.

ve'nially, adv., véniellement.

venial'ity, n., vénialité, f.

veni're ou **veni're-fa'cias** (vi-nî-ri-fé-shi-ass), n., (jur.) ordre de convocation; ordre de comparaître, m.

ven'ison (-iz'n), n., venaison, f., chevreuil, m.

ven'om (vè'n'eume), n., venin; poison, m.

ven'omous (vè'n'eu'm'-), adj., (of animals) venimeux; (of plants) vénéneux; (fig.) empoisonné, dangereux; méchant, venimeux.

ven'omously, adv., d'une manière venimeuse; méchamment.

ven'omousness, n., venimosité; nature venimeuse; nature vénéneuse; (fig.) poison, venin, f.

ve'nous (vî-), adj., (anat.) veineux.

vent, v.a., (fig.) donner issue à, éventer; donner passage à; donner carrière à; donner cours à; donner un libre cours à; exhaler; décharger, faire éclater; satisfaire.

vent, *n.*, issue; ouverture, *f.*; passage, *m.*; (of a gun) lumière, *f.*; (of a cask) trou de fausset, *m.*; (publication) publication; (emission) issue; (utterance) articulation; carrière, *f.*, cours, libre cours, *m.* To give —to; *donner carrière* à, *donner un libre cours* à, *s'abandonner* à. —-hole; *soupirail*; *aspirateur de pompe*; (of a cask) *trou de fausset, m.* —peg; *fausset de tonneau, m.*

ven'tiduct (-deuk'te), *n.*, soupirail, *m.*; (arch.) ventouse, *f.*

ven'tilate, *v.a.*, aérer, ventiler; donner de l'air à; (agri.) vanner; (fig.) discuter; élucider, examiner; ventiler.

ventila'tion (vè'n-ti-lé-), *n.*, ventilation, aération, *f.*; aérage; (agri.) vannage, *m.*; (fig.) examen; discussion, élucidation, *f.*

ven'tilator (vè'n-ti-lé-teur), *n.*, ventilateur, *m.*, ventouse, *f.*

ventos'ity (vè'n-tôss'-), *n.*, (ant.) ventosité; flatuosité, *f.*

ven'tral, *adj.*, ventral.

ven'tricle (vè'n-tri-k'l), *n.*, ventricule, *m.*

ventril'oquism (-kwiz'm), *n.*, ventriloquie, *f.*

ventril'oquist (-kwiste), *n.*, ventriloque, *m.*

ven'ture (vè'n't'ioure), *n.*, aventure, *f.*; risque, hasard, *m.*; chance; (com.) pacotille, *f.* At a —; *à l'aventure; au hasard.*

ven'ture (vè'n'tioure), *v.a.*, aventurer, risquer, hasarder, gager. Nothing — nothing have; *qui ne risque rien n'a rien.*

ven'ture, *v.n.*, se hasarder à, s'aventurer; se risquer; (to presume) s'aviser **de**; ne pas hésiter à. I — to say that . . . ; *je n'hésite pas à dire que* . . . Nothing — nothing have; (prov.) *qui ne risque rien n'a rien.* To — on; *se risquer* **sur, dans**; *se hasarder* **sur, dans**; *s'aventurer* **sur, dans**; *entreprendre; s'engager* **dans**. To — to; *oser; se hasarder* à; *prendre sur soi* **de**. To — beyond; *s'aventurer, se hasarder* (*d'aller*) *au delà* **de**.

ven'turer, *n.*, personne aventureuse, *f.*

ven'turesome (vè'n'tiour-seume), **ven'turous**, *adj.*, aventureux; hasardeux, audacieux.

ven'turesomely, *adv.*, aventureusement, d'une manière aventureuse.

ven'turously, *adv.*, aventureusement, audacieusement; hardiment.

ven'turousness, *n.*, caractère aventureux, *m.*; hardiesse, audace, *f.*

ven'ue (vè'n'iou), *n.* To lay a —; (jur.) *nommer le tribunal qui doit juger une action.* To change the —; *changer la saisie (d'une cause).*

Ve'nus (vî-), *n.*, (myth., astron.) Vénus, *f.* —'s comb; (bot.) *peigne de Vénus, m., aiguille de berger, f.* —'s looking-glass; *miroir de Vénus, m.*

vera'cicus (vi-ré-sheusse), *adj.*, vrai, véridique.

vera'city (vî-), *n.*, véracité; véridicité; vérité, *f.*

veran'da (vi-), *n.*, **veran'dah**, véranda; marquise, *f.*

verb (veurbe), *n.*, verbe, *m.*

ver'bal (veur-), *adj.*, verbal, de vive voix; oral; (literal) mot à mot, littéral; (gram.) verbal.

ver'bally (veur-), *adv.*, verbalement; de vive voix, oralement; (literally) mot à mot, littéralement.

verba'tim (veur-bé-), *adv.*, textuellement, mot pour mot, à la lettre.

verbe'na (veur-bi-), *n.*, (bot.) verveine, *f.*

ver'biage (-bi-èdje), *n.*, verbiage, *m.*

verbose' (vèr-bôce), *adj.*, verbeux; (of style) diffus.

verbose'ly, *adv.*, verbeusement, diffusément.

verbos'ity (vèr-bôss'-), *n.*, verbosité; (of style) diffusion, *f.*

ver'dant (veur-), *adj.*, verdoyant, vert; fleurissant; **(inexperienced**, etc.) simple, crédule, innocent.

verd'-antique, *n.*, patine, *f.*; vert antique, vert d'Egypte, *m.*

ver'derer (veur-deur'-), *n.*, (of the royal forests) verdier, *m.*

ver'dict (veur-), *n.*, verdict; (fig.) jugement, arrêt, *m.*, opinion, *f.* To give, *ou* bring in, a —; *rendre*, ou *prononcer, un verdict.*

ver'digris (-griss), *n.*, vert-de-gris, *m.*

ver'dure (veurd'ieur), *n.*, verdure, *f.*

verge (veurdje), *n.*, verge, *f.*; (arch.) fût, *m.*; (horl.) verge, *f.*; (gard.) bord, *m.*, bordure, *f.*; (brink) bord, *m.*, extrémité; (of a forest) lisière, *f.* On the — of setting out; *à la veille de partir.* To be on the — of ruin; *être sur le penchant de sa ruine; être à deux doigts de sa perte.* On the — of committing a bad action; *parvenu au bord d'une mauvaise action* (V. Hugo).

verge (veurdje), *v.n.*, pencher **vers**; incliner **vers**. To — on, to be —ing on; *approche-* **de.**

ver'ger (veurdj'-), *n.*, sacristain, bedeau, porte-verge; huissier à verge, *m.*

ver'ifiable (-faï-a-b'l), *adj.*, vérifiable.

verifica'tion (vèr'i-fi-ké-), *n.*, vérification, *f.*

ver'ificative, *adj.*, vérificatif.

ver'ifier (vèr'i-faï-), *n.*, vérificateur, *f.*

ver'ify, *v.a.*, vérifier; prouver, constater, établir.

ver'ily (vèr'-), *adv.*, en vérité, vraiment.

verisim'ilar (vèr'i-ci'm'-), *adj.*, vraisemblable, probable.

verisimil'itude (vè'ri-ci-mil'i-tioude), *n.*, vraisemblance, probabilité, apparence de vérité, *f.*

ver'itable (vèr'i-ta-b'l), *adj.*, véritable.

ver'itably, *adv.*, véritablement.

ver'ity (vèr'-), *n.*, vérité; véracité, *f.* Of a —; *en vérité.*

ver'juice (veur-djiouce), *n.*, verjus, *m.*

vermicel'li (veur-mi-tshèl'i), *n.*, vermicelle, *m.* — soup; *potage*, ou *consommé, au vermicelle.*

vermic'ular (vèr'mik'iou-), *adj.*, vermiculaire; (arch.) vermiculé.

ver'micule (veur-mi-kioule), *n.*, vermisseau, *m.*

ver'mifuge (veur-mi-fioudje), *n.*, vermifuge, *m.*

vermill'ion (veur-), *n.*, vermillon, *m.*

vermill'ion, *v.a.*, vermillonner.

ver'min (veur-), *n.*, vermine, *f.* — killer; *mort aux rats, f.*, insecticide, *m.*

vernac'ular (veur-nak'iou-), *adj.*, natal, du pays; national; naturel; indigène; (disease) endémique, du pays. One's own —; *sa propre langue, sa langue maternelle.*

ver'nal (veur-), *adj.*, du printemps; printanier; (bot.) vernal; (fig.) de la jeunesse.

vero'nica (vi-), *n.*, (bot.) véronique, *f.*

ver'satile (veur-sa-tile), *adj.*, tournant; mobile; (bot.) versatile, oscillant; (changeable) changeant, versatile; (talent, etc.) souple, flexible.

versatil'ity (-n., mobilité; (variableness) versatilité; (talent, etc.) flexibilité, souplesse, *f.*

verse (veurse), *n..*, vers; (poet.) vers, *m.pl.*, poésie, *f.*; (Bible) verset; (of a song) couplet, *m.* To give chapter and —; *donner des preuves authentiques.*

versed (veurste), *adj.*, versé **dans**, exercé **dans**, expert **dans.**

ver'sicle, *n.*, petit verset; versicule (used in plural), *m.*

versifica'tion (-si-fi-ké-), *n.*, versification, *f.*

ver'sifier (-si-faï-), *n.*, versificateur, rimeur, *m.*

ver'sify (-si-faïe), *v.n.*, versifier, faire des vers.

ver'sify, *v.a.*, mettre en vers.

ver'sion (veur-sheu'ne), *n.*, version, *f.*

verst, *n.*, verste, *f.*

ver'sus (veur-), *prep.*, (jur.) contre.

ver'tebra (veur-ti-), *n.*, (*vertebræ*) (anat.) vertèbre, *f.*

ver'tebral (veur-ti-), *adj.*, (anat.) vertébral.

ver'tebrate (veur-tî-), *n.*, (zoöl.) vertébré, *m.*

ver'tebrate *ou* **ver'tebrated** (veur-tî-), *adj.*, (zoöl.) vertébré.

ver'tebrates (-brétse) *ou* **vertebra'ta**, *n.pl.*, (zoöl.) vertébrés, animaux vertébrés, *m.pl.*

ver'tex (veur-tèkse), *n.*, (*vertices*) sommet, haut, faîte ; (astron.) zénith, *m.*

ver'tical (veur-), *adj.*, vertical ; (of the sun) vertical, au zénith. — circle ; (astron.) *méridien*, *cercle azimutal* ou *vertical*, *m.*

ver'tically, *adv.*, verticalement.

ver'ticalness (-), *n.*, verticalité, *f.*

ver'ticil (veur-), *n.*, (bot.) verticille, *m.*

ver'tigo (veur- *ou* vèr-), *n.*, vertige, *m.*

ver'y (vèr'-), *adj.*, vrai ; véritable ; même ; seul, simple ; (b.s.) même. The — best ; *tout ce qu'il y a de mieux*, or (as adjective) *meilleur*. The — worst ; *tout ce qu'il y a de pire*. This — day ; *ce jour même, aujourd'hui même* ; (starting from) *dès aujourd'hui*. This — evening ; *pas plus tard que ce soir, ce soir même* ; (starting from) *dès ce soir*. The — thought makes me shudder; *la seule pensée m'en fait frémir*. The — thing; *la chose même*. I have the — thing for you ; *j'ai votre affaire* (V. Hugo). That's the — thing ; *c'est cela même !* The — man ; *l'homme même*. The — same ; *identiquement le même*. At the — same time ; *précisément au même instant*.

ver'y, *adv.*, fort, bien, très. — well ; *bien, très bien*. So —; *si*.

ves'icle (vès'i-k'l), *n.*, (anat.) vésicule, *f.*

vesic'ular (vi-cik'iou-), *adj.*, vésiculaire.

ves'per (vès-), *n.*, Vénus, étoile du soir, *f.* ; (evening) soir, *m.* *pl.*, vêpres, *f.pl.*

ves'sel (vès-), *n.*, vase, vaisseau ; réceptacle ; (nav.) vaisseau, bâtiment, navire, *m.*

ves'signon (vès'sig-neu'ne), *n.*, (vet.) vessigon, *m.*

vest, *n.*, gilet, *m.* ; veste, *f.*

vest, *v.a.*, vêtir, revêtir ; investir ; assigner, déterminer ; (money) placer.

vest, *v.n.*, être dévolu à, échoir à. The right is —ed in the Crown ; *le droit appartient à*, ou *réside dans, la couronne*. To be —ed in ; *être entre les mains de*.

ves'ta (match), *n.*, allumette-bougie, *f.*

ves'tal, *n.*, vestale, *f.*

ves'tal, *adj.*, de Vesta ; virginal, chaste.

vest'ed, *adj.*, fixe, déterminé ; (jur.) dévolu. — legacy ; *héritage dévolu*, *m.* — rights ; *droits substitués*, *m.pl.* — interests ; *intérêts inaliénables*, *m.pl.*

ves'tibule (vès-ti-bioule), *n.*, vestibule, *m.* ; antichambre, *f.*

ves'tige (vès-tidje), *n.*, vestige, *m.* ; trace, *f.*

vest'ment, *n.*, vêtement, *m.* *pl.* (of churches) vêtements sacerdotaux, *m.pl.*

ves'try, *n.*, (place) sacristie ; (assembly) conseil de fabrique, *m.*, assemblée paroissiale, *ou* de la commune, *f.*

ves'try-board (-bôrde), *n.*, fabrique, *f.* ; conseil de fabrique, *m.*

ves'try-clerk (-klârke), *n.*, secrétaire de la fabrique, *m.*

ves'try-man, *n.*, fabricien, *m.*

ves'try-meet'ing (-mît'-), *n.*, réunion du conseil de fabrique ; assemblée de la commune, de la paroisse, *f.*

ves'try-pew, *n.*, banc de l'œuvre, *m.*

ves'try-room, *n.*, sacristie, *f.*

ves'ture (vèst'ioure), *n.*, vêtement, *m.* ; robe ; parure, *f.*

vesu'vian (vi-ciou-), *adj.*, du Vésuve.

vetch, *n.*, (bot.) vesce, *f.*

vetch'y, *adj.*, qui abonde en vesce.

vet'eran (vèt'eur'-), *n.*, vétéran, *m.*

vet'eran (vèt'eur'-), *adj.*, aguerri, éprouvé, expérimenté ; vieux, ancien.

vet'erinary (vèt'eur'i-na-), *adj.*, vétérinaire. — surgeon ; *vétérinaire*, *m.*

ve'to (vî-), *n.*, veto, *m.*

ve'to, *v.a.*, mettre son veto à ; s'opposer à ; interdire, défendre.

vex (vèkse), *v.a.*, (to harass) affliger, tourmenter, vexer ; troubler ; (to irritate) irriter, vexer, fâcher, ennuyer, contrarier.

vexa'tion (vèks'é-), *n.*, affliction, *f.* ; tourment ; trouble, *m.* ; vexation ; (teasing, trouble) contrariété, *f.*, désagrément, chagrin, tourment, *m.*

vexa'tious (vèks'é-sheusse), *adj.*, vexatoire ; (irritating) irritant, fâcheux, ennuyeux, contrariant, vexant ; (harassing) fatigant.

vexa'tiously, *adv.*, d'une manière fâcheuse, d'une manière contrariante, d'une manière vexatoire.

vexa'tiousness, *n.*, caractère vexatoire, *m.* ; contrariété, *f.* ; ennui, *m.*

vexed (vèks'te), *adj.*, vexé, irrité, fâché ; (fig.) (of a question) épineux ; souvent débattu, sujet à controverse.

vex'ing, *adj.*, contrariant, vexant, ennuyeux.

vex'ingly, *adv.*, d'une manière contrariante.

vi'a (vaï-eu), *adv.*, par voie de, par, viâ.

vi'aduct (vaï-eu-deuk'te), *n.*, viaduc, *m.*

vi'al (vaï-al), *n.*, fiole, *f.* To pour out the —s of one's wrath upon one ; *tirer une vengeance éclatante de quelqu'un*.

vi'and (vaï-a'n'de), *n.*, viande, *f.* ; mets, *m.*

viat'icum (vaï-at'-), *n.*, provisions de route, *f.pl.* ; (c.rel.) viatique, *m.*

vi'brate (vaï-), *v.n.*, vibrer ; osciller ; vaciller.

vibra'tion (vaï-bré-), *n.*, oscillation ; (phys., mus.) vibration, *f.*

vi'brative *ou* **vi'bratory** (vaï-), *adj.*, vibrant ; de vibration ; oscillatoire, vibratoire.

vibur'num (vaï-beur-), *n.*, (bot.) viorne, *f.* (*m.* according to some writers).

vic'ar, *n.*, vicaire ; (of a parish) curé, *m.*

vic'arage (-èdje), *n.*, vicariat, *m.* ; vicairie ; (of a parish) cure, *f.*, presbytère, *m.*

vica'rial, *adj.*, vicarial ; du curé, de la cure.

vica'riate (vi-ké-), *n.*, vicariat, *m.*

vica'riate (vi-ké-), *adj.*, de vicaire.

vica'rious (vi-ké-), *adj.*, vicarial, de vicaire ; (fig.) de délégué ; de substitution.

vic'arship, *n.*, vicariat, *m.* ; cure, *f.*

vice (vaïce), *n.*, vice ; défaut ; (tool) étau, *m.* Free from — ; *exempt de vices ; sans défaut*.

vice (vaïce), *adv.*, en remplacement de. — admiral ; *vice-amiral*, *m.* —admiralty ; *vice-amirauté*, *f.* —agent ; *délégué*, *m.* —chamberlain ; *sous-chambellan*, *m.* —chancellor ; *vice-chancelier*, *m.* —consul ; *vice-consul*, *m.* —consulship ; *vice-consulat*, *m.* —legate ; *vice-légat*, *m.* —presidency ; *vice-présidence*, *f.* —president ; *vice-président*, *m.*

vicege'rency (-djî-), *n.*, vice-gérance, *f.*

vicege'rent, *n.*, vice-gérent ; (com.) vice-gérant, *m.*

vice'roy (vaïce-), *n.*, vice-roi, *m.*

vice'royalty, *n.*, vice-royauté, *f.*

vi'ce ver'sa (vaï-cî-veur-), *adv.*, vice versa.

vic'inage (-nèdje), *n.*, voisinage, *m.*

vicin'ity, *n.*, voisinage, *m.* ; proximité, *f.* ; alentours, environs, *m.pl.*

vi'cious (vish'euse), *adj.*, vicieux.

vi'ciously, *adv.*, vicieusement.

vi'ciousness, *n.*, nature vicieuse, *f.* ; vice, *m.*

vicis'situde (-tiode), *n.*, vicissitude, *f.* ; changement, *m.* ; revirement, *m.*

vic'tim, *n.*, victime, *f.* — to ; *victime de*. He fell a — to duty ; *il tomba victime du devoir*.

vic'timize (-'aïze), *v.a.*, victimer, duper.

vic'tor (-teur), *n.*, vainqueur, *m.*

vic'torine, *n.*, (dress) palatine, *f.*

victo'rious (-tô-), *adj.*, victorieux, de victoire.

victo'riously (-tô-), *adv.*, victorieusement, en vainqueur.

vic'tory, *n.*, victoire, *f.*

vict′ual (vit′t′l), *v.a.*, approvisionner ; avitailler ; ravitailler.

vict′ual, *v.n.*, faire ses vivres.

vict′ualer (vit′t′l′-), *n.*, pourvoyeur ; fournisseur de vivres ; (mil.) munitionnaire, vivrier (Bescherelle), *m.* Licensed —; *aubergiste ; marchand*, ou *débitant, de vin ; cabaretier, m.*

vict′ualing (vit′t′l′-), *n.*, avitaillement, ravitaillement, *m. ;* vivres, *m.pl.* — board ; *manutention, f.* —office ; *bureau des vivres, m.* — ship ; *vaisseau d'approvisionnement, m.*

vict′uals (vit′t′l′ze), *n.pl.*, vivres, aliments, *m.pl. ;* provisions, *f.pl. ;* manger, *m.sing. ;* (fam.) mangeaille, *f.*

vicugna ou **vicuña** (vi-kou′n′-), *n.*, (mam.) vigogne, *f.*

videl′icet (ab. of *videre licet*), *adv.*, savoir ; à savoir ; c'est-à-dire.

vie (vaïe), *v.n.*, rivaliser **de**, lutter de, (pers.) **avec** ; disputer **en** (things) ; le disputer à (pers.); faire assaut **de**. To — with; *se comparer* à; *entrer en rivalité* **avec**. While each to be the loudest —s ; *tandis qu'ils crient à qui mieux mieux*. To — with each other ; *rivaliser, rivaliser* **avec**; *à l'envi l'un de l'autre; c'est à qui* . . . They —d with each other as to who . . . ; *c'était à qui* . . . (V. Hugo).

view (viou), *v.a.*, regarder ; contempler ; considérer ; voir ; examiner ; inspecter ; explorer ; (to survey intellectually) envisager, considérer.

view (viou), *n.*, vue ; (persp.) vue, élévation ; (prospect) rue, perspective, scène, *f.*, coup d'œil, point de vue, *m. ;* (appearance) apparence, *f. ;* (examination by the eye) coup d'œil, regard ; (mental examination) aperçu, examen, *m. ;* (intention) intention, *f.*, but, dessein, *m. ;* (opinion) vue, opinion, pensée, appréciation, manière de voir, *f.* Bird's-eye —; (persp.) *plan à vol d'oiseau, m.* In —; *en vue*. With a — to ; *en vue* **de**, *dans l'intention, le but,* **de**. On — ; *exposé; qu'on peut voir, visiter ; ouvert au public.* Distance lends enchantment to the —; *la distance augmente le charme de la scène.* To take a correct — (of things) ; *envisager bien.* To take a different — ; (of a question, etc.) *apprécier différemment, envisager d'une autre manière.* Field of — ; (of a telescope) *champ, m.* Dissolving —s ; *fantasmagorie, f.* In — of ; *en considération* **de.** Point of — ; *point de vue, m.*

view′er (viou-eur), *n.*, spectateur, *m.*, spectatrice, *f.*

view′ing, *n.*, examen, *m. ;* inspection ; manière d'envisager, *f.*

view′less, *adj.*, invisible.

vig′il (-d′jil), *n.*, veille ; veillée ; (ecc.) vigile, *f.*

vig′ilance (vid′jil′-), *n.*, vigilance, *f.*

vig′ilant (vid′jil′-), *adj.*, vigilant ; éveillé ; circonspect ; soigneux.

vig′ilantly (vid′jil′-), *adv.*, avec vigilance.

vign′ette (vi′n′iète), *n.*, vignette, *f.*

vig′orous, *adj.*, vigoureux, fort.

vig′orously, *adv.*, vigoureusement, fortement.

vig′orousness, vig′or, *n.*, force, vigueur, *f.*

vile (vaïl), *adj.*, vil, abject, bas ; (of no value) sans prix, sans valeur.

vile′ly (vaïl′-), *adv.*, vilement, bassement, lâchement, honteusement.

vile′ness (vaïl′-), *n.*, avilissement, *m. ;* bassesse, abjection, *f.*

vilifica′tion (vil′i-fi-ké-), *n.*, rabaissement ; dénigrement, *m. ;* diffamation, *f.*

vil′ifier (vil′i-faï-), *n.*, diffamateur, *m.*

vil′ify (vil′i-faïe), *v.a.*, avilir, abaisser ; vilipender ; dénigrer.

vil′la, *n.*, villa ; maison de plaisance, *f.*

vil′ladom, *n.*, la bourgeoisie, *f.*, les classes moyennes, *f.pl.*

vil′lage (-lèdje), *n.*, village, *m.*

vil′lager, *n.*, villageois, *m.*, villageoise, *f.*

vil′lain (vil-lène), *n.*, scélérat, misérable, gredin ; (in feudal law) vilain, roturier, *m.*

vil′lainage, vil′lenage (vil-lè-nèdje), *m.*, servage, vilainage, *m. ;* servitude, *f.*

vil′lainous (vil-lè-), *adj.*, vil, infâme ; de scélérat ; (sorry) méchant, vilain, mauvais.

vil′lainously, *adv.*, vilement, bassement ; avec infamie ; horriblement, d'une manière infâme.

vil′lainy, *n.*, infamie, scélératesse, vilenie, *f.*

villos′ity (vil-loss′-), *n.*, (nat. hist.) villosité, *f.*

vil′lous ou **vil′lose**, *adj.*, villeux.

vin′cible (-ci-b′l), *adj.*, que l'on peut vaincre.

vinde′mial (-dī-), *adj.*, de la vendange.

vin′dicable (-ca-b′l), *adj.*, défendable ; justifiable, soutenable.

vin′dicate, *v.a.*, soutenir, défendre, justifier ; (to maintain) maintenir, soutenir, défendre.

vindica′tion (-di-ké-), *n.*, défense, justification, *f. ;* (of an opinion) maintien, *m.*

vin′dicator (-ké-teur), *n.*, défenseur ; soutien, *m.*

vin′dicatory, *adj.*, vengeur ; (justificatory) justificatif.

vindic′tive, *adj.*, vindicatif.

vindic′tively, *adv.*, d'une manière vindicative.

vindic′tiveness, *n.*, esprit de vengeance, *m.*

vine (vaïne), *n.*, vigne, *f. ;* (of plants) sarment, *m.* —branch ; *branche de vigne, f. ; sarment ; pampre, m.* — -clad ; *couvert,* ou *tapissé, de vignes.* —dresser ; *vigneron, m.* — -grub ; *charançon de la vigne, m.* — -estate ; *vignoble, m.* —leaf ; *feuille de vigne, f.* — grower ; *propriétaire de vignes, viticulteur, m.* —growing ; *viticulture, f.* —prop ; *échalas, m.* — -shoot ; *sarment, m.* —stock ; *cep, pied de vigne, m.*

vin′egar (vi′n′i-), *n.*, vinaigre, *m. ;* (fig.) aigreur, *f.* —cruet ; *vinaigrier, m. ; burette* à *vinaigre, f.* —maker ; *vinaigrier, m.* —tree ; (bot.) *sumac des corroyeurs, vinaigrier, m.*

vin′ery (vaï′n′ri), *n.*, serre à vignes, *f.*

vine′yard (vi′n′-), *n.*, vigne, *f. ;* vignoble, *m.*

vinicul′tural, *adj.*, vinicole.

vin′iculture, *n.*, viniculture, *f.*

vi′nose (-nôce) ou **vi′nous** (-neusse), *adj.*, vineux.

vinos′ity, *n.*, caractère vineux, *m. ;* vinosité, *f.*

vint′age (vi′n′tèdje), *n.*, crû, *m. ;* vendange ; (wine produced by one crop of grapes) vinée, récolte de vin, *f. ;* (time of gathering) vendanges, *f.pl.*

vint′ager (-tèdj′-), *n.*, vendangeur, *m.*

vint′ner, *n.*, cabaretier, marchand de vin, *m.*

vint′ry, *n.*, marché au vin ; entrepôt de vin, *m.*

vin′y (vaï-), *adj.*, de vigne ; de vignoble.

vi′ol (vaï-ol), *n.*, (mus.) viole, *f.*

vi′olable (vaï-o-la-b′l), *adj.*, qui peut être violé, violable.

vi′olate (vaï-), *v.a.*, violer ; (to ravish) violer ; faire violence à ; (to disturb) déranger, troubler ; (to profane) outrager, profaner.

viola′tion (vaï-o-lé-), *n.*, (of rules and regulations) violation, infraction, *f. ;* (rape) viol, *m.*

vi′olator (vaï-o-l′ét′eur), *n.*, violateur, *m.*, violatrice, *f. ;* infracteur, empiéteur, *m.*

vi′olence (vaï-o-), *n.*, violence, *f.* With — ; (of robbery) à *main armée.* To do — to ; *violenter ; faire violence à.* To do — to one's feelings ; *se faire violence, se forcer.* To use — ; *user de violence* **envers**, *employer la force.*

vi′olent (vaï-o-), *adj.*, violent ; (extorted) arraché par la violence ; (death) violent ; (extreme) extrême ; (pain) violent, grand, atroce. To lay — hands on one's self ; *attenter à ses jours.* To die a — death ; *mourir de mort violente.*

vi′olently (vaï-o-), *adv.*, avec violence.

vi′olet (vaï-o-), *n.*, (bot.) violette, *f.*

vi′olet (vaï-o-), *adj.*, (color) violet. —tribe ; *violacées, f.pl.* — powder ; *poudre de riz à la violette, f.*

violin' (vaï-o-), *n.*, violon, *m.*

violin'ist (vaï-o-), *n.*, violoniste, *m.f.*; violon, *m.*

vi'olist (vaï-o-), *n.*, (mus.) violiste, *m.*

violoncel'list (vi-o-lo'n'sèl'-), *n.*, violoncelliste, *m.*

violoncel'lo (-sèl-lô), *n.*, violoncelle, *m.*; basse, *f.* One-stringed —; *trompette marine, f.*

vi'per (vaï-), *n.*, vipère, *f.*

vi'perine (vaï-peur'aïne), *adj.*, vipérin; de vipère; venimeux.

vi'perous (vaï-), *adj.*, de vipère; venimeux; (malignant) malfaisant.

vi'per's-bugloss, *n.*, vipérine, *f.*

vi'per's-grass (vaï-peur'z'grâce), *n.*, (bot.) scorsonère, *f.*

vira'go (vi-ré-gô), *n.*, guerrière; virago, *f.*; dragon de femme, *m.*

vir'elay, *n.*, virelai, *m.*

virgil'ian (veur-djil'-), *adj.*, virgilien.

vir'gin (veur-dji'ne), *n.*, vierge, *f.*

vir'gin, *adj.*, vierge; virginal, de vierge.

vir'ginal, *adj.*, virginal, de vierge.

virgin'ity, *n.*, virginité, *f.*

vir'gin's-bower (veur-dji'n'z'baou'eur), *n.*, (bot.) clématite commune *ou* des haies, *f.*

vir'go, *n.*, (astron.) la Vierge, *f.*

virid'ity, *n.*, verdeur, fraîcheur, *f.*

vir'ile, *adj.*, viril, mâle.

viril'ity, *n.*, virilité; nature virile, *f.*

vir'tu (veur-tiou), *n.*, goût des arts, *m.* Articles of —; *objets d'art, m.pl.*

vir'tual (veur-tiou-), *adj.*, virtuel. — force; *force potentielle, virtuelle, f.*

virtual'ity (veur-tiou-), *n.*, virtualité, *f.*

vir'tually (veur-tiou-), *adv.*, virtuellement, de fait; censément.

vir'tue (veur-tiou), *n.*, vertu; (quality of physical bodies) vertu, propriété, qualité; (excellence) excellence, valeur, *f.*, mérite, *m.* By, *ou* in, — of; *en vertu de; au moyen de.*

vir'tueless, *adj.*, sans vertu; dénué de mérite; sans valeur.

virtuo'so (veur-tiou-ô-çô), *n.*, (*virtuosi*) virtuose, *m.f.*

vir'tuous (veurt'iou-eusse), *adj.*, vertueux.

vir'tuously, *adv.*, vertueusement.

vir'tuousness, *n.*, vertu, *f.*

vir'ulence (vir'iou-), *n.*, virulence; violence; (fig.) aigreur, *f.*

vir'ulent, *adj.*, virulent; violent.

vir'ulently, *adv.*, avec virulence.

vir'us (vaï-), *n.*, (med.) virus, *m.*

vis, *n.*, (Latin) force, *f.* — inertiæ; *force d'inertie.* — major; *force majeure.*

vis'a, *n.*, visa, *m.* *v.a.*, viser.

vis'age (viz'èdje), *n.*, visage, *m.*; figure, *f.*

vis'aged, *adj.*, à, *ou* au, visage (de).

vis-a-vis' (viz'â-vi), *n.*, vis-à-vis, *m.*

vis'cera, *n.pl.*, viscères, *m.pl.*

vis'ceral (vis-ci-), *adj.*, (anat.) viscéral.

vis'cid, *adj.*, visqueux.

viscid'ity, *n.*, viscosité, *f.*

viscos'ity (-côss'-), *n.*, viscosité, *f.*

vis'count (vaï-caou'n'te), *n.*, vicomte, *m.*

viscount'ess (-caou'n't'-), *n.*, vicomtesse, *f.*

vis'countship *ou* **vis'county** (vaï-), *n.*, vicomté, *f.*

vis'cous (vis'keusse), *adj.*, visqueux, gluant, glutineux.

vis'cus, *n.*, (*viscera*) viscère, *m.*

Vish'nu (-nou), *n.*, Vishnou, *m.*

vis'ible (viz'i-b'l), *adj.*, visible; (apparent) visible, évident, clair, manifeste; (horizon) sensible.

vis'ibleness (viz'-), *n.*, visibilité, *f.*

vis'ibly (viz'-), *adv.*, visiblement; (rapidly) à vue d'œil.

Vis'igoth (viz'i-goth), *n.*, Visigoth, *m.*

vis'ion (vij'eune), *n.*, vision; vue; (in Scripture) vision, *f.*

vis'ional (-eu'n'-), *adj.*, de vision, de la vue.

vis'ionary (vij'eu'n'-), *adj.*, visionnaire; chimérique.

vis'ionary (vij'eu'n'-), *n.*, visionnaire, *m.f.*

vis'it (viz'-), *n.*, visite; (of one going to inspect) visite, inspection, tournée, *f.*; (a stay) séjour, *m.* To pay a —; *faire une visite, aller voir (par).* On a —; *en visite.*

vis'it (viz'-), *v.a.*, visiter; rendre (*ou* faire) visite à; (of doctors) voir; (in Scripture) visiter, éprouver. To — on, *ou* upon; (to vent) décharger **sur**, *se venger* **de** . . . **sur**, punir, châtier; reprocher **à**. She could only be —ed . . .; *on ne pouvait la voir que . . .; on ne pouvait lui faire visite que . . .*

vis'it, *v.n.*, faire des visites.

vis'itant (viz'-), *n.*, (rel.) visitant; visiteur, *m.*

visita'tion (viz'i-té-), *n.*, visite; (jur.) inspection; (in Scripture) épreuve, affliction, *f.* By the — of God; (of death) subitement.

vis'iting (viz'-), *n.*, visite, *f.*; visites, *f.pl.*

vis'iting, *adj.*, en visite, de visite. — card; *carte de visite, f.* — master; *professeur externe, m.*

vis'itor (viz'it'eur), *n.*, visiteur, *m.*, (official) inspecteur, *m.* *pl.*, monde, *m.sing.* She has —s; *elle a du monde.*

vis'or (viz'eur), *n.*, masque, *m.*; (of a helmet) visière, *f.*

vis'ored (viz'eurde), *adj.*, masqué.

vis'ta, *n.*, échappée de vue; (of woods) percée, éclaircie; (fig.) perspective, *f.*

vis'ual (vij'iou-), *adj.*, visuel.

vi'tal (vaï-), *adj.*, vital; de vie; (air) respirable; (essential) vital, capital, essentiel. — organ; *partie vitale, f.*

vital'ity (vaï-), *n.*, vitalité; vie, *f.*

vi'talize (vaï-tal'aïze), *v.a.*, vivifier; donner la vie à; animer.

vi'tally (vaï-), *adv.*, vitalement.

vi'tals (vaï-talze), *n.pl.*, parties vitales, *ou* nobles, *f.pl.*; (fig.) sein, *m.*; entrailles, *f.pl.*

vit'iate (vish'i-), *v.a.*, gâter, corrompre; (jur.) vicier.

vitia'tion (vish'i-é-), *n.*, viciation, altération; corruption; (jur.) invalidation, *f.*

vit'reous (vit'ri-), *adj.*, de verre; (min., chem.) vitreux; (anat., phys.) vitré.

vitrifac'tion (vit'ri-fak'-), *n.*, vitrification, *f.*

vit'rifiable (vit'ri-faï-a-b'l), *adj.*, vitrifiable, vitrescible.

vit'rify (vit'ri-faï), *v.a.*, vitrifier.

vit'rify, *v.n.*, se vitrifier.

vit'riol (vit'-), *n.*, vitriol, *m.* Oil of —; *huile de vitriol, f., acide sulfurique, m.*

vitriol'ic, *adj.*, sulfurique, vitriolique.

vit'riolize (-'aïze), *v.a.*, convertir en sulfate.

vit'uline (vit'iou-laïne), *adj.*, de veau.

vitu'perable, *adj.*, blâmable, répréhensible.

vitu'perate, *v.a.*, blâmer; censurer; condamner, vilipender; faire des reproches à.

vitupera'tion, *n.*, blâme, reproche, *m.*, injures, *f.pl.*

vitu'perative, *adj.*, de blâme, de reproche.

viva'cious (vi-vé-sheusse), *adj.*, vif; vivace; animé.

viva'ciously, *adv.*, vivement, avec vivacité.

viva'ciousness *ou* **viva'city**, *n.*, vivacité, *f.*

vi'vary (vaï-), *n.*, vivier, *m.*; (warren) garenne, *f.*

vi'va vo'ce, *adv.*, de vive voix. — examination; *examen oral, m.*

viv'id, *adj.*, vif, animé, ardent; (striking) frappant; (color) vif, éclatant.

viv'idly, *adv.*, vivement; avec force; d'une manière frappante; avec ardeur; (with brightness) avec éclat.

viv'idness, *n.*, vivacité, *f.*; feu, *m.*; ardeur; (of colors) ardeur, *f.*, éclat, *m.*

vivifica'tion (vi-vi-fi-ké-), *n.*, vivification, *f.*

viv'ify (vi-vif'aïe), *v.a.*, vivifier, animer.

viv'ifying (vi-vi-faï-igne), *adj.*, vivifiant.

vivip'arous (vi-vip'-), *adj.*, vivipare.

viv'isect, *v.n.*, opérer par vivisection.

vivisec'tion, *n.*, vivisection, *f.*

viv'isector, *n.*, vivisecteur.

vix'en (vik's'n), *n.*, (female fox) renarde ; (quarrelsome woman) mégère, *f.*

vix'enish, *adj.*, de mégère, acariâtre.

viz., (ab. of *videlicet, viderelicet*), *adv.*, savoir ; c'est-à-dire.

vizier' (viz'îre), *n.*, vizir, *m.*

vizier'ate, *n.*, vizirat, viziriat, *m.*

voc'able (vô-ca-b'l), *n.*, mot, vocable, *m.*

vocab'ulary (vo-cab'iou-), *n.*, vocabulaire, *m.*

vocab'ulist, *n.*, auteur d'un vocabulaire, *m.*

vo'cal (vô-) *ou* **vocal'ic**, *adj.*, vocal ; de la voix ; (having a voice) doué de la parole.

vo'calist (vô-), *n.*, chanteur, *m.*, vocaliste, *m.f.*

vocaliza'tion (vô-cal'aïzé-), *n.*, (mus.) vocalisation, *f.*

vo'calize, *v.n.*, vocaliser.

vo'cally (vô-), *adv.*, par la voix ; verbalement.

voca'tion (vo-ké-), *n.*, vocation ; profession, *f.* ; état, emploi, métier ; (summons) appel, *m.*

voc'ative, *n.*, vocatif, *m.* In the —; *au vocatif.*

vocif'erate (-'eur'-), *v.a.* and *n.*, vociférer.

vocifera'tion (-'eur'é-), *n.*, vocifération, *f.*

vocif'erous, *adj.*, qui vocifère ; bruyant.

vocif'erously, *adv.*, en vociférant, bruyamment.

vogue (vôghe), *n.*, vogue, mode, *f.* In —; *en vogue* ; *à la mode.* To bring into — ; *mettre en vogue*, ou *à la mode.* To be in —; *avoir la vogue.*

voice (voïce), *n.*, voix, *f.*, (language) langage, *m.*, paroles, *f.pl.* ; (sound) son, *m.* ; (vote) voix, *f.*, suffrage, vote, *m.* ; (gram.) voix, *f.* At the top of one's —; *à tue-tête.* Without a dissentient —; *à l'unanimité des voix.* With one —; *d'une commune voix, unanimement.* My — failed me ; *la voix me manqua.* To know by the — ; *reconnaître à la voix.* His — is cracking ; *sa voix mue.* To know how to manage one's —; *savoir moduler sa voix.*

voice (voïce), *v.a.*, former la voix de ; régler le ton **de**; (to vote) voter; (to report) rapporter. To —; (public opinion) *refléter, exprimer, interpréter.*

voice'less, *adj.*, sans voix ; sans vote.

void (voïde), *v.a.*, vider ; évacuer, quitter ; (to send out) jeter, verser ; rejeter ; (to annul) annuler, rendre nul ; (to leave vacant) laisser vacant.

void, *adj.*, vide ; vacant ; (null) nul, de nul effet ; (free) libre ; (of legacies) caduc ; (vain) vain, idéal. Null and —; (com.) *nul et non avenu.* To render —; *rendre nul, annuler.* — of ; *dépourvu* **de** ; *dénué* **de**.

void (voïde), *n.*, vide ; espace vide, *m.*

void'able (voïd'a-b'l), *adj.*, qui peut être annulé, rejeté ; annulable.

void'ance (voïd'-), *n.*, évacuation ; (ejection) expulsion d'un bénéfice ; vacance ; défaite, *f.*

vol'atile (-taïle), *adj.*, qui vole, volant ; (fickle) inconstant, volage, léger ; (thoughtless) étourdi ; (chem.) volatil.

volatil'ity (-til'-), *n.*, légèreté.

volatiliza'tion (-til'aïzé-), *n.*, volatilisation, *f.*

vol'atilize (-til'aïze), *v.a.*, volatiliser.

vol'atilize, *v.n.*, se volatiliser.

volcan'ic, *adj.*, volcanique ; volcanisé.

volca'no (-ké-nô), *n.*, volcan, *m.*

vole (vôle), *n.*, (cards) vole, *f.* ; (mam.) campagnol, *m.*

voli'tion (-lish'eune), *n.*, volition ; volonté, *f.*

vol'ley, *n.*, (of musketry) décharge, salve ; (of cannon) volée; (for salute) salve ; (of abuse)

volée, bordée, *f.*, torrent, *m.* ; (of blows) volée ; (of stones, etc.) grêle, *f.* To fire a —; *faire une décharge de mousqueterie* ; *tirer une volée* ; (salute) *tirer une salve.* — firing ; *feu de peloton,* ou *de bataillon, m.*

vol'ley, *v.a.*, (at lawn tennis) renvoyer sans bond.

vol'leyed (vol-lide), *adj.*, (at tennis) renvoyé sans bond.

Vol'scian, *adj.*, volsque.

volt, *n.*, (fenc. ; man.) volte, *f.* ; (elect.) volt, *m.*

vol'ta (-tâ), *n.*, (mus.) volta, *f.*

volta'ic (-taïke), *adj.*, voltaïque, de Volta.

volubil'ity (vol'iou-), *n.*, volubilité ; rotation, révolution ; (of the tongue) volubilité de langue, volubilité, garrulité, *f.*

vol'uble (vol'iou-b'l), *adj.*, qui tourne ; en rotation ; (pers.) qui parle avec volubilité ; (of the tongue) délié, bien pendu ; (of speech) facile, coulant, abondant.

vol'ubly, *adv.*, avec volubilité.

vol'ume (vol'ieume), *n.*, (geom.) volume, *m.* ; masse, *f.* ; (book) volume, tome ; (of smoke) tourbillon ; (of the voice) volume, *m.*, étendue, portée, *f.* That speaks —s ; *cela dit beaucoup.* That speaks —s for him ; *cela dit beaucoup en sa faveur.*

vol'umed (vol'ieu'm'de), *adj.*, formé en volume. A three- — novel ; *un roman en trois volumes.*

volu'minous (vo-liou-), *adj.*, volumineux ; (writer) fécond, diffus.

volu'minously (vo-liou-), *adv.*, d'une manière volumineuse, en masse.

volu'minousness (vo-liou-), *n.*, étendue, dimension ; grosseur, *f.*

vol'untarily (vol'eu'n'-), *adv.*, volontairement ; spontanément ; de bonne volonté.

vol'untariness (vol'eu'n'-), *n.*, spontanéité, *f.*

vol'untary (vol'eu'n'-), *adj.*, volontaire ; spontané ; (free) libre, indépendant ; (done by design) volontaire, intentionnel, fait avec intention. — oath; *serment extrajudiciaire, m.*

vol'untary, *n.*, (mus.) improvisation, *f.*, prélude, solo d'orgue, *m.*

volunteer' (vol'eu'n'tîre), *n.*, volontaire, *m.*

volunteer', *v.a.*, offrir volontairement.

volunteer', *v.n.*, s'engager comme volontaire ; s'offrir ; offrir ses services.

volup'tuary (vo-leupt'iou-), *n.*, voluptueux, épicurien, *m.*

volup'tuous (vo-leupt'iou-eusse), *adj.*, voluptueux.

volup'tuously, *adv.*, voluptueusement.

volup'tuousness, *n.*, volupté, voluptuosité, *f.*

volute' (vo-lioute), *n.*, (arch.) zoöl.) volute, *f.*

volut'ed, *adj.*, voluté.

volu'tion (vo-liou-), *n.*, spirale, *f.*

vom'ic, *adj.*, vomique. — nut ; (bot.) *noix vomique, f.*

vom'ica, *n.*, (med.) vomique, *f.*

vom'it, *n.*, vomissement, *m.*, matières vomies, *f.pl.* ; (pharm.) vomitif, *m.*

vom'it, *v.a.*, vomir, rendre ; (fig.) vomir, émettre.

vom'it, *v.n.*, vomir.

vom'iting, *n.*, vomissement ; rejet, *m.*

vom'itory, *adj.*, vomitif, émétique.

vom'itory, *n.*, vomitif, émétique, *m.*

vora'cious (vo-ré-sheusse), *adj.*, vorace ; dévorant ; (of the appetite) dévorant, d'enfer ; (fig.) avide, dévorant.

vora'ciously, *adv.*, avec voracité.

vora'ciousness *ou* **vora'city**, *n.*, voracité, *f.*

vor'tex, *n.*, (vortices) tourbillon, *m.*

vor'tical, *adj.*, tournoyant ; tourbillonnant ; en rond, en tourbillon.

vo'tary, *n.*, **vo'taress**, *f.*, sectateur, *m.*, sectatrice, *f.* ; adorateur ; zélateur ; amateur ; partisan, ami, admirateur, *m.*

vo'tary (vô-), *adj.*, votif.

vote (vôte), *n.*, vote, *m.*; voix; opinion, *f.*; suffrage, *m.*; décision, résolution, *f.*; (ticket) bulletin, *m.*; (ballot) boule, *f.* To put to the —; *mettre aux voix.* To go to the —, *ou* put (it) to the —; *aller aux voix.* To pass a — of thanks to; *voter des remercîments à.*

vote (vôte), *v.a.*, voter; élire; déclarer.

vote, *v.n.*, voter.

vot'er (vôt'-), *n.*, votant, *m.*

vot'ing, *n.*, scrutin, vote, *m.* — paper; *bulletin de vote, m.*

vo'tive (vô-), *adj.*, voué, votif.

vouch (vaoutshe), *v.a.*, prendre à témoin, attester; (to affirm) garantir, affirmer; attester; (to confirm) attester, prouver; (jur.) appeler en garantie

vouch, *v.n.*, témoigner **de**, répondre **de**, garantir. To — for the success of any one; *se porter garant du succès de quelqu'un.*

vouchee' (vaoutsh'î), *n.*, caution; personne appelée en garantie, *f.*

vouch'er (vaoutsh'-), *n.*, garant, *m.*; (document) garantie, preuve, *f.*, titre, *m.*; pièce justificative, *f.*; (ticket) billet, *m.*; entrée, passe, *f.*; laisser-passer, *m.*; (jur.) demande en garantie, *f.*

vouch'or (vaoutsh'-), *n.*, (jur.) demandeur en garantie, *m.*, demanderesse en garantie, *f.*

vouchsafe' (vaoutsh'séfe), *v.a.*, permettre; daigner, accorder.

vouchsafe', *v.n.*, daigner; condescendre.

vouchsafe'ment, *n.*, condescendance, *f.*, don, *m.*; faveur, *f.*

vow (vaou), *n.*, vœu, *m.*

vow (vaou), *v.a.*, vouer **à**, dévouer **à**, consacrer **à**.

vow, *v.n.*, faire un vœu, faire vœu **de**, faire des vœux; jurer, protester **contre**.

vow'el (vaou'èl), *n.*, voyelle, *f.*

vow'eled (vaou'èlde), *adj.*, formé de voyelles.

voy'age (voi-yèdje), *n.*, voyage par mer, *m.*; traversée, *f.* Pleasant — to you! *bon voyage!* Outward —; *voyage d'aller.* Home —; *voyage de retour.* On a —; *en voyage, en mer.*

voy'age (voi-yèdje), *v.n.* V. **travel.**

voy'ager, *n.*, voyageur, *m.*, voyageuse, *f.*

vul'canite, *n.*, caoutchouc vulcanisé, *m.*

vul'gar (veul-), *n.*, bas peuple; vulgaire, *m.*

vul'gar (veul-), *adj.*, vulgaire, commun, ordinaire, du peuple; grossier, trivial; de mauvais goût.

vul'garism (veul-gar'iz'm), *n.*, vulgarité, *f.*, vulgarisme, *m.*; expression vulgaire, *f.*

vulgar'ity (veul-), *n.*, vulgarité; grossièreté, *f.*; mauvais ton, mauvais goût, *m.*; (mean condition) bassesse, nature vulgaire, condition vulgaire, *f.*

vul'garize (-'aïze), *v.a.*, populariser, vulgariser.

vul'garly, *adv.*, vulgairement; communément; avec mauvais goût, avec mauvais ton; grossièrement; (meanly) bassement.

Vul'gate (veul-), *n.*, Vulgate, *f.*

vulnerabil'ity, *n.*, vulnérabilité, *f.*

vul'nerable (veul'neur'a-b'l), *adj.*, vulnérable, que l'on peut blesser.

vul'nerably, *adv.*, vulnérablement.

vul'nerary (veul-neur'-), *adj.*, vulnéraire.

vul'pine (veul-païne), *adj.*, de renard; rusé.

vul'ture (veult'ieur), *n.*, (orni.) vautour, *m.*

vul'turine (-aïne), *adj.*, de vautour; rapace.

W

w, vingt-troisième lettre de l'alphabet, w, *m.*

wab'ble (wôb'b'l), *v.n.*, vaciller, branler; aller en zigzag, zigzaguer; (of a horse) se bercer.

wab'bling, *n.*, balancement, *m.*; (of horses) bercement, *m.* adj., branlant; irrégulier.

wab'blingly, *adv.*, en branlant.

wad (wode), *n.*, bourre (for fire-arms); (little bundle) touffe, *f.*, paquet, *m.*

wad (wode), *v.a.*, (fire-arms) bourrer; (a garment) garnir **de** ouate, ouater.

wad'ded (wod'dède), *adj.*, ouaté (with, **de**).

wad'ding (wod'-), *n.*, ouate; (of fire-arms) bourre, *f.*

wad'dle (wod'd'l), *v.n.*, se dandiner, se balancer; se tortiller; (fig.) patauger, *m.*

wad'dling (wod'd'l-), *n.*, dandinement, *m.*

wad'dlingly, *adv.*, en se dandinant.

wade (wéde), *v.a.*, (to ford) traverser à gué, passer à gué.

wade, *v.n.*, marcher dans l'eau, dans la vase, dans le sable, etc.; passer à gué; (to move with difficulty) se traîner, avancer péniblement. To — in the mud; *patauger dans la boue.* To — through; *traverser, passer; marcher* **dans;** (fig.) *examiner laborieusement, en détail; étudier à fond;* (to master) *venir à bout* **de.**

wad'er (wéd'-) *ou* **wad'ing-bird** (-beurde), *n.*, (orni.) échassier, *m.*

wad'-hook (-houke), *n.*, (artil.) tire-bourre, *m.*

wa'fer (wé-), *n.*, pain à cacheter, *m.*; (c. rel.) hostie; (cake) oublie, *f.*, plaisir, *m.*

wa'fer (wé-), *v.a.*, mettre un pain à cacheter **à,** cacheter.

waf'fle (wof'f'l), *n.*, gaufre, *f.* — -iron; *gaufrier, m.*

waft (wâfte), *v.a.*, porter, transporter. To — on high; *faire flotter vers les cieux; porter au ciel;* (to buoy up) *soutenir.*

waft, *v.n.*, flotter dans l'air, sur l'eau.

wag (wâg), *n.*, badin, plaisant, farceur, *m.*; (fam.) loustic, *m.*

wag, *v.a.*, branler, remuer; mouvoir; agiter; (tail of a dog) remuer, agiter.

wag, *v.n.*, remuer, se mouvoir, bouger, branler; (to pack off) (fam.) décamper, déguerpir, partir.

wage (wédje), *v.a.*, (war) faire, soutenir. To — war with; *faire la guerre* **à.**

wa'ger (wédj'-), *n.*, gageure, *f.*; pari; (deposited) gage, sujet, *m.* To lay a —; *faire un pari, faire une gageure; gager, parier.*

wa'ger (wédj'-), *v.a.*, gager, parier.

wa'gerer (wédj'-), *n.*, parieur, gageur, *m.*

wa'ges (wé'djize), *n.pl.*, (of servants) gages, *m.pl.*; (of workmen) salaire, *m.*, paye, *f.*; (fig.) salaire, prix, *m.*; récompense, *f.* Week's —; *semaine, f.*

wag'gery (wag'gheur'i), *n.*, espièglerie; plaisanterie, malice, *f.*

wag'ging (wag'ghigne), *n.*, remuement, branlement, *m.*

wag'gish (wag-ghish), *adj.*, badin, malin, espiègle; plaisant, facétieux; (of things) d'espiègle. — trick; *espièglerie, plaisanterie, farce, f.; tour d'espiègle, m.*

wag'gishly, *adv.*, plaisamment; avec espièglerie, d'une manière badine, pour badiner.

wag'gishness, *n.*, espièglerie, malice, plaisanterie, farce, *f.*

wag'gle (wag'g'l), *v.n.*, frétiller, se remuer, remuer.

wag'gle, *v.a.*, remuer.

wag'on (wag-gheune), *n.*, charrette, chariot; wagon; voiture de roulage, *f.*; (milit.) caisson, fourgon; (railw.) wagon, *m.* — -master; (milit.) *vaguemestre, m.*

wag'on, *v.a.*, charrier, charroyer, voiturer.

wag'onage (-'èdje), *n.*, prix de roulage; roulage, *m.*

wag'oner, *n.*, roulier, voiturier, *m.*

wag'oning, *n.*, charriage; roulage, *m.*

wag'on-train (-tré'n), *n. sing.*, train des équipages, *m.*

wag'tail (-téle), *n.*, (orni.) hochequeue, *m.*, bergeronnette, *f.*

waif (wéfe), *n.*, épave, *f.* The —s and strays; (children) *les petits va nu-pieds, les enfants abandonnés; les gens sans asile et sans abri,* m.pl.

wail (wéle), *v.a.* V. **bewail.**

wail, *v.n.*, pleurer, gémir, se lamenter.

wail *ou* **wail'ing**, *n.*, lamentation, plainte, *f.*, gémissement, *m.*

wail'ful (-foule), *adj.*, plaintif, lamentable.

wain (wé'ne), *n.*, chariot. Charles's Wain (astron.) *grand Chariot,* m., *grande Ourse,* f.

wain'age, *n.*, charriage, charroi, *m.*

wain'-bote (-bôte), *n.*, bois de charronnage, *m.*

wain'scot (wé'n'scote), *n.*, boiserie, *f.*, lambris, *m.*

wain'scot, *v.a.*, lambrisser **de**; boiser **de.**

wain'scoting, *n.*, lambrissage, *m.*, boiserie, *f.*; (material) bois de lambris, *m.*

waist (véste), *n.*, ceinture, taille, *f.*; milieu du corps, *m.*; (nav.) coursive, *f.*, entre-deux, *m.*

waist'band, *n.*, ceinture (of trousers, etc.), *f.*

waist'coat (-côte), *n.*, gilet, *m.*

waist'coating (-côt'-), *n.*, étoffe pour gilets, *f.*

wait (wéte), *n.*, embûche, *f.*; embûches, *f.pl.*; embuscade, *f.*; guet-apens, piège, *m.* To lie in —; *être, se tenir, en embuscade; être à l'affût.* To lie in — for; *dresser des embûches* **à,** *tendre un guet-apens* **à.**

wait (wéte), *v.n.*, attendre; (at table, etc.) servir. To keep —ing; *faire attendre.* Not to — to be told; *ne pas se le faire répéter.* To — for; *attendre, attendre* **après**; (to watch) *guetter,* surveiller. To —on, upon; (of servants, etc.) *servir;* (to call upon) *aller* **chez**, *se rendre* **chez,** *auprès* **de**; *faire une visite* **à**, *rendre visite* **à**, *présenter ses respects* **à**; *rendre ses devoirs* **à**; (to accompany) *accompagner, suivre;* (to look towards) *être dirigé* **vers**; *se tourner* **vers**; (to attend) *faire attention* **à**; *écouter.*

wait, *v.a.*, attendre. To — dinner for a person; *retarder le dîner pour quelqu'un.*

wait'er, *n.*, garçon (of public-house, coffee-house); domestique; (tray) plateau, *m.* Dumb-—; *servante, f.*

wait'ing, *n.*, attente, *f.*; (attendance) service, *m.* In —; (in attendance) *de service.* Lady in —; *dame d'honneur,* f.

wait'ing-maid (-méde), *n.*, femme de chambre, *f.*

wait'ing-room (-roume), *n.*, salle d'attente, *f.*

wait'ing-woman (-woum'-), *n.*, femme de chambre; (of a princess) camériste, *f.*

wait'ress, *n.*, fille (d'hôtel, etc.), fille de service; demoiselle de restaurant, *f.*

waits (wétse), *n.pl.*, musiciens ambulants (de la Noël), *m.pl.*

waive (wéve), *v.a.*, (to put off) écarter, éloigner; mettre de côté, mettre à l'écart; (to relinquish) abandonner; se désister **de**, retirer; renoncer **à**; ne pas insister **sur.**

wake (wéke), *n.*, veille, veillée, *f.*; (nav.) sillage, *m.*, eaux, *f.pl.*; (village fete) fête de village, veillée; (fig.) suite; trace, *f.* In the — of the vessel; *dans le sillage du vaisseau.* On the — of; (fig.) *à la suite* **de**; *sur les traces* **de.**

wake, *v.a.*, éveiller, réveiller.

wake, *v.n.*, (to sit up) veiller; (from sleep) s'éveiller, se réveiller.

wake'ful (-foule), *adj.*, éveillé; (vigilant) vigilant.

wake'fully, *adv.*, sans dormir; avec vigilance.

wake'fulness, *n.*, insomnie; veille, *f.*

wak'en (wék'n), *v.a.*, éveiller, réveiller.

wak'en, *v.n.*, s'éveiller, se réveiller. V. **awaken.**

wak'er (wék'-), *n.*, veilleur, personne qui veille.

wak'ing (wék'-), *n.*, veille, *f.*; réveil, *m.*

wak'ing, *adj.*, éveillé, qui ne dort pas.

wale (wéle), *n.*, raie, marque; (of cloth) côte, *f.*; (nav.) préceinte, *f.* Gun—; (nav.) *plat-bord,* m.

Wales, *n. proper*, Pays de Galles, *m.* Prince of —; *Prince de Galles.*

walk (wôke), *n.*, marche; (for pleasure) promenade, *f.*, tour, *m.*; (place) promenade, *f.*, promenoir, *m.*; (path) allée, avenue; (for business) course; (gait) démarche, allure, *f.*, port, marcher; (of a horse) pas, *m.*, allure, *f.*; (fig.) voie, sphère, région, carrière, *f.*, chemin, domaine, département; rang, *m.*, classe, *f.* At a —; *au pas.* To go out for a —; *aller se promener, faire une promenade.* To take a —; *faire un tour de promenade.* To take out for a —; *mener promener.*

walk (wôke), *v.n.*, marcher; (not to ride) aller à pied; (to come on foot) venir à pied; (for pleasure) se promener; (of a horse) aller au pas, marcher. We —ed thirty miles; *nous fîmes* (or *avons fait*) *trente milles à pied.* To — on; *continuer de marcher.* To — over; *parcourir à pied.* To — after; *suivre.* To — down; *descendre.* To — into; *entrer* **dans.** To — in; *entrer.* To ask, to beg, any one to — in; *faire entrer.* To — off, away; *s'en aller, s'éloigner; partir, décamper; faire mine de s'en aller; s'écarter.* To — out; *sortir; se promener.* To ask, to desire any one to — out; *faire sortir.* To — up; *monter, s'approcher.* To ask, to beg, any one to — up; *faire monter.* To — up and down; *se promener en long et en large.* To — the rounds; (mil.) *faire la ronde.*

walk, *v.a.*, marcher **dans**, parcourir, courir, traverser à pied; (any distance) faire à pied; (a horse) mettre au pas, faire aller au pas. To — the hospitals; *étudier la médecine; suivre les cours de clinique.* To — the streets; *se promener par les rues;* (b.s.) *battre le pavé; faire le trottoir.*

walk'er, *n.*, marcheur, *m.*; marcheuse, *f.*; piéton, *m.*; promeneur, *m.*, promeneuse, *f.* Shop —; *inspecteur de magasin, m.*

walk'ing, *n.*, marche; promenade à pied, *f.*

walk'ing, *adj.*, ambulant; de marche, de promenade. At a — pace; *au pas.* It is bad — (on account of snow); *il fait mauvais marcher.*

walk'ing-dress, *n.*, (of ladies) toilette de ville, *f.*; (of men) costume de ville, *m.*

walk'ing-place, *n.*, promenade, *f.*; (covered) promenoir, *m.*

walk'ing-shoes, *n.pl.*, souliers de promenade, de fatigue, *m.pl.*

walk'ing-staff (-stâfe) *ou* **walk'ing-stick**, *n.*, canne, *f.*; (for the blind) bâton; (for pilgrims) bourdon, *m.*

walk'ing-ticket, *n.*, congé, renvoi, *m.* To give any one his —; *donner son congé à quelqu'un; signifier à quelqu'un son renvoi.*

wall (wôl), *n.*, muraille, *f.*; mur; (rampart) mur, *m.*, muraille, *f.*, (fig.) rempart; (for fruit) espalier, *m.* Party—; *mur mitoyen.* Within the —s; *dans l'enceinte des murs, intra-muros.* To give the —; *céder le haut du pavé* **à.** To go to the —; *avoir le dessous; succomber;* (com.) *faire banqueroute.* To hang by the —; *rester sans emploi.*

wall, *v.a.*, murer, entourer de murs. To — up; *boucher, murer.*

Walla'chian, *adj.*, Valaque.

wall'-creeper, *n.*, (orni.) grimpereau, *m.*

wal'let (wôl-), *n.*, sac, havresac; bissac, *m.*, besace, *f.*

wall'-eye (-aïe), *n.*, (med.) glaucome; (vet.) œil vairon, *m.*

wall'-eyed (-aïde), *adj.*, (of horses) qui a l'œil vairon.

wall'-flower (-flaoueur), *n.*, giroflée jaune, ravenelle, *f.*; violier, *m.* To be a —; (fig.) *faire tapisserie, ou galerie.*

wall'-fruit (-froute), *n.*, fruit d'espalier, *m.*

wall'ing, *n.*, maçonnerie de murs, *f.*; muraillement, *m.*, murs, *m.pl.*, murailles, *f.pl.*

Walloon' (wal'loune), *n.*, Wallon, *m.*, Wallonne, *f.*

Walloon', *adj.*, wallon.

Walloon', *n.*, wallon (language), *m.*

wal'lop, *v.a.*, rosser; tanner la peau, le cuir, à.

wal'loping, *n.*, rossée, volée de coups, roulée, *f.*

wal'low (wŏl-lô), *v.n.*, se vautrer, se rouler; croupir. To — in; *se vautrer dans, se rouler dans.*

wal'low (wŏl-lô), *n.*, dandinement, balancement. *m.*

wal'lower, *n.*, créature qui se roule, qui se vautre.

wall'-paper, *n.*, papier de tenture, *m.*

wall'-plate, *n.*, sablière, *f.*

wall'-sided (-saïd'-), *adj.*, aux côtés perpendiculaires.

wall'-tree (-trî), *n.*, arbre en espalier, *m.*

wall'-wort (-weurte), *n.*, (bot.) pariétaire, hièble, *f.*

wal'nut (wol-neute), *n.*, noix, *f.* — wood; noyer, *m.*

wal'nut-peel (-pîle), *n.*, brou de noix, *m.*

wal'nut-shell, *n.*, coquille de noix, *f.*

wal'nut-table, table en noyer, *f.*

wal'nut-tree (-trî), *n.*, (bot.) noyer, *m.*

wal'rus (wol-), *n.*, (mam.) morse, cheval marin, *m.*, vache marine, *f.*

waltz (wŏltz), *n.*, valse, *f.*

waltz (wŏltz), *v.n.*, valser.

waltz'er, *n.*, valseur, *m.*, valseuse, *f.*

waltz'ing, *n.*, valse, *f.*

wam'ble (wo'm'b'l), *v.n.*, se soulever.

wam'bling, *n.*, soulèvement de cœur, *m.*

wan (wŏ'n), *adj.*, blême, pâle; blafard.

wand (wŏ'n'de), *n.*, baguette; verge, *f.*; (staff) bâton, *m.* Mercury's —; *caducée, m.*

wan'der (wŏ'n'd'-), *v.n.*, errer, rôder, vaguer; s'égarer; (in mind) divaguer; (to be delirious) avoir le délire, délirer; battre la campagne (Daudet). To—about; *errer dans, parcourir ; errer partout, courir çà et là; courir de tous côtés.* To — from; *s'écarter de, s'éloigner de, sortir de; quitter.* To — over; *errer dans.* His thoughts began to —; *il commença à battre la campagne, à divaguer.* To — into; *se perdre, s'égarer dans.*

wan'derer, *n.*, rôdeur, vagabond, *m.*, vagabonde, *f.*; fugitif, *m.*, fugitive, *f.*

wan'dering, *n.*, course, course vagabonde, errante, *f.*; voyage; (in mind) égarement, *m.*, distraction, divagation, *f.*; (deviation) écart, *m.*, divagation, *f.*; (delirium) délire, *m.*

wan'dering, *adj.*, errant, vagabond; distrait, divaguant. The — Jew; *le juif errant.*

wan'deringly, *adv.*, d'une manière errante; d'une manière distraite; en rôdant.

wane (wé'n), *n.*, déclin; (of the moon) décours, décroissement, *m.*; (fig.) décadence, décroissance, *f.*; déclin, *m.* On the —; *sur son déclin;* (fig.) *sur le retour.*

wane (wé'n), *v.n.*, (of the moon) décroître; diminuer; (fig.) décliner, s'altérer, baisser, s'affaiblir.

wan'ly (wŏ'n'-), *adv.*, avec pâleur.

wan'ness (wŏ'n'nèce), *n.*, pâleur, *f.*; teint blême, *m.*

wan'nish (wŏ'n'-), *adj.*, pâlot, un peu hâve, un peu terne.

want (wŏ'n'te), *n.*, besoin, *m.*; nécessité, *f.*; (lack) manque, défaut; (poverty) besoin, dénûment, *m.*; indigence, misère, *f.* To be, *ou* to stand, in — of; *avoir besoin de;* (not to have) *manquer de.* For — of; *faute de, manque de; à défaut de.* In —; *dans le besoin, dans la misère; dans la gêne.* I have no — for it; *je n'en ai pas besoin ou il ne me servirait de rien; il ne me serait d'aucun usage.*

want (wŏ'n'te), *v.a.*, avoir besoin de; (not to have) manquer de; être dépourvu de, être dénué

de; (pers.) demander; avoir besoin de; (to wish for) désirer; vouloir; demander; avoir envie de. A carriage was much —ed; *une voiture était indispensable, ou nécessaire;* ou *il fallait une voiture (à tout prix).* These men are —ed by the police; *la police est aux trousses de ces hommes.* —ed a . . .; *on demande un . . ., on a besoin d'un . . .* You are —ed; *on vous demande.* I —you; *j'ai besoin de vous.* A scapegoat was —ed; *il fallait un bouc émissaire.* What do you — of me? *que me voulez-vous? que désirez-vous, que voulez-vous de moi?* You shall — nothing; *vous ne manquerez de rien.* I sadly —; *j'ai grand besoin de.* A thing much —ed; *une chose dont on a grand besoin.*

want, *v.n.*, manquer; (to wish) vouloir, désirer. It —s; (it requires) *il faut;* (it is short of) *il manque, il s'en faut de.* It —s ten minutes to one; *il est une heure moins dix minutes.* All that is —ing is to . . .; *tout ce qu'il faut, ou tout ce qui est nécessaire, c'est de . . .* To be —ing; *manquer.* Two spoons are —ing; *il manque deux cuillers.* To be —ing in; (to fail) *manquer à, de;* (to be without) *manquer de.* There —s a leaf; *il manque un feuillet.* There —s but little; *peu s'en faut, il s'en faut peu.* I — you to do . . .; *je désire que vous fassiez . . .* I —ed to tell you; *je voulais vous dire.* The rogue —ed to deceive me; *le coquin voulait me tromper.*

want'ing, *adj.*, qui manque. To be found —; *se trouver, ou être trouvé, en défaut.*

want'less, *adj.*, sans besoins; riche.

wan'ton (wŏ'n'teune), *adj.*, (playful) badin, folâtre, follet; (floating) flottant, qui flotte au gré du vent; (wicked) méchant, fait par malice, par méchanceté; gratuit, systématique, insigne, brutal; (of the tongue) indiscret, sans frein; (unchaste) dérégé, licencieux, libertin, lascif, dissolu; (luxuriant) exubérant, luxuriant.

wan'ton (wŏ'n'teune), *n.*, libertin, *m.*, libertine, *f.*; débauché, *m.*

wan'ton (wŏ'n'teune), *v.n.*, flotter au gré du vent; folâtrer; s'ébattre; se jouer, se réjouir, badiner; faire le libertin.

wan'tonly, *adv.*, de gaîté de cœur; en folâtrant, par malice, inconsidérément; gratuitement; d'une manière déréglée; licencieusement; par libertinage.

war (wore), *n.*, guerre, *f.* Secretary of State for —; *ministre de la guerre, m.* Naval —; *guerre maritime, f.* At —; *en guerre avec.* To inure to —; *aguerrir.* Inured to —; *aguerri.* To declare — against; *déclarer la guerre à.* To go to — with; to wage — against, upon; *faire la guerre à.* — to the knife; *guerre à mort.* Articles of —; *code pénal militaire, m.sing.* There is — between them over this; (fig.) *ils en sont à couteaux tirés.*

war (wore), *v.n.*, faire la guerre à; combattre; lutter contre.

war'ble (wor'b'l), *v.a.n.*, gazouiller, chanter; (fig.) murmurer.

war'bler, *n.*, (orni.) chanteur; oiseau chanteur, *m.*; fauvette, *f.*

war'bling (wor-), *n.*, ramage, gazouillement; chant, *m.*

war'bling, *adj.*, harmonieux, mélodieux.

war'blingly, *adv.*, mélodieusement.

war'-cry (wor-craïe) *ou* **war'-whoop** (-houpe), *n.*, cri de guerre, *m.*

ward (worde), *n.*, (minor) pupille, *m.f.*; (guardianship) tutelle; (fenc.) act of guarding of a lock) garde; (of hospitals) salle, *f.*; (of a school) quartier, *m.*; (of a town) arrondissement, *m.* To keep watch and —; *faire le guet.*

ward, *v.n.*, être sur ses gardes; parer les coups.

ward (off) (worde-), *v.a.*, parer, éviter; écarter; détourner; repousser.

ward'en (word'n), *n.*, gardien; gouverneur;

garde ; (of prisons) directeur ; (of a university) recteur ; (of a college) proviseur, directeur, *m.*

ward'enship, *n.*, place de gardien, de directeur, *f.* ; office de gouverneur, de directeur, etc., *m.*

ward'er, *n.*, garde ; gardien, *m.*

ward'mote (-môte), *n.*, conseil d'arrondissement, *n.*

ward'robe (-rôbe), *n.*, (for dresses, etc.) garderobe ; (furniture) armoire, *f.* ; (in schools) vestiaire, *m.* ; lingerie, *f.* — dealer ; *revendeuse à la toilette*, *f.* — woman ; (in schools) *lingère*, *f.*

ward'-room (-roume), *n.*, (nav.) carré des officiers, *m.* —mess ; *table des officiers*, *f.*

ward'ship, *n.*, tutelle ; minorité, pupillarité, *f.*

ware (wère), *n.*, marchandise, denrée, *f.* ; produit, article, objet, *m.* China— ; *porcelaine*, *f.* Small —s ; *petits objets*, *m.pl.*

ware (wère), *v.a.* V. **wear**, *v.a.*

ware'house (-haouce), *n.*, magasin ; entrepôt, *m.* Bonded — ; *entrepôt de douane*, *m.* Italian — ; *magasin de pâtes d'Italie, magasin de comestibles*, *m.*

ware'house (-haouce), *v.a.*, emmagasiner, mettre en magasin ; (at the custom-house) entreposer.

ware'house-keep'er (-kîp-), *n.*, entreposeur ; garde-magasin, *m.*

ware'houseman, *n.*, garde-magasin ; (owner of a warehouse) marchand en gros, *m.*

ware'house-rent, *n.*, magasinage ; loyer, *m.*

ware'housing, *n.*, emmagasinage ; magasinage ; (at the custom-house) entreposage, *m.*

war'fare (wor-fére), *n.*, vie militaire ; guerre ; lutte, *f.* ; combats, *m.pl.*

war'-horse, *n.*, cheval de bataille, *m.*

wa'rily (wé-), *adv.*, prudemment, sagement, avec précaution ou circonspection.

wa'riness (wé-), *n.*, prudence, circonspection, *f.*

war'like (wor-laïke), *adj.*, militaire, guerrier, martial, belliqueux.

war'likeness, *n.*, caractère belliqueux, *m.*

warm (worme), *adj.*, chaud ; (fig.) zélé, ardent ; passionné, vif, animé ; (of welcome) chaleureux. To be — ; (pers.) *avoir chaud* ; (of the weather) *faire chaud*. It is very — ; *il fait très-chaud.* — work ; *rude, forte, chaude besogne.* To keep oneself — ; *se tenir chaudement.* To keep one — ; (of clothes) *tenir chaud.* To get — ; *chauffer, se réchauffer* ; (of the weather) *commencer à faire chaud* ; (of persons) *s'échauffer* ; *s'animer.* To make — ; *chauffer, réchauffer.*

warm (worme), *v.a.*, chauffer ; échauffer ; (a bed) bassiner ; réchauffer. To — again, up ; *réchauffer.* To — any one's ears ; *frotter les oreilles à* (Molière : *Le Médecin malgré lui*).

warm, *v.n.*, chauffer, réchauffer ; (oneself) se chauffer, se réchauffer ; (fig.) s'animer.

war-material, *n.*, matériel de guerre, *m.*

warm'ing, *n.*, action de chauffer, de s'échauffer, *f.* To give a — to ; *chauffer.*

warm'ing-apparatus, *n.*, appareil de chauffage, *m.*

warm'ing-pan, *n.*, bassinoire, *f.* ; (fig.) intérimaire, *m.f.* ; bouche-trou, *m.*

war'-minister, *n.*, ministre de la guerre, *m.*

warm'ly, *adv.*, chaudement ; chaleureusement, passionnément, vivement.

warmth (worm'th), *n.*, chaleur ; (fig.) ardeur, *f.*, zèle, *m.*, chaleur, vivacité, *f.*

warn (worne), *v.a.*, avertir **de** ; prévenir **de** ; faire savoir **à**, notifier **à**. He had —ed him about ; *il lui avait dit de se garder de.* To — against ; *prémunir* **contre**, *précautionner* **contre**, *mettre sur ses gardes* **contre**. To — any one off the premises ; *signifier à quelqu'un qu'il ait à se retirer.*

warn'ing, *n.*, avis, avertissement, *m.* ; alarme, leçon, *f.* ; (to leave) **congé** ; (of a clock) avant-

quart, *m.* To give — to ; *avertir ; donner avis* **à**. To give — to leave ; *donner congé*. To get — ; (to leave or quit) *recevoir son congé.*

war'-office (wor-), *n.*, bureaux du ministère de la guerre, *m.pl.* ; ministère de la guerre, *m.*

warp (worpe), *n.*, (weaving) chaîne, *f.* ; (nav.) grelin, *m.*, touée, *f.*

warp (worpe), *v.a.*, (inweaving) ourdir ; (wood) faire déjeter, faire tourmenter, travailler ; (nav.) touer ; (arch.) gauchir ; (to influence) influencer ; (to pervert) fausser, pervertir.

warp, *v.n.*, se cambrer, se déjeter ; plier ; travailler, gauchir ; (to deviate) dévier **de** ; s'écarter **de** ; (nav.) se touer.

warp'er, *n.*, ourdisseur, *m.*

warp'ing, *n.*, (in weaving) ourdissage, *m.* ; of wood) cambrure, *f.* ; déjettement, gauchissement.

warp'ing-mill, *n.*, machine à ourdir, *f.*

war'rant (wôr-), *n.*, autorisation, autorité, *f.* ; ordre, pouvoir, mandat, *m.* ; garantie ; justification, *f.* ; garant ; (for payment) mandat, *m.* ; (to arrest) mandat d'amener, mandat d'arrêt, *m.* Death— ; *ordre d'exécution.* Search— ; *mandat de perquisition.* — of attorney ; *procuration*, *f.* —officer ; *adjudant sous-officier*, *m.*

war'rant (wor'-), *v.a.*, garantir ; certifier, attester, assurer ; autoriser ; (to answer for) justifier, répondre **de** ; (to secure) garantir, défendre ; (com.) garantir.

war'rantable (-'a-b'l), *adj.*, justifiable, soutenable, autorisé, légitime.

war'rantableness, *n.*, caractère justifiable, *m.* ; légitimité, *f.*

war'rantably, *adv.*, d'une manière justifiable, légitimement.

warrantee' (wor'ra'n'tî), *n.*, (jur.) garanti, *m.*

war'ranter *ou* **warrantor'**, *n.*, garant, *m.* ; caution ; personne qui autorise ; (jur.) mandant, commettant, *m.*

war'ranting, *n.*, cautionnement, *m.* *adj.*, (fig.) qui autorise, qui justifie.

war'ranty (wor'-), *n.*, garantie ; autorisation, *f.* ; pouvoir ; droit ; cautionnement, *m.*

war'ranty, *v.a.*, garantir.

war'ren (wor'-), *n.*, garenne, *f.*

war'rener (wor'rè'n'-), *n.*, garennier, *m.*

war'rior (wor'rieur), *n.*, guerrier, militaire, soldat, *m.*

war'-song, *n.*, chant de guerre, *m.*

wart (worte), *n.*, verrue, *f.*, poireau, *m.* ; (bot.) excroissance, *f.*

wart'-cress, *n.*, (bot.) corne-de-cerf, *f.*

wart'wort (wort'weurte), *n.*, (bot.) éclaire, *f.* ; réveille-matin, *m.*

wart'y (wort'-), *adj.*, plein de verrues ; verruqueux ; comme une verrue.

wa'ry (wé-), *adj.*, avisé, sage, prévoyant ; prudent.

wash (woshe), *n.*, (of linen) blanchissage, savonnage, *m.* ; lessive, *f.*, lavage ; (paint., drawing) lavis, *m.* ; (med.) lotion, eau, *f.* ; (for toilet) cosmétique, *m.* ; (slight layer) couche légère, *f.* ; enduit, *m.* ; (dirty water) lavure, eau de vaisselle ; (of thin soup) lavasse, *f.* ; (distilleries) liqueur à distiller, *f.* ; (of an oar) plat, *m.* ; pale, *f.* ; (of the sea) clapotement, *m.* ; (of a vessel) eau, *f.* ; sillage, *m.*

wash (woshe), *v.a.*, laver ; (to bathe) mouiller, baigner, laver, arroser ; (in lye) lessiver ; (linen) blanchir, savonner ; (a horse) guéer ; (paint.) laver. I was —ed on to the rock ; *les vagues me jetèrent sur le rocher.* To — one's hands ; *se laver les mains.* To — one's hands ; (of the business) (fig.) *s'en laver les mains ; retirer son épingle du jeu ; n'avoir plus rien à y voir.* To — clean ; *laver bien.* To — away, off ; *enlever en lavant ; nettoyer, laver, effacer* ; (to carry away) *enlever, emporter, entraîner* ; (a stain) *enlever.* To — down ; *laver, nettoyer* ; (of food, with wine, etc.) *arroser*. To — up ; *laver ;* (on shore) *rejeter sur le rivage*. To — over ; (of the waves) *submerger*. To — over with gold ; *dorer*.

wash, *v.n.*, se laver ; se baigner ; (of a wash-erwoman, etc.) blanchir, savonner. To — for any one ; *blanchir quelqu'un*. To — off ; *disparaître, deteindre, s'effacer à l'eau*. That stuff —es ; *cette étoffe se lave*.

wash'able, *adj.*, qui peut se laver, lavable.

wash'-ball (-bôl), *n.*, savonnette, *f.*

wash'-board (-bôrde), *n.*, (carp.) plinthe, *f.*

wash'er, *n.*, laveur, *m.*, laveuse ; (machine) machine à laver, *f.*

wash'erwoman, *n.*, blanchisseuse, *f.*

wash'-ba'sin (-bés'n), *n.*, cuvette, *f.*

wash'-stand, *n.*, lavabo, *m.*

wash'-house (-haouce), *n.*, lavoir, *m.* ; buanderie, *f.*

wash'ing, *n.*, blanchissage, lavage, *m.* ; (in lye) lessive ; (pers.) ablution ; (med.) lotion, *f.*

wash'ing-machine (-ma-shîne), *n.*, machine à blanchir, *f.*

wash'-leather (-lèth'-), *n.*, peau de chamois, *f.*

wash'-stand, *n.*, toilette, *f. ;* (small) lavabo, *m.*

wash'-tub, *n.*, baquet, cuvier, *m.*

wash'y (wosh'i), *adj.*, flasque ; humide, mouillé ; faible. — stuff ; *lavasse, f.*

wasp (wospe), *n.*, (ent.) guêpe, *f.*

wasp'-fly (-flaïe), *n.*, (ent.) mouche-guêpe, *f.*

wasp'ish (wosp'-), *adj.*, maussade, bourru ; irascible, irritable ; piquant.

wasp'ishly, *adv.*, avec irritation ; d'une manière piquante.

wasp'ishness, *n.*, humeur bourrue, irritabilité, maussaderie, *f.*

wasp's'-nest, *n.*, guêpier, *m.*

was'sail (wos's'l), *n.*, bière sucrée aromatisée ; (drunken bout) partie de débauche, bombance, orgie, ribote, *f.* The — bowl ; *la coupe du festin*.

was'sail (wos's'l), *v.n.*, faire bombance, faire ripaille.

was'sailer, *n.*, riboteur, ripailleur, *m.*

waste (wéste), *n.*, perte, *f. ;* déchet ; (extravagance) gaspillage, *m.*, perte, prodigalité ; (useless expense) dépense inutile, *f. ;* (jur.) dégât, *m.*, dégradation, *f. ;* (land) désert, *m.*, terre inculte, terre en friche ; solitude, *f. ;* (tech.) tropplein ; (print., bookselling) défet, *m.* — lands ; *terrains vagues ; pays perdus, m.pl.* (V. Hugo). To go, *ou* run, to — ; *se dissiper, se perdre, tomber en ruine*. It is mere — of money ; *c'est de l'argent perdu, ou jeté par la fenêtre*. It is mere — of time ; *c'est simplement perdre son, ou le, temps*. Willful — makes woful want ; (prov.) *les folles dépenses refroidissent la cuisine*.

waste (wéste), *adj.*, inutile, mauvais, de rebut, sans valeur ; (ruined) ruiné, ravagé, dévasté ; (not used) non employé, perdu ; (of land) inculte, en friche. — paper ; *papier de rebut, m. ;* (print.) *maculature, f.* —paper basket; *panier au papier, panier au rebut, m.* To lay —; *ravager, dévaster, ruiner*.

waste (wéste), *v.a.*, (to squander) gaspiller, perdre, prodiguer, dissiper ; (to exhaust) consumer, user, épuiser ; (to spoil) gâter, détériorer, dégrader ; (to ruin) ravager, dévaster, ruiner ; (to sacrifice) prodiguer, sacrifier ; (time) perdre ; (com.) donner un déchet de. To — paper ; *gâcher, brouiller, barbouiller, du papier*. I —d my time over it ; *je l'ai fait en pure perte*. — not, want not ; (prov.) *qui ne gaspille pas, toujours trouve*.

waste, *v.n.*, s'user, se consumer, s'épuiser, maigrir, dépérir ; se dissiper, se perdre ; (com.) produire du déchet. To — away ; *dépérir, se consumer, s'user, s'épuiser ; se perdre ;* (to lose flesh) *maigrir à vue d'œil*.

waste'-book (-bouke), *n.*, brouillard, *m.*

wast'ed, *adj.*, dépensé en pure perte ; gaspillé, perdu, prodigué ; (diminished) diminué ; (exhausted) épuisé.

waste'ful (-foule), *adj.*, dissipateur, prodigue ; ruineux, en pure perte, inutile ; destructeur.

waste'fully, *adv.*, prodigalement; en pure perte, inutilement.

waste'fulness, *n.*, dissipation, prodigalité, perte, *f. ;* gaspillage, *m.*

waste'-pipe (-païpe), *n.*, tuyau de trop-plein, *m.*

wast'er, *n.*, prodigue, gaspilleur, *m.*

waste'-silk, *n.*, déchets de soie, *m.pl.*

waste'-weir (-wère), *n.*, déversoir de superficie, *m.*

wast'ing, *adj.*, qui consume, qui use, qui épuise. *n.*, dégât, *m. ;* perte, *f. ;* gaspillage ; (of the body) dépérissement, *m.*, consomption, *f. ;* (of a country) dévastation, *f.*

watch (wotshe), *n.*, montre ; (attendance without sleep) veille ; (attention) attention, garde, vigilance, surveillance ; (sentry) sentinelle, *f.*, garde, *m. ;* (milit.) garde ; (guard) garde, *f.*, poste, guet ; (nav.) quart, *m.* By my —; *à ma montre*. To be upon the — ; *être, se tenir, sur ses gardes, être à l'affût, être aux aguets, avoir l'œil au guet ;* (nav.) *être de quart*. It was my — ; *j'étais de quart ;* (milit.) *être de garde, monter la garde*. To be upon the — for ; *guetter, épier*. To keep — ; *veiller, avoir l'œil au guet*. To keep a good, *ou* strict, — ; *faire bonne garde*. To keep good — over (a person) ; *surveiller de près*. To lie on the — for ; *être à l'affût de ; être aux aguets* pour. Bill of —; (nav.) *rôle de quart, m.*

watch (wotshe), *v.n.*, (not to sleep) veiller ; (to be attentive) veiller, être attentif, prendre garde, être aux aguets ; être, se tenir sur ses gardes ; (to keep guard) veiller, faire le guet, faire la garde ; (nav.) faire le quart. To — for ; (occasion) *attendre, épier, guetter ;* (person) *attendre à l'affût*. To — over ; *veiller, veiller* sur, *surveiller*. To — with ; (an invalid) *veiller, veiller auprès* de, *garder*.

watch, *v.a.*, veiller sur, veiller, surveiller de près; observer de près; prendre garde à ; guetter, épier, attendre ; garder à vue.

watch'-bill, *n.*, (nav.) rôle de quart, *m.*

watch'-box, *n.*, guérite, *f.*

watch'-case (-kéce), *n.*, boîte de montre, *f.*

watch'-chain, *n.*, chaîne de montre, *f.*

watch'-dog, *n.*, chien de garde, *m.*

watch'er (wotsh'-), *n.*, surveillant, inspecteur, *m. ;* (to an invalid) garde, garde-malade, *m.f.*, veilleur ; (nav.) guetteur, *m.*

watch'-fire (-faïeur), *n.*, feu de bivouac, *m.*

watch'ful (-foule), *adj.*, soigneux, vigilant, attentif, en éveil ; sur ses gardes ; (mindful of) en garde contre.

watch'fully, *adv.*, vigilamment.

watch'fulness, *n.*, vigilance ; (want of sleep) insomnie, privation de sommeil, *f.*, veilles, *f.pl. ;* (over a person) surveillance, *f.*

watch'-glass (-glâce), *n.*, verre de montre ; (nav.) sablier de quart, *m.*

watch'-guard (-gârde), *n.*, chaîne de sûreté, chaîne de montre, *f.*

watch'-house (-haouce), *n.*, corps de garde, *m.*

watch'ing (wotsh'-), *n.*, veille, insomnie ; (fig.) surveillance, observation ; vigilance, *f.*

watch'-light (-laïte), *n.*, veilleuse, *f.*

watch'-maker, *n.*, horloger, *m.*

watch'-making (-mék'-), *n.*, horlogerie, *f.*

watch'man, *n.*, homme de guet, garde, *m. ;* sentinelle, *f. ;* gardien de nuit ; (schools, hotels, etc.) veilleur, *m.* — ! what of the night ? *veilleur ! que dit la nuit ?*

watch'-pocket, *n.*, gousset (de montre) ; (for a bed) porte-montre, *m.*

watch'-spring, *n.*, ressort de montre, *m.*

watch'-stand, *n.*, porte-montre, *m.*

watch'-tower (-taoueur), *n.*, tour d'observation; guérite, *f.*

watch'-word (-weurde), *n.*, mot d'ordre, *m.*

watch'-work (-weurke), *n.*, (horl.) mouvement (de montre), *m.*

wa'ter (wo-), *n.*, eau; (tide) marée; (of diamonds) eau, *f.*, lustre; (class) ordre, rang, *m.*, volée; (urine) eau, urine, *f.* *adj.*, d'eau, à eau; hydraulique. By —; *par eau.* Under —; *sous l'eau; submergé.* — *carnival; fête aquatique, f.* Fresh —; *eau fraîche; (not salt) eau douce.* Salt— ; *eau salée, eau de mer.* Sea— ; *eau de mer.* Spring— ; *eau de source.* Hard —; *eau crue, dure.* Holy—— ; *eau bénite.* High——; *haute marée, haute mer, marée haute.* Low——; *marée basse, mer basse, f., basses eaux, f.pl.* Low — mark; *niveau des basses eaux; étiage, m.* It is high—, low— —; *la marée est haute, basse.* To take in —; (to leak) (nav.) *faire eau.* To hold —; *tenir l'eau; être solide.* To take in fresh —; *faire de l'eau.* To be of the first —; (of diamonds) *être de première eau;* (fig.) *être de la plus haute volée, du premier rang.* — on the brain; *hydrocéphale, f.* To be in hot —; *être dans le pétrin;* (in trouble) *être dans l'embarras.* To get into hot —; *se faire, ou s'attirer, une mauvaise affaire; se mettre dans le pétrin.* To let in —; (of shoes, etc.) *prendre l'eau.* To hold —; (fig. of an argument) *supporter l'examen.* To draw ten feet of —; *avoir dix pieds de tirant d'eau.* To fish in troubled —s; *pêcher en eau trouble.*

wa'ter, *v.a.*, arroser, mouiller; (animal) donner à boire à, abreuver; (to mix) mettre de l'eau **dans** ; (stuffs) moirer. To — one's wine; *tempérer son vin;* (fig.) *mettre de l'eau dans son vin.*

wa'ter (wo-), *v.n.*, (to weep) pleurer; (to draw water) puiser de l'eau; (nav., faire de l'eau, faire aiguade. To make one's mouth —; *faire venir l'eau à la bouche.* My mouth —s; *l'eau m'en vient à la bouche.*

wa'terage (wo-teur'èdje), *n.*, prix du transport par eau; transport par eau, *m.*

wa'ter-bailiff (-bé-life), *n.*, garde-port, inspecteur des halles à poisson; (of rivers) garde-pêche, *m.*

wa'ter-bearer (-bèr'-), *n.*, (astron.) Verseau; (pers.) porteur d'eau, *m.*

wa'ter-bed, *n.*, matelas à eau, *m.*

wa'ter-blow'ing-machine (- biô - igne - ma-shîne), *n.*, (metal.) trompe, *f.*

wa'ter-borne, *adj.*, (nav.) à flot; (fig.) porté sur l'eau.

wa'ter-bottle, *n.*, carafe, *f.*

wa'ter-cal'trops, *n.*, (bot.) châtaigne d'eau, macre, *f.*

wa'ter-can, *n.*, broc à eau, *m.*

wa'ter-carriage, *n.*, transport par eau, *m.*

wa'ter-carrier, *n.*, porteur d'eau, *m.*

wa'ter-cart, *n.*, voiture d'arrosement, *f.*

wa'ter-closet (-cloz'-), *n.*, cabinet d'aisances, cabinet, *m.*, lieux, *m.pl.*

wa'ter-color (-keul'leur), *n.*, aquarelle, *f.* — drawing; *aquarelle, peinture à l'aquarelle, f.* — painter; *peintre d'aquarelles, aquarelliste, m.*

wa'ter-course (-côrse), *n.*, cours d'eau; canal, conduit pour l'écoulement des eaux; (jur.) droit de puisage, *m.;* (hydr.) chute d'eau, *f.*

wa'ter-cress, *n.*, cresson, cresson de fontaine, *m.*

wa'ter-cure, *n.*, (med.) hydrothérapie, *f.*

wa'ter-dog, *n.*, barbet, caniche, terre-neuve, *m.* He is a good —; *il va bien à l'eau.*

wa'ter-drain (-dré'ne), *n.*, canal d'écoulement, *m.*

wa'ter-drain'age (-'èdje), *n.*, écoulement des eaux, *m.*

wa'ter-drink'er, *n.*, buveur d'eau, *m.*

wa'tered (wo-teurde), *adj.*, arrosé; (of stuffs) moiré.

wa'ter-engine (-è'n'djine), *n.*, machine, *ou* pompe hydraulique, *f.*

wa'terer (wo-teur'-), *n.*, arroseur; (of silks) moireur, *m.*

wa'ter-fall (-fôl), *n.*, cascade; chute d'eau, *f.*

wa'ter-fowl (-faoule), *n.*, poule d'eau, *f.*

wa'ter-gate, *n.*, vanne d'écluse, *f.*

wa'ter-gauge (-ghédje), *n.*, indicateur de la hauteur de l'eau, flotteur; tube de niveau, *m.*

wa'ter-god, *n.*, dieu aquatique, *m.*

wa'ter-gruel (-grou-), *n.*, gruau à l'eau, *m.*

wa'ter-hen, *n.*, poule d'eau, *f.*

wa'teriness (wo-teur'-), *n.*, humidité; aquosité; (med.) sérosité, *f.*

wa'tering (wo-teur'-), *n.*, arrosage; (of streets) arrosement; (of animals) abreuvage; (of stuffs) moiré, moirage, *m.;* (nav.) action de faire de l'eau; provision d'eau douce, *f.*

wa'tering-can, *n.*, arrosoir, *m.*

wa'tering-cart, *n.*, voiture d'arrosement, *f.*

wa'tering-en'gine (-è'n'djine), *n.*, pompe d'irrigation, d'arrosement, *f.;* irrigateur, *m.*

wa'tering-place, *n.*, eaux, *f.pl.;* (inland) ville d'eaux; ville de bains, *f.;* bains d'eaux minérales, *m.pl.;* ville au bord de la mer, *f.;* ville de bains de mer, *m.pl.;* (for animals) abreuvoir, *m.;* (nav.) aiguade, *f.*

wa'tering-pot, *n.*, arrosoir, *m.*

wa'tering-trough (-trofe), *n.*, auge, *f.;* abreuvoir, *m.*

wa'terish (wo-teur'-), *adj.*, aqueux.

wa'terishness, *n.*, (med.) sérosité; **nature** aqueuse, *f.*

wa'ter-jug, *n.*, pot à eau, *m.;* cruche à eau, *f.*

wa'terless, *adj.*, sans eau.

wa'ter-level, *n.*, niveau d'eau, *m.*

wa'ter-lily, *n.*, (bot.) nénuphar, *m.*

wa'ter-line (-laîne), *n.*, ligne de flottaison, *f.*

wa'ter-logged (-log'de), *adj.*, (nav.) engagé, à moitié engagé dans l'eau; à moitié plein d'eau.

wa'terman, *n.*, batelier, marinier; (at a ferry) passeur, *m.*

wa'ter-mark (-mârke), *n.*, niveau des eaux; (on paper) filigrane, *m.*, vergeure, *f.* High, low —; *niveau des hautes eaux, des eaux basses.*

wa'ter-marked (-mârk'te), *adj.*, à filigrane.

wa'ter-melon (-mèl'-), *n.*, melon d'eau, *m.;* pastèque, *f.*

wa'ter-met'er, *n.*, compteur à eau, *m.*

wa'ter-mill, *n.*, moulin à eau, *m.*

wa'ter-nymph, *n.*, (myth.) naïade, *f.*

wa'ter-pipe, *n.*, conduit d'eau; (for tobacco) narguilé, *m.*

wa'ter-plant, *n.*, plante aquatique, *f.*

wa'ter-plug, *n.*, robinet, *m.;* bouche d'eau, *f.*

wa'ter-poise (-poîze), *n.*, (phys.) hydromètre, *m.*

wa'ter-post, *n.*, poteau d'arrosement, *m.*, borne-fontaine, *f.*

wa'ter-pot, *n.*, pot à eau, *m.*

wa'ter-power (-paoueur), *n.*, force hydraulique, *f.*

wa'ter-pres'sure (-prèsh'eur), *n.*, pression de l'eau, *f.* —engine; *presse hydraulique, f.*

wa'ter-proof (-proufe), *adj.*, imperméable à l'eau; à l'épreuve de l'eau.

wa'ter-proof, *n.*, manteau imperméable, *m.*

wa'ter-ram, *n.*, bélier hydraulique, *m.*

wa'ter-rat, *n.*, rat d'eau, *m.*

wa'ter-rate, *n.*, contribution pour l'eau à domicile, *f.*

wa'ter-sail (-séle), *n.*, (nav.) bonnette, *f.*

wa'ter's edge, *n.*, extrême bord de l'eau, *m.*

wa'tershed, *n.*, (geog.) ligne de partage des eaux, *f.*, versant, *m.*

wa'ter-shoot (wo-teur-shoute), *n.*, (arch.) gargouille, *f.*

wa'ter-side, *adj.*, riverain.

wa'ter-side, *n.*, bord de l'eau, *m.*

wa'ter-span'iel, *n.*, épagneul d'eau, *m.*

wa'ter-spout (-spaoute), *n.*, (at sea) trombe, *f.* ; typhon, *m.* ; (of a house) gouttière, *f.* ; (jet) jet d'eau, *m.*

wa'ter-sta'tion (-sté-), *n.*, station à prendre de l'eau, *f.*

wa'ter-sump, *n.*, (mines) puisard, *m.*

wa'ter-supply', *n.*, approvisionnement d'eau, *n.* ; (of waterworks in towns) distribution des eaux, *f.*

wa'ter-table (-téb'l), *n.*, (arch.) pierre en saillie pour l'écoulement de l'eau, *f.*

wa'ter-tank, *n.*, réservoir (d'eau), *m.* ; citerne, *f.*

wa'ter-tight (-taïte), *adj.*, imperméable à l'eau ; (nav.) étanche (V. Hugo).

wa'ter-trough, *n.*, abreuvoir, *m.*

wa'ter-way, *n.*, cours d'eau ; débouché, *m.* ; (canal) section ; (of a ship) gouttière, *f.*

wa'ter-wheel (-hwîl), *n.*, roue hydraulique ; roue de moulin, *f.*

wa'ter-wings (-wign'ze), *n.pl.*, perré, *m.*

wa'ter-works (-weurkse), *n.*, eaux, *f.pl.*, ouvrages hydrauliques, *m.pl.* ; établissement pour la distribution des eaux, *m.* ; machine hydraulique, *f.*

wa'ter-worn, *adj.*, usé par les eaux.

wa'ter-wort (-weurte), *n.*, (bot.) élatine, *f.*

wa'tery (wo-teur'-), *adj.*, (poet.) humide ; liquide ; aqueux ; humecté, mouillé, plein d'eau ; marin, des eaux ; (of a grave) au fond des eaux. — gods ; *dieux marins, ou des eaux, m.pl.*

wat'tle (wot't'l), *n.*, (branch) brindille ; (hurdle) claie ; (of a cock, a fish) barbe, *f.*, barbillon, *m.*

wat'tle (wot't'l), *v.a.*, entourer de claies ; tresser, entrelacer ; lier avec de petites branches.

wave (wéve), *n.*, vague, *f.* ; flot, *m.* ; onde, lame ; (phys.) ondulation ; (on stuffs) moire, *f.* ; (on ground) pli, *m.*, ondulation, *f.* ; (of the hand) signe, *m.* ; (fig.) flot, caprice, *m.*

wave (wéve), *v.a.*, sillonner, rendre raboteux, rendre inégal ; (to brandish) agiter, brandir ; (to beckon) faire signe **de** ; (to reject, to waive) rejeter, repousser ; (to put off, to waive) éloigner ; (to relinquish, to waive) abandonner ; se désister **de**, retirer ; ne pas insister **sur**.

wave, *v.n.*, ondoyer, onduler, flotter ; (to move) s'agiter, se mouvoir, flotter, tournoyer, faire signe ; (to waver) balancer, hésiter.

waved (wév'de), *adj.*, ondulé ; (of stuffs) ondé ; (of lines) trempé.

wave'less, *adj.*, sans vagues ; calme, uni.

wa'ver (wév'eure), *v.n.*, chanceler ; vaciller ; flotter, balancer, être indécis, incertain, irrésolu.

wa'verer (wév'eur'-), *n.*, inconstant, *m.*, inconstante ; personne indécise, personne irrésolue, *f.*, esprit vacillant, *m.*

wa'vering (wév'eur'-), *adj.*, inconstant ; indécis, vacillant, incertain, irrésolu.

wa'veringly, *adv.*, en vacillant, en hésitant.

wa'veringness, *n.*, vacillation ; indécision, *f.*

wav'ing (wév'-), *n.*, ondoiement, *m.*, ondulation, *f.*, mouvement, balancement, *m.*

wav'y (wév'-), *adj.*, ondoyant, qui s'élève en ondes ; onduleux ; ondulé ; (of lines) tremblé.

wax, *n.*, cire ; (shoemaking) poix ; (fig., fam.) rage, colère, *f.*

wax, *v.a.*, cirer, enduire de cire ; bougier.

wax, *v.n.*, croître, s'accroître ; devenir, se faire. To — wroth ; *se mettre en colère.*

wax'-candle (-ca'n'd'l), *n.*, bougie, *f.*

wax'-chandler (-tsha'n'd'l-), *n.*, fabricant de bougies, cirier, *m.*

wax'en (waks'n), *adj.*, de cire.

wax'-light (-laïte), *n.*, bougie, *f.*

wax'-taper (-té-), *n.*, bougie, *f.* ; cierge, *m.*

wax'-tree (-trî), *n.*, (bot.) cirier, arbre à cire, *m.*

wax'-work (-weurke), *n.*, figure de cire, *f.* ; ouvrage de cire, *m.*

wax'y, *adj.*, (of potatoes) cireux, qui ressemble à la cire ; (fig.) en colère.

way (wé), *n.*, chemin, *m.* ; route, voie, *f.* ; (passage) chemin, passage, *m.*, place, issue, *f.* ; (direction) côté, sens, *m.*, direction ; (habit) habitude ; (manner) manière, façon, guise, mode, idée, fantaisie, *f.*, genre, *m.* ; (custom) coutume, *f.*, usage ; (means, system) moyen, système, expédient, *m.*, voie, méthode ; (conduct) conduite, manière d'agir, *f.* ; (state) état, *m.*, passe, *f.* ; (free scope) cours, libre cours ; (line of business) genre, *m.*, partie ; (fig.) voie, *f.*, chemin, *m.* The —s of Providence ; *les voies de la Providence.* — in ; *entrée, f.* — out ; *sortie ; issue, f.* — through ; *passage, m.* The — up ; *chemin pour monter.* Cross— ; *chemin de traverse.* By—; *chemin détourné.* Milky— ; *voie lactée.* By the —; *en passant, soit dit en passant, à propos.* On the — ; *en chemin, en route, chemin faisant.* Right of — ; *droit de passage, m.* The right — ; *le bon chemin ;* (fig.) *le bon moyen, la bonne manière.* The wrong —; *le mauvais chemin ; de la mauvaise manière, à rebours, de travers.* In this, *ou* that, — ; *de cette manière, ainsi.* By a long — ; (by far) *à beaucoup près, de beaucoup.* Evil —s ; *déportements, m.pl. ; mauvaise conduite, f.* In a fair —to ; *en passe* **de**, *en voie* **de**. In no — ; *nullement, d'aucune façon, tant s'en faut.* In one's own — ; *à sa façon, à sa guise.* In its —; *dans son genre.* Is this the —? *est-ce ici le chemin, ou la route,* **de**...? Is this the — that...? (fig.) *est-ce ainsi que...?* A — of his own ; *une manière à lui* (V. Hugo). —s and customs ; *us et coutumes, m.pl.* — and means ; *voies et moyens, m.pl.* The committee of —s and means ; *la commission du budget.* Under — ; (nav.) *en marche.* To go the right — to work ; *s'y prendre bien.* Out of the — ; *de côté ; à l'écart ; écarté ;* (strange) *étrange, extraordinaire ;* (hidden) *caché.* To keep, *ou* to be, out of the — ; *se cacher, se tenir éloigné, caché, à l'écart.* Out of the —! *en arrière ! gare ! rangez-vous !* Get out of the —; *ôtez-vous du chemin, de là.* To get any one out of the — ; *éloigner quelqu'un.* Make — ! *clear the —! faites place !* Go your — ; *passez votre chemin.* To be, to stand in the — ; *embarrasser, gêner, faire obstacle à, barrer le passage à.* He is in my — ; *il m'embarrasse, ou me gêne.* To be, *ou* to keep, in the — ; (to be near) *se tenir à portée.* To walk a long — ; *faire beaucoup de chemin.* To get under — ; (nav.) *appareiller* (V. Hugo). To lead the — ; *marcher en tête.* To lose one's —; *s'égarer, se perdre.* Half —; *à moitié chemin.* Over the — ; *vis-à-vis, en face ; de l'autre côté du chemin, de la rue.* That — ; *de ce côté-là, par là ;* (that manner) *de cette manière-là.* This —; *de ce côté-ci, par ici.* Which —? *de quel côté ? par où ? de quelle manière ?* To cut, to force one's — ; *se frayer, s'ouvrir un chemin, un passage.* To make the best of one's — ; *aller, ou se rendre, en toute hâte.* To work one's — towards ; *s'ouvrir un chemin* **vers**, *se diriger* **vers**. To be in a bad — ; *être au-dessous de ses affaires ; être dans de mauvais draps.* To feel one's — ; *marcher, ou aller, à tâtons ;* (fig.) *sonder le terrain.* To find one's — ; *trouver son chemin.* To find one's — into ; *s'introduire* **dans**, *ou* **de** ; *s'insinuer* **dans**. To get into the — of it ; (a thing) *s'y faire ; en prendre l'habitude.* By — of ; *en guise* **de**, *par forme* **de**. In my own — ; *à ma manière, ou guise.* To find a — to ; *trouver moyen* **de**. She will have her own — ; *elle veut être la maîtresse ; elle veut agir à sa fantaisie, faire ses volontés, faire à sa tête.* To go one's own — ; *aller son train ; faire comme on l'entend ; agir à sa guise.* To clear the — ; *débarrasser la voie, le chemin.* To clear the — for ; (fig.) *préparer la voie* **pour**. In the — of ; (in the matter of) *en matière* **de** ; *quant*

à. This —, my child ; *par ici, mon enfant.* — there ! —! *place par là !* To give —; *céder ; se laisser fléchir ;* (of troops) *reculer ; lâcher pied.* To go the — of all flesh ; *trépasser ; aller ad patres.* To go on one's —; (to pass by) *passer son chemin.* We are going your —; *nous allons de votre côté.* To pay one's — ; *ne pas s'endetter ; joindre les deux bouts.* To see one's —; *voir son chemin ;* (fig.) y *voir clair ;* (to) *voir la possibilité* **de.** To go the right — to work ; *savoir s'y prendre.* To go the wrong — to work ; *s'y prendre mal.* To make head—; *faire du chemin ; avancer ;* (fig.) *faire des progrès.* To make — (for); *laisser passer, se ranger.* To stand out of the — ; *s'ôter du chemin, se ranger ; se garer ; se tenir à l'écart.* To lead the —; *marcher en tête ; ouvrir la marche.* To bar, *ou* stop, the —; *barrer le passage ;* (of cabs, carts, etc.) *gêner la circulation.* Not to know which — to turn ; *ne savoir où donner de la tête, ou sur quel pied danser, ou à quel saint se vouer.* To make one's —; *faire son chemin.* Where there is a will there is a —; *vouloir c'est pouvoir ; qui veut la fin veut les moyens.* To take one's own —; *suivre son penchant, son inclination.*

way'-bill, *n.,* liste de voyageurs (d'une diligence), feuille de route, *f.*

way'faring (-fèr'-), *adj.,* qui voyage, en voyage.

way'lay, *v.a.,* guetter ; guetter au passage ; dresser un guet-apens **à.**

way'layer (-lé-eur), *n.,* personne qui dresse un guet-apens, qui se tient en embuscade, *f.*

way'less, *adj.,* sans chemins ; sans routes.

way'side, *adj.,* au bord de la route.

way'ward (-warde), *adj.,* fantasque ; capricieux ; entêté ; méchant.

way'wardly, *adv.,* méchamment ; avec humeur ; obstinément, avec entêtement.

way'wardness, *n.,* humeur capricieuse ; méchanceté, *f. ;* entêtement, obstination, *m.*

way'worn, *adj.,* (l.u.) harassé, épuisé par la route.

we (wî), *pron.,* nous ; (used indefinitely) on.

weak (wîke), *adj.,* faible ; infirme, débile ; léger ; (gram.) faible ; (of the sight) sensible. — side ; *côté faible ; faible, m.* To grow —; *s'affaiblir.* The —est go to the wall ; (prov.) *les battus payent l'amende.*

weak'en (wî-k'n), *v.a.,* affaiblir ; débiliter ; atténuer, diminuer ; (drinks) couper, étendre.

weak'ener, *n.,* débilitant, *m.*

weak'ening (wî-k'n'-), *n.,* affaiblissement, *m. ;* débilitation, *f.*

weak'ening, *adj.,* affaiblissant ; débilitant.

weak'-headed (-hèd'-), *adj.,* qui a la tête faible.

weak'-hearted (-hârt'-), *adj.,* peu courageux, poltron, pusillanime ; mou, sans cœur.

weak'ling (wîk'-), *n.,* être faible, être débile, *m.*

weak'ly (wîk'-), *adj.,* faible ; infirme ; débile.

weak'ly, *adv.,* faiblement ; débilement ; sans force.

weak'ness (wîk'-), *n.,* faiblesse ; débilité, *f. ;* (fig.) faible, *m.* Every one has his —; *tout le monde a son faible, son côté faible.*

weak'-sighted (-saït'-), *adj.,* qui a la vue faible.

weak'-spirited, *adj.,* mou, inanimé ; sans courage, sans cœur ; pusillanime.

weal (wîl), *n.,* bien, bien-être ; bonheur, *m.* *V.* **wale.** The public — ; *le bien public.*

wealth (wèlth), *n.,* richesse, opulence, fortune, *f.,* richesses, *f.pl. ;* biens, *m.pl.*

wealth'iness (wèlth'-), *n.,* opulence, *f.*

wealth'y (wèlth'-), *adj.,* riche, opulent.

wean (wîn), *v.a.,* sevrer ; (to alienate) (fig.) détacher **de,** aliéner **de,** priver **de.** Being —ed ; (of a child) *en sevrage.*

wean'ing, *n.,* sevrage, *m.*

wean'ling (wî'n'-), *n.,* (l.u.) enfant sevré ; animal sevré, *m.*

weap'on (wèp'p'n), *n.,* arme, défense, *f.*

weap'onless, *adj.,* sans armes, désarmé.

wear (wère), *n.,* (act of wearing) user, usage, *m. ;* (clothing) mode, *f. ;* (of money) frai, *m. ;* (waste by wearing) usure, *f.,* dépérissement, *m.* Of good — ; *d'un bon user.* The worse for —; *usé, ne servant plus, inutile ; de rebut.* — and tear ; *usure, détérioration, f. ; frais d'entretien, m.pl.* To have in — ; *porter.*

wear *ou* **weir** (wère), *n.,* barrage ; déversoir, *m. ;* (for fish) nasse, *f.*

wear (wère), *v.a.,* (preterit, Wore ; past part., Worn) (clothes) porter, avoir ; (to put on) mettre ; (to use by wear) user ; (to tire) lasser, fatiguer, harasser ; (to consume) consumer ; (nav.) faire virer. To — away ; *user ; consumer ;* (to deface) *effacer.* To — out ; *miner, épuiser ;* (time) *passer péniblement ;* (to tire) *lasser, harasser ;* (clothes) *user.* He —s my patience out ; *il m'impatiente, il lasse ma patience.* To — oneself into ; *se plier* **à.**

wear, *v.n.,* s'user ; se consumer. To — away, off ; *s'user, dépérir ; se consumer ; perdre ses forces ;* (to get effaced) *s'effacer ;* (of time) *se passer, s'écouler, se dissiper.* To — out ; *s'user.* Not to — out ; *être inusable.* To — well ; *être d'un bon user ;* (pers.) *ne pas vieillir ; porter bien son âge ; se conserver.* To — badly ; (of things) *n'être pas d'un bon user.* To — off ; *s'effacer, disparaître.*

wear'able (wèr-a-b'l), *adj.,* portable, mettable.

wear'er, *n.,* personne qui porte, *f.* Were I the — of … ; *si j'avais, ou je portais …*

wear'ied (wî-ride), *adj.,* fatigué ; ennuyé, las.

wear'ily (wî-), *adv.,* d'une manière fatigante, ennuyeusement.

wear'iness (wî-), *n.,* fatigue, lassitude, *f. ;* ennui, *m.*

wear'isome (wî-), *adj.,* ennuyeux ; fatigant ; fastidieux, lassant.

wear'isomely (wî-), *adv.,* ennuyeusement ; fastidieusement.

wear'isomeness (wî-), *n.,* nature fatigante, nature ennuyeuse, *f. ;* ennui, *m.*

wear'y (wî-ri), *v.a.,* lasser, ennuyer, fatiguer. To — out ; *harasser, excéder, exténuer.*

wear'y (wî-), *adj.,* las, ennuyé, fatigué ; (of things) fatigant, ennuyeux.

wea'sand (wî-z'n'de), *n.,* trachée-artère, *f.*

wea'sel (wî-z'l), *n.,* (zoöl.) belette, *f.*

weath'er (wèth'-), *n.,* temps ; (nav.) vent, côté du vent, *m. ;* (storm) tempête, *f.* It is fine — ; *il fait beau temps, il fait beau.* In fine — ; *quand le temps est beau ; quand il fait beau, ou beau temps.* In such — ; *par le temps qu'il fait.* In this — ; *par un temps pareil.* In all —s ; *par tous les temps.* In such, *ou* this, cold — ; *par le froid qu'il fait.* In such hot —, *ou* in this heat ; *par la chaleur qu'il fait.* In very cold — ; *dans les grands froids.* In very hot — ; *dans les grandes chaleurs.* It is beautiful, delightful — ; *il fait un temps superbe, charmant.* It is cloudy, rainy — ; *il fait un temps couvert, pluvieux.* Foggy — ; *temps de brouillard.* In rainy — ; *dans les temps de pluie.* What — is it ; *quel temps fait-il !* Stormy — ; *temps d'orage ;* (nav.) *gros temps.* — permitting ; *si le temps le permet.* In stress of — ; *dans les gros temps ; en cas de détresse.*

weath'er (wèth'-), *v.a.,* (a tempest) résister **à** ; lutter **contre** ; tenir tête **à** ; surmonter ; (a cape) doubler ; (nav.) gagner le vent **de,** *ou* passer au vent **de.** To — out ; (fig.) *lutter, tenir ferme jusqu'au bout.*

weath'er-beaten (-bît'n), *adj.,* battu par l'orage, par la tempête ; exténué, usé, épuisé.

weath'er-board, n., auvent, larmier, (nav.) bardis ou bardi, m.

weath'er-boarding (-bôrd'-), n., plancher pour abriter des maisons en construction; (nav.) bordage supplémentaire, m.

weath'er-bound (-baou'n'de), adj., arrêté, ou retenu, par le mauvais temps.

weath'er-cock, n., girouette, f.

weath'er-driven (-driv'n), adj., chassé par la tempête.

weath'er-eye, n. To keep one's — open; (fig.) être sur ses gardes; avoir l'œil au guet; ne pas perdre la tête.

weath'er-gauge (-ghédje), n., (nav.) avantage du vent, m. To get the —; prendre le dessus du vent.

weath'er-glass (-glâce), n., baromètre, m.

weath'er-hardened, adj., endurci aux mauvais temps.

weath'ering (wèth'eur'-), n., (geol.) action des éléments sur, f.

weath'er-most (-môste), adj., (nav.) le plus au vent.

weath'er-out (-aoute), v.a., tenir tête à; sortir sain et sauf, ou vainqueur de, (fig.) surmonter.

weath'er-proof (-proufe) adj., à l'épreuve du temps, de la tempête.

weath'er-quar'ter, n., côté du vent, m.

weath'er-report', n., bulletin météorologique, m.

weath'er-shore, terre au vent, f.

weath'er-side, n., (nav.) côté du vent, m.

weath'er-wise (-waîze), adj., qui prévoit le temps.

weath'er-worn, adj., usé par la tempête (V. Hugo); ou usé par les intempéries des saisons.

weave (wîve), v.a., (preterit, Wove; past part., Woven) tisser, faire au métier; tresser, entrelacer; (fig.) entremêler, unir, mêler (à ou avec).

weav'er (wîv'-), n., tisserand, m.

weav'ing (wîv'-), n., tissage, m.

weaz'ened (wîz'-), adj., ratatiné, ridé; maigre, décharné.

web (wèbe), n., tissu, m.; (for girths) sangle, f.; (fig.) tissu, enchaînement, m.; (in the eye) taie; (of water-fowls) membrane palmaire; (of a spider) toile; (of a feather) barbe, f.; (of a coulter) tranchant, m.

webbed (wèb'de), **web'by,** adj., palmé.

web'bing, n., tissu, m.; (of a chair, bed, etc.) sangle, f.

web'-cloth, n., tissu, ou tricot, palmé, m.

web'-footed (-fout'-), adj., palmipède, aux pieds palmés.

wed (wède), v.a., épouser; se marier avec; (fig.) unir, attacher, marier (à ou avec).

wed, v.n., se marier.

wed'ded, adj., marié à; (of love) conjugal, légitime; (fig.) fortement attaché à; entaché de.

wed'ding, n., noce, f.; noces, f.pl.; mariage, m. adj., de noce, de noces, de mariage. — breakfast; déjeuner de noce. — day; jour de mariage, m. On his — day; le jour de son mariage. — dress; robe de noce, f. — favors; faveurs, f.pl. — guests; invités de la noce, m.pl. — party; noce, f. — presents; cadeaux de noce, m.pl.; corbeille de mariage, f. — ring; alliance, f.; anneau nuptial, m. — tour; voyage de noces, m.

wedge (wèdje), n., coin; (metal.) lingot; (masonry) louveteau, m. The thin end of the —; (fig.) le premier pas; un pied de pris; le commencement.

wedge, v.a., serrer pour un coin; caler, fixer au moyen de coins; forcer; fendre. To — in; pousser, faire entrer; intercaler, insérer; caler, assujettir; serrer, presser. We were —d in the crowd; la foule nous serrait de tous côtés. To be —d in between; (of property, estates) être enclavé, ou resserré, entre.

wedge'-shaped (-shépte), adj., en forme de coin; (anat., bot.) cunéiforme.

wed'lock, n., mariage, hymen, m. Born in —; légitime. Born out of —; né hors mariage.

Wednes'day (wè'n'z'-), n., mercredi, m. Ash- —; mercredi des cendres.

wee (wî), adj., petit, tout petit, mignon. A — bit, a — mite; (pop.) un petit peu. A — drop; (pop.) un petit verre; un doigt; une goutte.

weed (wîde), n., mauvaise herbe, f.; (pop.) cigare, m. Widow's —s; vêtements de deuil, m.pl.

weed (wîde), v.a., sarcler; arracher les mauvaises herbes de; (fig.) purifier, nettoyer, extirper, purger, épurer. To — out; extirper, déraciner, enlever; débarrasser de.

weed'er (wîd'-), n., sarcleur; (fig.) destructeur, extirpateur, m.; (tool) sarcloir, m.

weed'-hook (-houke), **-fork,** n., sarcloir, m.

weed'ing, n., sarclage, m.; (fig.) épuration, f.; triage, m.

weed'y (wîd'-), adj., plein de mauvaises herbes.

week (wîke), n., semaine, f. This day —; (future) d'aujourd'hui en huit; (past) il y a aujourd'hui huit jours. A — ago, ou back; il y a huit jours. Yesterday —; il y a eu hier huit jours. Every —; tous les huit jours, toutes les semaines. In a —; (future) dans huit jours. In the course of the —; dans la huitaine. Passion —; la semaine de la Passion. Holy —; la semaine sainte. In a — of Sundays (i.e. never); la semaine des trois (quatre) jeudis.

week'-day, n., jour ouvrable, jour ouvrier, m.

week'ly (wîk'-), adv., toutes les semaines, chaque semaine; tous les huit jours.

week'ly, adj., de chaque semaine; (of newspapers) hebdomadaire.

ween (wî'n), v.n., (poet.) penser, croire, estimer, imaginer.

weep (wîpe), v.n., (preterit and past part., Wept) pleurer, verser des larmes; gémir, se plaindre. To — for; pleurer. To — bitterly; pleurer à chaudes larmes, pleurer amèrement.

weep, v.a., pleurer, pleurer sur; (tears) verser, répandre des larmes. To — for joy; pleurer de joie.

weep'er (wîp'-), n., pleureur, m., pleureuse; (band of cambric) pleureuse, f.

weep'ing (wîp'-), n., pleurs, m.pl.; larmes, f.pl.

weep'ing, adj., qui pleure, éploré; (bot.) pleureur. — willow; saule pleureur, m.

weep'ingly, adv., en pleurant.

wee'ver (wî-veur), n., (ich.) vive, f.

wee'vil (wî-), n., (ent.) calandre, f.; charançon, m.

wee'viled, adj., charançonné.

weft (wèfte), n., trame, f.; tissu, m.

weigh (wê), v.a., peser; (fig.) examiner, juger, peser, balancer; bien considérer; (anchor) lever. To — down; peser plus que; affaisser; (to oppress) surcharger, accabler; (fig.) l'emporter sur, surpasser. —ed down with age; accablé de vieillesse. To — out; peser en petites quantités.

weigh, v.n., peser, avoir un poids de; avoir du poids, avoir de la valeur; (nav.) lever l'ancre. To — upon; peser sur; être à charge à. To — with; avoir du poids aux yeux de. To — down; s'affaisser, s'abaisser; (of scales) pencher. To — against; (fig.) l'emporter sur.

weigh'able (wê-a-b'l), adj., pesable.

weigh'age (wê-èdje), n., pesage, m.

weigh'-bridge, n., pont à bascule, m.

weigh'er (wê-eur), n., peseur, m., peseuse, f.

weigh'ing (wê-igne), n., pesage, m.; pesée, f.

weigh'ing-machine (-ma-shîne), *n.*, bascule, *f.*

weigh'ing-room, *n.*, (at races) enceinte du pesage, *f.*

weight (wè-te), *n.*, poids, *m.;* pesanteur; (fig.) importance, valeur, *f.;* poids, *m.* By —; *au poids.* Of —; *de poids; important, grave, sérieux.* Gross —; (com.) *poids brut.* Net —; *poids net.* For its — in gold; *au poids de l'or.* To be worth one's — in gold; *valoir son pesant d'or.*

weight'ily (wêt'-), *adv.*, pesamment, lourdement; gravement; fortement; avec poids.

weight'iness (wêt'-), *n.*, poids, *m.;* pesanteur; importance, valeur, gravité, force, *f.*

weight'y *adj.*, pesant, lourd, de poids; (fig.) fort, solide, (important) important, grave, sérieux. — reasons; *des raisons puissantes.*

weir (wère), *n.*, barrage, déversoir, *m.*

weird, *adj.*, fantastique, étrange; sombre; magique; charmant; surnaturel. The — sisters; *les Parques, f.pl.*

weird'ness, *n.*, étrangeté, magie, *f.;* charme fascinateur, *m.*

wel'come (wèl-keume), *n.*, bienvenue; gracieuse réception, *f.;* bon accueil, *m.* To bid (any one) — ; *souhaiter la bienvenue à.* To give a good, a hearty — to; *faire un accueil cordial à.* We met with a poor —; *on nous fit un triste accueil, une triste réception.*

wel'come (wèl-keume), *adj.*, bienvenu; bien accueilli; bien reçu; (of things) agréable, acceptable, heureux, bon, bien reçu. To be a — guest everywhere; *être le bienvenu partout.* Do it and —! *à vous permis; que rien ne vous empêche; vous êtes parfaitement le maître de* ... To be — to do (anything); *être libre de.* You are — to it; *c'est bien à votre service.* It is very —; *c'est très acceptable, ce n'est pas de refus.* — news; *des nouvelles agréables.*

wel'come! *int.*, soyez le bienvenu.

wel'come (wèl-keume), *v.a.*, souhaiter la bienvenue à; bien accueillir; faire bon accueil à; recevoir très bien, fêter.

wel'comer, *n.*, personne qui fait bon accueil, *f.*

weld (wèlde), *v.a.*, joindre, incorporer; unir; (metal) souder; (fig.) amalgamer.

weld. *n.*, (bot.) gaude, *f.*

weld'ing, *n.*, soudure, *f.*

wel'fare (wèl-fère), *n.*, bien-être, bonheur, bien, *m.;* prospérité, *f.*

wel'kin (wèl-k'i'n), *n.*, (poet.) ciel, *m.;* voûte céleste, *f.;* régions de l'air. *f.pl.*

well, *n.*, puits, *m.;* fontaine, *f.;* réservoir d'eau; (of a fishing-boat) réservoir, *m.;* (fig.) source, *f.;* (of a carriage) coffre, *m.;* (of a boat) sentine, *f.* Draining —; *puisard, m.*

well, *adj.*, en bonne santé; (fortunate) bien, bon, heureux; (advantageous) utile, profitable; (cured) rétabli, remis, guéri; (in favor) en faveur. — off; *bien dans ses affaires; dans une bonne position; heureux; à l'aise.* To be —; (in health) *se porter bien, être bien portant, être en bonne santé, être bien.* To be very —; *aller très bien; se porter à ravir.* All is — that ends —; *la fin couronne l'œuvre; tout est bien, qui finit bien.* To be — with; *être en bons termes avec, ou en faveur auprès de.* To be — to do; *être à son aise, avoir de la fortune.* To get —; *se rétablir, se remettre.* To make — again; *guérir, rétablir.* To get — to do; *réussir; faire sa fortune,* (fam.) *faire ses foins.* That is all very —; *tout cela est bel et bon.* — I never; *pas possible! —; eh bien, quoi! eh bien, après! dame! ma foi! enfin! mais.* To be — enough off; *n'avoir pas à se plaindre.*

well, *adv.*, bien; très; fort; comme il faut. — and good, *à la bonne heure.* — nigh; *presque.* As — as; *aussi bien que.* To speak — of; *dire du bien de, parler favorablement de.* To wish

one —; *souhaiter du bien à quelqu'un.* Let — alone; *le mieux est l'ennemi du bien.* — done is half done; (prov.) *a moitié fait qui commence bien.* I cannot — ...; *il ne m'est guère possible de* ...; *je ne puis guère* ... We might as — be ...; *autant vaudrait être* ...; *autant vaudrait que nous fussions* ... You might as — say ...; *autant vaudrait dire* ...

well, *v.a.*, jaillir (de, out of).

well'aday! *int.*, hélas!

well'-appointed, *adj.*, bien équippé; (fam.) chic.

well'-balanced, *adj.*, bien équilibré.

well'being (-bî-igne), *n.*, bien-être, bonheur, *m.;* prospérité, *f.*

well'-born, *adj.*, de naissance, bien né, qui a de la naissance; (of a horse) qui a de la race.

well'-bred, *adj.*, poli, bien élevé.

well'-conducted, *adj.*, (pers.) sage, qui se conduit bien; (of things) bien mené, bien conduit, bien dirigé.

well'-doer (-dou'eur), *n.*, personne qui fait le bien, *f.*, bienfaiteur, *m.*

well'-doing (-dou-igne), *n.*, bienfaisance, *f.;* accomplissement de ses devoirs, *m.*

well'-done! *int.*, bien fait! fort bien! (of meat) bien cuit.

well'-drain, *n.*, puits d'écoulement, *m.*

well'-drilled, *adj.*, bien exercé.

well'-favored (-fé-veurde), *adj.*, beau, bien fait.

well'-founded, *adj.*, bien fondé.

well'-grounded, *adj.*, (of fears, etc.) bien fondé; (of language) possédant bien les principes.

well'-informed (-i'n'form'de), *adj.*, instruit, très instruit; (of facts) bien informé, bien renseigné.

well'-knit, *adj.*, compact; bien fait; solide; bien proportionné.

well'-mannered (-man'neurde), *adj.*, de bon ton, de bonnes manières, poli, bien élevé.

well'-meaning (-mî'n'-), *adj.*, bien intentionné; honnête.

well'-meant (-mè'n'te), *adj.*, fait à bonne intention.

well'-met! (-mète), *int.*, heureuse rencontre! To be hail-fellow — with everybody; *traiter tout le monde de pair à compagnon.*

well'-minded (-maï'n'dède), *adj.*, bien disposé.

well'-read (-rède), *adj.*, instruit, qui a beaucoup lu.

well'-room, *n.*, (nav.) sentine, *f.*

wells, *n.pl.*, eaux minérales, *f.pl.*

well'-sinker, *n.*, puisatier, *m.*

well'-sized, *adj.*, de grande dimension.

well'-spent, *adj.*, bien employé.

well'-spoken (-spôk'n), *adj.*, (pers.) qui parle bien, beau parleur; (of things) bien dit, bien tourné.

well'-spring, *n.*, source, *f.*

well'-taught, *adj.*, instruit; bien enseigné.

well'-timed (-taï'm'de), *adj.*, à propos; fait à propos.

well'-to-do, *adj.*, à son aise.

well'-tried (-traïde), *adj.*, à toute épreuve; à l'épreuve.

well'-wisher, *n.*, ami, *m.*, amie, *f.;* protecteur, *m.*, protectrice; personne qui souhaite, *ou* veut, du bien à, *f.;* partisan, *m.*

well'-worn, *adj.*, usé; vieux.

Welsh (wèltshe), *adj.*, gallois; du pays de Galles. —man; *Gallois, m.* —woman; *Galloise, f.*

Welsh, *n.*, gallois (language), *m.*

welsh'-rabbit *ou* **-rarebit**, *n.*, rôtie au fromage, *f.*

welt, *n.*, bord, *m.*, bordure, bande; (of leather) trépointe, *f.*

welt, *v.a.*, border, garnir.

welt′er, *v.n.*, se vautrer, se rouler **dans**; nager, être baigné, noyé **dans**. —ing in his blood; *baigné*, ou *noyé*, **dans** *son sang*.

wen (wè′ne), *n.*, (med.) tumeur enkystée, loupe, *f.*; (on the neck) goître, *m.*

wench, *n.*, fille; donzelle; (dirty) souillon, *f.*

wend, *v.n.* and *a.*, aller; aller et venir. To — one′s way; *poursuivre son chemin; se diriger* **vers**; *diriger sa course* **vers**.

were′wolf (wīr′-), *n.*, loup garou, *m.*

west (wèste), *n.*, ouest, occident, couchant, *m.*

west, *adj.*, occidental, d′ouest, de l′ouest. — wind; *vent d′ouest*, *m.*

west, *adv.*, à l′occident, à l′ouest.

west′erly (-′eur-) *ou* **west′ern** (-′eur′n), *adj.*, occidental; d′ouest; de l′ouest.

west′erly, *adv.*, vers l′occident, vers l′ouest, à l′ouest.

west′ern, *adj.*, occidental, d′ouest, de l′ouest, d′Occident; (of aspect) à l′ouest. The — Church; *l′Eglise d′Occident, l′Eglise romaine*, *f.* The — islands; *les Antilles*, *f.pl.* Great — Railway; *Chemin de fer de l′Ouest*, *m.*

west′ward, *adv.*, à l′ouest; **vers**, *ou* à, l′occident.

west′wardly, *adv.*, en se dirigeant vers l′ouest.

wet, *n.*, humidité, *f.*; (weather) temps pluvieux, *m.*, pluie, *f.* Do not stay out in the —; *ne vous exposez pas à la pluie.*

wet, *adj.*, mouillé; humide; (of the weather) pluvieux, humide; (of the hands) moite. — through, *ou* dripping —; *mouillé jusqu′aux os;* (fam.) *trempé comme une soupe; trempé.* It is —; *il fait mauvais temps, il pleut.* — dock; *bassin à flot*, *m.* — paint; *peinture fraîche*, *f.*

wet, *v.a.*, mouiller; tremper; humecter; arroser; (print.) tremper. To — one′s whistle; *s′humecter le gosier.*

weth′er (wèth′-), *n.*, mouton, *m.*

wet′ness, *n.*, humidité, *f.*; état pluvieux, *m.*

wet′-nurse (-neurse), *n.*, nourrice, *f.*

wet′ting, *n.*, trempée, *f.*; (print.) trempage, *m.* —board; *ais*, *m.* —room; (print.) *tremperie*, *f.* —trough; (print.) *baquet à tremper*, *m.*

wet′tish, *adj.*, un peu humide, moite.

whack, *n.*, grand coup, *m.*; taloche, *f.*

whale (hwéle), *n.*, baleine, *f.* —fin; *fanon de baleine*, *m.* —fishery; *pêche de la baleine*, *f.* —louse; (ent.) *cyame, pou de baleine*, *m.* — tribe; *cétacés*, *m.pl.*

whale′-boat, *n.*, baleinière, *f.*

whale′bone, *n.*, (com.) baleine, *f.*

whale′man, *n.*, baleinier, pêcheur de baleine, *m.*

whale′-oil, *n.*, huile de baleine, *f.*

whal′er (hwél′eure), *n.*, baleinier; navire baleinier; (man) baleinier, pêcheur de baleine, *m.*

whap, *n.*, coup fort; horion, *m.*

whap′per, *n.*, chose immense; masse; (lie) bourde, *f.* That′s a —; *en voilà une forte, par exemple.*

whap′ping, *n.*, raclée.

whap′ping, *adj.*, énorme, fier; (of lies) fameux.

wharf (hworfe), *n.*, (wharfs ou wharves) quai, embarcadère, débarcadère (de rivière); (for goods) entrepôt, *m.*

wharf (hworfe), *v.a.*, munir d′un quai.

wharf′age (-′édje), *n.*, quayage; droit de quai, *m.*

wharf′inger (-′in′djeure), *n.*, propriétaire de quai; gardien de quai, *m.*

what, *relative pron.*, (as subject) ce qui, quoi; (interrogatively) qu′est-ce qui; (as object) ce que, quoi, que; (interrogatively) qu′est-ce que, que, quoi; (whatever) quoi que ce soit, (that of which) ce dont (genitive); ce à quoi

(dative). — it is; *ce que c′est.* To know — ′s —; *connaître les couleurs, en savoir long; ne pas se moucher du pied.* — not; (after an enumeration) *et cætera.* Mr. —′s-his-name; *Monsieur Chose;* (fam.) *machin.* — little there was of novelty; *le peu qu′il y avait de nouveau.* Why then, I tell you —; *eh bien! je vais vous dire.* — then? *et après?* — not; *et le reste; et tout ce qui s′ensuit!* — with exile, poverty; *sans compter l′exil, la pauvreté.* I will tell you —; *je vous dirai ce que c′est.* Give me — I want; *donnez-moi ce dont j′ai besoin, ou ce qu′il me faut.* — of that? *qu′est-ce que cela fait?* — do you take me for? *pour qui me prenez-vous?* For —? *pourquoi? pourquoi faire?* That′s — it is; *voilà ce que c′est.* — I like best; *ce que j′aime le mieux.* —! can you not? *quoi! ou comment! ne le pouvez-vous pas?* — though it were so? *hé bien quoi! quand même cela serait?* — is done cannot be undone; (prov.) *à chose faite, point de remède.* —′s one man′s meat is another man′s poison; *ce qui nuit à l′un sert à l′autre.*

what, *adj. pron.*, quel, *m.sing.*, quelle, *f.sing.*; (exc.) que de, combien de. — ... soever; *quelque ... que ; quelque ... que ce soit.* — manner of man was ...; *quel homme c′était que ...* (V. Hugo). — a to-do! *quelle affaire!*

whatev′er (-′èv′-), *pron.*, quoi que ce soit; quelque ... que; quelque; (all that) tout ce qui; (as object) tout ce que. Of no use —; *absolument inutile.* — renders human nature amiable; *tout ce qui rend la nature humaine aimable.* He had no part — in it; *il n′y prit aucune part.* — you do, do it well; *quoi que vous fassiez, faites-le bien.* — restraints are laid; *quelques entraves que l′on impose.* — they are; *quels qu′ils soient.*

what′not, *n.*, étagère, *f.*

wheat (hwîte), *n.*, froment; blé, *m.*

wheat′-ear (-′îre), *n.*, (orni.) motteux, culblanc, *m.*

wheat′en (hwît′n), *adj.*, de froment, de blé.

wheat′-grass (-grâce), *n.*, (bot.) chiendent, *m.*

wheat′-worm (-weurme), *n.*, cécidomye, *m.*

whee′dle (hwîd′d′l), *v.a.*, cajoler; flagorner; enjôler; amadouer; câliner. To — one out of some money; *soutirer* (fam. *carotter*) *de l′argent à quelqu′un.*

whee′dler, *n.*, cajoleur, flagorneur, enjôleur, câlin, *m.*

whee′dling, *n.*, cajolerie, flagornerie, câlinerie, *f.* *adj.*, cajoleur, câlin.

wheel (hwîle), *n.*, roue, *f.*; (circular body) corps rond, *m.*; (nav.) barre; (torture) roue, *f.*; (for spinning) rouet, filoir, *m.*; (revolution) révolution, *f.*; (turning about) tour, cercle, *m.*; (of an umbrella) noix, *f.*; (fireworks) soleil, *m.* Cog —; *roue du gouvernail, roue dentée*, *f.* Fly —; *volant*, *m.* Driving —; *roue motrice*, *f.* — and axle; *treuil*, *m.* — of fortune; *roue de la fortune*, *f.* — of life; *zootrope*, *m.* To go as upon —s; *aller comme sur des roulettes; aller bon train.* To break upon the —; *rompre sur la roue.* To put one′s shoulder to the —; *pousser à la roue.* To break a fly on the —; *tirer sa poudre aux moineaux.* —s within —s; *des complications sans fin*, *f.pl.*; *un imbroglio où l′on ne pas s′y reconnaître.* The man at the —; (fig.) *l′homme à la tête des affaires.* The — went over his body; *la voiture lui passa sur le corps.* To lock the —; *enrayer; mettre le sabot à.*

wheel (hwîlc), *v.a.*, rouler; faire tourner; (in a barrow) brouetter; (to convey) voiturer, transporter, conduire, mener; (to provide with a wheel) mettre une roue à.

wheel, *v.n.*, rouler sur des roues; (to move round) tourner, se tourner; (of things) tourner, se mouvoir en rond; (to roll forward) s′avancer en roulant; (milit.) faire une conversion. To —

about ; *tourner ; faire une pirouette ;* (milit.) *faire une conversion ; faire demi-tour ; faire volte-face ;* (a child, etc.) *promener en petite voiture.*

wheel'-animalcules, *n.pl.,* rotifères, *m.pl.*

wheel'barrow (-bar'rô), *n.,* brouette, *f.*

wheel'-carriage, *n.,* voiture à roues, *f.*

wheel'-chair, *n.,* chaise roulante, *f.*

wheeled (hwîl'de), *adj.,* à roues. Four-— carriage ; *voiture à quatre roues, f.*

wheel'er (hwîl'-), *n.,* rouleur, *m. ;* (horse) cheval de brancard, brancardier, limonier, timonier, *m.* Four-— ; *flacre, m. ; voiture à quatre roues, f.*

wheel'ing, *n.,* transport sur roue ; roulage, *m. ;* (milit.) conversion, *f.*

wheel'-race (-réce), *n.,* (tech.) voie de la roue, *f.*

wheel'-shaped (-shép'te), *adj.,* en forme de roue ; (bot.) rotacé.

wheel'-work (-weurke), *n.sing.,* rouages, *m.pl. ;* charronnage, *m.*

wheel'-wright (-raïte), *n.,* charron, *m.*

wheeze (hwîze), *v.n.,* siffler en respirant, respirer avec bruit ; être asthmatique.

wheez'ing (hwîz'-), *n.,* sifflement, *m.,* respiration sifflante, *f.*

wheez'y, *adj.,* poussif.

whelk (hwèlke), *n.,* (conch.) buccin ; pou de roque, *m.* (V. Hugo).

whelm (hwèlme), *v.a.,* submerger ; (fig.) ensevelir, accabler, renverser, engloutir.

whelp (hwèlpe), *v.n.,* (of dogs, etc.) chienner ; faire ses petits ; mettre bas.

whelp, *n.,* petit ; (bear) ourson ; (lion) lionceau ; (wolf) louveteau ; (nav.) taquet, *m.*

when (hwè'ne), *adv.,* quand, lorsque, au moment où ; que, où ; (= then) alors. (Implying *futurity* it always takes the *future* in French :) — I come ; *quand je viendrai.* — you are ; *quand vous serez.* The — ; (since then) *depuis ce temps-là.* The day — I saw him ; *le jour où je l'ai vu.* At that age — ; *à cette époque de la vie* **où.** — dining ; *quand on dîne.* — visiting ; *quand on est en visite* **chez.** One day — ; *un jour* **que,** ou **où.** — in doubt, do nothing ; (prov.) *dans le doute abstiens-toi.* — Greek meets Greek then comes the tug of war ; (prov.) *fin contre fin, gare la bombe.* — thieves fall out, honest men get to their own ; *quand les voleurs se battent, les larcins se découvrent.* — the world was young ; *du temps que Berthe filait.*

whence, *adv.,* d'où ; de là.

whencesoev'er (hwè'n'ce-sô-èv'-), *adv.,* de quelque lieu, côté, endroit, part, que ce soit ; quelle qu'en soit la cause, l'origine.

whenev'er (-èv'-) *ou* **whensoev'er** (-sô-èv'-), *adv.,* toutes les fois que, quand ; dans quelque temps que ; dès que, sitôt que, à n'importe quel moment que.

where (hwère), *adv.,* où. Any-— ; *dans quelque endroit que ce soit ; n'importe où.* Not any-— ; *nulle part.* Every-— ; *partout.* Some-— ; *quelque part.* Else-— ; *ailleurs.*

where'about (-'abaoute) *ou* **where'abouts** (-'abaoutse), *adv.,* où ; à peu près ; (concerning which) au sujet de quoi.

where'abouts, *n.pl.,* demeure, *f.,* logis, *m.* To know the — of some one ; *savoir où quelqu'un est* (ou *était*) ou *se trouve, se trouvait.*

whereas' (-'aze), *adv.,* au lieu que ; tandis que ; (considering) vu que ; (jur.) considérant que, attendu que.

whereat', *adv.,* à quoi, de quoi, dont ; sur quoi ; là-dessus. — are you offended ? *de quoi vous offensez-vous?* — he left abruptly ; *sur quoi il partit subitement.*

whereby' (-baïe), *adv.,* par lequel ; par où ; par quoi.

where'fore, *adv.,* pourquoi, c'est pourquoi ; donc. The whys and —s ; *les pourquoi, m.pl.*

wherein' (-'i'n), *adv.,* en quoi, dans quoi, dans lequel, où.

whereof' (-'ove), *adv.,* dont, de quoi, duquel.

whereon' (hwèr'o'ne), *adv.,* sur quoi, sur lequel ; là-dessus.

wheresoev'er. *V.* **wherever.**

whereto' (-tou), *adv.,* à quoi, auquel ; où.

whereupon' (-eup'o'ne), *adv.,* sur quoi ; sur lequel.

wherev'er (hwèr'èv'eure), *adv.,* partout où, n'importe où ; en quelque lieu que ce soit ; où que.

wherewith' (hwèr'withe) *ou* **wherewithal'** (-'with'ôl), *adv.,* avec quoi, avec lequel ; de quoi. To have not the —al to ; *n'avoir pas les moyens* **de,** ou *de quoi.* To find the —al ; *fournir les moyens* (**de**), ou *l'argent nécessaire.*

wher'ry (hwèr'-), *n.,* bateau, bac, *m.*

whet (hwète), *v.a.,* aiguiser ; affiler ; repasser ; affûter ; (fig.) aiguiser, exciter, irriter.

whet (hwète), *n.,* aiguisement ; repassage ; (stimulant) excitant, stimulant, *m.*

wheth'er (hwèth'eure), *conj.,* soit, soit que ; si, que. — or no ; *bon gré, mal gré.* — . . . or ; *soit . . . soit ; que ce soit . . . ou ; soit que . . . soit que ; si . . . ou ; que . . . ou.* — he does it or not ; *qu'il le fasse ou non.* The question is — . . . ; *la question est de savoir si . . .*

whet'stone (-stône), *n.,* pierre à aiguiser, *f.*

whet'ter (hwèt'-), *n.,* aiguiseur, *m. ;* (fig.) stimulant, aiguillon, *m.*

whet'ting, *n.,* aiguisement, *m.*

whey (hwê), *n.,* petit-lait, *m.*

whey'ish (hwê-ishe), *adj.,* qui tient du petit-lait, séreux.

which (hwitshe), *relative pron.,* qui, *m.f. ;* lequel, *m.sing.,* laquelle, *f.sing. ;* lesquels, *m.pl.,* lesquelles, *f.pl. ;* (object) que ; (that which) ce qui ; (object) ce que, *m.* Take — you will ; *prenez celui que vous voudrez.* — is — ; *lequel des deux est le bon, le vrai.* I cannot tell — is — ; *je ne saurais les distinguer l'un de l'autre ;* (of things) *je ne puis m'y reconnaître.* Of, from — ; *dont, m.f.sing., pl. ; duquel, m.sing., de laquelle, f.sing. ; desquels, m.pl., desquelles, f.pl.* To— ; *auquel, m.sing., à laquelle, f.sing. ; auxquels, m.pl., auxquelles, f.pl. ; à quoi.* In — ; *dans lequel ; où.*

which, *adj.,* quel, *m.sing.,* quelle, *f.sing. ;* quels, *m.pl.,* quelles, *f.pl. ;* lequel, *m.sing.,* laquelle, *f.sing. ;* lesquels, *m.pl.,* lesquelles, *f.pl.* With — words she hurried into the house ; *à ces mots* (ou *en disant cela,* ou *avec cela,*) *elle se hâta d'entrer dans la maison.*

whichev'er (-èv'-), *pron.,* lequel, *m.sing.,* laquelle, *f.sing. ;* lesquels, *m.pl.,* lesquelles, *f.pl. ;* quelque . . . que ; celui, *ou* celle que ; lequel que ce soit que. Take — road you please ; *prenez le chemin que vous voudrez.*

whichsoev'er. *V.* **whichev'er.**

whiff, *n.,* bouffée, haleine, *f. ;* souffle, *m. ;* (ich.) cardine, *f. V.* **puff.**

whiff, *v.a.,* lancer en bouffées.

whif'fle (hwif'f'l), *v.n.,* tourner à tous vents ; changer.

whif'fler, *n.,* girouette, *f.*

whif'fling, *n.,* prévarication, *f.,* détour, *m.*

Whig (hwig), *n.,* whig, *m.*

Whig'gery (-gheuri) *ou* **Whig'gism** (-ghiz'm), *n.,* whiggisme, *m. ;* opinion des whigs, *f.*

while (hwaïle), *n.,* temps, *m. ;* durée, *f. ;* moment, instant, *m.* The— ; *en attendant.* All this — ; *pendant ce temps-là ; pendant tout ce temps-là.* A little, a long — ago ; *il y a peu de temps, il y a longtemps.* For a — ; *pour un temps.* A little — ; *un moment ; quelques moments.* All the — ; *tout le temps.* Between —s ; *entre temps, par moments, par intervalles.* It is not worth — ; *cela n'en vaut pas la peine.* It is worth — to ; *cela vaut la peine* **de.**

while (hwaïle), *v.a.*, passer, faire passer. To — away the time ; *tuer le temps.*

while (hwaïle) *ou* **whilst** (hwaïlste), *adv.*, (during the time that) pendant que ; (implying contrast) tandis que ; en même temps que ; (as long as) tant que, aussi longtemps que ; (before a present participle) tout en. — walking up and down ; *tout en allant et venant.* — doing ; *tout en faisant.* — there 's life, there 's hope ; *qui a temps a vie.*

whil'om (hwaïl'eume), *adv.*, jadis.

whim (hwime), *n.*, caprice, *m.* ; fantaisie, lubie, *f.* ; (capstan) treuil, cabestan, *m.*

whim'brel, *n.*, (orni.) courlieu, petit courlis, *m.*

whim'per, *v.n.*, se plaindre, geindre, pleurnicher.

whim'pering, *n.*, plainte, *f.*, pleurnichement, *m.*

whim'sical (hwi'm'zi-), *adj.*, fantasque, capricieux, bizarre.

whim'sically (-zi-cal'-), *adv.*, capricieusement, fantasquement, bizarrement.

whim'sicalness *ou* **whimsical'ity** (-zi-cal'-), *n.*, caractère capricieux, *m.*, bizarrerie, *f.*

whin, *n.*, ajonc ; genêt épineux, *m.*

whin'-chat, *n.*, (orni.) tarier, *m.*

whine (hwaïne), *v.n.*, se plaindre, gémir, se lamenter, geindre, pleurnicher ; (of animals) se plaindre.

whine (hwaïne), *n.*, pleurnichement, gémissement, *m.* ; plainte mêlée de pleurs ; (of animals) plainte, *f.*

whin'er (hwaï'n'-), *n.*, pleurnicheur, *m.*

whin'ing (hwaï'n'-), *n.*, plaintes, lamentations, *f.pl.* ; gémissements, *m.pl.*

whin'ing, *adj.*, plaintif, lamentable, dolent.

whin'ingly, *adv.*, en pleurnichant, d'un ton plaintif, en gémissant.

whin'ny (hwi'n'-), *v.n.*, hennir.

whin'stone (-stône), *n.*, (min.) trapp, *m.*

whip, *v.a.*, fouetter ; (to flog) fouetter ; donner le fouet à ; (to take up) enlever ; (needlework) surjeter ; faire un surjet à ; (wheat, etc.) battre ; (fig.) fouetter, flageller, châtier, fustiger. To —; (a stream) *fouetter.* To — away, *ou* off ; *chasser à coups de fouet ;* (to take away) *enlever vivement.* To — down ; *faire descendre à coups de fouet ;* (to take down) *faire descendre vite.* To — in ; *faire entrer à coups de fouet ;* (to put in) *rentrer vite.* To — into ; *passer rapidement* **dans.** To — off ; *chasser à coups de fouet ;* (to take off) *ôter vite.* To — on ; *faire avancer à coups de fouet ;* (a garment) *passer vite.* To — out ; *faire sortir à coups de fouet.* To — out of ; *expulser* **de.** To — up ; *faire monter à coups de fouet ;* (to pick up) *ramasser vivement, grimper vivement, saisir ;* (to construct) *bâcler.*

whip, *v.n.*, courir bien vite. To — away ; *partir au plus vite, décamper.* How he —s along ! *comme il court !* To — down ; *descendre vivement.* To — into ; *entrer vivement* **dans.** To — off ; *partir au plus vite ; s'enfuir.* To — out ; *sortir promptement, s'esquiver.*

whip, *n.*, fouet ; (nav.) palan ; (Parliamentary) chef de file ; appel fait aux membres d'un parti, *m.* ; (for riding) cravache, *f.* To be a good —; *savoir bien conduire.* To be a bad — ; *ne pas savoir conduire* ou *conduire mal.* To give any one the—; *donner le fouet à quelqu'un.* To come — and spur ; *venir ventre à terre, à bride abattue.*

whip'-cord, *n.*, fouet, *m.*

whip'-graft (-grâfte), *v.a.*, greffer à l'anglaise.

whip'-grafting, *n.*, greffe anglaise, *f.*

whip'-hand, *n.*, dessus ; (advantage) dessus, avantage, *m.* To have the — ; *avoir barres* **sur ;** *tenir le haut bout.*

whip'-lash, *n.*, mèche de fouet, *f.*

whip'per, *n.*, fouetteur, *m.*

whip'per-in, *n.*, piqueur ; (leader) chef de file, *m.*

whip'per-snap'per, *n.*, petit homme méprisable, petit bout d'homme ; (fam.) cascaret, *m.*

whip'ping, *n.*, coups de fouet, *m.pl.* ; action de fouetter ; flagellation, *f.* ; fouet, *m.* ; fustigation, *f.* To give a good — to ; *donner le fouet* à ; *fouetter d'importance.*

whip'ping-post (-pôste), *n.*, poteau pour les condamnés à la fustigation, *m.*

whip'ping-top, *n.*, (toy) sabot, *m.*

whip'ple-tree (hwip'pl-trî), *n.*, palonnier, *m.*

whip'-poor-will, *n.*, (orn.) engoulevent, *m.*

whip'saw (-sô), *n.*, scie à scier de long, *f.*

whip'-shaped, *adj.*, en forme de fouet.

whip'-staff (-stâfe), *n.*, (nav.) manivelle, *f.*

whip'ster, *n.*, homme agile, actif, *m.*

whir (hweur), *v.n.*, tourner avec bruit ; (of partridges, etc.) bourrir.

whirl (hweurle), *v.a.*, faire tourner ; tourner rapidement. To — away ; *emporter rapidement.*

whirl (hweurle), *v.n.*, pirouetter ; tournoyer ; tourbillonner.

whirl (hweurle), *n.*, tournoiement ; tourbillonnement ; tourbillon, *m.* ; rotation, *f.* ; (bot.) verticille ; (rope-making) émerillon, *m.* ; (plaything) pirouette, *f.*

whirl'igig (hweurl'i-ghighe), *n.*, pirouette ; (fig.) vicissitude, *f.*, changement, *m.*

whirl'pool (-poule) *ou* **whirl'pit**, *n.*, tourbillon ; tournant d'eau, gouffre, *m.*

whirl'wind (hweurl'wi'n'de), *n.*, tourbillon ; cyclone ; siphon, *m.* ; trombe, *f.* To reap the —; *récolter la tempête.*

whir'ring (hweur'-), *n.*, bruit de roue ; (of pheasants, etc.) bourrissement, *m.*

whisk, *n.*, vergette, époussette, *f.* ; (cook.) fouet à blancs d'œufs, *m.*

whisk, *v.a.*, vergeter ; épousseter ; (cook.) fouetter ; (fig.) remuer, agiter, fouetter. To — away ; *enlever vivement, entraîner rapidement, faire disparaître.* To — off ; (to toss off : of drinks) *avaler d'un trait.* —ed eggs ; *œufs à la neige, m.pl.*

whisk, *v.n.*, passer rapidement.

whis'ker, *n.*, favori, *m.* ; (of animals) moustache, *f.*

whis'kered (hwisk'eurde), *adj.*, à favoris ; (of animals) à moustaches.

whis'kerless, *adj.*, sans favoris.

whis'ky, *n.*, whiskey, *m.* ; eau-de-vie de grains, *f.*

whis'per, *n.*, chuchotement, *m.* ; (rumor) rumeur, *f.* ; bruit qui court ; murmure, *m.* In a —; *tout bas ; à voix basse ;* (fig.) *à l'oreille.*

whis'per, *v.a.*, chuchoter ; dire à l'oreille ; murmurer ; couler, souffler ; dire tout bas ; parler bas **à.** To — remarks ; *faire des observations à voix basse.*

whis'per, *v.n.*, chuchoter, murmurer, parler bas.

whis'perer, *n.*, chuchoteur, *m.*

whis'pering, *n.*, chuchoterie, *f.* ; chuchotement ; murmure ; (fig.) bruit, *m.*, rumeur, *f.*

whis'pering-gal'lery, *n.*, galerie acoustique, *f.*

whis'peringly, *adv.*, en chuchotant, tout bas.

whist, *n.*, (game) whist, *m.* A rubber of —; *un robre ; une partie (liée) de whist.*

whist ! *int.*, chut ! silence !

whis'tle (hwis's'l), *n.*, sifflement ; coup de sifflet ; (of the wind) sifflement, bruissement ; (throat) gosier, bec ; (instrument) sifflet, *m.* To wet one's — ; *s'humecter le gosier.* Ready at his — to array themselves round him ; *prêts, au moindre signal de sa part, à se ranger sous ses étendards.*

whis'tle (hwis's'l), *v.a.*, (to a dog) siffler ; appeler en sifflant. To — after, *ou* for ; *siffler ;* (fig.) *courir après.* — for it ! *attendez-vous y !*

whis′tle, v.n., siffler; bruire. The wind —s through the forest; *le vent bruit à travers la forêt.*

whis′tle-fish, n., (ich.) mustelle, f.

whis′tler (hwis′s′l′eure), n., siffleur, m.

whis′tling (hwis′s′l′igne), n., sifflement, coup de sifflet, m.

whis′tling, adj., sifflant.

whit, n., iota, point, atome, brin, m. Every —; *de tout point; absolument.* To be every — as; *être à tous égards; être tout aussi.* — Monday; *lundi de la Pentecôte, m.* Not a —; *pas le moins du monde, nullement, pas du tout.*

white (hwaïte), n., blanc; (of an egg) blanc, m., albumine, f.; (of wood) aubier, m.

white (hwaïte), adj., blanc; (fig.) sans tache, pur. — with; *blanc de, pâle de; blême de.* To get —; *blanchir;* (fig.) pâlir, blêmir. As — as a sheet; *blanc comme un linge.*

white′-bait (-béte), n., blanchaille, f.

white′-beam-tree (-bî′m′trî), n., (bot.) alisier blanc, m.

white′-ear (-ïre), n., (orni.) motteux; culblanc, m.

white′-faced, adj., au visage pâle.

white′ feather, n. To show the —; *payer de lâcheté; se conduire en poltron.*

white′-foot (-foute), n., balzane, f.

white′-footed, adj., balzan.

white′ friar, n., carme, m.

white′-heart, n., (cherry) guigne blanche, f.

white′-heat, n., (phys., chem., metal.) chaleur blanche, incandescence, f. At —; *chauffé à blanc; incandescent.*

white′-horse-fish, n., (ich.) raie cendrée, f.

white′-lead (-lède), n.,(chem.) blanc de plomb, m.; céruse, f.

white′ lie, n., mensonge excusable, m.

white′-lime, n., blanc de chaux, m.

white′-livered (-liveur′de), adj., pâle, blême; poltron.

white′-meat (-mîte), n., laitage, m.; (poultry, etc.) viande blanche, f.

whit′en (hwaït′n), v.a., blanchir; (mas.) blanchir à la chaux, badigeonner.

whit′en, v.n., blanchir.

whit′ening, n., blanchiment; (the substance) blanc d'Espagne, m.

white′ness (hwaït′-), n., blancheur; pâleur, (fig.) pureté, f.

white′-smith, n., ferblantier, m.

white′-swelling (-swèl′-), n., tumeur blanche, f.

white′-tail (-téle), n., (orni.) motteux; culblanc, m.

white′-thorn (-thorne), n., aubépine, épine blanche, f.

white′-throat (-thrôte), n., (orni.) fauvette babillarde, ou grise, f.

white′wash (-woshe), n., lait ou blanc de chaux; (mas.) badigeon, m.; (pharm.) eau blanche, f.

white′wash (-woshe), v.a., blanchir à la chaux; (mas.) blanchir, badigeonner; (fig.) réhabiliter, disculper; (of debts) purger (de dettes); passer l'éponge **sur.**

white′washer, n., badigeonneur, blanchisseur à la colle, m.

white′washing, n., blanchiment, blanchissage, m.

whith′er (hwith′-), adv., où, de quel côté.

whith′ersoever (hwith′eur-sô-èv′-), adv., partout, n'importe où; à quelque endroit que ce soit.

whit′ing (hwaït′-), n., blanc d'Espagne; (ich.) merlan, m.

whit′ish (hwaït′-), adj., blanchâtre.

whit′ishness (hwaït′-), n., couleur blanshâtre, f.

whit′low (hwit′lô), n., panaris, mal d'aven-

ture, m. — -grass; *drave, f.* — -wort; *paronyque argentée, f.*

Whit′sun (hwit′seune), adj., de la Pentecôte.

Whit′sun′day, n., jour, ou dimanche, de la Pentecôte, m.

Whit′suntide (-taïde), n., Pentecôte, f.

whit′y-brown (hwaït-ti-braou′ne), adj., brun, brunâtre; pâle, (of paper) bulle; (of bread) bis-blanc.

whiz, v.a., siffler.

whiz, whiz′zing, n., sifflement, m.

who (hou), pron., qui. As — should say; *comme qui dirait.*

whoev′er (hou-èv′-), pron., quiconque; qui que ce soit; qui; celui qui; toute personne qui; qui que (followed by subjunc.). — he may be; *quel qu'il soit.* — you are; *qui que vous soyez.*

whole (hôle), adj., entier, tout; intact; complet; total; (sound) sain; bien portant; (not ground) en grains. — meal; *bisaille, f.* — morocco; (book-binding) maroquin plein, m. — calf; *veau plein, m.* A — year; *tout un an, un an entier.* A — hour; *une grande heure.* The — country; *le pays entier, tout le pays.* The — world; *le monde entier (tout le monde is everybody).* The — show; (pop.) *toute la boutique, tout le tremblement; tout le diable et son train.*

whole (hôle), n., tout; total, montant; ensemble, m.; totalité, f. The — of us; *nous tous.* On the —; *en somme; à tout prendre.*

whole′sale (hôl′séle), n., vente en gros, f.; commerce de gros, m., masse, f. adj., général. By —; *en gros;* (fig.) *en masse.*

whole′some (hôl′cume), adj., (salubrious) sain, salubre; (salutary) salutaire; (useful) utile; (pleasing) agréable; (fig.) salutaire, sain, moral.

whole′somely, adv., salubrement; sainement.

whole′someness, n., salubrité; (of food) nature salutaire; (salutariness) nature salutaire, utilité; (fig.) nature salutaire, moralité, pureté, f.

whol′ly (hôl′li), adv., entièrement; complètement; tout à fait; exclusivement.

whom (houme), pron., que; (indirect object and direct object, of persons only) qui; (of persons and things) lequel, m.sing., laquelle, f.sing., lesquels, m.pl., lesquelles, f.pl. Of —, from —; *de qui; dont; desquels; desquelles.*

whomsoev′er (-sô-èv′-), pron., qui que ce soit, quiconque, qui.

whoop (houpe), n., huée, f.; cri, m.; (orni.) huppe, f.

whoop (houpe), v.a.n., huer, crier.

whoop′ing (houp′-), n., huées, f.pl.; cris, m. pl.

whoop′ing-cough (-côfe), n., coqueluche, f.

whose (houze), pron., dont, de qui, m.f.sing. pl.; duquel, m.sing., de laquelle, f.sing.; desquelles, m.pl., desquelles, f.pl.; à qui, que. The man — house I see; *l'homme dont je vois la maison.* — house is this? **à qui** est cette maison? — work is this? **de qui** est cet ouvrage? The men — hatreds only ruin them; *les hommes* **que** *leurs haines ne font que perdre.*

whosoev′er (house-çô-èv′-), pron., de ou à qui que ce soit, n'importe à qui.

whosoev′er, pron. V. **whoever.**

why (hwaïe), adv., pourquoi. — not? *pourquoi pas?* — is it that? *comment se fait-il que?*

why, exc., eh bien, mais, c'est que, ma foi! — then! *eh bien!*

wick (wike), n., mèche, f. — holder; *lamperon, m.*

wick′ed (wik′ède), adj., méchant, pervers; criminel; (mischievous) méchant, malin. — thing; *méchanceté, f.* The —; *les méchants, m.pl.*

wick′edly (wik′èd′-), adv., méchamment; par méchanceté.

wick′edness (wik′èd-), n., méchanceté, perversité; immoralité; (mischievousness) méchanceté, malice, f.

wick'en-tree (wik'n-trî), *n.*, (bot.) sorbier des oiseaux, *m.*

wick'er (wik'eur), *n.*, osier, *m.* —work; *clayonnage, m.*

wick'er, *adj.*, d'osier, en osier; clissé.

wick'et (wik'ète), *n.*, guichet, *m.* ; (at cricket) barres, *f.pl.*

wide (waïde), *adj.*, large ; large **de** ; (having great extent) grand, ample, étendu ; immense ; (distant) éloigné. A table three feet —; *une table large de trois pieds ; une table de trois pieds de large, de largeur.* — of the mark; *loin du but.* The statement is — of the truth; *l'assertion est loin de la réalité,* ou *loin de la vérité.* To open —; *ouvrir tout grand ; ouvrir à deux battants* (V. Hugo); (the eyes) *écarquiller.*

wide (waïde), *adv.*, loin, au loin ; largement. Far and —; *au loin, de tous les côtés.*

wide'-awake, *adj.*, tout, *ou* bien, éveillé ; (fig.) sur ses gardes. — eyes ; *yeux tout grands ouverts.*

wide'-awake, *m.*, feutre à bords relevés, *m.*

wide'ly (waïd'-), *adv.*, au large ; au loin ; grandement, largement. — known ; *bien connu.*

wid'en (waïd'n), *v.a.*, élargir, étendre, agrandir.

wid'en, *v.n.*, s'élargir, s'étendre, s'agrandir.

wide'ness (waïd'-), *n.*, largeur ; grandeur ; étendue, *f.*

wid'ening (waïd'-), *n.*, élargissement, agrandissement, *m.*

wide'-spread *ou* **-spread'ing**, *adj.*, étendu, qui s'étend au loin ; général ; répandu ; vaste, immense.

widg'eon (widj'o'n), *n.*, (orni.) canard siffleur, *m.*, sarcelle, *f.*

wid'ow (widô'), *n.*, veuve, *f.* — hunter; *coureur de veuves, m.*

wid'ow (widô'), *v.a.*, rendre veuve, *ou* veuf.

wid'owed (widô'd), *adj.*, veuf **de** ; privé **de**. — of his hopes; *veuf de ses espérances* (Hégésippe Moreau).

wid'ower (widô-eur), *n.*, veuf, *m.*

wid'owhood (widô-houde), *n.*, veuvage, *m.*

width, *n.*, largeur, grandeur, étendue, *f.*

wield (wîl'de), *v.a.*, manier ; tenir ; porter.

wield'able, *adj.*, maniable.

wield'er, *n.*, celui qui manie.

wife (waïfe), *n.*, femme, épouse, *f.* To take a —; *prendre femme, se marier.* "The merry wives of Windsor"; *les joyeuses commères de Windsor* (Shakespeare).

wife'less (waïf'-), *adj.*, sans femme, sans épouse, non marié.

wife'ly, wife'-like (waïf'-), *adj.*, de femme, d'épouse, conjugal.

wig, *n.*, perruque, *f.*

wig'-block, *n.*, tête à perruque, *f.*

wigged, *adj.*, à perruque, portant perruque.

wig'ging, *n.*, savon, *m.* To give a —; (fam.) *donner un savon à ; laver la tête à.*

wight (waïte), *n.*, personne, *f.*, être, personnage, individu, *m.* The poor little —; *le pauvre petit,* ou *gosse* (Daudet).

wig'-maker, *n.*, perruquier, *m.*

wig'wam (wig-wŏ'me), *n.*, (among Red Indians) cahute, chaumière, hutte, *f.*

wild (waïlde), *n.*, désert ; lieu sauvage, *m.*; solitude, *f.*

wild (waïlde), *adj.*, sauvage ; (desert) sauvage, inculte ; (not civilized) sauvage ; (savage) sauvage, farouche ; (turbulent) turbulent, violent, tumultueux ; (ungoverned) impétueux, violent, furieux, déchaîné ; (mad) (of projects, etc.) extravagant ; (inconstant) inconstant, capricieux, changeant ; (inordinate) licencieux, déréglé ; (uncouth) étrange, bizarre ; (irregular) déréglé ; désordonné ; (of the look) hagard, égaré, effaré ; (of fire-arms) erratique, peu précis ; (of plants, fruit) sauvage. — girl ; *étourdie, écervelée, f.* —

beast ; *bête féroce ; bête sauvage, f.* To grow —; (of plants) *croître à l'état sauvage.* To be —; (about anything) *bisquer* **de.** To run —; (of children) *vagabonder ;* (fig.) *se déchaîner, ne pas connaître de bornes.* To sow one's — oats ; *jeter sa gourme.* — horses would not make me speak ; *je me ferais tirer à quatre avant de parler.* To look —; *avoir l'air effaré.* He is on a — goose chase ; *il court après la lune,* ou *il cherche midi à quatorze heures.* A — goose chase ; (fig.) *une folle entreprise.* A — shot ; *un coup perdu, m.* He lets his imagination run —; *il laisse trotter son imagination (comme elle veut).*

wil'derness (wil'deur-), *n.*, désert ; lieu désert, *m.*; solitude ; (fig.) multitude, infinité, *f.*

wild'-fire (waïld'faïeure), *n.*, feu grégeois ; (vet.) érésipèle, *m.* ; (med.) dartre vive, *f.* Like —; *comme l'éclair.*

wild'ly (waïld'li), *adv.*, (without cultivation) sans culture, à l'état sauvage ; (without tameness) d'une manière farouche ; (with disorder) avec désordre ; (irregularly) d'une manière désordonnée ; (heedlessly) étourdiment, follement ; à tort et à travers ; (extravagantly) avec extravagance. To stare —; *regarder d'un air égaré, d'un air hagard, d'un air effaré.*

wild'ness (waïld'-), *n.*, (savage state) état sauvage ; (uncultivated state) état inculte, état sauvage, *m.*; (savageness) nature farouche, férocité ; (irregularity) folie, extravagance, *f.*; dérèglement, désordre, *m.* ; (alienation of mind) aliénation mentale, *f.* ; (of the look) égarement, *m.*; (of the winds) impétuosité, violence ; (of children) turbulence ; (of the passions) licence, *f.*, dérèglement, *m.*

wile (waïle), *n.*, artifice, *m.* ; ruse, fourberie, *f.*

will'ful (wil-foule), *adj.*, volontaire ; opiniâtre ; obstiné, têtu, entier ; (of horses) difficile, rétif ; (of things) volontaire, fait à dessein, prémédité, fait avec préméditation. — waste makes woful want ; (prov.) *les folles dépenses refroidissent la cuisine.*

will'fully, *adv.*, opiniâtrément ; avec entêtement ; obstinément ; à dessein ; avec intention ; (jur.) avec préméditation.

will'fulness, *n.*, caractère volontaire, *m.* ; obstination, opiniâtreté, *f.* ; entêtement, *m.*

wi'lily (waï-li-li), *adv.*, astucieusement.

wi'liness (waï-li-), *n.*, fourberie, ruse, astuce, *f.*

will, *n.*, volonté, *f.* ; vouloir ; (desire) désir, souhait, *m.* ; (pleasure) volonté, *f.*, bon plaisir, gré ; (power) pouvoir ; (divine determination) arrêt ; (jur.) testament, *m.* Last — and testament ; *dernières volontés, f.pl. ; testament, m.* At —; *à volonté; à discrétion; à son gré.* Against one's —; *à contre gré.* What is your —? *quel est votre bon plaisir ; quel est votre désir ? que désirez-vous ?* To bear any one good- —; *vouloir du bien à quelqu'un.* To bear any one ill- —; *vouloir du mal à quelqu'un; en vouloir à quelqu'un.* Good —; *bonne volonté ; bienveillance, sympathie ;* (in a commercial sense) *clientèle, f.* Ill —; *mauvaise volonté ; malveillance, f.* To have one's —; *faire sa volonté ; avoir ce qu'on désire, faire à sa tête, à sa guise.* To work one's —; *agir à sa volonté, à sa discrétion.* With a —; *de bon cœur ; avec entrain.* To have a — of one's own; *vouloir bien ce qu'on veut.* To work with a —; *travailler avec ardeur, avec zèle.* Where there's a — there's a way ; *qui veut la fin veut les moyens,* ou *avec de la bonne volonté on trouve toujours le moyen,* ou *vouloir, c'est pouvoir.* The — is as good as the deed, *l'intention est réputée pour le fait.*

will, *v.a.*, vouloir ; ordonner, commander ; (by testament) léguer ; disposer de (par testament).

will, *v.auxil.*, (preterit, Would). **Will** when not sign of the future is not translated. **The English infinitive which follows it is translated by the present indicative ; e.g :** Trade oftentimes —

genius fetter ; *le commerce parfois entrave le génie.* When **will** is the sign of the future, it is not translated, but the English infinitive becomes the future indicative in French. **Will** used emphatically may be translated by **vouloir** : *e.g.* I — not do it ; *je ne veux pas le faire* ou *je n'en ferai rien.* Whether he — or no ; *bon gré, mal gré.* Do as you —; *faites comme vous l'entendez.* Do what he —; *il a beau faire,* ou *quoi qu'il fasse.* What — you have me do ? *que voulez-vous que je fasse ?*

Wil′liam(-pear), *n.*, Guillaume bon-chrétien, *m.*

will′ing, *adj.*, bien disposé, de bonne volonté; complaisant ; (voluntary) volontaire. — to ; désireux **de** ; empressé **de** ; disposé **à**. — or not ; *bon gré, mal gré.* To be —; *vouloir, vouloir bien; être ,disposé* **à**. To be able and —; *pouvoir et vouloir.* To be — to; *être disposé* **à**. God —; *s'il plaît à Dieu.*

will′ingly (will′ign′li), *adv.*, volontiers ; de bon cœur ; de bonne volonté ; volontairement.

will′ingness (will′ign′nèce), *n.*, bonne volonté, *f.*; bon vouloir, *m.*; complaisance, *f.*; consentement, *m.* — to ; *bonne disposition* **à**, *f.*; *penchant* **à** ; *empressement* **à**, *m.*

will-o′-the-wisp ou **will-with-a-wisp**, *n.*, feu follet, *m.*

wil′low (wil′lô), *n.*, saule, *m.* Weeping-—; *saule de Babylone ; saule pleureur,* m. —weed ; *salicaire, f.*

wil′low-ground (-graou′n′de), *n.*, saussaie, *f.*
wil′low-herb (-eurbe), *n.*, (bot.) laurier Saint-Antoine, *m.*

wil′lowy (wil′lô-i), *adv.*, couvert de saules.

wil′ly-nil′ly, *adv.*, bon gré, mal gré.

wi′ly (waï-li), *adj.*, rusé, fin, astucieux, fourbe.

wim′ble (wi′m′b′l), *n.*, vilebrequin, *m.*

wim′ble (wi′m′b′l), *v.a.*, faire un trou avec un vilebrequin.

wim′ple, *n.*, guimpe, *f.* ; voile, *m.*

win, *v.a.*, (*preterit* and *past part.*, Won) (a battle) gagner ; (a prize, a victory) remporter ; (fig.) gagner, séduire.

win, *v.n.*, gagner ; triompher, vaincre. To — upon ; *gagner, séduire ;* (to gain ground) *faire des progrès* **dans**, *gagner du terrain* **dans.** To — back ; *regagner.*

wince, *v.n.*, reculer ; tressaillir ; sourciller ; (of horses) ruer, se cabrer.

win′cer, *n.*, animal qui rue, qui se cabre, *m.*

winch, *n.*, manivelle, *f.* ; treuil, *m.*

wind (wind), *n.*, vent, souffle, *m.*; (breath) respiration, haleine, *f.*; (flatulence) vent, *m.*, flatuosité ; (vet.) tympanite, *f.*; (fig.) vent, *m.*, fumée, *f.* In the —; *au vent;* (fig.) *dans l'air.* A breath of —; *un souffle de vent.* High —; *grand vent.* The — is very high ; *il vente très fort,* ou *il fait grand vent.* The trade —s ; *les vents alizés.* To sail before the —; (nav.) *courir vent arrière.* To sail close to the — ; *pincer le vent.* To sail against the —; *avoir vent debout.* To get the —; (of a ship) *gagner le vent.* Between — and water ; *à fleur d'eau.* — and water tight ; *clos et bien couvert.* It is an ill — that blows no one any good ; *à quelque chose malheur est bon.* To get — of ; *éventer ; avoir vent* **de.** To raise the —; *battre monnaie, faire ressource.* To get —; *s'ébruiter, se répandre, s'éventer.* There is something in the —; *il y a quelque chose qui se mitonne.* To take the — out of any one's sails ; *aller sur les brisées de quelqu'un.* To sow the — and reap the whirl—; *semer le vent et récolter la tempête.*

wind (wind), *v.a.*, éventer, exposer au vent, à l'air ; (hunt.) halener, avoir vent **de**, flairer ; (to take the breath away) faire perdre haleine à, (a horse) essouffler.

wind (waïnd), *v.a.*, (*preterit* and *past part.*, Wound) (to turn) tourner ; (to turn round some object) rouler, enrouler, dévider ; (to change) changer ; (to enfold) envelopper, enrouler ; (round) contourner. To — into ; *insinuer* **dans**, *glisser* **dans.** To — off ; *dérouler ; dévider.* To — up ; *rouler, entortiller ;* (to bring to a settlement) *régler, terminer, finir ;* (com.) *liquider ;* (to raise by degrees) *élever peu à peu ;* (clocks, etc.) *monter, remonter ;* (fig.) *préparer, apprêter.*

wind (waînde), *v.n.*, se rouler, s'enrouler, s'entortiller ; (to turn) tourne ; faire un détour ; (to change) changer, varier ; (to turn around something) s'enlacer, circuler, tourner ; (to have a circular direction) serpenter, aller en spirale ; (to proceed in flexures) serpenter, tourner. To — out of ; *sortir* **de.** To — up ; *se remonter.* The play —s up in this way ; *voici le dénoûment de la pièce, de l'intrigue.* He wound up by saying ; *il finit,* ou *il se résuma, en disant.*

wind′age (-èdje), *n.*, (artil.) vent, *m.*
wind′-bore (-bôre), *n.*, tuyau à vent, *m.*
wind′-bound (-baou′n′de), *adj.*, arrêté par les vents contraires.
wind′-chest (-tshèste), *n.*, (mus sommier, *m.*
wind′ed, *adj.*, hors d'haleine, essoufflé. A long-— speech ; *un discours interminable, ennuyeux, à perte d'haleine.*
wind′er (waï′n′d′-), *n.*, dévideur, *m.*, dévideuse, *f.* ; (thing) dévidoir, *m.* ; (bot.) plante grimpante, *f.* ; (o. a clock, etc.) remontoir, *m.*
wind′er (wi′n′deur), *n.*, (vulgar) coup qui fait perdre haleine, *m.*
wind′fall (wi′n′d′fôle), *n.*, fruit, ou arbre, abattu par le vent, abatis, *m.* ; (fig.) bonne aubaine, *f.*
wind′fallen, *adj.*, abattu par le vent.
wind′-flower (-flaoueur), *n.*, anémone, *f.*
wind′-gall (-gôle), *n.*, (vet.) molette, *f.*
wind′-gauge (-ghèdje), *n.*, anémomètre, *m.*
wind′-gun (-gheune), *n.*, fusil à vent, *m.*
wind′iness, *n.*, nature venteuse ; (flatulence) flatuosité ; (fig.) enflure, boursouflure, *f.*
wind′ing (waï′n′d′-), *n.*, sinuosité, *f.* ; méandre, détour, circuit, *m.*
wind′ing (waï′n′d′-), *adj.*, sinueux, tortueux, tournant ; (of a staircase) en limaçon.
wind′ing-engine (waï′n′dign′è′n′djine), *n.*, machine de tour, *f.*
wind′ing-sheet (waï′n′dign′shîte), *n.*, suaire, linceul, *m.*
wind′-instrument (wi′n′d′i′n′striou-), *n.*, instrument à vent, *m.*
wind′lass (wi′n′d′lâsse), *n.*, treuil ; (nav.) guindeau, cabestan, *m.*
wind′-mill, *n.*, moulin à vent, *m.*
win′dow (wi′n′dô), *n.*, fenêtre, croisée ; ouverture ; (of carriages) glace ; (of shops) vitrine, *f.* ; montre ; étalage, jour ; (of a church) vitrail, *m.*, verrière, *f.* Out of the —; *par la fenêtre ;* (of a carriage) *par la portière.* Sash —; *fenêtre à guillotine, f.* In the —; (of trade) *à l'étalage, à la montre, à la devanture.* Ticket —; (rail.) *guichet, m.* To break the —s ; *casser les vitres.* To let down the —; (of a carriage) *baisser la glace.* To put up the —; *lever la glace.*
win′dow, *v.a.*, garnir de fenêtres.
win′dow-blind (-blaï′n′de), *n.*, jalousie, persienne, *f.* ; (of carriages) store, *m.*
win′dow-curtain (-keur-tine), *n.*, rideau de fenêtre, *m.*
win′dow-dresser, *n.*, étalagiste, *m.*
win′dow-fastener, *n.*, espagnolette, *f.*
win′dow-frame, *n.*, dormant de fenêtre, châssis dormant, *m.*
win′dow-glass, *n.*, verre à vitres, *m.*
win′dowless, *adj.*, sans fenêtres.
win′dow-pane, *n.*, carreau, *m.* ; vitre, *f.*
win′dow-sash, *n.*, châssis de fenêtre, *m.*
win′dow-seat (-sîte), *n.*, saillie intérieure de fenêtre, avance, banquette, *f.*
win′dow-shutter (-sheut′-), *n.*, volet ; contrevent, *m.*

win'dow-sill, n., appui de fenêtre, m.

win'dow-strap, n., (of a vehicle) bricole, f.

win'dow-tax, n., impôt des portes et fenêtres, m.

wind'pipe (wi'n'd'païpe), n., (anat.) trachée-artère ; trachée, f. ; (mines) conduit aérien, m.

wind'-sail (-séle), n., manche à air, f.

wind'-tight (-taïte), adj., imperméable à l'air, étanche.

wind'ward, to, adv., (nav.) au vent. The — Islands ; Les Iles du Vent, f.pl.

wind'ward, n., côté du vent, m.

wind'y (wi'n'd'-), adj., du vent ; (tempestuous) venteux ; (flatulent) venteux, flatueux ; (fig.) creux, vain, vide. It is — ; il fait du vent.

wine (waïne), n., vin ; (fig.) vin, m., boisson, ivresse, f. Light — ; petit vin, m.; piquette, f.; (at school) abondance, f.

wine'-bag, n., outre à vin, f. ; (pers.) sac à vin, m.

wine'-bibber, n., buveur, biberon, ivrogne, m.

wine'-bibbing, n., (la) boisson, f.

wine'-bin, n., porte-bouteilles, m.

wine'-bottle, n., bouteille à vin, f.

wine'-broker (-brôk'-), n., courtier en vins, m.

wine'-cask, n., tonneau, m., barrique à vin, f., baril, m.

wine'-cellar, n., cave, f.

wine'-cooler, n., seau à frapper, ou rafraîchissoir à vin, m.

wine'-country, n., pays vignoble, m.

wine'-dealer, n., marchand de vin, m.

wine'-district, n., pays vignoble, m.

wine'-glass (-glâce), n., verre à vin, m.

wine'-grower (-grô-eur), n., propriétaire de vignes, viticulteur, m.

wine'-growing (-grô-igne), adj., viticole.

wine'-growing, n., culture de la vigne, viticulture, f.

wine'-list, n., carte des vins, f.

wine'-making (-mék'-), n., vinification ; fabrication du vin, f.

wine'-market, n., halle aux vins, f.

wine'-merchant (-meur'tsha'n'te), n., négociant en vins, m.

wine'-press, n., pressoir, m.

wine'-shop, n., boutique de marchand de vin, f. ; cabaret, m.

wine'-stone (-stône), n., tartre brut, m.

wine'-strainer (-stré'n'-), n., passe-vin, m.

wine'-taster (-tést'-), n., dégustateur ; (inst.) tâte-vin, m.

wine'-vault, n., caveau à vin, m., caveaux, m.pl.

wing (wigne), n., aile ; (flight) course, f., vol, m. ; (theat.) coulisse, f. On, ou upon, the — ; au vol. Stretch, ou expanse, of — ; envergure, f. Upon the —s of the wind ; sur les ailes du vent ; avec la plus grande hâte. — wardrobe ; (furniture) garde-robe à plusieurs portes, f. Under the — of ; (fig.) sous la protection de.

wing (wigne), v.a., garnir d'ailes ; (to transport by flight) transporter sur ses ailes ; (to wound in the wing) frapper à l'aile, blesser à l'aile. To — one's flight ; s'envoler ; prendre son vol, son essor.

wing, v.n., se diriger à tire d'aile.

winged (wign'de), adj., ailé ; rapide ; (wounded) blessé à l'aile ; (bot.) à ailes ; ailé.

wing'less (wign'-), adj., (zoöl.) aptère ; qui n'a pas d'ailes.

wing'let (wign'lète), n., (zoöl.) petite aile ; aile rudimentaire, ailette, f.

wing'-rib, n., (of beef) côte d'aloyau, f.

wing'-shell, n., (ent.) élytre, m.f.

wing'y (wign'i), adj., ailé, rapide ; vain.

wink (wign'ke), n., clin d'œil, m. Not to sleep a — ; ne pas fermer l'œil (de la nuit). To have forty —s ; sommeiller, faire un petit somme.

wink, v.n., cligner l'œil ; clignoter ; (of a

light) vaciller, trembler. To — at ; faire signe de l'œil à ; (to connive at) fermer les yeux sur, tolérer, passer sur.

wink'er, n., (for horses) œillère, f.

wink'ing, n., clignement, clignotement ; clignement d'yeux ; (fig.) clignement d'œil, signe de l'œil, m. ; connivence, f.

wink'ing, adj., qui cligne l'œil, clignotant ; qui fait signe de l'œil ; (of a light) vacillant, tremblant.

wink'ingly, adv., en clignotant.

win'ner, n., personne qui gagne, f. ; (horse-racing, lottery, etc.) gagnant f. ; (in a race or match, etc.) vainqueur, m.

win'ning, n., gain, m. pl., gain, m.sing.

win'ning, adj., gagnant ; vainqueur ; (attractive) qui gagne le cœur, séduisant, enchanteur. — game ; la belle. — post ; (at races) poteau d'arrivée, but, m.

win'now (wi'n'nô), v.a., vanner ; éventer ; (to examine) examiner, sasser ; (to separate) séparer, diviser, éplucher, trier.

win'now, v.n., vanner.

win'nower (wi'n'nô-eur), n., vanneur, m.

win'nowing (wi'n'nô-igne), n., vannage ; (fig.) examen, triage, m.

win'ter (wi'n'teur), n., hiver ; (print.) sommier, m. adj., d'hiver. In — ; en hiver. In the — time ; dans l'hiver.

win'ter, v.n., hiverner, passer l'hiver à.

win'ter, v.a., conserver pendant l'hiver ; nourrir pendant l'hiver.

win'ter-berry (-bèr'ri), n., (bot.) apalachine, f.

win'ter-cherry (-tshèr'-), n., coqueret, m.

win'ter crop, n., semis d'hiver, m.

win'ter-fallow (-fal-lô), v.a., (agri.) hiverner.

win'ter-garden, n., jardin d'hiver, m.

win'ter-ground (-graou'n'de), v.a., (agri.) conserver, ou couvrir, pendant l'hiver.

win'tering, n., hivernage, m. — place ; ville d'hivernage, f.

win'terly, adj., d'hiver, propre à l'hiver.

win'ter-season (-sî-z'n), n., saison d'hiver, f.

win'ter-weed (-wîde), n., (bot.) véronique à feuilles de lierre, f.

win'try, adj., d'hiver, hyémal, hiémal ; sévère ; glacial, rude.

win'y (waï-ni), adj., vineux, de vin.

wipe (waïpe), n., action d'essuyer ; (jeer) lardon, brocard, coup de patte, m. ; (blow) taloche, tape, f.

wipe (waïpe), v.a., essuyer ; nettoyer ; (to cleanse) purifier. — off, away ; essuyer, ôter, enlever ; (fig.) effacer.

wip'er (waïp'-), n., linge, torchon, m.

wire (waïeur), n., fil de métal, fil de fer, fil d'archal ; (of a cage) barreau, m. A — ; une dépêche. Telegraphic — ; fil télégraphique, m. To pull the —s ; (fig.) tenir les ficelles. Barbed — ; ronce artificielle, f., fil de fer barbelé, m.

wire (waïeur), v.a., attacher, lier avec un fil de métal ; griller ; (telegraph) envoyer, télégraphier.

wire' blind, n., store en toile métallique, m.

wire' bridge, n., pont en fil de fer, m.

wire'draw (waïeur-drô), v.a., (preterit, Wiredrew ; past part., Wiredrawn) tréfiler ; étendre, allonger ; passer à la filière ; (fig.) étendre, étirer, alambiquer.

wire'-drawer (waïeur-drô-eur), n., tireur, tréfileur, m.

wire'-drawing (waïeur-drô-igne), n., tréfilerie, f.

wire'-gauze (-gôze), n., gaze métallique, f.

wire'-grass (-grâce), n., (bot.) paturin comprimé, m.

wire'-guard (-gârde), n., grillage, garde-feu, m.

wire'-heel (-hîle), n., (vet.) seime au talon, f.

wire'-mark (-mârke), n., (paper) vergeure, f.

wire'-mill, n., tréfilerie, f.

wire'-puller, *n.*, meneur politique, *m.; * qui tient les ficelles.

wire'-ribbon (-rib'bo'n), *n.*, cannetille, *f.*

wire' rope, *n.*, cordage métallique, *m.*

wire'-work (-weurke), *n.*, grillage en fil métallique; réseau, treillis, *m.*

wire'-worker, *n.*, grillageur, *m.*

wire'-working (-weurk'-), *n.*, tréfilerie, *f.*

wire'-worm, *n.*, (zoöl.) iule, *m.*

wi'ry (waïeur'-), *adj.*, en fil métallique; en filigrane; (fig.) sec et nerveux; souple.

wis'dom (wiz'deume), *n.*, sagesse; prudence, *f.* — tooth; *dent de sagesse, f.*

wise (waïze), *adj.*, sage; (discreet) discret, sage, prudent; (grave) grave, sage. — man; *homme sensé, m.* — men of the East; *mages, les trois rois, m.pl.* To be none the —r for it; *n'en être pas plus avancé.* A word to the — is enough; (prov.) *à bon entendeur peu de paroles.*

wise (waïze), *n.*, manière, façon, sorte, guise, *f.* In no —; *en aucune manière; en aucune façon.* In this —; *de cette manière ou façon, ainsi qu'il suit.* To look —; *avoir l'air grave;* (ironically) *avoir l'air entendu, capable.*

wise'acre (waïz'a-keur), *n.*, prétendu sage, benêt, sot, imbécile, pédant, *m.*

wise'ly (waïz'-), *adv.*, sagement; prudemment.

wish, *n.*, souhait, désir, *m.*, envie, *f.; * vœu, *m.*, intention, demande, *f.* Good —es; *bons souhaits.* Best —es; *meilleurs souhaits; tous* (mes, nos, vos, leurs) *vœux de bonheur.* Have your —; *qu'il soit fait selon votre désir, comme vous voudrez.* To have one's —; *avoir ce qu'on désire.* If —ea were horses, beggars would ride; (prov.) *avec un* **si** *on mettrait Paris dans une bouteille.*

wish, *v.a.*, souhaiter; désirer; vouloir; faire des vœux **pour.** To — any one to the devil; *envoyer quelqu'un à tous les diables.* To — well to; *vouloir du bien à.* To — any one a pleasant journey; *souhaiter un bon voyage à.*

wish, *v.n.*, souhaiter; désirer; vouloir. To — for; *souhaiter, désirer; demander.* I — I could; *je voudrais pouvoir.* I — to know; *je désire savoir.* I — him to be; *je veux qu'il soit* (*vouloir que* always takes the **subj.**). I — I was . . . ; *je voudrais être . . .*

wish'er, *n.*, personne qui souhaite, qui désire, *f.*

wish'ful (-foule), *adv.*, désireux **de**, avide **de;** qui exprime le désir **de.**

wish'fully, *adv.*, avec désir; vivement, ardemment, passionnément.

wish'-wash, *n.*, lavasse, *f.* [consistance.

wish'y-washy, *adj.*, faible, pauvre; sans

wisp, *n.*, torchon, bouchon de paille, *m.*, touffe d'herbe, *f.* Will o' the —; *feu follet, m.*

wista'ria, *n.*, glycine, *f.*

wist'ful (-foule), *adj.*, attentif; pensif; (wishful) désireux, ardent; d'envie, de regret.

wist'fully, *adv.*, attentivement; d'une manière pensive; d'un œil d'envie; ardemment, vivement.

wit, *v.a.*, savoir. To —; *savoir; c'est à dire, par exemple.*

wit, *n.*, esprit; (intellect) esprit, entendement, jugement, génie, *m.; * (pers.) personne spirituelle, *f.*, bel esprit; (man of genius) grand esprit, homme de génie, homme d'esprit, *m.* —s, *pl.*, esprit, *m.*, raison, tête, *f.*, sens, bon sens, *m.* To drive any one out of his —s; *faire perdre la tête à quelqu'un.* To have lost one's —s; *avoir perdu la tête, l'esprit, la raison; être hors de son bon sens.* To frighten any one out of his —s; *faire une peur horrible à quelqu'un.* To be at one's —s' ends; *être au bout de son latin; ne plus savoir à quel saint se vouer; ne savoir que faire* (V. Hugo). To live by one's —s; (b.s.) *vivre d'industrie, d'expédients.*

witch, *n.*, sorcière, magicienne, *f.* To be no —; *n'être pas sorcier; n'avoir pas inventé la poudre.*

witch'craft (witsh'crâfte), *n.*, sorcellerie, magie, *f.; * maléfice; sortilège; sort, *m.*

witch'ery, *n.*, sorcellerie, *f.; * sortilège; (fig.) charme, enchantement, *m.; * (fascination) fascination, *f.*

with (*with*), *prep.*, avec; de; en; (at) de; (by means of) par; (who has, who have) à, au, à la, aux; (among persons, bodies of men) auprès **de;** (among nations, etc.) chez, parmi; (in the house of) chez; (in the estimation of) auprès **de;** (after same) que. To be — any one; *être avec quelqu'un.* To write — a pen; *écrire avec une plume.* — the right hand; *de la main droite.* — steady steps; *d'un pas ferme.* — care! *fragile!* — him; *à ses yeux.* To cover —; *couvrir* **de.** To hold, to love — all one's might; *tenir, aimer de toute sa force.* The lady — blue eyes; *la dame aux yeux bleus.* — arms in one's hands; *les armes à la main.* — study; *par l'étude.* I am disgusted, enchanted — that; *je suis dégoûté, enchanté,* **de** cela. Angry —; *fâché* **contre.** Lighted — gas; *éclairé au gaz.* A room — plastered walls; *une salle aux murs crépis.* — which words; *à ces mots.* Imbued —; *imbu* **de;** *pénétré* **de.** Content —; *content* **de.** To abound —; *abonder* **en.** — a view to; *en vue* **de,** *avec l'intention* **de.** What do you want — her? *que voulez-vous d'elle?* que *lui voulez-vous?* I shall be — you in a moment; *je suis à vous dans un instant.* (Sometimes **with** is not translated.) To meet —; *voir, rencontrer, trouver.* To inspire one — confidence; *inspirer la confiance à quelqu'un.* To sleep — one's eyes open; *dormir les yeux ouverts.* To speak — one's hands in one's pockets; *parler les mains dans les poches.*

withal' (with'ôl), *adv.*, avec tout cela, en outre, ensemble; aussi, de plus; en même temps.

withdraw' (with'drô), *v.a.*, (preterit, Withdrew; past part., Withdrawn) retirer, rappeler, éloigner **de.** To — one's word; *retirer sa parole.*

withdraw', *v.n.*, se retirer, s'éloigner **de.** To — from; *s'en aller* **de,** *s'éloigner* **de;** (softly) *s'esquiver* **de.**

withdraw'al, *n.*, retraite, *f.; * (taking away) retrait, *m.*

withdraw'ing, *n.*, (of troops, etc.) rappel, *m.; * (of help, etc.) privation, (retreat) retraite, *f.*

withe (withe), *n.*, osier, pleyon, *m.*, hart, *f.*

with'er (with'eur), *v.a.*, flétrir; dessécher.

with'er (with'eur), *v.n.*, se dessécher; se flétrir, se faner; dépérir; languir.

with'er-band (-eur-), *n.*, arçon de selle, *m.*, bande de garrot, *f.*

with'ering (with'eur'-), *adj.*, qui se flétrit; (blasting) brûlant; (sarcastic) écrasant, foudroyant; dédaigneux, méprisant.

with'eringly, *adv.*, d'un air écrasant; d'une manière flétrissante.

with'ers (with'eurze), *n.pl.*, (horse) garrot, *m.sing.*

with'er-wrung, *adj.*, (of a horse) égarrotté.

withhold' (with'hôlde), *v.a.*, (preterit and past part., Withheld) retenir, arrêter, différer; comprimer, refuser; (information) tenir secret; cacher **à;** ne pas publier, ne pas communiquer **à.** To — from; *s'abstenir* **de.**

withhold'er (with'hêld'-), *n.*, détenteur **de,** *m.*

withhold'ing, **withhold'ment**, *n.*, refus, *m.; * détention, *f.*

within' (with'i'n), *prep.*, dans, en; (of time) dans, en, dans l'espace **de;** (of past time) depuis; (of future time) dans, en, d'ici **à;** dans l'espace **de,** dans un délai **de;** (not exceeding) au-dessous **de,** à moins **de.** — one's reach; *à sa portée.* — reach of; *à portée* **de.** To live — one's income; *ne pas dépenser plus que son revenu.* — a life-time; *en moins d'une vie d'homme.* — the

memory of; *au souvenir* **de**; *de mémoire* **de**. —
eighty or a hundred yards; *à moins de quatre-vingts ou cent pas*. — a pound or so; *à une livre près*. — a week; *en dedans d'une semaine*. —
November 15 and 18; *entre le 15 et le 18 novembre*. — it; *au dedans; en dedans*.

within' (with'i'ne), *adv.*, en, *ou* au, dedans;
à l'intérieur; intérieurement; (in the house) à la maison, chez soi.

without' (with'aoute), *prep.*, sans; (outside) hors **de**, en dehors **de**. To be better —; *se trouver mieux* **sans**.

without' (with'aoute), *conj.*, à moins que, sans que; (unless) à moins que (with *ne* and subj.).
— his knowing it; *sans qu'il le sache*. — I send for it; *à moins que je ne l'envoie chercher*.

without' (with'aoute), *adv.*, en dehors, dehors, par dehors; à l'extérieur; extérieurement.

withstand' (with-), *v.a.*, résister à, combattre; s'opposer à. There is no —ing him; *impossible de lui résister; on ne peut*, ou *ne saurait, rien lui refuser*.

withstand'ing (with-), *n.*, résistance, opposition, *f.*

with'y (with'i), *adj.*, d'osier; de pleyon.

wit'less, *adj.*, sans esprit; sot.

wit'lessly, *adv.*, sans esprit; sottement.

wit'ling, *n.*, petit esprit; sot; bel-esprit, *m.*

wit'ness, *n.*, (pers.) témoin; (testimony) témoignage, *m.* To bear — to; *témoigner* **de**, rendre *témoignage* **de**. To call to —; *prendre à témoin; appeler en témoignage*. To be called as a —; *être cité comme témoin*. In the — box; *sur le banc des témoins*. — for the prosecution; *témoin à charge, m.* — for the defense; *témoin à décharge, m.*

wit'ness, *v.a.*, témoigner; être témoin **de**; voir, voir faire; assister à. To self-—; (a signature) *certifier véritable*.

wit'ness, *v.n.*, témoigner; porter témoignage, déposer.

wit'ted, *adj.* (in compounds) à l'esprit . . .

wit'ticism (-ciz'm), *n.*, trait d'esprit, bon mot, *m.*

wit'tily, *adv.*, spirituellement, avec esprit.

wit'tiness, *n.*, esprit, caractère spirituel, *m.*

wit'tingly, *adv.*, sciemment; à dessein.

wit'ty, *adj.*, spirituel; (sarcastic) piquant, sarcastique, mordant.

wiz'ard, *n.*, sorcier, magicien, *m.*

woad (wôde), *n.*, pastel, *m.*, guède, *f.*

woe (wô), *n.*, malheur, *m.*; peine, douleur, *f.*; chagrin, *m.*; (curse) malédiction, *f.*

woe! (wô), *int.*, malheur! — to whom . . . ; *malheur à qui . . . !*

woe'begone (wô-bi-), *adj.*, accablé de douleur, désolé.

wo'ful (wô-foule), *adj.*, triste, désolé, malheureux, affligé; (mournful) malheureux, triste, affligeant, douloureux; (paltry) triste, piteux, méchant.

wo'fully (wô-foul'-), *adv.*, tristement; douloureusement; cruellement.

wolf (woulfe), *n.*, loup, *m.* She-—; *louve, f.*
Young —; *louveteau, m.* Dark as a —'s mouth; *noir comme dans un four*. To cry —; *crier au loup*. To be as hungry as a —; *avoir une faim de loup*. To keep the — from the door; *être à l'abri du besoin, écarter la faim*. To see a —; *devenir muet de crainte*.

wolf'-dog, *n.*, chien-loup, *m.*

wolf'-fish, *n.*, (ich.) loup de mer, bars, *m.*

wolf'ish (woulf'-), *adj.*, de loup; rapace, vorace.

wolf's'-bane, *n.*, (bot.) aconit, *m.*

wolf's'-claw (-clô), *n.*, (bot.) lycopode, *m.*

wom'an (woum'-), *n.*, (*women*) femme; (seller of . . .) marchande (**de** . . .), *f.* — must have her way; *ce que femme veut Dieu le veut*. — is fickle ever; *souvent femme varie, bien fol est qui s'y fie*

(François I.). —'s instinct; *l'esprit primesautier d'une femme* (Montaigne).

wom'an-hater (-hét'-), *n.*, ennemi du sexe, *m.*

wom'anhood (-houde), *n.*, état, *ou* âge, de femme, *m.*

wom'anish, *adj.*, féminin; (effeminate) efféminé.

wom'anize (-aïze), *v.a.*, efféminer, amollir.

wom'ankind (-kaï'n'de), *n.*, le sexe, *m.*; les femmes, *f.pl.*

wom'an-like (-laïke), *adj.*, de, *ou* comme, une femme.

wom'anly, *adj.*, de femme; féminin.

wom'anly, *adv.*, en femme, comme une femme. So —; *si femme*.

womb (woume), *n.*, utérus, *m.*; matrice, *f.*; (fig.) sein, *m.*, entrailles, *f.pl.*, flancs, *m.pl.*

wom'en (wim'è'ne), *n.pl.* V. **woman**, *n.*

won'der (weu'n'd'-), *v.n.*, s'étonner; être étonné, être surpris; (to doubt) être curieux de savoir. To — at; *s'étonner* **de**; *être étonné* **de**; *s'émerveiller* **de**. To — whether; *se demander* **si**. I do not — at it; *cela ne me surprend, ne m'étonne pas*. I could not sufficiently — at the intrepidity which he showed; *je ne pouvais me lasser d'admirer le courage dont il fit preuve*.

won'der (weu'n'd'-), *n.*, étonnement, *m.*; surprise, admiration; (cause of wonder) merveille, *f.*; (miracle) miracle, prodige, *m.*, merveille, *f.* No —! *ce n'est pas étonnant!* ou *ce n'est pas surprenant*. For a —; *chose étonnante, f.* It is a — that; *il est étonnant* **que** (with subjunctive). To do, ou work, —s; *faire des prodiges*, ou *faire merveille*. It is a — to see you; *c'est merveille de vous voir*. A nine days' —; *la merveille d'un jour*; ou *d'une mort récente, une vieille nouvelle* (A. de Musset). It is a — he was not killed; *c'est merveille qu'il n'ait pas été tué*. You have done —s; *vous avez fait des merveilles*. To promise —s; *promettre monts et merveilles*. The — is that . . . ; *ce qu'il y a d'étonnant c'est que . . .*

won'derer, *n.*, admirateur, *m.*

won'derful (-foule), *adj.*, étonnant; surprenant; merveilleux, prodigieux. — to tell; *chose surprenante*; ô merveille! The — part of the matter is . . . ; *le merveilleux de l'affaire*, ou la merveille, c'est que . . .

won'derfully, *adv.*, étonnamment; merveilleusement; prodigieusement. — well; *à merveille; merveilleusement bien*.

won'derfulness, *n.*, nature étonnante, *f.*; merveilleux, prodigieux, *m.*

won'derment, *n.*, étonnement, *m.*

won'der-struck (-streuke), *adj.*, frappé d'étonnement; émerveillé.

won'der-worker (weurk'-), *n.*, faiseur de prodiges, *m.*

won'der-working (-weurk'-), *adj.*, qui fait des merveilles, des miracles.

won'drous (weu'n'd'-), *adj.*, merveilleux; prodigieux; étonnant, surprenant.

won'drously, *adv.*, étonnamment; prodigieusement; merveilleusement.

wont (weu'n'te), *adj.*, accoutumé, habitué, habituel.

wont (weu'n'te), *v.n.*, avoir coutume **de**, être habitué à.

won't, *v.i.*, (a contraction of **will not**). V. **will**.

wont'ed (weu'n't'-), *adj.*, accoutumé, habituel, ordinaire.

wont'edness (weu'n't'-), *n.*, habitude, coutume, *f.*

woo (wou), *v.a.*, faire la cour à, l'amour à; rechercher en mariage; courtiser; (fig.) demander, solliciter, inviter.

woo (wou), *v.n.*, courtiser; faire la cour.

wood (woude), *n.*, bois; (forest) bois, *m.*, forêt, *f.* In the —; (of wine, etc.) *dans le fût, en tonneau*.

wood'-ashes (-ash'ize), *n.pl.*, cendres de bois, *f.pl.*

wood'bind *ou* **wood'bine** (-baïne), *n.*, chèvrefeuille des bois, *m.*

wood'-bound (-baou'n'de), *adj.*, entouré de bois.

wood'-carver, *n.*, sculpteur, *ou* graveur, sur bois, *m.*

wood'-chopper, *n.*, merlin; (pers.) fendeur de bois, *m.*

wood'cock, *n.*, (orni.) bécasse, *f.*

wood'-cut (-keute), *n.*, gravure sur bois, *f.*

wood'-cutter (-keut'-), *n.*, bûcheron, *m.*

wood'-cutting (-keut'-), *n.*, coupe des bois, du bois, *f.*; gravure sur bois, *f.*

wood'ed (woud'-), *adj.*, boisé.

wood'en, *adj.*, de bois, en bois; (clumsy) gauche. — ship; *navire en bois, m.* — walls; *murailles en bois, f.pl.*; (ships) navires, vaisseaux, *m.pl.*

wood'-engraver (-è'n'grév'-), *n.*, graveur sur bois, *m.*

wood'-engraving (-è'n'grév'-), *n.*, gravure sur bois, *f.*

wood'-fire, *n.*, feu de bois, *m.*

wood'-house *ou* **-shed** (-haouce), *n.*, bûcher (place), *m.*

wood'land, *n.*, pays boisé, *m.*; forêt, *f.*; bois, *m.*

wood'land, *adj.*, des bois; sylvestre.

wood'less, *adj.*, sans bois, sans forêts.

wood'-lock, *n.*, (nav.) clef de gouvernail, *f.*

wood'-louse (-laouce), *n.*, (zoöl.) cloporte, *m.*

wood'man, *n.*, garde forestier; bûcheron, *m.*

wood'-merchant (-meur'tchan'te), *n.*, marchand de bois, *m.*

wood'-mouse (-maousse), *n.*, mulot, *m.*

wood'-note (-nôte), *n.*, chant sauvage, *m.*, musique sauvage, *f.*

wood'-nymph (-nim'fe), *n.*, nymphe des bois, dryade, *f.*

wood'-paving, *n.*, pavage en bois, *m.*

wood'pecker (-pèk'-), *n.*, (orni.) pic, pivert, *m.*

wood'-pigeon (-pidj'eune), *n.*, pigeon ramier, *m.*

wood'-pile (-païle), *n.*, pile de bois, *f.*

wood'-reeve (-rîve), *n.*, inspecteur de forêt, garde-bois, *m.*

wood'-ruff, *n.*, (bot.) aspérule, *f.*

wood'-shavings, *n.pl.*, copeaux, *m.pl.*

wood'-sorrel, *n.*, oseille sauvage, *f.*

wood'-work (-weurke), *n.*, boisage, *m.*, boiserie, charpente, *f.*

wood'y, *adj.*, boisé; (ligneous) ligneux; (pertaining to woods) des bois, des forêts.

wood'-yard (-yârde), *n.*, chantier de bois à brûler, *m.*

woo'er (wou-eur), *n.*, prétendant, soupirant, galant, amant, *m.*

woof (woufe), *n.*, trame; (texture) étoffe, *f.*, tissu, *m.*

woo'ing, *n.*, cour, *f.*

woo'ingly (wou-ign'-), *adv.*, amoureusement, avec amour.

wool (woule), *n.*, laine; (bot.) laine, *f.*, poil, duvet, *m.*; (hair) cheveux crépus, *m.pl.* Great cry and little —; *beaucoup de bruit à propos de rien.*

wool'-ball, *n.*, pelote de laine, *f.*

wool'-comber (-côm'eur), *n.*, cardeur de laine, *m.*

woold (woulde), *v.a.*, (nav.) rouster, roster.

woold'er (would'-), *n.*, (nav.) jumelle, *f.*

woold'ing (would'-), *n.*, (nav.) rousture, rosture, *f.*

wool'-driver (-draïv'-), *n.*, marchand de laines, *m.*

wooled (woul'de), *adj.*, à laine.

wool'en (woul'è'ne), *n.*, étoffe de laine, *f.*

wool'en (woul'è'ne), *adj.*, de laine; drapé.

wool'en-cloth (-cloth), *n*, drap, *m.*

wool'en-draper (-drép'-), *n.*, marchand de drap; drapier, *m.*

wool'en-goods, *n.*, lainages, *m.pl.*; étoffes de laine, *f.pl.*, lainerie, *f.*

wool'-gathering (-gath'eur'-), *n.*, absence d'esprit, *f.* To go, *ou* be, a —; *avoir l'esprit aux talons; être distrait; battre la campagne.*

wool'liness (woul'-), *n.*, qualité, nature laineuse, *f.*

wool'ly (woul'-), *adj.*, laineux; (resembling wool) qui ressemble à de la laine; (clothed with wool) couvert de laine; (fleecy) cotonneux; (of the hair) crépu, frisé. — head; *nègre, m.*

wool'-pack, *n.*, balle de laine, *f.*

wool'-sack, *n.*, ballot de laine; (seat of the Lord Chancellor) sac de laine, *m.*; (fig.) dignité de Lord Chancelier, *f.*

wool'-sorter, *n.*, trieur de laine, *m.*

wool'-staple (-sté'p'l), *n.*, marché à laines, *m.*

wool'-stapler, *n.*, marchand de laines, *m.*

wool'-winder (-waï'n'd'-), *n.*, emballeur de laines, *m.*

wool'-work, *n.*, tapisserie, *f.*

wootz (woutse), *n.*, acier wootz, *ou* indien, *m.*

word (weurde), *n.*, mot, *m.*; parole, *f.*; (letters written or printed, short discourse) mot, *m.*; (dispute) dispute, *f.*, mots, *m.pl.*, paroles, *f.pl.*; (promise) promesse, parole, *f.*; (signal, milit.) mot, mot d'ordre; (tidings) avis, *m.*, nouvelle; (declaration) déclaration, affirmation; (of God) parole, *f.*; (2d pers. of the Trinity) Verbe, *m.*; (proverb) proverbe, dicton, mot; (gram.) mot, *m.* —s, *f.pl.*, (discourse) paroles, *f.pl.*; (dispute) dispute, altercation, discussion, *f.*, paroles, injures, *f.pl.*, mots, *m.pl.* With these —s; *à ces mots.* In these —s; *en ces termes.* In other —; *en d'autres termes.* Vain, idle —s; *paroles en l'air.* A grating —; *un mot dur.* By — of mouth; *de vive voix; verbalement.* To speak a good — for; *dire un mot en faveur de, un mot de recommandation pour.* To be a man of one's —; *être homme de parole.* He is a man of few —; *c'est un homme qui parle, ou dit, peu.* Take my — for it; *croyez m'en.* To send — to; *envoyer dire à; faire dire à; donner avis à.* To write — to; *faire savoir à; mander à, écrire à.* To bring —; *venir dire.* To leave —; *dire; prévenir.* To break one's —; *manquer à sa parole.* To speak the —; *trancher le mot.* A — to the wise; *à bon entendeur salut.* To be as good as one's —; *tenir parole; être de parole.* To eat one's —s; *rétracter ce qu'on a dit; rétracter ses paroles.* To have a — with a person; *dire deux mots à quelqu'un.* To have —s; *avoir des mots, échanger des reproches, se quereller, se disputer.* I take you at your —; *je vous prends au mot.* — for —; (in translating) *mot à mot;* (in repeating) *mot pour mot.*

word (weurde), *v.a.*, exprimer; énoncer; écrire; rédiger. Thus —ed; *ainsi conçu.*

word'-book (-bouke), *n.*, vocabulaire, lexique, *m.*

word'-catcher, *n.*, puriste, *m.f.*, éplucheur de mots, *m.*, qui chicane sur les mots.

word'iness, *n.*, prolixité, verbosité, *f.*

word'ing (weurd'-), *n.*, expression, énonciation; rédaction, teneur, *f.*, style; (of a problem) énoncé, *m.*

word'less (weurd'-), *adj.*, sans parole; silencieux.

word'-painter, *n.*, qui excelle dans la description.

word'-painting, *n.*, vive description, *f.*

word'y (weurd'-), *adj.*, verbeux, diffus.

work (weurke), *v.n.*, (*preterit* and *past part.*, Worked, Wrought) travailler; (to act) fonctionner, aller, jouer, agir; (tech.) jouer; (to operate) opérer, agir, avoir de l'effet; (to ferment) fermenter, travailler; (to be agitated) s'agiter, se remuer, se mouvoir; (of a ship) travailler, fatiguer. To — hard; *piocher, travailler dur, ferme.* To — into; *entrer* **dans** . . . *peu à peu;* *pénétrer* **dans;** *s'introduire* **dans.** To — up; *monter; s'élever.* To — like a dog; *travailler comme quatre.* To — upon; *travailler, exciter, influencer; agir* **sur.**

work, *v.a.,* travailler; (to shape) travailler, façonner; (to lead, to influence) conduire, amener, pousser; (to make by action or violence) faire, se faire, se créer; (to employ) mettre en œuvre, exercer, faire travailler; (to produce) produire, faire, opérer; (to embroider) broder; (to cause to ferment) faire fermenter, faire travailler; (print.) tirer; (a machine, a mill, etc.) faire aller, faire mouvoir, manœuvrer; (a ship) manœuvrer; (a mine, a railway, etc.) exploiter. To — one's self up to; *s'exciter, se monter, s'élever* **à.** We have —ed up all our material; *nous avons employé tous nos matériaux.* To — up an article; *élaborer un article.* To — one's way through; *se frayer, s'ouvrir un passage, un chemin.* To — to death; *tuer de travail.* To — a horse to death; *surmener;* (fam.) *crever.* To — down; *réduire.* To — in; *insinuer, faire entrer* (à *force d'efforts).* To — off; *user; employer; achever;* (print.) *tirer.* To — up; *fabriquer, travailler, employer;* (to excite) *soulever, exciter, enflammer.* To — up with; *mélanger* **avec.** To — out; *effectuer par son travail; accomplir par ses efforts;* (a debt) *acquitter une dette par son travail; payer en travail;* (a problem) *résoudre; effectuer; accomplir; venir à bout* **de.** To — one's self up; *se monter, s'exalter.*

work (weurke), *n.,* travail; labeur; (work done) ouvrage, travail, *m.,* besogne; (embroidery) broderie; (awkward performance) mauvaise besogne, *f.,* gâchis, *m.;* (action) action, œuvre, *f.;* (feat) travail, *m.;* (effect) œuvre, *f.,* effet, (of an engine) mécanisme, *m.;* (operation) opération; (lit.) (whole work) œuvre, *f.,* (single work) ouvrage, *m. pl.,* (manu.) fabrique, usine, *f.sing.;* (fort.) travaux, *m.pl.;* (horl.) mouvement, *m.sing.* Day's —; *journée, f.;* — of art; *œuvre d'art, f.* It is a — of time; *c'est un ouvrage qui exige du temps; c'est un ouvrage de longue haleine.* — of love; *œuvre d'amour, f., plaisir, m.* He made me a piece of —; *il me fit une scène, une affaire.* To go, *ou* set, to —; *s'y prendre.* This is the way to go to —; *voici la manière de s'y prendre.* Maid of all —; *bonne à tout faire, f.* To be at —; *être à l'ouvrage, être à travailler.* To be out of —; *chômer, être sans travail.* To throw out of —; *faire chômer.* To cut out — for; *tailler de la besogne* **à.** To set to —; *se mettre au travail, ou à l'ouvrage.* To know how to set to —; *savoir s'y prendre.* To set any one to —; *faire aller, mettre en marche.* To get through a deal of —; *abattre de la besogne.* What a piece of —! *quel gâchis! quel malheur!* What a piece of — is a man! (Shakespeare); *quel problème que l'homme!*

work'able (weurk'a-b'l), *adj.,* maniable; ouvrable; (mines, etc.) exploitable.

work'-bag, *n.,* sac à ouvrage; cabas, *m.*

work'-basket, *n.,* corbeille à ouvrage, *f.*

work'-bench, *n.,* établi, *m.*

work'-box, *n.,* boîte à ouvrage, *f.*

work'-day, *n.,* V. **working-day.**

worked (weurk'te), *adj.,* brodé.

work'er, *n.,* ouvrier; travailleur, *m.*

work'fellow (-fèl-lô), *n.,* compagnon de travail, *m.*

work'-house (-haouce), *n.,* asile des pauvres; hospice, *m.* To come to the —; *aller mourir à l'hôpital.*

work'ing, *n.,* travail; ouvrage; labeur; (of machines) fonctionnement, jeu, *m.;* (operation) opération, *f.,* exécution; effet, *m.;* (fermentation) travail, *m.,* fermentation; (of mines, etc.)

exploitation; (fig.) œuvre, opération, *f.;* (print.) tirage, *m.*

work'ing-barrel (-bar-rèle), *n.,* corps de pompe, *m.*

work'ing-capital, *n.,* fonds de roulement, *m.pl.;* capital d'exploitation, *m.*

work'ing-day, *n.,* jour ouvrable, *m.*

work'ing-place, *n.,* champ d'exploitation, *m.*

work'ing-point (-poï'n'te), *n.,* point de fatigue, *m.*

work'ing-stock, *n.,* matériel d'exploitation, *m.*

work'man, *n.,* ouvrier, artisan, *m.* A bad — always blames his tools; (prov.) *mauvais ouvrier n'a jamais bons outils.*

work'manlike, *adj.,* d'ouvrier habile; bien fait, bien travaillé.

work'manly, *adv.,* en ouvrier; habilement.

work'manship, *n.,* ouvrage; travail, *m.;* œuvre; main d'œuvre, façon, exécution, *f.* Of exquisite —; *d'un travail exquis.*

work'-people (-pî-p'l), *n.pl.,* ouvriers, *m.pl.*

work'-shop, *n.,* atelier (for workmen), *m.*

work'-table (-té-b'l), *n.,* table à ouvrage, *f.*

work'-woman (-woum'-) *n.,* ouvrière, *f.*

work'-yard (-yârde), *n.,* chantier, *m.*

world (weurl'de), *n.,* monde; (course of life) monde, *m.,* vie, *f.;* (time) temps, *m.,* siècles, *m.pl.;* (fig.) monde, *m.,* foule, multitude, *f.* — without end; *éternellement; jusqu'à la fin des siècles.* Nothing in the —; *rien au monde,* (at all) *rien du tout.* A — of good; *beaucoup de bien ou un bien infini.* For the, *ou* for all the, —; *pour tout au monde; pour tout l'or du monde;* (exactly) *exactement.* All the — over; *dans le monde entier.* The best fellow in the —; *le meilleur garçon du monde.* What in the — is the matter with you? *que diantre avez-vous?* To begin the —; *débuter dans le monde;* *commencer la vie.* To come into the —; *venir au monde, voir le jour.* The next —; *l'autre monde, m.; la vie future.* The whole — sprang to arms (Macaulay); *le monde entier courut aux armes.* Such is the — *ou* such is the way of the —; *ainsi va le monde.*

world'liness, *n.,* mondanité; frivolité, *f.;* amour des plaisirs, *m.*

world'ling (weurld'-), *n.,* mondain, *m.*

world'ly (weurld'-), *adj.,* mondain; du monde; positif, frivole.

world'ly-mind'ed (-maï'n'd'-), *adj.,* mondain.

world'ly-mind'edness, *n.,* mondanité, *f.*

world'-wide, *adj.,* universel, répandu partout. He has a — reputation; *il jouit d'une réputation universelle.*

worm (weurme), *n.,* ver, *m.;* chenille, larve, *f.;* (remorse) ver rongeur, remords; (of a screw) filet; (artil.) tire-bourre; (tech.) tire-étoupe; (chem.) serpentin; (debased being) vermisseau, ver de terre, *m.*

worm (weurme), *v.a.,* miner; (fire-arm) débourrer; (tech.) tarauder; (a rope) congréer. To — out; *tirer* **de,** *arracher* **à.** To — one's self into; *se glisser, s'insinuer, se faufiler* **dans.**

worm, *v.n.,* ramper.

worm'-bit, *n.,* mèche à vis, *f.*

worm'-eaten (-ît'n), *adj.,* vermoulu; rongé, *ou* piqué, *ou* mangé des vers.

worm'-grass, *n.,* (bot.) spigélie; petite joubarbe, trique-madame, herbe aux vers, *f.*

worm'-hole (-hôle), *n.,* vermoulure, piqûre, *f.*

worm'-like (-laïke), *adj.,* vermiculaire; comme un ver.

worm'-powder (-paou-deur), *n.,* poudre vermifuge, *f.*

worm'-preventer (-pri-vè'n't'-), *n.,* (nav.) serpenteau, *m.*

worm'-screw (-scrou), *n.,* tire-bourre, *m.*

worm'-seed (-sîde), *n.,* santonine, *f.;* semen-contra, *m.*

worm'-shaped (-shép'te), adj., vermiculaire, vermiforme.

worm'wood (weurm'woude), n., absinthe, f.

worm'y (weurm'-), adj., verreux; plein de vers; (groveling) rampant.

worn, adj., usé; (of clothes in fashion) porté. — out; exténué (with, **de**).

wor'ried, adj., tourmenté, harassé; obsédé.

wor'rier (weur-ri-), n.,f.; taquin, tourment, m.

wor'ry (weur'-), v.a., tracasser, tourmenter, taquiner; (to harass) harasser, échiner; obséder; harceler; (to tear) (of dogs, etc.) déchirer.

wor'ry, v.n., se faire du mauvais sang; se tracasser; se faire de la bile.

worse (weurse), adj., plus mauvais; pire; (of persons ill) plus malade, plus mal; (more wicked) plus méchant. — and —; de pire en pire. — than ever; pire que jamais. To get, ou be taken, —; aller plus mal; empirer. To make —; aggraver, exaspérer, irriter.

worse (weurse), adv., plus mal; pis; plus fort. Far —; bien pis. — and worse; de mal en pis. — than ever; pis que jamais. All the —; d'autant plus mal. To be —; (of health) aller plus mal. To be — than . . .; (with adjective) être plus que . . . To be the — for; se trouver plus mal **de**, ou se ressentir **de**. To be none the — for (it); ne pas s'en trouver plus mal; ne pas s'en ressentir. So much the —; tant pis. Far —; bien pire. To begin again — than ever; recommencer de plus belle.

wor'ship (weur-), n., culte, m.; adoration, f.; service; (title) honneur, m. Your, his —; Monsieur le maire (V. Hugo).

wor'ship (weur-), v.a., adorer, rendre un culte à; (fig.) honorer.

wor'ship, v.n., adorer; adorer Dieu.

wor'shiper (weur-ship'-), n., adorateur, m.

wor'shipful (-foule), adj., honorable; digne.

wor'shipfully, adv., avec honneur; respectueusement.

wor'shiping, n., culte, m.; adoration, f.

worst (weurste), adj., le plus mauvais; le pire.

worst (weurste), n., le plus mauvais, le pire, le plus méchant; le plus mal, le pis, dessous, désavantage, m. To have, ou get, the — of it; avoir le dessous; être battu; succomber. At the —; au pis; au plus mal, au pis aller. The — of it is that . . . ; le pis de l'affaire, c'est que . . . Let us suppose the —; mettons les choses au pis. If the — comes to the —; au pis aller. Do your —; faites ce que vous voudrez.

worst, adv., le pis, le plus mal, le plus fort.

worst (weurste), v.a., battre, vaincre, défaire; l'emporter **sur**. To be worsted; être battu; avoir le dessous.

worst'ed (weurst'ède), n., laine filée; estame, f.

wort (weurte), n., (beer) moût, m.; (bot.) herbe, plante, f.

worth (weurth), n., prix, m.; valeur, f.; mérite, m.; (after a sum of money) pour. To have one's money's —; en avoir pour son argent. — makes the man; la valeur d'un homme dépend uniquement de son mérite. I have bought twenty dollars' — of grain; j'ai acheté pour cent francs de blé.

worth (weurth), adj., qui vaut; égal; qui mérite; qui est riche, ou digne, **de**; de valeur. It is — having; cela n'est pas à dédaigner. To be —; valoir. To be — while; valoir la peine **de**, mériter **de**. He is — a million est riche d'un million. That is — seeing; ∩ vaut la peine, cela mérite d'être vu. — reading; qui vaut la peine, qui vaut d'être lu. — knowing; bon à savoir. To be — having; avoir de la valeur. Not to be — having; sans valeur; ne valoir rien. To be — one's weight in gold; valoir son pesant d'or. Not to be — a brass farthing; n'avoir pas un sou vaillant. To ride, ou gallop, for all one's —; aller, ou galoper, à tombeau ouvert.

worth'ily (weur-thi-), adv., dignement, honorablement; à juste titre.

worth'iness (weur-thi-), n., valeur, f., mérite, m.; vertu, f.

worth'less (weurth'-), adj., sans valeur; de nulle valeur; sans mérite; méprisable, vil, qui ne vaut rien.

worth'lessness (weurth'-), n., manque de valeur, m.; mauvaise qualité; (fig.) bassesse, indignité, f.

worth'y (weur-thi), n., homme illustre, m.; célébrité; (neol.) sommité, f.

worth'y (weur-thi), adj., digne, noble; honorable; (fam.) brave. — of; digne **de**; qui mérite.

would (woude). V. **will**. When used emphatically **would** is translated by **vouloir**. When it is the sign of the conditional or of the imperfect subjunctive, the English infinitive is translated by the conditional or imperfect subjunctive in French. When it is the sign of the imperfect indicative, the English infinitive is translated by the imperfect indicative in French, and **would** itself is not translated. He — read all day; il lisait pendant toute la journée. Sometimes **would**, although the sign of the Conditional, is not followed by the infinitive in English. In that case it is translated by the Conditional of **faire**, e.g.: he received the present as it was anticipated that he —; il reçut le présent comme on pensait qu'il **ferait**. I warned him, but he — do it; je l'ai averti, mais il a voulu le faire tout de même. You — have it; so don't blame me; vous l'avez voulu; ne m'en veuillez pas alors. I thought I — try; j'ai voulu essayer. I thought I — (i.e. had better) speak to him before seeing you; j'ai cru devoir lui parler, ou j'ai cru que je ferais mieux de lui parler, avant de vous voir. — to God; plût à Dieu. What — you have had him do against three? I — have had him die; que vouliez-vous qu'il fût contre trois? Qu'il mourût! (Corneille).

would'-be (woud'bf), adj., prétendu, soi-disant; manqué; qui voulait, aurait voulu être.

wound (wou'n'de), n., blessure, plaie, f.

wound (wou'n'de), v.a., blesser; faire une blessure à; (fig.) (to offend) blesser, offenser.

wound'ing, n., action de blesser, f.; blessures, f.pl.

wrack (rake), n., (bot.) varech, varec, m.

wrack'-grass (-grâce), n., algue marine, f.

wran'gle (ragn'g'l), n., dispute, querelle, f.; chamaillis, m.

wran'gle (ragn'g'l), v.n., se disputer, se quereller, se chamailler.

wran'gler, n., disputeur, querelleur, m., querelleuse, f.; (Cambridge) lauréat en mathématiques, m.

wran'glesome, adj., querelleur.

wran'gling, n., dispute, f.; chamaillis, m.

wrap (rape), v.a., rouler, enrouler; envelopper (in, **dans**; with, **de**); entortiller; plier. To — in; plonger **dans**, envelopper **de**. To be —ped in; être plongé **dans**, être enveloppé **de**. To — up; envelopper, ployer. To be —ped up in; être absorbé **dans**; (in a woman) être engoué **de**.

wrap'per (rap'-), n., (envelope) enveloppe, f.; (garment) peignoir, m.; (for packing) toile d'emballage; (for MS.) chemise; (for newspapers) bande; (print.) couverture, f. Stamped —; (post) bande timbrée. In a —; sous bande.

wrap'ping, n., enveloppe, couverture, f. — paper; papier d'emballage, m.

wrasse (race), n., (ich.) labre, m.

wrath (rôth), n., courroux, m.; colère, fureur, f.

wrath'ful (rôth'foule), adj., courroucé, furieux, irrité.

wrath'fully (rŏth'-), *adv.*, avec courroux ; avec colère.

wreak (rîke), *v.a.*, exécuter ; décharger, faire peser ; assouvir, satisfaire. To — one's vengeance on, *ou* upon ; *tirer vengeance* **de**, ou *se venger* **de**.

wreath (rîth), *n.*, guirlande, couronne, tresse, *f.*; feston, *m.*

wreathe (rîth), *v.a.*, (twist) enrouler, entortiller ; entrelacer **de**; tresser **de**; couronner, *ou* ceindre, **de**.

wreathe (rîthe), *v.n.*, s'entrelacer ; s'enrouler ; tourbillonner.

wreathed (rîth'de), *adj.*, entrelacé ; entouré de guirlandes. — column ; *colonne torse, f.*

wreath'ing (rîth'-), *n.*, entrelacement, *m.*

wreck (rèke), *n.*, naufrage ; (ruins of a ship) navire naufragé, *m.*, épave, *f.*, débris d'un naufrage, *m.pl.*; (fig.) naufrage, *m.*, débris, *m.pl.*, destruction, ruine, ombre, *f.* This man is a perfect — ; *cet homme est l'ombre de lui-même.* To go to — and ruin ; (pers.) *se perdre ; courir à sa perte ;* (of things) *tomber en ruine.*

wreck (rèke), *v.a.*, faire faire naufrage à ; jeter à la côte ; (to ruin) ruiner, perdre. The vessel was —ed ; *le vaisseau fit naufrage.*

wreck'age (-), *n.*, débris du naufrage, *m.pl.*; épaves, *f.pl.*

wrecked (rèk'te), *adj.*, naufragé. To be — ; *faire naufrage.* — with loss of all hands ; *perdu corps et biens.*

wren (rèn), *n.*, (orni.) roitelet, *m.*

wrench (rè'n'she), *n.*, torsion, *f.*; arrachement, *m.*; (sprain) entorse ; (to unscrew) clef, *f.*

wrench (rè'n'she), *v.a.*, arracher (pers., à ; things, **de**) (en tordant) ; forcer, fausser ; (to sprain) se fouler.

wrest (rèste), *v.a.*, arracher à (from a person) ; (to distort) tordre ; torturer, fausser, forcer.

wres'tle (rès's'l), *v.n.*, lutter.

wres'tler (rès-'l'-), *n.*, lutteur, athlète, *m.*

wres'tling (rès's'l'-), *n.*, lutte, lutte corps à corps, *f.*, assaut, *m.*

wretch (rètshe), *n.*, malheureux, *m.*, -euse, *f.*; infortuné, *m.*, infortunée, *f.*; pauvre diable, *m.*; pauvre créature, *f.*; (scoundrel) misérable, *m.f.*, scélérat, *m.*

wretch'ed (rètsh'ède), *adj.*, malheureux, infortuné ; (despicable) méprisable, misérable, vil ; (paltry) triste, méchant ; (calamitous) calamiteux, malheureux.

wretch'edly (rètsh'èd'-), *adv.*, malheureusement ; dans la misère ; misérablement ; tristement ; (despicably) d'une manière méprisable, indignement.

wretch'edness (rètsh'èd'-), *n.*, misère, pauvreté, infortune, *f.*; (unhappiness) malheur, *m.*, souffrance, misère, infortune ; (scantiness) pauvreté ; (despicableness) nature méprisable, nature vile, *f.*

wrig'gle (rig'g'l), *v.n.*, se tortiller, se remuer ; frétiller, s'agiter, se démener. To — into ; *se fourrer* **dans**, s'insinuer **dans**. To — out ; *s'échapper ; échapper* **à**; *sortir* **de** (*en se démenant*), *avec efforts, avec difficulté ;* (fig.) *faire tous ses efforts, mettre tout en usage pour* **rompre**. To — away from ; *s'échapper comme une anguille* **de**.

wrig'gle, *v.a.*, tortiller, fourrer. To — one's way ; *se faufiler.*

wrig'gle (rig'g'l), **wrig'gling**, *n.*, tortillement, remûment, remuement, *m.*

wrig'gler, *n.*, qui se tortille, qui se remue.

wright (raïte), *n.*, ouvrier, artisan ; constructeur **de**, *m.* Wheel— ; *charron, m.* Ship— ; *charpentier de navire ; constructeur de vaisseaux, m.*

wring (rigne), *v.a.*, (*preterit* and *past part.*, Wrung) tordre ; (a secret, money, etc.) arracher ; presser ; serrer ; (to distress) torturer, déchirer, tourmenter ; (to distort) fausser, torturer ; (a mast) forcer. To — one's hands in despair ; *se tordre les mains* **de** *désespoir.* To — the heart ; *déchirer le cœur.* —ing wet ; *trempé jusqu'aux os.*

wring'-bolt (-bôlte), *n.*, (nav.) cheville de presse, *f.*

wring'er (rign'-), *n.*, qui tord ; (machine) tordeuse, *f.*

wring'ing, *n.*, torsion, *f.*; action de se tordre (les mains) ; tourment ; (fig.) déchirement, *m.*, torture, *f.*

wring'-stave (-stéve), *n.*, (nav.) bridole, *f.*

wrin'kle (rign'k'l), *n.*, (in garments) pli, faux pli, *m.*; (in the face ; bot.) ride, *f.*, pli, *m.* To know a — or two ; *en savoir plus d'une.* It is a — worth having ; *c'est bon à savoir.* Do you want a — ? Well, here's one ; *voulez-vous le mot?* Eh bien, le voici ; (fam.) *voulez-vous une ficelle?* Eh bien, en voici une !

wrin'kle (rign'k'l), *v.n.*, se rider.

wrin'kle, *v.a.*, rider ; plisser ; (the brow) froncer.

wrin'kled (rign'k'l'de), *adj.*, ridé ; froncé ; (bot.) plissé, chiffonné.

wrist (riste), *n.*, poignet ; (anat.) carpe, *m.*

wrist'-band (-ba'n'de), *n.*, poignet, *m.*

writ (rite), *n.*, (of parliament) lettre de convocation, *f.*; (jur.) exploit judiciaire, mandat, *m.*, ordonnance ; assignation, *f.* Holy — ; *l'Ecriture sainte, f.* To serve a — on any one ; *signifier une assignation* (à comparaître) **à** *quelqu'un.*

write (raïte), *v.a.*, (*preterit*, Wrote ; *past part.*, Written) écrire ; (to engrave) graver, tracer. To — again to ; *récrire* **à.** To — down ; *marquer ; mettre en écrit ; coucher par écrit ;* (to decry) *décrier, abîmer.* To — for ; (of things) *écrire pour demander ;* (of persons) *mander par écrit.* To — to say that . . . ; *écrire que . . .* To — off ; *écrire au courant de la plume ;* (to deduct) *défalquer, déduire ;* (com.) (of debts) *passer au compte de profits et pertes.* To — out ; *rédiger ; écrire entièrement ;* (to transcribe) *transcrire, copier.* To — out in full ; *écrire en toutes lettres, ou d'un bout à l'autre.* To — over again ; *récrire.* To — un— (to praise) *faire l'éloge de, faire mousser.*

writ, *past. part.*, (*V.* **written**) écrit ; par écrit. — large ; *écrit en toutes lettres ; clairement visible.*

write, *v.n.*, écrire ; transcrire ; (to be a clerk) faire les écritures, la correspondance. To — for ; (to send for) *mander ; faire venir.*

writ'er (raït'-), *n.*, écrivain ; (of a letter) auteur ; (author) écrivain, auteur ; (clerk) commis aux écritures, expéditionnaire, *m.*

writhe (raïthe), *v.a.*, tordre.

writhe (raïthe), *v.n.*, se tordre ; se débattre.

writ'ing (raït'-), *n.*, écriture, *f.*, (anything written) écrit ; (book) écrit, ouvrage, *m.*; (inscription) inscription, *f.* In — ; par écrit. — materials ; *fournitures de bureau, f.pl.; objets pour écrire, m.pl.*

writ'ing-book (-bouke), *n.*, cahier d'écriture, *m.*, cahier, *m.*

writ'ing-case, *n.*, papeterie, *f.*

writ'ing-copy, *n.*, exemple d'écriture, *m.*

writ'ing-desk, *n.*, pupitre, secrétaire, *m.*

writ'ing-master (-mâs-), *n.*, maître d'écriture, *m.*

writ'ing-pad, *n.*, sous-main, buvard, *m.*

writ'ing-table (-té-b'l), *n.*, table à écrire, *f.*; bureau, *m.*

writ'ten (rit't'n), *adj.*, écrit ; par écrit.

wrong (rogne), *adj.*, faux ; fautif, vicieux ; mauvais ; (not what is wanted) ne . . . pas . . . qu'il faut ; (erroneous) erroné, faux, inexact. — side ; *l'envers, m.* — side outward ; *à l'envers.* That is the — one ; *ce n'est pas celui-là qu'il faut.* That's the — trunk, the — train, the — street, etc. ; *ce n'est pas la malle, le train, la rue,* etc. To be — ; (pers.) *avoir tort ;* (of things) *être fautif, être mal, être mauvais ;* (improper) *n'être pas convenable, bienséant ;* (of watches) *aller mal.*

n'être pas à l'heure. That is — ! *c'est mal !* To do the — work, to bring the — book, to take the — street, etc. ; *se tromper d'ouvrage, de livre, de rue,* etc.

wrong (rogne), *adv.*, mal, à tort, à faux ; injustement ; de travers, inexactement.

wrong (rogne), *n.*, mal, *m.* ; (injury done to another) injustice, *f.*, mal, tort, dommage, préjudice, *m.* To be —; *avoir tort.* I am in the —; *j'ai tort.* To do —; *faire une mauvaise action ; faire du tort à.*

wrong (rogne), *v.a.*, faire du tort à ; nuire à ; préjudicier à, léser ; (to do injustice to by imputation) faire tort à ; faire injure à ; être injuste **envers.**

wrong'-doer (-dou'eur), *n.*, pervers, méchant ; auteur d'un tort, d'un préjudice, *m.*

wrong'-doing (-dou'igne), *n.*, mal, *m.*

wrong'ful (-foule), *adj.*, injuste ; (injurious) nuisible, préjudiciable ; injuste.

wrong'fully, *adv.*, à tort ; injustement.

wrong'headed (-hèd'-), *adj.*, qui a mauvaise tête, qui a l'esprit de travers.

wrong'headedness (-hèd'-), *n.*, extravagance ; mauvaise tête, *f. ;* travers d'esprit, *m.*

wrong'ly (ro'gn'-), *adv.*, injustement ; avec injustice ; mal, à tort.

wroth (rôth), *adj.*, en colère, irrité, courroucé. To wax —; *se mettre* (ou *entrer*) *en colère ; s'indigner ; se fâcher.*

wrought (rôte), *adj.*, travaillé, façonné ; (of textile fabrics) ouvré. — iron ; *fer battu,* ou *forgé.* — iron plate ; *tôle, f.*

wry (raïe), *adj.*, de travers ; tordu, tors ; (fig.) oblique, détourné, faux ; torturé, forcé. To pull a — face ; *faire la grimace.*

wry'neck (raïe-nèke), *n.*, cou de travers ; torticolis ; (orni.) torcol, *m.*

wry'-necked (-nèk'te), *adj.*, qui a le cou de travers, qui a le torticolis.

wych'-elm, *n.*, orme de montagne, *m.*

wynd (waïn'de), *n.*, (an alley) ruelle, *f.*

wy'vern, *n.*, givre, guivre, *f.*

X

x, vingt-quatrième lettre de l'alphabet, **x**, *m.*

xe'bec (zî-bèke), *n.*, (nav.) chebec, *m.*

xeroph'agy (zi-rof'a-dji), *n.*, xérophagie, *f.*

xiph'ias (zif'i-asse), *n.*, (ich.) xiphias, espadon, *m.*, épée de mer, *f. ;* (astron.) Xiphias, *m.*

x rays, *n.*, rayons x, *m.pl.*

xyst (ziste) *ou* **xys'tos** (zist'-), *n.*, (Greek and Rom. antiq.) xyste, *m.*

xys'ter (zis-teur), *n.*, (surg.) rugine, *f.*

Y

y, vingt-cinquième lettre de l'alphabet, **y**, *m.*

yacht (yote), *n.*, yacht, *m.*

yacht'ing, *n.*, voyage, *m.*, *ou* promenade, *f.*, en yacht.

yacht'ing-jacket, *n.*, vareuse, *f. ;* saute-en-barque, *m.*

yacht'-race, *n.*, course de yachts, *f.*

yak, *n.*, (zoöl.) yak, *m.*

yam, *n.*, (bot.) igname, *f.*

Yan'kee (ya'gn'ki), *n.*, yankee, Américain, *m.*

yard (yârde), *n.*, cour ; (of a prison) cour, *f.*, préau ; (work-yard) chantier, *m. ;* (nav.) vergue, *f. ;* (measure) yard (mètre 0·912), *m.* — arm ; *taquet, bout de vergue, m.* — stick ; *mesure d'un yard, f.* Fifty —s off ; *à cinquante pas.*

yarn (yârne), *n.*, fil, *m. ;* laine filée, *f. ;* (of a rope) fil, cordon ; (nav.) fil de caret ; (long story) conte à dormir debout, *m.* To spin a long —; *débiter une longue histoire ; en conter long.*

yat'aghan, *n.*, yatagan, *m.* (y *aspirate*).

yaw (yô). *n.*, (nav.) embardée, *f.*

yaw (yô), *v.n.*, (nav.) embarder, donner des embardées.

yawl (yôl), *n.*, yole, *f.* (y *aspirate*).

yawn *ou* **yawn'ing** (yô'n'-), *n.*, bâillement, *m. ;* (ant.) ouverture, *f.*

yawn (yô'n), *v.n.*, bâiller ; (to open wide) s'ouvrir tout grand.

yawn'er (yô'n'-), *n.*, bâilleur, *m.*, bâilleuse, *f.*

yawn'ing (yô'n'-), *adj.*, qui bâille, endormi, assoupi ; (fig.) béant, ouvert, entr'ouvert. The — abyss ; *le gouffre béant, entr'ouvert.*

ycleped' *ou* **yclept'** (i-clèp'te), *adj.*, appelé.

ye (yî), *pron.pl.*, vous.

yea (yé ou yî), *adv.*, oui ; vraiment ; en vérité ; oui-da.

yea (yé *ou* yî), *n.*, vote affirmatif, *m.*

yean (yî'ne), *v.n.*, agneler, mettre bas.

yean'ling (yî'n'-), *n.*, agneau, agnelet, *m.*

year (yîre), *n.*, (unit) an ; (connected with events, and the year in which one is) année, *f. ;* (age) âge, *m.* New —; *nouvel an.* Every —; *chaque année* ou *tous les ans.* Every two —s ; *tous les deux ans.* One — with another ; *une année dans l'autre ; bon an mal an.* From — to —; *d'année en année.* For —s together ; *plusieurs années de suite ; pour des années.* To be ten —s old ; *avoir dix ans.* By the —; *par an ; à l'année.* So much a —; *tant par an.* To be in —s ; *être âgé.* In the — of our Lord ; *l'an du Seigneur.* Academic —; *l'année scolaire.* Half-—; *semestre, m.* Four times a —; *quatre fois par an.* Five thousand a —; *cinq mille livres de rente.* — after —; *d'année en année.* —s and —s ago ; *il y a bien des années.* To grow in —s ; *avancer en âge.* To wish any one a happy New —; *souhaiter la bonne année à quelqu'un.* I wish you a happy New —; (fam.) *je vous la souhaite bonne.*

year'-book (-bouke), *n.*, recueil annuel de jurisprudence ; annuaire, *m.*

year'ling (yîr'-), *adj.*, antenois, âgé d'un an.

year'ling (yîr'-), *n.*, antenois, *m.*

year'ly (yîr'-), *adj.*, annuel, d'un an.

year'ly (yîr'-), *adv.*, annuellement, tous les ans.

yearn (yeurne), *v.n.*, être ému, s'émouvoir. To — after ; *soupirer* **après**, *avoir envie de ; désirer ardemment ; se laisser aller à des émotions (des élans) de tendresse* **pour.**

yearn'ing (yeurn'-), *n.*, élan de tendresse ; élan de l'âme, *m. ;* entrailles, *f.pl. ;* émotion ; compassion ; aspiration ; envie, *f.*, désir ardent, *m.*

yeast (yîste), *n.*, levure, *f. ;* levain, ferment, *m.*

yell, *n.*, hurlement, cri, *m.*

yell, *v.n.*, hurler, pousser des hurlements.

yell'ing, *n.*, hurlements, *m.pl.*

yel'low (yèl'lô), *n.*, jaune, *m.* To become —; *devenir jaune ; jaunir.* To make —; *jaunir.*

yel'low, *adj.*, jaune. — as a guinea ; *jaune comme un coing.*

yel'low (yèl-lô), *v.a.*, jaunir.

yel'low-blos'somed (-blos'seu'm'de), *adj.*, à fleurs jaunes.

yel'low-ham'mer (-), *n.*, bruant, verdier, *m.*

yel'lowish (yèl-lô-ishe), *adj.*, jaunâtre.

yel'lowness, *n.*, couleur jaune, *f.*

yel'low-wort (-weurte), *n.*, (bot.) chlore, *f.*

yelp (yèlpe), *v.n.*, glapir ; (of dogs) japper.

yelp'ing, *n.*, glapissement ; (of dogs) jappement, *m.*

yeo'man (yô-), *n.*, yeoman ; gros fermier, fermier-propriétaire ; garde national à cheval ; (nav.) magasinier, *m.* — of the guard ; *garde à pied, m.* The yeomen of the guard ; *les cent gardes.* —'s work ; *œuvre d'homme de cœur, f.*

yeo'manry (yô-), *n.*, corps des fermiers, *m. ;* garde nationale à cheval ; milice à cheval, *f.*

yes (yèss), *adv.*, oui ; (in reply to a negative remark) si, si fait. You have not done it. —, I have ; *vous ne l'avez pas fait. Si, je l'ai fait ;*

(fam.) *si fait*. To say — ; (*i.e.* to consent) *dire oui ;* (to affirm) *dire que oui* ou *si.* — sir! — sir! *on y va, Monsieur! ou voilà, voilà, Monsieur!*

yes'terday (yès-teur-), *n.*, hier. — evening ; *hier soir, hier au soir.* Day before — evening ; *avant hier soir.* — was Sunday ; *c'était hier dimanche.* In the course of — ; *dans la journée d'hier.* We are not born of — ; *nous ne sommes pas nés d'hier.* The day before — ; *avant-hier* (*matin* ou *soir*). [nuit, la nuit dernière, *f.*

yes'ter-night (yès-teur-naïte), *n.*, (l.u.) cette

yet (yète), *adv.*, encore ; déjà. As — ; *jusqu'ici, jusqu'à présent.* Not as — ; *pas encore.*

yet (yète), *conj.*, pourtant, cependant, toutefois, malgré cela.

yew (you), *n.*, (bot.) if, *m.*

yield (yîlde), *v.a.*, (of crops, etc.) produire ; donner ; rapporter ; (to exhibit) montrer, offrir ; (to grant) accorder, rendre ; (to resign) rendre, livrer ; (to surrender) livrer, céder, abandonner ; (to emit) émettre, exhaler. To — up ; *rendre, livrer.* To — up the ghost ; *rendre le dernier soupir, rendre l'âme.*

yield, *v.n.*, se rendre ; céder ; fléchir. To — to ; *se rendre* **à**, *céder* **à** ; (to temptation) *succomber* **à** ; (to comply with) *accéder* **à**, *se rendre* **à** ; (of inferiors) *se soumettre* **à**.

yield, *n.*, produit, rapport, rendement, *m.*

yield'ing, *adj.*, qui cède facilement ; complaisant, accommodant, facile, souple.

yield'ing (yîld'-), *n.*, reddition, *f. ;* abandon, consentement, *m. ;* soumission, *f.*

yield'ingly, *adv.*, facilement.

yield'ingness, *n.*, caractère accommodant, *m. ;* complaisance, *f.*

yoke (yôke), *v.a.*, mettre au joug ; atteler au joug ; atteler ; (to enslave) subjuguer, asservir ; réduire à l'esclavage ; (to confine) enchaîner, lier. To — with ; *accoupler* **avec.**

yoke, *n.*, joug ; attelage (de deux), *m. ;* (pair) paire, *f.*, couple, *m. ;* (nav.) barre de gouvernail ; (for carrying pails) courge, *f. ;* (fig.) joug, *m. ;* (blouse) empiècement, *m.*

yok'el, *n.*, rustre, campagnard, *m.*

yoke'-elm (-èl'me), *n.*, (bot.) charme, *m.* **e**

yoke'-fellow (-fèl'lô) ou **yoke'-mate,** *n.*, (of animals) camarade d'attelage ; (of men) compagnon de servitude, *m.*

yoke'-ox, *n.*, bœuf de labour, *m.*

yolk (yôke), *n.*, jaune d'œuf ; (of sheep) suint, *m.* The — of an egg ; *un jaune d'œuf.*

yon, *adv.* (ant.). *V.* **yonder.**

yond'er (yo'n'deur), *adv.*, dans le lointain ; là, là-bas ; là-haut.

yond'er (yo'n'deur), *adj.*, à quelque distance ; lointain, éloigné, qui est là-bas ; ce, cet, cette, ces. — castle ; *ce château-là ; le château que vous voyez là-bas.*

yore (yôre), *adv.*, longtemps. In days of — ; *autrefois, jadis. ; dans les jours d'autrefois ; au temps jadis.*

you, *pron.*, vous ; tu ; te, toi ; (indefinite) on. — English ; *vous autres Anglais.* — stupid ! *imbécile que vous êtes !* If I were — ; *si j'étais que de vous ;* ou *si j'étais à votre place.*

young (yeugne), *adj.*, jeune ; (inexperienced) novice ; neuf, inexpérimenté ; (fig.) naissant. — ones ; (of animals) *petits, m.pl.* To grow — again ; *rajeunir.* To make — again ; *rajeunir.*

young (yeugne), **the,** *n.pl.*, les jeunes gens, *m.pl. ;* la jeunesse, *f. ;* les petits, *m.pl.* With — ; (of animals) *pleine.*

young'er (yeugn'gheur), *adj.*, plus jeune ; (of two brothers, etc.) cadet. To grow — and — ; *rajeunir de plus en plus.* In my — days ; *quand j'étais plus jeune.* We don't grow — every day ; *nous ne rajeunissons pas ; ou nous vieillissons tous les jours.*

young'est (yeugn'ghèste), *adj.*, le plus jeune.

young'ish (yeugn'ish), *adj.*, un peu jeune, assez jeune.

young'ling (-'ligne), *n.*, jeune animal, *m.*

young'ster (yeugn'steur), *n.*, jeune homme ; gamin ; blanc-bec ; novice, *m.* — at school ; *écolier, m.*

your, *adj.*, votre, *m.f.sing. ;* vos, *pl.m.f. ;* ton, *m.sing.*, ta, *f.sing. ;* tes, *pl.m.f.* (if not intimate with). — father ; *monsieur votre père.* — mother ; *madame votre mère.*

yours (yourze), *pron.*, le vôtre, *m.sing. ;* la vôtre, *f.sing. ;* les vôtres, *pl.m.f. ;* à vous ; le tien, *m.sing.*, la tienne, *f.sing. ;* les tiens, *m.pl.*, les tiennes, *f.pl. ;* à toi. — truly, sincerely ; *tout, ou bien, à vous ; votre tout dévoué.* — affectionately ; *à vous de cœur.*

yourself' (your-sèlfe), **yourselves',** *pron.*, vous-même ; toi-même ; te, toi, vous ; vous-mêmes.

youth (youth), *n.*, jeunesse, adolescence, *f. ;* (young person) jeune homme, adolescent, *m.* The fountain of — ; *la fontaine de jouvence.* Crabbed age and — . . . ; *jeunesse folâtre et vieillesse revêche* . . .

youth'ful (-foule), *adj.*, jeune ; de jeunesse ; de la jeunesse ; (fresh) frais, vert, vigoureux.

youth'fully, *adv.*, en jeune homme, en jeune fille.

youth'fulness, *n.*, jeunesse, *f.*

yuc'ca (yeuk'-), *n.*, (bot.) yucca, *m.*

yule(tide) (youle), *n.*, fêtes de Noël, *f.* — log ; *bûche de Noël, m.*

Z

z, vingt-sixième lettre de l'alphabet, z, *m.*

zac'cho (zak'kô), *n.*, socle, *m.*

za'ny (zé-), *n.*, zani, bouffon, *m.*

zeal (zîl), *n.*, zèle, *m.*

zeal'less (zîl'-), *adj.*, sans zèle.

zeal'ot (zèl'ote), *n.*, partisan aveugle ; fanatique, zélateur, *m.*

zeal'otry (zèl'-), *n.*, zèle aveugle ; fanatisme, *m.*

zeal'ous (zèl'leusse), *adj.*, zélé ; ardent.

zeal'ously (zèl'leus'-), *adv.*, avec zèle ; ardemment.

zeal'ousness (zèl'leus'-), *n.*, zèle, *m.*

ze'bra (zî-), *n.*, (mam.) zèbre, *m.*

ze'bu (zî-biou), *n.*, (mam.) zébu, *m.*

zed, *n.*, z, *m.*

zena'na, *n.*, appartement des femmes (dans les familles mahométanes) ; harem ; sérail, *m.*

Zend'avesta, *n.*, Zend-Avesta, *m.*

ze'nith (zî-nith), *n.*, zénith ; (fig.) point culminant, comble, sommet, apogée, *m.*

zeph'yr (zèf'eur), *n.*, zéphyr ; Zéphyre, *m.*

ze'ro (zî-rô), *n.*, zéro ; rien, *m.*

zest (zèste), *n.*, zeste ; (relish) goût, *m.*, saveur ; (juice of orange-peel) essence, *f.;* (fig.) piquant, plaisir, *m. ;* ardeur, *f.* To give a — to ; *relever le goût* **de**, *assaisonner ; donner du piquant* **à.**

zig'zag, *n.*, zigzag, *m.*

zig'zag, *adj.*, en zigzag.

zig'zag, *v.a.*, former en zigzags.

zig'zag, *v.n.*, aller en zigzag ; zigzaguer ; former des zigzags.

zig'zagging (-zag'ghigne), *n.*, direction en zigzag, *f. ;* zigzags, *m.pl.*

zinc (zign'ke), *n.*, zinc, *m.*

zinc, *v.a.*, zinguer.

zinc'king, *n.*, zingage, *m.*

zincog'raphy, *n.*, gravure sur zinc, *f.*

zinc'-roofing, *n.*, toiture de zinc, *f.* [*m.*

zinc'-sheets, *n.pl.*, zinc en feuilles, *ou* laminé,

zinc-trade *ou* **-works,** *n.*, zinguerie, *m.*

zinc'-worker, *n.*, zingueur, *m.*

zith'er, *n.*, cithare, *f.*

zo'diac (zô-), *n.*, zodiaque, *m.*

zodi'acal (zô-daï-a-), *adj.*, zodiacal.

zone (zône), *n.*, zone; (girdle) ceinture, *f.*
zoned (zô'n'de), *adj.*, à ceinture; (nat. hist.) zoné.

zoög'eny (zo-odj'i-ni), *n.*, zoogénie, *f.*
zoög'rapher (zo-o-), *n.*, zoographe, *m.*
zoögraph'ic *ou* **zoögraph'ical** (zo-o-), *adj.*, zoographique.
zoög'raphy (zo-o-), *n.*, zoographie, *f.*
zool'atry (zo-o-), *n.*, zoolâtrie, *f.*
zo'ölite (zô-o-laïte), *n.*, zoolithe, *m.*
zoölog'ical (zo-ol-odj'-), *adj.*, zoologique. — gardens; *jardin des plantes, m.*

zoölog'ically (zo-ol-odj'-), *adv.*, d'après les principes de la zoologie; zoologiquement.
zoöl'ogist (zo-ol-odj'-), *n.*, zoologiste, **zoo-**logue, *m.*
zoöl'ogy (zo-ol-odji), *n.*, zoologie, *f.*
zoötom'ical (zo-o-), *adj.*, zootomique.
zoöt'omist (zo o-), *n.*, zootomiste, *m.*
zoöt'omy (-zo-o-), *n.*, zootomie, *f.*
zounds ! (zaou'n'dze), *int.*, parbleu ! morbleu ! diable ! sapristi !
Zu'lu (zou-lou), *n.*, Zoulou, *m. & adj.*
zymot'ic, *adj.*, zymotique.

VOCABULARY
OF
PROPER NAMES.

[For many names wanting here, but which only differ from the French by a letter in their last or penultinate syllable, or in which there is no difference at all, the reader is referred to the two Vocabularies at the end of French-English Part.]

A

Aaron, Aaron, *m.*
Abel, Abel, *m.*
Abigail, Abigaïl, Abigail, *f.*
Abraham, Abraham, *m.*
Absalom, Absalon, *m.*
Acastus, Acaste, *m.*
Achates, Achate, *m.*
Achilles, Achille, *m.*
Actæon, Actéon, *m.*
Ada, Ada, *f.*
Adam, Adam, *m.*
Adelaïde, Adélaïde, *f.*
Adolphus, Adolphe, *m.*
Adrastus, Adraste, *m.*
Adrian, Adrien, *m.*
Ægeus, Égée, *m.*
Ægisthus, Égisthe, *m.*
Æneas, Énée, *m.*
Æolus, Éole, *m.*
Æschylus, Eschyle, *m.*
Æsculapius, Esculape, *m.*
Æsop, Esope, *m.*
Agatha, Agathe, *f.*
Agesilaus, Agésilas, *m.*
Aglaia, Aglaé, *f.*
Agnes, Agnès, *f.*
Agricola, Agricola, *m.*
Agrippina, Agrippine, *f.*
Ahab, Achab, *m.*
Albert, Albert, *m.*
Alcæus, Alcée, *m.*
Alcestis, Alceste, *f.*
Alcibiades, Alcibiade, *m.*
Alcides, Alcide, *m.*
Alexander, Alexandre, *m.*
Alexis, Alexis, *m.*
Alfred, Alfred, *m.*
Alice, Alice, *f.*
Allen, Alain, *m.*
Alpheus, Alphée, *m.*
Alphonso, Alphonse, *m.*
Ambrose, Ambroise, *m.*
Amelia, Amélie, *f.*
Americus Vesputius, *n.,* Améric Vespuce, *m.*
Amos, Amos, *m.*
Amphitryon, Amphitryon, *m.*
Amurath, Amurat, *m.*
Amy, Aimée, *f.*
Anacharsis, Anacharsis, *m.*
Anacreon, Anacréon, *m.*
Anastasius, Anastase, *m.*
Anaxagoras, Anaxagore, *m.*
Anchises, Anchise, *m.*
Andrew, André, *m.*
Andromache, Andromaque, *f.*
Andromeda, Andromède, *f.*
Andronicus, (Livius) Andronicus, *m.*

Andronicus, (Constantinople) Andronique, *m.*
Angelina, Angéline, *f.*
Angelus, Ange, *m.*
Anicetus, Anicet, *m.*
Anna *or* Anne, Anne, *f.*
Annibal. *V.* Hannibal.
Annon, Hannon, *m.*
Anselmo, Anselme, *m.*
Antæus, Antée, *m.*
Anthony, Antoine, *m.*
Antigone, Antigone, *f.*
Antigonus, Antigone, *m.*
Antisthenes, Antisthène, *m.*
Antoinette, Antoinette, *f.*
Antonia, Antonine, *f.*
Antoninus, Antonin, *m.*
Antonius, Antoine, *m.*
Antony, Antoine, *m.*
Apelles, Apelle, *m.*
Apollina, Apolline, *f.*
Apollo, Apollon, *m.*
Appian, Appien, *m.*
Apuleius, Apulée, *f.*
Arabella, Arabelle, *f.*
Arcesilaus, Arcésilas, *m.*
Archibald, Archambaud, *m.*
Archimedes, Archimède, *m.*
Arethusa, Aréthuse, *f.*
Argus, Argus, *m.*
Ariadne, Ariane, *f.*
Ariovistus, Arioviste, *m.*
Aristides, Aristide, *m.*
Aristophanes, Aristophane, *m.*
Aristotle, Aristote, *m.*
Arnold, Arnaud, *m.*
Arrian, Arrien, *m.*
Arsenius, Arsène, *m.*
Artaxerxes, Artaxerxès, *m.*
Artemisia, Artémise, *f.*
Arthur, Arthur, *m.*
Ascanius, Ascagne, *m.*
Asclepiades, Asclépiade, *m.*
Asmodeus, Asmodée, *m.*
Aspasia, Aspasie, *f.*
Astræa, Astrée, *f.*
Astyages, Astyage, *m.*
Atalanta, Atalante, *f.*
Athanasius, Athanase, *m.*
Atreus, Atrée, *m.*
Attila, Attila, *m.*
Augias, Augias, *m.*
Augustin, Augustin, *m.*
Augustus, Auguste, *m.*
Aulus-Gellius, Aulu-Gelle, *m.*
Aurelia, Aurélie, *f.*
Aurelian, Aurélien, *m.*
Aurelius, Aurélius, *m.* Marcus —; *Marc Aurèle.*
Aurora, Aurore, *f.*
Ausonius, Ausone, *m.*

Austin, Augustin, *m.*
Aventine, Aventin, *m.*
Avicenna, Avicenne, *m.*
Avitus, Avit, *m.*

B

Baal, Baal, *m.*
Bajazeth, Bajazet, *m.*
Baliol, Baliol, Bailleul, *m.*
Balthasar, Balthasar, *m.*
Baptist, Baptiste, *m.*
Barbara, Barbe, *f.*
Barbarossa, Barberousse, *m.*
Barnabas, Barnabé, *m.*
Barnaby, Barnabé, *m.*
Bartholomew, Barthélemy, *m.*
Basil, Basile, *m.*
Beatrix, Béatrice, *f.*
Beelzebub, Belzébuth, *m.*
Belisarius, Bélisaire, *m.*
Bellona, Bellone, *f.*
Belshazzar, Balthasar, *m.*
Benedict, Benoît, *m.*
Benjamin, Benjamin, *m.*
Bernardine, Bernardin, *m.*
Bertha, Berthe, *f.*
Bertram, Bertrand, *m.*
Bessie, Élise, Lise, *f.*
Blaize, Blaise, *m.*
Blanche, Blanche, *f.*
Blasius, Blaise, *m.*
Boreas, Borée, *m.*
Bridget, Brigitte, *f.*

C

Cæpio, Cépion, *m.*
Cæsar, César, *m.*
Cæsarius, Césaire, *m.*
Cain, Caïn, *m.*
Calixtus, Calixte, *m.*
Calliope, Calliope, *f.*
Callisthenes, Callisthène, *m.*
Calypso, Calypso, *f.*
Cambyses, Cambyse, *m.*
Camilla, Camille, *f.*
Camillus, Camille, *m.*
Canute, Canut, *m.*
Caroline, Caroline, *f.*
Cassander, Cassandre, *m.*
Cassandra, Cassandre, *f.*
Cassius, Cassius, *m.*
Catharine, Catherine, *f.*
Catiline, Catilina, *m.*
Cato, Caton, *m.*
Catullus, Catulle, *m.*
Cecilia, Cécile, *f.*
Celestine, Célestin, *m.*
Celsus, Celse, *m.*

Cerberus, Cerbère, m.
Ceres, Cérès, f.
Charlemagne, Charlemagne, m.
Charles, Charles, m. — the Fifth (Spain); Charles-Quint. m.
Charlotte, Charlotte, f.
Christ, Christ, m.
Christian, Chrétien, m.
Christian, (Denmark) Christian, m.
Christina, Christine, f.
Christopher, Christophe, m.
Cicely, Cécile, f.
Cicero, Cicéron, m.
Cincinnatus, Cincinnatus, m.
Circe, Circé, f.
Clara, Clara, Claire, f.
Clarissa, Clarisse, f.
Claudia, Claude, f.
Claudian, Claudien, m.
Claudius, Claude, m.
Clement, Clément, m.
Clementina, Clémentine, f.
Cleopatra, Cléopatre, f.
Cletus, Clet, m.
Clio, Clio, f.
Clodoald, Cloud, Clodoald, m.
Cloelia, Clélie, f.
Clotilda, Clotilde, f.
Clytemnestra, Clytemnestre, f.
Columbus, Colomb, m.
Commodus, Commode, m.
Constantine, Constantin, m.
Coriolanus, Coriolan, m.
Cornelia, Cornélie, f.
Cornelius, Cornélius, Corneille, m.
Crispin, Crépin, m.
Croesus, Crésus, m.
Cunegund, Cunégonde, f.
Cupid, Cupidon, m.
the Curiatii, les Curiaces, m.pl.
Curio, Curion, m.
Cybela, or Cybele, Cybèle, f.
Cyprian, Cyprien, m.
Cyrus, Cyrus, m.

D

Dædalus, Dédale, m.
Damian, Damien, m.
Damocles, Damoclès, m.
Darius, Darius, m. — Codomanus; Darius Codoman.
David, David, m.
Deborah, Débora, f.
Dejanira, Déjanire, f.
Delia, Délie, f.
Democritus, Démocrite, m.
Demosthenes, Démosthène, m.
Dennis, Denis, m.
Diana, Diane, f.
Dido, Didon, f.
Diocletian, Dioclétien, m.
Diodorus, Diodore, m. — Siculus; Diodore de Sicile.
Diogenes, Diogène, m. — Laertius; Diogène Laerce, or de Laerte.
Diomedes, Diomède, m.
Dion Cassius, Dion Cassius, m.
Dionysius, Denys, m.
Dominic, Dominique, m.
Domitian, Domitien, m.
Donatius, Donatien, m.
Donatus, Donat, m.
Dorothy, Dorothée, f.
Draco, Dracon, m.
Drusilla, Drusille, f.

E

Edmund, n., Edmond, m.
Edward, n., Edouard, m.
Egeria, n., Égérie, f.
Eleanor, n., Éléonore, f.
Elia, n., Élie, m.
Elias, Elijah, n., Élie, m.
Eligius, n., Éloi, m.
Elisha, n., Élisée, m.
Eliza, n., Élise, Elisa, f.
Elizabeth, n., Élisabeth, f.
Eloïsa, n., Héloïse, f.
Emilius, n., Émile, m.
Emily, n., Émilie, f.
Emmanuel, Emmanuel, m.
Epicurus, n., Épicure, m.
Erasmus, n., Érasme, m.
Erebus, n., Érèbe, m.
Esther, n., Esther, f.
Euclid, n., Euclide, m.
Eugenia, n., Eugénie, f.
Eulalia, n., Eulalie, f.
Euphrasia, n., Euphrasie, f.
Euripides, n., Euripide, m.
Europa, n., Europe, f.
Euryale, n., Euryale, f.
Euryalus, n., Euryale, m.
Eurydice, n., Eurydice, f.
Eusebius, n., Eusèbe, m.
Eustace, n., Eustache, m.
Eutropius, n., Eutrope, m.
Evander, n., Évandre, m.
Eve, n., Ève, f.
Ezekiel, n., Ézéchiel, m.
Ezra, n., Esdras, m.

F

Fabian, Fabien, m.
Fanny, Françoise, Fanny, f.
Faustinus, Faustin, m.
Felix, Félix, m.
Ferdinand, Ferdinand, m.
Firmianus, Firmin, m.
Flavian, Flavien, m.
Flora, Flore, f.
Fortuna, Fortune, f.
Frances, Françoise, f.
Francis, François, m.
Frederick, Frédéric, m.
Fulvia, Fulvie, f.

G

Gabinius, Gabin, m.
Gaetano, Gaétan, Gaetano, m.
Galatea, Galatée, f.
Galileo, Galilée, m.
Ganymede, Ganymède, m.
Geoffrey, Geoffroi, m.
Genseric, Genséric, m.
George, Georges, m.
Georgina, Georgina, Georgette, f.
Germanus, Germain, m.
Germans, Germain, m.
Gertrude, Gertrude, f.
Gervaise, Gervais, m.
Gideon, Gédéon, m.
Giles, Gilles, m.
Glycera, Glycère, f.
Godfrey, Godefroi, Godefroy, m.
Goodwin, Gédouin, m.
Gordian, Gordien, m.
the Gracchi, les Gracques, m.
Gratian, Gratien, m.

Gregory, Grégoire, m.
Grimalkin, Grippeminaud, Raminagrobis, m.
Grizzle, Aliboron, m.
Guercino, le Guerchin, m.
Guido, le Guide, m. — Aretinus, Guy Arétin.
Gustavus, Gustave, m.

H

Habakkuk, n., Habacuc, m.
Hagar, Agar, f.
Haggai, Aggée, m.
Ham, Cham, m.
Hamilcar, Amilcar, m.
Hannah, Anna, f.
Hannibal, Annibal, m.
Hardicanute, Canut le Hardi, m.
Harriet, Henriette, f.
Harry, Henri, m.
Hebe, Hébé, f.
Hecate, Hécate, f.
Hecuba, Hécube, f.
Helen, Helena, Hélène, f.
Heliodorus, Héliodore, m.
Heliogabalus, Héliogabale, m.
Heloisa, Héloïse, f.
Henrietta, Henriette, f.
Henry, Henri, m.
Hercules, Hercule, m.
Hermione, Hermione, f.
Herod, Hérode, m.
Herodian, Hérodien, m.
Herodotus, Hérodote, m.
Hesiod, Hésiode, m.
Hezekiah, Ézéchias, m.
Hiero, Hiéron, m.
Hieronymus, Hiéronyme, Jérôme, m.
Hilary, Hilaire, m.
Hippocrates, Hippocrate, m.
Hippolytus, Hippolyte, m.
Hippomenes, Hippomène, m.
Hodge, Jacques Bonhomme, m.
Holofernes, Holopherne, m.
Homer, Homère, m.
Honorius, Honoré, m.
Horace, Horace, m.
the Horatii, les Horaces, m.
Horatio, Horace, m.
Hortensia, Hortense, f.
Hosea, Osée, m.
Hyacinthus, Hyacinthe, m.
Hugh, Hugues, m.
Hymen, Hymenæus, Hymen, Hyménée, m.
Hyperides, Hypéride, m.
Hyperion, Hypérion, m.
Hyrcanus, Hyrcan, m.
Hystaspes, Hystaspe. Darius —; Darius, fils d'Hystaspe, m.

I

Icarus, Icare, m.
Ignatius, Ignace, m.
Iphigenia, Iphigénie, f.
Irene, Irène, f.
Isaac, Isaac, m.
Isabella, Isabelle, f.
Isaiah, Isaïe, m.
Ishmael, Ismaël, m.
Isidorus, Isidore, m.
Isis, Isis, f.
Israel, Israël, m.
Ivanhoe, Ivanhoé, m.
Ixion, Ixion, m.

J

Jack, Jean, Jeannot, *m.*
Jacob, Jacob, *m.*
James, Jacques, James, *m.*
Jane, Jeanne, *f.*
Janet, Jeannette, Jeanneton, *f.*
Jansenius, Jansénius, *m.*
Janus, Janus, *m.*
Jasper, Gaspard, *m.*
Jean, Jeanne, *f.*
Jeffrey, Geoffroy, *m.*
Jehoshaphat, Josaphat, *m.*
Jehovah, Jéhovah, *m.*
Jehu, Jéhu, *m.*
Jenny, Jeannette, Jenny, *f.*
Jephthah, Jephté, *m.*
Jeremiah, Jérémie (le prophète), *m.*
Jeremy, Jérémie, *m.*
Jerome, Jérôme, *m.*
Jesus, Jésus, *m.* — Christ; *Jésus-Christ.*
Jezebel, Jézabel, *f.*
Jim *or* Jem, Jacquot, *m.*
Joan, Jeanne, *f.* — of Arc; *Jeanne d'Arc.*
Job, Job, *m.*
John, Jean, *m.*
Johnny, Jeannot, *m.*
Jonah, Jonas, *m.*
Joseph, Joseph, *m.*
Josephine, Joséphine, *f.*
Josephus, Josèphe, *m.*
Joshua, Josué, *m.*
Josiah, Josias, *m.*
Jove, Jupiter, *m.*
Judah, Juda, *m.*
Judas, Jude; Judas, *m.* — Iscariot; *Judas Iscariote.*
Juggernaut, Jagrenat, *m.*
Julia, Julie, *f.*
Julian, Julien, *m.*
Juliana, Julienne, *f.*
Juliet, Juliette, *f.*
Julius, Jules, *m.*
Junia, Junie, *f.*
Juno, Junon, *f.*
Jupiter, Jupiter, *m.* — Olympius; *Jupiter Olympien.*
Justinian, Justinien, *m.*
Justus, Juste, *m.*
Juvenal, Juvénal, *m.*

K

Katharine, Kate, Kitty, Catherine, *f.*

L

Ladislaus, Ladislas, *m.*
Laelia, Lélie, *f.*
Laertes, Laerte, *m.*
Laertius, Laerce, *m.*
Landrik, Landry, Landri, Landry, *m.*
Latona, Latone, *f.*
Launcelot, Lancelot, *m.*
Laura, Laure, *f.*
Laurence, Lawrence, Laurent, *m.*, Laurence, *f.*
Lavinia, Lavinie, *f.*
Lazarus, Lazare, *m.*
Leah, Lia, *f.*
Leander, Léandre, *m.*
Leda, Léda, *f.*
Leo, Léon, *m.*
Leon, Léon, *m.*
Leonard, Léonard, *m.*

Leonardo da Vinci, Léonard de Vinci, *m.*
Leonia, Léonie, *f.*
Leonidas, Léonidas, *m.*
Leonora, Léonore, *f.*
Leontius, Léonce, *m.*
Leopold, Léopold, *m.*
Lepidus, Lépide, *m.*
Lewis, Louis, *m.*
Linnæus, Linné, *m.*
Livia, Livie, *f.*
Livy, Tite-Live, *m.*
Lizzie, Lise, Lisette, *f.*
Longinus, Longin, *m.*
Lot, Loth, *m.*
Lothario, Lothaire, *m.*
Louie, Louison, *f.*
Louisa, Louise, *f.*
Lucan, Lucain, *m.*
Lucian, Lucien, *m.*
Lucifer, Lucifer, *m.*
Lucilla, Lucille, *f.*
Lucinda, Lucinde, *f.*
Lucretia, Lucrèce, *f.*
Lucretius, Lucrèce, *m.*
Lucy, Lucie, *f.*
Luke, Luc, *m.*
Lycurgus, Lycurgue, *m.*
Lydia, Lydie, *f.*
Lysander, Lysandre, *m.*
Lysippus, Lysippe, *m.*

M

Mab, Mab, *f.*
Macarius, Macaire, *m.*
the Maccabees, les Maccabées, *m.pl.*
Maccabeus, Maccabée, *m.*
Machiavelli, Machiavel, *m.*
Macrobius, Macrobe, *m.*
Madeline, Madeleine, *f.*
Maecenas, Mécène, *m.*
Maggie, Margot, *f.*
Magdalen, Madeleine, *f.*
Mahomet, Mahomet, *m.*
Malachi, Malachy, Malachie, *m.*
Manasseh, Manassé, (the king) Manassès, *m.*
Manfred, Mainfroi, Manfred, *m.*
Marcellinus, Marcellin, *m.*
Marcus Aurelius, Marc-Aurèle, *m.*
Margaret, Marguerite, *f.*
Marius, Marius, *m.*
Mark, Marc, *m.*
Mars, Mars, *m.*
Martha, Marthe, *f.*
Mary, Marie, *f.*
Matilda, Mathilde, *f.*
Matthew, Mathieu, *m.*
Matthias, Mathias, *m.*
Maud, Madelon, *f.*
Maurice, Maurice, *m.*
Maximian, Maximien, *m.*
Maximilian, Maximilien, *m.*
Maximus, Maxime, *m.*
Mecœnas, Mécène, *m.*
Medea, Médée, *f.*
Medici, Médicis, *m.f.*
Medusa, Méduse, *f.*
Melchizedek, Melchisédech, *m.*
Melpomene, Melpomène, *f.*
Menelaus, Ménélas, *m.*
Mephistopheles, Méphistophélès, *m.*
Mercury, Mercure, *m.*
Messalina, Messaline, *f.*
Methuselah, Mathusalem, *m.*

Micah, Michée, *m.*
Michael, Michel, *m.* — Angelo; *Michel-Ange.*
Milo, Milon, *m.*
Miltiades, Miltiade, *m.*
Minerva, Minerve, *f.*
Mithridates, Mithridate, *m.*
Mohammed, Mahomet, *m.*
Molly, Manon, Marion, Manette, *f.*
Monica, Monique, *f.*
Mordecai, Mardochée, *m.*
Morpheus, Morphée, *m.*
Morrice, Morris, Maurice, *m.*
Moses, Moïse, *m.*

N

Nancy, Nance, Nanette, *f.*
Naomi, Noémi, *f.*
Napoleon, Napoléon, *m.*
Narcissus, Narcisse, *m.*
Nathan, Nathan, *m.*
Nebuchadnezzar, Nabuchodonosor, *m.*
Nehemiah, Néhémie, *m.*
Nemesis, Némésis, *f.*
Neoptolemus, Néoptolème, *m.*
Neptune, Neptune, *m.*
Nereus, Nérée, *m.*
Nero, Néron, *m.*
Nicephorus, Nicéphore, *m.*
Nicodemus, Nicodème, *m.*
Nicholas, Nicolas, *m.*
Nimrod, Nemrod, *m.*
Niobe, Niobé, *f.*
Noah, Noé, *m.*

O

Obadiah, Abdias, *m.*
Oceanus, (myth.) Océan, *m.*
Octavia, Octavie, *f.*
Octavius, Octave, *m.*
Odoacer, Odoacre, *m.*
Œdipus, Œdipe, *m.*
Oliver, Olivier, *m.*
Olivia, Olivie, *f.*
Olympia, Olympe, *f.*
Onesimus, Onésime, *m.*
Ophelia, Ophélie, *f.*
Orestes, Oreste, *m.*
Orlando, Roland, *m.*
Orpheus, Orphée, *m.*
Osiris, Osiris, *m.*
Otho, Othon, *m.*
Ovid, Ovide, *m.*
Owen, Ouen, *m.*

P

Palaeologus, Paléologue, *m.*
Pamphylus, Pamphyle, *m.*
Pancras, Pancrace, *m.*
Pandora, Pandore, *f.*
Paracelsus, Paracelse, *m.*
the Parcæ, les Parques, *f.pl.*
Paris (pah-riss), Pâris, *m.*
Parmenio, Parménion, *m.*
Patrick, Patrice, Patrick, *m.*
Patrocles, Patrocle, *m.*
Paul, Paul, *m.*
Paulina, Pauline, *f.*
Paulinus, Paulin, *m.*
Paulus-Æmilius, Paul-Émile, *m.*
Pegasus, Pégase, *m.*
Pelagia, Pélagie, *f.*
Pelagius, Pélage, *m.*
Peleus, Pélée, *m.*

Penelope, Pénélope, f.
Pentheus, Penthée, m.
Pepin, Pépin, m. — the Short; Pépin le Bref.
Periander, Périandre, m.
Pericles, Périclès, m.
Perpetua, Perpétue, f.
Perseus, Persée, m.
Persius, Perse, m.
Perugino, le Pérugin, m.
Peter, Pierre, m.
Petrarch, Pétrarque, m.
Petronilla, Pétronille, f.
Petronius, Pétrone, m.
Phædra, Phèdre, f.
Phædrus, Phèdre, m.
Pharaoh, Pharaon, m.
Phaethon, Phaéton, m.
Pharnaces, Pharnace, m.
Philip, Philippe, m. — the Bold; Philippe le Hardi. — the Fair; Philippe le Bel.
Philippa, Philippe, f.
Phœbe, Phébé, f.
Phœbus, Phébus, m.
Phryne, Phryné, f.
Pindar, Pindare, m.
Pisistratus, Pisistrate, m.
Pius, Pie, m.
Plato, Platon, m.
Plautus, Plaute, m.
Pliny, Pline, m. — the Elder; Pline l'Ancien. — the Younger; Pline le Jeune.
Plutarch, Plutarque, m.
Pluto, Pluton, m.
Polybius, Polybe, m.
Polynices, Polynice, m.
Polymnia, Polymnie, f.
Polyphemus, Polyphème, m.
Pomona, Pomone, f.
Pompey, Pompée, m.
Pontius Pilate, Ponce Pilate, m.
Poppæa, Poppée, f.
Porphyry, Porphyre, m.
Potiphar, Putiphar, m.
Praxiteles, Praxitèle, m.
Priam, Priam, m.
Priapus, Priape, m.
Priscilla, Priscille, f.
Procopius, Procope, m.
Prometheus, Prométhée, m.
Propertius, Properce, m.
Proserpine, Proserpine, f.
Proteus, Protée, m.
Psyche, Psyché, f.
Ptolemy, Ptolémée, m.
Pylades, Pylade, m.
Pyramus, Pyrame, m.
Pyrrhus, Pyrrhus, m.
Pythagoras, Pythagore, m.

Q

Quintilian, Quintilien, m.
Quintus Curtius, Quinte-Curce, m.
Quixote, Quichotte, m. Don—; Don Quichotte.

R

Radegund, Radegonde, f.
Ralph, Raoul, m.
Randolph, Randolphe, m.
Raphael, Raphaël, m.
Raymund, Raymond, m.
Rebecca, Rébecca, f.
Reginald, Renaud, m.

Regulus, Régulus, m.
Remus, Rémus, m.
Remy, Rémi, m.
Reuben, Ruben, m.
Rhea, Rhée, f.
Richard, Richard, m.
Robert, Robert, m.
Roland, Roland, m.
Romano (Giulio), Jules Romain, m.
Romanus, Romain, m.
Romeo, Roméo, m.
Romulus, Romulus, m.
Rosa, Rose, Rose, f.
Rosaline, Rosalie, f.
Rosamund, Rosemonde, Rosamonde, f.
Rosinante, Rossinante, m.
Rowland, Roland, m.
Roxana, Roxane, f.

S

Sabina, Sabine, f.
Sallust, Salluste, m.
Samson, Samson, m.
Sancho Panza, Sancho Pança, m.
Santa Claus, Le Petit Noël, m.
Sappho, Sapho, f.
Sarah, Sara, f.
Sardanapalus, Sardanapale, m.
Satan, Satan, m.
Saturn, Saturne, m.
Saturninus (St.), n., Saturnin, Sernin, m.
Saul, Saül, m.
Savonarola, Savonarole, m.
Scipio, Scipion, m. — Africanus; Scipion l'Africain.
Sebastian, Sébastien, m.
Sejanus, Séjan, m.
Semiramis, Séminaris, f.
Seneca, Sénèque, m.
Septimius, Septime, m.
Sesostris, Sésostris, m.
Severus, Sévère, m.
Shem, Sem, m.
Sigismund, Sigismond, m.
Silenus, Silène, m.
Silvan, Silvain, m.
Silvester, Silvestre, Sylvestre, m.
Silvia, Silvie, f.
Simeon, Siméon, m.
Simonides, Simonide, m.
Sisyphus, Sisyphe, m.
Sixtus, Sixte, m. — the Fifth; Sixte-Quint.
Socrates, Socrate, m.
Socinus, Socin, m.
Solomon, Salomon, m.
Sophia, Sophie, f.
Sophocles, Sophocle, m.
Stanislaus, Stanislas, m.
Statius, Stace, m.
Stephen, Étienne, m.
Strabo, Strabon, m.
Suetonius, Suétone, m.
Sulpicius, Sulpice, m.
Susan, or Susannah, Susanne, Suzanne, f.
Susy, Susey, Susette, Suzon, f.

T

Tacitus, Tacite, m.
Tamerlane, Tamerlan, m.
Tancred, Tancrède, f.
Tantalus, Tantale, m.

Tarquin, Tarquinius, Tarquin, m. — Superbus; Tarquin le Superbe. — Priscus; Tarquin l'Ancien.
Tasso, le Tasse, m.
Telemachus, Télémaque, m.
Terentius, Térence, m.
Tereus, Térée, m.
Terpsichore, Terpsichore, f.
Tertullian, Tertullien, m.
Thales, Thalès, m.
Thalia, Thalie, f.
Themistocles, Thémistocle, m.
Theobald, Thibaut, m.
Theocritus, Théocrite, m.
Theodora, Théodore, Théodora, f.
Theodorus, Théodore, m.
Theophilus, Théophile, m.
Theophrastus, Théophraste, m.
Theresa, Thérèse, f.
Thersites, Thersite, m.
Theseus, Thésée, m.
Thisbe, Thisbé, f.
Thomas, Thomas, m. — Aquinas; Thomas d'Aquin.
Thrasybulus, Thrasybule, m.
Thucydides, Thucydide, m.
Thyestes, Thyeste, m.
Tiberius, Tibère, m.
Tibullus, Tibulle, m.
Timotheus, Timothée, m.
Timothy, Timothée, m.
Tintoretto, le Tintoret, m.
Titian, le Titien, m.
Titus, Titus, m. — Livius; Tito-Live.
Tobias, Tobie, m.
Trajan, Trajan, m. — 's Column; la colonne Trajane.
Tullia, Tullie, f.
Tully, Cicéron, m.
Tyrtæus, Tyrtée, m.

U

Ugolino, Ugolin, m.
Ulrica, Ulrique, f.
Ulysses, Ulysse, m.
Urania, Uranie, f.
Urban, Urbain, m.
Uriah, Urie, m.
Ursula, Ursule, f.

V

Valentine, Valentin, m., Valentine, f.
Valeria, Valérie, f.
Valerian, Valérien, m.
Valerius, Valère, m.
Varro, Varron, m.
Venus, Vénus, f.
Veronese, Véronèse, m.
Veronica, Véronique, f.
Verres, Verrès, m.
Vertumnus, Vertumne, m.
Vespasian, Vespasien, m.
Vespucci (Amerigo), Vespuce (Améric).
Victoria, Victoire, Victoria, f.
Victorian, Victorien, m.
Vincent, Vincent, m.
Virgil, Virgile, m.
Virginia, Virginie, f.
Vishnu, Vishnou, m.
Vitruvius, Vitruve, m.
Vivian, Vivien, m., Vivienne, f.
Volscian, Volsque, m.
Vulcan, Vulcain, m.

W

Walter, Gautier, Walter, *m.*
Wenceslas, Venceslas, *m.*
Wicliffe, Wiclef, *m.*
Wilfrid, Vilfrid, *m.*
Wilhelmina, Wilhelmine, *f.*
William, Guillaume, *m.* — the Conqueror; *Guillaume le Conquérant.* —Rufus; *Guillaume le Roux.*

X

Xanthippus, Xanthippe, *m.*
Xenophon, Xénophon, *m.*
Xerxes, Xerxès, *m.*

Z

Zaccheus, Zachée, *m.*
Zachariah, Zacharie, *m.*

Zebadiah, **Zebedee**, Zébédée, *m.*
Zedekiah, Sédécias, *m.*
Zeno, Zénon, *m.*
Zenobia, Zénobie, *f.*
Zephyrus, Zéphyre, *m.*
Zerubbabel, Zorobabel, *m.*
Zoe, Zoé, *f.*
Zoilus, Zoïle, *m.*
Zoroaster, Zoroastre, *m.*
Zuinglius, Zwingle, *m.*

VOCABULARY

OF

GEOGRAPHICAL NAMES.

A

Aargau, Argovie, *f.*
Abdera, Abdère, *f.*
the **Abruzzi,** les Abruzzes, *f. pl.*
Abruzzo, l'Abruzze, *f.*
Abyssinia, l'Abyssinie, *f.*
Acadia, Acadie, *f.*
Achaia, Achaïe, *f.*
Acre, Acre, St. Jean d'Acre, *m.*
Adrianople, Andrinople, *f.*
the **Adriatic,** la mer Adriatique, *f.*
the **Ægean Sea,** la mer Egée, *f.*
Ægina, Egine, *f.*
Æolia, l'Éolie, *f.*
Afghanistan, l'Afghanistan, *m.*
Africa, Afrique, *f.*
Agincourt, Azincourt, *m.*
Alba, Albe, *f.*
Albania, Albanie, *f.*
Alderney, Aurigny, *m.*
Aleppo, Alep, *m.*
Alexandretta, Alexandrette, *f.*
Alexandria, Alexandrie, *f.*
Algeria, Algérie, *f.*
Algiers, Alger, *m.*
the **Alps,** les Alpes, *f.pl.*
the **Amazon,** (riv.) l'Amazone, Maragnon, *m.*
America, Amérique, *f.*
Amoor, Amour, *m.*
Anatolia, Anatolie, *f.*
Ancona, Ancone, *f.*
Andalusia, Andalousie, *f.*
Andes, Andes, *f.pl.*
Andorra, Andorre, *f.*
Angiers, Angers, *m.*
Antananarivo, Tananarive, *m.*
Antigua, Antigoa, *m.*
the **Antilles,** les Antilles, *f.pl.*
the Greater —; *les Grandes Antilles.* *the* Lesser —; *les Petites Antilles.*
Antioch, Antioche, *f.*
Antwerp, Anvers, *m.*
the **Apennines,** les Apennins, *m.pl.*
the **Appalachians,** les monts Appalaches, *m.pl.*
Apulia, Pouille, Apulie, *f.*
Aquilea, Aquilée, *f.*
Aquitaine, l'Aquitaine, *f.*
Arabia, Arabie, *f.* — Deserta; *l'Arabie Déserte.* — Felix; *l'Arabie Heureuse.* — Petræa; *l'Arabie Pétrée.*
Arcadia, Arcadie, *f.*
Archangel, Archangel, *m.*
the **Archipelago,** l'Archipel, *m.*
the **Argentine Republic,** la République Argentine, *or* l'Argentine, *f.*; les Etats-Unis du Rio de la Plata, *m.pl.*
Argolis, l'Argolide, *f.*

Armenia, l'Arménie, *f.*
Asia, l'Asie, *f.* — Minor; *l'Asie-Mineure.*
Assyria, Assyrie, *f.*
the **Asturias,** les Asturies, *f.pl.*
Asuncion, l'Assomption, *f.*
Athens, Athènes, *f.*
Atlas, Atlas, *m.*
Attica, Attique, *f.*
Augsburg, Augsbourg, *m.*
Australasia, l'Australasie, *f.*
Australia, l'Australie, *f.*
Austria, l'Autriche, *f.*
Austria - Hungary, l'empire Austro-Hongrois, *m.*
the **Aventine Hill,** le Mont Aventin, *m.*
the **Averno,** l'Averne, *m.*
Azof, Azof, Azov, *m.*
the **Azores,** les Açores, *f.pl.*

B

Babylon, Babylone, *f.*
Baden Baden, Bade, *m.*
Baffin's Bay, la mer de Baffin, *f.*
Bagdad, Bagdad, *f.*
the **Bahama Islands,** les îles Bahama, les Lucayes, *f.pl.*
the **Balearic Islands,** les îles Baléares, *f.pl.*
the **Baltic,** la mer Baltique, *f.*
Baluchistan. *V.* **Beloochistan.**
Barbadoes, la Barbade, *f.*
Barbary, la Barbarie, *f.* The — States; *les États Barbaresques, m.pl.*
Barcelona, Barcelone, *f.*
Barcelonetta, Barcelonette (Spain), *f.*
Barcelonette, Barcelonnette (France), *f.*
Basel, *or* **Basle,** Bâle, *m.,f.*
Bavaria, la Bavière, *f.*
Bearn, le Béarn, *m.*
Belgium, la Belgique, *f.*
Beloochistan, Béloutchistan, *m.*
Bengal, le Bengale, *m.* *the* Bay of —; *le Golfe du Bengale.*
Berlin, Berlin, *m.*
the **Bermudas,** les îles Bermudes, *f.pl.*
Bern, Berne, *f.*
the **Bernese Alps,** les Alpes Bernoises, *f.pl.*
Bethlehem, Bethléem, *m.*
Beyrut, Beyrouth, *m.*
Biscay, la Biscaye, *f.* *the* Bay of —; *le Golfe de Gascogne, m.*
the **Black Forest,** la Forêt Noire, *f.*
Blanco (Cape), le Cap Blanc, *m.*
Bohemia, la Bohême, *f.*

Bokhara, (state) la Boukharie, *f.*; (city) Boukhara, *m.*
Bolivia, la Bolivie, *f.*
Bologna, Bologne, *f.*
Bombay, Bombay, *m.*
Bosnia, la Bosnie, *f.*
the **Bosphorus,** le Bosphore, le canal de Constantinople, *m.*
Bothnia, la Bothnie, *f.*
Bourbon (island), l'île de la Réunion, l'île Bourbon, *f.*
Brabant, Brabant, *m.*
Brazil, le Brésil, *m.*
Bremen, Brême, *f.*
Brindisi, Brindes, Brindisi, *m.*
Britain, la Grande Bretagne, *f.* New —; *la Nouvelle Bretagne.*
the **British Channel,** la Manche, *f.*
the **British Isles,** les îles Britanniques, *f.pl.*
Brittany, la Bretagne (France), *f.*
Brussels, Bruxelles, *f.*
Bucharest, Bukarest, Bucharest, *m.*
Bucharia, la Boukharie, *f.*
Buda, Bude, *f.*
Bulgaria, la Bulgarie, *f.*
Burgundy, la Bourgogne, *f.*
Burmah, l'Empire Birman, *m.*
Byzantium, Byzance, *f.*

C

Cabul, Caboul, *m.*
Cadiz, Cadix, *m.*
Caffraria, la Cafrerie, *f.*
Cairo, le Caire, *m.*
Calabria, la Calabre, *f.*
Calais, Calais, *m.*
Calcutta, Calcutta, *f.*
Caledonia, la Calédonie, *f.*
California, la Californie, *f.*
Calvary, le Calvaire, *m.*
Cambodia, le Cambodge, *m.*
Campania, la Campanie, *f.*
Campeachy, Campêche, *m.*
Canaan, Chanaan, *m.*
Canada, Canada, *m.*
the **Canary Islands,** les îles Canaries, *f.pl.*
Candia, Candie, Crète, *f.*
Cannæ, Cannes (*des anciens*), *f.*
Canterbury, Cantorbéry.
Capetown, le Cap, *m.;* la ville du Cap, *f.* *the* **Cape of Good Hope;** *le cap de Bonne Espérance.* Cape Colony; *la Colonie du Cap.*
Capernaum, Capharnaüm, *m.*
the **Capitoline Hill,** le Mont Capitoline, *m.*
Cappadocia, la Cappadoce, *f.*

Capua, Capoue, *f.*

the **Caribbean,** la mer des Antilles, *f.*

the **Caribbee Islands,** les Antilles, les îles Caraïbes, *f.pl.*

Carinthia, la Carinthie, *f.*

the **Carnatic,** le Karnatic, *m.*

the **Carnic Alps,** les Alpes Carniques, *f.pl.*

Carolina, la Caroline, *f.*

Carniola, la Carniole, *f.*

the **Carpathians,** les Monts Karpathes, les Carpathes, *m.pl.*

Cartagena, Carthagène, *f.*

Carthage, Carthage, *f.*

Cashmere, le Cachemire, *m.*

the **Caspian,** la mer Caspienne, *f.*

Castile, la Castille, *f.*

Catalonia, la Catalogne, *f.*

the **Caucasus,** le Caucase, *m.*

Cephalonia, Céphalonie, *f.*

Cettinje, Cettigne, *f.*

Ceylon, l'île de Ceylan, *f.*

Chalcedon, Chalcédoine, *f.*

Chaldea, la Chaldée, *f.*

Chamouny, Chamouny, Chamonix, *m.*

Champagne, la Champagne, *f.*

Chandernagore, Chandernagor, *m.*

the **Channel Islands,** *pl.*, les îles du Canal *or* de la Manche; les îles anglo-normandes, *f.pl.*

Charybdis, Charybde, *f.*

Chile, Chili, *m.*

China, Chine, *f.* The — Sea ; *la mer de Chine.*

Cilicia, la Cilicie, *f.*

Circassia, la Circassie, *f.*

Coburg, Cobourg, *m.*

Cochin-China, la Cochin-chine, *f.*

the **Cocytus,** le Cocyte, *m.*

Colchis, Colchide, *f.*

Colombia, la Colombie, *f.*

the **Congo,** le Congo, *m.*

Connecticut, Connecticut, *m.*

Constantina, Constantine, *f.*

Constantinople, Constantinople, *f.*

Cook's Strait, *n.*, le détroit de Cook, *m.*

the **Coral Sea,** la mer de Corail, *f.*

Cordova, Cordoue, *f.*

Corea, la Corée, *f.*

Corfu, Corfou (isle) *f.*, (town) *m.*

Corinth, Corinthe, *f.*

Cornwall, le Cornouailles, *m.*

Corsica, la Corse, *f.*

Corunna, la Corogne, *f.*

the **Cottian Alps,** les Alpes Cottiennes, *f.pl.*

Cracow, Cracovie, *f.*

Cremona, Crémone, *f.*

Crete, la Crète, Candie, *f.*

the **Crimea,** la Crimée, *f.*

Croatia, la Croatie, *f.*

Cuma, Cumæ, Cumes, *f.*

the **Cyclades,** *pl.*, les Cyclades, *f.pl.*

Cyprus, l'île de Chypre, *f.*

Cythera, Cythère, *f.*

D

Dacia, la Dacie, *f.*

Dalmatia, la Dalmatie, *f.*

Damascus, Damas, *m.*

Damietta, Damiette, *f.*

Danube, le Danube, *m.*

Danzig, Dantzick, *m.*

the **Dardanelles,** les Dardanelles, *f.pl.*

Dauphiny, le Dauphiné, *m.*

Davis Strait, le détroit de Davis, *m.*

the **Dead Sea,** la mer Morte, *f.*

the **Deccan,** le Décan, Dekhan, *m.*

Delos, Délos, *f.*

Delphi, Delphes, *f.*

Denmark, le Danemark, *m.*

Dominica, Dominique, *f.*

the **Dominican Republic,** Saint-Domingue, *m.*

Dover, Douvres, *m.* *the* Straits of — ; *le Pas-de-Calais, m.*

Dresden, Dresde, *f.*

Dunkirk, Dunkerque, *m.*

E

Ebro, l'Èbre, *m.*

Ecuador, la République de l'Équateur, *f.*

Edinburgh, Édimbourg, *m.*

Egypt, l'Égypte, *f.*

Elba, l'île d'Elbe, *f.*

the **Elbe,** (riv.) l'Elbe, *m.*

Elsinore, Elseneur, *m.*

the **Engadine,** l'Engadine, *f.*

England, l'Angleterre, *f.* New — ; *la nouvelle Angleterre.*

the **English Channel,** la Manche, *f.*

Eolia, *f.*, l'Éolie, *f.*

Ephesus, Éphèse, *f.*

Epidaurus, Epidaure, *f.*

Epirus, Épire, *f.*

Erie, (lake) le lac Érié, *m.*

Erin, Irlande, *f.*

Estremadura, l'Estrémadure, *f.*

Ethiopia, l'Éthiopie, *f.*

Etna, l'Etna, *m.* Mount — ; *le mont Etna.*

Etruria, l'Étrurie, *f.*

Euboea, l'île de Négrepont, l'Eubée, *f.*

the **Euphrates,** l'Euphrate, *m.*

Europe, l'Europe, *f.*

the **Euxine,** le Pont-Euxin, *m.*

F

the **Falkland Islands,** les îles Malouines *or* Falkland, *f.pl.*

the **Faroe Islands,** les îles Féroë, *f.pl.*

Ferrara, Ferrare, *f.*

Ferro, l'île de Fer, *f.*

Finland, la Finlande, *f.*

Flanders, la Flandre, *f.*

Flushing, la Flessingue, *m.*

the **Forth,** le Forth. The Frith, *or* Firth, of — ; *le Golfe de Forth.*

France, la France, *f.*

Franconia, la Franconie, *f.*

Frankfort, Francfort, *m.* — on the Main ; *Francfort-sur-le-Mein.*

Freiburg (Black Forest), Fribourg, *m.*

Friburg (Switzerland), Fribourg, *m.*

the **Friendly Islands,** *n.pl.*, les îles des Amis, *f.pl.*

Friesland, la Frise, *f.*

Friuli, Frioul, *m.*

Frontigniac, Frontignan, *m.*

G

Gaboon, Gabon, *m.*

Gaeta, Gaète, *f.*

Galicia, la Galicie (Austria); Galice (Spain), *f.*

Galilee, la Galilée, *f.*

Gallia, la Gaule, *f.*

the **Ganges,** le Gange, *m.*

Gascony, la Gascogne, *f.*

Gaul, la Gaule, *f.*

Geneva, Genève, *f.*

Genoa, Gênes, *f.*

Georgia, la Géorgie, *f.*

Germania, la Germanie, *f.*

the **German Ocean,** la mer du Nord, *f.*

Germany, l'Allemagne, *f.*

Ghent, Gand, *m.*

the **Giant's Causeway,** la Chaussée des Géants, *f.*

Gibraltar, Gibraltar, *m.*

Gilead, Giléad, Galaad.

Gironde, la Gironde, *f.*

Gloucester, Glocester, *m.*

the **Gold Coast,** la côte d'Or (Guinea), *f.*

Golgotha, le Golgotha, *m.*

Gomorrah, Gomorrhe, *f.*

Gothland, la Gothie, *f.*

Gottingen, Gottingue, Goettingue, *m.*

the **Grain Coast,** la côte des Graines, *f.*

Granada, la Grenade, *f.*

the **Granicus,** le Granique, *m.*

Greece, la Grèce, *f.*

Greenland, le Groënland, *m.*

Groningen, Groningue, *m.*

Guadaloup, la Guadeloupe, *f.*

Guelders, la Gueldre, *f.*

Guernsey, Guernesey, *f.*

Guiana, la Guyane, *f.*

Guinea, la Guinée, *f.* New — ; *la Nouvelle Guinée.*

Gujerat, Guzzerat, *m.*

the **Gulf of Lions,** le Golfe du Lion, *m.*

the **Gulf - Stream,** le Gulf-Stream, le courant du Golfe, *m.*

H

Habsburg, Habsbourg, *m.*

the **Hague,** la Haye, *f.*

Hainault, le Hainaut, *m.*

Halicarnassus, Halicarnasse, *f.*

Hamburg, Hambourg, *m.*

Hanoi, Hanoï, Kescho, *m.*

Hanover, le Hanovre, *m.*

the **Hanse Towns,** les villes Hanséatiques, *f.pl.*

Hapsburg, Hapsbourg, *f.*

Havana, Havannah, la Havane, *f.*

Havre, le Havre, *m.*

Hawaii, Hawaï, *m.*

Hayti, Haïti, *f.*

the **Hebrides,** les Hébrides, *f.pl.* The New — ; *les Nouvelles-Hébrides.*

Hebrus, l'Hèbre, *m.*

Hellespont, l'Hellespont, *m.*

Helvetia, l'Helvétie, *f.*

Herat, Hérat, m.
Herculaneum, Herculanum, m.
Herzegovina, la Herzégovine, f.
Hesperia, l'Hespérie, f.
Hibernia, l'Hibernie, f.
Himalaya, l'Himalaya, m.
Hindostan, l'Hindoustan, m.
Holland, la Hollande, f.
Homburg, Hombourg, m.
Horn (Cape), le Cap Horn, m.
Hudson's Bay, la baie or mer d'Hudson, f.
Hungary, la Hongrie, f.
the Hydaspes, l'Hydaspe, m.
Hymettus (Mount), le mont Hymette, m.
Hyrcania, l'Hyrcanie, f.

I

Iberia, l'Ibérie, f.
the Icarian Sea, la mer Icarienne, f.
Iceland, l'Islande, f.
Illyria, l'Illyrie, f.
India, Inde, f., les Indes Orientales, f.pl.
Indies, les Indes, f.pl. the East —; les Indes Orientales. the West —; les Indes Occidentales.
Indo-China, l'Indo-Chine, f.
the Indus (river), le Sind, m.
Ionia, Ionie, f.
the Ionian Islands, les îles Ioniennes, f.pl.
Ireland, l'Irlande, f.
the Irish Sea, la mer d'Irlande, f.
Italy, l'Italie, f.
Ithaca, l'île d'Ithaque, f.
the Ivory Coast, la côte d'Ivoire, f.

J

Jamaica, la Jamaïque, f.
Japan, le Japon, m.
Jena, Iéna, f.
Jerusalem, Jérusalem, f.
the Jordan, le Jourdain, m.
Judæa, la Judée, f.
Judah, Juda, m.
Juggernaut, Jagrenat, m.
Jutland, le Jutland, m.

K

Kabul, Kaboul, Caboul, m.
Kaffraria, la Cafrarie, f.
Kalat, Kélat, m.
Kamchatka, le Kamtchatka, m.
Kandahar, Candahar, m.
the Kuriles, les îles Kouriles, f.

L

the Laccadive Islands, les Laquedives; les îles Laquedives, f.pl.
Lacedæmon, Lacédémone, f.
Laconia, Laconie, f.
Lancaster, Lancastre, m.
Land's End, Pointe de Cornouailles, f.; cap Land's end, cap Finisterre, m.

Lapland, la Laponie, f.
Lebanon, le Liban, m.
the Leeward Islands, les îles sous le Vent, f.pl.
Leghorn, Livourne, f.
Leipsic, Leipsick, Leipzig, m.
the Levant, le Levant, m.
Leyden, Leyde, f.
Liburnia, la Liburnie, f.
Libya, la Libye, f.
Liege, Liège, f.
Limburg, Limbourg, m.
Lisbon, Lisbonne, f.
Lithuania, la Lithuanie, f.
Livonia, la Livonie, f.
Lizard Point, the Lizard, le Cap Lizard, m.
Locris, la Locride, f.
the Loire (river), la Loire, f.
Lombardy, la Lombardie, f.
London, Londres, m.
Loretto, Lorette, f.
Lorraine, la Lorraine, f.
Louisiana, la Louisiane, f.
the Low Countries, les Pays-Bas, m.pl.
the Lucaya Islands, les Lucayes, f.pl.
Lucca, Lucques, f.
Luconia, Luçon, m.
Luneburg, le Lunebourg, m.
Lusatia, la Lusace, f.
Lutetia (old Paris), Lutèce, f.
Luxemburg, le Luxembourg, m.
Lyons, Lyon, m.

M

the Maas, la Meuse, f.
Macedonia, la Macédoine, f.
Madagascar, Madagascar, f.
Madeira, la Madère, f.
Madrid, le Madrid, m.
Magdeburg, Magdebourg, m.
Mahee, Mahé, m.
Magellan, (Straits of), le détroit de Magellan, m.
the Main (river), le Mein, m.
Maine, le Maine, m.
Mainz, Mayence, f.
Majorca, l'île de Majorque, f.
the Malay Archipelago, Malaysia, Malaisie, f.
Maldive Archipelago, les Maldives, f.pl.
Malta, Malte, f.
Man (the Isle of), l'île de Man.
Manchuria, la Mandchourie, f.
Manila, Manille, f.
Mantua, Mantoue, f.
the Mariana Islands, les îles Mariannes, f.pl.
Marmora (the Sea of), la mer de Marmara, f.
the Marquesas, les îles Marquises, f.pl.
Marseilles, Marseille, f.
Martinique, la Martinique, f.
the Matterhorn, le Mont Cervin, m.
Mauritius, l'île Maurice, l'île de France, f.
Mecca, la Mecque, f.
Mechlin, Malines, f.
Mecklenburg, le Mecklembourg, m.
the Mediterranean, la Méditerranée, f.
Mekon, Cambodge, Mékong, m.

Mentone, Menton, m.
Mentz, Mayence, f.
the Mersey, le Mersey, f.
Messina, Messine, f. the Straits of —; le phare de Messine, m.
Mexico, le Mexique, m.; (city) Mexico, m.
Milan, Milan, m.
Milanese, le Milanais, m.
Minorca, la Minorque, f.
Minturnæ, Minturnes, f.
the Mississippi, le Mississippi, m.
the Missouri, le Missouri, m.
Mocha, Mokha, Moka, f.
Modena, Modène, f.
Modenese, le Modénois, m.
Moldavia, la Moldavie, f.
the Moluccas, les Moluques, f.pl.
Mongolia, la Mongolie, f.
Mont Blanc, le Mont Blanc, m.
Montreal, Montréal, m.
Moravia, la Moravie, f.
the Morea, la Morée, f.
Morocco, le Maroc, m.
Moscow, Moscou, m.
Mosul, Mossoul, f.
Mulhausen, Mulhouse, m.
Munich, Munich, m.
Murcia, la Murcie, f.
Muscovy, la Moscovie, f.
Mycenæ, Mycènes, f.
Mysore, le Maïssour, le Mysore, m.

N

Nanking, Nankin, m.
Nantes, Nantes, f.
Naples, Naples, f.
Natal, Terre de Natal, la Natalie, f.
Nauplia, Nauplie, f.
Navarino, Navarin, m.
Navarre, la Navarre, f.
Negroland, la Nigritie, f.
Negropont, la Négrepont, f.
Nepal, Népaul, m.
the Netherlands, les Pays-Bas, m.pl.; la Néerlande.
New Caledonia, la Nouvelle-Calédonie, f.
Newfoundland, Terre-Neuve, f.
New Orleans, la Nouvelle Orléans, f.
New South Wales, la Nouvelle-Galles du Sud, f.
New Zealand, la Nouvelle-Zélande, f.
New Zembla, la Nouvelle-Zemble, f.
Niagara, le Niagara, m.
Nicæa, Nicée, f.
Nice (France), Nice, f.
Niger, le Niger, m.
Nile, le Nil, m.
Nimeguen, Nimègue, m.
Nineveh, Ninive, f.
Nismes, Nîmes, f.
the Noric Alps, les Alpes Noriques, f.pl.
Normandy, la Normandie, f.
the North Sea, la mer du Nord, or d'Allemagne, f.
Norway, la Norvège, f.
Nova Scotia, la Nouvelle-Ecosse, f.

Nova Zembla, la Nouvelle-Zemble, *f.*
Nubia, la Nubie, *f.*
Numidia, la Numidie, *f.*
Nuremberg, Nuremberg, *m.*

O

Ocean, Océan, *m.*
Oceania, Océanie, *f.*
the **Ohio,** l'Ohio, *m.*
Oldenburg, Oldenbourg, *m.*
Olympus, l'Olympe, *m.* Mount
— ; *le Mont Olympe.*
Oporto, Oporto, Porto, *m.*
the **Orange River Colony,** la
Colonie du fleuve Orange, *f.*
the **Oregon,** l'Orégon, *m.*
the **Orinoco,** l'Orénoque, *m.*
the **Orkneys,** les Orcades, *f.pl.*
Orleans, Orléans, *m.;* New
— ; *la Nouvelle-Orléans, f.*
Osnabruck, Osnabruck, *m.*
Ostend, Ostende, *m.*
Ostia, Ostie, *f.*
Otaheite, Taïti, Otahiti, *f.*
Otranto, Otrante, *m.*
the **Ottoman Empire,** l'Empire
Ottoman, *m.*
Oude, (province) l'Oude, *m.;*
(town) Oude, *f.*
Owhyee, Hawaïi, *f.*

P

the **Pacific,** l'Océan Pacifique,
m.
the **Pactolus,** le Pactole, *m.*
Padua, Padoue, *f.*
the **Palatinate,** le Palatinat, *m.*
the **Palatine Hill,** le Mont Pala-
tin, *m.*
Palermo, Palerme, *f.*
Palestine, la Palestine, *f.*
Palmyra, Palmyre, *f.*
Palus-Mæotis, les Palus Méo-
tides, *m.pl.*
Pampeluna, Pamplona, Pam-
pelune, *f.*
Pamphylia, la Pamphylie, *f.*
Panama, le Panama, *m.*
Pannonia, la Pannonie, *f.*
Papua, la Papouasie, la Nou-
velle-Guinée, *f.*
Paris, Paris *(parree), m.*
Parma, Parme, *f.*
Parnassus, la Parnasse, *f.*
Patagonia, la Patagonie, *f.*
Paula, Paule, *f.*
Pausilippo, Pausilippe, *m.*
Pavia, Pavie, *f.*
Pekin, Pékin, *m.*
the **Pelew Islands,** *n.pl.,* les îles
Pelew, les îles Palao, *f.pl.*
the **Peloponnesus,** le Pélopon-
nèse, *m.*
Pennsylvania, la Pensylvanie,
f.
Pergamus, Pergame, *f.*
Pernambuco, Pernambouc,
Fernambouc, *m.*
Persia, la Perse, *f.*
the **Persian Gulf,** le golfe Per-
sique, *m.*
Peru, le Pérou, *m.*
Pharsalia, Pharsale, *f.*
Philadelphia, Philadelphie, *f.*
Philippi, Philippes, *f.*

the **Philippine Islands,** les, *or*
les îles, Philippines, *f.pl.*
Phocæa, Phocée, *f.*
Phocis, la Phocide, *f.*
Phœnicia, la Phénicie, *f.*
Phrygia, la Phrygie, *f.*
Piacenza, Plaisance, *f.*
Picardy, la Picardie, *f.*
Piedmont, le Piémont, *m.*
Pindus, le Pinde, *m.*
the **Piræus,** le Pirée, *m.*
Pisa, Pise, *f.*
Placentia, Plaisance, *f.*
the **Plata, Plate** (the river), la
Plata, *f.,* le Rio de la Plata, *m.*
the **Po,** le Pô, *m.*
Poland, la Pologne, *f.*
Poltava, Pultava, *m.*
Polynesia, la Polynésie, *f.*
Pomerania, la Poméranie, *f.*
Pompeii, Pompéi, *f.*
Pondicherry, Pondichéry, *m.*
the **Pontine Marshes,** *pl.,* les
marais Pontins, *m.pl.*
Pontus, le Pont, *m.*
Porto. *V.* **Oporto.**
Portugal, le Portugal, *m.*
Presburg, Presbourg, *m.*
Pretoria, Prétoria, *f.*
the **Propontis,** la Propontide, *f.*
Prussia, la Prusse, *f.*
Pultowa. *V.* **Poltava.**
Punjab, le Pundjab, *m.*
the **Pyrenees,** les Pyrénées,
f.pl.

Q

Quebec, Québec, *m.*
Queensland, le Queensland, *m.*

R

Ragusa, Raguse, *f.*
Rangoon, Rangoun, *m.*
Ratisbon, Ratisbonne, *f.*
Ravenna, Ravenne, *f.*
the **Red Sea,** la mer Rouge, *f.*
Reykjavik, Reikiavik, *m.*
Rheims, Reims, *m.*
Rhine, le Rhin, *m. the* Lower
—; *le Bas-Rhin. the* Upper —;
le Haut-Rhin.
Rhone, le Rhone, *m.*
the **Riphæi,** *pl.,* les Monts Ri-
phées *or* Hyperboréens, *m.pl.*
the **River Plate,** la Plata, *f.*
the **Riviera,** la Rivière, la
Riviéra.
the **Rocky Mountains,** les
Montagnes Rocheuses, *f.pl.*
Rome, Rome, *f.*
Rosetta, Rosette, *f.*
Roumania, la Roumanie, *f.*
Roumelia, la Roumélie, *f.*
the **Rubicon,** le Rubicon, *m.*
Russia, la Russie, *f.* — in Europe; *la Russie d'Europe.* —
in Asia; *la Russie d'Asie.*

S

Sabina, Sabine, *f.*
Saguntum, Sagonte, *f.*
the **Sahara,** le Sahara, *m.*
Saigon, Saigon, *m.*
Saint Albans, Saint Alban, *m.*

Saint Angelo, Saint-Ange, *m.*
Saint George's Channel, le
Canal Saint-George, *m.*
Saint Helena, Sainte-Hélène, *f.*
Saint Iago (in Spain), St. Jac-
ques de Compostelle.
Saint Petersburg, Saint-
Pétersbourg, *m.*
the **Saint Lawrence,** le Saint-
Laurent, *m.*
Salamanca, Salamanque, *f.*
Salamis, Salamine, *f.*
Salerno, Salerne, *f.*
Salonica, Salenique, *f.*
Salzburg, Salzbourg, *m.*
Samarcand, Samarcande, *f.*
Samaria, Samarie, *f.*
San Domingo, Saint-Domingue,
m.
San Francisco, San-Francisco,
m.
San Marin, Saint-Marin, *m.*
Santiago, Santiago, *m.*
the **Saone,** la Saône, *f.*
Saragossa, Saragosse, *f.*
Sardinia, Sardaigne, *f.*
Sardis, Sardes, *f.*
Savoy, la Savoie, *f.*
Saxony, la Saxe, *f.*
Scandinavia, la Scandinavie, *f.*
Schaffhausen, Schaffhouse, *f.*
the **Scheldt,** l'Escaut, *f.*
Schwarzburg, Schwarzbourg,
m.
the **Scilly Isles,** les îles Sorlin-
gues, *f.pl.*
Sclavonia, la Slavonie, l'Escla-
vonie, *f.*
Scotland, l'Écosse, *f.*
Scythia, la Scythie, *f.*
Sebastopol, Sébastopol, *m.*
Segovia, Ségovie, *f.*
the **Seine,** la Seine, *f.*
Seleucis, Séleucie, *f.*
Senegal, le Senégal, *m.*
Senegambia, Sénégambie, *f.*
Servia, Serbie, *f.*
Severn, la Severn, la Severne, *f.*
the **Seychelles,** les îles Sey-
chelles, *m.*
Shanghae, Shang-haï, Chang-
haï, *m.*
Sheba, Saba, *f.*
She. *V.* **Xeres.**
the **...lands,** les îles Shet-
lan...
Siberia, Sibérie, *f.*
Sicily, la Sicile, *f.*
Silesia, la Silésie, *f.*
Silistria, la Silistrie, *f.*
Sinai (Mount), le Mont Sinaï, *m.*
Sinde, *n.,* Sindhya, *m.;* (river)
le Sind, *m.*
Singapore, Singapour, *m.*
Sluys, l'Écluse (Holland), *f.*
Smyrna, Smyrne, *f.*
the **Society Islands,** *the* **Society
Isles,** les îles de la Société,
f.pl.
Socotra, l'île Socotora, *f.*
Sodom, Sodome, *f.*
Solway Firth, le Golfe de Sol-
way, *m.*
the **Soudan,** le Soudan, *m.*
the **South-African Republic,**
la République Sud-Africaine, *f.*
South Australia, l'Australie
du Sud, *f.*
Spain, l'Espagne, *f.*
Sparta, Sparte, *f.*

Speier, Speyer, Spire, m.
the **Spice Islands,** pl., les Moluques, f.pl.
Spitzbergen, Spitzberg, m.
Steinkerk, Steinkerque, m.
Strasburg, Strasbourg, m.
Suabia, la Souabe, f.
the **Sunda Islands,** *the* **Sunda Isles,** l'archipel de la Sonde, m.
Superior (Lake), le lac Supérieur, m.
Surat, Surate, f.
Susa, Suse, f.
Sweden, la Suède, f.
Switzerland, la Suisse, f.
Syracuse, Syracuse, f.
Syria, la Syrie, f.

T

Table Bay, la baie de la Table, f.
Table Mountain, le mont de la Table, m.
the **Tagus,** le Tage, m.
Tahiti. V. Otaheite.
Tangier, Tangiers, Tanger, m.
Taranto, Tarente, f.
Tarragona, Tarragone, f.
Tartarus, le Tartare, m.
Tartary, la Tartarie, f.
Tasmania, la Tasmanie, la Terre de Van-Diemen, f.
Teheran, Téhéran, m.
Tempe (*the* Vale of), la vallée de Tempé, f.
Teneriffe, Ténériffe, l'île Ténériffe. *the* Peak of —; *le* pic de Ténériffe.
Terra Firma, Terre-Ferme, f.
Tessin, le Tessin, m.
the **Thames,** la Tamise, f.
Thebes, Thèbes, f.
Thermopylæ, les Thermopyles, f.pl.
Thessaly, la Thessalie, f.
Thibet, le Thibet, Tibet, m.
Thrace, la Thrace, f.
Thurgau, la Thurgovie, f.
Thuringia, la Thuringe, f.
the **Tiber,** le Tibre, m.
Tiberias (*the* Lake of), le lac de Tibériade, le lac de Génézareth, m.
Ticino, le Tessin, m.
Tierra del Fuego, la Terre de Feu, f.
the **Tigris,** le Tigre, m.
Tilsit, Tilsitt, m.
Timbucto, le Tombouctou, f.
Tobago, l'île de Tabago, f.
Toledo, Tolède, f.
Tonquin, le Tonkin *or* le Tonquin, m.
Tortona, Tortone, f.

Touraine, la Touraine, f.
the **Transvaal,** le Transvaal, m.
Transylvania, la Transylvanie, f.
Trasimene (*the* Lake of), le lac Trasimène, m.
Turkestan, le Turkestan, m.
Trebizond, Trébizonde, f.
Trent, Trente, f.
Treport, le Tréport, m.
Treves, Trèves, m.
Treviso, Trévise, f.
Triest, Trieste, m. or f.
Trinidad, la Trinité, f.
Tripoli, Tripoli, m.
the **Troad, Troas,** la Troade, f., Troas, m.
Troy, Troie, f.
Tunis, Tunis, f.
Tunisia, la Tunisie, f.
Turin, Turin, m.
Turkey, la Turquie, f. — in Europe; *la Turquie d' Europe.* — in Asia; *la Turquie d'Asie.*
Tuscany, la Toscane, f.
the **Tweed,** la Tweed, f.
Tyne, la Tyne, f.
Tyre, Tyr, f.
Tyrol, le Tyrol, m.

U

the **Ukraine,** l'Ukraine, f.
Umbria, l'Ombrie, f.
the **United Kingdom,** le Royaume-Uni, m.
the **United Provinces,** les Provinces-Unies, f.pl.
the **United States,** les États-Unis, m.pl.
Upsala, Upsal, m.
the **Ural Mountains,** les Monts Ourals, m.pl.
Urbino, Urbin, m.
Uruguay, l'Uruguay, m.
Ushant, Ouessant, m.
Utica, Utique, f.

V

the **Valdaï Hills,** le plateau de Valdaï, m.
Valencia, Valence, f.
Valletta, la Valette, f.
Vancouver Island, l'île Vancouver, f.
Van Diemen's Land, la Terre de Van Diémen, Tasmanie, f.
the **Vendee,** la Vendée, f.
Venetia, la Vénétie, f.
Venice, Venise, f.
Vercelli, Verceil, m.
Cape **Verd,** le Cap Vert, m.
Cape **Verd Islands,** les îles du Cap Vert, f.pl.

Verona, Vérone, f.
Vesuvius, le Vésuve, m.
Viburg, Viborg, m.
Vicenza, Vicence, f.
Vienna, Vienne, f.
Virginia, la Virginie, f.
the **Virgin Islands,** les îles Vierges, f.pl.
Vistula, la Vistule, f.
Viterbo, Viterbe, f.
Vittoria, Vitoria, f.
the **Vosges,** les Vosges, f.pl.

W

Wales, le Pays de Galles, m. New —; *la Nouvelle-Galles,* f. North —; *la Galle du Nord,* f. South —; *la Galle du Sud.*
Wallachia, la Valachie, f.
Warsaw, Varsovie, f.
Waterloo, Waterloo, m.
Western Australia, l'Australie occidentale, f.
Western Islands, les Hébrides, f.pl.
Westphalia, la Westphalie, f.
the **White Sea,** la mer Blanche, f.
Wight (*the* **Isle of**), l'île de Wight, f.
the **Windward Islands,** les îles du Vent, f.pl.
Wurtemberg, le Wurtemberg, m.
Wurzburg, Wurtzbourg, m.

X

the **Xanthus,** le Xanthe, m.
Xeres, Xérès, Xérez de la Frontera.

Y

the **Yang-tsze-Kiang,** le fleuve Bleu ; le Yang-tsé-Kiang, m.
the **Yellow River,** le fleuve Jaune ; le Hoang-ho, m.
the **Yellow Sea,** la mer Jaune, f.
Yucatan, le Yucatan, m.

Z

the **Zambesi,** le Zambèse, m.
Zealand, Zélande, f. New- —; la Nouvelle-Zélande, f.
Zion (Mount), Sion, m.
Zululand, le Zoulouland, m.
Zurich, Zurich, m.
the **Zuyder** *or* **Zuider Zee,** le Zuyderzée, m.